The New International Atlas
Der Neue Internationale Atlas
El Nuevo Atlas Internacional
Le Nouvel Atlas International
O Nôvo Atlas Internacional

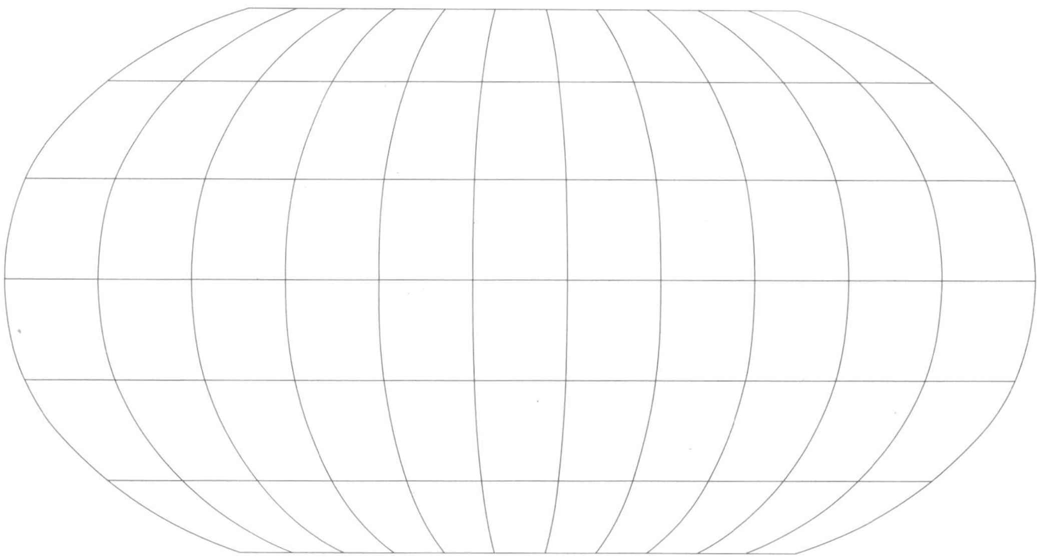

Kümmerly + Frey

ADVISERS AND CONSULTANTS

The editors wish to express their special appreciation to these geographers, cartographers, and regional specialists who assisted in the refinement of the basic concepts of the atlas or who participated in the review of many of the regional maps.

ALLGEMEINE UND KARTOGRAPHISCHE BERATER

Die Herausgeber möchten ihren besonderen Dank den Geographen, Kartographen und Landeskundlern aussprechen, die mitgeholfen haben bei der Klärung des Atlaskonzepts oder beteiligt waren an der Durchsicht vieler Regionalkarten.

ASESORES Y CONSULTORES

Los redactores quieren expresar su más profundo agradecimiento a los geógrafos, cartógrafos y especialistas en mapas regionales, que han colaborado en la determinación exacta de los conceptos básicos del atlas o que han participado en la revisión de gran número de los mapas regionales.

CONSEILLERS ET CONSULTANTS

Les éditeurs veulent exprimer ici leur gratitude aux géographes, cartographes et spécialistes régionaux qui ont collaboré à la mise au point de la conception de base de l'Atlas ou qui ont participé à la révision de nombreuses cartes régionales.

CONSELHEIROS E CONSULTORES

Os editores desejam expressar seu profundo agradecimento aos geógrafos, cartógrafos e especialistas regionais que assistiram no refinamento dos conceitos básicos do atlas ou que tenham participado na revisão de um grande número de mapas regionais.

International Planning Conference
Internationale Planungskonferenz
Conferencia Internacional de Consultores
Conférence Internationale de Planning
Conferência Internacional de Consultores

Dr. MANLIO CASTIGLIONI
Italy

Dr. ARCH C. GERLACH
United States

Dr. Ir. CORNELIS KOEMAN
Netherlands

Dr. ANDRÉ LIBAULT
Brazil

Brig. D. E. O. THACKWELL
United Kingdom

ROBERT J. VOSKUIL
United States

Dr. AKIRA WATANABE
Japan

Map Advisers
Kartographische Berater
Consejeros Cartográficos
Conseillers Cartographes
Conselheiros Cartográficos

Europe
Prof. Dr. EMIL MEYNEN
Germany

Dr. SANDOR RADO
Hungary

Asia
Dr. HISASHI SATO
Japan

Australia
R. O. BUCHANAN
United Kingdom

Anglo-America
Dr. ARCH C. GERLACH
United States

Latin America
Dr. ANDRÉ LIBAULT
Brazil

Dra. CONSUELO SOTO MORA
Mexico

Dr. JORGE A. VIVÓ ESCOTO
Mexico

Metropolitan Area Maps
Prof. HAROLD M. MAYER
United States

Rand McNally
Corporate Advisory Group
Thomas J. Hermes
Dennis O'Shea
Carl Mapes, Ph.D.
Bruce C. Ogilvie, Ph.D.
Paul T. Tiddens

The New International Atlas

Revised Edition, 1993.

Printed in the United States of America

ISBN 3-259-04099-4

International Atlas Staff
Redaktion des Internationalen Atlasses
Personal del Atlas Internacional
Personnel de l'Atlas International
Redação do Atlas Internacional

RAND McNALLY

Publisher
Andrew McNally III
Andrew McNally IV

Editorial and Cartographic Direction
Russell L. Voisin
Michael W. Dobson, Ph.D.
Jon M. Leverenz

Art and Design Direction
Chris Arvetis
Gordon Hartshorne

Coordination
V. Patrick Healy
Arlen H. Winterfeld
John E. Zych

Geographic Research and Index
Susan Hudson
Keith Jennerjohn
Felix A. Lopez
Raymond T. Tobiaski
Richard L. Forstall (Consultant)

Cartographic Editorial
Robert K. Argersinger
Winifred V. Farbman

Cartographic Compilation
Ernest A. Dahl
Esther A. Grene
Lynn N. Jasmer
Han Sik Lee
Nina Lusterman
Jill M. Stift
Larry K. Tyler

Cartographic Production
Patty Porter
Ronald Peters
Barbara Smith
Walter E. Erck
Joseph H. Funke
Ruthe Garner
Raymond J. Nitch

Composition and Typesetting
Sam Wilen
Rajani Veeramachaneni

Terrain Illustrators
Ivan Barcaba
Evelyn Mitchell
Mary Jo Schrader

MONDADORI McNALLY GmbH, Stuttgart

General Manager
Helmut Schaub
and Cartographic Staff

CARTOGRAPHIA, Budapest

Coordinator
Ervin Földi
and Cartographic Staff

ESSELTE MAP SERVICE, Stockholm

Editorial and Cartographic Direction
Paul R. Kraske,
Jürgen Jansch,
and Cartographic Staff

GEORGE PHILIP & SON, London

Editorial and Cartographic Direction
Harold Fullard,
A. G. Poynter,
and Cartographic Staff

TEIKOKU-SHOIN CO., LTD., Tokyo

Supervisor
Kimio Moriya
and Cartographic Staff

Foreword

THE HISTORY OF MAPS is as old as travel, discovery, and curiosity about the world. Since the earliest times, cartographers have served mariners with guidance for their explorations, monarchs with portraits of their territories, and scholars with a record of the earth's surface. Today, maps play an even more important role by providing men with the evidence of the ties which link the world's countries and peoples to one another.

The prime function of a map is to portray the earth's surface and the patterns of human occupance that have developed upon it. If a map were no more than an objective record, it would not need revision; however, a map is more than just a simple picture. Greatly reduced in scale from the reality it represents, it must abstract and generalize from that reality, selecting and interpreting the facts deemed to be of greatest significance. Thus, not only must cartography map new regions of the world, but it must also reflect a steady improvement in the techniques of portraying geographic information for the user.

The present century has offered a great challenge to map makers. Not only has it witnessed the increasing demand for specialized map information from governments, teachers, and scientists, it has also seen growing numbers of non-specialists eager to use maps in their business, for travel, or simply for enjoyment.

The Editors of *The International Atlas* feel, then, that a new work should be more than an updated version of older ones. The goal should be to produce an atlas of the greatest possible value and interest to a wide range of specialists and laymen. In this Foreword, we call the attention of users to several aspects which are new to the traditional framework of atlas publishing. The two most significant of these are the internationality of its planning and execution, and the designing of the maps as components of five distinctive series.

From the beginning, this Atlas has been international in concept, planning, editorial policy, and production. It was felt by Rand McNally & Company that there would be important gains in source material and expertise from the participation of organizations with previous cartographic experience in widely varying regions of the world. The advice and guidance of the senior personnel of these organizations has borne out this belief, although Rand McNally & Company as publisher has retained prime responsibility.

The editorial policies of the Atlas have been established with international use in mind, being designed for those whose native tongue is German, Spanish, French or Portuguese, as well as English. This international approach has been carried into the maps through the utilization of the metric system of measurement, and particularly by a strong emphasis on the use of local forms for geographic names. Essentially all names are in the local language, and English is used only for names of major features which extend across international borders. The names of countries appear on most of the maps both in English and in the locally official forms.

Generic terms for physical features (mountain, island, cape, etc.) also appear in their local forms, not in English. Short glossaries translating the most common of these terms appear in the margins of most maps. There is also a comprehensive glossary of all the generic terms. In the index to the Atlas, translation of generic terms is aided by the use of a system of symbols.

The coverage of the world's regions has also been planned with international utilization in mind. The space allotted to each region reflects its relative economic and cultural significance on the world scene, as well as its total population and area. There is an approximate balance between Anglo-America, Europe, and Asia, each with over one-fifth of the total map pages. Africa, Oceania, and Latin America together account for the remaining one-third. The index maps on pages xiii-xv show the map coverage according to scale.

The second of the Atlas' significant new aspects is the planning of the maps as components of five separate series. Each series has a distinctive style and content. In the first of these series, the continents are portrayed at 1:24,000,000 in natural colors, as they might appear from about 4,000 miles in space. The series also includes maps of the oceans at 1:48,000,000 and the world at 1:75,000,000.

In the next series, the major world regions are uniformly portrayed at 1:12,000,000 (190 miles to the inch). These maps are primarily political in style and content. The third series covers virtually the entire inhabited area of the earth at either 1:6,000,000 (95 miles to the inch), for the less dense regions, or 1:3,000,000 (47 miles to the inch), for Europe, most of North America, and the densest portions of South and East Asia. Physical and cultural detail are given approximately equal emphasis in this series.

In the fourth series, the scale of 1:1,000,000 (16 miles to the inch) has been used to portray key regions in each continent, selected for their exceptional importance, high population density, or complexity of development. The emphasis is on cultural detail, though shaded relief also appears. A final series maps the world's major urban areas at 1:300,000 (4.7 miles to the inch). This series emphasizes the complex patterns characteristic of large urban areas, omitting relief portrayal.

Each of the map series is comprehensive in a significant sense. The first three are territorially comprehensive, except for a few remote areas, and the last two are comprehensive for the most densely settled regions of the earth.

The sequence of maps in the Atlas begins with the series of world, continent, and ocean maps. Next are the three series of regional maps, arranged within major regions from smallest scale (1:12,000,000) to largest scale (1:1,000,000). The metropolitan map series (1:300,000) has been kept together in one section following the regional maps.

The individual map layouts have usually been planned to portray geographic and economic regions rather than individual countries. Thus there are maps of the Iberian Peninsula and of Southeastern Europe, but no separate maps of Portugal or Romania. In a few instances, this has necessitated the omission of some small portion of the region or country described in the map title. Inset maps have also been avoided, though exceptions have been made to portray some isolated islands or island groups.

The map symbols used for given features (Legend to Maps, pages x-xii) are generally alike on all of the map scales, though reduced in size on smaller scales. The symbols most often used have been arranged on page xi.

No aspect of map design has shown more dramatic advances in recent years than the cartographic rendering of relief. The Editors believe that the most effective method to depict this is the bird's-eye view or hill shading technique, which uses variation from light through dark tones to indicate slope and shape of relief features pictorially. This Atlas uses shaded relief on all but one of its five map series. On the 1:6,000,000 and 1:3,000,000 maps, it appears in combination with altitude tints, which show variations in elevation by means of light reflection, hue and intensity.

In the concluding portion of the Atlas are various tables and summaries for general reference. Next is the comprehensive glossary of geographic terms (pages 289-295). The World Information Table (pages 296-299) lists the area, population, and political status for each major political unit. The world's largest metropolitan areas are listed on page 300, followed by a comprehensive list of the world's major cities with population (pages 301-316). Finally, the Index provides map location references—map page, latitude and longitude—for more than 160,000 names.

Vorwort

DIE GESCHICHTE DER KARTE ist so alt wie das Reisen, die Entdeckungsfahrten und die Wissbegier über die Welt. Seit alten Zeiten haben Kartographen den Seefahrern mit Unterlagen für ihre Erkundungen gedient, den Herrschern Aufnahmen ihres Besitzes und den Gelehrten Darstellungen der Erdoberfläche geliefert. Heute spielen Karten eine noch bedeutendere Rolle, weil sie den Menschen vor Augen führen, wie eng die Länder und Völker der Welt miteinander verbunden sind.

Wichtigste Aufgabe einer Karte ist es, die Oberfläche der Erde und die vom Menschen geschaffenen Formen darzustellen. Wäre eine Karte nichts anderes als eine objektive Bestandsaufnahme, brauchte sie nicht bearbeitet zu werden; eine Karte ist jedoch mehr als nur ein Bild. Da sie eine vielfache Verkleinerung der Wirklichkeit wiedergibt, muss sie abstrahieren und durch Auswahl und Symbolisierung der wesentlichsten Tatsachen vereinfachen. So hat die Kartographie neue Regionen der Erde aufzunehmen und den neuesten Stand der Darstellung geographischer Informationen für den Benutzer aufzuzeigen.

Unser Jahrhundert bedeutet für die Kartographen eine grosse Herausforderung. Karten werden nicht nur in zunehmendem Masse von Regierungen, Wissenschaftlern und Pädagogen gefordert, sondern auch von interessierten Laien, die in ihrem Beruf, auf Reisen oder einfach zu ihrer Freude Karten benutzen.

Die Herausgeber des *Internationalen Atlas* meinen, dass ein neues Atlaswerk mehr sein sollte als nur die laufend gehaltene Ausgabe eines alten. Das Ziel sollte sein, einen Atlas von höchstem Gebrauchswert und Interesse sowohl für Fachleute als auch Laien zu schaffen.

In diesem Sinne möchten wir auf Besonderheiten hinweisen, die sich von dem traditionallen Aufbau eines Atlas wesentlich unterscheiden. Die beiden wichtigsten sind die Internationalität in Planung und Ausführung sowie die einheitliche Gestaltung der Karten zu fünf Gruppen.

Von Anfang an war dieser Atlas international in Planung, Redaktion und Herstellung. Rand McNally & Company war überzeugt, dass die Beteiligung von Partnern aus verschiedenen Teilen der Welt mit ihrer kartographischen Erfahrung einen grossen Gewinn an Quellen und Rat ergeben würde. Der Rat und die Mitarbeit dieser Fachleute haben diese Ansicht voll bestätigt, wobei Rand McNally als Verleger die letzte Entscheidung zufiel.

Die redaktionelle Bearbeitung des Atlas erfolgte mit Blick auf einen internationalen Interessentenkreis, vor allem aber für Benutzer, deren Muttersprache Deutsch, Spanisch, Französisch, Portugiesisch oder Englisch ist. Diese internationale Einstellung zeigt sich im Karteninhalt selbst, in der Benutzung des metrischen Masssystems und vor allem in der Bevorzugung der lokalen Schreibweise geographischer Namen. Grundsätzlich werden alle Namen in der Landessprache wiedergegeben; nur Namen grösserer Objekte, die sich über nationale Grenzen erstrecken, erscheinen in Englisch. Die Ländernamen stehen auf den meisten Karten sowohl in Englisch als auch in der offiziellen nationalen Form.

Namen für physische Objekte (Berg, Insel, Kap usw.) sind ebenfalls in ihrer lokalen Form wiedergegeben, nicht in Englisch. Die am häufigsten vorkommenden Begriffe stehen am Rande der meisten Karten erläutert. Der Atlas enthält ausserdem ein umfangreiches Verzeichnis aller Gattungsbegriffe. Im Register wird das Verständnis dieser Gattungsbegriffe durch ein System von Symbolen erleichtert.

Die Kartenausschnitte der verschiedenen Regionen der Erde wurden gleichfalls mit Blick auf einen internationalen Benutzerkreis gewählt. In diesem Atlas entspricht der einer Region zugemessene Kartenanteil ihrer relativen wirtschaftlichen und kulturellen Bedeutung in der Welt wie ihrer Gesamtbevölkerung und Fläche. Auf Anglo-Amerika, Europa und Asien entfällt mit je etwas mehr als einem Fünftel der Gesamtkartenzahl ungefähr der gleiche Anteil. Das verbleibende Drittel teilen sich Afrika, Australien, Ozeanien und Lateinamerika. Auf den Seiten XIII-XV sind die Karteauschnitte den Massstäben entsprechend auf Übersichtskarten ersichtlich.

Die zweite wesentliche Besonderheit des Atlas ist seine Gliederung der Karten in fünf charakteristische Gruppen. Jede Gruppe ist gekennzeichnet durch einen bestimmten Stil und Inhalt. In der ersten Gruppe werden die Kontinente (1:24 Mill.) abgebildet, wie sie sich aus einer ungefähren Entfernung von 6 500 km aus dem Weltraum darbieten. Diese Gruppe schliesst Karten der Ozeane (1:48 Mill.) und der Erde (1:75 Mill.) ein. In der folgenden Gruppe werden Grossregionen einheitlich (1:12 Mill.) dargestellt. Diese Karten sind in erster Linie politische Karten. Die dritte Serie deckt im wesentlichen das bewohnte Gebiet der Erde, entweder 1:6 Mill. für weniger dicht besiedelte Gebiete oder 1:3 Mill. für Europa, den Grossteil von Nordamerika und die dichtest besiedelten Teile Süd- und Ostasiens. Physische und kulturgeographische Einzelheiten werden in ungefähr gleichem Umfang wiedergegeben.

Für die vierte Gruppe wurde der Massstab 1:1 Mill. gewählt, um zentrale Räume jedes Kontinents abzubilden; sie sind entsprechend ihrer aussergewöhnlichen Bedeutung, hohen Bevölkerungsdichte oder komplexen Entwicklung gewählt. Betont werden kulturgeographische Einzelheiten, dazu enthalten die Karten eine Reliefschummerung. Die letzte Gruppe umfasst die bedeutendsten Stadtregionen der Erde (1:300 000). Diese Serie hebt das charakteristische, komplexe Gefüge grosser städtischer Ballungsgebiete hervor; auf Reliefdarstellung wurde verzichtet.

Jede der Kartenserien ist in sich abgeschlossen: Die ersten drei sind in bezug auf die Landflächen umfassend, ausgenommem einige entlegene Gebiete; die zwei letzten sind es hinsichtlich der Darstellung der dichtest besiedelten Räume der Erde.

Der Atlas beginnt mit der Gruppe der Welt-, Kontinent- und Ozeankarten. Es folgen drei Gruppen Regionalkarten, innerhalb jeder Grossregion geordnet vom kleinsten Massstab (1:12 Mill.) zum grössten (1:1 Mill.). Die Serie der Stadtregionen (1:300 000) wurde in einem einzigen Kapitel zusammengefasst, im Anschluss an die Regionalkarten.

Die Festlegung der einzelnen Kartenausschnitte zielte gewöhnlich mehr darauf ab, geographische und wirtschaftliche Regionen darzustellen als einzelne Staaten. Es gibt daher eine Karte der Iberischen Halbinsel oder von Südosteuropa, aber keine Einzelkarte von Portugal oder Rumänien. In einigen Fällen sind hierdurch kleinere Flächen des Landes oder der Region nicht erfasst, die im Kartentitel genannt sind. Die Verwendung von Einsatzkärtchen wurde möglichst vermieden, dennoch waren Ausnahmen erforderlich, um entlegene Inseln oder Inselgruppen darstellen zu können.

Die Kartensignaturen für bestimmte Objekte (Zeichenerklärung Seite X-XII) gleichen sich im allgemeinen in allen Massstäben, auch wenn sie in Karten kleinerer Massstäbe verkleinert sind. Die am häufigsten vorkommenden Signaturen sind auf Seite XI dargestellt.

Auf kaum einem Gebiet der Kartengestaltung gab es in den vergangenen Jahren so eindrucksvolle Fortschritte wie auf dem der Geländedarstellung. Die Herausgeber glauben, dass die wirkungsvollste Darstellungsmethode die Reliefschummerung ist. Sie benutzt Tonabstufungen von Hell zu Dunkel, um Neigungen und Geländeformen plastisch hervorzuheben. Dieser Atlas bringt die Schummerung bei vier der fünf Kartenserien. In den Karten 1:6 und 1:3 Mill. wird sie kombiniert mit farbigen Höhenschichten, die unterschiedliche Höhenlagen durch ihren Farb- und Tonwert abgestuft wiedergeben.

Der letzte Teil des Atlas enthält zahlreiche Tabellen und Übersichten. Auf Seite 289-295 folgt eine Zusammenstellung geographischer Begriffe. In einer Länderübersicht (Seite 296-299) sind Daten über Fläche, Bevölkerung und politischen Status der wichtigsten politischen Einheiten zusammengefasst. Die grössten Stadtregionen der Erde werden auf Seite 300 dargestellt. Weiter folgt eine umfangreiche Liste der wichtigsten Weltstädte mit Einwohnerzahlen (Seite 301-316). Im Register werden für über 160 000 Namen die Kartenseite sowie die geographische Länge und Breite aufgeführt.

Prefacio

LA HISTORIA DE LOS MAPAS es tan antigua como la de los viajes, los descubrimientos y la curiosidad del hombre por el mundo. Desde hace mucho tiempo los cartógrafos han proporcionado guías a los navegantes en sus exploraciones, descripciones de sus territorios a los monarcas y registros de la superficie de la tierra a los eruditos. Más importante todavía es el papel que desempeñan los mapas en la actualidad, proporcionando al hombre en todas partes prueba de los lazos que vinculan entre sí a los diferentes países y pueblos del globo.

La función primordial de un mapa es la representación de la superficie de la tierra y de los patrones de ocupación humana que se han desarrollado sobre ella. Si un mapa no fuera sino un registro objetivo, no necesitaría ser revisado; sin embargo, un mapa es algo más que una simple representación gráfica. Representando una realidad enormemente reducida a escala, el mapa, forzosamente, debe abstraer y generalizar de esa realidad, seleccionando e interpretando los hechos que se juzguen de mayor significación. En consecuencia, la cartografía no debe limitarse al trazo de mapas de las nuevas regiones del mundo, sino que debe reflejar en ellos un continuo adelanto en las técnicas de representación de la información geográfica en provecho de quien los utiliza.

El siglo actual ha venido a presentar a los cartógrafos una desafiante tarea. Es época que no sólo ha presenciado una creciente demanda de información cartográfica especializada por parte de los gobiernos, maestros y científicos, sino que durante ella ha surgido un público cada vez mayor de gentes no especializadas, ávidas de aprovechar los mapas en sus negocios y viajes o que los adquieren simplemente por placer.

Los directores del *Atlas Internacional* consideran, por lo tanto, que una nueva obra debe ser algo más que una versión al día de trabajos anteriores. El objetivo debe ser producir un atlas del mayor valor e interés posibles para un vasto número de especialistas y de legos en la materia. En este prefacio, queremos llamar la atención de quienes consulten esta obra sobre varias innovaciones introducidas en el diseño tradicional de un atlas. De ellas, las más significativas son la internacionalidad de su preparación, y el diseño de los mapas como componentes de cinco series con características propias.

Desde un principio, este atlas ha tenido carácter internacional en cuanto a su concepto básico, su planeamiento, política editorial y producción. Rand McNally y Compañía consideró que con la participación de organizaciones con experiencia en cartografía en una gran variedad de regiones del mundo, se obtendría importante progreso en cuanto a fuentes de material y de conocimientos. Esta creencia originó el asesoramiento y guía recibidos del personal directivo de estas organizaciones, aunque Rand McNally y Compañía ha retenido la responsabilidad principal como casa editora.

Las normas o política editorial del atlas se ha establecido teniendo en cuenta su uso internacional, y éste ha sido diseñado para el público de habla alemana, española, francesa, portuguesa e inglesa. Este carácter internacional se introdujo en los mapas mediante la utilización del sistema métrico y en particular, dando marcada preferencia al uso de vocablos locales en la nomenclatura. Virtualmente todo nombre se da en el idioma de la localidad, usándose el inglés únicamente en la identificación de elementos geográficos de mayor importancia que se extienden a través de las fronteras internacionales. En la mayoría de los mapas, los nombres de los países aparecen en inglés y en la forma oficial localmente utilizada.

Los términos genéricos de geografía física (montañas, islas, cabos, etc.), también aparecen en el idioma local, no en inglés. Al margen de la mayoría de los mapas se incluyen breves glosarios con la traducción de los más comunes de dichos términos. Se incluye también un glosario completo de los términos genéricos y en el índice del atlas, mediante un sistema de símbolos, se facilita la traducción de los mismos.

Igualmente, la amplitud que el atlas da a las distintas regiones del mundo, fue preparada con un criterio de utilización internacional. El espacio asignado a cada región refleja su posición económica y cultural relativa dentro del escenario mundial, así como su población y superficie. El resultado de esto ha sido el equilibrio aproximado resultante entre Angloamérica, Europa y Asia, ocupando, cada cual, más de la quinta parte del total de páginas dedicadas a mapas. Africa, Oceanía y América Latina juntas, cubren el resto del volumen. Los mapas índices, en las páginas xiii a xv, muestran, a escala, la extensión de las regiones que los mapas comprenden.

El segundo de los nuevo aspectos significativos del atlas, es el planeamiento de los mapas como componentes de cinco series separadas. Cada serie tiene un estilo y contenido propios. En la primera de estas series, los continentes están representados a una escala de 1:24 000 000, en colores naturales, como aparecerían al observar la tierra desde el espacio a una distancia de cerca de 6 500 kilómetros. La serie incluye también mapas de los océanos a escala 1:48 000 000 y del mundo a escala 1:75 000 000.

En la serie siguiente, las principales regiones del mundo están uniformemente representadas a escala 1:12 000 000 (120 km por cm). Estos mapas son básicamente políticos en su estilo y contenido. La tercera serie cubre prácticamente el total de la superficie habitada de la tierra, a una de dos escalas: 1:6 000 000 (60 km por cm), para las regiones menos densas, o 1:3 000 000 (30 km por cm), para Europa, la mayor parte de Norteamérica y las regiones de mayor densidad de población del Sur y Sureste de Asia. En esta serie se hace aproximadamente igual énfasis a los detalles de orden físico y cultural.

En la cuarta serie se ha usado la escala 1:1 000 000 (10 km por cm), para representar las regiones más notables en cada continente, seleccionadas por su excepcional importancia, alta densidad de población o complejidad de desarrollo. Acá, el énfasis es en el detalle cultural aunque también aparece el relieve utilizando la técnica de sombreado. La serie final la componen los mapas de las principales áreas urbanas del mundo a una escala de 1:300 000 (3 km por cm). Esta serie recalca los complejos patrones culturales característicos de las grandes áreas urbanas, omitiendo la representación del relieve.

Cada una de las series es en sí una serie integral desde el punto de vista de significación. Las tres primeras, con excepción de unas cuantas áreas remotas, son territorialmente completas; las dos últimas, son completas en cuanto a las regiones más densamente pobladas de la tierra.

La sucesión de los mapas en el atlas principia con la serie del mundo, los continentes y los océanos. Luego vienen las tres series de mapas regionales distribuídos dentro de cada región principal, de la escala menor, (1:12 000 000), a la escala mayor, (1:1 000 000). La serie de mapas de áreas metropolitanas (1:300 000), se ofrece en una sección, inmediatamente después de los mapas regionales.

En general, el trazado de cada mapa se hizo con miras a representar regiones geográficas y económicas, y no necesariamente países individuales. Así, el atlas contiene mapas de la Península Ibérica y de Europa Sudoriental, pero no mapas separados de Portugal o de Rumania. En unos pocos casos, esto impuso la necesidad de omitir alguna pequeña porción de la región o país descrito en el título del mapa. También se evitó la inserción de mapas detallando determinada área, aunque se hicieron excepciones para representar algunas islas o grupos de islas.

Los símbolos utilizados para ciertos elementos (Leyenda para Mapas, páginas x a xii), son en general similares en todas las escalas, aunque reducidos en tamaño en los mapas de escala más pequeña. Los usados más frecuentemente se encuentran en la página xi.

En ningún aspecto del diseño cartográfico se han hecho progresos tan notables en años recientes como en la representación del relieve del terreno. Los editores opinan, sin embargo, que el método más efectivo en este sentido es la vista a vuelo de pájaro o técnica de sombreado: la variación de tonos claros a obscuros indica gráficamente la pendiente y la configuración del relieve. Este atlas utiliza el sombreado en cuatro de las cinco series de mapas. En los mapas a escala 1:6 000 000 y 1:3 000 000, el sombreado se combina con tintes que indican los cambios de altitud mediante reflexión de la luz, colorido e intensidad variables.

En la última parte del atlas se ofrecen varias tablas y resúmenes para consulta. En seguida se encuentra un glosario completo de términos geográficos (páginas 289-295). La Tabla de Información Mundial, (páginas 296 a 299), muestra el área, la población y la situación de cada una de las principales unidades políticas. La lista de las áreas metropolitanas más grandes del mundo aparece en la página 300, y está seguida por una lista completa de las principales ciudades del mundo con indicación del número de habitantes, (páginas 301-316). Finalmente, el índice ofrece referencias para localizar en los mapas más de 160 000 nombres: página del mapa, latitud y longitud.

Avant-propos

L'HISTOIRE DES CARTES géographiques remonte aussi loin que celle des voyages, des découvertes et du sentiment de curiosité touchant le globe terrestre. Depuis les temps les plus reculés, les cartographes ont servi les marins en les aidant à s'orienter dans leurs voyages d'explorations, les monarques en leur fournissant des représentations de leurs territoires, les savants en les documentant sur la surface terrestre. De nos jours, les cartes jouent un rôle plus important encore, en ce qu'elles procurent aux hommes l'évidence tangible des liens joignant les uns aux autres peuples et nations du monde.

La fonction primordiale d'une carte consiste à représenter la surface du globe et la répartition des concentrations humaines qui s'y sont développées. Une carte ne fût-elle qu'un document objectif, point ne serait besoin de la réviser; mais justement, elle constitue bien davantage qu'une simple image. Considérablement réduite relativement à la réalité qu'elle représente, elle doit abstraire et généraliser à partir de cette réalité, par la sélection et l'interprétation des données jugées les plus significatives. De sorte que la cartographie doit non seulement établir les cartes des nouvelles régions du globe, mais il lui faut en outre refléter les progrès constants des techniques d'exposé de la documentation géographique à l'intention du lecteur.

Le siècle actuel a porté un défi suprême aux cartographes. Non seulement en ce que l'on y est témoin d'une demande toujours croissante de cartes à l'usage des spécialistes, de la part des gouvernements, des professeurs et des savants, mais aussi bien en ce que l'on y constate une proportion de plus en plus élevée de non-initiés avides d'utiliser des cartes de vulgarisation pour leurs affaires, leurs voyages, ou simplement leur plaisir.

Les Editeurs de *L'Atlas International* estiment, dès lors, qu'un nouvel ouvrage se doit d'être plus qu'une ancienne version mise à jour. Le but qu'ils se proposent consiste à sortir un atlas qui soit du plus haut intérêt et de la plus profonde valeur pour un vaste public de spécialistes et de profanes. Les Editeurs attirent l'attention des lecteurs sur plusieurs innovations apportées ici au cadre traditionnel de publication des atlas. Deux des plus significatives de ces innovations résident dans l'internationalisation de la conception et de l'exécution d'une part, d'autre part dans la disposition des cartes réparties en cinq séries distinctives.

Envisagé et entrepris sur un mode international dès le début, cet Atlas s'est développé selon une conception, une forme éditoriale et une réalisation du même ordre. Rand McNally & Company jugeait que de sérieux avantages—apports importants en matériaux de documentation et en connaissances spécialisées faisant autorité—résulteraient d'une collaboration avec des organisations possédant de longue date une expérience cartographique des régions les plus diversifiées du globe. Les avis et les opinions émanant du personnel de cadres de ces organisations ont corroboré iette conviction, encore que Rand McNally en tant que société d'édition en assume la responsabilité principale.

D'usage international, destiné à des lecteurs de langue allemande, espagnole , française ou portugaise, tout autant qu'anglaise, cet Atlas a dû être édité sous une forme qui tînt compte de sa raison d'être. Cette conception internationale de l'Atlas a été réalisée sur les cartes elles-mêmes avec d'une part l'utilisation du système métrique, avec d'autre part l'emploi délibéré des noms géographiques sous leur forme nationale. Essentiellement, tous les noms apparaissent sous leur forme nationale, l'anglais n'étant utilisé que pour les noms d'importantes structures du relief qui s'étendent par-delà les frontières internationales. Sur la plupart des cartes, les noms des pays apparaissent à la fois en anglais et sous leur forme nationale officielle.

Les termes génériques désignant des structures de relief (montagne, île, cap, etc.) apparaissent également sous leur forme nationale, et non pas en anglais. En marge de la plupart des cartes, de courtes listes lexicales donnent la traduction des plus communs de ces termes. En outre, un glossaire donne tous les termes génériques dont la traduction se trouve par ailleurs facilitée grâce au système de symboles décrit dans l'Index de l'Atlas.

La répartition des régions du globe a été également déterminée en tenant compte de l'usage international qu'il sera fait de l'Atlas. L'espace attribué à chaque région reflète son importance économique et culturelle relative dans le monde, aussi bien que sa superficie et sa population. Il y a un équilibre approximatif entre l'Amérique du Nord, l'Europe et l'Asie, chacune avec plus d'un cinquième de la totalité des pages. L'Afrique, l'Océanie et l'Amérique du Sud occupent le tiers restant. Les cartes index des pages xiii-xv présentent la répartition des cartes en fonction de l'échelle à laquelle elles sont reproduites.

La seconde des innovations importantes de cet Atlas réside dans la conception des cartes en tant qu'éléments constitutifs de cinq séries séparées. Style et contenu distinctifs caractérisent nettement chacune de ces cinq séries. Dans la première, les continents sont représentés à l'échelle de 1:24 000 000, en couleurs naturelles, tels qu'ils apparaîtraient, vus de l'espace, à 6 500 km. Cette série comprend également les cartes de océans à l'échelle de 1:48 000 000 et du monde à l'échelle de 1:75 000 000.

Dans la série suivante, les régions majeures du globe sont représentées de facon uniforme à l'échelle de 1:12 000 000 (120 km au cm). Par leur style et leur contenu, celles-ci sont essentiellement des cartes politiques. Dans la troisième série, virtuellement toute las surface habitée de la terre est représentée, soit à l'échelle de 1:6 000 000 (60 km au cm) pour les régions de moindre densité de population, soit à l'échelle de 1:3 000 000 (30 km au cm) pour l'Europe, la plus grande partie de l'Amérique du Nord et les portions de plus forte densité du Sud et de l'Est de l'Asie. Dans cette série, une importance à peu près égale a été accordée aux détails physiques et aux détails culturels.

Dans la quatrième série, l'échelle de 1:1 000 000 (10 km au cm) a été employée pour représenter certaines régions-clefs de chaque continent, choisies pour leur importance exceptionnelle, leur densité de population, ou la complexité de leur développement. L'accent porte sur les détails culturels, bien que le relief ombré apparaisse également. Une série finale souligne la répartition culturelle complexe, caractéristique des vastes zones urbaines, omettant le relief.

Chacune de ces séries est complète dans un mode significatif. Les trois premières sont complètes du point de vue territorial, exception faite de quelques lointaines contrées, et les deux dernières sont complètes en ce qui concerne les régions du globe de plus forte densité de population.

La succession des cartes de l'Atlas s'ouvre avec la série qui comprend les cartes du monde, des continents, et des océans. A sa suite, viennent les trois séries de cartes régionales disposées pour chaque région principale depuis les plus petites échelles (1:12 000 000), aux plus grandes (1:1 000 000). La série des cartes métropolitaines est groupée en une section qui fait suite aux cartes régionales.

La répartition individuelle des cartes a généralement été conçue en fonction des régions géographiques et économiques, plutôt qu'en fonction des frontières politiques nationales. De sorte qu'il y a des cartes de la Péninsule Ibérique et de l'Europe du Sud-Est, mais pas de cartes séparées pour le Portugal ou la Roumanie. Dans quelques cas, ceci a nécessité l'omission de quelque petite portion de la région ou du pays décrit dans le titre de la carte. Les insertions d'extensions ont également été évitées, encore que plusieurs exceptions aient été faites pour représenter certaines îles isolées ou certains groupes d'îles.

Les symboles employés sur les cartes sont en général identiques pour toutes les échelles de cartes, quoique de taille réduite sur les cartes à petite échelle. Les symboles les plus fréquemment employés ont été réunis à la page xi.

Aucun de aspects de la réalisation des cartes n'a fait de progrès plus prodigieux durant ces dernières années que la représentation cartographique du relief. Les Editeurs estiment que la méthode la plus efficace est celle de la "vue à vol d'oiseau", ou technique du relief ombré; celle-ci utilise toute la gamme des tons, des plus clairs aux plus foncés, pour indiquer picturalement l'inclinaison des pentes et la forme des structures du relief. Le relief ombré apparaît sur quatre des cinqu séries de cartes. Sur les cartes au 1:6 000 000e et au 1:3 000 000e, il apparaît en combinaison avec les teintes d'altitude qui indiquent les variations d'élévation au moyen de la réflexion de la lumière, de la nuance et de l'intensité.

Dans la dernière partie de l'Atlas, qui constitue sa conclusion, se trouvent divers tableaux de récapitulations et de références. A sa suite se trouve le lexique complet des termes géographiques (pages 289-295). Puis une table d'informations mondiales donne la liste de toutes les unités politiques principales, avec superficie, population et statut politique de chacune (pages 296-299). La liste des plus importants centres urbains du monde est à la page 300. A la suite de cette table se trouve une liste complète des principales villes du monde avec leur population (pages 301-316). Enfin, l'Index fournit des références de cartes—numéros de pages, longitude et latitude—pour permettre de situer plus de 160 000 noms géographiques.

Prefácio

A HISTÓRIA DOS MAPAS é tão antiga quanto as das viagens, descobertas, e curiosidades sobre o mundo. Desde os primórdios tempos, cartógrafos têm servido à marinheiros orientando-os em suas explorações, monarcas com reproduções dos seus territórios, e acadêmicos com o registro da superfície da terra. Hoje, os mapas têm um papel mais importante-ainda, fornecendo ao homem provas das ligações que unem os países e os povos do mundo.

A função fundamental do mapa é de retratar a superfície da terra e os padrões da ocupação humana que sobre ela se desenvolveu. Se o mapa não fosse nada mais que um registro objetivo, não necessitaria de revisão; contudo, um mapa é mais do que um simples retrato. Grandemente reduzido em escala, em relação à realidade que representa, ele deve absorver e ao mesmo tempo generalizar a realidade, selecionando e interpretando os fatos supostamente de maior significado. Portanto, não somente é preciso que o cartógrafo registre novas regiões do mundo, mas também tente refletir um melhoramento contínuo nas técnicas de retratamento de informação geográfica para o usuário.

O século atual tem oferecido um grande desafio para confeccionadores de mapas. Não há somente o testemunho da crescente demanda por mapas de informações especializadas, pelos governos, professores e cientistas, mas também tem-se notado um número crescente de leigos, ansiosos em usar mapas em seus negócios, viagens, ou simplesmente como-passatempo.

Os Editores do *Atlas Internacional* sentem, que um novo trabalho deveria ser mais do que uma versão renovada dos trabalhos anteriores. O objetivo deveria ser de produzir um atlas de máximo valor e interêsse possível, para uma grande gama de especialistas e leigos. Neste prefácio, chamamos a atenção dos usuários para os vários aspectos-que são novos para os esquemas tradicionais de publicação de atlas. Os dois mais significantes são: a internacionalidade do seu planejamento e execução, e o arranjo de mapas como componentes de cinco séries distintas.

Desde o início, o atlas tem sido internacional em conceito, planejamento, política editorial e produção. Rand McNally & Company sentiu que haveriam ganhos importantes na fonte de material e conhecimento,, pela participação de organizações com experiências cartográficas anteriores, nas mais diversas regiões do mundo. O conselho e orientação do quadro pessoal dessas organizações têm comprovado esta crença, apesar da Rand McNally & Company, como editor, ter retido a responsabilidade principal.

As políticas editoriais do Atlas têm sido estabelecidas visando o uso internacional, sendo designado para aqueles cuja língua nativa é Alemão, Espanhol, Francês ou Português, bem como Inglês. Essa técnica internacional tem sido executada em mapas, através da utilização do sistema métrico de medidas, e particularmente, pela grande ênfase no uso dos estilos locais para nomes geográficos. Essencialmente, todos os nomes estão em linguagem local, e o Inglês é usado somente para nomes de acidentes geográficos importantes, que se extendam através de fronteiras internacionais. Os nomes dos países-aparecem na maioria dos mapas, em Inglês, e em linguagem oficial local.

Termos genéricos para características físicas (montanhas, ilhas, cabos, etc.) aparecem também nas suas formas locais, não em Inglês. Pequenos glossários traduzindo estes têrmos mais comuns aparecem nas margens da maioria dos mapas. Há também um glossário completo de todos os termos genéricos. No índice dos atlas, a tradução dos termos genéricos é auxiliada pelo uso de um sistema de símbolos.

A cobertura das regiões do mundo tem sido visando a utilização internacional. O espaço atribuído para cada região reflete seu relativo significado econômico e cultural no cenário mundial, bem como sua população e área. Há um balanço aproximado entre Anglo-América, Europa e Ásia, cada qual com mais de um quinto do total de páginas. África, Oceania e América Latina, juntos, contam com o restante um terço. O mapa índice nas páginas xiii-xv mostra a cobertura do mapa de acordo com a escala.

Um novo aspecto secundário do Atlas, é o planejamento de mapas como componentes de cinco séries separadas. Cada série tem um estilo e conteúdo distinto. Na primeira dessas séries, os continentes são ilustrados em 1:24 000 00 em cores naturais, tal como elas apareceriam a 6.500 km de espaço. A série também inclui mapas dos oceanos em 1:48 000 000 e do mundo em 1:75 000 000.

Na série seguinte, as regiões principais do mundo estão uniformemente ilustradas em 1:12 000 000 (120 km por cm). Estes mapas são principalmente políticos no estilo e conteúdo. A terceira série virtualmente, cobre toda a área habitada da terra em 1:6 000 000 (60 km por cm) para as regiões menos densas, ou 1:3 000 000 (47 km por cm) para Europa, maioria da América do Norte, e a mais densa porção do Sul e Leste da Ásia. É dado ênfase de igual valor aos detalhes físicos e culturais nesta série.

Na quarta série, a escala de 1:1 000 000 (10 km por cm) tem sido usada para ilustrar regiões chaves em cada continente, selecionado pela sua excepcional importância, alta densidade populacional ou complexidade de desenvolvimento. A ênfase está no detalhe cultural, apesar de relêvo sombreado também aparecer. A série final mapeia as principais áreas urbanas mundiais em 1:300 000 (3 km por cm). Esta série enfatiza padrões complexos característicos de grandes áreas urbanas, omitindo a ilustração do relêvo.

Cada série de mapas é completa em um determinado senso. As três primeiras são territorialmente completas, exceto as poucas áreas remotas, e as duas últimas são também completas para as regiões mais densamente habitadas da terra.

A sequência de mapas no Atlas começa com a série de mapas do mundo, continentes e oceanos. Em seguida, estão as três séries de mapas regionais, arranjados dentro de regiões principais de escala mínima (1:12 000 000) para escala máxima (1:1 000 000). As séries de mapas metropolitanos (1:300 000) têm sido mantidas juntas em uma secção seguindo os mapas regionais.

As apresentações individuais dos mapas têm sido normalmente planejadas para ilustrar regiões geográficas e econômicas em vez de países individuais. Portanto, existem mapas da Península Ibérica e do Sudeste Europeu, mas não existem mapas separados para Portugal ou Romênia. Em alguns casos, foi necessária a omissão de pequena porção de uma região ou país, descrito no título do mapa. Têm sido evitados os mapas embutidos, apesar de terem sido feitas exceções para ilustrar algumas ilhas ou grupos de ilhas isolados.

Os símbolos dos mapas usados para as características dadas (legendas para mapas, páginas x-xii) são geralmente semelhantes em todas as escalas dos mapas, apesar de serem reduzidos em tamanho nas escalas menores. Os símbolos mais usados foram dispostos na página xi.

Nenhum aspecto de apresentação de mapas, mostrou-se mais dramático recentemente, do que a reprodução cartográfica do relêvo. Os editores acreditam que o método mais efetivo para representá-lo é a reprodução vista do alto ou a técnica do sombreamento das colinas, que usa variações de tonalidades claras para escuras, para indicar o declive e a forma dos aspectos dos relêvos, por meio de ilustrações. Este Atlas usa relêvo sombreado em todas as cinco séries de mapas, com exceção de uma. Nos mapas de 1:6 000 000 e 1:3 000 000, aparece em combinação com variações de cores das altitudes, que mostram variações em elevação por meio de reflexão da luz, matiz e intensidade.

Na porção conclusiva do Atlas, estão várias tabelas e sumários para referências gerais. Em seguida, está um glossário completo de termos geográficos (páginas 289-295). A tabela de informação mundial (páginas 296-299). Registra a área, população e "status" político para cada unidade política principal. As maiores áreas metropolitanas do mundo, estão relacionadas na página 300. É seguido por uma lista completa das principais cidades do mundo, com as respectivas populações (páginas 301-316). Finalmente, o índice dá referências para a localização do mapa—página do mapa, latitude e longitude—com mais de 160 000 nomes.

SUMMARY OF CONTENTS

ADVISERS, CONTRIBUTORS, EDITORS AND STAFF ii
FOREWORD iii
SUMMARY OF CONTENTS vi
LIST OF MAPS vi–vii
LEGEND TO MAPS x–xii
WORLD AND REGIONAL INDEX MAPS xiii–xv
SELECTED MAP REFERENCES xvi
WORLD SCENE xvii–xl
MAPS (see *List of Maps,* vi–vii) 1–288
World, Ocean, and Continent Maps 1–19
Regional Maps 20–258
Metropolitan Area Maps 259–288
GLOSSARY AND ABBREVIATIONS OF GEOGRAPHICAL TERMS 289–295
WORLD INFORMATION TABLE 296–299
METROPOLITAN AREAS TABLE 300
POPULATIONS OF CITIES AND TOWNS 301–316
INDEX 317

INHALTSVERZEICHNIS

BERATER, MITARBEITER, HERAUSGEBER UND REDAKTION ii
VORWORT iii–iv
INHALTSVERZEICHNIS vi
KARTENVERZEICHNIS vii
ZEICHENERKLÄRUNG x–xii
WELT- UND REGIONALE INDEXKARTEN xiii–xv
REGISTER WICHTIGER GEOGRAPHISCHER NAMEN xvi
WELT-PANORAMA xvii–xl
KARTEN (siehe *Kartenverzeichnis,* vii) 1–288
Weltkarten, Karten der Ozeane und Erdteile 1–19
Regionalkarten 20–258
Karten von Stadtregionen 259–288
VERZEICHNIS UND ABKÜRZUNGEN GEOGRAPHISCHER BEGRIFFE 289–295
WELT-INFORMATIONSTABELLE 296–299
TABELLE DER STADTREGIONEN 300
EINWOHNERZAHLEN VON GROSS-STÄDTEN 301–316
REGISTER 317

SUMARIO DEL CONTENIDO

ASESORES, COLABORADORES, REDACTORES Y AYUDANTES ii
PREFACIO iv
SUMARIO DEL CONTENIDO vi
LISTA DE MAPAS vii–viii
LEYENDAS PARA MAPAS x–xii
INDICE DE LOS MAPAS DEL MUNDO Y REGIONALES xiii–xv
SELECCIONES DE REFERENCIAS DE LOS MAPAS xvi
PERSPECTIVA DEL MUNDO xvii–xl
MAPAS (véase *Lista de Mapas,* vii–viii) 1–288
Mapas del Mundo, Océanos y Continentes 1–19
Mapas Regionales 20–258
Mapas de las Áreas Metropolitanas 259–288
GLOSARIO Y ABREVIACIONES DE TÉRMINOS GEOGRÁFICOS 289–295
TABLA DE INFORMACIÓN MUNDIAL 296–299
TABLA DE LAS ÁREAS METROPOLITANAS 300
HABITANTES EN LAS CIUDADES Y POBLACIONES 301–316
INDICE 317

TABLE DES MATIÈRES

CONSEILLERS, COLLABORATEURS, RÉDACTEURS ET PERSONNEL ii
AVANT-PROPOS iv–v
TABLE DES MATIÈRES vi
LISTE DES CARTES viii–ix
LÉGENDE DES CARTES x–xii
INDEX DES CARTES DU MONDE ET DES CARTES RÉGIONALES xiii–xv
INDEX CARTOGRAPHIQUE ABRÉGÉ xvi
LE MONDE AUJOURD'HUI xvii–xl
CARTES (voir *Liste des Cartes,* viii–ix) 1–288
Cartes du Monde, des Océans et des Continents 1–19
Cartes Régionales 20–258
Cartes des Zones Métropolitaines 259–288
GLOSSAIRE ET ABRÉVIATIONS DE TERMES GÉOGRAPHIQUES 289–295
TABLE D'INFORMATIONS MONDIALES 296–299
TABLE DES ZONES MÉTROPOLITAINES 300
POPULATION DES GRANDS CENTRES ET DES VILLES 301–316
INDEX 317

SUMÁRIO

EDITORES, ASSESSORES E COLABORADORES ii
PREFÁCIO v
SUMÁRIO vi
LISTA DE MAPAS ix
LEGENDAS DOS MAPAS x–xii
ÍNDICE DES MAPAS DO MUNDO E REGIONAIS xiii–xv
REFERÊNCIAS A MAPAS SELECIONADAS xvi
PERSPECTIVA DO MUNDO xvii–xl
MAPAS (ver a *Lista de Mapas,* ix) 1–288
Mapas do mundo, dos oceanos e dos continentes 1–19
Mapas regionais 20–258
Mapas das áreas metropolitanas 259–288
GLOSSÁRIO E ABREVIAÇÕES DE TERMOS GEOGRÁFICOS 289–295
TABELA DE INFORMAÇÕES MUNDIAIS 296–299
TABELA DAS ÁREAS METROPOLITANAS 300
POPULAÇAÕ DOS CENTROS URBANOS 301–316
ÍNDICE 317

List of Maps

WORLD, OCEAN and CONTINENT MAPS

* Introduction 1
1:75 World: Political 2–3
1:75 World: Physical 4–5
1:48 Pacific and Indian Oceans 6–7
1:48 Atlantic Ocean 8
1:24 Antarctica 9
1:24 Europe and Africa 10–11
1:24 Asia 12–13
1:24 Australia and Oceania 14–15
1:24 North America 16–17
1:24 South America 18–19

REGIONAL MAPS

Introduction 20–21

Eurasia

1:12 Europe 22–23
1:6 Northern Europe 24–25
1:3 Southern Scandinavia 26–27
1:3 British Isles 28–29
1:3 Central Europe 30–31
1:3 France and the Alps 32–33
1:3 Spain and Portugal 34–35
1:3 Italy 36–37
1:3 Southeastern Europe 38–39
1:1 Stockholm - Karlstad 40
1:1 København - Malmö - Kiel 41
1:1 London - Birmingham - Cardiff 42–43
1:1 Dublin - Manchester - Newcastle upon Tyne 44–45
1:1 Glasgow - Edinburgh - Aberdeen 46–47
1:1 Dublin - Belfast - Cork 48–49
1:1 Paris - London - Bruxelles 50–51
1:1 Amsterdam - Düsseldorf - Hamburg 52–53
1:1 Berlin - Hamburg - Praha 54–55
1:1 Bruxelles - Frankfurt - Stuttgart 56–57
1:1 Zürich - Genève - Strasbourg 58–59
1:1 Nürnberg - München 60
1:3 Wien - Brno - Linz 61
1:1 Lyon - Marseille - Milano 62–63
1:1 München - Venezia - Firenze 64–65
1:1 Roma - Firenze - Napoli 66–67
1:1 Napoli - Messina - Bari 68–69
1:1 Palermo - Catania - Messina 70
1:1 Cagliari - Sassari 71
1:12 Northwest Asia 72–73
1:12 Northeast Asia 74–75
1:3 Baltic and Moscow Regions 76–77
1:3 Ukraine 78–79
1:3 Volga Region 80–81
1:1 Moskva - Tula - Tver' 82
1:1 Doneck - Lugansk - Rostov 83
1:3 Caucasus and Transcaucasia 84
1:3 Tashkent Region 85
1:6 Central Russia and Kazakhstan 86–87
1:6 Lake Baikal Region 88
1:6 Far Eastern Russia 89
1:12 China, Japan and Korea 90–91
1:3 Japan 92–93
1:1 Tōkyō - Nagoya - Kyōto 94–95
1:1 Ōsaka - Hiroshima - Fukuoka 96–97
1:3 Northeast China and Korea 98–99
1:3 East and Southeast China 100–101
1:6 Interior China 102–103
1:1 Shenyang -Fushun (Mukden - Fushun) 104
1:1 Beijing - Tianjin (Peking - Tientsin) 105
1:1 Shanghai - Nanjing (Shanghai - Nanking) 106
1:1 Chongqing - Chengdu (Chungking - Chengtu) 107
1:6 Southeast Asia 108–109
1:6 Burma, Thailand and Indochina 110–111
1:6 Malaysia and Western Indonesia 112–113
1:3 Malaya, Singapore and Northern Sumatra 114
1:3 Java • Lesser Sunda Islands 115
1:3 Philippines 116–117
1:12 India, Pakistan and Southwest Asia 118–119
1:6 Northern India and Pakistan 120–121
1:6 Southern India and Sri Lanka 122
1:3 Punjab and Kashmir 123
1:3 Ganges Lowland and Nepal 124–125
1:1 Calcutta - Dhaka - Jamshedpur 126–127
1:6 The Middle East 128–129
1:3 Turkey and Cyprus 130–131
1:1 Yerushalayim - Dimashq (Jerusalem - Damascus) 132–133

Africa

1:12 Western North Africa 134–135
1:12 Eastern North Africa 136–137
1:12 Southern Africa 138–139
1:6 Egypt and Sudan 140–141
1:1 Al-Qāhirah - As-Suways (Cairo - Suez) 142–143
1:6 Ethiopia, Somalia and Yemen 144–145
1:6 Libya and Chad 146–147
1:6 Northwestern Africa 148–149
1:6 West Africa 150–151
1:6 Western Congo Basin 152–153
1:6 East Africa and Eastern Congo Basin 154–155
1:6 Southern Africa and Madagascar 156–157
1:3 South Africa 158–159

Australia/Oceania

1:12 Australia 160–161
1:6 Western and Central Australia 162–163
1:6 Northern Australia and New Guinea 164–165
1:6 Eastern Australia 166–167
1:1 Perth • Adelaide 168
1:1 Melbourne - Geelong - Ballarat 169
1:1 Sydney - Newcastle 170
1:1 Brisbane • Canberra 171
1:3 New Zealand 172–173
Various Scales
Islands of the Pacific 174–175

Anglo America

1:12 Canada 176–177
1:12 United States 178–179
1:6 Alaska and Yukon 180–181
1:6 Southwestern Canada 182–183
1:6 South-Central Canada 184–185
1:6 Southeastern Canada 186–187
1:3 Northeastern United States 188–189
1:6 Great Lakes Region 190–191
1:6 Southeastern United States 192–193
1:6 Mississippi Valley 194–195
1:6 Southern Great Plains 196–197
1:6 Northern Great Plains 198–199
1:6 Southern Rocky Mountains 200–201
1:6 Northwestern United States 202–203
1:6 California and Nevada 204–205
1:1 Montréal - Québec 206
1:1 Boston - New York - Albany 207
1:1 New York - Philadelphia - Washington - Norfolk 208–209
1:1 New York - Buffalo 210–211
1:1 Toronto - Ottawa 212–213
1:1 Pittsburgh - Cleveland - Detroit 214–215
1:1 Chicago - Detroit - Milwaukee 216–217
1:1 Indianapolis - Cincinnati - Louisville 218
1:1 St. Louis - Springfield 219
1:1 Miami - Tampa - Orlando 220–221
1:1 Houston - Dallas - Austin 222–223
1:1 Vancouver - Seattle - Portland 224–225
1:1 San Francisco - Reno - Bakersfield 226–227
1:1 Los Angeles - San Diego 228
Various Scales
Hawaii 229

Latin America

1:12 Middle America 230–231
1:6 Mexico 232–233
1:3 Central Mexico 234–235
1:3 Central America 236–237
1:6 Caribbean Region 238–239
Various Scales
Islands of the West Indies 240–241
1:12 Northern South America 242–243
1:12 Southern South America 244–245
1:6 Colombia, Ecuador, Venezuela and Guyana 246–247
1:6 Peru, Bolivia and Western Brazil 248–249
1:6 Northeastern Brazil 250–251
1:6 Central Argentina and Chile 252–253
1:6 Southern Argentina and Chile 254
1:6 Southeastern Brazil 255
1:1 Rio de Janeiro - São Paulo 256–257
1:1 Buenos Aires - Montevideo 258

METROPOLITAN AREA MAPS (1:300,000)

Introduction 259
London 260
Paris 261
Manchester - Liverpool 262
Ruhr Area 263
Berlin • Wien • Budapest 264
Sankt Peterburg • Moskva 265
Madrid • Milano • Lisboa • Barcelona 266
Roma • Athínai • İstanbul • Tehrān 267
Tōkyō - Yokohama 268

*Scale in millions

Krung Thep (Bangkok) • Thanh Pho Ho Chi Minh (Saigon) • Jakarta • Shanghai • T'aipei • Manila 269
Ōsaka - Kōbe - Kyōto 270
Beijing (Peking) • Sŏul • Singapore • Hong Kong 271
Delhi • Bombay • Calcutta 272
Lagos • Kinshasa - Brazzaville • Al-Qāhirah (Cairo) • Johannesburg 273
Sydney • Melbourne 274
Montréal • Toronto 275
New York 276–277
Chicago 278
Cleveland • Pittsburgh 279
Los Angeles 280
Detroit - Windsor 281
San Francisco - Oakland - San Jose 282
Boston 283
Buffalo - Niagara Falls • Baltimore • Washington 284
Philadelphia 285
Ciudad de México • La Habana • Caracas • Lima • Santiago 286
Rio de Janeiro • São Paulo 287
Buenos Aires 288

Kartenverzeichnis

WELTKARTEN, KARTEN DER OZEANE UND ERDTEILE

* Einleitung 1
1:75 Erde: Politisch 2–3
1:75 Erde: Physisch 4–5
1:48 Pazifischer und Indischer Ozean 6–7
1:48 Atlantischer Ozean 8
1:24 Antarktis 9
1:24 Europa und Afrika 10–11
1:24 Asien 12–13
1:24 Australien und Ozeanien 14–15
1:24 Nordamerika 16–17
1:24 Südamerika 18–19

REGIONALKARTEN

Einleitung 20–21

Eurasien

1:12 Europa 22–23
1:6 Nordeuropa 24–25
1:3 Südskandinavien 26–27
1:3 Britische Inseln 28–29
1:3 Mitteleuropa 30–31
1:3 Frankreich und die Alpen 32–33
1:3 Spanien und Portugal 34–35
1:3 Italien 36–37
1:3 Südosteuropa 38–39
1:1 Stockholm - Karlstad 40
1:1 København - Malmö - Kiel 41
1:1 London - Birmingham - Cardiff 42–43
1:1 Dublin - Manchester - Newcastle upon Tyne 44–45
1:1 Glasgow - Edinburgh - Aberdeen 46–47
1:1 Dublin - Belfast - Cork 48–49
1:1 Paris - London - Bruxelles 50–51
1:1 Amsterdam - Düsseldorf - Hamburg 52–53
1:1 Berlin - Hamburg - Praha 54–55
1:1 Bruxelles - Frankfurt - Stuttgart 56–57
1:1 Zürich - Genève - Strasbourg 58–59
1:1 Nürnberg - München 60
1:3 Wien - Brno - Linz 61
1:1 Lyon - Marseille - Milano 62–63
1:1 München - Venezia - Firenze 64–65
1:1 Roma - Firenze - Napoli 66–67
1:1 Napoli - Messina - Bari 68–69
1:1 Palermo - Catania - Messina 70
1:1 Cagliari - Sassari 71
1:12 Nordwestasien 72–73
1:12 Nordostasien 74–75
1:3 Baltenland und Mittelrussland 76–77
1:3 Ukraine 78–79
1:3 Wolgagebiet 80–81
1:1 Moskva - Tula - Tver' 82
1:1 Doneck - Lugansk - Rostov 83
1:3 Kaukasus und Transkaukasien 84
1:3 Taschkentgebiet 85
1:6 Mittelrussland und Kasachstan 86–87
1:6 Baikalseegebiet 88
1:6 Russlands Ferne Osten 89
1:12 China, Japan und Korea 90–91
1:3 Japan 92–93
1:1 Tōkyō - Nagoya - Kyōto 94–95
1:1 Ōsaka - Hiroshima - Fukuoka 96–97
1:3 Nordostchina und Korea 98–99
1:3 Ost- und Südostchina 100–101
1:6 Innerchina 102–103
1:1 Shenyang -Fushun (Mukden - Fushun) 104
1:1 Beijing - Tianjin (Peking - Tientsin) 105
1:1 Shanghai - Nanjing (Shanghai - Nanking) 106
1:1 Chongqing - Chengdu (Chungking - Chengtu) 107
1:6 Südostasien 108–109
1:6 Burma, Thailand und Indochina 110–111
1:6 Malaysia und westliches Indonesien 112–113
1:3 Malaya, Singapur und Nordsumatra 114
1:3 Java • Kleine Sundainseln 115
1:3 Philippinen 116–117
1:12 Indien, Pakistan und Südwestasien 118–119
1:6 Nordindien und Pakistan 120–121
1:6 Südindien und Sri Lanka 122
1:3 Pandschab und Kaschmir 123
1:3 Gangestiefland und Nepal 124–125
1:1 Calcutta - Dhaka - Jamshedpur 126–127
1:6 Vorderasien 128–129
1:3 Türkei und Zypern 130–131
1:1 Yerushalayim - Dimashq (Jerusalem - Damascus) 132–133

Afrika

1:12 West Nordafrika 134–135
1:12 Ost Nordafrika 136–137
1:12 Südafrika 138–139
1:6 Ägypten und Sudan 140–141
1:1 Al-Qāhirah - As-Suways (Cairo - Suez) 142–143
1:6 Äthiopien, Somalia und Jemen 144–145
1:6 Libyen und Tschad 146–147
1:6 Nordwestafrika 148–149
1:6 Westafrika 150–151
1:6 Westliches Kongobecken 152–153
1:6 Ostafrika und Östliches Kongobecken 154–155
1:6 Südafrika und Madagaskar 156–157
1:3 Republik Südafrika 158–159

Australien/Ozeanien

1:12 Australien 160–161
1:6 West-und Mittelaustralien 162–163
1:6 Nordaustralien und Neuguinea 164–165
1:6 Ostaustralien 166–167
1:1 Perth • Adelaide 168
1:1 Melbourne - Geelong - Ballarat 169
1:1 Sydney - Newcastle 170
1:1 Brisbane • Canberra 171
1:3 Neuseeland 172-173
verschiedene Massstäbe
Pazifische Inseln 174–175

Anglo-Amerika

1:12 Kanada 176–177
1:12 Vereinigte Staaten 178–179
1:6 Alaska und Yukon 180–181
1:6 Südwestkanada 182–183
1:6 Südliches Mittelkanada 184–185
1:6 Südostkanada 186–187
1:3 Nordöstliche Vereinigte Staaten 188–189
1:6 Grosse Seen-Region 190–191
1:6 Südöstliche Vereinigte Staaten 192–193
1:6 Mississippi-Tiefland 194–195
1:6 Südliche Grosse Ebenen 196–197
1:6 Nördliche Grosse Ebenen 198–199
1:6 Südliches Felsengebirge 200–201
1:6 Nordwestliche Vereinigte Staaten 202–203
1:6 Kalifornien und Nevada 204–205
1:1 Montréal - Québec 206
1:1 Boston - New York - Albany 207
1:1 New York - Philadelphia - Washington - Norfolk 208–209
1:1 New York - Buffalo 210–211
1:1 Toronto - Ottawa 212–213
1:1 Pittsburgh - Cleveland - Detroit 214–215
1:1 Chicago - Detroit - Milwaukee 216–217
1:1 Indianapolis - Cincinnati - Louisville 218
1:1 St. Louis - Springfield 219
1:1 Miami - Tampa - Orlando 220–221
1:1 Houston - Dallas - Austin 222–223
1:1 Vancouver - Seattle - Portland 224–225
1:1 San Francisco - Reno - Bakersfield 226–227
1:1 Los Angeles - San Diego 228
verschiedene Massstäbe
Hawaii 229

Latein-Amerika

1:12 Mittelamerika 230–231
1:6 Mexiko 232–233
1:3 Mittelmexiko 234–235
1:3 Zentralamerika 236–237
1:6 Mittelamerikanische Inselwelt 238–239
verschiedene Massstäbe
Westindische Inseln 240–241
1:12 Südamerika, nördlicher Teil 242–243
1:12 Südamerika, südlicher Teil 244–245
1:6 Kolumbien, Ecuador, Venezuela und Guayana 246–247
1:6 Peru, Bolivien und westliches Brasilien 248–249
1:6 Nordostbrasilien 250–251
1:6 Mittelargentinien und Mittelchile 252–253
1:6 Südliches Argentinien und südliches Chile 254
1:6 Südostbrasilien 255
1:1 Rio de Janeiro - São Paulo 256–257
1:1 Buenos Aires - Montevideo 258

KARTEN VON STRADTREGIONEN (1:300 000)

Einleitung 259
London 260
Paris 261
Manchester - Liverpool 262
Ruhr Area 263
Berlin • Wien • Budapest 264
Sankt Peterburg • Moskva 265
Madrid • Milano • Lisboa • Barcelona 266
Roma • Athínai • İstanbul • Tehrān 267
Tōkyō - Yokohama 268
Krung Thep (Bangkok) • Thanh Pho Ho Chi Minh (Saigon) • Jakarta • Shanghai • T'aipei • Manila 269
Ōsaka - Kōbe - Kyōto 270
Beijing (Peking) • Sŏul • Singapore • Hong Kong 271
Delhi • Bombay • Calcutta 272
Lagos • Kinshasa - Brazzaville • Al-Qāhirah (Cairo) • Johannesburg 273
Sydney • Melbourne 274
Montréal • Toronto 275
New York 276–277
Chicago 278
Cleveland • Pittsburgh 279
Los Angeles 280
Detroit - Windsor 281
San Francisco - Oakland - San Jose 282
Boston 283
Buffalo - Niagara Falls • Baltimore • Washington 284
Philadelphia 285
Ciudad de México • La Habana • Caracas • Lima • Santiago 286
Rio de Janeiro • São Paulo 287
Buenos Aires 288

* Massstab in Millionen

Lista de Mapas

MAPAS DEL MUNDO, OCÉANOS Y CONTINENTES

* Introducción 1
1:75 Mundo: Político 2–3
1:75 Mundo: Físico 4–5
1:48 Océanos Pacífico e Indico 6–7
1:48 Océano Atlántico 8
1:24 Antártida 9
1:24 Europa y África 10–11
1:24 Asia 12–13
1:24 Australia y Oceanía 14–15
1:24 América del Norte 16–17
1:24 América del Sur 18–19

MAPAS REGIONALES

Introducción 20–21

Eurasia

1:12 Europa 22–23
1:6 Europe Septentrional 24–25
1:3 Escandinavia Meridional 26–27
1:3 Islas Británicas 28–29
1:3 Europa Central 30–31
1:3 Francia y los Alpes 32–33
1:3 España y Portugal 34–35
1:3 Italia 36–37
1:3 Europa Sud-oriental 38–39
1:1 Stockholm - Karlstad 40
1:1 København - Malmö - Kiel 41
1:1 London - Birmingham - Cardiff 42–43
1:1 Dublin - Manchester - Newcastle upon Tyne 44–45
1:1 Glasgow - Edinburgh - Aberdeen 46–47
1:1 Dublin - Belfast - Cork 48–49
1:1 Paris - London - Bruxelles 50–51
1:1 Amsterdam - Düsseldorf - Hamburg 52–53
1:1 Berlin - Hamburg - Praha 54–55
1:1 Bruxelles - Frankfurt - Stuttgart 56–57
1:1 Zürich - Genève - Strasbourg 58–59
1:1 Nürnberg - München 60
1:3 Wien - Brno - Linz 61
1:1 Lyon - Marseille - Milano 62–63
1:1 München - Venezia - Firenze 64–65
1:1 Roma - Firenze - Napoli 66–67
1:1 Napoli - Messina - Bari 68–69
1:1 Palermo - Catania - Messina 70
1:1 Cagliari - Sassari 71
1:12 Asia Nor-occidental 72–73
1:12 Asia Nor-oriental 74–75
1:3 Regiones de Báltico y de Moscú 76–77
1:3 Ucrania 78–79
1:3 Región del Volga 80–81
1:1 Moskva - Tula - Tver' 82
1:1 Doneck - Lugansk - Rostov 83
1:3 Cáucaso y Transcaucasia 84
1:3 Región de Tachkent 85
1:6 Rusia Central e Kazajstan 86–87
1:6 Región del Lago Baikal 88

*Escala en millones

1:6 Extremo Oriente Ruso 89
1:12 China, Japón y Corea 90–91
1:3 Japón 92–93
1:1 Tōkyō - Nagoya - Kyōto 94–95
1:1 Ōsaka - Hiroshima - Fukuoka 96–97
1:3 China Nor-oriental y Corea 98–99
1:3 Este y Sudeste de la China 100–101
1:6 China Interior 102–103
1:1 Shenyang -Fushun (Mukden - Fushun) 104
1:1 Beijing - Tianjin (Peking - Tientsin) 105
1:1 Shanghai - Nanjing (Shanghai - Nanking) 106
1:1 Chongqing - Chengdu (Chungking - Chengtu) 107
1:6 Asia Sud-oriental 108–109
1:6 Birmania, Siam e Indochina 110–111
1:6 Malasia e Indonesia Occidental 112–113
1:3 Malaya, Singapur y Sumatra Septentrional 114
1:3 Java • Islas Menores de la Sonda 115
1:3 Filipinas 116–117
1:12 India, Pakistán y Asia Sud-occidental 118–119
1:6 India Septentrional y Pakistán 120–121
1:6 India Meridional y Sri Lanka 122
1:3 Punjab y Cachemira 123
1:3 Llanuras del Ganges y Nepal 124–125
1:1 Calcutta - Dhaka - Jamshedpur 126–127
1:6 El Medio Oriente 128–129
1:3 Turquía y Chipre 130–131
1:1 Yerushalayim - Dimashq (Jerusalem - Damascus) 132–133

África

1:12 Región Occidental de Africa Septentrional 134–135
1:12 Región Oriental de Africa Septentrional 136–137
1:12 África Meridional 138–139
1:6 Egipto y Sudán 140–141
1:1 Al-Qāhirah - As-Suways (Cairo - Suez) 142–143
1:6 Etiopía, Somalía y Yemen 144–145
1:6 Libia y el Chad 146–147
1:6 África Nor-occidental 148–149
1:6 África Occidental 150–151
1:6 Cuenca Occidental del Congo 152–153
1:6 África Oriental y Cuenca Oriental del Congo 154–155
1:6 África Meridional y Madagascar 156–157
1:3 Sudáfrica 158–159

Australia/Oceanía

1:12 Australia 160–161
1:6 Australia Centro-occidental 162–163
1:6 Australia Septentrional y Nueva Guinea 164–165
1:6 Australia Oriental 166–167
1:1 Perth • Adelaide 168
1:1 Melbourne - Geelong - Ballarat 169
1:1 Sydney - Newcastle 170
1:1 Brisbane • Canberra 171
1:3 Nueva Zelanda 172-173
Varias Escalas
Islas del Pacífico 174–175

América Anglosajona

1:12 Canadá 176–177
1:12 Estados Unidos 178–179
1:6 Alaska y Yukón 180–181
1:6 Canadá Sud-occidental 182–183
1:6 Centro Meridional del Canadá 184–185
1:6 Canadá Sud-oriental 186–187
1:3 Nor-este de los Estados Unidos 188–189
1:6 Región de los Grandes Lagos 190–191
1:6 Sud-este de los Estados Unidos 192–193
1:6 Valle del Misisipí 194–195
1:6 Grandes Llanos: zona meridional 196–197
1:6 Grandes Llanos: zona septentrional 198–199
1:6 Montañas Rocosas: zona meridional 200–201
1:6 Nor-oeste de los Estados Unidos 202–203
1:6 California y Nevada 204–205
1:1 Montréal - Québec 206
1:1 Boston - New York - Albany 207
1:1 New York - Philadelphia - Washington - Norfolk 208–209
1:1 New York - Buffalo 210–211
1:1 Toronto - Ottawa 212–213
1:1 Pittsburgh - Cleveland - Detroit 214–215
1:1 Chicago - Detroit - Milwaukee 216–217
1:1 Indianapolis - Cincinnati - Louisville 218
1:1 St. Louis - Springfield 219
1:1 Miami - Tampa - Orlando 220–221
1:1 Houston - Dallas - Austin 222–223
1:1 Vancouver - Seattle - Portland 224–225
1:1 San Francisco - Reno - Bakersfield 226–227
1:1 Los Angeles - San Diego 228
Varias Escalas
Hawaii 229

América Latina

1:12 México, Centroamérica y Las Antillas 230–231
1:6 México 232–233
1:3 México Central 234–235
1:3 América Central 236–237
1:6 Región del Caribe 238–239
Varias Escalas
Islas de las Antillas 240–241
1:12 América del Sur: zona septentrional 242–243
1:12 América del Sur: zona meridional 244–245
1:6 Colombia, Ecuador, Venezuela y Guyana 246–247
1:6 Perú, Bolivia y Brasil Occidental 248–249
1:6 Brasil Nor-oriental 250–251
1:6 Argentina y Chile: zonas centrales 252–253
1:6 Argentina y Chile: zonas meridionales 254
1:6 Brazil Sud-oriental 255
1:1 Rio de Janeiro - São Paulo 256–257
1:1 Buenos Aires - Montevideo 258

MAPAS DE LAS ÁREAS METROPOLITANAS (1:300 000)

Introducción 259
London 260
Paris 261
Manchester - Liverpool 262
Ruhr Area 263
Berlin • Wien • Budapest 264
Sankt Peterburg • Moskva 265
Madrid • Milano • Lisboa • Barcelona 266
Roma • Athínai • İstanbul • Tehrān 267
Tōkyō - Yokohama 268
Krung Thep (Bangkok) • Thanh Pho Ho Chi Minh (Saigon) • Jakarta • Shanghai • T'aipei • Manila 269
Ōsaka - Kōbe - Kyōto 270
Beijing (Peking) • Sŏul • Singapore • Hong Kong 271
Delhi • Bombay • Calcutta 272
Lagos • Kinshasa - Brazzaville • Al-Qāhirah (Cairo) • Johannesburg 273
Sydney • Melbourne 274
Montréal • Toronto 275
New York 276–277
Chicago 278
Cleveland • Pittsburgh 279
Los Angeles 280
Detroit - Windsor 281
San Francisco - Oakland - San Jose 282
Boston 283
Buffalo - Niagara Falls • Baltimore • Washington 284
Philadelphia 285
Ciudad de México • La Habana • Caracas • Lima • Santiago 286
Rio de Janeiro • São Paulo 287
Buenos Aires 288

*Escala en millones

Liste des Cartes

CARTES DU MONDE, DES OCÉANS ET DES CONTINENTS

* Introduction 1
1:75 Monde: Politique 2–3
1:75 Monde: Physique 4–5
1:48 Océans Pacifique et Indien 6–7
1:48 Océan Atlantique 8
1:24 Antarctique 9
1:24 Europe et Afrique 10–11
1:24 Asie 12–13
1:24 Australie et Océanie 14–15
1:24 Amérique du Nord 16–17
1:24 Amérique du Sud 18–19

CARTES RÉGIONALES

Introduction 20–21

Eurasie

1:12 Europe 22–23
1:6 Europe Septentrionale 24–25
1:3 Scandinavie Méridionale 26–27
1:3 Îles Britanniques 28–29
1:3 Europe Centrale 30–31
1:3 France et Alpes 32–33
1:3 Espagne et Portugal 34–35
1:3 Italie 36–37
1:3 Europe du Sud-Est 38–39
1:1 Stockholm Karlstad 40
1:1 København - Malmö - Kiel 41
1:1 London - Birmingham - Cardiff 42–43
1:1 Dublin - Manchester - Newcastle upon Tyne 44–45
1:1 Glasgow - Edinburgh - Aberdeen 46–47
1:1 Dublin - Belfast - Cork 48–49
1:1 Paris - London - Bruxelles 50–51
1:1 Amsterdam - Düsseldorf - Hamburg 52–53
1:1 Berlin - Hamburg - Praha 54–55
1:1 Bruxelles - Frankfurt - Stuttgart 56–57
1:1 Zürich - Genève - Strasbourg 58–59
1:1 Nürnberg - München 60
1:3 Wien - Brno - Linz 61
1:1 Lyon - Marseille - Milano 62–63
1:1 München - Venezia - Firenze 64–65
1:1 Roma - Firenze - Napoli 66–67
1:1 Napoli - Messina - Bari 68–69
1:1 Palermo - Catania - Messina 70
1:1 Cagliari - Sassari 71
1:12 Asie du Nord-Ouest 72–73
1:12 Asie du Nord-Est 74–75
1:3 Républiques Baltes et la Région de Moscou 76–77
1:3 Ukraine 78–79
1:3 Région de la Volga 80–81
1:1 Moskva - Tula - Tver' 82
1:1 Doneck - Lugansk - Rostov 83
1:3 Caucasie et Transcaucasie 84
1:3 Région de Tachkent 85
1:6 Russie Centrale et Kazakhstan 86–87
1:6 Région du Lac Baïkal 88
1:6 Extrême-Orient Russe 89
1:12 Chine, Japon et Corée 90–91
1:3 Japon 92–93
1:1 Tōkyō - Nagoya - Kyōto 94–95
1:1 Ōsaka - Hiroshima - Fukuoka 96–97
1:3 Nord-Est de la Chine et Corée 98–99
1:3 Chine de l'Est et du Sud-Est 100–101
1:6 Chine Intérieure 102–103
1:1 Shenyang -Fushun (Mukden - Fushun) 104
1:1 Beijing - Tianjin (Peking - Tientsin) 105
1:1 Shanghai - Nanjing (Shanghai - Nanking) 106
1:1 Chongqing - Chengdu (Chungking - Chengtu) 107
1:6 Asie du Sud-Est 108–109
1:6 Birmanie, Thaïlande et Indochine 110–111
1:6 Malaisie et Indonésie Occidentale 112–113
1:3 Malaya, Singapour et Sumatra Septentrional 114
1:3 Java • Petites Îles de la Sonde 115
1:3 Philippines 116–117
1:12 Inde, Pakistan et Asie du Sud-Ouest 118–119
1:6 Inde Septentrionale et Pakistan 120–121
1:6 Inde Méridionale et Sri Lanka 122
1:3 Punjab et Cachemire 123
1:3 Plaine du Gange et Népal 124–125
1:1 Calcutta - Dhaka - Jamshedpur 126–127
1:6 Le Moyen-Orient 128–129
1:3 Turquie et Chypre 130–131
1:1 Yerushalayim Dimashq (Jerusalem - Damascus) 132–133

Afrique

1:12 Afrique du Nord Occidentale 134–135
1:12 Afrique du Nord Orientale 136–137
1:12 Afrique Méridionale 138–139
1:6 Égypte et Soudan 140–141
1:1 Al-Qāhirah - As-Suways (Cairo - Suez) 142–143
1:6 Ethiopie, Somalie et Yemen 144–145
1:6 Libye et Tchad 146–147
1:6 Afrique du Nord-Ouest 148–149
1:6 Afrique Occidentale 150–151
1:6 Bassin du Congo, partie Occidentale 152–153
1:6 Afrique Orientale et Bassin du Congo, partie Orientale 154–155
1:6 Afrique Méridionale et Madagascar 156–157
1:3 Afrique du Sud 158–159

Australie/Océanie

1:12 Australie 160–161
1:6 Australie Occidentale et Centrale 162–163
1:6 Australie Septentrionale et Nouvelle Guinée 164–165
1:6 Australie Orientale 166–167
1:1 Perth • Adelaide 168
1:1 Melbourne - Geelong - Ballarat 169
1:1 Sydney - Newcastle 170
1:1 Brisbane • Canberra 171
1:3 Nouvelle Zélande 172–173
Echelles Variées
Îles du Pacifique 174–175

Amérique Anglo-Saxonne

1:12 Canada 176–177
1:12 États-Unis 178–179
1:6 Alaska et Yukon 180–181
1:6 Sud-Ouest du Canada 182–183
1:6 Canada Central, partie Méridionale 184–185
1:6 Sud-Est du Canada 186–187
1:3 Nord-Est des États-Unis 188–189
1:6 Région des Grands Lacs 190–191
1:6 Sud-Est des États-Unis 192–193
1:6 Vallée du Mississippi 194–195
1:6 Grandes Plaines, partie Méridionale 196–197
1:6 Grandes Plaines, partie Septentrionale 198–199
1:6 Montagnes Rocheuses, partie Méridionale 200–201
1:6 Nord-Ouest des États-Unis 202–203
1:6 Californie et Névada 204–205
1:1 Montréal - Québec 206

*Echelle en millions

1:1 Boston - New York - Albany 207
1:1 New York - Philadelphia - Washington - Norfolk 208–209
1:1 New York - Buffalo 210–211
1:1 Toronto - Ottawa 212–213
1:1 Pittsburgh - Cleveland - Detroit 214–215
1:1 Chicago - Detroit - Milwaukee 216–217
1:1 Indianapolis - Cincinnati - Louisville 218
1:1 St. Louis - Springfield 219
1:1 Miami - Tampa - Orlando 220–221
1:1 Houston - Dallas - Austin 222–223
1:1 Vancouver - Seattle - Portland 224–225
1:1 San Francisco - Reno - Bakersfield 226–227
1:1 Los Angeles - San Diego 228
Echelles Variées
Hawaï 229

Amérique Latine

1:12 Mexique, Amérique Centrale et Région des Caraïbes 230 –231
1:6 Mexique 232–233
1:3 Mexique Central 234–235
1:3 Amérique Centrale 236–237
1:6 Région des Caraïbes 238–239
Echelles Variées
Îles des Antilles 240–241
1:12 Amérique du Sud Septentrionale 242–243
1:12 Amérique du Sud Méridionale 244–245
1:6 Colombie, Équateur, Venezuela et Guyane 246–247
1:6 Pérou, Bolivie et Brésil Occidental 248–249
1:6 Nord-Est du Brésil 250–251
1:6 Argentine et Chili, parties Centrales 252–253
1:6 Argentine et Chili, parties Méridionales 254
1:6 Sud-Est du Brésil 255
1:1 Rio de Janeiro - São Paulo 256–257
1:1 Buenos Aires - Montevideo 258

CARTES DES ZONES MÉTROPOLITAINES (1:300 000)

Introduction 259
London 260
Paris 261
Manchester - Liverpool 262
Ruhr Area 263
Berlin • Wien • Budapest 264
Sankt Peterburg • Moskva 265
Madrid • Milano • Lisboa • Barcelona 266
Roma • Athínai • İstanbul • Tehrān 267
Tōkyō - Yokohama 268
Krung Thep (Bangkok) • Thanh Pho Ho Chi Minh (Saigon) • Jakarta • Shanghai • T'aipei • Manila 269
Ōsaka - Kōbe - Kyōto 270
Beijing (Peking) • Sŏul • Singapore • Hong Kong 271
Delhi • Bombay • Calcutta 272
Lagos • Kinshasa - Brazzaville • Al-Qāhirah (Cairo) • Johannesburg 273
Sydney • Melbourne 274
Montréal • Toronto 275
New York 276–277
Chicago 278
Cleveland • Pittsburgh 279
Los Angeles 280
Detroit - Windsor 281
San Francisco - Oakland - San Jose 282
Boston 283
Buffalo - Niagara Falls • Baltimore • Washington 284
Philadelphia 285
Ciudad de México • La Habana • Caracas • Lima • Santiago 286
Rio de Janeiro • São Paulo 287
Buenos Aires 288

* Echelle en millions

Lista de Mapas

MAPAS DO MUNDO, DOS OCEANOS E DOS CONTINENTES

* Introdução 1
1:75 Mundo: Político 2–3
1:75 Mundo: Físico 4–5
1:48 Oceanos Pacífico e Indico 6–7
1:48 Oceano Atlântico 8
1:24 Antártida 9
1:24 Europa e África 10–11
1:24 Ásia 12–13
1:24 Austrália e Oceania 14–15
1:24 América do Norte 16–17
1:24 América do Sul 18–19

MAPAS REGIONAIS

Introdução 20–21

Eurásia

1:12 Europa 22–23
1:6 Europa Setentrional 24–25
1:3 Escandinávia Meridional 26–27
1:3 Ilhas Britânicas 28–29
1:3 Europa Central 30–31
1:3 França e os Alpes 32–33
1:3 Espanha e Portugal 34–35
1:3 Itália 36–37
1:3 Europa Sul-oriental 38–39
1:1 Stockholm - Karlstad 40
1:1 København - Malmö - Kiel 41
1:1 London - Birmingham - Cardiff 42–43
1:1 Dublin - Manchester - Newcastle upon Tyne 44–45
1:1 Glasgow - Edinburgh - Aberdeen 46–47
1:1 Dublin - Belfast - Cork 48–49
1:1 Paris - London - Bruxelles 50–51
1:1 Amsterdam - Düsseldorf - Hamburg 52–53
1:1 Berlin - Hamburg - Praha 54–55
1:1 Bruxelles - Frankfurt - Stuttgart 56–57
1:1 Zürich - Genève - Strasbourg 58–59
1:1 Nürnberg - München 60
1:3 Wien - Brno - Linz 61
1:1 Lyon - Marseille - Milano 62–63
1:1 München - Venezia - Firenze 64–65
1:1 Roma - Firenze - Napoli 66–67
1:1 Napoli - Messina - Bari 68–69
1:1 Palermo - Catania - Messina 70
1:1 Cagliari - Sassari 71
1:12 Ásia do Norte Ocidental 72–73
1:12 Ásia do Norte Oriental 74–75
1:3 Regiões do Báltico e de Moscou 76–77
1:3 Ucrânia 78–79
1:3 Região do Volga 80–81
1:1 Moskva - Tula - Tver' 82
1:1 Doneck - Lugansk - Rostov 83
1:3 Cáucaso e Transcaucásia 84
1:3 Região do Taschkent 85
1:6 Rússia Central e Casaquistão 86–87
1:6 Região do Lago Baikal 88
1:6 Extremo Oriente Russo 89
1:12 China, Japão e Coréia 90–91
1:3 Japão 92–93
1:1 Tōkyō - Nagoya - Kyōto 94–95
1:1 Ōsaka - Hiroshima - Fukuoka 96–97
1:3 Nordeste da China e Coréia 98–99
1:3 Leste e Sudeste da China 100–101
1:6 China Interior 102–103
1:1 Shenyang -Fushun (Mukden - Fushun) 104
1:1 Beijing - Tianjin (Peking - Tientsin) 105
1:1 Shanghai - Nanjing (Shanghai - Nanking) 106
1:1 Chongqing - Chengdu (Chungking - Chengtu) 107
1:6 Sudeste Asiático 108–109
1:6 Birmânia, Tailândia e Indochina 110–111
1:6 Malásia e Indonésia Ocidental 112–113
1:3 Malaia, Cingapura e Sumatra Setentrional 114
1:3 Java • Ilhas Menores da Sonda 115
1:3 Filipinas 116–117
1:12 Índia, Paquistão e Ásia do Sudoeste 118–119
1:6 Índia Setentrional e Paquistão 120–121
1:6 Índia Meridional e Sri Lanka 122
1:3 Punjab e Cachemira 123
1:3 Planície do Ganges e Nepal 124–125
1:1 Calcutta - Dhaka - Jamshedpur 126–127
1:6 Oriente Médio 128–129
1:3 Turquia e Chipre 130–131
1:1 Yerushalayim - Dimashq (Jerusalem - Damascus) 132–133

África

1:12 África do Norte Ocidental 134–135
1:12 África do Norte Oriental 136–137
1:12 África Meridional 138–139
1:6 Egito e Sudão 140–141
1:1 Al-Qāhirah - As-Suways (Cairo - Suez) 142–143
1:6 Etiópia, Somália e Iêmen 144–145
1:6 Líbia e Tchad 146–147
1:6 África Norte-ocidental 148–149
1:6 África Ocidental 150–151
1:6 Bacia Ocidental do Congo 152–153
1:6 África Oriental e Bacia Oriental do Congo 154–155
1:6 África Meridional e Madagascar 156–157
1:3 África do Sul 158–159

Austrália/Oceania

1:12 Austrália 160–161
1:6 Austrália Ocidental e Central 162–163
1:6 Austrália Setentrional e Nova Guiné 164–165
1:6 Austrália Oriental 166–167
1:1 Perth • Adelaide 168
1:1 Melbourne - Geelong - Ballarat 169
1:1 Sydney - Newcastle 170
1:1 Brisbane • Canberra 171
1:3 Nova Zelândia 172–173
Várias Escalas
Ilhas do Pacífico 174–175

América Anglosaxônica

1:12 Canadá 176–177
1:12 Estados Unidos 178–179
1:6 Alasca e Yukon 180–181
1:6 Canadá: Sudoeste 182–183
1:6 Canadá Central, parte meridional 184–185
1:6 Canadá: Sudeste 186–187
1:3 Estados Unidos: Nordeste 188–189
1:6 Região dos Grandes Lagos 190–191
1:6 Estados Unidos: Sudeste 192–193
1:6 Vale do Mississippi 194–195
1:6 Grandes Planícies: zona meridional 196–197
1:6 Grandes Planícies: zona setentrional 198–199
1:6 Montanhas Rochosas: zona meridional 200–201
1:6 Noroeste dos Estados Unidos 202–203
1:6 Califórnia e Nevada 204–205
1:1 Montréal Québec 206
1:1 Boston - New York - Albany 207
1:1 New York - Philadelphia - Washington - Norfolk 208–209
1:1 New York - Buffalo 210–211
1:1 Toronto - Ottawa 212–213
1:1 Pittsburgh - Cleveland - Detroit 214–215
1:1 Chicago - Detroit - Milwaukee 216–217
1:1 Indianapolis - Cincinnati - Louisville 218
1:1 St. Louis - Springfield 219
1:1 Miami - Tampa - Orlando 220–221
1:1 Houston - Dallas - Austin 222–223
1:1 Vancouver - Seattle - Portland 224–225
1:1 San Francisco - Reno - Bakersfield 226–227
1:1 Los Angeles - San Diego 228
Várias Escalas
Havaí 229

América Latina

1:12 México, América Central e Antilhas 230–231
1:6 México 232–233
1:3 México Central 234–235
1:3 América Central 236–237
1:6 Região do Caribe 238–239
Várias Escalas
Ilhas do Caribe (Índias Ocidentais) 240–241
1:12 América do Sul: zona setentrional 242–243
1:12 América do Sul: zona meridional 244–245
1:6 Colômbia, Equador, Venezuela e Guiana 246–247
1:6 Peru, Bolívia e Brasil Ocidental 248–249
1:6 Brasil: Nordeste 250–251
1:6 Argentina e Chile: zonas centrais 252–253
1:6 Argentina e Chile: zonas meridionais 254
1:6 Brasil: Sudeste 255
1:1 Rio de Janeiro - São Paulo 256–257
1:1 Buenos Aires - Montevideo 258

MAPAS DAS ÁREAS METROPOLITANAS (1:300 000)

Introdução 259
London 260
Paris 261
Manchester - Liverpool 262
Ruhr Area 263
Berlin • Wien • Budapest 264
Sankt Peterburg • Moskva 265
Madrid • Milano • Lisboa • Barcelona 266
Roma • Athínai • İstanbul • Tehrān 267
Tōkyō - Yokohama 268
Krung Thep (Bangkok) • Thanh Pho Ho Chi Minh (Saigon) • Jakarta • Shanghai • T'aipei • Manila 69
Ōsaka - Kōbe - Kyōto 270
Beijing (Peking) • Sŏul • Singapore • Hong Kong 271
Delhi • Bombay • Calcutta 272
Lagos • Kinshasa - Brazzaville • Al-Qāhirah (Cairo) • Johannesburg 273
Sydney • Melbourne 274
Montréal • Toronto 275
New York 276–277
Chicago 278
Cleveland • Pittsburgh 279
Los Angeles 280
Detroit - Windsor 281
San Francisco - Oakland - San Jose 282
Boston 283
Buffalo - Niagara Falls • Baltimore • Washington 284
Philadelphia 285
Rio de Janeiro • São Paulo 287
Buenos Aires 288

*Escalas em milhões

Legend to Maps/Zeichenerklärung
Leyendas Para Mapas/Légende des Cartes/Legendas dos Mapas

The design and color of the map symbols are consistent throughout the Regional and Metropolitan Area maps, although the size of the symbol varies with scale. An asterisk marks those symbols which appear only on the 1:300,000 scale maps. Symbols for inhabited localities, boundaries, and capitals are given on page xi.

The symbol 80-81→ in the margin of a map directs the reader to a map of the adjoining area.

A separate legend on page 1 identifies the land and submarine features which appear on the World, Ocean, and Continent maps.

Der Entwurf und die Farbe der Kartensymbole sind einheitlich für alle Regionalkarten und Karten von Stadtregionen, während die Grösse des Symbols sich mit dem Massstab ändert. Ein Stern kennzeichnet diejenigen Symbole, welche nur auf den Karten im Massstab 1:300 000 erscheinen. Symbole für bewohnte Orte, für Grenzen und Hauptstädte sind auf Seite xi angeführt.

Kennzeichen 80-81→ am Rande einer Karte ist ein Hinweis für den Leser, die Karte eines angrenzenden Gebietes nachzuschlagen.

Eine andere Legende auf Seite 1 identifiziert die Land- und untermeerischen Phänomene, die auf den Weltkarten, Karten der Ozeane und Erdteile erscheinen.

El diseño y el color de los símbolos cartográficos son uniformes para todas los mapas regionales y de las áreas metropolitanas, aunque el tamaño del símbolo varía según la escala. Un asterisco distingue los símbolos que aparecen sólo en los mapas a 1:300 000. Los símbolos de lugares poblados, de límites y de capitales se hallan en la página xi.

El símbolo 80-81→ al margen de un mapa dirige al lector a un mapa del área adyacente.

Otra leyenda, en la página 1, identifica la topografía terrestre y submarina que se encuentra en los mapas del Mundo, Océanos y Continentes.

La couleur et la forme des symboles cartographiques des cartes régionales et des cartes des zones métropolitaines sont identiques, bien que la grandeur des signes varie selon l'échelle. Un astérisque accompagne les symboles qui n'apparaissent que sur les cartes au 1:300 000. La légende des signes conventionnels pour les lieux habités, les frontières et les capitales se trouve à la page xi.

Le symbole 80-81→ en marge d'une carte renvoie le lecteur à une carte de la région voisine.

Pour les cartes du monde, des océans et des continents une légende séparée, à la page 1, donne le sens des symboles représentant les paysages continentaux et les formes de relief sous-marin.

A cor e a forma dos símbolos cartográficos dos mapas regionais e das áreas metropolitanas são idênticos, ainda que a dimensão do símbolo varie segundo a escala. Um asterisco distingue os símbolos que só aparecem nos mapas da escala de 1:300 000. As legendas dos símbolos convencionais dos lugares povoados, fronteiras e capitais encontram-se à pág. xi.

O símbolo 80-81→ à margem de um mapa, remete o leitor a um mapa da região vizinha.

Nos mapas do mundo, dos oceanos e dos continentes uma legenda separada, na pág. 1, indica o sentido dos símbolos representativos das paisagens continentais e das formas do relevo submarino.

Hydrographic Features / Hydrographische Objekte / Elementos Hidrográficos
Données Hydrographiques / Acidentes Hidrográficos

Symbol	Meaning
	Shoreline/Uferlinie **Línea costanera/Trait de côte** **Linha costeira**
	Undefined or Fluctuating Shoreline **Unbestimmte oder Veränderliche Uferlinie** **Línea costanera indefinida o fluctuante** **Trait de côte indéfini ou fluctuant** **Linha costeira indefinida ou flutuante**
Amur	**River, Stream/Fluss, Strom** **Río, Corriente/Rivière, Cours d'eau** **Rio, curso d'água**
	Intermittent Stream/Periodischer Fluss **Corriente intermitente/Cours d'eau périodique** **Rio, curso d'água intermitente**
SALTO ANGEL	**Rapids, Falls/Stromschnellen, Wasserfälle** **Rápidos, Cascadas/Rapides, Chutes d'eau** **Corredeiras, quedas d'água**
764 ▽	**Depth of Water/Wassertiefe** **Profundidad del agua/Profondeur bathymétrique** **Profundidade da água**
8428 ▼	**Greatest Depth** (Atlantic, Indian, Pacific oceans) **Grösste Tiefe** (Atlantischer, Indischer, Pazifischer Ozean) **Profundidad más grande** (Océanos Atlántico, Índico, Pacífico) **Profondeur maximum** (océans Atlantique, Indien, Pacifique) **Profundidade máxima** (oceanos Atlântico, Índico, Pacífico)
Canal du Midi	**Navigable Canal/Schiffbarer Kanal** **Canal navegable/Canal navigable** **Canal navegável**
	Irrigation or Drainage Canal **Be- oder Entwässerungskanal** **Canal de irrigación o desagüe** **Canal d'irrigation ou de drainage** **Canal de irrigação ou drenagem**
Los Angeles Aqueduct	**Aqueduct/Aquädukt** **Acueducto/Aqueduc** **Aqueduto**
	Pier, Breakwater/Landungsbrücke, Wellenbrecher **Embarcadero, Rompeolas/Jetée, Brise-lames** **Cais, Quebra-mar**
GREAT BARRIER REEF	**Reef/Riff** **Arrecife/Récif** **Recife**
Kumdah∘	**Uninhabited Oasis/Unbewohnte Oase** **Oasis deshabitado/Oasis inhabitée** **Oásis desabitado**
L. Victoria	**Lake, Reservoir/See, Stausee** **Lago, Embalse/Lac, Réservoir** **Lago, reservatório** (represa)
	Intermittent Lake, Reservoir **Periodischer See, Stausee** **Lago o Embalse intermitente** **Lac ou Réservoir périodique** **Lago, reservatório** (represa) **intermitente**
Tuz Gölü	**Salt Lake/Salzsee** **Lago salado/Lac salé** **Lago salgado**
	Dry Lake Bed/Trockener Seeboden **Lecho de lago seco/Fond de lac asséché** **Leito de lago seco**
The Everglades	**Swamp/Sumpf** **Pantano/Marais** **Pântano**
RIMO GLACIER	**Glacier/Gletscher** **Glaciar/Glacier** **Geleira**
(395)	**Lake Surface Elevation** **Seehöhe** **Elevación del lago** **Cote du niveau du lac** **Altitude do nível do lago**

Topographic Features / Topographische Objekte / Elementos Topográficos
Données Topographiques / Acidentes Topográficos

Symbol	Meaning
Matterhorn 4478 △	**Elevation Above Sea Level** **Höhe über dem Meeresspiegel** **Elevatión sobre el nivel del mar** **Cote au-dessus du niveau de la mer** **Altitude acima do nível do mar**
76 ▽	**Elevation Below Sea Level** **Höhe unter dem Meeresspiegel** **Elevación bajo del nivel del mar** **Cote au-dessous du niveau de la mer** **Altitude abaixo do nível do mar**
Mount Cook 3764 ▲	**Highest Elevation in Country** **Höchster Punkt des Landes** **Elevación más alta en el país** **Cote la plus élevée d'un pays** **Altitude mais elevada de um país**
133 ▼	**Lowest Elevation in Country** **Tiefster Punkt des Landes** **Elevación más baja en el país** **Cote la plus basse d'un pays** **Altitude mais baixa de um país**
(106)	**Elevation of City** **Höhenangabe einer Stadt** **Elevación de ciudad** **Altitude d'une ville** **Altitude de uma cidade**
Khyber Pass 1067	**Mountain Pass/Pass** **Paso/Col de montagne** **Passo** (de montanha)
*	**Rock/Fels** **Roca/Rocher** **Rocha**
	Lava/Lava **Lava/Lave** **Lava**
	Sand Area/Sandgebiet **Area de arena/Région sableuse, Erg** **Região arenosa, Erg**
	Salt Flat/Salzebene **Salar/Dépression salée** **Depressão salgada**
A N D E S KUNLUN SHAN	**Mountain Range, Plateau, Valley, etc.** **Gebirge, Hochebene, Tal, usw.** **Sierra, Meseta, Valle, etc.** **Chaîne de montagnes, Plateau, Vallée, etc.** **Cadeia de montanhas. Planalto, Vale etc.**
BAFFIN ISLAND NUNIVAK ISLAND	**Island** **Insel** **Isla** **Île** **Ilha**
POLUOSTROV KAMČATKA CABO DE HORNOS	**Peninsula, Cape, Point, etc.** **Halbinsel, Kap, Landspitze, usw.** **Península, Cabo, Punta, etc.** **Péninsule, Cap, Pointe, etc.** **Península, Cabo, Ponta etc.**

Elevations and depths are given in meters
Höhen und Tiefen sind in Metern angegeben
Elevaciones y profundidades se dan en metros
Cotes et profondeurs sont indiquées en mètres
Altitudes e profundidades são apresentadas em metros

Highest Elevation and Lowest Elevation of a continent are underlined
Höchster und tiefster Punkt innerhalb eines Erdteils sind unterstrichen
Elevación más alta y más baja de un continente se subrayan
La cote la plus haute et la cote la plus basse d'un continent sont soulignées
As altitudes mais e menos elevadas de um continente são sublinhadas

Inhabited Localities / Bewohnte Orte / Lugares Poblados / Lieux Habités / Lugares Habitados

The symbol represents the number of inhabitants within the locality/Die Signatur entspricht der Einwohnerzahl des Ortes
El símbolo representa el número de habitantes dentro del lugar/Le symbole représente le nombre d'habitants de la localité
O símbolo representa o número de habitantes do lugar

1:300,000 / 1:3,000,000 / 1:1,000,000 / 1:6,000,000	1:12,000,000	1:24,000,000 / 1:48,000,000
0—10,000	0—50,000	0—100,000
10,000—25,000	50,000—100,000	100,000—1,500,000
25,000—100,000	100,000—250,000	>1,500,000
100,000—250,000	250,000—1,000,000	
250,000—1,000,000	>1,000,000	
>1,000,000		

The size of type indicates the relative economic and political importance of the locality
Die Schriftgrösse entspricht der relativen wirtschaftlichen und politischen Bedeutung des Ortes
El tamaño del tipo de imprenta indica la relativa importancia económica y política del lugar
La dimension des caractères indique l'importance économique et politique relative d'une localité
A dimensão dos caracteres tipográficos indica a importância econômica e política relativa do lugar

Écommoy Lisieux Rouen
Trouville Orléans PARIS

Hollywood / Westminster — Section of a City, Neighborhood/Stadtteil, Nachbarschaft
Sección de una ciudad, Barrio/Arrondissement, Quartier
Seção de uma cidade, Bairro

Northland Center — * Major Shopping Center/Haupteinkaufszentrum/Mercado principal
Centre commercial important/Centro comercial importante

BYRD — Scientific Station/Wissenschaftliche Station/Estación científica
Station scientifique/Estação científica

Bi'r Safājah — Inhabited Oasis/Bewohnte Oase/Oasis habitado
Oasis habitée/Oásis habitado

Kumdah — Uninhabited Oasis/Unbewohnte Oase/Oasis deshabitado
Oasis inhabitée/Oásis desabitado

Urban Area (area of continuous industrial, commercial, and residential development)
Stadtgebiet (ausgedehntes industrie-, Geschäfts- und Wohngebiet)
Zona urbanizada (área de desarrollo industrial, comercial y residencial)
Zone urbanisée (zone d'occupation continue par des industries, des commerces, des habitations)
Zona urbanizada (área de ocupação contínua por indústrias, estabelecimentos comerciais e habitações)

* Major Industrial Area/Hauptindustriegebiet/Zona principal industrial
Région industrielle importante/Zona industrial importante

* Wooded Area/Wald/Área de bosque
Région boisée/Área verde

* Local Park or Recreational Area/Park oder Erholungsgebiet
Parque municipal o área de recreo/Parc municipal ou zone de loisirs
Parque municipal ou área de lazer

Political Boundaries / Politische Grenzen / Límites Políticos / Frontières Politiques / Fronteiras e Limites

International (First-order political unit) /**Staatsgrenze** (Politische Einheit erster Ordnung)
Internacionales (Unidad política de primer orden) /**Internationales** (Entités politiques de premier ordre)
Internacionais (Unidade política de primeiro nível)

1:1,000,000 — 1:300,000 / 1:3,000,000 / 1:6,000,000 — 1:24,000,000 / 1:48,000,000 — 1:12,000,000

HUNGARY

Demarcated, Undemarcated, and Administrative
Markiert, unmarkiert, verwaltungstechnisch
Demarcado, No demarcado, y Administrativo
Délimitées, Non-délimitées, Administratives
Delimitados, Não delimitados, Administrativos

Disputed de facto/Umstritten de facto
Disputado de hecho/Contestées de facto
Contestados de fato

Disputed de jure/Umstritten de jure
Disputado de derecho/Contestées de jure
Contestados de direito

Indefinite or Undefined/Unklar oder Unbestimmt
Indefinido o No determinado/Imprécises ou Non définies
Imprecisos ou Não definidos

Demarcation Line/Demarkationslinie
Línea de demarcación/Ligne de démarcation
Linha de demarcação

Capitals of Political Units
Hauptstädte politischer Einheiten
Capitales de Unidades Políticas
Capitales d'Entités Politiques
Capitais de Unidades Políticas

BUDAPEST — Independent Nation
Unabhängiger Staat
Nación independiente
État indépendant
Estado independente

Cayenne — Dependency (Colony, protectorate, etc.)
Abhängiges Gebiet (Kolonie, Protektorat, usw.)
Dependencia (Colonia, protectorado, etc.)
Territoire dépendant (Colonie, protectorat, etc.)
Dependência (Colônia, protetorado, etc.)

GALAPAGOS (Ecuador) — Administering Country
Verwaltender Staat
País administrador
Pays administrateur
País administrador

Internal/Verwaltungsgrenze/Internos/Intérieures/Limites Internos

PERNAMBUCO — **State, Province, etc.** (Second-order political unit)
Land, Provinz, usw. (Politische Einheit zweiter Ordnung)
Estado, Provincia, etc. (Unidad política de segundo orden)
État, Province, etc. (Subdivision administrative de deuxième ordre)
Estado, Província, etc. (Unidade política de segundo nível)

SIENA / WESTCHESTER — **County, Oblast, etc.** (Third-order political unit)/**Grafschaft, Oblast, usw.** (Politische Einheit dritter Ordnung)
Condado, Oblast, etc. (Unidad política de tercer orden)
Comté, Oblast, etc. (Subdivision administrative de troisième ordre)
Condado, Oblast, etc. (Unidade política de terceiro nível)

ISERLOHN — **Okrug, Kreis, etc.** (Fourth-order political unit)/**Okrug, Kreis, usw.** (Politische Einheit vierter Ordnung)
Okrug, Kreis, etc. (Unidad política de cuarto orden)
Okrug, Kreis, etc. (Subdivision administrative de quatrième ordre)
Okrug, Kreis, etc. (Unidade política de quarto nível)

City or Municipality (may appear in combination with another boundary symbol)
Stadt oder Gemeinde (kann zusammen mit einem anderen Begrenzungssymbol erscheinen)
Ciudad o Municipio (puede aparecer en combinación con otro símbolo de límite)
Ville ou Municipalité (peut paraître en combinaison avec un autre symbole de limites politiques)
Cidade ou Municipalidade (Pode aparecer em combinação com outro símbolo de limite político)

Recife — State, Province, etc./Land, Provinz, usw.
Estado, Provincia, etc./État, Province, etc.
Estado, Província, etc.

Ambāla / Johnstown — County, Oblast, etc./Grafschaft, Oblast, usw.
Condado, Oblast, etc./Comté, Oblast, etc.
Condado, Oblast, etc.

Iserlohn — Okrug, Kreis, etc./Okrug, Kreis, usw.
Okrug, Kreis, etc./Okrug, Kreis, etc.
Okrug, Kreis, etc.

NORMANDIE — **Historical Region** (No boundaries indicated)
Historische Landschaft (Grenzen werden nicht gezeigt)
Región Histórica (Sin indicación de límites)
Région Historique (Sans indication de frontières)
Região Histórica (Sem indicação de fronteiras)

Legend to Maps/Zeichenerklärung
Leyendas Para Mapas/Légende des Cartes/Legendas dos Mapas

Transportation / Verkehr / Transporte / Transports / Transporte

Road/Strasse/Camino/Route/Rodovia	1:300,000	1:1,000,000	1:3,000,000 1:6,000,000	1:12,000,000
Primary/Erster Ordnung/Principal/de premier ordre/Principal	PASSAIC EXPWY. (I-80)	PENNSYLVANIA TURNPIKE		
Secondary/Zweiter Ordnung/Secundario/de second ordre/Secundária	BERLINER RING			
Tertiary/Dritter Ordnung/Terciario/de troisième ordre/Terciária				
Minor Road, Trail/Weg, Pfad Rodera, Vereda/Route secondaire, Piste/Caminho, trilha				

Railway/Eisenbahn/Ferrocarril/Voie ferrée/Ferrovia				
Primary/Hauptbahn/Principal/Principale/Principal	CANADIAN NATIONAL	SANTA FE		
Secondary/Sonstige Bahn/Secundario/Secondaire/Secundária				
*Rapid Transit/Schnellverkehr/Tránsito rápido/Métro/Trânsito rápido (metrô)				
Airport/Flughafen/Aeropuerto/Aéroport/Aeroporto	LONDON (HEATHROW) AIRPORT	DULLES INTERNATIONAL AIRPORT		
*Rail or Air Terminal/Bahnhof oder Flughafengebäude Terminal ferroviaria o aéro/Gare ou aérogare Terminal ferroviário ou aéreo (estação)	SÜD-BAHNHOF			

REICHS-BRÜCKE — Bridge/Brücke/Puente/Pont/Ponte

GREAT ST. BERNARD TUNNEL — Tunnel/Tunnel/Túnel/Tunnel/Túnel

Houston Ship Channel — Shipping Channel/Schiffahrtsrinne
Canal maritimo/Chenal maritime
Canal marítimo

Canal du Midi — Navigable Canal/Schiffbarer Kanal
Canal navegable/Canal navigable
Canal navegável

Intracoastal Waterway/Küstenschiffahrtsweg
Via fluvial Intracostera/Canal côtier
Via costeira interna

TO MALMÖ — Ferry/Fähre
Balsadera/Bac
Balsa

Miscellaneous Cultural Features / Sonstige Objekte / Elementos Culturales Misceláneos
Éléments Culturels Divers / Acidentes Culturais Diversos

PARQUE NACIONAL LANÍN — National or State Park or Monument
National- oder Naturpark oder Denkmal
Parque o Monumento nacional o provincial
Parc ou Monument national ou régional
Parque ou Monumento nacional ou regional

EDISON NAT. HIST. SITE — National or State Historic(al) Site, Memorial
Historische Stätte, Gedenkstätte
Sitio histórico nacional o provincial, Monumento
Site historique national ou régional, Mémorial
Sitio histórico nacional ou regional, Monumento histórico

SEMINOLE IND. RES. — Indian Reservation/Indianerreservation
Reserva de indios/Réserve indienne
Reserva indígena

FORT DIX — Military Installation/Militäranlage
Instalación militar/Installation militaire
Instalação militar

GREENWOOD CEMETERY — * Cemetery/Friedhof
Cementerio/Cimetière/Cemitério

SORBONNE — Point of Interest (Battlefield, museum, temple, university, etc.)
Sehenswürdigkeit (Schlachtfeld, Museum, Tempel, Universität, usw.)
Punto de interés (Campo de batalla, museo, templo, universidad, etc.)
Curiosité (Champ de bataille, musée, temple, université, etc.)
Pontos de interesse (Campo de batalha, museu, templo, universidade, etc.)

STEPHANSDOM — Church, Monastery/Kirche, Kloster
Iglesia, Monasterio/Église, Monastère
Igreja, Mosteiro

UXMAL — Ruins/Ruinen/Ruinas/Ruines/Ruínas

WINDSOR CASTLE — Castle/Burg, Schloss/Castillo/Château/Castelo

* Lighthouse/Leuchtturm
Faro/Phare/Farol

ASWĀN DAM — Dam/Damm/Presa/Barrage
Represa (barragem)

* Lock/Schleuse/Esclusa
Écluse/Eclusa

Crib — * Water Intake Crib/Wasseraufnahmestation
Toma de agua/Prise d'eau/Captação de água

Quarry or Surface Mine
Steinbruch oder Tagebau
Cantera o Mina de hoyo abierto
Carrière ou Mine à ciel ouvert
Pedreira ou mina a céu aberto

Subsurface Mine/Bergwerk
Mina subterránea/Mine souterraine
Mina subterrânea

* Oil Well/Ölbohrturm
Pozo de petróleo/Puits de pétrole
Poço de petróleo

Metric-English Equivalents / Umrechnung metrischer Masse in englische Masse / Métrico-Equivalentes Ingleses
Equivalences métriques des mesures anglaises / Equivalentes métricos das medidas inglesas

Areas represented by one square centimeter at various map scales
Flächen die einem cm² in den verschiedenen Kartenmassstäben entsprechen
Áreas representados por un centímetro cuadrado a varias escalas de mapas
Surface représentée par un cm² aux échelles indiquées
Áreas representadas por cm² nas escalas indicadas nos mapas

1:300,000 9 km² 3.48 square miles	1:6,000,000 3,600 km² 1,390 square miles	1:48,000,000 230,400 km² 88,934 square miles
1:1,000,000 100 km² 39 square miles	1:12,000,000 14,400 km² 5,558 square miles	
1:3,000,000 900 km² 348 square miles	1:24,000,000 57,600 km² 22,234 square miles	

Meter=3.28 feet — Meter² (m²)=10.76 square feet

Kilometer=0.62 mile — Kilometer² (km²)=0.39 square mile

Elevation tints shown only on 1:3,000,000 and 1:6,000,000 scale maps
Höhenschichten erscheinen nur auf Karten im Massstab 1:3 000 000 und 1:6 000 000
Se indica las tintas de elevación sólo en los mapas de escala 1:3 000 000 y 1:6 000 000
Teintes hypsométriques exprimées seulement sur cartes à 1:3 000 000 et 1:6 000 000
Indicaram-se as graduações de cor hipsométricas somente nos mapas de escalas 1:3 000 000 e 1:6 000 000

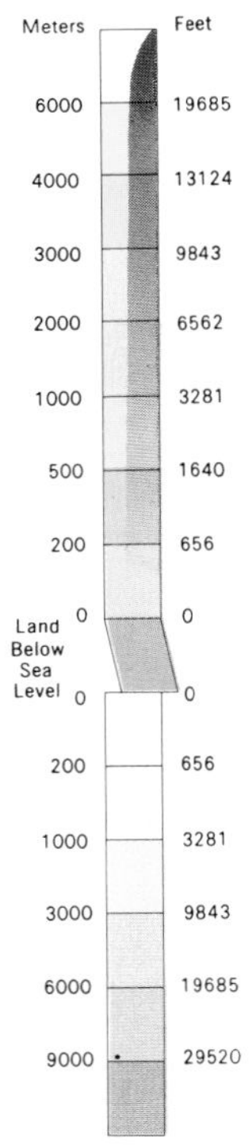

Meters
Feet
6000
19685
4000
13124
3000
9843
2000
6562
1000
3281
500
1640
200
656
0
0
Land Below Sea Level
0
0
200
656
1000
3281
3000
9843
6000
19685
9000
29520

Alternate Names / Alternative Namensformen / Nombres Alternativos
Variantes Toponymiques / Variantes Toponímicas

MOSKVA
MOSCOW

Basel
Bâle

English or second official language names are shown in reduced size lettering
Englische Namen oder Namen in einer zweiten offiziellen Sprache erscheinen in kleineren Schriftgrössen
Los nombres en inglés o un segundo idioma oficial se muestran en tipo de imprenta mas pequeño
Les toponymes en anglais ou dans la seconde langue officielle sont indiqués en caractères plus petits
Os topônimos em inglês ou num segundo idioma oficial aparecem em tipologia menor

VOLGOGRAD
(STALINGRAD)

Ventura
(San Buenaventura)

Historical or other alternates in the local language are shown in parentheses
Historische oder alternative Namensformen einheimischen Sprache erscheinen in Klammern
Los nombres históricos y alternativos locales se muestran en paréntesis
Les noms historiques de lieux ou les variantes toponymiques locales sont mis entre parenthèses
Os topônimos históricos ou as variantes toponímicas locais aparecem entre parênteses

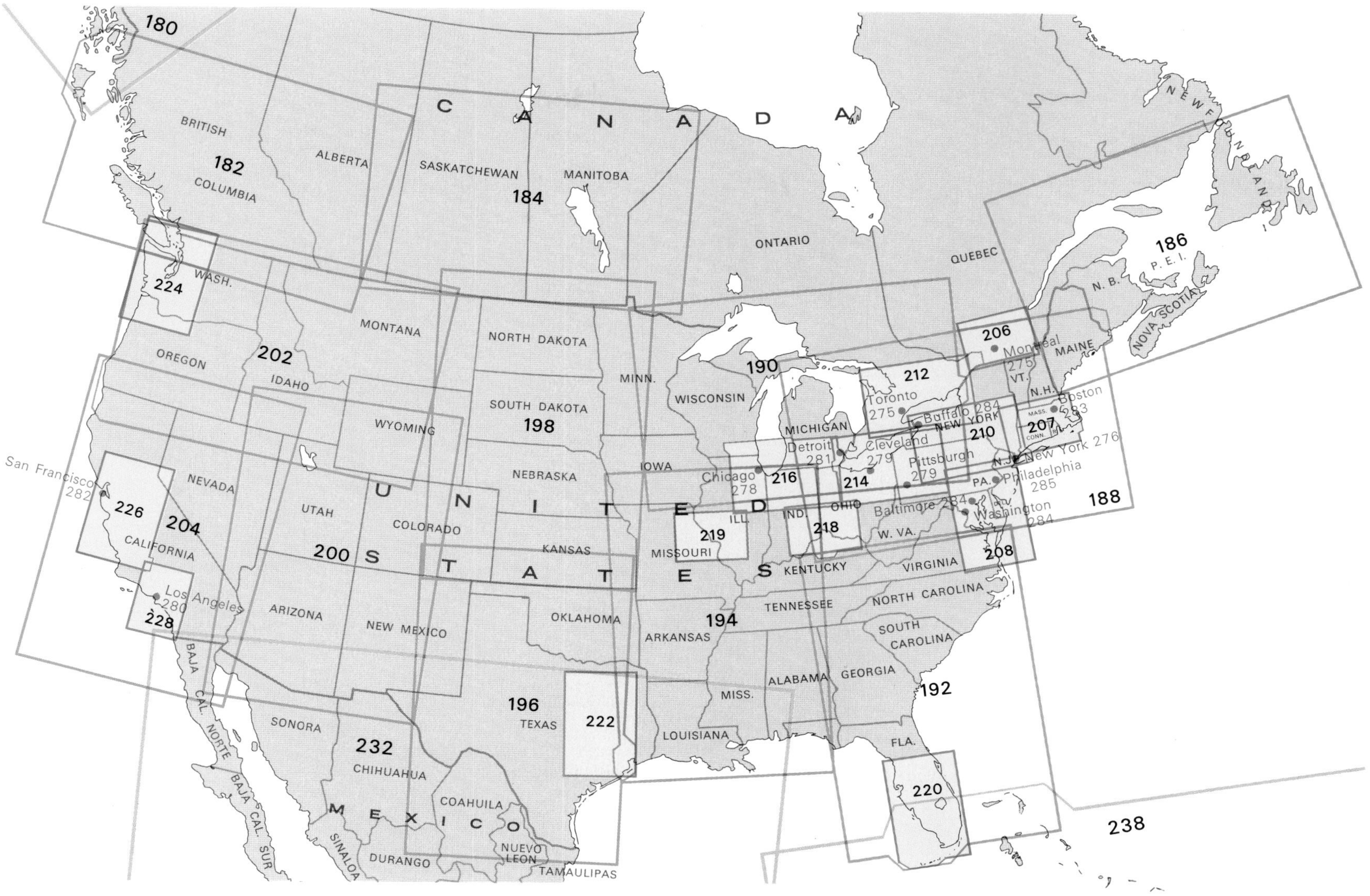
180
CANADA
BRITISH COLUMBIA
182
ALBERTA
SASKATCHEWAN
184
MANITOBA
NEWFOUNDLAND
ONTARIO
QUEBEC
186
P.E.I.
N.B.
NOVA SCOTIA
WASH.
224
MONTANA
NORTH DAKOTA
OREGON
202
IDAHO
206
Montréal 275
VT.
MAINE
190
MINN.
WISCONSIN
212
Toronto 275
N.H.
Boston 283
SOUTH DAKOTA
198
WYOMING
MICHIGAN
Buffalo 284
NEW YORK
210
MASS.
207
CONN.
Detroit 281
Cleveland 279
New York 276
Pittsburgh 279
N.J.
Philadelphia 285
San Francisco 282
NEVADA
NEBRASKA
IOWA
Chicago 278
216
214
PA.
188
226
204
UTAH
COLORADO
UNITED STATES
ILL.
IND.
OHIO
Baltimore 284
Washington 284
219
218
W. VA.
CALIFORNIA
200
KANSAS
MISSOURI
KENTUCKY
VIRGINIA
208
Los Angeles 280
228
ARIZONA
NEW MEXICO
OKLAHOMA
194
TENNESSEE
NORTH CAROLINA
ARKANSAS
SOUTH CAROLINA
BAJA CAL. NORTE
ALABAMA
GEORGIA
MISS.
192
196
TEXAS
222
SONORA
232
CHIHUAHUA
LOUISIANA
FLA.
220
BAJA CAL. SUR
MEXICO
COAHUILA
SINALOA
DURANGO
NUEVO LEON
TAMAULIPAS
238

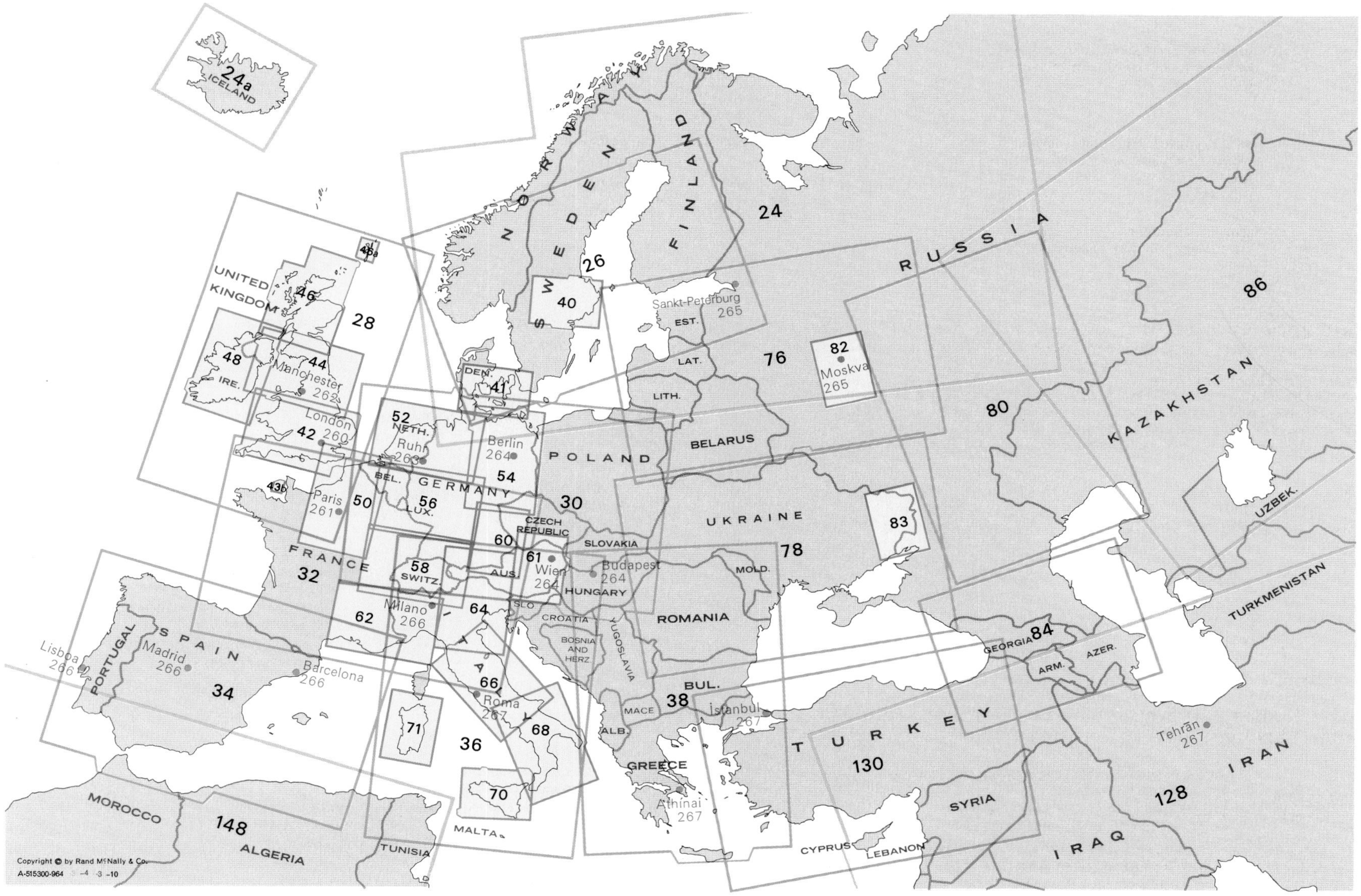
24a
ICELAND
NORWAY
SWEDEN
FINLAND
24
26
40
48a
UNITED KINGDOM
46
28
Sankt-Peterburg 265
EST.
RUSSIA
86
48
IRE.
44
Manchester 262
LAT.
76
82
Moskva 265
DEN.
41
LITH.
80
KAZAKHSTAN
London 260
52
NETH.
Ruhr 263
42
Berlin 264
POLAND
BELARUS
54
BEL.
GERMANY
43b
Paris 261
50
56
LUX.
30
UKRAINE
83
CZECH REPUBLIC
UZBEK.
FRANCE
32
58
SWITZ.
60
61
SLOVAKIA
Wien 264
AUS.
Budapest 264
HUNGARY
78
MOLD.
SLO.
CROATIA
ROMANIA
TURKMENISTAN
62
Milano 266
64
BOSNIA AND HERZ.
YUGOSLAVIA
GEORGIA
84
ARM.
AZER.
Lisboa 266
PORTUGAL
SPAIN
Madrid 266
Barcelona 266
ITALY
66
Roma 267
BUL.
38
MACE.
İstanbul 267
34
71
36
68
ALB.
TURKEY
130
Tehrān 267
GREECE
IRAN
70
Athínai 267
SYRIA
128
MOROCCO
148
ALGERIA
TUNISIA
MALTA
CYPRUS
LEBANON
IRAQ

181a
180
ALASKA
GREENLAND
ICELAND
24a
Atlantic
Ocean
182
184
186
CANADA
202
198
190
188
204
200
UNITED STATES
194
196
192
BERMUDA
240a
BAHAMAS
240b
229b 229c
229a
229d
HAWAII
232
MEXICO
234
Ciudad de México
286
240p
238
240m
240c
241o
240d
241f
241g
241n
240e
241h
241s
241k
241r
241q
Caribbean Sea
HONDURAS
GUAT.
SALVADOR
NICARAGUA
236
COSTA RICA
Caracas
286
VENEZUELA
Pacific
Ocean
246
COLOMBIA
ECUADOR
GALAPAGOS ISLANDS
246a
250
BRAZIL
Lima
286
PERU
248
BOLIVIA
255
SAMOA ISLANDS
175a
174y
PARAGUAY
São Paulo
287
256
Rio de Janeiro
287
252
URUGUAY
258
Santiago
286
Buenos Aires
288
CHILE
ARGENTINA
254
AZORES
148a
CAPE VERDE
150a
UNITED KINGDOM
28
26
30
32
FRANCE
SPAIN
34
36
MOROCCO
148
ALGERIA
LIBYA
WESTERN SAHARA
MAURITANIA
MALI
NIGER
146
SENEGAL
150
CHAD
GUINEA
NIGERIA
IVORY COAST
GHANA
Lagos
273
CAMEROON
GABON
CONGO
152
ANGOLA

MAP COVERAGE / KARTENAUSSCHNITTE
CONTENIDO DEL ATLAS / TABLEAU D'ASSEMBLAGE
ABRANGÊNCIA DO MAPA

Map Scale

Manila 269 • 1:300,000

1:1,000,000 | 1:6,000,000

1:3,000,000 | 1:12,000,000

148 **Page Reference / Seitenangabe**
Página de Referencia / Page de Référence / Página de Referência

Enlarged maps of Anglo-America and Europe on page xiii.
Vergrösserte Karten von Anglo-Amerika und Europa auf Seite xiii.
Mapas aumentados de América Anglosajona y Europa, página xiii.
Cartes à grande échelle de l'Amérique anglo-saxonne et de l'Europe à la page xiii.
Mapas ampliados da América Anglo-saxônica e da Europa, página xiii.

World, Ocean, and Continent maps on pages 2-19.
Weltkarten, Karten der Ozeane und Erdteile auf Seiten 2-19.
Mapas del Mundo, Océanos y Continentes, páginas 2-19.
Cartes du Monde, des Océans et des Continents aux pages 2-19.
Mapas do Mundo, dos Oceanos e dos Continentes, páginas 2-19.

Additional Pacific Ocean Island maps on pages 174-175.
Zusätzliche Karten der Inseln des Pazifischen Ozeans auf Seite 174-175.
Mapas adicionales de las Islas del Océano Pacifico, páginas174-175.
Cartes supplémentaires des Îles de l'Océan Pacifique aux pages 174-175.
Mapas suplementares das ilhas do Oceano Pacífico, páginas 174-175.

RUSSIA
Pacific Ocean
24
76
80
86
88
89
92a
92
94
96
KAZAKHSTAN
MONGOLIA
KOREA
104
105
98
Beijing (Peking) 271
93b
UKRAINE
78
Black Sea
Caspian Sea
84
85
UZBEKISTAN
TURKMENISTAN
KYRG.
TAJIKISTAN
CHINA
Shanghai 269
106
100
102
107
174m
175d
TURKEY
130
SYRIA
IRAQ
128
IRAN
Tehrān 267
AFGHANISTAN
123
120
PAKISTAN
Delhi 272
NEPAL
124
Taipei 269
TAIWAN
Hong Kong
132
Al-Qāhirah (Cairo) 273
142
EGYPT
KUWAIT
SAUDI ARABIA
INDIA
Calcutta 272
126
BURMA
LAOS
VIETNAM
THAILAND
Krung Thep (Bangkok) 269
CAMBODIA
Thanh-pho Ho Chi Minh (Saigon) 269
Manila 269
116
PHILIPPINES
175c
TRUK ISLANDS
175b
PALAU ISLANDS
Red Sea
OMAN
140
SUDAN
ERITREA
YEMEN
DJIBOUTI
Bombay 272
122
110
SRI LANKA
144
ETHIOPIA
SOMALIA
MALAYSIA
BRUNEI
114
Singapore 271
BORNEO
112
CELEBES
SUMATRA
INDONESIA
PAPUA NEW GUINEA
NEW GUINEA
KENYA
UGANDA
RWANDA
BURUNDI
Jakarta 269
115a
JAVA
LESSER SUNDA ISLANDS
115b
SOLOMON ISLANDS
175e
164
TANZANIA
154
Indian Ocean
COMOROS
157a
ZAMBIA
MALAWI
MOZAMBIQUE
ZIMBABWE
MADAGASCAR
157b
157c
MAURITIUS
RÉUNION
VANUATU
175f
175g
FIJI
NEW CALEDONIA
AUSTRALIA
162
171a
166
168a
168b
170
Sydney 274
171b
169
Melbourne
TASMANIA
SWAZILAND
LESOTHO
158
NEW ZEALAND
172

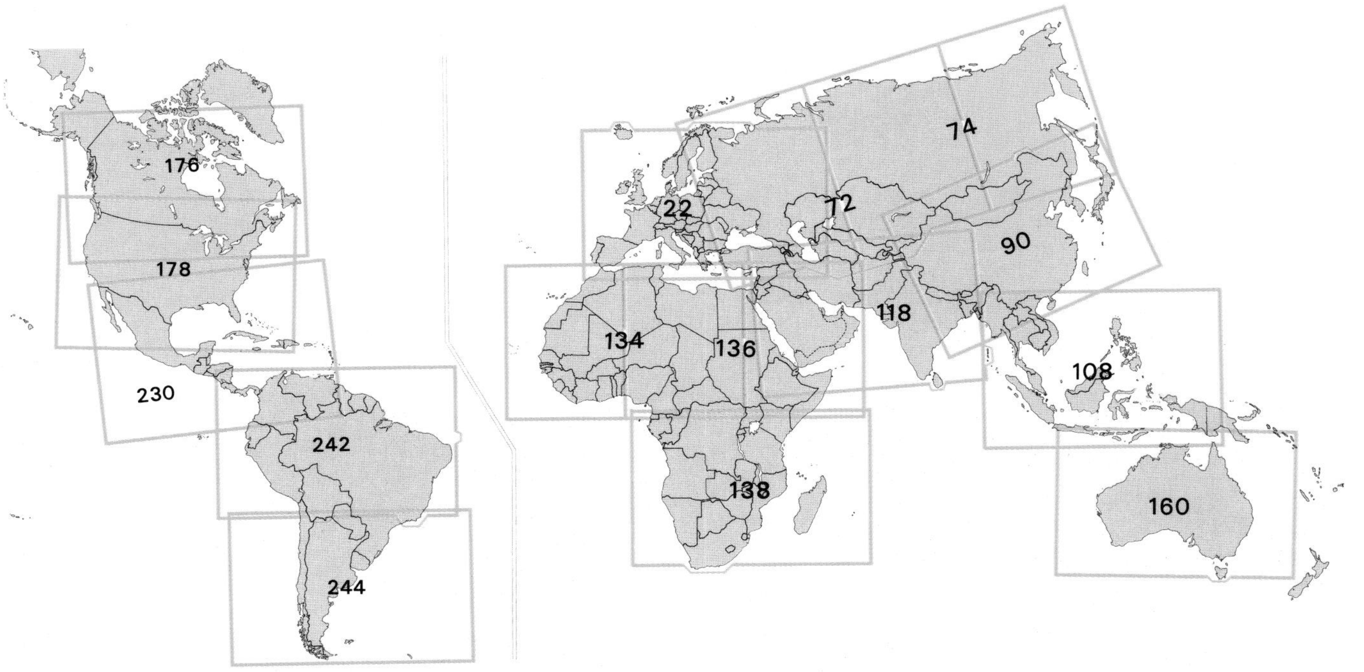
74
176
22
72
90
178
118
134
136
108
230
242
138
160
244

Adriatic Sea 36-37
Aegean Sea 39
Afars and Issas, see Djibouti
Afghanistan 118-119
Africa 10-11
Alabama 195
Alaska 180-181
Albania 38-39
Alberta 184-185
Aleutian Islands 180-181
Algeria 148-149
Alps 33
American Samoa 175a
Andaman and Nicobar Islands 110-111
Andes 18-19
Andorra 35
Angola 152-153
Anguilla 239
Antarctica 9
Antigua and Barbuda 239
Appalachian Mountains 17
Arabian Peninsula 118
Arabian Sea 118-119
Aral Sea 86
Arctic Ocean 16
Argentina 244-245
Arizona 201
Arkansas 194-195
Armenia 84
Aruba 241s
Ascension 11
Asia 12-13
Asia Minor 23
Atlantic Ocean 8
Atlas Mountains 134-135
Australia 160-161
Australian Capital Territory 171b
Austria 30-31
Azerbaijan 84
Azores 148a
Bahamas 238-239
Bahrain 129
Baikal, Lake 88
Balearic Islands 35
Balkhash, Lake 87
Baltic Sea 24
Bangladesh 121
Barbados 241g
Belarus 76
Belgium 30
Belize 233
Bengal, Bay of 13
Benin 151
Bering Sea 16
Bermuda 240a
Bhutan 121
Bismarck Archipelago 165
Black Sea 23
Bolivia 248-249
Bophuthatswana 156-157
Borneo 112-113
Bosnia and Herzegovina 36
Botswana 156-157
Brazil 242-245
British Columbia 182-183
British Honduras, see Belize
British Solomon Islands, see Solomon Islands
British Virgin Islands 240m
Brunei 113
Bulgaria 38-39
Burkina Faso 150-151
Burma 110-111
Burundi 154
California 204-205
Cambodia 110-111
Cameroon 135
Canada 176-177
Canary Islands 148
Cape Verde 150a
Caribbean Sea 238-239
Caroline Islands 14-15
Caspian Sea 72
Cayman Islands 238
Celebes 113
Central African Republic 135
Central America 236-237
Ceylon, see Sri Lanka
Chad 146-147
Channel Islands 43b
Chile 244
China 90-91
Ciskei 159
Cocos (Keeling) Islands 13
Colombia 246-247
Colorado 199-201
Comoros 157a
Congo 152
Congo, Democratic Republic of the, see Zaire
Connecticut 207
Cook Islands 15
Corsica 36-37
Costa Rica 237
Crete 39
Croatia 36
Cuba 240p
Curacao 241s
Cyprus 130-131
Czech Republic 30-31
Dahomey, see Benin
Delaware 208-209
Denmark 26
Djibouti 144
Dominica 240d
Dominican Republic 239
Ecuador 246
Egypt 140
El Salvador 236
England 28-29
Equatorial Guinea 152
Erie, Lake 214-215
Eritrea 144
Estonia 76
Ethiopia 144-145
Europe 22-23
Faeroe Islands 22
Falkland Islands 254
Fiji 175g
Finland 24-25
Florida 193
France 32-33
French Guiana 250
French Polynesia 15
Gabon 152
Galapagos Islands 246a
Gambia 150
Georgia (U.S.) 192-193
Georgia 84
Germany 30-31
Ghana 151
Gibraltar 34
Gobi Desert 90-91
Great Britain, see United Kingdom
Great Lakes 190-191
Greece 39
Greenland 16
Grenada 241k
Guadeloupe 241o
Guam 174p
Guatemala 236
Guernsey 43b
Guinea 150
Guinea-Bissau 150
Guyana 247
Haiti 238-239
Hawaii 229d
Himalayas 120-121
Hispaniola 238-239
Holland, see Netherlands
Honduras 236-237
Hong Kong 271d
Hudson Bay 176-177
Hungary 31
Huron, Lake 191
Iceland 24a
Idaho 202-203
Illinois 190, 194
India 119
Indiana 194
Indian Ocean 6
Indonesia 108-109
Inner Mongolia 90-91
Iowa 190, 199
Iran 128-129
Iraq 128
Ireland 48-49
Isle of Man 44
Israel 132-133
Italy 36-37
Ivory Coast 150-151
Jamaica 241q
Japan 92-93
Java 115a
Jersey 43b
Jordan 128
Kansas 199
Kazakhstan 72-73
Kentucky 192, 194
Kenya 154
Kiribati 15
Korea, North 99
Korea, South 99
Kuwait 128
Kyrgyzstan 85
Labrador 177
Laos 110
Latvia 76
Lebanon 128
Lesotho 159
Liberia 150
Libya 146-147
Liechtenstein 59
Lithuania 76
Louisiana 195
Luxembourg 56
Macau 101
Macedonia 38-39
Madagascar 157b
Madeira Islands 148
Maine 186
Malagasy Republic, see Madagascar
Malawi 155
Malaysia 112-113
Maldives 13
Mali 134-135
Malta 37
Manchuria 89
Manitoba 184-185
Maritime Provinces 186-187
Marshall Islands 15
Martinique 240e
Maryland 188-189
Massachusetts 207
Mauritania 134
Mauritius 157c
Mayotte 157a
Mediterranean Sea 10
Melanesia 14-15
Mexico 232-233
Mexico, Gulf of 231-232
Michigan 190-191
Michigan, Lake 190-191
Micronesia, Federated States of 14-15
Middle East 128-129
Midway Islands 174g
Minnesota 190, 198
Mississippi 195
Missouri 194
Moldova 78
Monaco 63
Mongolia 90-91
Montana 198, 202-203
Montserrat 239
Morocco 148-149
Mozambique 138-139
Myanmar, see Burma
Namibia 156
Nauru 174b
Nebraska 199
Nepal 124-125
Netherlands 52-53
Netherlands Antilles 241s
Nevada 204-205
New Brunswick 186
New Caledonia 175f
Newfoundland 187
New Guinea 164-165
New Hampshire 189
New Hebrides, see Vanuatu
New Jersey 208, 211
New Mexico 196, 201
New South Wales 166-167
New York 188-189
New Zealand 172-173
Nicaragua 236-237
Niger 134-135
Nigeria 135
Niue 174v
Norfolk Island 174c
North America 16-17
North Carolina 192
North Dakota 198
Northern Ireland 48-49
Northern Mariana Islands 14
Northern Territory 160-161
North Sea 22
Northwest Territories 176-177
Norway 24-25
Nova Scotia 186-187
Nyasa, Lake 155
Ohio 188
Oklahoma 196
Oman 118
Ontario 176-177, 188-189
Ontario, Lake 212-213
Oregon 202
Orkney Islands 46
Pacific Ocean 6-7
Pakistan 120
Palau 14
Palestine 132-133
Panama 246
Papua New Guinea 165
Paraguay 249, 252-253
Pennsylvania 188-189
Persian Gulf 128-129
Peru 242
Philippines 116-117
Pitcairn 174e
Poland 31
Polynesia 15
Portugal 34
Portuguese Guinea, see Guinea-Bissau
Prince Edward Island 186
Puerto Rico 240m
Qatar 129
Quebec 177, 189
Queensland 161
Red Sea 137
Reunion 157c
Rhode Island 207
Rhodesia, see Zimbabwe
Rocky Mountains 16-17
Romania 38
Russia 72-75
Rwanda 154
Sahara Desert 134-135
St. Helena 11
St. Kitts and Nevis 239
St. Lucia 241f
St. Pierre and Miquelon 187
St. Vincent and the Grenadines 241h
San Marino 66
Sao Tome and Principe 152
Sardinia 71
Saskatchewan 184-185
Saudi Arabia 118
Scandinavia 24
Scotland 46-47
Senegal 150
Seychelles 139
Shetland Islands 46a
Siberia 74-75
Sicily 70
Sierra Leone 150
Singapore 271c
Sinkiang 90
Slovakia 31
Slovenia 36
Society Islands 15
Solomon Islands 175e
Somalia 144-145
South Africa 156-157
South America 18-19
South Australia 163
South Carolina 192
South China Sea 108
South Dakota 198-199
South Georgia 245
Southwest Africa, see Namibia
Spain 34-35
Spanish Sahara, see Western Sahara
Sri Lanka 122
Sudan 140-141
Sumatra 108
Superior, Lake 190-191
Suriname 250
Swaziland 159
Sweden 24
Switzerland 58-59
Syria 128
Taiwan 101
Tajikistan 72
Tanganyika, Lake 154-155
Tanzania 154-155
Tasmania 167
Tennessee 192, 194-195
Texas 196-197
Thailand 110-111
Tibet 90
Tierra del Fuego 254
Togo 151
Tokelau 15
Tonga 15
Transcaucasia 84
Transkei 159
Transvaal 156-157
Trinidad and Tobago 241r
Tristan da Cunha 8
Tunisia 149
Turkey 130-131
Turkmenistan 72
Turks and Caicos Islands 239
Tuvalu 15
Uganda 154
Ukraine 78-79
United Arab Emirates 129
United Kingdom 28-29
United States 178-179
Ural Mountains 72-73
Uruguay 253
Utah 200-201
Uzbekistan 72
Vanuatu 175f
Vatican City 267a
Venda 157
Venezuela 246-247
Vermont 189
Victoria 167
Victoria, Lake 154
Vietnam 110-111
Virginia 188, 192
Virgin Islands 240m
Wake Island 174a
Wales 29
Wallis and Futuna 15
Washington 202
Western Australia 162
Western Sahara 148
Western Samoa 175a
West Indies 238-239
West Virginia 188, 192
White Russia, see Belarus
White Sea 25
Wisconsin 190
Wyoming 198-200, 202
Yellow Sea 91
Yemen 118
Yugoslavia 38-39
Yukon 181
Zaire 138
Zambia 138-139
Zanzibar 154
Zimbabwe 155

World Scene

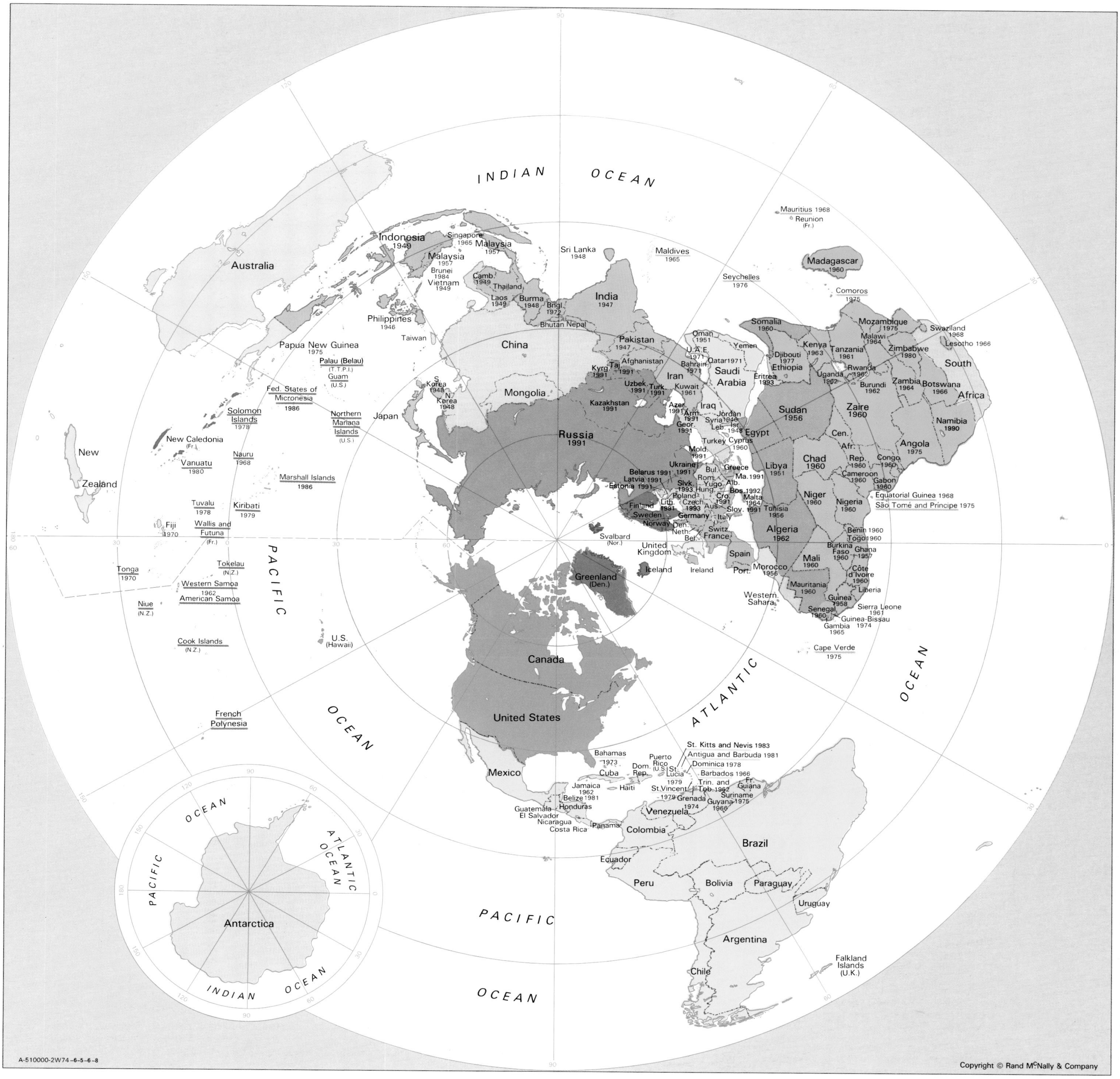

INDIAN OCEAN
ATLANTIC OCEAN
PACIFIC OCEAN
PACIFIC
OCEAN
Australia
Indonesia 1949
Singapore 1965
Malaysia 1957
Brunei 1984
Vietnam 1949
Camb. 1949
Thailand
Laos 1949
Burma 1948
Bngl. 1972
Bhutan
Nepal
Sri Lanka 1948
Maldives 1965
India 1947
Philippines 1946
Taiwan
China
Mongolia
Papua New Guinea 1975
Palau (Belau) (T.T.P.I.)
Guam (U.S.)
Fed. States of Micronesia 1986
Northern Mariana Islands (U.S.)
S. Korea 1948
N. Korea 1948
Japan
Solomon Islands 1978
New Caledonia (Fr.)
Nauru 1968
Vanuatu 1980
Marshall Islands 1986
New Zealand
Tuvalu 1978
Kiribati 1979
Fiji 1970
Wallis and Futuna (Fr.)
Tonga 1970
Tokelau (N.Z.)
Western Samoa 1962
American Samoa
Niue (N.Z.)
Cook Islands (N.Z.)
U.S. (Hawaii)
French Polynesia
Russia 1991
Kazakhstan 1991
Kyrg. 1991
Taj. 1991
Uzbek. 1991
Turk. 1991
Afghanistan
Pakistan 1947
Iran
Oman 1951
U.A.E. 1971
Qatar 1971
Bahrain 1971
Kuwait 1961
Saudi Arabia
Yemen
Iraq
Azer. 1991
Arm. 1991
Geor. 1991
Syria 1946
Jordan 1946
Leb. 1943
Isr. 1948
Turkey
Cyprus 1960
Egypt
Mold. 1991
Ukraine 1991
Belarus 1991
Latvia 1991
Estonia 1991
Lith. 1991
Poland
Czech. 1993
Slvk. 1993
Hung.
Rom.
Bul.
Greece
Yugo.
Alb.
Ma. 1991
Cro. 1991
Bos. 1992
Slov. 1991
Aus.
Malta 1964
Finland
Sweden
Norway
Germany
Den.
Neth.
Bel.
Switz.
France
Italy
Svalbard (Nor.)
United Kingdom
Ireland
Iceland
Greenland (Den.)
Spain
Port.
Morocco 1956
Western Sahara
Tunisia 1956
Algeria 1962
Libya 1951
Mauritania 1960
Mali 1960
Niger 1960
Chad 1960
Sudan 1956
Eritrea 1993
Djibouti 1977
Ethiopia
Somalia 1960
Kenya 1963
Tanzania 1961
Uganda 1962
Rwanda 1962
Burundi 1962
Zaire 1960
Cen. Afr. Rep. 1960
Congo 1960
Cameroon 1960
Gabon 1960
Equatorial Guinea 1968
São Tomé and Príncipe 1975
Nigeria 1960
Benin 1960
Togo 1960
Burkina Faso 1960
Ghana 1957
Côte d'Ivoire 1960
Liberia
Guinea 1958
Sierra Leone 1961
Senegal 1960
Guinea-Bissau 1974
Gambia 1965
Cape Verde 1975
Mozambique 1975
Malawi 1964
Zimbabwe 1980
Zambia 1964
Botswana 1966
Swaziland 1968
Lesotho 1966
South Africa
Namibia 1990
Angola 1975
Madagascar 1960
Comoros 1975
Seychelles 1976
Mauritius 1968
Reunion (Fr.)
Canada
United States
Mexico
Bahamas 1973
Cuba
Jamaica 1962
Haiti
Dom. Rep.
Puerto Rico (U.S.)
Belize 1981
Guatemala
Honduras
El Salvador
Nicaragua
Costa Rica
Panama
St. Kitts and Nevis 1983
Antigua and Barbuda 1981
Dominica 1978
St. Lucia 1979
Barbados 1966
St. Vincent 1979
Grenada 1974
Trin. and Tob. 1962
Fr. Guiana
Suriname 1975
Guyana 1966
Venezuela
Colombia
Ecuador
Peru
Brazil
Bolivia
Paraguay
Uruguay
Argentina
Chile
Falkland Islands (U.K.)
Antarctica
A-510000-2W74-6-5-6-8
Copyright © Rand McNally & Company

Intergovernmental Organizations: May 1, 1993

The admission of scores of new countries to the world community after World War II, indicated on the map above by the dates of their independence, created certain opportunities for these new countries that had formerly been the prerogative of a much smaller community of independent states. Until the 19th century, the countries to which international law was applicable was confined to the principal states of Europe and such others, like those of the Americas, as had asserted their independence and right to be treated as equals, or those older kingdoms and states like Siam and Ethiopia that had preserved their independence in an era of colonialism and had, perforce, to be treated as equals in treaty relationships. But equality as a matter of international law does not constitute equality of opportunity, identity of national interest, or safety from aggression. Consequently, despite the aims and achievements of the United Nations, there remains the need for intergovernmental organizations as a means for small *and* large countries to promote economic advancement, military security, or to assert their cultural identity with a stronger voice than a single country might possess. The organizations shown represent some of the principal regional and mutual-interest organizations created to advance those interests.

- European Community (EC)
- Organization of American States (OAS)
- Colombo Plan
- Colombo Plan and OAS
- Commonwealth of Independent States
- Nordic Council
- Nordic Council and EC
- Arab League
- Organization of African Unity (OAU)
- Arab League and OAU
- South Pacific Commission (SPC)
- Colombo Plan and SPC
- Colombo Plan, EC and SPC
- Other Countries

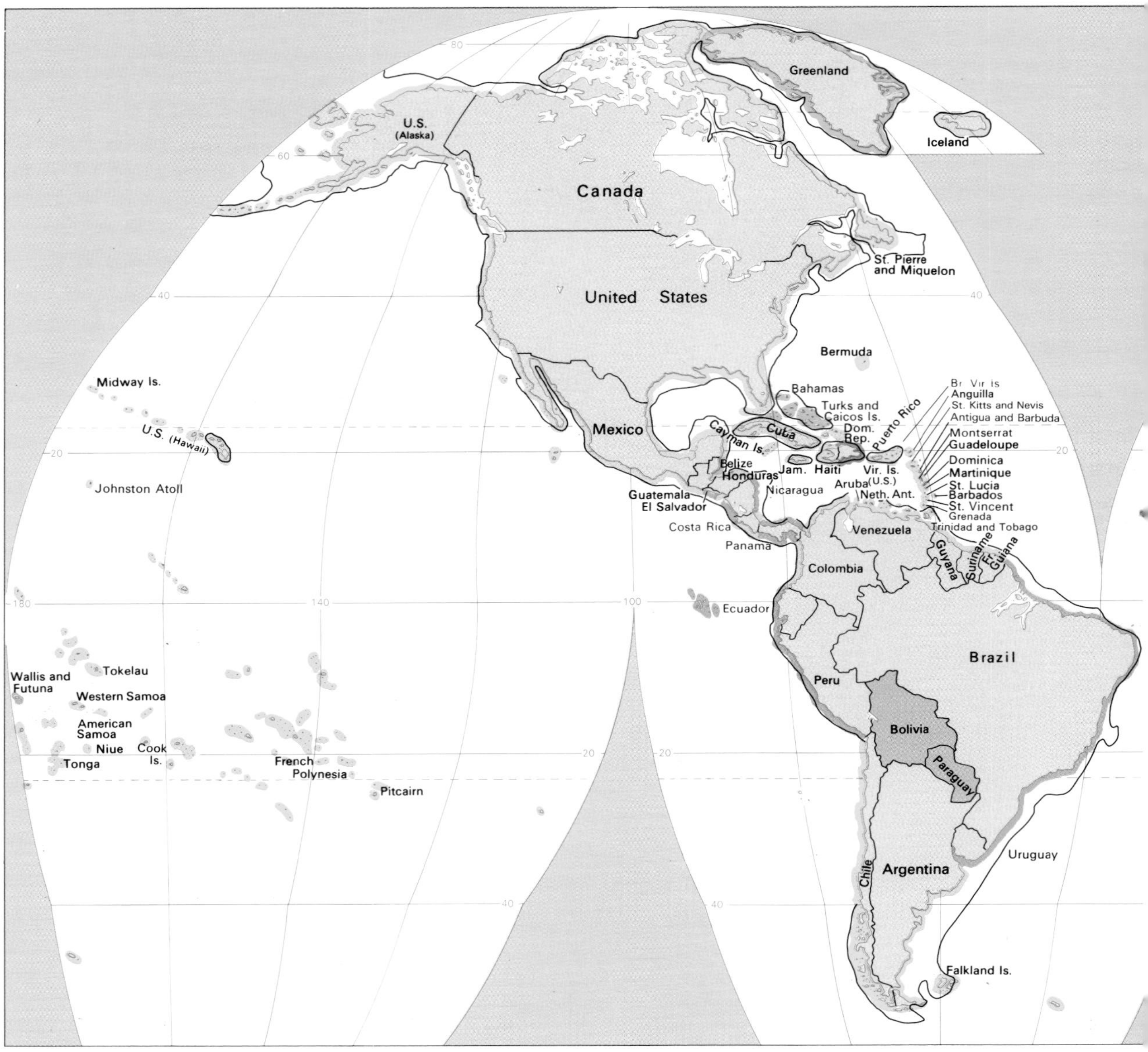
Greenland
Iceland
U.S. (Alaska)
Canada
St. Pierre and Miquelon
United States
Bermuda
Midway Is.
U.S. (Hawaii)
Bahamas
Turks and Caicos Is.
Dom. Rep.
Puerto Rico
Br. Vir. Is.
Anguilla
St. Kitts and Nevis
Antigua and Barbuda
Montserrat
Guadeloupe
Dominica
Martinique
St. Lucia
Barbados
St. Vincent
Grenada
Trinidad and Tobago
Mexico
Cayman Is.
Cuba
Belize
Honduras
Jam.
Haiti
Vir. Is. (U.S.)
Aruba
Neth. Ant.
Johnston Atoll
Guatemala
El Salvador
Nicaragua
Costa Rica
Panama
Venezuela
Guyana
Suriname
Fr. Guiana
Colombia
Ecuador
Wallis and Futuna
Tokelau
Western Samoa
American Samoa
Niue
Cook Is.
Tonga
French Polynesia
Pitcairn
Brazil
Peru
Bolivia
Paraguay
Chile
Argentina
Uruguay
Falkland Is.

Seaward Claims

Common territorial sea claims

- 3 nautical miles
- 6 nautical miles
- 12 nautical miles

Less common claims

- 4 nautical miles
- 10 nautical miles
- Over 12 nautical miles
- Unusual claim

Other features

- Landlocked countries
- Continental shelf

Note: Territorial claims of outlying islands to their offshore waters are the same as those of the administering country.

The growth of international law on the legal status of the portions of the seas claimed by coastal states probably began in the early 17th century, when conflicting claims to parts of the high seas by colonial and exploring European sea powers induced the Dutch jurist Hugo Grotius to write *Mare liberum* (1609), on the concept of the "free, or open, sea." His work was answered in 1617-18 by John Selden's *Mare clausum*, proposing that the seas were as subject to property rights and claims as land areas. The first successful synthesis of the two positions was Cornelis van Bynkershoek's *De dominio maris* (1702) in which he suggested that the seaward limit of a national claim should be that of its effective land-based control (the distance of a cannon-shot, three nautical miles). Though never universally accepted, that standard persisted well into the twentieth century.

After World War II, however, both traditional sea-based economic activity—fishing, commercial navigation—and activities made newly possible or intensified by technological change—exploitation of the seabed, pollution, scientific investigation—led coastal states to make increasingly wider claims to both territorial seas, those wholly subject to national law, and to zones in which some, but not all, sovereign rights were claimed, usually to protect economic, but especially fishing, interests. The first Law of the Sea Conference in 1958 attempted under UN auspices to codify international law in these areas. More than 14 years later at the final meeting of the Third Conference, a text representing the efforts of some 150 countries was opened for signature on Dec. 10, 1982 as the *United Nations Convention on the Law of the Sea*. Accessions were deposited that day by 119 states to a document providing definitions, guidelines, procedures, and institutions to govern a wide range of maritime law and activities.

Among the subjects relating to sovereignty delimited by the Convention were sections defining the rights, jurisdiction, and duties of coastal states in matters relating to the territorial sea, the right of innocent passage, international straits, archipelagic (island) states, exclusive economic zones (EEZ's), the continental shelf, the high seas, as well as access to, and use of, areas of the sea beyond the jurisdiction of a single national power.

Territorial sea may be claimed up to a distance of 12 nautical miles (n.m.) from either the shoreline of a coastal state (measured from low water on navigational charts), or from a straight baseline defined by the state when its shoreline is very irregular, as is that of Norway. Waters directly connected to the sea behind this baseline are called internal waters, and include bays (which may be closed at the mouth by a single baseline if they are less than 24 n.m. wide, and river mouths and estuaries. A zone contiguous to the territorial sea not wider than 24 n.m. beyond the baselines defining the territorial sea is defined in which states may exercise *limited* control for customs, immigration, fiscal, or sanitary reasons. Another zone, defined in relation to the continental shelf (the seaward prolongation of the coastal landmass beneath the sea) permits extension of the national sovereignty over the seabed and subsoil of the zone to the edge of the continental margin (the lower termination of the continental slope and rise) for purposes of exploration, scientific study, or economic exploitation of either biological or mineral resources.

In areas of the seas where coastal states lie in close proximity, the seaward extension of a national boundary may necessitate the drawing or negotiation of an international boundary in the sea. Where claims permissible under the Convention overlap, as in the Persian Gulf, median lines must be drawn so as to accommodate each state's maximum claim without disadvantaging bordering states.

The table opposite provides a description of the nature of current national claims to territorial seas and of the economic, usually fishing, zones that have been declared *within* the permissible 200-n.m. limits of the potential EEZ permitted by the Convention.

Offshore zones

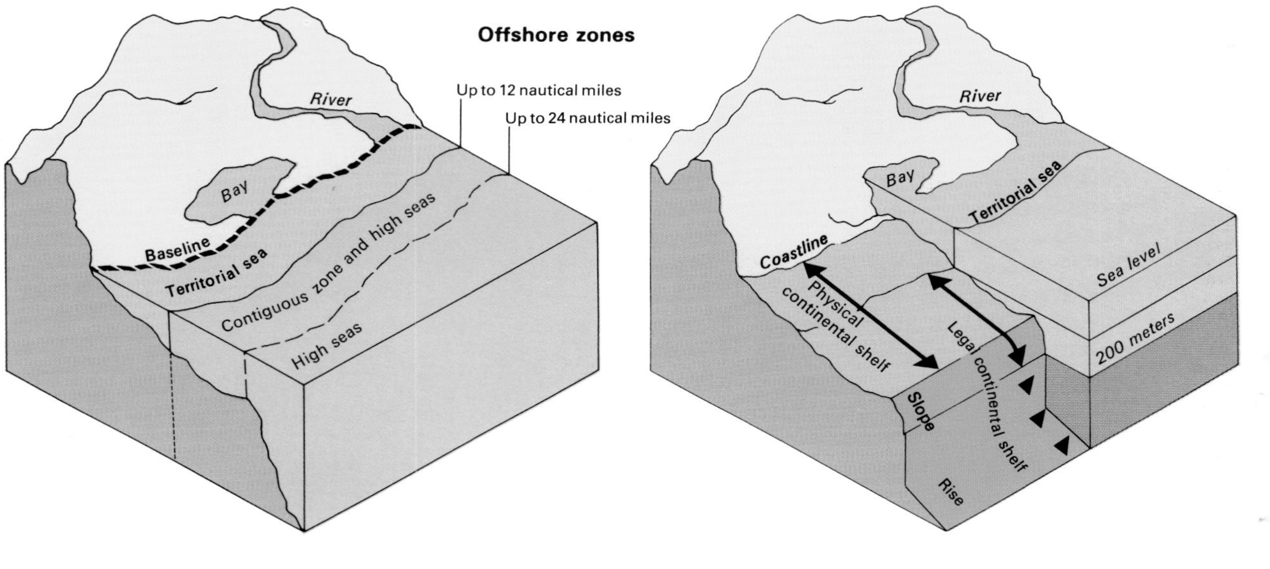
River
Up to 12 nautical miles
Up to 24 nautical miles
Bay
Baseline
Territorial sea
Contiguous zone and high seas
High seas
River
Bay
Territorial sea
Coastline
Physical continental shelf
Legal continental shelf
Sea level
200 meters
Slope
Rise

Irregular coastline of Norway

Norway measures its territorial sea from a straight baseline, which in general runs along the outer fringe of offshore islands and coastal promontories. The Law of the Sea Convention permits this type of claim in the case of highly irregular coastlines fringed with islands. In other cases the coastal features do not justify such claims to additional waters, and the claims may not be recognized.

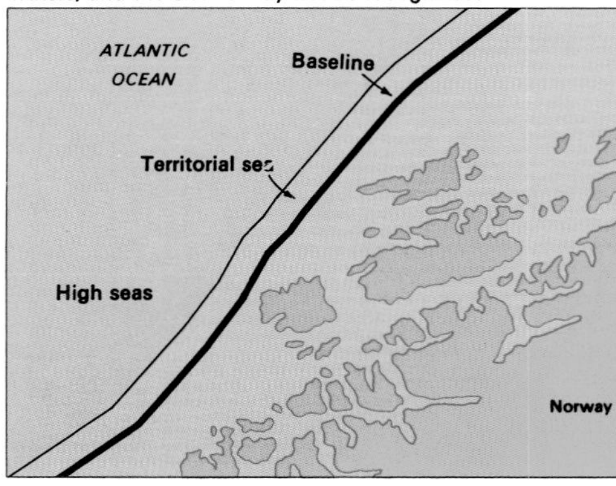
ATLANTIC OCEAN
Baseline
Territorial sea
High seas
Norway

Overlapping claims in the Persian Gulf

The waters of the Persian Gulf are less than 200 meters in depth and the entire seabed is continental shelf. To determine the extent of jurisdiction that each state has over the resources of the seabed beyond its territorial sea, the Law of the Sea Convention provides for median lines, measured from the same baseline as the territorial sea. The median lines divide the continental shelf between opposite and adjacent states.

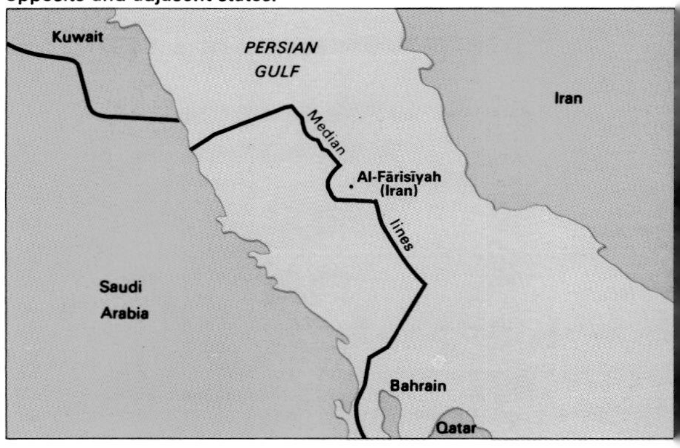
Kuwait
PERSIAN GULF
Iran
Median lines
Al-Fārisīyah (Iran)
Saudi Arabia
Bahrain
Qatar

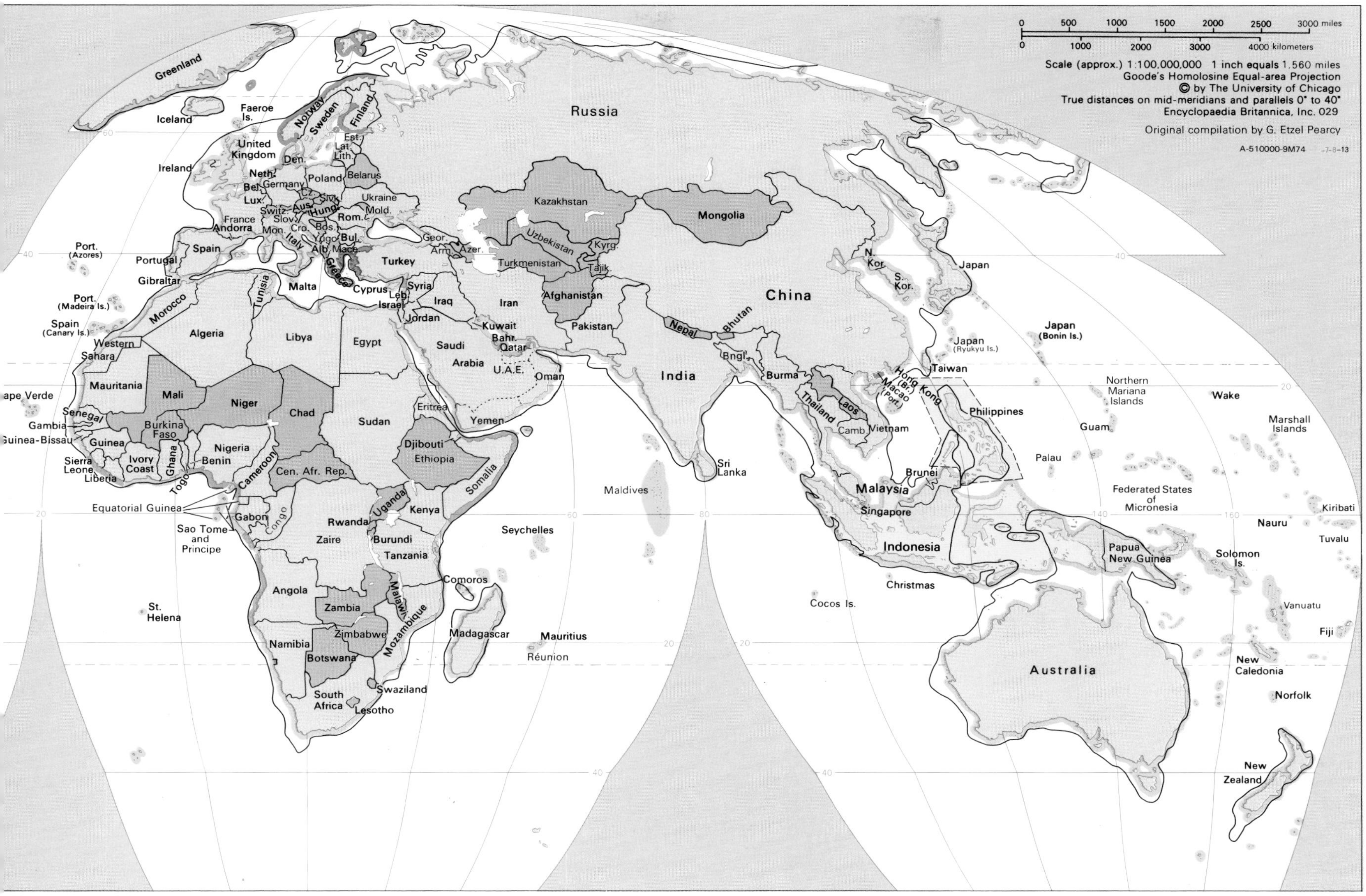

0 500 1000 1500 2000 2500 3000 miles
0 1000 2000 3000 4000 kilometers
Scale (approx.) 1:100,000,000 1 inch equals 1,560 miles
Goode's Homolosine Equal-area Projection
© by The University of Chicago
True distances on mid-meridians and parallels 0° to 40°
Encyclopaedia Britannica, Inc. 029
Original compilation by G. Etzel Pearcy
A-510000-9M74
Greenland
Iceland
Faeroe Is.
Norway
Sweden
Finland
Russia
United Kingdom
Ireland
Den.
Est.
Lat.
Lith.
Poland
Belarus
Neth.
Germany
Bel.
Lux.
Ukraine
Mold.
France
Switz.
Slov.
Andorra
Mon.
Cro.
Bos.
Rom.
Bul.
Yugo.
Alb.
Mac.
Italy
Greece
Spain
Portugal
Port. (Azores)
Gibraltar
Port. (Madeira Is.)
Spain (Canary Is.)
Morocco
Tunisia
Malta
Cyprus
Leb.
Israel
Syria
Iraq
Jordan
Turkey
Geor.
Arm.
Azer.
Kazakhstan
Uzbekistan
Turkmenistan
Kyrg.
Tajik.
Afghanistan
Iran
Pakistan
Kuwait
Bahr.
Qatar
Saudi Arabia
U.A.E.
Oman
Yemen
Mongolia
China
N. Kor.
S. Kor.
Japan
Japan (Ryukyu Is.)
Japan (Bonin Is.)
Taiwan
Nepal
Bhutan
India
Bngl.
Burma
Thailand
Laos
Camb.
Vietnam
Hong Kong (Br.)
Macao (Port.)
Philippines
Sri Lanka
Maldives
Malaysia
Singapore
Brunei
Indonesia
Christmas
Cocos Is.
Northern Mariana Islands
Guam
Palau
Wake
Marshall Islands
Federated States of Micronesia
Nauru
Kiribati
Papua New Guinea
Solomon Is.
Tuvalu
Vanuatu
Fiji
New Caledonia
Norfolk
Australia
New Zealand
Western Sahara
Algeria
Libya
Egypt
Mauritania
Mali
Niger
Chad
Sudan
Eritrea
Djibouti
Ethiopia
Somalia
Cape Verde
Senegal
Gambia
Guinea-Bissau
Guinea
Burkina Faso
Sierra Leone
Liberia
Ivory Coast
Ghana
Togo
Benin
Nigeria
Cameroon
Cen. Afr. Rep.
Equatorial Guinea
Sao Tome and Principe
Gabon
Congo
Zaire
Uganda
Kenya
Rwanda
Burundi
Tanzania
Seychelles
Comoros
Angola
Zambia
Malawi
Mozambique
Zimbabwe
Namibia
Botswana
Madagascar
Mauritius
Réunion
South Africa
Swaziland
Lesotho
St. Helena

Political unit	Territorial sea claim*	Fishing claim*†
Albania	12 A	
Algeria	12 A	
Angola	20 A	200
Antigua and Barbuda	12	200 D
Argentina	12 A	200 D
Aruba	12 B	
Australia	12 A	200
Bahamas	3	200
Bahrain	3	
Bangladesh	12 A	200 D
Barbados	12	200 D
Belgium	12	E
Belize	3	
Benin	200	
Bermuda	3 B	200
Brazil	200 A	
Brunei	12	200
Bulgaria	12 A	200 D
Burma	12 A	200 D
Cambodia	12 A	200 D
Cameroon	50 A	
Canada	12 A	200
Cape Verde	12 C	200 D
Chile	12 A	200 D
China	12 A	
Colombia	12 A	200 D
Comoros	12 C	200 D
Congo	200	
Cook Islands	12 B	200 D
Costa Rica	12	200 D
Cuba	12 A	200 D
Cyprus	12	
Denmark	3 A	200
Djibouti	12	200 D
Dominica	12	200 D
Dominican Republic	6 A	200 D
Ecuador	200 A	
Egypt	12 A	200 D
El Salvador	200	
Equatorial Guinea	12	200 D
Eritrea	12 A	
Faeroe Islands	3 B	200
Falkland Islands	3	200
Fiji	12 C	200 D
Finland	4 A	12
France	12 A	200 D
French Guiana	12 B	200 D
French Polynesia	12 B	200 D
Gabon	12	200 D
Gambia	12	200
Germany	3-16 A	200
Ghana	12	200 D
Gibraltar	3 B	
Greece	6	
Greenland	3 B	200
Grenada	12	200 D
Guatemala	12 A	200 D
Guinea	12 A	200 D
Guinea-Bissau	12 A	200 D
Guyana	12	200
Haiti	12 A	200 D
Honduras	12	200 D
Hong Kong	3 B	
Iceland	12 A	200 D
India	12	200 D
Indonesia	12 C	200 D
Iran	12 A	50
Iraq	12	
Ireland	12 A	200
Israel	12	
Italy	12	
Ivory Coast	12	200 D
Jamaica	12	
Japan	12	200
Jordan	3	
Kenya	12 A	200 D
Kiribati	12	200 D
Korea, North	12	200 D
Korea, South	12 A	
Kuwait	12 A	
Lebanon	12	
Liberia	200	
Libya	12 A	
Madagascar	12 A	200 D
Malaysia	12 A	200 D
Maldives	12	37-310 D
Malta	12 A	25
Marshall Islands	12	200 D
Mauritania	12 A	200 D
Mauritius	12 A	200 D
Mexico	12 A	200 D
Micronesia, Fed. States of	12	200 D
Monaco	12	
Morocco	12 A	200 D
Mozambique	12 A	200 D
Namibia	12	200 D
Nauru	12	200
Netherlands	12 A	200
Netherlands Antilles	12	
New Caledonia	12 B	200 D
New Zealand	12	200 D
Nicaragua	200	
Nigeria	30	200 D
Northern Mariana Islands	12 B	200 D
Norway	4 A	200 D
Oman	12 A	200 D
Pakistan	12	200 D
Palau	12 B	200 D
Panama	200 A	
Papua New Guinea	12 C	200
Peru	200	
Philippines		200 D
Poland	12 A	E
Portugal	12 A	200 D
Puerto Rico	12 B	200 D
Qatar	3	E
Romania	12	200 D
St. Kitts and Nevis	12	200 D
St. Lucia	12	200 D
St. Pierre and Miquelon	12 B	200 D
St. Vincent and the Grenadines	12	200 D
Sao Tome and Principe	12 C	200 D
Saudi Arabia	12 A	
Senegal	12 A	200 D
Seychelles	12	200 D
Sierra Leone	200	
Singapore	3	
Solomon Islands	12 C	200 D
Somalia	200 A	
South Africa	12	200
Soviet Union (former)	12 A	200 D
Spain	12 AC	200 D
Sri Lanka	12 A	200 D
Sudan	12 A	
Suriname	12	200 D
Sweden	12 A	E
Syria	35 A	
Taiwan	12	200 D
Tanzania	12 A	200 D
Thailand	12 A	200 D
Togo	30	200 D
Tonga	12 A	200 D
Trinidad and Tobago	12	200 D
Tunisia	12 A	
Turkey	6-12 A	12
Tuvalu	12	200 D
United Arab Emirates	3	F
United Kingdom	12 A	200
United States	12	200 D
Uruguay	200	
Vanuatu	12 C	200 D
Venezuela	12 A	200 D
Vietnam	12 A	200 D
Western Samoa	12	200 D
Yemen	12	
Yugoslavia	12 A	
Zaire	12	200 D

* Nautical miles
† When claim is beyond the territorial sea.
Data as of December 31, 1990.

A. Measured from a straight baseline.
B. Same as that of administering country.
C. Extends beyond a perimeter drawn around archipelago.

D. Exclusive economic zone.
E. Fishing rights extend to median line with neighboring countries.
F. Exclusive econ. zone extends to median line with neighboring countries.

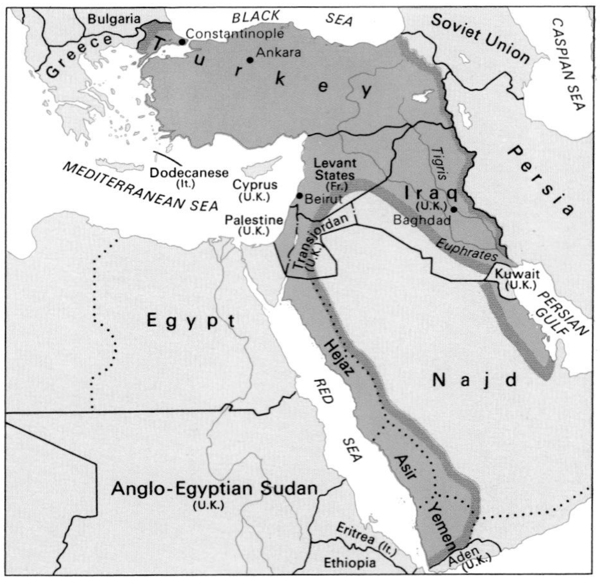
Bulgaria
BLACK SEA
Soviet Union
CASPIAN SEA
Constantinople
Ankara
Greece
Turkey
Persia
Dodecanese (It.)
Cyprus (U.K.)
Levant States (Fr.)
Beirut
Iraq (U.K.)
Baghdad
Tigris
Euphrates
MEDITERRANEAN SEA
Palestine (U.K.)
Transjordan (U.K.)
Kuwait (U.K.)
PERSIAN GULF
Egypt
Hejaz
RED SEA
Najd
Asir
Yemen
Anglo-Egyptian Sudan (U.K.)
Eritrea (It.)
Ethiopia
Aden (U.K.)

Dissolution of the Ottoman Empire

- Ottoman Empire 1913
- Administrative boundaries (1923) as a result of WW I settlements; dotted are indefinite

Germany
Poland
Prague
Czechoslovakia
Danube
Vienna
Liech.
Switz.
Austria
Budapest
Hungary
Romania
Kingdom of the Serbs, Croats, and Slovenes
Danube
ADRIATIC SEA
Italy
Bulgaria
Albania
Greece
TYRRHENIAN SEA

Dissolution of Austria-Hungary

- Austria-Hungary 1913
- Administrative boundaries (1923) as a result of WW I settlements

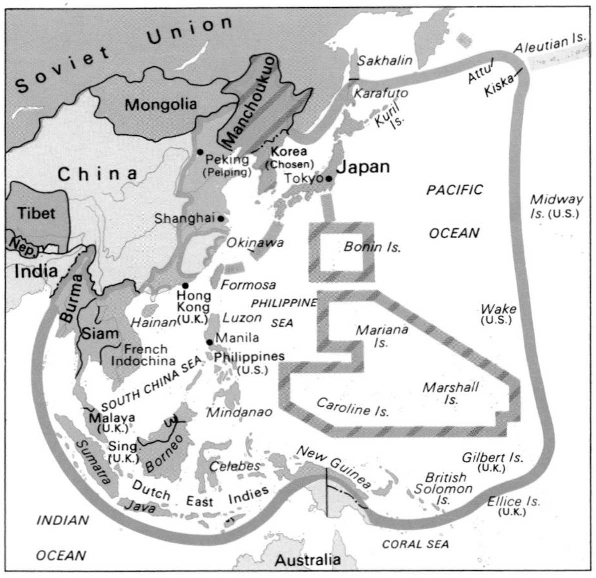
Soviet Union
Aleutian Is.
Sakhalin
Attu
Kiska
Mongolia
Manchoukuo
Karafuto
Kuril Is.
China
Peking (Peiping)
Korea (Chosen)
Tokyo
Japan
PACIFIC OCEAN
Midway Is. (U.S.)
Tibet
Shanghai
Nepal
India
Okinawa
Bonin Is.
Formosa
Hong Kong (U.K.)
Hainan
Luzon
PHILIPPINE SEA
Wake (U.S.)
Burma
Siam
French Indochina
Manila
Philippines (U.S.)
Mariana Is.
SOUTH CHINA SEA
Marshall Is.
Malaya (U.K.)
Mindanao
Caroline Is.
Sing. (U.K.)
Borneo
Sumatra
Celebes
New Guinea
Gilbert Is. (U.K.)
British Solomon Is.
Dutch East Indies
Java
Ellice Is. (U.K.)
INDIAN OCEAN
Australia
CORAL SEA

Japanese Expansion World War II

- Japan 1939
- Japanese dependencies 1939
- Maximum occupation
- Neutral states
- States joining Allies 1945

Iceland*
Faeroe Is.* (Den.)
Norway
Sweden
Finland
OCEAN
United Kingdom
Ireland
Den.
Danzig
Moscow
Neth.
London
Berlin
Ger.
Warsaw
Soviet Union
Poland
Germany
ATLANTIC
Bel.
Paris
Lux.
France
Liech.
Hung.
Switz.
Romania
Port.
Spain
Italy
Yugoslavia
Bulgaria
BLACK SEA
Rome
Alb.
Turkey
Greece
Tangier
Sp. Mor.
Morocco
MEDITERRANEAN SEA
Syria*
Iraq*
Cyprus (U.K.)
Leb.
Tunisia (Fr.)
Malta (U.K.)
Palestine (U.K.)
Algeria*
Libya (It.)
Egypt
Trans-jordan (U.K.)

Axis Expansion World War II

- Germany 1939
- Other Axis Powers 1940-45
- Maximum occupation
- Neutral states
- States joining Allies 1943-45

*Occupied by Allies

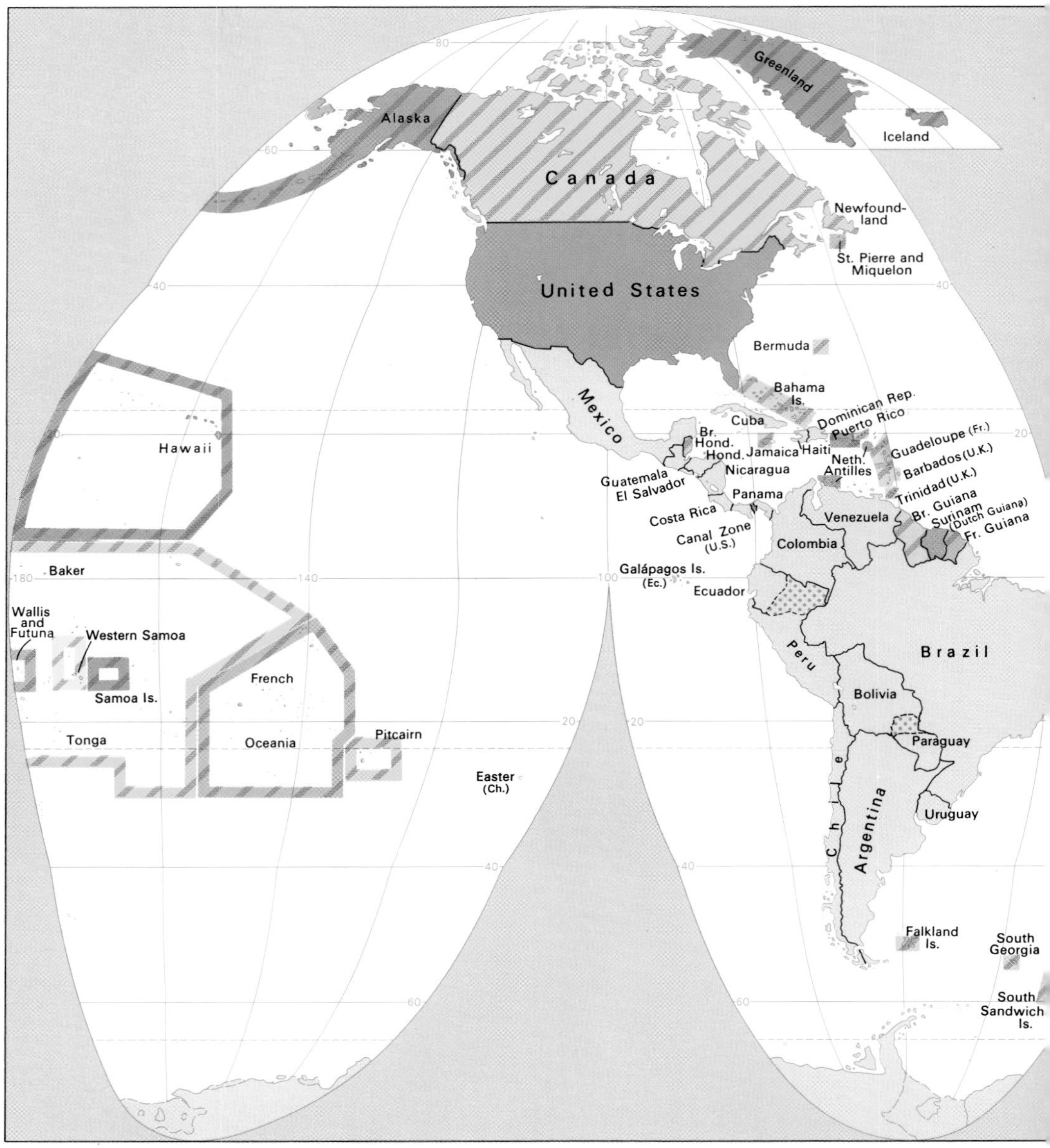
Greenland
Iceland
Alaska
Canada
Newfoundland
St. Pierre and Miquelon
United States
Bermuda
Hawaii
Mexico
Bahama Is.
Cuba
Dominican Rep.
Puerto Rico
Haiti
Br. Hond.
Jamaica
Guadeloupe (Fr.)
Neth. Antilles
Barbados (U.K.)
Nicaragua
Guatemala
El Salvador
Trinidad (U.K.)
Panama
Venezuela
Br. Guiana
Surinam (Dutch Guiana)
Fr. Guiana
Costa Rica
Canal Zone (U.S.)
Colombia
Baker
Galápagos Is. (Ec.)
Ecuador
Wallis and Futuna
Western Samoa
Peru
Brazil
Samoa Is.
French
Oceania
Bolivia
Tonga
Pitcairn
Paraguay
Easter (Ch.)
Chile
Argentina
Uruguay
Falkland Is.
South Georgia
South Sandwich Is.

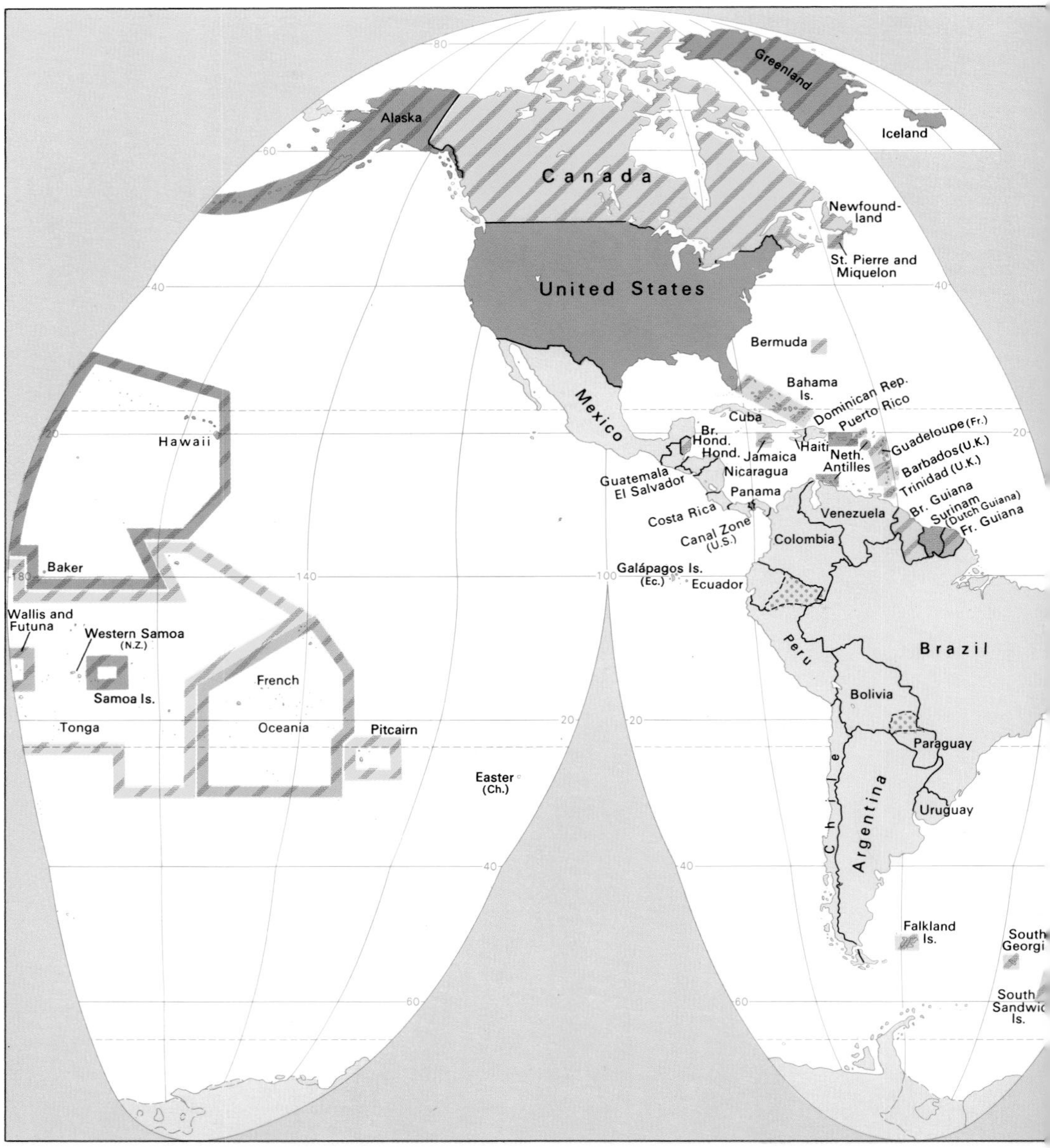
Greenland
Iceland
Alaska
Canada
Newfoundland
St. Pierre and Miquelon
United States
Bermuda
Hawaii
Mexico
Bahama Is.
Cuba
Dominican Rep.
Puerto Rico
Haiti
Br. Hond.
Jamaica
Guadeloupe (Fr.)
Neth. Antilles
Barbados (U.K.)
Nicaragua
Guatemala
El Salvador
Trinidad (U.K.)
Panama
Venezuela
Br. Guiana
Surinam (Dutch Guiana)
Fr. Guiana
Costa Rica
Canal Zone (U.S.)
Colombia
Baker
Galápagos Is. (Ec.)
Ecuador
Wallis and Futuna
Western Samoa (N.Z.)
Peru
Brazil
Samoa Is.
French
Oceania
Bolivia
Tonga
Pitcairn
Paraguay
Easter (Ch.)
Chile
Argentina
Uruguay
Falkland Is.

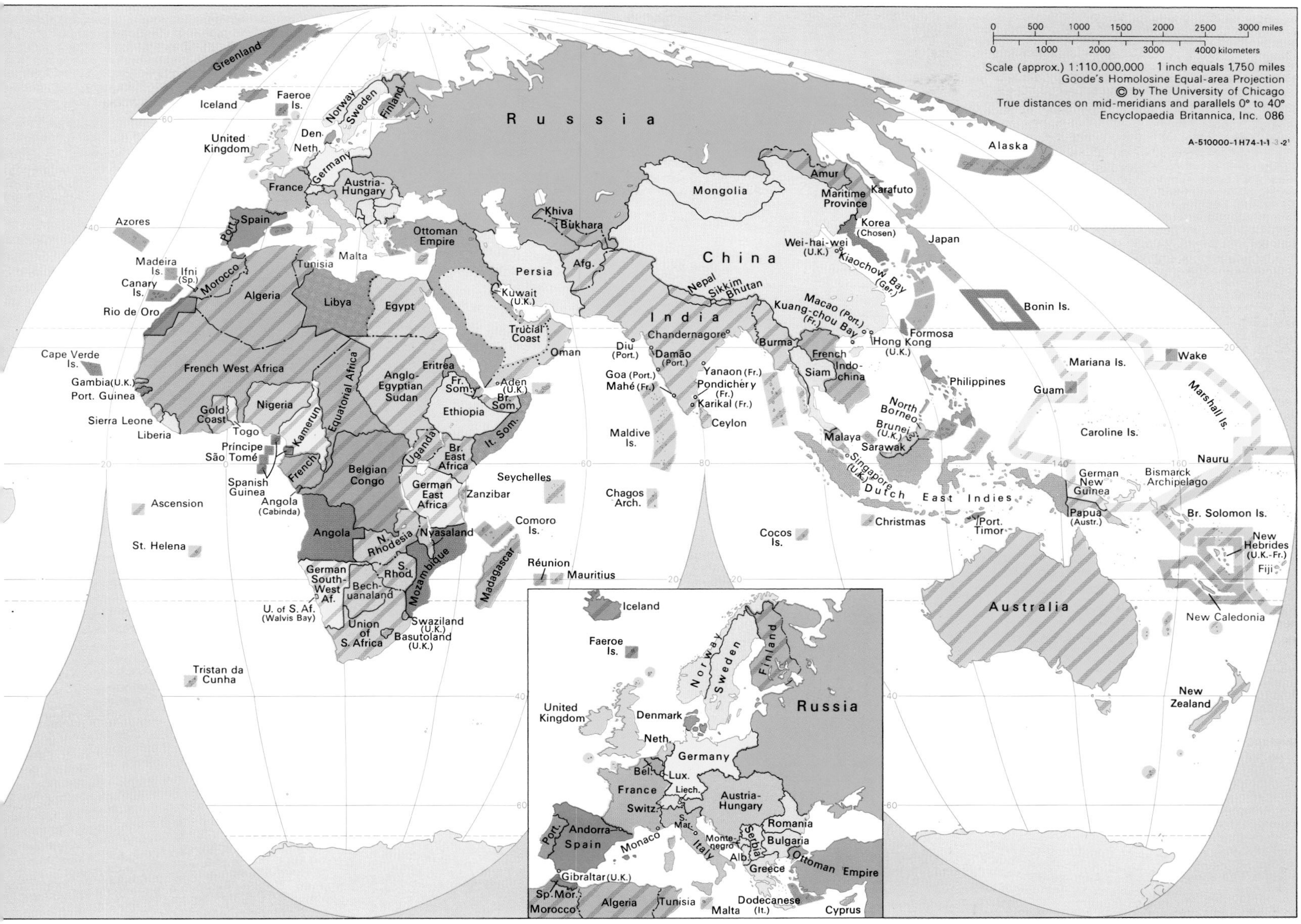
0 500 1000 1500 2000 2500 3000 miles
0 1000 2000 3000 4000 kilometers
Scale (approx.) 1:110,000,000 1 inch equals 1,750 miles
Goode's Homolosine Equal-area Projection
© by The University of Chicago
True distances on mid-meridians and parallels 0° to 40°
Encyclopaedia Britannica, Inc. 086
A-510000-1H74-1-1
Greenland
Iceland
Faeroe Is.
Norway
Sweden
Finland
United Kingdom
Den.
Neth.
Germany
France
Austria-Hungary
Russia
Alaska
Amur
Maritime Province
Karafuto
Mongolia
Korea (Chosen)
Japan
Azores
Spain
Port.
Ottoman Empire
Khiva
Bukhara
Madeira Is.
Ifni (Sp.)
Canary Is.
Rio de Oro
Morocco
Tunisia
Malta
Algeria
Libya
Egypt
Persia
Afg.
China
Wei-hai-wei (U.K.)
Kiaochow Bay (Ger.)
Nepal
Sikkim
Bhutan
Kuwait (U.K.)
Trucial Coast
Oman
India
Chandernagore
Macao (Port.)
Kuang-chou Bay (Fr.)
Bonin Is.
Formosa
Hong Kong (U.K.)
Burma
Diu (Port.)
Damão (Port.)
Goa (Port.)
Mahé (Fr.)
Yanaon (Fr.)
Pondichéry (Fr.)
Karikal (Fr.)
Ceylon
French Indo-china
Siam
Philippines
Mariana Is.
Wake
Guam
Marshall Is.
Cape Verde Is.
French West Africa
Gambia (U.K.)
Port. Guinea
Sierra Leone
Liberia
Gold Coast
Togo
Nigeria
Kamerun
Anglo-Egyptian Sudan
Eritrea
Fr. Som.
Aden (U.K.)
Br. Som.
Ethiopia
It. Som.
Equatorial Africa
Uganda
Br. East Africa
Maldive Is.
North Borneo
Brunei (U.K.)
Sarawak
Malaya
Singapore (U.K.)
Caroline Is.
Nauru
Príncipe
São Tomé
Spanish Guinea
French
Belgian Congo
German East Africa
Zanzibar
Seychelles
Chagos Arch.
Dutch East Indies
German New Guinea
Bismarck Archipelago
Ascension
Angola (Cabinda)
Angola
N. Rhodesia
Nyasaland
Comoro Is.
Cocos Is.
Christmas
Port. Timor
Papua (Austr.)
Br. Solomon Is.
St. Helena
German South-West Af.
Bech-uanaland
S. Rhod.
Mozambique
Madagascar
Réunion
Mauritius
New Hebrides (U.K.-Fr.)
Fiji
U. of S. Af. (Walvis Bay)
Union of S. Africa
Swaziland (U.K.)
Basutoland (U.K.)
Australia
New Caledonia
Tristan da Cunha
New Zealand
Iceland
Faeroe Is.
Norway
Sweden
Finland
United Kingdom
Denmark
Russia
Neth.
Germany
Bel.
Lux.
France
Liech.
Austria-Hungary
Switz.
Romania
Port.
Andorra
Spain
Monaco
Mar.
Italy
Monte-negro
Serbia
Bulgaria
Alb.
Greece
Ottoman Empire
Gibraltar (U.K.)
Sp. Mor.
Morocco
Algeria
Tunisia
Malta
Dodecanese (It.)
Cyprus

The World January 1, 1914

- United Kingdom
  - Related areas
- France
  - Related areas
- Portugal
  - Related areas
- Spain
  - Related areas
- Netherlands
  - Related areas
- Belgium
  - Related areas
- Germany
  - Related areas
- Denmark
  - Related areas
- Japan
  - Related areas
- Italy
  - Related areas
- United States
  - Related areas
- Ottoman Empire
- Russia
  - Related areas
- Austria-Hungary
- Countries without related areas
- Disputed areas
- Intercolonial boundary

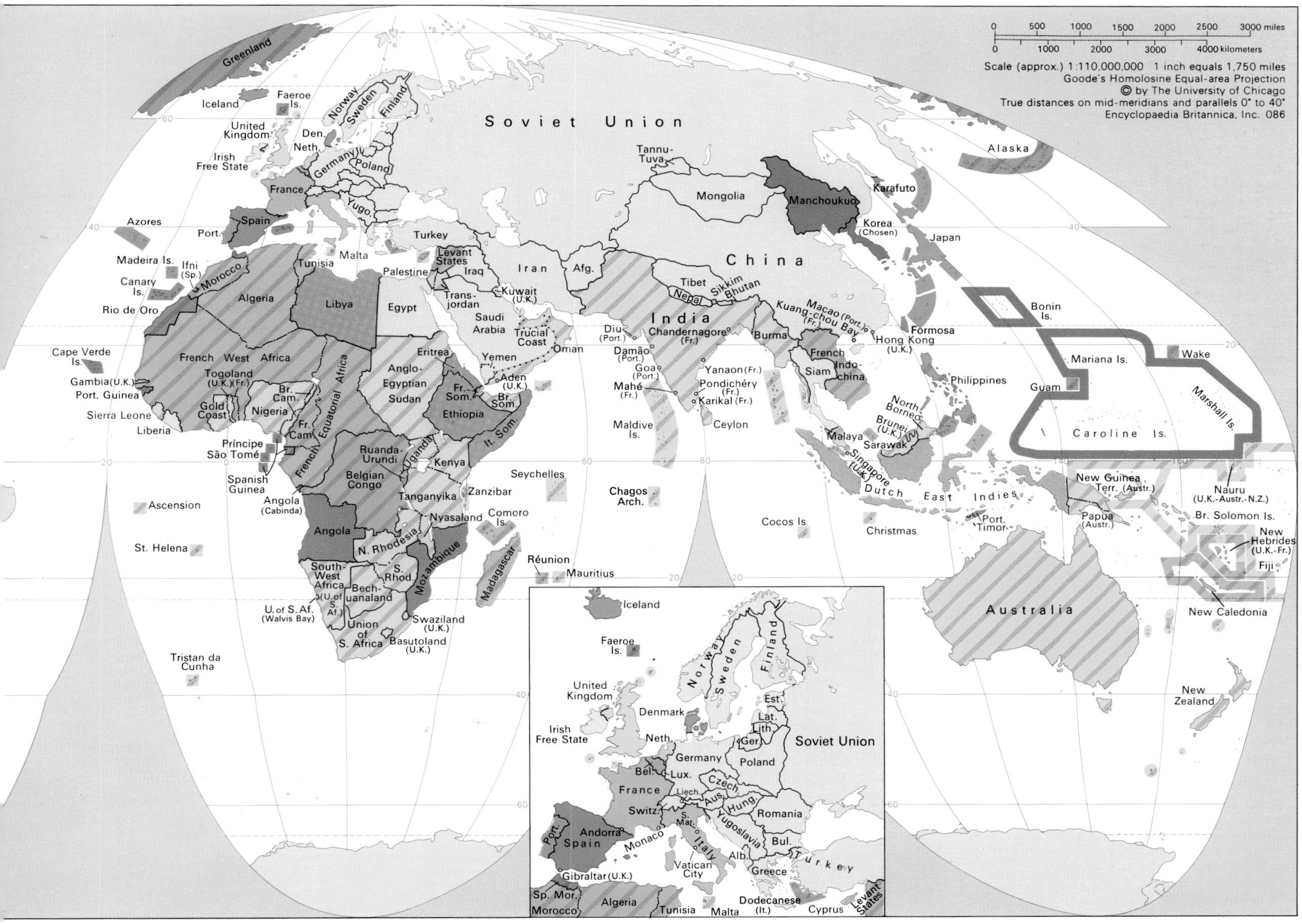
0 500 1000 1500 2000 2500 3000 miles
0 1000 2000 3000 4000 kilometers
Scale (approx.) 1:110,000,000 1 inch equals 1,750 miles
Goode's Homolosine Equal-area Projection
© by The University of Chicago
True distances on mid-meridians and parallels 0° to 40°
Encyclopaedia Britannica, Inc. 086
Greenland
Iceland
Faeroe Is.
Norway
Sweden
Finland
United Kingdom
Den.
Neth.
Irish Free State
Germany
Poland
France
Yugo.
Soviet Union
Tannu-Tuva
Alaska
Mongolia
Manchoukuo
Karafuto
Korea (Chosen)
Japan
Azores
Port.
Spain
Turkey
Madeira Is.
Ifni (Sp.)
Canary Is.
Rio de Oro
Morocco
Tunisia
Malta
Palestine
Levant States
Iraq
Iran
Afg.
China
Tibet
Sikkim
Bhutan
Nepal
Algeria
Libya
Egypt
Trans-jordan
Kuwait (U.K.)
Saudi Arabia
Trucial Coast
Oman
India
Chandernagore (Fr.)
Macao (Port.)
Kuang-chou Bay (Fr.)
Bonin Is.
Formosa
Hong Kong (U.K.)
Burma
Diu (Port.)
Damão (Port.)
Goa (Port.)
Mahé (Fr.)
Yanaon (Fr.)
Pondichéry (Fr.)
Karikal (Fr.)
Ceylon
French Indo-china
Siam
Philippines
Mariana Is.
Wake
Guam
Marshall Is.
Caroline Is.
Cape Verde Is.
French West Africa
Togoland (U.K.)(Fr.)
Gambia (U.K.)
Port. Guinea
Sierra Leone
Liberia
Gold Coast
Nigeria
Br. Cam.
Fr. Cam.
Anglo-Egyptian Sudan
Eritrea
Yemen
Aden (U.K.)
Fr. Som.
Br. Som.
Ethiopia
It. Som.
Equatorial Africa
French
Uganda
Kenya
Ruanda-Urundi
Belgian Congo
Príncipe
São Tomé
Spanish Guinea
Maldive Is.
North Borneo
Brunei (U.K.)
Sarawak
Malaya
Singapore (U.K.)
Dutch East Indies
New Guinea Terr. (Austr.)
Nauru (U.K.-Austr.-N.Z.)
Br. Solomon Is.
Tanganyika
Zanzibar
Seychelles
Chagos Arch.
Ascension
Angola (Cabinda)
Angola
Nyasaland
Comoro Is.
Cocos Is
Christmas
Port. Timor
Papua (Austr.)
St. Helena
N. Rhodesia
South West Africa (U. of S. Af.)
Bech-uanaland
S. Rhod.
Mozambique
Madagascar
Réunion
Mauritius
New Hebrides (U.K.-Fr.)
Fiji
U. of S. Af. (Walvis Bay)
Union of S. Africa
Swaziland (U.K.)
Basutoland (U.K.)
Australia
New Caledonia
Tristan da Cunha
New Zealand
Iceland
Faeroe Is.
Norway
Sweden
Finland
United Kingdom
Irish Free State
Denmark
Est.
Lat.
Lith.
Ger.
Soviet Union
Neth.
Germany
Poland
Bel.
Lux.
Czech.
France
Liech.
Aus.
Hung.
Switz.
Romania
Yugoslavia
Port.
Andorra
Spain
Monaco
Mar.
Italy
Bul.
Vatican City
Alb.
Greece
Turkey
Gibraltar (U.K.)
Sp. Mor.
Morocco
Algeria
Tunisia
Malta
Dodecanese (It.)
Cyprus
Levant States

The World January 1, 1937

- United Kingdom
  - Related areas
- France
  - Related areas
- Portugal
  - Related areas
- Spain
  - Related areas
- Netherlands
  - Related areas
- Belgium
  - Related areas
- Denmark
  - Related areas
- Japan
  - Related areas
- Italy
  - Related areas
- United States
  - Related areas
- Countries without related areas
- Disputed areas
- Intercolonial boundary

Population

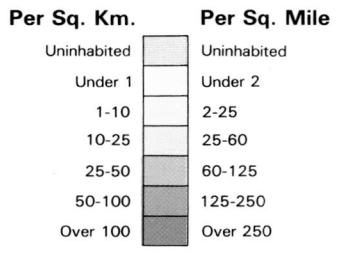

Per Sq. Km.		Per Sq. Mile
Uninhabited		Uninhabited
Under 1		Under 2
1-10		2-25
10-25		25-60
25-50		60-125
50-100		125-250
Over 100		Over 250

- • Metropolitan areas over 2,000,000 population
- o Metropolitan areas 1,000,000 to 2,000,000 population

Some cities are identified by initial letter only.

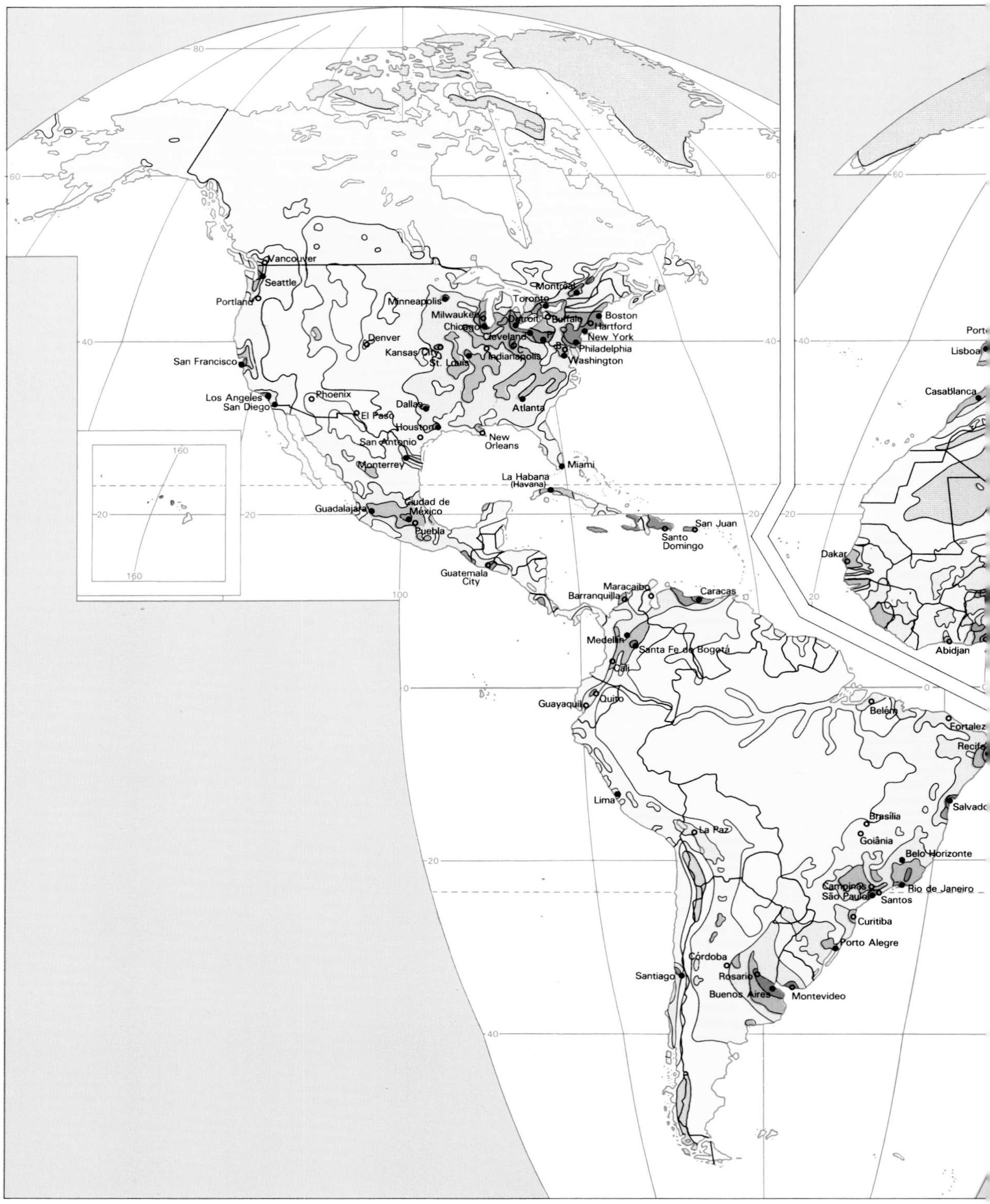

80
60
40
20
0
20
40
160
100
Vancouver
Seattle
Portland
San Francisco
Los Angeles
San Diego
Phoenix
Denver
Minneapolis
Milwaukee
Chicago
Detroit
Toronto
Montreal
Buffalo
Cleveland
Boston
Hartford
New York
Philadelphia
Washington
Kansas City
St. Louis
Indianapolis
Dallas
El Paso
Houston
San Antonio
Atlanta
New Orleans
Miami
Monterrey
La Habana
(Havana)
Guadalajara
Ciudad de México
Puebla
San Juan
Santo Domingo
Guatemala City
Maracaibo
Barranquilla
Caracas
Medellín
Santa Fe de Bogotá
Cali
Quito
Guayaquil
Lima
Belém
Fortalez
Recife
Salvado
Brasília
Goiânia
Belo Horizonte
La Paz
Campinas
São Paulo
Santos
Rio de Janeiro
Curitiba
Porto Alegre
Córdoba
Santiago
Rosario
Buenos Aires
Montevideo
Dakar
Abidjan
Casablanca
Lisboa
Porto

The numbers and distribution of human beings on their planet and the forms that their occupance takes are controlled by a variety of factors. The main population map opposite focuses on identifying the location and density of the most populous regions and cities of the earth. The Urbanization inset highlights the propensity of man to congregate in cities and the group of "age pyramids" below illustrates some of the diversity that is concealed within apparently simple population totals.

Population

The patterns of distribution shown display certain characteristics worldwide: relative densities decline with altitude (and the capacity of the land to support higher densities); settlement patterns follow rivers, or focus on harbours opening on large bodies of water connecting populous, economically interrelated areas; populations tend to fill up contiguous areas of similar topographical and climatic opportunity, whether in coastal plains, intermontane basins, along railroad right-of-ways, or in biologically and climatically defined regions of similar soil, vegatative response, or access from more populous areas.

The main map also identifies the largest cities of the world, distinguishing between those of 1-2 million and more than 2 million population. The selection of cities is determined by the concept of "city proper," that is, usually the smallest contiguous civilly or adminstratively defined and named entity. The meaning of the concept in terms of local practice worldwide, however, is considerable. A city of 100,000 may in one country be a single social, economic, and administrative place, bound together fully by its transportation infrastructure and representing a single *urban* entity in its population's collective mind. A city of the same apparent size in another country, however, might represent something more nearly characterizable as 100 villages of 1,000 persons, pursuing separate economic activities in separate neighbourhoods, often poorly interconnected, sometimes still predominately rural in terms of economic activity, and perhaps not universally understood by its own people as the greater place seen by others.

Urbanization

The concept of "urban" exemplified on the inset map of urbanization is particularly elusive in international studies of population, as most countries have their own definition of the concept, appropriate to local conditions and discourse, but often unsuitable for international comparisons. It is that local concept which is mapped here. Size is a useful indicator as to whether a place is classifiable as "urban," but as indicated above, the "size" of a place, even in the presence of administrative requirements may be misleading. Japan defines a place as "urban" if it has 50,000 or more population and meets certain criteria for their location within the city. A smaller country with a less hospitable landscape, like Iceland or Norway, might, by the same token, define a place as small as 200 as "urban" if it had predominately non-rural employment patterns, administrative function, or its houses were closer together than some set distance. The concept of "metropolitan area," or urban areas contiguous with a central city that are economically dependent on it is also complex and interpreted differently thorughout the world. The inset map of urbanization extends the city proper concept of the main map by showing metropolitan areas of more than 2 million. As can be seen from comparison of the two maps, sometimes high urbanization may correlate with relatively low numbers or densities of population. This occurs when the majority of a population lives in large settlements, rather than distributed across an entire landscape and may happen either because of localized economic and employment opportunities in the city, or because the countryside is unsuitable for agricultural or other exploitation. The strong correlation, however, is still between highly populous areas and large cities.

Age and sex composition

Among the characteristics of a population having the greatest significance both in terms of current needs and future trends, the age and sex composition of a population is perhaps the most important. Several examples are presented at the right of a graphic called an "age pyramid," which summarizes the relative proportion of males and females in each age cohort of a population. These examples, drawn by five-year age groups, often illuminate the effects on the whole population of the recent history of the relative growth or diminution of smaller parts of the whole: war losses, emigration of the young for work abroad, natural causes like disasters.
The origins of the concern of many countries and organizations with uncontrolled population growth may be inferred from examples like Brazil, where the high proportion of young people means enormous numbers (both absolutely and relatively) in or near their childbearing years resulting in growth rates for the total population that can outrun the far more difficult-to-attain economic growth rates that determine the relative prosperity of a country. Japan, on the other hand, shows a pattern typical of a demographically mature population, that is, a population which is growing slowly or not at all, resulting in lower, more predictable, and more economically supportable demographic rates, but also foreshadowing the movement of large numbers of its people into the pensionable and financially dependent age groups without large numbers of younger workers to support them. The Japanese example also shows, in a somewhat smoothed form, the effects of some of the viscissitudes of Twentieth century history on the relative size of certain age groups.

Age and sex composition

- Male
- Female

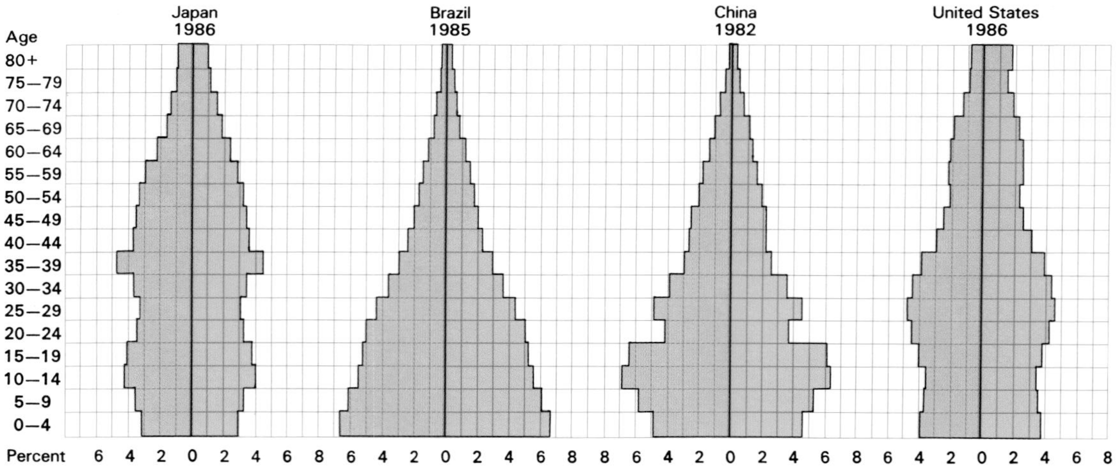

Japan
1986
Brazil
1985
China
1982
United States
1986
Age
80+
75—79
70—74
65—69
60—64
55—59
50—54
45—49
40—44
35—39
30—34
25—29
20—24
15—19
10—14
5—9
0—4
Percent
6 4 2 0 2 4 6 8 6 4 2 0 2 4 6 8 8 6 4 2 0 2 4 6 8 6 4 2 0 2 4 6 8

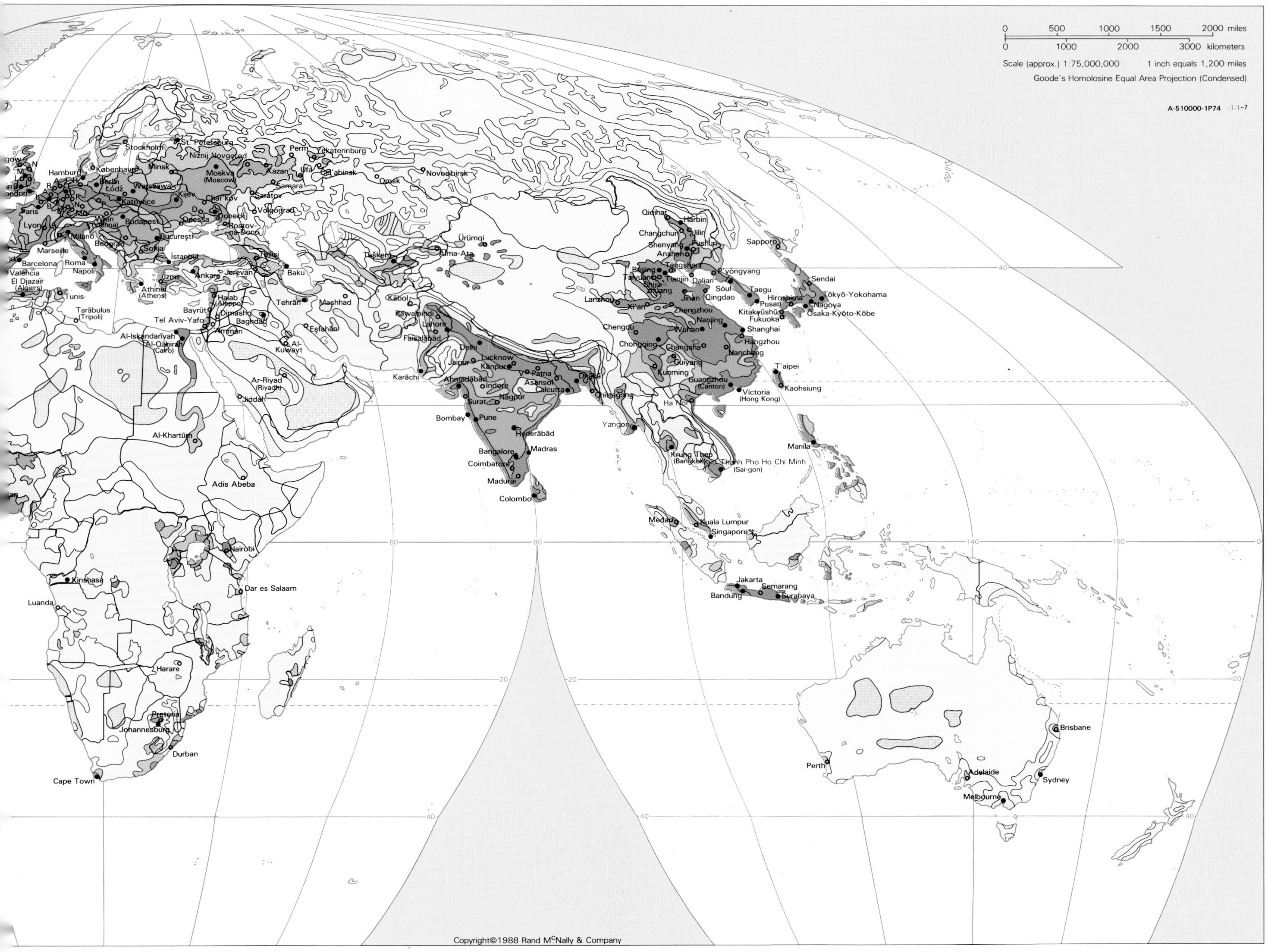
0 500 1000 1500 2000 miles
0 1000 2000 3000 kilometers
Scale (approx.) 1:75,000,000 1 inch equals 1,200 miles
Goode's Homolosine Equal Area Projection (Condensed)
A-510000-1P74
Stockholm
St. Peterburg
Nižnij Novgorod
Perm'
Jekaterinburg
Čel'abinsk
Omsk
Novosibirsk
Hamburg
København
Minsk
Moskva
(Moscow)
Kazan'
Ufa
Samara
Saratov
Berlin
Łódź
Warszawa
Katowice
Kijev
Char'kov
Paris
Lyon
Wien
Budapest
Milano
Beograd
Odessa
Doneck
Rostov-na-Donu
Volgograd
Bucureşti
Sofija
Barcelona
Marseille
Roma
Napoli
Valencia
El Djazair
(Algiers)
Tunis
Tarābulus
(Tripoli)
İstanbul
Ankara
İzmir
Athínai
(Athens)
Tbilisi
Jerevan
Baku
Halab
(Aleppo)
Dimashq
Bayrūt
Tel Aviv-Yafo
'Ammān
Baghdād
Tehrān
Mashhad
Eşfahān
Al-Iskandarīyah
Al-Qāhirah
(Cairo)
Al-Kuwayt
Ar-Riyāḍ
(Riyadh)
Jiddah
Al-Kharṭūm
Adis Abeba
Nairobi
Kinshasa
Dar es Salaam
Luanda
Harare
Pretoria
Johannesburg
Durban
Cape Town
Taškent
Alma-Ata
Ürümqi
Kābol
Rawalpindi
Lahore
Faisalābād
Karāchi
Delhi
Jaipur
Lucknow
Kānpur
Patna
Ahmadābād
Indore
Asansol
Calcutta
Dhaka
Nāgpur
Surat
Bombay
Pune
Chittagong
Hyderābād
Madras
Bangalore
Coimbatore
Madurai
Colombo
Yangon
Krung Thep
(Bangkok)
Thanh Pho Ho Chi Minh
(Sai-gon)
Ha Noi
Medan
Kuala Lumpur
Singapore
Jakarta
Bandung
Semarang
Surabaya
Qiqihar
Harbin
Changchun
Jilin
Shenyang
Fushun
Anshan
Tangshan
Beijing
Tianjin
Dalian
Taiyuan
Shijiazhuang
Jinan
Qingdao
P'yŏngyang
Sŏul
Taegu
Pusan
Lanzhou
Xi'an
Zhengzhou
Nanjing
Shanghai
Wuhan
Hangzhou
Chengdu
Chongqing
Changsha
Nanchang
Guiyang
Kunming
Guangzhou
(Canton)
Victoria
(Hong Kong)
T'aipei
Kaohsiung
Manila
Sapporo
Sendai
Tōkyō-Yokohama
Nagoya
Hiroshima
Kitakyūshū
Fukuoka
Ōsaka-Kyōto-Kōbe
Brisbane
Perth
Adelaide
Sydney
Melbourne
Copyright©1988 Rand McNally & Company

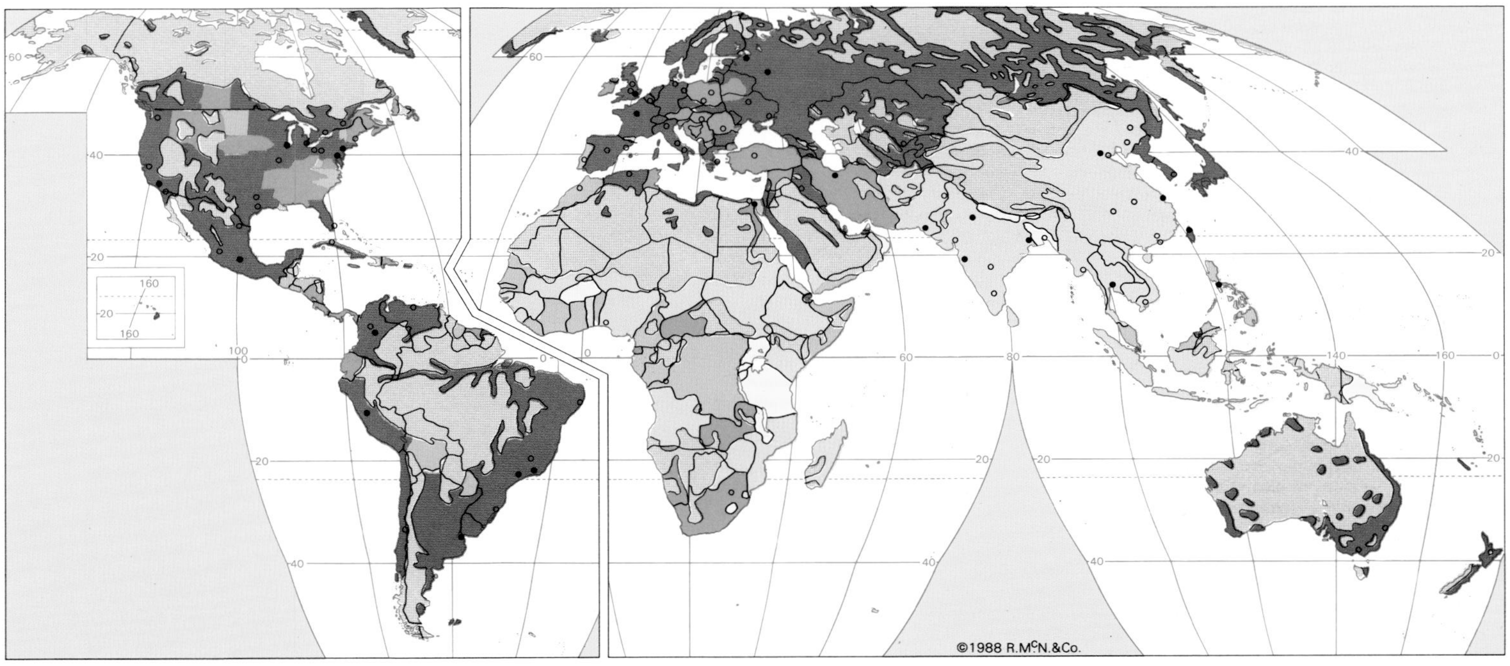
©1988 R.McN.&Co.

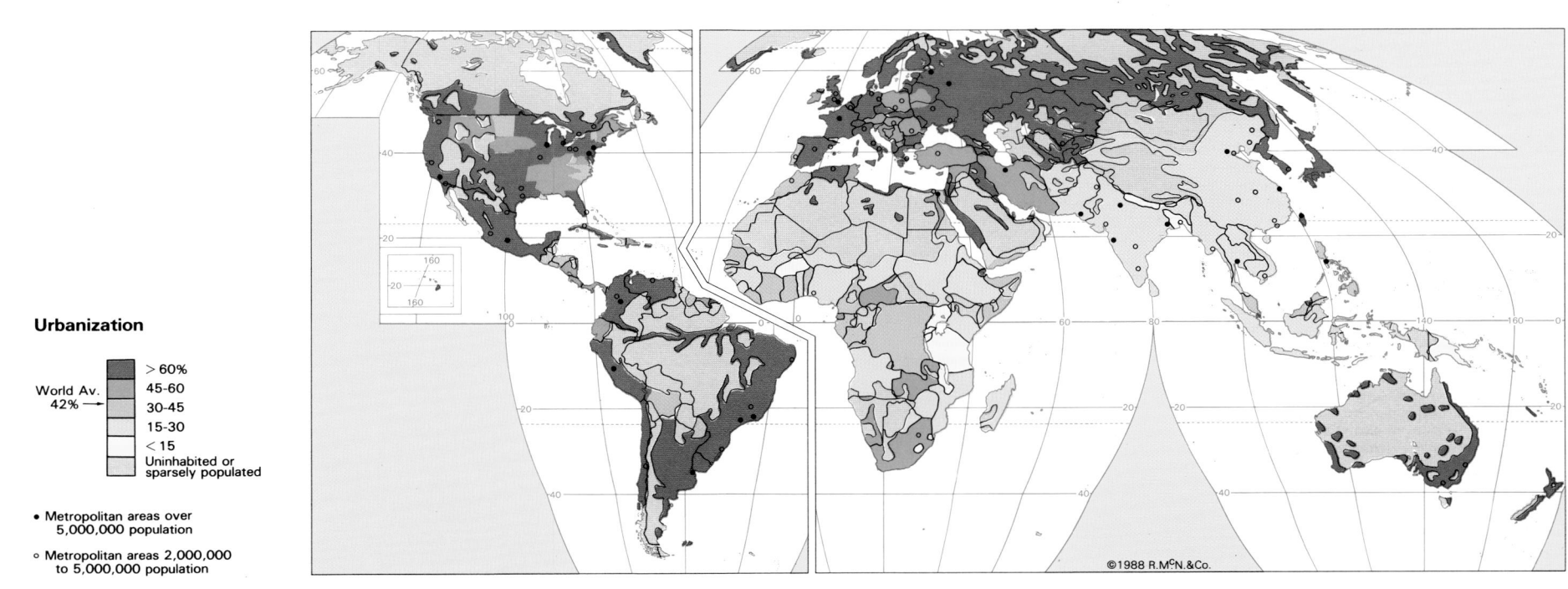

Urbanization

World Av. 42% →

- >60%
- 45-60
- 30-45
- 15-30
- <15
- Uninhabited or sparsely populated

• Metropolitan areas over 5,000,000 population

∘ Metropolitan areas 2,000,000 to 5,000,000 population

Religions

The majority of the inhabitants in each of the areas colored on the map share the religious tradition indicated. Letter symbols show religious traditions shared by at least 25% of the inhabitants within areal units no smaller than one thousand square miles. Therefore minority religions of city-dwellers have generally not been represented.

R Roman Catholicism
P Protestantism
E Eastern Orthodox religions (including Armenian, Coptic, Ethiopian, Greek, and Russian Orthodox)
M Mormonism
C Christianity, undifferentiated by branch (chiefly mingled Protestantism and Roman Catholicism, neither predominant)
I Islam, predominantly Sunni
Sh Islam, predominantly Shia
Theravada Buddhism
L Lamaism
H Hinduism
J Judaism
Ch Chinese religions*
Ja Japanese religions*
Korean religions*
Vietnamese religions*
T Simple ethnic (tribal) religions
Sk Sikhism
Areas long under Communist regimes; traditional religions often subject to official restraint
Uninhabited

***In certain Eastern Asian areas, most of the people have plural religious affiliations. Chinese, Korean, and Vietnamese religions include Mahayana Buddhism, Taoism, Confucianism, and folk cults. The Japanese religions include Shinto and Mahayana Buddhism.**

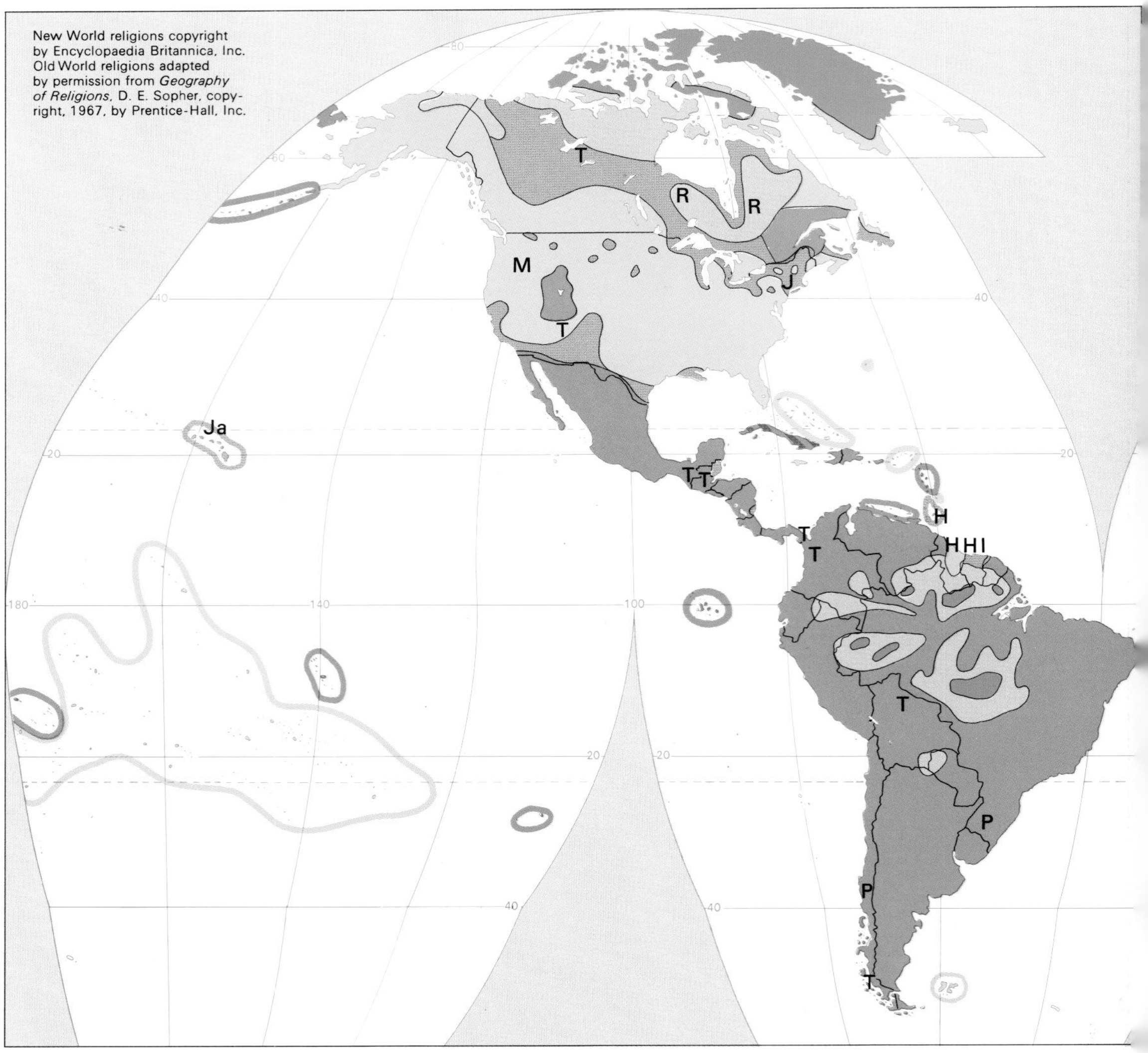
New World religions copyright by Encyclopaedia Britannica, Inc.
Old World religions adapted by permission from *Geography of Religions*, D. E. Sopher, copyright, 1967, by Prentice-Hall, Inc.
T
R
R
M
J
T
Ja
T T
H
H H I
T
T
T
P
P
T

Languages

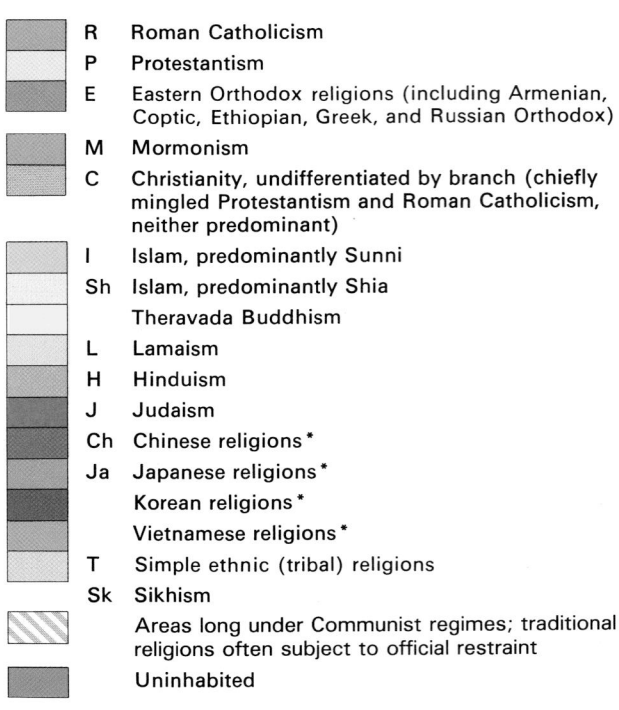

Languages of Europe

The following languages are ranked in descending order by number of speakers. Languages spoken by more than 4.5 million people are indicated by color. Others listed, spoken by fewer than 4.5 million persons, are named on the map.

Russian
German
Italian
English
French
Ukrainian
Polish
Spanish
Romanian
Serbo-Croatian
Dutch-Flemish
Hungarian
Portuguese
Czech
Belorussian
Greek
Bulgarian
Swedish
Catalan
Danish
Turkish
Slovak
Albanian
Finnish
All others

Norwegian
Lithuanian
Chuvash
Slovenian
Macedonian
Latvian
Mordvinian
Estonian
Breton

Basque
Irish-Gaelic
Mari
Welsh
Friulian
Komi
Frisian
Sardinian
Maltese

Karelian
Icelandic
Adyge
Scots-Gaelic
Romansh
Lappish
Lusatian
Ladin

Quechua

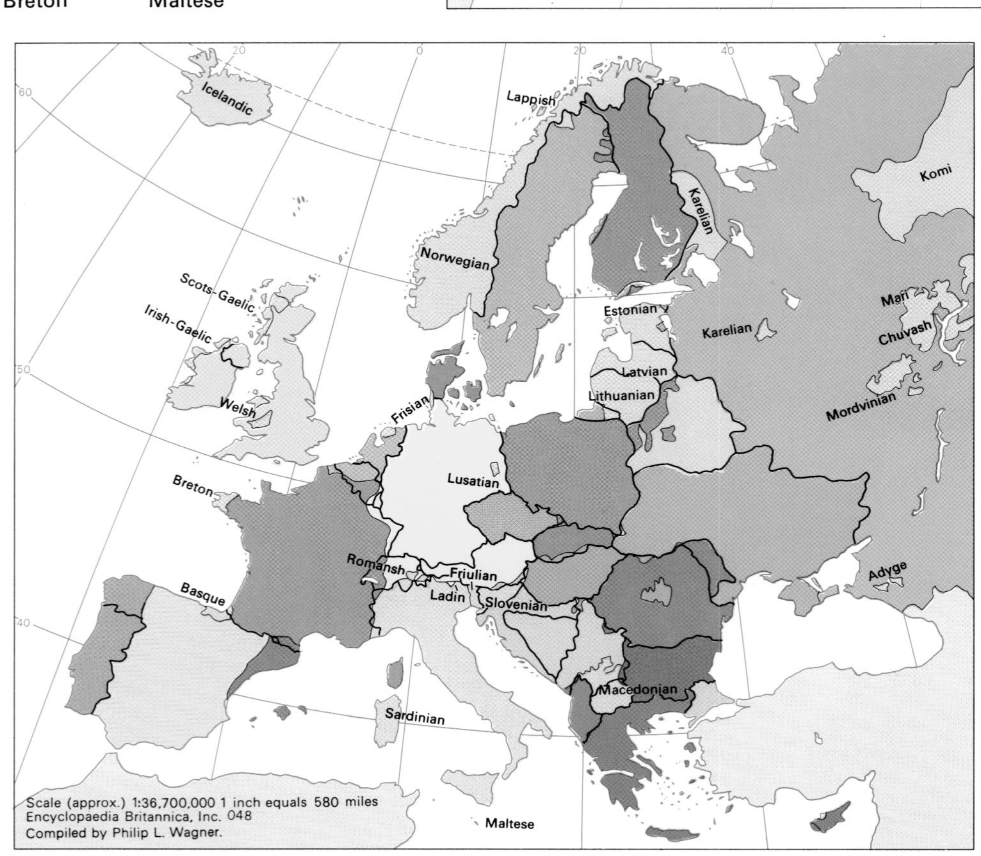
Icelandic
Lappish
Komi
Karelian
Norwegian
Scots-Gaelic
Irish-Gaelic
Estonian
Karelian
Mari
Chuvash
Latvian
Lithuanian
Welsh
Frisian
Mordvinian
Lusatian
Breton
Romansh
Friulian
Ladin
Slovenian
Adyge
Basque
Macedonian
Sardinian
Maltese
Scale (approx.) 1:36,700,000 1 inch equals 580 miles
Encyclopaedia Britannica, Inc. 048
Compiled by Philip L. Wagner.

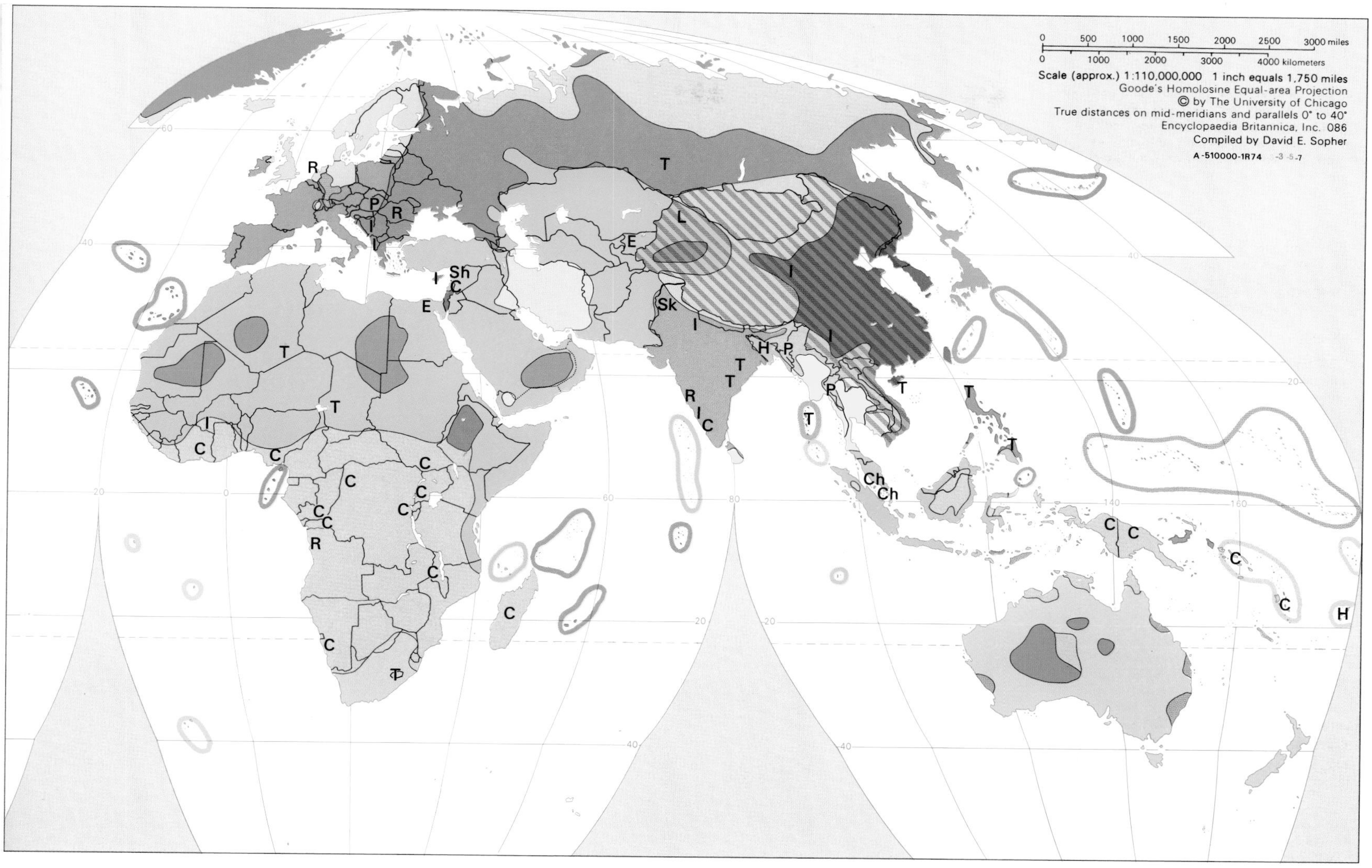

0 500 1000 1500 2000 2500 3000 miles
0 1000 2000 3000 4000 kilometers
Scale (approx.) 1:110,000,000 1 inch equals 1,750 miles
Goode's Homolosine Equal-area Projection
© by The University of Chicago
True distances on mid-meridians and parallels 0° to 40°
Encyclopaedia Britannica, Inc. 086
Compiled by David E. Sopher
A-510000-1R74

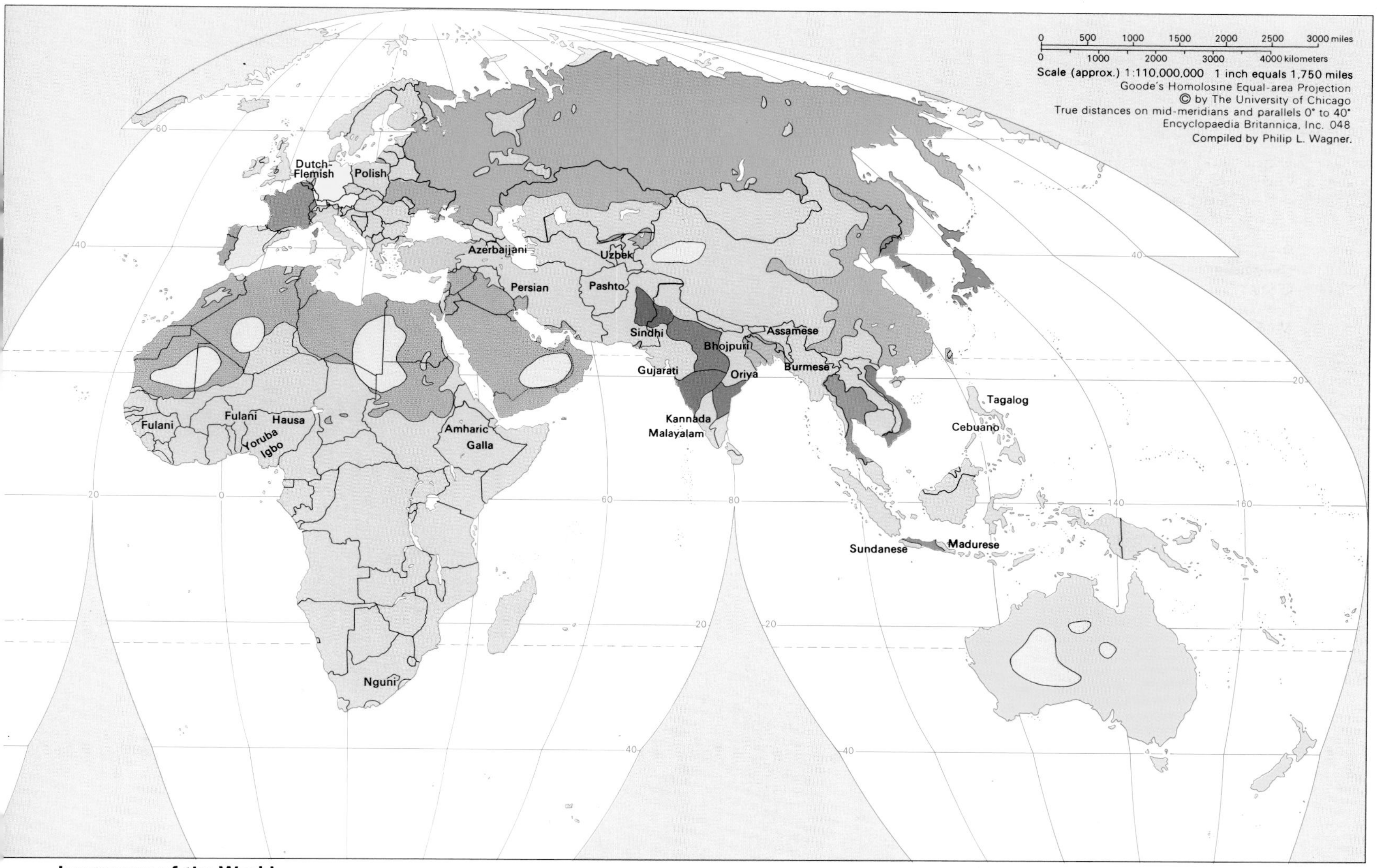

0 500 1000 1500 2000 2500 3000 miles
0 1000 2000 3000 4000 kilometers
Scale (approx.) 1:110,000,000 1 inch equals 1,750 miles
Goode's Homolosine Equal-area Projection
© by The University of Chicago
True distances on mid-meridians and parallels 0° to 40°
Encyclopaedia Britannica, Inc. 048
Compiled by Philip L. Wagner.
Dutch-Flemish
Polish
Azerbaijani
Uzbek
Persian
Pashto
Sindhi
Bhojpuri
Assamese
Gujarati
Oriya
Burmese
Kannada
Malayalam
Tagalog
Cebuano
Fulani
Fulani
Hausa
Yoruba
Igbo
Amharic
Galla
Sundanese
Madurese
Nguni

Languages of the World

The following languages are ranked in descending order by number of speakers. Languages spoken by more than 40 million persons are indicated by color. Others listed, spoken by 10-40 million persons, are named on the map.

Chinese
Spanish
English
Hindi
Bengali
Arabic
Russian
Portuguese
Japanese
German
Punjabi
Javanese
Korean
Telugu
Marathi
French
Italian
Tamil
Vietnamese
Urdu
Turkish
Ukrainian
Thai
All others
Uninhabited

Polish
Gujarati
Malayalam
Kannada
Oriya
Burmese
Persian
Hausa
Sundanese
Bhojpuri
Yoruba
Dutch-Flemish
Pashtu
Fulani
Igbo
Uzbek
Galla
Cebuano
Azerbaijani
Nguni
Tagalog
Assamese
Sindhi
Amharic
Madurese

Agricultural Regions

- Cash crop and livestock farming
- Cash crop farming, grain or cotton dominant
- Crop and livestock farming with cash products minor
- Livestock ranching
- Dairying
- Mediterranean agriculture
- Specialized horticulture
- Plantation agriculture
- Intensive subsistence tillage, rice dominant
- Intensive subsistence tillage, with no dominant crop
- Rudimental sedentary farming
- Shifting cultivation
- Nomadic herding
- No agriculture

The agricultural systems classified and mapped here represent the primary *agricultural,* rather than economic, activity in the areas shown, since in many developed countries farm population may now constitute less than 5 percent of the total population. No particular level of technology is implied by the classification, as reindeer herding can be carried out with dogs or snowmobiles, crops be irrigated with bucket wheels or electric pumps, dairy cows milked by hand or by machine. Much of the activity shown is controlled, or more specifically, limited by topography and climate. Thus while it is easier to farm on flat land, terracing can create flat land where none exists; intermediate slopes can either be cropped by special techniques, as in Switzerland, or planted in a crop like tea or wine grapes for which slope, or attitude toward the sun and other climatic elements might determine the crop's success. Density of natural vegetation usually declines with altitude and rainfall and so livestock ranching can take place in the compass of a North American feedlot, an Australian cattle station, or a Papua New Guinean butterfly farm. Among the types of occupance listed, "Mediterranean" agriculture may be the least familiar to North Americans. It refers to a system developed in the Mediterranean basin's hot, dry summers that concentrates on hardy tree crops (olive, citrus) or vines (grape), interspersed with small plantings of vegetables or grain; few livestock are kept except in uplands, though small ruminants like goats may be kept lower down.

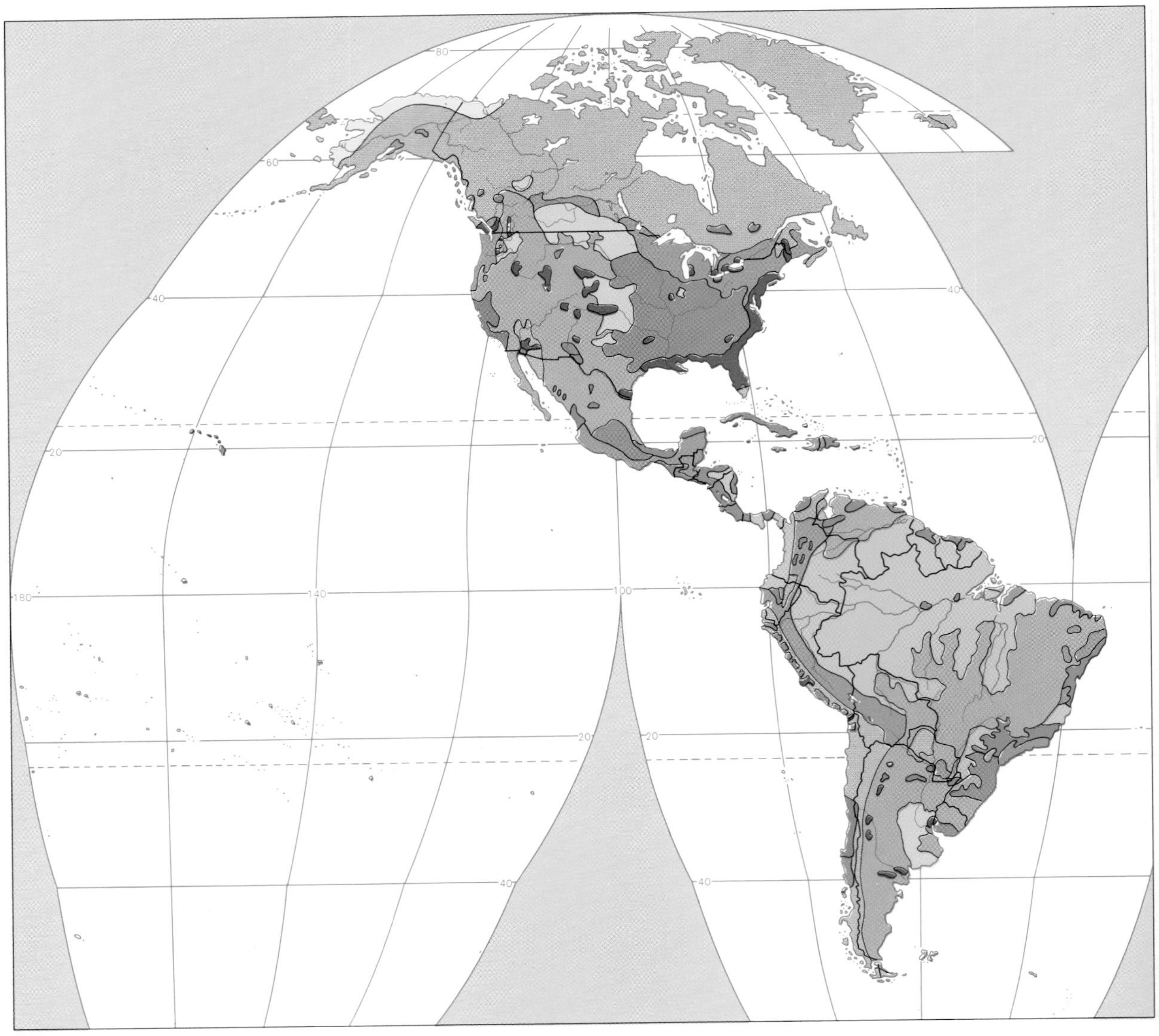

Forests and Fisheries

Forests

- Conifers: cedar, fir, hemlock, pine, redwood, spruce
- Regions of exploitation
- Tropical hardwoods: ebony, mahogany, rosewood, teak
- Regions of exploitation
- Temperate hardwoods: hickory, maple, oak, poplar, walnut, and some mixed hardwoods and conifers
- Regions of exploitation

Fisheries

- Pelagic fishing regions: anchoveta, anchovy, herring, menhaden, pilchard, sardine, sprat, tuna
- Ground fishing regions: cod, haddock, hake, horse mackerel, mackerel, pollack, redfish
- Mixed ground and pelagic fishing regions
- Shellfish: clam, crab, lobster, mussel, oyster, scallop, shrimp, squid

Two principal *commercial* activities are summarized on the map opposite: forestry, classified by type of forests exploited, and fisheries, classified by type of fishing grounds. Three forest types are shown, classified by the woods of chief economic interest within them, rather than by the predominant vegetation. For example, while the softwood conifers listed may actually predominate in many of the regions shown, there are very few areas where the temperate or tropical hardwoods listed will actually constitute the predominant or characteristic tree. Commercial exploitation concentrates on regions where the tree stock has reached economically significant size, is not diluted by other, uneconomical woods, and where transportation infrastructure permits economical removal.

Of the ocean fisheries shown, the term 'Pelagic' refers to near-surface fisheries, either near-shore or on the high seas. 'Ground' fisheries are those which exploit bottom-dwelling fish, or shellfish but should not be confused with the term 'fishing grounds,' which may be either pelagic or ground. The types of fish listed are the principal species exploited in terms of quantities landed. Ocean areas of greatest biological diversity may support both kinds of fish populations, such as those of the Grand Banks of Newfoundland. Commercial whaling is no longer significant although some traditional whaling from small boats still takes place.

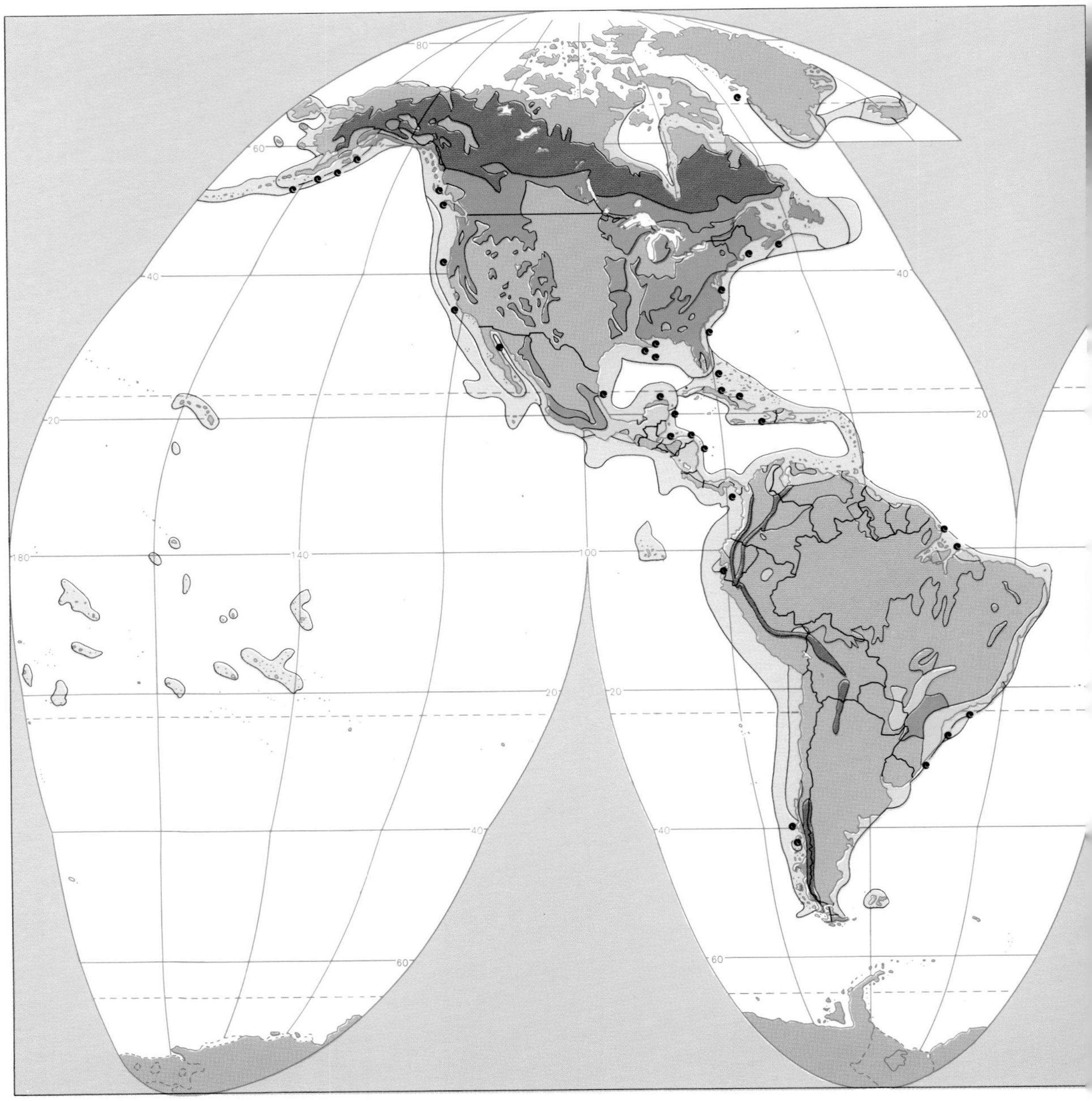

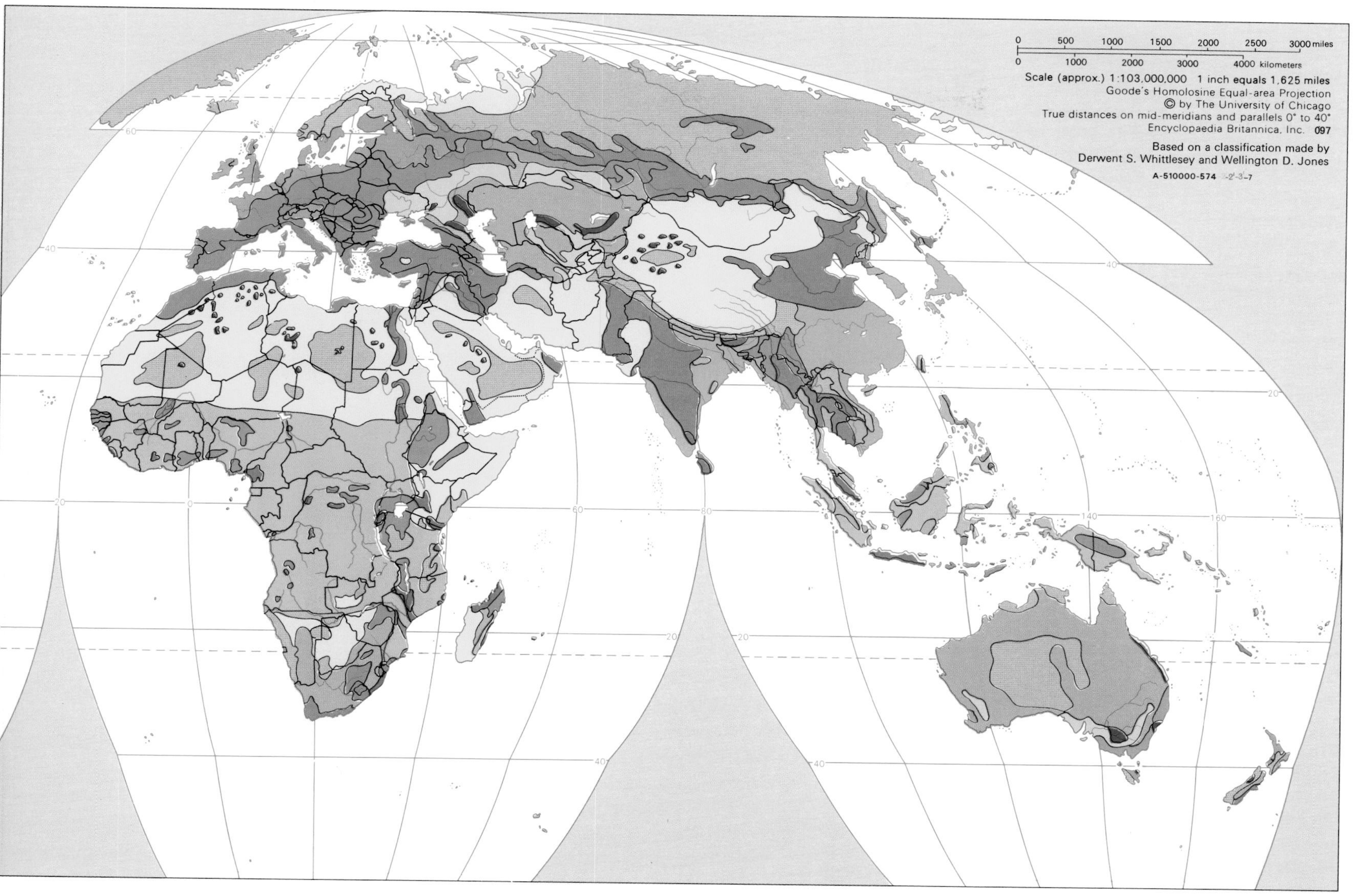
0 500 1000 1500 2000 2500 3000 miles
0 1000 2000 3000 4000 kilometers
Scale (approx.) 1:103,000,000 1 inch equals 1,625 miles
Goode's Homolosine Equal-area Projection
© by The University of Chicago
True distances on mid-meridians and parallels 0° to 40°
Encyclopaedia Britannica, Inc. 097
Based on a classification made by
Derwent S. Whittlesey and Wellington D. Jones
A-510000-574

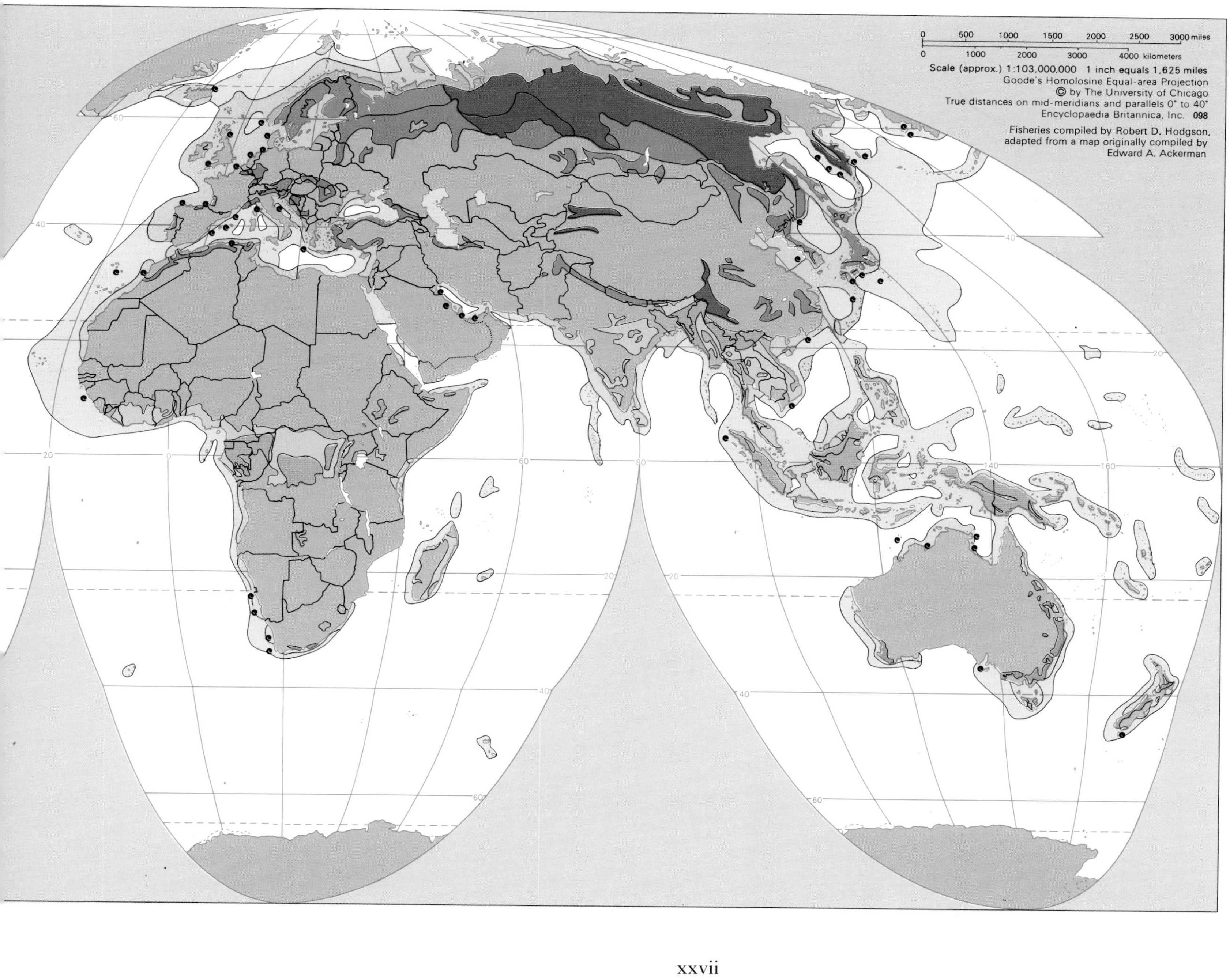
0 500 1000 1500 2000 2500 3000 miles
0 1000 2000 3000 4000 kilometers
Scale (approx.) 1:103,000,000 1 inch equals 1,625 miles
Goode's Homolosine Equal-area Projection
© by The University of Chicago
True distances on mid-meridians and parallels 0° to 40°
Encyclopaedia Britannica, Inc. 098
Fisheries compiled by Robert D. Hodgson,
adapted from a map originally compiled by
Edward A. Ackerman

Minerals

4-year world average production shown in graphs. Producing areas shown on maps

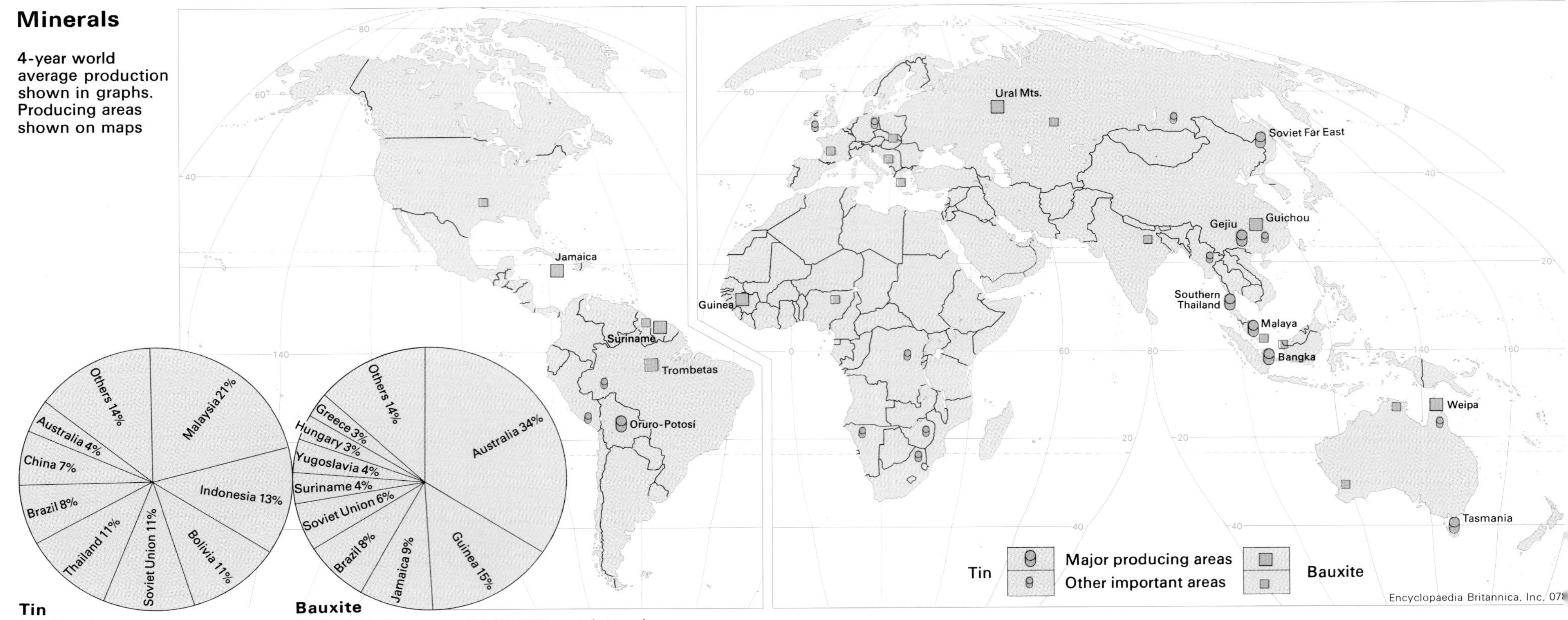
Others 14%
Malaysia 21%
Indonesia 13%
Bolivia 11%
Soviet Union 11%
Thailand 11%
Brazil 8%
China 7%
Australia 4%
Others 14%
Australia 34%
Guinea 15%
Jamaica 9%
Brazil 8%
Soviet Union 6%
Suriname 4%
Yugoslavia 4%
Hungary 3%
Greece 3%
Ural Mts.
Soviet Far East
Jamaica
Guinea
Suriname
Trombetas
Oruro-Potosí
Gejiu
Guichou
Southern Thailand
Malaya
Bangka
Weipa
Tasmania
Tin
Major producing areas
Other important areas
Bauxite
Encyclopaedia Britannica, Inc. 07

Tin
222,200 short tons
(201,600 metric tons)

Bauxite
91,290,000 short tons (82,817,000 metric tons)

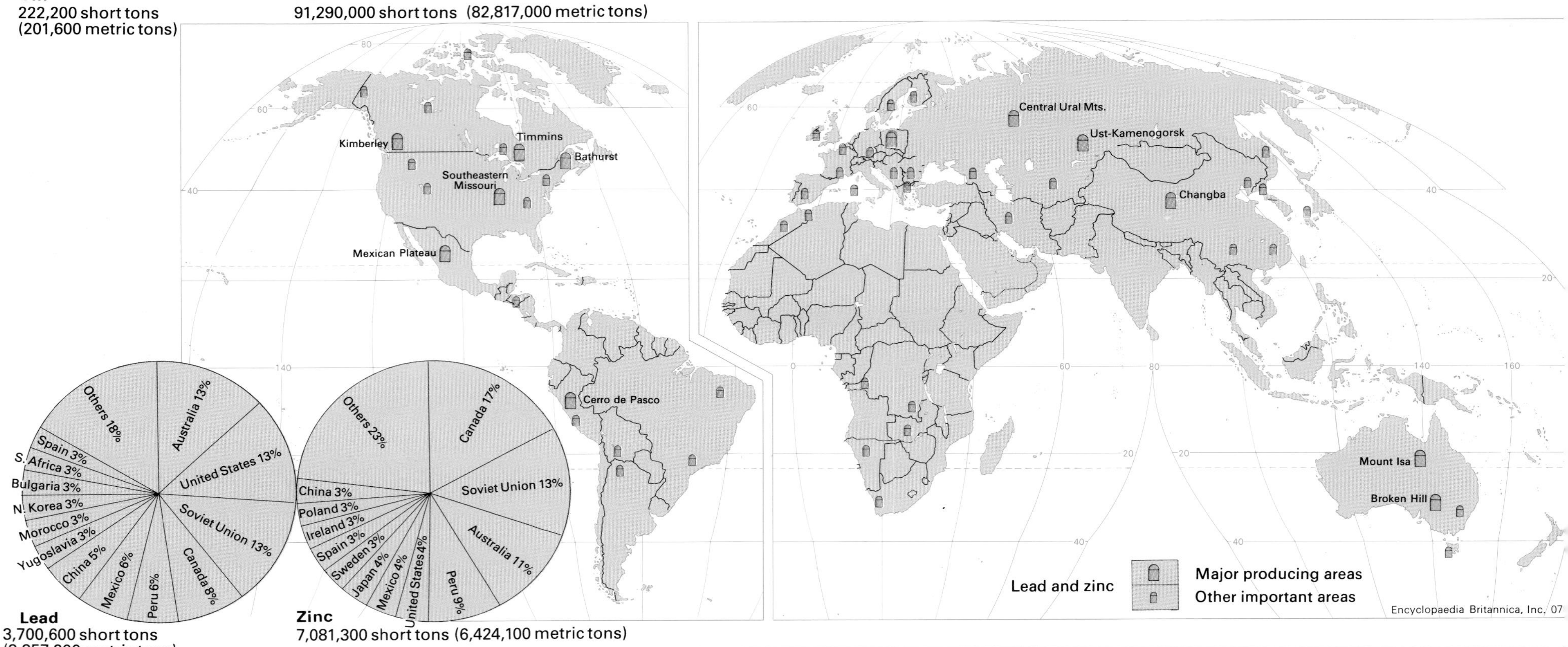
Others 18%
Australia 13%
United States 13%
Soviet Union 13%
Canada 8%
Peru 6%
Mexico 6%
China 5%
Yugoslavia 3%
Morocco 3%
N. Korea 3%
Bulgaria 3%
S. Africa 3%
Spain 3%
Others 23%
Canada 17%
Soviet Union 13%
Australia 11%
Peru 9%
United States 4%
Mexico 4%
Japan 4%
Sweden 3%
Spain 3%
Ireland 3%
Poland 3%
China 3%
Kimberley
Timmins
Bathurst
Southeastern Missouri
Mexican Plateau
Cerro de Pasco
Central Ural Mts.
Ust-Kamenogorsk
Changba
Mount Isa
Broken Hill
Lead and zinc
Major producing areas
Other important areas
Encyclopaedia Britannica, Inc. 07

Lead
3,700,600 short tons
(3,357,200 metric tons)

Zinc
7,081,300 short tons (6,424,100 metric tons)

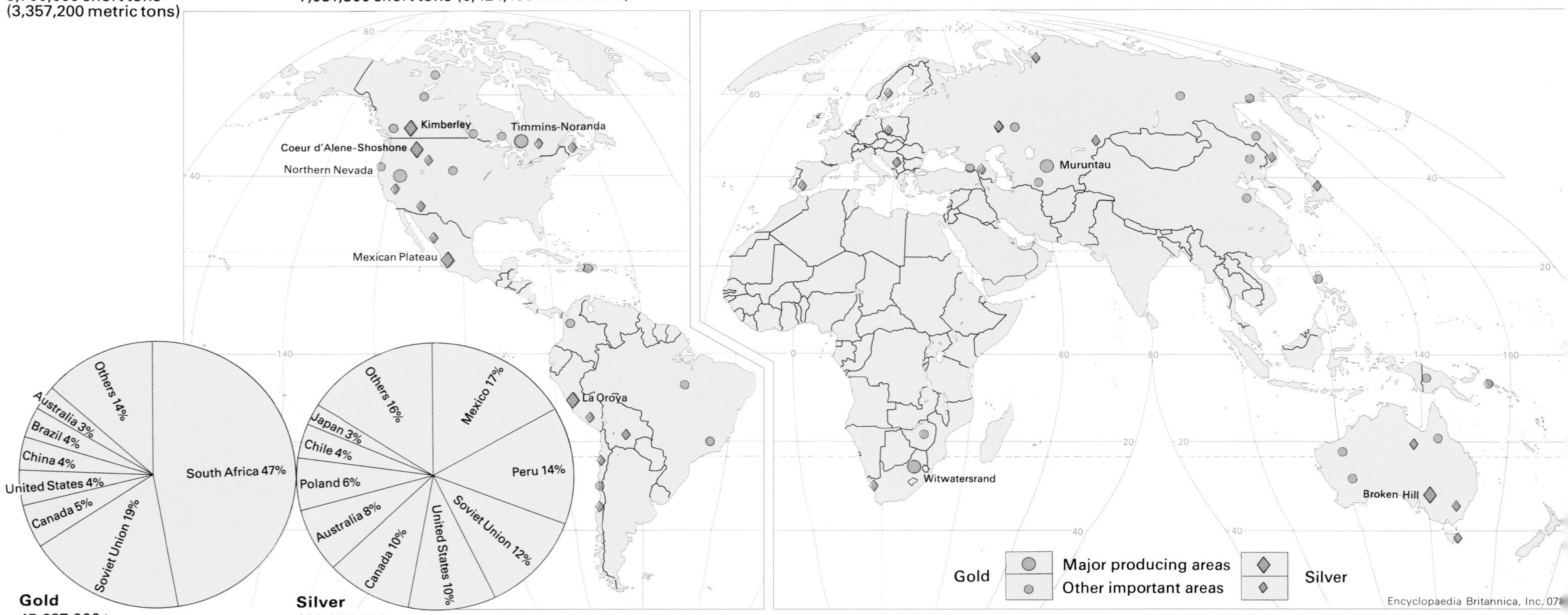
Others 14%
South Africa 47%
Soviet Union 19%
Canada 5%
United States 4%
China 4%
Brazil 4%
Australia 3%
Others 16%
Mexico 17%
Peru 14%
Soviet Union 12%
United States 10%
Canada 10%
Australia 8%
Poland 6%
Chile 4%
Japan 3%
Kimberley
Timmins-Noranda
Coeur d'Alene-Shoshone
Northern Nevada
Mexican Plateau
La Oroya
Muruntau
Witwatersrand
Broken Hill
Gold
Major producing areas
Other important areas
Silver
Encyclopaedia Britannica, Inc. 07

Gold
45,687,000 troy ounces
(1,421,000 kilograms)

Silver
400,634,000 troy ounces
(12,461,000 kilograms)

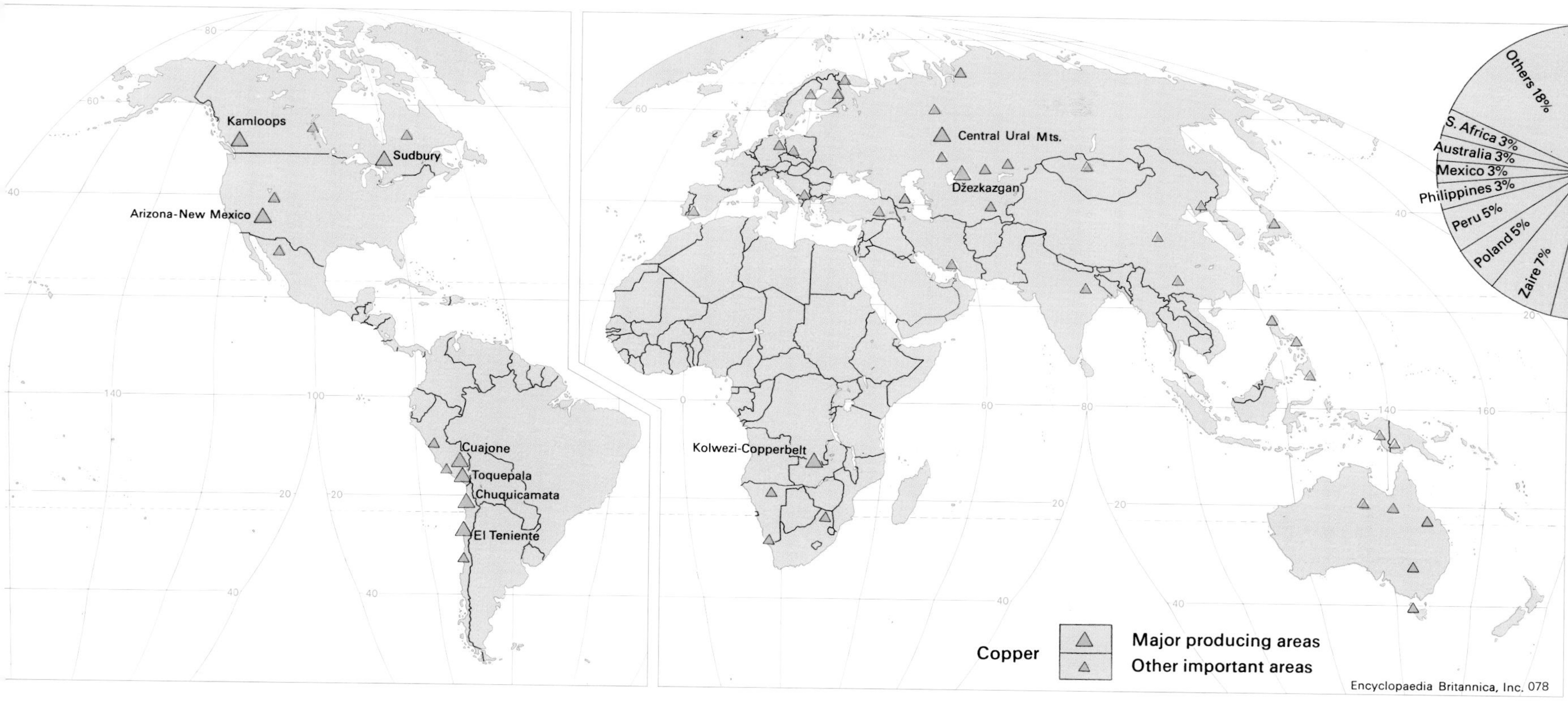
Kamloops
Sudbury
Arizona-New Mexico
Cuajone
Toquepala
Chuquicamata
El Teniente
Central Ural Mts.
Džezkazgan
Kolwezi-Copperbelt
Copper
Major producing areas
Other important areas
Encyclopaedia Britannica, Inc. 078

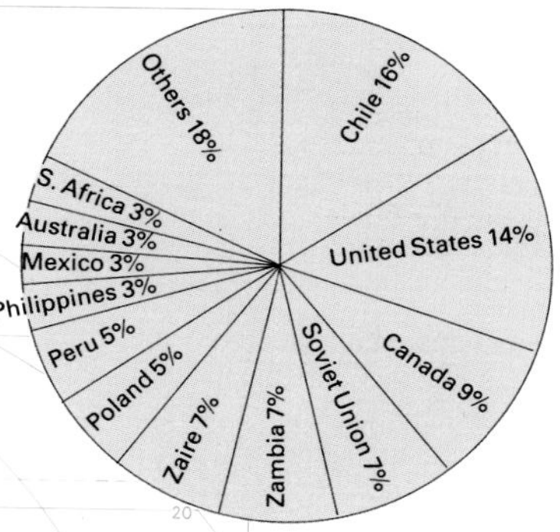
Chile 16%
United States 14%
Canada 9%
Soviet Union 7%
Zambia 7%
Zaire 7%
Poland 5%
Peru 5%
Philippines 3%
Mexico 3%
Australia 3%
S. Africa 3%
Others 18%

Copper
8,661,600
short tons
(7,857,700
metric tons)

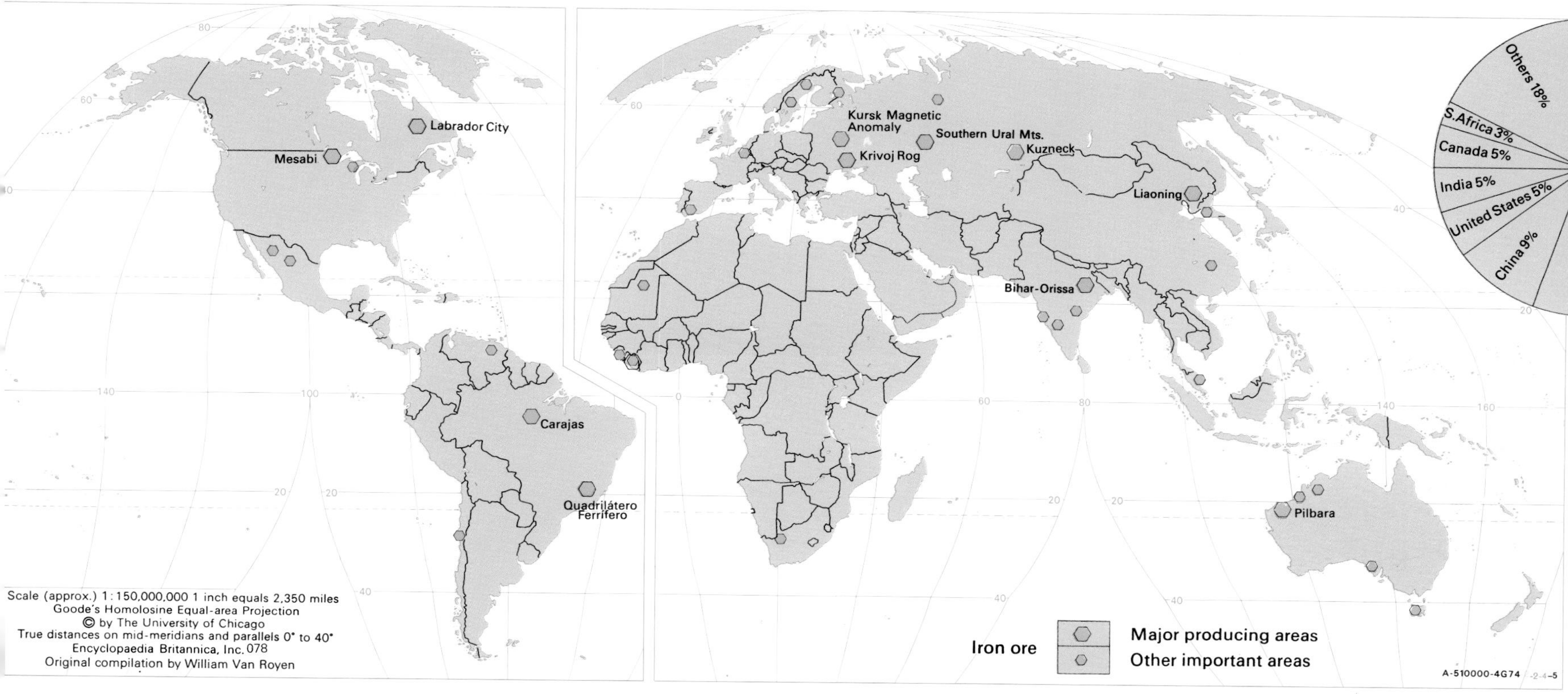
Labrador City
Mesabi
Carajas
Quadrilátero Ferrífero
Kursk Magnetic Anomaly
Krivoj Rog
Southern Ural Mts.
Kuzneck
Liaoning
Bihar-Orissa
Pilbara
Scale (approx.) 1:150,000,000 1 inch equals 2,350 miles
Goode's Homolosine Equal-area Projection
© by The University of Chicago
True distances on mid-meridians and parallels 0° to 40°
Encyclopaedia Britannica, Inc. 078
Original compilation by William Van Royen
Iron ore
Major producing areas
Other important areas
A-510000-4G74

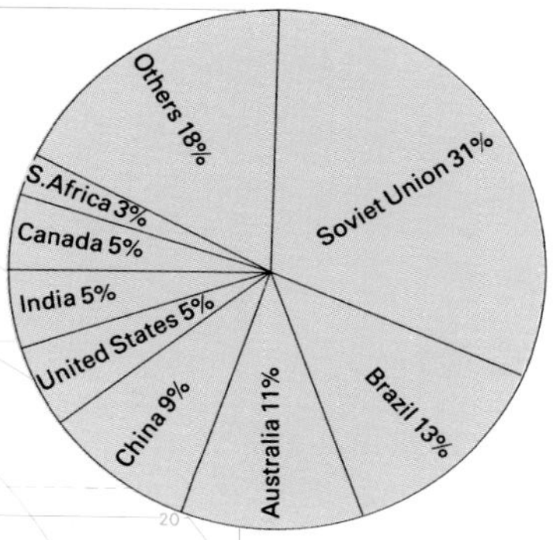
Soviet Union 31%
Brazil 13%
Australia 11%
China 9%
United States 5%
India 5%
Canada 5%
S. Africa 3%
Others 18%

Iron ore
883,984,900
short tons
(801,937,600
metric tons)

Ferroalloying Minerals

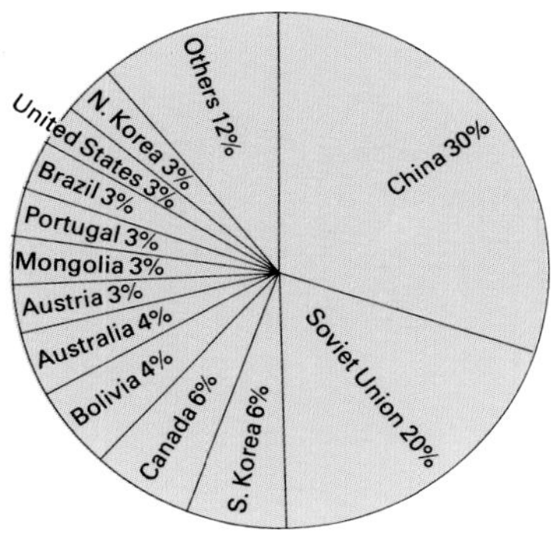
China 30%
Soviet Union 20%
S. Korea 6%
Canada 6%
Bolivia 4%
Australia 4%
Austria 3%
Mongolia 3%
Portugal 3%
Brazil 3%
United States 3%
N. Korea 3%
Others 12%

Tungsten
49,900 short tons
(45,300 metric tons)

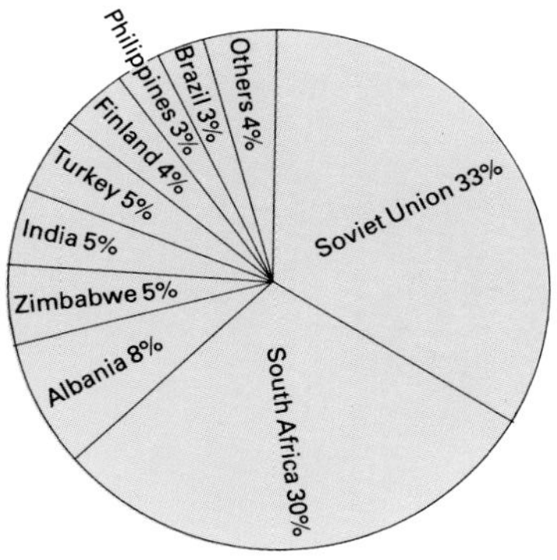
Soviet Union 33%
South Africa 30%
Albania 8%
Zimbabwe 5%
India 5%
Turkey 5%
Finland 4%
Philippines 3%
Brazil 3%
Others 4%

Chromite
9,779,500 short tons
(8,871,800 metric tons)

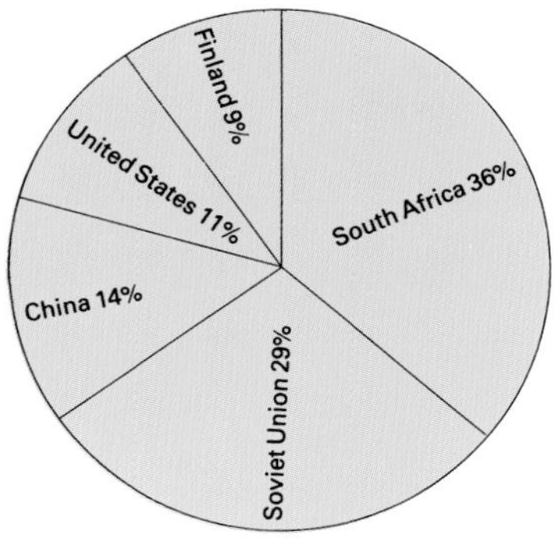
South Africa 36%
Soviet Union 29%
China 14%
United States 11%
Finland 9%

Vanadium
36,200 short tons
(32,900 metric tons)

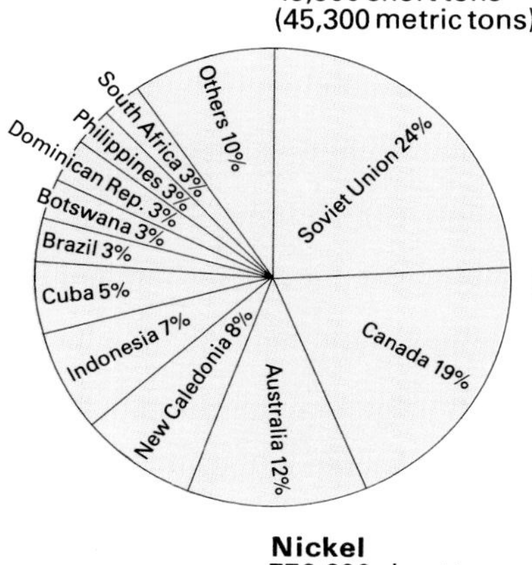
Soviet Union 24%
Canada 19%
Australia 12%
New Caledonia 8%
Indonesia 7%
Cuba 5%
Brazil 3%
Botswana 3%
Dominican Rep. 3%
Philippines 3%
South Africa 3%
Others 10%

Nickel
776,600 short tons
(704,500 metric tons)

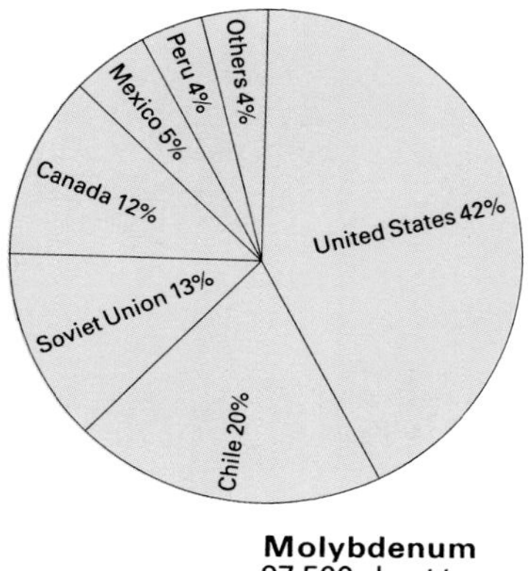
United States 42%
Chile 20%
Soviet Union 13%
Canada 12%
Mexico 5%
Peru 4%
Others 4%

Molybdenum
97,500 short tons
(88,400 metric tons)

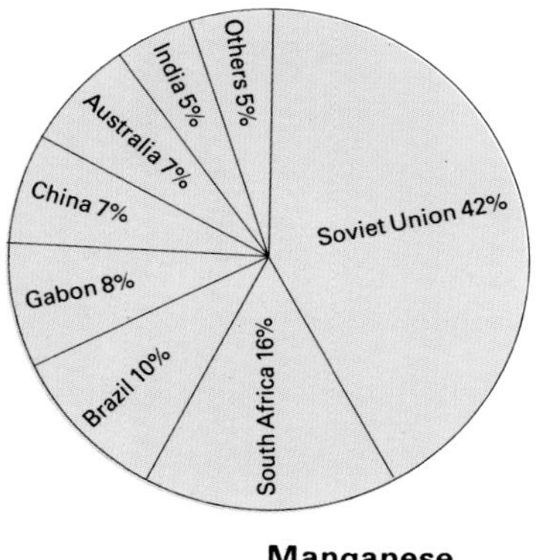
Soviet Union 42%
South Africa 16%
Brazil 10%
Gabon 8%
China 7%
Australia 7%
India 5%
Others 5%

Manganese
25,960,000 short tons
(23,550,500 metric tons)

Energy Production and Consumption

Unit of measure is metric tons coal equivalent (m.t.c.e.)

Production

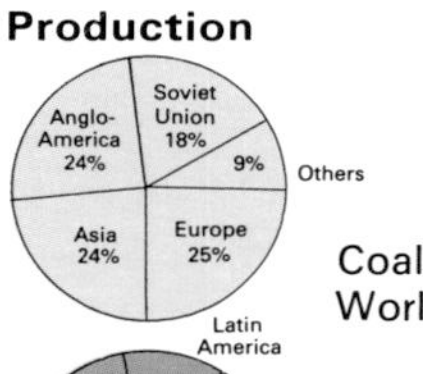
Anglo-America 24%
Soviet Union 18%
9%
Others
Asia 24%
Europe 25%
Latin America

Coal and lignite
World total: 2,712,000,000

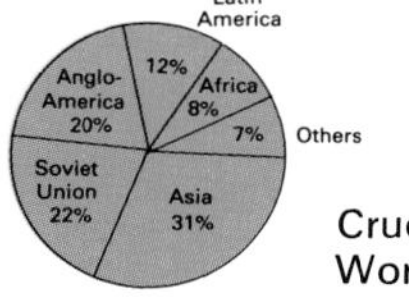
Anglo-America 20%
12%
Africa 8%
7%
Others
Soviet Union 22%
Asia 31%

Crude petroleum
World total: 4,035,000,000

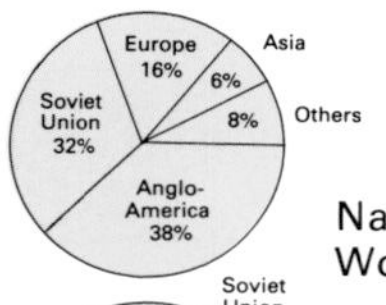
Europe 16%
Asia
6%
8%
Others
Soviet Union 32%
Anglo-America 38%

Natural gas
World total: 1,852,000,000

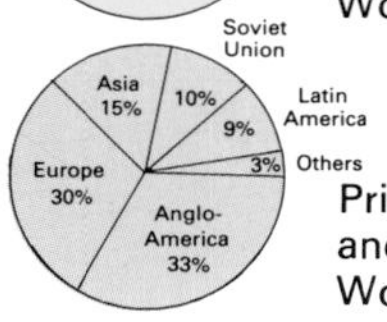
Soviet Union
Asia 15%
10%
Latin America
9%
3%
Others
Europe 30%
Anglo-America 33%

Primary electricity (hydro-, geothermal, and nuclear)
World total: 334,000,000

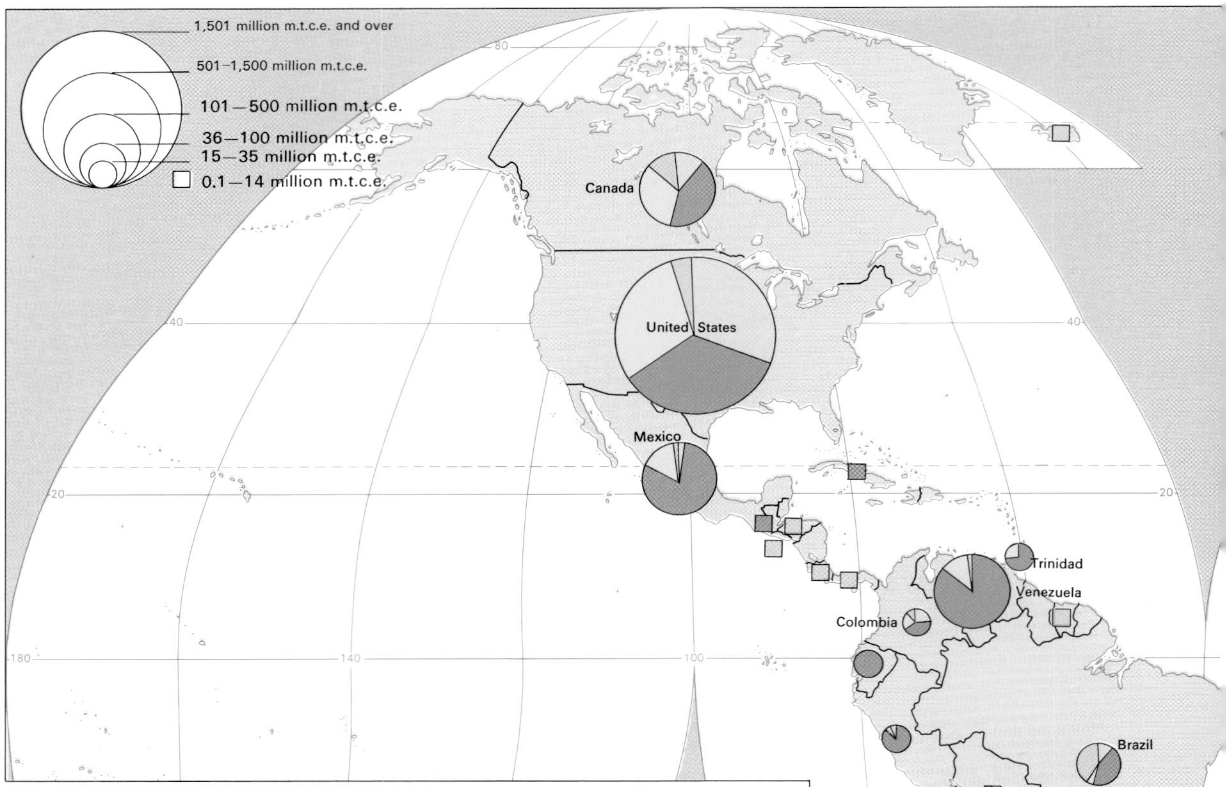
1,501 million m.t.c.e. and over
501–1,500 million m.t.c.e.
101–500 million m.t.c.e.
36–100 million m.t.c.e.
15–35 million m.t.c.e.
0.1–14 million m.t.c.e.
Canada
United States
Mexico
Trinidad
Venezuela
Colombia
Brazil
Argentina

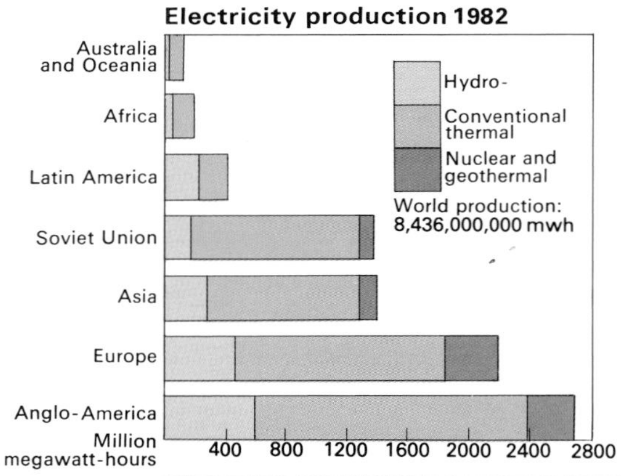
Electricity production 1982
Australia and Oceania
Africa
Latin America
Soviet Union
Asia
Europe
Anglo-America
Hydro-
Conventional thermal
Nuclear and geothermal
World production: 8,436,000,000 mwh
Million megawatt-hours
400
800
1200
1600
2000
2400
2800

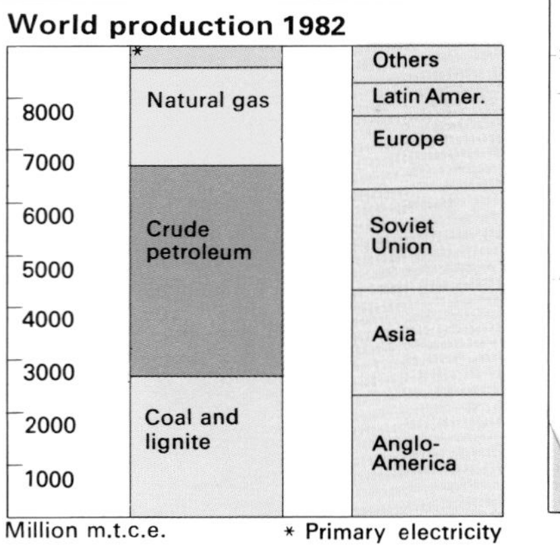
World production 1982
*
Natural gas
Crude petroleum
Coal and lignite
Others
Latin Amer.
Europe
Soviet Union
Asia
Anglo-America
8000
7000
6000
5000
4000
3000
2000
1000
Million m.t.c.e.
* Primary electricity

Table of equivalents

Coal, anthracite and bituminous	1 metric ton = 1.0 m.t.c.e.
Lignite	1 metric ton = 0.3 – 0.6 m.t.c.e.
Petroleum	1 metric ton = 1.5 m.t.c.e.
Natural gas	1,000 cubic meters = 1.33 m.t.c.e.
Hydro-, geothermal, and nuclear electricity	1.0 megawatt-hour = 0.125 m.t.c.e.

Potential energy of 1 metric ton of coal equals 28,000,000 B.T.U.

Consumption

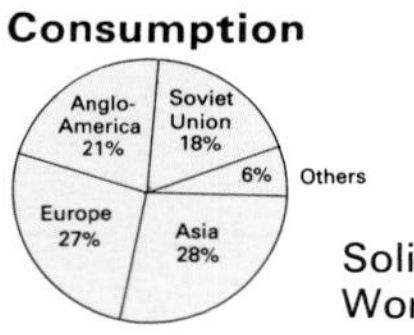
Anglo-America 21%
Soviet Union 18%
6%
Others
Europe 27%
Asia 28%

Solid fuels
World total: 2,693,000,000

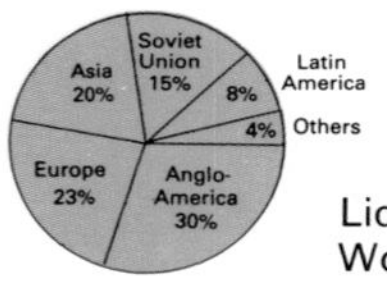
Asia 20%
Soviet Union 15%
8%
Latin America
4%
Others
Europe 23%
Anglo-America 30%

Liquid fuels
World total: 3,543,000,000

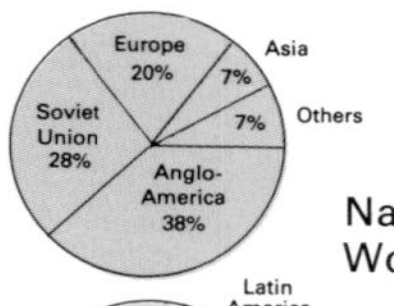
Europe 20%
Asia
7%
7%
Others
Soviet Union 28%
Anglo-America 38%

Natural and manufactured gas
World total: 1,836,000,000

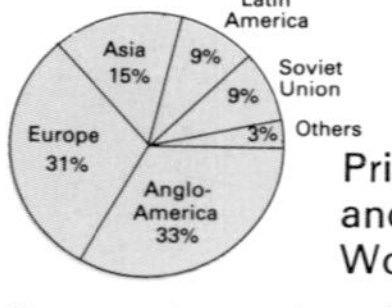
Latin America
Asia 15%
9%
Soviet Union
9%
3%
Others
Europe 31%
Anglo-America 33%

Primary electricity (hydro-, geothermal, and nuclear)
World total: 334,000,000

Consumption totals exclude noncommercial fuels, fuels consumed by vessels engaged in international trade, and nonfuel petroleum products.

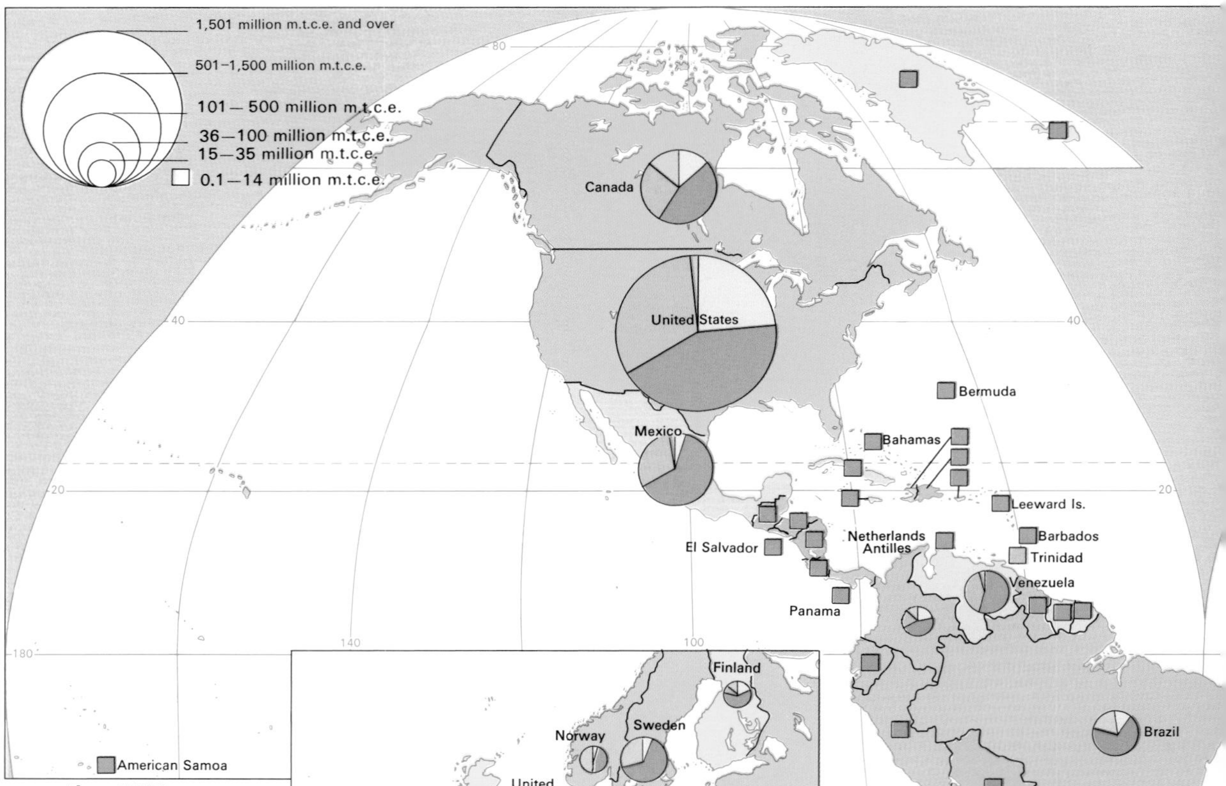
1,501 million m.t.c.e. and over
501–1,500 million m.t.c.e.
101–500 million m.t.c.e.
36–100 million m.t.c.e.
15–35 million m.t.c.e.
0.1–14 million m.t.c.e.
Canada
United States
Mexico
Bermuda
Bahamas
Leeward Is.
Barbados
Trinidad
Netherlands Antilles
El Salvador
Panama
Venezuela
Brazil
Argentina
American Samoa
Finland
Norway
Sweden
United Kingdom
Denmark
Neth.
Belgium-Luxembourg
Germany
Poland
Czechoslovakia
Austria
France
Switz.
Hungary
Romania
Yugoslavia
Spain
Italy
Bulgaria
Malta

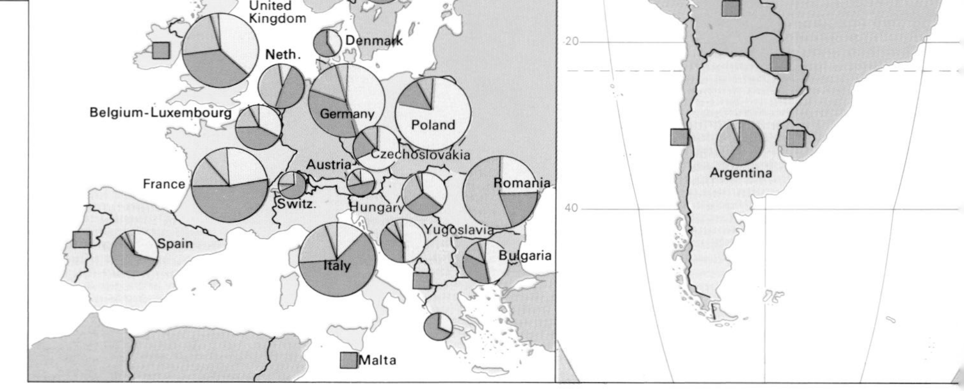

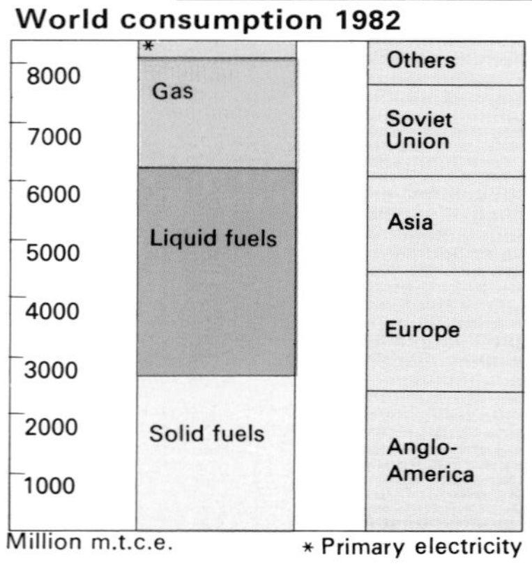
World consumption 1982
*
Gas
Liquid fuels
Solid fuels
Others
Soviet Union
Asia
Europe
Anglo-America
8000
7000
6000
5000
4000
3000
2000
1000
Million m.t.c.e.
* Primary electricity

Per capita consumption

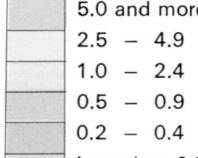

- 5.0 and more
- 2.5 – 4.9
- 1.0 – 2.4
- 0.5 – 0.9
- 0.2 – 0.4
- Less than 0.2

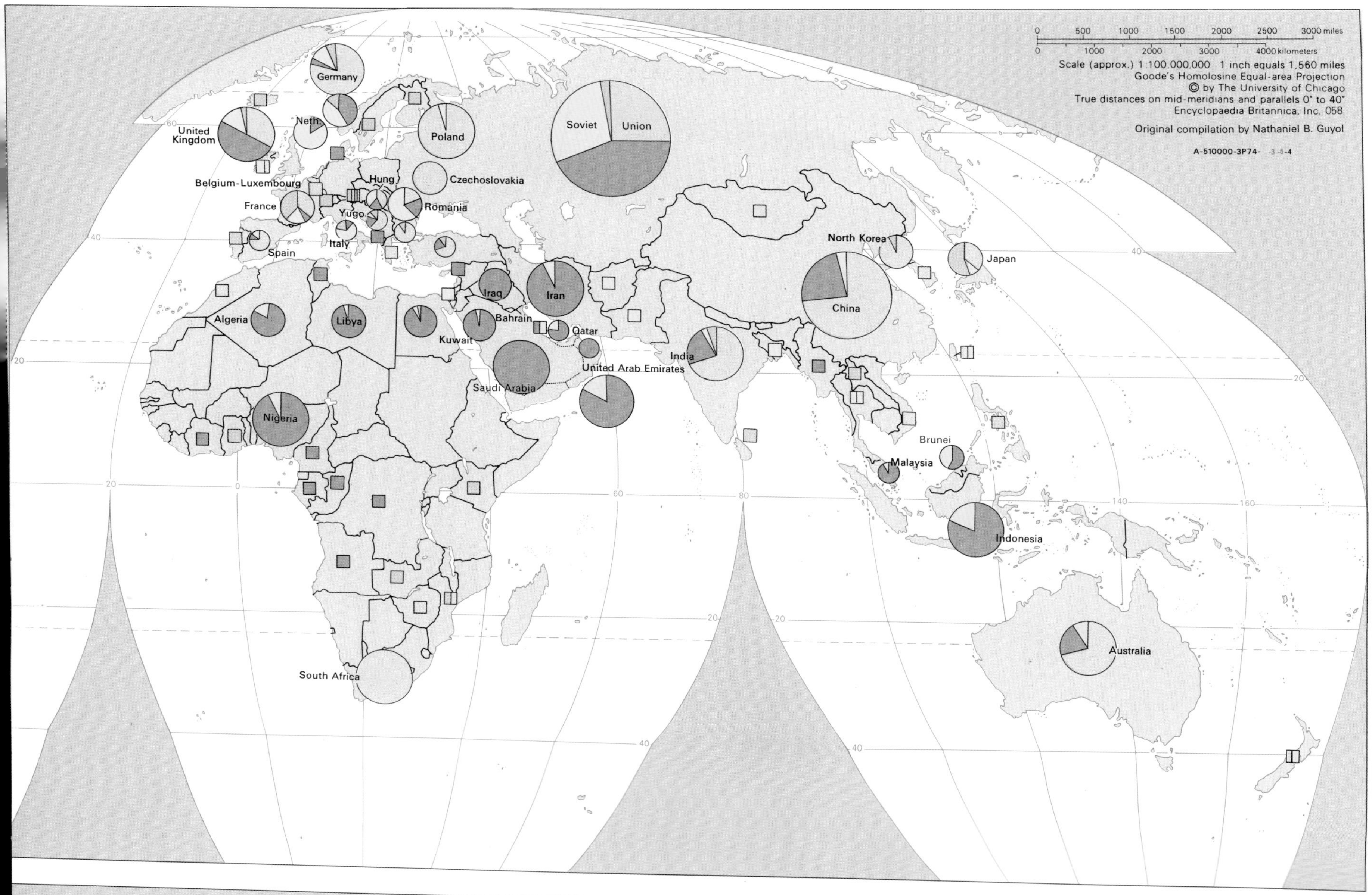
0 500 1000 1500 2000 2500 3000 miles
0 1000 2000 3000 4000 kilometers
Scale (approx.) 1:100,000,000 1 inch equals 1,560 miles
Goode's Homolosine Equal-area Projection
© by The University of Chicago
True distances on mid-meridians and parallels 0° to 40°
Encyclopaedia Britannica, Inc. 058
Original compilation by Nathaniel B. Guyol
A-510000-3P74-
Germany
United Kingdom
Neth.
Poland
Soviet
Union
Czechoslovakia
Belgium-Luxembourg
Hung
France
Romania
Yugo
Italy
Spain
Iraq
Iran
North Korea
Japan
China
Algeria
Libya
Kuwait
Bahrain
Qatar
India
United Arab Emirates
Saudi Arabia
Nigeria
Brunei
Malaysia
Indonesia
Australia
South Africa

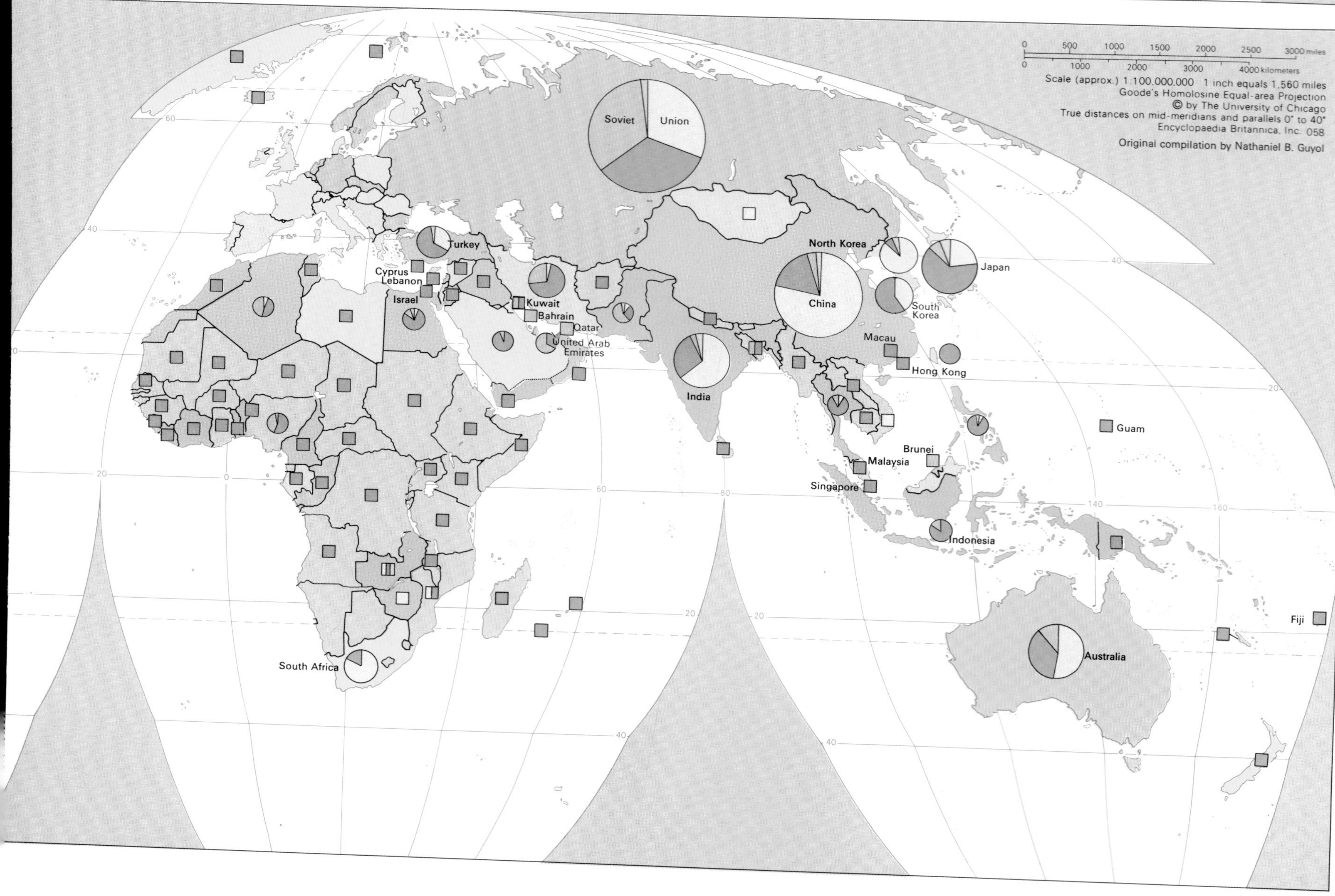
0 500 1000 1500 2000 2500 3000 miles
0 1000 2000 3000 4000 kilometers
Scale (approx.) 1:100,000,000 1 inch equals 1,560 miles
Goode's Homolosine Equal-area Projection
© by The University of Chicago
True distances on mid-meridians and parallels 0° to 40°
Encyclopaedia Britannica, Inc. 058
Original compilation by Nathaniel B. Guyol
Soviet
Union
Turkey
North Korea
Japan
Cyprus
Lebanon
Israel
Kuwait
Bahrain
Qatar
United Arab Emirates
China
South Korea
Macau
Hong Kong
India
Guam
Brunei
Malaysia
Singapore
Indonesia
Fiji
Australia
South Africa

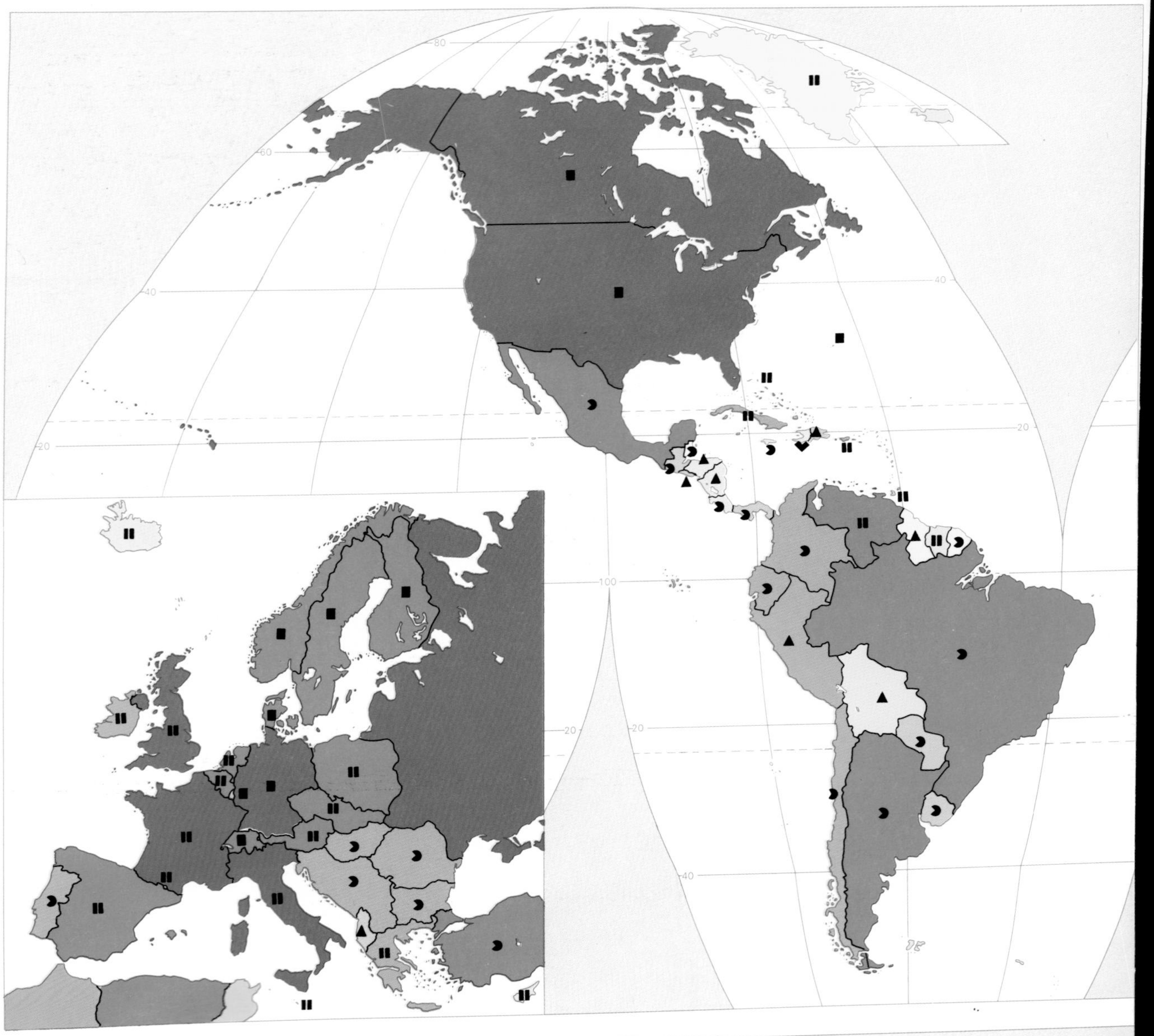

Gross National Product

Total per country at market price In billions of U.S. dollars	Number of countries
300–3,670	9
50–300	26
10–50	28
3–10	34
1–3	32
Less than 1	21
No data available	

Per capita In U.S. dollars		Number of countries
■	10,000–22,300	19
▮▮	3,000–10,000	33
◗	1,000–3,000	32
▲	400–1,000	30
❤	200–400	27
●	Less than 200	15

International Trade

otal per country billions of U.S. dollars	Number of countries
100–560	10
30–100	18
10–30	25
3–10	19
–3	33
ss than 1	46
data available	

	Number of countries
45,000	11
,000	25
0	27
	18
	36
	39

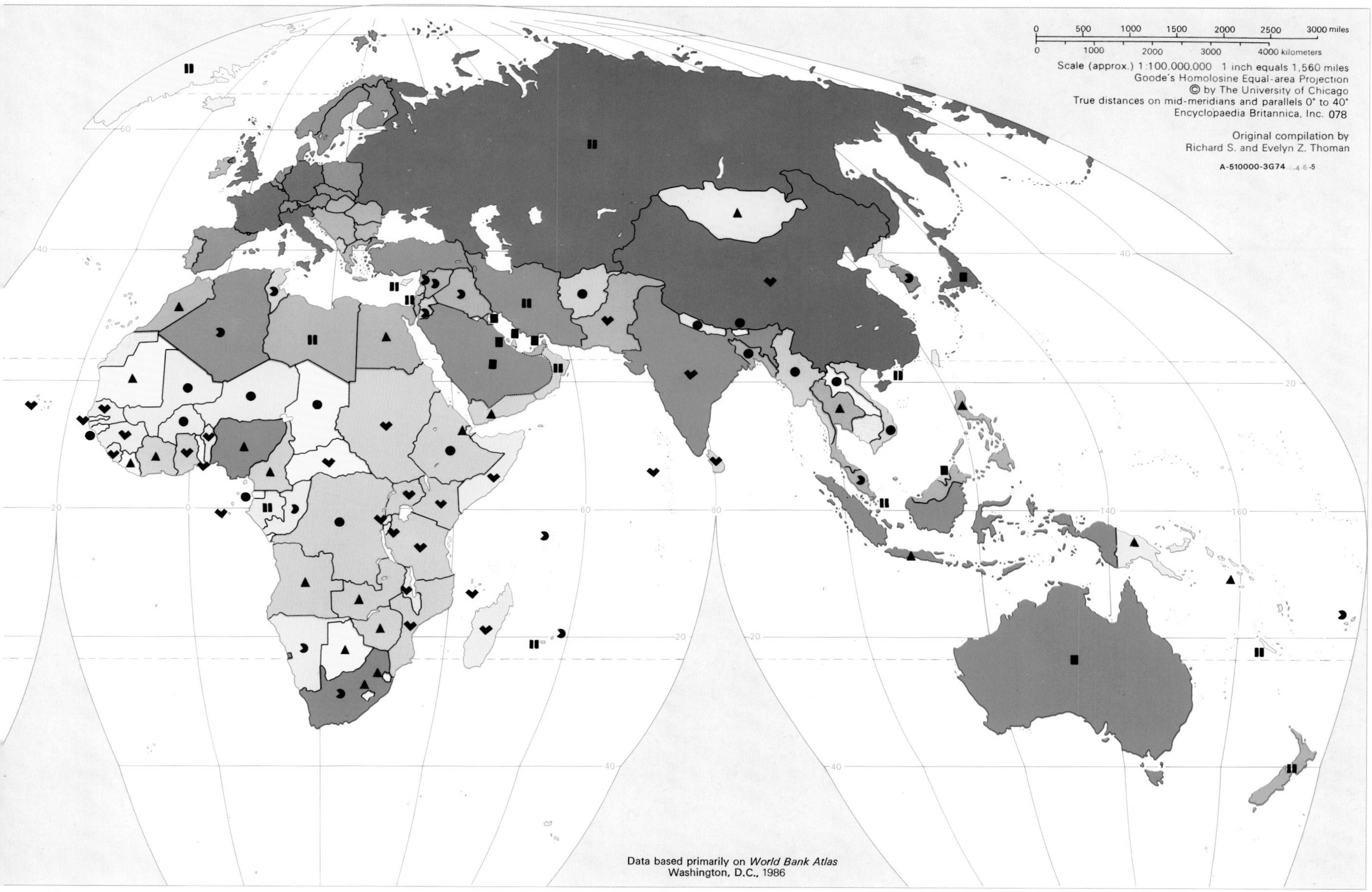
0 500 1000 1500 2000 2500 3000 miles
0 1000 2000 3000 4000 kilometers
Scale (approx.) 1:100,000,000 1 inch equals 1,560 miles
Goode's Homolosine Equal-area Projection
© by The University of Chicago
True distances on mid-meridians and parallels 0° to 40°
Encyclopaedia Britannica, Inc. 078
Original compilation by
Richard S. and Evelyn Z. Thoman
A-510000-3G74-4-6-5
Data based primarily on *World Bank Atlas*
Washington, D.C., 1986

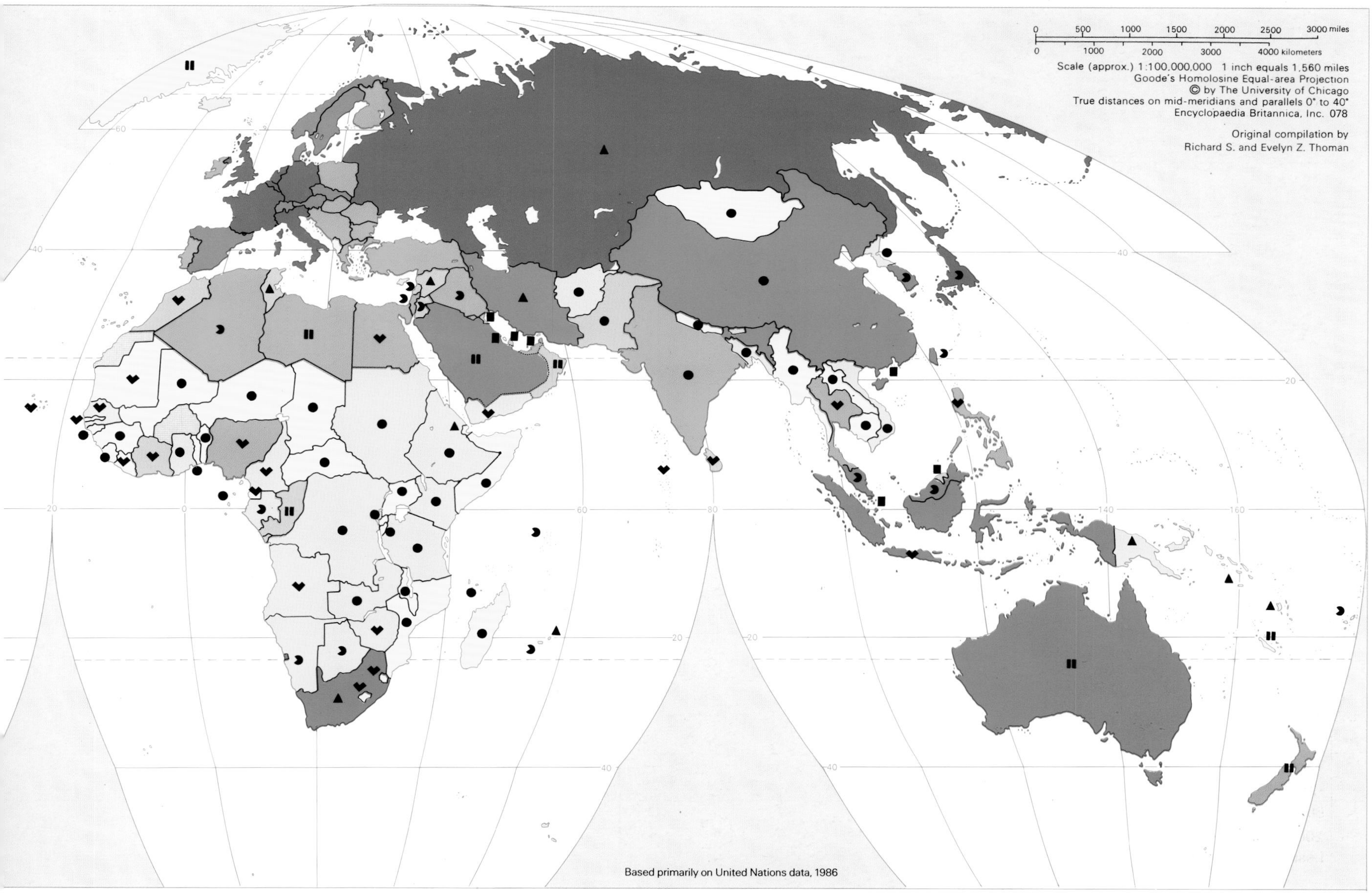
0 500 1000 1500 2000 2500 3000 miles
0 1000 2000 3000 4000 kilometers
Scale (approx.) 1:100,000,000 1 inch equals 1,560 miles
Goode's Homolosine Equal-area Projection
© by The University of Chicago
True distances on mid-meridians and parallels 0° to 40°
Encyclopaedia Britannica, Inc. 078
Original compilation by
Richard S. and Evelyn Z. Thoman
Based primarily on United Nations data, 1986

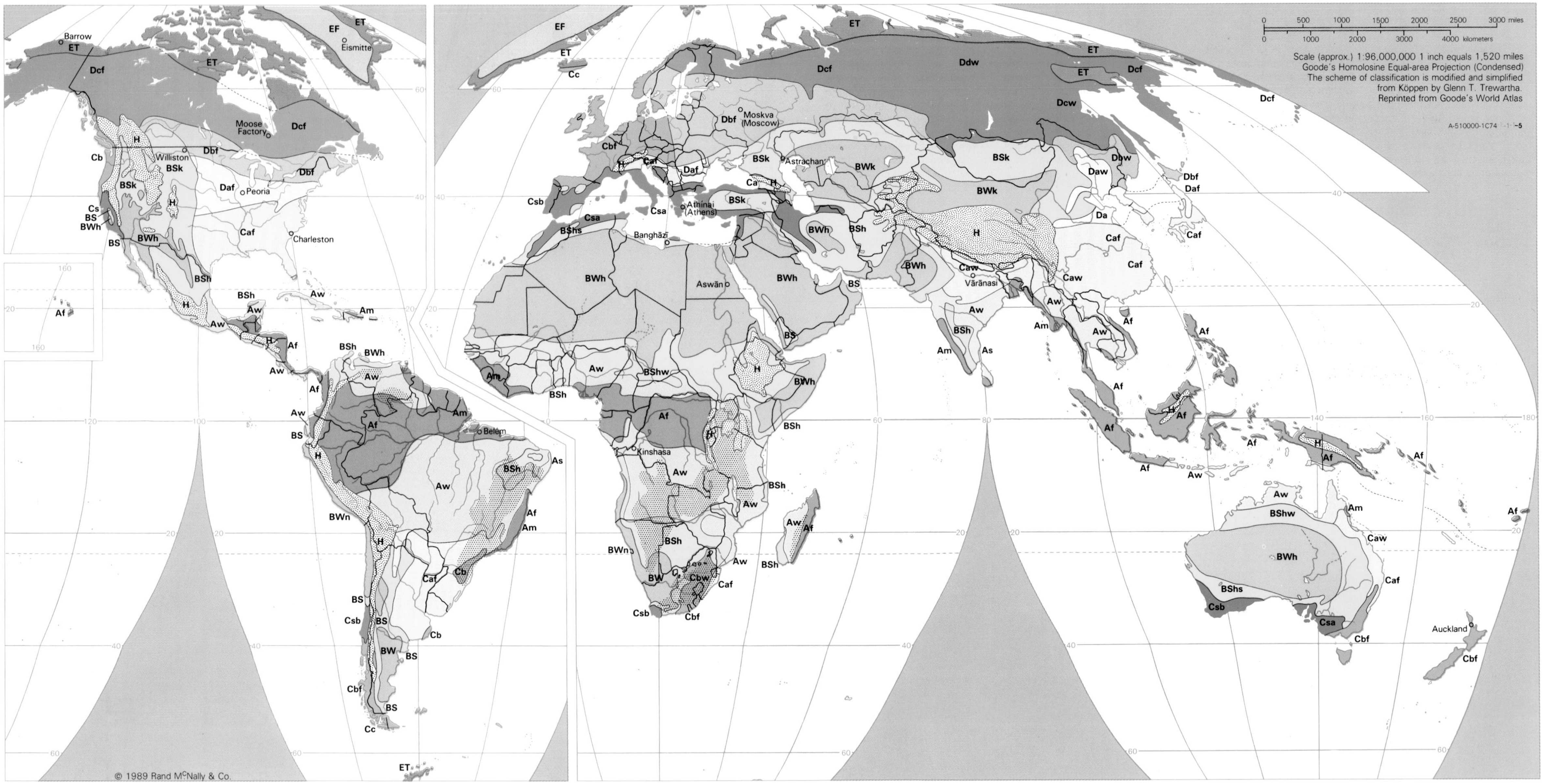
Scale (approx.) 1:96,000,000 1 inch equals 1,520 miles
Goode's Homolosine Equal-area Projection (Condensed)
The scheme of classification is modified and simplified
from Köppen by Glenn T. Trewartha.
Reprinted from Goode's World Atlas
A-510000-1C74 -1- -5
© 1989 Rand McNally & Co.
Barrow
Eismitte
Moose Factory
Williston
Peoria
Charleston
Belém
Moskva (Moscow)
Astrachan'
Athinai (Athens)
Banghāzī
Aswān
Kinshasa
Vārānasi
Auckland

Climate

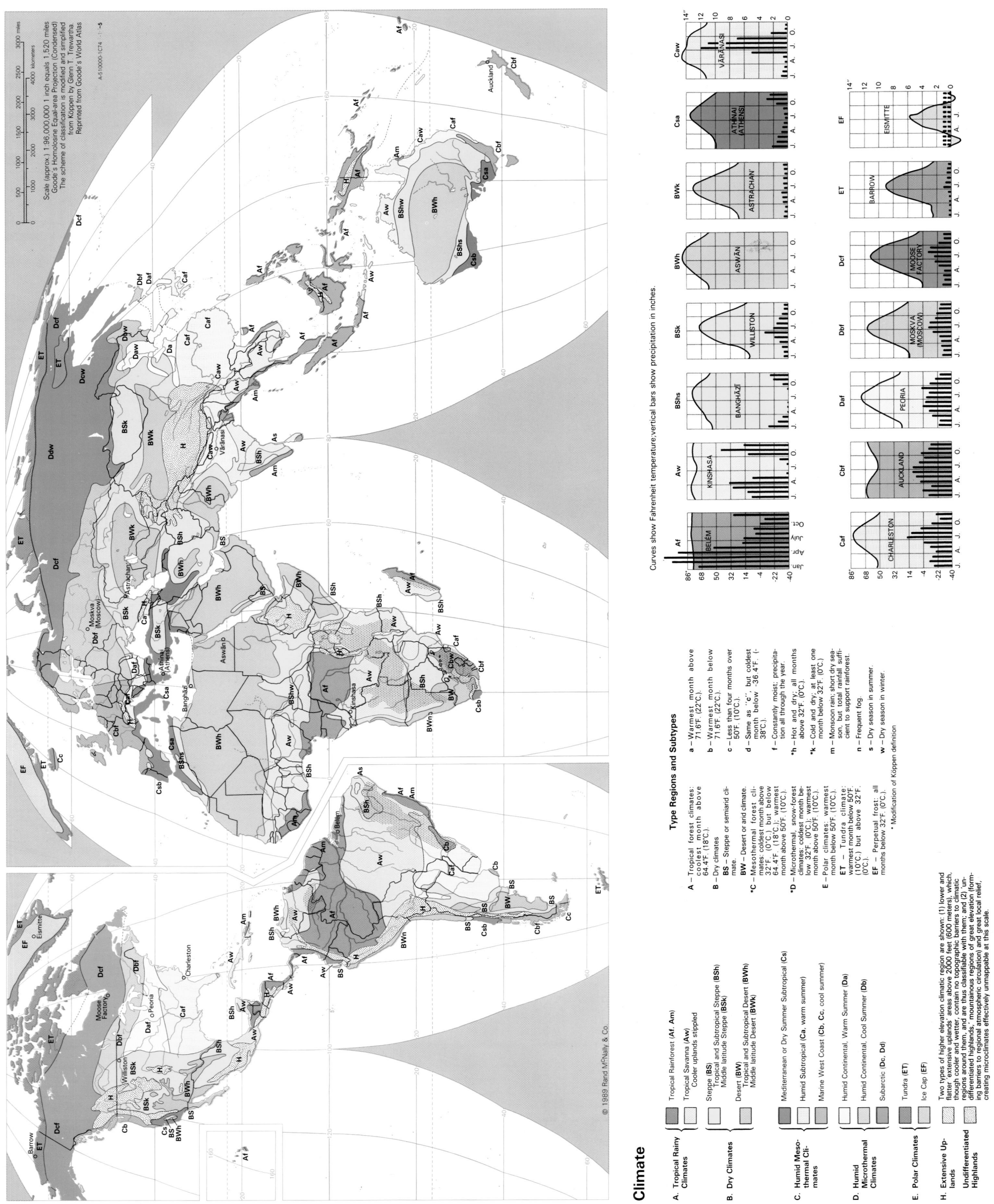

A. **Tropical Rainy Climates**
- Tropical Rainforest (**Af. Am**)
- Tropical Savanna (**Aw**)
  - Cooler uplands stippled

B. **Dry Climates**
- Steppe (**BS**)
  - Tropical and Subtropical Steppe (**BSh**)
  - Middle latitude Steppe (**BSk**)
- Desert (**BW**)
  - Tropical and Subtropical Desert (**BWh**)
  - Middle latitude Desert (**BWk**)

C. **Humid Mesothermal Climates**
- Mediterranean or Dry Summer Subtropical (**Cs**)
- Humid Subtropical (**Ca**, warm summer)
- Marine West Coast (**Cb, Cc**, cool summer)

D. **Humid Microthermal Climates**
- Humid Continental, Warm Summer (**Da**)
- Humid Continental, Cool Summer (**Db**)
- Subarctic (**Dc, Dd**)

E. **Polar Climates**
- Tundra (**ET**)
- Ice Cap (**EF**)

H. **Extensive Uplands**

Undifferentiated Highlands

Two types of higher elevation climatic region are shown: (1) lower and flatter 'extensive uplands' areas above 2000 feet (600 meters), which, though cooler and wetter, contain no topographic barriers to climatic regions around them, and are thus classifiable with them; and (2) 'undifferentiated highlands,' mountainous regions of great elevation (forming barriers to regional atmospheric circulation) and great local relief, creating microclimates effectively unmappable at this scale.

Type Regions and Subtypes

A – Tropical forest climates: coolest month above 64.4°F. (18°C.).

B – Dry climates

BS – Steppe or semiarid climate.

BW – Desert or arid climate.

*C – Mesothermal forest climates: coldest month above 32°F. (0°C.) but below 64.4°F. (18°C.); warmest month above 50°F. (10°C.).

*D – Microthermal, snow-forest climates: coldest month below 32°F. (0°C.); warmest month above 50°F. (10°C.).

E – Polar climates: warmest month below 50°F. (10°C.).

ET – Tundra climate: warmest month below 50°F. (10°C.) but above 32°F. (0°C.).

EF – Perpetual frost: all months below 32°F. (0°C.).

a – Warmest month above 71.6°F. (22°C.).

b – Warmest month below 71.6°F. (22°C.).

c – Less than four months over 50°F. (10°C.).

d – Same as "c", but coldest month below -36.4°F. (-38°C.).

f – Constantly moist; precipitation all through the year.

*h – Hot and dry; all months above 32°F. (0°C.).

*k – Cold and dry; at least one month below 32°F. (0°C.)

m – Monsoon rain; short dry season, but total rainfall sufficient to support rainforest.

n – Frequent fog.

s – Dry season in summer.

w – Dry season in winter.

* Modification of Köppen definition

Curves show Fahrenheit temperature; vertical bars show precipitation in inches.

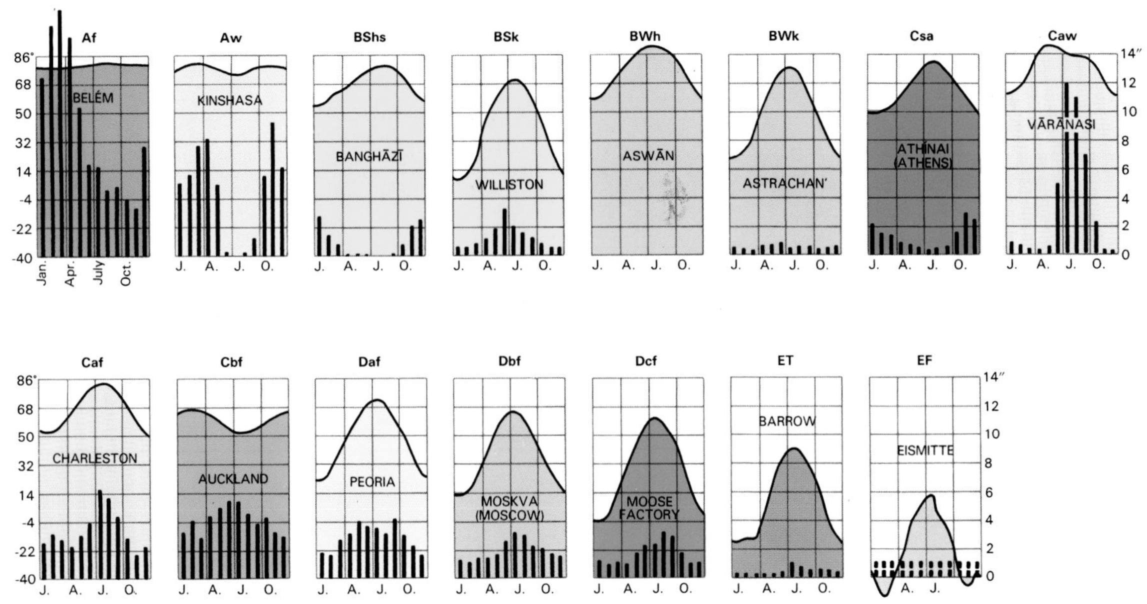
Af
BELÉM
Aw
KINSHASA
BShs
BANGHĀZĪ
BSk
WILLISTON
BWh
ASWĀN
BWk
ASTRACHAN'
Csa
ATHINAI (ATHENS)
Caw
VĀRĀNASI
Caf
CHARLESTON
Cbf
AUCKLAND
Daf
PEORIA
Dbf
MOSKVA (MOSCOW)
Dcf
MOOSE FACTORY
ET
BARROW
EF
EISMITTE
Jan. Apr. July Oct.
J. A. J. O.

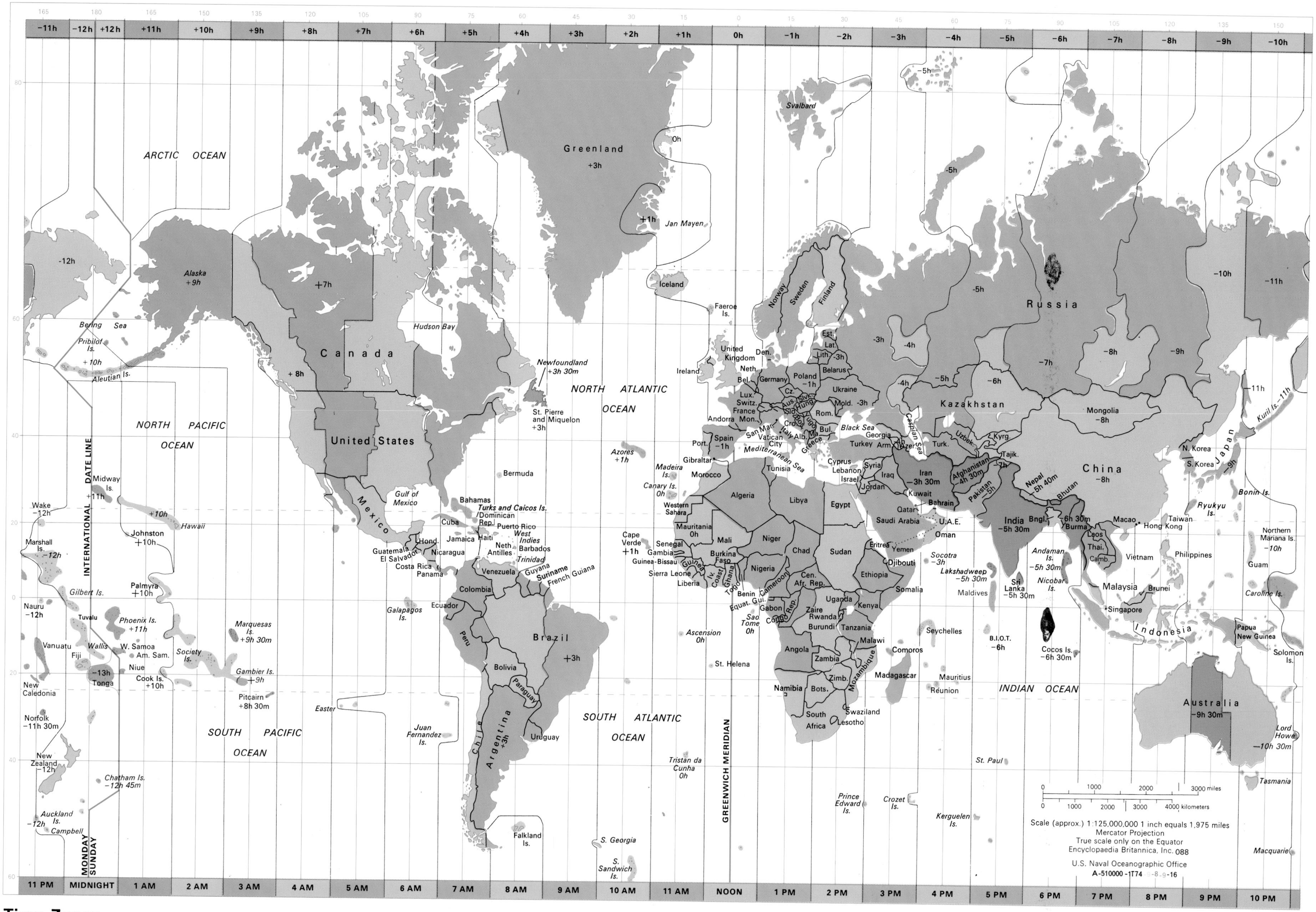
-11h -12h +12h +11h +10h +9h +8h +7h +6h +5h +4h +3h +2h +1h 0h -1h -2h -3h -4h -5h -6h -7h -8h -9h -10h
11 PM MIDNIGHT 1 AM 2 AM 3 AM 4 AM 5 AM 6 AM 7 AM 8 AM 9 AM 10 AM 11 AM NOON 1 PM 2 PM 3 PM 4 PM 5 PM 6 PM 7 PM 8 PM 9 PM 10 PM
ARCTIC OCEAN
NORTH PACIFIC OCEAN
SOUTH PACIFIC OCEAN
NORTH ATLANTIC OCEAN
SOUTH ATLANTIC OCEAN
INDIAN OCEAN
INTERNATIONAL DATE LINE
MONDAY
SUNDAY
GREENWICH MERIDIAN
Greenland +3h
Alaska +9h
Canada
+7h
+8h
Hudson Bay
United States
Mexico
Gulf of Mexico
Newfoundland +3h 30m
St. Pierre and Miquelon +3h
Bermuda
Iceland
Jan Mayen
Svalbard
Russia
China -8h
Mongolia -8h
Kazakhstan
India -5h 30m
Nepal 5h 40m
Iran -3h 30m
Afghanistan -4h 30m
Australia -9h 30m
Brazil +3h
Argentina +3h
Japan -9h
Bering Sea
Aleutian Is.
Hawaii
Midway Is. +11h
Johnston +10h
Wake -12h
Marshall Is. -12h
Nauru -12h
Gilbert Is.
Tuvalu
Phoenix Is. +11h
Palmyra +10h
Vanuatu
Fiji
Wallis
W. Samoa
Am. Sam.
Niue
Tonga -13h
Cook Is. +10h
Society Is.
Marquesas Is. +9h 30m
Gambier Is. +9h
Pitcairn +8h 30m
Easter
Juan Fernandez Is.
Galapagos Is.
New Caledonia
Norfolk -11h 30m
New Zealand -12h
Chatham Is. -12h 45m
Auckland Is. -12h
Campbell
Faeroe Is.
Azores +1h
Madeira Is.
Canary Is. 0h
Cape Verde +1h
Ascension 0h
St. Helena
Tristan da Cunha 0h
S. Georgia
S. Sandwich Is.
Falkland Is.
Prince Edward Is.
Crozet Is.
Kerguelen Is.
St. Paul
B.I.O.T. -6h
Cocos Is. -6h 30m
Andaman Is. -5h 30m
Nicobar Is.
Lakshadweep -5h 30m
Maldives
Sri Lanka -5h 30m
Seychelles
Mauritius
Réunion
Comoros
Madagascar
Lord Howe -10h 30m
Tasmania
Macquarie
Solomon Is.
Papua New Guinea
Northern Mariana Is. -10h
Guam
Caroline Is.
Bonin Is.
Ryukyu Is.
Kuril Is. -11h
Scale (approx.) 1:125,000,000 1 inch equals 1,975 miles
Mercator Projection
True scale only on the Equator
Encyclopaedia Britannica, Inc. 088
U.S. Naval Oceanographic Office
A-510000-1T74 -8-9-16

Time Zones

- Standard time zone of even-numbered hours from Greenwich time
- Standard time zone of odd-numbered hours from Greenwich time
- Time varies from the standard time zone by half an hour
- Time varies from the standard time zone by other than half an hour

h m hours, minutes

The standard time zone system, fixed by international agreement and by law in each country, is based on a theoretical division of the globe into 24 zones of 15° longitude each. The mid-meridian of each zone fixes the hour for the entire zone. The zero time zone extends 7½° east and 7½° west of the Greenwich meridian, 0° longitude. Since the earth rotates toward the east, time zones to the west of Greenwich are earlier, to the east, later.

Plus and minus hours at the top of the map are added to or subtracted from local time to find Greenwich time. Local standard time can be determined for any area in the world by adding one hour for each time zone counted in an easterly direction from one's own, or by subtracting one hour for each zone counted in a westerly direction. To separate one day from the next, the 180th meridian has been designated as the international date line. On both sides of the line the time of day is the same, but west of the line it is one day later than it is to the east.

Countries that adhere to the international zone system adopt the zone applicable to their location. Some countries, however, establish time zones based on political boundaries, or adopt the time zone of a neighboring unit. For all or part of the year some countries also advance their time by one hour, thereby utilizing more daylight hours each day.

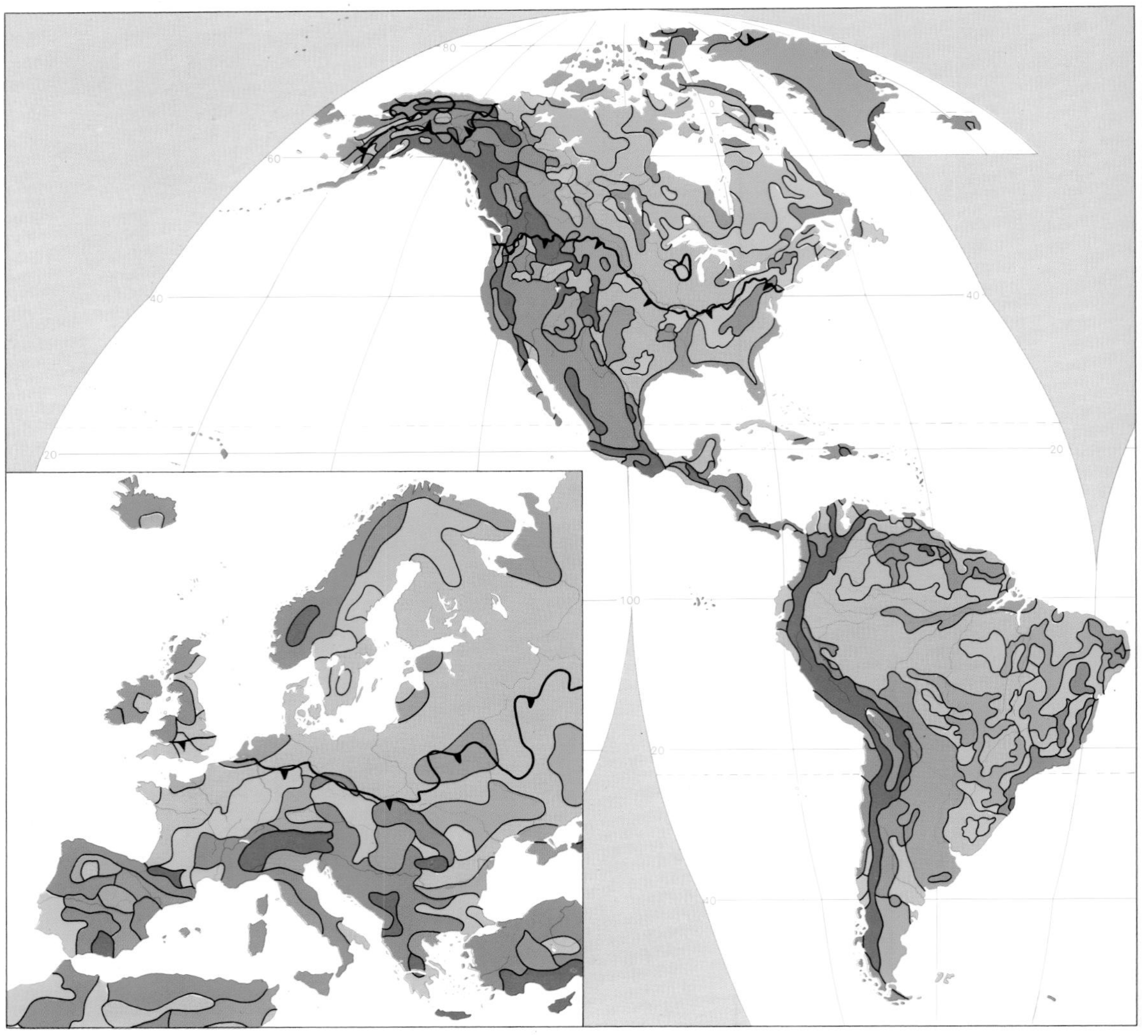

Surface Configuration

Smooth lands

- Level plains: nearly all slopes gentle; local relief less than 100 ft. (30 m.)
- Irregular plains: majority of slopes gentle; local relief 100-300 ft. (30-90 m.)

Broken lands

- Tablelands and plateaus: majority of slopes gentle, with the gentler slopes on the uplands; local relief more than 300 ft. (90 m.)
- Hill-studded plains: majority of slopes gentle, with the gentler slopes in the lowlands; local relief 300-1,000 ft. (90-300 m.)
- Mountain-studded plains: majority of slopes gentle, with the gentler slopes in the lowlands; local relief more than 1,000 ft. (300 m.)

Rough lands

- Hill lands: steeper slopes predominate; local relief less than 1,000 ft. (300 m.)
- Mountains: steeper slopes predominate; local relief 1,000-5,000 ft. (300-1,500 m.)
- Mountains of great relief: steeper slopes predominate; local relief more than 5,000 ft. (1,500 m.)

Other surfaces

- Ice caps: permanent ice
- Maximum extent of glaciation

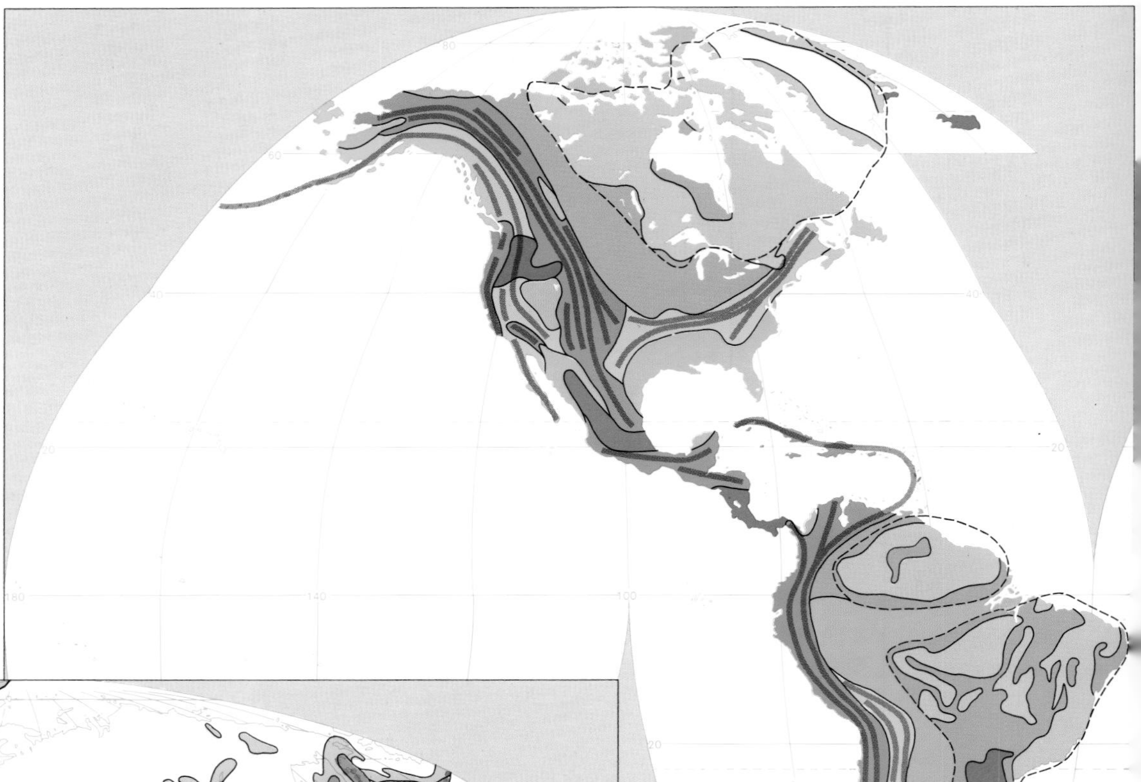

Earth Structure and Tectonics

- Precambrian stable shield areas
- Exposed Precambrian rock
- Paleozoic and Mesozoic flat-lying sedimentary rocks
- Principal Paleozoic and Mesozoic folded areas
- Cenozoic sedimentary rocks
- Principal Cenozoic folded areas
- Lava plateaus
- Major trends of folding

Geologic time chart

Precambrian—from formation of the earth (at least 4 billion years ago) to 600 million years ago

Paleozoic—from 600 million to 200 million years ago

Mesozoic—from 200 million to 70 million years ago

Cenozoic—from 70 million years ago to present time

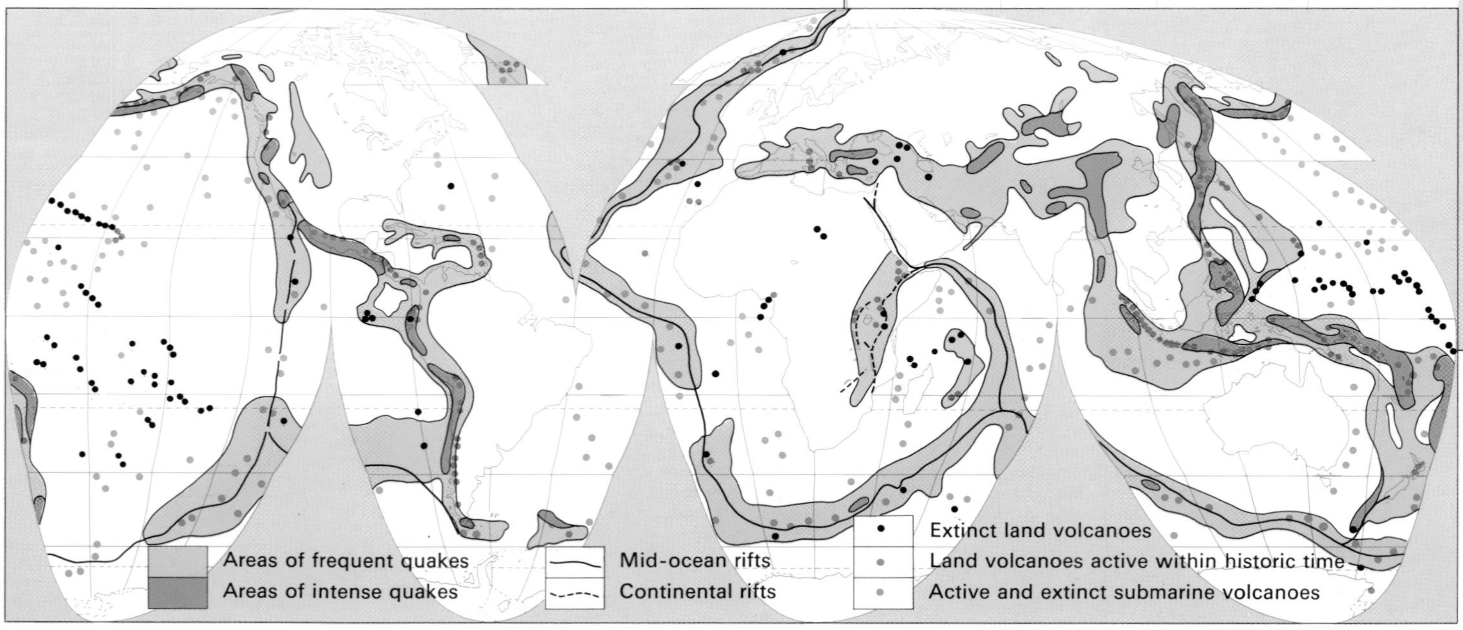
Areas of frequent quakes
Areas of intense quakes
Mid-ocean rifts
Continental rifts
Extinct land volcanoes
Land volcanoes active within historic time
Active and extinct submarine volcanoes

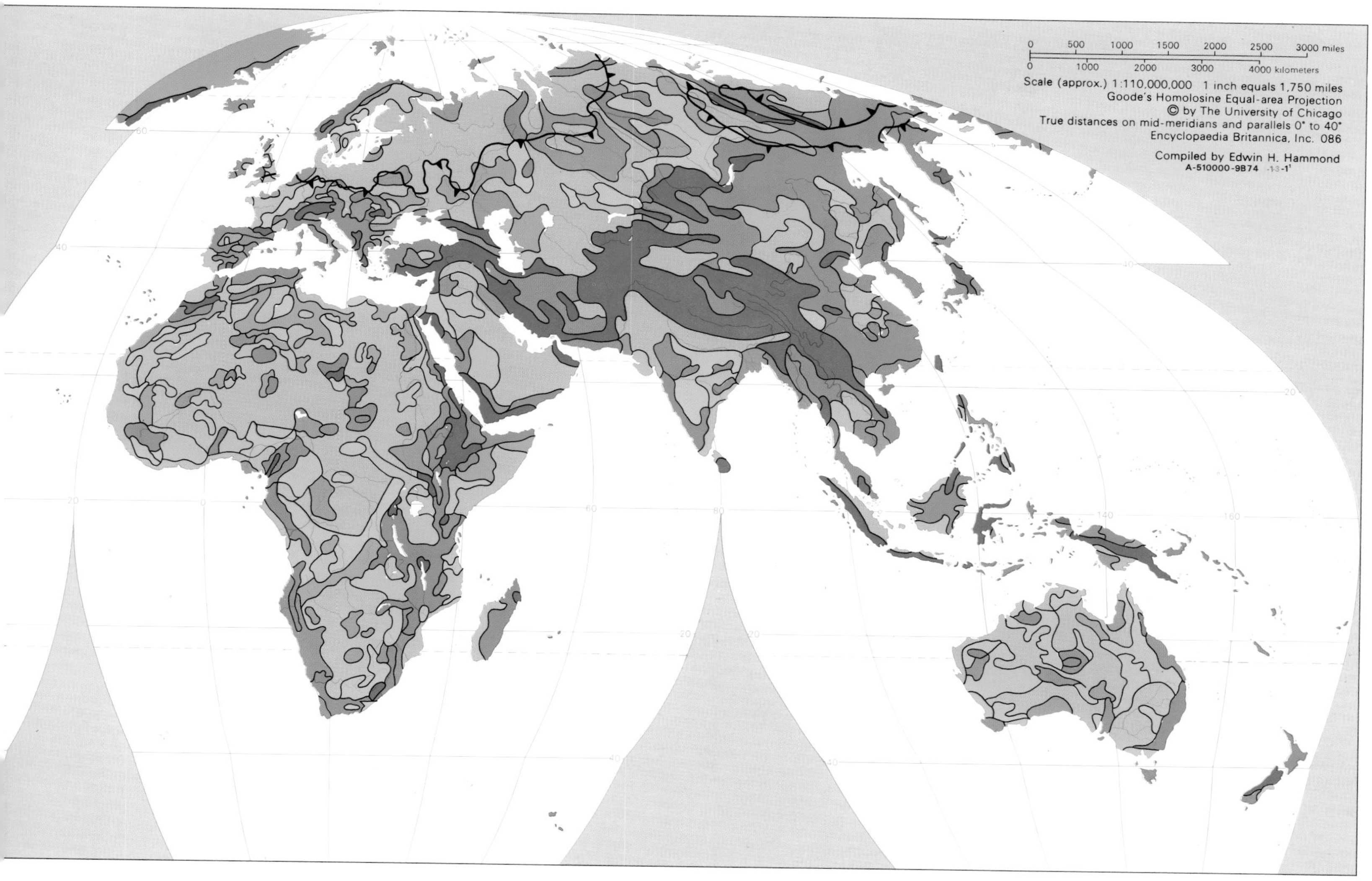
0 500 1000 1500 2000 2500 3000 miles
0 1000 2000 3000 4000 kilometers
Scale (approx.) 1:110,000,000 1 inch equals 1,750 miles
Goode's Homolosine Equal-area Projection
© by The University of Chicago
True distances on mid-meridians and parallels 0° to 40°
Encyclopaedia Britannica, Inc. 086
Compiled by Edwin H. Hammond
A-510000-9B74

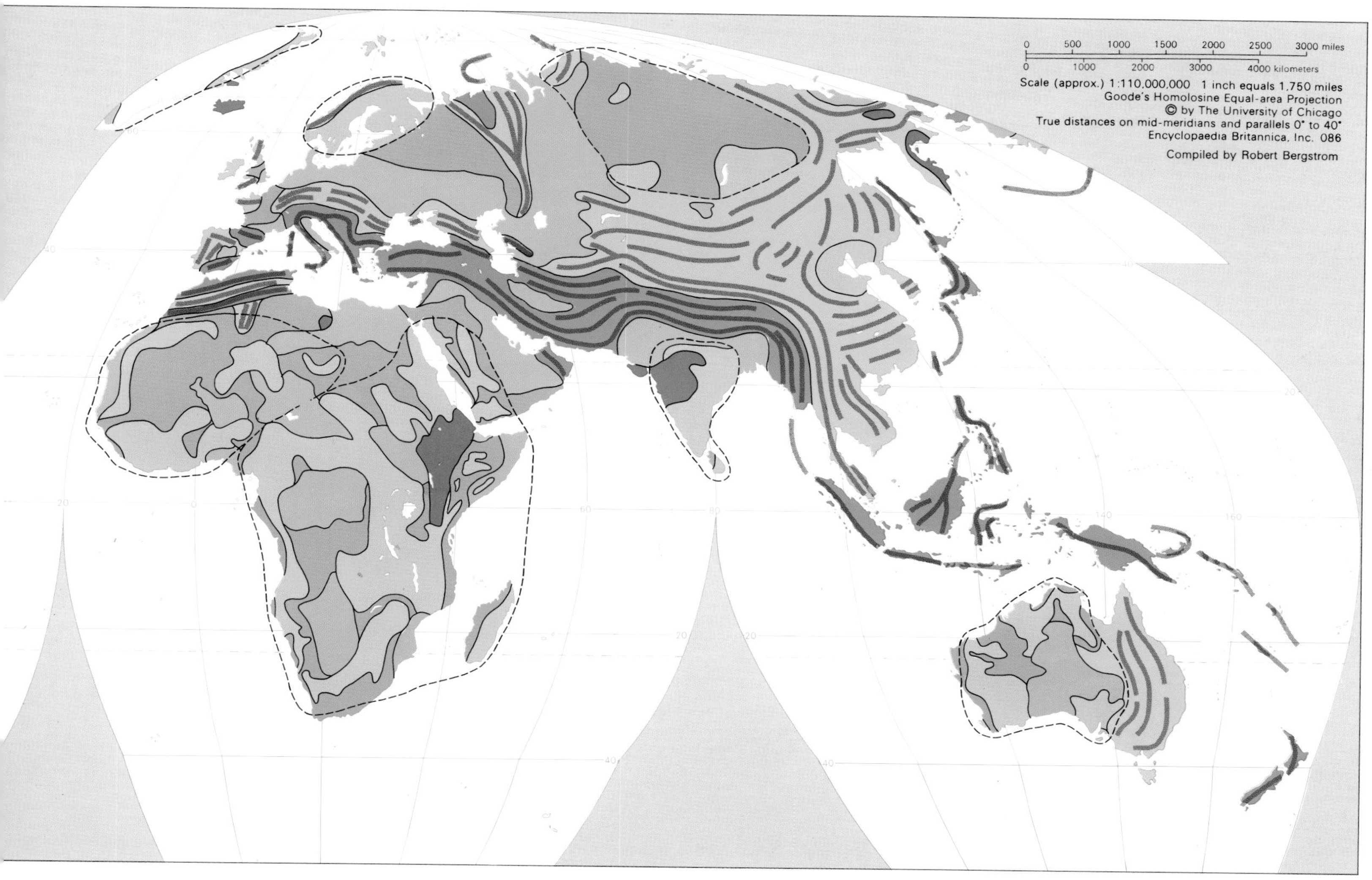
0 500 1000 1500 2000 2500 3000 miles
0 1000 2000 3000 4000 kilometers
Scale (approx.) 1:110,000,000 1 inch equals 1,750 miles
Goode's Homolosine Equal-area Projection
© by The University of Chicago
True distances on mid-meridians and parallels 0° to 40°
Encyclopaedia Britannica, Inc. 086
Compiled by Robert Bergstrom

Development of the earth's structure

The earth is in process of constant transformation. Movements in the hot, dense interior of the earth result in folding and fracture of the crust and transfer of molten material to the surface. As a result, large structures such as mountain ranges, volcanoes, lava plateaus, and rift valleys are created. The forces that bring about these structural changes are called *tectonic forces*.

The present continents have developed from stable nuclei, or *shields*, of ancient (Precambrian) rock. Erosive forces such as water, wind, and ice have worn away particles of the rock, depositing them at the edges of the shields, where they have accumulated and ultimately become sedimentary rock. Subsequently, in plaees, these extensive areas of flat-lying rock have been elevated, folded, or warped, by the action of tectonic forces, to form mountains. The shape of these mountains has been altered by later erosion. Where the forces of erosion have been at work for a long time, the mountains tend to have a low relief and rounded contours, like the Appalachians. Mountains more recently formed are high and rugged, like the Himalayas.

The map above depicts some of the major geologic structures of the earth and identifies them according to the period of their formation. A geologic time chart is included in the legend. The inset map shows the most important areas of earthquakes, rifts, and volcanic activity. Comparison of all the maps will show the close correlation between present-day mountain systems, recent (Cenozoic) mountain-building, and the areas of frequent earthquakes and active volcanoes.

Natural Vegetation

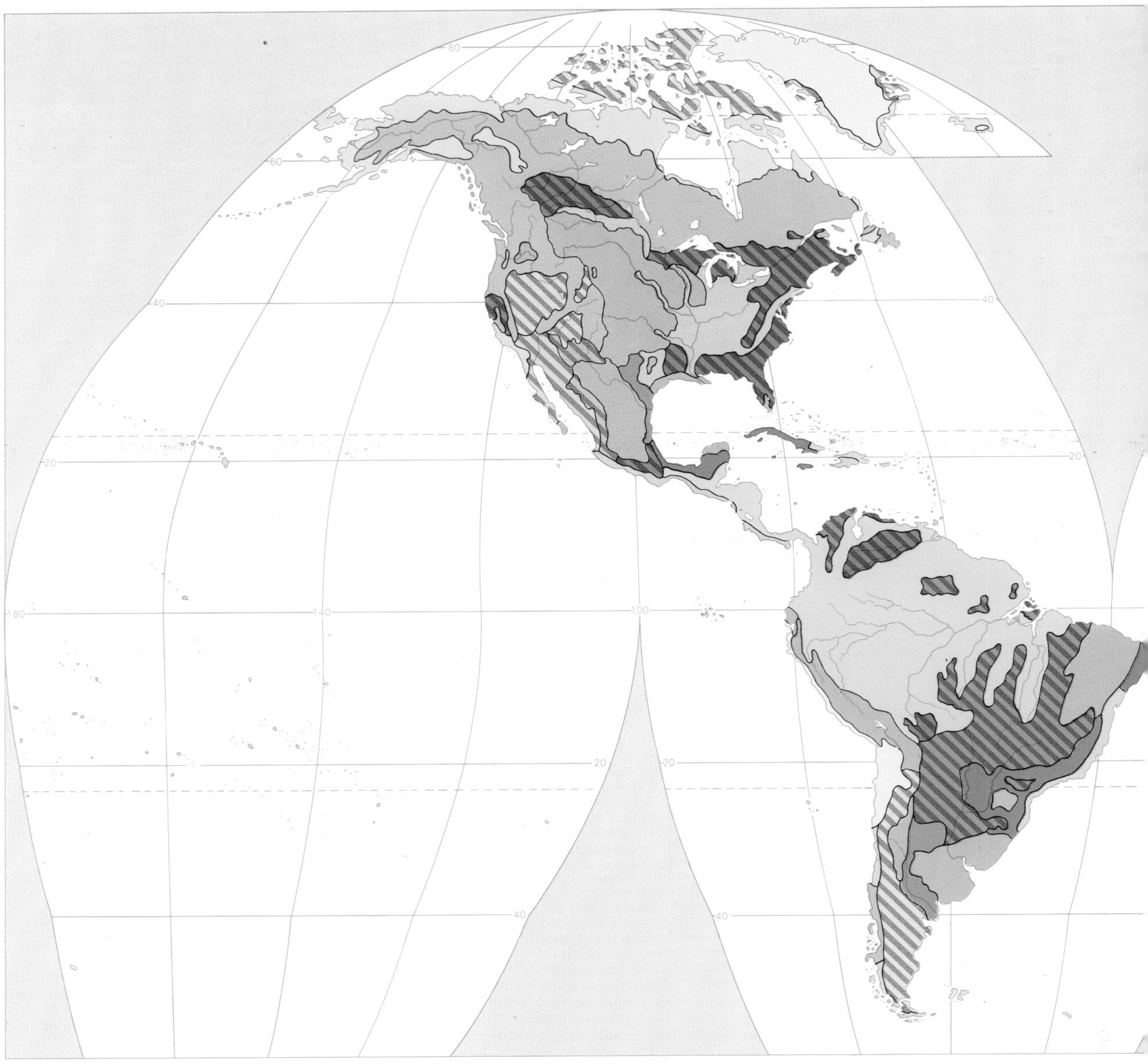
80
60
40
20
180
140
100
20
40

Broad-leaved evergreen vegetation
- Broad-leaved evergreen forest
- Broad-leaved evergreen shrub formation
- Scattered broad-leaved evergreen shrubs
- Scattered broad-leaved evergreen dwarf shrubs

Broad-leaved deciduous vegetation
- Broad-leaved deciduous forest
- Broad-leaved deciduous shrub formation
- Scattered broad-leaved deciduous shrubs
- Scattered broad-leaved deciduous dwarf shrubs

Coniferous vegetation
- Needle-leaved evergreen forest
- Scattered needle-leaved evergreen trees
- Needle-leaved deciduous forest

Mixed vegetation without grass
- Forest of broad-leaved evergreen and deciduous trees
- Forest of broad-leaved and needle-leaved evergreen trees
- Broad-leaved deciduous forests with broad-leaved evergreen shrubs
- Forest of broad-leaved deciduous and needle-leaved evergreen trees

Mixed vegetation with grass
- Grassland with scattered broad-leaved evergreen trees
- Grassland with broad-leaved evergreen shrubs
- Grassland with scattered broad-leaved deciduous trees
- Grassland with broad-leaved deciduous shrubs

Grassland, tundra, barren
- Grassland
- Patches of grass
- Lichens and grasses
- Lichens and mosses
- Barren

Soils

80
60
40
20
180
140
100
20
40

- Tundra soils of frigid climates; commonly with permanently frozen subsoil; supports dwarf shrubs, mosses, and lichens; some used for reindeer pasture
- Podzolic soils of humid, cool climates; covered with predominantly coniferous forest; some farming, mainly subsistence
- Podzolic soils of humid, temperate climates; originally covered with predominantly deciduous forest, much of it removed to accommodate extensive general farming, industry, and cities
- Podzolic soils of humid, warm climates; covered with coniferous or mixed forest; general farming
- Chernozemic soils of subhumid and semiarid, cool to tropical climates; supports mainly grasslands; extensive grain and livestock farming
- Latosolic soils of humid or wet-dry tropical and subtropical climates; supports forest or savanna; shifting cultivation with some plantation agriculture
- Grumusolic soils of humid to semiarid and temperate to tropical climates, with distinct wet and dry seasons; mainly grass-covered; livestock and grain farming
- Desertic soils of arid climates; includes many areas of shallow, stony soils; sparse cover of shrubs and grass, some suitable for grazing; fertile if irrigated; dry farming possible in some areas
- Mountain soils of all climates; shallow, stony; barren, grass-covered, or forested, depending on climate; includes many areas of other soils
- Alluvial soils of all climates; deposited by water in flood plains and deltas of rivers; intensive farming in most temperate and some tropical regions (many smaller areas not shown)
- Ice cap of polar regions

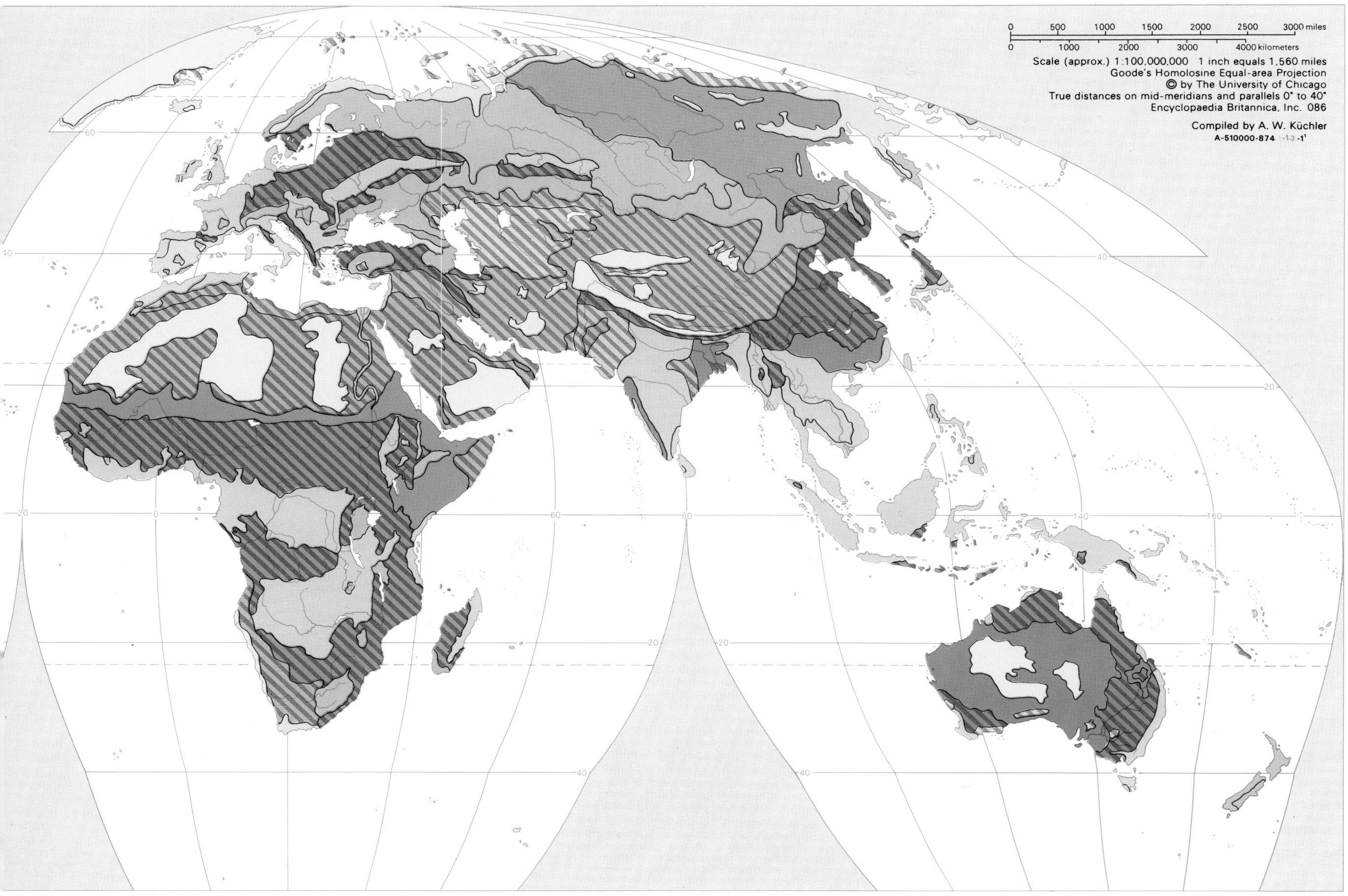
0 500 1000 1500 2000 2500 3000 miles
0 1000 2000 3000 4000 kilometers
Scale (approx.) 1:100,000,000 1 inch equals 1,560 miles
Goode's Homolosine Equal-area Projection
© by The University of Chicago
True distances on mid-meridians and parallels 0° to 40°
Encyclopaedia Britannica, Inc. 086
Compiled by A. W. Küchler
A-510000-874 1-13-1'
60
40
20
0
20
40
60
80
140
160

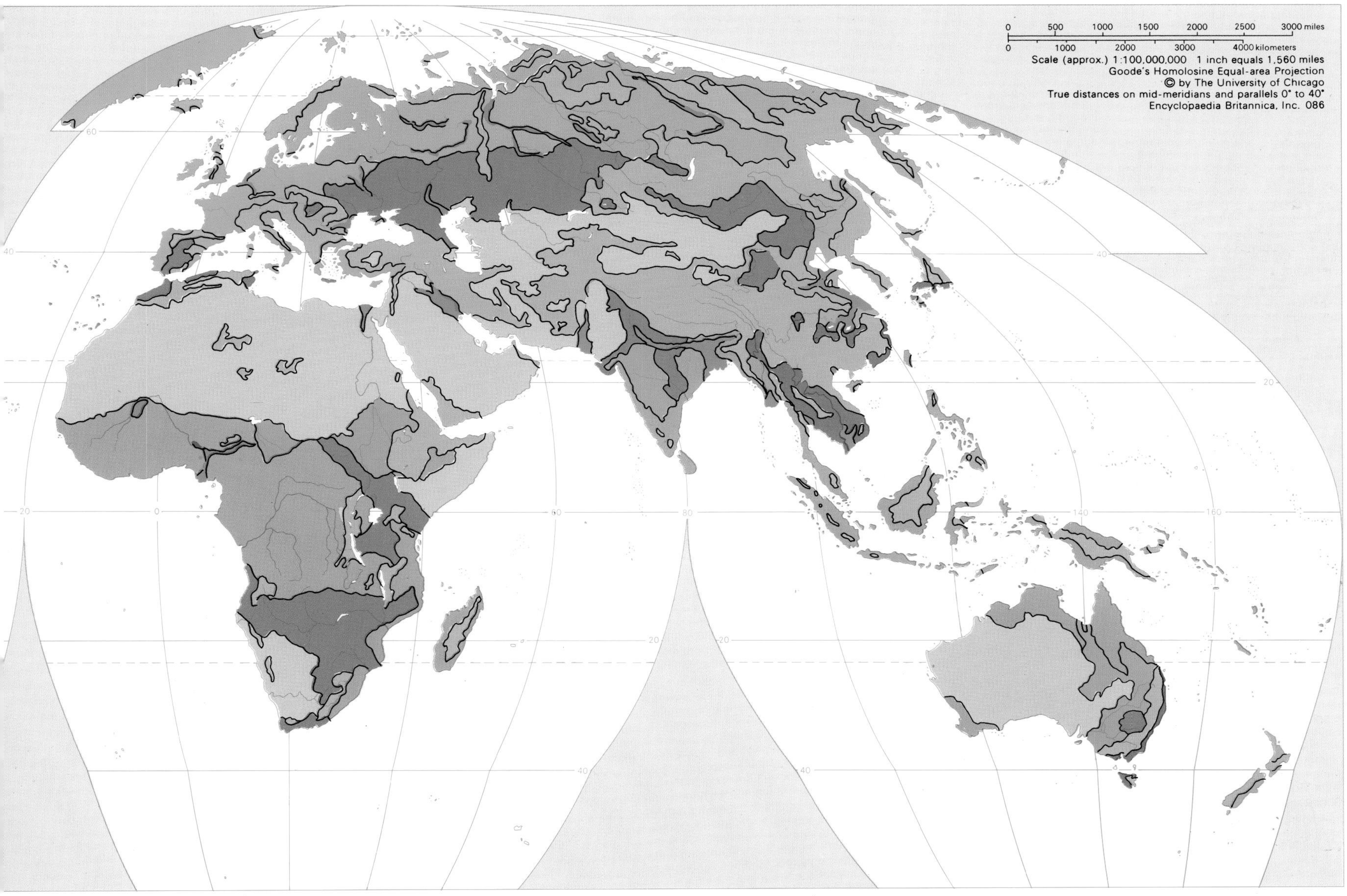
0 500 1000 1500 2000 2500 3000 miles
0 1000 2000 3000 4000 kilometers
Scale (approx.) 1:100,000,000 1 inch equals 1,560 miles
Goode's Homolosine Equal-area Projection
© by The University of Chicago
True distances on mid-meridians and parallels 0° to 40°
Encyclopaedia Britannica, Inc. 086
60
40
20
0
20
40
60
80
140
160

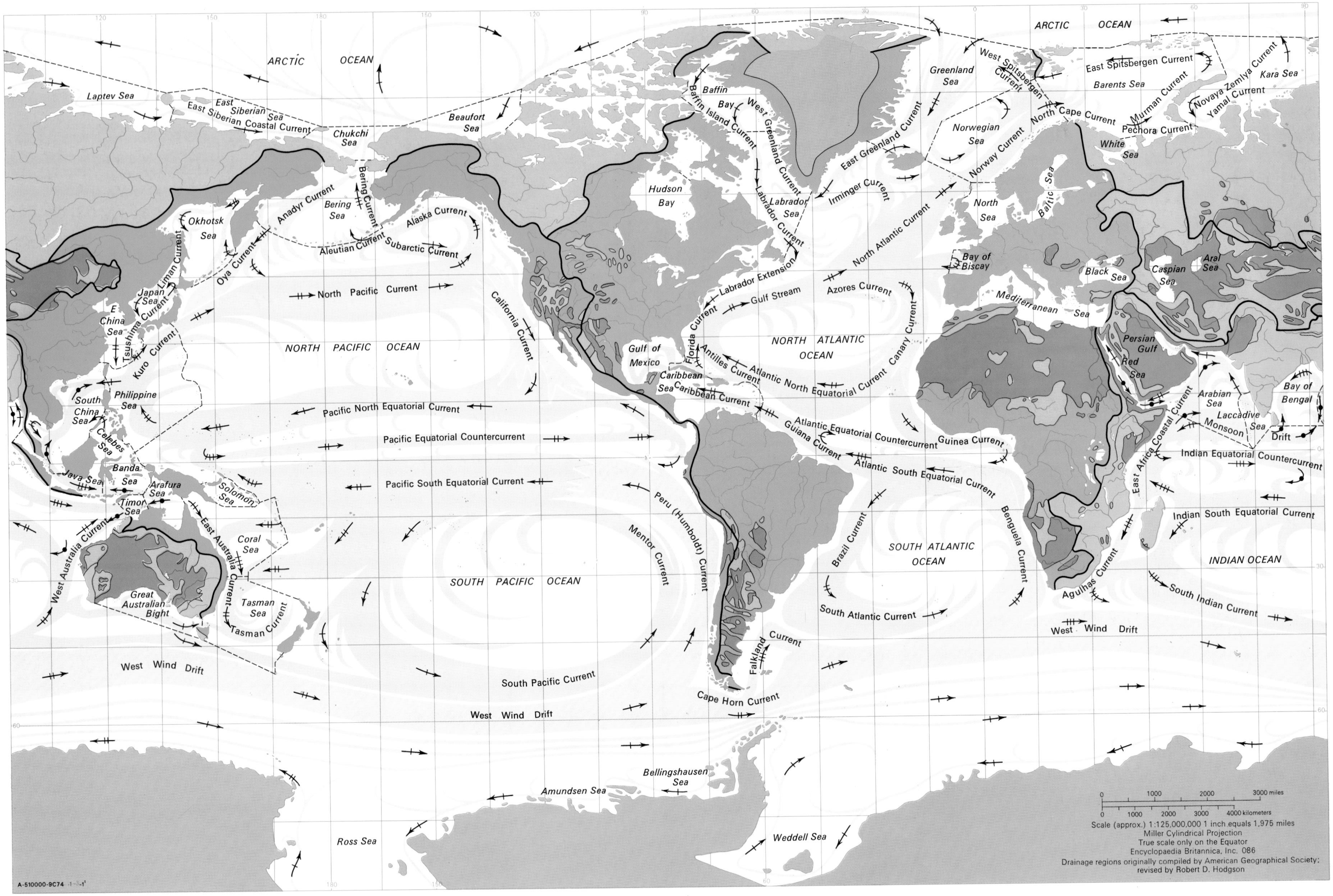
ARCTIC OCEAN
Laptev Sea
East Siberian Sea
East Siberian Coastal Current
Chukchi Sea
Beaufort Sea
Baffin Bay
Baffin Island Current
West Greenland Current
East Greenland Current
Greenland Sea
West Spitsbergen Current
East Spitsbergen Current
Barents Sea
Kara Sea
Novaya Zemlya Current
Yamal Current
Murman Current
Pechora Current
White Sea
North Cape Current
Norwegian Sea
Norway Current
Irminger Current
Labrador Sea
Labrador Current
Hudson Bay
Okhotsk Sea
Oya Current
Anadyr Current
Bering Sea
Bering Current
Aleutian Current
Alaska Current
Subarctic Current
Liman Current
Japan Sea
Tsushima Current
E China Sea
Kuro Current
North Pacific Current
NORTH PACIFIC OCEAN
California Current
Philippine Sea
South China Sea
Celebes Sea
Java Sea
Banda Sea
Arafura Sea
Timor Sea
Solomon Sea
Coral Sea
Pacific North Equatorial Current
Pacific Equatorial Countercurrent
Pacific South Equatorial Current
West Australia Current
East Australia Current
Great Australian Bight
Tasman Sea
Tasman Current
SOUTH PACIFIC OCEAN
Mentor Current
Peru (Humboldt) Current
South Pacific Current
West Wind Drift
Cape Horn Current
Falkland Current
Amundsen Sea
Bellingshausen Sea
Ross Sea
Weddell Sea
Gulf of Mexico
Caribbean Sea
Caribbean Current
Florida Current
Antilles Current
Gulf Stream
Labrador Extension
North Atlantic Current
Azores Current
NORTH ATLANTIC OCEAN
Atlantic North Equatorial Current
Canary Current
Atlantic Equatorial Countercurrent
Guiana Current
Guinea Current
Atlantic South Equatorial Current
Brazil Current
SOUTH ATLANTIC OCEAN
Benguela Current
South Atlantic Current
North Sea
Baltic Sea
Bay of Biscay
Mediterranean Sea
Black Sea
Caspian Sea
Aral Sea
Persian Gulf
Red Sea
Arabian Sea
Laccadive Sea
Monsoon Drift
Bay of Bengal
East Africa Coastal Current
Indian Equatorial Countercurrent
Indian South Equatorial Current
INDIAN OCEAN
Agulhas Current
South Indian Current
West Wind Drift
0 1000 2000 3000 miles
0 1000 2000 3000 4000 kilometers
Scale (approx.) 1:125,000,000 1 inch equals 1,975 miles
Miller Cylindrical Projection
True scale only on the Equator
Encyclopaedia Britannica, Inc. 086
Drainage regions originally compiled by American Geographical Society; revised by Robert D. Hodgson
A-510000-9C74

Drainage Regions and Ocean Currents

Currents during Northern Hemisphere winter
- Cold current
- Warm current
- Indicates a current that reverses direction during Northern Hemisphere summer

Speed of current
(1 knot=1 nautical mile[6,076 ft.] per hour)
- Less than 0.5 knots
- 0.5–0.8 knots
- Greater than 0.8 knots
- Limits of seas

Drainage regions
Surface drainage reaching an Ocean
- Outline of oceanic drainage regions
- Atlantic Ocean
- Pacific Ocean
- Indian Ocean
- Arctic Ocean
- Surface drainage not reaching an ocean
- Arid regions
- Ice cap

THIS SECTION OPENS with World Political and World Physical maps at the scale of 1:75,000,000. There follow maps of the Pacific, Indian, and Atlantic oceans at the scale 1:48,000,000, the largest scale at which the total expanse of these bodies of water could be portrayed. Finally, a series of continent relief maps at the scale of 1:24,000,000 show a global view of the earth as it would appear from about 4,000 miles in space. The Azimuthal Equal-Area projection is used for the 1:24,000,000 maps, the scale being approximately that of a globe 20 inches in diameter.

The colors of the continent maps portray the land areas as if viewed from space during the growing season, without regard to the fact that the growing seasons are not concurrent in all areas. Underwater features and varying water depths are represented by shaded relief and different color tones. The result is a strong physical portrait of the earth's major land and submarine forms. The legend below shows how these different kinds of terrain and vegetation have been represented. The names of physical features—plateaus, basins, mountain ranges, seas, rivers, lakes, gulfs, trenches, bays, islands—predominate on these maps.

DIESER KARTENTEIL BEGINNT mit politischen und physischen Weltkarten im Massstab 1:75 Millionen. Dann folgen Karten des Pazifischen, Indischen und Atlantischen Ozeans in 1:48 Millionen, dem grössten Massstab, in dem diese Wasserflächen in ihrer ganzen Ausdehnung abgebildet werden konnten. Schliesslich folgt eine Reihe von Reliefkarten der Erdteile in 1:24 Millionen. Sie geben eine Übersicht der Erde, wie sie aus einer Entfernung von ungefähr 6 400 Kilometer aus dem Weltraum gewonnen würde. Den Karten im Massstab 1:24 Millionen liegt ein flächentreuer azimutaler Entwurf zugrunde, dieser Massstab entspricht ungefähr dem eines Globus von 50 cm Durchmesser.

Die Farben der Erdteilkarten bilden jedes Landgebiet so ab, wie es in der Vegetationsperiode aus der Vogelperspektive erschiene, ohne zu berücksichtigen, dass die Vegetationsperioden nicht in allen Gebieten gleichzeitig eintreten. Die Gliederung des Meeresbodens und die unterschiedlichen Meerestiefen werden durch Schummerung und verschiedene Farbstufen dargestellt. Das Ergebnis ist eine anschauliche physische Darstellung der wichtigsten terrestrischen und untermeerischen Formen der Erde. Die untenstehende Zeichenerklärung zeigt, wie diese verschiedenen Geländeformen und Vegetationsgebiete veranschaulicht werden. Namen physischer Objekte—Hochebenen, Becken, Gebirgszüge, Meere, Flüsse, Seen, Buchten, Gräben, Inseln—herrschen in diesen Karten vor.

ESTA SECCIÓN DA PRINCIPIO con los Mapas Políticos y Físicos del Mundo, a una escala de 1:75 000 000. A continuación están los mapas de los océanos Pacífico, Indico y Atlántico a una escala de 1:48 000 000, que es la mayor escala utilizable para la representación de esas masas de agua en toda su extensión. Por último, una serie de mapas del relieve de los continentes, a una escala de 1:24 000 000, proporcionan una vista global de la tierra tal como se apreciaría desde el espacio a una distancia aproximada de 6 400 kilómetros. La proyección azimutal equiárea se usa, para los mapas de 1:24 000 000, a una escala según la cual la tierra se reduciría a un globo de unos 50 cm de diámetro.

Los colores utilizados en los mapas de los continentes representan las diversas regiones de la tierra tal como se verían desde el espacio durante la estación en que la vegetación se desarrolla, sin tomar en cuenta que este fenómeno no se produce simultáneamente en todas las áreas. Las estructuras características del fondo marino y las variaciones de profundidad de los océanos se representan mediante relieve sombreado y distintos matices de color. El resultado es una imagen elocuente de las formas terrestres y submarinas más notables del planeta. La leyenda abajo explica cómo se representan estos diferentes tipos de terreno y vegetación. En estos mapas predomina la nomenclatura de elementos físicos: mesetas, cuencas, sierras, mares, ríos, lagos, golfos, bahías, trincheras, islas.

CETTE PARTIE comprend d'abord des cartes du monde politique et du monde physique à l'échelle de 1:75 000 000. Viennent ensuite les cartes des océans Pacifique, Indien et Atlantique à l'échelle de 1:48 000 000, la plus grande échelle qui a permis la reproduction complète de ces étendues d'eau. Pour terminer, une série de cartes en relief des continents à l'échelle de 1:24 000 000 donne une vue globale de la terre, telle qu'elle apparaîtrait vue de l'espace à une distance d'environ 6 400 kilomètres. La projection azimutale équivalente a été utilisée pour les cartes au 1:24 000 000ᵉ, dont l'échelle équivaut à celle d'un globe de 50 cm de diamètre environ.

Les couleurs des cartes font apparaître les continents tels qu'on les verrait de l'espace, pendant la saison de croissance végétale, mais sans tenir compte du fait que cette saison n'apparaît pas partout simultanément. Le relief sous-marin est représenté par un estompage et la profondeur des océans par une variation de la couleur. Il en résulte une reproduction vigoureuse des principaux paysages continentaux et des principales formes sous-marines. La légende ci-dessous indique de quelle façon ils sont cartographiés. Les noms d'éléments topographiques tels que plateaux, bassins, chaînes de montagnes, mers, cours d'eau, lacs, golfes, baies, crêtes, îles et fosses océaniques, prédominent dans ces cartes.

ESTA SEÇÃO PRINCIPIA com os mapas políticos e físicos do Mundo, em escala de 1:75 000 000. Seguem-se os mapas dos oceanos Pacífico, Índico e Atlântico na escala de 1:48 000 000, a maior escala que se pode utilizar para a representação dessas massas de água em toda a sua extensão. Finalmente, uma série de mapas de relevo dos continentes, na escala de 1:24 000 000, proporciona uma visão global da Terra tal como apareceria do espaço a uma distância aproximada de cerca de 6 400 km. A projeção azimutal equiárea foi usada para os mapas da escala de 1:24 000 000, segundo a qual a Terra se apresentaria como um globo de cerca de 50 cm de diâmetro.

As cores utilizadas nos mapas dos continentes representam as massas terrestres tal como apareceriam vistas do espaço durante a estação do crescimento vegetal, sem levar em conta que este fenômeno não se produz simultaneamente em todas as regiões. As características do fundo do mar e as variações de profundidade das águas são representadas por um relevo sombreado e por diferentes matizes de cor. O resultado proporciona uma imagem física eloqüente das principais formas terrestres e submarinas da Terra. As legendas abaixo explicam como foram representados os diversos tipos de terreno e de vegetação. Nestes mapas predomina a nomenclatura dos elementos físicos: planaltos, bacias, cadeias de montanhas, mares, rios, lagos, golfos, baías, fossas, ilhas.

Land Features / Land Phänomene / Elementos de la Tierra
Paysages Continentaux / Acidentes Continentais

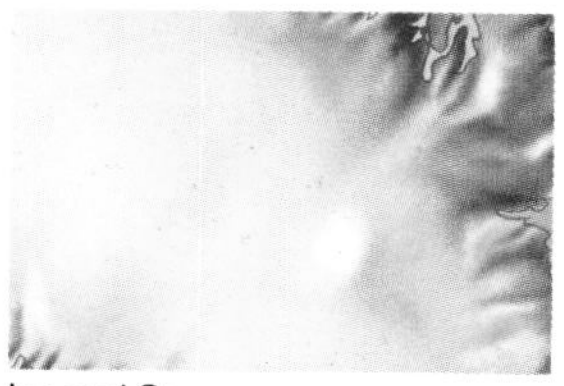
Ice and Snow
Eis und Schnee
Hielo y nieve
Glace et neige
Gelo e neve

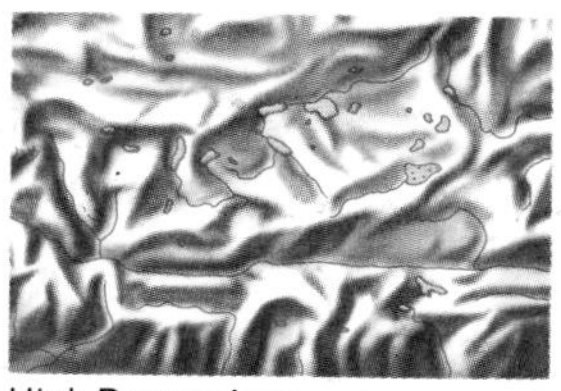
High Barren Area
Hochgebirgswüste
Alta zona árida
Région haute et aride
Alta zona árida

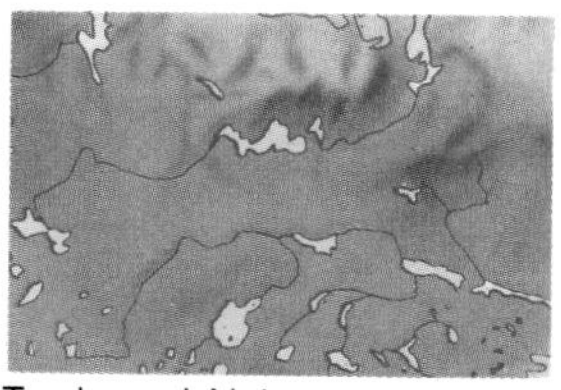
Tundra and Alpine
Tundra und Alpine Vegetation
Tundra y alpina
Toundra et végétation alpine
Tundra e vegetação alpina

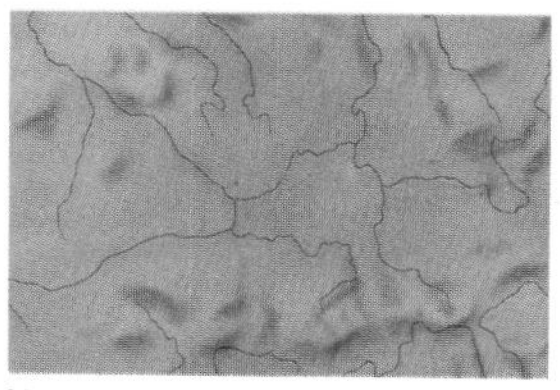
Needleleaf Trees
Nadelwälder
Coníferas
Forêt de conifères
Coníferas

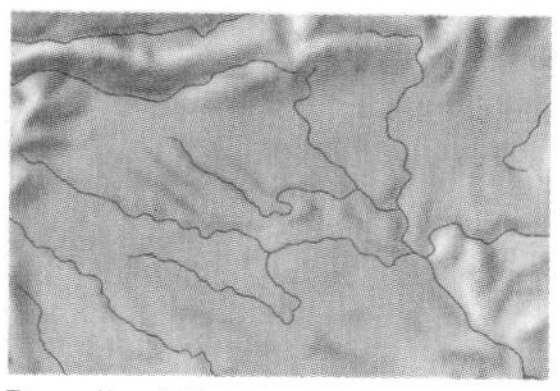
Broadleaf Trees
Laubwälder
Árboles de hojas anchas
Forêt à feuilles caduques
Árvores de folhas caducas

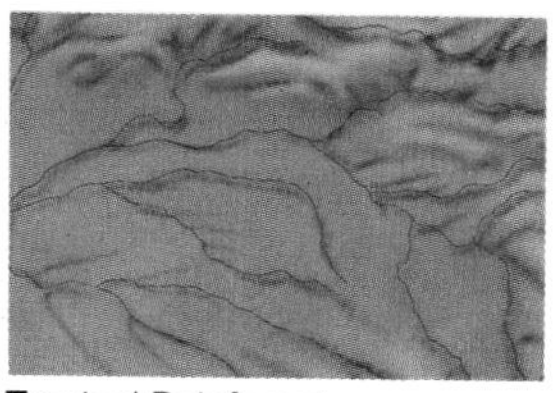
Tropical Rainforest
Tropischer Regenwald
Bosque tropical lluvioso
Forêt tropicale humide
Floresta tropical úmida

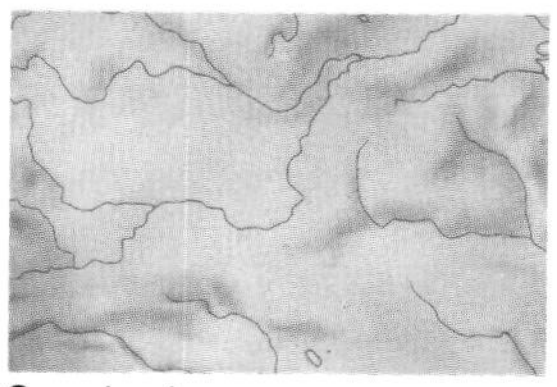
Grassland
Grasland
Pradera
Formations herbacées
Pradaria

Dry Scrub
Trockenes Buschland
Matorral
Brousse sèche
Caatinga

Desert
Wüste
Desierto
Désert
Deserto

Submarine Features / Untermeerische Phänomene
Elementos Submarinos / Formes de Relief Sous-marin / Acidentes do Revelo Submarino

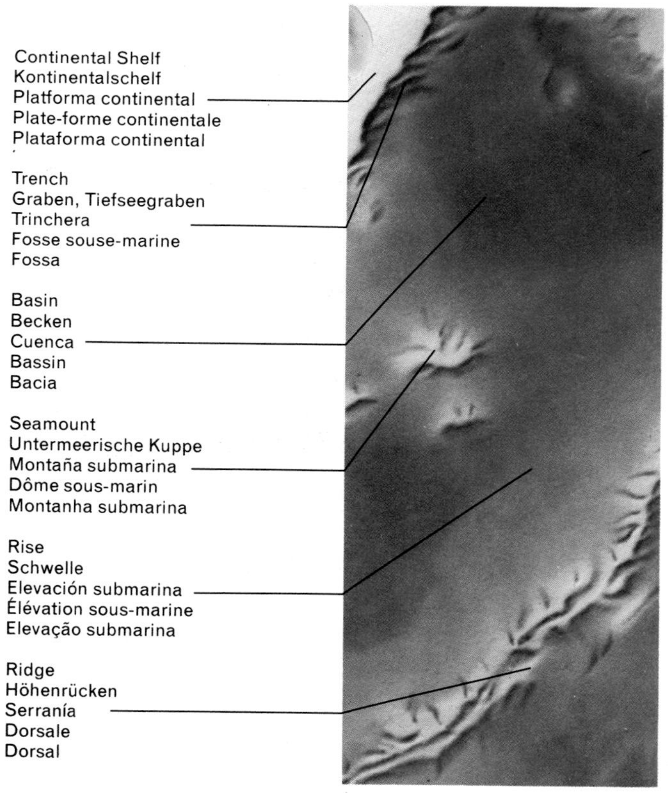
Continental Shelf
Kontinentalschelf
Platforma continental
Plate-forme continentale
Plataforma continental
Trench
Graben, Tiefseegraben
Trinchera
Fosse souse-marine
Fossa
Basin
Becken
Cuenca
Bassin
Bacia
Seamount
Untermeerische Kuppe
Montaña submarina
Dôme sous-marin
Montanha submarina
Rise
Schwelle
Elevación submarina
Élevation sous-marine
Elevação submarina
Ridge
Höhenrücken
Serranía
Dorsale
Dorsal

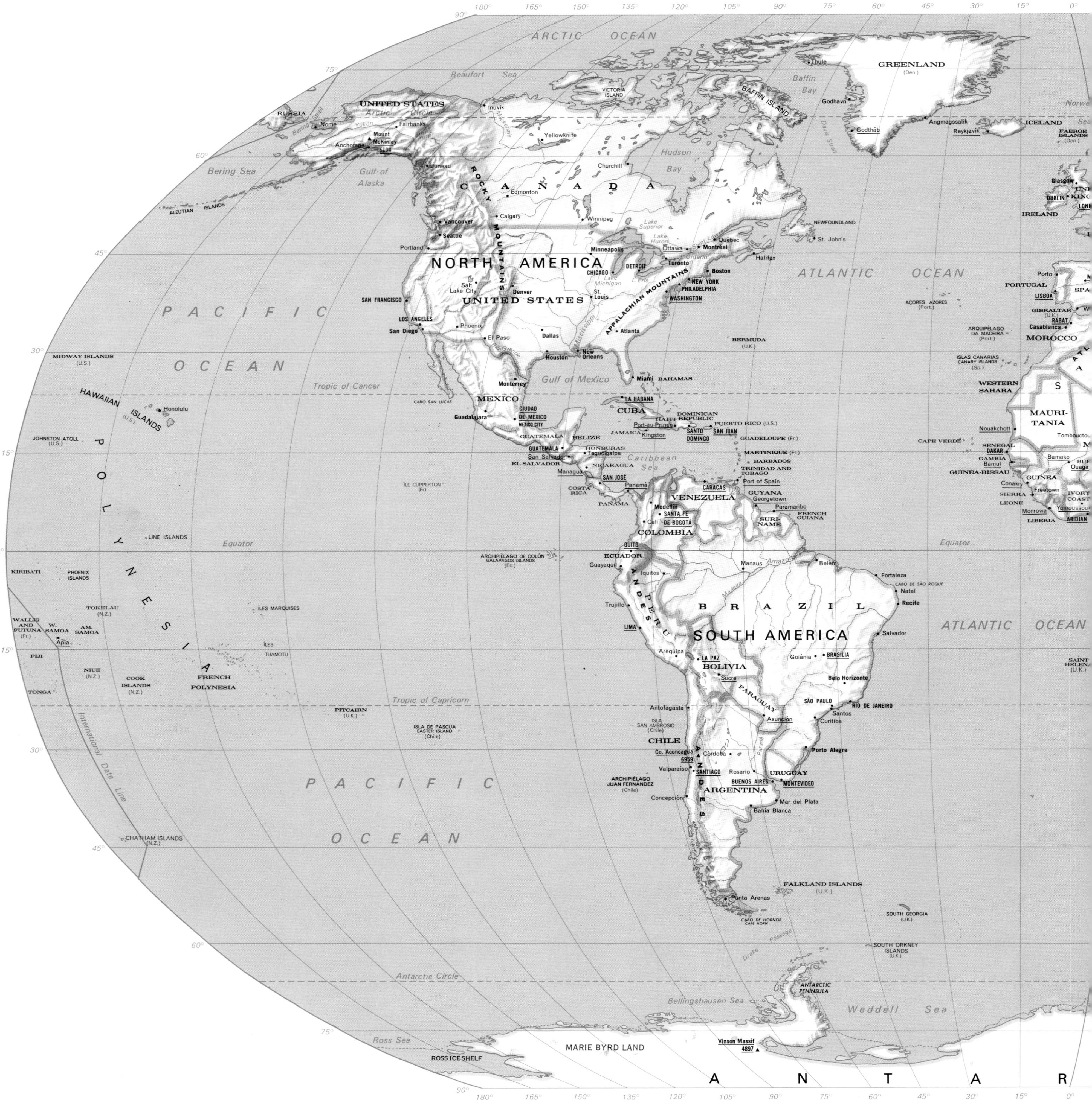
ARCTIC OCEAN
Beaufort Sea
GREENLAND (Den.)
Baffin Bay
BAFFIN ISLAND
VICTORIA ISLAND
Hudson Bay
Bering Sea
Gulf of Alaska
ALEUTIAN ISLANDS
RUSSIA
UNITED STATES
Mount McKinley 6194
C A N A D A
ROCKY MOUNTAINS
NORTH AMERICA
UNITED STATES
APPALACHIAN MOUNTAINS
NEWFOUNDLAND
ICELAND
IRELAND
PORTUGAL
MOROCCO
ATLANTIC OCEAN
PACIFIC OCEAN
MIDWAY ISLANDS (U.S.)
HAWAIIAN ISLANDS (U.S.)
JOHNSTON ATOLL (U.S.)
Tropic of Cancer
Gulf of Mexico
MEXICO
CUBA
JAMAICA
HAITI
DOMINICAN REPUBLIC
PUERTO RICO (U.S.)
BERMUDA (U.K.)
BAHAMAS
BELIZE
GUATEMALA
HONDURAS
EL SALVADOR
NICARAGUA
COSTA RICA
PANAMA
Caribbean Sea
VENEZUELA
GUYANA
SURINAME
FRENCH GUIANA
COLOMBIA
ECUADOR
PERU
BRAZIL
SOUTH AMERICA
BOLIVIA
PARAGUAY
CHILE
ARGENTINA
URUGUAY
ANDES
Equator
POLYNESIA
LINE ISLANDS
KIRIBATI
PHOENIX ISLANDS
TOKELAU (N.Z.)
WALLIS AND FUTUNA (Fr.)
W. SAMOA
AM. SAMOA
FIJI
TONGA
NIUE (N.Z.)
COOK ISLANDS (N.Z.)
FRENCH POLYNESIA
ÎLES MARQUISES
ÎLES TUAMOTU
PITCAIRN (U.K.)
ISLA DE PASCUA EASTER ISLAND (Chile)
Tropic of Capricorn
International Date Line
CHATHAM ISLANDS (N.Z.)
FALKLAND ISLANDS (U.K.)
SOUTH GEORGIA (U.K.)
SOUTH ORKNEY ISLANDS (U.K.)
Drake Passage
Antarctic Circle
ANTARCTIC PENINSULA
Bellingshausen Sea
Weddell Sea
Ross Sea
ROSS ICE SHELF
MARIE BYRD LAND
Vinson Massif 4897
A N T A R

ARCTIC OCEAN
Barents Sea
Karskoje more
more Laptevych
Arctic Circle
Sea of Okhotsk
Bering Sea
Sea of Japan
Black Sea
Caspian Sea
Mediterranean Sea
Red Sea
Arabian Sea
Bay of Bengal
South China Sea
Philippine Sea
PACIFIC OCEAN
MICRONESIA
MELANESIA
Equator
Tropic of Cancer
Tropic of Capricorn
INDIAN OCEAN
Coral Sea
Tasman Sea
SOUTHERN OCEAN
Antarctic Circle
International Date Line
Mozambique Channel
Gulf of Carpentaria
ZEML'A FRANCA-IOSIFA
NOVAJA ZEML'A
NOVOSIBIRSKIJE OSTROVA
RUSSIA
EUROPE
ASIA
AFRICA
KAZAKHSTAN
MONGOLIA
CHINA
GOBI
ALTAI
TIEN SHAN
HIMALAYAS
URAL'SKIJE GORY
JAPAN
N. KOREA
S. KOREA
TURKEY
IRAN
IRAQ
SYRIA
LEB.
ISR.
JORDAN
KUWAIT
SAUDI ARABIA
QATAR
UNITED ARAB EMIRATES
OMAN
YEMEN
AFGHANISTAN
PAKISTAN
INDIA
NEPAL
BHUTAN
BNGL.
BURMA
THAILAND
LAOS
VIETNAM
CAMB.
MALAYSIA
BRUNEI
PHILIPPINES
INDONESIA
PAPUA NEW GUINEA
AUSTRALIA
NEW ZEALAND
TASMANIA
NORTH ISLAND
SOUTH ISLAND
NEW CALEDONIA (Fr.)
SOLOMON ISLANDS
VANUATU
FIJI
KIRIBATI
NAURU
TUVALU
MARSHALL ISLANDS
FEDERATED STATES OF MICRONESIA
NORTHERN MARIANA ISLANDS (U.S.)
GUAM (U.S.)
PALAU (U.S.)
WAKE ISLAND (U.S.)
NORFOLK ISLAND (Austl.)
OGASAWARA-GUNTŌ (Japan)
NANSEI-SHOTŌ
TAIWAN
SRI LANKA
MALDIVES
SEYCHELLES
BRITISH INDIAN OCEAN TERRITORY
ANDAMAN ISLANDS (India)
NICOBAR ISLANDS (India)
COCOS ISLANDS (Austl.)
CHRISTMAS ISLAND (Austl.)
MADAGASCAR
MAURITIUS
REUNION (Fr.)
ÎLES KERGUÉLEN (Fr.)
SWEDEN
FINLAND
NORWAY
POLAND
GERMANY
CZECH REP.
SLVK.
HUNG.
AUS.
SLO.
CRO.
BOS.
YUGO.
ROM.
MOLD.
BUL.
ALB.
MA.
GREECE
ITALY
TUNISIA
ALGERIA
LIBYA
EGYPT
SUDAN
CHAD
NIGER
NIGERIA
CAMEROON
CEN. AFR. REP.
EQUATORIAL GUINEA
GABON
CONGO
ZAIRE
UGANDA
KENYA
RWANDA
BURUNDI
TANZANIA
ETHIOPIA
ERITREA
DJIBOUTI
SOMALIA
ANGOLA
ZAMBIA
MALAWI
ZIMBABWE
MOZAMBIQUE
BOTSWANA
NAMIBIA
SOUTH AFRICA
LESOTHO
SWAZILAND
ESTONIA
LAT.
LITH.
BELARUS
UKRAINE
GEOR.
ARMENIA
AZER.
TURKMENISTAN
UZBEKISTAN
KYRG.
TAJIK.
MALTA
Hammerfest
Narvik
Murmansk
Archangel'sk
Vorkuta
Salechard
Dikson
Chatanga
Noril'sk
Igarka
Tiksi
Verchojansk
Jakutsk
Lensk
Magadan
Ochotsk
Anadyr'
Petropavlovsk-Kamčatskij
Nikolajevsk
OSTROV SACHALIN
KURIL'SKIJE OSTROVA
ALEUTIAN IS. (U.S.)
Chabarovsk
Harbin
Vladivostok
Sapporo
Sendai
TŌKYŌ
HONSHŪ
ŌSAKA
Fukuoka
Pusan
SŎUL
P'YŎNGYANG
Dalian
Shenyang
BEIJING
PEKING
Tianjin
Qingdao
Hohhot
Lanzhou
Xi'an
Nanjing
Wuhan
SHANGHAI
Chengdu
Chongqing
Changsha
Fuzhou
T'AIPEI
Guangzhou
HONG KONG (U.K.)
Kunming
HA-NOI
Lhasa
Ürümqi
Shache
ULAANBAATAR
Čita
Irkutsk
ozero Bajkal
Krasnojarsk
Novosibirsk
Omsk
Karaganda
ALMA-ATA
TAŠKENT
KĀBUL
Islāmābād
Rāwalpindi
Lahore
DELHI
New Delhi
Kāthmāndau
THIMPHU
Mount Everest 8848
DHAKA
CALCUTTA
Karāchi
Ahmadābād
BOMBAY
Hyderābād
Bangalore
Madras
Cochin
COLOMBO
YANGON
KRUNG THEP
BANGKOK
Phnum Pénh
Thanh Pho Ho Chi Minh
MANILA
Davao
Medan
KUALA LUMPUR
SINGAPORE
SUMATERA
BORNEO
SULAWESI
Palembang
Banjarmasin
JAKARTA
Surabaya
JAWA
Ujungpandang
TIMOR
Mount Wilhelm 4509
NEW GUINEA
Port Moresby
CAPE YORK
Darwin
Cairns
Rockhampton
Brisbane
Alice Springs
Perth
Adelaide
Melbourne
Canberra
Sydney
Mount Kosciusko 2228
Hobart
Auckland
Wellington
Christchurch
Nouméa
Suva
MOSKVA
Sankt-Peterburg
ST. PETERSBURG
Nižnij Novgorod
Perm'
Jekaterinburg
Čel'abinsk
Samara
Volgograd
Astrachan'
gora El'brus 5642
KIJEV
HELSINKI
STOCKHOLM
KØBENHAVN
BERLIN
Bonn
WARSZAWA
WIEN
BUDAPEST
BEOGRAD
BUCUREŞTI
SOFIJA
İstanbul
ANKARA
ATHINAI
ROMA
Milano
Napoli
ALPS
TUNIS
TARĀBULUS
TRIPOLI
Banghāzī
Al-Iskandarīyah
Alexandria
AL-QĀHIRAH
CAIRO
Aswān
BAGHDĀD
TEHRĀN
Eşfahān
Ābādān
BAKU
AR-RIYĀḌ
Makkah
Masqaţ
Şan'ā'
Adan
SUQUṬRĀ (Yem.)
Djibouti
ADIS ABEBA
AL-KHARṬŪM
N'Djamena
Kano
Yaounde
Douala
Libreville
Bangui
KAMPALA
NAIROBI
Kilimanjaro 5895
Mombasa
Zanzibar
DAR ES SALAAM
Dodoma
Bujumbura
Lake Tanganyika
KINSHASA
Brazzaville
LUANDA
Lobito
Lubumbashi
Lusaka
Lilongwe
HARARE
Muqdisho
ANTANANARIVO
Windhoek
Walvisbaai (S. Afr.)
Gaborone
PRETORIA
Johannesburg
MAPUTO
Durban
CAPE TOWN
Port Elizabeth
CAPE AGULHAS
ENDERBY LAND
WILKES LAND
ANTARCTICA
30° 45° 60° 75° 90° 105° 120° 135° 150° 165° 180°
Copyright © by Rand McNally & Co.
Map prepared by Rand McNally & Co.
A-510000-264 20-18-38

Kilometers 0 1000 2000 3000 Km.
Statute Miles 0 1000 2000 3000 Mi.

One centimeter represents 750 kilometers.
One inch represents approximately 1200 miles.
Robinson Projection
Scale 1:75,000,000

ARCTIC OCEAN
GRØNLAND
Baffin Bay
Beaufort Sea
Hudson Bay
Bering Sea
Chukchi Sea
Gulf of Alaska
ALEUTIAN BASIN
ALEUTIAN TRENCH
Labrador Sea
LABRADOR BASIN
ICELAND
C A N A D A
N O R T H
A M E R I C A
U N I T E D S T A T E S
ROCKY MOUNTAINS
APPALACHIAN MOUNTAINS
Mount McKinley 6194
Pikes Peak 4301
CHICAGO
NEW YORK
Montreal
LOS ANGELES
Houston
Gulf of Mexico
MEXICO
CIUDAD DE MÉXICO
Caribbean Sea
GREATER ANTILLES
WEST INDIES
Tropic of Cancer
NORTH AMERICAN BASIN
Sargasso Sea
ATLANTIC OCEAN
MID-ATLANTIC RIDGE
NEWFOUNDLAND BASIN
WEST EUROPEAN BASIN
AZORES PLATEAU
CAPE VERDE BASIN
GUIANA BASIN
SIERRA LEONE BASIN
MENDOCINO FRACTURE ZONE
MURRAY FRACTURE ZONE
CLARION FRACTURE ZONE
CLIPPERTON FRACTURE ZONE
P A C I F I C
O C E A N
HAWAIIAN ISLANDS
HAWAIIAN RIDGE
P O L Y N E S I A
CENTRAL PACIFIC BASIN
Equator
SOUTH
A M E R I C A
B R A Z I L
VENEZUELA
COLOMBIA
BOLIVIA
PARAGUAY
URUGUAY
Amazon
A N D E S
Chimborazo 6310
Nevado Huascarán 6768
LIMA
SÃO PAULO
RIO DE JANEIRO
BUENOS AIRES
SANTIAGO
Cerro Aconcagua 6959
PATAGONIA
Tropic of Capricorn
EAST PACIFIC RISE
CHILE RISE
SOUTHWEST PACIFIC BASIN
SOUTHEAST PACIFIC BASIN
ARGENTINE BASIN
BRAZIL BASIN
FALKLAND ISLANDS
Scotia Sea
Drake Passage
SOUTH SHETLAND ISLANDS
SOUTH ORKNEY ISLANDS
Antarctic Circle
Bellingshausen Sea
Amundsen Sea
Weddell Sea
Ross Sea
MARIE BYRD LAND
ROSS ICE SHELF
RONNE ICE SHELF
FILCHNER ICE SHELF
Vinson Massif 4897
International Date Line
A N T

ARCTIC OCEAN
SEVERNAJA ZEML'A
NOVOSIBIRSKIJE OSTROVA
more Laptevych
Karskoje more
Barents Sea
Vostočno-Sibirskoje more
East Siberian Sea
Arctic Circle
SREDNESIBIRSKOJE
SIBERIA
PLOSKOGORJE
ZAPADNO-
SIBIRSKAJA
RAVNINA
SIBIR'
RUSSIA
MOSKVA
SANKT-PETERBURG
Baltic Sea
SWEDEN
FINLAND
POLAND
BELARUS
UKRAINE
GERMANY
EUROPE
ROMANIA
ITALY
Black Sea
Caspian Sea
KAZAKHSTAN
ASIA
MONGOLIA
GOBI
CHINA
BEIJING
Sea of Okhotsk
Bering Sea
ALEUTIAN BASIN
ALEUTIAN TRENCH
KURIL TRENCH
EMPEROR SEAMOUNTS
International Date Line
NORTHWEST PACIFIC BASIN
Sea of Japan
JAPAN
TŌKYŌ
Yellow Sea
SHANGHAI
East China Sea
PACIFIC OCEAN
Tropic of Cancer
HONG KONG
TAIWAN
Philippine Sea
PHILIPPINE BASIN
PHILIPPINES
MARIANA TRENCH
MICRONESIA
MID-PACIFIC MOUNTAINS
MARSHALL ISLANDS
EAST MARIANA BASIN
CAROLINE ISLANDS
WEST CAROLINE BASIN
EAST CAROLINE BASIN
Equator
South China Sea
VIETNAM
THAILAND
BURMA
INDOCHINA
MALAYSIA
BORNEO
SUMATERA
JAKARTA
INDONESIA
SULAWESI
NEW GUINEA
PAPUA NEW GUINEA
SOLOMON ISLANDS
Coral Sea
MELANESIA
Arafura Sea
Gulf of Carpentaria
AUSTRALIA
GREAT SANDY DESERT
GIBSON DESERT
GREAT VICTORIA DESERT
GREAT DIVIDING RANGE
Sydney
Perth
Great Australian Bight
SOUTH AUSTRALIAN BASIN
TASMANIA
Tasman Sea
TASMAN BASIN
NEW ZEALAND
NORTH ISLAND
SOUTH ISLAND
SOUTHERN OCEAN
SOUTHEAST INDIAN RIDGE
SOUTH INDIAN BASIN
INDIAN OCEAN
WHARTON BASIN
NINETYEAST RIDGE
MID-INDIAN BASIN
MID-INDIAN RIDGE
SOUTHWEST INDIAN RIDGE
CROZET BASIN
MADAGASCAR BASIN
MASCARENE ISLANDS
Tropic of Capricorn
MADAGASCAR
Mozambique Channel
SOMALI BASIN
ARABIAN BASIN
CARLSBERG RIDGE
Arabian Sea
Bay of Bengal
INDIA
SRI LANKA
PAKISTAN
HIMALAYAS
Mount Everest 8848
TIBET
IRAN
IRAQ
SAUDI ARABIA
ARABIAN PENINSULA
Persian Gulf
Red Sea
Gulf of Aden
TURKEY
Mediterranean Sea
EGYPT
LIBYA
SUDAN
CHAD
NIGER
NIGERIA
ETHIOPIA
ADIS ABEBA
SOMALIA
CENTRAL AFRICAN REPUBLIC
ZAIRE
KINSHASA
TANZANIA
Kilimanjaro 5895
ANGOLA
ZAMBIA
ZIMBABWE
MOZAMBIQUE
NAMIBIA
BOTSWANA
SOUTH AFRICA
CAPE TOWN
Johannesburg
AFRICA
AGULHAS BASIN
ATLANTIC-INDIAN RIDGE
ATLANTIC-INDIAN BASIN
Antarctic Circle
ENDERBY LAND
AMERICAN HIGHLAND
WILKES LAND
VICTORIA LAND
Ross Sea
ROSS ICE SHELF
Mount Kirkpatrick 4528
EN MAUD LAND
ANTARCTICA
Copyright © by Rand McNally & Co.
Map prepared by Rand McNally & Co.
30° 45° 60° 75° 90° 105° 120° 135° 150° 165° 180°

Kilometers 0 1000 2000 3000 Km.

Statute Miles 0 1000 2000 3000 Mi.

One centimeter represents 750 kilometers.
One inch represents approximately 1200 miles.
Robinson Projection
Scale 1:75,000,000

GREENLAND
Greenland Sea
Barents Sea
ICELAND
Norwegian Sea
Arctic Circle
NORWEGIAN BASIN
FINLAND
SWEDEN
NORWAY
UNITED KINGDOM
IRELAND
North Sea
DENMARK
POLAND
GERMANY
FRANCE
SPAIN
ITALY
UKRAINE
BELARUS
HUNGARY
ROMANIA
BULGARIA
Black Sea
TURKEY
ASIA MINOR
MEDITERRANEAN SEA
TUNISIA
LIBYA
EGYPT
SAHARA
Tropic of Cancer
SUDAN
ETHIOPIA
SOMALIA
KENYA
TANZANIA
ZAMBIA
ZIMBABWE
MOZAMBIQUE
BOTSWANA
NAMIBIA
SOUTH AFRICA
MADAGASCAR
Mozambique Channel
AFRICA
Equator
SAUDI ARABIA
YEMEN
OMAN
IRAN
IRAQ
SYRIA
JORDAN
ISRAEL
Caspian Sea
Aral'skoje more
KAZAKHSTAN
UZBEK.
TURKM.
AFGHANISTAN
PAKISTAN
INDIA
NEPAL
BHUTAN
BNGL.
BURMA
HIMALAYAS
TIBET
TIENYSHAN
MONGOLIA
GOBI
CHINA
KUNLUN SHAN
QING ZANG GAOYUAN
URAL'SKIJE GORY
URAL MOUNTAINS
RUSSIA
ZAPADNO-SIBIRSKAJA RAVNINA
SIBERIA
SREDNESIBIRSKOJE PLOSKOGORJE
Lena
Sea of Okhotsk
JAPAN
N. KOREA
S. KOREA
Yellow Sea
East China Sea
Sea of Japan
TAIWAN
Philippine Sea
PHILIPPINES
South China Sea
THAILAND
INDOCHINA
VIETNAM
CAMB.
MALAYSIA
BORNEO KALIMANTAN
SUMATERA
SULAWESI CELEBES
GREATER SUNDA ISLANDS
INDONESIA
JAVA TRENCH
NEW GUINEA
PAPUA NEW GUINEA
Arafura Sea
Timor Sea
Gulf of Carpentaria
Coral Sea
AUSTRALIA
GREAT SANDY DESERT
GIBSON DESERT
SIMPSON DESERT
GREAT VICTORIA DESERT
GREAT DIVIDING RANGE
GREAT BARRIER REEF
Great Australian Bight
TASMANIA
ARABIAN SEA
Bay of Bengal
SRI LANKA
MALDIVES
ARABIAN BASIN
SOMALI BASIN
CARLSBERG RIDGE
CHAGOS-LACCADIVE PLATEAU
MID-INDIAN BASIN
NINETY EAST RIDGE
NORTH AUSTRALIAN BASIN
WHARTON BASIN
PERTH BASIN
BROKEN RIDGE
INDIAN OCEAN
Tropic of Capricorn
MASCARENE BASIN
MASCARENE PLATEAU
SEYCHELLES
MAURITIUS
REUNION
MADAGASCAR BASIN
MADAGASCAR PLATEAU
MOZAMBIQUE PLATEAU
SOUTHWEST INDIAN RIDGE
MID-INDIAN RIDGE
CROZET BASIN
AGULHAS BASIN
SOUTH AUSTRALIAN BASIN
SOUTHERN OCEAN
SOUTHEAST INDIAN RIDGE
SOUTH INDIAN BASIN
KERGUELEN PLATEAU
ATLANTIC-INDIAN RIDGE
ATLANTIC-INDIAN BASIN
Antarctic Circle
ENDERBY LAND
AMERY ICE SHELF
AMERICAN HIGHLAND
WILKES LAND
ANTARCTICA
PRINCESS MARTHA COAST

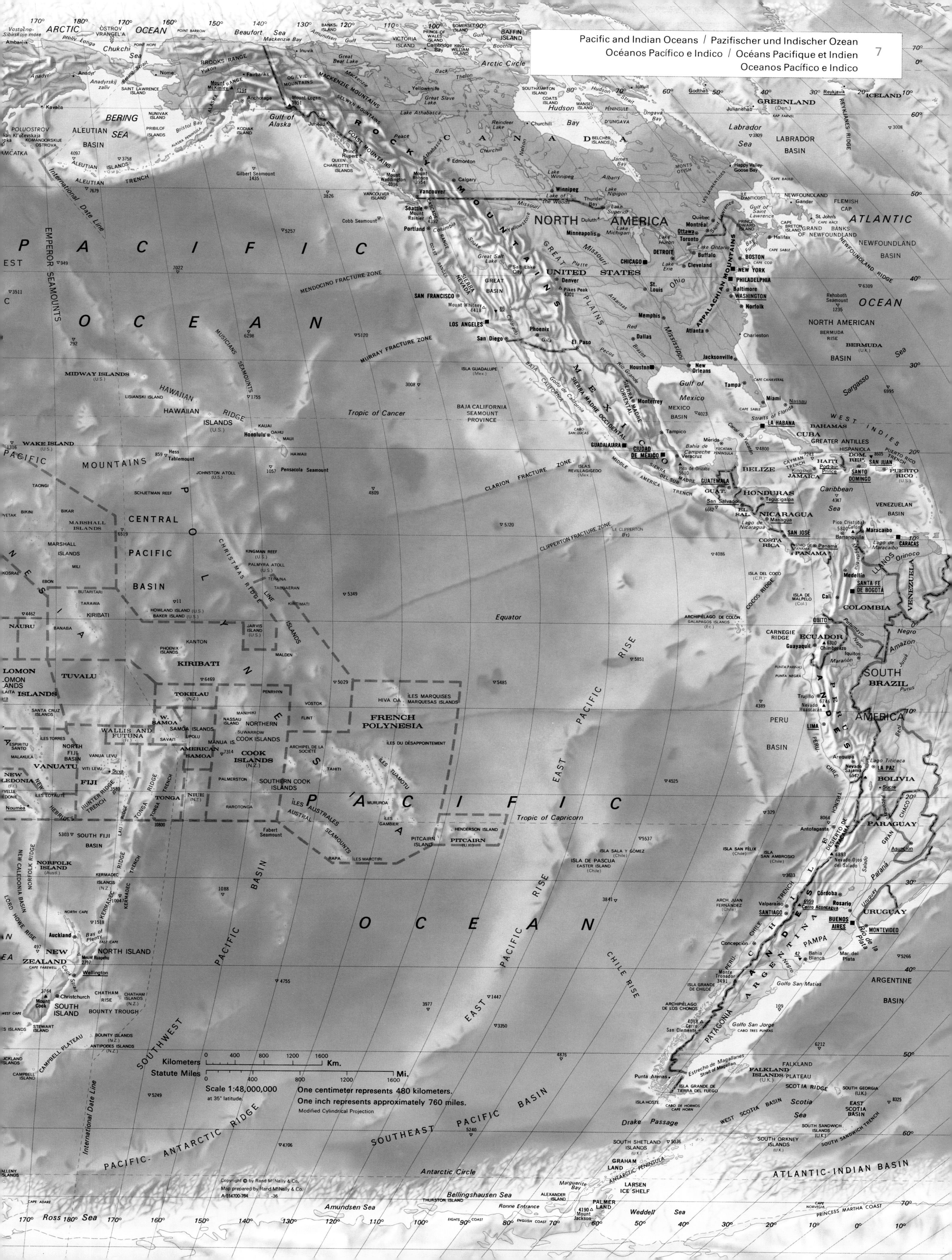
ARCTIC OCEAN
Beaufort Sea
Chukchi Sea
BERING SEA
ALEUTIAN BASIN
ALEUTIAN TRENCH
Gulf of Alaska
International Date Line
EMPEROR SEAMOUNTS
P A C I F I C O C E A N
MENDOCINO FRACTURE ZONE
MURRAY FRACTURE ZONE
MUSICIANS SEAMOUNTS
MIDWAY ISLANDS (U.S.)
HAWAIIAN RIDGE
HAWAIIAN ISLANDS (U.S.)
Honolulu
Tropic of Cancer
BAJA CALIFORNIA SEAMOUNT PROVINCE
WAKE ISLAND (U.S.)
MID-PACIFIC MOUNTAINS
CLARION FRACTURE ZONE
CLIPPERTON FRACTURE ZONE
CENTRAL PACIFIC BASIN
MARSHALL ISLANDS
CHRISTMAS RIDGE
LINE ISLANDS
KIRIBATI
NAURU
TUVALU
Equator
TOKELAU (N.Z.)
W. SAMOA
AMERICAN SAMOA
WALLIS AND FUTUNA (Fr.)
FIJI
VANUATU
TONGA
NIUE (N.Z.)
COOK ISLANDS (N.Z.)
FRENCH POLYNESIA
ÎLES MARQUISES
PITCAIRN
P A C I F I C O C E A N
Tropic of Capricorn
EAST PACIFIC RISE
ISLA DE PASCUA EASTER ISLAND (Chile)
CHILE RISE
SOUTH FIJI BASIN
NORFOLK ISLAND (Austl.)
KERMADEC TRENCH
TONGA TRENCH
SOUTHWEST PACIFIC BASIN
NEW ZEALAND
NORTH ISLAND
SOUTH ISLAND
Auckland
Wellington
Christchurch
CHATHAM RISE
BOUNTY TROUGH
CAMPBELL PLATEAU
PACIFIC-ANTARCTIC RIDGE
SOUTHEAST PACIFIC BASIN
Antarctic Circle
Amundsen Sea
Bellingshausen Sea
Ross Sea
Weddell Sea
ANTARCTIC PENINSULA
Drake Passage
Scotia Sea
SOUTH GEORGIA (U.K.)
FALKLAND ISLANDS (U.K.)
ATLANTIC-INDIAN BASIN
C A N A D A
ROCKY MOUNTAINS
NORTH AMERICA
UNITED STATES
Hudson Bay
Vancouver
Seattle
Portland
SAN FRANCISCO
LOS ANGELES
San Diego
Phoenix
Denver
Winnipeg
Minneapolis
CHICAGO
DETROIT
Toronto
Ottawa
Montréal
Québec
BOSTON
NEW YORK
PHILADELPHIA
WASHINGTON
Atlanta
Dallas
Houston
New Orleans
Miami
Gulf of Mexico
M E X I C O
CIUDAD DE MEXICO
GUADALAJARA
Monterrey
LA HABANA
CUBA
BAHAMAS
JAMAICA
HAITI
DOM. REP.
SANTO DOMINGO
PUERTO RICO (U.S.)
BELIZE
GUATEMALA
HONDURAS
NICARAGUA
COSTA RICA
PANAMA
Caribbean Sea
VENEZUELA
CARACAS
COLOMBIA
SANTA FE DE BOGOTÁ
ECUADOR
QUITO
PERU
LIMA
BOLIVIA
LA PAZ
SOUTH AMERICA
BRAZIL
Amazon
PARAGUAY
Asunción
CHILE
SANTIAGO
ARGENTINA
BUENOS AIRES
URUGUAY
MONTEVIDEO
PATAGONIA
PERU-CHILE TRENCH
ATLANTIC OCEAN
NORTH AMERICAN BASIN
BERMUDA (U.K.)
Sargasso Sea
WEST INDIES
GREATER ANTILLES
ARGENTINE BASIN
GREENLAND (Den.)
ICELAND
LABRADOR BASIN
Labrador Sea
NEWFOUNDLAND
NEWFOUNDLAND BASIN
Kilometers 0 400 800 1200 1600 Km.
Statute Miles 0 400 800 1200 1600 Mi.
Scale 1:48,000,000 at 35° latitude
One centimeter represents 480 kilometers.
One inch represents approximately 760 miles.
Modified Cylindrical Projection
Copyright © by Rand McNally & Co.
Map prepared by Rand McNally & Co.

8 Atlantic Ocean / Atlantischer Ozean / Océano Atlántico / Océan Atlantique / Oceano Atlântico

GREENLAND
Baffin Bay
Labrador Sea
Norwegian Sea
Barents Sea
North Sea
Hudson Bay
NORTH AMERICA
CANADA
UNITED STATES
ICELAND
FAEROE IS.
UNITED KINGDOM
IRELAND
FRANCE
SPAIN
PORTUGAL
GERMANY
POLAND
RUSSIA
EUROPE
FINLAND
SWEDEN
NORWAY
DENMARK
ITALY
ROMANIA
TURKEY
ASIA MINOR
Black Sea
Caspian Sea
Mediterranean Sea
SYRIA
IRAQ
LEBANON
ISRAEL
JORDAN
SAUDI ARABIA
EGYPT
LIBYA
ALGERIA
MOROCCO
WESTERN SAHARA
MAURITANIA
MALI
NIGER
CHAD
SUDAN
SAHARA
SUDAN
SENEGAL
GAMBIA
GUINEA-BISSAU
GUINEA
SIERRA LEONE
LIBERIA
IVORY COAST
BURKINA FASO
GHANA
TOGO
BENIN
NIGERIA
CAMEROON
CENTRAL AFRICAN REPUBLIC
ETHIOPIA
KENYA
UGANDA
RWANDA
BURUNDI
TANZANIA
GABON
CONGO
ZAIRE
ANGOLA
ZAMBIA
MOZAMBIQUE
ZIMBABWE
NAMIBIA
BOTSWANA
SWAZILAND
LESOTHO
SOUTH AFRICA
AFRICA
ATLANTIC OCEAN
NORTH AMERICAN BASIN
Sargasso Sea
WEST EUROPEAN BASIN
NEWFOUNDLAND BASIN
LABRADOR BASIN
MID-ATLANTIC RIDGE
CAPE VERDE BASIN
GUIANA BASIN
SIERRA LEONE BASIN
GUINEA BASIN
BRAZIL BASIN
ANGOLA BASIN
CAPE BASIN
ARGENTINE BASIN
AGULHAS BASIN
WALVIS RIDGE
RIO GRANDE RISE
BROMLEY PLATEAU
Tropic of Cancer
Tropic of Capricorn
Equator
Arctic Circle
Antarctic Circle
Gulf of Mexico
Caribbean Sea
MEXICO
CUBA
BAHAMAS
HAITI
DOM. REP.
JAMAICA
PUERTO RICO
BELIZE
HONDURAS
NICARAGUA
COSTA RICA
PANAMA
VENEZUELA
COLOMBIA
GUYANA
SURINAME
FRENCH GUIANA
ECUADOR
PERU
BRAZIL
BOLIVIA
PARAGUAY
URUGUAY
ARGENTINA
CHILE
SOUTH AMERICA
FALKLAND ISLANDS
PATAGONIA
PAMPA
ANDES
PACIFIC OCEAN
INDIAN OCEAN
Scotia Sea
Weddell Sea
Drake Passage
SOUTH GEORGIA
SOUTH SANDWICH ISLANDS
SOUTH ORKNEY ISLANDS
SOUTH SHETLAND ISLANDS
ANTARCTICA
Kilometers 0 400 800 1200 1600 Km.
Statute Miles 0 400 800 1200 1600 Mi.
Scale 1:48,000,000 at 35° latitude.
One centimeter represents 480 kilometers.
One inch represents approximately 760 miles.
Modified Cylindrical Projection
Copyright © by Rand McNally & Co.
Map prepared by Rand McNally & Co.
A-513700-764 - 32

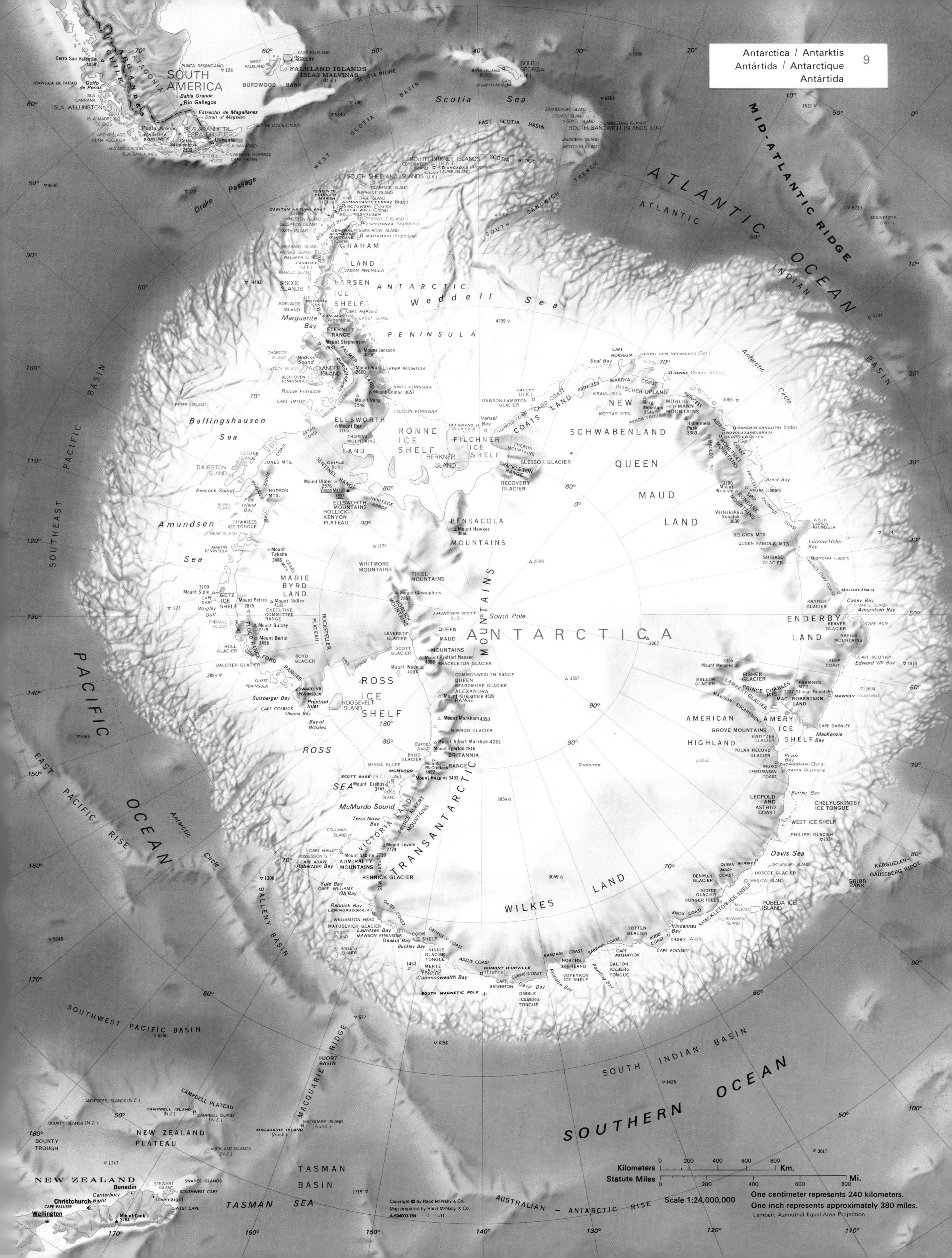
SOUTH AMERICA
PATAGONIA
CHILE
ANDES
Cerro San Valentín 4058
PENÍNSULA DE TAITAO
Golfo de Penas
ISLA WELLINGTON
Bahía Grande
Río Gallegos
Estrecho de Magallanes
Strait of Magellan
ISLA GRANDE DE TIERRA DEL FUEGO
Punta Arenas
Ushuaia
Cerro Sarmiento 2300
CABO DE HORNOS
CAPE HORN
ISLA DE LOS ESTADOS
FALKLAND ISLANDS
ISLAS MALVINAS
(U.K.)
EAST FALKLAND
WEST FALKLAND
Stanley
BURDWOOD BANK
SCOTIA RIDGE
Scotia Sea
SOUTH GEORGIA
(U.K.)
EAST SCOTIA BASIN
SOUTH SANDWICH ISLANDS (U.K.)
SOUTH SANDWICH TRENCH
SOUTH ORKNEY ISLANDS
SOUTH SHETLAND ISLANDS
WEST SCOTIA BASIN
Drake Passage
MID-ATLANTIC RIDGE
ATLANTIC OCEAN
ATLANTIC INDIAN BASIN
SOUTH ATLANTIC
BOUVETØYA
GRAHAM LAND
JASON PENINSULA
LARSEN ICE SHELF
ANTARCTIC PENINSULA
Weddell Sea
BISCOE ISLANDS
ADELAIDE ISLAND
Marguerite Bay
ETERNITY RANGE
Mount Stephenson 2981
Mount Jackson 4190
CHARCOT ISLAND
Wilkins Sound
ALEXANDER ISLAND
PALMER LAND
George VI Sound
KEMP PENINSULA
Mount Ward 2600
SMITH PENINSULA
Mount Coman 3657
BEETHOVEN PENINSULA
LATADY ISLAND
Ronne Entrance
ENGLISH COAST
Mount Vang 1548
DODSON PENINSULA
PETER I ISLAND
Bellingshausen Sea
ELLSWORTH LAND
Mount Rex 1105
THOMAS MOUNTAINS
RONNE ICE SHELF
BERKNER ISLAND
FILCHNER ICE SHELF
Vahsel Bay
THURSTON ISLAND
Peacock Sound
JONES MTS.
SENTINEL RANGE
Vinson Massif 4897
Mount Ulmer 2576
HUDSON MTS.
ELLSWORTH MOUNTAINS
HERITAGE RANGE
HOLLICK-KENYON PLATEAU
Pine Island Bay
THWAITES ICE TONGUE
Amundsen Sea
MARTIN PENINSULA
Mount Takahe 3486
MARIE BYRD LAND
Mount Siple 3100
GETZ ICE SHELF
Wrigley Gulf
Mount Petras 2875
Mount Sidley 4181
EXECUTIVE COMMITTEE RANGE
FLOOD RANGE
Mount Bursey 2779
Mount Berlin 3498
HULL GLACIER
ROCKEFELLER PLATEAU
FORD RANGES
BALCHEN GLACIER
EDWARD VII PENINSULA
Sulzberger Bay
Okuma Bay
Prestrud Inlet
Bay of Whales
ROOSEVELT ISLAND
ROSS ICE SHELF
ROSS SEA
COATS LAND
LUITPOLD COAST
CAIRD COAST
HALLEY (U.K.)
DAWSON-LAMBTON GLACIER
THERON MOUNTAINS
SHACKLETON RANGE
SLESSOR GLACIER
RECOVERY GLACIER
PENSACOLA MOUNTAINS
Mount Hawkes 3660
WHITMORE MOUNTAINS
THIEL MOUNTAINS
Mount Glossopteris 2867
HORLICK MOUNTAINS
AMUNDSEN-SCOTT (U.S.)
South Pole
QUEEN MAUD MOUNTAINS
LEVERETT GLACIER
SCOTT GLACIER
Mount Fridtjof Nansen 4068
SHACKLETON GLACIER
Mount Wade 4084
COMMONWEALTH RANGE
QUEEN ALEXANDRA RANGE
BEARDMORE GLACIER
Mount Kirkpatrick 4528
Mount Markham 4350
NIMROD GLACIER
Mount Albert Markham 4282
Mount Egerton 2816
BRITANNIA RANGE
BYRD GLACIER
MINNA BLUFF
Mount McClintock 3492
Mount Huggins 3433
SCOTT BASE (N.Z.)
MCMURDO (U.S.)
Mount Erebus 3743
ROSS ISLAND
McMurdo Sound
Terra Nova Bay
COULMAN ISLAND
VICTORIA LAND
PRINCE ALBERT MOUNTAINS
TRANSANTARCTIC MOUNTAINS
Mount Levick 2774
CAPE HALLETT
POSSESSION IS.
CAPE ADARE
Robertson Bay
Mount Sabine 3719
ADMIRALTY MOUNTAINS
RENNICK GLACIER
Yule Bay
CAPE WILLIAMS
Ob' Bay
Rennick Bay
OATES COAST
WILLIAMSON HEAD
MATUSEVICH GLACIER
Lauritzen Bay
MAWSON PENINSULA
Deakin Bay
COOK ICE SHELF
GEORGE V COAST
Buckley Bay
NINNIS GLACIER TONGUE
BALLENY ISLANDS
MERTZ GLACIER TONGUE
ADÉLIE COAST
Commonwealth Bay
DUMONT D'URVILLE (France)
CLARIE COAST
CAPE BICKERTON
SOUTH MAGNETIC POLE
Davis Bay
DIBBLE ICEBERG TONGUE
Porpoise Bay
VOYEYKOV ICE SHELF
NORTHS HIGHLAND
BANZARE COAST
SABRINA COAST
CAPE MIKHAYLOV
DALTON ICEBERG TONGUE
Paulding Bay
WILKES LAND
TOTTEN GLACIER
BUDD COAST
CASEY (Austl.)
Vincennes Bay
CAPE POINSETT
KNOX COAST
SHACKLETON ICE SHELF
BOWMAN ISLAND
BUNGER HILLS
SCOTT GLACIER
DENMAN GLACIER
QUEEN MARY COAST
MIRNYY
POBEDA ICE ISLAND
ROSCOE GLACIER
MASSON ISLAND
Davis Sea
DRYGALSKI ISLAND
PHILIPPI GLACIER
WEST ICE SHELF
CHELYUSKINTSY ICE TONGUE
Barrier Bay
LEOPOLD AND ASTRID COAST
INGRID CHRISTENSEN COAST
DAVIS (Australia)
ZHONGSHAN (China)
Prydz Bay
AMERY ICE SHELF
MacKenzie Bay
CAPE DARNLEY
POLAR RECORD GLACIER
KREITZER GLACIER
GROVE MOUNTAINS
AMERICAN HIGHLAND
MAWSON ESCARPMENT
LAMBERT GLACIER
PRINCE CHARLES MTS.
MAC. ROBERTSON LAND
FRAMNES MTS.
MAWSON (Australia)
MELLOR GLACIER
FISHER GLACIER
Mount Menzies 3355
KEMP COAST
Edward VIII Bay
CAPE BOOTHBY
NAPIER MOUNTAINS
CAPE ANN
ENDERBY LAND
BEAVER GLACIER
Amundsen Bay
Casey Bay
RAYNER GLACIER
MOLODEZHNAJA
PRINCE OLAV COAST
SYOWA (Japan)
Lützow-Holm Bay
SHIRASE GLACIER
RIISER-LARSEN PENINSULA
QUEEN FABIOLA MTS.
BELGICA MTS.
PRINCE HARALD COAST
Breid Bay
ASUKA (Japan)
SØR RONDANE MOUNTAINS
Vørterkaka Nunatak 3630
Mount Widerøe 3180
QUEEN MAUD LAND
SCHWABENLAND
NEW SCHWABENLAND
WOHLTHAT MOUNTAINS
HUMBOLDT MTS.
ASTRID COAST
PRINCESS RAGNHILD COAST
Habermehl Peak 3300
DAKSHIN GANGOTRI (India)
NOVOLAZAREVSKAJA
GEORG FORSTER (Ger.)
MÜHLIG-HOFMANN MOUNTAINS
Borg Mountain 2546
PENCK TROUGH
RITSCHER UPLAND
PRINCESS MARTHA COAST
KRAUL MTS.
KOTTAS MTS.
SANAE (South Africa)
GEORG VON NEUMAYER (Ger.)
Seal Bay
CAPE NORVEGIA
Antarctic Circle
ANTARCTICA
INDIAN OCEAN
KERGUELEN-GAUSSBERG RIDGE
GRIBB BANK
SOUTH INDIAN BASIN
SOUTHERN OCEAN
AUSTRALIAN - ANTARCTIC RISE
TASMAN SEA
TASMAN BASIN
SOUTHWEST PACIFIC BASIN
MACQUARIE RIDGE
HJORT BASIN
MACQUARIE ISLAND (Austl.)
CAMPBELL PLATEAU
CAMPBELL ISLAND (N.Z.)
ANTIPODES ISLANDS (N.Z.)
BOUNTY ISLANDS (N.Z.)
BOUNTY TROUGH
NEW ZEALAND PLATEAU
AUCKLAND ISLANDS (N.Z.)
NEW ZEALAND
Christchurch
Canterbury Bight
Dunedin
Invercargill
STEWART ISLAND
SNARES ISLANDS
Wellington
CAPE PALLISER
Mount Cook 3764
BALLENY BASIN
PACIFIC OCEAN
EAST PACIFIC RISE
SOUTHEAST PACIFIC BASIN
Kilometers 0 200 400 600 800 Km.
Statute Miles 0 200 400 600 Mi.
Scale 1:24,000,000
One centimeter represents 240 kilometers.
One inch represents approximately 380 miles.
Lambert Azimuthal Equal-Area Projection
Copyright © by Rand McNally & Co.
Map prepared by Rand McNally & Co.
A-594000-764

ATLANTIC OCEAN
EUROPE
ASIA
RUSSIA
MID-ATLANTIC RIDGE
WEST EUROPEAN BASIN
GREENLAND
ICELAND
CANADA
Labrador Sea
Norwegian Sea
Barents Sea
Greenland Sea
North Sea
Baltic Sea
Black Sea
Caspian Sea
Mediterranean Sea
Red Sea
Bay of Biscay
URAL'SKIJE GORY
URAL MOUNTAINS
KAZAKHSTAN
UZBEKISTAN
TURKMENISTAN
TURKEY
ASIA MINOR
SYRIA
IRAQ
IRAN
SAUDI ARABIA
ARABIAN PENINSULA
EGYPT
LIBYA
ALGERIA
TUNISIA
MOROCCO
WESTERN SAHARA
MAURITANIA
MALI
NIGER
SAHARA
FRANCE
SPAIN
PORTUGAL
ITALY
GERMANY
POLAND
UNITED KINGDOM
IRELAND
SWEDEN
NORWAY
FINLAND
UKRAINE
BELARUS
HUNGARY
ROMANIA
BULGARIA
GREECE
AUSTRIA
CZECH REP.
SLOVAKIA
DENMARK
Tropic of Cancer
Arctic Circle
MOSKVA
SANKT-PETERBURG
LONDON
PARIS
BERLIN
ROMA
MADRID
LISBOA
WARSZAWA
KIJEV
MINSK
STOCKHOLM
HELSINKI
KØBENHAVN
AMSTERDAM
BRUXELLES
WIEN
PRAHA
BUDAPEST
BUCUREŞTI
SOFIJA
BEOGRAD
ATHINAI
İSTANBUL
ANKARA
AL-QĀHIRAH
TEHRĀN
BAGHDĀD
AR-RIYĀD
TUNIS
EL DJAZAÏR
RABAT
TARĀBULUS

INDIAN OCEAN
ATLANTIC OCEAN
SOMALI BASIN
MASCARENE BASIN
MADAGASCAR BASIN
MADAGASCAR PLATEAU
MOZAMBIQUE PLATEAU
NATAL BASIN
AGULHAS PLATEAU
SOUTHWEST INDIAN RIDGE
CAPE BASIN
CAPE RISE
WALVIS RIDGE
ANGOLA BASIN
GUINEA BASIN
GUINEA RISE
SIERRA LEONE BASIN
SIERRA LEONE RISE
BRAZIL BASIN
MID-ATLANTIC RIDGE
Equator
Tropic of Capricorn
Gulf of Aden
Gulf of Guinea
Bight of Benin
Bight of Biafra
Mozambique Channel
SOMALIA
ETHIOPIA
KENYA
UGANDA
RWANDA
BURUNDI
TANZANIA
ZAIRE
CONGO
GABON
CAMEROON
CENTRAL AFRICAN REPUBLIC
NIGERIA
BENIN
TOGO
GHANA
IVORY COAST
LIBERIA
SIERRA LEONE
GUINEA
GUINEA-BISSAU
BURKINA FASO
ANGOLA
ZAMBIA
MALAWI
MOZAMBIQUE
ZIMBABWE
BOTSWANA
NAMIBIA
SOUTH AFRICA
LESOTHO
SWAZILAND
MADAGASCAR
COMOROS
SEYCHELLES
MAURITIUS
REUNION (Fr.)
EQUAT. GUI.
SAO TOME AND PRINCIPE
SAINT HELENA (U.K.)
ADIS ABEBA
NAIROBI
KAMPALA
DAR ES SALAAM
KINSHASA
LUANDA
HARARE
MAPUTO
PRETORIA
CAPE TOWN
ANTANANARIVO
LAGOS
ACCRA
ABIDJAN
Kilometers
Statute Miles
Scale 1:24,000,000
One centimeter represents 240 kilometers.
One inch represents approximately 380 miles.
Lambert Azimuthal Equal-Area Projection
Copyright © by Rand McNally & Co.
Map prepared by Rand McNally & Co.
A-519394-764 34

ARCTIC
OCEAN
North Pole
ATLANTIC
OCEAN
GREENLAND
ICELAND
Reykjavík
Denmark Strait
Greenland Sea
Norwegian Sea
Barents Sea
Kara Sea
Karskoje more
Laptev Sea
East Siberian Sea
Chukchi Sea
Bering Sea
Bering Strait
Sea of Okhotsk
Sea of Japan
Yellow Sea
EAST CHINA SEA
Caspian Sea
Black Sea
Aral Sea
Baltic Sea
Gulf of Bothnia
North Sea
Mediterranean Sea
Arctic Circle
SVALBARD
ZEMLJA FRANCA-JOSIFA
FRANZ JOSEF LAND
NOVAJA ZEMLJA
SEVERNAJA ZEMLJA
NOVOSIBIRSKIJE OSTROVA
OSTROV VRANGEL'A
ALEUTIAN ISLANDS
KURIL'SKIJE OSTROVA
KURIL ISLANDS
OSTROV SACHALIN
HOKKAIDO
HONSHU
KYUSHU
UNITED STATES
UNITED KINGDOM
IRELAND
NORWAY
SWEDEN
FINLAND
DENMARK
NETHERLANDS
BELGIUM
GERMANY
POLAND
CZECH REP.
SLOVAKIA
HUNGARY
ROMANIA
BULGARIA
UKRAINE
BELARUS
LITH.
LAT.
EST.
MOLD.
TURKEY
ASIA MINOR
SYRIA
IRAQ
IRAN
JORDAN
KUWAIT
SAUDI ARABIA
GEORGIA
KAZAKHSTAN
UZBEKISTAN
TURKMENISTAN
KYRGYZSTAN
TAJIKISTAN
AFGHANISTAN
MONGOLIA
NORTH KOREA
SOUTH KOREA
JAPAN
CHINA
RUSSIA
SIBERIA
EUROPE
ASIA
URAL'SKIJE GORY
URAL MOUNTAINS
ZAPADNO-SIBIRSKAJA RAVNINA
SREDNESIBIRSKOJE PLOSKOGORJE
CHREBET ČERSKOGO
SAJAN MOUNTAINS
ALTAI
TIEN SHAN
KUNLUN SHAN
ALTUN SHAN
HINDU KUSH
PAMIR
TARIM PENDI
QAIDAM PENDI
GOBI
DA HINGAN LING
SICHOTE-ALIN
BOL'ŠOJ KAVKAZ
CAUCASUS
LONDON
DUBLIN
BRUXELLES
AMSTERDAM
BERLIN
PRAHA
WIEN
BUDAPEST
WARSZAWA
KØBENHAVN
OSLO
STOCKHOLM
HELSINKI
TALLINN
RIGA
VILNIUS
MINSK
KIEV
MOSKVA
MOSCOW
SANKT-PETERBURG
ST. PETERSBURG
BUCUREŞTI
SOFIJA
BEOGRAD
ISTANBUL
ANKARA
TBILISI
JEREVAN
BAKU
TEHRĀN
BAGHDĀD
DIMASHQ
'AMMĀN
BAYRŪT
AL-KUWAYT
KĀBOL
TAŠKENT
ALMA-ATA
BIŠKEK
DUŠANBE
AŠCHABAD
ULAANBAATAR
BEIJING
TIANJIN
SHANGHAI
NANJING
WUHAN
XI'AN
SHENYANG
SÕUL
P'YONGYANG
ŌSAKA
Sapporo
Vladivostok
Chabarovsk
Irkutsk
Novosibirsk
Omsk
Jekaterinburg
Čel'abinsk
Perm'
Kazan'
Samara
Volgograd
Murmansk
Archangel'sk
Jakutsk
Magadan
Noril'sk
Krasnojarsk
Lena
Jenisej
Ob'
Amur
Volga
Huang
Irtyš

INDIAN OCEAN
ARABIAN SEA
Bay of Bengal
Andaman Sea
SOUTH CHINA SEA
GREATER SUNDA ISLANDS
INDONESIA
INDIA
PAKISTAN
BANGLADESH
BURMA
THAILAND
CAMBODIA
LAOS
MALAYSIA
PHILIPPINES
SRI LANKA
MALDIVES
SEYCHELLES
MAURITIUS
MADAGASCAR
SOMALIA
ETHIOPIA
YEMEN
OMAN
ARABIAN PENINSULA
AR-RUB' AL-KHĀLĪ
AUSTRALIA
DELHI
New Delhi
BOMBAY
CALCUTTA
MADRAS
BANGALORE
KARĀCHI
DHAKA
YANGON
RANGOON
KRUNG THEP
BANGKOK
HA NOI
SINGAPORE
JAKARTA
MANILA
HONG KONG
Colombo
Mogadisho
ANTANANARIVO
Tropic of Cancer
Tropic of Capricorn
Equator
CARLSBERG RIDGE
MID-INDIAN RIDGE
NINETYEAST RIDGE
BROKEN RIDGE
SOUTHWEST INDIAN RIDGE
WHARTON BASIN
MASCARENE PLATEAU
CHAGOS-LACCADIVE PLATEAU
SOMALI BASIN
MADAGASCAR BASIN
JAVA TRENCH
Kilometers
Statute Miles
Scale 1:24,000,000
One centimeter represents 240 kilometers.
One inch represents approximately 380 miles.
Lambert Azimuthal Equal-Area Projection

ASIA
CHINA
HIMALAYAS
INDIA
BURMA
LAOS
VIETNAM
THAILAND
CAMBODIA
INDOCHINA
MALAYSIA
BRUNEI
SINGAPORE
INDONESIA
SUNDA ISLANDS
GREATER SUNDA ISLANDS
PHILIPPINES
TAIWAN
PAPUA NEW GUINEA
AUSTRALIA
CHONGQING
Chengdu
Changsha
Nanchang
Wenzhou
Fuzhou
Guiyang
Kunming
Liuzhou
Nanning
Xiamen
GUANGZHOU CANTON
VICTORIA
HONG KONG (U.K.)
Macau (Port.)
Zhanjiang
Ha Noi
Hai Phong
Haikou
HAINAN DAO
Mandalay
Viangchan
Chiang Mai
Udon Thani
Da Nang
Mawlamyine
KRUNG THEP BANGKOK
Phnum Penh
THANH PHO HO CHI MINH (SAIGON)
T'AIPEI
MANILA
Quezon City
Cebu
Davao
Manado
George Town
Medan
Kuala Lumpur
Kuching
Bandar Seri Begawan
Balikpapan
Banjarmasin
Ujungpandang
Padang
Palembang
JAKARTA
Bandung
SURABAYA
Dili
Jayapura
Port Moresby
Lae
Rabaul
Darwin
Cairns
Townsville
Rockhampton
Brisbane
Newcastle
SYDNEY
Canberra
MELBOURNE
Launceston
Hobart
Adelaide
Perth
Broome
Kalgoorlie
Alice Springs
Mount Isa
Broken Hill
Carnarvon
Birdum
East China Sea
SOUTH CHINA SEA
PHILIPPINE SEA
PHILIPPINE BASIN
WEST MARIANA BASIN
MARIANA ISLANDS
NORTHERN MARIANA ISLANDS (U.S.)
GUAM (U.S.)
EAST MARIANA BASIN
MARIANA TRENCH
Challenger Deep 10915
CAROLINE ISLANDS
CAROLINE BASIN
WEST CAROLINE BASIN
EAST CAROLINE BASIN
FEDERATED STATES OF MICRONESIA
PALAU ISLANDS
PALAU (T.T.P.I.)
YAP TRENCH
PHILIPPINE TRENCH
Sulu Sea
Celebes Sea
Laut Jawa
Java Sea
Laut Flores
Banda Sea
Arafura Sea
ARAFURA SHELF
Timor Sea
TIMOR TROUGH
SAHUL SHELF
Gulf of Carpentaria
Gulf of Thailand
Gulf of Tonkin
Strait of Malacca
Torres Strait
CORAL SEA BASIN
GREAT BARRIER REEF
QUEENSLAND PLATEAU
BISMARCK ARCHIPELAGO
NEW BRITAIN
NEW GUINEA
MOLUCCAS
SULAWESI CELEBES
BORNEO KALIMANTAN
SUMATERA SUMATRA
JAWA JAVA
NUSA TENGGARA
SUNDA SHELF
JAVA TRENCH
CHRISTMAS ISLAND (Austl.)
COCOS ISLANDS (Austl.)
NORTH AUSTRALIAN BASIN
EXMOUTH PLATEAU
WHARTON BASIN
INDIAN OCEAN
PERTH BASIN
SOUTH AUSTRALIAN BASIN
Great Australian Bight
SOUTHERN OCEAN
BROKEN RIDGE
DIAMANTINA FRACTURE ZONE
TASMAN
KIMBERLEY PLATEAU
BARKLY TABLELAND
GREAT SANDY DESERT
TANAMI DESERT
GIBSON DESERT
GREAT VICTORIA DESERT
NULLARBOR PLAIN
SIMPSON DESERT
MACDONNELL RANGES
GREAT DIVIDING RANGE
ARNHEM LAND
CAPE YORK PENINSULA
Tropic of Cancer
Tropic of Capricorn
Equator
Kilometers 0 200 400 600 800 Km.
Statute Miles 0 200 400 600 800 Mi.
Scale 1:24,000,000
One centimeter represents 240 kilometers.
One inch represents approximately 380 miles.
Lambert Azimuthal Equal-Area Projection
Copyright © by Rand McNally & Co.
Map prepared by Rand McNally & Co.

International Date Line
MIDWAY ISLANDS (U.S.)
KURE ATOLL
PEARL AND HERMES ATOLL
LISIANSKI ISLAND
LAYSAN ISLAND
GARDNER PINNACLES
FRENCH FRIGATE SHOALS
NECKER ISLAND
NIHOA
HAWAIIAN ISLANDS (U.S.)
HAWAIIAN RIDGE
NECKER RIDGE
KAUAI
NIIHAU
OAHU
Honolulu
MOLOKAI
LANAI
MAUI
Hilo
HAWAII
Mauna Kea 4205
KA LAE
UNITED STATES
FRACTURE ZONE
MOLOKAI
Tropic of Cancer
Guadalupe Seamount
Paul Seamount
Hess Tablemount
Horizon Tablemount
Swordfish Seamount
Karin Seamount
Pensacola Seamount
JOHNSTON ATOLL (U.S.)
Cape Johnson Tablemount
SCHJETMAN REEF
WAKE ISLAND (U.S.)
PACIFIC MOUNTAINS
MARSHALL ISLANDS
TAONGI
BIKINI
BIKAR
ENEWETAK
RONGELAP
UTIRIK
WOTHO
AILUK
WOTJE
UJELANG
UJAE
KWAJALEIN
LAE
LIB
NAMU
RALIK CHAIN
RATAK CHAIN
MALOELAP
ARNO
AILINGLAPALAP
MAJURO
JALUIT
MILI
KILI
EBON
NAMORIK
PINGELAP
KOSRAE
MARSHALL ISLANDS
CENTRAL PACIFIC BASIN
PACIFIC OCEAN
CHRISTMAS RIDGE
KINGMAN REEF (U.S.)
PALMYRA ATOLL (U.S.)
TERAINA
TABUAERAN
KIRITIMATI
JARVIS ISLAND (U.S.)
LINE ISLANDS
POLYNESIA
MELANESIAN BASIN
NAURU
BUTARITARI
TARAWA
ABEMAMA
KURIA
KIRIBATI
BANABA
NONOUTI
BERU
NIKUNAU
TABITEUEA
ONOTOA
TAMANA
ARORAE
HOWLAND ISLAND (U.S.)
BAKER ISLAND (U.S.)
WINSLOW REEF
KIRIBATI
PHOENIX ISLANDS
KANTON
ENDERBURY
BIRNIE
RAWAKI
NIKUMARORO
ORONA
MANRA
MALDEN
STARBUCK
Equator
SOLOMON ISLANDS
TUVALU
NANUMEA
NIUTAO
NANUMANGA
NUI
VAITUPU
NUKUFETAU
FUNAFUTI
NUKULAELAE
NIULAKITA
TOKELAU (N.Z.)
ATAFU
NUKUNONU
FAKAOFO
SWAINS ISLAND
AMERICAN SAMOA
SAMOA ISLANDS
Combe Seamount
Home Seamount
WALLIS AND FUTUNA (Fr.)
ÎLES WALLIS
ÎLE FUTUNA
ÎLES DE HORNE
WESTERN SAMOA
SAVAI'I
Apia
UPOLU
Pago Pago
TUTUILA
MANUA ISLANDS
ROSE ISLAND
SAMOA BASIN
NASSAU ISLAND
NORTHERN COOK ISLANDS
MANIHIKI
SUWARROW
PENRHYN
VOSTOK
CAROLINE
FLINT
Merlin Seamount
MALAITA
GUADALCANAL
SAN CRISTOBAL
NENDO
UTUPUA
VANIKOLO
SANTA CRUZ ISLANDS
SANTA CRUZ BASIN
RENNELL
ÎLES TORRES
ÎLES BANKS
VANUA LAVA
SANTA MARIA
ESPIRITU SANTO
MAEWO
PENTECÔTE
MALAKULA
AMBRYM
EPI
ÉFATÉ
Port Vila
ERROMANGO
TANNA
ANATOM
VANUATU
NEW HEBRIDES
NORTH FIJI BASIN
ROTUMA
FIJI ISLANDS
VANUA LEVU
TAVEUNI
LAU GROUP
VITI LEVU
Suva
Koro Sea
KANDAVU ISLAND
FIJI
LAU BASIN
NEW CALEDONIA (Fr.) NOUVELLE CALÉDONIE
OUVÉA
LIFOU
ÎLES LOYAUTÉ
MARÉ
Nouméa
NEW HEBRIDES TRENCH
ÎLE HUNTER
HUNTER TRENCH
HUNTER RIDGE
TOKU ISLAND
VAVA'U GROUP
TONGA ISLANDS
TONGATAPU GROUP
TONGATAPU
Nuku'alofa
EUA
'ATA
TONGA
TONGA TRENCH
TONGA RIDGE
LAU RIDGE
NIUE (N.Z.)
TAFAHI
COOK ISLANDS (N.Z.)
PALMERSTON
AITUTAKI
MANUAE
TAKUTEA
MITIARO
ATIU
MAUKE
RAROTONGA
MANGAIA
SOUTHERN COOK ISLANDS
MOTU ONE
MANUAE
MAUPIHAA
BORA-BORA
TAHAA
RAIATEA
MOOREA
TAHITI
Papeete
MEHETIA
TETIAROA
MAKATEA
MATAIVA
KAUKURA
FAKARAVA
SOCIETY RIDGE
ÎLES DE LA SOCIÉTÉ
SOCIETY ISLANDS
ÎLES TUAMOTU
TUAMOTU RIDGE
TUAMOTU ARCHIPELAGO
ÎLES DU DÉSAPPOINTEMENT
ÎLES DU ROI GEORGES
ÎLE TIKEI
RAROIA
TAKAROA
MAKEMO
HIKUERU
MARUTEA
HARAIKI
ANAA
AMANU
RAVAHERE
NEGONEGO
MANUHANGI
HAO
AHUNUI
VANAVANA
TEMATAGI
FRENCH POLYNESIA
ÎLES MARIA
RIMATARA
RURUTU
ÎLES AUSTRALES
ÎLE TUPUAI
RAIVAVAE
AUSTRAL SEAMOUNTS
Tropic of Capricorn
RAPA
ÎLES MAROTIRI
Fabert Seamount
Ozbourn Seamount
SOUTH FIJI BASIN
NEW CALEDONIA BASIN
NORFOLK RIDGE
NORFOLK ISLAND (Austl.)
LORD HOWE ISLAND (Austl.)
LORD HOWE RISE
KERMADEC RIDGE
KERMADEC TRENCH
RAOUL ISLAND
KERMADEC
CURTIS ISLAND
KERMADEC ISLANDS
Currituck Seamount
Seafox Seamount
Louisville Seamount
Burton Seamount
LOUISVILLE RIDGE
SOUTHWEST PACIFIC BASIN
THREE KINGS IS.
NORTH CAPE
TAUROA POINT
GREAT BARRIER ISLAND
Auckland
Bay of Plenty
EAST CAPE
NEW ZEALAND
NORTH ISLAND
New Plymouth
Mount Ruapehu 2797
CAPE EGMONT
Napier
Hawke Bay
CAPE FAREWELL
Tasman Sea
Wellington
CAPE PALLISER
Cook Strait
Mount Cook 3764
Christchurch
SOUTH ISLAND
Canterbury Bight
CHATHAM RISE
CHATHAM ISLAND
CHATHAM ISLANDS (N.Z.)
BOUNTY TROUGH
WEST CAPE
Dunedin
Invercargill
SOUTH WEST CAPE
STEWART ISLAND
SNARES ISLANDS
BOUNTY ISLANDS (N.Z.)
CAMPBELL PLATEAU
ANTIPODES ISLANDS (N.Z.)
TASMAN BASIN
6890
1316
1477
859
1057
4809
6519
11
4462
5349
1737
6469
5029
1188
6879
8322
9175
3580
7314
4846
10800
5303
10047
1518
8009
1088
497
5267
4755
160°
170°
180°
170°
160°
150°
140°
130°
40°
30°
20°
10°
0°

ARCTIC
OCEAN
North Pole
3910
GREENLAND
(Den.)
ICELAND
Reykjavik
Norwegian Sea
NORWEGIAN BASIN
LOFOTEN BASIN
Greenland Sea
GREENLAND BASIN
Barents Sea
Kara Sea
Karskoje more
SVALBARD
SPITSBERGEN
ZEMLJA FRANCA-IOSIFA
FRANZ JOSEF LAND
NOVAJA ZEMLJA
SEVERNAJA ZEMLJA
NOVOSIBIRSKIE OSTROVA
more Laptevych
Laptev Sea
Vostočno-Sibirskoje more
East Siberian Sea
Chukchi Sea
Beaufort Sea
BERING SEA
Bering Strait
Sea of Okhotsk
ALEUTIAN TRENCH
ALEUTIAN ISLANDS
ATLANTIC OCEAN
IRMINGER BASIN
REYKJANES RIDGE
LABRADOR BASIN
Labrador Sea
Davis Strait
Baffin Bay
BAFFIN ISLAND
Hudson Bay
Hudson Strait
QUEEN ELIZABETH ISLANDS
ELLESMERE ISLAND
DEVON ISLAND
VICTORIA ISLAND
BANKS ISLAND
CANADA
ALASKA
UNITED STATES
BROOKS RANGE
MACKENZIE MOUNTAINS
Gulf of Alaska
GULF OF ALASKA SEAMOUNT PROVINCE
EUROPE
FINLAND
SWEDEN
NORWAY
DENMARK
UNITED KINGDOM
FAEROE ISLANDS
North Sea
Baltic Sea
Gulf of Bothnia
Gulf of Finland
MOSKVA
MOSCOW
SANKT-PETERBURG
Helsinki
Stockholm
Oslo
København
ASIA
RUSSIA
SIBERIA
URAL'SKIJE GORY
VERCHOJANSKIJ CHREBET
CHREBET ČERSKOGO
POLUOSTROV KAMČATKA
Arctic Circle

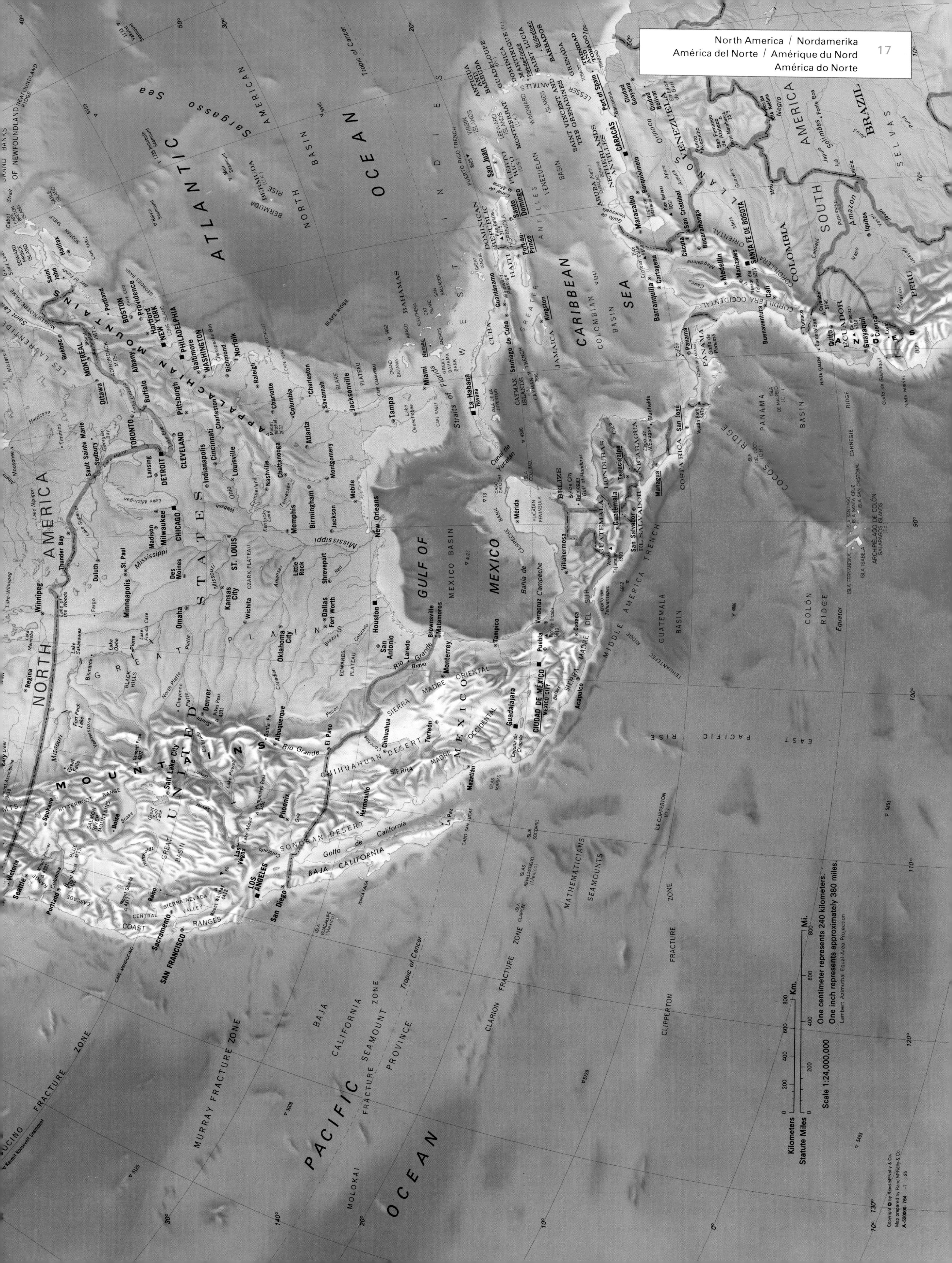
NORTH AMERICA
SOUTH AMERICA
UNITED STATES
MEXICO
ATLANTIC OCEAN
PACIFIC OCEAN
GULF OF MEXICO
CARIBBEAN SEA
Sargasso Sea
WEST INDIES
GREAT PLAINS
ROCKY MOUNTAINS
APPALACHIAN MOUNTAINS
SIERRA MADRE ORIENTAL
SIERRA MADRE OCCIDENTAL
SIERRA MADRE DEL SUR
CHIHUAHUAN DESERT
SONORAN DESERT
BAJA CALIFORNIA
Golfo de California
NORTH AMERICAN BASIN
MEXICO BASIN
COLOMBIAN BASIN
VENEZUELAN BASIN
GUATEMALA BASIN
PANAMA BASIN
MIDDLE AMERICA TRENCH
EAST PACIFIC RISE
COCOS RIDGE
CARNEGIE RIDGE
COLÓN RIDGE
CLARION FRACTURE ZONE
CLIPPERTON FRACTURE ZONE
MURRAY FRACTURE ZONE
MOLOKAI FRACTURE ZONE
MATHEMATICIANS SEAMOUNTS
BAJA CALIFORNIA SEAMOUNT PROVINCE
Tropic of Cancer
Equator
CIUDAD DE MÉXICO
WASHINGTON
NEW YORK
PHILADELPHIA
CHICAGO
LOS ANGELES
SAN FRANCISCO
DETROIT
BOSTON
TORONTO
MONTRÉAL
Ottawa
La Habana
CARACAS
SANTA FE DE BOGOTÁ
Quito
Panamá
Kingston
Port-au-Prince
Santo Domingo
San Juan
Guatemala
San Salvador
Tegucigalpa
Managua
San José
Belmopan
Nassau
COLOMBIA
VENEZUELA
ECUADOR
PERU
BRAZIL
CUBA
HAITI
JAMAICA
BAHAMAS
NICARAGUA
HONDURAS
GUATEMALA
EL SALVADOR
COSTA RICA
PANAMA
BELIZE

Kilometers 0 200 400 600 800 Km.
Statute Miles 0 200 400 600 800 Mi.
Scale 1:24,000,000
One centimeter represents 240 kilometers.
One inch represents approximately 380 miles.
Lambert Azimuthal Equal-Area Projection

NORTH AMERICA
UNITED STATES
ROCKY MTS.
APPALACHIAN MOUNTAINS
GREAT PLAINS
OZARK PLATEAU
EDWARDS PLATEAU
Des Moines
Omaha
CHICAGO
CLEVELAND
Pittsburgh
NEW YORK
PHILADELPHIA
Baltimore
WASHINGTON
Chesapeake Bay
LONG ISLAND
GEORGES BANK
Indianapolis
Cincinnati
Charleston
Louisville
Kansas City
ST. LOUIS
Denver
Cheyenne
Pikes Peak 4301
Wichita
Santa Fe
Albuquerque
Oklahoma City
Little Rock
Memphis
Nashville
Chattanooga
Richmond
Norfolk
Raleigh
Charlotte
Columbia
Atlanta
Birmingham
Montgomery
Savannah
Charleston
Jackson
Shreveport
Dallas
Fort Worth
El Paso
Houston
San Antonio
Laredo
Brownsville
New Orleans
Mobile
Jacksonville
Tampa
Miami
Lake Okeechobee
CAPE HATTERAS
CAPE LOOKOUT
CAPE FEAR
CAPE CANAVERAL
CAPE SABLE
BLAKE PLATEAU
BLAKE RIDGE
Mississippi
Missouri
Ohio
Platte
North Platte
South Platte
Arkansas
Canadian
Red
Brazos
Colorado
Pecos
Rio Grande
Bravo
Tennessee
Cumberland
Wabash
MEXICO
SIERRA MADRE ORIENTAL
SIERRA MADRE DEL SUR
Monterrey
Matamoros
Torreón
Tampico
Guadalajara
Laguna de Chapala
CIUDAD DE MEXICO
MEXICO CITY
Puebla
Veracruz
Pico de Orizaba 5610
Oaxaca
Villahermosa
Acapulco
Mérida
YUCATAN PENINSULA
Bahía de Campeche
CAMPECHE BANK
Golfo de Tehuantepec
GULF OF MEXICO
MEXICO BASIN
Canal de Yucatán
Straits of Florida
BAHAMAS
GRAND BAHAMA
ABACO
ELEUTHERA
CAT ISLAND
SAN SALVADOR
ANDROS
GREAT BAHAMA BANK
Nassau
CUBA
La Habana
Havana
ISLA DE LA JUVENTUD
Santiago de Cuba
Guantánamo
CAYMAN ISLANDS (U.K.)
CAYMAN TRENCH
Windward Passage
JAMAICA
Kingston
HAITI
Port-au-Prince
HISPANIOLA
Pico Duarte 3175
DOMINICAN REPUBLIC
Santo Domingo
Canal de la Mona
PUERTO RICO (U.S.)
San Juan
PUERTO RICO TRENCH
GREAT INAGUA
VIRGIN ISLANDS
WEST INDIES
GREATER ANTILLES
LESSER ANTILLES
ANTIGUA AND BARBUDA
MONTSERRAT (U.K.)
LEEWARD ISLANDS
GUADELOUPE (Fr.)
DOMINICA
MARTINIQUE (Fr.)
Fort-de-France
WINDWARD ISLANDS
SAINT LUCIA
BARBADOS
Bridgetown
SAINT VINCENT AND THE GRENADINES
GRENADA
TRINIDAD AND TOBAGO
TOBAGO
TRINIDAD
Port of Spain
ARUBA (Neth.)
CURAÇAO
BONAIRE
NETHERLANDS ANTILLES
CARIBBEAN SEA
VENEZUELAN BASIN
COLOMBIAN BASIN
BELIZE
Belize City
Belmopan
Gulf of Honduras
GUATEMALA
Guatemala
Volcán Tajumulco 4220
HONDURAS
Tegucigalpa
EL SALVADOR
San Salvador
NICARAGUA
Managua
Lago de Nicaragua
Bluefields
Coco
COSTA RICA
San José
Volcán Barú 3475
PANAMA
Panamá
Colón
ISTMO DE PANAMÁ
Golfo de Panamá
MIDDLE AMERICA TRENCH
TEHUANTEPEC RIDGE
GUATEMALA BASIN
PANAMA BASIN
COCOS RIDGE
ISLA DEL COCO (C.R.)
ISLA DE MALPELO (Col.)
COLÓN RIDGE
CARNEGIE RIDGE
ARCHIPIÉLAGO DE COLÓN
GALAPAGOS ISLANDS (Ec.)
ISLA ISABELA
ISLA FERNANDINA
ISLA SANTA CRUZ
ISLA SAN CRISTÓBAL
ISLA SANTIAGO
Equator
NORTH AMERICAN BASIN
BERMUDA (U.K.)
BERMUDA RISE
Sargasso Sea
ATLANTIC OCEAN
MID-ATLANTIC RIDGE
Tropic of Cancer
Kelvin Seamount
Rehoboth Seamount 1235
Muir Seamount
Yakutat Seamount 1133
Great Meteor Tablemount 269
AZORES PLATEAU
AÇORES
AZORES (Port.)
FLORES
TERCEIRA
PICO
SÃO MIGUEL
SANTA MARIA
CAPE VERDE BASIN
GUIANA BASIN
SOUTH AMERICA
VENEZUELA
CARACAS
Maracaibo
Lago de Maracaibo
Golfo de Venezuela
Barquisimeto
Barcelona
Ciudad Bolívar
Ciudad Guayana
Orinoco
Apure
Meta
Arauca
LLANOS
San Cristóbal
Pico Bolívar 5007
Puerto Ayacucho
San Fernando de Atabapo
Cerro Marahuaca 2579
Embalse de Guri
SALTO ÁNGEL
ANGEL FALLS
Pico da Neblina 3014
COLOMBIA
SANTA FE DE BOGOTÁ
Barranquilla
Cartagena
Pico Cristóbal Colón 5800
Cúcuta
Bucaramanga
Medellín
Manizales
Nevado del Tolima 5215
Cali
Buenaventura
CORDILLERA OCCIDENTAL
CORDILLERA ORIENTAL
CORDILLERA CENTRAL
Magdalena
Cauca
Guaviare
Mitú
Caquetá
Putumayo
GUYANA
Georgetown
Cuyuni
Essequibo
Mount Roraima 2875
PAKARAIMA MTS.
KAIETEUR FALL
SURINAME
Paramaribo
FRENCH GUIANA
Cayenne
TUMUC-HUMAC MTS.
Oiapoque
CABO ORANGE
ECUADOR
Quito
Cayambe 5790
Chimborazo 6310
Guayaquil
Golfo de Guayaquil
Cuenca
Loja
Esmeraldas
PUNTA GALERA
Tumaco
Napo
PERU
Iquitos
Marañón
Ucayali
Chiclayo
Cajamarca
Trujillo
Huaraz
Nevado Huascarán 6768
Nevado Yerupajá 6634
Cerro de Pasco
Huancayo
Pucallpa
LIMA
Cuzco
Ica
Puerto Maldonado
Lago Titicaca
Puno
Nevado Coropuna
Nevado Illampu
PUNTA PARIÑAS
PUNTA NEGRA
PUNTA CABALLAS
PERU-CHILE TRENCH
ANDES
BRAZIL
SELVAS
Amazon
Amazonas
Negro
Branco
Boa Vista
Japurá
Içá
Solimões
Fonte Boa
Javari
Yavari
Leticia
Juruá
Purus
Madeira
Aripuanã
Manaus
Represa Balbina
Tapajós
Óbidos
Santarém
Porto de Moz
Xingu
Iriri
Jari
Macapá
Amapá
ILHA DE MARACÁ
ILHA CAVIANA DE FORA
CABO MAGUARI
ILHA DE MARAJÓ
Pará
Belém
Tocantins
Araguaia
Marabá
São Luís
Parnaíba
Teresina
Fortaleza
ATOL DAS ROCAS
ILHA FERNANDO DE NORONHA (Braz.)
CABO DE SÃO ROQUE
Natal
Campina Grande
João Pessoa
PONTA DO SEIXAS
Recife
Caruaru
Maceió
Penedo
Aracaju
Salvador
Paulistana
Juàzeiro
São Francisco
Represa de Sobradinho
Barra
Carolina
CHAPADA DAS MANGABEIRAS
Porto Nacional
ILHA DO BANANAL
SA. DO CACHIMBO
São Manuel
SA. FORMOSA
Juruena
Porto Velho
Rio Branco
Guajará-Mirim
Riberalta
Cobija
Beni
Mamoré
Madre de Dios
Guaporé
Itenes
Trinidad
Mato Grosso
Cuiabá
PLANALTO
Brasília
Pico das Almas 1836
Paraguaçu
Itabuna

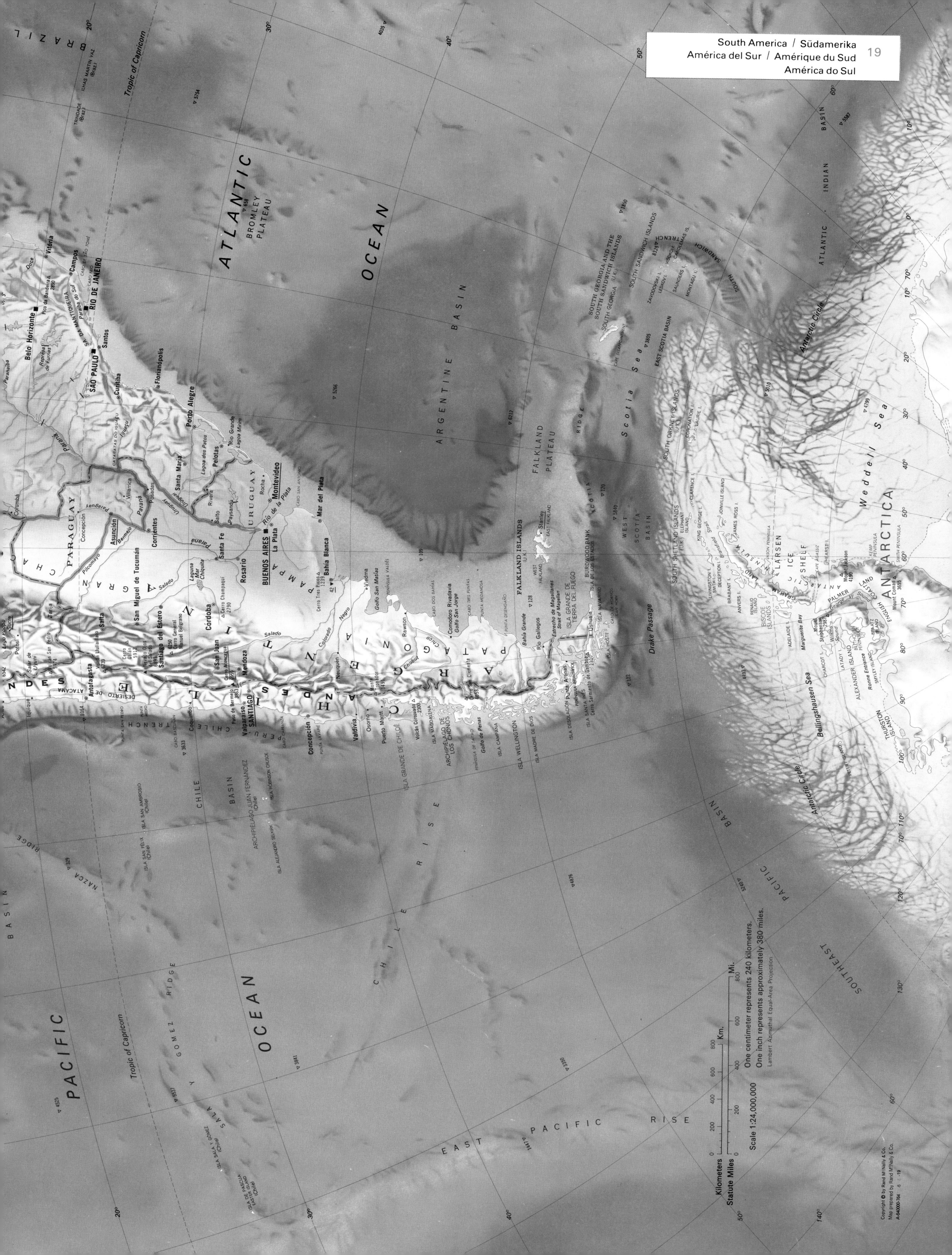
ATLANTIC
OCEAN
PACIFIC
OCEAN
ARGENTINE BASIN
BROMLEY PLATEAU
FALKLAND PLATEAU
FALKLAND ISLANDS
Scotia Sea
Weddell Sea
ANTARCTICA
Drake Passage
Bellingshausen Sea
Antarctic Circle
Tropic of Capricorn
CHILE RISE
EAST PACIFIC RISE
SOUTHEAST PACIFIC BASIN
CHILE BASIN
ATLANTIC INDIAN BASIN
SOUTH GEORGIA AND THE SOUTH SANDWICH ISLANDS
SOUTH SANDWICH ISLANDS
SOUTH SHETLAND ISLANDS
SOUTH ORKNEY ISLANDS
PATAGONIA
PAMPA
GRAN CHACO
PARAGUAY
URUGUAY
BUENOS AIRES
Montevideo
SANTIAGO
SÃO PAULO
RIO DE JANEIRO
Kilometers
Statute Miles
Scale 1:24,000,000
One centimeter represents 240 kilometers.
One inch represents approximately 380 miles.
Lambert Azimuthal Equal-Area Projection

THE REGIONAL MAPS consist of three basic series, each distinctive in style, but using common symbols to ensure ease of understanding (see Legend to Maps, pages x-xii). Every major land region, continent or subcontinent, is introduced by one or more maps at the scale of 1:12,000,000. There follow maps at 1:6,000,000 and 1:3,000,000 which cover the region in sections, in greater detail. Except for scale, the 1:6,000,000 and 1:3,000,000 maps are alike. Finally, selected areas of special importance in the region are shown at 1:1,000,000. Each scale is identified by a color bar, and a locater map with the same color may be found in the margin of the map page. A sample area at each of the scales, including centimeter-kilometer and inch-mile equivalents, appears on page 21.

The three basic series differ in content and emphasis. The 1:12,000,000 maps, which are primarily political, present an overview of each region. They show national boundaries and, in some cases, subordinate administrative subdivisions as well. These introductory maps make it possible to compare location, areal extent, and shape among the nations of the world. The distribution of cities, towns and metropolitan areas is shown in the context of broad physical configurations. A selection of the most important railways and highways also appears.

The 1:6,000,000 and 1:3,000,000 maps together constitute about half of the map pages and provide the basic reference coverage of the Atlas. They show sections of regions in great detail—in some cases individual countries (Japan and New Zealand), in others, parts of countries (central Mexico), in still others, larger regions (the Middle East). The more densely settled areas appear at the larger 1:3,000,000 scale, the remaining areas at 1:6,000,000. Maps at these two scales present political and cultural information against the background of a detailed physical portrait of the terrain, which is depicted by both shaded relief and a spectrum of altitude tints. Bathymetric tints are used to show offshore water depths. The transportation pattern shown includes major railways, two classes of roads, and airports that offer either international or jet service. The names and boundaries of political subdivisions are given for selected countries.

In the 1:1,000,000 series, strategic areas that are of special interest because of economic importance, dense settlement, or both, appear in even greater detail. This series is designed to show the pattern of cities, towns, roads, railways, bridges, airports, dams, reservoirs, and other interrelated features reflecting man's dense occupancy in these areas. The most important parks, places of historical interest, and recreational facilities are indicated. Three classes of highways and two classes of railways are shown, and major roads are named. All features are portrayed against a topographic background of shaded relief.

Inhabited places on the regional maps are classified in two distinct ways. Cities and towns of different *population size* are distinguished by the *size and shape of the symbol* that locates the place. The symbol reflects the population within the municipal or corporate limits, exclusive of any suburbs. In countries where the limits of a municipality include rural areas, the symbol represents only the urban or agglomerated population. The *relative political and economic importance* of a place which may be independent of the number of its inhabitants, is indicated by the *size of type* in which its name appears.

DIE REGIONALKARTEN bestehen aus drei Serien, die im Stil verschieden sind, der besseren Lesbarkeit halber aber gemeinsame Kartensignaturen verwenden (siehe "Zeichenerklärung" S. x-xii). Jede Grossregion, jeder Kontinent oder Subkontinent werden durch eine oder mehrere Karten im Massstab 1:12 Millionen eingeleitet. Es folgen sodann Karten in den Massstäben 1:6 und 1:3 Millionen, welche die Region in Teilen und grösseren Einzelheiten darstellen. Die Karten in 1:6 Millionen und 1:3 Millionen unterscheiden sich nur im Massstab. Schliesslich werden ausgewählte Gebiete von besonderer Bedeutung innerhalb der Region in 1:1 Million dargestellt. Jede Massstabsangabe ist durch ein Farbfeld gekennzeichnet, und ein Lagekärtchen in derselben Farbe erscheint am Rand der Kartenseite. Kartenausschnitte als Beispiele für jeden dieser Massstäbe mit Angabe des Verhältnisses Zentimeter zu Kilometer und Zoll zu Meilen sind auf Seite 21 aufgeführt.

Die drei Kartenreihen unterscheiden sich in Inhalt und Betonung. Die Karten im Massstab 1:12 Millionen, die vor allem politische Karten sind, geben einen Überblick über jede Region. Sie zeigen die Staatsgrenzen und in manchen Fällen auch die Grenzen von nachgeordneten Verwaltungseinheiten. Diese einführenden Karten ermöglichen einen Vergleich der Lage, Ausdehnung und Gestalt der Staaten der Erde. Die Verteilung der städtischen Ballungsgebiete, Grossstädte und Städte wird in ihrem Zusammenhang mit dem grossräumigen Formenschatz des Reliefs dargestellt. Gezeigt wird auch eine Auswahl der wichtigsten Eisenbahnlinien und Fernverkehrsstrassen.

Die Karten 1:6 Millionen und 1:3 Millionen machen zusammen mehr als die Hälfte der Kartenseiten aus und bilden den grundlegenden Teil des Atlas. Sie zeigen sehr inhaltsreiche Ausschnitte von Regionen—in einigen Fällen einzeln Länder (Japan und Neuseeland), in anderen Landesteile (Zentralmexiko) und wieder anderen Grossräume (Mittlerer Osten).

Die dichter besiedelten Gebiete sind im Massstab 1:3 Millionen dargestellt, die übrigen Gebiete im Massstab 1:6 Millionen. Die Karten in diesen beiden Massstäben liefern politische und kulturgeographische Informationen vor dem Hintergrund einer detaillierten Geländedarstellung, gekennzeichnet durch Reliefschummerung und eine Skala von Höhenschichten. Tiefenstufen werden verwendet, um die Meerestiefen jenseits der Küsten zu gliedern. Das abgebildete Verkehrsnetz umfasst wichtige Eisenbahnlinien, zwei Klassen von Strassen und Flughäfen, die entweder im internationalen Verkehr oder von Düsenflugzeugen angeflogen werden. Die Verwaltungsgliederung wird für eine grosse Zahl von Staaten gezeigt.

In der Kartenserie 1:1 Million sind mit noch zahlreicheren Einzelheiten zentrale Räume dargestellt, denen infolge ihrer wirtschaftlichen Bedeutung, dichten Besiedlung oder durch beide Faktoren bedingt besonderes Interesse zukommt. Diese Kartenserie wurde entwikelt, um die Verteilung der Grossstädte, Städte, Strassen, Eisenbahnen, Brücken, Flughäfen, Dämme, Stauseen und anderer Objekte zu zeigen, die Ausdruck sind für die dichte Besiedlung. Verzeichnet sind auch die wichtigsten Parks, Örtlichkeiten von historischem Interesse und Erholungsstätten. Drei Strassenklassen und zwei Klassen von Eisenbahnlinien werden unterschieden. Die Darstellung ist mit einer Reliefschummerung unterlegt.

Die Siedlungen auf den Regionalkarten sind auf zwei bestimmte Arten klassifiziert. Grossstädte und Städte unterschiedlicher *Einwohnerzahl* sind durch *Grösse und Form der Signatur* unterschieden, die den Ort lokalisiert. Die Signatur entspricht der Zahl der Einwohner innerhalb der Stadtgrenzen, schliesst also nicht eingemeindete Vororte aus. In Staaten, in denen ländliche Gebiete in die Stadtgemeinden einbezogen sind, entsprechen die Signaturen nur der in den zentralen Siedlungen ansässigen Bevölkerung. Die *relative politische und wirtschaftliche Bedeutung* eines Ortes, die von der Zahl seiner Einwohner unabhängig sein kann, ist ausgedrückt durch die *Schriftgrösse,* in welcher der Ortsname erscheint.

LOS MAPAS REGIONALES integran tres series básicas, cada una con su estilo propio; pero los símbolos usados son en todas los mismos para facilitar su comprensión (véanse las Leyendas para Mapas, páginas x-xii). Cada una de las grandes regiones, continentes o subcontinentes, se presenta a través de uno o varios mapas a la escala de 1:12 000 000. A continuación hay mapas a escalas de 1:6 000 000 y 1:3 000 000 que presentan la región correspondiente en secciones, con mayores detalles. Con excepción de su escala, los mapas de 1:6 000 000 y 1:3 000 000 tienen las mismas características. Por ultimo, aparecen a la escala de 1:1 000 000 áreas de cada región seleccionadas por su importancia. Cada escala se identifica por una barra de color, y un mapa-guía con el mismo color se presenta en el margen de la página de cada mapa. La página 21 ofrece como ejemplo un área-muestra a cada una de las escalas, incluyendo equivalentes en centímetros-kilómetros y pulgadas-millas.

Las tres series básicas son diferentes en contenido y en énfasis. Los mapas a escala de 1:12 000 000, fundamentalmente políticos, ofrecen una vista general de cada región. Indican las fronteras nacionales y, en algunos casos, las subdivisiones administrativas secundarias. Son mapas introductivos que permiten comparar la ubicación, extensión territorial y forma de las distintas naciones. La distribución de ciudades, poblados y áreas metropolitanas se aprecia en un contexto físico esbozado a grandes rasgos. Los detalles incluyen una selección de las vías férras y las carreteras más importantes.

Las series de mapas a 1:6 000 000 y a 1:3 000 000 ocupan entre ambas cerca de la mitad de los mapas del atlas y en ellas se concentra el material de consulta básico de la obra. Los mapas muestran secciones de regiones en gran detalle: en algunos casos países enteros, como Japón y Nueva Zelandia; en otros, partes de países, como el centro de México; y en otros, regiones mas extensas, como el Medio Oriente. Las áreas con mayor densidad de establecimientos humanos se presentan a una escala mayor, la de 1:3 000 000, y las demás a la escala de 1:6 000 000. En estas dos escalas los mapas contienen información política y cultural, sobre un fondo que ilustra en detalle la configuración física del terreno, utilizando sombreado para el relieve y toda una gama de tintes para indicar las altitudes. Un colorido batimétrico señala las variaciones de profundidad en el suelo marino. El esquema de las vías de comunicación incluye las principales vías férreas, dos clases de caminos, y los aeropuertos que ofrecen servicio nacional o internacional de jets. Las subdivisiones políticas secundarias se dan para una selección de varios países.

En la serie de mapas de 1:1 000 000, las áreas estratégicas de especial interés por su importancia económica, su densidad de población, o ambos factores combinados, aparecen aún con mayor detalle. Esta serie se diseñó para mostrar la distribución de ciudades, poblados, caminos, vías férreas, puentes, aeropuertos, presas, embalses y otros elementos similares, que reflejan la densidad de la ocupación humana. También se consignan los parques más importantes, los sitios de interés histórico, los campos de recreo, tres clases de carreteras, y dos de ferrocarriles, se da los nombres de los caminos más importantes. Todos estos elementos aparecen sobre un fondo topográfico de relieve sombreado.

En los mapas regionales se hacen dos clasificaciones distintas de los lugares habitados. Las ciudades y las poblaciones *de diferente densidad de habitantes* se distinguen por la *forma y tamaño del símbolo* que las localiza en el mapa. Este símbolo refleja el tamaño de la población dentro de sus límites municipales, sin tomar en cuenta los suburbios. En los países donde los límites de una municipalidad incluyen áreas rurales, el símbolo se limita a representar el conglomerado urbano de habitantes. La *importancia económica y política de un lugar,* la cual puede ser independiente del número de sus habitantes, se indica mediante el *tamaño del tipo de imprenta* en que aparece su nombre.

LES CARTES RÉGIONALES sont de trois types principaux, chacun d'un style différent mais avec des symboles communs pour faciliter la compréhension (voir la légende des cartes pages x-xii). Chaque grande région, continent ou subcontinent, est représentée par une ou plusieurs cartes à l'échelle de 1:12 000 000e. Viennent ensuite des cartes au 1:6 000 000e et au 1:3 000 000e qui couvrent la région par sections plus détaillées; hormis la différence d'échelle, ces cartes sont semblables. Enfin, des secteurs particulièrement importants sont représentés au 1:1 000 000e. À chaque échelle correspond une bande colorée et une carte repère de même couleur, dans la marge de chaque page. Un échantillon de cartes aux diverses échelles est représenté à droite. Chaque carte est accompagnée d'une double échelle graphique donnant les rapports centimètre/kilomètre et inch/mille correspondants.

Les trois catégories de cartes diffèrent par le contenu et par ce qu'elles mettent en relief. Les cartes au 1:12 000 000e, qui sont essentiellement politiques, donnent un apercu général de chaque région. Elles indiquent les frontières nationales et, dans certains cas, les subdivisions administratives intérieures. Ces cartes d'introduction permettent de comparer la localisation, la superficie et la forme des pays du monde. La répartition des villes et des zones métropolitaines y apparaît dans le cadre des grandes régions naturelles. Les routes et les voies ferrées les plus importantes y figurent également.

Les cartes au 1:6 000 000e et au 1:3 000 000e forment la moitié de l'Atlas et en constituent la série cartographique essentielle. Elles représentent de façon plus détaillée une partie de pays (centre du Mexique), ou encore des régions plus vestes (Moyen-Orient) ou, parfois, des pays entiers (Japon, Nouvelle-Zélande). Les régiones les plus peuplées sont représentées à plus grande échelle (1;3 000 000e) que les autres (1:6 000 000e). Ces cartes offrent des informations d'ordre politique et culturel sur un fond topographique précis où le relief est indiqué à la fois par un estompage et par des variations de couleur. Différentes teintes de bleu sont utilisées pour symboliser les profondeurs marines. Les réseaux de transport représentés comprennent les principales voies ferrées, deux catégories de routes et les aéroports internationaux ou desservis par des avions à réaction. Les subdivisions politiques d'un certain nombre de pays sont aussi tracées.

Dans la série de cartes au 1:1 000 000e, des régions très importantes, soit du fait de leur densité de population, soit du fait de leur rôle économique, sont représentées d'une manière encore plus détaillée. L'objectif de cette série de cartes est de montrer la répartition des villes, routes, voies ferrées, ponts, aéroports, barrages, lacs de barrages et autres données associées qui traduisent la densité de l'occupation humaine dans ces régions. Les parcs les plus importants, les sites historiques essentiels et les centres de loisirs sont indiqués. Toutes les informations se détachent sur un fond topographique où le relief apparaît en estompage.

Les centres urbains des cartes régionales sont classés de deux manières différentes. *L'importance de la population* des villes est indiquée par *la dimension et la forme du symbole* qui les situe sur la carte. Seule la population comprise dans les limites municipales est prise en considération; dans les pays où des espaces ruraux sont inclus dans les limites d'une municipalité, seule la population urbaine entre en ligne de compte. *L'importance politique et économique relative* d'une ville, qui n'est pas nécessairement liée au nombre d'habitants, est indiquée par la dimension des caractères qui composent son nom.

OS MAPAS REGIONAIS compreendem três séries básicas, cada uma em estilo diferente, mas que empregam os mesmos símbolos para facilitar sua compreensão (Ver as *Legendas dos mapas*, pág. x-xii). Os mapas de cada uma das principais regiões terrestres, continentes ou subcontinentes, são introduzidos por um ou mais mapas na escala 1:12 000 000. Em seguida, vêm mapas, nas escalas de 1:6 000 000 e 1:3 000 000, que apresentam, com maiores detalhes, seções da região considerada. Exceto quanto à escala, os mapas de 1:6 000 000 e 1:3 000 000 têm as mesmas características. Finalmente, aparecem, na escala de 1:1 000 000, os mapas das áreas mais importantes da região considerada. A cada escala corresponde uma barra colorida e um indicador da mesma cor, que se encontra à margem da página de cada mapa. À página 21, acha-se um exemplo de cada escala, bem como a equivalência das relações centímetro/quilômetro e polegada/milha.

As três séries básicas de mapas são diferentes quanto ao conteúdo e à apresentação. Os mapas em escala de 1:12 000 000, que são essencialmente políticos, oferecem uma visão geral de cada região. Indicam as fronteiras nacionais e, em alguns casos, as subdivisões administrativas internas. Esses mapas servem de introdução e permitem avaliar e comparar a posição, superfície e forma dos países do Mundo. Neles está claramente indicada a distribuição das cidades e outros centros urbanos, bem como as principais características da configuração do solo. Encontra-se neles também uma seleção das ferrovias e rodovias mais importantes.

A série de mapas das escalas de 1:6 000 000 e de 1:3 000 000 constituem o principal material de referência do Atlas e representa cerca de metade do conjunto de mapas. Entre eles há mapas detalhados de parte de um país (centro do México), de um país inteiro (Japão e a Nova Zelândia) ou de uma região mais extensa (Oriente Médio). As áreas de maior densidade demográfica são apresentadas em escala maior, a de 1:3 000 000, e as demais, na de 1:6 000 000. Nessas duas escalas, os mapas fornecem informações de ordem política e cultural sobre um fundo que indica a configuração detalhada das particularidades físicas do solo, cujo relevo se destaca por contrastes de sombras e cores. Diversos matizes do azul traduzem o mapa batimétrico da profundidade ao largo das costas. Indicam também os aeroportos internacionais, as principais ferrovias, duas categorias de rodovias. As subdivisões políticas internas de numerosos países estão igualmente assinalados.

Na série de mapas da escala de 1:1 000 000, certas áreas, de interesse estratégico conjugado à importância econômica, densidade demográfica, ou ambos os elementos combinados, aparecem em forma ainda mais detalhada. O objetivo dessa série é representar a distribuição dos grandes centros urbanos, cidades, rodovias, ferrovias, pontes, aeroportos, represas, reservatórios e outras características associadas às grandes densidades demográficas. Indicam-se, também, os parques mais importantes, os lugares de interesse histórico, as áreas de lazer, três categorias de rodovias, e duas de ferrovias; e a nomenclatura dos grandes itinerários rodoviários. Todos esses elementos destacam-se sobre um fundo topográfico do relevo, executado em matizes das diversas cores.

Nos mapas regionais, assinalam-se os centros urbanos de dois modos. A *grandeza da população* das grandes cidades e dos centros urbanos secundários é representada pela *dimensão e forma do símbolo* que as localiza no mapa. O símbolo só reflete a população situada dentro de limites administrativos, sem levar em conta os subúrbios. Nos países onde os limites de uma municipalidade incluem zonas rurais, o símbolo representa apenas a população. A *importância política e econômica* de uma cidade, que não se relaciona necessariamente com o número de seus habitantes, é indicada pela *dimensão* dos caracteres tipográficos com que se compõe o seu nome.

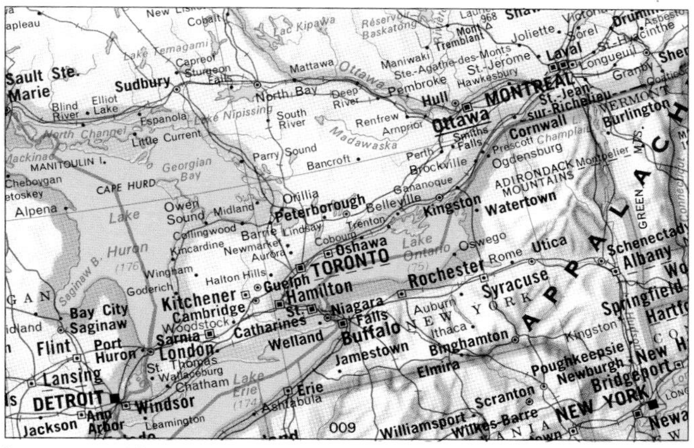
Sault Ste. Marie
Sudbury
Ottawa
MONTREAL
Kingston
Watertown
Rochester
Syracuse
TORONTO
Hamilton
Kitchener
Buffalo
Niagara Falls
London
Sarnia
DETROIT
Windsor
Erie
Jamestown
Binghamton
Scranton
Wilkes-Barre
Williamsport
Albany
Schenectady
Utica
Burlington
NEW YORK

0 200 400 600 Km.
0 200 400 600 Mi.

Scale 1:12,000,000
One centimeter represents 120 kilometers.
One inch represents approximately 190 miles.

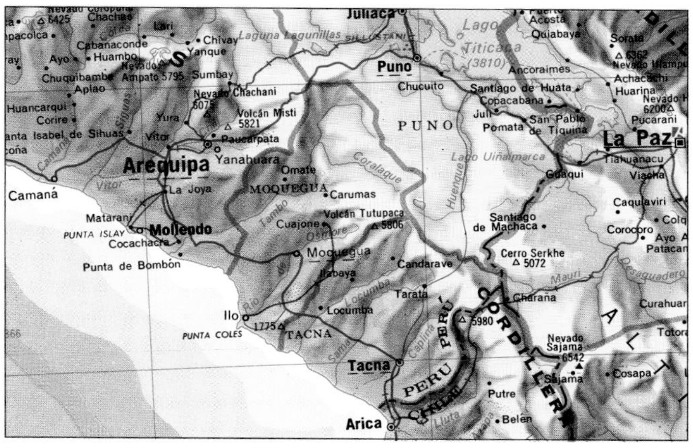
Juliaca
Puno
PUNO
La Paz
Arequipa
Moquegua
Mollendo
Ilo
Tacna
TACNA
Arica
Camaná
PERU
Cerro Serkhe
5072

0 100 200 300 Km.
0 100 200 300 Mi.

Scale 1:6,000,000
One centimeter represents 60 kilometers.
One inch represents approximately 95 miles.

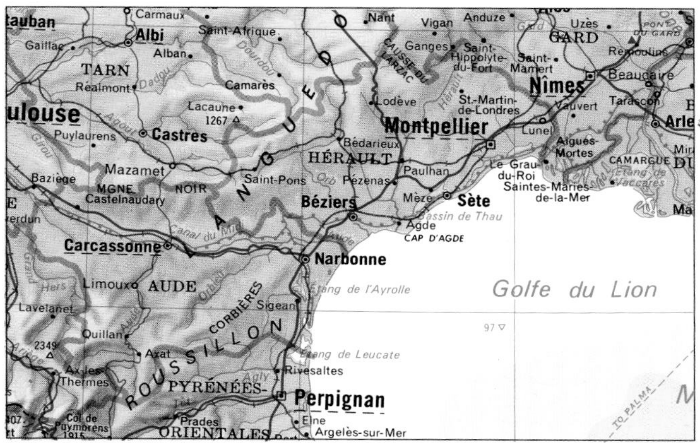
Albi
TARN
Castres
Mazamet
Montpellier
HÉRAULT
Nîmes
Sète
Béziers
Carcassonne
AUDE
Narbonne
Golfe du Lion
Perpignan
PYRÉNÉES-ORIENTALES
Arles

0 50 100 150 Km.
0 50 100 150 Mi.

Scale 1:3,000,000
One centimeter represents 30 kilometers.
One inch represents approximately 47 miles.

Preston
Blackburn
Southport
Chorley
Bolton
Bury
Rochdale
Wigan
Oldham
Salford
MANCHESTER
St. Helens
LIVERPOOL
Birkenhead
Warrington
Widnes
Stockport
Wilmslow

0 10 20 30 40 50 Km.
0 10 20 30 40 50 Mi.

Scale 1:1,000,000
One centimeter represents 10 kilometers.
One inch represents approximately 16 miles.

ICELAND
Reykjavík
NORWEGIAN SEA
Arctic Circle
FAEROE ISLANDS (Den.)
SHETLAND ISLANDS
ORKNEY ISLANDS
ROCKALL (U.K.)
HEBRIDES
ATLANTIC OCEAN
IRELAND
DUBLIN
SCOTLAND
UNITED KINGDOM
GREAT BRITAIN
NORTH SEA
LONDON
CELTIC SEA
English Channel
ISLE OF MAN
CHANNEL ISLANDS
NORWAY
Oslo
SWEDEN
DENMARK
KØBENHAVN COPENHAGEN
Skagerrak
NETHERLANDS
AMSTERDAM
BELGIUM
BRUXELLES
LUXEMBOURG
GERMANY
BERLIN
FRANCE
PARIS
Bay of Biscay
SWITZERLAND
AUSTRIA
WIEN VIENNA
CZECH REP.
PRAHA PRAGUE
SLOVENIA
CROATIA
BOSNIA AND HERZEGOVINA
HUNGARY
ITALY
ROMA
CORSE CORSICA (Fr.)
SARDEGNA SARDINIA (It.)
Tyrrhenian Sea
SICILIA SICILY
MALTA
Valletta
SPAIN
MADRID
PORTUGAL
LISBOA LISBON
ANDORRA
MONACO
ILLES BALEARS BALEARIC ISLANDS
MEDITERRANEAN SEA
MOROCCO
RABAT
ALGERIA
EL DJAZAÏR ALGIERS
TUNISIA
TUNIS
ATLAS MOUNTAINS
Gibraltar (U.K.)
Ceuta (Sp.)
Melilla (Sp.)
Copyright © by Rand McNally & Co.
Map prepared by Esselte Map Service AB, Stockholm.

MAP FORM	-älven	gora	île	islands	-øya	ozero	sea	vodochranilišče
ENGLISH	river	mountain	island	islands	island	lake	sea	reservoir
DEUTSCH	Fluss	Berg	Insel	Inseln	Insel	See	Meer	Stausee
ESPAÑOL	río	montaña	isla	islas	isla	lago	mar	embalse
FRANÇAIS	rivière	montagne	île	îles	île	lac	mer	réservoir
PORTUGUÊS	rio	montanha	ilha	ilhas	ilha	lago	mar	reservatório

Map continues pages 134-135

BARENTS SEA
Murmansk
Archangel'sk
Beloje more
White Sea
KARELIJA
FINLAND
Helsinki
Tampere
Oulu
Petrozavodsk
SANKT-PETERBURG
ST. PETERSBURG
(LENINGRAD)
Tallinn
ESTONIA
Tartu
Pskov
Novgorod
RIGA
LATVIA
LITHUANIA
Vilnius
Kaunas
MINSK
BELARUS
Gomel'
Vitebsk
Smolensk
MOSCOW MOSKVA
Tver'
Jaroslavl'
Kostroma
Vologda
Čerepovec
Ivanovo
Vladimir
Nižnij Novgorod
Kazan'
Čeboksary
RUSSIA
KOMI
Syktyvkar
Kirov
Perm'
Iževsk
Ufa
Samara
Toljatti
Uljanovsk
Penza
Saratov
Volgograd
(Stalingrad)
Astrachan'
Jekaterinburg (Sverdlovsk)
Čel'abinsk
Magnitogorsk
Orenburg
Orsk
URAL'SKIJE GORY
URAL MOUNTAINS
ZAPADNO SIBIRSKAJA RAVNINA
Tumen'
Kurgan
KAZAKHSTAN
Ural'sk
Akt'ubinsk
Aralskoje more
Aral Sea
CASPIAN SEA
UZBEK.
TURKMENISTAN
Kursk
Orel
Tula
Br'ansk
Voronež
Lipeck
Tambov
Char'kov
KIJEV KIEV
UKRAINE
Poltava
Dnepropetrovsk
DONECK
Zaporožje
L'vov
Vinnica
Odessa
Kišin'ov
MOLDOVA
Rostov-na-Donu
Krasnodar
Stavropol'
KALMYKIJA
Groznyj
Machačkala
BOL'ŠOJ KAVKAZ CAUCASUS
TBILISI
GEORGIA
ARMENIA
JEREVAN
AZERBAIJAN
BAKU
BLACK SEA
Sevastopol'
Simferopol'
Azovskoje more
Sea of Azov
ROMANIA
BUCUREŞTI
BUCHAREST
Constanța
BULGARIA
SOFIJA
Varna
İstanbul
ANKARA
TURKEY
İzmir
Adana
Konya
Kayseri
Erzurum
Trabzon
Samsun
Diyarbakır
ASIA MINOR
ATHINAI ATHENS
Thessaloniki
KRÍTI
CRETE
NORTH CYPRUS
Nicosia
CYPRUS
SYRIA
Halab
Aleppo
Ḥamāh
IRAQ
BAGHDĀD
Al-Mawşil
Mosul
Kirkūk
IRAN
TEHRĀN
Tabrīz
Hamadān
Qom
Eşfahān
Rasht

Map continues pages 72-73

Map continues pages 118-119

Kilometers 0 200 400 600 Km.

Statute Miles 0 200 400 600 Mi.

Scale 1:12,000,000

One centimeter represents 120 kilometers.
One inch represents approximately 190 miles.
Miller Oblated Stereographic Projection

Northern Europe / Nordeuropa / Europe Septentrional
Europe Septentrionale / Europa Setentrional

a

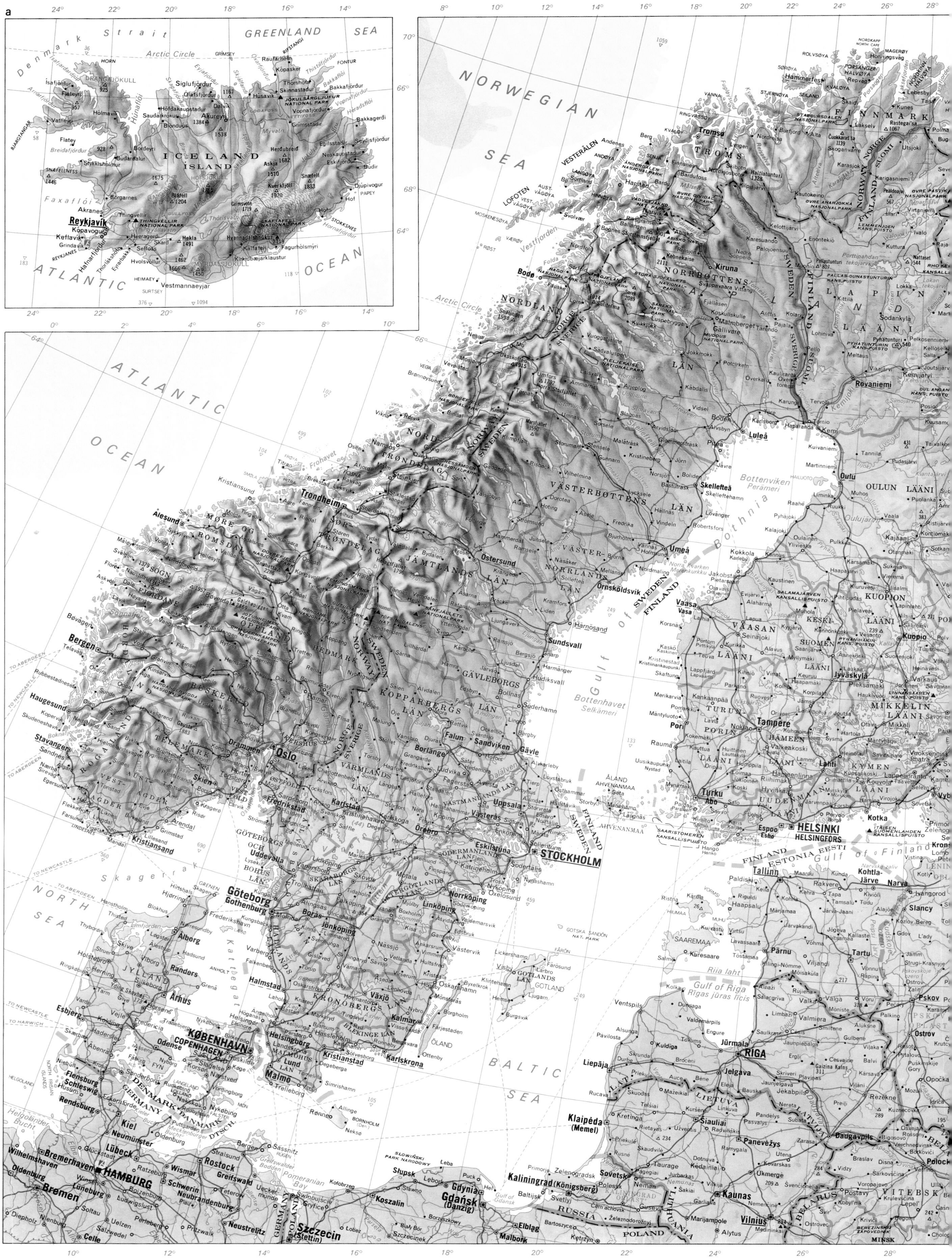
GREENLAND SEA
Denmark Strait
Arctic Circle
ICELAND
ISLAND
Reykjavík
Akureyri
Vestmannaeyjar
ATLANTIC OCEAN
NORWEGIAN SEA
ATLANTIC OCEAN
NORTH SEA
Skagerrak
Kattegat
BALTIC SEA
Gulf of Bothnia
Gulf of Finland
Gulf of Riga
Bottenviken
Bottenhavet
FINNMARK
TROMS
NORDLAND
NORRBOTTENS LÄN
LAPIN LÄÄNI
OULUN LÄÄNI
VÄSTERBOTTENS LÄN
JÄMTLANDS LÄN
VÄSTERNORRLANDS LÄN
GÄVLEBORGS LÄN
KOPPARBERGS LÄN
VÄRMLANDS LÄN
HEDMARK
OPPLAND
BUSKERUD
TELEMARK
ROGALAND
HORDALAND
SOGN OG FJORDANE
MØRE OG ROMSDAL
SØR-TRØNDELAG
NORD-TRØNDELAG
VAASAN LÄÄNI
KUOPION LÄÄNI
KESKI-SUOMEN LÄÄNI
HÄMEEN LÄÄNI
TURUN-PORIN LÄÄNI
UUDENMAAN LÄÄNI
KYMEN LÄÄNI
MIKKELIN LÄÄNI
NORWAY
SWEDEN
FINLAND
DENMARK
ESTONIA
LATVIA
LIETUVA
LITHUANIA
POLAND
RUSSIA
BELARUS
GERMANY
Oslo
STOCKHOLM
HELSINKI
HELSINGFORS
KØBENHAVN
COPENHAGEN
Tallinn
RIGA
Vilnius
Bergen
Trondheim
Göteborg
Gothenburg
Malmö
Tampere
Turku
Åbo
Oulu
Umeå
Luleå
Tromsø
Hammerfest
Kiruna
Rovaniemi
Kaunas
Klaipėda (Memel)
Kaliningrad (Königsberg)
Gdańsk (Danzig)
Gdynia
Szczecin (Stettin)
HAMBURG
Bremen
Kiel
Lübeck
Rostock
Århus
Ålborg
Esbjerg
Stavanger
Kristiansand
Ålesund
Norrköping
Linköping
Uppsala
Västerås
Örebro
Gävle
Sundsvall
Östersund
Daugavpils
Liepāja
Jelgava
Šiauliai
Panevėžys
Pärnu
Tartu
Narva
Pskov
Kuopio
Jyväskylä
Vaasa
Pori
Lahti
Kotka
GOTLAND
ÅLAND AHVENANMAA
SAAREMAA
BORNHOLM
ÖLAND

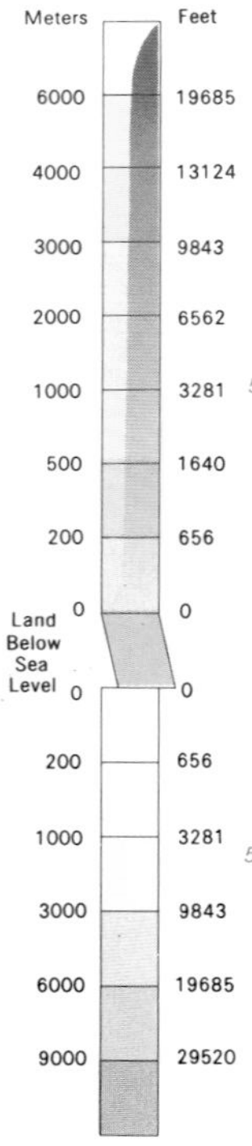
Meters
Feet
6000 19685
4000 13124
3000 9843
2000 6562
1000 3281
500 1640
200 656
0 0
Land Below Sea Level
0 0
200 656
1000 3281
3000 9843
6000 19685
9000 29520

MAP FORM	-älven	-fjorden	guba	-joki	-jökull	lääni	-øya	ozero
ENGLISH	river	fjord, lake	bay	river	glacier	province	island	lake
DEUTSCH	Fluss	Fjord, See	Bucht	Fluss	Gletscher	Provinz	Insel	See
ESPAÑOL	río	fiordo, lago	bahía	río	glaciar	provincia	isla	lago
FRANÇAIS	rivière	fjord, lac	baie	rivière	glacier	province	île	lac
PORTUGUÊS	rio	fiorde, lago	baía	rio	geleira	província	ilha	lago

BARENTS SEA
BARENCEVO MORE
PEČORSKOJE MORE
OSTROV KOLGUJEV
Češskaja guba
White Sea
Beloje more
Dvinskaja guba
Onežskaja guba
Kandalakšskij zaliv
POLUOSTROV KANIN
Kanin Nos
Murmansk
Severomorsk
Kola
Apatity
Kirovsk
Kandalakša
Mončegorsk
Olenegorsk
Kem'
Belomorsk
Segeža
Onega
Severodvinsk
Archangel'sk
Novodvinsk
Mezen'
Narjan-Mar
Nar'jan-Mar
Vorkuta
Inta
Pečora
Uchta
Sosnogorsk
Syktyvkar
Kotlas
Velikij Ust'ug
Petrozavodsk
Kondopoga
Medvežjegorsk
Vologda
Čerepovec
Jaroslavl'
Kostroma
Rybinsk
Kirov
Slobodskoj
Kirovo-Čepeck
Glazov
Iževsk
Votkinsk
Sarapul
Solikamsk
Kudymkar
Omutninsk
Joškar-Ola
Čeboksary
Kazan'
Zelenodol'sk
Nižnekamsk
Naberežnyje Čelny
Al'metjevsk
Leninogorsk
Bugul'ma
Dimitrovgrad
Uljanovsk
Toljatti
Samara
Novokujbyševsk
Čapajevsk
Syzran'
Saransk
Penza
Arzamas
Nižnij Novgorod
Gorky
Dzeržinsk
Vladimir
Kovrov
Ivanovo
Kinešma
Murom
Moskva
Moscow
Tver'
Klin
Sergijev Posad
Noginsk
Orechovo-Zujevo
Kolomna
Serpuchov
Tula
Kaluga
Obninsk
Rjazan'
Smolensk
Vjaz'ma
Rževn
Velikije Luki
Staraja Russa
Novgorod
Boroviči
Sankt-Peterburg
St. Petersburg
Volchov
Tichvin
Kiriši
Ladožskoje ozero
Lake Ladoga
Onežskoje ozero
Rybinskoje vodochranilišče
Gor'kovskoje vodochranilišče
Kujbyševskoje vodochranilišče
Saratovskoje vodochranilišče
Čeboksarskoje vodochranilišče
Kamskoje vodochranilišče
KARELIJA
KOMI
NENECKIJ
MARIJ EL
ČUVAŠIJA
TATARSTAN
UDMURTIJA
MORDOVIJA
Arctic Circle
URAL MOUNTAINS
URAL'SKIJE GORY
POLJARNYJ URAL
TIMANSKIJ KRJAŽ
BOL'ŠEZEMEL'SKAJA TUNDRA
Pečora
Mezen'
Vyčegda
Suchona
Dvina
Volga
Kama
Oka
Copyright © by Rand McNally & Co.
Map compiled by Rand McNally GmbH, Stuttgart
Map produced by Rand McNally & Co.
A-573000-764
32° 34° 36° 38° 40° 42° 44° 46° 48° 50° 52° 54° 56° 58° 60° 62° 64° 66°
66° 64° 62° 60° 58° 56° 54°

Map continues pages 86-87

Map continues pages 76-77

Kilometers 0 100 200 300 Km.

Statute Miles 0 100 200 300 Mi.

Scale 1:6,000,000

One centimeter represents 60 kilometers.
One inch represents approximately 95 miles.
Lambert Conformal Conic Projection

NORWEGIAN SEA
NORTH SEA
Skagerrak
Kattegat
NORWAY NORGE
SWEDEN SVERIGE
DENMARK DANMARK
GERMANY DTSCH
MØRE OG ROMSDAL
SOGN OG FJORDANE
HORDALAND
SØR-TRØNDELAG
OPPLAND
HEDMARK
BUSKERUD
TELEMARK
ROGALAND
AUST-AGDER
VEST-AGDER
VESTFOLD
AKERSHUS
ØSTFOLD
JÄMTLANDS LÄN
HÄRJEDALEN
KOPPARBERGS LÄN
DALARNA
DALECARLIA
VÄRMLANDS LÄN
ÖREBRO LÄN
VÄSTMANLANDS LÄN
UPPSALA
SÖDERMANLANDS LÄN
SÖDERMANLAND
ÖSTERGÖTLANDS LÄN
SKARABORGS LÄN
ÄLVSBORGS LÄN
GÖTEBORGS OCH BOHUS LÄN
HALLANDS LÄN
JÖNKÖPINGS LÄN
KALMAR LÄN
KRONOBERGS LÄN
SMÅLAND
BLEKINGE LÄN
KRISTIANSTADS LÄN
MALMÖHUS LÄN
GOTLANDS LÄN
ÖLAND
JOTUNHEIMEN
HARDANGERVIDDA
DOVREFJELL
Ålesund
Molde
Kristiansund
Trondheim
Bergen
Haugesund
Stavanger
Kristiansand
Arendal
Skien
Porsgrunn
Drammen
Oslo
Lillehammer
Hamar
Moss
Sarpsborg
Fredrikstad
Halden
Karlstad
Karlskoga
Örebro
Västerås
Uppsala
STOCKHOLM
Södertälje
Eskilstuna
Norrköping
Linköping
Nyköping
Motala
Jönköping
Borås
Trollhättan
Uddevalla
Göteborg
Gothenburg
Mölndal
Halmstad
Helsingborg
Landskrona
Malmö
Lund
Trelleborg
Kristianstad
Karlskrona
Kalmar
Växjö
Visby
Falun
Borlänge
Sandviken
Frederikshavn
Skagen
Ålborg
Randers
Viborg
Silkeborg
Herning
Århus
Horsens
Vejle
Esbjerg
Kolding
Fredericia
Odense
FYN
SJÆLLAND
KØBENHAVN
COPENHAGEN
Helsingør
Roskilde
Næstved
LOLLAND
FALSTER
MØN
BORNHOLM
Rønne
Flensburg
Schleswig
Kiel
Rendsburg
Neumünster
SCHLESWIG-HOLSTEIN

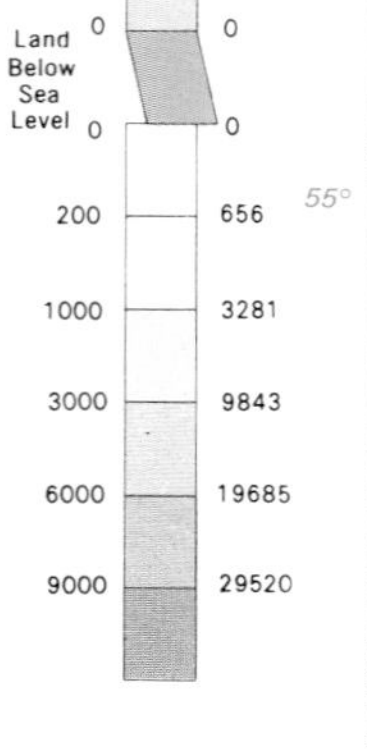
Meters
Feet
6000 19685
4000 13124
3000 9843
2000 6562
1000 3281
500 1640
200 656
0 0
Land Below Sea Level
0 0
200 656
1000 3281
3000 9843
6000 19685
9000 29520

Map continues pages 30-31

MAP FORM	-älven	bugt	-fjället	-fjell	-fjorden	-järvi	-joki	-ö, -ön	-sjön	-vesi
ENGLISH	river	bay	mountain	mountain	fjord, lake	lake	river	island	lake	lake
DEUTSCH	Fluss	Bucht	Berg	Berg	Fjord, See	See	Fluss	Insel	See	See
ESPAÑOL	río	bahía	montaña	montaña	fiordo, lago	lago	río	isla	lago	lago
FRANÇAIS	rivière	baie	montagne	montagne	fjord, lac	lac	rivière	île	lac	lac
PORTUGUÊS	rio	baía	montanha	montanha	fiorde, lago	lago	rio	ilha	lago	lago

Map compiled by Esselte Map Service AB, Stockholm.
Map produced by Rand McNally & Co.
A-554400-764 -6 -5 -11

Map continues pages 24-25

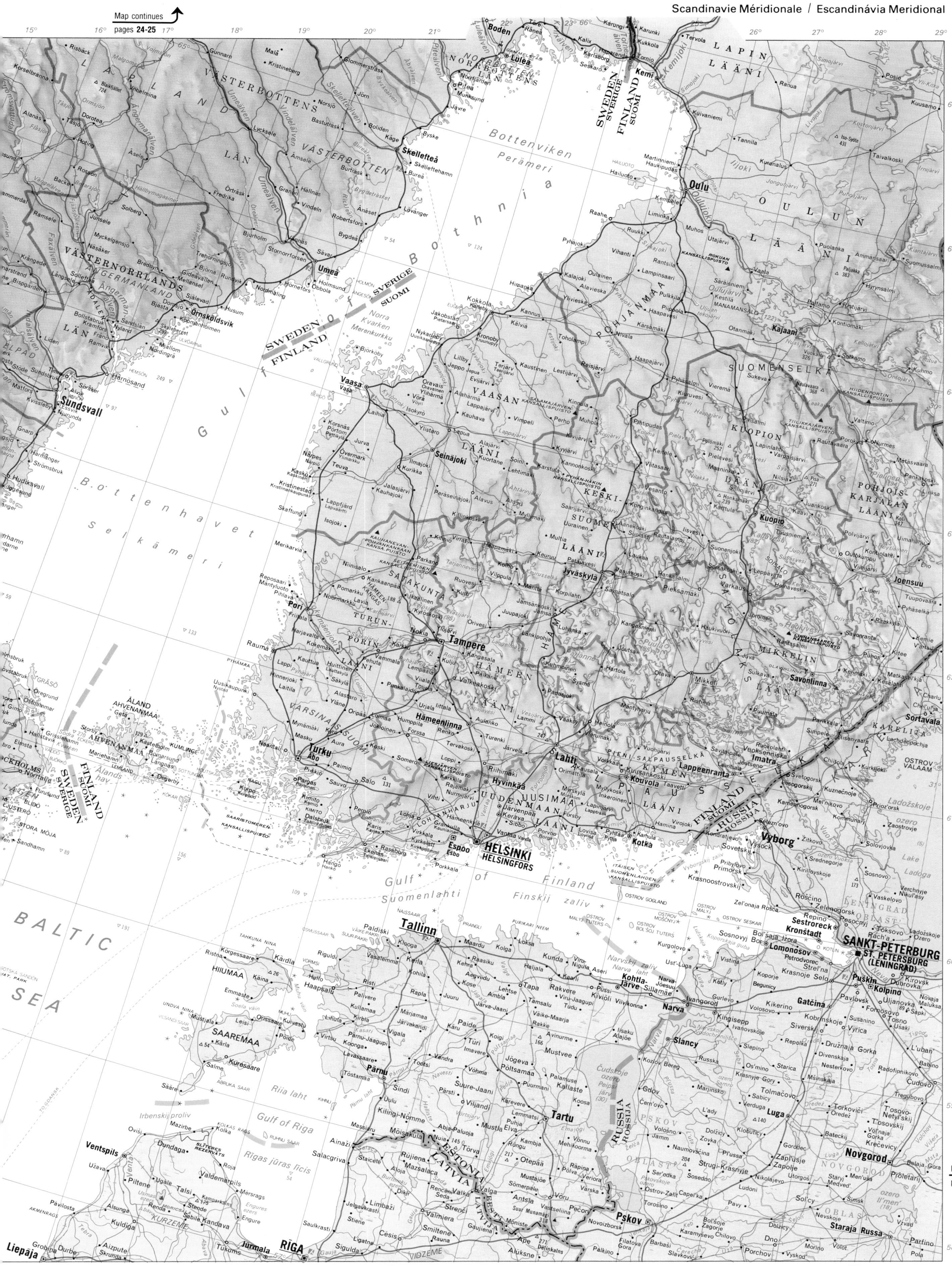
Bottenviken
Perämeri
Gulf of Bothnia
Bottenhavet
Selkämeri
Gulf of Finland
Suomenlahti
Finskij zaliv
BALTIC SEA
Gulf of Riga
Rīgas jūras līcis
Riia laht
SWEDEN SVERIGE
FINLAND SUOMI
RUSSIA ROSSIJA
ESTONIA
LATVIA
HELSINKI HELSINGFORS
Tallinn
RĪGA
SANKT-PETERBURG ST. PETERSBURG (LENINGRAD)
Oulu
Tampere
Turku Åbo
Vaasa Vasa
Umeå
Sundsvall
Luleå
Kuopio
Jyväskylä
Lahti
Pori
Vyborg
Tartu
Pskov
Novgorod
Pärnu
Liepāja
Ventspils
Jūrmala
SAAREMAA
HIIUMAA
ÅLAND AHVENANMAA
LAPIN LÄÄNI
OULUN LÄÄNI
VAASAN LÄÄNI
KUOPION LÄÄNI
KESKI-SUOMEN LÄÄNI
MIKKELIN LÄÄNI
HÄMEEN LÄÄNI
TURUN-PORIN LÄÄNI
UUDENMAAN LÄÄNI
KYMEN LÄÄNI
POHJOIS-KARJALAN LÄÄNI
VÄSTERBOTTENS LÄN
VÄSTERNORRLANDS LÄN
NORRBOTTENS LÄN
SUOMENSELKÄ
SALPAUSSELKÄ
KARELIA
Ladožskoje ozero
Lake Ladoga
Čudskoje ozero
Peipsi järv

Map continues pages 76-77

Map continues pages 76-77

Kilometers 0 50 100 150 Km.
Statute Miles 0 50 100 150 Mi.

Scale 1:3,000,000

One centimeter represents 30 kilometers.
One inch represents approximately 47 miles.
Conic Projection, Two Standard Parallels

British Isles / Britische Inseln / Islas Británicas
Îles Britanniques / Ilhas Britânicas

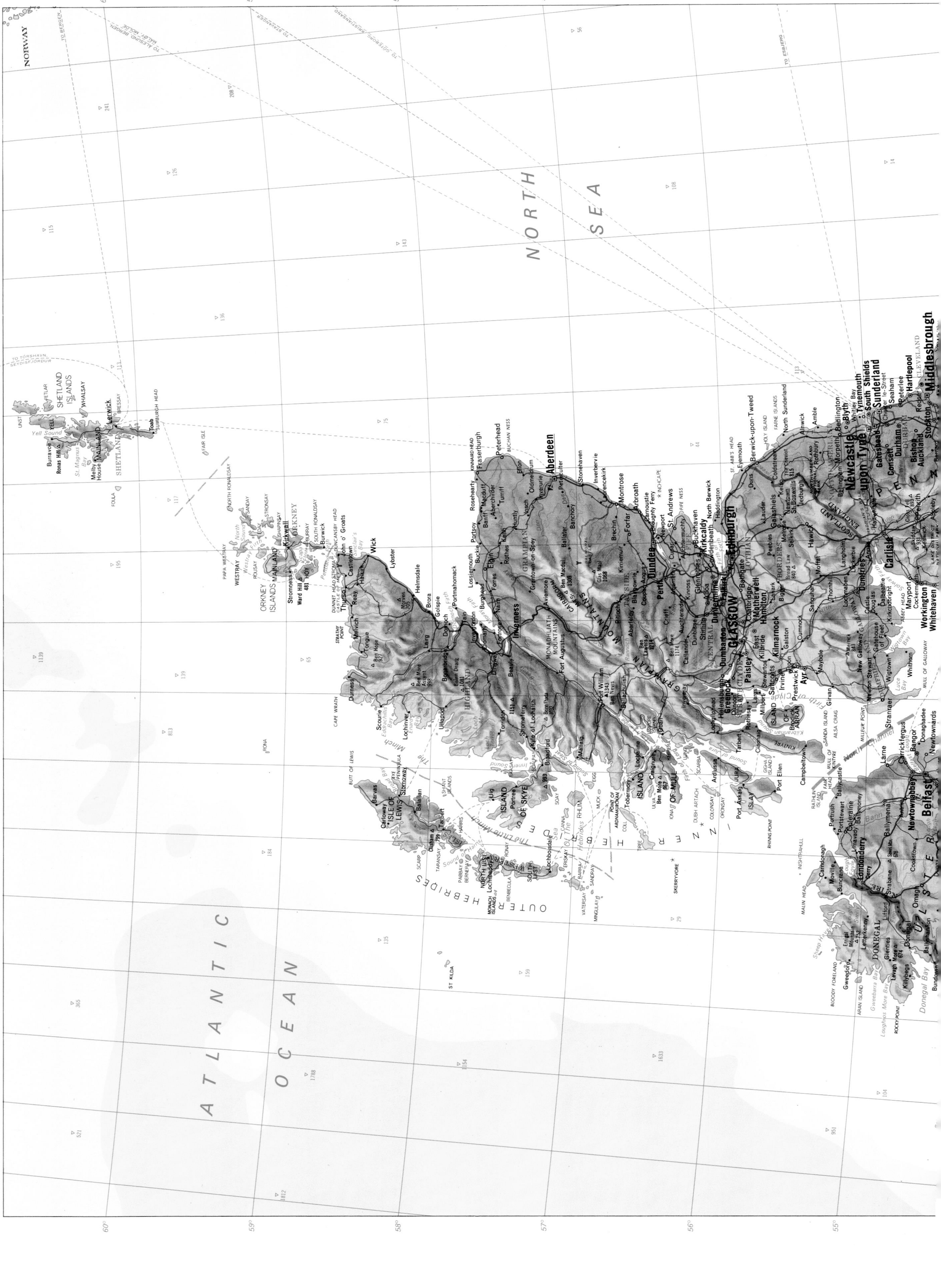
NORTH SEA
ATLANTIC OCEAN
NORWAY
SHETLAND ISLANDS
ORKNEY ISLANDS
OUTER HEBRIDES
Aberdeen
Edinburgh
GLASGOW
Dundee
Inverness
Newcastle upon Tyne
Sunderland
Middlesbrough
Carlisle
Belfast
Londonderry

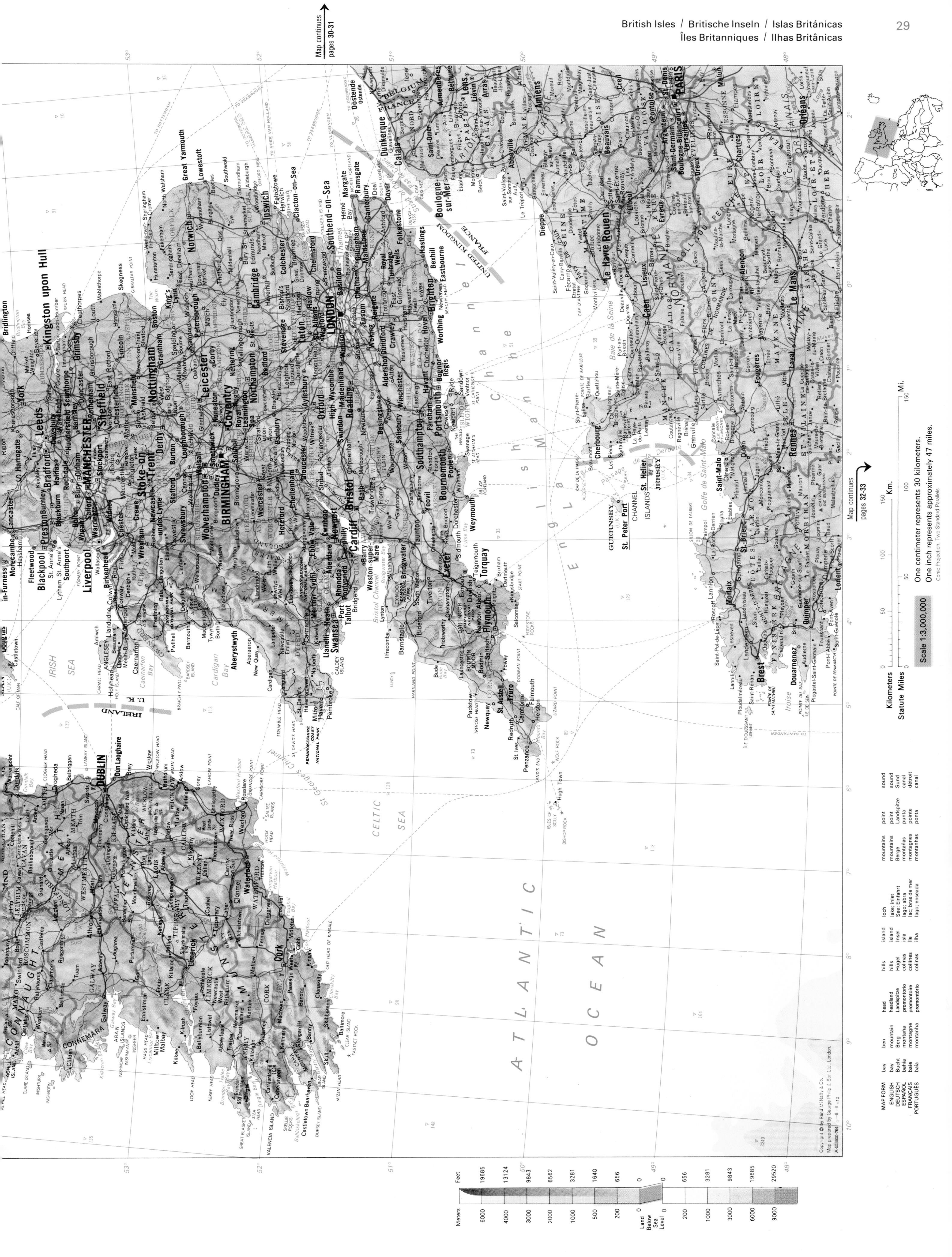
Map continues pages 30-31
Map continues pages 32-33
ATLANTIC OCEAN
CELTIC SEA
IRISH SEA
English Channel
La Manche
St. George's Channel
Bristol Channel
UNITED KINGDOM
FRANCE
BELGIUM
IRELAND
U.K.
DUBLIN
LONDON
PARIS
BIRMINGHAM
MANCHESTER
Scale 1:3,000,000
One centimeter represents 30 kilometers.
One inch represents approximately 47 miles.
Conic Projection, Two Standard Parallels
Kilometers
Statute Miles
MAP FORM / ENGLISH / DEUTSCH / ESPAÑOL / FRANÇAIS / PORTUGUÊS
bay / bay / Bucht / bahía / baie / baía
ben / mountain / Berg / montaña / montagne / montanha
head / headland / Landspitze / promontorio / promontoire / promontório
hills / hills / Hügel / colinas / collines / colinas
island / island / Insel / isla / île / ilha
loch / lake; inlet / See; Einfahrt / lago; abra / lac; bras de mer / lago; enseada
mountains / mountains / Berge / montañas / montagnes / montanhas
point / point / Landspitze / punta / pointe / ponta
sound / sound / Sund / canal / détroit / canal
Copyright © by Rand McNally & Co.
Map prepared by George Philip & Son Ltd., London.
Meters / Feet
Land Below Sea Level

Map continues pages 26-27

Map continues pages 28-29

NORTH SEA
FRISIAN ISLANDS
NORTH FRISIAN ISLANDS
Deutsche Bucht
Helgoländer Bucht
OSTFRIESISCHE INSELN
WADDENEILANDEN
IJsselmeer (Zuider Zee)
Markermeer
Kieler Bucht
Mecklenburger Bucht
DENMARK
GERMANY
NETHERLANDS
BELGIUM
FRANCE
LUXEMBOURG
SWITZERLAND
AUSTRIA
LIECHTENSTEIN
Flensburg
Kiel
Lübeck
Rostock
HAMBURG
Bremerhaven
Bremen
Schwerin
Groningen
Leeuwarden
Den Helder
AMSTERDAM
Haarlem
's-Gravenhage
The Hague
Utrecht
Rotterdam
Arnhem
Eindhoven
Antwerpen
Gent
BRUXELLES
BRUSSEL
Lille
Liège
Hannover
Braunschweig
Magdeburg
Osnabrück
Münster
Bielefeld
Dortmund
Essen
Duisburg
Düsseldorf
Wuppertal
Köln
Bonn
Aachen
Kassel
Göttingen
Halle
Leipzig
Erfurt
Koblenz
Frankfurt a. M.
Wiesbaden
Mainz
Darmstadt
Mannheim
Ludwigshafen
Heidelberg
Karlsruhe
Stuttgart
Würzburg
Nürnberg
Regensburg
Augsburg
MÜNCHEN
MUNICH
Ulm
Luxembourg
Trier
Saarbrücken
Metz
Nancy
Strasbourg
Reims
Troyes
Dijon
Besançon
Mulhouse
Freiburg
Basel
Bâle
Zürich
Bern
Luzern
Lausanne
Genève
Innsbruck
Bolzano
Bozen
Merano
SCHLESWIG-HOLSTEIN
NIEDERSACHSEN
MECKLENBURG-VORPOMMERN
NORDRHEIN-WESTFALEN
RHEINLAND-PFALZ
SAARLAND
HESSEN
THÜRINGEN
SACHSEN-ANHALT
BADEN-WÜRTTEMBERG
BAYERN
ALPS
JURA
ARDENNES
EIFEL
HUNSRÜCK
SCHWARZWALD
BLACK FOREST
Rhein
Bodensee
Lake Constance
Lac Léman
Copyright by Rand McNally & Company
Made in U.S.A.

Meters	Feet
6000	19685
4000	13124
3000	9843
2000	6562
1000	3281
500	1640
200	656
0	0
Land Below Sea Level	
0	0
200	656
1000	3281
3000	9843
6000	19685
9000	29520

MAP FORM	Bucht	Gebirge	jezioro	Kanal	park narodowy	See	Wald
ENGLISH	bay	range	lake, lagoon	canal	national park	lake	forest, mountains
DEUTSCH	Bucht	Gebirge	See, Haff	Kanal	Nationalpark	See	Wald
ESPAÑOL	bahia	sierra	lago, laguna	canal	parque national	lago	bosque, montañas
FRANÇAIS	baie	chaîne	lac, lagune	canal	parc national	lac	forêt, montagnes
PORTUGUÊS	baia	serra	lago, laguna	canal	parque nacional	lago	floresta, montanhas

Kilometers 0 50 100 150 Km.
Statute Miles 0 50 100 150 Mi.

Scale 1:3,000,000

One centimeter represents 30 kilometers.
One inch represents approximately 47 miles.
Conic Projection, Two Standard Parallels.

BALTIC SEA
Pomeranian Bay
Gulf of Gdansk
Kaliningrad (Königsberg)
RUSSIA
LITHUANIA
POLAND
BELARUS
GERMANY
CZECH REPUBLIC
SLOVAKIA
AUSTRIA
HUNGARY
SLOVENIA
CROATIA
ROMANIA
UKRAINE
SERBIA
Gdańsk (Danzig)
Gdynia
Szczecin (Stettin)
Bydgoszcz
Toruń
Poznań
WARSZAWA WARSAW
Łódź
Wrocław (Breslau)
Kraków
Katowice
Lublin
Białystok
Dresden
Leipzig
PRAHA PRAGUE
Brno
Ostrava
WIEN VIENNA
Bratislava
BUDAPEST
Graz
Linz
Košice
Miskolc
Debrecen
Szeged
Pécs
Oradea
Arad
C A R P A T H I A N M O U N T A I N S
14°
15°
16°
17°
18°
19°
20°
21°
22°
23°
24°
54°
53°
52°
51°
50°
49°
48°
47°
46°

Map continues pages 76-77

Map continues pages 78-79

p continues
ies 36-37

France and the Alps / Frankreich und die Alpen / Francia y los Alpes
France et Alpes / França e os Alpes

Map continues pages 28-29

English Channel
La Manche
ATLANTIC OCEAN
Bay of Biscay
Golfe de Saint-Malo
Baie de la Seine
Strait of Dover
Pas de Calais
UNITED KINGDOM
FRANCE
CHANNEL ISLANDS
GUERNSEY (UK)
St. Peter Port
JERSEY (UK)
St. Helier
Southampton
Portsmouth
Bournemouth
Brighton
Plymouth
Exeter
Torquay
Dover
Folkestone
Hastings
Eastbourne
Dunkerque
Calais
Boulogne-sur-Mer
BRUXEL
Gent
Lille
Roubaix
Amiens
Dieppe
Le Havre
Rouen
Cherbourg
Caen
Évreux
PARIS
Versailles
Brest
Quimper
Morlaix
Saint-Malo
Saint-Brieuc
Lorient
Vannes
Rennes
Le Mans
Laval
Alençon
Chartres
Orléans
Tours
Blois
Angers
Nantes
Saint-Nazaire
Cholet
Saumur
Poitiers
La Rochelle
Rochefort
Niort
Limoges
Angoulême
Bordeaux
Arcachon
Périgueux
Bergerac
Agen
Montauban
Toulouse
Albi
Rodez
Clermont-Ferrand
Vichy
Bourges
Nevers
Auxerre
Montpellier
Béziers
Narbonne
Carcassonne
Perpignan
Sète
Tarbes
Pau
Bayonne
Biarritz
Anglet
Dax
Mont-de-Marsan
Donostia San Sebastián
Bilbao
Santander
Vitoria Gasteiz
Pamplona
Burgos
Logroño
Miranda de Ebro
ANDORRA
Andorra
PYRÉNÉES
MASSIF CENTRAL
BRETAGNE
NORMANDIE
LANDES
GASCOGNE

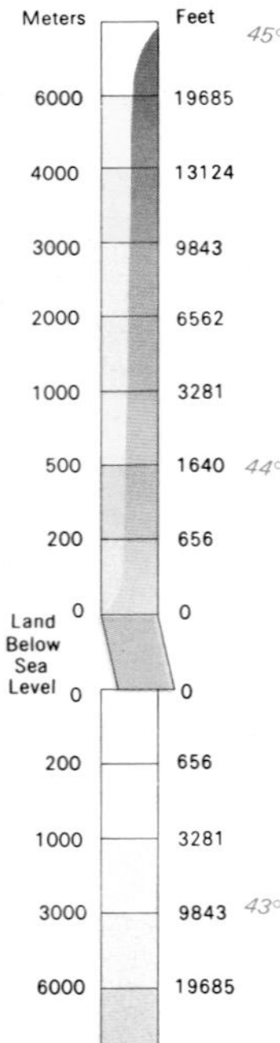

Meters
Feet
6000
19685
4000
13124
3000
9843
2000
6562
1000
3281
500
1640
200
656
0
0
Land Below Sea Level
0
0
200
656
1000
3281
3000
9843
6000
19685
9000
29520

Map continues pages 34-35

MAP FORM	canal	cap	île	lago	mont (e)	monts	pointe	See
ENGLISH	canal	cape	island	lake	mount	mountains	point	lake
DEUTSCH	Kanal	Kap	Insel	See	Berg	Berge	Landspitze	See
ESPAÑOL	canal	cabo	isla	lago	monte	montes	punta	lago
FRANÇAIS	canal	cap	île	lac	mont	monts	pointe	lac
PORTUGUÊS	canal	cabo	ilha	lago	monte	montes	ponta	lago

Map continues pages 30-31

MEDITERRANEAN SEA
LIGURIAN SEA
ADRIATIC SEA
Gulf of Venice
Marseille
Toulon
Nice
Cannes
Genova
Torino
MILANO
Venezia
Bologna
Firenze
Lyon
Genève
Lausanne
Bern
Basel
Zürich
Strasbourg
Stuttgart
München
Nürnberg
Frankfurt a. M.
Köln
Bonn
Aachen
Liège
Luxembourg
Mannheim
Karlsruhe
Innsbruck
Salzburg
Trieste
PRAHA
Chemnitz
Dijon
Besançon
Grenoble
Copyright © by Rand McNally & Co.
Map prepared by Rand McNally GmbH, Stuttgart.
A-559495-764

Map continues pages 36-37

Kilometers 0 50 100 150 Km.
Statute Miles 0 50 100 150 Mi.

Scale 1:3,000,000

One centimeter represents 30 kilometers.
One inch represents approximately 47 miles.
Lambert Conformal Conic Projection

Spain and Portugal / Spanien und Portugal / España y Portugal
Espagne et Portugal / Espanha e Portugal

Bay of Biscay
ATLANTIC
OCEAN
ATLANTIC
OCEAN
ALBORÁN SEA
Golfo de Cádiz
CORDILLERA CANTÁBRICA
ASTURIAS
CANTABRIA
GALICIA
CASTILLA LEÓN
CASTILLA LA MANCHA
EXTREMADURA
ANDALUCÍA
MADRID
LA RIOJA
SISTEMA CENTRAL
SISTEMA IBÉRICO
SIERRA MORENA
SISTEMAS BÉTICOS
SIERRA NEVADA
SPAIN ESPAÑA
PORTUGAL
MINHO
TRÁS-OS-MONTES
BEIRA
ESTREMADURA
ALENTEJO
ALGARVE
MOROCCO AL-MAGREB
RIF
La Coruña
El Ferrol del Caudillo
Santiago de Compostela
Lugo
Oviedo
Gijón
Avilés
Santander
Bilbao
Vitoria
Burgos
León
Palencia
Valladolid
Zamora
Salamanca
Segovia
Ávila
Soria
Logroño
Guadalajara
MADRID
Alcalá de Henares
Getafe
Leganés
Aranjuez
Toledo
Talavera de la Reina
Plasencia
Cáceres
Badajoz
Mérida
Ciudad Real
Puertollano
Valdepeñas
Tomelloso
Córdoba
Jaén
Linares
Úbeda
Granada
Almería
Málaga
Sevilla
Seville
Huelva
Cádiz
San Fernando
Jerez de la Frontera
El Puerto de Santa María
Algeciras
La Línea
Gibraltar (U.K.)
Strait of Gibraltar
Ceuta (Sp.)
Tanger
Tétouan
Larache
Ksar-el-Kebir
Al-Hoceima
Melilla (Sp.)
Nador
Orense
Pontevedra
Vigo
Viana do Castelo
Braga
Porto
Vila Nova de Gaia
Aveiro
Coimbra
Leiria
Santarém
LISBOA LISBON
Setúbal
Évora
Beja
Faro
Bay of Biscay
Copyright © by Rand McNally & Co.
Map prepared by Rand McNally GmbH, Stuttgart.
A-559900-764

Meters	Feet
6000	19685
4000	13124
3000	9843
2000	6562
1000	3281
500	1640
200	656
0	0
Land Below Sea Level	
0	0
200	656
1000	3281
3000	9843
6000	19685
9000	29520

ESPAÑOL	bahía	cabo	isla	embalse	puerto	punta	ría	sierra
ENGLISH	bay	cape	island	reservoir	port	point	estuary	mountains
DEUTSCH	Bucht	Kap	Insel	Stausee	Hafen	Landspitze	Trichtermündung	Berge
FRANÇAIS	baie	cap	île	réservoir	port	pointe	estuaire	montagnes
PORTUGUÊS	baía	cabo	ilha	reservatório	porto	ponta	estuário	serra

Map continues
pages 32-33

Toulouse
Montpellier
Nîmes
Avignon
Marseille
Toulon
Nice
Cannes
Perpignan
Narbonne
Carcassonne
Béziers
Sète
Golfe du Lion
PYRÉNÉES
ANDORRA
CATALUNYA
Zaragoza
Huesca
Lleida
Girona
BARCELONA
L'Hospitalet de Llobregat
Tarragona
DELTA DE L'EBRE
Castelló de la Plana
València
Golf de València
Alacant
Murcia
Cartagena
MENORCA
MALLORCA MAJORCA
Palma
Maó
Ciutadella
EIVISSA IBIZA
FORMENTERA
ILLES BALEARS
BALEARIC ISLANDS
MEDITERRANEAN SEA
EL DJAZAÏR ALGIERS
Wahran Oran
Tizi-Ouzou
Bejaïa (Bougie)
Jijel
Sétif
Batna
Ech Cheliff
Mestghanem
Sidi bel Abbès
ALGERIA
ALGÉRIE
ATLAS TELLIEN
MOUNTAINS
PLAINE DU HODNA

Map continues
pages 148-149

Kilometers 0 50 100 150 Km.
Statute Miles 0 50 100 150 Mi.

Scale 1:3,000,000

One centimeter represents 30 kilometers.
One inch represents approximately 47 miles.
Conic Projection, Two Standard Parallels

Map continues pages 38-39

Map continues pages 30-31

ADRIATIC SEA
LIGURIAN SEA
Gulf of Venice
BUDAPEST
Bratislava
WIEN
VIENNA
MÜNCHEN
MUNICH
Zagreb
Ljubljana
Sarajevo
Split
Dubrovnik
Trieste
Venezia
Venice
MILANO
MILAN
Torino
Turin
Genova
Genoa
Bologna
Firenze
Florence
Ancona
Pescara
Nice
Cannes
Bastia
CORSE
CORSICA
Livorno
Leghorn
Zürich
Basel
Bâle
Bern
Berne
Lausanne
Innsbruck
Salzburg
Graz
Linz
Rijeka
Verona
Padova
Trento
Bolzano
Parma
Modena
Rimini
Perugia
Siena
Pisa
ITALY
ITALIA
FRANCE

Map continues pages 32-33

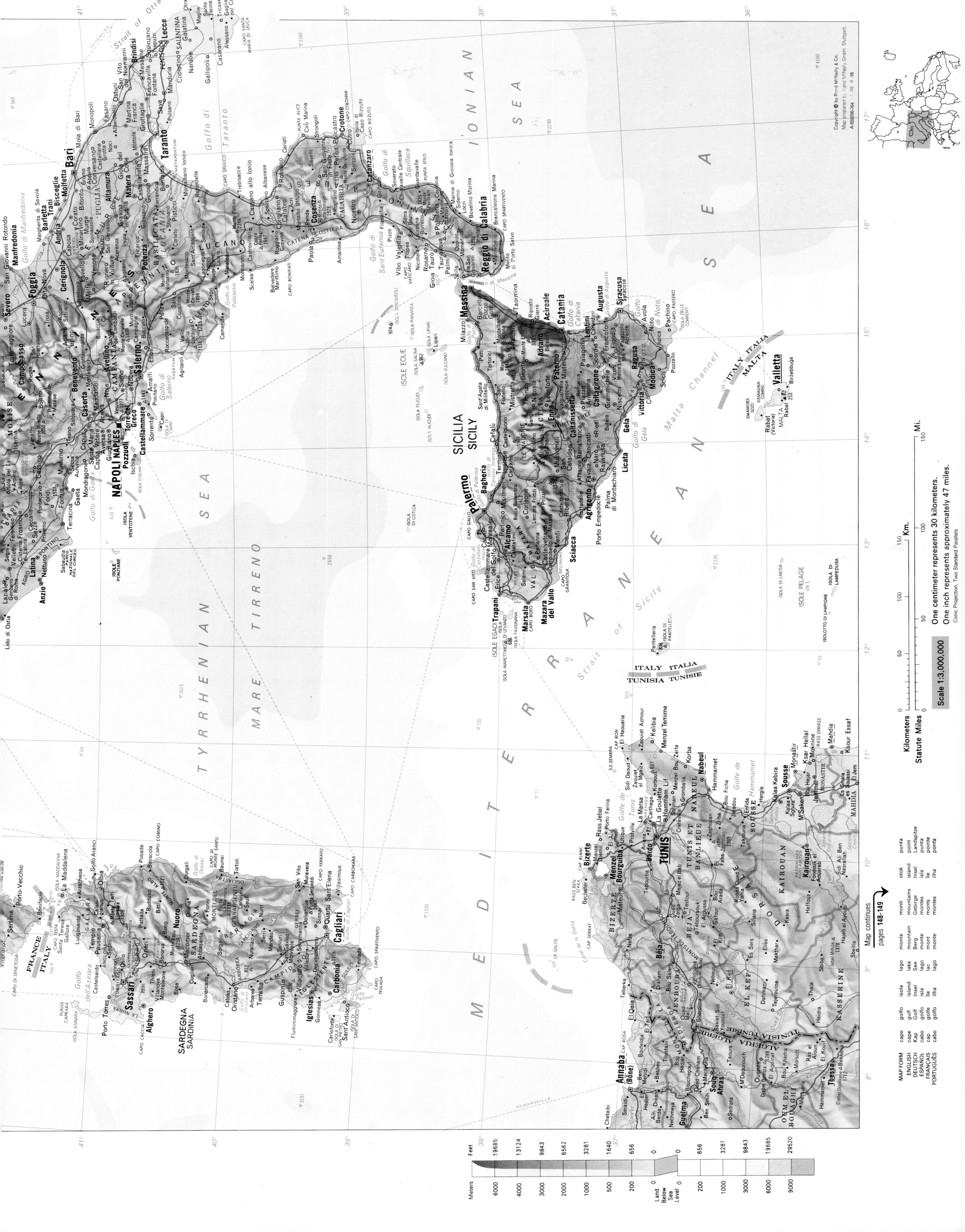
TYRRHENIAN SEA
MARE TIRRENO
IONIAN SEA
MEDITERRANEAN SEA
SICILIA
SICILY
SARDEGNA
SARDINIA
MALTA
Strait of Sicily
Malta Channel
Strait of Otranto
Golfo di Taranto
ITALY ITALIA
TUNISIA TUNISIE
FRANCE
ITALY
Palermo
Messina
Catania
Cagliari
Sassari
NAPOLI NAPLES
Bari
Taranto
Reggio di Calabria
TUNIS
Valletta
Scale 1:3,000,000
One centimeter represents 30 kilometers.
One inch represents approximately 47 miles.
Conic Projection, Two Standard Parallels
Kilometers
Statute Miles
Map continues pages 148-149
Copyright © by Rand McNally & Co.
Map prepared by Rand McNally GmbH, Stuttgart.
Feet
Meters
Land Below Sea Level
MAP FORM
ENGLISH
DEUTSCH
ESPAÑOL
FRANÇAIS
PORTUGUÊS

Map continues pages 78-79

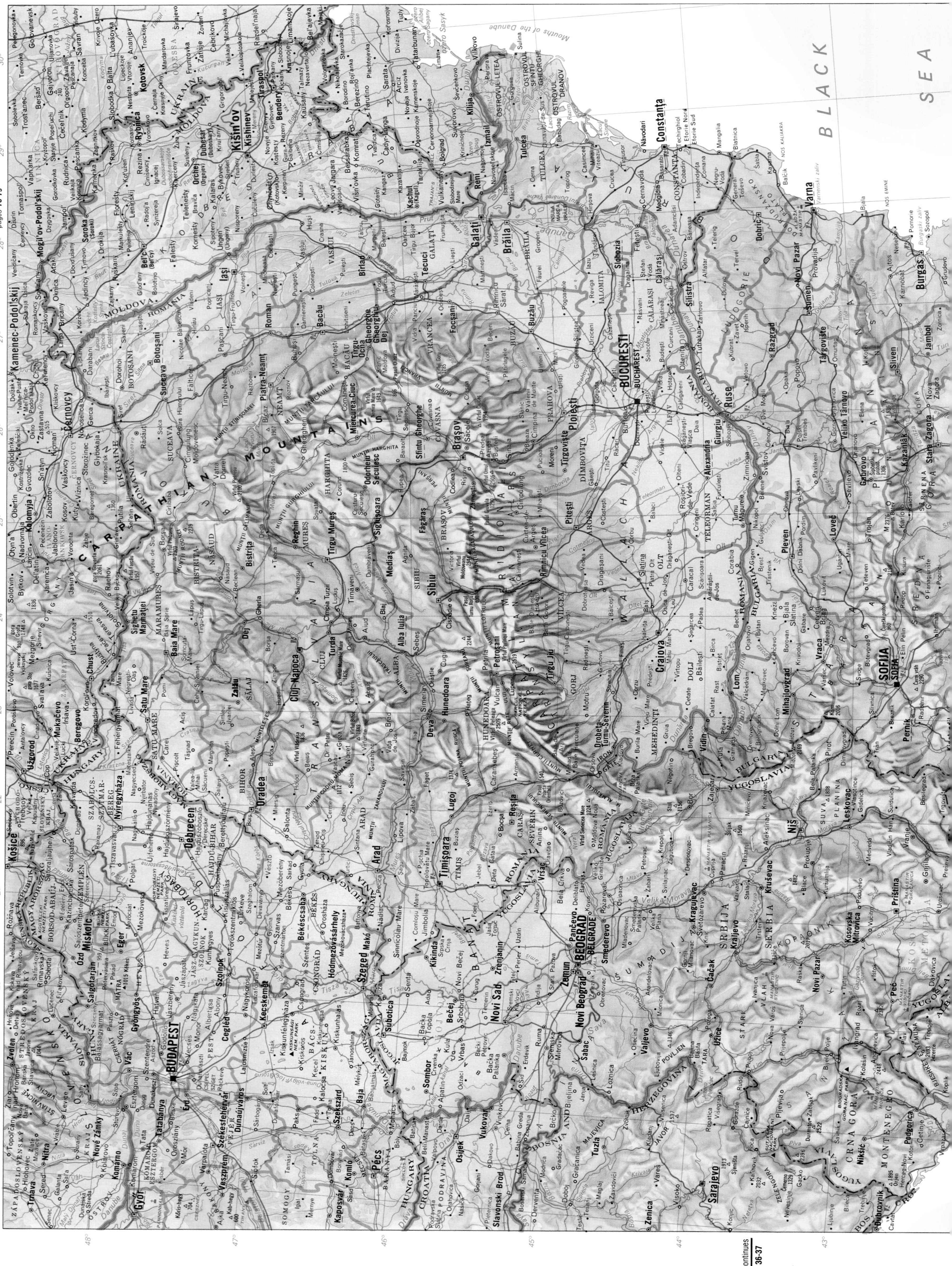
BLACK SEA
CARPATHIAN MOUNTAINS
BUCUREŞTI
BUDAPEST
BEOGRAD
SOFIJA

Kilometers 0 50 100 150 Km.
Statute Miles 0 50 100 150 Mi.

Scale 1:3,000,000

One centimeter represents 30 kilometers.
One inch represents approximately 47 miles.
Conic Projection, Two Standard Parallels

MAP FORM	ákra	kólpos	lacul	limni	manastir	munții	prohod	sea
ENGLISH	cape	bay	lake	lake	monastery	mountains	pass	sea
DEUTSCH	Kap	Bucht	See	See	Kloster	Berge	Pass	Meer
ESPAÑOL	cabo	bahía	lago	lago	monasterio	montañas	paso	mar
FRANÇAIS	cap	baie	lac	lac	monastère	montagnes	col	mer
PORTUGUÊS	cabo	baía	lago	lago	mosteiro	montanhas	passo	mar

Map continues pages 30-31

Map continues pages 36-37

Map continues pages 130-131

AEGEAN SEA
IONIAN SEA
MEDITERRANEAN SEA
ADRIATIC SEA
Strait of Otranto
IONIAN ISLANDS
KIKLÁDHES CYCLADES
D'HODHEKÁNISOS DODECANESE
KRÍTI CRETE
Sea of Crete
Sea of Marmara
ISTANBUL
Bursa
İzmir (Smyrna)
Thessaloníki Salonika
ATHÍNAI ATHENS
Piraiévs Piraeus
Pátrai
Lárisa
Vólos
Ioánnina
Kérkira
Tiranë
Durrës
Vlorë
Elbasan
Bitola
Prilep
Skopje
Edirne
Iráklion
Khaniá
Ródhos Rhodes
RÓDHOS RHODES
LÉSVOS LESBOS
KHÍOS CHOS
SÁMOS
LÍMNOS
THÁSOS
ÁYION ÓROS
PELOPÓNNISOS PELOPONNESUS
RHODOPE MOUNTAINS
TURKEY TÜRKİYE
GREECE ELLÁS
ITALY
Bandırma
Çanakkale
Balıkesir
Manisa
Kavála
Kateríni
Lamía
Kalámai
Kíthira
Otranto
Gallipoli del Capo

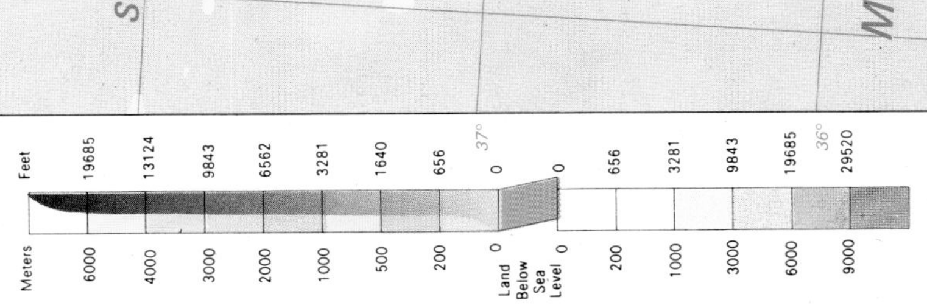
Feet
19685
13124
9843
6562
3281
1640
656
0
Meters
6000
4000
3000
2000
1000
500
200
0
Land Below Sea Level
0
200
1000
3000
6000
9000
0
656
3281
9843
19685
29520

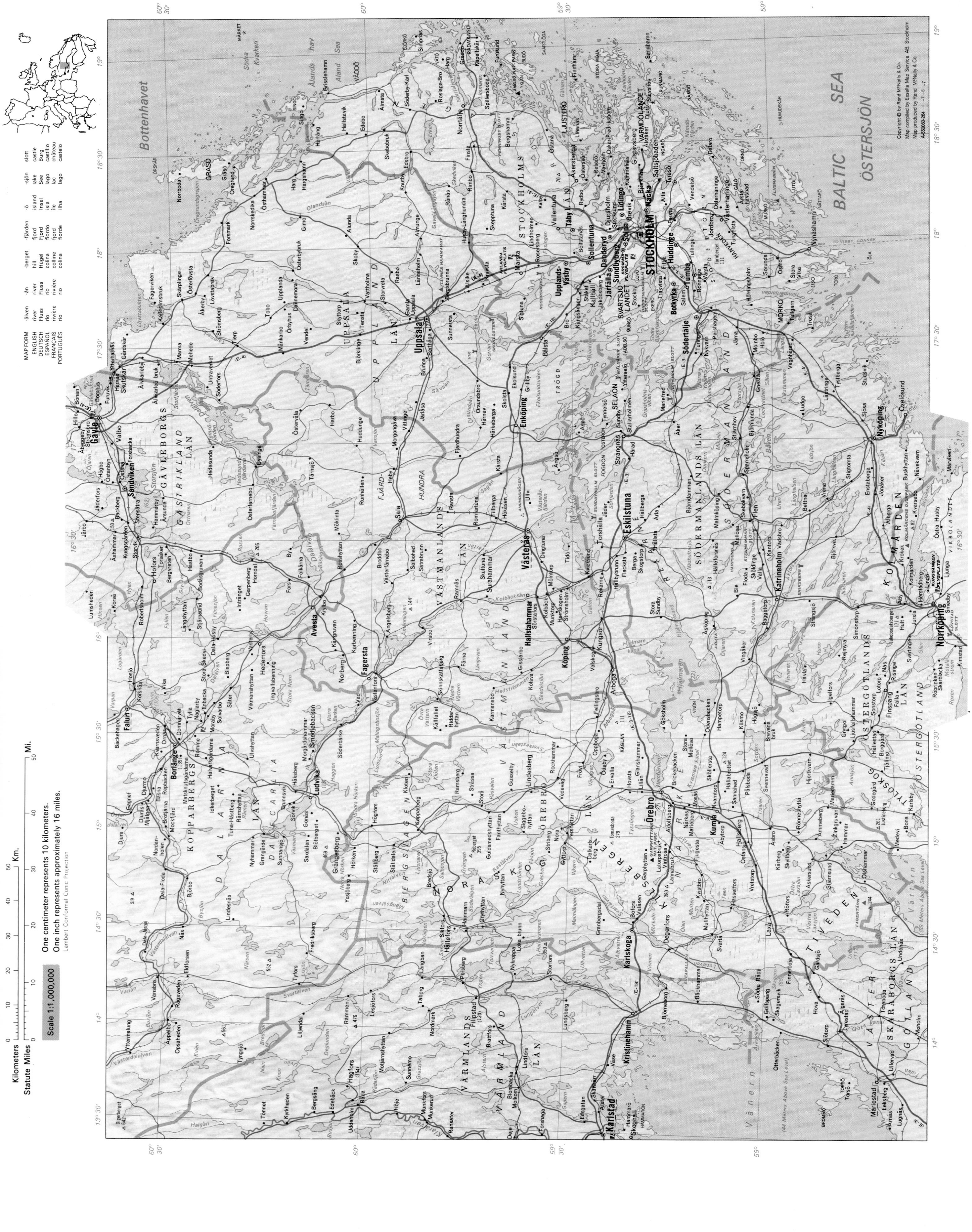

Kilometers 0 10 20 30 40 50 Km.
Statute Miles 0 10 20 30 40 50 Mi.
Scale 1:1,000,000
One centimeter represents 10 kilometers.
One inch represents approximately 16 miles.
Lambert Conformal Conic Projection
MAP FORM -älven -ån -berget -fjärden -ö -sjön slott
ENGLISH river river hill fjord island lake castle
DEUTSCH Fluss Fluss Hügel Fjord Insel See Burg
ESPAÑOL río río colina fiordo isla lago castillo
FRANÇAIS rivière rivière colline fjord île lac château
PORTUGUÊS rio rio colina fiorde ilha lago castelo
Bottenhavet
BALTIC SEA
ÖSTERSJÖN
STOCKHOLM
Uppsala
Gävle
Västerås
Eskilstuna
Örebro
Norrköping
Nyköping
Karlstad
Vänern
Copyright © by Rand McNally & Co.
Map compiled by Esselte Map Service AB, Stockholm.
Map produced by Rand McNally & Co.

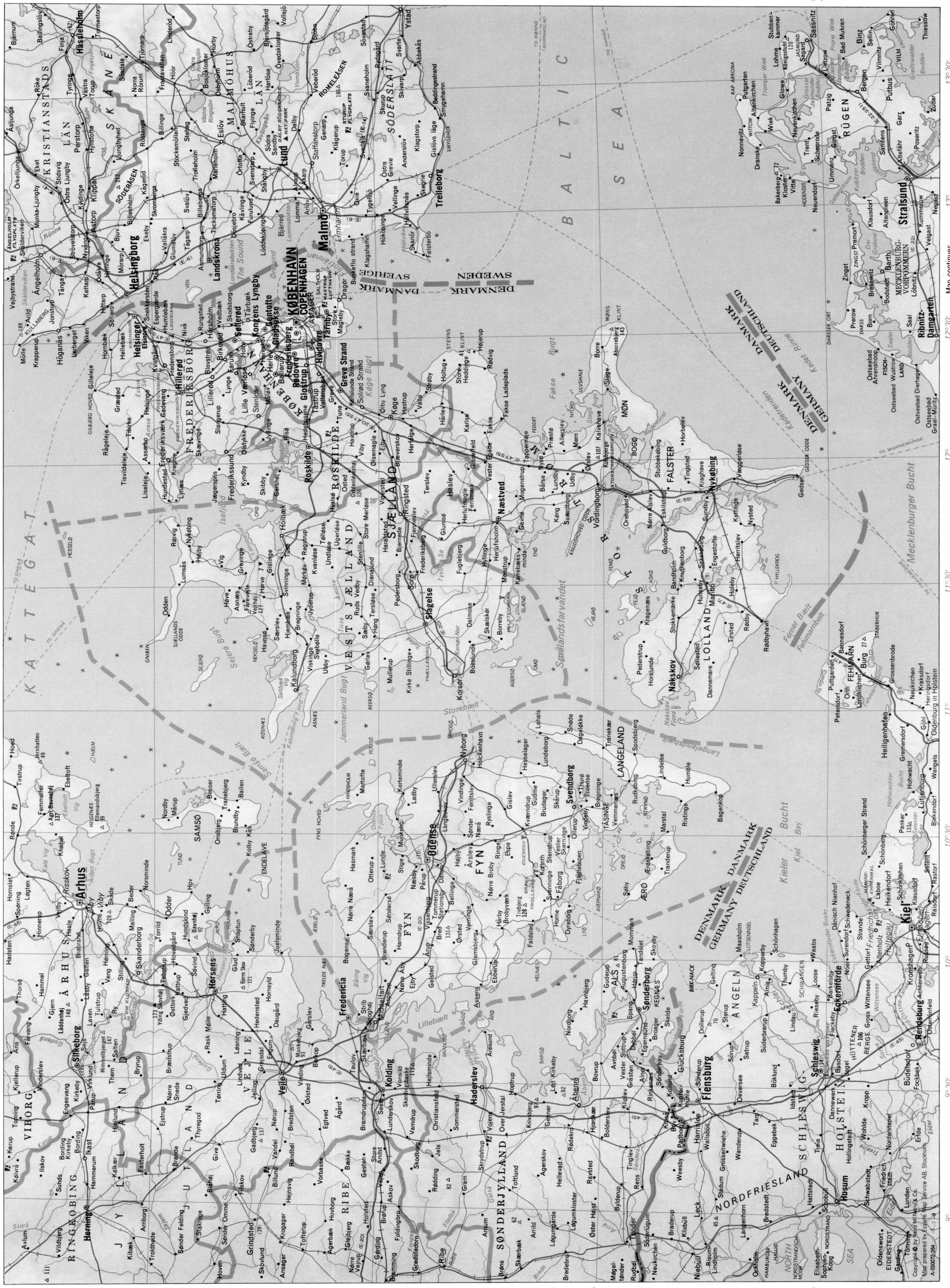
Map continues pages 54-55
Kilometers
Statute Miles
Scale 1:1,000,000
One centimeter represents 10 kilometers.
One inch represents approximately 16 miles.
Lambert Conformal Conic Projection
KATTEGAT
BALTIC SEA
DANMARK
SVERIGE
DEUTSCHLAND
GERMANY
SWEDEN
DENMARK
København
Malmö
Kiel

Map continues pages 48-49

Saint George's Channel
Cardigan Bay
Bristol Channel
Carmarthen Bay
Tremadog Bay
Lyme Bay
TORBAY
E N G
CAMBRIAN MOUNTAINS
SNOWDONIA NATIONAL PARK
PEMBROKESHIRE COAST NATIONAL PARK
BRECON BEACONS NATIONAL PARK
EXMOOR
DARTMOOR
BODMIN MOOR
Wrexham
Stoke-on-Trent
Shrewsbury
Wolverhampton
Worcester
Hereford
Gloucester
Aberystwyth
Cardigan
Carmarthen
Haverfordwest
Pembroke
Llanelli
Swansea
Neath
Port Talbot
Rhondda
Merthyr Tydfil
Pontypridd
Caerphilly
Newport
Cardiff
Penarth
Barry
Bristol
Bath
Weston-super-Mare
Bridgwater
Taunton
Yeovil
Barnstaple
Bideford
Exeter
Torquay
Plymouth
Newquay
Truro
Falmouth
Penzance
Weymouth
Dorchester
a
ISLES OF SCILLY
ATLANTIC OCEAN

ENGLISH	bay	drain	forest	head	hill	isle	marsh	point	vale
DEUTSCH	Bucht	Abzugsgraben	Wald	Landspitze	Hügel	Insel	Marsch	Landspitze	Tal
ESPAÑOL	bahía	acquia	bosque	promontorio	colina	isla	pantano	punta	valle
FRANÇAIS	baie	drainage	forêt	promontoire	colline	île	marais	pointe	dépression
PORTUGUÊS	baía	drenagem	floresta	promontório	colina	ilha	pântano	ponta	vale

Map continues pages 44-45

NORTH SEA
The Wash
Nottingham
Derby
Leicester
Coventry
Northampton
Peterborough
Cambridge
Norwich
Great Yarmouth
Lowestoft
Ipswich
Colchester
Chelmsford
Bedford
Luton
Oxford
Reading
LONDON
Southend-on-Sea
Margate
Canterbury
Maidstone
Dover
Folkestone
Hastings
Eastbourne
Brighton
Worthing
Portsmouth
Southampton
Winchester
Salisbury
Bournemouth
Swindon
ISLE OF WIGHT
CHANNEL
Strait of Dover
GUERNSEY (U.K.)
St. Peter Port
JERSEY (U.K.)
St. Helier
CHANNEL ISLANDS

Map continues pages 50-51

Kilometers 0 10 20 30 40 50 Km.

Statute Miles 0 10 20 30 40 50 Mi.

Scale 1:1,000,000

One centimeter represents 10 kilometers.
One inch represents approximately 16 miles.

Lambert Conformal Conic Projection

Map continues pages 46-47

North Channel
SCOTLAND
NORTHERN IRELAND
IRISH SEA
IRELAND ÉIRE
UNITED KINGDOM
ISLE OF MAN (U.K.)
Belfast
Newtownabbey
Bangor
Larne
Ballymena
Coleraine
Londonderry Derry
Lisburn
Lurgan
Portadown
Armagh
Newry
Dundalk Dún Dealgan
Drogheda Droichead Átha
DUBLIN BAILE ÁTHA CLIATH
Dún Laoghaire
Bray
Wicklow
Arklow
Douglas
Ayr
Kilmarnock
Irvine
Stranraer
Dumfries
Workington
Whitehaven
Barrow-in-F
Holyhead
Bangor
Caernarfon
Llandudno
Colwyn Bay
Rhyl
ANGLESEY
Caernarfon Bay
Luce Bay
Solway Firth
Dundalk Bay
MOURNE MTS.
WICKLOW MOUNTAINS
Lough Neagh
Lough Foyle
DONEGAL
MONAGHAN
CAVAN
LOUTH
MEATH
KILDARE
DUBLIN
WICKLOW
CARLOW
WEXFORD
GALLOWAY
CARRICK
STRATHCLYDE
ISLAND OF ARRAN
KINTYRE
SNOWDONIA NATIONAL PARK
LLEYN PENINSULA
Copyright © by Rand McNally & Co.
Map prepared by Rand McNally & Co.
A-556600-264

Map continues pages 48-49

MAP FORM	bay	dale	firth	forest	head	loch	moor	water
ENGLISH	bay	dale	estuary	forest	head	lake; inlet	moor	water (lake, river)
DEUTSCH	Bucht	Weites Tal	Trichtermündung	Wald	Landspitze	See; Einfahrt	Moor	See, Fluss
ESPAÑOL	bahía	valle	estuario	bosque	promontorio	lago; abra	páramo	lago, río
FRANÇAIS	baie	vallée	estuaire	forêt	promontoire	lac; bras de mer	lande	lac, rivière
PORTUGUÊS	baía	vale	estuário	floresta	promontório	lago; enseada	pântano	lago, rio

NORTH SEA
NEWCASTLE UPON TYNE
Gateshead
South Shields
Sunderland
Carlisle
Durham
Hartlepool
Middlesbrough
Stockton-on-Tees
Darlington
Whitby
Scarborough
Bridlington
York
Harrogate
Lancaster
Kendal
Penrith
Berwick-upon-Tweed
Hawick
Selkirk
Galashiels
Alnwick
Morpeth
Blyth
NORTHUMBERLAND NATIONAL PARK
CHEVIOT HILLS
NORTH YORK MOORS
NORTH YORK MOORS NATIONAL PARK
VALE OF PICKERING
YORKSHIRE DALES NATIONAL PARK
LAKE DISTRICT NATIONAL PARK
FLAMBOROUGH HEAD
Kingston upon Hull
Grimsby
Cleethorpes
Scunthorpe
Doncaster
LEEDS
Bradford
Halifax
Huddersfield
Wakefield
Dewsbury
Barnsley
Sheffield
Rotherham
Chesterfield
Mansfield
Nottingham
Derby
Lincoln
Gainsborough
Newark-on-Trent
Grantham
Boston
Skegness
Spalding
King's Lynn
The Wash
Preston
Blackburn
Burnley
Blackpool
Bolton
Wigan
Rochdale
Oldham
MANCHESTER
Salford
Stockport
LIVERPOOL
St. Helens
Warrington
Widnes
Chester
Crewe
Stoke-on-Trent
Macclesfield
Stafford
Burton upon Trent
Loughborough
Melton Mowbray
Wrexham
Whitchurch
Spurn Head
Humber
TO BERGEN, ÅLESUND, MÅLØY, MOLDE
TO STAVANGER
TO GÖTEBORG, KRISTIANSAND
TO ESBJERG
TO ROTTERDAM, ZEEBRUGGE

Map continues pages 42-43

Kilometers 0 10 20 30 40 50 Km.

Statute Miles 0 10 20 30 40 50 Mi.

Scale 1:1,000,000

One centimeter represents 10 kilometers.

One inch represents approximately 16 miles.

Lambert Conformal Conic Projection

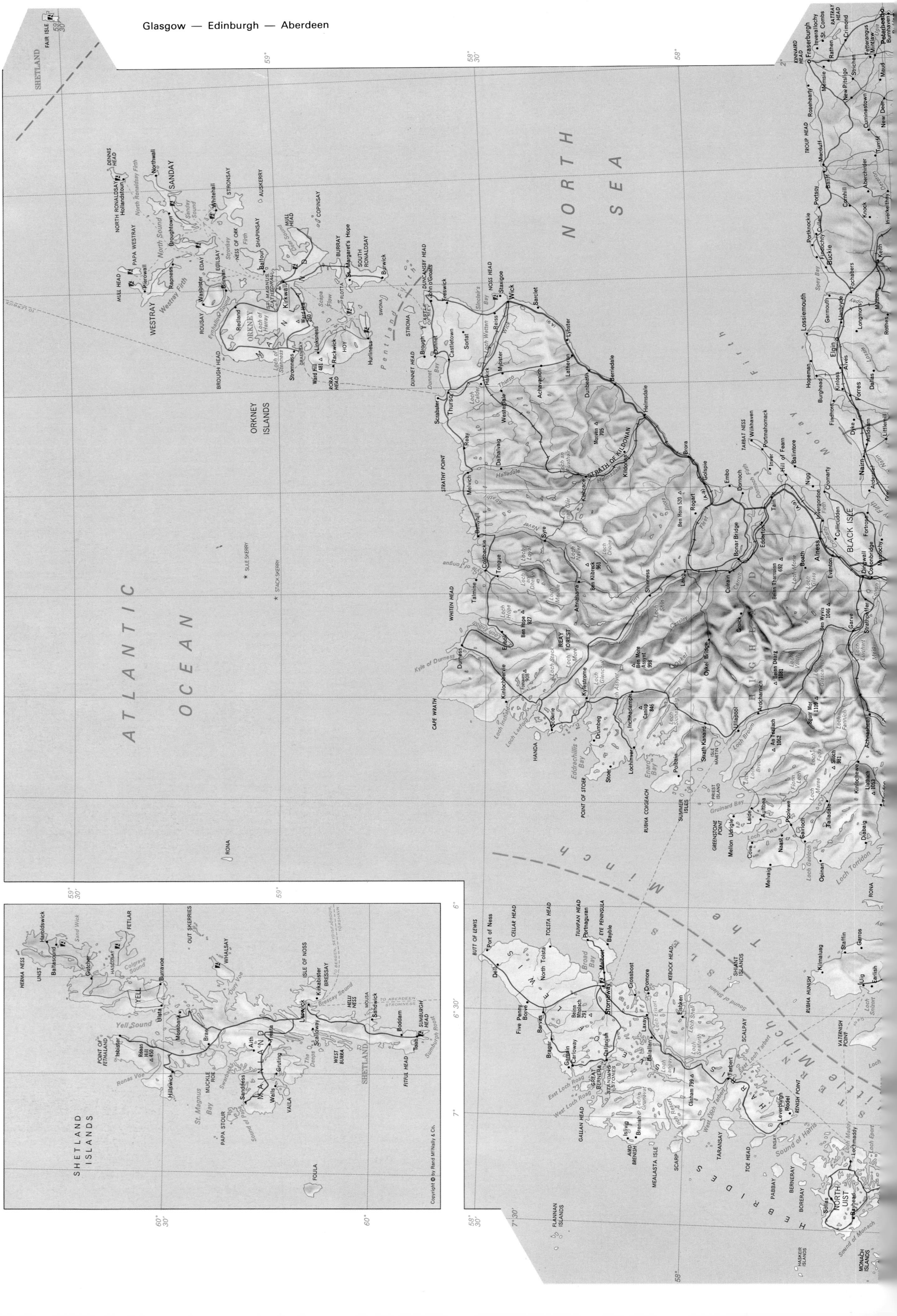
ATLANTIC OCEAN
NORTH SEA
ORKNEY ISLANDS
SHETLAND ISLANDS
SHETLAND
FAIR ISLE
WESTRAY
PAPA WESTRAY
NORTH RONALDSAY
SANDAY
STRONSAY
EDAY
ROUSAY
SHAPINSAY
COPINSAY
AUSKERRY
HOY
FLOTTA
BURRAY
SOUTH RONALDSAY
SWONA
STROMA
Kirkwall
Stromness
St. Margaret's Hope
Pentland Firth
Thurso
Wick
John o'Groats
DUNNET HEAD
DUNCANSBY HEAD
CAPE WRATH
Durness
Tongue
Helmsdale
Brora
Golspie
Dornoch
Tain
Invergordon
Dingwall
BLACK ISLE
Nairn
Forres
Elgin
Lossiemouth
Buckie
Banff
Fraserburgh
Peterhead
Moray Firth
Ullapool
Lochinver
Kylestrome
Scourie
Kinlochbervie
Lairg
Bonar Bridge
Gairloch
Poolewe
Loch Torridon
The Minch
The Little Minch
OUTER HEBRIDES
LEWIS
HARRIS
Stornoway
Tarbert
Leverburgh
BUTT OF LEWIS
Port of Ness
NORTH UIST
Lochmaddy
Sound of Harris
FLANNAN ISLANDS
SHIANT ISLANDS
SCALPAY
Uig
Staffin
UNST
YELL
FETLAR
WHALSAY
BRESSAY
MAINLAND
Lerwick
Scalloway
Sandwick
Baltasound
Yell Sound
St. Magnus Bay
PAPA STOUR
FOULA
FITFUL HEAD
SUMBURGH HEAD
FAIR ISLE
SULE SKERRY
STACK SKERRY
RONA
Copyright © by Rand McNally & Co.

NORTH SEA
OUTER HEBRIDES
INNER HEBRIDES
Sea of the Hebrides
SKYE
LOCHABER
BADENOCH
RAMPIAN
FOREST OF ATHOLL
STRATHMORE
SIDLAW HILLS
OCHIL HILLS
FIFE
LENNOX
CENTRAL
COWAL
KNAPDALE
KINTYRE
CUNNINGHAME
STRATHCLYDE
TWEEDDALE
BORDERS
LAMMERMUIR
LAUDERDALE
TEVIOTDALE
CHEVIOT HILLS
SCOTLAND
ENGLAND
NORTHUMBERLAND NATIONAL PARK
DUMFRIES AND GALLOWAY
JURA
ISLAY
ISLAND OF MULL
ISLAND OF ARRAN
IRELAND
Aberdeen
Dundee
Perth
Stirling
Glasgow
Edinburgh
Kirkcaldy
Dunfermline
Fort William
Oban
Inverness
Ayr
Greenock
Motherwell
Hamilton
Kilmarnock
Berwick-upon-Tweed
Campbeltown
Montrose
Arbroath
Stonehaven
St. Andrews
Copyright © by Rand McNally & Co.
Map prepared by Rand McNally & Co.
A-553500-264 -7 -7 -9
Map continues pages 48-49
Map continues pages 44-45

MAP FORM	bay	ben, beinn	firth	head	loch	sound	water
ENGLISH	bay	mountain	estuary	head	lake; inlet	sound	water (river)
DEUTSCH	Bucht	Berg	Trichtermündung	Landspitze	See; Einfahrt	Sund	Fluss
ESPAÑOL	bahía	montaña	estuario	promontorio	lago; abra	canal	río
FRANÇAIS	baie	montagne	estuaire	promontoire	lac; bras de mer	détroit	rivière
PORTUGUÊS	baía	montanha	estário	promontório	lago; enseada	canal	rio

Kilometers 0 10 20 30 40 50 Km.

Statute Miles 0 10 20 30 40 50 Mi.

Scale 1:1,000,000

One centimeter represents 10 kilometers.

One inch represents approximately 16 miles.

Lambert Conformal Conic Projection

Map continues pages 46-47

Map continues pages 44-45

SCOTLAND
NORTHERN IRELAND
North Channel
ATLANTIC
OCEAN
IRISH SEA
Belfast
Londonderry
Derry
Coleraine
Ballymena
Larne
Bangor
Newtownards
Lisburn
Lurgan
Portadown
Armagh
Newry
Dundalk
Dún Dealgan
Drogheda
Droichead Átha
Navan
Omagh
Strabane
Enniskillen
Donegal
Sligo
Sligeach
Ballina
Castlebar
Westport
Newport
Cavan
Monaghan
Longford
Roscommon
Campbeltown
ULSTER
DONEGAL
SPERRIN MTS.
MOURNE MTS.
BLUE STACK MTS.
DERRYVEAGH MTS.
NEPHIN BEG RANGE
SLIEVE GAMPH
Lough Neagh
Lough Foyle
Lough Swilly
Donegal Bay
Clew Bay
ACHILL ISLAND
CLARE ISLAND
INISHOWEN
MONAGHAN
CAVAN
LOUTH
MEATH
LEITRIM
LONGFORD
ROSCOMMON
SLIGO
MAYO
CONNAUGHT
U.K.
IRELAND
EIRE
55°30'
55°
54°30'
54°
6°
6°30'
7°
7°30'
8°
8°30'
9°
9°30'
10°
10°30'

Map continues pages 42-43

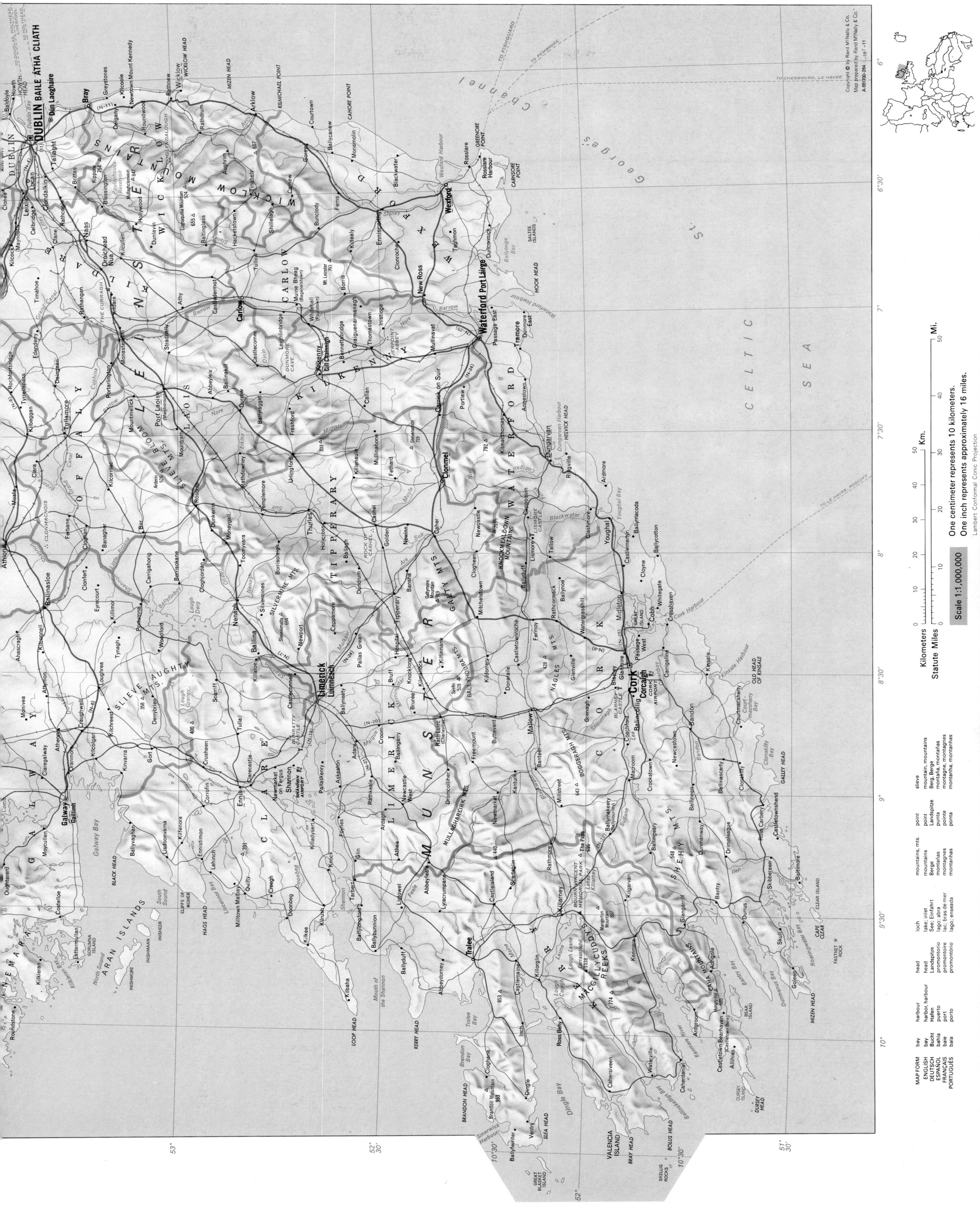
DUBLIN BAILE ÁTHA CLIATH
Belfast
Cork Corcaigh
Limerick Luimneach
Waterford Port Láirge
Galway Gaillimh
Kilkenny Cill Chainnigh
Wexford
Wicklow
Arklow
Carlow
Clonmel
Tralee
Killarney
Shannon
Athlone
Dungarvan
Youghal
Mallow
Bray
Dún Laoghaire
LEINSTER
MUNSTER
WICKLOW MOUNTAINS
KNOCKMEALDOWN MOUNTAINS
GALTY MTS.
SLIEVE BLOOM
SILVERMINE MTS.
BOGGERAGH MTS.
NAGLES MTS.
SHEHY MTS.
CAHA MOUNTAINS
MACGILLYCUDDY'S REEKS
MULLAGHAREIRK MTS.
SLIEVE AUGHTY MTS.
ARAN ISLANDS
VALENCIA ISLAND
GREAT BLASKET ISLAND
CAPE CLEAR
FASTNET ROCK
OLD HEAD OF KINSALE
St. George's Channel
CELTIC SEA
Galway Bay
Dingle Bay
Bantry Bay
Cork Harbour
Waterford Harbour
Wexford Harbour
TO FISHGUARD
TO PEMBROKE
TO CHERBOURG, LE HAVRE
TO LE HAVRE, ROSCOFF
TO HOLYHEAD
53°
52° 30'
52°
51° 30'
6°
6°30'
7°
7°30'
8°
8°30'
9°
9°30'
10°
10°30'
Copyright © by Rand McNally & Co.
Map prepared by Rand McNally & Co.
A-557000-264 -1-7-11
Scale 1:1,000,000
Kilometers
Statute Miles
One centimeter represents 10 kilometers.
One inch represents approximately 16 miles.
Lambert Conformal Conic Projection
MAPFORM | bay | harbour | head | loch | mountains, mts. | point | slieve
ENGLISH | bay | harbor, harbour | head | lake; inlet | mountains | point | mountain, mountains
DEUTSCH | Bucht | Hafen | Landspitze | See; Einfahrt | Berge | Landspitze | Berg, Berge
ESPAÑOL | bahía | puerto | promontorio | lago; abra | montañas | punta | montaña, montañas
FRANÇAIS | baie | port | promontoire | lac; bras de mer | montagnes | pointe | montagne, montagnes
PORTUGUÊS | baía | porto | promontório | lago; enseada | montanhas | ponta | montanha, montanhas

Map continues pages 56-57

Map continues pages 52-53

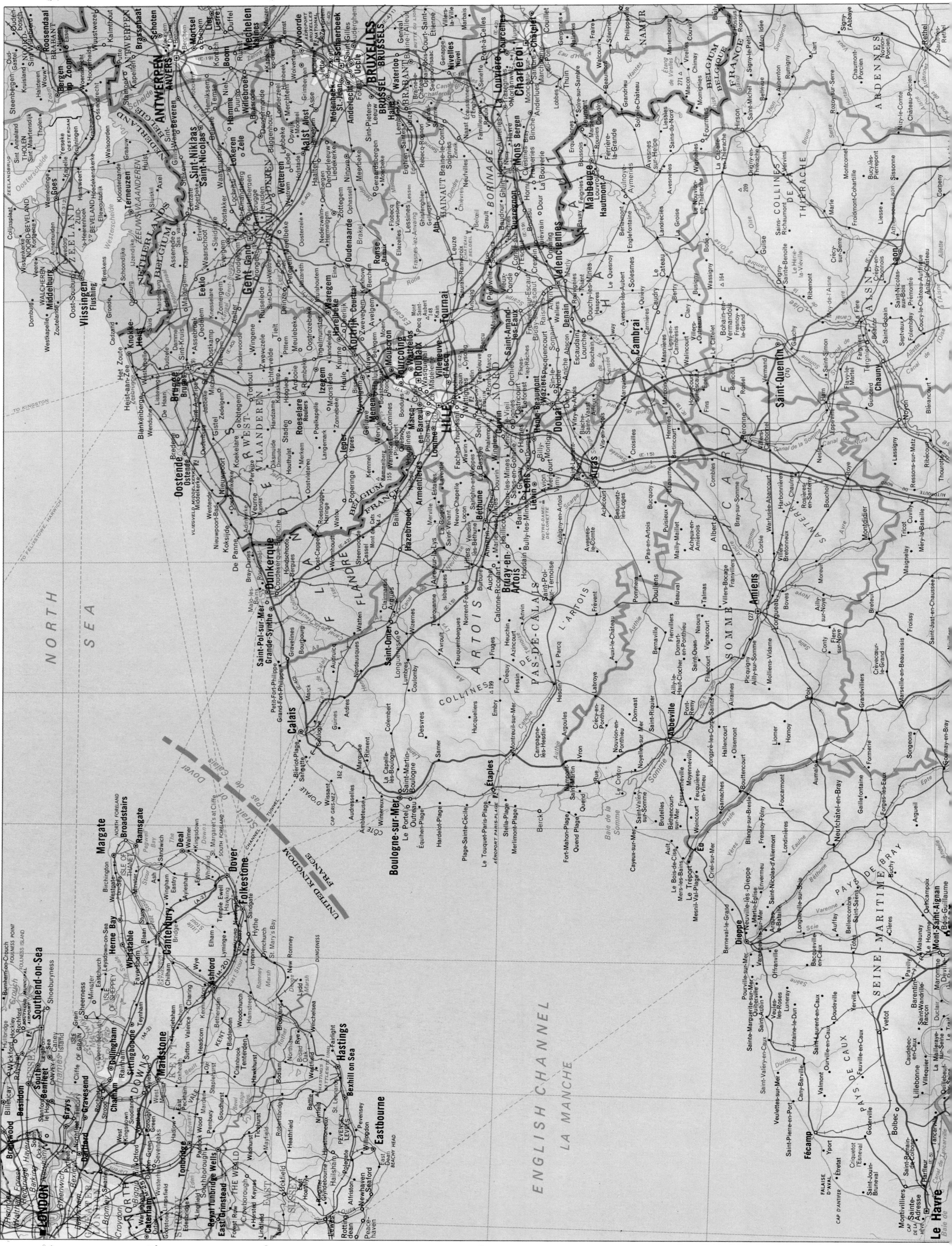
NORTH SEA
ENGLISH CHANNEL
LA MANCHE
Strait of Dover
Pas de Calais
UNITED KINGDOM
FRANCE
BELGIUM
NEDERLAND
LONDON
Dover
Folkestone
Canterbury
Margate
Ramsgate
Hastings
Eastbourne
Maidstone
Calais
Boulogne-sur-Mer
Dunkerque
Oostende
Brugge
Gent
Antwerpen
Bruxelles
Lille
Amiens
Abbeville
Dieppe
Le Havre
Fécamp
Saint-Quentin
Cambrai
Arras
Valenciennes
Charleroi
Mons
Tournai
Kortrijk
Vlissingen
Laon
ARDENNES
SEINE-MARITIME
SOMME
PAS-DE-CALAIS
NORD
ARTOIS
PICARDIE
FLANDRE

Map continues pages 42-43

Map continues pages 58-59

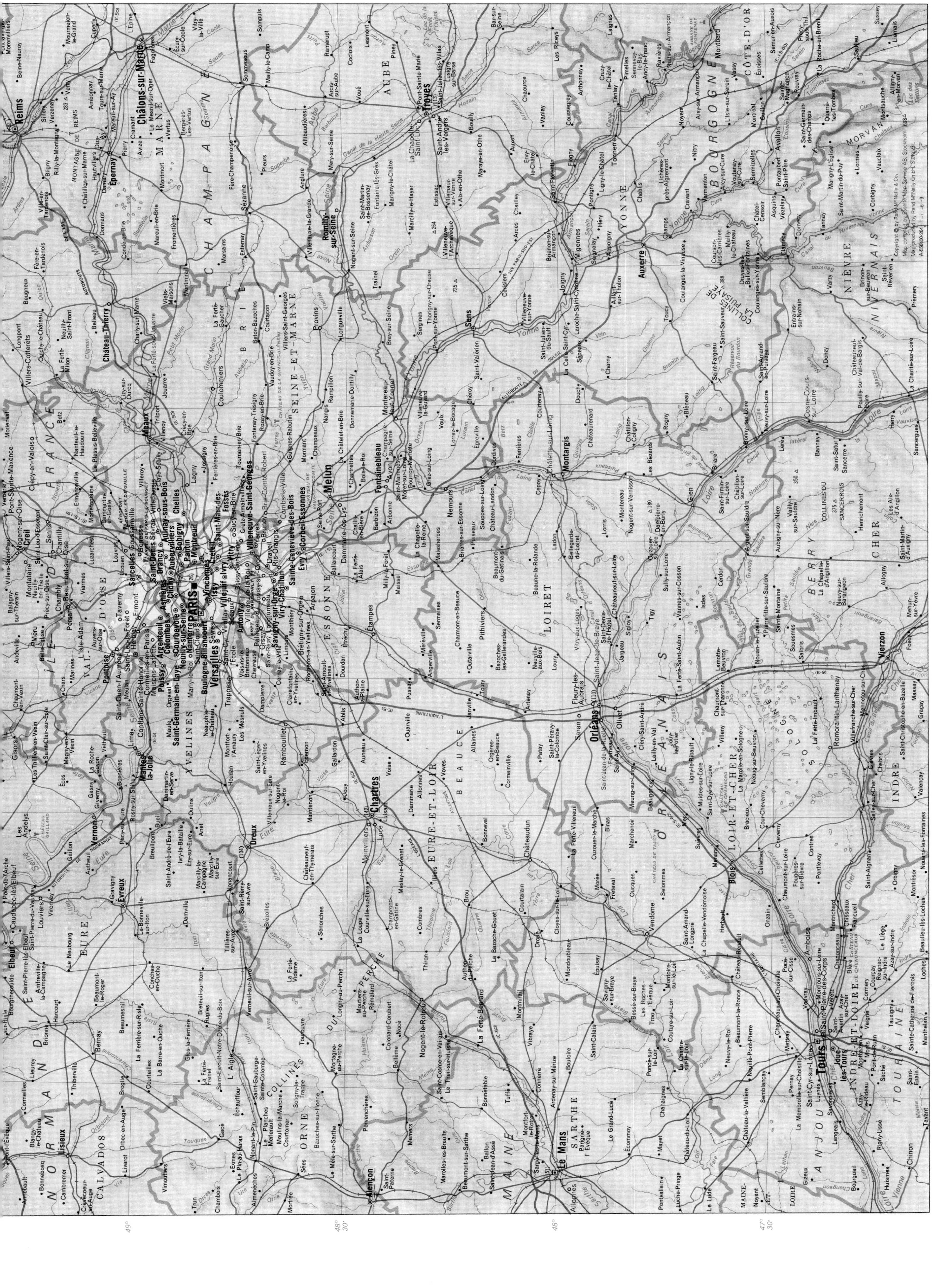
PARIS
Reims
Châlons-sur-Marne
Troyes
Auxerre
Sens
Melun
Fontainebleau
Montargis
Orléans
Chartres
Évreux
Dreux
Le Mans
Alençon
Tours
Blois
Vierzon
Versailles
Meaux
Château-Thierry
Épernay
Lisieux
CHAMPAGNE
BRIE
BEAUCE
SOLOGNE
BERRY
TOURAINE
MAINE
NORMANDIE
BOURGOGNE
MORVAN
ÎLE-DE-FRANCE
LOIRET
YONNE
AUBE
MARNE
ESSONNE
YVELINES
SEINE-ET-MARNE
EURE-ET-LOIR
LOIR-ET-CHER
INDRE-ET-LOIRE
SARTHE
ORNE
CALVADOS
EURE
CHER
INDRE
NIÈVRE
CÔTE-D'OR
Loire
Seine

FRANÇAIS aéroport canal cap château collines réservoir, rés.
ENGLISH airport canal cape castle hills reservoir
DEUTSCH Flughafen Kanal Kap Burg Hügel Stausee
ESPAÑOL aeropuerto canal cabo castillo colinas embalse
PORTUGUÊS aeroporto canal cabo castelo colinas reservatório

Kilometers 0 10 20 30 40 50 Km.
Statute Miles 0 10 20 30 40 50 Mi.

Scale 1:1,000,000
One centimeter represents 10 kilometers.
One inch represents approximately 16 miles.
Lambert Conformal Conic Projection

NORTH SEA
FRISIAN
WADDENEILANDEN
Waddenzee
IJsselmeer (Zuiderzee)
Markermeer
GERMANY
NETHERLANDS
NEDERLAND
BELGIUM
BELGIE
DEUTSCHLAND
TEXEL
VLIELAND
TERSCHELLING
AMELAND
SCHIERMONNIKOOG
FRIESLAND
GRONINGEN
DRENTHE
OVERIJSSEL
GELDERLAND
FLEVOLAND
NOORD-HOLLAND
ZUID-HOLLAND
UTRECHT
ZEELAND
NOORD-BRABANT
LIMBURG
ANTWERPEN
FLANDERS
Den Helder
Alkmaar
IJmuiden
Haarlem
AMSTERDAM
Hilversum
Utrecht
Amersfoort
Leiden
's-Gravenhage
The Hague
Delft
ROTTERDAM
Gouda
Dordrecht
Breda
Tilburg
's-Hertogenbosch
Eindhoven
Helmond
Venlo
Nijmegen
Arnhem
Apeldoorn
Deventer
Zwolle
Lelystad
Leeuwarden
Groningen
Assen
Meppel
Hoogeveen
Almelo
Hengelo
Enschede
Emmen
Harlingen
Sneek
Heerenveen
Drachten
Vlissingen
Flushing
Middelburg
Bergen op Zoom
Roosendaal
Terneuzen
ANTWERPEN
ANVERS
Gent
Gand
Sint Niklaas
Mechelen
Malines
Turnhout
Lokeren
Mönchen-gladbach
Krefeld
Duisburg
Neuss
Viersen
Kleve
Emmerich
Wesel
Roermond
Weert
Mol
Herentals
Geel
Oss
Harderwijk
Ede
Zutphen
Doetinchem
Veenendaal
Culemborg
Tiel
Gorinchem
Schiedam
Vlaardingen
Maassluis
Zaanstad
Purmerend
Hoorn
Enkhuizen
Bergen
Castricum
Heemskerk
Beverwijk
Zandvoort
Noordwijk aan Zee
Katwijk aan Zee
Wassenaar
Hoek van Holland
Spijkenisse
Hellevoetsluis
Zierikzee
Goes
Kampen
Urk
Emmeloord
Wolvega
Steenwijk
Bussum
Huizen
Soest
Zeist
Nieuwegein
Woerden
Alphen aan den Rijn
Zoetermeer
Rijswijk
Voorburg
Capelle
Waalwijk
Oosterhout
Veldhoven
Geldrop
Boxtel
Valkenswaard
Lommel
Schoten
Brasschaat
Zele
Hamme
Temse
Eeklo
Ruiselede
TO HARWICH
TO HARWICH, KINGSTON

DEUTSCH	Gebirge	Kanal	Moor	Naturpark	Stausee	Talsperre	Wald
ENGLISH	range	canal	moor	reserve	reservoir	dam	forest, mountains
ESPAÑOL	sierra	canal	páramo	reserva	embalse	presa	bosque, montañas
FRANÇAIS	chaîne	canal	lande	réserve	réservoir	barrage	forêt, montagnes
PORTUGUÊS	serra	canal	pântano	reserva natural	reservatório	represa	floresta, montanhas

Map continues pages 50-51

Map continues pages 56-57

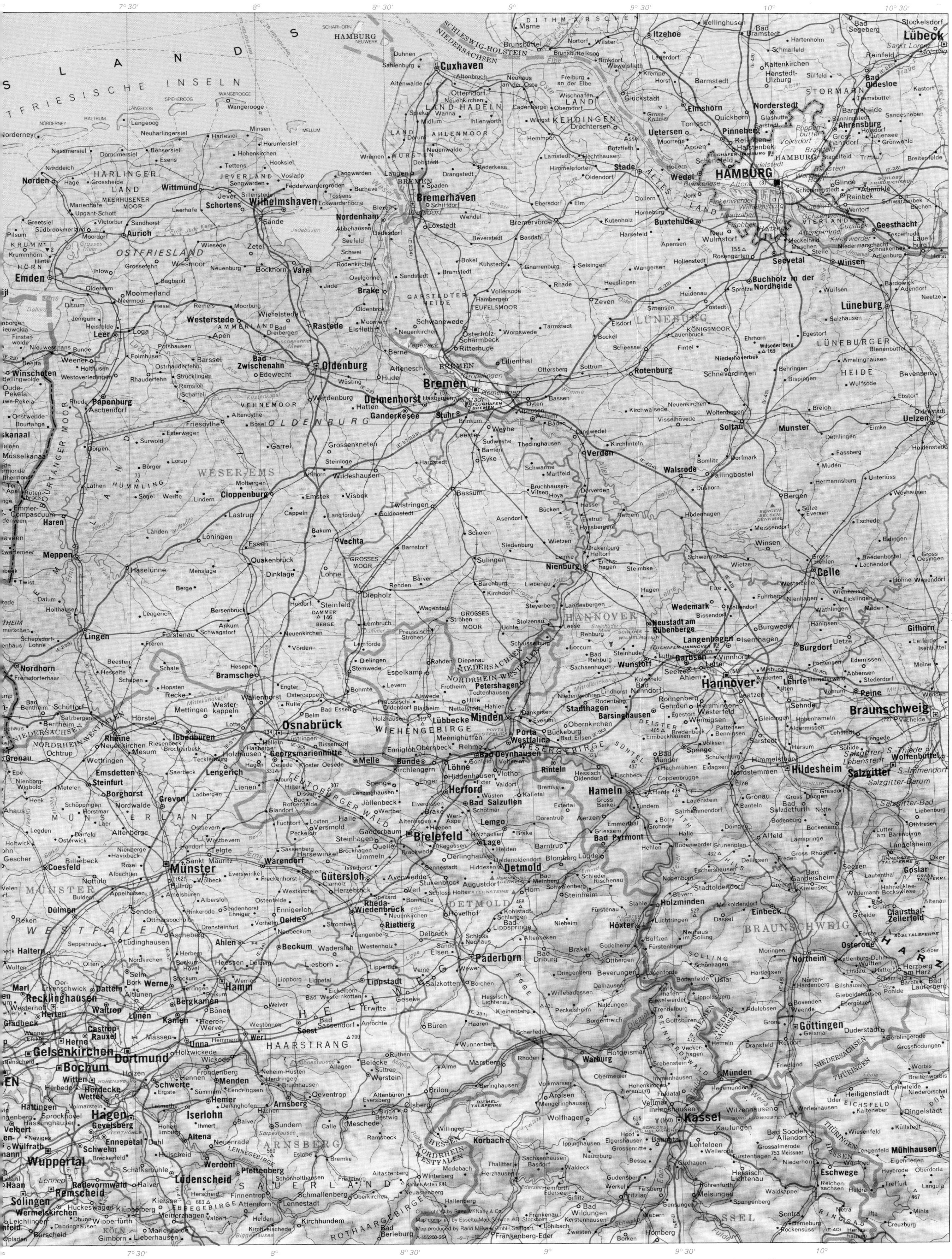
7° 30'
8°
8° 30'
9°
9° 30'
10°
10° 30'
Hamburg
Lübeck
Cuxhaven
Bremerhaven
Wilhelmshaven
Emden
Oldenburg
Bremen
Delmenhorst
Lüneburg
Celle
Hannover
Braunschweig
Hildesheim
Salzgitter
Osnabrück
Bielefeld
Detmold
Paderborn
Münster
Hamm
Dortmund
Bochum
Gelsenkirchen
Recklinghausen
Hagen
Wuppertal
Remscheid
Solingen
Lüdenscheid
Iserlohn
Göttingen
Kassel
Hameln
Minden
Herford
Gütersloh
Lingen
Meppen
Nordhorn
Rheine
Celle
Uelzen
Soltau
Verden
Nienburg
Cloppenburg
Vechta
Stade
Norderstedt
Pinneberg
Elmshorn
Itzehoe
Bad Oldesloe
Geesthacht
Buxtehude
Osterode
Northeim
Einbeck
Höxter
Holzminden
Warburg
Korbach
Eschwege
Mühlhausen
Heiligenstadt
Goslar
Wolfenbüttel
Peine
Burgdorf
Lehrte
Gifhorn
OSTFRIESISCHE INSELN
OSTFRIESLAND
LÜNEBURGER HEIDE
HARZ
SOLLING
SAUERLAND
ROTHAARGEBIRGE
TEUTOBURGER WALD
WIEHENGEBIRGE
HAARSTRANG
WESTFALEN
NIEDERSACHSEN
NORDRHEIN-WESTFALEN
HESSEN
THÜRINGEN
SCHLESWIG-HOLSTEIN
Copyright © by Rand McNally & Co.
Map compiled by Esselte Map Service AB, Stockholm
Map produced by Rand McNally GmbH, Stuttgart
7° 30'
8°
8° 30'
9° 30'
10°

Map continues pages 54-55

Kilometers 0 10 20 30 40 50 Km.
Statute Miles 0 10 20 30 40 50 Mi.

Scale 1:1,000,000

One centimeter represents 10 kilometers.
One inch represents approximately 16 miles.
Lambert Conformal Conic Projection

BALTIC SEA
Pomeranian Bay
Mecklenburger Bucht
Kieler Bucht
POMMERN
MECKLENBURG
MECKLENBURGISCHE SEENPLATTE
UCKERMARK
BARNIM
HAVELLAND
PRIGNITZ
ALTMARK
WENDLAND
RÜGEN
FEHMARN
POLSKA
DEUTSCHLAND
POLAND
GERMANY
BERLIN
HAMBURG
Szczecin (Stettin)
Rostock
Stralsund
Greifswald
Wismar
Schwerin
Lübeck
Kiel
Neubrandenburg
Potsdam
Lüneburg
Wittenberge
Stendal

Map continues page 41

Map continues pages 52-53

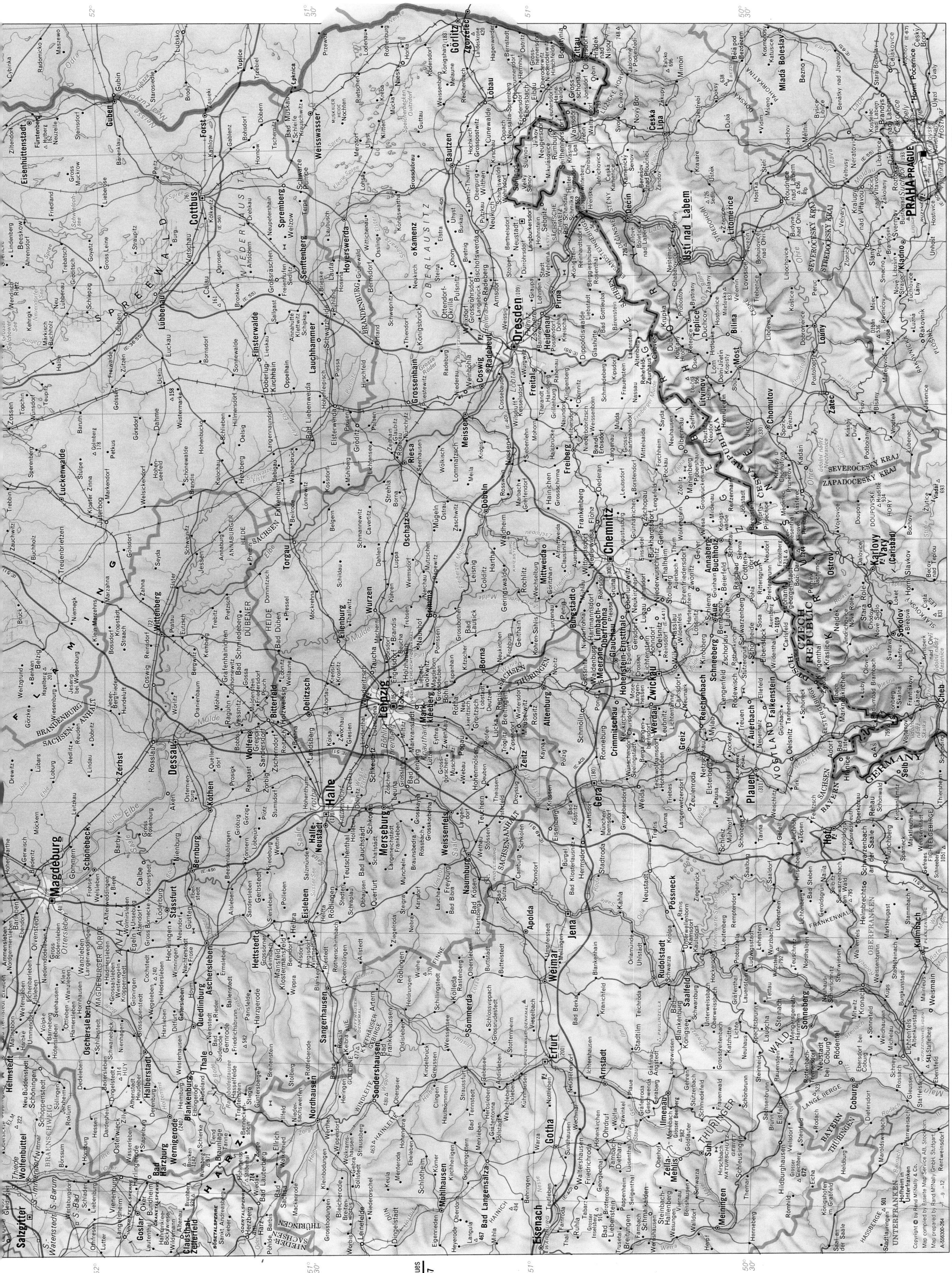
Berlin
Magdeburg
Halle
Leipzig
Dresden
Chemnitz
Zwickau
Plauen
Erfurt
Weimar
Jena
Gera
Gotha
Eisenach
Dessau
Cottbus
Görlitz
Bautzen
Praha
PRAHA PRAGUE
Ústí nad Labem
Děčín
Teplice
Most
Chomutov
Karlovy Vary (Carlsbad)
Cheb
Kladno
Liberec
Mladá Boleslav
Coburg
Hof
CZECH REPUBLIC
ČESKÁ REPUBLIKA
GERMANY
SACHSEN
THÜRINGEN
BAYERN
SACHSEN-ANHALT
BRANDENBURG
HARZ
SPREEWALD
OBERLAUSITZ
VOGTLAND
FLÄMING
DÜBENER HEIDE
LANGE BERGE
HASSBERGE
UNTERFRANKEN
OBERFRANKEN
FRANKENWALD
THÜRINGER WALD
Elbe
Saale
Mulde
Main

Map continues page 60

Map continues pages 56-57

Scale 1:1,000,000

Kilometers 0 10 20 30 40 50 Km.
Statute Miles 0 10 20 30 40 50 Mi.

One centimeter represents 10 kilometers.
One inch represents approximately 16 miles.
Lambert Conformal Conic Projection

DEUTSCH	Berg, Bg.	Bodden	Bucht	Gebirge	Heide	Kanal	See	Talsperre
ENGLISH	mountain	bay	bay	range	heath	canal	lake	dam
ESPAÑOL	montaña	bahía	bahía	sierra	matorral	canal	lago	presa
FRANÇAIS	montagne	baie	baie	chaîne	lande	canal	lac	barrage
PORTUGUÊS	montanha	baía	baía	serra	charneca	canal	lago	represa

Map continues pages 52-53

Map continues pages 50-51

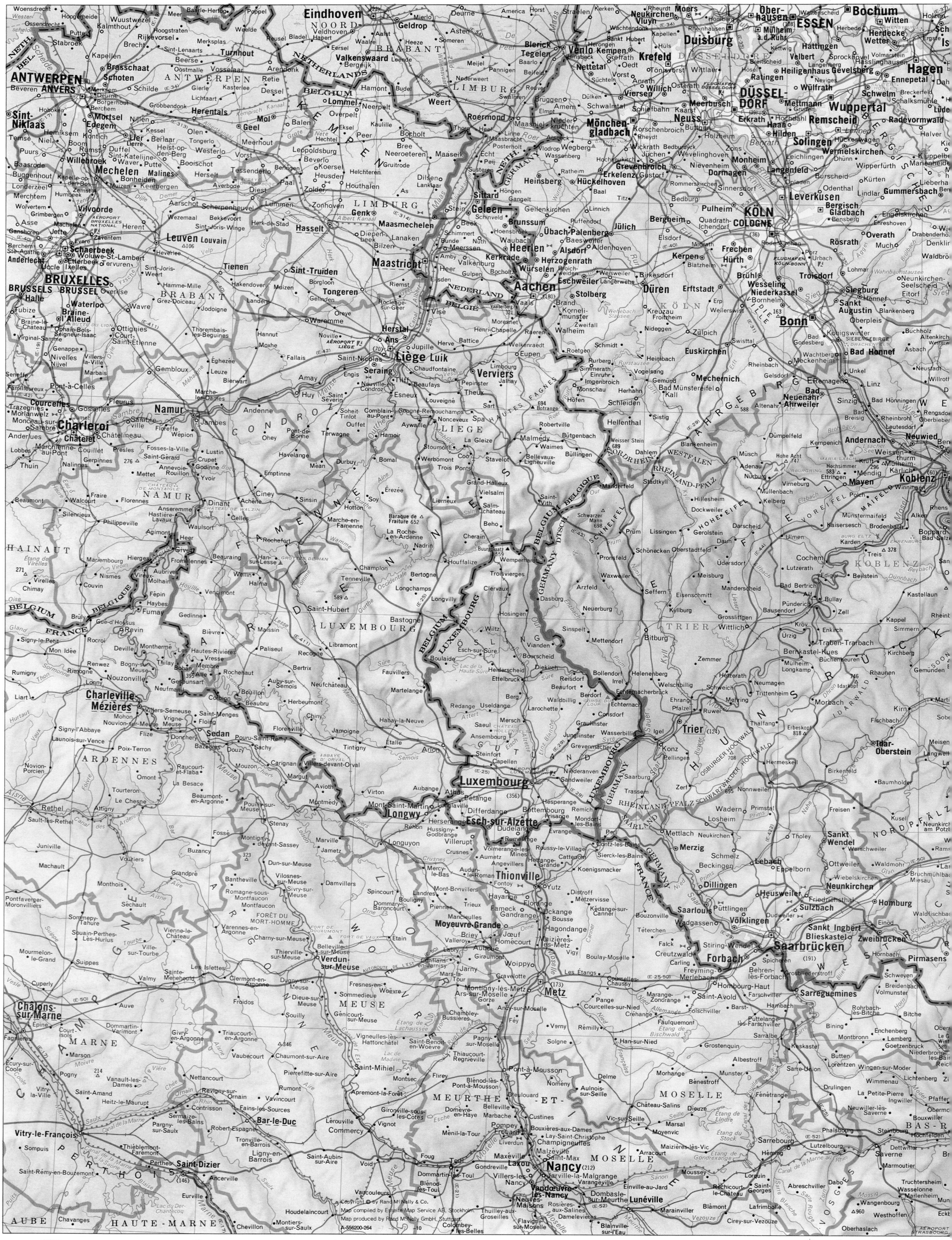
4° 30'
5°
5° 30'
6°
6° 30'
7°
7° 30'
51°
50° 30'
50°
49° 30'
49°
48° 30'
Eindhoven
Bochum
ESSEN
Duisburg
Krefeld
Hagen
Wuppertal
DÜSSEL-DORF
Mönchen-gladbach
Solingen
Leverkusen
KÖLN COLOGNE
Bonn
ANTWERPEN ANVERS
Mechelen Malines
Leuven Louvain
BRUXELLES BRUSSEL
Hasselt
Maastricht
Aachen
Düren
Liège Luik
Verviers
Namur
Charleroi
Koblenz
Trier
LUXEMBOURG
Luxembourg
Charleville-Mézières
Sedan
Longwy
Esch-sur-Alzette
Thionville
Metz
Saarbrücken
Nancy
Verdun-sur-Meuse
Bar-le-Duc
Châlons-sur-Marne
Vitry-le-François
Saint-Dizier
Lunéville
Forbach
Saarlouis
BELGIUM
NETHERLANDS
GERMANY
FRANCE
Copyright © by Rand McNally & Co.
Map compiled by Esselte Map Service AB, Stockholm.
Map produced by Rand McNally GmbH, Stuttgart

Map continues pages 58-59

MAP FORM	aéroport	Berg	canal	château	étang	Gebirge	Naturpark	Stausee
ENGLISH	airport	mountain	canal	castle	pond	range	reserve	reservoir
DEUTSCH	Flughafen	Berg	Kanal	Burg	Teich	Gebirge	Naturpark	Stausee
ESPAÑOL	aeropuerto	montaña	canal	castillo	charca	cordillera	reserva	embalse
FRANÇAIS	aéroport	montagne	canal	château	étang	chaîne	réserve	réservoir
PORTUGUÊS	aeroporto	montanha	canal	castelo	lagoa	cordilheira	reserva	reservatório

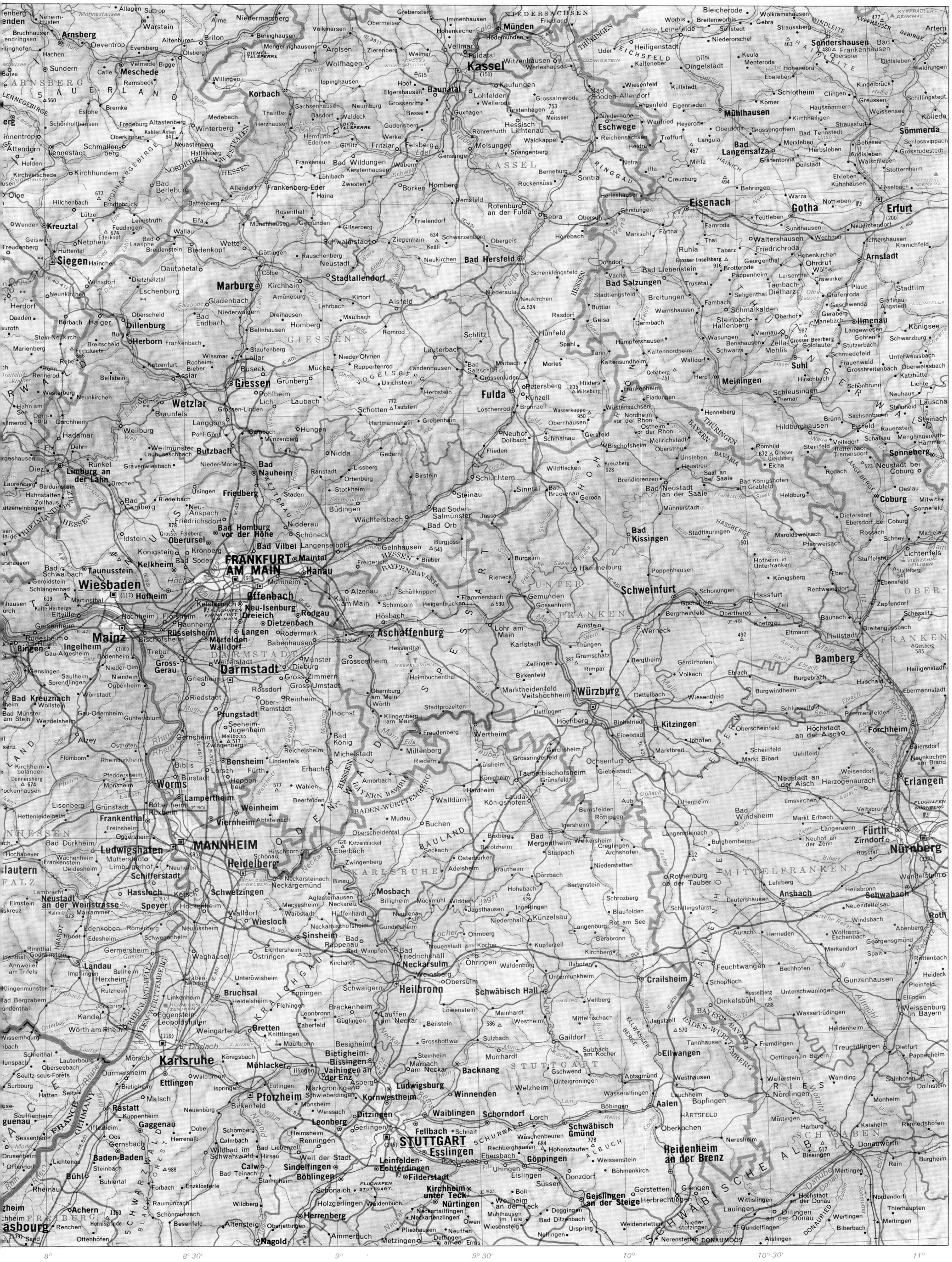

Kassel
Münden
Arnsberg
Meschede
Korbach
Marburg
Giessen
Wetzlar
Siegen
Dillenburg
Herborn
Fulda
Bad Hersfeld
Eisenach
Gotha
Erfurt
Mühlhausen
Eschwege
Bad Langensalza
Sondershausen
Sömmerda
Arnstadt
Ilmenau
Suhl
Meiningen
Bad Salzungen
Coburg
Sonneberg
Bad Kissingen
Schweinfurt
Bamberg
Würzburg
Kitzingen
Erlangen
Fürth
Nürnberg
Schwabach
Ansbach
Crailsheim
Aalen
Heidenheim an der Brenz
Schwäbisch Gmünd
Schwäbisch Hall
Heilbronn
Göppingen
Esslingen
STUTTGART
Ludwigsburg
Pforzheim
Karlsruhe
Rastatt
Baden-Baden
Heidelberg
MANNHEIM
Ludwigshafen
Worms
Darmstadt
Aschaffenburg
Offenbach
FRANKFURT AM MAIN
Hanau
Wiesbaden
Mainz
Bad Kreuznach
Bad Homburg vor der Höhe
Friedberg
Bad Nauheim
Limburg an der Lahn
Speyer
Landau
Neustadt an der Weinstrasse
Bruchsal
Sinsheim
Mosbach
Bad Mergentheim
Rothenburg ob der Tauber
Dinkelsbühl
Nördlingen
Ellwangen
Donauwörth
Map continues pages 54-55
Map continues page 60

Map continues pages 54-55

Map continues page 60

Kilometers 0 10 20 30 40 50 Km.

Statute Miles 0 10 20 30 40 50 Mi.

Scale 1:1,000,000

One centimeter represents 10 kilometers.
One inch represents approximately 16 miles.
Lambert Conformal Conic Projection

Map continues pages 50-51

MARNE
MEUSE
MEURTHE-ET-MOSELLE
MOSELLE
AUBE
HAUTE-MARNE
VOSGES
HAUTE-SAÔNE
CÔTE-D'OR
DOUBS
JURA
SAÔNE-ET-LOIRE
AIN
RHÔNE
HAUTE-SAVOIE
SAVOIE
FRANCE
SWITZERLAND
SUISSE
VAUD
FRIBOURG
NEUCHÂTEL
BERN
Nancy
Lunéville
Saint-Dizier
Chaumont
Épinal
Saint-Dié
Colmar
Mulhouse
Belfort
Montbéliard
Basel
Langres
Dijon
Besançon
Vesoul
Dole
Beaune
Chalon-sur-Saône
Le Creusot
Montceau-les-Mines
Lons-le-Saunier
Mâcon
Bourg-en-Bresse
Villefranche
LYON
Villeurbanne
Oyonnax
Pontarlier
La Chaux-de-Fonds
Neuchâtel
Biel
Bern
Fribourg
Yverdon
Lausanne
Vevey
Montreux
Genève
Geneva
Annemasse
Annecy
Sion
Lake Geneva
Lac Léman
Lac de Genève
Copyright © by Rand McNally & Co.

MAP FORM	col	Horn	lago	mont	passo	piz, -zo	See	Spitze	val
ENGLISH	pass	peak	lake	mount	pass	peak	lake	peak	valley
DEUTSCH	Pass	Horn	See	Berg	Pass	Gipfel	See	Spitze	Tal
ESPAÑOL	paso	pico	lago	monte	paso	pico	lago	pico	valle
FRANÇAIS	col	cime	lac	mont	col	cime	lac	cime	val
PORTUGUÊS	passo	pico	lago	monte	passo	pico	lago	pico	vale

Map continues pages 56-57

Strasbourg
Kehl
Offenburg
Lahr
Freiburg im Breisgau
Emmendingen
Baden-Baden
Sindelfingen
Böblingen
Göppingen
Heidenheim an der Brenz
Kirchheim unter Teck
Nürtingen
Geislingen an der Steige
Herrenberg
Tübingen
Reutlingen
Rottenburg am Neckar
Nagold
Horb am Neckar
Ulm
Neu-Ulm
Augsburg
Friedberg
Balingen
Albstadt
Rottweil
Schramberg
Ehingen
Biberach an der Riss
Memmingen
Kaufbeuren
Landsberg am Lech
Villingen-Schwenningen
Tuttlingen
Sigmaringen
Singen (Hohentwiel)
Radolfzell
Konstanz
Friedrichshafen
Ravensburg
Weingarten
Leutkirch
Kempten
Lindau
Wangen im Allgäu
Sonthofen
Füssen
Bregenz
Dornbirn
Lustenau
Feldkirch
Vaduz
Schaffhausen
Winterthur
Baden
Wettingen
Aarau
Olten
Zofingen
Zürich
Uster
Sankt Gallen
Zug
Luzern
Emmenbrücke
Schwyz
Chur
Bellinzona
Locarno
Lugano
Domodossola
Verbania
Varese
Como
Lecco
Sondrio
SCHWÄBISCHE ALB
SCHWARZWALD
SCHWABEN
GERMANY
SWITZERLAND
AUSTRIA
ITALY
LIECHTENSTEIN
THURGAU
AARGAU
ZÜRICH
SCHWYZ
GLARUS
URI
LUZERN
TICINO
GRAUBÜNDEN
VORARLBERG
TIROL
Bodensee
Lake Constance
Lago Maggiore
Lago di Como
Lago di Lugano
RÄTISCHE ALPEN
GLARNER ALPEN
LECHTALER ALPEN
ALPI OROBIE

Map continues page 60

Map continues pages 64-65

Map continues pages 62-63

Kilometers 0 10 20 30 40 50 Km.

Statute Miles 0 10 20 30 40 50 Mi.

Scale 1:1,000,000

One centimeter represents 10 kilometers.
One inch represents approximately 16 miles.

Lambert Conformal Conic Projection

Map continues pages 54-55

Map continues pages 56-57

Map continues pages 58-59

Map continues page 61

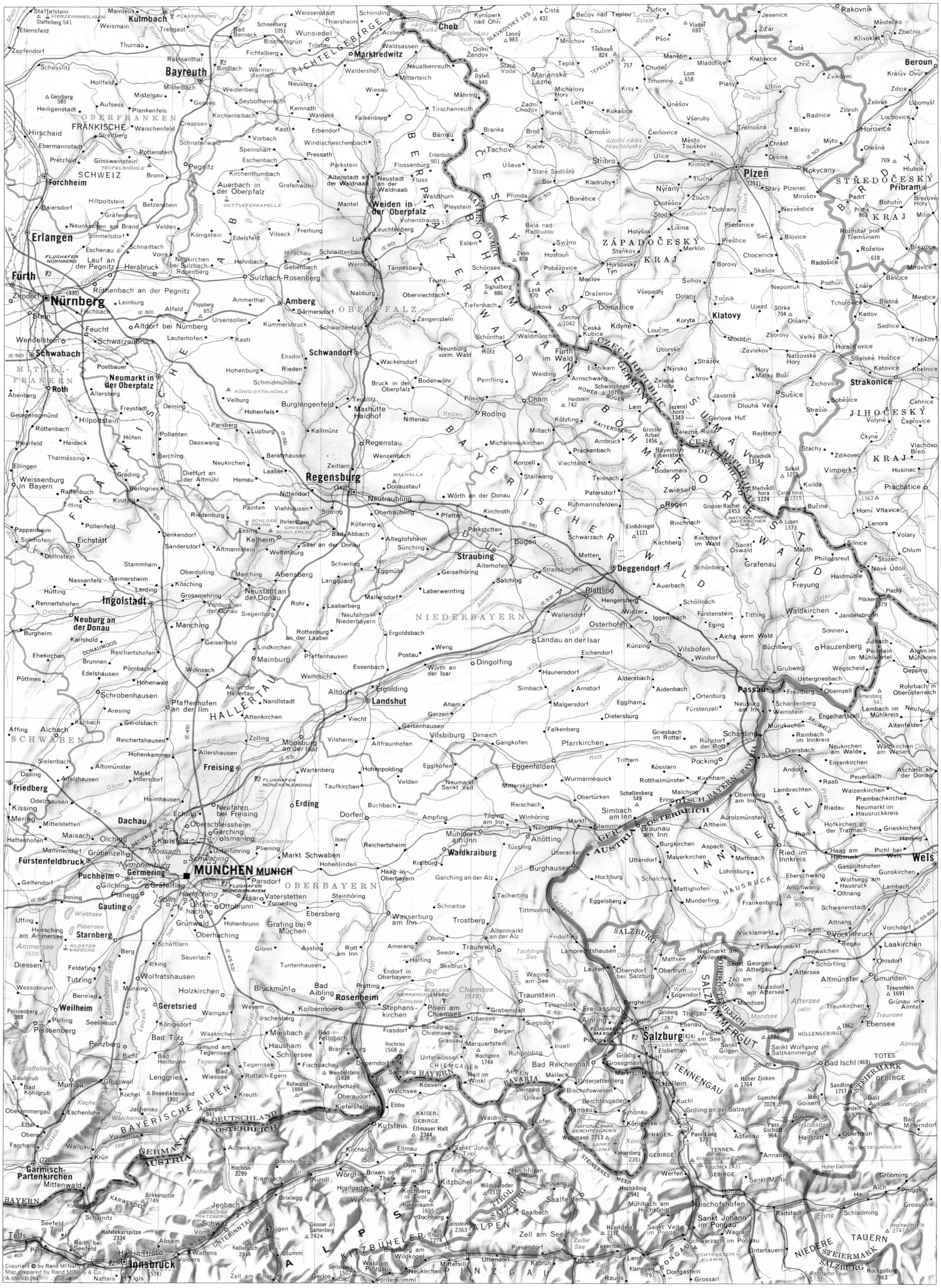

Kulmbach
Bayreuth
Cheb
Marktredwitz
Weiden in der Oberpfalz
Erlangen
Fürth
Nürnberg
Amberg
Schwandorf
Regensburg
Ingolstadt
Landshut
Straubing
Deggendorf
Passau
Freising
Dachau
München
Rosenheim
Salzburg
Innsbruck
Plzeň
Klatovy
Strakonice
Wels
Garmisch-Partenkirchen
O B E R F R A N K E N
O B E R P F A L Z
N I E D E R B A Y E R N
O B E R B A Y E R N
S C H W A B E N
DEUTSCHLAND
ÖSTERREICH
GERMANY
AUSTRIA
CZECH REPUBLIC
BAYERISCHER WALD
ŠUMAVA
BÖHMERWALD
BAYERISCHE ALPEN
A L P S

Map continues pages 64-65

DEUTSCH	Berg	Gebirge	Pass	Schloss	See
ENGLISH	mountain	range	pass	castle	lake
ESPAÑOL	montaña	sierra	paso	castillo	lago
FRANÇAIS	montagne	chaîne	col	château	lac
PORTUGUÊS	montanha	serra	passo	castelo	lago

Kilometers 0 10 20 30 40 50 Km.

Statute Miles 0 10 20 30 40 50 Mi.

Scale 1:1,000,000

One centimeter represents 10 kilometers.
One inch represents approximately 16 miles.
Modified Polyconic Projection

Map continues page 60

continues s 64-65

14°
14° 30'
15°
15° 30'
16°
16° 30'
49°
48° 30'
48°
47° 30'
47°
46° 30'
17°
Brno (227)
Třebíč
Jindřichův Hradec
České Budějovice (386)
JIHOČESKÝ KRAJ
JIHOMORAVSKÝ KRAJ
Znojmo
Břeclav
Mikulov
Valtice
ČESKÁ REPUBLIK
ÖSTERREICH
CZECH REPUBLIC
AUSTRIA
WALDVIERTEL
WEINVIERTEL
MÜHLVIERTEL
BOHEMIAN FOREST
BÖHMER WALD
ŠUMAVA
Freistadt
Linz (266)
Leonding
Wels
Traun
Steyr
Enns
Amstetten
OBERÖSTERREICH
NIEDERÖSTERREICH
WACHAU
Krems an der Donau
Sankt Pölten (267)
Melk
Zwettl (520)
Horn
Hollabrunn
Mistelbach
Stockerau
Korneuburg
Klosterneuburg
WIEN (170)
VIENNA
Schwechat
Mödling
Baden
Bratislava (164)
SLOVAKIA
SLOVENSKÁ REPUBLIKA
ZÁPADOSLOVENSKÝ KRAJ
MALÉ KARPATY
WIENERWALD
Wiener Neustadt
Eisenstadt
Neusiedler See
Mosonmagyaróvár
Sopron (212)
GYŐR-MOSON-SOPRON
MAGYARORSZÁG
BURGENLAND
Oberwart
Szombathely (216)
VAS
Körmend
Szentgotthárd
Zalaegerszeg
ZALA
AUSTRIA
HUNGARY
Graz (364)
STEIERMARK
Leoben
Bruck an der Mur
Kapfenberg
Mürzzuschlag
Judenburg
Liezen
NIEDERE TAUERN
ALPS
HOCHSCHWAB
Eisenerz
Wolfsberg
Leibnitz
KÄRNTEN
Klagenfurt (446)
Völkermarkt
KARAWANKEN
KARAVANKE
ÖSTERREICH
SLOVENIJA
AUSTRIA
SLOVENIA
Maribor (274)
Ptuj
SLOVENSKE GORICE
PREKOMURJE
Murska Sobota
CROATIA
HRVATSKA
MEDUMURJE
Čakovec
Titovo Velenje
Danube
Donau
Drava
Mura
Copyright © 1980, 1987 by Rand McNally & Co.
Map prepared by Rand McNally & Co.

DEUTSCH	Alpe, -n	Berg	Gebirge	Sattel	Schloss	Wald
ENGLISH	mountains	mountain	range	saddle	castle	forest; mountains
ESPAÑOL	montañas	montaña	sierra	paso	castillo	bosque; montañas
FRANÇAIS	montagnes	montagne	chaîne	col	château	forêt; montagnes
PORTUGUÊS	montanhas	montanha	serra	passo	castelo	Floresta; montanhas

Kilometers 0 10 20 30 40 50 Km.

Statute Miles 0 10 20 30 40 50 Mi.

Scale 1:1,000,000

One centimeter represents 10 kilometers.
One inch represents approximately 16 miles.

Lambert Conformal Conic Projection

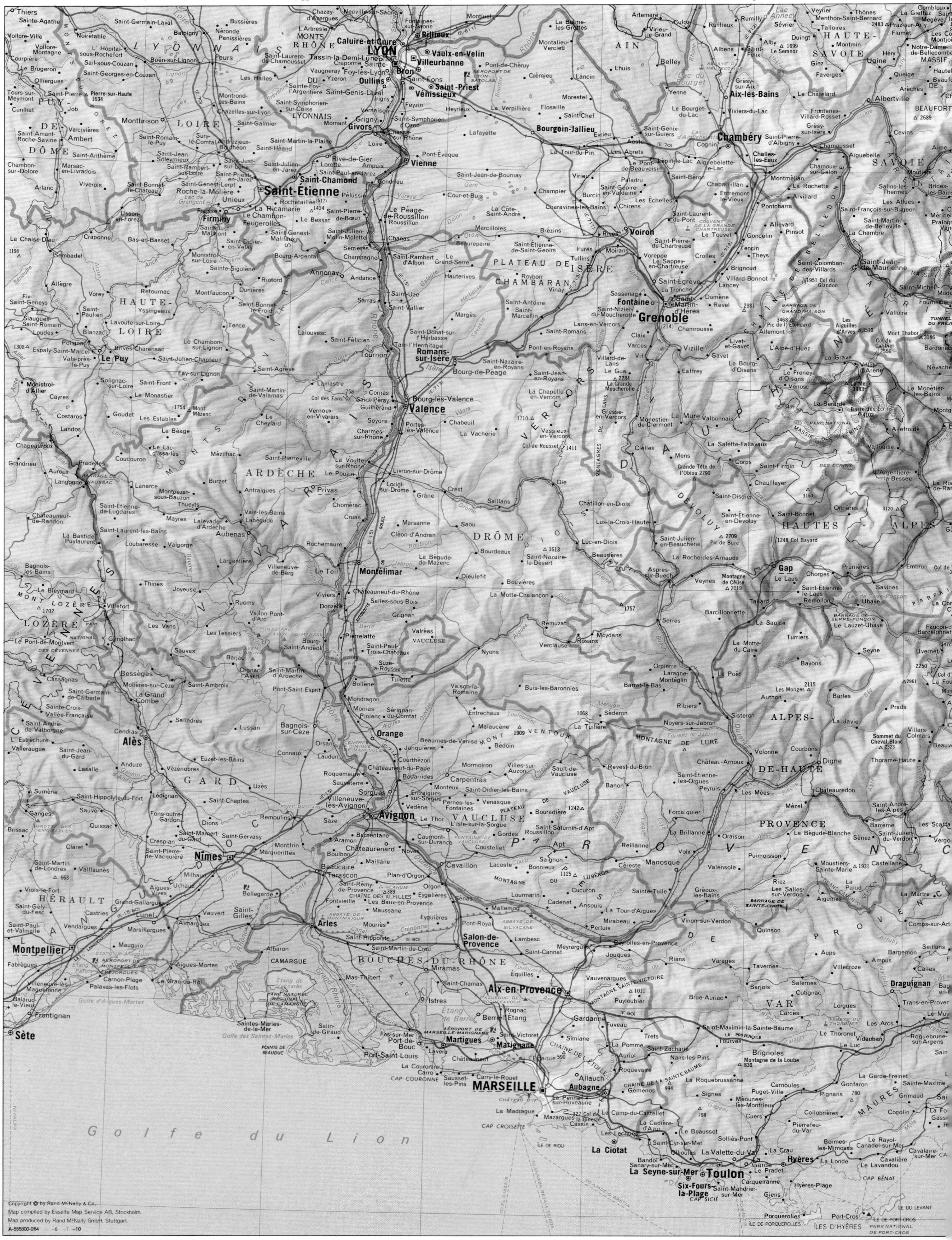

4°
4°30'
5°
5°30'
6°
6°30'
45° 30'
45°
44° 30'
44°
43° 30'
43°
LYON
Villeurbanne
Vénissieux
Saint-Étienne
Firminy
Vienne
Grenoble
Chambéry
Aix-les-Bains
Voiron
Valence
Romans-sur-Isère
Montélimar
Le Puy
Alès
Nîmes
Avignon
Orange
Arles
Montpellier
Sète
Salon-de-Provence
Aix-en-Provence
MARSEILLE
Aubagne
La Ciotat
Toulon
La Seyne-sur-Mer
Hyères
Draguignan
Digne
Gap
LYONNAIS
LOIRE
HAUTE-LOIRE
ARDÈCHE
DRÔME
VAUCLUSE
GARD
HÉRAULT
BOUCHES-DU-RHÔNE
VAR
ISÈRE
AIN
SAVOIE
HAUTE-SAVOIE
HAUTES-ALPES
ALPES-DE-HAUTE-PROVENCE
LOZÈRE
CAMARGUE
PLATEAU DE CHAMBARAN
VERCORS
DAUPHINÉ
PROVENCE
Golfe du Lion
Golfe d'Aigues-Mortes
Golfe des Saintes-Maries
ÎLES D'HYÈRES
Copyright © by Rand McNally & Co.
Map compiled by Esselte Map Service AB, Stockholm.
Map produced by Rand McNally GmbH, Stuttgart.
A-555900-264 -6 -7 -10

MAP FORM	abbaye	capo	col	île, î.	lac, l.	monte	passo	pic	val (-le)
ENGLISH	abbey	cape	pass	island	lake	mountain	pass	peak	valley
DEUTSCH	Abtei	Kap	Pass	Insel	See	Berg	Pass	Gipfel	Tal
ESPAÑOL	abadia	cabo	paso	isla	lago	montaña	paso	pico	valle
FRANÇAIS	abbaye	cap	col	île	lac	montagne	col	cime	val
PORTUGUÊS	abadia	cabo	passo	ilha	lago	montanha	passo	pico	vale

Map continues pages 58-59

TORINO TURIN
MILANO MILAN
GENOVA GENOA
Golfo di Genova
Ligurian Sea
Mar Ligure
MEDITERRANEAN SEA
RIVIERA DI PONENTE
RIVIERA DI LEVANTE
APPENNINO LIGURE
ALPI MARITTIME
ALPES MARITIMES
Nice
Monaco
San Remo
Savona
Alessandria
Asti
Cuneo
Novara
Vercelli
Pavia
Piacenza
Bergamo
La Spezia

Map continues pages 64-65

Kilometers 0 10 20 30 40 50 Km.

Statute Miles 0 10 20 30 40 50 Mi.

Scale 1:1,000,000

One centimeter represents 10 kilometers.

One inch represents approximately 16 miles.

Lambert Conformal Conic Projection

Map continues page 61

Map continues page 60

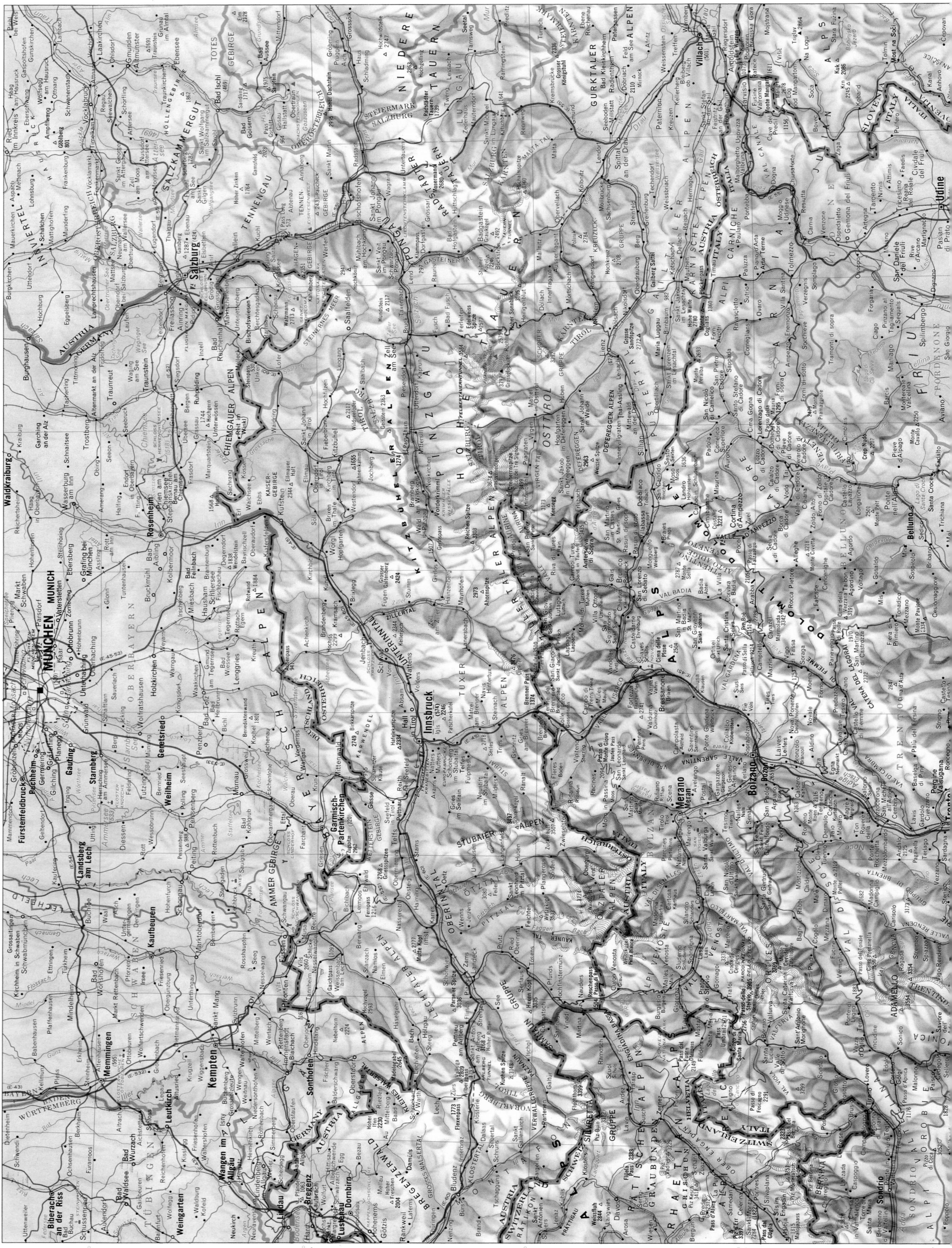
MÜNCHEN MUNICH
Salzburg
Innsbruck
Bolzano Bozen
Merano Meran
Udine
Belluno
Kempten
Rosenheim
Villach
Garmisch-Partenkirchen
Memmingen
Kaufbeuren
Landsberg am Lech
Weilheim
Starnberg
Lindau
Bregenz
Dornbirn
Sondrio
AUSTRIA
GERMANY
ITALY
SWITZERLAND
SLOVENIA
HOHE TAUERN
NIEDERE TAUERN
KITZBÜHELER ALPEN
DOLOMITI

Map continues pages 58-59

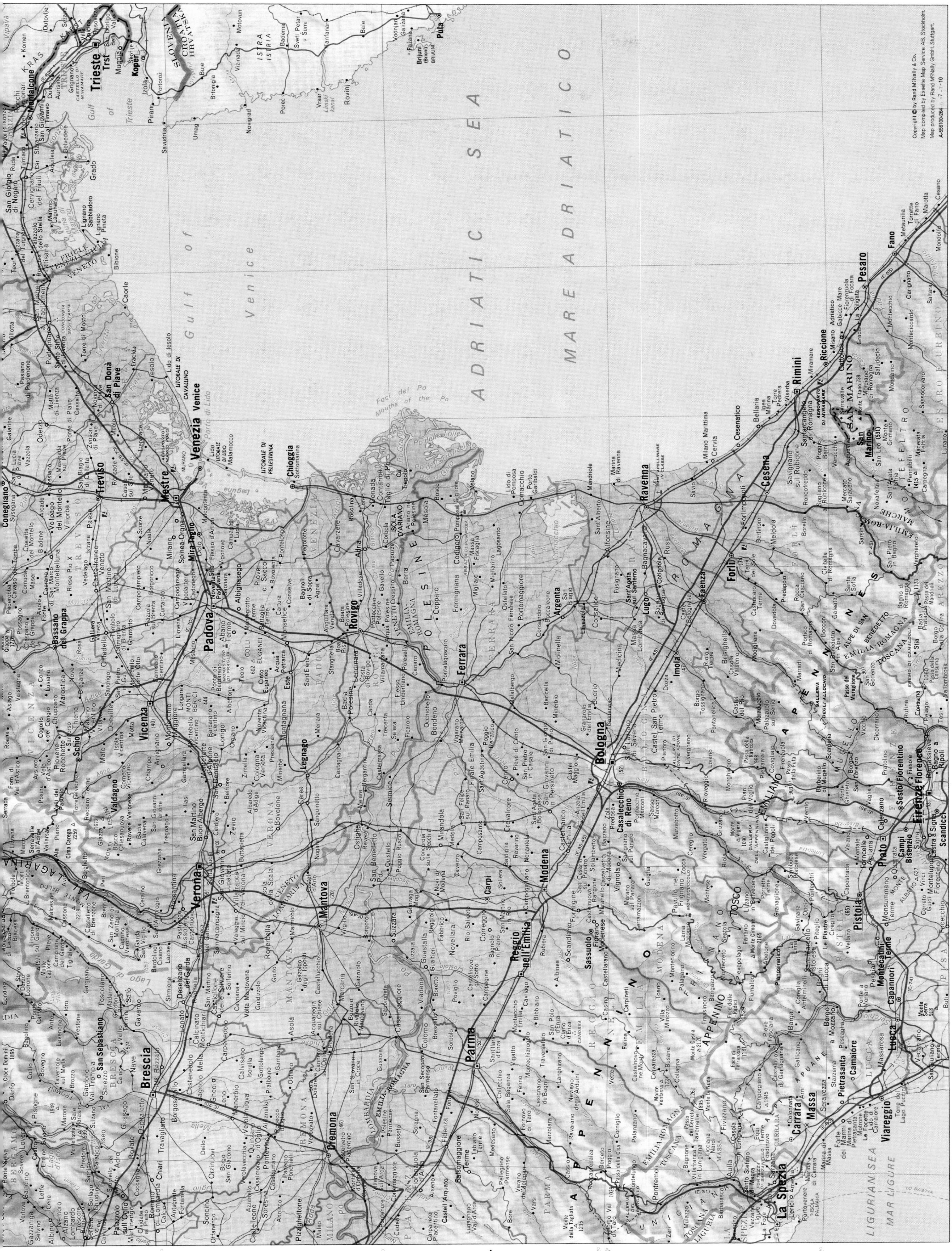
ADRIATIC SEA
MARE ADRIATICO
Gulf of Venice
Gulf of Trieste
Foci del Po
Mouths of the Po
LIGURIAN SEA
MAR LIGURE
APPENNINO
Venezia
Venice
Padova
Verona
Vicenza
Treviso
Trieste
Bologna
Ferrara
Ravenna
Rimini
Modena
Parma
Mantova
Brescia
Cremona
Firenze
Pistoia
Prato
Lucca
La Spezia
Pesaro
San Marino
Rovigo
Chioggia
Forlì
Cesena
Reggio nell'Emilia

Map continues pages 62-63

Map continues pages 66-67

Copyright © by Rand McNally & Co.
Map compiled by Esselte Map Service AB, Stockholm.
Map produced by Rand McNally GmbH, Stuttgart.
A-556100-364 -7-7-10

MAP FORM	ENGLISH	DEUTSCH	ESPAÑOL	FRANÇAIS	PORTUGUÊS
Alpen	mountains	Alpen	montañas	montagnes	montanhas
Berg	mountain	Berg	montaña	montagne	montanha
cima	peak	Gipfel	pico	cime	pico
Gebirge	range	Gebirge	sierra	chaîne	serra
monte	mountain	Berg	montaña	montagne	montanha
piz	peak	Gipfel	pico	cime	pico
Schloss	castle	Schloss	castillo	château	castelo
See	lake	See	lago	lac	lago
Spitze	peak	Spitze	pico	cime	pico

Kilometers 0 10 20 30 40 50 Km.
Statute Miles 0 10 20 30 40 50 Mi.

Scale 1:1,000,000

One centimeter represents 10 kilometers.
One inch represents approximately 16 miles.
Lambert Conformal Conic Projection

Map continues pages 64-65

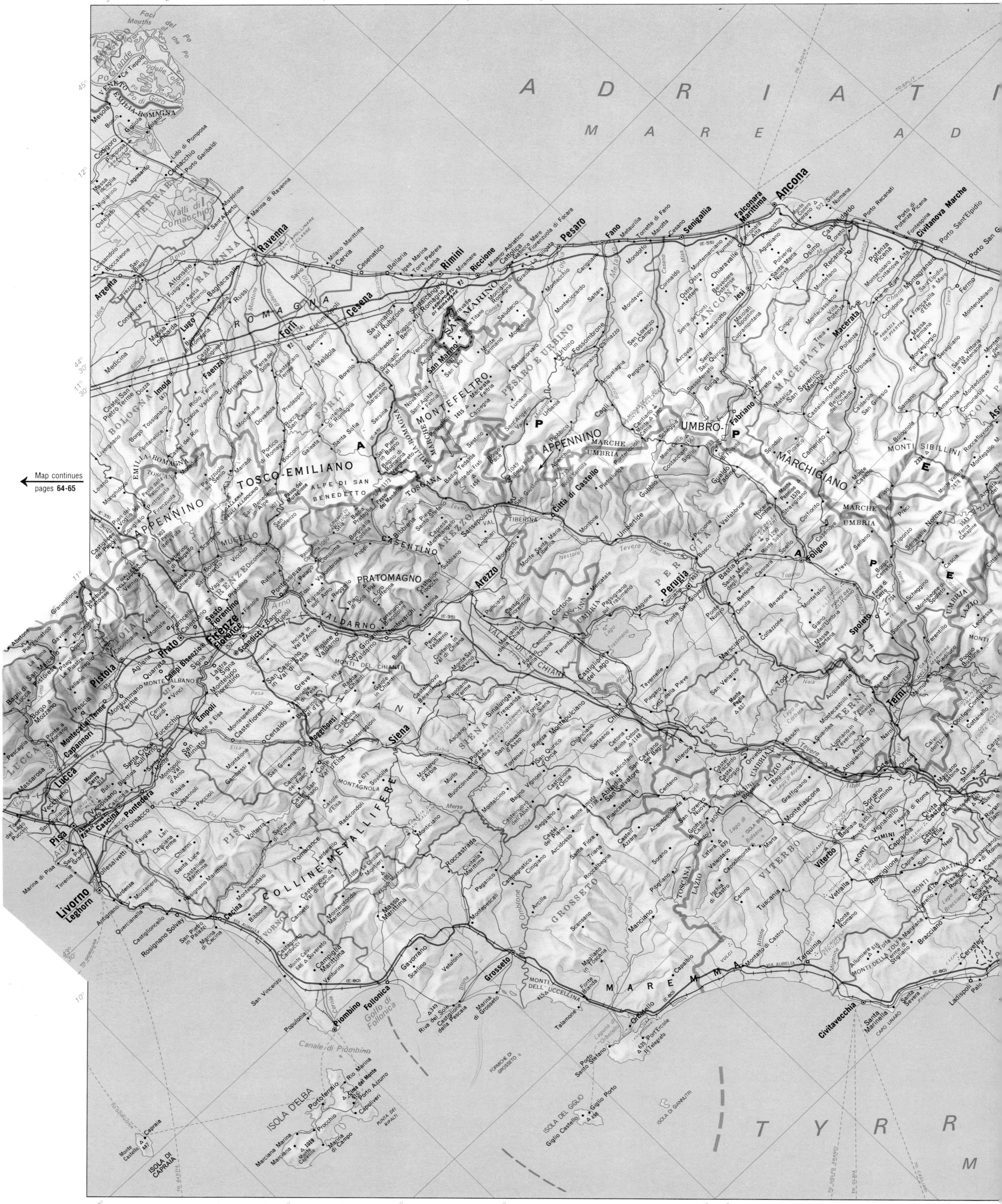

ADRIATI
MARE AD
TYRR
Ancona
Pesaro
Rimini
Riccione
Ravenna
Forlì
Cesena
Senigallia
Fano
Civitanova Marche
Macerata
Jesi
Fabriano
Imola
Faenza
Lugo
Argenta
SAN MARINO
MONTEFELTRO
ROMAGNA
APPENNINO TOSCO-EMILIANO
ALPE DI SAN BENEDETTO
PRATOMAGNO
CASENTINO
MUGELLO
VALDARNO
Arezzo
Perugia
Città di Castello
Gubbio
Foligno
Spoleto
Terni
Assisi
MONTI SIBILLINI
APPENNINO UMBRO-MARCHIGIANO
Firenze
Florence
Prato
Pistoia
Lucca
Pisa
Livorno
Leghorn
Empoli
Siena
Poggibonsi
MONTI DEL CHIANTI
COLLINE METALLIFERE
Grosseto
Piombino
Follonica
Orvieto
Viterbo
Civitavecchia
MAREMMA
ISOLA D'ELBA
Portoferraio
ISOLA DEL GIGLIO
ISOLA DI CAPRAIA
Canale di Piombino
Golfo di Follonica
Lago Trasimeno
Lago di Bolsena
Lago di Vico
Lago di Bracciano
MONTI CIMINI
MONTI SABATINI
Foci del Po
Valli di Comacchio

MAP FORM	golfo	isola	lago	monte	monti	passo	punta
ENGLISH	gulf	island	lake	mountain	mountains	pass	point
DEUTSCH	Golf	Insel	See	Berg	Berge	Pass	Landspitze
ESPAÑOL	golfo	isla	lago	montaña	montañas	paso	punta
FRANÇAIS	golfe	île	lac	montagne	montagnes	col	pointe
PORTUGUÊS	golfo	ilha	lago	montanha	montanhas	passo	ponta

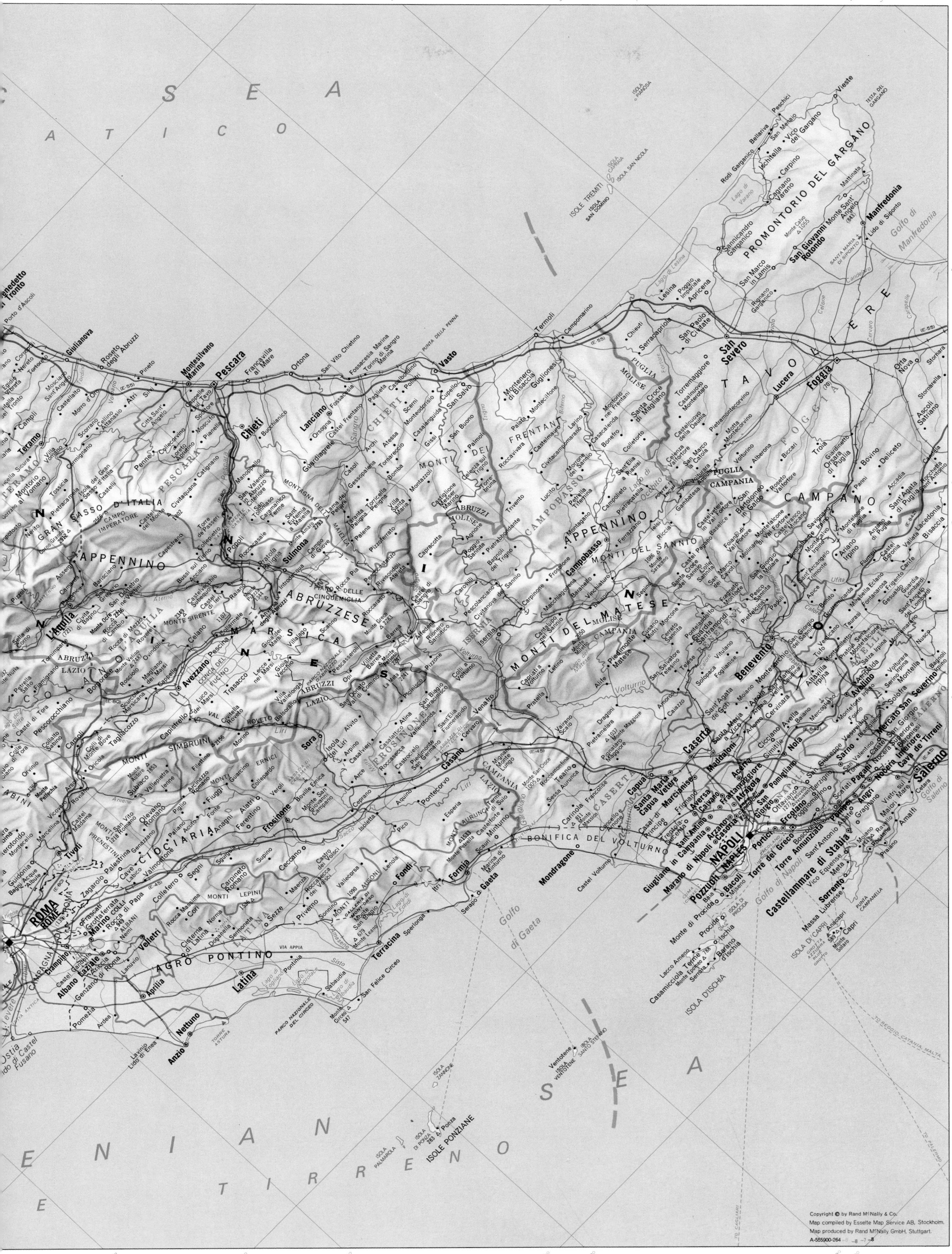
SEA
PROMONTORIO DEL GARGANO
TAVOLIERE
APPENNINO CAMPANO
MONTI DEL MATESE
MONTI DEL SANNIO
ABRUZZESE
MARSICA
CIOCIARIA
AGRO PONTINO
BONIFICA DEL VOLTURNO
TIRRENO
Golfo di Gaeta
Golfo di Napoli
Golfo di Salerno
Golfo di Manfredonia
ISOLE TREMITI
ISOLE PONZIANE
ISOLA D'ISCHIA
ISOLA DI CAPRI
ROMA
NAPOLI
NAPLES
Pescara
Chieti
Lanciano
Vasto
Termoli
San Severo
Foggia
Lucera
Manfredonia
Vieste
Campobasso
Benevento
Caserta
Avellino
Salerno
Latina
Frosinone
Sora
Cassino
Formia
Gaeta
Terracina
Anzio
Nettuno
Velletri
Tivoli
Teramo
L'Aquila
Avezzano
Sulmona
Isernia
Pozzuoli
Castellammare di Stabia
Sorrento
Capri
Ischia
Giulianova

Map continues pages 68-69

Kilometers 0 10 20 30 40 50 Km.
Statute Miles 0 10 20 30 40 50 Mi.

Scale 1:1,000,000
One centimeter represents 10 kilometers.
One inch represents approximately 16 miles.
Lambert Conformal Conic Projection

ADRIATIC SEA
MARE ADRIATICO
CROATIA
ITALY
TYRRHEN
Bari
Napoli
Salerno
Foggia
Taranto
Matera
Potenza
Manfredonia
Barletta
Benevento
Caserta
Campobasso
Avellino
Sorrento
Golfo di Salerno
Golfo di Gaeta
Golfo di Manfredonia
PROMONTORIO DEL GARGANO
APPENNINO LUCANO
PIANA DEL SELE
VALLO DI DIANO
BONIFICA DEL VOLTURNO
ISOLE TREMITI
ISOLA D'ISCHIA
ISOLA DI CAPRI

Map continues pages **66-67**

MAP FORM	capo	golfo	isola	lago	monte	monti	punta
ENGLISH	cape	gulf	island	lake	mountain	mountains	point
DEUTSCH	Kap	Golf	Insel	See	Berg	Berge	Landspitze
ESPAÑOL	cabo	golfo	isla	lago	montaña	montañas	punta
FRANÇAIS	cap	golfe	île	lac	montagne	montagnes	pointe
PORTUGUÊS	cabo	golfo	ilha	lago	montanha	montanhas	ponta

Strait of Otranto
Lecce
Otranto
Galatina
Nardò
Copertino
Gallipoli
PENISOLA SALENTINA
Golfo di Taranto
IONIAN SEA
MARE IONIO
Crotone
Cirò Marina
Rossano
Corigliano Calabro
SILA GRANDE
SILA PICCOLA
Cosenza
Catanzaro
Golfo di Squillace
Golfo di Sant'Eufemia
Nicastro
Vibo Valentia
Tropea
Golfo di Gioia
Gioia Tauro
Palmi
Reggio di Calabria
CALABRIA
SICILIA
SICILY
Messina
MARE TIRRENO
Stromboli

Map continues page 70

Kilometers 0 10 20 30 40 50 Km.

Statute Miles 0 10 20 30 40 50 Mi.

Scale 1:1,000,000

One centimeter represents 10 kilometers.
One inch represents approximately 16 miles.

Lambert Conformal Conic Projection

Map continues pages 68-69

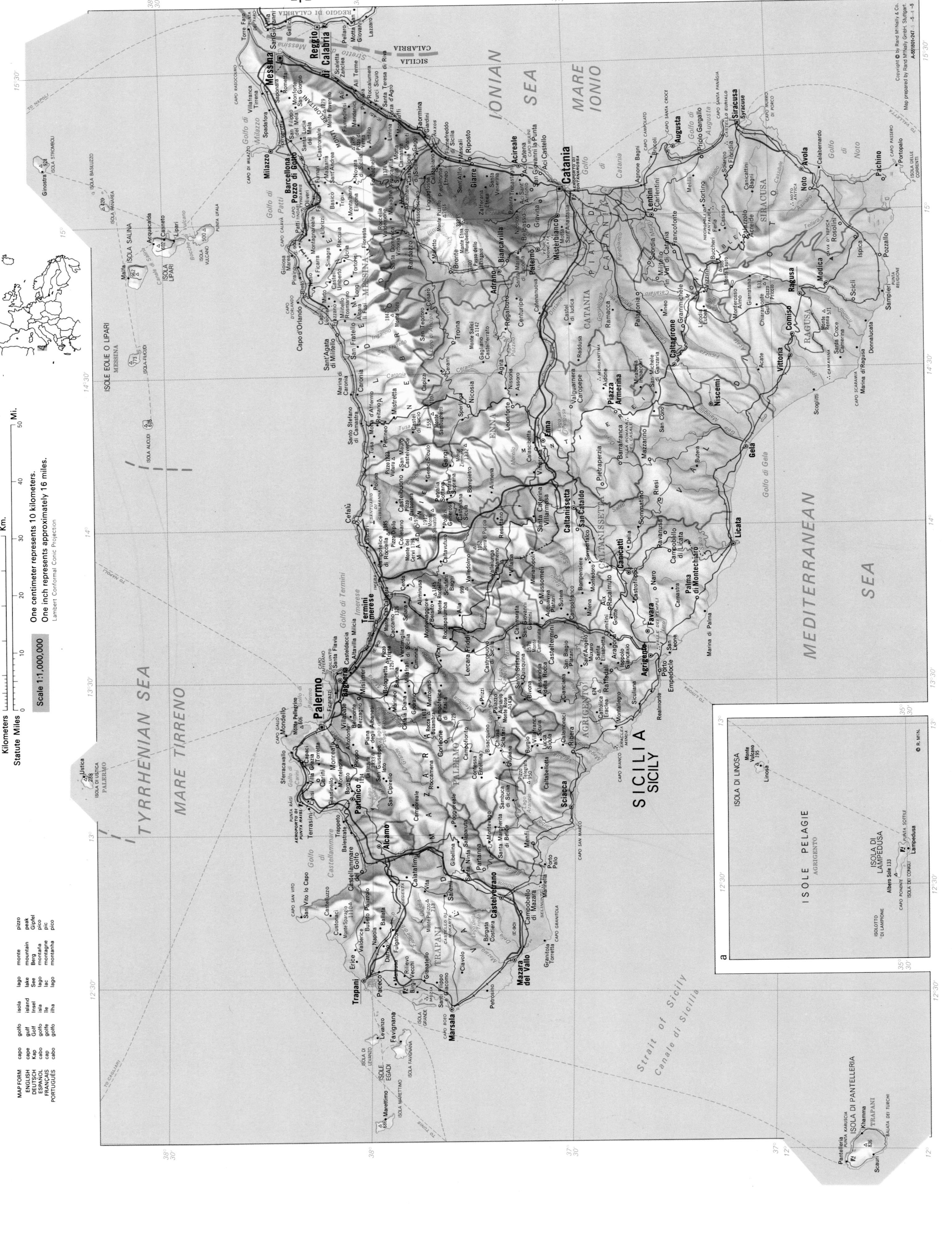
Kilometers
Statute Miles
Scale 1:1,000,000
One centimeter represents 10 kilometers.
One inch represents approximately 16 miles.
Lambert Conformal Conic Projection
MAP FORM capo golfo isola lago monte pizzo
ENGLISH cape gulf island lake mountain peak
DEUTSCH Kap Golf Insel See Berg Gipfel
ESPAÑOL cabo golfo isla lago montaña pico
FRANÇAIS cap golfe île lac montagne pic
PORTUGUÊS cabo golfo ilha lago montanha pico
TYRRHENIAN SEA
MARE TIRRENO
IONIAN SEA
MARE IONIO
MEDITERRANEAN SEA
SICILIA
SICILY
Strait of Sicily
Canale di Sicilia
ISOLE EOLIE O LIPARI
ISOLE EGADI
ISOLE PELAGIE
ISOLA DI LINOSA
ISOLA DI LAMPEDUSA
ISOLA DI PANTELLERIA
CALABRIA
Palermo
Catania
Messina
Reggio di Calabria
Siracusa
Ragusa
Trapani
Marsala
Agrigento
Caltanissetta
Enna
Gela
Licata
Termini Imerese
Cefalù
Milazzo
Acireale
Augusta
Copyright © by Rand McNally & Co.
Map prepared by Rand McNally GmbH, Stuttgart.

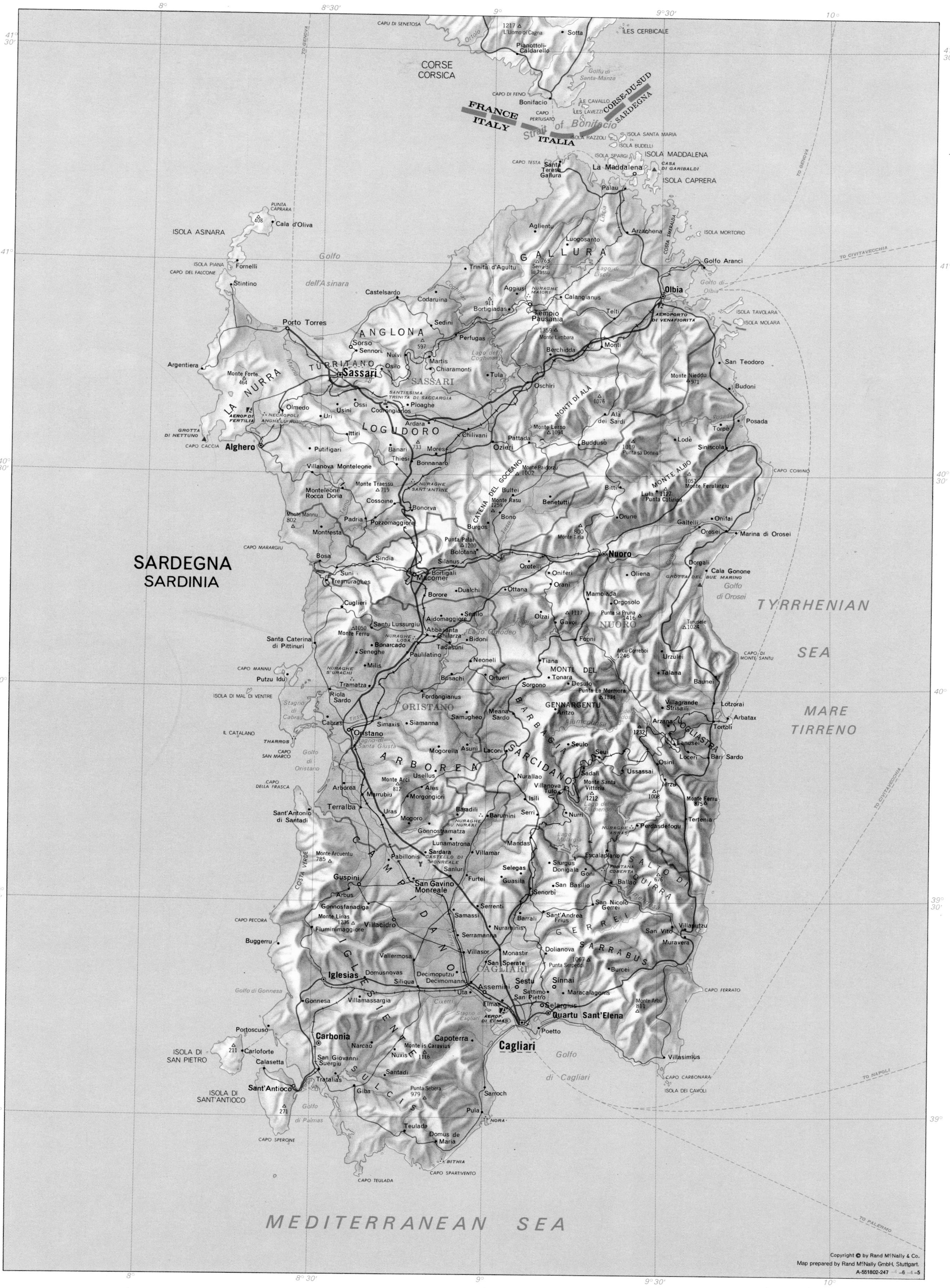
CORSE
CORSICA
FRANCE
ITALY
CORSE-DU-SUD
SARDEGNA
Strait of Bonifacio
ITALIA
Bonifacio
Sotta
ÎLES CERBICALE
Golfo di Santa-Manza
CAPO DI FENO
CAPO DI SENETOSA
Pianottoli-Caldarello
ÎLE CAVALLO
ÎLES LAVEZZI
CAPO PERTUSATO
ISOLA SANTA MARIA
ISOLA RAZZOLI
ISOLA BUDELLI
ISOLA SPARGI
ISOLA MADDALENA
CASA DI GARIBALDI
ISOLA CAPRERA
CAPO TESTA
Santa Teresa Gallura
La Maddalena
Palau
Arzachena
COSTA SMERALDA
ISOLA MORTORIO
Aglientu
Luogosanto
G A L L U R A
Trinità d'Agultu
Golfo Aranci
Olbia
Golfo di Olbia
ISOLA TAVOLARA
ISOLA MOLARA
AEROPORTO DI VENAFIORITA
Telti
Calangianus
Tempio Pausania
Aggius
NURAGHE MAIORI
Bortigiadas
Monte Limbara
Berchidda
Monti
San Teodoro
Budoni
Posada
Torpè
Siniscola
Lodè
Alà dei Sardi
MONTI DI ALA
Oschiri
Tula
Lago del Coghinas
Perfugas
Sedini
Castelsardo
Codaruina
ANGLONA
Sorso
Sennori
Nulvi
Osilo
Martis
Chiaramonti
Porto Torres
TURRITANO
Sassari
SASSARI
Stintino
Fornelli
ISOLA PIANA
CAPO DEL FALCONE
ISOLA ASINARA
PUNTA CAPRARA
Cala d'Oliva
Golfo dell'Asinara
Argentiera
Monte Forte
LA NURRA
Olmedo
Uri
Usini
Ossi
Codrongianos
Ploaghe
SANTISSIMA TRINITÀ DI SACCARGIA
AEROP. DI FERTILIA
NECROPOLI ANGHELU RUJU
GROTTA DI NETTUNO
CAPO CACCIA
Alghero
Ittiri
LOGUDORO
Ardara
Chilivani
Ozieri
Pattada
Monte Lerno
Budduso
Putifigari
Banari
Thiesi
Mores
Bonnanaro
Villanova Monteleone
Monte Raidorzu
CATENA DEL GOCEANO
Monte Traessu
NURAGHE SANT'ANTINE
Monteleone Rocca Doria
Cossoine
Bultei
Monte Rasu
Benetutti
Bitti
MONTE ALBO
Monte Ferulargiu
Lula
Punta Catirina
Onifai
Orune
Galtellì
Orosei
Marina di Orosei
CAPO COMINO
Monte Mannu
Padria
Pozzomaggiore
Bonorva
Bono
Burgos
Montresta
Punta Palai
Bolotana
Monte Tiria
Nuoro
CAPO MARARGIU
SARDEGNA
SARDINIA
Bosa
Sindia
Silanus
Orotelli
Oniferi
Orani
Oliena
Dorgali
Cala Gonone
GROTTA DEL BUE MARINO
Golfo di Orosei
Suni
Tresnuraghes
Macomer
Bortigali
Borore
Dualchi
Ottana
Mamoiada
Orgosolo
Punta sa Pruna
TYRRHENIAN SEA
Cuglieri
Santu Lussurgiu
Aidomaggiore
Sedilo
Lago Omodeo
Olzai
Gavoi
NUORO
Fonni
Monte Ferru
Abbasanta
Ghilarza
Tadasuni
Bidoni
NURAGHE LOSA
Bonarcado
Seneghe
Paulilatino
Santa Caterina di Pittinuri
Milis
NURAGHE S'URACHI
CAPO MANNU
Putzu Idu
Tramatza
Neoneli
Ortueri
Busachi
Tiana
MONTI DEL GENNARGENTU
Tonara
Desulo
Sorgono
Punta La Marmora
Arcu Correboi
Urzulei
Talana
Baunei
CAPO DI MONTE SANTU
ISOLA DI MAL DI VENTRE
Stagno di Cabras
Cabras
Riola Sardo
Fordongianus
ORISTANO
Oristano
Simaxis
Siamanna
Samugheo
Meana Sardo
Aritzo
BARBAGIA
Villagrande Strisaili
Lotzorai
Arbatax
Tortolì
Arzana
Lanusei
OGLIASTRA
MARE TIRRENO
IL CATALANO
THARROS
CAPO SAN MARCO
Golfo di Oristano
Stagno di Santa Giusta
ARBOREA
Mogorella
Asuni
Laconi
SARCIDANO
Seulo
Seui
Ussassai
Loceri
Bari Sardo
Osini
Jerzu
CAPO DELLA FRASCA
Arborea
Monte Arci
Usellus
Ales
Marrubiu
Morgongiori
Nurallao
Villanova Tulo
Isili
Sadali
Monte Santa Vittoria
Monte Ferru
Tertenia
Terralba
Sant'Antonio di Santadi
Uras
Mogoro
Baradili
Barumini
NURAGHE SU NURAXI
Serri
Nurri
Gonnostramatza
Perdasdefogu
Lunamatrona
Sardara
Pabillonis
CASTELLO DI MONREALE
Villamar
Mandas
Escalaplano
Monte Arcuentu
COSTA VERDE
CAMPIDANO
Sanluri
Furtei
Selegas
Guasila
Siurgus Donigala
Goni
Ballao
SALTO DI QUIRRA
PUNTA CORONGIU
Guspini
Arbus
San Gavino Monreale
Senorbì
San Basilio
San Nicolò Gerrei
Gonnosfanadiga
Monte Linas
Villacidro
Fluminimaggiore
Serrenti
Samassi
Barrali
Sant'Andrea Frius
GERREI
Villaputzu
San Vito
Muravera
CAPO PECORA
Buggerru
Serramanna
Nuraminis
Villasor
Monastir
San Sperate
Dolianova
SARRABUS
Punta Serpeddì
Burcei
IGLESIENTE
Vallermosa
Iglesias
Domusnovas
Siliqua
Decimoputzu
Decimomannu
CAGLIARI
Sestu
Sinnai
Settimo San Pietro
Maracalagonis
Golfo di Gonnesa
Gonnesa
Villamassargia
Uta
Assemini
Elmas
AEROP. DI ELMAS
Selargius
Quartu Sant'Elena
Monte Arbu
CAPO FERRATO
Stagno di Cagliari
Cixerri
Portoscuso
Carbonia
Capoterra
Poetto
Cagliari
ISOLA DI SAN PIETRO
Carloforte
Narcao
Nuxis
Monte is Caravius
San Giovanni Suergiu
SULCIS
Santadi
Calasetta
Villasimius
Golfo di Cagliari
CAPO CARBONARA
ISOLA DEI CAVOLI
ISOLA DI SANT'ANTIOCO
Sant'Antioco
Tratalias
Giba
Punta Sebera
Sarroch
Golfo di Palmas
Pula
NORA
CAPO SPERONE
Teulada
Domus de Maria
BITHIA
CAPO SPARTIVENTO
CAPO TEULADA
MEDITERRANEAN SEA
TO GENOVA
TO CIVITAVECCHIA
TO NAPOLI
TO PALERMO
8°
8°30'
9°
9°30'
10°
41° 30'
41°
40° 30'
40°
39° 30'
39°
Copyright © by Rand McNally & Co.
Map prepared by Rand McNally GmbH, Stuttgart.
A-551802-247

MAP FORM	capo	golfo	isola	lago, l.	monte
ENGLISH	cape	gulf	island	lake	mountain
DEUTSCH	Kap	Golf	Insel	See	Berg
ESPAÑOL	cabo	golfo	isla	lago	montaña
FRANÇAIS	cap	golfe	île	lac	montagne
PORTUGUÊS	cabo	golfo	ilha	lago	montanha

Kilometers 0 10 20 30 40 50 Km.

Statute Miles 0 10 20 30 40 50 Mi.

Scale 1:1,000,000

One centimeter represents 10 kilometers.
One inch represents approximately 16 miles.

Lambert Conformal Conic Projection

FINLAND
ESTONIA
LATVIA
LITHUANIA
POLAND
BELARUS
UKRAINE
HUNGARY
ROMANIA
MOLDOVA
GEORGIA
TURKEY
IRAN
AZERBAIJAN
KAZAKHSTAN
UZBEKISTAN
TURKMENISTAN
TAJIKISTAN
KYRGYZSTAN
AFGHANISTAN
BLACK SEA
CASPIAN SEA
(28 Meters Below Sea Level)
Beloje more
White Sea
Azovskoje more
Sea of Azov
Aral'skoje more
Aral Sea
ozero Balchaš
Lake Balkhash
(342)
KARAKUMY
KAZACHSKIJ MELKOSOPOČNIK
BETPAK-DALA
USTJURT
PRIKASPIJSKAJA NIZMENNOST'
KAVKAZ
CAUCASUS
KOLSKIJ POLUOSTROV
DASHT-E KAVIR
DASHT-E LUT
ALBORZ
KOPETDAG
TURGAJSKAJA
BUDAPEST
BUCUREŞTI
HELSINKI
TALLINN
RIGA
VILNIUS
MINSK
KIEV
MOSKVA
MOSCOW
SANKT-PETERBURG
(LENINGRAD)
TBILISI
JEREVAN
BAKU
TEHRĀN
AŠCHABAD
TAŠKENT
DUŠANBE
BIŠKEK
ALMA-ATA
Murmansk
Archangel'sk
Novgorod
Smolensk
Kazan'
Perm'
Jekaterinburg
Čeljabinsk
Samara (Kujbyšev)
Saratov
Volgograd (Stalingrad)
Astrachan'
Rostov-na-Donu
Odessa
Sevastopol'
Doneck
Char'kov
Voronež
Nižnij Novgorod (Gor'kij)
Orenburg
Ufa
Mashhad
Eşfahān
Tabrīz
Samarkand
Buchara
Kermān
Herāt
20°
25°
30°
35°
40°
45°
55°
60°
65°
70°
80°

Map continues
pages 22-23

Map continues
pages 118-119

MAP FORM	chrebet	gora	guba	mys	ostrov	ozero	poluostrov	proliv	vodochranilišče
ENGLISH	range	mountain	bay	cape	island	lake	peninsula	strait	reservoir
DEUTSCH	Gebirge	Berg	Bucht	Kap	Insel	See	Halbinsel	Meeresstrasse	Stausee
ESPAÑOL	sierra	montaña	bahía	cabo	isla	lago	península	estrecho	embalse
FRANÇAIS	chaîne	montagne	baie	cap	île	lac	péninsule	détroit	réservoir
PORTUGUÊS	serra	montanha	baía	cabo	ilha	lago	península	estreito	reservatório

KARSKOJE MORE
KARA SEA
MORE LAPTEVYCH
LAPTEV SEA
NOVAJA ZEMLJA
SEVERNAJA ZEMLJA
POLUOSTROV TAJMYR
GORY BYRRANGA
SEVERO - SIBIRSKAJA NIZMENNOST'
PLATO PUTORANA
SREDNE-SIBIRSKOJE PLOSKOGORJE
SIBERIA SIBIR'
JAKUTIJA
RUSSIA
ZAPADNO-SIBIRSKAJA RAVNINA
JAMALO-NENECKIJ
STANOVOJE NAGORJE
STANOVOY MOUNTAINS
BURJATIJA
ZAPADNYJ SAJAN
SAJAN MOUNTAINS
TUVA
ALTAJ
MONGOL ALTAJN NURUU
CHANGAJN NURUU
MONGOLIA
CHINA
XINJIANG UYGUR ZIZHIQU
SINKIANG
Noril'sk
Novosibirsk
Krasnojarsk
Irkutsk
Ulan-Ude
Ulaanbaatar
Omsk
Tomsk
Barnaul
Bratsk
Čita
Kemerovo
Novokuzneck
Semipalatinsk
Ust'-Kamenogorsk
Abakan
Kyzyl
Vorkuta
Surgut
Salechard
Dudinka
Chatanga
Mirnyj
Lensk
Olëkminsk
Vitim
Bodajbo
Ozero Bajkal
Lake Baikal
Lena
Jenisej
Ob'
Copyright © by Rand McNally & Co.
Map prepared by Esselte Map Service AB, Stockholm.
A-579594-264

Map continues pages 74-75

Map continues pages 90-91

Kilometers 0 200 400 600 Km.
Statute Miles 0 200 400 600 Mi.

Scale 1:12,000,000

One centimeter represents 120 kilometers.
One inch represents approximately 190 miles.
Lambert Conformal Conic Projection

BARENTS SEA
NOVAJA ZEML'A
KARSKOJE MORE
KARA SEA
MORE LAPTEVYH
LAPTEV SEA
SEVERNAJA ZEML'A
POLUOSTROV TAJMYR
GORY BYRRANGA
SEVERO-SIBIRSKAJA NIZMENNOST'
POLUOSTROV JAMAL
GYDANSKIJ POLUOSTROV
JAMALO-NENECKIJ
NENECKIJ
URAL'SKIJE GORY
ZAPADNO-SIBIRSKAJA RAVNINA
SIBERIA
SREDNE-SIBIRSKOJE PLOSKOGORJE
PLATO PUTORANA
RUSSIA
STANOVOJE NAGORJE
STANOVOY MOUNTAINS
BURJATIJA
JABLONOVYJ CHREBET
VOSTOČNYJ SAJAN
SAJAN MOUNTAINS
ZAPADNYJ SAJAN
TUVA
CHAKASIJA
ALTAJ
KAZAKHSTAN
MONGOLIA
CHINA
XINJIANG UYGUR ZIZHIQU
JUNGGAR PENDI
Noril'sk
Dudinka
Dikson
Vorkuta
Salechard
Surgut
Omsk
Novosibirsk
Tomsk
Kemerovo
Barnaul
Novokuzneck
Krasnojarsk
Bratsk
Irkutsk
Ulan-Ude
Čita
Abakan
Bijsk
Semipalatinsk
Pavlodar
Ust'-Kamenogorsk
Ulaanbaatar
Darchan
Jenisej
Lena
Ob'
Copyright © by Rand McNally & Co.
Map prepared by Esselte Map Service AB, Stockholm.

Map continues pages 72-73

Map continues pages 90-91

MAP FORM	chrebet	gora	guba	mys	ostrov	ozero	poluostrov	proliv	vodochranilišče
ENGLISH	range	mountain	bay	cape	island	lake	peninsula	strait	reservoir
DEUTSCH	Gebirge	Berg	Bucht	Kap	Insel	See	Halbinsel	Meeresstrasse	Stausee
ESPAÑOL	sierra	montaña	bahia	cabo	isla	lago	peninsula	estrecho	embalse
FRANÇAIS	chaîne	montagne	baie	cap	île	lac	péninsule	détroit	réservoir
PORTUGUÊS	serra	montanha	baia	cabo	ilha	lago	peninsula	estreito	reservatório

Kilometers 0 200 400 600 Km.
Statute Miles 0 200 400 600 Mi.

Scale 1:12,000,000

One centimeter represents 120 kilometers.
One inch represents approximately 190 miles.
Lambert Conformal Conic Projection

ALASKA
UNITED STATES
Chukchi Sea
Bering Strait
OSTROV VRANGEL'A
VOSTOČNO-SIBIRSKOJE MORE
EAST SIBERIAN SEA
NOVOSIBIRSKIJE OSTROVA
OSTROV KOTEL'NYJ
OSTROV NOVAJA SIBIR'
OSTROVA DE-LONGA
OSTROV BOL'ŠOJ L'ACHOVSKIJ
Arctic Circle
SAINT LAWRENCE ISLAND
NUNIVAK ISLAND
SAINT MATTHEW ISLAND
ČUKOTSKIJ POLUOSTROV
EKIATAPSKIJ CHREBET
AN'UJSKIJ CHREBET
ANADYRSKOJE PLOSKOGORJE
Anadyrskij zaliv
Provideniya
Anadyr'
Bering Sea
KOR'AKSKOJE NAGORJE
PENŽINSKIJ CHREBET
KOLYMSKAJA NIZMENNOST'
JUKAGIRSKOJE PLOSKOGORJE
MOMSKIJ CHREBET
CHREBET ČERSKOGO
CHREBET SUNTAR-CHAJATA
CHREBET SETTE-DABAN
JAKUTIJA
SIBERIA
Jakutsk
Magadan
Ochotsk
Ajan
zaliv Šelichova
KAMČATKA
POLUOSTROV KAMČATKA
KAMCHATKA
SREDINNYJ CHREBET
KOMANDORSKIJE OSTROVA
Petropavlovsk-Kamčatskij
SEA OF OKHOTSK
OCHOTSKOJE MORE
KURIL'SKIJE OSTROVA
KURIL ISLANDS
Habomai, Shikotan, Kunashiri, and Etorofu, occupied since 1945, are claimed by Japan pending a final peace treaty.
ALDANSKOJE NAGORJE
STANOVOJ CHREBET
CHREBET DŽUGDŽUR
ŠANTARSKIJE OSTROVA
OSTROV SACHALIN
SAKHALIN
Južno-Sachalinsk
La Perouse Strait
Tatarskij proliv
SICHOTE-ALIN'
BUREINSKIJ CHREBET
Komsomol'sk-na-Amure
Chabarovsk
Blagoveščensk
Svobodnyj
Birobidžan
JEVREJ
Vladivostok
Nachodka
Ussurijsk
Harbin
Qiqihar
MANCHURIA
CHINA
HEILONGJIANG
NEI MONGGOL ZIZHIQU
DA HINGGAN LING
XIAO HINGGAN LING
JILIN
SEA OF JAPAN
HOKKAIDŌ
Sapporo
Asahikawa
Hakodate
JAPAN
HONSHŪ
Aomori
PACIFIC OCEAN

Map continues pages 26-27

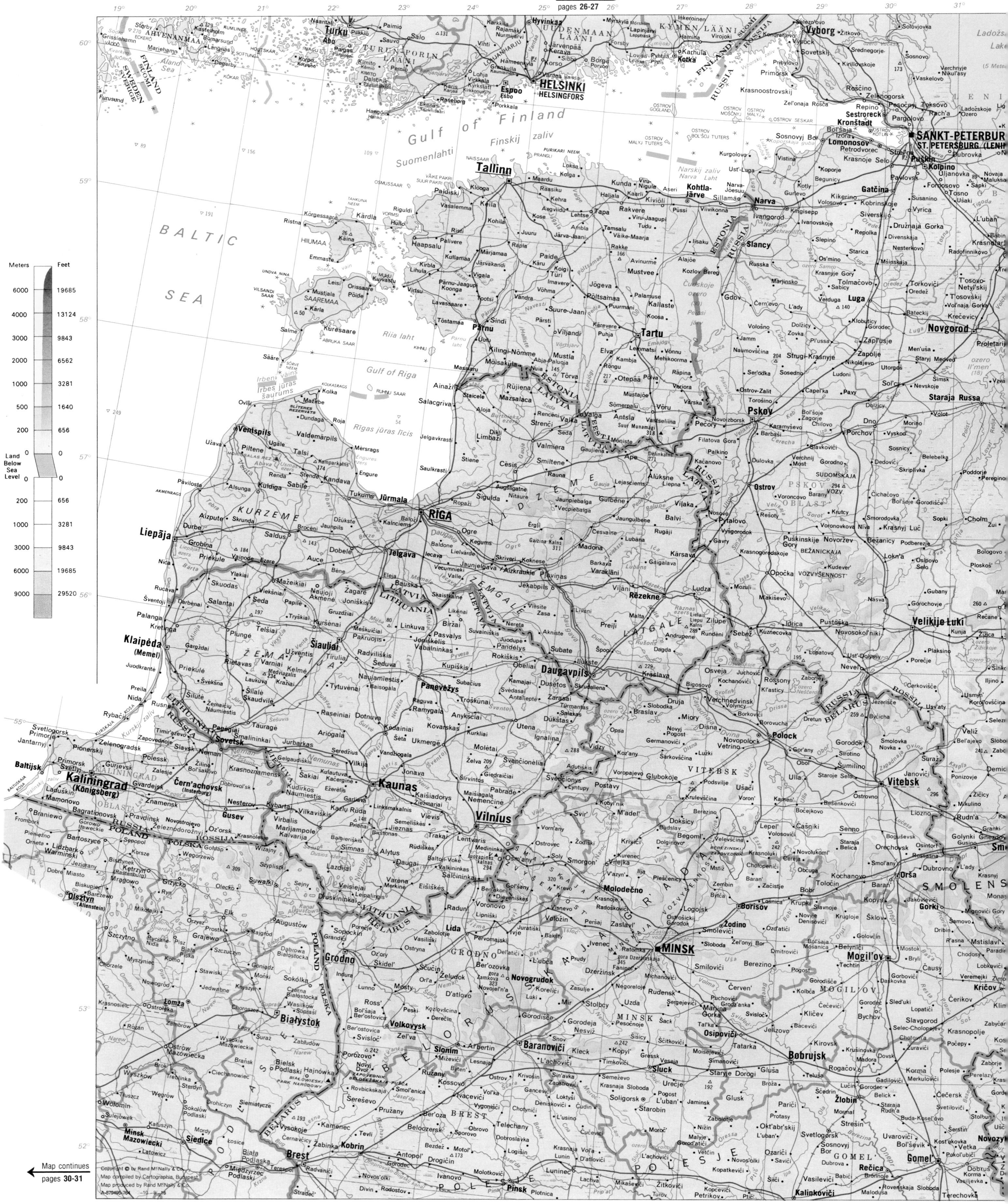
Meters
Feet
6000
19685
4000
13124
3000
9843
2000
6562
1000
3281
500
1640
200
656
0
0
Land Below Sea Level
200
656
1000
3281
3000
9843
6000
19685
9000
29520
BALTIC SEA
Gulf of Finland
Suomenlahti
Finskij zaliv
Gulf of Riga
Rīgas jūras līcis
Riia laht
HELSINKI HELSINGFORS
SANKT-PETERBURG
Tallinn
RĪGA
Vilnius
MINSK
Kaunas
Kaliningrad (Königsberg)
Pskov
Novgorod
Vitebsk
Grodno
Białystok
Brest
Tartu
Daugavpils
Klaipėda (Memel)
Liepāja
Ventspils
Šiauliai
ESTONIA
LATVIA
LITHUANIA
BELARUS
RUSSIA
POLAND
POLSKA
FINLAND SUOMI
SWEDEN SVERIGE
KURZEME
VIDZEME
ZEMGALE
LATGALE
ŽEMAITIJA
SMOLENSK
Copyright © by Rand McNally & Co.
Map compiled by Cartographia, Budapest
Map produced by Rand McNally & Co.

Map continues pages 30-31

MAP FORM	gr'ada	ostrov, o.	ozero, o.	vodochranilišče, vdchr.	vozvyšennost', vozv.	zaliv	zapovednik, zapov.
ENGLISH	ridge	island	lake	reservoir	upland	gulf; bay	reserve
DEUTSCH	Höhenrücken	Insel	See	Stausee	Bergland	Golf; Bucht	Reservat
ESPAÑOL	lomerío	isla	lago	embalse	tierras altas	golfo; bahía	reserva
FRANÇAIS	crête	île	lac	réservoir	hautes terres	golfe; baie	réserve
PORTUGUÊS	cordilheira	ilha	lago	reservatório	terras altas	golfo; baía	reserva

Map continues pages 24-25

MOSKVA
MOSCOW
NIŽNIJ NOVGOROD (GOR'KIJ)
Jaroslavl'
Kostroma
Ivanovo
Vladimir
Vologda
Čerepovec
Rybinsk
Tver' (Kalinin)
Tula
Kaluga
R'azan'
Br'ansk
Orel
Lipeck
Tambov
Jelec
Dzeržinsk
Kovrov
Murom
Kolomna
Serpuchov
Novomoskovsk
Mičurinsk
Tichvin
Boroviči
Ržev
Vyšnij Voloček
Toržok
Sergijev Posad
Podol'sk
Obninsk
Rostov
Uglič
Kinešma
Sokol
Galič
Vjaz'ma
Roslavl'
Kirov
Safonovo
Kimry
Dubna
Klin
Mytišči
Elektrostal'
Orechovo-Zujevo
Noginsk
Ramenskoje
Žukovskij
Domodedovo
Aleksin
Kašira
Stupino
Ozery
Zarajsk
Kasimov
Sasovo
Moršansk
Kotovsk
Rasskazovo
Kirsanov
Jefremov
Mcensk
Livny
Gus'-Chrustal'nyj
Vyksa
Kulebaki
Pavlovo
Balachna
Bor
Gorodec
Zavolžje
VOLOGODSKAJA OBLAST'
JAROSLAVSKAJA OBLAST'
MOSKOVSKAJA OBLAST'
VLADIMIRSKAJA OBLAST'
KALUŽSKAJA OBLAST'
TULSKAJA OBLAST'
RJAZANSKAJA OBLAST'
TAMBOVSKAJA OBLAST'
LIPECKAJA OBLAST'
OREL OBLAST'
BR'ANSKAJA OBLAST'
KURSK OBLAST'
VORONEZ OBLAST'
KOSTROMA OBLAST'
IVANOVO OBLAST'
SREDNERUSSKAJA VOZVYŠENNOST'
SMOLENSKO-MOSKOVSKAJA VOZVYŠENNOST'
VALDAJSKAJA VOZVYŠENNOST'
OKSKO-DONSKAJA RAVNINA
VEPSOVSKAJA VOZVYŠENNOST'
RUSSIA
UKRAINE
Rybinskoje vodochranilišče
Volga
Oka
Moskva
Kl'az'ma
Dnepr
Don
Desna

Map continues pages 80-81

Map continues pages 78-79

Kilometers 0 50 100 150 Km.
Statute Miles 0 50 100 150 Mi.

Scale 1:3,000,000
One centimeter represents 30 kilometers.
One inch represents approximately 47 miles.
Lambert Conformal Conic Projection

Map continues pages 30-31

KIJEV
KIEV
L'vov
Lublin
Kiši'nov
Kishinev
BUCUREŞTI
BUCHAREST
Constanţa
Vinnica
Žitomir
Rovno
Ivano-Frankovsk
Černovcy
Cluj-Napoca
Iaşi
Galaţi
Brăila
Ploieşti
Braşov
Sibiu
Craiova
Debrecen
Oradea
Košice
Radom
Kielce
Rzeszów
Przemyśl
Tarnów
Pinsk
Mozyr'
Gomel'
Korosten'
Berdičev
Chmel'nickij
Bel'cy
Tiraspol'
Bendery
Izmail
Ruse
Silistra
Vidin
UKRAINE
ROMANIA
POLAND
BELARUS
HUNGARY
MOLDOVA
BULGARIA
TRANSYLVANIA
WALLACHIA
CARPATII MERIDIONALI
TRANSYLVANIAN ALPS
VOLYNSKAJA VOZVYŠENNOST'
PODOL'SKAJA VOZVYŠENNOST'
PRIDNEPROVSKAJA VOZVYŠENNOST'
KIJEVSKOJE VODOCHRANILIŠČE
Mouths of the Danube
Danube
21°
22°
23°
24°
25°
26°
27°
28°
29°
30°
44°
45°
46°
47°
48°
49°
50°
51°

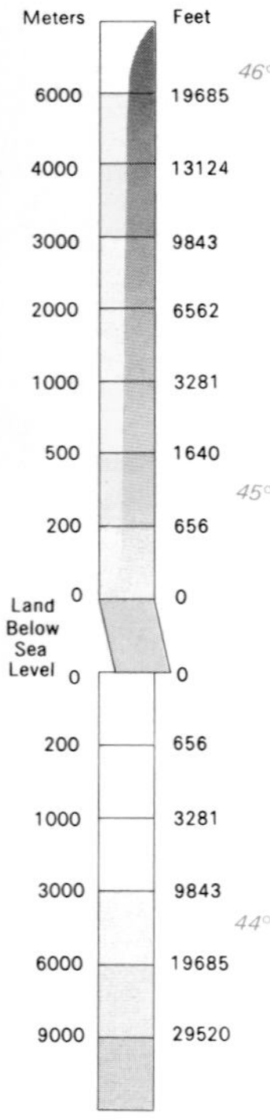
Meters
Feet
6000
19685
4000
13124
3000
9843
2000
6562
1000
3281
500
1640
200
656
0
0
Land Below Sea Level
0
0
200
656
1000
3281
3000
9843
6000
19685
9000
29520

MAP FORM	gora	liman	mys	nizmennost', nizm.	ozero	vozvyšennost', vozv.	zaliv
ENGLISH	mountain	bay	cape	plain	lake	upland	bay
DEUTSCH	Berg	Bucht	Kap	Ebene	See	Bergland	Bucht
ESPAÑOL	montaña	bahía	cabo	llanno	lago	tierras altas	bahía
FRANÇAIS	montagne	baie	cap	plaine	lac	hautes terres	baie
PORTUGUÊS	montanha	baía	cabo	planície	lago	terras altas	baía

Map continues pages 38-39

Map continues pages 76-77

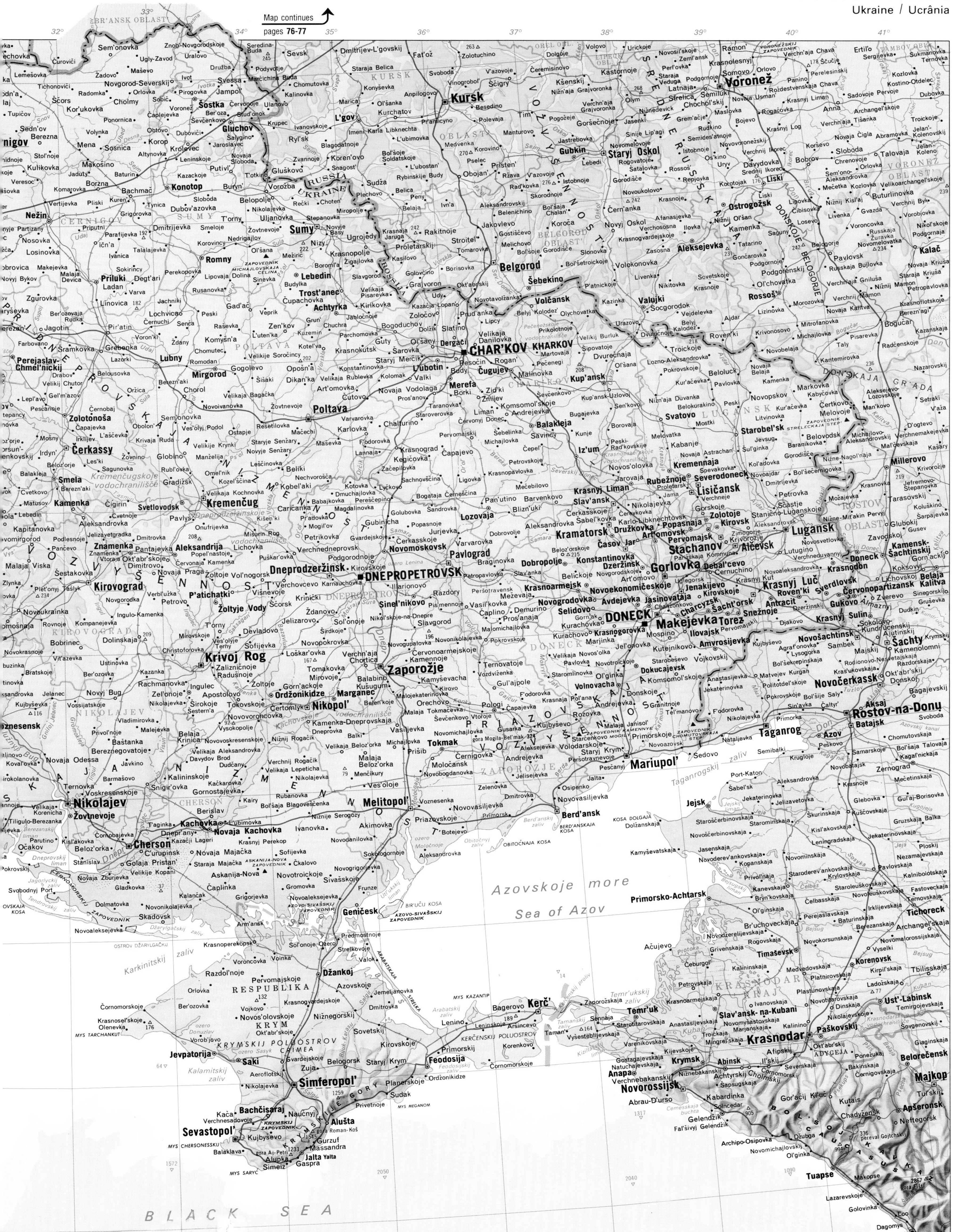
BR'ANSK OBLAST'
KURSK
Kursk
Voronež
Stary Oskol
Belgorod
Sumy
Konotop
Gluchov
Romny
Priluki
Lubny
Mirgorod
Poltava
Čerkassy
Kremenčug
Kirovograd
Krivoj Rog
Nikolajev
Cherson
Nikopol'
Zaporožje
Melitopol'
DNEPROPETROVSK
Dneprodzeržinsk
Pavlograd
ČHAR'KOV KHARKOV
Izjum
Lisičansk
Severodoneck
Lugansk
Kramatorsk
Slav'ansk
Gorlovka
DONECK
Makejevka
Mariupol'
Berd'ansk
Taganrog
Rostov-na-Donu
Novočerkassk
Šachty
Azovskoje more
Sea of Azov
Džankoj
Jevpatorija
Simferopol'
Sevastopol'
Jalta Yalta
Feodosija
Kerč'
Anapa
Novorossijsk
Krasnodar
Majkop
Tuapse
Soči
BLACK SEA
ČORNOJE MORE
KRYM
RESPUBLIKA
KRASNODAR KRAJ
ROSTOV OBLAST'
RUSSIA
UKRAINE
Lambert Conformal Conic Projection

Map continues pages 80-81

Map continues page 84

Kilometers 0 50 100 150 Km.
Statute Miles 0 50 100 150 Mi.

Scale 1:3,000,000
One centimeter represents 30 kilometers.
One inch represents approximately 47 miles.
Lambert Conformal Conic Projection

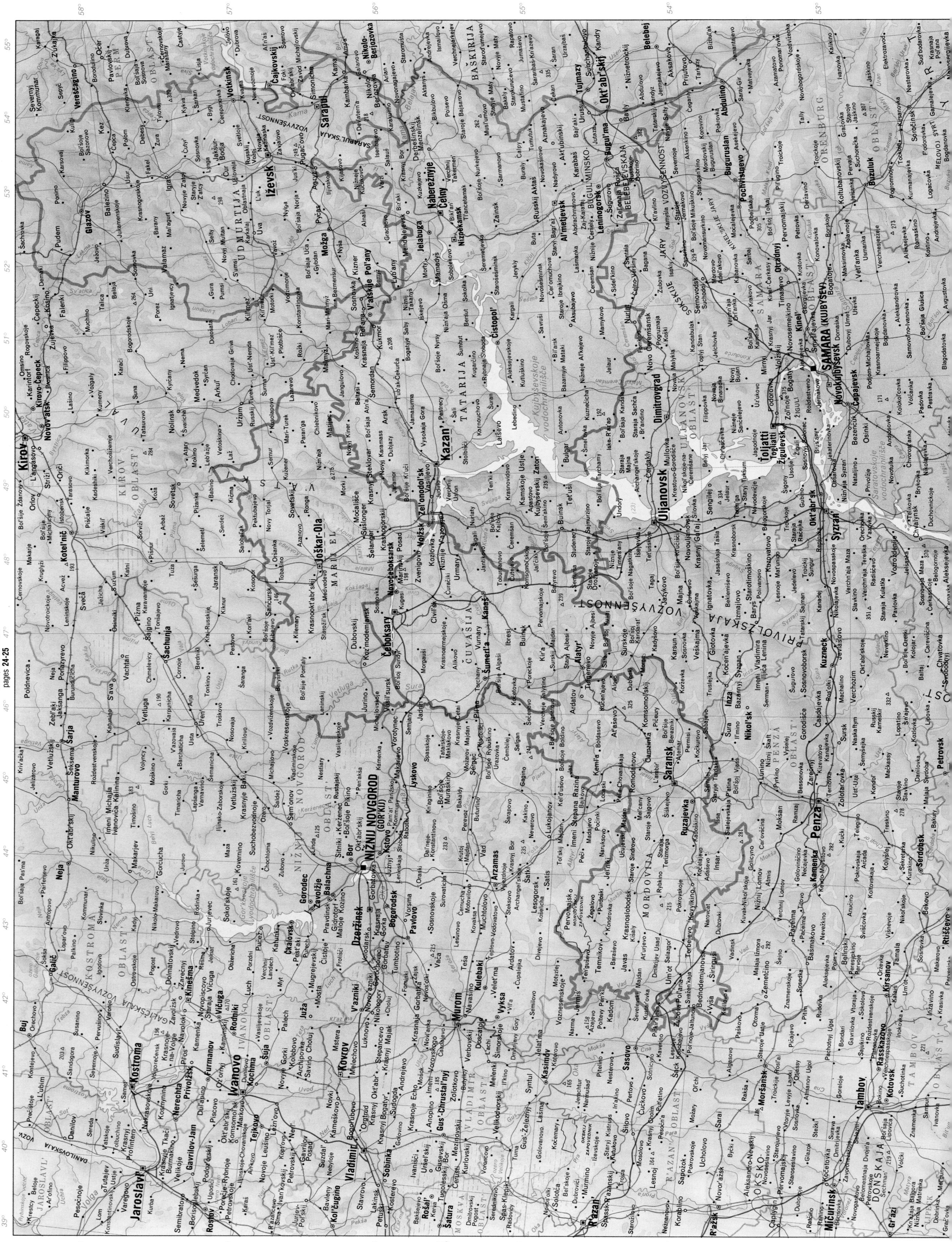
Kirov
Iževsk
Kazan'
Nižnij Novgorod (Gor'kij)
Samara (Kujbyšev)
Ul'janovsk
Penza
Saransk
Čeboksary
Joškar-Ola
Kostroma
Jaroslavl'
Ivanovo
Vladimir
Tambov
Toljatti
Syzran'
Dimitrovgrad
Naberežnyje Čelny
Al'metjevsk
Oktjabr'skij
Arzamas
Murom
Kovrov
Dzeržinsk
Glazov
Votkinsk
Sarapul
Buguruslan
Buzuluk
Novokujbyševsk
Čapajevsk
Kuzneck
Kirsanov
Rasskazovo
Mičurinsk
Kotovsk
Moršansk
Rjazan'
Sasovo
Vyksa
Kineshma
Šuja
Sergač
Alatyr'
Kanaš
Novočeboksarsk
Zelenodol'sk
Čistopol'
Bugul'ma
Leninogorsk
Nižnekamsk
Jelabuga
Mozga
Sarapul
Kujbyševskoje vodochranilišče
Gor'kovskoje vodochranilišče
Saratovskoje vodochranilišče
Volga
Kama
Vjatka
Oka
Sura
Moksa
UDMURTIJA
TATARIJA
ČUVAŠIJA
MORDOVIJA
MARI EL
BAŠKIRIJA
KIROV OBLAST'
NIŽNIJ NOVGOROD OBLAST'
KOSTROMA OBLAST'
IVANOVO OBLAST'
VLADIMIR OBLAST'
JAROSLAVL' OBLAST'
RJAZAN' OBLAST'
TAMBOV OBLAST'
PENZA OBLAST'
UL'JANOVSK OBLAST'
SAMARA OBLAST'
ORENBURG OBLAST'
PERM OBLAST'
PRIVOLŽSKAJA VOZVYŠENNOST'
GALIČSKAJA VOZVYŠENNOST'
BUGUL'MINSKO-BELEBEJEVSKAJA VOZVYŠENNOST'
OKSKO-DONSKAJA
39°
40°
41°
42°
43°
44°
45°
46°
47°
48°
49°
50°
51°
52°
53°
54°
55°
56°
57°
58°

Map continues
pages 24-25

Map continues
pages 76-77

Map continues pages 86-87

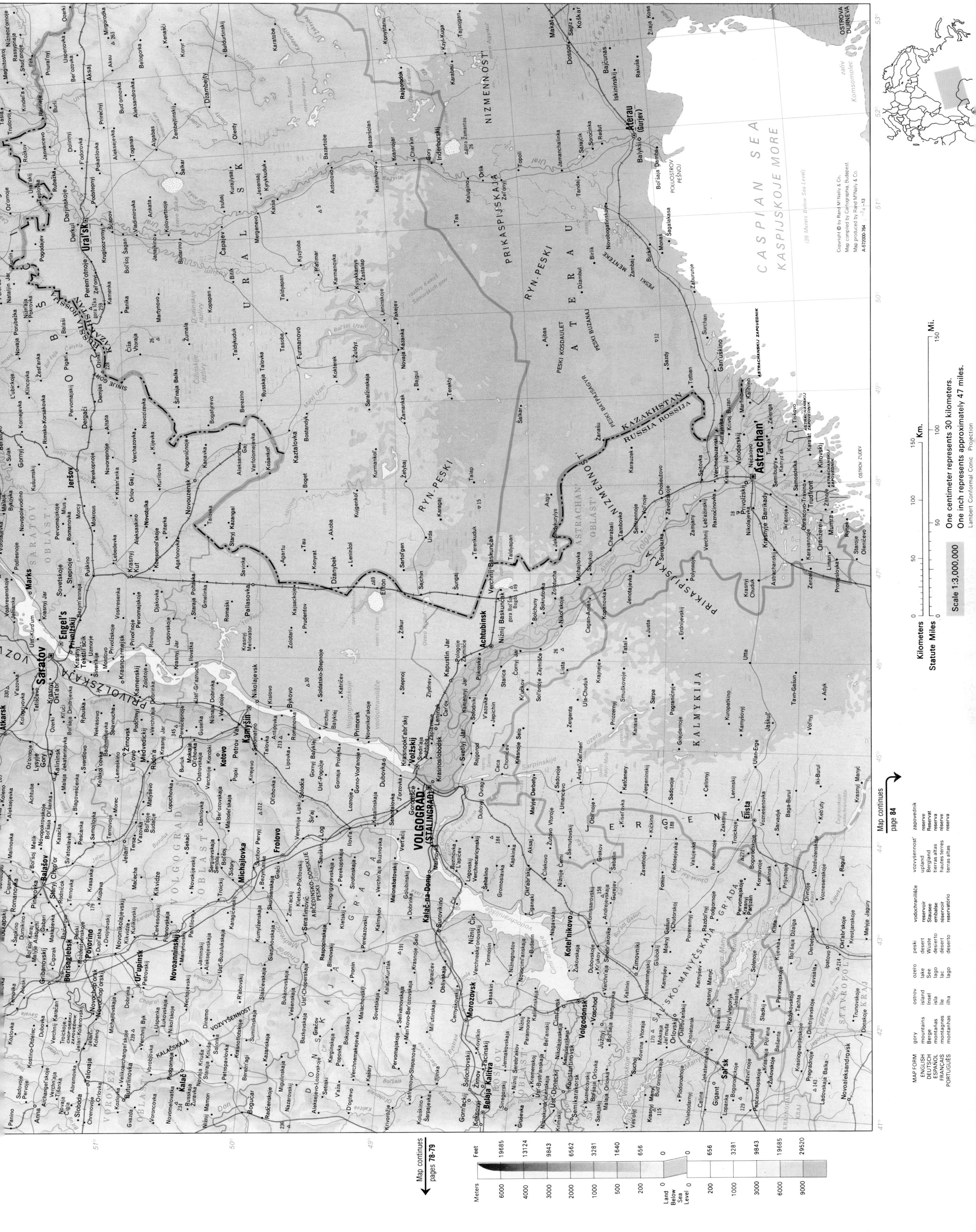
Saratov
Volgograd (Stalingrad)
Astrachan'
Ural'sk
Aterau (Gurjev)
Engel's
Kamyšin
Elista
Achtubinsk
Volžskij
Caspian Sea
Kaspijskoje More
Prikaspijskaja Nizmennost'
Ryn-Peski
Kalmykija
Kazakhstan
Russia Rossija
Scale 1:3,000,000
Kilometers
Statute Miles
One centimeter represents 30 kilometers.
One inch represents approximately 47 miles.
Lambert Conformal Conic Projection
MAP FORM / ENGLISH / DEUTSCH / ESPAÑOL / FRANÇAIS / PORTUGUÊS
gory / mountains / Berge / montañas / montagnes / montanhas
ostrov / island / Insel / isla / île / ilha
ozero / lake / See / lago / lac / lago
peski / desert / Wüste / desierto / désert / deserto
vodochranilišče / reservoir / Stausee / embalse / réservoir / reservatório
vozvyšennost' / upland / Bergland / tierras altas / hautes terres / terras altas
zapovednik / reserve / Reservat / reserva / réserve / reserva
Feet
Meters
Land Below Sea Level
Copyright © by Rand McNally & Co.
Map compiled by Cartographia, Budapest.
Map produced by Rand McNally & Co.
A-572000-764 -1-1-13

Map continues page 84

Map continues pages 78-79

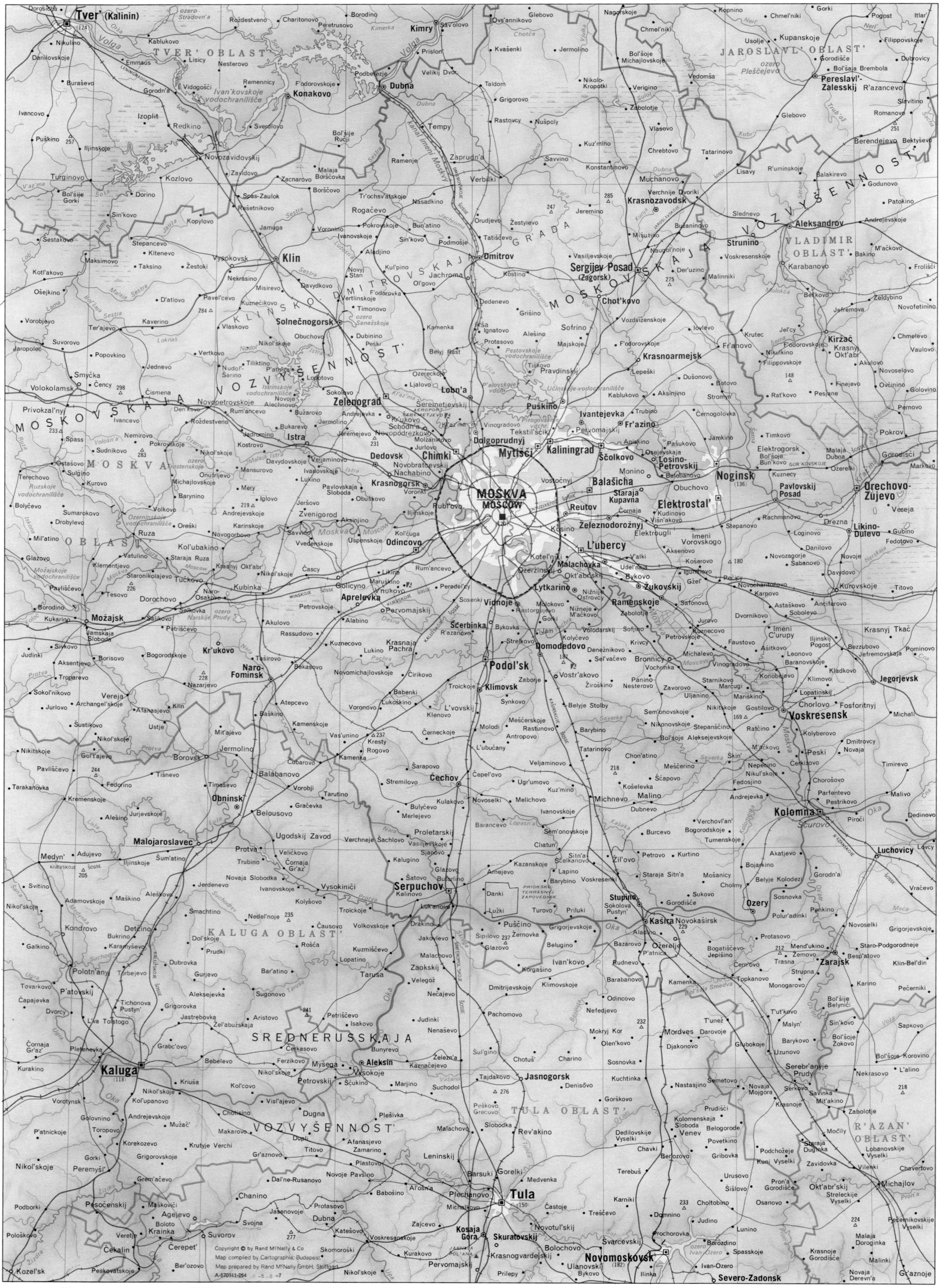
36°
36°30′
37°
37°30′
38°
38°30′
39°
56° 30′
56°
55° 30′
55°
54° 30′
Tver′ (Kalinin)
TVER′ OBLAST′
Volga
Kimry
Dubna
Konakovo
Ivan′kovskoje vodochranilišče
Kanal imeni Moskvy
Klin
Dmitrov
Sergijev Posad (Zagorsk)
Pereslavl′-Zalesskij
JAROSLAVL′ OBLAST′
VLADIMIR OBLAST′
Aleksandrov
Strunino
Krasnozavodsk
Chot′kovo
Solnečnogorsk
Zelenograd
Lobn′a
Puškino
Ivantejevka
Fr′azino
Krasnoarmejsk
KLINSKO-DMITROVSKAJA GR′ADA
MOSKOVSKAJA VOZVYŠENNOST′
Volokolamsk
Istra
Chimki
Dolgoprudnyj
Mytišči
Kaliningrad
Ščolkovo
Noginsk
Elektrostal′
Orechovo-Zujevo
Pavlovskij Posad
Balašicha
Reutov
Železnodorožnyj
L′ubercy
Dedovsk
Krasnogorsk
MOSKVA
MOSCOW
MOSKVA OBLAST′
Odincovo
Zvenigorod
Ruza
Možajsk
Tučkovo
Golicyno
Kubinka
Aprelevka
Vidnoje
Lytkarino
Žukovskij
Ramenskoje
Dzeržinskij
Ščerbinka
Domodedovo
Podol′sk
Klimovsk
Naro-Fominsk
Borovsk
Obninsk
Malojaroslavec
Čechov
Serpuchov
Kašira
Stupino
Ozery
Kolomna
Voskresensk
Bronnicy
Egorjevsk
Luchovicy
Zarajsk
Oka
Protva
Kaluga
KALUGA OBLAST′
SREDNERUSSKAJA VOZVYŠENNOST′
Aleksin
Tarusa
Jasnogorsk
TULA OBLAST′
Tula
Kosaja Gora
Ščokino
Novomoskovsk
Venev
Severo-Zadonsk
Suvorov
Lichvin
R′AZAN′ OBLAST′
Michajlov
Serebr′anyje Prudy
Kozel′sk
PRIOKSKO-TERRASNYJ ZAPOVEDNIK
Copyright © by Rand McNally & Co.
Map compiled by Cartographia, Budapest.
Map prepared by Rand McNally GmbH, Stuttgart.
A-570311-264 -5 -3 -7

MAP FORM	gr′ada	ozero	vodochranilišče, vdchr.	vozvyšennost′	zapovednik
ENGLISH	ridge	lake	reservoir	upland	reserve
DEUTSCH	Höhenrücken	See	Stausee	Bergland	Reservat
ESPAÑOL	lomerio	lago	embalse	tierras altas	reserva
FRANÇAIS	crête	lac	réservoir	hautes terres	réserve
PORTUGUÊS	cordilheira	lago	reservatório	terras altas	reserva

Kilometers 0 10 20 30 40 50 Km.

Statute Miles 0 10 20 30 40 50 Mi.

Scale 1:1,000,000

One centimeter represents 10 kilometers.
One inch represents approximately 16 miles.
Lambert Conformal Conic Projection

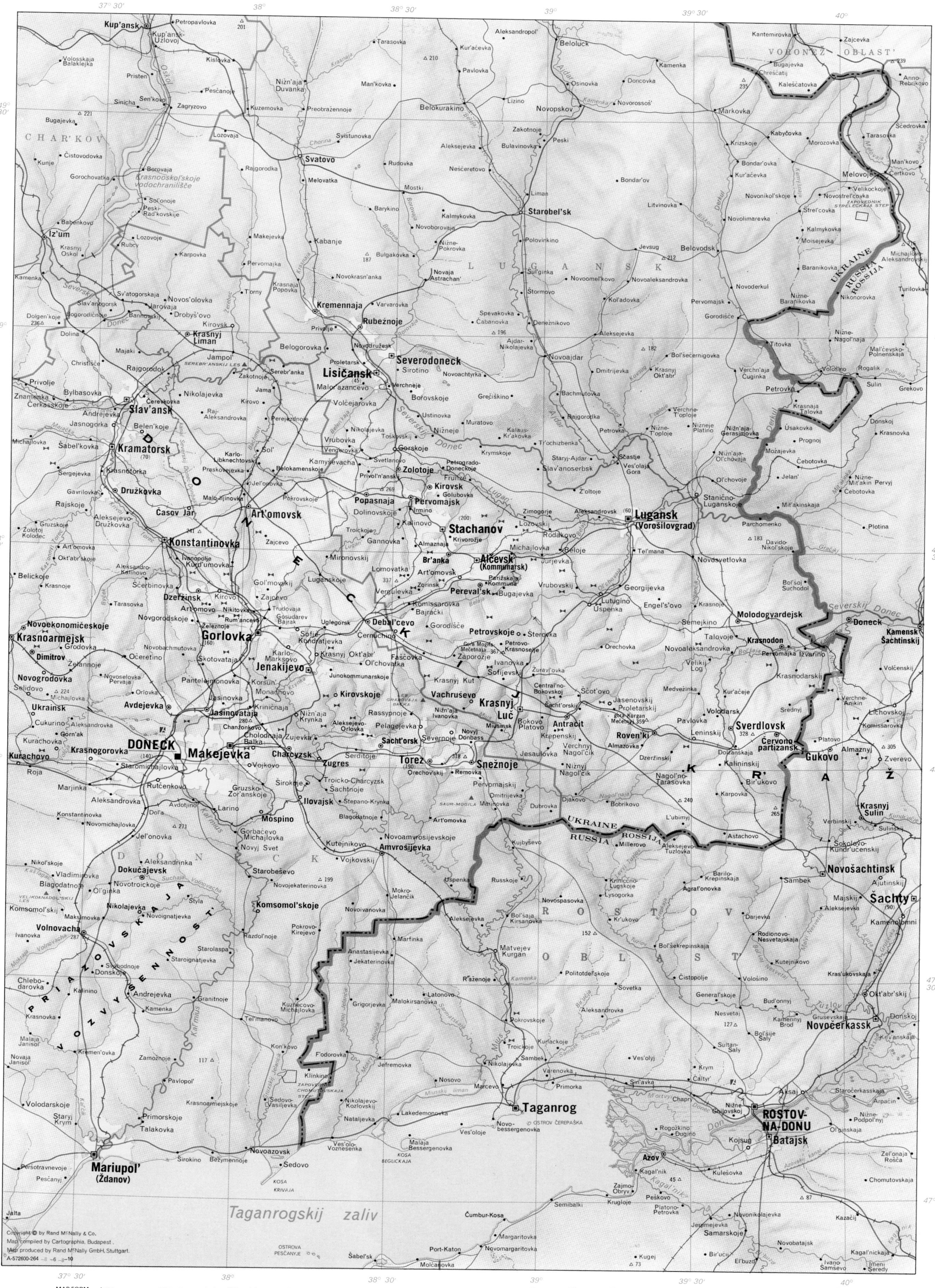
Kup'ansk
Kup'ansk-Uzlovoj
Petropavlovka
Tarasovka
Kur'ačevka
Aleksandropol'
Beloluck
Kantemirovka
Zajcevka
VORONEŽ OBLAST'
Bugajevka
Kamenka
Osinovka
Doncovka
Kalešcatovka
Volosskaja Balakleja
Kislovka
Pristen'
Oskol
Pavlovka
Man'kovka
Nižn'aja Duvanka
Pesčanoje
Sen'kovo
Sinicha
Zagryzovo
Kuzemovka
Preobraženoje
Belokurakino
Lizino
Novopskov
Novorossoš'
Markovka
Anno-Rebrikovo
Bugajevka
CHAR'KOV
Lozovaja
Svistunovka
Zakotnoje
Peski
Kabyčovka
Tarasovka
Ščedrovka
Čistovodovka
Kunje
Svatovo
Rudovka
Aleksejevka
Bulavinovka
Krizskoje
Morozovka
Man'kovo
Gorochovatka
Borovaja
Krasnooskol'skoje vodochranilišče
Rajgorodka
Melovatka
Nesčeretovo
Bondar'ovka
Bondar'ov
Melovoje
Čertkovo
Sol'onoje
Peski-Rad'kovskije
Mostki
Liman
Kur'ačevka
Velikokoje
Litvinovka
Novonikol'skoje
Novostrel'covka
Babenkovo
Barykino
Kalmykovka
Starobel'sk
Strel'covka
Iz'um
Lozovoje
Novoborovaja
Makejevka
Novolimarevka
Kalmykovka
Rubcy
Krasnyj Oskol
Kabanje
Nižne-Pokrovka
Polovinkino
Moisejevka
Karpovka
Bulgakovka
Jevsug
Belovodsk
Mychajlo-Aleksandrovskij
Pervomajka
Kamenka
Novokrasn'anka
Novaja Astrachan'
Sul'gina
Novoomel'kovo
Novoaleksandrovka
Baranikovka
LUGANSK
Severskij Donec
Sv'atogorskaja
Novos'olovka
Torny
Krasnaja Popovka
Stormovo
Novoderkul
Turilovka
UKRAINE
RUSSIA
ROSSIJA
Slav'anogorsk
Jarovaja
Kremennaja
Varvarovka
Nižne-Baranikovka
Nikonorovka
Dolgen'koje
Bogorodičnoje
Drobyš'ovo
Bannovskij
Kol'adovka
Pervomajsk
Gorodišče
Rubežnoje
Spevakovka
Čabanovka
Deneznikovo
Dolina
Krasnyj Liman
Kirovsk
Privolje
Aleksejevka
Titovka
Nizne-Nagol'naja
Majaki
Christišče
Jampol'
Belogorovka
Novodružesk
Proletarsk
Severodoneck
Sirotino
Ajdar-Nikolajevka
Novoajdar
Bol'šecernigovka
Mal'čevsko-Polnenskaja
Rajgorodok
Zakotnoje
Lisičansk
Novoachtyrka
Dmitrijevka
Krasnyj Okt'abr'
Verchn'aja Cuginka
Rogalik
Vološino
Sulin
Privolje
Bylbasovka
Jama
Malorjazancevo
Verchneje
Borovskoje
Grečiškino
Bachmutovka
Petrovka
Grekovo
Znamenka
Čerkasskoje
Nikolajevka
Slav'ansk
Čerevkovka
Raj-Aleksandrovka
Kirovo
Volčejarovka
Krasnaja Talovka
Andrejevka
Perejezdnoje
Ustinovka
Muratovo
Rajgorodka
Verchne-T'oploje
Donskoj
Jasnogorka
Belen'koje
Nižneje
Kalaus-Kr'akovka
Nižne-T'oploje
Nižneje Platino
Nižn'aja-Gerasimovka
Usakovka
Krasnovka
Michajlovka
Šabel'kovka
Kramatorsk
Nikolajevka
Toškovskij
Vrubovka
Gorskoje
Krymskoje
Tr'ochizbenka
Petrovka
Prognoj
DONECK
Karlo-Libknechtovskij
Sol'
Kamyševacha
Svetlanovo
Staryj Ajdar
Ščastje
Nižn'aja-Ol'chovaja
Možajevka
Sergejevka
Krasnotorka
Praskovejevka
Belokamenskoje
Petrogrado-Doneckoje
Zolotoje
Slav'anoserbsk
Ves'olaja Gora
Čebotovka
Jel'onovka
Privol'nanskij
Frunze
Ol'chovoje
Jelan'
Nizne-Mit'akin Pervyj
Gavrilovka
Družkovka
Kirovsk
Golubovka
Z'oltoje
Čebotovka
Malo-Iljinovka
Pokrovskoje
Popasnaja
Pervomajsk
Staničn-Luganskoje
Rajskoje
Časov Jar
Art'omovsk
Dolinovskoje
Irmino
Zimogorje
Aleksandrovsk
Lugansk
(Vorošilovgrad)
Mit'akinskaja
Aleksejevo-Družkovka
Kalinovo
Stachanov
Parchomenko
Plotina
Gruzskoje
Zolotoj Kolodec
Konstantinovka
Zajcevo
Troickoje
Lozovskij
Krivorožje
Rodakovo
Davido-Nikol'skoje
Art'omovka
Gannovka
Almaznaja
Michajlovka
Beloje
Tel'mana
Okt'abr'skoje
Ivanopolje
Kurd'umovka
Mironovskij
Br'anka
Alčevsk
(Kommunarsk)
Jurjevka
Novosvetlovka
Belickoje
Aleksandro-Kalinovo
Lomovatka
Art'omovsk
Parižskaja Kommuna
Vrubovskij
Georgijevka
Bol'soj Suchodol
Krasnoje
Ščerbinovka
Gol'movskij
Luganskoje
Vergulevka
Zorinsk
Pereval'sk
Bugajevka
Lutugino
Engel's'ovo
Uspenka
Tarasovka
Dzeržinsk
Kirovo
Zajcevo
Komissarovka
Bajrački
Krasnoje
Molodogvardejsk
Severskij Donec
Doneck
Kamensk Šachtinskij
Artemovo
Nikitovka
Trudovaja
Gosudarev Bajrak
Uglegorsk
Debal'cevo
Gorodišče
Novoekonomičeskoje
Novgorodskoje
Rum'ancevo
Petrovskoje
Sterovka
Semejkino
Krasnoarmejsk
Grodovka
Gorlovka
Sofije-Kondratjevka
Černuchino
Gora Mogila
Mečetnaja
Petrovo-Krasnosel'je
Talovoje
Krasnodon
Orechovka
Novoaleksandrovka
Dimitrov
Novobachmutovka
Karlo-Marksovo
Krasnyj Okt'abr'
Zaporožje
Pervomajka
Izvarino
Želannoje
Očeretino
Skotovataja
Fascovka
Ol'chovatka
Ivanovka
Velikij Log
Volčenskij
Novogrodovka
Novoselovka Pervaja
Panteleimonovka
Jenakijevo
Junokommunarskoje
Krasnyj Kut
Sofijevskij
Žuravl'ovka
Krasnodarskij
Selidovo
Orlovka
Korsun'
Central'no-Bokovskoj
Ščot'ovo
Michajlovka
Monachovo
Kirovskoje
Vachruševo
Krasnyj Luč
Šachtorskij
Jasenovskij
Medvežinka
Kur'ačeje
Verchne-Anikin
Ukrainsk
Jasinovka
Avdejevka
Jasinovataja
Krinichnaja
Nižn'aja Krynka
Rassypnoje
Nižn'aja-Ivanovka
Proletarskij
Gora Kurgan Mečetnaja
Volodarsk
Srednyj
Cukurino
Aleksandrovka
Gorn'ak
Chanžonkovo
Aleksejevo-Orlovka
Pelagejevka
Bokovo-Platovo
Miusinsk
Antracit
Pavlovka
Leninskij
Sverdlovsk
Lichovskoj
Komissarovka
Kurachovka
Cholodnaja Balka
Zujevka
Sacht'orsk
Severnoje
Novyj Donbass
Krepenskij
Verchnij Nagol'čik
Roven'ki
Červono partizansk
Platovo
Almaznyj
Kurachovo
Krasnogorovka
DONECK
Makejevka
Charcyzsk
Serditoje
Torez
Snežnoje
Jesaulovka
Almazovka
Dzeržinskij
Dolžanskaja
Kalininskij
Gukovo
Zverevo
Roja
Staromichajlovka
Vojkovo
Zugres
Orechovskij
Removka
Nižnyj Nagol'čik
Nagol'no-Tarasovka
Bir'ukovo
Marjinka
Rutčenkovo
Širokoje
Troicko-Charcyzsk
Šachtnoje
Pervomajskij
Omitrijevka
Karpovka
Krasnyj Sulin
Aleksandrovka
Gruzsko-Zor'anskoje
Ilovajsk
Stepano-Krynka
Saur-Mogila
Marinovka
Dubrovka
Djakovo
Bobrikovo
Avdotjino
Larino
Konstantinovka
Novomichajlovka
Dol'a
Mospino
Blagodatnoje
Art'omovka
L'ubimyj
Verbinskij
Sulinskij
Jel'onovka
Gorbačevo Michajlovka
Novoamvrosijevskoje
Kujbyševo
Astachovo
Sokolovo-Kundr'učenskij
Nikol'skoje
Aleksandrinka
Novyj Svet
Kutejnikovo
Amvrosijevka
Millerovo
Aleksejevo-Tuzlovka
Novošachtinsk
Dokučajevsk
Vojkovskij
Uspenka
Russkoje
Krinično-Lugskoje
Barilo-Krepinskaja
Sambek
Ajutinskij
Vladimirovka
Blagodatnoje
Novotroickoje
Starobeševo
Novojekaterinovka
Mokro-Jelančik
Lysogorka
Agrafonovka
Majskij
Šachty
Ol'ginka
Stylja
Komsomol'skoje
Novospasovka
Aleksejevka
Nikolajevka
Novoignatjevka
Novoivanovka
Aleksejevka
Bol'šaja Kirsanovka
ROSTOV
Kr'ukovo
Darjevka
Kamenolomni
Komsomol'skij
Maksimovka
Pokrovo-Kirejevo
Volnovacha
Ivanovka
Razdol'noje
Marfinka
Rodionovo-Nesvetajskaja
Bol'šekrepinskaja
Starolaspa
Staroignatjevka
Anastasijevka
Jekaterinovka
Matvejev Kurgan
OBLAST'
Kutejnikovo
Svobodnoje
Donskoje
Politotdel'skoje
Čistopolje
Vološino
Kras'ukovskaja
Chlebodarovka
Andrejevka
Granitnoje
R'aženoje
Sovetka
General'skoje
Bud'onnyj
Okt'abr'skij
Kalinino
Latonovo
Malokirsanovka
Kamenka
Kuznecovo-Michajlovka
Grigorjevka
Aleksandrovka
Nesvetaj
Kamennyj Brod
Gruševskaja
Novočerkassk
Donskoj
Krasnovka
Tel'manovo
Pokrovskoje
Bol'šije Saly
Malaja Janisol'
Kon'kovo
Troickoje
Kurlackoje
Sultan-Saly
Kr'ukovo
Kremen'ovka
Novaja Janisol'
F'odorovka
Jefremovka
Sambek
Ves'olyj
Krym
Zamožnoje
Nikolajevka
Varenovka
Primorka
Čaltyr'
Pavlopol'
Klinkino
Zapovednik Chomutovskaja Step'
Novovo
Marcevo
Sin'avka
Aksaj
Starocerkasskaja
Arpačin
Volodarskoje
Krasnoarmejskoje
Sedovo-Vasiljevka
Nikolajevo-Kozlovskij
Miusskij liman
Taganrog
Chapry
Nižne-Gnilovskoj
ROSTOV-NA-DONU
Nižne-Podpol'nyj
Staryj Krym
Primorskoje
Nataljevka
Lakedemonovka
Novo-bessergenovka
Ostrov Čerepaška
Ves'oloje
Rogožkino
Dugino
Ol'ginskaja
Talakovka
Ves'olo-Voznesenka
Malaja Bessergenovka
Kojsug
Batajsk
Zel'onaja Rošča
Mariupol'
(Ždanov)
Širokino
Bezymennoje
Novoazovsk
Sedovo
Kosa Beglickaja
Azov
Kagal'nik
Kulešovka
Chomutovskaja
Peresravnevoje
Pesčanyj
Kosa Krivaja
Zajmo-Obryv
Kagal'nik
Peškovo
Jalta
Taganrogskij zaliv
Semibalki
Krugloje
Platono-Petrovka
Novonikolajevka
Kazačij
Čumbur-Kosa
Jeremejevka
Samarskoje
Margaritovka
Ostrova Pesčanyje
Port-Katon
Novomargaritovka
Kugej
Novobatajsk
Kagal'nickaja
Šabel'sk
Molčanovka
Bir'učij
El'buzd
Ivano-Samsevo
Ilmen' Seredy
Copyright © by Rand McNally & Co.
Map compiled by Cartographia, Budapest.
Map produced by Rand McNally GmbH, Stuttgart.
A-572600-264
37° 30'
38°
38° 30'
39°
39° 30'
40°
49° 30'
49°
48° 30'
48°
47° 30'
47°

MAP FORM	kosa	ostrov, o.	vodochranilišče, vdchr.	vozvyšennost', vozv.	zaliv	zapovednik, zapov
ENGLISH	spit	island	reservoir	upland	bay	reserve
DEUTSCH	Landzunge	Insel	Stausee	Bergland	Bucht	Reservat
ESPAÑOL	lengua de tierra	isla	embalse	tierras altas	bahía	reserva
FRANÇAIS	flèche	île	réservoir	hautes terres	baie	réserve
PORTUGUÊS	ponta de terra	ilha	reservatório	terras altas	baía	reserva

Kilometers 0 10 20 30 40 50 Km.

Statute Miles 0 10 20 30 40 50 Mi.

Scale 1:1,000,000

One centimeter represents 10 kilometers.
One inch represents approximately 16 miles.
Lambert Conformal Conic Projection

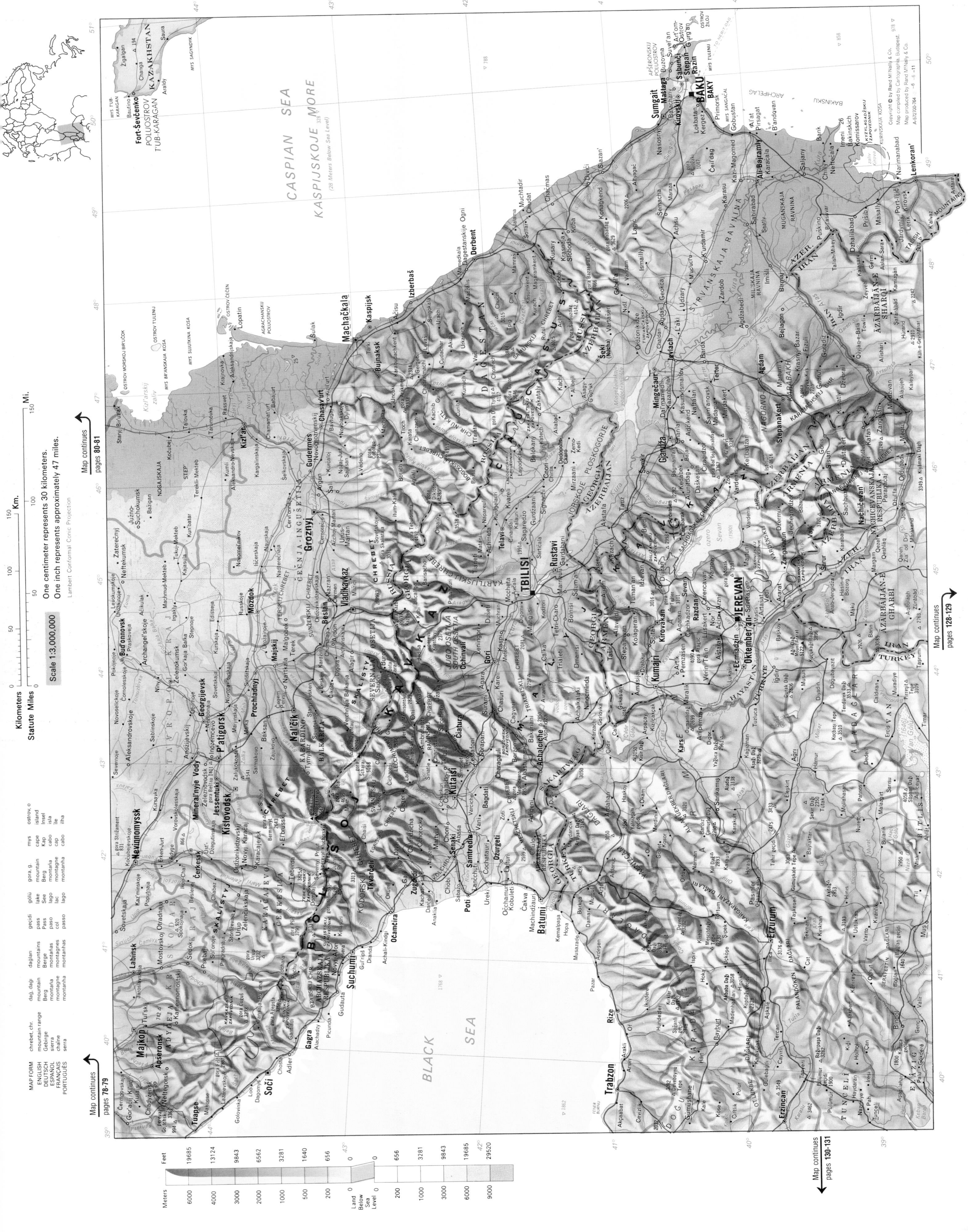
Kilometers 0 50 100 150 Km.
Statute Miles 0 50 100 150 Mi.
Scale 1:3,000,000
One centimeter represents 30 kilometers.
One inch represents approximately 47 miles.
Lambert Conformal Conic Projection
Map continues pages 78-79
Map continues pages 80-81
Map continues pages 128-129
Map continues pages 130-131
CASPIAN SEA
KASPIJSKOJE MORE
(28 Meters Below Sea Level)
BLACK SEA
TBILISI
JEREVAN
BAKU
Feet 19685 13124 9843 6562 3281 1640 656 0 0 656 3281 9843 19685 29520
Meters 6000 4000 3000 2000 1000 500 200 0 Land Below Sea Level 0 200 1000 3000 6000 9000
Copyright © by Rand McNally & Co.

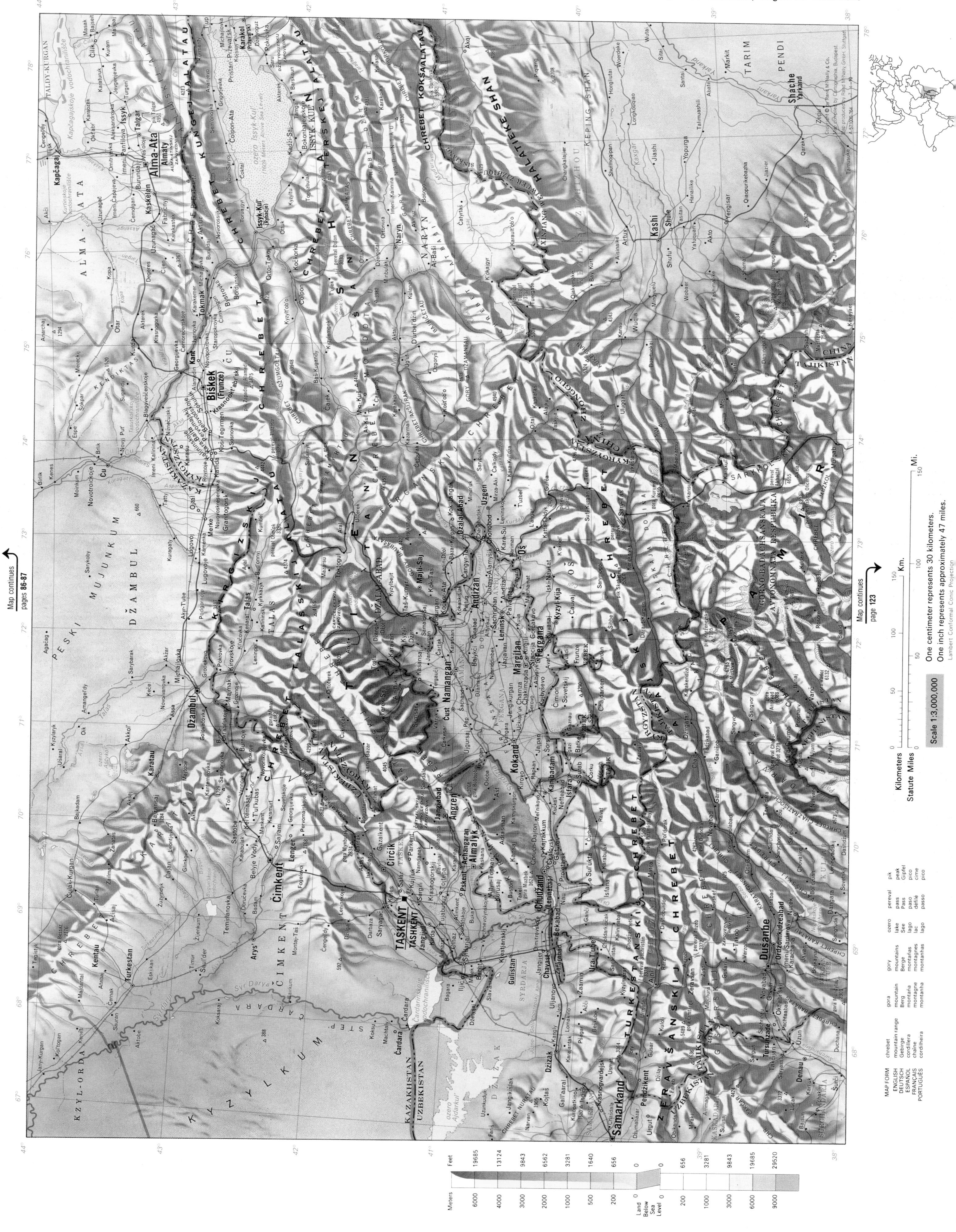
Map continues pages 86-87
Map continues page 123
TAŠKENT
Biškek (Frunze)
Alma-Ata
Almaty
Dušanbe
Samarkand
Kashi
Kokand
Namangan
Andižan
Fergana
Čimkent
Džambul
Turkestan
Leninabad
Chudžand
KAZAKHSTAN
UZBEKISTAN
TAJIKISTAN
CHINA
TARIM PENDI
Scale 1:3,000,000
One centimeter represents 30 kilometers.
One inch represents approximately 47 miles.
Lambert Conformal Conic Projection
Kilometers
Statute Miles
MAP FORM
ENGLISH
DEUTSCH
ESPAÑOL
FRANÇAIS
PORTUGUÊS
chrebet
mountain range
Gebirge
cordillera
chaîne
cordilheira
gora
mountain
Berg
montaña
montagne
montanha
gory
mountains
Berge
montañas
montagnes
montanhas
ozero
lake
See
lago
lac
lago
pereval
pass
Pass
paso
défilé
passo
pik
peak
Gipfel
pico
cime
pico
Meters
Feet
Land Below Sea Level

Map continues pages 72-73

Map continues pages 24-25

Map continues pages 80-81

Perm'
Kirov
Ufa
Orenburg
SAMARA
Kazan'
JEKATERINBURG (SVERDLOVSK)
ČEL'ABINSK
Magnitogorsk
Kurgan
T'umen'
Petropavlovsk
Kustanaj
Akt'ubinsk
Orsk
Ural'sk
Aral'sk
Kzyl-Orda
Džezkazgan
Celinograd
Kokčetav
Turkestan
Novokazalinsk
Arkalyk
Atbasar
Nižnij Tagil
Iževsk
Naberežnyje Čelny
Sterlitamak
Zlatoust
Miass
Troick
Rudnyj
Lisakovsk
Novotroick
Gaj
Mednogorsk
Buzuluk
Buguruslan
Oktʼabrʼskij
Almetjevsk
Leninogorsk
Bugulʼma
Dimitrovgrad
Novokujbyševsk
Solikamsk
Berezniki
Serov
Krasnoturjinsk
Karpinsk
Severouralʼsk
Kungur
Čajkovskij
Sarapul
Glazov
Votkinsk
Pervouralʼsk
Kamensk-Uralʼskij
Šadrinsk
Išim
Tobolʼsk
Irbit
Kyštym
Satka
Beloreck
Salavat
Kumertau
Išimbaj
URALʼSKIJE GORY
BAŠKIRIJA
UDMURTIJA
TATARIJA
KAZAKHSTAN
UZBEKISTAN
RUSSIA
ROSSIJA
Aral Sea
Caspian Sea
KYZYLKUM
TURGAJSKOJE PLATO
PRIARALʼSKIJE KARAKUMY
PLATO USTJURT
MANGISTAU
KARAKALPAK RESPUBLIKA
Copyright © by Rand McNally & Co.
Map compiled by Cartographia, Budapest.
Map produced by Rand McNally & Co.
A-579500-764

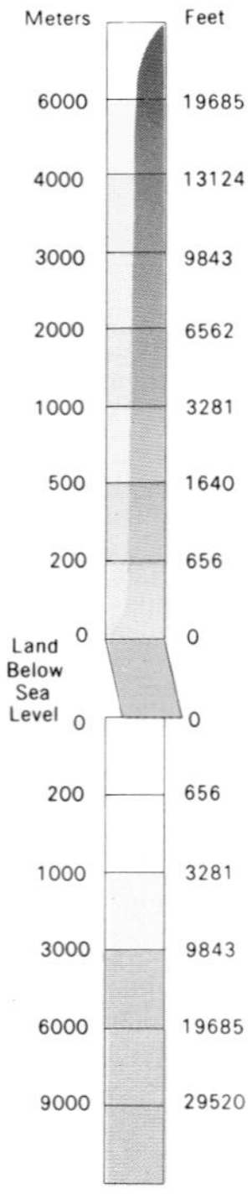
Meters
Feet
6000 19685
4000 13124
3000 9843
2000 6562
1000 3281
500 1640
200 656
0 0
Land Below Sea Level
0 0
200 656
1000 3281
3000 9843
6000 19685
9000 29520

Map continues page 85

MAP FORM	chrebet	gora	hu	ozero	plato	porog
ENGLISH	mountain range	mountain	lake	lake	plateau	waterfall
DEUTSCH	Gebirge	Berg	See	See	Hochebene	Wasserfall
ESPAÑOL	cordillera	montaña	lago	lago	meseta	cascada
FRANÇAIS	chaîne	montagne	lac	lac	plateau	chute d'eau
PORTUGUÊS	cordilheira	montanha	lago	lago	planalto	queda d'água

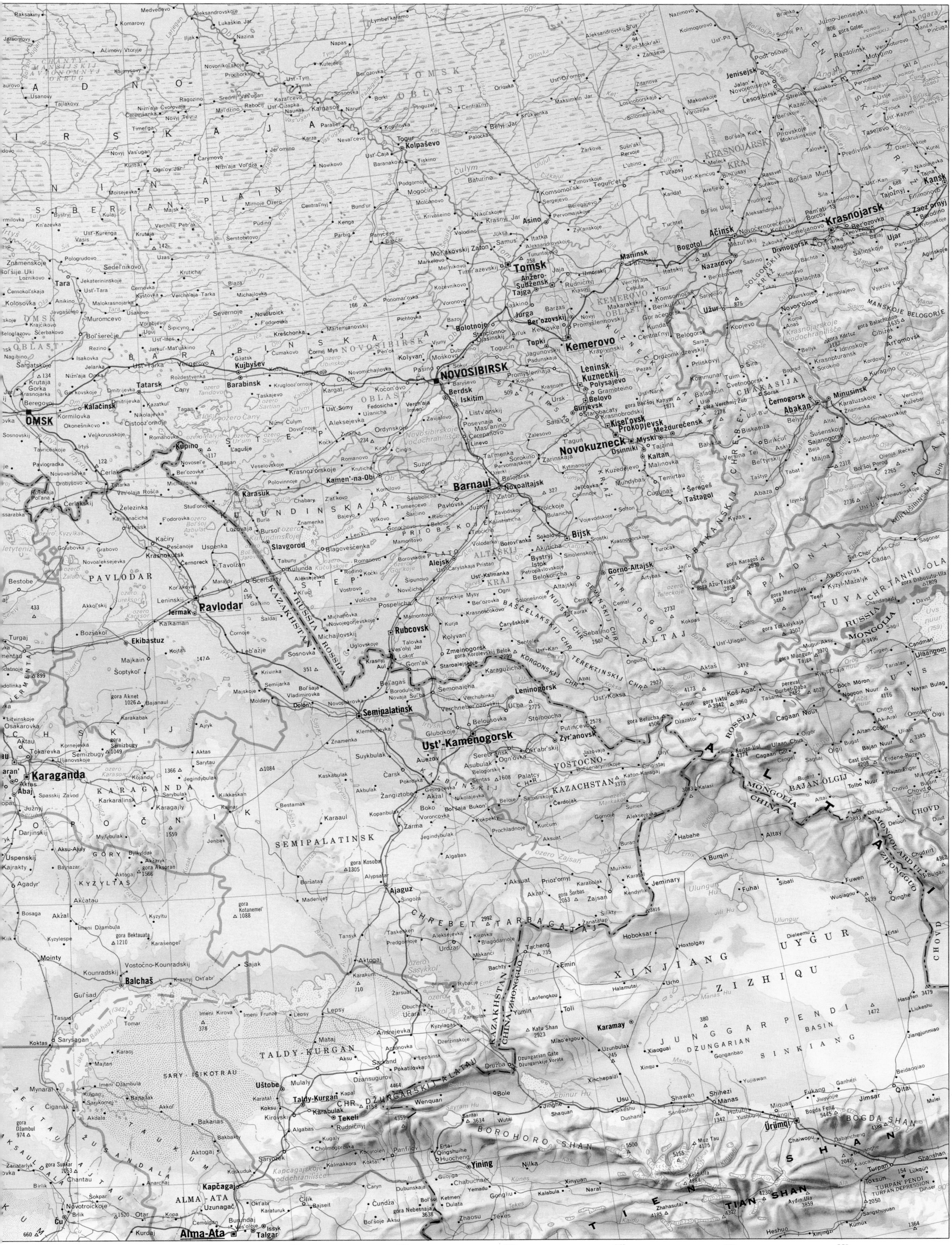
NOVOSIBIRSK
Tomsk
Kemerovo
Novokuzneck
Barnaul
Bijsk
Krasnojarsk
Abakan
Omsk
Pavlodar
Semipalatinsk
Ust'-Kamenogorsk
Karaganda
Balchaš
Alma-Ata
Ürümqi
Rubcovsk
Gorno-Altajsk
Kolpaševo
T O M S K O B L A S T'
N O V O S I B I R S K A J A O B L A S T'
K E M E R O V O O B L A S T'
A L T A J S K I J K R A J
K R A S N O J A R S K I J K R A J
P A V L O D A R
S E M I P A L A T I N S K
K A R A G A N D A
T A L D Y - K U R G A N
A L M A - A T A
X I N J I A N G U Y G U R Z I Z H I Q U
J U N G G A R P E N D I
DZUNGARIAN BASIN
T U V A
MONGOLIA
CHINA
KAZAKHSTAN
RUSSIA
B O G D A S H A N
T I A N S H A N
B O R O H O R O S H A N
A L T A J
W E S T S I B E R I A N P L A I N
K U L U N D I N S K A J A S T E P'
A L T A I
Ob'
Irtyš
Jenisej

Map continues page 88

Kilometers 0 100 200 300 Km.
Statute Miles 0 100 200 300 Mi.

Scale 1:6,000,000

One centimeter represents 60 kilometers.
One inch represents approximately 95 miles.
Lambert Conformal Conic Projection

Map continues page 89

RUSSIA
MONGOLIA
CHINA
Baikal
Irkutsk
Ulan-Ude
Čita
Krasnojarsk
Bratsk
Ulaanbaatar
Kyzyl
BURJATIJA
IRKUTSK OBLAST'
TUVA
JAKUTIJA
STANOVOJE NAGORJE
VITIMSKOJE PLOSKOGORJE
JABLONOVYJ CHREBET
VOSTOČNYJ SAJAN
ZAPADNYJ SAJAN
SAJANY MOUNTAINS
OLËKMINSKIJ STANOVIK
CHENTIJ NURUU
CHANGAJN NURUU
SELENGE
TÖV
Copyright © by Rand McNally & Co.
Map compiled by Cartographia, Budapest.
Map produced by Rand McNally & Co.

Map continues pages 74-75

Map continues pages 102-103

Map continues pages 86-87

Kilometers 0 100 200 300 Km.
Statute Miles 0 100 200 300 Mi.

Scale 1:6,000,000

One centimeter represents 60 kilometers.
One inch represents approximately 95 miles.
Lambert Conformal Conic Projection

MAP FORM	chrebet	gora	nuruu	nuur	ozero, o.	porog	uul
ENGLISH	mountain range	mountain	mountain range	lake	lake	waterfall	mountains
DEUTSCH	Gebirge	Berg	Gebirge	See	See	Wasserfall	Berge
ESPAÑOL	cordillera	montaña	cordillera	lago	lago	cascada	montañas
FRANÇAIS	chaîne	montagne	chaîne	lac	lac	chute d'eau	montagnes
PORTUGUÊS	cordilheira	montanha	cordilheira	lago	lago	queda d'água	montanhas

Feet	19685	13124	9843	6562	3281	1640	656	0		0	656	3281	9843	19685	29520
Meters	6000	4000	3000	2000	1000	500	200	0	Land Below Sea Level	0	200	1000	3000	6000	9000

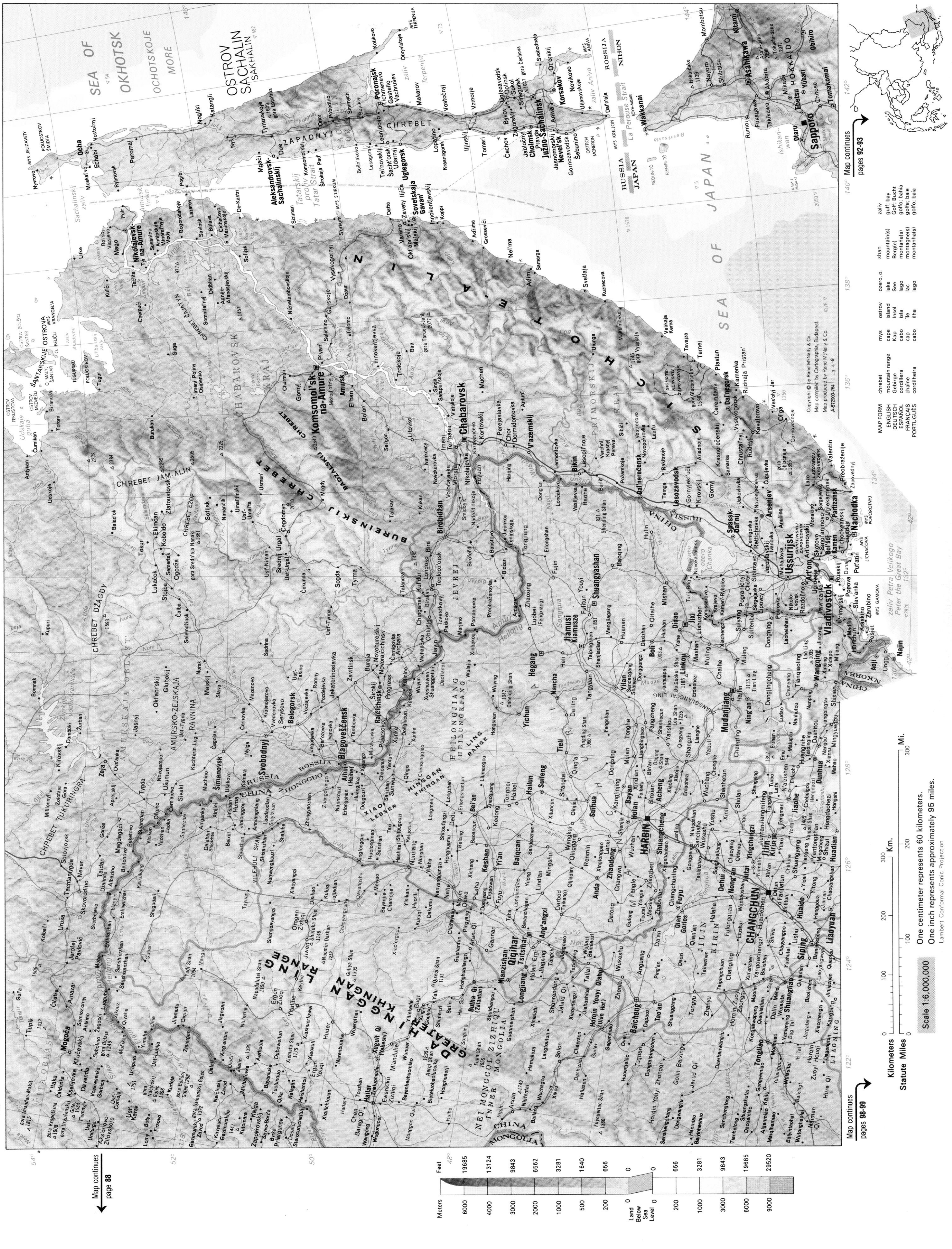
SEA OF OKHOTSK
OCHOTSKOJE MORE
OSTROV SACHALIN SAKHALIN
SEA OF JAPAN
HOKKAIDŌ
CHABAROVSK KRAJ
PRIMORSKIJ KRAJ
AMURSKAJA OBLAST'
HEILONGJIANG
JILIN KIRIN
NEI MONGGOL ZIZHIQU INNER MONGOLIA
GREATER KHINGAN RANGE
DA HINGGAN LING
LESSER KHINGAN RANGE
XIAO HINGGAN LING
SICHOTE-ALIN'
BUREINSKIJ CHREBET
CHREBET DŽAGDY
CHREBET TUKURINGRA
CHREBET JAM-ALIN'
RUSSIA / CHINA
ROSSIJA / ZHONGGUO
RUSSIA / JAPAN
ROSSIJA / NIHON
CHINA / MONGOLIA
NORTH KOREA
Chabarovsk
Komsomol'sk-na-Amure
Vladivostok
Harbin
Changchun
Blagoveščensk
Južno-Sachalinsk
Sapporo
Qiqihar
Map continues pages 74-75
Map continues page 88
Map continues pages 92-93
Map continues pages 98-99
Scale 1:6,000,000
One centimeter represents 60 kilometers.
One inch represents approximately 95 miles.
Lambert Conformal Conic Projection
Kilometers
Statute Miles
Copyright © by Rand McNally & Co.
Map compiled by Cartographia, Budapest.
Map produced by Rand McNally & Co.
MAP FORM / ENGLISH / DEUTSCH / ESPAÑOL / FRANÇAIS / PORTUGUÊS
chrebet / mountain range / Gebirge / cordillera / chaîne / cordilheira
mys / cape / Kap / cabo / cap / cabo
ostrov / island / Insel / isla / île / ilha
ozero, o. / lake / See / lago / lac / lago
shan / mountain(s) / Berg(e) / montaña(s) / montagne(s) / montanha(s)
zaliv / gulf; bay / Golf; Bucht / golfo; bahía / golfe; baie / golfo; baía
Meters / Feet
Land / Below Sea Level

Map continues pages 74-75

RUSSIA
KAZAKHSTAN
BETPAK-DALA
KYRGYZSTAN
TIEN SHAN
XINJIANG UYGUR ZIZHIQU
SINKIANG
TARIM PENDI
TAKLIMAKAN SHAMO
KURUKTAG
ALTUN SHAN
KUNLUN SHAN
XIZANG ZIZHIQU
TIBET
QAIDAM PENDI
QINGHAI
TSINGHAI
BAYAN HAR SHAN
TANGGULA SHAN
NYAINQENTANGLHA SHAN
GANGDISE SHAN
HIMALAYA
NEPAL
BHUTAN
BANGLADESH
INDIA
BURMA
LAOS
THAILAND
VIETNAM
MONGOLIA
GOBI
ALTAJ
MONGOL ALTAJN NURUU
CHANGAJN NURUU
JUNGGAR PENDI
BEI SHAN
QILIAN SHAN
SICHUAN
SZECHWAN
YUNNAN
GUIZHOU
KWEICHOW
GANSU
KANSU
NINGXIA HUIZU ZIZHIQU
BAY OF BENGAL
SUNDARBANS
EASTERN GHATS
Alma-Ata
Bišhkek
Ürümqi
Lhasa
Kathmandu
Dhaka
Calcutta
Chengdu
Kunming
Lanzhou
Xining
Mandalay
Chittagong
Patna
Lucknow
Kanpur
Allahabad
Varanasi
Ha Noi
Vientiane
Chiang Mai
Irkutsk
Angarsk
Ust'-Kamenogorsk
Kashi
Shache
Yining
Guiyang
Map continues pages 118-119

MAP FORM	bandao	dao	hu	-jima	pendi	shan	-shima
ENGLISH	peninsula	island	lake	island	basin	mountain(s)	island
DEUTSCH	Halbinsel	Insel	See	Insel	Becken	Berg(e)	Insel
ESPAÑOL	peninsula	isla	lago	isla	cuenca	montaña(s)	isla
FRANÇAIS	péninsule	île	lac	île	bassin	montagne(s)	île
PORTUGUÊS	península	ilha	lago	ilha	bacia	montanha(s)	ilha

RUSSIA
SEA OF OKHOTSK
OSTROV SACHALIN
SAKHALIN
Chabarovsk
Vladivostok
Blagoveščensk
Svobodnyj
Nachodka
Ussurijsk
Čita
MANCHURIA
HEILONGJIANG
HEILUNGKIANG
JILIN
KIRIN
LIAONING
Harbin
Qiqihar
Tsitsihar
Changchun
Jilin
Mudanjiang
Jiamusi
Hegang
Yichun
SHENYANG
MUKDEN
Fushun
Anshan
Dandong
Dalian
Lüshun (Port Arthur)
NEI MONGGOL ZIZHIQU
INNER MONGOLIA
DA HINGGAN LING
XIAO HINGGAN LING
Hohhot
Baotou
Zhangjiakou
Kalgan
BEIJING
PEKING
TIANJIN
TIENTSIN
Tangshan
Shijiazhuang
Taiyuan
SHANXI
SHANSI
HEBEI
HOPEH
SHANDONG
SHANTUNG
Jinan
Tsinan
Qingdao
Tsingtao
Yantai
Chefoo
Zibo
Zhengzhou
Kaifeng
Luoyang
Xuzhou
HENAN
HONAN
JIANGSU
KIANGSU
ANHUI
ANHWEI
Hefei
Nanjing
Wuxi
Suzhou
SHANGHAI
Hangzhou
Ningbo
HUBEI
HUPEH
WUHAN
Yichang
HUNAN
Changsha
Xiangtan
Hengyang
Nanchang
JIANGXI
KIANGSI
ZHEJIANG
CHEKIANG
Wenzhou
FUJIAN
FUKIEN
Fuzhou
Xiamen
Amoy
Quanzhou
Zhangzhou
Shantou
Swatow
GUANGZHOU
CANTON
Kowloon
VICTORIA
HONG KONG
Macau
Haikou
NORTH KOREA
P'YONGYANG
Ch'ŏngjin
Hamhŭng
Kimch'aek
SOUTH KOREA
SOUL
SEOUL
Inch'ŏn
Taejŏn
Taegu
Kwangju
Pusan
CHEJU-DO
SEA OF JAPAN
Yellow Sea
Korea Bay
Bo Hai
JAPAN
HOKKAIDO
Sapporo
Asahikawa
Hakodate
Aomori
Sendai
Niigata
HONSHU
TOKYO
Yokohama
Kawasaki
Nagoya
Kyoto
Kobe
OSAKA
Hiroshima
SHIKOKU
KYUSHU
Kitakyushu
Fukuoka
Nagasaki
Kumamoto
Kagoshima
La Perouse Strait
RYUKYU ISLANDS
NANSEI-SHOTO
Naha
OKINAWA-JIMA
EAST CHINA SEA
T'AIPEI
Chilung
Kaohsiung
T'ainan
TAIWAN
Tropic of Cancer
PACIFIC OCEAN
PHILIPPINE SEA
Bashi Channel
Luzon Strait
BATAN ISLANDS
BABUYAN ISLANDS
PHILIPPINES
LUZON
SOUTH CHINA SEA
Copyright © by Rand McNally & Co.
Map prepared by Esselte Map Service AB, Stockholm.

Map continues pages 108-109

Kilometers 0 200 400 600 Km.
Statute Miles 0 200 400 600 Mi.

Scale 1:12,000,000
One centimeter represents 120 kilometers.
One inch represents approximately 190 miles.
Lambert Conformal Conic Projection

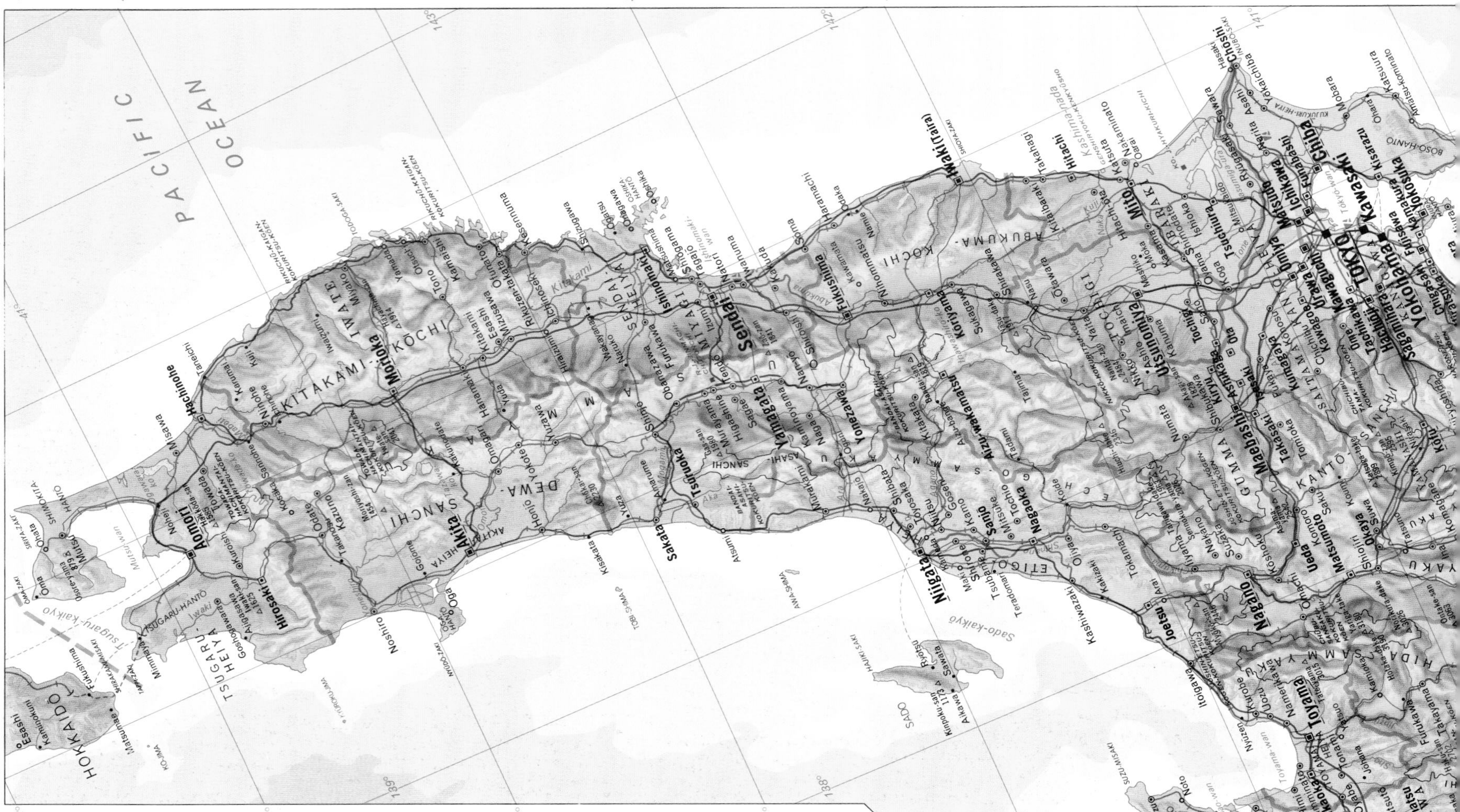
PACIFIC OCEAN
HONSHŪ
TOKYO
Sendai
Niigata
Aomori
Akita
Morioka
Yokohama
Kawasaki
Chiba
Kanazawa
SADO
HOKKAIDŌ

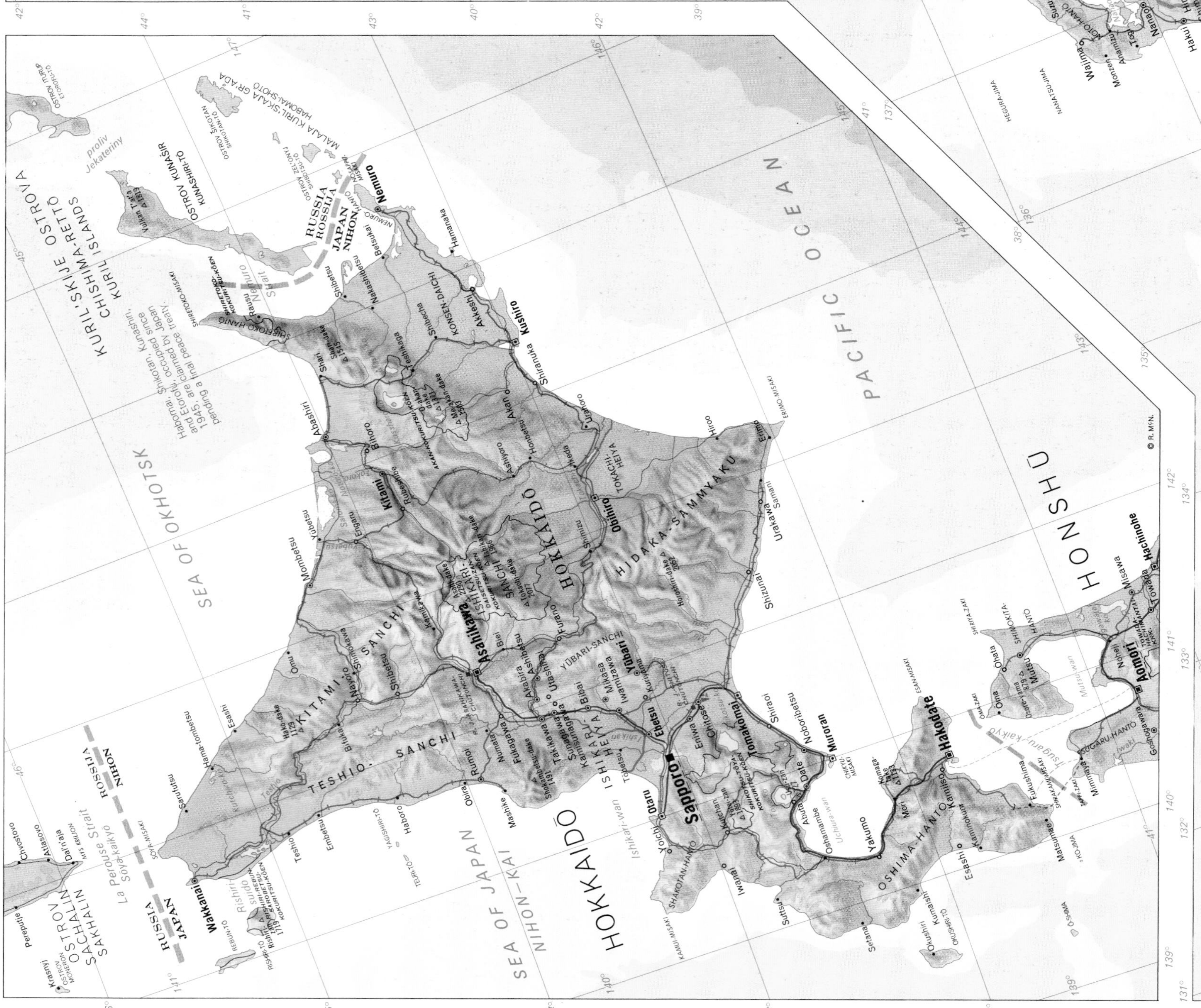
SEA OF OKHOTSK
KURIL'SKIJE OSTROVA
CHISHIMA-RETTŌ
KURIL ISLANDS
Habomai, Shikotan, Kunashiri, and Etorofu, occupied since 1945, are claimed by Japan, pending a final peace treaty.
PACIFIC OCEAN
HOKKAIDŌ
SEA OF JAPAN
NIHON-KAI
HONSHŪ
RUSSIA
JAPAN
La Perouse Strait
Sōya-kaikyō
Sapporo
Asahikawa
Hakodate
Kushiro
Nemuro
Wakkanai
Obihiro
Kitami
Muroran
Otaru
Aomori
OSTROV SACHALIN
SAKHALIN

a

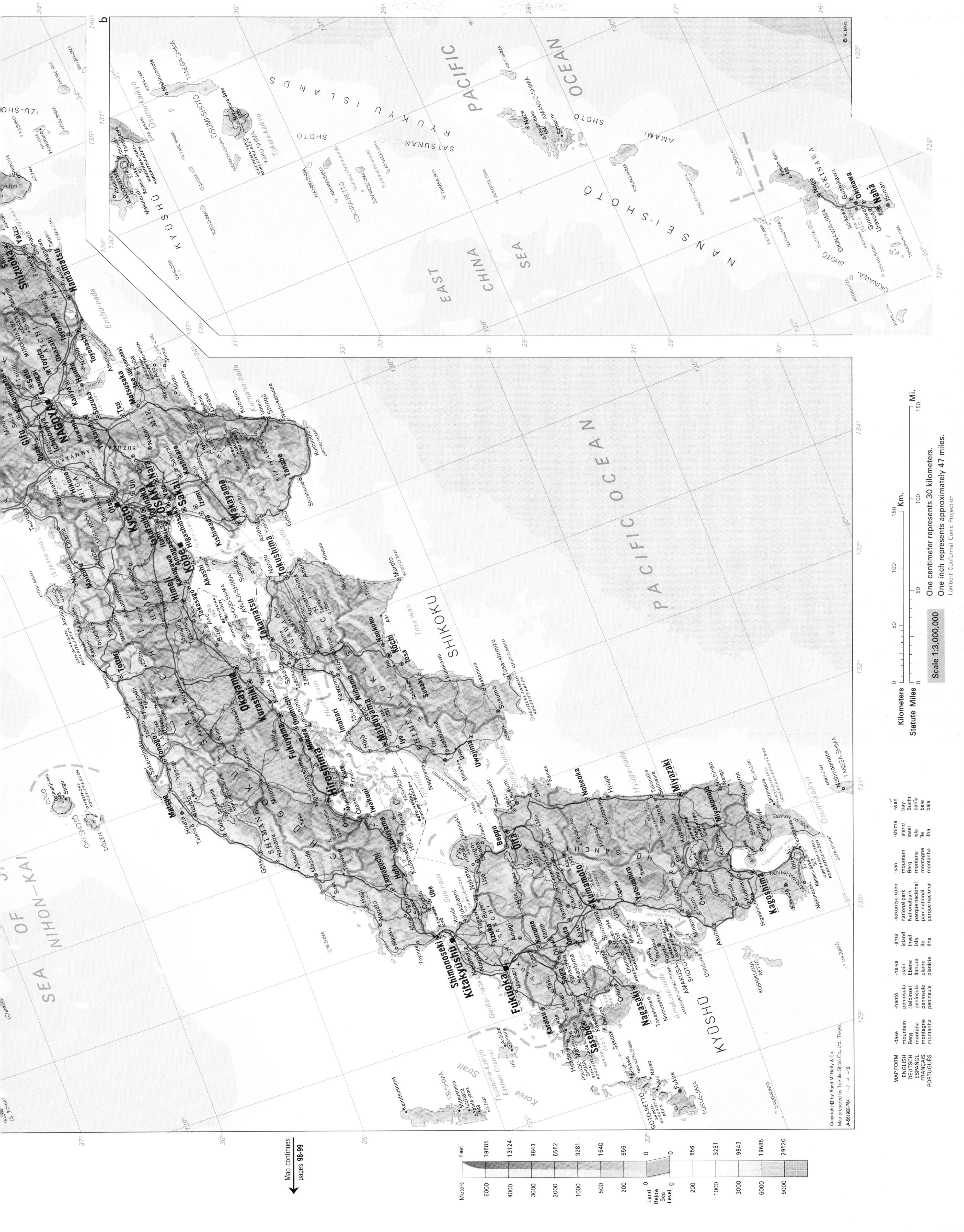
SEA OF JAPAN
NIHON-KAI
PACIFIC OCEAN
EAST CHINA SEA
KYŪSHŪ
SHIKOKU
RYUKYU ISLANDS
NANSEI-SHOTŌ
SATSUNAN-SHOTŌ
AMAMI-SHOTŌ
OKINAWA-SHOTŌ
ŌSUMI-SHOTŌ
TOKARA-RETTŌ
Korea Strait
Tsushima-kaikyō
Eastern Channel
TSUSHIMA
GOTŌ-RETTŌ
OKI-SHOTŌ
Naha
Okinawa
Shimonoseki
Kitakyūshū
Fukuoka
Nagasaki
Sasebo
Kumamoto
Kagoshima
Miyazaki
Ōita
Hiroshima
Okayama
Matsue
Tottori
Takamatsu
Matsuyama
Kōchi
Tokushima
Kōbe
Ōsaka
Kyōto
Nara
Wakayama
Nagoya
Gifu
Shizuoka
Hamamatsu
Map continues pages 98-99
Meters
Feet
Land Below Sea Level
Kilometers
Statute Miles
Scale 1:3,000,000
One centimeter represents 30 kilometers.
One inch represents approximately 47 miles.
Lambert Conformal Conic Projection
MAP FORM -dake -hantō -heiya -jima -kokuritsu-kōen -san -shima -wan
ENGLISH mountain peninsula plain island national park mountain island bay
DEUTSCH Berg Halbinsel Ebene Insel Nationalpark Berg Insel Bucht
ESPAÑOL montaña península llanura isla parque nacional montaña isla bahía
FRANÇAIS montagne péninsule plaine île parc national montagne île baie
PORTUGUÊS montanha península planície ilha parque nacional montanha ilha baía
Copyright © by Rand McNally & Co.
Map prepared by Teikoku Shoin Co., Ltd. Tokyo
© R.McN.

SEA OF JAPAN
NIHON-KAI
Toyama-wan
Wakasa-wan
Ise-wan
Mikawa-wan
Enshū-nada
Biwa-ko
NOTO-HANTŌ
Kanazawa
Toyama
Takaoka
Fukui
Tsuruga
Gifu
Nagoya
KYŌTO
ŌSAKA
Nara
Ōtsu
Yokkaichi
Tsu
Matsusaka
Ise (Uji-yamada)
Toyohashi
Hamamatsu
Okazaki
Toyota
Ichinomiya
Ōgaki
Takayama
Matsumoto
Nagano
Suwa
Iida
Nakatsugawa
Komatsu
Kaga
Nanao
Itoigawa
Joetsu
HIDA-SAMMYAKU
KISO-SAMMYAKU
AKAISHI-SAMMYAKU
RYŌHAKU-SANCHI
SUZUKA-SAMMYAKU
HIDA-KŌCHI
HONSHŪ
136°
136°30'
137°
137°30'
138°
37°
36°30'
36°
35°30'
35°

Map continues pages 96-97

MAP FORM	-dake	-hantō	-kokutei-kōen	-misaki	-san	-tōge	-wan	-yama	-zaki
ENGLISH	mountain	peninsula	national park	cape	mountain	pass	bay	mountain	point
DEUTSCH	Berg	Halbinsel	Nationalpark	Kap	Berg	Pass	Bucht	Berg	Landspitze
ESPAÑOL	montaña	península	parque nacional	cabo	montaña	paso	bahía	montaña	punta
FRANÇAIS	montagne	péninsule	parc national	cap	montagne	col	baie	montagne	pointe
PORTUGUÊS	montanha	península	parque nacional	cabo	montanha	passo	baía	montanha	ponta

TŌKYŌ
KAWASAKI
YOKOHAMA
Chiba
Utsunomiya
Maebashi
Takasaki
Mito
Hitachi
Iwaki (Taira)
Shirakawa
Nikkō
Kiryū
Ashikaga
Ōta
Isesaki
Kumagaya
Chichibu
Kawagoe
Ōmiya
Urawa
Koshigaya
Kasukabe
Noda
Kashiwa
Matsudo
Ichikawa
Funabashi
Narashino
Hachiōji
Tachikawa
Fuchū
Mitaka
Musashino
Sagamihara
Machida
Yamato
Atsugi
Hiratsuka
Fujisawa
Kamakura
Yokosuka
Odawara
Hakone
Numazu
Mishima
Fuji
Fujinomiya
Shimizu
Kōfu
Gotemba
Otsuki
Tsuru
Fuji-yoshida
Itō
Atami
Shimoda
Tateyama
Kisarazu
Mobara
Chōshi
Sawara
Narita
Sakura
Tsuchiura
Ishioka
Koga
Oyama
Tochigi
Kanuma
Numata
Tōkamachi
Nagaoka
Ōshima
Tōkyō-wan
Sagami-wan
Sagami-nada
Suruga-wan
Kashima-nada
KANTŌ HEIYA
BŌSŌ-HANTŌ
IZU-HANTŌ
IZU-SHOTŌ
HONSHŪ
PACIFIC OCEAN
FUKUSHIMA
NIIGATA
TOCHIGI
IBARAKI
GUMMA
SAITAMA
CHIBA
TŌKYŌ
KANAGAWA
YAMANASHI
SHIZUOKA
NAGANO
Copyright © by Rand McNally & Co.
Map prepared by Teikoku-Shoin Co., Ltd., Tokyo.
A-566500-264

Kilometers 0 10 20 30 40 50 Km.

Statute Miles 0 10 20 30 40 50 Mi.

Scale 1:1,000,000

One centimeter represents 10 kilometers.
One inch represents approximately 16 miles.
Lambert Conformal Conic Projection

SEA OF JAPAN
NIHON-KAI
KYŪSHŪ
HIROSHIMA
KITAKYŪSHŪ
FUKUOKA
Shimonoseki
Yamaguchi
Matsuyama
Hagi
Masuda
Hamada
Izumo
Oda
Tokuyama
Iwakuni
Kure
Ube
Hōfu
Ōita
Beppu
Nakatsu
Usa
Kurume
Ōmuta
Uwajima
Yawatahama
Suō-nada
Iyo-nada
Uwa-kai
Hibiki-nada
Hiroshima-wan
Beppu-wan
Aki-nada
SETO-NAIKAI-KOKURITSU-KŌEN
NISHI-CHŪGOKU-SANCHI-KOKUTEI-KŌEN
KITA-NAGATO-KAIGAN-KOKUTEI-KŌEN
AKIYOSHI-DAI
KUNISAKI-HANTŌ
SADA-MISAKI-HANTŌ
HŌYO-SHOTŌ
TSUKUSHI-SANCHI
TSUKUSHI-HEIYA
ASO-KOKURITSU-KŌEN
YAMA-HITA-HIKO-SAN-KOKUTEI-KŌEN
EHIME
KŌCHI
SHIMANE
YAMAGUCHI
130° 30′
131°
131° 30′
132°
132° 30′
35° 30′
35°
34° 30′
34°
33° 30′
33°

MAP FORM	-jima	-misaki	-san	-sen	-shima	-tōge	-yama	-zen
ENGLISH	island	cape	mountain	mountain	island	pass	mountain	mountain
DEUTSCH	Insel	Kap	Berg	Berg	Insel	Pass	Berg	Berg
ESPAÑOL	isla	cabo	montaña	montaña	isla	paso	montaña	montaña
FRANÇAIS	île	cap	montagne	montagne	île	col	montagne	montagne
PORTUGUÊS	ilha	cabo	montanha	montanha	ilha	passo	montanha	montanha

133°30'
134°
134°30'
135°
135°30'
Map continues pages 94-95
HONSHU
SHIKOKU
PACIFIC OCEAN
SAN'IN-KAIGAN-KOKURITSU-KŌEN
SETO-NAIKAI-KOKURITSU-KŌEN
DAISEN-OKI-KOKURITSU-KŌEN
TANGO-HANTŌ
Wakasa-wan
WAKASA-WAN KOKUTEI-KŌEN
Miho-wan
Harima-nada
Ōsaka-wan
Hiuchi-nada
Mizushima-nada
Tosa-wan
Kii-suidō
KII-HANTŌ
AWAJI-SHIMA
SHŌDO-SHIMA
IESHIMA-SHOTŌ
BISAN-SHOTŌ
SHIWAKU-SHOTŌ
SANUKI-SAMMYAKU
SHIKOKU-SANCHI
KYŌTO
ŌSAKA
KOBE
Ōtsu
Nara
Himeji
Okayama
Kurashiki
Fukuyama
Onomichi
Takamatsu
Tokushima
Kōchi
Wakayama
Tottori
Yonago
Sakaiminato
Kurayoshi
Maizuru
Fukuchiyama
Ayabe
Toyooka
Tsuyama
Niihama
Kanonji
Marugame
Sakaide
Naruto
Anan
Muroto
Susaki
Saijo
Iyo-mishima
Kawanoe
Akashi
Kakogawa
Takasago
Nishinomiya
Amagasaki
Itami
Toyonaka
Suita
Takatsuki
Ibaraki
Hirakata
Neyagawa
Moriguchi
Higashiōsaka
Yao
Sakai
Kishiwada
Izumi
Kawachi-nagano
Sumoto
Tanabe
Gobō
Arida
Kainan
Kameoka
Nishiwaki
Ono
Miki
Aioi
Akō
Bizen
Tamano
Kojima
Takahashi
Niimi
Shingū
Kasai
Kaizuka
Izumi-sano
Izumi-ōtsu
Takaishi
Mihara
Matsubara
Fujiidera
Habikino
Kashiwara
Yamato-takada
Kashihara
Sakurai
Tenri
Yamato-kōriyama
Ikoma
Daitō
Gose
Muko
Nagaokakyō
Uji
Jōyō
Yawata
Kadoma
Mino
Ikeda
Kawanishi
Takarazuka
Ashiya
Sanda
Tatsuno
Shirahama
MUROTO-ZAKI
ASHIZURI

Kilometers 0 10 20 30 40 50 Km.

Statute Miles 0 10 20 30 40 50 Mi.

Scale 1:1,000,000

One centimeter represents 10 kilometers.

One inch represents approximately 16 miles.

Lambert Conformal Conic Projection

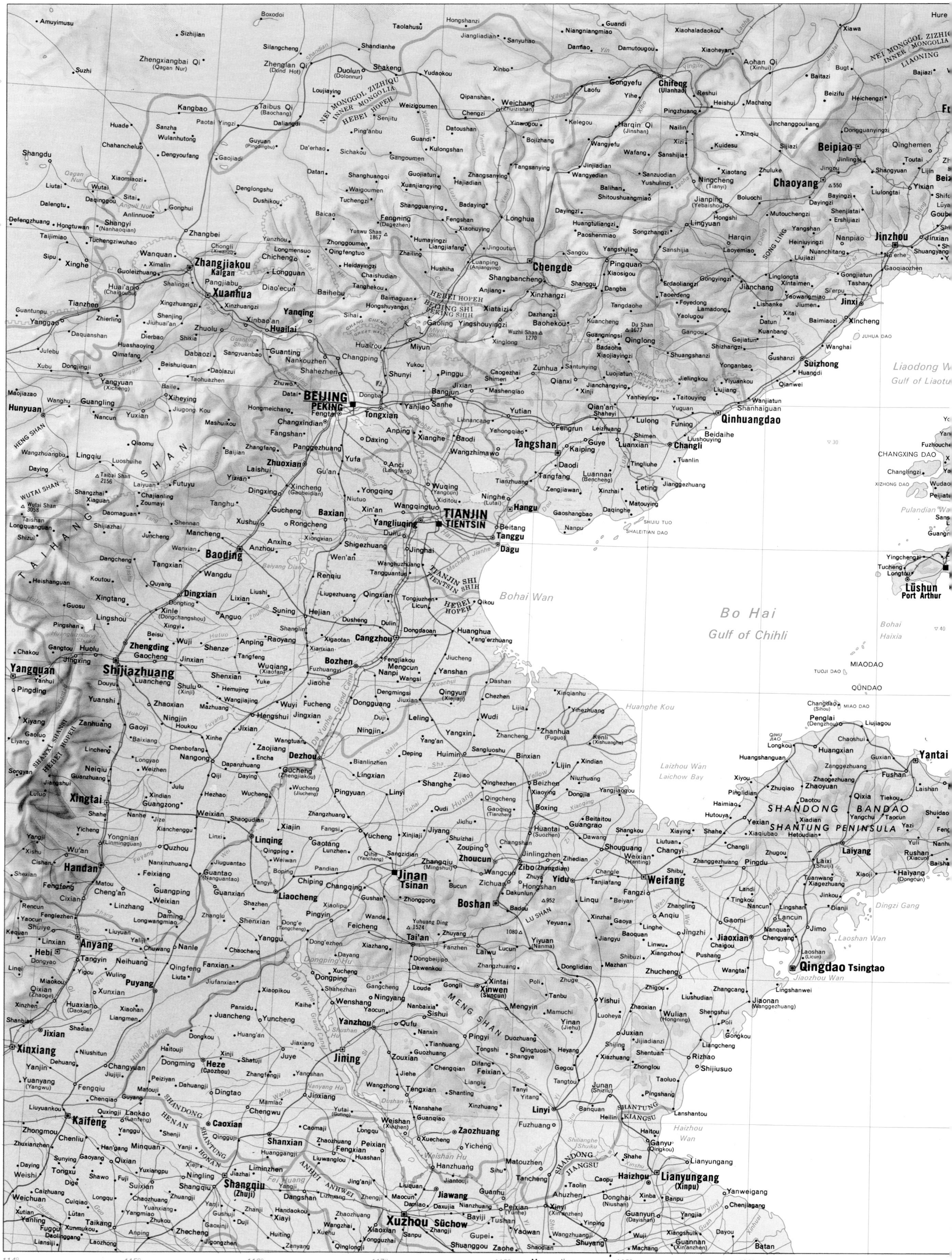
NEI MONGGOL ZIZHIQU
INNER MONGOLIA
HEBEI HOPEH
LIAONING
BEIJING SHI PEKING SHIH
TIANJIN SHI TIENTSIN SHIH
SHANXI SHANSI
SHANDONG
HENAN HONAN
ANHUI ANHWEI
JIANGSU KIANGSU
BEIJING
PEKING
TIANJIN
TIENTSIN
Zhangjiakou
Kalgan
Xuanhua
Chengde
Chifeng
(Ulanhad)
Chaoyang
Beipiao
Jinzhou
Jinxi
Suizhong
Qinhuangdao
Shanhaiguan
Tangshan
Tanggu
Dagu
Baoding
Dingxian
Shijiazhuang
Yangquan
Xingtai
Handan
Anyang
Xinxiang
Kaifeng
Shangqiu
Xuzhou
Süchow
Jining
Yanzhou
Tai'an
Jinan
Tsinan
Zibo
Boshan
Weifang
Yantai
Qingdao
Tsingtao
Lianyungang
(Xinpu)
Lüshun
Port Arthur
Dezhou
Cangzhou
Heze
(Caozhou)
Linyi
Zaozhuang
Puyang
Liaocheng
Linqing
Hengshui
Bo Hai
Gulf of Chihli
Bohai Wan
Liaodong Wan
Gulf of Liaotung
Laizhou Wan
Laichow Bay
Huanghe Kou
Jiaozhou Wan
Haizhou Wan
SHANDONG BANDAO
SHANTUNG PENINSULA
TAIHANG SHAN
MENG SHAN
HENG SHAN
WUTAI SHAN
SONG LING
Grand Canal
Huang
114°
115°
116°
117°
118°
119°
120°
121°
34°
35°
36°
37°
38°
39°
40°
41°
42°

Map continues pages 102-103

Map continues pages 100-101

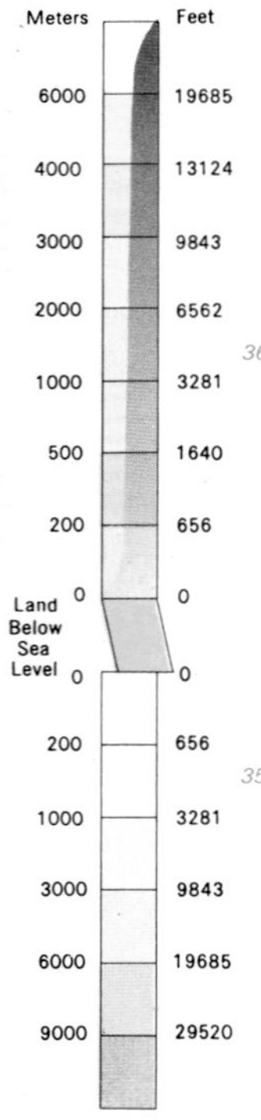
Meters
Feet
6000
19685
4000
13124
3000
9843
2000
6562
1000
3281
500
1640
200
656
0
0
Land Below Sea Level
0
0
200
656
1000
3281
3000
9843
6000
19685
9000
29520

MAP FORM	dao	-do	-gang	hu	kukrip kongwŏn	-san	shan	wan
ENGLISH	island	island	river	lake	national park	mountain	mountain(s)	bay
DEUTSCH	Insel	Insel	Fluss	See	Nationalpark	Berg	Berg(e)	Bucht
ESPAÑOL	isla	isla	río	lago	parque nacional	montaña	montaña(s)	bahía
FRANÇAIS	île	île	rivière	lac	parc national	montagne	montagne(s)	baie
PORTUGUÊS	ilha	ilha	rio	lago	parque nacional	montanha	montanha(s)	baía

Map continues page 89

SEA OF JAPAN
Korea Bay
YELLOW SEA
MANCHURIA
SHENYANG
MUKDEN
FUSHUN
Anshan
Dandong
P'YONGYANG
SŎUL
SEOUL
Inch'ŏn
Pusan
Taegu
Kwangju
Taejŏn
Wŏnsan
Hamhŭng
Ch'ŏngjin
Kimch'aek
Kaesŏng
Namp'o
Sinŭiju
Mokp'o
Ulsan
Chŏnju
Masan
Chinju
Yŏsu
TSUSHIMA
Korea Strait
Western Channel
Eastern Channel
Copyright © by Rand McNally & Co.
Map compiled by Cartographia, Budapest.
Map produced by Rand McNally & Co.
A-564400-764

Map continues pages 92-93

Kilometers 0 50 100 150 Km.

Statute Miles 0 50 100 150 Mi.

Scale 1:3,000,000

One centimeter represents 30 kilometers.

One inch represents approximately 47 miles.

Lambert Conformal Conic Projection

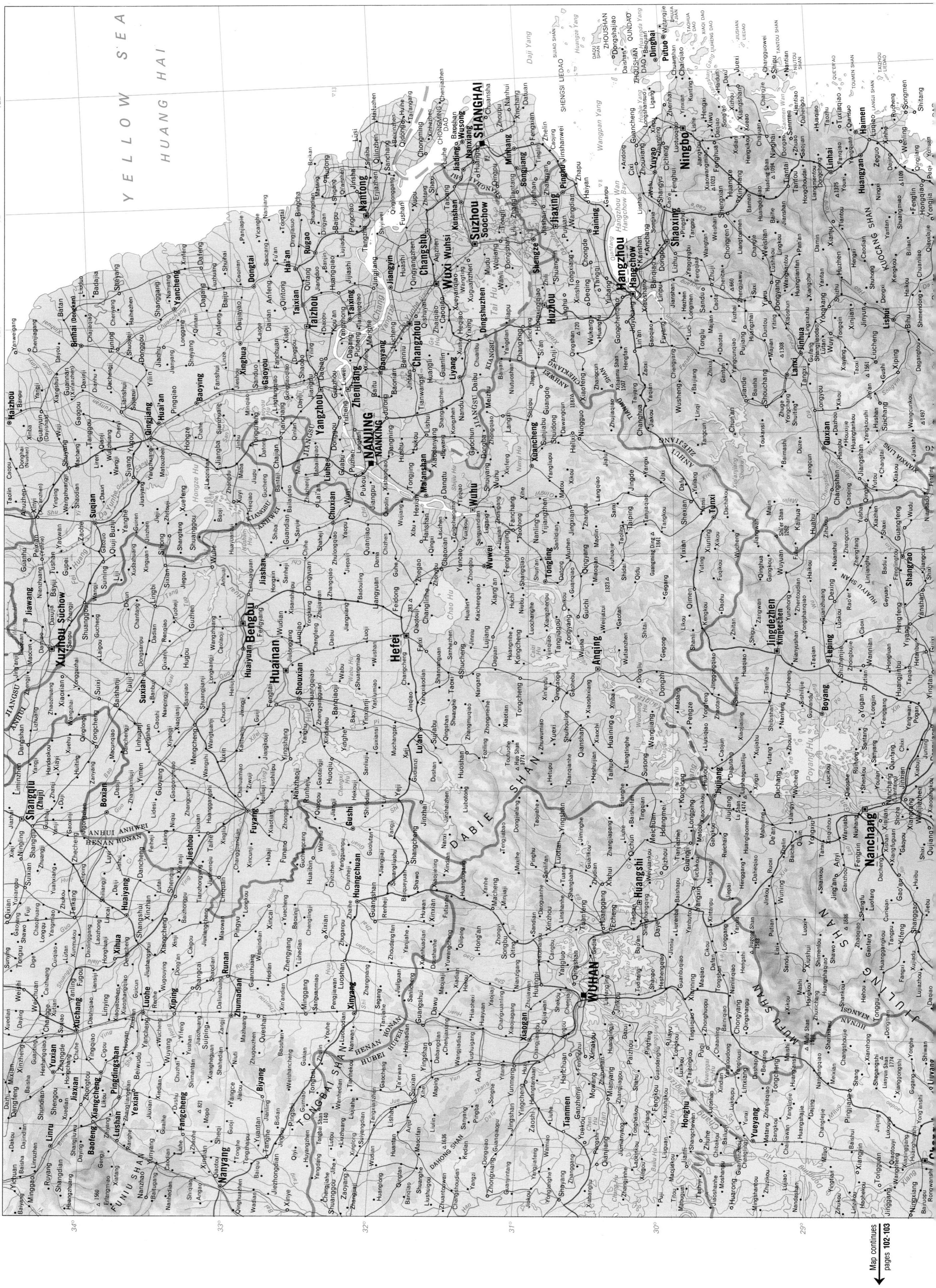
YELLOW SEA
HUANG HAI
SHANGHAI
NANJING
NANKING
WUHAN
Hangzhou
Hefei
Nanchang
Suzhou
Wuxi
Changzhou
Ningbo
Bengbu
Huainan
Anqing
Jingdezhen
Xuzhou
DABIE SHAN
TONGBAI SHAN
FUNIU SHAN
MUFU SHAN
JIULING SHAN
Tai Hu
Chao Hu
Poyang Hu
ANHUI ANHWEI
HENAN HONAN
JIANGSU
ZHEJIANG
HUBEI HUPEH
HUNAN
122°
121°
120°
119°
118°
117°
116°
115°
114°
113°
34°
33°
32°
31°
30°
29°

Map continues pages 98-99

Map continues pages 102-103

Scale 1:3,000,000
One centimeter represents 30 kilometers.
One inch represents approximately 47 miles.
Lambert Conformal Conic Projection
Kilometers
Statute Miles
EAST CHINA SEA
SOUTH CHINA SEA
PACIFIC OCEAN
TAIWAN
Taiwan Strait
TAIWAN HAIHSIA
CHINA
ZHONGGUO
Tropic of Cancer
HONG KONG
Luzon Strait
Feet
Meters
Land Below Sea Level
MAP FORM
ENGLISH
DEUTSCH
ESPAÑOL
FRANÇAIS
PORTUGUÊS
Copyright © by Rand McNally & Co.
Map compiled by Cartographia, Budapest.
Map produced by Rand McNally & Co.

Map continues pages 98-99

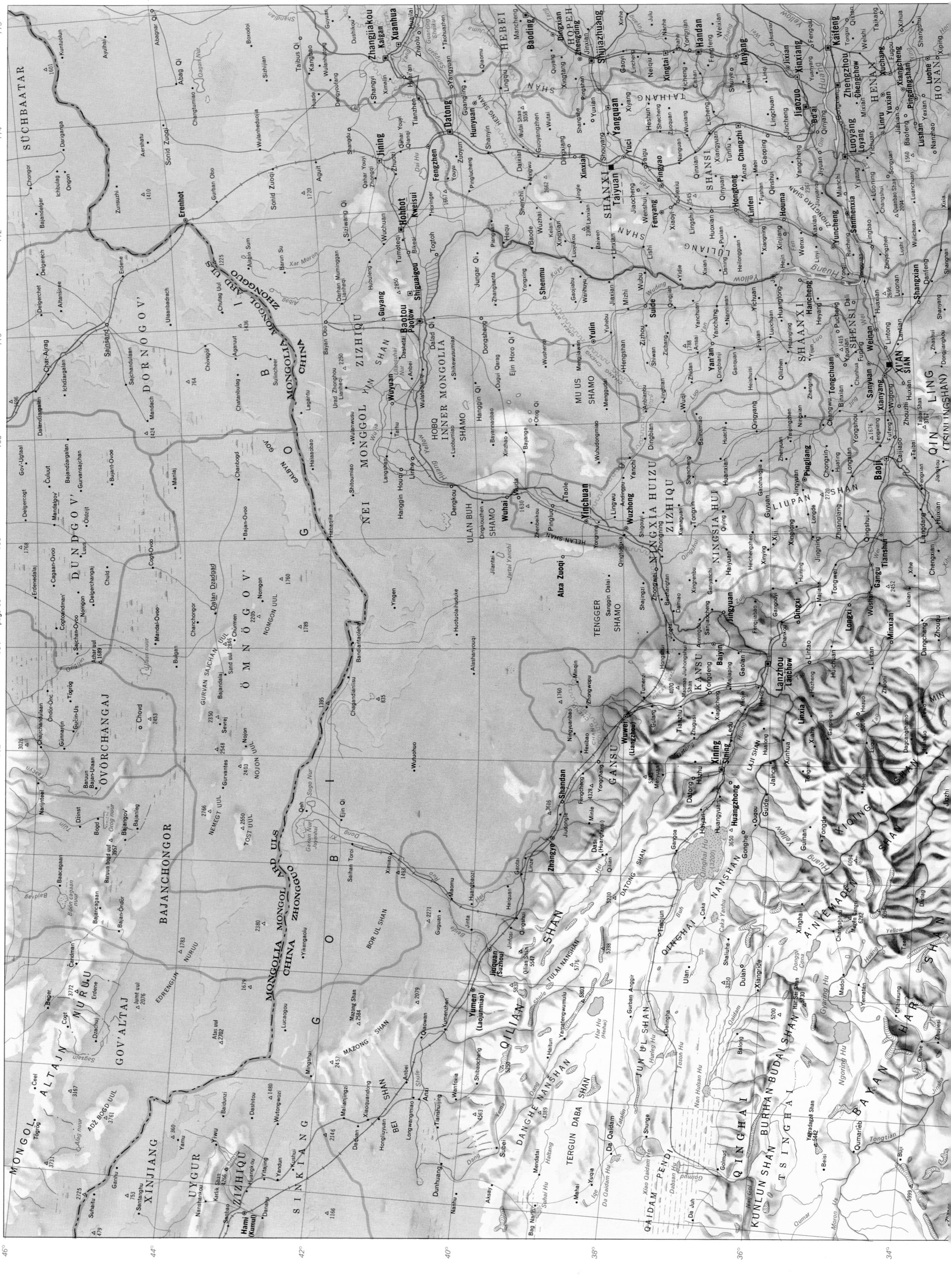
SÜCHBAATAR
DORNOGOV'
DUNDGOV'
ÖMNÖGOV'
ÖVÖRCHANGAJ
BAJANCHONGOR
GOV'-ALTAJ
MONGOL ALTAJN NURUU
GURVAN SAJCHAN UUL
MONGOLIA
MONGOL ARD ULS
CHINA
ZHONGGUO
GOBI
NEI MONGGOL ZIZHIQU
INNER MONGOLIA
YIN SHAN
HOBQ SHAMO
MU US SHAMO
TENGGER SHAMO
ULAN BUH SHAMO
NINGXIA HUIZU ZIZHIQU
NINGSIA HUI
GANSU
KANSU
QINGHAI
TSINGHAI
QILIAN SHAN
QAIDAM PENDI
KUNLUN SHAN
BURHAN BUDAI SHAN
BAYAN HAR SHAN
XINJIANG UYGUR ZIZHIQU
SINKIANG
SHANXI
SHANSI
SHAANXI
SHENSI
HEBEI
HOPEH
HENAN
HONAN
QIN LING
LÜLIANG SHAN
TAIHANG SHAN
Erenhot
Hohhot
Baotou
Datong
Taiyuan
Shijiazhuang
Baoding
Zhangjiakou
Yinchuan
Lanzhou
Xining
Xi'an
Zhengzhou
Luoyang
Kaifeng
Yan'an
Yulin
Wuwei
Zhangye
Jiuquan
Yumen
Hami
Baiyin
Tianshui
Baoji
Golmud
Dunhuang

Map continues page 88

Map continues pages 100-101

Scale 1:6,000,000
One centimeter represents 60 kilometers.
One inch represents approximately 95 miles.
Lambert Conformal Conic Projection
Kilometers
Statute Miles
Km.
Mi.
Map continues pages 110-111
Map continues pages 120-121
MAP FORM / ENGLISH / DEUTSCH / ESPAÑOL / FRANÇAIS / PORTUGUÊS
dao / island / Insel / isla / île / ilha
hu / lake / See / lago / lac / lago
ling / mountains / Berge / montañas / montagnes / montanhas
shamo / desert / Wüste / desierto / désert / deserto
shan / mountain(s) / Berg(e) / montaña(s) / montagne(s) / montanha(s)
shuiku / reservoir / Stausee / embalse / réservoir / reservatório
Feet
Meters
Land Below Sea Level
SOUTH CHINA SEA
Gulf of Tonkin
HAINAN DAO
HUNAN
GUIZHOU
SICHUAN
YUNNAN
GUANGXI ZHUANGZU ZIZHIQU
GUANGDONG
HUBEI
XIZANG ZIZHIQU
BURMA
VIETNAM
LAOS
THAILAND
WUHAN
CHONGQING
CHENGDU
KUNMING
GUIYANG
GUANGZHOU (CANTON)
Ha-noi
Mandalay

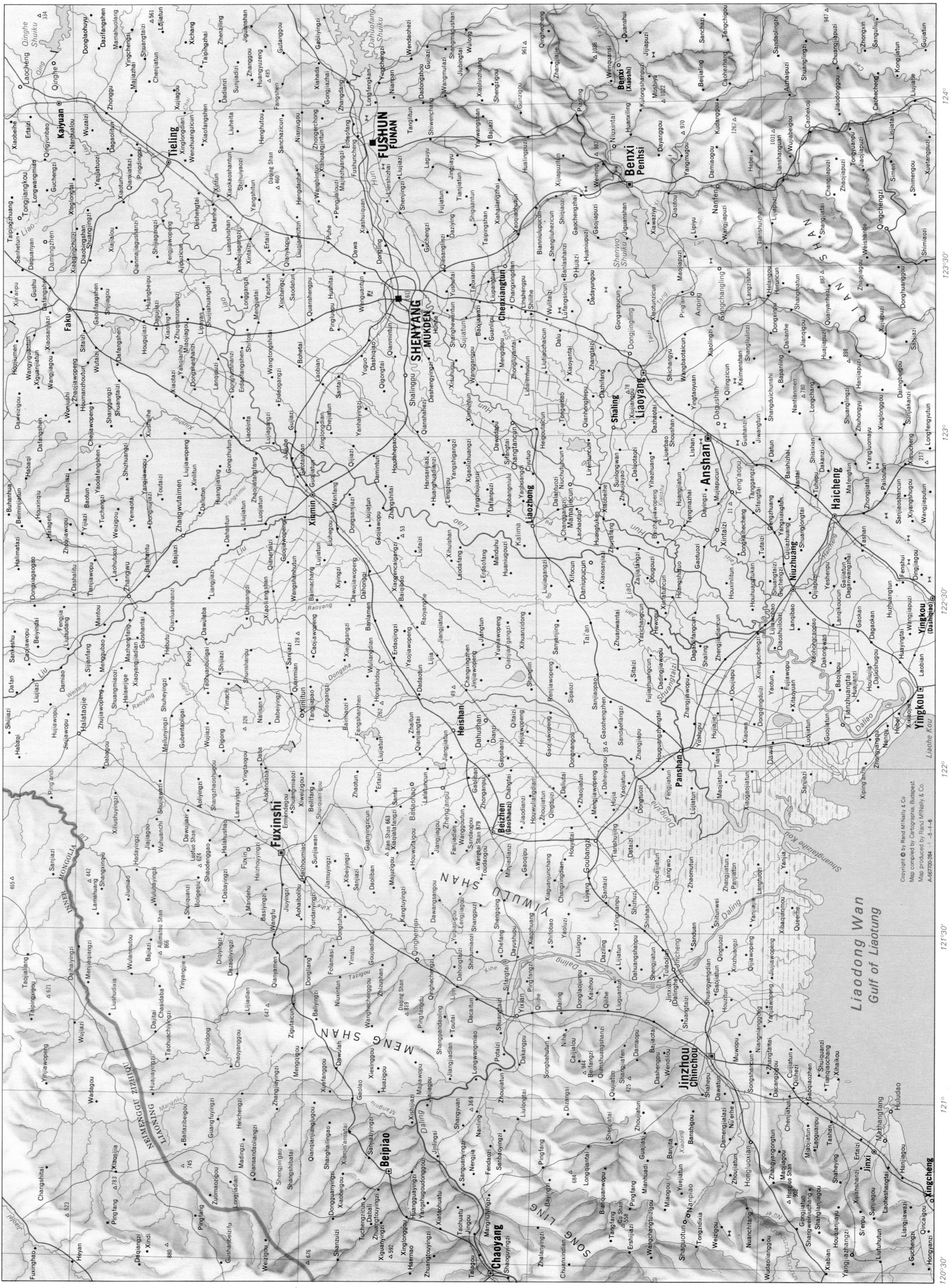

SHENYANG
MUKDEN
FUSHUN
FUNAN
Anshan
Liaoyang
Benxi
Penhsi
Fuxinshi
Jinzhou
Chinchou
Yingkou
Tieling
Kaiyuan
Fakü
Xinmin
Haicheng
Panshan
Beizhen
Heishan
Beipiao
Chaoyang
Jinxi
Xingcheng
Dashiqiao
Niuzhuang
Liaozhong
Chenxiangtun
Liaodong Wan
Gulf of Liaotung
YIWULÜ SHAN
MENG SHAN
SONG LING
NEIMENGGU ZIZHIQU
LIAONING
INNER MONGOLIA
Liao
Hun
Taizi
Daling
Xiaoling
Liu
Raoyang
Liaohe Kou
Shuangtaizihe Kou
Dahuofang Shuiku
Shenwo Shuiku
Qinghe Shuiku

Kilometers 0 10 20 30 40 50 Km.
Statute Miles 0 10 20 30 40 50 Mi.

Scale 1:1,000,000
One centimeter represents 10 kilometers.
One inch represents approximately 16 miles.
Modified Polyconic Projection

MAP FORM	kou	shan	shuiku	wan
ENGLISH	estuary	mountain(s)	reservoir	bay
DEUTSCH	Trichtermündung	Berg(e)	Stausee	Bucht
ESPAÑOL	estuario	montaña(s)	embalse	bahía
FRANÇAIS	estuaire	montagne(s)	réservoir	baie
PORTUGUÊS	estuário	montanha(s)	reservatório	baía

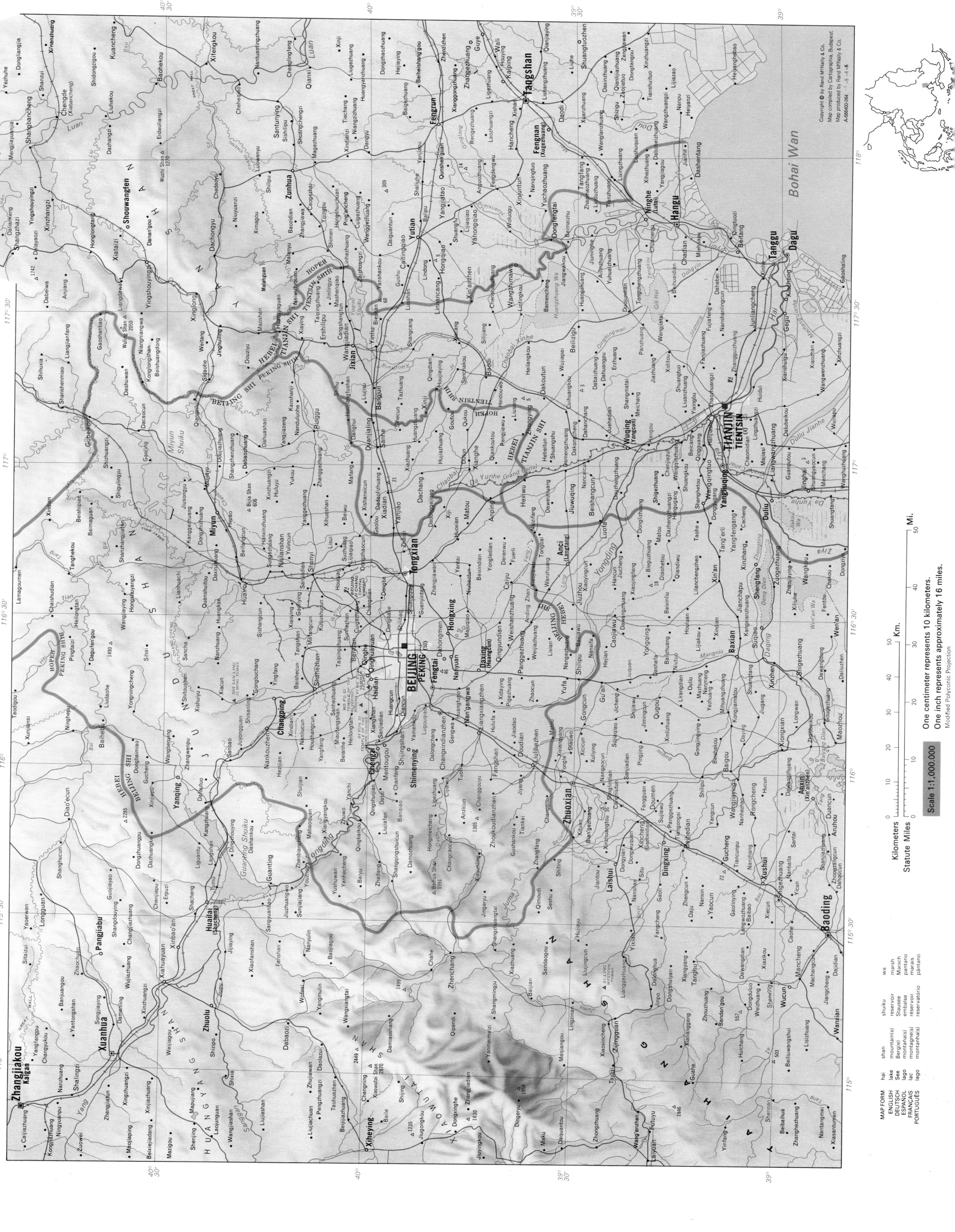
Beijing (Peking)
Tianjin (Tientsin)
Tangshan
Chengde
Zhangjiakou (Kalgan)
Xuanhua
Baoding
Tanggu
Dagu
Hangu
Tongxian
Miyun
Huairou
Changping
Yanqing
Daxing (Huangcun)
Fengtai
Haidian
Zhuoxian
Anci (Langfang)
Bohai Wan
Guanting Shuiku
Miyun Shuiku
Yongding
Chaobai
Da Yunhe (Grand Canal)
Beijing Shi
Tianjin Shi
Hebei
Kilometers
Statute Miles
Scale 1:1,000,000
One centimeter represents 10 kilometers.
One inch represents approximately 16 miles.
Modified Polyconic Projection
Copyright © by Rand McNally & Co.
Map compiled by Cartographia, Budapest.
Map produced by Rand McNally & Co.
MAP FORM: hai, shan, shuiku, wa
ENGLISH: lake, mountain(s), reservoir, marsh
DEUTSCH: See, Berg(e), Stausee, Marsch
ESPAÑOL: lago, montaña(s), embalse, pantano
FRANÇAIS: lac, montagne(s), réservoir, marais
PORTUGUÊS: lago, montanha(s), reservatório, pântano

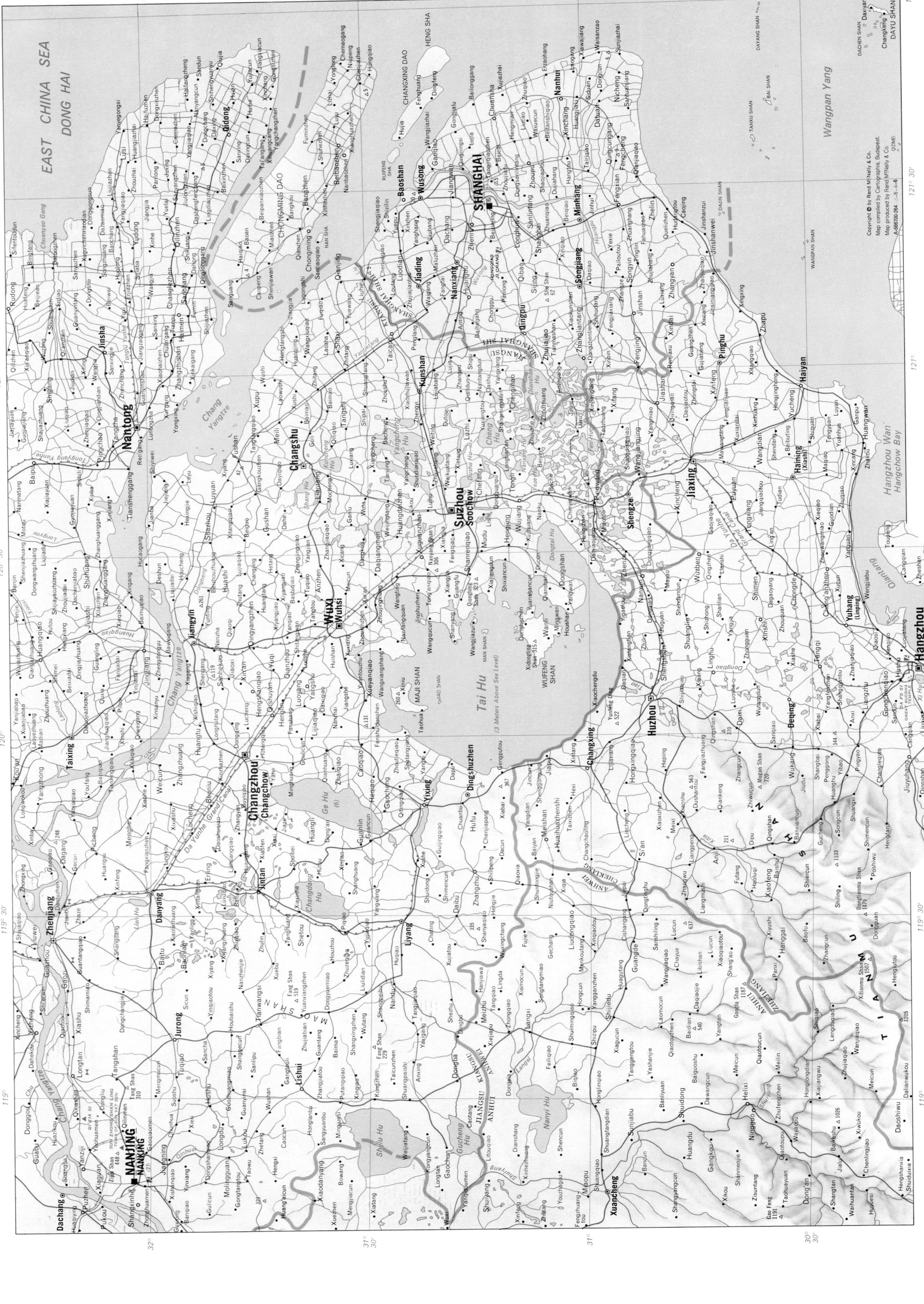
EAST CHINA SEA
DONG HAI
Wangpan Yang
Hangzhou Wan
Hangchow Bay
SHANGHAI
NANJING
NANKING
Suzhou
Soochow
Wuxi
Wuhsi
Changzhou
Changchow
Hangzhou
Hangchow
Nantong
Zhenjiang
Tai Hu
(3 Meters Above Sea Level)
Chang Yangtze
CHONGMING DAO
Scale 1:1,000,000
Kilometers
Statute Miles
One centimeter represents 10 kilometers.
One inch represents approximately 16 miles.
Lambert Conformal Conic Projection
MAP FORM dao hu sha shan si wan
ENGLISH island lake island mountain(s); island temple bay
DEUTSCH Insel See Insel Berg(e); Insel Tempel Bucht
ESPAÑOL isla lago isla montaña(s); isla templo bahía
FRANÇAIS île lac île montagne(s); île temple baie
PORTUGUÊS ilha lago ilha montanha(s); ilha templo baía
Copyright © by Rand McNally & Co.
Map compiled by Cartographia, Budapest.
Map produced by Rand McNally & Co.

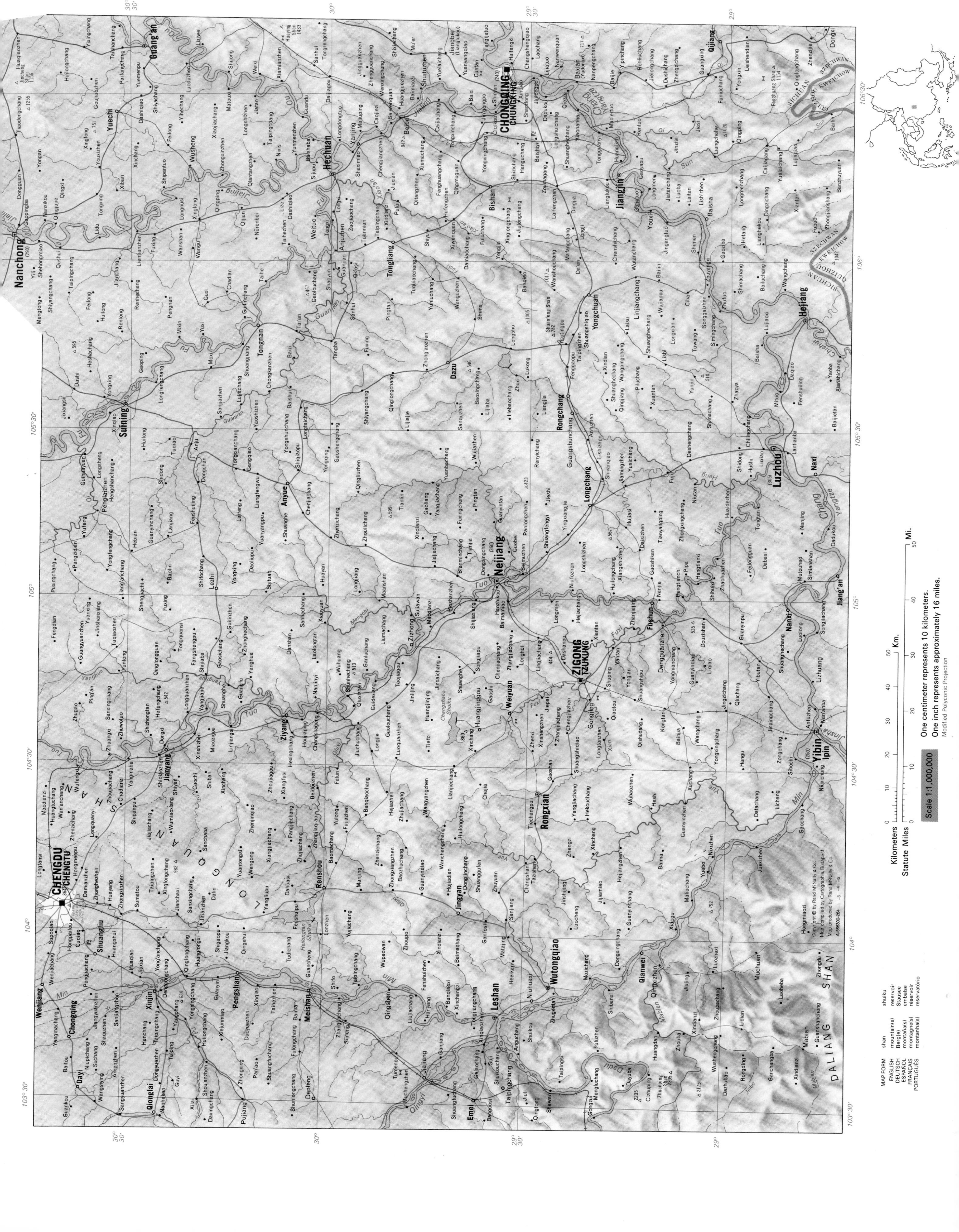
CHENGDU
CHENGTU
CHONGQING
CHUNGKING
Nanchong
Hechuan
Suining
Neijiang
ZIGONG
TZUKUNG
Luzhou
Yibin
Ipin
Leshan
Meishan
Jiangjin
Yongchuan
Kilometers
Statute Miles
Scale 1:1,000,000
One centimeter represents 10 kilometers.
One inch represents approximately 16 miles.
Modified Polyconic Projection
Copyright © by Rand McNally & Co.
Map compiled by Cartographia, Budapest.
Map produced by Rand McNally & Co.
MAP FORM shan shuiku
ENGLISH mountain(s) reservoir
DEUTSCH Berg(e) Stausee
FRANÇAIS montagne(s) réservoir
ESPAÑOL montaña(s) embalse
PORTUGUÊS montanha(s) reservatório

Map continues pages 90-91

Map continues pages 118-119

CHINA
YUNNAN
GUANGXI
Nanning
GUANGZHOU
CANTON
HONG KONG
VICTORIA
HAINAN
Haikou
BANGLADESH
Chittagong
INDIA
BURMA
Mandalay
YANGON
RANGOON
LAOS
HA NOI
Hai Phong
Viangchan (Vientiane)
Louangphrabang
THAILAND
KRUNG THEP
BANGKOK
CAMBODIA
Phnum Pénh
VIETNAM
Da Nang
Hue
THANH PHO HO CHI MINH (SAIGON)
Gulf of Tonkin
BAY OF BENGAL
ANDAMAN SEA
ANDAMAN ISLANDS (India)
NICOBAR ISLANDS (India)
Gulf of Thailand
SOUTH CHINA SEA
XISHA QUNDAO
PARACEL ISLANDS
SPRATLY ISLANDS
MALAYSIA
KUALA LUMPUR
George Town (Pinang)
SINGAPORE
BRUNEI
Bandar Seri Begawan
SUMATERA
SUMATRA
Medan
Padang
Palembang
BORNEO
KALIMANTAN
Pontianak
Banjarmasin
INDONESIA
GREATER SUNDA ISLANDS
LAUT JAWA
JAVA SEA
JAKARTA
BANDUNG
Semarang
Yogyakarta
SURABAYA
JAWA
JAVA
INDIAN OCEAN
CHRISTMAS ISLAND (Austl.)
Equator
Copyright © by Rand McNally & Co.
Map prepared by Esselte Map Service AB, Stockholm.
A-569800-264 -11-9-15

MAP FORM	gulf	gunung	island	kepulauan	pulau	sea	selat	strait
ENGLISH	gulf	mountain	island	islands	island	sea	strait	strait
DEUTSCH	Golf	Berg	Insel	Inseln	Insel	Meer	Meeresstrasse	Meeresstrasse
ESPAÑOL	golfo	montaña	isla	islas	isla	mar	estrecho	estrecho
FRANÇAIS	golfe	montagne	île	îles	île	mer	détroit	détroit
PORTUGUÊS	golfo	montanha	ilha	ilhas	ilha	mar	estreito	estreito

Tropic of Cancer
TAIWAN
T'AIWAN
Hualien
T'aitung
P'ingtung
Bashi Channel
Luzon Strait
BATAN ISLANDS
BABUYAN ISLANDS
Balintang Channel
Laoag
Tuguegarao
Ilagan
LUZON
Baguio
Dagupan
Cabanatuan
San Fernando
Quezon City
Cavite
San Pablo
Lucena
Batangas
Calapan
MINDORO
Naga
Mayon Volcano
Legaspi
Sorsogon
PHILIPPINES
SAMAR
Catbalogan
Tacloban
LEYTE
PANAY
Roxas
Kalibo
Iloilo
Bacolod
Cebu
NEGROS
BOHOL
Dumaguete
Surigao
Butuan
Cagayan de Oro
MINDANAO
Ozamiz
Iligan
Zamboanga
Cotabato
Davao
General Santos
Moro Gulf
Davao Gulf
Jolo
SULU ARCHIPELAGO
CAPE SAN AGUSTIN
P H I L I P P I N E
S E A
P A C I F I C
O C E A N
OKINO-TORI-SHIMA
(Japan)
FARALLON DE PAJAROS
MAUG ISLANDS
ASUNCION ISLAND
NORTHERN MARIANA ISLANDS
(U.S.)
MARIANA
ISLANDS
AGRIHAN
PAGAN
ALAMAGAN
GUGUAN
SARIGAN
ANATAHAN
FARALLON DE MEDINILLA
SAIPAN
TINIAN
AGUIJAN
ROTA
Agana
GUAM
(U.S.)
ULITHI
FAIS
YAP
FEDERATED STATES OF MICRONESIA
NGULU
SOROL
GAFERUT
FARAULEP
OLIMARAO
WOLEAI
IFALIK
EAURIPIK
KAYANGEL ISLANDS
PALAU ISLANDS
BABELTHUAP
Koror
PELELIU
ANGAUR
C A R O L I N E   I S L A N D S
SONSOROL ISLANDS
PULO ANNA
MERIR
PALAU BELAU
(T.T.P.I.)
TOBI
HELEN ISLAND
KEPULAUAN ASIA
KEPULAUAN MAPIA
KEPULAUAN AYU
Equator
C E L E B E S
S E A
KEPULAUAN TALAUD
KEPULAUAN SANGIHE
Manado
Tondano
Gorontalo
MINAHASA
Ternate
Tidore
HALMAHERA
MOROTAI
LAUT MALUKU
MOLUCCA SEA
M A L U K U
Laut Halmahera
Halmahera Sea
KEPULAUAN OBI
KEPULAUAN SULA
KEPULAUAN BANGGAI
Teluk Tomini
Kendari
BUTON
Baubau
SULAWESI
LAUT SERAM
CERAM SEA
SERAM
BURU
Ambon
Sorong
WAIGEO
JAZIRAH DOBERAI
Manokwari
Fakfak
BIAK
PULAU YAPEN
Teluk Cenderawasih
Jayapura (Sukarnapura)
PEGUNUNGAN VAN REES
PEGUNUNGAN MAOKE
Puncak Jaya
5030
Puncak Trikora
4750
Puncak Mandala
4760
NEW GUINEA
PAPUA NEW GUINEA
Vanimo
Aitape
Wewak
Angoram
Sepik
Mount Wilhelm
4509
Mount Hagen
4368
Mount Giluwe
Mount Bosavi
2397
Lake Murray
Kikori
Fly
Balimo
Gulf of Papua
Daru
Merauke
PULAU YOS SUDARSO
Kokenau
Tanahmerah
KEPULAUAN KAI
Tual
KEPULAUAN ARU
Dobo
L A U T   B A N D A
BANDA SEA
KEPULAUAN TANIMBAR
YAMDENA
Saumlaki
KEPULAUAN BABAR
KEPULAUAN LETI
KEPULAUAN BARAT DAYA
WETAR
FLORES
Ende
Maumere
Larantuka
Kalabahi
ALOR
Dili
TIMOR
Kupang
Soe
SUMBA
Waingapu
Laut Sawu
Savu Sea
T I M O R   S E A
A R A F U R A   S E A
TANJUNG VALS
Torres Strait
CAPE YORK PENINSULA
CAPE YORK
PRINCE OF WALES ISLAND
A U S T R A L I A
CAPE WESSEL
CAPE CROKER
GREAT BARRIER REEF
125°
130°
135°
140°
145°
20°
15°
10°
5°
0°
Map continues pages 160-161
Kilometers
0
200
400
600
Km.
Statute Miles
0
200
400
600
Mi.
Scale 1:12,000,000
One centimeter represents 120 kilometers.
One inch represents approximately 190 miles.
Lambert Conformal Conic Projection

Kilometers 0 100 200 300 Km.
Statute Miles 0 100 200 300 Mi.

Scale 1:6,000,000

One centimeter represents 60 kilometers.
One inch represents approximately 95 miles.
Lambert Conformal Conic Projection

Map continues pages 102-103

MAP FORM	dao	gunung	island	kepulauan	khao	kyun	pulau	shan
ENGLISH	island	mountain	island	islands	mountain	island	island	mountain(s)
DEUTSCH	Insel	Berg	Insel	Inseln	Berg	Insel	Insel	Berg(e)
ESPAÑOL	isla	montaña	isla	islas	montaña	isla	isla	montaña(s)
FRANÇAIS	île	montagne	île	îles	montagne	île	île	montagne(s)
PORTUGUÊS	ilha	montanha	ilha	ilhas	montanha	ilha	ilha	montanha(s)

Map continues pages 120-121

SOUTH CHINA SEA
Gulf of Tonkin
BAY OF BENGAL
Gulf of Martaban
HAINAN DAO
GUANGDONG
GUANGXI ZHUANGZU ZIZHIQU
YUNNAN
GUIZHOU
HUNAN
YANGON (RANGOON)
HA NOI
Mandalay
Kunming
Viangchan (Vientiane)
Da Nang
Hue
Chittagong
BANGLADESH
BURMA
LAOS
THAILAND
VIETNAM

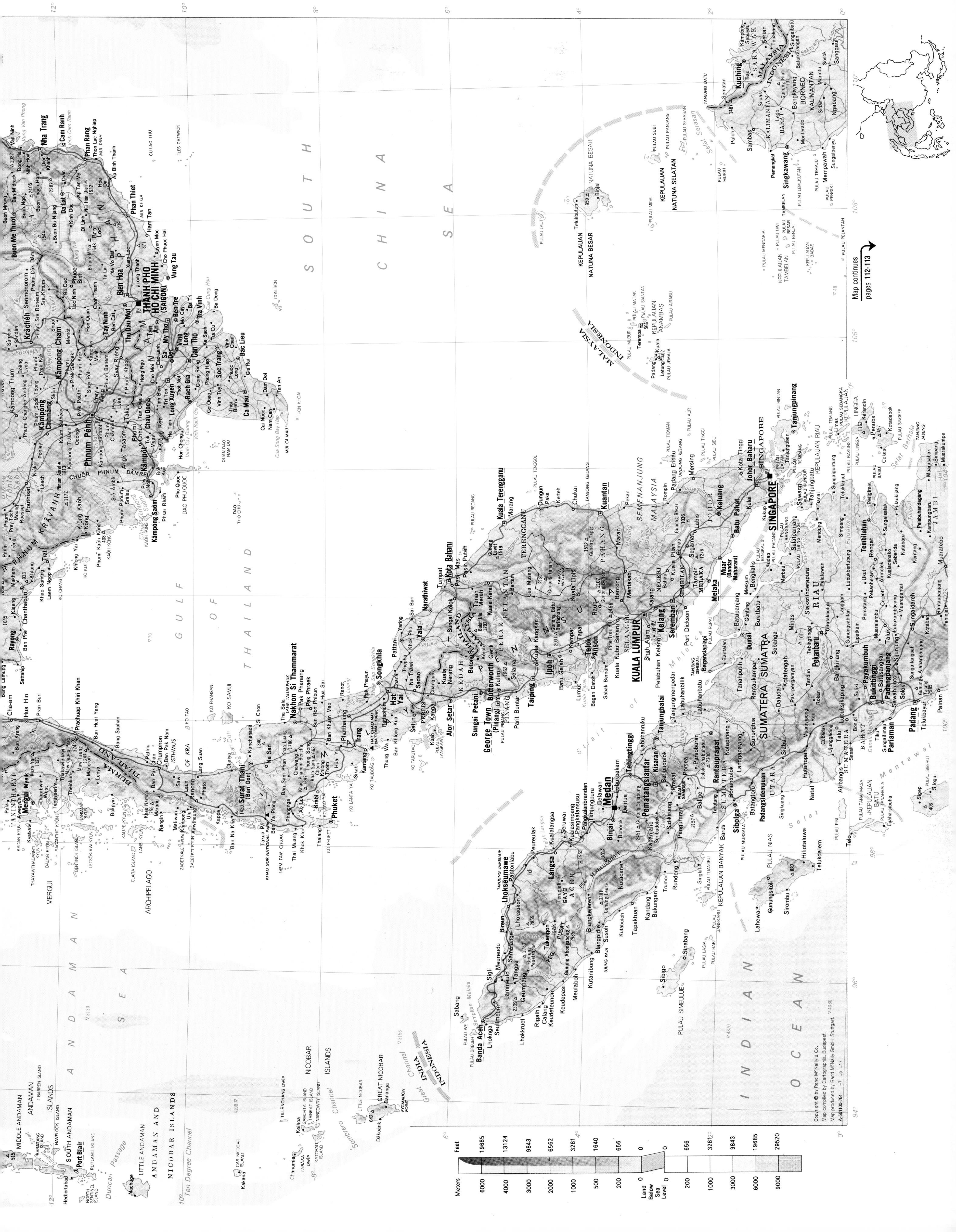
SOUTH CHINA SEA
GULF OF THAILAND
ANDAMAN SEA
INDIAN OCEAN
Strait of Malacca
Great Channel
Ten Degree Channel
Duncan Passage
Sombrero Channel
MERGUI ARCHIPELAGO
ANDAMAN AND NICOBAR ISLANDS
NICOBAR ISLANDS
SUMATERA
MALAYSIA
SEMENANJUNG MALAYSIA
INDONESIA
BURMA
THAILAND
KEPULAUAN RIAU
KEPULAUAN NATUNA SELATAN
KEPULAUAN ANAMBAS
NATUNA BESAR
BORNEO
KALIMANTAN
SARAWAK
THANH PHO HO CHI MINH (SAIGON)
Phnum Pénh
KUALA LUMPUR
SINGAPORE
Medan
Padang
Pekanbaru
George Town (Pinang)
Kuantan
Kuala Terengganu
Kota Baharu
Johor Baharu
Melaka
Ipoh
Hat Yai
Songkhla
Nakhon Si Thammarat
Surat Thani
Phuket
Banda Aceh
Kuching
Port Blair
Map continues pages 112-113
Feet
19685
13124
9843
6562
3281
1640
656
0
Meters
6000
4000
3000
2000
1000
500
200
0
Land Below Sea Level
Copyright © by Rand McNally & Co.
Map compiled by Cartographia, Budapest.
Map produced by Rand McNally GmbH, Stuttgart.
A-561100-764

Map continues pages 110-111

SOUTH CHINA SEA
INDIAN OCEAN
LAUT JAVA
SUMATERA
SUMATRA
SEMENANJUNG MALAYSIA
KALIMANTAN
JAWA
JAVA
SINGAPORE
Songkhla
Hat Yai
Pattani
Narathiwat
Yala
THAILAND
MALAYSIA
Kota Baharu
Alor Setar
George Town (Pinang)
Butterworth
Kuala Terengganu
KELANTAN
TERENGGANU
Taiping
Ipoh
PERAK
Teluk Anson
Kuantan
PAHANG
Kuala Lumpur
SELANGOR
Klang
Seremban
NEGERI SEMBILAN
MELAKA
Melaka
Muar (Bandar Maharani)
Batu Pahat
Keluang
JOHOR
Johor Baharu
Mersing
KEPULAUAN NATUNA BESAR
KEPULAUAN ANAMBAS
KEPULAUAN NATUNA SELATAN
KEPULAUAN TAMBELAN
KEPULAUAN RIAU
KEPULAUAN LINGGA
Tanjungpinang
Pekanbaru
RIAU
Dumai
Bukittinggi
Payakumbuh
Padangpanjang
Pariaman
Padang
SUMATERA BARAT
JAMBI
Jambi
Palembang
SUMATERA SELATAN
Prabumulih
Lahat
Bengkulu
BENGKULU
LAMPUNG
Kotabumi
Tanjungkarang-Telukbetung
PULAU BANGKA
Pangkalpinang
BELITUNG
Tanjungpandan
KEPULAUAN MENTAWAI
PULAU ENGGANO
Selat Sunda
Sunda Strait
JAKARTA
Serang
Bogor
Sukabumi
Cianjur
BANDUNG
Garut
Tasikmalaya
Cirebon
Tegal
Pekalongan
Semarang
Kudus
Salatiga
Purwokerto
Cilacap
Magelang
Yogyakarta
Surakarta
Madiun
Kediri
JAWA BARAT
JAWA TENGAH
KEPULAUAN KARIMUNJAWA
Pontianak
Singkawang
Kuching
Sibu
Ketapang
Sukadana
KEPULAUAN KARIMATA
Selat Karimata
Karimata Strait
BARAT
Equator
CHRISTMAS ISLAND (Austr.)
Flying Fish Cove
100°
102°
104°
106°
108°
110°
112°

Meters	Feet
6000	19685
4000	13124
3000	9843
2000	6562
1000	3281
500	1640
200	656
0	0
Land Below Sea Level	
0	0
200	656
1000	3281
3000	9843
6000	19685
9000	29520

MAP FORM	danau	gunung	kepulauan	pegunungan	pulau	selat	tanjung	teluk
ENGLISH	lake	mountain	islands	mountains	island	strait	cape	bay
DEUTSCH	See	Berg	Inseln	Berge	Insel	Meeresstrasse	Kap	Bucht
ESPAÑOL	lago	montaña	islas	montañas	isla	estrecho	cabo	bahía
FRANÇAIS	lac	montagne	îles	montagnes	île	détroit	cap	baie
PORTUGUÊS	lago	montanha	ilhas	montanhas	ilha	estreito	cabo	baía

Map continues pages 116-117

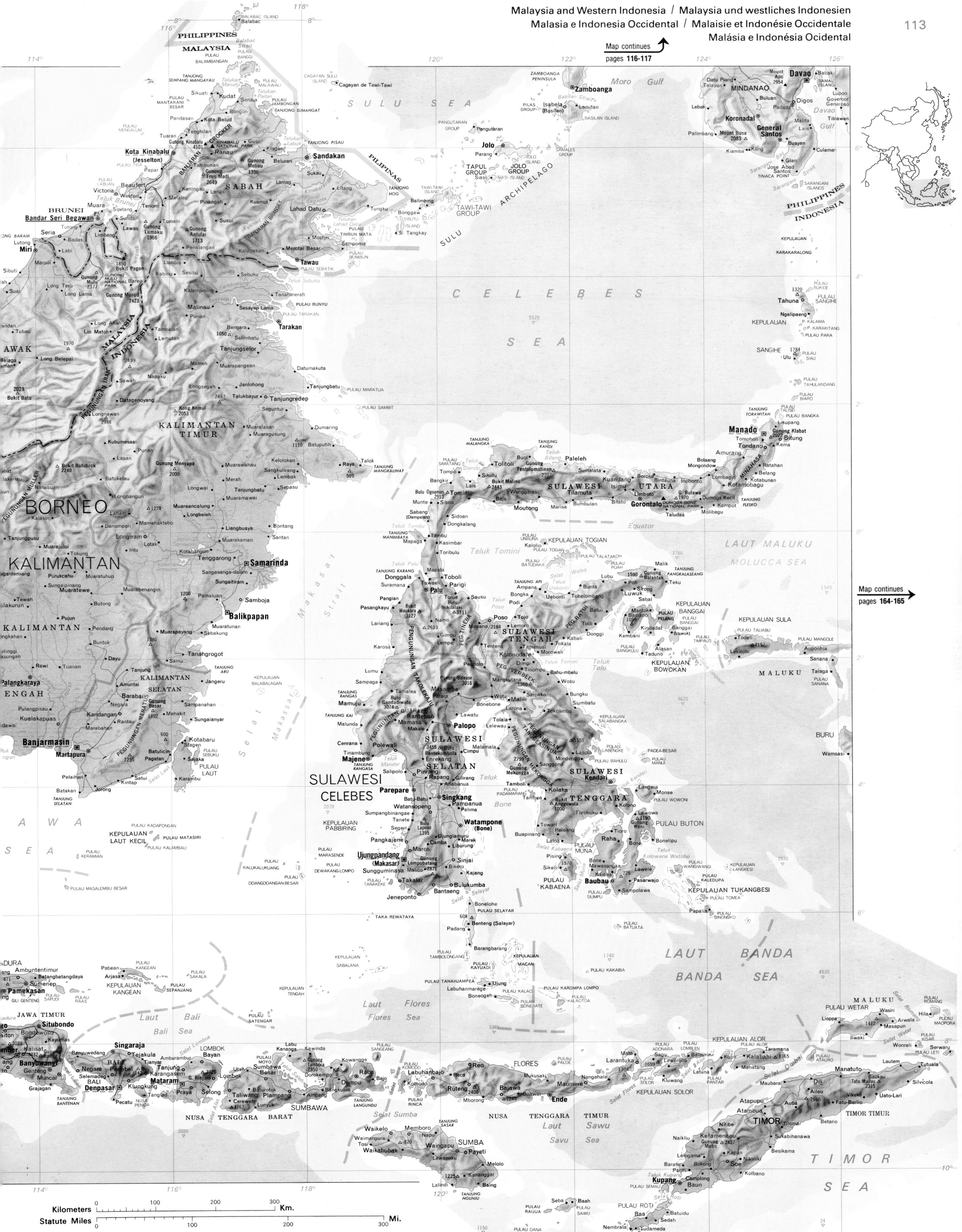
PHILIPPINES
MALAYSIA
SULU SEA
Moro Gulf
Zamboanga
MINDANAO
Davao
Davao Gulf
General Santos
Jolo
SULU ARCHIPELAGO
TAWI-TAWI GROUP
PILIPINAS
SABAH
Kota Kinabalu (Jesselton)
Sandakan
Tawau
BRUNEI
Bandar Seri Begawan
Miri
Tarakan
CELEBES SEA
KALIMANTAN TIMUR
BORNEO
KALIMANTAN
Samarinda
Balikpapan
Banjarmasin
KALIMANTAN SELATAN
Makasar Strait
Selat Makassar
Manado
SULAWESI UTARA
Gorontalo
Teluk Tomini
Equator
LAUT MALUKU
MOLUCCA SEA
Palu
SULAWESI TENGAH
SULAWESI SELATAN
SULAWESI CELEBES
Kendari
SULAWESI TENGGARA
Ujungpandang (Makasar)
Teluk Bone
PULAU BUTON
Baubau
KEPULAUAN BANGGAI
KEPULAUAN SULA
BURU
MALUKU
KEPULAUAN TUKANGBESI
LAUT BANDA
BANDA SEA
JAWA SEA
Laut Flores
Flores Sea
Laut Bali
Bali Sea
JAWA TIMUR
BALI
Denpasar
LOMBOK
Mataram
SUMBAWA
NUSA TENGGARA BARAT
FLORES
Ende
SUMBA
NUSA TENGGARA TIMUR
Laut Sawu
Savu Sea
TIMOR
Kupang
Dili
TIMOR TIMUR
KEPULAUAN ALOR
PULAU WETAR
TIMOR SEA
Kilometers 0 100 200 300 Km.
Statute Miles 0 100 200 300 Mi.

Map continues pages 164-165

Scale 1:6,000,000
One centimeter represents 60 kilometers.
One inch represents approximately 95 miles.
Mercator Projection

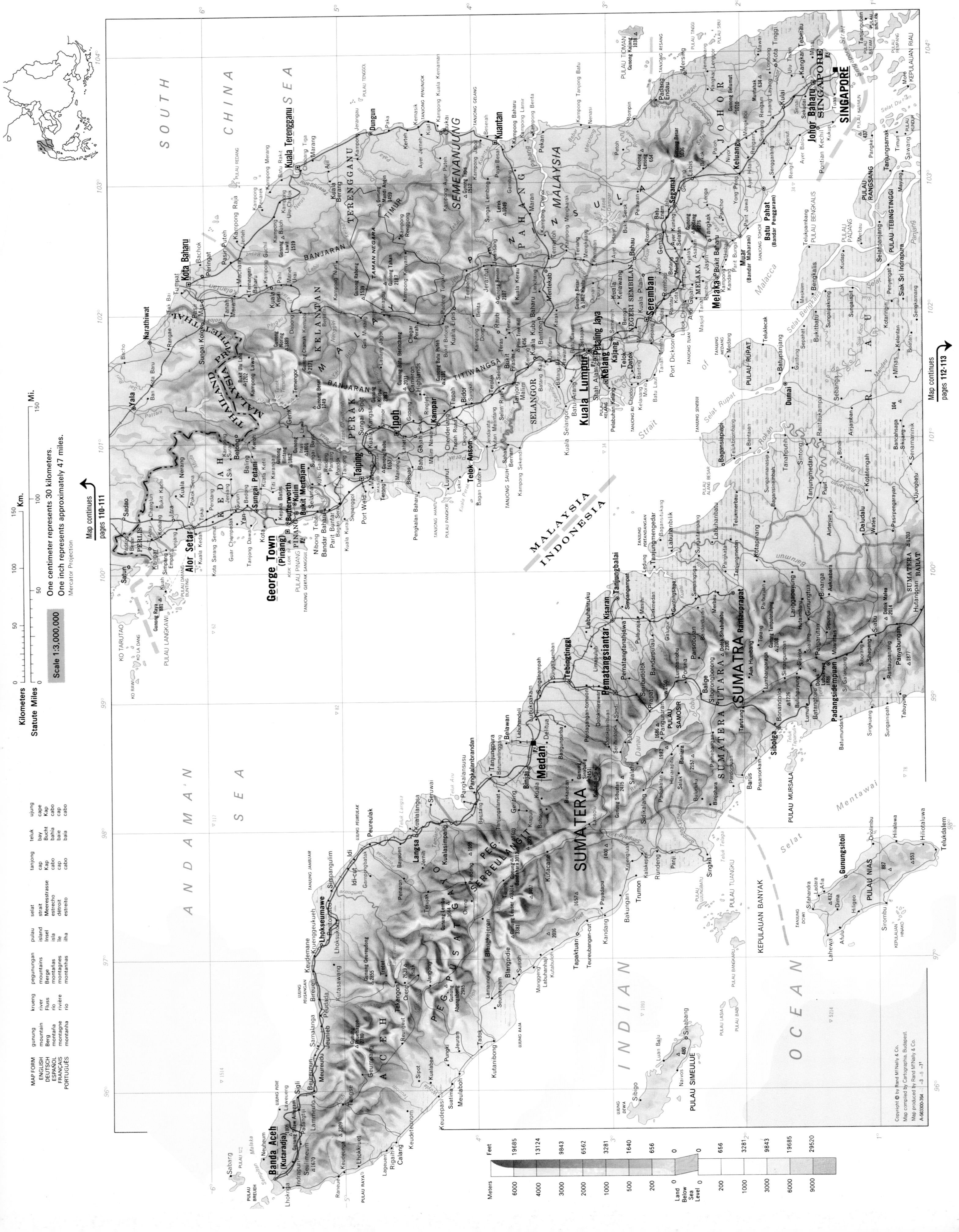
SOUTH CHINA SEA
ANDAMAN SEA
INDIAN OCEAN
MALAYSIA
INDONESIA
SUMATERA
SINGAPORE
Kuala Lumpur
George Town (Pinang)
Ipoh
Medan
Banda Aceh (Kutaradja)
Kuala Terengganu
Kota Baharu
Kuantan
Seremban
Melaka
Johor Baharu
Pematangsiantar
Tebingtinggi
Sibolga
Padangsidempuan
Kilometers 0 50 100 150 Km.
Statute Miles 0 50 100 150 Mi.
Scale 1:3,000,000
One centimeter represents 30 kilometers.
One inch represents approximately 47 miles.
Mercator Projection
Map continues pages 110-111
Map continues pages 112-113
MAP FORM / ENGLISH / DEUTSCH / ESPAÑOL / FRANÇAIS / PORTUGUÊS
gunung / mountain / Berg / montaña / montagne / montanha
krueng / river / Fluss / rio / rivière / rio
pegunungan / mountains / Berge / montañas / montagnes / montanhas
pulau / island / Insel / isla / île / ilha
selat / strait / Meeresstrasse / estrecho / détroit / estreito
tanjong / cap / Kap / cabo / cap / cabo
teluk / bay / Bucht / bahía / baie / baía
ujung / cape / Kap / cabo / cap / cabo
Feet 19685 13124 9843 6562 3281 1640 656 0 0 656 3281 9843 19685 29520
Meters 6000 4000 3000 2000 1000 500 200 0 Land Below Sea Level 0 200 1000 3000 6000 9000
Copyright © by Rand McNally & Co.
Map compiled by Cartographia, Budapest.
Map produced by Rand McNally & Co.

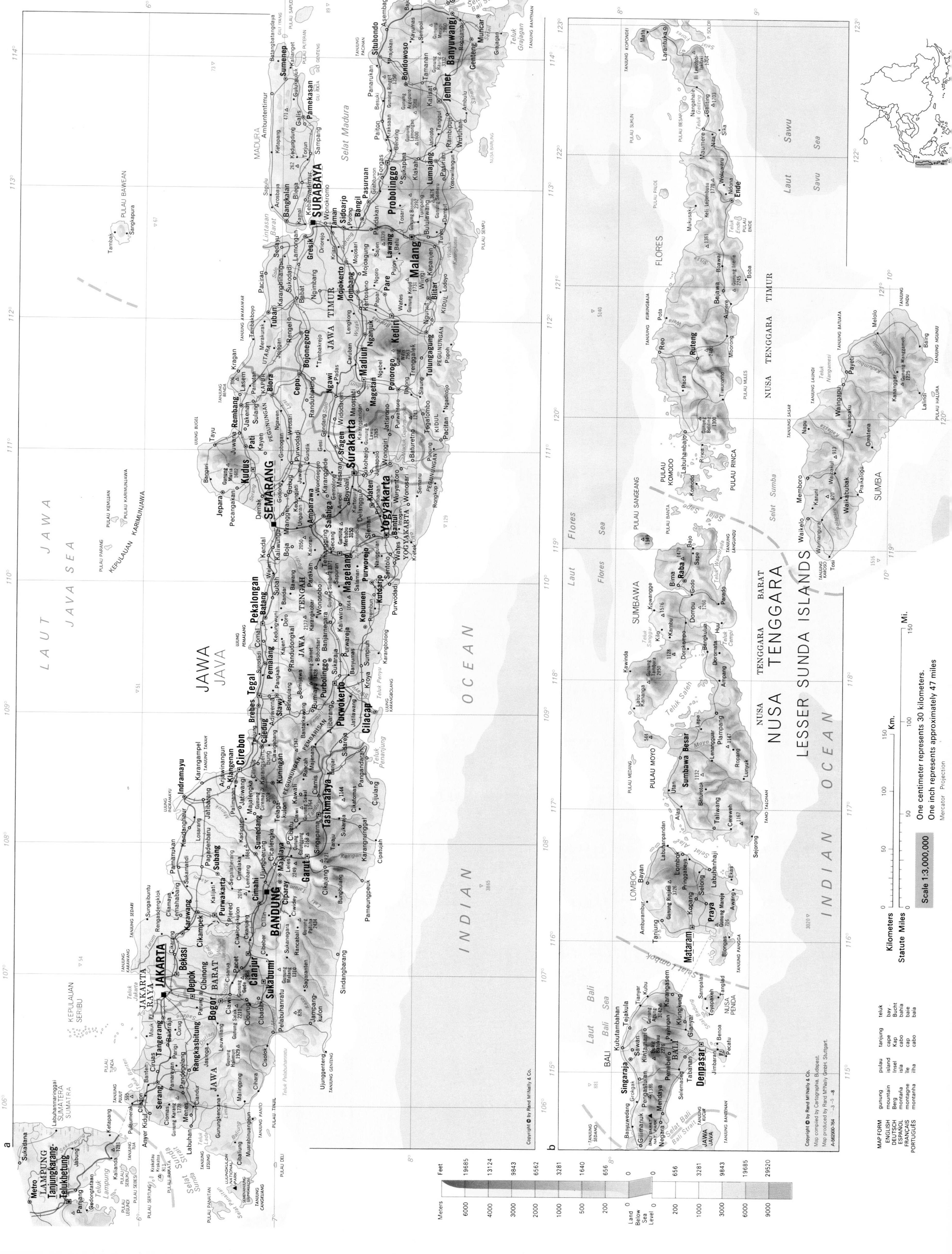
a
b
LAUT JAWA
JAVA SEA
JAWA
JAVA
INDIAN OCEAN
JAKARTA
BANDUNG
SEMARANG
SURABAYA
Yogyakarta
Surakarta
Malang
Cirebon
Tegal
Pekalongan
MADURA
Selat Madura
BALI
LOMBOK
SUMBAWA
FLORES
SUMBA
NUSA TENGGARA
LESSER SUNDA ISLANDS
Laut Flores
Flores Sea
Laut Sawu
Sawu Sea
Denpasar
Mataram
Sumbawa Besar
Ende
Scale 1:3,000,000
One centimeter represents 30 kilometers.
One inch represents approximately 47 miles
Mercator Projection
Kilometers
Statute Miles
MAP FORM
ENGLISH
DEUTSCH
ESPAÑOL
FRANÇAIS
PORTUGUÊS
gunung mountain Berg montaña montagne montanha
pulau island Insel isla île ilha
tanjung cape Kap cabo cap cabo
teluk bay Bucht bahía baie baía
Meters
Feet
Land Below Sea Level
Copyright © by Rand McNally & Co.
Map compiled by Cartographia, Budapest.
Map produced by Rand McNally GmbH, Stuttgart.

Kilometers 0 50 100 150 Km.
Statute Miles 0 50 100 150 Mi.

Scale 1:3,000,000

One centimeter represents 30 kilometers.
One inch represents approximately 47 miles.

Lambert Conformal Conic Projection

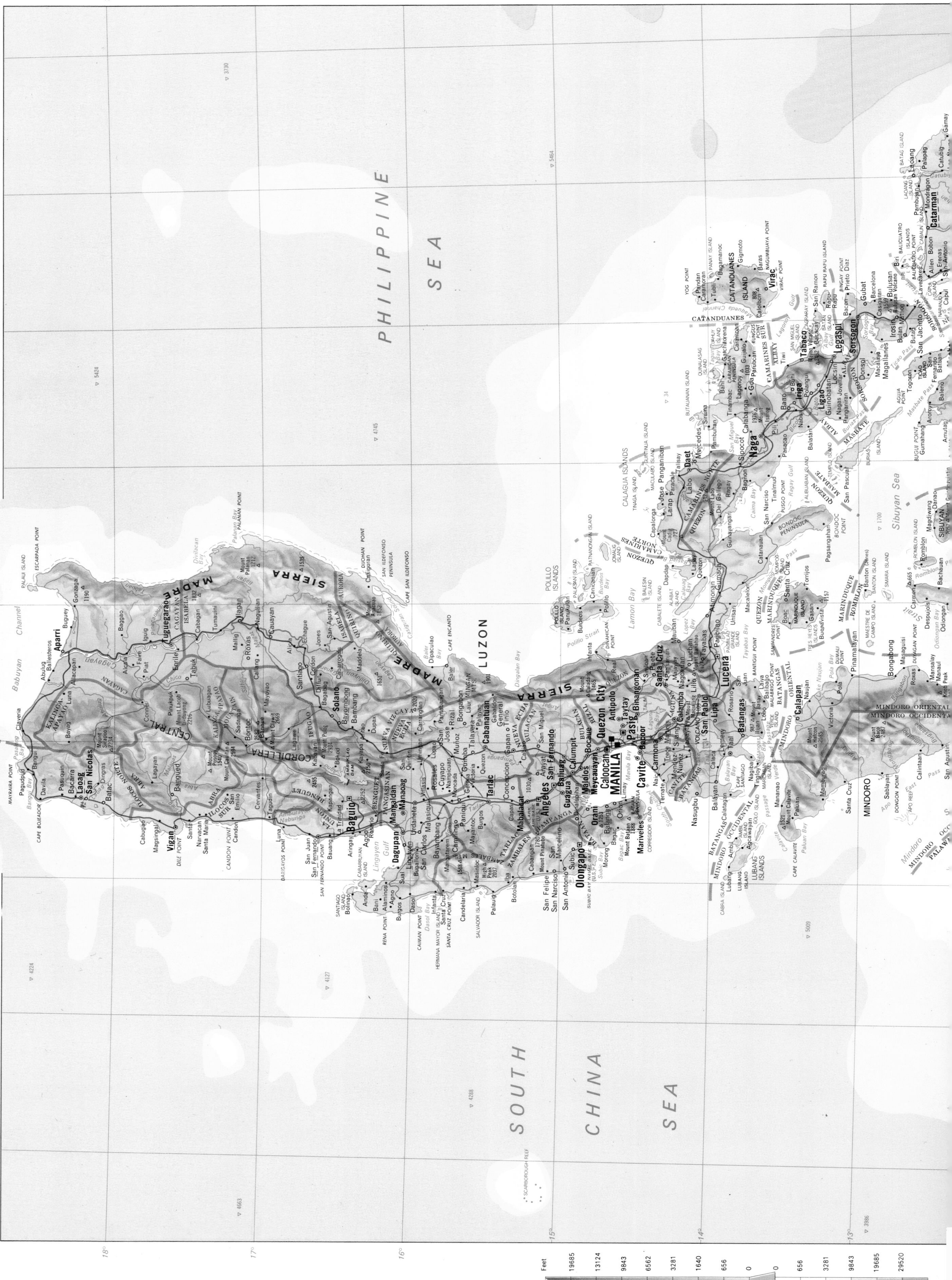
PHILIPPINE SEA
SOUTH CHINA SEA
LUZON
MANILA
Quezon City
BABUYAN ISLANDS
Luzon Strait
Babuyan Channel
SIERRA MADRE
CORDILLERA CENTRAL
Lingayen Gulf
Manila Bay
Lamon Bay
CATANDUANES
MINDORO
MINDORO ORIENTAL
MINDORO OCCIDENTAL
MARINDUQUE
MASBATE
Sibuyan Sea
Polillo Strait
POLILLO ISLANDS
CALAGUA ISLANDS
SCARBOROUGH REEF

MAP FORM	bay	channel	island, i.	mount, mt.	passage	peak, pk.	point	strait
ENGLISH	bay	channel	island	mount	passage	peak	point	strait
DEUTSCH	Bucht	Kanal	Insel	Berg	Durchfahrt	Gipfel	Landspitze	Meeresstrasse
ESPAÑOL	bahía	canal	isla	montaña	pasaje	pico	punta	estrecho
FRANÇAIS	baie	détroit	île	mont	passage	cime	pointe	détroit
PORTUGUÊS	baía	canal	ilha	montanha	passagem	pico	ponta	estreito

Feet	19685	13124	9843	6562	3281	1640	656	0	0	656	3281	9843	19685	29520
Meters	6000	4000	3000	2000	1000	500	200	0 Land Below Sea Level	0	200	1000	3000	6000	9000

MINDANAO
SULU SEA
CELEBES SEA
Moro Gulf
Davao
Zamboanga
Cebu
Iloilo
Bacolod
Tacloban
Cagayan de Oro
Butuan
Puerto Princesa
PALAWAN
NEGROS
PANAY
BOHOL
SULU ARCHIPELAGO
Sandakan
PHILIPPINES PILIPINAS
MALAYSIA
Copyright © by Rand McNally & Co.
Map continues pages 112-113

Map continues pages 22-23

Map continues pages 134-135

CASPIAN SEA
TURKMENISTAN
KARAKUM
TURKEY
ASIA MINOR
SYRIA
LEBANON
ISRAEL
JORDAN
IRAQ
IRAN
DASHT-E KAVĪR
DASHT-E LŪT
KUWAIT
SAUDI ARABIA
AN-NAFŪD
NAJD
AL-HIJAZ
QATAR
BAHRAIN
UNITED ARAB EMIRATES
OMAN
AR-RUB' AL-KHĀLĪ
YEMEN
ERITREA
DJIBOUTI
ETHIOPIA
SOMALIA
RED SEA
Gulf of Aden
Gulf of Oman
Tropic of Cancer
INDIAN
ARAB
TBILISI
JEREVAN
BAKU
TEHRĀN
BAGHDAD
DIMASHQ DAMASCUS
BAYRŪT BEIRUT
AMMAN
AL-KUWAYT
AR-RIYĀḌ RIYADH
Ad-Dawhah Doha
Al-Manāmah
Abū Zaby Abu Dhabi
Masqaṭ Muscat
Ṣan'ā'
Adan Aden
Asmera
Djibouti
Makkah Mecca
Jiddah Jeddah
Al-Madīnah Medina
Mashhad
Eṣfahān
Shīrāz
Tabrīz
Ankara
Halab Aleppo
Al-Mawṣil Mosul
Al-Başrah Basra
Dubayy
Herāt
Nicosia
Yerushalayim Jerusalem
Tel Aviv-Yafo

MAP FORM	gulf	jabal	jazīrat	range	ra's	shan
ENGLISH	gulf	mountain	island	range	cape	mountain(s)
DEUTSCH	Golf	Berg	Insel	Gebirge	Kap	Berg(e)
ESPAÑOL	golfo	montaña	isla	sierra	cabo	montaña(s)
FRANÇAIS	golfe	montagne	île	chaîne	cap	montagne(s)
PORTUGUÊS	golfo	montanha	ilha	serra	cabo	montanha(s)

Kilometers 0 200 400 600 Km.
Statute Miles 0 200 400 600 Mi.

Scale 1:12,000,000

One centimeter represents 120 kilometers.
One inch represents approximately 190 miles.
Lambert Conformal Conic Projection

Map continues pages 72-73

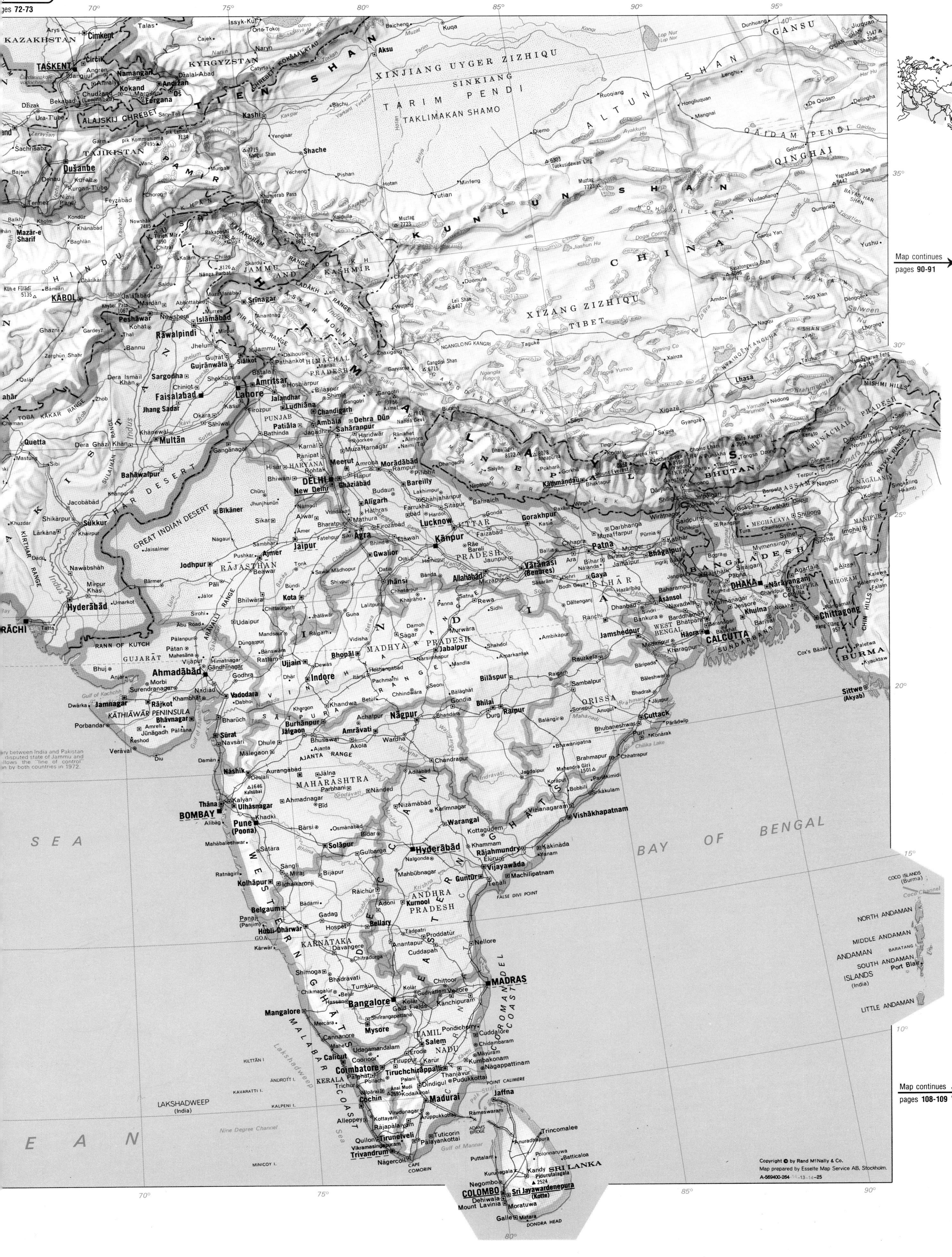
KAZAKHSTAN
KYRGYZSTAN
TAJIKISTAN
XINJIANG UYGUR ZIZHIQU
SINKIANG
TARIM PENDI
TAKLIMAKAN SHAMO
TIEN SHAN
ALTUN SHAN
QAIDAM PENDI
QINGHAI
GANSU
KUNLUN SHAN
CHINA
XIZANG ZIZHIQU
TIBET
JAMMU AND KASHMIR
HIMACHAL PRADESH
PUNJAB
HARYANA
UTTAR PRADESH
RAJASTHAN
GREAT INDIAN DESERT
THAR DESERT
GUJARAT
MADHYA PRADESH
MAHARASHTRA
ANDHRA PRADESH
KARNATAKA
TAMIL NADU
KERALA
ORISSA
BIHAR
WEST BENGAL
NEPAL
BHUTAN
BANGLADESH
BURMA
SRI LANKA
HINDU KUSH
HIMALAYAS
KARAKORAM RANGE
WESTERN GHATS
EASTERN GHATS
MALABAR COAST
COROMANDEL COAST
BAY OF BENGAL
SEA
LAKSHADWEEP (India)
ANDAMAN ISLANDS (India)
NORTH ANDAMAN
MIDDLE ANDAMAN
SOUTH ANDAMAN
LITTLE ANDAMAN
Port Blair
DELHI
New Delhi
BOMBAY
CALCUTTA
MADRAS
Bangalore
Hyderābād
Ahmadābād
Kānpur
Lucknow
Nāgpur
Jaipur
Agra
Vārānasi (Benares)
Patna
DHAKA
Chittagong
Lahore
Faisalabad
Multān
Rawalpindi
Islāmābād
Peshāwar
KĀBOL
Srinagar
Quetta
Hyderābād
Sukkur
Lhasa
Kāthmāndau
COLOMBO
Sri Jayawardenepura (Kotte)
Jaffna
Trivandrum
Cochin
Madurai
Coimbatore
Mangalore
Goa
Pune (Poona)
Sūrat
Vadodara
Rājkot
Jamnagar
Indore
Bhopāl
Jabalpur
Raipur
Cuttack
Vishākhapatnam
Vijayawāda
Dušanbe
Taškent
Kashi
Copyright © by Rand McNally & Co.
Map prepared by Esselte Map Service AB, Stockholm.

Map continues pages 90-91

Map continues pages 108-109

Map continues pages 128-129

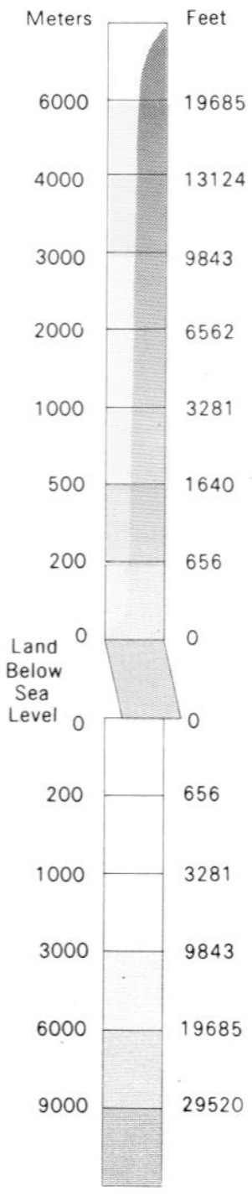
Meters
Feet
6000
19685
4000
13124
3000
9843
2000
6562
1000
3281
500
1640
200
656
0
0
Land Below Sea Level
0
0
200
656
1000
3281
3000
9843
6000
19685
9000
29520

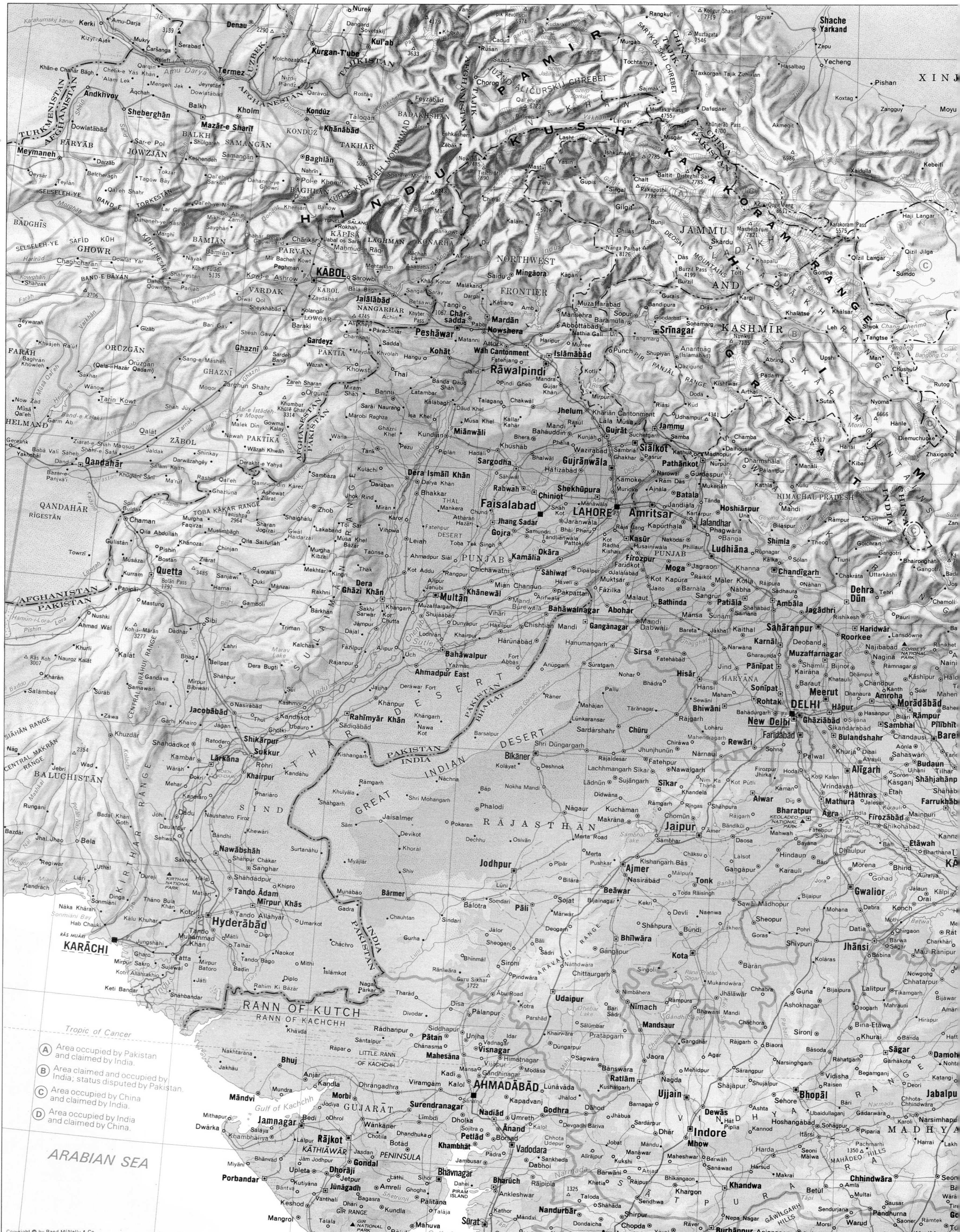
ARABIAN SEA
Tropic of Cancer
RANN OF KUTCH
RANN OF KACHCHH
GREAT INDIAN DESERT
THAR DESERT
HINDU KUSH
PAMIR
KARAKORAM RANGE
GREAT HIMALAYA RANGE
PAKISTAN
INDIA
AFGHANISTAN
KASHMIR
JAMMU AND KASHMIR
NORTHWEST FRONTIER
PUNJAB
SIND
BALUCHISTAN
RAJASTHAN
GUJARAT
KATHIAWAR PENINSULA
MADHYA
HIMACHAL PRADESH
HARYANA
KĀBOL
Peshāwar
Rawalpindi
Islāmābād
LAHORE
Amritsar
DELHI
New Delhi
KARĀCHI
Hyderābād
Quetta
Qandahār
Multān
Faisalabad
Jaipur
AHMADĀBĀD
Indore
Bhopāl
Nāgpur
Srīnagar
A Area occupied by Pakistan and claimed by India.
B Area claimed and occupied by India; status disputed by Pakistan.
C Area occupied by China and claimed by India.
D Area occupied by India and claimed by China.
Copyright © by Rand McNally & Co.
Map prepared by George Philip & Son Ltd., London.
A-565200-764 -8 -7-19

MAP FORM	co	feng	hu	range	shan	shankou	yumco
ENGLISH	lake	peak	lake	range	mountain(s)	pass	lake
DEUTSCH	See	Gipfel	See	Gebirge	Berg(e)	Pass	See
ESPAÑOL	lago	pico	lago	sierra	montaña(s)	paso	lago
FRANÇAIS	lac	cime	lac	chaîne	montagne(s)	col	lac
PORTUGUÊS	lago	pico	lago	serra	montanha(s)	passo	lago

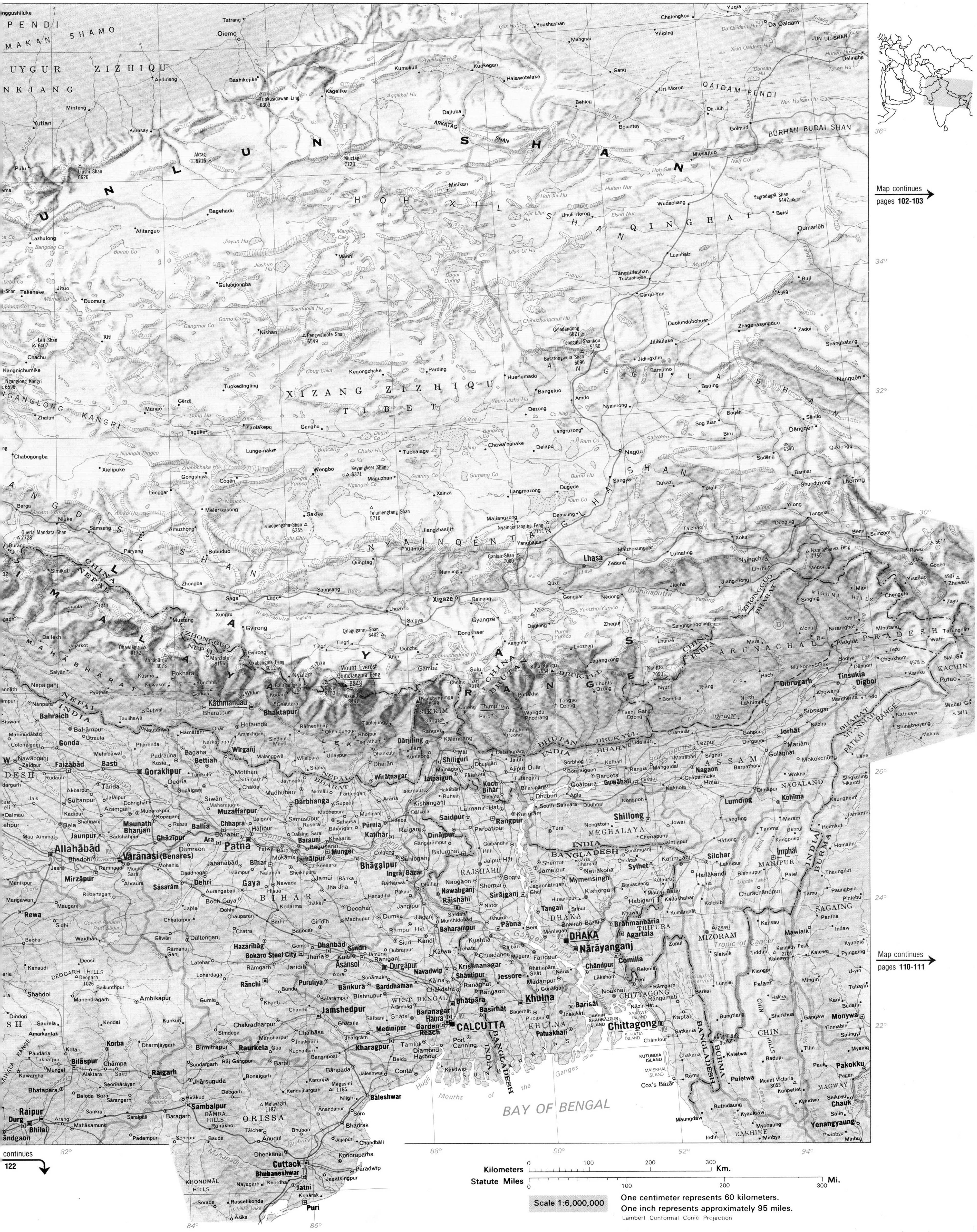
KUNLUN SHAN
HOH XIL SHAN
QINGHAI
QAIDAM PENDI
BURHAN BUDAI SHAN
XIZANG ZIZHIQU
TIBET
NYAINQÊNTANGLHA SHAN
GANGDISE SHAN
HIMALAYA
GREAT HIMALAYA RANGE
NEPAL
BHUTAN
SIKKIM
ARUNACHAL PRADESH
ASSAM
MEGHALAYA
NAGALAND
MANIPUR
MIZORAM
TRIPURA
BANGLADESH
BIHAR
ORISSA
WEST BENGAL
BURMA
CHIN HILLS
BAY OF BENGAL
Mouths of the Ganges
Tropic of Cancer
Lhasa
Kathmandu
Thimphu
DHAKA
CALCUTTA
Patna
Allahābād
Vārānasi (Benares)
Chittagong
Khulna
Cuttack
Bhubaneshwar
Puri
Mount Everest
Qomolangma Feng
8848
Brahmaputra
Ganges
UYGUR ZIZHIQU
XINJIANG
TAKLIMAKAN SHAMO
Map continues pages 102-103
Map continues pages 110-111
continues 122

Kilometers 0 100 200 300 Km.
Statute Miles 0 100 200 300 Mi.

Scale 1:6,000,000
One centimeter represents 60 kilometers.
One inch represents approximately 95 miles.
Lambert Conformal Conic Projection

Southern India and Sri Lanka / Südindien und Sri Lanka / India Meridional y Sri Lanka
Inde Méridionale et Sri Lanka / Índia Meridional e Sri Lanka

Map continues pages 120-121

Surendranagar
Indore
Nāgpur
BOMBAY
Pune (Poona)
HYDERĀBĀD
Warangal
Vishākhapatnam
Vijayawāda
BANGALORE
MADRAS
Mysore
Mangalore
Calicut
Coimbatore
Cochin
Madurai
Trivandrum
Nagercoil
Jaffna
Trincomalee
Anurādhapura
Batticaloa
Kandy
COLOMBO
Sri Jayawardenepura (Kotte)
Galle
SRI LANKA
LAKSHADWEEP
MALDIVES
ARABIAN SEA
BAY OF BENGAL
INDIAN OCEAN
Gulf of Mannar
Palk Strait
Nine Degree Channel
Eight Degree Channel
Laksadweep Sea
Copyright © by Rand McNally & Co.
Map prepared by George Philip & Son Ltd. London
A-565300-764

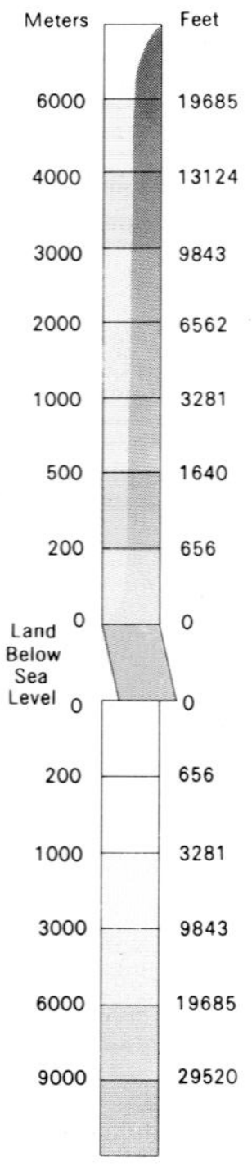

Meters
Feet
6000
19685
4000
13124
3000
9843
2000
6562
1000
3281
500
1640
200
656
0
0
Land Below Sea Level
0
0
200
656
1000
3281
3000
9843
6000
19685
9000
29520

ENGLISH	atoll	hills	island	lagoon	lake	range	reservoir
DEUTSCH	Atoll	Hügel	Insel	Haff	See	Gebirge	Stausee
ESPAÑOL	atolón	colinas	isla	laguna	lago	sierra	embalse
FRANÇAIS	atoll	collines	île	lagune	lac	chaîne	réservoir
PORTUGUÊS	atol	colinas	ilha	laguna	lago	serra	reservatório

Kilometers 0 100 200 300 Km.
Statute Miles 0 100 200 300 Mi.

Scale 1:6,000,000

One centimeter represents 60 kilometers.
One inch represents approximately 95 miles.
Lambert Conformal Conic Projection

Map continues page 85

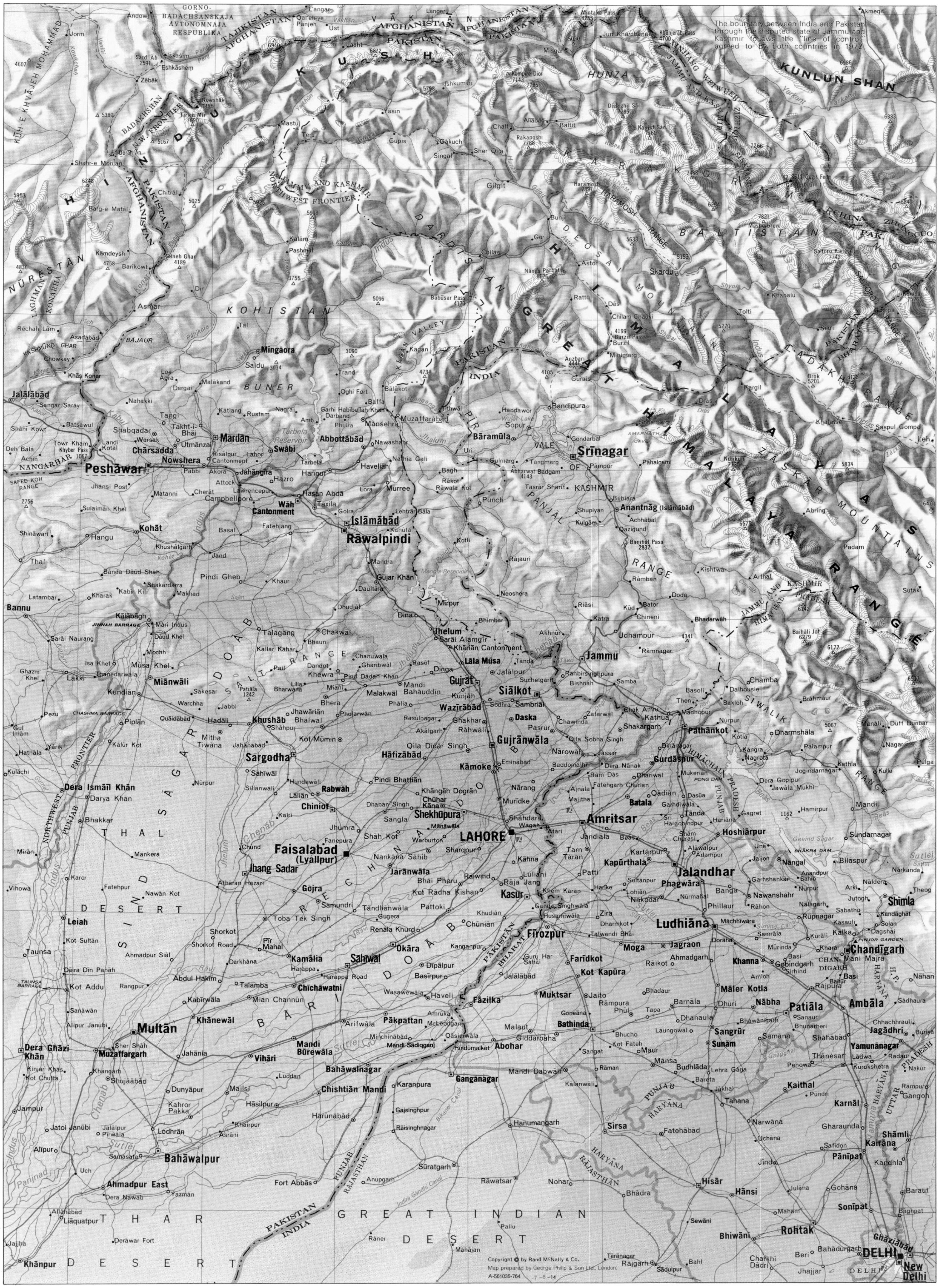
The boundary between India and Pakistan through the disputed state of Jammu and Kashmir follows the "line of control" agreed to by both countries in 1972.
HINDU KUSH
KARAKORAM RANGE
KUNLUN SHAN
GREAT HIMALAYA RANGE
ZASKAR MOUNTAINS
LADAKH RANGE
PIR PANJAL RANGE
SIWALIK RANGE
SALT RANGE
THAL DESERT
GREAT INDIAN DESERT
THAR DESERT
SIND SAGAR DOAB
RECHNA DOAB
BARI DOAB
VALE OF KASHMIR
KOHISTAN
BALTISTAN
HUNZA
Peshāwar
Islāmābād
Rāwalpindi
Srīnagar
Jammu
Lahore
Amritsar
Faisalabad (Lyallpur)
Multān
Bahāwalpur
Jalandhar
Ludhiāna
Chandīgarh
Shimla
Patiāla
Ambāla
Delhi
New Delhi
Copyright by Rand McNally & Co.
Map prepared by George Philip & Son Ltd., London.
A-561035-764

Map continues pages 124-125

Meters	Feet
6000	19685
4000	13124
3000	9843
2000	6562
1000	3281
500	1640
200	656
0	0
Land Below Sea Level 0	0
200	656
1000	3281
3000	9843
6000	19685
9000	29520

MAP FORM	airport	doāb	glacier	pass	range	sar
ENGLISH	airport	upland	glacier	pass	range	mountain
DEUTSCH	Flughafen	Bergland	Gletscher	Pass	Gebirge	Berg
ESPAÑOL	aeropuerto	tierras altas	glaciar	paso	sierra	montaña
FRANÇAIS	aéroport	hautes terres	glacier	col	chaîne	montagne
PORTUGUÊS	aeroporto	terras altas	geleira	passo	serra	montanha

Kilometers 0 50 100 150 Km.
Statute Miles 0 50 100 150 Mi.

Scale 1:3,000,000

One centimeter represents 30 kilometers.
One inch represents approximately 47 miles.
Lambert Conformal Conic Projection

Ganges Lowland and Nepal / Gangestiefland und Nepal / Llanuras del Ganges y Nepal
Plaine du Gange et Népal / Planície do Ganges e Nepal

Map continues page 123

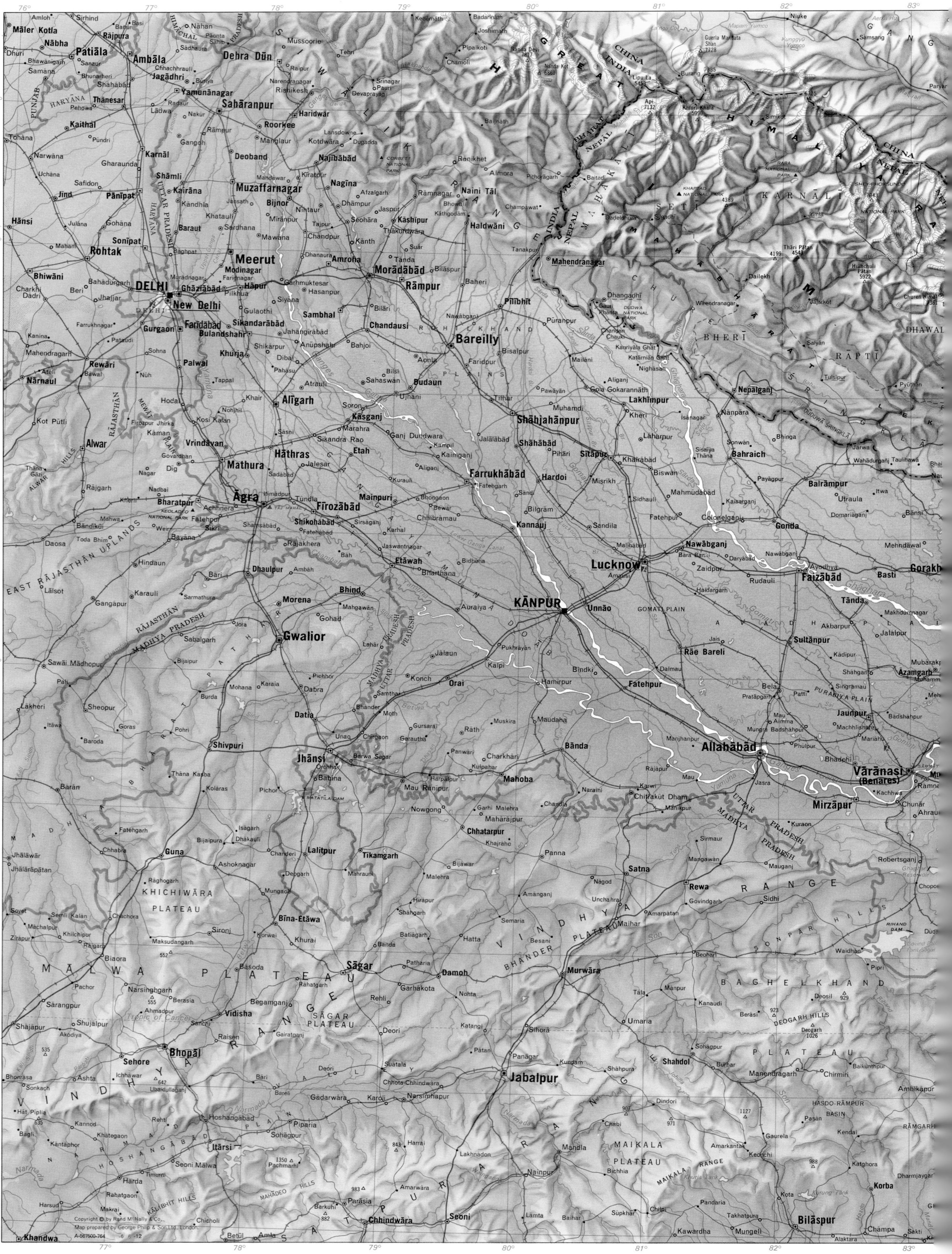

DELHI
New Delhi
Meerut
Morādābād
Bareilly
Shāhjahānpur
Lucknow
KĀNPUR
Allahābād
Vārānasi (Benares)
Āgra
Mathura
Alīgarh
Gwalior
Jhānsi
Sāgar
Bhopāl
Jabalpur
Bilāspur
Dehra Dūn
Sahāranpur
Muzaffarnagar
Ambāla
Patiāla
Rohtak
Alwar
Etāwah
Farrukhābād
Fīrozābād
Faizābād
Gonda
Bahraich
Mahendranagar
Nepālganj
Rewa
Satna
Murwāra
Mirzāpur
Jaunpur
Rāe Bareli
Sultānpur
Fatehpur
Bānda
Mahoba
Shivpuri
Guna
Lalitpur
Tikamgarh
Chhatarpur
Damoh
Vidisha
Sehore
Itārsi
Hoshangābād
Chhindwāra
Seoni
Mandla
Korba
Khandwa
GREAT HIMALAYA
SIWALIK RANGE
EAST RĀJASTHĀN UPLANDS
KHICHIWĀRA PLATEAU
MĀLWA PLATEAU
SAGAR PLATEAU
VINDHYA RANGE
BHANDER PLATEAU
MAIKALA PLATEAU
BAGHELKHAND PLATEAU
SĀTPURA RANGE
GOMATI PLAIN
Tropic of Cancer
CHINA
INDIA
NEPAL
UTTAR PRADESH
MADHYA PRADESH
RĀJASTHĀN
HARYĀNA
PUNJAB
HIMĀCHAL PRADESH
Copyright © by Rand McNally & Co.
Map prepared by George Philip & Son Ltd., London.

Meters / Feet

Meters	Feet
6000	19685
4000	13124
3000	9843
2000	6562
1000	3281
500	1640
200	656
0	0
Land Below Sea Level	
0	0
200	656
1000	3281
3000	9843
6000	19685
9000	29520

MAP FORM	hills	plains	plateau	range	shan	yumco
ENGLISH	hills	plains	plateau	range	mountains	lake
DEUTSCH	Hügel	Ebenen	Hochebene	Gebirge	Berge	See
ESPAÑOL	colinas	llanos	meseta	sierra	montañas	lago
FRANÇAIS	collines	plaines	plateau	chaîne	montagnes	lac
PORTUGUÊS	colinas	planícies	planalto	serra	montanhas	lago

Kilometers 0 50 100 150 Km.
Statute Miles 0 50 100 150 Mi.

Scale 1:3,000,000

One centimeter represents 30 kilometers.
One inch represents approximately 47 miles.
Lambert Conformal Conic Projection

NYAINQÊNTANGLHA SHAN
XIZANG
TIBET
ZIZHIQU
LABUCHONG SHAN
GREAT HIMALAYA RANGE
Mount Everest 8848
Kānchenjunga 8598
Lhasa
Xigazê
Gyangzê
Thimphu
Kāthmāndau
Bhaktapur
Pokhara
Dārjiling
Gangtok
SIKKIM
BHUTAN
DRUK-YUL
ZHONGGUO
CHINA
INDIA
BHARAT
NEPAL
BANGLADESH
MEGHĀLAYA
ASSAM
BIHĀR
WEST BENGAL
UTTAR PRADESH
ORISSA
Patna
Gaya
Muzaffarpur
Darbhanga
Bhāgalpur
Munger
Jamshedpur
Rānchi
Bokāro Steel City
Dhanbād
Āsansol
Durgāpur
Barddhamān
CALCUTTA
Haora
Kharagpur
Medinīpur
Shiliguri
Rājshāhi
Dhaka (Dacca)
Nārāyanganj
Mymensingh
Comilla
Khulna
Barisāl
Jessore
Rangpur
Dinājpur
CHOTA NAGPUR PLATEAU
RĀNCHI PLATEAU
HAZĀRĪBĀG PLATEAU
RĀJMAHĀL HILLS
GANGES DELTA
Tropic of Cancer
Ganges
Brahmaputra
Meghna
Hugli
BAY OF BENGAL
Mouths of the Ganges
84°
85°
86°
87°
88°
89°
90°
91°
22°
23°
24°
25°
26°
27°
28°
29°
30°

86° 30′
87°
87° 30′
88°
24°
23° 30′
23°
22° 30′
22°
21° 30′
Tropic of Cancer
Madhupur
Dumka
Nalhāti
Giridih
Rāmpur Hāt
Jiāganj
Murshidābād
Baharampur
RĀJMAHAL HILLS
Morākhi Reservoir
Maithon Reservoir
Jāmtāra
Kāndi
Chittaranjan
BIHĀR
WEST BENGAL
Dhanbād
Jharia
Sindri
Kulti
Kumardhubi
Pānchet Reservoir
Āsānsol
Rānīganj
Durgāpur
Sūri
Bolpur
Dubrājpur
Katwa
Chās
Raghunāthpur
Ādra
Puruliya
Bānkura
Bishnupur
Barddhamān
Navadwīp
Kālna
Mēmāri
Jamshedpur
Ghātsila
Ārāmbāg
Ghātāl
Chandrakona
Medinīpur
Kharagpur
Jhārgrām
Hāora
Hugli-Chinsurah
Chandannagar
Bhadreswar
Champdāni
Baidyabāti
Serāmpore
Rishra
Konnagar
Uttarpara-Kotrung
Bally
Baranagar
Garden Reach
Behāla
Budge Budge
Ulubāria
Tamlūk
Mahishādal
Diamond Harbour
Haldī
Contai
Jaleshwar
Bāripada
Bāleshwar
BIHĀR
ORISSA
WEST BENGAL
ORISSA
MIDNAPORE PLAIN
KĀNTHI COASTAL PLAIN
BHĀGĪRATHI PLAIN
RĀRH PLAIN
GARHJĀT HILLS
SĀGAR ISLAND
Ganga Sāgar
Hugli
Dāmodar
Ajay
Kāsai
Subarnarekha
Rūpnārāyan
Dwārkeswar
GRAND TRUNK ROAD
EASTERN RAILWAY
SOUTH EASTERN RAILWAY

MAP FORM	bay	canal	char	delta	island	plain
ENGLISH	bay	canal	island	delta	island	plain
DEUTSCH	Bucht	Kanal	Insel	Delta	Insel	Ebene
ESPAÑOL	bahía	canal	isla	delta	isla	llanura
FRANÇAIS	baie	canal	île	delta	île	plaine
PORTUGUÊS	baía	canal	ilha	delta	ilha	planície

89°
89° 30′
90°
90° 30′
24°
23° 30′
23°
22° 30′
22°
21° 30′
Bāgātipāra
Barāigrām
Ullāpāra
Saidābād
Gala
Pākundia
Debīpur
Chārghāt
Ārāni
Chātmohar
Garādaha
Betil
Sthal
Tangail
Basāil
Karatia
Pāthrāil
Masua
Ulusara
Kātiādi
Duāigaon
Majlispur
Lālpur
Nāopāra
Gopālpur
Faridpur
Shāhzādpur
Sripur
Jalangi
RĀJSHĀHI
KHULNA
Raita
Ishurdi
Dāsuria
Āighāria
Pāchh Elāsin
Jāmurki
Mirzāpur
Kāliākair
Kāpāsia
Rājendrapur
Manohardi
Char Lakhpur
Sibpur
Mathurāpur
Sāra
Pāksey
Bera
Sānthia
Nākālia
Nagarpur
Daulatpur
Bheramāra
Ganges
Pābna
Chhanka
Pakrāganj
Karimpur
Chandipur
Mirpur
Padma
Kāshināthpur
Sujānagar
Dulāi
Bāliāti
Kāsimpur
Dhirāsrām
Jaydebpur
Pubāil
Rāipura
Āmla
Kushtia
Jagati
Kumārkhāli
Hogalbāria
Poradaha
Sātbāria
Tilli
Ghior
Mahādebpur
Chāndar
Mānikganj
Dhāmrai
Tongi
Kāliganj
Narsinghdi
Dānga
Biraba
Kāthuli
Ālampur
Barkhanpur
Shivalaya
Sābhār
Meherpur
Āmjhupi
Alamdanga
Khoksa
Pāngsa
Rājbāri
Kālikāpur
Singair
Gulshan
Mīrpur
ZIA INTERNATIONAL AIRPORT
Rupganj
Ārāihāzar
Bānchhārāmpur
Gobra
Gauribaradia
Bankhari
Āyubnagar
DHAKA
DACCA
Bākhrābād
Sailkupa
Rāmdia
Bānibaha
Morghar
Harirāmpur
Natudaha
Chuādanga
Nāgirat
Bāliākāndi
Nawābganj
Rohitpur
Baidyer Bāzār
Dāmurhuda
Harinākunda
Sonāpur
Dāriāpur
Fatulla
Nārāyanganj
Bhātai
Sripur
Naliagrām
Baharpur
Faridpur
Dohār
Boalia
Sādhuhāti
Jhenida
Chandanpratāp
Kāmārkhāli Ghāt
Gārākhola
Madhukhāli
Kānaipur
Krishnapur
Srinagar
Munshiganj
Gumti
Nayāgaon
Dārsana
BHARAT
Bishaykhāli
Māgura
Baksir Chāndpur
Bangeswardi
Tālma
Sadarpur
Bāisrasi
Daudkāndi
Elliotganj
Naldanga
Kāliganj
Binodepur
Ghoshpur
Bāghia
Rājābāri
DHAKA
CHITTAGONG
Tropic of Cancer
Jibannagar
Dhaneswargāti
Muhammadpur
Kotchāndpur
Mohanpur
Bhushana
Bhānga
Hanskhāli
Bagula
Mahespur
Ārpāra
Mangalpaita
Phulbāria
Sibchar
Matlab Bāzār
Kachua
Bunagāti
Nahāta
Sāhasrail
Muksudpur
Naria
Kedārpur
Sālikha
Mathurāpur
Nārikelbāria
Alfādanga
Masura
Chaugācha
North Singa
Nabaganga
Gohāla
Hājīganj
Chāndpur
Dattapulia
Kāsiāni
Kamranga
Churāmankāti
Bāgherpāra
Raghunāthpur
Jalirpār
Pālang
Bāghāt
Bagdaha
Bhātiapara Ghāt
Mādāripur
Bishahari
Jessore
Narāil
Lohāgara
Bāje Phukura
Kanakeswar
Gāngnāpur
Rupdia
Jangal Bādhāl
Hānār Char
Jhikergacha
Dhopākhola
Dighalia
Baghia Bil
Faridganj
Rāmganj
Chandra Dighalia
Kālkini
Gosairhāt
Sridharpur
Meghna
Gopālnagar
Char Hāim
Rāipur
Bangaon
Buruz Bāgān
Manirāmpur
Nawāpāra
Kālia
Ulpur
Kājulia
Medakul
Abhaynagar
Gopālganj
Safipur
CHITTAGONG
KHULNA
Chaubaria
Phultala
Kotwālipāra
Gaurnadi
Char Bansi
Dattapāra
Chāndpara
Mobārakpur
Durbādānga
Lakshmīpur
Gaighata
Kesabpur
Terakhāda
Mahilāra
Deopāra
Bārākpur
DHAKA
KHULNA
Mollāhāt
Satla Bil
Gobardānga
Dhāmura
Muladi
Patghāti
Nalgora
Kālāroa
Miksimil
Daulatpur
Senhāti
Mehendiganj
Dumuria
Naihāti
Mātibhānga
Swarupnagar
Khulna
Kurmani
Iluhār
Bānaripāra
Kāzir Char
Sānkdaha
Mulghar
Bhattapratāp
Sonādugi
Tala
Hāntālbunia
Naoāpara
Singāti
Makrampur
Swarupkāti
Bāduria
Paläspol
Sātkhira
Kapilmuni
Jātrāpur
Nazirpur
Barisāl
Bhola
Arbālia
Kālikāpur
Gaurambha
Kachua
Jhālakāti
Daulatkhān
Deganga
Basīrhāt
Budhhāta
Bāgerhāt
Kaukhāli
Nālchiti
Medua
Shāhbāzpur
Pānkhāli
Gilatala
Banagrām
Pirojpur
Jaynagar
Tāki
Debhāta
Hāsnābād
Paikgācha
Rāmpāl
Rājāpur
Bākarganj
Bhātsala
Chaitāl
Asāsuni
BANGLADESH
INDIA
Umedpur
Barahānuddin
Jatarpur
Amādi
Mīrzākalu
Tazumuddin
Haldibunia
Morrelganj
Bhandāria
Bibi Chini
Āngāria
DAKHIN SHĀHBĀZPUR ISLAND
Kāliganj
Kālinagar
Jiudhara
Bauphal
Rājbāri
Maulala
Pratāpnagar
Betāgi
Baga
Kālaia
Debir Char
Mirzāganj
Nūrnagar
Syāmnagar
Raenda
Bamna
Patuākhāli
Lālmohan
Sandeshkhāli
Iswaripur
Sarankhola
Mathbaria
Badura
Dasmina
BHARAT
Basanti
Kabadak
Phuljhuri
Ulānia
Tetulia
Gosāba
Bārguna
Amtāli
Galāchipa
Bara Doāni
Pātua
DONMĀNICK ISLANDS
Chhota Baisdia
Kalāpāra
Tetulbāria
Lālua
KUKURI MUKURI CHAR
CHAR LAKSHMI
RABNABĀD ISLANDS
U N D A R B A N S
PUTNEY ISLAND
DALHOUSIE ISLAND
BANGADUNI ISLAND
BAY OF BENGAL
Copyright © by Rand McNally & Co.
Map prepared by George Philip & Son Ltd., London.
A-567900-264

Kilometers 0 10 20 30 40 50 Km.

Statute Miles 0 10 20 30 40 50 Mi.

Scale 1:1,000,000

One centimeter represents 10 kilometers.

One inch represents approximately 16 miles.

Lambert Conformal Conic Projection

Map continues page 84

Map continues pages 130-131

ANKARA
Konya
Kayseri
Sivas
Erzurum
Adana
Gaziantep
Diyarbakır
Tabrīz
JEREVAN
Halab Aleppo
Al-Mawṣil Mosul
Kirkūk
Dayr az-Zawr
DIMASHQ DAMASCUS
BEIRUT BAYRŪT
Tripoli
Nicosia
NORTH CYPRUS KUZEY KIBRIS
CYPRUS KIPROS
The Turkish Republic of Northern Cyprus unilaterally declared its independence on November 15, 1983.
MEDITERRANEAN SEA
LEBANON LUBNĀN
Area occupied by Israel since June 1967
ISRAEL YISRA'EL
PALESTINE
TEL AVIV-YAFO
Yerushalayim Jerusalem
'AMMĀN
BAGHDĀD
Al-Basrah
AL-KUWAYT
Bur Sa'īd Port Said
As-Suways Suez
AR-RIYĀḌ RIYADH
Al-Madīnah Medina
Ḥā'il
Tabūk
AN-NAFŪD
SYRIAN DESERT
AL-HIJĀZ
RED SEA
AL-BAHR AL-AHMAR
Tropic of Cancer
Meters
Feet
6000 19685
4000 13124
3000 9843
2000 6562
1000 3281
500 1640
200 656
0 0
Land Below Sea Level
0 0
200 656
1000 3281
3000 9843
6000 19685
9000 29520

Map continues pages 140-141

Map continues pages 144-145

MAP FORM	harrat	jabal	jazīreh	kūh	ra's	sabkhat	wādī
ENGLISH	lava flow	mountain	island	mountain	cape	salt marsh	wadi
DEUTSCH	Lavastrom	Berg	Insel	Berg	Kap	Salzmarsch	Wadi
ESPAÑOL	corriente de lava	montaña	isla	montaña	cabo	pantano salado	uadi
FRANÇAIS	coulée de lave	montagne	île	montagne	cap	marais salé	wadi
PORTUGUÊS	corrente de lava	montanha	ilha	montanha	cabo	pântano salgado	uádi

CASPIAN SEA
(28 Meters Below Sea Level)
BAKU
Krasnovodsk
Nebit-Dag
Kizyl-Arvat
BALKAN
TAŠAUZ
K A R A K U M Y
C E N T R A L ' N Y J E
Aščabad
Ashgabat
Mary
Čardžou
Buchara
Kagan
Karši
UZBEKISTAN
TURKMENISTAN
TURKMENISTAN IRAN IRĀN
KOPETDAG
Mashhad
Gorgān
Sārī
Qazvīn
TEHRĀN
RESHTEH-YE KŪHHĀ-YE ALBORZ
ELBURZ MOUNTAINS
Semnān
SEMNĀN
DASHT-E KAVĪR
Qom
Kāshān
Eṣfahān
Isfahan
EṢFAHĀN
YAZD
Yazd
KHORĀSĀN
DASHT-E LŪT
Kermān
K E R M Ā N
Shīrāz
FĀRS
BŪSHEHR
Bandar-e Būshehr
HORMOZGĀN
Bandar-e 'Abbās
Strait of Hormuz
SĪSTĀN VA BALŪCHESTĀN
Zāhedān
Zābol
BALUCHISTAN
CHĀGAI HILLS
CENTRAL MAKRĀN RANGE
MAKRAN COAST
SANDY DESERT
Herāt
HERĀT
FARĀH
Farāh
HELMAND
RĪGESTĀN
Qandahār
QANDAHĀR
NĪMRŪZ
DASHT-E MĀRGOW
AFGHANISTAN
PAKISTAN
Mazār-e Sharīf
Sheberghān
Meymaneh
SAFĪD KŪH
Persian Gulf
Arabian Gulf
BAHRAIN
AL-BAḤRAYN
Al-Manāmah
QATAR
Ad-Dawḥah
Doha
Abū Ẓaby
Abu Dhabi
Dubayy
UNITED ARAB EMIRATES
AL-IMĀRĀT AL-'ARABĪYAH AL-MUTTAḤIDAH
OMAN
'UMĀN
Masqaṭ
Muscat
AL-ḤAJAR AL-GHARBĪ
AL-JABAL AL-AKHḌAR
Gulf of Oman
Tropic of Cancer
Map continues pages 120-121
Copyright © by Rand McNally & Co.
Map prepared by George Philip & Son Ltd., London.

Kilometers 0 100 200 300 Km.
Statute Miles 0 100 200 300 Mi.

Scale 1:6,000,000
One centimeter represents 60 kilometers.
One inch represents approximately 95 miles.
Lambert-Conformal Conic Projection

Map continues pages 38-39

BLACK
MEDITERRANEAN SEA
İSTANBUL
ANKARA
İZMİR
Bursa
Eskişehir
Konya
Antalya
Adapazarı
İzmit
Kütahya
Afyon
Denizli
Isparta
Burdur
Muğla
Aydın
Manisa
Balıkesir
Çanakkale
Edirne
Tekirdağ
Zonguldak
Bolu
Nicosia
Lefkoşa
Lefkosia
Lárnax
Lemesós
Rhodes
Ródhos
Marmara Denizi
Sea of Marmara
Antalya Körfezi
Gulf of Antalya
Gökova Körfezi
TAURUS MOUNTAINS
NORTH CYPRUS
KUZEY KIBRIS
CYPRUS
KİPROS
The Turkish Republic of Northern Cyprus unilaterally declared its independence on November 15, 1983.
Copyright © by Rand McNally & Co.
Map prepared by George Philip & Son Ltd., London.

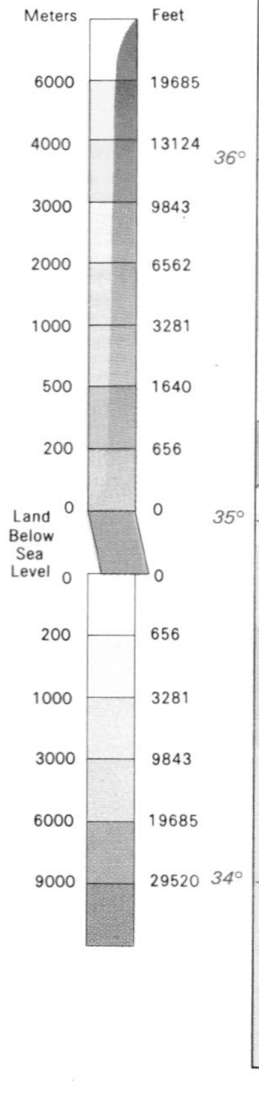
Meters
Feet
6000 19685
4000 13124
3000 9843
2000 6562
1000 3281
500 1640
200 656
0 0
Land Below Sea Level
0 0
200 656
1000 3281
3000 9843
6000 19685
9000 29520

MAP FORM	burnu	dağ, dagı	dağları	gölü	jabal	körfezi	sabkhat
ENGLISH	cape	mountain	mountains	lake	mountains	bay, gulf	salt marsh
DEUTSCH	Kap	Berg	Berge	See	Berge	Bucht, Golf	Salzmarsch
ESPAÑOL	cabo	montaña	montañas	lago	montañas	bahía, golfo	pantano salado
FRANÇAIS	cap	montagne	montagnes	lac	montagnes	baie, golfe	marais salé
PORTUGUÊS	cabo	montanha	montanhas	lago	montanhas	baia, golfo	pântano salgado

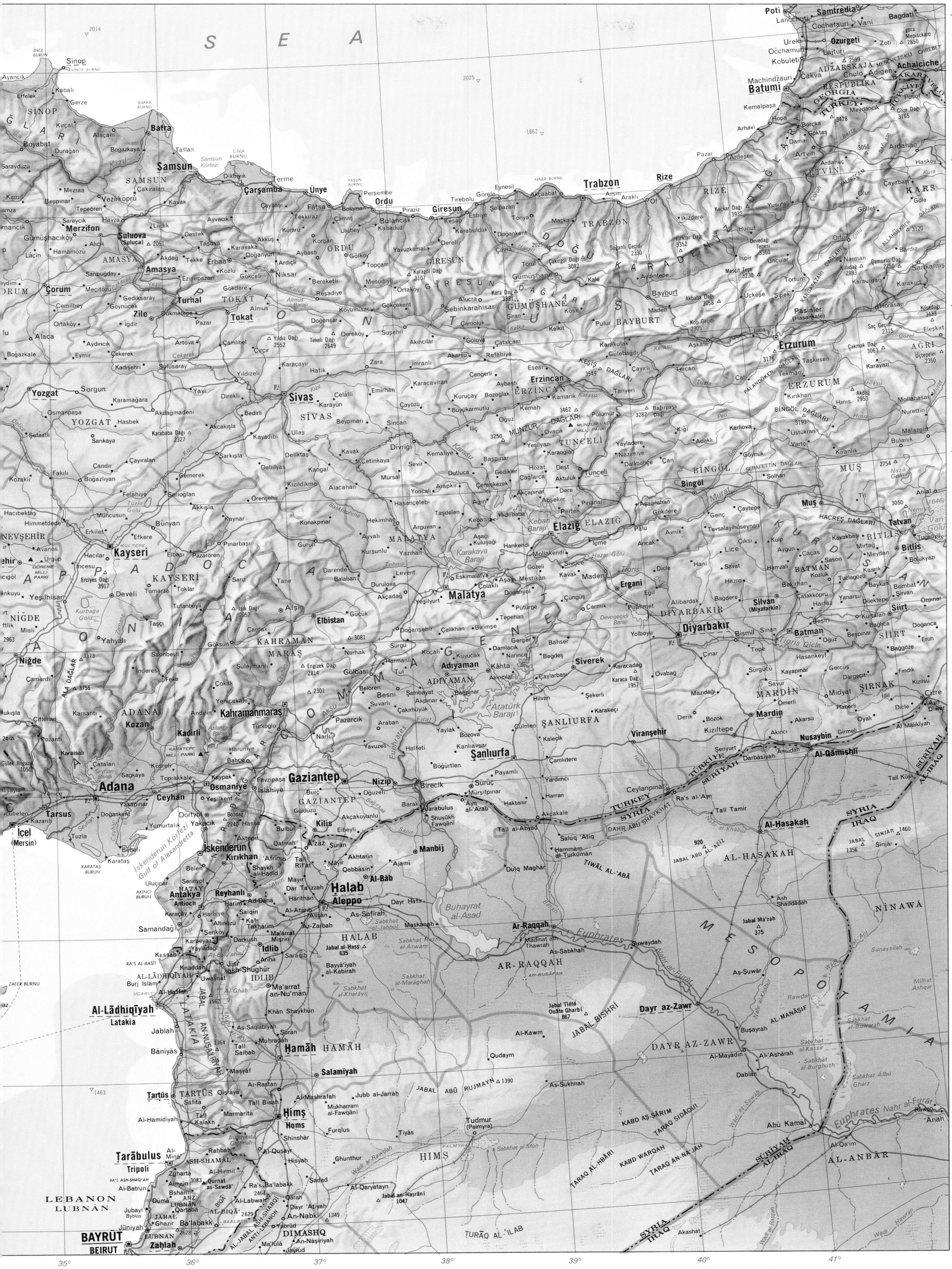
SEA
Sinop
Samsun
Bafra
Ordu
Giresun
Trabzon
Rize
Batumi
Poti
Artvin
Erzurum
Kars
Amasya
Tokat
Sivas
Yozgat
Kayseri
Erzincan
Malatya
Elazığ
Tunceli
Bingöl
Muş
Bitlis
Tatvan
Diyarbakır
Batman
Siirt
Mardin
Adıyaman
Kahramanmaraş
Gaziantep
Şanlıurfa
Adana
Tarsus
Ceyhan
İçel
(Mersin)
Niğde
Kozan
Osmaniye
Kilis
Halab
Aleppo
İskenderun
Antakya
Idlib
Al-Lādhiqīyah
Latakia
Ḩamāh
Ḩimş
Homs
Ţarābulus
Tripoli
BAYRŪT
BEIRUT
DIMASHQ
Tudmur
(Palmyra)
Ar-Raqqah
Dayr az-Zawr
Al-Ḩasakah
Al-Qāmishlī
Abū Kamāl
Euphrates
LEBANON
LUBNĀN
SYRIA
TURKEY
GEORGIA
IRAQ
MESOPOTAMIA
KAPPADOKIA
KOMMAGENE
PONTUS
KURDISTAN
DOĞU KARADENİZ DAĞLARI
Atatürk Barajı
Keban Barajı
Iskenderun Körfezi
Gulf of Alexandretta
Buhayrat al-Asad

Map continues page 84

Map continues pages 128-129

Kilometers 0 50 100 150 Km.

Statute Miles 0 50 100 150 Mi.

Scale 1:3,000,000

One centimeter represents 30 kilometers.
One inch represents approximately 47 miles.
Conic Projection, Two Standard Parallels

MEDITERRANEAN
SEA
DIMASHQ DAMASCUS
BAYRŪT BEIRUT
'AMMĀN
TEL AVIV-YAFO
Hefa Haifa
Netanya
Area occupied by Israel.
A Area occupied by United Nations Disengagement Observer Force since 1974.
B Golan Heights area. Occupied by Israel since 1967. Unilaterally annexed by Israel, 1981.
C West Bank area. Unilaterally annexed by Jordan, 1950. Occupied by Israel since 1967. Status to be determined.
D East Jerusalem portion of West Bank. Unilaterally annexed by Israel, 1980.
E Gaza Strip. Occupied by Israel since 1967. Status to be determined.

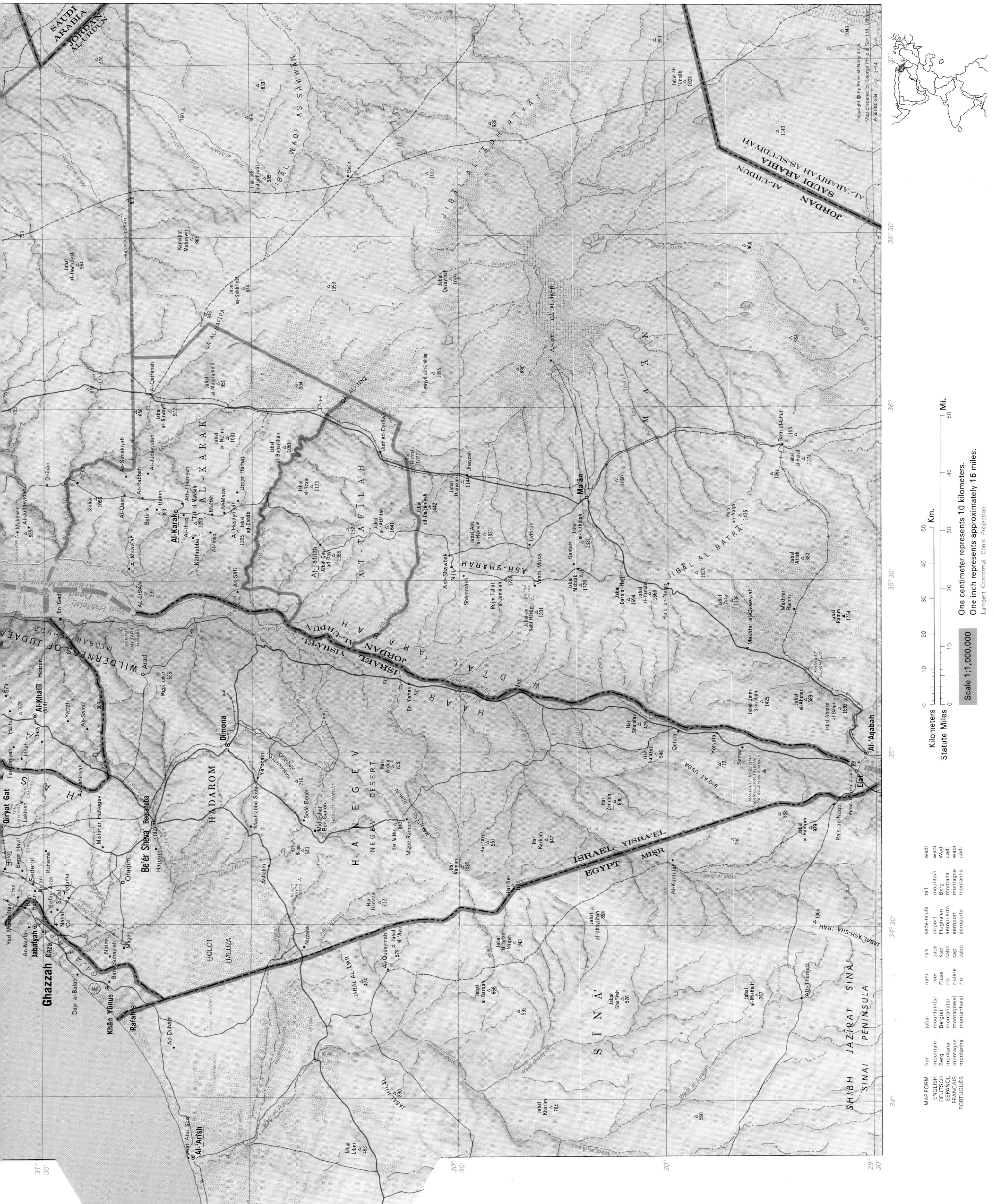
SAUDI ARABIA
JORDAN AL-URDUN
AL-'ARABIYAH AS-SU'ŪDIYAH
ISRAEL YISRA'EL
EGYPT MIṢR
JIBĀL WAQF AṢ-ṢAWWĀN
JIBĀL AL-'ĀDHIRIYĀT
QĀ' AL-JAFR
AL-KARAK
AṬ-ṬAFĪLAH
ASH-SHARAH
JIBĀL AL-BATRĀ'
WĀDĪ AL-'ARABAH
HA'ARAVA
HANEGEV
NEGEV DESERT
HADAROM
WILDERNESS OF JUDAEA
SĪNĀ'
SHIBH JAZĪRAT SĪNĀ'
SINAI PENINSULA
Ghazzah
Gaza
Khān Yūnus
Rafaḥ
Al-'Arīsh
Be'ér Sheva'
Beersheba
Dimona
Al-Khalīl
Hebron
Al-Karak
Aṭ-Ṭafīlah
Ma'ān
Al-'Aqabah
Elat
Yam HaMelah
Dead Sea
Al-Baḥr al-Mayyit
Scale 1:1,000,000
Kilometers
Statute Miles
Km.
Mi.
One centimeter represents 10 kilometers.
One inch represents approximately 16 miles.
Lambert Conformal Conic Projection
MAP FORM har jabal nahr ra's sede te'ufa tall wadi
ENGLISH mountain mountain(s) river cape airport mountain wadi
DEUTSCH Berg Berg(e) Fluss Kap Flughafen Berg Wadi
ESPAÑOL montaña montaña(s) río cabo aeropuerto montaña uadi
FRANÇAIS montagne montagne(s) rivière cap aéroport montagne wadi
PORTUGUÊS montanha montanha(s) rio cabo aeroporto montanha uádi
Copyright © by Rand McNally & Co.
Map prepared by George Philip & Son Ltd., London

Western North Africa / West Nordafrika / Región Occidental de Africa Septentrional
Afrique du Nord Occidentale / África do Norte Ocidental

ATLANTIC
OCEAN
ARQUIPÉLAGO DA MADEIRA
MADEIRA ISLANDS
(Portugal)
Funchal
ISLAS CANARIAS
CANARY ISLANDS
(Spain)
Santa Cruz de Tenerife
Las Palmas de Gran Canaria
Western Sahara has been occupied by Morocco
Tropic of Cancer
WESTERN SAHARA
El Aaiún
Dakhla
MOROCCO
RABAT
Casablanca
Marrakech
Fès
Meknès
Agadir
Tanger
Gibraltar (U.K.)
Ceuta (Sp.)
Tétouan
SPAIN
Málaga
ATLAS
MAURITANIA
Nouakchott
Nouâdhibou
SAHARA
MALI
Tombouctou
Bamako
CAPE VERDE
Praia
Mindelo
SENEGAL
DAKAR
Saint-Louis
Thiès
Kaolack
GAMBIA
Banjul
GUINEA-BISSAU
Bissau
ARQUIPÉLAGO DOS BIJAGÓS
GUINEA
Conakry
SIERRA LEONE
Freetown
LIBERIA
Monrovia
IVORY COAST
ABIDJAN
BURKINA FASO
Ouagadougou
Bobo Dioulasso
GHANA
Kumasi
ACCRA
Sekondi-Takoradi
Equator
Copyright © by Rand McNally & Co.
Map prepared by Esselte Map Service AB, Stockholm.
A-589491-264

MAP FORM	bahr, baḥr	chott	jabal	lake	mountains	oued	wahât
ENGLISH	river, sea	salt marsh	mountain(s)	lake	mountains	wadi	oasis
DEUTSCH	Fluss, Meer	Salzmarsch	Berg(e)	See	Berge	Wadi	Oase
ESPAÑOL	río, mar	pantano salado	montaña(s)	lago	montañas	uadi	oasis
FRANÇAIS	rivière, mer	marais salé	montagne(s)	lac	montagnes	wadi	oasis
PORTUGUÊS	rio, mar	pântano salgado	montanha(s)	lago	montanhas	uádi	oásis

Map continues
pages 22-23

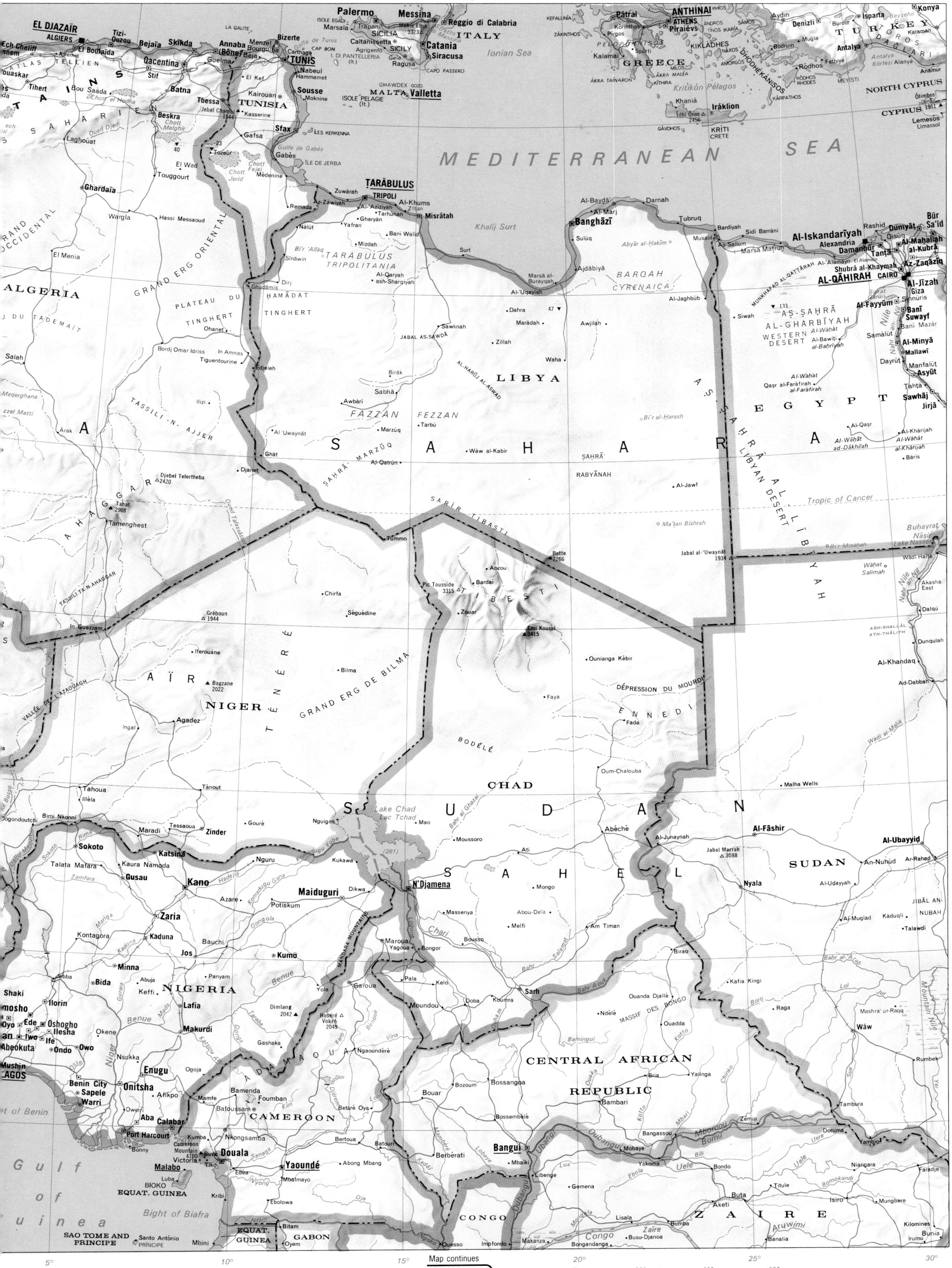
MEDITERRANEAN SEA
Ionian Sea
ITALY
SICILIA
SICILY
Palermo
Messina
Reggio di Calabria
Catania
Siracusa
MALTA
Valletta
GREECE
ATHENS
Piraiévs
KRITI
CRETE
Iráklion
TURKEY
Konya
Antalya
NORTH CYPRUS
CYPRUS
Lemesós
Kritikón Pélagos
Rhódos
TUNISIA
TUNIS
Sfax
Sousse
Gabès
Kairouan
Bizerte
Golfe de Gabès
EL DJAZAÏR
ALGIERS
Annaba
Skikda
Qacentina
Batna
Biskra
Touggourt
Ghardaïa
ALGERIA
GRAND ERG ORIENTAL
PLATEAU DU TINGHERT
TASSILI-N-AJJER
AHAGGAR
Tamenghest
TARĀBULUS
TRIPOLI
Misrātah
Banghāzī
Khalīj Surt
LIBYA
FEZZAN
Sabhā
Marzūq
BARQAH
CYRENAICA
EGYPT
AL-QĀHIRAH
CAIRO
Al-Iskandarīyah
Alexandria
Asyūt
Nile
WESTERN DESERT
LIBYAN DESERT
AṢ-ṢAḤRĀ AL-LĪBĪYAH
Lake Nasser
Tropic of Cancer
SAHARA
TIBESTI
Emi Koussi 3415
TÉNÉRÉ
GRAND ERG DE BILMA
AÏR
NIGER
Agadez
Zinder
Tahoua
CHAD
BODÉLÉ
ENNEDI
Lake Chad
Lac Tchad
N'Djamena
Abéché
Faya
SUDAN
SAHEL
Al-Fāshir
Nyala
Al-Ubayyiḍ
NIGERIA
Kano
Kaduna
Zaria
Maiduguri
Sokoto
Jos
Ilorin
Oshogho
Ibadan
LAGOS
Benin City
Onitsha
Enugu
Port Harcourt
Calabar
Makurdi
Minna
CAMEROON
Yaoundé
Douala
Garoua
Ngaoundéré
ADAMAOUA
CENTRAL AFRICAN REPUBLIC
Bangui
Berbérati
Bambari
Sarh
Moundou
EQUAT. GUINEA
Malabo
BIOKO
GABON
CONGO
ZAIRE
SAO TOME AND PRINCIPE
Gulf of Guinea
Bight of Biafra
Benue
Niger
Ubangi
Uele

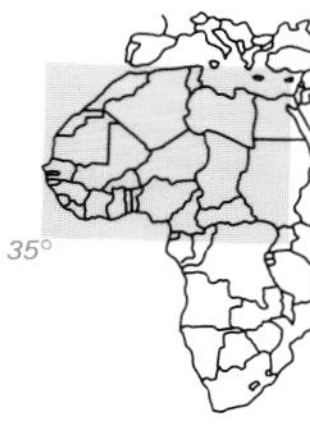

Map continues
pages 136-137

Map continues
pages 138-139

Kilometers 0 200 400 600 Km.
Statute Miles 0 200 400 600 Mi.

Scale 1:12,000,000
One centimeter represents 120 kilometers.
One inch represents approximately 190 miles.
Miller Oblated Stereographic Projection

Map continues pages 22-23

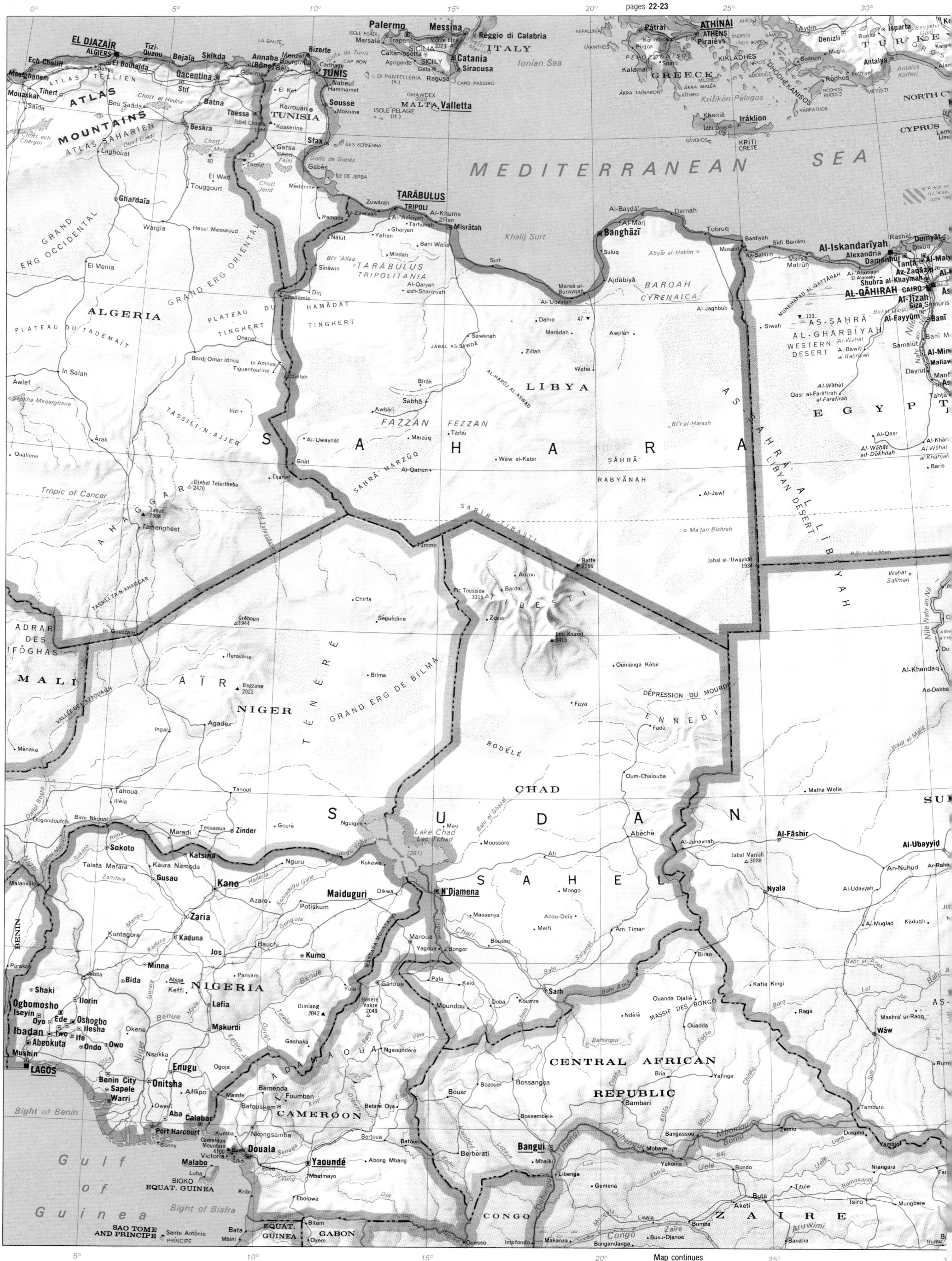
MEDITERRANEAN SEA
ALGERIA
LIBYA
EGYPT
NIGER
CHAD
NIGERIA
CAMEROON
CENTRAL AFRICAN REPUBLIC
TUNISIA
ITALY
GREECE
MALI
BENIN
CONGO
GABON
ZAIRE
EQUAT. GUINEA
SAO TOME AND PRINCIPE
S A H A R A
S U D A N
S A H E L
ATLAS MOUNTAINS
GRAND ERG OCCIDENTAL
GRAND ERG ORIENTAL
GRAND ERG DE BILMA
TÉNÉRÉ
AÏR
AHAGGAR
TIBESTI
ENNEDI
BODÉLÉ
FAZZĀN FEZZAN
LIBYAN DESERT
WESTERN DESERT
Gulf of Guinea
Bight of Benin
Bight of Biafra
Tropic of Cancer
Lake Chad
EL DJAZAÏR ALGIERS
TUNIS
TARĀBULUS TRIPOLI
AL-QĀHIRAH CAIRO
N'Djamena
Lagos
Yaoundé
Bangui
Valletta
Palermo
Messina
Catania
Banghāzī
Misrātah
Al-Iskandarīyah Alexandria
Kano
Zaria
Kaduna
Ibadan
Douala
Maiduguri
Zinder
Agadez
Sabhā
Ghardaïa
Tamenghest
Abéché
Sarh
Al-Fāshir
Nyala
Map continues pages 134-135

Map continues pages 138-139

MAP FORM	bahr, baḥr	chott	jabal	lake	mountains	oued	ra's; ras	wāhāt
ENGLISH	river, sea	salt marsh	mountain(s)	lake	mountains	wadi	cape	oasis
DEUTSCH	Fluss, Meer	Salzmarsch	Berg(e)	See	Berge	Wadi	Kap	Oase
ESPAÑOL	río, mar	pantano salado	montaña(s)	lago	montañas	uadi	cabo	oasis
FRANÇAIS	rivière, mer	marais salé	montagne(s)	lac	montagnes	wadi	cap	oasis
PORTUGUÊS	rio, mar	pântano salgado	montanha(s)	lago	montanhas	uádi	cabo	oásis

IRAN
IRAQ
SYRIA
JORDAN
KUWAIT
SAUDI ARABIA
QATAR
BAHRAIN
UNITED ARAB EMIRATES
OMAN
YEMEN
ERITREA
ETHIOPIA
DJIBOUTI
SOMALIA
KENYA
UGANDA
AFGHANISTAN
PAKISTAN
BALUCHISTAN
BAGHDĀD
AR-RIYĀD
RIYADH
AL-KUWAYT
DIMASHQ
DAMASCUS
AMMAN
Yerushalayim Jerusalem
Makkah Mecca
Al-Madīnah Medina
Jiddah Jeddah
Ṣan'ā'
Adan Aden
Asmera
ADIS ABEBA
ADDIS ABABA
Muqdisho Mogadishu
Djibouti
AL-KHARṬŪM
KHARTOUM
Bur Sūdān Port Sudan
Ad-Dawḥah Doha
Al-Manāmah
Abū Ẓaby Abu Dhabi
Dubayy Dubai
Masqaṭ Muscat
Eṣfahān
Shīrāz
Kermān
Yazd
Ahvāz
Abādān
Al-Baṣrah Basra
Al-Mawṣil Mosul
Ḥalab Aleppo
Ḥimṣ
AN-NAFŪD
AD-DAHNĀ'
AR-RUB' AL-KHĀLĪ
ḤAḌRAMAWT
OGADEN
Persian Gulf
Gulf of Oman
Gulf of Aden
RED SEA
ARABIAN SEA
INDIAN OCEAN
SUQUṬRĀ SOCOTRA (Yemen)
Tropic of Cancer
Equator
Copyright © by Rand McNally & Co.
Map prepared by Esselte Map Service AB, Stockholm.

Map continues pages 118-119

Kilometers 0 200 400 600 Km.
Statute Miles 0 200 400 600 Mi.

Scale 1:12,000,000
One centimeter represents 120 kilometers.
One inch represents approximately 190 miles.
Miller Oblated Stereographic Projection

Map continues pages 136-137

5° 10° 15° 20° 25° 30°
0° 5° 10° 15° 20° 25° 30°
SAO TOME AND PRINCIPE
PRINCIPE
Santo António
SÃO TOMÉ
São Tomé
ANNOBÓN (Equat. Gui.)
EQUATORIAL GUINEA
CAMEROON
Bata
Mbini
Bitam
Oyem
Libreville
GABON
CAP LOPEZ
Port Gentil
Lambaréné
Ogooué
Omboué
Fougamou
Iguéla
Setté Cama
Mayumba
Lastoursville
Koulamoutou
Franceville
Moanda
Mouila
Ndendé
Tchibanga
Makokou
Mékambo
CONGO
Ouesso
Impfondo
Owando
Makoua
Mossaka
Gamboma
Djambala
Zanaga
Mossendjo
Sibiti
Dolisie
Madingou
Brazzaville
Kayes
Pointe-Noire
CABINDA (Angola)
Cabinda
KINSHASA (LÉOPOLDVILLE)
Madimba
Kenge
Mbanza Ngungu
Boma
Matadi
Muanda
Banana
Soyo
Zaire
Congo
Ubangi
Mbandaka (Coquilhatville)
Ingende
Bikoro
Lac Tumba
Lukolela
Bolobo
Lac Mai-Ndombe
Inongo
Kiri
Mushie
Bandundu
Nioki
Kutu
Oshwe
Lokolama
ZAIRE
Basankusu
Bolomba
Befale
Bongandanga
Lisala
Bumba
Busu-Djanoa
Basoko
Banalia
Aruwimi
Bafwasende
Kisangani (Stanleyville)
STANLEY FALLS
Ubundu
Opala
Lomami
Lualaba
Lubutu
Punia
Kasese
Kindu
Kalima
Pangi
Kibombo
Kasongo
Lomela
Ikela
Bokungu
Boende
Tshuapa
Dekese
Kole
Lodja
Bena-Dibele
Sankuru
Kasai
Kwango
Kwilu
Masi Manimba
Lusanga
Idiofa
Ilebo
Mweka
Lusambo
Lubefu
Tshofa
Kikwit
Gungu
Luebo
Djokupunda
Demba
Kananga (Luluabourg)
Kabinda
Mbuji-Mayi (Bakwanga)
Dibaya
Tshikapa
Makumbi
Popokabaka
Feshi
Kasongo-Lunda
Kahemba
Luiza
Kaniama
Kabalo
Kongolo
Kalemie (Albertville)
Lake Tanganyika
Manono
Kabongo
Kamina
Bukama
Luena
Lubudi
Kapanga
Sandoa
Dilolo
Kasaji
Kolwezi
Likasi (Jadotville)
Lubumbashi (Elisabethville)
KATANGA
Mitwaba
Pweto
Lake Mweru
Kasenga
Kipushi
Mwinilunga
Solwezi
Chililabombwe
Chingola
Mufulira
Kitwe
Luanshya
Ndola
ZAMBIA
Kabwe (Broken Hill)
Lusaka
Mumbwa
Kaoma
Mongu
Kalabo
Senanga
Livingstone
Kazungula
Sesheke
Choma
Kalomo
Mazabuka
Kariba
Lake Kariba
Zambezi
Bukavu
Kigali
RWANDA
BURUNDI
Bujumbura
Uvira
Kigoma
Ujiji
Kisenyi
Goma
Rutshuru
Lake Kivu
Lake Edward
Lake George
Kasese
Fort Portal
Beni
Butembo
Kilomines
Bunia
Irumu
Masaka
Mbarara
Kabale
Gitega
Mpanda
Sumbawanga
Kipili
Kawambwa
Mansa
Lake Bangweulu
Serenje
Mbala
MONTS MITUMBA
N'zeto
Nova Caipemba
Ambriz
Uíge
Negage
Sanza Pombo
Damba
Maquela do Zombo
Nóqui
M'banza Congo
Cuango
Camabatela
Marimba
LUANDA
PONTA DAS PALMEIRINHAS
Barra do Cuanza
Caxito
Catete
N'dalatando
Dondo
Muxima
Malanje
Cuanza
Cacolo
Cambundi-Catembo
Saurimo
Chitato
Camissombo
Chiluage
Muconda
Luau
ANGOLA
Porto Amboim
Gabela
Sumbe
Waku Kundo
Lobito
Benguela
Serra Môco 2620
Bailundo
Huambo (Nova Lisboa)
Kuito
Camacupa
Munhango
Luena
Caála
Ganda
Caconda
Chitembo
CABO DE SANTA MARIA
Lucira
Kuvango
Menongue
Cangombe
Lumbala N'guimbo
Mussuma
Lukulu
Bibala
Lubango
Capelongo
Cassinga
Cuito-Cuanavale
Cuando
Cubango
Namibe
Tombua
PONTA DA MARCA
Humbe
Xangongo
Ondjiva
Foz do Cunene
Cunene
Chitado
Mavinga
Neriquinha
Calundo
Cazombo
Calunda
Balovale
ATLANTIC OCEAN
KAOKO VELD
NAMIB DESERT
Rehoboth
Ondangwa
OVAMBOLAND
Etosha Pan
Namutoni
CAPE FRIA
Sesfontein
Okaukuejo
Tsumeb
Grootfontein
Otavi
Outjo
Otjiwarongo
Brandberg 2574
NAMIBIA
Omaruru
Karibib
Usakos
Okahandja
DAMARALAND
Swakopmund
Walvisbaai
Walvis Bay (S. Afr.)
Windhoek
Gobabis
Epukiro
Tropic of Capricorn
Rehoboth
Tsumis Park
HOLLANDSBIRD ISLAND
Mariental
Maltahöhe
Gibeon
GREAT NAMAQUALAND
Koes
Bethanien
Keetmanshoop
Lüderitz
Aus
Guibes
Seeheim
Aroab
HUNSBERGE
Karasburg
Warmbad
Oranjemund
Alexander Bay
Orange
Port Nolloth
Cuangar
Dirico
CAPRIVI ZIPFEL
Shakawe
KAUKAU VELD
OKAVANGO DELTA
MABABE DEPRESSION
Maun
Tsau
Toteng
Lake Ngami
Makgadikgadi
Lake Xau
Ghanzi
BOTSWANA
Tshwaane
KALAHARI DESERT
Lehututu
Tshane
Khakhea
Molepolole
Mochudi
Gaborone
Kanye
Lobatse
Mmabatho
Mafikeng
Tshabong
Serowe
Palapye
Mahalatswe
Shoshong
Francistown
Plumtree
Bulawayo
Gwanda
West Nicholson
Mwenezi
Beitbridge
Messina
Tuli
Shashe
Old Tate
ZIMBABWE
Hwange
Gwai
Gweru
Kwekwe
Mvuma
Shurugwi
Zvishavane
Masvingo
Chinhoyi
Chegutu
Bindura
VENDA
Thohoyandou
Louis Trichardt
Pietersburg
Potgietersrus
Thabazimbi
Nylstroom
Warmbad
BOPHUTHATSWANA
PRETORIA
Rustenburg
Zeerust
Krugersdorp
JOHANNESBURG
Germiston
Benoni
Springs
Potchefstroom
Klerksdorp
Vereeniging
Vanderbijlpark
Witbank
Belfast
Nelspruit
Marble Hall
Lydenburg
Ermelo
Standerton
Piet Retief
SWAZILAND
Mbabane
Vryburg
Hotazel
Kuruman
Sishen
Bloemhof
Odendaalsrus
Welkom
Kroonstad
Heilbron
Vrede
Volksrust
Newcastle
Utrecht
Vryheid
Bethlehem
Harrismith
Ladysmith
Estcourt
Greytown
Virginia
Kimberley
Bloemfontein
Warrenton
Ficksburg
Maseru
LESOTHO
Thabana-Ntlenyana 3482
Pietermaritzburg
Durban
Upington
Kakamas
Pofadder
BUSHMAN LAND
Kenhardt
Okiep
Springbok
Grootvloer
Prieska
Hopetown
Jagersfontein
Verneukpan
Brandvlei
SOUTH AFRICA
De Aar
Britstown
Carnarvon
Victoria West
Colesberg
Burgersdorp
Barkly East
Aliwal North
Garies
Bitterfontein
Calvinia
Vanrhynsdorp
Klawer
Clanwilliam
Lambert's Bay
Sutherland
NUWEVELDBERGE
Beaufort West
Graaff-Reinet
Kompasberg 2504
Murraysburg
Middelburg
Noupoort
Steynsburg
Sterkstroom
Tarkastad
Cradock
Queenstown
TRANSKEI
Umtata
Idutywa
Port Shepstone
Port Edward
Port Saint Johns
Kokstad
Harding
Matatiele
Umzinto
Qacha's Nek
Saldanha
Piketberg
Malmesbury
Tulbagh
Worcester
Paarl
CAPE TOWN KAAPSTAD
Stellenbosch
Simon's Town
CAPE OF GOOD HOPE
Hermanus
Bredasdorp
CAPE AGULHAS
Laingsburg
GREAT KAROO
GROOT-SWARTBERGE
LITTLE KAROO
Montagu
Swellendam
Mosselbaai
George
Knysna
Oudtshoorn
Willowmore
Somerset East
Kirkwood
Klipplaat
Uitenhage
Port Elizabeth
Humansdorp
CAPE SAINT FRANCIS
Grahamstown
Alicedale
Port Alfred
East London Oos-Londen
King William's Town
CISKEI
Bisho
Fort Beaufort
Cathcart
Drakensberg

MAP FORM	cape	île	island	lake	mountains	plateau
ENGLISH	cape	island	island	lake	mountains	plateau
DEUTSCH	Kap	Insel	Insel	See	Berge	Hochebene
ESPAÑOL	cabo	isla	isla	lago	montañas	meseta
FRANÇAIS	cap	île	île	lac	montagnes	plateau
PORTUGUÊS	cabo	ilha	ilha	lago	montanhas	planalto

INDIAN OCEAN
Equator
Tropic of Capricorn
SOMALIA
KENYA
NAIROBI
Mombasa
Tanga
Zanzibar
DAR ES SALAAM
SERENGETI PLAIN
MASAI STEPPE
YATTA PLATEAU
Arusha
Moshi
Kilimanjaro 5895
Lake Nyasa
Lake Malawi
Lilongwe
Blantyre
Zomba
MOZAMBIQUE
Nampula
Nacala
Moçambique
Quelimane
Beira
Inhambane
Mocímboa da Praia
Pemba
CABO DELGADO
COMOROS
Moroni
ARCHIPEL DES COMORES
MAYOTTE (Fr.)
Dzaoudzi
Mozambique Channel
MADAGASCAR
ANTANANARIVO
Antsiranana
CAP D'AMBRE
MASSIF DU TSARATANANA
Maromokotro 2876
Mahajanga
Toamasina
Antsirabe
Fianarantsoa
Toliara
Morondava
Manakara
Farafangana
Taolanaro
CAP SAINTE-MARIE
SEYCHELLES
Victoria
MAHÉ ISLAND
AMIRANTE ISLANDS (Sey.)
ALDABRA ISLAND (Sey.)
ÎLE EUROPA (Reunion)
BASSAS DA INDIA (Reunion)
ÎLE TROMELIN (Reunion)
AGALEGA ISLANDS (Mauritius)
Port Louis
Curepipe
MAURITIUS
Saint-Denis
REUNION (Fr.)
MASCARENE ISLANDS
Copyright © by Rand McNally & Co.
Map prepared by Esselte Map Service AB, Stockholm.

Kilometers 0 200 400 600 Km.
Statute Miles 0 200 400 600 Mi.

Scale 1:12,000,000
One centimeter represents 120 kilometers.
One inch represents approximately 190 miles.
Miller Oblated Stereographic Projection

Map continues pages 128-129

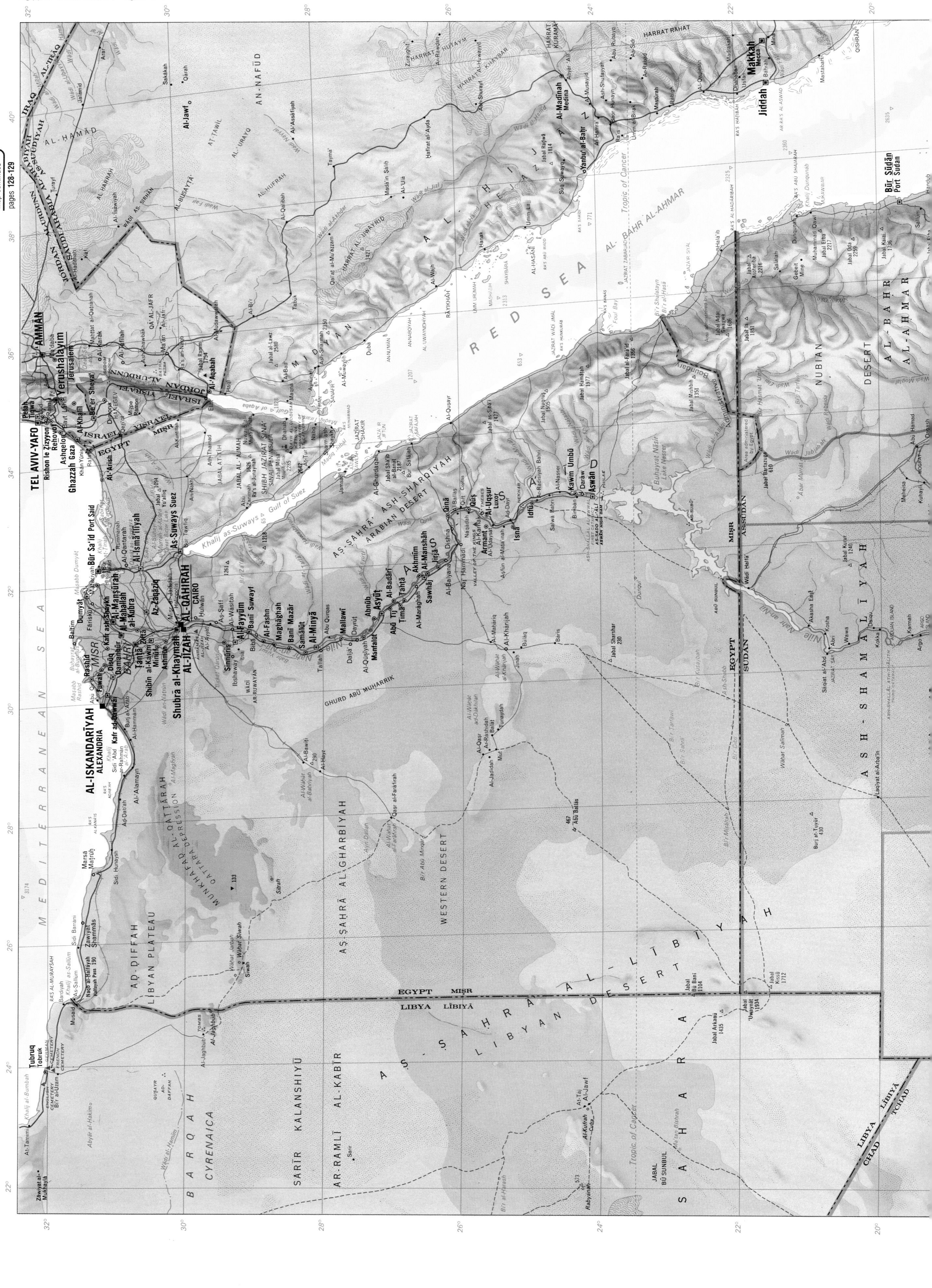
MEDITERRANEAN SEA
RED SEA
AL-BAHR AL-AHMAR
AL-QAHIRAH
CAIRO
AL-ISKANDARIYAH
ALEXANDRIA
AL-JIZAH
Shubra al-Khaymah
Bur Sa'id Port Said
As-Suways Suez
Al-Isma'iliyah
Dumyat
Tanta
Al-Mahallah al-Kubra
Al-Mansurah
Az-Zaqaziq
Al-Fayyum
Bani Suwayf
Al-Minya
Asyut
Sawhaj
Qina
Al-Uqsur Luxor
Aswan
Marsa Matruh
Tubruq Tobruk
TEL AVIV-YAFO
Yerushalayim Jerusalem
'AMMAN
Al-'Aqabah
Makkah Mecca
Jiddah
Al-Madinah Medina
Yanbu' al-Bahr
Bur Sudan Port Sudan
EGYPT MISR
LIBYA LIBIYA
ISRAEL
JORDAN
SAUDI ARABIA
WESTERN DESERT
ARABIAN DESERT
LIBYAN DESERT
LIBYAN PLATEAU
QATTARA DEPRESSION
NUBIAN DESERT
SINAI PENINSULA
Gulf of Suez
Tropic of Cancer
Buhayrat Nasir Lake Nasser
CYRENAICA
BARQAH
AL-KUFRAH
AL-HIJAZ

Map continues pages 144-145

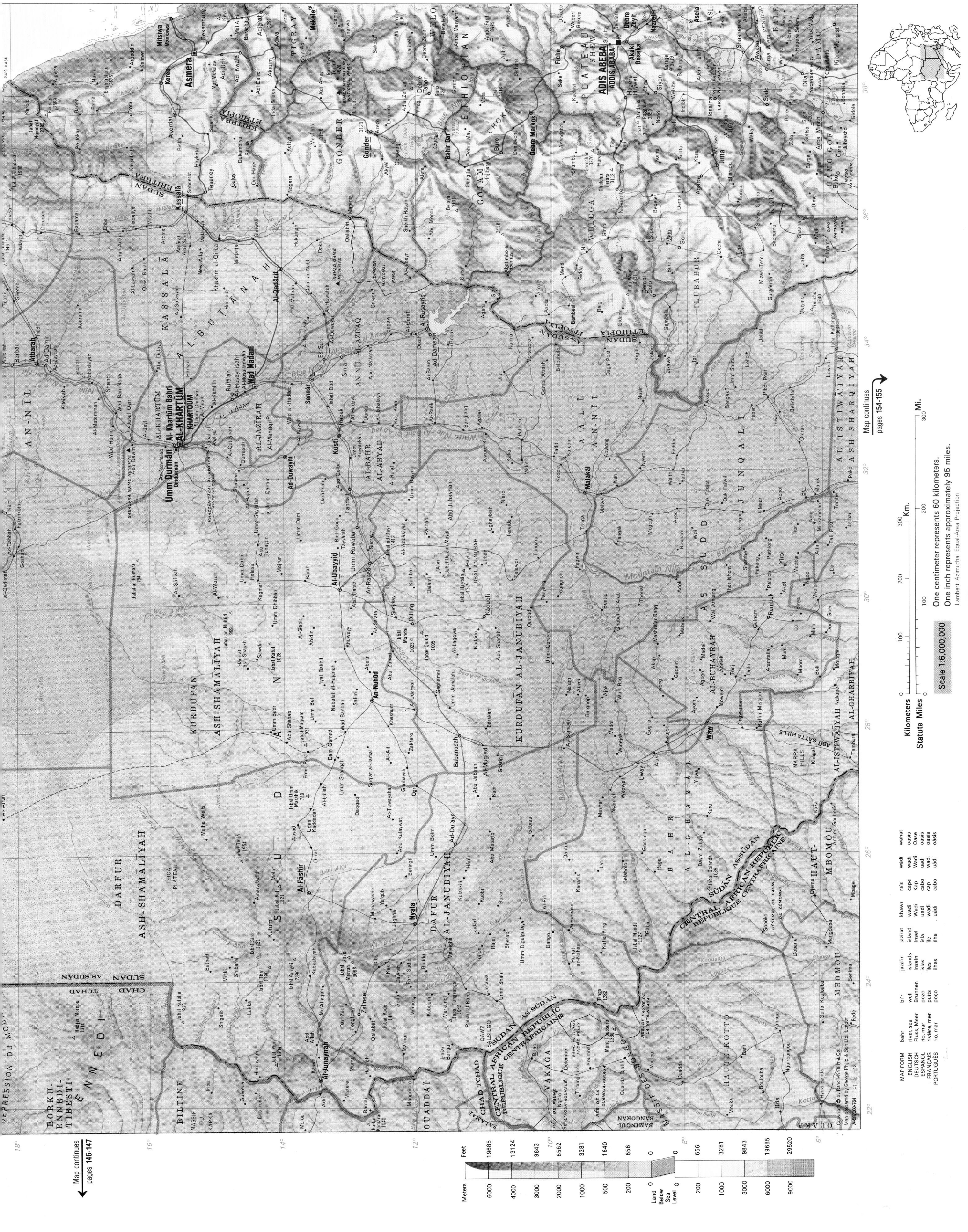
Scale 1:6,000,000
One centimeter represents 60 kilometers.
One inch represents approximately 95 miles.
Lambert Azimuthal Equal-Area Projection
Kilometers
Statute Miles
Km.
Mi.
MAP FORM / ENGLISH / DEUTSCH / ESPAÑOL / FRANÇAIS / PORTUGUÊS
bahr: river, sea / Fluss, Meer / río, mar / rivière, mer / rio, mar
bi'r: well / Brunnen / pozo / puits / poço
jazā'ir: islands / Inseln / islas / îles / ilhas
jazīrat: island / Insel / isla / île / ilha
khawr: wadi / Wadi / uadi / wadi / uadi
ra's: cape / Kap / cabo / cap / cabo
wadi: wadi / Wadi / uadi / wadi / uadi
wāhāt: oasis / Oase / oasis / oasis / oasis
Feet
Meters
Land Below Sea Level
AL-KHARTŪM
Umm Durmān
Al-Khartūm Bahrī
Asmera
ADIS ABEBA
Kassalā
Wad Madanī
Al-Ubayyid
Malakāl
Waw
Nyala
Al-Fāshir
Al-Junaynah
Kūstī
Sannār
KURDUFĀN
DĀRFŪR
AS-SUDD
BAHR AL-GHAZĀL
ETHIOPIAN PLATEAU
CENTRAL AFRICAN REPUBLIC
RÉPUBLIQUE CENTRAFRICAINE
CHAD
TCHAD
ERITREA
ETHIOPIA
White Nile
Blue Nile
Mountain Nile

Map continues pages 154-155

Map continues pages 146-147

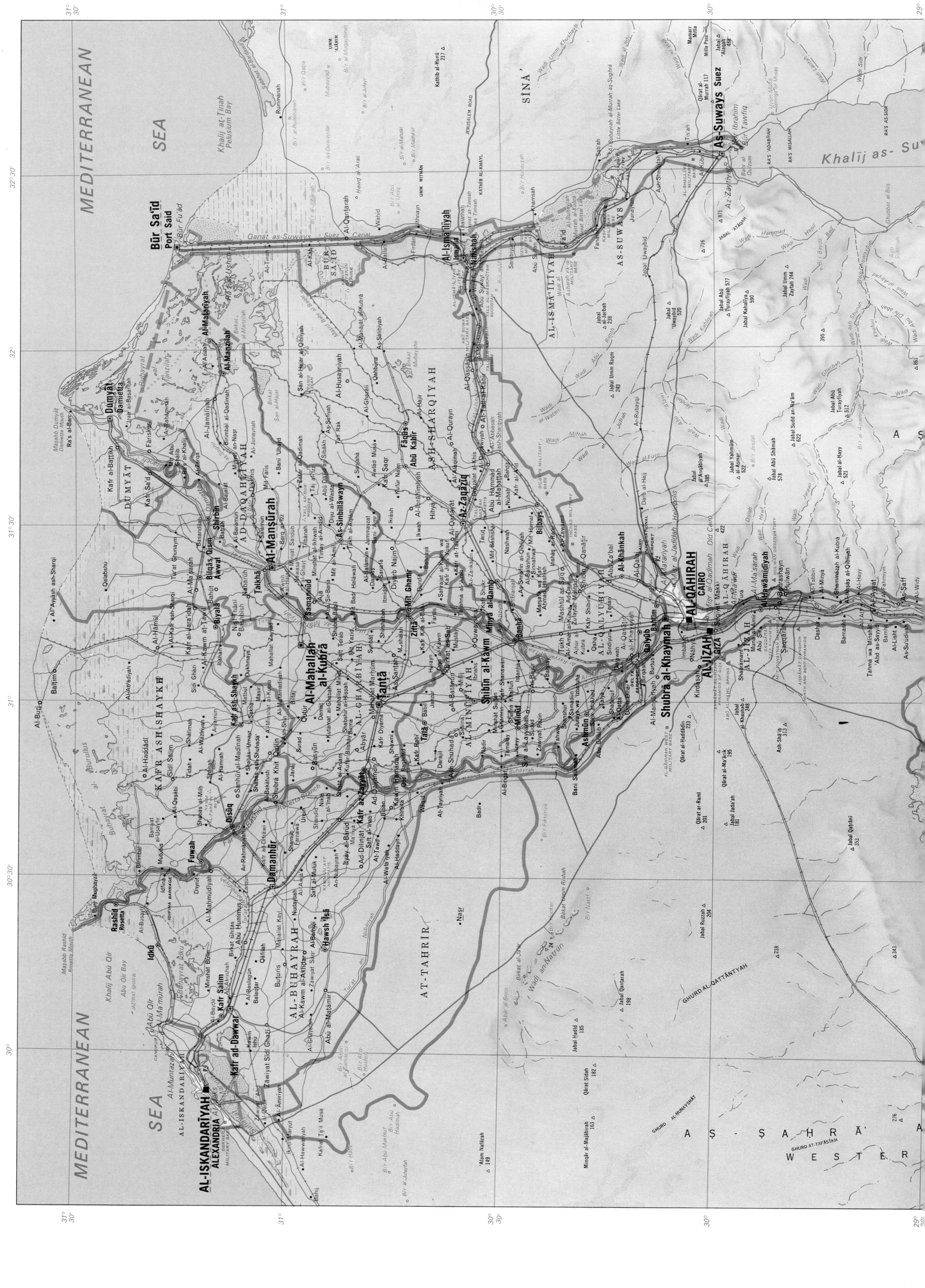
MEDITERRANEAN SEA
MEDITERRANEAN SEA
Būr Sa'īd
Port Said
Al-Iskandarīyah
Alexandria
Dumyāṭ
Damietta
Rashīd
Rosetta
Al-Qāhirah
Cairo
Al-Jīzah
Gīza
As-Suways
Suez
Al-Ismā'īlīyah
Ismailia
Al-Manṣūrah
Ṭanṭā
Az-Zaqāzīq
Damanhūr
Al-Maḥallah al-Kubrā
Shubrā al-Khaymah
Kafr ad-Dawwār
Kafr ash-Shaykh
Sīnā'
Khalīj as-Suways
Qanāt as-Suways
Suez Canal
Aṣ-Ṣaḥrā' al-Gharbīyah
At-Taḥrīr
Wādī an-Naṭrūn
Khalīj at-Tīnah
Pelusium Bay
Khalīj Abū Qīr
Abu Qir Bay
Buḥayrat Maryūṭ
Buḥayrat al-Burullus
Buḥayrat al-Manzilah

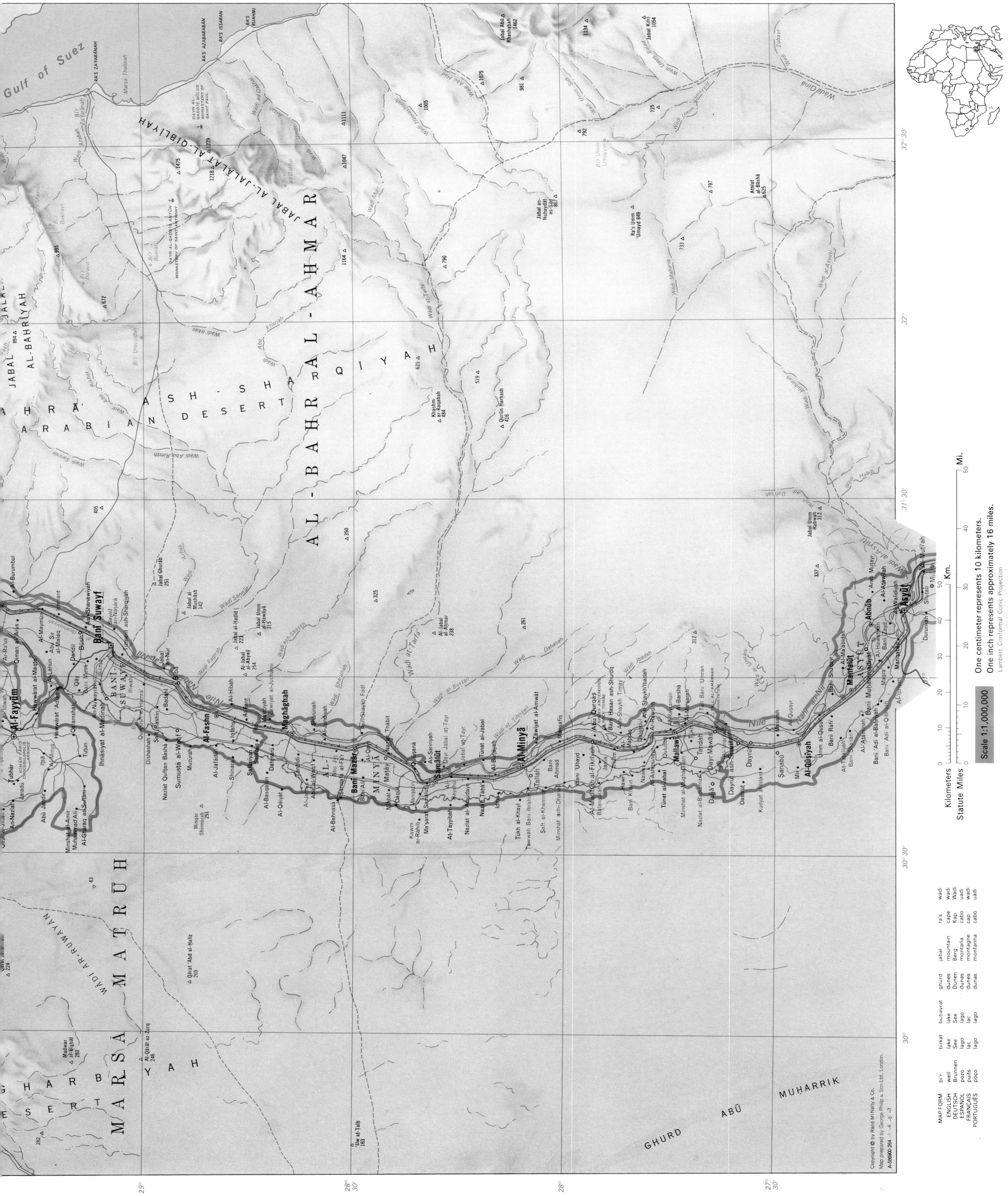
Gulf of Suez
JABAL AL-JALĀLAT AL-QIBLIYAH
AL-BAHR AL-AHMAR
ARABIAN DESERT
ASH-SHARQIYAH
MARSĀ MATRŪH
WADI AR-RUWAYAN
GHURD ABŪ MUHARRIK
Al-Fayyūm
Banī Suwayf
Al-Fashn
Maghāghah
Banī Mazār
Samālūt
Al-Minyā
Abū Qurqās
Mallawī
Manfalūt
Al-Qūsīyah
Asyūt
Nile
Kilometers
Statute Miles
Km.
Mi.
Scale 1:1,000,000
One centimeter represents 10 kilometers.
One inch represents approximately 16 miles.
Lambert Conformal Conic Projection
MAP FORM: bi'r, birkat, buhayrat, ghurd, jabal, ra's, wadi
ENGLISH: well, lake, lake, dunes, mountain, cape, wadi
DEUTSCH: Brunnen, See, See, Dunen, Berg, Kap, Wadi
ESPAÑOL: pozo, lago, lago, dunas, montaña, cabo, uadi
FRANÇAIS: puits, lac, lac, dunes, montagne, cap, wadi
PORTUGUÊS: poço, lago, lago, dunas, montanha, cabo, uadi
Copyright © by Rand McNally & Co.
Map prepared by George Philip & Son Ltd., London.

RED SEA
AL-BAHR AL-AHMAR
Gulf of Aden
AR-RUB' AL-KHALI
SAUDI ARABIA
YEMEN
ERITREA
ETHIOPIA
DJIBOUTI
SUDAN
EGYPT
Makkah
Jiddah
Şan'ā'
'Adan
Al-Mukallā
Al-Hudaydah
Asmera
Djibouti
Bür Südān
Port Sudan
Berbera
Bahir Dar
Gonder
Mekele
Dese
Kassalā
Wad Madanī
Atbarah
Al-Qadārif

Map continues pages 128-129

Map continues pages 140-141

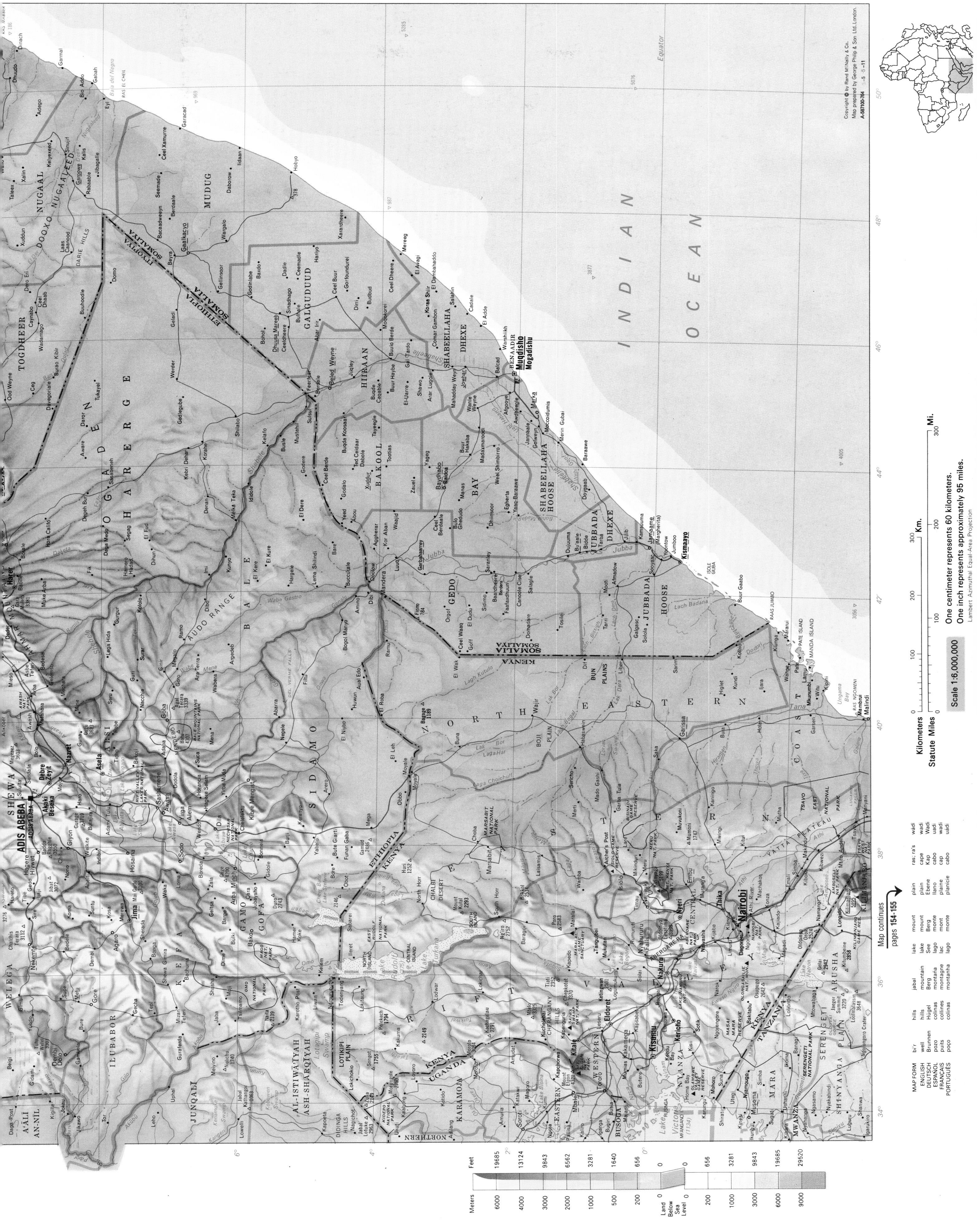
INDIAN OCEAN
ETHIOPIA
SOMALIA
KENYA
TANZANIA
UGANDA
ADIS ABEBA
Mugdisho
Mogadishu
Nairobi
Kismaayo
Marka
Hobyo
Gaalkacyo
Equator
MUDUG
GALGUDUUD
HIIRAAN
BAKOOL
BAY
GEDO
SHABEELLAHA DHEXE
SHABEELLAHA HOOSE
JUBBADA DHEXE
JUBBADA HOOSE
OGADEN
HARERGE
BALE
SIDAMO
GAMO GOFA
KEFA
ILUBABOR
WELEGA
SHEWA
NORTH EASTERN
COAST
RIFT VALLEY
Lake Turkana
Lake Victoria
Scale 1:6,000,000
Kilometers
Statute Miles
One centimeter represents 60 kilometers.
One inch represents approximately 95 miles.
Lambert Azimuthal Equal-Area Projection
Map continues pages 154-155
Copyright © by Rand McNally & Co.
Map prepared by George Philip & Son, Ltd. London.
A-587100-764
Feet
Meters
Land Below Sea Level

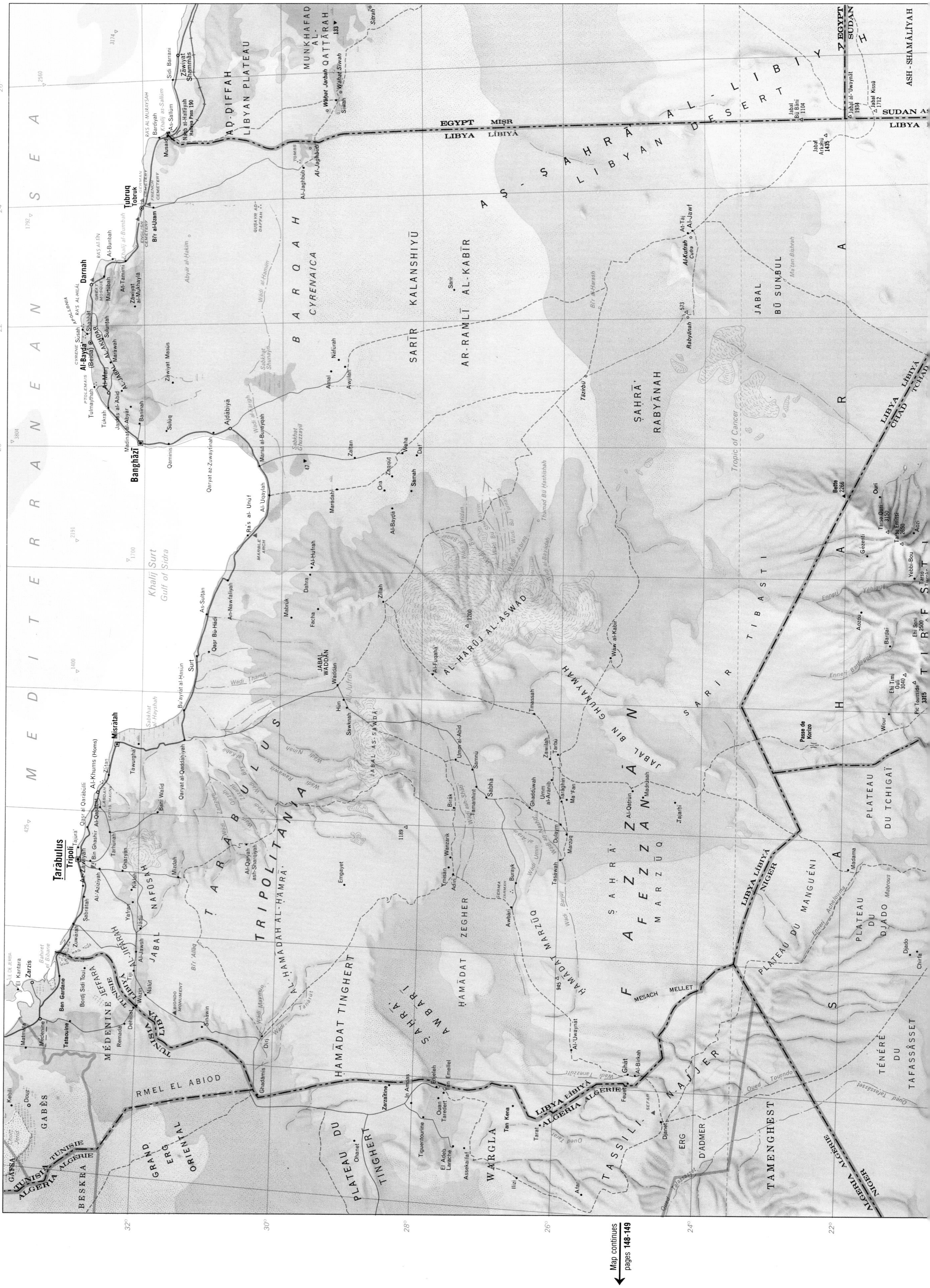
MEDITERRANEAN SEA
Ṭarābulus
Tripoli
Misrātah
Banghāzī
Darnah
Ṭubruq
Tobruk
Al-Bayḍā'
Surt
Ajdābiyā
Khalīj Surt
Gulf of Sidra
TARĀBULUS
TRIPOLITANIA
BARQAH
CYRENAICA
FEZZĀN
AL-HARŪJ AL-ASWAD
AS-SAHRĀ' AL-LĪBIYAH
LIBYAN DESERT
AD-DIFFAH
LIBYAN PLATEAU
SARĪR KALANSHIYŪ
Sabhā
Marzūq
Awbārī
Ghadāmis
Ghāt
Al-Kufrah
Siwah
Tropic of Cancer
EGYPT
LIBYA
SUDAN
NIGER
ALGERIA
TUNISIA
TIBESTI

Map continues pages 148-149

Map continues pages 140-141

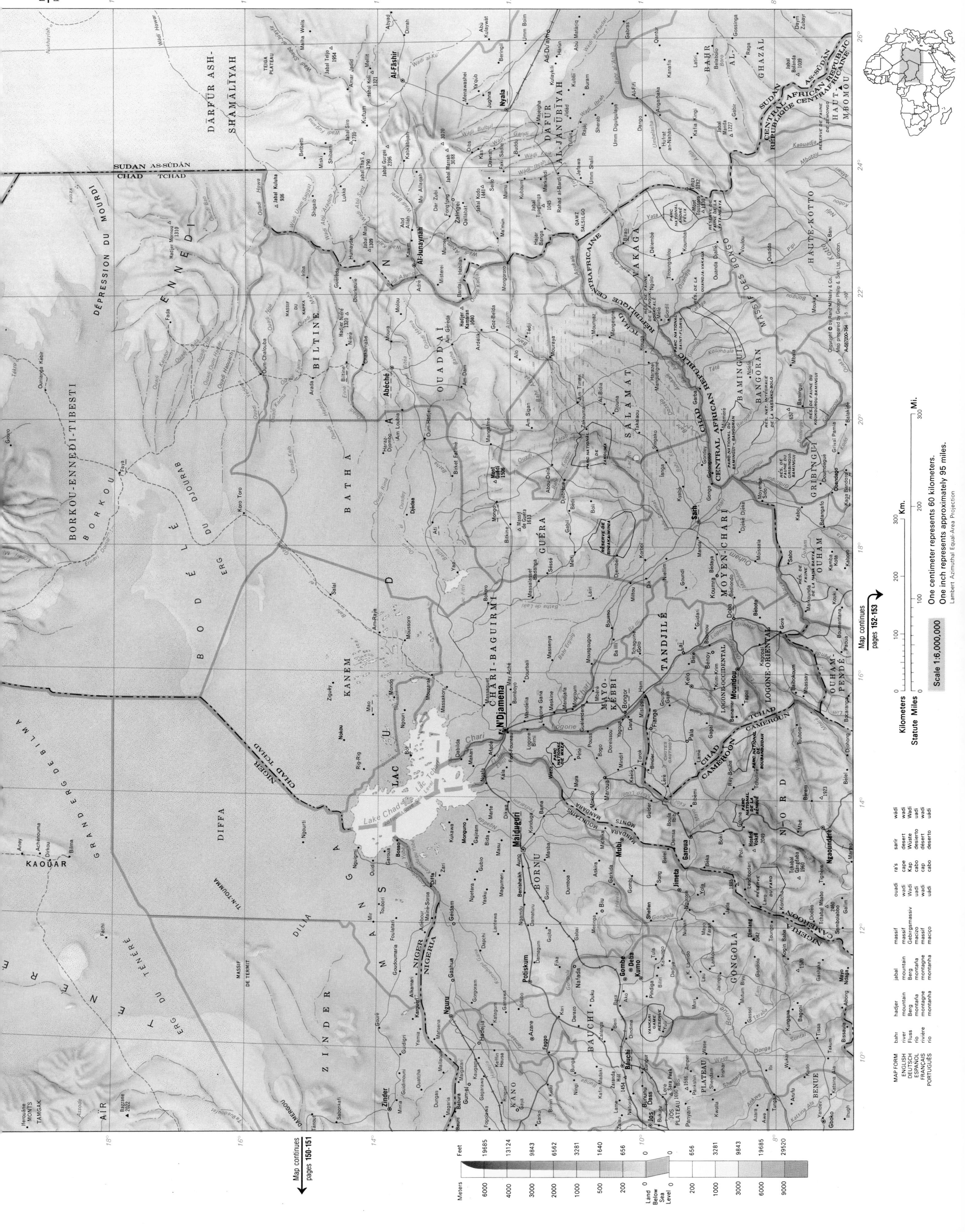
Scale 1:6,000,000
One centimeter represents 60 kilometers.
One inch represents approximately 95 miles.
Lambert Azimuthal Equal-Area Projection
Kilometers
Statute Miles

Map continues pages 152-153

Map continues pages 150-151

Map continues pages 34-35

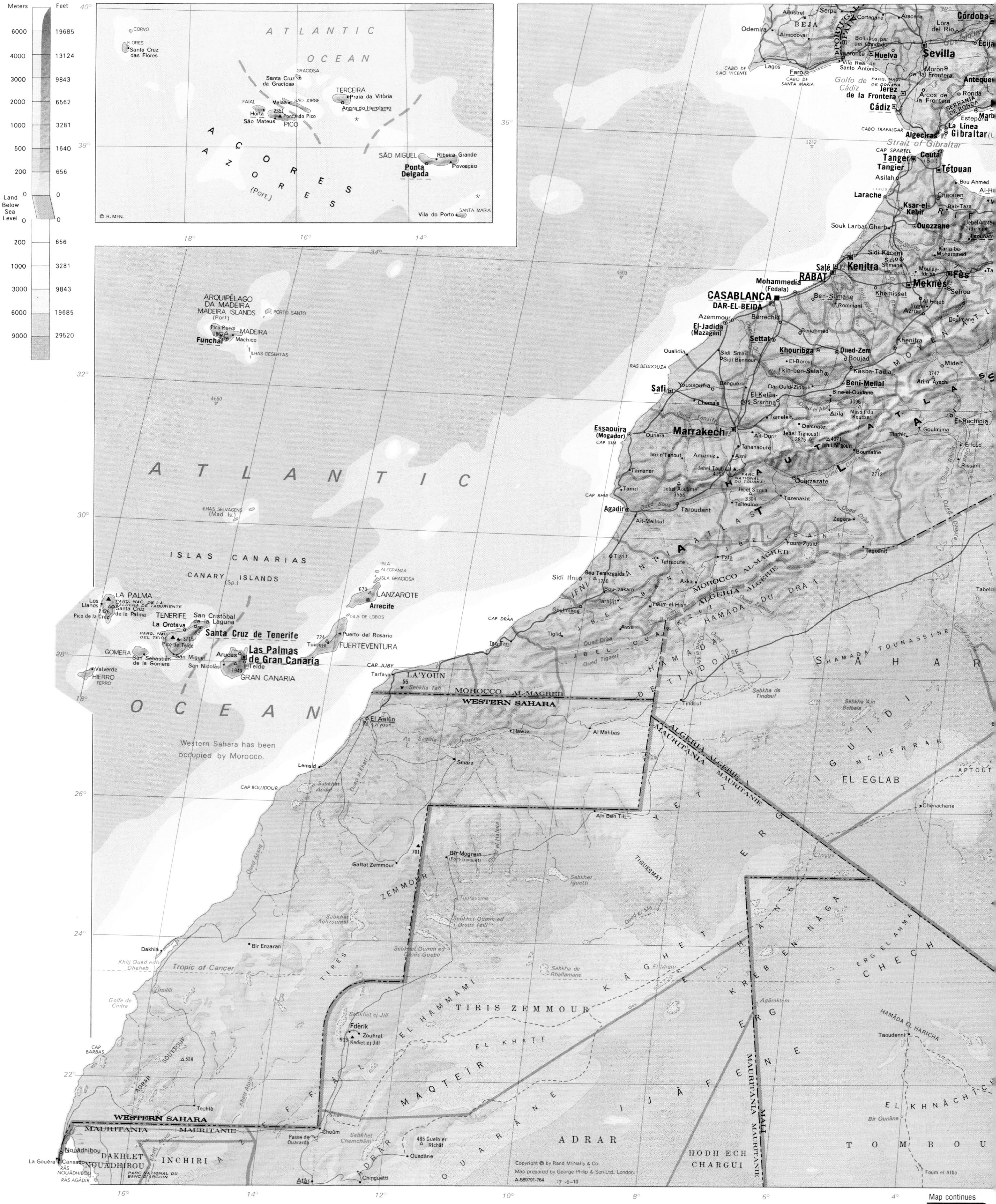
a
Meters
Feet
6000
19685
4000
13124
3000
9843
2000
6562
1000
3281
500
1640
200
656
Land Below Sea Level
ATLANTIC OCEAN
AÇORES
AZORES
(Port.)
SÃO MIGUEL
Ponta Delgada
TERCEIRA
PICO
ARQUIPÉLAGO DA MADEIRA
MADEIRA ISLANDS
(Port.)
Funchal
ISLAS CANARIAS
CANARY ISLANDS
(Sp.)
Santa Cruz de Tenerife
Las Palmas de Gran Canaria
LANZAROTE
FUERTEVENTURA
GRAN CANARIA
Western Sahara has been occupied by Morocco.
Sevilla
Córdoba
Cádiz
Gibraltar
Strait of Gibraltar
Tanger
Ceuta
Tétouan
RABAT
Kenitra
Fès
Meknès
CASABLANCA
DAR-EL-BEIDA
El-Jadida
(Mazagan)
Safi
Essaouira
(Mogador)
Marrakech
Agadir
MOROCCO AL-MAGREB
WESTERN SAHARA
ALGERIA ALGÉRIE
MAURITANIA MAURITANIE
LA'YOUN
El Aaiún
Smara
Dakhla
Tropic of Cancer
TIRIS ZEMMOUR
ADRAR
INCHIRI
DAKHLET NOUADHIBOU
Nouadhibou
HODH ECH CHARGUI
MALI
EL EGLAB
Tindouf
Copyright © by Rand McNally & Co.
Map prepared by George Philip & Son Ltd., London.

MAP FORM	cap	chott	djebel	erg	hamada	jbel	oued	sebkha
ENGLISH	cape	intermittent lake	mountain	sand desert	desert	mountain	wadi	salt flat
DEUTSCH	Kap	periodischer See	Berg	Sandwüste	Wüste	Berg	Wadi	Salzebene
ESPAÑOL	cabo	lago intermitente	montaña	desierto arenoso	desierto	montaña	uadi	salar
FRANÇAIS	cap	lac périodique	montagne	désert de sable	désert	montagne	wadi	saline
PORTUGUÊS	cabo	lago intermitente	montanha	deserto arenoso	deserto	montanha	uádi	salina

Map continues pages 150-151

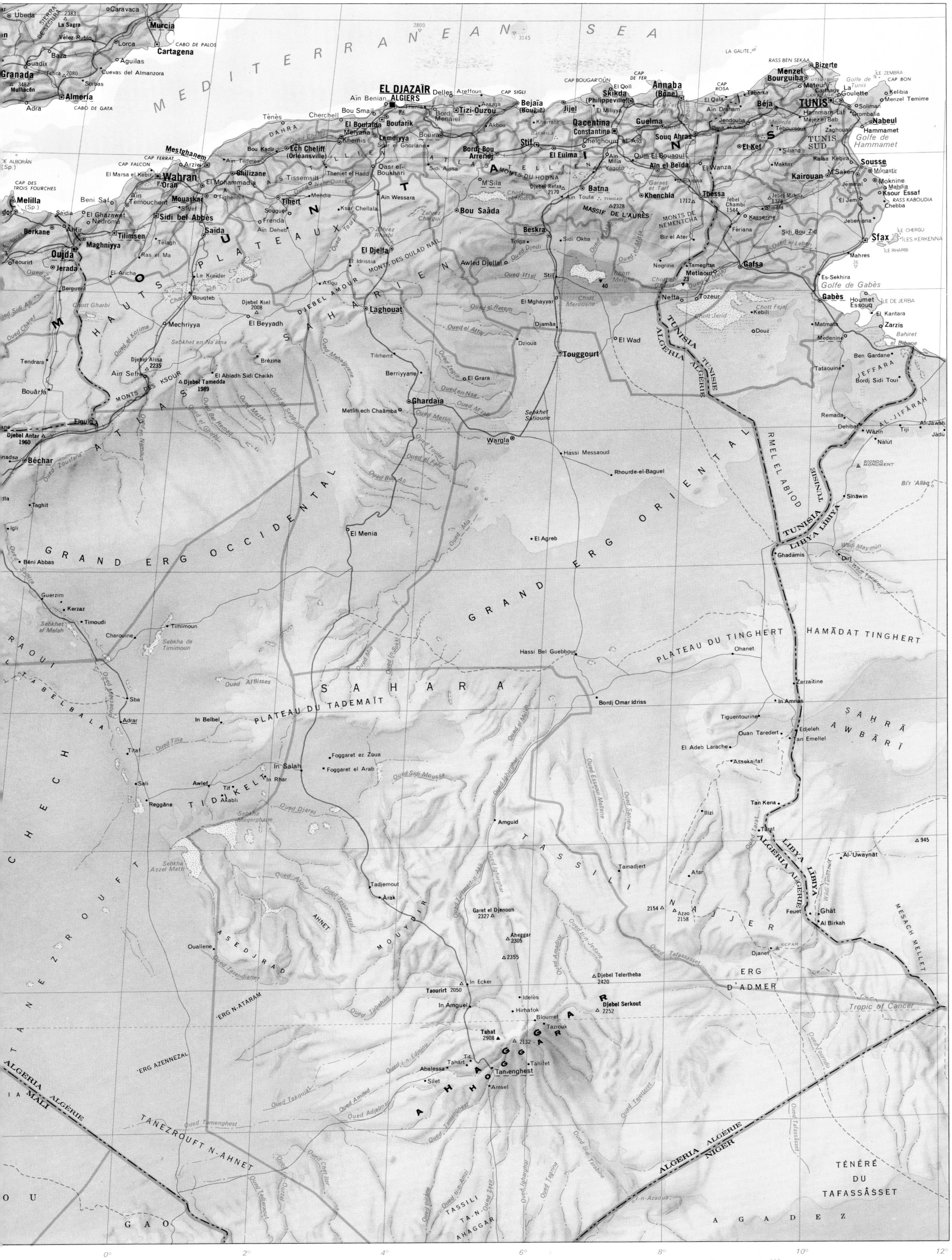
MEDITERRANEAN SEA
EL DJAZAÏR
ALGIERS
Annaba (Bône)
Bizerte
TUNIS
Qacentina
Constantine
Wahran
Oran
Sidi bel Abbès
Tilimsen
Oujda
Murcia
Cartagena
Granada
Almería
Melilla
Bejaïa (Bougie)
Skikda (Philippeville)
Tizi-Ouzou
Blida
Sétif
Batna
Biskra
Sousse
Sfax
Kairouan
Gabès
Gafsa
Tozeur
Nefta
Touggourt
Wargla
Ghardaïa
Laghouat
El Djelfa
Bou Saâda
Béchar
El Menia
Hassi Messaoud
Ghadāmis
In Salah
Adrar
Reggâne
Timimoun
Tamanrasset
Djanet
Ghāt
Illizi
In Amenas
GRAND ERG OCCIDENTAL
GRAND ERG ORIENTAL
S A H A R A
PLATEAU DU TADEMAÏT
PLATEAU DU TINGHERT
HAMĀDAT TINGHERT
T A S S I L I
A H A G G A R
TANEZROUFT N-AHNET
ERG D'ADMER
TÉNÉRÉ DU TAFASSÂSSET
A G A D E Z
G A O
SAHRĀ AWBĀRĪ
Tropic of Cancer
ALGERIA ALGÉRIE
TUNISIA TUNISIE
LIBYA LIBYE
NIGER
MALI
Golfe de Gabès
Golfe de Hammamet
Chott Melrhir
Chott Djerid
Chott ech Chergui
HAUTS PLATEAUX
SAHARIEN
ATLAS
Tahat 2908
Djebel Serkout 2252
Djebel Telertheba 2420

Map continues pages 146-147

Kilometers 0 100 200 300 Km.
Statute Miles 0 100 200 300 Mi.

Scale 1:6,000,000
One centimeter represents 60 kilometers.
One inch represents approximately 95 miles.
Lambert Azimuthal Equal-Area Projection

DAKHLET NOUADHIBOU
INCHIRI
ADRAR
ADÂFER EL ABIOD
TAGANT
HODH ECH CHARGUI
MALI
MAURITANIA
MAURITANIE
Nouakchott
TRARZA
BRAKNA
GORGOL
GUIDIMAKA
HODH EL GHARBI
Saint-Louis
Louga
Thiès
DAKAR
Diourbel
Kaolack
FERLO
KAYES
KOULIKORO
SÉGOU
Bamako
SIKASSO
Banjul (Bathurst)
GAMBIA
SENEGAL
SÉNÉGAL
TAMBACOUNDA
KOLDA
Ziguinchor
Bissau
GUINEA-BISSAU
GUINÉ-BISSAU
ARQUIPÉLAGO DOS BIJAGÓS
GUINEA
GUINÉE
FOUTA DJALON
Conakry
SIERRA LEONE
Freetown
NORTHERN
EASTERN
SOUTHERN
LIBERIA
Monrovia
IVORY COAST
CÔTE D'IVOIRE
ABIDJAN
Bouaké
Yamoussoukro
Korhogo
San Pédro
ATLANTIC OCEAN
GRAIN COAST
IVORY COAST
Meters
Feet
6000 19685
4000 13124
3000 9843
2000 6562
1000 3281
500 1640
200 656
0 0
Land Below Sea Level
200 656
1000 3281
3000 9843
6000 19685
9000 29520
a
SANTO ANTÃO
SÃO VICENTE
SÃO NICOLAU
SAL
BOA VISTA
MAIO
SANTIAGO
FOGO
BRAVA
Praia
CAPE VERDE
CABO VERDE
ATLANTIC
OCEAN
Copyright © by Rand McNally & Co.
Map prepared by George Philip & Son Ltd., London.

MAP FORM	coast	dhar	game reserve	ilha	lac	monts	mountains	vallée
ENGLISH	coast	escarpment	game reserve	island	lake	mountains	mountains	valley
DEUTSCH	Küste	Landstufe	Wildpark	Insel	See	Berge	Berge	Tal
ESPAÑOL	costa	escarpa	vedado de caza	isla	lago	montes	montañas	valle
FRANÇAIS	côte	escarpement	réserve à gibier	île	lac	monts	montagnes	vallée
PORTUGUÊS	costa	escarpa	reserva de caça	ilha	lago	montes	montanhas	vale

continues
es 148-149

ADRAR
TAMENGHEST
ADRAR DES IFÔGHAS
GAO
TALAK
AGADEZ
AÏR
TAHOUA
TÉGAMA
DAMERGOU
ZINDER
MARADI
NIAMEY
DOSSO
SOKOTO
KATSINA
KANO
KADUNA
BAUCHI
NIGER
PLATEAU
FEDERAL CAPITAL TERRITORY
KWARA
OYO
OGUN
ONDO
BENDEL
ANAMBRA
IMO
RIVERS
CROSS RIVER
BENUE
GONGOLA
BORGOU
ATAKORA
ZOU
MONO
ATLANTIQUE
NORTHERN
UPPER WEST
UPPER EAST
BRONG-AHAFO
ASHANTI
EASTERN
VOLTA
CENTRAL
WESTERN
SUD-OUEST
LITTORAL
ALGERIA
ALGÉRIE
MALI
NIGER
BURKINA FASO
NIGERIA
BENIN
TOGO
GHANA
IVORY COAST
CAMEROON
EQUATORIAL GUINEA
BIOKO
Niamey
Ouagadougou
Gao
Agadez
Zinder
Maradi
Tahoua
Sokoto
Kano
Zaria
Kaduna
Jos
Bauchi
Minna
Ilorin
Ogbomosho
Oshogbo
Ibadan
Abeokuta
Lagos
Porto-Novo
Cotonou
Lomé
Accra
Tema
Kumasi
Tamale
Cape Coast
Sekondi-Takoradi
Benin City
Enugu
Onitsha
Port Harcourt
Calabar
Douala
Buea
Malabo
Makurdi
Lokoja
SLAVE COAST
Bight of Benin
GOLD COAST
GULF OF GUINEA
NIGER DELTA
Bight of Biafra
Lake Volta
Kainji Lake

Map continues
pages 146-147

Map continues
pages 152-153

Kilometers 0 100 200 300 Km.
Statute Miles 0 100 200 300 Mi.

Scale 1:6,000,000
One centimeter represents 60 kilometers.
One inch represents approximately 95 miles.
Lambert Azimuthal Equal-Area Projection

Map continues pages 146-147

CENTRAL AFRICAN REPUBLIC
CAMEROON
CONGO
ZAIRE
GABON
EQUATORIAL GUINEA
SAO TOME AND PRINCIPE
Gulf of Guinea
Bight of Biafra
Bangui
Yaoundé
Douala
Malabo
Libreville
Port Gentil
Brazzaville
KINSHASA (LÉOPOLDVILLE)
Mbandaka (Coquilhatville)
Bandundu
Enugu
Calabar
Port Harcourt
Equator

Map continues pages 150-151

Map continues pages 154-155

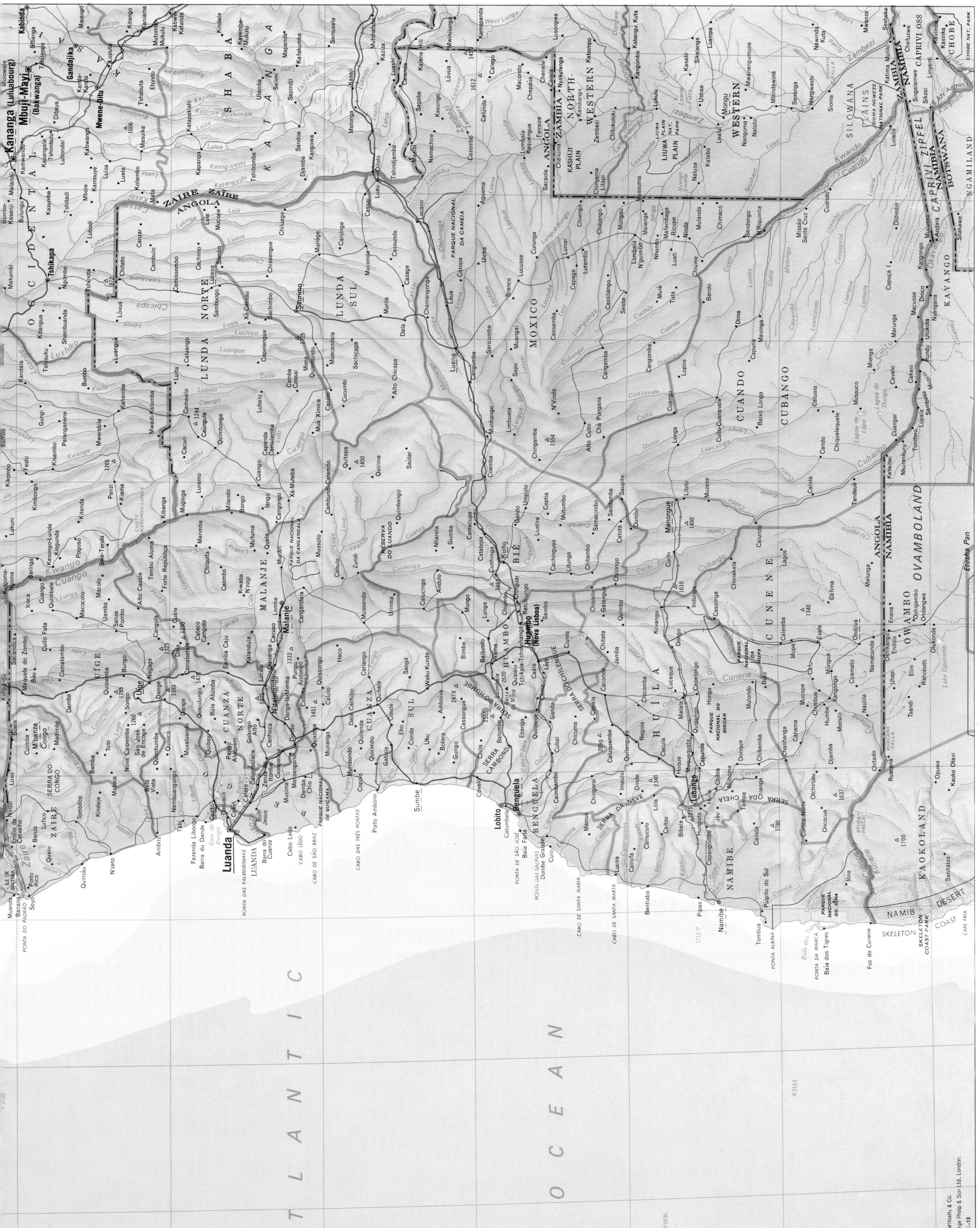
ATLANTIC
OCEAN
ANGOLA
ZAIRE
ZAMBIA
NAMIBIA
BOTSWANA
Luanda
Lobito
Benguela
Huambo (Nova Lisboa)
Malanje
Kananga (Luluabourg)
Mbuji-Mayi (Bakwanga)
Tshikapa
Lubango
Namibe
Menongue
Luena
Cabinda
OVAMBOLAND
KAOKOLAND
NAMIB DESERT
SKELETON COAST
Etosha Pan
Zambezi
Cunene
Cuanza
Kwango
CAPRIVI ZIPFEL
NORTH-WESTERN
WESTERN
SHABA
KATANGA
MOXICO
CUANDO CUBANGO
HUÍLA
BIÉ
CUNENE
LUNDA NORTE
LUNDA SUL
UÍGE
CUANZA NORTE
CUANZA SUL
BENGUELA
NAMIBE
MALANJE
ZAIRE
Copyright © by Rand McNally & Co.
Map prepared by George Philip & Son Ltd. London.

Map continues pages 156-157

Kilometers 0 100 200 300 Km.

Statute Miles 0 100 200 300 Mi.

Scale 1:6,000,000

One centimeter represents 60 kilometers.
One inch represents approximately 95 miles.
Lambert Azimuthal Equal Area Projection

MAP FORM	cabo	falls	île	lac	lagune	monts	ponta	serra
ENGLISH	cape	waterfall	island	lake	lagoon	mountains	point	mountains
DEUTSCH	Kap	Wasserfall	Insel	See	Haff	Berge	Landspitze	Berge
ESPAÑOL	cabo	cascada	isla	lago	laguna	montes	punta	sierra
FRANÇAIS	cap	chute d'eau	île	lac	lagune	monts	pointe	montagnes
PORTUGUÊS	cabo	queda d'água	ilha	lago	laguna	montes	ponta	serra

Meters	Feet
6000	19685
4000	13124
3000	9843
2000	6562
1000	3281
500	1640
200	656
0	0
Land Below Sea Level 0	0
200	656
1000	3281
3000	9843
6000	19685
9000	29520

East Africa and Eastern Congo Basin / Ostafrika und Östliches Kongobecken / África Oriental y Cuenca Oriental del Congo
Afrique Orientale et Bassin du Congo, partie Orientale / África Oriental e Bacia Oriental do Congo

Map continues pages 144-145

Map continues pages 140-141

Kilometers 0 100 200 300 Km.
Statute Miles 0 100 200 300 Mi.

Scale 1:6,000,000

One centimeter represents 60 kilometers.
One inch represents approximately 95 miles.
Lambert Azimuthal Equal-Area Projection

ENGLISH	falls	game reserve	island	lake	mountains	national park	plain	swamp
DEUTSCH	Wasserfall	Wildreservat	Insel	See	Berge	Nationalpark	Ebene	Sumpf
ESPAÑOL	cascada	vedado de caza	isla	lago	montañas	parque nacional	llano	pantano
FRANÇAIS	chute d'eau	réserve à gibier	île	lac	montagnes	parc national	plaine	marais
PORTUGUÊS	queda d'água	reserva de caça	ilha	lago	montanhas	parque nacional	planície	pântano

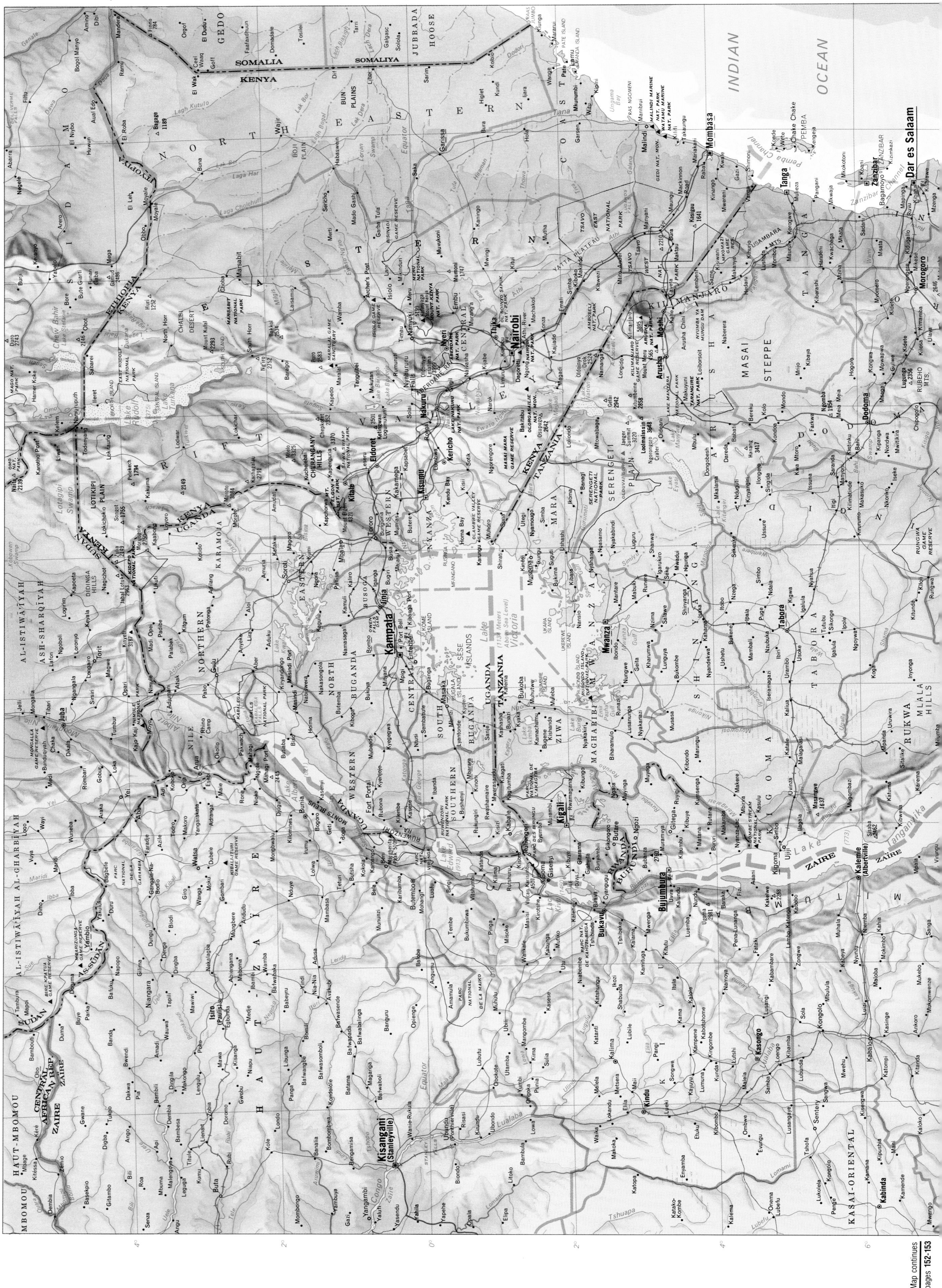

INDIAN OCEAN
SOMALIA
KENYA
ETHIOPIA
SUDAN
UGANDA
TANZANIA
RWANDA
BURUNDI
ZAIRE
CENTRAL AFRICAN REP.
Nairobi
Mombasa
Kampala
Dar es Salaam
Kigali
Bujumbura
Kisangani (Stanleyville)
Lake Victoria
Lake Tanganyika
Lake Rudolf
KILIMANJARO
MASAI STEPPE
SERENGETI PLAIN

Map continues pages 152-153

MOZAMBIQUE CHANNEL
Map continues pages 156-157
MOZAMBIQUE
ZAMBIA
ZIMBABWE
MALAWI
TANZANIA
Lake Nyasa (Lake Malawi)
Feet
Meters
Land Below Sea Level

Map continues pages 152-153

ATLANTIC OCEAN
NAMIB DESERT
KALAHARI DESERT
KAOKOLAND
OVAMBOLAND
OWAMBO
KAVANGO
CAPRIVI STRIP
ETOSHA NATIONAL PARK
DAMARALAND
GREAT NAMAQUALAND
NAMALAND
KEETMANSHOOP
KARASBURG
LITTLE NAMAQUALAND
BUSHMAN LAND
GHANZI
NGAMILAND
KWENENG
KGALAGADI
BECHUANALAND
GRIQUALAND WEST
ORANJE-VRYSTAAT
ORANGE FREE
GREAT KARROO
NAMIBIA
BOTSWANA
SOUTH AFRICA
SUID-AFRIKA
ANGOLA
ZAMBIA
ZIMBABWE
Windhoek
Swakopmund
Walvis Bay
Lüderitz
Upington
Kimberley
Bloemfontein
Gaborone
Mafikeng
Klerksdorp
CAPE TOWN
KAAPSTAD
Port Elizabeth
Grahamstown
Livingstone
Tropic of Capricorn
Meters
Feet
Land Below Sea Level
Copyright © by Rand McNally & Co.
Map prepared by George Philip & Son Ltd., London.
A-589292-764

Kilometers 0 100 200 300 Km.
Statute Miles 0 100 200 300 Mi.

Scale 1:6,000,000

One centimeter represents 60 kilometers.
One inch represents approximately 95 miles.
Lambert Azimuthal Equal-Area Projection

MAP FORM	bay	berg, berge	cape	game reserve	ilha	lake	national park
ENGLISH	bay	mountain, mountains	cape	game reserve	island	lake	national park
DEUTSCH	Bucht	Berg, Berge	Kap	Wildpark	Insel	See	Nationalpark
ESPAÑOL	bahía	montaña, montañas	cabo	vedado de caza	isla	lago	parque nacional
FRANÇAIS	baie	montagne, montagnes	cap	réserve à gibier	île	lac	parc national
PORTUGUÊS	baía	montanha, montanhas	cabo	reserva de caça	ilha	lago	parque nacional

Map continues pages 154-155

HARARE (SALISBURY)
MAPUTO
PRETORIA
DURBAN
Beira
Quelimane
Chimoio
Xai-Xai
Pietermaritzburg
Mbabane
SWAZILAND
ZIMBABWE
MOZAMBIQUE
SOUTH AFRICA
NATAL
MOZAMBIQUE CHANNEL
INDIAN OCEAN
Tropic of Capricorn
MADAGASCAR
MADAGASIKARA
ANTANANARIVO
Mahajanga
Toamasina
Antsiranana
Fianarantsoa
Toliara
a
COMOROS
COMORES
Moroni
MAYOTTE (Fr.)
Dzaoudzi
b
c
MAURITIUS
Port Louis
REUNION
Saint-Denis
MASCARENE ISLANDS
Bophuthatswana, Ciskei, Transkei, and Venda are not internationally recognized.
© R. McN.

Map continues pages 156-157

19°
20°
21°
22°
23°
24°
25°
26°
27°
28°
29°
30°
31°
32°
33°
34°
18°
SOUTH AFRICA
SUID AFRIKA
NAMIBIA
BOTSWANA
KALAHARI GEMSBOK NATIONAL PARK
KGALAGADI
KEETMANSHOOP
K A L A H A R I
D E S E R T
BECHUANALAND
BOPHUTHATSWANA
GRIQUALAND WEST
WARMBAD
BUSHMAN LAND
GHAAPPLATO
KURUMANHEUWELS
LANGBERG
ASBESBERG
KAREEBERGE
NUWEVELDBERGE
GREAT KARROO
GROOT KARROO
ROGGEVELDBERGE
SNEEUBERG
SWARTRUGGENS
OLIFANTSRIVIERBERGE
GROOT SWARTBERGE
KOUGABERGE
OUTENIEKWABERGE
LITTLE KARROO
WITTEBERGE
HEX RIVIERBERGE
HANTAMSBERG
GROOT KARASBERGE
Koes
Tshabong
Morokweng
Donegal
Ewbank
Twee Rivieren
Kines West
Aroab
Koopan-Noord
Askham
Beginsel
Witdraai
Khuis
Aansluit
Severn
Vanzylsrus
Sonstraal
Kuruman
Hotazel
Tsineng
Cardington
Wesselsvlei
Battlemount
Vryburg
Gannahoek
Ganyesa
Tlhakgameng
Stella
Setlagodi
Dirkiesrus
Peachdale
Narubis
Kochena
Klipdam
Tränental
Schroffenstein
Koopan-Suid
Obobogorap
Noenieput
Tsaraxaibis
Davignab
Klein-Karas
Grünau
Kanus
Vrouenspan
Bokhara
Karasburg
Nieuwefontein
Ukamas
Dabegabis
Ariamsvlei
Doorndam
Grondneus
Rooidam
Langklip
Lutzputs
Upington
Karos
Lambrechts Drift
Louisvale
Trooilapspan
Kalkwerf
Keimoes
Kanoneiland
Kalkmond
Augrabies
AUGRABIES FALLS NATIONAL PARK
Kakamas
Orange
Warmbad
Onseepkans
Nous
Bladgrond
Klipbakken
Wegdraai
Rooilyf
Kleinbegin
Groblershoop
Goodhouse
Pella
Pofadder
Aggeneis
Namies
N'Rougas
Voordeelspan
Putsonderwater
Kenhardt
Marydale
Koegas
Niekerkshoop
Bakenkop
Springfield
Abrahamsdam
Griekwastad
Douglas
Campbell
Schmidtsdrif
Barkly West
Kimberley
Postmasburg
Pretoriusvlei
Matsap
Sishen
Olifantshoek
Lohatlha
Daniëlskuil
Koopmansfontein
Silver Streams
Delportshoop
Ulco
Windsorton
Warrenton
Vaalhartsdam
Reivilo
Bethlehem
Schweizer-Reneke
Taung
Pudimoe
Buxton
Hartswater
Jan Kempdorp
Andalusia
Ganspan
Boetsap
Winton
Dibeng
Appleby
Vroeggedeel
Gakarosa
Modderrivier
Ritchie
Jacobsdal
Salt Lake
Higgs' Hope
Koffiefontein
Belmont
Remhoogte
Prieska
Hopetown
Wanda
Oranjerivier
Luckhoff
Brakputs
Boomrivier
Vleikolk
Sononder
Bundu
Redlands
Strydenburg
Kraankuil
Diemansputs
Nelspoortjie
Grootvloer
Verneukpan
Zooafskolk
Gamoep
Kalkstasie
Granaatboskolk
Verneukpan
De Naauwte
Omdraaisvlei
Sodium
Petrusville
Potfontein
Philippolis
Korga
Onderstedorings
Poortjie
Gannapan
Vanwyksvlei
Houtkraal
Philipstown
Buchuberg
Buchufontein
Klein-Soutpan
Brandvlei
Britstown
De Aar
Waterdale
Colesberg
Aalwynsfontein
Garies
Botersleegte
Garskolk
Muldersvlei
Vosburg
Lekkeroog
Kaalspruit
Grasbult
Carnarvon
Deelfontein
Mynfontein
Hanover Road
Hanover
Wildfontein
Sakrivier
Van Reenen's Plaats
Loeriesfontein
Pampoenpoort
Sterkaar
Merriman
Skerpioensdrif
Bitterfontein
Nuwerus
Klipwerf
Kootjieskolk
Williston
Sterling
Brakpoort
Victoria West
Hutchinson
Richmond
Middelburg
Komkans
Brandkop
Nieuwoudtville
Calvinia
Loxton
Ockies
Dassiefontein
Koekenaap
Lutzville
Vredendal
Vanrhynsdorp
Klawer
Doringbaai
Juriesfontein
Merwede
Kompasberg
Nieu Bethesda
Bethesdaweg
Sandheuwel
Fraserburg
Good Hope
Three Sisters
Murraysburg
Middelpos
Die Boss
Prinshof
Rosedene
Nelspoort
VALLEY OF DESOLATION NATIONAL MONUMENT
Graaff-Reinet
Adendorp
Lambert's Bay
Graafwater
Leipoldtville
Elandsbaai
BABOON POINT
Clanwilliam
Wuppertal
Elandsvlei
Honderfontein
Bontberg
Excelda
Beaufort West
Sutherland
Bo-Wadrif
Bulwater
Aberdeen
Kendrew
Pearston
Redelinghuys
Sneeuberg
Citrusdal
Letjiesbos
Merweville
Bakoondfontein
Vinkekuil
Leeu-Gamka
Aurora
Velddrif
CAPE COLUMBINE
Tulpfontein
Bokfontein
Koringplaas
Kruidfontein
Rietbron
Jansenville
Piketberg
Vredenburg
Saldanha
Koringberg
De Hoek
Porterville
Prince Albert Road
Dwyka
Seekoegat
Kommandokraal
Strydomsvlei
Volstruisleegte
Klipplaat
Mount Stewart
Hillandale
Langebaan
Hopefield
Moorreesburg
Saldanhabaai
Laingsburg
Matjiesfontein
Prince Albert
Klaarstroom
Willowmore
Steytlerville
Baroe
YSTERFONTEINPUNT
Darling
Riebeek-Wes
Riebeek-Kasteel
Gouda
Saron
Tulbagh
Hottentotskloof
Prince Alfred Hamlet
Ceres
Touwsrivier
Konstabel
Spreeufontein
Seweweekspoort
Ladismith
Zoar
Kruisrivier
Cango Caves
De Rust
Dysselsdorp
Zaaimansdal
DASSENEILAND
Malmesbury
Mamre
Hermon
Wolseley
De Doorns
Anysberg
Calitzdorp
Oudtshoorn
Uniondale
BOKPUNT
Philadelphia
Wellington
Worcester
Rawsonville
Boerboonfontein
Montagu
Klein Karroo
Vanwyksdorp
Daskop
Avontuur
Haarlem
Joubertina
Patensie
Hankey
Melkbosstrand
Bloubergstrand
Paarl
Durbanville
Kraaifontein
Robertson
Ashton
Bonnievale
Lemoenshoek
Barrydale
Muiskraal
Holgate
Jonkersberg
Blanco
George
Bergplaas
Wilderness
Kruisvallei
TSITSIKAMMA FOREST AND COASTAL NAT. PARK
Kareedouw
Kruisfontein
ROBBENEILAND
Table Bay
Parow
Bellville
Franschhoek
McGregor
Stellenbosch
Villiersdorp
Suurbraak
Herbertsdale
Groot-Brakrivier
Pacaltsdorp
Knysna
Keurboomsrivier
Plettenbergbaai
Stormsrivier
Humansdorp
Jeffreys Bay
CAPE TOWN
KAAPSTAD
Table Mtn. 1086
Wynberg
Strand
Somerset West
Genadendal
Greyton
Stormsvlei
Swellendam
Heidelberg
Riversdale
Mosselbaai
Mossel Bay
CAPE SAINT BLAIZE
WALKER POINT
CAPE SEAL
CAPE SAINT FRANCIS
Houtbaai
Kommetjie
Simon's Town
Vishoek
Valsbaai
Gordon's Bay
Grabouw
Caledon
Riviersonderend
BONTEBOK NATIONAL PARK
Askraal
Albertinia
Riethuiskraal
Vleesbaai
KAAP VACCA
Avondrust
Stilbaai
CAPE BARRACOUTA
CAPE OF GOOD HOPE NATURE RESERVE
CAPE OF GOOD HOPE
KAAP DIE GOEIE HOOP
KAAPPUNT
KAAP HANGKLIP
Kleinmond
Betty's Bay
Hermanus
Protem
Klipdale
Malgas
Vermaaklikheid
Witsand
Saint Sebastian Bay
KAAP INFANTE
Wydgelee
Napier
Stanford
Bredasdorp
Skipskop
Walker Bay
Baardskeerdersbos
Elim
Gansbaai
DANGER POINT
Viljoenshof
Waenhuiskrans
DYER ISLAND
QUOIN POINT
Struisbaai
Agulhas
CAPE AGULHAS
Meters
Feet
6000
19685
4000
13124
3000
9843
2000
6562
1000
3281
500
1640
200
656
0
0
Land Below Sea Level
0
0
200
656
1000
3281
3000
9843
6000
19685
9000
29520

MAP FORM	bay	berge	cape	dam	game reserve	national park	pass	point
ENGLISH	bay	mountains	cape	dam	game reserve	national park	pass	point
DEUTSCH	Bucht	Berge	Kap	Damm	Wildpark	Nationalpark	Pass	Landspitze
ESPAÑOL	bahía	montañas	cabo	presa	vedado de caza	parque nacional	paso	punta
FRANÇAIS	baie	montagnes	cap	barrage	réserve à gibier	parc national	col	pointe
PORTUGUÊS	baía	montanhas	cabo	represa	reserva de caça	parque nacional	passo	ponta

Pretoria
JOHANNESBURG
Soweto
Maputo (Lourenço Marques)
MOZAMBIQUE
MOÇAMBIQUE
Mbabane
SWAZILAND
LESOTHO
Maseru
DRAKENSBERG
Pietermaritzburg
DURBAN
Ladysmith
Harrismith
Bethlehem
Kroonstad
Welkom
Klerksdorp
Potchefstroom
Vereeniging
Standerton
Newcastle
Dundee
Richard's Bay
Umtata
TRANSKEI
CISKEI
KAFFRARIA
TEMBULAND
Queenstown
King William's Town
East London
Oos-Londen
Grahamstown
Port Alfred
Elizabeth
INDIAN
OCEAN
WILD COAST
Bophuthatswana, Ciskei, Transkei, and Venda are not internationally recognized.
Copyright © by Rand McNally & Co.
Map prepared by George Philip & Son Ltd., London.
A-584600-764

Kilometers 0 50 100 150 Km.
Statute Miles 0 50 100 150 Mi.

Scale 1:3,000,000

One centimeter represents 30 kilometers.
One inch represents approximately 47 miles.
Lambert Conformal Conic Projection

Map continues
pages 108-109

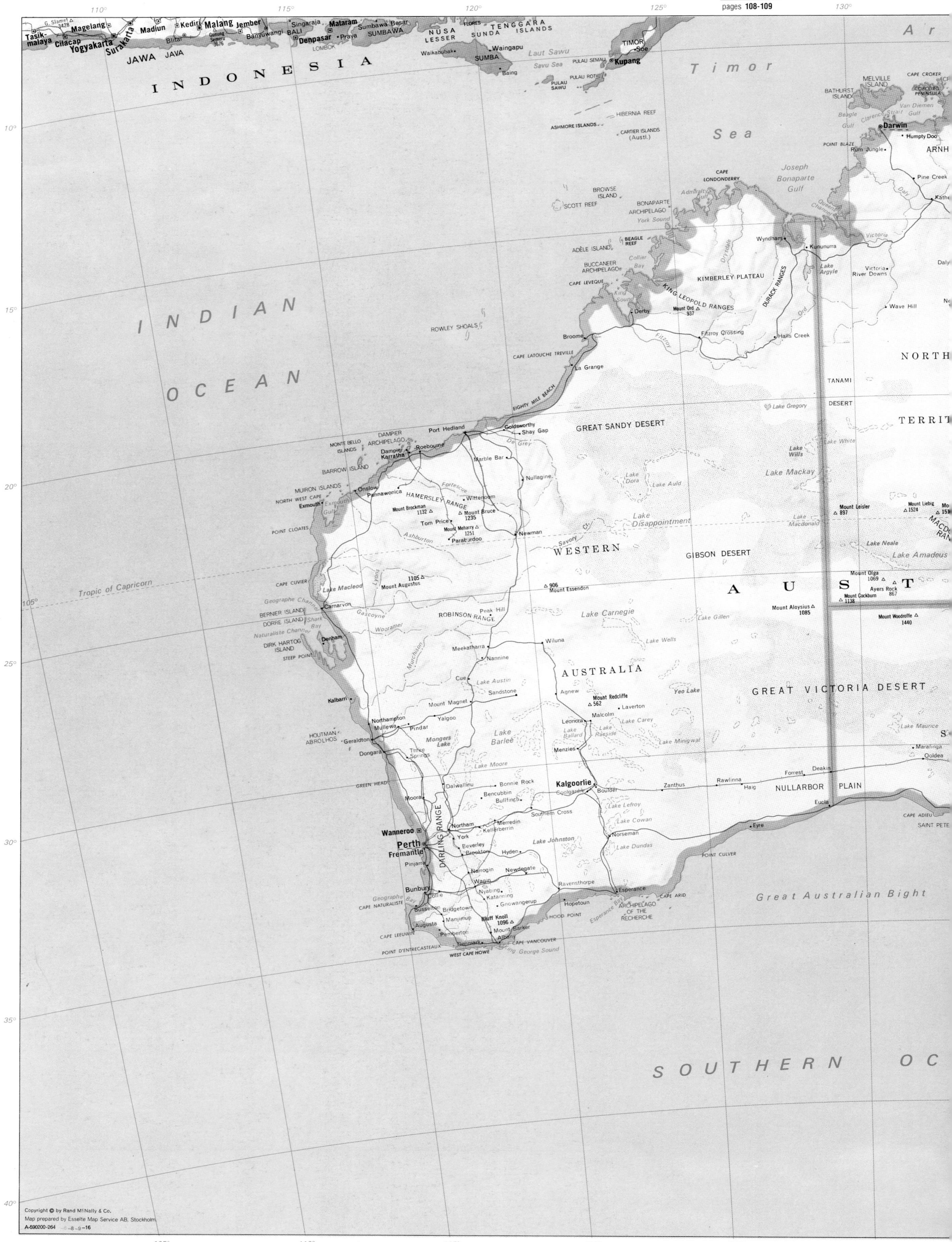
INDONESIA
JAWA
Yogyakarta
Surakarta
Magelang
Madiun
Kediri
Malang
Jember
Blitar
Cilacap
Tasikmalaya
Banyuwangi
Singaraja
BALI
Denpasar
Mataram
LOMBOK
Sumbawa Besar
SUMBAWA
NUSA TENGGARA
LESSER SUNDA ISLANDS
FLORES
SUMBA
Waingapu
Waikabubak
Baing
Laut Sawu
Savu Sea
PULAU SEMAU
Kupang
TIMOR
Soe
PULAU ROTI
PULAU SAWU
Timor Sea
HIBERNIA REEF
ASHMORE ISLANDS
CARTIER ISLANDS (Austl.)
CAPE LONDONDERRY
Joseph Bonaparte Gulf
BROWSE ISLAND
SCOTT REEF
BONAPARTE ARCHIPELAGO
York Sound
Admiralty Gulf
ADÈLE ISLAND
BEAGLE REEF
Collier Bay
BUCCANEER ARCHIPELAGO
CAPE LEVEQUE
King Sound
Derby
KIMBERLEY PLATEAU
KING LEOPOLD RANGES
Mount Ord 937
DURACK RANGES
Wyndham
Kununurra
Lake Argyle
Victoria River Downs
Wave Hill
Fitzroy Crossing
Halls Creek
Ord
ROWLEY SHOALS
Broome
CAPE LATOUCHE TREVILLE
La Grange
EIGHTY MILE BEACH
INDIAN OCEAN
MELVILLE ISLAND
BATHURST ISLAND
CAPE CROKER
COBOURG PENINSULA
Van Diemen Gulf
Beagle Gulf
Clarence Strait
Darwin
Humpty Doo
POINT BLAZE
Rum Jungle
Pine Creek
Katherine
ARNH
NORTH
TERRIT
TANAMI DESERT
Lake Gregory
Lake White
GREAT SANDY DESERT
Port Hedland
Goldsworthy
Shay Gap
De Grey
MONTE BELLO ISLANDS
DAMPIER ARCHIPELAGO
Roebourne
Dampier
Karratha
Marble Bar
Nullagine
BARROW ISLAND
MUIRON ISLANDS
NORTH WEST CAPE
Onslow
Exmouth
Exmouth Gulf
Pannawonica
Fortescue
HAMERSLEY RANGE
Wittenoom
Mount Brockman 1132
Mount Bruce 1235
Tom Price
Mount Meharry 1251
Paraburdoo
Ashburton
Newman
POINT CLOATES
Lake Wills
Lake Mackay
Lake Dora
Lake Auld
Lake Disappointment
Lake Macdonald
Mount Leisler 897
Mount Liebig 1524
Savory Ck.
WESTERN AUSTRALIA
GIBSON DESERT
Lake Neale
Lake Amadeus
Mount Olga 1069
Ayers Rock 867
Mount Cockburn 1138
Mount Woodroffe 1440
Tropic of Capricorn
CAPE CUVIER
Lake Macleod
Lyons
1105
Mount Augustus
906 Mount Essendon
Mount Aloysius 1085
Geographe Channel
Carnarvon
BERNIER ISLAND
DORRE ISLAND
Shark Bay
Naturaliste Channel
DIRK HARTOG ISLAND
STEEP POINT
Denham
Gascoyne
Wooramel
ROBINSON RANGE
Peak Hill
Lake Carnegie
Lake Gillen
Lake Wells
Wiluna
Meekatharra
Nannine
Murchison
Cue
Lake Austin
Sandstone
Agnew
Mount Redcliffe 562
Laverton
Yeo Lake
GREAT VICTORIA DESERT
Kalbarri
Mount Magnet
Northampton
Mullewa
Pindar
Yalgoo
Leonora
Malcolm
Lake Ballard
Lake Raeside
Lake Carey
Lake Minigwal
Lake Maurice
HOUTMAN ABROLHOS
Geraldton
Dongara
Three Springs
Mongers Lake
Lake Barlee
Menzies
Lake Moore
GREEN HEAD
Dalwallinu
Bonnie Rock
Bencubbin
Bullfinch
Kalgoorlie
Coolgardie
Boulder
Zanthus
Rawlinna
Haig
Forrest
Deakin
NULLARBOR PLAIN
Maralinga
Ooldea
Eucla
Moora
DARLING RANGE
Wanneroo
Perth
Fremantle
Pinjarra
Northam
York
Merredin
Kellerberrin
Southern Cross
Lake Lefroy
Lake Cowan
Norseman
Lake Johnston
Lake Dundas
Beverley
Brookton
Hyden
Narrogin
Newdegate
Wagin
Bunbury
Collie
Nyabing
Katanning
Gnowangerup
Ravensthorpe
Esperance
CAPE ARID
ARCHIPELAGO OF THE RECHERCHE
Hopetoun
HOOD POINT
Esperance Bay
Geographe Bay
CAPE NATURALISTE
Busselton
Bridgetown
Manjimup
Bluff Knoll 1096
Mount Barker
Augusta
Pemberton
CAPE LEEUWIN
Denmark
Albany
CAPE VANCOUVER
King George Sound
POINT D'ENTRECASTEAUX
WEST CAPE HOWE
Eyre
POINT CULVER
CAPE ADIEU
SAINT PETE
Great Australian Bight
SOUTHERN OC
110° 115° 120° 125° 130°
105° 110° 115° 120° 125° 130°
10° 15° 20° 25° 30° 35° 40°

ENGLISH	bay	cape	island	lake	mount	point	range	reef
DEUTSCH	Bucht	Kap	Insel	See	Berg	Landspitze	Gebirge	Riff
ESPAÑOL	bahía	cabo	isla	lago	montaña	punta	cordillera	arrecife
FRANÇAIS	baie	cap	île	lac	mont	pointe	chaîne	récif
PORTUGUÊS	baía	cabo	ilha	lago	monte	ponta	cordilheira	recife

Coral Sea
Solomon Sea
PACIFIC OCEAN
Tasman Sea
Gulf of Carpentaria
Gulf of Papua
Torres Strait
Bass Strait
Tropic of Capricorn
NEW GUINEA
PAPUA NEW GUINEA
Port Moresby
SOLOMON ISLANDS
Honiara
GUADALCANAL
Mt. Makarakomburu 2447
RENNELL
LOUISIADE ARCHIPELAGO
D'ENTRECASTEAUX ISLANDS
KIRIWINA ISLANDS
CAPE YORK PENINSULA
Thursday Island
Bamaga
CAPE YORK
GREAT BARRIER REEF
GREAT DIVIDING RANGE
GREAT ARTESIAN BASIN
GREY RANGE
GREGORY RANGE
SIMPSON DESERT
STURT STONY DESERT
QUEENSLAND
NEW SOUTH WALES
VICTORIA
AUSTRALIA
TASMANIA
A.C.T.
Canberra
Lake Eyre North
Lake Eyre South
Lake Torrens
Lake Frome
FLINDERS RANGE
Saint Mary Peak 1180
BARRIER RANGE
SNOWY MTS.
Mount Kosciusko 2228
Mount Bogong 1986
Bartle Frere 1622
Mount Kiangarow 1146
Mount Ossa 1617
Round Mountain 1583
GROOTE EYLANDT
WELLESLEY ISLANDS
MORNINGTON ISLAND
BENTINCK ISLAND
FRASER ISLAND
MORETON ISLAND
NORTH STRADBROKE ISLAND
KANGAROO ISLAND
KING ISLAND
FLINDERS ISLAND
FURNEAUX GROUP
CAPE BARREN ISLAND
HUNTER ISLAND
MARIA ISLAND
LORD HOWE ISLAND (N.S.W.)
BALLS PYRAMID (N.S.W.)
MIDDLETON REEF
ELIZABETH REEF
WILLIS GROUP (Austl.)
CHILCOTT ISLAND (Austl.)
DIAMOND ISLETS (Austl.)
TREGOSSE ISLETS (Austl.)
BIRD ISLET (Austl.)
CATO ISLAND
WRECK REEF
KENN REEF
SAUMAREZ REEF
MELLISH REEF
MARION REEF
ÎLES CHESTERFIELD (N. Cal.)
CAYE DE L'OBSERVATOIRE (N. Cal.)
ÎLE DE SABLE (N. Cal.)
OSPREY REEF
BOUGAINVILLE REEF
HOLMES REEF
FLINDERS REEFS
CAPRICORN GROUP
BUNKER GROUP
SWAIN REEFS
Cairns
Cooktown
Townsville
Mackay
Rockhampton
Gladstone
Bundaberg
Maryborough
Brisbane
Southport
Toowoomba
Ipswich
Mount Isa
Cloncurry
Longreach
Charleville
Roma
Bourke
Broken Hill
Wilcannia
Dubbo
Tamworth
Armidale
Grafton
Lismore
Coffs Harbour
Port Macquarie
Newcastle
Maitland
SYDNEY
Parramatta
Campbelltown
Wollongong
Bathurst
Orange
Goulburn
Queanbeyan
Wagga Wagga
Albury
Mildura
Bendigo
Ballarat
Geelong
MELBOURNE
Moe
Morwell
Warrnambool
Portland
Mount Gambier
Adelaide
Elizabeth
Port Augusta
Port Pirie
Whyalla
Port Lincoln
Launceston
Devonport
Burnie
Hobart
Queenstown
Oodnadatta
Birdsville
Innamincka
Tibooburra
135°
140°
145°
150°
155°
160°
165°
15°
20°
25°
30°
35°
40°

Kilometers 0 200 400 600 Km.
Statute Miles 0 200 400 600 Mi.

Scale 1:12,000,000

One centimeter represents 120 kilometers.
One inch represents approximately 190 miles.
Lambert Conformal Conic Projection

Western and Central Australia / West-und Mittelaustralien / Australia Centro-occidental
Australie Occidentale et Centrale / Austrália Ocidental e Central

INDIAN OCEAN
GREAT SANDY DESERT
GIBSON DESERT
LITTLE SANDY DESERT
WESTERN AUSTRALIA
Tropic of Capricorn
Lake Disappointment
Lake Carnegie
Lake Moore
Lake Barlee
Lake Way
Lake Dora
HAMERSLEY RANGE
CHICHESTER RANGE
KENNEDY RANGE
ROBINSON RANGE
DARLING RANGE
STIRLING RANGE
KING LEOPOLD
Broome
Derby
Port Hedland
Dampier
Karratha
Roebourne
Onslow
Exmouth
Carnarvon
Shark Bay
Denham
Kalbarri
Geraldton
Dongara
Meekatharra
Wiluna
Newman
Tom Price
Wittenoom
Mount Magnet
Cue
Leonora
Laverton
Menzies
Kalgoorlie
Boulder
Coolgardie
Norseman
Esperance
Ravensthorpe
Hopetoun
Albany
Denmark
Walpole
Pemberton
Manjimup
Bridgetown
Busselton
Margaret River
Bunbury
Collie
Harvey
Mandurah
Pinjarra
Rockingham
Kwinana
Fremantle
Perth
Stirling
Wanneroo
Northam
York
Merredin
Southern Cross
Narrogin
Katanning
Wagin
Kondinin
Hyden
ROTTNEST ISLAND
GARDEN ISLAND
HOUTMAN ABROLHOS
DIRK HARTOG ISLAND
BERNIER ISLAND
DORRE ISLAND
BARROW ISLAND
MONTE BELLO ISLANDS
DAMPIER ARCHIPELAGO
ROWLEY SHOALS
ARCHIPELAGO OF THE RECHERCHE
CAPE LEEUWIN
CAPE NATURALISTE
POINT D'ENTRECASTEAUX
NORTH WEST CAPE
EIGHTY MILE BEACH
RUDALL RIVER NATIONAL PARK
HAMERSLEY RANGE NATIONAL PARK
Meters / Feet
6000 19685
4000 13124
3000 9843
2000 6562
1000 3281
500 1640
200 656
0 0
Land Below Sea Level
0 0
200 656
1000 3281
3000 9843
6000 19685
9000 29520

ENGLISH	bay	cape	creek, cr.	island, i.	lake, l.	mount	point	range
DEUTSCH	Bucht	Kap	Bach	Insel	See	Berg	Landspitze	Gebirge
ESPAÑOL	bahía	cabo	riachuelo	isla	lago	montaña	punta	cordillera
FRANÇAIS	baie	cap	crique	île	lac	mont	pointe	chaîne
PORTUGUÊS	baía	cabo	riacho	ilha	lago	monte	ponta	cordilheira

Map continues pages 164-165

NORTHERN TERRITORY
SOUTH AUSTRALIA
QUEENSLAND
NEW SOUTH WALES
VICTORIA
TANAMI DESERT
SIMPSON DESERT
VICTORIA DESERT
NULLARBOR PLAIN
BARKLY TABLELAND
CHANNEL COUNTRY
Great Australian Bight
Gulf of Carpentaria
Spencer Gulf
Gulf St Vincent
Lake Eyre North
Lake Amadeus
Lake Mackay
Lake Torrens
Lake Gairdner
Lake Frome
MACDONNELL RANGES
MUSGRAVE RANGES
FLINDERS RANGES
GAWLER RANGES
PETERMANN RANGES
EYRE PENINSULA
YORKE PENINSULA
WOOMERA PROHIBITED AREA
Alice Springs
Tennant Creek
Mount Isa
Broken Hill
Port Augusta
Whyalla
Port Pirie
Port Lincoln
Adelaide
Ceduna
Coober Pedy
Oodnadatta
Woomera
Eucla
Birdsville
Boulia
Camooweal
Halls Creek
Uluru Nat. Park
Ayers Rock 867
Mount Olga 1069
Burketown
Cloncurry
Mildura

Map continues pages 166-167

Kilometers 0 100 200 300 Km.
Statute Miles 0 100 200 300 Mi.

Scale 1:6,000,000
One centimeter represents 60 kilometers.
One inch represents approximately 95 miles.
Lambert Conformal Conic Projection

Map continues pages 112-113

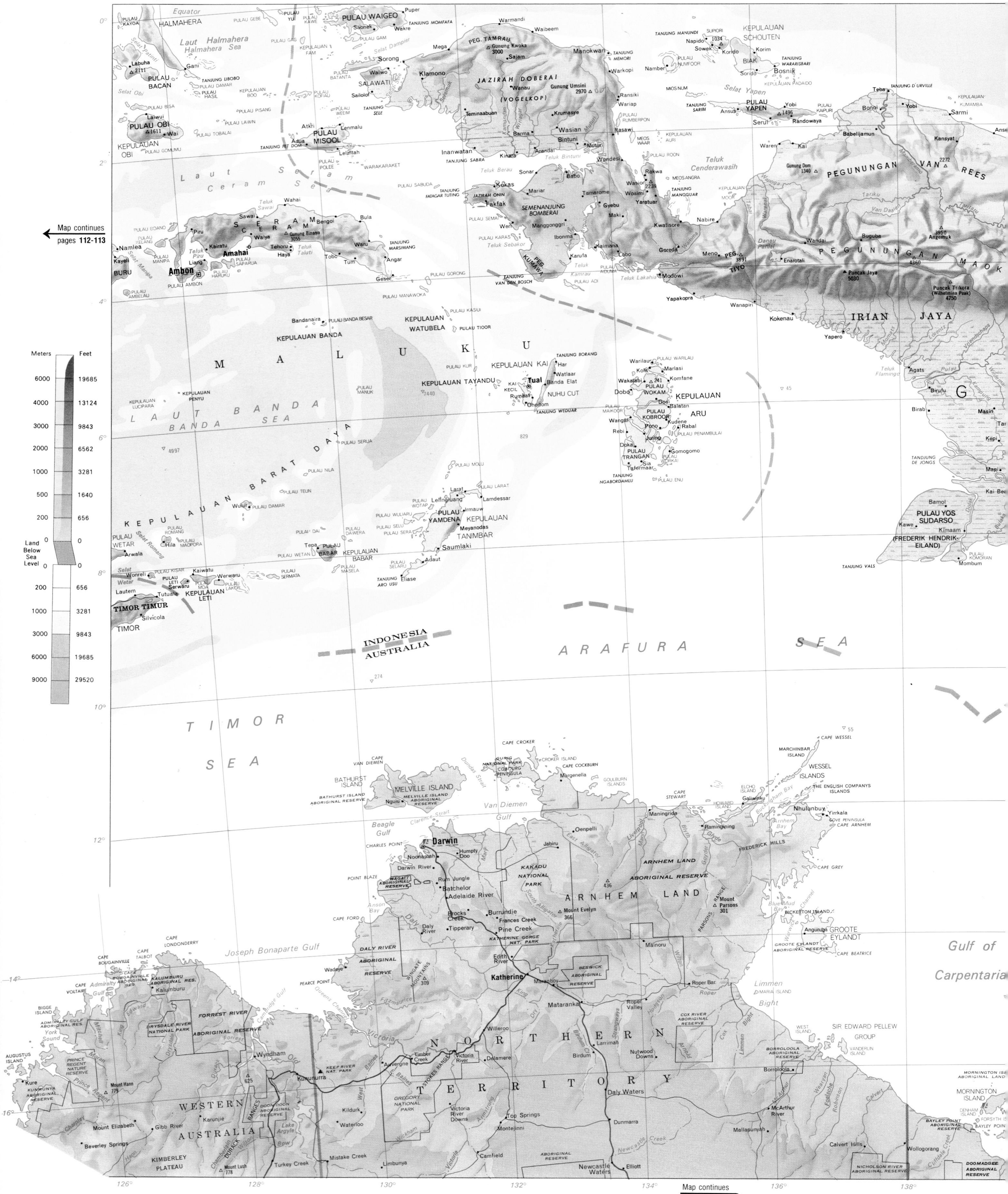
Meters
Feet
6000
19685
4000
13124
3000
9843
2000
6562
1000
3281
500
1640
200
656
0
0
Land Below Sea Level
0
0
200
656
1000
3281
3000
9843
6000
19685
9000
29520
128°
130°
132°
134°
136°
138°
126°
Equator
HALMAHERA
Laut Halmahera
Halmahera Sea
PULAU WAIGEO
PULAU BACAN
PULAU OBI
KEPULAUAN OBI
PULAU MISOOL
Sorong
SALAWATI
JAZIRAH DOBERAI
(VOGELKOP)
Manokwari
KEPULAUAN SCHOUTEN
BIAK
PULAU YAPEN
Teluk Cenderawasih
PEGUNUNGAN VAN REES
Laut Seram
Ceram Sea
SERAM
Gunung Binaiya 3055
Ambon
Amahai
BURU
Fakfak
SEMENANJUNG BOMBERAI
PEGUNUNGAN MAOKE
Puncak Jaya 5030
Puncak Trikora (Wilhelmina Peak) 4750
IRIAN JAYA
MALUKU
KEPULAUAN BANDA
KEPULAUAN WATUBELA
KEPULAUAN KAI
Tual
KEPULAUAN TAYANDU
LAUT BANDA
BANDA SEA
KEPULAUAN ARU
KEPULAUAN BARAT DAYA
PULAU YAMDENA
KEPULAUAN TANIMBAR
Saumlaki
PULAU WETAR
KEPULAUAN BABAR
KEPULAUAN LETI
TIMOR TIMUR
TIMOR
PULAU YOS SUDARSO
(FREDERIK HENDRIK EILAND)
Merauke
INDONESIA
AUSTRALIA
ARAFURA SEA
TIMOR SEA
BATHURST ISLAND
MELVILLE ISLAND
Van Diemen Gulf
Beagle Gulf
Darwin
WESSEL ISLANDS
Nhulunbuy
CAPE ARNHEM
ARNHEM LAND
ABORIGINAL RESERVE
KAKADU NATIONAL PARK
GROOTE EYLANDT
Gulf of Carpentaria
Joseph Bonaparte Gulf
Katherine
Mataranka
Roper Bar
SIR EDWARD PELLEW GROUP
NORTHERN TERRITORY
Daly Waters
Borroloola
Wyndham
Kununurra
WESTERN AUSTRALIA
KIMBERLEY PLATEAU
Newcastle Waters
Elliott
MORNINGTON ISLAND

Map continues pages 162-163

MAP FORM	bay	cape	island	kepulauan	mount	pulau	range	tanjung
ENGLISH	bay	cape	island	islands	mount	island	range	cape
DEUTSCH	Bucht	Kap	Insel	Inseln	Berg	Insel	Gebirge	Kap
ESPAÑOL	bahía	cabo	isla	islas	montaña	isla	cordillera	cabo
FRANÇAIS	baie	cap	île	îles	mont	île	chaîne	cap
PORTUGUÊS	baía	cabo	ilha	ilhas	monte	ilha	cordilheira	cabo

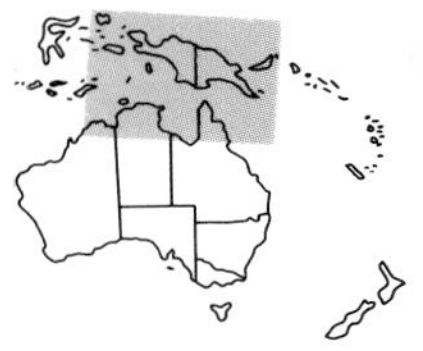

PACIFIC OCEAN
BISMARCK ARCHIPELAGO
BISMARCK SEA
SOLOMON SEA
CORAL SEA
Gulf of Papua
Torres Strait
INDONESIA
PAPUA NEW GUINEA
AUSTRALIA
MANUS
NEW IRELAND
WEST NEW BRITAIN
EAST NEW BRITAIN
WEST SEPIK
EAST SEPIK
MADANG
ENGA
WESTERN HIGHLANDS
SOUTHERN HIGHLANDS
EASTERN HIGHLANDS
CHIMBU
GULF
WESTERN
MOROBE
NORTHERN
CENTRAL
MILNE BAY
CAPE YORK PENINSULA
QUEENSLAND
GREAT DIVIDING RANGE
GREAT BARRIER REEF
GREAT BARRIER REEF MARINE PARK
CORAL SEA ISLANDS TERRITORY
Jayapura (Sukarnapura)
Wewak
Madang
Lae
Rabaul
Port Moresby
Cairns
Equator
Copyright © by Rand McNally & Co.
Map prepared by George Philip & Son Ltd., London.
A-593000-764

Map continues pages 166-167

Kilometers 0 100 200 300 Km.
Statute Miles 0 100 200 300 Mi.

Scale 1:6,000,000

One centimeter represents 60 kilometers.
One inch represents approximately 95 miles.
Lambert Conformal Conic Projection

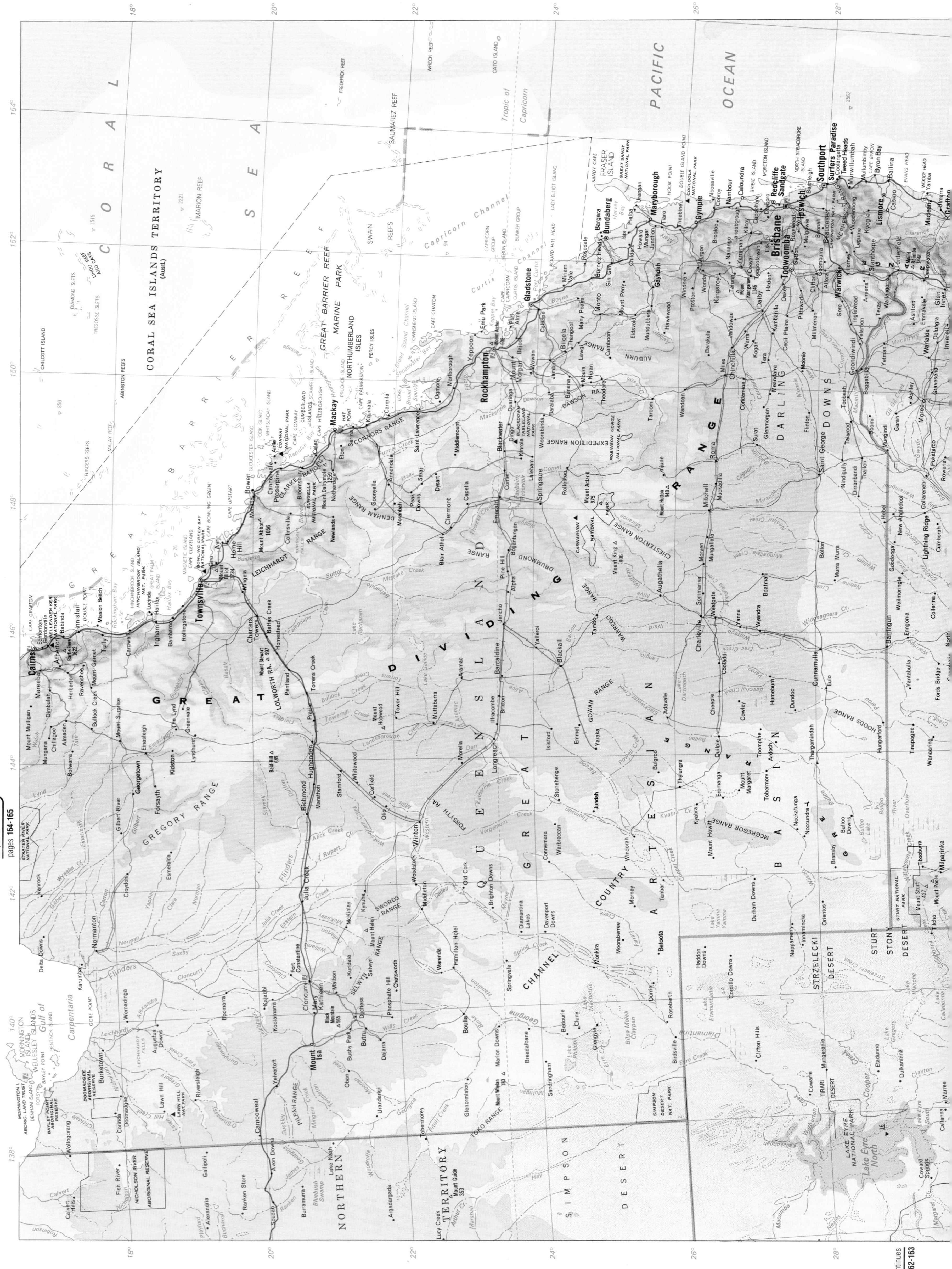
CORAL SEA
CORAL SEA ISLANDS TERRITORY (Austl.)
PACIFIC OCEAN
GREAT BARRIER REEF
GREAT BARRIER REEF MARINE PARK
Tropic of Capricorn
GREAT DIVIDING RANGE
GREAT ARTESIAN BASIN
QUEENSLAND
NORTHERN TERRITORY
SIMPSON DESERT
STRZELECKI DESERT
STURT STONY DESERT
DARLING DOWNS
CHANNEL COUNTRY
GREGORY RANGE
Gulf of Carpentaria
Brisbane
Townsville
Cairns
Rockhampton
Mackay
Gladstone
Bundaberg
Toowoomba
Mount Isa
Longreach
Charleville
Roma

Map continues pages 164-165

Map continues pages 162-163

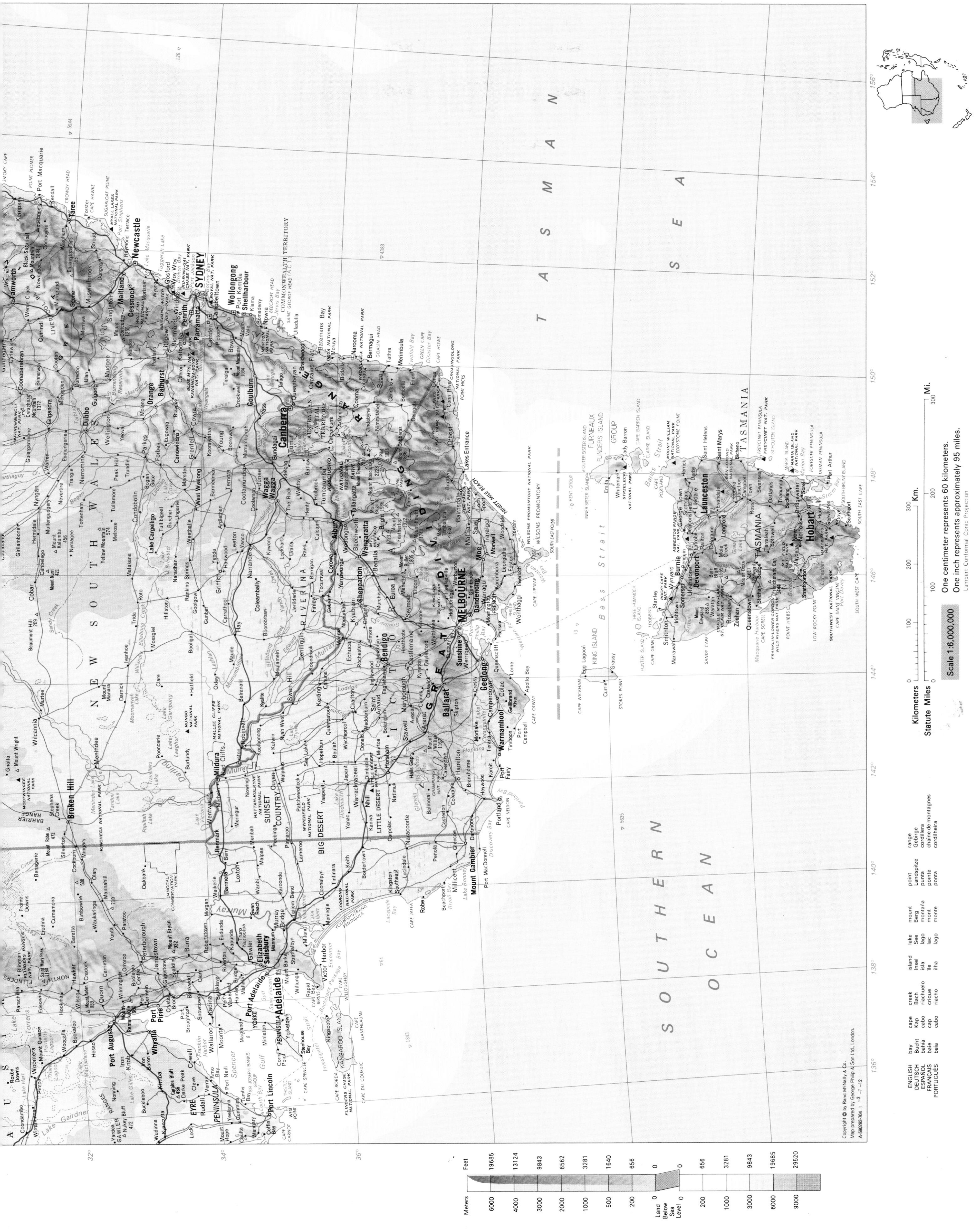
NEW SOUTH WALES
VICTORIA
TASMANIA
SOUTH AUSTRALIA
TASMAN SEA
SOUTHERN OCEAN
GREAT DIVIDING RANGE
Bass Strait
SYDNEY
MELBOURNE
Canberra
Adelaide
Hobart
Newcastle
Wollongong
Geelong
Ballarat
Bendigo
Launceston
Broken Hill
Mildura
Wagga Wagga
Albury
Port Augusta
Whyalla
Port Lincoln
Mount Gambier
Dubbo
Tamworth
Port Macquarie
KANGAROO ISLAND
KING ISLAND
FLINDERS ISLAND
FURNEAUX GROUP
WILSONS PROMONTORY
EYRE PENINSULA
YORKE PENINSULA
AUSTRALIAN CAPITAL TERRITORY
COMMONWEALTH TERRITORY
RIVERINA
Murray
Darling
Kilometers 0 100 200 300 Km.
Statute Miles 0 100 200 300 Mi.
Scale 1:6,000,000
One centimeter represents 60 kilometers.
One inch represents approximately 95 miles.
Lambert Conformal Conic Projection
ENGLISH bay cape creek island lake mount point range
DEUTSCH Bucht Kap Bach Insel See Berg Landspitze Gebirge
ESPAÑOL bahía cabo riachuelo isla lago montaña punta cordillera
FRANÇAIS baie cap crique île lac mont pointe chaîne de montagnes
PORTUGUÊS baía cabo riacho ilha lago monte ponta cordilheira
Meters 6000 4000 3000 2000 1000 500 200 0 Land Below Sea Level 0 200 1000 3000 6000 9000
Feet 19685 13124 9843 6562 3281 1640 656 0 0 656 3281 9843 19685 29520

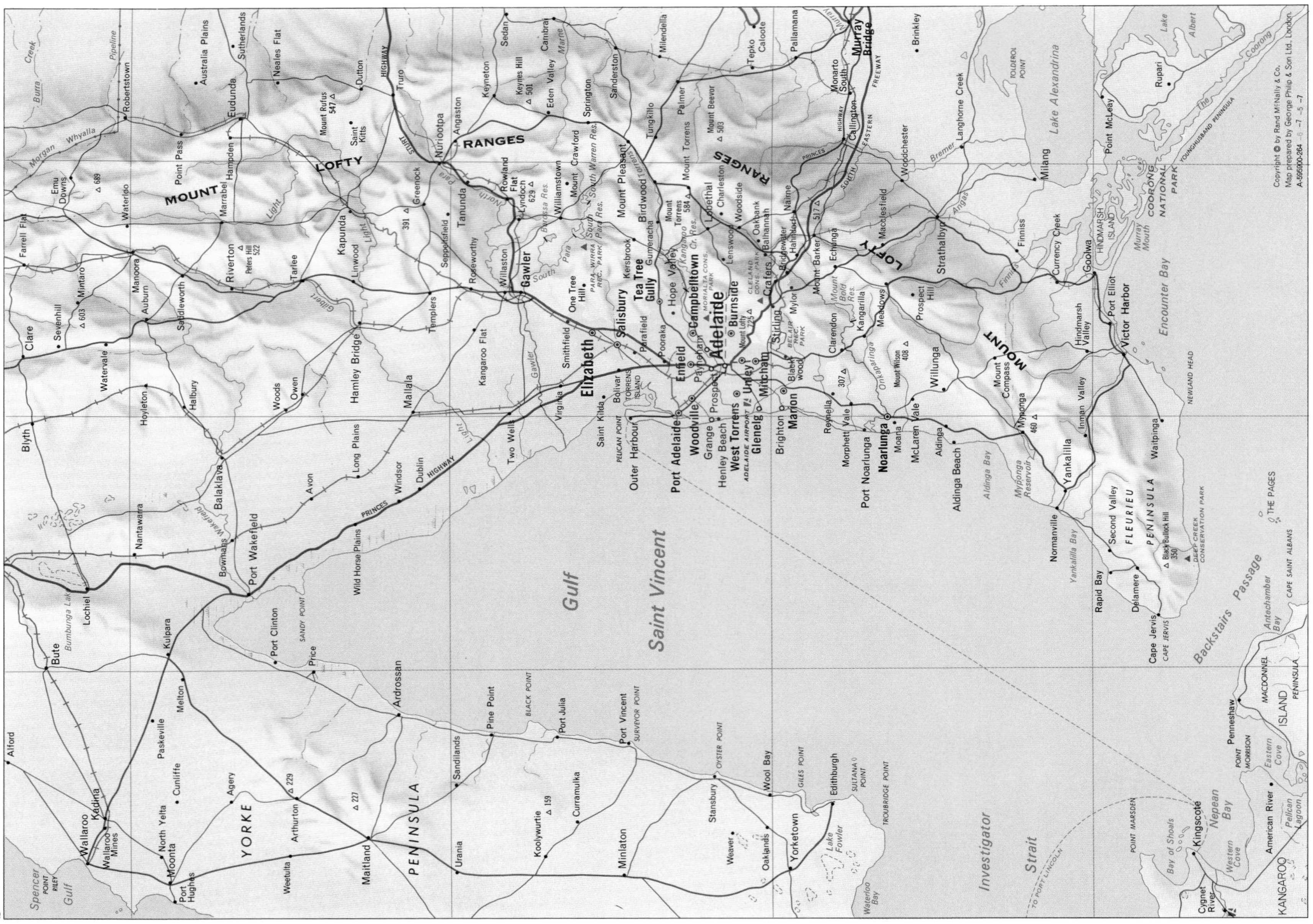
b
Gulf Saint Vincent
Investigator Strait
Spencer Gulf
Backstairs Passage
Encounter Bay
Lake Alexandrina
YORKE PENINSULA
FLEURIEU PENINSULA
MOUNT LOFTY RANGES
KANGAROO ISLAND
Adelaide
Port Adelaide
Elizabeth
Salisbury
Gawler
Glenelg
Noarlunga
Murray Bridge
Victor Harbor
Kingscote
Port Wakefield
Moonta
Wallaroo
Kadina
Maitland
Yorketown
Edithburgh
Ardrossan
Copyright © by Rand McNally & Co.

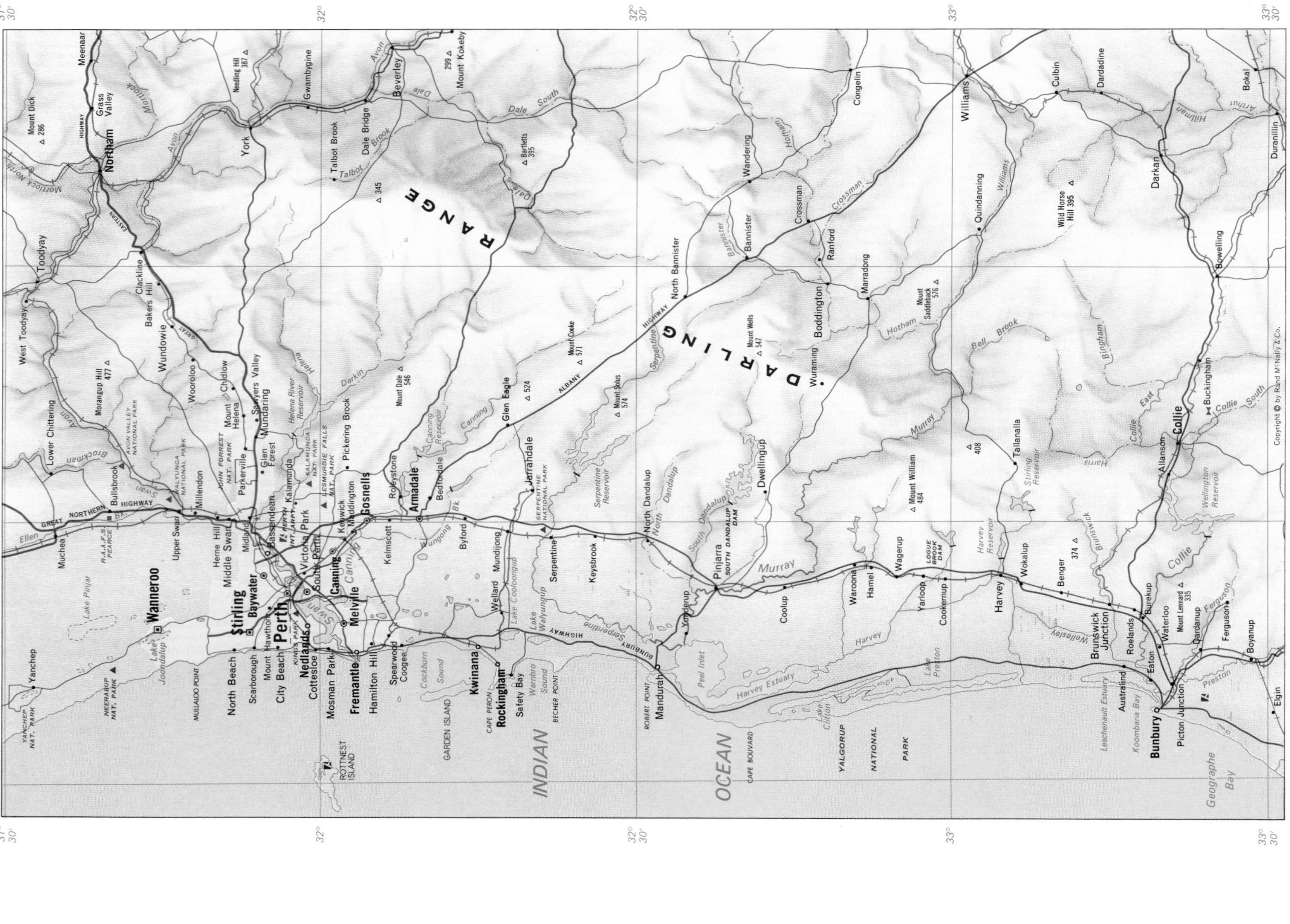
a
INDIAN OCEAN
DARLING RANGE
Perth
Fremantle
Stirling
Wanneroo
Kwinana
Rockingham
Mandurah
Pinjarra
Armadale
Gosnells
Northam
York
Toodyay
Bunbury
Collie
Harvey
Williams
Geographe Bay
Peel Inlet
Copyright © by Rand McNally & Co.

Kilometers 0 10 20 30 40 50 Km.

Statute Miles 0 10 20 30 40 50 Mi.

Scale 1:1,000,000

One centimeter represents 10 kilometers.
One inch represents approximately 16 miles.

Lambert Conformal Conic Projection

ENGLISH:	bay, b.	cape	dam	gulf	island	lake, l.	peninsula	point
DEUTSCH	Bucht	Kap	Damm	Golf	Insel	See	Halbinsel	Landspitze
ESPAÑOL	bahía	cabo	diques	golfo	isla	lago	península	punta
FRANÇAIS	baie	cap	barrage	golfe	île	lac	péninsule	pointe
PORTUGUÊS	baía	cabo	barragem	golfo	ilha	lago	península	ponta

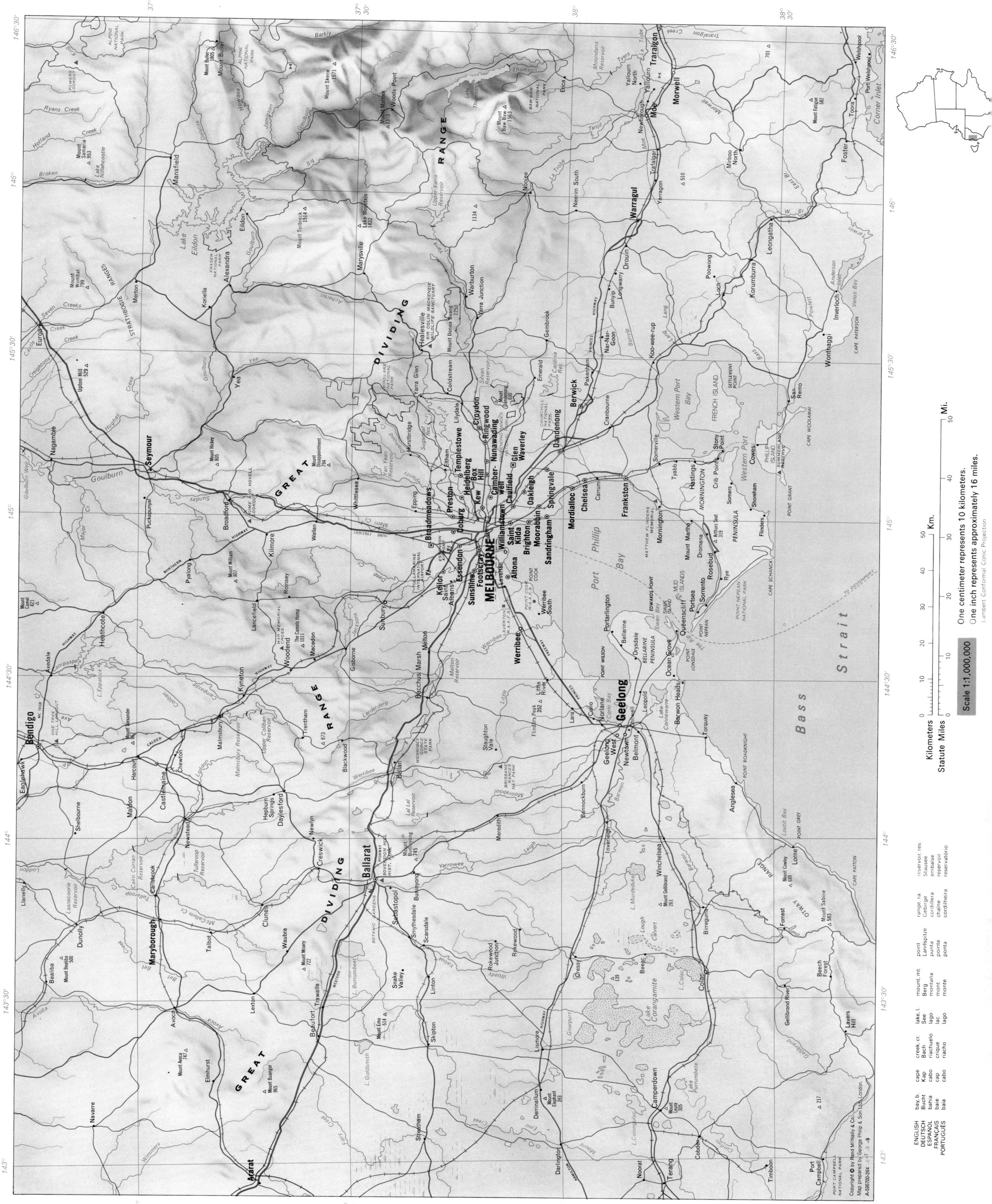
MELBOURNE
Geelong
Ballarat
Bendigo
Seymour
Warragul
Traralgon
Morwell
Moe
Frankston
Dandenong
Werribee
Colac
Camperdown
Ararat
Maryborough
Castlemaine
Port Phillip Bay
Bass Strait
GREAT DIVIDING RANGE
MORNINGTON PENINSULA
BELLARINE PENINSULA
FRENCH ISLAND
PHILLIP ISLAND
Western Port
Lake Eildon
Lake Corangamite
Kilometers 0 10 20 30 40 50 Km.
Statute Miles 0 10 20 30 40 50 Mi.
Scale 1:1,000,000
One centimeter represents 10 kilometers.
One inch represents approximately 16 miles.
Lambert Conformal Conic Projection
ENGLISH bay, b. cape creek, cr. lake, l. mount, mt. point range, ra. reservoir res.
DEUTSCH Bucht Kap Bach See Berg Landspitze Gebirge Stausee
ESPAÑOL bahía cabo riachuelo lago monte punta cordillera embalse
FRANÇAIS baie cap crique lac mont pointe chaîne réservoir
PORTUGUÊS baía cabo riacho lago monte ponta cordilheira reservatório
Copyright © by Rand McNally & Co.
Map prepared by George Philip & Son Ltd., London.

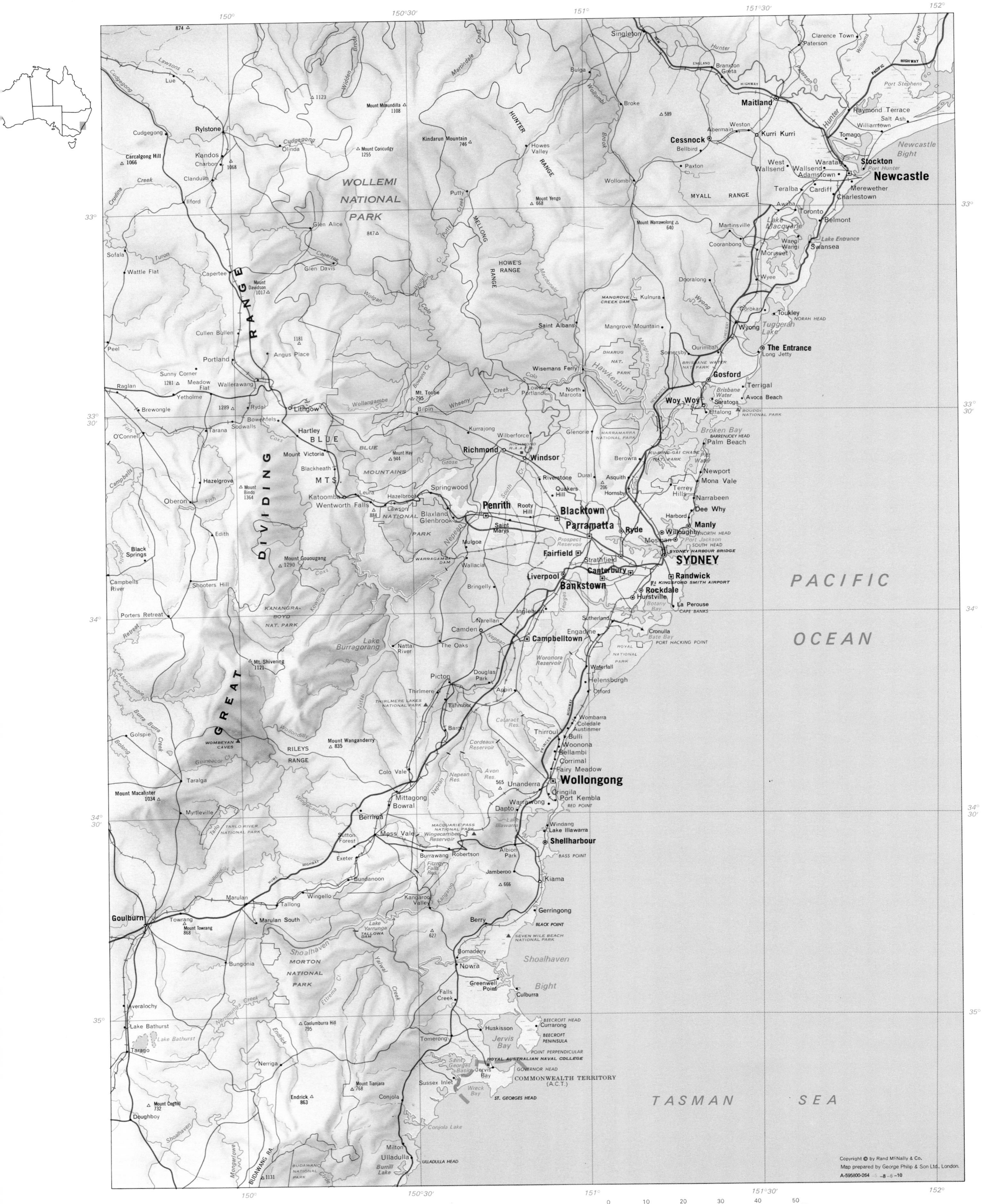

PACIFIC
OCEAN
TASMAN SEA
SYDNEY
Newcastle
Wollongong
Parramatta
Blacktown
Bankstown
Penrith
Liverpool
Campbelltown
Gosford
Maitland
Cessnock
Goulburn
Nowra
Singleton
Lithgow
Katoomba
Richmond
Windsor
Manly
Randwick
Rockdale
Ryde
Shellharbour
Kiama
The Entrance
Stockton
WOLLEMI NATIONAL PARK
GREAT DIVIDING RANGE
BLUE MTS.
BLUE MOUNTAINS NATIONAL PARK
HUNTER RANGE
MELLONG RANGE
HOWE'S RANGE
MYALL RANGE
RILEYS RANGE
KANANGRA-BOYD NAT. PARK
MORTON NATIONAL PARK
ROYAL NATIONAL PARK
Lake Burragorang
Lake Macquarie
Tuggerah Lake
Broken Bay
Botany Bay
Port Jackson
Jervis Bay
Shoalhaven Bight
Newcastle Bight
Port Stephens
Hawkesbury
Hunter
Nepean
Shoalhaven
SYDNEY HARBOUR BRIDGE
KINGSFORD SMITH AIRPORT
ROYAL AUSTRALIAN NAVAL COLLEGE
COMMONWEALTH TERRITORY (A.C.T.)
150°
150°30'
151°
151°30'
152°
33°
33° 30'
34°
34° 30'
35°
Copyright © by Rand McNally & Co.
Map prepared by George Philip & Son Ltd., London.

ENGLISH	bight	creek, cr.	head	mount	range	reservoir, res.
DEUTSCH	Bucht	Bach	Vorgebirge	Berg	Gebirge	Stausee
ESPAÑOL	ensenada pequeña	riachuelo	promontorio	montaña	cordillera	estanque
FRANÇAIS	anse	crique	promontoire	mont	chaîne	réservoir
PORTUGUÊS	enseada	riacho	promontório	monte	cordilheira	reservatório

Kilometers 0 10 20 30 40 50 Km.

Statute Miles 0 10 20 30 40 50 Mi.

Scale 1:1,000,000

One centimeter represents 10 kilometers.

One inch represents approximately 16 miles.

Lambert Conformal Conic Projection

a

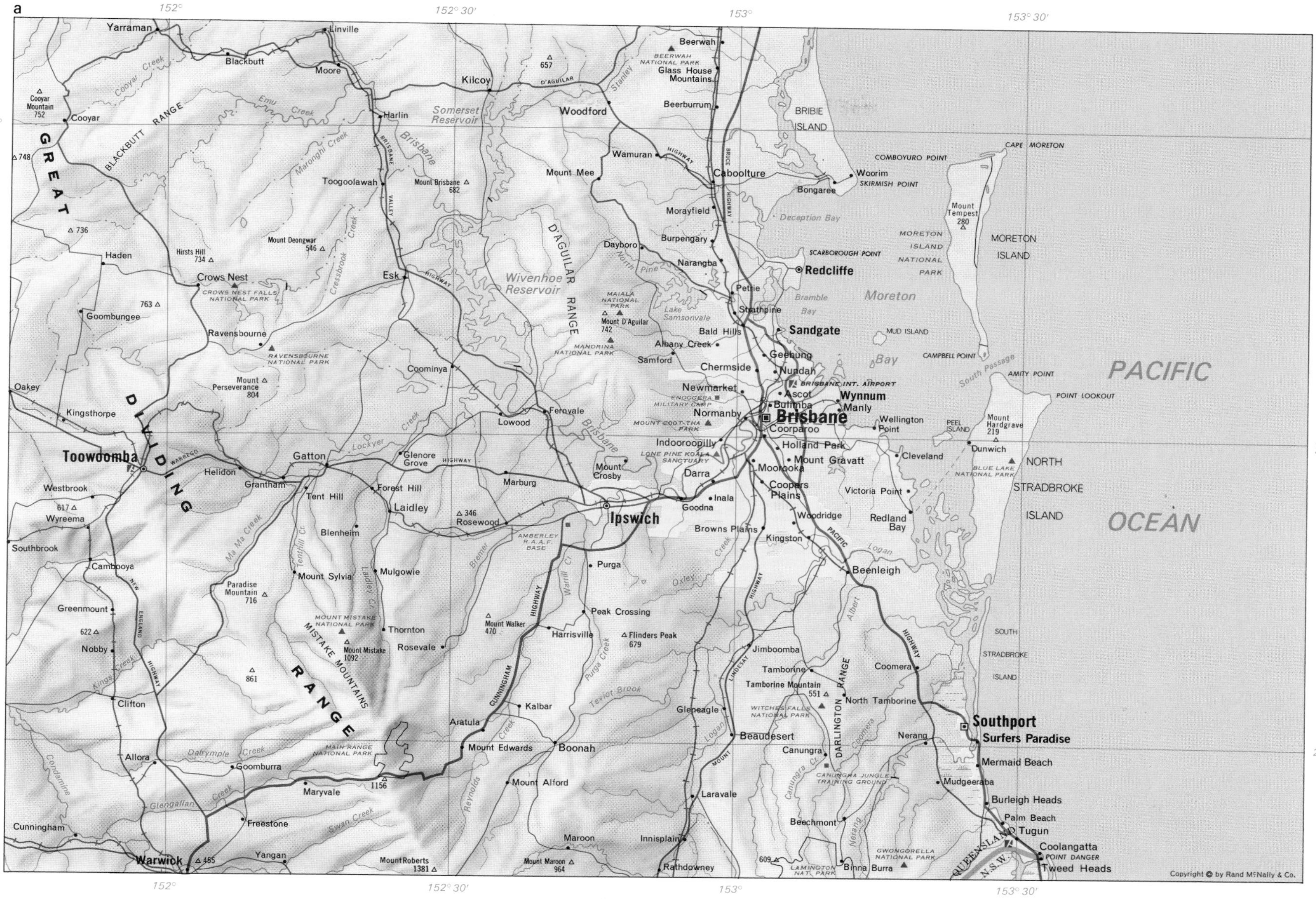
PACIFIC
OCEAN
Brisbane
Ipswich
Toowoomba
Redcliffe
Sandgate
Wynnum
Manly
Southport
Surfers Paradise
Warwick
Gatton
Esk
Kilcoy
Woodford
Caboolture
Beenleigh
Beaudesert
Boonah
Laidley
Coolangatta
Tweed Heads
Burleigh Heads
Palm Beach
Tugun
Mermaid Beach
Cleveland
Dunwich
Redland Bay
MORETON ISLAND
NORTH STRADBROKE ISLAND
SOUTH STRADBROKE ISLAND
BRIBIE ISLAND
Moreton Bay
GREAT DIVIDING RANGE
MISTAKE MOUNTAINS
D'AGUILAR RANGE
DARLINGTON RANGE
BLACKBUTT RANGE
QUEENSLAND
N.S.W.
Copyright © by Rand McNally & Co.

b

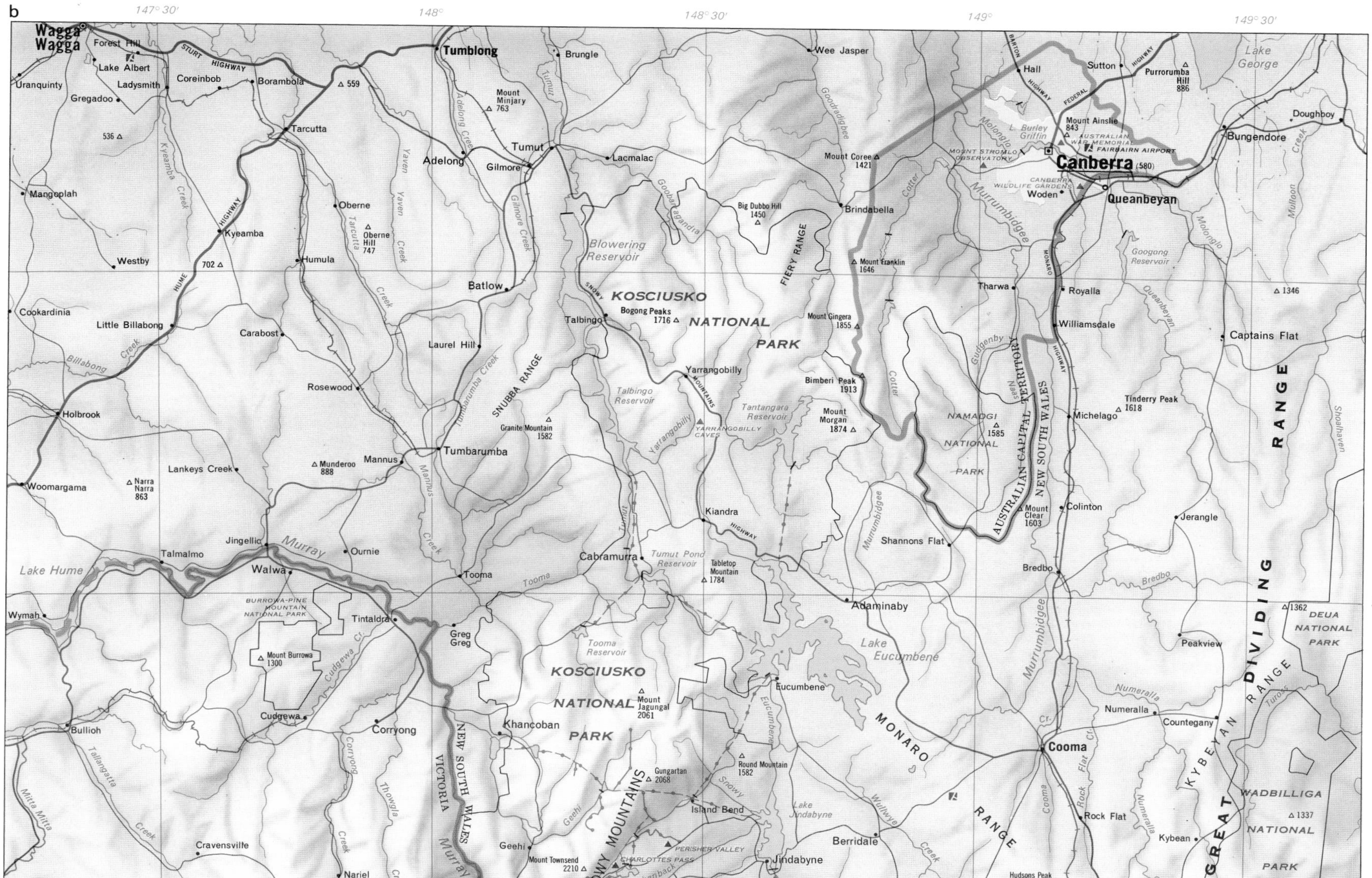
Wagga Wagga
Canberra
Queanbeyan
Tumut
Tumbarumba
Cooma
Jindabyne
Adaminaby
Holbrook
Tarcutta
Tumblong
Batlow
Adelong
Corryong
Khancoban
Thredbo Village
Berridale
Captains Flat
Bungendore
Michelago
Bredbo
KOSCIUSKO NATIONAL PARK
SNOWY MOUNTAINS
AUSTRALIAN CAPITAL TERRITORY
NEW SOUTH WALES
VICTORIA
MONARO RANGE
GREAT DIVIDING RANGE
Lake Eucumbene
Lake Hume
Murray
Murrumbidgee
Mount Kosciusko 2228
Copyright © by Rand McNally & Co.
Map prepared by George Philip & Son Ltd., London.

ENGLISH	creek	island	mount	peak	point	range	reservoir
DEUTSCH	Bach	Insel	Berg	Gipfel	Landspitze	Gebirge	Stausee
ESPAÑOL	riachuelo	isla	montaña	pico	punta	cordillera	embalse
FRANÇAIS	crique	île	mont	cime	pointe	chaîne	réservoir
PORTUGUÊS	riacho	ilha	monte	pico	ponta	cordilheira	reservatório

Kilometers 0 10 20 30 40 50 Km.
Statute Miles 0 10 20 30 40 50 Mi.

Scale 1:1,000,000

One centimeter represents 10 kilometers.
One inch represents approximately 16 miles.
Lambert Conformal Conic Projection

New Zealand / Neuseeland / Nueva Zelanda
Nouvelle Zélande / Nova Zelândia

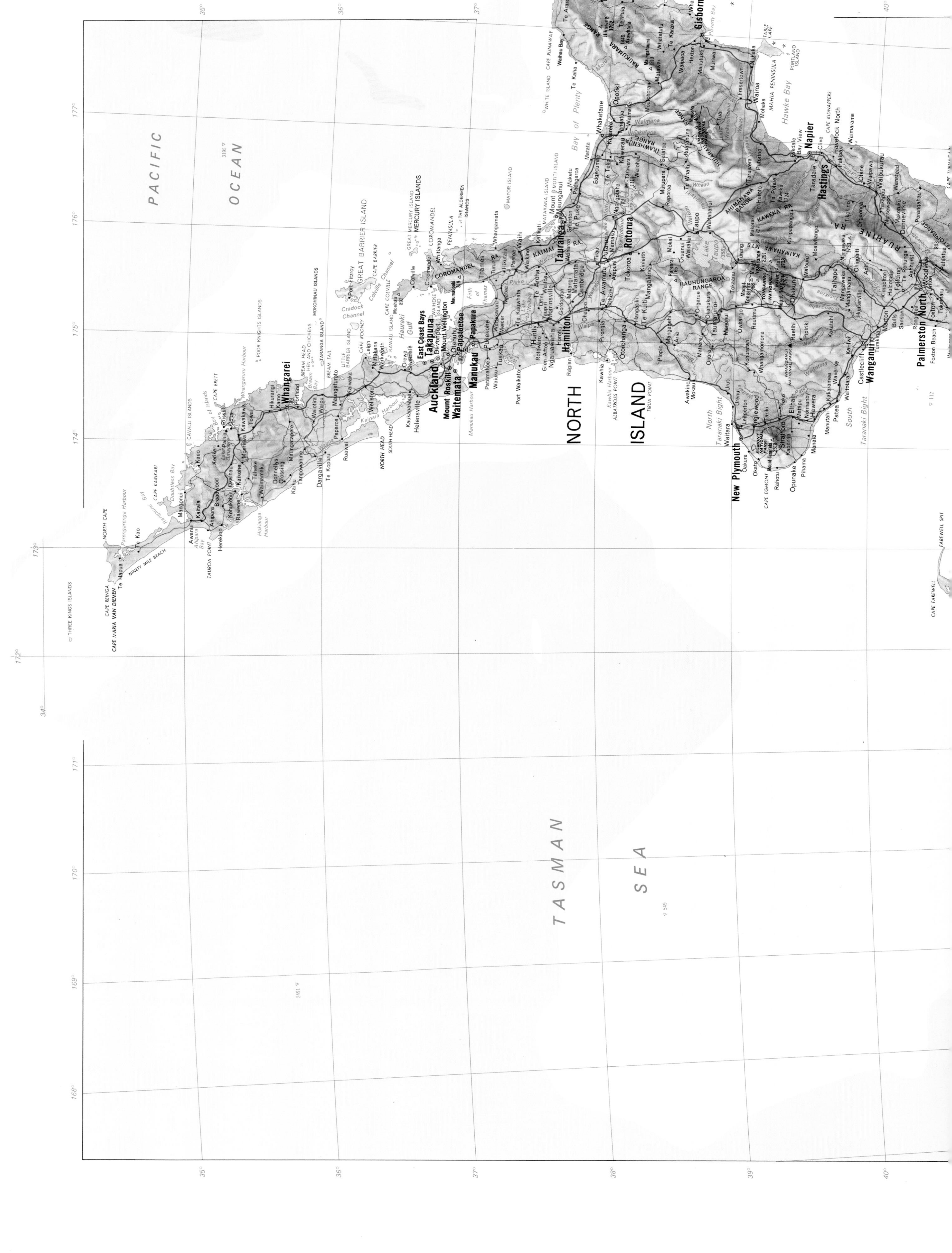
PACIFIC
OCEAN
TASMAN
SEA
NORTH
ISLAND
Bay of Plenty
Hawke Bay
Auckland
Manukau
Hamilton
Tauranga
Rotorua
Taupo
Gisborne
Napier
Hastings
Whangarei
New Plymouth
Wanganui
Palmerston North
Dargaville
CAPE REINGA
NORTH CAPE
THREE KINGS ISLANDS
GREAT BARRIER ISLAND
MERCURY ISLANDS
COROMANDEL PENINSULA
MAHIA PENINSULA
CAPE EGMONT
EAST CAPE
Taranaki Bight
Kaipara Harbour
Hokianga Harbour
Ninety Mile Beach
Hauraki Gulf
Firth of Thames
CAPE FAREWELL
FAREWELL SPIT

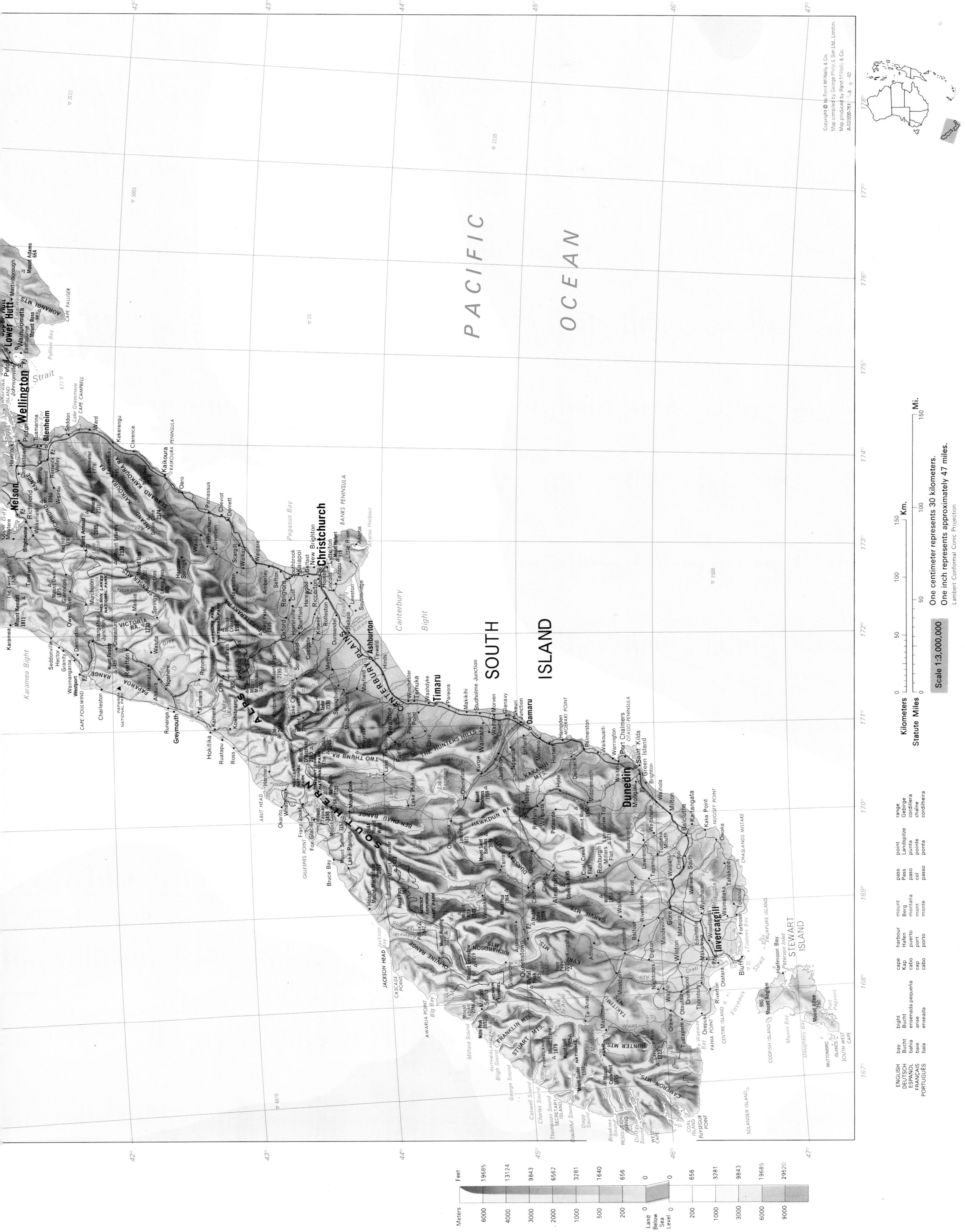
PACIFIC OCEAN
SOUTH ISLAND
STEWART ISLAND
Canterbury Bight
Pegasus Bay
Karamea Bight
Foveaux Strait
Cook Strait
SOUTHERN ALPS
CANTERBURY PLAINS
BANKS PENINSULA
OTAGO PENINSULA
KAIKOURA PENINSULA
Wellington
Lower Hutt
Nelson
Blenheim
Christchurch
Timaru
Ashburton
Oamaru
Dunedin
Invercargill
Greymouth
Westport
Queenstown
Scale 1:3,000,000
Kilometers
Statute Miles
0 50 100 150 Km.
0 50 100 150 Mi.
One centimeter represents 30 kilometers.
One inch represents approximately 47 miles.
Lambert Conformal Conic Projection
ENGLISH bay bight cape harbour mount pass point range
DEUTSCH Bucht Bucht Kap Hafen Berg Pass Landspitze Gebirge
ESPAÑOL bahía ensenada pequeña cabo puerto montaña paso punta cordillera
FRANÇAIS baie anse cap port mont col pointe chaîne
PORTUGUÊS baía enseada cabo porto monte passo ponta cordilheira
Feet 19685 13124 9843 6562 3281 1640 656 0 0 656 3281 9843 19685 29520
Meters 6000 4000 3000 2000 1000 500 200 0 Land Below Sea Level 0 200 1000 3000 6000 9000

a 166°35′ 166°40′ 19° 20′ 19° 15′

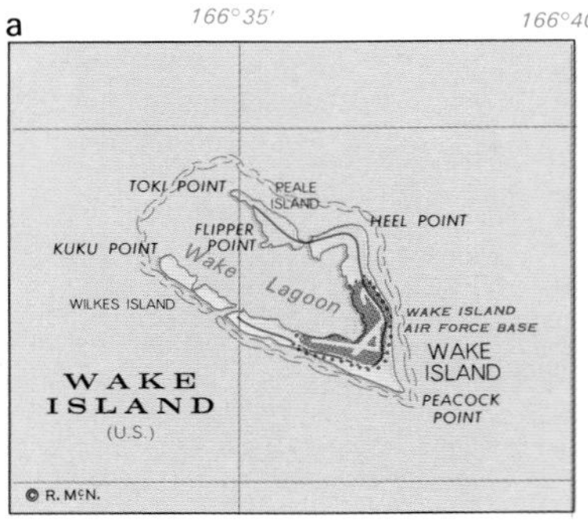
TOKI POINT
PEALE ISLAND
HEEL POINT
FLIPPER POINT
KUKU POINT
Wake Lagoon
WILKES ISLAND
WAKE ISLAND AIR FORCE BASE
WAKE ISLAND
WAKE ISLAND
(U.S.)
PEACOCK POINT
© R. McN.

b 166°55′ 0° 30′

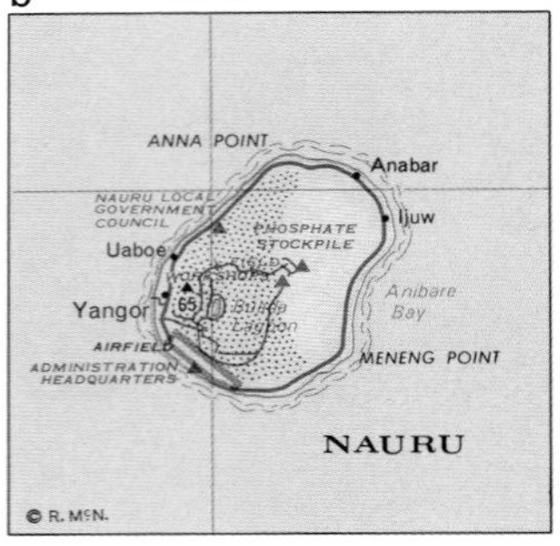
ANNA POINT
Anabar
Ijuw
NAURU LOCAL GOVERNMENT COUNCIL
PHOSPHATE STOCKPILE
Uaboe
Yangor
Anibare Bay
AIRFIELD
ADMINISTRATION HEADQUARTERS
MENENG POINT
NAURU
© R. McN.

c 167°55′ 168° 29° 29° 5′

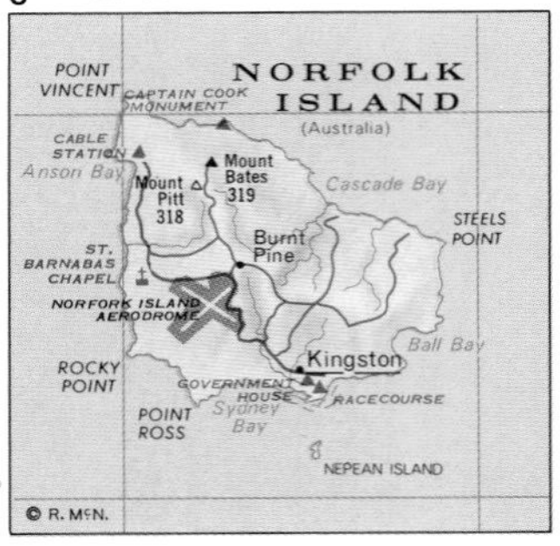
POINT VINCENT
CAPTAIN COOK MONUMENT
NORFOLK ISLAND
(Australia)
CABLE STATION
Anson Bay
Mount Pitt 318
Mount Bates 319
Cascade Bay
ST. BARNABAS CHAPEL
Burnt Pine
STEELS POINT
NORFOLK ISLAND AERODROME
Ball Bay
ROCKY POINT
Kingston
GOVERNMENT HOUSE
RACECOURSE
POINT ROSS
Sydney Bay
NEPEAN ISLAND
© R. McN.

d 169°35′ 0° 50′ 0° 55′

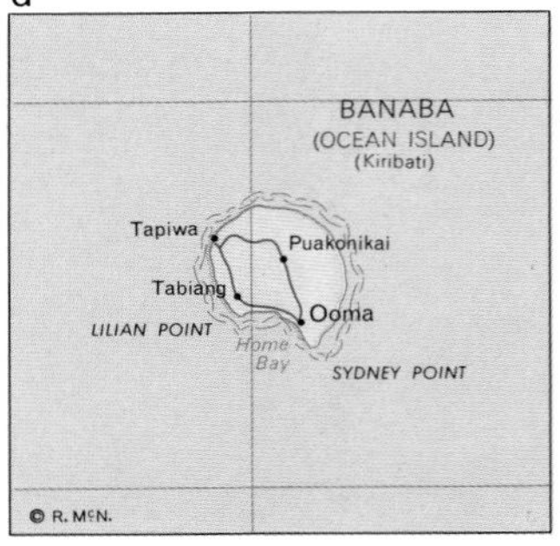
BANABA
(OCEAN ISLAND)
(Kiribati)
Tapiwa
Puakonikai
Tabiang
Ooma
LILIAN POINT
Home Bay
SYDNEY POINT
© R. McN.

e 130°5′

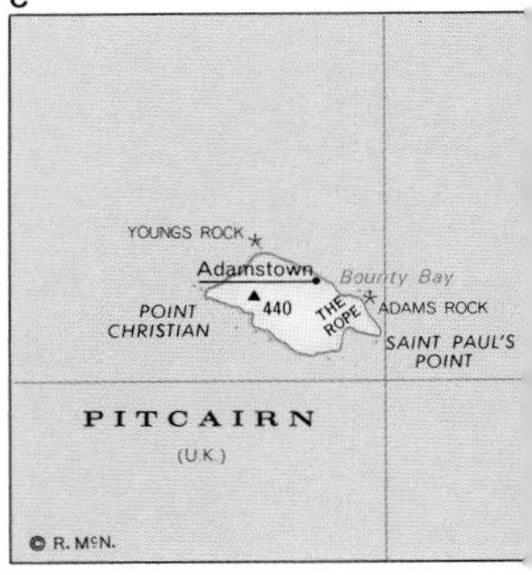
YOUNGS ROCK
Adamstown
Bounty Bay
POINT CHRISTIAN
440
THE HOPE
ADAMS ROCK
SAINT PAUL'S POINT
PITCAIRN
(U.K.)
© R. McN.

f 24° 50′ 24° 45′

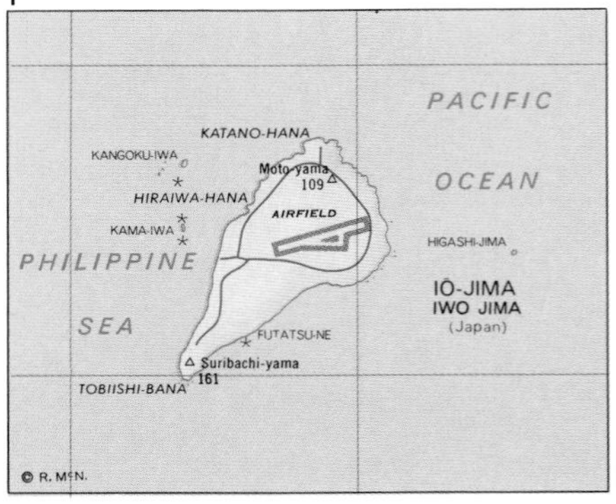
PACIFIC
OCEAN
KATANO-HANA
KANGOKU-IWA
Moto-yama 109
HIRAIWA-HANA
AIRFIELD
KAMA-IWA
HIGASHI-JIMA
PHILIPPINE
SEA
IŌ-JIMA
IWO JIMA
(Japan)
FUTATSU-NE
Suribachi-yama 161
TOBIISHI-BANA
© R. McN.

g 28° 15′ 28° 10′

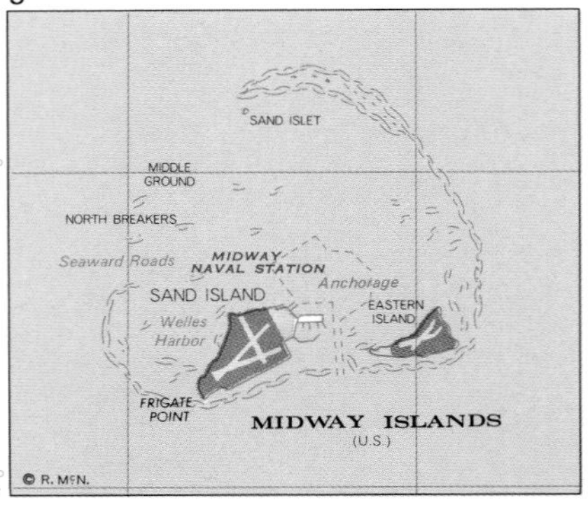
SAND ISLET
MIDDLE GROUND
NORTH BREAKERS
Seaward Roads
MIDWAY NAVAL STATION
Anchorage
SAND ISLAND
Welles Harbor
EASTERN ISLAND
FRIGATE POINT
MIDWAY ISLANDS
(U.S.)
© R. McN.

h 2° 50′

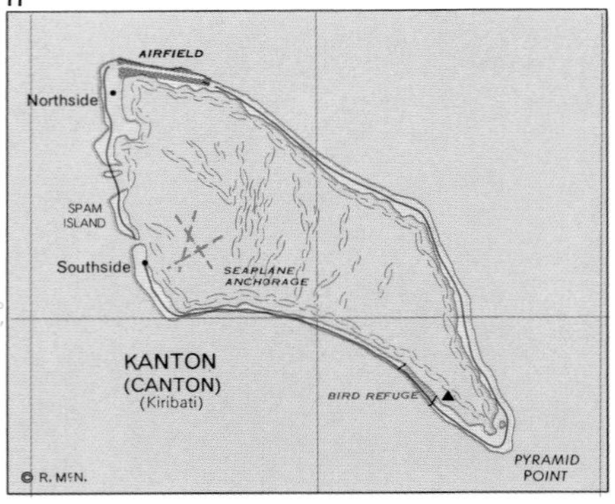
AIRFIELD
Northside
SPAM ISLAND
Southside
SEAPLANE ANCHORAGE
KANTON
(CANTON)
(Kiribati)
BIRD REFUGE
PYRAMID POINT
© R. McN.

k

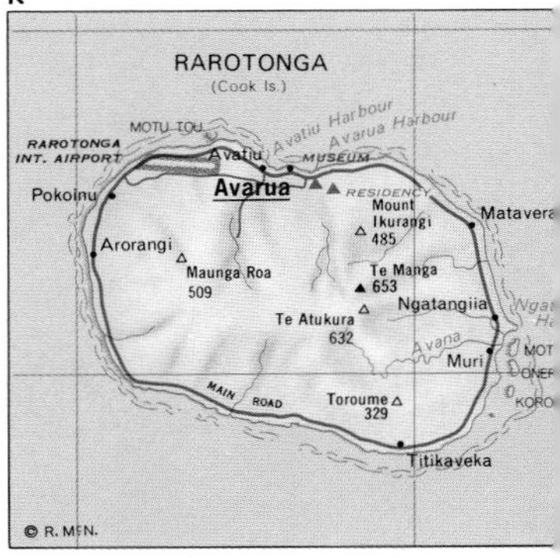
RAROTONGA
(Cook Is.)
MOTU TOU
Avatiu Harbour
Avarua Harbour
RAROTONGA INT. AIRPORT
Avatiu
MUSEUM
Avarua
RESIDENCY
Pokoinu
Mount Ikurangi 485
Matavera
Arorangi
Maunga Roa 509
Te Manga 653
Ngatangiia
Te Atukura 632
Avana
Muri
MAIN ROAD
Toroume 329
Titikaveka
© R. McN.

141°15′ 141°20′ 177°25′ 177°20′ 171°45′ 171°40′ 171°35′ 159°50′ 159°45′

Kilometers 0 5 10 15 Km.
Statute Miles 0 5 10 15 Mi.

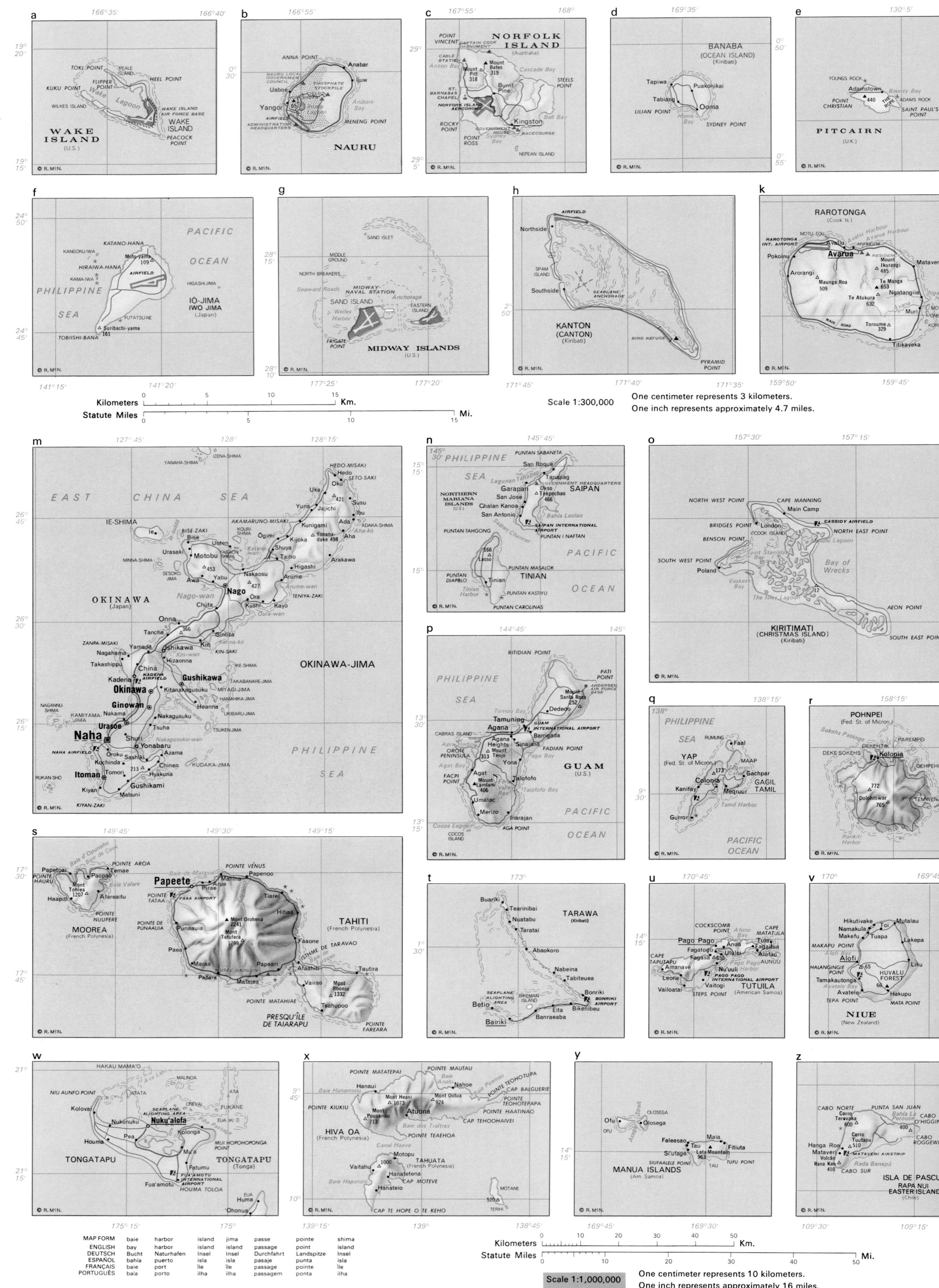

Scale 1:300,000
One centimeter represents 3 kilometers.
One inch represents approximately 4.7 miles.

m 127°45′ 128° 128°15′ 26° 45′ 26° 30′ 26° 15′

IZENA-SHIMA
YANAHA-SHIMA
HEDO-MISAKI
Hedo
Oku
SETO-SAKI
EAST CHINA SEA
Uka
421
Susu
Yuna
Jajichi
Ibu
IE-SHIMA
AKAMARUNO-MISAKI
Ada
ADAKA-SHIMA
Ie
BISE-ZAKI
Kunigami
Bise
Ōgimi
Yonaha-dake 498
Aha
Urasaki
Unten
Kijoka
Shuya
Motobu
Taiho
Arakawa
MINNA-SHIMA
Higashi
453
SESOKO-JIMA
Awa
Yabu
Nakaosu
427
Arume
Nago
Ora
Nago-wan
Kushi
Kayo
OKINAWA
(Japan)
Chuta
TENIYA-ZAKI
Oura-wan
Onna
366
Tancha
Ginoza
ZANPA-MISAKI
Yamada
Ishikawa
Kin
Nagahama
Kin-wan
KIN-SAKI
Takashippu
Hizaonna
China
IKEI-SHIMA
OKINAWA-JIMA
Kadena
KADENA AIRFIELD
Gushikawa
TAKABANARE-JIMA
Okinawa
Kitanakagusuku
MIYAGI-JIMA
HAMAHIKA-JIMA
NAGANNU-SHIMA
Ginowan
Heanna
KAMIYAMA-JIMA
Nakama
Nakagusuku
UKIBARU-JIMA
Urasoe
Tsuha
TSUKEN-JIMA
Naha
Shuri
NAHA AIRFIELD
Yonabaru
PHILIPPINE SEA
Oroku
Azama
Sashiki
Kochinda
Chinen
KUDAKA-JIMA
Tomori
213
Itoman
Hyakuna
KURKAN-SHO
Kiyan
Gushikami
Mabuni
KIYAN-ZAKI
© R. McN.

n 145°45′ 15° 15′ 15°

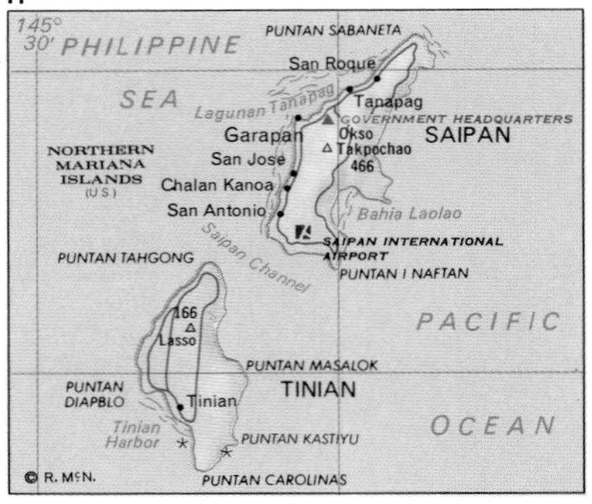
PUNTAN SABANETA
PHILIPPINE
SEA
San Roque
Tanapag
GOVERNMENT HEADQUARTERS
Garapan
Okso Takpochao 466
SAIPAN
NORTHERN MARIANA ISLANDS
(U.S.)
San Jose
Chalan Kanoa
San Antonio
Bahia Laolao
SAIPAN INTERNATIONAL AIRPORT
PUNTAN TAHGONG
PUNTAN I NAFTAN
Saipan Channel
PACIFIC
166
Lasso
PUNTAN MASALOK
TINIAN
PUNTAN DIAPBLO
Tinian
OCEAN
Tinian Harbor
PUNTAN KASTIYU
PUNTAN CAROLINAS
© R. McN.

o 157°30′ 157°15′

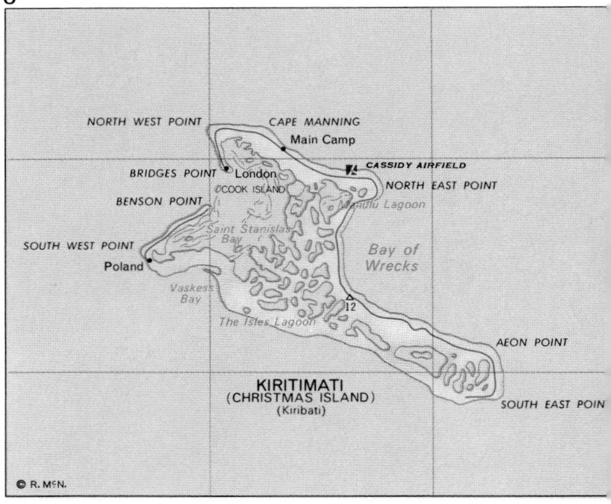
NORTH WEST POINT
CAPE MANNING
Main Camp
CASSIDY AIRFIELD
BRIDGES POINT
London
COOK ISLAND
NORTH EAST POINT
BENSON POINT
Lagoon
Saint Stanislas Bay
SOUTH WEST POINT
Bay of Wrecks
Poland
Vaskess Bay
The Isles Lagoon
12
AEON POINT
KIRITIMATI
(CHRISTMAS ISLAND)
(Kiribati)
SOUTH EAST POINT
© R. McN.

p 144°45′ 145° 13° 30′ 13° 15′

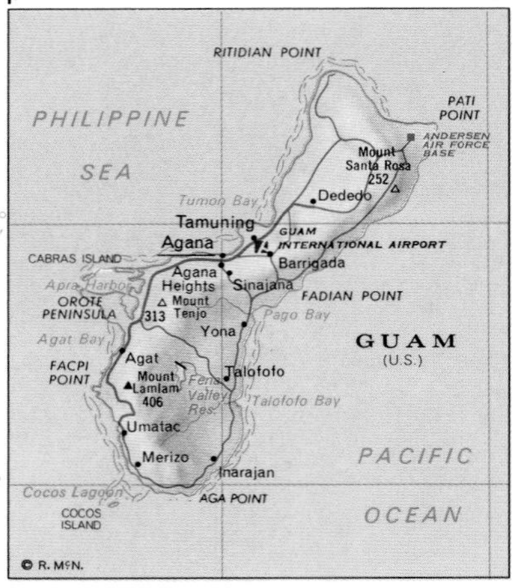
RITIDIAN POINT
PATI POINT
PHILIPPINE
SEA
ANDERSEN AIR FORCE BASE
Mount Santa Rosa 252
Dededo
Tumon Bay
Tamuning
Agana
GUAM INTERNATIONAL AIRPORT
CABRAS ISLAND
Barrigada
Apra Harbor
Agana Heights
Sinajana
OROTE PENINSULA
Mount Tenjo 313
FADIAN POINT
Pago Bay
Yona
GUAM
(U.S.)
Agat Bay
FACPI POINT
Agat
Mount Lamlam 406
Talofofo
Talofofo Bay
Umatac
PACIFIC
Merizo
Inarajan
Cocos Lagoon
COCOS ISLAND
AGA POINT
OCEAN
© R. McN.

q 138°15′ 9° 30′

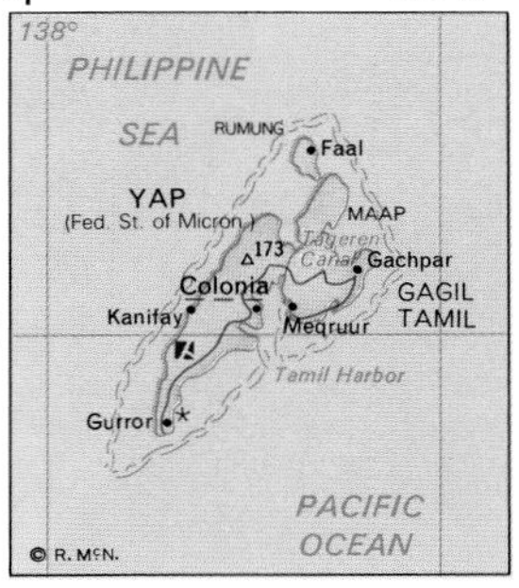
PHILIPPINE
SEA
RUMUNG
Faal
YAP
(Fed. St. of Micron.)
MAAP
173
Gachpar
Colonia
GAGIL TAMIL
Kanifay
Maqruur
Tamil Harbor
Gurror
PACIFIC
OCEAN
© R. McN.

r 158°15′

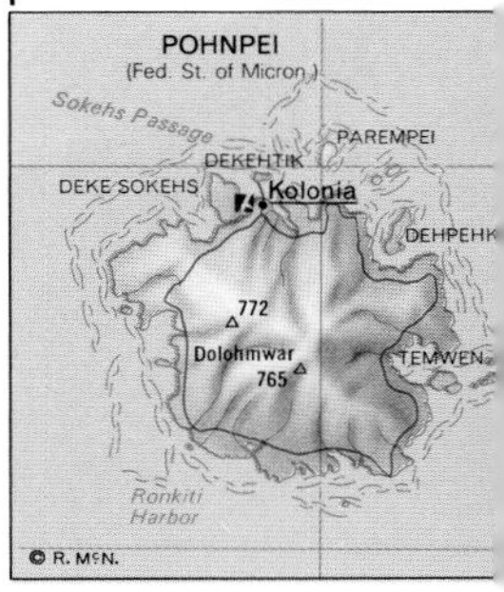
POHNPEI
(Fed. St. of Micron.)
Sokehs Passage
PAREMPEI
DEKE SOKEHS
DEKEHTIK
Kolonia
DEHPEHEI
772
TEMWEN
Dolohmwar 765
Ronkiti Harbor
© R. McN.

s 149°45′ 149°30′ 149°15′ 17° 30′ 17° 45′

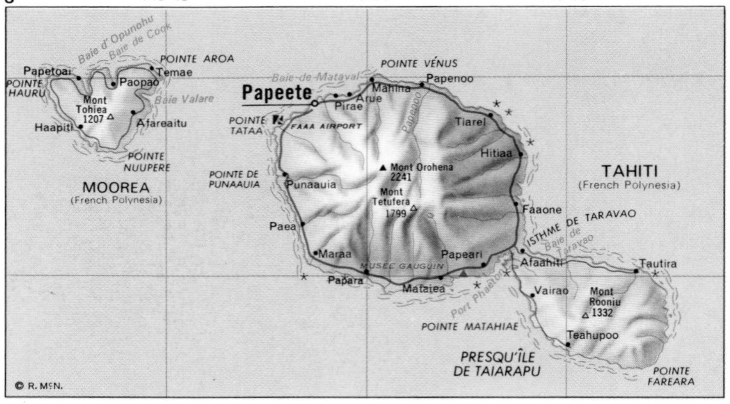
Baie d'Opunohu
Baie de Cook
POINTE AROA
Papetoai
Temae
POINTE HAURU
Paopao
POINTE VÉNUS
Papenoo
Mont Tohiea 1207
Baie Valare
Papeete
Mahina
Arue
Pirae
Haapiti
Afareaitu
POINTE TATAA
FAAA AIRPORT
Tiarei
POINTE NUUPERE
MOOREA
(French Polynesia)
Hitiaa
Mont Orohena 2241
POINTE DE PUNAAUIA
Punaauia
TAHITI
(French Polynesia)
Mont Tetufera 1799
Paea
Faaone
TARAVAO
ISTHME DE TARAVAO
Mataiea
Papeari
MUSÉE GAUGUIN
Papara
Afaahiti
Tautira
Vairao
Mont Ronui 1332
POINTE MATAHIAE
Teahupoo
PRESQU'ILE DE TAIARAPU
POINTE FAREARA
© R. McN.

t 173° 1° 30′

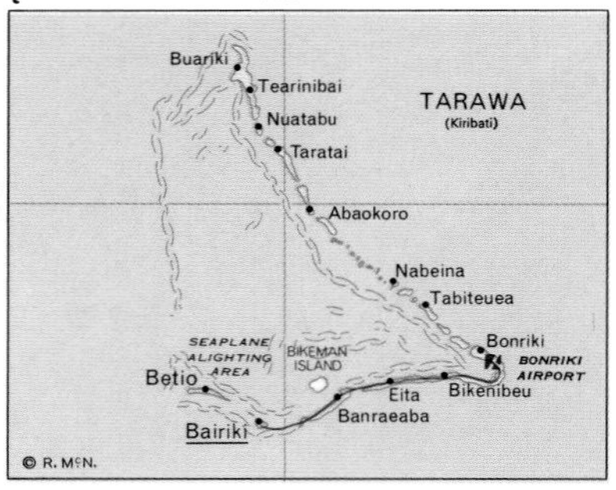
Buariki
Tearinibai
Nuatabu
Taratai
TARAWA
(Kiribati)
Abaokoro
Nabeina
Tabiteuea
SEAPLANE ALIGHTING AREA
BIKEMAN ISLAND
Bonriki
BONRIKI AIRPORT
Betio
Eita
Bikenibeu
Bairiki
Banraeaba
© R. McN.

u 170°45′ 14° 15′

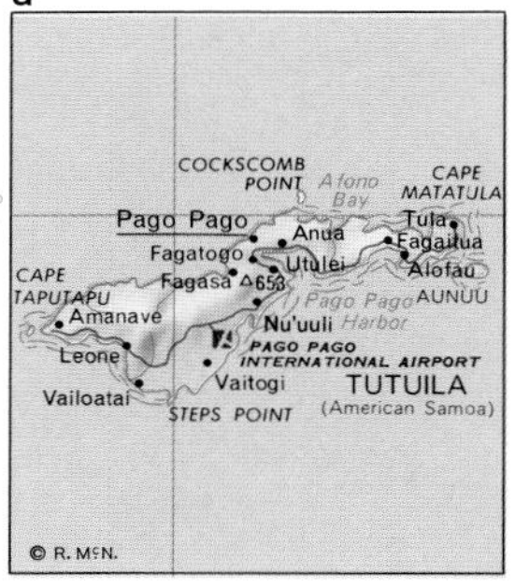
COCKSCOMB POINT
Afono Bay
CAPE MATATULA
Pago Pago
Tula
Fagatogo
Aua
Faga'itua
CAPE TAPUTAPU
Fagasa 650
Utulei
Alofau
AUNUU
Amanave
Pago Pago Harbor
Leone
Nu'uuli
PAGO PAGO INTERNATIONAL AIRPORT
Vailoatai
Vaitogi
TUTUILA
(American Samoa)
STEPS POINT
© R. McN.

v 170° 169°45′

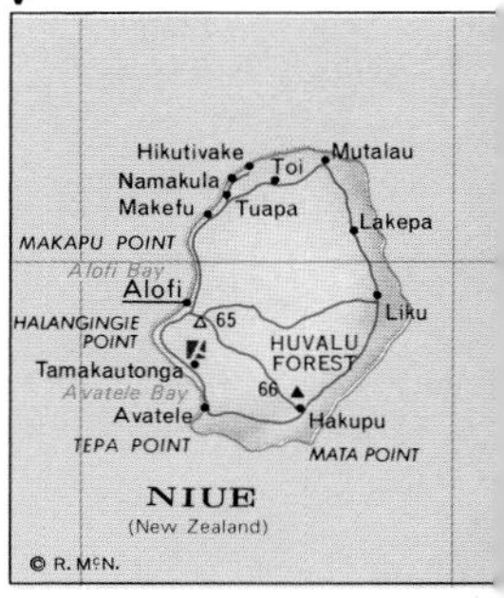
Hikutavake
Mutalau
Namukulu
Toi
Makefu
Tuapa
Lakepa
MAKAPU POINT
Alofi Bay
Alofi
HALANGINGIE POINT
65
Liku
HUVALU FOREST
Tamakautonga
66
Avatele Bay
Avatele
Hakupu
TEPA POINT
MATA POINT
NIUE
(New Zealand)
© R. McN.

w 21° 21° 15′

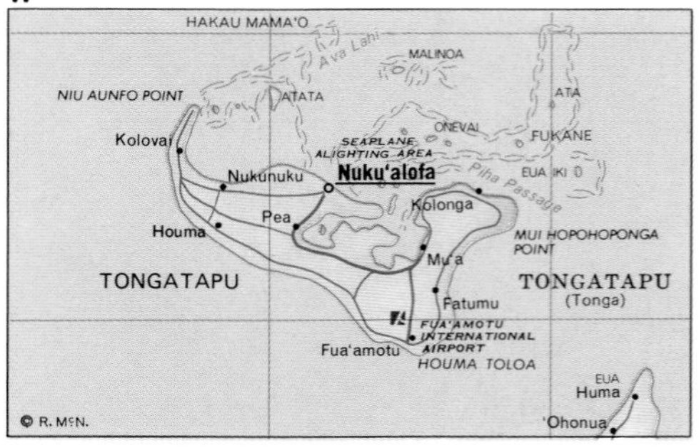
HAKAU MAMA'O
MALINOA
NIU AUNFO POINT
ATATA
ATA
Kolovai
SEAPLANE ALIGHTING AREA
ONEVAI
FUKAVE
Nukunuku
Nuku'alofa
EUA IKI
Piha Passage
Kolonga
Houma
Pea
MUI HOPOHOPONGA POINT
TONGATAPU
Mu'a
TONGATAPU
(Tonga)
Fatumu
FUA'AMOTU INTERNATIONAL AIRPORT
Fua'amotu
HOUMA TOLOA
EUA
Huma
'Ohonua
© R. McN.

x 9° 45′ 10°

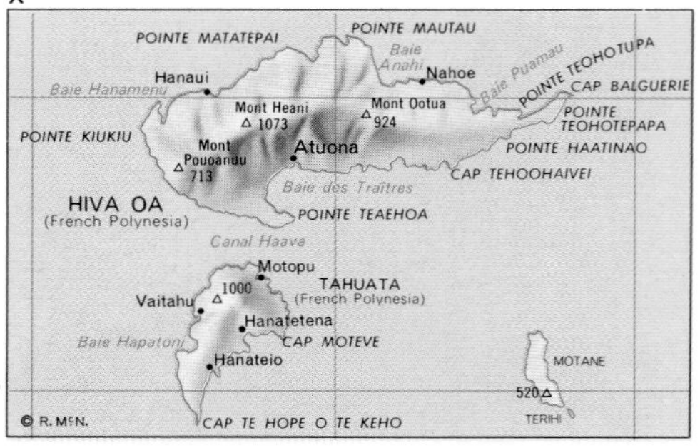
POINTE MATATEPAI
POINTE MAUTAU
Baie Anaho
Nahoe
POINTE TEOHOTUPA
CAP BALGUERIE
Hanaui
Baie Hanamenu
Mont Heani 1073
Mont Ootua 924
Baie Puamau
POINTE TEOHOTEPAPA
POINTE KIUKIU
Mont Pouoanuu 713
Atuona
POINTE HAATINAIO
CAP TEHOOHAIVEI
Baie des Traîtres
HIVA OA
(French Polynesia)
POINTE TEAEHOA
Canal Haava
Motopu
1000
TAHUATA
(French Polynesia)
Vaitahu
Hanatetena
Baie Hapatoni
CAP MOTEVE
Hanateio
MOTANE
520
TERIHI
CAP TE HOPE O TE KEHO
© R. McN.

y 14° 15′

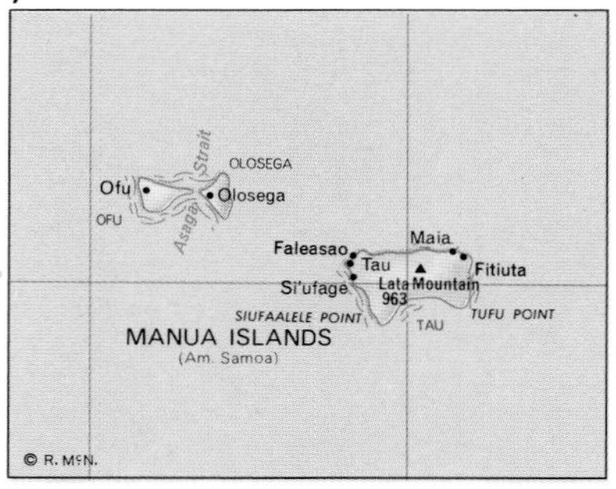
Asaga Strait
OLOSEGA
Ofu
Olosega
OFU
Faleasao
Maia
Tau
Fitiuta
Lata Mountain 963
Si'ufaga
SIUFAALELE POINT
TAU
TUFU POINT
MANUA ISLANDS
(Am. Samoa)
© R. McN.

z

CABO NORTE
PUNTA SAN JUAN
Cerro Terevaka 600
Bahía La Pérouse
CABO O'HIGGINS
400
CABO ROGGEWEEN
Cerro Tuutapu 510
Hanga Roa
Mataveri
MATAVERI AIRSTRIP
Volcán Rano Kau 410
Rada Benepú
CABO SUR
ISLA DE PASCUA
RAPA NUI
EASTER ISLAND
(Chile)
© R. McN.

175°15′ 175° 139°15′ 139° 138°45′ 169°45′ 169°30′ 109°30′ 109°15′

MAP FORM	baie	harbor	island	jima	passe	pointe	shima
ENGLISH	bay	harbor	island	island	passage	point	island
DEUTSCH	Bucht	Naturhafen	Insel	Insel	Durchfahrt	Landspitze	Insel
ESPAÑOL	bahía	puerto	isla	isla	pasaje	punta	isla
FRANÇAIS	baie	port	île	île	passage	pointe	île
PORTUGUÊS	baía	porto	ilha	ilha	passagem	ponta	ilha

Kilometers 0 10 20 30 40 50 Km.
Statute Miles 0 10 20 30 40 50 Mi.

Scale 1:1,000,000
One centimeter represents 10 kilometers.
One inch represents approximately 16 miles.
Transverse Mercator Projection

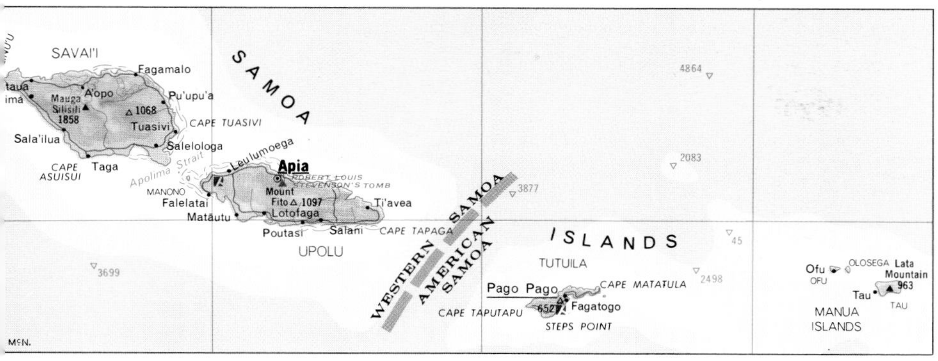
SAVAI'I
SAMOA
Fagamalo
A'opo
Pu'upu'a
Mauga Silisili 1858
1068
Tuasivi
CAPE TUASIVI
Sala'ilua
Salelologa
CAPE ASUISUI
Taga
Apolima Strait
Leulumoega
Apia
MANONO
Falelatai
Matautu
Mount Fito 1097
Lotofaga
Ti'avea
Poutasi
Salani
CAPE TAPAGA
UPOLU
WESTERN SAMOA
AMERICAN SAMOA
ISLANDS
TUTUILA
Pago Pago
CAPE MATATULA
Fagatogo
CAPE TAPUTAPU
STEPS POINT
Ofu
OLOSEGA
Lata Mountain 963
Tau
MANUA ISLANDS
172°
171°
170°

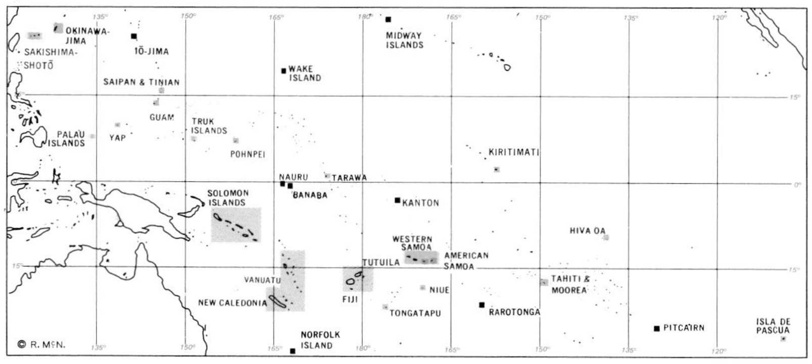
OKINAWA-JIMA
SAKISHIMA-SHOTŌ
IŌ-JIMA
MIDWAY ISLANDS
WAKE ISLAND
SAIPAN & TINIAN
GUAM
PALAU ISLANDS
YAP
TRUK ISLANDS
POHNPEI
KIRITIMATI
NAURU
TARAWA
BANABA
SOLOMON ISLANDS
KANTON
HIVA OA
WESTERN SAMOA
TUTUILA
AMERICAN SAMOA
VANUATU
FIJI
NIUE
TAHITI & MOOREA
NEW CALEDONIA
TONGATAPU
RAROTONGA
NORFOLK ISLAND
PITCAIRN
ISLA DE PASCUA
© R. McN.

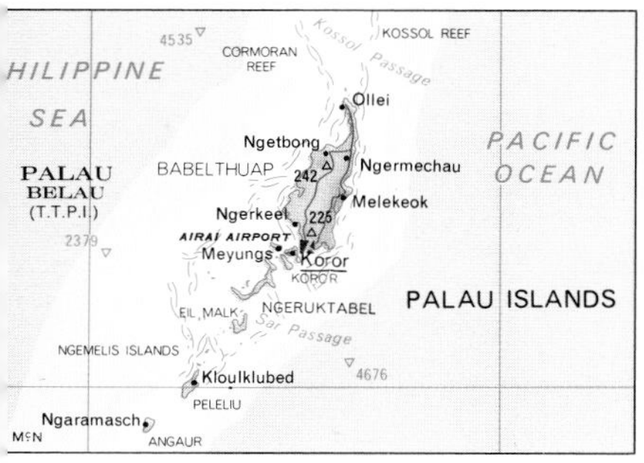
KOSSOL REEF
CORMORAN REEF
PHILIPPINE SEA
Ollei
Ngetbong
PACIFIC OCEAN
PALAU BELAU (T.T.P.I.)
BABELTHUAP
Ngermechau
Melekeok
Ngerkeel
AIRAI AIRPORT
Meyungs
Koror
NGERUKTABEL
PALAU ISLANDS
Kloulklubed
PELELIU
Ngaramasch
ANGAUR
134°
135°

c

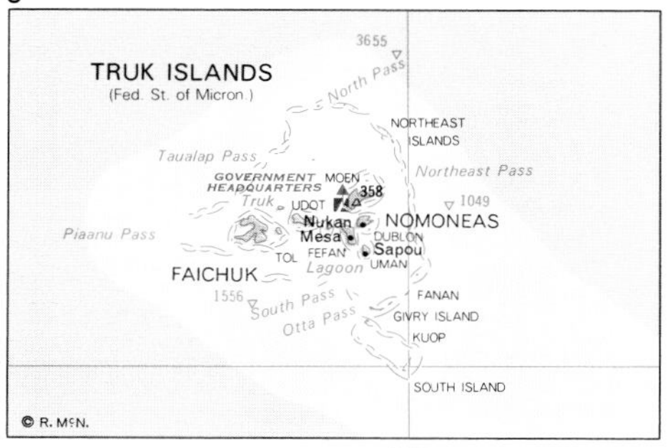
TRUK ISLANDS
(Fed. St. of Micron.)
NORTHEAST ISLANDS
Northeast Pass
GOVERNMENT HEADQUARTERS
MOEN
Nukan
Mesa
NOMONEAS
FAICHUK
DUBLON
Sapou
FEFAN
UMAN
Truk Lagoon
FANAN
South Pass
Otta Pass
GIVRY ISLAND
KUOP
SOUTH ISLAND
© R. McN.
152°

d

SAKISHIMA-SHOTŌ
EAST CHINA SEA
IKEMA-JIMA
Karimata
Irabu
Hirara
SHIMOJI-JIMA
Shimoji
Guskube
MIYAKO-JIMA
MINNA-SHIMA
Tarama
TARAMA-SHIMA
YAEYAMA RETTŌ
MIYAKO-RETTŌ
Yonaguni
YONAGUNI-SHIMA
Hirano
Kabira
Funakuyā
Ueharu
IRIOMOTE-JIMA
KOHAMA-JIMA
ISHIGAKI-SHIMA
TAKE-SHIMA
Miyara
Amitori
470
526
Ishigaki
OKINAWA
(Japan)
Toyohara
Ōtomi
KURO-SHIMA
NAKANOUGAN-JIMA
PHILIPPINE SEA
HATERUMA-SHIMA
© R. McN.
123°
124°
125°
25°
24°

Kilometers 0 50 100 150 Km.
Statute Miles 0 50 100 150 Mi.

Scale 1:3,000,000
One centimeter represents 30 kilometers.
One inch represents approximately 47 miles.
Lambert Conformal Conic Projection

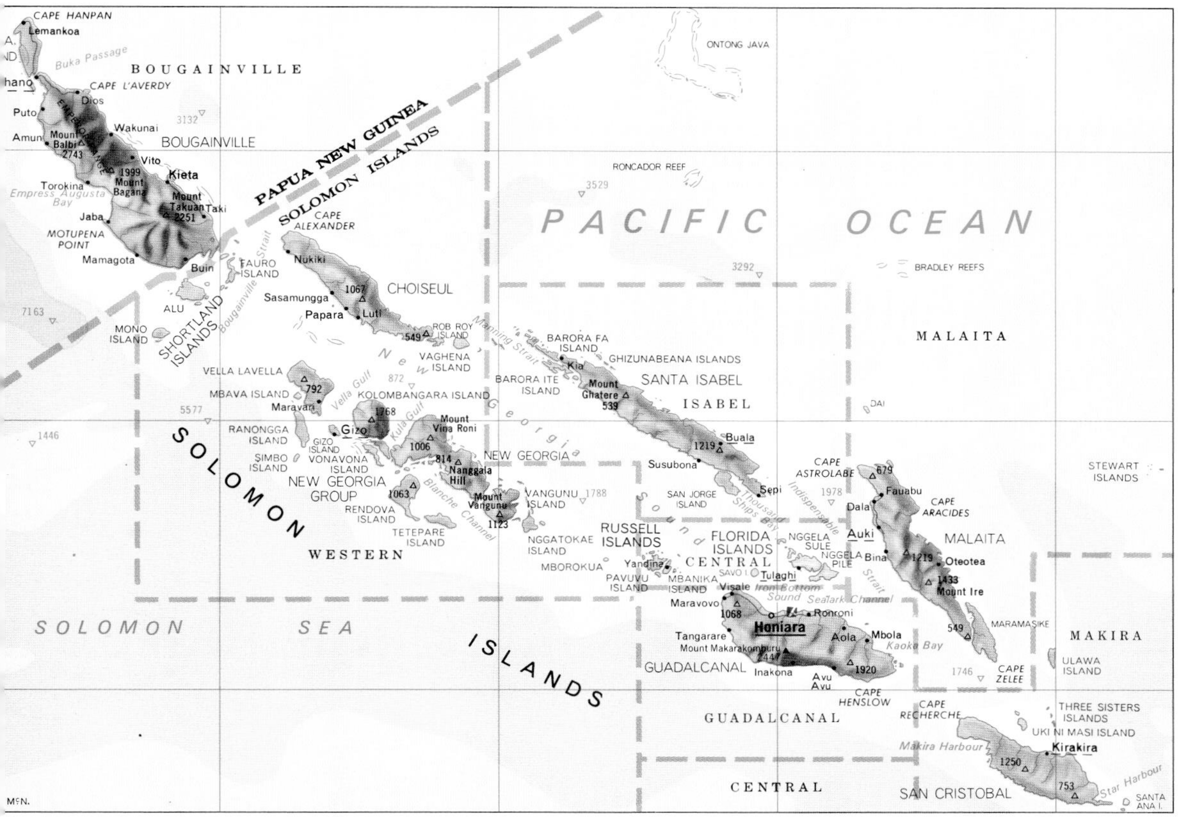
CAPE HANPAN
Lemankoa
Buka Passage
BOUGAINVILLE
CAPE L'AVERDY
Wakunai
BOUGAINVILLE
Kieta
Torokina
Empress Augusta Bay
Jaba
MOTUPENA POINT
Mamagota
Buin
PAPUA NEW GUINEA
SOLOMON ISLANDS
CAPE ALEXANDER
ONTONG JAVA
RONCADOR REEF
PACIFIC OCEAN
BRADLEY REEFS
FAURO ISLAND
Nukiki
CHOISEUL
Sasamungga
Papara
ALU
MONO ISLAND
SHORTLAND ISLANDS
ROB ROY ISLAND
BARORA FA ISLAND
GHIZUNABEANA ISLANDS
MALAITA
VAGHENA ISLAND
VELLA LAVELLA
BARORA ITE ISLAND
Mount Ghatere
SANTA ISABEL
ISABEL
MBAVA ISLAND
KOLOMBANGARA ISLAND
RANONGGA ISLAND
Gizo
Buala
SIMBO ISLAND
VONAVONA ISLAND
NEW GEORGIA
NEW GEORGIA GROUP
Susubona
STEWART ISLANDS
RENDOVA ISLAND
TETEPARE ISLAND
VANGUNU ISLAND
SAN JORGE ISLAND
Sepi
CAPE ASTROLABE
Fauabu
SOLOMON
WESTERN
RUSSELL ISLANDS
FLORIDA ISLANDS
NGGELA SULE
NGGELA PILE
Dala
Auki
CAPE ARACIDES
MALAITA
Oteotea
Mount Ire
Bina
NGGATOKAE ISLAND
MBOROKUA
PAVUVU ISLAND
Yandina
MBANIKA ISLAND
CENTRAL
SAVO
Tulaghi
Visale
Sealark Channel
Maravovo
Honiara
Rorroni
SOLOMON SEA
ISLANDS
Tangarare
Mount Makarakomburu
Aola
Mbola
GUADALCANAL
Inakona
Avu Avu
CAPE HENSLOW
CAPE ZELEE
ULAWA ISLAND
MAKIRA
MARAMASIKE
THREE SISTERS ISLANDS
UKI NI MASI ISLAND
CAPE RECHERCHE
Kirakira
Makira Harbour
GUADALCANAL
CENTRAL
SAN CRISTOBAL
SANTA ANA I.
156°
158°
160°
162°

f

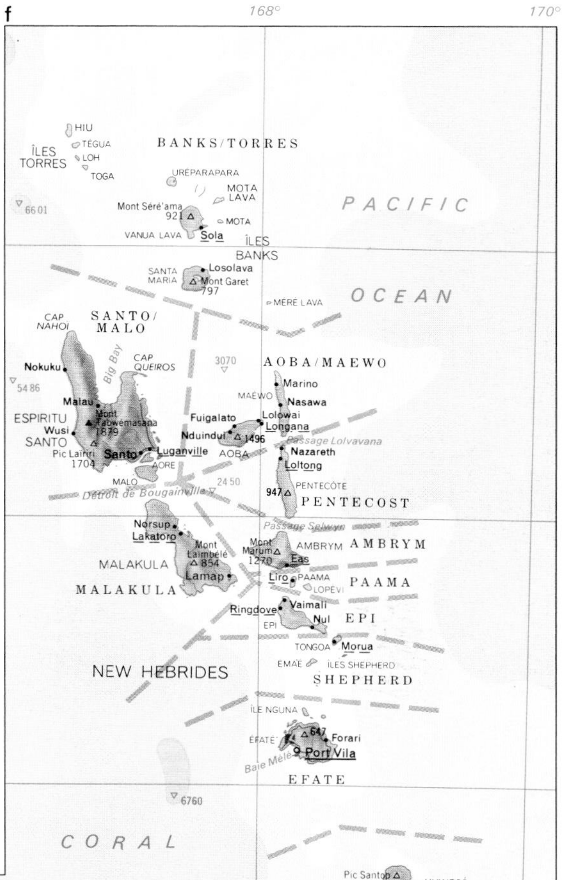
HIU
TEGUA
LOH
TOGA
ÎLES TORRES
BANKS/TORRES
UREPARAPARA
MOTA LAVA
MOTA
Mont Sérétama
VANUA LAVA
Sola
ÎLES BANKS
PACIFIC
SANTA MARIA
Losolava
Mont Garet 797
MERE LAVA
OCEAN
CAP NAHOI
SANTO/MALO
CAP QUIROS
AOBA/MAEWO
Nokuku
MAEWO
Marino
Malau
Nasawa
Mont Tabwemasana 1879
ESPIRITU SANTO
Wusi
Fuigalato
Lolowai
Longana
Pic Lairiri
Santo
Luganville
AOBA
Passage Lolvavana
Nazareth
Loltong
AORE
MALO
Détroit de Bougainville
PENTECOTE
Norsup
Lakatoro
Mont Lambrele
Mont Marum
AMBRYM
AMBRYM
MALAKULA
Lamap
Eas
MALAKULA
Lito
PAAMA
PAAMA
LOPEVI
Ringdove
Vaimali
EPI
Nul
EPI
TONGOA
Morua
NEW HEBRIDES
EMAE
ÎLES SHEPHERD
SHEPHERD
ÎLE NGUNA
Forari
Port Vila
EFATE
Baie Mélé
EFATE
168°
170°
14°
16°
18°

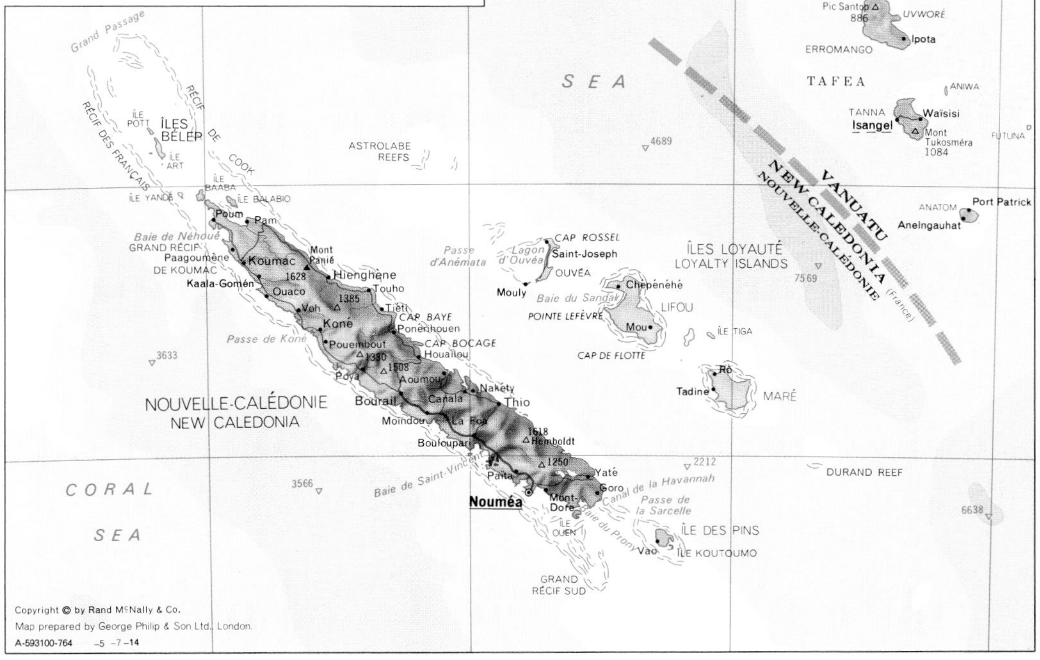
CORAL
SEA
Pic Santop 886
UVWORÉ
Ipota
ERROMANGO
TAFEA
ANIWA
TANNA
Waisisi
Isangel
Mont Tukosméra 1084
FUTUNA
ANATOM
Port Patrick
Anelngauhat
VANUATU
NEW CALEDONIA
NOUVELLE-CALÉDONIE (France)
Grand Passage
RÉCIF DES FRANÇAIS
RÉCIF DE COOK
ÎLES BELEP
ÎLE ART
ÎLE POTT
ASTROLABE REEFS
ÎLE YANDÉ
ÎLE BAABA
ÎLE BALABIO
Poum
Pam
Baie de Néhoué
GRAND RÉCIF DE KOUMAC
Paagoumène
Koumac
Kaala-Gomen
Mont Panié 1628
Hienghène
Ouaco
Touho
CAP ROSSEL
Saint-Joseph
Passe d'Anémata
Lagon d'Ouvéa
OUVÉA
ÎLES LOYAUTÉ
LOYALTY ISLANDS
Chépénéhé
Mouly
Baie du Santal
POINTE LEFÈVRE
LIFOU
Koné
CAP BAYE
Ponérihouen
Passe de Koné
Pouembout
CAP BOCAGE
Houaïlou
Mou
ÎLE TIGA
CAP DE FLOTTE
Poya
Bourail
Canala
Nakety
Thio
Tadine
Ro
MARÉ
NOUVELLE-CALÉDONIE
NEW CALEDONIA
Moindou
La Foa
Boulouparis
Mont Humboldt 1618
Baie de Saint Vincent
Yaté
Goro
Canal de la Havannah
Païta
Mont Dore
Passe de la Sarcelle
Nouméa
ÎLE OUEN
ÎLE DES PINS
Vao
ÎLE KOUTOUMO
GRAND RÉCIF SUD
DURAND REEF
CORAL
SEA
164°
166°
168°
170°
20°
22°

Copyright © by Rand McNally & Co.
Map prepared by George Philip & Son Ltd., London.
A-593100-764 -5 -7 -14

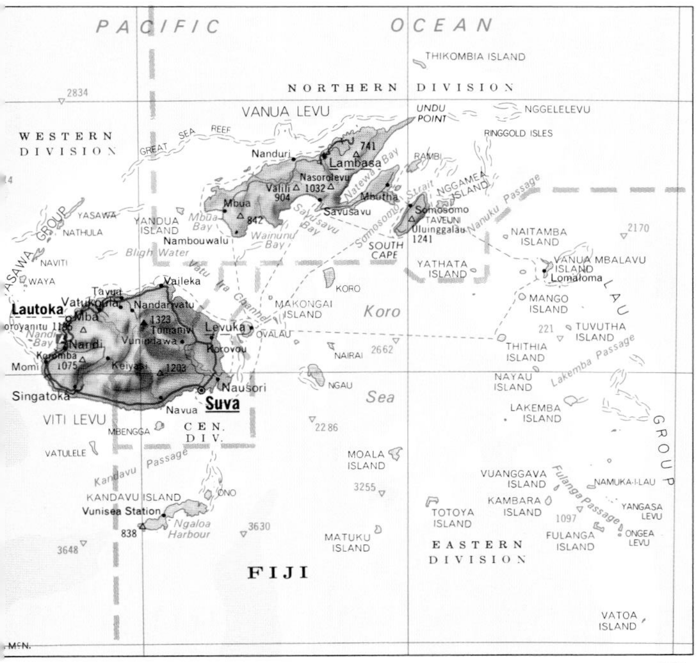
PACIFIC OCEAN
THIKOMBIA ISLAND
NORTHERN DIVISION
VANUA LEVU
UNDU POINT
NGGELELEVU
RINGGOLD ISLES
WESTERN DIVISION
GREAT SEA REEF
Nanduri
Lambasa
Nasorolevu
Vaili
Mbua
Savusavu
Somosomo
TAVEUNI
Uluinggalau
YASAWA GROUP
YANDUA ISLAND
Nambouwalu
NAITAMBA ISLAND
SOUTH CAPE
YATHATA ISLAND
VANUA MBALAVU
Lomaloma
NAVITI
WAYA
Vaileka
Tavua
Lautoka
Nandarivatu
Levuka
MAKONGAI ISLAND
KORO
Koro
MANGO ISLAND
TUVUTHA ISLAND
LAU
Nandi
Momi
OVALAU
NAIRAI
THITHIA ISLAND
Singatoka
Nausori
Suva
NGAU
Sea
NAYAU ISLAND
VITI LEVU
Navua
CEN. DIV.
LAKEMBA ISLAND
Lakemba Passage
VATULELE
MOALA ISLAND
KANDAVU ISLAND
Vunisea Station
Ngaloa Harbour
ONO
MATUKU ISLAND
TOTOYA ISLAND
VUANGGAVA ISLAND
KAMBARA ISLAND
NAMUKA-I-LAU
YANGASA LEVU
ONGEA LEVU
FULANGA ISLAND
EASTERN DIVISION
FIJI
VATOA ISLAND
GROUP
178°
180°
178°
16°

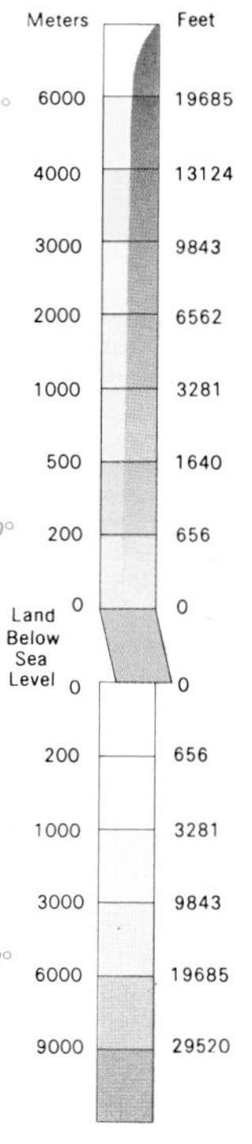
Meters
Feet
6000
19685
4000
13124
3000
9843
2000
6562
1000
3281
500
1640
200
656
Land 0
0
Below Sea Level 0
0
200
656
1000
3281
3000
9843
6000
19685
9000
29520

MAP FORM	bay	cape	île	lagoon	mount	point	passage	strait
ENGLISH	bay	cape	island	lagoon	mount	point	passage	strait
DEUTSCH	Bucht	Kap	Insel	Haff	Berg	Landspitze	Durchfahrt	Meeresstrasse
ESPAÑOL	bahía	cabo	isla	laguna	montaña	punta	pasaje	estrecho
FRANÇAIS	baie	cap	île	lagune	mont	pointe	passage	détroit
PORTUGUÊS	baia	cabo	ilha	laguna	monte	ponta	passagem	estreito

Kilometers 0 100 200 300 Km.
Statute Miles 0 100 200 300 Mi.

Scale 1:6,000,000
One centimeter represents 60 kilometers.
One inch represents approximately 95 miles.
Lambert Conformal Conic Projection

Beaufort Sea
Gulf of Alaska
PACIFIC OCEAN
UNITED STATES
CANADA
ALASKA RANGE
NORTHWEST
ROCKY MOUNTAINS
COAST MOUNTAINS
COLUMBIA MOUNTAINS
MACKENZIE MTS
SELWYN MTS.
OGILVIE MTS.
PELLY MOUNTAINS
BRITISH COLUMBIA
ALBERTA
SASKATCHEWAN
MANITOBA
WASHINGTON
OREGON
IDAHO
MONTANA
WYOMING
NORTH DAKOTA
SOUTH DAKOTA
MINNESOTA
NEBRASKA
UTAH
COLORADO
IOWA
CALIFORNIA
CASCADE RANGE
SIERRA NEVADA
GREAT BASIN
BITTERROOT RANGE
VICTORIA ISLAND
BANKS ISLAND
MELVILLE ISLAND
PRINCE OF WALES ISLAND
QUEEN CHARLOTTE ISLANDS
VANCOUVER ISLAND
Fairbanks
Anchorage
Whitehorse
Yellowknife
Fort Nelson
Fort St. John
Dawson Creek
Prince George
Prince Rupert
Edmonton
Calgary
Lethbridge
Saskatoon
Regina
Moose Jaw
Winnipeg
Brandon
Vancouver
Victoria
Seattle
Tacoma
Spokane
Portland
Salem
Eugene
Boise
Missoula
Great Falls
Helena
Butte
Billings
Bismarck
Fargo
Grand Forks
Minneapolis
Rapid City
Pierre
Sioux Falls
Sioux City
Casper
Cheyenne
Salt Lake City
Ogden
Provo
Reno
Sacramento
SAN FRANCISCO
Oakland
San Jose
Fresno
Idaho Falls
Pocatello
Twin Falls
Medford
Klamath Falls
Eureka

ENGLISH	bay	cape	island	lake, l.	mountains, mts.	point	range	strait
DEUTSCH	Bucht	Kap	Insel	See	Berge	Landspitze	Gebirge	Meeresstrasse
ESPAÑOL	bahía	cabo	isla	lago	montañas	punta	sierra	estrecho
FRANÇAIS	baie	cap	île	lac	montagnes	pointe	chaîne	détroit
PORTUGUÊS	baía	cabo	ilha	lago	montanhas	ponta	serra	estreito

Map continues
pages 178-179

GREENLAND
KALAALLIT NUNAAT
(Denmark)
Baffin Bay
Davis Strait
Labrador Sea
ATLANTIC OCEAN
Hudson Bay
Foxe Basin
Hudson Strait
Ungava Bay
James Bay
DEVON ISLAND
Lancaster Sound
BAFFIN ISLAND
SOUTHAMPTON ISLAND
PÉNINSULE D'UNGAVA
QUEBEC
LABRADOR
NEWFOUNDLAND
ONTARIO
NEW BRUNSWICK
NOVA SCOTIA
PRINCE EDWARD ISLAND
Gulf of St. Lawrence
Gulf of Maine
APPALACHIAN MTS.
ST. PIERRE AND MIQUELON (Fr.)
CAPE BRETON ISLAND
ÎLE D'ANTICOSTI
All islands within Hudson Bay, James Bay, and Ungava Bay lie within Northwest Territories
Iqaluit
Chicoutimi
Quebec
Trois-Rivières
Montreal
Ottawa
Toronto
Hamilton
Kingston
Sudbury
Timmins
Thunder Bay
Sault Ste. Marie
Halifax
Sydney
Moncton
Saint John
Charlottetown
St. John's
Corner Brook
Gander
Sept-Îles
Boston
New York
Philadelphia
Buffalo
Rochester
Syracuse
Albany
Portland
Detroit
Cleveland
Chicago
Milwaukee
Lake Superior
Lake Huron
Lake Erie
Lake Ontario
Lake Michigan
Copyright © by Rand McNally & Co.
Map prepared by Rand McNally & Co.
A-520200-264

Kilometers 0 200 400 600 Km.

Statute Miles 0 200 400 600 Mi.

Scale 1:12,000,000

One centimeter represents 120 kilometers.

One inch represents approximately 190 miles.

Lambert Conformal Conic Projection

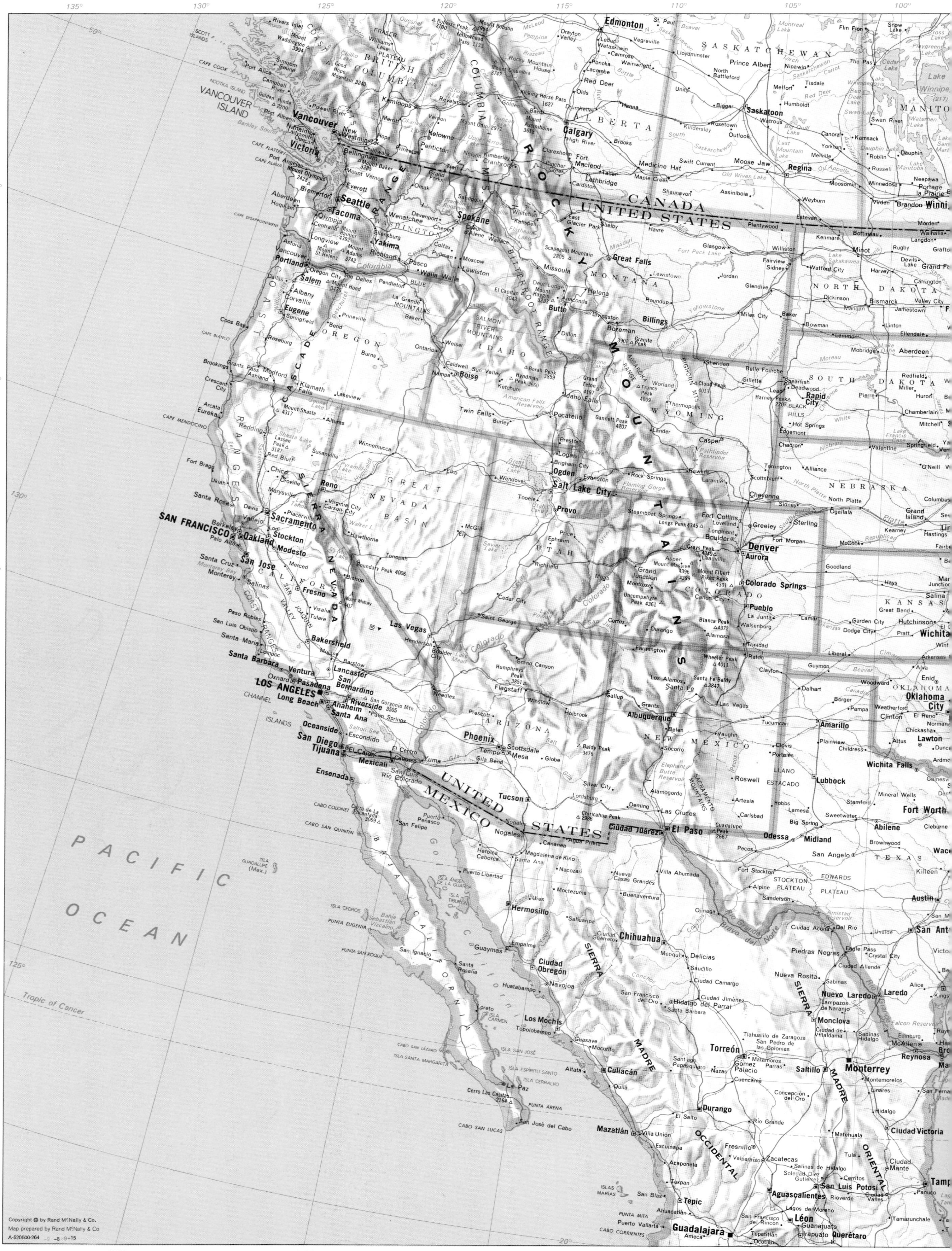
PACIFIC OCEAN
CANADA
UNITED STATES
MEXICO
VANCOUVER ISLAND
BRITISH COLUMBIA
ALBERTA
SASKATCHEWAN
ROCKY MOUNTAINS
COAST RANGES
CASCADE RANGE
SIERRA NEVADA
GREAT BASIN
WASHINGTON
OREGON
IDAHO
MONTANA
WYOMING
NEVADA
UTAH
COLORADO
CALIFORNIA
ARIZONA
NEW MEXICO
NORTH DAKOTA
SOUTH DAKOTA
NEBRASKA
KANSAS
OKLAHOMA
TEXAS
SIERRA MADRE OCCIDENTAL
SIERRA MADRE ORIENTAL
Edmonton
Calgary
Vancouver
Victoria
Seattle
Tacoma
Spokane
Portland
Salem
Eugene
Boise
Great Falls
Helena
Billings
Salt Lake City
Reno
Sacramento
SAN FRANCISCO
Oakland
San Jose
Fresno
Bakersfield
Las Vegas
LOS ANGELES
Long Beach
San Diego
Tijuana
Mexicali
Phoenix
Tucson
Albuquerque
El Paso
Ciudad Juárez
Denver
Colorado Springs
Cheyenne
Oklahoma City
Wichita
Lubbock
Amarillo
Odessa
San Antonio
Austin
Fort Worth
Chihuahua
Hermosillo
Culiacán
Mazatlán
Durango
Torreón
Monterrey
Saltillo
Nuevo Laredo
Zacatecas
Aguascalientes
San Luis Potosí
Guadalajara
León
Querétaro
Tropic of Cancer

ENGLISH	bay	cape	desert	island	lake	mountains	peak	range
DEUTSCH	Bucht	Kap	Wüste	Insel	See	Berge	Gipfel	Gebirge
ESPAÑOL	bahía	cabo	desierto	isla	lago	montañas	pico	sierra
FRANÇAIS	baie	cap	désert	île	lac	montagnes	cime	chaîne
PORTUGUÊS	baía	cabo	deserto	ilha	lago	montanhas	pico	serra

Map continues pages 230-231

Map continues
pages 176-177

ATLANTIC OCEAN
GULF OF MEXICO
CARIBBEAN SEA
WEST INDIES
BAHAMAS
APPALACHIAN MOUNTAINS
ONTARIO
QUÉBEC
NEW YORK
WASHINGTON
PHILADELPHIA
BOSTON
MONTREAL
TORONTO
CHICAGO
DETROIT
Atlanta
Miami
New Orleans
LA HABANA HAVANA
BERMUDA (U.K.)
Tropic of Cancer
Straits of Florida
Gulf of Saint Lawrence
Gulf of Maine
CAYMAN IS. (U.K.)
HISPANIOLA
TURKS AND CAICOS ISLANDS (U.K.)

Kilometers 0 200 400 600 Km.
Statute Miles 0 200 400 600 Mi.

Scale 1:12,000,000

One centimeter represents 120 kilometers.
One inch represents approximately 190 miles.
Albers Conical Equal-Area Projection

ARCTIC
Chukchi Sea
BERING SEA
Anadyrskij zaliv
Norton Sound
Bristol Bay
Kuskokwim Bay
PACIFIC
RUSSIA
ROSSIJA
UNITED STATES
International Date Line
Arctic Circle
Bering Strait
SEWARD PENINSULA
BROOKS
DE LONG MOUNTAINS
LISBURNE PENINSULA
BAIRD MOUNTAINS
SCHWATKA MOUNTAINS
KUSKOKWIM
KILBUCK MOUNTAINS
AHKLUN MOUNTAINS
ALEUTIAN ISLANDS
ANDREANOF ISLANDS
FOX ISLANDS
ISLANDS OF FOUR MOUNTAINS
KRENITZIN ISLANDS
PRIBILOF ISLANDS
SAINT LAWRENCE ISLAND
SAINT MATTHEW ISLAND
NUNIVAK ISLAND
UNIMAK ISLAND
UNALASKA ISLAND
UMNAK ISLAND
SHUMAGIN ISLANDS
ČUKOTSKIJ POLUOSTROV
ANADYRSKAJA NIZMENNOST
ANADYRSKOJE PLOSKOGORJE
EKVYVATAPSKIJ CHREBET
Barrow
Wainwright
Point Hope
Kotzebue
Nome
Unalakleet
Bethel
Anadyr'
Providenija
Gambell
Savoonga
Dillingham
Port Heiden
Cold Bay
Dutch Harbor
Unalaska
Adak
Meters
6000
4000
3000
2000
1000
500
200
0
Land Below Sea Level
0
200
1000
3000
6000
9000
Feet
19685
13124
9843
6562
3281
1640
656
0
0
656
3281
9843
19685
29520
ENGLISH bay cape island, i. lake, l. mount, mt. peak, pk. point volcano
DEUTSCH Bucht Kap Insel See Berg Gipfel Landspitze Vulkan
ESPAÑOL bahía cabo isla lago monte punta punta volcán
FRANÇAIS baie cap île lac mont cime pointe volcan
PORTUGUÊS baía cabo ilha lago monte pico ponta vulcão

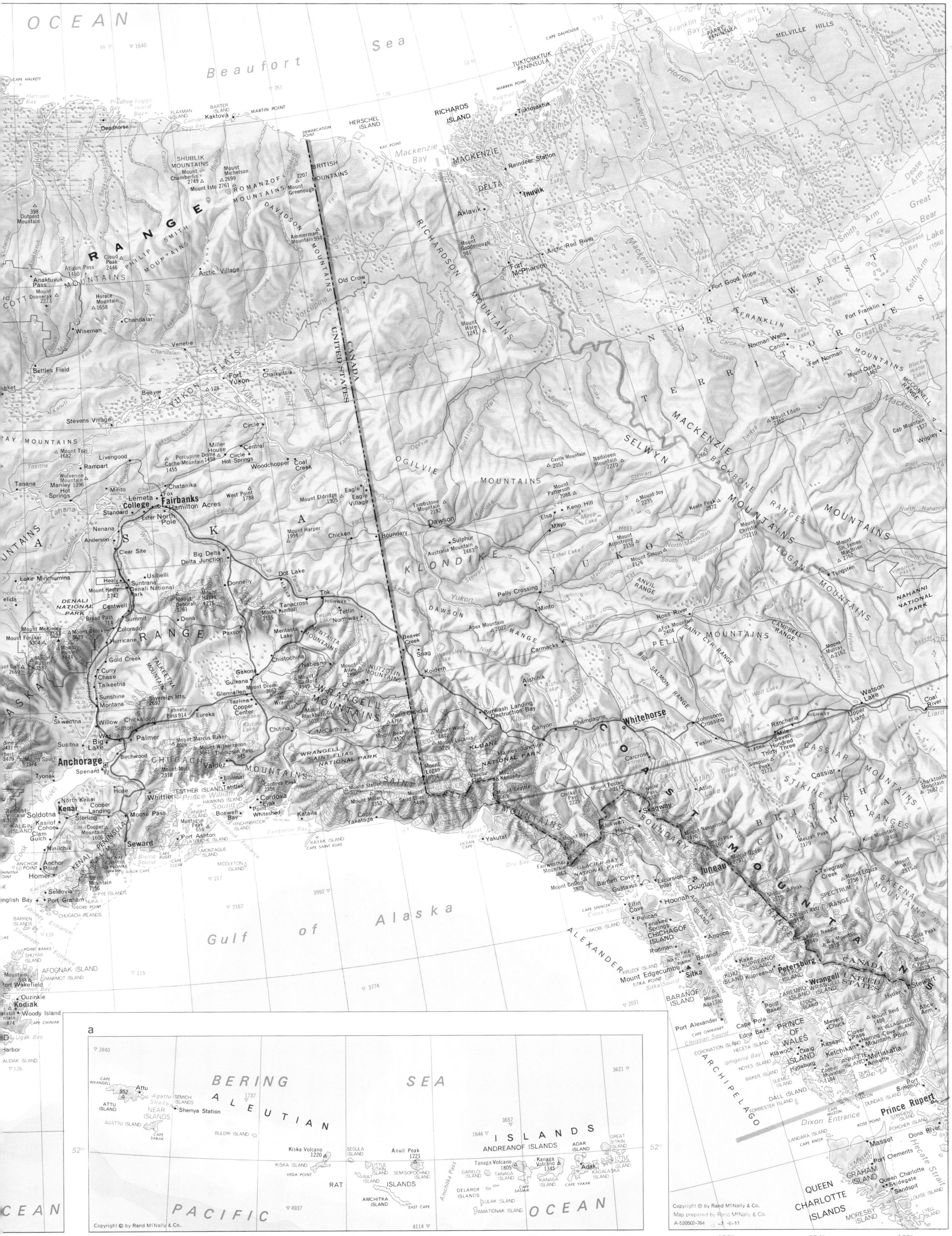
OCEAN
Beaufort Sea
RANGE
BROOKS
Kaktovik
Deadhorse
BRITISH MOUNTAINS
RICHARDSON MOUNTAINS
UNITED STATES
CANADA
MACKENZIE DELTA
Inuvik
Aklavik
Fort McPherson
Arctic Red River
Old Crow
Arctic Village
Fort Yukon
YUKON FLATS
Fairbanks
College
North Pole
Circle
Eagle
Dawson
KLONDIKE
OGILVIE MOUNTAINS
SELWYN MOUNTAINS
MACKENZIE MOUNTAINS
NORTHWEST TERRITORIES
YUKON
Norman Wells
Fort Norman
Fort Good Hope
Fort Franklin
Tok
Delta Junction
Healy
DENALI NATIONAL PARK
Mount McKinley 6194
ALASKA RANGE
WRANGELL MOUNTAINS
CHUGACH MOUNTAINS
SAINT ELIAS MOUNTAINS
Mount Logan 6050
KLUANE NATIONAL PARK
WRANGELL-SAINT ELIAS NATIONAL PARK
Anchorage
Palmer
Wasilla
Valdez
Cordova
Seward
Kenai
Homer
Kodiak
AFOGNAK ISLAND
Whitehorse
Watson Lake
Ross River
Carmacks
Skagway
Haines
Juneau
Sitka
Petersburg
Wrangell
Ketchikan
Prince Rupert
COAST MOUNTAINS
CASSIAR MOUNTAINS
BRITISH COLUMBIA
ALEXANDER ARCHIPELAGO
PRINCE OF WALES ISLAND
QUEEN CHARLOTTE ISLANDS
NAHANNI NATIONAL PARK
Gulf of Alaska
Yakutat
a
BERING SEA
ALEUTIAN ISLANDS
ANDREANOF ISLANDS
RAT ISLANDS
NEAR ISLANDS
Attu
Adak
Kiska Volcano 1220
PACIFIC OCEAN
Copyright © by Rand McNally & Co.

Map continues pages 176-177

Map continues pages 182-183

Kilometers 0 100 200 300 Km.
Statute Miles 0 100 200 300 Mi.

Scale 1:6,000,000

One centimeter represents 60 kilometers.
One inch represents approximately 95 miles.
Lambert Conformal Conic Projection

Southwestern Canada / Südwestkanada / Canadá Sud-occidental
Sud-Ouest du Canada / Canadá: Sudoeste

Map continues pages 180-181

Meters
Feet
6000
19685
4000
13124
3000
9843
2000
6562
1000
3281
500
1640
200
656
0
0
Land Below Sea Level
0
0
200
656
1000
3281
3000
9843
6000
19685
9000
29520
PACIFIC
OCEAN
Queen Charlotte Sound
Dixon Entrance
Hecate Strait
QUEEN CHARLOTTE ISLANDS
GRAHAM ISLAND
MORESBY ISLAND
Prince Rupert
Kitimat
COAST MOUNTAINS
PACIFIC RANGES
KITIMAT RANGES
HAZELTON MOUNTAINS
SKEENA MOUNTAINS
OMINECA MOUNTAINS
NECHAKO PLATEAU
FRASER PLATEAU
TWEEDSMUIR PROVINCIAL PARK
VANCOUVER ISLAND
VANCOUVER
Victoria
Nanaimo
Port Alberni
Powell River
Prince George
Quesnel
Bellingham
Port Angeles
Mount Waddington 3994
U.S.
CANADA
UNITED STATES
Strait of Juan de Fuca
Copyright © by Rand McNally & Co.
Map prepared by Rand McNally & Co.
A-520220-764

ENGLISH	creek	Indian reserve	inlet	island	lake, l.	mountain	peak	provincial park	sound
DEUTSCH	Bach	Indianerreservation	Einfahrt	Insel	See	Berg	Gipfel	Provinz-Park	Sund
ESPAÑOL	riachuelo	reserva de Indios	abra	isla	lago	montaña	pico	parque de provincia	sonda
FRANÇAIS	crique	réserve indienne	bras de mer	île	lac	montagne	cime	parc provincial	détroit
PORTUGUÊS	riacho	reserva indigena	enseada	ilha	lago	montanha	pico	parque provincial	estreito

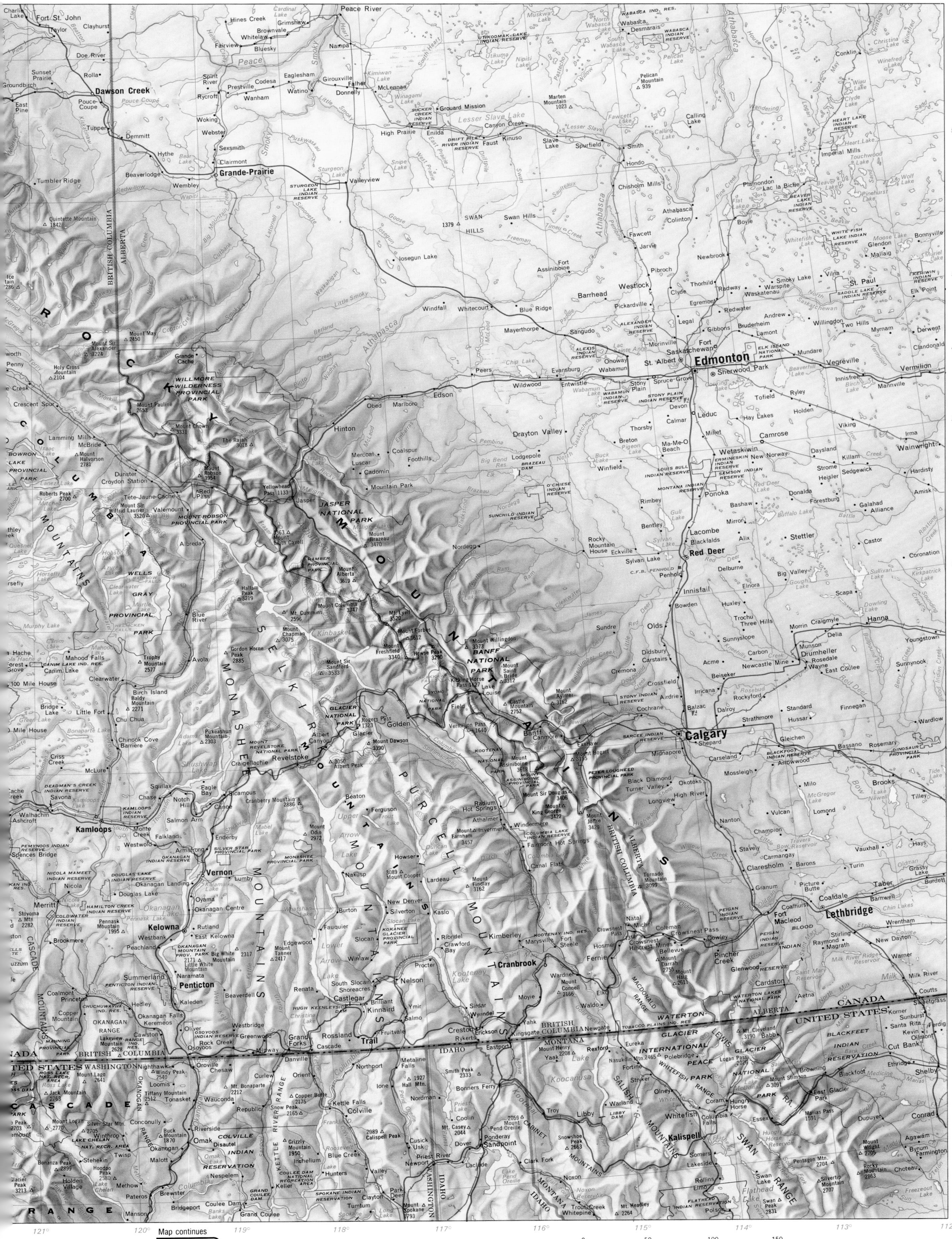
Peace River
Fort St. John
Dawson Creek
Grande-Prairie
Grande Cache
Valleyview
Lesser Slave Lake
Slave Lake
High Prairie
Swan Hills
Athabasca
Whitecourt
Barrhead
Westlock
Edmonton
St. Albert
Sherwood Park
Vegreville
Vermilion
Wainwright
Camrose
Wetaskiwin
Leduc
Drayton Valley
Edson
Hinton
Jasper
JASPER NATIONAL PARK
Ponoka
Lacombe
Red Deer
Innisfail
Olds
Drumheller
Hanna
Calgary
Banff
Canmore
BANFF NATIONAL PARK
Golden
Revelstoke
GLACIER NATIONAL PARK
Kamloops
Vernon
Kelowna
Penticton
Nelson
Trail
Cranbrook
Kimberley
Fernie
Lethbridge
Fort Macleod
Medicine Hat
Okotoks
High River
Cardston
Kalispell
Whitefish
Libby
Sandpoint
Colville
Omak
ROCKY MOUNTAINS
COLUMBIA MOUNTAINS
SELKIRK MOUNTAINS
MONASHEE MOUNTAINS
PURCELL MOUNTAINS
CASCADE RANGE
BRITISH COLUMBIA
ALBERTA
CANADA
UNITED STATES
WASHINGTON
IDAHO
MONTANA

Map continues pages 184-185

Map continues pages 202-203

Kilometers 0 50 100 150 Km.
Statute Miles 0 50 100 150 Mi.

Scale 1:3,000,000

One centimeter represents 30 kilometers.
One inch represents approximately 47 miles.
Lambert Conformal Conic Projection

Fort McMurray
Anzac
GREGOIRE LAKE INDIAN RESERVE
La Loche
Buffalo Narrows
PETER POND LAKE INDIAN RESERVE
Peter Pond Lake
Churchill Lake
Conklin
Ile-à-la-Crosse
Pinehouse Lake
LAC LA RONGE PROVINCIAL PARK
La Ronge
Lac la Ronge
Pelican Narrows
Island Falls
Deschambault Lake
WAPAWEKKA HILLS 767
Flin Flon
Denare Beach
Beauval
LA PLONGE INDIAN RESERVE
CANOE LAKE INDIAN RESERVE
MOSTOOS HILLS
Primrose Lake
Imperial Mills
Plamondon
Lac la Biche
Boyle
BEAVER LAKE INDIAN RESERVE
HEART LAKE INDIAN RESERVE
COLD LAKE INDIAN RESERVE
MEADOW LAKE PROVINCIAL PARK
Cold Lake
Grand Centre
Bonnyville
Glendon
Mallaig
WHITE FISH LAKE INDIAN RESERVE
Doré Lake
THUNDER HILLS 730
Molanosa
Green Lake
Meadow Lake
Waskatenau
Smoky Lake
Warspite
Vilna
St. Paul
KEHIWIN INDIAN RESERVE
SADDLE LAKE INDIAN RESERVE
Andrew
Willingdon
Elk Point
Two Hills
Myrnam
Mundare
ELK ISLAND NATIONAL PARK
Vegreville
Derwent
Innisfree
Clandonald
Tofield
Ryley
Holden
Vermilion
Mannville
Kitscoty
Lloydminster
Marwayne
PRINCE ALBERT NATIONAL PARK
Montreal Lake
MONTREAL LAKE INDIAN RESERVE
CUB HILLS 741
NIPAWIN PROVINCIAL PARK
Big River
Leoville
Spiritwood
Shell Lake
Medstead
Glaslyn
Turtleford
Mervin
Edam
Meota
Maidstone
Paynton
Delmas
Lashburn
Viking
Daysland
Killam
Irma
Strome
Heisler
Sedgewick
Forestburg
Wainwright
Edgerton
Hardisty
Galahad
Alliance
Amisk
Chauvin
Metiskow
Provost
Castor
Coronation
NEUTRAL HILLS 861
Consort
Scapa
Macklin
Evesham
Senlac
Unity
Wilkie
Scott
Cut Knife
North Battleford
Battleford
Hafford
Krydor
Blaine Lake
Marcelin
Leask
Shellbrook
Prince Albert
STURGEON LAKE INDIAN RESERVE
Smeaton
Choiceland
Snowden
White Fox
Nipawin
Carrot River
Aylsham
Arborfield
Zenon Park
Ridgedale
Kinistino
Birch Hills
Weldon
Gronlid
Star City
Melfort
Tisdale
Crooked River
Peesane
Mistatim
Hudson Bay
Prairie River
PASQUIA HILLS
Wildcat Hill 782
Duck Lake
Rosthern
Waldheim
Hague
Radisson
Borden
Langham
Dalmeny
Warman
Saskatoon
Aberdeen
Cudworth
Wakaw
Saint-Louis
Domremy
Saint-Brieux
Pleasantdale
Naicam
Spalding
Humboldt
Bruno
Watson
Quill Lake
Wadena
Kelvington
Rose Valley
Porcupine Plain
Preeceville
Sturgis
Invermay
Endeavour
Biggar
Perdue
Asquith
Landis
Luseland
Kerrobert
Fusilier
Altario
Hanna
Sedalia
Youngstown
Chinook
Cereal
Sunnynook
Oyen
Sibbald
Alsask
Flaxcombe
Coleville
Smiley
Dodsland
Plenty
Herschel
Kindersley
Brock
Rosetown
Zealandia
Harris
Delisle
Clavet
Colonsay
Allan
Dundurn
Hanley
Kenaston
Young
Watrous
Manitou Beach
Lanigan
Jansen
Dafoe
Kandahar
Wynyard
Elfros
Foam Lake
Buchanan
Canora
TOUCHWOOD HILLS
Nokomis
Semans
Raymore
Punnichy
Wishart
Sheho
Theodore
Yorkton
Finnegan
Acadia Valley
Eatonia
Elrose
Milden
Conquest
Outlook
Dinsmore
Hawarden
Bladworth
Davidson
Imperial
Govan
Quinton
Kelliher
Ituna
Willowbrook
Wardlow
Empress
Bindloss
Leader
Prelate
Sceptre
THE COTEAU
Dunblane
Elbow
Lucky Lake
Beechy
Riverhurst
Kyle
Craik
Strasbourg
Holdfast
Earl Grey
Southey
Cupar
Dysart
Lipton
Goodeve
Melville
Brooks
Tilley
Burstall
Abbey
Cabri
GREAT SAND HILLS
Hilda
Fox Valley
Pennant Station
Hazlet
Stewart Valley
Leinan
Central Butte
Tugaske
Eyebrow
Chamberlain
Regina Beach
Silton
Craven
Lumsden
Balcarres
Abernethy
Lemberg
Neudorf
Grayson
Esterhazy
Suffield
Hays
Redcliff
Medicine Hat
Golden Prairie
Webb
Swift Current
Herbert
Morse
Chaplin
Caron
Mortlach
Moose Jaw
Belle-Plaine
Pense
Pilot Butte
Regina
Qu'Appelle
Indian Head
McLean
Wolseley
Grenfell
Broadview
Bow Island
Irvine
Walsh
Seven Persons
Burdett
Tompkins
Gull Lake
Maple Creek
Piapot
Wymark
McMahon
Blumenhof
Hodgeville
Coderre
Rouleau
Lajord
Vibank
Kendal
Glenavon
Kipling
Simmie
CYPRESS HILLS PROVINCIAL PARK
1462
1392
Foremost
Manyberries
Admiral
Ponteix
Vanguard
Gravelbourg
Mossbank
Ardill
Avonlea
Wilcox
Milestone
Lewvan
Francis
Truax
Lang
Yellow Grass
Fillmore
MOOSE MOUNTAIN PROVINCIAL PARK
Handsworth
Instow
Shaunavon
Cadillac
Aneroid
Kincaid
Meyronne
Mazenod
Congress
Limerick
Lafleche
Assiniboia
Ormiston
Pangman
Weyburn
Stoughton
Arcola
Kisbey
Eastend
Ravenscrag
Senate
Consul
Govenlock
Frontier
Climax
Orkney
Val-Marie
Masefield
Pinto Butte 1049
Mankota
Wood Mountain 1021
Scout Lake
Lisieux
Willow Bunch
Fife Lake
Viceroy
Ogema
Bengough
Ceylon
Radville
Midale
Halbrite
Griffin
Lampman
Tribune
Estevan
Bienfait
Frobisher
Torquay
Roche-Percée
North Portal
Rockglen
Big Beaver
Minton
Coronach
Hogeland
Turner
Morgan
Loring
Whitewater
Opheim
Richland
Ambrose
Crosby
Columbus
Flaxton
West Butte 2128
Mount Brown 2121
SWEET GRASS HILLS
Joplin
Rudyard
Chester
Gildford
ALBERTA
SASKATCHEWAN
MONTANA
NORTH DAKOTA
CANADA
UNITED STATES
Copyright © by Rand McNally & Co.
Map prepared by Rand McNally & Co.
A-630218-764

Meters	Feet
6000	19685
4000	13124
3000	9843
2000	6562
1000	3281
500	1640
200	656
0	0
Land Below Sea Level 0	0
200	656
1000	3281
3000	9843
6000	19685
9000	29520

Map continues pages 182-183

Map continues pages 202-203

Map continues pages 198-199

ENGLISH	creek, cr.	hills	Indian reserve	island, i.	lake, l.	provincial park
DEUTSCH	Bach	Hügel	Indianerreservation	Insel	See	Provinz-Park
ESPAÑOL	riachuelo	colinas	reserva de Indios	isla	lago	parque de provincia
FRANÇAIS	crique	collines	réserve indienne	île	lac	parc provincial
PORTUGUÊS	riacho	colinas	reserva indígena	ilha	lago	parque provincial

Lake Winnipeg
(217)
Lake Winnipegosis
(253)
Lake Manitoba
(248)
Cedar Lake
Winnipeg
Brandon
Portage-la-Prairie
Thompson
Kenora
Dryden
International Falls
Selkirk
Dauphin
Gillam
Lynn Lake
Flin Flon
The Pas
Gods Lake
Island Lake
Red Sucker Lake
Sandy Lake
Lac Seul
Sioux Lookout
Red Lake
Lake of the Woods
Nelson
Churchill
Hayes
Severn
Gods
Assiniboine
MANITOBA
ONTARIO
MINNESOTA
CANADA
UNITED STATES
WETIKO HILLS
RIDING MOUNTAIN NATIONAL PARK
DUCK MOUNTAIN
Port Nelson
York Factory
Norway House
Berens River
Oxford House
Shamattawa
Poplar Hill
Pikangikum
Grand Rapids
Gimli
Steinbach
Morden
Winkler
Neepawa
Minnedosa
Virden
Souris
Emerson
101°
100°
99°
98°
97°
96°
95°
94°
93°
92°
91°
90°
56°
55°
54°
53°
52°
51°
50°
49°

Map continues pages 190-191

Kilometers 0 50 100 150 Km.
Statute Miles 0 50 100 150 Mi.

Scale 1:3,000,000

One centimeter represents 30 kilometers.
One inch represents approximately 47 miles.
Lambert Conformal Conic Projection

72°
71°
70°
69°
68°
67°
66°
65°
64°
63°
51°
50°
49°
48°
47°
46°
45°
44°
Mont de Babel
Réservoir Manicouagan
Lac Manouane
Réservoir Pipmuacan
Sept-Îles
Moisie
Clarke City
Port-Cartier
Rivière-Pentecôte
Islets-Caribou
Baie-Trinité
Godbout
Baie-Comeau
Hauterive
Betsiamites
Forestville
Portneuf-sur-Mer
Sault-au-Mouton
Tadoussac
Alma
Kenogami
Arvida
Jonquière
Chicoutimi
La Baie
Laterrière
Rivière-au-Tonnerre
Magpie
Mingan
Havre-St-Pierre
Baie-Johan-Beetz
Aguanish
MINGAN ARCHIPELAGO NAT. PARK
Détroit de Jacques-Cartier
Baie-Ste-Claire
Port-Menier
ÎLE D'ANTICOSTI
Rivière-de-la-Chaloupe
Détroit d'Honguedo
Saint Laurent
Saint Lawrence
Ste.-Anne-des-Monts
Cap-Chat
Ste.-Marthe-de-Gaspé
Rivière-à-Claude
Madeleine-Centre
Pointe-à-la-Frégate
St.-Yvon
Matane
Ste.-Félicité
Mont-Joli
Rimouski
Bic
St.-Fabien
Trois-Pistoles
Amqui
Causapscal
PÉNINSULE DE LA GASPÉSIE
PARC NATIONAL DE FORILLON
Gaspé
Fontenelle
Percé
St.-Gabriel-de-Gaspé
Grande-Rivière
Chandler
Newport
New-Richmond
Nouvelle
Caplan
Bonaventure
New-Carlisle
Matapédia
Campbellton
Dalhousie
Jacquet River
Chaleur Bay
Miscou Centre
Lamèque
Shippegan
Caraquet
Grande-Anse
Beresford
Bathurst
St.-Isidore
Tracadie
Neguac
Miramichi Bay
Chatham
Newcastle
Rivière-du-Loup
Cabano
Clermont
La Malbaie
Baie-St-Paul
St.-Siméon
Kedgwick
St.-Quentin
Edmundston
Madawaska
St.-Basile
Rivière-Verte
Fort Kent
Van Buren
St.-Leonard
Grand Falls
Stockholm
Caribou
Presque Isle
Fort Fairfield
Washburn
Ashland
Mars Hill
Bridgewater
Houlton
Woodstock
Hartland
Perth-Andover
Plaster Rock
Doaktown
Boiestown
Renous
Rogersville
Richibucto
Rexton
Buctouche
Notre-Dame
Shediac
Moncton
Dieppe
Petitcodiac
Sackville
Amherst
Oxford
Springhill
Parrsboro
Truro
New Glasgow
Stellarton
Westville
Pictou
Antigonish
Charlottetown
Summerside
PRINCE EDWARD ISLAND
Northumberland Strait
Fredericton
Oromocto
Marysville
Nashwaaksis
Chipman
Minto
Sussex
Hampton
Rothesay
Saint John
St. Martins
Grand Bay
McAdam
St. Stephen
Calais
St. Andrews
Eastport
Lubec
Machias
Cutler
Bay of Fundy
GRAND MANAN ISLAND
Digby
Annapolis Royal
Bridgetown
Middleton
Kentville
Wolfville
Windsor
Berwick
Kingston
Halifax
Dartmouth
Lunenburg
Bridgewater
Liverpool
Brooklyn
Shelburne
Lockeport
Barrington
Pubnico
Yarmouth
NOVA SCOTIA
Québec
Lévis
Lauzon
Ste.-Foy
Beauport
Montmagny
St.-Pamphile
Lac-Frontière
St.-Georges
Beauceville
Lac-Mégantic
Jackman
Greenville
Millinocket
East Millinocket
Patten
Island Falls
Sherman Mills
Lincoln
Bangor
Brewer
Old Town
Orono
Ellsworth
Bar Harbor
ACADIA NATIONAL PARK
Belfast
Camden
Rockland
Thomaston
Waldoboro
Wiscasset
Bath
Brunswick
Freeport
Yarmouth
Portland
South Portland
Cape Elizabeth
Old Orchard Beach
Biddeford
Saco
Kennebunk
Ogunquit
Cape Porpoise
Lewiston
Auburn
Augusta
Gardiner
Hallowell
Waterville
Winslow
Skowhegan
Madison
Pittsfield
Newport
Dexter
Guilford
Bingham
Farmington
Wilton
Rumford
Mexico
Dixfield
Bethel
Norway
Oxford
Mechanic Falls
Gulf of Maine
APPALACHIAN MOUNTAINS
NOTRE DAME MOUNTAINS
MAINE
NEW BRUNSWICK
QUÉBEC
UNITED STATES
CANADA
Mount Katahdin
BAXTER STATE PARK
Moosehead L.
Sable
CAPE SABLE ISLAND
SEAL ISLAND

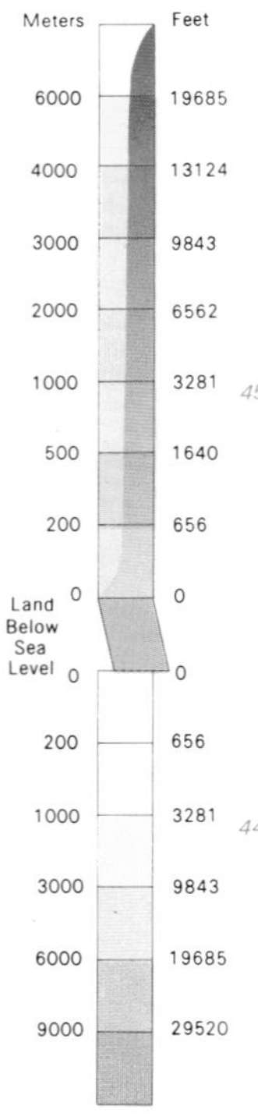
Meters
Feet
6000
19685
4000
13124
3000
9843
2000
6562
1000
3281
500
1640
200
656
0
0
Land Below Sea Level
0
0
200
656
1000
3281
3000
9843
6000
19685
9000
29520

Map continues pages 188-189

ENGLISH	bay	cape	dam	island	lake, l.	mountain	point	strait
DEUTSCH	Bucht	Kap	Damm	Insel	See	Berg	Landspitze	Meeresstrasse
ESPAÑOL	bahía	cabo	presa	isla	lago	montaña	punta	estrecho
FRANÇAIS	baie	cap	barrage	île	lac	montagne	pointe	détroit
PORTUGUÊS	baía	cabo	represa	ilha	lago	montanha	ponta	estreito

LABRADOR
SEA
ATLANTIC
OCEAN
NEWFOUNDLAND
LONG RANGE MOUNTAINS
SAINT PIERRE AND MIQUELON
(France)
SAINT-PIERRE-ET-MIQUELON
Saint-Pierre
Miquelon
Langlade
Gulf of Saint Lawrence
Cabot Strait
QUÉBEC
NEWF.
NEWFOUNDLAND
CANADA
Corner Brook
St. John's
Sydney
North Sydney
Sydney Mines
Glace Bay
New Waterford
Dominion
Port Morien
CAPE BRETON ISLAND
CAPE BRETON HIGHLANDS NATIONAL PARK
Louisbourg
FORTRESS OF LOUISBOURG NATIONAL HISTORIC PARK
Gabarus
Fourchu
St. Peters
L'Ardoise
Arichat
ISLE MADAME
Canso
Guysborough
Larrys River
Chedabucto Bay
West Bay
Iona
Mabou
Judique
Inverness
Margaree Harbour
Chéticamp
Grand-Étang
Pleasant Bay
Dingwall
Ingonish
CAPE NORTH
CAPE SAINT LAWRENCE
CAPE SMOKEY
Aspy Bay
SCATARIE ISLAND
Mira Bay
ST. PAUL ISLAND (N.S.)
SABLE ISLAND (N.S.)
Channel-Port-aux-Basques
CAPE RAY
Burnt Island
Isle-aux-Morts
Rose-Blanche
La Poile
Grand Bruit
Burgeo
Ramea
RAMEA ISLANDS
Grey River
François
Cape la Hune
Pass Island
Hermitage
Harbour Breton
Belleoram
English Harbour West
Garnish
Grand Bank
Fortune
Lamaline
Lawn
St. Lawrence
Burin
Marystown
Creston
BURIN PENINSULA
Fortune Bay
Placentia Bay
Placentia
Argentia
Dunville
Colinet
Mount Carmel
AVALON PENINSULA
St. Mary's Bay
St. Mary's
St. Bride's
Branch
CAPE SAINT MARY'S
St. Vincent's
St. Shotts
Trepassey
Portugal Cove South
CAPE RACE
MISTAKEN POINT
Renews
Ferryland
Cape Broyle
Tors Cove
Witless Bay
Bay Bulls
Petty Harbour
CAPE SPEAR
Torbay
Pouch Cove
CAPE SAINT FRANCIS
Wabana
BELL ISLAND
Conception Bay
Carbonear
Harbour Grace
Upper Island Cove
Spaniard's Bay
Bay Roberts
Brigus
Whitbourne
Winterton
Heart's Content
Hant's Harbour
Old Perlican
Bay de Verde
BACCALIEU ISLAND
GRATES POINT
Trinity Bay
Hickman's Harbour
RANDOM ISLAND
Shoal Harbour
Clarenville
Sunnyside
Come by Chance
Port Blandford
Lethbridge
Musgravetown
Princeton
Port Rexton
TERRA NOVA NATIONAL PARK
Little Catalina
Catalina
Port Union
Elliston
Bonavista
CAPE BONAVISTA
Bonavista Bay
Keels
Eastport
Salvage
Glovertown
Gambo
Middle Brook
Hare Bay
St. Brendan's
Gander
Glenwood
Appleton
Gander Bay
Carmanville
Doting Cove
Lumsden
CAPE FREELS
Newtown
Wesleyville
Valleyfield
Greenspond
Trinity
FOGO ISLAND
Fogo
Joe Batt's Arm
CAPE FOGO
Change Islands
FUNK ISLAND
WADHAM ISLANDS
Hamilton Sound
Twillingate
NEW WORLD ISLAND
Summerford
Boyd's Cove
Birchy Bay
Campbellton
Lewisporte
Northern Arm
Botwood
Norris Arm
Bishop's Falls
Grand Falls
Windsor
Badger
Millertown Junction
Millertown
Buchans
EXPLOITS DAM
Bay of Exploits
Point Leamington
Notre Dame Bay
Little Bay Islands
Beaumont
Fortune Harbour
Port Anson
Pilley's Island
Robert's Arm
Springdale
King's Point
Rattling Brook
Burlington
Green Bay
Nippers Harbour
Westport
Baie Verte
Pacquet
La Scie
Shoe Cove
Round Harbour
CAPE SAINT JOHN
Seal Cove
Fleur-de-Lys
White Bay
Jackson's Arm
Hampden
Sandy Lake
Little Harbour Deep
Harbour Deep
Williamsport
Hooping Harbour
Englee
Canada Bay
Roddickton
Conche
GROAIS ISLAND
GREY ISLANDS
BELL ISLAND
HORSE ISLANDS
St. Anthony
Hare Bay
Raleigh
CAPE BAULD
QUIRPON ISLAND
L'ANSE-AUX-MEADOWS NAT. HIST. PARK
Pistolet Bay
Cook's Harbour
West St. Modeste
Red Bay
Belle Isle
Forteau
Blanc Sablon
Middle-Bay
Bradore-Bay
Flower's Cove
St. Barbe
Brig Bay
Bartletts Harbour
Saint John Bay
Port Saunders
Ingornachoix Bay
POINTE RICHE
River of Ponds
Blue Mountain
Daniel's Harbour
Portland Creek Pond
Parson's Pond
Cow Head
Saint Pauls Inlet
GROS MORNE NATIONAL PARK
Gros Morne
Rocky Harbour
Bonne Bay
Norris Point
Woody Point
Trout River
Mount Saint Gregory
Bay of Islands
Lark Harbour
Cox's Cove
Deer Lake
Pasadena
Howley
Main Topsail
Old Man Mountain
Grand Lake
Spruce Brook
Stephenville
Stephenville Crossing
Port au Port
Piccadilly
Lourdes
Port au Port Bay
PORT AU PORT PENINSULA
LONG POINT
CAPE SAINT GEORGE
Saint George's Bay
St. George's
BARACHOIS POND PROVINCIAL PARK
Flat Bay
Mount Howley
Robinson
St. David's
Codroy Pond
South Branch
Codroy
CAPE ANGUILLE
Doyles
Tompkins
Table Mountain
BLUE HILLS OF COUTEAU
Red Indian Lake
Victoria Lake
Meelpaeg Lake
Jeddore Lake
St. Alban's
Head Bay d'Espoir
Mount Sylvester
Gisborne Lake
Terrenceville
Davis Cove
Rencontre East
Pool's Cove
Gaultois
McCallum
Pushthrough
Richard's Harbour
Petit Forte
Merasheen
Fox Harbour
Sawyers Hill
Ship Cove
Red Bay
Vieux-Fort
Salmon-Bay
Port-St-Servan
Shekatika
St-Augustin-Saguenay
ÎLES MONGER
Baie des Hal Hal
La Tabatière
Baie-des-Moutons
Tête-à-la-Baleine
Pointe-à-Maurier
Washicoutai
La-Romaine
Kégashka
Wolf-Bay
CAP WHITTLE
ÎLES DE LA MADELEINE (Qué.)
Grand-Entrée
Lac Robertson
Lac Brûlé
Lac Montgevelles
Lac Musquaro
Lac Kegashka
Lac Coxipi
Lac Chevreuil
Lac Atikonipi
Lac Fonteneau
Lac Briçonnet

Kilometers 0 50 100 150 Km.
Statute Miles 0 50 100 150 Mi.

Scale 1:3,000,000

One centimeter represents 30 kilometers.
One inch represents approximately 47 miles.
Lambert Conformal Conic Projection

Map continues pages 190-191

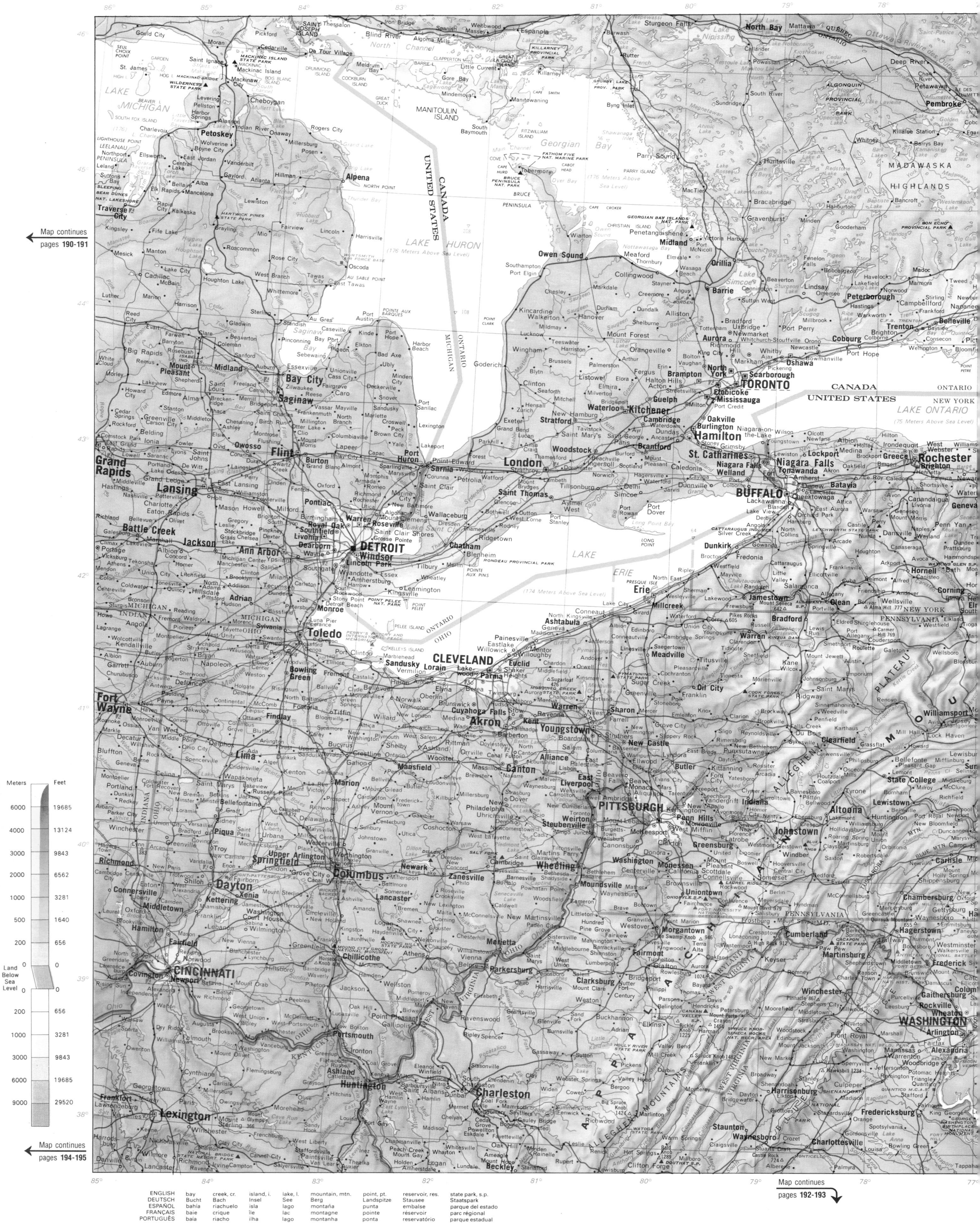
Meters Feet
6000 19685
4000 13124
3000 9843
2000 6562
1000 3281
500 1640
200 656
Land 0 0
Below Sea Level 0 0
200 656
1000 3281
3000 9843
6000 19685
9000 29520
LAKE MICHIGAN
LAKE HURON
Georgian Bay
LAKE ERIE
LAKE ONTARIO
CANADA
UNITED STATES
MANITOULIN ISLAND
BRUCE PENINSULA
MADAWASKA HIGHLANDS
ALLEGHENY MOUNTAINS
TORONTO
DETROIT
CLEVELAND
PITTSBURGH
CINCINNATI
BUFFALO
WASHINGTON
Rochester
Toledo
Columbus
Dayton
Lexington
Charleston
Flint
Lansing
Grand Rapids
Fort Wayne
Akron
Youngstown
Erie
Hamilton
London
Kitchener
Windsor
Saginaw
Bay City
Alpena
Sarnia
Altoona
Johnstown
Morgantown
Hagerstown
North Bay
Pembroke
Orillia
Barrie
Peterborough

Map continues pages 194-195

Map continues pages 192-193

ENGLISH	bay	creek, cr.	island, i.	lake, l.	mountain, mtn.	point, pt.	reservoir, res.	state park, s.p.
DEUTSCH	Bucht	Bach	Insel	See	Berg	Landspitze	Stausee	Staatspark
ESPAÑOL	bahía	riachuelo	isla	lago	montaña	punta	embalse	parque del estado
FRANÇAIS	baie	crique	île	lac	montagne	pointe	réservoir	parc régional
PORTUGUÊS	baía	riacho	ilha	lago	montanha	ponta	reservatório	parque estadual

Map continues
pages 186-187

Trois-Rivières
Sherbrooke
MONTRÉAL
Ottawa
Laval
Plattsburgh
Burlington
Montpelier
Augusta
Bangor
Lewiston
Portland
Gulf
of
Maine
Manchester
Concord
BOSTON
Worcester
Springfield
Providence
Hartford
New Haven
Bridgeport
Albany
Schenectady
Syracuse
Binghamton
Utica
Scranton
Wilkes-Barre
Allentown
Newark
NEW YORK
Paterson
Trenton
PHILADELPHIA
Camden
Wilmington
Atlantic City
Long Island Sound
Cape Cod Bay
Massachusetts Bay
ATLANTIC
OCEAN
DELMARVA PENINSULA
ADIRONDACK MOUNTAINS
CATSKILL MOUNTAINS
WHITE MOUNTAINS
GREEN MOUNTAINS
Copyright © by Rand McNally & Co.
Map prepared by Rand McNally & Co.
A-520696-764

Kilometers 0 50 100 150 Km.

Statute Miles 0 50 100 150 Mi.

Scale 1:3,000,000

One centimeter represents 30 kilometers.

One inch represents approximately 47 miles.

Albers Conical Equal-Area Projection

Map continues pages 184-185

Map continues pages 198-199

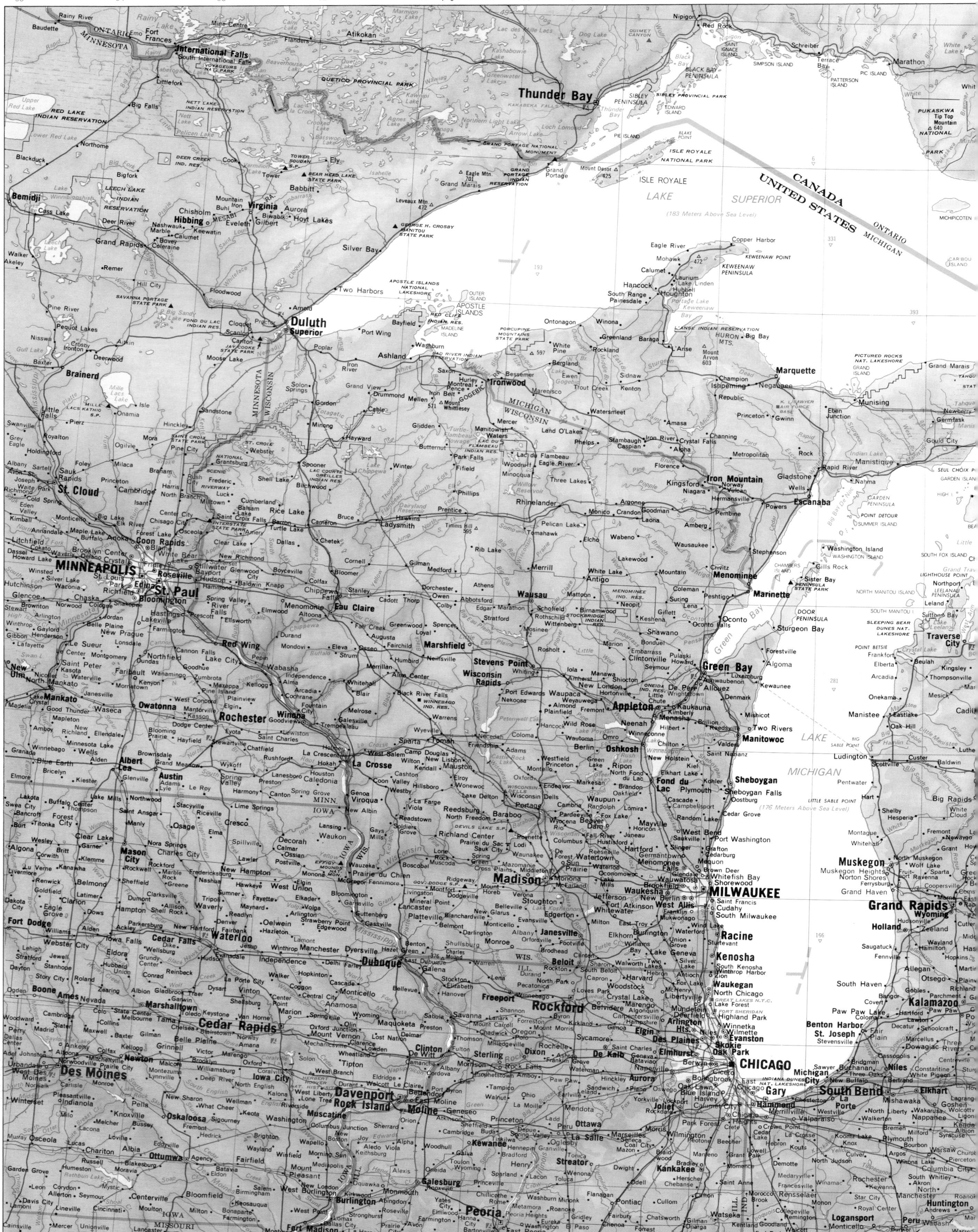
Thunder Bay
Duluth
Superior
MINNEAPOLIS
St. Paul
St. Cloud
Rochester
Eau Claire
La Crosse
Green Bay
Appleton
Oshkosh
Madison
MILWAUKEE
Racine
Kenosha
Rockford
CHICAGO
Gary
South Bend
Peoria
Davenport
Rock Island
Moline
Cedar Rapids
Des Moines
Waterloo
Dubuque
Grand Rapids
Kalamazoo
Muskegon
LAKE SUPERIOR
LAKE MICHIGAN
CANADA
UNITED STATES
ONTARIO
MICHIGAN
MINNESOTA
WISCONSIN
IOWA
ILL.
MISSOURI
Copyright © by Rand McNally & Co.
Map prepared by Rand McNally & Co.

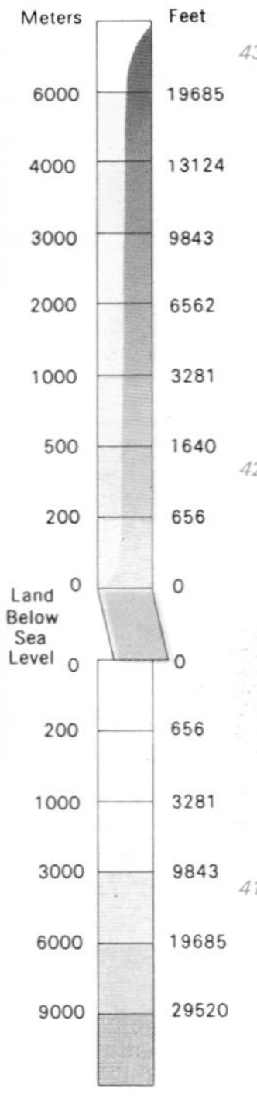
Meters
Feet
6000
19685
4000
13124
3000
9843
2000
6562
1000
3281
500
1640
200
656
0
0
Land Below Sea Level
0
0
200
656
1000
3281
3000
9843
6000
19685
9000
29520

Map continues pages 194-195

ENGLISH	bay	creek, cr.	Indian reservation	island, i.	lake, l.	point	reservoir, res.	state park, s.p.
DEUTSCH	Bucht	Bach	Indianerreservation	Insel	See	Landspitze	Stausee	Staatspark
ESPAÑOL	bahía	riachuelo	reserva de Indios	isla	lago	punta	embalse	parque del estado
FRANÇAIS	baie	crique	réserve indienne	île	lac	pointe	réservoir	parc régional
PORTUGUÊS	baía	riacho	reserva indígena	ilha	lago	ponta	reservatório	parque estadual

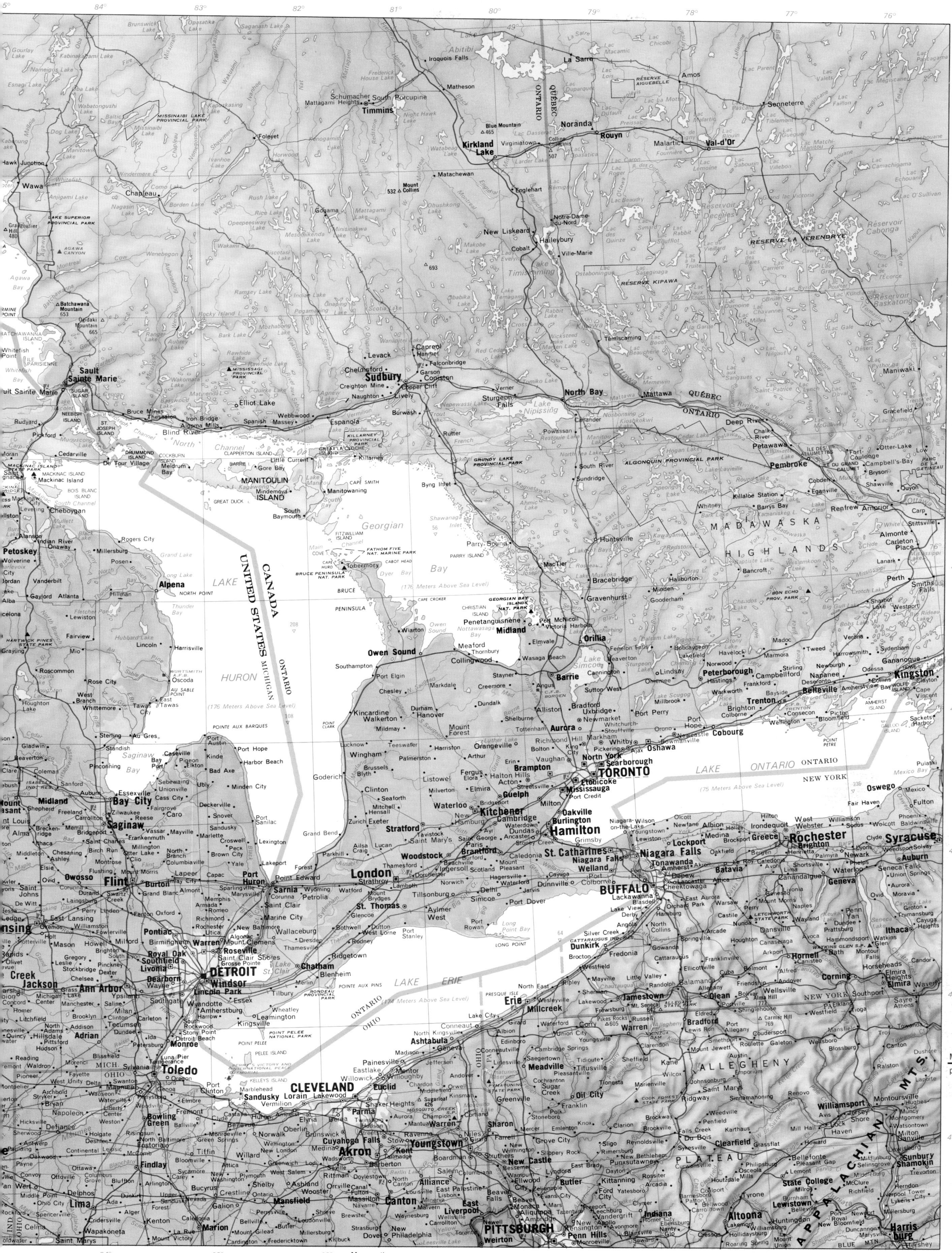
LAKE HURON
(176 Meters Above Sea Level)
Georgian Bay
(176 Meters Above Sea Level)
LAKE ONTARIO
(75 Meters Above Sea Level)
LAKE ERIE
(174 Meters Above Sea Level)
Saginaw Bay
North Channel
CANADA
UNITED STATES
ONTARIO
QUÉBEC
MICHIGAN
NEW YORK
OHIO
MADAWASKA HIGHLANDS
ALLEGHENY PLATEAU
APPALACHIAN MTS.
MANITOULIN ISLAND
BRUCE PENINSULA
ALGONQUIN PROVINCIAL PARK
RÉSERVE LA VÉRENDRYE
RÉSERVE KIPAWA
Réservoir Baskatong
Lake Nipissing
Lake Simcoe
Lake Timiskaming
Sault Sainte Marie
Sudbury
Timmins
Kirkland Lake
Rouyn
Noranda
Val-d'Or
North Bay
Pembroke
Orillia
Barrie
Owen Sound
TORONTO
Hamilton
St. Catharines
Niagara Falls
Kitchener
London
Windsor
DETROIT
Flint
Saginaw
Bay City
Toledo
CLEVELAND
Akron
Youngstown
Erie
BUFFALO
Rochester
Syracuse
Kingston
PITTSBURGH
Harrisburg
Williamsport
84° 83° 82° 81° 80° 79° 78° 77° 76°
49° 48° 47° 46° 45° 44° 43° 42° 41°

Map continues pages 188-189

Map continues pages 188-189

Kilometers 0 50 100 150 Km.
Statute Miles 0 50 100 150 Mi.

Scale 1:3,000,000

One centimeter represents 30 kilometers.
One inch represents approximately 47 miles.
Albers Conical Equal-Area Projection

Southeastern United States / Südöstliche Vereinigte Staaten / Sud-este de los Estados Unidos
Sud-Est des États-Unis / Estados Unidos: Sudeste

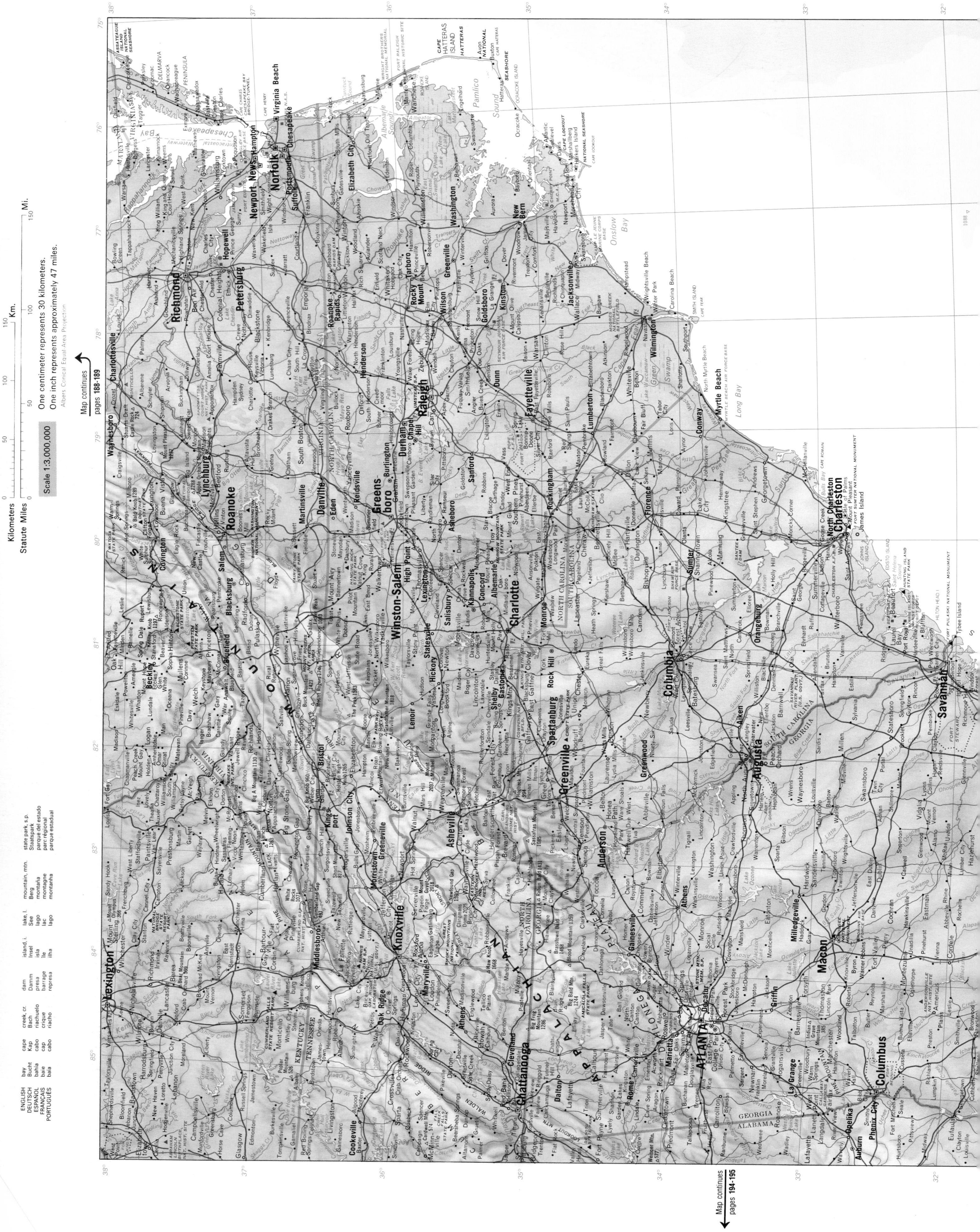
Kilometers
Statute Miles
Scale 1:3,000,000
One centimeter represents 30 kilometers.
One inch represents approximately 47 miles.
Albers Conical Equal Area Projection
ENGLISH bay cape creek, cr. dam island, i. lake, l. mountain, mtn. state park, s.p.
DEUTSCH Bucht Kap Bach Damm Insel See Berg Staatspark
ESPAÑOL bahía cabo riachuelo presa isla lago montaña parque del estado
FRANÇAIS baie cap crique barrage île lac montagne parc régional
PORTUGUÊS baía cabo riacho represa ilha lago montanha parque estadual
Richmond
Norfolk
Virginia Beach
Raleigh
Charlotte
Columbia
Atlanta
Knoxville
Chattanooga
Savannah
Charleston
Wilmington
Augusta
Macon
Columbus
Greensboro
Winston-Salem
Roanoke
Lexington
Asheville

Map continues pages 188-189

Map continues pages 194-195

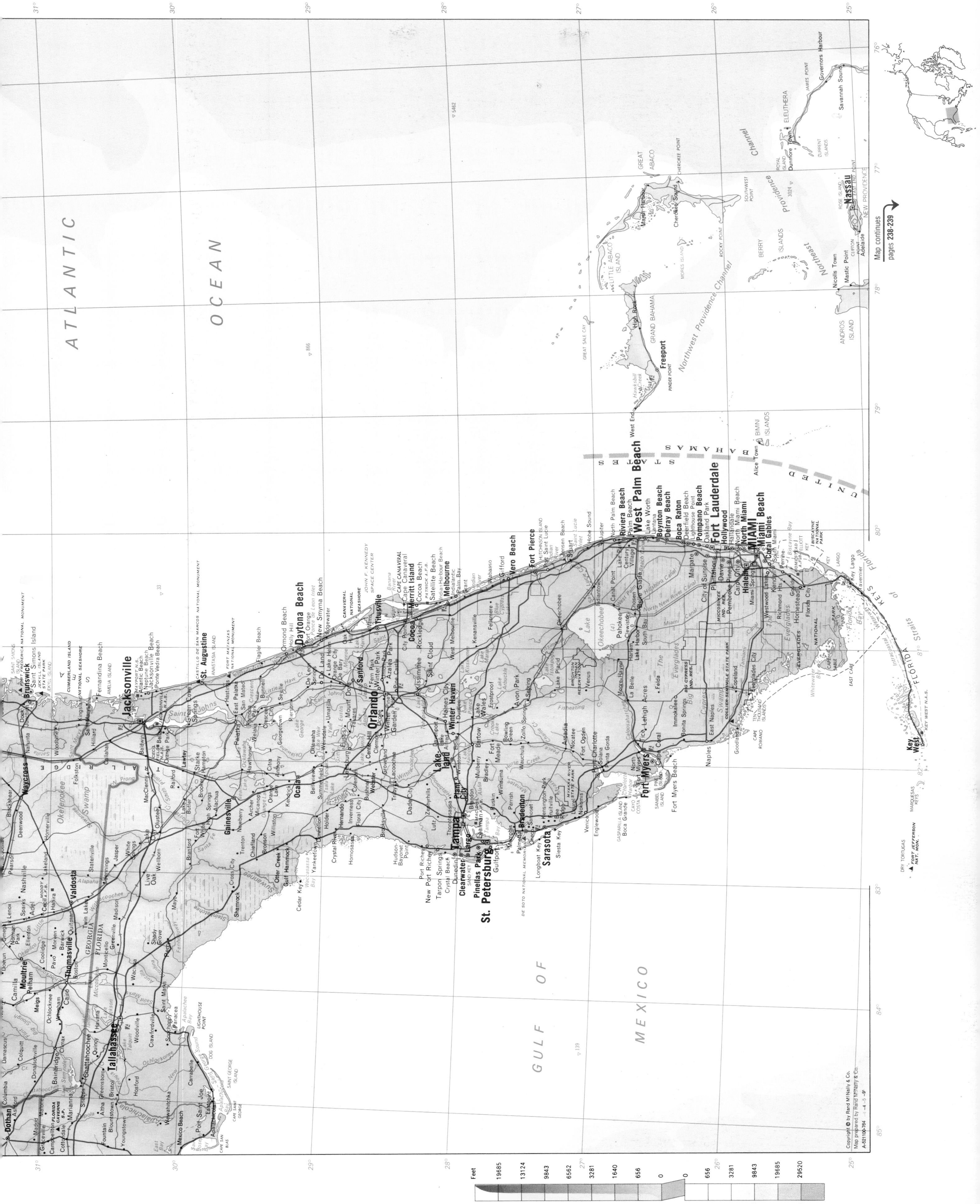
ATLANTIC
OCEAN
GULF OF
MEXICO
Jacksonville
Saint Augustine
Daytona Beach
Orlando
Tampa
St. Petersburg
Clearwater
Sarasota
Bradenton
Fort Myers
Gainesville
Ocala
Tallahassee
Melbourne
Fort Pierce
West Palm Beach
Boca Raton
Fort Lauderdale
Hollywood
MIAMI
Miami Beach
Hialeah
Key West
Valdosta
Thomasville
Waycross
Brunswick
Lake Okeechobee
The Everglades
GRAND BAHAMA
Freeport
GREAT ABACO
Nassau
NEW PROVIDENCE
ANDROS ISLAND
BIMINI ISLANDS
Northwest Providence Channel
Northeast Providence Channel
BERRY ISLANDS
ELEUTHERA
UNITED STATES
BAHAMAS
Straits of Florida
FLORIDA KEYS
Map continues pages 238-239
Feet
Meters
Land Below Sea Level
Copyright © by Rand McNally & Co.
Map prepared by Rand McNally & Co.

Map continues pages 188-189

Map continues pages 190-191

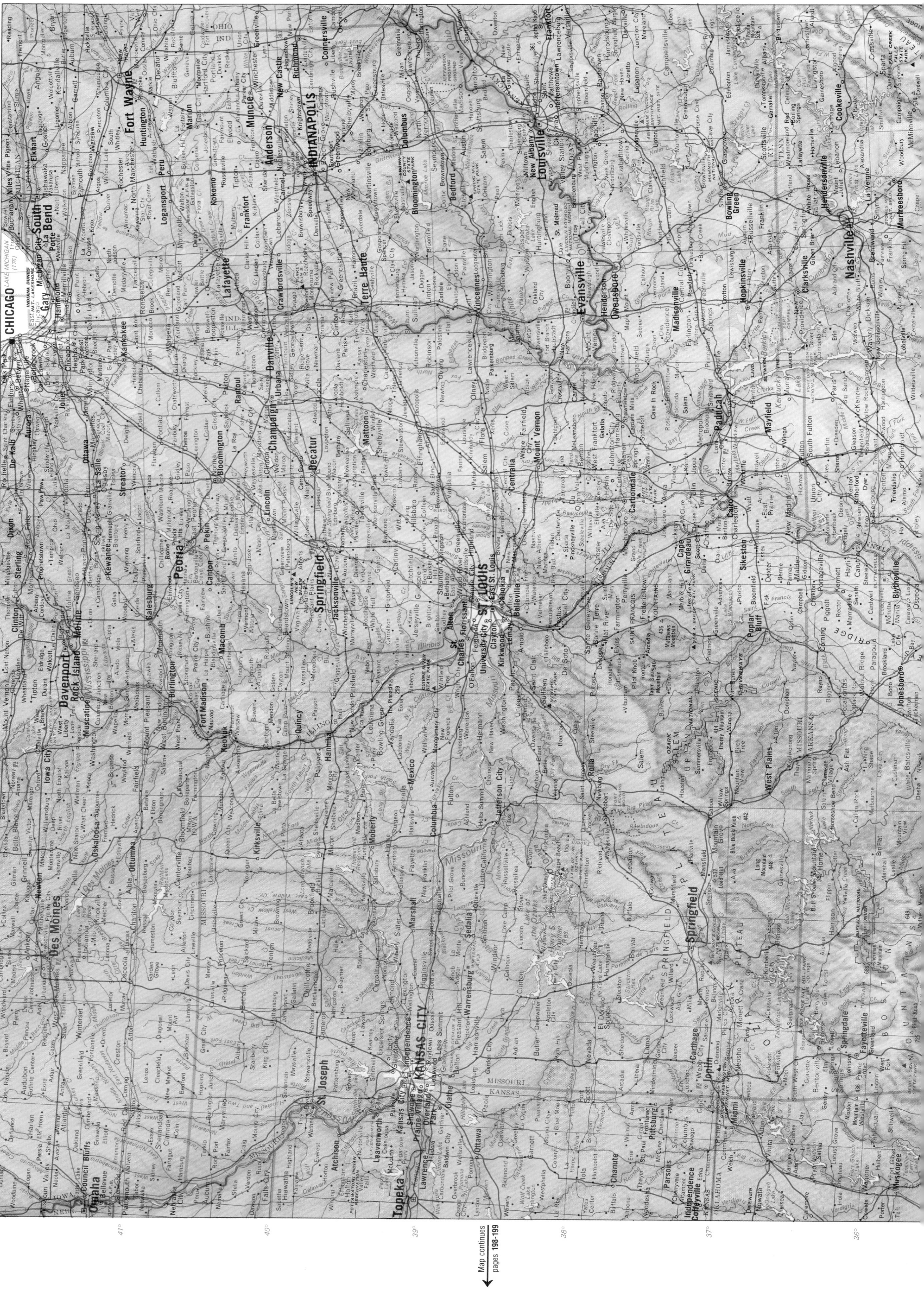
CHICAGO
INDIANAPOLIS
ST LOUIS
KANSAS CITY
Louisville
Nashville
Springfield
Des Moines
Omaha
Topeka
Fort Wayne
Evansville
Peoria

Map continues pages 198-199

Map continues pages 192-193

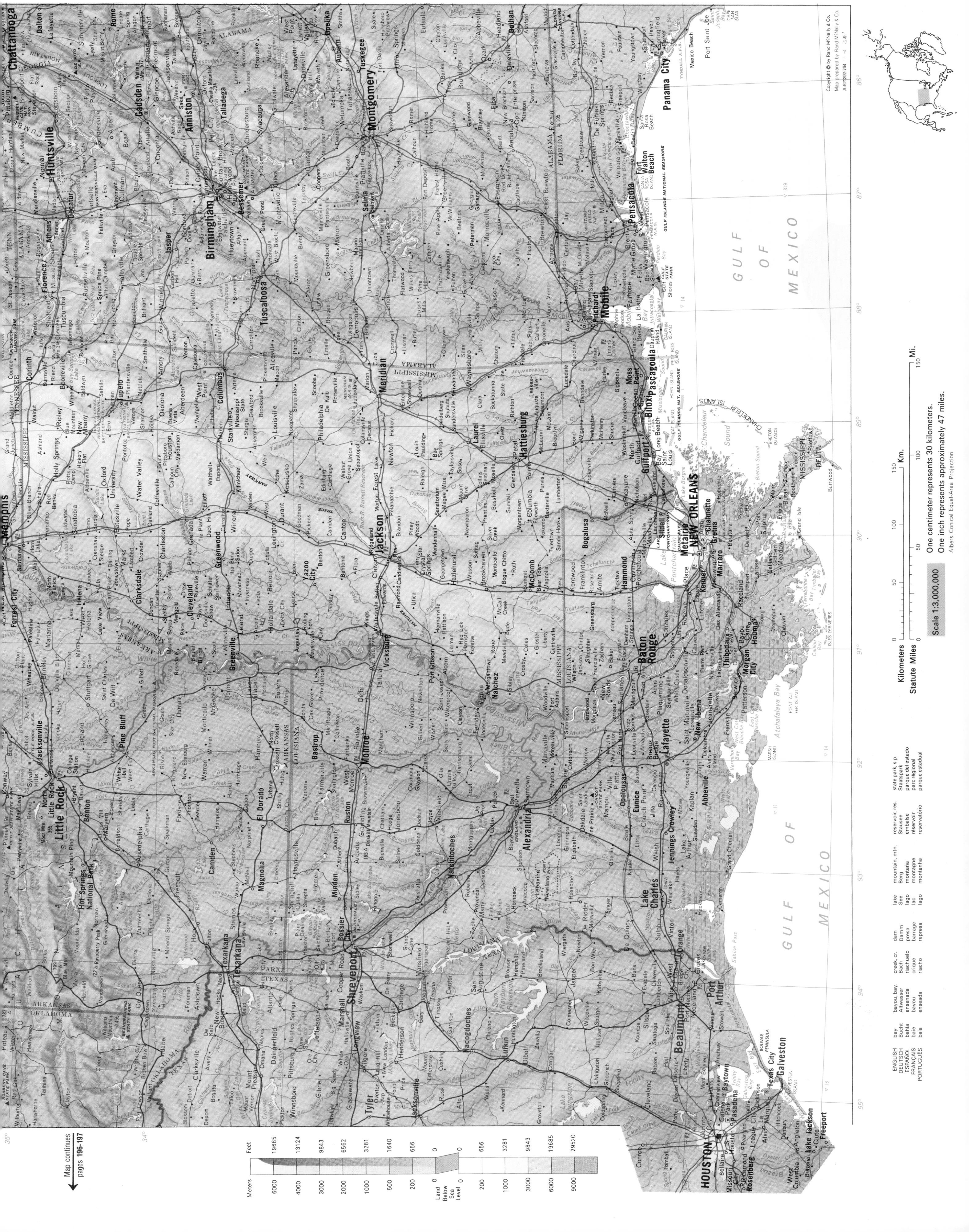
GULF OF MEXICO
Scale 1:3,000,000
One centimeter represents 30 kilometers.
One inch represents approximately 47 miles.
Albers Conical Equal-Area Projection
Kilometers
Statute Miles
Copyright © by Rand McNally & Co.
Memphis
Jackson
Montgomery
Birmingham
New Orleans
Baton Rouge
Shreveport
Little Rock
Mobile
Houston
Beaumont
Lafayette
Alexandria
Monroe
Chattanooga
Huntsville

Map continues pages 196-197

Map continues pages 194-195

Map continues pages 198-199

MISSOURI
KANSAS
OKLAHOMA
TEXAS
COLORADO
NEW MEXICO
Wichita
Hutchinson
Tulsa
Oklahoma City
Amarillo
Lubbock
Wichita Falls
Lawton
Fort Worth
DALLAS
Pueblo
Trinidad
Roswell
Abilene
Dodge City
Garden City
Emporia
Enid
Clovis
LLANO ESTACADO
GYPSUM HILLS
FLINT HILLS

Map continues pages 200-201

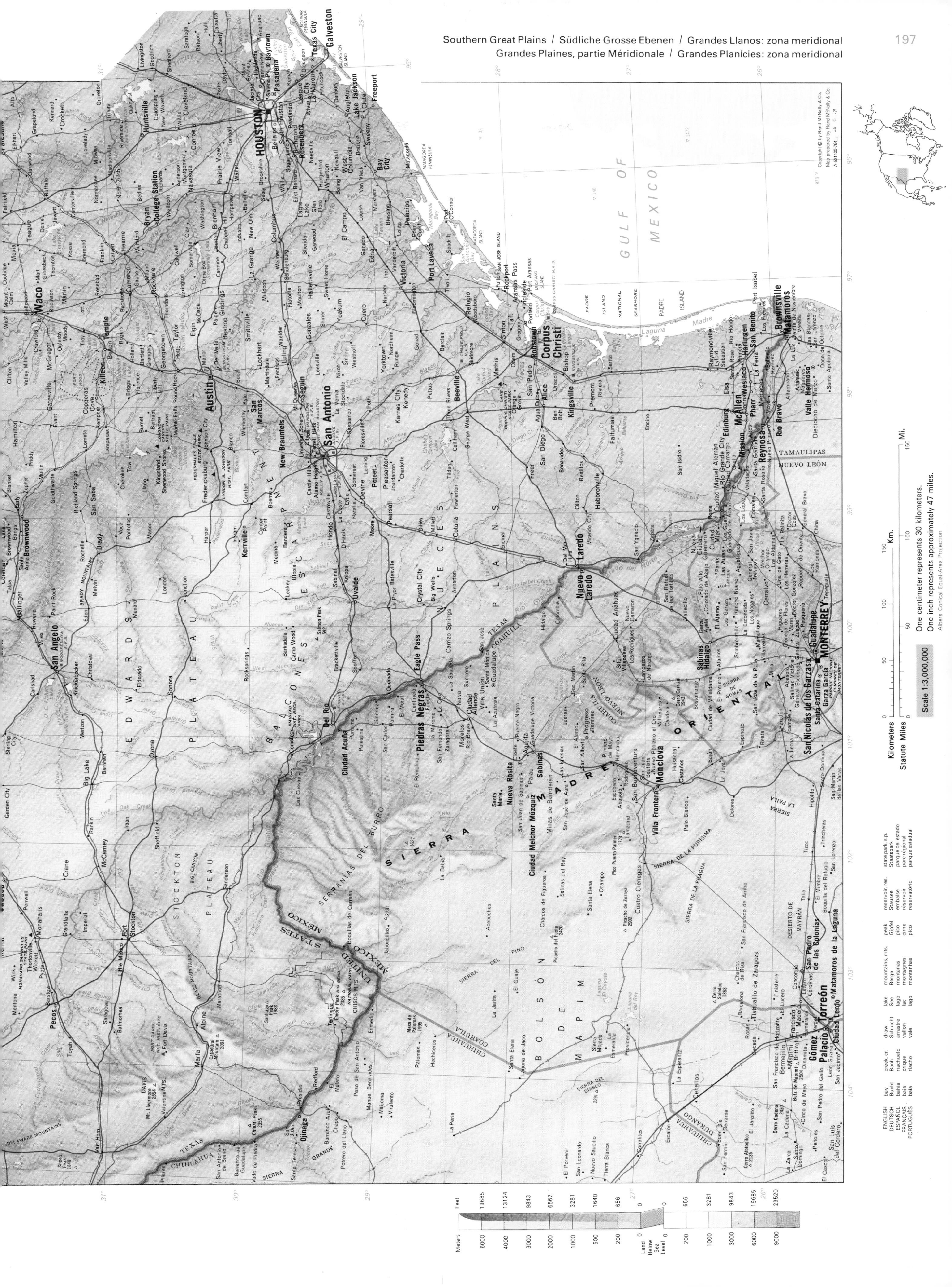
GULF OF MEXICO
Scale 1:3,000,000
One centimeter represents 30 kilometers.
One inch represents approximately 47 miles.
Albers Conical Equal-Area Projection
Kilometers
Statute Miles
Copyright © by Rand McNally & Co.
Map prepared by Rand McNally & Co.
ENGLISH bay creek, cr. draw lake mountains, mts. peak reservoir, res. state park, s.p.
DEUTSCH Bucht Bach Schlucht See Berge Gipfel Stausee Staatspark
ESPAÑOL bahía riachuelo arrastre lago montañas pico embalse parque del estado
FRANÇAIS baie cirque vallon lac montagnes cime reservoir parc regional
PORTUGUÊS baía riacho vale lago montanhas pico reservatório parque estadual
Meters
Feet
Land Below Sea Level

Map continues pages 190-191

Map continues pages 184-185

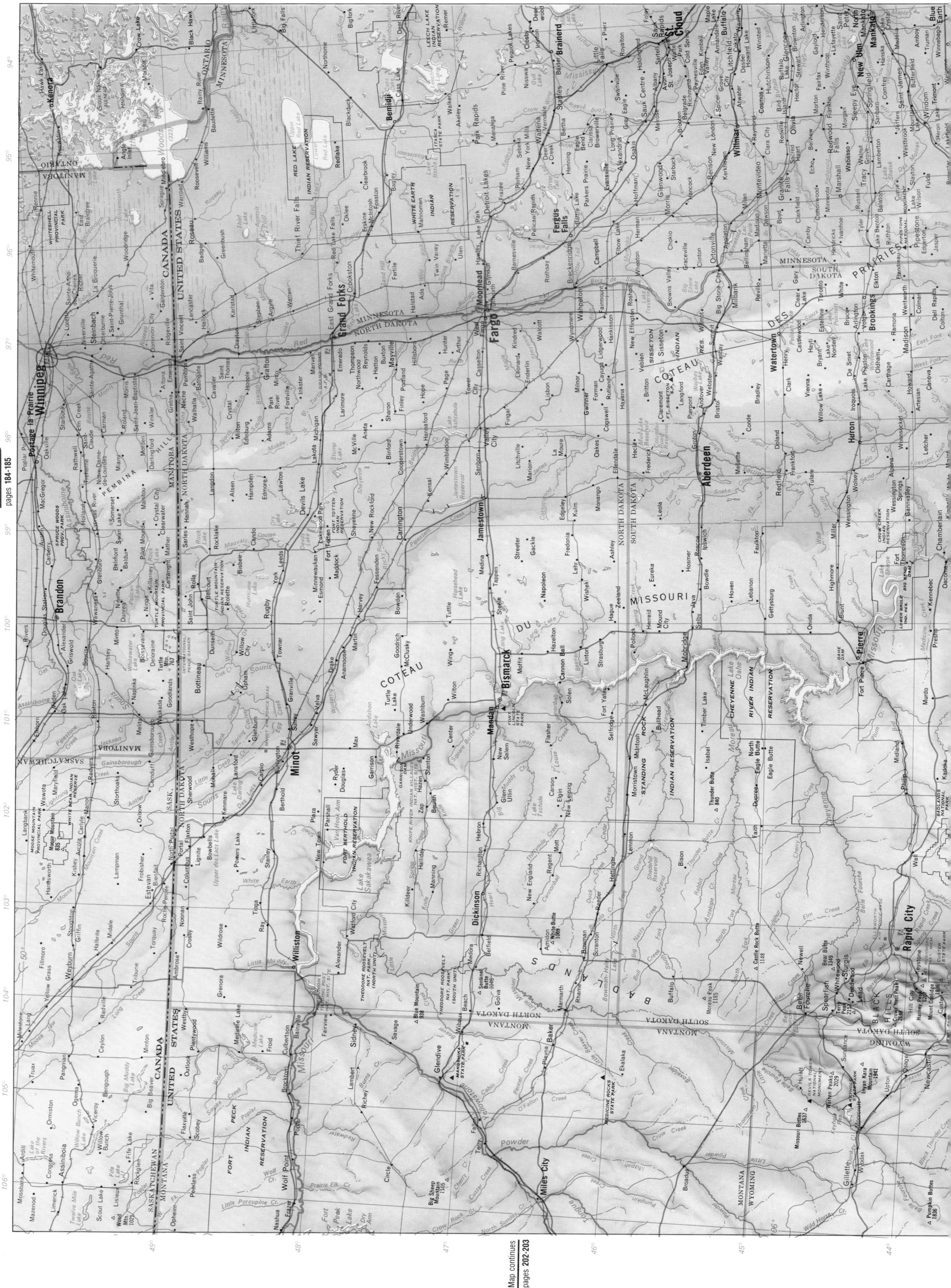
Winnipeg
Portage la Prairie
Brandon
Minot
Bismarck
Mandan
Fargo
Moorhead
Grand Forks
Jamestown
Dickinson
Williston
Aberdeen
Pierre
Rapid City
Miles City
St. Cloud
Brainerd
Bemidji
Huron
Watertown
Brookings
MINNESOTA
NORTH DAKOTA
SOUTH DAKOTA
MONTANA
WYOMING
MANITOBA
SASKATCHEWAN
ONTARIO
CANADA
UNITED STATES

Map continues pages 202-203

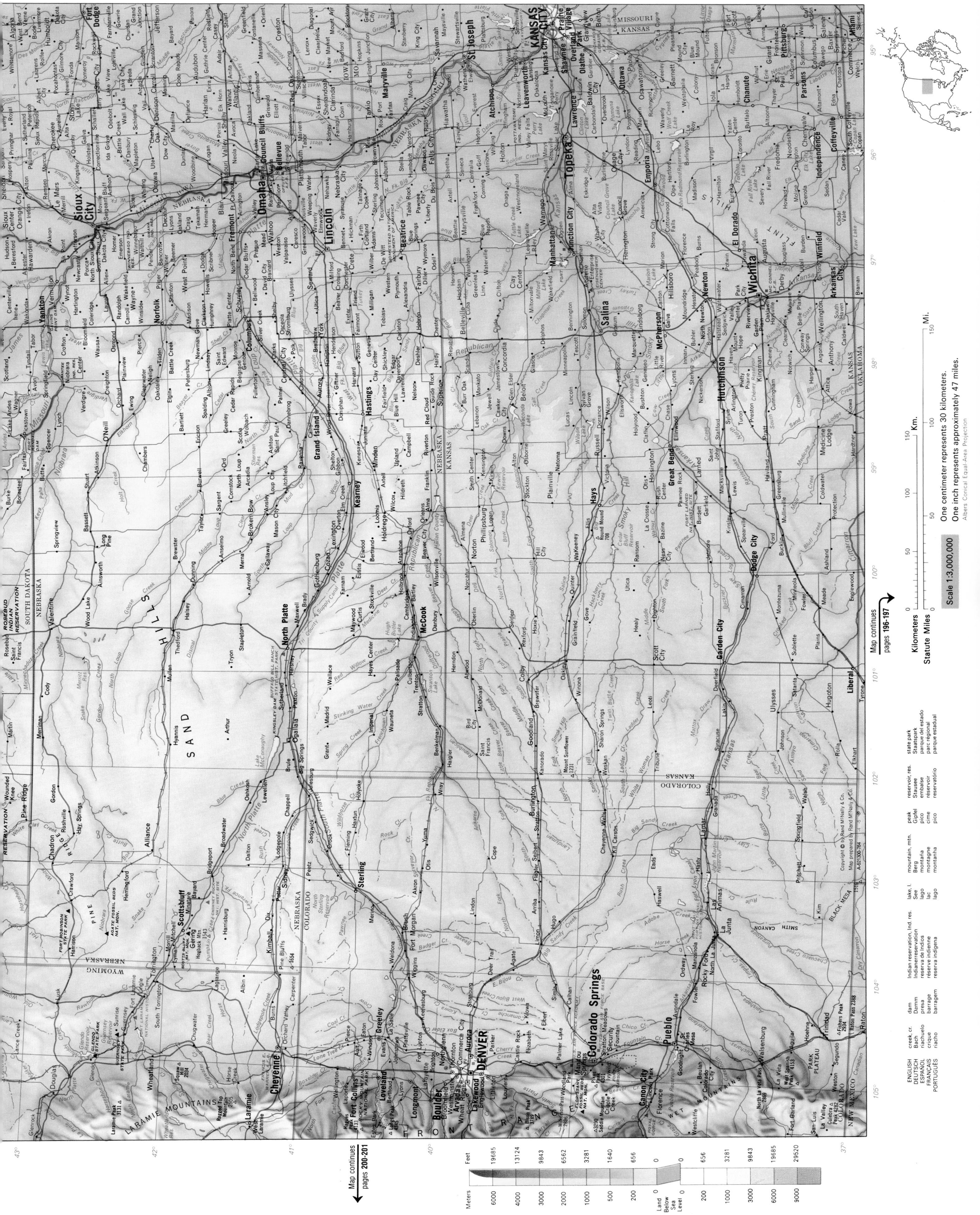
Scale 1:3,000,000
One centimeter represents 30 kilometers.
One inch represents approximately 47 miles.
Albers Conical Equal-Area Projection
Kilometers
Statute Miles
Map continues pages 194-195
Map continues pages 196-197
Map continues pages 200-201
ENGLISH DEUTSCH ESPAÑOL FRANÇAIS PORTUGUÊS
creek, cr. Bach riachuelo ruisseau riacho
dam Damm presa barrage barragem
Indian reservation, Ind. res. Indianerreservation reserva de indios reserve indienne reserva indígena
lake, l. See lago lac lago
mountain, mtn. Berg montaña montagne montanha
peak Gipfel pico cime pico
reservoir, res. Stausee embalse reservoir reservatório
state park Staatspark parque del estado parc régional parque estadual
Copyright © by Rand McNally & Co.
Map prepared by Rand McNally & Co.
Feet
Meters
Land Below Sea Level

Map continues pages 198-199

Map continues pages 202-203

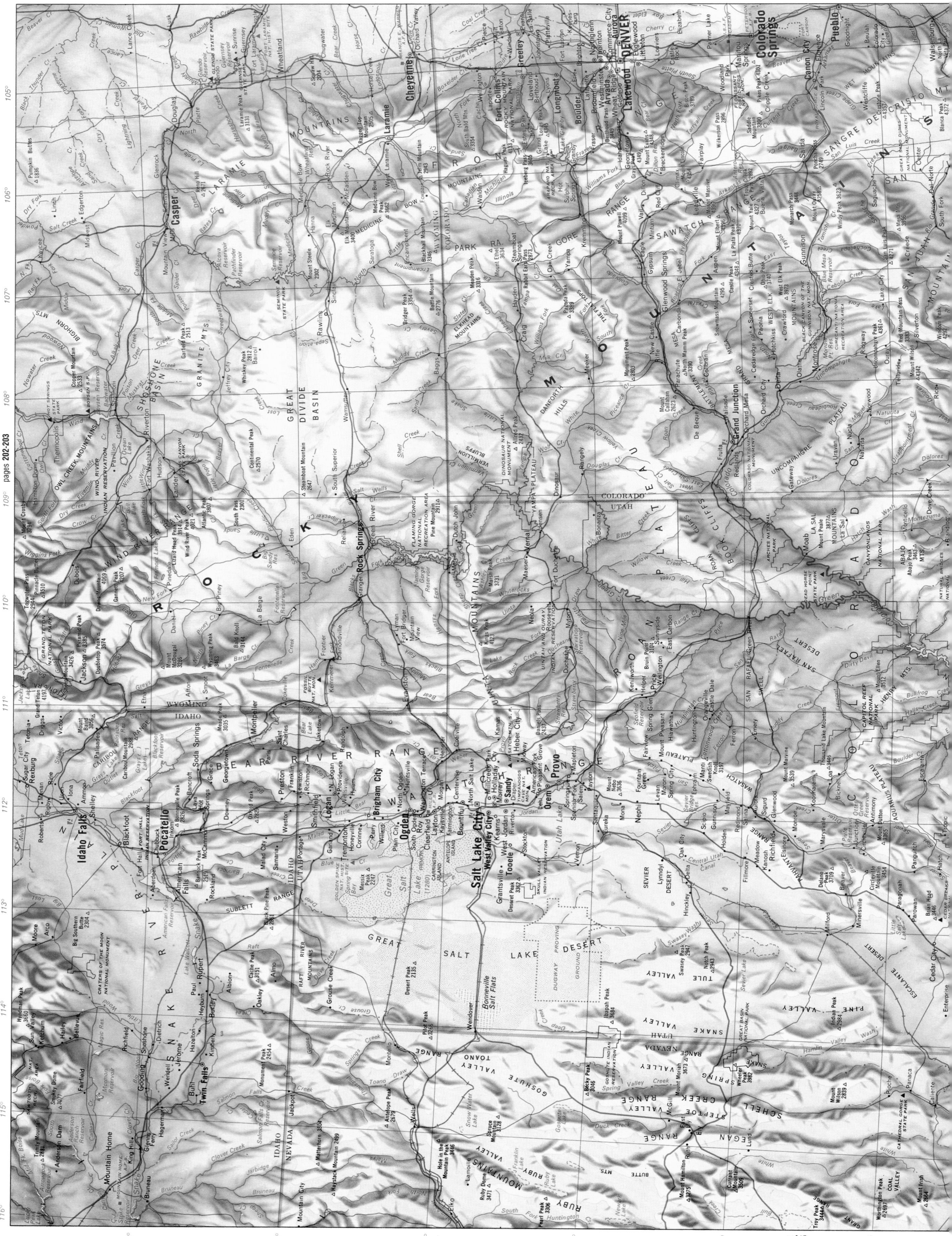
ROCKY MOUNTAINS
GREAT DIVIDE BASIN
GREAT SALT LAKE DESERT
SNAKE RIVER PLAIN
WASATCH RANGE
UINTA MOUNTAINS
WIND RIVER RANGE
LARAMIE MOUNTAINS
MEDICINE BOW MOUNTAINS
COLORADO PLATEAU
SAWATCH RANGE
SANGRE DE CRISTO MTS
SAN JUAN MOUNTAINS
DENVER
Boulder
Colorado Springs
Pueblo
Grand Junction
Cheyenne
Laramie
Casper
Rock Springs
Salt Lake City
Ogden
Provo
Logan
Brigham City
Pocatello
Idaho Falls
Twin Falls
Great Salt Lake
Utah Lake
WYOMING
IDAHO
UTAH
COLORADO
NEVADA
43°
42°
41°
40°
39°
38°
105°
106°
107°
108°
109°
110°
111°
112°
113°
114°
115°
116°

Map continues pages 204-205

Map continues pages 196-197

Scale 1:3,000,000
One centimeter represents 30 kilometers.
One inch represents approximately 47 miles.
Kilometers
Statute Miles
ENGLISH creek, cr. Indian reservation lake mountains national monument, nat. mon. peak reservoir, res. wash
DEUTSCH Bach Indianerreservation See Berge Nationaldenkmal Gipfel Stausee Trockenfluss
ESPAÑOL riachuelo reserva de indios lago montañas monumento nacional pico embalse uadi
FRANÇAIS crique réserve indienne lac montagnes monument national cime réservoir wadi
PORTUGUÊS riacho reserva indígena lago montanhas monumento nacional pico reservatório uádi
Feet
Meters
Land Below Sea Level

Northwestern United States / Nordwestliche Vereinigte Staaten / Nor-oeste de los Estados Unidos
Nord-Ouest des États-Unis / Noroeste dos Estados Unidos

Map continues pages 182-183

125° 124° 123° 122° 121° 120° 119° 118° 117° 116°
49° 48° 47° 46° 45° 44° 43° 42° 41°
BRITISH COLUMBIA
CANADA
UNITED STATES
WASHINGTON
OREGON
IDAHO
CALIFORNIA
NEVADA
PACIFIC OCEAN
Vancouver
Victoria
Strait of Juan de Fuca
Bellingham
Everett
SEATTLE
Tacoma
Olympia
Aberdeen
Hoquiam
Bremerton
Port Angeles
OLYMPIC MTS.
OLYMPIC NATIONAL PARK
Mount Rainier 4392
Mount Adams 3742
Mount Hood 3426
Yakima
Ellensburg
Wenatchee
Moses Lake
Richland
Pasco
Kennewick
Walla Walla
Spokane
Coeur d'Alene
Pullman
Moscow
Lewiston
Clarkston
Penticton
Trail
Nelson
Cranbrook
COLUMBIA BASIN
CASCADE RANGE
BLUE MOUNTAINS
WALLOWA MOUNTAINS
HELLS CANYON
COAST RANGES
PORTLAND
Vancouver
Longview
The Dalles
Pendleton
Salem
Corvallis
Albany
Eugene
Springfield
Bend
Redmond
Prineville
Baker
La Grande
Ontario
Boise
Nampa
Caldwell
Coos Bay
Roseburg
Grants Pass
Medford
Ashland
Klamath Falls
Lakeview
Burns
HARNEY BASIN
HARNEY
ALVORD DESERT
STEENS MOUNTAIN
Crescent City
Eureka
Arcata
Yreka
Redding
Mount Shasta 4317
Alturas
Winnemucca
KLAMATH MOUNTAINS
SALMON MOUNTAINS
Humboldt
SNAKE RIVER PLATEAU

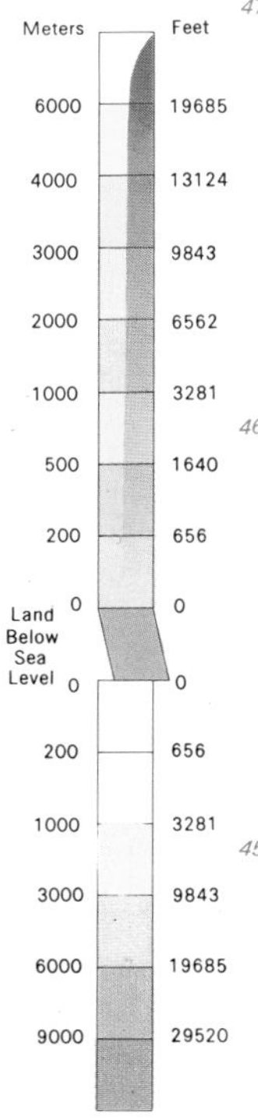

Meters
Feet
6000 19685
4000 13124
3000 9843
2000 6562
1000 3281
500 1640
200 656
0 0
Land Below Sea Level
0 0
200 656
1000 3281
3000 9843
6000 19685
9000 29520

Map continues pages 204-205

ENGLISH	creek, cr.	Indian reservation	lake, l.	mountain, mtn.	pass	peak	range	reservoir, res.
DEUTSCH	Bach	Indianerreservation	See	Berg	Pass	Gipfel	Gebirge	Stausee
ESPAÑOL	riachuelo	reserva de Indios	lago	montaña	paso	pico	sierra	embalse
FRANÇAIS	crique	réserve indienne	lac	montagne	col	cime	chaîne	réservoir
PORTUGUÊS	riacho	reserva indígena	lago	montanha	passo	pico	serra	reservatório

Map continues pages 184-185

CANADA
UNITED STATES
ALBERTA
SASKATCHEWAN
BRITISH COLUMBIA
MONTANA
IDAHO
WYOMING
UTAH
COLORADO
Great Falls
Helena
Missoula
Butte
Anaconda
Bozeman
Billings
Havre
Kalispell
Lewistown
Miles City
Sheridan
Casper
Cody
Idaho Falls
Pocatello
Twin Falls
Logan
Ogden
Brigham City
Rock Springs
Rawlins
Missouri
Yellowstone
YELLOWSTONE NATIONAL PARK
GRAND TETON NAT. PARK
GLACIER NATIONAL PARK
BIGHORN BASIN
GREAT DIVIDE BASIN
GREAT SALT LAKE DESERT
SNAKE RIVER PLAIN
ROCKY MOUNTAINS
WIND RIVER RANGE
BIG BELT MOUNTAINS
ABSAROKA RANGE
BEARTOOTH MTS.
BIGHORN MOUNTAINS
Copyright © by Rand McNally & Co.
Map prepared by Rand McNally & Co.
A-520597-764

Map continues pages 198-199

Map continues pages 200-201

Kilometers 0 50 100 150 Km.
Statute Miles 0 50 100 150 Mi.

Scale 1:3,000,000
One centimeter represents 30 kilometers.
One inch represents approximately 47 miles.
Albers Conical Equal-Area Projection

Map continues pages 200-201

Map continues pages 202-203

GREAT SALT LAKE DESERT
SNAKE RIVER PLAIN
COLUMBIA PLATEAU
GREAT BASIN
IDAHO
NEVADA
OREGON
CALIFORNIA
UTAH
CASCADE RANGE
COAST RANGES
SIERRA NEVADA
KLAMATH MOUNTAINS
SACRAMENTO VALLEY
SAN FRANCISCO
Sacramento
Reno
Carson City
Stockton
Oakland
Eureka
Redding
Medford
Klamath Falls
Twin Falls
Winnemucca
Elko
Ely
Tonopah
Roseburg
Coos Bay
Grants Pass
Ashland
Santa Rosa
Modesto
BLACK ROCK DESERT
ALVORD DESERT
HARNEY BASIN
RUBY MOUNTAINS
SHOSHONE RANGE
TOIYABE RANGE
SMOKY VALLEY
EGAN RANGE
SCHELL CREEK RANGE
TUSCARORA MOUNTAINS
INDEPENDENCE MOUNTAINS
SANTA ROSA RANGE
WARNER MOUNTAINS
YOSEMITE NATIONAL PARK

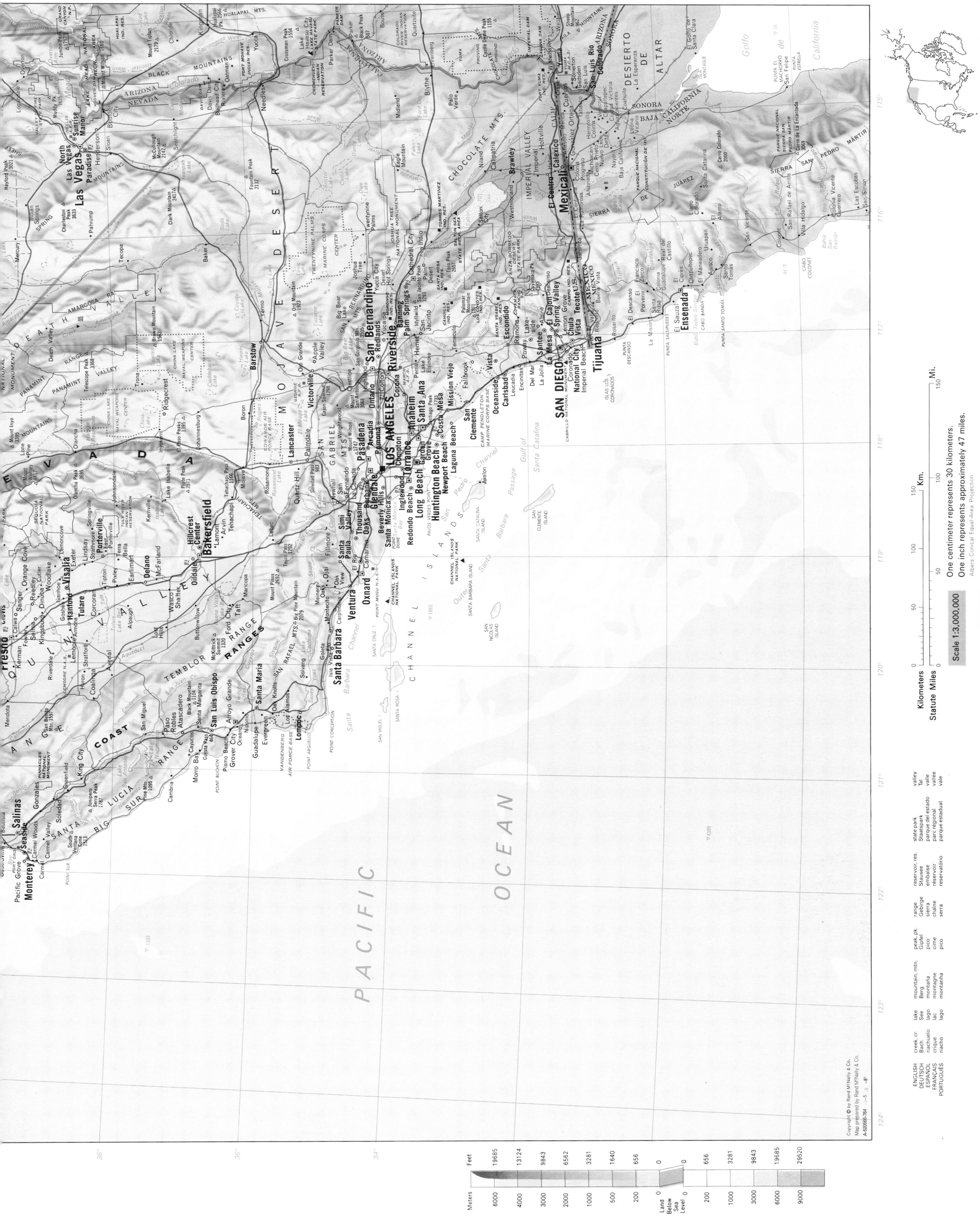
PACIFIC OCEAN
MOJAVE DESERT
DEATH VALLEY
SAN JOAQUIN VALLEY
SIERRA NEVADA
IMPERIAL VALLEY
CHOCOLATE MTS.
DESIERTO DE ALTAR
CHANNEL ISLANDS
LOS ANGELES
SAN DIEGO
Las Vegas
San Bernardino
Riverside
Bakersfield
Santa Barbara
Mexicali
Tijuana
Ensenada
Kilometers 0 50 100 150 Km.
Statute Miles 0 50 100 150 Mi.
Scale 1:3,000,000
One centimeter represents 30 kilometers.
One inch represents approximately 47 miles.
Albers Conical Equal-Area Projection
ENGLISH creek, cr. lake mountain, mtn. peak, pk. range reservoir, res. state park valley
DEUTSCH Bach See Berg Gipfel Gebirge Stausee Staatspark Tal
ESPAÑOL riachuelo lago montaña pico sierra embalse parque del estado valle
FRANÇAIS ruisseau lac montagne cime chaîne réservoir parc régional vallée
PORTUGUÊS riacho lago montanha pico serra reservatório parque estadual vale
Copyright © by Rand McNally & Co.
Map prepared by Rand McNally & Co.
Feet 19685 13124 9843 6562 3281 1640 656 0 0 656 3281 9843 19685 29520
Meters 6000 4000 3000 2000 1000 500 200 0 Land Below Sea Level 0 200 1000 3000 6000 9000

Québec
Trois-Rivières
Sherbrooke
MONTRÉAL
St-Hyacinthe
Drummondville
Granby
Sorel
Joliette
Shawinigan
St-Jérôme
Cornwall
Lévis
Ste-Foy
Laval
Longueuil
St-Jean-sur-Richelieu
Valleyfield
Thetford Mines
Victoriaville
CANADA
UNITED STATES
QUÉBEC
VERMONT
NEW YORK
NEW HAMPSHIRE
ONTARIO

FRANÇAIS	aéroport	barrage	île	lac	montagne	parc	réservoir, rés.	rivière, r.
ENGLISH	airport	dam	island	lake	mountain	park	reservoir	river
DEUTSCH	Flughafen	Damm	Insel	See	Berg	Park	Stausee	Fluss
ESPAÑOL	aeropuerto	presa	isla	lago	montaña	parque	embalse	río
PORTUGUÊS	aeroporto	represa	ilha	lago	montanha	parque	reservatório	rio

Kilometers 0 10 20 30 40 50 Km.

Statute Miles 0 10 20 30 40 50 Mi.

Scale 1:1,000,000

One centimeter represents 10 kilometers.
One inch represents approximately 16 miles.

Lambert Conformal Conic Projection

Map continues pages 212-213

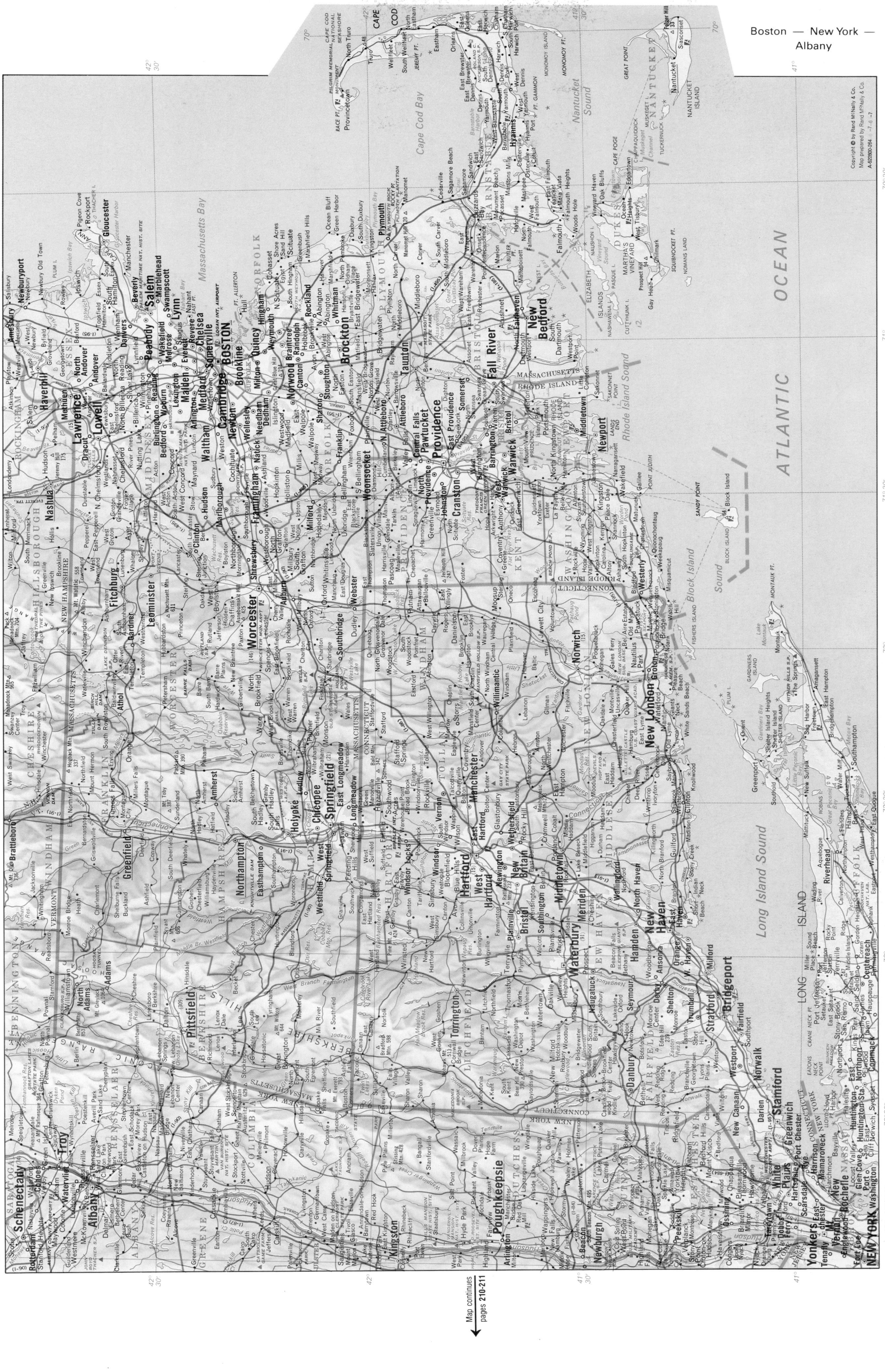
ATLANTIC OCEAN
Long Island Sound
Block Island Sound
Rhode Island Sound
Nantucket Sound
Cape Cod Bay
Massachusetts Bay
Copyright © by Rand McNally & Co.
Map prepared by Rand McNally & Co.
A-522800-264 -7-6 -7
Kilometers
Statute Miles
Scale 1:1,000,000
One centimeter represents 10 kilometers.
One inch represents approximately 16 miles.
Lambert Conformal Conic Projection
ENGLISH bay island, I. lake, I. mountain, mtn. point, pt. pond reservoir, res. sound
DEUTSCH Bucht Insel See Berg Landspitze Teich Stausee Sund
ESPAÑOL bahía isla lago montaña punta estanque embalse sonda
FRANÇAIS baie île lac montagne pointe étang réservoir détroit
PORTUGUÊS baía ilha lago montanha ponta lagoa reservatório estreito

Map continues pages 208-209

Map continues pages 210-211

Map continues pages 210-211

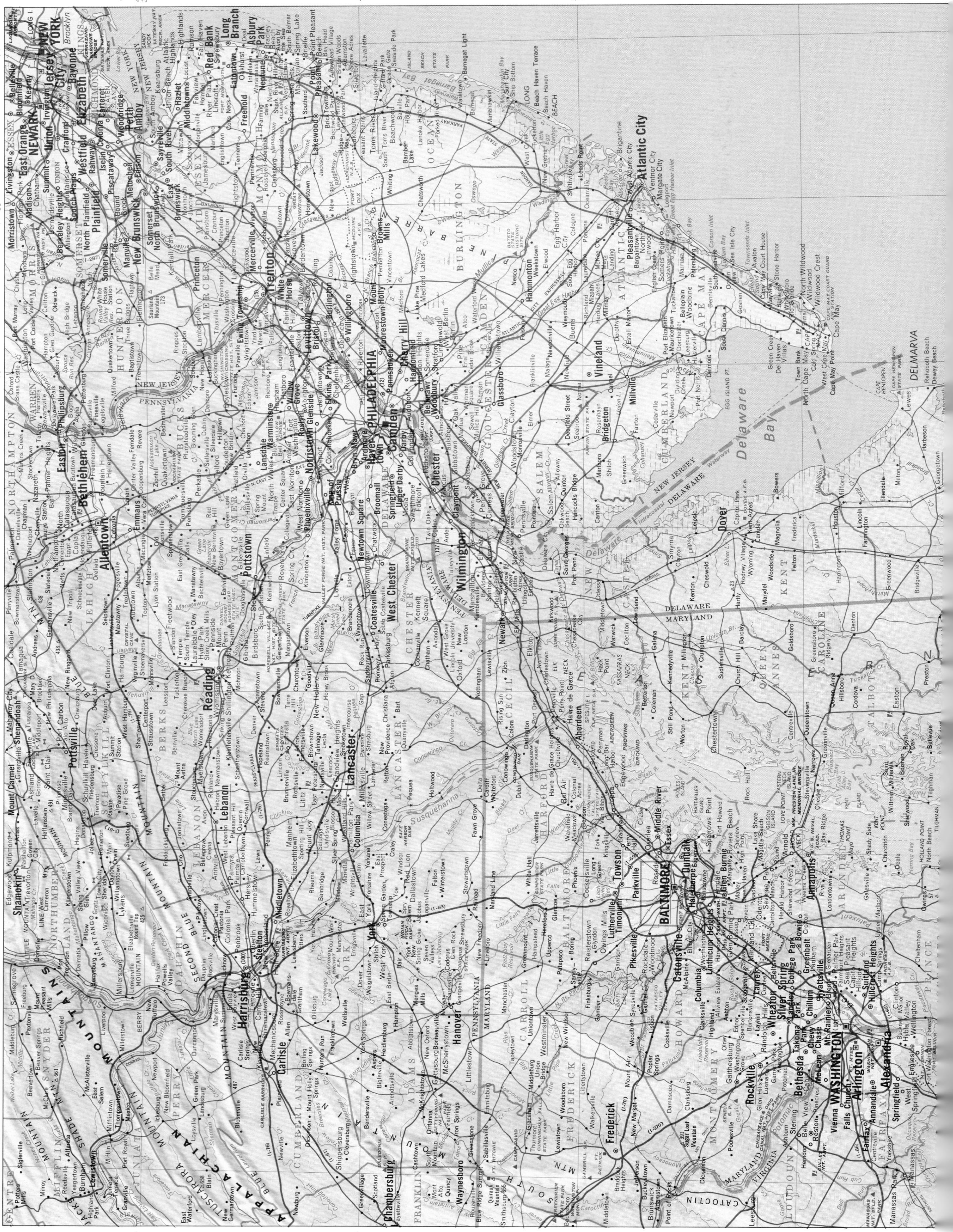
NEW YORK
Jersey City
Newark
Elizabeth
Trenton
PHILADELPHIA
Camden
Chester
Wilmington
Atlantic City
Vineland
Allentown
Bethlehem
Reading
Lancaster
York
Harrisburg
BALTIMORE
WASHINGTON
Arlington
Alexandria
Annapolis
Dover
Delaware Bay
NEW JERSEY
PENNSYLVANIA
MARYLAND
DELAWARE
DELMARVA

ATLANTIC
OCEAN
Chesapeake
Bay
Potomac
PENINSULA
WICOMICO
DORCHESTER
WORCESTER
SOMERSET
ACCOMACK
NORTHAMPTON
MARYLAND
VIRGINIA
NORTH CAROLINA
Salisbury
Fredericksburg
Richmond
Petersburg
Williamsburg
Hampton
Newport News
Norfolk
Portsmouth
Chesapeake
Virginia Beach
Suffolk
ASSATEAGUE ISLAND NATIONAL SEASHORE
Chincoteague Bay
Tangier Sound
Intracoastal Waterway
Dismal Swamp
ENGLISH airport, arpt. bay creek, cr. inlet island, i. mountain point, pt. reservoir, res. state park
DEUTSCH Flughafen Bucht Bach Einfahrt Insel Berg Landspitze Stausee Naturpark
ESPAÑOL aeropuerto bahía riachuelo abra isla montaña punta embalse parque provincial
FRANÇAIS aéroport baie crique bras de mer île montagne pointe réservoir parc régional
PORTUGUÊS aeroporto baía riacho enseada ilha montanha ponta reservatório parque estadual
Kilometers
Statute Miles
Scale 1:1,000,000
One centimeter represents 10 kilometers.
One inch represents approximately 16 miles.
Lambert Conformal Conic Projection
Copyright © by Rand McNally & Co.
Map prepared by Rand McNally & Co.

Map continues pages 212-213

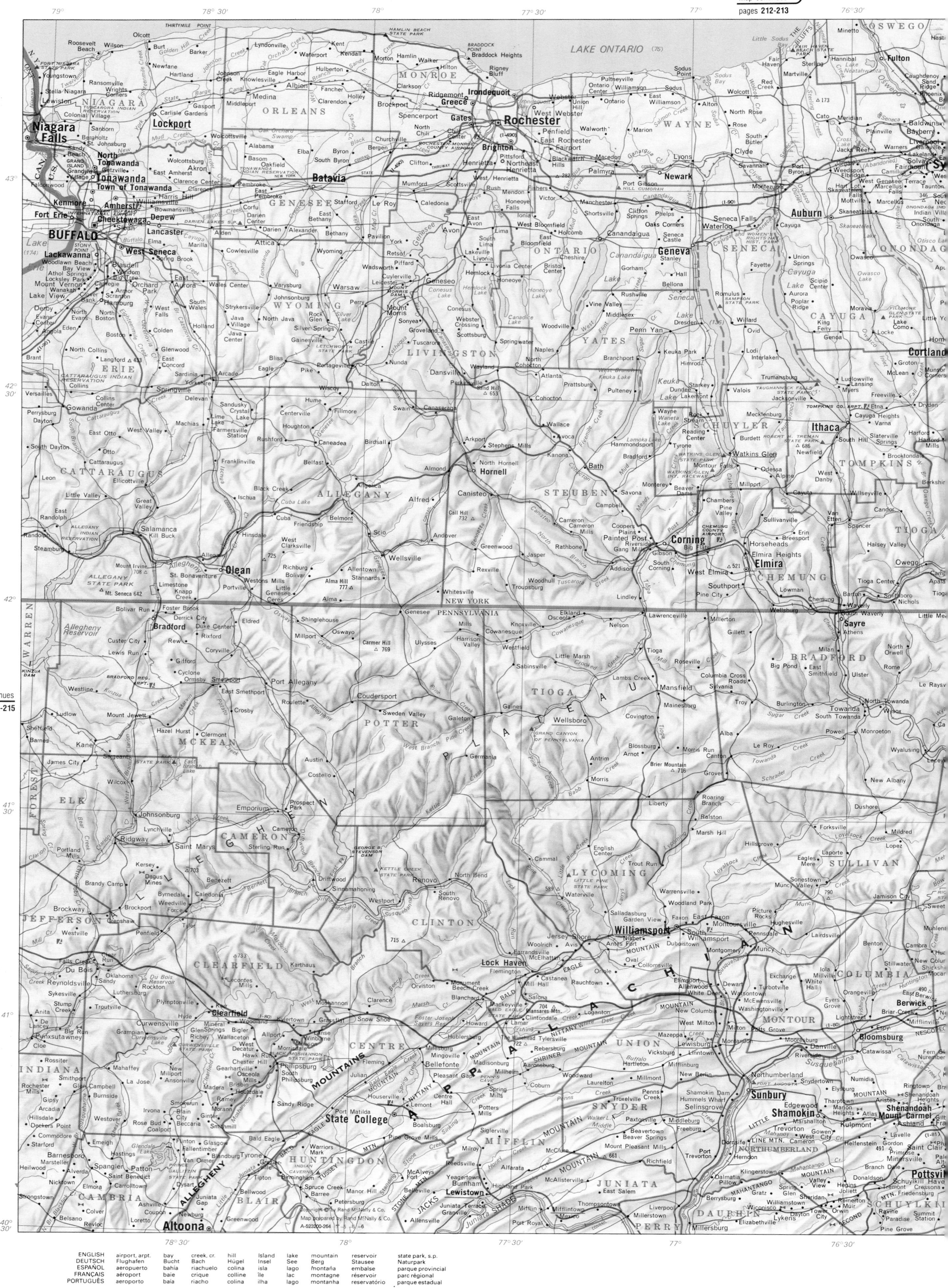

79°
78°30'
78°
77°30'
77°
76°30'
43°
42° 30'
42°
41° 30'
41°
40° 30'
LAKE ONTARIO (75)
Niagara Falls
BUFFALO
Lockport
Rochester
Batavia
Geneva
Auburn
Ithaca
Elmira
Corning
Hornell
Olean
Bradford
Williamsport
State College
Altoona
Clearfield
Lock Haven
Sunbury
Shamokin
Bloomsburg
Cortland
Sayre
Towanda
Wellsboro
NIAGARA
ORLEANS
MONROE
WAYNE
GENESEE
ONTARIO
SENECA
CAYUGA
ERIE
WYOMING
LIVINGSTON
YATES
SCHUYLER
TOMPKINS
CATTARAUGUS
ALLEGANY
STEUBEN
CHEMUNG
TIOGA
NEW YORK
PENNSYLVANIA
WARREN
MCKEAN
POTTER
TIOGA
BRADFORD
SULLIVAN
LYCOMING
CLINTON
CAMERON
ELK
FOREST
JEFFERSON
CLEARFIELD
CENTRE
UNION
MONTOUR
COLUMBIA
SNYDER
MIFFLIN
JUNIATA
HUNTINGDON
BLAIR
CAMBRIA
INDIANA
NORTHUMBERLAND
SCHUYLKILL
DAUPHIN
PERRY
ALLEGHENY PLATEAU
APPALACHIAN
Map prepared by Rand McNally & Co.

Map continues pages 214-215

ENGLISH	airport, arpt.	bay	creek, cr.	hill	island	lake	mountain	reservoir	state park, s.p.
DEUTSCH	Flughafen	Bucht	Bach	Hügel	Insel	See	Berg	Stausee	Naturpark
ESPAÑOL	aeropuerto	bahía	riachuelo	colina	isla	lago	montaña	embalse	parque provincial
FRANÇAIS	aéroport	baie	crique	colline	île	lac	montagne	réservoir	parc régional
PORTUGUÊS	aeroporto	baía	riacho	colina	ilha	lago	montanha	reservatório	parque estadual

ADIRONDACK MOUNTAINS
HAMILTON
FULTON
HERKIMER
MONTGOMERY
SCHENECTADY
SARATOGA
WASHINGTON
RENSSELAER
ALBANY
SCHOHARIE
OTSEGO
MADISON
CHENANGO
DELAWARE
GREENE
COLUMBIA
ULSTER
DUTCHESS
SULLIVAN
ORANGE
PUTNAM
WESTCHESTER
ROCKLAND
LITCHFIELD
FAIRFIELD
BERKSHIRE
WAYNE
PIKE
MONROE
CARBON
LACKAWANNA
NORTHAMPTON
LEHIGH
BERKS
BUCKS
HUNTERDON
SOMERSET
MORRIS
SUSSEX
WARREN
PASSAIC
BERGEN
ESSEX
UNION
MIDDLESEX
NASSAU
SUFFOLK
KINGS
QUEENS
BRONX
RICHMOND
CATSKILL MOUNTAINS
POCONO MOUNTAINS
TACONIC RANGE
Rome
Utica
Oneida
Amsterdam
Gloversville
Saratoga Springs
Glens Falls
Schenectady
Troy
Albany
Pittsfield
Oneonta
Binghamton
Hudson
Kingston
Poughkeepsie
Newburgh
Middletown
Danbury
Scranton
Wilkes-Barre
Hazleton
Allentown
Bethlehem
Easton
Stamford
Bridgeport
Norwalk
White Plains
Yonkers
Paterson
Newark
Jersey City
Elizabeth
NEW YORK
Long Island Sound
ATLANTIC OCEAN
VERMONT
MASSACHUSETTS
CONNECTICUT
NEW YORK
NEW JERSEY
PENNSYLVANIA

Map continues page 207

Map continues pages 208-209

Kilometers 0 10 20 30 40 50 Km.

Statute Miles 0 10 20 30 40 50 Mi.

Scale 1:1,000,000

One centimeter represents 10 kilometers.
One inch represents approximately 16 miles.
Lambert Conformal Conic Projection

81°
80° 30'
80°
79° 30'
79°
78° 30'
45° 30'
45°
44° 30'
44°
43° 30'
43°
Georgian Bay
(176 Meters Above Sea Level)
Nottawasaga Bay
Lake Simcoe
LAKE ERIE
(174 Meters Above Sea Level)
Long Point Bay
CANADA
UNITED STATES
ONTARIO
NEW YORK
PARRY SOUND
MUSKOKA
HALIBURTON
NIPISSING
VICTORIA
DURHAM
YORK
PEEL
SIMCOE
DUFFERIN
GREY
BRUCE
HURON
PERTH
WELLINGTON
WATERLOO
HALTON
HAMILTON-WENTWORTH
OXFORD
BRANT
MIDDLESEX
ELGIN
HALDIMAND-NORFOLK
NIAGARA
ERIE
TORONTO
North York
Scarborough
East York
York
Etobicoke
Mississauga
Brampton
Oakville
Burlington
Hamilton
Stoney Creek
Kitchener
Waterloo
Cambridge (Galt)
Guelph
Brantford
Woodstock
London
Saint Thomas
Stratford
Owen Sound
Collingwood
Midland
Barrie
Orillia
Oshawa
Whitby
Ajax
Pickering
Newmarket
Aurora
Richmond Hill
Markham
Vaughan
Saint Catharines
Niagara Falls
Welland
Port Colborne
Fort Erie
BUFFALO
Lockport
Lackawanna
Tonawanda
Cheektowaga
Lindsay
Huntsville
Bracebridge
Gravenhurst
Parry Sound
Simcoe
Copyright © by Rand McNally & Co.
Map prepared by Rand McNally & Co.
A-523300-264 -5 -5 -7

Map continues pages 214-215

ENGLISH	airport	bay	canal	channel	creek, cr.	Indian reservation	island	lake, l.	point
DEUTSCH	Flughafen	Bucht	Kanal	Kanal	Bach	Indianerreservation	Insel	See	Landspitze
ESPAÑOL	aeropuerto	bahía	canal	canal	riachuelo	reserva de Indios	isla	lago	punta
FRANÇAIS	aéroport	baie	canal	canal	crique	réserve indienne	île	lac	pointe
PORTUGUÊS	aeroporto	baía	canal	canal	riacho	reserva indígena	ilha	lago	ponta

Map continues page 206

ONTARIO
(75 Meters Above Sea Level)
ONTARIO
NEW YORK
Ottawa
Hull
Gatineau
Kingston
Belleville
Trenton
Cobourg
Rochester
Syracuse
Utica
Rome
Oswego
Watertown
Auburn
Geneva
Batavia
Ogdensburg
Brockville
Smiths Falls
Perth
Renfrew
Arnprior
Carleton Place
Almonte
Nepean
Gloucester
Kemptville
Prescott
Gananoque
Picton
Napanee
Deseronto
Campbellford
Bancroft
Fulton
Oneida
Newark
Greece
Irondequoit
Brighton
LANARK
FRONTENAC
LEEDS AND GRENVILLE
OTTAWA-CARLETON
PRINCE EDWARD
JEFFERSON
OSWEGO
ONEIDA
ONONDAGA
WAYNE
MONROE
LIVINGSTON
SENECA
CAYUGA
CORTLAND
MADISON
LEWIS
ST. LAWRENCE
HASTINGS
MADAWASKA HIGHLANDS
RENFREW

Map continues pages 210-211

Kilometers 0 10 20 30 40 50 Km.
Statute Miles 0 10 20 30 40 50 Mi.

Scale 1:1,000,000

One centimeter represents 10 kilometers.
One inch represents approximately 16 miles.
Lambert Conformal Conic Projection

Map continues pages 216-217

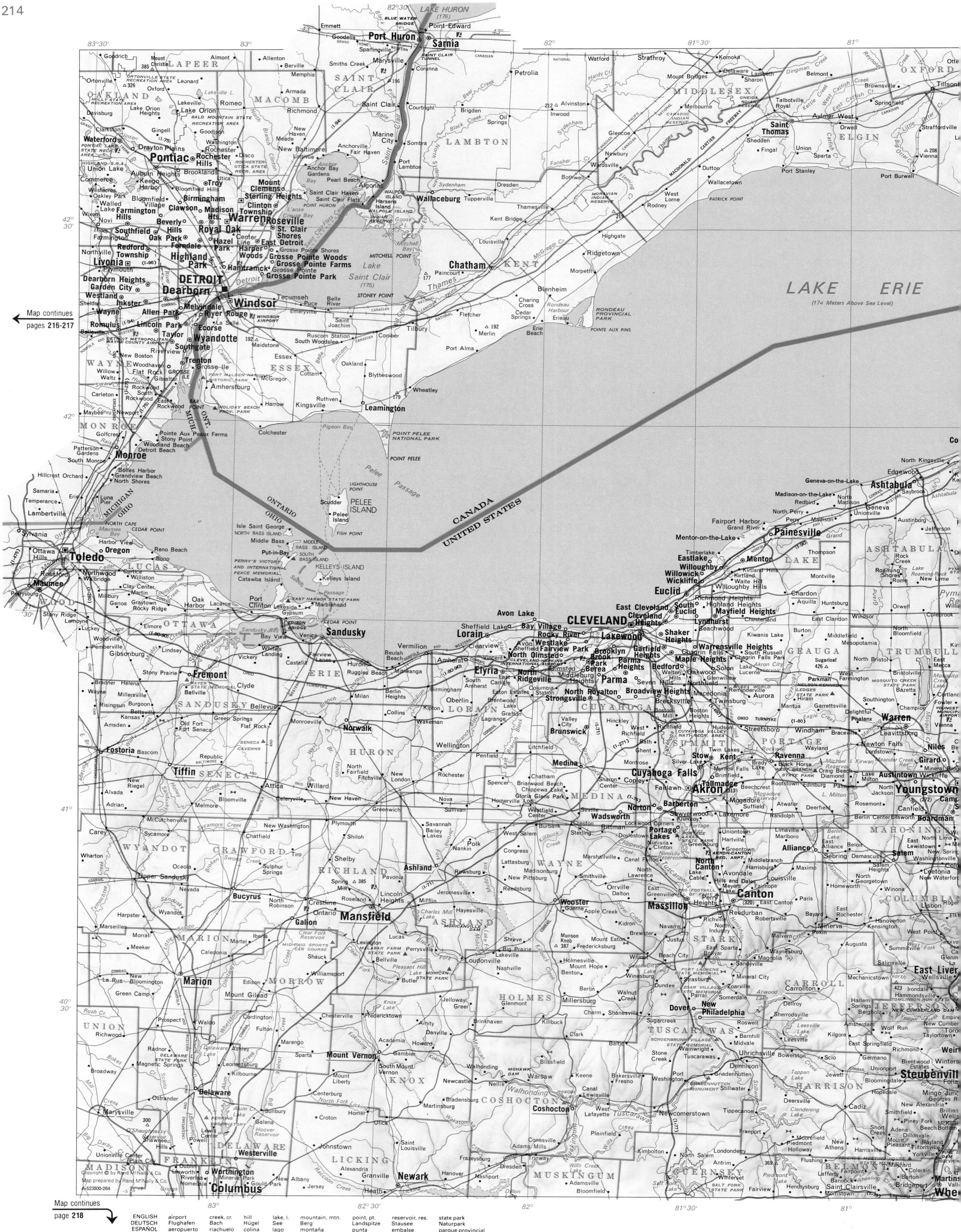
LAKE HURON
LAKE ERIE
(174 Meters Above Sea Level)
Lake Saint Clair
(175)
CANADA
UNITED STATES
ONTARIO
OHIO
MICH.
ONT.
MICHIGAN
Port Huron
Sarnia
DETROIT
Dearborn
Windsor
Pontiac
Warren
Royal Oak
Chatham
Leamington
Toledo
Monroe
Sandusky
CLEVELAND
Lakewood
Lorain
Elyria
Parma
Euclid
Ashtabula
Painesville
Akron
Canton
Cuyahoga Falls
Youngstown
Warren
Mansfield
Massillon
Marion
Columbus
Delaware
Newark
Mount Vernon
Coshocton
New Philadelphia
Steubenville
Fremont
Tiffin
Fostoria
Ashland
Wooster
Norwalk
Medina
PELEE ISLAND
POINT PELEE NATIONAL PARK
KELLEYS ISLAND
LAMBTON
KENT
ESSEX
ELGIN
MIDDLESEX
OXFORD
SAINT CLAIR
MACOMB
OAKLAND
LAPEER
WAYNE
MONROE
LUCAS
WOOD
OTTAWA
SANDUSKY
ERIE
LORAIN
CUYAHOGA
GEAUGA
LAKE
ASHTABULA
TRUMBULL
PORTAGE
SUMMIT
MEDINA
HURON
SENECA
WYANDOT
CRAWFORD
RICHLAND
ASHLAND
WAYNE
STARK
MAHONING
COLUMBIANA
CARROLL
HARRISON
TUSCARAWAS
HOLMES
KNOX
MORROW
MARION
UNION
DELAWARE
LICKING
COSHOCTON
MUSKINGUM
GUERNSEY
BELMONT
FRANKLIN
MADISON
Copyright © by Rand McNally & Co.
Map prepared by Rand McNally & Co.
A-523500-264
83°30'
83°
82°30'
82°
81°30'
81°
42°30'
42°
41°30'
41°
40°30'

Map continues page 218

ENGLISH	DEUTSCH	ESPAÑOL	FRANÇAIS	PORTUGUÊS
airport	Flughafen	aeropuerto	aéroport	aeroporto
creek, cr.	Bach	riachuelo	crique	riacho
hill	Hügel	colina	colline	colina
lake, l.	See	lago	lac	lago
mountain, mtn.	Berg	montaña	montagne	montanha
point, pt.	Landspitze	punta	pointe	ponta
reservoir, res.	Stausee	embalse	réservoir	reservatório
state park	Naturpark	parque provincial	parc régional	parque estadual

Map continues pages 212-213

CANADA
UNITED STATES
ONTARIO
NEW YORK
PENNSYLVANIA
HALDIMAND
NIAGARA
GENESEE
ERIE
WYOMING
LIVINGSTON
CHAUTAUQUA
CATTARAUGUS
ALLEGANY
STEUBEN
WARREN
MCKEAN
POTTER
CRAWFORD
FOREST
ELK
CAMERON
MERCER
VENANGO
CLARION
JEFFERSON
CLEARFIELD
CLINTON
LAWRENCE
BUTLER
ARMSTRONG
INDIANA
CENTRE
ALLEGHENY
BEAVER
CAMBRIA
BLAIR
HUNTINGDON
MIFFLIN
WASHINGTON
WESTMORELAND
SOMERSET
BEDFORD
FULTON
FAYETTE
FRANKLIN
ALLEGHENY PLATEAU
ALLEGHENY MOUNTAINS
APPALACHIAN MOUNTAINS
BUFFALO
Erie
Jamestown
Olean
Bradford
Warren
Meadville
Oil City
Franklin
New Castle
Butler
PITTSBURGH
McKeesport
Washington
Greensburg
Johnstown
Altoona
State College
Indiana
Hornell
Dunkirk
Allegheny Reservoir
Long Point Bay
80°
79°30′
79°
78°30′
78°
42°
42° 30′
41° 30′
41°
40° 30′

Map continues pages 210-211

Kilometers 0 10 20 30 40 50 Km.

Statute Miles 0 10 20 30 40 50 Mi.

Scale 1:1,000,000

One centimeter represents 10 kilometers.
One inch represents approximately 16 miles.
Lambert Conformal Conic Projection

LAKE MICHIGAN
(176 Meters Above Sea Level)
Madison
Sun Prairie
Watertown
Waukesha
MILWAUKEE
Wauwatosa
West Allis
Whitefish Bay
Shorewood
Cudahy
South Milwaukee
Oak Creek
Franklin
Greenfield
Brookfield
Menomonee Falls
Glendale
Janesville
Beloit
Whitewater
Racine
Kenosha
Rockford
Loves Park
Belvidere
Waukegan
North Chicago
Lake Forest
Highland Park
Deerfield
Glenview
Evanston
Skokie
Des Plaines
Schaumburg
Elgin
De Kalb
Saint Charles
Wheaton
Naperville
Aurora
Bolingbrook
Joliet
CHICAGO
Oak Park
Cicero
Berwyn
Elmhurst
Lombard
Glen Ellyn
Downers Grove
Hinsdale
La Grange
Evergreen Park
Oak Lawn
Calumet City
Hammond
East Chicago
Gary
Hobart
Portage
Merrillville
Valparaiso
Michigan City
La Porte
Chesterton
Crown Point
La Salle
Peru
Ottawa
Streator
Kankakee
Pontiac
Bloomington
Normal
Paxton
Rantoul
Watseka
Rensselaer
Monticello
Delphi
West Lafayette
Lafayette
Frankfort
Logansport
Benton Harbor
Saint Joseph
Plymouth
Muskegon
DODGE
WASHINGTON
OZAUKEE
WAUKESHA
JEFFERSON
DANE
GREEN
ROCK
WALWORTH
RACINE
KENOSHA
WISCONSIN
ILLINOIS
INDIANA
WINNEBAGO
BOONE
MCHENRY
LAKE
OGLE
DE KALB
KANE
COOK
DU PAGE
LEE
KENDALL
WILL
LA SALLE
GRUNDY
KANKAKEE
LIVINGSTON
IROQUOIS
FORD
MC LEAN
WOODFORD
MARSHALL
DE WITT
PIATT
CHAMPAIGN
VERMILION
LAKE
PORTER
LA PORTE
STARKE
JASPER
NEWTON
PULASKI
FULTON
CASS
WHITE
BENTON
CARROLL
WARREN
TIPPECANOE
FOUNTAIN
CLINTON
BERRIEN
Copyright © by Rand McNally & Co.
Map prepared by Rand McNally & Co.
A-523000-264
89°
88°30'
88°
87°30'
87°
86°30'
42°
41°

Map continues
page 219

ENGLISH	airport	creek, cr.	ditch	lake, l.	reservoir	state park, s.p.
DEUTSCH	Flughafen	Bach	Graben	See	Stausee	Naturpark
ESPAÑOL	aeropuerto	riachuelo	acequia	lago	embalse	parque provincial
FRANÇAIS	aéroport	crique	fossé	lac	réservoir	parc régional
PORTUGUÊS	aeroporto	riacho	fosso	lago	reservatório	parque estadual

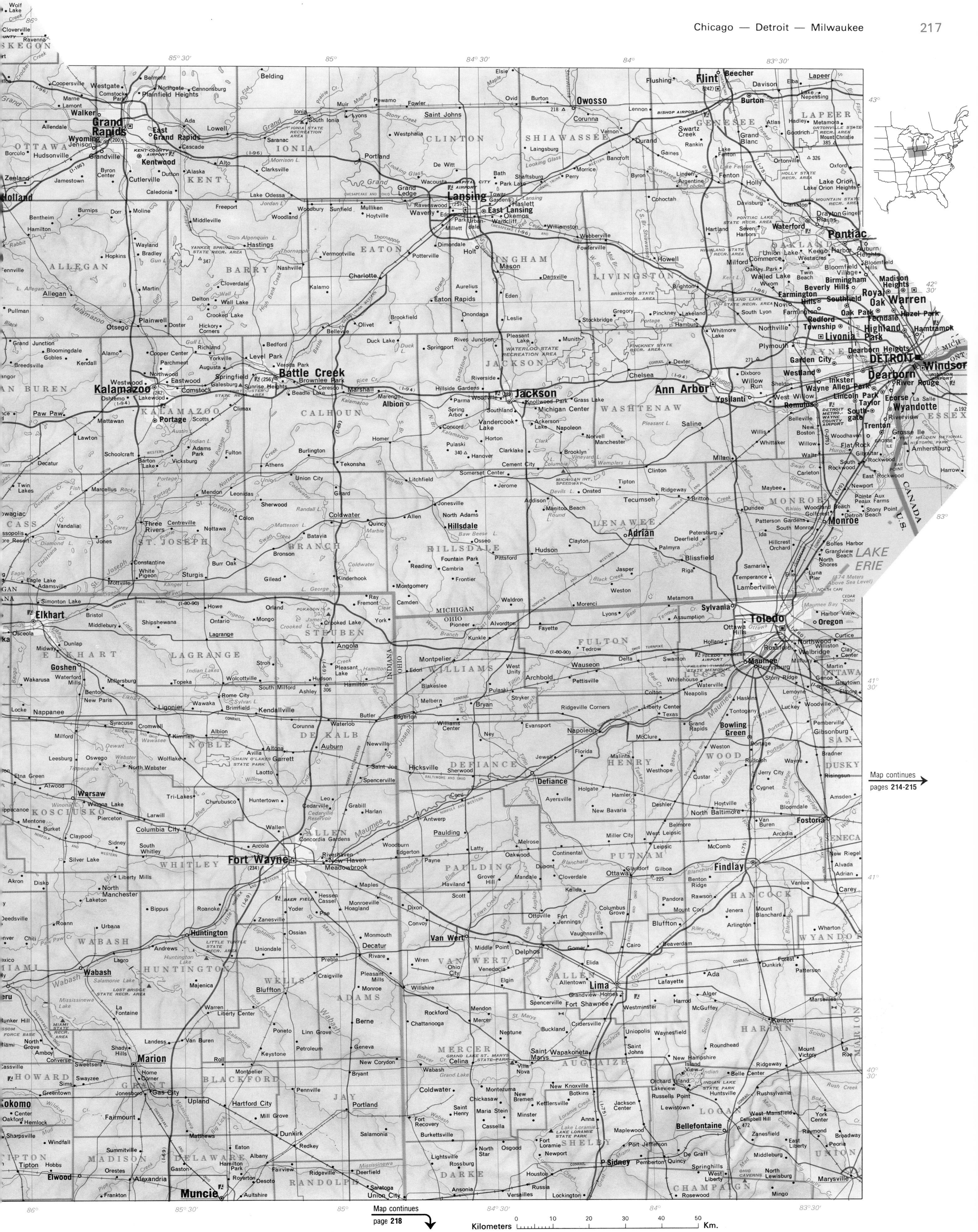
Grand Rapids
Kalamazoo
Battle Creek
Lansing
East Lansing
Jackson
Ann Arbor
Flint
Owosso
Pontiac
Detroit
Windsor
Dearborn
Livonia
Toledo
Elkhart
Fort Wayne
Marion
Muncie
Lima
Findlay
Defiance
Adrian
Monroe
Hillsdale
Coldwater
Huntington
Wabash
Kokomo
OTTAWA
KENT
IONIA
CLINTON
SHIAWASSEE
GENESEE
LAPEER
ALLEGAN
BARRY
EATON
INGHAM
LIVINGSTON
OAKLAND
WAYNE
VAN BUREN
KALAMAZOO
CALHOUN
JACKSON
WASHTENAW
CASS
ST. JOSEPH
BRANCH
HILLSDALE
LENAWEE
MONROE
ELKHART
LAGRANGE
STEUBEN
WILLIAMS
FULTON
LUCAS
NOBLE
DE KALB
DEFIANCE
HENRY
WOOD
KOSCIUSKO
WHITLEY
ALLEN
PAULDING
PUTNAM
HANCOCK
WABASH
HUNTINGTON
WELLS
ADAMS
VAN WERT
ALLEN
HARDIN
GRANT
BLACKFORD
JAY
MERCER
AUGLAIZE
LOGAN
HOWARD
MADISON
DELAWARE
RANDOLPH
DARKE
SHELBY
CHAMPAIGN
UNION
MICHIGAN
INDIANA
OHIO
CANADA
U.S.
LAKE ERIE
ESSEX
85° 30′
85°
84° 30′
84°
83° 30′
86°
83°
43°
42° 30′
42°
41° 30′
41°
40° 30′

Map continues pages 214-215

Map continues page 218

Kilometers 0 10 20 30 40 50 Km.

Statute Miles 0 10 20 30 40 50 Mi.

Scale 1:1,000,000

One centimeter represents 10 kilometers.
One inch represents approximately 16 miles.
Lambert Conformal Conic Projection

Map continues pages 214-215

Map continues pages 216-217

ENGLISH	airport	creek, cr.	dam	lake	reservoir, res.	ridge	state park
DEUTSCH	Flughafen	Bach	Damm	See	Stausee	Höhenrücken	Naturpark
ESPAÑOL	aeropuerto	riachuelo	presa	lago	embalse	serranía	parque provincial
FRANÇAIS	aéroport	crique	barrage	lac	réservoir	crête	parc régional
PORTUGUÊS	aeroporto	riacho	represa	lago	reservatório	cordilheira	parque estadual

Kilometers 0 10 20 30 40 50 Km.
Statute Miles 0 10 20 30 40 50 Mi.

Scale 1:1,000,000

One centimeter represents 10 kilometers.
One inch represents approximately 16 miles.
Lambert Conformal Conic Projection

INDIANAPOLIS
CINCINNATI
Louisville
Dayton
Columbus
Springfield
Richmond
Hamilton
Middletown
Muncie
Anderson
Bloomington
Columbus
Bedford
Madison
Portsmouth
Chillicothe
Frankfort
Maysville
OHIO
INDIANA
KENTUCKY

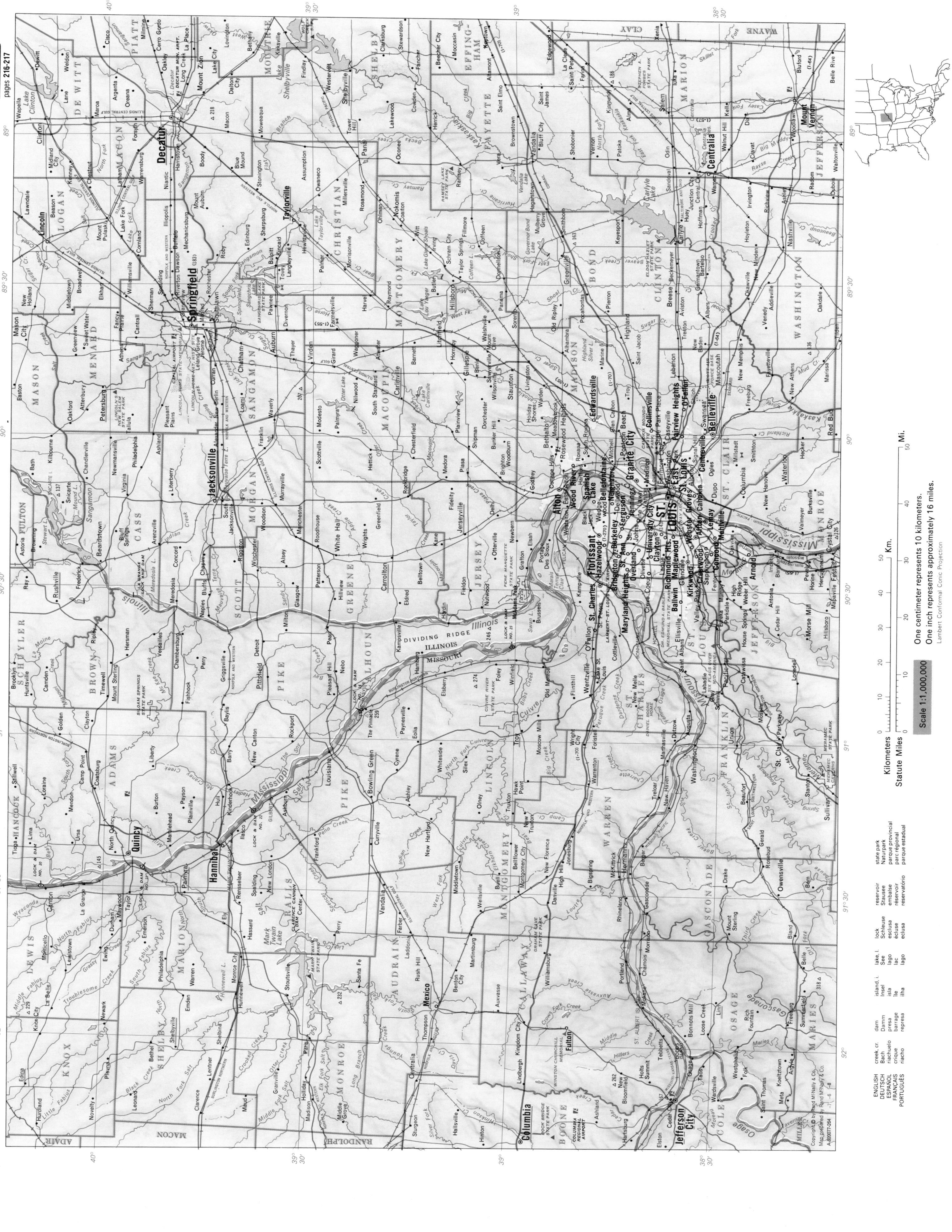
Map continues pages 216-217
Scale 1:1,000,000
One centimeter represents 10 kilometers.
One inch represents approximately 16 miles.
Lambert Conformal Conic Projection
Kilometers
Statute Miles
ENGLISH creek, cr. dam island, i. lake, l. lock reservoir state park
DEUTSCH Bach Damm Insel See Schleuse Stausee Naturpark
ESPAÑOL riachuelo presa isla lago esclusa embalse parque provincial
FRANÇAIS crique barrage île lac écluse réservoir parc régional
PORTUGUÊS riacho represa ilha lago eclusa reservatório parque estadual
Copyright © by Rand McNally & Co.
Map prepared by Rand McNally & Co.
ST. LOUIS
Springfield
Decatur
Jacksonville
Quincy
Hannibal
Jefferson City
Columbia
Mexico
Belleville
East St. Louis
Alton
Centralia
Mississippi
Missouri
Illinois
Kaskaskia
DIVIDING RIDGE ILLINOIS MISSOURI

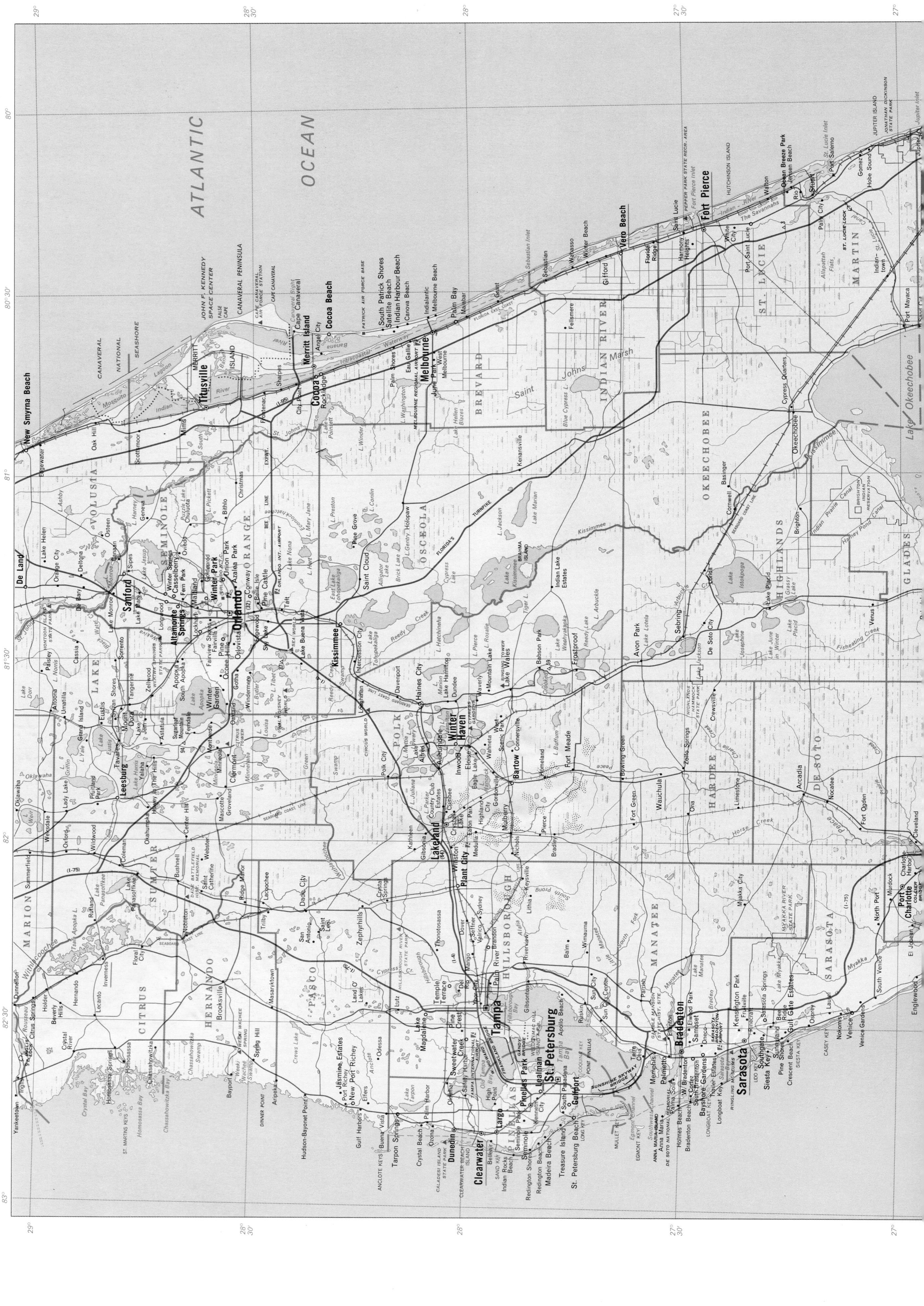
Kilometers 0 10 20 30 40 50 Km.
Statute Miles 0 10 20 30 40 50 Mi.
Scale 1:1,000,000
One centimeter represents 10 kilometers.
One inch represents approximately 16 miles.
Lambert Conformal Conic Projection
ENGLISH bay canal cape creek, cr. inlet island key lake, l. swamp
DEUTSCH Bucht Kanal Kap Bach Einfahrt Insel Klippe See Sumpf
ESPAÑOL bahía canal cabo riachuelo abra isla cayo lago pantano
FRANÇAIS baie canal cap crique bras de mer île caye lac marais
PORTUGUÊS baía canal cabo riacho enseada ilha recife lago pântano
ATLANTIC OCEAN

GULF OF MEXICO
Florida Bay
Palm Beach
West Palm Beach
Lake Worth
Lantana
Boynton Beach
Delray Beach
Highland Beach
Boca Raton
Deerfield Beach
Pompano Beach
Lighthouse Point
Margate
Coral Springs
Fort Lauderdale
Lauderdale-by-the-Sea
Oakland Park
Wilton Manors
Lauderhill
Lauderdale Lakes
City of Sunrise
Plantation
Davie
Dania
Hollywood
West Hollywood
Pembroke Pines
Miramar
Hallandale
Golden Beach
North Miami Beach
North Miami
Bay Harbor Islands
Surfside
Miami Beach
MIAMI
Hialeah
Miami Springs
Opa-Locka
Carol City
Coral Gables
South Miami
Key Biscayne
Kendall
Perrine
Cutler Ridge
Goulds
Princeton
Naranja
Homestead
Florida City
Leisure City
Westwood Lakes
Olympia Heights
Richmond Heights
South Miami Heights
Sweetwater
Belle Glade
South Bay
Clewiston
Harlem
La Belle
Immokalee
Felda
Corkscrew
Alva
Lehigh Acres
Fort Myers
North Fort Myers
Fort Myers Shores
Fort Myers Villas
Fort Myers Beach
Tanglewood
Cape Coral
Sanibel
Captiva
Saint James City
Estero
Bonita Springs
Naples Park
North Naples
Naples
East Naples
Golden Gate
Marco
Goodland
Everglades City
Chokoloskee
Copeland
Ochopee
Monroe
Flamingo
Key Largo
Tavernier
Plantation
Islamorada
Marathon
Big Pine Key
Key West
Stock Island
PALM BEACH
BROWARD
HENDRY
COLLIER
LEE
DADE
MONROE
The Everglades
EVERGLADES NATIONAL PARK
BISCAYNE NATIONAL PARK
BIG CYPRESS NATIONAL PRESERVE
MICCOSUKEE INDIAN RESERVATION
BIG CYPRESS INDIAN RESERVATION
HOLLYWOOD INDIAN RESERVATION
COLLIER-SEMINOLE STATE PARK
JOHN PENNEKAMP CORAL REEF STATE PARK
TAMIAMI TRAIL
Big Cypress Swamp
Corkscrew Swamp
Fakahatchee Strand
TEN THOUSAND ISLANDS
CAPE SABLE
FLORIDA KEYS
SEVENMILE BRIDGE
DRY TORTUGAS
FORT JEFFERSON NATIONAL MONUMENT
MARQUESAS KEYS
Copyright © by Rand McNally & Co.
Map prepared by Rand McNally & Co.

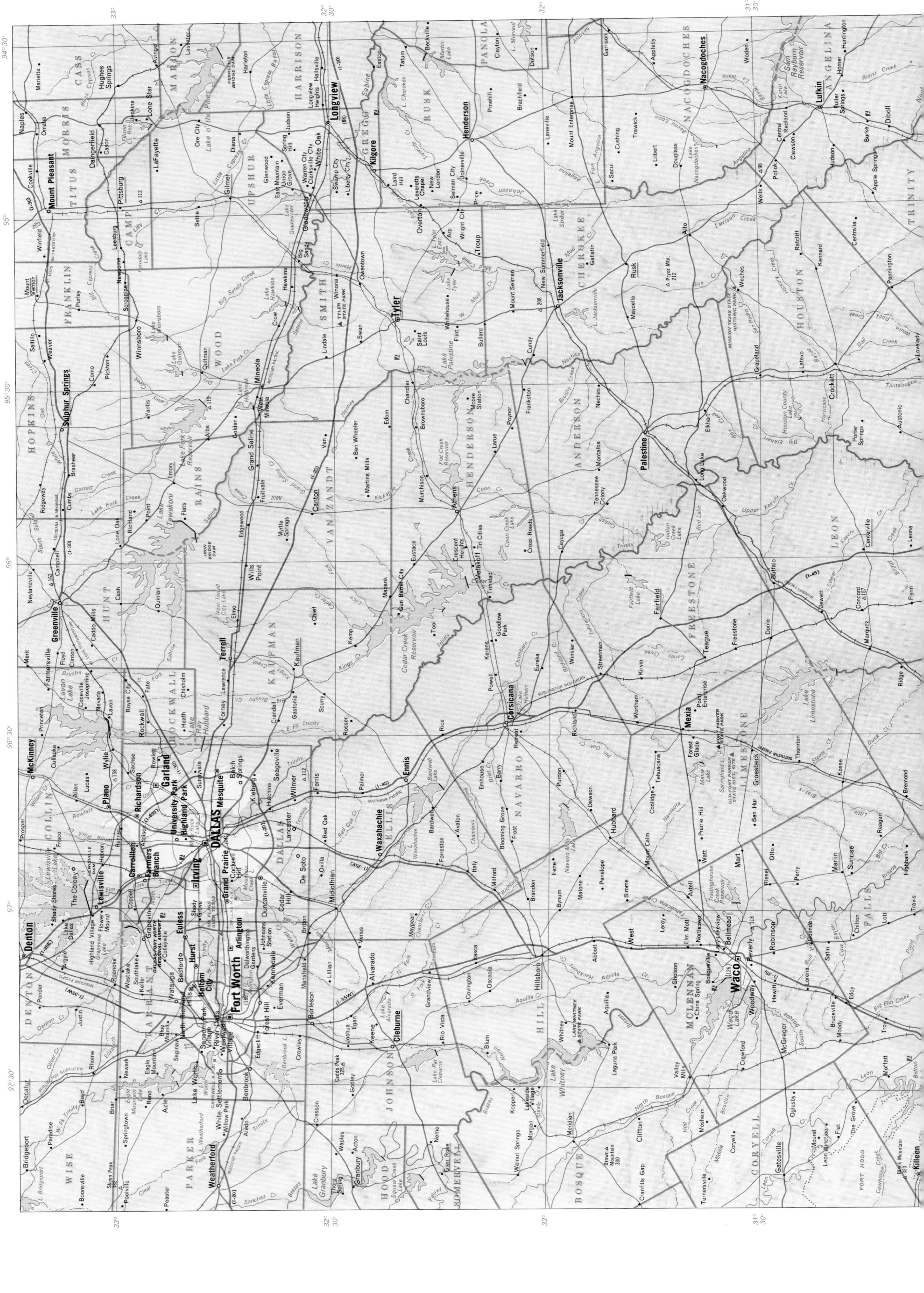
DALLAS
Fort Worth
Waco
Tyler
Longview
Palestine
Corsicana
Denton
McKinney
Greenville
Sulphur Springs
Mount Pleasant
Nacogdoches
Lufkin
Jacksonville
Athens
Terrell
Waxahachie
Cleburne
Weatherford
Killeen
Mexia
Crockett
Henderson
Kilgore
Ennis
Hillsboro
Arlington
Garland
Mesquite
Irving
Plano
Richardson
Grand Prairie
Lewisville
Carrollton
Canton
Kaufman
Fairfield
Rusk
Mineola
Gatesville
Marlin
Groesbeck
Teague

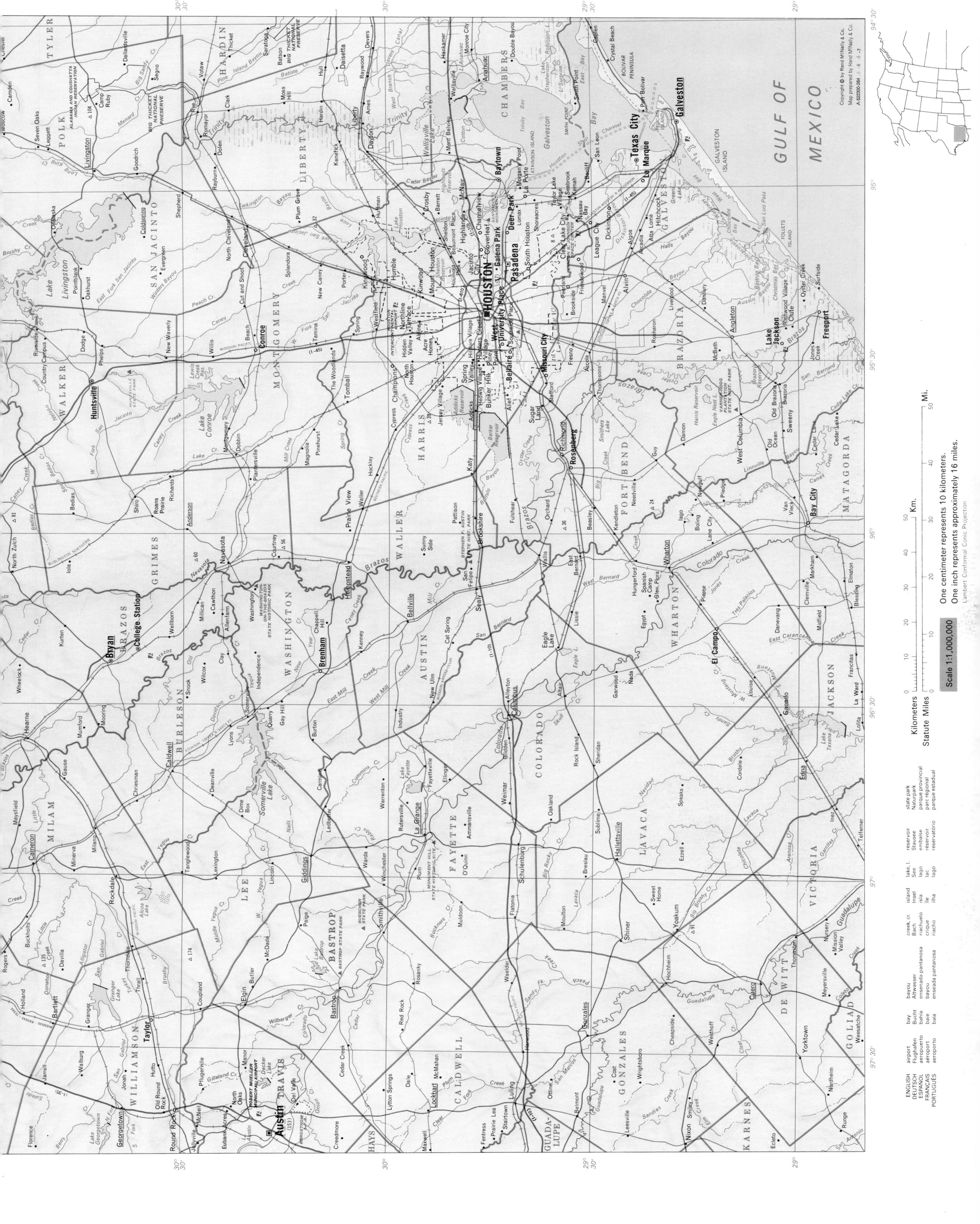
HOUSTON
Galveston
Texas City
Pasadena
Baytown
Conroe
Huntsville
Bryan
College Station
Brenham
Bay City
Freeport
Austin
Georgetown
Taylor
GULF OF MEXICO
GALVESTON ISLAND
BOLIVAR PENINSULA
WALKER
MONTGOMERY
LIBERTY
CHAMBERS
HARRIS
GALVESTON
BRAZORIA
FORT BEND
WALLER
GRIMES
WASHINGTON
AUSTIN
COLORADO
WHARTON
MATAGORDA
JACKSON
LAVACA
FAYETTE
BASTROP
TRAVIS
WILLIAMSON
MILAM
BURLESON
BRAZOS
LEE
CALDWELL
GONZALES
DE WITT
VICTORIA
GOLIAD
KARNES
HAYS
GUADALUPE
SAN JACINTO
POLK
TYLER
HARDIN
Scale 1:1,000,000
One centimeter represents 10 kilometers.
One inch represents approximately 16 miles.
Lambert Conformal Conic Projection
Kilometers
Statute Miles
Km.
Mi.
ENGLISH airport bay bayou creek, cr. island lake, l. reservoir state park
DEUTSCH Flughafen Bucht Altwasser Bach Insel See Stausee Naturpark
ESPAÑOL aeropuerto bahía enseada pantanosa riachuelo isla lago embalse parque estatal
FRANÇAIS aéroport baie bayou crique île lac réservoir parc régional
PORTUGUÊS aeroporto baía enseada pantanosa riacho ilha lago reservatório parque estadual
Copyright © by Rand McNally & Co.
Map prepared by Rand McNally & Co.

VANCOUVER
New Westminster
Burnaby
North Vancouver
Richmond
Strait of Georgia
Victoria
Esquimalt
Oak Bay
Nanaimo
Port Alberni
Duncan
Ladysmith
Chemainus
VANCOUVER ISLAND
BRITISH COLUMBIA
WASHINGTON
CANADA
UNITED STATES
Strait of Juan de Fuca
Bellingham
Mount Vernon
Anacortes
Everett
SEATTLE
Bremerton
Renton
Tacoma
Port Angeles
Port Townsend
Chilliwack
Abbotsford
Mission City
Blaine
WHATCOM
SKAGIT
SNOHOMISH
KING
CHELAN
OKANOGAN
MASON
CLALLAM
OLYMPIC MOUNTAINS
OLYMPIC NATIONAL PARK
CASCADE MOUNTAINS
WENATCHEE MOUNTAINS
SAN JUAN ISLANDS
WHIDBEY ISLAND
Puget Sound
Hood Canal
SEYMOUR RANGE
VANCOUVER ISLAND RANGES
PACIFIC RIM NATIONAL PARK
NORTH CASCADES NATIONAL PARK
ROSS LAKE NATIONAL RECREATION AREA
49°
48° 30'
48°
47° 30'
121°
121° 30'
122°
122° 30'
123°
123° 30'
124°
124° 30'

PACIFIC
OCEAN
PORTLAND
Vancouver
Salem
Longview
Kelso
Astoria
Aberdeen
Hoquiam
Centralia
Chehalis
The Dalles
Hood River
Oregon City
Gresham
Beaverton
Hillsboro
McMinnville
Tillamook
Seaside
WASHINGTON
OREGON
CLATSOP
COLUMBIA
WASHINGTON
YAMHILL
POLK
MARION
CLACKAMAS
MULTNOMAH
HOOD RIVER
WASCO
SHERMAN
KLICKITAT
SKAMANIA
CLARK
COWLITZ
LEWIS
PIERCE
THURSTON
PACIFIC
WAHKIAKUM
TILLAMOOK
LINCOLN
YAKIMA
Mt. Rainier
Mount Saint Helens
Mt. Adams
Mount Hood
MT. RAINIER NATIONAL PARK
YAKIMA INDIAN RESERVATION
WARM SPRINGS INDIAN RESERVATION
TOUTLE MOUNTAIN RANGE
Columbia
Willamette
Deschutes

Scale 1:1,000,000

One centimeter represents 10 kilometers.
One inch represents approximately 16 miles.

Lambert Conformal Conic Projection

Kilometers 0 10 20 30 40 50 Km.

Statute Miles 0 10 20 30 40 50 Mi.

ENGLISH	DEUTSCH	ESPAÑOL	FRANÇAIS	PORTUGUÊS
bay	Bucht	bahía	baie	baía
cape	Kap	cabo	cap	cabo
channel	Kanal	canal	canal	canal
creek, cr.	Bach	riachuelo	crique	riacho
island, I.	Insel	isla	île	ilha
lake, L.	See	lago	lac	lago
mount	Berg	monte	mont	monte
peak	Gipfel	pico	cime	pico
strait	Meeresstrasse	estrecho	détroit	estreito

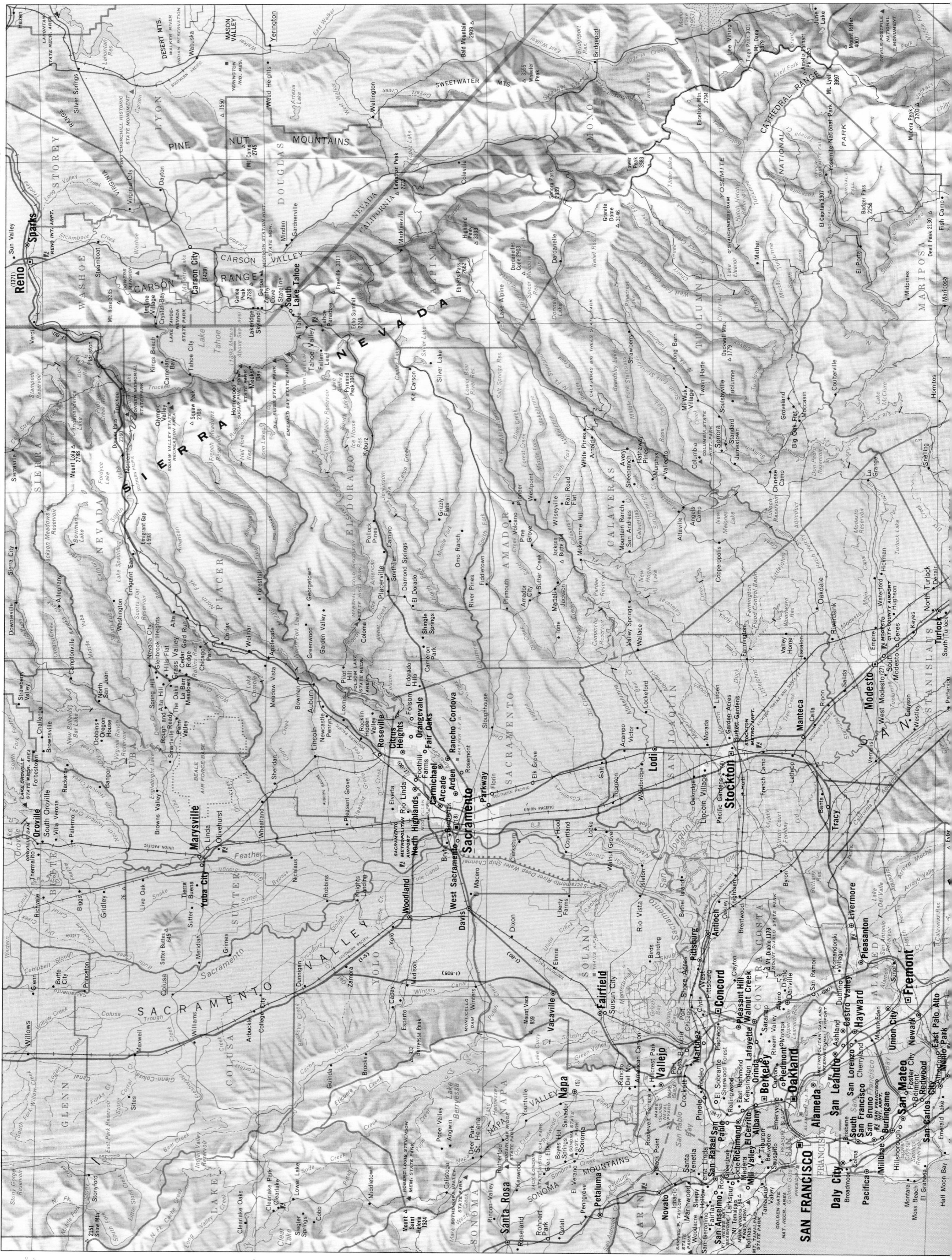
Reno
Sparks
Carson City
Lake Tahoe
South Lake Tahoe
SIERRA NEVADA
Sacramento
Stockton
Modesto
Lodi
Tracy
Manteca
Marysville
Yuba City
Oroville
Auburn
Placerville
Woodland
Davis
Fairfield
Vacaville
Vallejo
Napa
Santa Rosa
Petaluma
Oakland
Berkeley
Alameda
San Leandro
Hayward
Fremont
San Mateo
Daly City
SAN FRANCISCO
Concord
Walnut Creek
Antioch
Pittsburg
Livermore
Pleasanton
SACRAMENTO VALLEY
YOSEMITE NATIONAL PARK
CARSON RANGE
PINE NUT MOUNTAINS
SWEETWATER MTS.
CATHEDRAL RANGE
Yerington
Minden
Gardnerville
Roseville
Citrus Heights
Willows
Colusa
Mount Saint Helena 1324
Sonora
Mariposa

PACIFIC OCEAN
Monterey Bay
Santa Cruz
Watsonville
Salinas
Monterey
Pacific Grove
Seaside
Carmel
Gilroy
Hollister
Los Gatos
Saratoga
King City
Soledad
Greenfield
Gonzales
San Lucas
San Ardo
Paso Robles
Atascadero
San Luis Obispo
Morro Bay
Cambria
Fresno
Clovis
Madera
Chowchilla
Los Banos
Firebaugh
Mendota
Kerman
Coalinga
Avenal
Hanford
Visalia
Tulare
Lemoore
Corcoran
Delano
Wasco
Shafter
Bakersfield
Oildale
SANTA CRUZ MOUNTAINS
GABILAN RANGE
DIABLO RANGE
SANTA LUCIA RANGE
SIERRA DE SALINAS
SALINAS VALLEY
SAN JOAQUIN VALLEY
SANTA CLARA VALLEY
COAST RANGES
KETTLEMAN HILLS
CHOLAME HILLS
TEMBLOR RANGE
CARRIZO PLAIN
BIG SUR
MERCED
MADERA
FRESNO
KINGS
TULARE
KERN
SAN BENITO
MONTEREY
SAN LUIS OBISPO
Copyright © by Rand McNally & Co.
Map prepared by Rand McNally & Co.
A-522500-264

Map continues page 228

ENGLISH	bay	canal	creek, cr.	lake, l.	mountain, mtn.	pass	range	reservoir	slough
DEUTSCH	Bucht	Kanal	Bach	See	Berg	Pass	Gebirge	Stausee	verlandende Wasserfläche
ESPAÑOL	bahía	canal	riachuelo	lago	montaña	paso	sierra	embalse	pantano
FRANÇAIS	baie	canal	crique	lac	montagne	col	chaîne	réservoir	fondrière
PORTUGUÊS	baía	canal	riacho	lago	montanha	passo	serra	reservatório	pântano

Kilometers 0 10 20 30 40 50 Km.
Statute Miles 0 10 20 30 40 50 Mi.

Scale 1:1,000,000

One centimeter represents 10 kilometers.
One inch represents approximately 16 miles.
Lambert Conformal Conic Projection

Map continues
pages 226-227

119°
118°30'
118°
117°30'
117°
35°
34°30'
34°
33°30'
33°
32°30'
Bakersfield
Hillcrest Center
SAN JOAQUIN VALLEY
SIERRA NEVADA
TEHACHAPI MOUNTAINS
Tehachapi
Mojave
MOJAVE DESERT
EDWARDS AIR FORCE BASE
ANTELOPE VALLEY
Lancaster
Palmdale
Victorville
Barstow
SAN BERNARDINO MOUNTAINS
SAN GABRIEL MTS.
VENTURA
Ventura (San Buenaventura)
Oxnard
Port Hueneme
Santa Paula
Fillmore
Camarillo
Thousand Oaks
Simi Valley
San Fernando
Burbank
Glendale
Pasadena
LOS ANGELES
Santa Monica
Beverly Hills
East Los Angeles
Inglewood
Torrance
Long Beach
Garden Grove
Anaheim
Santa Ana
Huntington Beach
Newport Beach
Laguna Beach
Pomona
Ontario
San Bernardino
Riverside
Corona
Norco
Redlands
Banning
Hemet
Lake Elsinore
Temecula
Mission Viejo
San Clemente
Oceanside
Carlsbad
Escondido
Vista
San Marcos
Encinitas
Del Mar
Poway
La Jolla
El Cajon
La Mesa
San Diego
Coronado
National City
Chula Vista
Imperial Beach
Tijuana
U.S.
MEX.
Santa Monica Bay
San Pedro Channel
SANTA CATALINA ISLAND
Avalon
SAN CLEMENTE ISLAND
SANTA BARBARA ISLAND
PACIFIC OCEAN
Gulf of Santa Catalina
Outer Santa Barbara Passage
Copyright © by Rand McNally & Co.
Map prepared by Rand McNally & Co.
A-522600-264

ENGLISH	canyon	creek, cr.	lake, l.	mountain, mtn.	pass	peak	point	reservoir, res
DEUTSCH	Cañon	Bach	See	Berg	Pass	Gipfel	Landspitze	Stausee
ESPAÑOL	cañón	riachuelo	lago	montaña	paso	pico	punta	embalse
FRANÇAIS	canyon	crique	lac	montagne	col	cime	pointe	réservoir
PORTUGUÊS	canhão	riacho	lago	montanha	passo	pico	ponta	reservatório

Kilometers 0 10 20 30 40 50 Km.

Statute Miles 0 10 20 30 40 50 Mi.

Scale 1:1,000,000

One centimeter represents 10 kilometers.
One inch represents approximately 16 miles.

Lambert Conformal Conic Projection

a

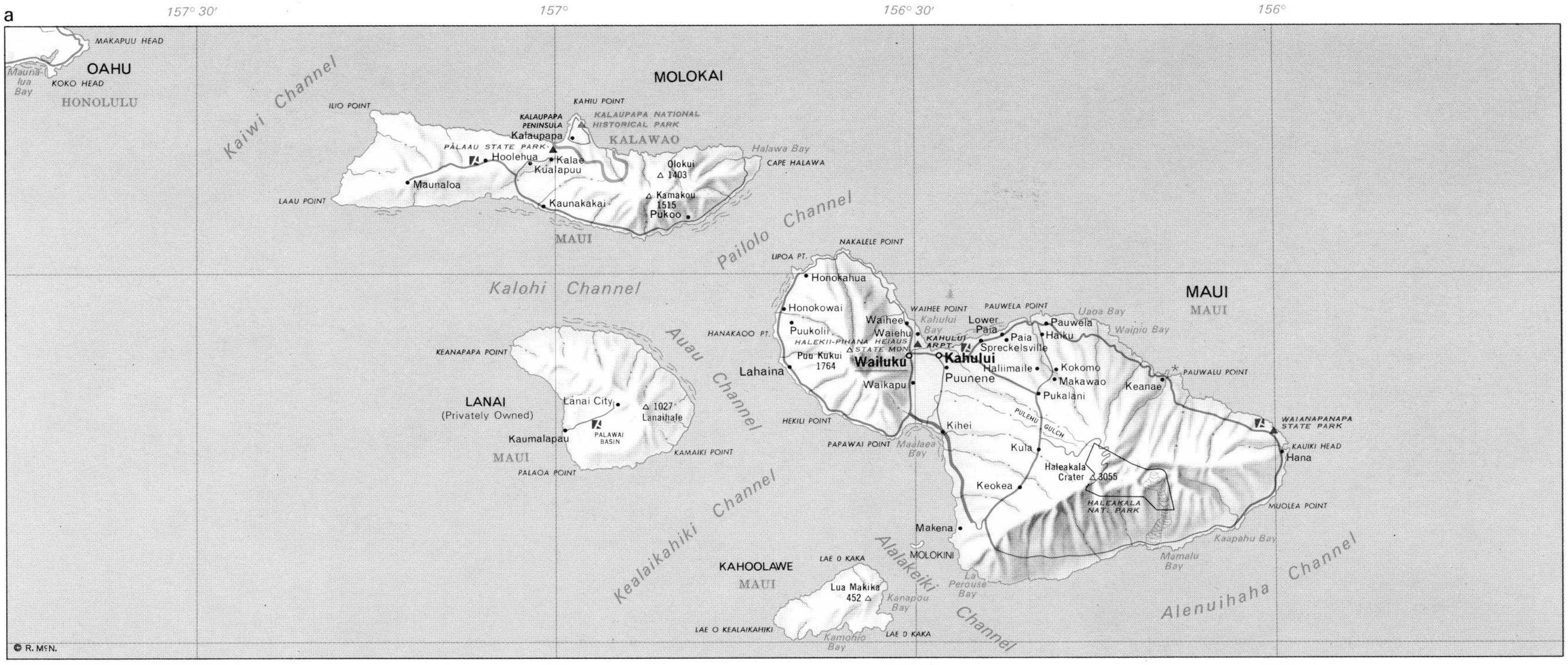
OAHU
HONOLULU
MAKAPUU HEAD
KOKO HEAD
Kaiwi Channel
MOLOKAI
KALAUPAPA NATIONAL HISTORICAL PARK
KALAWAO
Kalaupapa
Hoolehua
Kalae
Kualapuu
Maunaloa
Kaunakakai
Olokui 1403
Kamakou 1515
Pukoo
MAUI
Halawa Bay
CAPE HALAWA
LAAU POINT
ILIO POINT
Pailolo Channel
Kalohi Channel
Auau Channel
NAKALELE POINT
LIPOA PT.
Honokahua
Honokowai
Puukolii
Puu Kukui 1764
Lahaina
Wailuku
Kahului
Waihee
Waiehu
Waikapu
Puunene
Lower Paia
Paia
Spreckelsville
Pauwela
Haiku
Haliimaile
Makawao
Kokomo
Pukalani
Keanae
Kihei
Kula
Keokea
Haleakala Crater 3055
HALEAKALA NATL. PARK
Makena
MOLOKINI
Hana
KAUIKI HEAD
WAIANAPANAPA STATE PARK
PAUWELA POINT
PAUWALU POINT
Uaoa Bay
Waipio Bay
Kahului Bay
Maalaea Bay
La Perouse Bay
Kaupahu Bay
Mamalu Bay
MUOLEA POINT
LANAI
(Privately Owned)
Lanai City
1027 Lanaihale
Kaumalapau
PALAWAI BASIN
KEANAPAPA POINT
KAMAIKI POINT
PALAOA POINT
HEKILI POINT
PAPAWAI POINT
Kealaikahiki Channel
KAHOOLAWE
LAE O KAKA
Lua Makika 452
Kanapou Bay
Kamohio Bay
LAE O KEALAIKAHIKI
Alalakeiki Channel
Alenuihaha Channel
© R. McN.

b

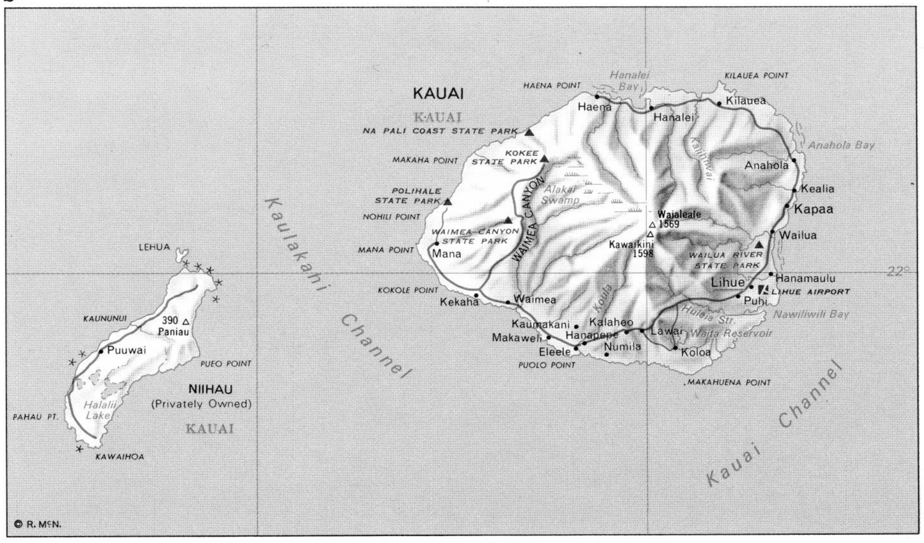
KAUAI
HAENA POINT
Hanalei Bay
KILAUEA POINT
Haena
Hanalei
Kilauea
NA PALI COAST STATE PARK
KOKEE STATE PARK
POLIHALE STATE PARK
WAIMEA CANYON STATE PARK
Anahola
Anahola Bay
Kealia
Kapaa
Wailua
Waialeale 1569
Kawaikini 1598
Lihue
Hanamaulu
LIHUE AIRPORT
Mana
Kekaha
Waimea
Kaumakani
Makaweli
Hanapepe
Eleele
Kalaheo
Lawai
Koloa
Numila
Puhi
Nawiliwili Bay
PUOLO POINT
MAKAHUENA POINT
Kaulakahi Channel
Kauai Channel
LEHUA
NIIHAU
(Privately Owned)
Puuwai
390 Paniau
KAWAIHOA
© R. McN.

c

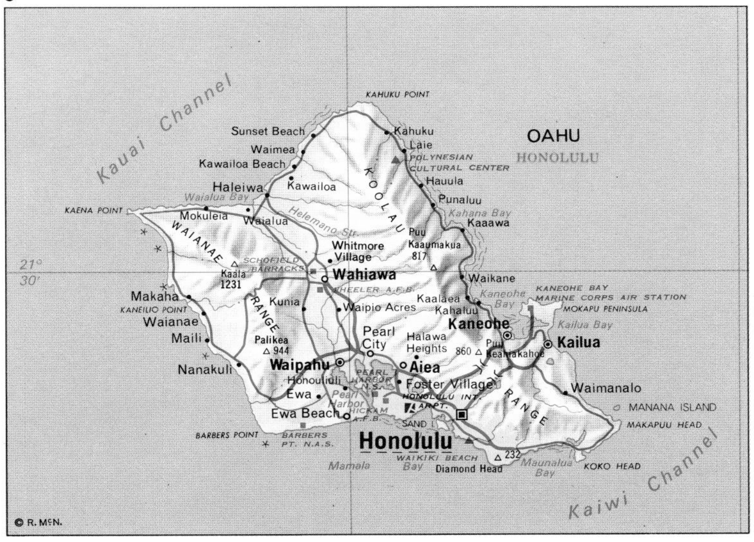
OAHU
HONOLULU
Kauai Channel
KAHUKU POINT
Kahuku
Laie
POLYNESIAN CULTURAL CENTER
Hauula
Punaluu
Kaaawa
Sunset Beach
Waimea
Kawailoa Beach
Haleiwa
Kawailoa
Mokuleia
Waialua
KAENA POINT
Whitmore Village
Wahiawa
Kaala 1231
Kunia
Waipio Acres
Makaha
Waianae
Maili
Nanakuli
Palikea 944
Waipahu
Pearl City
Aiea
Honolulu
Ewa
Ewa Beach
Kaneohe
Kailua
Waimanalo
Waikane
Kahaluu
Kaalaea
Halawa Heights
Foster Village
Diamond Head
MAKAPUU HEAD
KOKO HEAD
MANANA ISLAND
BARBERS POINT
Kaiwi Channel
© R. McN.

Kilometers 0 10 20 30 40 50 Km.
Statute Miles 0 10 20 30 40 50 Mi.

Scale 1:1,000,000
One centimeter represents 10 kilometers.
One inch represents approximately 16 miles.
Lambert Conformal Conic Projection

d

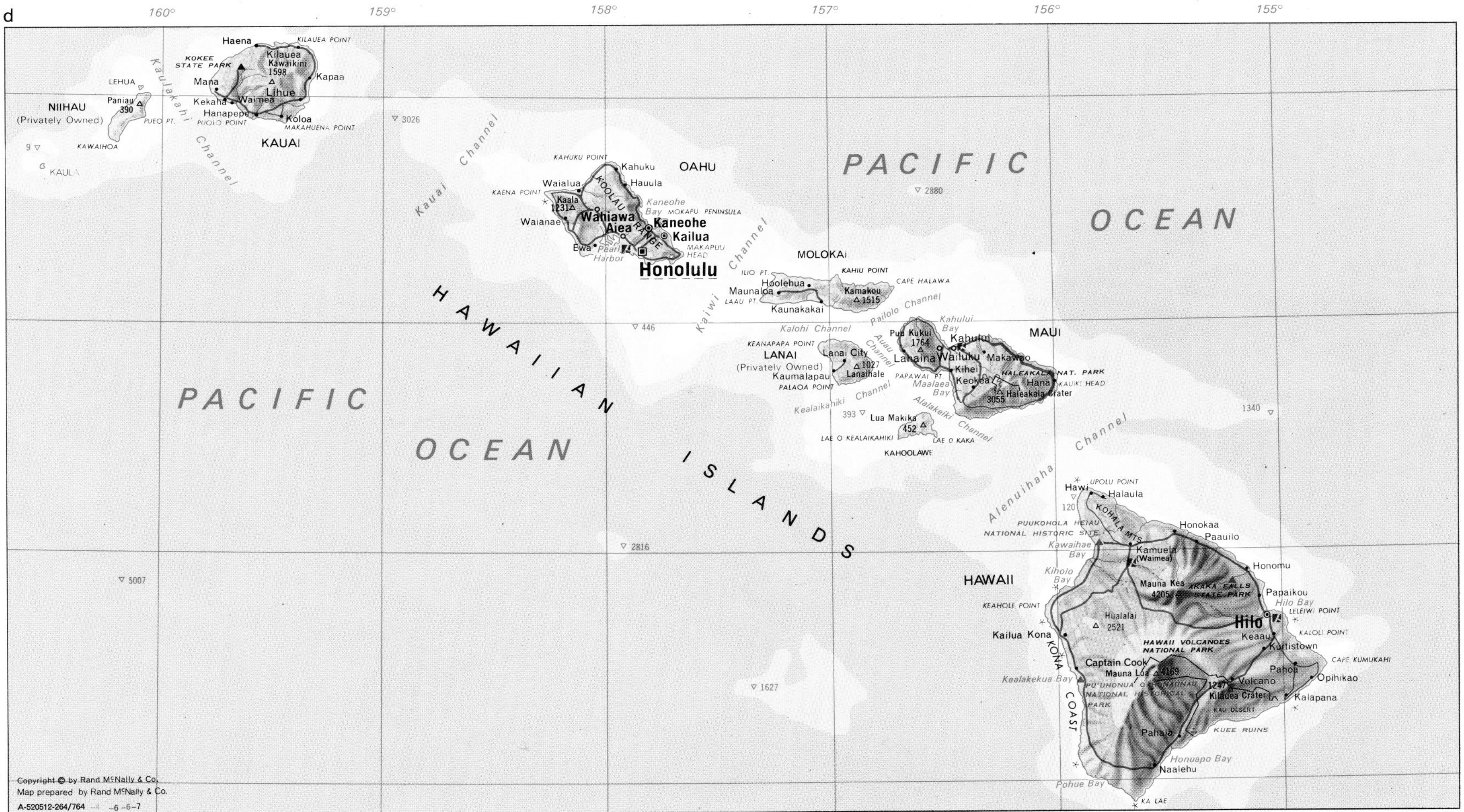
PACIFIC OCEAN
HAWAIIAN ISLANDS
NIIHAU
(Privately Owned)
KAUAI
OAHU
Honolulu
MOLOKAI
LANAI
MAUI
KAHOOLAWE
HAWAII
Hilo
Kailua Kona
Mauna Kea 4205
Mauna Loa 4169
Hualalai 2521
HAWAII VOLCANOES NATIONAL PARK
Kilauea Crater
Naalehu
KA LAE
Copyright © by Rand McNally & Co.
Map prepared by Rand McNally & Co.
A-520512-264/764 -6-6-7

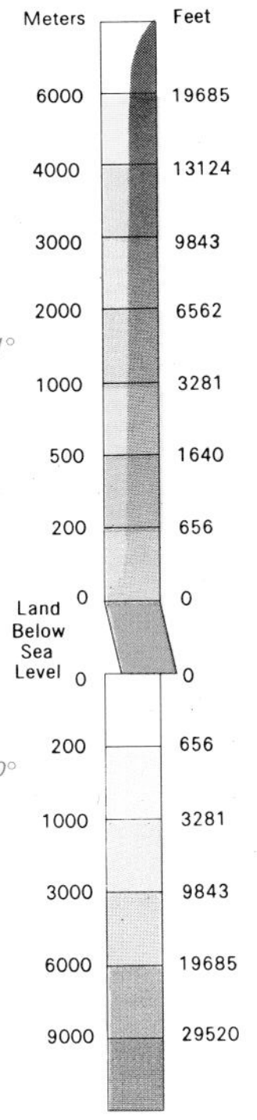
Meters
Feet
6000 19685
4000 13124
3000 9843
2000 6562
1000 3281
500 1640
200 656
0 0
Land Below Sea Level
200 656
1000 3281
3000 9843
6000 19685
9000 29520

ENGLISH	bay	channel	head	mount	point	state park, s.p.
DEUTSCH	Bucht	Kanal	Landspitze	Berg	Landspitze	Staatspark
ESPAÑOL	bahía	canal	promontorio	monte	punta	parque del estado
FRANÇAIS	baie	détroit	promontoire	mont	pointe	parc régional
PORTUGUÊS	baía	canal	promontório	monte	ponta	parque estadual

Kilometers 0 50 100 150 Km.
Statute Miles 0 50 100 150 Mi.

Scale 1:3,000,000
One centimeter represents 30 kilometers.
One inch represents approximately 47 miles.
Lambert Conformal Conic Projection

Map continues pages 178-179

UNITED STATES
MEXICO
GULF OF MEXICO
PACIFIC OCEAN
SIERRA MADRE OCCIDENTAL
SIERRA MADRE ORIENTAL
SIERRA MADRE DEL SUR
Golfo de California
BAJA CALIFORNIA
Tropic of Cancer
EDWARDS PLATEAU
TEXAS
NEW MEXICO
ARIZONA
OKLAHOMA
ARKANSAS
LOUISIANA
MISSISSIPPI
YUCATAN PENINSULA
GUATEMALA
BELIZE
EL SALVADOR
ISLAS REVILLAGIGEDO
ÎLE CLIPPERTON (Fr.)
Bahía de Campeche
Golfo de Tehuantepec
CIUDAD DE MEXICO
MEXICO CITY
San Diego
Tijuana
Mexicali
Ensenada
Phoenix
Tucson
Albuquerque
El Paso
Ciudad Juárez
Hermosillo
Chihuahua
Ciudad Obregón
Culiacán
Mazatlán
Durango
Torreón
Monterrey
Saltillo
Nuevo Laredo
Laredo
San Antonio
Austin
Houston
Dallas
Fort Worth
Oklahoma City
Tulsa
Little Rock
Memphis
Shreveport
Jackson
Baton Rouge
New Orleans
Mobile
Corpus Christi
Brownsville
Matamoros
Tampico
San Luis Potosí
Aguascalientes
Guadalajara
León
Querétaro
Morelia
Puebla
Veracruz
Acapulco
Oaxaca
Mérida
Campeche
Villahermosa
Tuxtla Gutiérrez
Tapachula
GUATEMALA
San Salvador
Santa Ana
Belize City
San Pedro Sula
115°
110°
105°
100°
95°
90°
30°
25°
20°
15°
10°
5°

ESPAÑOL	cabo	cordillera	golfo	isla, i.	lago, l.	punta	sierra	volcán, vol.
ENGLISH	cape	mountains	gulf	island	lake	point	mountains	volcano
DEUTSCH	Kap	Berge	Golf	Insel	See	Landspitze	Berge	Vulkan
FRANÇAIS	cap	montagnes	golfe	île	lac	pointe	montagnes	volcan
PORTUGUÊS	cabo	cordilheira	golfo	ilha	lago	ponta	serra	vulcão

ATLANTIC OCEAN
Sargasso Sea
BERMUDA (U.K.)
Hamilton
Tropic of Cancer
Straits of Florida
BAHAMAS
Nassau
ANDROS
ELEUTHERA
TURKS AND CAICOS ISLANDS (U.K.)
Grand Turk
WEST INDIES
GREATER ANTILLES
LA HABANA HAVANA
CUBA
ISLA DE LA JUVENTUD
CAYMAN IS. (U.K.)
George Town
JAMAICA
Kingston
HAITI
Port-au-Prince
DOMINICAN REPUBLIC
SANTO DOMINGO
HISPANIOLA
PUERTO RICO (U.S.)
San Juan
VIRGIN ISLANDS
BRITISH VIRGIN ISLANDS
ANGUILLA (U.K.)
ANTIGUA AND BARBUDA
Saint John's
SAINT KITTS AND NEVIS
Basseterre
MONTSERRAT (U.K.)
GUADELOUPE (Fr.)
Basse-Terre
DOMINICA
Roseau
MARTINIQUE (Fr.)
Fort-de-France
SAINT LUCIA
Castries
BARBADOS
Bridgetown
SAINT VINCENT AND THE GRENADINES
Kingstown
GRENADA
Saint George's
TRINIDAD AND TOBAGO
Port of Spain
LESSER ANTILLES
ARUBA (Neth.)
Oranjestad
NETHERLANDS ANTILLES
Willemstad
CARIBBEAN SEA
CARACAS
VENEZUELA
COLOMBIA
SANTA FE DE BOGOTÁ
BRAZIL
GUYANA
COSTA RICA
SAN JOSÉ
PANAMÁ
Panamá
Atlanta
Charleston
Jacksonville
Miami
Tampa
St. Petersburg
Norfolk
Charlotte
APPALACHIAN MTS.

Map continues pages 242-243

Kilometers 0 200 400 600 Km.
Statute Miles 0 200 400 600 Mi.

Scale 1:12,000,000
One centimeter represents 120 kilometers.
One inch represents approximately 190 miles.
Oblique Conic Conformal Projection

San Diego
Tijuana
Mexicali
Yuma
San Luis Rio Colorado
ARIZONA
Tucson
NEW MEXICO
Las Cruces
El Paso
Ciudad Juárez
Nogales
UNITED STATES
MEXICO
Ensenada
Golfo de Santa Clara
Puerto Peñasco
San Felipe
Caborca
BAJA CALIFORNIA NORTE
SONORA
Hermosillo
Guaymas
Ciudad Obregón
Navojoa
Los Mochis
CHIHUAHUA
Chihuahua
Delicias
Hidalgo del Parral
Golfo de California
BAJA CALIFORNIA
BAJA CALIFORNIA SUR
Santa Rosalía
Mulegé
Loreto
SIERRA DE LA GIGANTA
Ciudad Constitución
La Paz
Todos Santos
San José del Cabo
San Lucas
CABO SAN LUCAS
Tropic of Cancer
SIERRA MADRE OCCIDENTAL
SINALOA
Culiacán
Mazatlán
DURANGO
Durango
Torreón
Gómez Palacio
NAYARIT
Tepic
ISLAS MARÍAS
Puerto Vallarta
JALISCO
Guadalajara
Ciudad Guzmán
Colima
Tecomán
COLIMA
PACIFIC
OCEAN
ISLAS REVILLAGIGEDO (Mex.)
ISLA SOCORRO
ISLA CLARIÓN (Mex.)
ISLA SAN BENEDICTO
ISLA ROCA PARTIDA

Meters	Feet
6000	19685
4000	13124
3000	9843
2000	6562
1000	3281
500	1640
200	656
0	0
Land Below Sea Level 0	0
200	656
1000	3281
3000	9843
6000	19685
9000	29520

ESPAÑOL	bahía	cerro	isla	laguna	presa	punta	río	sierra
ENGLISH	bay	mountain	island	lagoon	reservoir	point	river	mountains
DEUTSCH	Bucht	Berg	Insel	Haff	Stausee	Landspitze	Fluss	Berge
FRANÇAIS	baie	montagne	île	lagune	réservoir	pointe	rivière	montagnes
PORTUGUÊS	baía	montanha	ilha	laguna	reservatório	ponta	rio	serra

Kilometers 0 100 200 300 Km.
Statute Miles 0 100 200 300 Mi

Scale 1:6,000,000
One centimeter represents 60 kilometers.
One inch represents approximately 95 miles.
Lambert Conformal Conic Projection

GULF
OF
MEXICO
Bahía de Campeche
Golfo de Tehuantepec
Tropic of Cancer
TEXAS
LOUISIANA
MISSISSIPPI
ALABAMA
EDWARDS
PLATEAU
NUEVO LEÓN
TAMAULIPAS
SAN LUIS POTOSÍ
QUERÉTARO
HIDALGO
MÉXICO
MORELOS
PUEBLA
VERACRUZ
OAXACA
GUERRERO
MICHOACÁN
TABASCO
CHIAPAS
CAMPECHE
YUCATÁN
QUINTANA ROO
YUCATAN PENINSULA
PENÍNSULA DE YUCATÁN
SIERRA MADRE ORIENTAL
SIERRA MADRE DEL SUR
SIERRA MADRE DE CHIAPAS
ISTMO DE TEHUANTEPEC
MEXICO
GUATEMALA
BELIZE
HONDURAS
Dallas
Fort Worth
Arlington
Abilene
Waco
Austin
San Antonio
Houston
Galveston
Beaumont
Port Arthur
Corpus Christi
Laredo
Nuevo Laredo
Brownsville
Matamoros
McAllen
Reynosa
Monterrey
Saltillo
Ciudad Victoria
Tampico
Ciudad Madero
San Luis Potosí
Querétaro
León
Morelia
CIUDAD DE MÉXICO
MEXICO CITY
Toluca
Puebla
Cuernavaca
Chilpancingo de los Bravo
Acapulco
Xalapa
Veracruz
Orizaba
Oaxaca
Coatzacoalcos
Minatitlán
Villahermosa
Ciudad del Carmen
Campeche
Mérida
Progreso
Cancún
Cozumel
Chetumal
Belize City
Belmopan
Tuxtla Gutiérrez
Tapachula
GUATEMALA
Quetzaltenango
San Pedro Sula
Shreveport
Jackson
Baton Rouge
New Orleans
Mobile
Gulfport
Biloxi
Lafayette
Lake Charles
Alexandria
Monroe
Meridian
Hattiesburg
Map continues
pages 238-239
Map continues
pages 236-237

Map continues pages 232-233

Durango
Mazatlán
SIERRA MADRE OCCIDENTAL
Zacatecas
Aguascalientes
San Luis Potosí
Tepic
GUADALAJARA
León
Guanajuato
Irapuato
Querétaro
Celaya
Morelia
Colima
Manzanillo
Puerto Vallarta
Acapulco
Lázaro Cárdenas
Uruapan del Progreso
PACIFIC OCEAN
Copyright © by Rand McNally & Co.
Map prepared by Rand McNally & Co.
A-531695-764 -3 -5 -8

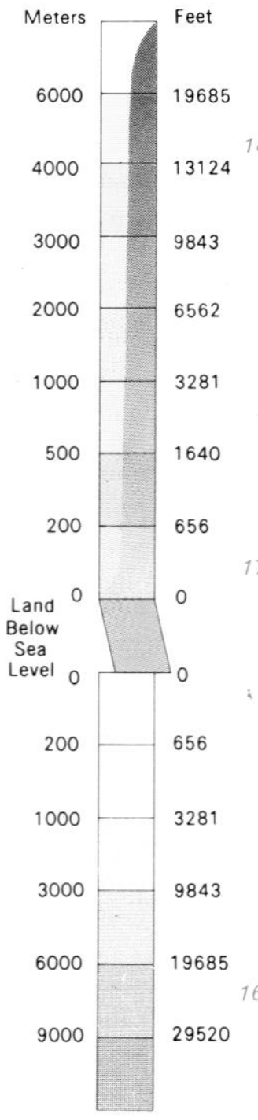
Meters
Feet
6000 19685
4000 13124
3000 9843
2000 6562
1000 3281
500 1640
200 656
0 0
Land Below Sea Level
0 0
200 656
1000 3281
3000 9843
6000 19685
9000 29520

ESPAÑOL	arroyo	boca	cerro	lago	laguna	punta	río	sierra	volcán
ENGLISH	brook	entrance	butte	lake	lagoon	point	river	ranges	volcano
DEUTSCH	Bach	Einfahrt	Restberg	See	Haff	Landspitze	Fluss	Bergketten	Vulkan
FRANÇAIS	ruisseau	entrée	butte	lac	lagune	pointe	rivière	chaîne	volcan
PORTUGUÊS	riacho	entrada	cerro	lago	laguna	ponta	rio	serra	vulcão

GULF OF MEXICO
Bahía de Campeche
Tropic of Cancer
Golfo de Tehuantepec
ISTMO DE TEHUANTEPEC
SIERRA MADRE DEL SUR
SIERRA MADRE DE CHIAPAS
TAMAULIPAS
VERACRUZ
SAN LUIS POTOSÍ
HIDALGO
PUEBLA
TLAXCALA
MORELOS
GUERRERO
OAXACA
TABASCO
CHIAPAS
CIUDAD DE MÉXICO
MEXICO CITY
Ciudad Victoria
Ciudad Mante
Ciudad Madero
Tampico
Villa Cuauhtémoc
Pánuco
Tamuín
El Higo
Tempoal de Sánchez
Tantoyuca
Naranjos
Cerro Azul
Huejutla de Reyes
Túxpan
Poza Rica
Papantla
Gutiérrez Zamora
Nautla
Martínez de la Torre
Misantla
Teziutlán
Altotonga
Xalapa
Coatepec
Zempoala
José Cardel
Veracruz
Boca del Río
Alvarado
Córdoba
Orizaba
Ciudad Mendoza
Fortín
Huatusco
Soledad de Doblado
Tierra Blanca
Tlacotalpan
Cosamaloapan
San Andrés Tuxtla
Santiago Tuxtla
Catemaco
Acayucan
Coatzacoalcos
Cosoleacaque
Minatitlán
Las Choapas
Agua Dulce
Cárdenas
Comalcalco
Villahermosa
Frontera
Teapa
Pachuca
Tulancingo
Huauchinango
Xicotepec de Juárez
Actopan
Apizaco
Tlaxcala
Puebla
Atlixco
Cholula
Tehuacán
Izúcar de Matamoros
Cuautla
Nezahualcóyotl
Oaxaca
Tuxtepec
Loma Bonita
Juchitán de Zaragoza
Salina Cruz
Santo Domingo Tehuantepec
Matías Romero
Tonalá
Arriaga
Tuxtla Gutiérrez
San Cristóbal de las Casas
Puerto Escondido
Puerto Ángel
Pinotepa Nacional
Huajuapan de León
Tlaxiaco
Miahuatlán de Porfirio Díaz
Ejutla de Crespo
Ocotlán de Morelos
Puerto Arista
Pijijiapan
Mapastepec
Laguna Madre
Laguna Morales
Laguna de Chairel
Laguna de Tamiahua
Laguna Tampamachoco
Laguna Superior
Laguna Inferior
Presa Vicente Guerrero
Presa Nezahualcóyotl
Presa Miguel Alemán
Pánuco
Tamesí
ISLA JUAN RAMÍREZ
CABO ROJO
ISLA DE LOBOS
PUNTA ZEMPOALA
PUNTA ANTÓN LIZARDO
PUNTA ROCA PARTIDA
PUNTA MALDONADO
PUNTA CORNETA
Pico de Orizaba 5610
3646
2836
1474
118
105
84

Map continues pages 232-233
Map continues pages 236-237

Kilometers 0 50 100 150 Km.
Statute Miles 0 50 100 150 Mi.

Scale 1:3,000,000
One centimeter represents 30 kilometers.
One inch represents approximately 47 miles.
Lambert Conformal Conic Projection

Map continues
pages 232-233

Map continues
pages 234-235

92°
91°
90°
89°
88°
87°
15°
14°
13°
12°
11°
10°
9°
8°
MEXICO
GUATEMALA
BELIZE
HONDURAS
EL SALVADOR
PETÉN
CHIAPAS
SIERRA MADRE DE CHIAPAS
ALTA VERAPAZ
BAJA VERAPAZ
IZABAL
QUICHÉ
HUEHUETENANGO
SAN MARCOS
TOTONICAPÁN
QUETZALTENANGO
SOLOLÁ
CHIMALTENANGO
SUCHITEPÉQUEZ
RETALHULEU
ESCUINTLA
SANTA ROSA
JUTIAPA
JALAPA
CHIQUIMULA
ZACAPA
EL PROGRESO
SIERRA DE LAS MINAS
COPÁN
OCOTEPEQUE
SANTA BÁRBARA
CORTÉS
YORO
ATLÁNTIDA
COMAYAGUA
INTIBUCÁ
LEMPIRA
LA PAZ
FRANCISCO MORAZÁN
EL PARAÍSO
VALLE
CHOLUTECA
CHINANDEGA
LEÓN
ESTELÍ
MADRIZ
NUEVA SEGOVIA
Gulf of Honduras
Golfo de Fonseca
Tapachula
Quetzaltenango
Retalhuleu
Mazatenango
Escuintla
GUATEMALA
Antigua Guatemala
Cobán
Puerto Barrios
Puerto Cortés
San Pedro Sula
El Progreso
La Ceiba
Tela
Comayagua
Siguatepeque
Tegucigalpa
Danlí
Choluteca
Santa Ana
San Salvador
Sonsonate
Acajutla
La Libertad
San Miguel
San Vicente
Usulután
Zacatecoluca
La Unión
Chinandega
León
Managua
Corinto
Puerto Sandino
Comitán de Domínguez
Livingston
Roatán
Utila
ISLAS DE LA BAHÍA
ISLA DE ROATÁN
PACIFIC
OCEAN
Meters
Feet
6000
19685
4000
13124
3000
9843
2000
6562
1000
3281
500
1640
200
656
0
0
Land Below Sea Level
0
0
200
656
1000
3281
3000
9843
6000
19685
9000
29520
Copyright © by Rand McNally & Co.
Map prepared by Rand McNally & Co.
A-533600-764

ESPAÑOL	bahía	cerro	cordillera	isla	lago	laguna	punta	sierra	volcán
ENGLISH	bay	mountain	mountains	island	lake	lagoon	point	mountains	volcano
DEUTSCH	Bucht	Berg	Berge	Insel	See	Haff	Landspitze	Berge	Vulkan
FRANÇAIS	baie	montagne	montagnes	île	lac	lagune	pointe	montagnes	volcan
PORTUGUÊS	baía	montanha	cordilheira	ilha	lago	laguna	ponta	serra	vulcão

CARIBBEAN SEA
LA MOSQUITIA
GRACIAS A DIOS
MONTAÑAS DE COLÓN
COSTA DE MOSQUITOS
CORDILLERA ISABELIA
CORDILLERA DARIENSE
ZELAYA
MATAGALPA
JINOTEGA
BOACO
CHONTALES
CORDILLERA CHONTALEÑA
SERRANÍAS DE YOLAINA
RÍO SAN JUAN
Lago de Nicaragua
NICARAGUA
COSTA RICA
PANAMÁ
ALAJUELA
HEREDIA
GUANACASTE
CARTAGO
SAN JOSÉ
LIMÓN
PUNTARENAS
BOCAS DEL TORO
CHIRIQUÍ
VERAGUAS
COCLÉ
COLÓN
HERRERA
LOS SANTOS
SAN ANDRÉS Y PROVIDENCIA (Colombia)
Cabo Gracias a Dios
Puerto Cabezas
Bluefields
San José
Puerto Limón
Puntarenas
David
Colón
Panamá
Golfo de los Mosquitos
Golfo de Panamá
Golfo de Chiriquí
Golfo Dulce
Golfo de Nicoya
ARCHIPIÉLAGO DE BOCAS DEL TORO
CAYOS MISKITOS
ISLAS DEL MAÍZ (Nic.)
San Andrés
ISLA DE PROVIDENCIA
ISTMO DE PANAMÁ

CAYO DE SERRANILLA (Colombia)

Map continues pages 246-247

Kilometers 0 50 100 150 Km.
Statute Miles 0 50 100 150 Mi.

Scale 1:3,000,000

One centimeter represents 30 kilometers.
One inch represents approximately 47 miles.
Lambert Conformal Conic Projection

Caribbean Region / Mittelamerikanische Inselwelt / Región del Caribe
Région des Caraïbes / Região do Caribe

GULF OF MEXICO
Straits of Florida
UNITED STATES
FLORIDA
Fort Myers
West Palm Beach
Fort Lauderdale
MIAMI
Miami Beach
Coral Gables
Hialeah
Hollywood
Key Largo
Key West
Florida Keys
Nassau
NEW PROVIDENCE
ANDROS
ELEUTHERA
GRAND BAHAMA
ABACO
EXUMA
GREAT BAHAMA BANK
LA HABANA
HAVANA
Matanzas
Cárdenas
Pinar del Río
Santa Clara
Cienfuegos
Sancti Spíritus
Ciego de Ávila
Camagüey
Holguín
Bayamo
Manzanillo
Santiago de Cuba
Guantánamo
CUBA
ISLA DE LA JUVENTUD
(ISLA DE PINOS)
Golfo de Batabanó
Canal de Yucatán
YUCATÁN
QUINTANA ROO
Cancún
Cozumel
YUCATAN PENINSULA
PENÍNSULA DE YUCATÁN
CAYMAN ISLANDS
(U.K.)
George Town
GREATER
WEST
Montego Bay
JAMAICA
Kingston
Spanish Town
Blue Mountain Peak
ISLAS DE LA BAHÍA
Roatán
Gulf of Honduras
La Ceiba
Tegucigalpa
HONDURAS
NICARAGUA
LA MOSQUITIA
Managua
León
Granada
Lago de Nicaragua
Bluefields
SAN ANDRÉS Y PROVIDENCIA
(Col.)
COSTA RICA
SAN JOSÉ
Puerto Limón
PANAMÁ
Colón
Panamá
ISTMO DE PANAMÁ
Barranquilla
Cartagena
CARIBBEAN
PACIFIC OCEAN
Copyright © by Rand McNally & Co.
Map prepared by Rand McNally & Co.
A-530100-764

Map continues pages 232-233

Map continues pages 236-237

Meters	Feet
6000	19685
4000	13124
3000	9843
2000	6562
1000	3281
500	1640
200	656
0	0
Land Below Sea Level 0	0
200	656
1000	3281
3000	9843
6000	19685
9000	29520

MAP FORM	bahia	cabo	cerro	channel	golfo	isla	passage	pico	punta
ENGLISH	bay	cape	mountain	channel	gulf	isle	passage	peak	point
DEUTSCH	Bucht	Kap	Berg	Kanal	Golf	Insel	Durchfahrt	Gipfel	Landspitze
ESPAÑOL	bahía	cabo	cerro	canal	golfo	isla	pasaje	pico	punta
FRANÇAIS	baie	cap	montagne	détroit	golfe	île	passage	cime	pointe
PORTUGUÊS	baía	cabo	montanha	canal	golfo	ilha	passagem	pico	ponta

ATLANTIC OCEAN
Sargasso Sea
Tropic of Cancer
TURKS AND CAICOS ISLANDS
(U.K.)
CAICOS ISLANDS
GREAT INAGUA
SILVER BANK
INDIES
HAITI
HAÏTI
Cap-Haïtien
Port-de-Paix
Gonaïves
Saint-Marc
Port-au-Prince
Pétionville
Jacmel
HISPANIOLA
Santiago
La Vega
San Francisco de Macorís
SANTO DOMINGO
San Pedro de Macorís
La Romana
Higüey
Barahona
DOMINICAN REPUBLIC
REPÚBLICA DOMINICANA
PUERTO RICO
(U.S.)
SAN JUAN
Arecibo
Mayagüez
Bayamón
Caguas
Ponce
Guayama
Canal de la Mona
VIRGIN ISLANDS
(U.S.)
BRITISH VIRGIN ISLANDS
Road Town
Charlotte Amalie
Christiansted
Frederiksted
SAINT CROIX
ANGUILLA
(U.K.)
The Valley
Marigot
Philipsburg
SAINT KITTS AND NEVIS
Basseterre
Charlestown
ANTIGUA AND BARBUDA
Saint John's
MONTSERRAT
(U.K.)
Plymouth
GUADELOUPE
(Fr.)
Pointe-à-Pitre
Basse-Terre
DOMINICA
Roseau
MARTINIQUE
(Fr.)
Fort-de-France
SAINT LUCIA
Castries
SAINT VINCENT AND THE GRENADINES
Kingstown
BARBADOS
Bridgetown
GRENADA
Saint George's
LEEWARD ISLANDS
WINDWARD ISLANDS
LESSER ANTILLES
ANTILLES
SEA
ARUBA
(Neth.)
Oranjestad
NETHERLANDS ANTILLES
NEDERLANDSE ANTILLEN
CURAÇAO
BONAIRE
Willemstad
Kralendijk
LA GUAJIRA
Riohacha
Golfo de Venezuela
Punto Fijo
Coro
FALCÓN
Maracaibo
Lago de Maracaibo
ZULIA
Cabimas
Ciudad Ojeda
Barquisimeto
LARA
Valencia
Maracay
CARACAS
DISTRITO FEDERAL
Maiquetía
Puerto Cabello
Barcelona
Puerto la Cruz
Cumaná
SUCRE
Carúpano
ISLA DE MARGARITA
NUEVA ESPARTA
Porlamar
MONAGAS
Maturín
ANZOÁTEGUI
El Tigre
Calabozo
GUÁRICO
PORTUGUESA
COJEDES
TRUJILLO
Valera
Guanare
DELTA AMACURO
Tucupita
TRINIDAD AND TOBAGO
TRINIDAD
TOBAGO
Port of Spain
San Fernando
Scarborough
Gulf of Paria
Serpents Mouth
72°
70°
68°
66°
64°
62°
60°
24°
22°
20°
18°
16°
14°
12°
10°

Map continues pages 246-247

Kilometers 0 100 200 300 Km.
Statute Miles 0 100 200 300 Mi.

Scale 1:6,000,000
One centimeter represents 60 kilometers.
One inch represents approximately 95 miles.
Lambert Conformal Conic Projection

a

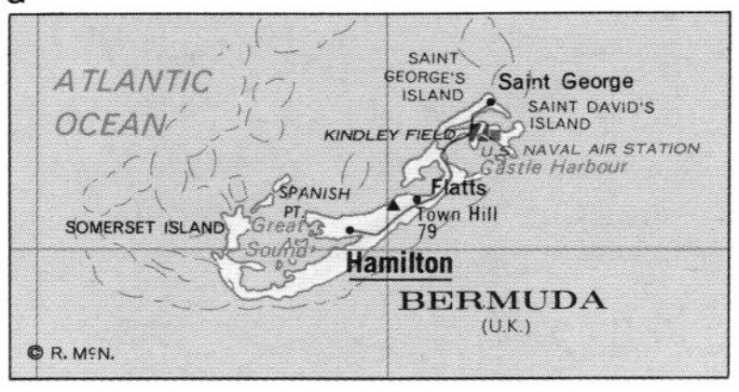
ATLANTIC OCEAN
Saint George
Hamilton
BERMUDA
(U.K.)

b

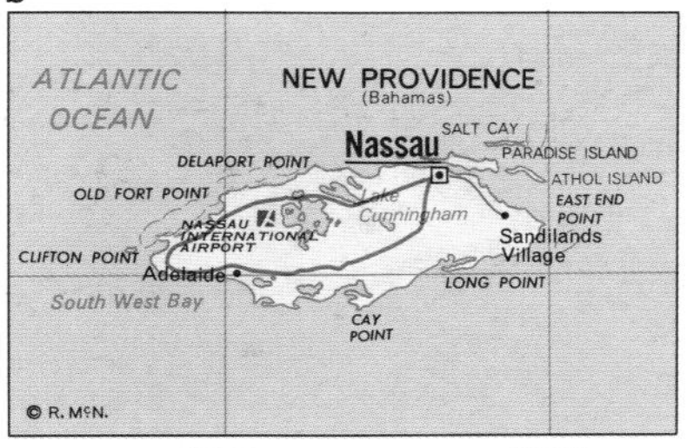
ATLANTIC OCEAN
NEW PROVIDENCE
(Bahamas)
Nassau
South West Bay

c

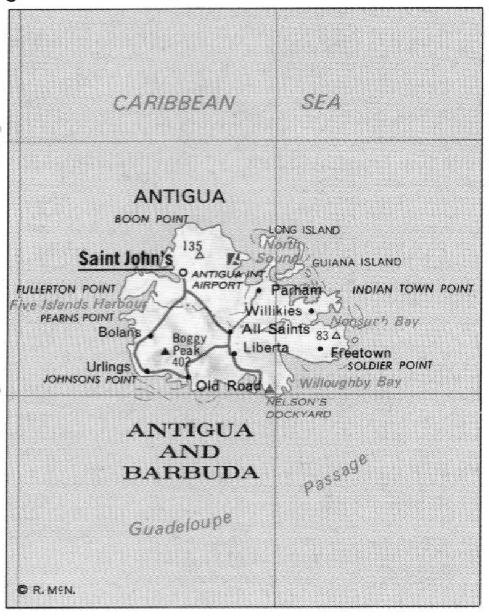
CARIBBEAN SEA
ANTIGUA
Saint John's
ANTIGUA AND BARBUDA
Guadeloupe Passage

d

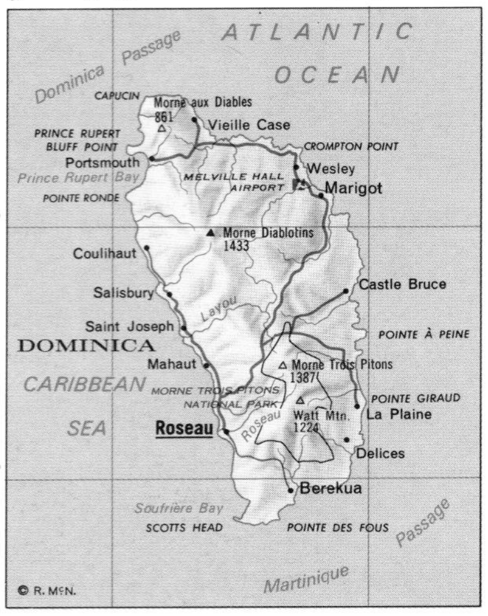
ATLANTIC OCEAN
Dominica Passage
DOMINICA
CARIBBEAN SEA
Roseau
Martinique Passage

e

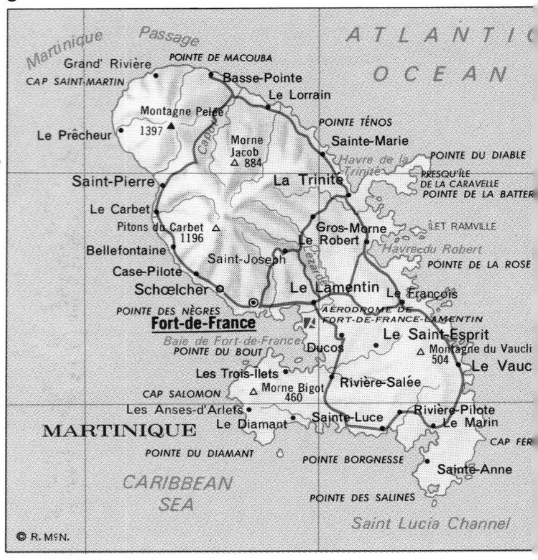
ATLANTIC OCEAN
Martinique Passage
Fort-de-France
MARTINIQUE
CARIBBEAN SEA
Saint Lucia Channel

m

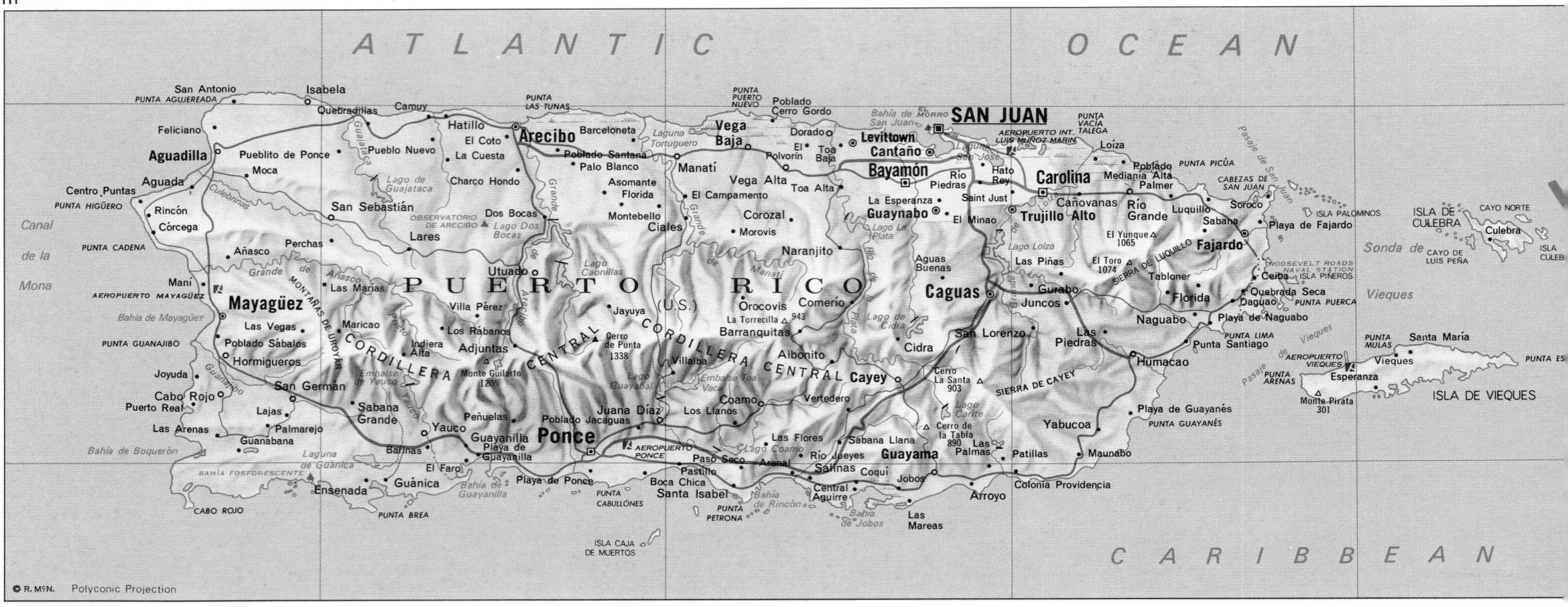
ATLANTIC OCEAN
SAN JUAN
PUERTO RICO
(U.S.)
CORDILLERA CENTRAL
Mayagüez
Ponce
Caguas
Arecibo
Bayamón
ISLA DE CULEBRA
ISLA DE VIEQUES
CARIBBEAN
Polyconic Projection

p

GULF OF MEXICO
LA HABANA
HAVANA
Matanzas
Pinar del Río
Cienfuegos
Santa Clara
Sancti Spíritus
ARCHIPIÉLAGO DE SABANA
Nicholas Channel
Golfo de Batabanó
ISLA DE LA JUVENTUD
(ISLA DE PINOS)
Nueva Gerona
ARCHIPIÉLAGO DE LOS CANARREOS
Golfo de Guanahacabibes
CARIBBEAN SEA
CAYMAN ISLANDS
(U.K.)

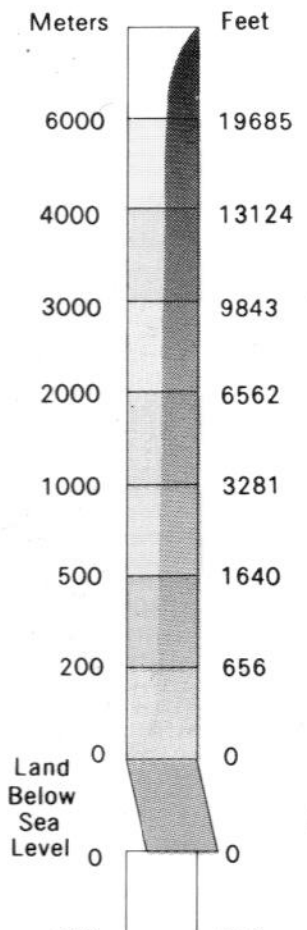
Meters
Feet
6000 19685
4000 13124
3000 9843
2000 6562
1000 3281
500 1640
200 656
0 0
Land Below Sea Level
0 0
200 656
1000 3281
3000 9843
6000 19685
9000 29520

MAP FORM	bahía	cayo	channel	ensenada	golfo	island	mount	passage	point
ENGLISH	bay	cay	channel	bayou	gulf	island	mount	passage	point
DEUTSCH	Bucht	Klippe	Kanal	Altwasser	Golf	Insel	Berg	Durchfahrt	Landspitze
ESPAÑOL	bahía	cayo	canal	ensenada	golfo	isla	montaña	pasaje	punta
FRANÇAIS	baie	caye	détroit	bayou	golfe	île	mont	passage	pointe
PORTUGUÊS	baía	baixio	canal	enseada	golfo	ilha	montanha	passagem	ponta

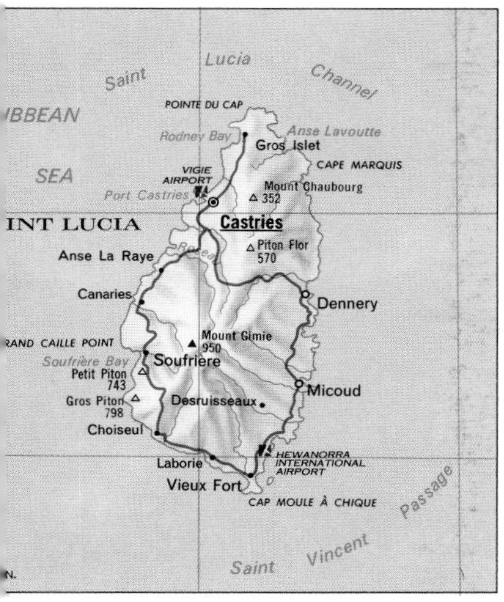
Saint Lucia Channel
SEA
SAINT LUCIA
Castries
Gros Islet
Dennery
Soufrière
Micoud
Vieux Fort
Saint Vincent Passage

g

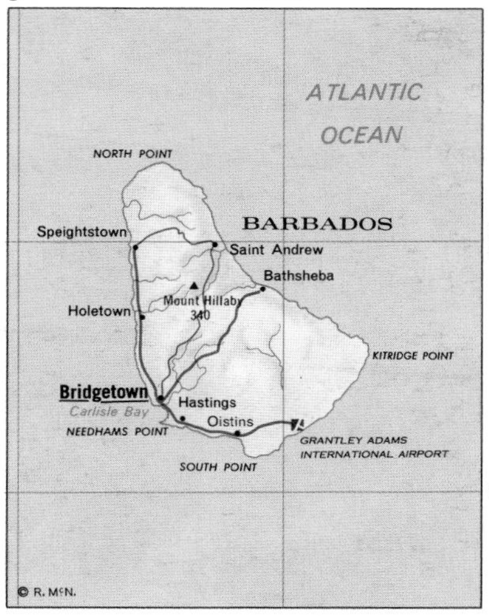
ATLANTIC OCEAN
BARBADOS
Speightstown
Holetown
Bridgetown
Bathsheba
Hastings
Oistins
© R. McN.

h

Saint Vincent Passage
CARIBBEAN SEA
SAINT VINCENT
Kingstown
SAINT VINCENT AND THE GRENADINES
BEQUIA
GRENADINES
© R. McN.

k

CARIBBEAN SEA
Victoria
Sauteurs
Grenville
Saint George's
GRENADA
© R. McN.

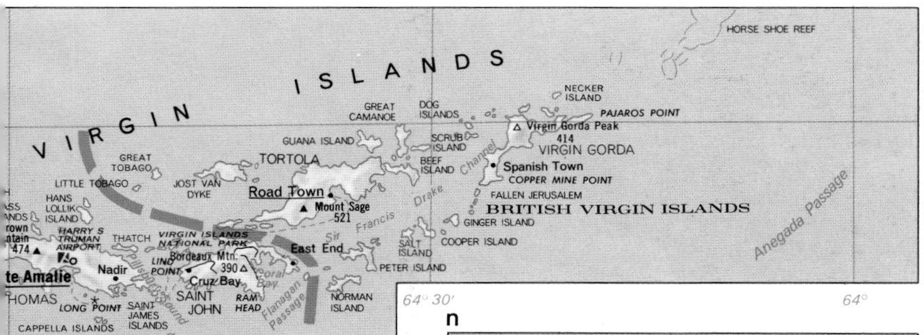
VIRGIN ISLANDS
TORTOLA
Road Town
VIRGIN GORDA
BRITISH VIRGIN ISLANDS
Charlotte Amalie
SAINT JOHN
VIRGIN ISLANDS (U.S.)
SEA

n

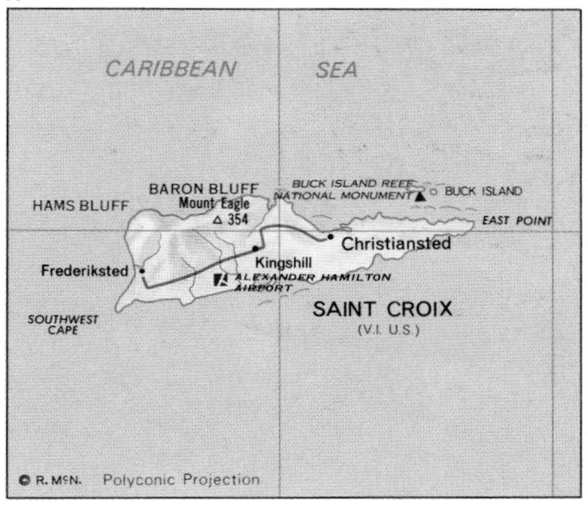
CARIBBEAN SEA
Frederiksted
Kingshill
Christiansted
SAINT CROIX
(V.I. U.S.)
© R. McN. Polyconic Projection

o

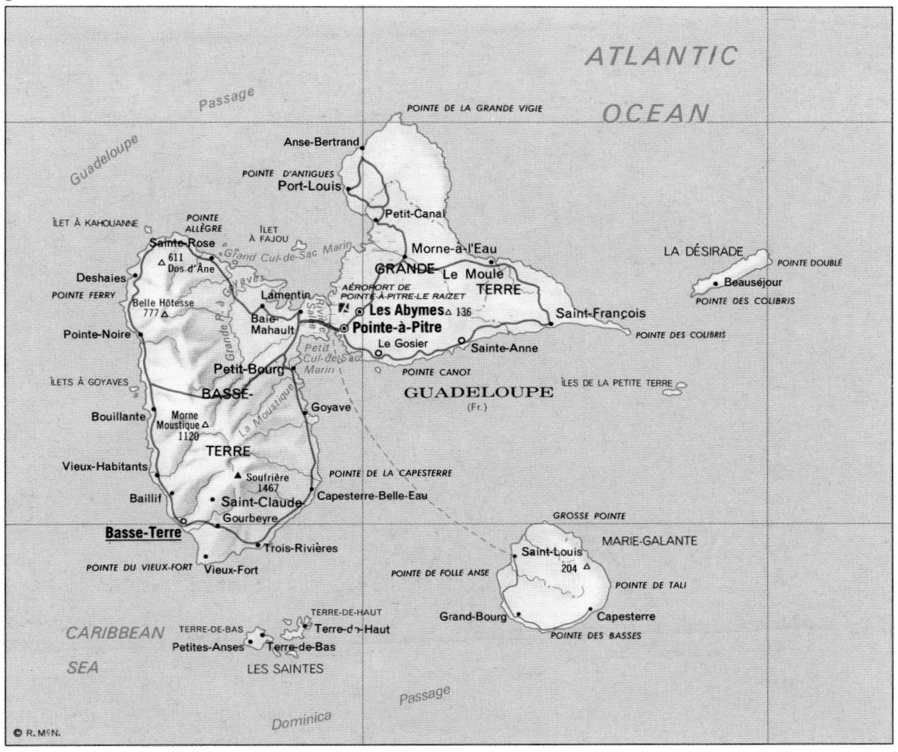
ATLANTIC OCEAN
Anse-Bertrand
Port-Louis
Petit-Canal
Morne-à-l'Eau
GRANDE-TERRE
Le Moule
Les Abymes
Pointe-à-Pitre
Le Gosier
Sainte-Anne
Saint-François
LA DÉSIRADE
GUADELOUPE (Fr.)
BASSE-TERRE
Basse-Terre
Capesterre-Belle-Eau
MARIE-GALANTE
Grand-Bourg
LES SAINTES
CARIBBEAN SEA
© R. McN.

Kilometers 0 10 20 30 40 50 Km.
Statute Miles 0 10 20 30 40 50 Mi.

Scale 1:1,000,000

One centimeter represents 10 kilometers.
One inch represents approximately 16 miles.
Transverse Mercator Projection (except as noted)

q

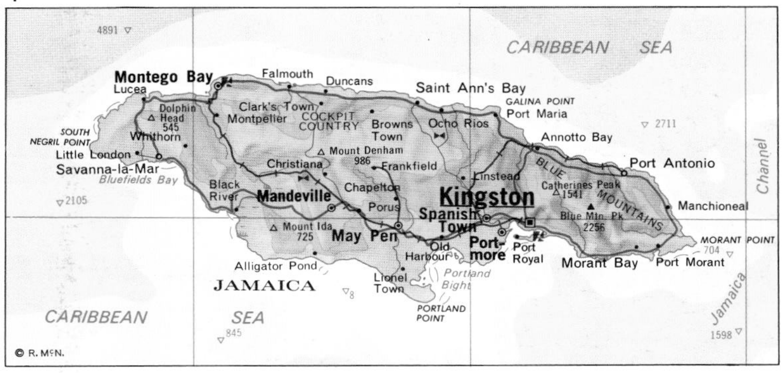
CARIBBEAN SEA
Montego Bay
Falmouth
Saint Ann's Bay
Ocho Rios
Port Antonio
Mandeville
May Pen
Spanish Town
Kingston
Portmore
JAMAICA
© R. McN.

ATLANTIC OCEAN
GREAT BAHAMA BANK
Nuevitas
Camagüey
Las Tunas
Holguín
Banes
Moa
Manzanillo
Bayamo
Palma Soriano
Guantánamo
Baracoa
Santiago de Cuba
GRANMA
SIERRA MAESTRA

r

TOBAGO
Scarborough
CARIBBEAN SEA
Port of Spain
Arima
San Fernando
TRINIDAD AND TOBAGO
Gulf of Paria
Serpents Mouth
VENEZUELA
ATLANTIC OCEAN
© R. McN.

s

CARIBBEAN SEA
ARUBA (Neth.)
Oranjestad
NETHERLANDS ANTILLES
NEDERLANDSE ANTILLEN
CURAÇAO
Willemstad
BONAIRE
Kralendijk
Punto Fijo
Coro
VENEZUELA
© R. McN.

Kilometers 0 50 100 150 Km.
Statute Miles 0 50 100 150 Mi.

Scale 1:3,000,000

One centimeter represents 30 kilometers.
One inch represents approximately 47 miles.
Lambert Conformal Conic Projection

Northern South America / Südamerika, nördlicher Teil / América del Sur: zona septentrional
Amérique du Sud Septentrionale / América do Sul: zona setentrional

Map continues
pages 230-231

CARIBBEAN SEA
PACIFIC OCEAN
NICARAGUA
COSTA RICA
PANAMA
COLOMBIA
VENEZUELA
ECUADOR
PERU
BOLIVIA
CHILE
ARGENTINA
AMAZONAS
ACRE
RONDÔNIA
SELVA
LLANOS
RORAIMA
LA GRAN SABANA
ARUBA (Neth.)
NETHERLANDS ANTILLES
LESSER ANTILLES
SAINT VINCENT AND THE GRENADINES
Managua
SAN JOSÉ
Panamá
SANTA FE DE BOGOTÁ
CARACAS
QUITO
LIMA
LA PAZ
Sucre
Barranquilla
Cartagena
Medellín
Cali
Maracaibo
Valencia
Barquisimeto
Guayaquil
Cuenca
Iquitos
Trujillo
Chiclayo
Arequipa
Cusco
Cochabamba
Santa Cruz de la Sierra
Porto Velho
Rio Branco
Equator
Amazon
Orinoco
Lago Titicaca
CORDILLERA OCCIDENTAL
CORDILLERA CENTRAL
CORDILLERA ORIENTAL
CORDILLERA REAL
ALTIPLANO
Copyright © by Rand McNally & Co.
Map prepared by Esselte Map Service AB, Stockholm.
A-549100-264 -8-6-15

Kilometers 0 200 400 600 Km.
Statute Miles 0 200 400 600 Mi.

Scale 1:12,000,000

One centimeter represents 120 kilometers.
One inch represents approximately 190 miles.
Oblique Conic Conformal Projection

ATLANTIC OCEAN
Equator
Tropic of Capricorn
SURINAME
FRENCH GUIANA
Georgetown
Paramaribo
Cayenne
TUMUC-HUMAC MTS.
AMAPÁ
Macapá
ILHA DE MARAJÓ
Belém
São Luís
Fortaleza
Teresina
PARÁ
Santarém
Represa de Tucuruí
MARANHÃO
PIAUÍ
CEARÁ
RIO GRANDE DO NORTE
Natal
João Pessoa
Recife
PERNAMBUCO
ALAGOAS
Maceió
SERGIPE
Aracaju
BAHIA
Salvador
Feira de Santana
SERRA DO CACHIMBO
TOCANTINS
B R A Z I L
ILHA DO BANANAL
MATO GROSSO
PLANALTO DO MATO GROSSO
Cuiabá
GOIÁS
BRASÍLIA
Goiânia
Anápolis
PLANALTO CENTRAL
MINAS GERAIS
Belo Horizonte
Uberlândia
ESPÍRITO SANTO
Vitória
MATO GROSSO DO SUL
Campo Grande
Corumbá
SÃO PAULO
Campinas
Santos
RIO DE JANEIRO
Niterói
Juiz de Fora
Amazon
Amazonas
Tocantins
Xingu
Tapajós
São Francisco
ATOL DAS ROCAS
ILHA FERNANDO DE NORONHA (Brazil)
MAP-FORM / ENGLISH / DEUTSCH / ESPAÑOL / FRANÇAIS / PORTUGUÊS
cerro / mountain / Berg / montaña / montagne / montanha
cordillera / range / Gebirge / cordillera / chaîne / cordilheira
ilha / island / Insel / isla / île / ilha
lago / lake / See / lago / lac / lago
nevado / mountain / Berg / montaña / montagne / montanha
peninsula / peninsula / Halbinsel / peninsula / péninsule / peninsula
serra / mountains / Berge / montañas / montagnes / montanhas

Map continues pages 244-245

Map continues
pages 242-243

PACIFIC OCEAN
CHILE
ARGENTINA
BOLIVIA
PARAGUAY
GRAN CHACO
PATAGONIA
ANDES
DESIERTO DE ATACAMA
CORDILLERA DOMEYKO
PUNA DE ATACAMA
Tropic of Capricorn
ISLA SAN FÉLIX (Chile)
ISLA SAN AMBROSIO (Chile)
ARCHIPIÉLAGO JUAN FERNÁNDEZ (Chile)
ISLA ALEJANDRO SELKIRK ISLA MÁS AFUERA
ISLA ROBINSON CRUSOE ISLA MÁS A TIERRA
Antofagasta
Calama
Tocopilla
Salta
San Salvador de Jujuy
San Miguel de Tucumán
Santiago del Estero
Asunción
Corrientes
Resistencia
Formosa
La Serena
Coquimbo
Córdoba
San Juan
Mendoza
Santa Fe
Paraná
Rosario
Valparaíso
Viña del Mar
SANTIAGO
BUENOS AIRES
Rancagua
Talca
Chillán
Concepción
Talcahuano
San Rafael
Mar del Plata
Bahía Blanca
Neuquén
Temuco
Valdivia
Osorno
Puerto Montt
ISLA GRANDE DE CHILOÉ
ARCHIPIÉLAGO DE LOS CHONOS
PENÍNSULA DE TAITAO
Trelew
Rawson
Comodoro Rivadavia
Golfo San Jorge
Puerto Deseado
Puerto San Julián
Río Gallegos
Bahía Grande
Puerto Natales
Punta Arenas
ISLA GRANDE DE TIERRA DEL FUEGO
Ushuaia
CABO DE HORNOS
CAPE HORN
ISLA DE LOS ESTADOS
FALKLAND ISLANDS (U.K.)
WEST FALKLAND
Copyright © by Rand McNally & Co.
Map prepared by Esselte Map Service AB, Stockholm.
A-549200-264

MAP FORM	cerro, co.	golfo	ilha	isla	lago	lagoa	monte	salar
ENGLISH	butte	gulf	island	isle	lake	lake	mountain	saltflat
DEUTSCH	Restberg	Golf	Insel	Insel	See	See	Berg	Salzebene
ESPAÑOL	cerro	golfo	isla	isla	lago	lago	montaña	salobral
FRANÇAIS	butte	golfe	île	île	lac	lac	montagne	salina
PORTUGUÊS	colina	golfo	ilha	ilha	lago	lago	montanha	salina

55°
50°
45°
40°
35°
30°
20°
25°
30°
35°
40°
45°
15°
SÃO PAULO
MINAS GERAIS
ESPÍRITO SANTO
RIO DE JANEIRO
Ribeirão Preto
Araraquara
São Carlos
Presidente Prudente
Marília
Bauru
Rio Claro
Limeira
Piracicaba
Campinas
Jundiaí
Sorocaba
SÃO PAULO
Santo André
São Vicente
Santos
São José dos Campos
Volta Redonda
Petrópolis
Nova Iguaçu
Niterói
RIO DE JANEIRO
Juiz de Fora
Poços de Caldas
Campos
Londrina
Maringá
B R A Z I L
PARANÁ
Ponta Grossa
Curitiba
Paranaguá
Cascavel
Foz do Iguaçu
Joinvile
Blumenau
Itajaí
SANTA CATARINA
Florianópolis
Lages
Erexim
Passo Fundo
RIO GRANDE DO SUL
Santa Maria
Caxias do Sul
São Leopoldo
Porto Alegre
Pelotas
Rio Grande
Bagé
Tropic of Capricorn
TRINDADE (Brazil)
ILHAS MARTIN VAZ (Brazil)
A T L A N T I C
O C E A N
SOUTH GEORGIA AND THE SOUTH SANDWICH ISLANDS (U.K.)
SHAG ROCKS (S. Georgia)
BLACK ROCK (S. Georgia)
BIRD ISLAND
SOUTH GEORGIA
ANNENKOV ISLAND
2934 Mount Paget
CAPE DISAPPOINTMENT
CLERKE ROCKS
55°
50°
Kilometers 0 200 400 600 Km.
Statute Miles 0 200 400 600 Mi.

Scale 1:12,000,000

One centimeter represents 120 kilometers.
One inch represents approximately 190 miles.
Oblique Conic Conformal Projection

Map continues pages 238-239

CARIBBEAN SEA
PACIFIC OCEAN
NICARAGUA
COSTA RICA
PANAMÁ
COLOMBIA
VENEZUELA
ECUADOR
PERÚ
BRASIL
Barranquilla
Santa Marta
Cartagena
Maracaibo
Medellín
Cali
Manizales
Pereira
SANTA FE DE BOGOTÁ
Bucaramanga
Cúcuta
Buenaventura
Popayán
Pasto
Tumaco
Esmeraldas
QUITO
Guayaquil
Cuenca
Machala
Loja
Iquitos
Panamá
Colón
Puerto Limón
David
a
PACIFIC OCEAN
ARCHIPIÉLAGO DE COLÓN
GALÁPAGOS ISLANDS
GALÁPAGOS (Ec.)
Equator
Copyright © by Rand McNally & Co.
Map prepared by Rand McNally & Co.

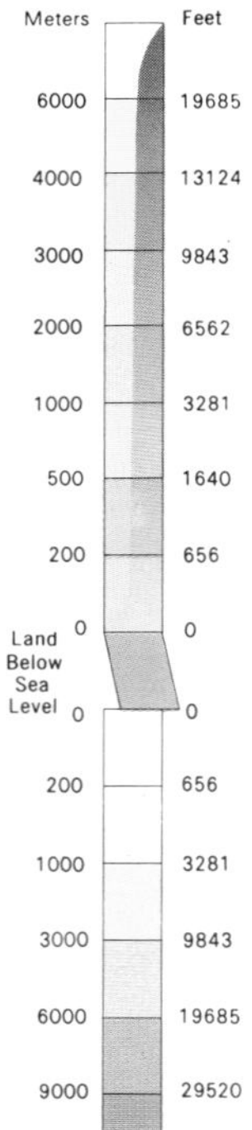
Meters
Feet
6000
19685
4000
13124
3000
9843
2000
6562
1000
3281
500
1640
200
656
0
0
Land Below Sea Level
0
0
200
656
1000
3281
3000
9843
6000
19685
9000
29520

Map continues pages 248-249

MAP FORM	bahía	cabo	cerro, co.	golfo	igarapé	isla, i.	lago, l.	punta	volcán, vol.
ENGLISH	bay	cape	butte	gulf	river	island	lake	point	volcano
DEUTSCH	Bucht	Kap	Restberg	Golf	Fluss	Insel	See	Landspitze	Vulkan
ESPAÑOL	bahía	cabo	cerro	golfo	río	isla	lago	punta	volcán
FRANÇAIS	baie	cap	butte	golfe	rivière	île	lac	pointe	volcan
PORTUGUÊS	baía	cabo	colina	golfo	rio	ilha	lago	ponta	vulcão

Map continues
pages 238-239

ATLANTIC
OCEAN
LESSER ANTILLES
GRENADA
TRINIDAD AND TOBAGO
Port of Spain
CARACAS
Valencia
Maracay
Barcelona
Cumaná
Maturín
Ciudad Guayana
Ciudad Bolívar
San Fernando
Puerto Ayacucho
Georgetown
New Amsterdam
Boa Vista
Manaus
BOLÍVAR
AMAZONAS
RORAIMA
PARÁ
VENEZUELA
COLOMBIA
BRAZIL
GUYANA
SURINAME
PAKARAIMA MOUNTAINS
SIERRA PARIMA
KAMOA MOUNTAINS
ACARAI MOUNTAINS
Orinoco
Negro
Amazon
Equator

Map continues
pages 250-251

Kilometers 0 100 200 300 Km.
Statute Miles 0 100 200 300 Mi.

Scale 1:6,000,000

One centimeter represents 60 kilometers.
One inch represents approximately 95 miles.
Oblique Conic Conformal Projection

PACIFIC
OCEAN
LORETO
UCAYALI
ACRE
AMAZONAS
SAN MARTÍN
HUÁNUCO
PASCO
JUNÍN
LIMA
ANCASH
HUANCAVELICA
AYACUCHO
APURÍMAC
CUSCO
AREQUIPA
MOQUEGUA
TACNA
PUNO
ICA
MADRE DE DIOS
DESIERTO DE SECHURA
CORDILLERA OCCIDENTAL
CORDILLERA CENTRAL
CORDILLERA ORIENTAL
CORDILLERA DE VILCABAMBA
CORDILLERA DE HUANZO
SERRA DO DIVISOR
CORD. ULTRAORIENTAL
PAMPA DEL SACRAMENTO
GRAN PAJONAL
PARQUE NACIONAL DEL MANU
LIMA
Callao
Chosica
Huacho
Chimbote
Trujillo
Chiclayo
Piura
Sullana
Paita
Cajamarca
Huaraz
Huánuco
Cerro de Pasco
La Oroya
Huancayo
Ayacucho
Cusco
Arequipa
Mollendo
Ica
Pisco
Nazca
Chincha Alta
Pucallpa
Iquitos
Cruzeiro do Sul
Juliaca
Puno
Tacna
Arica
Iquique
Tocopilla
Meters
Feet
6000 19685
4000 13124
3000 9843
2000 6562
1000 3281
500 1640
200 656
0 0
Land Below Sea Level
0 0
200 656
1000 3281
3000 9843
6000 19685
9000 29520
Copyright © by Rand McNally & Co.
Map prepared by Rand McNally & Co.
A-549792-764

MAP FORM	cerro	cordillera	isla, i.	lago, l.	nevado	punta	rio	serra
ENGLISH	mountain	mountains	island	lake	mountain	point	river	mountains
DEUTSCH	Berg	Berge	Insel	See	Berg	Landspitze	Fluss	Berge
ESPAÑOL	montaña	montañas	isla	lago	nevado	punta	rio	sierra
FRANÇAIS	montagne	montagnes	île	lac	montagne	pointe	rivière	montagnes
PORTUGUÊS	montanha	montanhas	ilha	lago	pico nevado	ponta	rio	serra

Map continues pages 246-247

AMAZONAS
SELVAS
PARÁ
SERRA DO CACHIMBO
RONDÔNIA
SERRA DOS PACAÁS NOVOS
SERRA DOS APIACÁS
SERRA DO NORTE
SERRA DO TOMBADOR
MATO GROSSO
PLANALTO DO MATO GROSSO
CHAPADA DOS PARECIS
PANDO
BENI
SANTA CRUZ
COCHABAMBA
CHUQUISACA
TARIJA
POTOSÍ
CHACO BOREAL
GRAN CHACO
ALTO PARAGUAY
NUEVA ASUNCIÓN
BOQUERÓN
CONCEPCIÓN
AMAMBAY
MATO GROSSO DO SUL
PANTANAL MATOGROSSENSE
BRAZIL
BOLIVIA
BRASIL
PARAGUAY
ARGENTINA
SALTA
JUJUY
CORDILLERA REAL
ALTIPLANO
Salar de Uyuni
Lago Poopó
Porto Velho
Rio Branco
Ji-Paraná
Ariquemes
Vilhena
Humaitá
Manicoré
Cuiabá
Várzea Grande
Cáceres
Rondonópolis
Corumbá
Campo Grande
Ponta Porã
Dourados
Pedro Juan Caballero
Trinidad
Cochabamba
Santa Cruz de la Sierra
Sucre
Potosí
Oruro
Tarija
Madeira
Mamoré
Guaporé
Paraguai
Juruena
Purus
Beni
66°
64°
62°
60°
58°
56°
6°
8°
10°
12°
14°
16°
18°
20°
22°

Map continues pages 250-251

Map continues page 255

Map continues pages 252-253

Kilometers 0 100 200 300 Km.
Statute Miles 0 100 200 300 Mi.

Scale 1:6,000,000
One centimeter represents 60 kilometers.
One inch represents approximately 95 miles.
Oblique Conic Conformal Projection

Map continues
pages 246-247

Paramaribo
Cayenne
Nieuw Amsterdam
New Amsterdam
Corriverton
CORONIE
NICKERIE
SARAMACCA
PARA
MAROWIJNE
COMMEWIJNE
WANICA
BROKOPONDO
SAINT-LAURENT-DU-MARONI
CAYENNE
SIPALIWINI
EAST BERBICE-CORENTYNE
GUYANA
SURINAME
FRENCH GUIANA
GUYANE FRANÇAISE
BRASIL
BRAZIL
TUMUC-HUMAC MOUNTAINS
KAYSER GEBERGTE
WILHELMINA GEB.
ORANJE GEB.
AMAPÁ
PARQUE NACIONAL DO CABO ORANGE
CABO ORANGE
Macapá
ILHA DE MARAJÓ
Belém
Equator
Amazonas
Amazon
AMAZONAS
Santarém
Óbidos
Parintins
Itacoatiara
Altamira
Itaituba
PARQUE NACIONAL DA AMAZÔNIA
RODOVIA TRANSAMAZÔNICA
P A R Á
Xingu
Tapajós
Tocantins
Represa de Tucuruí
Tucuruí
Marabá
SERRA DOS CARAJÁS
MARANHÃO
Imperatriz
Araguaína
Araguaia
Conceição do Araguaia
SERRA DO CACHIMBO
SERRA DOS APIACÁS
SERRA DO TOMBADOR
MATO GROSSO
SERRA FORMOSA
SERRA DO RONCADOR
ILHA DO BANANAL
PARQUE NACIONAL DO ARAGUAIA
SERRA DO ESTRONDO
TOCANTINS
CHAPADA DAS MANGABEIRAS
SERRA DO PENITENTE
Porto Nacional
Gurupi
Alta Floresta
Cachimbo
Gradaús
Carajás
Meters
Feet
6000
19685
4000
13124
3000
9843
2000
6562
1000
3281
500
1640
200
656
0
0
Land Below Sea Level
0
0
200
656
1000
3281
3000
9843
6000
19685
9000
29520
58°
56°
54°
52°
50°
48°
46°
2°
4°
6°
8°
10°
12°

Map continues
pages 248-249

Map continues
page 255

MAP FORM	cabo	cachoeira, cach.	ilha, i.	lago, l.	riacho	ribeirão, rão.	rio, r.	serra, sa.
ENGLISH	cape	waterfall	island	lake	creek	creek	river	mountains
DEUTSCH	Kap	Wasserfall	Insel	See	Bach	Bach	Fluss	Berge
ESPAÑOL	cabo	cascada	isla	lago	riachuelo	riachuelo	río	montañas
FRANÇAIS	cap	chute d'eau	île	lac	crique	crique	rivière	montagnes
PORTUGUÊS	cabo	queda d'água	ilha	lago	riacho	riacho	rio	montanhas

ATLANTIC
OCEAN
Equator
FORTALEZA
Natal
João Pessoa
RECIFE
Olinda
Maceió
Aracaju
Teresina
CEARÁ
RIO GRANDE DO NORTE
PARAÍBA
PERNAMBUCO
ALAGOAS
SERGIPE
PIAUÍ
BAHIA
Parnaíba
Sobral
Caucaia
Maranguape
Mossoró
Juazeiro do Norte
Crato
Campina Grande
Caruaru
Garanhuns
Arcoverde
Petrolina
Juazeiro
Paulo Afonso
Picos
Floriano
Caxias
Senhor do Bonfim
Alagoinhas
Represa de Sobradinho
ATOL DAS ROCAS
ILHA FERNANDO DE NORONHA (Brazil)
CABO DE SÃO ROQUE
Copyright © by Rand McNally & Co.
Map prepared by Rand McNally & Co.

Kilometers 0 100 200 300 Km.
Statute Miles 0 100 200 300 Mi.

Scale 1:6,000,000

One centimeter represents 60 kilometers.
One inch represents approximately 95 miles.
Oblique Conic Conformal Projection

Map continues pages 248-249

PACIFIC
OCEAN
Tropic of Capricorn
ANDES
PUNA DE ATACAMA
DESIERTO DE ATACAMA
CORDILLERA DOMEYKO
GRAN CHACO
CHACO AUSTRAL
BOLIVIA
CHILE
ARGENTINA
POTOSÍ
TARIJA
BOQUERÓN
JUJUY
SALTA
ANTOFAGASTA
ATACAMA
TUCUMÁN
CATAMARCA
SANTIAGO DEL ESTERO
LA RIOJA
CÓRDOBA
SAN JUAN
COQUIMBO
VALPARAÍSO
MENDOZA
SAN LUIS
LA PAMPA
NEUQUÉN
RÍO NEGRO
BUENOS
MAULE
BIOBÍO
LA ARAUCANÍA
Antofagasta
Calama
Chuquicamata
Tocopilla
San Salvador de Jujuy
Salta
San Miguel de Tucumán
Santiago del Estero
Copiapó
La Serena
Coquimbo
La Rioja
San Juan
Córdoba
Mendoza
Viña del Mar
Valparaíso
SANTIAGO
Rancagua
San Luis
Río Cuarto
Villa María
Talca
Chillán
Talcahuano
Concepción
Los Angeles
Temuco
Neuquén
Santa Rosa
Bahía Blanca
Copyright © by Rand McNally & Co.
Map prepared by Rand McNally & Co.
A-540191-764

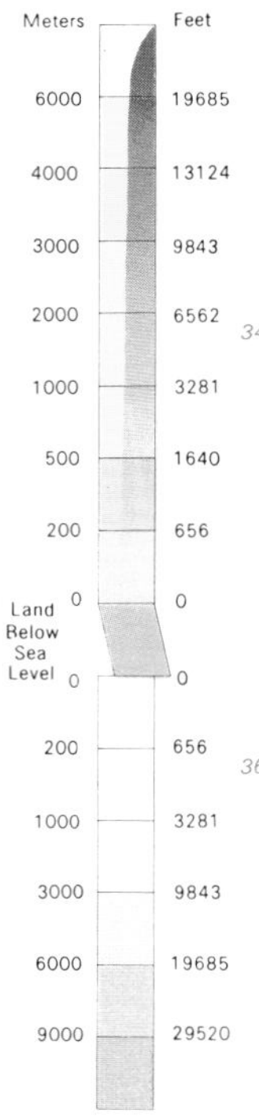
Meters
Feet
6000 19685
4000 13124
3000 9843
2000 6562
1000 3281
500 1640
200 656
Land Below Sea Level
0 0
0 0
200 656
1000 3281
3000 9843
6000 19685
9000 29520

Map continues page 254

MAP FORM	cabo	cerro	cuchilla	ilha	laguna	punta	salar	sierra	volcán
ENGLISH	cape	mountain	hills	island	lagoon; lake	point	saltflat	mountains	volcano
DEUTSCH	Kap	Berg	Hügel	Insel	Haff; See	Landspitze	Salzebene	Berge	Vulkan
ESPAÑOL	cabo	cerro	cuchilla	isla	laguna	punta	salobral	sierra	volcán
FRANÇAIS	cap	montagne	collines	île	lagune; lac	pointe	salina	montagnes	volcan
PORTUGUÊS	cabo	montanha	colina	ilha	laguna	ponta	salina	serra	vulcão

Map continues
page 255

ATLANTIC
OCEAN
PORTO ALEGRE
MONTEVIDEO
BUENOS AIRES
SÃO PAULO
Curitiba
Florianópolis
Asunción
La Plata
Mar del Plata
Santos
Campinas
Pelotas
Rio Grande
Corrientes
Posadas
Uruguaiana
Santa Maria
Paysandú
Concepción
Necochea
Tandil
RIO GRANDE DO SUL
SANTA CATARINA
PARANÁ
SÃO PAULO
MATO GROSSO DO SUL
CORRIENTES
MISIONES
ITAPÚA
CONCEPCIÓN
PRESIDENTE HAYES
Lagoa dos Patos
Lagoa Mirim
Bahía Samborombón
Río de la Plata

Kilometers 0 100 200 300 Km.
Statute Miles 0 100 200 300 Mi.

Scale 1:6,000,000
One centimeter represents 60 kilometers.
One inch represents approximately 95 miles.
Oblique Conic Conformal Projection

Map continues pages 252-253

PACIFIC
OCEAN
ATLANTIC
OCEAN
FALKLAND ISLANDS
(U.K.)
LA ARAUCANÍA
LOS LAGOS
AISÉN DEL GENERAL CARLOS IBÁÑEZ DEL CAMPO
MAGALLANES Y DE LA ANTÁRTICA CHILENA
LA PAMPA
BUENOS AIRES
RÍO NEGRO
NEUQUÉN
CHUBUT
SANTA CRUZ
PATAGONIA
ISLA GRANDE DE TIERRA DEL FUEGO
ISLA GRANDE DE CHILOÉ
ARCHIPIÉLAGO DE LOS CHONOS
ISLA WELLINGTON
ISLA SANTA INÉS
ISLA RIESCO
ISLA NAVARINO
ISLA HOSTE
ISLAS WOLLASTON
CABO DE HORNOS
CAPE HORN
WEST FALKLAND
EAST FALKLAND
Stanley
Temuco
Valdivia
Osorno
La Unión
Puerto Montt
Ancud
Castro
Quellón
Esquel
Trelew
Rawson
Puerto Madryn
Comodoro Rivadavia
Puerto Deseado
Puerto San Julián
Río Gallegos
Puerto Natales
Punta Arenas
Río Grande
Ushuaia
Puerto Williams
Neuquén
Cipolletti
General Roca
San Carlos de Bariloche
Viedma
Carmen de Patagones
San Antonio Oeste
Bahía Blanca
Punta Alta
Coihaique
Cochrane
Golfo San Matías
Golfo San Jorge
Bahía Grande
Golfo de Penas
Golfo Corcovado
Strait of Magellan
ARGENTINA
CHILE
Copyright © by Rand McNally & Co.
Map prepared by Rand McNally & Co.

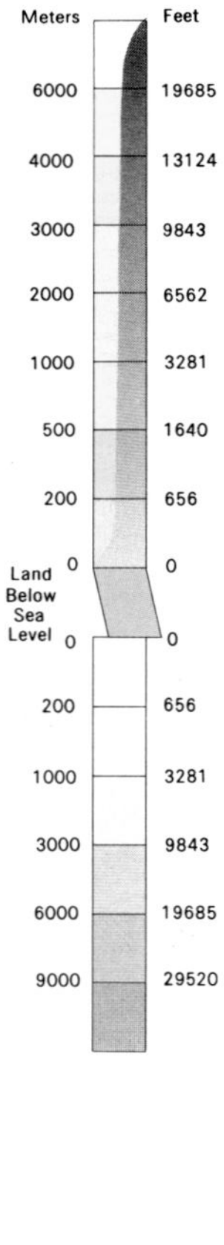
Meters
Feet
6000
19685
4000
13124
3000
9843
2000
6562
1000
3281
500
1640
200
656
0
0
Land Below Sea Level
0
0
200
656
1000
3281
3000
9843
6000
19685
9000
29520

MAP FORM	bahia	cabo	cerro	isla	lago	monte	punta
ENGLISH	bay	cape	mountain, hill	isle	lake	mountain	point
DEUTSCH	Bucht	Kap	Berg, Hügel	Insel	See	Berg	Landspitze
ESPAÑOL	bahía	cabo	cerro	isla	lago	monte	punta
FRANÇAIS	baie	cap	montagne, colline	île	lac	montagne	pointe
PORTUGUÊS	baía	cabo	montanha, colina	ilha	lago	monte	ponta

Kilometers 0 100 200 300 Km.
Statute Miles 0 100 200 300 Mi.

Scale 1:6,000,000

One centimeter represents 60 kilometers.
One inch represents approximately 95 miles.
Oblique Conic Conformal Projection

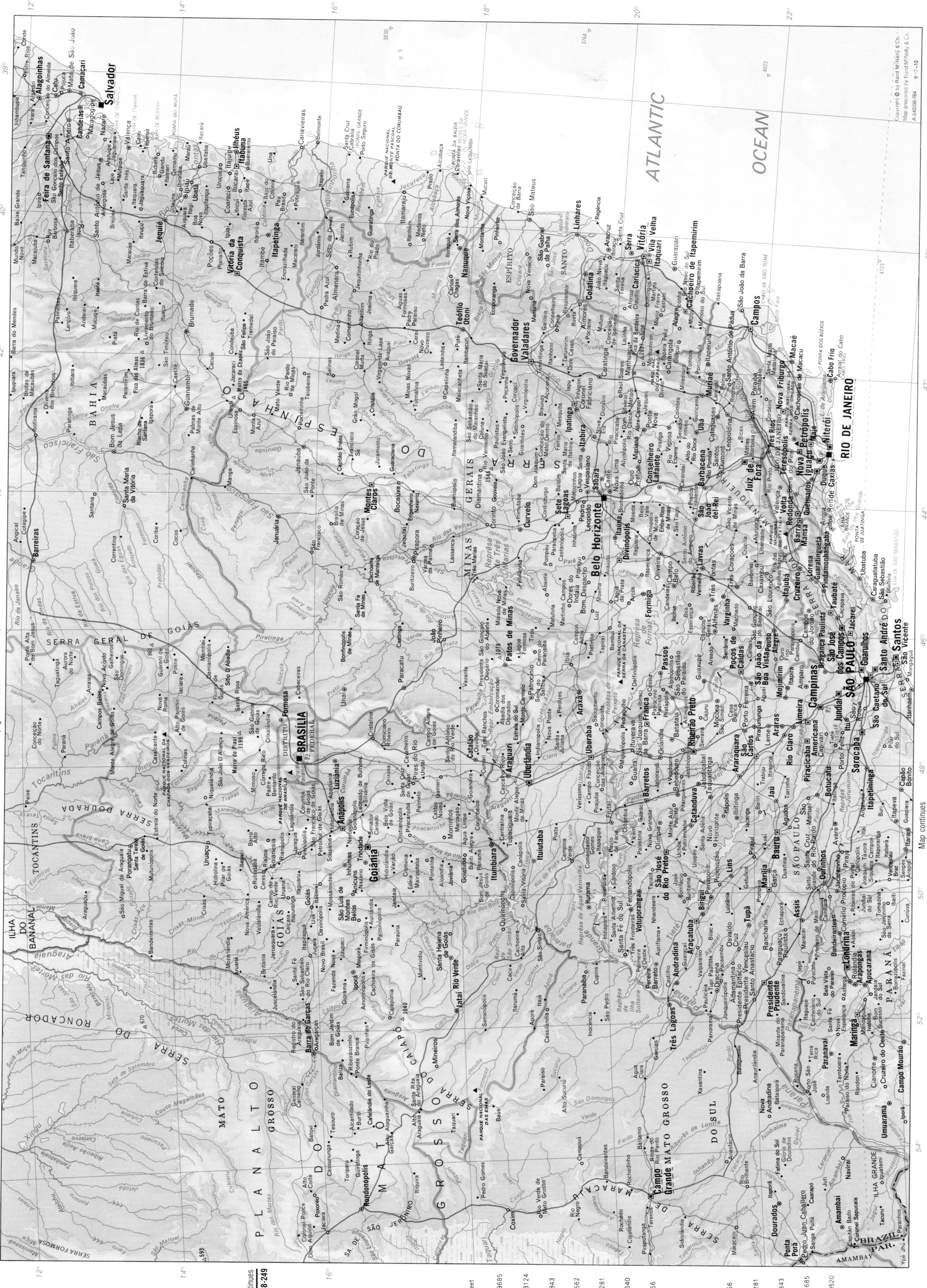
ATLANTIC
OCEAN
Salvador
Feira de Santana
Ilhéus
Itabuna
Jequié
Vitória da Conquista
BAHIA
ESPINHAÇO
Vitória
Vila Velha
Cachoeiro de Itapemirim
Colatina
Linhares
Governador Valadares
Teófilo Otoni
Montes Claros
Belo Horizonte
Juiz de Fora
Petrópolis
Niterói
RIO DE JANEIRO
Campos
Nova Friburgo
Volta Redonda
São José dos Campos
Taubaté
SÃO PAULO
Santos
São Vicente
Santo André
Guarulhos
Campinas
Jundiaí
Sorocaba
Piracicaba
Ribeirão Preto
Uberaba
Uberlândia
Araguari
Patos de Minas
Divinópolis
Franca
Barretos
São José do Rio Preto
Bauru
Marília
Araçatuba
Presidente Prudente
Londrina
Maringá
Apucarana
Campo Grande
Dourados
Ponta Porã
Rondonópolis
BRASÍLIA
DISTRITO FEDERAL
Goiânia
Anápolis
Luziânia
Formosa
GOIÁS
SERRA GERAL DE GOIÁS
SERRA DOURADA
SERRA DO RONCADOR
ILHA DO BANANAL
TOCANTINS
MATO GROSSO
PLANALTO DO MATO GROSSO
MATO GROSSO DO SUL
SERRA DE MARACAJU
SERRA DE CAIAPÓ
PARANÁ
MINAS GERAIS
SERRA DA MANTIQUEIRA
ESPÍRITO SANTO
BRAZIL
PAR.
AMAMBAY

MAP FORM	ENGLISH	DEUTSCH	ESPAÑOL	FRANÇAIS	PORTUGUÊS
cabo	cape	Kap	cabo	cap	cabo
cachoeira, cach.	waterfall	Wasserfall	cascada	chute d'eau	cascata
ilha, i.	island	Insel	isla	île	ilha
lagoa	lake	See	lago	lac	lago
parque nacional	reservation	Reservat	parque nacional	parc national	parque nacional
ponta	point	Landspitze	punta	pointe	ponta
ribeirão, rão.	creek	Bach	riachuelo	crique	riacho
rio, r.	river	Fluss	río	rivière	rio
serra	mountains	Berge	sierra	montagnes	serra

Scale 1:6,000,000
One centimeter represents 60 kilometers.
One inch represents approximately 95 miles.
Kilometers 0 100 200 300
Statute Miles 0 100 200 300
Oblique Conic Conformal Projection

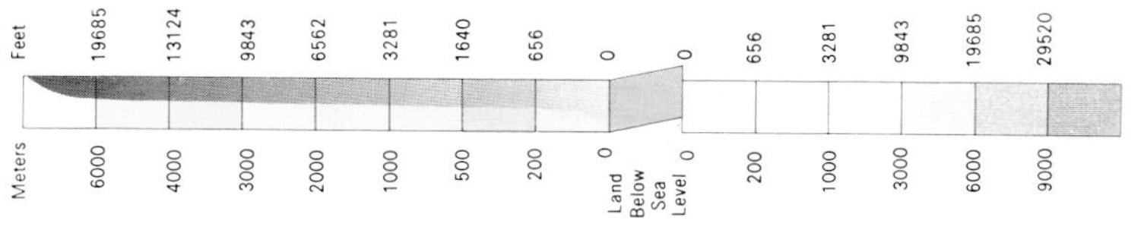
Feet
19685
13124
9843
6562
3281
1640
656
0
Meters
6000
4000
3000
2000
1000
500
200
0
Land Below Sea Level
656
3281
9843
19685
29520
200
1000
3000
6000
9000

Map continues pages 250-251
Map continues pages 252-253
Map continues pages 248-249

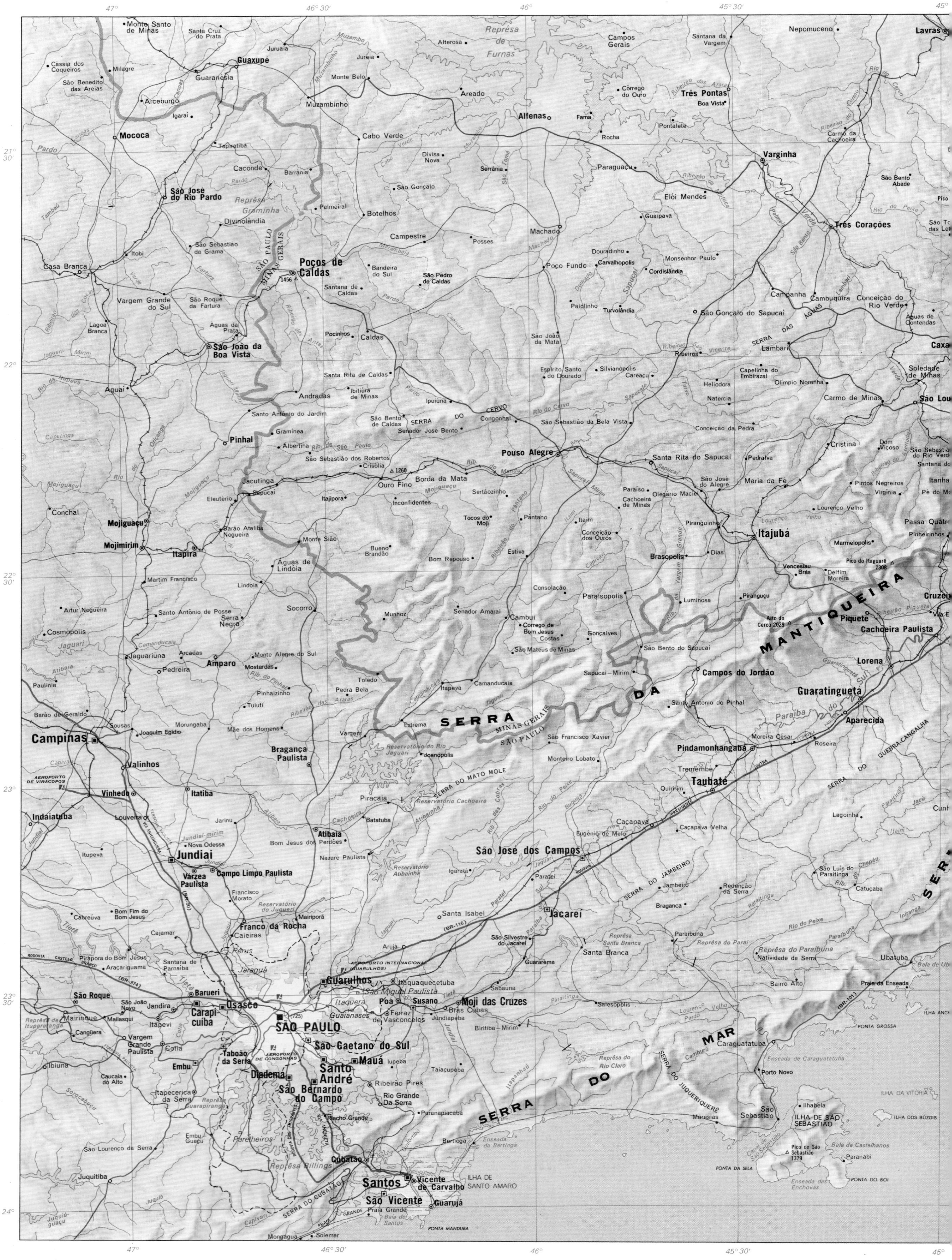
47°
46° 30′
46°
45° 30′
45°
21° 30′
22°
22° 30′
23°
23° 30′
24°
Monte Santo de Minas
Santa Cruz do Prata
Juruaia
Guaxupé
Cássia dos Coqueiros
Milagre
Guaranésia
São Benedito das Areias
Arceburgo
Igaraí
Mococa
Muzambinho
Monte Belo
Jureia
Alterosa
Represa de Furnas
Campos Gerais
Santana da Vargem
Nepomuceno
Lavras
Areado
Córrego do Ouro
Três Pontas
Boa Vista
Alfenas
Fama
Pontalete
Rocha
Carmo da Cachoeira
Cabo Verde
Tapiratiba
Divisa Nova
Serrânia
Varginha
Paraguaçu
Caconde
Barrânia
São Gonçalo
São José do Rio Pardo
Represa Graminha
Palmeiral
Botelhos
Elói Mendes
Divinolândia
Guaipava
Três Corações
São Bento Abade
Machado
Campestre
Posses
São Sebastião da Grama
Itobi
SÃO PAULO
MINAS GERAIS
Poços de Caldas
1456
Douradinho
Carvalhópolis
Monsenhor Paulo
Casa Branca
Bandeira do Sul
São Pedro de Caldas
Poço Fundo
Cordislândia
Vargem Grande do Sul
São Roque da Fartura
Santana de Caldas
Campanha
Cambuquira
Conceição do Rio Verde
Paiolinho
Turvolândia
São Gonçalo do Sapucaí
Águas de Contendas
Lagoa Branca
Aguas da Prata
Pocinhos
Caldas
São João da Mata
SERRA DAS ÁGUAS
Lambari
São João da Boa Vista
Ribeiros
Espírito Santo do Dourado
Silvianópolis
Careaçu
Capelinha do Embirazal
Soledade de Minas
Santa Rita de Caldas
Heliodora
Olímpio Noronha
Aguaí
Andradas
Ibitiúra de Minas
Ipuiuna
Natercia
Carmo de Minas
São Lourenço
Santo Antônio do Jardim
São Bento de Caldas
SERRA DO CERVO
Congonhal
São Sebastião da Bela Vista
Senador José Bento
Conceição da Pedra
Pinhal
Gramínea
Albertina
Cristina
Dom Viçoso
São Sebastião do Rio Verde
São Sebastião dos Robertos
Crisólia
Pouso Alegre
Santa Rita do Sapucaí
Pedralva
1260
Jacutinga
Ouro Fino
Borda da Mata
São José do Alegre
Maria da Fé
Pintos Negreiros
Virgínia
Sapucaí
Sertãozinho
Paraíso
Olegário Maciel
Cachoeira de Minas
Eleutério
Itajiporã
Inconfidentes
Lourenço Velho
Conchal
Tocos do Moji
Pântano
Itaim
Piranguinho
Passa Quatro
Mojiguaçu
Barão Ataliba Nogueira
Conceição dos Ouros
Itajubá
Mojimirim
Itapira
Monte Sião
Bueno Brandão
Estiva
Brasópolis
Dias
Marmelópolis
Bom Repouso
Pico do Itaguaré 2308
Águas de Lindóia
Vencesiau Brás
Delfim Moreira
Martim Francisco
Lindóia
Consolação
Paraisópolis
Luminosa
Piranguçu
Cruzeiro
Artur Nogueira
Santo Antônio de Posse
Socorro
Munhoz
Senador Amaral
Alto do Cerco 2028
Piquete
Serra Negra
Cambuí
Córrego do Bom Jesus
Costas
Cosmópolis
Gonçalves
Cachoeira Paulista
Jaguariúna
Arcadas
Monte Alegre do Sul
São Mateus de Minas
São Bento do Sapucaí
SERRA DA MANTIQUEIRA
Pedreira
Amparo
Mostardas
Lorena
Paulínia
Pinhalzinho
Toledo
Sapucaí-Mirim
Campos do Jordão
Pedra Bela
Itapeva
Camanducaia
Guaratinguetá
Tuiuti
Santo Antônio do Pinhal
Barão de Geraldo
Morungaba
Aparecida
Campinas
Sousas
Joaquim Egídio
Mãe dos Homens
Vargem
Extrema
São Francisco Xavier
Moreira César
Roseira
Bragança Paulista
Reservatório do Rio Jaguari
Joanópolis
Pindamonhangaba
Valinhos
Monteiro Lobato
SERRA DO QUEBRA-CANGALHA
AEROPORTO DE VIRACOPOS
SERRA DO MATO MOLE
Tremembé
Taubaté
Vinhedo
Itatiba
Piracaia
Reservatório Cachoeira
Quiririm
Indaiatuba
Louveira
Jarinu
Batatuba
Caçapava
Lagoinha
Atibaia
Eugênio de Melo
Caçapava Velha
Nova Odessa
Bom Jesus dos Perdões
Itupeva
Jundiaí
Nazaré Paulista
São José dos Campos
Várzea Paulista
Campo Limpo Paulista
Reservatório Atibainha
Igaratá
Paraitinga
São Luís do Paraitinga
Francisco Morato
Paratei
SERRA DO JAMBEIRO
Jambeiro
Redenção da Serra
Catuçaba
Reservatório do Juqueri
Bragança
Bom Fim do Bom Jesus
Cabreúva
Mairiporã
Santa Isabel
Jacareí
Franco da Rocha
Caieiras
Cajamar
São Silvestre do Jacareí
Paraibuna
Represa Santa Branca
Represa do Paraí
Represa do Paraibuna
Natividade da Serra
Perus
Arujá
Santa Branca
Pirapora do Bom Jesus
Santana de Parnaíba
Araçariguama
Jaraguá
AEROPORTO INTERNACIONAL (GUARULHOS)
Guararema
Ubatuba
Guarulhos
Itaquaquecetuba
São Roque
Barueri
São Miguel Paulista
Sabaúna
Praia da Enseada
Bairro Alto
São João Novo
Jandira
Carapicuíba
Osasco
Itaquera
Poá
Suzano
Moji das Cruzes
Salesópolis
Mairinque
Mailasqui
Itapevi
(725)
Guaianases
Ferraz de Vasconcelos
Brás Cubas
Jundiapeba
Biritiba-Mirim
Represa de Itupararanga
Cangüera
SÃO PAULO
PONTA GROSSA
Vargem Grande Paulista
Cotia
São Caetano do Sul
SERRA DO MAR
Caraguatatuba
Ibiúna
Embu
Taboão da Serra
AEROPORTO DE CONGONHAS
Santo André
Mauá
Ipuela
Enseada de Caraguatatuba
Caucaia do Alto
Diadema
Ribeirão Pires
Taiaçupeba
Represa do Rio Claro
Porto Novo
Itapecerica da Serra
Represa Guarapiranga
São Bernardo do Campo
Rio Grande da Serra
SERRA DO JUQUERIQUERÊ
ILHA DA VITÓRIA
Paranapiacaba
Ilhabela
Riacho Grande
Maresias
São Sebastião
ILHA DE SÃO SEBASTIÃO
ILHA DOS BÚZIOS
Embu-Guaçu
Parelheiros
Bertioga
Enseada da Bertioga
Bala de Castelhanos
São Lourenço da Serra
Represa Billings
Cubatão
Pico de São Sebastião 1379
Paranabi
PONTA DA SELA
Juquitiba
Santos
Vicente de Carvalho
ILHA DE SANTO AMARO
PONTA DO BOI
Enseada das Enchovas
SERRA DO CUBATÃO
São Vicente
Guarujá
Praia Grande
PONTA MANDUBA
Mongaguá
Solemar

MAP FORM	baía	enseada	ilha	pico	ponta	represa	ribeirão	rio	serra
ENGLISH	bay	bay	island	peak	point	reservoir	stream	river	mountains
DEUTSCH	Bucht	Bucht	Insel	Gipfel	Landspitze	Stausee	Bach	Fluss	Berge
ESPAÑOL	bahía	bahía	isla	pico	punta	estanque	corriente de agua	río	sierra
FRANÇAIS	baie	baie	île	cime	pointe	réservoir	cours d'eau	rivière	montagnes
PORTUGUÊS	baía	enseada	ilha	pico	ponta	represa	ribeirão	rio	serra

THIS SECTION CONSISTS of 60 maps of the world's major metropolitan areas, at the scale of 1:300,000. The maps show the generalized land-use patterns in and around each city—the total urban extent, major industrial areas, parks and preserves, and wooded areas. Airports are shown, as are many details of the highway and rail transportation networks. Selected points of interest appear, such as Fisherman's Wharf and Chinatown in San Francisco, the Welcome monument in Jakarta, the Temple of the Jade Buddha in Shanghai, and the Cristo Redentor statue in Rio de Janeiro.

The maps name and locate a great number of towns, villages, and suburbs, and also sections or neighborhoods within limits of the larger cities. Prominent physical features, including elevations, named and unnamed, have been indicated to give a general impression of the local topography. Shaded relief has been omitted, however, to permit display of such details as streams, parks, airport runways, important public buildings and monuments, and the names of major streets. The corporate limits of major cities are also outlined. For the symbols used on these maps see the Legend to Maps.

Maps of major world cities usually vary widely in scale, and heretofore have not been consistent in design and coverage. For this section, a special effort has been made to portray these varied metropolitan areas in as standard and comparable a fashion as possible. However, for a few cities (notably several in Asia) there has not been adequate source material to include certain information, such as major industrial areas and corporate limits.

The order of presentation is generally regional, with some exceptions where for ease of comparison major capitals or industrial centers or cities located in similar physical surroundings have been juxtaposed. Many American cities and some European cities, with their lower densities and more extensive areas, require larger maps than do Asiatic cities of comparable population. The total land area and population within the confines of each map are stated in the margin as a further aid to comparison.

DIESER KARTENTEIL UMFASST 60 Karten der bedeutendsten Stadtregionen der Erde im Massstab 1:300 000. Die Karten zeigen in generalisierter Form die Landnutzung in und um jede Stadt: die gesamte Ausdehnung des verstädterten Gebietes, wichtige Industriegebiete, Parks, Landflächen in Gemeinbesitz und Wald. Flughäfen werden ebenso dargestellt wie viele Einzelheiten des Strassen- und Eisenbahnnetzes. Bekannte Sehenswürdigkeiten sind eingetragen wie die "Fisherman's Wharf" und "Chinatown" in San Francisco, das Willkomm-Denkmal in Jakarta, der Tempel des Jade-Buddhas in Shanghai und die "Cristo Redentor"-Statue in Rio de Janeiro.

Die Karten verzeichnen Name and Lage einer grossen Zahl von Städten, Dörfern, Vororten ebenso wie eingemeindete Ortsteile bei grösseren Städten. Hervortretende physische Formen wie benannte und unbenannte Erhebungen sind aufgenommen, um eine allgemeine Vorstellung des lokalen Reliefs zu geben. Auf die Schummerung wurde jedoch verzichtet, um klar solche Einzelheiten wie Flüsse, Parks, Start- und Landebahnen der Flughäfen, bedeutende öffentliche Gebäude und Denkmäler sowie die Namen der wichtigsten Strassen herausstellen zu können. Eingetragen sind ferner die Gemeindegrenzen der wichtigsten Städte. Zu den auf diesen Karten verwendeten Signaturen siehe "Zeichenerklärung".

Karten der bedeutendsten Weltstädte differieren normalerweise sehr stark in ihren Massstäben und sind daher uneinheitlich in ihrer Gestaltung und Begrenzung. Deshalb wurde in diesem Kartenteil besonderer Wert darauf gelegt, die verschiedenen städtischen Ballungsgebiete in möglichst einheitlicher und vergleichbarer Form darzustellen. Für einige Städte, vor allem mehrere asiatische, war das Quellenmaterial jedoch nicht ausreichend genug, um gewisse Informationen wie Hauptindustriegebiete oder Stadtgrenzen einzutragen.

Im allgemeinen sind diese Karten nach regionalen Gesichtspunkten geordnet. Um Vergleiche zu erleichtern wurden einige Ausnahmen gemacht, indem wichtige Hauptstädte, Industriezentren oder Städte in vergleichbarer landschaftlicher Lage einander gegenübergestellt wurden. Viele americkanische und einige europäische Städte mit ihrer geringen Bevölkerungsdichte, aber ausgedehnteren Fläche erfordern eine grössere Kartenfläche als asiatische Städte von vergleichbarer Bevölkerungszahl. Die gesamte Landfläche und die Bevölkerung innerhalb des dargestellten Gebietes ist am Kartenrand verzeichnet als ein weiteres Hilfsmittel für Vergleiche.

INTEGRAN ESTA SECCION 60 mapas de las áreas metropolitanas más importantes del mundo, a la escala de 1:300 000. Los mapas muestran los patrones de uso del suelo dentro de cada ciudad y en sus alrededores—la extensión total del conglomerado urbano, las principales áreas industriales, parques y reservas, y zonas boscosas. Aparecen los aeropuertos, así como muchos otros detalles de las redes de carreteras y ferrocarriles. Se seleccionaron también puntos de interés, como el Muelle de los Pescadores y el Barrio Chino de San Francisco, el monumento de Bienvenida de Jakarta, el Templo del Buda de Jade de Shanghai y la estatua del Cristo Redentor de Rio de Janeiro.

Los mapas incluyen los nombres y la ubicación de gran número de ciudades, poblaciones menores, suburbios, e inclusive barrios y distritos de algunas de las ciudades más importantes. Las características físicas sobresalientes, e incluso algunas elevaciones con o sin nombre, están indicados para dar una impresión general de la topografía local. Se omitió sin embargo el relieve sombreado, lo cual permite mostrar detalles como ríos y arroyos, parques, pistas de aterrizaje, edificios y monumentos públicos notables y los nombres de las calles principales. También están marcados los límites territoriales de las ciudades más grandes. Para la interpretación de los símbolos usados en estos mapas, véanse Leyendas para Mapas.

Los mapas de las ciudades más importantes del mundo varían generalmente en escala, y hasta ahora no han sido consistentes ni en diseño ni en contenido. En esta sección hemos hecho un esfuerzo de presentar las distintas áreas metropolitanas en la forma más uniforme posible, para facilitar sus comparaciones. Para algunas ciudades (la mayoría de ellas en Asia), no fué posible obtener de las propias fuentes material adecuado para la inclusión de ciertos datos, tales como las mayores áreas industriales y los límites municipales.

Los mapas de áreas metropolitanas se presentan por regiones, a excepción de unos cuantos que aparecen yuxtapuestos para facilitar la comparación entre grandes capitales, o centros comerciales, o ciudades ubicadas en contextos físicos similares. Muchas ciudades de América y algunas ciudades de Europa, por su baja densidad de población y su área extensa, requieren mapas más grandes que los ocupados por ciudades asiáticas con poblaciones comparables. Al margen de cada mapa se anotaron el área total y la población de territorio representado, lo cual facilita también las comparaciones.

CETTE PARTIE COMPREND 60 cartes des principales zones métropolitaines à l'échelle du 1:300 000e. Les cartes représentent les principaux types d'occupation du sol des villes et de leurs environs, c'est-à-dire de toute la zone urbanisée, les principales zones industrielles, les parcs et réserves naturelles, et les régions boisées. Les aéroports sont aussi représentés ainsi que de nombreux éléments des réseaux routier et ferroviaire. Certains lieux particulièrement intéressants sont indiqués, tels que le quai des pêcheurs et la ville chinoise à San Francisco, le monument de la Bienvenue à Jakarta, le temple du Bouddha de Jade à Shanghai et la statue du Christ Rédempteur à Rio de Janeiro.

Les cartes permettent de localiser un grand nombre de villes, villages et banlieues, ainsi que des quartiers de grandes villes. Les caractéristiques topographiques notables, comme les hauteurs sont indiquées même si elles ne portent pas de nom, pour donner une idée du site de l'aire métropolitaine. L'estompage du relief est omis cependant pour permettre de représenter cours d'eau, parcs, pistes d'envol des aéroports, monuments et bâtiments publics importants, noms des principales rues, ainsi que les limites municipales des grandes villes. (Pour la signification des symboles voir légende.)

En général, les échelles des cartes des grandes villes du monde varient considérablement, et jusqu'ici la présentation et le contenu de ces cartes n'étaient pas comparables. Dans cette partie de l'Atlas, un effort spécial a été fait pour représenter les diverses zones métropolitaines de manière aussi homogène que possible. Cependant, dans certains cas (en Asie notamment), les documents de base n'étaient pas assez complets pour qu'il fût possible d'inclure avec précision des données comme les zones industrielles et les limites municipales.

L'ordre de présentation est régional, avec des exceptions quand, pour faciliter les comparaisons, de grandes capitales de grands centres industriels ou encore des villes possédant un même environnement naturel, sont juxtaposés. Beaucoup de villes américaines et quelques villes européennes ont une faible densité de population et une étendue considérable; elles requièrent, par conséquent, des cartes plus grandes que des villes asiatiques de population similaire. La superficie et la population de chaque carte sont indiquées dans la marge.

INTEGRAM ESTA SEÇÃO 60 mapas das áreas metropolitanas mais importantes do mundo, em escala de 1:300 000. Os mapas mostram os principais tipos de uso do solo em cada cidade e seus arredores, seja, a extensão total da zona urbanizada, as principais áreas industriais, os parques e reservas, e as áreas florestais. Mostram os aeroportos, e muitos detalhes das redès rodo e ferroviária. Indicam também pontos de interesse, selecionados, tais como o Cais dos Pescadores e o Bairro Chinês de San Francisco, o monumento de Boasvindas, em Jakarta, o templo do Buda de Jade, em Shanghai, e a Estátua do Cristo Redentor, no Rio de Janeiro.

Os mapas apresentam o nome e a localização de grande número de cidades, vilas e subúrbios, e incluem bairros das cidades mais importantes. Foram indicadas as características físicas principais, inclusive elevações, com ou sem nome, com o objetivo de proporcionar uma idéia geral da topografia local. No entanto, omitiu-se o sombreado do relevo, para permitir a indicação de detalhes tais como cursos d'água, parques, pistas de aeroportos, edifícios públicos e monumentos notáveis, e os nomes das principais ruas, bem como os limites municipais das grandes cidades. Para a interpretação dos símbolos usados nesses mapas, ver as *Legendas dos mapas*.

Os mapas das cidades mais importantes do mundo variam consideravelmente, de modo geral, quanto à escala, e até o presente não são comparáveis nem na forma de apresentação nem no conteúdo. Nesta seção, fez-se um esforço especial para representar as diversas áreas metropolitanas do modo mais uniforme e comparável possível. No entanto, para algumas cidades, a maioria das quais da Ásia, não foi possível obter fontes fidedignas de informações, tais como áreas industriais principais e limites municipais.

A ordem de apresentação dos mapas das áreas metropolitanas é geralmente regional, exceto em certos casos em que, para facilidade de comparação, capitais ou centros industriais e cidades importantes localizadas em meio físico semelhante foram justapostos. Muitas cidades da América e algumas da Europa, por sua baixa densidade demográfica e áreas mais extensas, exigem mapas maiores que as cidades asiáticas de população comparável. À margem de cada mapa indicam-se a área terrestre e a população total do território representado, também para maior facilidade de comparação.

Kilometers 0 5 10 15 Km.

Statute Miles 0 5 10 15 Mi.

Scale 1:300,000

One centimeter represents 3 kilometers.
One inch represents approximately 4.7 miles.

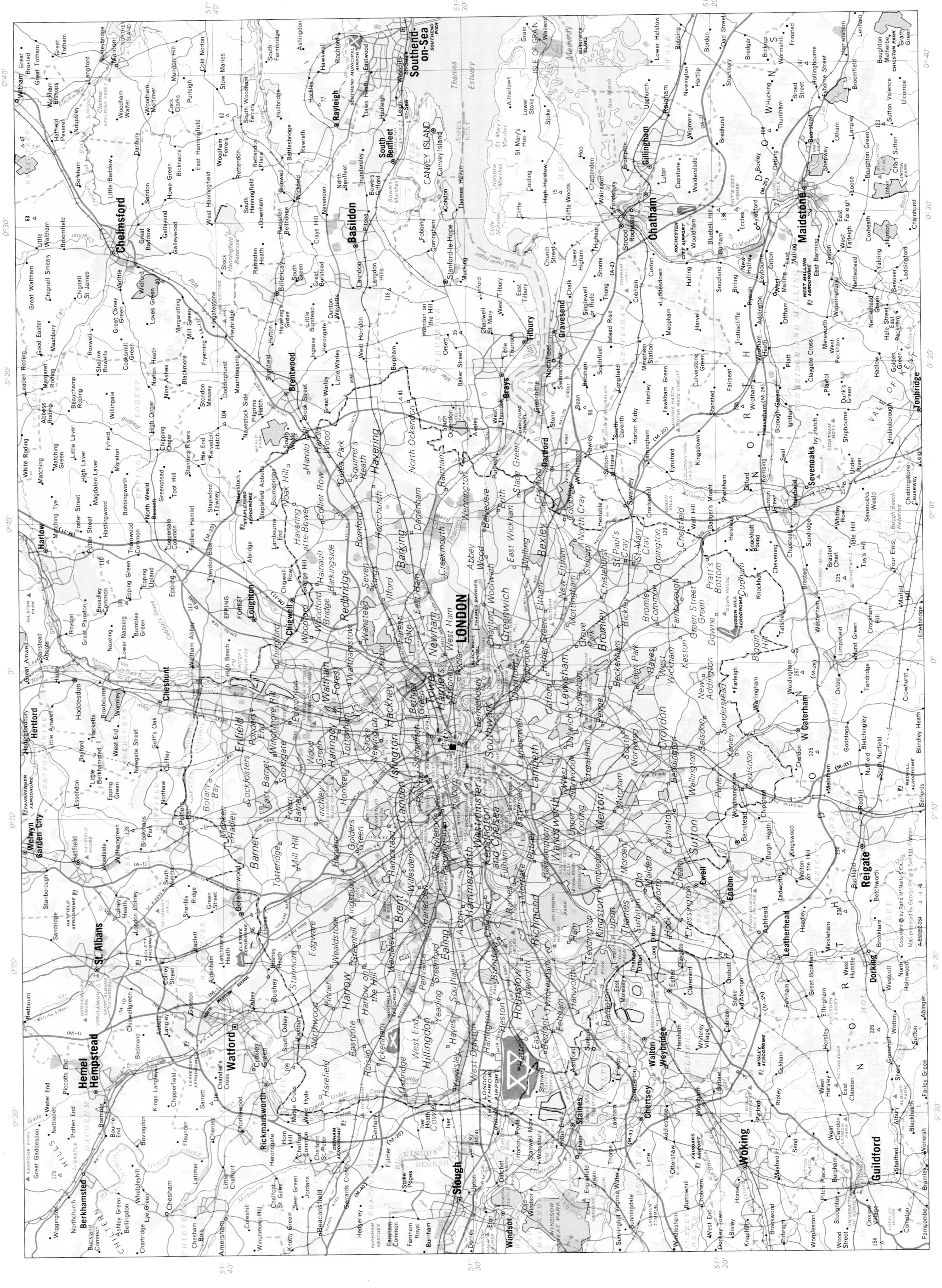
LONDON
Chelmsford
Southend-on-Sea
Basildon
Brentwood
Harlow
St. Albans
Watford
Hemel Hempstead
Welwyn Garden City
Hertford
Cheshunt
Chatham
Gillingham
Maidstone
Gravesend
Dartford
Sevenoaks
Tonbridge
Reigate
Guildford
Woking
Slough
Windsor
Staines
Epsom
Leatherhead
Dorking
Croydon
Rickmansworth
Berkhamsted
Chesham
Amersham
Thames
Copyright © by Rand McNally & Co.
Map produced by George Philip & Son Ltd, London

ENGLISH	DEUTSCH	ESPAÑOL	FRANÇAIS	PORTUGUÊS
aerodrome	Flughafen	aeropuerto	aéroport	aeroporto
canal	Kanal	canal	canal	canal
castle	Burg	castillo	château	castelo
palace	Palast	palacio	palais	palácio
park	Park	parque	parc	parque
race course	Rennbahn	hipódromo	champ de course	hipódromo
road	Landstrasse	camino	route	rodovia
station	Bahnhof	estación	gare	estação

AREA 6,400 km²
POPULATION 10,325,000

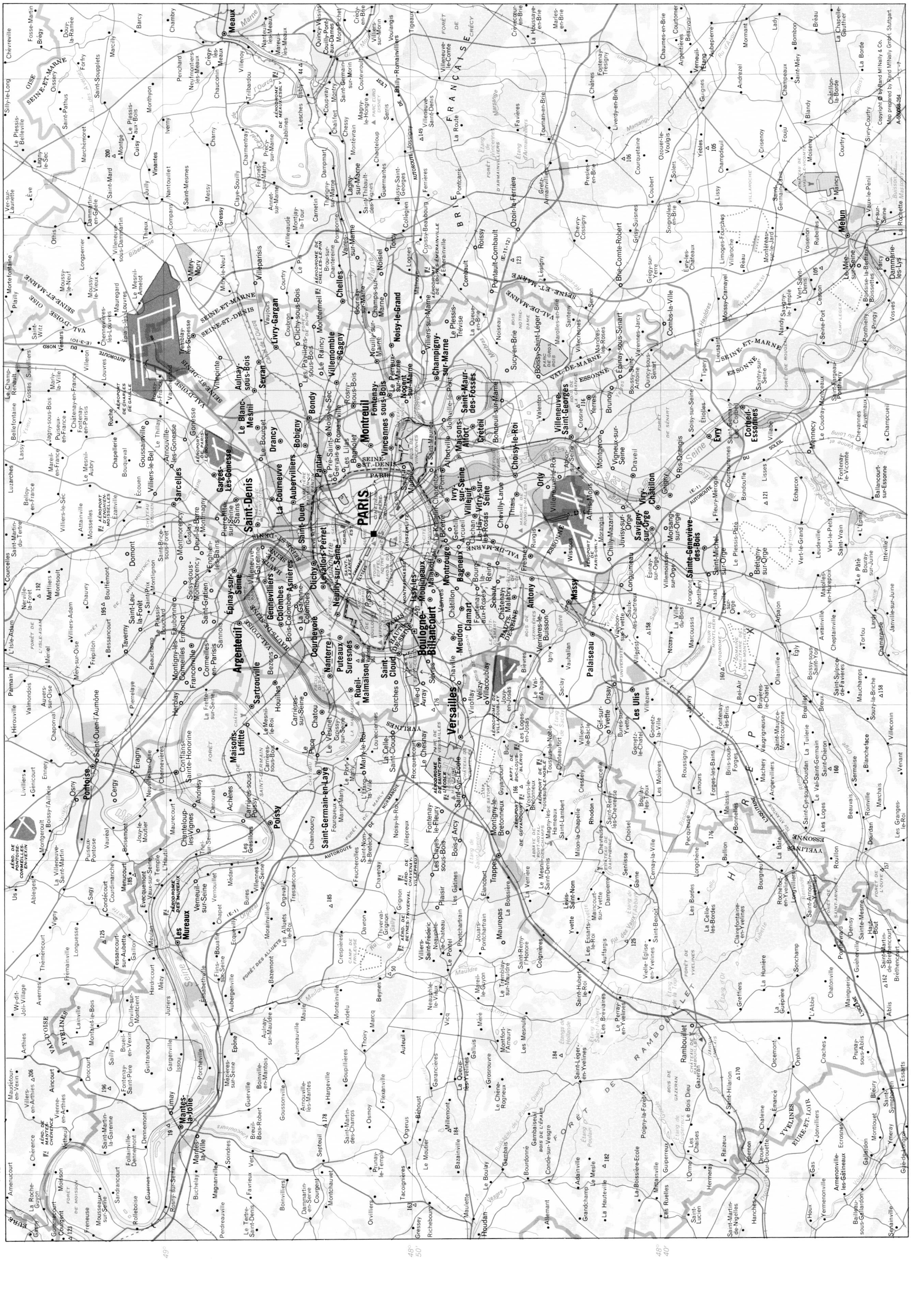

AREA 6,500 km²
POPULATION 9,800,000

FRANÇAIS	aérodrome	bois	château	étang	forêt	ruisseau
ENGLISH	airport	woods	castle	pond	forest	brook
DEUTSCH	Flughafen	Gehölz	Burg	Teich	Wald	Bach
ESPAÑOL	aeropuerto	bosques	castillo	charca	bosque	arroyo
PORTUGUÊS	aeroporto	bosques	castelo	lagoa	floresta	arroio

Kilometers 0 5 10 15 Km.
Statute Miles 0 5 10 15 Mi.

Scale 1:300,000
One centimeter represents 3 kilometers.
One inch represents approximately 4.7 miles.

IRISH SEA
Liverpool Bay
MANCHESTER
LIVERPOOL
Blackpool
Preston
Blackburn
Burnley
Accrington
Halifax
Huddersfield
Rochdale
Oldham
Bury
Bolton
Wigan
St. Helens
Warrington
Widnes
Runcorn
Stockport
Salford
Stretford
Sale
Ashton-under-Lyne
Birkenhead
Wallasey
Bootle
Southport
Chester
Ellesmere Port
Macclesfield
Northwich
Crosby
Formby
Ormskirk
Skelmersdale
Chorley
Leyland
Darwen
Rawtenstall
Bacup
Todmorden
Glossop
Buxton
Lytham St. Anne's
Wilmslow
Altrincham
Heswall
Flint
Holywell
PEAK DISTRICT NATIONAL PARK
ENGLAND
WALES

Kilometers 0 5 10 15 Km.
Statute Miles 0 5 10 15 Mi.

Scale 1:300,000
One centimeter represents 3 kilometers.
One inch represents approximately 4.7 miles.

ENGLISH	DEUTSCH	ESPAÑOL	FRANÇAIS	PORTUGUÊS
bank	Bank	banco	banc	banco
canal	Kanal	canal	canal	canal
hill	Hügel	colina	colline	colina
moor	Ried	páramo	lande	charneca
park	Park	parque	parc	parque
railway station	Bahnhof	terminal ferroviaria	gare	estação ferroviária
reservoir	Stausee	estanque	réservoir	reservatório
tower	Turm	torre	tour	torre

AREA 5,650 km²
POPULATION 6,275,000

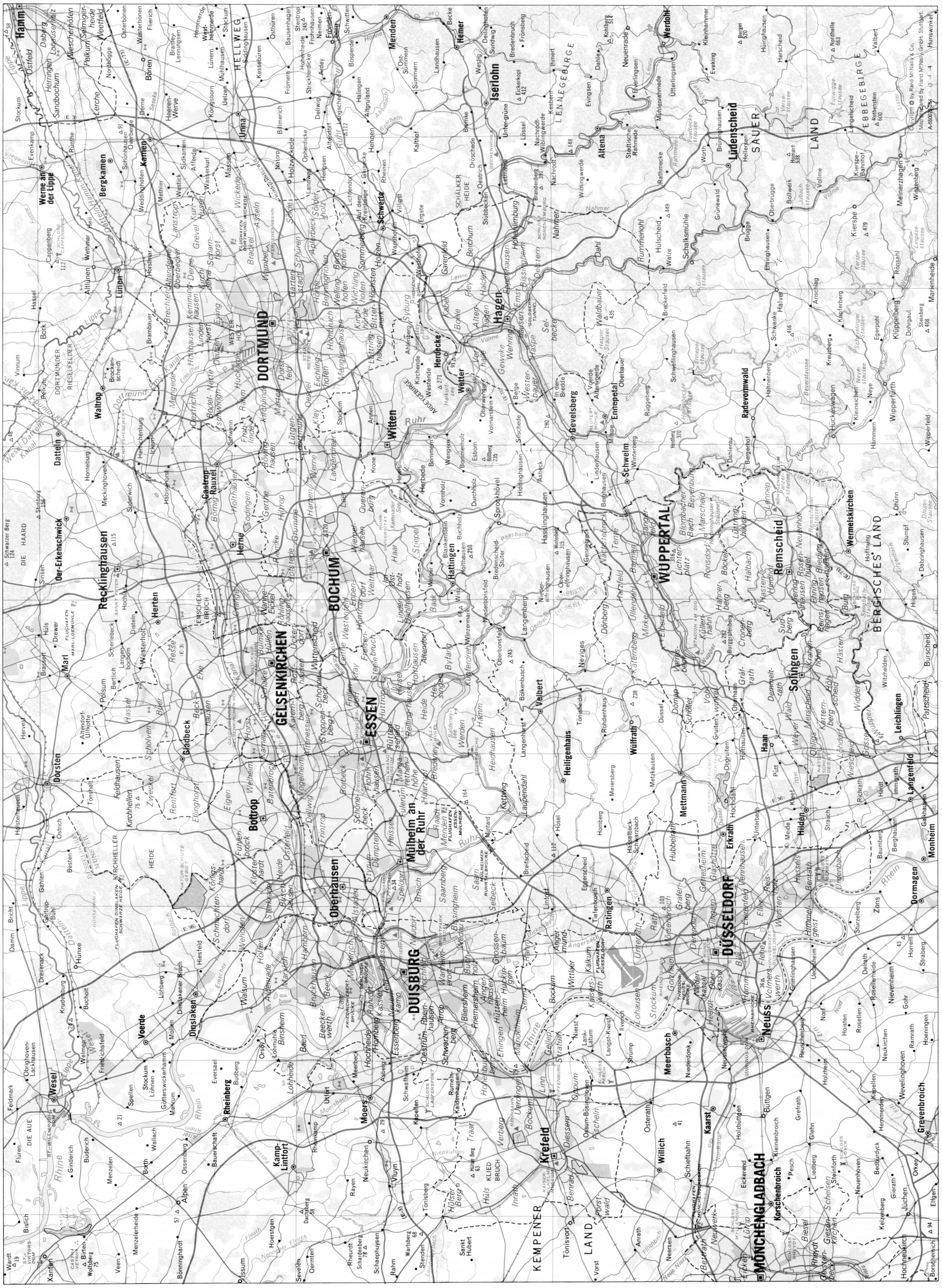
Hamm
Werne an der Lippe
Bergkamen
Kamen
Unna
Lünen
Dortmund
Menden
Hemer
Iserlohn
Werdohl
Altena
Lüdenscheid
Schwerte
Hagen
Herdecke
Wetter
Witten
Datteln
Waltrop
Castrop-Rauxel
Herne
Bochum
Recklinghausen
Oer-Erkenschwick
Herten
Marl
Gelsenkirchen
Gladbeck
Essen
Bottrop
Dorsten
Oberhausen
Mülheim an der Ruhr
Duisburg
Dinslaken
Voerde
Wesel
Moers
Kamp-Lintfort
Rheinberg
Krefeld
Willich
Meerbusch
Neuss
Düsseldorf
Ratingen
Velbert
Heiligenhaus
Wülfrath
Mettmann
Erkrath
Hilden
Haan
Solingen
Langenfeld
Leichlingen
Monheim
Dormagen
Grevenbroich
Kaarst
Mönchengladbach
Korschenbroich
Wuppertal
Remscheid
Wermelskirchen
Radevormwald
Schwelm
Gevelsberg
Ennepetal
Hattingen
Sprockhövel
Rhein
Ruhr
Lippe
Hellweg
Sauerland
Lennegebirge
Ebbegebirge
Bergisches Land
Kempener Land
Die Haard
Die Aue
Kirchheller Heide

AREA: 6,500 km²
POPULATION: 8,450,000

DEUTSCH	Bach	Berg	Flughafen	Heide	Kanal	Schloss	Stausee
ENGLISH	creek	mountain	airport	heath	canal	castle	reservoir
ESPAÑOL	riachuelo	montana	aeropuerto	matorral	canal	castillo	estanque
FRANÇAIS	ruisseau	montagne	aéroport	lande	canal	château	réservoir
PORTUGUÊS	riacho	montanha	aeroporto	charneca	canal	castelo	reservatório

Kilometers 0 5 10 15 Km.
Statute Miles 0 5 10 15 Mi.

Scale 1:300,000
One centimeter represents 3 kilometers.
One inch represents approximately 4.7 miles.

a

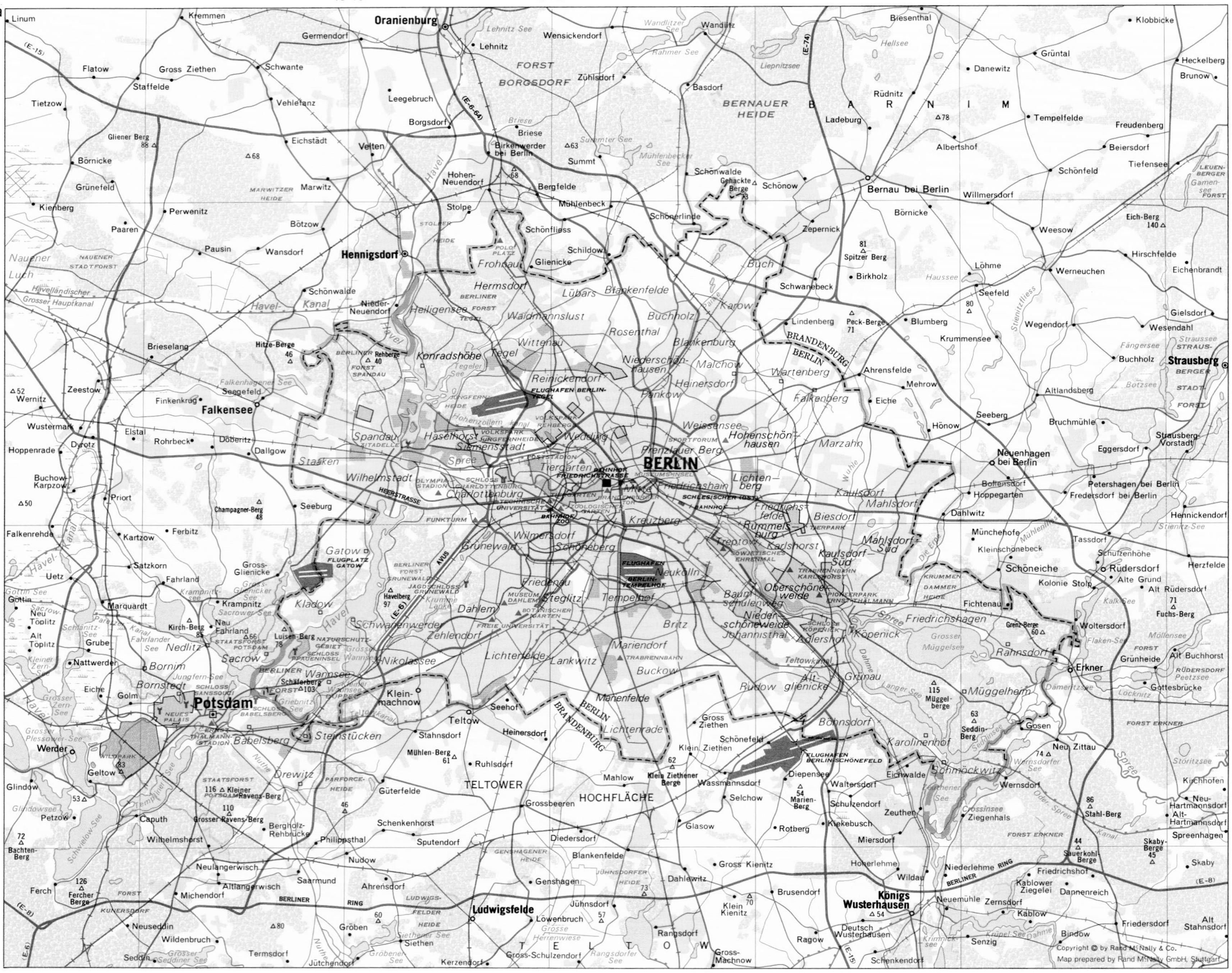

Oranienburg
Hennigsdorf
Falkensee
Potsdam
BERLIN
Spandau
Charlottenburg
Tiergarten
Wilmersdorf
Schöneberg
Kreuzberg
Neukölln
Tempelhof
Steglitz
Zehlendorf
Pankow
Reinickendorf
Weissensee
Köpenick
Treptow
Lichtenberg
Marzahn
Hellersdorf
Strausberg
Erkner
Bernau bei Berlin
Königs Wusterhausen
Ludwigsfelde
Werder
FLUGHAFEN BERLIN-TEGEL
FLUGHAFEN BERLIN-SCHÖNEFELD
FLUGHAFEN TEMPELHOF
FLUGPLATZ GATOW
BERNAUER HEIDE
FORST BORGSDORF
BARNIM
TELTOWER HOCHFLÄCHE
BERLINER RING
Copyright © by Rand McNally & Co.
Map prepared by Rand McNally GmbH, Stuttgart.

b

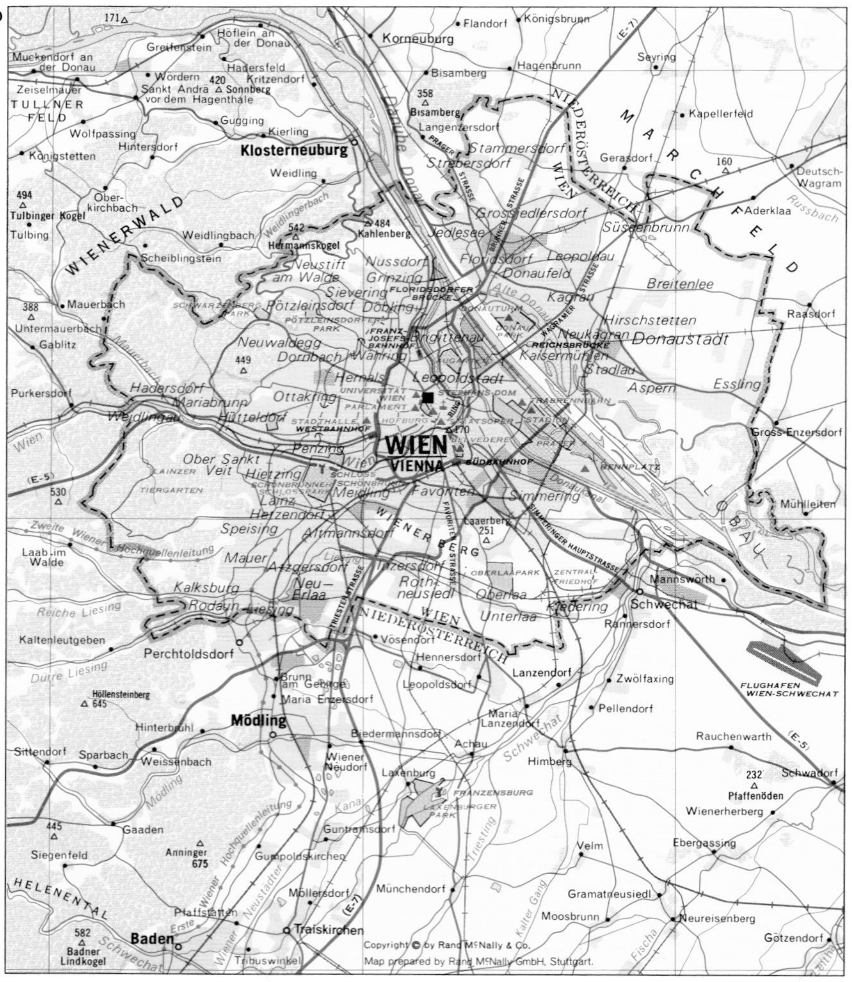

WIEN
VIENNA
Klosterneuburg
Korneuburg
Mödling
Baden
Schwechat
Floridsdorf
Donaustadt
Döbling
Ottakring
Hietzing
Favoriten
Simmering
Liesing
WIENERWALD
MARCHFELD
NIEDERÖSTERREICH
FLUGHAFEN WIEN-SCHWECHAT
Copyright © by Rand McNally & Co.
Map prepared by Rand McNally GmbH, Stuttgart.

c

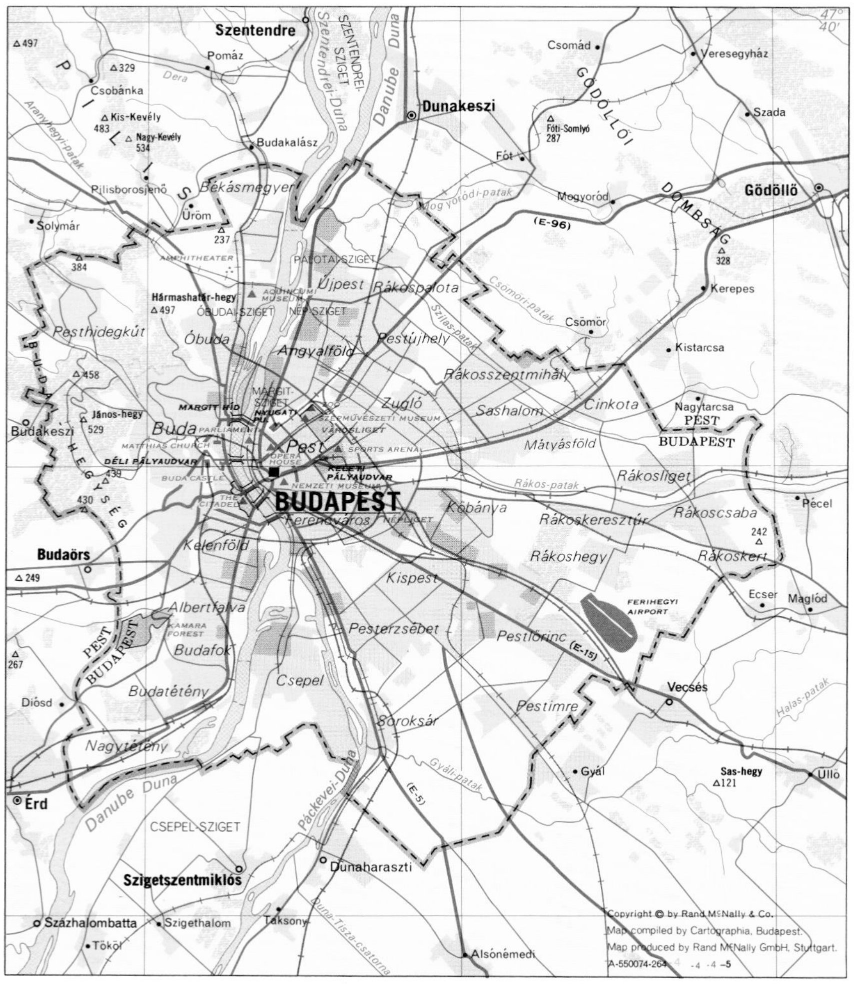

BUDAPEST
Buda
Pest
Óbuda
Újpest
Csepel
Kispest
Pesterzsébet
Szentendre
Dunakeszi
Gödöllő
Budaörs
Érd
Szigetszentmiklós
Vecsés
FERIHEGYI AIRPORT
CSEPEL SZIGET
Danube
Duna
GÖDÖLLŐI DOMBSÁG
PILIS
BUDAI HEGYSÉG
Copyright © by Rand McNally & Co.
Map compiled by Cartographia, Budapest
Map produced by Rand McNally GmbH, Stuttgart.
A-550074-264

	AREA (km²)	POPULATION
BERLIN	3,700	3,550,000
WIEN	1,300	1,825,000
BUDAPEST	1,300	2,450,000

MAP FORM	Berg	Berge	hegy	Heide	Schloss	See	sziget
ENGLISH	hill	hills	mountain	heath	castle	lake	island
DEUTSCH	Berg	Berge	Berg	Heide	Schloss	See	Insel
ESPAÑOL	colina	colinas	montaña	matorral	castillo	lago	isla
FRANÇAIS	colline	collines	montagne	lande	château	lac	île
PORTUGUÊS	colina	colinas	montanha	charneca	castelo	lago	ilha

Kilometers 0 5 10 15 Km.
Statute Miles 0 5 10 15 Mi.

Scale 1:300,000
One centimeter represents 3 kilometers.
One inch represents approximately 4.7 miles.

a

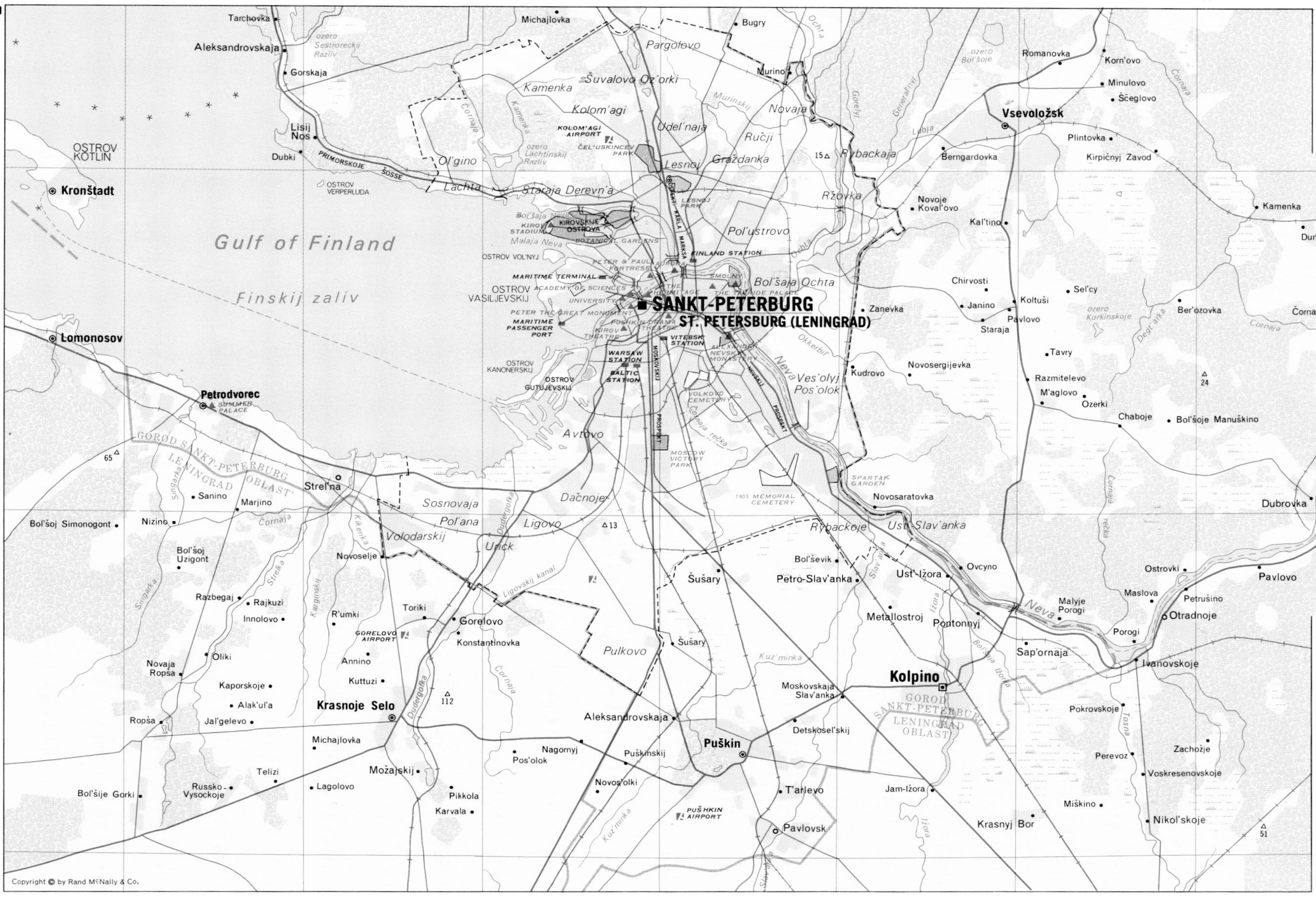

29° 50′
30°
30° 10′
30° 20′
30° 30′
30° 40′
30° 50′
60°
59° 50′
59° 40′
31°
Gulf of Finland
Finskij zaliv
OSTROV KOTLIN
Kronštadt
Lomonosov
Petrodvorec
SUMMER PALACE
Strel'na
SANKT-PETERBURG
ST. PETERSBURG (LENINGRAD)
OSTROV VASIL'JEVSKIJ
Neva
Kolpino
Puškin
Pavlovsk
Krasnoje Selo
Vsevoložsk
Šlissel'burg
Kirovsk
Otradnoje
Sestroreck
Pargolovo
Lachta
Ol'gino
Murino
Novaja
Kupčino
Volodarskij
Gorelovo
PULKOVO AIRPORT
PUŠKIN AIRPORT
Ladožskoje ozero
Lake Ladoga
GOROD SANKT-PETERBURG
LENINGRAD OBLAST'
Copyright © by Rand McNally & Co.

b

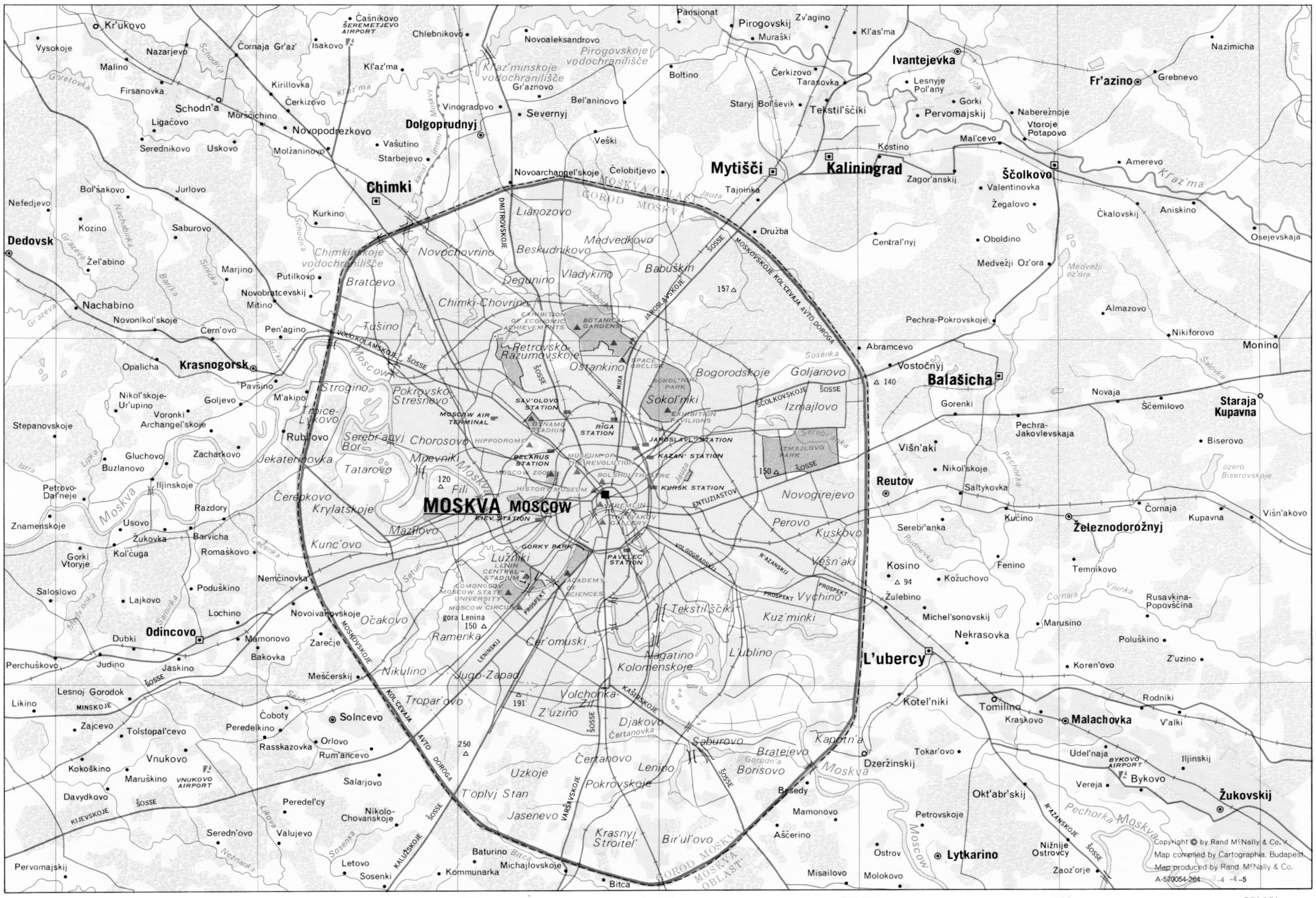

37° 10′
37° 20′
37° 30′
37° 40′
37° 50′
38°
38° 10′
55° 50′
55° 40′
MOSKVA MOSCOW
Chimki
Mytišči
Kaliningrad
Ščolkovo
Fr'azino
Ivantejevka
Dolgoprudnyj
Krasnogorsk
Dedovsk
Odincovo
Solncevo
Balašicha
Reutov
Železnodorožnyj
L'ubercy
Lytkarino
Malachovka
Žukovskij
Dzeržinskij
Moskva
ŠEREMETJEVO AIRPORT
VNUKOVO AIRPORT
BYKOVO AIRPORT
MOSKOVSKAJA KOL'CEVAJA AVTO DOROGA
GOROD MOSKVA
MOSKVA OBLAST'
Copyright © by Rand McNally & Co.
Map compiled by Cartographia, Budapest
Map produced by Rand McNally & Co.
A-530054-264 -4 -4-5

	AREA (km²)	POPULATION
SANKT-PETERBURG	2,800	4,850,000
MOSKVA	3,200	9,950,000

MAP FORM	ostrov	ozero	stadion	vodochranilišče	vokzal
ENGLISH	island	lake	stadium	reservoir	rail terminal
DEUTSCH	Insel	See	Stadion	Stausee	Bahnhof
ESPAÑOL	isla	lago	estadio	estanque	terminal ferroviaria
FRANÇAIS	île	lac	stade	réservoir	gare
PORTUGUÊS	ilha	lago	estádio	reservatório	estação ferroviária

Kilometers 0 5 10 15 Km.

Statute Miles 0 5 10 15 Mi.

Scale 1:300,000

One centimeter represents 3 kilometers.
One inch represents approximately 4.7 miles.

Kilometers 0 5 10 15 Km.

Statute Miles 0 5 10 15 Mi.

Scale 1:300,000

One centimeter represents 3 kilometers.
One inch represents approximately 4.7 miles

	AREA (km²)	POPULATION
MADRID	1,250	3,875,000
MILANO	1,900	3,975,000
LISBOA	1,150	2,150,000
BARCELONA	950	3,825,000

MAP FORM	aeroporto	arroyo	estacion	ponta	ribeira	riera
ENGLISH	airport	brook	station	point	creek	creek
DEUTSCH	Flughafen	Bach	Bahnhof	Landspitze	Bach	Bach
ESPAÑOL	aeropuerto	arroyo	estación	punta	riachuelo	riera
FRANÇAIS	aéroport	ruisseau	gare	pointe	crique	crique
PORTUGUÊS	aeroporto	arroio	estação	ponta	riacho	riacho

a

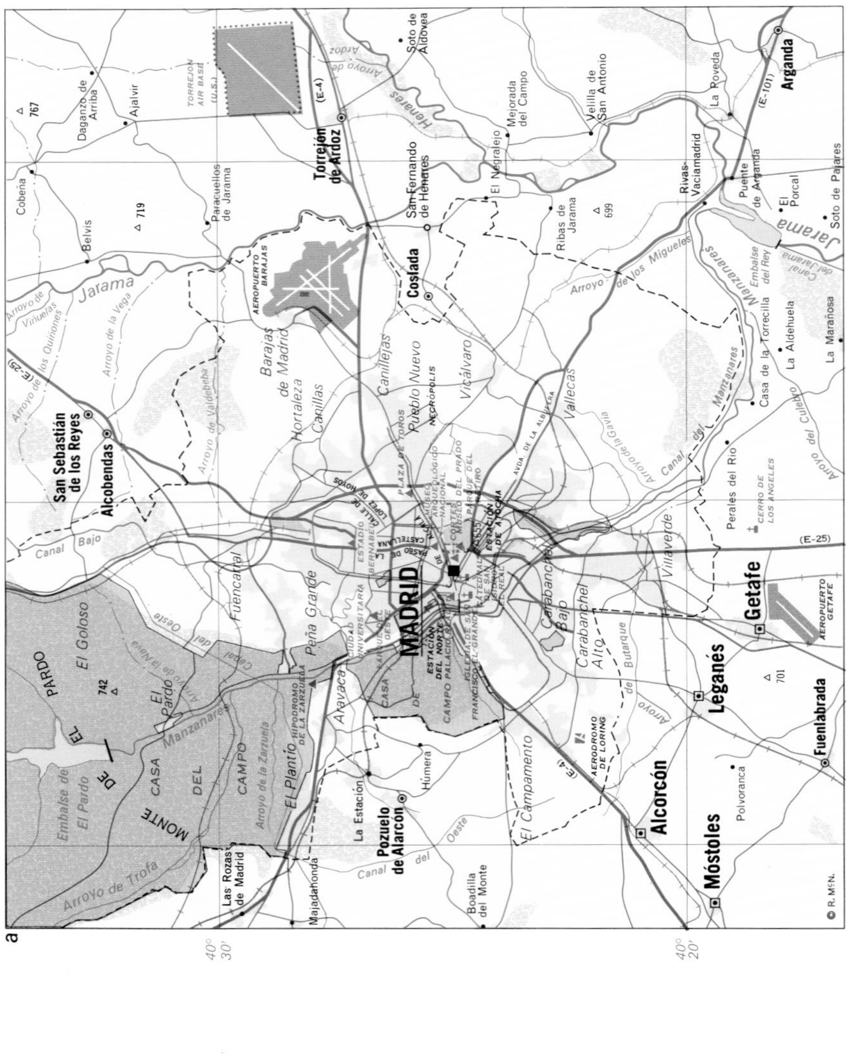
MADRID
Alcorcón
Móstoles
Getafe
Leganés
Torrejón de Ardoz
© R. MCN.

b

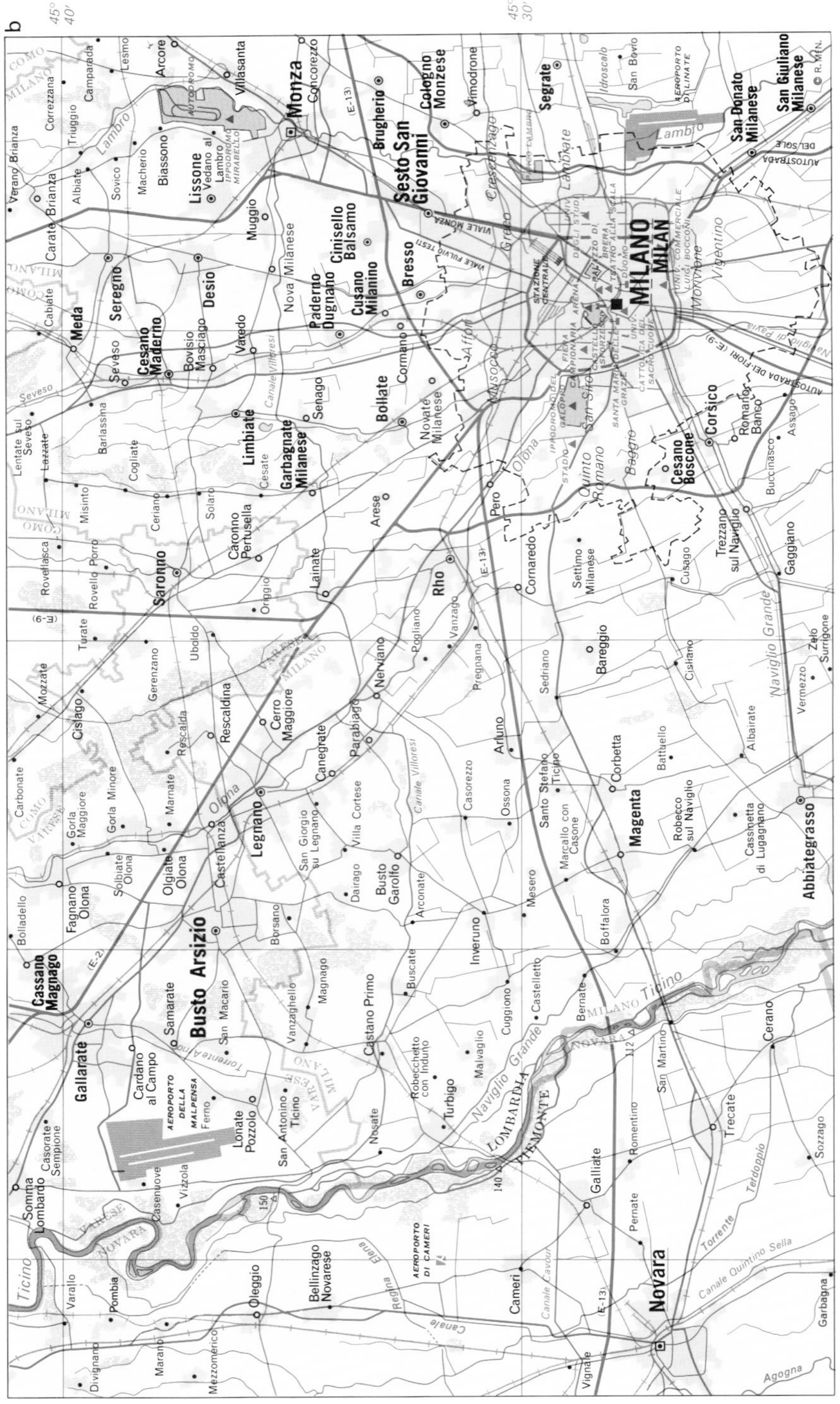
MILANO
MILAN
Monza
Novara
Busto Arsizio
Legnano
Sesto San Giovanni
© R. MCN.

c

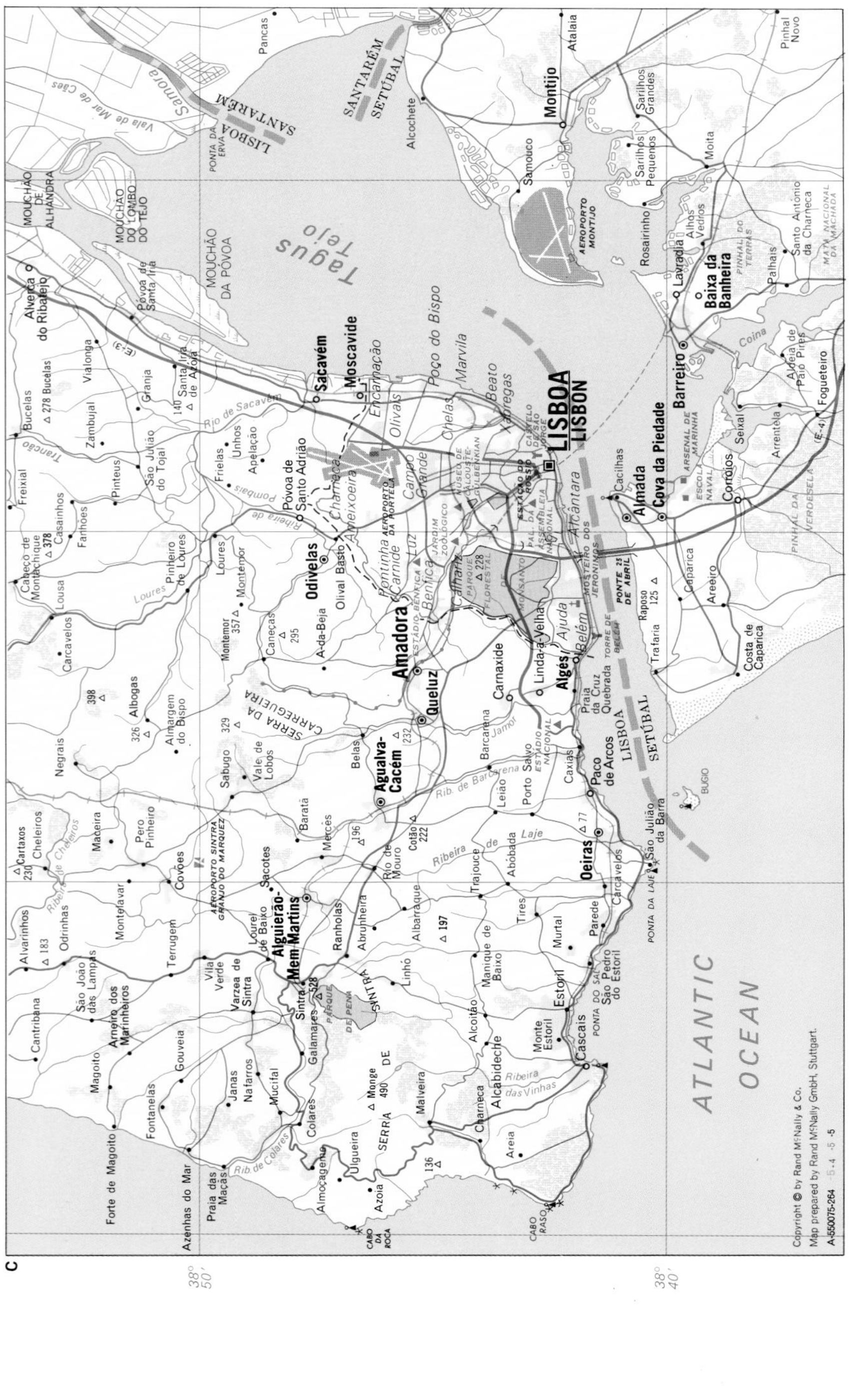
LISBOA
LISBON
Tagus Tejo
ATLANTIC OCEAN
Amadora
Queluz
Barreiro

d

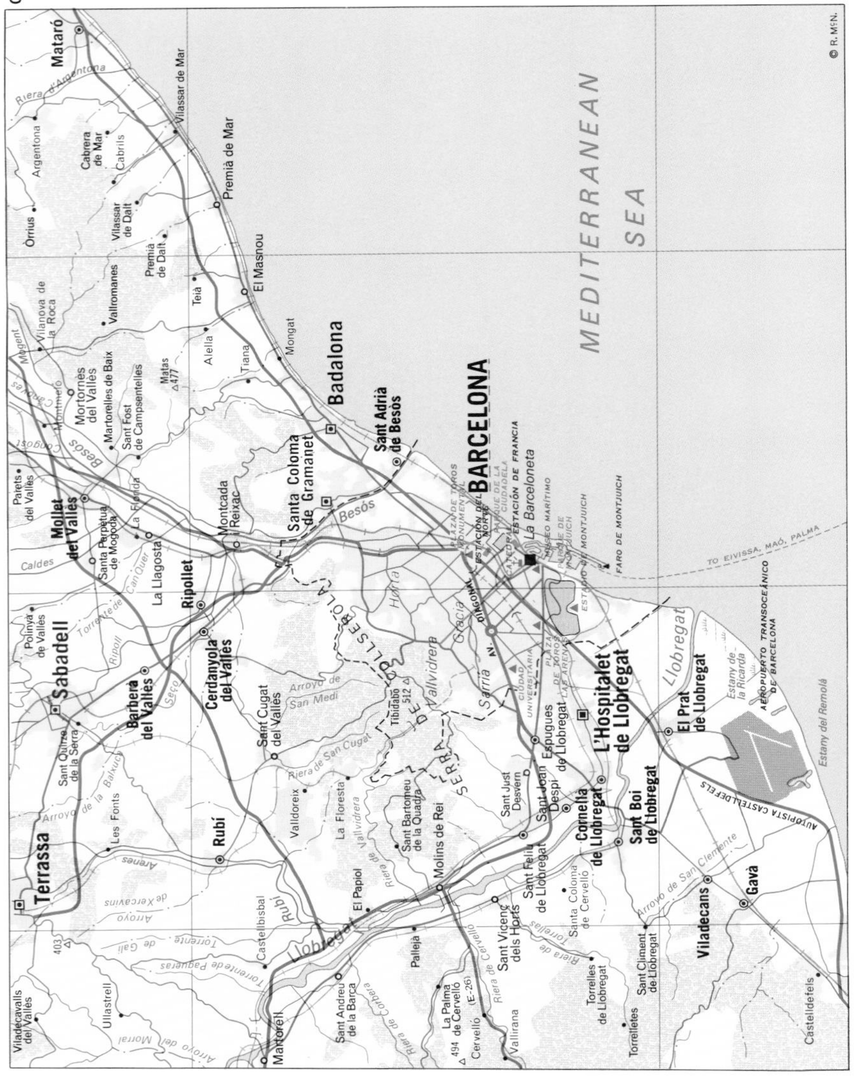
BARCELONA
MEDITERRANEAN SEA
Badalona
Sabadell
Terrassa
L'Hospitalet de Llobregat
© R. MCN.

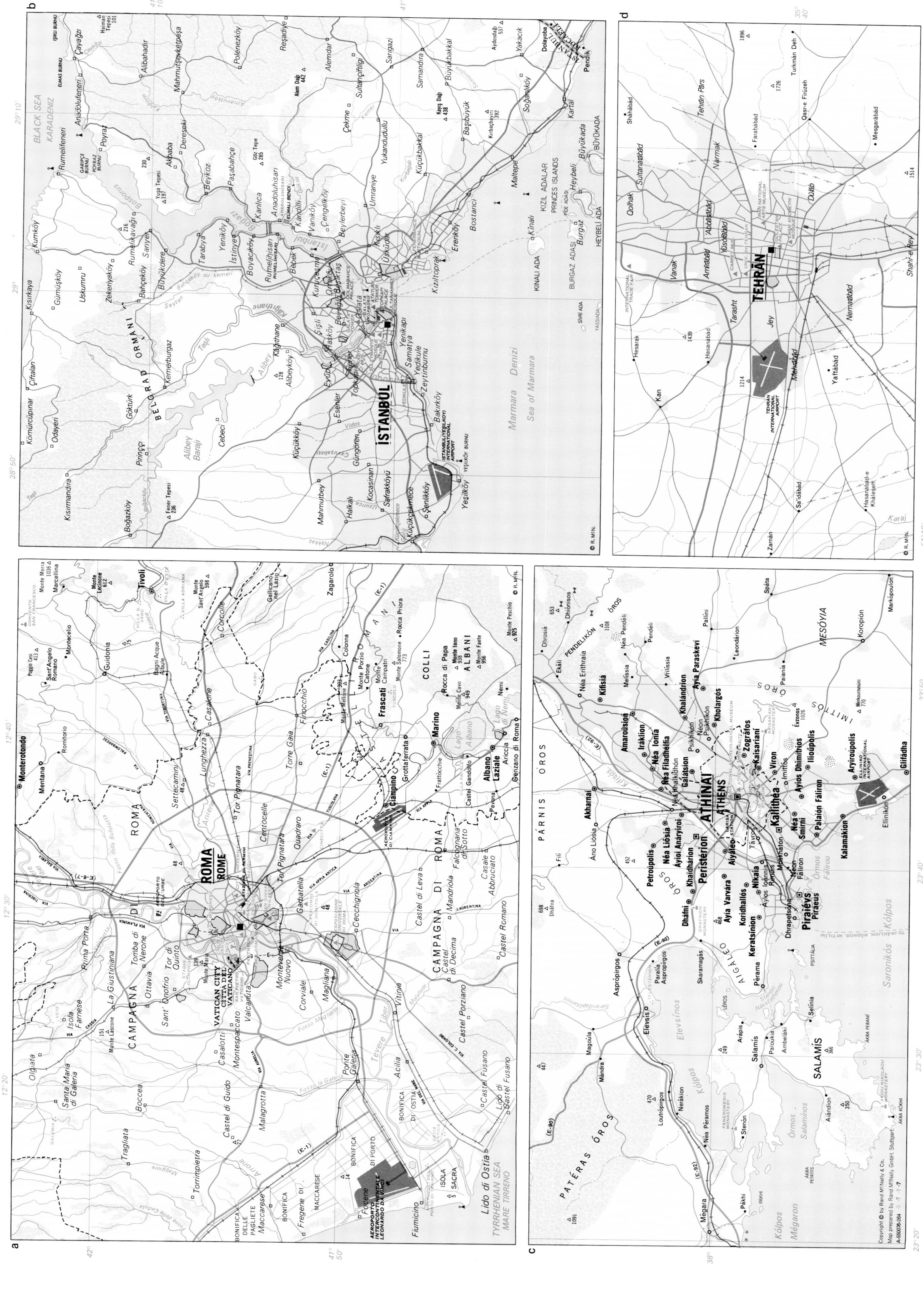
a
ROMA
ROME
VATICAN CITY
CITTÀ DEL VATICANO
TYRRHENIAN SEA
MARE TIRRENO
b
İSTANBUL
BLACK SEA
KARADENİZ
Marmara Denizi
Sea of Marmara
c
ATHÍNAI
ATHENS
PIRAIÉVS
Piraeus
SALAMÍS
Saronikós Kólpos
d
TEHRĀN

	AREA (km²)	POPULATION
ROMA	2,000	3,250,000
ATHÍNAI	1,100	3,350,000
İSTANBUL	1,300	4,300,000
TEHRĀN	950	5,200,000

MAP FORM	ada	burnu	camii	deresi	fosso	moni	monte
ENGLISH	island	cape	mosque	river	brook	monastery	mount
DEUTSCH	Insel	Kap	Moschee	Fluss	Bach	Kloster	Berg
ESPAÑOL	isla	cabo	mezquita	río	arroyo	monasterio	monte
FRANÇAIS	île	cap	mosquée	rivière	ruisseau	monastère	mont
PORTUGUÊS	ilha	cabo	mesquita	rio	arroio	mosteiro	monte

Scale 1:300,000
One centimeter represents 3 kilometers.
One inch represents approximately 4.7 miles.

Kilometers 0 5 10 15 Km.
Statute Miles 0 5 10 15 Mi.

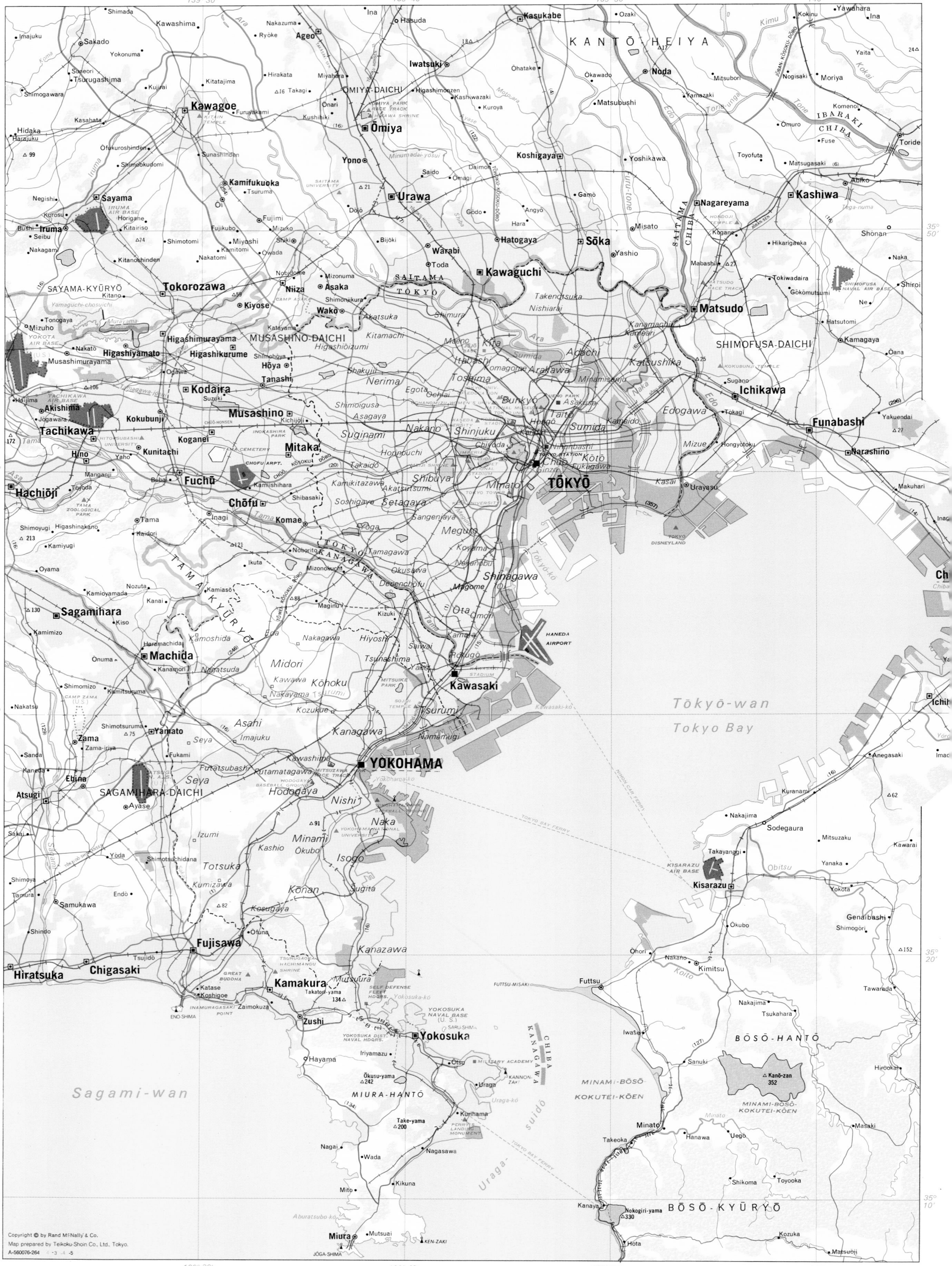

139° 30'
139° 40'
139° 50'
140°
35° 50'
35° 40'
35° 30'
35° 20'
35° 10'
KANTŌ-HEIYA
Kasukabe
Iwatsuki
Noda
Kawagoe
Ōmiya
Ageo
Urawa
Kashiwa
Nagareyama
Koshigaya
Sōka
Warabi
Kawaguchi
Matsudo
Tokorozawa
Sayama
Iruma
Kiyose
Niiza
Asaka
Wakō
Higashimurayama
Higashikurume
Higashiyamato
Kodaira
Musashino
Mitaka
Akishima
Tachikawa
Kokubunji
Koganei
Hino
Kunitachi
Hachiōji
Fuchū
Chōfu
Komae
Ichikawa
Funabashi
Narashino
Urayasu
TŌKYŌ
Chūō
Shinjuku
Shibuya
Minato
Shinagawa
Meguro
Setagaya
Suginami
Nakano
Nerima
Itabashi
Kita
Adachi
Katsushika
Edogawa
Sumida
Taitō
Bunkyō
Toshima
Arakawa
Kōtō
Ōta
MUSASHINO-DAICHI
SAYAMA-KYŪRYŌ
TAMA-KYŪRYŌ
SHIMOFUSA-DAICHI
Sagamihara
Machida
Kawasaki
HANEDA AIRPORT
TOKYO DISNEYLAND
Tōkyō-wan
Tokyo Bay
YOKOHAMA
Yamato
Zama
Ebina
Atsugi
SAGAMIHARA-DAICHI
Fujisawa
Chigasaki
Hiratsuka
Kamakura
Zushi
Yokosuka
Miura
MIURA-HANTŌ
Sagami-wan
Uraga-suidō
Kisarazu
Futtsu
Kimitsu
BŌSŌ-HANTŌ
BŌSŌ-KYŪRYŌ
MINAMI-BŌSŌ KOKUTEI-KŌEN
Kanō-zan 352
Nokogiri-yama 330
Copyright © by Rand McNally & Co.
Map prepared by Teikoku-Shoin Co., Ltd., Tokyo.
A-560076-264

AREA (km²): 5,350
POPULATION: 24,350,000

MAP FORM	air base	camp	-daichi	-kō	-shima	temple	-yama
ENGLISH	air base	camp	plateau	harbor	island	temple	mountain
DEUTSCH	Luftstützpunkt	Lager	Hochebene	Hafen	Insel	Tempel	Berg
ESPAÑOL	base aérea	campo	meseta	puerto	isla	templo	montaña
FRANÇAIS	base aérienne	camp	plateau	port	île	temple	montagne
PORTUGUÊS	base aérea	campo	planalto	porto	ilha	templo	montanha

Kilometers 0 5 10 15 Km.
Statute Miles 0 5 10 15 Mi.

Scale 1:300,000

One centimeter represents 3 kilometers.
One inch represents approximately 4.7 miles.

a

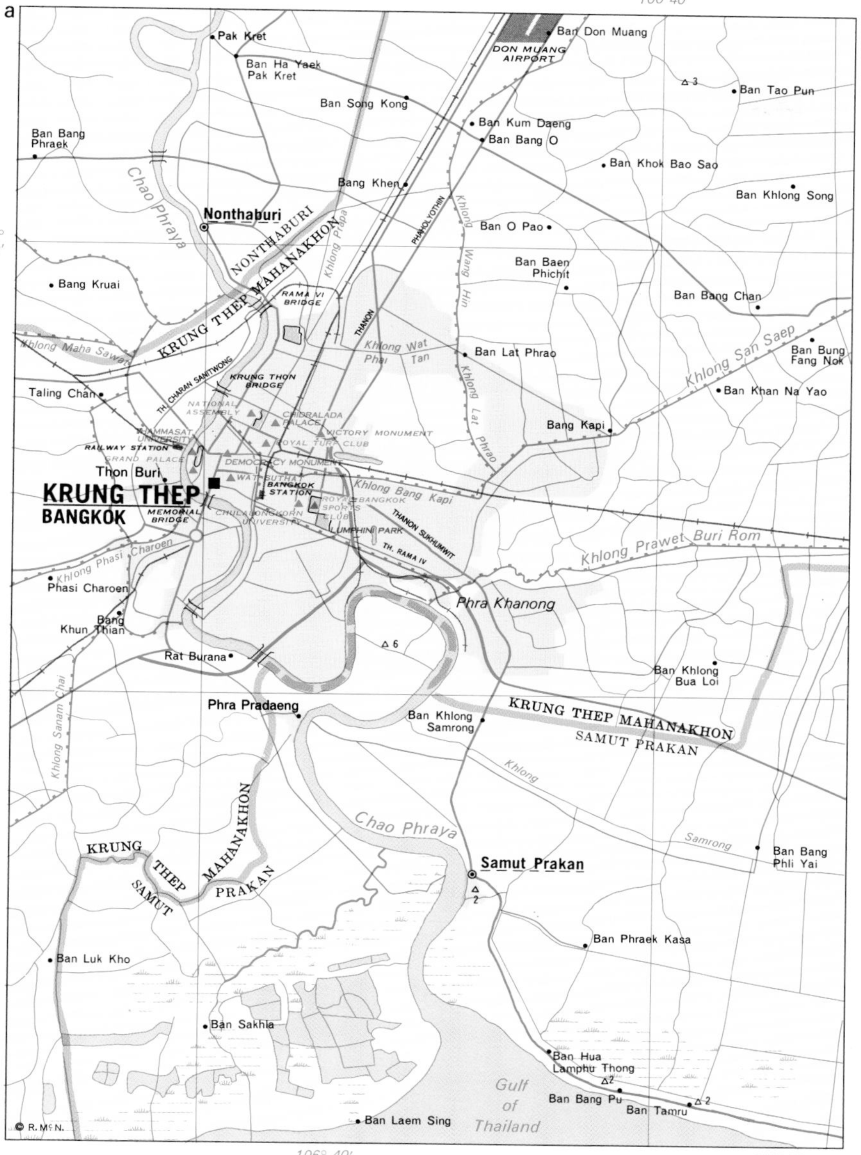
KRUNG THEP
BANGKOK
Nonthaburi
Thon Buri
Phra Pradaeng
Samut Prakan
Chao Phraya
Gulf of Thailand
Pak Kret
Ban Don Muang
DON MUANG AIRPORT
Bang Kruai
Taling Chan
Phasi Charoen
Rat Burana
Ban Luk Kho
Ban Sakhla
Ban Laem Sing
KRUNG THEP MAHANAKHON
SAMUT PRAKAN
NONTHABURI
Bang Khen
Bang Kapi
Phra Khanong
Ban Khlong Samrong
Ban Phraek Kasa
Ban Bang Pu
Ban Tamru
© R. McN.

b

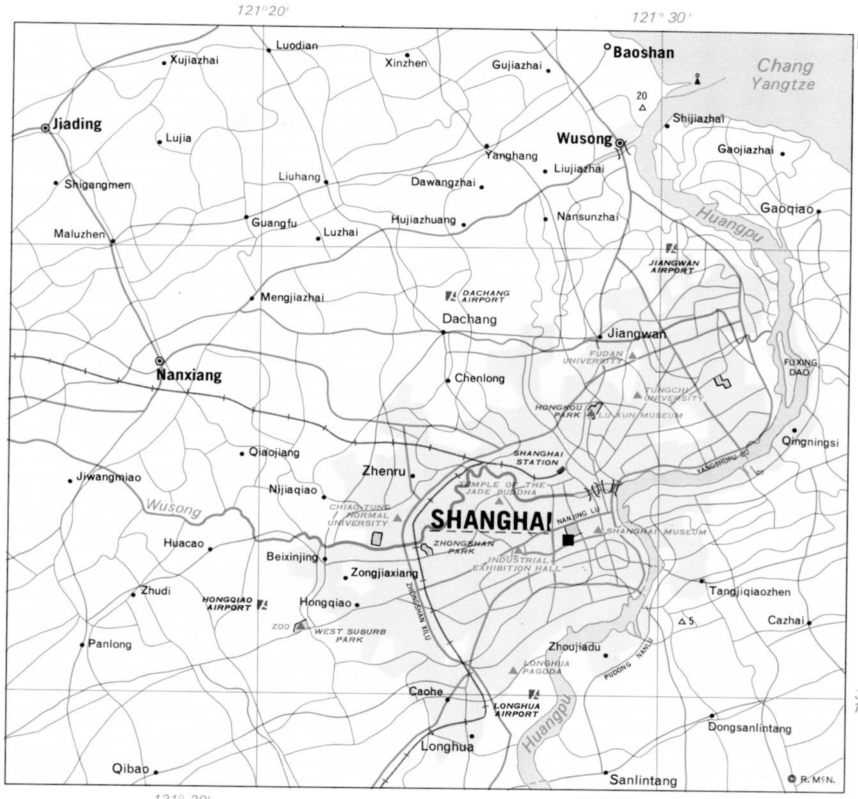
SHANGHAI
Baoshan
Chang Yangtze
Jiading
Wusong
Nanxiang
Huangpu
Jiangwan
Dachang
JIANGWAN AIRPORT
DACHANG AIRPORT
HONGQIAO AIRPORT
LONGHUA AIRPORT
Zhenru
Wusong
Longhua
Qibao
Sanlintang
Gaoqiao
Qingningsi
© R. McN.

d

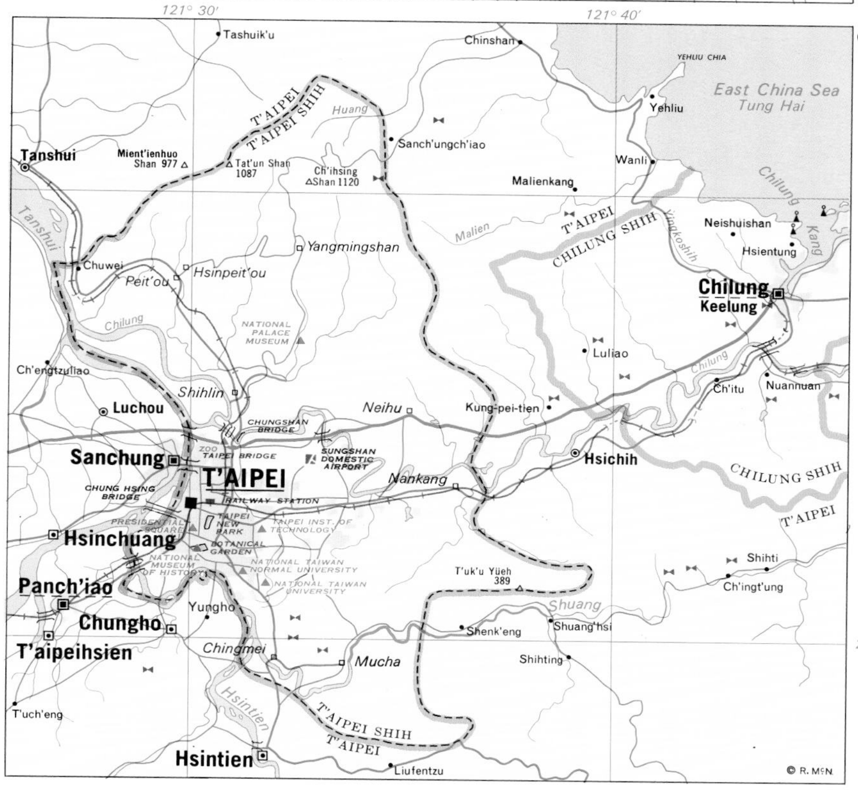
T'AIPEI
East China Sea
Tung Hai
Tanshui
Chilung
Keelung
Sanchung
Hsinchuang
Panch'iao
Chungho
T'aipeihsien
Hsintien
Shihlin
Luchou
Hsichih
Neihu
Nankang
Mucha
Yangmingshan
SUNGSHAN DOMESTIC AIRPORT
T'AIPEI SHIH
T'AIPEI
CHILUNG SHIH
© R. McN.

c

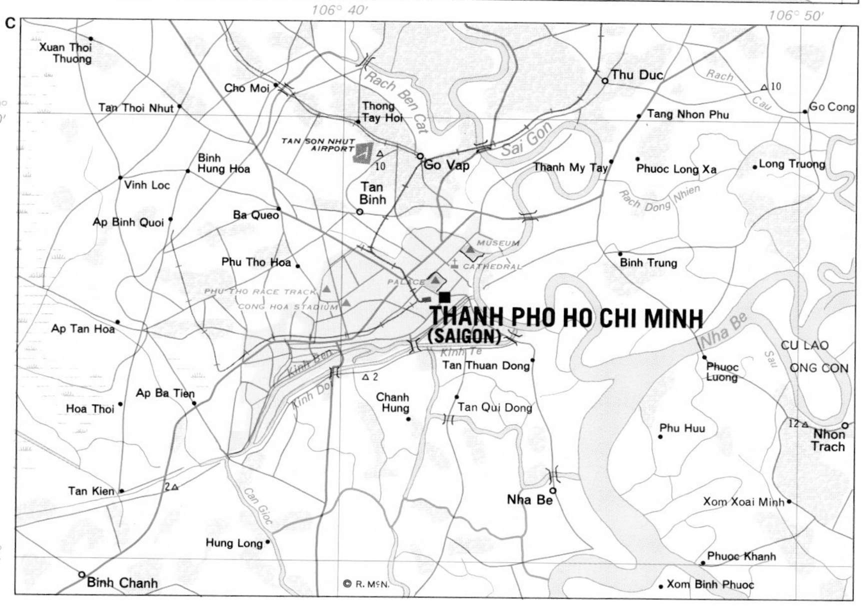
THANH PHO HO CHI MINH
(SAIGON)
Thu Duc
Go Vap
Tan Binh
TAN SON NHUT AIRPORT
Sai Gon
Nha Be
Binh Chanh
Tan Thuan Dong
Chanh Hung
Phuoc Long Xa
Nhon Trach
CU LAO
ONG CON
© R. McN.

e

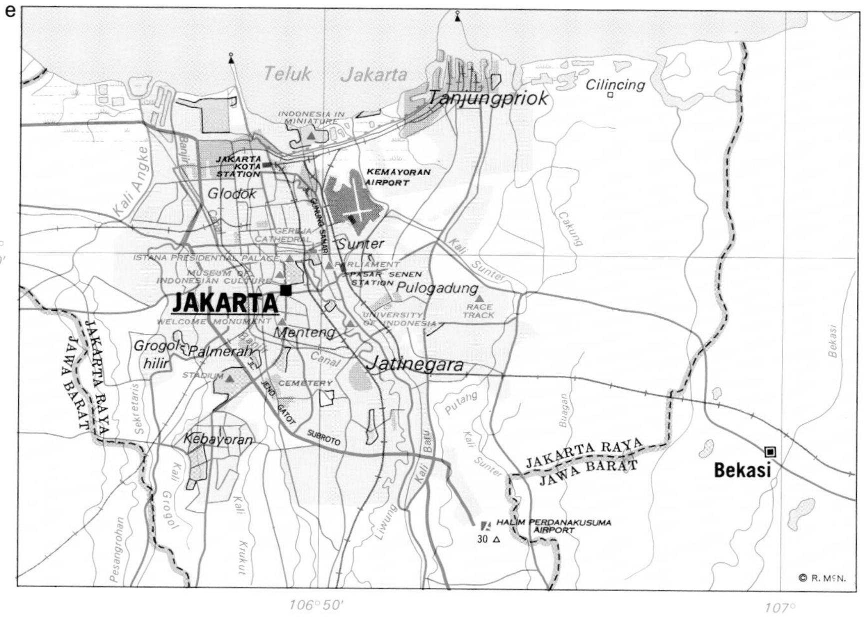
JAKARTA
Teluk Jakarta
Tanjungpriok
Cilincing
KEMAYORAN AIRPORT
Glodok
Sunter
Pulogadung
Menteng
Jatinegara
Kebayoran
Bekasi
JAKARTA RAYA
JAWA BARAT
HALIM PERDANAKUSUMA AIRPORT
© R. McN.

f

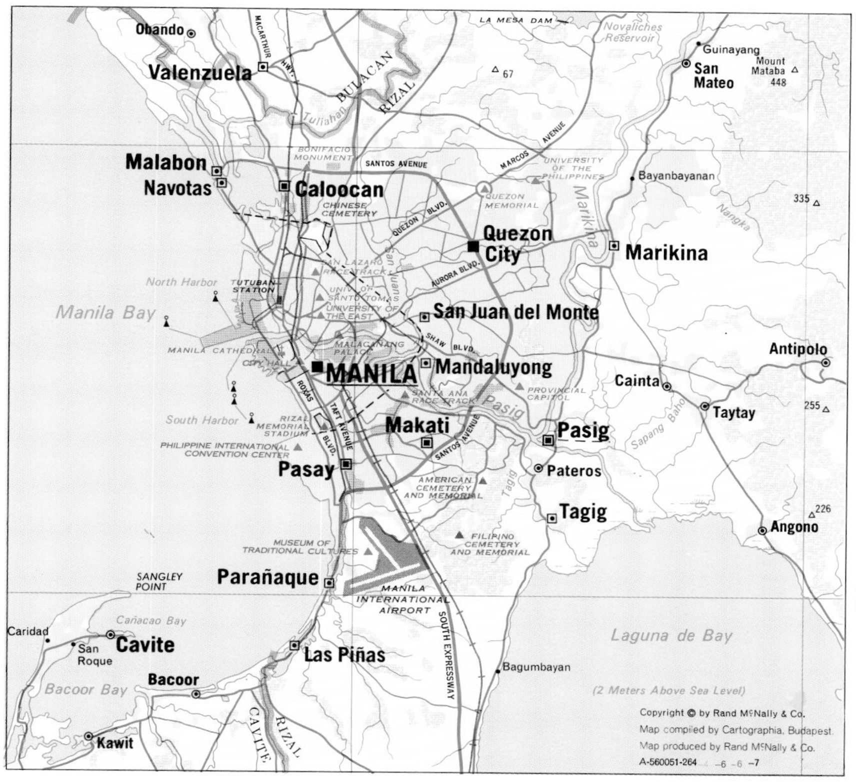
MANILA
Quezon City
Caloocan
Malabon
Navotas
Valenzuela
Obando
San Mateo
Marikina
San Juan del Monte
Mandaluyong
Makati
Pasay
Pasig
Pateros
Tagig
Parañaque
Las Piñas
Cavite
Bacoor
Kawit
Antipolo
Cainta
Taytay
Angono
Manila Bay
Laguna de Bay
Bacoor Bay
MANILA INTERNATIONAL AIRPORT
(2 Meters Above Sea Level)
Copyright © by Rand McNally & Co.
Map compiled by Cartographia, Budapest.
Map produced by Rand McNally & Co.
A-560051-264 -6 -6 -7

	AREA (km²)	POPULATION
KRUNG THEP (BANGKOK)	1,450	5,300,000
SAI-GON	750	2,400,000
JAKARTA	700	6,450,000
SHANGHAI	1,000	8,400,000
T'AIPEI	950	4,125,000
MANILA	650	5,900,000

MAP FORM	kali	khlong	monument	shan
ENGLISH	stream	stream	monument	mountain
DEUTSCH	Bach	Bach	Denkmal	Berg
ESPAÑOL	corriente de agua	corriente de agua	monumento	montaña
FRANÇAIS	cours d'eau	cours d'eau	monument	montagne
PORTUGUÊS	corrente de água	corrente de água	monumento	montanha

Kilometers 0 5 10 15 Km.

Statute Miles 0 5 10 15 Mi.

Scale 1:300,000

One centimeter represents 3 kilometers.

One inch represents approximately 4.7 miles.

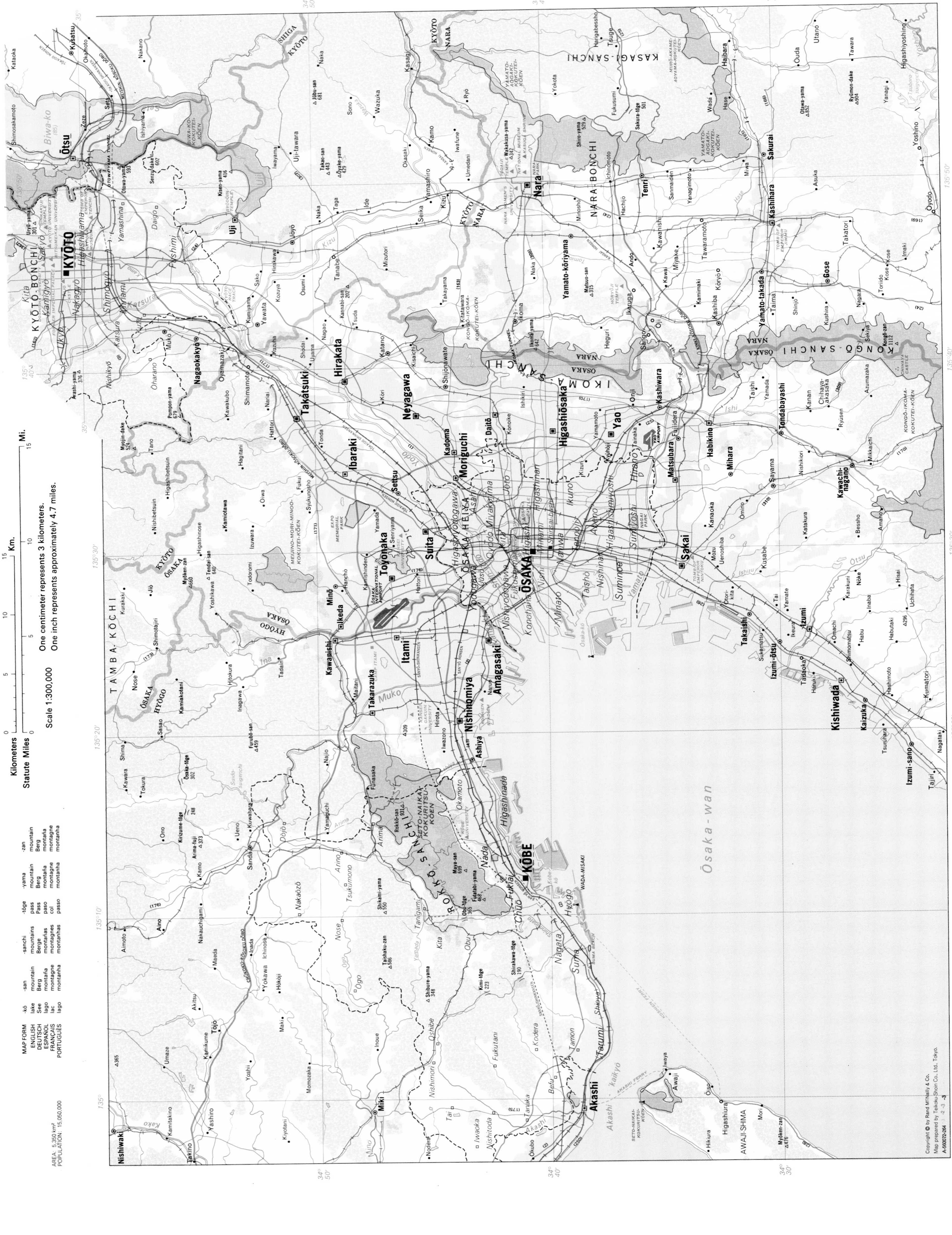
Kilometers 0 5 10 15 Km.
Statute Miles 0 5 10 15 Mi.
Scale 1:300,000
One centimeter represents 3 kilometers.
One inch represents approximately 4.7 miles.
MAP FORM -kō -san -sanchi -tōge -yama -zan
ENGLISH lake mountain mountains pass mountain mountain
DEUTSCH See Berg Berge Pass Berg Berg
ESPAÑOL lago montaña montañas paso montaña montaña
FRANÇAIS lac montagne montagnes col montagne montagne
PORTUGUÊS lago montanha montanhas passo montanha montanha
AREA 5,350 km²
POPULATION 15,050,000
KYŌTO
Ōtsu
Biwa-ko
Uji
Nara
Tenri
Sakurai
Kashihara
Yamato-takada
Gose
Takatsuki
Hirakata
Neyagawa
Ibaraki
Suita
Toyonaka
Ikeda
Itami
Takarazuka
Nishinomiya
Amagasaki
Ashiya
KŌBE
ŌSAKA
Sakai
Kishiwada
Akashi
Miki
Nishiwaki
Ōsaka-wan
AWAJI-SHIMA
KYŌTO-BONCHI
NARA-BONCHI
KASAGI-SANCHI
IKOMA-SANCHI
KONGŌ-SANCHI
ROKKŌ-SANCHI
TAMBA-KŌCHI
Copyright © by Rand McNally & Co.
Map prepared by Teikoku-Shoin Co. Ltd., Tokyo.

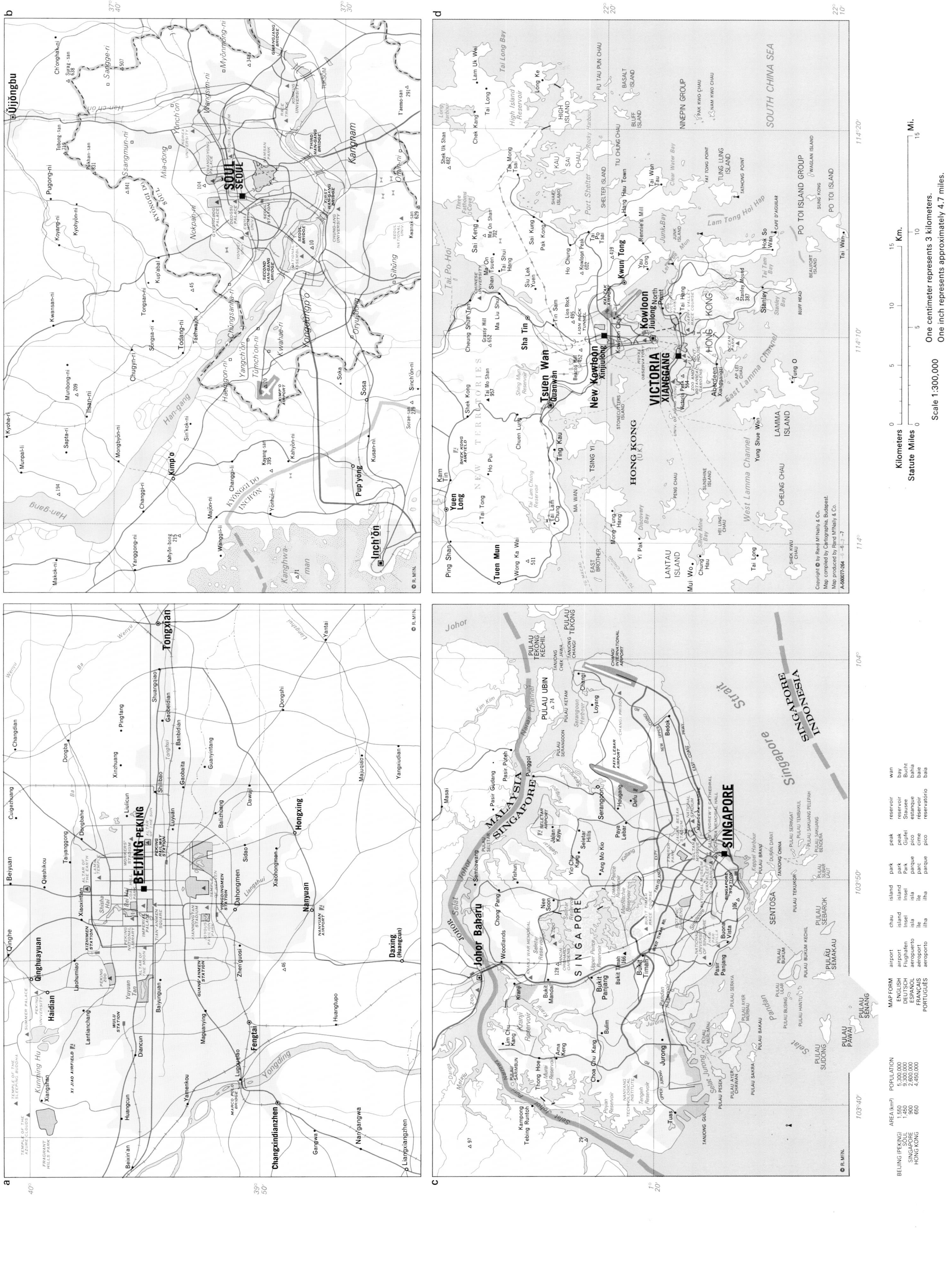
a
BEIJING PEKING
Tongxian
Fengtai
Haidian
Changxindianzhen
Daxing (Huangcun)
b
SŎUL SEOUL
Inch'ŏn
Kimp'o
Ŭijŏngbu
c
SINGAPORE
Johor Baharu
MALAYSIA
SINGAPORE
INDONESIA
Singapore Strait
d
VICTORIA XIANGGANG
Kowloon Jiulong
New Kowloon Xinjiulong
Tsuen Wan Quanwan
Sha Tin
Tuen Mun
Yuen Long
HONG KONG (U.K.)
LANTAU ISLAND
LAMMA ISLAND
SOUTH CHINA SEA
Scale 1:300,000
One centimeter represents 3 kilometers.
One inch represents approximately 4.7 miles.
Kilometers 0 5 10 15 Km.
Statute Miles 0 5 10 15 Mi.
Copyright © by Rand McNally & Co.
Map compiled by Cartographia, Budapest.
Map produced by Rand McNally & Co.
© R.McN.
AREA (km²) POPULATION
BEIJING (PEKING) 1,550 5,300,000
SŎUL 1,450 9,300,000
SINGAPORE 900 2,500,000
HONG KONG 650 4,450,000
MAP FORM airport chau island park peak reservoir wan
ENGLISH airport island island park peak reservoir bay
DEUTSCH Flughafen Insel Insel Park Gipfel Stausee Bucht
ESPAÑOL aeropuerto isla isla parque pico embalse bahía
FRANÇAIS aéroport île île parc cime réservoir baie
PORTUGUÊS aeroporto ilha ilha parque pico reservatório baía

Kilometers 0 5 10 15 Km.
Statute Miles 0 5 10 15 Mi.

Scale 1:300,000
One centimeter represents 3 kilometers.
One inch represents approximately 4.7 miles.

	AREA (km²)	POPULATION
DELHI	1,400	5,500,000
BOMBAY	1,050	8,250,000
CALCUTTA	3,100	11,200,000

ENGLISH	DEUTSCH	ESPAÑOL	FRANÇAIS	PORTUGUÊS
airport	Flughafen	aeropuerto	aéroport	aeroporto
dock	Dock	muelle	quai	cais
island	Insel	isla	île	ilha
lake	See	lago	lac	lago
point	Punkt	punta	pointe	ponta
railroad station	Bahnhof	terminal ferroviaria	gare	estação ferroviária
road	Landstrasse	camino	route	rodovia
temple	Tempel	templo	temple	templo

b

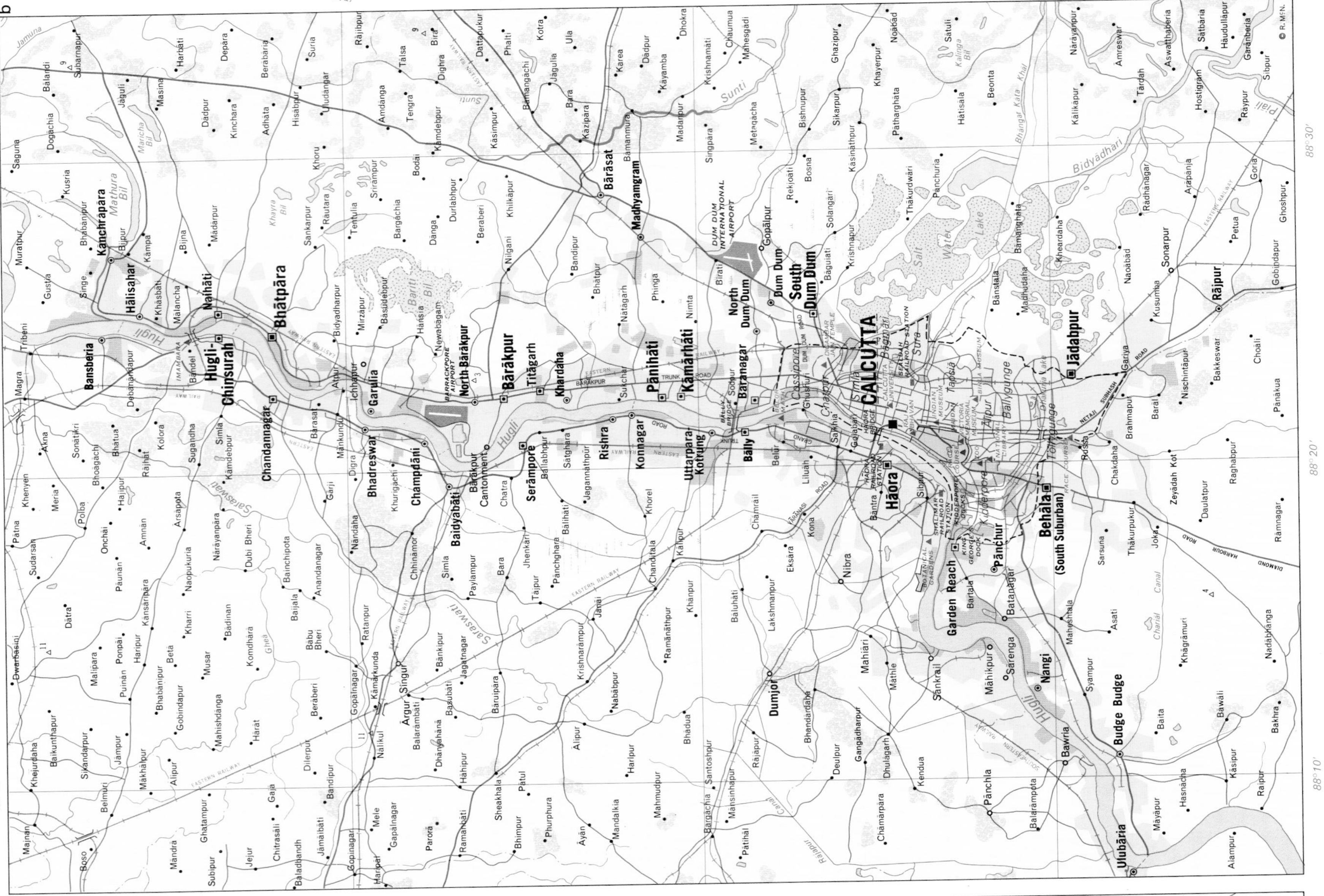
CALCUTTA
Hāora
Bhātpāra
Bārākpur
Dum Dum
Behāla (South Suburban)
Budge Budge
Garden Reach
Hugli
DUM DUM INTERNATIONAL AIRPORT
© R.M/N.

a

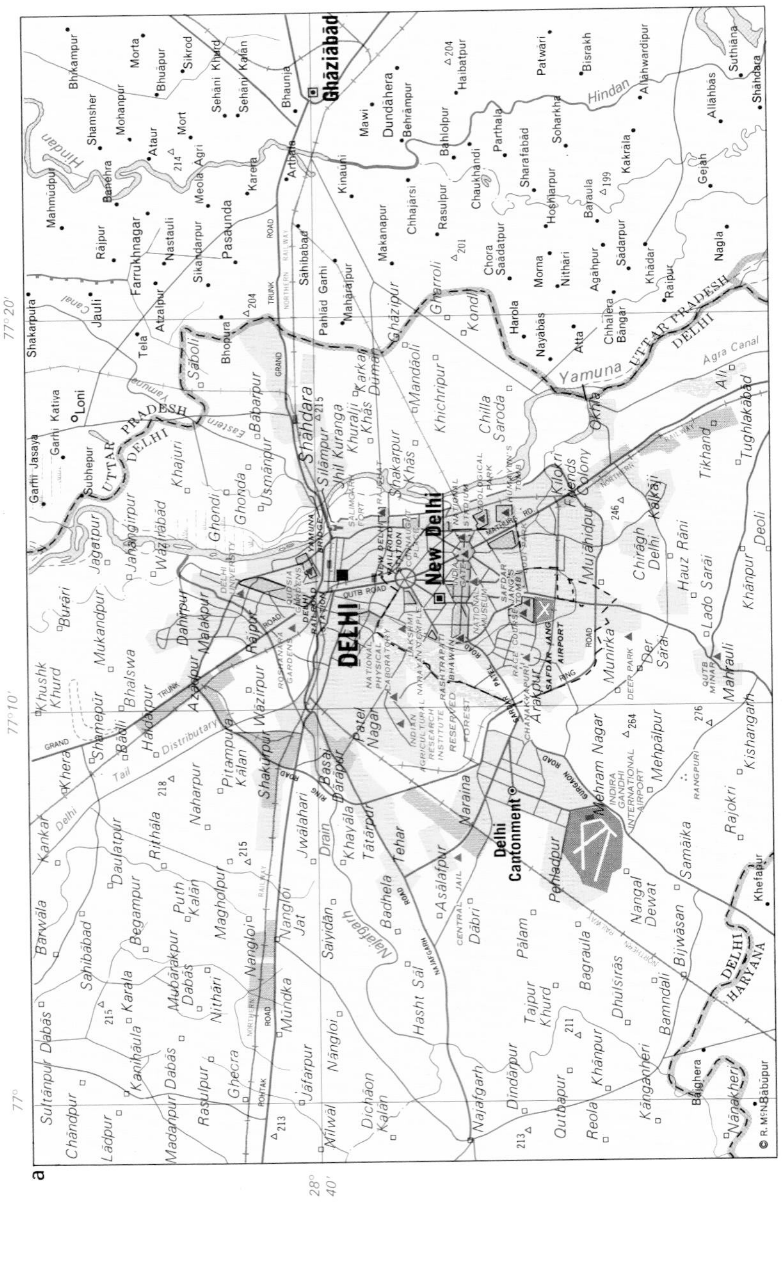
DELHI
New Delhi
Ghāziābād
Delhi Cantonment
Yamuna
UTTAR PRADESH
DELHI
HARYANA
© R. M/N.

c

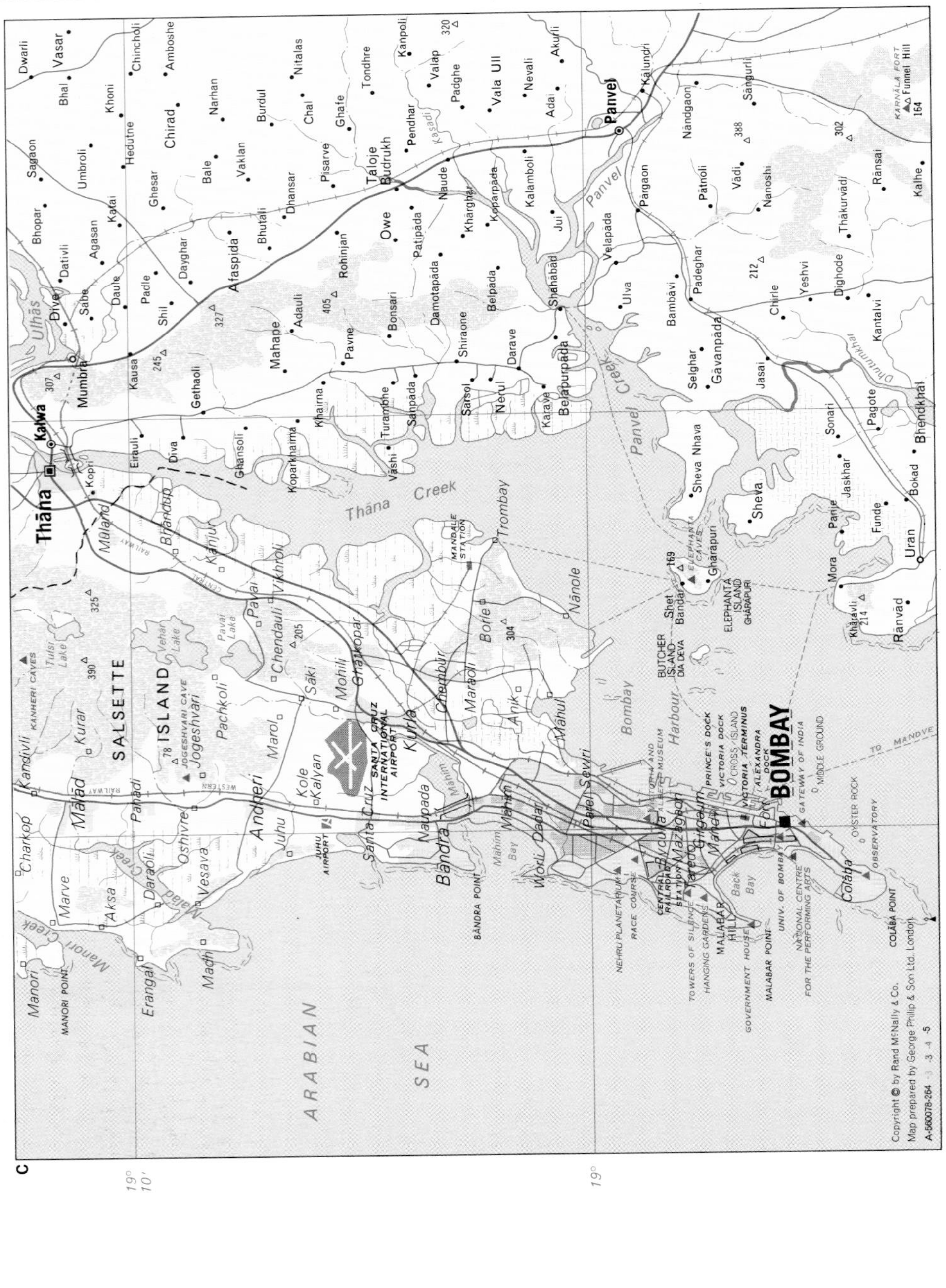
BOMBAY
Thāna
SALSETTE ISLAND
ARABIAN SEA
Thāna Creek
Bombay Harbour
SANTA CRUZ INTERNATIONAL AIRPORT
Copyright © by Rand McNally & Co.
Map prepared by George Philip & Son Ltd. London

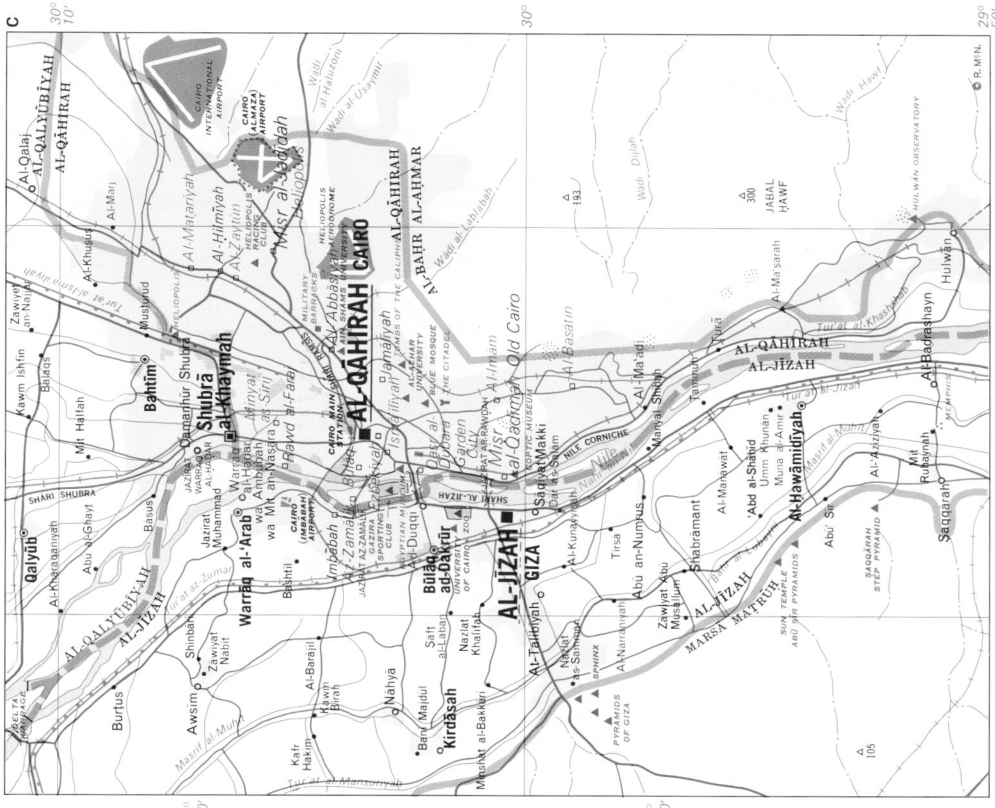
c

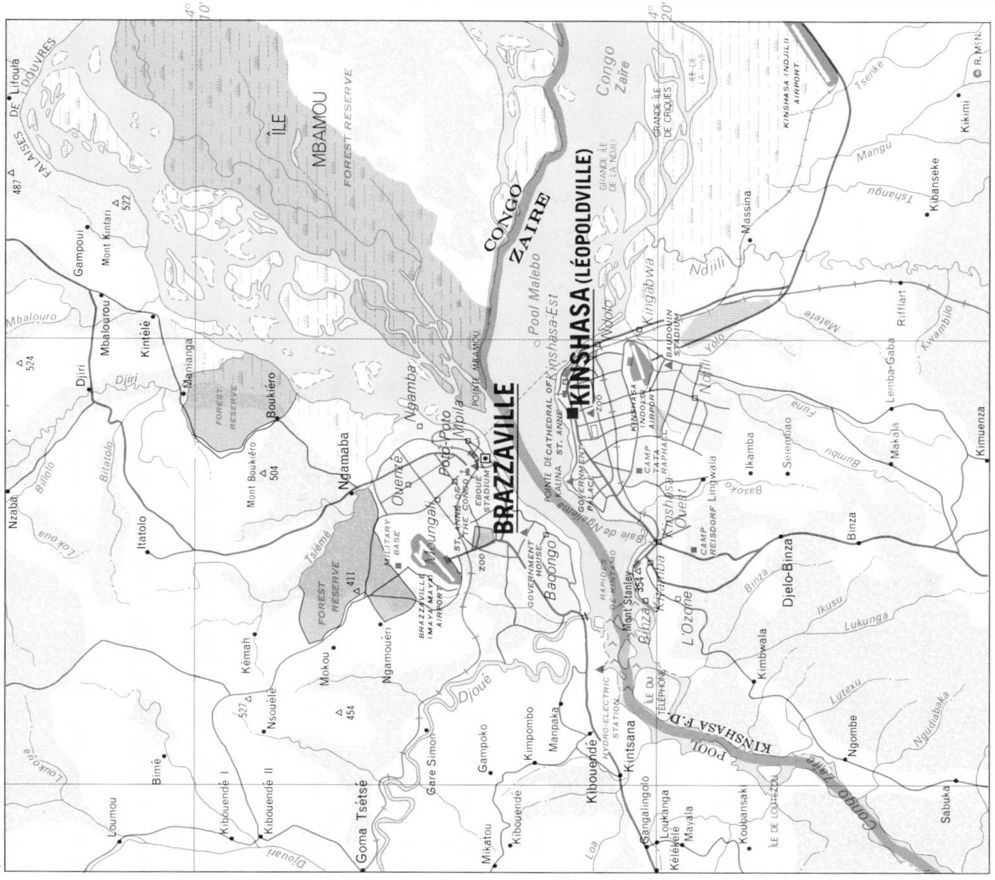
b

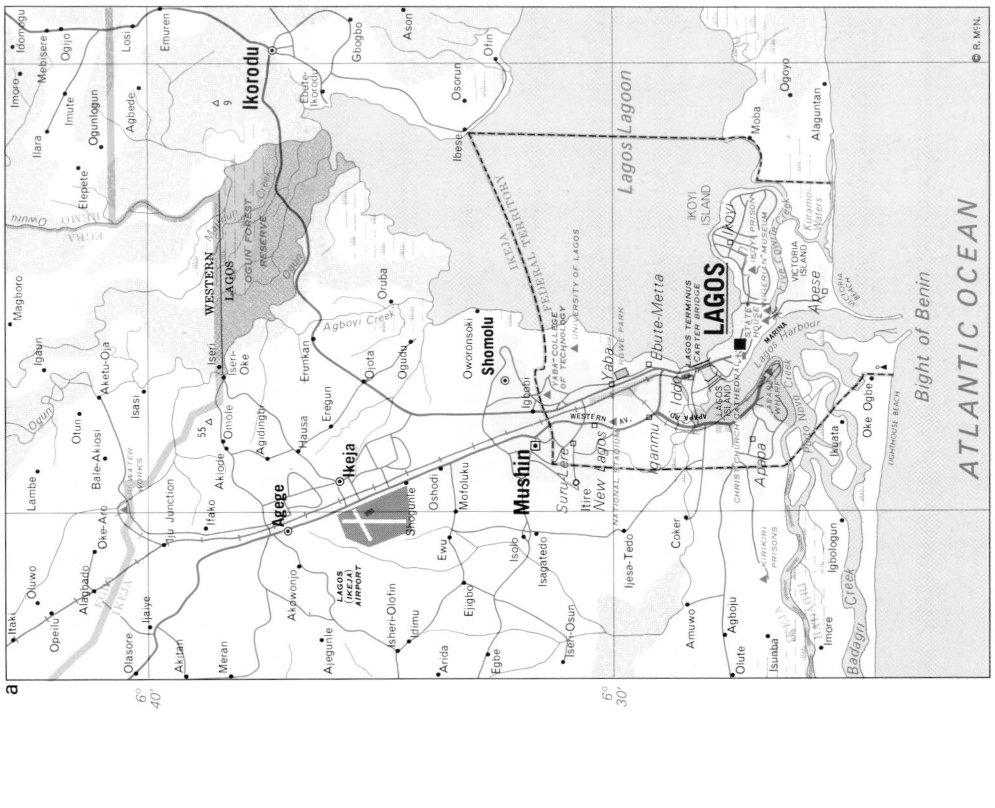
a

d

	AREA (km²)	POPULATION
LAGOS	750	2,400,000
KINSHASA–BRAZZAVILLE	1,150	2,750,000
AL-QĀHIRAH (CAIRO)	1,200	8,900,000
JOHANNESBURG	2,650	3,300,000

MAP FORM	airport	creek	dam	île	park	race course	tur'at	wadi
ENGLISH	airport	creek	dam	island	park	race course	canal	wadi
DEUTSCH	Flughafen	Bach	Damm	Insel	Park	Rennbahn	Kanal	Wadi
ESPAÑOL	aeropuerto	riachuelo	presa	isla	parque	hipódromo	canal	uadi
FRANÇAIS	aéroport	crique	barrage	île	parc	champ de course	canal	wadi
PORTUGUÊS	aeroporto	riacho	represa	ilha	parque	hipódromo	canal	uádi

Kilometers 0 5 10 15 Km.
Statute Miles 0 5 10 15 Mi.

Scale 1:300,000
One centimeter represents 3 kilometers.
One inch represents approximately 4.7 miles.

a

150° 40'
150° 50'
151°
151° 10'
151° 20'
33° 40'
33° 50'
34°
Riverstone
Schofields
Penrith
Blacktown
Parramatta
Holroyd
Fairfield
Liverpool
Bankstown
Auburn
Strathfield
Ryde
Willoughby
Manly
Mosman
North Sydney
SYDNEY
Leichhardt
Woollahra
Waverley
Randwick
Ashfield
Marrickville
Canterbury
Botany
Rockdale
Hurstville
Kogarah
Sutherland
Campbelltown
Camden
Cronulla
Botany Bay
PACIFIC
OCEAN
Copyright © by Rand McNally & Co.

b

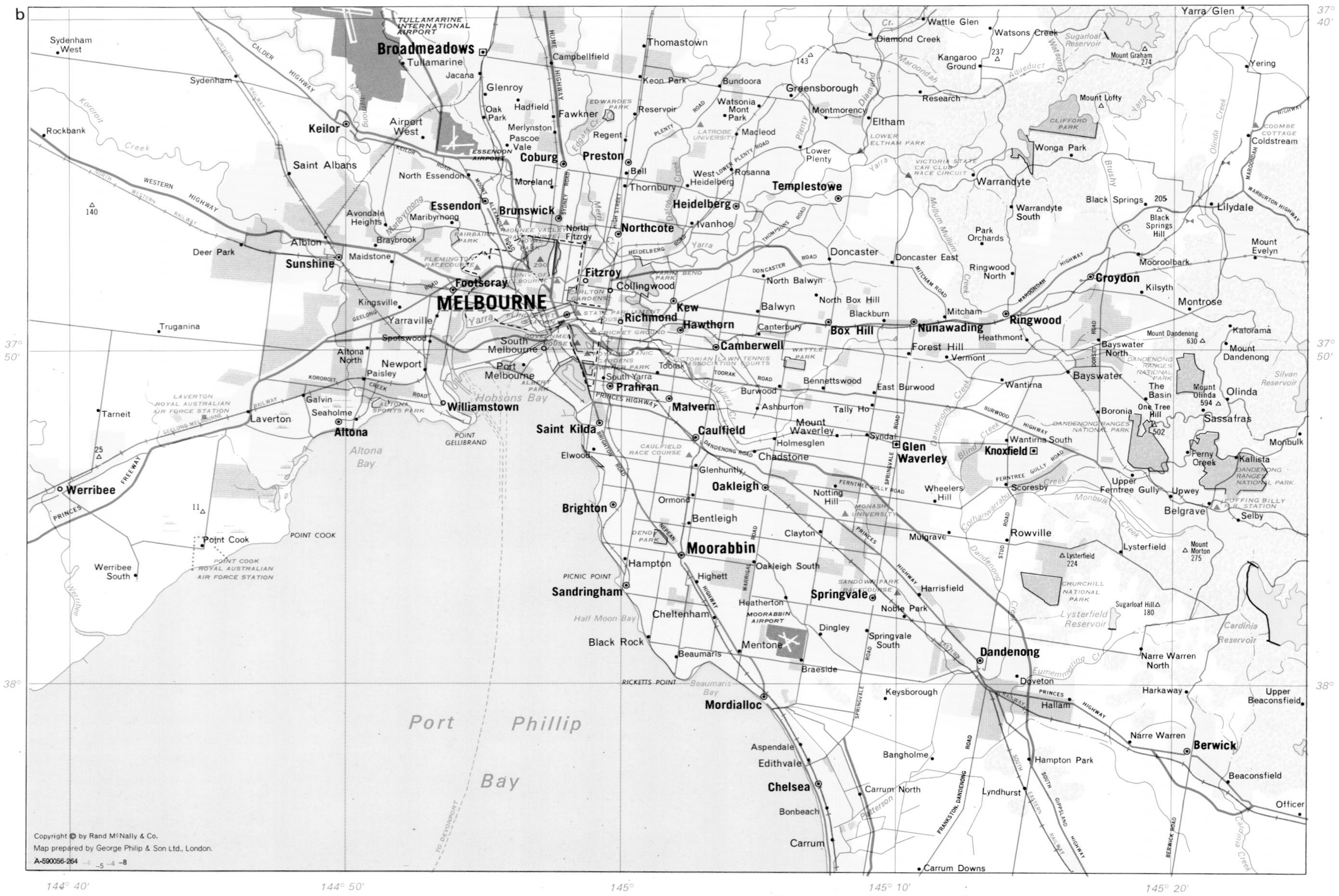
37° 40'
37° 50'
38°
144° 40'
144° 50'
145°
145° 10'
145° 20'
TULLAMARINE INTERNATIONAL AIRPORT
Broadmeadows
Keilor
Coburg
Preston
Essendon
Brunswick
Northcote
Heidelberg
Templestowe
Sunshine
Footscray
MELBOURNE
Fitzroy
Collingwood
Richmond
Kew
Hawthorn
Camberwell
Box Hill
Nunawading
Ringwood
Croydon
Williamstown
Altona
Werribee
Prahran
Malvern
Caulfield
Saint Kilda
Brighton
Oakleigh
Waverley
Knoxfield
Moorabbin
Sandringham
Springvale
Dandenong
Mordialloc
Chelsea
Berwick
Port Phillip Bay
Copyright © by Rand McNally & Co.
Map prepared by George Philip & Son Ltd., London.
A-590056-264

	AREA (km²)	POPULATION
MELBOURNE	2,600	2,425,000
SYDNEY	2,800	2,850,000

ENGLISH	bay, b.	bridge	creek, cr.	highway	point	road
DEUTSCH	Bucht	Brücke	Bach	Landstrasse	Landspitze	Landstrasse
ESPAÑOL	bahía	puente	riachuelo	camino	punta	camino
FRANÇAIS	baie	pont	crique	route	pointe	route
PORTUGUÊS	baía	ponte	riacho	rodovia	ponta	rodovia

Kilometers 0 5 10 15 Km.

Statute Miles 0 5 10 15 Mi.

Scale 1:300,000

One centimeter represents 3 kilometers.

One inch represents approximately 4.7 miles.

a

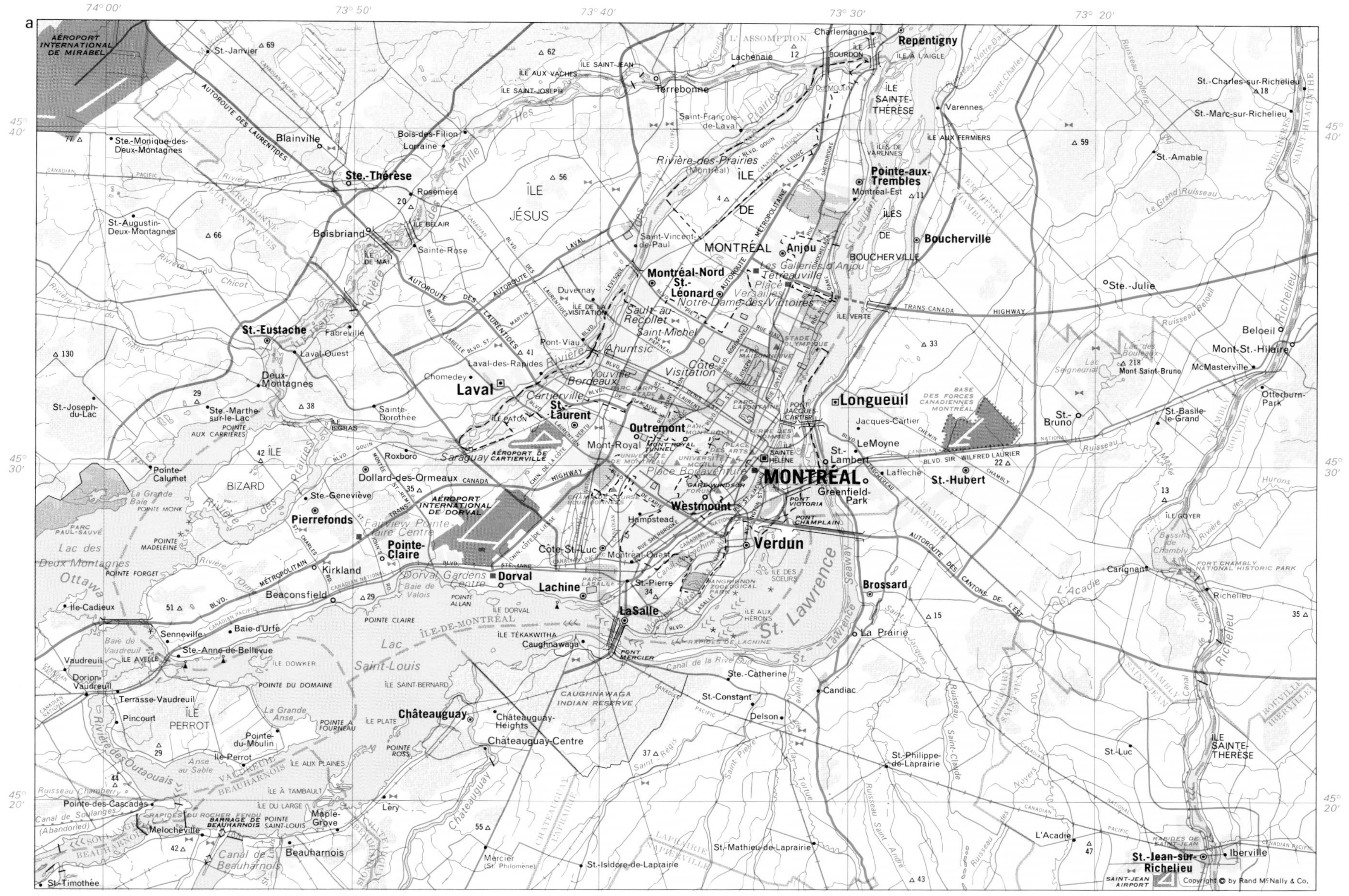
74° 00'
73° 50'
73° 40'
73° 30'
73° 20'
45° 40'
45° 30'
45° 20'
AÉROPORT INTERNATIONAL DE MIRABEL
St.-Janvier
Charlemagne
Repentigny
Lachenaie
Terrebonne
Blainville
Ste.-Thérèse
Rosemère
Bois-des-Filion
Lorraine
ÎLE JÉSUS
Boisbriand
Sainte-Rose
Ste.-Monique-des-Deux-Montagnes
St.-Augustin-Deux-Montagnes
ÎLE SAINTE-THÉRÈSE
Varennes
St.-Charles-sur-Richelieu
St.-Marc-sur-Richelieu
St.-Amable
Pointe-aux-Trembles
Montréal-Est
ÎLES DE BOUCHERVILLE
Boucherville
ÎLE DE MONTRÉAL
Anjou
Montréal-Nord
St.-Léonard
Saint-Vincent-de-Paul
Duvernay
St.-Eustache
Fabreville
Laval-Ouest
Deux-Montagnes
St.-Joseph-du-Lac
Ste.-Marthe-sur-le-Lac
Pont-Viau
Laval-des-Rapides
Chomedey
Laval
Sainte-Dorothée
St.-Laurent
Outremont
Mont-Royal
Longueuil
St.-Lambert
LeMoyne
Jacques-Cartier
St.-Hubert
Greenfield-Park
Laflèche
Ste.-Julie
Beloeil
Mont-St.-Hilaire
McMasterville
St.-Bruno
St.-Basile-le-Grand
Otterburn-Park
MONTRÉAL
Westmount
Verdun
Roxboro
Dollard-des-Ormeaux
Pointe-Calumet
ÎLE BIZARD
Ste.-Geneviève
Pierrefonds
AÉROPORT INTERNATIONAL DE DORVAL
Pointe-Claire
Dorval
Lachine
Côte-St-Luc
Montréal-Ouest
Hampstead
LaSalle
Kirkland
Beaconsfield
Baie-d'Urfé
Senneville
Ste.-Anne-de-Bellevue
Ile-Cadieux
Lac des Deux Montagnes
Lac Saint-Louis
St. Lawrence
Brossard
La Prairie
Candiac
Ste.-Catherine
St.-Constant
Delson
Caughnawaga
CAUGHNAWAGA INDIAN RESERVE
Châteauguay
Châteauguay-Heights
Châteauguay-Centre
Vaudreuil
Dorion-Vaudreuil
Terrasse-Vaudreuil
Pincourt
ÎLE PERROT
Pointe-du-Moulin
Île-Perrot
Pointe-des-Cascades
Melocheville
Maple-Grove
Beauharnois
Léry
Mercier
St.-Isidore-de-Laprairie
St.-Mathieu-de-Laprairie
St.-Philippe-de-Laprairie
St.-Luc
L'Acadie
St.-Jean-sur-Richelieu
Iberville
Carignan
Richelieu
St.-Timothée
Copyright © by Rand McNally & Co.

b

79° 50'
79° 40'
79° 30'
79° 20'
79° 10'
43° 50'
43° 40'
43° 30'
Caledon East
Mono Road Station
Bolton
Richmond Hill
Markham
Pickering
Ajax
Teston
Maple
Richvale
Buttonville
Unionville
Kleinburg
Nashville
Vellore
Sherwood
Sandhill
Wildfield
Elder Mills
Pine Grove
Vaughan
Edgeley
Concord
Thornhill
Langstaff
Hagerman Corners
Milliken
Armadale
Cherrywood
Dunbarton
Fairport
Fairport Beach
Rosebank Station
Port Union
Tullamore
Castlemore
Stanley Mills
Ebenezer
Claireville
Woodhill
North York
Willowdale
Agincourt
Scarborough
Maryvale
Wexford
West Hill
Snelgrove
Nortonville
Bramalea
Malton
LESTER B. PEARSON INTERNATIONAL AIRPORT
Brampton
Mount Charles
Pleasant
Springbrook
Norval
Huttonsville
Churchville
Meadowvale
Britannia
Derry West
Rexdale
Thistletown
Weston
Mount Dennis
York
Leaside
Don Mills
East York
Scarborough Bluffs
Birch Cliff
TORONTO
Etobicoke
Islington
Swansea
Mimico
New Toronto
Long Branch
Summerville
Burnhamthorpe
Streetsville
Mississauga
Port Credit
Erindale
Hornby
Omagh
Trafalgar
Glenarchy
Boyne
Oakville
LAKE ONTARIO
(75 Meters Above Sea Level)
CANADA
UNITED STATES
Copyright © by Rand McNally & Co.
Map prepared by Rand McNally & Co.
A-520080-264 -3 -4 -5

	AREA (km²)	POPULATION
MONTRÉAL	3,100	2,875,000
TORONTO	2,100	2,850,000

MAP FORM	île	park	rapides	rivière	ruisseau
ENGLISH	island	park	rapids	river	brook
DEUTSCH	Insel	Park	Stromschnellen	Fluss	Bach
ESPAÑOL	isla	parque	rápidos	río	arroyo
FRANÇAIS	île	parc	rapides	rivière	ruisseau
PORTUGUÊS	ilha	parque	rápidos	rio	arroio

Kilometers 0 5 10 15 Km.
Statute Miles 0 5 10 15 Mi.

Scale 1:300,000
One centimeter represents 3 kilometers.
One inch represents approximately 4.7 miles.

74°40′
74°30′
74°20′
74°10′
74°
41° 10′
41°
40° 50′
40° 40′
40° 30′
40° 20′
NEW YORK
NEW JERSEY
Newark
Paterson
Passaic
Clifton
Hackensack
Jersey City
Elizabeth
Plainfield
Morristown
New Brunswick
Edison
Perth Amboy
STATEN ISLAND
Hoboken
Bayonne
Princeton
Somerville
Sayreville
East Brunswick
Red Bank
Raritan Bay
Sandy Hook Bay
Lower Bay
Brooklyn
Manhattan
Queens
Suffern
New City
Ramapo Mts.
Hamburg Mts.
Watchung
Union
Summit
Livingston
Montclair
Bloomfield
Irvington
Orange
Wayne
Paramus
Teaneck
Fort Lee
Linden
Rahway
Westfield
Cranford
Piscataway
Keansburg
Middletown
Hazlet
Matawan
Great Swamp National Wildlife Refuge
Newark International Airport

AREA: 8,900 km²
POPULATION: 15,800,000

ENGLISH	bay	brook, br.	creek	harbor	island	lake, l.	point	pond
DEUTSCH	Bucht	Bach	Bach	Hafen	Insel	See	Landspitze	Teich
ESPAÑOL	bahía	arroyo	riachuelo	puerto	isla	lago	punta	charca
FRANÇAIS	baie	ruisseau	ruisseau	port	île	lac	pointe	étang
PORTUGUÊS	baía	arroio	riacho	porto	ilha	lago	ponta	lagoa

73°40'
73°30'
73°20'
73°10'
41° 10'
41°
40° 50'
40° 40'
40° 30'
40° 20'
Bridgeport
Fairfield
Westport
Norwalk
New Canaan
Darien
Stamford
Greenwich
Port Chester
Rye
Harrison
White Plains
Scarsdale
Hartsdale
Mamaroneck
Larchmont
New Rochelle
Pelham
Eastchester
Tuckahoe
Valhalla
Pleasantville
Chappaqua
Briarcliff Manor
Thornwood
Armonk
Hawthorne
Elmsford
Purchase
Long Island Sound
Sound
Island
Long
NEW YORK
CONNECTICUT
WESTCHESTER
FAIRFIELD
Glen Cove
Oyster Bay
Huntington
Huntington Station
Northport
East Northport
Commack
Smithtown
Kings Park
San Remo
St. James
Stony Brook
Setauket
Port Jefferson
Port Jefferson Station
Terryville
Centereach
Selden
Coram
Lake Grove
Hauppauge
Ronkonkoma
Lake Ronkonkoma
Holbrook
Medford
Farmingville
Patchogue
North Patchogue
Bohemia
Sayville
Bayport
Islip
Central Islip
East Islip
Bay Shore
Brentwood
Deer Park
West Babylon
North Babylon
Babylon
Lindenhurst
Copiague
Amityville
Massapequa
Wantagh
Seaford
Bellmore
Merrick
Freeport
Baldwin
Oceanside
Rockville Centre
Lynbrook
Valley Stream
Hempstead
West Hempstead
Garden City
Mineola
Westbury
Hicksville
Plainview
Syosset
Jericho
Levittown
Bethpage
Farmingdale
Melville
Dix Hills
Wyandanch
Manhasset
Great Neck
Port Washington
Roslyn
Flushing
Bayside
Jamaica
Hollis
Elmont
Franklin Square
Long Beach
Point Lookout
Lido Beach
Inwood
Lawrence
Far Rockaway
JOHN F. KENNEDY INTERNATIONAL AIRPORT
LONG ISLAND
LONG
ISLAND
Smithtown Bay
Oyster Bay
Huntington Bay
Great South Bay
South Oyster Bay
Fire Island Inlet
FIRE ISLAND
FIRE ISLAND NATIONAL SEASHORE
Ocean Beach
Davis Park
ROBERT MOSES STATE PARK
JONES BEACH STATE PARK
West Gilgo Beach
ATLANTIC OCEAN
Copyright © by Rand McNally & Co.
Map prepared by Rand McNally & Co.
A-520060-264

Kilometers 0 5 10 15 Km.

Statute Miles 0 5 10 15 Mi.

Scale 1:300,000

One centimeter represents 3 kilometers.

One inch represents approximately 4.7 miles.

88°
87° 50'
87° 40'
87° 30'
87° 20'
42° 20'
42° 10'
42°
41° 50'
41° 40'
41° 30'
LAKE MICHIGAN
(176 Meters Above Sea Level)
ILLINOIS
INDIANA
Waukegan
North Chicago
GREAT LAKES NAVAL TRAINING CENTER
Round Lake Park
Round Lake
Hainesville
Grayslake
Gages Lake
Wildwood
Wilson
Park City
Countryside Manor
Green Oaks
North Hills
Libertyville
Knollwood
Lake Bluff
Rondout
Mundelein
Ivanhoe
Wauconda
Diamond Lake
Sylvan Lake
Lake Forest
Gilmer
Indian Creek
Mettawa
Timber Lake
Hawthorn Woods
Vernon Hills
FORT SHERIDAN
Forest Lake
Half Day
Del Mar Woods
Highwood
Lake Zurich
Prairie View
Bannockburn
Highland Park
Kildeer
Aptakisic
Long Grove
Lincolnshire
Deer Park
Horatio Gardens
Deerfield
Barrington
Barrington Woods
Riverwoods
Buffalo Grove
Wheeling
Glencoe
Inverness
Palatine
Northbrook
Winnetka
South Barrington
Prospect Heights
Arlington Heights
Northfield
Kenilworth
Wilmette
Rolling Meadows
Plum Grove Estates
Mount Prospect
Glenview
Hoffman Estates
Evanston
Schaumburg
Des Plaines
Morton Grove
Skokie
Niles
Park Ridge
Elk Grove Village
CHICAGO-O'HARE INTERNATIONAL AIRPORT
Lincolnwood
Roselle
Medinah
Rosemont
Keeneyville
Itasca
Bloomingdale
Wood Dale
Bensenville
Harwood Heights
Norridge
Schiller Park
Glendale Heights
Addison
Franklin Park
River Grove
Elmwood Park
Carol Stream
Glen Ellyn Countryside
Stone Park
Melrose Park
North Glen Ellyn
Lombard
Elmhurst
Villa Park
River Forest
Oak Park
Glen Ellyn
Glen Oak
Wheaton
Berkeley
Hillside
Bellwood
Maywood
Forest Park
CHICAGO
York Center
Broadview
Berwyn
Cicero
Westchester
Highland Hills
Butterfield
North Riverside
Oak Brook
La Grange Park
Brookfield
Riverside
Valley View
La Grange
Lyons
Stickney
Forest View
Downers Grove
Westmont
Hinsdale
Western Springs
Lisle
Clarendon Hills
La Grange Highlands
Golfview Hills
McCook
Countryside
Summit
Indian Head Park
Hodgkins
Woodridge
Willowbrook
Bedford Park
Nottingham Park
Bridgeview
Darien
Burr Ridge
Justice
Burbank
Tristate Village
Willow Springs
Roberts Park
Hickory Hills
Oak Lawn
Hometown
Evergreen Park
Bolingbrook
Palos Hills
Chicago Ridge
Worth
Merrionette Park
Lemont
Hastings
Palos Park
Palos Heights
Alsip
Whiting
Romeoville
Blue Island
Calumet Park
Riverdale
Hegewisch
Robbins
Posen
Dolton
Burnham
East Chicago
Crestwood
Midlothian
Calumet City
Orland Park
Oak Forest
Harvey
Phoenix
Hammond
Gary
Markham
South Holland
Lockport
Westhaven
Tinley Park
Hazel Crest
East Hazel Crest
Thornton
Lansing
Munster
Highland
Crest Hill
Homewood
Homewood Acres
Marley
Country Club Hills
Flossmoor
Ross
Joliet
Arbury Hills
Sunny Crest
Glenwood
Ingalls Park
Cherry Hill
Mokena
Crawford Countryside
Olympia Fields
Hollybrook
Lynwood
Griffith
Chicago Heights
East Chicago Heights
Schererville
New Lenox
Lincolnwood Hills
Lincoln Estates
Frankfort
Matteson
Dyer
Merrillville
Copyright by Rand McNally & Co.
Map prepared by Rand McNally & Co.

ENGLISH	airport	creek, cr.	harbor	lake, l.	park	woods
DEUTSCH	Flughafen	Bach	Hafen	See	Park	Gehölz
ESPAÑOL	aeropuerto	riachuelo	puerto	lago	parque	bosques
FRANÇAIS	aéroport	crique	port	lac	parc	bois
PORTUGUÊS	aeroporto	riacho	porto	lago	parque	bosques

Kilometers 0 5 10 15 Km.

Statute Miles 0 5 10 15 Mi.

Scale 1:300,000

One centimeter represents 3 kilometers.

One inch represents approximately 4.7 miles.

a

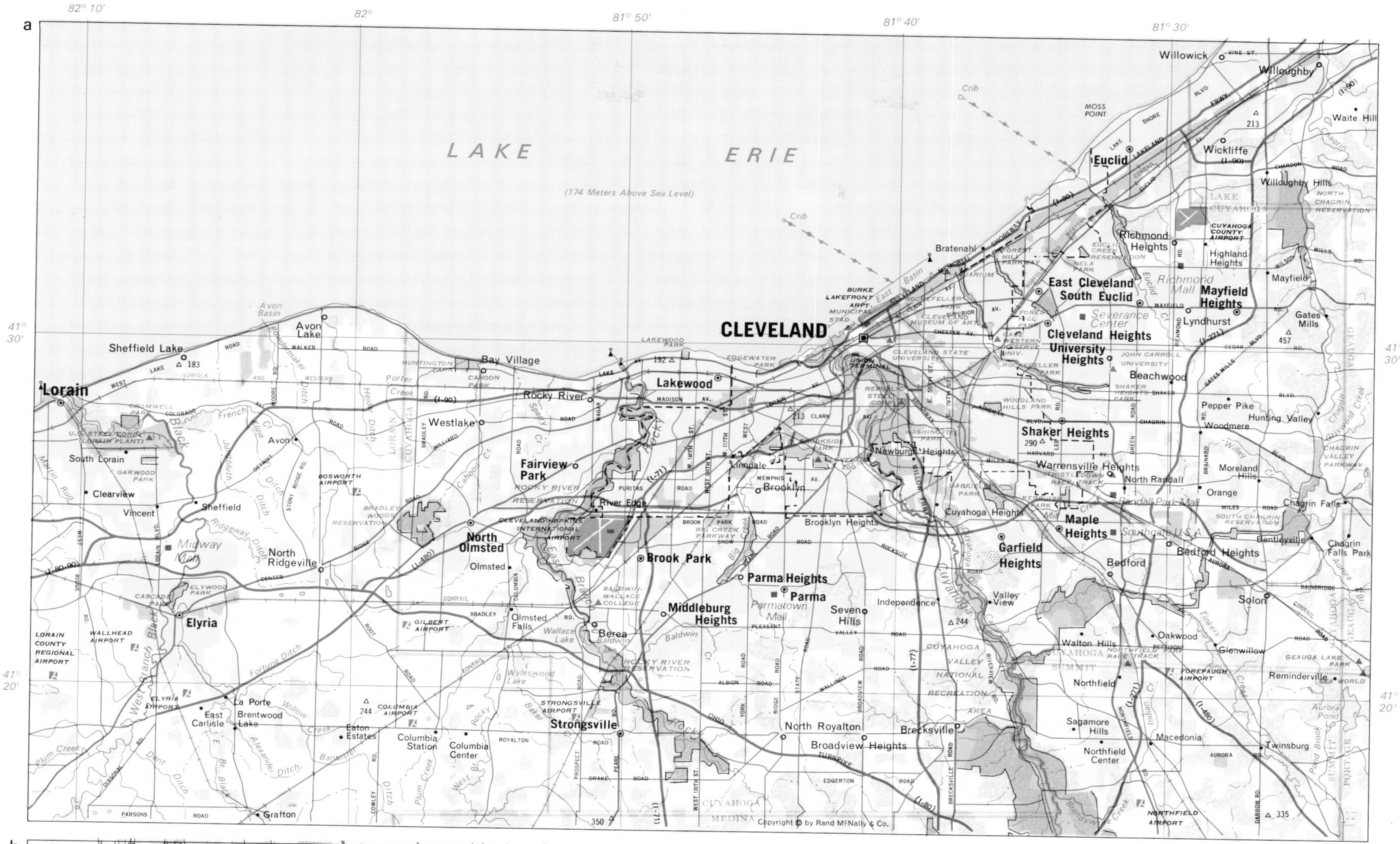
LAKE ERIE
(174 Meters Above Sea Level)
CLEVELAND
Lorain
Sheffield Lake
Avon Lake
Bay Village
Rocky River
Lakewood
Westlake
Avon
Fairview Park
North Olmsted
Olmsted Falls
Berea
Brook Park
Parma Heights
Parma
Middleburg Heights
Strongsville
North Royalton
Broadview Heights
Brecksville
Seven Hills
Independence
Garfield Heights
Maple Heights
Bedford
Solon
Shaker Heights
Cleveland Heights
University Heights
East Cleveland
South Euclid
Euclid
Richmond Heights
Mayfield Heights
Lyndhurst
Beachwood
Willowick
Willoughby
Wickliffe
Elyria
North Ridgeville
Sheffield
Clearview
Vincent
South Lorain
Grafton
Columbia Station
Columbia Center
Eaton Estates
La Porte
Macedonia
Twinsburg
Northfield
Chagrin Falls
Copyright © by Rand McNally & Co.

b

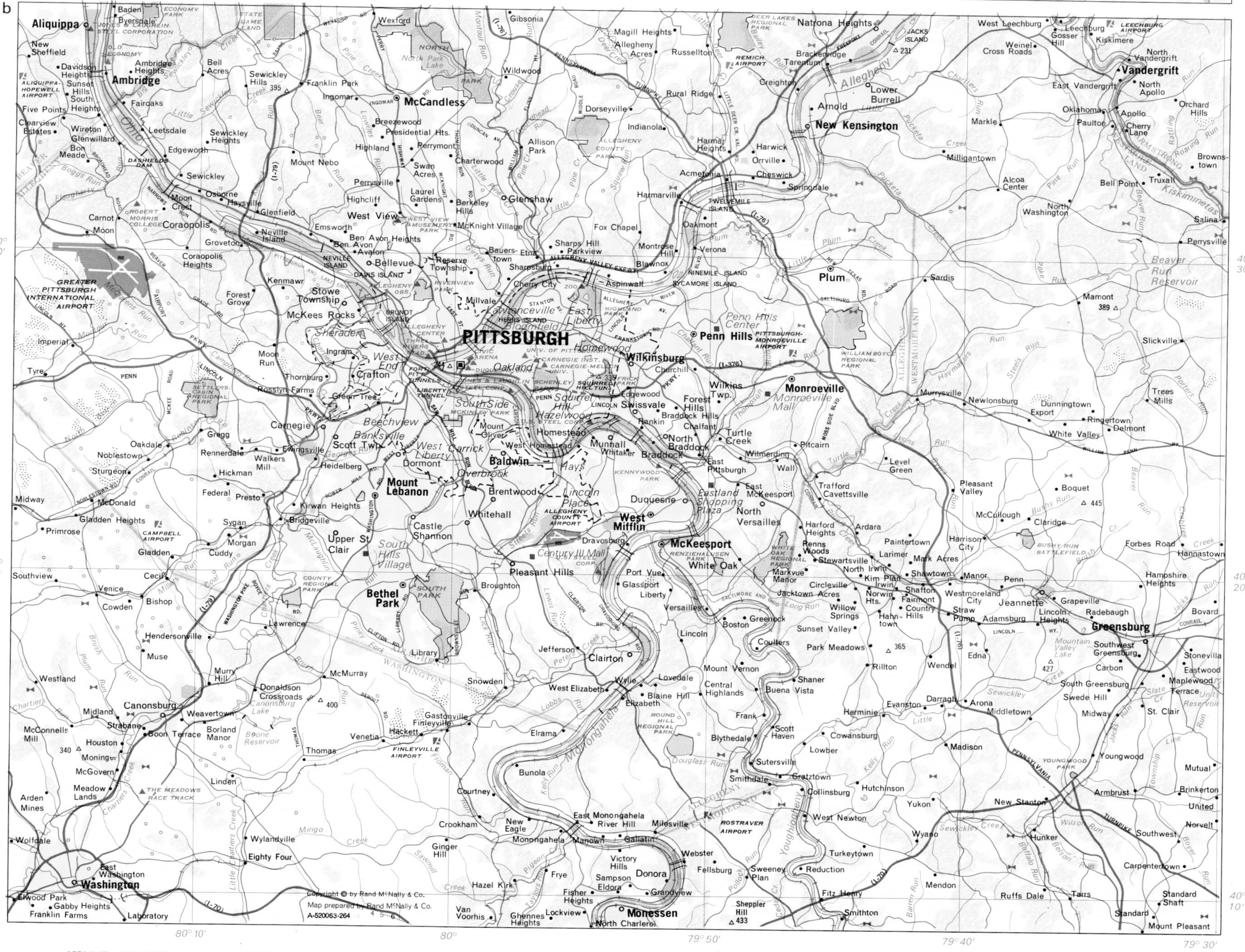
PITTSBURGH
Aliquippa
Ambridge
Sewickley
Coraopolis
GREATER PITTSBURGH INTERNATIONAL AIRPORT
McCandless
Bellevue
Wilkinsburg
Penn Hills
Plum
New Kensington
Vandergrift
Monroeville
Mount Lebanon
Baldwin
Bethel Park
West Mifflin
McKeesport
Clairton
White Oak
Greensburg
Jeannette
Canonsburg
Washington
Monessen
Donora
Charleroi
Carnegie
Crafton
Upper St. Clair
Pleasant Hills
Elizabeth
Irwin
North Irwin
Murrysville
Copyright © by Rand McNally & Co.
Map prepared by Rand McNally & Co.
A-520063-264

	AREA (km²)	POPULATION
CLEVELAND	1,900	1,850,000
PITTSBURGH	3,800	1,950,000

ENGLISH	creek, cr.	ditch	island	lake, l.	park	reservoir	run
DEUTSCH	Bach	Graben	Insel	See	Park	Stausee	Bach
ESPAÑOL	riachuelo	acequia	isla	lago	parque	embalse	arroyo
FRANÇAIS	crique	fossé	île	lac	parc	réservoir	ruisseau
PORTUGUÊS	riacho	fosso	ilha	lago	parque	reservatório	córrego

Kilometers 0 5 10 15 Km.
Statute Miles 0 5 10 15 Mi.

Scale 1:300,000
One centimeter represents 3 kilometers.
One inch represents approximately 4.7 miles.

LOS ANGELES
PACIFIC OCEAN
SAN GABRIEL MOUNTAINS
SANTA MONICA MOUNTAINS
SANTA ANA MOUNTAINS
SAN FERNANDO VALLEY
PUENTE HILLS
CHINO HILLS
SAN JOSE HILLS
Santa Monica Bay
San Pedro Bay
San Pedro Channel
Pasadena
Glendale
Burbank
Beverly Hills
Santa Monica
Inglewood
Long Beach
Anaheim
Santa Ana
Pomona
Ontario
Fullerton
Torrance
Whittier
Downey
Norwalk
East Los Angeles
Redondo Beach
Seal Beach
Garden Grove
Orange
Upland
Montclair
Claremont
Azusa
Covina
West Covina
El Monte
Alhambra
Monterey Park
Compton
Lakewood
Cerritos
Huntington Park
Gardena
Hawthorne
Manhattan Beach
Hermosa Beach
Rancho Palos Verdes
Culver City
West Hollywood
Altadena
Arcadia
Monrovia
Glendora
San Dimas
La Verne
Chino
Diamond Bar
Yorba Linda
Placentia
Brea
La Habra
Buena Park
Cypress
Westminster
Fountain Valley
Stanton
Tustin
Carson
Paramount
Bellflower
Bell Gardens
Pico Rivera
Montebello
Rosemead
Temple City
San Gabriel
South Pasadena
Northridge
San Fernando
Sepulveda
Van Nuys
Sherman Oaks
Encino
Tarzana
Canoga Park
Woodland Hills
Chatsworth
Topanga
Malibu
Pacific Palisades
Venice
Marina del Rey
El Segundo
Wilmington
San Pedro
118°30′
118°20′
118°10′
118°
117°50′
117°40′
34°10′
34°
33°50′

Kilometers 0 5 10 15 Km.
Statute Miles 0 5 10 15 Mi.

Scale 1:300,000
One centimeter represents 3 kilometers.
One inch represents approximately 4.7 miles.

ENGLISH	canyon	college	creek	dam	hills	mount	park	peak	reservoir
DEUTSCH	Cañon	College	Bach	Damm	Hügel	Berg	Park	Gipfel	Stausee
ESPAÑOL	cañón	escuela	riachuelo	diques	colinas	montaña	parque	pico	estanque
FRANÇAIS	canyon	collège	crique	barrage	collines	mont	parc	cime	réservoir
PORTUGUÊS	canhão	colégio	riacho	represa	colinas	monte	parque	pico	reservatório

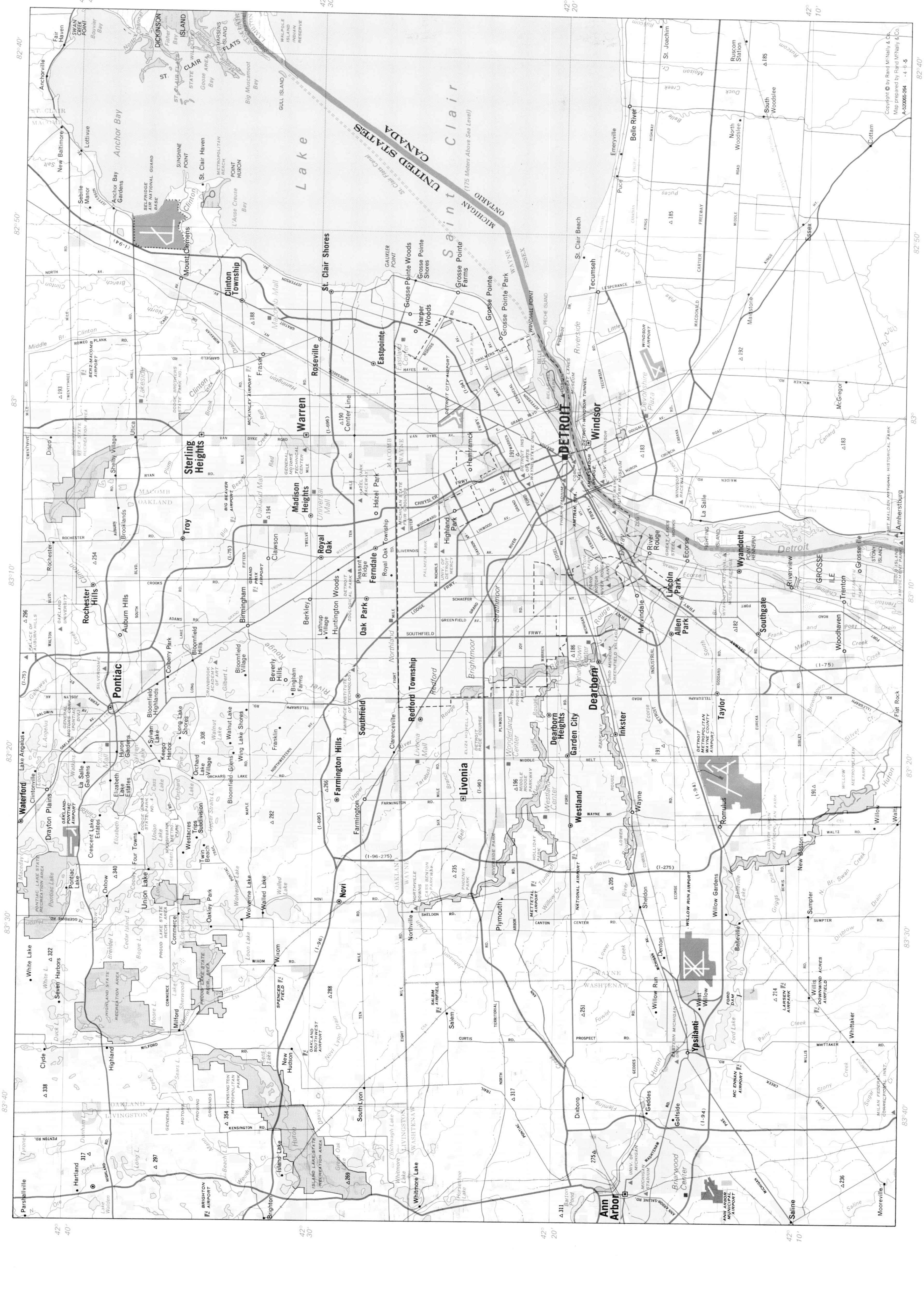

DETROIT
Windsor
UNITED STATES
CANADA
MICHIGAN
ONTARIO
Lake Saint Clair
Detroit
Pontiac
Warren
Sterling Heights
Troy
Royal Oak
Southfield
Livonia
Dearborn
Westland
Ann Arbor
Ypsilanti
Novi
Farmington Hills
Rochester Hills
Clinton Township
St. Clair Shores
Eastpointe
Roseville
Madison Heights
Ferndale
Hamtramck
Highland Park
Redford Township
Garden City
Inkster
Taylor
Lincoln Park
Allen Park
Southgate
Wyandotte
Trenton
Romulus
Belleville
Plymouth
Northville
Tecumseh
Amherstburg
Essex

Kilometers 0 5 10 15 Km.
Statute Miles 0 5 10 15 Mi.

Scale 1:300,000

One centimeter represents 3 kilometers.
One inch represents approximately 4.7 miles.

ENGLISH	bay	channel	creek, cr.	island	lake, l.	point
DEUTSCH	Bucht	Kanal	Bach	Insel	See	Landspitze
ESPAÑOL	bahía	canal	riachuelo	isla	lago	punta
FRANÇAIS	baie	détroit	crique	île	lac	pointe
PORTUGUÊS	baía	canal	riacho	ilha	lago	ponta

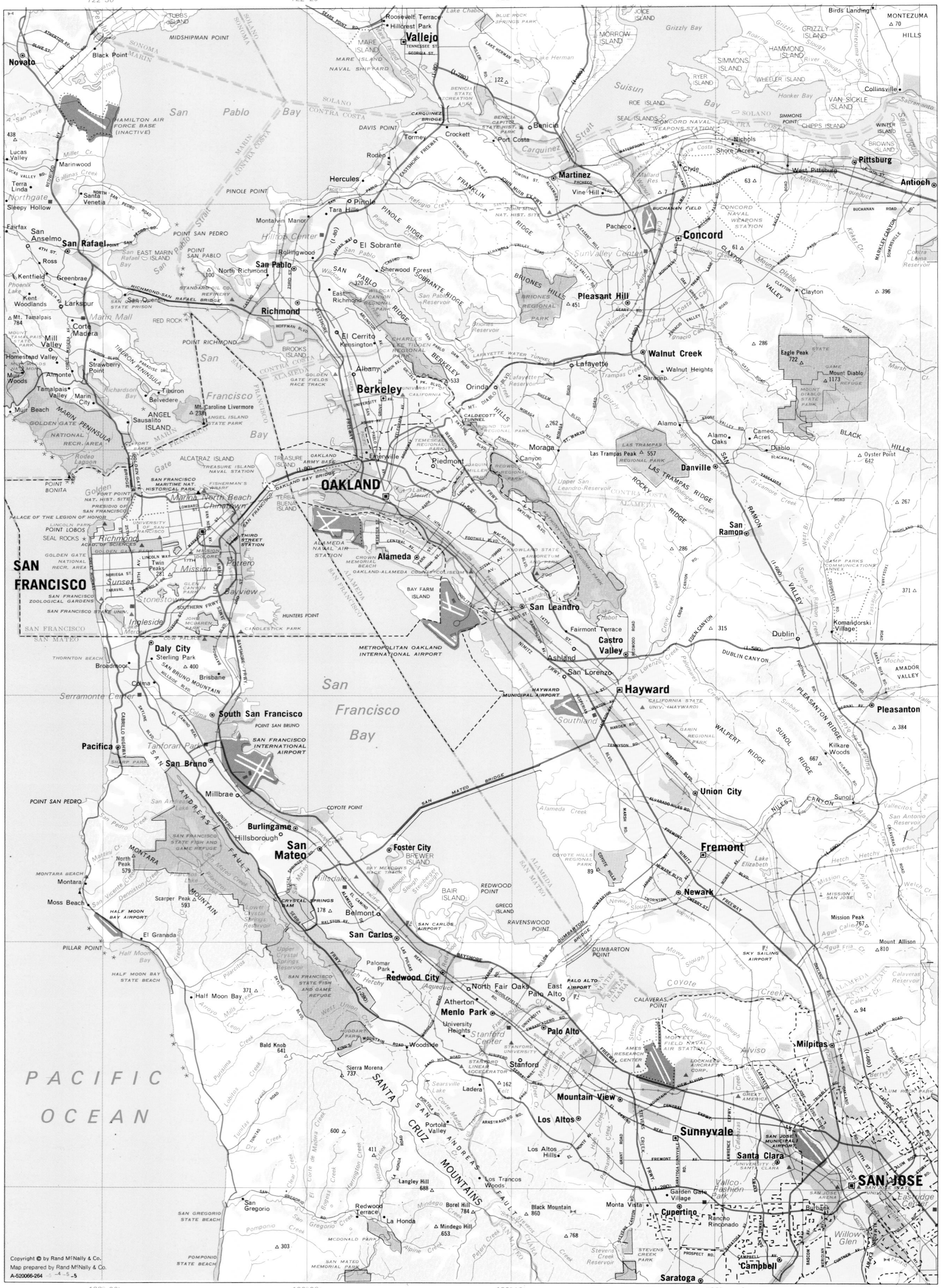

122°30′
122°20′
122°10′
122°
121°50′
38°
37° 50′
37° 40′
37° 30′
37° 20′
Novato
San Pablo Bay
Vallejo
Suisun Bay
Benicia
Martinez
Pittsburg
Antioch
Concord
Pleasant Hill
Walnut Creek
San Rafael
Richmond
Berkeley
OAKLAND
SAN FRANCISCO
Alameda
San Leandro
Hayward
Castro Valley
Daly City
South San Francisco
San Francisco Bay
Pacifica
San Bruno
Burlingame
San Mateo
Foster City
Redwood City
Menlo Park
Palo Alto
Mountain View
Sunnyvale
Santa Clara
SAN JOSE
Milpitas
Fremont
Union City
Newark
Pleasanton
Dublin
San Ramon
Danville
Cupertino
Campbell
Saratoga
Los Altos
Half Moon Bay
PACIFIC OCEAN
SANTA CRUZ MOUNTAINS
SAN ANDREAS FAULT
Mount Diablo

ENGLISH	bay	beach	creek, cr.	island	lake	point	reservoir
DEUTSCH	Bucht	Strand	Bach	Insel	See	Punkt	Stausee
ESPAÑOL	bahia	playa	riachuelo	isla	lago	punta	estanque
FRANÇAIS	baie	plage	crique	île	lac	pointe	réservoir
PORTUGUÊS	baia	praia	riacho	ilha	lago	ponta	reservatório

Kilometers 0 5 10 15 Km.
Statute Miles 0 5 10 15 Mi.

Scale 1:300,000

One centimeter represents 3 kilometers.
One inch represents approximately 4.7 miles.

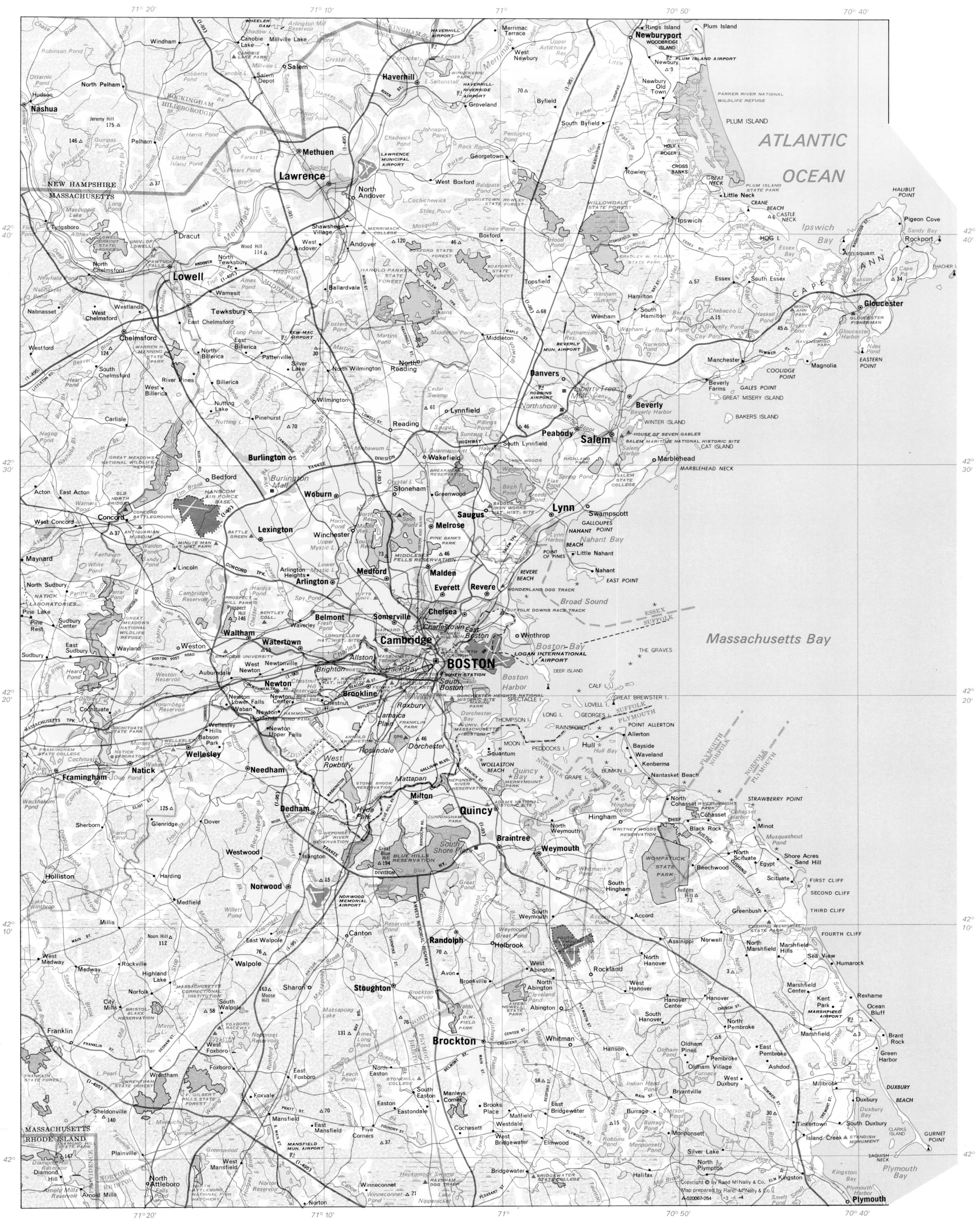
71° 20'
71° 10'
71°
70° 50'
70° 40'
42° 40'
42° 30'
42° 20'
42° 10'
42°
ATLANTIC OCEAN
Massachusetts Bay
Ipswich Bay
Cape Ann
Broad Sound
Nahant Bay
Boston Bay
Boston Harbor
Quincy Bay
Hingham Bay
Plymouth Bay
Duxbury Bay
Kingston Bay
NEW HAMPSHIRE
MASSACHUSETTS
RHODE ISLAND
ROCKINGHAM
HILLSBOROUGH
ESSEX
MIDDLESEX
SUFFOLK
NORFOLK
PLYMOUTH
BRISTOL
BOSTON
Cambridge
Lawrence
Lowell
Haverhill
Methuen
Newburyport
Nashua
Salem
Lynn
Peabody
Beverly
Danvers
Gloucester
Rockport
Marblehead
Swampscott
Saugus
Melrose
Malden
Medford
Everett
Revere
Chelsea
Somerville
Arlington
Belmont
Watertown
Waltham
Newton
Brookline
Lexington
Woburn
Winchester
Burlington
Wakefield
Reading
Stoneham
Concord
Bedford
Wellesley
Needham
Natick
Framingham
Dedham
Milton
Quincy
Braintree
Weymouth
Hingham
Hull
Norwood
Westwood
Walpole
Canton
Randolph
Stoughton
Brockton
Holbrook
Rockland
Abington
Whitman
Sharon
Foxboro
Wrentham
Franklin
Norfolk
Medfield
Millis
Medway
Holliston
Sherborn
Dover
Plymouth
Kingston
Duxbury
Marshfield
Scituate
Cohasset
Hanover
Pembroke
Halifax
Bridgewater
Easton
Mansfield
North Attleboro
Plainville
Andover
North Andover
Tewksbury
Chelmsford
Billerica
Wilmington
Dracut
Tyngsboro
Westford
Carlisle
Acton
Maynard
Sudbury
Wayland
Weston
Lincoln
Ipswich
Rowley
Newbury
Georgetown
Groveland
Boxford
Topsfield
Hamilton
Wenham
Essex
Manchester
Middleton
Lynnfield
Nahant
Winthrop
LOGAN INTERNATIONAL AIRPORT
BLUE HILLS RESERVATION
MIDDLESEX FELLS RESERVATION
PLUM ISLAND
PARKER RIVER NATIONAL WILDLIFE REFUGE
Copyright © by Rand McNally & Co.
Map prepared by Rand McNally & Co.
A-520067-264

AREA: 5,150 km²
POPULATION: 3,625,000

ENGLISH	bay	brook	island, i.	lake, l.	point	pond	reservation
DEUTSCH	Bucht	Bach	Insel	See	Landspitze	Teich	Reservat
ESPAÑOL	bahía	arroyo	isla	lago	punta	charca	parque nacional
FRANÇAIS	baie	ruisseau	île	lac	pointe	étang	réservation
PORTUGUÊS	baía	arroio	ilha	lago	ponta	lagoa	parque nacional

Kilometers 0 5 10 15 Km.
Statute Miles 0 5 10 15 Mi.

Scale 1:300,000
One centimeter represents 3 kilometers.
One inch represents approximately 4.7 miles.

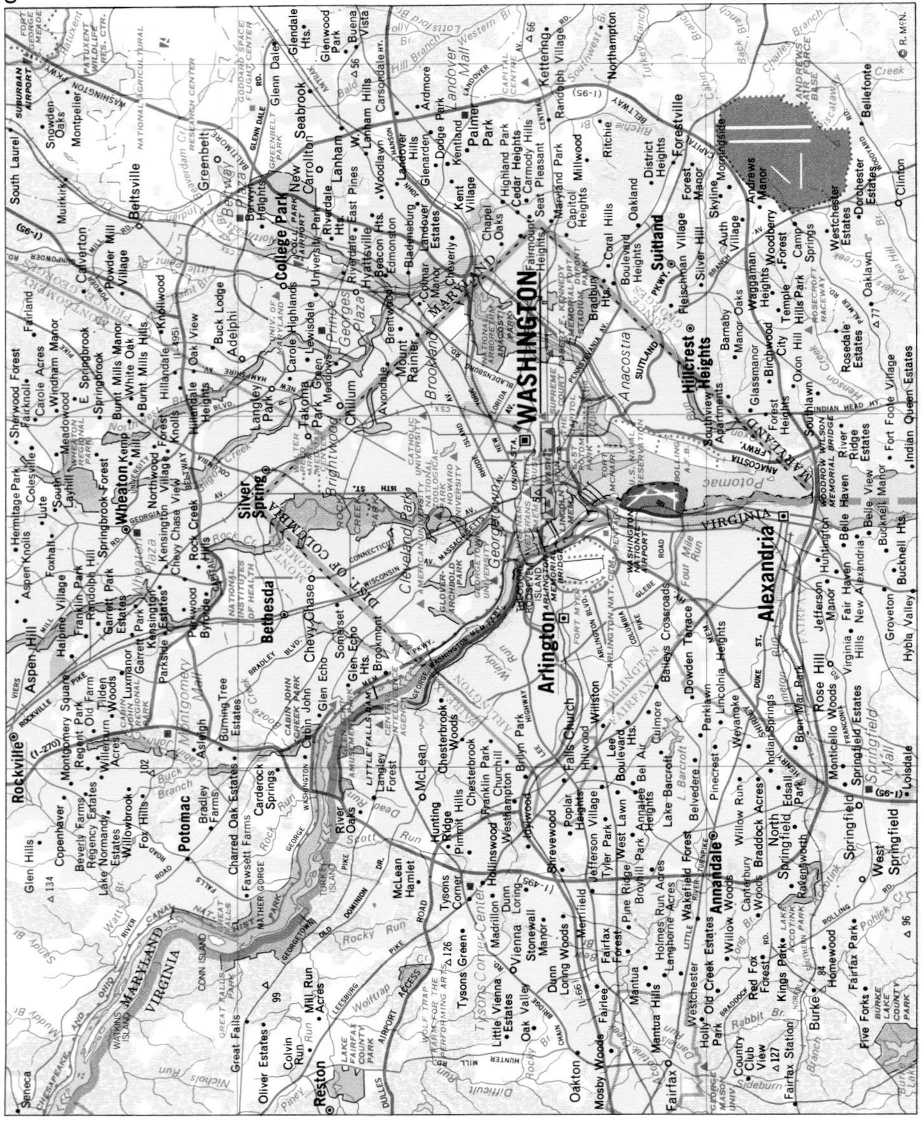

Kilometers 0 5 10 15 Km.
Statute Miles 0 5 10 15 Mi.

Scale 1:300,000
One centimeter represents 3 kilometers.
One inch represents approximately 4.7 miles.

ENGLISH	DEUTSCH	ESPAÑOL	FRANÇAIS	PORTUGUÊS
airport	Flughafen	aeropuerto	aéroport	aeroporto
bridge	Brücke	puente	pont	ponte
creek, cr.	Bach	riachuelo	crique	riacho
island, i.	Insel	isla	île	ilha
park	Park	parque	parc	parque
point	Landspitze	punta	pointe	ponta
run	Bach	arroyo	ruisseau	córrego
university	Universität	universidad	université	universidade

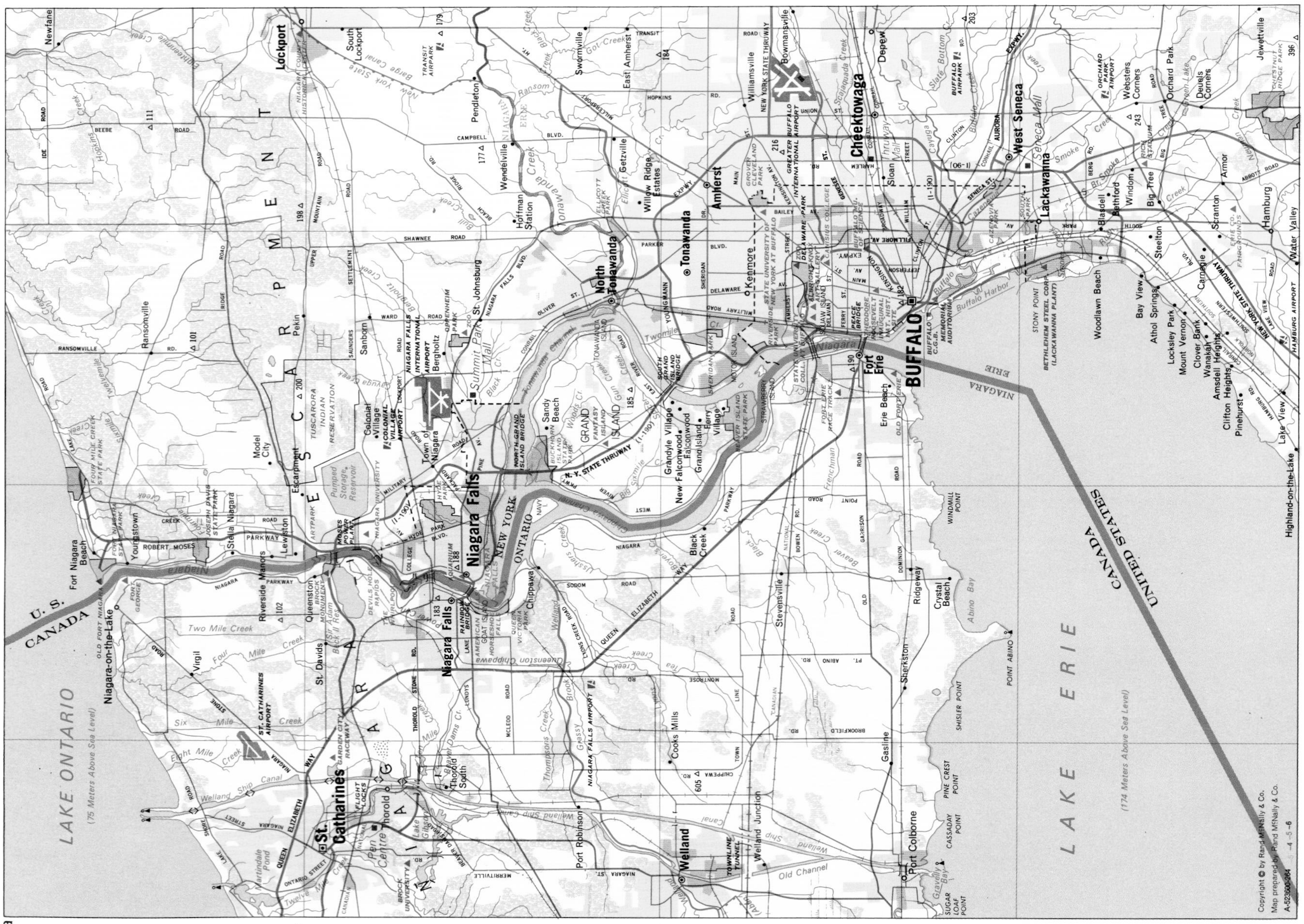

PHILADELPHIA
Camden
Trenton
Wilmington
Chester
Norristown
WHARTON STATE FOREST
DELAWARE
NEW JERSEY
PENNSYLVANIA
Copyright © by Rand McNally & Co.
Map prepared by Rand McNally & Co.

Kilometers 0 5 10 15 Km.
Statute Miles 0 5 10 15 Mi.

Scale 1:300,000
One centimeter represents 3 kilometers.
One inch represents approximately 4.7 miles.

ENGLISH	airport	bridge	college	creek, cr.	island, i.	lake, l.	run	state park
DEUTSCH	Flughafen	Brücke	College	Bach	Insel	See	Bach	Staatspark
ESPAÑOL	aeropuerto	puente	escuela	riachuelo	isla	lago	arroyo	parque del estado
FRANÇAIS	aéroport	pont	collège	crique	île	lac	ruisseau	parc régional
PORTUGUÊS	aeroporto	ponte	escola	riacho	ilha	lago	córrego	parque estadual

a

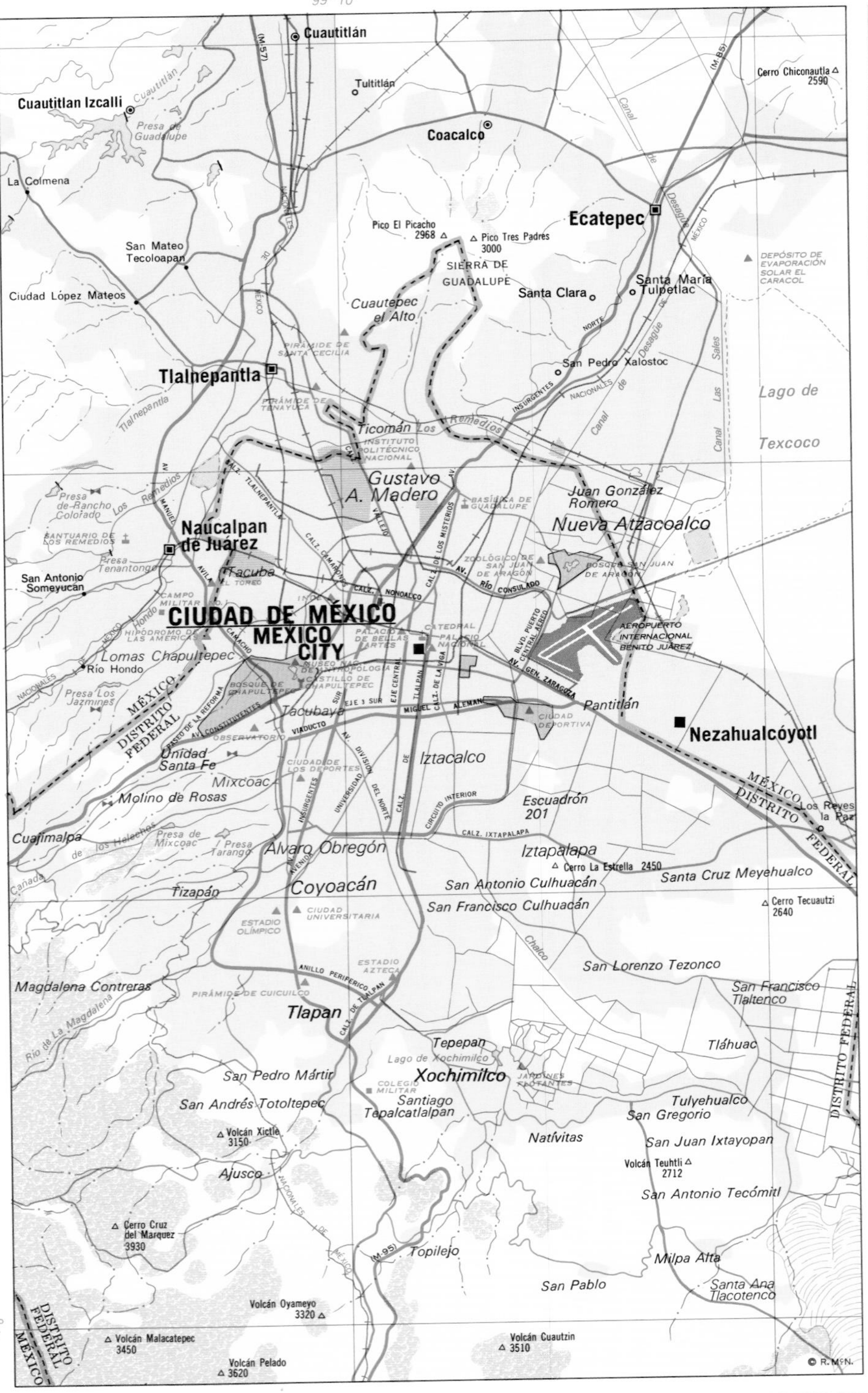

CIUDAD DE MÉXICO
MEXICO CITY
Cuautitlán
Cuautitlan Izcalli
Tultitlán
Coacalco
Ecatepec
Tlalnepantla
Santa Clara
Santa María Tulpetlac
San Pedro Xalostoc
Lago de Texcoco
Gustavo A. Madero
Juan González Romero
Nueva Atzacoalco
Naucalpan de Juárez
Lomas Chapultepec
Río Hondo
Tacubaya
Pantitlán
Nezahualcóyotl
Iztacalco
Mixcoac
Escuadrón 201
Iztapalapa
Álvaro Obregón
Coyoacán
Cuajimalpa
Tizapán
San Antonio Culhuacán
San Francisco Culhuacán
Santa Cruz Meyehualco
Magdalena Contreras
San Lorenzo Tezonco
Tlalpan
Xochimilco
Tláhuac
San Pedro Mártir
San Andrés Totoltepec
Santiago Tepalcatlalpan
San Gregorio
Tulyehualco
Nativitas
San Juan Ixtayopan
Ajusco
San Antonio Tecómitl
Topilejo
Milpa Alta
San Pablo
Santa Ana Tlacotenco
Volcán Oyameyo 3320
Volcán Malacatepec 3450
Volcán Pelado 3620
Volcán Cuautzin 3510
Cerro Chiconautla 2590
Pico Tres Padres 3000
Sierra de Guadalupe
DISTRITO FEDERAL
MÉXICO
© R. McN.

b

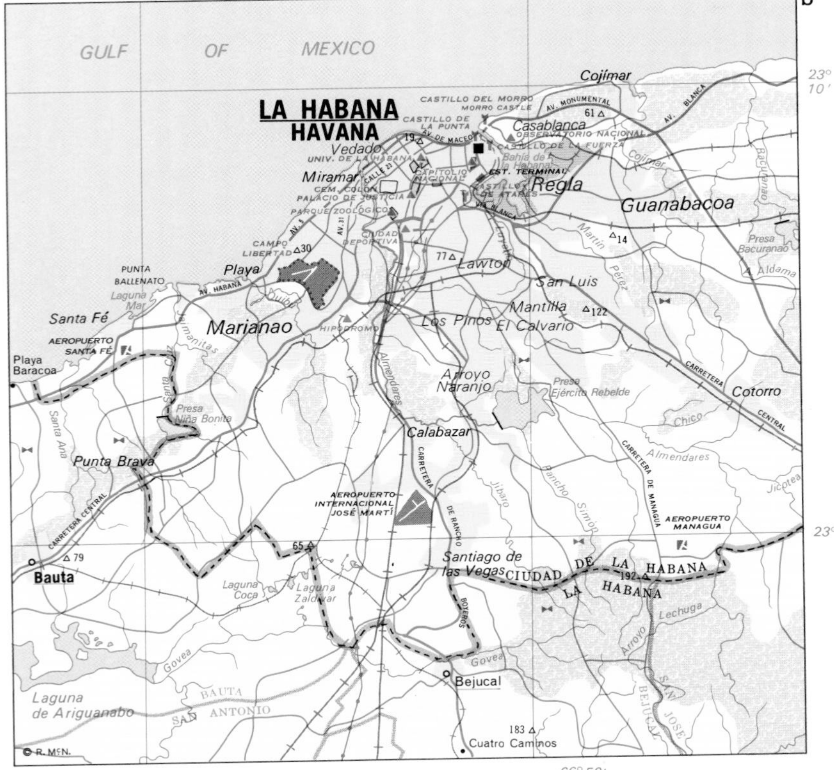

GULF OF MEXICO
LA HABANA
HAVANA
Cojímar
Casablanca
Regla
Guanabacoa
Vedado
Miramar
Playa
Lawton
San Luis
Mantilla
Marianao
Santa Fé
Los Pinos
El Calvario
Playa Baracoa
Arroyo Naranjo
Cotorro
Calabazar
Punta Brava
Bauta
Santiago de las Vegas
Bejucal
Laguna de Ariguanabo
Cuatro Caminos
© R. McN.

c

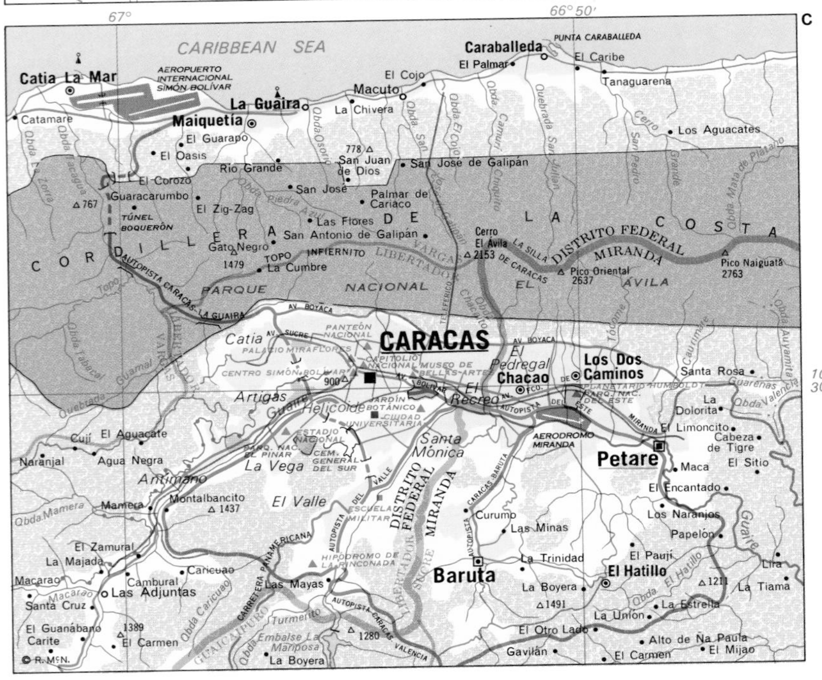

CARIBBEAN SEA
Caraballeda
Catia La Mar
Macuto
La Guaira
Maiquetía
Tanaguarena
CORDILLERA DE LA COSTA
PARQUE NACIONAL EL ÁVILA
DISTRITO FEDERAL
MIRANDA
CARACAS
Catia
El Pedregal
Chacao
Los Dos Caminos
Petare
Artigas
La Vega
Santa Mónica
El Valle
Antímano
Baruta
El Hatillo
Las Adjuntas
Pico Naiguatá 2763
© R. McN.

d

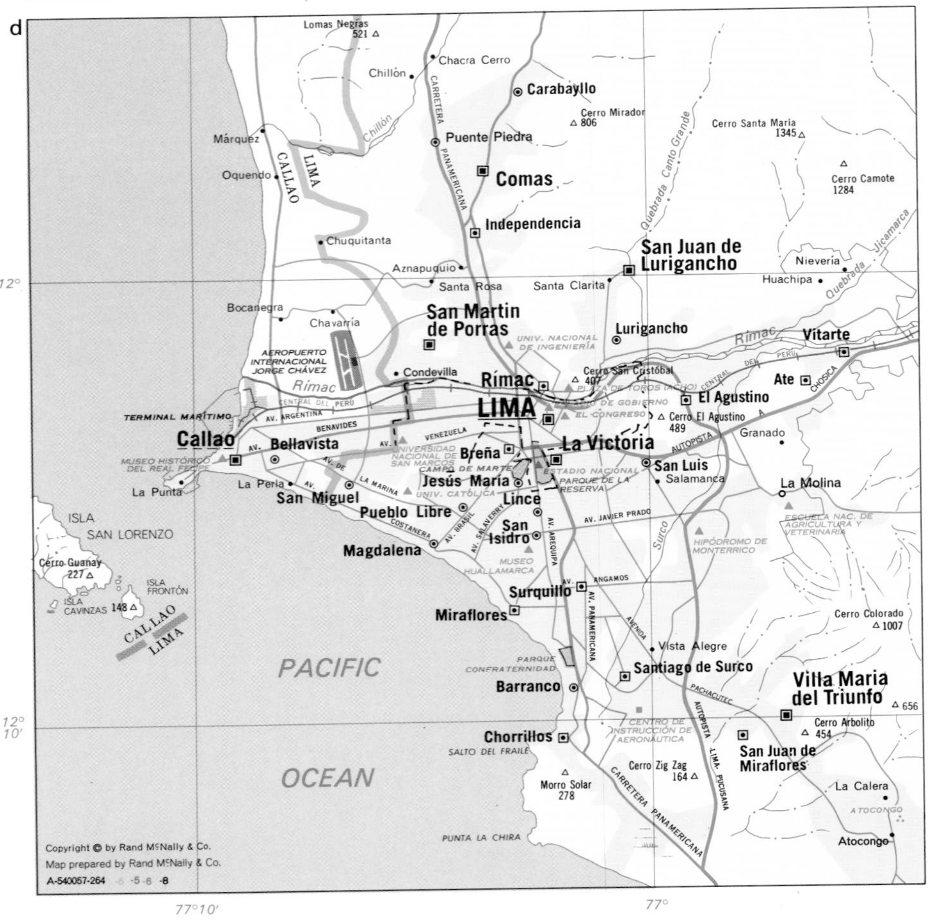

LIMA
Carabayllo
Puente Piedra
Comas
Independencia
San Juan de Lurigancho
San Martín de Porras
Lurigancho
Vitarte
Ate
Callao
Bellavista
La Perla
La Punta
Rímac
El Agustino
La Victoria
Breña
Jesús María
San Luis
San Miguel
Pueblo Libre
Lince
San Isidro
Magdalena
La Molina
Surquillo
Miraflores
Santiago de Surco
Barranco
Villa María del Triunfo
Chorrillos
San Juan de Miraflores
Isla San Lorenzo
PACIFIC OCEAN
Atocongo

e

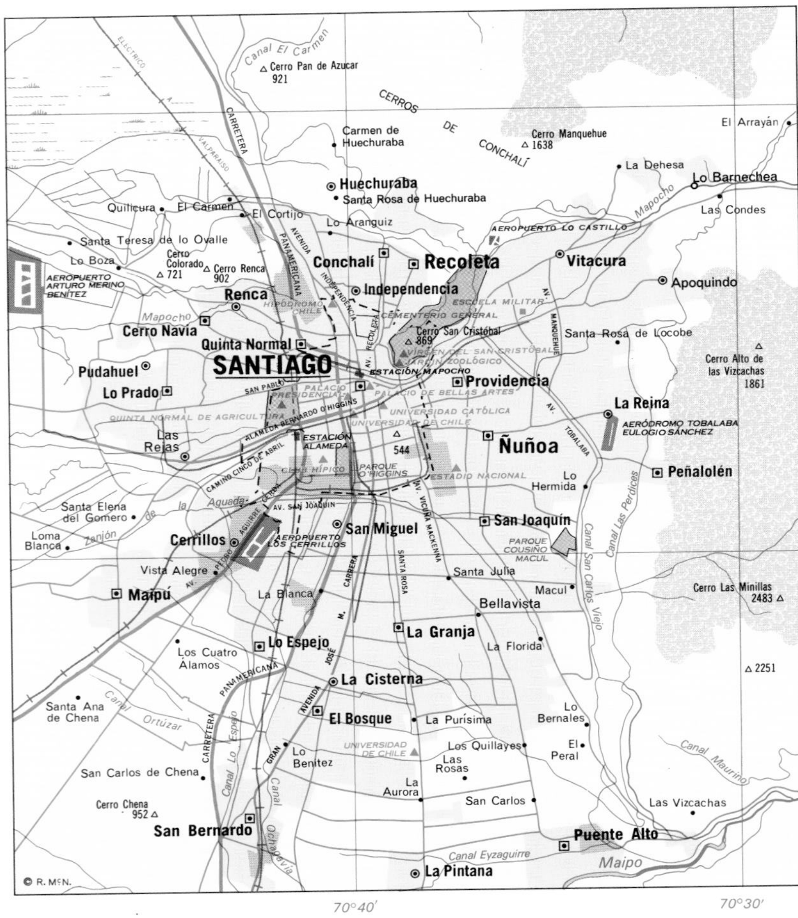

SANTIAGO
Huechuraba
Conchalí
Recoleta
Vitacura
Lo Barnechea
Renca
Independencia
Cerro Navia
Quinta Normal
Pudahuel
Lo Prado
Providencia
La Reina
Ñuñoa
Peñalolén
Cerrillos
San Miguel
San Joaquín
Maipú
Lo Espejo
La Granja
La Cisterna
El Bosque
San Bernardo
La Pintana
Puente Alto
© R. McN.

ESPAÑOL	arroyo	castillo	isla	laguna	presa	quebrada
ENGLISH	brook	castle	island	lagoon	reservoir	creek
DEUTSCH	Bach	Burg	Insel	Haff	Stausee	Bach
FRANÇAIS	ruisseau	château	île	lagune	réservoir	crique
PORTUGUÊS	arroio	castelo	ilha	laguna	reservatório	riacho

Kilometers 0 5 10 15 Km.

Statute Miles 0 5 10 15 Mi.

Scale 1:300,000

One centimeter represents 3 kilometers.
One inch represents approximately 4.7 miles.

a

43°30'
43°20'
43°10'
43°
22° 40'
22° 50'
23°
Queimados
Nova Iguaçu
Belford Roxo
Mesquita
Coelho da Rocha
Duque de Caxias
São João de Meriti
Nilópolis
São Mateus
Olinda
Campos Elísios
Magé
Cava
Guia de Pacobaíba
São Gonçalo
Neves
Sete Pontes
Niterói
RIO DE JANEIRO
Baía de Guanabara
ILHA DO GOVERNADOR
AEROPORTO INTERNACIONAL (GALEÃO)
ILHA DE PAQUETÁ
SERRA DE MADUREIRA
SERRA DA MISERICÓRDIA
Pico da Tijuca 1022
PARQUE NACIONAL DA TIJUCA
Pão de Açúcar 404 Sugar Loaf
Morro do Corcovado 704
Copacabana
Ipanema
Leblon
Botafogo
Tijuca
Jacarepaguá
Campo Grande
Bangu
Realengo
Santíssimo
Inhoaíba
Cosmos
Ilha
Vargem Grande
Barra da Tijuca
PONTA DO MARISCO
PRAIA DOS BANDEIRANTES
RESTINGA DA MARAMBAIA
ILHA DO BOM JARDIM
Morro de Guaratiba 355
ILHA RASA DA GUARATIBA
PONTA DA PRAIA FUNDA
ILHAS CAGARRAS
ILHA RASA
ILHA REDONDA
ATLANTIC
OCEAN
Copyright © by Rand McNally & Co.

b

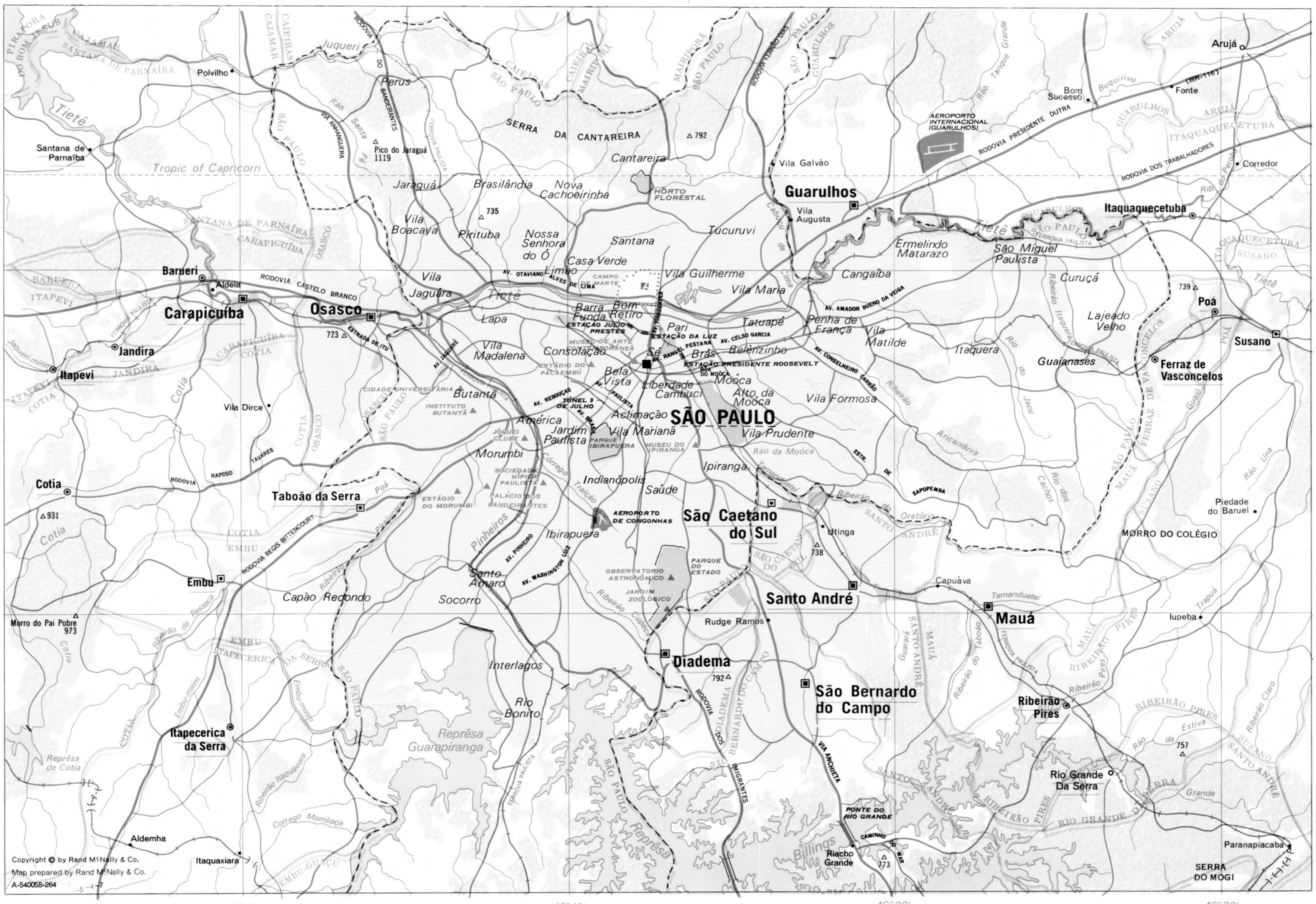
Polvilho
Santana de Parnaíba
Tietê
Tropic of Capricorn
SERRA DA CANTAREIRA
Pico do Jaraguá 1119
Cantareira
HORTO FLORESTAL
AEROPORTO INTERNACIONAL (GUARULHOS)
Guarulhos
Arujá
Itaquaquecetuba
Barueri
Carapicuíba
Osasco
Jandira
Itapevi
Vila Dirce
Cotia
Taboão da Serra
Embu
Morro do Pai Pobre 973
Itapecerica da Serra
Aldemha
Itaquaxiara
SÃO PAULO
Butantã
Morumbi
Ibirapuera
AEROPORTO DE CONGONHAS
São Caetano do Sul
Santo André
Mauá
Diadema
São Bernardo do Campo
Ribeirão Pires
Rio Grande Da Serra
Paranapiacaba
SERRA DO MOGI
Poá
Susano
Ferraz de Vasconcelos
Guaianases
Santo Amaro
Socorro
Interlagos
Capão Redondo
Represa Guarapiranga
Billings
Riacho Grande
Rudge Ramos
MORRO DO COLÉGIO
Copyright © by Rand McNally & Co.
Map prepared by Rand McNally & Co.
A-540058-264
46°50'
46°40'
46°30'
46°20'
23° 30'
23° 40'

PORTUGUÊS	ilha	lagoa, l.	morro	ponta	reservatório	ribeirão, raõ.
ENGLISH	island	lagoon	hill	point	reservoir	creek
DEUTSCH	Insel	Haff	Hügel	Landspitze	Stausee	Bach
ESPAÑOL	isla	laguna	colina	punta	embalse	riachuelo
FRANÇAIS	île	lagune	colline	pointe	réservoir	crique

Kilometers 0 5 10 15 Km.
Statute Miles 0 5 10 15 Mi.

Scale 1:300,000
One centimeter represents 3 kilometers.
One inch represents approximately 4.7 miles.

Kilometers 0 5 10 15 Km.
Statute Miles 0 5 10 15 Mi.
Scale 1:300,000
One centimeter represents 3 kilometers.
One inch represents approximately 4.7 miles.

ESPAÑOL	ENGLISH	DEUTSCH	FRANÇAIS	PORTUGUÊS
aeropuerto	airport	Flughafen	aéroport	aeroporto
arroyo	brook	Bach	ruisseau	arroio
estación	station	Bahnhof	gare	estação
isla	island	Insel	île	ilha
parque	park	Park	parc	parque
punta	point	Landspitze	pointe	ponta

RÍO DE LA PLATA
URUGUAY
COLONIA
Colonia del Sacramento
Real de San Carlos
ARGENTINA
BUENOS AIRES
La Plata
Berisso
Ensenada
Quilmes
Avellaneda
Lanús
Lomas de Zamora
Almirante Brown (Adrogué)
Berazategui
Florencio Varela
Esteban Echeverría (Monte Grande)
San Justo
Morón
Merlo
Moreno
General Sarmiento (San Miguel)
General San Martín
Caseros (Tres de Febrero)
Vicente López
San Isidro
San Fernando
Tigre
Belén de Escobar
AEROPUERTO INTERNACIONAL DE EZEIZA
Río de la Matanza
Copyright © by Rand McNally & Co.
Map prepared by Rand McNally & Co.
A-540003-284

THE MAP FORM column of the glossary lists in alphabetical order the geographical terms, including any abbreviations, that appear on the maps. Terms preceded by a hyphen are those which commonly appear as endings in map names (for example, -san in Fuji-san, -älven in Dalälven). The languages of the terms are identified by abbreviations in *italics* (see Abbreviations of Language Names below). The glossary provides the English, German, Spanish, French, and Portuguese equivalent for each term.

As a rule, the translations were made from the map form to English, then from English into the other four languages. Since the glossary terms and translations refer to specific map features, some may vary from the customary dictionary definitions of the terms.

IN DER SPALTE "Geographische Begriffe" werden alle Begriffe und Abkürzungen in alphabetischer Ordnung aufgeführt, die in den Karten erscheinen. Begriffe mit vorgesetztem Bindestrich erscheinen normalerweise als Wortendungen in Kartennamen (z.B. -san in Fuji-san, -älven in Dalälven). In *Kursivschrift* sind die jeweiligen Abkürzungen angegeben für die Sprachen, in denen der Begriff wiedergegeben ist (siehe unten: Abkürzungen der Sprachen). Das Verzeichnis gibt für jeden Begriff den entsprechenden Ausdruck in englisch, deutsch, spanisch, französisch, und portugiesisch.

In der Regel wurde der Begriff in der Karte ins Englische übersetzt und dann vom Englischen in die vier anderen Sprachen. Da die Begriffe und Übersetzungen sich auf bestimmte Objekte in der Karte beziehen, können einige von ihnen von den in den üblichen Wörterbüchern aufgeführten Begriffsbestimmungen abweichen.

LOS TÉRMINOS GEOGRÁFICOS que aparecen en los mapas, incluyendo abreviaciones, son presentados en la columna de Términos Geográficas del Glosario, en orden alfabético. Los términos que están precedidos por un guión aparecen frecuentemente como terminaciones de los nombres en los mapas (por ejemplo, -san en Fuji-san, -älvan en Dalälven). Los idiomas que representan los términos están identificados por medio de abreviaciones en *cursiva* (véase abajo, Abreviaciones de los Idiomas Extranjeros). El Glosario provee el equivalente para cada término en inglés, alemán, español, francés y portugués.

Generalmente las traducciones están hechas de las formas originales de la terminología de los mapas que aparecen primero en inglés, y luego se traducen a las otras cuatro lenguas. Algunos términos y traducciones pueden aparecer distintas a las usadas en los diccionarios generales porque se refieren a los rasgos particulares de los mapas.

LE GLOSSAIRE cite par ordre alphabétique les termes géographiques et les abréviations utilisées. Les mots précédés d'un tiret sont des suffixes (par exemple, -san dans Fuji-san, -älven dans Dalälven). La langue d'origine du nom cité est indiquée par une abréviation en *italique* (voir Abréviations des noms de langues, ci-dessous). Le Glossaire donne chaque nom en anglais, allemand, espagnol, français, et portugais.

En général, les termes géographiques des cartes ont d'abord été traduits en anglais, puis de l'anglais dans les quatre autres langues. Les définitions de certains termes sont adaptées aux particularités de l'Atlas. Il peut arriver qu'elles diffèrent des définitions habituelles données par les dictionnaires.

A COLUNA 'TERMINOLOGIA', do *Glossário*, contém todos os termos geográficos que figuram nos mapas, em ordem alfabética e com as respectivas abreviações. Os termos precedidos por um hífen são os que freqüentemente aparecem nos mapas como sufixos de nomes tais como *-san* (em Fuji-san), *-älven* (em Dalälven). As línguas em que os termos são expressos estão identificadas por abreviações em *grifo* (ver abaixo, 'Abreviações das línguas estrangeiras'). O Glossário fornece o equivalente de cada termo em inglês, alemão, espanhol, português e francês.

De modo geral, as traduções foram feitas das formas originais da terminologia usada nos mapas para o inglês, e, em seguida, do inglês para as outras quatro línguas. Uma vez que os termos geográficos e traduções do *Glossário* referem-se a acidentes específicos de cada mapa, é possível que algumas definições sejam diferentes das consignadas nos dicionários gerais das línguas.

Abbreviations of Language Names / Abkürzungen der Nationalsprachen / Abreviaciones de los Idiomas Extranjeros / Abréviations des Noms de Langues / Abreviações dos Idiomas Estrangeiros

	ENGLISH	DEUTSCH	ESPAÑOL	FRANÇAIS	PORTUGUÊS
Afk.	Afrikaans	Afrikaans	Africano	Afrikaans	Afrikaans
Alb.	Albanian	Albanisch	Albanesa	Albanais	Albanês
Ara.	Arabic	Arabisch	Árabe	Arabe	Árabe
Ber.	Berber	Berberisch	Bereber	Berbère	Berbere
Ben.	Bengali	Bengali	Bengali	Bengali	Bengali
Blg.	Bulgarian	Bulgarisch	Búlgaro	Bulgare	Búlgaro
Bur.	Burmese	Burmanisch	Birmano	Birman	Birmanês
Cat.	Catalan	Katalanisch	Catalán	Catalan	Catalão
Cbd.	Cambodian	Kambodschanisch	Camboyano	Cambodgien	Cambojano
Ch.	Chinese	Chinesisch	Chino	Chinois	Chinês
Czech	Czech	Tschechisch	Checo	Tchèque	Tcheco
Dan.	Danish	Dänisch	Danés	Danois	Dinamarquês
Du.	Dutch	Niederländisch	Holandés	Néerlandais	Holandês
Eng.	English	Englisch	Inglés	Anglais	Inglês
Est.	Estonian	Estnisch	Estonio	Esthonien	Estoniano
Finn.	Finnish	Finnisch	Finés	Finnois	Finlandês
Flm.	Flemish	Flämisch	Flamenco	Flamand	Flamengo
Fr.	French	Französisch	Francés	Français	Francês
Gae.	Gaelic	Gälisch	Gaélico	Gaélique	Gaélico
Ger.	German	Deutsch	Alemán	Allemand	Alemão
Gr.	Greek	Griechisch	Griego	Grec	Grego
Hau.	Hausa	Haussa	Hausa	Haoussa	Haussa
Heb.	Hebrew	Hebräisch	Hebreo	Hébreu	Hebraico
Hung.	Hungarian	Ungarisch	Húngaro	Hongrois	Húngaro
Ice.	Icelandic	Isländisch	Islandés	Islandais	Islandês
Indon.	Indonesian	Indonesisch	Indonesio	Indonésien	Indonésio
It.	Italian	Italienisch	Italiano	Italien	Italiano

	ENGLISH	DEUTSCH	ESPAÑOL	FRANÇAIS	PORTUGUÊS
Jap.	Japanese	Japanisch	Japonés	Japonais	Japonês
Kor.	Korean	Koreanisch	Coreano	Coréen	Coreano
Lao.	Laotian	Laotisch	Laosiano	Laotien	Laosiano
Lapp.	Lappish	Lappisch	Lapón	Lapon	Lapão
Latv.	Latvian	Lettisch	Letón	Letton	Letão
Lith.	Lithuanian	Litauisch	Lituano	Lithuanien	Lituano
Mal.	Malay	Malaiisch	Malayo	Malais	Malaio
Mong.	Mongolian	Mongolisch	Mogol	Mongol	Mongol
Nor.	Norwegian	Norwegisch	Norvego	Norvégien	Norueguês
Pas.	Pashto	Paschtu	Pushtu	Pachtou	Pachtu
Per.	Persian	Persisch	Persa	Persan	Persa
Pol.	Polish	Polnisch	Polaco	Polonais	Polonês
Poly.	Polynesian	Polynesisch	Polinesio	Polynésien	Polinésio
Port.	Portuguese	Portugiesisch	Portugués	Portugais	Português
Rom.	Romanian	Rumänisch	Rumano	Roumain	Romeno
Rus.	Russian	Russisch	Ruso	Russe	Russo
S./C.	Serbo-Croatian	Serbokroatisch	Servio-croata	Serbo-croate	Servo-croata
Sin.	Sinhalese	Singhalesisch	Cingalés	Cinghalais	Cingalês
Slo.	Slovak	Slowakisch	Eslovaco	Slovaque	Eslovaco
Sp.	Spanish	Spanisch	Español	Espagnol	Espanhol
Swe.	Swedish	Schwedisch	Sueco	Suédois	Sueco
Thai	Thai	Thai	Tai	Thaï	Tailandês
Tib.	Tibetan	Tibetisch	Tibetano	Tibétain	Tibetano
Tur.	Turkish	Türkisch	Turco	Turc	Turco
Viet.	Vietnamese	Vietnamesisch	Vietnamita	Vietnamien	Vietnamita
Welsh	Welsh	Walisisch	Galés	Gallois	Galês

A

ENGLISH	DEUTSCH	Map Form Geographische Begriffe Términos Geográficos Termes Géographiques Termos Geográficos	ESPAÑOL	FRANÇAIS	PORTUGUÊS
river	Fluss	**-å** *Dan., Nor., Swe.*	río	rivière	rio
brook	Bach	**a., arroyo** *Sp.*	arroyo	ruisseau	córrego
river	Fluss	**āb** *Per.*	río	rivière	rio
army base	Heeres-stützpunkt	**a.b., army base** *Eng.*	base del ejército	base d'armée	base militar
well	Brunnen	**ābār** *Ara.*	pozo	puits	poço
abbey	Abtei	**abb., abbazia** *It.*	abadía	abbaye	abadia
abbey	Abtei	**abbaye** *Fr.*	abadía	abbaye	abadia
abbey	Abtei	**abbazia** *It.*	abadía	abbaye	abadia
abbey	Abtei	**abbey** *Eng.*	abadía	abbaye	abadia
aboriginal reserve	Eingeborenen-schutzgebiet	**aboriginal reserve** *Eng.*	zona de aborígenes	réserve d'indigènes	reserva indígena
abbey	Abtei	**Abtei** *Ger.*	abadía	abbaye	abadia
ditch	Graben	**acequia** *Sp.*	acequia	fossé	fosso
reservoir	Stausee	**ačude** *Port.*	embalse	réservoir	açude
island(s)	Insel(n)	**ada(lar)** *Tur.*	isla(s)	île(s)	ilha(s)
island	Insel	**adası** *Tur.*	isla	île	ilha
mountains	Berge	**adrar** *Ber.*	montañas	montagnes	montanhas
Atomic Energy Commission	Atomenergie-kommission	**A.E.C., Atomic Energy Commission** *Eng.*	Comisión de Energía Atomica	Commission de l'Énergie Atomique	Comissão de Energia Atômica
airport	Flughafen	**aérd., aérodrome** *Fr.*	aeródromo	aérodrome	aeródromo
airport	Flughafen	**aeródromo** *Port., Sp.*	aeródromo	aérodrome	aeródromo
airport	Flughafen	**aeroparque** *Sp.*	aeroparque	aéroport	aeroporto
airport	Flughafen	**aéroport** *Fr.*	aeropuerto	aéroport	aeroporto
airport	Flughafen	**aeroporto** *It., Port.*	aeropuerto	aéroport	aeroporto
airport	Flughafen	**aeropuerto** *Sp.*	aeropuerto	aéroport	aeroporto
air force base	Luftwaffen-stützpunkt	**a.f.b., air force base** *Eng.*	base aeronáutica	base aérienne	base aérea
wadi	Wadi	**ahzar** *Ara.*	uadi	wadi	uádi
peak	Gipfel	**aiguille** *Fr.*	pico	aiguille	pico
air base	Luftstützpunkt	**air base** *Eng.*	base aérea	base aérienne	base aérea
airfield	Flugplatz	**airfield** *Eng.*	camp de aviación	aérodrome	campo de pouso
air force base	Luftwaffen-stützpunkt	**air force base** *Eng.*	base aeronáutica	base aérienne	base aérea
airport	Flughafen	**airport** *Eng.*	aeropuerto	aéroport	aeroporto
cape	Kap	**ákra, akrotírion** *Gr.*	cabo	cap	cabo
hill	Hügel	**'alam, 'alāmat** *Ara.*	colina	colline	colina
avenue	Allee	**alameda** *Sp.*	alameda	avenue	avenida
alps	Alpen	**alpes** *Fr.*	alpes	alpes	alpes
alps	Alpen	**alpi** *It.*	alpes	alpes	alpes
mountains, hills	Berge, Hügel	**altos** *Sp.*	altos	montagnes, collines	montanhas, colinas
river	Fluss	**-älv,-älven** *Swe.*	río	rivière	rio
amusement park	Vergnügungs-park	**amusement park** *Eng.*	parque de diversiones	parc récréatif	parque de diversões
river	Fluss	**-ån** *Swe.*	río	rivière	rio
anchorage	Ankerplatz	**anchorage** *Eng.*	ancladero	ancrage	ancoradouro
bay	Bucht	**angra** *Sp.*	angra	baie	baía
cove	kleine Bucht	**anse** *Fr.*	ensenada	anse	enseada
bay	Bucht	**ao** *Ch.*	bahía	baie	baía
bay	Bucht	**ao** *Thai*	bahía	baie	baía
aqueduct	Aquädukt	**aqueduc** *Fr.*	acueducto	aqueduc	aqueduto
aqueduct	Aquädukt	**aqueduct** *Eng.*	acueducto	aqueduc	aqueduto
archipelago	Archipel	**archipel** *Fr.*	archipiélago	archipel	arquipélago
archipelago	Archipel	**archipelag** *Rus.*	archipiélago	archipel	arquipélago
archipelago	Archipel	**archipelago** *Eng.*	archipiélago	archipel	arquipélago
archipelago	Archipel	**archipiélago** *Sp.*	archipiélago	archipel	arquipélago
arm	Arm	**arm** *Eng.*	brazo	bras	braço de rio
army base	Heeres-stützpunkt	**army base** *Eng.*	base del ejército	base d'armée	base militar
airport	Flughafen	**arpt., aéroport** *Fr.* **aeroporto** **aeropuerto** **airport**	aeropuerto	aéroport	aeroporto
archipelago	Archipel	**arquipélago** *Port.*	archipiélago	archipel	arquipélago
reef	Riff	**arrecife** *Sp.*	arrecife	récif	recife
brook	Bach	**arroyo** *Sp.*	arroyo	ruisseau	córrego, arroio
hills	Hügel	**-ås,-åsen** *Swe.*	colinas	collines	colinas
ridge	Höhenrücken	**'assâbet** *Ara.*	sierra	crête	serra
atoll	Atoll	**atol** *Port.*	atolón	atoll	atol
atoll	Atoll	**atoll** *Eng., Fr.*	atolón	atoll	atol
auditorium	Auditorium	**aud., auditorium** *Eng.*	auditorio	auditorium	auditório
race course	Rennbahn	**autodrome** *Fr.*	autódromo	autodrome	autódromo
race course	Rennbahn	**autodromo** *It.*	autódromo	autodrome	autódromo
expressway	Autobahn	**autopista** *Sp.*	autopista	autoroute	via expressa

ENGLISH	DEUTSCH	Map Form / Geographische Begriffe / Términos Geográficos / Termes Géographiques / Termos Geográficos	ESPAÑOL	FRANÇAIS	PORTUGUÊS
avenue	Allee	**av., avenida** *Port., Sp.*	avenida	avenue	avenida
		avenue			
channel	Kanal	**ava** *Poly.*	canal, estrecho	canal, détroit	canal, estreito
avenue	Allee	**avenida** *Port., Sp.*	avenida	avenue	avenida
spring	Quelle	**'ayn** *Ara.*	manantial	source	manancial, fonte

B

ENGLISH	DEUTSCH	Map Form	ESPAÑOL	FRANÇAIS	PORTUGUÊS
bay	Bucht	**baai** *Du.*	bahía	baie	baía
strait	Meeresstrasse	**bab** *Ara.*	estrecho	détroit	estreito
brook, creek	Bach	**Bach** *Ger.*	arroyo, riachuelo	ruisseau, crique	córrego, arroio
hill	Hügel	**-backen** *Swe.*	colina	colline	colina
bay	Bucht	**badia** *Cat.*	bahía	baie	baía
desert	Wüste	**bādiyat** *Ara.*	desierto	désert	deserto
strait	Meeresstrasse	**bælt** *Dan.*	estrecho	détroit	estreito
bay	Bucht	**bahía** *Sp.*	bahía	baie	baía
inlet	Einfahrt	**bahiret** *Ara.*	abra	bras de mer	enseada, estuário
railroad station	Bahnhof	**Bahnhof** *Ger.*	estacíon de ferrocarril	gare	estação ferroviária
river, sea	Fluss, Meer	**bahr, bahr** *Ara.*	río, mar	rivière, mer	rio, mar
reservoir	Stausee	**bahrat** *Ara.*	embalse	réservoir	reservatório
bay	Bucht	**baía** *Port.*	bahía	baie	baía
bay	Bucht	**baie** *Fr.*	bahía	baie	baía
reef, sand bar	Riff, Sandbarre	**bajo** *Sp.*	bajo	récif, banc de sable	recife, banco de areia
gorge	Schlucht	**balka** *Rus.*	garganta	gorge	garganta
dome	Kuppe	**ballon** *Fr.*	domo	ballon	domo
marsh	Marsch	**balta** *Rom.*	pantano	marais	pântano
cape	Kap	**-bana** *Jpn.*	cabo	cap	cabo
marsh	Marsch	**bañados** *Sp.*	bañados	marais	pântano
island	Insel	**-banare** *Jpn.*	isla	île	ilha
bank	Bank	**banco** *Sp.*	banco	banc	banco
peninsula	Halbinsel	**bandao** *Ch.*	península	péninsule	península
bank	Bank	**bank** *Eng.*	banco	banc	banco
shoal	Untiefe	**-banken** *Swe.*	bajo	haut-fond	escolho
sand bar	Sandbarre	**barra** *Sp.*	barra	banc de sable	banco de areia
dam	Damm	**barrage** *Fr.*	presa	barrage	represa
ravine	Tobel	**barranca** *Sp.*	barranca	ravin	ravina
air base	Luftstützpunkt	**base aérea** *Sp.*	base aérea	base aérienne	base aérea
basilica	Basilika	**basílica** *Sp.*	basílica	basilique	basílica
basilica	Basilika	**basilique** *Fr.*	basílica	basilique	basílica
basin	Becken	**basin** *Eng.*	cuenca	bassin	bacia
basin	Becken	**bassin** *Fr.*	cuenca	bassin	bacia
marsh	Marsch	**batakliği** *Tur.*	pantano	marais	pântano
river	Fluss	**batang** *Indon.*	río	rivière	rio
river	Fluss	**batha** *Ara.*	río	rivière	rio
marsh	Marsch	**bāţlāq** *Per.*	pantano	marais	pântano
battlefield	Schlachtfeld	**battlefield** *Eng.*	campo de batalla	champ de bataille	campo de batalha
mountain	Berg	**batu** *Mal.*	montaña	montagne	montanha
bay	Bucht	**bay** *Eng.*	bahía	baie	baía
bayou	Altwasser	**bayou** *Fr., Eng.*	ensenada pantanosa	bayou	enseada pantanosa
beach	Strand	**beach** *Eng.*	playa	plage	praia
mountain	Berg	**bein, beinn** *Gae.*	montaña	montagne	montanha
snowcapped mountains	Schneegipfel	**belogorje** *Rus.*	nevados	montagnes neigeuses	picos nevados
mountain	Berg	**ben** *Gae.*	montaña	montagne	montanha
mountain, hill	Berg	**Berg** *Ger.*	montaña, colina	montagne, colline	montanha, colina
mountains	Gebirge	**-berg** *Afk.*	montañas	montagnes	montanhas
hill(s), mountain(s)	Hügel, Berg(e)	**-berg** *Swe.*	colina(s), montaña(s)	colline(s), montagne(s)	colina(s), montanha(s)
mountains	Berge	**Berge** *Ger.*	montañas	montagnes	montanhas
mountains	Berge	**-berge** *Afk.*	montañas	montagnes	montanhas
hills, mountains	Hügel, Berge	**-bergen** *Swe.*	colinas, montañas	collines, montagnes	colinas, montanhas
hill, mountain	Hügel, Berg	**-berget** *Swe.*	colina, montaña	colline, montagne	colina, montanha
upland	Bergland	**Bergland** *Ger.*	tierras altas	hautes terres	terras altas
battlefield	Schlachtfeld	**bfld., battlefield** *Eng.*	campo de batalla	champ de bataille	campo de batalha
mountain, hill	Berg	**Bg., Berg** *Ger.*	montaña, colina	montagne, colline	montanha, colina
bridge	Brücke	**bge., bridge** *Eng.*	puente	pont	ponte
bight (bay)	Bucht	**bight** *Eng.*	bahía	baie	baía, enseada
bill (point)	Landspitze	**bill** *Eng.*	punta	pointe	ponta
valley	Tal	**biq'at** *Heb.*	valle	vallée	vale
well	Brunnen	**bi'r** *Ara.*	pozo	puits	poço
lake	See	**birkat** *Ara.*	lago	lac	lago
mountains	Berge	**bjeshkët** *Alb.*	montañas	montagnes	montanhas
brook	Bach	**bk., brook** *Eng.*	arroyo	ruisseau	córrego, arroio
upland	Bergland	**blaenau** *Welsh*	tierras altas	hautes terres	terras altas
bluff(s)	Steilufer	**bluff(s)** *Eng.*	acantilado(s)	falaise(s)	falésia(s)
boulevard	Boulevard	**blvd., boulevard** *Fr., Eng.*	bulevar	boulevard	bulevar
mountain	Berg	**b'nom** *Viet.*	montaña	montagne	montanha
river mouth	Flussmündung	**boca** *Sp.*	boca	embouchure	foz
river mouth, pass	Flussmündung, Pass	**bocca** *It.*	boca, paso	embouchure, col	foz, passo
bay	Bucht	**bocht** *Du.*	bahía	baie	baía
bay	Bodden	**Bodden** *Ger.*	bahía	baie	baía
lake	See	**bœng** *Cbd.*	lago	lac	lago
bog	Moor	**bog** *Eng.*	pantano	fondrière	pântano
strait	Meeresstrasse	**boğazı** *Tur.*	estrecho	détroit	estreito
range	Gebirge	**bogd** *Mong.*	sierra	chaîne	cordilheira
woods	Gehölz	**bois** *Fr.*	bosque	bois	bosque
enclosed basin	Becken	**bolsón** *Sp.*	bolsón	bassin fermée	bacia fechada
forest	Wald	**bory** *Pol.*	bosque	forêt	floresta
forest	Wald	**bosque** *Sp.*	bosque	forêt	floresta
boulevard	Boulevard	**boulevard** *Fr., Eng.*	boulevar	boulevard	bulevar
branch	Arm	**br., branch** *Eng.*	brazo	bras	braço
stream distributary	Flussarm	**bratul** *Rom.*	brazo de río	bras	braço de rio
breakwater	Wellenbrecher	**breakwater** *Eng.*	rompeolas	brise-lames	quebra-mar
glacier	Gletscher	**-breen** *Nor.*	glaciar	glacier	geleira
bridge	Brücke	**bridge** *Eng.*	puente	pont	ponte
marsh	Bruch	**Bruch** *Ger.*	pantano	marais	pântano
bridge	Brücke	**Brücke** *Ger.*	puente	pont	ponte
bridge	Brücke	**brug** *Du.*	puente	pont	ponte
bay	Bucht	**Bucht** *Ger.*	bahía	baie	baía
bay	Bucht	**buchta** *Rus.*	bahía	baie	baía
mountain	Berg	**bufa** *Sp.*	bufa	montagne	montanha
bay	Bucht	**bugt** *Dan.*	bahía	baie	baía
lake	See	**buhayrah** *Ara.*	lago	lac	lago
lake, lagoon	See, Lagune, Haff	**buhayrat** *Ara.*	lago, laguna	lac, lagune	lago, laguna
mountain, hill	Berg, Hügel	**bukit** *Indon., Mal.*	montaña, colina	montagne, colline	montanha, colina
bay	Bucht	**-bukten** *Swe.*	bahía	baie	baía
mountain	Berg	**bulu** *Indon.*	montaña	montagne	montanha
castle	Burg	**Burg** *Ger.*	castillo	château	castelo
hill	Hügel	**burj** *Ara.*	colina	colline	colina
brook	Bach	**burn** *Gae.*	riachuelo	crique	riacho
cape	Kap	**burnu, burun** *Tur.*	cabo	cap	cabo
bay	Busen	**Busen** *Ger.*	bahía	baie	baía
butte(s)	Restberg(e)	**butte(s)** *Eng., Fr.*	butte(s)	butte(s)	colina, outeiro

C

ENGLISH	DEUTSCH	Map Form	ESPAÑOL	FRANÇAIS	PORTUGUÊS
cape	Kap	**c., cabo** *Sp.*	cabo	cap	cabo
		cap			
		cape			
street	Strasse	**c., calle** *Sp.*	calle	rue	rua
peaks	Gipfel	**cabezas** *Sp.*	cabezas	cimes	picos
cape	Kap	**cabo** *Port., Sp.*	cabo	cap	cabo
waterfall	Wasserfall	**cachoeira** *Port.*	cascada	chute d'eau	cachoeira
street	Strasse	**calle** *Sp.*	calle	rue	rua
parkway	Ferienstrasse	**calzada** *Sp.*	calzada	allée de parc	alameda de parque

ENGLISH	DEUTSCH	Map Form / Geographische Begriffe / Términos Geográficos / Termes Géographiques / Termos Geográficos	ESPAÑOL	FRANÇAIS	PORTUGUÊS
mosque	Moschee	**camıı** *Tur.*	mezquita	mosqée	mesquita
road	Landstrasse	**camino** *Sp.*	camino	route	rodovia
camp	Lager	**camp** *Eng., Fr.*	campo	camp	campo
plain	Ebene	**campo** *It.*	llanura	plaine	planície
brook, ravine	Bach, Tobel	**cañada** *Sp.*	cañada	ruisseau, ravin	ravina
canal	Kanal	**canal** *Eng.*	canal	canal	canal
canal, channel	Kanal	**canal** *Fr., Port., Sp.*	canal	canal	canal
canal, channel	Kanal	**canale** *It.*	canal	canal	canal
stream distributary	Flussarm	**caño** *Sp.*	caño	bras	braço de rio, igarapé
canyon	Cañon	**cañón** *Sp.*	cañón	canyon	canhão
canyon	Cañon	**canyon** *Eng.*	cañón	canyon	canhão
plateau	Hochebene	**cao nguyen** *Viet.*	meseta	plateau	planalto
cape	Kap	**cap** *Fr., Cat.*	cabo	cap	cabo
cape	Kap	**cape** *Eng.*	cabo	cap	cabo
capitol	Kapitol	**capitolio** *Sp.*	capitolio	capitole	capitólio
cape	Kap	**capo** *It.*	cabo	cap	cabo
captain	Kapitän	**capt., captain** *Eng.*	capitán	capitaine	capitão
highway	Strasse	**carretera** *Sp.*	carretera	route	rodovia
valley	Tal	**carse** *Gae.*	valle	vallée	vale
waterfall	Wasserfall	**cascada** *Sp.*	cascada	chute d'eau	queda d'água
waterfall	Wasserfall	**cascata** *It.*	cascada	chute d'eau	queda d'água
castle	Burg, Schloss	**castel, castello** *It.*	castillo	château	castelo
castle	Burg, Schloss	**castelo** *Port.*	castillo	château	castelo
castle	Burg, Schloss	**castillo** *Sp.*	castillo	château	castelo
castle	Burg, Schloss	**castle** *Eng.*	castillo	château	castelo
cataracts	Katarakten	**cataratas** *Port., Sp.*	cataratas	cataractes	cataratas
cathedral	Kathedrale	**catedral** *Sp.*	catedral	cathédrale	catedral
range	Gebirge	**catena** *Sp.*	catena	chaîne	cordilheira
cathedral	Kathedrale	**cathedral** *Eng.*	catedral	cathédrale	catedral
causeway	Dammweg	**causeway** *Eng.*	calzada	chaussée	calçada
upland	Bergland	**causse** *Fr.*	tierras altas	causse	terras altas
cave(s)	Höhle(n)	**cave(s)** *Eng.*	cueva(s)	caverne(s)	caverna(s)
cay (islet)	Klippe	**cay** *Eng.*	cayo	caye	baixio
cay(s), islet(s)	Klippe(n)	**cayo(s)** *Sp.*	cayo(s)	caye(s)	baixio(s)
cemetery	Friedhof	**cementerio** *Sp.*	cementerio	cimetière	cemitério
cemetery	Friedhof	**cemetery** *Eng.*	cementerio	cimetière	cemitério
mountain(s), hill(s)	Berg(e), Hügel	**cerro(s)** *Sp.*	cerro(s)	montagne(s), colline(s)	montanha(s), colina(s)
range	Gebirge	**chaîne** *Fr.*	sierra	chaîne	cordilheira
channel	Kanal	**channel** *Eng.*	canal, estrecho	canal, détroit	canal, estreito
hills	Hügel	**chapada** *Port.*	colinas	collines	chapada
island	Insel	**char** *Ben.*	isla	île	ilha
castle	Burg, Schloss	**château** *Fr.*	castillo	château	castelo
road	Landstrasse	**chemin** *Fr.*	camino	chemin	rodovia
bay	Bucht	**chhâk** *Cbd.*	bahía	baie	baía
lake	See	**chi** *Ch.*	lago	lac	lago
harbor, harbour	Hafen	**chiang** *Ch.*	puerto	port	porto
cape	Kap	**chiao** *Ch.*	cabo	cap	cabo
road	Landstrasse	**chin., chemin** *Fr.*	camino	chemin	rodovia
river	Fluss	**-ch'ŏn** *Kor.*	río	rivière	rio
reservoir	Stausee	**-chŏsuji** *Kor.*	embalse	réservoir	reservatório
intermittent lake, salt marsh	periodischer See, Salzmarsch	**chott** *Ara.*	lago intermitente, pantano salado	lac périodique, marais salé	lago intermitente, pântano salgado
range	Gebirge	**chr., chrebet** *Rus.*	sierra	chaîne	cordilheira
mountains	Berge	**chuŏr phnum** *Cbd.*	montañas	montagnes	montanhas
church	Kirche	**church** *Eng.*	iglesia	église	igreja
waterfalls	Wasserfälle	**chutes** *Fr.*	cascadas	chutes d'eau	quedas d'água
marsh	Marsch	**ciénaga** *Sp.*	ciénaga	marais	pântano
peak	Gipfel	**cima** *It., Sp.*	cima	cime	pico
peak	Gipfel	**cime** *Fr.*	cima	cime	pico
cemetery	Friedhof	**cimetière** *Fr.*	cementerio	cimetière	cemitério
city	Stadt	**città** *It.*	ciudad	ville	cidade
city	Stadt	**city** *Eng.*	ciudad	ville	cidade
city	Stadt	**ciudad** *Sp.*	ciudad	ville	cidade
claypan	Tonpfanne	**claypan** *Eng.*	capa de arcilla	couche argilleuse	camada de argila
cliff(s)	Kliff(e)	**cliff(s)** *Eng.*	risco(s)	falaise(s)	falésia(s)
lake	See	**co** *Tib.*	lago	lac	lago
mountain	Berg	**co** *Viet.*	montaña	montagne	montanha
mountain, hill	Berg, Hügel	**co., cerro** *Sp.*	cerro	montagne, colline	montanha, colina
coast	Küste	**coast** *Eng.*	costa	côte	costa
coast guard station	Küstenwacht-station	**coast guard station** *Eng.*	estación de los guardacostas	station des gardescôte	estação de guarda costeira
pass	Pass	**col** *Fr.*	paso	col	passo
college	Hochschule	**colegio** *Sp.*	colegio	collège	colégio
hill(s)	Hügel	**colina(s)** *Sp.*	colina(s)	colline(s)	colina(s)
college	Hochschule	**coll., college** *Eng.*	colegio	collège	colégio
hills	Hügel	**colli** *It.*	colinas	collines	colinas
hills	Hügel	**colline** *It.*	colinas	collines	colinas
hills	Hügel	**collines** *Fr.*	colinas	collines	colinas
common	Gemeindeland	**common** *Eng.*	campo común	commune	terra comum
islands	Inseln	**con** *Viet.*	islas	îles	ilhas
plain	Ebene	**conca** *It.*	llanura	plaine	planície
convent	Nonnenkloster	**convent** *Eng.*	convento	couvent	convento
convent	Nonnenkloster	**convento** *It., Port., Sp.*	convento	couvent	convento
range	Gebirge	**cord., cordillera** *Sp.*	cordillera	chaîne	cordilheira
mountain	Berg	**corno** *It.*	montaña	montagne	montanha
brook	Bach	**córrego** *Port.*	arroyo	ruisseau	córrego
coast	Küste	**costa** *Sp.*	costa	côte	costa
coast, hills	Küste, Hügel	**côte** *Fr.*	costa, colinas	côte	costa, colinas
hills	Hügel	**coteau** *Fr.*	colinas	coteau	colinas
coulee	breite Schlucht	**coulee** *Eng.*	rambla	coulée	barranco
coulee	breite Schlucht	**coulee** *Fr.*	rambla	coulée	barranco
county park	Park	**county park** *Eng.*	parque del condado	parc de comté	parque de condado
convent	Nonnenkloster	**couvent** *Fr.*	convento	couvent	convento
cove	kleine Bucht	**cove** *Eng.*	ensenada	anse	enseada
brook	Bach	**cr., creek** *Eng.*	riachuelo	crique	riacho
crag	Felsspitze	**crag** *Eng.*	despeñadero	pointe de rocher	despenhadeiro
crater	Krater	**crater** *Eng.*	cráter	cratère	cratera
crater	Krater	**cratère** *Fr.*	cráter	cratère	cratera
creek	Bach	**creek** *Eng.*	riachuelo	crique	riacho
peak	Gipfel	**croda** *It.*	pico	cime	pico
canal	Kanal	**csatorna** *Hung.*	canal	canal	canal
bay	Bucht	**cua** *Viet.*	bahía	baie	baía
hills, ridge	Hügel, Höhenrücken	**cuchilla** *Sp.*	cuchilla	collines, crête	coxilha
caves	Höhen	**cuevas** *Sp.*	cuevas	cavernes	cavernas
cove	kleine Bucht	**cul-de-sac** *Fr.*	ensenada	cul-de-sac	enseada
mountains	Berge	**culmea** *Rom.*	montañas	montagnes	montanhas
summit	Gipfel	**cumbre** *Sp.*	cumbre	sommet	cume

D

ENGLISH	DEUTSCH	Map Form	ESPAÑOL	FRANÇAIS	PORTUGUÊS
mountain	Berg	**dağ, dağı** *Tur.*	montaña	montagne	montanha
mountains	Berge	**dāgh** *Per.*	montañas	montagnes	montanhas
mountains	Berge	**dağlar, dağları** *Tur.*	montañas	montagnes	montanhas
hill	Hügel	**dahr** *Ara.*	colina	colline	colina
plateau	Hochebene	**-dai, -daichi** *Jpn.*	meseta	plateau	planalto
mountain	Berg	**-dake** *Jpn.*	montaña	montagne	montanha
valley	Tal	**-dal, -dalen** *Nor., Swe.*	valle	vallée	vale
dale	weites Tal	**dale** *Eng.*	valle ancho	vallée large	vale aberto
dam	Damm	**dam** *Eng.*	presa	barrage	represa
lake	See	**danau** *Indon.*	lago	lac	lago
island	Insel	**dao** *Ch., Viet.*	isla	île	ilha
marsh	Marsch	**daqq** *Per.*	pantano	marais	pântano
lake	See	**daryācheh** *Per.*	lago	lac	lago
desert	Wüste	**dasht** *Per.*	desierto	désert	deserto
monastery	Kloster	**dayr** *Ara.*	monasterio	monastère	mosteiro

ENGLISH	DEUTSCH	Map Form Geographische Begriffe Términos Geográficos Termes Géographiques Termos Geográficos	ESPAÑOL	FRANÇAIS	PORTUGUÊS
deep	Tiefe	**deep** *Eng.*	fosa marina	fossé marin	fossa submarina
delta	Delta	**delta** *Eng., Fr., Sp.*	delta	delta	delta
sea	Meer	**deniz, denizi** *Tur.*	mar	mer	mar
monument	Denkmal	**Denkmal** *Ger.*	monumento	monument	monumento
pass	Pass	**deo** *Viet.*	paso	col	passo
depression	Senke	**depression** *Eng.*	depresión	dépression	depressão
river	Fluss	**deresi** *Tur.*	río	rivière	rio
desert	Wüste	**desert** *Eng.*	desierto	désert	deserto
desert	Wüste	**desierto** *Sp.*	desierto	désert	deserto
strait	Meeresstrasse	**détroit** *Fr.*	estrecho	détroit	estreito
escarpment	Landstufe	**dhar** *Ara.*	escarpa	escarpement	escarpa
canal	Kanal	**dhiórix** *Gr.*	canal	canal	canal
lake, marsh	See, Marsch	**dian** *Ch.*	lago, pantano	lac, marais	lago, pântano
channel	Kanal	**diep** *Du.*	canal, estrecho	canal, détroit	canal, estreito
dike	Deich	**dijk** *Du.*	dique	digue	dique
district	Distrikt	**district** *Eng.*	distrito	district	distrito
district	Distrikt	**distrito** *Sp.*	distrito	district	distrito
ditch	Graben	**ditch** *Eng.*	acequia	fossé	fosso
mountain(s)	Berg(e)	**djebel** *Ara.*	montaña(s)	montagne(s)	montanha(s)
fjord	Fjord	**-djúp** *Ice.*	fiordo	fjord	fiorde
channel, sound	Kanal, Sund	**-djupet** *Swe.*	canal, sonda	canal, détroit	canal, estreito
zoo	Zoo	**djurpark** *Swe.*	parque zoológico	zoo	jardim zoológico
island	Insel	**-do** *Kor.*	isla	île	ilha
interfluve	Erhebung	**doāb** *Per.*	interfluvio	interfluve	interflúvio
dock	Dock	**dock** *Eng.*	muelle	quai	doca
mountain	Berg	**doi** *Thai*	montaña	montagne	montanha
valley	Tal	**dolina** *Rus.*	valle	vallée	vale
mountain	Berg	**dolok** *Indon.*	montaña	montagne	montanha
hills	Hügel	**dombrovidék** *Hung.*	colinas	collines	colinas
hills	Hügel	**dombvidék** *Hung.*	colinas	collines	colinas
peak	Gipfel	**dos** *Fr.*	pico	dos	pico
downs (hills)	Hügelland	**downs** *Eng.*	colinas	collines	terras baixas (colinas)
drive	Fahrweg	**dr., drive** *Eng.*	calzada	avenue	avenida
drain (water-course)	Abzugsgraben	**drain** *Eng.*	desaguadero	drainage	escoadouro
draw (ravine)	kleines Tal	**draw** *Eng.*	valle pequeño	ravine	bacia, vale
drive	Fahrweg	**drive** *Eng.*	calzada	avenue	avenida
dry lake	Trockensee	**dry lake** *Eng.*	lago seco	lac asséché	lago seco
dunes	Dünen	**dunes** *Eng., Fr.*	dunas	dunes	dunas

E

ENGLISH	DEUTSCH	Map Form	ESPAÑOL	FRANÇAIS	PORTUGUÊS
east	Ost	**e., east** *Eng.*	este	est	leste
school	Schule	**école** *Fr.*	escuela	école	escola
mountain	Berg	**-egga** *Nor.*	montaña	montagne	montanha
memorial	Ehrenmal	**Ehrenmal** *Ger.*	monumento	memorial	monumento
river	Fluss	**-elv,-elva** *Nor.*	río	rivière	rio
reservoir	Stausee	**embalse** *Sp.*	embalse	réservoir	reservatório
pier	Landungsbrücke	**embarcadero** *Sp.*	embarcadero	jetée	cais
valley	Tal	**'emeq** *Heb.*	valle	vallée	vale
monument	Denkmal	**emlékmű** *Hung.*	monumento	monument	monumento
spring	Quelle	**'en** *Heb.*	manantial	source	fonte, manancial
cove	kleine Bucht	**enseada** *Port.*	ensenada	anse	enseada
cove	kleine Bucht	**ensenada** *Sp.*	ensenada	anse	enseada
entrance	Einfahrt	**entrance** *Eng.*	entrada	entrée	entrada
forest	Wald	**erdö** *Hung.*	bosque	forêt	floresta
sand desert	Sandwüste	**erg** *Ara.*	desierto arenoso	désert de sable	deserto arenoso
escarpment	Landstufe	**escarpment** *Eng.*	escarpa	escarpement	escarpa
school	Schule	**escuela** *Sp.*	escuela	école	escola
highland	Hochland	**espigão** *Port.*	región montañosa	pays montagneux	espigão
station	Bahnhof, Stützpunkt	**est., estação** *Port.*	estación	station	estação
		estación			
stadium	Stadion	**estadio** *Sp.*	estadio	stade	estádio
reservoir	Stausee	**estanque** *Sp.*	estanque	réservoir	reservatório
estuary	Trichtermündung	**estero** *Sp.*	estero	estuaire	estuário
road	Landstrasse	**estr., estrada** *Port.*	camino	route	estrada
strait	Meeresstrasse	**estrecho** *Sp.*	estrecho	détroit	estreito
estuary	Trichtermündung	**estuary** *Eng.*	estuario	estuaire	estuário
pond	Teich	**étang** *Fr.*	charca	étang	lagoa, açude
expressway	Autobahn	**expy., expressway** *Eng.*	autopista	autoroute	via expressa
island	Insel	**-ey** *Ice.*	isla	île	ilha
lake	See	**ežeras** *Lith.*	lago	lac	lago
lake	See	**ezers** *Latv.*	lago	lac	lago

F

ENGLISH	DEUTSCH	Map Form	ESPAÑOL	FRANÇAIS	PORTUGUÊS
faculty (school)	Fakultät	**faculté** *Fr.*	facultad	faculté	faculdade
fairground	Ausstellungsgelände	**fairground** *Eng.*	campo para ferias	champ de foire	terreno para feiras
cliff	Kliff	**falaise** *Fr.*	risco	falaise	falésia
fall(s) (waterfall)	Wasserfall	**falls(s)** *Eng.*	cascada	chute d'eau	queda d'água
waterfall	Fall	**Fall** *Ger.*	cascada	chute d'eau	queda d'água
waterfall	Wasserfall	**-fallet** *Swe.*	cascada	chute d'eau	queda d'água
river	Fluss	**far'** *Ara.*	río	rivière	rio
lighthouse	Leuchtturm	**faro** *Sp.*	faro	phare	farol
upland	Bergland	**farsh** *Ara.*	tierras altas	hautes terres	terras altas
fell (mountain, hill)	ödes Hügelland	**fell** *Eng.*	colina rocosa	colline rocheuse	colina rochosa
mountain	Berg	**-fell** *Ice.*	montaña	montagne	montanha
mountain	Berg	**feng** *Ch.*	montaña	montagne	montanha
upland	Bergland	**fennsík** *Hung.*	tierras altas	hautes terres	terras altas
ferry	Fähre	**ferry** *Eng.*	balsadera	bac	balsa
lake	See	**fertö** *Hung.*	lago	lac	lago
fortress	Feste	**Feste** *Ger.*	fortaleza	fort	fortaleza
estuary, strait	Trichtermündung, Meeresstrasse	**firth** *Gae.*	estuario, estrecho	estuaire, détroit	estuário, estreito
mountain(s)	Berg(e)	**fjäll(en)** *Swe.*	montaña(s)	montagne(s)	montanha(s)
mountain	Berg	**fjället** *Swe.*	montaña	montagne	montanha
fjord	Fjord	**fjärden** *Swe.*	fiordo	fjord	fiorde
mountain	Berg	**-fjell, -fjellet** *Nor.*	montaña	montagne	montanha
mountain	Berg	**-fjöll** *Ice.*	montaña	montagne	montanha
fjord	Fjord	**-fjord** *Nor.*	fiordo	fjord	fiorde
fjord, lake	Fjord, See	**-fjorden** *Nor., Swe.*	fiordo, lago	fjord, lac	fiorde, lago
fjord, bay	Fjord, Bucht	**-fjörđur** *Ice.*	fiordo, bahía	fjord, baie	fiorde, baía
fork	Arm	**fk., fork** *Eng.*	brazo	bras	braço de rio
flat	Flachland	**flat** *Eng.*	llano	plat	planície
river	Fluss	**-fljót** *Ice.*	río	rivière	rio
bay	Bucht	**-flói** *Ice.*	bahía	baie	baía
flood control basin	Hochwasserrückhaltebecken	**flood control basin** *Eng.*	cuenca para controlar la inundación	bassin de contrôle d'inondation	bacia de controle de inundações
airport	Flughafen	**Flughafen** *Ger.*	aeropuerto	aéroport	aeroporto
airport	Flugplatz	**Flugplatz** *Ger.*	aeropuerto	aérodrome	aeroporto
airport	Flughafen	**flygplats** *Swe.*	aeródromo	aérodrome	aeródromo
river mouth, pass	Flussmündung, Pass	**foce** *It.*	desembocadura, paso	embouchure, col	desembocadura, foz, passo
canal	Kanal	**föcsatorna** *Hung.*	canal	canal	canal
glacier	Gletscher	**-fonn** *Nor.*	glaciar	glacier	geleira
spring	Quelle	**fontaine** *Fr.*	manantial	fontaine	fonte, manancial
pass	Pass	**forca** *It.*	paso	col	passo

ENGLISH	DEUTSCH	Map Form Geographische Begriffe Términos Geográficos Termes Géographiques Termos Geográficos	ESPAÑOL	FRANÇAIS	PORTUGUÊS
inlet	Förde	**Förde** *Ger.*	abra	bras de mer	enseada, estuário
foreland	Vorland	**foreland** *Eng.*	promontorio	promontoire	promontório
forest	Wald	**forest** *Eng.*	bosque	forêt	floresta
forest reserve	Waldreservat	**forest reserve** *Eng.*	reserva de bosque	réserve forestière	reserva florestal
forest	Wald	**forêt** *Fr.*	bosque	forêt	floresta
waterfall	Wasserfall	**-forsen** *Swe.*	cascada	chute d'eau	queda d'água
forest	Forst	**Forst** *Ger.*	bosque	forêt	floresta
fort	Fort	**fort** *Eng., Fr.*	fuerte	fort	forte
waterfall	Wasserfall	**-foss** *Ice.*	cascada	chute d'eau	queda d'água
waterfall	Wasserfall	**-fossen** *Nor.*	cascada	chute d'eau	queda d'água
brook	Bach	**fosso** *It.*	arroyo	ruisseau	córrego
pass	Pass	**foum** *Ara.*	paso	col	passo
fracture zone	Bruchzone	**fracture zone** *Eng.*	zona de fractura	zone de faille	zona de fratura
freeway	Autobahn	**frwy., freeway** *Eng.*	autopista	autoroute	via expressa
fort	Fort	**ft., fort** *Eng., Fr.*	fuerte	fort	forte
stream distributary	Flussarm	**furo** *Port.*	brazo de río	bras	furo

G

ENGLISH	DEUTSCH	Map Form	ESPAÑOL	FRANÇAIS	PORTUGUÊS
mountain, hill	Berg, Hügel	**g., gora** *Rus.*	montaña, colina	montagne, colline	montanha, colina
mountain	Berg	**g., gunong** *Mal.*	montaña	montagne	montanha
		gunung			
mountain	Berg	**-gai'sa** *Lapp.*	montaña	montagne	montanha
tunnel	Tunnel	**galleria** *It.*	túnel	tunnel	túnel
gallery	Galerie	**gallery** *Eng.*	galería	galerie	galeria
game farm	Wildfarm	**game farm** *Eng.*	criadero de caza	ferme de gibier	fazenda de caça
game park	Wildpark	**game park** *Eng.*	vedado de caza	parc à gibier	parque de caça
game refuge	Wildgehege	**game refuge** *Eng.*	refugio de caza	refuge de gibier	refúgio de caça
game reserve	Wildreservat	**game reserve** *Eng.*	vedado de caza	réserve à gibier	reserva de caça
game sanctuary	Wildschutzgebiet	**game sanctuary** *Eng.*	vedado de caza	réserve à gibier	santuário de caça
bay	Bucht	**gang** *Ch.*	bahía	baie	baía
river	Fluss	**-gang** *Kor.*	río	rivière	rio
gap	Pass	**gap** *Eng.*	paso	col	passo
intermittent lake	periodischer See	**garaet** *Ara.*	lago intermitente	lac périodique	lago intermitente
garden	Garten	**gard., garden** *Eng.*	jardín	jardin	jardim
gardens	Gärten	**gardens** *Eng.*	jardines	jardins	jardins
mountain	Berg	**garet** *Ara.*	montaña	montagne	montanha
lake	See	**-gata** *Jpn.*	lago	lac	lago
gate	Tor	**gate** *Eng.*	puerta	porte	portão
mountain torrent	Wildbach	**gave** *Fr.*	torrente	gave	torrente
range	Gebirge	**gebergte** *Du.*	sierra	chaîne	cordilheira
range	Gebirge	**Gebirge** *Ger.*	sierra	chaîne	cordilheira
pass	Pass	**geçidi** *Tur.*	paso	col	passo
oasis, well	Oase, Brunnen	**ghadīr** *Ara.*	oasis, pozo	oasis, puits	oásis, poço
mountains	Gebirge	**ghar** *Pas.*	montañas	montagnes	montanhas
spring	Quelle	**ghayl** *Ara.*	manantial	source	manancial
bay	Bucht	**ghubbat** *Ara.*	bahía	baie	baía
dunes	Dünen	**ghurd** *Ara.*	dunas	dunes	dunas
island	Insel	**gili** *Indon.*	isla	île	ilha
peak	Gipfel	**Gipfel** *Ger.*	pico	cime	pico
hill	Hügel	**giva't** *Heb.*	colina	colline	colina
bay	Bucht	**gji** *Alb.*	bahía	baie	baía
glacier	Gletscher	**glacier** *Eng., Fr.*	glaciar	glacier	geleira
lake	See	**göl** *Tur.*	lago	lac	lago
bald mountains	kahle Berge	**gol'cy** *Rus.*	montañas calvas	monts chauves	montanhas calvas
gulf	Golf	**golf** *Cat.*	golfo	golfe	golfo
golf course	Golfplatz	**golf course** *Eng.*	campo de golf	champ de golf	campo de golfe
gulf	Golf	**golfe** *Fr.*	golfo	golfe	golfo
bay	Bucht	**golfete** *Sp.*	golfete	baie	baía
gulf	Golf	**golfo** *It., Sp.*	golfo	golfe	golfo
lake	See	**gölü** *Tur.*	lago	lac	lago
mountain, hill	Berg, Hügel	**gora** *Rus.*	montaña, colina	montagne, colline	montanha, colina
mountains	Berge	**gora** *S./C.*	montañas	montagnes	montanhas
mountain	Berg	**góra** *Pol.*	montaña	montagne	montanha
gorge	Schlucht	**gorge** *Eng., Fr.*	garganta	gorge	garganta
mountains, hills	Berge, Hügel	**gorje** *S./C.*	montañas, colinas	montagnes, collines	montanhas, colinas
ruins	Ruinen	**gorodišče** *Rus.*	ruinas	ruines	ruínas
mountains, hills	Berge, Hügel	**gory** *Rus.*	montañas, colinas	montagnes, collines	montanhas, colinas
mountains	Berge	**góry** *Pol.*	montañas	montagnes	montanhas
sinkhole	Schluckloch	**gouffre** *Fr.*	sumidero	gouffre	sumidouro
wadi	Wadi	**goulbin** *Hau.*	uadi	wadi	uádi
ditch	Graben	**Graben** *Ger.*	acequia	fossé	fosso
ridge	Höhenrücken	**gr'ada** *Rus.*	sierra	crête	cordilheira
mountain	Berg	**gradište** *Blg.*	montaña	montagne	montanha
ridges	Höhenrücken	**gr'ady** *Rus.*	sierras	crêtes	cordilheira
general	General	**gral., general** *Eng., Sp.*	general	général	geral
ridge	Grat	**Grat** *Ger.*	sierra	crête	cordilheira
grotto	Grotte	**grotta** *It.*	gruta	grotte	gruta
grotto	Grotte	**grotte** *Fr.*	gruta	grotte	gruta
group	Gruppe	**group** *Eng.*	grupo	groupe	grupo
island	Insel	**-grund** *Swe.*	isla	île	ilha
group	Gruppe	**grupo** *Sp.*	grupo	groupe	grupo
group	Gruppe	**groppo** *It.*	grupo	groupe	grupo
pass	Pass	**guan** *Ch.*	paso	col	passo
bay	Bucht	**guba** *Rus.*	bahía	baie	baía
mountain	Berg	**guelb** *Ara.*	montaña	montagne	montanha
gulch	Wildbachschlucht	**gulch** *Eng.*	quebrada	ravin	quebrada
gulf	Golf	**gulf** *Eng.*	golfo	golfe	golfo
mountain	Berg	**gunong** *Mal.*	montaña	montagne	montanha
mountain	Berg	**gunung** *Indon.*	montaña	montagne	montanha
islands	Inseln	**-guntō** *Jpn.*	islas	îles	ilhas

H

ENGLISH	DEUTSCH	Map Form	ESPAÑOL	FRANÇAIS	PORTUGUÊS
upland	Bergland	**hadabat** *Ara.*	tierras altas	hautes terres	terras altas
mountain	Berg	**hadjer** *Ara.*	montaña	montagne	montanha
lagoon	Haff	**Haff** *Ger.*	laguna	lagune	laguna
sea, lake	Meer, See	**hai** *Ch.*	mar, lago	mer, lac	mar, lago
strait	Meeresstrasse	**haixia** *Ch.*	estrecho	détroit	estreito
reef	Riff	**hakau** *Poly.*	arrecife	récif	recife
peninsula	Halbinsel	**Halbinsel** *Ger.*	península	péninsule	península
hall	Halle	**hall** *Eng., Fr.*	salón	hall	hall
peninsula	Halbinsel	**-halvøya** *Nor.*	península	péninsule	península
beach	Strand	**-hama** *Jpn.*	playa	plage	praia
desert	Wüste	**hamada** *Ara.*	desierto	désert	deserto
plateau	Hochebene	**hammādat** *Ara.*	meseta	plateau	planalto
lake, marsh	See, Marsch	**hāmūn** *Per.*	lago, pantano	lac, marais	lago, pântano
point	Landspitze	**-hana** *Jpn.*	punta	pointe	ponta
peninsula	Halbinsel	**-hantō** *Jpn.*	península	péninsule	península
mountain, hill	Berg, Hügel	**har** *Heb.*	montaña, colina	montagne, colline	montanha, colina
harbor, harbour	Hafen	**harbor, harbour** *Eng.*	puerto	port	porto
mountains, hills	Berge, Hügel	**hare** *Heb.*	montañas, colinas	montagnes, collines	montanhas, colinas
ridge	Höhenrücken	**-harju** *Finn.*	sierra	crête	cordilheira
lava flow	Lavastrom	**harrat** *Ara.*	corriente de lava	coulée de lave	corrente de lava
hills	Hügel	**hauteurs** *Fr.*	colinas	hauteurs	colinas
sea, bay	Meer, Bucht	**-hav** *Swe.*	mar, bahía	mer, baie	mar, baía
harbor, harbour	Hafen	**havre** *Fr.*	puerto	havre	porto
oasis	Oase	**hawd** *Ara.*	oasis	oasis	oásis
lake	See	**hawr** *Ara.*	lago	lac	lago

ENGLISH	DEUTSCH	Map Form Geographische Begriffe Términos Geográficos Termes Géographiques Termos Geográficos	ESPAÑOL	FRANÇAIS	PORTUGUÊS
harbor, harbour	Hafen	**hbr., harbor, harbour** *Eng.*	puerto	port	porto
headquarters	Hauptquartier	**hdqrs., headquarters** *Eng.*	cuartel general	guartier général	quartel-general
river	Fluss	**he** *Ch.*	río	rivière	rio
head (headland)	Landspitze	**head** *Eng.*	promontorio	promontoire	promontório
heath	Heide	**heath** *Eng.*	matorral	lande	charneca
mountain(s)	Berg(e)	**hegy(ség)** *Hung.*	montaña(s)	montagne(s)	montanha(s)
heath	Heide	**Heide** *Ger.*	matorral	lande	charneca
plain	Ebene	**-heiya** *Jpn.*	llanura	plaine	planície
hills	Hügel	**-heuwells** *Afk.*	colinas	collines	colinas
highland	Hochland	**highland** *Eng.*	región montañosa	pays montagneux	terras altas
highway	Strasse	**highway** *Eng.*	carretera	route	rodovia
hill(s)	Hügel	**hill(s)** *Eng.*	colina(s)	colline(s)	colina(s)
race course	Rennbahn	**hipódromo** *Sp.*	hipódromo	hippodrome	hipódromo
race course	Rennbahn	**hippodrome** *Fr.*	hipódromo	hippodrome	hipódromo
historical	historisch	**hist., historical** *Eng.*	histórico	historique	histórico
historical park	historischer Park	**historical park** *Eng.*	parque histórico	parc historique	parque histórico
historic(al) site	historische Stätte	**historic(al) site** *Eng.*	sitio histórico	site historique	sítio histórico
Her Majesty's Air Station (U.K.)	Luftwaffenstützpunkt (V.K.)	**H.M.A.S., Her Majesty's Air Station** *Eng.*	Real Estación Aeronáutica (R.U.)	Station Aérienne Royale (R.U.)	Estação Aérea Real (R.U.)
river	Fluss	**ho** *Ch.*	río	rivière	rio
reservoir	Stausee	**-ho** *Kor.*	embalse	réservoir	reservatório
mountain	Berg	**-hø** *Nor.*	montaña	montagne	montanha
plateau	Hochebene	**Hochebene** *Ger.*	meseta	plateau	planalto
forest	Hochwald	**Hochwald** *Ger.*	bosque	forêt	floresta
mountain	Berg	**-högarna** *Swe.*	montaña	montagne	montanha
height	Höhe	**Höhe** *Ger.*	altura	hauteur	elevação
cave(s)	Höhle(n)	**Höhle(n)** *Ger.*	cueva(s)	caverne(s)	caverna(s)
island	Insel	**-holm** *Dan.*	isla	île	ilha
hook	Haken	**hook** *Eng.*	gancho	crochet	cabo, promontório
mountain	Berg	**hora** *Czech, Slo.*	montaña	montagne	montanha
point, peak	Horn	**Horn** *Ger.*	punta, pico	pointe, cime	ponta, pico
ruin	Ruine	**ḥorva** *Heb.*	ruina	ruine	ruína
mountains	Berge	**hory** *Czech, Slo.*	montañas	montagnes	montanhas
hospital	Krankenhaus	**hospital** *Eng., Sp.*	hospital	hôpital	hospital
point	Landspitze	**houma** *Poly.*	punta	pointe	ponta
house	Haus	**house** *Eng.*	casa	maison	casa
island	Insel	**hsü** *Ch.*	isla	île	ilha
lake, reservoir	See, Stausee	**hu** *Ch.*	lago, embalse	lac, réservoir	lago, reservatório
hill	Hügel	**Hügel** *Ger.*	colina	colline	colina
cape	Huk	**Huk** *Ger.*	cabo	cap	cabo
cape	Huk	**-huk** *Swe.*	cabo	cap	cabo
highway	Strasse	**hy., highway** *Eng.*	carretera	route	rodovia

I

ENGLISH	DEUTSCH	Map Form	ESPAÑOL	FRANÇAIS	PORTUGUÊS
island	Insel	**i., isla** *Sp.* **island**	isla	île	ilha
icefield	Eisdecke	**icefield** *Eng.*	helero	champ de glace	geleira
ice shelf	Schelfeis	**ice shelf** *Eng.*	corniza glacial	barrière de glace	banco de gelo
ice tongue	Eiszunge	**ice tongue** *Eng.*	lengua de glaciar	langue glaciaire	língua de geleira
dunes	Dünen	**idehan** *Ber.*	dunas	dunes	dunas
river	Fluss	**ig., igarapé** *Port.*	río	rivière	igarapé
church	Kirche	**iglesia** *Sp.*	iglesia	église	igreja
lake	See	**-ike** *Jpn.*	lago	lac	lago
island(s)	Insel(n)	**île(s)** *Fr.*	isla(s)	île(s)	ilha(s)
islet(s)	kleine Insel(n)	**îlet(s)** *Fr.*	isleta(s)	îlet(s)	ilhota(s)
island(s)	Insel(n)	**ilha(s)** *Port.*	isla(s)	île(s)	ilha(s)
islet(s)	kleine Insel(n)	**ilhéu(s)** *Port.*	isleta(s)	îlot(s)	ilhéu(s)
island	Insel	**illa** *Cat.*	isla	île	ilha
islands	Inseln	**illes** *Cat.*	islas	îles	ilhas
hill, upland	Hügel, Bergland	**'ilw** *Ara.*	colina, tierras altas	colline, hautes terres	colina, terras altas
hill	Hügel	**'ilwat** *Ara.*	colina	colline	colina
Indian reservation	Indianer-reservation	**Ind. res., Indian reservation** *Eng.*	reserva de Indios	réserve indienne	reserva indígena
inlet	Einfahrt	**inlet** *Eng.*	abra	bras de mer	enseada
island(s)	Insel(n)	**Insel(n)** *Ger.*	isla(s)	île(s)	ilha(s)
institute	Institut	**inst., institute** *Eng.*	instituto	institut	instituto
international	international	**int., international** *Eng.*	internacional	international	internacional
race course	Rennbahn	**ippodromo** *It.*	hipódromo	hippodrome	hipódromo
wadi	Wadi	**irhazer** *Ber.*	uadi	wadi	uádi
dunes	Dünen	**'irq** *Ara.*	dunas	dunes	dunas
islands	Inseln	**is., islands** *Eng.* **islas**	islas	îles	ilhas
island	Insel	**isla** *Sp.*	isla	île	ilha
island(s)	Insel(n)	**island(s)** *Eng.*	isla(s)	île(s)	ilha(s)
islands	Inseln	**islas** *Sp.*	islas	îles	ilhas
isle(s)	Insel(n)	**isle(s)** *Eng.*	isla(s)	île(s)	ilha(s)
islet(s)	kleine Insel(n)	**islet(s)** *Eng.*	isleta(s)	îlot(s)	ilhota(s)
islet	kleine Insel	**islote** *Sp.*	islote	îlot	ilhota
island	Insel	**isola** *It.*	isla	île	ilha
islands	Inseln	**isole** *It.*	islas	îles	ilhas
islet	kleine Insel	**isolotto** *It.*	isleta	îlot	ilhota
isthmus	Landenge	**isthme** *Fr.*	istmo	isthme	istmo
isthmus	Landenge	**isthmus** *Eng.*	istmo	isthme	istmo
isthmus	Landenge	**istmo** *Sp.*	istmo	isthme	istmo
island	Insel	**-iwa** *Jpn.*	isla	île	ilha

J

ENGLISH	DEUTSCH	Map Form	ESPAÑOL	FRANÇAIS	PORTUGUÊS
mountain(s)	Berg(e)	**jabal** *Ara.*	montaña(s)	montagne(s)	montanha(s)
cave	Höhle	**jama** *S./C.*	cueva	caverne	caverna
caves	Höhlen	**jame** *S./C.*	cuevas	cavernes	cavernas
garden	Garten	**jardin** *Fr.*	jardín	jardin	jardim
garden	Garten	**jardín** *Sp.*	jardín	jardin	jardim
gardens	Gärten	**jardines** *Sp.*	jardines	jardins	jardins
lake	See	**järv** *Est.*	lago	lac	lago
lake	See	**-järvi** *Finn.*	lago	lac	lago
mountains	Berge	**jary** *Rus.*	montañas	montagnes	montanhas
lake	See	**-jaur** *Lapp.*	lago	lac	lago
islands	Inseln	**jazā'ir** *Ara.*	islas	îles	ilhas
peninsula	Halbinsel	**jazirah** *Indon.*	península	péninsule	península
island	Insel	**jazīrat** *Ara.*	isla	île	ilha
island	Insel	**jazīreh** *Per.*	isla	île	ilha
reservoir	Stausee	**jazovir** *Blg.*	embalse	réservoir	reservatório
mountain(s)	Berg(e)	**jbel** *Ara.*	montaña(s)	montagne(s)	montanha(s)
lake	See	**jezero** *S./C.*	lago	lac	lago
lake, lagoon	See, Lagune, Haff	**jezioro** *Pol.*	lago, laguna	lac, lagune	lago, laguna
river	Fluss	**jiang** *Ch.*	río	rivière	rio
cape	Kap	**jiao** *Ch.*	cabo	cap	cabo
mountains	Berge	**jibāl** *Ara.*	montañas	montagnes	montanhas
island	Insel	**-jima** *Jpn.*	isla	île	ilha
saddle (pass)	Joch	**Joch** *Ger.*	paso	col	passo
river	Fluss	**-joki** *Finn.*	río	rivière	rio
glacier	Gletscher	**-jokulen** *Nor.*	glaciar	glacier	geleria
glacier	Gletscher	**-jökull** *Ice.*	glaciar	glacier	geleria
gulf	Golf	**jūras līcis** *Latv.*	golfo	golfe	golfo
islands	Inseln	**juzur** *Ara.*	islas	îles	ilhas

K

ENGLISH	DEUTSCH	Map Form	ESPAÑOL	FRANÇAIS	PORTUGUÊS
mountains	Berge	**kabīr** *Per.*	montañas	montagnes	montanhas
dunes	Dünen	**kahal** *Ara.*	dunas	dunes	dunas
sea	Meer	**-kai** *Jpn.*	mar	mer	mar
strait	Meeresstrasse	**-kaikyō** *Jpn.*	estrecho	détroit	estreito
mountain	Berg	**-kaise** *Lapp.*	montaña	montagne	montanha
navy installation	Anlage de Marine	**ka.j., kaijō-jieitai** *Jpn.*	estación de la marina	installation navale	instalação naval
brook	Bach	**kali** *Indon.*	riachuelo	crique	riacho
mountain	Berg	**kalns** *Latv.*	montaña	montagne	montanha
ridge	Kamm	**Kamm** *Ger.*	sierra	crête	serra
canal	Kanal	**kanaal** *Du.*	canal	canal	canal
canal, channel	Kanal	**Kanal** *Ger.*	canal	canal	canal
canal, channel	Kanal	**kanal** *Rus., S./C., Swe.*	canal	canal	canal
canal, channel	Kanal	**kanał** *Pol.*	canal	canal	canal
canal, channel	Kanal	**kanalen** *Swe.*	canal	canal	canal
canal, channel	Kanal	**kanava** *Finn.*	canal	canal	canal
pass	Pass	**kandao** *Pas.*	paso	col	passo
river	Fluss	**-kang** *Kor.*	río	rivière	rio
moor	Moor	**-kangas** *Finn.*	páramo	lande	charneca
national park	Nationalpark	**kansallis-puisto** *Finn.*	parque nacional	parc national	parque nacional
island	Insel	**kaoh** *Cbd.*	isla	île	ilha
cape	Kap	**Kap** *Ger.*	cabo	cap	cabo
gorge	Schlucht	**kapija** *S./C.*	garganta	gorge	garganta
cape	Kap	**-kapp** *Nor.*	cabo	cap	cabo
dunes	Dünen	**kathīb** *Ara.*	dunas	dunes	dunas
desert	Wüste	**kavīr** *Per.*	desierto	désert	deserto
mountain	Berg	**kawlat** *Ara.*	montaña	montagne	montanha
hill	Hügel	**kawm** *Ara.*	colina	colline	colina
mountain	Berg	**keḍiet** *Ara.*	montaña	montagne	montanha
lake	See	**kenohan** *Indon.*	lago	lac	lago
cape	Kap	**kep** *Alb.*	cabo	cap	cabo
islands	Inseln	**kepulauan** *Indon.*	islas	îles	ilhas
key(s), cay(s)	Klippe(n)	**key(s)** *Eng.*	cayo(s)	caye(s)	baixio(s)
intermittent lake	periodischer See	**khabrat** *Ara.*	lago intermitente	lac périodique	lago intermitente
gulf	Golf	**khalīj** *Ara.*	golfo	golfe	golfo
mountain	Berg	**khao** *Bur., Thai*	montaña	montagne	montanha
mountain	Berg	**khashm** *Ara.*	montaña	montagne	montanha
wadi	Wadi	**khatt** *Ara.*	uadi	wadi	uádi
wadi, river	Wadi, Fluss	**khawr** *Ara.*	uadi, río	wadi, rivière	uádi, rio
dam	Damm	**khazzān** *Ara.*	presa	barrage	represa
river, canal	Fluss, Kanal	**khlong** *Thai*	río, canal	rivière, canal	rio, canal
dunes	Dünen	**khubb** *Ara.*	dunas	dunes	dunas
kill (river, channel)	Fluss, Kanal	**kill** *Eng.*	río, canal	rivière, canal	rio, canal
cemetery	Friedhof	**kladb., kladbišče** *Rus.*	cementerio	cimetière	cemitério
cloister	Kloster	**klasztory** *Pol.*	claustro	cloître	claustro, convento
cloister, monastery	Kloster	**Kloster** *Ger.*	claustro, monasterio	cloître, monastère	claustro, mosteiro
knob	Kuppe	**knob** *Eng.*	protuberancia	bosse	cerro, colina
island	Insel	**ko** *Thai*	isla	île	ilha
lake, lagoon	See, Lagune, Haff	**-ko** *Jpn.*	lago, laguna	lac, lagune	lago, laguna
harbor, harbour	Hafen	**-kō** *Jpn.*	puerto	port	porto
highland	Hochland	**-kōchi** *Jpn.*	región montañosa	pays montagneux	terras altas
mountain	Kogel	**Kogel** *Ger.*	montaña	montagne	montanha
plateau	Hochebene	**-kogen** *Jpn.*	meseta	plateau	planalto
mountains	Berge	**koh** *Per.*	montañas	montagnes	montanhas
air force installation	Anlage der Luftwaffe	**ko.j., kōkū-jieitai** *Jpn.*	estación aeronáutica	installation aérienne	instalação da força aérea
national park	Nationalpark	**-kokuritsu-kōen** *Jpn.*	parque nacional	parc national	parque nacional
national park	Nationalpark	**-kokutei-kōen** *Jpn.*	parque nacional	parc national	parque nacional
bay	Bucht	**kólpos** *Gr.*	bahía	baie	baía
mountain	Berg	**kong** *Indon.*	montaña	montagne	montanha
peak	Kopf	**Kopf** *Ger.*	pico	cime	pico
bridge	Brücke	**köprüsü** *Tur.*	puente	pont	ponte
gulf, bay	Golf, Bucht	**körfezi** *Tur.*	golfo, bahía	golfe, baie	golfo, baía
spit	Landzunge	**kosa** *Rus.*	lengua de tierra	flèche	ponta de terra
rapids	Stromschnellen	**-koski** *Finn.*	rápidos	rapides	rápidos
pass	Pass	**kotal** *Per.*	paso	col	passo
basin	Becken	**kotlina** *Pol.*	cuenca	bassin	bacia
bay, pass	Bucht, Pass	**kou** *Ch.*	bahía, paso	baie, col	baía, passo
ridge	Höhenrücken	**kr'až** *Rus.*	sierra	crête	serra
escarpment	Landstufe	**kreb** *Ara.*	escarpa	escarpement	escarpa
fort	Fort	**krepost'** *Rus.*	fuerte	fort	forte
national park	Nationalpark	**krk., kokuritsu-kōen** *Jpn.*	parque nacional	parc national	parque nacional
national park	Nationalpark	**ktk., kokutei-kōen** *Jpn.*	parque nacional	parc national	parque nacional
bay	Bucht	**kuala** *Mal.*	bahía	baie	baía
mountain(s)	Berg(e)	**kūh(ha)** *Per.*	montaña(s)	montagne(s)	montanha(s)
hill	Hügel	**-kulle** *Swe.*	colina	colline	colina
dome	Kuppe	**Kuppe** *Ger.*	domo	dôme	domo
strait	Meeresstrasse	**-kurkku** *Finn.*	estrecho	détroit	estreito
channel	Kanal	**kyle** *Gae.*	canal, estrecho	canal, détroit	canal, estreito
island	Insel	**kyun** *Bur.*	isla	île	ilha
hills	Hügel	**-kyūryū** *Jpn.*	colinas	collines	colinas

L

ENGLISH	DEUTSCH	Map Form	ESPAÑOL	FRANÇAIS	PORTUGUÊS
lake	See	**l., lac** *Fr.* **lago lagoa lake**	lago	lac	lago, lagoa
pass	Pass	**la** *Tib.*	paso	col	passo
province	Provinz	**lääni** *Finn.*	provincia	province	província
lake(s)	See(n)	**lac(s)** *Fr.*	lago(s)	lac(s)	lago(s)
lake	See	**lacul** *Rom.*	lago	lac	lago
cape	Kap	**laem** *Thai*	cabo	cap	cabo
lagoon, lake	Lagune, Haff, See	**lag., laguna** *Sp.*	laguna	lagune, lac	laguna
lake	See	**lago** *It., Port., Sp.*	lago	lac	lago
lake, lagoon	See, Lagune, Haff	**lagoa** *Port.*	lago, laguna	lac, lagune	lagoa
lagoon	Lagune, Haff	**lagoon** *Eng.*	laguna	lagune	laguna
lakes	Seen	**lagos** *Port., Sp.*	lagos	lacs	lagos
lagoon, lake	Lagune, Haff, See	**laguna** *Sp.*	laguna	lagune, lac	laguna, lago
lagoon	Lagune, Haff	**lagune** *Fr.*	laguna	lagune	laguna
bay	Bucht	**laht** *Est.*	bahía	baie	baía
gulf	Golf	**-lahti** *Finn.*	golfo	golfe	golfo
lake(s)	See(n)	**lake(s)** *Eng.*	lago(s)	lac(s)	lago(s)
county	Grafschaft	**län** *Swe.*	condado	comté	condado
lake	Lanke (See)	**Lanke** *Ger.*	lago	lac	lago
sea	Meer	**laut** *Indon.*	mar	mer	mar
lava flow	Lavastrom	**lava flow** *Eng.*	corriente de lava	coulée de lave	corrente de lava
hill, mountain	Hügel, Berg	**law** *Gae.*	colina, montaña	colline, montagne	colina, montanha
mountains, forest	Berge, Wald	**les** *Czech*	montañas, bosque	montagnes, forêt	montanhas, floresta
forest	Wald	**les** *Rus.*	bosque	forêt	floresta
level (plain)	Niveau (Ebene)	**level** *Eng.*	nivel (llano)	niveau (plaine)	planície
islands	Inseln	**liedao** *Ch.*	islas	îles	ilhas
lighthouse	Leuchtturm	**lighthouse** *Eng.*	faro	phare	farol
estuary	Trichtermündung	**liman** *Rus.*	estuario	estuaire	estuário
bay	Bucht	**limanı** *Tur.*	bahía	baie	baía
lake	See	**límni** *Gr.*	lago	lac	lago
mountain(s), peak	Berg(e), Gipfel	**ling** *Ch.*	montaña(s), pico	montagne(s), pic	montanha(s), pico
plain(s)	Ebene(n)	**llano(s)** *Sp.*	llano(s)	plaine(s)	planície(s)

ENGLISH	DEUTSCH	Map Form / Geographische Begriffe / Términos Geográficos / Termes Géographiques / Termos Geográficos	ESPAÑOL	FRANÇAIS	PORTUGUÊS
lake, reservoir	See, Stausee	**llyn** *Welsh*	lago, embalse	lac, réservoir	lago, reservatório
lake, inlet	See, Einfahrt	**loch** *Gae.*	lago, abra	lac, bras de mer	lago, angra
lock	Schleuse	**lock** *Eng.*	esclusa	écluse	eclusa
lock and dam	Damm mit Schleuse	**lock and dam** *Eng.*	presa y esclusa	écluse et barrage	represa e eclusa
gorge	Schlucht	**log** *Rus.*	garganta	gorge	garganta
mountain	Berg	**loi** *Bur.*	montaña	montagne	montanha
hills	Hügel	**lomas** *Sp.*	lomas	collines	colinas
lake	See	**lough** *Gae.*	lago	lac	lago
lowland	Tiefland	**lowland** *Eng.*	tierra baja	terrain bas	terras baixas
marsh	Luch (Bruch)	**Luch** *Ger.*	pantano	marais	pântano
island	Insel	**-luoto** *Finn.*	isla	île	ilha

M

ENGLISH	DEUTSCH	Map Form	ESPAÑOL	FRANÇAIS	PORTUGUÊS
mountains	Berge	**m., munţii** *Rom.*	montañas	montagnes	montanhas
island	Insel	**-maa** *Est.*	isla	île	ilha
strait	Meeresstrasse	**madīq** *Ara.*	estrecho	détroit	estreito
river	Fluss	**mae** *Thai*	río	rivière	rio
depression	Senke	**makhtesh** *Heb.*	depresión	dépression	depressão
bay	Bucht	**-man** *Kor.*	bahía	baie	baía
monastery	Kloster	**manastir** *S./C.*	monasterio	monastère	mosteiro
sea	Meer	**mar** *Sp., It.*	mar	mer	mar
marsh	Marsch	**marais** *Fr.*	pantano	marais	pântano
sea	Meer	**mare** *It.*	mar	mer	mar
marine corps air station	Flugstützpunkt des Marine-Corps	**marine corps air station** *Eng.*	estación aeronáutica de la infantería de marina	station aérienne de fusiliers marins	estação aérea de fuzileiros navais
marine corps base	Marine-Corps-Stützpunkt	**marine corps base** *Eng.*	base de la infantería de marina	base de fusiliers marins	base de fuzileiros navais
bay	Bucht	**marsā** *Ara.*	bahía	baie	baía
marsh	Marsch	**Marsch** *Ger.*	pantano	marais	pântano
marsh(es)	Marsch(en)	**marsh(es)** *Eng.*	pantano(s)	marais	pântano(s)
river mouth	Flussmündung	**maṣabb** *Ara.*	desembocadura	embouchure	desembocadura
canal	Kanal	**masrif** *Ara.*	canal	canal	canal
massif	Gebirgsmassiv	**massif** *Eng., Fr.*	macizo	massif	maciço
marine corps air station	Flugstützpunkt des Marine-Corps	**m.c.a.s., marine corps air station**	estación aeronáutica de la infantería de marina	station aérienne de fusiliers marins	estação aérea de fuzileiros navais
marine corps base	Marine-Corps-Stützpunkt	**m.c.b., marine corps base** *Eng.*	base de la infantería de marina	base de fusiliers marins	base de fuzileiros navais
meadow	Wiese	**meadow** *Eng.*	prado	prairie	pradaria
dunes	Dünen	**médanos** *Sp.*	médanos	dunes	dunas
sea, lake	Meer	**Meer** *Ger.*	mar, lago	mer, lac	mar, lago
sea, lake	Meer	**-meer** *Afk., Du.*	mar, lago	mer, lac	mar, lago
hills	Hügel	**melkosopočnik** *Rus.*	colinas	collines	colinas
memorial	Gedenkstätte	**mem., memorial** *Eng.*	monumento	mémorial	monumento
peninsula	Halbinsel	**menanjung** *Indon.*	península	péninsule	península
sea	Meer	**mer** *Fr.*	mar	mer	mar
mesa	Tafelberg	**mesa** *Sp.*	mesa	mesa	mesa
plateau	Hochebene	**meseta** *Sp.*	meseta	plateau	planalto
middle	Mittel-	**mid., middle** *Eng.*	medio	moyen	médio, central
spit	Landzunge	**mierzeja** *Pol.*	lengua de tierra	flèche	ponta de terra
bay	Bucht	**mifraz** *Heb.*	bahía	baie	baía
mines	Bergwerke	**mikhrot** *Heb.*	minas	mines	minas
military	militärisch	**mil., military** *Eng.*	militar	militaire	militar
harbor, harbour	Hafen	**-minato** *Jpn.*	puerto	port	porto
mine	Bergwerk	**mine** *Eng., Fr.*	mina	mine	mina
mountain	Berg	**-mine** *Jpn.*	montaña	montagne	montanha
cliff	Kliff	**minqār** *Ara.*	risco	falaise	falésia
cape	Kap	**-misaki** *Jpn.*	cabo	cap	cabo
mission	Mission	**mission** *Eng., Fr.*	misión	mission	missão
monument	Denkmal	**mon., monument** *Eng., Fr.*	monumento	monument	monumento
monastery	Kloster	**monasterio** *Sp.*	monasterio	monastère	mosteiro
monastery	Kloster	**monastero** *It.*	monasterio	monastère	mosteiro
monastery	Kloster	**monastery** *Eng.*	monasterio	monastère	mosteiro
monastery	Kloster	**moni** *Gr.*	monasterio	monastère	mosteiro
mount	Berg	**mont** *Fr.*	monte	mont	monte
mountain	Berg	**montagna** *It.*	montaña	montagne	montanha
mountain(s)	Berg(e)	**montagne(s)** *Fr.*	montaña(s)	montagne(s)	montanha(s)
mountain(s)	Berg(e)	**montaña(s)** *Sp.*	montaña(s)	montagne(s)	montanha(s)
mount	Berg	**monte** *It., Port., Sp.*	monte	mont	monte
mountains	Berge	**montes** *Port., Sp.*	montes	monts	montes
mountains	Berge	**monti** *It.*	montes	monts	montes
mountains	Berge	**monts** *Fr.*	montes	monts	montes
monument	Denkmal	**monument** *Eng., Fr.*	monumento	monument	monumento
moor	Moor	**moor** *Eng.*	páramo	lande	pântano
moor	Moor	**Moor** *Ger.*	páramo	lande	pântano
sea	Meer	**more** *Rus.*	mar	mer	mar
mountain	Berg	**-mori** *Jpn.*	montaña	montagne	montanha
mountain	Berg	**morne** *Fr.*	montaña	morne	montanha
hill, mountain	Hügel, Berg	**morro** *Port., Sp.*	morro	colline, montagne	morro
mosque	Moschee	**mosque** *Eng.*	mezquita	mosquée	mesquita
island, rock	Insel, Fels	**motu** *Poly.*	isla, roca	île, rocher	ilha, rochedo
island	Insel	**mouchão** *Port.*	isla	île	mouchão
mound	Erdhügel	**mound** *Eng.*	montículo	tertre	montículo
mount	Berg	**mount** *Eng.*	monte	mont	monte
mountain(s)	Berg(e)	**mountain(s)** *Eng.*	montaña(s)	montagne(s)	montanha(s)
mouth (river mouth)	Mündung	**mouth** *Eng.*	desembocadura	embouchure	desembocadura
mount	Berg	**mt., mount** *Eng.*	monte	mont	monte
mountain	Berg	**mtn., mountain** *Eng.*	montaña	montagne	montanha
mountains	Berge	**mts., mountains** *Eng.*	montañas	montagnes	montanhas
point	Landspitze	**mui** *Viet.*	punta	pointe	ponta
headland	Landspitze	**mull** *Gae.*	promontorio	promontoire	promontório
depression	Senke	**munkhafad** *Ara.*	depresión	dépression	depressão
mountain	Berg	**muntele** *Rom.*	montaña	montagne	montanha
mountains	Berge	**munţii** *Rom.*	montañas	montagnes	montanhas
museum	Museum	**museo** *It., Sp.*	museo	musée	museu
museum	Museum	**Museum** *Ger.*	museo	musée	museu
museum	Museum	**museum** *Eng.*	museo	musée	museu
museum	Museum	**múzeum** *Hung.*	museo	musée	museu
museum	Museum	**muzej** *Rus.*	museo	musée	museu
cape	Kap	**mys** *Rus.*	cabo	cap	cabo

N

ENGLISH	DEUTSCH	Map Form	ESPAÑOL	FRANÇAIS	PORTUGUÊS
north	Nord	**n., north** *Eng.*	norte	nord	norte
sea, gulf	Meer, Golf	**-nada** *Jpn.*	mar, golfo	mer, golfe	mar, golfo
desert	Wüste	**nafūd** *Ara.*	desierto	désert	deserto
plateau, mountains	Hochebene, Berge	**nagorje** *Rus.*	meseta, montañas	plateau, montagnes	planalto, montanhas
river	Fluss	**nahr** *Ara.*	río	rivière	rio
sea	Meer	**-naikai** *Jpn.*	mar	mer	mar
salt flat	Salzebene	**namakzār** *Per.*	salar	saline	salina
narrows	Meeresenge	**narrows** *Eng.*	angostura	goulet	estreito
peninsula	Halbinsel	**-näs** *Swe.*	península	péninsule	península
naval air station	Flugstützpunkt der Marine	**n.a.s., naval air station** *Eng.*	estación aeronáutica de la marina	station de forces aériennes navales	estação aérea da marinha
National Aeronautics and Space Administration	Nationale Aeronautik-und Weltraum-Behörde	**N.A.S.A., National Aeronautics and Space Administration** *Eng.*	Administración Nacional Aeronáutica y Espacial	Administration Nationale de l'Espace et Aéronautique	Administração Nacional do Espaço e Aeronâutica
national park	Nationalpark	**nasjonal park** *Nor.*	parque nacional	parc national	parque nacional
national	national	**nat., national** *Eng., Fr.*	nacional	national	nacional
national battlefield site	Schlachtfeld	**national battlefield site** *Eng.*	campo de batalla nacional	champ de bataille national	campo de batalha nacional
national cemetery	Nationalfriedhof	**national cemetery** *Eng.*	cementerio nacional	cimetière national	cemitério nacional
national forest	Wald in Gemeinbesitz	**national forest** *Eng.*	bosque nacional	forêt nationale	floresta nacional
national historical park	Park an historischer Stätte	**national historical park** *Eng.*	parque histórico nacional	parc historique national	parque histórico nacional
national historical site	historische Stätte	**national historical site** *Eng.*	lugar histórico nacional	site historique national	sítio histórico nacional
national laboratory	staatliche Forschungs-anstalt	**national laboratory** *Eng.*	laboratorio nacional	laboratoire national	laboratório nacional
national memorial	nationale Gedenkstätte	**national memorial** *Eng.*	monumento nacional	memorial national	monumento nacional
national military park	Park bei einem Schlachtfeld	**national military park** *Eng.*	parque militar nacional	parc militaire national	parque militar nacional
national monument	National-denkmal	**national monument** *Eng.*	monumento nacional	monument national	monumento nacional
national park	Nationalpark	**national park** *Eng.*	parque nacional	parc nationale	parque nacional
national recreation area	Ausflugsgebiet	**national recreation area** *Eng.*	campo nacional de recreo	région de récréation national	área de lazer nacional
national seashore	öffentlicher Badestrand	**national seashore** *Eng.*	playa nacional	plage nationale	praia nacional
reserve	Naturpark	**Naturpark** *Ger.*	reserva natural	réserve naturelle	reserva natural
nature reserve	Naturschutzgebiet	**Naturschutzgebiet** *Ger.*	reserva natural	réserve naturelle	reserva natural
naval air station	Flugstützpunkt der Marine	**naval air station** *Eng.*	estación aeronáutica de la marina	station de forces aériennes navales	estação aérea da marinha
naval base	Flottenstützpunkt	**naval base** *Eng.*	base naval	base navale	base naval
naval station	Marinestation	**naval station** *Eng.*	estación naval	station navale	estação naval
naval base	Flottenstützpunkt	**n.b., naval base** *Eng.*	base naval	base navale	base naval
rock	Fels	**-ne** *Jpn.*	roca	rocher	rochedo
neck	Landenge	**neck** *Eng.*	istmo	isthme	istmo
necropolis (cemetery)	Friedhof	**necrópolis** *Sp.*	necrópolis	nécropole	necrópole
cape	Kap	**neem** *Est.*	cabo	cap	cabo
peninsula, point	Halbinsel, Landspitze	**-nes** *Ice., Nor.*	península, punta	péninsule, pointe	península, ponta
promontory	Vorgebirge	**ness** *Gae.*	promontorio	promontoire	promontório
snowcapped mountain(s)	Schneegipfel	**nev.(s)., nevado(s)** *Sp.*	nevado(s)	montagne(s) neigeuse(s)	pico(s) nevado(s)
mountain	Berg	**ngoc** *Viet.*	montaña	montagne	montanha
cape	Kap	**nina** *Est.*	cabo	cap	cabo
islands	Inseln	**nísoi** *Gr.*	islas	îles	ilhas
island	Insel	**nísos** *Gr.*	isla	île	ilha
lowland	Tiefland	**nizina** *Rus.*	tierra baja	terrain bas	terras baixas
lowland	Tiefland	**nižina** *Slo.*	tierra baja	terrain bas	terras baixas
lowland	Tiefland	**nizmennost'** *Rus.*	tierra baja	terrain bas	terras baixas
cape	Kap	**nos** *Blg.*	cabo	cap	cabo
naval station	Marinestation	**n.s., naval station** *Eng.*	estación naval	station navale	estação naval
nature reserve	Naturschutzgebiet	**Nsg., Naturschutzgebiet** *Ger.*	reserva natural	réserve naturelle	reserva natural
mountain	Berg	**nui** *Viet.*	montaña	montagne	montanha
lake	See	**-numa** *Jpn.*	lago	lac	lago
mountains	Berge	**nuruu** *Mong.*	montañas	montagnes	montanhas
island	Insel	**nusa** *Indon.*	isla	île	ilha
lake	See	**nuur** *Mong.*	lago	lac	lago

O

ENGLISH	DEUTSCH	Map Form	ESPAÑOL	FRANÇAIS	PORTUGUÊS
island	Insel	**-ø** *Dan., Nor.*	isla	île	ilha
island	Insel	**-ö** *Swe.*	isla	île	ilha
island	Insel	**o., ostrov** *Rus.*	isla	île	ilha
islands	Inseln	**-öarna** *Swe.*	islas	îles	ilhas
oasis	Oase	**oasis** *Eng., Fr., Sp.*	oasis	oasis	oásis
observatory	Observatorium	**observatorio** *Sp.*	observatorio	observatoire	observatório
observatory	Observatorium	**observatory** *Eng.*	observatorio	observatoire	observatório
ocean	Ozean	**ocean** *Eng.*	océano	océan	oceano
island	Insel	**-ön** *Swe.*	isla	île	ilha
mountains	Berge	**óri** *Gr.*	montañas	montagnes	montanhas
bay	Bucht	**órmos** *Gr.*	bahía	baie	baía
mountain(s)	Berg(e)	**óros** *Gr.*	montaña(s)	montagne(s)	montanha(s)
island(s)	Insel(n)	**ostrov(a)** *Rus.*	isla(s)	île(s)	ilha(s)
island	Insel	**ostrovul** *Rom.*	isla	île	ilha
islands	Inseln	**otoci** *S./C.*	islas	îles	ilhas
island	Insel	**otok** *S./C.*	isla	île	ilha
wadi	Wadi	**ouadi** *Ara.*	uadi	wadi	uádi
wadi	Wadi	**oued** *Ara.*	uadi	wadi	uádi
outlet	Abfluss	**outlet** *Eng.*	desagüe	débouché	escoadouro
island	Insel	**-øy, -øya** *Nor.*	isla	île	ilha
lake	See	**oz., ozero** *Rus.*	lago	lac	lago
lakes	Seen	**ozera** *Rus.*	lagos	lacs	lagos

P

ENGLISH	DEUTSCH	Map Form	ESPAÑOL	FRANÇAIS	PORTUGUÊS
hills	Hügel	**pahorkatina** *Czech*	colinas	collines	colinas
palace	Palast	**pal., palace** *Eng.*	palacio	palais	palácio
palace	Palast	**palacio** *Sp.*	palacio	palais	palácio
palace	Palast	**palais** *Fr.*	palacio	palais	palácio
palace	Palast	**palazzo** *It.*	palacio	palais	palácio
palace	Palast	**paleis** *Du.*	palacio	palais	palácio
railroad station	Bahnhof	**pályaudvar** *Hung.*	estacíon ferrocarril	gare	estação ferroviária
monument	Denkmal	**pam'atnik** *Rus.*	monumento	monument	monumento
plain	Ebene	**pampa** *Sp.*	pampa	plaine	pampa
basin	Becken	**pánev** *Czech*	cuenca	bassin	bacia
swamp	Sumpf	**pantanal** *Port., Sp.*	pantanal	marais	pantanal
marsh, swamp, reservoir	Marsch, Sumpf, Stausee	**pantano** *Sp.*	pantano	marais, réservoir	Pântano
moor	Moor	**páramo** *Sp.*	páramo	lande	pântano
park	Park	**parc** *Fr.*	parque	parc	parque
national park	Nationalpark	**parc national** *Fr.*	parque nacional	parc national	parque nacional
park	Park	**parco** *It.*	parque	parc	parque
national park	Nationalpark	**parco nazionale** *It.*	parque nacional	parc national	parque nacional
provincial park	Naturpark	**parc provincial** *Fr.*	parque de la provincia	parc provincial	parque provincial
park	Park	**Park** *Ger.*	parque	parc	parque
park	Park	**park** *Eng.*	parque	parc	parque
national park	Nationalpark	**park narodowy** *Pol.*	parque nacional	parc national	parque nacional
parkway	Ferienstrasse	**parkway** *Eng.*	calzada	allée de parc	alameda de parque
park	Park	**parque** *Port., Sp.*	parque	parc	parque
national park	Nationalpark	**parq. nac., parque nacional** *Port., Sp.*	parque nacional	parc national	parque nacional
beach	Strand	**part** *Hung.*	playa	plage	praia
strait	Meeresstrasse	**pas** *Fr.*	estrecho	détroit	estreito
passage	Durchfahrt	**pasaje** *Sp.*	pasaje	passage	passagem
pass	Pass	**paso** *Sp.*	paso	col	passo
pass	Pass	**Pass** *Ger.*	paso	col	passo
pass	Pass	**pass** *Eng.*	paso	col	passo
passage	Durchfahrt	**passage** *Eng., Fr.*	pasaje	passage	passagem
passage	Durchfahrt	**passe** *Fr.*	pasaje	passe	passagem
pass	Pass	**passo** *It.*	paso	col	passo
pass	Pass	**pasul** *Rom.*	paso	col	passo
brook	Bach	**patak** *Hung.*	riachuelo	crique	riacho
peak(s)	Gipfel	**peak(s)** *Eng.*	pico(s)	pic(s)	pico(s)
cave	Höhle	**pećina** *S./C.*	cueva	caverne	caverna
mountain	Berg	**pedra** *Port.*	montaña	montagne	montanha

ENGLISH	DEUTSCH	Map Form Geographische Begriffe Términos Geográficos Termes Géographiques Termos Geográficos	ESPAÑOL	FRANÇAIS	PORTUGUÊS
mountains	Berge	**peg., pegunungan** *Indon.*	montañas	montagnes	montanhas
sea	Meer	**pélagos** *Gr.*	mar	mer	mar
peninsula	Halbinsel	**pen., peninsula** *Eng.*	península	péninsule	península
peak, rock	Gipfel, Fels	**peña** *Sp.*	peña	pic, rocher	penha
peak, large rock	Gipfel, grosser Fels	**peñasco** *Sp.*	peñasco	pic, rocher	penhasco
basin	Becken	**pendi** *Ch.*	cuenca	bassin	bacia
peninsula	Halbinsel	**peninsula** *Eng.*	península	péninsule	península
peninsula	Halbinsel	**península** *Sp.*	península	péninsule	península
peninsula	Halbinsel	**péninsule** *Fr.*	península	péninsule	península
rock	Fels	**peñón** *Sp.*	peñón	rocher	rochedo
pass	Pass	**pereval** *Rus.*	paso	col	passo
strait	Meeresstrasse	**pertuis** *Fr.*	estrecho	pertuis	estreito
sand desert	Sandwüste	**peski** *Rus.*	desierto arenoso	désert de sable	deserto arenoso
mountain	Berg	**phnum** *Cbd.*	montaña	montagne	montanha
mountain	Berg	**phou** *Lao.*	montaña	montagne	montanha
mountain	Berg	**phu** *Thai*	montaña	montagne	montanha
cape	Kap	**pi** *Ch.*	cabo	cap	cabo
plain	Ebene	**piano** *It.*	llanura	plaine	planície
peak	Gipfel	**pic** *Fr.*	pico	pic	pico
peak	Gipfel	**picacho** *Sp.*	picacho	pic	pico
peak	Gipfel	**picco** *It.*	pico	pic	pico
peak(s)	Gipfel	**pico(s)** *Port., Sp.*	pico(s)	pic(s)	pico(s)
pier	Landungs-brücke	**pier** *Eng.*	embarcadero	jetée	cais
mountain	Berg	**-piggen** *Nor.*	montaña	montagne	montanha
peak	Gipfel	**pik** *Rus.*	pico	pic	pico
forest	Wald	**pinhal** *Port.*	bosque	forêt	pinhal
peak	Gipfel	**pique** *Fr.*	pico	pique	pico
pyramid	Pyramide	**pirámide** *Sp.*	pirámide	pyramide	pirâmide
peak(s)	Gipfel	**piton(s)** *Fr.*	pico(s)	piton(s)	pico(s)
peak	Gipfel	**piz, pizzo** *It.*	pico	pic	pico
peak	Gipfel	**pk., peak** *Eng.*	pico	pic	pico
parkway	Ferienstrasse	**pkwy., parkway** *Eng.*	calzada	allée de parc	avenida
plain	Ebene	**plain** *Eng.*	llanura	plaine	planície
plain	Ebene	**plaine** *Fr.*	llanura	plaine	planície
plains	Ebenen	**plains** *Eng.*	llanura	plaines	planícies
plateau	Hochebene	**planalto** *Port.*	meseta	plateau	planalto
planetarium	Planetarium	**planetario** *Sp.*	planetario	planétarium	planetário
planetarium	Planetarium	**planetarium** *Eng.*	planetario	planétarium	planetário
mountain, range	Berg, Gebirge	**planina** *S./C.*	montaña, sierra	montagne, chaîne	montanha, cordilheira
plateau	Hochebene	**plateau** *Eng., Fr.*	meseta	plateau	planalto
plateau	Hochebene	**plato** *Afk., Blg., Rus.*	meseta	plateau	planalto
beach	Strand	**playa** *Sp.*	playa	plage	praia
square	Platz	**plaza** *Sp.*	plaza	place	praça
plateau	Hochebene	**plošina** *Czech*	meseta	plateau	planalto
plateau	Hochebene	**ploskogorje** *Rus.*	meseta	plateau	planalto
pass	Pass	**poarta** *Rom.*	paso	col	passo
hill	Hügel	**poggio** *It.*	colina	colline	colina
point	Landspitze	**point** *Eng.*	punta	pointe	ponta
point	Landspitze	**pointe** *Fr.*	punta	pointe	ponta
island	Insel	**pol** *Du.*	isla	île	ilha
plain, basin	Ebene, Becken	**polje** *S./C.*	llanura, cuenca	plaine, bassin	planície, bacia
peninsula	Halbinsel	**poluostrov** *Rus.*	península	péninsule	península
peninsula	Halbinsel	**poluotok** *S./C.*	península	péninsule	península
pond	Teich	**pond** *Eng.*	charca	étang	lago
peak	Gipfel	**-pong** *Kor.*	pico	cime	pico
bridge	Brücke	**pont** *Fr.*	puente	pont	ponte
point	Landspitze	**ponta, pontal** *Port.*	punta	pointe	ponta, pontal
bridge	Brücke	**ponte** *Port.*	puente	pont	ponte
pool	Tümpel	**pool** *Eng.*	charco	étang	charco
rapids	Stromschnellen	**porog** *Rus.*	rápidos	rapides	rápidos
port	Hafen	**port** *Eng., Fr.*	puerto	port	porto
port	Hafen	**porto** *It.*	puerto	port	porto
strait	Meeresstrasse	**porthmós** *Gr.*	estrecho	détroit	estreito
provincial park	Naturpark	**p.p., provincial park** *Eng.*	parque de la provincia	parc provincial	parque provincial
beach	Strand	**praia** *Port.*	playa	plage	praia
reservoir	Stausee	**přehr., přehradová nádrž** *Czech*	embalse	réservoir	reservatório
reservoir, dam	Stausee, Damm	**presa** *Sp.*	presa	réservoir, barrage	represa
peninsula	Halbinsel	**presqu'île** *Fr.*	península	presqu'île	península
reservoir	Stausee	**priehradová nádrẓ** *Slo.*	embalse	réservoir	reservatório
pass	Pass	**priesmyk** *Slo.*	paso	col	passo
prison	Gefängnis	**prison** *Eng.*	prisión	prison	prisão
pass	Pass	**prohod** *Blg.*	paso	col	passo
strait	Meeresstrasse	**proliv** *Rus.*	estrecho	détroit	estreito
promontory	Vorgebirge	**promontorio** *It., Sp.*	promontorio	promontoire	promontório
promontory	Vorgebirge	**promontory** *Eng.*	promontorio	promontoire	promontório
provincial park	Naturpark	**prov. park, provincial park** *Eng.*	parque de la provincia	parc provincial	parque provincial
reservoir	Stausee	**prudy** *Rus.*	embalse	réservoir	reservatório
pass	Pass	**průsmyk** *Czech*	paso	col	passo
pass	Pass	**przełęcz** *Pol.*	paso	col	passo
cape	Kap	**przylądek** *Pol.*	cabo	cap	cabo
point	Landspitze	**pt., point** *Eng.*	punta	pointe	ponta
railroad station	Bahnhof	**pu., pályaudvar** *Hung.*	estación de ferrocarril	gare	estação ferroviária
port	Hafen	**puerto** *Sp.*	puerto	port	porto
peak	Gipfel	**puig** *Cat.*	pico	cime	pico
island	Insel	**pulau** *Indon., Mal.*	isla	île	ilha
upland	Bergland	**puna** *Sp.*	puna	hautes terres	terras altas
peak	Gipfel	**puncak** *Indon.*	pico	cime	pico
point	Landspitze	**punt** *Du.*	punta	pointe	ponta
point, peak	Landspitze, Gipfel	**punta** *It., Sp.*	punta	pointe, cime	ponta
point	Landspitze	**puntilla** *Sp.*	puntilla	pointe	ponta pequena
forest	Wald	**puszcza** *Pol.*	bosque	forêt	floresta
pyramid	Pyramide	**pyramid** *Eng.*	pirámide	pyramide	pirâmide

Q

ENGLISH	DEUTSCH	Map Form	ESPAÑOL	FRANÇAIS	PORTUGUÊS
salt flat	Salzebene	**qāʿ** *Ara.*	salar	saline	salina
canal	Kanal	**qanāt** *Ara.*	canal	canal	canal
hill	Hügel	**qārat** *Ara.*	colina	colline	colina
hills	Hügel	**qārāt** *Ara.*	colinas	collines	colinas
dunes	Dünen	**qawz** *Ara.*	dunas	dunes	dunas
brook	Bach	**qbda., quebrada** *Sp.*	quebrada	crique	arroio
mountain	Berg	**qolleh** *Per.*	montaña	montagne	montanha
canal	Kanal	**-qu** *Ch.*	canal	canal	canal
quarry	Steinbruch	**quarry** *Eng.*	cantera	carrière	pedreira
brook	Bach	**quebrada** *Sp.*	quebrada	crique	arroio
rapids	Stromschnellen	**quedas** *Port.*	rápidos	rapides	quedas
islands	Inseln	**qundao** *Ch.*	islas	îles	ilhas
hill	Hügel	**qūr** *Ara.*	colina	colline	colina
mountain	Berg	**qurnat** *Ara.*	montaña	montagne	montanha

R

ENGLISH	DEUTSCH	Map Form	ESPAÑOL	FRANÇAIS	PORTUGUÊS
river	Fluss	**r., rio** *Port.* **río** **river** **rivière**	río	rivière	rio
range	Gebirge	**ra., range** *Eng.*	sierra	chaîne	cordilheira
Royal Australian Air Force Station	Luftwaffen-stützpunkt (Austl.)	**R.A.A.F.S., Royal Australian Air Force Station** *Eng.*	Real Estación Aeronáutica (Austl.)	Station Aérienne Royale (Austl.)	Real Estação da Força Aérea Australiana
race course	Rennbahn	**race course** *Eng.*	hipódromo	champ de course	hipódromo
race track	Rennbahn	**race track** *Eng.*	hipódromo	champ de course	hipódromo
raceway	Rennbahn	**raceway** *Eng.*	hipódromo	champ de course	hipódromo
river	Fluss	**rach** *Viet.*	río	rivière	rio
anchorage	Ankerplatz	**rada** *Sp.*	rada	ancrage	ancoradouro
cape	Kap	**rags** *Latv.*	cabo	cap	cabo
railroad	Eisenbahn	**railroad** *Eng.*	ferrocarril	chemin de fer	ferrovia
railway	Eisenbahn	**railway** *Eng.*	ferrocarril	chemin de fer	ferrovia
railway station	Bahnhof	**railway station** *Eng.*	estacíon de ferrocarril	gare	estação ferroviária
dunes	Dünen	**ramlat** *Ara.*	dunas	dunes	dunas
range(s)	Gebirge	**range(s)** *Eng.*	sierra(s)	chaîne(s)	cordilheira(s)
river	Fluss	**rão., ribeirão** *Port.*	río	rivière	rio, ribeirão
rapids	Stromschnellen	**rapides** *Fr.*	rápidos	rapides	rápidos
rapids	Stromschnellen	**rapids** *Eng.*	rápidos	rapides	rápidos
wadi	Wadi	**raqabat** *Ara.*	uadi	wadi	uádi
cape	Kap	**ras, ra's** *Ara.*	cabo	cap	cabo
cape	Kap	**rās** *Per.*	cabo	cap	cabo
ravine	Tobel	**ravine** *Eng.*	barranca	ravin	ravina
plain	Ebene	**ravnina** *Rus.*	llanura	plaine	planície
canal	Kanal	**rayyāḥ** *Ara.*	canal	canal	canal
flood plain	Überschwem-mungsebene	**razlivy** *Rus.*	llanura de inundación	lit d'inondation	planície de inunda-ção
road	Landstrasse	**rd., road** *Eng.*	camino	route	rodovia
reef	Riff	**récif** *Fr.*	arrecife	récif	recife
reefs	Riffe	**recifes** *Port.*	arrecifes	récifs	recifes
reefs	Riffe	**récifs** *Fr.*	arrecifes	récifs	recifes
reef(s)	Riff(e)	**reef(s)** *Eng.*	arrecife(s)	récif(s)	recife(s)
regional park	Regionalpark	**regional park** *Eng.*	parque regional	parc régional	parque regional
mountain	Berg	**-rei** *Jpn.*	montaña	montagne	montanha
race course	Rennbahn	**Rennbahn** *Ger.*	hipódromo	champ de course	hipódromo
dam, reservoir	Damm, Stausee	**represa** *Port.*	presa, embalse	barrage, réservoir	represa
airport	Flughafen	**repülötér** *Hung.*	aeropuerto	aéroport	aeroporto
reservoir	Stausee	**res., reservoir** *Eng.*	embalse	réservoir	reservatório
reservation	Reservat	**reservation** *Eng.*	reservación	réservation	reserva
reservoir	Stausee	**reservatório** *Port.*	embalse	réservoir	reservatório
reserve	Reservat	**reserve** *Eng.*	reserva	réserve	reserva
reserve	Reservat	**réserve** *Fr.*	reserva	réserve	reserva
game reserve	Wildreservat	**réserve de chasse** *Fr.*	vedado de caza	réserve de chasse	reserva de caça
reservoir	Stausee	**reservoir** *Eng.*	embalse	réservoir	reservatório
reservoir	Stausee	**réservoir** *Fr.*	embalse	réservoir	reservatório
beach	Strand	**restinga** *Port.*	playa	plage	praia
islands	Inseln	**-retto** *Jpn.*	islas	îles	ilhas
ria (inlet)	Ria	**ría** *Sp.*	ría	ria	ria
brook	Bach	**riacho** *Port., Sp.*	riacho	crique	riacho
brook	Bach	**riachuelo** *Sp.*	riachuelo	crique	riacho
brook	Bach	**rib., ribeira** *Port.*	riachuelo	crique	ribeira
river	Fluss	**ribeirão** *Port.*	río	rivière	ribeirão
ridge	Höhenrücken	**ridge** *Eng.*	sierra	crête	serra
moor	Ried	**Ried** *Ger.*	páramo	lande	pântano
brook	Bach	**riera** *Sp., Cat.*	riera	crique	riacho
national museum	Reichsmuseum	**rijksmuseum** *Du.*	museo nacional	musée national	museu nacional
army installation	Anlage des Heeres	**rikujō-jieitai** *Jpn.*	estación del ejército	installation militaire	instalação militar
river	Fluss	**rio** *Port.*	río	rivière	rio
river	Fluss	**río** *Sp.*	río	rivière	rio
river	Fluss	**riozinho** *Port.*	río	rivière	riozinho
rise (submarine)	Schwelle (untermeer-ische)	**rise** *Eng.*	elevación (submarina)	élévation (sous-marine)	elevação (submarina)
river	Fluss	**river** *Eng.*	río	rivière	rio
brook	Bach	**rivera** *Sp.*	rivera	ruisseau	córrego
coast	Küste	**riviera** *It.*	costa	côte	costa
river	Fluss	**rivière** *Fr.*	río	rivière	rio
army installation	Anlage des Heeres	**r.j., rikujō-jieitai** *Jpn.*	estación del ejército	installation militaire	instalação do exército
road	Landstrasse	**road** *Eng.*	camino	route	rodovia
roads (anchorage)	Ankerplatz	**roads** *Eng.*	ancladero	ancrage	ancoradouro
rock	Fels	**roca** *Sp.*	roca	rocher	rochedo
rock, mountain	Fels, Berg	**rocca** *It.*	roca, montaṇa	rocher, montagne	rochedo, montanha
rock(s)	Fels(en)	**rock(s)** *Eng.*	roca(s)	rocher(s)	rochedo(s)
cape	Kap	**rt** *S./C.*	cabo	cap	cabo
brook	Bach	**rû** *Fr.*	arroyo	rû	córrego
mountains	Berge	**rudohorie** *Slo.*	montañas	montagnes	montanhas
brook	Bach	**ruisseau** *Fr.*	arroyo	ruisseau	córrego
mountain	Berg	**rujm** *Ara.*	montaña	montagne	montanha
run (stream)	Bach	**run** *Eng.*	arroyo	ruisseau	córrego

S

ENGLISH	DEUTSCH	Map Form	ESPAÑOL	FRANÇAIS	PORTUGUÊS
south	Süd	**s., south** *Eng.*	sur	sud	sul
range	Gebirge	**sa., serra** *Port.*	sierra	chaîne	cordilheira
island	Insel	**saar** *Est.*	isla	île	ilha
savanna	Savanne	**sabana** *Sp.*	sabana	savane	savana
salt marsh, lagoon	Salzmarsch, Lagune, Haff	**sabkhat** *Ara.*	pantano salado, laguna	marais salé, lagune	pântano salgado, laguna
dam	Damm	**sadd** *Ara.*	presa	barrage	represa
wadi	Wadi	**saguia** *Ara.*	uadi	wadi	uádi
desert	Wüste	**ṣaḥrā'** *Ara.*	desierto	désert	deserto
cape	Kap	**-saki** *Jpn.*	cabo	cap	cabo
salt flat	Salzebene	**salar** *Sp.*	salar	saline	salina
salt marsh, salt flat	Salzmarsch, Salzebene	**salina(s)** *Sp.*	salina(s)	marais salé, saline	salina(s)
salt marsh, salt flat	Salzmarsch, Salzebene	**salines** *Fr.*	pantano salado, salinas, salar	salines	pântano salgado, salinas
salt flat	Salzebene	**salt flat** *Eng.*	salar	saline	salina
salt lake	Salzsee	**salt lake** *Eng.*	lago salado	lac salé	lago salgado
salt marsh	Salzmarsch	**salt marsh** *Eng.*	pantano salado	marais salé	pântano salgado
waterfall	Wasserfall	**salto(s)** *Port., Sp.*	salto(s)	chute d'eau	salto(s)
reservoir	Stausee	**samudra** *Sin.*	embalse	réservoir	reservatório
range	Gebirge	**-sammyaku** *Jpn.*	sierra	chaîne	cordilheira
mountain	Berg	**-san** *Jpn., Kor.*	montaña	montagne	montanha
mountains	Berge	**-sanchi** *Jpn.*	montañas	montagnes	montanhas
mountains	Berge	**-sanmaek** *Kor.*	montañas	montagnes	montanhas
shrine	Schrein	**santuario** *It., Sp.*	santuario	châsse	santuário
mountain	Berg	**sar** *Pas.*	montaña	montagne	montanha
island	Insel	**sari** *Est.*	isla	île	ilha
desert	Wüste	**sarīr** *Ara.*	desierto	désert	deserto
saddle (pass)	Sattel	**Sattel** *Ger.*	paso	col	passo
strait	Meeresstrasse	**šaurums** *Latv.*	estrecho	détroit	estreito
waterfall	Wasserfall	**saut** *Fr.*	cascada	saut	queda d'água
castle	Schloss	**Schloss** *Ger.*	castillo	château	castelo
gorge	Schlucht	**Schlucht** *Ger.*	garganta	gorge	garganta
school	Schule	**school** *Eng.*	escuela	école	escola
sea	Meer	**sea** *Eng.*	mar	mer	mar
seamount	untermeerische Kuppe	**seamount** *Eng.*	montaña submarina	montagne sous-marine	montanha submarina
sea scarp	Abbruch	**sea scarp** *Eng.*	cantil	escarpement sous-marine	escarpa submarina
dry lake	Trockensee	**sebjet** *Ara.*	lago seco	lac asséché	lago seco
salt flat	Salzebene	**sebkha** *Ara.*	salar	saline	salina
intermittent lake	periodischer See	**sebkra** *Ara.*	lago intermitente	lac périodique	lago intermitente
salt marsh	Salzmarsch	**sebkret** *Ara.*	pantano salado	marais salé	pântano salgado
airport	Flughafen	**sede-teʿufa** *Heb.*	aeropuerto	aéroport	aeroporto
saddle (pass)	Sattel	**sedlo** *Czech*	paso	col	passo
lake(s)	See(n)	**See(n)** *Ger.*	lago(s)	lac(s)	lago(s)
strait	Meeresstrasse	**selat** *Indon.*	estrecho	détroit	estreito
peninsula	Halbinsel	**semenanjung** *Indon.*	península	péninsule	península
seminary	Seminar	**seminary** *Eng.*	seminario	séminaire	seminário
mountain	Berg	**-sen** *Jpn.*	montaña	montagne	montanha
sound	Sund	**seno** *Sp.*	seno	détroit	estreito

ENGLISH	DEUTSCH	Map Form Geographische Begriffe Términos Geográficos Termes Géographiques Termos Geográficos	ESPAÑOL	FRANÇAIS	PORTUGUÊS
mountains	Gebirge	**serra** *Cat.*	montañas	montagnes	montanhas
range, mountain	Gebirge, Berg	**serra** *Port.*	sierra	chaîne, montagne	serra
ridge(s)	Höhenrücken	**serranía(s)** *Sp.*	serranía(s)	crête(s)	serrania(s)
island	Insel	**sha** *Ch.*	isla	île	ilha
rapids	Stromschnellen	**shallāl** *Ara.*	rápidos	rapides	rápidos
desert	Wüste	**shamo** *Ch.*	desierto	désert	deserto
mountain(s), island	Berg(e), Insel	**shan** *Ch.*	montaña(s), isla	montagne(s), île	montanha(s), ilha
pass	Pass	**shankou** *Ch.*	paso	col	passo
mountains	Berge	**shanmo** *Ch.*	montañas	montagnes	montanhas
bay	Bucht	**sharm** *Ara.*	bahía	baie	baía
peninsula	Halbinsel	**shibh jazīrat** *Ara.*	península	péninsule	península
island	Insel	**-shima** *Jpn.*	isla	île	ilha
reef	Riff	**-shō** *Jpn.*	arrecife	récif	recife
shoal(s)	Untiefe(n)	**shoal(s)** *Eng.*	bajo(s)	haut-fond(s)	baixio(s)
islands	Inseln	**-shotō** *Jpn.*	islas	îles	ilhas
shrine	Schrein	**shrine** *Eng.*	santuario	châsse	santuário
river	Fluss	**shui** *Ch.*	río	rivière	rio
reservoir	Stausee	**shuiku** *Ch.*	embalse	réservoir	reservatório
strait	Meeresstrasse	**shuitao** *Ch.*	estrecho	détroit	estreito
temple	Tempel	**si** *Ch.*	templo	temple	templo
range, ridge	Gebirge, Höhenrücken	**sierra** *Sp.*	sierra	chaîne, crête	serra
rapids	Stromschnellen	**šivera** *Rus.*	rápidos	rapides	rápidos
lake	See	**-sjø** *Nor.*	lago	lac	lago
lakes	Seen	**-sjöarna** *Swe.*	lagos	lacs	lagos
lake	See	**-sjøen** *Nor.*	lago	lac	lago
lake, bay	See, Bucht	**-sjön** *Swe.*	lago, bahía	lac, baie	lago, baía
island	Insel	**skär** *Swe.*	isla	île	ilha
forest	Wald	**-skog, -skogen** *Swe.*	bosque	forêt	floresta
mountain	Berg	**slieve** *Gae.*	montaña	montagne	montanha
castle	Schloss	**slot** *Du.*	castillo	château	castelo
castle	Schloss	**slott** *Swe.*	castillo	château	castelo
slough (swamp)	verlandende Wasserfläche	**slough** *Eng.*	pantano	fondrière	pântano, brejo
ridge	Höhenrücken	**snía., serranía** *Sp.*	serranía	crête	serrania
snowfield	Schneefeld	**snowfield** *Eng.*	ventisquero	champ de neige	campo de neve
lake	See	**-sø** *Dan.*	lago	lac	lago
sound	Sund	**sonda** *Sp.*	sonda	détroit	estreito
sound	Sund	**sound** *Eng.*	sonda	détroit	estreito
cave, tunnel	Höhle, Tunnel	**souterrain** *Fr.*	cueva, túnel	souterrain	caverna, túnel
state park	Naturpark	**s.p., state park** *Eng.*	parque provincial	parc régional	parque estadual
cave	Höhle	**špilja** *S./C.*	cueva	caverne	caverna
spit	Landzunge	**spit** *Eng.*	lengua de tierra	flèche	ponta de terra
peak	Spitze	**Spitze** *Ger.*	pico	cime	pico
spring	Quelle	**spr., spring** *Eng.*	manantial	source	fonte, manancial
square	Platz	**sq., square** *Eng.*	plaza	place	praça
range, ridge	Gebirge, Höhenrücken	**srra., sierra** *Sp.*	sierra	chaîne, crête	serra
saint	Sankt	**st., saint** *Eng., Fr.*	san, santa, santo	saint	são, santa, santo
street	Strasse	**st., street** *Eng.*	calle	rue	rua
saint	Sankt	**sta., santa** *Port., Sp.*	santa	sainte	santa
station	Bahnhof, Stützpunkt	**sta., station** *Eng., Fr.*	estación	station	estação
stadium	Stadion	**stad., stadium** *Eng.*	estadio	stade	estádio
stadium	Stadion	**stadio** *It.*	estadio	stade	estádio
stadium	Stadion	**Stadion** *Ger.*	estadio	stade	estádio
stadium	Stadion	**stadion** *Rus.*	estadio	stade	estádio
stadium	Stadion	**stadium** *Eng.*	estadio	stade	estádio
state beach	öffentlicher Badestrand	**state beach** *Eng.*	playa provincial	plage régionale	praia estadual
state forest	Wald in Gemeinbesitz	**state forest** *Eng.*	bosque provincial	forêt régionale	floresta estadual
state historical park	Park an historischer Stätte	**state historical park** *Eng.*	parque histórico provincial	parc historique régional	parque histórico estadual
state park	Naturpark	**state park** *Eng.*	parque provincial	parc régional	parque estadual
state recreation area	Ausflugsgebiet	**state recreation area** *Eng.*	zona de recreo provincial	zone récréative regionale	área de lazer estadual
station	Bahnhof, Stützpunkt	**station** *Eng., Fr.*	estación	station	estação
reservoir	Stausee	**Stausee** *Ger.*	embalse	réservoir	reservatório
station	Bahnhof, Stützpunkt	**stazione** *It.*	estación	station	estação
saint	Sankt	**ste., sainte** *Fr.*	santa	sainte	santa
mountains	Berge	**stěny** *Czech*	montañas	montagnes	montanhas
steppe	Steppe	**step'** *Rus.*	estepa	steppe	estepe
peak	Gipfel	**štít** *Slo.*	pico	cime	pico
saint	Sankt	**sto., santo** *Port., Sp.*	santo	saint	santo
strait(s)	Meeresstrasse	**strait(s)** *Eng.*	estrecho	détroit	estreito
stream	Strom	**stream** *Eng.*	corriente de agua	cours d'eau	curso d'água
street	Strasse	**street** *Eng.*	calle	rue	rua
strait	Meeresstrasse	**stretto** *It.*	estrecho	détroit	estreito
stream	Strom	**Strom** *Ger.*	corriente de agua	cours d'eau	curso d'água
stream	Strom	**-ström, -strömmen** *Swe.*	corriente de agua	cours d'eau	curso d'água
river	Fluss	**-su** *Kor.*	río	rivière	rio
channel	Kanal	**-suidō** *Jpn.*	canal, estrecho	canal, détroit	canal, estreito
sound	Sund	**Sund** *Ger.*	sonda	détroit	estreito
sound	Sund	**-sund** *Swe.*	sonda	détroit	estreito
swamp	Sumpf	**swamp** *Eng.*	pantano	marais	pântano
ridge	Höhenrücken	**syrt** *Tur.*	sierra	crête	serra
island	Insel	**sziget** *Hung.*	isla	île	ilha

T

ENGLISH	DEUTSCH	Map Form	ESPAÑOL	FRANÇAIS	PORTUGUÊS
tableland	Tafelland	**tableland** *Eng.*	mesa, altiplano	plateau	planalto
woods	Gehölz	**taillis** *Fr.*	bosque	taillis	bosque
reef	Riff	**taka** *Indon.*	arrecife	récif	recife
mountain	Berg	**-take** *Jpn.*	montaña	montagne	montanha
waterfall	Wasserfall	**-taki** *Jpn.*	cascada	chute d'eau	queda d'água
valley	Tal	**Tal** *Ger.*	valle	vallée	vale
mountain	Berg	**tall** *Ara.*	montaña	montagne	montanha
mountain, hill	Berg, Hügel	**tallat** *Ara.*	montaña, colina	montagne, colline	montanha, colina
hills	Hügel	**tallāt** *Ara.*	colinas	collines	colinas
dam	Talsperre	**Talsperre** *Ger.*	presa	barrage	represa
point	Landspitze	**-tangar, -tangi** *Ice.*	punta	pointe	ponta
cape	Kap	**tanjong** *Mal.*	cabo	cap	cabo
cape	Kap	**tanjung** *Indon.*	cabo	cap	cabo
island	Insel	**tao** *Ch.*	isla	île	ilha
hills	Hügel	**ţaraq** *Ara.*	colinas	collines	colinas
lake	See	**tasek** *Mal.*	lago	lac	lago
lake	See	**tasik** *Indon.*	lago	lac	lago
plateau	Hochebene	**tassili** *Ber.*	meseta	plateau	planalto
mountain	Berg	**taung** *Bur.*	montaña	montagne	montanha
range	Gebirge	**taungdan** *Bur.*	sierra	chaîne	cordilheira
theatre	Theater	**teatro** *It., Sp.*	teatro	théâtre	teatro
bay	Bucht	**teluk** *Indon.*	bahía	baie	baía
temple	Tempel	**temple** *Eng., Fr.*	templo	temple	templo
church	Kirche	**templom** *Hung.*	iglesia	église	igreja
desert	Wüste	**ténéré** *Ber.*	desierto	désert	deserto
peak, hill	Gipfel, Hügel	**tepe, tepesi** *Tur.*	pico, colina	cime, colline	pico, colina
territory	Territorium	**territory** *Eng.*	territorio	territoire	território
lagoon	Lagune, Haff	**thale** *Thai*	laguna	lagune	laguna
mountains	Berge	**thiu khao** *Thai*	montañas	montagnes	montanhas
mountain	Berg	**-tind,-tinderne** *Nor.*	montaña	montagne	montanha
ridge	Höhenrücken	**ţiwāl** *Ara.*	sierra	crête	serra
mountain	Berg	**-tjåkko, tjöure** *Lapp.*	montaña	montagne	montanha
island	Insel	**-to** *Kor.*	isla	île	ilha
island	Insel	**-tō** *Jpn.*	isla	île	ilha
lake	See	**tó** *Hung.*	lago	lac	lago
pass	Pass	**-tōge** *Jpn.*	paso	col	passo
island	Insel	**tokong** *Mal.*	isla	île	ilha
lake	See	**tônlé** *Cbd.*	lago	lac	lago
mountain torrent	Wildbach	**torrente** *It., Sp.*	torrente	torrent	torrente
tower	Turm	**tower** *Eng.*	torre	tour	torre
turnpike	gebührenpflichtige Autobahn	**tpk., turnpike** *Eng.*	camino con peaje	grande route à péage	rodovia com pedágio
lake	See	**-träsk** *Swe.*	lago	lac	lago
trench	Tiefseegraben	**trench** *Eng.*	trinchera	tranchée	fossa submarina
trough	Tiefseegraben	**trough** *Eng.*	trinchera	tranchée	fossa submarina
volcano	Vulkan	**tulūl** *Ara.*	volcán	volcan	vulcão
tunnel	Tunnel	**túnel** *Sp.*	túnel	tunnel	túnel
tunnel	Tunnel	**tunnel** *Eng., Fr.*	túnel	tunnel	túnel
hill, mountain	Hügel, Berg	**-tunturi** *Finn.*	colina, montaña	colline, montagne	colina, montanha
island	Insel	**tuo** *Ch.*	isla	île	ilha
canal	Kanal	**tur'at** *Ara.*	canal	canal	canal
turnpike	gebührenpflichtige Autobahn	**turnpike** *Eng.*	camino con peaje	grande route à péage	rodovia com pedágio

U-V

ENGLISH	DEUTSCH	Map Form	ESPAÑOL	FRANÇAIS	PORTUGUÊS
cape	Kap	**ujung** *Indon.*	cabo	cap	cabo
lagoon	Lagune, Haff	**-umi** *Jpn.*	laguna	lagune	laguna
United Nations	Vereinte Nationen	**U.N., United Nations** *Eng.*	Naciones Unidas	Nations Unies	Nações Unidas
canal	Kanal	**-unga** *Jpn.*	canal	canal	canal
university	Universität	**univ., universidad** *Sp.* **universidade università university**	universidad	université	universidade
university	Universität	**Universität** *Ger.*	universidad	université	universidade
university	Universität	**université** *Fr.*	universidad	université	universidade
university	Universität	**universitet** *Rus.*	universidad	université	universidade
upland	Bergland	**upland** *Eng.*	tierras altas	hautes terres	terras altas
lake	See	**-ura** *Jpn.*	lago	lac	lago
mountain(s)	Berg(e)	**uul** *Mong.*	montaña(s)	montagne(s)	montanha(s)
elevation(s)	Höhe(n)	**uval(y)** *Rus.*	altura(s)	élévation(s)	elevação(ões)
spring	Quelle	**'uyūn** *Ara.*	manantial	source	fonte, manancial
hill	Hügel	**-vaara** *Finn.*	colina	colline	colina
strait	Meeresstrasse	**väin** *Est.*	estrecho	détroit	estreito
valley	Tal	**val** *Fr., It.*	valle	val	vale
valley	Tal	**valle** *It., Sp.*	valle	vallée	vale
valley	Tal	**vallée** *Fr.*	valle	vallée	vale
waterfall	Wasserfall	**vallen** *Du.*	cascada	chute d'eau	queda d'água
valley	Tal	**valley** *Eng.*	valle	vallée	vale
valley	Tal	**vallon** *Fr.*	valle	vallon	vale
lake	See	**-vatn** *Ice., Nor.*	lago	lac	lago
lake	See	**-vatnet** *Nor.*	lago	lac	lago
lake	See	**-vattnett** *Swe.*	lago	lac	lago
reservoir	Stausee	**vdchr., vodochranilišče** *Rus.*	embalse	réservoir	reservatório
hills	Hügel	**-veden** *Swe.*	colinas	collines	colinas
upland	Bergland	**verch** *Rus.*	tierras altas	hautes terres	terras altas
lake	See	**-vesi** *Finn.*	lago	lac	lago
viaduct	Viadukt	**viaducto** *Sp.*	viaducto	viaduc	viaduto
plateau	Hochebene	**-vidda** *Nor.*	meseta	plateau	planalto
gulf	Golf	**-viken** *Swe.*	golfo	golfe	golfo
bay	Bucht	**vinh** *Viet.*	bahía	baie	baía
mountain	Berg	**vîrful** *Rom.*	montaña	montagne	montanha
airport	Flughafen	**vliegveld** *Du.*	aeropuerto	aéroport	aeroporto
channel	Kanal	**vliet** *Du.*	canal, estrecho	canal, détroit	canal, estreito
canal	Kanal	**vodnyj put'** *Rus.*	canal	canal	canal
reservoir	Stausee	**vodochranilišče** *Rus.*	embalse	réservoir	reservatório
railroad station	Bahnhof	**vokzal** *Rus.*	estación de ferrocarril	gare	estação ferroviária
volcano	Vulkan	**vol., volcán** *Sp.* **volcano**	volcán	volcan	vulcão
pass	Pass	**vorota** *Rus.*	paso	col	passo
upland	Bergland	**vozvyšennost'** *Rus.*	tierras altas	hautes terres	terras altas
mountain	Berg	**vrăh** *Blg.*	montaña	montagne	montanha
mountains	Berge	**vrchovina** *Czech, Slo.*	montañas	montagnes	montanhas
mountains	Berge	**vrchy** *Slo.*	montañas	montagnes	montanhas
peak	Gipfel	**vrh** *S./C.*	pico	cime	pico
volcano	Vulkan	**vulkan** *Rus.*	volcán	volcan	vulcão
bay	Bucht	**vung** *Viet.*	bahía	baie	baía
mountain, hill	Berg, Hügel	**-vuori** *Finn.*	montaña, colina	montagne, colline	montanha, colina

W-Z

ENGLISH	DEUTSCH	Map Form	ESPAÑOL	FRANÇAIS	PORTUGUÊS
west	West	**w., west** *Eng.*	oeste	ouest	oeste
marsh	Marsch	**wa** *Ch.*	pantano	marais	pântano
wadi	Wadi	**wādī** *Ara.*	uadi	wadi	uádi
oasis	Oase	**wāḥat, wāḥāt** *Ara.*	oasis	oasis	oásis
forest, mountains	Wald	**Wald** *Ger.*	bosque, montaṇas	forêt, montagnes	floresta, montanhas
bay	Bucht	**wan** *Ch., Jap.*	bahía	baie	baía
wash	Wadi	**wash** *Eng.*	uadi	wadi	uádi
waterfalls	Wasserfälle	**Wasserfälle** *Ger.*	cascadas	chutes d'eau	quedas d'água
water (lake, river)	Wasser (See, Fluss)	**water** *Eng.*	agua (lago, río)	eau (lac, rivière)	água (lago, rio)
waterway	Wasserstrasse	**waterway** *Eng.*	canal	canal	canal
pond	Weiher	**Weiher** *Ger.*	charca	étang	charco
well	Brunnen	**well** *Eng.*	pozo	puits	poço
bay	Wiek	**Wiek** *Ger.*	bahía	baie	baía
woods	Gehölz	**woods** *Eng.*	bosque	bois	bosque
water (lake, river)	Wasser (See, Fluss)	**wr., water** *Eng.*	agua (lago, río)	eau (lac, rivière)	água (lago, rio)
strait	Meeresstrasse	**xia** *Ch.*	estrecho	détroit	estreito
lake, sea	See, Meer	**yam** *Heb.*	lago, mar	lac, mer	lago, mar
mountain	Berg	**-yama** *Jpn.*	montaña	montagne	montanha
bay	Bucht	**yang** *Ch.*	bahía	baie	baía
peninsula	Halbinsel	**yarımadası** *Tur.*	península	péninsule	península
mountain	Berg	**yebel** *Ara.*	montaña	montagne	montanha
rock, island	Fels, Insel	**yen** *Ch.*	roca, isla	rocher, île	rochedo, ilha
mountains	Berge	**yoma** *Bur.*	montañas	montagnes	montanhas
island	Insel	**yu** *Ch.*	isla	île	ilha
lake	See	**yumco** *Tib.*	lago	lac	lago
canal	Kanal	**yunhe** *Ch.*	canal	canal	canal
intermittent lake	periodischer See	**zahrez** *Ara.*	lago intermitente	lac périodique	lago intermitente
point	Landspitze	**-zaki** *Jpn.*	punta	pointe	ponta
lagoon	Lagune, Haff	**zalew** *Pol.*	laguna	lagune	laguna
gulf, bay	Golf, Bucht	**zaliv** *Rus.*	golfo, bahía	golfe, baie	golfo, baía
reserve	Reservat	**zapov., zapovednik** *Rus.*	reserva	réserve	reserva
sea, lake	Meer, See	**zee** *Du.*	mar, lago	mer, lac	mar, lago
autonomous province	autonome Provinz	**zizhiqu** *Ch.*	provincia autónoma	province autonome	província autônoma
zoo	Zoo	**zoo** *Eng.*	parque zoológico	zoo	jardim zoológico

THIS TABLE gives the area, population, population density, capital, and political status for every country in the world. The political units listed are categorized by political status in the last column of the table, as follows: A—independent countries; B—internally independent political entities which are under the protection of another country in matters of defense and foreign affairs; C—colonies and other dependent political units; and D—the major administrative subdivisions of Australia, Canada, China, the United Kingdom, and the United States. For comparison, the table also includes the continents and the world. For units categorized B, the names of protecting countries are specified in the political-status column. For units categorized C, the names of administering countries are given in parentheses in the first column.

The populations are estimates for January 1, 1993, made by Rand McNally on the basis of official data, United Nations estimates, and other available information.

IN DIESER ÜBERSICHT sind Fläche, Bevölkerung, Bevölkerungsdichte, Hauptstadt und politischer Status für jedes Land der Erde aufgeführt. Die politischen Einheiten sind in der letzten Spalte der Tabelle nach ihrem politischen Status wie folgt gegliedert: A—souveräne Staaten; B—innenpolitisch unabhängige Länder unter der Protektion eines anderen Landes in Angelegenheiten der Aussenpolitik und Verteidigung; C—Kolonien oder anderweitig abhängige Gebiete; D—die wichtigsten Verwaltungseinheiten von Australien, Kanada, China, dem Vereinigten Königreich und den Vereinigten Staaten. Für Vergleiche enthält die Übersicht auch Angaben über die Kontinente und die Welt. Für die unter B eingestuften Einheiten ist der Name des Schutzstaates in der Spalte Politischer Status aufgeführt. Für die unter C eingestuften Gebiete steht der Name des die Verwaltung ausübenden Landes in Klammern in der ersten Spalte.

Die Bevölkerungsangaben sind Schätzungen zum 1. Januar 1993, die Rand McNally auf der Grundlage amtlicher Zahlen, Schätzungen der Vereinten Nationen und anderer zugänglicher Informationen berechnet hat.

EL CUADRO ABAJO incluye la extensión, población y densidad de población, la capital y el estado político de todos los países del mundo. Las entidades políticas nombradas están clasificadas de acuerdo a su estado político en la última columna de la tabla, de esta manera: A—países independientes; B—entidades políticas internamente independientes las cuales se encuentran bajo la protección de otro país en cuanto a asuntos de defensa nacional y relaciones con el extranjero; C—colonias y otras entidades políticas dependientes; y D—las mayores subdivisiones administrativas de Australia, Canadá, China, el Reino Unido, y los Estados Unidos. Para servir de medida comparativa, el cuadro también incluye los continentes y el mundo. Para las entidades de la clasificación B, los nombres de los países protectores están especificados en la columna de estado político. Para las unidades bajo la categoría C, los nombres de los países administradores se encuentran entre paréntesis en la primera columna.

Las poblaciones son los estimados de Rand McNally, tomados el 1o. de Enero de 1993, en base a datos oficiales, estimados de las Naciones Unidas y varias otras informaciones disponibles.

CETTE TABLE donne, pour chaque pays du monde, les renseignements suivants: superficie, population, densité de population, capitale, statut politique. Les entités politiques sont classées, selon leur statut, dans la dernière colonne du tableau: A—pays indépendants; B—entités politiques indépendants intérieurement, mais qui se trouvent sous la protection d'un autre pays pour leur défense et leurs relations extérieures; C—colonies et autres entités politiques dépendantes; D—principales subdivisions administratives de l'Australie, du Canada, de la Chine, du Royaume-Uni, des États-Unis. Pour permettre les comparaisons, la table comprend aussi les continents et le monde. Pour les entités politiques de la catégorie B, les noms des pays protecteurs sont spécifiés dans la colonne "statut politique". Pour celles de la catégorie C, les noms des pays administrateurs sont mis entre parenthèses dans la première colonne.

Les chiffres concernant la population sont des estimations au 1er janvier 1993, établies par Rand McNally, d'après les sources officielles, les estimations des Nations Unies et autres informations disponibles.

A TABELA que se segue apresenta a área, a população, a densidade demográfica, a capital e o estatuto político de todos os países do mundo. As unidades políticas relacionadas na tabela estão classificadas de acordo com o respectivo estatuto político na última coluna, do seguinte modo: A—países independentes; B—unidades políticas internamente independentes mas que se encontram sob a proteção de outro país no tocante a assuntos de defesa nacional e negócios extrenos; C—colônias e outras unidades políticas dependentes; e D—subdivisões administrativas principais da Austrália, Canadá, China, Reino Unido e Estados Unidos. Para fins de comparabilidade, a tabela também inclui os continentes e o mundo. No tocante ás unidades classificadas em B, os nomes dos países protetores estão especificados na coluna relativa ao estatuto político. Para as unidades da categoria C, os nomes dos países administradores figuram entre parênteses na primeira coluna.

Os dados relativos à população são estimativas de Rand McNally para 1 de janeiro de 1993, com base em dados oficiais, estimativas das Nações Unidas e outras informações disponíveis.

NAME / NAME / NOMBRE / NOM / NOME — English / Englisch / Inglés / Anglais / Inglês	Local / Einheimisch / Local / Local / Local	AREA / FLÄCHE / AREA / SUPERFICIE / ÁREA sq. km.	sq. mi.	POPULATION / BEVÖLKERUNG / POBLACIÓN / POPULATION / POPULAÇÃO	DENSITY PER / BEVÖLKERUNGSDICHTE PRO / DENSIDAD POR / DENSITÉ / DENSIDADE POR sq. km.	sq. mi.	CAPITAL / HAUPSTADT / CAPITAL / CAPITALE / CAPITAL	POLITICAL STATUS / POLITISCHER STATUS / ESTADO POLITICO / STATUS POLITIQUE / ESTATUTO POLITICO
†Afghanistan	Afghānestān	652,225	251,826	16,290,000	25	65	Kābol	A
Africa	. . .	30,300,000	11,700,000	668,700,000	22	57	. . .	. . .
Alabama, U.S.	Alabama	135,775	52,423	4,128,000	30	79	Montgomery	D
Alaska, U.S.	Alaska	1,700,139	656,424	564,000	0.3	0.9	Juneau	D
†Albania	Shqipëri	28,748	11,100	3,305,000	115	298	Tiranë	A
Alberta, Can.	Alberta	661,190	255,287	2,839,000	4.3	11	Edmonton	D
†Algeria	Algérie (French) / Djazaïr (Arabic)	2,381,741	919,595	26,925,000	11	29	El Djazaïr (Algiers)	A
American Samoa (U.S.)	American Samoa (English) / Amerika Samoa (Samoan)	199	77	52,000	261	675	Pago Pago	C
Andorra	Andorra	453	175	56,000	124	320	Andorra	B(Sp., Fr.)
†Angola	Angola	1,246,700	481,354	10,735,000	8.6	22	Luanda	A
Anguilla	Anguilla	91	35	7,000	77	200	The Valley	B(U.K.)
Anhwei, China	Anhui	139,000	53,668	58,440,000	420	1,089	Hefei	D
Antarctica	. . .	14,000,000	5,400,000	(1)	. . .	. . .	. . .	. . .
†Antigua and Barbuda	Antigua and Barbuda	442	171	77,000	174	450	St. John's	A
†Argentina	Argentina	2,780,400	1,073,519	32,950,000	12	31	Buenos Aires and Viedma (5)	A
Arizona, U.S.	Arizona	295,276	114,006	3,872,000	13	34	Phoenix	D
Arkansas, U.S.	Arkansas	137,742	53,182	2,410,000	17	45	Little Rock	D
†Armenia	Hayastan	29,800	11,506	3,429,000	115	298	Jerevan	A
Aruba	Aruba	193	75	65,000	337	867	Oranjestad	B(Neth.)
Asia	. . .	44,900,000	17,300,000	3,337,800,000	74	193	. . .	. . .
†Australia	Australia	7,682,300	2,966,155	16,965,000	2.2	5.7	Canberra	A
Australian Capital Territory, Austl.	Australian Capital Territory	2,400	927	282,000	118	304	Canberra	D
†Austria	Österreich	83,856	32,377	7,899,000	94	244	Wien (Vienna)	A
†Azerbaijan	Azerbajdžan	86,600	33,436	7,510,000	87	225	Baku (Baky)	A
†Bahamas	Bahamas	13,939	5,382	265,000	19	49	Nassau	A
†Bahrain	Al-Baḥrayn	691	267	561,000	812	2,101	Al-Manāmah	A
†Bangladesh	Bangladesh	143,998	55,598	120,850,000	839	2,174	Dhaka (Dacca)	A
†Barbados	Barbados	430	166	258,000	600	1,554	Bridgetown	A
†Belarus	Byelarus'	207,600	80,155	10,400,000	50	130	Minsk	A
†Belgium	Belgique (French) / België (Flemish)	30,518	11,783	10,030,000	329	851	Bruxelles (Brussels)	A
†Belize	Belize	22,963	8,866	186,000	8.1	21	Belmopan	A
†Benin	Bénin	112,600	43,475	5,083,000	45	117	Porto-Novo and Cotonou	A
Bermuda (U.K.)	Bermuda	54	21	60,000	1,111	2,857	Hamilton	C
†Bhutan	Druk-Yul	46,500	17,954	1,680,000	36	94	Thimphu	B(India)
†Bolivia	Bolivia	1,098,581	424,165	7,411,000	6.7	17	La Paz and Sucre	A
Bophuthatswana (2)	Bophuthatswana	40,509	15,641	2,525,000	62	161	Mmabatho	B(S. Afr.)
†Bosnia and Herzegovina	Bosna i Hercegovina	51,129	19,741	4,375,000	86	222	Sarajevo	A
†Botswana	Botswana	582,000	224,711	1,379,000	2.4	6.1	Gaborone	A
†Brazil	Brasil	8,511,996	3,286,500	159,630,000	19	49	Brasília	A
British Columbia, Can.	British Columbia (English) / Colombie-Britannique (French)	947,800	365,948	3,665,000	3.9	10	Victoria	D
British Indian Ocean Territory (U.K.)	British Indian Ocean Territory	60	23	(1)	. . .	. . .	. . .	C
British Virgin Islands (U.K.)	British Virgin Islands	153	59	13,000	85	220	Road Town	C
†Brunei	Brunei	5,765	2,226	273,000	47	123	Bandar Seri Begawan	A
†Bulgaria	Bâlgarija	110,912	42,823	8,842,000	80	206	Sofija (Sofia)	A
†Burkina Faso	Burkina Faso	274,200	105,869	9,808,000	36	93	Ouagadougou	A
†Burma	Myanmar	676,577	261,228	43,070,000	64	165	Yangon (Rangoon)	A
†Burundi	Burundi	27,830	10,745	6,118,000	220	569	Bujumbura	A
California, U.S.	California	424,002	163,707	31,310,000	74	191	Sacramento	D
†Cambodia	Kâmpŭchéa	181,035	69,898	8,928,000	49	128	Phnum Pénh (Phnom Penh)	A
†Cameroon	Cameroun (French) / Cameroon (English)	475,442	183,569	12,875,000	27	70	Yaoundé	A
†Canada	Canada	9,970,610	3,849,674	30,530,000	3.1	7.9	Ottawa	A
†Cape Verde	Cabo Verde	4,033	1,557	404,000	100	259	Praia	A
Cayman Islands (U.K.)	Cayman Islands	259	100	29,000	112	290	George Town	C
†Central African Republic	République centrafricaine	622,984	240,535	3,068,000	4.9	13	Bangui	A
†Chad	Tchad	1,284,000	495,755	5,297,000	4.1	11	N'Djamena	A
Chekiang, China	Zhejiang	101,800	39,305	43,150,000	424	1,098	Hangzhou	D
†Chile	Chile	756,626	292,135	13,635,000	18	47	Santiago	A
†China (excl. Taiwan)	Zhongguo	9,556,100	3,689,631	1,179,030,000	123	320	Beijing (Peking)	A
Christmas Island (Austl.)	Christmas Island	135	52	900	6.7	17	The Settlement	C
Ciskei (2)	Ciskei	7,760	2,996	1,105,000	142	369	Bisho	B(S. Afr.)
Cocos (Keeling) Islands (Austl.)	Cocos (Keeling) Islands	14	5.4	500	36	93	. . .	C
†Colombia	Colombia	1,141,748	440,831	34,640,000	30	79	Santa Fe de Bogotá	A
Colorado, U.S.	Colorado	269,620	104,100	3,410,000	13	33	Denver	D
†Comoros (excl. Mayotte)	Comores (French) / Al-Qumur (Arabic)	2,235	863	503,000	225	583	Moroni	A
†Congo	Congo	342,000	132,047	2,413,000	7.1	18	Brazzaville	A
Connecticut, U.S.	Connecticut	14,358	5,544	3,358,000	234	606	Hartford	D
Cook Islands	Cook Islands	236	91	18,000	76	198	Avarua	B(N.Z.)
†Costa Rica	Costa Rica	51,100	19,730	3,225,000	63	163	San José	A
†Croatia	Hrvatska	56,538	21,829	4,793,000	85	220	Zagreb	A
†Cuba	Cuba	110,861	42,804	10,900,000	98	255	La Habana (Havana)	A
†Cyprus (excl. North Cyprus)	Kípros (Greek) / Kıbrıs (Turkish)	5,896	2,276	527,000	89	232	Nicosia (Levkosía)	A
Cyprus, North	Kuzey Kıbrıs	3,355	1,295	193,000	58	149	Nicosia (Lefkoşa)	A
†Czech Republic	Česká Republika	78,864	30,450	10,335,000	131	339	Praha (Prague)	A

NAME / NAME / NOMBRE / NOM / NOME English / Englisch Inglés / Anglais / Inglês	Local / Einheimisch Local / Local / Local	AREA / FLÄCHE AREA / SUPERFICIE / ÁREA sq. km.	sq. mi.	POPULATION BEVÖLKERUNG POBLACIÓN POPULATION POPULAÇÃO	DENSITY PER BEVÖLKERUNGSDICHTE PRO / DENSIDAD POR DENSITÉ / DENSIDADE POR sq. km.	sq. mi.	CAPITAL HAUPTSTADT CAPITAL CAPITALE CAPITAL	POLITICAL STATUS POLITISCHER STATUS ESTADO POLÍTICO STATUS POLITIQUE ESTATUTO POLÍTICO
Delaware, U.S.	Delaware	6,447	2,489	692,000	107	278	Dover	D
†Denmark	Danmark	43,093	16,638	5,169,000	120	311	København (Copenhagen)	A
District of Columbia, U.S.	District of Columbia	177	68	590,000	3,333	8,676	Washington	D
†Djibouti	Djibouti	23,200	8,958	396,000	17	44	Djibouti	A
†Dominica	Dominica	790	305	88,000	111	289	Roseau	A
†Dominican Republic	República Dominicana	48,442	18,704	7,591,000	157	406	Santo Domingo	A
†Ecuador	Ecuador	283,561	109,484	11,055,000	39	101	Quito	A
†Egypt	Mişr	1,001,449	386,662	57,050,000	57	148	Al-Qāhirah (Cairo)	A
†El Salvador	El Salvador	21,041	8,124	5,635,000	268	694	San Salvador	A
England, U.K.	England	130,478	50,378	48,235,000	370	957	London	D
†Equatorial Guinea	Guinea Ecuatorial	28,051	10,831	394,000	14	36	Malabo	A
Eritrea	Eritrea	93,679	36,170	3,425,000	37	95	Asmera	A
†Estonia	Eesti	45,100	17,413	1,613,000	36	93	Tallinn	A
†Ethiopia	Ityopiya	1,157,603	446,953	51,715,000	45	116	Adis Abeba	A
Europe	. . .	9,900,000	3,800,000	694,900,000	70	183	. . .	. . .
Faeroe Islands	Føroyar	1,399	540	49,000	35	91	Tórshavn	B(Den.)
Falkland Islands (U.K.) (3)	Falkland Islands	12,173	4,700	2,100	0.2	0.4	Stanley	C
†Fiji	Fiji (French / Viti (Fijian)	18,274	7,056	754,000	41	107	Suva	A
†Finland	Suomi (Finnish) / Finland (Swedish)	338,145	130,559	5,074,000	15	39	Helsinki (Helsingfors)	A
Florida, U.S.	Florida	170,313	65,758	13,630,000	80	207	Tallahassee	D
†France (excl. Overseas Departments)	France	547,026	211,208	57,570,000	105	273	Paris	A
French Guiana (Fr.)	Guyane française	91,000	35,135	131,000	1.4	3.7	Cayenne	C
French Polynesia (Fr.)	Polynésie française	3,521	1,359	208,000	59	153	Papeete	C
Fukien, China	Fujian	120,000	46,332	31,160,000	260	673	Fuzhou	D
†Gabon	Gabon	267,667	103,347	1,115,000	4.2	11	Libreville	A
†Gambia	Gambia	10,689	4,127	916,000	86	222	Banjul	A
Georgia, U.S.	Georgia	153,953	59,441	6,795,000	44	114	Atlanta	D
†Georgia	Sakartvelo	69,700	26,911	5,593,000	80	208	Tbilisi	A
†Germany	Deutschland	356,955	137,822	80,590,000	226	585	Berlin and Bonn	A
†Ghana	Ghana	238,533	92,098	16,445,000	69	179	Accra	A
Gibraltar (U.K.)	Gibraltar	6.0	2.3	32,000	5,333	13,913	Gibraltar	C
†Greece	Ellás	131,957	50,949	10,075,000	76	198	Athínai (Athens)	A
Greenland	Kalaallit Nunaat (Eskimo) / Grønland (Danish)	2,175,600	840,004	57,000	. . .	0.1	Godthåb (Nuuk)	B(Den.)
†Grenada	Grenada	344	133	97,000	282	729	St. George's	A
Guadeloupe (incl. Dependencies) (Fr.)	Guadeloupe	1,780	687	413,000	232	601	Basse-Terre	C
Guam (U.S.)	Guam	541	209	143,000	264	684	Agana	C
†Guatemala	Guatemala	108,889	42,042	9,705,000	89	231	Guatemala	A
Guernsey (incl. Dependencies)	Guernsey	78	30	58,000	744	1,933	St. Peter Port	B(U.K.)
†Guinea	Guinée	245,857	94,926	7,726,000	31	81	Conakry	A
†Guinea-Bissau	Guiné-Bissau	36,125	13,948	1,060,000	29	76	Bissau	A
†Guyana	Guyana	214,969	83,000	737,000	3.4	8.9	Georgetown	A
Hainan, China	Hainan	34,000	13,127	6,820,000	201	520	Haikou	D
†Haiti	Haïti	27,750	10,714	6,509,000	235	608	Port-au-Prince	A
Hawaii, U.S.	Hawaii	28,313	10,932	1,159,000	41	106	Honolulu	D
Heilungkiang, China	Heilongjiang	469,000	181,082	36,685,000	78	203	Harbin	D
Honan, China	Henan	167,000	64,479	88,890,000	532	1,379	Zhengzhou	D
†Honduras	Honduras	112,088	43,277	5,164,000	46	119	Tegucigalpa	A
Hong Kong (U.K.)	Hong Kong (English) / Xianggang (Chinese)	1,072	414	5,580,000	5,205	13,478	Hong Kong (Victoria)	C
Hopeh, China	Hebei	190,000	73,359	63,500,000	334	866	Shijiazhuang	D
Hunan, China	Hunan	210,000	81,081	63,140,000	301	779	Changsha	D
†Hungary	Magyarország	93,033	35,920	10,305,000	111	287	Budapest	A
Hupeh, China	Hubei	187,400	72,356	56,090,000	299	775	Wuhan	D
†Iceland	Ísland	103,000	39,769	260,000	2.5	6.5	Reykjavík	A
Idaho, U.S.	Idaho	216,456	83,574	1,026,000	4.7	12	Boise	D
Illinois, U.S.	Illinois	150,007	57,918	11,640,000	78	201	Springfield	D
†India (incl. part of Jammu and Kashmir)	India (English) / Bharat (Hindi)	3,203,975	1,237,062	873,850,000	273	706	New Delhi	A
Indiana, U.S.	Indiana	94,328	36,420	5,667,000	60	156	Indianapolis	D
†Indonesia	Indonesia	1,948,732	752,410	186,180,000	96	247	Jakarta	A
Inner Mongolia, China	Nei Monggol	1,183,000	456,759	22,340,000	19	49	Hohhot	D
Iowa, U.S.	Iowa	145,754	56,276	2,821,000	19	50	Des Moines	D
†Iran	Īrān	1,638,057	632,457	60,500,000	37	96	Tehrān	A
†Iraq	Al-ʿIrāq	438,317	169,235	18,815,000	43	111	Baghdād	A
†Ireland	Ireland (English) / Éire (Gaelic)	70,285	27,137	3,525,000	50	130	Dublin (Baile Átha Cliath)	A
Isle of Man	Isle of Man	572	221	70,000	122	317	Douglas	B(U.K.)
†Israel (excl. Occupied Areas)	Yisra'el (Hebrew) / Isrā'īl (Arabic)	20,770	8,019	4,593,000	221	573	Yerushalayim (Jerusalem)	A
Israeli Occupied Areas (4)	. . .	7,632	2,947	2,461,000	322	835	. . .	. . .
†Italy	Italia	301,277	116,324	56,550,000	188	486	Roma (Rome)	A
†Ivory Coast	Côte d'Ivoire	322,500	124,518	13,765,000	43	111	Abidjan and Yamoussoukro (5)	A
†Jamaica	Jamaica	10,991	4,244	2,412,000	219	568	Kingston	A
†Japan	Nihon	377,801	145,870	124,710,000	330	855	Tōkyō	A
Jersey	Jersey	116	45	85,000	733	1,889	St. Helier	B(U.K.)
†Jordan	Al-Urdun	91,000	35,135	3,632,000	40	103	'Ammān	A
Kansas, U.S.	Kansas	213,110	82,282	2,539,000	12	31	Topeka	D
Kansu, China	Gansu	450,000	173,746	23,280,000	52	134	Lanzhou	D
†Kazakhstan	Kazakhstan	2,717,300	1,049,156	17,190,000	6.3	16	Alma-Ata (Almaty)	A
Kentucky, U.S.	Kentucky	104,665	40,411	3,745,000	36	93	Frankfort	D
†Kenya	Kenya	582,646	224,961	26,635,000	46	118	Nairobi	A
Kiangsi, China	Jiangxi	166,600	64,325	39,270,000	236	610	Nanchang	D
Kiangsu, China	Jiangsu	102,600	39,614	69,730,000	680	1,760	Nanjing (Nanking)	D
Kiribati	Kiribati	811	313	76,000	94	243	Bairiki	A
Kirin, China	Jilin	187,000	72,201	25,630,000	137	355	Changchun	D
†Korea, North	Chosŏn-minjujuŭi-inmīn-konghwaguk	120,538	46,540	22,450,000	186	482	P'yŏngyang	A
†Korea, South	Taehan-min'guk	99,016	38,230	43,660,000	441	1,142	Sŏul (Seoul)	A
†Kuwait	Al-Kuwayt	17,818	6,880	2,388,000	134	347	Al-Kuwayt (Kuwait)	A
Kwangsi Chuang, China	Guangxi Zhuangzu	236,300	91,236	43,975,000	186	482	Nanning	D
Kwangtung, China	Guangdong	178,000	68,726	65,380,000	367	951	Guangzhou (Canton)	D
Kweichow, China	Guizhou	170,000	65,637	33,745,000	199	514	Guiyang	D
†Kyrgyzstan	Kyrgyzstan	198,500	76,641	4,613,000	23	60	Biškek (Frunze)	A
†Laos	Lao	236,800	91,429	4,507,000	19	49	Viangchan (Vientiane)	A
†Latvia	Latvija	63,700	24,595	2,737,000	43	111	Rīga	A
†Lebanon	Lubnān	10,400	4,015	3,467,000	333	864	Bayrūt (Beirut)	A
†Lesotho	Lesotho	30,355	11,720	1,873,000	62	160	Maseru	A
Liaoning, China	Liaoning	145,700	56,255	41,035,000	282	729	Shenyang (Mukden)	D
†Liberia	Liberia	99,067	38,250	2,869,000	29	75	Monrovia	A
†Libya	Lībiyā	1,759,540	679,362	4,552,000	2.6	6.7	Tarābulus (Tripoli)	A
†Liechtenstein	Liechtenstein	160	62	30,000	188	484	Vaduz	A
†Lithuania	Lietuva	65,200	25,174	3,804,000	58	151	Vilnius	A
Louisiana, U.S.	Louisiana	134,275	51,843	4,282,000	32	83	Baton Rouge	D
†Luxembourg	Luxembourg (French) / Lezebuurg (Luxembourgish)	2,586	998	392,000	152	393	Luxembourg	A
Macau (Port.)	Macau	17	6.6	477,000	28,059	72,273	Macau	C
†Macedonia	Makedonija	25,713	9,928	2,179,000	85	219	Skopje	A
†Madagascar	Madagasikara (Malagasy) / Madagascar (French)	587,041	226,658	12,800,000	22	56	Antananarivo	A
Maine, U.S.	Maine	91,653	35,387	1,257,000	14	36	Augusta	D
†Malawi	Malaŵi	118,484	45,747	9,691,000	82	212	Lilongwe	A
†Malaysia	Malaysia	334,758	129,251	18,630,000	56	144	Kuala Lumpur	A
†Maldives	Maldives	298	115	235,000	789	2,043	Male'	A
†Mali	Mali	1,248,574	482,077	8,754,000	7.0	18	Bamako	A
†Malta	Malta	316	122	360,000	1,139	2,951	Valletta	A
Manitoba, Can.	Manitoba	649,950	250,947	1,221,000	1.9	4.9	Winnipeg	D
†Marshall Islands	Marshall Islands	181	70	51,000	282	729	Majuro (island)	A
Martinique (Fr.)	Martinique	1,100	425	372,000	338	875	Fort-de-France	C
Maryland, U.S.	Maryland	32,135	12,407	4,975,000	155	401	Annapolis	D

NAME / NAME / NOMBRE / NOM / NOME English / Englisch Inglés / Anglais / Inglês	Local / Einheimisch Local / Local / Local	AREA / FLÄCHE AREA / SUPERFICIE / ÁREA sq. km.	sq. mi.	POPULATION BEVÖLKERUNG POBLACIÓN POPULATION POPULAÇÃO	DENSITY PER BEVÖLKERUNGSDICHTE PRO / DENSIDAD POR DENSITÉ / DENSIDADE POR sq. km.	sq. mi.	CAPITAL HAUPSTADT CAPITAL CAPITALE CAPITAL	POLITICAL STATUS POLITISCHER STATUS ESTADO POLITICO STATUS POLITIQUE ESTATUTO POLITICO
Massachusetts, U.S.	Massachusetts	27,337	10,555	6,103,000	223	578	Boston	D
†Mauritania	Mauritanie (French) / Mūrītāniyā (Arabic)	1,025,520	395,956	2,092,000	2.0	5.3	Nouakchott	A
†Mauritius (incl. Dependencies)	Mauritius	2,040	788	1,096,000	537	1,391	Port Louis	A
Mayotte (Fr.) [6]	Mayotte	374	144	89,000	238	618	Dzaoudzi and Mamoudzou [5]	C
†Mexico	México	1,967,183	759,534	86,170,000	44	113	Ciudad de México (Mexico City)	A
Michigan, U.S.	Michigan	250,738	96,810	9,488,000	38	98	Lansing	D
†Micronesia, Federated States of	Federated States of Micronesia	702	271	117,000	167	432	Kolonia and Paliker [5]	A
Midway Islands (U.S.)	Midway Islands	5.2	2.0	500	96	250	. . .	C
Minnesota, U.S.	Minnesota	225,182	86,943	4,513,000	20	52	St. Paul	D
Mississippi, U.S.	Mississippi	125,443	48,434	2,616,000	21	54	Jackson	D
Missouri, U.S.	Missouri	180,546	69,709	5,231,000	29	75	Jefferson City	D
†Moldova	Moldova	33,700	13,012	4,474,000	133	344	Kišin'ov (Chişinău)	A
Monaco	Monaco	1.9	0.7	31,000	16,316	44,286	Monaco	A
†Mongolia	Mongol Ard Uls	1,566,500	604,829	2,336,000	1.5	3.9	Ulaanbaatar (Ulan Bator)	A
Montana, U.S.	Montana	380,850	147,046	821,000	2.2	5.6	Helena	D
Montserrat (U.K.)	Montserrat	102	39	13,000	127	333	Plymouth	C
†Morocco (excl. Western Sahara)	Al-Magrib	446,550	172,414	27,005,000	60	157	Rabat	A
†Mozambique	Moçambique	799,380	308,642	15,795,000	20	51	Maputo	A
†Namibia (excl. Walvis Bay)	Namibia	823,144	317,818	1,603,000	1.9	5.0	Windhoek	A
Nauru	Nauru (English) / Naoero (Nauruan)	21	8.1	10,000	476	1,235	Yaren District	A
Nebraska, U.S.	Nebraska	200,358	77,358	1,615,000	8.1	21	Lincoln	D
†Nepal	Nepāl	147,181	56,827	20,325,000	138	358	Kāṭhmāṇḍau	A
†Netherlands	Nederland	41,864	16,164	15,190,000	363	940	Amsterdam and 's-Gravenhage (The Hague)	A
Netherlands Antilles	Nederlandse Antillen	800	309	191,000	239	618	Willemstad	B(Neth.)
Nevada, U.S.	Nevada	286,368	110,567	1,308,000	4.6	12	Carson City	D
New Brunswick, Can.	New Brunswick (English) / Nouveau-Brunswick (French)	73,440	28,355	824,000	11	29	Fredericton	D
New Caledonia (Fr.)	Nouvelle-Calédonie	19,058	7,358	177,000	9.3	24	Nouméa	C
Newfoundland, Can.	Newfoundland (English) / Terre-Neuve (French)	405,720	156,649	641,000	1.6	4.1	St. John's	D
New Hampshire, U.S.	New Hampshire	24,219	9,351	1,154,000	48	123	Concord	D
New Jersey, U.S.	New Jersey	22,590	8,722	7,898,000	350	906	Trenton	D
New Mexico, U.S.	New Mexico	314,939	121,598	1,590,000	5.0	13	Santa Fe	D
New South Wales, Austl.	New South Wales	801,600	309,500	5,770,000	7.2	19	Sydney	D
New York, U.S.	New York	141,089	54,475	18,350,000	130	337	Albany	D
†New Zealand	New Zealand	270,534	104,454	3,477,000	13	33	Wellington	A
†Nicaragua	Nicaragua	129,640	50,054	3,932,000	30	79	Managua	A
†Niger	Niger	1,267,000	489,191	8,198,000	6.5	17	Niamey	A
†Nigeria	Nigeria	923,768	356,669	91,700,000	99	257	Lagos and Abuja	A
Ningsia Hui, China	Ningxia Huizu	66,400	25,637	4,820,000	73	188	Yinchuan	D
Niue	Niue	258	100	1,700	6.6	17	Alofi	B(N.Z.)
Norfolk Island (Austl.)	Norfolk Island	36	14	2,600	72	186	Kingston	C
North America	. . .	24,700,000	9,500,000	438,200,000	18	46	. . .	. . .
North Carolina, U.S.	North Carolina	139,397	53,821	6,846,000	49	127	Raleigh	D
North Dakota, U.S.	North Dakota	183,123	70,704	632,000	3.5	8.9	Bismarck	D
Northern Ireland, U.K.	Northern Ireland	14,121	5,452	1,604,000	114	294	Belfast	D
Northern Mariana Islands	Northern Mariana Islands	477	184	48,000	101	261	Saipan (island)	B(U.S.)
Northern Territory, Austl.	Northern Territory	1,346,200	519,771	176,000	0.1	0.3	Darwin	D
Northwest Territories, Can.	Northwest Territories (English) / Territoires du Nord-Ouest (French)	3,426,320	1,322,910	61,000	. . .	. . .	Yellowknife	D
†Norway (incl. Svalbard and Jan Mayen)	Norge	386,975	149,412	4,308,000	11	29	Oslo	A
Nova Scotia, Can.	Nova Scotia (English) / Nouvelle-Écosse (French)	55,490	21,425	1,007,000	18	47	Halifax	D
Oceania (incl. Australia)	. . .	8,500,000	3,300,000	26,700,000	3.1	8.1	. . .	. . .
Ohio, U.S.	Ohio	116,103	44,828	11,025,000	95	246	Columbus	D
Oklahoma, U.S.	Oklahoma	181,049	69,903	3,205,000	18	46	Oklahoma City	D
†Oman	'Umān	212,457	82,030	1,617,000	7.6	20	Masqaṭ (Muscat)	A
Ontario, Can.	Ontario	1,068,580	412,581	11,265,000	11	27	Toronto	D
Oregon, U.S.	Oregon	254,819	98,386	2,949,000	12	30	Salem	D
†Pakistan (incl. part of Jammu and Kashmir)	Pākistān	879,902	339,732	123,490,000	140	363	Islāmābād	A
Palau	Palau (English) / Belau (Palauan)	508	196	16,000	31	82	Koror and Melekeok [5]	B(U.S.)
†Panama	Panamá	75,517	29,157	2,555,000	34	88	Panamá	A
†Papua New Guinea	Papua New Guinea	462,840	178,704	3,737,000	8.1	21	Port Moresby	A
†Paraguay	Paraguay	406,752	157,048	5,003,000	12	32	Asunción	A
Peking, China	Beijing	16,800	6,487	11,290,000	672	1,740	Beijing (Peking)	D
Pennsylvania, U.S.	Pennsylvania	119,291	46,058	12,105,000	101	263	Harrisburg	D
†Peru	Perú	1,285,216	496,225	22,995,000	18	46	Lima	A
†Philippines	Philippines (English) / Pilipinas (Tagalog)	300,000	115,831	65,500,000	218	565	Manila	A
Pitcairn (incl. Dependencies) (U.K.)	Pitcairn	49	19	50	1.0	2.6	Adamstown	C
†Poland	Polska	312,683	120,728	38,330,000	123	317	Warszawa (Warsaw)	A
†Portugal	Portugal	91,985	35,516	10,660,000	116	300	Lisboa (Lisbon)	A
Prince Edward Island, Can.	Prince Edward Island (English) / Île-du Prince-Édouard (French)	5,660	2,185	152,000	27	70	Charlottetown	D
Puerto Rico	Puerto Rico	9,104	3,515	3,594,000	395	1,022	San Juan	B(U.S.)
†Qatar	Qatar	11,427	4,412	492,000	43	112	Ad-Dawḥah (Doha)	A
Quebec, Can.	Québec	1,540,680	594,860	7,725,000	5.0	13	Québec	D
Queensland, Austl.	Queensland	1,727,200	666,876	3,000,000	1.7	4.5	Brisbane	D
Reunion (Fr.)	Réunion	2,510	969	633,000	252	653	Saint-Denis	C
Rhode Island, U.S.	Rhode Island	4,002	1,545	1,026,000	256	664	Providence	D
†Romania	România	237,500	91,699	23,200,000	98	253	Bucureşti (Bucharest)	A
†Russia	Rossija	17,075,400	6,592,849	150,500,000	8.8	23	Moskva (Moscow)	A
†Rwanda	Rwanda	26,338	10,169	7,573,000	288	745	Kigali	A
St. Helena (incl. Dependencies) (U.K.)	St. Helena	314	121	7,000	22	58	Jamestown	C
†St. Kitts and Nevis	St. Kitts and Nevis	269	104	40,000	149	385	Basseterre	A
†St. Lucia	St. Lucia	616	238	153,000	248	643	Castries	A
St. Pierre and Miquelon (Fr.)	Saint-Pierre-et-Miquelon	242	93	7,000	29	75	Saint-Pierre	C
†St. Vincent and the Grenadines	St. Vincent and the Grenadines	388	150	116,000	299	773	Kingstown	A
†San Marino	San Marino	61	24	23,000	377	958	San Marino	A
†Sao Tome and Principe	São Tomé e Príncipe	964	372	134,000	139	360	São Tomé	A
Saskatchewan, Can.	Saskatchewan	652,330	251,866	1,099,000	1.7	4.4	Regina	D
†Saudi Arabia	Al-'Arabīyah as-Su'ūdīyah	2,149,690	830,000	15,985,000	7.4	19	Ar-Riyāḍ (Riyadh)	A
Scotland, U.K.	Scotland	78,789	30,421	5,145,000	65	169	Edinburgh	D
†Senegal	Sénégal	196,712	75,951	7,849,000	40	103	Dakar	A
†Seychelles	Seychelles	453	175	70,000	155	400	Victoria	A
Shanghai, China	Shanghai	6,200	2,394	13,875,000	2,238	5,796	Shanghai	D
Shansi, China	Shanxi	156,000	60,232	29,865,000	191	496	Taiyuan	D
Shantung, China	Shandong	153,000	59,074	87,840,000	574	1,487	Jinan	D
Shensi, China	Shaanxi	205,000	79,151	34,215,000	167	432	Xi'an (Sian)	D
†Sierra Leone	Sierra Leone	72,325	27,925	4,424,000	61	158	Freetown	A
†Singapore	Singapore	636	246	2,812,000	4,421	11,431	Singapore	A
Sinkiang Uighur, China	Xinjiang Uygur	1,600,000	617,764	15,755,000	9.8	26	Ürümqi	D
†Slovakia	Slovenská Republika	49,035	18,933	5,287,000	108	279	Bratislava	A
†Slovenia	Slovenija	20,251	7,819	1,965,000	97	251	Ljubljana	A
†Solomon Islands	Solomon Islands	28,370	10,954	366,000	13	33	Honiara	A
†Somalia	Somaliya	637,657	246,201	6,000,000	9.4	24	Muqdisho (Mogadishu)	A
†South Africa (incl. Walvis Bay)	South Africa (English) / Suid-Afrika (Afrikaans)	1,123,226	433,680	33,040,000	29	76	Pretoria, Cape Town, and Bloemfontein	A

NAME / NAME / NOMBRE / NOM / NOME English / Englisch Inglés / Anglais / Inglês	Local / Einheimisch Local / Local / Local	AREA / FLÄCHE AREA / SUPERFICIE / ÁREA sq. km.	sq. mi.	POPULATION BEVÖLKERUNG POBLACIÓN POPULATION POPULAÇÃO	DENSITY PER BEVÖLKERUNGSDICHTE PRO / DENSIDAD POR DENSITÉ / DENSIDADE POR sq. km.	sq. mi.	CAPITAL HAUPSTADT CAPITAL CAPITALE CAPITAL	POLITICAL STATUS POLITISCHER STATUS ESTADO POLITICO STATUS POLITIQUE ESTATUTO POLITICO
South America	. . .	17,800,000	6,900,000	310,700,000	17	45	. . .	. . .
South Australia, Austl.	South Australia	984,000	379,925	1,410,000	1.4	3.7	Adelaide	D
South Carolina, U.S.	South Carolina	82,898	32,007	3,616,000	44	113	Columbia	D
South Dakota, U.S.	South Dakota	199,745	77,121	718,000	3.6	9.3	Pierre	D
South Georgia and the South Sandwich Islands (U.K.)	South Georgia and the South Sandwich Islands	3,755	1,450	(1)	. . .	. . .	. . .	C
†Spain	España	504,750	194,885	39,155,000	78	201	Madrid	A
Spanish North Africa (Sp.) (7)	Plazas de Soberanía en el Norte de África	32	12	144,000	4,500	12,000	. . .	C
†Sri Lanka	Sri Lanka	64,652	24,962	17,740,000	274	711	Colombo and Sri Jayawardenapura	A
†Sudan	As-Sūdān	2,505,813	967,500	28,760,000	11	30	Al-Kharṭūm (Khartoum)	A
†Suriname	Suriname	163,820	63,251	413,000	2.5	6.5	Paramaribo	A
†Swaziland	Swaziland	17,364	6,704	925,000	53	138	Mbabane and Lobamba	A
†Sweden	Sverige	449,964	173,732	8,619,000	19	50	Stockholm	A
Switzerland	Schweiz (German) / Suisse (French) / Svizzera (Italian)	41,293	15,943	6,848,000	166	430	Bern (Berne)	A
†Syria	Sūrīyah	185,180	71,498	14,070,000	76	197	Dimashq (Damascus)	A
Szechwan, China	Sichuan	570,000	220,078	111,470,000	196	507	Chengdu	D
Taiwan	T'aiwan	36,002	13,900	20,985,000	583	1,510	T'aipei	A
†Tajikistan	Tajikistan	143,100	55,251	5,765,000	40	104	Dušanbe	A
†Tanzania	Tanzania	945,087	364,900	28,265,000	30	77	Dar es Salaam and Dodoma (5)	A
Tasmania, Austl.	Tasmania	67,800	26,178	456,000	6.7	17	Hobart	D
Tennessee, U.S.	Tennessee	109,158	42,146	5,026,000	46	119	Nashville	D
Texas, U.S.	Texas	695,676	268,601	17,610,000	25	66	Austin	D
†Thailand	Prathet Thai	513,115	198,115	58,030,000	113	293	Krung Thep (Bangkok)	A
Tibet, China	Xizang	1,220,000	471,045	2,235,000	1.8	4.7	Lhasa	D
Tientsin, China	Tianjin	11,300	4,363	9,170,000	812	2,102	Tianjin (Tientsin)	D
†Togo	Togo	56,785	21,925	4,030,000	71	184	Lomé	A
Tokelau (N.Z.)	Tokelau	12	4.6	1,800	150	391	. . .	C
Tonga	Tonga	747	288	103,000	138	358	Nuku'alofa	A
Transkei (2)	Transkei	43,553	16,816	4,845,000	111	288	Umtata	B(S. Afr.)
†Trinidad and Tobago	Trinidad and Tobago	5,128	1,980	1,307,000	255	660	Port of Spain	A
Tsinghai, China	Qinghai	720,000	277,994	4,585,000	6.4	16	Xining	D
†Tunisia	Tunisie (French) / Tunis (Arabic)	163,610	63,170	8,495,000	52	134	Tunis	A
†Turkey	Türkiye	779,452	300,948	58,620,000	75	195	Ankara	A
†Turkmenistan	Turkmenistan	488,100	188,456	3,884,000	8.0	21	Aščhabad (Ashgabat)	A
Turks and Caicos Islands (U.K.)	Turks and Caicos Islands	500	193	13,000	26	67	Grand Turk	C
Tuvalu	Tuvalu	26	10	10,000	385	1,000	Funafuti	A
†Uganda	Uganda	241,139	93,104	17,410,000	72	187	Kampala	A
†Ukraine	Ukrayina	603,700	233,090	51,990,000	86	223	Kijev (Kiev)	A
†United Arab Emirates	Al-Imārāt al-'Arabīyah al-Muttaḥidah	83,600	32,278	2,590,000	31	80	Abū Ẓaby (Abu Dhabi)	A
†United Kingdom	United Kingdom	244,154	94,269	57,890,000	237	614	London	A
†United States	United States	9,809,431	3,787,425	256,420,000	26	68	Washington	A
†Uruguay	Uruguay	177,414	68,500	3,151,000	18	46	Montevideo	A
Utah, U.S.	Utah	219,902	84,904	1,795,000	8.2	21	Salt Lake City	D
†Uzbekistan	Uzbekiston	447,400	172,742	21,885,000	49	127	Taškent (Toshkent)	A
†Vanuatu	Vanuatu	12,190	4,707	157,000	13	33	Port Vila	A
Vatican City	Città del Vaticano	0.4	0.2	800	2,000	4,000	Città del Vaticano (Vatican City)	A
Venda (2)	Venda	6,198	2,393	732,000	118	306	Thohoyandou	B(S. Afr.)
†Venezuela	Venezuela	912,050	352,145	19,085,000	21	54	Caracas	A
Vermont, U.S.	Vermont	24,903	9,615	590,000	24	61	Montpelier	D
Victoria, Austl.	Victoria	227,600	87,877	4,273,000	19	49	Melbourne	D
†Vietnam	Viet Nam	330,036	127,428	69,650,000	211	547	Ha Noi	A
Virginia, U.S.	Virginia	110,771	42,769	6,411,000	58	150	Richmond	D
Virgin Islands (U.S.)	Virgin Islands	344	133	104,000	302	782	Charlotte Amalie	C
Wake Island (U.S.)	Wake Island	7.8	3.0	200	26	67	. . .	C
Wales, U.K.	Wales	20,766	8,018	2,906,000	140	362	Cardiff	D
Wallis and Futuna (Fr.)	Wallis et Futuna	255	98	17,000	67	173	Mata-Utu	C
Washington, U.S.	Washington	184,674	71,303	5,052,000	27	71	Olympia	D
Western Australia, Austl.	Western Australia	2,525,500	975,101	1,598,000	0.6	1.6	Perth	D
Western Sahara	. . .	266,000	102,703	200,000	0.8	1.9	El Aaiún (Laayone)	. . .
†Western Samoa	Western Samoa (English) / Samoa i Sisifo (Samoan)	2,831	1,093	197,000	70	180	Apia	A
West Virginia, U.S.	West Virginia	62,759	24,231	1,795,000	29	74	Charleston	D
Wisconsin, U.S.	Wisconsin	169,653	65,503	5,000,000	29	76	Madison	D
Wyoming, U.S.	Wyoming	253,349	97,818	462,000	1.8	4.7	Cheyenne	D
†Yemen	Al-Yaman	527,968	203,850	12,215,000	23	60	Ṣan'ā'	A
Yugoslavia	Jugoslavija	102,173	39,449	10,670,000	104	270	Beograd (Belgrade)	A
Yukon Territory, Can.	Yukon Territory	483,450	186,661	31,000	0.1	0.2	Whitehorse	D
Yunnan, China	Yunnan	394,000	152,124	38,450,000	98	253	Kunming	D
†Zaire	Zaïre	2,345,095	905,446	39,750,000	17	44	Kinshasa	A
†Zambia	Zambia	752,614	290,586	8,475,000	11	29	Lusaka	A
†Zimbabwe	Zimbabwe	390,759	150,873	10,000,000	26	66	Harare (Salisbury)	A
WORLD	. . .	150,100,000	57,900,000	5,477,000,000	36	95	. . .	. . .

† Member of the United Nations (1992).
. . . None, or not applicable.
(1) No permanent population.
(2) Bophuthatswana, Ciskei, Transkei, and Venda are not recognized by the United Nations.
(3) Claimed by Argentina.
(4) Includes West Bank, Golan Heights, and Gaza Strip.
(5) Future capital.
(6) Claimed by Comoros.
(7) Comprises Ceuta, Melilla, and several small islands.

† Mitglied der Vereinten Nationen (1992).
. . . Kein(e), oder nicht anwendbar.
(1) Bevölkerungszahl schwankend.
(2) Bophuthatswana, Ciskei, Transkei und Venda von Vereinten Nationen nicht anerkannt.
(3) Von Argentinien beansprucht.
(4) Westufer, Golan-Höhen und Gazastreifen einbegriffen.
(5) Zukünftige Hauptstadt.
(6) Von Komoren beansprucht.
(7) Umfasst Ceuta, Melilla und mehrere kleine Inseln.

† Miembro de las Naciones Unidas (1992).
. . . Ninguno, o no se aplica.
(1) Sin población permanente.
(2) Bophuthatswana, Ciskei, Transkei y Venda no reconocido por las Naciones Unidas.
(3) Reclamado por la Argentina.
(4) Incluye la ribera oeste, las alturas de Golán y la franja de Gaza.
(5) Capital futura.
(6) Reclamado por las Comores.
(7) Comprende Ceuta, Melilla y various islas pequeñas.

† Membre des Nations Unies (1992).
. . . Pas d'information, ou pas applicable.
(1) Pas de population permanente.
(2) Bophuthatswana, Ciskei, Transkei et Venda non reconnaissent pas les Nations Unies.
(3) Revendiqué par l'Argentine.
(4) Y compris Cisjordanie, hauteurs de Golan et la bande de Gaza.
(5) Capitale future.
(6) Revendiqué par les Comores.
(7) Inclus Ceuta, Melilla et plusieurs petites îles.

† Membro das Nações Unidas (1992).
. . . Inexistente ou não aplicável.
(1) Sem população permanente.
(2) Bophuthatswana, Ciskei, Transkei e Venda não son reconhecido pelas Nações Unidas.
(3) Reivindicado pela Argentina.
(4) Incluindo a margem oeste, as colinas de Golan e a faixa de Gaza.
(5) Capital futuro.
(6) Reivindicado pelas Comores.
(7) Compreende Ceuta, Melilla e várias ilhas pequenas.

THIS TABLE lists the major metropolitan areas of the world according to their estimated population on January l, 1993. For convenience in reference, the areas are grouped by major region with the total for each region given. The number of areas by population classification is given in parentheses with each size group.

For ease of comparison, each metropolitan area has been defined by Rand McNally according to consistent rules. A metropolitan area includes a central city, neighboring communities linked to it by continuous built-up areas, and more distant communities if the bulk of their population is supported by commuters to the central city. Some metropolitan areas have more than one central city; in such cases each central city is listed.

IN DIESER TABELLE sind die Hauptmetropolen der Welt verzeichnet, gemessen nach ihrer Bevölkerung, die nach dem Stand vom 1. Januar 1993 geschätzt wurde. Zur besseren Übersicht sind die Zonen nach grösseren Regionen gruppiert, wobei die Gesamtzahl für jede Region angegeben ist. Die Anzahl der Zonen ist nach Bevölkerung klassifiziert und in Klammern hinter denen nach Grössen sortierten Gruppen angegeben.

Zum einfacheren Vergleich ist jede Metropole von Rand McNally nach übereinstimmenden Massstäben definiert worden. Eine Metropole schliesst eine zentrale Stadt mit benachbarten Gemeinden, die mit ihr durch ununterbrochen bebaute Gebiete verbunden sind ein, sowie weiter entfernte Gemeinden, wenn der grösste Teil ihrer Bevölkerung von den Pendlern unterhalten wird. Einige Metropolen haben mehr als eine zentrale Stadt; in solchen Fällen ist jede dieser zentralen Städte angeführt.

ESTA TABLA indica las principales áreas metropolitanas del mundo, de acuerdo con su población calculada al 1 de enero de 1993. Para facilitar las referencias, las áreas se han agrupado por regiones principales, indicándose el total para cada región. El número de áreas, clasificadas por población, se indica entre paréntesis en los grupos de cada tamaño.

Para facilitar las comparaciones, Rand McNally ha definido cada área metropolitana de acuerdo con reglas consistentes. Un área metropolitana incluye una ciudad central, localidades vecinas vinculadas con ella mediante sectores construídos y contínuos, y localidades más distantes, si el grueso de su población lo constituye un núcleo que diariamente viaja a la ciudad central. Algunas áreas metropolitanas incluyen más de una ciudad central; en tales casos se indica cada una dichas ciudades.

CETTE TABLE contient la liste des aires métropolitaines les plus considérables dans le monde pour ce qui est du peuplement a la date du 1 er janvier 1993. Afin de faciliter la consultation, on a groupé les aires par grandes régions en indiquant la population totale pour chaque région, et, entre parenthéses, le nombre d'aires comprises dans celle-ci.

Afin de rendre plus faciles les comparaisons, Rand McNally a défini chaque aire métropolitaine selorègles cohérentes: une aire métropolitaine englobe une citè centrale ou métropole et l'environnement urbain continu qui s'y rattache; elle inclut également des agglomérations éloignées de la métropole lorsque la population de ces dernières est pour sa májorité constituée d'habitants se rendant quotidiennement dans la cité ou est situé le lieu de travail de ceux-ci. On trouvera quelques aires métropolitaines pourvues de plus d'une métropole. Dans ce cas, chaque métropole est mentionnée.

A TABELA que se segúe relaciona as principais áreas metropolitanas do mundo, de acordo com as respectivas populações, estimadas para 1 de janeiro de 1993. Para facilidade de referência, as áreas metropolitanas foram agrupadas dentro das regiões maiores, indicando-se, entre parênteses, os totais de cada região maior e o número de áreas metropolitanas, classificadas segundo a população, compreendidas em cada uma.

Para fins de comparabilidade, Rand McNally definiu cada área metropolitana de acordo com regras uniformes. Uma área metropolitana inclui uma cidade central, as localidades vizinhas ligadas a ela por áreas construídas contínuas, e as localidades mais distantes, desde que a maior parte de suas respectivas populações dependa economicamente da cidade central e que para ela viaje diariamente. Algumas áreas metropolitanas incluem mais de uma cidade central; em tais casos, indicam-se ambas as cidades.

CLASSIFICATION KLASSIFIZIERT CLASIFICADAS CLASSIFICATION CLASSIFICAÇÃO	ANGLO-AMERICA ANGLO-AMERIKA AMÉRICA ANGLOSAJONA AMÉRIQUE ANGLO-SAXONNE AMÉRICA ANGLO-SAXÔNICA	LATIN AMERICA LATEIN-AMERIKA AMÉRICA LATINA AMÉRIQUE LATINE AMÉRICA LATINA	WESTERN EUROPE WESTEUROPA EUROPA OCCIDENTAL EUROPE OCCIDENTALE EUROPA OCIDENTALE	EASTERN EUROPE-RUSSIA OSTEUROPA-RUSSLAND EUROPA ORIENTAL-RUSIA EUROPE ORIENTALE-RUSSIE EUROPA ORIENTAL-RÚSSIA	WEST ASIA WESTASIEN ASIA OCCIDENTAL ASIE OCCIDENTALE ÁSIA OCIDENTAL	EAST ASIA OSTASIEN ASIA ORIENTAL ASIE ORIENTALE ÁSIA ORIENTAL	AFRICA-OCEANIA AFRIKA-OZEANIEN AFRICA-OCEANÍA AFRIQUE-OCÉANIE ÁFRICA-OCEANIA
Over 15,000,000 (6)	New York	Ciudad de México (Mexico City) São Paulo				Ōsaka-Kōbe-Kyōto Sŏul (Seoul) Tōkyō-Yokohama	
10,000,000-15,000,000 (13)	Los Angeles	Buenos Aires Rio de Janeiro	London Paris	Moskva (Moscow)	Bombay Calcutta Delhi-New Delhi	Jakarta Manila Shanghai	Al-Qāhirah (Cairo)
5,000,000-10,000,000 (21)	Chicago Philadelphia-Trenton-Wilmington San Francisco-Oakland-San Jose	Lima Santa Fe de Bogotá Santiago	Essen-Dortmund-Duisburg (Ruhr Area)	Sankt-Peterburg (St. Petersburg)	Dhaka (Dacca) İstanbul Karāchi Madras Tehrān	Beijing (Peking) Krung Thep (Bangkok) Nagoya T'aipei Tianjin (Tientsin) Victoria (Hong Kong)	Johannesburg Lagos
3,000,000-5,000,000 (37)	Boston Dallas-Fort Worth Detroit-Windsor Houston Miami-Fort Lauderdale Montréal San Diego-Tijuana Toronto Washington	Belo Horizonte Caracas Guadalajara Porto Alegre	Barcelona Berlin Madrid Milano (Milan) Roma (Rome)	Athínai (Athens) Kijev (Kiev)	Ahmadābād Baghdād Bangalore Hyderābād Lahore	Guangzhou (Canton) Pusan Shenyang (Mukden) Singapore Thanh Pho Ho Chi Minh (Saigon) Wuhan Yangon (Rangoon)	Al-Iskandarīyah (Alexandria) Casablanca Kinshasa Melbourne Sydney
2,000,000-3,000,000 (64)	Atlanta Baltimore Cleveland Minneapolis-St. Paul Phoenix Pittsburgh St. Louis Seattle-Tacoma	Fortaleza La Habana (Havana) Medellín Monterrey Recife Salvador San Juan Santo Domingo	Amsterdam Birmingham Bruxelles (Brussels) Frankfurt am Main Hamburg Leeds-Bradford Lisboa (Lisbon) Liverpool Manchester München (Munich) Napoli (Naples) Stuttgart Wien (Vienna)	București (Bucharest) Budapest Char'kov (Kharkov) Doneck-Makejevka Katowice-Bytom-Gliwice Nižnij Novgorod (Gorky) Warszawa (Warsaw)	Ankara Baku Colombo Dimashq (Damascus) İzmir Kānpur Pune (Poona) Taškent	Bandung Changchun Chengdu (Chengtu) Chongqing (Chungking) Dalian (Dairen) Fukuoka Harbin Kuala Lumpur Nanjing (Nanking) P'yongyang Sapporo-Otaru Surabaya Taegu Xi'an (Sian)	Abidjan Adis Abeba Al-Kharṭūm-Umm Durmān (Khartoum-Omdurman) Cape Town Durban El Djazaïr (Algiers)
1,500,000-2,000,000 (48)	Cincinnati Denver El Paso-Ciudad Juárez Portland Vancouver	Brasília Cali Curitiba Guatemala Guayaquil Montevideo San José	Glasgow København (Copenhagen) Köln (Cologne) Mannheim Stockholm	Beograd (Belgrade) Dnepropetrovsk Jekaterinburg (Sverdlovsk) Minsk Novosibirsk	'Amman Ar-Riyad (Riyadh) Bayrūt (Beirut) Chittagong Faisalabad Ḥalab (Aleppo) Jaipur Jiddah Kābol (Kabul) Lucknow Mashhad Nāgpur Rāwalpindi-Islāmābād Surat Tbilisi Tel Aviv-Yafo	Hiroshima-Kure Jinan (Tsinan) Kaohsiung Kitakyūshū-Shimonoseki Medan Qingdao (Tsingtao) Taiyuan	Accra Dakar Rabat-Salé
1,000,000-1,500,000 (119)	Buffalo-Niagara Falls-St. Catharines Columbus Hartford-New Britain Indianapolis Kansas City Milwaukee New Orleans Norfolk-Newport News Sacramento St. Petersburg-Clearwater San Antonio	Asuncíon Barranquilla Belém Campinas Córdoba Goiânia La Paz Manaus Maracaibo Puebla Quito Rosario San Salvador Santos Valencia Vitória	Antwerpen (Antwerp) Dublin (Baile Átha Cliath) Düsseldorf Hannover Helsinki Lille-Roubaix Lyon Marseille Newcastle-Sunderland Nürnberg Porto Rotterdam Sevilla Torino (Turin) Valencia	Čel'abinsk (Chelyabinsk) Łódź Kazan' Kraków Krasnojarsk Odessa Omsk Perm Praha (Prague) Rīga Rostov-na-Donu Samara (Kuybyshev) Saratov Sofija (Sofia) Ufa Volgograd Voronež	Adana Agra Allahābād Al-Kuwayt (Kuwait) Alma-Ata Asansol Bhopāl Cochin Coimbatore Esfahān Indore Jerevan Ludhiāna Madurai Patna Shīrāz Tabrīz Vadodara Vārānasi (Benares) Vishākhapatnam	Anshan Baotou Changsha Fushun Guiyang Hangzhou Ha Noi Jilin (Kirin) Kunming Kwangju Lanzhou Nanchang Palembang Qiqihar (Tsitsihar) Semarang Sendai Shijiazhuang Shizuoka-Shimizu Taejŏn Tangshan Ujungpandang Ürümqi Zhengzhou Zibo	Adelaide Antananarivo Brisbane Dar es Salaam Douala Harare Ibadan Kampala Luanda Lusaka Maputo Nairobi Perth Pretoria Ṭarābulus (Tripoli) Tunis
Total/Gesamtzahl Total/Total/Total (308)	38	42	41	33	57	64	33

ALL URBAN CENTERS of 50,000 or more population and many other important or well-known cities and towns are listed in the following table. The populations are from recent censuses (designated C) or official estimates (designated E) for the dates specified. For a few cities, only unofficial estimates are available (designated U). For comparison, the total population of each country is also given. For each country, the date stated for the total population also applies to the cities, except those for which another date is specified.

Population estimates for 1993 for countries may be found in the World Information Table.

A population figure in parentheses and preceded by a star (★) is the population of a city's entire metropolitan area. To permit meaningful comparisons of metropolitan areas, these have been defined by Rand McNally according to consistent rules (see introduction to Metropolitan Areas Table), and in some cases may differ somewhat from the officially recognized metropolitan areas. Where a town is located within the metropolitan area of another city, that city's name is given in parentheses preceded by a star (★). The capital of a country is denoted by CAPITAL letters.

ALLE STÄDTISCHEN ZENTREN mit 50 000 oder mehr Einwohnern und zahlreiche andere bedeutende oder bekannte Städte sind in der folgenden Tabelle zusammengestellt. Die Bevölkerungszahlen stammen von neuesten Zählungen (mit C gekennzeichnet) oder amtlichen Schätzungen (E) zu den angegebenen Zeitpunkten. Für einige wenige Städte waren lediglich inoffizielle Schätzungen erhältlich (U). Zu Vergleichszwecken ist ferner die Gesamtbevölkerung jedes Landes angegeben. Das Bezugsjahr für die Einwohnerzahl eines Landes betrifft auch die Städte mit Ausnahme jener, bei denen ein anderes Datum angegeben ist.

Schätzungen der Bevölkerungszahlen der Länder für 1993 finden sich in der Welt-Informationstabelle.

Bevölkerungszahlen in Klammern mit vorangestelltem Stern (★) beziehen sich auf die gesamte Stadtregion einer Stadt. Um sinnvolle Vergleiche von Stadtregionen zu ermöglichen, wurden diese von Rand McNally nach einheitlichen Regeln festgelegt (siehe Einleitung: Tabelle der Stadtregionen), weshalb sie in einigen Fällen etwas von der offiziellen Abgrenzung von Stadtregionen abweichen können. Ist eine Stadt in die Stadtregion einer anderen Grossstadt einbezogen, so wird der Name der Stadtregion mit vorangestelltem Stern (★) in Klammern aufgeführt. Die Hauptstadt eines Landes wird durch GROSSBUCHSTABEN hervorgehoben.

TODAS LOS CENTROS URBANOS de 50 000 habitantes o más y muchos otros de importancia así como bien conocidas ciudades y pueblos están incluídos en la tabla que se presenta a continuación. El número de habitantes indicados está tomado del censo más reciente (cifras identificadas con la letra C) o estimados oficiales (E) para las fechas especificadas. Para algunas ciudades, sólo existen informes no oficiales (U). Para medida de comparación, la población total de cada país se encuentra incluída también.

Para permitir una comparación, se da la población total de cada país, referente al mismo año que se usa para las ciudades principles, excepto para aquellas en las que se especifica otra fecha. El número de habitantes para 1993 para los países, se encuentra en la Tabla de Información Mundial.

La segunda cifra para la población que aparece en paréntesis y está precedida por una estrella (★) constituye la población de un área metropolitana entera. Para permitir comparaciones validas de áreas metropolitanas, éstas fueron definidas por Rand McNally siguiendo las reglas establecidas para estos propósitos (véase la Introducción a la Tabla de las Areas Metropolitanas), y en algunas ocasiones pueden ser un poco distintas de las áreas metropolitanas oficialmente reconocidas. Cuando una población se encuentra dentro de los límites de un área metropolitana de otra ciudad, el nombre de ésta se da entre paréntesis precedido por una (★). La capital de un país se indica con letras MAYÚSCULAS.

TOUTES LES VILLES de plus de 50 000 habitants et des villes moins peuplées, mais cèlèbres ou importantes, sont mentionnées dans la table ci-dessous. Les chiffres donnant la population proviennent de recensements récents (référence C), ou d'estimations officielles (référence E), aux dates indiquées. Pour quelques villes, on dispose seulement d'estimations non officielles (référence U). La population totale de chaque pays est également donnée, ce qui permet des comparaisons. Dans chaque pays, la date des renseignements est identique pour les villes et le pays, sauf indication contraire.

On trouvera dans la table d'informations mondiales les estimations de la population en 1993 pour chaque pays.

Les chiffres entre parenthèses, précédés d'une étoile (★), indiquent la population de l'ensemble de la zone métropolitaine. Pour permettre d'établir des comparaisons significatives entre les zones métropolitaines, ces dernières ont été définies selon des critères uniformes par Rand McNally & Company (voir l'introduction à la table des zones métropolitaines). Parfois, les limites des zones métropolitaines ainsi définies diffèrent des limites officielles. Quand une ville fait partie de la zone métropolitaine d'une autre ville, le nom de celle-ci, précédé d'une étoile (★), est mis entre parenthèses. Le nom des capitales de pays est écrit en lettres MAJUSCULES.

TODOS OS CENTROS URBANOS de 50 000 habitantes e mais, bem como muitas outras cidades e vilas importantes ou muito conhecidas figuram na tabela que se apresenta em sequida. Os dados relativos à população referem-se a censos recentes (identificadas com a letra C), ou a estimativas oficiais (E) nas datas indicadas. Para algumas cidades só existem estimativas não oficiais (U). Para fins de comparabilidade, apresenta-se também a população total de cada país.

Para cada país, a data de referência da população total aplica-se também às cidades exceto quando especificado em contrário. As estimativas da população dos países para 1993 encontra-se na *Tabela de informaçoes mundiais.*

Um dado de população apresentado entre parênteses e precedido por uma estrela (★), refere-se à população de toda a área metropolitana. Para fins de comparabilidade, as áreas metropolitanas foram definidas por Rand McNally segundo regras coerentes (ver a 'Introdução' à *Tabela das áreas metropolitanas),* e em certos casos podem ser um pouco diferentes das áreas metropolitanas oficialmente reconhecidas. Quando um centro urbano esta localizado dentro dos limites da área metropolitana de outro, seu nome figura entre parênteses precedido por uma estrela (★). A capital de um país é indicada por letras MAIÚSCULAS.

AFGHANISTAN / Afghānestān	
1988 E	17,672,000
Herāt	177,300
Jalālābād (1982E)	58,000
• KĀBOL	1,424,400
Kondūz (1982E)	57,000
Mazār-e Sharīf	130,600
Qandahār	225,500
ALBANIA / Shqipëri	
1989 C	3,182,400
Durrës	82,700
Elbasan	80,700
Korçë	63,600
Shkodër	79,900
• TIRANË	238,100
Vlorë	71,700
ALGERIA / Algérie / Djazaïr	
1987 C	23,038,942
Aïn el Beïda	61,997
Aïn Oussera	44,270
Aïn Témouchent	47,479
Annaba (Bône)	305,526
Bab Ezzouar (★El Djazaïr)	55,211
Barika	56,488
Batna	181,601
Béchar	107,311
Bejaïa (Bougie)	114,534
Beskra	128,281
Bordj Bou Arrerid	84,264
Bordj el Kiffan (★El Djazaïr)	61,035
Boufarik	41,305
Bou Saâda	66,688
Ech Cheliff (Orléansville)	129,976
El Boulaïda	170,935
• EL DJAZAÏR (ALGIERS) (★2,547,983)	1,507,241
El Djelfa	84,207
El Eulma	67,933
El Wad	70,073
Ghardaïa	89,415
Ghilizane	80,091
Guelma	77,821
Jijel	62,793
Khemis	55,335
Khenchla	69,743
Laghouat	67,214
Lemdiyya	85,195
Maghniyya	52,275
Messaad	47,460
Mestghanem	114,037
Mouaskar	64,691
M'Sila	65,805
Qacentina	440,842
Saïda	80,825
Sidi bel Abbès	152,778
Skikda	128,747
Souq Ahras	83,015
Stif	170,182
Tbessa	107,559
Tihert	95,821
Tilimsen	126,882
Tizi-Ouzou	61,163
Touggourt	70,645
Wahran	628,558
Wargla	81,721
AMERICAN SAMOA / Amerika Samoa	
1980 C	32,279
• PAGO PAGO	3,075
ANDORRA	
1991 E	54,507
• ANDORRA	20,437
ANGOLA	
1989 E	9,739,100
Benguela (1983E)	155,000
Huambo (Nova Lisboa) (1983E)	203,000
Lobito (1983E)	150,000
• LUANDA	1,459,900
Lubango (1984E)	95,915
Namibe (1981E)	100,000
ANGUILLA	
1984 C	6,680
South Hill	961
• THE VALLEY	1,042
ANTIGUA AND BARBUDA	
1977 E	72,000
• SAINT JOHN'S	24,359
ARGENTINA	
1991 C	32,608,687
Almirante Brown (★Buenos Aires)	449,105
Avellaneda (★Buenos Aires)	346,620
Bahía Blanca (1980C)	223,818
Berazategui (★Buenos Aires)	243,690
Berisso (★Buenos Aires)	74,012
• BUENOS AIRES (★10,800,000)	2,960,976
Campana (★Buenos Aires) (1980C)	54,832
Caseros (Tres de Febrero) (★Buenos Aires)	349,221
Comodoro Rivadavia (1980C)	96,817
Concordia (1980C)	94,222
Córdoba (★1,260,000)	1,179,067
Corrientes (1980C)	180,612
Ensenada (★Buenos Aires)	48,524
Esteban Echeverría (★Buenos Aires)	276,017
Florencio Varela (★Buenos Aires)	253,554
Formosa (1980C)	93,603
General San Martín (★Buenos Aires)	407,506
General Sarmiento (San Miguel) (★Buenos Aires)	646,891
Godoy Cruz (★Mendoza)	179,502
Gualeguaychú (1980C)	51,400
Junín (1980C)	62,458
Lanús (★Buenos Aires)	466,755
La Plata (★Buenos Aires)	542,567
La Rioja (1980C)	67,043
Las Heras (★Mendoza) (1980C)	101,579
Lomas de Zamora (★Buenos Aires)	572,769
Mar del Plata (1980C)	414,696
Mendoza (★650,000)	121,696
Mercedes (1980C)	50,992
Merlo (★Buenos Aires)	390,031
Moreno (★Buenos Aires)	287,188
Morón (★Buenos Aires)	641,541
Necochea (1980C)	51,069
Neuquén (1980C)	90,089
Olavarría (1980C)	64,097
Paraná (1980C)	161,638
Pergamino (1980C)	68,612
Pilar (★Buenos Aires)	130,177
Posadas (1980C)	143,889
Presidencia Roque Sáenz Peña (1980C)	49,341
Punta Alta (1980C)	56,620
Quilmes (★Buenos Aires)	509,445
Rafaela (1980C)	53,273
Resistencia (1980C)	220,104
Río Cuarto (1980C)	110,254
Rosario (★1,190,000)	1,078,374
Salta (1980C)	260,744
San Carlos de Bariloche (1980C)	48,980
San Fernando (★Buenos Aires)	144,761
San Fernando del Valle de Catamarca (★90,000) (1980C)	78,799
San Francisco (★58,536) (1980C)	51,932
San Isidro (★Buenos Aires)	299,022
San Juan (★300,000)	119,399
San Justo (★Buenos Aires)	1,121,164
San Lorenzo (★Rosario) (1980C)	96,891
San Luis (1980C)	70,999
San Miguel de Tucumán (★525,000) (1980C)	392,888
San Nicolás de los Arroyos (1980C)	98,495
San Rafael (1980C)	70,959
San Salvador de Jujuy (1980C)	124,950
Santa Fe (1980C)	292,165
Santiago del Estero (★200,000) (1980C)	148,758
San Vincente (★Buenos Aires)	74,890
Tandil (1980C)	79,429
Tigre (★Buenos Aires)	256,005
Trelew (1980C)	52,372
Vicente López (★Buenos Aires)	289,142
Villa Krause (★San Juan) (1980C)	66,693
Villa María (1980C)	67,560
Villa Nueva (★Mendoza)	222,081
Zárate (1980C)	67,143
ARMENIA / Hayastan	
1989 C	3,283,000
Abovjan (1987E)	53,000
Ečmiadzin (★Jerevan) (1987E)	53,000
• JEREVAN (★1,315,000)	1,199,000
Kirovakan (1987E)	169,000
Kumajri	120,000
Razdan (1987E)	56,000
ARUBA	
1987 E	64,763
• ORANJESTAD	19,800
AUSTRALIA	
1989 E	16,833,100
Adelaide (★1,036,747)	12,340
Albury (★66,530)	40,730
Auburn (★Sydney)	49,950
Ballarat (★80,090)	36,680
Bankstown (★Sydney)	158,750
Bayswater (★Perth)	46,426
Bendigo (★67,920)	32,050
Berwick (★Melbourne)	64,100
Blacktown (★Sydney)	210,900
Blue Mountains (★Sydney)	70,800
Box Hill (★Melbourne)	47,700
Brisbane (★1,273,511)	744,828
Broadmeadows (★Melbourne)	105,500
Brunswick (★Melbourne)	41,100
Camberwell (★Melbourne)	87,700
Campbelltown (★Sydney)	139,500
CANBERRA (★271,362) (1986C)	247,194
Canning (★Perth)	69,104
Canterbury (★Sydney)	135,200
Caulfield (★Melbourne)	70,100
Coburg (★Melbourne)	54,500
Cockburn (★Perth)	49,802
Coffs Harbour	47,890
Dandenong (★Melbourne)	59,400
Darwin (★73,300)	63,900
Doncaster (★Melbourne)	107,300
Enfield (★Adelaide)	64,058
Essendon (★Melbourne)	55,300
Fairfield (★Sydney)	176,350

▲ Population of an entire municipality, commune, or district, including rural area.
• Largest city in country.
★ Population or designation of the metropolitan area, including suburbs.
C Census. E Official estimate. U Unofficial estimate.

▲ Bevölkerung eines ganzen städtischen Verwaltungsgebietes, eines Kommunalbezirkes oder eines Distrikts, einschliesslich ländlicher Gebiete.
• Grösste Stadt des Landes.
★ Bevölkerung oder Bezeichnung der Stadtregion einschliesslich Vororte.
C Volkszählung. E Offizielle Schätzung. U Inoffizielle Schätzung.

▲ Población de un municipio, comuna o distrito entero, incluyendo sus áreas rurales.
• Ciudad más grande de un país.
★ Población o designación de un área metropolitana, incluyendo los suburbios.
C Censo. E Estimado oficial. U Estimado no oficial.

▲ Population d'une municipalité, d'une commune ou d'un district, zone rurale incluse.
• Ville la plus peuplée du pays.
★ Population de l'agglomération (ou nom de la zone métropolitaine englobante).
C Recensement. E Estimation officielle. U Estimation non officielle.

▲ População de um municipio, comuna ou distrito, inclusive as respectivas áreas rurais.
• Maior cidade de um país.
★ População ou indicação de uma área metropolitana.
C Censo. E Estimativa oficial. U Estimativa não oficial.

Footscray (★Melbourne)	48,700
Frankston (★Melbourne)	90,500
Geelong (★148,980)	13,190
Gosford	126,600
Gosnells (★Perth)	71,862
Heidelberg (★Melbourne)	63,500
Hobart (★181,210)	47,280
Holroyd (★Sydney)	82,500
Hurstville (★Sydney)	66,350
Ipswich (★Brisbane)	75,283
Keilor (★Melbourne)	103,700
Knox (★Melbourne)	121,300
Kogarah (★Sydney)	47,850
Lake Macquarie (★Newcastle)	161,700
Launceston (★92,350)	32,150
Leichhardt (★Sydney)	58,950
Liverpool (★Sydney)	99,750
Logan (★Brisbane)	142,222
Mackay (★50,885)	22,583
Malvern (★Melbourne)	43,400
Marion (★Adelaide)	74,631
Marrickville (★Sydney)	84,650
Melbourne (★3,039,100)	55,300
Melville (★Perth)	85,590
Mitcham (★Adelaide)	63,301
Moorabbin (★Melbourne)	98,900
Newcastle (★425,610)	130,940
Noarlunga (★Adelaide)	77,352
Northcote (★Melbourne)	49,100
North Sydney (★Sydney)	53,400
Nunawading (★Melbourne)	96,400
Oakleigh (★Melbourne)	57,600
Parramatta (★Sydney)	134,600
Penrith (★Sydney)	152,650
Perth (★1,158,387)	82,413
Prahran (★Melbourne)	43,900
Preston (★Melbourne)	82,000
Randwick (★Sydney)	119,200
Redcliffe (★Brisbane)	48,123
Rockdale (★Sydney)	88,200
Rockhampton (★61,694)	58,890
Ryde (★Sydney)	94,400
Saint Kilda (★Melbourne)	46,400
Salisbury (★Adelaide)	106,129
Shoalhaven	64,070
Southport (★254,861)	135,408
South Sydney (★Sydney)	74,100
Springvale (★Melbourne)	88,700
Stirling (★Perth)	181,556
Sunshine (★Melbourne)	97,700
• Sydney (★3,623,550)	9,800
Tea Tree Gully (★Adelaide)	82,324
Toowoomba	81,071
Townsville (★111,972)	83,339
Wagga Wagga	52,180
Wanneroo (★Perth)	163,324
Waverley (★Melbourne)	126,300
Waverley (★Sydney)	61,850
West Torrens (★Adelaide)	44,711
Willoughby (★Sydney)	53,950
Wollongong (★236,690)	174,770
Woodville (★Adelaide)	82,590
Woollahra (★Sydney)	53,850

AUSTRIA / Österreich

1991 C	7,812,100
Bruck an der Mur (★52,000)	14,155
Graz (★325,000)	232,155
Innsbruck (★185,000)	114,996
Klagenfurt (★115,000)	89,502
Leoben (★52,000)	28,504
Linz (★335,000)	202,855
Neunkirchen (★45,000)	10,334
Salzburg (★220,000)	143,971
Sankt Pölten (★67,000)	49,805
Steyr (★65,000)	39,542
Villach (★65,000)	55,165
Wels (★76,000)	53,042
• WIEN (VIENNA) (★1,875,000)	1,533,176

AZERBAIJAN

1991 E	7,136,600
Ali-Bajramly	61,500
• BAKU (BAKY) (★2,020,000)	1,080,500
Gjandža	282,200
Mingečaur	90,900
Nachičevan'	61,700
Šeki (Nucha)	63,200
Stepanakert	55,200
Sumgait (★Baku)	236,200

BAHAMAS

1990 C	254,685
Freeport (▲171,542)	28,200
• NASSAU	141,000

BAHRAIN / Al-Baḥrayn

1988 E	473,000
• AL-MANĀMAH (★273,000) (1986E)	82,700
Al-Muharraq (★Al-Manāmah)	78,000
Jidd Hafs (★Al-Manāmah)	48,000

BANGLADESH

1981 C	87,119,965
Barisāl	172,905
Begamganj	69,623
Bhairab Bāzār	63,563
Bogra	68,749
Brāhmanbāria	87,570
Chāndpur	85,656
Chittagong (★1,391,877)	980,000
Chuādanga	76,000
Comilla	184,132
• DHAKA (DACCA) (★3,430,312)	2,365,695
Dinājpur	96,718
Farīdpur	66,579
Gopālpur	31,725
Gulshan (★Dhaka)	215,444
Jamālpur	91,815
Jessore	148,927
Jhenida	47,953
Khulna	648,359
Kishorganj	52,302
Kurīgrām	47,641
Kushtia	74,892
Mādārīpur	63,917
Mīrpur (★Dhaka)	349,031
Mymensingh	190,991
Naogaon	52,975
Nārāyanganj (★Dhaka)	405,562
Narsinghdi	76,841
Nawābganj	87,724
Noākhāli	59,065
Pābna	109,065
Patuākhāli	48,121
Rājshāhi	253,740
Rangpur	153,174
Saidpur	126,608
Sātkhira	52,156
Sherpur	48,214
Sirājganj	106,774
Sītākunda (★Chittagong)	237,520
Sylhet	168,371
Tangail	77,518
Tongi (★Dhaka)	94,580

BARBADOS

1980 C	244,228
• BRIDGETOWN (★115,000)	7,466

BELARUS

1991 E	10,260,400
Baranoviči	166,700
Bobrujsk	223,000
Borisov	150,200
Brest	277,000
Gomel'	503,300
Grodno	284,800
Lida	95,000
• MINSK (★1,694,000)	1,633,600
Mogil'ov	363,000
Molodečno	93,500
Mozyr'	103,000
Novopolock	96,600
Orša	125,300
Pinsk	123,800
Polock	78,700
Rečica	69,400
Sluck	60,100
Soligorsk	96,000
Vitebsk	361,500
Žlobin	60,800
Žodino	56,000

BELGIUM / België / Belgique

1987 E	9,864,751
Aalst (Alost) (★Bruxelles)	77,113
Anderlecht (★Bruxelles)	88,849
Antwerpen (★1,100,000)	479,748
Bastogne (▲11,699)	6,900
Brugge (Bruges) (★223,000)	117,755
• BRUXELLES (★2,385,000)	136,920
Charleroi (★480,000)	209,395
Etterbeek (★Bruxelles)	44,240
Forest (★Bruxelles)	48,266
Genk (★Hasselt)	61,391
Gent (Gand) (★465,000)	233,856
Hasselt (★290,000)	65,563
Ixelles (★Bruxelles)	76,241
Kortrijk (Courtrai) (★202,000)	76,216
La Louvière (★147,000)	76,340
Leuven (Louvain) (★173,000)	84,583
Liège (Luik) (★750,000)	200,891
Mechelen (Malines) (★121,000)	75,808
Molenbeek-St.-Jean (★Bruxelles)	69,764
Mons (Bergen) (★242,000)	89,697
Mouscron (★Lille, France)	53,713
Namur (★147,000)	102,670
Oostende (Ostende) (★122,000)	68,318
Roeselare (Roulers)	51,963
Saint-Gilles (★Bruxelles)	42,482
Schaerbeek (★Bruxelles)	104,919
Seraing (★Liège)	61,731
Sint-Niklaas (Saint-Nicolas)	68,082
Spa	9,645
Tournai (Doornik) (▲66,998)	44,900
Uccle (★Bruxelles)	75,876
Verviers (★101,000)	53,498
Waterloo (★Bruxelles)	25,232
Woluwe-Saint-Lambert (Sint-Lambrechts-Woluwe) (★Bruxelles)	47,887

BELIZE

1990 C	184,340
• Belize City	43,621
BELMOPAN	5,256

BENIN / Bénin

1984 E	3,825,000
Abomey	53,000
• COTONOU	478,000
Parakou	92,000
PORTO-NOVO	164,000

BERMUDA

1985 E	56,000
• HAMILTON (★15,000)	1,676

BHUTAN / Druk-Yul

1982 E	1,333,000
• THIMPHU	12,000

BOLIVIA

1990 E	7,314,000
Cochabamba	413,300
• LA PAZ	1,125,600
Montero	
Oruro	207,700
Potosí	120,100
Santa Cruz de la Sierra	696,100
SUCRE	101,400
Tarija	74,600
Trinidad	51,900

BOPHUTHATSWANA

1987 E	1,819,242
• Ga-Rankuwa (1980C)	48,300
Mafikeng (★16,000) (1980C)	6,500
MMABATHO (★Mafikeng) (1977E)	9,062

BOSNIA AND HERZEGOVINA / Bosna i Hercegovina

1987 E	4,400,464
Banja Luka (▲193,890)	130,900
• SARAJEVO (▲479,688)	341,200
Tuzla (▲129,967)	67,300
Zenica (▲144,869)	67,500

BOTSWANA

1991 C	1,325,291
Francistown	65,026
• GABORONE	133,791
Selebi Phikwe	39,769

BRAZIL / Brasil

1985 E	135,564,395
Alagoinhas (▲116,959)	87,500
Alegrete (▲71,898)	56,700
Alvorada (★Porto Alegre) (1989E)	115,465
Americana	156,030
Anápolis	225,840
Apucarana (▲92,812)	73,700
Aracaju	360,013
Araçatuba	129,304
Araguari (▲96,035)	84,300
Arapiraca (▲147,879)	91,400
Araraquara (▲145,042)	87,500
Araras (▲71,652)	59,900
Araxá	61,418
Assis (▲74,238)	63,100
Atibaia (▲81,263) (1989E)	64,200
Bacabal (▲97,633) (1989E)	51,600
Bagé (▲106,155)	70,800
Barbacena (▲99,337)	80,200
Barra do Piraí (▲78,189)	55,700
Barra Mansa (★Volta Redonda)	149,200
Barretos	80,202
Bauru	220,105
Bayeux (★João Pessoa)	67,182
Belém (★1,200,000)	1,116,578
Belford Roxo (★Rio de Janeiro)	340,700
Belo Horizonte (★2,950,000)	2,114,429
Betim (★Belo Horizonte)	96,810
Birigui (▲71,527) (1989E)	63,660
Blumenau	192,074
Boa Vista (▲74,493) (1989E)	48,700
Botucatu (▲71,139)	62,600
Bragança Paulista (▲105,099)	76,300
BRASÍLIA	1,567,709
Cabo (▲134,748) (1989E)	62,000
Caçapava (▲64,213)	56,600
Cáceres (▲92,370) (1989E)	51,700
Cachoeira do Sul (▲91,492)	58,900
Cachoeirinha (★Porto Alegre)	73,117
Cachoeiro de Itapemirim (▲138,156)	95,000
Campina Grande	279,929
Campinas (★1,125,000)	841,016
Campo Grande	384,398
Campos (▲366,716)	187,900
Campos Elísios (★Rio de Janeiro)	188,200
Canoas (★Porto Alegre)	261,222
Carapicuíba (★São Paulo)	265,856
Carazinho (▲62,108)	48,500
Cariacica (★Vitória)	74,300
Carpina (▲71,753) (1989E)	48,000
Caruaru (▲190,794)	152,100
Cascavel (▲200,485)	123,100
Castanhal (▲89,703)	71,200
Cataguases (▲62,080) (1989E)	50,900
Catanduva (▲80,309)	71,400
Caucaia (★Fortaleza)	78,500
Cavaleiro (★Recife)	106,600
Caxias (▲148,230)	66,300
Caxias do Sul	266,809
Chapecó (▲100,997)	64,200
Coelho da Rocha (★Rio de Janeiro)	164,400
Colatina (▲106,260)	58,600
Colombo (★Curitiba)	65,900
Conselheiro Lafaiete	77,958
Contagem (★Belo Horizonte)	152,700
Corumbá (▲80,666)	65,800
Crato (▲86,371)	52,700
Criciúma (▲128,410)	85,900
Cruz Alta (▲71,817)	58,300
Cruzeiro	63,918
Cubatão (★Santos)	98,322
Cuiabá (▲279,651)	220,400
Curitiba (★1,700,000)	1,279,205
Diadema (★São Paulo)	320,187
Divinópolis	139,940
Dourados (▲123,757)	89,200
Duque de Caxias (★Rio de Janeiro)	353,200
Embu (★São Paulo)	119,791
Erechim (▲70,709)	54,300
Esteio (★Porto Alegre)	58,964
Feira de Santana (▲355,201)	278,600
Ferraz de Vasconcelos (★São Paulo)	68,831
Florianópolis (★365,000)	178,400
Fortaleza (★1,825,000)	1,582,414
Foz do Iguaçu (▲182,101)	124,900
Franca	182,820
Garanhuns	73,100
Goiânia (★1,130,000) (1989E)	1,038,187
Governador Valadares (▲216,957)	192,300
Guaratinguetá (▲93,534)	80,400
Guarujá (★Santos)	83,500
Guarulhos (★São Paulo)	571,700
Ijuí (▲82,064)	64,400
Ilhéus (▲145,810)	79,400
Imperatriz (▲235,453)	119,500
Ipatinga (★270,000)	149,100
Ipiíba (★Rio de Janeiro)	116,200
Itabira (▲81,771)	66,300
Itabuna (▲167,543)	142,200
Itajaí	104,232
Itajubá (▲69,675)	61,500
Itapecerica da Serra (★São Paulo)	65,500
Itapetininga (▲105,512)	76,700
Itapeva (▲92,122) (1989E)	51,400
Itapevi (★São Paulo)	66,825
Itaquaquecetuba (★São Paulo)	91,366
Itaquari (★Vitória)	163,900
Itatiba (▲58,508) (1989E)	49,700
Itaúna	61,446
Itú (▲92,786)	77,900
Ituiutaba (▲85,365)	74,900
Itumbiara (▲78,844)	57,200
Jaboatão (★Recife)	82,900
Jaboatão (★Recife) (1989E)	94,000
Jacareí	149,061
Jataí (▲65,383) (1989E)	49,700
Jaú (▲92,547)	74,500
Jequié (▲127,070)	92,100
João Monlevade (1989E)	60,731
João Pessoa (★550,000)	348,500
Joinvile	302,877
Juàzeiro (★Petrolina)	78,600
Juazeiro do Norte	159,806
Juiz de Fora	349,720
Jundiaí (▲313,652)	268,900
Lajes (▲143,246)	103,600
Lavras	52,100
Leme (▲65,006) (1989E)	55,900
Limeira	186,986
Linhares (▲122,453)	53,400
Lins (▲59,479) (1989E)	51,700
Londrina (▲346,676)	296,400
Lorena	63,230
Luziânia (▲98,408)	71,400
Macapá (▲168,839)	109,400
Maceió	482,195
Majé (▲225,398) (1989E)	49,600
Manaus	809,914
Marabá (▲133,559)	92,700
Marília (▲136,187)	116,100
Maringá	196,871
Mauá (★São Paulo)	269,321
Mesquita (★Rio de Janeiro)	161,300
Mogi das Cruzes (▲255,636)(★São Paulo) (1989E)	155,900
Mojiguaçu (▲91,994)	81,800
Mojimirim (▲63,313)	52,300
Monjolo (★Rio de Janeiro)	113,900
Montes Claros (▲214,472)	183,500
Mossoró (▲158,723)	128,300
Muriaé (▲80,466)	57,600
Muribeca dos Guararapes (★Recife) (1989E)	196,000
Natal	510,106
Neves (★Rio de Janeiro)	163,600
Nilópolis (★Rio de Janeiro)	112,800
Niterói (★Rio de Janeiro)	441,684
Nova Friburgo (▲143,529)	103,500
Nova Iguaçu (★Rio de Janeiro)	592,800
Novo Hamburgo (★Porto Alegre)	167,744
Olinda (★Recife)	316,600
Osasco (★São Paulo)	591,568
Ourinhos (▲65,841)	58,100
Paranaguá (▲94,809)	82,300
Paranavaí (▲75,511)	60,900
Parnaíba (▲116,206)	90,200
Parque Industrial (★Belo Horizonte)	228,400
Passo Fundo (▲137,843)	117,500
Passos (▲79,393)	65,500
Patos	74,298
Patos de Minas (▲99,027)	69,000
Paulo Afonso (▲86,182)	75,300
Pelotas (▲277,730)	210,300
Petrolina (★225,000)	92,100
Petrópolis (▲284,535)(★Rio de Janeiro) (1989E)	173,600
Pindamonhangaba (▲86,990)	64,100
Pinheirinho (★Curitiba)	51,600
Piracicaba (▲252,079)	211,000
Poá (★São Paulo)	66,006
Poços de Caldas	100,004
Ponta Grossa	223,154
Porto Alegre (★2,600,000)	1,272,121
Porto Velho (▲202,011)	152,700
Pouso Alegre (▲65,958)	58,300
Praia Grande (★Santos)	67,800
Presidente Prudente	155,883
Queimados (★Rio de Janeiro)	113,700
Recife (★2,625,000)	1,287,623
Ribeirão Preto	383,125
Rio Branco (▲145,486)	109,800
Rio Claro	129,859
Rio de Janeiro (★10,150,000)	5,603,388
Rio do Sul (1989E)	48,860
Rio Grande	164,221
Rio Verde (▲92,954)	59,400
Rondonópolis (▲101,642)	65,500
Salto (1989E)	59,561
Salvador (★2,050,000)	1,804,438
Santa Bárbara d'Oeste	95,818
Santa Cruz do Sul (▲115,288)	60,300
Santa Maria (▲196,827)	163,900
Santana do Livramento (▲70,489)	60,100
Santarém (▲226,618)	120,800
Santa Rita (★João Pessoa)	60,100
Santa Rosa (▲66,925) (1989E)	51,500
Santo André (★São Paulo)	635,129
Santo Ângelo (▲107,559)	57,700
Santos (★1,065,000)	460,100
São Bernardo do Campo (★São Paulo)	562,485
São Borja (▲71,317) (1989E)	50,600
São Caetano do Sul (★São Paulo)	171,005
São Carlos	140,383
São Gonçalo (★Rio de Janeiro)	262,400
São João da Boa Vista (▲61,653)	50,400
São João del-Rei (▲74,385)	61,400
São João de Meriti (★Rio de Janeiro)	241,700
São José do Rio Preto	229,221
São José dos Campos	372,578
São José dos Pinhais (★Curitiba)	64,100
São Leopoldo (★Porto Alegre)	114,065
São Lourenço da Mata (★Recife)	65,936
São Luís (★600,000)	227,900
• São Paulo (★15,175,000)	10,063,110
São Vicente (★Santos)	239,778
Sapucaia do Sul (★Porto Alegre)	91,820
Sertãozinho (▲72,441) (1989E)	60,100
Sete Lagoas	121,418
Sete Pontes (★Rio de Janeiro)	72,300
Sobral (▲112,275)	69,400
Sorocaba	327,468
Susano (★São Paulo)	128,924
Taboão da Serra (★São Paulo)	122,112
Tatuí (▲69,358)	56,000
Taubaté	205,120
Teófilo Otoni (▲126,265)	82,700
Teresina (★525,000)	425,300
Teresópolis (▲115,859)	92,600
Timon (★Teresina)	68,300
Três Rios (▲93,902) (1989E)	61,900
Tubarão (▲82,082)	70,400
Tupã (▲65,867) (1989E)	51,400
Ubá (▲67,166) (1989E)	53,700
Uberaba	244,875
Uberlândia	312,024
Uruguaiana (▲105,862)	91,500
Varginha	74,630
Várzea Grande (▲124,188) (1989E)	64,600

▲ Population of an entire municipality, commune, or district, including rural area.
• Largest city in country.
★ Population or designation of the metropolitan area, including suburbs.
C Census. E Official estimate. U Unofficial estimate.

▲ Bevölkerung eines ganzen städtischen Verwaltungsgebietes, eines Kommunalbezirkes oder eines Distrikts, einschliesslich ländlicher Gebiete.
• Grösste Stadt des Landes.
★ Bevölkerung oder Bezeichnung der Stadtregion einschliesslich Vororte.
C Volkszählung. E Offizielle Schätzung. U Inoffizielle Schätzung.

Vicente de Carvalho (★Santos)	102,700
Vila Velha (★Vitória)	91,900
Vitória (★735,000)	201,500
Vitória da Conquista (▲198,150)	145,800
Vitória de Santo Antão (▲100,450)	67,800
Volta Redonda (★375,000)	219,267

BRITISH VIRGIN ISLANDS

1980 C	12,034
• ROAD TOWN	2,479

BRUNEI

1981 C	192,832
• BANDAR SERI BEGAWAN (★64,000)	22,777
Seria	23,415

BULGARIA / Bâlgarija

1989 E	8,986,636
Asenovgrad	
Blagoevgrad	74,236
Burgas	200,464
Dimitrovgrad	57,102
Dobrič	112,582
Gabrovo	80,930
Haskovo	93,609
Jambol	97,414
Kârdžali	58,995
Kazanlâk	63,776
Kjustendil	55,620
Loveč	50,872
Mihajlovgrad	55,203
Pazardžik	83,451
Pernik	97,930
Pleven	136,287
Plovdiv	364,162
Razgrad	56,494
Ruse	190,720
Silistra	56,907
Sliven	109,432
• SOFIJA (★1,205,000)	1,136,875
Stara Zagora	158,151
Šumen	107,973
Varna	306,300
Veliko Târnovo	71,709
Vidin	65,892
Vraca	81,992

BURKINA FASO

1985 C	7,964,705
Bobo Dioulasso	228,668
Koudougou	51,926
• OUAGADOUGOU	441,514
Ouahigouya	38,902

BURMA / Myanmar

1983 C	34,124,908
Bago (Pegu)	150,528
Chauk	51,437
Dawei (Tavoy)	69,882
Henzada	82,005
Kale	52,628
Lashio	88,590
Magway	54,881
Mandalay	532,949
Mawlamyine (Moulmein)	219,961
Maymyo	63,782
Meiktila	96,496
Mergui (Myeik)	88,600
Mogok	49,392
Monywa	106,843
Myingyan	77,060
Myitkyinā	56,427
Nyaunglebin	55,194
Pakokku	71,860
Pathein (Bassein)	144,096
Prome (Pyè)	83,332
Pyinmana	52,962
Sagaing	46,212
Shwebo	52,185
Sittwe (Akyab)	107,621
Taunggyi	108,231
Thaton	61,790
Toungoo	65,861
• YANGON (RANGOON) (★2,800,000)	2,705,039
Yenangyaung	62,582

BURUNDI

1990 C	5,356,266
• BUJUMBURA	226,628

CAMBODIA / Kâmpŭchéa

1990 E	8,567,582
Bătdâmbâng	94,412
Kâmpóng Saôm	67,452
• PHNUM PÉNH	477,874
Prey Vêng	41,456
Siĕmréab	76,434
Sisŏphŏn	67,041
Ta Khmau	34,947

CAMEROON / Cameroun

1986 E	10,446,409
Bafoussam (1985E)	89,000
Bamenda (1985E)	72,000
• Douala	1,029,731
Foumban (1985E)	50,000
Garoua (1985E)	96,000
Kumba (1985E)	67,000
Maroua	103,653
Ngaoundéré (1985E)	61,000
Nkongsamba	123,149
YAOUNDÉ	653,670

CANADA

1986 C	25,354,064

CANADA: ALBERTA

1986 C	2,375,278
Calgary (★671,326)	636,104
Edmonton (★785,465)	573,982
Lethbridge	58,841
Medicine Hat (★50,734)	41,804
Red Deer	54,425

CANADA: BRITISH COLUMBIA

1986 C	2,889,207
Burnaby (★Vancouver)	145,161
Coquitlam (★Vancouver) (1991C)	84,021
Delta (★Vancouver) (1991C)	88,978
Kamloops	61,773
Kelowna (★89,730)	61,213
Matsqui (★88,420)	51,449
Nanaimo (★60,420)	49,029
Prince George	67,621
Richmond (★Vancouver)	108,492
Saanich (★Victoria) (1991C)	95,577
Surrey (★Vancouver) (1991C)	245,173
Vancouver (★1,380,729)	431,147
Victoria (★255,547)	66,303

CANADA: MANITOBA

1986 C	1,071,232
Winnipeg (★625,304)	594,551

CANADA: NEW BRUNSWICK

1986 C	710,422
Fredericton (★65,768)	44,352
Moncton (★102,084)	55,468
Saint John (★121,265)	76,381

CANADA: NEWFOUNDLAND

1986 C	568,349
Saint John's (★161,901)	96,216

CANADA: NORTHWEST TERRITORIES

1986 C	52,238
Yellowknife	11,753

CANADA: NOVA SCOTIA

1986 C	873,199
Dartmouth (★Halifax)	65,243
Halifax (★295,990)	113,577
Sydney (★119,470)	27,754

CANADA: ONTARIO

1986 C	9,113,515
Barrie (★67,703)	48,287
Brampton (★Toronto)	188,498
Brantford (★90,521)	76,146
Burlington (★Hamilton)	116,675
Cambridge (Galt) (★Kitchener)	79,920
Cornwall (★51,719)	46,425
East York (★Toronto)	101,085
Etobicoke (★Toronto)	302,973
Gloucester (★Ottawa)	89,810
Guelph (★85,962)	78,235
Hamilton (★557,029)	306,728
Kingston (★122,350)	55,050
Kitchener (★311,195)	150,604
London (★342,302)	269,140
Markham (★Toronto)	114,597
Mississauga (★Toronto)	374,005
Nepean (★Ottawa)	95,490
Niagara Falls (★Saint Catharines)	72,107
North Bay (★57,422)	50,623
North York (★Toronto)	556,297
Oakville (★Toronto)	87,107
Oshawa (★203,543)	123,651
OTTAWA (★819,263)	300,763
Peterborough (★87,083)	61,049
Saint Catharines (★343,258)	123,455
Sarnia (★85,700)	49,033
Sault Sainte Marie (★101,800) (1991C)	81,476
Scarborough (★Toronto)	484,676
Sudbury (★148,877)	88,717
Thunder Bay (★122,217)	112,272
• Toronto (★3,427,168)	612,289
Vaughan (★Toronto)	65,058
Waterloo (★Kitchener)	58,718
Windsor (★253,988)	193,111
York (★Toronto)	135,401

CANADA: PRINCE EDWARD ISLAND

1986 C	126,646
Charlottetown (★53,868)	15,776

CANADA: QUÉBEC

1986 C	6,540,276
Beauport (★Québec)	62,869
Brossard (★Montréal)	57,441
Charlesbourg (★Québec)	68,996
Chicoutimi (★158,468)	61,083
Drummondville (★56,283)	36,020
Gatineau (★Ottawa)	81,244
Hull (★Ottawa)	58,722
Jonquière (★Chicoutimi)	58,467
La Salle (★Montréal)	75,621
Laval (★Montréal)	284,164
Longueuil (★Montréal)	125,441
Montréal (★2,921,357)	1,015,420
Montréal-Nord (★Montréal)	90,303
Québec (★603,267)	164,580
Sainte-Foy (★Québec)	69,615
Saint-Hubert (★Montréal)	66,218
Saint-Jean-sur-Richelieu (★59,958)	34,745
Saint-Laurent (★Montréal)	67,002
Saint-Léonard (★Montréal)	75,947
Shawinigan (★61,965)	21,470
Sherbrooke (★129,960)	74,438
Trois-Rivières (★128,888)	50,122
Verdun (★Montréal)	60,246

CANADA: SASKATCHEWAN

1986 C	1,010,198
Regina (★186,521)	175,064
Saskatoon (★200,665)	177,641

CANADA: YUKON

1986 C	23,504
Whitehorse	15,199

CAPE VERDE / Cabo Verde

1990 C	341,491
Mindelo	47,109
• PRAIA	61,644

CAYMAN ISLANDS

1988 E	25,900
• GEORGE TOWN	13,700

CENTRAL AFRICAN REPUBLIC / République centrafricaine

1984 E	2,517,000
• BANGUI	473,817
Bouar (1982E)	48,000

CHAD / Tchad

1988 E	5,428,000
Abéché	40,000
Moundou	100,000
• N'DJAMENA	500,000
Sarh	76,835

CHILE

1982 C	11,329,736
Antofagasta (1990E)	218,800
Apoquindo (★Santiago)	175,735
Arica (1990E)	177,300
Calama	81,684
Cerrillos (★Santiago)	67,013
Cerro Navia (★Santiago)	137,777
Chillán (1990E)	146,000
Concepción (★710,000) (1990E)	306,500
Conchalí (★Santiago)	157,884
Copiapó	69,045
Coquimbo	62,186
Coronel (★Concepción)	65,918
Curicó	60,550
El Bosque (★Santiago)	143,717
Huechuraba (★Santiago)	56,313
Independencia (★Santiago)	86,724
Iquique (1990E)	148,500
La Cisterna (★Santiago)	95,863
La Florida (★Santiago)	191,883
La Granja (★Santiago)	109,168
La Pintana (★Santiago)	73,932
La Reina (★Santiago)	80,452
La Serena (1990E)	105,600
Las Rejas (★Santiago)	147,918
Linares	46,433
Lo Espejo (★Santiago)	124,462
Lo Prado (★Santiago)	103,575
Los Ángeles	70,529
Lota (★Concepción)	47,133
Macul (★Santiago)	113,100
Maipú (★Santiago)	114,117
Ñuñoa (★Santiago)	168,919
Osorno (1990E)	117,400
Ovalle	43,023
Pedro Aguirre Cerda (★Santiago)	145,207
Peñalolén (★Santiago)	137,298
Providencia (★Santiago)	115,449
Pudahuel (★Santiago)	97,578
Puente Alto (★Santiago) (1990E)	187,400
Puerto Montt (1990E)	106,500
Punta Arenas (1990E)	120,000
Quilpué (★Valparaíso) (1990E)	107,400
Quinta Normal (★Santiago)	128,989
Rancagua (1990E)	190,400
Recoleta (★Santiago)	164,292
Renca (★Santiago)	93,928
San Antonio	61,486
San Bernardo (★Santiago) (1990E)	188,200
San Joaquín (★Santiago)	123,904
San Miguel (★Santiago)	88,764
San Ramón (★Santiago)	99,410
• SANTIAGO (★4,100,000)	232,667
Talca (1990E)	164,500
Talcahuano (★Concepción) (1990E)	246,900
Temuco (1990E)	211,700
Valdivia (1990E)	113,500
Vallenar	38,375
Valparaíso (★690,000) (1990E)	276,800
Villa Alemana (★Valparaíso)	55,766
Viña del Mar (★Valparaíso) (1990E)	281,100
Vitacura (★Santiago)	72,038

CHINA / Zhongguo

1988 E	1,103,983,000
Abagnar Qi (▲100,700) (1986E)	71,700
Acheng (1985E)	100,304
Aihui (▲135,000) (1986E)	76,700
Aksu (▲345,900) (1986E)	143,100
Altay (▲141,700) (1986E)	62,800
Anci (Langfang) (▲522,800) (1986E)	122,100
Anda (▲425,500) (1986E)	130,200
Ankang (1985E)	89,188
Anqing (▲433,900) (1986E)	213,200
Anshan	1,330,000
Anshun (▲214,700) (1986E)	128,800
Anyang (▲541,900) (1986E)	361,200
Baicheng (▲282,000) (1986E)	198,600
Baiquan (1985E)	50,996
Baiyin (▲301,900) (1986E)	157,100
Baoding (▲535,100) (1986E)	423,200
Baoji (▲359,500) (1986E)	286,200
Baoshan (▲688,400) (1986E)	52,300
Baotou (Paotow)	1,130,000
Baoying (1985E)	50,479
Bei'an (▲440,500) (1986E)	199,500
Beihai (▲175,900) (1986E)	119,000
BEIJING (PEKING) (★7,200,000)	6,710,000
Beipiao (▲603,700) (1986E)	180,900
Bengbu (▲612,600) (1986E)	403,900
Benxi (Penhsi)	860,000
Bijie (1985E)	54,871
Binxian (▲177,900) (1986E)	86,700
Binxian (1982C)	127,326
Boli (1985E)	61,990
Bose (▲271,400) (1986E)	82,000
Boshan (1975U)	100,000
Boxian (1985E)	63,222
Boxing (1982C)	57,554
Boyang (1985E)	60,688
Butha Qi (Zalantun) (▲389,500) (1986E)	111,300
Cangshan (Bianzhuang) (1982C)	79,334
Cangzhou (▲293,600) (1986E)	196,700
Changchun (▲2,000,000)	1,822,000
Changde (▲220,800) (1986E)	178,200
Changge (1982C)	67,002
Changji (▲233,400) (1986E)	110,500
Changqing (1982C)	65,094
Changsha	1,230,000
Changshou (1985E)	51,923
Changshu (▲998,000) (1986E)	281,300
Changtu (1985E)	49,937
Changyi (1982C)	64,513
Changzhi (▲463,400) (1986E)	273,000
Changzhou (Changchow) (1986E)	522,700
Chao'an (▲1,214,500) (1986E)	265,400
Chaoxian (▲739,500) (1986E)	116,800
Chaoyang, Guangdong prov. (1985E)	85,968
Chaoyang, Liaoning prov. (▲318,900) (1986E)	180,300
Chengde (▲330,400) (1986E)	226,600
Chengdu (Chengtu) (▲2,960,000)	1,884,000
Chenghai (1985E)	50,631
Chenxian (▲191,900) (1986E)	143,500
Chifeng (Ulanhad) (▲882,900) (1986E)	299,000
Chongqing (Chungking) (▲2,890,000)	2,502,000
Chuxian (▲365,000) (1986E)	113,300
Chuxiong (▲379,400) (1986E)	67,700
Da'an (1985E)	70,552
Dachangzhen (1975U)	50,000
Dalian (Dairen)	2,280,000
Dandong (1986E)	579,800
Daqing (▲880,000)	640,000
Dashiqiao (1985E)	68,898
Datong (▲1,040,000)	810,000
Datong (1985E)	55,529
Dawa (1985E)	142,581
Daxian (▲209,400) (1986E)	142,000
Dehui (1985E)	60,247
Dengfeng (1982C)	49,746
Deqing (1982C)	48,726
Deyang (▲753,400) (1986E)	184,800
Dezhou (▲276,200) (1986E)	161,300
Didao (1975U)	50,000
Dinghai (1985E)	50,161
Dongchuan (Xincun) (▲275,100) (1986E)	67,400
Dongguan (▲1,208,500) (1986E)	254,900
Dongsheng (▲121,300) (1986E)	57,500
Dongtai (1985E)	65,788
Dongying (▲514,400) (1986E)	178,100
Dukou (▲551,200) (1986E)	380,200
Dunhua (▲448,000) (1986E)	217,100
Duyun (▲386,600) (1986E)	123,800
Echeng (▲938,000) (1986E)	217,400
Enshi (▲679,000) (1986E)	84,300
Erenhot (1986E)	7,200
Ergun Zuoqi (1985E)	55,970
Feixian (1982C)	73,246
Fengcheng (1985E)	66,745
Foshan (▲312,700) (1986E)	243,500
Fujin (1985E)	60,948
Fuling (▲973,500) (1986E)	166,300
Fushun (Funan)	1,290,000
Fuxian (Wafangdian) (▲960,700) (1986E)	246,200
Fuxin	700,000
Fuyang (▲195,200) (1986E)	143,400
Fuyu, Heilongjiang prov. (1985E)	48,670
Fuyu, Jilin prov. (1985E)	98,373
Fuzhou, Fujian prov. (▲1,240,000)	910,000
Fuzhou, Jiangxi prov. (▲171,800) (1986E)	106,700
Gaixian (1985E)	67,587
Ganhe (1985E)	48,128
Ganzhou (▲346,000) (1986E)	191,600
Gaoqing (Tianzhen) (1982C)	70,411
Gaoyou (1985E)	57,844
Gejiu (Kokiu) (▲341,700) (1986E)	193,600
Golmud (1986E)	60,300
Gongchangling (1982C)	49,281
Guanghua (▲420,000) (1986E)	104,400
Guangyuan (▲805,500) (1986E)	162,200
Guangzhou (Canton) (▲3,420,000)	3,100,000
Guanxian, Shandong prov. (1982C)	49,782
Guanxian, Sichuan prov. (1985E)	65,039
Guilin (Kweilin) (▲457,500) (1986E)	324,200
Guixian (1985E)	61,970
Guiyang (Kweiyang) (▲1,430,000)	1,030,000
Haicheng (▲984,800) (1986E)	210,700
Haifeng (1985E)	50,401
Haikou (▲289,600) (1986E)	209,200
Hailar (▲163,549) (1986E)	180,000
Hailin (1985E)	58,909
Hailong (Meihekou) (▲534,200) (1986E)	117,500
Hailun (1985E)	83,448
Haiyang (Dongcun) (1982C)	77,098
Hami (Kumul) (▲270,300) (1986E)	146,400
Hancheng (▲304,200) (1986E)	66,600
Handan (▲1,030,000)	870,000
Hangu (1975U)	100,000
Hangzhou (Hangchow)	1,290,000
Hanzhong (▲415,000) (1986E)	151,700
Harbin	2,710,000
Hebi (▲321,600) (1986E)	158,500
Hechi (▲266,800) (1986E)	74,400
Hechuan (1985E)	65,237
Hefei (▲930,000)	740,000
Hegang (1986E)	588,300
Helong (1985E)	62,665
Hengshui (▲286,500) (1986E)	83,100
Hengyang (▲601,300) (1986E)	419,200
Heshan (▲109,600) (1986E)	42,000
Heze (Caozhou) (▲1,001,500) (1986E)	115,400
Hohhot (▲830,000)	670,000
Hongjiang (▲67,000) (1986E)	54,300
Horqin Youyi Qianqi (Ulan Hot) (▲192,100) (1986E)	129,100
Hotan (▲122,800) (1986E)	71,700
Houma (▲158,500) (1986E)	67,000
Huadian (1985E)	75,183
Huai'an (1985E)	65,673
Huaibei (▲447,200) (1986E)	252,100
Huaide (▲899,400) (1986E)	187,600
Huaihua (▲427,100) (1986E)	102,000
Huainan (▲1,110,000)	700,000
Huaiyin (Wangying) (▲382,500) (1986E)	201,700
Huanan (1985E)	66,596
Huanggang (1982C)	65,961
Huangshi (▲431,713) (1986E)	451,900
Huayun (Huarong) (▲313,500) (1986E)	81,000
Huinan (Chaoyang) (1985E)	52,429
Huizhou (▲182,100) (1986E)	117,000
Hulan (1985E)	74,989
Hunjiang (Badaojiang) (▲687,700) (1986E)	442,600
Huzhou (▲964,400) (1986E)	208,500
Jiading (1985E)	60,718

▲ Población de un municipio, comuna o distrito entero, incluyendo sus áreas rurales.
• Ciudad más grande de un país.
★ Población o designación de un área metropolitana, incluyendo los suburbios.
C Censo. E Estimado oficial. U Estimado no oficial.

▲ Population d'une municipalité, d'une commune ou d'un district, zone rurale incluse.
• Ville la plus peuplée du pays.
★ Population de l'agglomération (ou nom de la zone métropolitaine englobante).
C Recensement. E Estimation officielle. U Estimation non officielle.

▲ População de um município, comuna ou distrito, inclusive as respectivas áreas rurais.
• Maior cidade de um país.
★ População ou indicação de uma área metropolitana.
C Censo. E Estimativa oficial. U Estimativa não oficial.

Jiamusi (Kiamusze) (▲557,700) (1986E)	429,800
Ji'an (▲184,300) (1986E)	132,200
Jiangling (1985E)	77,887
Jiangmen (▲231,700) (1986E)	168,800
Jiangyin (1985E)	66,476
Jiangyou (1985E)	72,663
Jian'ou (1985E)	55,180
Jiaohe (1985E)	51,504
Jiaojiang (▲385,200) (1986E)	82,300
Jiaoxian (1985E)	51,869
Jiaozuo (▲509,900) (1986E)	335,400
Jiawang (1975U)	50,000
Jiaxing (▲686,500) (1986E)	210,200
Jiayuguan (▲102,100) (1986E)	73,800
Jiexiu (1985E)	51,300
Jieyang (1985E)	98,531
Jilin (Kirin)	1,200,000
Jinan (Tsinan) (▲2,140,000)	1,546,000
Jinchang (Baijiazui) (▲136,000) (1986E)	90,500
Jincheng (▲612,700) (1986E)	99,900
Jingdezhen (Kingtechen) (▲569,700) (1986E)	304,000
Jingmen (▲946,500) (1986E)	227,000
Jinhua (▲799,900) (1986E)	147,800
Jining, Nei Monggol prov. (1986E)	163,300
Jining, Shandong prov. (▲765,700) (1986E)	222,600
Jinshi (▲219,700) (1986E)	73,700
Jinxi (▲634,300) (1986E)	223,100
Jinxian (1985E)	95,761
Jinzhou (Chinchou) (▲810,000)	710,000
Jishou (▲194,500) (1986E)	59,500
Jishu (1985E)	75,587
Jiujiang (▲382,300) (1986E)	248,500
Jiuquan (Suzhou) (▲269,900) (1986E)	56,300
Jiutai (1985E)	63,021
Jixi (▲820,000)	700,000
Jixian (1985E)	59,725
Juancheng (1982C)	54,110
Junan (Shizilu) (1982C)	90,222
Junxian (▲423,400) (1986E)	97,000
Juxian (1982C)	51,666
Kaifeng (▲629,100) (1986E)	458,800
Kaili (▲342,100) (1986E)	96,600
Kaiping (1985E)	54,145
Kaiyuan (▲342,100) (1986E)	96,600
Kaiyuan (1985E)	85,762
Karamay (▲168,868) (1986E)	185,300
Kashi (▲194,500) (1986E)	146,300
Keshan (1985E)	65,088
Korla (▲219,000) (1986E)	129,400
Kunming (▲1,550,000)	1,310,000
Kunshan (1985E)	44,645
Kuqa (1985E)	63,847
Kuytun (1986E)	60,200
Laiwu (▲1,041,800) (1986E)	143,500
Langxiang (1985E)	64,658
Lanxi (1985E)	53,236
Lanxi (▲606,800) (1986E)	70,500
Lanzhou (Lanchow) (▲1,420,000)	1,297,000
Lechang (1986E)	56,913
Lengshuijiang (▲277,600) (1986E)	101,700
Lengshuitan (▲362,000) (1986E)	60,900
Leshan (▲972,300) (1986E)	307,300
Lhasa (▲107,700) (1986E)	84,400
Lianyungang (Xinpu) (▲459,400) (1986E)	288,000
Liaocheng (▲724,300) (1986E)	119,000
Liaoyang (▲576,900) (1986E)	442,600
Liaoyuan (▲771,577) (1986E)	370,400
Liling (▲856,300) (1986E)	107,100
Linfen (▲530,100) (1986E)	157,600
Lingling (▲515,300) (1986E)	72,700
Lingyuan (1985E)	66,825
Linhai (1985E)	52,653
Linhe (▲365,900) (1986E)	99,800
Linkou (1985E)	52,936
Linqing (▲603,000) (1986E)	87,000
Linqu (1982C)	84,196
Linxia (▲150,200) (1986E)	72,900
Linyi (▲1,365,000) (1986E)	190,000
Liuzhou	680,000
Longjiang (1985E)	51,156
Longyan (▲378,500) (1986E)	114,500
Loudi (▲254,300) (1986E)	84,200
Lu'an (▲163,400) (1986E)	122,600
Lufeng (1985E)	53,015
Luohe (▲159,100) (1986E)	102,300
Luoyang (Loyang) (▲1,090,000)	760,000
Luzhou (▲360,300) (1986E)	237,800
Ma'anshan (▲367,000) (1986E)	258,900
Manzhouli (1986E)	116,600
Maoming (▲434,900) (1986E)	118,600
Meixian (▲740,600) (1986E)	169,100
Mengyin (1982C)	70,602
Mianyang, Sichuan prov. (▲848,500) (1986E)	233,900
Minhang (1975U)	60,000
Mishan (1985E)	54,919
Mixian (1982C)	64,776
Mudanjiang (▲580,982)	650,000
Nahe (1985E)	49,725
N'aizishen (1985E)	51,982
Nancha (1975U)	50,000
Nanchang (▲1,260,000)	1,090,000
Nanchong (▲238,100) (1986E)	158,000
Nanjing (Nanking)	2,390,000
Nanning (▲1,000,000)	720,000
Nanpiao (1982C)	67,274
Nanping (▲420,800) (1986E)	157,100
Nantong (▲411,000) (1986E)	308,800
Nanyang (▲294,800) (1986E)	199,400
Neihuang (1982C)	56,039
Neijiang (▲298,500) (1986E)	191,100
Ning'an (1985E)	49,334
Ningbo (▲1,050,000)	570,000
Ningyang (1982C)	55,424
Nong'an (1985E)	55,966
Nunjiang (1985E)	59,276
Orogen Zizhiqi (1985E)	48,042
Panshan (▲343,100) (1986E)	248,100
Panshi (1985E)	59,270
Pingdingshan (▲819,900) (1986E)	363,200
Pingliang (▲362,500) (1986E)	85,400
Pingxiang, Jiangxi prov. (▲1,286,700) (1986E)	368,700
Pingyi (1982C)	89,373
Pingyin (1982C)	62,827
Potou (▲456,100) (1986E)	59,000
Puqi (1985E)	65,239
Putian (▲265,400) (1986E)	64,600
Putuo (1985E)	50,962
Puyang (▲1,086,100) (1986E)	131,000
Qian Gorlos (1985E)	79,494
Qingdao (Tsingtao)	1,300,000
Qinggang (1985E)	43,075
Qingjiang, Jiangsu prov. (▲246,617) (1982C)	150,000
Qingjiang, Jiangxi prov. (1985E)	42,698
Qingyuan (1985E)	51,756
Qinhuangdao (Chinwangtao) (▲436,000) (1986E)	307,500
Qinzhou (▲923,400) (1986E)	97,100
Qiqihar (Tsitsihar) (▲1,330,000)	1,180,000
Qitaihe (▲309,900) (1986E)	166,400
Qixia (1982C)	54,158
Qixian (1982C)	53,041
Quanzhou (Chuanchou) (▲436,000) (1986E)	157,000
Qujing (▲758,000) (1986E)	135,000
Quxian (▲704,800) (1986E)	124,000
Raoping (1985E)	54,831
Rizhao (▲970,300) (1986E)	93,300
Rongcheng (1982C)	52,878
Rugao (1985E)	50,643
Rui'an (1985E)	57,993
Sanmenxia (Shanxian) (▲150,000) (1986E)	79,000
Sanming (▲214,300) (1986E)	144,900
• Shanghai (★9,300,000)	7,220,000
Shangqiu (Zhuji) (▲199,400) (1986E)	135,400
Shangrao (▲142,500) (1986E)	113,000
Shangshui (1982C)	50,191
Shantou (Swatow) (▲790,000)	560,000
Shanwei (1985E)	61,234
Shaoguan (▲344,892) (1986E)	363,100
Shaowu (▲266,700) (1986E)	81,400
Shaoxing (▲250,900) (1986E)	167,100
Shaoyang (▲465,900) (1986E)	218,600
Shashi (1986E)	253,700
Shenxian (1982C)	50,208
Shenyang (Mukden) (▲4,370,000)	3,910,000
Shenzhen (▲231,900) (1986E)	189,600
Shiguaigou (1975U)	50,000
Shihezi (▲549,300) (1987E)	304,700
Shijiazhuang	1,220,000
Shiyan (▲332,600) (1986E)	227,300
Shizuishan (▲317,400) (1986E)	225,500
Shouguang (1982C)	83,400
Shuangcheng (1985E)	91,163
Shuangliao (1985E)	67,326
Shuangyashan (1986E)	427,300
Shuicheng (▲2,216,500) (1986E)	363,500
Shulan (1986E)	50,582
Shunde (1985E)	50,262
Siping (▲357,800) (1986E)	280,100
Sishui (1982C)	82,990
Songjiang (1985E)	71,864
Songjianghe (1985E)	53,023
Suifenhe (▲21,700) (1986E)	13,900
Suihua (▲732,100) (1986E)	200,400
Suileng (1985E)	68,399
Suining (▲1,174,900) (1986E)	118,500
Suixian (▲1,281,600) (1986E)	187,700
Suqian (1985E)	50,742
Suxian (▲218,600) (1986E)	123,300
Suzhou (Soochow)	740,000
Tai'an (▲1,325,400) (1986E)	215,900
Taiyuan (▲1,980,000)	1,700,000
Taizhou (▲210,800) (1987E)	143,200
Tancheng (1982C)	61,857
Tangshan (▲1,440,000)	1,080,000
Tao'an (1985E)	76,269
Tengxian (1985E)	53,254
Tianjin (Tientsin) (▲5,540,000)	4,950,000
Tianshui (▲953,200) (1986E)	209,500
Tiefa (▲146,367) (1982C)	60,000
Tieli (1985E)	102,527
Tieling (▲454,100) (1986E)	326,100
Tongchuan (▲393,200) (1986E)	268,900
Tonghua (▲367,400) (1986E)	290,200
Tongliao (▲253,100) (1986E)	190,100
Tongling (▲216,400) (1986E)	182,900
Tongren (1985E)	50,307
Tongxian (1985E)	97,168
Tumen (▲99,700) (1986E)	77,600
Tunxi (▲104,500) (1986E)	61,800
Turpan (▲196,800) (1986E)	52,300
Ürümqi (▲1,147,300)	1,060,000
Wangkui (1985E)	52,021
Wangqing (1985E)	61,237
Wanxian (▲280,800) (1986E)	138,700
Weifang (▲1,042,200) (1986E)	312,500
Weihai (▲220,800) (1986E)	83,000
Weinan (▲699,400) (1986E)	111,300
Weishan (Xiazhen) (1982C)	57,932
Weixian (Hanting) (1982C)	50,180
Wenzhou (▲530,600) (1986E)	372,200
Wuchang (1985E)	64,403
Wuhai (1986E)	266,000
Wuhan	3,570,000
Wuhu (▲502,200) (1986E)	396,000
Wulian (Hongning) (1982C)	51,718
Wusong (1982C)	64,017
Wuwei (Liangzhou) (▲804,000) (1986E)	115,500
Wuxi (Wuhsi)	880,000
Wuzhong (▲402,400) (1986E)	48,600
Wuzhou (Wuchow) (▲261,500) (1986E)	194,800
Xiaguan (▲395,800) (1986E)	112,100
Xiamen (Amoy) (▲546,400) (1986E)	343,700
Xi'an (Sian) (▲2,580,000)	2,210,000
Xiangfan (▲421,200) (1986E)	314,900
Xiangtan (▲511,100) (1986E)	389,500
Xianning (▲402,200) (1986E)	122,200
Xianyang (▲641,800) (1986E)	285,900
Xiaogan (▲1,204,400) (1986E)	125,500
Xiaoshan (1985E)	63,074
Xichang (▲161,000) (1986E)	105,000
Xinghua (1985E)	75,573
Xinglongzhen (1982C)	52,961
Xingtai (▲350,800) (1986E)	265,600
Xinhui (1985E)	77,381
Xining (Sining)	620,000
Xinmin (1985E)	47,900
Xintai (▲1,157,300) (1986E)	171,400
Xinwen (Suncun) (1975U)	50,000
Xinxian (▲398,600) (1986E)	74,200
Xinxiang (▲540,500) (1986E)	411,000
Xinyang (▲234,200) (1986E)	169,100
Xinyu (▲610,600) (1986E)	140,200
Xuancheng (1985E)	52,387
Xuanhua (1975U)	140,000
Xuanwei (1982C)	70,081
Xuchang (▲247,200) (1986E)	167,800
Xuguit Qi (Yakeshi) (1986E)	390,000
Xuzhou (Süchow)	860,000
Yaan (▲277,600) (1986E)	89,200
Yan'an (▲259,800) (1986E)	86,700
Yancheng (▲1,251,400) (1986E)	258,400
Yangcheng (1982C)	57,255
Yangjiang (1986E)	91,433
Yangquan (▲478,900) (1986E)	295,100
Yangzhou (▲417,300) (1986E)	321,500
Yanji (▲216,900) (1986E)	175,000
Yanji (Longjing) (1985E)	55,035
Yanling (1982C)	52,679
Yantai (Chefoo) (▲717,300) (1986E)	327,000
Yanzhou (1985E)	48,972
Yaxian (Sanya) (▲321,700) (1986E)	70,500
Yi'an (1986E)	54,253
Yibin (Ipin) (▲636,500) (1986E)	218,800
Yichang (Ichang) (1986E)	410,500
Yichuan (1982C)	58,914
Yichun, Heilongjiang prov.	840,000
Yichun, Jiangxi prov. (▲770,200) (1986E)	132,600
Yidu (1985E)	54,838
Yilan (1985E)	50,436
Yima (▲84,800) (1986E)	53,700
Yinan (Jiehu) (1982C)	67,803
Yinchuan (▲396,900) (1986E)	268,200
Yingchengzi (1985E)	59,072
Yingkou (▲480,000) (1986E)	366,900
Yingtan (▲116,200) (1986E)	64,500
Yining (Kuldja) (▲232,000) (1986E)	153,200
Yiyang (▲365,000) (1986E)	155,300
Yiyuan (Nanma) (1982C)	53,800
Yong'an (▲269,000) (1986E)	105,100
Yongchuan (1985E)	70,444
Yuci (▲420,700) (1986E)	171,000
Yueyang (▲411,300) (1986E)	239,500
Yulin, Guangxi Zhuangzu prov. (▲1,228,800) (1986E)	115,600
Yulin, Shaanxi prov. (1985E)	51,610
Yumen (Laojunmiao) (▲160,100) (1986E)	84,300
Yuncheng, Shandong prov. (1982C)	54,262
Yuncheng, Shansi prov. (▲434,900) (1986E)	87,000
Yunyang (1982C)	54,903
Yushu (1985E)	57,222
Yuyao (▲772,700) (1986E)	169,700
Zaozhuang (▲1,592,000) (1986E)	292,200
Zhangjiakou (Kalgan) (▲640,000)	500,000
Zhangye (▲394,200) (1986E)	73,000
Zhangzhou (Longxi) (▲310,400) (1986E)	159,400
Zhanjiang (▲920,900) (1986E)	335,500
Zhaodong (1985E)	99,836
Zhaoqing (Gaoyao) (▲187,600) (1986E)	145,700
Zhaotong (▲546,600) (1986E)	77,500
Zhaoyuan (1985E)	42,426
Zhaoyuan (1982C)	56,389
Zhengzhou (Chengchow) (▲1,580,000)	1,150,000
Zhenjiang (1986E)	412,400
Zhongshan (Shiqizhen) (▲1,059,700) (1986E)	238,700
Zhoucun (1975U)	50,000
Zhoukouzhen (▲220,400) (1986E)	110,500
Zhuhai (▲155,000) (1986E)	88,800
Zhumadian (▲149,500) (1986E)	99,400
Zhuoxian (1985E)	54,523
Zhuzhou (Chuchow) (▲499,600) (1986E)	344,800
Zibo (Zhangdian) (▲2,370,000)	840,000
Zigong (Tzukung) (▲909,300) (1986E)	361,700
Zixing (▲334,300) (1986E)	97,100
Ziyang (1985E)	57,349
Zouping (1982C)	49,274
Zouxian (1985E)	61,578
Zunyi (▲347,600) (1986E)	236,600

CISKEI

1986 E	882,200
BISHO	2,850
• Mdantsane (★East London, S. Afr.)	242,823

COLOMBIA

1985 C	27,867,326
Armenia	187,130
Barrancabermeja	137,406
Barranquilla (★1,140,000)	899,781
Bello (★Medellín)	212,861
Bucaramanga (★550,000)	352,326
Buenaventura	160,342
Buga	82,992
Cali (★1,400,000)	1,350,565
Cartagena	531,426
Cartago	97,791
Ciénaga	56,860
Cúcuta (★445,000)	379,478
Dos Quebradas (★Pereira)	101,480
Duitama	56,390
Envigado (★Medellín)	91,391
Florencia	66,430
Floridablanca (★Bucaramanga)	143,824
Girardot	70,078
Ibagué	292,965
Itagüí (★Medellín)	137,623
Magangué	49,160
Maicao	46,033
Malambo (★Barranquilla)	52,584
Manizales (★330,000)	299,352
Medellín (★2,095,000)	1,468,089
Montería	157,466
Neiva	194,556
Ocaña	51,443
Palmira	175,186
Pasto	197,407
Pereira (★390,000)	233,271
Popayán	141,964
• SANTA FE DE BOGOTÁ (★4,260,000)	3,982,941
Santa Marta	177,922
Sincelejo	120,537
Soacha (★Santa Fe de Bogotá)	109,051
Sogamoso	64,437
Soledad (★Barranquilla)	165,791
Tuluá	99,721
Tunja	93,792
Valledupar	142,771
Villa Rosario (★Cúcuta)	63,615
Villavicencio	178,685
Zipaquirá	45,676

COMOROS / Al-Qumur / Comores

1990 E	452,742
• MORONI	23,432

CONGO

1989 C	2,188,367
• BRAZZAVILLE	693,712
Dolisie	57,991
Pointe-Noire	350,139

COOK ISLANDS

1986 C	18,155
• AVARUA	9,678

COSTA RICA

1988 E	2,851,000
Alajuela (▲34,556) (1984C)	29,273
Desamparados (★San José) (1984C)	43,352
Puerto Limón (▲62,600)	40,400
Puntarenas (1984C)	29,224
• SAN JOSÉ (★670,000)	278,600

CROATIA / Hrvatska

1987 E	4,673,517
Osijek (▲162,490)	106,800
Rijeka (▲199,282)	166,400
Split	191,074
• ZAGREB	697,925

CUBA

1991 E	10,694,465
Bayamo	139,061
Camagüey	286,404
Cárdenas (▲84,590)	69,800
Cárdenas (1981C)	59,352
Ciego de Ávila	101,620
Cienfuegos	136,233
Florida	51,442
Guantánamo	215,864
Holguín	236,967
• LA HABANA (HAVANA) (★2,210,000)	2,119,059
Las Tunas	126,678
Manzanillo	108,668
Matanzas	119,510
Morón	49,793
Palma Soriano (▲124,543)	66,600
Pinar del Río	136,303
Sancti Spíritus	97,522
Santa Clara	203,753
Santiago de Cuba	434,541

CYPRUS / Kıbrıs / Kípros

1982 C	512,097
Lárnax (Larnaca) (★48,330)	35,823
Lemesós (Limassol) (★107,161)	74,782
• NICOSIA (LEVKOSÍA) (★185,000)	48,221

CYPRUS, NORTH / Kuzey Kıbrıs

1985 E	160,287
Gazimağusa (Famagusta)	19,428
• NICOSIA (LEFKOŞA)	37,400

CZECH REPUBLIC / Česká Republika

1991 C	10,298,731
Brno (★450,000)	387,986
Česká Lípa	39,667
České Budějovice (★114,000)	97,283
Český Těšín (★Třinec)	28,737
Cheb	31,847
Chomutov (★80,000)	53,191
Děčín (★72,000)	55,112
Frýdek-Místek (★Ostrava)	65,067
Havířov (★Ostrava)	86,267
Hodonín	30,736
Hradec Králové (★113,000)	99,889
Jablonec nad Nisou (★Liberec)	45,918
Jihlava	52,271
Karlovy Vary (Carlsbad)	56,291
Karviná (★Ostrava)	68,368
Kladno (★88,500)	71,735
Kolín	31,582
Kroměříž (★38,500)	28,962
Liberec (★175,000)	101,934
Litvínov (★Most)	29,085
Mladá Boleslav	44,471
Most (★135,000)	70,675
Nový Jičín	29,028
Olomouc (★126,000)	105,690
Opava (★78,000)	63,601
Orlová (★Ostrava)	36,307
Ostrava (★760,000)	327,553
Pardubice	94,857
Písek	29,542
Plzeň (★210,000)	173,129
• PRAHA (★1,328,000)	1,212,010
Přerov	51,341
Příbram	36,869
Prostějov	50,102
Šumperk	30,446
Tábor (★55,500)	36,329
Teplice (★94,000)	53,039
Třebíč	39,348
Třinec (★87,500)	45,189
Trutnov	31,957
Ústí nad Labem (★115,000)	99,739
Valašské Meziříčí	28,153
Vsetín	31,584
Zlín (★124,000)	84,634
Znojmo	39,910

DENMARK / Danmark

1992 E	5,162,126
Ålborg (▲156,614)	115,200
Århus (▲267,873)	207,300
Ballerup (★København)	45,476
Esbjerg (▲81,843)	72,200
Fredericia (▲46,617)	28,700
Frederiksberg (★København)	86,372

▲ Population of an entire municipality, commune, or district, including rural area.
• Largest city in country.
★ Population or designation of the metropolitan area, including suburbs.
C Census. **E** Official estimate. **U** Unofficial estimate.

▲ Bevölkerung eines ganzen städtischen Verwaltungsgebietes, eines Kommunalbezirkes oder eines Distrikts, einschliesslich ländlicher Gebiete.
• Grösste Stadt des Landes.
★ Bevölkerung oder Bezeichnung der Stadtregion einschliesslich Vororte.
C Volkszählung. **E** Offizielle Schätzung. **U** Inoffizielle Schätzung.

Gentofte (★København) 66,077
Gladsakse (★København) 60,604
Helsingør (Elsinore) (★København) 56,794
Horsens (▲55,123) 47,200
Hvidovre (★København) 48,754
• KØBENHAVN (★1,670,000) 464,566
Kolding (▲57,982) 42,700
Kongens Lyngby (★København) 49,612
Odense (▲179,487) 142,800
Randers 61,440
Rønne 15,236
Roskilde (▲50,158)(★København) 40,700
Vejle (▲51,845) 45,700

DJIBOUTI

1976 E 226,000
• DJIBOUTI 120,000

DOMINICA

1984 E 77,000
• ROSEAU 9,348

DOMINICAN REPUBLIC / República Dominicana

1990 E 7,169,800
Barahona 80,400
La Romana 147,800
La Vega 192,300
Mao 58,400
Puerto Plata 94,900
San Cristóbal 137,500
San Francisco de Macorís 165,300
San Juan [de la Maguana] 129,700
San Pedro de Macorís 144,300
Santiago [de los Caballeros] 489,500
• SANTO DOMINGO 2,411,900

ECUADOR

1990 C 9,648,189
Ambato 124,166
Babahoyo 50,285
Cuenca 194,981
Eloy Alfaro (★Guayaquil) 82,359
Esmeraldas 98,558
• Guayaquil (★1,508,444) 1,508,444
Ibarra 80,991
La Libertad 53,108
Loja 94,305
Machala 144,197
Manta 125,505
Milagro 93,637
Portoviejo 132,937
Quevedo 86,910
QUITO (★1,300,000) 1,100,847
Riobamba 94,505
Santo Domingo de los Colorados 114,422

EGYPT / Miṣr

1986 C 48,205,049
Abnūb 48,519
Abū Kabīr 69,509
Abū Tīj 48,711
Akhmīm 70,602
Al-'Arīsh 67,638
Al-Fayyūm 212,523
Al-Hawāmidīyah (★Al-Qāhirah) 73,060
Al-Iskandarīyah (Alexandria) (★3,350,000) 2,917,327
Al-Ismā'īlīyah (★235,000) 212,567
Al-Jīzah (Giza) (★Al-Qāhirah) 1,870,508
Al-Maḥallah al-Kubrā 358,844
Al-Manṣūrah (★375,000) 316,870
Al-Manzilah 55,090
Al-Maṭarīyah 74,554
Al-Minyā 179,136
• AL-QĀHIRAH (CAIRO) (★9,300,000) 6,052,836
Al-Qanāṭir al-Khayrīyah 48,909
Al-Uqṣur (Luxor) 125,404
Armant 54,650
Ashmūn 54,450
As-Sinbillāwayn 60,285
As-Suways (Suez) 326,820
Aswān 191,461
Asyūṭ 273,191
Az-Zaqāzīq 245,496
Bahtīm (★Al-Qāhirah) 275,807
Banhā 115,571
Banī Mazār 47,964
Banī Suwayf 151,813
Bilbays 96,540
Bilqās Qism Awwal 73,162
Biyalā 47,781
Būlāq ad-Dakrūr (★Al-Qāhirah) 148,787
Būr Sa'īd (Port Said) 399,793
Būsh 54,482
Damanhūr 190,840
Disūq 78,119
Dumyāṭ (Damietta) 89,498
Fāqūs 48,625
Hawsh 'Īsā (1980C) 53,619
Idkū 70,729
Jirjā 70,899
Kafr ad-Dawwār (★Al-Iskandarīyah) 195,102
Kafr ash-Shaykh 102,910
Kafr az-Zayyāt 58,061
Kawm Umbū 52,131
Maghāghah 50,807
Mallawī 99,062
Manfalūṭ 52,644
Marsā Maṭrūḥ 43,192
Minūf 69,883
Mīt Ghamr (★100,000) 92,253
Qalyūb 86,684
Qinā 119,794
Rashīd (Rosetta) 52,014
Rummānah 50,014
Samālūṭ 62,404
Sāqiyat Makkī 51,062
Sawhāj 132,965
Shibīn al-Kawm 132,751
Shubrā al-Khaymah (★Al-Qāhirah) 710,794
Sinnūris 55,323
Ṭahṭā 58,516
Ṭalkhā (★Al-Manṣūrah) 55,757
Ṭanṭā 334,505
Ṭimā 47,223
Warrāq al-'Arab (★Al-Qāhirah) 127,108
Ziftā (★Mīt Ghamr) 69,050

EL SALVADOR

1985 E 5,337,896
Delgado (★San Salvador) 67,684
Mejicanos (★San Salvador) 91,465
Nueva San Salvador (★San Salvador) 53,688
San Miguel 88,520
• SAN SALVADOR (★920,000) 462,652
Santa Ana 137,879
Soyapango (★San Salvador) 60,000

EQUATORIAL GUINEA / Guinea Ecuatorial

1983 C 300,000
• MALABO 31,630

ERITREA

1987 2,951,000
• ASMERA (1988E) 319,353
Mitsiwa (1984C) 15,441

ESTONIA / Eesti

1991 E 1,581,800
Kohtla-Järve 74,700
Narva 83,000
Pärnu 54,200
• TALLINN 481,500
Tartu 115,300

ETHIOPIA / Ityopiya

1986 E 44,927,000
• ADIS ABEBA (★1,760,000) (1988E) 1,686,300
Akaki Beseka (★Adis Abeba) 59,000
Awasa (1984C) 36,169
Bahir Dar 60,000
Debre Zeyit 56,000
Dese 77,000
Dire Dawa 107,000
Gonder 88,000
Harer 68,000
Jima 67,000
Mekele 66,000
Nazret 83,000

FAEROE ISLANDS / Føroyar

1990 E 47,946
• TÓRSHAVN 14,767

FALKLAND ISLANDS

1986 C 1,916
• STANLEY 1,200

FIJI

1986 C 715,375
Lautoka (★39,057) 28,728
• SUVA (★141,273) 69,665

FINLAND / Suomi

1992 E 5,029,002
Espoo (Esbo) (★Helsinki) 175,670
• HELSINKI (HELSINGFORS) (★1,040,000) 497,542
Joensuu 48,182
Jyväskylä (★93,000) (1990E) 67,026
Kotka 56,515
Kouvola (★53,821) 32,066
Kuopio 81,593
Lahti (★108,000) 93,414
Lappeenranta 55,358
Oulu (★121,000) (1990E) 102,280
Pori 76,432
Tampere (★241,000) 173,797
Turku (Åbo) (★228,000) 159,403
Vaasa (Vasa) 53,764
Vantaa (Vanda) (★Helsinki) 157,274

FRANCE

1990 C 56,614,493
Aix-en-Provence (★Marseille) 123,842
Ajaccio 58,315
Albi (★54,359) 46,579
Alès (★76,856) 41,037
Amiens (★156,120) 131,872
Angers (★208,282) 141,404
Angoulême (★102,908) 42,876
Annecy (★126,729) 49,644
Antibes (★Cannes) 63,248
Antony (★Paris) 57,771
Argenteuil (★Paris) 93,096
Arles (★54,309) 39,000
Armentières (★57,738) 25,219
Arras (★79,607) 38,983
Asnières [-sur-Seine] (★Paris) 71,850
Aubervilliers (★Paris) 67,557
Aulnay-sous-Bois (★Paris) 82,314
Avignon (★181,136) 86,939
Bastia (★52,446) 37,845
Bayonne (★164,378) 40,051
Beauvais (★57,704) 54,190
Belfort (★77,844) 50,125
Besançon (★122,623) 113,828
Béthune (★261,535) 24,556
Béziers (★76,304) 70,996
Blois (★65,132) 49,318
Bondy (★Paris) 46,676
Bordeaux (★760,000) 210,336
Boulogne-Billancourt (★Paris) 101,743
Boulogne-sur-Mer (★91,249) 43,678
Bourg-en-Bresse (★55,784) 40,972
Bourges (★94,731) 75,609
Brest (★201,480) 147,956
Brive-la-Gaillarde (★64,379) 49,765
Bruay-en-Artois (★Béthune) 24,927
Caen (★191,490) 112,846
Calais (★101,768) 75,309
Cambrai (★48,133) 33,092
Cannes (★335,647) 68,676
Carcassonne 43,470
Castres (★46,482) 44,812
Châlons-sur-Marne (★61,452) 48,423
Chalon-sur-Saône (★77,764) 54,575
Chambéry (★103,283) 54,120
Champigny-sur-Marne (★Paris) 79,486
Charleville-Mézières (★67,213) 57,008
Chartres (★85,933) 39,595
Châteauroux (★67,090) 50,969
Châtellerault (★36,298) 34,678
Cherbourg (★92,045) 27,121
Cholet 55,132
Clamart (★Paris) 47,227
Clermont-Ferrand (★254,416) 136,181
Clichy (★Paris) 48,030
Cognac (★27,468) 19,528
Colmar (★83,816) 63,498
Colombes (★Paris) 78,513
Compiègne (★67,057) 41,896
Courbevoie (★Paris) 65,389
Creil (★97,119) 31,956
Créteil (★Paris) 82,088
Denain (★Valenciennes) 19,544
Dieppe (★43,348) 35,894
Dijon (★230,451) 146,703
Douai (★199,562) 42,175
Drancy (★Paris) 60,707
Dunkerque (★190,879) 70,331
Elbeuf (★53,886) 16,604
Épinal (★62,140) 36,732
Épinay-sur-Seine (★Paris) 48,762
Évreux (★57,968) 49,103
Évry (★Paris) 45,531
Fontainebleau (★35,706) 15,714
Fontenay-sous-Bois (★Paris) 51,868
Forbach (★98,758) 27,076
Fréjus (★73,967) 41,486
Gennevilliers (★Paris) 44,818
Grenoble (★404,733) 150,758
Hagondange (★112,061) 8,222
Hayange (★Thionville) 15,638
Issy-les-Moulineaux (★Paris) 46,127
Ivry-sur-Seine (★Paris) 53,619
La Rochelle (★100,264) 71,094
La Seyne-sur-Mer (★Toulon) 59,968
Laval (★56,855) 50,473
Le Blanc-Mesnil (★Paris) 46,956
Le Havre (★253,627) 195,854
Le Mans (★189,107) 145,502
Lens (★323,174) 35,017
Le Puy (★43,499) 21,743
Levallois-Perret (★Paris) 47,548
Lille (★1,050,000) 172,142
Limoges (★170,065) 133,464
Longwy (★41,300) 15,439
Lorient (★115,488) 59,271
Lourdes 16,300
Lyon (★1,335,000) 415,487
Mâcon (★46,714) 37,275
Maisons-Alfort (★Paris) 53,375
Mantes-la-Jolie (★Paris) 45,087
Marseille (★1,225,000) 800,550
Martigues (★Marseille) 31,300
Maubeuge (★102,772) 34,989
Meaux (★63,006) 48,305
Melun (★107,705) 35,319
Menton (★Monaco, Monaco) 29,141
Mérignac (★Bordeaux) 57,273
Metz (★193,117) 119,594
Meudon (★Paris) 45,339
Montargis (★52,804) 15,020
Montbéliard (★117,510) 29,005
Montceau-les-Mines (★47,283) 22,999
Montluçon (★63,018) 44,248
Montpellier (★248,303) 207,996
Montreuil-sous-Bois (★Paris) 94,754
Moulins (★41,715) 22,799
Moyeuvre-Grande (★Hagondange) 9,203
Mulhouse (Mülhausen) (★223,856) 108,357
Nancy (★329,447) 99,351
Nanterre (★Paris) 84,565
Nantes (★496,078) 244,995
Neuilly-sur-Seine (★Paris) 61,768
Nevers (★58,915) 41,968
Nice (★516,740) 342,439
Nîmes (★138,527) 128,471
Niort (★65,792) 57,012
Noisy-le-Grand (★Paris) 54,032
Noisy-le-Sec (★Paris) 36,309
Orléans (★243,153) 105,111
Orly (★Paris) 21,646
Pantin (★Paris) 47,303
• PARIS (★10,275,000) 2,152,423
Pau (★144,674) 82,157
Périgueux (★63,322) 30,280
Perpignan (★157,873) 105,983
Pessac (★Bordeaux) 51,055
Poissy (★Paris) 36,745
Poitiers (★107,625) 78,894
Quimper (★65,954) 59,437
Reims (★206,437) 180,620
Rennes (★245,065) 197,536
Roanne (★77,160) 41,756
Rodez (★39,017) 24,701
Romans-sur-Isère (★49,212) 32,734
Roubaix (★Lille) 97,746
Rouen (★380,161) 102,723
Rueil-Malmaison (★Paris) 66,401
Saint-Brieuc (★83,861) 44,752
Saint-Chamond (★81,795) 38,878
Saint-Denis (★Paris) 89,988
Saint-Dizier (★40,097) 33,552
Saint-Étienne (★313,338) 199,396
Saint-Lô (★2,760) 21,546
Saint-Malo 48,057
Saint-Maur-des-Fossés (★Paris) 77,206
Saint-Nazaire (★131,511) 64,812
Saint-Ouen (★Paris) 42,343
Saint-Quentin (★71,113) 60,644
Sarcelles (★Paris) 56,833
Sartrouville (★Paris) 50,329
Sevran 48,478
Soissons (★46,168) 29,829
Strasbourg (★415,000) 252,338
Suresnes (★Paris) 35,998
Tarbes (★77,787) 47,566
Thionville (★132,413) 39,712
Toulon (★437,553) 167,619
Toulouse (★650,000) 358,688
Tourcoing (★Lille) 93,765
Tours (★282,152) 129,509
Troyes (★122,763) 59,255
Valence (★107,965) 63,437
Valenciennes (★338,392) 38,441
Vénissieux (★Lyon) 60,444
Verdun-sur-Meuse (★26,711) 20,753
Versailles (★Paris) 87,789
Vichy (★61,566) 27,714
Villefranche (★55,249) 29,542
Villejuif (★Paris) 48,405
Villeneuve-d'Ascq (★Lille) 65,320
Villeurbanne (★Lyon) 116,872
Vitry-sur-Seine (★Paris) 82,400
Wattrelos (★Lille) 43,675

FRENCH GUIANA / Guyane française

1982 C 73,022
• CAYENNE 38,091

FRENCH POLYNESIA / Polynésie française

1988 C 188,814
• PAPEETE (★80,000) 23,555

GABON

1985 E 1,312,000
Franceville 58,800
Lambaréné 49,500
• LIBREVILLE 235,700
Port Gentil 124,400

GAMBIA

1983 C 687,817
• BANJUL (★160,000) 44,188
Brikama 19,624

GEORGIA

1991 E 5,464,200
Batumi 137,500
Gori 70,100
Kutaisi 238,200
Poti (1979C) 51,100
Rustavi (★Tbilisi) 161,900
Suchumi 120,000
• TBILISI (★1,460,000) 1,279,000
Zugdidi 50,600

GERMANY / Deutschland

1991 E 79,753,227
Aachen (★540,000) 241,861
Aalen (★78,000) 64,781
Ahlen 54,169
Albstadt 49,021
Alsdorf (★Aachen) 46,935
Altenburg 48,926
Amberg 43,111
Arnsberg 75,864
Aschaffenburg (★150,000) 34,098
Augsburg (★420,000) 256,877
Baden-Baden 51,849
Bad Homburg (★Frankfurt am Main) 51,820
Bad Oeynhausen 46,475
Bad Salzuflen (★Herford) 53,771
Bamberg (★122,000) 70,521
Bautzen 48,588
Bayreuth (★87,000) 72,345
Bergheim (★Köln) 58,146
Bergisch Gladbach (★Köln) 104,037
Bergkamen (★Essen) 49,761
BERLIN (★4,150,000) 3,433,695
Bielefeld (★535,000) 319,037
Bitterfeld (★105,000) 17,988
Bocholt 68,936
Bochum (★Essen) 396,486
BONN (★575,000) 292,234
Bottrop (★Essen) 118,936
Brandenburg 89,889
Braunschweig (★320,000) 258,833
Bremen (★790,000) 551,219
Bremerhaven (★180,000) 130,446
Castrop-Rauxel (★Essen) 79,037
Celle 72,260
Chemnitz (★500,000) 294,244
Coburg 44,246
Cottbus 125,891
Cuxhaven 56,090
Dachau (★München) 35,387
Darmstadt (★315,000) 138,920
Delmenhorst (★Bremen) 75,154
Dessau (★138,000) 96,754
Detmold 70,074
Dinslaken (★Essen) 65,313
Dormagen (★Köln) 58,260
Dorsten (★Essen) 78,035
Dortmund (★Essen) 599,055
Dresden (★870,000) 490,571
Duisburg (★Essen) 535,447
Düren (★108,000) 86,508
Düsseldorf (★1,225,000) 575,794
Eberswalde 52,586
Eisenach 45,220
Eisenhüttenstadt 50,216
Emden 50,735
Erfurt 208,989
Erlangen (★Nürnberg) 102,440
Eschweiler (★Aachen) 54,675
• Essen (★5,050,000) 626,973
Esslingen (★Stuttgart) 91,685
Euskirchen 49,654
Flensburg (★98,000) 86,977
Frankenthal (★Mannheim) 46,966
Frankfurt am Main (★1,935,000) 644,865
Frankfurt an der Oder 86,131
Freiberg 48,609
Freiburg (★235,000) 191,029
Friedrichshafen 54,129
Fulda (★74,000) 56,289
Fürth (★Nürnberg) 103,362
Garbsen (★Hannover) 60,776
Garmisch-Partenkirchen 26,837
Gelsenkirchen (★Essen) 293,714
Gera 129,037
Giessen (★155,000) 74,497
Gladbeck (★Essen) 80,267
Göppingen (★155,000) 54,957
Görlitz 72,237
Goslar (★72,000) 46,251
Gotha 54,525
Göttingen 121,831
Greifswald 66,251
Grevenbroich (★Düsseldorf) 60,835
Gummersbach 50,965
Gütersloh (★Bielefeld) 86,807
Hagen (★Essen) 214,449
Halberstadt 45,364
Halle (★455,000) 310,234
Hamburg (★2,385,000) 1,652,363
Hameln (★65,000) 58,539
Hamm 179,639
Hanau (★Frankfurt am Main) 86,913
Hannover (★1,000,000) 513,010
Hattingen (★Essen) 58,241
Heidelberg (★Mannheim) 136,796

▲ Población de un municipio, comuna o distrito entero, incluyendo sus áreas rurales.
• Ciudad más grande de un país.
★ Población o designación de un área metropolitana, incluyendo los suburbios.
C Censo. **E** Estimado oficial. **U** Estimado no oficial.

▲ Population d'une municipalité, d'une commune ou d'un district, zone rurale incluse.
• Ville la plus peuplée du pays.
★ Population de l'agglomération (ou nom de la zone métropolitaine englobante).
C Recensement. **E** Estimation officielle. **U** Estimation non officielle.

▲ População de um município, comuna ou distrito, inclusive as respectivas áreas rurais.
• Maior cidade de um país.
★ População ou indicação de uma área metropolitana.
C Censo. **E** Estimativa oficial. **U** Estimativa não oficial.

Heidenheim (★80,000)	50,532
Heilbronn (★245,000)	115,843
Herford (★120,000)	63,893
Herne (★Essen)	178,132
Herten (★Essen)	69,245
Hilden (★Düsseldorf)	54,782
Hildesheim (★126,000)	105,291
Hof	52,913
Hoyerswerda	64,888
Hürth (★Köln)	50,808
Ingolstadt (★145,000)	105,489
Iserlohn	96,314
Jena	102,518
Kaiserslautern (★130,000)	99,351
Kamen (★Essen)	46,160
Karlsruhe (★505,000)	275,061
Kassel (★375,000)	194,268
Kempten (Allgäu)	61,906
Kerpen (★Köln)	57,337
Kiel (★325,000)	245,567
Kleve	45,963
Koblenz (★170,000)	108,733
Köln (★1,810,000)	953,551
Konstanz	75,089
Krefeld (★Essen)	244,020
Landshut	59,066
Langenfeld (★Düsseldorf)	53,455
Langenhagen (★Hannover)	47,432
Leipzig (★720,000)	511,079
Leverkusen (★Köln)	160,919
Lingen	49,137
Lippstadt	62,345
Lübeck (★250,000)	214,758
Lüdenscheid	79,401
Ludwigsburg (★Stuttgart)	82,343
Ludwigshafen (★Mannheim)	162,173
Lüneburg	61,870
Lünen (★Essen)	87,845
Magdeburg (★400,000)	278,807
Mainz (★Wiesbaden)	179,486
Mannheim (★1,525,000)	310,411
Marburg	74,146
Marl (★Essen)	91,467
Meerbusch (★Düsseldorf)	52,104
Menden	56,527
Merseburg (★Halle)	42,905
Minden (★121,000)	78,145
Moers (★Essen)	104,595
Mönchengladbach (★410,000)	259,436
Mülheim an der Ruhr (★Essen)	177,681
München (Munich) (★1,900,000)	1,229,026
Münster	259,438
Neubrandenburg	89,284
Neumünster	80,743
Neunkirchen/Saar (★125,000)	51,536
Neuss (★Düsseldorf)	147,019
Neustadt an der Weinstrasse	51,988
Neu-Ulm (★Ulm)	46,264
Neuwied (★157,000)	62,075
Norderstedt (★Hamburg)	68,450
Nordhausen	46,422
Nordhorn	49,359
Nürnberg (★1,065,000)	493,692
Oberhausen (★Essen)	223,840
Offenbach (★Frankfurt am Main)	114,992
Offenburg	52,964
Oldenburg	143,131
Osnabrück (★270,000)	163,168
Paderborn	120,680
Passau	50,328
Peine	46,654
Pforzheim (★230,000)	112,944
Pirmasens	47,680
Pirna (★Dresden)	41,798
Plauen	71,774
Potsdam (★Berlin)	139,794
Ratingen (★Düsseldorf)	91,007
Ravensburg (★75,000)	45,650
Recklinghausen (★Essen)	125,060
Regensburg (★180,000)	121,691
Remscheid (★Wuppertal)	123,155
Reutlingen (★170,000)	103,687
Rheine	70,452
Riesa	45,440
Rosenheim	56,340
Rostock	248,088
Rüsselsheim (★Wiesbaden)	59,430
Saarbrücken (★365,000)	191,694
Saarlouis (★115,000)	38,160
Salzgitter	114,355
Sankt Augustin (★Bonn)	51,886
Schwäbisch Gmünd	60,081
Schwedt	50,633
Schweinfurt (★105,000)	54,483
Schwerin	127,447
Schwerte (★Essen)	50,696
Siegburg (★175,000)	35,441
Siegen (★192,000)	109,174
Sindelfingen (★Stuttgart)	58,805
Solingen (★Wuppertal)	165,401
Speyer	46,553
Stendal	48,532
Stolberg (★Aachen)	57,231
Stralsund	72,780
Stuttgart (★2,005,000)	579,988
Suhl	54,731
Trier (★122,000)	97,835
Troisdorf (★Siegburg)	64,430
Tübingen	80,372
Ulm (★215,000)	110,529
Unna (★Essen)	61,552
Velbert (★Essen)	89,253
Viersen (★Mönchengladbach)	77,453
Villingen-Schwenningen	78,218
Weimar	60,326
Wesel	59,631
Wetzlar (★96,000)	51,737
Wiesbaden (★790,000)	260,301
Wilhelmshaven (★122,000)	90,561
Wismar	55,509
Witten (★Essen)	105,403
Wittenberg	49,682
Wolfenbüttel (★Braunschweig)	52,032
Wolfsburg	128,510
Worms (★Mannheim)	76,503
Wuppertal (★845,000)	383,660
Würzburg (★195,000)	127,777
Zweibrücken (★100,000)	33,918
Zwickau (★180,000)	114,632

GHANA

1987 E	13,577,538
• ACCRA (★1,390,000)	949,113
Ashiaman (★Accra) (1984C)	49,427
Cape Coast (1984C)	86,620
Koforidua (1984C)	54,400
Kumasi (★540,000)	385,192
Obuasi (1984C)	60,146
Sekondi (★175,352) (1984C)	32,355
Tafo (★Kumasi) (1984C)	50,432
Takoradi (★Sekondi) (1984C)	61,527
Tamale (★168,091)	151,069
Tema (★Accra)	109,975
Teshie (★Accra) (1984C)	62,954

GIBRALTAR

1988 E	30,077
• GIBRALTAR	30,077

GREECE / Ellás

1981 C	9,740,417
Aiyáleo (★Athínai) (1991C)	79,560
Akharnaí (1991C)	60,062
Amaroúsion (★Athínai) (1991C)	63,619
Ampelókipoi (★Thessaloníki)	40,033
• ATHÍNAI (ATHENS) (★3,096,775) (1991E)	748,110
Áyios Dhimítrios (★Athínai) (1991C)	57,387
Ermoúpolis (★16,595)	13,876
Galátsion (★Athínai) (1991C)	56,972
Glifádha (★Athínai) (1991C)	62,310
Ilioúpolis (★Athínai) (1991C)	72,623
Ioánnina (1991C)	56,496
Iráklion (★110,958)	102,398
Kalámai (★43,235)	42,075
Kalamariá (★Thessaloníki)	51,676
Kallithéa (★Athínai) (1991C)	110,738
Kardhítsa (1991C)	30,451
Kateríni (★39,895)	38,404
Kavála (1991C)	58,576
Keratsínion (★Athínai) (1991C)	71,845
Khalándrion (★Athínai) (1991C)	72,286
Khalkís (1991C)	51,482
Khaniá (★61,976)	47,451
Khíos (★29,742)	24,070
Koridhallós (★Athínai) (1991C)	63,033
Kórinthos (Corinth) (1991C)	28,903
Lárisa (★125,623) (1991C)	113,426
Návplion (1991C)	11,453
Néa Ionía (★Athínai) (1991C)	60,364
Néa Liósia (★Athínai) (1991C)	78,029
Neápolis (★Thessaloníki)	31,464
Néa Smírni (★Athínai) (1991C)	69,319
Níkaia (★Athínai) (1991C)	87,924
Palaión Fáliron (★Athínai) (1991C)	60,974
Pátrai (★154,596)	142,163
Peristérion (★Athínai) (1991C)	145,854
Piraiévs (Piraeus) (★Athínai) (1991C)	169,622
Ródhos (Rhodes) (1991C)	43,619
Sérrai (1991C)	50,875
Spárti (Sparta) (★14,388)	12,975
Thessaloníki (Salonika) (★706,180)	406,413
Tríkala (1991C)	48,810
Trípolis (1991C)	21,772
Véroia (1991C)	38,871
Víron (★Athínai) (1991C)	57,149
Vólos (★107,407)	71,378
Zográfos (★Athínai) (1991C)	78,570

GREENLAND / Grønland / Kalaallit Nunaat

1990 E	55,558
Egedesminde (Aasiaat)	3,308
• GODTHÅB (NUUK)	12,217
Holsteinsborg (Sisimiut)	4,871

GRENADA

1991 C	90,691
• SAINT GEORGE'S (★25,000)	4,439

GUADELOUPE

1982 C	328,400
BASSE-TERRE (★26,600)	13,656
Les Abymes (★Pointe-à-Pitre)	56,165
• Pointe-à-Pitre (★83,000)	25,310

GUAM

1990 C	133,152
• AGANA (★50,000)	1,139

GUATEMALA

1989 E	8,935,395
Escuintla	60,673
• GUATEMALA (★1,400,000)	1,057,210
Quetzaltenango	88,769

GUERNSEY

1991 C	58,867
• SAINT PETER PORT (★36,000)	16,648

GUINEA / Guinée

1986 E	6,225,000
• CONAKRY	800,000
Kankan	100,000
Kindia	80,000
Labé	110,000
Nzérékoré (1983C)	55,356

GUINEA-BISSAU / Guiné-Bissau

1988 E	945,000
• BISSAU	125,000

GUYANA

1983 E	918,000
• GEORGETOWN (★188,000)	78,500

HAITI / Haïti

1987 E	5,531,802
Cap-Haïtien	72,161
Gonaïves	37,034
• PORT-AU-PRINCE (★880,000)	797,000

HONDURAS

1988 C	4,376,839
Choluteca	53,799
El Progreso	55,523
La Ceiba	68,289
San Pedro Sula	279,356
• TEGUCIGALPA	551,606

HONG KONG

1986 C	5,395,997
Kowloon (Jiulong) (★Victoria)	774,781
Kwai Chung (★Victoria)	131,362
New Kowloon (Xinjiulong) (★Victoria)	1,526,910
Sha Tin (★Victoria)	355,810
Sheung Shui	87,206
Tai Po	119,679
Tsuen Wan (Quanwan) (★Victoria)	514,241
Tuen Mun (★Victoria)	262,458
• VICTORIA (★4,770,000) (1991C)	1,250,993
Yuen Long	75,740

HUNGARY / Magyarország

1991 C	10,354,842
Békéscsaba (▲67,691)	58,900
• BUDAPEST (★2,515,000)	2,018,035
Debrecen	213,927
Dunaújváros	58,874
Eger	62,474
Győr	129,598
Hódmezővásárhely (▲51,180)	42,800
Kaposvár	71,368
Kecskemét (▲103,568)	82,000
Miskolc	194,033
Nagykanizsa	53,700
Nyíregyháza (▲114,596)	88,800
Ózd	43,020
Pécs	170,023
Salgótarján	47,500
Sopron	55,140
Szeged	176,135
Székesfehérvár	109,106
Szolnok	78,661
Szombathely	85,702
Tatabánya	73,854
Vác	33,858
Veszprém	64,277
Zalaegerszeg	62,357

ICELAND / Ísland

1991 E	259,577
Akureyri	14,436
• REYKJAVÍK (★149,482)	99,623

INDIA / Bharat

1991 C	844,324,222
Abohar	107,016
Achalpur	96,216
Ādilābād	84,233
Adītyapur (★Jamshedpur)	78,184
Ādoni	135,718
Agartala	157,636
Āgra (★955,684)	899,195
Āgra Cantonment (★Āgra)	49,975
Ahmadābād (★3,297,655)	2,872,865
Ahmadnagar (★221,710)	181,015
Āīzawl	154,343
Ajmer	401,930
Akola	327,946
Akot	65,670
Alandur (★Madras)	125,009
Alīgarh	479,978
Ālīpur Duār (★103,512)	65,945
Allahābād (★858,213)	806,447
Alleppey (★264,887)	174,606
Alwal (★Hyderābād)	66,064
Alwar (★211,162)	206,107
Amalner	76,406
Ambājogāi	57,054
Ambāla	119,535
Ambāla Cantonment (★Ambāla Sadar)	48,903
Ambāla Sadar (★139,615)	90,712
Ambāsamudram (★59,527)	33,860
Ambattur (★Madras)	223,332
Ambikāpur (★53,228)	50,278
Āmbūr	75,728
Amrāvati	433,746
Amreli (★69,279)	67,740
Amritsar	709,456
Amroha	136,893
Anakāpalle	84,362
Ānand (★168,776)	110,144
Anantapur	174,792
Anjār	51,207
Ankleshwar (★78,064)	51,708
Ara	156,871
Arakkonam	71,500
Arcot (★114,884)	45,193
Arni	54,881
Aruppukkottai	78,184
Asansol (★763,845)	261,836
Ashoknagar-Kalyangarh (★Hābra)	96,315
Āttūr	55,529
Auraiya	50,771
Aurangābād (★592,052)	572,034
Avadi (★Madras)	180,291
Āzamgarh	78,382
Badagara (★102,429)	72,441
Bagaha	64,574
Bāgalkot	76,819
Bahādurgarh (★57,195)	56,484
Baharampur (★126,303)	115,036
Bahraich	135,352
Baidyabāti (★Calcutta)	90,601
Bālāghāt (★67,113)	62,164
Balāngīr	70,014
Bāleshwar (★102,504)	86,116
Ballarpur (★92,438)	83,511
Ballia	84,758
Bālly (★Calcutta)	73,265
Bālly (★Calcutta)	181,978
Balrāmpur	60,077
Bālurghāt (★126,199)	119,829
Bānda	97,227
Bangalore (★4,086,548)	2,650,659
Bangaon	79,433
Bānkura	114,927
Bansberia (★Calcutta)	93,447
Bānswāra (★67,952)	66,676
Banūr	55,660
Bāpatla	62,688
Bārākpur (★Calcutta)	133,429
Bārān	57,703
Baranagar (★Calcutta)	223,770
Bārāsat (★Calcutta)	102,648
Baraut	67,673
Barddhamān	244,789
Bareilly (★607,652)	583,473
Bargarh	51,135
Bāripada (★68,895)	49,569
Bārmer	69,385
Barnāla	75,387
Bārsi	88,774
Basīrhāt	101,652
Basti	87,512
Batala (★106,062)	88,896
Bathinda	159,114
Beāwar (★106,715)	105,357
Begusarai (★83,907)	71,362
Bela	66,845
Belampalli	66,608
Belgaum (★401,619)	325,639
Bellary	245,758
Bettiah	92,583
Betūl	63,489
Bhadohi	63,590
Bhadrak	76,390
Bhadrāvati (★149,131)	55,413
Bhadrāvati New Town (★Bhadrāvati)	74,864
Bhadreswar (★Calcutta)	72,414
Bhāgalpur (★261,855)	254,993
Bhandāra	71,762
Bharatpur (★156,844)	148,506
Bharūch (★138,246)	132,312
Bhātpāra (★Calcutta)	304,298
Bhavāni (★97,020)	35,202
Bhāvnagar (★403,521)	400,636
Bhawānipatna	51,014
Bhilai (★688,670)	389,601
Bhīlwāra	183,791
Bhīmavaram	125,495
Bhind	109,731
Bhiwandi (★391,670)	378,546
Bhiwāni	121,449
Bhopāl	1,063,662
Bhubaneshwar	411,542
Bhuj (★110,734)	91,901
Bhusāwal (★159,459)	144,804
Bīd	112,351
Bīdar (★130,804)	107,542
Bihār	200,976
Bijāpur (★193,038)	186,846
Bijnor (★73,570)	66,156
Bīkāner	415,355
Bilāspur (★233,570)	190,911
Bilīmora (★50,940)	46,366
Birlapur (★65,333)	20,239
Birnagar (★92,108)	20,014
Bishnupur	56,119
Bodhan	64,386
Bodināyakkanūr	66,028
Bokāro Steel City (★415,686)	350,540
Bolpur	52,866
Bombay (★12,571,720)	9,909,547
Botād	64,491
Brahmapur	210,585
Brajrajnagar	69,548
Budaun	116,706
Budge Budge (★Calcutta)	73,361
Bulandshahr	126,737
Buldāna	52,738
Bulsār (★111,759)	57,903
Būndi	65,016
Burhānpur	172,809
• Calcutta (★11,605,833)	4,388,262
Calicut (★800,913)	419,531
Cannanore (★Tellicherry)	65,233
Chāībāsa	56,657
Chākdaha	74,780
Chakradharpur (★48,329)	33,263
Chālisgaon	77,346
Champdāni (★Calcutta)	98,818
Chandannagar (★Calcutta)	122,351
Chandausi	82,733
Chandīgarh (★574,646)	502,992
Chāndpur	55,829
Chandrapur	225,841
Changanācheri	52,448
Channapatna	55,210
Chāpra	136,824
Chās	65,146
Chhatarpur (★75,515)	72,745
Chhindwāra (★96,852)	93,731
Chidambaram (★68,819)	58,927
Chikmagalūr	60,814
Chilakalūrupet	79,081
Chingleput	53,784
Chintāmani	50,376
Chīrāla (★142,654)	80,837
Chitradurga (★103,345)	87,053
Chittaranjan (★58,338)	47,148
Chittaurgarh	71,566
Chittoor	133,233
Chopda	49,112
Chūru (★82,818)	82,430
Cochin (★1,139,543)	564,038
Coimbatore (★1,135,549)	853,402
Contai	53,425
Coonoor (★99,615)	47,100
Cuddalore	143,774
Cuddapah (★215,545)	121,422
Cuttack (★439,273)	402,390
Dabgram	146,917
Dabhoi	50,619
Dāhod (★96,568)	66,444
Dāltenganj	56,408
Damoh (★105,032)	95,553
Dānāpur (★Patna)	84,104
Dandeli	52,699
Darbhanga	218,274
Darjiling	73,088
Datia	65,565
Dāvangere (★287,114)	265,971
Dehra Dūn (★367,411)	270,028
Dehri	94,526
Delhi (★8,375,188)	7,174,755
Delhi Cantonment (★Delhi)	94,326
Deoband	62,461
Deoghar (★85,846)	76,322
Deolāli Cantonment (★Nāsik)	51,115
Deoria	81,943
Dewās	163,699
Dhamtari	69,273
Dhanbad (★817,549)	151,334
Dhār	59,089
Dhārāpuram	48,392
Dharmapuri	59,070
Dharmavaram	78,747
Dhaulpur	68,524
Dholka (★54,351)	49,855
Dhorāji (★79,414)	77,683
Dhrāngadhra	54,281
Dhuburi	65,861
Dhule	277,957
Dibrugarh (★123,885)	118,374
Dimāpur	56,918

▲ Population of an entire municipality, commune, or district, including rural area.
• Largest city in country.
★ Population or designation of the metropolitan area, including suburbs.
C Census. **E** Official estimate. **U** Unofficial estimate.

▲ Bevölkerung eines ganzen städtischen Verwaltungsgebietes, eines Kommunalbezirkes oder eines Distrikts, einschliesslich ländlicher Gebiete.
• Grösste Stadt des Landes.
★ Bevölkerung oder Bezeichnung der Stadtregion einschliesslich Vororte.
C Volkszählung. **E** Offizielle Schätzung. **U** Inoffizielle Schätzung.

Dindigul	182,293
Dīsa	61,888
Dod Ballāpur	54,468
Dum Dum (★Calcutta)	40,942
Durg (★Bhilai)	150,513
Durgāpur	415,986
Elūru	212,918
Erode (★357,427)	158,774
Etah	78,424
Etāwah	124,032
Faizābād (★177,505)	125,012
Farīdābād New Township (★Delhi)	613,828
Farīdkot	56,038
Farrukhābād (★207,783)	193,624
Fatehpur	117,203
Fathpur	66,398
Fāzilka	57,386
Fīrozābād (★270,534)	215,089
Fīrozpur	77,505
Fīrozpur Cantonment	53,691
Gadag	133,918
Gāndhidham	104,392
Gāndhinagar	121,746
Ganga Ghat	50,520
Gangānagar	161,377
Gangāpur (★68,982)	53,784
Gangāwati (★81,108)	64,807
Gangtok	24,971
Gārulia (★Calcutta)	80,872
Gaya (★293,971)	291,220
Ghāziābād (★519,508)	460,949
Ghāzīpur	77,069
Girīdīh	77,912
Godhra (★100,363)	96,514
Gokāk	52,037
Gonda	106,078
Gondal (★81,533)	80,506
Gondia	109,271
Gopichettipālaiyam	48,349
Gorakhpur	489,850
Gudivāda	101,635
Gudiyāttam (★89,966)	82,652
Gūdūr	55,962
Gulbarga (★309,962)	303,139
Guna (★	100,389
Guntakal	107,560
Guntūr	471,020
Gurdāspur	54,575
Gurgaon (★134,639)	120,790
Guruvayur (★118,626)	20,209
Guwāhāti	577,591
Gwalior (★720,068)	692,982
Hābra (★196,457)	100,142
Hājīpur	87,669
Haldwāni	102,744
Hālisahar (★Calcutta)	113,670
Hānsi	59,638
Hanumāngarh (★82,717)	78,504
Hāora (★Calcutta)	946,732
Hāpur	146,591
Hardoi	88,632
Haridwār (★188,961)	148,882
Harihar	66,660
Hassan (★108,458)	90,719
Hāthras	113,653
Hazārībāg	97,712
Himatnagar	50,929
Hindaun	60,761
Hindupur	104,635
Hinganghāt	78,709
Hingoli	54,444
Hisār (★180,774)	172,873
Hoshangābād	70,820
Hoshiārpur	122,528
Hospet (★134,935)	96,499
Hubli-Dhārwār	647,640
Hugli-Chinsurah (★Calcutta)	142,388
Hyderābād (★4,280,261)	2,991,884
Ichalkaranji (★235,854)	214,835
Imphāl (★200,615)	196,268
Indore (★1,104,065)	1,086,673
Ingrāj Bāzār (★176,991)	139,018
Itānagar	17,320
Itārsi (★85,706)	78,700
Jabalpur (★887,188)	739,961
Jabalpur Cantonment (★Jabalpur)	56,742
Jagādhri (★Yamunānagar)	67,371
Jagdalpur (★84,553)	65,544
Jagtiāl	67,965
Jahānābād	51,846
Jaipur (★1,514,425)	1,454,678
Jalandhar	519,530
Jālgaon	241,603
Jālna	174,958
Jalpāiguri	67,495
Jamālpur	86,123
Jamkhandi	48,111
Jammu (★223,361) (1981C)	206,135
Jamnagar (★365,464)	325,475
Jamshedpur (★834,535)	461,212
Jaora (★55,986)	54,960
Jaunpur	136,287
Jaypur	65,582
Jetpur (★95,290)	73,556
Jhānsi (★368,590)	301,304
Jharia (★Dhanbād)	69,542
Jhārsuguda	65,022
Jhunjhunūn	71,972
Jīnd	85,307
Jodhpur	648,621
Jorhāt (★111,584)	57,998
Jūnāgadh (★166,755)	130,132
Kadaiyanallūr	68,805
Kadiri	63,428
Kagaznagar	57,653
Kairāna	56,083
Kaithal	71,294
Kākināda (★327,407)	279,875
Kalamassery (★Cochin)	54,313
Kālol (★92,320)	81,916
Kalyān (★Bombay)	1,014,062
Kāmāreddi	48,641
Kāmārhāti (★Calcutta)	266,625
Kambam	51,987
Kāmthi (★131,837)	78,586
Kānchipuram (★169,813)	145,028
Kānchrāpāra (★Calcutta)	100,059
Kānnangād (★118,180)	57,133
Kannauj	59,650
Kānpur (★2,111,284)	1,958,282
Kānpur Cantonment (★Kānpur)	93,109
Kapra (★Hyderābād)	87,607
Kapūrthala (1981C)	63,083
Karād	56,705
Kāraikāl	61,875
Kāraikkudi (★110,473)	71,599
Kāranja	48,857
Karauli	48,961
Karīmnagar	148,349
Karnāl (★176,120)	173,742
Karūr (★110,605)	73,428
Kārwār	51,011
Kāsaragod	50,123
Kāsganj	75,610
Kāshīpur	69,889
Katihār (★154,101)	135,348
Kātwa	55,535
Kāvali	65,804
Kāyankulam	67,170
Keshod	50,164
Khadki Cantonment (★Pune)	78,046
Khambhāt (★89,813)	76,724
Khāmgaon	73,705
Khammam (★148,646)	127,812
Khandwa	145,111
Khanna	72,140
Kharagpur (★279,736)	189,101
Kharagpur Railway Settlement (★Kharagpur)	881,253
Khardaha	88,278
Khargone	66,776
Khurja	80,384
Kishanganj	64,462
Kishangarh Bās	81,944
Koch Bihār (★92,628)	71,028
Kodarma	53,560
Kohīma	53,122
Kolār	83,219
Kolār Gold Fields (★156,398)	72,481
Kolhāpur (★417,286)	405,118
Konnagar (★Calcutta)	62,214
Korba	124,365
Kota	536,444
Kot Kapūra	62,403
Kottagūdem (★102,061)	80,420
Kottayam (★166,178)	62,829
Kovilpatti	77,967
Krishnagiri	60,252
Krishnanagar	120,918
Kukatpalle (★Hyderābād)	185,378
Kulti (★Asansol)	108,930
Kumārapālaiyam (★Bhavāni)	57,532
Kumbakonam (★150,502)	139,449
Kundla (★65,732)	64,762
Kurasia (★71,638)	15,828
Kurichi (★Coimbatore)	63,688
Kurnool (★274,795)	236,313
Lādnūn	48,174
Lakhīmpur	79,549
Lalitpur (1981C)	55,756
Lalitpur	79,891
Lātūr	197,164
Luckeesarai	53,198
Lucknow (★1,642,134)	1,592,010
Lucknow Cantonment (★Lucknow)	50,124
Ludhiāna	1,012,062
Machilīpatnam (Bandar)	159,007
Madanapalle	73,729
Madgaon (Margao) (★72,070)	58,745
Mādhavaram (★Madras)	49,005
Madhubani	53,543
Madras (★5,361,468)	3,795,028
Madurai (★1,093,702)	951,696
Mahbūbnagar	116,775
Mahesāna (★109,540)	87,889
Mahoba	56,152
Mahuva (★63,837)	59,675
Mainpuri	76,696
Makrāna (★66,654)	59,648
Malappuram (★142,203)	49,690
Malaut	56,856
Mālegaon	342,431
Māler Kotla	88,587
Malkajgiri (★Hyderābād)	126,066
Malkāpur	51,302
Mancheriyal	52,626
Mandsaur	95,758
Mandya	119,970
Mangalagiri	59,276
Mangalore (★425,785)	272,819
Mango (★Jamshedpur)	110,024
Manjeri	69,335
Manmād	61,257
Mannārgudi	56,563
Mānsa	55,088
Mathura (★233,235)	226,850
Maunath Bhanjan	136,447
Mawāna	51,644
Māyūram	77,042
Medinīpur	125,098
Meerut (★846,954)	752,078
Meerut Cantonment (★Meerut)	94,876
Melappālaiyam (★Tirunelveli)	68,318
Mettuppālaiyam	63,217
Mhow (★83,649)	74,852
Mira Bhayandar (★Bombay)	175,372
Miraj (★Sāngli)	121,564
Miryalaguda	65,836
Mirzāpur	169,368
Modinagar (★124,197)	102,307
Moga (★110,867)	108,213
Mokāma	59,519
Morādābād (★432,434)	416,836
Morbi (★120,107)	90,349
Morena	147,095
Mormugao (★91,285)	83,209
Motihāri (★82,965)	77,440
Mubārakpur (★62,721)	45,388
Muktsar	66,377
Munger	150,042
Murwāra	163,390
Muzaffarnagar (★247,729)	240,057
Muzaffarpur	240,450
Mysore (★652,246)	480,006
Nābha	54,079
Nadiād (★170,018)	166,852
Nagaon	93,324
Nāgappattinam (★99,024)	86,155
Nāgaur	68,088
Nagda	79,405
Nāgercoil	189,482
Nagīna	58,494
Nāgpur (★1,661,409)	1,622,225
Naihāti (★Calcutta)	132,032
Najībābād	66,842
Nalasopara (★Bombay)	67,548
Nalgonda	84,674
Nānded (★308,853)	274,626
Nandurbār	78,364
Nandyāl	120,171
Nangi (★Calcutta)	52,909
Narasapur	56,358
Narasaraopet	88,766
Nārnaul	51,880
Nāshik (★722,139)	646,896
Navadwip (★156,117)	125,247
Navsāri (★190,019)	125,980
Nawābganj (★77,613)	64,719
Nawāda	53,075
Nawalgarh	51,168
Nedumangād	49,864
Neemuch (★90,460)	81,397
Nellore	316,445
New Bārākpur (★Calcutta)	63,857
New Bombay (★Bombay)	307,297
NEW DELHI (★Delhi)	294,149
Neyveli (★126,494)	117,471
Nipāni	51,622
Nirmal	57,777
Nizāmābād	240,924
North Bārākpur (★Calcutta)	100,513
North Dum Dum (★Calcutta)	151,298
Ongole (★128,128)	100,544
Orai	98,640
Osmānābād	67,980
Pālakodu	56,972
Palani (★75,948)	68,747
Pālanpur (★90,231)	80,620
Pālayankottai (★Tirunelveli)	97,662
Pālghāt (★179,695)	122,964
Pāli	136,797
Pallavaram (★Madras)	111,194
Palwal	59,127
Palwancha	52,892
Panaji (Panjim) (★85,199)	42,915
Pandharpur	79,798
Pānihāti (★Calcutta)	275,359
Pānīpat	191,010
Panruti	51,424
Panvel	58,845
Paramakkudi	72,105
Parbhani	190,235
Parli	72,573
Pātan (★97,025)	96,109
Pathānkot (★147,130)	142,862
Patiāla (★268,521)	253,341
Patna (★1,098,572)	916,980
Pattukkottai	57,909
Payyannūr	64,011
Periyakulam	46,739
Petlād	48,546
Phagwāra (★88,855)	83,702
Pīlībhīt	106,329
Pilkhua	50,218
Pimpri-Chinchwad (★Pune)	515,962
Pollāchi (★127,180)	87,012
Pondicherry (★401,337)	202,648
Ponmalai (★Tiruchchirāppalli)	70,196
Ponnāni	51,754
Ponnūru Nidubrolu	54,352
Porbandar (★160,043)	116,546
Port Blair	74,810
Proddatūr	133,860
Pudukkottai	98,619
Puliyangudi	53,206
Pune (Poona) (★2,485,014)	1,559,558
Pune Cantonment (★Pune)	81,978
Puri	124,835
Pūrnia (★135,995)	114,189
Puruliya	92,574
Pusad	55,919
Quilon (★362,402)	139,717
Qutubullapur (★Hyderābād)	105,380
Rabkavi Banhatti	60,607
Rāe Bareli	130,101
Rāichūr (★170,500)	157,477
Raiganj (★159,675)	151,454
Raigarh (★92,569)	89,166
Raipur (★461,851)	437,887
Rājahmundry (★403,781)	326,071
Rājapālaiyam	114,042
Rajendranagar (★Hyderābād)	83,849
Rajhara-Jharandalli	55,928
Rājkot (★651,007)	556,137
Rāj Nāndgaon	125,394
Rājpur (★86,390)	61,121
Rājpura	70,886
Rāmanagaram	50,411
Rāmanāthapuram	52,654
Rāmgarh (★82,186)	51,138
Rāmpur	242,752
Rānāghāt (★126,611)	64,244
Rānchi (★614,454)	598,498
Rānībennur	67,419
Rānīganj (★155,644)	62,014
Ratangarh	55,078
Ratlām (★195,752)	183,370
Ratnāgiri	56,512
Raurkela (★398,692)	215,489
Raurkela Civil Township (★Raurkela)	140,192
Rāyagāda	48,352
Rewa	128,918
Rewāri	75,294
Rishīkesh (★71,510)	44,399
Rishra (★Calcutta)	102,649
Robertson Pet (★Kolār Gold Fields)	67,900
Rohtak	215,844
Roorkee (★90,116)	80,236
Rudrapur	61,067
Sāgar (★256,878)	195,106
Sahāranpur	373,904
Saharsa	80,071
Sahaswān	51,067
Sāhibganj	49,133
Salem (★573,685)	363,934
Sāmalkot	48,727
Sambalpur (★192,917)	130,766
Sambhal	150,012
Sangamner	48,895
Sangareddi	50,098
Sāngli (★363,728)	193,181
Sangrūr	56,374
Sankarankovil	48,739
Sardārshahr	67,969
Sarni	84,201
Sāsarām	98,220
Sātāra	95,133
Satna (★160,191)	156,321
Sawāi Mādhopur (★77,561)	72,037
Secunderābād Cantonment (★Hyderābād)	167,461
Sehore	71,437
Seoni	64,302
Serampore (★Calcutta)	137,087
Serilungampalle (★Hyderābād)	72,648
Shahdol (★60,572)	55,554
Shāhjahānpur (★260,260)	237,663
Shāmli	70,347
Shāntipur	109,911
Shikohābād	63,240
Shiliguri	226,677
Shillong (★222,273)	130,691
Shimoga (★192,647)	178,882
Shivpuri	108,271
Shrirampur (★79,042)	71,356
Siddhapur (★51,586)	50,858
Siddipet	54,020
Sikandarābād	61,035
Sīkar	148,235
Silchar	115,045
Silvassa	11,720
Simla (★109,860)	81,463
Sindri (★Dhānbād)	72,349
Sircilla	50,012
Sirsa	112,542
Sītāmarhi (★67,320)	44,910
Sītāpur	120,595
Siuri	54,274
Sivakāsi (★102,139)	65,556
Siwān	81,092
Solāpur (★620,499)	603,870
Sonīpat	142,992
South Dum Dum (★Calcutta)	230,507
Srīkākulam	88,684
Srikalahasti	61,575
Srīnagar (★606,002) (1981C)	594,775
Srīrangam (★Tiruchchirāppalli)	69,928
Srīvilliputtūr	68,543
Sujāngarh	70,393
Sultānpur	76,567
Sūrat (★1,517,076)	149,643
Surendranagar (★166,309)	105,973
Suriāpet	60,563
Tādepallegūdem	88,979
Tādpatri	71,043
Talipparamba	60,242
Tāmbaram (★Madras)	106,590
Tānda	69,989
Tanuku	62,877
Tellicherry (★463,951)	103,577
Tenāli	143,836
Tenkāsi	55,044
Tezpur	54,999
Thāna (★Bombay)	796,620
Thānesar	81,275
Thanjāvūr	200,216
Theni-Allinagaram	65,958
Thiruvārūr	49,194
Thrippunithura (★Cochin)	51,032
Tīkamgarh	54,130
Tindivanam	61,715
Tinsukia	73,760
Tiruchchirāppalli (★711,120)	386,628
Tiruchengodu	62,903
Tirunelveli (★365,932)	135,762
Tirupati (★189,030)	174,393
Tiruppattūr	54,884
Tiruppur (★305,546)	235,076
Tirūr	49,450
Tiruvalla	54,745
Tiruvannāmalai	108,291
Tirūvottiyūr (★Madras)	167,851
Titāgarh (★Calcutta)	113,831
Tonk	100,020
Trichūr (★274,898)	73,849
Trivandrum (★825,682)	523,733
Ttruchchendūr (★75,400)	27,363
Tumkūr (★179,497)	138,598
Tuticorin (★284,193)	205,105
Udagamandalam	81,726
Udaipur	307,682
Udamalpet	58,643
Udgīr	70,409
Ujjain	366,787
Ulhāsnagar (★Bombay)	368,822
Ulubāria	155,188
Unjha	50,947
Unnāo	107,246
Upleta	51,553
Uppal Kalan (★Hyderābād)	75,039
Uttarpara-Kotrung (★Calcutta)	100,867
Vadodara (★1,115,390)	1,021,084
Vālpārai	106,289
Vāniyambādi (★92,097)	72,282
Vārānasi (Benares) (★1,026,467)	925,962
Vasai (Bassein) (★83,572)	39,741
Veerappanchattiram (★Erode)	61,598
Vejalpur (★Ahmadābād)	89,053
Vellore (★304,713)	172,467
Verāval (★119,995)	93,826
Vidisha	92,917
Vijayawāda (★845,305)	701,351
Vikramasingapuram	49,034
Viluppuram	88,916
Viramgām	51,089
Virār (★Bombay)	57,581
Virudunagar	70,951
Vishākhapatnam (★1,051,918)	750,024
Visnagar (★59,693)	57,834
Vizianagaram (★176,125)	159,461
Vriddhāchalam	52,763
Wadhwan (★Surendranager)	49,773
Warangal (★466,877)	446,760
Wardha	102,974
Wāshīm	49,133
Yamunānagar (★219,642)	144,250
Yavatmāl (★121,834)	108,591
Yemmiganur	65,118

INDONESIA

1990 C	179,378,946
Ambon (▲275,888)	205,193
Balikpapan	344,147
Banda Aceh (Kuturaja) (▲184,650)	143,360
Bandung (★2,220,000)	2,058,122
Banjarmasin	480,737
Banyuwangi (1980C)	90,378
Batang (1980C)	49,328
Bekasi (★Jakarta) (1980C)	144,290
Bengkulu	170,183
Binjai (▲181,866)	127,184
Blitar (★150,000)	118,933
Bogor (★560,000)	271,341

▲ Población de un municipio, comuna o distrito entero, incluyendo sus áreas rurales.
• Ciudad más grande de un país.
★ Población o designación de un área metropolitana, incluyendo los suburbios.
C Censo. **E** Estimado oficial. **U** Estimado no oficial.

▲ Population d'une municipalité, d'une commune ou d'un district, zone rurale incluse.
• Ville la plus peuplée du pays.
★ Population de l'agglomération (ou nom de la zone métropolitaine englobante).
C Recensement. **E** Estimation officielle. **U** Estimation non officielle.

▲ População de um município, comuna ou distrito, inclusive as respectivas áreas rurais.
• Maior cidade de um país.
★ População ou indicação de uma área metropolitana.
C Censo. **E** Estimativa oficial. **U** Estimativa não oficial.

Bojonegoro (1980C)	57,483
Bukittinggi	83,753
Cianjur (1980C)	105,655
Cibinong (1980C)	87,580
Cilacap (1980C)	127,017
Cimahi (★Bandung) (1971C)	72,367
Ciparay (1980C)	66,854
Cirebon (★275,000)	254,477
Denpasar (1980C)	159,233
Depok (★Jakarta) (1980C)	126,693
Dili (▲123,475)	10,900
Garut (1980C)	145,624
Genteng (1980C)	59,481
Gorontalo (▲119,745)	94,058
Gresik (1980C)	86,418
• JAKARTA (★10,000,000)	8,227,746
Jambi	339,786
Jayapura (Sukarnapura) (1980C)	60,641
Jember (1980C)	171,284
Jombang (1980C)	58,800
Karawang (1980C)	72,195
Kediri	249,538
Kisaran (1980C)	58,129
Klangenang (1980C)	64,013
Klaten (1980C)	117,560
Kudus (1980C)	154,478
Kupang (1980C)	84,587
Lumajang (1980C)	58,495
Madiun (★200,000)	170,050
Magelang (★160,000)	123,156
Majalaya (1980C)	87,474
Malang	695,089
Manado	320,600
Mataram (1980C)	210,485
Medan	1,730,052
Mojokerto	99,707
Muncar (1980C)	47,009
Padang (▲631,263)	477,064
Padangsidempuan (1980C)	56,984
Palangkaraya	112,511
Palembang	1,144,047
Pangkalpinang	113,129
Pare (1980C)	47,262
Parepare (▲101,421)	84,093
Pasuruan (★190,000)	152,075
Pati (1980C)	50,159
Payakumbuh (▲90,838)	50,475
Pekalongan (★380,000)	242,714
Pekanbaru	398,621
Pemalang (1980C)	72,663
Pematangsiantar (★250,000)	219,316
Ponorogo (1980C)	55,523
Pontianak	396,658
Pringsewu (1980C)	56,115
Probolinggo (▲176,906)	131,077
Purwakarta (1980C)	61,995
Purwokerto (1980C)	143,787
Salatiga	98,012
Samarinda (▲407,174)	334,851
Semarang	1,249,230
Serang (1980C)	78,209
Sibolga	71,559
Sidoarjo (1980C)	56,090
Singaraja (1980C)	53,368
Singkawang (1980C)	58,693
Situbondo (1980C)	58,299
Sorong (1980C)	52,041
Subang (1980C)	52,041
Sukabumi (★225,000)	119,938
Surabaya	2,473,272
Surakarta (★590,000)	503,827
Taman (1980C)	64,358
Tangerang (1980C)	97,091
Tanjungbalai	107,751
Tanjungkarang-Telukbetung (▲636,418)	457,927
Tanjungpinang	105,820
Tarakan (1980C)	46,657
Tasikmalaya (1980C)	192,267
Tebingtinggi	116,749
Tegal (★450,000)	229,553
Tembilahan (1980C)	52,140
Tuban (1980C)	48,558
Tulungagung (1980C)	91,585
Ujungpandang (Makasar)	944,372
Yogyakarta (★510,000)	412,059

IRAN / Īrān

1986 C	49,445,010
Ābādān (1976C)	296,081
Āghā Jārī (1982E)	64,000
Ahar (1982E)	52,000
Ahvāz	579,826
Alīgūdarz	53,843
Āmol	118,242
Andīmeshk (1982E)	53,000
Arāk	265,349
Ardabīl	281,973
Bābol	115,320
Bākhtarān (Kermānshāh)	560,514
Bandar-e 'Abbās	201,642
Bandar-e Anzalī (Bandar-e Pahlavī) (1982E)	83,000
Bandar-e Būshehr	120,787
Bandar-e Māh Shahr (1982E)	88,000
Behbahān (1982E)	84,000
Bīrjand (1982E)	68,000
Bojnūrd (1982E)	82,000
Borāzjān (1982E)	53,000
Borūjerd	183,879
Dezfūl	151,420
Do Rūd (1982E)	52,000
Emāmshahr (Shāhrūd) (1982E)	68,000
Eşfahān (★1,175,000)	986,753
Eslāmābād (1982E)	71,000
Eslāmshahr (★Tehrān)	215,129
Fasā (1982E)	67,000
Gonbad-e Qābūs (1982E)	75,000
Gorgān	139,430
Hamadān	272,499
Īlām (1982E)	75,000
Jahrom (1982E)	68,000
Karaj (★Tehrān)	275,100
Kāshān	138,599
Kāzerūn (1982E)	63,000
Kermān	257,284
Khomeynīshahr (★Eşfahān)	104,647
Khorramābād	208,592
Khorramshahr (1976C)	146,706
Khvorāsgān	51,155
Khvoy	115,343
Mahābād (1982E)	63,000
Malāyer	103,640
Marāgheh	100,679
Marand (1982E)	59,000
Marv Dasht (1982E)	72,000
Mashhad	1,463,508
Masjed-e Soleymān	104,787
Mehr Shānī	57,477
Mīāndoāb (1982E)	52,000
Mīāneh (1982E)	57,000
Najafābād	129,058
Naqadeh	52,275
Neyshābūr	109,258
Orūmīyeh (Reẓā'īyeh)	300,746
Qā'emshahr	109,288
Qarchaqah	77,957
Qazvīn	248,591
Qom	543,139
Qomsheh (1982E)	67,000
Qūchān (1982E)	61,000
Rafsanjān (1982E)	61,000
Rāmhormoz (1982E)	53,000
Rasht	290,897
Sabzevār	129,103
Sanandaj	204,537
Saqqez (1982E)	76,000
Sārī	141,020
Semnān (1982E)	54,000
Shahr-e Kord (1982E)	63,000
Shīrāz	848,289
Shīrvān	48,688
Shūshtar	65,840
Sīrjān (1982E)	67,000
Tabrīz	971,482
• TEHRĀN (★7,500,000)	6,042,584
Torbat-e Heydarīyeh (1982E)	62,000
Varāmīn (1982E)	51,000
Yazd	230,483
Zābol (1982E)	58,000
Zāhedān	281,923
Zanjān	215,261
Zarrīn Shahr (1982E)	69,000

IRAQ / Al 'Irāq

1985 E	15,584,987
Ad-Dīwānīyah (1970E)	62,300
Al-'Amārah	131,785
Al-Başrah	616,700
Al-Hillah	215,249
Al-Kūt	73,022
Al-Mawşil	570,926
An-Najaf	242,603
An-Nāşirīyah	138,842
Ar-Ramādī	137,388
As-Samāwah	75,293
As-Sulaymānīyah	279,424
• BAGHDĀD (1987C)	3,841,268
Ba'qūbah	114,516
Irbīl	333,903
Karbalā'	184,574
Kirkūk (1970E)	207,900

IRELAND / Éire

1986 C	3,540,643
Cork (★173,694)	133,271
• DUBLIN (BAILE ĀTHA CLIATH) (★1,140,000)	502,749
Dún Laoghaire (★Dublin)	54,715
Galway	47,104
Limerick (★76,557)	56,279
Waterford (★41,054)	39,529

ISLE OF MAN

1991 C	69,788
• DOUGLAS (★30,000)	22,214

ISRAEL / Isrā'īl / Yisra'el

1991 E	4,713,800
Ashdod	83,900
Ashqelon	59,700
Bat Yam (★Tel Aviv-Yafo)	141,300
Be'ér Sheva (Beersheba)	122,000
Bene Beraq (★Tel Aviv-Yafo)	116,700
Elat	26,300
Giv'atayim (★Tel Aviv-Yafo)	46,600
Hefa (★450,000)	245,900
Herzliyya (★Tel Aviv-Yafo)	77,200
Holon (★Tel Aviv-Yafo)	156,700
Kefar Sava (★Tel Aviv-Yafo)	61,100
Lod (Lydda) (★Tel Aviv-Yafo)	43,300
Nazerat (Nazareth) (★77,000)	53,600
Netanya (★Tel Aviv-Yafo)	132,200
Petah Tiqwa (★Tel Aviv-Yafo)	144,000
Ra'anana (★Tel Aviv-Yafo)	53,600
Ramat Gan (★Tel Aviv-Yafo)	119,500
Rehovot (★Tel Aviv-Yafo)	80,300
Rishon LeẔiyyon (★Tel Aviv-Yafo)	139,500
• Tel Aviv-Yafo (★1,735,000)	339,400
YERUSHALAYIM (AL-QUDS) (JERUSALEM) (★560,000)	524,500

ISRAELI OCCUPIED TERRITORIES

1991 E	1,704,900
Al-Quds (Jerusalem) (★Yerushalayim) (1976E)	90,000
Arīḥā (Jericho) (1967C)	6,829
Bayt Lahm (Bethlehem) (1971E)	25,000
• Ghazzah (1967C)	118,272
Khān Yūnis (1967C)	52,997
Nābulus (1971E)	64,000
Rafah (1967C)	49,812

ITALY / Italia

1991 C	56,411,290
Afragola (★Napoli)	59,940
Alessandria (▲93,351) (1990E)	74,000
Altamura	57,462
Ancona (1990E)	103,268
Andria	82,556
Arezzo (▲91,623) (1990E)	74,200
Asti (▲74,497) (1990E)	62,800
Avellino	54,343
Aversa (★Napoli)	50,361
Bari (★475,000)	341,273
Barletta	86,215
Benevento (▲62,683)	51,900
Bergamo (★345,000)	115,655
Biella (1990E)	50,993
Bitonto	49,792
Bologna (★525,000) (1990E)	411,803
Bolzano (1990E)	100,380
Brescia (1990E)	196,766
Brindisi	91,778
Busto Arsizio (★Milano)	77,001
Cagliari (★305,000) (1990E)	211,719
Caltanissetta (1990E)	62,853
Campobasso (▲51,307) (1990E)	44,400
Carpi (▲60,794) (1990E)	49,600
Carrara (★Massa) (1990E)	68,480
Caserta	68,811
Casoria (▲79,315)(★Napoli)	57,800
Castellammare di Stabia (★Napoli)	68,720
Catania (★550,000)	330,037
Catanzaro (1990E)	103,802
Cava de'Tirreni (★Salerno)	52,610
Cerignola	54,971
Cesena (▲89,497) (1990E)	72,200
Chieti (1990E)	57,535
Cinisello Balsamo (★Milano)	75,606
Civitavecchia	50,856
Collegno (★Torino)	47,192
Cologno Monzese (★Milano)	50,853
Como (★165,000)	85,955
Cosenza (★150,000) (1990E)	104,483
Cremona (1990E)	75,160
Crotone (▲61,813) (1990E)	54,300
Cuneo (▲55,838) (1990E)	47,900
Empoli (▲42,790)	32,300
Ercolano (★Napoli)	60,869
Ferrara (▲140,600) (1990E)	110,700
Firenze (★640,000)	402,316
Foggia	155,042
Foligno (▲53,518) (1990E)	42,500
Forlì (▲109,755) (1990E)	90,600
Gela (1990E)	79,718
Genova (Genoa) (★805,000)	675,639
Giugliano in Campania (★Napoli)	59,091
Grosseto (▲71,373) (1990E)	57,000
Imola (▲62,352) (1990E)	48,800
Imperia (1990E)	41,278
L'Aquila (▲67,818) (1990E)	43,100
La Spezia (★185,000)	101,701
Latina (▲105,543)	72,700
Lecce (1990E)	102,344
Lecco	45,859
Legnano (★Milano)	50,068
Livorno (1990E)	171,265
Lucca (1990E)	86,437
Manfredonia	58,157
Mantova (▲54,228) (1990E)	46,800
Marsala	77,218
Massa (★145,000) (1990E)	67,779
Matera (1990E)	54,872
Messina (1990E)	274,846
Mestre (▲317,837)(★Venezia) (1990E)	181,900
• Milano (Milan) (★3,750,000)	1,371,008
Modena (1990E)	177,501
Molfetta	66,658
Moncalieri (★Torino)	58,433
Monopoli (▲43,019)	33,100
Monza (★Milano)	121,151
Napoli (Naples) (★2,875,000)	1,024,601
Nicastro (▲69,660) (1990E)	53,700
Nocera Inferiore	49,021
Novara (1990E)	103,349
Padova (★270,000) (1990E)	218,186
Palermo	697,162
Parma (1990E)	173,991
Pavia (1990E)	80,073
Perugia (▲150,576) (1990E)	109,500
Pesaro (▲90,341) (1990E)	78,700
Pescara (1990E)	128,553
Piacenza	102,252
Pisa (1990E)	101,500
Pistoia (▲87,275)	73,900
Pordenone (1990E)	50,222
Portici (★Napoli)	67,824
Potenza (▲68,499) (1990E)	58,800
Pozzuoli (▲75,706)(★Napoli)	67,100
Prato (★215,000)	165,364
Quartu Sant'Elena (1990E)	60,852
Ragusa (1990E)	69,423
Ravenna (▲136,724) (1990E)	87,000
Reggio di Calabria (1990E)	178,496
Reggio nell'Emilia (▲131,880) (1990E)	108,800
Rho (★Milano)	51,646
Rimini (▲130,896) (1990E)	114,800
Rivoli (★Torino)	51,884
ROMA (★3,175,000)	2,693,383
Salerno (★250,000)	153,436
San Benedetto del Tronto (1990E)	45,220
San Giorgio a Cremano (★Napoli)	62,168
San Remo (1990E)	59,247
San Severo	55,376
Sassari (1990E)	120,011
Savona (★112,000) (1990E)	68,997
Scandicci (★Firenze)	53,264
Sesto Fiorentino (★Firenze)	46,899
Sesto San Giovanni (★Milano)	85,175
Siena (1990E)	57,745
Siracusa (1990E)	125,444
Taranto	232,200
Teramo (▲52,490) (1990E)	36,100
Terni (▲109,809) (1990E)	93,400
Torino (★1,550,000)	961,916
Torre Annunziata (★Napoli)	50,346
Torre del Greco (★Napoli)	101,456
Trani	49,337
Trapani (▲69,273)	59,700
Trento (▲102,124) (1990E)	83,100
Treviso (1990E)	83,886
Trieste (Triest) (1990E)	231,047
Udine (★126,000) (1990E)	98,322
Varese	85,461
Venezia (Venice) (★420,000) (1990E)	85,100
Vercelli (1990E)	50,207
Verona (1990E)	258,946
Viareggio (▲60,559) (1990E)	51,500
Vicenza (1990E)	109,333
Vigevano (1990E)	61,380
Viterbo (▲60,213) (1990E)	48,700
Vittoria (1990E)	56,970

IVORY COAST / Côte d'Ivoire

1983 E	9,300,000
• ABIDJAN	1,950,000
Bouaké	275,000
Daloa (1986E)	120,000
Korhogo	125,000
Man (1986E)	59,000
YAMOUSSOUKRO	80,000

JAMAICA

1990 E	2,392,000
• KINGSTON (★820,000)	661,600
Montego Bay (▲155,700)	80,500
Portmore (★Kingston) (1982C)	73,426
Spanish Town (▲358,600)(★Kingston)	96,100

JAPAN / Nihon

1990 C	123,611,541
Abiko (★Tōkyō)	120,629
Ageo (★Tōkyō)	194,952
Aizu-wakamatsu	119,084
Akashi (★Ōsaka)	270,728
Akigawa (★Tōkyō)	50,388
Akishima (★Tōkyō)	105,375
Akita	302,359
Akō	51,131
Amagasaki (★Ōsaka)	498,998
Anan (▲59,045)	47,000
Anjō	142,217
Aomori	287,813
Arao (★Ōmuta)	59,508
Asahikawa	359,069
Asaka (★Tōkyō)	103,621
Ashikaga	167,687
Ashiya (★Ōsaka)	87,528
Atami	47,290
Atsugi (★Tōkyō)	197,292
Ayase (★Tōkyō)	77,926
Beppu	130,323
Bisai (★Nagoya)	55,881
Chiba (★Tōkyō)	829,467
Chichibu	60,916
Chigasaki (★Tōkyō)	201,672
Chikushino (★Fukuoka)	70,303
Chiryū (★Nagoya)	54,061
Chita (★Nagoya)	75,434
Chitose	78,947
Chōfu (★Tōkyō)	197,680
Chōshi	85,138
Daitō (★Ōsaka)	126,460
Dazaifu (★Fukuoka)	62,408
Ebetsu (★Sapporo)	97,201
Ebina (★Tōkyō)	105,816
Eniwa	55,613
Fuchū (★Tōkyō)	209,419
Fuchū	45,738
Fuchū	50,061
Fuji (★370,000)	222,500
Fujieda (★Shizuoka)	119,815
Fujiidera (★Ōsaka)	65,924
Fujimi (★Tōkyō)	94,858
Fujinomiya (★Fuji)	117,093
Fujioka (▲60,983)	50,100
Fujisawa (★Tōkyō)	350,335
Fuji-yoshida	54,802
Fukaya (▲94,023)	75,600
Fukuchiyama (▲66,506)	56,700
Fukui	252,750
Fukuoka (★1,750,000)	1,237,107
Fukushima	277,526
Fukuyama	365,615
Funabashi (★Tōkyō)	533,273
Furukawa (▲64,227)	51,200
Fussa (★Tōkyō)	58,053
Gamagōri	84,819
Gifu	410,318
Ginowan (1985C)	69,206
Ginowan	75,899
Gotemba	79,560
Gushikawa	54,026
Gyōda	83,181
Habikino (★Ōsaka)	115,035
Hachinohe	241,065
Hachiōji (★Tōkyō)	466,373
Hadano (★Tōkyō)	155,619
Hagi	50,619
Hakodate	307,251
Hamada	49,139
Hamakita	81,159
Hamamatsu	534,624
Hanamaki (▲70,514)	55,000
Handa (★Nagoya)	99,550
Hannō (★Tōkyō)	73,216
Hashima	61,460
Hasuda (★Tōkyō)	59,703
Hatogaya (★Tōkyō)	56,441
Hatsukaichi (★Hiroshima)	63,441
Hekinan	65,901
Higashihiroshima (★Hiroshima)	94,206
Higashikurume (★Tōkyō)	113,800
Higashimatsuyama	84,395
Higashimurayama (★Tōkyō)	134,002
Higashiōsaka (★Ōsaka)	518,251
Higashiyamato (★Tōkyō)	75,124
Hikari (★Tokuyama)	47,613
Hikone	99,518
Himeji (★660,000)	454,360
Himi (▲60,768)	51,400
Hino (★Tōkyō)	165,935
Hirakata (★Ōsaka)	390,790
Hiratsuka (★Tōkyō)	245,944
Hirosaki (▲174,710)	133,800
Hiroshima (★1,575,000)	1,085,677
Hita (▲64,694)	57,100
Hitachi	202,145
Hōfu	117,639
Honjō	59,094
Hōya (★Tōkyō)	95,148
Hyūga	58,448
Ibaraki (★Ōsaka)	254,080
Ichihara (★Tōkyō)	257,717
Ichikawa (★Tōkyō)	436,597
Ichinomiya (★Nagoya)	262,434
Ichinoseki (▲61,971)	50,100
Iida (▲91,859)	64,700
Iizuka (★110,000)	83,133
Ikeda (★Ōsaka)	104,219
Ikoma (★Ōsaka)	99,598
Imabari	123,114
Imari (▲60,887)	50,000
Ina (▲60,063)	49,500
Inagi (★Tōkyō)	58,593
Inazawa (★Nagoya)	96,277
Inuyama (★Nagoya)	69,803
Iruma (★Tōkyō)	137,585
Isahaya	90,678
Ise (Uji-yamada)	104,162
Isehara (★Tōkyō)	89,568
Isesaki	115,939
Ishinomaki	121,980
Itami (★Ōsaka)	186,132
Itō	71,223
Iwaki (Taira)	355,817
Iwakuni	109,534
Iwamizawa	80,423
Iwata	83,521
Iwatsuki (★Tōkyō)	106,462

▲ Population of an entire municipality, commune, or district, including rural area.
• Largest city in country.
★ Population or designation of the metropolitan area, including suburbs.
C Census. **E** Official estimate. **U** Unofficial estimate.

▲ Bevölkerung eines ganzen städtischen Verwaltungsgebietes, eines Kommunalbezirkes oder eines Distrikts, einschliesslich ländlicher Gebiete.
• Grösste Stadt des Landes.
★ Bevölkerung oder Bezeichnung der Stadtregion einschliesslich Vororte.
C Volkszählung. **E** Offizielle Schätzung. **U** Inoffizielle Schätzung.

Izumi (★Sendai)	124,216
Izumi (★Ōsaka)	146,105
Izumi-ōtsu (★Ōsaka)	67,037
Izumi-sano (★Ōsaka)	88,862
Izumo (▲82,680)	69,600
Joetsu	130,114
Jōyō (★Ōsaka)	84,770
Kadoma (★Ōsaka)	142,288
Kaga	69,199
Kagoshima	536,685
Kainan (★Wakayama)	48,598
Kaizuka (★Ōsaka)	79,236
Kakamigahara	129,682
Kakegawa (▲72,795)	59,000
Kakogawa (★Ōsaka)	239,803
Kamagaya (★Tōkyō)	95,052
Kamaishi	52,483
Kamakura (★Tōkyō)	174,299
Kameoka	85,283
Kamifukuoka (★Tōkyō)	58,753
Kanazawa	442,872
Kani (★Nagoya)	80,012
Kanoya (▲77,652)	61,500
Kanuma (▲90,044)	74,900
Karatsu (▲79,206)	70,500
Kariya (★Nagoya)	120,121
Kasai	51,789
Kasaoka (▲59,618)	52,700
Kashihara (★Ōsaka)	115,556
Kashiwa (★Tōkyō)	305,060
Kashiwara (★Ōsaka)	76,819
Kashiwazaki (▲88,309)	75,300
Kasuga (★Fukuoka)	88,703
Kasugai (★Nagoya)	266,599
Kasukabe (★Tōkyō)	188,809
Katano (★Ōsaka)	65,311
Katsuta	109,826
Kawachi-nagano (★Ōsaka)	108,770
Kawagoe (★Tōkyō)	304,860
Kawaguchi (★Tōkyō)	438,667
Kawanishi (★Ōsaka)	141,254
Kawasaki (★Tōkyō)	1,173,606
Kesennuma	65,578
Kimitsu (▲89,243)	76,100
Kiryū	126,443
Kisarazu	123,434
Kishiwada (★Ōsaka)	188,553
Kitaibaraki	51,092
Kitakyūshū (★1,525,000)	1,026,467
Kitami	107,247
Kitamoto (★Tōkyō)	63,933
Kiyose (★Tōkyō)	67,540
Kōbe (★Ōsaka)	1,477,423
Kōchi	317,090
Kodaira (★Tōkyō)	164,021
Kōfu	200,630
Koga (★Tōkyō)	58,227
Koganei (★Tōkyō)	105,888
Kokubunji (★Tōkyō)	100,958
Komae (★Tōkyō)	74,197
Komaki (★Nagoya)	124,441
Komatsu	106,072
Kōnan (★Nagoya)	93,836
Kōnosu (★Tōkyō)	72,436
Kōriyama	314,651
Koshigaya (★Tōkyō)	285,280
Kudamatsu (★Tokuyama)	53,029
Kuki (★Tōkyō)	66,852
Kumagaya	152,122
Kumamoto	579,305
Kunitachi (★Tōkyō)	65,830
Kurashiki	414,692
Kure (★Hiroshima)	216,717
Kuroiso (▲52,346)	41,900
Kurume	228,350
Kusatsu (★Ōsaka)	94,766
Kushiro	205,640
Kuwana (★Nagoya)	97,911
Kyōto (★Ōsaka)	1,461,140
Machida (★Tōkyō)	349,030
Maebashi	286,261
Maizuru	96,329
Marugame	75,607
Matsubara (★Ōsaka)	135,921
Matsudo (★Tōkyō)	456,211
Matsue	142,931
Matsumoto	200,723
Matsusaka	118,727
Matsuyama	443,317
Mihara	85,518
Miki (★Ōsaka)	76,509
Minō (★Ōsaka)	122,133
Misato (★Tōkyō)	128,377
Mishima (★Numazu)	105,419
Mitaka (★Tōkyō)	165,555
Mito	234,970
Miura (★Tōkyō)	52,441
Miyako	58,505
Miyakonojō (▲130,155)	106,200
Miyazaki	287,367
Mobara	83,437
Moriguchi (★Ōsaka)	157,365
Morioka	235,440
Moriyama	58,561
Mukō (★Ōsaka)	52,932
Munakata	68,267
Muroran (★195,000)	117,852
Musashimurayama (★Tōkyō)	65,555
Musashino (★Tōkyō)	139,069
Mutsu	48,470
Nabari	68,933
Nagahama	55,482
Nagano	347,036
Nagaoka	185,938
Nagaokakyō (★Ōsaka)	77,193
Nagareyama (★Tōkyō)	140,059
Nagasaki	444,616
Nagoya (★4,800,000)	2,154,664
Naha	304,896
Nakama (★Kitakyūshū)	49,216
Nakatsu	66,383
Nakatsugawa	53,722
Nanao	50,101
Nara (★Ōsaka)	349,356
Narashino (★Tōkyō)	151,472
Narita	86,708
Naruto	64,577
Naze	46,309
Neyagawa (★Ōsaka)	256,521
Niigata	486,087
Niihama	129,151
Niitsu (▲64,005)	55,700
Niiza (★Tōkyō)	138,919
Nishinomiya (★Ōsaka)	426,919
Nishio	95,198

▲ Población de un municipio, comuna o distrito entero, incluyendo sus áreas rurales.
• Ciudad más grande de un país.
★ Población o designación de un área metropolitana, incluyendo los suburbios.
C Censo. **E** Estimado oficial. **U** Estimado no oficial.

Nobeoka	130,615
Noboribetsu (★Muroran)	55,575
Noda (★Tōkyō)	114,476
Nōgata	62,532
Noshiro (▲55,915)	47,800
Numazu (★495,000)	211,731
Obihiro	167,389
Ōbu (★Nagoya)	69,721
Ōdate (▲68,196)	58,500
Odawara	193,415
Ōgaki	148,281
Ōita	408,502
Ōkawa	45,705
Okaya	59,854
Okayama	593,742
Okazaki	306,821
Okegawa (★Tōkyō)	69,030
Okinawa (1985C)	101,210
Okinawa	105,852
Ōme (★Tōkyō)	125,945
Ōmi-hachiman (★Ōsaka)	66,068
Ōmiya (★Tōkyō)	403,779
Ōmura	73,437
Ōmuta (★225,000)	150,461
Ōnojō (★Fukuoka)	75,217
Onomichi	97,104
Ōsaka (★16,900,000)	2,623,831
Ōta	139,801
Otaru (★Sapporo)	163,215
Ōtsu (★Ōsaka)	260,004
Owariashi (★Nagoya)	65,676
Oyama (▲142,263)	120,000
Sabae	62,284
Saga	169,964
Sagamihara (★Tōkyō)	531,562
Saijō	56,823
Saiki	52,325
Sakado (★Tōkyō)	95,736
Sakai (★Ōsaka)	807,859
Sakaide	63,878
Sakata	100,808
Saku (▲62,005)	50,000
Sakura (★Tōkyō)	144,688
Sakurai	60,261
Sanda (▲64,560)Ōsaka)	54,500
Sanjō	85,824
Sano	83,484
Sapporo (★1,900,000)	1,671,765
Sasebo	244,693
Satte	54,339
Sayama (★Tōkyō)	157,307
Sayama (★Ōsaka)	54,323
Seki	68,386
Sendai, Kagoshima pref. (▲71,736)	58,000
Sendai, Miyagi pref. (★1,175,000)	918,378
Sennan (★Ōsaka)	60,054
Seto	126,343
Settsu (★Ōsaka)	87,465
Shibata (▲78,168)	63,600
Shijōnawate (★Ōsaka)	50,036
Shiki (★Tōkyō)	63,492
Shimada (▲73,809)	64,500
Shimizu (★Shizuoka)	241,524
Shimodate (▲66,030)	54,100
Shimonoseki (★Kitakyūshū)	262,643
Shiogama (★Sendai)	62,025
Shizuoka (★975,000)	472,199
Sōka (★Tōkyō)	206,129
Suita (★Ōsaka)	345,187
Suwa	52,465
Suzuka	174,103
Tachikawa (★Tōkyō)	152,817
Tagajō (★Sendai)	58,456
Tagawa	57,701
Tajimi (★Nagoya)	94,036
Takaishi (★Ōsaka)	65,084
Takamatsu	329,695
Takaoka (★220,000)	175,469
Takarazuka (★Ōsaka)	201,863
Takasago (★Ōsaka)	93,267
Takasaki	236,463
Takatsuki (★Ōsaka)	359,867
Takayama	65,245
Takefu	70,188
Takikawa	49,591
Tama (★Tōkyō)	144,490
Tamano	73,240
Tanabe (▲69,861)	59,100
Tanashi (★Tōkyō)	75,141
Tatebayashi	76,223
Tenri	68,818
Tochigi	86,216
Toda (★Tōkyō)	87,600
Tōkai (★Nagoya)	97,359
Toki	64,946
Tokoname (★Nagoya)	51,784
Tokorozawa (★Tōkyō)	303,047
Tokushima	263,336
Tokuyama (★250,000)	110,900
• TŌKYŌ (★30,300,000)	8,163,127
Tomakomai	160,116
Tondabayashi (★Ōsaka)	110,444
Toride (★Tōkyō)	81,667
Tosu	55,878
Tottori	142,477
Toyama	321,459
Toyoake (★Nagoya)	62,156
Toyohashi	337,988
Toyokawa	111,731
Toyonaka (★Ōsaka)	409,843
Toyota	332,336
Tsu	157,178
Tsuchiura	127,470
Tsuruga	68,039
Tsuruoka	99,891
Tsushima (★Nagoya)	59,345
Tsuyama	89,405
Ube (★230,000)	175,052
Ueda	119,435
Ueno (▲60,239)	51,400
Uji (★Ōsaka)	177,018
Uozu	49,516
Urasoe	89,993
Urawa (★Tōkyō)	418,267
Urayasu (★Tōkyō)	115,675
Usa (▲50,830)	38,600
Ushiku	60,698
Utsunomiya	426,809
Uwajima	68,034
Wakayama (★495,000)	396,554
Wakkanai	48,232
Wakō (★Tōkyō)	56,891
Warabi (★Tōkyō)	73,620

▲ Population d'une municipalité, d'une commune ou d'un district, zone rurale incluse.
• Ville la plus peuplée du pays.
★ Population de l'agglomération (ou nom de la zone métropolitaine englobante).
C Recensement. **E** Estimation officielle. **U** Estimation non officielle.

Yachiyo (★Tōkyō)	148,615
Yaizu (★Shizuoka)	112,188
Yamagata	249,493
Yamaguchi	129,467
Yamato (★Tōkyō)	194,870
Yamato-kōriyama (★Ōsaka)	92,948
Yamato-takada (★Ōsaka)	68,236
Yao (★Ōsaka)	277,724
Yashio (★Tōkyō)	72,474
Yatsushiro (▲108,135)	88,300
Yawata (★Ōsaka)	75,761
Yokkaichi	274,184
Yokohama (★Tōkyō)	3,220,350
Yokosuka (★Tōkyō)	433,361
Yonago	131,453
Yonezawa	94,763
Yono (★Tōkyō)	79,058
Yotsukaidō (★Tōkyō)	72,157
Yukuhashi	65,713
Zama (★Tōkyō)	112,100
Zushi (★Tōkyō)	56,705

JERSEY

1991 C	84,082
• SAINT HELIER (★46,500)	28,123

JORDAN / Al-Urdun

1989 E	3,111,000
Al-Baq'ah (★'Ammān)	63,985
• 'AMMĀN (★1,625,000)	936,300
Ar-Ruṣayfah (★'Ammān)	72,580
As-Salt	47,585
Az-Zarqā' (★'Ammān)	318,055
Irbid	167,785

KAZAKHSTAN

1991 E	16,793,100
Aktau	169,000
Akt'ubinsk	266,600
• ALMA-ATA (ALMATY) (★1,190,000)	1,156,200
Arkalyk	64,900
Aterau	156,700
Balchaš	87,600
Čelinograd	286,000
Čimkent	438,800
Džambul	312,300
Džetygara	48,900
Džezkazgan	111,100
Ekibastuz	138,900
Karaganda	608,600
Kentau	65,100
Kokčetav	143,300
Kustanaj	233,900
Kzyl-Orda	158,200
Leninogorsk	69,500
Leninsk	73,000
Pavlodar	342,500
Petropavlovsk	248,300
Rudnyj	128,800
Šachtinsk	65,300
Saptajev	61,400
Šaran'	62,600
Ščučinsk	56,000
Semipalatinsk	344,700
Taldy-Kurgan	136,100
Turkestan	81,200
Ural'sk	214,000
Ust'-Kamenogorsk	332,900
Žanatas	53,000
Zyr'anovsk	53,800

KENYA

1990 E	24,870,000
Eldoret (1979C)	50,503
Kisumu (1984E)	167,100
Machakos (1983E)	92,300
Meru (1979C)	72,049
Mombasa	537,000
• NAIROBI	1,505,000
Nakuru (1984E)	101,700

KIRIBATI

1990 C	72,298
BAIRIKI	2,226
• Bikenibeu	5,055

KOREA, NORTH / Chosŏn-minjujuŭi-inmĭn-konghwaguk

1981 E	18,317,000
Ch'ŏngjin	490,000
Haeju (1983E)	213,000
Hamhŭng (1970E)	150,000
Hŭngnam (1967E)	260,000
Kaesŏng	259,000
Kanggye (1967E)	130,000
Kimch'aek (Sŏngjin) (1967E)	265,000
Namp'o	241,000
• P'YŎNGYANG (★1,600,000)	1,283,000
Sinŭiju	305,000
Songnim (1944C)	53,035
Wŏnsan	398,000

KOREA, SOUTH / Taehan-min'guk

1990 C	43,520,199
Andong	116,932
Ansan (★Sŏul)	252,157
Anyang (★Sŏul)	480,668
Bucheon (★Sŏul)	667,777
Changsŭngp'o	48,614
Changwŏn (★Masan)	323,138
Chech'on	102,037
Cheju	232,687
Chinhae	120,207
Chinju	258,365
Chŏmch'on	47,802
Ch'ŏnan	211,382
Ch'ŏngju	497,429
Chŏnju	86,850
Chŏnju, Chŏlla Pukdo prov.	517,104
Ch'unch'ŏn	174,153
Ch'ungju	129,994
Ch'ungmu	92,159
Hanam (★Sŏul)	101,278
Inch'ŏn (★Sŏul)	1,818,293
Iri	203,401
Kangnŭng	152,605
Kimch'ŏn	81,349
Kimhae	106,166
Kimje	55,136
Kongju	65,195
Kumi	206,101
Kŭmsŏng (1985C)	58,897
Kunp'o (★Sŏul)	99,956
Kunsan	218,216
Kwachŏn (★Sŏul)	72,328
Kwangju	1,144,695
Kwangmyŏng (★Sŏul)	328,803
Kyŏngju	141,895
Kyŏngsan	60,524
Masan (★625,000)	496,639
Mikŭm (★Sŏul)	74,688
Miryang	52,995
Mokp'o	253,423
Naju	55,306
Namwŏn	63,121
Ŏnyang	66,379
Osan	59,492
P'ohang	318,595
Pusan (★3,800,000)	3,797,566
P'yŏngt'aek	79,238
Samch'ŏnp'o	62,824
Sangju	51,875
Shihŭng (★Sŏul)	107,190
Sŏgwipo	88,292
Sŏkch'o	73,796
Sŏngnam (★Sŏul)	540,764
Songtan	77,460
Sŏsan	55,930
• SŎUL (SEOUL) (★15,850,000)	10,627,790
Sunch'ŏn	167,209
Suwŏn (★Sŏul)	644,968
T'aebaek	89,770
Taech'ŏn	56,922
Taegu	2,228,834
Taejŏn	1,062,084
Tongduchŏn	71,448
Tonghae	89,162
Tongkwang	70,118
Ŭijŏngbu (★Sŏul)	212,368
Ŭiwang	96,892
Ulsan	682,978
Wŏnju	173,013
Yŏch'ŏn	63,802
Yŏngch'ŏn	48,890
Yŏngju	84,335
Yŏsu	173,164

▲ População de um municipio, comuna ou distrito, inclusive as respectivas áreas rurais.
• Maior cidade de um país.
★ População ou indicação de uma área metropolitana.
C Censo. **E** Estimativa oficial. **U** Estimativa não oficial.

KUWAIT / Al-Kuwayt

1985 C	1,697,301
Abraq Khīṭān (★Al-Kuwayt)	45,120
Al-Aḥmadī (★285,000)	26,899
Al-Farwānīyah (★Al-Kuwayt)	68,701
Al-Fuḥayḥīl (★Al-Aḥmadī)	50,081
Al-Jahrah (★Al-Kuwayt)	111,222
• AL-KUWAYT (★1,375,000)	44,335
As-Sālimīyah (★Al-Kuwayt)	153,359
Aṣ-Ṣulaybīyah (★Al-Kuwayt)	51,314
Hawallī (★Al-Kuwayt)	145,126
Qalīb ash-Shuyūkh (★Al-Kuwayt)	114,771
South Khīṭān (★Al-Kuwayt)	69,256
Subahiya (★Al-Aḥmadī)	60,787

KYRGYZSTAN

1991 E	4,422,200
• BIŠKEK	631,300
Džalal-Abad	79,900
Kara-Balta	55,000
Karakol (Prževal'sk)	64,300
Oš	238,200
Tokmak	71,200

LAOS / Lao

1985 C	3,584,803
Savannakhét (1975E)	53,000
• VIANGCHAN (VIENTIANE)	377,409

LATVIA / Latvija

1991 E	2,680,500
Daugavpils	129,000
Jelgava	74,500
Jūrmala (★Rīga)	66,500
Liepāja	114,900
• RĪGA (★1,005,000)	910,200
Ventspils	50,400

LEBANON / Lubnān

1982 E	2,637,000
• BAYRŪT (★1,675,000)	509,000
Ṣaydā	105,000
Ṣūr (Tyre) (1970E)	12,500
Ṭarābulus (Tripoli) (★950,000)	198,000

LESOTHO

1986 C	1,577,536
• MASERU	109,382

LIBERIA

1986 E	2,221,000
• MONROVIA	465,000

LIBYA / Lībiyā

1988 E	3,772,500
Al-Baydā (Beida) (1984C)	67,120
Banghāzī	446,250
Darnah (1984C)	62,179
Misrātah	121,669
• ṬARĀBULUS (TRIPOLI)	591,062
Ṭubruq (Tobruk) (1984C)	75,282

LIECHTENSTEIN

1992 E	29,386
• VADUZ	4,887

LITHUANIA / Lietuva

1989 C	3,690,000
Alytus (1987E)	71,000
Kaunas	423,000
Klaipėda (Memel)	204,000
Panevėžys	126,000
Šiauliai	145,000
• VILNIUS	582,000

LUXEMBOURG

1991 C	384,062

Esch-sur-Alzette (★83,000)	24,012
• LUXEMBOURG (★136,000)	75,377

MACAU

1989 E	452,300
• MACAU	452,300

MACEDONIA / Makedonija

1987 E	2,064,581
Bitola (▲143,090)	76,200
• SKOPJE (▲547,214)	444,900

MADAGASCAR / Madagasikara

1988 E	11,238,000
• ANTANANARIVO	1,250,000
Antsirabe (▲100,000)	52,700
Antsiranana	220,000
Fianarantsoa	300,000
Mahajanga	200,000
Toamasina	230,000
Toliara	150,000

MALAWI / Malaŵi

1987 C	7,982,607
• Blantyre	331,588
LILONGWE	233,973

MALAYSIA

1980 C	13,136,109
Alor Setar	69,435
Batu Pahat	64,727
Butterworth (★George Town)	77,982
George Town (Pinang) (★495,000)	248,241
Ipoh	293,849
Johor Baharu (★Singapore)	246,395
Kelang	192,080
Keluang	50,315
Kota Baharu	167,872
Kota Kinabalu (Jesselton)	55,997
• KUALA LUMPUR (★1,475,000)	919,610
Kuala Terengganu	180,296
Kuantan	131,547
Kuching	72,555
Melaka	87,494
Miri	52,125
Muar (Bandar Maharani)	65,151
Petaling Jaya (★Kuala Lumpur)	207,805
Sandakan	70,420
Seremban	132,911
Sibu	85,231
Taiping	146,000
Telok Anson	49,148

MALDIVES

1990 C	213,215
• MALE'	55,130

MALI

1987 C	7,696,348
• BAMAKO	658,275
Gao	54,874
Kayes	48,216
Koutiala	48,010
Mopti	73,979
Ségou	88,877
Sikasso	73,050
Tombouctou (Timbuktu)	31,925

MALTA

1991 E	355,910
• VALLETTA (★215,000)	9,199

MARSHALL ISLANDS

1980 C	30,873
• Jarej-Uliga-Delap	8,583

MARTINIQUE

1982 C	328,566
• FORT-DE-FRANCE (★116,017)	99,844

MAURITANIA / Mauritanie / Mūrītāniyā

1987 E	2,007,000
• NOUAKCHOTT	285,000

MAURITIUS

1989 E	1,081,669
Beau Bassin-Rose Hill (★Port Louis)	94,236
Curepipe (★Port Louis)	66,704
• PORT LOUIS (★420,000)	141,870
Quatre Bornes (★Port Louis)	65,759
Vacoas-Phoenix (★Port Louis)	56,335

MAYOTTE

1985 E	67,205
• DZAOUDZI (★6,979)	5,865

MEXICO / México

1990 C	81,249,645
Acámbaro	52,248
Acapulco [de Juárez]	515,374
Aguascalientes	440,425
Apatzingán de la Constitución	76,643
Apodaca	103,364
Atlixco	74,233
Buenavista	114,653
Campeche	150,518
Cancún	167,730
Cárdenas	61,017
Celaya	214,856
Chalco (★Ciudad de México)	224,190
Chetumal	94,158
Chicoloapan de Juárz	57,306
Chihuahua	516,153
Chilpancingo de los Bravo	97,165
Chimalhuacán	235,587
Cholula [de Rivadabia] (★Puebla)	53,673
Ciudad Acuña	52,983
Ciudad del Carmen	83,806
• CIUDAD DE MÉXICO (★14,100,000)	8,235,744
Ciudad Guzmán	72,619
Ciudad Hidalgo	48,476
Ciudad Juárez (★El Paso, Tex., U.S.A.)	789,522
Ciudad Lerdo (★Torreón)	46,593
Ciudad López Mateos	315,059
Ciudad Madero (★Tampico)	160,331
Ciudad Mante	76,799
Ciudad Obregón	219,980
Ciudad Valles	91,402
Ciudad Victoria	194,996
Coacalco	151,255
Coatzacoalcos	198,817
Colima	106,967
Comitan de Dominguez	48,299
Comondú	74,346
Córdoba	130,695
Cortazar	45,579
Cuauhtémoc	69,895
Cuautitlán Izcalli (★Ciudad de México)	313,238
Cuernavaca	279,187
Culiacán	415,046
Delicias	87,412
Durango	348,036
Ecatepec (★Ciudad de México)	1,218,135
Ensenada	169,426
Fresnillo	75,118
Garza García (★Monterrey)	113,017
Gómez Palacio (★Torreón)	164,092
Guadalajara (★2,325,000)	1,650,042
Guadalupe	46,433
Guadalupe (★Monterrey)	535,332
Guamúchil	49,635
Guanajuato	73,108
Guasave	49,338
Guaymas	87,484
Hermosillo	406,417
Heroica Zitácuaro	66,983
Hidalgo del Parral	88,197
Iguala	83,412
Irapuato	265,042
Ixtapaluca	115,711
Jiutepec	82,845
Juchitán de Zaragoza	53,666
Lagos de Moreno	63,646
La Paz	137,641
La Piedad de Cabadas	62,625
Las Choapas	43,868
Las Truchas	53,581
León	758,279
Los Mochis	162,659
Los Reyes la Paz	134,544
Manzanillo	67,697
Matamoros (★Brownsville, Tex., U.S.A.)	266,055
Matehuala	54,713
Mazatlán	262,705
Mérida	523,422
Metepec	116,203
Mexicali (★460,000)	438,377
Minatitlán	142,060
Monclova	177,792
Monterrey (★2,015,000)	1,068,996
Morelia	428,486
Naucalpan de Juárez (★Ciudad de México)	845,960
Navojoa	82,618
Nezahualcóyotl (★Ciudad de México)	1,255,456
Nogales	105,873
Nuevo Laredo (★Laredo, Tex., U.S.A.)	218,413
Oaxaca [de Juárez]	212,818
Ocotlán	62,595
Orizaba (★215,000)	114,216
Pachuca	174,013
Papantla [de Olarte]	46,075
Piedras Negras	96,178
Poza Rica	151,739
Puebla (★1,200,000)	1,007,170
Puerto Vallarta	93,503
Querétaro	385,503
Reynosa	265,663
Río Bravo	67,092
Sahuayo de José María Morelos	50,463
Salamanca	123,190
Salina Cruz	61,656
Saltillo	420,947
San Andrés Tuxtla	49,658
San Cristóbal de las Casas	73,388
San Francisco del Rincón	52,291
San Juan del Río	61,652
San Luis Potosí (★600,000)	489,238
San Luis Río Colorado	95,461
San Martín Texmelucan	57,519
San Miguel de Allende	48,935
San Nicolás de los Garza (★Monterrey)	436,603
San Pablo de las Salinas	84,217
Santa Catarina (★Monterrey)	162,707
Silao	50,828
Soledad de Graciano Sanchez	123,943
Tampico (★440,000)	272,690
Tapachula	138,858
Tecomán	60,938
Tehuacán	139,450
Temixco	65,058
Tepatitlán de Morelos	54,036
Tepic	206,967
Texcoco [de Mora] (★Ciudad de México)	74,194
Tijuana (★San Diego, Calif., U.S.A.)	698,752
Tlalnepantla (★Ciudad de México)	702,270
Tlaquepaque (★Guadalajara)	328,031
Tlaxcala [de Xicoténcatl]	50,486
Toluca [de Lerdo]	327,865
Tonalá	151,190
Torreón (★690,000)	439,436
Tulancingo	75,477
Tuxpan	69,224
Tuxtepec	62,788
Tuxtla Gutiérrez	289,626
Uruapan del Progreso	187,623
Valle de Santiago	56,009
Veracruz [Llave] (★540,000)	438,821
Villa Frontera	58,216
Villahermosa	261,231
Villa Nicolás Romero	148,342
Xalapa	279,451
Zacatecas	100,051
Zamora de Hidalgo	109,751
Zapopan (★Guadalajara)	668,323

MICRONESIA, FEDERATED STATES OF

1985 E	94,534
• KOLONIA	6,306

MOLDOVA

1991 E	4,366,300
Bel'c'	164,900
Bendery	141,500
Kišin'ov	676,700
Rybnica	62,900
Tiraspol'	186,000

MONACO

1990 C	29,972
• MONACO (★87,000)	29,972

MONGOLIA / Mongol Ard Uls

1989 E	2,040,000
Darchan (1985E)	69,800
• ULAANBAATAR	548,400

MONTSERRAT

1980 C	11,606
• PLYMOUTH	1,568

MOROCCO / Al-Magreb

1982 C	20,419,555
Agadir	110,479
Beni-Mellal	95,003
Berkane	60,490
• Casablanca (Dar-el-Beida) (★2,475,000)	2,139,204
El-Jadida (Mazagan)	81,455
Fès (★535,000)	448,823
Kenitra	188,194
Khemisset	58,925
Khouribga	127,181
Ksar-el-Kebir	73,541
Larache	63,893
Marrakech (★535,000)	439,728
Meknès (★375,000)	319,783
Mohammedia (Fedala) (★Casablanca)	105,120
Nador	62,040
Oued-Zem	58,744
Oujda	260,082
RABAT (★980,000)	518,616
Safi	197,309
Salé (★Rabat)	289,391
Settat	65,203
Sidi Kacem	55,833
Sidi Slimane	50,457
Tanger (Tangier) (★370,000)	266,346
Tan-Tan	41,451
Taza	77,216
Temera (★Rabat)	48,644
Tétouan	199,615

MOZAMBIQUE / Moçambique

1989 E	15,326,476
Beira	291,604
Chimoio (1986E)	86,928
Inhambane (1986E)	64,274
• MAPUTO	1,069,727
Nacala	101,615
Nampula	197,309
Pemba (1986E)	50,215
Quelimane	78,520
Tete (1986E)	56,178
Xai-Xai (1986E)	51,620

NAMIBIA

1988 E	1,760,000
• WINDHOEK	114,500

NAURU / Naoero

1987 E	8,000

NEPAL / Nepāl

1981 C	15,022,839
Bhaktapur	48,472
• KĀTHMĀNDAU (★320,000)	235,160
Wirātnagar	93,544

NETHERLANDS / Nederland

1991 E	15,010,000
Alkmaar (★124,000)	90,767
Almelo	62,664
Alphen aan den Rijn	62,404
Amersfoort	101,966
Amstelveen (★Amsterdam)	70,337
• AMSTERDAM (★1,875,000)	702,686
Apeldoorn	148,195
Arnhem (★305,000)	131,707
Assen	50,353
Bergen op Zoom	46,897
Breda (★163,000)	124,792
Delft (★'s-Gravenhage)	89,369
Den Helder	61,463
Deventer	67,473
Dordrecht (★209,000)	110,472
Ede (▲94,721)	50,000
Eindhoven (★384,000)	192,810
Emmen (▲92,896)	36,900
Enschede (★252,000)	146,509
Geleen (★179,000)	33,833
Gouda	65,918
Groningen (★208,000)	168,701
Haarlem (★Amsterdam)	149,464
Haarlemmermeer (▲98,070)(★Amsterdam)	13,600
Heerlen (★267,500)	94,304
Helmond	69,968
Hengelo (★Enschede)	76,377
Hilversum (★Amsterdam)	84,602
Hoorn	58,202
IJmuiden (★Amsterdam)	60,129
Kerkrade (★Heerlen)	53,276
Leeuwarden	85,697
Leiden (★190,000)	111,927
Maastricht (★163,000)	117,398
Nieuwegein (★Utrecht)	58,912
Nijmegen (★242,000)	145,646
Oss	51,688
Purmerend (★Amsterdam)	61,056
Ridderkerk (★Rotterdam)	45,990
Rijswijk (★'s-Gravenhage)	47,709
Roosendaal	60,732
Rotterdam (★1,120,000)	582,238
Schiedam (★Rotterdam)	70,206
'S-GRAVENHAGE (THE HAGUE) (★772,000)	444,256
's-Hertogenbosch (★200,000)	92,052
Soest (★Amersfoort)	41,415
Spijkenisse (★Rotterdam)	69,103
Tilburg (★233,000)	158,839
Utrecht (★527,000)	231,232
Veenendaal	49,689
Venlo (★87,000)	64,386
Vlaardingen (★Rotterdam)	73,711
Vlissingen (Flushing) (▲43,799)	25,100
Zaanstad (★Amsterdam)	130,684
Zeist (★Utrecht)	59,363
Zoetermeer (★'s-Gravenhage)	99,094
Zwolle	95,574

NETHERLANDS ANTILLES / Nederlandse Antillen

1990 E	189,687
• WILLEMSTAD (★130,000) (1981C)	31,883

NEW CALEDONIA / Nouvelle-Calédonie

1989 C	164,173
• NOUMÉA (★97,581)	65,110

NEW ZEALAND

1991 C	3,434,950
• Auckland (★855,571)	315,668
Christchurch (★307,179)	292,858
Dunedin	116,577
Hamilton (★148,625)	101,448
Invercargill	56,148
Lower Hutt (★Wellington)	94,540
Manukau (★Auckland)	226,147
Napier (★110,216)	51,645
Palmerston North (★70,951)	70,318
Rotorua (★53,702)	45,144
Takapuna (★Auckland)	74,360
Tauranga (★70,803)	46,308
Waitemata (★Auckland)	136,716
WELLINGTON (★350,000)	150,301
Whangarei (★44,183)	40,101

NICARAGUA

1985 E	3,272,100
Chinandega	75,000
Granada (1981E)	64,642
León	101,000
• MANAGUA	682,000
Masaya	75,000
Matagalpa	68,000

NIGER

1988 C	7,250,383
Agadez	50,164
Maradi	112,965
• NIAMEY	398,265
Tahoua	51,607
Zinder	120,892

NIGERIA

1987 E	101,907,000
Aba	239,800
Abakaliki	56,800
Abeokuta	341,300
Ado-Ekiti	287,000
Afikpo	65,790
Agege	83,810
Akure	129,600
Amaigbo	53,690
Apomu	49,570
Aramoko	48,280
Asaba	47,410
Awka	88,800
Azare	50,020
Bauchi	68,840
Benin City	183,200
Bida	100,200
Calabar	139,800
Deba	110,600
Duku	52,880
Ede	245,200
Effon-Alaiye	122,300
Ejigbo	84,570
Emure-Ekiti	58,750
Enugu	252,500
Epe	80,560
Erin-Oshogbo	59,940
Eruwa	49,140
Fiditi	49,440
Gboko	49,390
Gbongan	53,990
Gombe	86,120
Gusau	126,200
Ibadan	1,144,000
Idah	50,550
Idanre	56,080
Ife	237,000
Ifon-Oshogbo	65,980
Igbasa-Odo	48,040
Igboho	85,230
Igbo-Ora	68,060
Igede-Ekiti	56,570
Ihiala	73,240
Ijebu-Igbo	78,680
Ijebu-Ode	124,900
Ijero-Ekiti	76,420
Ikare	112,500
Ikerre	195,400
Ikire	94,450
Ikirun	144,900
Ikole	71,860
Ikorodu	147,700
Ikot Ekpene	69,440
Ila	210,800
Ilawe-Ekiti	147,300
Ilesha	302,100
Ilobu	159,000
Ilorin	380,000
Inisa	95,630
Ipoti-Ekiti	53,220
Ise-Ekiti	82,580
Iseyin	173,500
Iwo	289,100
Jega (1985E)	47,000
Jimeta	66,130
Jos	164,700
Kaduna	273,200
Kano	538,300
Katsina	165,000
Kaura Namoda	52,910
Keffi	57,790
Kishi	77,210
Kumo	118,200
Lafia	97,810
Lafiagi	57,580
• LAGOS (★3,800,000)	1,213,000

▲ Population of an entire municipality, commune, or district, including rural area.
• Largest city in country.
★ Population or designation of the metropolitan area, including suburbs.
C Census. **E** Official estimate. **U** Unofficial estimate.

▲ Bevölkerung eines ganzen städtischen Verwaltungsgebietes, eines Kommunalbezirkes oder eines Distrikts, einschliesslich ländlicher Gebiete.
• Grösste Stadt des Landes.
★ Bevölkerung oder Bezeichnung der Stadtregion einschliesslich Vororte.
C Volkszählung. **E** Offizielle Schätzung. **U** Inoffizielle Schätzung.

Lalupon	56,130
Lere	49,670
Maiduguri	255,100
Makurdi	98,350
Minna	109,300
Mubi	51,190
Mushin (★Lagos)	266,100
Nguru	78,770
Nsukka	47,760
Ode-Ekiti	48,910
Offa	157,500
Ogbomosho	582,900
Oka	114,400
Oke-Mesi	55,040
Okwe	52,550
Olupona	65,720
Ondo	135,300
Onitsha	298,200
Opobo	64,620
Oron	62,260
Oshogbo	380,800
Owerri (1985E)	37,000
Owo	146,600
Oyan	50,930
Oyo	204,700
Pindiga	64,130
Port Harcourt	327,300
Potiskum	56,490
Sapele	111,200
Shagamu	93,610
Shaki	139,000
Shomolu (★Lagos)	120,700
Sokoto	163,700
Ugep	81,910
Umuahia	52,550
Uyo	60,500
Warri	100,700
Zaria	302,800

NIUE

1989 C	2,267
• ALOFI	706

NORTHERN MARIANA ISLANDS

1980 C	16,780
• Chalan Kanoa	2,678
Garapan	2,063

NORWAY / Norge

1987 E	4,190,000
Bærum (★Oslo) (1985E)	83,000
Bergen (★239,000)	209,320
Drammen (★73,000) (1985E)	50,700
Fredrikstad (★52,000) (1983E)	27,618
Hammerfest (1983E)	7,208
Kristiansand (1985E)	62,200
Narvik (1983E)	19,080
• OSLO (★720,000)	452,415
Skien (★77,981) (1985E)	46,700
Stavanger (★132,000) (1985E)	94,200
Tromsø (1985E)	47,800
Trondheim	135,010
Louga (1988C)	52,763

OMAN / 'Umān

1983 E	1,131,000
• MASQAṬ (MUSCAT)	30,000
Maṭrah (1971E)	14,000
Ṣūr	30,000

PAKISTAN / Pākistān

1981 C	84,253,644
Abbottābād (★65,996)	32,188
Ahmadpur East	56,979
Attock (★39,986)	26,233
Bahāwalnagar	74,533
Bahāwalpur (★180,263)	152,009
Bannu (★43,210)	35,170
Bhakkar	41,934
Chārsadda	62,530
Chīchāwatni	50,241
Chiniot	105,559
Chishtiān Mandi	61,959
Daska	55,555
Dera Ghāzi Khān	102,007
Dera Ismāīl Khān (★68,145)	64,358
Drigh Road Cantonment (★Karāchi)	56,742
Faisalabad (Lyallpur)	1,104,209
Gojra	68,000
Gujrānwāla (★658,753)	600,993
Gujrānwāla Cantonment (★Gujrānwāla)	57,760
Gujrāt	155,058
Hāfizābād	83,464
Hyderābād (★800,000)	702,539
Hyderābād Cantonment (★Hyderābād)	48,990
ISLĀMABAD (★Rāwalpindi)	204,364
Jacobābād	79,365
Jarānwāla	69,459
Jhang Sadar	195,558
Jhelum (★106,462)	92,646
Kamālia	61,107
Kāmoke	71,097
• Karāchi (★5,300,000)	4,901,627
Karāchi Cantonment (★Karāchi)	181,981
Kasūr	155,523
Khairpur	61,447
Khānewāl	89,090
Khānpur	70,589
Khāriān Cantonment (★51,506)	16,042
Khushāb	56,274
Kohāt (★77,604)	55,832
Lahore (★3,025,000)	2,707,215
Lahore Cantonment (★Lahore)	245,474
Lārkāna	123,890
Leiah	51,482
Malir Cantonment (★Karāchi)	47,588
Mandi Būrewāla	86,311
Mardān (★147,977)	141,842
Miānwāli	59,159
Mingāora	88,078
Mīrpur Khās	124,371
Multān (★732,070)	696,316
Muzaffargarh	53,000
Nawābshāh	102,139
Nowshera (★74,913)	38,875
Okāra (★153,483)	127,455
Pākpattan	69,820
Peshāwar (★566,248)	506,896
Peshāwar Cantonment (★Peshāwar)	59,352
Quetta (★285,719)	244,842
Rahīmyār Khān (★132,635)	119,036
Rāwalpindi (★1,040,000)	457,091
Rāwalpindi Cantonment (★Rāwalpindi)	337,752
Sādiqābād	63,935
Sāhīwal	150,954
Sargodha (★291,362)	231,895
Sargodha Cantonment (★Sargodha)	59,467
Shekhūpura	141,168
Shikārpur	88,138
Shorkot (★50,568)	18,533
Siālkot (★302,009)	258,147
Sukkur	190,551
Tando Ādam	62,744
Turbat	52,337
Vihāri	53,799
Wāh Cantonment	122,335
Wazīrābād	62,725

PALAU / Belau

1986 C	13,873
• KOROR	8,629

PANAMA / Panamá

1990 C	2,315,047
Balboa (★Panamá)	1,214
Colón (★96,000)	54,469
David	65,635
• PANAMÁ (★770,000)	411,549
San Miguelito (★Panamá)	242,529

PAPUA NEW GUINEA

1990 C	3,534,038
Lae	78,265
• PORT MORESBY	193,242
Rabaul	16,883

PARAGUAY

1992 C	4,123,550
• ASUNCIÓN (★700,000)	502,426
Caaguazú	38,200
Capiatá	83,189
Ciudad del Este	133,896
Encarnación	55,359
Fernando de la Mora (★Asunción)	95,287
Lambaré (★Asunción)	99,681
Mariano Roque Alonso	39,240
Pedro Juan Caballero	53,601
San Lorenzo (★Asunción)	133,311

PERU / Perú

1981 C	17,031,221
Arequipa (★446,942)	108,023
Ayacucho (★69,533)	57,432
Barranco (★Lima)	46,478
Breña (★Lima)	112,398
Cajamarca	62,259
Callao (★Lima)	264,133
Cerro de Pasco (★66,373)	55,597
Chiclayo (★279,527)	213,095
Chimbote	223,341
Chorrillos (★Lima)	141,881
Chosica	65,139
Cuzco (★184,550)	89,563
Huacho	43,398
Huancayo (★164,954)	84,845
Huánuco	61,812
Ica	114,786
Iquitos	178,738
Jesús María (★Lima)	83,179
Juliaca	87,651
La Victoria (★Lima)	270,778
• LIMA (★4,608,010)	371,122
Lince (★Lima)	80,456
Magdalena (★Lima)	55,535
Miraflores (★Lima)	103,453
Pisco	55,604
Piura (★207,934)	144,609
Pucallpa	112,263
Pueblo Libre (★Lima)	83,985
Puno	67,397
Rimac (★Lima)	184,484
San Isidro (★Lima)	71,203
San Martin de Porras (★Lima)	404,856
Santiago de Surco (★Lima)	146,636
Sullana	89,037
Surquillo (★Lima)	134,158
Tacna	97,173
Talara	57,351
Trujillo (★354,301)	202,469
Tumbes	47,936
Vitarte (★Lima)	145,504

PHILIPPINES / Pilipinas

1990 C	60,477,000
Angeles	236,000
Antipolo (▲68,912) (1980C)	54,117
Bacolod	364,000
Bacoor (★Manila) (1980C)	90,364
Baguio	183,000
Baliuag (1980C)	70,555
Biñan (★Manila) (1980C)	83,684
Binangonan (1980C)	80,980
Bislig (▲81,615) (1980C)	49,498
Bocaue (1980C)	49,693
Butuan (▲228,000)	99,000
Cabanatuan (▲173,000)	75,700
Cagayan de Oro (▲340,000)	255,000
Cainta (★Manila) (1980C)	59,025
Calamba (▲121,175) (1980C)	72,359
Caloocan (★Manila)	746,000
Carmona (★Manila) (1980C)	65,014
Cavite (★195,000)	92,000
Cebu (★825,000)	610,000
Cotabato	127,000
Dagupan	122,000
Davao (▲850,000)	569,300
Dumaguete	80,000
General Santos (Dadiangas) (▲250,000)	157,600
Guagua (1980C)	72,609
Iloilo	311,000
Isabela (Basilan) (▲49,891) (1980C)	11,491
Jolo (1980C)	52,429
Lapu-Lapu (Opon)	146,000
Las Piñas (★Manila) (1984E)	190,364
Legaspi (▲121,000)	63,000
Lucena	151,000
Mabalacat (▲80,966) (1980C)	54,988
Makati (★Manila) (1984E)	408,991
Malabon (★Manila) (1984E)	212,930
Malolos (1980C)	95,699
Mandaluyong (★Manila) (1984E)	226,670
Mandaue (★Cebu)	180,000
Mangaldan (1980C)	50,434
• MANILA (★9,650,000)	1,587,000
Marawi	92,000
Marikina (★Manila) (1984E)	248,183
Meycauayan (★Manila) (1980C)	83,579
Muntinglupa (★Manila) (1984E)	172,421
Naga	115,000
Navotas (★Manila) (1984E)	146,899
Olongapo	192,000
Pagadian (▲107,000)	52,400
Parañaque (★Manila) (1984E)	252,791
Pasay (★Manila)	354,000
Pasig (★Manila) (1984E)	318,853
Puerto Princesa (▲92,000)	52,000
Quezon City (★Manila)	1,632,000
San Fernando (1980C)	110,891
San Juan del Monte (★Manila) (1984E)	139,126
San Pablo (▲161,000)	83,900
San Pedro (1980C)	74,556
Santa Cruz (1980C)	60,620
Santa Rosa (★Manila) (1980C)	64,325
Tacloban	138,000
Tagbilaran	56,000
Tagig (★Manila) (1984E)	130,719
Taytay (★Manila) (1980C)	75,328
Valenzuela (★Manila) (1984E)	275,725
Zamboanga (▲444,000)	107,000

PITCAIRN

1988 C	59
• ADAMSTOWN	59

POLAND / Polska

1991 E	38,183,200
Będzin (★Katowice)	76,200
Bełchatów	57,400
Biała Podlaska	53,100
Białystok	270,600
Bielsko-Biała	181,300
Bydgoszcz	381,500
Bytom (Beuthen) (★Katowice)	231,200
Chełm	66,400
Chorzów (★Katowice)	131,900
Częstochowa	258,000
Dąbrowa Górnicza (★Katowice)	136,900
Dzierżoniów (Reichenbach) (★89,000)	38,000
Elbląg (Elbing)	126,100
Ełk	52,400
Gdańsk (Danzig) (★909,000)	465,100
Gdynia (★Gdańsk)	251,500
Gliwice (Gleiwitz) (★Katowice)	214,200
Głogów	73,300
Gniezno	70,400
Gorzów Wielkopolski (Landsberg an der Warthe)	124,300
Grudziądz	102,300
Inowrocław	77,700
Jastrzębie-Zdrój	103,700
Jaworzno (★Katowice)	99,500
Jelenia Góra (Hirschberg)	93,400
Kalisz	106,200
• Katowice (★2,778,000)	366,800
Kędzierzyn Kozle	71,700
Kielce	214,200
Konin	80,300
Koszalin (Köslin)	108,700
Kraków (★828,000)	750,500
Krosno	49,700
Legionowo (★Warszawa)	50,400
Legnica (Liegnitz)	105,200
Leszno	58,300
Łódź (★1,061,000)	848,200
Łomża	59,300
Lubin	82,300
Lublin (★389,000)	351,400
Mielec	61,800
Mysłowice (★Katowice)	93,800
Nowy Sącz	78,200
Olsztyn (Allenstein)	162,900
Opole (Oppeln)	128,400
Ostrołęka	50,700
Ostrowiec Świętokrzyski	78,600
Ostrów Wielkopolski	73,300
Pabianice (★Łódź)	75,200
Piekary Śląskie (★Katowice)	68,500
Piła (Schneidemühl)	72,300
Piotrków Trybunalski	81,000
Płock	123,400
Poznań (★672,000)	590,100
Pruszków (★Warszawa)	53,700
Przemyśl	68,500
Puławy	85,700
Racibórz (Ratibor)	64,400
Radom	228,500
Radomsko	50,400
Ruda Śląska (★Katowice)	171,000
Rybnik	144,000
Rzeszów	153,000
Siedlce	72,000
Siemianowice Śląskie (★Katowice)	81,100
Skarżysko-Kamienna	50,900
Słupsk (Stolp)	101,200
Sopot (★Gdańsk)	46,700
Sosnowiec (★Katowice)	259,400
Stalowa Wola	70,000
Starachowice	56,600
Stargard Szczeciński (Stargard in Pommern)	71,000
Starogard Gdański	49,500
Suwałki	61,300
Świdnica (Schweidnitz)	63,300
Świętochłowice (★Katowice)	60,500
Świnoujście (Swinemünde)	43,300
Szczecin (Stettin) (★449,000)	413,400
Tarnów	121,200
Tarnowskie Góry (★Katowice)	74,100
Tczew	59,500
Tomaszów Mazowiecki	69,900
Toruń	202,300
Tychy (★Katowice)	191,700
Wałbrzych (Waldenburg) (★207,000)	141,000
WARSZAWA (★2,323,000)	1,655,700
Włocławek	122,200
Wodzisław Śląski	111,800
Wrocław (Breslau)	643,200
Zabrze (Hindenburg) (★Katowice)	205,000
Zamość	61,800
Zawiercie	56,600
Zgierz (★Łódź)	59,000
Zielona Góra (Grünberg)	114,100
Żory	67,000

PORTUGAL

1981 C	9,833,014
Amadora (★Lisboa)	95,518
Barreiro (★Lisboa)	50,863
Braga	63,033
Coimbra	74,616
• LISBOA (★2,250,000)	807,167
Ponta Delgada	21,187
Porto (★1,225,000)	327,368
Setúbal	77,885
Vila Nova de Gaia (★Porto)	62,469

PUERTO RICO

1990 C	3,522,037
Arecibo (★160,500)	49,545
Bayamón (▲220,262)(★San Juan)	202,103
Caguas (▲133,447)(★San Juan)	92,429
Carolina (▲177,806)(★San Juan)	162,404
Guaynabo (▲92,886)(★San Juan)	73,385
Mayagüez (★200,600)	83,010
Ponce (★232,700)	159,151
• SAN JUAN (★1,877,000)	426,832

QATAR / Qaṭar

1986 C	369,079
• AD-DAWHAH (DOHA) (★310,000)	217,294
Ar-Rayyān (★Ad-Dawḥah)	91,996

REUNION / Réunion

1982 C	515,814
• SAINT-DENIS (▲109,072)	84,400

ROMANIA / România

1992 C	22,760,449
Alba Iulia	71,254
Alexandria	58,582
Arad	190,088
Bacău	204,495
Baia Mare	148,815
Bîrlad	77,009
Bistrița	87,793
Botoșani	126,204
Brăila	234,706
Brașov	323,835
• BUCUREȘTI (BUCHAREST) (★2,300,000)	2,064,474
Buzău	148,247
Călărași	76,886
Cluj-Napoca	328,008
Constanța	350,476
Craiova	303,520
Deva	78,366
Drobeta-Turnu Severin	115,526
Focșani	101,296
Galați	325,788
Giurgiu	74,236
Hunedoara	81,198
Iași	342,994
Lugoj	50,983
Medgidia	46,586
Mediaș	64,488
Miercurea-Ciuc	46,029
Onești	59,008
Oradea	220,848
Petroșani (★76,000)	52,532
Piatra Neamț	123,175
Pitești	179,479
Ploiești (★310,000)	252,073
Reșița	96,798
Rîmnicu Vîlcea	113,356
Roman	80,192
Satu Mare	131,859
Sfîntu-Gheorghe	68,070
Sibiu	169,696
Slatina	85,336
Slobozia	55,614
Suceava	114,355
Tecuci	46,735
Timișoara	334,278
Tîrgoviște	97,876
Tîrgu Jiu	98,267
Tîrgu-Mureș	163,625
Tulcea	97,500
Turda	61,135
Vaslui	80,151
Zalău	68,322

RUSSIA

1991 E	148,542,700
Abakan	157,300
Achtubinsk	50,800
Ačinsk	122,000
Alapajevsk	50,300
Alatyr'	47,700
Aleksandrov	68,600
Aleksin	74,200
Al'metjevsk	132,700
Amursk	59,600
Anapa	55,900
Angarsk	268,500
Anžero-Sudžensk	107,000
Apatity	88,600
Archangel'sk	420,400
Armavir	162,200
Arsenjev	71,200
Art'om	70,100
Arzamas	111,800
Asbest	84,900
Astrachan'	511,900
Azov	80,700
Balakovo	201,300
Balašicha (★Moskva)	137,600
Balašov	97,300
Barnaul (★673,000)	606,800
Batajsk (★Rostov-na-Donu)	93,300
Belebej	54,500
Belgorod	311,400

▲ Población de un municipio, comuna o distrito entero, incluyendo sus áreas rurales.
• Ciudad más grande de un país.
★ Población o designación de un área metropolitana, incluyendo los suburbios.
C Censo. **E** Estimado oficial. **U** Estimado no oficial.

▲ Population d'une municipalité, d'une commune ou d'un district, zone rurale incluse.
• Ville la plus peuplée du pays.
★ Population de l'agglomération (ou nom de la zone métropolitaine englobante).
C Recensement. **E** Estimation officielle. **U** Estimation non officielle.

▲ População de um municipio, comuna ou distrito, inclusive as respectivas áreas rurais.
• Maior cidade de um país.
★ População ou indicação de uma área metropolitana.
C Censo. **E** Estimativa oficial. **U** Estimativa não oficial.

Belogorsk	74,300
Beloreč̌ensk	51,900
Beloreck	73,100
Belovo	92,900
Berdsk (★Novosibirsk)	80,400
Berezniki	199,700
Berezovskiy	51,900
Bijsk	234,600
Birobidžan	86,300
Blagoveščensk	211,000
Bor (★Nižnij Novgorod)	64,500
Borisoglebsk	72,100
Boroviči	62,800
Br'ansk	458,900
Bratsk	259,400
Bud'onnovsk	57,500
Bugul'ma	91,100
Buguruslan	54,100
Buj	62,900
Bujnaksk	57,900
Buzuluk	85,100
Čajkovskij	88,300
Čapajevsk	96,000
Čebarkul'	50,700
Čeboksary	436,000
Čechov	60,200
Čel'abinsk (★1,325,000)	1,148,300
Čeremchovo	73,600
Čerepovec	315,900
Čerkessk	117,000
Černogorsk	79,700
Chabarovsk	613,300
Chasavjurt	72,800
Chimki (★Moskva)	135,500
Cholmsk	51,800
Čistopol'	66,600
Čita	376,300
Čusovoj	58,000
Derbent	81,500
Dimitrovgrad	127,000
Dmitrov	65,600
Dolgoprudnyj (★Moskva)	71,100
Domodedovo (★Moskva)	56,300
Doneck	48,900
Dubna	67,200
Dzeržinsk (★Nižnij Novgorod)	286,700
Elektrostal'	153,000
Elista	92,700
Engel's (★Saratov)	183,600
Fr'azino (★Moskva)	54,000
Furmanov	45,900
Gatčina (★Sankt-Peterburg)	80,600
Gelendžik	48,600
Georgijevsk	63,700
Georgiu-Dež	54,600
Glazov	106,000
Gorno-Altajsk	47,500
Gr'azi	47,700
Groznyj	401,400
Gubkin	76,400
Gukovo	67,700
Gus'-Chrustal'nyj	77,000
Inta	60,900
Irbit	51,300
Irkutsk	640,500
Išim	65,900
Išimbaj	71,000
Iskitim	68,700
Ivanovo	482,200
Ivantejevka (★Moskva)	53,200
Iževsk	646,800
Jakutsk	193,300
Jarcevo	54,000
Jaroslavl'	638,100
Jefremov	56,600
Jegorjevsk	74,200
Jejsk	79,400
Jelec	121,300
Jelizovo	48,700
Jermolajevo	65,600
Jessentuki	86,300
Joškar-Ola	247,800
Jurga	94,000
Južno-Sachalinsk	164,000
Kaliningrad (Königsberg)	408,100
Kaliningrad (★Moskva)	161,500
Kaluga	315,500
Kamensk-Šachtinskij	73,100
Kamensk-Ural'skij	208,700
Kamyšin	124,400
Kanaš	56,100
Kandalakša	54,300
Kansk	109,900
Kaspijsk	61,900
Kazan' (★1,165,000)	1,107,300
Kemerovo	520,700
Kimry	62,000
Kinel'	33,800
Kinešma	104,900
Kingisepp	50,600
Kiriši	53,100
Kirov	491,200
Kirovo-Čepeck	95,600
Kisel'ovsk (★Prokopjevsk)	126,900
Kislovodsk	116,800
Kizel	36,600
Klimovsk (★Moskva)	57,600
Klin	95,100
Klincy	71,200
Kogalym	48,200
Kol'čugino	45,600
Kolomna	163,500
Kolpino (★Sankt-Peterburg)	144,500
Komsomol'sk-na-Amure	318,800
Kopejsk (★Čel'abinsk)	78,300
Korkino	44,800
Korsakov	45,300
Kostroma	281,800
Kotlas	68,900
Kovrov	161,900
Krasnodar	631,200
Krasnogorsk (★Moskva)	91,700
Krasnojarsk	924,400
Krasnokamensk	57,800
Krasnokamsk	67,000
Krasnoturjinsk	67,200
Krasnoufimsk	46,100
Krasnoural'sk	34,800
Krasnyj Sulin	43,200
Kropotkin	76,600
Krymsk	51,100
Kstovo (★Nižnij Novgorod)	65,300
Kujbyšev	51,600
Kungur	81,800
Kurgan	363,800
Kursk	433,300
Kušva	43,300
Kuzneck	100,000
Kyzyl	88,000
Labinsk	58,600
Leninogorsk	63,300
Leninsk-Kuzneckij	133,400
Lesosibirsk	69,300
Lipeck	460,100
Livny	52,600
Lobn'a (★Moskva)	61,000
L'ubercy (★Moskva)	164,900
Lys'va	77,800
Lytkarino (★Moskva)	51,700
Machačkala	333,500
Magadan	154,900
Magnitogorsk	443,900
Majkop	152,500
Mcensk	49,200
Meleuz	55,200
Meždurečensk	107,500
Miass	169,700
Michajlovka	58,700
Mičurinsk	109,400
Mineral'nyje Vody	72,500
Minusinsk	74,200
Mončegorsk	68,100
Moršansk	50,500
• MOSKVA (MOSCOW) (★13,150,000)	8,801,500
Murmansk	472,900
Murom	126,000
Mytišči (★Moskva)	153,900
Naberežnyje Čelny	510,100
Nachodka	164,500
Nadym	52,200
Nal'čik	240,600
Naro-Fominsk	58,800
Nazarovo	65,200
Neftejugansk	65,500
Ner'ungri	77,200
Nevinnomyssk	123,300
Nikolo-Berjozovka	110,500
Nižnekamsk	196,200
Nižnevartovsk	247,400
Nižnij Novgorod (Gorky) (★2,025,000)	1,445,000
Nižnij Tagil	439,200
Njagan	59,800
Noginsk	122,700
Nojabr'sk	88,900
Noril'sk	169,000
Novgorod	233,800
Novoaltajsk (★Barnaul)	55,200
Novočeboksarsk	119,300
Novočerkassk	188,500
Novodvinsk	50,300
Novokujbyševsk (★Samara)	113,200
Novokuzneck	601,900
Novomoskovsk, Tula oblast' (★365,000)	145,800
Novorossijsk	188,600
Novošachtinsk	107,300
Novosibirsk (★1,600,000)	1,446,300
Novotroick	107,600
Novyj Urengoj	93,600
Obninsk	103,700
Odincovo (★Moskva)	128,400
Okt'abr'skij	106,700
Omsk (★1,190,000)	1,166,800
Orechovo-Zujevo (★205,000)	136,800
Orel	345,200
Orenburg	556,500
Orsk	272,200
Osinniki	63,200
Otradnyj	49,600
Partizansk	50,000
P'atigorsk	131,100
Pavlovo	72,200
Pavlovskij Posad	70,800
Pečora	65,500
Penza	551,100
Perm' (★1,180,000)	1,110,400
Pervoural'sk	143,700
Petrodvorec (★Sankt-Peterburg)	83,800
Petropavlovsk-Kamčatskij	272,900
Petrozavodsk	277,400
Podol'sk (★Moskva)	208,500
Polevskoj	71,900
Prochladnyj	58,500
Prokopjevsk (★410,000)	272,600
Pskov	207,500
Puškin (★Sankt-Peterburg)	95,300
Puškino (★Moskva)	75,800
Ramenskoje	88,800
Rasskazovo	49,800
R'azan'	527,200
Reutov (★Moskva)	68,900
Revda	66,000
Roslavl'	60,700
Rossoš'	58,900
Rostov-na-Donu (★1,165,000)	1,027,600
Rubcovsk	172,500
Ruzajevka	52,100
Rybinsk	252,600
Ržev	70,900
Šachty	227,700
Šadrinsk	87,500
Safonovo	56,300
Sajanogorsk	53,000
Salavat	151,400
Sal'sk	61,700
Samara (★1,505,000)	1,257,300
Sankt-Peterburg (Saint Petersburg) (★5,525,000)	4,466,800
Saransk	319,600
Sarapul	110,600
Saratov (★1,155,000)	911,100
Satka	51,100
Ščelkovo (★Moskva)	109,600
Ščokino	68,800
Šelechov	48,600
Sergijev Posad (Zagorsk)	115,600
Serov	103,800
Serpuchov	141,200
Severodvinsk	251,500
Severomorsk	66,200
Slav'ansk-Na-Kubani	58,500
Smolensk	349,800
Soči	341,500
Sokol	46,700
Solikamsk	110,200
Solnečnogorsk (★Moskva)	56,700
Sosnovyj Bor	56,700
Spassk-Dal'nij	61,100
Staryj Oskol	181,900
Stavropol'	328,300
Sterlitamak	252,200
Stupino	74,600
Šuja	69,000
Surgut	261,100
Sverdlovsk, Sverdlovsk oblast' (★1,620,000)	1,375,400
Svetlogorsk	71,600
Svobodnyj	80,900
Syktyvkar	224,000
Syzran'	174,900
Taganrog	293,600
Talnach	65,600
Tambov	309,600
Temirtau	213,100
Tichoreck	67,600
Tichvin	71,800
Tobol'sk	96,800
Toljatti	654,700
Tomsk	505,600
Toržok	50,500
Troick	89,800
Tuapse	63,800
Tujmazy	59,800
Tula (★640,000)	543,600
Tulun	53,700
T'umen'	494,200
Tver'	455,300
Tyndinskij	64,700
Uchta	112,100
Ufa (★1,118,000)	1,097,000
Uglič	40,000
Ulan-Ude	362,400
Uljanovsk	648,300
Usinsk	52,300
Usolje-Sibirskoje	106,800
Ussurijsk	160,200
Ust'-Ilimsk	112,200
Ust'-Kut	61,800
Uzlovaja (★Novomoskovsk)	34,000
V'az'ma	59,900
Velikije Luki	115,400
Verchn'aja Pyšma (★Sverdlovsk)	53,500
Verchn'aja Salda	55,100
Vičuga	49,700
Vidnoje (★Moskva)	56,900
Vladikavkaz	306,000
Vladimir	355,600
Vladivostok	648,000
Volchov	50,100
Volgodonsk	180,700
Volgograd (Stalingrad) (★1,360,000)	1,007,300
Vologda	289,200
Vol'sk	65,500
Volžsk	62,000
Volžskij (★Volgograd)	278,400
Vorkuta	117,400
Voronež	900,000
Voskresensk	81,400
Votkinsk	104,500
Vyborg	81,100
Vyksa	62,200
Vyšnij Voločok	64,600
Zarinsk	51,800
Zelenograd (★Moskva)	162,700
Železnodorožnyj (★Moskva)	99,300
Železnogorsk	89,200
Zel'onodol'sk	97,000
Žigulevsk	45,000
Zlatoust	208,200
Žukovskij	101,300

RWANDA

1991 C	6,762,145
• KIGALI (1990C)	232,733

SAINT HELENA

1987 C	5,644
• JAMESTOWN	1,413

SAINT KITTS AND NEVIS

1980 C	44,404
• BASSETERRE	14,725
Charlestown	1,771

SAINT LUCIA

1987 E	142,342
• CASTRIES	53,933

SAINT PIERRE AND MIQUELON / Saint-Pierre-et-Miquelon

1982 C	6,041
• SAINT-PIERRE	5,371

SAINT VINCENT AND THE GRENADINES

1987 E	112,589
• KINGSTOWN (★28,936)	19,028

SAN MARINO

1988 E	22,304
• SAN MARINO	2,777

SAO TOME AND PRINCIPE / São Tomé e Príncipe

1970 C	73,631
• SÃO TOMÉ	17,380

SAUDI ARABIA / Al-'Arabīyah as-Su'ūdīyah

1980 E	9,229,000
Abhā (1974C)	30,150
Ad-Dammām	200,000
Al-Hufūf (1974C)	101,271
Al-Khubar (1974C)	48,817
Al-Madīnah (Medina)	290,000
Al-Mubarraz (1974C)	54,325
AR-RIYĀD (RIYADH)	1,250,000
At-Tā'if	300,000
Buraydah (1974C)	69,940
Hā'il (1974C)	40,502
• Jiddah (Jeddah)	1,300,000
Khamīs Mushayt (1974C)	49,581
Makkah (Mecca)	550,000
Najran (1974C)	47,501
Tabūk (1974C)	74,825

SENEGAL / Sénégal

1988 C	6,892,720
• DAKAR	1,490,450
Diourbel	77,548
Kaolack	152,007
Saint-Louis	160,689
Thiès	184,902
Ziguinchor	124,283

SEYCHELLES

1984 E	64,718
• VICTORIA	23,000

SIERRA LEONE

1985 C	3,515,812
Bo	59,768
• FREETOWN (★525,000)	469,776
Kenema	52,473
Koidu	82,474
Makeni	49,038

SINGAPORE

1990 C	2,690,100
• SINGAPORE (★3,025,000)	2,690,100

SLOVAKIA / Slovenská Republika

1991 C	5,268,935
Banská Bystrica	85,007
• BRATISLAVA	441,453
Komárno	37,370
Košice	234,840
Martin	58,338
Michalovce	38,866
Nitra	89,888
Nové Zámky	42,851
Poprad	52,878
Považská Bystrica	39,801
Prešov	87,788
Prievidza	53,393
Spišská Nová Ves	39,187
Trenčín	56,733
Trnava	71,641
Žilina	83,853
Zvolen	41,935

SLOVENIA / Slovenija

1987 E	1,936,606
• LJUBLJANA (▲316,607)	233,200
Maribor (▲187,651)	107,400

SOLOMON ISLANDS

1986 C	285,176
• HONIARA	30,413

SOMALIA / Somaliya

1984 E	5,423,000
Berbera	65,000
Hargeysa	70,000
Kismaayo	70,000
Marka	60,000
• MUQDISHO	600,000

SOUTH AFRICA / Suid-Afrika

1985 C	23,385,645
Alberton (★Johannesburg)	66,155
Alexandra (★Johannesburg)	67,276
Atteridgeville (★Pretoria)	73,439
Bellville (★Cape Town)	68,915
Benoni (★Johannesburg)	94,926
Bloemfontein (★235,000)	104,381
Boksburg (★Johannesburg)	110,832
Botshabelo (★Bloemfontein)	95,625
Brakpan (★Johannesburg)	46,416
CAPE TOWN (KAAPSTAD) (★1,790,000)	776,617
Carletonville (★120,499)	97,874
Daveyton (★Johannesburg)	99,056
Diepmeadow (★Johannesburg)	192,682
Durban (★1,550,000)	634,301
East London (Oos-Londen) (★320,000)	85,699
Edendale (★Pietermaritzburg)	47,001
Elsies River (★Cape Town)	70,067
Empumalanga (★Durban)	47,938
Evaton (★Vereeniging)	52,559
Galeshewe (★Kimberley)	63,238
Germiston (★Johannesburg)	116,718
Grassy Park (★Cape Town)	50,193
Guguleto (★Cape Town)	63,893
• Johannesburg (★3,650,000)	632,369
Kagiso (★Johannesburg)	50,647
Katlehong (★Johannesburg)	137,745
Kayamnandi (★Port Elizabeth)	220,548
Kempton Park (★Johannesburg)	87,721
Kimberley (★145,000)	74,061
Klerksdorp (★205,000)	48,947
Krugersdorp (★Johannesburg)	73,767
Kwa Makuta (★Durban)	71,378
Kwa Mashu (★Durban)	111,593
Kwanobuhle (★Port Elizabeth)	52,376
Kwa-Thema (★Johannesburg)	78,640
Ladysmith (★31,670)	25,102
Lekoa (Shapeville) (★Vereeniging)	218,392
Madadeni (★Newcastle)	65,832
Mamelodi (★Pretoria)	127,033
Mangaung (★Bloemfontein)	79,851
Ntuzuma (★Durban)	61,834
Nyanga (★Cape Town)	148,882
Ozisweni (★Newcastle)	51,934
Paarl (★Cape Town)	63,671
Parow (★Cape Town)	60,294
Pietermaritzburg (★230,000)	133,809
Pinetown (★Durban)	55,770
Port Elizabeth (★690,000)	272,844
PRETORIA (★960,000)	443,059
Randburg (★Johannesburg)	74,347
Randfontein (★Johannesburg)	43,763
Roodepoort-Maraisburg (★Johannesburg)	141,764
Sandton (★Johannesburg)	86,089
Soshanguve (★Pretoria)	68,598
Soweto (★Johannesburg)	521,948
Springs (★Johannesburg)	68,235
Tembisa (★Johannesburg)	149,282
Thabong (★Welkom)	43,470
Uitenhage (★Port Elizabeth)	54,987
Umlazi (★Durban)	194,933
Vanderbijlpark (★Vereeniging)	59,865
Vereeniging (★525,000)	60,584
Verwoerdburg (★Pretoria)	49,891
Vosloosrus (★Johannesburg)	52,061
Walvisbaai (Walvis Bay) (★16,607)	9,687
Welkom (★215,000)	54,488
Westonaria (★Johannesburg)	46,523

▲ Population of an entire municipality, commune, or district, including rural area.
• Largest city in country.
★ Population or designation of the metropolitan area, including suburbs.
C Census. **E** Official estimate. **U** Unofficial estimate.

▲ Bevölkerung eines ganzen städtischen Verwaltungsgebietes, eines Kommunalbezirkes oder eines Distrikts, einschliesslich ländlicher Gebiete.
• Grösste Stadt des Landes.
★ Bevölkerung oder Bezeichnung der Stadtregion einschliesslich Vororte.
C Volkszählung. **E** Offizielle Schätzung. **U** Inoffizielle Schätzung.

SPAIN / España

1988 E	39,217,804
Alacant (Alicante)	261,051
Albacete	125,997
Alcalá de Guadaira	50,935
Alcalá de Henares (★Madrid)	150,021
Alcobendas (★Madrid)	73,455
Alcoi (Alcoy)	66,074
Alcorcón (★Madrid)	139,796
Algeciras	99,528
Almería	157,644
Avilés (★131,000)	87,811
Badajoz (▲122,407)	106,400
Badalona (★Barcelona)	225,229
Baracaldo (★Bilbao)	113,502
Barcelona (★4,040,000)	1,714,355
Bilbao (★985,000)	384,733
Burgos	160,561
Cáceres	71,598
Cádiz (★240,000)	156,591
Cartagena (▲172,710)	70,000
Castelló de la Plana	131,809
Ciudad Real	56,300
Córdoba	302,301
Cornellà de Llobregat (★Barcelona)	86,866
Coslada (★Madrid)	68,765
Donostia (San Sebastián) (★285,000)	177,622
Dos Hermanas (▲68,456)	60,600
Elda	56,756
El Ferrol del Caudillo (★129,000)	86,503
El Prat de Llobregat (★Barcelona)	64,193
El Puerto de Santa María (▲62,285)	49,900
Elx (Elche) (▲180,256)	158,300
Fuenlabrada (★Madrid)	128,872
Gernika-Lumo (Guernica y Luno) (▲17,836) (1981C)	12,214
Getafe (★Madrid)	135,367
Gijón	262,156
Granada	263,334
Granollers (★Barcelona)	49,045
Guadalajara	61,309
Huelva	137,826
Irún	54,886
Jaén	106,435
Jerez de la Frontera (▲183,007)	156,200
La Coruña	248,862
La Línea	60,956
Las Palmas de Gran Canaria (▲366,347)	319,000
Leganés (★Madrid)	168,403
León (★159,000)	136,558
L'Hospitalet de Llobregat (★Barcelona)	278,449
Linares	58,622
Lleida (Lérida) (▲109,795)	91,500
Logroño	119,038
Lugo (▲78,795)	68,700
• MADRID (★4,650,000)	3,102,846
Málaga	574,456
Manresa	65,607
Mataró	100,817
Mérida	52,368
Móstoles (★Madrid)	181,648
Murcia (▲314,124)	149,800
Orense	106,042
Oviedo (▲190,073)	168,900
Palencia	76,692
Palma (▲314,608)	249,000
Pamplona	180,598
Parla (★Madrid)	66,253
Portugalete (★Bilbao)	57,813
Puertollano	52,284
Reus	83,800
Rubí (★Barcelona)	48,807
Sabadell (★Barcelona)	189,489
Salamanca	159,342
San Baudilio de Llobrega (★Barcelona)	77,502
San Cristóbal de la Laguna (▲111,533)	25,900
San Fernando (★Cádiz)	81,975
San Sebastián de los Reyes (★Madrid)	51,653
Santa Coloma de Gramanet (★Barcelona)	136,042
Santa Cruz de Tenerife	215,228
Santander (▲190,795)	166,800
Santiago de Compostela (▲88,110)	68,800
Santurce-Antiguo (★Bilbao)	52,334
Segovia	54,402
Sevilla (★945,000)	663,132
Talavera de la Reina	68,158
Tarragona (▲109,586)	63,500
Tarrasa (★Barcelona)	161,410
Toledo	59,551
Torrejón de Ardoz (★Madrid)	83,267
Torrent (★València)	55,751
València (★1,270,000)	743,933
Valladolid	331,461
Vigo (▲271,128)	179,500
Vitoria (Gasteiz)	204,264
Zamora	62,047
Zaragoza	582,239

SPANISH NORTH AFRICA / Plazas de Soberanía en el Norte de África

1988 E	122,905
• Ceuta	67,188
Melilla	55,717

SRI LANKA

1989 E	16,806,000
Battaramulla (★Colombo) (1981C)	56,535
Batticaloa	50,000
• COLOMBO (★2,050,000)	612,000
Dehiwala-Mount Lavinia (★Colombo)	193,000
Galle	83,000
Jaffna	128,000
Kandy	103,000
Moratuwa (★Colombo)	166,000
Negombo	64,000
SRI JAYAWARDENEPURA (KOTTE) (★Colombo)	108,000
Trincomalee	49,000

SUDAN / As-Sūdān

1983 C	20,594,197
Al-Fāshir	84,298
• AL-KHARṬŪM (★1,450,000)	473,597
Al-Kharṭūm Baḥrī (★Al-Kharṭūm)	340,857
Al-Qaḍārif	116,876
Al-Ubayyiḍ	137,582
ʿAṭbarah	72,836
Būr Sūdān (Port Sudan)	206,038
Jūbā	84,377
Kassalā	141,429
Kūstī	89,135
Nyala	111,693
Umm Durmān (Omdurman) (★Al-Kharṭūm)	526,192
Wad Madanī	145,015
Wāw	90,960

SURINAME

1988 E	392,000
• PARAMARIBO (★296,000)	241,000
Wanica (★Paramaribo)	55,000

SWAZILAND

1986 C	712,131
LOBAMBA	
Manzini (★30,000)	18,084
• MBABANE	38,290

SWEDEN / Sverige

1991 E	8,590,630
Borås	101,766
Eskilstuna	89,765
Gävle (▲88,568)	67,900
Göteborg (★710,894)	433,042
Halmstad (▲80,061)	51,300
Helsingborg	109,267
Huddinge (★Stockholm)	73,829
Järfälla (★Stockholm)	56,359
Jönköping	111,486
Karlstad	76,467
Linköping	122,268
Luleå	68,412
Lund (★Malmö)	87,681
Malmö (★445,000)	233,887
Mölndal (★Göteborg)	52,028
Nacka (★Stockholm)	64,056
Norrköping	120,522
Örebro	120,944
Södertälje (★Stockholm)	81,786
Sollentuna (★Stockholm)	51,377
Solna (★Stockholm)	51,841
• STOCKHOLM (★1,449,972)	674,452
Sundsvall (▲93,808)	50,800
Täby (★Stockholm)	56,714
Trollhättan	51,047
Tumba (★Stockholm)	68,542
Umeå (▲91,258)	59,500
Uppsala	167,508
Västerås	119,761
Växjö (▲69,547)	46,000

SWITZERLAND / Schweiz / Suisse / Svizzera

1990 E	6,673,850
Aarau (★58,903)	15,881
Arbon (★41,639)	12,284
Baden (★71,769)	14,545
Basel (Bâle) (★575,000)	169,587
BERN (BERNE) (★298,363)	134,393
Biel (Bienne) (★83,133)	52,023
Fribourg (Freiburg) (★59,141)	33,962
Genève (Geneva) (★470,000)	165,404
Lausanne (★263,442)	122,600
Locarno (★42,350)	14,149
Lugano (★94,800)	26,055
Luzern (★163,026)	59,115
Neuchâtel (★66,457)	32,509
Sankt Gallen (★126,845)	73,191
Schaffhausen (★53,501)	33,956
Thun (★78,978)	37,707
Vevey (★65,074)	15,207
Winterthur (★110,000) (1991E)	86,496
Zug (★68,698)	21,467
• Zürich (★870,000) (1991E)	347,634

SYRIA / Sūrīyah

1988 E	11,338,000
Al-Ḥasakah (1981C)	73,426
Al-Lādhiqīyah (Latakia)	249,000
Al-Qāmishlī	126,236
Ar-Raqqah	113,000
Darʿā (1981C)	49,534
Dārayyā (★Dimashq)	53,204
Dayr az-Zawr	112,000
• DIMASHQ (DAMASCUS) (★2,000,000)	1,326,000
Dūmā (★Dimashq)	66,130
Ḥalab (Aleppo) (★1,335,000)	1,261,000
Ḥamāh	222,000
Ḥimṣ	447,000
Idlib (1981C)	51,682
Jaramānah (★Dimashq)	96,681
Kābir aṣ Ṣaghīr	47,728
Madīnat ath Thawrah	58,151
Salamīyah	46,844
Ṭarṭūs (1981C)	52,589

TAIWAN / T'aiwan

1991 E	20,352,966
Changhua (▲215,224)	165,000
Chiai (1992E)	258,713
Chilung (1992E)	357,000
Chungho (★T'aipei)	374,339
Chungli	269,804
Chutung (1988E)	104,797
Fangshan (★Kaohsiung)	290,777
Fengyüan (▲151,642)	121,100
Hsichih (★T'aipei) (1980C)	70,031
Hsinchu (1992E)	330,576
Hsinchuang (★T'aipei)	299,174
Hsintien (★T'aipei)	225,517
Hualien	107,552
Ilan (▲81,751) (1980C)	70,900
Kangshan (1980C)	78,049
Kaohsiung (★1,845,000) (1992E)	1,401,239
Lotung (1980C)	57,925
Lukang (1980C)	72,019
Miaoli (1980C)	81,500
Nant'ou (1980C)	84,038
P'ingchen (★T'aipei)	147,030
P'ingtung (▲210,801)	172,400
Sanchung (★T'aipei)	375,996
Shulin (★T'aipei)	111,993
Tach'i (1980C)	67,209
T'aichung (1992E)	785,182
T'ainan (1992E)	692,116
• T'AIPEI (★6,130,000) (1992)	2,706,453
T'aipeihsien (★T'aipei)	538,954
T'aitung (▲108,196)	79,100
Taoyüan	241,263
T'oufen (1980C)	66,536
T'uch'eng (▲136,928)T'aipei)	80,300
Yangmei (1980C)	84,353
Yüanlin (▲121,251)	53,200
Yungho (★T'aipei)	249,736
Yungkang (▲136,705)	70,900

TAJIKISTAN

1991 E	5,358,300
Chudžand (Leninabad)	164,500
• DUŠANBE	582,400
Kul'ab	79,300
Kurgan-T'ube	58,400

TANZANIA

1984 E	21,062,000
Arusha	69,000
• DAR ES SALAAM	1,300,000
Dodoma	54,000
Iringa	67,000
Kigoma (1978C)	50,044
Mbeya	93,000
Morogoro	72,000
Moshi	62,000
Mtwara (1978C)	48,510
Mwanza (1978C)	110,611
Tabora	87,000
Tanga	121,000
Ujiji (1967C)	21,369
Zanzibar (1985E)	133,000

THAILAND / Prathet Thai

1988 E	54,960,917
Chiang Mai	164,030
Chon Buri	47,286
Hat Yai	138,046
Khon Kaen	131,340
• KRUNG THEP (BANGKOK) (★7,025,000) (1989E)	5,845,152
Nakhon Ratchasima	204,982
Nakhon Sawan	105,220
Nakhon Si Thammarat	72,407
Nonthaburi (★Krung Thep)	218,354
Pattaya	56,402
Phitsanulok	77,675
Phra Nakhon Si Ayutthaya	60,847
Sakon Nakhon	25,110
Samut Prakan (★Krung Thep)	73,327
Samut Sakhon	53,984
Saraburi	61,206
Songkhla	84,433
Trang	48,042
Ubon Ratchathani	100,374
Udon Thani	81,202
Yala	67,383

TOGO

1987 E	3,148,000
• LOMÉ	500,000
Sokodé	55,000

TOKELAU

1986 C	1,690

TONGA

1986 C	94,535
• NUKUʿALOFA	21,265

TRANSKEI

1987 E	3,081,770
• UMTATA (1978E)	30,000

TRINIDAD AND TOBAGO

1990 C	1,234,388
• PORT OF SPAIN (★370,000)	50,878
San Fernando (★75,000)	30,092

TUNISIA / Tunis / Tunisie

1984 C	6,975,450
Ariana (★Tunis)	98,655
Bardo (★Tunis)	65,669
Ben Arous (★Tunis)	52,105
Bizerte	94,509
Gabès	92,258
Gafsa	60,970
Hammam Lif (★Tunis)	47,009
Houmt Essouk	92,269
Kairouan	72,254
Kasserine	47,606
La Goulette (★Tunis)	61,609
Menzel Bourguiba	51,399
Sfax (★310,000)	231,911
Sousse (★160,000)	83,509
• TUNIS (★1,225,000)	596,654
Zarzis	49,063

TURKEY / Türkiye

1990 C	56,473,035
Adana	916,150
Adapazarı	171,225
Adıyaman	100,045
Afyon	95,643
Ağrı	58,038
Akhisar	73,944
Aksaray	90,698
Akşehir	51,746
Alanya	52,460
Amasya	57,288
ANKARA (★2,650,000)	2,559,471
Antakya (Antioch)	123,871
Antalya	378,208
Aydın	107,011
Bafra	65,600
Balıkesir	170,589
Bandırma	77,444
Batman	147,347
Bilecik	23,273
Bolu	60,789
Burdur	56,432
Bursa	834,576
Çanakkale	53,995
Ceyhan	85,308
Cizre	50,023
Çorlu	74,681
Çorum	116,810
Darıca	53,560
Denizli	204,118
Diyarbakır	381,144
Düzce	61,878
Edirne	102,345
Elazığ	204,603
Elbistan	54,741
Ereğli, Konya prov.	74,283
Ereğli, Zonguldak prov.	63,987
Erzincan	91,772
Erzurum	242,391
Esenyurt (★İstanbul)	70,280
Eskişehir	413,082
Gaziantep	603,434
Gebze (★İstanbul)	159,116
Gelibolu	18,670
Gemlik	50,237
Giresun	67,604
Gölcük	64,911
Gümüşhane	26,014
Hakkâri	30,407
İçel (Mersin)	422,357
İnegöl	71,120
İskenderun	154,807
Isparta	112,117
• İstanbul (★7,550,000)	6,620,241
İzmir (★1,900,000)	1,757,414
İzmit	256,882
Kadirli	55,061
Kahramanmaraş	228,129
Karabük	105,373
Karaman	76,525
Kars	78,455
Kastamonu	51,560
Kayseri	421,362
Kilis	82,882
Kırıkhan	68,601
Kırıkkale	185,431
Kırşehir	73,538
Kızıltepe	60,134
Konya	513,346
Körfez	65,786
Kozan	54,451
Kütahya	130,994
Lüleburgaz	52,384
Malatya	281,776
Manisa	158,928
Mardin	53,005
Muş	44,019
Nazilli	80,277
Nevşehir	52,719
Niğde	55,035
Nizip	58,604
Nusaybin	49,671
Ödemiş	51,620
Ordu	102,107
Osmaniye	123,307
Polatlı	60,158
Rize	52,031
Salihli	70,861
Samsun	303,979
Şanlıurfa	276,528
Siirt	68,320
Silvan (Miyafarkin)	59,865
Sinop	25,537
Sivas	221,512
Siverek	63,049
Söke	50,866
Soma	49,977
Sultanbeyli (★İstanbul)	82,298
Tarsus	187,508
Tatvan	54,071
Tekirdağ	80,442
Tokat	83,058
Trabzon	143,941
Tunceli	24,513
Turgutlu	73,634
Turhal	68,384
Uşak	105,270
Van	153,111
Viranşehir	57,461
Yalova (★İstanbul)	65,823
Yozgat	50,335
Zonguldak (★220,000)	116,725

TURKMENISTAN

1991 E	3,714,100
• AŠCHABAD (ASHGABAT)	412,200
Čardžou	166,400
Krasnovodsk	59,500
Mary	94,900
Nebit-Dag	89,100
Tašauz	117,000

TURKS AND CAICOS ISLANDS

1990 C	11,465
• GRAND TURK	3,691

TUVALU

1979 C	7,349
• FUNAFUTI	2,191

UGANDA

1991 C	16,582,700
Jinja	60,979
• KAMPALA	773,463
Masaka	49,070
Mbale	53,634

UKRAINE / Ukrayina

1991 E	5,194,440
Achtyrka	52,300
Alčevsk (★Stachanov)	126,000
Aleksandrija	104,900
Antracit (★Krasnyj Luč)	72,800
Art'omovsk	90,800
Belaja Cerkov'	204,400
Belgorod-Dnestrovskij	56,800
Berd'ansk	138,700
Berdičev	93,400
Borispol' (★Kijev)	52,700
Br'anka (★Stachanov)	64,500
Brovary (★Kijev)	84,800
Čerkassy	302,200
Černigov	305,700
Černovcy	258,800
Červonograd	74,000

▲ Población de un municipio, comuna o distrito entero, incluyendo sus áreas rurales.
• Ciudad más grande de un país.
★ Población o designación de un área metropolitana, incluyendo los suburbios.
C Censo. **E** Estimado oficial. **U** Estimado no oficial.

▲ Population d'une municipalité, d'une commune ou d'un district, zone rurale incluse.
• Ville la plus peuplée du pays.
★ Population de l'agglomération (ou nom de la zone métropolitaine englobante).
C Recensement. **E** Estimation officielle. **U** Estimation non officielle.

▲ População de um municipio, comuna ou distrito, inclusive as respectivas áreas rurais.
• Maior cidade de um país.
★ População ou indicação de uma área metropolitana.
C Censo. **E** Estimativa oficial. **U** Estimativa não oficial.

Charcyzsk (★Doneck)	69,300
Char'kov (★2,050,000)	1,622,800
Cherson	365,400
Chmel'nickij	244,500
Dimitrov (★Krasnoarmejsk)	371,800
Dneprodzeržinsk (★Dnepropetrovsk)	284,400
Dnepropetrovsk (★1,600,000)	1,189,300
Doneck (★2,125,000)	1,121,300
Drogobyč	79,200
Družkovka (★Kramatorsk)	74,400
Džankoj	54,500
Dzeržinsk (★Gorlovka)	50,500
Energodar	51,500
Fastov	54,400
Feodosija	85,600
Gorlovka (★700,000)	336,600
Iljičovsk (★Odessa)	56,000
Ivano-Frankovsk	241,000
Izmail	95,100
Iz'um	64,800
Jalta	89,300
Jenakijevo (★Gorlovka)	120,100
Jevpatorija	110,500
Kaluš	69,400
Kamenec-Podol'skij	104,900
Kerč'	178,300
• KIJEV (★3,250,000)	263,500
Kirovograd	277,900
Kolomyja	66,200
Komsomol'sk	56,000
Konotop	97,700
Konstantinovka	107,800
Korosten'	67,500
Kovel'	69,700
Kramatorsk (★515,000)	201,300
Krasnoarmejsk (★180,000)	73,300
Krasnodon (★165,000)	54,800
Krasnyj Luč (★320,000)	113,400
Kremenčug	240,600
Krivoj Rog	724,000
Lisičansk (★415,000)	126,400
Lozovaja	74,100
Lubny	60,300
Luck	209,500
Lugansk (Vorošilovgrad) (★650,000)	503,900
L'vov	802,200
Makejevka (★Doneck)	423,900
Marganec	54,700
Mariupol' (Ždanov)	521,800
Melitopol'	176,900
Mukačevo	88,000
Nežin	82,000
Nikolajev	511,600
Nikopol'	159,000
Novaja Kachovka	59,000
Novograd-Volynskij	56,100
Novomoskovsk, Dnepropetrovsk oblast'	76,600
Novovolynsk	56,400
Odessa (★1,185,000)	1,100,700
Pavlograd	134,300
Pervomajsk	83,800
Pervomajsk (★Stachanov)	52,000
Poltava	320,100
Priluki	72,900
Romny	57,700
Roven'ki	58,500
Rovno	239,300
Rubežnoje (★Lisičansk)	75,100
Šacht'orsk (★Torez)	73,100
Šepetovka	51,900
Sevastopol'	366,200
Severodoneck (★Lisičansk)	133,300
Simferopol'	352,600
Slav'ansk (★Kramatorsk)	137,100
Smela	81,200
Snežnoje (★Torez)	68,900
Šostka	95,200
Stachanov (★700,000)	112,700
Stryj	68,200
Sumy	303,300
Sverdlovsk, Vorosilovgrad oblast' (★145,000)	83,700
Svetlovodsk	57,900
Ternopol'	219,200
Torez (★320,000)	88,100
Uman'	97,700
Užgorod	122,600
Vinnica	380,900
Zaporožje	896,600
Žitomir	297,500
Žoltyje Vody	64,900

UNITED ARAB EMIRATES / Al-Imārāt al-'Arabīyah al-Muttaḥidah

1980 C	980,000
ABŪ ZABY (ABU DHABI)	242,975
Al-'Ayn	101,663
Ash-Shāriqah	125,149
• Dubayy	265,702
Ra's al-Khaymah	42,000

UNITED KINGDOM

1981 C	55,678,079

UNITED KINGDOM: ENGLAND

1981 C	46,220,955
Aldershot (★London)	53,665
Ashton-under-Lyne (★Manchester)	43,605
Aylesbury	51,999
Barnsley	76,783
Barrow-in-Furness	50,174
Basildon (★London)	94,800
Basingstoke	73,027
Bath	84,283
Bebington (★Liverpool)	62,618
Bedford	75,632
Beeston and Stapleford (★Nottingham)	64,785
Benfleet (★London)	50,783
Birkenhead (★Liverpool)	99,075
Birmingham (★2,675,000)	1,013,995
Blackburn (★221,900)	109,564
Blackpool (★280,000)	146,297
Bognor Regis	50,323
Bolton (★Manchester)	143,960
Bootle	70,860
Bournemouth (★315,000)	142,829
Bracknell (★London)	52,257
Bradford (★Leeds)	293,336
Brentwood (★London)	51,212
Brighton (★420,000)	134,581
Bristol (★630,000)	413,861
Burnley (★160,000)	76,365
Burton upon Trent	59,040
Bury (★Manchester)	61,785
Bury Saint Edmunds	30,563
Camberley see Frimley and Camberley	
Cambridge	87,111
Cannock (★Birmingham)	54,503
Canterbury	34,546
Carlisle	72,206
Carlton (★Nottingham)	46,053
Chatham (★London)	65,835
Cheadle and Gatley (★Manchester)	59,478
Chelmsford (★London)	91,109
Cheltenham	87,188
Cheshunt (★London)	49,616
Chester	80,154
Chesterfield (★127,000)	73,352
Clacton-on-Sea	39,618
Colchester	87,476
Corby	48,704
Coventry (★645,000)	318,718
Crawley (★London)	80,113
Crewe	59,097
Crosby (★Liverpool)	54,103
Darlington	85,519
Dartford (★London)	62,032
Derby (★275,000)	218,026
Dewsbury (★Leeds)	49,612
Doncaster	74,727
Dover	33,461
Dudley (★Birmingham)	186,513
Dunstable (★Luton)	48,436
Durham	38,105
Eastbourne	86,715
Eastleigh (★Southampton)	58,585
Ellesmere Port (★Liverpool)	65,829
Epsom and Ewell (★London)	65,830
Esher / Molesey (★London)	46,688
Exeter	88,235
Fareham / Portchester (★Portsmouth)	55,563
Farnborough (★London)	48,063
Folkestone	42,949
Frimley and Camberley (★London)	45,108
Gateshead (★Newcastle)	91,429
Gillingham (★London)	92,531
Gloucester (★115,000)	106,526
Gosport (★Portsmouth)	69,664
Gravesend (★London)	53,450
Grays (★London)	45,881
Greasby / Moreton (★Liverpool)	56,410
Great Yarmouth	54,777
Grimsby (★145,000)	91,532
Guildford (★London)	61,509
Halesowen (★Birmingham)	57,533
Halifax	76,675
Harlow (★London)	79,150
Harrogate	63,637
Hartlepool (★Middlesbrough)	91,749
Hastings	74,979
Havant (★Portsmouth)	50,098
Hemel Hempstead (★London)	80,110
Hereford	48,277
Hertford (★London)	21,350
High Wycombe (▲156,800)	69,575
Hove (★Brighton)	65,587
Huddersfield (▲377,400)	147,825
Huyton-with-Roby (★Liverpool)	62,011
Ipswich	129,661
Keighley (★Leeds)	49,188
Kidderminster	50,385
Kingston upon Hull (★350,000)	322,144
Kingswood (★Bristol)	54,736
Kirkby (★Liverpool)	52,825
Lancaster	43,902
Leeds (★1,540,000)	445,242
Leicester (★495,000)	324,394
Lincoln	79,980
Littlehampton	46,028
Liverpool (★1,525,000)	538,809
• LONDON (★11,100,000)	6,574,009
Loughborough	44,895
Lowestoft	59,430
Luton (★220,000)	163,209
Macclesfield	47,525
Maidenhead (★London)	59,809
Maidstone	86,067
Manchester (★2,775,000)	437,612
Mansfield (★198,000)	71,325
Margate	53,137
Middlesbrough (★580,000)	158,516
Middleton (★Manchester)	51,373
Milton Keynes	36,886
Newcastle-under-Lyme (★Stoke-on-Trent)	73,208
Newcastle upon Tyne (★1,300,000)	199,064
Northampton	154,172
Norwich (★230,000)	169,814
Nottingham (★655,000)	273,300
Nuneaton (★Coventry)	60,337
Oldbury / Smethwick (★Birmingham)	153,268
Oldham (★Manchester)	107,095
Oxford (★230,000)	113,847
Penzance	18,501
Peterborough	113,404
Plymouth (★290,000)	238,583
Poole (★Bournemouth)	122,815
Portsmouth (★485,000)	174,218
Preston (★250,000)	166,675
Ramsgate	36,678
Reading (★200,000)	194,727
Redditch (★Birmingham)	61,639
Reigate / Redhill (★London)	48,241
Rochdale (★Manchester)	97,292
Rotherham (★Sheffield)	122,374
Royal Leamington Spa (★Coventry)	56,552
Royal Tunbridge Wells	57,699
Rugby	59,039
Runcorn (★Liverpool)	63,995
Saint Albans (★London)	76,709
Saint Helens	114,397
Sale (★Manchester)	57,872
Salford (★Manchester)	96,525
Salisbury	36,890
Scarborough	36,665
Scunthorpe	79,043
Sheffield (★710,000)	470,685
Shrewsbury	57,731
Slough (★London)	106,341
Solihull (★Birmingham)	93,940
Southampton (★415,000)	211,321
Southend-on-Sea (★London)	155,720
Southport (★Liverpool)	88,596
South Shields (★Newcastle)	86,488
Stafford	60,915
Staines (★London)	51,949
Stapleford see Beeston and Stapleford	
Stevenage	74,757
Stockport (★Manchester)	135,489
Stockton-on-Tees (★Middlesbrough)	86,699
Stoke-on-Trent (★440,000)	272,446
Stourbridge (★Birmingham)	55,136
Stratford-upon-Avon	20,941
Stretford (★Manchester)	47,522
Sunderland (★Newcastle)	195,064
Sutton Coldfield (★Birmingham)	102,572
Swindon	127,348
Tamworth	63,260
Taunton	47,793
Torquay (★112,400)	54,430
Wakefield (★Leeds)	74,764
Wallasey (★Liverpool)	62,465
Walsall (★Birmingham)	177,923
Walton and Weybridge (★London)	50,031
Warrington	81,366
Washington (★Newcastle)	48,856
Waterlooville (★Portsmouth)	57,296
Watford (★London)	109,503
West Bromwich (★Birmingham)	153,725
Weston-super-Mare	60,821
Weybridge see Walton and Weybridge	
Widnes	55,973
Wigan (★Manchester)	88,725
Woking (★London)	92,667
Wolverhampton (★Birmingham)	263,501
Worcester	75,466
Worthing (★Brighton)	90,687
York (★145,000)	123,126

UNITED KINGDOM: NORTHERN IRELAND

1990 E	1,589,400
Bangor (★Belfast)	72,600
Belfast (★685,000)	295,100
Castlereagh (★Belfast)	58,100
Londonderry (Derry)	100,500
Lurgan (★63,000)	20,991
Newtownabbey (★Belfast)	72,900

UNITED KINGDOM: SCOTLAND

1990 E	5,102,400
Aberdeen	211,080
Ayr (★100,000) (1981C)	48,493
Clydebank (★Glasgow) (1981C)	51,832
Coatbridge (1981C)	50,831
Cumbernauld (★Glasgow)	50,700
Dundee	172,860
Dunfermline (★125,817) (1981C)	52,105
East Kilbride (★Glasgow)	70,500
Edinburgh (★630,000)	434,520
Falkirk (★148,171) (1981C)	36,372
Glasgow (★1,800,000)	689,210
Greenock (★101,000) (1981C)	58,436
Hamilton (★Glasgow) (1981C)	51,666
Irvine (★94,000)	56,000
Kilmarnock (★84,000) (1981C)	51,799
Kirkcaldy (★148,171) (1981C)	46,356
Motherwell (★Glasgow) (1981C)	30,616
Paisley (★Glasgow) (1981C)	84,330
Perth (1981C)	41,916
Stirling (★61,000) (1981C)	36,640

UNITED KINGDOM: WALES

1981 C	2,790,462
Cardiff (★625,000)	262,313
Cwmbran (★Newport)	44,592
Llanelli	45,336
Merthyr Tydfil	38,893
Neath (★Swansea)	48,687
Newport (★310,000)	115,896
Pontypool (★Newport)	36,064
Port Talbot (★130,000)	40,078
Rhondda (★Cardiff)	70,980
Swansea (★275,000)	172,433
Wrexham	39,929

UNITED STATES

1990 C	248,709,873

UNITED STATES: ALABAMA

1990 C	4,040,587
Anniston (★116,034)	26,623
Auburn (★61,100)	33,830
Birmingham (★907,810)	265,968
Decatur (★131,556)	48,761
Dothan (★130,964)	53,589
Florence (★131,327)	36,426
Gadsden (★99,840)	42,523
Huntsville (★238,912)	159,789
Mobile (★476,923)	196,278
Montgomery (★292,517)	187,106
Tuscaloosa (★150,522)	77,759

UNITED STATES: ALASKA

1990 C	550,043
Anchorage (★248,400)	226,338
Fairbanks (★59,500)	30,843
Juneau	26,751

UNITED STATES: ARIZONA

1990 C	3,665,228
Chandler (★Phoenix)	90,533
Glendale (★Phoenix)	148,134
Mesa (★Phoenix)	288,091
Nogales (★Nogales, Mexico)	19,489
Phoenix (★2,122,101)	900,013
Scottsdale (★Phoenix)	130,069
Tempe (★Phoenix)	141,865
Tucson (★666,880)	405,390
Yuma (★106,895)	54,923

UNITED STATES: ARKANSAS

1990 C	2,350,725
Fayetteville (★113,409)	42,099
Fort Smith (★175,911)	72,798
Hot Springs National Park (★56,500)	32,462
Jonesboro (★49,300)	46,535
Little Rock (★513,117)	175,795
North Little Rock (★Little Rock)	61,741
Pine Bluff (★85,487)	57,140

UNITED STATES: CALIFORNIA

1990 C	29,760,021
Alameda (★Oakland)	76,459
Alhambra (★Los Angeles)	82,106
Anaheim (★2,410,556)(★Los Angeles)	266,406
Antioch (★Oakland)	62,195
Arden (★Sacramento)	62,900
Bakersfield (★543,477)	174,820
Baldwin Park (★Los Angeles)	69,330
Bellflower (★Los Angeles)	61,815
Berkeley (★Oakland)	102,724
Buena Park (★Anaheim)	68,784
Burbank (★Los Angeles)	93,643
Calexico (★Mexicali, Mexico)	18,633
Camarillo (★Oxnard)	52,303
Carlsbad (★San Diego)	63,126
Carmichael (★Sacramento)	48,702
Carson (★Los Angeles)	83,995
Cerritos (★Los Angeles)	53,240
Chico (★182,120)	40,079
Chino (★Riverside)	59,682
Chula Vista (★San Diego)	135,163
Citrus Heights (★Sacramento)	112,800
Clovis (★Fresno)	50,323
Compton (★Los Angeles)	90,454
Concord (★Oakland)	111,348
Corona (★Riverside)	76,095
Costa Mesa (★Anaheim)	96,357
Cucamonga (★Riverside)	101,409
Daly City (★San Francisco)	92,311
Diamond Bar (★Los Angeles)	53,672
Downey (★Los Angeles)	91,444
East Los Angeles (★Los Angeles)	126,379
El Cajon (★San Diego)	88,693
El Monte (★Los Angeles)	106,209
El Toro (★Anaheim)	62,685
Escondido (★San Diego)	108,635
Eureka (★89,800)	27,025
Fairfield (★Vallejo)	77,211
Fontana (★Riverside)	87,535
Fountain Valley (★Anaheim)	53,691
Fremont (★Oakland)	173,339
Fresno (★667,490)	354,202
Fullerton (★Anaheim)	114,144
Gardena (★Los Angeles)	49,847
Garden Grove (★Anaheim)	143,050
Glendale (★Los Angeles)	180,038
Hacienda Heights (★Los Angeles)	58,200
Hawthorne (★Los Angeles)	71,349
Hayward (★Oakland)	111,498
Hemet (★Riverside)	36,094
Huntington Beach (★Anaheim)	181,519
Huntington Park (★Los Angeles)	56,065
Inglewood (★Los Angeles)	109,602
Irvine (★Anaheim)	110,330
La Habra (★Anaheim)	51,266
Lakewood (★Los Angeles)	73,557
La Mesa (★San Diego)	52,931
Lancaster (★189,300)(★Los Angeles)	97,291
Livermore (★Oakland)	56,741
Lodi (★Stockton)	51,874
Lompoc (★Santa Barbara)	37,649
Long Beach (★Los Angeles)	429,433
Los Angeles (★14,531,529)	3,485,398
Lynwood (★Los Angeles)	61,945
Merced (★178,403)	56,216
Milpitas (★San Jose)	50,686
Mission Viejo (★Anaheim)	72,820
Modesto (★370,522)	164,730
Montebello (★Los Angeles)	59,564
Monterey (★Salinas)	31,954
Monterey Park (★Los Angeles)	60,738
Mountain View (★San Jose)	67,460
Napa (★Vallejo)	61,842
National City (★San Diego)	54,249
Newport Beach (★Anaheim)	66,643
Norwalk (★Los Angeles)	94,279
Oakland (★2,082,914)(★San Francisco)	372,242
Oceanside (★San Diego)	128,398
Ontario (★Riverside)	133,179
Orange (★Anaheim)	110,658
Oxnard (★669,016)(★Los Angeles)	142,216
Palm Springs (★Riverside)	40,181
Palo Alto (★San Jose)	55,900
Pasadena (★Los Angeles)	131,591
Pico Rivera (★Los Angeles)	59,177
Pleasanton (★Oakland)	50,553
Pomona (★Los Angeles)	131,723
Porterville (★Visalia)	29,563
Rancho Cordova (★Sacramento)	48,731
Redding (★147,036)	66,462
Redlands (★Riverside)	60,394
Redondo Beach (★Los Angeles)	60,167
Redwood City (★San Francisco)	66,072
Rialto (★Riverside)	72,388
Richmond (★Oakland)	87,425
Riverside (★2,588,793)(★Los Angeles)	226,505
Rosemead (★Los Angeles)	51,638
Sacramento (★1,481,102)	369,365
Salinas (★355,660)	108,777
San Bernardino (★Riverside)	164,164
San Diego (★2,949,000)	1,110,549
San Francisco (★6,253,311)	723,959
San Jose (★1,497,577)(★San Francisco)	782,248
San Leandro (★Oakland)	68,223
San Mateo (★San Francisco)	85,486
Santa Ana (★Anaheim)	293,742
Santa Barbara (★369,608)	85,571
Santa Clara (★San Jose)	93,613
Santa Cruz (★229,734)(★San Francisco)	49,040
Santa Maria (★Santa Barbara)	61,284
Santa Monica (★Los Angeles)	86,905
Santa Rosa (★388,222)(★San Francisco)	113,313
Santee (★San Diego)	52,902
Simi Valley (★Oxnard)	100,217
South Gate (★Los Angeles)	86,284
South San Francisco (★San Francisco)	54,312
South Whittier (★Los Angeles)	51,100
Spring Valley (★San Diego)	54,600
Stockton (★480,628)	210,943

▲ Population of an entire municipality, commune, or district, including rural area.
• Largest city in country.
★ Population or designation of the metropolitan area, including suburbs.
C Census. **E** Official estimate. **U** Unofficial estimate.

▲ Bevölkerung eines ganzen städtischen Verwaltungsgebietes, eines Kommunalbezirkes oder eines Distrikts, einschliesslich ländlicher Gebiete.
• Grösste Stadt des Landes.
★ Bevölkerung oder Bezeichnung der Stadtregion einschliesslich Vororte.
C Volkszählung. **E** Offizielle Schätzung. **U** Inoffizielle Schätzung.

Sunnyvale (★San Jose)	117,229
Thousand Oaks (★Oxnard)	104,352
Torrance (★Los Angeles)	133,107
Tustin (★Anaheim)	50,689
Union City (★Oakland)	53,762
Upland (★Riverside)	63,374
Vacaville (★Vallejo)	71,479
Vallejo (★451,186)(★San Francisco)	109,199
Ventura (San Buenaventura) (★Oxnard)	92,575
Visalia (★311,921)	75,636
Vista (★San Diego)	71,872
Walnut Creek (★Oakland)	60,569
Watsonville (★Santa Cruz)	31,099
West Covina (★Los Angeles)	96,086
Westminster (★Anaheim)	78,118
Whittier (★Los Angeles)	77,671
Yorba Linda (★Anaheim)	52,422
Yuba City (★122,643)	27,437

UNITED STATES: COLORADO

1990 C	3,294,394
Arvada (★Denver)	89,235
Aurora (★Denver)	222,103
Boulder (★225,339)(★Denver)	83,312
Colorado Springs (★397,014)	281,140
Denver (★1,848,319)	467,610
Fort Collins (★186,136)	87,758
Grand Junction (★85,200)	29,034
Greeley (★131,821)	60,536
Lakewood (★Denver)	126,481
Longmont (★Boulder)	51,555
Loveland (★Fort Collins)	37,352
Pueblo (★123,051)	98,640
Thornton (★Denver)	55,031
Westminster (★Denver)	74,625

UNITED STATES: CONNECTICUT

1990 C	3,287,116
Bridgeport (★443,722)(★New York, N.Y.)	141,686
Bristol (★79,488)(★Hartford)	60,640
Danbury (★187,867)(★New York, N.Y.)	65,585
East Hartford (★Hartford)	50,452
Fairfield (★Bridgeport)	53,418
Greenwich (★Stamford)	58,441
Hamden (★New Haven)	53,100
Hartford (★1,085,837)	139,739
Manchester (★Hartford)	51,000
Meriden (★New Haven)	59,479
Milford (★Bridgeport)	48,168
New Britain (★148,188)(★Hartford)	75,491
New Haven (★530,180)	130,474
New London (★266,819)	28,540
Norwalk (★127,378)(★New York, N.Y.)	78,331
Stamford (★202,557)(★New York, N.Y.)	108,056
Stratford (★Bridgeport)	49,389
Torrington (★58,800)	33,687
Waterbury (★221,629)	108,961
West Hartford (★Hartford)	59,100
West Haven (★New Haven)	54,021

UNITED STATES: DELAWARE

1990 C	666,168
Dover (★78,900)	27,630
Wilmington (★Philadelphia, Pa.)	71,529

UNITED STATES: DISTRICT OF COLUMBIA

1990 C	606,900
WASHINGTON (★3,923,574)	606,900

UNITED STATES: FLORIDA

1990 C	12,937,926
Boca Raton (★West Palm Beach)	61,492
Brandon (★Tampa)	57,985
Cape Coral (★Fort Myers)	74,991
Carol City (★Miami)	52,800
City of Sunrise (★Fort Lauderdale)	64,407
Clearwater (★Tampa)	98,784
Daytona Beach (★370,712)	61,921
De Land (★Daytona Beach)	16,491
Fort Lauderdale (★1,255,488)(★Miami)	149,377
Fort Myers (★335,113)	45,206
Fort Pierce (★251,071)	36,830
Fort Walton Beach (★143,776)	21,471
Gainesville (★204,111)	84,770
Hialeah (★Miami)	188,004
Hollywood (★Fort Lauderdale)	121,697
Jacksonville (★906,727)	635,230
Kendall (★Miami)	53,100
Lakeland (★405,382)	70,576
Largo (★Tampa)	65,674
Melbourne (★398,978)	59,646
Miami (★3,192,582)	358,548
Miami Beach (★Miami)	92,639
Naples (★152,099)	19,505
Ocala (★194,833)	42,045
Orlando (★1,072,748)	164,693
Panama City (★126,994)	34,378
Pembroke Pines (★Fort Lauderdale)	65,452
Pensacola (★344,406)	58,165
Plantation (★Fort Lauderdale)	66,692
Pompano Beach (★Fort Lauderdale)	72,411
Saint Petersburg (★Tampa)	238,629
Sarasota (★277,776)	50,961
Tallahassee (★233,598)	124,773
Tampa (★2,067,959)	280,015
Venice (★Sarasota)	16,922
West Palm Beach (★863,518)	67,643
Winter Haven (★Lakeland)	24,725

UNITED STATES: GEORGIA

1990 C	6,478,216
Albany (★112,561)	78,122
Athens (★156,267)	45,734
Atlanta (★2,833,511)	394,017
Augusta (★396,809)	44,639
Columbus (★243,072)	178,681
Macon (★281,103)	106,612
Rome (★74,900)	30,326
Savannah (★242,622)	137,560
Valdosta (★64,000)	39,806
Warner Robins (★Macon)	43,726

UNITED STATES: HAWAII

1990 C	1,108,229
Hilo (★47,600)	37,808
Honolulu (★836,231)	365,272

UNITED STATES: IDAHO

1990 C	1,006,749
Boise (★205,775)	125,738
Idaho Falls (★72,700)	43,929
Lewiston (★44,300)	28,082
Nampa (★70,500)	28,365
Pocatello (★56,700)	46,080

UNITED STATES: ILLINOIS

1990 C	11,430,602
Arlington Heights (★Chicago)	75,460
Aurora (★356,884)(★Chicago)	99,581
Bloomington (★129,180)	51,972
Champaign (★173,025)	63,502
Chicago (★8,065,633)	2,783,726
Cicero (★Chicago)	67,436
Danville (★68,000)	33,828
Decatur (★117,206)	83,885
De Kalb (★52,200)	34,925
Des Plaines (★Chicago)	53,223
East Saint Louis (★Saint Louis, Mo.)	40,944
Elgin (★Aurora)	77,010
Evanston (★Chicago)	73,233
Galesburg (★40,600)	33,530
Joliet (★389,650)(★Chicago)	76,836
Kankakee (★96,255)	27,575
Mount Prospect (★Chicago)	53,170
Naperville (★Chicago)	85,351
Oak Lawn (★Chicago)	56,182
Oak Park (★Chicago)	53,648
Peoria (★339,172)	113,504
Quincy (★50,600)	39,681
Rockford (★283,719)	139,426
Schaumburg (★Chicago)	68,586
Skokie (★Chicago)	59,432
Springfield (★189,550)	105,227
Waukegan (★Chicago)	69,392
Wheaton (★Chicago)	51,464

UNITED STATES: INDIANA

1990 C	5,544,159
Anderson (★130,669)	59,459
Bloomington (★108,978)	60,633
Columbus (★59,000)	31,802
Elkhart (★156,198)	43,627
Evansville (★278,990)	126,272
Fort Wayne (★363,811)	173,072
Gary (★604,526)(★Chicago, Il.)	116,646
Hammond (★Gary)	84,236
Indianapolis (★1,249,822)	731,327
Kokomo (★96,946)	44,962
Lafayette (★130,598)	43,764
Marion (★76,900)	32,618
Michigan City (★55,600)	33,822
Muncie (★119,659)	71,035
Richmond (★64,100)	38,705
South Bend (★247,052)	105,511
Terre Haute (★130,812)	57,483

UNITED STATES: IOWA

1990 C	2,776,755
Ames (★65,400)	47,198
Cedar Rapids (★168,767)	108,751
Clinton (★39,600)	29,201
Council Bluffs (★Omaha, Ne.)	54,315
Davenport (★350,861)	95,333
Des Moines (★392,928)	193,187
Dubuque (★86,403)	57,546
Iowa City (★96,119)	59,738
Mason City	29,040
Sioux City (★115,018)	80,505
Waterloo (★146,611)	66,467

UNITED STATES: KANSAS

1990 C	2,477,574
Hutchinson (★46,800)	39,308
Kansas City (★Kansas City, Mo.)	149,767
Lawrence (★81,798)	65,608
Manhattan (★47,400)	37,712
Olathe (★Kansas City, Mo.)	63,352
Overland Park (★Kansas City, Mo.)	111,790
Salina (★42,700)	42,303
Topeka (★160,976)	119,883
Wichita (★485,270)	304,011

UNITED STATES: KENTUCKY

1990 C	3,685,296
Bowling Green (★59,100)	40,641
Covington (★Cincinnati, Oh.)	43,264
Frankfort	25,968
Lexington (★348,428)	225,366
Louisville (★952,662)	269,063
Owensboro (★87,189)	53,549
Paducah (★63,000)	27,256

UNITED STATES: LOUISIANA

1990 C	4,219,973
Alexandria (★131,556)	49,188
Baton Rouge (★528,264)	219,531
Bossier City (★Shreveport)	52,721
Houma (★182,842)	96,982
Kenner (★New Orleans)	72,033
Lafayette (★208,740)	94,440
Lake Charles (★168,134)	70,580
Metairie (★New Orleans)	149,428
Monroe (★142,191)	54,909
New Iberia (★49,000)	31,828
New Orleans (★1,238,816)	496,938
Shreveport (★334,341)	198,525

UNITED STATES: MAINE

1990 C	1,227,928
Augusta (★56,700)	21,325
Bangor (★88,745)	33,181
Lewiston (★88,141)	39,757
Portland (★215,281)	64,358

UNITED STATES: MARYLAND

1990 C	4,781,468
Annapolis (★Baltimore)	33,187
Baltimore (★2,382,172)	736,014
Bethesda (★Washington, D.C.)	62,936
Columbia (★Baltimore)	75,883
Cumberland (★101,643)	23,706
Dundalk (★Baltimore)	65,800
Hagerstown (★121,393)	35,445
Salisbury (★72,400)	20,592
Silver Spring (★Washington, D.C.)	76,046
Towson (★Baltimore)	49,445
Wheaton (★Washington, D.C.) (1989)	58,300

UNITED STATES: MASSACHUSETTS

1990 C	6,016,425
Amherst (★44,700)	17,824
Boston (★4,171,643)	574,283
Brockton (★189,478)(★Boston)	92,788
Brookline (★Boston)	54,718
Cambridge (★Boston)	95,802
Chicopee (★Springfield)	56,632
Fall River (★157,272)(★Providence, R.I.)	92,703
Fitchburg (★102,797)	41,194
Framingham (★Boston)	64,989
Haverhill (★Lawrence)	51,418
Lawrence (★393,516)(★Boston)	70,207
Lowell (★273,067)(★Boston)	103,439
Lynn (★Salem)	81,245
Malden (★Boston)	53,884
Medford (★Boston)	57,407
New Bedford (★175,641)	99,922
Newton (★Boston)	82,585
Northampton (★Springfield)	29,289
Pittsfield (★79,250)	48,622
Quincy (★Boston)	84,985
Somerville (★Boston)	76,210
Springfield (★529,519)	156,983
Taunton (★59,700)	49,832
Waltham (★Boston)	57,878
Weymouth (★Boston)	54,063
Worcester (★436,905)	169,759

UNITED STATES: MICHIGAN

1990 C	9,295,297
Ann Arbor (★282,937)(★Detroit)	109,592
Battle Creek (★135,982)	53,540
Benton Harbor (★161,378)	12,818
Clinton Township (★Detroit)	77,900
Dearborn (★Detroit)	89,286
Dearborn Heights (★Detroit)	60,838
Detroit (★4,665,236)	1,027,974
East Lansing (★Lansing)	50,677
Farmington Hills (★Detroit)	74,652
Flint (★430,459)	140,761
Grand Rapids (★688,399)	189,126
Holland (★Grand Rapids)	30,745
Jackson (★149,756)	37,446
Kalamazoo (★223,411)	80,277
Lansing (★432,674)	127,321
Livonia (★Detroit)	100,850
Monroe (★62,600)(★Detroit)	22,902
Muskegon (★158,983)	40,283
Pontiac (★Detroit)	71,166
Port Huron (★Sarnia, Canada)	33,694
Redford Township (★Detroit)	54,387
Roseville (★Detroit)	51,412
Royal Oak (★Detroit)	65,410
Saginaw (★399,320)	69,512
Saint Clair Shores (★Detroit)	68,107
Sault Sainte Marie	14,689
Southfield (★Detroit)	75,728
Sterling Heights (★Detroit)	117,810
Taylor (★Detroit)	70,811
Troy (★Detroit)	72,884
Warren (★Detroit)	144,864
Westland (★Detroit)	84,724
Wyoming (★Grand Rapids)	63,891

UNITED STATES: MINNESOTA

1990 C	4,375,099
Bloomington (★Minneapolis)	86,335
Brooklyn Park (★Minneapolis)	56,381
Burnsville (★Minneapolis)	51,288
Coon Rapids (★Minneapolis)	52,978
Duluth (★239,971)	85,493
Mankato (★48,400)	31,477
Minneapolis (★2,464,124)	368,383
Plymouth (★Minneapolis)	50,889
Rochester (★106,470)	70,745
Saint Cloud (★190,921)	48,812
Saint Paul (★Minneapolis)	272,235

UNITED STATES: MISSISSIPPI

1990 C	2,573,216
Biloxi (★197,125)	46,319
Columbus (★52,100)	23,799
Greenville (★48,500)	45,226
Gulfport (★Biloxi)	40,775
Hattiesburg (★71,600)	41,882
Jackson (★395,396)	196,637
Laurel (★47,300)	18,827
Meridian (★60,600)	41,036
Natchez (★45,700)	19,460
Pascagoula (★115,243)	25,899
Vicksburg (★43,500)	20,908

UNITED STATES: MISSOURI

1990 C	5,117,073
Cape Girardeau (★59,100)	34,438
Columbia (★112,379)	69,101
Florissant (★Saint Louis)	51,206
Independence (★Kansas City)	112,301
Jefferson City (★60,100)	35,481
Joplin (★134,910)	40,961
Kansas City (★1,566,280)	435,146
Saint Charles (★Saint Louis)	54,555
Saint Joseph (★83,083)	71,852
Saint Louis (★2,444,099)	396,685
Springfield (★240,593)	140,494

UNITED STATES: MONTANA

1990 C	799,065
Billings (★113,419)	81,151
Butte (★33,900)	33,336
Great Falls (★77,691)	55,097
Helena	24,569
Missoula (★65,700)	42,918

UNITED STATES: NEBRASKA

1990 C	1,578,385
Grand Island (★42,200)	39,386
Lincoln (★213,641)	191,972
Omaha (★618,262)	335,795

UNITED STATES: NEVADA

1990 C	1,201,833
Carson City	40,443
Henderson (★Las Vegas)	64,942
Las Vegas (★741,459)	258,295
Paradise (★Las Vegas)	124,682
Reno (★254,667)	133,850
Sparks (★Reno)	53,367
Sunrise Manor (★Las Vegas)	95,362

UNITED STATES: NEW HAMPSHIRE

1990 C	1,109,252
Concord (★73,300)	36,006
Manchester (★147,809)	99,567
Nashua (★180,557)(★Boston, Ma.)	79,662
Portsmouth (★223,578)	25,925

UNITED STATES: NEW JERSEY

1990 C	7,730,188
Atlantic City (★319,416)	37,986
Bayonne (★Jersey City)	61,444
Bloomfield (★Newark)	45,061
Brick Township (★New York, N.Y.)	66,473
Camden (★Philadelphia, Pa.)	87,492
Cherry Hill (★Philadelphia, Pa.)	69,319
Clifton (★New York, N.Y.)	71,742
East Orange (★Newark)	73,552
Edison (★New York, N.Y.)	88,680
Elizabeth (★Newark)	110,002
Irvington (★Newark)	59,774
Jersey City (★553,099)(★New York, N.Y.)	228,537
Middletown (★New York, N.Y.)	62,298
Newark (★1,824,321)(★New York, N.Y.)	275,221
Passaic (★New York, N.Y.)	58,041
Paterson (★New York, N.Y.)	140,891
Trenton (★325,824)(★Philadelphia, Pa.)	88,675
Union (★Newark)	50,024
Union City (★Jersey City)	58,012
Vineland (★138,053)(★Philadelphia, Pa.)	54,780

UNITED STATES: NEW MEXICO

1990 C	1,515,069
Albuquerque (★480,577)	384,736
Farmington (★50,300)	33,997
Las Cruces (★135,510)	62,126
Roswell (★50,600)	44,654
Santa Fe (★117,043)	55,859

UNITED STATES: NEW YORK

1990 C	17,990,455
Albany (★874,304)	101,082
Auburn (★52,900)	31,258
Binghamton (★264,497)	53,008
Buffalo (★1,189,288)	328,123
Cheektowaga (★Buffalo)	84,387
Elmira (★95,195)	33,724
Glens Falls (★118,539)	15,023
Hempstead (★New York)	49,453
Irondequoit (★Rochester)	52,322
Ithaca (★82,700)	29,541
Jamestown (★141,895)	34,681
Kingston (★88,200)	23,095
Levittown (★New York)	53,286
Lockport (★57,500)(★Buffalo)	24,426
Mount Vernon (★New York)	67,153
Newburgh (★102,300)(★New York)	26,454
New Rochelle (★New York)	67,265
● New York (★18,087,251)	7,322,564
Niagara Falls (★220,756)(★Buffalo)	61,840
Poughkeepsie (★259,462)	28,844
Rochester (★1,002,410)	231,636
Schenectady (★Albany)	65,566
Syracuse (★659,864)	163,860
Troy (★Albany)	54,269
Utica (★316,633)	68,637
West Seneca (★Buffalo)	47,866
Yonkers (★New York)	188,082

UNITED STATES: NORTH CAROLINA

1990 C	6,628,637
Asheville (★174,821)	61,607
Burlington (★108,213)	39,498
Charlotte (★1,162,093)	395,934
Durham (★Raleigh)	136,611
Fayetteville (★274,566)	75,695
Gastonia (★Charlotte)	54,732
Goldsboro (★94,200)	40,709
Greensboro (★942,091)	183,521
Hickory (★221,700)	28,301
High Point (★Greensboro)	69,496
Jacksonville (★149,838)	30,013
Kannapolis (★Charlotte)	29,696
Raleigh (★735,480)	207,951
Rocky Mount (★83,400)	48,997
Salisbury (★Charlotte)	23,087
Wilmington (★120,284)	55,530
Winston-Salem (★Greenboro)	143,485

UNITED STATES: NORTH DAKOTA

1990 C	638,800
Bismarck (★83,831)	49,256
Fargo (★153,296)	74,111
Grand Forks (★70,683)	49,425
Minot (★39,800)	34,544

UNITED STATES: OHIO

1990 C	10,347,115
Akron (★657,575)(★Cleveland)	223,019
Alliance (★Canton)	23,376
Ashtabula (★40,900)	21,633
Brunswick (★Cleveland)	28,230
Canton (★394,106)	84,161
Cincinnati (★1,744,124)	364,040
Cleveland (★2,759,823)	505,616
Cleveland Heights (★Cleveland)	54,052
Columbus (★1,377,419)	632,910
Dayton (★951,270)	182,044
East Liverpool (★44,400)	13,654
Elyria (★Lorain)	56,746
Euclid (★Cleveland)	54,875

▲ Población de un municipio, comuna o distrito entero, incluyendo sus áreas rurales.
● Ciudad más grande de un país.
★ Población o designación de un área metropolitana, incluyendo los suburbios.
C Censo. **E** Estimado oficial. **U** Estimado no oficial.

▲ Population d'une municipalité, d'une commune ou d'un district, zone rurale incluse.
● Ville la plus peuplée du pays.
★ Population de l'agglomération (ou nom de la zone métropolitaine englobante).
C Recensement. **E** Estimation officielle. **U** Estimation non officielle.

▲ População de um município, comuna ou distrito, inclusive as respectivas áreas rurais.
● Maior cidade de um país.
★ População ou indicação de uma área metropolitana.
C Censo. **E** Estimativa oficial. **U** Estimativa não oficial.

Hamilton (★291,479)(★Cincinnati)	61,368
Kettering (★Dayton)	60,569
Lakewood (★Cleveland)	59,718
Lancaster (★Columbus)	34,507
Lima (★154,340)	45,549
Lorain (★271,126)(★Cleveland)	71,245
Mansfield (★126,137)	50,627
Marion (★53,900)	34,075
Middletown (★107,200)(★Cincinnati)	46,022
Newark (★Columbus)	44,389
Parma (★Cleveland)	87,876
Portsmouth (★64,300)	22,676
Sandusky (★79,800)	29,764
Springfield (★Dayton)	70,487
Steubenville (★142,523)	22,125
Toledo (★614,128)	332,943
Warren (★Youngstown)	50,793
Youngstown (★492,619)	95,732
Zanesville (★67,800)	26,778

UNITED STATES: OKLAHOMA

1990 C	3,145,585
Broken Arrow (★Tulsa)	58,043
Edmond (★Oklahoma City)	52,315
Enid (★56,735)	45,309
Lawton (★111,486)	80,561
Midwest City (★Oklahoma City)	52,267
Muskogee (★49,500)	37,708
Norman (★Oklahoma City)	80,071
Oklahoma City (★958,839)	444,719
Tulsa (★708,954)	367,302

UNITED STATES: OREGON

1990 C	2,842,321
Beaverton (★Portland)	53,310
Corvallis (★98,700)	44,757
Eugene (★282,912)	112,669
Gresham (★Portland)	68,235
Medford (★146,389)	46,951
Portland (★1,477,895)	437,319
Salem (★278,024)	107,786

UNITED STATES: PENNSYLVANIA

1990 C	11,881,643
Abington (★Philadelphia)	59,300
Allentown (★686,688)	105,090
Altoona (★130,542)	51,881
Bensalem (★Philadelphia)	56,788
Bethlehem (★Allentown)	71,428
Bristol (★Philadelphia)	57,129
Butler (★86,500)	15,714
Coatesville (★93,400)(★Philadelphia)	11,038
Erie (★275,572)	108,718
Hanover (★York)	14,399
Harrisburg (★587,986)	52,376
Haverford (★Philadelphia)	49,848
Hazleton (★Scranton)	24,730
Johnstown (★241,247)	28,134
Lancaster (★422,822)	55,551
Lebanon (★Harrisburg)	24,800
Lower Merion Township (★Philadelphia)	58,003
New Castle (★68,400)	28,334
Oil City (★42,000)	11,949
Penn Hills (★Pittsburgh)	51,430
Philadelphia (★5,899,345)	1,585,577
Pittsburgh (★2,242,798)	369,879
Pottstown (★88,300)(★Philadelphia)	21,831
Pottsville (★54,200)	16,603
Reading (★336,523)	78,380
Scranton (★734,175)	81,805
Sharon (★121,003)	17,493
State College (★123,786)	38,923
Uniontown (★53,200)(★Pittsburgh)	12,034
Upper Darby (★Philadelphia)	84,054
Washington (★66,000)(★Pittsburgh)	15,864
Wilkes-Barre (★Scranton)	47,523
Williamsport (★118,710)	31,933
York (★417,848)	42,192

UNITED STATES: RHODE ISLAND

1990 C	1,003,464
Cranston (★Providence)	76,060
East Providence (★Providence)	50,380
Newport (★64,500)	28,227
Pawtucket (★329,384)(★Providence)	72,644
Providence (★1,141,510)	160,728
Warwick (★Providence)	85,427

UNITED STATES: SOUTH CAROLINA

1990 C	3,486,703
Anderson (★145,196)	26,184
Charleston (★506,875)	80,414
Columbia (★453,331)	98,052
Florence (★114,344)	29,813
Greenville (★640,861)	58,282
North Charleston (★Charleston)	70,218
Rock Hill (★Charlotte, N.C.)	41,643
Spartanburg (★Greenville)	43,467
Sumter (★90,300)	41,943

UNITED STATES: SOUTH DAKOTA

1990 C	696,004
Pierre	12,906
Rapid City (★81,343)	54,523
Sioux Falls (★123,809)	100,814

UNITED STATES: TENNESSEE

1990 C	4,877,185
Bristol (★Johnson City)	23,421
Chattanooga (★433,210)	152,466
Clarksville (★169,439)	75,494
Jackson (★77,982)	48,949
Johnson City (★436,047)	49,381
Kingsport (★Johnson City)	36,365
Knoxville (★604,816)	165,121
Memphis (★981,747)	610,337
Murfreesboro (★Nashville)	44,922
Nashville (★985,026)	487,969

UNITED STATES: TEXAS

1990 C	16,986,510
Abilene (★119,655)	106,654
Amarillo (★187,547)	157,615
Arlington (★Fort Worth)	261,721
Austin (★781,572)	465,622
Baytown (★Houston)	63,850
Beaumont (★361,226)	114,323
Brownsville (★460,000)	98,962
Bryan (★121,862)	55,002
Carrollton (★Dallas)	82,169
College Station (★Bryan)	52,456
Corpus Christi (★349,894)	257,453
Dallas (★3,885,415)	1,006,877
Denton (★Dallas)	66,270
El Paso (★650,000)	515,342
Fort Worth (★1,332,053)(★Dallas)	447,619
Freeport (★88,600)(★Houston)	11,389
Galveston (★217,399)(★Houston)	59,070
Garland (★Dallas)	180,650
Grand Prairie (★Dallas)	99,616
Harlingen (★Brownsville)	48,735
Houston (★3,711,043)	1,630,553
Irving (★Dallas)	155,037
Killeen (★255,301)	63,535
Laredo (★354,000)	122,899
Longview (★162,431)	70,311
Lubbock (★222,636)	186,206
Lufkin (★56,000)	30,206
McAllen (★383,545)	84,021
Mesquite (★Dallas)	101,484
Midland (★106,611)	89,443
Odessa (★118,934)	89,699
Pasadena (★Houston)	119,363
Plano (★Dallas)	128,713
Port Arthur (★Beaumont)	58,724
Richardson (★Dallas)	74,840
San Angelo (★98,458)	84,474
San Antonio (★1,302,099)	935,933
Sherman (★95,021)	31,601
Temple (★Killeen)	46,109
Texarkana (★120,132)	31,656
Tyler (★151,309)	75,450
Victoria (★74,361)	55,076
Waco (★189,123)	103,590
Wichita Falls (★122,378)	96,259

UNITED STATES: UTAH

1990 C	1,722,850
Logan (★60,300)	32,762
Ogden (★Salt Lake City)	63,909
Orem (★Provo)	67,561
Provo (★263,590)	86,835
Salt Lake City (★1,072,227)	159,936
Sandy (★Salt Lake City)	75,058
West Valley City (★Salt Lake City)	86,976

UNITED STATES: VERMONT

1990 C	562,758
Burlington (★131,439)	39,127
Montpelier (★52,800)	8,247
Rutland (★53,000)	18,230

UNITED STATES: VIRGINIA

1990 C	6,187,358
Alexandria (★Washington, D.C.)	111,183
Annandale (★Washington, D.C.)	50,975
Arlington (★Washington, D.C.)	170,936
Charlottesville (★131,107)	40,341
Chesapeake (★Norfolk)	151,976
Danville (★108,711)	53,056
Hampton (★Norfolk)	133,793
Lynchburg (★142,199)	66,049
Martinsville (★67,100)	16,162
Newport News (★Norfolk)	170,045
Norfolk (★1,396,107)	261,229
Portsmouth (★Norfolk)	103,907
Richmond (★865,640)	203,056
Roanoke (★224,477)	96,397
Suffolk (★Norfolk)	52,141
Virginia Beach (★Norfolk)	393,069

UNITED STATES: WASHINGTON

1990 C	4,866,692
Bellevue (★Seattle)	86,874
Bellingham (★127,780)	52,179
Bremerton (★189,731)	38,142
Everett (★Seattle)	69,961
Lakes District (★Tacoma)	58,412
Longview (★67,100)	31,499
Olympia (★161,238)	33,840
Pasco (★Richland)	20,337
Seattle (★2,559,164)	516,259
Spokane (★361,364)	177,196
Tacoma (★586,203)(★Seattle)	176,664
Yakima (★188,823)	54,827

UNITED STATES: WEST VIRGINIA

1990 C	1,793,477
Beckley (★64,300)	18,296
Charleston (★250,454)	57,287
Clarksburg (★53,800)	18,059
Fairmont (★53,700)	20,210
Huntington (★312,529)	54,844
Morgantown (★71,500)	25,879
Parkersburg (★149,169)	33,862
Wheeling (★159,301)	34,882

UNITED STATES: WISCONSIN

1990 C	4,891,769
Appleton (★315,121)	65,695
Beloit (★Janesville)	35,573
Eau Claire (★137,543)	56,856
Fond du Lac (★52,400)	37,757
Green Bay (★194,594)	96,466
Janesville (★139,510)	52,133
Kenosha (★128,181) (★Chicago, Il.)	80,352
La Crosse (★97,904)	51,003
Madison (★367,085)	191,262
Manitowoc (★57,300)	32,520
Milwaukee (★1,607,183)	628,088
Oshkosh (★Appleton)	55,006
Racine (★175,034)(★Milwaukee)	84,298
Sheboygan (★103,877)	49,676
Waukesha (★Milwaukee)	56,958
Wausau (★115,400)	37,060
Wauwatosa (★Milwaukee)	49,366
West Allis (★Milwaukee)	63,221

UNITED STATES: WYOMING

1990 C	453,588
Casper (★61,226)	46,742
Cheyenne (★73,142)	50,008

URUGUAY

1985 C	2,955,241
Las Piedras (★Montevideo)	58,288
Melo	42,615
Mercedes	36,702
Minas	34,661
• MONTEVIDEO (★1,550,000)	1,251,647
Paysandú	76,191
Rivera	57,316
Salto	80,823

UZBEKISTAN

1991 E	20,708,200
Almalyk	116,400
Andižan	298,300
Angren	132,600
Bekabad	82,800
Buchara	249,600
Chodžeili	61,200
Čirčik (★Taškent)	158,400
Denau	49,300
Džizak	110,900
Fergana	226,500
Gulistan	56,900
Jangijul'	56,900
Kagan	49,800
Karši	168,000
Kattakurgan	59,600
Kokand	175,000
Margilan	124,900
Namangan	319,200
Navoi	111,600
Nukus	179,600
Šachrisabz	53,200
Samarkand	370,500
• TAŠKENT (TASHKENT) (★2,325,000)	2,113,300
Termez	90,400
Urgenč	130,400

VANUATU

1989 C	142,944
• PORT VILA (★23,000)	19,311

VATICAN CITY / Città del Vaticano

1988 E	766

VENDA

1985 C	459,819
Makwarela	3,712
• Shayandima	4,853
THOHOYANDOU	3,641

VENEZUELA

1990 C	18,105,265
Acarigua (1981C)	91,662
Barcelona	109,061
Barinas	152,853
Barquisimeto	602,622
Baruta (★Caracas) (1981C)	200,063
Cabimas (1981C)	140,435
Cagua (1981C)	53,704
Calabozo (1981C)	61,995
• CARACAS (★3,600,000)	18,245,892
Carora (1981C)	58,694
Carúpano (1981C)	64,579
Catia La Mar (★Caracas) (1981C)	87,916
Chacao (★Caracas) (1981C)	72,703
Ciudad Bolívar	225,846
Ciudad Guayana (1981C)	314,497
Ciudad Ojeda (Lagunillas) (1981C)	83,565
Coro	124,616
Cumaná	212,492
El Limón (1981C)	65,122
El Tigre (1981C)	73,595
Guacara (1981C)	72,727
Guanare	83,380
Guarenas (★Caracas) (1981C)	101,742
La Asunción	16,585
La Victoria (1981C)	70,828
Los Dos Caminos (★Caracas) (1981C)	63,346
Los Teques (★Caracas)	143,519
Maiquetía (★Caracas) (1981C)	66,056
Maracaibo	1,207,513
Maracay	354,428
Mariara (1981C)	47,242
Maturín	207,382
Mérida	167,992
Petare (★Caracas) (1981C)	395,715
Porlamar (1981C)	51,079
Pozuelos (1981C)	80,342
Puerto Ayacucho	35,865
Puerto Cabello (1981C)	71,759
Puerto la Cruz (1981C)	53,881
Punto Fijo (1981C)	71,114
San Carlos	50,339
San Cristóbal	220,697
San Felipe	65,793
San Fernando	72,733
San Juan de los Morros	67,645
Trujillo	32,683
Tucupita	40,946
Turmero (1981C)	111,186
Valencia	903,076
Valera (1981C)	102,068
Valle de la Pascua (1981C)	55,761

VIETNAM / Viet Nam

1989 C	64,411,668
Bac Giang	50,879
Bac Lieu	83,483
Bien Hoa	273,879
Buon Me Thuot	97,044
Ca Mau	81,901
Cam Pha	105,336
Can Tho (1978C)	208,078
Chau Doc	50,935
Da Lat	102,583
Da Nang	369,734
Hai Duong	53,370
Hai Phong (▲1,447,523)	351,919
HA NOI (★1,275,000)	905,939
Hoa Binh	69,323
Hon Gai	123,102
Hue	211,718
Long Xuyen	128,814
Minh Hai (1979C)	72,517
My Tho	104,724
Nam Dinh	165,629
Nha Trang	213,460
Phan Rang	71,111
Phan Thiet	114,236
Play Cu	76,991
Qui Nhon	159,852
Rach Gia	137,784
Sa Dec	50,733
Soc Trang (1979C)	74,967
Soc Trang	87,899
Tan An	50,288
Thai Binh	57,640
Thai Nguyen	124,871
Thanh Hoa	84,951
• Thanh Pho Ho Chi Minh (Saigon) (★3,300,000)	2,796,229
Tra Vinh	47,785
Tuy Hoa	54,081
Uong Bi	49,595
Viet Tri	73,347
Vinh	110,793
Vinh Long	81,620
Vung Tau	123,528
Yen Bai	58,645

VIRGIN ISLANDS OF THE UNITED STATES

1990 C	101,809
• CHARLOTTE AMALIE (★32,000)	12,331

WALLIS AND FUTUNA / Wallis et Futuna

1983 E	12,408
• MATĀ'UTU	815
Ono (1976C)	624

WESTERN SAHARA

1982 E	142,000
• EL AAIÚN	93,875

WESTERN SAMOA / Samoa i Sisifo

1981 C	156,349
• APIA	33,170

YEMEN / Al-Yaman

1990 E	15,267,000
'Adan (★318,000) (1984E)	176,100
Al-Hudaydah (1986C)	155,110
Al-Mukallā (1984E)	58,000
• SAN'Ā' (1986C)	427,150
Ta'izz (1986C)	178,043

YUGOSLAVIA / Jugoslavija

1987 E	10,342,020
• BEOGRAD (★1,400,000)	1,130,000
Kragujevac (▲171,609)	94,800
Niš (▲240,219)	168,400
Novi Sad (▲266,772)	176,000
Pančevo (★Beograd)	62,700
Podgorica (▲145,163)	82,500
Priština (▲244,830)	125,400
Subotica (▲153,306)	100,500
Zrenjanin (▲140,009)	65,400

ZAIRE / Zaïre

1984 C	30,729,443
Bandundu	63,642
Beni	44,141
Boma	197,617
Bukavu	167,950
Bumba	51,197
Bunia	59,598
Butembo	73,312
Gandajika	64,878
Gemena	63,052
Goma	77,908
Ilebo (Port-Francqui)	53,877
Isiro	78,268
Kalemie (Albertville)	73,528
Kamina	62,789
Kananga (Luluabourg)	298,693
Kikwit	149,296
Kindu	66,812
• KINSHASA (LÉOPOLDVILLE) (1986E)	3,000,000
Kipushi	53,207
Kisangani (Stanleyville)	317,581
Kolwezi	416,122
Likasi (Jadotville)	213,862
Lubumbashi (Élisabethville)	564,830
Matadi	138,798
Mbandaka (Coquilhatville)	137,291
Mbuji-Mayi (Bakwanga)	486,235
Mwene-Ditu	94,560
Tshikapa	116,016
Uvira	74,432

ZAMBIA

1990 C	7,818,447
Chililabombwe (Bancroft) (★76,848)	35,200
Chingola	167,954
Kabwe (Broken Hill)	166,519
Kalulushi	75,197
Kitwe (★338,207)	247,100
Livingstone	82,218
Luanshya (★146,275)	79,500
• LUSAKA	982,362
Mufulira (★152,944)	85,000
Ndola	376,311

ZIMBABWE

1983 E	7,740,000
Bulawayo (1982C)	495,317
Chitungwiza (★Harare)	202,000
Gweru (1982C)	78,940
• HARARE (★890,000)	681,000
Mutare (1982C)	75,358

▲ Population of an entire municipality, commune, or district, including rural area.
• Largest city in country.
★ Population or designation of the metropolitan area, including suburbs.
C Census. E Official estimate.
U Unofficial estimate.

▲ Bevölkerung eines ganzen städtischen Verwaltungsgebietes, eines Kommunalbezirkes oder eines Distrikts, einschliesslich ländlicher Gebiete.
• Grösste Stadt des Landes.
★ Bevölkerung oder Bezeichnung der Stadtregion einschliess lich Vororte.
C Volkszählung. E Offizielle Schätzung.
U Inoffizielle Schätzung.

▲ Población de un municipio, comuna o distrito entero, incluyendo sus áreas rurales.
• Ciudad más grande de un país.
★ Población o designación de un área metropolitana, incluyendo los suburbios.
C Censo. E Estimado oficial.
U Estimado no oficial.

▲ Population d'une municipalité, d'une commune ou d'un district, zone rurale incluse.
• Ville la plus peuplée du pays.
★ Population de l'agglomération (ou nom de la zone métropolitaine englobante).
C Recensement. E Estimation officielle.
U Estimation non officielle.

▲ População de um municipio, comuna ou distrito, inclusive as respectivas áreas rurais.
• Maior cidade de um país.
★ População ou indicação de uma área metropolitana.
C Censo. E Estimativa oficial.
U Estimativa não oficial.

The index includes in a single alphabetical list some 170,000 names appearing on the maps. Each name is followed by a page reference to one or more maps and by the location of the feature on the map, in coordinates of latitude and longitude. If a page contains several maps, a lowercase letter identifies the particular map. The page reference for two-page maps is always to the left-hand page.

Most map features are indexed to the largest-scale map on which they appear. However, a feature usually is not indexed to a Metropolitan Area map if it is also shown on another map where it can be seen in a broader setting. Countries, mountain ranges, and other extensive features are generally indexed to the largest-scale map that shows them in their entirety.

The order in which index information is presented is shown in the English, German, Spanish, French, and Portuguese headings at the center of each two-page spread.

For example:

ENGLISH

Name	Page	Lat.°′	Long.°′

The features indexed are of three types: *point*, *areal*, and *linear*. For *point* features (for example, cities, mountain peaks, dams), latitude and longitude coordinates give the location of the point on the map. For *areal* features (countries, mountain ranges, etc.), the coordinates generally indicate the approximate center of the feature. For *linear* features (rivers, canals, aqueducts), the coordinates locate a terminating point—for example, the mouth of a river, or the point at which a feature reaches the map margin.

Name Forms Names in the index, as on the maps, are generally in the local language and insofar as possible are spelled according to official practice. Diacritical marks are included, except that those used to indicate tone, as in Vietnamese, are usually not shown. Most features that extend beyond the boundaries of one country have no single official name, and these are usually named in English. Many English, German, Spanish, French, and Portuguese names, which may not be shown on the maps, appear in the index as cross references. All cross references are indicated by the symbol →. A name that appears in a shortened version on the map due to space limitations is given in full in the index, with the portion that is omitted on the map enclosed in brackets, for example, Acapulco [de Juárez].

Transliteration For names in languages not written in the Roman alphabet, the locally official transliteration system has been used where one exists. Thus, names in Russia and Bulgaria have been transliterated according to the systems adopted by the academies of science of these countries. Similarly, the transliteration for mainland Chinese names follows the Pinyin system, which has been officially adopted in mainland China. For languages with no one locally accepted transliteration system, notably Arabic, transliteration in general follows closely a system adopted by the United States Board on Geographic Names.

Alphabetization Names are alphabetized in the order of the letters of the English alphabet. Spanish *ll* and *ch*, for example, are not treated as distinct letters. Furthermore, diacritical marks are disregarded in alphabetization—German or Scandinavian *ä* or *ö* are treated as *a* or *o*.

The names of physical features may appear inverted, since they are always alphabetized under the proper, not the generic, part of the name, thus: "Gibraltar, Strait of ɰ." Otherwise every entry, whether consisting of one word or more, is alphabetized as a single continuous entity. "Lakeland," for example, appears after "La Crosse" and before "La Salle." Names beginning with articles (Le Havre, Den Helder, Al-Qāhirah, As-Suways) are not inverted. Names beginning with "St." and "Sainte" are alphabetized as though spelled "Saint."

In the case of identical names, towns are listed first, then political divisions, then physical features. Entries that are completely identical (including symbols, discussed below) are distinguished by abbreviations of their official country names and are sequenced alphabetically by country name. The many duplicate names in Canada, the United Kingdom, and the United States are further distinguished by abbreviations of the names of their primary subdivisions. (See list of abbreviations on pages 319-320).

Abbreviation and Capitalization Abbreviation and styling have been standardized for all languages. A period is used after every abbreviation even when this may not be the local practice. The abbreviation "St." is used only for "Saint." "Sankt" and other forms of the term are spelled out.

All names are written with an initial capital letter except for a few Dutch names, such as 's-Gravenhage. Capitalization of noninitial words in a name generally follows local practice.

Symbols The symbols that appear in the index represent graphically the broad categories of the features named, for example, ∧ for mountain (Everest, Mount ∧). An abbreviated key to the symbols, in the five atlas languages, appears at the foot of each pair of index pages. Superior numbers following some symbols in the index indicate finer distinctions, for example, $\wedge^{1}$ for volcano (Fuji-san $\wedge^{1}$). A complete list of the symbols and superior numbers is given on page I•1.

Das Register umfasst in alphabetischer Anordnung etwa 170 000 in den Karten erscheinende Namen. Nach jedem Namen folgt die Seitenangabe zu einer oder mehreren Karten und die Lageangabe des Objektes in der Karte mit geographischer Länge und Breite. Enthält eine Seite mehrere Karten, so wird die betreffende Karte durch einen Kleinbuchstaben gekennzeichnet. Die Seitenangabe für Doppelseiten bezieht sich immer auf die linke Seite.

Die Verweise für die meisten Objekte in den Karten beziehen sich auf die Karte mit dem grössten Massstab. Normalerweise werden jedoch Verweise auf Objekte in den Karten der Stadtregionen nicht gegeben, wenn sie auf einer anderen Karte in grösserem Zusammenhang dargestellt sind. Die Lageangaben für Länder, Gebirgszüge und andere ausgedehnte Objekte beziehen sich allgemein auf die Karte grössten Massstabes, die sie in ihrer ganzen Ausdehnung zeigt.

Die Anordnung, in welcher die Lageangabe erfolgt, geht aus den englischen, deutschen, spanischen, französischen und portugiesischen Überschriften in der Mitte jeder Doppelseite hervor.

Zum Beispiel:

DEUTSCH

Name	Seite	Breite°′	Länge°′ E = Ost

Die aufgeführten Objekte gliedern sich in drei Gruppen: *punkt-*, *flächen-* und *linienförmige* Objekte. Bei *punktförmigen* Objekten (z.B. Städte, Berge, Dämme) beziehen sich die Angaben nach Länge und Breite auf die Signatur in der Karte. Bei *flächenhaften* Objekten (Länder, Gebirgszüge usw.) verweisen die Koordinaten im allgemeinen auf das ungefähre Zentrum des Objektes. Bei *linienhaften* Objekten (Flüsse, Kanäle, Wasserleitungen) beziehen sich die Koordinaten auf einen bestimmten Punkt, z.B. die Mündung eines Flusses oder den Punkt, an dem das Objekt den Kartenrand schneidet.

Namengebung Wie in den Karten so sind auch im Register die Namen im allgemeinen in der örtlichen Namensform wiedergegeben und soweit als möglich in der amtlichen Schreibweise. Diakritische Zeichen wurden gesetzt; sie wurden nur dort weggelassen, wo sie, wie im Vietnamesischen, Tonhöhen kennzeichnen. Meist haben Objekte, die sich über die Grenzen eines Landes hinaus erstrecken, keinen einzelnen offiziellen Namen; normalerweise sind sie daher englisch beschriftet. Viele englische, deutsche, spanische, französische und portugiesische Namensformen, die nicht in den Karten enthalten sind, erscheinen im Register als Kreuzverweis. Alle Kreuzverweise werden durch das Symbol → gekennzeichnet. Namen, die aus Platzgründen in abgekürzter Form in der Karte erscheinen, werden im Register voll ausgeschrieben, wobei der auf der Karte weggelassene Teil in Klammern gesetzt ist, z.B. Acapulco [de Juárez].

Transkription Für die Transkription von Namen aus Sprachen, die nicht im lateinischen Alphabet geschrieben werden, wurde das offizielle Transkriptionssystem benutzt, sofern ein solches vorhanden ist. So wurden die Namen in Russland und in Bulgarien nach dem von den wissenschaftlichen Akademien dieser Länder angewandten System transkribiert. Entsprechend wurden die Namen auf dem chinesischen Festland nach dem Pinyin-System übertragen, das offiziell in der Volksrepublik China eingeführt wurde. Bei Sprachen, für die ein allgemein anerkanntes Transkriptionssystem nicht vorliegt, vor allem für Arabisch, erfolgte die Transkription in enger Anlehnung an das vom United States Board on Geographic Names angewandte System.

Alphabetische Ordnung Die alphabetische Ordnung der Namen entspricht der Reihenfolge der Buchstaben im englischen Alphabet. So werden z.B. das spanische *ll* und *ch* nicht als besondere Buchstaben behandelt. Ferner wurden diakritische Zeichen beim Alphabetisieren nicht berücksichtigt, das deutsche oder skandinavische *ä* oder *ö* als *a* oder *o* behandelt.

Physische Objekte können umgestellt erscheinen, da sie immer nach dem Eigennamen und nicht nach dem Gattungsbegriff eingeordnet wurden, z.B. "Gibraltar, Strait of ɰ." Ansonsten wurde jeder Eintrag, ob er aus einem Wort oder aus mehreren besteht, als eine einzige Einheit behandelt. So ist z.B. "Lakeland" nach "La Crosse," aber vor "La Salle" aufgeführt. Namen, die mit einem Artikel beginnen, wurden nicht umgestellt (Le Havre, Den Helder, Al-Qāhirah, As-Suways). Namen, die mit "St." und "Sainte" beginnen, sind der Schreibweise "Saint" nach eingeordnet.

Wo Namensgleichheit besteht, werden zunächst die Städte aufgeführt, dann politische Einheiten und schliesslich physische Objekte. Eintragungen, die vollkommen identisch sind (einschliesslich der weiter unten erläuterten Symbole), werden durch Hinzufügung der Abkürzung des offiziellen Ländernamens unterschieden und sind den Ländernamen nach alphabetisch geordnet. Die zahlreichen identischen Namen in Kanada, dem Vereinigten Königreich und den Vereinigten Staaten sind darüber hinaus noch durch Abkürzungen der obersten Verwaltungseinheit unterschieden. (Siehe Verzeichnis der Abkürzungen, Seite 319-320).

Abkürzungen und Grossschreibung Abkürzung und Schreibweise wurden für alle Sprachen vereinheitlicht. Nach jeder Abkürzung steht ein Punkt, auch wenn dies nicht der jeweiligen Gepflogenheit entspricht. Die Abkürzung "St." wird ausschliesslich für "Saint" gebraucht. "Sankt" und andere Formen dieses Begriffes werden ausgeschrieben.

Der erste Buchstabe eines Namens wird gross geschrieben, ausgenommen einige holländische Namen wie 's-Gravenhage. Die Grossschreibung der weiteren Worte eines zusammengesetzten Namens folgt im allgemeinen der landesüblichen Schreibweise.

Symbole Die im Register verwendeten Symbole veranschaulichen graphisch die zahlreichen Kategorien der benannten Objekte, z.B. ∧ = Berg (Everest, Mount ∧). Eine kurzgefasste Erläuterung der Symbole erscheint in jeder der fünf Sprachen des Atlas am Fusse jeder Doppelseite des Registers. Hochgestellte Ziffern hinter Symbolen im Register bezeichnen feinere Unterscheidungen, z.B. $\wedge^{1}$ = Vulkan (Fuji-san $\wedge^{1}$). Eine vollständige Übersicht der Symbole und hochgestellten Ziffern findet sich auf Seite I•1.

El índice contiene en una sola lista alfabética, alrededor de 170 000 nombres que aparecen en los mapas. Después de cada nombre está indicada la página o las páginas de referencia, en los cuales se encuentran los mismos, y las coordinadas de la latitud y la longitud del lugar del rasgo. Si una página contiene various mapas, letras minúsculas identifican el mapa correspondiente. Para mapas que ocupan dos páginas, la página de referencia siempre es la de la izquierda.

La mayoría de los nombres que figuran en el índice, se efiere a los mapas en la escala más grande. Sin embargo, un nombre no se refiere en un mapa metropolitano si ya aparece en otro mapa, donde se muestra en un marco de mayor proporción. Los países, sierras y otros rasgos extensivos se refieren generalmente en el índice en los mapas de escalas mayores en que se muestran completos.

En orden en que la información del índice se presenta, aparece en un encabezamiento al centro de cada par de páginas, en inglés, alemán, español, francés y portugués.

Por ejemplo:

ESPAÑOL

Nombre	Página	Lat.°′	Long.°′ W = Oeste

Los rasgos anotados en el índice son de tres tipos: *el punto, el área y la extensión linear.* Para rasgos que indican *el punto* (como por ejemplo, las ciudades, picos de montañas, presas), las coordinadas de latitud y longitud indican la posición exacta del punto sobre el mapa. Respecto a *las áreas* (como países, sierras, etc.), las coordinadas indican usualmente el centro aproximado del rasgo particular. En cuanto a *los rasgos lineares* (ríos, canales, acueductos) las coordinadas indican los puntos terminales, por ejemplo, la boca de un río, o el punto en que un rasgo físico alcanza el margen del mapa.

Las Formas de los Nombres Los nombres que aparecen en el índice, así como también en los mapas, se dan en general en el idioma local, y en tanto que es posible siguen la ortografía oficialmente aceptada. Incluímos también marcas diacríticas, excepto las que se usan para indicar tono, como en la lengua vietnamita. A causa de que la mayoría de los rasgos que se extienden más allá de las fronteras de un país no tienen un solo nombre oficial, éstos se denominan usualmente en inglés. Muchos nombres, en inglés, alemán, español, francés y portugués, que pueden no figurar en el mapa, se dan como referencia de una página a otra en el índice. Todas las referencias que pasan a otras páginas se indican con el símbolo →. Un nombre que aparece en el mapa en forma abreviada, debido a la limitación de espacio, en el índice figura en su forma completa, poniendo entre paréntesis angulares la parte omitida en el mapa, por ejemplo Acapulco [de Juárez].

"Trasliteración" Para los nombres escritos en los idiomas que no usan el alfabeto latino, el sistema oficial de trasliteración ha sido utilizado donde localmente existe. Así, los nombres de Rusia y de Bulgaria se trasliteran conforme a los sistemas aceptados por las academias de las ciencias de sus respectivos países. De la misma manera, la trasliteración de los nombres en chino continental siguen el sistema Pinyin que ha sido oficialmente adoptado en este país. Para idiomas sin ningún sistema localmente aceptado de trasliteración, particularmente para el árabe, éstos se trasliteran usando por lo general un sistema adoptado por el United States Board on Geographic Names.

Alfabetización Los nombres se han ordenado de acuerdo con el alfabeto inglés. Las letras del alfabeto en español *ll* y *ch* por ejemplo, no se han considerado letras separadas. Además, los signos diacríticos no se toman en cuenta en la alfabetización — en alemán o escadinavo letras *ä* u *ö* se tratan como *a* u *o*.

Los nombres de los rasgos físicos algunas veces se invierten, ya que se ordenan alfabéticamente según la parte propia y no genérica del nombre. Así por ejemplo, en el caso del Estrecho de Gibraltar aparece: Gibraltar, Strait of ʉ. Por lo demás, cada renglón, sea una palabra o una frase, se alfabetiza como una unidad. Por ejemplo, "Lakeland" aparece después de "La Crosse" y antes de "La Salle." Los nombres que comienzan con artículos (Le Havre, Den Helder, Al-Qāhirah, As-Suways) no están invertidos. Nombres que empiezan con "St." y "Sainte" se alfabetizan como "Saint".

En los casos de nombres idénticos, las poblaciones aparecen primero, las divisiones políticas después y finalmente los rasgos físicos. En caso de ser completamente idénticos (incluyendo los símbolos, discutidos más abajo) se distinguen por medio de abreviaciones de los nombres oficiales de los países a que pertenecen y son puestos en orden alfabético, de acuerdo al nombre de cada país. Hay muchos nombres duplicados en Canadá, el Reino Unido y los Estados Unidos de América, y éstos se distinguen además, por sus subdivisiones primarias. (Vease abajo, la lista de abreviaciones en las páginas 319-320).

Abreviaciones y Mayúsculas Las abreviaciones y el uso de las mayúsculas se han hecho uniformes para todos los idiomas. Se usa un punto al final de la abreviación, aun cuando en algunos casos no sea ésta la práctica local. La abreviación "St." se usa sólo para "Saint." Las otras formas del mismo término, como "Sankt," se escriben completas.

La mayúscula se usa al comienzo de todos los nombres a excepción de algunos holandeses, como 's-Gravenhage. Las palabras que no son iniciales, se dan con mayúscula o minúscula, según la práctica local.

Símbolos Los símbolos que aparecen en el índice representan gráficamente las grandes categorías do los rasgos que se han ido nombrando, por ejemplo, ʌ para montaña (Everest, Mount ʌ). Una clave abreviada para los símbolos aparece en los cinco idiomas del atlas al pie de cada par de páginas del índice. Los números que siguen más arriba del símbolo indican alguna diferencia más precisa, pro ejemplo, ʌ^1 para un volcán (Fuji- san ʌ^1). Una lista completa de símbolos y números superiores aparece en la página I•1.

L'index rassemble en une seule liste alphabétique, quelque 170 000 noms qui figurent sur les cartes. Chaque nom est suivi d'un renvoi à une ou plusieurs pages de cartes et de coordonnées géographiques qui permettent de localiser ce qu'il désigne. Si une page contient plusieurs cartes, une lettre minuscule permet d'identifier chaque carte. Pour les cartes en double page, la référence indiquée est toujours celle de la page de gauche.

En général, l'index renvoie aux cartes où l'information recherchée est reproduite à la plus grande échelle; cependant, les cartes de zones métropolitaines ne sont pas utilisées si le terme géographique figure sur une autre carte dans un contexte plus large. Pour les éléments de grande dimension comme les pays et les chaînes de montagnes, l'index renvoie généralement à la carte à grande échelle qui les représente en entier.

L'ordre des informations de l'index est rappelé en tête de chaque double page dans les cinq langues: anglais, allemand, espagnol, français et portugais.

Par exemple:

FRANÇAIS

Nom	Page	Lat.°′	Long.°′ W = Ouest

Les termes de l'index désignent des réalités géographiques de type *ponctuel, spatial* ou *linéaire.* Leur position est déterminée par les coordonnées géographiques du lieu quand les données sont de type *ponctuel* (villes, sommets, barrages, etc.), quand elles sont de type *spatial* (pays, chaînes de montagnes, etc.) par les coordonnées du centre approximatif de la zone considérée, et, quand elles sont du type *linéaire* (aqueducs, canaux, etc.) par les coordonnées soit d'un point terminal comme l'embouchure d'un cours d'eau, soit du point où les limites de la carte les interrompent.

Forme des Toponymes Les noms de l'index comme ceux des cartes sont généralement reproduits dans la langue locale et, dans la mesure du possible, selon leur orthographe officielle. Les signes diacritiques sont conservés, à l'exclusion de ceux qui servent à indiquer le ton, comme en vietnamien. La plupart des données géographiques qui s'étendent au-delà des frontières d'un pays sont nommées souvent en anglais, car elles n'ont pas de nom officiel unique. Beaucoup de noms anglais, allemands, espagnols, français et portugais, qui ne se trouvent pas sur les cartes, sont cités dans l'index sous forme de renvois. Tous les renvois sont signalés par le symbole (→). Un nom écrit sur la carte sous forme abrégée, par manque de place, figure en entier dans l'index; la partie omise est entre crochets, par exemple: Acapulco [de Juárez].

Transcription des Noms Pour les noms qui viennent de langues n'utilisant pas l'alphabet romain, le système local et officiel de transcription a été utilisé là où il existait. Ainsi, les noms russes et bulgares ont été transcrits selon les systèmes adoptés par les académies des sciences de ces pays. De même, pour la transcription des noms de la Chine continentale, on a employé le système Pinyin, officiellement adopté en Chine continentale. Pour les langues qui n'ont pas de système officiel de transcription en alphabet romain, notamment l'arabe, la transcription suit généralement de près le système adopté par le United States Board on Geographic Names (Comité américain pour les noms géographiques).

Ordre Alphabétique Les noms sont classés dans l'ordre de l'alphabet anglais. Les *ll* et *ch* espagnols, par exemple, ne sont pas traités comme des lettres séparées. De plus, on ne tient pas compte des signes diacritiques: le *ä* et le *ö* allemand ou scandinave correspondent au *a* et *o* sans tréma.

Les noms des données physiques peuvent se trouver inversés car ils sont toujours classés suivant le nom propre. Exemple: "Gibraltar, Strait of ʉ." Par ailleurs, les noms composés d'un ou plusieurs mots sont considérés comme une seule entité. Exemple: "Lakeland" est inscrit après "La Crosse" et avant "La Salle." Les noms qui commencent par un article (Le Havre, Den Helder, Al-Qāhirah, As-Suways) ne sont pas inversés. Les noms qui commencent par "St." ou "Sainte" sont classés comme s'ils s'écrivaient "Saint."

Dans le cas de noms identiques, les villes sont inscrites d'abord, puis les divisions politiques, et ensuite les données physiques. Les noms qui sont tout à fait identiques (y compris les symboles qui s'y rapportent) se distinguent par leur pays d'origine, noté en abrégé dans l'ordre alphabétique. Les noms que l'on rencontre plusieurs fois, au Canada, au Royaume-Uni et aux Etats-Unis se distinguent grâce à l'abréviation de la première subdivision administrative de ce pays (voir la liste des abréviations de la page 319-320).

Abréviations et Majuscules L'usage des abréviations a été standardisé pour toutes les langues. Un point suit chaque abréviation, même quand ce n'est pas l'usage dans certaines langues. L'abréviation "St." sert uniquement pour le mot "Saint." "Sankt" et les autres formes du mot "Saint" sont écrites en entier.

Tous les noms commencent par une majuscule, sauf quelques noms des Pays-Bas comme 's-Gravenhage. Certains noms prennent une majuscule, même s'ils ne se trouvent pas au début du terme; on a adopté, en général, l'orthographe locale.

Symboles Les symboles utilisés dans l'index donnent une représentation graphique des réalités géographiques mentionnées. Par exemple, ʌ pour une montagne (Everest, Mount ʌ). Une explication abrégée des symboles dans les cinq langues de l'Atlas se trouve au bas de chaque double page de l'index. Les indices qui accompagnent certains symboles permettent une distinction plus précise. Par exemple, ʌ^1 pour volcan (Fujisan ʌ^1). Une liste complète des symboles et indices est donnée à la page I•1.

O Índice contém, numa só lista alfabética, cerca de 170,000 nomes que figuram nos mapas. Segue-se a cada nome a referência a um ou mais mapas e a localização do acidente geográfico no mapa pelas respectivas coordenadas de latitude e longitude. A referência a mapas que ocupam duas páginas fica sempre na página da esquerda. A maior parte dos acidentes geográficos estão indexados no mapa em que aparecem em escala maior. No entanto, um acidente geográfico não é geralmente indexado num mapa de Área Metropolitana se também figura em outro mapa em que aparece em contexto mais amplo. Os países, cordilheiras e outros acidentes geográficos de maior extensão estão geralmente indexados no mapa em escala maior que os apresente em seu todo.

A ordem em que as informações são apresentadas no Índice figura no cabeçalho, a cada duas páginas, em inglês, alemão, espanhol, francês e PORTUGUÊS.

Por exemplo:

PORTUGUÊS

Nome	Página	Lat.°′	Long.°′ W = Oeste

Os acidentes indexados são de três tipos: *Ponto, espacial* (área) e *linear* (extensão). Para acidentes que indicam *pontos* (como, por exemplo, cidades, picos de montanhas, represas), as coordenadas de latitude e longitude indicam a posição exata do ponto no mapa. No que se refere aos *acidentes espaciais* (como países, cordilheiras etc.), as coordenadas geralmente indicam o centro aproximado do acidente específico. Quanto aos *acidentes lineares* (rios, canais, aquedutos), as coordenadas localizam os pontos terminais, como, por exemplo, a foz de um rio, ou o ponto em que um acidente físico atinge a margem do mapa.

Formas dos nomes Os nomes que aparecem no Índice, assim como também nos mapas, são geralmente apresentados na língua local, e tanto quanto possível, seguem a ortografia oficial. Usam-se, também, os sinais diacríticos, exceto os que indicam tom, como na língua vietnamita. A maioria dos acidentes geográficos que se estendem além das fronteiras de um só país não possuem um nome oficial único; nesses casos, estão geralmente indicados em inglês. Muitos nomes em inglês, alemão, espanhol, português e francês podem não figurar nos mapas, mas aparecem no Índice como referências remissivas. Todas essas referências são indicadas pelo símbolo (→). Um nome que aparece no mapa em forma abreviada devido a limitações de espaço, figura no Índice em sua forma completa, com a parte omitida no mapa entre chaves (por exemplo, Acapulco [de Juárez]).

Transliteração Para os nomes escritos em línguas que não usam o alfabeto latino, foi utilizado o sistema oficial de transliteração, sempre que este existia. Assim, os nomes da Rússia e da Bulgária foram transliterados de acordo com os sistemas adotados pelas academias de ciências desses países. Do mesmo modo, a transliteração dos nomes da China continental seguem o sistema Pinyin, que foi oficialmente adotado nesse país. Para as línguas que não possuem um sistema de transliteração adotado oficialmente, em especial o árabe, a transliteração geralmente segue de perto o sistema adotado pelo Conselho de Nomes Geográficos dos Estados Unidos (United States Board on Geographic Names).

Alfabetação Os nomes foram ordenados de acordo com o alfabeto inglês. Por exemplo, o espanhol *ll* e *ch* não foram considerados como letras separadas. Ademais, os sinais diacríticos não foram considerados na alfabetação. Por exemplo, em alemão ou escandinavo as letras *ä* ou *ö* foram tratradas como *a* ou *o*.

Os nomes dos acidentes físicos podem aparecer, às vezes, invertidos, já que foram sempre alfabetados pela parte específica e não genérica do nome, como, por exemplo, *Gibraltar, estreito de* ʉ. Por outro lado, cada entrada do Índice, quer constituída por uma só palavra ou mais de uma, foi alfabetada como uma unidade contínua. Por exemplo, "Lakeland" aparece depois de "La Grosse" e antes de "La Salle". Os nomes que começam por artigo (Le Havre, Den Helder, Al-Qāhirah, As-Suways) não são invertidos. Os nomes que começam por "St." e "Sainte" são alfabetados como se fossem soletrados "Saint".

Nos casos de nomes idênticos, as cidades estão relacionadas em primeiro lugar; depois as divisões políticas e em seguida os acidentes físicos. As entradas completamente idênticas (inclusive símbolos, mencionados mais abaixo), distinguem-se pelas abreviaturas dos nomes oficiais dos países a que pertencem e são arrolados na ordem alfabética do nome do país. Os muitos nomes repetidos no Canadá, no Reino Unido e nos Estados Unidos, são ainda diferenciados pelas abreviaturas dos nomes das respectivas subdivisões primárias (Ver a lista de abreviaturas, das páginas 319-320).

Abreviações e uso de maiúsculas As abreviaturas e o estilo foram normalizados em todas as línguas. Usa-se um ponto depois de cada abreviatura, mesmo que não seja essa a prática local. A abreviatura "St." só é usada para "Saint". As outras formas do termo, tal como "Sankt", são escritas por extenso.

Todos os nomes são escritos com a inicial maiúscula exceto em alguns nomes holandeses, como 's-Gravenhage. O uso de maiúsculas em palavras não iniciais de um nome segue geralmente a prática local.

Símbolos Os símbolos que aparecem no Índice representam graficamente as grandes categorias dos acidentes indicados, por exemplo, ʌ para montanha (Everest, Mount ʌ). Uma chave abreviada dos símbolos nas cinco línguas do Atlas figura no pé de cada par de páginas do Índice. Os números altos que acompanham certos símbolos do Índice indicam diferenças mais precisas, como, por examplo, ʌ^1 para vulcão (Fuji-san ʌ^1). Uma lista completa de símbolos e números altos aparece à pág. I•1.

	LOCAL NAME	ENGLISH	DEUTSCH	ESPAÑOL	FRANÇAIS	PORTUGUÊS
Ab., Can.	Alberta	Alberta	Alberta	Alberta	Alberta	Alberta
Afg.	Afghānestān	Afghanistan	Afghanistan	Afganistán	Afghanistan	Afeganistão
Afr.	. . .	Africa	Afrika	Africa	Afrique	África
Ak., U.S.	Alaska	Alaska	Alaska	Alaska	Alaska	Alasca
Al., U.S.	Alabama	Alabama	Alabama	Alabama	Alabama	Alabama
Alg.	Algérie / Djazaïr	Algeria	Algerien	Argelia	Algérie	Argélia
Am. Sam.	American Samoa / Amerika Samoa	American Samoa	Amerikanisch-Samoa	Samoa Americana	Samoa américaines	Samoa Americana
And.	Andorra	Andorra	Andorra	Andorra	Andorre	Andorra
Ang.	Angola	Angola	Angola	Angola	Angola	Angola
Anguilla	Anguilla	Anguilla	Anguilla	Anguilla	Anguilla	Anguilla
Ant.	. . .	Antarctica	Antarktis	Antártida	Antarctique	Antártida
Antig.	Antigua and Barbuda	Antigua and Barbuda	Antigua und Barbuda	Antigua y Barbuda	Antigua-et-Barbuda	Antígua e Barbuda
Ar., U.S.	Arkansas	Arkansas	Arkansas	Arkansas	Arkansas	Arkansas
Arg.	Argentina	Argentina	Argentinien	Argentina	Argentine	Argentina
Ar. Su.	Al-'Arabīyah as-Su'ūdīyah	Saudi Arabia	Saudi-Arabien	Arabia Saudita	Arabie saoudite	Arábia Saudita
Aruba	Aruba	Aruba	Aruba	Aruba	Aruba	Aruba
Asia	. . .	Asia	Asien	Asia	Asie	Ásia
Austl.	Australia	Australia	Australien	Australia	Australie	Austrália
Az., U.S.	Arizona	Arizona	Arizona	Arizona	Arizona	Arizona
Azer.	Azerbaijan	Azerbaijan	Aserbaidschan	Azerbaidján	Azerbaïdjan	Azerbaijão
Ba.	Bahamas	Bahamas	Bahamas	Bahamas	Bahamas	Bahamas
Bahr.	Al-Baḥrayn	Bahrain	Bahrain	Bahrein	Bahreïn	Bahrein
Barb.	Barbados	Barbados	Barbados	Barbados	Barbade	Barbados
B.C., Can.	British Columbia / Colombie-Britannique	British Columbia	Britisch Kolumbien	Columbia Británica	Colombie britannique	Colúmbia Britânica
Bdi.	Burundi	Burundi	Burundi	Burundi	Burundi	Burundi
Bel.	Belgique / België	Belgium	Belgien	Bélgica	Belgique	Bélgica
Belize	Belize	Belize	Belize	Belice	Bélize	Belize
Bela.	Belarus	Belarus	Belorussland	Bielorrusia	Biélorussie	Bielorrússia
Bénin	Bénin	Benin	Benin	Benin	Bénin	Benin
Ber.	Bermuda	Bermuda	Bermuda	Bermudas	Bermudes	Bermudas
B.I.O.T.	British Indian Ocean Territory	British Indian Ocean Territory	Britisch-Indien Ozean-Territorium	Territorio Británico del Océano Indico	Territoire britannique de l'océan Indien	Território Britânico do Oceano Indico
Blg.	Bâlgarija	Bulgaria	Bulgarien	Bulgaria	Bulgarie	Bulgária
Bngl.	Bangladesh	Bangladesh	Bangladesch	Bangladesh	Bangladesh	Bangladesh
Bol.	Bolivia	Bolivia	Bolivien	Bolivia	Bolivie	Bolívia
Boph.	Bophuthatswana	Bophuthatswana	Bophuthatswana	Bophuthatswana	Bophuthatswana	Bophuthatswana
Bos.	Bosna i Hercegovina	Bosnia and Hercegovina	Bosnien und Herzegowina	Bosnia y Herzegovina	Bosnie et Herzégovine	Bósnia e Herzegovina
Bots.	Botswana	Botswana	Botswana	Botswana	Botswana	Botsuana
Bra.	Brasil	Brazil	Brasilien	Brasil	Brésil	Brasil
Bru.	Brunei	Brunei	Brunei	Brunei	Brunéi	Brunei
Br. Vir. Is.	British Virgin Islands	British Virgin Islands	Britische Jungferninseln	Islas Vírgenes Británicas	Îles Vierges britanniques	Virgens Britânicas, Ilhas
Burkina	Burkina Faso	Burkina Faso	Burkina Faso	Burkina Faso	Burkina Faso	Burkina Faso
Ca., U.S.	California	California	Kalifornien	California	Californie	Califórnia
Cam.	Cameroun / Cameroon	Cameroon	Kamerun	Camerún	Cameroun	Camarão
Can.	Canada	Canada	Kanada	Canadá	Canada	Canadá
Cay. Is.	Cayman Islands	Cayman Islands	Caiman-Inseln	Islas Caimán	Îles Caïmanes	Cayman, Ilhas
Centraf.	République centrafricaine	Central African Republic	Zentralafrikanische Republik	República Centroafricana	République centrafricaine	Centro-Africana, República
Česká	Česká Republika	Czech Republic	Tschechische Republik	República Checa	République Tcheque	República Tcheca
Chile	Chile	Chile	Chile	Chile	Chili	Chile
Christ. I.	Christmas Island	Christmas Island	Weihnachtsinsel	Isla Christmas	Île Christmas	Christmas, Ilha
Ciskei	Ciskei	Ciskei	Ciskei	Ciskei	Ciskei	Ciskei
C. Iv.	Côte d'Ivoire	Ivory Coast	Elfenbeinküste	Costa de Marfil	Côte d'Ivoire	Costa do Marfim
C.M.I.K.	Chosŏn-minjujuŭi-inmīn-konghwaguk	Korea, North	Nordkorea	Corea del Norte	Corée du Nord	Coréia do Norte
Co., U.S.	Colorado	Colorado	Colorado	Colorado	Colorado	Colorado
Cocos Is.	Cocos (Keeling) Islands	Cocos (Keeling) Islands	Cokos-Inseln	Islas Cocos (Keeling)	Îles Cocos (Keeling)	Cocos (Keeling), Ilhas
Col.	Colombia	Colombia	Kolumbien	Colombia	Colombie	Colômbia
Comores	Comores / Al-Qumur	Comoros	Komoren	Comoras	Comores	Comores
Congo	Congo	Congo	Kongo	Congo	Congo	Congo
Cook Is.	Cook Islands	Cook Islands	Cook-Inseln	Islas Cook	Îles Cook	Cook, Ilhas
C.R.	Costa Rica	Costa Rica	Costa Rica	Costa Rica	Costa Rica	Costa Rica
Ct., U.S.	Connecticut	Connecticut	Connecticut	Connecticut	Connecticut	Connecticut
Cuba	Cuba	Cuba	Kuba	Cuba	Cuba	Cuba
C.V.	Cabo Verde	Cape Verde	Kap Verde	Cabo Verde	Cap-Vert	Cabo Verde
Dan.	Danmark	Denmark	Dänemark	Dinamarca	Danemark	Dinamarca
D.C., U.S.	District of Columbia	District of Columbia	District of Columbia	District of Columbia	District of Columbia	Distrito de Columbia
De., U.S.	Delaware	Delaware	Delaware	Delaware	Delaware	Delaware
Dji.	Djibouti	Djibouti	Djibouti	Djibouti	Djibouti	Djibouti
Dom.	Dominica	Dominica	Dominica	Dominica	Dominique	Dominica
Dtsch.	Deutschland	Germany	Deutschland	Alemania	Allemagne	Alemanha
D.Y.	Druk-Yul	Bhutan	Bhutan	Bhután	Bhoutan	Butã
Ec.	Ecuador	Ecuador	Ecuador	Ecuador	Équateur	Equador
Eesti	Eesti	Estonia	Estland	Estonia	Estonie	Estónia
Ellás	Ellás	Greece	Griechenland	Grecia	Grèce	Grécia
El Sal.	El Salvador	El Salvador	El Salvador	El Salvador	El Salvador	El Salvador
Eng., U.K.	England	England	England	Inglaterra	Angleterre	Inglaterra
Erit.	Eritrea	Eritrea	Eritrea	Eritrea	Erythrée	Eritréia
Esp.	España	Spain	Spanien	España	Espagne	Espanha
Europe	. . .	Europe	Europa	Europa	Europe	Europa
Falk. Is.	Falkland Islands	Falkland Islands	Falkland-Inseln	Islas Malvinas	Îles Falkland	Falkland, Ilhas
Fiji	Fiji	Fiji	Fidschi	Fiji	Fidji	Fiji (Fidji)
Fl., U.S.	Florida	Florida	Florida	Florida	Floride	Flórida
Før.	Føroyar	Faeroe Islands	Färöer	Islas Feroe	Îles Féroé	Faeroe, Ilhas
Fr.	France	France	Frankreich	Francia	France	França
Ga., U.S.	Georgia	Georgia	Georgia	Georgia	Georgie	Geórgia
Gabon	Gabon	Gabon	Gabun	Gabón	Gabon	Gabão
Gam.	Gambia	Gambia	Gambia	Gambia	Gambie	Gâmbia
Ghana	Ghana	Ghana	Ghana	Ghana	Ghana	Gana
Gib.	Gibraltar	Gibraltar	Gibraltar	Gibraltar	Gibraltar	Gibraltar
Gren.	Grenada	Grenada	Grenada	Granada	Grenade	Grenada
Guad.	Guadeloupe	Guadeloupe	Guadeloupe	Guadalupe	Guadeloupe	Guadalupe
Guam	Guam	Guam	Guam	Guam	Guam	Guam
Guat.	Guatemala	Guatemala	Guatemala	Guatemala	Guatemala	Guatemala
Guernsey	Guernsey	Guernsey	Guernsey	Guernsey	Guernesey	Guernsey
Gui.-B.	Guiné-Bissau	Guinea-Bissau	Guinea-Bissau	Guinea-Bissau	Guinée-Bissau	Guiné-Bissau
Gui. Ecu.	Guinea Ecuatorial	Equatorial Guinea	Äquatorial-guinea	Guinea Ecuatorial	Guinée équatoriale	Guiné Equatorial
Guinée	Guinée	Guinea	Guinea	Guinea	Guinée	Guiné
Guy.	Guyana	Guyana	Guyana	Guyana	Guyane	Guiana
Guy. fr.	Guyane française	French Guiana	Französisch-Guayana	Guayana Francesa	Guyane française	Guiana Francesa
Haï.	Haïti	Haiti	Haiti	Haití	Haïti	Haiti
Haya.	Hayastan	Armenia	Armenien	Armenia	Arménie	Arménia
Hi., U.S.	Hawaii	Hawaii	Hawaii	Hawaii	Hawaii	Havaí
H.K.	Hong Kong	Hong Kong	Hongkong	Hong Kong	Hong-Kong	Hong Kong
Hond.	Honduras	Honduras	Honduras	Honduras	Honduras	Honduras
Hrv.	Hrvatska	Croatia	Kroatien	Croacia	Croatie	Croácia
Ia., U.S.	Iowa	Iowa	Iowa	Iowa	Iowa	Iowa

	LOCAL NAME	ENGLISH	DEUTSCH	ESPAÑOL	FRANÇAIS	PORTUGUÊS
I.A.M.	Al-Imārāt al-'Arabīyah al-Muttaḥidah	United Arab Emirates	Vereinigte Arabische Emirate	Emiratos Arabes Unidos	Émirats arabes unis	Emirados Árabes Unidos
Id., U.S.	Idaho	Idaho	Idaho	Idaho	Idaho	Idaho
Il., U.S.	Illinois	Illinois	Illinois	Illinois	Illinois	Illinois
In., U.S.	Indiana	Indiana	Indiana	Indiana	Indiana	Indiana
India	India / Bharat	India	Indien	India	Inde	Índia
Indon.	Indonesia	Indonesia	Indonesien	Indonesia	Indonésie	Indonésia
I. of Man	Isle of Man	Isle of Man	Insel Man	Isla de Man	Île de Man	Man, Ilha de
Īrān	Īrān	Iran	Iran	Irán	Iran	Irã
'Īrāq	Al-'Īrāq	Iraq	Irak	Iraq	Iraq	Iraque
Ire.	Ireland / Éire	Ireland	Irland	Irlanda	Irlande	Irlanda
Ísland	Ísland	Iceland	Island	Islandia	Islande	Islândia
Isr. Occ.	. . .	Israeli Occupied Areas	Von Israel besetztes Gebiet	Áreas ocupadas por Israel	Territoires occupés par Israël	Áreas occupadas por Israel
It.	Italia	Italy	Italien	Italia	Italie	Itália
Ityo.	Ityopiya	Ethiopia	Äthiopien	Etiopía	Éthiopie	Etiópia
Jam.	Jamaica	Jamaica	Jamaika	Jamaica	Jamaïque	Jamaica
Jersey	Jersey	Jersey	Jersey	Jersey	Jersey	Jersey
Jugo.	Jugoslavija	Yugoslavia	Jugoslawien	Yugoslavia	Yougoslavie	Iugoslávia
Kal. Nun.	Kalaallit Nunaat / Grønland	Greenland	Grönland	Groenlandia	Groenland	Groenlândia
Kâm.	Kâmpŭchéa	Cambodia	Kambodscha	Camboya	Cambodge	Camboja
Kaz.	Kazachstan	Kazakhstan	Kasachstan	Kazajstán	Kazakhstan	Cazaquistão
Kenya	Kenya	Kenya	Kenia	Kenya	Kenya	Quênia
Kıbrıs	Kuzey Kıbrıs	Cyprus, North	Türkische Republik Nordzypern	República Turca de Chipre del Norte	République turque du Nord de Chypre	República Turca do Norte de Chipre
Kípros	Kípros / Kıbrıs	Cyprus	Zypern	Chipre	Chypre	Chipre
Kiribati	Kiribati	Kiribati	Kiribati	Kiribati	Kiribati	Kiribati
Ks., U.S.	Kansas	Kansas	Kansas	Kansas	Kansas	Kansas
Kuwayt	Al-Kuwayt	Kuwait	Kuwait	Kuwait	Koweït	Kuwait
Ky., U.S.	Kentucky	Kentucky	Kentucky	Kentucky	Kentucky	Kentucky
Kyrg.	Kyrgyzstan	Kyrgyzstan	Kirgisistan	Kirguizia	Kirghizistan	Quirguizão
La., U.S.	Louisiana	Louisiana	Louisiana	Luisiana	Louisiane	Louisiana
Lao	Lao	Laos	Laos	Laos	Laos	Lao
Lat.	Latvija	Latvia	Lettland	Letonia	Lettonie	Letónia
Leso.	Lesotho	Lesotho	Lesotho	Lesotho	Lesotho	Lesoto
Liber.	Liberia	Liberia	Liberia	Liberia	Libéria	Libéria
Lībiyā	Lībiyā	Libya	Libyen	Libia	Libye	Líbia
Liech.	Liechtenstein	Liechtenstein	Liechtenstein	Liechtenstein	Liechtenstein	Liechtenstein
Liet.	Lietuva	Lithuania	Litauen	Lituania	Lithuanie	Lituânia
Lubnān	Lubnān	Lebanon	Libanon	Líbano	Liban	Líbano
Lux.	Luxembourg	Luxembourg	Luxemburg	Luxemburgo	Luxembourg	Luxemburgo
Ma., U.S.	Massachusetts	Massachusetts	Massachusetts	Massachusetts	Massachusetts	Massachusetts
Macau	Macau	Macau	Macao	Macao	Macao	Macau
Mac.	Makedonija	Macedonia	Makedonien	Macedonia	Macédoine	Macedonia
Madag.	Madagasikara / Madagascar	Madagascar	Madagaskar	Madagascar	Madagascar	Madagascar
Magreb	Al-Magreb	Morocco	Marokko	Marruecos	Maroc	Marrocos
Magy.	Magyarország	Hungary	Ungarn	Hungría	Hongrie	Hungria
Malaŵi	Malaŵi	Malawi	Malawi	Malawi	Malawi	Malaui
Malay.	Malaysia	Malaysia	Malaysia	Malasia	Malaisie	Malásia
Mald.	Maldives	Maldives	Malediven	Maldivas	Maldives	Maldivas
Mali	Mali	Mali	Mali	Malí	Mali	Mali
Malta	Malta	Malta	Malta	Malta	Malte	Malta
Marsh. Is.	Marshall Islands	Marshall Islands	Marshall Islands	Islas Marshall	Îles Marshall	Marshall Islands
Mart.	Martinique	Martinique	Martinique	Martinica	Martinique	Martinica
Maur.	Mauritanie / Mūrītāniyā	Mauritania	Mauretanien	Mauritania	Mauritanie	Mauritânia
Maus.	Mauritius	Mauritius	Mauritius	Mauricio	Maurice	Maurício
Mayotte	Mayotte	Mayotte	Mayotte	Mayotte	Mayotte	Mayotte
Mb., Can.	Manitoba	Manitoba	Manitoba	Manitoba	Manitoba	Manitoba
Md., U.S.	Maryland	Maryland	Maryland	Maryland	Maryland	Maryland
Me., U.S.	Maine	Maine	Maine	Maine	Maine	Maine
Méx.	México	Mexico	Mexiko	México	Mexique	México
Mi., U.S.	Michigan	Michigan	Michigan	Michigan	Michigan	Michigan
Micron.	Federated States of Micronesia	Micronesia, Federated States of	Federated States of Micronesia	Estado Federal de Micronesia	États fédérés de Micronésie	Federated States of Micronesia
Mid. Is.	Midway Islands	Midway Islands	Midway-Inseln	Islas Midway	Îles Midway	Midway, Ilhas
Miṣr	Miṣr	Egypt	Ägypten	Egipto	Égypte	Egito
Mn., U.S.	Minnesota	Minnesota	Minnesota	Minnesota	Minnesota	Minnesota
Mo., U.S.	Missouri	Missouri	Missouri	Misuri	Missouri	Missouri
Moç.	Moçambique	Mozambique	Mosambik	Mozambique	Mozambique	Moçambique
Mol.	Moldova	Moldova	Moldawien	Moldavia	Moldavie	Moldávia
Monaco	Monaco	Monaco	Monaco	Mónaco	Monaco	Mônaco
Mong.	Mongol Ard Uls	Mongolia	Mongolei	Mongolia	Mongolie	Mongólia
Monts.	Montserrat	Montserrat	Montserrat	Montserrat	Montserrat	Montserrat
Ms., U.S.	Mississippi	Mississippi	Mississippi	Misisipi	Mississippi	Mississippi
Mt., U.S.	Montana	Montana	Montana	Montana	Montana	Montana
Mya.	Myanmar	Burma	Birma	Birmania	Birmanie	Birmânia
N.A.	. . .	North America	Nordamerika	América del Norte	Amérique du Nord	América do Norte
Namibia	Namibia	Namibia	Namibia	Namibia	Namibie	Namíbia
Nauru	Nauru / Naoero	Nauru	Nauru	Nauru	Nauru	Nauru
N.B., Can.	New Brunswick / Nouveau-Brunswick	New Brunswick	Neubraunschweig	Nueva Brunswick	Nouveau-Brunswick	Nova Brunswick
N.C., U.S.	North Carolina	North Carolina	Nord Karolina	Carolina del Norte	Caroline du Nord	Carolina do Norte
N. Cal.	Nouvelle-Calédonie	New Caledonia	Neukaledonien	Nueva Caledonia	Nouvelle Calédonie	Nova Caledônia
N.D., U.S.	North Dakota	North Dakota	Nord Dakota	Dakota del Norte	Dakota du Nord	Dakota do Norte
Ne., U.S.	Nebraska	Nebraska	Nebraska	Nebraska	Nebraska	Nebraska
Ned.	Nederland	Netherlands	Niederlande	Países Bajos	Pays-Bas	Países Baixos
Ned. Ant.	Nederlandse Antillen	Netherlands Antilles	Niederländische Antillen	Antillas Neerlandesas	Antilles néerlandaises	Antilhas Holandesas
Nepāl	Nepāl	Nepal	Nepal	Nepal	Népal	Nepal
Nf., Can.	Newfoundland / Terre-Neuve	Newfoundland	Neufundland	Terranova	Terre-Neuve	Terra Nova
N.H., U.S.	New Hampshire	New Hampshire	New Hampshire	Nuevo Hampshire	New Hampshire	Nova Hampshire
Nic.	Nicaragua	Nicaragua	Nicaragua	Nicaragua	Nicaragua	Nicarágua
Nig.	Nigeria	Nigeria	Nigeria	Nigeria	Nigéria	Nigéria
Niger	Niger	Niger	Niger	Níger	Niger	Níger
Nihon	Nihon	Japan	Japan	Japón	Japon	Japão
N. Ire., U.K.	Northern Ireland	Northern Ireland	Nordirland	Irlanda del Norte	Irlande du Nord	Irlanda do Norte
Niue	Niue	Niue	Niue	Niue	Nioué	Niue
N.J., U.S.	New Jersey	New Jersey	New Jersey	Nueva Jersey	New Jersey	Nova Jersey
N.M., U.S.	New Mexico	New Mexico	New Mexico	Nuevo México	Nouveau-Mexique	Nova México
N. Mar. Is.	Northern Mariana Islands	Northern Mariana Islands	Northern Mariana Islands	Islas Marianas	Îles Mariannes du Nord	Northern Mariana Islands
Nor.	Norge	Norway	Norwegen	Noruega	Norvège	Noruega
Norf. I.	Norfolk Island	Norfolk Island	Norfolk-Insel	Isla Norfolk	Île Norfolk	Norfolk, Ilha
N.S., Can.	Nova Scotia / Nouvelle-Écosse	Nova Scotia	Neu Schottland	Nueva Escocia	Nouvelle-Écosse	Nova Scotia
N.T., Can.	Northwest Territories / Territoires du Nord-Ouest	Northwest Territories	Nord-West Territorien	Territorios del Noroeste	Territoires du Nord-Ouest	Territórios do Noroeste
Nv., U.S.	Nevada	Nevada	Nevada	Nevada	Nevada	Nevada
N.Y., U.S.	New York	New York	New York	Nueva York	New York	Nova York

	LOCAL NAME	ENGLISH	DEUTSCH	ESPAÑOL	FRANÇAIS	PORTUGUÊS
N.Z.	New Zealand	New Zealand	Neuseeland	Nueva Zelanda	Nouvelle-Zélande	Nova Zelândia
Oc.	. . .	Oceania	Ozeanien	Oceanía	Océanie	Oceania
Oh., U.S.	Ohio	Ohio	Ohio	Ohio	Ohio	Ohio
Ok., U.S.	Oklahoma	Oklahoma	Oklahoma	Oklahoma	Oklahoma	Oklahoma
On., Can.	Ontario	Ontario	Ontario	Ontario	Ontario	Ontário
Or., U.S.	Oregon	Oregon	Oregon	Oregón	Oregon	Oregon
Öst.	Österreich	Austria	Österreich	Austria	Autriche	Austria
Pa., U.S.	Pennsylvania	Pennsylvania	Pennsylvanien	Pensilvania	Pennsylvanie	Pennsylvania
Pāk.	Pākistān	Pakistan	Pakistan	Pakistán	Pakistan	Paquistão
Palau	Palau / Belau	Palau	Palau	Palau	Palau (Belau)	Palau
Pan.	Panamá	Panama	Panama	Panamá	Panama	Panamá
Pap. N. Gui.	Papua New Guinea	Papua New Guinea	Papua-Neuguinea	Papua Nueva Guinea	Papouasie-Nouvelle Guinée	Papua-Nova Guiné
Para.	Paraguay	Paraguay	Paraguay	Paraguay	Paraguay	Paraguai
P.E., Can.	Prince Edward Island / Île-du-Prince-Édouard	Prince Edward Island	Prinz Edward-Insel	Isla Príncipe Eduardo	Île-du-Prince Édouard	Príncipe Eduardo, Ilha do
Perú	Perú	Peru	Peru	Perú	Pérou	Peru
Pil.	Pilipinas / Philippines	Philippines	Philippinen	Filipinas	Philippines	Filipinas
Pit.	Pitcairn	Pitcairn	Pitcairn	Pitcairn	Pitcairn	Pitcairn
Pol.	Polska	Poland	Polen	Polonia	Pologne	Polônia
Poly. fr.	Polynésie française	French Polynesia	Französisch-Polynesien	Polinesia Francesa	Polynésie française	Polinésia Francesa
Port.	Portugal	Portugal	Portugal	Portugal	Portugal	Portugal
P.Q., Can.	Québec	Quebec	Quebec	Quebec	Québec	Québec
P.R.	Puerto Rico	Puerto Rico	Puerto Rico	Puerto Rico	Porto Rico	Porto Rico
P.S.N.Á.	Plazas de Soberanía en el Norte de África	Spanish North Africa	Spanisch-Nordafrika	Plazas de Soberanía en el Norte de África	Afrique du Nord espagnole	África do Norte Espanhola
Qaṭar	Qaṭar	Qatar	Katar	Qatar	Qatar	Qatar
Rep. Dom.	República Dominicana	Dominican Republic	Dominikanische Republik	República Dominicana	République dominicaine	Dominicana, República
Réu.	Réunion	Reunion	Réunion	Reunión	Réunion	Reunião
R.I., U.S.	Rhode Island	Rhode Island	Rhode Island	Rhode Island	Rhode Island	Rhode Island
Rom.	România	Romania	Rumänien	Rumanía	Roumanie	Romênia
Ross.	Rossija	Russia	Russland	Rusia	Russie	Rússia
Rw.	Rwanda	Rwanda	Ruanda	Rwanda	Rwanda	Ruanda
S.A.	. . .	South America	Südamerika	América del Sur	Amérique du Sud	América do Sul
S. Afr.	South Africa / Suid-Afrika	South Africa	Südafrika	Sudáfrica	Afrique du Sud	África do Sul
Sak.	Sakartvelo	Georgia	Georgien	Georgia	Géorgie	Geórgia
S.C., U.S.	South Carolina	South Carolina	Süd Karolina	Carolina del Sur	Caroline du Sud	Carolina do Sul
Schw.	Schweiz / Suisse / Svizzera	Switzerland	Schweiz	Suiza	Suisse	Suíça
Scot., U.K.	Scotland	Scotland	Schottland	Escocia	Écosse	Escócia
S.D., U.S.	South Dakota	South Dakota	Süd Dakota	Dakota del Sur	Dakota du Sud	Dakota do Sul
Sén.	Sénégal	Senegal	Senegal	Senegal	Sénégal	Senegal
Sey.	Seychelles	Seychelles	Seschellen	Seychelles	Seychelles	Seychelles
Shq.	Shqipëri	Albania	Albanien	Albania	Albanie	Albânia
Sing.	Singapore	Singapore	Singapur	Singapur	Singapour	Cingapura
Sk., Can.	Saskatchewan	Saskatchewan	Saskatchewan	Saskatchewan	Saskatchewan	Saskatchewan
S.L.	Sierra Leone	Sierra Leone	Sierra Leone	Sierra Leona	Sierra Leone	Serra Leoa
S. Lan.	Sri Lanka	Sri Lanka	Sri Lanka	Sri Lanka	Sri Lanka	Sri Lanka
Slo.	Slovenija	Slovenia	Slowenien	Eslovenia	Slovénie	Eslovênia
Slov.	Slovensko	Slovakia	Slowakei	Eslovaquia	Slovaquie	Eslováquia
S. Mar.	San Marino	San Marino	San Marino	San Marino	Saint-Marin	San Marino
Sol. Is.	Solomon Islands	Solomon Islands	Salomonen	Islas Salomón	Îles Salomon	Salomão, Ilhas
Som.	Somaliya	Somalia	Somalia	Somalia	Somalie	Somália
St. Hel.	St. Helena	St. Helena	Sankt Helena	Santa Elena	Sainte-Hélène	Santa Helena
St. K./N.	St. Kitts and Nevis	St. Kitts and Nevis	Sankt Kitts und Nevis	San Kitts y Nevis	Saint-Kitts-et-Nevis	São Kitts e Nevis
St. Luc.	St. Lucia	St. Lucia	Sankt Lucia	Santa Lucía	Sainte-Lucie	Santa Lúcia
S. Tom./P.	São Tomé e Príncipe	Sao Tome and Principe	São Tomé und Principe	Santo Tomé y Princípe	Sao Tomé-et-Principe	São Tomé e Príncipe
St. P./M.	Saint-Pierre-et-Miquelon	St. Pierre and Miquelon	Saint-Pierre und Miquelon	San Pedro y Miquelón	Saint-Pierre-et-Miquelon	São Pedro e Miquelon
St. Vin.	St. Vincent and the Grenadines	St. Vincent and the Grenadines	Sankt Vincent und die Grenadinen	San Vicente y las Granadinas	Saint-Vincent-et-Grenadines	São Vicente e Granadinas

	LOCAL NAME	ENGLISH	DEUTSCH	ESPAÑOL	FRANÇAIS	PORTUGUÊS
Sūd.	As-Sūdān	Sudan	Sudan	Sudán	Soudan	Sudão
Suomi	Suomi / Finland	Finland	Finnland	Finlandia	Finlande	Finlândia
Sur.	Suriname	Suriname	Suriname	Suriname	Suriname	Suriname
Sūrīy.	Sūrīyah	Syria	Syrien	Siria	Syrie	Síria
Sve.	Sverige	Sweden	Schweden	Suecia	Suéde	Suécia
Swaz.	Swaziland	Swaziland	Swasiland	Swazilandia	Swaziland	Suazilândia
T.a.a.f.	Terres australes et antarctiques françaises	French Southern and Antarctic Territories	Französische Süd- und Antarktis-Gebiete	Tierras Australes y Antárticas Francesas	Terres australes et antarctiques françaises	Terras Austrais e Antárticas Francesas
Taehan	Taehan-min'guk	Korea, South	Südkorea	Corea del Sur	Corée du Sud	Coréia do Sul
T'aiwan	T'aiwan	Taiwan	Taiwan	Taiwán	Taïwan	Taiwan (Formosa)
Taj.	Tajikistan	Tajikistan	Tadschikistan	Tadjikistán	Tadjikistan	Tajiquistão
Tan.	Tanzania	Tanzania	Tansania	Tanzanía	Tanzanie	Tanzânia
Tchad	Tchad	Chad	Tschad	Chad	Tchad	Tchad
T./C. Is.	Turks and Caicos Islands	Turks and Caicos Islands	Turks- und Caicos-Inseln	Islas Turcas y Caicos	Îles Turques et Caïques	Turcas e Caicos, Ilhas
Thai	Prathet Thai	Thailand	Thailand	Tailandia	Thaïlande	Tailândia
Tn., U.S.	Tennessee	Tennessee	Tennessee	Tennessee	Tennessee	Tennessee
Togo	Togo	Togo	Togo	Togo	Togo	Togo
Tok.	Tokelau	Tokelau	Tokelau	Tokelau	Tokélaou	Tokelau
Tonga	Tonga	Tonga	Tonga	Tonga	Tonga	Tonga
Transkei	Transkei	Transkei	Transkei	Transkei	Transkei	Transkei
Trin.	Trinidad and Tobago	Trinidad and Tobago	Trinidad und Tobago	Trinidad y Tabago	Trinité-et-Tobago	Trinidad e Tobago
Tun.	Tunisie / Tunis	Tunisia	Tunesien	Túnez	Tunisie	Tunísia
Tür.	Türkiye	Turkey	Türkei	Turquía	Turquie	Turquia
Turk.	Turkmenistan	Turkmenistan	Turkmenistan	Turkmenia	Turkmenistan	Turquemenistão
Tuvalu	Tuvalu	Tuvalu	Tuvalu	Tuvalu	Tuvalu	Tuvalu
Tx., U.S.	Texas	Texas	Texas	Texas	Texas	Texas
Ug.	Uganda	Uganda	Uganda	Uganda	Ouganda	Uganda
U.K.	United Kingdom	United Kingdom	Vereinigtes Königreich	Reino Unido	Royaume-Uni	Reino Unido
Ukr.	Ukraina	Ukraine	Ukraine	Ucrania	Ukraine	Ucrânia
ʿUmān	ʿUmān	Oman	Oman	Omán	Oman	Omã
Ur.	Uruguay	Uruguay	Uruguay	Uruguay	Uruguay	Uruguai
Urd.	Al-Urdun	Jordan	Jordanien	Jordania	Jordanie	Jordânia
U.S.	United States	United States	Vereinigte Staaten	Estados Unidos	États-Unis	Estados Unidos
Ut., U.S.	Utah	Utah	Utah	Utah	Utah	Utah
Uzb.	Uzbekistan	Uzbekistan	Usbekistan	Uzbekistán	Ouzbekistan	Usbequistão
Va., U.S.	Virginia	Virginia	Virginia	Virginia	Virginie	Virgínia
Vanuatu	Vanuatu	Vanuatu	Vanuatu	Vanuatu	Vanuatu	Vanuatu
Vat.	Cittá del Vaticano	Vatican City	Vatikanstadt	Ciudad del Vaticano	Cité du Vatican	Vaticano
Ven.	Venezuela	Venezuela	Venezuela	Venezuela	Venezuela	Venezuela
Venda	Venda	Venda	Venda	Venda	Venda	Venda
Viet	Viet Nam	Vietnam	Vietnam	Viet Nam	Viet Nam	Vietnam
Vir. Is., U.S.	Virgin Islands (U.S.)	Virgin Islands (U.S.)	Amerikanische Jungferninseln	Islas Vírgenes (americanas)	Îles Vierges (américaines)	Virgens Americanas, Ilhas
Vt.	Vermont	Vermont	Vermont	Vermont	Vermont	Vermont
Wa., U.S.	Washington	Washington	Washington	Washington	Washington	Washington
Wake I.	Wake Island	Wake Island	Wake	Isla Wake	Île Wake	Wake
Wales, U.K.	Wales	Wales	Wales	Gales	Galles	Gales
Wal./F.	Wallis et Futuna	Wallis and Futuna	Wallis und Futuna	Wallis y Futuna	Wallis et Futuna	Wallis e Futuna
Wi., U.S.	Wisconsin	Wisconsin	Wisconsin	Wisconsin	Wisconsin	Wisconsin
W. Sah.	. . .	Western Sahara	Westliche Sahara	Sahara Occidental	Sahara occidental	Saara Ocidental
W. Sam.	Western Samoa / Samoa i Sisifo	Western Samoa	Westsamoa	Samoa Occidental	Samoa-Occidental	Samoa Ocidental
W.V., U.S.	West Virginia	West Virginia	West Virginia	Virginia Occidental	Virginie Occidentale	Virgínia Ocidental
Wy., U.S.	Wyoming	Wyoming	Wyoming	Wyoming	Wyoming	Wyoming
Yaman	Al-Yaman	Yemen	Jemen	Yemen	Yémen	Iêmen
Yis.	Yisra'el / Isrā'īl	Israel	Israel	Israel	Israël	Israel
Yk., Can.	Yukon Territory	Yukon Territory	Yukon	Yukón	Yukon	Yukon
Zaïre	Zaïre	Zaire	Zaire	Zaire	Zaïre	Zaire
Zam.	Zambia	Zambia	Sambia	Zambia	Zambie	Zâmbia
Zhg.	Zhongguo	China	China	China	Chine	China
Zimb.	Zimbabwe	Zimbabwe	Simbabwe	Zimbabwe	Zimbabwe	Zimbabwe

Key to Index Symbols

The symbols below represent the categories into which the physical and cultural features are classified in the Index. Broad categories appear in **boldface** type. Symbols with superior numbers identify subcategories.

Schlüssel zu den Symbolen des Registers

Die folgenden Symbole veranschaulichen die Kategorien, nach denen physische und kulturgeographische Objekte im Register geordnet sind. Die Oberbegriffe sind in **Fettdruck** hervorgehoben. Symbole mit hochgestellten Nummern kennzeichnen Unterbegriffe.

Clave de los Símbolos del Índice

Los símbolos abajo representan las categorías dentro de las cuales están clasificados los rasgos físicos y culturales que están incluídos en el Índice. Las grandes categorías aparecen en **negrilla**. Los símbolos que tienen números en su parte superior identifican las subcategorías.

Signification des Symboles de l'Index

Les symboles ci-dessous représentent les catégories sous lesquelles les données physiques et culturelles sont classées dans l'indes. Les symboles en caractèter **gras** correspondent aux catégories principales. Ceux suivis d'un indice désignent les subdivisions d'une même catégorie.

Chave dos Símbolos do Índice

Os símbolos abaixo representam as categorias em que estão classificados os acidentes físicos e culturais no Índice. As grandes categorias aparecem em **negrito**. Os símbolos acompanhados de números altos identificam as subcategorias.

ENGLISH	DEUTSCH	ESPANOL	FRANCAIS	PORTUGUES
∧ **Mountain**	∧ **Berg**	∧ **Montaña**	∧ **Montagne**	∧ **Montanha**
∧[1] Volcano	∧[1] Vulkan	∧[1] Volcán	∧[1] Volcan	∧[1] Vulcão
∧[2] Hill	∧[2] Hügel	∧[2] Colina	∧[2] Colline	∧[2] Colina
⋏ **Mountains**	⋏ **Gebirge**	⋏ **Montañas**	⋏ **Montagnes**	⋏ **Montanhas**
⋏[1] Plateau	⋏[1] Hochebene	⋏[1] Meseta	⋏[1] Plateau	⋏[1] Planalto
⋏[2] Hills	⋏[2] Hügel	⋏[2] Colinas	⋏[2] Collines	⋏[2] Colinas
)(**Pass**	)(**Paß**	)(**Paso**	)(**Col**	)(**Passo**
V **Valley, Canyon**	V **Tal, Cañon**	V **Valle, Cañón**	V **Vallée, Canyon**	V **Vale, Canhão**
≚ **Plain**	≚ **Ebene**	≚ **Llano**	≚ **Plaine**	≚ **Planície**
≚[1] Basin	≚[1] Becken	≚[1] Cuenca	≚[1] Bassin	≚[1] Bacia
≚[2] Delta	≚[2] Delta	≚[2] Delta	≚[2] Delta	≚[2] Delta
≻ **Cape**	≻ **Kap**	≻ **Cabo**	≻ **Cap**	≻ **Cabo**
≻[1] Peninsula	≻[1] Halbinsel	≻[1] Península	≻[1] Péninsule	≻[1] Península
≻[2] Spit, Sand Bar	≻[2] Landzunge, Sandbarre	≻[2] Lengua de Tierra, Bajo	≻[2] Flèche, Banc de sable	≻[2] Ponta de Terra, Banco de Areia
I **Island**	I **Insel**	I **Isla**	I **Île**	I **Ilha**
I[1] Atoll	I[1] Atoll	I[1] Atolón	I[1] Atoll	I[1] Atol
I[2] Rock	I[2] Fels	I[2] Roca	I[2] Rocher	I[2] Rochedo
II **Islands**	II **Inseln**	II **Islas**	II **Îles**	II **Ilhas**
II[1] Rocks	II[1] Felsen	II[1] Rocas	II[1] Rochers	II[1] Rochedos
± **Other Topographic Features**	± **Andere Topographische Objekte**	± **Otros Elementos Topográficos**	± **Autres données topographiques**	± **Outros Acidentes Topográficos**
±[1] Continent	±[1] Erdteil	±[1] Continente	±[1] Continent	±[1] Continente
±[2] Coast, Beach	±[2] Küste, Strand	±[2] Costa, Playa	±[2] Côte, Plage	±[2] Costa, Praia
±[3] Isthmus	±[3] Landenge	±[3] Istmo	±[3] Isthme	±[3] Istmo
±[4] Cliff	±[4] Kliff	±[4] Risco	±[4] Falaise	±[4] Falésia
±[5] Cave, Caves	±[5] Höhle, Höhlen	±[5] Cueva, Cuevas	±[5] Caverne, Cavernes	±[5] Caverna, Cavernas
±[6] Crater	±[6] Krater	±[6] Cráter	±[6] Cratère	±[6] Cratera
±[7] Depression	±[7] Senke	±[7] Depresión	±[7] Dépression	±[7] Depressão
±[8] Dunes	±[8] Dünen	±[8] Dunas	±[8] Dunes	±[8] Dunas
±[9] Lava Flow	±[9] Lavastrom	±[9] Corriente de Lava	±[9] Coulée de lave	±[9] Corrente de Lava
≏ **River**	≏ **Fluß**	≏ **Río**	≏ **Rivière, Fleuve**	≏ **Rio**
≏[1] River Channel	≏[1] Flussarm	≏[1] Brazo de Río	≏[1] Bras de rivière	≏[1] Canal de Rio
≊ **Canal**	≊ **Kanal**	≊ **Canal**	≊ **Canal**	≊ **Canal**
≊[1] Aqueduct	≊[1] Aquädukt	≊[1] Acueducto	≊[1] Aqueduc	≊[1] Aqueduto
∟ **Waterfall, Rapids**	∟ **Wasserfall, Stromschnellen**	∟ **Cascada, Rápidos**	∟ **Chute d'eau, Rapides**	∟ **Quedas d'água, Rápidos**
ʊ **Strait**	ʊ **Meeresstraße**	ʊ **Estrecho**	ʊ **Détroit**	ʊ **Estreito**
⊂ **Bay, Gulf**	⊂ **Bucht, Golf**	⊂ **Bahía, Golfo**	⊂ **Baie, Golfe**	⊂ **Baía, Golfo**
⊂[1] Estuary	⊂[1] Trichtermündung	⊂[1] Estuario	⊂[1] Estuaire	⊂[1] Estuário
⊂[2] Fjord	⊂[2] Fjord	⊂[2] Fiordo	⊂[2] Fjord	⊂[2] Fiorde
⊂[3] Bight	⊂[3] Bucht	⊂[3] Bahía	⊂[3] Baie	⊂[3] Enseada
⊜ **Lake, Lakes**	⊜ **See, Seen**	⊜ **Lago, Lagos**	⊜ **Lac, Lacs**	⊜ **Lago, Lagos**
⊜[1] Reservoir	⊜[1] Stausee	⊜[1] Embalse	⊜[1] Réservoir, Retenue	⊜[1] Reservatório
⁝⁝ **Swamp**	⁝⁝ **Sumpf**	⁝⁝ **Pantano**	⁝⁝ **Marais**	⁝⁝ **Pântano**
⍓ **Ice Features, Glacier**	⍓ **Eis- und Gletscherformen**	⍓ **Accidentes Glaciales, Glaciar**	⍓ **Formes glaciaires, Glacier**	⍓ **Acidentes Glaciares, Geleira**
⍑ **Other Hydrographic Features**	⍑ **Andere Hydrographische Objekte**	⍑ **Otros Elementos Hidrográficos**	⍑ **Autres données hydrographiques**	⍑ **Outros Acidentes Hidrográficos**
⍑[1] Ocean	⍑[1] Ozean	⍑[1] Océano	⍑[1] Océan	⍑[1] Oceano
⍑[2] Sea	⍑[2] Meer	⍑[2] Mar	⍑[2] Mer	⍑[2] Mar
⍑[3] Anchorage	⍑[3] Ankerplatz	⍑[3] Ancladero	⍑[3] Ancrage	⍑[3] Ancoradouro
⍑[4] Oasis, Well, Spring	⍑[4] Oase, Brunnen, Quelle	⍑[4] Oasis, Pozo, Manantial	⍑[4] Oasis, Puits, Source	⍑[4] Oásis, Poço, Fonte, Manancial

ENGLISH	DEUTSCH	ESPANOL	FRANCAIS	PORTUGUES
✣ **Submarine Features**	✣ **Untermeerische Objekte**	✣ **Accidentes Submarinos**	✣ **Formes de relief sous-marin**	✣ **Acidentes Submarinos**
✣[1] Depression	✣[1] Senke	✣[1] Depresión	✣[1] Dépression	✣[1] Depressão
✣[2] Reef, Shoal	✣[2] Riff, Untiefe	✣[2] Arrecife, Bajo	✣[2] Récif, Haut-fond	✣[2] Recife, Baixio
✣[3] Mountain, Mountains	✣[3] Berg, Gebirge	✣[3] Montaña, Montañas	✣[3] Montagne, Montagnes	✣[3] Montanha, Montanhas
✣[4] Slope, Shelf	✣[4] Abhang, Schelf	✣[4] Talud, Plataforma	✣[4] Talus, Plateau continental	✣[4] Talude, Plataforma
□ **Political Unit**	□ **Politische Einheit**	□ **Unidad Política**	□ **Entité politique**	□ **Unidade Política**
□[1] Independent Nation	□[1] Unabhängiger Staat	□[1] Nación Independiente	□[1] État indépendant	□[1] País Independente
□[2] Dependency	□[2] Abhängiges Gebiet	□[2] Dependencia	□[2] Dépendance	□[2] Dependência
□[3] State, Canton, Republic	□[3] Land, Kanton, Republik	□[3] Estado, Cantón, República	□[3] État, Canton, République	□[3] Estado, Cantão, República
□[4] Province, Region, Oblast	□[4] Provinz, Landschaft, Oblast	□[4] Provincia, Región, Oblast	□[4] Province, Région, Oblast	□[4] Província, Região, Oblast
□[5] Department, District, Prefecture	□[5] Département, Distrikt, Präfektur	□[5] Departamento, Distrito, Prefectura	□[5] Département, District, Préfecture	□[5] Departamento, Distrito, Prefeitura
□[6] County	□[6] Grafschaft	□[6] Condado	□[6] Comté	□[6] Condado
□[7] City, Municipality	□[7] Stadt, Stadtkreis	□[7] Ciudad, Municipalidad	□[7] Ville, Municipalité	□[7] Cidade, Municipalidade
□[8] Miscellaneous	□[8] Verschiedenes	□[8] Misceláneo	□[8] Divers	□[8] Diversos
□[9] Historical	□[9] Historisch	□[9] Histórico	□[9] Historique	□[9] Sítio Histórico
⊍ **Cultural Institution**	⊍ **Kulturelle Institution**	⊍ **Institución Cultural**	⊍ **Institution culturelle**	⊍ **Instituição Cultural**
⊍[1] Religious Institution	⊍[1] Religiöse Institution	⊍[1] Institución Religiosa	⊍[1] Institution religieuse	⊍[1] Instituição Religiosa
⊍[2] Educational Institution	⊍[2] Erziehungsinstitution	⊍[2] Institución Educacional	⊍[2] Établissement d'éducation	⊍[2] Estabelecimento de Ensino
⊍[3] Scientific, Industrial Facility	⊍[3] Wissenschaftliche, Industrielle Anlage	⊍[3] Institución Científica o Industrial	⊍[3] Établissement scientifique ou industriel	⊍[3] Estabelecimento Científico ou Industrial
⊥ **Historical Site**	⊥ **Historische Stätte**	⊥ **Sitio Histórico**	⊥ **Site historique**	⊥ **Sítio Histórico**
♠ **Recreational Site**	♠ **Erholungs- und Ferienort**	♠ **Sitio de Recreo**	♠ **Centre de loisirs**	♠ **Área de Lazer**
⊠ **Airport**	⊠ **Flughafen**	⊠ **Aeropuerto**	⊠ **Aéroport**	⊠ **Aeroporto**
■ **Military Installation**	■ **Militäranlage**	■ **Instalación Militar**	■ **Installation militaire**	■ **Instalação Militar**
⬥ **Miscellaneous**	⬥ **Verschiedenes**	⬥ **Misceláneo**	⬥ **Divers**	⬥ **Diversos**
⬥[1] Region	⬥[1] Region	⬥[1] Región	⬥[1] Région	⬥[1] Região
⬥[2] Desert	⬥[2] Wüste	⬥[2] Desierto	⬥[2] Désert	⬥[2] Deserto
⬥[3] Forest, Moor	⬥[3] Wald, Moor	⬥[3] Bosque, Páramo	⬥[3] Forêt, Lande	⬥[3] Floresta, Pântano
⬥[4] Reserve, Reservation	⬥[4] Reservat	⬥[4] Reserva, Reservación	⬥[4] Réserve	⬥[4] Reserva
⬥[5] Transportation	⬥[5] Verkehr	⬥[5] Transporte	⬥[5] Transport	⬥[5] Transporte
⬥[6] Dam	⬥[6] Damm	⬥[6] Presa	⬥[6] Barrage	⬥[6] Represa
⬥[7] Mine, Quarry	⬥[7] Bergwerk, Steinbruch	⬥[7] Mina, Cantera	⬥[7] Mine, Carrière	⬥[7] Mina, Pedreira
⬥[8] Neighborhood	⬥[8] Nachbarschaft	⬥[8] Barrio	⬥[8] Quartier	⬥[8] Arredores, Vizinhança
⬥[9] Shopping Center	⬥[9] Einkaufszentrum	⬥[9] Mercado	⬥[9] Centre commercial	⬥[9] Shopping Center

A

Aa ≏	**50**	51.01 N	2.06 E
Aach	**58**	47.50 N	8.51 E
Aachen	**56**	50.47 N	6.05 E
Aach im Allgäu	**58**	47.31 N	9.58 E
Aach-Linz	**58**	47.54 N	9.11 E
Aadorf	**58**	47.30 N	8.54 E
Aaiun → El Aaiún	**148**	27.09 N	13.12 W
Aalen	**56**	48.50 N	10.05 E
A'ālī an-Nīl □[4]	**140**	9.30 N	31.00 E
Aalsmeer	**52**	52.16 N	4.45 E
Aalst (Alost), Bel.	**50**	50.56 N	4.02 E
Aalst, Ned.	**52**	51.23 N	5.29 E
Aalten	**52**	51.56 N	6.35 E
Aalter	**50**	51.05 N	3.27 E
Aalwynsfontein	**158**	30.27 S	18.38 E
Äänekoski	**26**	62.36 N	25.44 E
Aansluit	**158**	26.44 S	22.28 E
Aar ≏	**56**	50.23 N	8.00 E
Aarau	**58**	47.23 N	8.03 E
Aarberg	**58**	47.03 N	7.16 E
Aarburg	**58**	47.19 N	7.54 E
Aardenburg	**52**	51.16 N	3.27 E
Aare ≏	**58**	47.37 N	8.13 E
Aareschlucht ♠	**58**	46.44 N	8.12 E
Aargau □[3]	**58**	47.30 N	8.10 E
Aarle-Rixtel	**52**	51.31 N	5.38 E
Aaronsburg	**210**	40.54 N	77.27 W
Aarschot	**56**	50.59 N	4.50 E
Aarwangen	**58**	47.15 N	7.46 E
Aazanèn	**34**	35.13 N	3.10 W
Aba, Nig.	**150**	5.06 N	7.21 E
Aba, Zaïre	**154**	3.52 N	30.14 E
Aba, Zhg.	**102**	33.06 N	101.59 E
Abā al-Bawl, Qurayn ∧[2]	**128**	24.56 N	51.13 E
Abā al-Waqf	**142**	28.35 N	30.46 E
Abā as-Su'ūd	**144**	17.29 N	44.08 E
Abacaxis ≏	**242**	3.54 S	58.47 W
Abaco I	**238**	26.28 N	77.05 W
Abacou, Pointe ≻	**238**	18.03 N	73.47 W
Abadab, Jabal ∧	**140**	18.53 N	35.59 E
Ābādān	**128**	30.20 N	48.16 E
Ābādeh	**128**	31.10 N	52.37 E
Abadia dos Dourados	**255**	18.28 S	47.24 W
Abadiânia	**255**	16.06 S	48.48 W
Abadla	**148**	31.01 N	2.44 W
Abaeté	**255**	19.09 S	45.27 W
Abaeté ≏	**255**	18.02 S	45.12 W
Abaetetuba	**250**	1.42 S	48.54 W
Abagajtuj	**88**	49.35 N	117.49 E
Abagnar Qi	**102**	43.58 N	116.04 E
Abag Qi	**102**	43.53 N	114.33 E
Abaí	**252**	26.01 S	55.57 W
Abaj, Kaz.	**86**	49.38 N	72.52 E
Abaj, Ross.	**86**	50.27 N	85.05 E
Abaji	**150**	8.28 N	6.57 E
Abajo Mountains ⋏	**200**	37.50 N	109.25 W
Abajo Peak ∧	**200**	37.51 N	109.28 W
Abak	**150**	4.57 N	7.47 E
Abakaliki	**150**	6.21 N	8.06 E
Abakan	**86**	53.43 N	91.26 E
Abakan ≏	**86**	53.43 N	91.30 E
Abakanovo	**76**	59.18 N	37.39 E
Abakanskij chrebet ⋏	**86**	52.20 N	88.50 E
Abala, Congo	**152**	1.21 S	15.30 E
Abala, Niger	**150**	14.56 N	3.26 E
Abalak, Niger	**150**	15.27 N	6.17 E
Abalak, Ross.	**86**	58.08 N	68.36 E
Abalemma, Vallée d' V	**150**	15.34 N	6.23 E
Abalessa	**148**	22.54 N	4.50 E
Aban	**88**	56.41 N	96.04 E
Abancay	**248**	13.35 S	72.55 W
Abanga ≏	**152**	0.20 S	10.30 E
Abano Terme	**64**	45.21 N	11.47 E
Abaokoro	**174t**	1.29 N	173.02 E
Abar Irir	**144**	4.53 N	46.10 E
Abar Kūh	**128**	31.08 N	53.17 E
Abarra	**144**	5.23 N	39.58 E
Abarracamento	**256**	22.12 S	43.30 W
Abaša	**84**	42.12 N	42.13 E
Abascay, Arroyo ≏	**258**	35.17 S	58.07 W
Abashiri	**92a**	44.01 N	144.17 E
Abasolo, Méx.	**196**	25.57 N	100.24 W
Abasolo, Méx.	**196**	27.12 N	101.24 W
Abasolo, Méx.	**204**	32.39 N	115.21 W
Abasolo, Méx.	**232**	25.18 N	104.40 W
Abasolo, Méx.	**232**	24.04 N	98.22 W
Abasolo, Méx.	**234**	20.27 N	101.32 W
Abasolo del Valle	**234**	17.44 N	95.29 W
Abasto	**258**	34.58 S	58.06 W
Abastumani	**84**	41.46 N	42.50 E
Abate	**85**	39.03 N	77.36 E
Abate Alonia, Lago di ⊜	**68**	41.01 N	15.45 E
Abatimbo el Gumas	**144**	10.36 N	35.13 E
Abatskij	**86**	56.18 N	70.28 E
Abau	**164**	10.11 S	148.42 E
Abava ≏	**76**	57.06 N	21.54 E
Abaya, Lake ⊜	**144**	6.20 N	37.55 E
Abay → Blue Nile ≏	**140**	15.38 N	32.31 E
Abayuba	**258**	34.51 S	56.14 W
Abaza	**86**	52.39 N	90.06 E
Abba	**152**	5.20 N	15.11 E
Abbabach ≏	**263**	51.28 N	7.41 E
Abbadia San Salvatore	**66**	42.53 N	11.41 E
'Abbāsābād ⬥[8]	**267d**	35.44 N	51.25 E
Abbasanta	**71**	40.08 N	8.49 E
Abbaye, Étang de l' ⊜	**261**	48.41 N	1.56 E
Abbé, Lac (Lake Abe) ⊜	**144**	11.06 N	41.50 E
Abbehausen	**52**	53.29 N	8.26 E
Abbekås	**41**	55.24 N	13.36 E
Abbensen	**52**	52.23 N	10.11 E
Abbert ≏	**48**	53.25 N	8.53 W
Abbess Roding	**260**	51.47 N	0.17 E
Abbeville, Fr.	**50**	50.06 N	1.50 E
Abbeville, Ga., U.S.	**192**	31.59 N	83.18 W
Abbeville, La., U.S.	**194**	29.58 N	92.08 W
Abbeville, Ms., U.S.	**194**	34.30 N	89.30 W
Abbeville, S.C., U.S.	**192**	34.10 N	82.22 W
Abbey	**184**	50.43 N	108.45 W
Abbeydorney	**48**	52.19 N	9.41 W
Abbeyfeale	**48**	52.24 N	9.18 W
Abbey Head ≻	**44**	54.46 N	3.58 W
Abbeyleix	**48**	52.55 N	7.20 W
Abbey Peak ∧	**164**	14.18 S	144.29 E
Abbey Wood ⬥[8]	**260**	51.29 N	0.08 E
Abbiategrasso	**62**	45.24 N	8.54 E
Abbot, Mount ∧	**166**	20.03 S	147.45 E
Abbots Bromley	**42**	52.48 N	1.52 W
Abbotsbury	**42**	50.40 N	2.36 W
Abbotsford, Austl.	**274a**	33.51 S	151.08 E
Abbotsford, B.C., Can.	**224**	49.03 N	122.17 W
Abbotsford, Wi., U.S.	**190**	44.56 N	90.18 W
Abbots Langley	**42**	51.43 N	0.25 W
Abbott, Arg.	**258**	35.17 S	58.48 W
Abbott, Tx., U.S.	**222**	31.53 N	97.04 W
Abbottābād	**123**	34.09 N	73.13 E
Abbott Butte ∧	**202**	42.57 N	122.33 W
Abbottstown	**208**	39.53 N	76.59 W
Abchazskaja Respublika □[3]	**84**	43.10 N	41.00 E
Abcoude	**52**	52.16 N	4.58 E
'Abd al-'Azīz, Jabal ⋏	**130**	36.25 N	40.20 E
'Abd al-Ḥafiẓ, Qārat ∧[2]	**142**	28.53 N	30.08 E
'Abd al-Kūrī I	**118**	12.12 N	52.13 E
'Abd Allāh	**140**	13.30 N	23.02 E
'Abd Allāh, Khawr ʊ	**128**	29.50 N	48.20 E
'Abd al-Shāhīd	**273c**	29.55 N	31.13 E
Ābdānān	**128**	32.58 N	47.26 E
Ábdēra ⊥	**38**	40.59 N	24.58 E
Abdrachmanovo	**80**	54.46 N	52.30 E
Abdul Hakīm	**123**	30.33 N	72.07 E
Abdulino	**80**	53.42 N	53.40 E
Abdulovo	**80**	54.16 N	53.27 E
Abe ≏	**94**	34.56 N	138.24 E
Abe, Lake (Lac Abbé) ⊜	**144**	11.06 N	41.50 E
Abéché	**146**	13.49 N	20.49 E
Abéjar	**34**	41.48 N	2.47 W
Abejonal, Cerro ∧	**236**	11.39 N	86.10 W
Abejorral	**246**	5.47 N	75.26 W
Abekr	**140**	12.43 N	28.55 E
Abelek	**140**	7.23 N	28.46 E
Abel Tasman National Park ♠	**172**	40.55 S	173.00 E
Abelti	**144**	8.10 N	37.34 E
Abemama I[1]	**14**	0.21 N	173.51 E
Abenberg	**56**	49.14 N	10.57 E
Abengourou	**150**	6.44 N	3.29 W
Abeno ⬥[8]	**270**	34.38 N	135.32 E
Abenójar	**34**	38.53 N	4.21 W
Åbenrå	**41**	55.02 N	9.26 E
Åbenrå Fjord ⊂	**41**	55.03 N	9.34 E
Abens ≏	**60**	48.51 N	11.46 E
Abensberg	**60**	48.49 N	11.51 E
Abeokuta	**150**	7.10 N	3.26 E
Aber	**154**	2.12 N	32.21 E
Aberaeron	**42**	52.15 N	4.15 W
Aberaman	**42**	51.42 N	3.25 W
Aberavon → Port Talbot	**42**	51.36 N	3.47 W
Abercarn	**42**	51.39 N	3.08 W
Aberchirder	**46**	57.33 N	2.38 W
Abercorn	**206**	45.02 N	72.40 W
Abercorn → Mbala	**154**	8.50 S	31.22 E
Abercrombie ≏	**170**	34.09 S	149.40 E
Aberdare	**42**	51.43 N	3.27 W
Aberdare National Park ♠	**154**	0.30 S	36.45 E
Aberdare Range ⋏	**154**	0.25 S	36.38 E
Aberdaron	**42**	52.49 N	4.43 W
Aberdeen, Sk., Can.	**184**	52.19 N	106.17 W
Aberdeen (Xianggangzi), H.K.	**271d**	22.15 N	114.09 E
Aberdeen, S. Afr.	**158**	32.29 S	24.05 E
Aberdeen, Scot., U.K.	**46**	57.10 N	2.04 W
Aberdeen, Id., U.S.	**202**	42.56 N	112.50 W
Aberdeen, Md., U.S.	**208**	39.30 N	76.09 W
Aberdeen, Ms., U.S.	**194**	33.49 N	88.32 W
Aberdeen, N.C., U.S.	**192**	35.07 N	79.25 W
Aberdeen, Oh., U.S.	**218**	38.39 N	83.45 W
Aberdeen, S.D., U.S.	**198**	45.27 N	98.29 W
Aberdeen, Wa., U.S.	**224**	46.58 N	123.48 W
Aberdeen Lake ⊜	**176**	64.27 N	99.00 W
Aberdeen Lake ⊜[1]	**194**	33.55 N	88.30 W
Aberdeen Proving Ground ■	**208**	39.25 N	76.10 W
Aberdour	**46**	56.03 N	3.19 W
Aberdulais	**42**	51.41 N	3.48 W
Aberdyfi	**42**	52.33 N	4.02 W
Aberfeldy	**46**	56.37 N	3.54 W
Aberfoyle	**46**	56.11 N	4.23 W
Abergavenny	**42**	51.50 N	3.00 W
Abergele	**44**	53.17 N	3.34 W
Abergwynfi	**42**	51.40 N	3.35 W
Abergynolwyn	**42**	52.40 N	3.58 W
Aberjona ≏	**283**	42.27 N	71.08 W
Abermain	**170**	32.49 S	151.25 E
Abernathy	**196**	33.50 N	101.51 W
Abernethy, Sk., Can.	**184**	50.45 N	103.25 W
Abernethy, Scot., U.K.	**46**	56.20 N	3.19 W
Aberporth	**42**	52.09 N	4.33 W
Abersoch	**42**	52.50 N	4.29 W
Abersychan	**42**	51.44 N	3.04 W
Abert, Lake ⊜	**202**	42.38 N	120.13 W
Abertillery	**42**	51.45 N	3.09 W
Aberuthven	**46**	56.19 N	3.39 W
Aberystwyth	**42**	52.25 N	4.05 W
Abessinien, Hochland von → Ethiopian Plateau ⋏[1]	**144**	9.00 N	38.00 E
Abetone	**66**	44.08 N	10.40 E
Abez'	**24**	66.32 N	61.42 E
Abhā	**144**	18.13 N	42.30 E
Abhar	**128**	36.09 N	49.13 E
Abharwat ∧	**123**	34.02 N	74.25 E
Abhayāpuri	**124**	26.20 N	90.40 E
Abhaynagar	**126**	23.01 N	89.28 E
Abiaca Creek ≏	**194**	33.20 N	90.15 W
Abid, Oued el ≏	**148**	32.18 N	7.03 W
Ābidīn	**140**	13.33 N	29.38 E
'Abīdīyah	**140**	18.14 N	33.57 E
Abidjan	**150**	5.19 N	4.02 W
'Ābid Mār, Tall ∧	**132**	32.26 N	36.42 E
Abiengama	**154**	2.35 N	27.46 E

Abiko 94 35.52 N 140.03 E
Abilene, Ks., U.S. 198 38.55 N 97.12 W
Abilene, Tx., U.S. 196 32.26 N 99.43 W
Abingdon, Eng., U.K. 42 51.41 N 1.17 W
Abingdon, Il., U.S. 190 40.48 N 90.24 W
Abingdon, Il., U.S. 194 40.48 N 90.24 W
Abingdon, Va., U.S. 192 36.42 N 81.58 W
Abinger 260 51.12 N 0.24 W
Abington, Ct., U.S. 207 41.51 N 72.00 W
Abington, Ma., U.S. 207 42.06 N 70.56 W
Abington, Pa., U.S. 208 40.07 N 75.07 W
Abington Reefs ✢[2] 166 18.00 S 149.36 E
Abino, Point › 212 42.50 N 79.05 W
Abino Bay c 284a 42.51 N 79.05 W
Abinsk 78 44.52 N 38.09 E
Abiod, Rmel el ⊥[8] 148 31.30 N 9.30 E
Abiquiu 200 36.12 N 106.19 W
Abiquiu Reservoir ⊜[1] 200 36.18 N 106.32 W
Abiseo ≃ 248 7.18 S 76.50 W
Abiseo, Parque Nacional ♦ 248 7.35 S 77.10 W
Abisko 24 68.20 N 18.51 E
Abisko Nationalpark ♦ 24 68.20 N 18.30 E
Abita Springs 194 30.28 N 90.02 W
Abitau ≃ 176 59.53 N 109.03 W
Abitibi ≃ 176 51.03 N 80.55 W
Abitibi, Lake ⊜ 190 48.42 N 79.45 W
Abiy Adi 144 13.26 N 39.05 E
Abiyata, Lake ⊜ 144 7.37 N 38.36 E
Abja-Paluoja 76 58.08 N 25.21 E
Ableiges 261 49.05 N 1.59 E
Ablis 50 48.31 N 1.50 E
Ablon-sur-Seine 261 48.43 N 2.25 E
Abnūb 142 27.16 N 31.09 E
Abóbada 266c 38.43 N 9.20 W
Abodom 150 5.32 N 0.49 W
Abohar 123 30.09 N 74.11 E
Aboisso 150 5.28 N 3.12 W
Abomey 150 7.11 N 1.59 E
Abondance 58 46.17 N 6.44 E
Abong 146 6.59 N 10.44 E
Abongabong, Gunung ∧ 114 4.15 N 96.48 E
Abong Mbang 152 3.59 N 13.10 E
Abonnema 150 4.43 N 6.47 E
Abony 30 47.11 N 20.01 E
Aborigen, pik ∧ 74 61.59 N 149.19 E
Aborlan 116 9.26 N 118.33 E
Aborrebjerg ∧[2] 41 54.59 N 12.32 E
Aboso 150 5.22 N 1.56 W
Abō-tōge)(94 36.11 N 137.35 E
Åbo → Turku 26 60.27 N 22.17 E
Abou 144 4.21 N 43.03 E
Abou-Deïa 146 11.27 N 19.17 E
Abounamy ≃ 250 4.24 N 54.26 W
Aboyne 46 57.05 N 2.50 W
Abra □[4] 116 17.35 N 120.50 E
Abra ≃ 116 17.31 N 120.23 E
Abraão 256 23.08 S 44.10 W
Abraham Lake ⊜[1] 182 52.15 N 116.23 W
Abraham Lincoln Birthplace National Historic Site ⊥ 194 37.32 N 85.44 W
Abrahamsdam 158 29.08 S 22.39 E
Abraka 150 5.50 N 6.05 E
Abram 262 53.31 N 2.35 W
Abramcevo 265b 55.50 N 37.50 E
Abramovka 78 51.12 N 41.01 E
Abramovskaja 24 65.11 N 51.43 E
Abram S. Hewitt State Forest ♦ 276 41.11 N 74.22 W
Abrantes 34 39.28 N 8.12 W
Abra Pampa 252 22.43 S 65.42 W
Abraq, Wādī al- V 146 26.27 N 18.48 E
Abrau-D'urso 78 44.43 N 37.37 E
Abra Vieja, Arroyo ≃ 288 34.26 S 58.34 W
Abre-Campo 255 20.18 S 42.29 W
Ábrego 246 8.05 N 73.13 W
Abreojos, Punta › 232 26.42 N 113.35 W
Abreschviller 58 48.38 N 7.06 E
Abreu e Lima 250 7.54 S 34.53 W
ʻAbrī, Sūd. 140 11.40 N 30.28 E
ʻAbrī, Sūd. 140 20.48 N 30.20 E
Abriachan 46 57.22 N 4.24 W
Abridge 260 51.39 N 0.07 E
Abriès 62 44.47 N 6.56 E
Abring 123 33.42 N 76.35 E
Abriola 68 40.30 N 15.49 E
Abrud 38 46.17 N 23.04 E
Abruka saar I 76 58.10 N 22.30 E
Abrunheira 266c 38.46 N 9.21 W
Abruzzi □[4] 66 42.20 N 13.45 E
Abruzzo, Parco Nazionale d' ♦ 66 41.45 N 13.45 E
Absam 64 47.18 N 11.30 E
Absaroka Range ⋏ 202 44.45 N 109.50 W
Absarokee 202 45.31 N 109.26 W
Abscon 50 50.20 N 3.18 E
Absdorf 61 48.24 N 15.59 E
Absecon 208 39.25 N 74.29 W
Absecon Bay c 208 39.24 N 74.28 W
Abşeker 130 38.55 N 39.11 E
Abtenau 64 47.33 N 13.21 E
Abtsgmünd 56 48.54 N 10.00 E
Abtsteinach 56 49.33 N 8.47 E
Abu 96 34.30 N 131.28 E
Abu ≃ 96 34.25 N 131.24 E
Abū Ahl ⊤[4] 128 34.06 N 43.45 E
Abū ʻAlāwī, Wādī V 142 30.07 N 31.51 E
Abū al-Ghayṭ 273c 30.09 N 31.11 E
Abū al-Ḥamām, Jabal ∧ 132 30.27 N 35.38 E
Abū al-Hawl (Sphinx) ⊥ 142 29.59 N 31.08 E
Abū ʻAlī I 128 27.20 N 49.33 E
Abū al-Khaṣīb 128 30.27 N 47.59 E
Abū al-Maṭāmīr 142 30.55 N 30.11 E
Abū al-ʻUrūq, Bi'r ⊤[4] 142 30.45 N 32.23 E
Abū an-Numrus 273c 29.57 N 31.12 E
Abū ʻAradeib, Wādī V 140 14.12 N 23.06 E
Abū ʻArīsh 144 16.57 N 42.50 E
Abū Ballās ∧[2] 140 24.26 N 27.39 E
Abū Daraj, Ra's › 142 29.23 N 32.34 E
Abū Dā'ūd, Ra's › 128 23.19 N 58.55 E
Abū Dā'ūd as-Sibākh 142 30.55 N 31.34 E
Abū Dawm 140 16.16 N 32.36 E
Abū Dawm, Wādī V 140 18.28 N 31.49 E
Abu Dhabi → Abū Ẓaby 128 24.28 N 54.22 E
Abū Dhi'ābah, Wādī V 142 29.37 N 32.06 E
Abū Dīs 140 19.08 N 33.34 E
Abū Dulayq 140 15.54 N 33.49 E
Abufari 248 5.25 S 62.59 W
Abū Gatta Hills ⋏[2] 140 6.06 N 27.44 E
Abū Gelba 140 13.11 N 31.52 E
Abū Ghālib 142 30.16 N 30.56 E
Abū Ḥabl, Khawr V 140 12.49 N 31.15 E
Abū Ḥād, Wādī V 142 28.20 N 32.49 E
Abū Ḥadīmah, Bi'r ⊤[4] 142 30.44 N 29.51 E
Abū Hamad 140 19.32 N 33.19 E
Abū Ḥammād al-Mahaṭṭah 142 30.32 N 31.40 E
Abū Ḥarāz, Sūd. 140 12.58 N 29.52 E
Abū Ḥarāz, Sūd. 140 19.04 N 32.07 E
Abū Ḥasan, Jabal ∧ 144 17.42 N 42.54 E
Abū Ḥummuṣ 142 31.06 N 30.19 E
Abū Ḥushsh, Bi'r ⊤[4] 142 30.49 N 29.57 E
Abuja 150 9.12 N 7.11 E
Abū Jābirah 140 11.04 N 26.51 E
Abū Jandīr 142 29.14 N 30.41 E
Abū Jirj 142 28.32 N 30.47 E
Abū Jubayhah 140 11.27 N 31.14 E
Abū Kabīr 142 30.44 N 31.40 E
Abū Kamāl 130 34.27 N 40.55 E
Abū Kharjah, Wādī V 142 28.38 N 31.44 E
Abū Khashabah, Jabal ∧ 142 28.08 N 32.52 E
Abūksāh 142 29.23 N 30.42 E
Abū Kulaywāt 140 12.20 N 26.00 E
Abukuma ≃ 92 38.02 N 140.56 E
Abukuma-kōchi ⋏ 92 37.30 N 140.45 E
Abū Latt I 144 19.58 N 40.08 E
Abulug 116 18.27 N 121.27 E
Abulug ≃ 116 18.29 N 121.25 E
Abū Madd, Ra's › 128 24.50 N 37.07 E
Abū Makhlūf, Bi'r ⊤[4] 142 30.45 N 29.42 E
Abū Maṭāriq 140 10.58 N 26.17 E
Abu Mendi 144 11.47 N 35.43 E
Abū Minqār, Bi'r ⊤[4] 140 26.30 N 27.35 E
Abumombazi 152 3.42 N 22.10 E
Abū Muḥammad, Bi'r ⊤[4] 132 29.43 N 34.13 E
Abū Muḥarrik, Ghurd ⊥[8] 140 27.50 N 29.40 E
Abū Mūsā I 128 25.52 N 55.03 E
Abuna 248 9.42 S 65.23 W
Abuná (Abunã) ≃ 248 9.41 S 65.23 W
Abū Naʻāmah 140 12.44 N 34.08 E
Abune Yosef ∧ 144 12.10 N 39.12 E
Abū Qardī, Qāʻ ≃ 132 32.08 N 37.11 E
Abü Qashsh 132 31.57 N 35.11 E
Abū Qīr •[8] 142 31.19 N 30.04 E
Abū Qīr, Khalīj (Abu Qir Bay) c 142 31.23 N 30.13 E
Abū Qurqāṣ 142 27.56 N 30.50 E
Aburatsubo-kō c 268 35.09 N 139.38 E
Abū Rimth, Wādī V, Miṣr 142 28.45 N 31.27 E
Abū Rimth, Wādī V, Miṣr 142 30.21 N 31.53 E
Abū Rīshat, Wādī V 142 28.54 N 31.37 E
Ābu Road 120 24.29 N 72.47 E
Abū Rubayq 128 23.44 N 39.42 E
Abū Rujmayn, Jabal ⋏ 130 34.52 N 38.20 E
Abū Sanṭ, Wādī V 140 14.11 N 23.06 E
Abū Shajarah, Ra's › 140 21.04 N 37.14 E
Abū Shāmah, Jabal ∧ 142 29.52 N 31.38 E
Abū Shanab, Sūd. 140 10.47 N 29.32 E
Abū Shanab, Sūd. 140 13.57 N 27.47 E
Abū Shaykhāt, Ḍahr ∧[2] 130 36.36 N 39.40 E
Abu Simbel → Abū Sunbul ⊥ 140 22.22 N 31.38 E
Abū Ṣīr 273c 29.53 N 31.13 E
Abu Ṣīr al-Malaq 142 29.15 N 31.05 E
Abū Ṣīr-Banā 142 30.55 N 31.15 E
Abū Ṣīr Pyramids ⊥ 273c 29.54 N 31.12 E
Abū Sulṭan 142 30.25 N 32.19 E
Abū Sunbul ⊥ 140 22.22 N 31.38 E
Abū Ṣuwayr al-Mahaṭṭah 142 30.34 N 32.07 E
Abū Ṣuwayr Military Base ■ 142 30.34 N 32.06 E
Abuta 92a 42.33 N 140.46 E
Abū Ṭabarī ⊤[4] 140 17.35 N 28.31 E
Abū Ṭarafah, Wādī V 132 30.12 N 36.13 E
Abut Head › 172 43.07 S 170.15 E
Abū Tīj 140 27.02 N 31.19 E
Abū Ṭunayṭin 140 14.24 N 31.01 E
Abū Ṭurayfīyah, Jabal ∧, Miṣr 142 29.58 N 32.06 E
Abū Ṭurayfīyah, Jabal ∧, Miṣr 142 29.42 N 31.49 E
Abū ʻUwayjilah ⊤[4] 132 30.50 N 34.07 E
Abuye Meda ∧ 144 10.28 N 39.44 E
Abuyog 116 10.45 N 125.01 E
Abū Zabad 140 12.21 N 29.15 E
Abū Zaʻbal 142 30.15 N 31.21 E
Abū Ẓaby (Abu Dhabi) 128 24.28 N 54.22 E
Abū Zanīmah 140 29.03 N 33.06 E
Abwong 140 9.07 N 32.12 E
Åby 40 58.40 N 16.11 E
Åby •[8] 41 56.09 N 10.10 E
Aby, Lagune c 150 5.15 N 3.14 W
Abyaḍ 140 13.46 N 26.28 E
Abyaḍ, Al-Baḥr al- → White Nile ≃ 140 15.38 N 32.31 E
Abyaḍ, Wādī al- V 142 29.38 N 32.13 E
Åbyälven ≃ 26 65.01 N 21.24 E
Abyār 142 30.50 N 30.52 E
Abyār ʻAlī 128 24.25 N 39.32 E
Åbybro 26 57.09 N 9.45 E
Abydos 162 21.25 S 118.54 E
Abyei 140 9.36 N 28.26 E
Åbyggeby 40 60.44 N 17.07 E
Åbytorp 40 59.07 N 15.04 E
Abzanovo 86 53.50 N 58.36 E
Acacías 246 3.59 N 73.46 W
Academia 214 40.25 N 82.28 W
Academy Corners 208 41.57 N 77.23 W
Academy of Sciences ʋ[3] 282 37.46 N 122.28 W
Acadia National Park ♦ 188 44.18 N 68.15 W
Acadia Valley 184 51.08 N 110.13 W
Acahay 252 25.55 S 57.09 W
Açailandia 250 4.57 S 47.29 W
Acajete 234 19.06 N 97.57 W
Acajutiba 250 11.40 S 38.01 W
Acajutla 236 13.36 N 89.50 W
Acala 234 16.34 N 92.48 W
Acalayong 152 1.05 N 9.40 E
Acámbaro 234 20.02 N 100.44 W
Acampo 226 38.10 N 121.13 W
Acandí 246 8.32 N 77.14 W
Acaponeta 234 22.30 N 105.22 W
Acaponeta ≃ 234 22.20 N 105.37 W
Acapulco [de Juárez] 234 16.51 N 99.55 W
Acará 250 1.57 S 48.11 W
Acará ≃ 250 1.40 S 48.25 W
Acará, Lago ⊜ 246 3.39 S 62.40 W
Acaraí ≃ 250 2.02 S 52.15 W
Acarai Mountains ⋏ 246 1.30 N 58.15 W
Acará-Mirim ≃ 250 1.58 S 48.12 W
Acaraú 250 2.53 S 40.07 W
Acaraú ≃ 250 2.51 S 40.08 W
Acaray ≃ 252 25.29 S 54.42 W
Acari, Bra. 250 6.31 S 36.38 W
Acarí, Perú 248 15.26 S 74.37 W
Acari ≃, Bra. 248 5.18 S 59.42 W
Acari ≃, Bra. 255 16.00 S 45.03 W
Acarí ≃, Perú 248 15.39 S 74.39 W
Acarigua 246 9.33 N 69.12 W
Acate 70 37.02 N 14.28 E
Acate ≃ 70 37.00 N 14.20 E
Acatic 234 20.47 N 102.53 W
Acatlán ≃ 234 18.04 N 98.19 W
Acatlán de Juárez 234 20.26 N 103.38 W
Acatlán de Osorio 234 18.12 N 98.03 W
Acatlán de Pérez Figueroa 234 18.32 N 96.37 W
Acatzingo [de Hidalgo] 234 18.59 N 97.47 W
Acay, Nevado de ∧ 252 24.21 S 66.12 W
Acayucan 234 17.57 N 94.55 W
Accadia 68 41.10 N 15.20 E
Acceglio 62 44.28 N 7.00 E
Aččen, mys › 180 64.45 N 175.30 W
Accettura 68 40.29 N 16.09 E
Aččhoj-Martan 84 43.11 N 45.18 E
Ačči 85 39.57 N 68.14 E
Acciano 66 42.10 N 13.43 E
Accokeek 208 38.40 N 77.02 W
Accomac 208 37.43 N 75.39 W
Accomack □[6] 208 37.45 N 75.40 W
Accord, Ma., U.S. 283 42.10 N 70.53 W
Accord, N.Y., U.S. 210 41.47 N 74.13 W
Accord Brook ≃ 283 42.10 N 70.53 W
Accord Pond ⊜ 283 42.10 N 70.53 W
Accotink Creek ≃ 284c 38.46 N 77.13 W
Accotink Creek, Bear Branch ≃ 284c 38.52 N 77.15 W
Accotink Creek, Long Branch ≃ 284c 38.48 N 77.13 W
Accoville 192 37.46 N 81.50 W
Accra 150 5.33 N 0.13 W
Accra □[4] 150 5.40 N 0.10 W
Accrington 44 53.46 N 2.21 W
Accumoli 66 42.42 N 13.15 E
Acebuches 232 28.15 N 102.43 W
Aceguá 252 31.52 S 54.09 W
Aceh □[4] 114 4.00 N 97.00 E
Aceh ≃ 114 5.36 N 95.20 E
Acerentia ⊥ 68 39.16 N 16.49 E
Acerenza 68 40.48 N 15.57 E
Acerno 68 40.44 N 15.03 E
Acerra 68 40.57 N 14.22 E
Acevedo 252 33.45 S 60.27 W
Achacachi 248 16.03 S 68.43 W
Achaguas 246 7.46 N 68.14 W
Achalciche 84 41.38 N 42.59 E
Achali-Kindgi 84 42.48 N 41.16 E
Achalkalaki 84 41.25 N 43.29 E
Achalpur 120 21.16 N 77.31 E
Achangaran 85 40.54 N 69.37 E
Achao 254 42.28 S 73.30 W
Achar 252 32.25 S 56.10 W
Acharacle 46 56.44 N 5.47 W
Achar uul ∧ 102 45.10 N 103.45 E
Achau 264b 48.05 N 16.23 E
Achavanich 46 58.22 N 3.24 W
Achelouma, Enneri V 146 21.55 N 13.35 E
Achêne 56 50.16 N 5.03 E
Acheng 89 45.32 N 126.59 E
Achenkirch 64 47.31 N 11.42 E
Achénouma 146 19.08 N 12.55 E
Achen Pass)(64 47.35 N 11.38 E
Achensee ⊜ 64 47.28 N 11.42 E
Achères 261 48.58 N 2.04 E
Achern 56 48.37 N 8.04 E
Acheron ≃, Austl. 169 37.14 S 145.42 E
Acheron ≃, N.Z. 172 42.24 S 172.58 E
Acheux-en-Amiénois 50 50.04 N 2.32 E
Achhābal 123 33.41 N 75.14 E
Achhnera 124 27.11 N 77.46 E
Achí, Col. 246 8.34 N 74.33 W
Achi, Nihon 94 35.27 N 137.45 E
Achiasi 150 5.52 N 1.00 W
Achicourt 50 50.16 N 2.46 E
Achigan, Lac de l' ⊜ 206 45.56 N 73.58 W
Achiguate ≃ 236 13.55 N 90.55 W
Achill 28 53.56 N 9.54 W
Achilles 208 37.17 N 76.27 W
Achill Head › 48 53.59 N 10.13 W
Achill Island I 48 54.00 N 10.00 W
Achill Sound 48 53.55 N 9.58 W
Achim 52 53.00 N 9.02 E
Achīn 120 34.08 N 70.42 E
Achiras 252 33.10 S 65.00 W
Achir-Ula, gora ∧ 88 50.21 N 94.31 E
Achmeta 84 42.02 N 45.13 E
Achnasaul 46 56.58 N 4.59 W
Achnasheen 46 57.35 N 5.06 W
Achol 140 6.34 N 31.31 E
Achosnich 46 56.45 N 6.06 W
Achsu 84 40.34 N 48.24 E
Achterwasser c 54 54.00 N 13.57 E
Achterwehr 41 54.19 N 9.57 E
Achthuizen 52 51.42 N 4.16 E
Achtuba 80 51.37 N 44.22 E
Achtuba ≃ 80 46.42 N 48.00 E
Achtubinsk 80 48.17 N 46.10 E
Achty 84 41.28 N 47.43 E
Achtyrka 78 50.19 N 34.55 E
Achtyrskij 78 44.52 N 38.20 E
Achuapa 236 13.03 N 86.35 W
Achur'an (Arpaçay) ≃ 84 40.06 N 43.39 E
Achwa ≃ 154 3.43 N 31.55 E
Ači 85 41.17 N 73.02 E
Aci Castello 70 37.33 N 15.08 E
Aci Catena 70 37.36 N 15.08 E
Acıgöl 130 38.35 N 34.31 E
Acı Göl ⊜ 130 37.50 N 29.54 E
Acikak 88 54.11 N 106.18 E
Ačikulak 84 44.34 N 44.50 E
Acilia •[8] 267a 41.47 N 12.22 E
Ačimovy Vtoryje 86 60.04 N 75.12 E
Ačinsk 86 56.17 N 90.30 E
Acıpayam 130 37.25 N 29.22 E
Acireale 70 37.37 N 15.10 E
Acîș 38 47.33 N 22.47 E
Ačisaj 85 43.35 N 68.53 E
Aci Sant'Antonio 70 37.36 N 15.07 E
Ačisu 84 42.38 N 47.40 E
Ačit 86 56.48 N 57.54 E
Ačit nuur ⊜ 86 49.30 N 90.30 E
Ackerly 196 32.32 N 101.43 W
Ackerman 194 33.18 N 89.10 W
Ackermanville 210 40.49 N 75.17 W
Ackerson Lake 216 42.11 N 84.20 W
Ackley 190 42.33 N 93.03 W
Acklins I 238 22.26 N 73.58 W
Acklins, Bight of c[3] 238 22.30 N 74.15 W
Acland, Mount ∧ 166 24.55 S 148.05 E
Acle 42 52.38 N 1.33 E
Aclimação •[8] 287b 23.34 S 46.37 W
Acme, Ab., Can. 182 51.30 N 113.30 W
Acme, Pa., U.S. 214 40.08 N 79.26 W
Acme, Wa., U.S. 224 48.43 N 122.12 W
Acmetonia 279b 40.32 N 79.49 W
Acobamba 248 12.48 S 74.34 W
Acolla 248 11.44 S 75.34 W
Acoma Indian Reservation •[4] 200 34.52 N 107.40 W
Acomayo, Perú 248 13.55 S 71.41 W
Acomayo, Perú 248 9.46 S 76.05 W
Aconcagua, Cerro ∧ 252 32.39 S 70.01 W
Aconchi 232 29.50 N 110.12 W
Aconibe 152 1.18 N 10.56 E
Acopiara 250 6.06 S 39.27 W
Açores (Azores) II 148a 38.30 N 28.00 W
Acoria 248 12.37 S 74.53 W
Acorizal 248 15.12 S 56.22 W
Acornhoek 156 24.37 S 31.02 E
Acosta 214 40.07 N 79.04 W
Acoyapa 236 11.58 N 85.10 W
Acoyapa ≃ 236 11.48 N 85.16 W
Acquabona, Passo di)(68 39.02 N 16.20 E
Acquacalda 70 38.31 N 14.57 E
Acqualagna 66 43.37 N 12.40 E
Acquanegra sul Chiese 64 45.10 N 10.26 E
Acquapendente 66 42.44 N 11.52 E
Acquappesa 68 39.29 N 15.57 E
Acquarossa 58 46.28 N 8.57 E
Acquasanta Terme 66 42.46 N 13.24 E
Acquasparta 66 42.41 N 12.33 E
Acquaviva 66 43.57 N 12.25 E
Acquaviva delle Fonti 68 40.54 N 16.50 E
Acquaviva Platani 70 37.34 N 13.42 E
Acqui Terme 62 44.41 N 8.28 E
Acra 210 42.19 N 74.03 W
Acraman, Lake ⊜ 162 32.02 S 135.26 E
Acre □[3] 248 9.00 S 70.00 W
Acre ≃ 248 8.45 S 67.22 W
Acre → ʻAkko 132 32.55 N 35.05 E
Acre Homes 222 29.53 N 95.27 W
Acri 68 39.29 N 16.23 E
Acropolis ⊥ 267c 37.58 N 23.43 E
Acrotambo, Cerro ∧ 248 8.50 S 76.50 W
Acton, On., Can. 212 43.37 N 80.02 W
Acton, Ca., U.S. 228 34.28 N 118.11 W
Acton, Ma., U.S. 207 42.29 N 71.26 W
Acton, Tx., U.S. 222 32.27 N 97.41 W
Acton •[8] 260 51.30 N 0.16 W
Acton Bridge 262 53.16 N 2.36 W
Acton Homes 158 28.36 S 29.26 E
Acton Lake ⊜ 218 39.34 N 84.45 W
Acton Turville 42 51.32 N 2.17 W
Acton-Vale 206 45.39 N 72.34 W
Actopan 234 20.16 N 98.56 W
Actopan ≃ 234 19.25 N 96.20 W
Açu 250 5.34 S 36.54 W
Açuã ≃ 248 7.12 S 64.11 W
Açucena 255 19.04 S 42.32 W
Acuitzio del Canje 234 19.29 N 101.20 W
Ačujevo 78 45.43 N 37.45 E
Acuña 252 29.55 S 57.58 W
Acurauá ≃ 248 7.37 S 70.48 W
Acurenam 152 1.02 N 10.40 E
Acushnet 207 41.41 N 70.55 W
Acuto 66 41.47 N 13.10 E
Acvež 80 58.21 N 47.46 E
Acworth 192 34.03 N 84.40 W
Ada, Ghana 150 5.47 N 0.24 E
Ada, Jugo. 38 45.48 N 20.08 E
Ada, Nihon 174m 26.44 N 128.19 E
Ada, Mi., U.S. 216 42.57 N 85.29 W
Ada, Mn., U.S. 198 47.18 N 96.31 W
Ada, Oh., U.S. 216 40.46 N 83.49 W
Ada, Ok., U.S. 196 34.46 N 96.40 W
Ada, Mount ∧ 180 56.41 N 134.41 W
Adaba 144 7.00 N 39.24 E
A-da-Beja 266c 38.47 N 9.14 W
ʻAdabīyah, Ra's › 142 29.52 N 32.30 E
Adachi •[8] 268 35.45 N 139.48 E
Adachi-yama ∧ 96 33.51 N 130.55 E
Adado, Ras › 144 11.20 N 48.40 E
Adâfer el Abioḍ •[1] 150 19.30 N 10.00 W
Adai 272c 19.01 N 73.08 E
Adailo 144 14.29 N 40.52 E
Adainville 261 48.43 N 1.39 E
Adair, Ia., U.S. 198 41.22 N 94.19 W
Adair, Ok., U.S. 196 36.26 N 95.16 W
Adair □[6] 219 40.08 N 92.22 W
Adair, Bahía de c 200 31.30 N 113.48 W
Adair, Cape › 176 71.24 N 71.13 W
Adairsville 192 34.22 N 84.56 W
Adairville 194 36.40 N 86.51 W
Adaja ≃ 34 41.32 N 4.52 W
Adajevka 86 51.47 N 62.06 E
Adak, Ross. 24 66.30 N 59.38 E
Adak, Ak., U.S. 180 51.54 N 176.35 W
Adaka-shima I 174m 26.45 N 128.20 E
Adak Island I 180 51.45 N 176.40 W
Adaklı 130 39.14 N 40.30 E
Ådalen V 26 63.10 N 17.16 E
Ādam 118 22.24 N 57.32 E
Adam, Mount ∧ 254 51.36 S 59.55 W
Adamantina 255 21.42 S 51.04 W
Adamaoua ⋏ 152 7.00 N 12.00 E
Adamawa → Adamaoua ⋏ 152 7.00 N 12.00 E
Adamclisi 38 44.05 N 27.57 E
Adamello ⋏ 64 46.10 N 10.35 E
Adaminaby 171b 36.03 S 148.43 E
Adami Tulu 144 7.52 N 38.42 E
Adamovka 86 51.32 N 59.56 E
Adamovskoje 82 54.52 N 35.57 E
Adamów 30 51.45 N 22.17 E
Ādampur 123 31.26 N 75.43 E
Adams, In., U.S. 218 39.22 N 85.33 W
Adams, Ma., U.S. 207 42.37 N 73.07 W
Adams, Mn., U.S. 190 43.33 N 92.43 W
Adams, Ne., U.S. 198 40.27 N 96.30 W
Adams, N.Y., U.S. 212 43.48 N 76.01 W
Adams, N.D., U.S. 198 48.25 N 98.04 W
Adams, Tn., U.S. 194 36.34 N 87.03 W
Adams, Wi., U.S. 190 43.57 N 89.49 W
Adams □[6], Il., U.S. 219 39.56 N 91.23 W
Adams □[6], In., U.S. 216 40.50 N 84.56 W
Adams □[6], Oh., U.S. 218 38.48 N 83.32 W
Adams □[6], Pa., U.S. 208 39.48 N 77.15 W
Adams ≃ 182 50.52 N 119.35 W
Adams, Mount ∧, N.Z. 172 41.19 S 175.46 E
Adams, Mount ∧, Wa., U.S. 224 46.12 N 121.28 W
Adams Bridge ✢[2] 122 9.04 N 79.37 E
Adamsburg 279b 40.19 N 79.40 W
Adams Center 212 43.51 N 76.00 W
Adams Creek ≃ 224 46.18 N 121.40 W
Adams Lake ⊜ 182 51.13 N 119.33 W
Adams Mills 214 40.09 N 81.57 W
Adams National Historic Site ⊥ 283 42.15 N 71.01 W
Adams Park 216 42.08 N 85.29 W
Adams Park ♦ 275b 43.48 N 79.09 W
Adams Peak ∧ 122 6.48 N 80.30 E
Adams Rock I[2] 174e 25.04 S 130.05 W
Adamston 208 40.02 N 74.05 W
Adamstown, Austl. 170 32.56 S 151.44 E
Adamstown, Pit. 174e 25.04 S 130.05 W
Adamstown, Md., U.S. 208 39.18 N 77.28 W
Adamstown, Pa., U.S. 208 40.14 N 76.03 W
Adamsville, P.Q., Can. 206 45.17 N 72.47 W
Adamsville, Mi., U.S. 216 41.47 N 86.00 W
Adamsville, Oh., U.S. 214 40.04 N 81.53 W
Adamsville, Pa., U.S. 214 41.31 N 80.22 W
Adamsville, Tn., U.S. 194 35.14 N 88.23 W
ʻAdan (Aden) 144 12.45 N 45.12 E
Adana 130 37.01 N 35.18 E
Adana □[4] 130 37.20 N 35.45 E
Adanero 34 40.56 N 4.36 W
Adapazarı 130 40.46 N 30.24 E
Adarama 140 17.05 N 34.54 E
Adare 48 52.34 N 8.48 W
Adare, Cape › 9 71.17 S 170.14 E
Adar Gwagwa, Jabal ∧ 140 22.15 N 35.20 E
Adarot 140 17.50 N 36.07 E
Adaševo 80 53.56 N 44.19 E
Adauli 272c 19.06 N 73.02 E
Adaut 164 8.08 S 131.07 E
Adavale 166 25.55 S 144.36 E
Adda ≃, It. 36 45.08 N 9.53 E
Adda ≃, Sūd. 140 9.51 N 24.50 E
Ad-Ḍabʻah 140 31.02 N 28.26 E
Ad-Dabbah 140 18.03 N 30.57 E
Ad-Dafīnah 128 23.18 N 41.58 E
Aḍ-Ḍafrah •[1] 128 23.25 N 53.25 E
Ad-Dahnā' •[2] 128 24.30 N 48.10 E
Ad-Daljamūn 142 30.48 N 30.50 E
Ad-Damazin 140 11.49 N 34.23 E
Ad-Dāmir 140 17.35 N 33.58 E
Ad-Dammām 128 26.26 N 50.07 E
Ad-Dāmūr 132 33.44 N 35.27 E
Ad-Dānā 130 36.13 N 36.46 E
Ad-Daqahlīyah □[4] 142 31.10 N 31.30 E
Ad-Darb 144 17.43 N 42.15 E
Ad-Dawādimī 128 24.28 N 44.18 E
Ad-Dawḥah (Doha) 128 25.17 N 51.32 E
Ad-Dayr, Miṣr 140 25.20 N 32.35 E
Ad-Dayr, Miṣr 142 30.20 N 31.16 E
Adderbury 42 52.00 N 1.17 W
Ad-Dibdibah •[1] 128 28.00 N 46.30 E
Addicks 222 29.47 N 95.39 W
Addicks Reservoir ⊜[1] 222 29.49 N 95.40 W
Addieville 219 38.23 N 89.29 W
Aḍ-Ḍiffah (Libyan Plateau) ⋏[1] 140 30.30 N 25.30 E
Ad-Dilam 128 23.59 N 47.12 E
Ad-Dilinjāt 142 30.50 N 30.30 E
Ad-Dīmās 132 33.35 N 36.05 E
Addingham 44 53.57 N 1.53 W
Addington 260 51.18 N 0.23 E
Addis 194 30.21 N 91.15 W
Addis Ababa → Adis Abeba 144 9.02 N 38.42 E
Addison, Il., U.S. 216 41.55 N 87.59 W
Addison, Mi., U.S. 216 41.59 N 84.21 W
Addison, N.Y., U.S. 210 42.06 N 77.14 W
Addison, Tx., U.S. 222 32.57 N 96.49 W
Addison Creek ≃ 278 41.51 N 87.51 W
Ad-Dīwānīyah 128 31.59 N 44.56 E
Addlestone 260 51.22 N 0.30 W
Addo 158 33.32 S 25.45 E
Addo Elephant National Park ♦ 158 33.29 S 25.46 E
Ad-Du'ayn 140 11.26 N 26.09 E
Aḍ-Ḍuhayr 132 31.11 N 34.08 E
Ad-Duqqī 273c 30.04 N 31.15 E
Ad-Duwayd 128 30.15 N 42.17 E
Ad-Duwaym 140 14.00 N 32.19 E
Ad-Duwayr 132 33.23 N 35.25 E
Adébour 146 13.20 N 11.54 E
Adego 144 8.58 N 49.35 E
Adel, Ga., U.S. 192 31.08 N 83.25 W
Adel, Ia., U.S. 190 41.36 N 94.01 W
Adelaida → Adelaide 168b 34.55 S 138.35 E
Adelaide, Austl. 168b 34.55 S 138.35 E
Adelaide, Ba. 240b 25.00 N 77.31 W
Adelaide, S. Afr. 158 32.42 S 26.20 E
Adelaide Airport ⊠ 168b 34.58 S 138.32 E
Adelaide Island I 9 67.15 S 68.30 W
Adelaide Peninsula ›[1] 176 68.09 N 97.45 W
Adelaide River 164 13.15 S 131.06 E
Adelanto 228 34.34 N 117.24 W
Adelbert Range ⋏ 164 4.35 S 145.10 E
Adelboden 58 46.30 N 7.33 E
Adelebsen 52 51.34 N 9.45 E
Adèle Island I 160 15.32 S 123.09 E
Adelfia 68 41.00 N 16.52 E
Adélie Coast ⊥[2] 9 67.00 S 139.00 E
Adelong 171b 35.19 S 148.03 E
Adelong Creek ≃ 171b 35.06 S 148.02 E
Adelphi 284c 39.00 N 76.58 W
Adelphia 208 40.13 N 74.15 W
Adelphi University ʋ[2] 276 40.43 N 73.36 W
Adelsheim 56 49.24 N 9.23 E
Adelsö I 40 59.23 N 17.30 E
Adelzhausen 60 48.21 N 11.08 E
Aden, Gulf of c 136 12.30 N 48.00 E
Adena 214 40.13 N 80.52 W
Aden → ʻAdan 144 12.45 N 45.12 E
Adenau 56 50.23 N 6.55 E
Adendorf 52 53.17 N 10.26 E
Adendorp 158 32.20 S 24.33 E
Ader ⋏[1] 150 14.50 N 5.15 E
Aderklaa 264b 48.17 N 16.32 E
Adéta 150 7.08 N 0.44 E
Adhāta 272b 22.52 N 88.32 E
ʻĀdhirīyāt, Jibāl al- ⋏[2] 132 30.25 N 36.48 E
Adi 154 3.24 N 30.48 E
Adi, Pulau I 164 4.18 S 133.26 E
Adiaké 150 5.16 N 3.17 W
Adi Arkay 144 13.27 N 37.57 E
Adi Dairo 144 14.23 N 38.12 E
Adieu, Cape › 162 31.59 S 132.09 E
Adigala 144 10.25 N 42.14 E
Adige (Etsch) ≃ 64 45.10 N 12.20 E
Adigeni 84 41.42 N 42.42 E
Adigrat 144 14.17 N 39.28 E
Adıgüzel Barajı ⊜[1] 130 38.10 N 29.15 E
Adi Keyih 144 14.51 N 39.22 E
Adi Kwala 144 14.38 N 38.50 E
Ādilābād 122 19.40 N 78.32 E
Adilang 154 2.44 N 33.29 E
Adilcevaz 84 38.44 N 42.44 E
Adimi 89 47.20 N 138.56 E
Adin 204 41.11 N 120.56 W
Adinkerke 50 51.04 N 2.36 E
Adirondack Mountains ⋏ 188 44.00 N 74.00 W
Adirondack Park ♦ 188 44.00 N 74.20 W
Adis Abeba (Addis Ababa) 144 9.02 N 38.42 E
Adis Zemen 144 12.07 N 37.47 E
Adi Ugri 144 14.53 N 38.49 E
Adiwerna 115a 6.56 S 109.07 E
Adıyaman 130 37.46 N 38.17 E
Adıyaman □[4] 130 37.45 N 38.30 E
Adjan 112 2.11 N 113.12 E
Adjelman, Oued V 148 22.09 N 3.47 E
Adjohon 150 6.42 N 2.28 E
Adjud 38 46.04 N 27.11 E
Adjumani 154 3.22 N 31.47 E
Adjuntas 240m 18.10 N 66.43 W
Adler 78 43.27 N 39.55 E
Adler Planetarium ʋ 278 41.52 N 87.37 W
Adlershof •[8] 264a 52.26 N 13.33 E
Adlington 44 53.37 N 2.36 W
Adlington Hall ⊥ 262 53.19 N 2.09 W
Adliswil 58 47.19 N 8.32 E
Admer, Erg d' •[2] 148 24.00 N 9.15 E
Admiral 184 49.43 N 108.01 W
Admiralitäts-Inseln → Admiralty Islands II 164 2.10 S 147.00 E
Admiralty Bay c, St. Vin. 241h 13.00 N 61.16 W
Admiralty Bay c, Ak., U.S. 180 70.53 N 155.45 W
Admiralty Gulf c 160 14.20 S 125.50 E
Admiralty Gulf Aboriginal Reserve •[4] 164 14.40 S 125.30 E
Admiralty Inlet c, N.T., Can. 176 73.00 N 86.00 W
Admiralty Inlet c, Wa., U.S. 224 48.05 N 122.39 W
Admiralty Island I, N.T., Can. 176 69.30 N 101.00 W
Admiralty Island I, Ak., U.S. 180 57.50 N 134.30 W
Admiralty Islands II 164 2.10 S 147.00 E
Admiralty Mountains ⋏ 9 71.45 S 168.30 E
Admont 61 47.34 N 14.27 E
Adna 224 46.38 N 123.04 W
Ado ≃ 94 35.19 N 136.05 E
Adobe Creek ≃, Ca., U.S. 282 37.26 N 122.06 W
Adobe Creek ≃, Co., U.S. 198 38.05 N 103.18 W
Ado-Ekiti 150 7.38 N 5.12 E
Adogawa 94 35.20 N 136.02 E
Adok 140 8.11 N 30.19 E
Adolfo López Mateos 232 28.28 N 107.20 W
Adolfo López Mateos, Presa ⊜[1] 232 25.13 N 107.25 W
Adolfsberg 40 59.15 N 15.10 E
Adolphus Reach ɥ 212 44.05 N 76.55 W
Adonara, Pulau I 112 8.20 S 123.10 E
Ādoni 122 15.38 N 77.17 E
Ado-Odo 150 6.36 N 2.56 E
Adorf 54 50.19 N 12.15 E
Adoua, Korén V 150 14.37 N 6.40 E
Adour ≃ 32 43.32 N 1.32 W
Adowa → Adwa 144 14.10 N 38.55 E
Adra, Esp. 34 36.44 N 3.01 W
Ādra, India 126 23.30 N 86.40 E
ʻAdrā, Sūrīy. 132 33.37 N 36.30 E
Adranga 154 2.54 N 30.26 E
Adrano 70 37.40 N 14.50 E
Adrar 148 27.54 N 0.17 W
Adrar □[4] 150 20.05 N 11.00 W
Adrar □[5] 148 26.00 N 1.00 W
Adrâr •[1] 134 20.30 N 13.30 W
Adraskan 128 33.39 N 62.16 E
Adrasman 85 40.38 N 69.58 E
Adré 146 13.28 N 22.12 E
Adrī 146 27.32 N 13.14 E
Adria 64 45.03 N 12.03 E
Adrian, Ga., U.S. 192 32.31 N 82.35 W
Adrian, Mi., U.S. 216 41.53 N 84.02 W
Adrian, Mn., U.S. 198 43.38 N 95.55 W
Adrian, Mo., U.S. 194 38.23 N 94.21 W
Adrian, Oh., U.S. 214 41.03 N 83.20 W
Adrian, Or., U.S. 202 43.44 N 117.04 W
Adrian, Pa., U.S. 214 40.53 N 79.32 W
Adrian, Tx., U.S. 196 35.16 N 102.40 W
Adrian, W.V., U.S. 188 38.54 N 80.16 W
Adrianople → Edirne 130 41.40 N 26.34 E
Adrianópolis 287a 22.39 S 43.30 W
Adrianovka 88 51.34 N 114.30 E
Adriatico, Mar → Adriatic Sea ⊤[2] 22 42.30 N 16.00 E
Adriatic Sea ⊤[2] 22 42.30 N 16.00 E
Adriatique, Mer → Adriatic Sea ⊤[2] 22 42.30 N 16.00 E
Adriatisches Meer → Adriatic Sea ⊤[2] 22 42.30 N 16.00 E
Adrigole 48 51.40 N 9.42 W
Adro 64 45.37 N 9.57 E
Adrogué → Almirante Brown 258 34.48 S 58.23 W
Adstock, Mont ∧ 206 46.02 N 71.12 W
Adua 164 1.55 S 129.50 E
Aduard 52 53.15 N 6.26 E
Adujevo 82 54.59 N 35.59 E
Aduku 154 2.01 N 32.43 E
A Dun ≃ 110 13.24 N 108.28 E
Adur ≃ 42 50.49 N 0.16 W
Adusa 154 1.23 N 28.01 E
Adutiškis 76 55.09 N 26.36 E
Advance 194 37.06 N 89.54 W
Adventure, Bahía ɥ 254 44.50 S 74.45 W
Advie 46 57.23 N 3.27 W
Advocate Harbour 186 45.20 N 64.47 W
Adwa 144 14.10 N 38.55 E
Adwick le Street 44 53.34 N 1.11 W
Adyča ≃ 74 68.13 N 134.41 E
Adyge 84 44.19 N 41.57 E
Adygea → Adygeja □[3] 72 45.00 N 40.00 E
Adygeja □[3] 72 45.00 N 40.00 E
Adyk 80 45.48 N 45.38 E
Adžarskaja Respublika □[3] 84 41.40 N 42.00 E
Adž Bogd uul ⋏ 102 44.52 N 95.10 E
Adžikend 84 40.31 N 46.21 E
Adžima 89 48.08 N 139.40 E
Adzopé 150 6.06 N 3.52 W
Adz'va ≃ 24 66.36 N 59.28 E
Adz'vavom 24 66.36 N 59.12 E
Ae, Water of ≃ 44 55.08 N 3.27 W
Æbelø I 41 55.38 N 10.12 E
Aegean Sea ⊤[2] 38 38.30 N 25.00 E
Aegerisee ⊜ 58 47.07 N 8.38 E
Aegina → Aíyina I 38 37.46 N 23.26 E
Aegviidu 76 59.17 N 25.37 E
Aek Humbang 114 1.59 N 99.11 E
Aeknabara 114 1.17 N 99.45 E
Aeon Point › 174o 1.46 N 157.11 W
Aerhuola 89 51.01 N 120.10 E
Aerku Hu ⊜ 120 30.43 N 82.55 E
Ærø I 41 54.53 N 10.20 E
Aeroflotskij 78 45.03 N 34.01 E
Aeron ≃ 42 52.14 N 4.16 W
Aeronáutica, Centro de Instrucción de ʋ[2] 286d 12.09 S 77.00 W
Ærøskøbing 41 54.53 N 10.25 E
Aerqi Shan ∧ 89 48.35 N 121.07 E
Aershatu 102 44.11 N 113.36 E
Aerzen 52 52.03 N 9.16 E
Aesch 58 47.28 N 7.36 E
Aeschi 58 46.40 N 7.42 E
Aetna 182 49.08 N 113.15 W
Afaahiti 174s 17.43 S 149.19 W
Afadé 146 12.14 N 14.38 E
Afadjoto ∧[2] 150 7.05 N 0.35 E
ʻAfak 128 32.04 N 45.15 E
Afan ≃ 42 51.35 N 3.48 W
Afanasjevka 78 50.47 N 38.36 E
Afanasjevo, Ross. 24 58.52 N 53.12 E
Afanasjevo, Ross. 82 54.20 N 37.01 E
Afanasjevo, Ross. 82 55.18 N 36.12 E
Afanasjevskoje 86 56.49 N 58.17 E
Afándou 38 36.17 N 28.10 E
Afar 148 25.30 N 8.22 E
Afareaitu 174s 17.33 S 149.47 W
Afars and Issas → Djibouti □[1] 144 11.30 N 43.00 E
Afaspida 272c 19.08 N 73.04 E
Afdem 144 9.28 N 41.00 E
Afferde, Dtsch. 52 52.06 N 9.25 E
Afferde, Dtsch. 263 51.34 N 7.39 E
Afféry 150 6.19 N 3.57 W
Affi 64 45.33 N 10.46 E
Affing 58 48.27 N 10.58 E
Afflisses, Oued V 148 28.29 N 1.09 E
Affoltern am Albis 58 47.17 N 8.27 E
Affori •[8] 266b 45.31 N 9.10 E
Affric ≃ 46 57.19 N 4.50 W
Affric, Glen V 46 57.17 N 4.56 W
Affton 219 38.33 N 90.19 W
Afghānestān → Afghanistan □[1] 118 33.00 N 65.00 E
Afghanistan (Afghānestān) □[1] 118 33.00 N 65.00 E
Afgooye 144 2.09 N 45.07 E
Afia 114 1.23 N 97.32 E
ʻAfīf 128 23.55 N 42.56 E
Afikpo 150 5.53 N 7.56 E
Afipskij 78 44.55 N 38.50 E
Afiqim 132 32.40 N 35.35 E
Åfjord 26 63.58 N 10.12 E
Aflao 150 6.05 N 1.08 E
Aflenz Kurort 61 47.32 N 15.14 E
Aflou 148 34.07 N 2.06 E
Afmadow 144 0.31 N 42.04 E
Afodo 144 10.14 N 34.39 E
Afogados da Ingazeira 250 7.45 S 37.39 W
Afognak Island I 180 58.15 N 152.30 W
Afollé ⋏[2] 150 16.55 N 10.25 W
Afonicha 24 68.13 N 53.17 E
Afono Bay c 174u 14.15 S 170.39 W
Afonso Arinos 256 22.00 S 43.20 W
Afonso Bezerra 250 5.30 S 36.30 W
Afonso Claudio 255 20.05 S 41.08 W
Afonsos, Campo dos ■ 287a 22.53 S 43.23 W
Afragola 68 40.55 N 14.18 E
Afram ≃ 150 7.00 N 0.52 W
Africa ⊥[1] 4 10.00 N 22.00 E
Africa ⊥[1] 10 10.00 N 22.00 E
Africa del Sur → South Africa □[1] 156 30.00 S 26.00 E
Africo 68 38.04 N 15.59 E
Afrika → Africa ⊥[1] 10 10.00 N 22.00 E
Afrikanda 24 67.25 N 32.43 E
ʻAfrīn 130 36.31 N 36.52 E
ʻAfrīn ≃ 130 36.22 N 36.28 E
Afrique → Africa ⊥[1] 10 10.00 N 22.00 E
Afrique du Sud (République d') → South Africa □[1] 156 30.00 S 26.00 E
Afritz 64 46.43 N 13.48 E
Afşin 130 38.15 N 36.55 E
Afsluitdijk •[5] 52 53.00 N 5.15 E
Afton, De., U.S. 285 39.49 N 75.29 W
Afton, Ia., U.S. 194 41.01 N 94.11 W
Afton, N.Y., U.S. 210 42.13 N 75.31 W
Afton, Ok., U.S. 196 36.41 N 94.57 W
Afton, Wi., U.S. 216 42.36 N 89.04 W
Afton, Wy., U.S. 200 42.43 N 110.55 W
Aftout •[1] 148 26.40 N 3.48 W
Afuá 250 0.10 S 50.23 W
ʻAfula 132 32.36 N 35.17 E
ʻAfula ʻIllit 132 32.38 N 35.20 E
Afulu 114 1.17 N 97.15 E
Afyon 130 38.45 N 30.33 E
Afyon □[4] 130 38.40 N 30.30 E
Afyonkarahisar → Afyon 130 38.45 N 30.33 E
Afzalgarh 124 29.24 N 78.41 E
Aga, Nor. 26 60.18 N 6.36 E
Aga, Ross. 88 51.12 N 115.10 E
Aga ≃ 88 51.30 N 115.50 E
Agačag 85 44.03 N 71.58 E

Symbols in the index entries represent the broad categories identified in the key at the right. Symbols with superior numbers (⋏[1]) identify subcategories (see complete key on page *I · 1).*

Symbole im Register stellen die rechts im Schlüssel erklärten Kategorien dar. Symbole mit hochgestellten Ziffern (⋏[1]) bezeichnen Unterabteilungen einer Kategorie (vgl. vollständiger Schlüssel auf Seite *I · 1).*

Los símbolos incluídos en el texto del índice representan las grandes categorias identificadas con la clave a la derecha. Los símbolos con numeros en su parte superior (⋏[1]) identifican las subcategorías (véase la clave completa en la página *I · 1).*

Les symboles de l'index représentent les catégories indiquées dans la légende à droite. Les symboles suivis d'un indice (⋏[1]) représentent des sous-catégories (voir légende complète à la page *I · 1).*

Os símbolos incluídos no texto do índice representam as grandes categorias identificadas com a chave à direita. Os símbolos com números em sua parte superior (⋏[1]) identificam as subcategorias (veja-se a chave completa à página *I · 1).*

English	Deutsch	Español	Français	Português
∧ Mountain	Berg	Montaña	Montagne	Montanha
⋏ Mountains	Gebirge	Montañas	Montagnes	Montanhas
)(Pass	Paß	Paso	Col	Passo
V Valley, Canyon	Tal, Cañon	Valle, Cañón	Vallée, Canyon	Vale, Canhão
≃ Plain	Ebene	Llano	Plaine	Planície
› Cape	Kap	Cabo	Cap	Cabo
I Island	Insel	Isla	Île	Ilha
II Islands	Inseln	Islas	Îles	Ilhas
⊥ Other Topographic Features	Andere Topographische Objekte	Otros Elementos Topográficos	Autres données topographiques	Outros acidentes topográficos

ESPAÑOL

Nombre	Página	Lat.°'	Long.°' W = Oeste
Ağaçören	130	38.52 N	33.56 E
Agadez	150	16.58 N	7.59 E
Agadez □[5]	146	19.45 N	12.00 E
Agadez, Ighazer oua-n- ∨	150	17.28 N	6.26 E
Agadir	148	30.26 N	9.36 W
Agadir □[4]	148	30.40 N	8.55 W
Agâdîr, Râs ›	148	20.34 N	16.32 W
Agadyr'	86	48.17 N	72.53 E
Agafonovka	80	50.36 N	47.26 E
Agāhpur	272a	28.34 N	77.22 E
Agaie	150	9.03 N	6.18 E
Ägäisches Meer → Aegean Sea ∓[2]	38	38.30 N	25.00 E
Agalak	140	11.01 N	32.42 E
Agalega Islands II	138	10.24 S	56.37 E
Agal Terara ∧	144	6.57 N	40.08 E
Agan ≃	72	61.23 N	74.35 E
Agana	174p	13.28 N	144.45 E
Agana Heights	174p	13.28 N	144.45 E
Agano ≃	92	37.57 N	139.08 E
Agapa	74	71.27 N	89.15 E
Aga Point ›	174p	13.15 N	144.43 E
Agapovka	86	53.18 N	59.28 E
Agar	120	23.42 N	76.01 E
Agara	84	42.03 N	43.49 E
Agâraktem ∓[4]	148	23.11 N	6.20 W
Ågård	41	55.35 N	9.26 E
Agaro	144	7.50 N	36.40 E
Agartala	120	23.49 N	91.16 E
Agartu	80	49.49 N	47.06 E
Agaru	140	10.59 N	34.44 E
Agaruut	102	43.10 N	109.26 E
Agasan	272c	19.11 N	73.04 E
Agassiz	224	49.14 N	121.46 W
Agassiz, Cape ›	9	68.29 S	62.56 W
Agassiz Pool ⊜	198	48.20 N	95.58 W
Agat	174p	13.24 N	144.39 E
Agat Bay ⊂	174p	13.24 N	144.39 E
Agate	198	39.27 N	103.56 W
Agate Beach	202	44.40 N	124.03 W
Agate Fossil Beds National Monument ♠	198	42.25 N	103.43 W
Agathonísion I	38	37.28 N	27.00 E
Agats	164	5.33 S	138.08 E
Agatsuma	94	36.34 N	138.50 E
Agatsuma ≃	94	36.30 N	139.01 E
Agatti Island I	122	10.50 N	72.12 E
Agattu Island I	181a	52.25 N	173.35 E
Agattu Strait ʊ	181a	52.35 N	173.25 E
Agawa	96	33.34 N	133.10 E
Agawa ≃	190	47.21 N	84.38 W
Agawa Bay ⊂	190	47.20 N	84.42 W
Agawa Canyon ∨	190	47.27 N	84.29 W
Agawam, Ma., U.S.	207	42.04 N	72.36 W
Agawam, Mt., U.S.	182	48.00 N	112.10 W
Agay	62	43.26 N	6.51 E
Agazzano	62	44.57 N	9.31 E
Agbaja	150	7.58 N	6.38 E
Agbede	273a	6.40 N	3.29 E
Agbélouvé	150	6.40 N	1.10 E
Agboju	273a	6.28 N	3.17 E
Agboville	150	5.56 N	4.13 W
Agboyi Creek ≃	273a	6.34 N	3.25 E
Agcawayan	116	13.46 N	120.16 E
Agdam	84	39.59 N	46.57 E
Agdaš	84	40.38 N	47.28 E
Agde	32	43.19 N	3.28 E
Agde, Cap d' ›	32	43.16 N	3.30 E
Agdžabedi	84	40.03 N	47.28 E
Agege	273a	6.37 N	3.20 E
Agejevo	82	54.10 N	36.29 E
Agematsu	94	35.47 N	137.42 E
Agen	32	44.12 N	0.37 E
Agency	190	40.59 N	92.18 W
Agency Lake ⊜	202	42.32 N	121.58 W
Ageo	94	35.58 N	139.36 E
Agepsta, gora ∧	84	43.32 N	40.30 E
Ager ≃	60	48.05 N	13.51 E
Agerbæk	41	55.36 N	8.48 E
Agerskov	41	55.07 N	9.08 E
Agersø I	41	55.12 N	11.12 E
Agery	168b	34.10 S	137.44 E
Ágfalva	61	47.41 N	16.31 E
Aggeneis	158	29.03 S	18.51 E
Agger ≃	56	50.48 N	7.11 E
Aggherar	144	4.03 N	42.40 E
Aggius	71	40.46 N	9.04 E
Aggstein ⊥	61	48.18 N	15.25 E
Aggteleki Nemzeti Park ♠	30	48.30 N	20.32 E
Āghā Jārī	128	30.42 N	49.50 E
Aghleam	48	54.08 N	10.07 W
Aghzoumal, Sabkhat ⊜	148	24.21 N	12.52 W
Agia	124	26.05 N	90.32 E
Agidingbi	273a	6.38 N	3.21 E
Agimont	56	50.10 N	4.48 E
Ağın	130	38.57 N	38.43 E
Agincourt ◆[8]	275b	43.48 N	79.17 W
Aginskoje, Ross.	86	55.15 N	94.55 E
Aginskoje, Ross.	88	51.06 N	114.32 E
Agira	70	37.39 N	14.31 E
Aglasterhausen	56	49.21 N	8.59 E
Ağlasun	130	37.40 N	30.32 E
Agliana	66	43.54 N	11.00 E
Agliano	62	44.47 N	8.15 E
Aglientu	71	41.05 N	9.07 E
Agly ≃	32	42.47 N	3.02 E
Agna	64	45.10 N	11.58 E
Agnadello	62	45.26 N	9.33 E
Agnes, Mount ∧	162	26.51 S	128.59 E
Agnes Lake ⊜	190	48.13 N	91.21 W
Agnew	162	28.01 S	120.30 E
Agnew Lake ⊜[1]	190	46.22 N	81.45 W
Agnews Hill ∧[2]	48	54.51 N	5.56 W
Agnibilékrou	150	7.08 N	3.12 W
Agnije-Afanasjevskij	89	51.57 N	138.45 E
Agnita	38	45.59 N	24.38 E
Agno, Pil.	116	16.07 N	119.48 E
Agno, Schw.	58	46.00 N	8.54 E
Agno ≃, It.	64	45.31 N	11.22 E
Agno ≃, Pil.	116	16.02 N	120.08 E
Agnone	66	41.48 N	14.22 E
Agnone Bagni ◆[8]	70	37.18 N	15.06 E
Ago	92	34.20 N	136.51 E
Agogna ≃	62	45.04 N	8.54 E
Agogo, Ghana	150	6.47 N	1.04 W
Agogo, Süd.	140	7.49 N	28.52 E
Agoo	116	16.20 N	120.22 E
Agordat → Akordat	144	15.33 N	37.53 E
Agordo	64	46.17 N	12.02 E
Agostinho Pôrto	287a	22.47 S	43.23 W
Agostitlán	234	19.33 N	100.41 W
Agou, Mont ∧	150	6.52 N	0.46 E
Agouna	150	7.34 N	1.42 E
Agoura Hills	228	34.08 N	118.44 W
Agout ≃	32	43.47 N	1.41 E
Agoza ⊥	146	18.30 N	23.45 E
Āgra	124	27.11 N	78.01 E
Āgra Canal ≊	272a	28.34 N	77.18 E
Agrachanskij poluostrov ›[1]	84	43.42 N	47.36 E
Agraciada	258	33.48 S	58.15 W
Agrado	246	2.15 N	75.46 W
Agraf'novka	83	47.45 N	39.29 E
Agramonte	240p	22.41 N	81.07 W
Agram → Zagreb	36	45.48 N	15.58 E
Agrate Brianza	62	45.34 N	9.21 E
Ágreda	34	41.51 N	1.56 W
Ağrı	84	39.44 N	43.03 E
Ağrı □[4]	84	39.30 N	43.15 E
Agri ≃	68	40.13 N	16.44 E
Agri Bavnehøj ∧[2]	41	56.14 N	10.33 E
Ağrı Dağı (Mount Ararat) ∧	84	39.42 N	44.18 E
Agrigento	70	37.18 N	13.35 E

FRANÇAIS

Nom	Page	Lat.°'	Long.°' W = Ouest
Agrigento □[4]	70	37.27 N	13.30 E
Agrihan I	108	18.46 N	145.40 E
Agrínion	38	38.37 N	21.24 E
Agrio ≃	252	38.21 S	69.43 W
Agropoli	68	40.21 N	15.00 E
Agro Pontino ◆[1]	66	41.25 N	12.55 E
Agryz	80	56.33 N	53.00 E
Agtuuganon, Mount ∧	116	7.48 N	126.12 E
Agua, Ilha d' I	287a	22.49 S	43.10 W
Agua, Volcán de ∧[1]	236	14.28 N	90.45 W
Água Branca, Bra.	250	9.17 S	37.55 W
Água Branca, Bra.	250	7.31 S	37.40 W
Água Branca, Bra.	250	5.53 S	42.38 W
Agua Brava, Laguna ⊂	234	22.10 N	105.32 W
Agua Caliente, Méx.	232	27.27 N	108.32 W
Agua Caliente, Méx.	234	23.20 N	105.20 W
Agua Caliente Creek ≃	282	37.29 N	121.56 W
Agua Caliente Grande	232	26.31 N	108.22 W
Aguacate	240p	22.59 N	81.49 W
Aguachica	246	8.19 N	73.38 W
Água Clara	255	20.27 S	52.52 W
Aguada	240m	18.23 N	67.11 W
Aguada, Zanjón de la ≃	286e	33.30 S	70.47 W
Aguada Cecilio	254	40.51 S	65.51 W
Aguada de Guerra	254	41.04 S	68.25 W
Aguada de Pasajeros	240p	22.23 N	80.51 W
Aguadas	246	5.37 N	75.27 W
Aguadilla	240m	18.26 N	67.09 W
Água Doce	252	27.00 S	51.33 W
Agua Dulce, Méx.	234	18.08 N	94.08 W
Aguadulce, Pan.	236	8.15 N	80.33 W
Agua Dulce, Ca., U.S.	228	34.30 N	118.23 W
Agua Dulce, Tx., U.S.	196	27.47 N	97.54 W
Agua Fria ≃	200	33.23 N	112.21 W
Agua Fria Creek ≃	282	37.28 N	121.56 W
Aguaí	256	22.04 S	46.58 W
Agualeguas	232	26.18 N	99.34 W
Água Limpa	255	18.06 S	48.46 W
Agualva-Cacém	266c	38.46 N	9.18 W
Aguán ≃	236	15.57 N	85.44 W
Aguanaval ≃	232	25.28 N	102.53 W
Agua Negra	286c	10.28 N	67.01 W
Aguanish	186	50.13 N	62.05 W
Aguanus ≃	186	50.13 N	62.05 W
Aguapeí ≃, Bra.	248	15.53 S	58.25 W
Aguapeí ≃, Bra.	255	21.03 S	51.47 W
Aguapey ≃	252	29.07 S	56.36 W
Água Preta, Igarapé ≃	246	1.41 S	63.48 W
Agua Prieta	232	31.18 N	109.34 W
Aguaragüe, Serranía de ⋏	248	21.30 S	63.40 W
Aguaray	252	22.16 S	63.44 W
Aguaray-Guazú ≃, Para.	252	24.47 S	57.19 W
Aguaray-Guazú ≃, Para.	252	24.05 S	56.40 W
Aguarico ≃	246	0.59 S	75.11 W
Aguaro-Guariquito, Parque Nacional ♠	246	8.10 N	66.50 W
Aguaruto	232	24.47 N	107.29 W
Aguas ≃	34	37.09 N	1.49 W
Águas, Serra das ∧	256	21.55 S	45.25 W
Aguasabon ≃	190	48.46 N	87.07 W
Águas Belas	250	9.07 S	37.07 W
Aguas Buenas	240m	18.15 N	66.06 W
Aguascalientes, Méx.	200	32.18 N	115.10 W
Aguascalientes, Méx.	234	21.53 N	102.18 W
Aguascalientes □[3]	234	22.00 N	102.30 W
Aguascalientes, Río de ≃	234	21.23 N	102.28 W
Aguas Corrientes	258	34.31 S	56.24 W
Águas da Prata	256	21.56 S	46.43 W
Águas de Contendas	256	21.54 S	45.01 W
Águas de Lindóia	256	22.29 S	46.39 W
Águas Formosas	255	17.05 S	40.57 W
Aguasvivas ≃	34	41.20 N	0.25 W
Agua Tibia ∧	228	33.24 N	116.59 W
Água Vermelha, Represa de ⊜[1]	255	20.00 S	50.00 W
Agua-Viva	256	21.41 S	42.33 W
Aguayo	252	31.40 S	65.54 W
Aguaytía ≃	248	8.08 S	74.37 W
Agua Zarca	200	31.10 N	110.59 W
Agu Bay ⊂	176	70.18 N	86.30 W
Agudos	255	22.28 S	49.00 W
Águeda	34	40.34 N	8.27 W
Águeda ≃	34	41.02 N	6.56 W
Aguelhok	150	19.28 N	0.52 E
Aguema	152	12.03 S	21.49 E
Aguenier, Lac ⊜	186	50.43 N	68.13 W
Agugliano	66	43.32 N	13.23 E
Agui	94	34.55 N	136.55 E
Aguié	150	13.30 N	7.47 E
Aguijan I	108	14.51 N	145.34 E
Aguila	200	33.56 N	113.10 W
Aguilar, Esp.	34	37.31 N	4.39 W
Aguilar, Co., U.S.	198	37.24 N	104.39 W
Aguilares, Arg.	252	27.26 S	65.37 W
Aguilares, El Sal.	236	13.58 N	89.12 W
Águilas	34	37.24 N	1.35 W
Aguililla	234	18.44 N	102.44 W
Aguirre ≃	246	8.28 N	61.02 W
Aguirre, Arroyo ≃	288	34.46 S	58.35 W
Aguirre, Bahía ⊂	254	54.57 S	65.50 W
Aguit	102	41.52 N	112.56 E
Aguita Zarc	234	23.10 N	104.28 W
Aguja, Cerro ∧	254	42.11 S	71.51 W
Aguja, Punta ›	248	5.48 S	81.06 W
Aguja Point ›	116	12.42 N	123.23 E
Agujas, Cabo de las → Agulhas, Cape ›	158	34.52 S	20.00 E
Agujereada, Punta ›	240m	18.31 N	67.08 W
Agujita	196	27.53 N	101.09 W
Agul ≃	88	55.44 N	95.41 E
Agulai	144	13.41 N	39.35 E
Agulhas	158	34.50 S	20.00 E
Agulhas, Cape ›	158	34.52 S	20.00 E
Agulhas Basin ✦[1]	8	47.00 S	27.00 E
Agulhas Negras	256	22.28 S	44.27 W
Agulhas Negras, Pico das ∧	256	22.23 S	44.38 W
Agulhas Plateau ✦[3]	10	40.00 S	26.00 E
Agung, Gunung ∧	115b	8.21 S	115.30 E
Aguni-jima I	93b	26.35 N	127.14 E
Agusan ≃	116	9.00 N	125.31 E
Agusan del Norte □[4]	116	9.00 N	125.30 E
Agusan del Sur □[4]	116	8.30 N	125.40 E
Agustín Codazzi	246	10.02 N	73.14 W
Agutaya	116	11.09 N	120.56 E
Agutaya Island I	116	11.09 N	120.58 E
Ağva	130	41.09 N	29.50 E
Agvali	84	42.33 N	46.06 E
Agwarra	150	10.42 N	4.35 E
Ägypten → Egypt □[1]	140	27.00 N	30.00 E
Aha	174m	26.43 N	128.17 E
Ahaggar (Hoggar) ⋏	148	23.00 N	6.30 E
Ahaggar, Tassili ta-n- ⋏[1]	148	21.00 N	6.00 E
Aha Hills ⋏[2]	156	19.45 S	21.10 E
Aha-kō ⊂	174m	26.43 N	128.18 E
Aham	60	48.32 N	12.28 E
Ahar	128	38.28 N	47.04 E
Ahar ≃	128	38.32 N	47.31 E
Ahascragh	48	53.24 N	8.20 W
Ahaura	172	42.21 S	171.32 E
Ahaura ≃	172	42.21 S	171.31 E
Ahaus	52	52.04 N	7.00 E
Ahe ≃	263	51.13 N	7.43 E
Aheggar ∧	148	24.43 N	5.39 E
Ahfir	148	34.57 N	2.17 W
Ahimanawa Range ⋏	172	39.00 S	176.27 E
Ahipara	172	35.10 S	173.10 E

PORTUGUÊS

Nome	Página	Lat.°'	Long.°' W = Oeste
Ahipara Bay ⊂	172	35.10 S	173.07 E
'Āhirah	132	32.53 N	36.28 E
Ahırlı	130	37.14 N	32.08 E
Ahklun Mountains ⋏	180	59.15 N	161.00 W
Ahlat, Tür.	128	38.45 N	42.29 E
Ahlat, Tür.	130	38.45 N	42.29 E
Ahlbeck	54	53.40 N	14.11 E
Ahlem	52	52.23 N	9.40 E
Ahlen	52	51.46 N	7.53 E
Ahlenberg	263	51.25 N	7.28 E
Ahlenmoor ◆[3]	52	53.40 N	8.45 E
Ahlhorn	52	52.54 N	8.14 E
Ahlsdorf	54	51.32 N	11.28 E
Ahmadābād	120	23.02 N	72.37 E
Aḥmadābād-e Sarjām	128	35.51 N	59.36 E
Aḥmad al-Bāqir, Jabal ∧	132	29.36 N	35.08 E
Ahmadgarh	123	30.41 N	75.50 E
Ahmadnagar	122	19.05 N	74.44 E
Ahmadpur, India	124	23.31 N	77.13 E
Ahmadpur, India	126	23.50 N	87.42 E
Ahmadpur East	123	29.09 N	71.16 E
Ahmadpur Siāl	123	30.41 N	71.46 E
Ahmad Wāl	120	29.25 N	65.56 E
Aḥmar, Al-Baḥr al- → Red Sea ∓[2]	136	20.00 N	38.00 E
Aḥmar, 'Erg el ◆[2]	148	23.30 N	4.54 W
Aḥmar, Jabal al- ∧	132	29.40 N	35.09 E
Ahmar Mountains ⋏	144	9.15 N	41.00 E
Ahmedabad → Ahmadābād	120	23.02 N	72.37 E
Ahmetli	130	38.31 N	27.57 E
Ahmic Lake ⊜	190	45.37 N	79.42 W
Ahnet ⋏	148	24.58 N	2.57 E
Ahnet, Tanezrouft n- ◆[2]	148	22.15 N	1.30 E
Ahoada	150	5.05 N	6.38 E
Ahoghill	48	54.51 N	6.22 W
Ahome	232	25.55 N	109.11 W
Ahon, Tarso ∧	146	20.23 N	18.18 E
Ahornspitz ∧	64	47.08 N	11.56 E
Ahoskie	192	36.17 N	76.59 W
Ahousat	182	49.17 N	126.04 W
Ahr ≃	56	50.33 N	7.17 E
Ahram	128	28.52 N	51.16 E
Ahrāmāt Dahshūr (North and Bent Pyramids) ⊥	142	29.48 N	31.13 E
Ahrāmāt Maydūm (Maydūm Pyramid) ⊥	142	29.23 N	31.10 E
Ahraura	124	25.01 N	83.01 E
Ahrensbök	54	54.00 N	10.34 E
Ahrensburg	52	53.40 N	10.14 E
Ahrensdorf, Dtsch.	54	52.10 N	14.05 E
Ahrensdorf, Dtsch.	264a	52.19 N	13.12 E
Ahrensfelde	264a	52.35 N	13.35 E
Ahrgebirge ⋏	56	50.30 N	6.50 E
Ahtanum	224	46.34 N	120.37 W
Ahtanum Creek ≃	202	46.32 N	120.31 W
Ahtanum Ridge ∧	224	46.30 N	120.50 W
Ähtäri	26	62.34 N	24.06 E
Ähtärinjärvi ⊜	26	62.40 N	24.03 E
Ähtävänjoki ≃	26	63.38 N	22.48 E
Ahtopol	38	42.06 N	27.57 E
Ahu	98	34.27 N	118.39 E
Ahuacatlán, Méx.	234	21.03 N	104.29 W
Ahuacatlán, Méx.	234	20.00 N	97.52 W
Ahuachapán	236	13.55 N	89.51 W
Ahuacuotzingo	234	17.42 N	98.56 W
Ahualulco de Mercado	234	20.42 N	103.59 W
Ahuijullo	234	19.05 N	103.05 W
Ahuijullo ≃	234	18.49 N	103.37 W
Ahumada, Méx.	204	32.30 N	115.30 W
Ahumada, Méx.	232	30.37 N	106.31 W
Ahun	32	46.05 N	2.05 E
Ahuntsic ◆[8]	275a	45.33 N	73.39 W
Ahunui I[1]	14	19.39 S	140.25 W
Ahuriri ≃	172	44.33 S	170.11 E
Åhus	26	55.55 N	14.17 E
Ahuzhen	98	34.27 N	118.39 E
Ahvāz	128	31.19 N	48.42 E
Ahvenanmaa □[4]	26	60.15 N	20.00 E
Ahwahnee	226	37.21 N	119.43 W
Aḥwar	144	13.31 N	46.42 E
Ahwa-ri	98	35.54 N	129.02 E
Ai ≃	98	40.13 N	124.30 E
Aialik Cape ›	180	59.42 N	149.31 W
Aiándion	267c	37.55 N	23.28 E
Aiapuá	246	4.29 S	62.04 W
Aiapuá, Lago ⊜	246	4.27 S	62.08 W
Aibag ≃	102	42.40 N	110.42 E
Aibonito	240m	18.08 N	66.16 W
Aich	64	47.25 N	13.49 E
Aichach	60	48.28 N	11.08 E
Aicha vorm Wald	60	48.41 N	13.18 E
Aichi □[5]	94	35.00 N	137.15 E
Aichi-kōgen-kokutei-kōen ♠	94	35.10 N	137.25 E
Aichi-yōsui ≊	94	34.42 N	136.57 E
Aichstetten	58	47.54 N	10.04 E
Aidenbach	60	48.34 N	13.06 E
Aidomaggiore	71	40.10 N	8.51 E
Aidone	70	37.25 N	14.27 E
Aidong	102	24.46 N	107.21 E
Aiduma, Pulau I	164	3.58 S	134.06 E
Aiea	229c	21.22 N	157.56 W
Aiello Calabro	68	39.07 N	16.10 E
Aigáleo Óros ∧[2]	267c	38.00 N	23.37 E
Aigburth ◆[8]	262	53.22 N	2.55 W
Aigen im Mühlkreis	60	48.39 N	13.58 E
Aigenmiao	89	43.36 N	120.50 E
Aigle	58	46.19 N	6.58 E
Aigle, Île à l' I	275a	45.42 N	73.28 W
Aigle, Lac à l' ⊜	186	51.12 N	65.25 W
Aignay-le-Duc	58	47.40 N	4.44 E
Aigre	32	45.54 N	0.01 E
Aiguá	252	34.12 S	54.45 W
Aiguebelette, Lac d' ⊜	62	45.33 N	5.48 E
Aiguebelette-le-Lac	62	45.32 N	5.49 E
Aiguebelle	62	45.32 N	6.18 E
Aiguebelle, Réserve ♠	190	48.33 N	78.45 W
Aigueperse	32	46.01 N	3.12 E
Aigues ≃	62	44.07 N	4.43 E
Aigues-Mortes	62	43.34 N	4.11 E
Aigues-Mortes, Golfe d' ⊂	62	43.31 N	4.03 E
Aigüestortes, Parc National d' ♠	34	42.30 N	1.01 E
Aigues-Vives	62	43.44 N	4.10 E
Aiguilles	62	44.47 N	6.52 E
Aiguines	62	43.46 N	6.15 E
Aigurande	32	46.26 N	1.50 E
Aihui (Heihe)	89	50.16 N	127.28 E
Aija	248	9.46 S	77.38 W
Aikawa, Nihon	92	38.02 N	138.15 E
Aikawa, Nihon	94	35.32 N	139.17 E
Aiken	192	33.33 N	81.43 W
Aikens Lake ⊜	184	51.12 N	95.20 W
Ailao Shan ⋏	102	24.08 N	101.25 E
Ailefroide	62	44.53 N	6.27 E
Aileron	162	22.39 S	133.20 E
Ailette ≃	50	49.35 N	3.10 E
Aileu	112	8.43 S	125.34 E
Ailimutou Shan ∧	104	42.19 N	121.25 E
Ailingen	58	47.41 N	9.29 E
Ailinglapalap I[1]	14	7.23 N	168.46 E
Ailinzhuang	105	39.27 N	117.36 E
Aillant-sur-Tholon	50	47.52 N	3.21 E
Aille ≃	62	43.26 N	6.30 E
Ailly-le-Haut-Clocher	50	50.05 N	2.00 E
Ailly-sur-Noye	50	49.45 N	2.22 E
Ailly-sur-Somme	50	49.55 N	2.12 E
Ailo	164	4.50 S	151.40 E
Ailsa Craig	190	43.08 N	81.33 W
Ailsa Craig I	44	55.16 N	5.07 W
Ailuk I[1]	14	10.20 N	169.56 E
Aim	74	58.50 N	134.12 E
Aimargues	62	43.41 N	4.12 E
Aime	62	45.33 N	6.39 E
Aimere	115b	8.50 S	120.52 E
Aimi	96	35.22 N	133.22 E
Aimogasta	252	28.33 S	66.49 W
Aimorés	255	19.30 S	41.04 W
Aimoto	270	34.59 N	135.10 E
Ain □[5]	32	46.10 N	5.20 E
Ain ≃	62	45.48 N	5.10 E
Aïn Arnat	34	36.11 N	5.19 E
Aïn Azel	34	35.49 N	5.31 E
Ainaži	76	57.52 N	24.21 E
'Aïn Belbela, Sebkha ≋	148	27.30 N	5.20 W
Aïn Benian	148	36.48 N	2.55 E
Aïn Ben Tili	148	26.00 N	9.32 W
Aïn Berda	36	36.39 N	7.35 E
Aïn Bessem	34	36.18 N	3.40 E
Aincourt	261	49.04 N	1.47 E
Aïn Defla	34	36.16 N	1.58 E
Aïn Deheb	148	34.51 N	1.33 E
Aïn Draham	148	36.47 N	8.42 E
Aine ≃	56	50.23 N	5.31 E
Aïn el Beïda	148	35.48 N	7.24 E
Aïn el Hadjel	34	35.40 N	3.53 E
Aïn el Kebira	34	36.22 N	5.30 E
Aïn Milia	148	36.02 N	6.34 E
Aino	270	34.57 N	135.10 E
Aino-shima I, Nihon	96	33.59 N	130.50 E
Aino-shima I, Nihon	96	33.45 N	130.23 E
Aïn Oulmène	34	35.55 N	5.18 E
Ainring	64	47.48 N	12.56 E
Ainsdale	44	53.36 N	3.02 W
Aïn Sefra	148	32.45 N	0.35 W
Ain Shams University ⊍[2]	273c	30.03 N	31.17 E
Ainslie, Mount ∧	171b	35.16 S	149.10 E
Ainslie Lake ⊜	186	46.08 N	61.12 W
Ainsworth, Eng., U.K.	262	53.35 N	2.22 W
Ainsworth, Ne., U.S.	198	42.33 N	99.51 W
Aïn Taghrout	34	36.08 N	5.05 E
Aïn Tedelès	148	36.00 N	0.18 E
Aïn Témouchent	148	35.18 N	1.08 W
Aïn Touta	148	35.23 N	5.54 E
Aintree	262	53.29 N	2.56 W
Aintree Race Course ♠	262	53.28 N	2.56 W
Aïn Wessara	148	35.27 N	2.54 E
Aïn Yagout	148	35.47 N	6.25 E
Aio	96	34.00 N	131.26 E
Aioi	96	34.48 N	134.28 E
Aiome	164	5.10 S	144.45 E
Aiora	34	39.04 N	1.03 W
Aipe	246	3.13 N	75.15 W
Aiquara	255	14.07 S	39.52 W
Aiquile	248	18.10 S	65.10 W
Aïr ⋏	150	18.00 N	8.30 E
Airabu, Pulau I	112	2.46 N	106.14 E
Airai Airport ⊠	175b	7.22 N	134.33 E
Airaines	50	49.58 N	1.57 E
Airão	246	1.56 S	61.22 W
Airasca	62	44.55 N	7.29 E
Airbangis	110	0.12 N	99.23 E
Airdikit	112	2.40 S	101.15 E
Airdrie, Ab., Can.	182	51.18 N	114.02 W
Airdrie, Scot., U.K.	46	55.52 N	3.59 W
Aire	32	43.42 N	0.16 W
Aire ≃, Fr.	56	49.19 N	4.49 E
Aire ≃, Eng., U.K.	44	53.44 N	0.54 W
Aire-sur-la-Lys	50	50.38 N	2.24 E
Air Force Island I	176	67.55 N	74.10 W
Airgegas	112	2.42 S	106.25 E
Airgin Sum	102	42.58 N	111.08 E
Airhaji	112	1.57 S	100.53 E
Airjamban	114	1.13 N	101.14 E
Airlie	166	20.16 S	148.43 E
Airmolek	112	0.22 S	102.17 E
Airmont	276	41.06 N	74.06 W
Airola	68	41.04 N	14.33 E
Airole	62	43.52 N	7.33 E
Airolo	58	46.32 N	8.37 E
Airor	46	57.04 N	5.46 W
Airport West	274b	37.44 S	144.53 E
Airtenang	112	3.08 S	101.43 E
Airterjun	114	1.20 N	100.27 E
Airuno	62	45.45 N	9.25 E
Airvault	32	46.50 N	0.08 W
Aisch ≃	60	49.46 N	11.01 E
Aisega	164	5.44 S	148.21 E
Aisén del General Carlos Ibáñez del Campo □[4]	254	46.30 S	73.30 W
Aisey-sur-Seine	58	47.45 N	4.35 E
Aishihik	180	61.35 N	137.30 W
Aishihik Lake ⊜	180	61.25 N	137.06 W
Ai-shima I	96	34.30 N	131.17 E
Aisinaike	85	39.47 N	75.47 E
Aislingen	56	48.30 N	10.27 E
Aisne □[5]	50	49.30 N	3.30 E
Aisne ≃	50	49.26 N	2.50 E
Aisne à la Marne, Canal de l' ≊	50	49.24 N	3.55 E
Aïssa, Djebel ∧	148	32.51 N	0.30 W
Aïssey	58	47.16 N	6.20 E
Aist ≃	61	48.14 N	14.35 E
Aisy-sur-Armançon	50	47.39 N	4.13 E
Aitana, Serra d' ∧	34	38.44 N	0.16 W
Aitape	164	3.08 S	142.21 E
Aiterach ≃	60	48.54 N	12.38 E
Aiterhofen	60	48.51 N	12.37 E
Aith	46a	60.16 N	1.23 W
Aitkin	190	46.31 N	93.42 W
Aït-Melloul	148	30.21 N	9.31 W
Aitolikón	38	38.27 N	21.22 E
Aït-Ourir	148	31.38 N	7.42 W
Aitrach	58	47.56 N	10.05 E
Aitutaki I[1]	14	18.52 S	159.45 W
Ait Youssef ou Ali	34	35.13 N	3.55 W
Aiuaba	250	6.38 S	40.07 W
Aiud	38	46.19 N	23.44 E
Aiún → El Aaiún	148	27.09 N	13.12 W
Aiuruoca	256	21.58 S	44.36 W
Aiuruoca ≃, Bra.	256	21.42 S	44.22 W
Aiuruoca ≃, Bra.	256	21.32 S	44.26 W
Aiva	287a	22.42 S	43.28 W
Aiviekste ≃	76	56.37 N	25.45 E
Aix, Mount ∧	224	46.47 N	121.15 W
Aix-en-Othe	50	48.13 N	3.44 E
Aix-en-Provence	62	43.32 N	5.26 E
Aix-la-Chapelle → Aachen	56	50.47 N	6.05 E
Aix-les-Bains	62	45.42 N	5.55 E
Aiyáleo	267c	37.59 N	23.41 E
Aiyang, Mount ∧	164	5.05 S	141.19 E
Aiyansh	182	55.17 N	129.03 W
Aíyina	38	37.44 N	23.27 E
Aíyina I	38	37.46 N	23.26 E
Aiyínion	38	40.30 N	22.33 E
Aíyion	38	38.15 N	22.05 E
Āīzawl	120	23.44 N	92.43 E
Aizhaipuzi	104	40.57 N	124.01 E
Aizkraukle	76	56.38 N	25.13 E
Aizpute	76	56.43 N	21.38 E
Aizu-bange	92	37.34 N	139.49 E
Aizu-wakamatsu	92	37.30 N	139.56 E
Aj ≃	86	56.08 N	57.40 E
Ajā	142	30.57 N	31.17 E
Ajā', Jabal ⋏	128	27.20 N	41.45 E
'Ajab Shīr	128	37.28 N	45.54 E
Ajaccio	36	41.55 N	8.44 E
Ajaguz	86	47.56 N	80.23 E
Ajaguz ≃	86	46.42 N	79.15 E
Ajajú ≃	246	0.59 N	72.20 W
Ajalpan	234	18.22 N	97.15 W
'Ajaltūn	132	33.58 N	35.41 E
Ajalvir	266a	40.32 N	3.29 W
'Ajamī	130	36.28 N	37.42 E
Ajan, Ross.	74	56.27 N	138.10 E
Ajan, Ross.	88	54.43 N	110.55 E
Ajan ≃	74	70.10 N	95.50 E
Ajana	162	27.57 S	114.38 E
Ajanta	122	20.32 N	75.45 E
Ajanta Range ⋏	122	20.30 N	76.00 E
Ajaokuta	150	7.28 N	6.39 E
Ajarani ≃	246	1.33 N	61.16 W
Ajasse	150	8.17 N	4.48 E
Ajasso	150	5.52 N	8.52 E
Ajat ≃	86	52.54 N	63.02 E
Ajax	212	43.51 N	79.02 W
Ajay ≃	126	23.39 N	88.08 E
Ajbas	80	47.51 N	49.37 E
Ajdābiyā	146	30.48 N	20.14 E
Ajdabul'	86	52.42 N	68.59 E
Ajdar	78	50.03 N	38.56 E
Ajdar ≃	78	48.42 N	39.13 E
Ajdarkul', ozero ⊜[1]	72	40.45 N	67.20 E
Ajdarly	86	44.32 N	65.50 E
Ajdar-Nikolajevka	83	48.58 N	38.58 E
Ajdovščina	64	45.53 N	13.53 E
Ajdyrlinskij	86	52.03 N	59.50 E
Ajegunle	273a	6.36 N	3.17 E
Ajgurka ≃	80	45.46 N	43.12 E
Ajgyrkol', ozero ⊜	80	48.15 N	52.50 E
Ajhūr al-Kubrā	142	30.18 N	31.09 E
Aji	96	34.23 N	134.08 E
Ajibar	144	10.52 N	38.40 E
Ajibarang	115a	7.25 S	109.04 E
Ajigasawa	92	40.47 N	140.12 E
'Ajīj, Wādī al- ∨	130	35.19 N	41.09 E
Ajijic	234	20.18 N	103.17 W
Ajil	114	5.05 N	103.05 E
Ājimganj	126	24.14 N	88.15 E
Ajimu	96	33.26 N	131.21 E
Ajipuzicun	104	42.16 N	123.33 E
Ajisu	96	34.00 N	131.22 E
Ajjer, Tassili-n- ⋏[1]	148	25.10 N	8.00 E
Ajka	30	47.07 N	17.34 E
Ajke, ozero ⊜	86	50.57 N	61.36 E
Ajkino	24	62.15 N	49.56 E
'Ajlūn	132	32.20 N	35.45 E
Ajlune	224	46.31 N	122.26 W
'Ajmah, Jabal al- ⋏	140	29.12 N	34.02 E
Ajmer	120	26.27 N	74.38 E
Ajnāla	123	31.51 N	74.48 E
Ajni	85	39.23 N	68.32 E
Ajo	200	32.22 N	112.51 W
Ajo, Cabo de ›	34	43.31 N	3.35 W
Ajok	140	9.15 N	28.27 E
Ajon, ostrov I	74	69.50 N	168.40 E
Ajoya	232	24.04 N	106.22 W
Aj-Petri, gora ∧	78	44.27 N	34.03 E
Ajrag nuur ⊜	88	48.54 N	93.28 E
'Ajramīyah, Bi'r al- ∓[4]	142	29.39 N	31.50 E
Ajrum	84	41.13 N	44.53 E
Ajryk	86	50.30 N	76.48 E
Ajsary	86	53.18 N	71.52 E
Ajtos	38	42.42 N	27.15 E
Ajuchitlán del Progreso	234	18.09 N	100.29 W
Ajuda ◆[8]	266c	38.43 N	9.12 W
Ajusco	204	31.35 N	116.25 W
Ajusco ◆[8]	286a	19.14 N	99.12 W
Ajuta ≃	83	47.34 N	40.07 E
Ajuterique	236	14.20 N	87.43 W
Ajutinskij	83	47.46 N	40.08 E
Ajuy	116	11.10 N	123.01 E
Ajuy Bay ⊂	116	11.10 N	123.02 E
Aka ≃	92	38.54 N	139.50 E
Akaba	150	7.57 N	1.03 E
Akabane	94	34.37 N	137.12 E
Akabira	92a	43.34 N	142.03 E
Akabli	148	26.42 N	1.22 E
Akabori	94	36.22 N	139.14 E
Akademii, zaliv ⊂	89	54.15 N	138.05 E
Akagera (Kagera) ≃	154	0.57 S	31.47 E
Akagera, Parc National de l' ♠	154	1.30 S	30.35 E
Akagi, Nihon	94	36.33 N	139.03 E
Akagi, Nihon	96	35.00 N	132.43 E
Akagi-san ∧	94	36.33 N	139.11 E
Akaishi-dake ∧	94	35.27 N	138.09 E
Akaishi-sammyaku ⋏	94	35.18 N	138.07 E
Akaka Falls State Park ♠	229d	19.52 N	155.09 W
Akaki Beseka	144	8.52 N	38.47 E
Akālgarh	123	32.16 N	73.49 E
Akalkot	122	17.32 N	76.13 E
Akamaruno-misaki ›	174m	26.44 N	128.09 E
Akámas, Akrotírion ›	130	35.06 N	32.17 E
Akan	92a	43.06 N	144.10 E
Akana-tōge)(	96	34.57 N	132.44 E
Akan-kokuritsu-kōen ♠	92a	43.30 N	144.15 E
Akaoka	96	33.32 N	133.43 E
Ak-Aral	86	49.10 N	90.57 E
Akaroa	172	43.48 S	172.58 E
Akaroa Harbour ⊂	172	43.50 S	172.56 E
Åkarp	41	55.39 N	13.07 E
Akarsu, Tür.	130	37.14 N	41.04 E
Akarsu, Tür.	130	39.56 N	38.38 E
Akasaki	96	35.31 N	133.38 E
'Akasha East	140	21.05 N	30.43 E
Akashat	130	33.45 N	39.58 E
Akashi	96	34.38 N	134.59 E
Akashi ≃	270	34.38 N	134.59 E
Akashi-kaikyō ʊ	96	34.37 N	135.02 E
Akashina	94	36.21 N	137.56 E
Akatani-ko ⊜[1]	94	36.43 N	138.54 E
Akatjevo	82	54.59 N	38.45 E
Akatova	76	55.09 N	31.48 E
Akatsuka ◆[8]	268	35.46 N	139.39 E
Akatsutsumi ◆[8]	268	35.39 N	139.39 E
Akbaba ◆[8]	267b	41.09 N	29.06 E
Akbaba Dağı ∧	130	40.12 N	40.51 E
Akbajtal	85	38.32 N	73.49 E
Akbajtal, pereval)(	85	38.32 N	73.40 E
Akbarpur, India	124	26.25 N	82.33 E
Akbarpur, India	124	24.39 N	83.58 E
Akbeit	86	51.38 N	70.02 E
Akbou	148	36.28 N	4.32 E
Akbulak, Kaz.	86	49.26 N	80.28 E
Akbulak, Ross.	86	51.01 N	55.37 E
Akbura ≃	85	40.39 N	72.36 E
Akçaabat	130	41.02 N	39.34 E
Akçadağ	130	38.21 N	37.59 E
Akçakale	130	36.41 N	38.56 E
Akcakışla	130	39.33 N	36.22 E
Akçakoca	130	41.05 N	31.09 E
Akçakoyunlu	130	36.46 N	37.38 E
Akçaova, Tür.	130	37.30 N	28.02 E
Akçaova, Tür.	130	41.03 N	29.57 E
Akçapınar	130	38.57 N	38.57 E
Akčatau	86	47.59 N	74.02 E
Akçay	130	36.36 N	29.45 E
Akçay ≃	130	37.50 N	28.15 E
Akchâr ◆[1]	150	20.00 N	14.30 W
Akči	85	44.00 N	76.20 E
Akdağ	130	40.43 N	36.00 E
Akdağ ∧	130	39.29 N	41.54 E
Akdağmadeni	130	39.40 N	35.54 E
Akdala	86	45.02 N	74.35 E
Akdoğan	130	35.06 N	33.41 E
Ak-Dovurak	86	51.16 N	90.31 E
Akechi	94	35.18 N	137.23 E
Akehama	96	33.19 N	132.26 E
Akeley	190	47.00 N	94.43 W
Aken	54	51.51 N	12.02 E
Akeno, Nihon	94	36.15 N	140.02 E
Akeno, Nihon	94	35.46 N	138.26 E
Åker	40	59.15 N	17.05 E
Akera ≃	84	39.09 N	46.51 E
Åkerby	40	60.25 N	17.46 E
Åkersberga	40	59.29 N	18.18 E
Akershus □[6]	26	60.00 N	11.10 E
Akersloot	52	52.34 N	4.44 E
Akespe	86	46.48 N	60.31 E
Aketi	152	2.44 N	23.46 E
Aketilepa	85	39.57 N	74.03 E
Aketu-Oja	273a	6.41 N	3.23 E
Åkforsån ≃	40	58.54 N	16.28 E
Akgöl ⊜	130	38.58 N	31.48 E
Akharnaí	38	38.05 N	23.44 E
Akhḍar, Al-Jabal al- ⋏, Lībiyā	146	32.30 N	21.30 E
Akhḍar, Al-Jabal al- ⋏, 'Umān	128	23.15 N	57.20 E
Akhelóös ≃	38	38.36 N	21.14 E
Akh Gol ⊜	84	39.33 N	44.47 E
Akhiok	180	56.57 N	154.10 W
Akhisar	130	38.55 N	27.51 E
Akhmīm	140	26.34 N	31.44 E
Akhnūr	123	32.54 N	74.44 E
Akhtarīn	130	36.31 N	37.20 E
Aki, Nihon	96	33.30 N	133.54 E
Aki, Nihon	96	33.28 N	131.43 E
Aki ≃, Nihon	94	35.41 N	139.21 E
Aki ≃, Nihon	96	33.30 N	133.55 E
Akiachak	180	60.55 N	161.27 W
Akiak	180	60.55 N	161.12 W
Akiéni	152	1.11 S	13.53 E
Akima	88	53.06 N	115.44 E
Akimiski Island I	176	53.00 N	81.20 W
Akimovka	78	46.42 N	35.09 E
Aki-nada ∓[2]	96	34.05 N	132.48 E
Akıncı	130	37.10 N	40.52 E
Akıncı Burun ›	130	36.19 N	35.47 E
Akıncılar, Tür.	130	40.06 N	38.21 E
Akıncılar, Tür.	130	37.45 N	38.50 E
Akiode	273a	6.38 N	3.21 E
Åkirkeby	26	55.04 N	14.56 E
Akishima	94	35.41 N	139.22 E
Akišma ≃	89	52.08 N	132.40 E
Akita	92	39.43 N	140.07 E
Akita-heiya ≋	92	39.45 N	140.10 E
Akitan	273a	6.39 N	3.16 E
Akitipa	150	8.17 N	6.16 E
Akitkan, chrebet ⋏	88	57.05 N	109.05 E
Akitsu, Nihon	96	34.19 N	132.50 E
Akitsu, Nihon	270	34.56 N	135.06 E
Akiyama	94	35.34 N	139.05 E
Akiyoshi-dai ⋏[1]	96	34.15 N	131.15 E
Akiyoshi-dai-kokutei-kōen ♠	96	34.15 N	131.17 E
Akiyoshi-do ⍛[5]	96	34.14 N	131.19 E
Akjar	86	51.50 N	58.14 E
Akjoujt	150	19.45 N	14.23 W
Akka	148	29.22 N	8.14 W
Akkala	86	43.43 N	59.31 E
Akkani	180	65.30 N	171.10 W
Akkerman → Belgorod-Dnestrovskij	78	46.12 N	30.20 E
Akkermanovka	86	51.11 N	58.12 E
Akkerwoude	52	53.17 N	5.58 E
Akkeshi	92a	43.02 N	144.51 E
Akkışla	130	39.00 N	36.11 E
'Akko (Acre)	132	32.55 N	35.05 E
Akkol', Kaz.	85	43.25 N	70.47 E
Akkol', Kaz.	86	45.02 N	75.40 E
Akkol', ozero ⊜	85	43.24 N	70.40 E
Akkol'skij	86	52.12 N	75.05 E
Akköy	130	37.29 N	27.15 E
Akkra → Accra	150	5.33 N	0.13 W
Akkrum	52	53.03 N	5.50 E
Ak-Kul'	85	41.41 N	74.16 E
Akkuş	130	40.49 N	37.01 E
Aklan □[4]	116	11.40 N	122.20 E
Aklan ≃	116	11.44 N	122.20 E
Aklan Point ›	116	11.44 N	122.22 E
Aklavik	180	68.12 N	135.00 W
'Aklé 'Aouâna ◆[1]	150	18.00 N	5.30 W
Akmeņrags ›	76	56.51 N	21.03 E
Akmeqit	120	37.01 N	76.59 E
Akmeşe	130	40.51 N	30.12 E
Akmuz	85	41.16 N	76.09 E
Ākna	272b	22.59 N	88.21 E
Aknet, gora ∧	86	50.51 N	75.40 E
Aknīste	76	56.10 N	25.45 E
Aknoul	148	34.43 N	3.49 W
Ako, Nig.	146	10.17 N	10.58 E
Akō, Nihon	96	34.45 N	134.24 E
Akoba	80	49.28 N	47.25 E
Akobo	140	7.47 N	33.01 E
Akobo (Akūbū) ≃	140	7.47 N	33.03 E
Akodiya	124	23.23 N	76.36 E
Akok, Cam.	152	2.46 N	10.18 E
Akok, Gabon	152	0.31 N	9.45 E
Akola	122	20.44 N	77.00 E
Akonolinga	152	3.47 N	12.15 E
Akop	140	8.21 N	29.05 E
Akor	150	14.53 N	6.58 W
Akora	123	34.00 N	72.08 E
Akordat	144	15.33 N	37.53 E
Akören	130	37.27 N	32.23 E
Akosombo Dam ◆[6]	150	6.16 N	0.03 E
Akot, India	120	21.11 N	77.04 E
Akot, Süd.	140	6.33 N	30.03 E
Akoupé	150	6.23 N	3.54 W
Akowonjo	273a	6.37 N	3.19 E
Akpatok Island I	176	60.25 N	68.00 W
Akpınar, Tür.	130	37.34 N	38.13 E
Akpınar, Tür.	130	39.17 N	33.40 E
Akqi	85	40.52 N	77.58 E
Åkrafjorden ⊂[2]	26	59.46 N	6.06 E
Akranes	24a	64.18 N	22.02 W
Åkrehamn	26	59.16 N	5.11 E
Akrítas, Ákra ›	38	36.43 N	21.54 E
Akrofuom	150	6.07 N	1.39 W
Akrokórinthos ⊥	38	37.54 N	22.56 E
Akron, Co., U.S.	198	40.09 N	103.12 W
Akron, In., U.S.	216	41.02 N	86.01 W
Akron, Ia., U.S.	198	42.49 N	96.33 W
Akron, N.Y., U.S.	210	43.01 N	78.29 W
Akron, Oh., U.S.	214	41.04 N	81.31 W
Akron, Pa., U.S.	208	40.09 N	76.12 W
Akron-Canton Regional Airport ⊠	214	40.55 N	81.27 W
Akron City Reservoir ⊜[1]	214	41.20 N	81.17 W
Akrotíri	130	34.36 N	32.57 E
Akša	88	50.16 N	113.17 E
Aksa ◆[8]	272c	19.10 N	72.48 E
Aksaj, Kaz.	80	51.09 N	53.00 E
Aksaj, Kaz.	85	43.22 N	70.12 E
Aksaj, Ross.	80	47.58 N	43.59 E
Aksaj, Ross.	83	47.15 N	39.52 E
Aksaj (Toxkan) ≃, Asia	85	40.55 N	78.16 E
Aksaj ≃, Ross.	83	47.15 N	39.53 E
Aksaj ≃, Ross.	84	43.32 N	46.51 E
Aksakovo	80	54.02 N	54.09 E
Aksaray	130	38.23 N	34.03 E
Aksaray □[4]	130	38.30 N	34.00 E
Aksarka	74	66.36 N	67.46 E
Akšatau	86	49.23 N	54.36 E
Aksaut ≃	84	43.55 N	41.42 E
Aksay	102	39.28 N	94.15 E
Aksayqin Hu ⊜	120	35.12 N	79.50 E
Akşehir	130	38.21 N	31.25 E
Akşehir Gölü ⊜	130	38.30 N	31.28 E
Akseki	130	37.02 N	31.48 E
Aksengir ≃	85	43.40 N	76.14 E
Aksenkino	80	53.59 N	53.06 E
Aksenovo	82	55.40 N	38.15 E
Aksentjevo	82	55.25 N	35.54 E
Akšij	86	47.37 N	55.56 E
Akšijrak, chrebet ⋏	85	41.20 N	74.15 E
Aksinjino, Ross.	82	55.44 N	36.59 E
Aksinjino, Ross.	82	56.02 N	38.12 E
Aks'onovo	88	58.51 N	101.43 E
Aks'onovo-Zilovskoje	88	53.04 N	117.32 E
Aksoran, gora ∧	86	48.27 N	75.32 E
Akstafa	84	41.08 N	45.28 E
Akstafa ≃	84	41.15 N	45.26 E
Aksu, Kaz.	80	50.56 N	53.06 E
Aksu, Kaz.	86	52.28 N	71.59 E
Aksu, Kaz.	86	45.37 N	79.30 E

Symbol	English	Deutsch	Español	Français	Português
≃	River	Fluß	Río	Rivière	Rio
≊	Canal	Kanal	Canal	Canal	Canal
∟	Waterfall, Rapids	Wasserfall, Stromschnellen	Cascada, Rápidos	Chute d'eau, Rapides	Cascata, Rápidos
ʊ	Strait	Meeresstraße	Estrecho	Détroit	Estreito
⊂	Bay, Gulf	Bucht, Golf	Bahía, Golfo	Baie, Golfe	Baía, Golfo
⊜	Lake, Lakes	See, Seen	Lago, Lagos	Lac, Lacs	Lago, Lagos
≋	Swamp	Sumpf	Pantano	Marais	Pântano
⊼	Ice Features, Glacier	Eis- und Gletscherformen	Accidentes Glaciales	Formes glaciaires	Acidentes glaciares
∓	Other Hydrographic Features	Andere Hydrographische Objekte	Otros Elementos Hidrográficos	Autres données hydrographiques	Outros acidentes hidrográficos
✦	Submarine Features	Untermeerische Objekte	Accidentes Submarinos	Formes de relief sous-marin	Acidentes submarinos
□	Political Unit	Politische Einheit	Unidad Politica	Entité politique	Unidade política
⊍	Cultural Institution	Kulturelle Institution	Institución Cultural	Institution culturelle	Institução cultural
⊥	Historical Site	Historische Stätte	Sitio Histórico	Site historique	Sitio histórico
♠	Recreational Site	Erholungs- und Ferienort	Sitio de Recreo	Centre de loisirs	Area de Lazer
⊠	Airport	Flughafen	Aeropuerto	Aéroport	Aeroporto
■	Military Installation	Militäranlage	Instalación Militar	Installation militaire	Instalação militar
◆	Miscellaneous	Verschiedenes	Misceláneo	Divers	Diversos

Aksu, Tür. 130 36.58 N 30.50 E
Aksu, Zhg. 90 41.10 N 80.20 E
Aksu ≐, Asia 85 43.22 N 73.54 E
Aksu ≐, Kaz. 86 46.20 N 78.15 E
Aksu ≐, Tür. 130 36.51 N 30.54 E
Aksu ≐, Tür. 130 37.25 N 36.54 E
Aksu-Ajuly 86 48.47 N 73.40 E
Aksuart, ozero ⊜ 86 51.24 N 64.28 E
Aksuat, Kaz. 86 51.32 N 64.34 E
Aksuat, Kaz. 86 47.45 N 82.40 E
Aksuat, Kaz. 86 48.16 N 83.50 E
Aksubajevo 80 54.52 N 50.50 E
Aksu-Džabaglinskij zapovednik ♦ 85 42.20 N 70.35 E
Aksum 144 14.08 N 38.43 E
Aktag ∧ 120 36.45 N 84.40 E
Aktal 85 41.25 N 75.03 E
Aktanyš 80 55.43 N 54.05 E
Aktas, Kaz. 85 42.57 N 70.04 E
Aktas, Kaz. 86 48.02 N 66.21 E
Aktas, Kaz. 86 49.47 N 72.59 E
Aktas, Kaz. 86 50.06 N 76.40 E
Aktaš, Ross. 86 50.18 N 87.44 E
Aktaš, Uzb. 85 41.38 N 69.44 E
Aktaş Gölü ⊜ 84 41.15 N 43.12 E
Aktasty 86 50.44 N 61.43 E
Aktau, Kaz. 72 43.35 N 51.05 E
Aktau, Kaz. 86 50.16 N 73.02 E
Aktau, gora ∧ 86 48.00 N 71.45 E
Aktepe 130 36.44 N 36.27 E
Akterek, Kaz. 85 43.22 N 75.18 E
Akterek, Kyrg. 85 42.14 N 77.45 E
Akto 85 39.08 N 75.57 E
Aktobe 85 43.13 N 67.46 E
Aktogaj, Kaz. 86 48.18 N 74.58 E
Aktogaj, Kaz. 86 46.57 N 79.40 E
Aktogaj, Kaz. 86 44.27 N 76.42 E
Aktubek 86 48.37 N 71.06 E
Akt'ubinsk 86 50.17 N 57.10 E
Akt'ubinsk □[8] 86 48.30 N 58.30 E
Akt'ubinskij 80 54.49 N 52.47 E
Aktuluk 130 39.03 N 39.32 E
Aktumsyk 86 46.40 N 57.19 E
Akt'uz 85 42.54 N 76.07 E
Aku 150 6.42 N 7.20 E
Akūbū (Akobo) ≐ 140 7.47 N 33.03 E
Akui ≐ 96 34.06 N 134.33 E
Akula 152 2.22 N 20.11 E
Akuliči Pervyje 76 53.11 N 33.13 E
Akulovo, Ross. 82 55.31 N 36.42 E
Akulovo, Ross. 82 56.05 N 38.59 E
Akumadan 150 7.24 N 1.57 W
Akune 92 32.01 N 130.11 E
Akun Island I 180 54.12 N 165.35 W
Akure 150 7.15 N 5.12 E
Akureyri 24a 65.44 N 18.08 W
Akurli 272c 19.01 N 73.08 E
Akuša 84 42.17 N 47.21 E
Akuse 150 6.06 N 0.08 E
Akuseki-jima I 93b 29.27 N 129.37 E
Akutan 180 54.08 N 165.46 W
Akutan Island I 180 54.10 N 165.55 W
Akutan Pass ⩌ 180 54.00 N 166.10 W
Akuticha 86 52.27 N 84.29 E
Akwa Ibom □[3] 150 4.50 N 7.50 E
Akwanga 150 8.55 N 8.23 E
Akwatia 150 6.04 N 0.49 W
Akwawa ∧[2] 150 6.27 N 0.25 W
Akwaya 152 6.30 N 9.40 E
Akyab → Sittwe 110 20.09 N 92.54 E
Akyazı 130 40.41 N 30.37 E
Akyel 144 12.33 N 37.04 E
Akyr-T'ube 85 42.59 N 72.07 E
Akyurt 130 40.08 N 33.06 E
Akžajkyn, ozero ⊜ 86 44.55 N 67.46 E
Akžal, Kaz. 86 47.47 N 74.02 E
Akžal, Kaz. 86 49.13 N 81.25 E
Akžar, Kaz. 85 43.08 N 71.38 E
Akžar, Kaz. 86 47.35 N 83.42 E
Akžaryk 86 48.34 N 75.30 E
Ål 26 60.38 N 8.34 E
Ala 64 45.45 N 11.00 E
Ala ≐ 86 42.42 N 89.12 E
Alà, Monti di ⋏ 71 40.40 N 9.14 E
Al-Ab'ādīyah 142 31.22 N 31.07 E
Alabama 210 43.06 N 78.23 W
Alabama □[3], U.S. 178 32.50 N 87.00 W
Alabama □[3], U.S. 194 32.50 N 87.00 W
Alabama ≐ 194 31.08 N 87.57 W
Alabama and Coushatta Indian Reservation ◆[4] 222 30.43 N 94.42 W
Alabaster 194 33.14 N 86.48 W
Alabat Island I 116 14.07 N 122.03 E
Al-'Abbāsah ash-Sharqīyah 142 30.32 N 31.43 E
Al-'Abbāsīyah 140 12.10 N 31.18 E
Al-'Abbāsīyah ◆[8] 273c 30.04 N 31.17 E
Alabino 82 55.31 N 37.01 E
Āl-'Ābis 144 18.04 N 43.10 E
Alabuga ≐ 85 41.26 N 74.41 E
Ala-Buka 85 41.23 N 71.30 E
Alaca 130 40.10 N 34.51 E
Alacahan 130 39.07 N 37.37 E
Alacalı 130 41.11 N 29.27 E
Alaçam 130 41.37 N 35.37 E
Alaçam Dağları ⋏ 130 39.20 N 28.32 E
Alacant 34 38.21 N 0.29 W
Alacant □[4] 34 38.30 N 0.45 W
Alaçatı 130 38.16 N 26.23 E
Alachadzy 84 43.14 N 40.18 E
Alachua 192 29.47 N 82.29 W
Alacrán, Arrecife ✦[2] 232 22.24 N 89.42 W
Alacranes, Presa ⊜[1] 240p 22.45 N 80.08 W
Aladağ 130 37.02 N 32.41 E
Aladağ ∧, Tür. 84 40.11 N 42.49 E
Aladağ ∧, Tür. 130 37.44 N 35.09 E
Aladağlar ⋏, Tür. 84 39.20 N 43.35 E
Ala Dağlar ⋏, Tür. 130 37.55 N 35.13 E
Al-'Adasīyah 132 32.40 N 35.37 E
Alà dei Sardi 71 40.39 N 9.20 E
Aladino 82 54.49 N 38.12 E
Aladinskij, porog ∟ 86 58.24 N 95.29 E
Ala di Stura 62 45.19 N 7.19 E
Aladjino 82 56.21 N 37.04 E
Aladža manastir ʊ[1] 38 43.17 N 28.01 E
Alafia ≐ 220 27.52 N 82.23 W
Alafia, South Prong ≐ 220 27.51 N 82.08 W
Alagbado 273a 6.41 N 3.18 E
Alagna Valsesia 62 45.51 N 7.56 E
Alag nuur ⊜ 102 45.09 N 94.28 E
Alagoa 256 22.10 S 44.38 W
Alagoa Grande 250 7.03 S 35.38 W
Alagoa Nova 250 7.04 S 35.46 W
Alagoas □[3] 250 9.00 S 36.00 W
Alagoinhas 255 12.07 S 38.26 W
Alagón 34 41.46 N 1.07 W
Alagón ≐ 34 39.44 N 6.53 W
Alaguntan 273a 6.26 N 3.30 E
Alah ≐ 116 6.53 N 124.33 E
Alahanpanjang 112 1.05 S 100.47 E
Alahärmä 26 63.14 N 22.51 E
Alaior 34 39.56 N 4.08 E
Al-Ait 140 12.22 N 27.27 E
Al-'Ajamīyīn 142 29.20 N 30.43 E
Alajärvi 26 63.00 N 23.49 E
Alajku 85 40.18 N 74.25 E
Alajõe 76 59.01 N 27.26 E
Alajskaja dolina V 85 39.30 N 73.00 E
Alajskij chrebet ⋏ 85 39.45 N 72.00 E
Alajuela 236 10.01 N 84.13 W
Alajuela □[4] 236 10.30 N 84.30 W
Alajuela, Lago ⊜[1] 236 9.15 N 79.35 W
Ālājūjeh 84 38.57 N 46.41 E
Alakai Swamp ≡ 229b 22.08 N 159.35 W
Alakamisy 157b 21.19 S 47.14 E
Alakanuk 180 62.41 N 164.37 W
Alaknanda ≐ 124 30.08 N 78.36 E
Alakol', ozero ⊜ 86 46.10 N 81.45 E
Al-'Akrīshah 142 31.08 N 30.09 E
Alaktara 124 22.01 N 82.26 E
Alak'ul'a 265a 59.44 N 29.56 E
Alakurtti 24 66.57 N 30.18 E
Al-'Āl 132 32.48 N 35.44 E
Alalakeiki Channel ⩌ 229a 20.35 N 156.30 W
Al-'Alamayn 140 30.49 N 28.57 E
Al-'Alāqimah 142 30.37 N 31.38 E
Alalaú ≐ 246 0.30 S 61.09 W
Al-'Amādīyah 128 37.06 N 43.29 E
Alamagan I 108 17.36 N 145.50 E
Al-'Amārah 128 31.50 N 47.09 E
Al-'Amār al-Kubrā 142 30.21 N 31.08 E
Alamata 144 12.25 N 39.33 E
Alamdānga 124 23.46 N 88.57 E
Alameda, Esp. 34 37.12 N 4.39 W
Alameda, Ca., U.S. 226 37.45 N 122.14 W
Alameda, N.M., U.S. 200 35.11 N 106.37 W
Alameda □[6] 226 37.35 N 121.55 W
Alameda, Estación ◆[5] 286e 33.27 S 70.41 W
Alameda Creek ≐ 226 37.35 N 122.09 W
Alameda Naval Air Station ■ 226 37.47 N 122.18 W
Alamedin 85 42.54 N 74.37 E
Alamein → Al-'Alamayn 140 30.49 N 28.57 E
Alamillo 200 31.02 N 110.35 W
Alaminos 116 16.10 N 119.59 E
Al-'Āmirīyah 142 31.01 N 29.48 E
'Alam Lek 128 37.02 N 65.57 E
Álamo, Méx. 234 20.55 N 97.41 W
Alamo, Ca., U.S. 226 37.51 N 122.02 W
Alamo, Ga., U.S. 192 32.08 N 82.46 W
Alamo, Mi., U.S. 216 42.22 N 85.43 W
Alamo, Nv., U.S. 204 37.21 N 115.09 W
Alamo, Tn., U.S. 194 35.47 N 89.07 W
Alamo ≐ 204 33.14 N 115.39 W
Alamo Creek ≐ 282 37.42 N 121.55 W
Alamo Creek, West Branch ≐ 282 37.45 N 121.55 W
Alamogordo 200 32.53 N 105.57 W
Alamogordo Creek ≐ 196 34.40 N 104.23 W
Alamo Heights 196 29.29 N 98.27 W
Alamo Indian Reservation ◆[4] 200 34.30 N 107.30 W
Alamo Lake ⊜[1] 200 34.20 N 113.30 W
Alamo Oaks 282 37.51 N 121.59 W
Alamor 246 4.02 S 80.02 W
Alamos, Méx. 196 26.25 N 100.25 W
Álamos, Méx. 232 27.01 N 108.56 W
Álamos, Río de los ≐ 196 27.53 N 101.12 W
Alamosa 200 37.28 N 105.52 W
Alamosa ≐ 200 37.22 N 105.46 W
Alamosa Creek ≐, N.M., U.S. 196 34.26 N 103.58 W
Alamosa Creek ≐, N.M., U.S. 200 33.20 N 107.21 W
Alamosa East 200 37.28 N 105.49 W
Álamos de Márquez 232 28.40 N 103.30 W
Ālampur, Bngl. 126 23.49 N 89.06 E
Alampur, India 272b 22.25 N 88.08 E
Alanäs 26 64.10 N 15.42 E
Al-'Ānāt 132 32.21 N 36.48 E
Al-Anbār □[4] 128 33.45 N 41.45 E
Aland 122 17.34 N 76.34 E
Åland (Ahvenanmaa) II 26 60.15 N 20.00 E
Aland ≐ 54 53.02 N 11.34 E
Åland-Inseln → Åland II 26 60.15 N 20.00 E
Ålands hav ⊤[2] 26 60.00 N 19.30 E
Alandur 122 13.02 N 80.15 E
Alangalang 116 11.12 N 124.51 E
Alang-besar, Pulau I 114 2.12 N 100.39 E
Alanje 236 8.24 N 82.33 W
Alano di Piave 64 45.55 N 11.52 E
Alanson 190 45.26 N 84.47 W
Alanya 130 36.33 N 32.01 E
Al-'Anz 132 32.23 N 36.38 E
Alaotra, Lac ⊜ 157b 17.30 S 48.30 E
Alapaha 192 31.23 N 83.13 W
Alapaha ≐ 192 30.26 N 83.06 W
Alapajevsk 86 57.52 N 61.42 E
Alaplı 130 41.11 N 31.24 E
Al-'Aqabah 132 29.31 N 35.00 E
'Alaqah, Jabal ∧ 142 29.59 N 32.53 E
Alaquines 234 22.08 N 99.36 W
Al-'Arabīyah as-Su'ūdīyah → Saudi Arabia □[1] 118 25.00 N 45.00 E
Alarcón 34 39.33 N 2.05 W
Alarcón, Embalse de ⊜[1] 34 39.36 N 2.10 W
Al-'Arīsh 132 31.08 N 33.48 E
Al-'Armah ⋏[1] 128 25.30 N 46.30 E
Alarobia Vohiposa 157b 20.59 S 47.09 E
Alas 115b 8.32 S 117.00 E
Alas ≐, Indon. 114 3.05 N 97.55 E
Alaš ≐, Ross. 86 51.15 N 90.54 E
Alas, Selat ⩌ 115b 8.40 S 116.40 E
Alasan 112 1.45 S 123.19 E
Alasdair, Sgurr ∧ 46 57.12 N 6.14 W
Alaşehir 130 38.21 N 28.32 E
Alashanyouqi 102 40.02 N 103.33 E
Al-'Ashārah 130 34.55 N 40.34 E
Al-Ashmūnayn 142 27.47 N 30.49 E
Alaska 216 42.50 N 85.29 W
Alaska □[3] 180 65.00 N 153.00 W
Alaska, Gulf of ⊂ 16 58.00 N 146.00 W
Alaska Peninsula >[1] 180 57.00 N 158.00 W
Alaska Range ⋏ 180 62.30 N 150.00 W
Al-'Assāfīyah 128 28.21 N 39.08 E
Alassio 62 44.00 N 8.10 E
Alastaro 26 60.56 N 22.55 E
Alastuey 258 34.25 S 59.13 W
Al'at, Azer. 84 39.57 N 49.25 E
Alat, Uzb. 128 39.26 N 63.48 E
Al-'Atāminah 142 27.20 N 30.50 E
Alatan'aola → Xin Barag Youqi 88 48.41 N 116.53 E
Al-Atārib 130 36.08 N 36.49 E
Al-Aṭāwilah 142 27.14 N 31.13 E
Al-'Aṭf 142 29.39 N 31.16 E
Al-'Athāmīn ⋏ 128 30.22 N 43.40 E
Alatna ≐ 180 66.34 N 152.34 W
Alatri 66 41.43 N 13.21 E
Al-'Aṭrūn 140 18.11 N 26.36 E
Alatyr' 80 54.51 N 46.36 E
Alatyr' ≐ 80 54.52 N 46.36 E
Alausí 246 2.12 S 78.50 W
Alava, Cape > 224 48.10 N 124.43 W
Alaverdi 84 41.08 N 44.39 E
Alavieska 26 64.10 N 24.18 E
Alavus 26 62.35 N 23.37 E
Alaw ≐ 44 53.18 N 4.32 W
Alaw, Llyn ⊜[1] 44 53.20 N 4.22 W
Alawa 150 10.20 N 6.39 E
Alāwalpur 123 31.26 N 75.39 E
Al-'Awjā' 142 30.58 N 30.32 E
Al-'Awsajīyah 128 26.49 N 41.41 E
'Ālayh 132 33.48 N 35.36 E
Al-'Ayn 128 24.13 N 55.46 E
Al-'Ayn ⊤[4] 140 16.36 N 29.19 E
Al-'Ayyāsh ash-Sharqī 142 31.33 N 31.13 E
Al-'Ayyāṭ 142 29.37 N 31.15 E
Alazani ≐ 84 41.05 N 46.40 E
Alazeja ≐ 74 70.51 N 153.34 E
Al-Azhar University ʊ[2] 273c 30.03 N 31.16 E
Al'Azīzah 142 31.11 N 31.57 E
Al-'Azīzīyah, Lībiyā 146 32.32 N 13.01 E
Al-'Azīzīyah, Miṣr 142 30.29 N 31.18 E
Al-'Azīzīyah, Miṣr 273c 29.52 N 31.15 E
Al-Azraq ◆[1] 132 31.52 N 36.50 E
Alb ≐ 58 47.35 N 8.08 E
Alba, It. 62 44.42 N 8.02 E
Alba, Mi., U.S. 190 44.58 N 84.58 W
Alba, Pa., U.S. 210 41.42 N 76.50 W
Alba, Tx., U.S. 222 32.48 N 95.38 W
Alba □[6] 38 46.15 N 23.30 E
Alba, Foum de)(148 20.27 N 3.36 W
Al-Bāb 130 36.22 N 37.31 E
Albacete 34 38.59 N 1.51 W
Albacete □[4] 34 38.50 N 1.50 W
Albachten 52 51.55 N 7.31 E
Albacina 66 43.21 N 13.01 E
Al-Bad' 128 28.25 N 35.04 E
Al-Badārī 140 26.59 N 31.25 E
Alba de Tormes 34 40.49 N 5.31 W
Al-Badrashayn 142 29.51 N 31.16 E
Ålbæk 26 57.36 N 10.25 E
Al-Bahnasā 142 28.32 N 30.39 E
Al-Baḥr al-Abyaḍ □[4] 140 13.15 N 32.25 E
Al-Baḥr al-Aḥmar □[4], Miṣr 142 28.45 N 32.00 E
Al-Baḥr al-Aḥmar □[4], Sūd. 140 20.00 N 35.15 E
Al-Baḥrayn → Bahrain □[1] 128 26.00 N 50.30 E
Albaida 34 38.51 N 0.31 W
Albairate 266b 45.25 N 8.56 E
Alba Iulia 38 46.04 N 23.35 E
Al-Bajalāt 142 31.10 N 31.37 E
Al-Bājūr 142 30.26 N 31.02 E
Al-Bakātūsh 142 31.03 N 30.48 E
Al-Balāmūn 142 30.49 N 31.26 E
Al-Balāshūn 142 30.26 N 31.26 E
Al-Ballaḥ 142 30.46 N 32.19 E
Al-Ballāṣ 140 26.01 N 32.46 E
Al-Balqā' □[8] 132 32.00 N 35.40 E
Al-Bālū'ah ⊜ 130 35.55 N 36.28 E
Al-Balyanā 140 26.14 N 32.00 E
Alban 32 43.54 N 2.28 E
Albanel, Lac ⊜ 176 50.55 N 73.12 W
Albanella 68 40.30 N 15.08 E
Albani, Colli ⋏[2] 66 41.45 N 12.45 E
Albania, Col. 246 1.21 N 75.57 W
Albania, Col. 246 11.01 N 72.40 W
Albania (Shqipëri) □[1], Europe 22 41.00 N 20.00 E
Albania (Shqipëri) □[1], Europe 38 41.00 N 20.00 E
Albanie → Albania □[1] 38 41.00 N 20.00 E
Albanien → Albania □[1] 38 41.00 N 20.00 E
Albano, Lago ⊜ 66 41.45 N 12.40 E
Albano, Monte ∧ 66 43.50 N 10.58 E
Albano di Lucania 68 40.35 N 16.02 E
Albano Laziale 66 41.44 N 12.39 E
Albany, Austl. 162 35.02 S 117.53 E
Albany, Ca., U.S. 226 37.53 N 122.17 W
Albany, Ga., U.S. 192 31.34 N 84.09 W
Albany, Il., U.S. 190 41.47 N 90.13 W
Albany, In., U.S. 216 40.18 N 85.14 W
Albany, Ky., U.S. 194 36.41 N 85.08 W
Albany, Mn., U.S. 190 45.37 N 94.34 W
Albany, Mo., U.S. 194 40.14 N 94.19 W
Albany, N.Y., U.S. 210 42.39 N 73.45 W
Albany, Oh., U.S. 188 39.13 N 82.12 W
Albany, Or., U.S. 202 44.38 N 123.06 W
Albany, Tx., U.S. 196 32.43 N 99.17 W
Albany, Wi., U.S. 190 42.42 N 89.26 W
Albany □[6] 210 42.39 N 73.45 W
Albany ≐ 176 52.17 N 81.31 W
Albany County Airport ⊠ 210 42.45 N 73.48 W
Albany Creek 171a 27.21 S 152.58 E
Albany Park ◆[8] 278 41.58 N 87.43 W
Al-Baq'ah 132 32.05 N 35.53 E
Al-Barājīl 273c 30.04 N 31.09 E
Al-Barāmūn 142 31.07 N 31.26 E
Albardón 252 31.26 S 68.32 W
Albaredo d'Adige 64 45.19 N 11.16 E
Al-Bāriḥah 132 32.34 N 35.50 E
Al-Barnūjī 142 30.56 N 30.23 E
Albaron 62 43.37 N 4.28 E
Albaron ∧ 62 45.20 N 7.07 E
Albarracín 34 40.25 N 1.26 W
Al-Barrah 128 24.55 N 45.52 E
Albarraque 266c 38.46 N 9.21 W
Al-Barshā 142 27.43 N 30.54 E
Al-Barun 140 11.44 N 33.30 E
Al-Basātīn ◆[8] 273c 29.59 N 31.16 E
Al-Baslaqūn 142 31.06 N 30.08 E
Al-Basqalūn 142 28.42 N 30.44 E
Al-Baṣrah (Basra) 128 30.30 N 47.47 E
Al-Baṣrah □[4] 128 30.20 N 47.35 E
Al-Batānūn 142 30.37 N 30.59 E
Al-Baṭḥā' 128 31.06 N 45.53 E
Al-Bāṭinah ◆[1] 128 23.45 N 57.20 E
Albatross Bay ⊂ 164 12.45 S 141.43 E
Albatross Point > 172 38.06 S 174.41 E
Al-Batrūn 130 34.15 N 35.39 E
Al-Baṭrūnah 132 33.39 N 36.02 E
Al-Bauga 140 18.16 N 33.55 E
Al-Bawīṭī 140 28.21 N 28.52 E
Albay □[4] 116 13.00 N 123.40 E
Al-Bayahū 142 28.16 N 30.44 E
Al-Bayḍā (Beida), Lībiyā 146 28.22 N 18.55 E
Al-Bayḍā' (Beida), Lībiyā 146 32.46 N 21.43 E
Al-Bayḍā', Miṣr 142 31.10 N 30.05 E
Albay Gulf ⊂ 116 13.10 N 124.00 E
Albazino 89 53.23 N 124.05 E
Albbruck 58 47.35 N 8.07 E
Albegna ≐ 66 42.30 N 11.11 E
Albemarle 192 35.13 N 80.13 W
Albemarle and Chesapeake Canal ≍ 208 36.43 N 76.15 W
Albemarle Sound ⩌ 192 36.03 N 76.12 W
Albenga 62 44.03 N 8.13 E
Albens 62 45.47 N 5.57 E
Alberche ≐ 34 39.58 N 4.46 W
Alberdi 252 26.10 S 58.09 W
Alberene 192 37.53 N 78.37 W
Alberga, Austl. 162 27.12 S 135.28 E
Ålberga, Sve. 40 58.44 N 16.34 E
Alberga Creek ≐ 162 27.06 S 135.33 E
Albergaria-a-Velha 34 40.42 N 8.29 W
Alberhill 228 33.44 N 117.23 W
Alberic 34 39.07 N 0.31 W
Alberni Inlet ⊂ 182 49.07 N 124.50 W
Alberobello 68 40.47 N 17.15 E
Alberona 68 41.26 N 15.07 E
Albero Sole ∧ 70a 35.31 N 12.32 E
Albers 219 38.33 N 89.37 W
Alberschwende 58 47.27 N 9.49 E
Albersloh 52 51.52 N 7.43 E
Albert 50 50.00 N 2.39 E
Albert ≐ 171a 27.42 S 153.15 E
Albert, Lake ⊜, Afr. 154 1.40 N 31.00 E
Albert, Lake ⊜, Austl. 166 35.38 S 139.17 E
Alberta 194 32.13 N 87.24 W
Alberta □[4], Can. 176 54.00 N 113.00 W
Alberta □[4], Can. 182 54.00 N 113.00 W
Alberta, Mount ∧ 182 52.18 N 117.28 W
Albert Canyon 182 51.08 N 117.52 W
Albert City 198 42.46 N 94.56 W
Albert Edward, Mount ∧ 164 8.23 S 147.24 E
Albert Edward Bay ⊂ 176 69.32 N 103.00 W
Albert Falls 158 29.27 S 30.25 E
Albertfalva ◆[8] 264c 47.27 N 19.02 E
Alberti 252 35.02 S 60.16 W
Al'bertin 76 53.05 N 25.23 E
Albertina 256 22.12 S 46.37 W
Albertinia 158 34.13 S 21.36 E
Albertirsa 30 47.15 N 19.38 E
Albert Kanaal (Canal Albert) ≍ 56 50.39 N 5.37 E
Albert Lea 190 43.38 N 93.22 W
Albert Markham, Mount ∧ 9 81.23 S 158.12 E
Albert Nile ≐ 154 3.36 N 32.02 E
Alberto, Lago → Albert, Lake ⊜ 154 1.40 N 31.00 E
Alberto Eduardo → Albert Edward, Mount ∧ 164 8.23 S 147.24 E
Alberton, P.E., Can. 186 46.49 N 64.04 W
Alberton, S. Afr. 273d 26.16 S 28.08 E
Alberton, Mt., U.S. 202 47.00 N 114.29 W
Albert Park ♦ 274b 37.51 S 144.57 E
Albert Peak ∧ 182 51.02 N 117.51 W
Albertshof 264a 52.42 N 13.40 E
Albertson 276 40.46 N 73.38 W
Albertson Brook ≐ 285 39.41 N 74.43 W
Albertson Brook, Blue Anchor Branch ≐ 285 39.42 N 74.49 W
Albertson Brook, Pump Branch ≐ 285 39.42 N 74.49 W
Albertville, Fr. 62 45.41 N 6.23 E
Albertville, Al., U.S. 194 34.16 N 86.12 W
Albertville → Kalemie 154 5.56 S 29.12 E
Albestroff 56 48.56 N 6.51 E
Albettone 64 45.21 N 11.35 E
Albi 32 43.56 N 2.09 E
Albia, Ia., U.S. 190 41.01 N 92.48 W
Albia, N.Y., U.S. 210 42.43 N 73.39 W
Albiate 266b 45.39 N 9.15 E
Al Bidia 146 10.33 N 20.13 E
Albidona 68 39.55 N 16.28 E
Albignasego 64 45.21 N 11.52 E
Albin 198 41.25 N 104.05 W
Albina 250 5.30 N 54.03 W
Albina, Ponta > 152 15.51 S 11.44 E
Albinea 64 44.37 N 10.36 E
Albino 62 45.46 N 9.47 E
Albion, Austl. 274b 37.47 S 144.49 E
Albion, B.C., Can. 224 49.11 N 122.33 W
Albion, Ca., U.S. 204 39.13 N 123.46 W
Albion, Id., U.S. 202 42.24 N 113.34 W
Albion, Il., U.S. 194 38.22 N 88.03 W
Albion, In., U.S. 216 41.23 N 85.25 W
Albion, Ia., U.S. 190 42.06 N 92.59 W
Albion, Mi., U.S. 216 42.14 N 84.45 W
Albion, Ne., U.S. 198 41.41 N 98.00 W
Albion, N.J., U.S. 285 39.47 N 74.56 W
Albion, N.Y., U.S. 210 43.14 N 78.11 W
Albion, Pa., U.S. 214 41.53 N 80.22 W
Albion, R.I., U.S. 207 41.57 N 71.27 W
Albion, Wa., U.S. 202 46.47 N 117.14 W
Albion, Wi., U.S. 216 42.52 N 89.04 W
Albion Airstrip ⊠ 285 39.46 N 74.58 W
Albion Park 170 34.34 S 150.47 E
Al-Biqā' □[4] 130 34.00 N 36.00 E
Al-Biqā' V 128 33.50 N 36.00 E
Al-Bi'r 128 28.50 N 36.19 E
Al-Bīrah 132 31.54 N 35.13 E
Al-Birīgāt 142 30.30 N 30.49 E
Al-Birk 144 18.13 N 41.33 E
Al-Birkah 146 24.54 N 10.11 E
Al-Birkah ⊤[4] 144 22.12 N 40.43 E
Albisola Marina 62 44.19 N 8.30 E
Albisola Superiore 62 44.20 N 8.31 E
Albizzate 62 45.43 N 8.44 E
Alblasserdam 52 51.52 N 4.40 E
Albo, Monte ∧ 71 40.32 N 9.35 E
Albocàsser 34 40.21 N 0.02 E
Albogas 266c 38.51 N 9.15 W
Alborán, Isla de I 34 35.58 N 3.02 W
Alborán Sea ⊤[2] 34 36.00 N 3.00 W
Ålborg 26 57.03 N 9.56 E
Ålborg Bugt ⊂ 26 56.45 N 10.30 E
Alborz, Reshteh-ye Kūhhā-ye (Elburz Mountains) ⋏ 128 36.00 N 53.00 E
Albreda 182 52.38 N 119.09 W
Albright-Knox Art Gallery ʊ 284a 42.56 N 78.53 W
Albrighton 42 52.38 N 2.16 W
Albuch ⋏ 56 48.15 N 9.50 E
Albuera 116 10.55 N 124.42 E
Albufeira 34 37.05 N 8.15 W
Ālbū Gharz, Sabkhat ⊜ 130 34.45 N 41.15 E
Al-Buḥayrah □[4], Miṣr 142 30.59 N 30.12 E
Al-Buḥayrah □[4], Sūd. 140 7.30 N 29.30 E
Albula ≐ 58 46.42 N 9.27 E
Al-Bunbah 146 32.24 N 23.08 E
Albuñol 34 36.47 N 3.12 W
Albuquerque, Bra. 248 19.23 S 57.26 W
Albuquerque, N.M., U.S. 200 35.05 N 106.39 W
Albuquerque, Cayos de II 236 12.10 N 81.50 W
Al-Buraymī 128 24.15 N 55.45 E
Alburg 206 44.58 N 73.18 W
Al-Burj 142 31.35 N 30.59 E
Al-Burjāyah 142 28.09 N 30.44 E
Alburno, Monte ∧ 68 40.33 N 15.17 E
Alburquerque 34 39.13 N 7.00 W
Alburtis 208 40.31 N 75.36 W
Al-Burumbul 142 29.19 N 31.14 E
Albury, Austl. 166 36.05 S 146.55 E
Albury, N.Z. 172 44.14 S 170.52 E
Albury, Eng., U.K. 260 51.13 N 0.30 W
Albury Park ♦ 260 51.13 N 0.29 W
Al-Buṣaylī 142 31.20 N 30.24 E
Al-Busayṭā' ≚ 128 29.30 N 38.45 E
Al-Buṭānah ◆[1] 140 15.00 N 34.40 E
Al-Buṭaynah 132 32.57 N 36.42 E
Al-Buwayḍah 132 32.28 N 36.04 E
Al-Buzūn 144 15.35 N 50.55 E
Albuzzano 62 45.11 N 9.16 E
Alby, Fr. 62 45.49 N 6.01 E
Alby, Sve. 26 62.30 N 15.28 E
Alca 248 15.08 S 72.46 W
Alcabideche 266c 38.44 N 9.24 W
Alcácer do Sal 34 38.22 N 8.30 W
Alcains 34 39.55 N 7.27 W
Alcala 116 17.54 N 121.39 E
Alcalá de Guadaira 34 37.20 N 5.50 W
Alcalá de Henares 34 40.29 N 3.22 W
Alcalá la Real 34 37.28 N 3.56 W
Alcalde 200 36.05 N 106.03 W
Alcamachi ≐ 248 16.08 S 66.50 W
Alcamo 70 37.59 N 12.58 E
Alčan ≐ 89 46.38 N 134.22 E
Alcanadre ≐ 34 41.37 N 0.12 E
Alcanar 34 40.33 N 0.29 E
Alcañices 34 41.42 N 6.21 W
Alcañiz 34 41.03 N 0.08 W
Alcântara, Bra. 250 2.24 S 44.24 W
Alcántara, Esp. 34 39.43 N 6.53 W
Alcantara, Pil. 116 12.16 N 122.03 E
Alcântara ◆[8] 266c 38.42 N 9.10 W
Alcantara ≐ 70 37.49 N 15.16 E
Alcántara, Embalse de ⊜[1] 34 39.45 N 6.25 W
Alcantarilla 34 37.58 N 1.13 W
Alcantilado 255 16.23 S 53.31 W
Alcara li Fusi 70 38.01 N 14.42 E
Alcaraz 34 38.40 N 2.29 W
Alcarrache ≐ 34 38.16 N 7.24 W
Alcatraz Island I 282 37.49 N 122.26 W
Alcaudete 34 37.36 N 4.05 W
Alcázar de San Juan 34 39.24 N 3.12 W
Alcazarquivir → Er-Rachidia 148 31.58 N 4.25 W
Alcester, Eng., U.K. 42 52.13 N 1.52 W
Alcester, S.D., U.S. 198 43.01 N 96.37 W
Alcester Island I 164 9.35 S 152.25 E
Alčevsk 83 48.30 N 38.47 E
Alcira (Gigena) 252 32.45 S 64.20 W
Alcoa 192 35.47 N 83.58 W
Alcoa Center 279b 40.33 N 79.39 W
Alcoa Lake ⊜[1] 222 30.34 N 97.03 W
Alcobaça, Bra. 255 17.30 S 39.13 W
Alcobaça, Port. 34 39.33 N 8.59 W
Alcobaça ≐ 255 17.32 S 39.12 W
Alcobendas 34 40.32 N 3.38 W
Alcochete 266c 38.45 N 8.58 W
Alcockspruit 158 27.55 S 30.01 E
Alcoi 34 38.42 N 0.28 W

ENGLISH

Name	Page	Lat.°′	Long.°′

Alcoi ≐ 34 38.59 N 0.09 W
Alcoitão 266c 38.44 N 9.24 W
Alcolea del Pinar 34 41.02 N 2.28 W
Alcolu 192 33.45 N 80.12 W
Alcomunga 234 18.25 N 97.02 W
Alconbury Brook ≐ 42 52.19 N 0.12 W
Alconchel 34 38.31 N 7.04 W
Alcony 218 40.01 N 84.04 W
Alcorcón 266a 40.21 N 3.50 W
Alcorn 194 31.52 N 91.09 W
Alcorta 252 33.32 S 61.07 W
Alcoutim 34 37.28 N 7.28 W
Alcova Reservoir ⊜[1] 200 42.32 N 106.45 W
Alcove 210 42.28 N 73.55 W
Alcove Reservoir ⊜[1] 210 42.29 N 73.57 W
Alcovy ≐ 192 33.26 N 83.50 W
Alcubierre 34 41.48 N 0.27 W
Alcúdia 34 39.52 N 3.07 E
Alcúdia, Badia d' ⊂ 34 39.48 N 3.13 E
Alcyon Lake ⊜ 285 39.44 N 75.08 W
Aldabra Island I 138 9.25 S 46.22 E
Aldama, Méx. 232 28.51 N 105.54 W
Aldama, Méx. 234 22.55 N 98.04 W
Aldama, Arroyo ≐ 286b 23.05 N 82.15 W
Aldan, Ross. 74 58.37 N 125.24 E
Aldan, Pa., U.S. 285 39.55 N 75.17 W
Aldan ≐ 74 63.28 N 129.35 E
Aldanskoje nagorje ⋏[1] 74 57.00 N 127.00 E
Aldbourne 42 51.31 N 1.37 W
Aldbrough 44 53.50 N 0.07 W
Aldbury 42 51.48 N 0.36 W
Alde ≐ 42 52.03 N 1.28 E
Aldea Apeleg 254 44.41 S 70.51 W
Aldeburgh 42 52.09 N 1.35 E
Aldeia de Paio Pires 266c 38.38 N 9.05 W
Aldeia Nova de Santo Bento 34 37.55 N 7.25 W
Aldeia Velha 256 22.47 S 42.55 W
Aldemha 287b 23.45 S 46.53 W
Alden, Il., U.S. 216 42.27 N 88.31 W
Alden, Ia., U.S. 190 42.31 N 93.22 W
Alden, Mn., U.S. 190 43.40 N 93.34 W
Alden, N.Y., U.S. 210 42.54 N 78.29 W
Alden, Pa., U.S. 210 41.10 N 76.00 W
Alden Center 212 42.55 N 78.32 W
Aldenham 260 51.40 N 0.21 W
Aldenhoven 56 50.53 N 6.16 E
Aldenrade ◆[8] 263 51.31 N 6.44 E
Alder, Ben ∧ 46 56.48 N 4.28 W
Alder Creek ≐ 202 45.50 N 119.56 W
Aldergrove 224 49.04 N 122.28 W
Alder Lake ⊜[1] 224 46.45 N 122.15 W
Alderley Edge 44 53.18 N 2.15 W
Aldermaston 42 51.23 N 1.09 W
Alderney I 43b 49.43 N 2.12 W
Alder Peak ∧ 226 35.53 N 121.22 W
Aldersbach 60 48.36 N 13.05 E
Aldershot 42 51.15 N 0.47 W
Alderson 192 37.44 N 80.38 W
Alderton 224 47.10 N 122.14 W
Alderwood Manor 224 47.49 N 122.17 W
Aldine 222 29.54 N 95.24 W
Aldinga 168b 35.17 S 138.29 E
Aldinga Bay ⊂ 168b 35.20 S 138.25 E
Aldinga Beach 168b 35.18 S 138.27 E
Aldingen 58 48.05 N 8.41 E
Aldino 64 46.23 N 11.20 E
Aldo Bonzi 288 34.42 S 58.31 W
Aldridge 42 52.36 N 1.55 W
Aldwell, Lake ⊜[1] 224 48.05 N 123.34 W
Alechovščina 76 60.25 N 33.52 E
Aled ≐ 44 53.14 N 3.34 W
Aledo, Il., U.S. 190 41.11 N 90.44 W
Aledo, Tx., U.S. 222 32.42 N 97.36 W
Alefa 144 11.57 N 36.52 E
Aleg 150 17.03 N 13.55 W
Alegranza, Isla I 148 29.23 N 13.30 W
Alegre 255 20.46 S 41.32 W
Alegre ≐ 248 15.01 S 59.57 W
Alegres Mountain ∧ 200 34.09 N 108.11 W
Alegrete 252 29.46 S 55.46 W
Alej ≐ 86 52.52 N 83.36 E
Alejandría → Al-Iskandarīyah 142 31.12 N 29.54 E
Alejandro, Isla → Alexander Island I 9 71.00 S 70.00 W
Alejandro Roca 252 33.21 S 63.43 W
Alejandro Selkirk, Isla (Isla Más Afuera) I 244 33.45 S 80.46 W
Alejo Ledesma 252 33.37 S 62.37 W
Alejsk 86 52.28 N 82.45 E
Aleknagik 180 59.17 N 158.38 W
Aleknagik, Lake ⊜ 180 59.20 N 158.45 W
Aleksandrija 78 48.40 N 33.07 E
Aleksandrijskaja 84 43.54 N 47.08 E
Aleksandrinka 83 47.47 N 37.41 E
Aleksandro-Kalinovo 83 48.25 N 37.40 E
Aleksandro-Nevskaja 84 43.55 N 46.35 E
Aleksandro-Nevskij 80 53.28 N 40.13 E
Aleksandropol' 83 49.42 N 38.50 E
Aleksandrov 82 56.24 N 38.43 E
Aleksandrov Gaj 80 50.09 N 48.34 E
Aleksandrovka, Kaz. 80 50.47 N 52.59 E
Aleksandrovka, Kaz. 85 43.27 N 77.20 E
Aleksandrovka, Kaz. 86 53.07 N 69.50 E
Aleksandrovka, Ross. 78 46.47 N 39.01 E
Aleksandrovka, Ross. 80 52.36 N 50.37 E
Aleksandrovka, Ross. 83 47.26 N 39.13 E
Aleksandrovka, Ross. 86 56.32 N 90.47 E
Aleksandrovka, Ross. 86 52.43 N 54.17 E
Aleksandrovka, Ukr. 78 48.43 N 36.55 E
Aleksandrovka, Ukr. 78 46.32 N 35.29 E
Aleksandrovka, Ukr. 78 48.57 N 32.14 E
Aleksandrovka, Ukr. 78 47.42 N 31.16 E
Aleksandrovka, Ukr. 83 47.55 N 37.35 E
Aleksandrovka, Ukr. 83 48.05 N 37.27 E
Aleksandrovsk 83 48.35 N 39.12 E
Aleksandrovskaja, Ross. 265a 60.03 N 29.59 E
Aleksandrovskaja, Ross. 265a 59.44 N 30.21 E
Aleksandrovskij 78 51.03 N 36.44 E
Aleksandrovskij Šl'uz 86 59.26 N 89.20 E
Aleksandrovskij Zavod 88 50.55 N 117.57 E
Aleksandrovskoje, Ross. 84 44.42 N 43.00 E
Aleksandrovskoje, Ross. 86 56.44 N 85.23 E
Aleksandrovskoje, Ross. 86 60.26 N 77.50 E
Aleksandrovsk-Sachalinskij 89 50.54 N 142.10 E
Aleksandrów Kujawski 30 52.52 N 18.42 E
Aleksandrów Łódzki 30 51.49 N 19.19 E
Aleksaskino 80 50.57 N 47.42 E
Aleksejevka, Kaz. 80 50.58 N 52.25 E
Aleksejevka, Kaz. 86 53.31 N 69.30 E
Aleksejevka, Kaz. 86 51.59 N 70.59 E
Aleksejevka, Kaz. 86 47.16 N 81.34 E
Aleksejevka, Kaz. 86 48.25 N 85.40 E
Aleksejevka, Ross. 78 50.37 N 38.42 E
Aleksejevka, Ross. 80 52.35 N 51.17 E
Aleksejevka, Ross. 80 51.49 N 43.56 E
Aleksejevka, Ross. 80 52.18 N 48.01 E
Aleksejevka, Ross. 80 53.02 N 42.46 E
Aleksejevka, Ross. 80 53.15 N 50.30 E
Aleksejevka, Ross. 82 54.41 N 36.34 E
Aleksejevka, Ross. 83 47.38 N 38.49 E
Aleksejevka, Ross. 83 47.41 N 39.54 E
Aleksejevka, Ross. 86 52.30 N 79.33 E
Aleksejevka, Ross. 86 54.31 N 81.08 E
Aleksejevka, Ross. 86 55.22 N 72.03 E
Aleksejevka, Ukr. 78 47.14 N 36.32 E
Aleksejevka, Ukr. 83 49.25 N 38.46 E
Aleksejevka, Ukr. 83 49.01 N 39.11 E
Aleksejevo-Družkovka 83 48.34 N 37.36 E

DEUTSCH

Name	Seite	Breite°′	Länge°′ E = Ost

Aleksejevo-Lozovskoje 78 49.24 N 40.39 E
Aleksejevo-Orlovka ◆[8] 83 48.04 N 38.25 E
Aleksejevo-Tuzlovka 83 47.50 N 39.24 E
Aleksejevsk 88 57.50 N 108.23 E
Aleksejevskaja 80 50.17 N 42.11 E
Aleksejevskoje 80 55.18 N 50.06 E
Aleksin 82 54.31 N 37.05 E
Aleksinac 38 43.32 N 21.43 E
Alella 266d 41.30 N 2.18 E
Alemanha → Germany □[1] 30 51.00 N 10.00 E
Alemania 252 25.36 S 65.38 W
Alemania → Germany □[1] 30 51.00 N 10.00 E
Alem Dağı ∧ 267b 41.04 N 29.12 E
Alemdar ◆[8] 267b 41.03 N 29.14 E
Além Paraíba 256 21.52 S 42.41 W
Alençon 50 48.26 N 0.05 E
Alenquer 250 1.56 S 54.46 W
Alentejo □[9] 34 38.00 N 8.00 W
Alenuihaha Channel ⩌ 229a 20.26 N 156.00 W
Aléoutiennes, Îles → Aleutian Islands II 180 52.00 N 176.00 W
Alep → Ḥalab 130 36.12 N 37.10 E
Aleppo → Ḥalab 130 36.12 N 37.10 E
Aléria 36 42.05 N 9.30 E
Alert 16 82.29 N 62.22 W
Alert Bay 182 50.35 N 126.55 W
Alès, Fr. 62 44.08 N 4.05 E
Ales, It. 71 39.46 N 8.49 E
Aleşd 38 47.04 N 22.24 E
Alešino, Ross. 82 56.09 N 37.45 E
Alešino, Ross. 82 55.04 N 36.05 E
Aleški 80 51.38 N 41.46 E
Aleškovo 82 54.53 N 36.23 E
Alessandria 62 44.54 N 8.37 E
Alessandria □[4] 62 44.49 N 8.42 E
Alessandria del Carretto 68 39.57 N 16.23 E
Alessandria della Rocca 70 37.34 N 13.27 E
Alessano 68 39.53 N 18.20 E
Ålestrup 26 56.42 N 9.30 E
Ålesund 26 62.28 N 6.09 E
Aletschhorn ∧ 58 46.28 N 8.00 E
Alëuten → Aleutian Islands II 180 52.00 N 176.00 W
Aleutianas, Islas → Aleutian Islands II 180 52.00 N 176.00 W
Aleutian Basin ✦[1] 16 57.00 N 177.00 E
Aleutian Islands II 180 52.00 N 176.00 W
Aleutian Range ⋏ 180 59.00 N 155.00 W
Aleutian Trench ✦[1] 6 51.00 N 170.00 W
Aleutka 74 45.57 N 150.10 E
Alevina, mys > 74 58.50 N 151.20 E
Ale Water ≐ 46 55.31 N 2.35 W
Alex 196 34.54 N 97.46 W
Alexander, Mb., Can. 184 49.50 N 100.17 W
Alexander, Il., U.S. 219 39.43 N 90.02 W
Alexander, N.Y., U.S. 210 42.54 N 78.16 W
Alexander, N.D., U.S. 198 47.50 N 103.38 W
Alexander ≐ 132 32.24 N 34.52 E
Alexander, Cape > 175e 6.35 S 156.30 E
Alexander, Mount ∧, Austl. 162 22.39 S 115.32 E
Alexander, Mount ∧, Austl. 169 36.59 S 144.18 E
Alexander Archipelago II 180 56.30 N 134.00 W
Alexander Bay 156 28.40 S 16.30 E
Alexander City 194 32.56 N 85.57 W
Alexander Dam ⊜[1] 273d 26.13 S 28.25 E
Alexander Ditch ≍ 279a 41.20 N 82.05 W
Alexander Hamilton Airport ⊠ 241n 17.42 N 64.48 W
Alexander Indian Reserve ◆[4] 182 53.48 N 113.58 W
Alexander Island I 9 71.00 S 70.00 W
Alexander Nevsky Monastery ʊ[1] 265a 59.55 N 30.24 E
Alexandra, Austl. 169 37.12 S 145.43 E
Alexandra, N.Z. 172 45.15 S 169.24 E
Alexandra, S. Afr. 273d 26.06 S 28.05 E
Alexandra ≐ 166 18.14 S 139.54 E
Alexandra Canal ≍ 274a 33.56 S 151.10 E
Alexandra Falls ∟ 176 60.29 N 116.18 W
Alexandra Park ♦ 262 53.27 N 2.15 W
Alexandra Park Race Course ♦ 260 51.36 N 0.08 W
Alexandretta, Gulf of → İskenderun Körfezi ⊂ 130 36.30 N 35.40 E
Alexandretta → İskenderun 130 36.37 N 36.07 E
Alexandria, Austl. 166 19.05 S 136.40 E
Alexandria, Bra. 250 6.25 S 38.01 W
Alexandria, B.C., Can. 182 52.38 N 122.27 W
Alexandria, On., Can. 206 45.19 N 74.38 W
Alexandria, Rom. 38 43.58 N 25.20 E
Alexandria, S. Afr. 158 33.40 S 26.24 E
Alexandria, Scot., U.K. 46 55.59 N 4.36 W
Alexandria, In., U.S. 216 40.15 N 85.40 W
Alexandria, Ky., U.S. 218 38.57 N 84.23 W
Alexandria, La., U.S. 194 31.18 N 92.26 W
Alexandria, Mn., U.S. 198 45.53 N 95.22 W
Alexandria, Mo., U.S. 194 40.21 N 91.27 W
Alexandria, Ne., U.S. 198 40.14 N 97.23 W
Alexandria, Oh., U.S. 214 40.05 N 82.37 W
Alexandria, Pa., U.S. 214 40.34 N 78.06 W
Alexandria, S.D., U.S. 198 43.39 N 97.46 W
Alexandria, Tn., U.S. 194 36.04 N 86.02 W
Alexandria, Va., U.S. 208 38.48 N 77.02 W
Alexandria → Al-Iskandarīyah 142 31.12 N 29.54 E
Alexandria Bay 212 44.20 N 75.55 W
Alexandrie → Al-Iskandarīyah 142 31.12 N 29.54 E
Alexandrina, Lake ⊜ 168b 35.26 S 139.10 E
Alexandroúpolis 38 40.50 N 25.52 E
Alexis 190 41.03 N 90.33 W
Alexis Creek 182 52.05 N 123.17 W
Alexis Indian Reserve ◆[4] 182 53.46 N 114.30 W
Alezio 68 40.04 N 18.03 E
Alf 56 50.03 N 7.07 E
Ālfādānga 126 23.18 N 89.42 E
Al-Fahmīyīn 142 29.36 N 31.17 E
Al-Fallūjah 128 33.20 N 43.46 E
Alfambra 34 40.33 N 1.02 W
Alfambra ≐ 34 40.21 N 1.07 W
Al-Fant 142 28.46 N 30.53 E
Alfarata 208 40.39 N 77.27 W
Al-Farḍah 144 14.51 N 48.27 E
Alfaro 34 42.11 N 1.45 W
Alfarràs 34 41.49 N 0.35 E
Al-Fāshir 140 13.38 N 25.21 E
Al-Fashn 142 28.49 N 30.54 E
Alfatar 38 43.57 N 27.17 E
Alfavaca, Ilha I 287a 23.02 S 43.18 W
Al-Fāw 128 29.58 N 48.29 E
Al-Fayyūm 142 29.19 N 30.50 E
Al-Fayyūm □[4] 142 29.19 N 30.48 E
Al-Fāzah 144 14.08 N 43.05 E
Alfbach ≐ 56 50.03 N 7.08 E
Alfedena 66 41.44 N 14.02 E
Alfeld, Dtsch. 52 51.59 N 9.50 E
Alfeld, Dtsch. 60 49.26 N 11.33 E
Alfenas 256 21.25 S 45.57 W
Alfianello 64 45.16 N 10.10 E
Al-Fifi 140 10.03 N 25.01 E
Alfiós ≐ 38 37.40 N 21.33 E

Symbols in the index entries represent the broad categories identified in the key at the right. Symbols with superior numbers (⋏[1]) identify subcategories (see complete key on page *I · 1).*

Symbole im Register stellen die rechts im Schlüssel erklärten Kategorien dar. Symbole mit hochgestellten Ziffern (⋏[1]) bezeichnen Unterabteilungen einer Kategorie (vgl. vollständiger Schlüssel auf Seite *I · 1).*

Los símbolos incluídos en el texto del índice representan las grandes categorias identificadas con la clave a la derecha. Los símbolos con numeros en su parte superior (⋏[1]) identifican las subcategorías (véase la clave completa en la página *I · 1).*

Les symboles de l'index représentent les catégories indiquées dans la légende à droite. Les symboles suivis d'un indice (⋏[1]) représentent des sous-catégories (voir légende complète à la page *I · 1).*

Os símbolos incluídos no texto do índice representam as grandes categorias identificadas com a chave à direita. Os símbolos com números em sua parte superior (⋏[1]) identificam as subcategorias (veja-se a chave completa à página *I · 1).*

∧ Mountain	Berg	Montaña	Montagne	Montanha
⋏ Mountains	Gebirge	Montañas	Montagnes	Montanhas
)(Pass	Paß	Paso	Col	Passo
V Valley, Canyon	Tal, Cañon	Valle, Cañón	Vallée, Canyon	Vale, Canhão
≚ Plain	Ebene	Llano	Plaine	Planície
> Cape	Kap	Cabo	Cap	Cabo
I Island	Insel	Isla	Île	Ilha
II Islands	Inseln	Islas	Îles	Ilhas
± Other Topographic Features	Andere Topographische Objekte	Otros Elementos Topográficos	Autres données topographiques	Outros acidentes topográficos

ESPAÑOL — Nombre | Página | Lat.°′ | Long.°′ W = Oeste
FRANÇAIS — Nom | Page | Lat.°′ | Long.°′ W = Ouest
PORTUGUÊS — Nome | Página | Lat.°′ | Long.°′ W = Oeste

Nombre / Nom / Nome	Página / Page	Lat.°′	Long.°′ W = Oeste / Ouest
Al-Firdān	142	30.41 N	32.20 E
Alföld ≡	30	47.00 N	20.00 E
Alfonsine	66	44.30 N	12.03 E
Alford, Austl.	168b	33.49 S	137.49 E
Alford, Eng., U.K.	44	53.16 N	0.10 E
Alford, Scot., U.K.	46	57.13 N	2.42 W
Alfortville	261	48.49 N	2.25 E
Ålfotbreen ⊓	26	61.45 N	5.40 E
Alfred, On., Can.	206	45.34 N	74.53 W
Alfred, Me., U.S.	188	43.28 N	70.43 W
Alfred, N.Y., U.S.	210	42.15 N	77.47 W
Alfred National Park ♠	166	37.35 S	149.20 E
Alfredo M. Terrazas	234	21.28 N	98.51 W
Alfreton	44	53.06 N	1.23 W
Alfriston	42	50.48 N	0.10 E
Alfta	26	61.21 N	16.05 E
Al-Fujayrah	128	25.06 N	56.21 E
Al-Fuqahā'	146	27.50 N	16.22 E
Al-Furzul	132	33.52 N	35.56 E
Alga	86	49.46 N	57.20 E
Algabas, Kaz.	80	50.39 N	52.07 E
Algabas, Kaz.	86	44.41 N	78.06 E
Algabas, Kaz.	86	48.21 N	81.39 E
Algači	88	50.43 N	117.47 E
Ålgarås	40	58.48 N	14.14 E
Ålgård	26	58.46 N	5.51 E
Al-Garef	140	12.03 N	34.19 E
Algarrobal	252	28.08 S	70.39 W
Algarrobo, Arg.	252	38.53 S	63.08 W
Algarrobo, Arg.	252	31.44 S	68.18 W
Algarrobo, Chile	252	33.22 S	71.40 W
Algarrobo del Águila	252	36.26 S	67.09 W
Algarve □ 9	34	37.10 N	8.15 W
Algás ≃	34	41.08 N	0.39 E
Algasovo	76	53.41 N	41.40 E
Al-Gebir	140	13.43 N	29.49 E
Algeciras, Col.	246	2.35 N	75.18 W
Algeciras, Esp.	34	36.08 N	5.30 W
Algemesí	34	39.11 N	0.26 W
Algena	144	17.19 N	38.31 E
Alger	216	40.42 N	83.50 W
Alger, Baie d' ⊂	34	36.50 N	3.15 E
Alger → El Djazaïr	148	36.47 N	3.03 E
Algeria (Algérie) □ 1, Afr.	134	28.00 N	3.00 E
Algeria (Algérie) □ 1, Afr.	148	28.00 N	3.00 E
Algérie → Algeria □ 1	148	28.00 N	3.00 E
Algerien → Algeria □ 1	148	28.00 N	3.00 E
Algermissen	52	52.15 N	9.58 E
Algés	266c	38.42 N	9.13 W
Al-Ghāb ⊜	130	35.30 N	36.18 E
Al-Gharaq as-Sulṭānī	142	29.08 N	30.42 E
Al-Gharbīyah □ 4	142	30.45 N	31.00 E
Al-Ghāriyah	132	32.23 N	36.39 E
Al-Ghāṭ	128	26.00 N	45.03 E
Al-Ghawr V	132	31.50 N	35.30 E
Al-Ghayatah	142	30.57 N	30.06 E
Al-Ghayḍah	118	16.12 N	52.15 E
Al-Ghazālah	128	26.48 N	41.19 E
Al-Ghazālī	142	30.49 N	31.49 E
Al-Ghāzīyah	132	33.31 N	35.22 E
Alghero	71	40.34 N	8.19 E
Al-Ghurayfah	128	24.00 N	56.29 E
Al-Ghurdaqah	140	27.14 N	33.50 E
Algier → El Djazaïr	148	36.47 N	3.03 E
Algiers → El Djazaïr	148	36.47 N	3.03 E
Alginet	34	39.16 N	0.28 W
Algoa	222	29.24 N	95.11 W
Algoabaai ⊂	158	33.50 S	25.50 E
Algodão, Ilha do I	256	23.13 S	44.36 W
Algodón ≃	246	2.23 S	71.56 W
Algodones	200	35.22 N	106.28 W
Algodor ≃	34	39.55 N	3.53 W
Algoma	190	44.36 N	87.25 W
Algoma Mills	190	46.10 N	82.50 W
Algona, Ia., U.S.	190	43.04 N	94.13 W
Algona, Wa., U.S.	224	47.16 N	122.15 W
Algonac	214	42.37 N	82.31 W
Algonquin	216	42.09 N	88.17 W
Algonquin Lake ⊜	216	42.40 N	85.20 W
Algonquin Provincial Park ♠	190	45.45 N	78.26 W
Algood	194	36.11 N	85.26 W
Algorta, Esp.	34	43.22 N	3.01 W
Algorta, Ur.	252	32.25 S	57.23 W
Alguierão-Mem Martins	266c	38.48 N	9.20 W
Al-Ḥaddādī	142	31.20 N	30.47 E
Al-Ḥaddayn	142	30.44 N	30.38 E
Al-Ḥadīthah	128	34.07 N	42.23 E
Al-Ḥaḍr	128	35.35 N	42.44 E
Al-Ḥaffah	130	35.35 N	36.02 E
Al-Ḥafīr Al-Fawqānī	132	33.42 N	36.28 E
Al-Ḥajālīj	140	14.36 N	31.54 E
Al-Ḥajarah ◆ 1	128	30.00 N	44.00 E
Al-Ḥajar al-Gharbī ⋏	128	24.10 N	56.15 E
Al-Ḥajar ash-Sharqī ⋏	128	22.45 N	59.00 E
Al Hajeb	148	33.43 N	5.13 W
Al-Ḥājir	142	30.41 N	31.49 E
Al-Ḥalfāyah	128	31.49 N	47.26 E
Al-Ḥamād ≡	128	32.00 N	39.30 E
Alhama de Granada	34	37.00 N	3.59 W
Alhama de Murcia	34	37.51 N	1.25 W
Al-Ḥamal ◆ 1	128	23.30 N	49.45 E
Alhambra, Ca., U.S.	228	34.05 N	118.07 W
Alhambra, Il., U.S.	219	38.53 N	89.44 W
Al-Ḥamīdīyah	130	34.43 N	35.56 E
Al-Ḥammām	140	30.50 N	29.23 E
Al-Ḥamrā', Ar. Su.	128	23.57 N	38.52 E
'Al-Ḥamrā', Lubnān	132	33.42 N	35.27 E
Al-Ḥamrah	142	31.10 N	30.52 E
Al-Ḥāmūl	142	31.19 N	31.10 E
Alhandra	250	7.26 S	34.54 W
Alhandra, Mouchão de I	266c	38.54 N	9.00 W
Al-Ḥarāk	132	32.44 N	36.18 E
Al-Ḥarīq	128	23.37 N	46.31 E
Al-Ḥārrah	132	33.03 N	36.00 E
Al-Ḥarrah ⊥ 9	128	31.00 N	38.30 E
Al-Ḥarūj al-Aswad ⋏ 2	146	27.00 N	17.10 E
Al-Ḥasakah	130	36.29 N	40.45 E
Al-Ḥasakah □ 8	130	36.30 N	41.00 E
Al-Ḥasānī I	128	24.58 N	37.05 E
Alhaurín el Grande	34	36.38 N	4.41 W
Al-Ḥawāmidīyah	273c	29.54 N	31.15 E
Al-Ḥawātah	140	13.25 N	34.38 E
Al-Ḥawātikah	142	27.16 N	31.01 E
Al-Ḥawrah	144	13.49 N	47.37 E
Al-Ḥawṭah	144	15.50 N	48.27 E
Al-Ḥawwārīyah	142	30.58 N	29.41 E
Al-Ḥayy, 'Irāq	128	32.10 N	46.03 E
Al-Ḥayy, Miṣr	142	29.39 N	31.18 E
Al-Ḥayyānīyah	128	28.38 N	42.45 E
Al-Ḥayz	140	28.02 N	28.39 E
Al-Ḥībah	142	28.45 N	30.55 E
Al-Ḥījānah	132	33.21 N	36.33 E
Al-Ḥijāz ◆ 1	118	24.30 N	38.30 E
Al-Ḥillah, 'Irāq	128	32.29 N	44.25 E
Al-Ḥillah, Sūd.	140	13.27 N	27.08 E
Al-Ḥilmīyah ◆ 8	273c	30.07 N	31.19 E
Al-Hindīyah	128	32.33 N	44.13 E
Al-Hirmil	130	34.23 N	36.23 E
Al-Ḥiṣn	132	32.29 N	35.52 E
Al-Hoceïma	148	35.15 N	3.55 W
Al-Hoceïma □ 4	148	35.00 N	4.30 W
Al Hoceïma, Baie d' ⊂	34	35.20 N	3.50 W
Alhos Vedros	266c	38.39 N	9.02 W
Alhucemas, Peñón de I	34	35.13 N	3.53 W
Al-Huḍayb	140	13.00 N	32.50 E
Al-Ḥudaydah	144	14.48 N	42.57 E
Al-Ḥufrah	146	29.10 N	18.02 E
Al-Ḥufrah ◆ 1	128	28.40 N	38.30 E
Al-Hufūf	128	25.22 N	49.34 E
Al-Ḥulwah	128	23.27 N	46.47 E
Al-Ḥumayshah	144	13.41 N	45.52 E
Al-Ḥumrah ◆ 1	128	23.20 N	54.30 E
Al-Ḥuṣayḥiṣah	140	14.44 N	33.18 E
Al-Ḥusaynīyah	142	30.52 N	31.55 E
Al-Ḥuṣaynīyah ▼ 4	144	17.48 N	44.27 E
Al-Ḥuwaylizah	132	33.02 N	35.51 E
Al-Ḥuwaymī	144	14.05 N	47.44 E
Al-Ḥuwayyiṭ	128	25.36 N	40.23 E
Alì	70	38.02 N	15.25 E
Ali ◆ 8	272a	28.31 N	77.18 E
'Ālī, As-Sadd al- (Aswān High Dam) ◆ 6	140	23.58 N	32.52 E
Alía, Esp.	34	39.27 N	5.13 W
Alia, It.	70	37.47 N	13.43 E
Aliabad, Azer.	84	41.29 N	46.37 E
'Alīābād, Īrān	128	36.57 N	54.59 E
Alīābād, Pāk.	123	36.18 N	74.37 E
Aliade	150	7.16 N	8.28 E
Aliaga, Esp.	34	40.40 N	0.42 W
Aliağa, Tür.	130	38.48 N	26.59 E
Aliákmon ≃	38	40.30 N	22.36 E
Aliákmonos, Tekhnití Límni ⊜ 1	38	40.15 N	22.00 E
Aliaksin, Cape ›	180	55.30 N	160.43 W
'Alī al-Gharbī	128	32.27 N	46.41 E
Aliança	250	7.35 S	35.13 W
Aliano	68	40.19 N	16.14 E
Alībāg	122	18.39 N	72.54 E
Alibahadır ◆ 8	267b	41.11 N	29.12 E
Ali-Bajramly	84	39.56 N	48.56 E
Alibardak	130	38.06 N	40.25 E
Alibates Flint Quarries National Monument ♠	196	35.35 N	101.39 W
Alibej, ozero ⊜	78	45.48 N	30.02 E
Alibejli	84	41.23 N	46.49 E
Alibey ≃	267b	41.03 N	28.56 E
Alibey Adası I	130	39.20 N	26.38 E
Alibey Barajı ⊜ 1	267b	41.07 N	28.55 E
Alibeyköy ◆ 8	267b	41.04 N	28.56 E
Alibijaban Island I	116	13.20 N	122.43 E
Alibori ≃	150	11.56 N	3.17 E
Al-Ibrāhīmīyah	142	30.57 N	31.35 E
Alibunar	38	45.05 N	20.58 E
Alicante → Alacant	34	38.21 N	0.29 W
Alice, Ciskei	158	32.47 S	26.50 E
Alice, Tx., U.S.	196	27.45 N	98.04 W
Alice ≃, Austl.	164	15.22 S	141.58 E
Alice ≃, Austl.	166	24.02 S	144.50 E
Alice, Punta ›	68	39.24 N	17.10 E
Alice Arm	182	55.29 N	129.29 W
Alicedale	158	33.19 S	26.05 E
Alice Downs	162	17.45 S	127.56 E
Alice Springs	162	23.42 S	133.53 E
Alice Superiore	62	45.28 N	7.47 E
Alice Town	238	25.44 N	79.17 W
Aliceville	194	33.07 N	88.09 W
Alicia, Pil.	116	16.45 N	121.42 E
Alicia, Pil.	116	7.30 N	122.55 E
Alıcık	130	40.49 N	35.21 E
Alick Creek ≃	166	20.25 S	142.00 E
Alicudi, Isola I	70	38.32 N	14.21 E
Alicurá, Embalse de ⊜ 1	254	40.40 S	71.00 W
Al-'Idwah	142	29.21 N	30.55 E
Alief	222	29.43 N	95.35 W
Alife	68	41.20 N	14.20 E
Al-Ifranj	132	31.11 N	35.41 E
Alīganj, India	124	28.07 N	80.36 E
Alīganj, India	124	27.30 N	79.11 E
Alīgarh	124	27.53 N	78.05 E
Alignements de Carnac ⊥	32	47.35 N	3.05 W
Alīgūdarz	128	33.24 N	49.41 E
Alijos, Islas II	232	24.57 N	115.44 W
'Alī Kheyl	120	33.57 N	69.43 E
Al-Ikhṣāṣ al-Qiblīyah	142	29.42 N	31.17 E
Al-Ikhwān II	118	12.08 N	53.10 E
Alikovo	80	55.45 N	46.45 E
Alima ≃	152	1.36 S	16.36 E
Al-Imām ◆ 8	273c	30.01 N	31.10 E
Al-Imārāt al-'Arabīyah al-Muttaḥidah → United Arab Emirates □ 1	128	24.00 N	54.00 E
Al-'Imārīyah	142	27.37 N	30.53 E
Alimena	70	37.42 N	14.07 E
Alimini Grande ⊜	68	40.12 N	18.27 E
Alimini Piccolo ⊜	68	40.10 N	18.27 E
Aliminusa	70	37.52 N	13.47 E
Alim Island I	164	2.55 S	147.05 E
Alimkent	85	40.58 N	69.11 E
Alimodian	116	10.49 N	122.26 E
Alindao	152	5.02 N	21.13 E
Alingsås	26	57.56 N	12.31 E
Alipur, India	272b	22.55 N	88.11 E
Ālipur, India	272b	22.43 N	88.12 E
Alīpur, Pāk.	123	29.23 N	70.55 E
Ālīpur ◆ 8	126	22.31 N	88.20 E
Alīpur Duār	124	26.29 N	89.44 E
Alīpur Janūbi	123	30.13 N	71.18 E
Aliquippa	214	40.38 N	80.14 W
Aliquippa-Hopewell Airport ⊠	279b	40.35 N	80.17 W
Alīrājpur	120	22.19 N	74.21 E
Al-'Irāq	132	31.05 N	35.39 E
Al-'Irāq → Iraq □ 1	128	33.00 N	44.00 E
Al-'Irqah	144	13.30 N	47.22 E
Ali-Sabieh	144	11.09 N	42.42 E
Al-'Īsāwīyah	128	30.38 N	37.53 E
Aliseda	34	39.26 N	6.41 W
Alise-Sainte-Reine	58	47.32 N	4.29 E
Alīshārī	84	39.02 N	47.15 E
Al-Iskandarīyah (Alexandria)	142	31.12 N	29.54 E
Al-Iskandarīyah □ 4	142	31.10 N	29.53 E
Al-Ismā'īlīyah (Ismailia)	142	30.35 N	32.16 E
Al-Ismā'īlīyah □ 4	142	30.30 N	32.15 E
Al-Ismā'īlīyah Military Base ■	142	30.35 N	32.14 E
Aliso Canyon V, Ca., U.S.	280	34.18 N	118.33 W
Aliso Canyon V, Ca., U.S.	280	33.53 N	117.40 W
Aliso Creek ≃	228	33.31 N	117.45 W
Al-Istiwā'īyah al-Gharbīyah □ 4	140	5.55 N	28.15 E
Al-Istiwā'īyah ash-Sharqīyah □ 4	154	4.30 N	33.00 E
Alistráti	38	41.04 N	23.57 E
Alitak, Cape ›	180	56.51 N	154.21 W
Alitak Bay ⊂	180	57.00 N	154.05 W
Alitanguo	120	35.10 N	83.30 E
Alì Terme	70	38.01 N	15.26 E
Alivérion	38	38.24 N	24.02 E
Aliwal North	158	30.45 S	26.45 E
Alix	182	52.24 N	113.11 W
Al-'Izzīyah	142	27.13 N	30.59 E
Al-Jabal al-Abyaḍ ∧ 2	142	28.46 N	31.00 E
Al-Jabal al-Aḥmar ∧ 2	142	28.19 N	31.07 E
Al-Jabalayn	140	12.36 N	32.48 E
Al-Jadīdah	140	25.34 N	28.51 E
Al-Jafādūn	142	28.50 N	30.48 E
Al-Jafr	132	30.18 N	36.13 E
Al-Jāfūrah ◆ 2	128	24.14 N	50.00 E
Al-Jaghbūb	146	29.45 N	24.31 E
Al-Jaghbūb ▼ 4	146	29.40 N	24.43 E
Al-Jahrah	128	29.20 N	47.40 E
Al-Jamālīyah	142	31.11 N	31.51 E
Al-Jarnūs	142	28.36 N	30.43 E
Al-Jawf, Ar. Su.	128	29.50 N	39.52 E
Al-Jawf, Lībiyā	146	24.11 N	23.19 E
Al-Jawsh	146	32.00 N	11.40 E
Al-Jaylī	140	16.01 N	32.36 E
Al-Jazā'ir → Algeria □ 1	148	28.00 N	3.00 E
Al-Jazīrah □ 4	140	14.30 N	33.20 E
Al-Jazīrah ◆ 1	140	14.25 N	33.00 E
Aljezur, Bra.	287a	22.40 S	43.36 W
Aljezur, Port.	34	37.19 N	8.48 W
Al-Jibāb	132	33.06 N	36.15 E
Al-Jifārah	128	23.59 N	45.11 E
Al-Jifārah (Jeffara) ≡	146	32.30 N	11.45 E
Al-Jīzah (Giza), Miṣr	142	30.01 N	31.13 E
Al-Jīzah, Urd.	132	31.43 N	35.58 E
Al-Jīzah □ 4	142	29.46 N	31.18 E
Al-Jubayl	128	27.01 N	49.40 E
Al-Jubayn	140	12.07 N	35.10 E
Aljucén ≃	34	38.56 N	6.25 W
Al-Judaydah	132	33.54 N	35.34 E
Al-Judayyidah, Urd.	132	31.32 N	35.39 E
Al-Judayyidah, Urd.	132	31.15 N	35.49 E
Al-Jufrah ▼ 4	146	29.10 N	16.00 E
Al-Julaydah ▼ 4	128	29.03 N	45.38 E
Al-Junaynah, Miṣr	142	31.06 N	31.41 E
Al-Junaynah, Sūd.	140	13.27 N	22.27 E
Al-Junaynah, Sūrīy.	132	32.54 N	36.44 E
Al-Jundīyah	142	28.34 N	30.50 E
Aljustrel	34	37.52 N	8.10 W
Al-Kāb	142	30.57 N	32.18 E
Al-Kabrit Military Base ■	142	30.15 N	32.29 E
Al-Kafr	132	32.38 N	36.38 E
Al-Kafr ash-Sharqī	142	37.17 N	31.10 E
Al-Kahfah	128	27.04 N	43.02 E
Alkali Creek ≃, Ab., Can.	184	50.52 N	110.30 W
Alkali Creek ≃, Wy., U.S.	202	43.16 N	107.40 W
Alkali Lake	182	51.47 N	122.14 W
Alkali Lake ⊜, Nv., U.S.	204	41.42 N	119.50 W
Alkali Lake ⊜, Or., U.S.	202	42.58 N	120.02 W
Alkamari	146	13.24 N	11.07 E
Al-Kāmilīn	140	15.05 N	33.11 E
Al-Karabah	140	18.33 N	33.42 E
Al-Karak	132	31.11 N	35.42 E
Al-Karak □ 8	132	31.10 N	35.45 E
Al-Karnak	140	25.43 N	32.39 E
Al-Kawah	140	13.44 N	32.30 E
Al-Kawd	144	13.05 N	45.22 E
Al-Kawm	130	35.11 N	38.52 E
Al-Kawm al-Akhḍar	142	30.58 N	30.17 E
Al-Kawm Aṭ-Ṭawīl	142	31.12 N	31.05 E
Alken	56	50.15 N	7.26 E
Al-Khabrā'	128	26.04 N	43.33 E
Al-Khābūrah	128	23.59 N	57.08 E
Al-Khafaqān ⊜	128	23.24 N	40.24 E
Al-Khalīl (Hebron)	132	31.32 N	35.06 E
Al-Khālis	128	33.49 N	44.32 E
Al-Khandaq	140	18.36 N	30.34 E
Al-Khānkah	142	30.13 N	31.21 E
Al-Kharaqānīyah	273c	30.10 N	31.10 E
Al-Khārijah	140	25.26 N	30.33 E
Al-Kharṭūm (Khartoum)	140	15.36 N	32.32 E
Al-Kharṭūm □ 4	140	15.45 N	32.30 E
Al-Kharṭūm Baḥrī	140	15.38 N	32.33 E
Al-Khaṣab	128	26.12 N	56.15 E
Al-Khatam ◆ 1	128	24.00 N	55.10 E
Al-Khirbah as-Samrā'	132	32.11 N	36.10 E
Al-Khiyām	132	33.19 N	35.36 E
Al-Khubar	128	26.17 N	50.12 E
Al-Khums (Homs)	146	32.39 N	14.16 E
Al-Khuraybah, Urd.	132	32.40 N	35.52 E
Al-Khuraybah, Yaman	144	15.06 N	48.19 E
Al-Khurmah	144	21.54 N	42.03 E
Al-Khushnīyah	132	33.00 N	35.48 E
Al-Khuṣūṣ	273c	30.09 N	31.19 E
Al-Kifl	128	32.14 N	44.22 E
Al-Kiswah	132	33.21 N	36.14 E
Alkmaar	52	52.37 N	4.44 E
Alkoven	61	48.17 N	14.06 E
Al-Kūbrī	142	30.02 N	32.33 E
Al-Kūfah	128	32.02 N	44.24 E
Al-Kufrah (Cufra) ▼ 4	146	24.20 N	23.15 E
Al-Kunayyisah	273c	29.59 N	31.11 E
Al-Kuntillah	140	30.00 N	34.41 E
Al-Kūt	128	32.25 N	45.49 E
Al-Kuwayt	128	29.20 N	47.59 E
Al-Kuwayt → Kuwait □ 1	128	29.30 N	47.45 E
Alkvettern ⊜	40	59.25 N	14.21 E
Allaben	210	42.07 N	74.22 W
Al-Labwah	130	34.12 N	36.21 E
Allacapan	116	18.15 N	121.35 E
Allach-Jun'	74	61.08 N	138.03 E
Allada	150	6.39 N	2.09 E
Al-Lādhiqīyah (Latakia)	130	35.31 N	35.47 E
Al-Lādhiqīyah □ 8	130	35.30 N	36.00 E
Allagash ≃	186	47.05 N	69.02 W
Allagen	56	51.28 N	8.14 E
Al-Lagowa	140	11.24 N	29.08 E
Allahābād, India	124	25.27 N	81.51 E
Allāhābād, Pāk.	123	28.57 N	70.53 E
Allāhbās	272a	28.31 N	77.25 E
Allahüekber Dağları ⋏	130	40.35 N	42.32 E
Al-Lāhūn	142	29.13 N	30.59 E
Allāhwardipur	272a	28.33 N	77.26 E
Allaines	50	48.12 N	1.50 E
Allaire State Park ♠	208	40.08 N	74.08 W
Allakaket	180	66.34 N	152.41 W
Allaman	58	46.28 N	6.24 E
Allamuchy	210	40.55 N	74.48 W
Allan	184	51.53 N	106.04 W
Allan, Pointe ›	275a	45.26 N	73.45 W
Allanche	32	45.14 N	2.56 E
Alland	61	48.03 N	16.05 E
Allan Island I	224	48.28 N	122.42 W
Allanmyo	110	19.22 N	95.13 E
Allanridge	158	27.55 S	26.44 E
Allanson	168a	33.20 S	116.06 E
Allanton	46	55.47 N	3.51 W
Allan Water ≃	46	56.08 N	3.56 W
Allapattah Flats ≡	220	27.29 N	82.34 W
'Allāq, Bi'r ▼ 4	146	31.05 N	11.42 E
'Allāqī, Wādī al- V	140	22.42 N	33.12 E
Allard, Lac ⊜	186	50.32 N	63.31 W
Allardt	194	36.22 N	84.53 W
Allariz	34	42.11 N	7.48 W
Allatoona Lake ⊜ 1	192	34.08 N	84.38 W
Allauch	62	43.20 N	5.29 E
Al-Layyah	140	16.16 N	35.25 E
Alldays	156	22.44 S	29.04 E
Alle, Bel.	56	49.51 N	4.58 E
Alle, Schw.	58	47.26 N	7.08 E
Ålleberg ∧ 2	26	58.08 N	13.36 E
Allegan	216	42.31 N	85.51 W
Allegan □ 6	216	42.35 N	85.53 W
Allegan, Lake ⊜	216	42.33 N	85.55 W
Allegany	210	42.05 N	78.29 W
Allegany □ 6	210	42.13 N	78.02 W
Allegany Indian Reservation ◆ 4	210	42.10 N	78.47 W
Allegany State Park ♠	210	42.04 N	78.44 W
Alleghany	226	39.28 N	120.51 W
Alleghe	64	46.24 N	12.01 E
Allegheny □ 6	214	40.26 N	79.59 W
Allegheny ≃	214	40.27 N	80.00 W
Allegheny Acres	279b	40.37 N	79.53 W
Allegheny Center ◗	279b	40.27 N	80.01 W
Allegheny County Airport ⊠	279b	40.21 N	79.56 W
Allegheny County Park ♠	279b	40.34 N	79.55 W
Allegheny Mountains ⋏	188	38.30 N	80.00 W
Allegheny Observatory ◗ 3	279b	40.29 N	80.01 W
Allegheny Plateau ⋏ 1	188	41.30 N	78.00 W
Allegheny Portage Railroad National Historic Site ⊥	214	40.28 N	78.32 W
Allegheny Reservoir ⊜ 1	214	42.00 N	78.56 W
Allègre	62	45.12 N	3.42 E
Allègre, Pointe ›	241o	16.22 N	61.45 W
Allemagne → Germany □ 1	30	51.00 N	10.00 E
Allemands, Lac Des ⊜	194	29.55 N	90.35 W
Allemanskraaldam ⊜ 1	158	28.16 S	27.07 E
Allemant	261	48.45 N	1.37 E
Allemont	62	45.08 N	6.02 E
Allen, Arg.	252	38.58 S	67.50 W
Allen, Pil.	116	12.30 N	124.17 E
Allen, Md., U.S.	208	38.17 N	75.41 W
Allen, Mi., U.S.	216	41.57 N	84.46 W
Allen, Ne., U.S.	198	42.24 N	96.50 W
Allen, Ok., U.S.	196	34.52 N	96.24 W
Allen, Pa., U.S.	208	40.10 N	77.05 W
Allen, S.D., U.S.	198	43.16 N	101.55 W
Allen, Tx., U.S.	222	33.06 N	96.40 W
Allen, Wa., U.S.	224	48.31 N	122.23 W
Allen □ 6, In., U.S.	216	41.04 N	85.09 W
Allen □ 6, Oh., U.S.	216	40.46 N	84.06 W
Allen ≃	44	54.58 N	2.19 W
Allen, Lough ⊜	48	54.08 N	8.08 W
Allen, Mount ∧, N.Z.	172	47.05 S	167.48 E
Allen, Mount ∧, Ak., U.S.	180	62.14 N	142.13 W
Allenby Bridge ◆ 5	132	31.52 N	35.52 E
Allendale, Il., U.S.	194	38.32 N	87.43 W
Allendale, Mi., U.S.	216	42.58 N	85.57 W
Allendale, N.J., U.S.	276	41.02 N	74.07 W
Allendale, S.C., U.S.	192	33.00 N	81.18 W
Allendale Town	44	54.54 N	2.15 W
Allende, Méx.	232	28.20 N	100.51 W
Allende, Méx.	234	18.09 N	94.16 W
Allendorf	56	51.02 N	8.38 E
Allenfarm	222	30.24 N	96.14 W
All England Lawn Tennis Club ♠	260	51.26 N	0.13 W
Allen Grove	216	42.35 N	88.41 W
Allen Park	216	42.15 N	83.12 W
Allenport, Pa., U.S.	214	40.20 N	77.53 W
Allenport, Pa., U.S.	214	40.06 N	79.51 W
Allensbach	58	47.43 N	9.03 E
Allenstein → Olsztyn	30	53.48 N	20.29 E
Allensville	214	40.32 N	77.49 W
Allenton, Mi., U.S.	214	42.55 N	82.57 W
Allenton, R.I., U.S.	207	41.32 N	71.28 W
Allentown, N.J., U.S.	208	40.10 N	74.35 W
Allentown, N.Y., U.S.	210	42.05 N	78.03 W
Allentown, Oh., U.S.	216	40.46 N	84.12 W
Allentown, Pa., U.S.	208	40.36 N	75.28 W
Allentsteig	61	48.42 N	15.20 E
Allenwood, N.J., U.S.	208	40.12 N	74.13 W
Allenwood, N.Y., U.S.	276	40.48 N	73.44 W
Allenwood, Pa., U.S.	210	41.07 N	76.54 W
Alleppey	122	9.29 N	76.19 E
Aller ≃	30	52.57 N	9.11 E
Allerona	66	42.49 N	11.58 E
Allersberg	60	49.15 N	11.15 E
Allershausen	60	48.26 N	11.36 E
Allerslev	41	55.05 N	12.03 E
Allerton, Ia., U.S.	190	40.42 N	93.21 W
Allerton, Ma., U.S.	283	42.18 N	70.53 W
Allerton ◆ 8	262	53.22 N	2.53 W
Allerton, Point ›	207	42.18 N	70.53 W
Allestree	42	52.57 N	1.29 W
Allevard	62	45.24 N	6.04 E
Alley Park ♠	276	40.45 N	73.44 W
Alleyton	222	29.43 N	96.29 W
Allgäu ◆ 1	58	47.35 N	10.10 E
Allgäuer Alpen ⋏	58	47.20 N	10.25 E
Allhallows	260	51.28 N	0.39 E
Alli ≃	68	38.51 N	16.40 E
Alliance, Ab., Can.	182	52.26 N	111.47 W
Alliance, Ne., U.S.	198	42.12 N	102.58 W
Alliance, Oh., U.S.	214	40.54 N	81.06 W
Allibaudières	50	48.35 N	4.07 E
Al-Lidām	144	20.29 N	44.50 E
Allier □ 5	32	46.25 N	3.00 E
Allier ≃, Fr.	32	46.58 N	3.04 E
Allier ≃, Fr.	62	45.05 N	3.35 E
Alligator ≃	192	35.58 N	75.58 W
Alligator Creek ≃, Ga., U.S.	192	31.58 N	82.22 W
Alligator Creek ≃, Tx., U.S.	222	30.42 N	97.07 W
Alligator Lake ⊜	220	28.13 N	81.13 W
Alligator Pond	241q	17.52 N	77.34 W
Alligny-en-Morvan	50	47.12 N	4.10 E
Allihies	48	51.38 N	10.03 W
Allinagaram	122	10.02 N	77.30 E
Allinge	26	55.16 N	14.49 E
Allington Castle ⊥	260	51.17 N	0.31 E
Al-Lisān › 1	132	31.17 N	35.28 E
Al-Lisht	142	29.34 N	31.14 E
Allison	190	42.45 N	92.47 W
Allison, Mount ∧	282	37.30 N	121.52 W
Allison Gulch V	280	34.16 N	117.44 W
Allison Park	214	40.34 N	79.57 W
Alliste	68	39.57 N	18.05 E
Alliston	212	44.09 N	79.52 W
Al-Līth	144	20.09 N	40.16 E
Allmendingen	58	48.20 N	9.43 E
Alloa	46	56.07 N	3.49 W
Allochio, Galleria degli ◆ 5	66	44.03 N	11.30 E
Allogny	50	47.13 N	2.19 E
Allonby	44	54.46 N	3.25 W
Alloné Abba	132	32.44 N	35.10 E
Allonnes, Dtsch.	50	47.58 N	0.09 E
Allonnes, Fr.	50	48.20 N	1.40 E
Allora	171a	28.02 S	151.59 E
Allos	62	44.14 N	6.38 E
Allott, Mount ∧ 2	162	26.06 S	124.46 E
Allouez	190	44.28 N	88.00 W
Alloway	208	39.33 N	75.21 W
Alloway Creek ≃	208	39.27 N	75.30 W
Allport	214	40.58 N	78.12 W
Allred Peak ∧	200	40.32 N	108.33 W
All Saints	240c	17.03 N	61.48 W
Allschwil	58	47.33 N	7.33 E
Allstedt	54	51.24 N	11.23 E
Allston ◆ 8	283	42.22 N	71.08 W
Alluets, Forêt des ♠	261	48.55 N	1.55 E
Al-Luḥayyah	144	15.42 N	42.42 E
Allumette Lake ⊜	190	45.53 N	77.13 W
Allumettes, Île des I	190	45.50 N	77.05 W
Allumiere	66	42.09 N	11.54 E
Allview Estates	208	39.12 N	76.51 W
Allyn	224	47.23 N	122.49 W
Alm ≃	60	48.05 N	13.55 E
Alma, N.B., Can.	186	45.36 N	64.57 W
Alma, P.Q., Can.	186	48.33 N	71.39 W
Alma, Ar., U.S.	194	35.28 N	94.13 W
Alma, Ga., U.S.	192	31.32 N	82.27 W
Alma, Il., U.S.	219	38.43 N	88.55 W
Alma, Ks., U.S.	198	39.01 N	96.17 W
Alma, Mi., U.S.	190	43.22 N	84.39 W
Alma, Ne., U.S.	198	40.05 N	99.21 W
Alma, N.Y., U.S.	210	42.01 N	78.03 W
Alma, Wi., U.S.	190	44.19 N	91.54 W
Al-Ma'ābidah	142	27.20 N	31.01 E
Al-Ma'ādī ◆ 8	142	29.58 N	31.15 E
Alma-Ata (Almaty)	85	43.15 N	76.57 E
Alma-Ata □ 8	86	44.00 N	77.00 E
Alma-Atinskij zapovednik ♠	85	43.10 N	77.25 E
Alma Center	190	44.26 N	90.54 W
Almada	34	38.41 N	9.09 W
Almaden, Austl.	166	17.20 S	144.41 E
Almadén, Esp.	34	38.46 N	4.50 W
Almadén de la Plata	34	37.52 N	6.04 W
Al-Madīnah (Medina)	128	24.28 N	39.36 E
Al-Madīnah al-Fikrīyah	142	27.56 N	30.49 E
Al-Madwar	132	32.17 N	36.00 E
Al-Mafāzah	140	13.36 N	34.33 E
Al-Mafraq	132	32.21 N	36.12 E
Al-Mafraq □ 8	132	32.15 N	36.30 E
Almafuerte	252	32.12 S	64.15 W
Al-Maghārīm	144	15.01 N	47.51 E
Al-Maghrah ▼ 4	140	30.14 N	28.56 E
Almagor	132	32.55 N	35.36 E
Almagre, Laguna ⊂	234	23.48 N	97.48 W
Al-Magreb → Morocco □ 1	148	32.00 N	5.00 W
Almagro	34	38.53 N	3.43 W
Almagro Island I	116	11.56 N	124.18 E
Al-Maḥallah al-Kubrā	142	30.58 N	31.10 E
Al-Maḥārīq	140	25.37 N	30.39 E
Al Mahbas	148	27.13 N	9.44 W
Alma Hill ∧ 2	210	42.03 N	78.01 W
Al-Maḥmūdīyah	142	31.11 N	30.32 E
Al-Maḥraṣ	142	27.49 N	30.48 E
Al-Maḥsamah	142	30.34 N	32.01 E
Al-Majdal	132	32.47 N	36.30 E
Al-Majma'ah	128	25.54 N	45.20 E
Almăjului, Munții ⋏	38	44.43 N	22.12 E
Al-Maks ◆ 8	142	31.09 N	29.51 E
Al-Mālikīyah	130	37.10 N	42.08 E
Almalyk	85	40.50 N	69.35 E
Al-Ma'mūrah ◆ 8	142	31.18 N	30.03 E
Al-Manāmah	128	26.13 N	50.35 E
Al-Manāqil	140	14.15 N	32.59 E
Al-Manāṣif ◆ 1	130	35.17 N	40.50 E
Al-Manāwāt	273c	29.55 N	31.14 E
Almanor, Lake ⊜	204	40.15 N	121.08 W
Almansa	34	38.52 N	1.05 W
Al-Manshāh	140	26.28 N	31.48 E
Al-Manṣūrah, Isr. Occ	132	33.08 N	35.48 E
Al-Manṣūrah, Miṣr	142	31.03 N	31.23 E
Al-Manṣūrīyah	142	30.08 N	31.05 E
Almanza	34	42.39 N	5.02 W
Al-Manzilah	142	31.09 N	31.56 E
Almanzor ∧	34	40.15 N	5.18 W
Almanzora ≃	34	37.14 N	1.46 W
Almar ≃	34	40.54 N	5.29 W
Al-Marāghah	140	26.42 N	31.36 E
Almargem do Bispo	266c	38.51 N	9.16 W
Al-Marj	146	32.30 N	20.54 E
Al-Marj ◆ 8	273c	30.09 N	31.20 E
Almas	250	11.33 S	47.09 W
Almaș ≃	38	47.14 N	23.19 E
Almas, Pico das ∧	255	13.33 S	41.56 W
Al-Ma'ṣarah, Miṣr	142	27.42 N	30.52 E
Al-Ma'ṣarah, Miṣr	142	31.13 N	31.19 E
Al-Ma'sarah ◆ 8	142	29.54 N	31.17 E
Al-Mashqūq	132	32.24 N	36.43 E
Al-Mashrafah	130	34.50 N	36.52 E
Al-Masīd	140	15.15 N	32.57 E
Almassora	34	39.57 N	0.03 W
Al-Matammah	140	16.43 N	33.22 E
Al-Maṭarīyah	142	31.11 N	32.02 E
Al-Maṭarīyah ◆ 8	142	30.07 N	31.19 E
Al-Matnah	140	13.47 N	35.03 E
Al-Mawṣil (Mosul)	128	36.20 N	43.08 E
Al-Mayādīn	130	35.01 N	40.27 E
Al-Maymūn	142	29.14 N	31.12 E
Almazán	34	41.29 N	2.32 W
Al-Mazār, Urd.	132	31.04 N	35.42 E
Almazar, Uzb.	85	40.59 N	68.54 E
Almaznaja ◆ 8	83	48.31 N	38.35 E
Almaznyj	83	48.02 N	40.03 E
Almazovka ◆ 8	83	48.04 N	39.18 E
Almazovo	265b	55.51 N	38.02 E
Al-Mazra'ah	132	31.16 N	35.31 E
Al-Mazzah	132	33.30 N	36.15 E
Alme	56	51.28 N	8.37 E
Almeer	52	52.20 N	5.14 E
Almeida	34	40.43 N	6.54 W
Almeirim, Bra.	250	1.32 S	52.34 W
Almeirim, Port.	34	39.12 N	8.38 W
Almelo	52	52.21 N	6.39 E
Almena	198	39.53 N	99.42 W
Almenara	255	16.11 S	40.42 W
Almenar de Soria	34	41.41 N	2.12 W
Almendares ≃	286b	23.08 N	82.25 W
Almendra, Embalse de ⊜ 1	34	41.15 N	6.10 W
Almendralejo	34	38.41 N	6.24 W
Almenêches	50	48.42 N	0.07 E
Al'menevo	86	54.57 N	63.34 E
Almenno San Salvatore	62	45.45 N	9.35 E
Almería	34	36.50 N	2.27 W
Almería □ 4	34	37.10 N	2.25 W
Almería, Golfo de ⊂	34	36.46 N	2.30 W
Al'metjevsk	80	54.53 N	52.20 E
Al'mež	24	60.03 N	48.03 E
Älmhult	26	56.33 N	14.08 E
Al-Midhnab	128	25.54 N	44.14 E
Al-Mīnā'	130	34.27 N	35.49 E
Almina, Punta ›	34	35.53 N	5.15 W
Almino Afonso	250	6.09 S	37.46 W
Al-Minshāt al-Kubrā	142	31.03 N	30.54 E
Al-Minūfīyah □ 4	142	30.30 N	31.00 E
Al-Minyā, Miṣr	142	28.06 N	30.45 E
Al-Minyā, Miṣr	142	29.45 N	31.18 E
Al-Minyā, Miṣr	142	29.14 N	30.45 E
Al-Minyā □ 4	142	28.26 N	30.42 E
Al-Miqdādīyah	128	33.59 N	44.56 E
Almira	202	47.42 N	118.56 W
Almirantazgo, Islas → Admiralty Islands II	164	2.10 S	147.00 E
Almirantazgo, Montes → Admiralty Mountains ⋏	9	71.45 S	168.30 E
Almirante	236	9.18 N	82.24 W
Almirante, Bahía de ⊂	236	9.20 N	82.18 W
Almirante Brown	258	34.48 S	58.23 W
Almirante Brown □ 5	288	34.50 S	58.20 W
Almirante Guillermo Brown, Parque ♠	288	34.40 S	58.28 W
Almirante Latorre	252	29.38 S	70.58 W
Almirante Montt, Golfo ʮ	254	51.55 S	72.45 W
Almirós	38	39.11 N	22.46 E
Almiroú, Kólpos ⊂	38	35.23 N	24.20 E
Al-Mismīyah	132	33.08 N	36.23 E
Almo	202	42.06 N	113.37 W
Almoçageme	266c	38.48 N	9.28 W
Almodôvar	34	37.31 N	8.04 W
Almodóvar del Campo	34	38.43 N	4.10 W
Almolonga	236	14.49 N	91.30 W
Almond, N.Y., U.S.	210	42.19 N	77.44 W
Almond, Wi., U.S.	190	44.15 N	89.24 W
Almond ≃, Scot., U.K.	46	55.58 N	3.18 W
Almond ≃, Scot., U.K.	46	56.25 N	3.27 W
Almondbank	46	56.24 N	3.33 W
Almondsbury	42	51.34 N	2.34 W
Almonesson	208	39.49 N	75.06 W
Almont	214	42.55 N	83.02 W
Almont ≃	261	48.32 N	2.40 E
Almonte, On., Can.	212	45.14 N	76.12 W
Almonte, Esp.	34	37.15 N	6.31 W
Almonte, Ca., U.S.	282	37.53 N	122.32 W
Almora	124	29.37 N	79.40 E
Almsee ⊜	64	47.45 N	13.57 E
Älmsta	40	59.58 N	18.48 E
Al-Mu'aḍḍamīyah	132	33.45 N	36.39 E
Al-Mubarraz, Ar. Su.	128	25.25 N	49.35 E
Al-Mubarraz, Ar. Su.	144	22.17 N	46.44 E
Al-Mudawwarah	128	29.19 N	35.59 E
Almudébar	34	42.03 N	0.35 W
Al-Muglad	140	11.02 N	27.44 E
Al-Muḥarraq	128	26.16 N	50.37 E
Al-Mukallā	144	14.32 N	49.08 E
Al-Mukhā (Mocha)	144	13.19 N	43.15 E
Al-Munājāt al-Kubrā	142	30.50 N	32.01 E
Almuñécar	34	36.43 N	3.41 W
Almunge	40	59.53 N	18.03 E
Al-Muntazah ◆ 8	142	31.17 N	30.01 E
Almus	130	40.23 N	36.55 E
Al-Musallamīyah	140	14.34 N	33.21 E
Al-Musayfirah	132	32.37 N	36.20 E
Al-Musayjīd	128	24.05 N	39.06 E
Al-Musayyib	128	32.47 N	44.18 E
Almus Barajı ⊜ 1	130	40.20 N	37.00 E
Al-Mushannaf	132	32.44 N	36.46 E
Al-Musharrak Qiblī	142	29.23 N	30.34 E
Al-Mutā'iyah	132	32.29 N	36.17 E
Al-Mu'tamadīyah	142	31.02 N	31.05 E
Al-Mutayn	132	33.54 N	35.44 E
Al-Muthannā □ 4	128	30.30 N	45.15 E
Al-Muṭī'ah	142	27.08 N	31.18 E
Al-Muwaqqar ⊥	132	31.49 N	36.06 E
Al-Muwassam	144	16.25 N	42.20 E
Al-Muwayh	144	22.45 N	41.36 E
Al-Muwayliḥ	128	27.41 N	35.27 E
Aln ≃	44	55.23 N	1.37 W
Alnarp	41	55.39 N	13.05 E
Al-Narrānīyah	273c	29.58 N	31.10 E
Al'n'aš	80	56.44 N	54.43 E
Alnaši	80	56.11 N	52.28 E
Al-Nasser	140	24.32 N	32.55 E
Alne ≃	42	52.13 N	1.52 W
Alness	46	57.41 N	4.15 W
Alnmouth	44	55.23 N	1.36 W
Alnön I	26	62.25 N	17.26 E
Alnor	41	54.55 N	9.36 E
Alnwick	44	55.25 N	1.42 W
Alnwick Indian Reserve ◆ 4	212	44.10 N	78.06 W
Alo	146	11.47 N	20.53 E
Aloândia	255	17.43 S	49.29 W
Alofau	174u	14.16 S	170.36 W
Alofi	174v	19.01 S	169.55 W
Alofi Bay ⊂	174v	19.01 S	169.56 W
Aloha	224	45.29 N	122.51 W
Aloha, Lake ⊜	226	38.52 N	120.09 W
Aloi	154	2.17 N	33.10 E
Aloja	76	57.46 N	24.53 E
Alondra	280	33.55 N	118.15 W
Along	120	28.18 N	94.39 E
Alónnisos	38	39.08 N	23.50 E
Alónnisos I	38	39.13 N	23.55 E
Alor, Kepulauan II	112	8.15 S	124.30 E
Alor, Pulau I	112	8.15 S	124.45 E
Alor, Selat ʮ	112	8.20 S	123.48 E
Álora	34	36.48 N	4.42 W
Alor Gajah	114	2.23 N	102.13 E
Alor Setar	114	6.07 N	100.22 E
Alor Star → Alor Setar	114	6.07 N	100.22 E
Alorton	219	38.36 N	90.08 W
Al'oškino	88	58.35 N	100.32 E
Al'ošn'a, Ross.	76	53.38 N	33.29 E
Al'ošn'a, Ross.	82	54.14 N	37.16 E
Alosno	34	37.33 N	7.07 W
Alost → Aalst	50	50.56 N	4.02 E
Alotau	164	10.14 S	150.30 E
Alouette ≃	224	49.16 N	122.42 W
Alouette Lake ⊜	224	49.19 N	122.28 W
Alovo	80	54.38 N	46.27 E
Aloxe-Corton	58	47.04 N	4.52 E
Aloysius, Mount ∧	162	26.01 S	128.34 E
Alpachiri	252	37.22 S	63.46 W
Alpaugh	226	35.53 N	119.29 W
Alpen	52	51.35 N	6.30 E
Alpena, Ar., U.S.	194	36.17 N	93.17 W
Alpena, Mi., U.S.	190	45.03 N	83.25 W
Alpena, S.D., U.S.	198	44.10 N	98.21 W
Alpen → Alps ⋏	32	46.25 N	10.00 E
Alpercatas ≃	250	6.02 S	44.19 W
Alpes → Alps ⋏	32	46.25 N	10.00 E
Alpes-de-Haute-Provence □ 5	62	44.10 N	6.00 E
Alpes Dináricos → Dinara ⋏	36	43.50 N	16.35 E
Alpes Maritimes □ 5	62	44.00 N	7.10 E
Alpes Marítimos → Maritime Alps ⋏	62	44.15 N	7.10 E
Alpes Transilvanos → Carpații Meridionali ⋏	38	45.30 N	24.15 E
Alpha, Austl.	166	23.39 S	146.38 E
Alpha, Il., U.S.	190	41.12 N	90.23 W
Alpha, Mi., U.S.	190	46.02 N	88.22 W
Alpha, N.J., U.S.	210	40.40 N	75.09 W
Alpharetta	192	34.04 N	84.17 W
Alphen aan den Rijn	52	52.07 N	4.40 E
Alphington	42	50.42 N	3.31 W
Alphin Pike ∧ 2	262	53.31 N	2.00 W
Alphonse Island I	138	7.00 S	52.45 E
Alpi, Monte ∧	68	40.07 N	15.59 E
Alpi → Alps ⋏	32	46.25 N	10.00 E
Alpiarça	34	39.15 N	8.35 W
Alpi Dinariche → Dinara ⋏	36	43.50 N	16.35 E
Alpignano	62	45.06 N	7.31 E
Alpilles, Chaîne des ⋏ 2	62	43.45 N	4.50 E
Alpine, Az., U.S.	200	33.50 N	109.08 W
Alpine, Ca., U.S.	204	32.50 N	116.47 W
Alpine, N.J., U.S.	276	40.57 N	73.55 W
Alpine, N.Y., U.S.	210	42.19 N	76.44 W
Alpine, Tx., U.S.	196	30.21 N	103.39 W
Alpine □ 6	226	38.41 N	119.47 W
Alpine Creek ≃	282	37.19 N	122.17 W
Alpine National Park ♠	166	37.00 S	147.15 E
Alpinópolis	255	20.52 S	46.23 W
Alpi Retiche → Rhaetian Alps ⋏	58	46.30 N	10.00 E
Alpirsbach	58	48.21 N	8.23 E
Alplaus Kill ≃	210	42.51 N	73.54 W
Alpnachstad	58	46.57 N	8.17 E
Alps ⋏	22	46.25 N	10.00 E
Alpsee ⊜	58	47.34 N	10.10 E
Alpu	130	39.47 N	30.58 E
Al-Qābil	128	23.57 N	55.48 E
Al-Qābūn	132	33.33 N	36.20 E
Al-Qadam	132	33.28 N	36.17 E
Al-Qaḍārif	140	14.02 N	35.24 E
Al-Qaḍīmah	144	22.21 N	39.09 E
Al-Qādisīyah □ 4	128	31.55 N	45.00 E
Al-Qāhirah (Cairo), Miṣr	142	30.03 N	31.15 E
Al-Qāhirah (Cairo), Miṣr	273c	30.03 N	31.15 E
Al-Qāhirah □ 4	142	30.02 N	31.17 E
Al-Qāhirah West Military Base ■	142	30.06 N	30.56 E
Al-Qaḥmah	144	18.00 N	41.41 E
Al-Qā'im	128	34.21 N	41.07 E
Al-Qā'īyah ▼ 4	128	26.27 N	45.35 E
Al-Qāiyāt	142	28.40 N	30.41 E
Al-Qalaj	142	30.11 N	31.21 E
Al-Qalībah	128	28.32 N	37.42 E
Al-Qalyūbīyah □ 4	142	30.18 N	31.18 E
Al-Qāmishlī	130	37.02 N	41.14 E
Al-Qanāṭir al-Khayrīyah	142	30.12 N	31.08 E
Al-Qanāyāt	142	30.37 N	31.28 E
Al-Qanṭarah	142	30.52 N	32.19 E
Al-Qaryah ash-Sharqīyah	146	30.24 N	13.36 E
Al-Qaryatayn	130	34.14 N	37.14 E
Al-Qaṣabāt	146	32.35 N	14.03 E
Al-Qaṣābī	142	31.16 N	30.41 E
Al-Qaṣr, Miṣr	140	25.42 N	28.53 E
Al-Qaṣr, Urd.	132	31.19 N	35.45 E
Al-Qaṣṣāṣīn	142	30.34 N	31.56 E
Al-Qaṭīf	128	26.33 N	50.00 E
Al-Qaṭrānah	132	31.15 N	36.03 E

Symbol	English	Deutsch	Español	Français	Português
≃	River	Fluß	Río	Rivière	Rio
≊	Canal	Kanal	Canal	Canal	Canal
⌊	Waterfall, Rapids	Wasserfall, Stromschnellen	Cascada, Rápidos	Chute d'eau, Rapides	Cascata, Rápidos
ʮ	Strait	Meeresstraße	Estrecho	Détroit	Estreito
⊂	Bay, Gulf	Bucht, Golf	Bahía, Golfo	Baie, Golfe	Baía, Golfo
⊜	Lake, Lakes	See, Seen	Lago, Lagos	Lac, Lacs	Lago, Lagos
≡	Swamp	Sumpf	Pantano	Marais	Pântano
⊓	Ice Features, Glacier	Eis- und Gletscherformen	Accidentes Glaciales	Formes glaciaires	Acidentes glaciares
▼	Other Hydrographic Features	Andere Hydrographische Objekte	Otros Elementos Hidrográficos	Autres données hydrographiques	Outros acidentes hidrográficos
✦	Submarine Features	Untermeerische Objekte	Accidentes Submarinos	Formes de relief sous-marin	Acidentes submarinos
□	Political Unit	Politische Einheit	Unidad Politica	Entité politique	Unidade política
◗	Cultural Institution	Kulturelle Institution	Institución Cultural	Institution culturelle	Instituição cultural
⊥	Historical Site	Historische Stätte	Sitio Histórico	Site historique	Sitio histórico
♠	Recreational Site	Erholungs- und Ferienort	Sitio de Recreo	Centre de loisirs	Area de Lazer
⊠	Airport	Flughafen	Aeropuerto	Aéroport	Aeroporto
■	Military Installation	Militäranlage	Instalación Militar	Installation militaire	Instalação militar
◆	Miscellaneous	Verschiedenes	Misceláneo	Divers	Diversos

Al-Qatrūn 146 24.56 N 14.38 E
Al-Qaṭṭā 142 30.13 N 30.58 E
Al-Qaṭṭāwīyah 142 30.33 N 31.40 E
Al-Qays 142 28.29 N 30.47 E
Al-Qayṣūmah 128 28.16 N 46.03 E
Al-Qir'awn 132 33.34 N 35.43 E
Al-Qiṣfah 132 32.38 N 35.52 E
Al-Quds → Yerushalayim 132 31.46 N 35.14 E
Alquízar 240p 22.48 N 82.35 W
Al-Qun'abah 132 33.08 N 35.40 E
Al-Qunayṭirah 132 33.07 N 35.49 E
Al-Qunayṭirah □[8] 132 33.00 N 35.50 E
Al-Qunfudhah 144 19.08 N 41.05 E
Al-Qurayn 142 30.37 N 31.44 E
Al-Qurayyah 132 32.32 N 36.36 E
Al-Qurnah 128 31.00 N 47.26 E
Al-Quṣaymah 132 30.40 N 34.22 E
Al-Quṣayr, Miṣr 128 26.06 N 34.17 E
Al-Quṣayr, Miṣr 142 27.27 N 30.52 E
Al-Quṣayr, Sūrīy. 130 34.31 N 36.35 E
Al-Qūṣīyah 142 27.26 N 30.49 E
Al-Quṭayfah 132 33.44 N 36.36 E
Al-Quṭaynah 140 14.52 N 32.21 E
Al-Quway'īyah 128 24.03 N 45.15 E
Al-Quwaysī 140 13.20 N 34.05 E
Alrø I 41 55.51 N 10.05 E
Alroy Downs 162 19.18 S 136.04 E
Als I 41 54.59 N 9.55 E
Alsace □[9] 58 48.30 N 7.30 E
Alsace, Ballon d' ∧ 58 47.50 N 6.51 E
Alsager 44 53.06 N 2.17 W
Alsask 184 51.23 N 109.59 W
Alsasua 34 42.54 N 2.10 W
Alsdorf 56 50.53 N 6.10 E
Alsea 202 44.22 N 123.35 W
Alsea ≃ 202 44.26 N 124.05 W
Alsek ≃ 180 59.10 N 138.10 W
Alsen 198 48.37 N 98.42 W
Alseno 64 44.54 N 9.59 E
Alsenz 56 49.43 N 7.49 E
Alsenz ≃ 56 49.49 N 7.51 E
Alsey 219 39.34 N 90.25 W
Alsfeld 56 50.45 N 9.16 E
Als Fjord c[2] 41 55.02 N 9.38 E
Alsh, Loch c 46 57.15 N 5.39 W
Al-Shallūfa Military Base ■ 142 30.03 N 32.32 E
Alsike 40 59.45 N 17.45 E
Alsina 252 33.54 S 59.23 W
Alsip 216 41.40 N 87.44 W
Alsleben 54 51.42 N 11.41 E
Alsónémedi 264c 47.19 N 19.10 E
Alstaden ✦[8] 263 51.28 N 6.50 E
Ålstäket 40 59.20 N 18.28 E
Alstätte 52 52.08 N 6.55 E
Alstead ≃ 184 55.50 N 107.26 W
Alster 40 59.24 N 13.36 E
Alster ≃ 52 53.36 N 9.59 E
Alsterbro 26 56.57 N 15.55 E
Alstern ⊜ 40 59.40 N 13.55 E
Alston 44 54.49 N 2.26 W
Alsunga 76 56.59 N 21.34 E
Alswede 52 52.20 N 8.33 E
Alt ≃ 44 53.32 N 3.03 W
Alta, Nor. 24 69.55 N 23.12 E
Älta, Sve. 40 59.16 N 18.11 E
Alta, Ca., U.S. 226 39.12 N 120.49 W
Alta, Ia., U.S. 198 42.40 N 95.17 W
Alta, Cachoeira ∟ 250 5.46 S 54.28 W
Alta, Mount ∧ 172 44.30 S 168.58 E
Altadena 228 34.11 N 118.07 W
Alta Floresta 250 9.57 S 56.06 W
Alta Gracia, Arg. 252 31.40 S 64.26 W
Altagracia, Nic. 236 11.34 N 85.35 W
Altagracia, Ven. 246 10.43 N 71.32 W
Altagracia de Orituco 246 9.52 N 66.23 W
Alta Hill 226 39.14 N 121.04 W
Al Tahoe 226 38.57 N 119.59 W
Altai ⛰ 90 48.00 N 90.00 E
Altair 222 29.34 N 96.28 W
Altaj, Mong. 86 48.18 N 89.35 E
Altaj (Jesönbulag), Mong. 90 46.20 N 96.18 E
Altaj, Ross. 86 53.27 N 91.48 E
Altaj □[3] 86 51.00 N 86.00 E
Altajskij 86 51.58 N 85.22 E
Alta Loma, Ca., U.S. 228 34.07 N 117.36 W
Alta Loma, Tx., U.S. 222 29.22 N 95.04 W
Altamaha ≃ 192 31.19 N 81.17 W
Altamira, Arg. 258 34.40 S 59.22 W
Altamira, Bra. 250 3.12 S 52.12 W
Altamira, Chile 252 25.47 S 69.51 W
Altamira, C.R. 236 10.30 N 84.23 W
Altamira, Méx. 234 22.24 N 97.55 W
Altamira, Las Cuevas de ⊥[5] 34 43.18 N 4.08 W
Altamirano, Arg. 258 35.21 S 58.09 W
Altamirano, Méx. 196 25.55 N 97.47 W
Altamont, Il., U.S. 219 39.03 N 88.44 W
Altamont, Ks., U.S. 198 37.11 N 95.17 W
Altamont, N.Y., U.S. 210 42.42 N 74.02 W
Altamont, Or., U.S. 202 42.12 N 121.44 W
Altamont, Tn., U.S. 194 35.25 N 85.43 W
Altamonte Springs 220 28.39 N 81.21 W
Altamura 68 40.50 N 16.33 E
Altamura, Isla I 232 25.00 N 108.10 W
Altan, Ross. 88 49.31 N 111.32 E
Altan, Ross. 88 49.53 N 109.04 E
Altanbulag, Mong. 88 50.19 N 106.30 E
Altanbulag, Mong. 88 47.41 N 106.22 E
Altan-Cögör 86 49.03 N 90.27 E
Altanširee 102 45.35 N 110.27 E
Altar 232 30.43 N 111.44 W
Altar ≃ 232 30.39 N 111.53 W
Altar, Desierto de ✦[2] 232 31.50 N 114.15 W
Altar de Los Sacrificios ⊥ 232 16.28 N 90.32 W
Altare 62 44.20 N 8.20 E
Altario 184 51.55 N 110.09 W
Altarnun 42 50.37 N 4.30 W
Altar of the Earth ⊍[1] 271a 39.57 N 116.24 E
Altar of the Moon ⊍[1] 271a 39.55 N 116.20 E
Altar of the Sun ⊍[1] 271a 39.54 N 116.27 E
Altar Wash V 200 32.05 N 111.19 W
Altaskij Kraj □[8] 86 52.30 N 83.00 E
Altastenberg 56 51.11 N 8.28 E
Altata, Méx. 232 24.38 N 107.55 W
Altata, Ross. 80 51.07 N 48.44 E
Alta Verapaz □[5] 236 15.40 N 90.00 W
Altavilla Irpina 68 41.00 N 14.47 E
Altavilla Milicia 70 38.02 N 13.32 E
Altavilla Silentina 68 40.32 N 15.08 E
Altaville 226 38.05 N 120.33 W
Alta Vista, Ks., U.S. 198 38.51 N 96.29 W
Altavista, Va., U.S. 192 37.06 N 79.17 W
Altay, Ross. 86 60.20 N 68.58 E
Altay, Zhg. 86 47.52 N 88.07 E
Altay → Altaj □[3] 86 51.00 N 86.00 E
Alt Buchhorst 264a 52.26 N 13.51 E
Altdöbern 54 51.39 N 14.02 E
Altdorf, Dtsch. 60 48.34 N 12.07 E
Altdorf, Schw. 58 46.53 N 8.39 E
Altdorf bei Nürnberg 60 49.23 N 11.21 E
Alte Donau ⊜ 264b 48.14 N 16.26 E
Alteelva ≃ 24 69.58 N 23.23 E
Altefähr 54 54.20 N 13.07 E
Alteglofsheim 60 48.55 N 12.12 E
Alte Grund 264a 52.28 N 13.47 E
Altena 56 51.17 N 7.40 E
Altenahr 56 50.31 N 6.59 E
Altenau 52 51.48 N 10.26 E
Altenbeken 52 51.46 N 8.56 E
Altenberg 54 50.46 N 13.45 E
Altenberge 52 52.03 N 7.27 E
Altenbruch 52 53.49 N 8.46 E
Altenbüren 56 51.23 N 8.30 E
Altenburg, Dtsch. 54 50.59 N 12.26 E
Altenburg, Öst. 61 48.38 N 15.35 E
Altenderne Oberbecker ✦[8] 263 51.35 N 7.33 E
Altendorf 263 51.29 N 7.40 E
Altendorf ✦[8] 263 51.25 N 7.06 E
Altendorf-Ulfkotte 263 51.38 N 7.00 E
Altenesch 52 53.08 N 8.37 E
Altenessen ✦[8] 263 51.29 N 7.00 E
Altenfelden 60 48.29 N 13.58 E
Altengamme ✦[8] 52 53.25 N 10.16 E
Altenhagen, Dtsch. 52 52.03 N 8.38 E
Altenhagen, Dtsch. 54 53.45 N 13.06 E
Altenhagen ✦[8] 263 51.22 N 7.28 E
Altenhof 54 52.55 N 13.43 E
Altenholz 41 54.24 N 10.07 E
Altenkirchen, Dtsch. 54 54.38 N 13.20 E
Altenkirchen (Westerwald), Dtsch. 56 50.41 N 7.38 E
Altenkrempe 54 54.08 N 10.49 E
Altenkunstadt 54 50.07 N 11.14 E
Altenmarkt an der Alz 60 48.00 N 12.32 E
Altenoythe 52 53.02 N 7.52 E
Altenpleen 54 54.21 N 12.57 E
Altenstadt an der Waldnaab 60 49.48 N 12.10 E
Altensteig 56 48.35 N 8.37 E
Altentreptow 54 53.42 N 13.14 E
Altenvoerde 263 51.18 N 7.22 E
Altenwalde 52 53.49 N 8.40 E
Altenweddingen 54 52.00 N 11.31 E
Alte Oder ≃ 54 52.52 N 14.09 E
Alter do Chão 34 39.12 N 7.40 W
Alterosa 256 21.15 S 46.08 W
Alter Rhein ≃ 263 51.35 N 6.36 E
Altes Land ✦[1] 52 53.33 N 9.38 E
Altevatnet ⊜ 24 68.32 N 19.30 E
Altfraunhofen 60 48.27 N 12.10 E
Altfriedland 54 52.38 N 14.12 E
Altglashütten 58 47.51 N 8.06 E
Alt-Glienicke ✦[8] 264a 52.25 N 13.32 E
Altgruland 263 51.27 N 7.41 E
Altha 192 30.34 N 85.07 W
Altham 262 53.47 N 2.21 W
Alt-Hartmannsdorf 264a 52.21 N 13.50 E
Althea Lake ⊜ 283 42.40 N 71.23 W
Altheim 60 48.15 N 13.13 E
Altheimer 194 34.19 N 91.50 W
Althofen 61 46.54 N 14.27 E
Altınekin 130 38.19 N 32.53 E
Altinho 250 8.29 S 36.04 W
Altınoluk 130 39.34 N 26.44 E
Altinópolis 255 21.02 S 47.23 W
Altınova 130 39.13 N 26.47 E
Altınözü 130 36.08 N 36.12 E
Altıntaş 130 39.04 N 30.07 E
Altınyaka 130 36.34 N 30.21 E
Altiplano ⛰[1] 248 18.00 S 68.00 W
Alt Käbelich 54 53.29 N 13.29 E
Altkirch 58 47.37 N 7.15 E
Altlandsberg 54 52.33 N 13.43 E
Altlangerwisch 264a 52.19 N 13.04 E
Altlewin 54 52.42 N 14.16 E
Altlüdersdorf 54 53.02 N 13.11 E
Altlünen 52 51.38 N 7.31 E
Altmannsdorf ✦[8] 264b 48.10 N 16.20 E
Altmannstein 60 48.54 N 11.39 E
Altmar 212 43.31 N 76.00 W
Altmark □[9] 54 52.40 N 11.20 E
Altmittweida 54 50.58 N 12.57 E
Altmühl ≃ 60 48.54 N 11.54 E
Altmünster 64 47.54 N 13.45 E
Altnaharra 46 58.16 N 4.27 W
Alto, Mi., U.S. 216 42.51 N 85.22 W
Alto, Tx., U.S. 222 31.39 N 95.04 W
Alto, Cerro ∧, Méx. 234 20.50 N 100.22 W
Alto, Cerro ∧, Ca., U.S. 226 35.25 N 120.43 W
Alto Anapu ≃ 250 2.15 S 51.27 W
Alto Araguaia 255 17.19 S 53.12 W
Alto Cauale 152 7.34 S 16.16 E
Alto Cedro 240p 20.31 N 75.58 W
Alto Chicapa 152 10.53 S 19.14 E
Alto Coité 255 15.47 S 54.20 W
Alto Cuito 152 13.27 S 18.49 E
Alto da Moóca ✦[8] 287b 23.34 S 46.35 W
Alto da Serra 256 22.53 S 44.14 W
Alto de las Vizcachas, Cerro ∧ 286e 33.25 S 70.26 W
Alto del Carmen 252 28.46 S 70.30 W
Alto de Ña Paula 286c 10.24 N 66.48 W
Alto do Rio Doce 255 21.02 S 43.25 W
Altofonte 70 38.03 N 13.18 E
Alto Garças 255 16.56 S 53.32 W
Alto Ligonha 154 15.30 S 38.20 E
Alto Longá 250 5.15 S 42.12 W
Alto Lucero 234 19.37 N 96.43 W
Alto Molócuè 154 15.38 S 37.42 E
Altomonte 68 39.42 N 16.08 E
Altomünster 60 48.23 N 11.15 E
Alton, On., Can. 212 43.52 N 80.04 W
Alton, Eng., U.K. 42 51.09 N 0.59 W
Alton, Il., U.S. 219 38.53 N 90.11 W
Alton, Ia., U.S. 198 42.59 N 96.00 W
Alton, Ks., U.S. 198 39.28 N 98.56 W
Alton, Ky., U.S. 218 38.04 N 84.55 W
Alton, Mo., U.S. 194 36.41 N 91.23 W
Alton, N.H., U.S. 188 43.27 N 71.13 W
Alton, N.Y., U.S. 210 43.13 N 76.59 W
Alton, R.I., U.S. 207 41.26 N 71.43 W
Altona, Austl. 162 27.34 S 120.00 E
Altona, Austl. 169 37.52 S 144.50 E
Altona, Mb., Can. 184 49.06 N 97.33 W
Altona, In., U.S. 216 41.21 N 85.09 W
Altona ✦[8] 52 53.32 N 9.56 E
Altona Bay c 274b 37.53 S 144.51 E
Altona North 274b 37.50 S 144.51 E
Altona Sports Park ♦ 274b 37.52 S 144.52 E
Altoona, Al., U.S. 194 34.01 N 86.19 W
Altoona, Fl., U.S. 220 28.57 N 81.38 W
Altoona, Ia., U.S. 190 41.39 N 93.28 W
Altoona, Ks., U.S. 198 37.31 N 95.39 W
Altoona, Pa., U.S. 214 40.31 N 78.23 W
Altoona, Wa., U.S. 224 46.16 N 123.39 W
Altoona, Wi., U.S. 190 44.48 N 91.26 W
Alto Pacajá ≃ 250 3.07 S 50.20 W
Alto Paraguai 248 14.30 S 56.31 W
Alto Paraguay □[5] 248 21.00 S 58.45 W
Alto Paraíso de Goiás 255 14.07 S 47.31 W
Alto Paraná □[5] 252 25.00 S 54.50 W
Alto Parnaíba 250 9.06 S 45.57 W
Alto Purús ≃ 248 9.34 S 70.36 W
Alto Río Mayo 254 45.35 S 71.06 W
Alto Río Senguer 254 45.02 S 70.50 W
Altos 250 5.03 S 42.28 W
Alto Santo 250 5.31 S 38.15 W
Alto Sucuriú 255 19.19 S 52.47 W
Altotonga 234 19.46 N 97.14 W
Altötting 60 48.13 N 12.40 E
Alto Volta → Burkina Faso □[1] 150 13.00 N 1.30 W
Alto Yurua ≃ 248 9.24 S 72.43 W
Altrincham 44 53.24 N 2.21 W
Alt Rüdersdorf 264a 52.28 N 13.49 E
Altruppin 54 52.56 N 12.50 E
Altshausen 58 47.56 N 9.32 E
Alt Stahnsdorf 264a 52.17 N 13.53 E
Altstätten 58 47.23 N 9.33 E
Alt Töplitz 264a 52.26 N 12.55 E
Altuchovo 76 52.40 N 34.20 E
Āltūn Kūprī 128 35.45 N 44.09 E
Altun Shan ⛰ 90 38.00 N 88.00 E
Alturas 204 41.29 N 120.32 W
Altus, Ar., U.S. 194 35.26 N 93.45 W
Altus, Ok., U.S. 196 34.38 N 99.20 W
Altus, Lake ⊜[1] 196 34.56 N 99.18 W
Altus Air Force Base ■ 196 34.40 N 99.16 W
Altusried 58 47.48 N 10.13 E
Altyagač 84 40.50 N 48.54 E
Altyaryk 85 40.23 N 71.30 E
Altykarasu 86 49.12 N 55.52 E
Altynaj 86 57.04 N 62.00 E
Altynasar ⊥ 86 45.10 N 63.07 E
Altynkul' 85 40.48 N 72.10 E
Altynovka 78 51.27 N 33.10 E
Altyntau 86 44.08 N 68.03 E
Altyn-Topkan 85 40.38 N 69.35 E
Alu I 175e 7.02 S 155.47 E
Al-Ubayyiḍ 140 13.11 N 30.13 E
Alubijid 116 8.35 N 124.29 E
Alucra 130 40.20 N 38.46 E
Al-'Udaysāt 140 25.35 N 32.29 E
Al-Uḍayyah 140 12.03 N 28.17 E
Aluk 140 8.26 N 27.27 E
Alūksne 76 57.25 N 27.03 E
Al-'Ulā 128 26.37 N 37.52 E
Alum Bank 214 40.14 N 78.34 W
Alum Creek ≃ 218 39.53 N 82.54 W
Alum Creek Lake ⊜[1] 214 40.15 N 82.58 W
Aluminé 254 39.13 S 70.57 W
Aluminé ≃ 254 39.50 S 70.53 W
Aluminé, Lago ⊜ 252 38.55 S 71.09 W
Alum Rock 226 37.21 N 121.49 W
Alum Rock Park ♦ 282 37.24 N 121.49 W
Alunda 40 60.04 N 18.05 E
Alunitdag 84 40.32 N 46.03 E
Alupka 78 44.26 N 34.03 E
Al-'Uqaylah 146 30.16 N 19.12 E
Al-'Uqayr 128 25.39 N 50.12 E
Al-Uqṣur (Luxor) 140 25.41 N 32.39 E
Al-'Urayq ⊥[8] 128 29.10 N 39.15 E
Al-'Urayq ✦[1] 128 24.47 N 42.55 E
Al-Urdun → Jordan □[1] 128 31.00 N 36.00 E
Al-Urdunn → Jordan ≃ 132 31.46 N 35.33 E
Alušta 78 44.42 N 34.24 E
Al-'Uṭayshān ⍑[4] 140 16.25 N 34.30 E
Al-'Uwaynāt 146 25.46 N 10.34 E
Al-'Uwaynidhīyah I 128 26.37 N 36.05 E
Al-'Uyaynah 128 24.54 N 46.23 E
Alva, Scot., U.K. 46 56.09 N 3.48 W
Alva, Fl., U.S. 220 26.42 N 81.36 W
Alva, Ok., U.S. 196 36.48 N 98.39 W
Alva ≃ 34 40.18 N 8.15 W
Alvada 214 41.03 N 83.24 W
Alvaiázere 34 39.49 N 8.23 W
Alvaneu-Bad 58 46.40 N 9.39 E
Älvängen 26 57.58 N 12.07 E
Alvanley 262 53.16 N 2.45 W
Alvarado, Méx. 234 18.46 N 95.46 W
Alvarado, Tx., U.S. 222 32.24 N 97.12 W
Alvarado, Lake ⊜[1] 222 32.23 N 97.15 W
Alvarães 246 3.12 S 64.50 W
Álvarez Jonte 258 35.19 S 57.28 W
Alvarinhos 266c 38.54 N 9.22 W
Álvaro Obregón 234 19.50 N 101.05 W
Alvaro Obregón ✦[8] 286a 19.21 N 99.12 W
Álvaro Obregón, Presa ⊜[1] 232 27.55 N 109.52 W
Alvastra ⊥ 26 58.18 N 14.39 E
Alvdal 26 62.07 N 10.39 E
Älvdalen 26 61.14 N 14.02 E
Alvear 252 29.06 S 56.33 W
Alvechurch 42 52.21 N 1.57 W
Alverca 34 38.54 N 9.02 W
Alverda 214 40.38 N 78.52 W
Alvernia, Mount ∧[2] 238 24.15 N 75.24 W
Alverton 214 40.08 N 79.35 W
Alves 46 57.38 N 3.27 W
Alvesta 26 56.54 N 14.33 E
Alveston 42 51.36 N 2.32 W
Alviano, Lago di ⊜[1] 66 42.36 N 12.15 E
Ålvik, Nor. 26 60.26 N 6.26 E
Alvik, Sve. 26 62.25 N 17.24 E
Alvin, Il., U.S. 216 40.19 N 87.37 W
Alvin, Tx., U.S. 222 29.25 N 95.14 W
Alvinópolis 255 20.06 S 43.03 W
Alvinston 214 42.49 N 81.52 W
Alviso ✦[8] 282 37.26 N 121.58 W
Alviso Slough ≃ 282 37.27 N 122.02 W
Alvito, It. 66 41.41 N 13.45 E
Alvito, Port. 34 38.15 N 7.59 W
Älvkarleby 40 60.34 N 17.27 E
Älvkarleö bruk 40 60.32 N 17.24 E
Alvord 196 33.22 N 97.42 W
Alvord Desert ✦[2] 202 42.30 N 118.25 W
Alvord Lake ⊜ 202 42.23 N 118.36 W
Alvordton 216 41.40 N 84.26 W
Alvra, Pass d')(58 46.35 N 9.50 E
Älvros 26 62.03 N 14.39 E
Älvsborgs Län □[6] 26 58.00 N 12.30 E
Älvsbyn 24 65.39 N 20.59 E
Älvsnabben ⊥ 40 58.59 N 18.10 E
Al-Wafā'īyah 142 30.46 N 30.36 E
Al-Wajh 128 26.15 N 36.26 E
Al-Wakrah 128 25.10 N 51.36 E
Al-Walīdīyah 142 27.12 N 31.10 E
Alwar 124 27.34 N 76.36 E
Alwar Hills ⛰[2] 124 27.20 N 76.15 E
Al-Wāṣifīyah 142 30.35 N 32.10 E
Al-Wāsiṭah 142 29.20 N 31.12 E
Alwaye 122 10.07 N 76.21 E
Al-Wazīrīyah 142 31.11 N 30.57 E
Al-Wazz 140 15.01 N 30.10 E
Alwen ≃ 44 52.58 N 3.24 W
Al-Widy 142 29.31 N 31.16 E
Alxa Zuoqi 102 38.50 N 105.32 E
Al-Yamāmah → As-Sulaymānīyah 128 24.09 N 47.19 E
Al-Yaman → Yemen □[1] 144 15.00 N 47.00 E
Al Yāmūn 132 32.29 N 35.14 E
Alygdžer 88 53.38 N 98.16 E
Alyn and Deeside □[8] 262 53.16 N 3.02 W
Alypsatar 86 48.03 N 80.21 E
Alyth 46 56.37 N 3.13 W
Alytus 76 54.24 N 24.03 E
Alz ≃ 60 48.16 N 12.49 E
Alzamaj 88 55.33 N 98.39 E
Alzano Lombardo 62 45.44 N 9.43 E
Al-Zarqa 142 31.13 N 31.38 E
Alzenau 56 50.05 N 9.04 E
Alzette ≃ 56 49.52 N 6.07 E
Alzey 56 49.45 N 8.07 E
Alzira (Alcira) 34 39.09 N 0.26 W
Amab, Khawr V 140 17.08 N 34.51 E
Amacayacu, Parque Nacional ♦ 246 3.45 S 70.10 W
Amacuro ≃ 246 8.32 N 60.28 W
Amacuzac ≃ 234 17.53 N 99.12 W
Amadeus, Lake ⊜ 162 24.50 S 130.45 E
Āmādi, Bngl. 126 22.28 N 89.19 E
Amadi, Zaïre 154 3.35 N 26.47 E
Amadjuak Lake ⊜ 176 65.00 N 71.00 W
Amador □[6] 226 38.21 N 120.46 W
Amadora 266c 38.45 N 9.14 W
Amador City 226 38.25 N 120.56 W
Amador Valley V 282 37.41 N 121.51 W
Amagansett 207 40.58 N 72.08 W
Amagasaki 96 34.43 N 135.25 E
Amagase 96 33.15 N 131.02 E
Amager I 41 55.37 N 12.37 E
Amagi 96 33.25 N 130.39 E
Amagi-san ∧ 94 34.51 N 139.00 E
Amagi-yugashima 94 34.53 N 138.56 E
Amagoi-dake ∧ 94 35.01 N 136.23 E
Amagunze 150 6.20 N 7.40 E
Amahai 164 3.20 S 128.55 E
Amaichá del Valle 252 26.36 S 65.55 W
Amaimon 164 5.10 S 145.25 E
Amajac ≃ 234 21.15 N 98.46 W
Amaka ≃ 236 14.14 N 85.07 W
Ama Keng 271c 1.24 N 103.42 E
Amak Island I 180 55.25 N 163.07 W
Amakusa-nada ⍑[2] 92 32.35 N 130.05 E
Amakusa-shotō II 92 32.20 N 130.15 E
Amakuso-Shimo-shima I 92 32.20 N 130.05 E
Amal, Libiyā 146 29.25 N 21.10 E
Åmål, Sve. 26 59.03 N 12.42 E
Amalāpuram 122 16.35 N 82.01 E
Amalat ≃ 88 54.49 N 115.12 E
Amalfi, Col. 246 6.55 N 75.04 W
Amalfi, It. 68 40.38 N 14.36 E
Amalia 158 27.16 S 25.03 E
Amaliás 38 37.49 N 21.23 E
Amalner 120 21.03 N 75.04 E
Amamaki-zan ∧ 94 36.25 N 140.09 E
Amambaí 255 23.05 S 55.13 W
Amambaí ≃ 255 23.22 S 53.56 W
Amambay □[5] 252 23.00 S 56.00 W
Amami-Ō-shima I 93b 28.15 N 129.20 E
Amami-shotō II 93b 28.16 N 129.21 E
Amamula 154 0.18 S 27.50 E
Amana 190 41.48 N 91.52 W
Amanã ≃, Bra. 250 4.25 S 57.34 W
Amana ≃, Ven. 238 9.45 N 62.39 W
Amanã, Lago ⊜ 246 2.35 S 64.40 W
Amanab 164 3.35 S 141.13 E
Amanave 174u 14.19 S 170.49 W
Amance 58 47.48 N 6.04 E
Amancey 58 47.02 N 6.05 E
Amancio 240p 20.49 N 77.35 W
Amanda 188 39.38 N 82.44 W
Amanda Park 224 47.28 N 123.54 W
Amandola 66 42.59 N 13.21 E
Amānganj 124 24.26 N 80.02 E
Amangel'dy, Kaz. 85 43.43 N 71.07 E
Amangel'dy, Kaz. 86 50.10 N 65.13 E
Amangel'dy, Kaz. 86 49.52 N 59.00 E
Åmänningen ⊜ 40 59.57 N 15.56 E
Amano 270 34.26 N 135.33 E
Amanotkel' 86 46.07 N 61.34 E
Amantea 68 39.08 N 16.05 E
Amantogaj 86 50.22 N 65.33 E
Amanu I[1] 14 17.48 S 140.46 W
Amanzimtofi 158 30.03 S 30.53 E
Amapá 250 2.03 N 50.48 W
Amapá □[3] 250 1.00 N 52.00 W
Amapa ≃ 234 18.18 N 96.19 W
Amapala 236 13.17 N 87.40 W
Amapala, Punta de > 236 13.10 N 87.54 W
Amapari ≃ 250 0.43 N 51.32 W
Amaraji 250 8.24 S 35.27 W
Amaral 287a 22.42 S 43.29 W
Amaramba, Lago ⊜ 154 14.30 S 35.55 E
Amarante 250 6.14 S 42.50 W
Amarante do Maranhão 250 5.36 S 46.45 W
Amaranth 184 50.36 N 98.43 W
Amarapura 110 21.54 N 96.03 E
Amărăștii-de-Jos 38 43.59 N 24.10 E
'Amārat Abū Sinn 140 15.21 N 35.45 E
Amarāvati ≃ 122 10.51 N 78.11 E
Amarda 126 21.47 N 87.08 E
Amareleja 34 38.12 N 7.14 W
Amares 34 41.38 N 8.21 W
Amargosa 255 13.02 S 39.36 W
Amargosa ≃ 204 36.13 N 116.48 W
Amargosa Range ⛰ 204 36.15 N 116.45 W
Amarillo 196 35.13 N 101.49 W
Amarillo, Mar → Yellow Sea ⍑[2] 90 36.00 N 123.00 E
'Amar Jadīd 140 14.28 N 25.14 E
Amarkantak 124 22.40 N 81.45 E
Amarnāth 122 19.11 N 73.10 E
Amarnāth Cave ⊥[5] 123 34.13 N 75.31 E
Amaro, Monte ∧ 66 42.05 N 14.05 E
Amaroúsion 267c 38.03 N 23.49 E
Amarpātan 124 24.19 N 80.59 E
Amarube-saki > 96 35.40 N 134.32 E
Amarume 92 38.50 N 139.55 E
Amarwāra 124 22.18 N 79.10 E
Amasa 190 46.13 N 88.26 W
Amaseno ≃ 66 41.34 N 13.13 E
Amasija 84 40.58 N 43.46 E
Amasra 130 41.45 N 32.24 E
Amasya 130 40.39 N 35.51 E
Amasya □[4] 130 40.45 N 35.30 E
Amataurá 246 3.29 S 68.06 W
Amatignak Island I 181a 51.15 N 179.08 W
Amatikulu 158 29.06 S 31.27 E
Amatique, Bahía de c 236 15.55 N 88.45 W
Amatitán 234 20.50 N 103.43 W
Amatitlán 236 14.29 N 90.37 W
Amatitlán, Lago de ⊜ 236 14.27 N 90.34 W
Amatlán de Cañas 234 20.52 N 104.27 W
Amatlán de los Reyes 234 18.50 N 96.55 W
Amatrice 66 42.38 N 13.17 E
Amatsu-kominato 94 35.07 N 140.10 E
Amau 164 10.02 S 148.34 E
Amausi 124 26.46 N 80.51 E
Amawalk 210 41.17 N 73.46 W
Amay 56 50.33 N 5.19 E
Ama-zaki > 94 37.08 N 136.40 E
Amazar 89 53.54 N 120.53 E
Amazon (Solimões) (Amazonas) ≃ 242 0.10 S 49.00 W
Amazonas □[3] 242 5.00 S 63.00 W
Amazonas □[5], Col. 246 1.00 S 72.00 W
Amazonas □[5], Perú 248 5.30 S 78.00 W
Amazonas □[8] 246 3.30 N 66.00 W
Amazonas → Amazon ≃ 242 0.10 S 49.00 W
Amazônia, Parque Nacional da ♦ 250 4.30 S 56.30 W
Amb 123 34.19 N 72.51 E
Ambāh 124 26.43 N 78.14 E
Ambahikily 157b 21.36 S 43.41 E
Ambahita 157b 24.01 S 45.16 E
Ambaí 287a 22.43 S 43.28 W
Ambājogāi 122 18.44 N 76.23 E
Ambakaka 157b 24.10 S 46.17 E
Ambāla 124 30.21 N 76.50 E
Ambāla Airport ⊠ 123 30.22 N 76.50 E
Ambalabe 157b 18.24 S 49.10 E
Ambalafany 157b 22.32 S 47.36 E
Ambalangoda 122 6.14 N 80.03 E
Ambalanjanakomby 157b 16.42 S 47.05 E
Ambalavao 157b 21.50 S 46.56 E
Ambam 152 2.23 N 11.17 E
Amba Maryam 144 11.26 N 39.17 E
Ambanja 157b 13.41 S 48.27 E
Ambar 248 10.44 S 77.16 W
Ambararata 157b 15.03 S 48.33 E
Ambarawa 115a 7.15 S 110.24 E
Ambarčik, Ross. 74 69.39 N 162.20 E
Ambarčik, Ross. 88 55.09 N 95.46 E
Ambargasta, Salinas de ≃ 252 29.15 S 64.30 W
Ambarijeby 157b 14.56 S 47.41 E
Ambarnyj 24 65.56 N 33.43 E
Ambaro, Baie d' c 157b 13.23 S 48.38 E
Ambāsamudram 122 8.42 N 77.28 E
Ambassador Bridge ✦[5] 281 42.20 N 83.05 W
Ambato, Ec. 246 1.15 S 78.37 W
Ambato, Madag. 157b 13.24 S 48.29 E
Ambato Boeny 157b 16.28 S 46.43 E
Ambatofinandrahana 157b 20.33 S 46.48 E
Ambatolampy 157b 19.23 S 47.25 E
Ambatomainty 157b 17.41 S 45.40 E
Ambatomanoina 157b 18.18 S 47.37 E
Ambatondrazaka 157b 17.50 S 48.25 E
Ambatosoratra 157b 17.34 S 48.32 E
Ambeláki 267c 37.57 N 23.32 E
Ambelau, Pulau I 164 3.51 S 127.12 E
Ámbelos, Ákra > 38 39.56 N 23.55 E
Ambenja 157b 15.17 S 46.58 E
Amber ≃ 44 53.04 N 1.29 W
Amberes → Antwerpen 50 51.13 N 4.25 E
Amberg, Dtsch. 60 49.27 N 11.52 E
Amberg, Wi., U.S. 190 45.30 N 87.59 W
Ambergris Cay I 232 18.03 N 87.56 W
Ambérieu-en-Bugey 58 45.57 N 5.21 E
Amberley 172 43.10 S 172.44 E
Amberley Royal Australian Air Force Base ■ 171a 27.37 S 152.41 E

ENGLISH

Name	Page	Lat.°′	Long.°′
Amberson	214	40.10 N	77.41 W
Ambert	62	45.33 N	3.45 E
Ambevongo	157b	15.27 S	47.27 E
Ambia	216	40.29 N	87.31 W
Ambidédi	150	14.35 N	11.47 W
Ambikānagar	126	22.57 N	86.46 E
Ambikāpur	124	23.07 N	83.12 E
Ambil	116	13.49 N	120.20 E
Ambil Island I	116	13.48 N	120.18 E
Ambilobe	157b	13.12 S	49.04 E
Ambinanindrano	157b	20.20 S	48.19 E
Ambinanitelo	157b	15.21 S	49.35 E
Ambinda	157b	16.25 S	45.52 E
Ambivy	157b	21.31 S	44.02 E
Ambjörby	26	60.30 N	13.10 E
Ambla	76	59.11 N	25.51 E
Amble	44	55.20 N	1.34 W
Ambler, Ak., U.S.	180	67.05 N	157.52 W
Ambler, Pa., U.S.	208	40.09 N	75.13 W
Ambleside	44	54.26 N	2.58 W
Ambleteuse	50	50.49 N	1.36 E
Amblève ≃	56	50.28 N	5.36 E
Ambo	248	10.07 S	76.10 W
Amboahangy	157b	24.15 S	46.22 E
Amboasary, Madag.	157b	18.26 S	48.16 E
Amboasary, Madag.	157b	25.02 S	46.23 E
Ambodifototra	157b	16.59 S	49.52 E
Ambodilazana	157b	18.06 S	49.10 E
Ambodiriana	157b	17.55 S	49.18 E
Ambohibary	157b	19.20 S	46.17 E
Ambohidratrimo	157b	18.50 S	47.26 E
Ambohidray	157b	18.36 S	48.18 E
Ambohimahamasina	157b	21.56 S	47.11 E
Ambohimahasoa	157b	21.07 S	47.13 E
Ambohimanga du Sud	157b	20.52 S	47.36 E
Ambohimitombo	157b	20.43 S	47.26 E
Amboina → Ambon	164	3.43 S	128.12 E
Amboise	50	47.25 N	0.59 E
Amboíva	152	11.32 S	14.44 E
Ambon	164	3.43 S	128.12 E
Ambon, Pulau I	164	3.40 S	128.10 E
Ambondro	157b	25.13 S	45.44 E
Ambonnay	50	49.04 N	4.10 E
Amboseli, Lake ⊜	154	2.37 S	37.08 E
Amboseli National Park ♦	154	2.30 S	37.15 E
Amboshe	272c	19.09 N	73.08 E
Ambositra	157b	20.31 S	47.15 E
Ambovombe	157b	25.11 S	46.05 E
Amboy, Il., U.S.	190	41.42 N	89.19 W
Amboy, In., U.S.	216	40.36 N	85.55 W
Amboy, Mn., U.S.	190	43.53 N	94.09 W
Amboy, Wa., U.S.	224	45.54 N	122.26 W
Ambre, Cap d' >	157b	11.57 S	49.17 E
Ambre, Montagne d' ∧	157b	12.30 S	49.10 E
Ambridge	214	40.35 N	80.13 W
Ambridge Heights	214	40.36 N	80.13 W
Ambridge Reservoir ⊜[1]	214	40.34 N	80.21 W
Ambrières	32	48.24 N	0.38 W
Ambriz	152	7.50 S	13.06 E
Ambrolauri	84	42.31 N	43.09 E
Ambronay	58	46.00 N	5.21 E
Ambrose	198	48.57 N	103.28 W
Ambrose Brook ≃	276	40.33 N	74.32 W
Ambrose Channel ʊ	276	40.32 N	74.02 W
Ambrosia Lake	200	35.25 N	107.49 W
Ambrym □[8]	175f	16.15 S	168.12 E
Ambrym I	175f	16.15 S	168.10 E
Ambuklao Dam ✦[6]	116	16.28 N	120.45 E
Ambulong Island I	116	12.12 N	121.01 E
Ambulu	115a	8.21 S	113.36 E
Ambuntentimur	115a	6.54 S	113.45 E
Ambunti	164	4.14 S	142.50 E
Āmbūr	122	12.47 N	78.42 E
Amburambur	115b	8.15 S	116.18 E
Amburayan Nabunga ≃	116	16.55 N	120.27 E
Amby	56	50.53 N	5.44 E
Amchitka Island I	181a	51.30 N	179.00 E
Amchitka Pass ʊ	181a	51.30 N	179.30 W
'Amd	144	15.18 N	48.00 E
Am-Dam	146	12.46 N	20.29 E
Āmdānga	272b	22.49 N	88.31 E
Amded, Oued V	148	22.09 N	3.15 E
Amden	58	47.09 N	9.11 E
Amderma	72	69.45 N	61.39 E
Amdo	120	32.18 N	91.04 E
Ameagle	188	37.56 N	81.25 W
Ameca	234	20.33 N	104.02 W
Ameca ≃	234	20.41 N	105.18 W
Amecameca [de Juárez]	234	19.07 N	98.46 W
Ameghino	252	34.50 S	62.27 W
Ameglia	64	44.04 N	9.57 E
Ameisberg ∧	60	48.33 N	13.50 E
Ameixoeira ✦[8]	266c	38.47 N	9.10 W
Ameland I	52	53.25 N	5.45 E
Amele	164	5.16 S	145.42 E
Amelia, It.	66	42.33 N	12.25 E
Amelia, Oh., U.S.	218	39.01 N	84.13 W
Amelia, Passo d')(	66	42.36 N	12.32 E
Amelia Court House	192	37.20 N	77.58 W
Amelia Earhart Peak ∧	226	37.47 N	119.17 W
Amelia Island I	192	30.37 N	81.27 W
Amelinghausen	52	53.08 N	10.13 E
Amelsbüren	52	51.53 N	7.37 E
Amendolara	68	39.57 N	16.35 E
Ameng	102	23.50 N	104.32 E
Amenia	210	41.50 N	73.33 W
Amenucourt	261	49.06 N	1.39 E
Āmer	120	26.59 N	75.52 E
Amerang	60	48.00 N	12.18 E
Amerevo	265b	55.55 N	38.03 E
America	52	51.26 N	5.59 E
América del Norte → North America ⊥[1]	16	45.00 N	100.00 W
América del Sur → South America ⊥[1]	18	15.00 S	60.00 W
American ≃, Ca., U.S.	226	38.36 N	121.30 W
American ≃, Wa., U.S.	224	46.58 N	121.08 W
American, Middle Fork ≃	226	38.55 N	121.02 W
American, North Fork ≃	226	38.43 N	121.09 W
American, South Fork ≃	226	38.43 N	121.09 W
Americana	255	22.45 S	47.20 W
American Canyon	226	38.10 N	122.15 W
American Cemetery and Memorial ✦	269f	14.33 N	121.03 E
American Falls	202	42.47 N	112.51 W
American Falls ∟	284a	43.05 N	79.04 W
American Falls Reservoir ⊜[1]	202	42.45 N	112.45 W
American Fork	200	40.22 N	111.47 W
American Highland ⛰[1]	9	72.30 S	78.00 E
American Lake ⊜	224	47.07 N	122.34 W
American Museum of Natural History ⊍	276	40.47 N	73.59 W
Americano	250	1.19 S	48.04 W
American River	168b	35.47 S	137.47 E
American Samoa □[2], Oc.	14	14.20 S	170.00 W
American Samoa □[2], Oc.	175a	14.20 S	170.00 W
American University ⊍[2]	284c	38.56 N	77.05 W
Américas, Hipódromo de las ♦	286a	19.26 N	99.13 W
Americus, Ga., U.S.	192	32.04 N	84.13 W
Americus, Ks., U.S.	198	38.30 N	96.15 W

DEUTSCH

Name	Seite	Breite°′	Länge°′ E = Ost
Amerikanisches Hochland → American Highland ⛰[1]	9	72.30 S	78.00 E
Ameringkogel ∧	61	47.04 N	14.48 E
Amérique du Nord → North America ⊥[1]	16	45.00 N	100.00 W
Amern	56	51.14 N	6.15 E
Amerongen	52	52.00 N	5.27 E
Amersfoort, Ned.	52	52.09 N	5.24 E
Amersfoort, S. Afr.	158	27.01 S	29.51 E
Amersham	42	51.40 N	0.38 W
Amery, Austl.	162	31.09 S	117.05 E
Amery, Mb., Can.	184	56.34 N	94.03 W
Amery, Wi., U.S.	190	45.18 N	92.21 W
Amery Ice Shelf ⊓	9	69.30 S	72.00 E
Ames, Ia., U.S.	190	42.02 N	93.37 W
Ames, N.Y., U.S.	210	42.50 N	74.36 W
Ames, Tx., U.S.	222	30.03 N	94.46 W
Amesbury, Eng., U.K.	42	51.10 N	1.45 W
Amesbury, Ma., U.S.	207	42.51 N	70.55 W
Ames Long Pond ⊜	283	42.05 N	71.07 W
Ames Nowell State Park ♦	283	42.07 N	70.59 W
Ames Pond ⊜	283	42.38 N	71.13 W
Ames Research Center ⊍[3]	282	37.25 N	122.04 W
Amet Sound ʊ	186	45.47 N	63.13 W
Amfíklia	38	38.38 N	22.35 E
Amfilokhía	38	38.51 N	21.10 E
Ámfissa	38	38.31 N	22.24 E
Amfreville-la-Campagne	50	49.13 N	0.57 E
Amfreville-les-Champs	50	49.19 N	1.19 E
Amga	74	60.53 N	132.00 E
Amga ≃	74	62.38 N	134.32 E
Am Géréda	146	12.52 N	21.10 E
Amguema	180	66.58 N	179.16 W
Amguema ≃	180	68.10 N	177.40 W
Amguid	148	26.26 N	5.22 E
Amgun' ≃	89	52.56 N	139.40 E
Amherst, N.S., Can.	186	45.49 N	64.14 W
Amherst, Ma., U.S.	207	42.22 N	72.31 W
Amherst, N.H., U.S.	207	42.51 N	71.37 W
Amherst, N.Y., U.S.	210	42.58 N	78.48 W
Amherst, Oh., U.S.	214	41.23 N	82.13 W
Amherst, Tx., U.S.	196	34.01 N	102.25 W
Amherst, Va., U.S.	192	37.35 N	79.03 W
Amherst, Wi., U.S.	190	44.27 N	89.17 W
Amherst, Mount ∧	162	18.11 S	126.59 E
Amherstburg	214	42.06 N	83.06 W
Amherstdale	188	37.47 N	81.48 W
Amherst Island I	212	44.08 N	76.45 W
Amherstview	212	44.13 N	76.38 W
Ami	94	36.02 N	140.14 E
Amianan Island I	108	21.07 N	121.57 E
Amiata, Monte ∧	66	42.53 N	11.37 E
Amicalola Falls State Park ♦	192	34.33 N	84.15 W
Amidon	198	46.28 N	103.19 W
Amiens, Austl.	166	28.35 S	151.49 E
Amiens, Fr.	50	49.54 N	2.18 E
Amili, India	120	28.26 N	95.52 E
Amili, Zhg.	120	28.25 N	95.52 E
Amīn as-Samālūsī, Bi'r ⍑[4]	142	29.52 N	30.02 E
Amīndīvi Islands II	122	11.23 N	72.23 E
Aminga	252	28.50 S	66.54 W
Amini Island I	122	11.07 N	72.44 E
Amino, Ityo.	144	4.31 N	41.49 E
Amino, Nihon	96	35.41 N	135.02 E
Aminuis	156	23.43 S	19.21 E
Amīrābād	128	36.04 N	54.10 E
Amīrābād ✦[8]	267d	35.43 N	51.23 E
Amirante Islands II	138	6.00 S	53.10 E
Amirauté, Îles de l' → Admiralty Islands II	164	2.10 S	147.00 E
Amisk	182	52.33 N	111.04 W
Amisk Lake ⊜	184	54.35 N	102.13 W
Amistad, Parque Internacional de la ♦	236	9.25 N	83.10 W
Amistad, Presa de la (Amistad Reservoir) ⊜[1]	196	29.34 N	101.15 W
Amistad National Recreation Area ♦	196	29.32 N	101.12 W
Amistad Reservoir (Presa de la Amistad) ⊜[1]	196	29.34 N	101.15 W
Amite	194	30.43 N	90.30 W
Amite ≃	194	30.12 N	90.35 W
Amite, East Fork ≃	194	30.58 N	90.51 W
Amiterno ⊥	66	42.21 N	13.42 E
Amitori	175d	24.18 N	123.41 E
Amity, Ar., U.S.	194	34.15 N	93.27 W
Amity, Oh., U.S.	214	40.03 N	83.17 W
Amity, Or., U.S.	224	45.06 N	123.12 W
Amity Point >	171a	27.24 S	153.27 E
Amityville	276	40.40 N	73.25 W
Amixtlán	234	20.03 N	97.48 W
Amizmiz	148	31.14 N	8.14 W
Āmjhori ∧	126	21.51 N	86.19 E
Āmjhupi	126	23.45 N	88.42 E
Āmla, Bngl.	126	23.54 N	88.56 E
Āmla, India	124	21.56 N	78.07 E
Āmlāgora	126	22.50 N	87.20 E
Amlekhgañj	124	27.17 N	84.59 E
Åmli	26	58.47 N	8.30 E
Amlia Island I	180	52.06 N	173.30 W
Amloh	124	30.37 N	76.14 E
Am Loubia	146	13.39 N	20.08 E
Amlwch	44	53.25 N	4.20 W
'Amm-Adām	140	16.22 N	36.06 E
Ammagan	85	38.56 N	67.15 E
'Ammān	132	31.57 N	35.56 E
'Ammān □[8]	132	31.45 N	36.15 E
Ammanford	42	51.48 N	3.59 W
Ämmänsaari	26	64.53 N	28.55 E
Ammansville	222	29.47 N	96.51 W
'Ammār, Tall ∧[2]	132	32.53 N	36.29 E
Ammarnäs	24	65.56 N	16.09 E
Ammaroo	162	21.45 S	135.15 E
Åmmeberg	40	58.52 N	15.00 E
Ammeloe	52	52.05 N	6.47 E
Ammendorf ✦[8]	54	51.25 N	11.59 E
Ammer ≃	64	47.57 N	11.08 E
Ammerån ≃	26	63.09 N	16.13 E
Ammerbuch	56	48.33 N	8.58 E
Ammer Gebirge ⛰	64	47.35 N	10.55 E
Ammerland ✦[1]	52	53.15 N	8.00 E
Ammerman Mountain ∧	180	68.21 N	141.03 W
Ammerschwihr	58	48.07 N	7.17 E
Ammersee ⊜	60	48.00 N	11.08 E
Ammerthal	60	49.26 N	11.45 E
Ammon	202	43.28 N	111.57 W
Ammonoosuc ≃	188	44.10 N	72.02 W
Amnān	272b	22.56 N	88.18 E
Amnat Charoen	110	15.51 N	104.38 E
Amnay ≃	116	12.58 N	120.46 E
Amne Machin Shan → A'nyêmaqên Shan ⛰	102	34.30 N	100.00 E
Amnicon ≃	190	46.41 N	91.52 W
Amnok-kang (Yalu) ≃	98	39.55 N	124.22 E
Amo ≃, Asia	124	26.16 N	89.36 E
Amo ≃, Zhg.	102	22.58 N	101.44 E
Āmol	128	36.23 N	52.20 E
Amolar	248	18.01 S	57.30 W
Amöneburg	56	50.48 N	8.55 E
Amorbach	56	49.39 N	9.13 E
Amorgós	38	36.50 N	25.54 E
Amorgós I	38	36.50 N	25.59 E
Amorim, Morro ∧[2]	287a	23.00 S	43.26 W
Amorinópolis	255	16.36 S	51.08 W
Amorosi	68	41.12 N	14.28 E
Amory	194	33.59 N	88.29 W

Symbols in the index entries represent the broad categories identified in the key at the right. Symbols with superior numbers (⛰[1]) identify subcategories (see complete key on page *I · 1*).

Symbole im Register stellen die rechts im Schlüssel erklärten Kategorien dar. Symbole mit hochgestellten Ziffern (⛰[1]) bezeichnen Unterteilungen einer Kategorie (vgl. vollständiger Schlüssel auf Seite *I · 1*).

Los símbolos incluídos en el texto del índice representan las grandes categorías identificadas con la clave a la derecha. Los símbolos con números en su parte superior (⛰[1]) identifican las subcategorías (véase la clave completa en la página *I · 1*).

Les symboles de l'index représentent les catégories indiquées dans la légende à droite. Les symboles suivis d'un indice (⛰[1]) représentent des sous-catégories (voir légende complète à la page *I · 1*).

Os símbolos incluídos no texto do índice representam as grandes categorias identificadas com a chave à direita. Os símbolos com números em sua parte superior (⛰[1]) identificam as subcategorias (veja-se a chave completa à página *I · 1*).

∧ Mountain	Berg	Montaña	Montagne	Montanha
⛰ Mountains	Gebirge	Montañas	Montagnes	Montanhas
)(Pass	Pass	Paso	Col	Passo
V Valley, Canyon	Tal, Cañon	Valle, Cañón	Vallée, Canyon	Vale, Canhão
≃ Plain	Ebene	Llano	Plaine	Planície
> Cape	Kap	Cabo	Cap	Cabo
I Island	Insel	Isla	Île	Ilha
II Islands	Inseln	Islas	Îles	Ilhas
⊥ Other Topographic Features	Andere Topographische Objekte	Otros Elementos Topográficos	Autres données topographiques	Outros acidentes topográficos

ESPAÑOL

Nombre	Página	Lat.°′	Long.°′ W = Oeste
Amos	190	48.35 N	78.07 W
Åmose ≏	41	55.35 N	11.18 E
Åmot, Nor.	26	59.35 N	8.00 E
Åmot, Nor.	26	59.54 N	9.54 E
Åmotfors	26	59.46 N	12.22 E
Amour, Djebel ⋏	148	34.00 N	2.15 E
Amour → Amur ≏	74	52.56 N	141.10 E
Amoy → Xiamen	100	24.28 N	118.07 E
Amozoc	234	19.02 N	98.03 W
Ampana	112	0.51 S	121.32 E
Ampanavoana	157b	15.41 S	50.22 E
Ampang	115b	8.47 S	118.00 E
Ampanihy	157b	24.42 S	44.45 E
Ampaoid, Mount ∧	116	7.57 N	125.41 E
Amparafaravola	157b	17.35 S	48.13 E
Amparihy, Madag.	157b	16.40 S	44.49 E
Amparihy, Madag.	157b	23.57 S	47.20 E
Amparo	256	22.42 S	46.45 W
Ampasibe	157b	22.56 S	46.58 E
Ampasinambo	157b	20.31 S	48.00 E
Ampasindava, Baie d' ⊂	157b	13.16 S	48.43 E
Ampasindava, Presq'île d' ≻[1]	157b	13.45 S	48.00 E
Ampato, Nevado ∧	248	15.50 S	71.52 W
Ampel	115a	7.27 S	110.32 E
Amper	150	9.20 N	9.43 E
Amper ≏	60	48.30 N	11.58 E
Ampezzo	64	46.25 N	12.48 E
Ampezzo, Valle d' V	64	46.30 N	12.10 E
Ampfing	60	48.16 N	12.25 E
Ampflwang	64	48.05 N	13.34 E
Amphion-les-Bains	58	46.23 N	6.32 E
Ampisikina	157b	12.57 S	49.49 E
Ampleforth	44	54.12 N	1.06 W
Ampollino, Lago ⊜	68	39.12 N	16.37 E
Ampombiantambo	157b	12.42 S	48.57 E
Amposta	34	40.43 N	0.35 E
Ampotaka	157b	25.03 S	44.41 E
Ampoza	157b	22.20 S	44.44 E
Ampthill	42	52.02 N	0.30 W
Ampuis	62	45.29 N	4.49 E
Ampus	62	43.36 N	6.23 E
Amqui	186	48.28 N	67.26 W
Āmr, Jabal al- ⋏	132	30.45 N	34.20 E
Amraoti → Amrāvati	120	20.56 N	77.45 E
Amrāvati	120	20.56 N	77.45 E
Am-Raya	146	14.00 N	16.35 E
Amreli	120	21.37 N	71.14 E
Āmreswar	272b	22.28 N	88.34 E
Amriswil	58	47.33 N	9.18 E
Amritsar	123	31.35 N	74.53 E
Amroha	124	28.55 N	78.28 E
Amrūka	123	30.19 N	73.53 E
Amrum I	30	54.39 N	8.21 E
Amsdell Heights	284a	42.45 N	78.54 W
Amsden	214	41.13 N	83.20 W
Amsel	148	22.37 N	5.26 E
Åmsele	26	64.32 N	19.20 E
Am Sigan	146	11.41 N	19.51 E
Amsoldingen	58	46.43 N	7.35 E
Amsteg	58	46.46 N	8.41 E
Amstel ≏	52	52.22 N	4.54 E
Amstelmeer ⊜	52	52.52 N	4.45 E
Amstelveen	52	52.18 N	4.51 E
Amsterdam, Ned.	52	52.22 N	4.54 E
Amsterdam, S. Afr.	158	26.35 S	30.45 E
Amsterdam, N.Y., U.S.	210	42.56 N	74.11 W
Amsterdam, Oh., U.S.	214	40.28 N	80.55 W
Amsterdam, Île I	6	37.52 S	77.32 E
Amsterdam-Rijnkanaal ≚	52	51.57 N	5.20 E
Amstetten	61	48.07 N	14.53 E
Amston	207	41.37 N	72.20 W
Āmta	126	22.35 N	88.01 E
Amt'ae-do I	98	34.50 N	126.07 E
Āmtala	126	23.55 N	88.27 E
Amtāli	126	22.08 N	90.14 E
Am Timan	146	11.02 N	20.17 E
Amtrak Station ⊸[5]	281	42.19 N	83.04 W
Amubri	236	9.31 N	82.56 W
'Āmūdah	130	37.05 N	40.54 E
Amu-Darja	128	37.53 N	65.15 E
Amu Darya (Amudarja) ≏	72	43.40 N	59.01 E
Amudat	154	1.57 N	34.57 E
Amugulang → Xin Barag Zuoqi	88	48.14 N	118.18 E
Amukta Island I	180	52.29 N	171.15 W
Amukta Pass ꭕ	180	52.25 N	172.00 W
Amulree	46	56.30 N	3.47 W
Amun	175e	5.57 S	154.45 E
Amundsen Bay ⊂	9	66.55 S	50.00 E
Amundsen Gulf ⊂	176	71.00 N	124.00 W
Amundsen-Scott ♁[3]	9	90.00 S	0.00
Amundsen Sea ⍑[2]	9	72.30 S	112.00 W
Amung, Mount ∧	164	7.26 S	146.36 E
Amungen ⊜	26	61.09 N	15.39 E
Amuntai	112	2.26 S	115.15 E
Amur (Heilong) ≏	74	52.56 N	141.10 E
'Amūr, Wādī V	140	18.56 N	33.34 E
Amurang	112	1.11 N	124.35 E
Amuria	154	2.01 N	33.38 E
Amursk	89	50.13 N	136.52 E
Amurskaja Oblast' □[8]	89	53.00 N	129.00 E
Amurskij liman ⊂	89	52.45 N	141.40 E
Amursko-Zejskaja ravnina ⋏[1]	89	52.30 N	128.30 E
Amurzet	89	47.42 N	131.05 E
Amutag	116	12.23 N	123.16 E
Amuwo	273a	6.28 N	3.18 E
Amuyimusu	98	42.25 N	113.21 E
Amuzhong	120	30.33 N	84.28 E
Amvamg	152	1.45 N	10.29 E
Amvrakikós Kólpos ⊂	38	39.00 N	21.00 E
Amvrosijevka	83	47.47 N	38.29 E
Amwom, Khawr V	140	7.50 N	31.13 E
Amyl ≏	86	53.47 N	92.54 E
Amyūn	130	34.18 N	35.49 E
Amz'a	80	56.13 N	54.23 E
Amzi, Oued ti-n- V	148	20.30 N	4.35 E
An	110	19.47 N	94.02 E
Anaa I[1]	14	17.25 S	145.30 W
Anabanua	112	3.57 S	120.04 E
Anabar	174b	0.30 S	166.57 E
Anabar ≏	74	73.08 N	113.36 E
'Anabtā	132	32.19 N	35.07 E
Anabuki	96	34.02 N	134.11 E
Anacapri	68	40.33 N	14.13 E
Anaco	246	9.27 N	64.28 W
Anacoco	194	31.15 N	93.20 W
Anacoco, Bayou ≏	194	30.52 N	93.34 W
Anaconda	202	46.07 N	112.56 W
Anaconda Range ⋏	202	45.55 N	113.30 W
Anacortes	224	48.30 N	122.36 W
Anacostia ⊸[8]	284c	38.52 N	76.59 W
Anacostia ≏	284c	38.52 N	77.01 W
Anacostia, Little Paint Branch ≏	284c	39.01 N	76.56 W
Anacostia, Northeast Branch ≏	284c	38.57 N	76.57 W
Anacostia, Paint Branch ≏	284c	38.58 N	76.55 W
Anacostia Park ♠	284c	38.54 N	76.58 W
Anacuao, Mount ∧	116	16.16 N	121.53 E
Anadarko	196	35.04 N	98.14 W
Anadia	250	9.42 S	36.18 W
Anadolufeneri ⊸[8]	267b	41.12 N	29.09 E
Anadoluhisarı ⊥	267b	41.04 N	29.03 E
Anadyr'	180	64.45 N	177.29 E
Anadyr' ≏	74	64.55 N	176.05 E
Anadyrskaja nizmennost' ≚	180	65.30 N	176.00 E
Anadyrskij liman ⊂	180	64.30 N	177.45 E
Anadyrskij zaliv ⊂	180	64.00 N	179.00 W

FRANÇAIS

Nom	Page	Lat.°′	Long.°′ W = Ouest
Anadyrskoje ploskogorje ⋏[1]	180	67.00 N	174.00 E
Anáfi I	38	36.21 N	25.50 E
Anagni	66	41.44 N	13.09 E
'Ānah	128	34.28 N	41.56 E
Anaheim	228	33.50 N	117.54 W
Anaheim Arena ♠	280	33.48 N	117.52 W
Anaheim Shopping Center ⊸[9]	280	33.51 N	117.56 W
Anaheim Stadium ♠	280	33.51 N	117.57 W
Anaheim Union Canal ≚	280	33.54 N	117.52 W
Anahi, Baie ⊂	174x	9.45 S	138.56 W
Anahim Lake	182	52.28 N	125.18 W
Anahola	229b	22.08 N	159.18 W
Anahola Bay ⊂	229b	22.09 N	159.18 W
Anáhuac, Méx.	196	25.48 N	97.45 W
Anáhuac, Méx.	232	27.14 N	100.09 W
Anáhuac, Méx.	232	28.25 N	106.40 W
Anahuac, Tx., U.S.	222	29.46 N	94.41 W
Anahuac, Lake ⊜	222	29.48 N	94.41 W
Anaimala	122	10.35 N	76.56 E
Ānai Mudi ∧	122	10.10 N	77.04 E
Anajás	250	0.59 S	49.57 W
Anajás, Ilha I	250	0.20 S	50.30 W
Anajatuba	250	3.16 S	44.37 W
Anakāpalle	122	17.41 N	83.01 E
Anaklia	84	42.24 N	41.34 E
Anaktuvuk ≏	180	69.32 N	151.30 W
Anaktuvuk Pass	180	68.10 N	151.50 W
Analalava	157b	14.38 S	47.45 E
Analapatsy	157b	25.10 S	46.42 E
Analavoka	157b	22.33 S	46.30 E
Analomink	210	41.03 N	75.13 W
Anamã	246	3.35 S	61.22 W
Anamã, Lago ⊜	246	3.32 S	61.35 W
Anama Bay	184	51.56 N	98.05 W
Ana María, Cayos de II	240p	21.29 N	78.46 W
Ana María, Golfo de ⊂	240p	21.25 N	78.40 W
Anambas, Kepulauan II	112	3.00 N	106.00 E
Anambra □[3]	150	6.30 N	7.20 E
Anambra ≏	150	6.11 N	6.46 E
Anamizu	94	37.14 N	136.54 E
Anamoose	198	47.52 N	100.14 W
Anamosa	190	42.06 N	91.17 W
Anamu ≏	250	0.56 N	57.03 W
Anamur	130	36.06 N	32.50 E
Anamur Burnu ≻	130	36.03 N	32.48 E
Anan, Nihon	94	35.19 N	137.49 E
Anan, Nihon	96	33.55 N	134.39 E
Ānand	120	22.34 N	72.56 E
Ananda	150	7.17 N	4.16 W
Anandanagar	272b	22.51 N	88.16 E
Ānandapur, India	120	21.14 N	86.07 E
Anandapur, India	126	22.34 N	87.25 E
Anandpur Sahib	123	31.15 N	76.30 E
Ananea	248	14.42 S	69.33 W
Ananindeua	250	1.22 S	48.23 W
Ananjev	78	47.40 N	29.55 E
Ananjevo	85	42.45 N	77.40 E
Anantapur	122	14.41 N	77.36 E
Anantnāg (Islāmābād)	123	33.44 N	75.09 E
Anao-aon	116	9.47 N	125.25 E
Anapa	78	44.53 N	37.19 E
Anapo ≏	70	47.03 N	15.16 E
Anápolis	255	16.20 S	48.58 W
Anapu ≏	250	1.53 S	50.53 W
Anapurus	250	3.40 S	43.06 W
Anār, Īrān	128	30.53 N	55.18 E
Anar, Kaz.	86	50.38 N	72.27 E
Anāra	126	23.28 N	86.33 E
Anārak	128	33.20 N	53.42 E
Anarchaj	85	44.02 N	75.15 E
Anār Darreh	128	32.46 N	61.39 E
Anaš	86	54.52 N	91.00 E
Anasagasti	258	35.01 S	59.24 W
Añasco	240m	18.17 N	67.08 W
Ånäset	26	64.16 N	21.03 E
Anastácio	255	21.31 S	54.08 W
Anastasia Island I	192	29.48 N	81.16 W
Anastasijevka	83	47.34 N	38.31 E
Anastasijevskaja	78	45.13 N	37.53 E
'Anātā	132	31.49 N	35.16 E
Anatahan I	108	16.22 N	145.40 E
Anatoljevka	78	46.48 N	31.13 E
Anatom I	175f	20.12 S	169.45 E
Añatuya	252	28.28 S	62.50 W
Anauá ≏	246	0.58 N	61.21 W
Anaurilândia	255	22.03 S	52.45 W
Anavilhanas, Arquipélago das II	246	2.42 S	60.45 W
Anawalt	192	37.20 N	81.26 W
Anbanjing	102	23.57 N	100.55 E
Anbei, Zhg.	102	40.45 N	96.06 E
Anbei, Zhg.	102	40.49 N	108.56 E
Anbianbu	102	37.39 N	108.11 E
Anbo	98	39.51 N	122.19 E
Anbu	100	23.28 N	116.44 E
Anbyŏn	98	39.03 N	127.32 E
Ancarano	66	42.50 N	13.44 E
Ancash □[5]	248	9.30 S	77.45 W
Ancaster, On., Can.	212	43.12 N	80.00 W
Ancaster, Eng., U.K.	44	52.59 N	0.32 W
Ancasti	252	28.49 S	65.30 W
Ancasti, Sierra de ⋏	252	28.50 S	65.39 W
Ance ≏, Fr.	62	45.17 N	4.08 E
Ance ≏, Fr.	62	44.58 N	3.40 E
Ancenis	32	47.22 N	1.11 W
Ancerville	58	48.38 N	5.02 E
Anchang	100	30.09 N	120.30 E
Anchau	150	10.59 N	8.23 E
Anchieta ⊸[8]	287a	22.49 S	43.24 W
Anchieta, Ilha I	256	23.33 S	45.04 W
Anch'ing → Anqing	100	30.31 N	117.02 E
Ancho, Canal ꭕ	254	49.54 S	74.23 W
Ancholme ≏	44	53.41 N	0.32 W
Anchor	216	40.34 N	88.32 W
Anchorage	180	61.13 N	149.54 W
Anchor Bay ⊂	214	42.38 N	82.45 W
Anchor Bay Gardens	214	42.39 N	82.49 W
Anchorena	252	35.41 S	65.27 W
Anchor Point	180	59.46 N	151.52 W
Anchor Point ≻	180	59.47 N	151.52 W
Anchorville	214	42.42 N	82.41 W
Anchuras	34	39.29 N	4.50 W
Anci (Langfang)	105	39.31 N	116.41 E
Ancien Ekalla	152	1.27 S	14.00 E
Ancien Goubéré	140	5.51 N	26.46 E
Ancienne-Lorette	206	46.48 N	71.21 W
Anciferovo, Ross.	76	58.58 N	34.01 E
Anciferovo, Ross.	82	55.33 N	38.49 E
Ancipa, Lago di ⊜	70	37.50 N	14.34 E
Anclitas, Cayo I	240p	20.48 N	78.54 W
Anclote ≏	220	39.59 N	88.49 W
Anclote Keys II	220	28.12 N	82.51 W
Ancón, Méx.	234	22.35 N	101.11 W
Ancón, Perú	248	11.47 S	77.11 W
Ancona, It.	66	43.38 N	13.30 E
Ancona, S. Afr.	158	27.40 S	26.32 E
Ancona □[4]	66	43.33 N	13.10 E
Ancón de Sardinas, Bahía de ⊂	246	1.30 N	79.00 W
Ancoraimes	248	15.54 S	68.58 W
Ancram	210	42.03 N	73.38 W
Ancre ≏	50	49.54 N	2.28 E
Ancrum	46	55.31 N	2.35 W
Ancuabe	154	12.58 S	39.54 E
Ancud	254	41.52 S	73.50 W
Ancud, Golfo de ⊂	254	42.05 S	73.00 W
Ancy-le-Franc	50	47.46 N	4.10 E
Ancy-sur-Moselle	56	49.03 N	6.04 E
Anda, Pil.	116	16.17 N	119.57 E
Anda, Zhg.	89	46.24 N	125.19 E
Andacollo, Arg.	252	37.11 S	70.41 W
Andacollo, Chile	252	30.14 S	71.06 W
Andahuaylas	248	13.39 S	73.23 W

PORTUGUÊS

Nome	Página	Lat.°′	Long.°′ W = Oeste
Andaingo	157b	18.12 S	48.17 E
Andāl	124	23.36 N	87.12 E
Andalgalá	252	27.36 S	66.19 W
Åndalo	64	46.10 N	11.00 E
Åndalsnes	26	62.34 N	7.42 E
Andalucía □[4]	34	37.30 N	4.30 W
Andalucía □[9]	34	37.36 N	4.30 W
Andalusia, Al., U.S.	194	31.19 N	86.29 W
Andalusia, Pa., U.S.	285	40.04 N	74.58 W
Andaman and Nicobar Islands □[8]	110	11.00 N	93.00 E
Andaman Basin ⊹[1]	12	10.00 N	94.00 E
Andamanen → Andaman Islands II	110	12.00 N	92.45 E
Andaman Islands II	110	12.00 N	92.45 E
Andaman Sea ⍑[2]	110	10.00 N	95.00 E
Andamarca, Bol.	248	18.49 S	67.31 W
Andamarca, Perú	248	11.46 S	74.44 W
Andamooka	166	30.27 S	137.12 E
Andance	62	45.14 N	4.47 E
Andapa	157b	14.39 S	49.39 E
Andara	152	18.03 S	21.27 E
Andaraí	255	12.48 S	41.20 W
Andaraí ⊸[8]	287a	22.56 S	43.15 W
Andarax ≏	34	36.48 N	2.26 W
Andaray	248	15.49 S	72.50 W
Andau	61	47.46 N	17.02 E
Andechs, Kloster ♁[1]	64	47.58 N	11.10 E
Andeer	58	46.36 N	9.26 E
Andelfingen	58	47.36 N	8.41 E
Andelle ≏	50	49.19 N	1.44 E
Andelot	58	48.15 N	5.18 E
Andelot-en-Montagne	58	46.51 N	5.56 E
Andelu	261	48.53 N	1.50 E
Anden → Andes ⋏	18	20.00 S	67.00 W
Andenes	24	69.16 N	16.08 E
Andenne	56	50.29 N	5.06 E
Andéranboukane	150	15.26 N	3.02 E
Ånderdalen Nasjonalpark ♠	24	69.14 N	17.17 E
Anderlecht	50	50.50 N	4.18 E
Anderlues	50	50.24 N	4.16 E
Andermatt	58	46.38 N	8.36 E
Andernach	56	50.26 N	7.24 E
Andersen Air Force Base ■	174p	13.35 N	144.56 E
Anderslöv	41	55.26 N	13.22 E
Anderson, Al., U.S.	194	34.55 N	87.15 W
Anderson, Ak., U.S.	180	64.21 N	149.10 W
Anderson, Ca., U.S.	204	40.26 N	122.17 W
Anderson, In., U.S.	218	40.06 N	85.40 W
Anderson, Mo., U.S.	194	36.39 N	94.26 W
Anderson, S.C., U.S.	192	34.30 N	82.39 W
Anderson, Tx., U.S.	222	30.29 N	95.59 W
Anderson □[6], Ky., U.S.	218	38.05 N	84.55 W
Anderson □[6], Tx., U.S.	222	31.47 N	95.40 W
Anderson ≏	180	69.43 N	128.58 W
Anderson, Mount ∧	224	47.43 N	123.20 W
Anderson Creek ≏	194	33.18 N	94.26 W
Anderson Dam	202	43.30 N	115.30 W
Anderson Inlet ⊂	169	38.39 S	145.48 E
Anderson Island I	224	47.10 N	122.42 W
Anderson Lake ⊜	182	50.41 N	122.07 W
Anderson Lake ⊜[1]	226	37.11 N	121.37 W
Anderson Peak ∧	228	34.08 N	116.53 W
Anderson Ranch Reservoir ⊜[1]	202	43.25 N	115.20 W
Andersonville	218	39.30 N	85.17 W
Andersonville National Historical Site ⊥	192	32.12 N	84.07 W
Anderstorp	26	57.17 N	13.38 E
Anderten	52	52.21 N	9.51 E
Anderton	262	53.17 N	2.32 W
Andes, Col.	246	5.40 N	75.53 W
Andes, N.Y., U.S.	210	42.12 N	74.47 W
Andes ⋏	18	20.00 S	67.00 W
Andes, Lake ⊜	198	43.11 N	98.27 W
Andeville	50	49.15 N	2.10 E
Andevoranto	157b	18.57 S	49.06 E
Andfjorden ꭕ	24	69.10 N	16.20 E
Andheri ⊸[8]	272c	19.07 N	72.51 E
Andhra Lake ⊜	122	18.54 N	73.32 E
Andhra Pradesh □[3]	122	16.00 N	79.00 E
Andijk	52	52.45 N	5.12 E
Andijskoje Kojsu ≏	84	42.47 N	46.48 E
Andikíthira I	38	35.52 N	23.18 E
Andilamena	157b	17.01 S	48.35 E
Andimákhia	38	36.48 N	27.07 E
Andīmeshk	128	32.27 N	48.21 E
Andingpu	102	37.58 N	107.02 E
Anding Zhan	105	39.38 N	116.29 E
Andíparos I	38	37.00 N	25.03 E
Andirá ≏	250	2.45 S	56.49 W
Andirá, Riozinho do ≏	248	9.21 S	67.31 W
Andırın	130	37.34 N	36.20 E
Andirlang	120	37.36 N	83.50 E
Andisleben	54	51.04 N	10.56 E
Ándissa	38	39.14 N	25.59 E
Andižan	85	40.45 N	72.22 E
Andižan □[4]	85	40.45 N	72.15 E
Andkhvoy	120	36.56 N	65.08 E
Andlau-au-Val	58	48.23 N	7.25 E
Ando	270	34.37 N	135.46 E
Andoam	164	12.40 S	141.55 E
Andoas	246	2.50 S	76.30 W
Andoga ≏	76	59.10 N	37.27 E
Andogskaja gr'ada ∧	76	59.25 N	37.30 E
Andolsheim	58	48.04 N	7.25 E
Andomskij Pogost	24	61.14 N	36.36 E
Andong, Taehan	98	36.35 N	128.44 E
Andong, Zhg.	100	30.16 N	121.13 E
Andong-chŏsuji ⊜[1]	98	36.41 N	128.49 E
Andong-ni	98	39.28 N	127.27 E
Andora	62	43.59 N	8.08 E
Andorf	60	48.23 N	13.35 E
Andorno Micca	62	45.37 N	8.03 E
Andorra	34	42.30 N	1.31 E
Andorra □[1], Europe	22	42.30 N	1.30 E
Andorra □[1], Europe	34	42.30 N	1.30 E
Andorre → Andorra □[1]	34	42.30 N	1.30 E
Andover, Eng., U.K.	42	51.13 N	1.28 W
Andover, Ct., U.S.	207	41.44 N	72.22 W
Andover, Me., U.S.	188	44.38 N	70.45 W
Andover, Ma., U.S.	207	42.39 N	71.08 W
Andover, N.J., U.S.	210	40.59 N	74.44 W
Andover, N.Y., U.S.	210	42.09 N	77.47 W
Andover, Oh., U.S.	214	41.36 N	80.34 W
Andover, S.D., U.S.	198	45.24 N	97.54 W
Andowj	123	37.02 N	71.27 E
Andøya I	24	69.08 N	15.54 E
Andradas	256	22.04 S	46.34 W
Andrade Pinto	256	22.14 S	43.22 W
Andradina	255	20.54 S	51.23 W
Andramasina	157b	19.11 S	47.35 E
Andranopasy	157b	21.17 S	43.44 E
Andranovory	157b	23.08 S	44.10 E
Andrate	62	45.32 N	7.53 E
Andreafsky ≏	180	62.02 N	163.16 W
Andreafsky, East Fork ≏	180	62.03 N	163.07 W
Andreanof Islands II	180	52.00 N	176.00 W
Andreapol'	76	56.39 N	32.15 E
Andreas, I. of Man	44	54.22 N	4.26 W
Andreas, Pa., U.S.	208	40.45 N	75.48 W
André Félix, Parc National ♠	146	9.25 N	23.20 E
Andrejevka, Kaz.	86	52.59 N	67.23 E
Andrejevka, Kaz.	86	45.50 N	80.35 E
Andrejevka, Ross.	80	55.42 N	54.23 E
Andrejevka, Ross.	80	52.19 N	51.55 E
Andrejevka, Ross.	82	55.59 N	37.08 E
Andrejevka, Ross.	82	55.07 N	38.37 E
Andrejevka, Ukr.	78	49.32 N	36.38 E
Andrejevka, Ukr.	78	47.06 N	36.35 E
Andrejevka, Ukr.	83	47.28 N	37.39 E
Andrejevka, Ukr.	83	48.49 N	37.33 E
Andrejevo	80	55.56 N	41.08 E
Andrejevo-Ivanovka	78	47.28 N	30.28 E
Andrejevsk	88	58.06 N	114.08 E
Andrejevskaja	80	47.21 N	43.02 E
Andrejevskoje, Ross.	82	54.23 N	36.12 E
Andrejevskoje, Ross.	82	56.24 N	39.01 E
Andrejevskoje, Ross.	82	55.46 N	36.35 E
Andrejkoviči	76	52.25 N	33.00 E
Andrelândia	256	21.44 S	44.18 W
Andrésy	261	48.59 N	2.04 E
Andretta	68	40.56 N	15.19 E
Andrew	182	53.53 N	112.21 W
Andrew, Mount ∧	162	32.52 S	122.56 E
Andrews, In., U.S.	216	40.51 N	85.36 W
Andrews, Mi., U.S.	216	41.57 N	86.22 W
Andrews, N.C., U.S.	192	35.12 N	83.49 W
Andrews, S.C., U.S.	192	33.18 N	79.17 W
Andrews, Tx., U.S.	196	32.19 N	102.32 W
Andrews Air Force Base ■	208	38.48 N	76.52 W
Andrews Manor	284c	38.49 N	76.54 W
Andrezel	261	48.37 N	2.49 E
Andrézieux Bouthéon	62	45.32 N	4.16 E
Andria	68	41.13 N	16.18 E
Andriamena	157b	17.26 S	47.30 E
Andriandampy	157b	22.45 S	45.41 E
Andriba	157b	17.36 S	46.55 E
Andrija, Otok I	36	43.02 N	15.45 E
Andrijevica	38	42.44 N	19.46 E
Androka	157b	25.02 S	44.05 E
Andronovskoje	76	60.39 N	34.46 E
Andropov → Rybinsk	76	58.03 N	38.52 E
Ándros	38	37.50 N	24.57 E
Andros I, Ba.	238	24.26 N	77.57 W
Ándros I, Ellás	38	37.45 N	24.42 E
Androscoggin ≏	188	43.55 N	69.55 W
Androsovka	80	52.41 N	49.35 E
Andros Town	238	24.43 N	77.47 W
Āndrott Island I	122	10.50 N	73.41 E
Andrupene	76	56.11 N	27.23 E
Andr'ušino	86	59.12 N	62.59 E
Andrušovka	78	50.01 N	29.01 E
Andrychów	30	49.52 N	19.21 E
Andudu	154	2.29 N	28.41 E
Andújar	34	38.03 N	4.04 W
Andulo	152	11.30 S	16.45 E
Anduze	62	44.03 N	3.59 E
Andžijevskij	84	44.14 N	43.05 E
Âne, Dos d' ∧	241o	16.19 N	61.46 W
Aneby	26	57.50 N	14.48 E
Anécho	150	6.14 N	1.36 E
Anecón Grande, Cerro ∧	254	41.25 S	70.16 W
Anefis i-n-Darane	150	18.03 N	0.36 E
Anegada I	238	18.45 N	64.20 W
Anegada, Bahía ⊂	254	40.15 S	62.15 W
Anegada Passage ꭕ	238	18.30 N	63.40 W
Anegam	200	32.22 N	112.01 W
Anegasaki	268	35.28 N	140.02 E
Anelngauhat	175f	20.14 S	169.44 E
Añelo	252	38.21 S	68.47 W
Anémata, Passe d' ꭕ	175f	20.31 S	166.12 E
Anepahan Peak ∧	116	9.40 N	118.25 E
Aneroid	184	49.43 N	107.20 W
Anet	50	48.51 N	1.26 E
Aneta	198	47.40 N	97.59 W
Aneto, Pico de ∧	34	42.38 N	0.40 E
Aney	146	19.24 N	12.56 E
Anfeng, Zhg.	100	32.44 N	120.24 E
Anfeng, Zhg.	100	33.06 N	120.08 E
Anfengqiao	100	26.41 N	118.08 E
Anfo	64	45.46 N	10.29 E
Anfu	100	27.23 N	114.37 E
Anfuzhen, Zhg.	107	28.47 N	104.41 E
Anfuzhen, Zhg.	107	29.21 N	105.28 E
Anga	88	53.58 N	106.12 E
Angamacutiro [de la Unión]	234	20.10 N	101.41 W
Angamos, Punta ≻	252	23.01 S	70.32 W
Angangueo	234	19.37 N	100.18 W
Ang'angxi	89	47.09 N	123.48 E
An'ganka	89	52.18 N	126.17 E
Angao	100	33.08 N	112.22 E
Angar	164	3.39 S	130.50 E
Angara ≏	88	58.06 N	93.00 E
Angara-Débou	150	11.19 N	3.03 E
Angarbaka	140	9.44 N	24.44 E
Āngāria	126	22.29 N	90.22 E
Angarsk	88	52.34 N	103.54 E
Angas ≏	168b	35.23 S	138.59 E
Angas Downs	162	24.49 S	132.14 E
Angas Hills ⋏[2]	162	22.55 S	128.00 E
Angastaco	252	25.38 S	66.11 W
Angaston	168b	34.30 S	139.02 E
Angat ≏	116	14.53 N	120.46 E
Angatuba	255	23.29 S	48.25 W
Angaul	88	53.49 N	100.18 E
Angaur I	175b	6.54 N	134.09 E
Angden Pass ⋊	124	29.43 N	86.17 E
Angduo	102	32.20 N	98.55 E
Ånge	26	62.31 N	15.37 E
Ángel, Salto (Angel Falls) ⌊	246	5.57 N	62.30 W
Angel Albino Corzo	234	15.55 N	92.43 W
Angel City	220	28.20 N	80.40 W
Ángel de la Guarda, Isla I	232	29.20 N	113.25 W
Angeles	116	15.09 N	120.35 E
Angeles National Forest ♠	280	34.15 N	117.56 W
Angel Etcheverry	258	35.02 S	58.04 W
Angel Falls → Ángel, Salto ⌊	246	5.57 N	62.30 W
Ängelholm	41	56.15 N	12.51 E
Ängelholm flygplats ⊠	41	56.20 N	12.51 E
Angelica	210	42.18 N	78.00 W
Angelina □[6]	222	31.17 N	94.42 W
Angelina ≏	194	30.53 N	94.12 W
Angelina, East Fork ≏	222	31.50 N	94.56 W
Angel Island I	282	37.52 N	122.26 W
Angellala Creek ≏	166	26.40 S	146.08 E
Angeln ⊸[1]	41	54.39 N	9.44 E
Angelo ≏	162	23.43 S	117.45 E
Angel R. Cabada	234	18.35 N	95.26 W
Ängelsberg	40	59.58 N	16.00 E
Angels Camp	226	38.04 N	120.33 W
Angels Creek ≏	226	38.01 N	120.33 W
Angelus, Lake ⊜	281	42.41 N	83.20 W
Angemuk ∧	164	3.30 S	138.34 E
Anger	61	47.16 N	15.42 E
Angera	62	45.46 N	8.35 E
Angerbach ≏	263	51.23 N	6.44 E
Angereb ≏	144	13.51 N	36.08 E
Angeren	52	51.55 N	5.58 E
Angerhausen ⊸[8]	263	51.23 N	6.44 E
Ångermanälven ≏	26	62.48 N	17.56 E
Ångermanland □[9]	26	63.30 N	18.05 E
Angermund ⊸[8]	263	51.20 N	6.47 E
Angermünde	54	53.01 N	14.00 E
Angern, Dtsch.	54	52.21 N	11.44 E
Angern, Öst.	61	48.22 N	16.50 E
Angers	32	47.28 N	0.33 W
Angerville	50	48.19 N	2.00 E
Angervilliers	261	48.36 N	2.04 E
Ängesön I	26	63.43 N	20.55 E
Angevillers	56	49.23 N	6.02 E
Anggowala, Bukit ∧	112	4.15 S	121.44 E
Anghelu Ruiu, Necropoli ⊥	71	40.38 N	8.20 E
Anghiari	66	43.32 N	12.03 E
Angical	255	12.00 S	44.42 W
Angical do Piauí	250	6.05 S	42.44 W
Angicos	250	5.40 S	36.36 W
Angier	192	35.30 N	78.44 W
Angijak Island I	176	65.40 N	62.15 W
Angikuni Lake ⊜	176	62.13 N	99.50 W
Angke, Kali ≏	269e	6.06 S	106.46 E
Angkor Wat ⊥	110	13.26 N	103.52 E
Ângk Tasaôm	110	11.01 N	104.41 E
Anglais, Baie des ⊂	186	49.15 N	68.07 W
Anglais, Jardin ♠	261	48.38 N	1.49 E
Anglais, Rivière des (English) ≏	206	45.13 N	73.50 W
Angle	42	51.41 N	5.06 W
Angle Inlet	198	49.21 N	95.04 W
Anglem, Mount ∧	172	46.44 S	167.56 E
Anglesea	169	38.25 S	144.11 E
Anglesey I	44	53.17 N	4.22 W
Anglet	32	43.29 N	1.31 W
Angleterre → England □[8]	28	52.30 N	1.30 W
Angleton	222	29.10 N	95.25 W
Anglezarke Moor ⊸[3]	262	53.40 N	2.33 W
Anglezarke Reservoir ⊜[1]	262	53.39 N	2.35 W
Angling ≏	184	56.45 N	93.36 W
Angling Lake ⊜	184	53.55 N	93.52 W
Anglona ⊸[1]	71	40.50 N	8.45 E
Anglo-Normandes, Îles → Channel Islands II	28	49.20 N	2.20 W
Anglure	50	48.35 N	3.49 E
Angmagssalik	176	65.36 N	37.41 W
Angmering	42	50.48 N	0.28 W
Ang Mo Kio	271c	1.22 N	103.51 E
Ango	154	4.02 N	25.52 E
Angoche	154	16.15 S	39.54 E
Angoche, Ilha I	154	16.20 S	39.50 E
Angohrān	128	26.35 N	57.54 E
Angol	252	37.48 S	72.43 W
Angola, In., U.S.	216	41.38 N	84.59 W
Angola, N.Y., U.S.	210	42.38 N	79.01 W
Angola □[1], Afr.	138	12.30 S	18.30 E
Angola □[1], Afr.	152	12.30 S	18.30 E
Angola Basin ⊹[1]	10	15.00 S	3.00 E
Angola Lake Shore	214	42.37 N	79.05 W
Angono	269f	14.31 N	121.09 E
Angoon	180	57.30 N	134.35 W
Angora → Ankara	130	39.56 N	32.52 E
Angoram	164	4.04 S	144.04 E
Angostura	232	25.22 N	108.11 W
Angostura, Presa de la ⊜[1]	234	16.10 N	92.40 W
Angostura → Ciudad Bolívar	246	8.08 N	63.33 W
Angostura Reservoir ⊜[1]	198	43.18 N	103.27 W
Angoulême	32	45.39 N	0.09 E
Angoumois □[9]	32	45.30 N	0.05 W
Angra, Meos I	164	2.42 S	134.50 E
Angra do Heroísmo	148a	38.39 N	27.13 W
Angra do Heroísmo □[5]	148a	38.50 N	27.30 W
Angra dos Reis	256	23.00 S	44.18 W
Angren	85	41.01 N	70.12 E
Angren ≏	85	40.48 N	68.53 E
Angri	68	40.44 N	14.34 E
Angrignon Zoological Park ♠	275a	45.26 N	73.36 W
Angrogna	62	44.50 N	7.13 E
Ängsö	40	59.32 N	16.51 E
Ängsö Nationalpark ♠	40	59.39 N	18.44 E
Ang Thong	110	14.35 N	100.27 E
Angu	154	3.33 N	24.28 E
Angu ≏	256	21.48 S	42.30 W
Angualasto	252	30.03 S	69.09 W
Anguang	89	45.31 N	123.45 E
Anguchang	107	29.30 N	103.39 E
Anguciana, Cerro ∧	236	8.50 N	83.07 W
Anguilas, Arroyo ≏	288	34.26 S	58.31 W
Anguilla	194	32.58 N	90.49 W
Anguilla □[2], N.A.	230	18.15 N	63.05 W
Anguilla □[2], N.A.	238	18.15 N	63.05 W
Anguilla Cays II	238	23.31 N	79.33 W
Anguillara Sabazia	66	42.05 N	12.16 E
Anguillara Veneta	64	45.08 N	11.53 E
Anguille, Cape ≻	186	47.55 N	59.25 W
Anguli Nur ⊜	98	41.13 N	114.32 E
Angumu	154	0.07 S	27.42 E
Anguo	98	38.25 N	115.19 E
Anguozhuang	105	39.44 N	117.59 E
Anguruga	164	14.00 S	136.29 E
Angus	212	44.19 N	79.53 W
Angus Place	170	33.20 S	150.06 E
Angustura	256	21.45 S	42.41 W
Angusville	184	50.44 N	101.01 W
Angwa ≏	154	15.51 S	30.35 E
Angwin	226	38.34 N	122.26 W
Angyalföld ⊸[8]	264c	47.33 N	19.05 E
Angyō	268	35.51 N	139.46 E
An Hai, Viet	110	15.13 N	108.56 E
Anhai, Zhg.	100	24.45 N	118.27 E
Anhalt □[9]	54	52.00 N	11.30 E
Anholt	52	51.52 N	6.27 E
Anholt I	26	56.42 N	11.34 E
Anhovo	64	46.03 N	13.37 E
Anhua	102	28.18 N	111.14 E
Anhuai	100	33.04 N	117.50 E
Anhui (Anhwei) □[4]	100	32.00 N	117.00 E
Anhŭng	98	36.41 N	126.10 E
Anhwei → Anhui □[4]	100	32.00 N	117.00 E
Aniak	180	61.35 N	159.33 W
Aniak ≏	180	61.34 N	159.30 W
Aniakchak National Monument ♠	180	56.50 N	157.50 W
Anibare Bay ⊂	174b	0.32 S	166.57 E
Aniche	50	50.20 N	3.15 E
Anicuns	255	16.28 S	49.58 W
Anié	150	7.45 N	1.12 E
Anié ≏	150	7.40 N	1.18 E
Anie, Pic d' ∧	32	42.57 N	0.43 W
Aniene ≏	66	41.56 N	12.30 E
Anif	64	47.45 N	13.04 E
Anik ⊸[8]	272c	19.02 N	72.53 E
Anikino, Ross.	86	56.32 N	73.56 E
Anikino, Ross.	88	53.26 N	120.20 E
Anikovo	76	59.23 N	43.45 E
Anil	250	2.32 S	44.14 W
Anil, Rio do ≏	287a	22.59 S	43.21 W
Animas	200	31.56 N	108.48 W
Animas ≏	200	36.43 N	108.13 W
Animas Peak ∧	200	31.35 N	108.47 W
Animas Valley V	200	31.45 N	108.50 W
Anin	110	15.40 N	97.46 E
Anina	38	45.05 N	21.51 E
Anipemza	84	40.27 N	43.37 E
Aniskino	82	55.54 N	38.06 E
Añisoc	152	1.51 N	10.46 E
Anita, Ia., U.S.	198	41.26 N	94.45 W
Anita, Pa., U.S.	214	41.00 N	78.58 W
Anıtkaya	130	38.57 N	30.18 E
Aniva	89	46.43 N	142.32 E
Aniva, mys ≻	89	46.01 N	143.25 E
Aniva, zaliv ⊂	89	46.16 N	142.48 E
Anivorano	157b	18.44 S	48.58 E
Anivorano Nord	157b	12.44 S	49.13 E
Aniwa I	175f	19.17 S	169.35 E
Anizy-le-Château	50	49.30 N	3.27 E
Anjad	120	22.02 N	75.03 E
Anjan	26	63.41 N	12.49 E
Anjangaon	120	21.10 N	77.18 E
Anjār, India	120	23.08 N	70.01 E
'Anjar, Lubnān	132	33.42 N	35.54 E
'Anjarah	132	32.18 N	35.45 E
Anjavimihavana	157b	12.32 S	49.16 E
Anji	106	30.43 N	119.41 E
Anjiabe	157b	12.07 S	49.20 E
Anjiang	105	40.45 N	117.38 E
Anjigami Lake ⊜	190	47.51 N	84.34 W
Anjō	94	34.57 N	137.05 E
Anjou	206	45.36 N	73.33 W
Anjou □[9]	32	47.20 N	0.30 W
Anjozorobe	157b	18.24 S	47.52 E
Anju, C.M.I.K.	98	39.36 N	125.40 E
Anju, Zhg.	100	31.45 N	113.11 E
Anju, Zhg.	107	30.21 N	105.27 E
Anjudin	24	62.33 N	58.12 E
Anjuzhen	107	29.59 N	106.02 E
Anka	150	12.07 N	5.55 E
Ankang	102	32.42 N	109.05 E
Ankara	130	39.56 N	32.52 E
Ankara □[4]	130	39.50 N	32.50 E
Ankara ≏	130	39.51 N	31.55 E
Ankaramena	157b	21.57 S	46.39 E
Ankaratra ⋏	157b	19.25 S	47.12 E
Ankarimbelo	157b	22.08 S	47.20 E
Ankaroaka ∧	157b	17.48 S	48.32 E
Ankarsrum	26	57.42 N	16.19 E
Ankasakasa	157b	16.21 S	44.52 E
Ankata	80	50.44 N	51.34 E
Ankavandra	157b	18.46 S	45.18 E
Ankazoabo	157b	22.18 S	44.31 E
Ankazobe	157b	18.21 S	47.07 E
Ankazomiriotra	157b	19.38 S	46.32 E
Ankeny	190	41.43 N	93.36 W
An Khe	110	13.57 N	108.39 E
Ankilimalinika	157b	22.58 S	43.45 E
Ankilizato	157b	20.25 S	45.01 E
Anking → Anqing	100	30.31 N	117.02 E
Ankisabe	157b	19.17 S	46.29 E
Anklam	54	53.51 N	13.41 E
Ankleshwar	120	21.36 N	73.00 E
Ankober	144	9.35 N	39.44 E
Ankoro	154	6.45 S	26.57 E
Ankororoka	157b	25.30 S	45.11 E
Ankou	100	25.03 N	113.24 E
An'kovo	80	56.57 N	39.57 E
Ankpa	150	7.23 N	7.37 E
Ankum	52	52.32 N	7.52 E
Ankwe ≏	150	8.03 N	9.26 E
Anlinnuoer	98	41.11 N	114.31 E
Anliu	100	23.42 N	115.42 E
Anloga	150	5.47 N	0.50 E
Anlong	102	25.02 N	105.31 E
Ânlóng Vêng	110	14.14 N	104.05 E
Anlu	100	31.17 N	113.40 E
Anma-do I	98	35.21 N	126.02 E
Ånmyŏn-do I	98	36.30 N	126.22 E
Ånn ⊜	26	63.16 N	12.34 E
Ann, Cape ≻, Ant.	9	66.10 S	51.22 E
Ann, Cape ≻, Ma., U.S.	283	42.39 N	70.38 W
Anna, Ross.	78	51.29 N	40.25 E
Anna, Il., U.S.	194	37.27 N	89.14 W
Anna, Oh., U.S.	216	40.23 N	84.10 W
Anna, Tx., U.S.	196	33.21 N	96.33 W
Anna, Lake ⊜[1]	188	38.04 N	77.45 W
Annaba (Bône)	148	36.54 N	7.46 E
Annaba □[5]	148	36.50 N	8.00 E
An-Nabaṭīyah □[4]	132	33.20 N	35.30 E
An-Nabaṭīyah at-Taḥtā	132	33.23 N	35.29 E
Annaberg, Öst.	61	47.52 N	15.22 E
Annaberg, Öst.	64	47.31 N	13.26 E
Annaberg-Buchholz	54	50.35 N	13.00 E
An-Nabī Shīt	132	33.52 N	36.07 E
An-Nabk	130	34.01 N	36.44 E
An-Nabqīyah I	128	26.44 N	36.01 E
Annaburg	54	51.44 N	13.03 E
Annaburger Heide ⊸[3]	54	51.40 N	13.05 E
An-Nafūd ⊸[2]	128	28.30 N	41.00 E
Annagassan	48	53.53 N	6.20 W
Annahütte	54	51.34 N	13.53 E
An-Najaf	128	31.59 N	44.20 E
An-Najaf □[4]	128	31.00 N	44.00 E
Annaka	94	36.19 N	138.54 E
An-Nakhl, Miṣr	140	29.55 N	33.45 E
An-Nakhl, Sūrīy.	132	33.00 N	36.07 E
Annalee ≏	48	54.03 N	7.24 W
Annalee Heights	208	38.51 N	77.10 W
Annalong	48	54.06 N	5.53 W
Anna Maria	220	27.31 N	82.44 W
Anna Maria Island I	220	27.30 N	82.43 W
An-Nāmir	132	32.47 N	36.13 E
Annamitique, Chaîne ⋏	110	17.00 N	106.00 E
Annam → Trung Phan □[9]	110	15.00 N	108.00 E
Annan	44	54.59 N	3.16 W
Annan ≏	44	54.59 N	3.16 W
Annanberg	164	4.55 S	144.40 E
Annandale, Austl.	166	21.57 S	148.22 E
Annandale, Mn., U.S.	190	45.15 N	94.07 W
Annandale, N.J., U.S.	210	40.38 N	74.52 W
Annandale, Va., U.S.	208	38.49 N	77.11 W
Annandale V	44	55.10 N	3.25 W
Annandale-on-Hudson	210	42.01 N	73.54 W
Anna Pink, Bahía ⊂	254	45.50 S	74.50 W
Anna Plains	162	19.17 S	121.37 E
Anna Point ≻	174b	0.30 S	166.56 E
Annapolis	208	38.58 N	76.29 W
Annapolis Basin ⊂	186	44.39 N	65.42 W
Annapolis Royal	186	44.45 N	65.31 W
Annapūrṇa ∧	124	28.34 N	83.50 E
Annapūrṇapratham ∧	124	28.31 N	84.08 E
An-Naqīrah ⍑[4]	128	27.53 N	48.15 E
Ann Arbor	216	42.16 N	83.43 W
Ann Arbor Municipal Airport ⊠	281	42.14 N	83.45 W
Anna Regina	246	7.16 N	58.30 W
Annaricken Brook ≏	285	40.03 N	74.42 W
An-Nāṣirīyah, 'Irāq	128	31.02 N	46.16 E
An-Nāṣirīyah, Sūrīy.	130	33.52 N	36.49 E
Annaspan ⊜	158	28.33 S	25.47 E
An-Nawfalāb	140	15.52 N	32.32 E
An-Nawfalīyah	146	30.47 N	17.50 E
An-Nazlah	132	31.32 N	34.29 E
An-Nazlat	142	29.19 N	30.39 E
Annbank	44	55.28 N	4.30 W
Annean, Lake ⊜	162	26.54 S	118.14 E
Anne Arundel □[6]	208	38.59 N	76.30 W
Annebault	50	49.15 N	0.04 E
Annecy	58	45.54 N	6.07 E
Annecy, Lac d' ⊜	58	45.51 N	6.11 E
Annecy-le-Vieux	58	45.55 N	6.09 E
Annemasse	58	46.12 N	6.15 E
Annen	263	51.27 N	7.22 E
Annenkov Island I	244	54.29 S	37.05 W
Annenskij Most	76	60.45 N	37.10 E
Annenskoje	86	53.08 N	60.26 E
Anner ≏	48	52.22 N	7.39 W
Annestown	48	52.08 N	7.17 W
Annet I	42a	49.54 N	6.21 W
Annet-sur-Marne	261	48.56 N	2.43 E
Annette	182	55.03 N	131.34 W
Annette Island I	182	55.10 N	131.28 W
Annevoie-Rouillon	56	50.21 N	4.50 E
Annezin	50	50.32 N	2.37 E
Annfield Plain	44	54.51 N	1.45 W
An Nhon	110	13.53 N	109.06 E
Anniangniang	89	51.33 N	125.49 E
Annicco	62	45.14 N	9.52 E
An-Nīl □[4]	140	19.00 N	33.00 E
An-Nīl al-Azraq □[4]	140	12.00 N	34.00 E
Anning	102	24.59 N	102.18 E
Anningdu	102	36.56 N	104.31 E
Anninger ∧	264b	48.03 N	16.15 E
Annino	265a	59.46 N	30.03 E
Anninskije Mineral'nyje Vody	89	52.44 N	140.12 E
Annisquam	283	42.39 N	70.41 W
Annisquam ≏	283	42.39 N	70.41 W
Anniston	194	33.39 N	85.49 W
Annobón I	138	1.25 S	5.36 E
Annonay	62	45.14 N	4.40 E
Annopol	30	50.54 N	21.52 E
Anno-Rebrikovo	83	49.36 N	40.12 E
Annot	62	43.58 N	6.40 E
Annotto Bay	241q	18.16 N	76.46 W

Symbol	English	Deutsch	Español	Français	Português
≏	River	Fluß	Río	Rivière	Rio
≚	Canal	Kanal	Canal	Canal	Canal
⌊	Waterfall, Rapids	Wasserfall, Stromschnellen	Cascada, Rápidos	Chute d'eau, Rapides	Cascata, Rápidos
ꭕ	Strait	Meeresstraße	Estrecho	Détroit	Estreito
⊂	Bay, Gulf	Bucht, Golf	Bahía, Golfo	Baie, Golfe	Baía, Golfo
⊜	Lake, Lakes	See, Seen	Lago, Lagos	Lac, Lacs	Lago, Lagos
≡	Swamp	Sumpf	Pantano	Marais	Pântano
⊓	Ice Features, Glacier	Eis- und Gletscherformen	Accidentes Glaciales	Formes glaciaires	Acidentes glaciares
⍑	Other Hydrographic Features	Andere Hydrographische Objekte	Otros Elementos Hidrográficos	Autres données hydrographiques	Outros acidentes hidrográficos
⊹	Submarine Features	Untermeerische Objekte	Accidentes Submarinos	Formes de relief sous-marin	Acidentes submarinos
□	Political Unit	Politische Einheit	Unidad Politica	Entité politique	Unidade política
♁	Cultural Institution	Kulturelle Institution	Institución Cultural	Institution culturelle	Instituição cultural
⊥	Historical Site	Historische Stätte	Sitio Histórico	Site historique	Sitio histórico
♠	Recreational Site	Erholungs- und Ferienort	Sitio de Recreo	Centre de loisirs	Area de Lazer
⊠	Airport	Flughafen	Aeropuerto	Aéroport	Aeroporto
■	Military Installation	Militäranlage	Instalación Militar	Installation militaire	Instalação militar
⊸	Miscellaneous	Verschiedenes	Misceláneo	Divers	Diversos

Name	Page	Lat.°′	Long.°′
Annsjön ⊜	40	58.48 N	15.26 E
An-Nubayrah	142	30.54 N	30.35 E
An-Nuhūd	140	12.42 N	28.26 E
An-Nuʿmān I	128	27.08 N	35.46 E
An-Nuʿmānīyah	128	32.32 N	45.25 E
An-Nuwayrah	142	29.06 N	30.59 E
Annville, Ky., U.S.	192	37.19 N	83.58 W
Annville, Pa., U.S.	208	40.19 N	76.30 W
Annweiler am Trifels	56	49.12 N	7.58 E
Anō	94	34.46 N	136.27 E
Anoia	68	38.27 N	16.05 E
Anoia ≃	34	41.28 N	1.56 E
Anoka	190	45.11 N	93.23 W
Áno Liósia	267c	38.05 N	23.42 E
Año Nuevo Bay c	226	37.07 N	122.19 W
Anopino	80	55.42 N	40.40 E
Anori, Bra.	246	3.47 S	61.38 W
Anorí, Col.	246	7.05 N	75.08 W
Anorotsangana	157b	13.56 S	47.55 E
Anosibe	157b	19.26 S	48.13 E
Anosyennes, Chaînes ⋀	157b	24.30 S	46.50 E
Anotaié ≃	250	3.29 N	52.04 W
Anpilogovo	78	51.47 N	36.01 E
Anping, Zhg.	98	38.16 N	115.30 E
Anping, Zhg.	98	34.01 N	115.07 E
Anping, Zhg.	100	26.33 N	113.22 E
Anping, Zhg.	104	41.11 N	123.26 E
Anping, Zhg.	105	39.43 N	116.53 E
Anpu	102	21.27 N	110.00 E
ʿAnqābīyah, Jabal al- ∧[2]	142	30.01 N	31.37 E
Anqing	100	30.31 N	117.02 E
Anqiu	98	36.25 N	119.10 E
Anrath	56	51.17 N	6.28 E
Anren, Zhg.	100	28.04 N	119.20 E
Anren, Zhg.	100	26.42 N	113.16 E
Anrenzhen	107	30.31 N	103.38 E
Anröchte	52	51.33 N	8.19 E
Ans, Bel.	56	50.39 N	5.32 E
Ans, Dan.	41	56.19 N	9.36 E
Ansager	41	55.42 N	8.45 E
Ansai	102	36.54 N	109.10 E
ʿAnṣār	132	33.23 N	35.21 E
Ansbach	56	49.17 N	10.34 E
Anschan → Anshan	104	41.08 N	122.59 E
Anschlag	263	51.10 N	7.29 E
Anse	58	45.56 N	4.43 E
Anseba ≃	144	17.03 N	37.24 E
Anse-Bertrand	241o	16.29 N	61.31 W
Anse-d'Hainault	238	18.30 N	74.27 W
Anse La Raye	241f	13.57 N	61.03 W
Anselmo	198	41.37 N	99.51 W
Anseremme	56	50.15 N	4.54 E
Anserma	246	5.13 N	75.48 W
Ansfelden	61	48.13 N	14.17 E
Anshan	104	41.08 N	122.59 E
Anshun	102	26.15 N	105.56 E
Ansina	252	31.54 S	55.28 W
Ansley	198	41.17 N	99.22 W
Anson	196	32.45 N	99.53 W
Anson Bay c, Austl.	164	13.20 S	130.06 E
Anson Bay c, Norf. I.	174c	29.01 S	167.55 E
Anson Creek ≃	212	44.53 N	79.03 W
Ansŏng	98	37.02 N	127.16 E
Ansongo	150	15.40 N	0.30 E
Ansonia, Ct., U.S.	207	41.20 N	73.04 W
Ansonia, Oh., U.S.	216	40.12 N	84.38 W
Ansonville, N.C., U.S.	192	35.06 N	80.06 W
Ansonville, Pa., U.S.	214	40.51 N	78.34 W
Ansouis	62	43.44 N	5.28 E
Ansted	188	38.08 N	81.05 W
Anstey	42	52.40 N	1.11 W
Anstruther	46	56.13 N	2.42 W
Anstruther Lake ⊜	212	44.45 N	78.12 W
Ansudu	164	2.08 S	139.20 E
Ansus	164	1.44 S	135.49 E
Anta, Bra.	256	22.03 S	42.59 W
Anta, Perú	248	13.29 S	72.09 W
Antabamba	248	14.19 S	72.55 W
Antakya (Antioch)	130	36.14 N	36.07 E
Antalaha	157b	14.53 S	50.16 E
Antalieptė	76	55.40 N	25.51 E
Antalovcy	78	48.38 N	22.31 E
Antalya	130	36.53 N	30.42 E
Antalya □[4]	130	37.00 N	31.00 E
Antalya, Gulf of → Antalya Körfezi c	130	36.30 N	31.00 E
Antalya Körfezi c	130	36.30 N	31.00 E
Antambohobe	157b	22.20 S	46.47 E
An Tan	110	15.26 N	108.39 E
Antanambao Manampotsy	157b	19.29 S	48.34 E
Antanambe	157b	16.26 S	49.52 E
Antananarivo	157b	18.55 S	47.31 E
Antananarivo □[4]	157b	19.00 S	47.00 E
Antanetibe	157b	18.27 S	46.42 E
Antanifotsy	157b	19.39 S	47.19 E
Antanimieva	157b	22.12 S	43.44 E
Antanimora	157b	24.49 S	45.40 E
Antar, Djebel ∧	148	31.57 N	1.56 W
Antarctica ±[1]	9	87.00 S	60.00 E
Antarctic Peninsula ≻[1]	9	69.30 S	65.00 W
Antarctique, Péninsule → Antarctic Peninsula ≻[1]	9	69.30 S	65.00 W
Antarctiques territoires britanniques → British Antarctic Territory □[2]	9	60.00 S	45.00 W
Antarktis → Antarctica ±[1]	9	87.00 S	60.00 E
Antártica, Península → Antarctic Peninsula ≻[1]	9	69.30 S	65.00 W
Antas	250	10.23 S	38.20 W
Antas, Ribeirão das ≃	256	21.47 S	46.36 W
Antas, Rio das ≃	252	29.04 S	51.21 W
An Teallach ∧	46	57.48 N	5.14 W
Antechamber Bay c	168b	35.48 S	138.05 E
Antegnate	62	45.29 N	9.47 E
Antela, Laguna de ⊜	34	42.07 N	7.41 W
Antelope Acres	228	34.44 N	118.19 W
Antelope Creek ≃, Nv., U.S.	204	40.00 N	117.24 W
Antelope Creek ≃, S.D., U.S.	198	45.19 N	102.27 W
Antelope Creek ≃, Wy., U.S.	198	43.29 N	105.23 W
Antelope Island I	202	40.57 N	112.12 W
Antelope Mine	154	21.02 S	28.27 E
Antelope Peak ∧	204	41.19 N	114.58 W
Antelope Reservoir ⊜[1]	202	42.54 N	117.13 W
Antelope Valley ∨	228	34.45 N	118.20 W
Antelope Wash ∨	204	39.33 N	116.17 W
Antenor Navarro	250	6.44 S	38.27 W
Antequera, Esp.	34	37.01 N	4.33 W
Antequera, Para.	252	24.08 S	57.07 W
Antero Reservoir ⊜[1]	200	39.00 N	105.55 W
Anterselva, Lago d' ⊜	64	46.53 N	12.10 E
Anterselva di Sopra	64	46.52 N	12.08 E
Antes Fort	210	41.12 N	77.14 W
Antetikireja	157b	14.42 S	47.29 E
Antevamena	157b	21.02 S	44.08 E
Antey-Saint-André	62	45.48 N	7.36 E
Anthéor	62	43.26 N	6.53 E
Anthon	198	42.23 N	95.51 W
Anthony, Fl., U.S.	192	29.17 N	82.06 W
Anthony, Ks., U.S.	198	37.09 N	98.01 W
Anthony, N.M., U.S.	200	32.00 N	106.36 W
Anthony, R.I., U.S.	207	41.41 N	71.32 W
Anthony, Tx., U.S.	200	31.59 N	106.36 W
Anthony Chabot Regional Park ♦	282	37.45 N	122.06 W
Anthony Creek ≃	188	37.54 N	80.20 W
Anthony Lagoon	162	17.59 S	135.32 E
Anthony Peak ∧	204	39.51 N	122.58 W
Anti-Atlas ⋀	148	30.00 N	8.30 W
Antibes	62	43.35 N	7.07 E
Antibes, Cap d' ≻	62	43.32 N	7.07 E
Anticosti, Île d' I	186	49.30 N	63.00 W
Antiesen ≃	60	48.22 N	13.24 E
Antietam Creek, West Branch ≃	208	39.41 N	77.37 W
Antietam National Battlefield ♦	188	39.24 N	77.47 W
Antifer, Cap d' ≻	50	49.41 N	0.10 E
Antignano	66	43.30 N	10.19 E
Antigo	190	45.08 N	89.09 W
Antigonish	186	45.35 N	61.55 W
Antigorio, Valle ∨	58	46.18 N	8.20 E
Antigua I	240c	17.03 N	61.48 W
Antigua and Barbuda □[1], N.A.	230	17.03 N	61.48 W
Antigua and Barbuda □[1], N.A.	240c	17.03 N	61.48 W
Antigua Guatemala	236	14.34 N	90.44 W
Antigua International Airport ⊠	240c	17.09 N	61.47 W
Antigues, Pointe d' ≻	241o	16.26 N	61.33 W
Antiguo Morelos	234	22.33 N	99.05 W
Anti-Lebanon → Sharqī, Al-Jabal ash- ⋀	132	33.35 N	36.00 E
Antilla, Arg.	252	26.07 S	64.36 W
Antilla, Cuba	240p	20.50 N	75.45 W
Antillas, Archipiélago de las → West Indies II	230	19.00 N	70.00 W
Antillas Holandesas → Netherlands Antilles □[2]	241s	12.15 N	69.00 W
Antilles hollandaise → Netherlands Antilles □[2]	241s	12.15 N	69.00 W
Antilles néerlandaises → Netherlands Antilles □[2]	241s	12.15 N	69.00 W
Antillo	70	37.58 N	15.15 E
Anṭilyās	132	33.55 N	35.35 E
Antímano ◆[8]	286c	10.28 N	66.59 W
Antimony	200	38.07 N	111.59 W
Anting	106	31.18 N	121.09 E
Antioch, Ca., U.S.	226	38.00 N	121.48 W
Antioch, Il., U.S.	216	42.28 N	88.05 W
Antioch → Antakya	130	36.14 N	36.07 E
Antioquia	246	6.33 N	75.50 W
Antioquia □[5]	246	7.00 N	75.30 W
Antipino, Ross.	76	55.55 N	33.16 E
Antipino, Ross.	86	57.49 N	66.34 E
Antipino, Ross.	86	59.01 N	55.10 E
Antipodes Islands II	9	49.40 S	178.47 E
Antipolo	116	14.35 N	121.10 E
Antipovka	80	49.50 N	45.20 E
Antiquarian Museum ✥	283	42.27 N	71.20 W
Antique □[4]	116	11.00 N	121.45 E
Antizana ∧[1]	246	0.30 S	78.08 W
Antler ≃	184	49.08 N	101.00 W
Antlers	196	34.13 N	95.37 W
Antoetra	157b	20.46 S	47.20 E
Antofagasta	252	23.39 S	70.24 W
Antofagasta □[4]	252	23.30 S	69.00 W
Antofagasta de la Sierra	252	26.04 S	67.25 W
Antofalla, Salar de ≚	252	25.44 S	67.45 W
Antofalla, Volcán ∧[1]	252	25.34 S	67.55 W
Antoing	50	50.34 N	3.27 E
Antolana ∧	157b	17.04 S	48.09 E
Antón, Pan.	236	8.24 N	80.16 W
Anton, Tx., U.S.	196	33.49 N	102.10 W
Anton Chico	200	35.12 N	105.08 W
Antongila, Helodrano c	157b	15.45 S	49.50 E
Antonia	219	38.21 N	90.27 W
Antonibe	157b	15.07 S	47.24 E
Antonina	252	25.27 S	48.43 W
Antonina do Norte	250	6.43 S	39.58 W
Antoniny	78	49.49 N	26.52 E
Antonio Amaro	232	24.16 N	104.01 W
Antonio Carboni	258	35.12 S	59.20 W
Antônio Carlos	256	21.19 S	43.45 W
Antonio de Biedma	254	47.29 S	66.30 W
Antonio Escobedo	234	20.46 N	103.57 W
Antônio Lemos	250	1.22 S	50.50 W
Antônio Prado	252	28.51 S	51.17 W
Antonito	200	37.05 N	106.00 W
Antón Lizardo, Punta ≻	234	19.03 N	95.58 W
Antonov	78	49.37 N	29.47 E
Antonovka, Kaz.	86	53.19 N	68.26 E
Antonovka, Kaz.	86	45.38 N	80.15 E
Antonovka, Ross.	80	54.55 N	49.30 E
Antonovo	80	49.23 N	51.47 E
Antony	50	48.45 N	2.18 E
Antopol'	76	52.12 N	24.47 E
Antou	100	26.07 N	118.11 E
Antracit	83	48.06 N	39.06 E
Antraigues	62	44.43 N	4.21 E
Antrain	32	48.27 N	1.29 W
Antratsit → Antracit	83	48.06 N	39.06 E
Antrift ≃	56	50.54 N	9.15 E
Antrim, N. Ire., U.K.	48	54.43 N	6.13 W
Antrim, Oh., U.S.	214	40.06 N	81.23 W
Antrim, Pa., U.S.	210	41.37 N	77.18 W
Antrodoco	66	42.25 N	13.05 E
Antronapiana	58	46.03 N	8.07 E
Antropologia, Museo Nacional de ✥	286a	19.25 N	99.11 W
Antropovo, Ross.	80	58.26 N	43.00 E
Antropovo, Ross.	82	55.15 N	37.39 E
Antsakabary	157b	15.03 S	48.56 E
Antsalova	157b	18.40 S	44.37 E
Antsenavolo	157b	21.24 S	48.03 E
Antsiafabositra	157b	17.18 S	46.57 E
Antsirabe, Madag.	157b	14.00 S	49.59 E
Antsirabe, Madag.	157b	15.57 S	48.58 E
Antsirabe, Madag.	157b	19.51 S	47.02 E
Antsiranana	157b	12.16 S	49.17 E
Antsiranana □[4]	157b	13.30 S	49.10 E
Antsla	76	57.50 N	26.32 E
Antsohihy	157b	14.52 S	47.59 E
Anttis	24	67.16 N	22.52 E
Antu (Songjiang)	98	42.32 N	128.18 E
Antufash, Jazīrat I	144	15.42 N	42.25 E
Antulai, Gunong ∧	112	4.40 N	116.21 E
Antun'	89	47.36 N	135.46 E
Antung → Dandong	98	40.08 N	124.20 E
Antuševo, Ross.	76	59.59 N	42.18 E
Antuševo, Ross.	76	59.54 N	37.40 E
Antwerp, N.Y., U.S.	212	44.11 N	75.36 W
Antwerp, Oh., U.S.	216	41.10 N	84.44 W
Antwerp → Antwerpen	50	51.13 N	4.25 E
Antwerpen (Anvers)	50	51.13 N	4.25 E
Antwerpen □[4]	56	51.10 N	4.50 E
Antykan	89	54.55 N	135.12 E
Anua	174u	14.16 S	170.40 W
Anučino, Ross.	80	52.58 N	43.52 E
Anučino, Ross.	89	43.58 N	133.02 E
Anugul	120	20.51 N	85.06 E
Anŭi	98	35.38 N	127.48 E
An'uj ≃	89	49.18 N	136.27 E
An'ujsk	74	68.18 N	161.38 E
An'ujskij chrebet ⋀, Ross.	74	67.30 N	166.00 E
Anujskij chrebet ⋀, Ross.	86	51.30 N	84.55 E
Anundshögen ⊥	40	59.38 N	16.37 E
Anūpgarh	123	29.11 N	73.13 E
Anūpshahr	124	28.22 N	78.16 E
Ānūr	126	22.55 N	87.39 E
Anuradhapura	122	8.21 N	80.23 E
Anversa degli Abruzzi	66	41.59 N	13.48 E
Anvers → Antwerpen	50	51.13 N	4.25 E
Anvers Island I	9	64.33 S	63.35 W
Anvik	180	62.40 N	160.12 W
Anvik ≃	180	62.39 N	160.14 W
Anvil Peak ∧	181a	52.00 N	179.35 E
Anvil Range ⋀	180	62.30 N	133.50 W
Anvin	50	50.27 N	2.15 E
Anxi, Zhg.	100	25.06 N	118.12 E
Anxi, Zhg.	100	25.15 N	115.06 E
Anxi, Zhg.	102	40.32 N	95.51 E
Anxi, Zhg.	106	30.25 N	120.01 E
Anxian	102	31.40 N	104.32 E
Anxiang	102	29.23 N	112.09 E
Anxin (Xin'anzhen)	105	38.55 N	115.55 E
Anxing	106	31.24 N	119.06 E
Anxious Bay c	162	33.25 S	134.35 E
Anyama	150	5.30 N	4.03 W
Anyang, Taehan	98	37.23 N	126.55 E
Anyang, Zhg.	98	36.06 N	114.21 E
Anyang ≃	98	36.01 N	114.46 E
Anyeke	154	2.24 N	32.31 E
A'nyêmaqên Shan ⋀	102	34.30 N	100.00 E
Anyer Kidul	115a	6.04 S	105.53 E
Anyi	100	28.50 N	115.31 E
Anykščiai	76	55.32 N	25.06 E
Anyox	182	55.25 N	129.49 W
Anysberg	158	33.31 S	20.46 E
Anyuan, Zhg.	100	26.36 N	116.38 E
Anyuan, Zhg.	100	27.37 N	113.54 E
Anyuan, Zhg.	100	25.08 N	115.28 E
Anyuanyi → Tianzhu	102	37.14 N	102.59 E
Anyue	107	30.06 N	105.21 E
Anza ≃	58	46.00 N	8.17 E
Anza-Borrego Desert State Park ♦	204	33.00 N	116.26 W
Anzac	184	56.27 N	111.02 W
Anzaldo	248	17.50 S	65.55 W
Anzano di Puglia	68	41.07 N	15.17 E
Anzbari ∧	123	34.40 N	74.50 E
Anze	102	36.11 N	112.16 E
Anžero-Sudžensk	86	56.07 N	86.00 E
Anzhen	106	31.36 N	120.28 E
Anzhou	105	38.52 N	115.49 E
Anzhuang	106	31.04 N	121.01 E
Anzi, It.	68	40.31 N	15.55 E
Anzi, Zaïre	152	0.52 S	23.24 E
Anzicun	105	39.46 N	115.50 E
Anzin	50	50.22 N	3.30 E
Anzio	66	41.27 N	12.37 E
Anzoátegui □[3]	246	9.00 N	64.30 W
Anzob	85	39.10 N	68.48 E
Anzob, pereval)(	85	39.07 N	68.52 E
Anzola dell'Emilia	64	44.33 N	11.11 E
Anzon ≃	62	45.45 N	3.57 E
Anžu, ostrova II	74	75.30 N	143.00 E
Aoba I	175f	15.25 S	167.50 E
Aoba / Maewo □[8]	175f	15.05 S	168.00 E
Aogaki	96	35.14 N	135.00 E
Aoga-shima I	90	32.28 N	139.46 E
Aohaibolihu	104	42.01 N	121.32 E
Aohandaba	104	42.05 N	121.59 E
Aohan Qi (Xinhui)	98	42.19 N	119.59 E
Aoíz	34	42.47 N	1.22 W
Aoji	98	42.31 N	130.23 E
Aojiang	100	27.37 N	120.33 E
Aojiao	100	23.37 N	117.26 E
Aola	175e	9.32 S	160.29 E
Aoliyingzi	104	42.14 N	121.58 E
Ao Luk	110	8.23 N	98.43 E
Aomar	34	36.30 N	3.47 E
Aomen → Macau	100	22.14 N	113.35 E
Aomori	92	40.49 N	140.45 E
Aonla	124	28.17 N	79.09 E
Aono-yama ∧	96	34.27 N	131.48 E
Aóös (Vijosë) ≃	38	40.37 N	19.20 E
A'opo	175a	13.29 S	172.30 W
Aôral, Phnum ∧	110	12.02 N	104.10 E
Aorangi Mountains ⋀	172	41.26 S	175.20 E
Aore I	175f	15.35 S	167.10 E
Aorere ≃	172	40.41 S	172.40 E
Aoshang	100	25.42 N	113.00 E
Ao-shima I, Nihon	96	33.44 N	132.29 E
Ao-shima I, Nihon	96	33.55 N	134.44 E
Aosta	62	45.44 N	7.20 E
Aosta □[4]	58	45.45 N	7.20 E
Aosta, Valle d' ∨	62	45.46 N	7.25 E
Aoste	62	45.35 N	5.36 E
Aotou	100	22.44 N	114.33 E
Aoudaghost ⊥	150	17.25 N	10.40 W
Aouderas	150	17.37 N	8.26 E
Aoudour, Oued ≃	34	35.02 N	5.02 W
Aouk, Bahr ≃	146	8.51 N	18.53 E
Aoukalé ≃	146	9.17 N	22.42 E
Aouk-Aoukalé, Réserve de Faune de l' ◆[4]	146	10.00 N	21.15 E
Aoukâr ◆[1]	150	18.00 N	9.30 W
Aoulime, Jebel ∧	148	30.48 N	8.50 W
Aoumou	175f	21.24 S	165.50 E
Aourou	150	14.57 N	11.35 W
Aoya	96	35.31 N	133.59 E
Aoyama	94	34.40 N	136.11 E
Aoyama-tōge)(	94	34.40 N	136.16 E
Aozi	146	21.04 N	18.41 E
Aozou	146	21.49 N	17.25 E
Apa ≃	252	22.06 S	58.00 W
Apache	196	34.53 N	98.21 W
Apache Junction	200	33.24 N	111.32 W
Apache Lake ⊜[1]	200	33.36 N	111.16 W
Apache Peak ∧	200	31.49 N	110.25 W
Apalachee ≃	192	33.32 N	83.17 W
Apalachee Bay c	192	30.00 N	84.13 W
Apalaches → Appalachian Mountains ⋀	178	41.00 N	77.00 W
Apalachicola	192	29.43 N	84.59 W
Apalachicola ≃	192	29.44 N	84.59 W
Apalachicola Bay c	192	29.40 N	85.00 W
Apalachin	210	42.04 N	76.09 W
Apam	150	5.17 N	0.44 W
Apan	234	19.43 N	98.25 W
Apanas, Laguna de ⊜[1]	236	13.11 N	85.59 W
Apango	234	17.44 N	99.20 W
Apapa ◆[8]	273a	6.27 N	3.22 E
Apapa Wharf ◆[5]	273a	6.23 N	3.23 E
Apaporis ≃	246	1.23 S	69.25 W
Aparados da Serra, Parque Nacional de ♦	252	29.30 S	50.32 W
Aparan	84	40.36 N	44.23 E
Aparecida	256	22.50 S	45.14 W
Aparima ≃	172	46.20 S	168.01 E
Aparri	116	18.22 N	121.39 E
Apartadó	246	7.54 N	76.39 W
Apaseo El Grande	234	20.33 N	100.41 W
Apastovo	80	55.11 N	48.30 E
Apatin	38	45.40 N	18.59 E
Apatity	24	67.34 N	33.18 E
Apatou	250	5.09 N	54.20 W
Apatzingán de la Constitución	234	19.05 N	102.21 W
Apaxtla de Castrejón	234	18.09 N	99.52 W
Apayacu ≃	246	3.19 S	71.51 W
Ap Ba Tien	269c	10.44 N	106.36 E
Ap Binh Quoi	269c	10.48 N	106.36 E
Ap Binh Thanh	110	11.11 N	108.42 E
Apcheron, Péninsule de l' → Apšeronskij poluostrov ≻[1]	84	40.30 N	50.00 E
Ape	76	57.32 N	26.40 E
Apeadero Funke	258	35.28 S	58.59 W
Apecchio	66	43.33 N	12.25 E
Ape Dale ∨	42	52.30 N	2.45 W
Apeganau Lake ⊜	184	55.35 N	99.35 W
Apelação	266c	38.49 N	9.08 W
Apeldoorn	52	52.13 N	5.58 E
Apeleg, Arroyo ≃	254	44.58 S	70.07 W
Apen	52	53.13 N	7.48 E
Apenes	224	49.16 N	124.41 W
Apeninos → Appennino ⋀	36	43.00 N	13.00 E
Apenninen → Appennino ⋀	36	43.00 N	13.00 E
Apennines → Appennino ⋀	36	43.00 N	13.00 E
Apennins → Appennino ⋀	36	43.00 N	13.00 E
Apensen	52	53.26 N	9.37 E
Apese ◆[8]	273a	6.25 N	3.25 E
Apetlon	61	47.45 N	16.50 E
Apex	192	35.43 N	78.51 W
Apex Mountain ∧	180	62.28 N	138.04 W
Api	154	3.40 N	25.26 E
Api ∧	124	30.00 N	80.57 E
Api, Tanjung ≻	112	0.48 S	121.39 E
Apía, Col.	246	5.05 N	75.58 W
Apia, W. Sam.	175a	13.50 S	171.44 W
Apiacá ≃	250	9.16 S	57.03 W
Apiacás, Serra dos ⋀[1]	248	10.15 S	57.15 W
Apiaí	252	24.31 S	48.50 W
Apiaú ≃	246	2.39 N	61.12 W
Apice	68	41.07 N	14.56 E
Apipilulco	234	18.11 N	99.41 W
Apishapa ≃	198	38.08 N	103.57 W
Apiti	172	39.58 S	175.53 E
Apizaco	234	19.25 N	98.09 W
Apizolaya	232	24.50 N	102.15 W
Aplahoué	150	6.56 N	1.41 E
Aplao	248	16.05 S	72.31 W
Ap Lei Chau I	271d	22.15 N	114.09 E
Aplerbeck ◆[8]	263	51.29 N	7.33 E
Aplinskij, porog ∟	88	58.28 N	100.32 E
Apo	234	19.25 N	102.25 W
Apo, Mount ∧	116	6.59 N	125.16 E
Apodi	250	5.39 S	37.48 W
Apodi ≃	250	4.56 S	37.10 W
Apo East Pass ⊍	116	12.40 N	120.40 E
Apoera	250	5.12 N	57.10 W
Apolakkiá	38	36.06 N	27.50 E
Apolda	54	51.01 N	11.31 E
Apolima Strait ⊍	175a	13.50 S	172.10 W
Apolinario Saravia	252	24.25 S	64.02 W
Apollo	214	40.34 N	79.34 W
Apollo Bay	166	38.45 S	143.40 E
Apollo Beach	220	27.45 N	82.25 W
Apollonia ⊥	146	32.54 N	21.58 E
Apolo	248	14.43 S	68.31 W
Apón ≃	246	10.06 N	72.23 W
Aponguao ≃	246	4.48 N	61.36 W
Apopa	236	13.48 N	89.11 W
Apopka	220	28.40 N	81.30 W
Apopka, Lake ⊜	220	28.37 N	81.38 W
Apoquindo	286e	33.24 S	70.32 W
Aporá	250	11.39 S	38.05 W
Aporé	255	18.58 S	52.01 W
Aporé ≃	255	19.27 S	50.57 W
Apo Reef ✢[2]	116	12.40 N	120.29 E
Aporema	250	1.14 N	50.49 W
Aporo	234	19.41 N	100.25 W
Apostle Islands II	190	46.50 N	90.30 W
Apostle Islands National Lakeshore ♦	190	46.55 N	91.00 W
Apóstoles	252	27.55 S	55.46 W
Apostolovo	78	47.39 N	33.44 E
Appalachen → Appalachian Mountains ⋀	178	41.00 N	77.00 W
Appalaches, Monts → Appalachian Mountains ⋀	178	41.00 N	77.00 W
Appalachia	192	36.54 N	82.46 W
Appalachian Mountains ⋀	178	41.00 N	77.00 W
Äppelbo	40	60.30 N	14.00 E
Appelhülsen	52	51.54 N	7.25 E
Appen	52	53.40 N	9.44 E
Appennino (Apennines) ⋀	36	43.00 N	13.00 E
Appennino, Galleria dell' ◆[5]	66	44.10 N	11.10 E
Appennino Abruzzese ⋀	66	42.00 N	14.00 E
Appennino Calabrese ⋀	68	39.00 N	16.30 E
Appennino Campano ⋀	66	41.30 N	15.00 E
Appennino Ligure ⋀	62	44.30 N	9.00 E
Appennino Lucano ⋀	68	40.30 N	16.00 E
Appennino Tosco-Emiliano ⋀	36	44.00 N	11.30 E
Appennino Umbro-Marchigiano ⋀	66	43.00 N	13.00 E
Appenzell	58	47.20 N	9.25 E
Appenzell-Ausser Rhoden □[3]	58	47.22 N	9.28 E
Appenzell-Inner Rhoden □[3]	58	47.18 N	9.25 E
Appiano (Eppan)	64	46.28 N	11.15 E
Appiano Gentile	62	45.44 N	8.59 E
Appin	170	34.12 S	150.47 E
Appingedam	52	53.18 N	6.52 E
Apple ≃, U.S.	190	42.11 N	90.14 W
Apple ≃, Wi., U.S.	190	45.09 N	92.45 W
Appleby, S. Afr.	158	27.39 S	22.36 E
Appleby, Eng., U.K.	44	54.36 N	2.29 W
Appleby, Tx., U.S.	222	31.43 N	94.36 W
Apple Creek	214	40.45 N	81.50 W
Apple Creek ≃, Il., U.S.	219	39.22 N	90.37 W
Apple Creek ≃, Mo., U.S.	194	37.35 N	89.32 W
Apple Creek ≃, N.D., U.S.	198	46.40 N	100.46 W
Applecross	46	57.25 N	5.49 W
Appledore	42	51.03 N	4.10 W
Applegate	226	39.06 N	120.59 W
Applegate ≃	202	42.26 N	123.27 W
Apple Hill	206	45.13 N	74.46 W
Apple Orchard Mountain ∧	192	37.31 N	79.31 W
Apples	58	46.34 N	6.25 E
Apple Springs	222	31.13 N	94.58 W
Appleton, Eng., U.K.	262	53.21 N	2.33 W
Appleton, Mn., U.S.	198	45.11 N	96.01 W
Appleton, Wa., U.S.	224	45.48 N	121.16 W
Appleton, Wi., U.S.	190	44.15 N	88.24 W
Appleton City	194	38.11 N	94.01 W
Apple Valley	228	34.30 N	117.11 W
Applewold	214	40.47 N	79.36 W
Appley Bridge	262	53.35 N	2.43 W
Appling	192	33.32 N	82.18 W
Appoigny	50	47.53 N	3.32 E
Appomattox	192	37.21 N	78.49 W
Appomattox ≃	192	37.18 N	77.18 W
Appomattox Court House National Historical Park ♦	192	37.23 N	78.48 W
Approuague ≃	250	4.38 N	51.58 W
Apra Harbor c	174p	13.27 N	144.38 E
Aprelevka	82	55.33 N	37.04 E
Aprel'sk	88	58.10 N	114.34 E
Aprel'skij	89	53.30 N	126.16 E
Apremont	58	46.13 N	5.40 E
Apremont-la-Forêt	56	48.51 N	5.38 E
Aprica, Passo d')(	64	46.09 N	10.09 E
Apricena	68	41.47 N	15.27 E
Aprigliano	68	39.14 N	16.20 E
April ≃	164	4.18 S	142.26 E
Aprilia	66	41.36 N	12.39 E
Apscheron → Apšeronskij poluostrov ≻[1]	84	40.30 N	50.00 E
Apšeronsk	84	44.28 N	39.44 E
Apšeronskij poluostrov ≻[1]	84	40.30 N	50.00 E
Apshawa	276	41.01 N	74.22 W
Apsley	212	44.45 N	78.06 W
Apt	62	43.53 N	5.24 E
Aptakisic	278	42.12 N	87.56 W
Ap Tan Hoa	269c	10.45 N	106.35 E
Ap Tan My	110	11.43 N	108.49 E
Aptos	226	36.58 N	121.53 W
Apuane, Alpi ⋀	64	44.09 N	10.15 E
Apuaú ≃	246	2.32 S	60.48 W
Apucarana	255	23.33 S	51.29 W
Apulia Station	210	42.49 N	76.05 W
Apure □[3]	246	7.10 N	68.50 W
Apure ≃	246	7.37 N	66.25 W
Apurímac □[5]	248	14.00 S	73.00 W
Apurímac ≃	248	11.48 S	74.03 W
Apurito	246	7.56 N	68.27 W
Āq ≃	84	38.59 N	45.27 E
Aqaba, Gulf of c	128	29.00 N	34.40 E
Aqabah, Wādī al- ∨	132	30.14 N	33.53 E
Āqbolāgh	84	38.54 N	44.32 E
Āqchah	120	36.56 N	66.11 E
ʿAqīq	140	18.14 N	38.12 E
ʿAqīq, Khalīj c	140	18.20 N	38.10 E
ʿAqīq, Wādī al- ∨	128	24.17 N	40.10 E
Aq Qalʿeh	128	37.01 N	54.30 E
Aqqikkol Hu ⊜	120	37.05 N	88.05 E
ʿAqrabah	132	33.06 N	36.00 E
ʿAqrah	128	36.45 N	43.54 E
Aquarius Plateau ⋀[1]	200	38.05 N	111.40 W
Aquasco	208	38.35 N	76.43 W
Aquashicola	210	40.49 N	75.35 W
Aquashicola Creek ≃	210	40.47 N	75.37 W
Äquatorial-Guinea → Equatorial Guinea □[1]	152	2.00 N	9.00 E
Aquebogue	207	40.56 N	72.37 W
Aqueduct Race Track ♦	276	40.40 N	73.50 W
Aquia Creek ≃	208	38.23 N	77.18 W
Aquiaulne ≃	50	47.37 N	2.30 E
Aquidabã	250	10.17 S	37.02 W
Aquidabã ≃	248	20.58 S	57.50 W
Aquidabán ≃	252	23.11 S	57.32 W
Aquidauana	248	20.28 S	55.48 W
Aquidauana ≃	248	19.44 S	56.50 W
Aquila, Méx.	234	18.36 N	103.30 W
Aquila, Schw.	58	46.31 N	8.57 E
Aquileia	64	45.46 N	13.22 E
Aquiles Serdán, Méx.	232	28.36 N	105.53 W
Aquiles Serdán, Méx.	232	25.38 N	97.50 W
Aquili, Cachoeira ∟	250	11.08 S	55.22 W
Aquilla, Oh., U.S.	214	41.34 N	81.09 W
Aquilla, Tx., U.S.	222	31.51 N	97.13 W
Aquilla Creek ≃	222	31.40 N	97.10 W
Aquilonia (S.M.)	68	41.00 N	15.29 E
Aquin	238	18.17 N	73.24 W
Aquincumi Museum ✥	264c	47.34 N	19.03 E
Aquino	66	41.30 N	13.42 E
Aquio ≃	246	2.42 N	67.34 W
Ara	124	25.34 N	84.40 E
Ara ≃, Esp.	34	42.25 N	0.09 E
Ara ≃, Ire.	48	52.24 N	7.56 W
Ara ≃, Nihon	92	38.09 N	139.25 E
Ara ≃, Nihon	94	35.39 N	139.51 E
Arab	194	34.19 N	86.29 W
ʿArab, Baḥr al- ≃	140	9.02 N	29.28 E
ʿArab, Khalīj al- c	140	30.55 N	29.05 E
Arab, Oued el ∨	148	34.41 N	6.31 E
Arab, Shatt al- ≃	128	29.57 N	48.34 E
ʿArab, Wādī al- ∨	132	32.35 N	35.35 E
ʿArabābād	128	33.02 N	57.41 E
ʿArabah, Wādī ∨	142	29.07 N	32.39 E
ʿArabah, Wādī al- (HaʿArava) ∨	132	30.10 N	35.10 E
Arabako □[4]	34	42.50 N	2.45 W
Araban	130	37.26 N	37.41 E
Arabatskaja strelka ≻[2]	78	45.40 N	35.00 E
Arabatskij zaliv c	78	45.20 N	35.30 E
Arabba	64	46.30 N	11.52 E
Arabelo	246	4.55 N	64.13 W
Arabi	194	29.57 N	90.00 W
Arabian Basin ✢[1]	12	11.30 N	65.00 E
Arabian Desert → Sharqīyah, Aṣ-Ṣaḥrā' ash- ◆[2]	140	28.00 N	32.00 E
Arabian Gulf → Persian Gulf c	128	27.00 N	51.00 E
Arabian Peninsula ≻[1]	12	25.00 N	45.00 E
Arabian Sea ▿[2]	118	15.00 N	65.00 E
Arabia Saudita → Saudi Arabia □[1]	118	25.00 N	45.00 E
Arabie, Mer d' → Arabian Sea ▿[2]	118	15.00 N	65.00 E
Arabie Saoudite → Saudi Arabia □[1]	118	25.00 N	45.00 E
Arabique, Péninsule → Arabian Peninsula ≻[1]	12	25.00 N	45.00 E
Arabisches Meer → Arabian Sea ▿[2]	118	15.00 N	65.00 E
Arab-Jengidža	84	39.29 N	44.58 E
ʿArab Muṭayr	142	27.16 N	31.14 E
Ara-Bure, porog ∟	88	53.00 N	100.12 E
Araç	130	41.15 N	33.21 E
Araçá ≃	246	0.25 S	62.55 W
Aracaju	250	10.55 S	37.04 W
Araçariguama	256	23.26 S	47.04 W
Aracataca	246	10.36 N	74.12 W
Aracati	250	4.34 S	37.46 W
Araçatuba	255	21.12 S	50.25 W
Araceli	116	10.33 N	119.59 E
Aracena	34	37.53 N	6.33 W
Arâches-les-Carroz	58	46.02 N	6.39 E
Arachino-seki ⊥	94	35.33 N	136.05 E
Araci	250	11.20 S	38.57 W
Aracides, Cape ≻	175e	8.39 S	161.01 E
Aracitaba	256	21.20 S	43.23 W
Aracoiaba	250	4.23 S	38.49 W
Aracruz	255	19.49 S	40.16 W
Araçuaí	255	16.52 S	42.04 W
Araçuaí ≃	255	16.46 S	42.02 W
Arad, Rom.	38	46.11 N	21.20 E
ʿArad, Yis.	132	31.15 N	35.13 E
Arad □[6]	38	46.20 N	21.40 E
Arada, Hond.	236	14.48 N	88.18 W
Arada, Tchad	146	15.01 N	20.40 E
Aradeo	68	40.08 N	18.08 E
Aradhíppou	130	34.57 N	33.35 E
Arafali	144	15.05 N	39.45 E
Arafune-san ∧	94	36.12 N	138.38 E
Arafura Sea ▿[2]	164	9.00 S	133.00 E
Arafura Shelf ✢[4]	14	10.00 S	137.00 E
Aragac, gora ∧	84	40.32 N	44.14 E
Aragarças	255	15.55 S	52.15 W
Arago, Cape ≻	202	43.18 N	124.25 W
Aragon	192	34.02 N	85.03 W
Aragón □[4]	34	41.30 N	0.30 W
Aragón ≃	34	42.13 N	1.44 W
Aragona	70	37.24 N	13.37 E
Aragua □[3]	246	10.00 N	67.10 W
Araguacema	250	8.50 S	49.34 W
Araguaçu	255	12.49 S	49.51 W
Aragua de Barcelona	246	9.28 N	64.49 W
Aragua de Maturín	246	9.58 N	63.29 W
Araguaia ≃	242	5.21 S	48.41 W
Araguaia, Braço Menor ≃	250	9.50 S	50.10 W
Araguaia, Parque Nacional do ♦	250	12.00 S	50.20 W
Araguaína	250	7.12 S	48.12 W
Araguainha	255	16.49 S	53.05 W
Araguao, Caño ≃[1]	246	9.15 N	60.50 W
Araguari	255	18.38 S	48.11 W
Araguari ≃, Bra.	250	1.15 N	49.55 W
Araguari ≃, Bra.	255	18.21 S	48.40 W
Araguatins	250	5.38 S	48.07 W
Aragvi ≃	84	41.50 N	44.43 E
ʿĀrah, Raʾs al- ≻	144	12.36 N	43.56 E
Arai, Nihon	94	37.01 N	138.15 E
Arai, Nihon	94	34.41 N	137.34 E
Ārāihāzar	126	23.47 N	90.40 E
Araioses	250	2.53 S	41.55 W
Ârak, Alg.	148	25.18 N	3.45 E
Arāk, Īrān	128	34.05 N	49.41 E
Araka	154	4.20 N	30.23 E
Arakamčečen, ostrov I	180	64.45 N	172.30 W
Arakan, porog ∟	88	57.35 N	96.36 E
Arakan Yoma ⋀	110	19.00 N	94.40 E
Arakawa, Nihon	94	35.57 N	139.02 E
Arakawa, Nihon	174m	26.39 N	128.15 E
Arakawa ◆[8]	268	35.47 N	139.47 E
Arakawa-dake ∧	94	35.30 N	138.10 E
Arákhova	38	38.29 N	22.35 E
Árakhthos ≃	38	39.01 N	21.03 E
Arakkonam	122	13.06 N	79.40 E
Araklı	130	40.57 N	40.03 E
Arakmeer, gora ∧	84	42.38 N	46.49 E
Arakpur ◆[8]	272a	28.35 N	77.10 E
Araks (Aras) ≃	84	39.56 N	48.28 E
Aral, Kyrg.	85	41.50 N	73.03 E
Aral, Kyrg.	85	42.32 N	72.40 E
Araldy	84	44.18 N	50.24 E
Aral Sea → Aral'skoje more ▿[2]	86	45.00 N	60.00 E
Aral'sk	86	46.48 N	61.40 E
Aral'skoje more (Aral Sea) ▿[2]	86	45.00 N	60.00 E
Aralsor, ozero ⊜, Kaz.	80	49.05 N	48.12 E
Aralsor, ozero ⊜, Kaz.	80	48.42 N	52.24 E
Aralsul'fat	86	46.50 N	61.58 E
Aramá ≃	250	1.06 S	50.40 W
Aramac	166	22.59 S	145.14 E
Aramac ≃	166	23.02 S	144.31 E
Aramari	255	12.04 S	38.30 W
Ārāmbāg	126	22.53 N	87.47 E
Aramberri	232	24.06 N	99.49 W
Aramia ≃	164	7.55 S	143.22 E
Aramon	62	43.53 N	4.41 E
Arampampa	248	17.55 S	66.04 W
Aramtalla	140	6.47 N	29.13 E
Ārān	128	34.04 N	51.29 E
Arana	258	35.00 S	57.54 W
Arancio, Lago ⊜	70	37.38 N	13.05 E
Aranda de Duero	34	41.41 N	3.41 W
Arandai	164	2.10 S	133.01 E
Arandas	234	20.42 N	102.21 W
Aranđelovac	38	44.18 N	20.35 E
Arandis	156	22.24 S	15.00 E
Aran Fawddwy ∧	42	52.47 N	3.41 W
Arang	120	21.12 N	81.58 E
Aranhegyi-patak ≃	264c	47.34 N	19.04 E
Ārāni, Bngl.	126	24.17 N	88.52 E
Arani, Bol.	248	17.34 S	65.46 W
Ārani, India	122	12.40 N	79.17 E
Aran Island I	48	54.58 N	8.33 W
Aran Islands II	48	53.07 N	9.43 W
Aranjuez	34	40.02 N	3.36 W
Aranos	156	24.09 S	19.09 E
Aransas ≃	196	28.04 N	97.14 W
Aransas Pass	196	27.54 N	97.08 W
Arantāngi	122	10.10 N	78.59 E
Arantina	256	21.56 S	44.15 W
Aranyaprathet	110	13.41 N	102.30 E
Arao	96	32.57 N	130.28 E
Araouane	150	18.54 N	3.33 W
Arapa, Laguna ⊜	248	15.10 S	70.01 W
Arapaho	196	35.34 N	98.57 W
Arapahoe	198	40.18 N	99.54 W
Arapaho National Recreation Area ♦	200	40.07 N	105.48 W
Arāpānja	272b	22.26 N	88.28 E
Arapawa Island I	172	41.11 S	174.19 E
Arapeí	256	22.41 S	44.27 W
Arapey	252	30.58 S	57.32 W
Arapey Chico ≃	252	30.57 S	57.30 W
Arapey Grande ≃	252	30.55 S	57.49 W
Arapiraca	250	9.45 S	36.39 W
Arapiri, Ilha I	250	2.04 S	54.56 W
Arápis	267c	37.59 N	23.32 E
Arapiuns ≃	250	2.18 S	55.00 W
Arapkir	130	39.03 N	38.30 E
Arapongas	255	23.23 S	51.27 W
Arapoti	255	24.08 S	49.50 W
Arapuni	172	38.04 S	175.39 E
Araquil ≃	34	42.48 N	1.45 W
ʿArʿar	128	30.59 N	41.02 E
ʿArʿar, Wādī ∨	128	31.23 N	42.26 E
Araracuara	246	0.38 S	72.15 W
Araranguá	252	28.56 S	49.29 W
Araraquara	255	21.47 S	48.10 W
Araras	255	22.22 S	47.23 W
Araras, Açude ⊜[1]	250	4.20 S	40.28 W
Araras, Ribeirão das ≃, Bra.	256	22.52 S	46.37 W
Araras, Ribeirão das ≃, Bra.	256	21.18 S	45.45 W
Ararat, Austl.	169	37.17 S	142.56 E
Ararat, Haya.	84	39.50 N	44.42 E
Ararat, Mount → Ağrı Dağı ∧	84	39.42 N	44.18 E
Arari	250	3.28 S	44.47 W
Arari, Lago ⊜	250	0.37 S	49.07 W
Arāria	124	26.08 N	87.24 E
Araripe	250	7.12 S	40.08 W
Araripe, Chapada do ⋀[1]	250	7.20 S	40.00 W
Araripina	250	7.33 S	40.34 W
Ararirá ≃	246	0.30 S	63.33 W
Arar Lugole	144	3.16 N	45.28 E
Araruama, Lagoa de c	255	22.53 S	42.12 W
Araruna	250	6.32 S	35.44 W
Aras (Araks) ≃	84	39.56 N	48.28 E
ʿAras, Ḥawḍ al- ▿[4]	142	30.51 N	32.32 E
Arashi-yama ∧[2]	270	35.01 N	135.40 E
Åråsviken c	40	59.02 N	14.01 E
Ara Terra	144	6.38 N	40.57 E
Áratos	38	41.05 N	25.33 E
Aratuípe	255	13.05 S	39.00 W
Aratula	171a	27.59 S	152.32 E
Arau	114	6.26 N	100.16 E
Arauá ≃, Bra.	246	4.06 S	63.36 W
Arauã ≃, Bra.	248	7.59 S	65.14 W
Arauá ≃, Bra.	248	5.40 S	60.48 W
Arauca	246	7.05 N	70.45 W
Arauca □[5]	246	6.40 N	71.00 W
Arauca ≃	246	7.24 N	66.35 W
Araucária	252	25.35 S	49.25 W
Arauco	252	37.15 S	73.19 W
Arauco, Golfo de c	252	37.11 S	73.25 W
Araújo, Ilha do I	256	23.09 S	44.42 W
Araújos	255	19.56 S	45.04 W
Arauquita	246	7.02 N	71.25 W
Araure	246	9.34 N	69.13 W
Aravaca ◆[8]	266a	40.28 N	3.46 W
Aravaipa Creek ≃	200	32.50 N	110.43 W
Arāvalli Range ⋀	120	25.00 N	73.30 E
Aravan	85	40.32 N	72.30 E
Arawata ≃	172	44.00 S	168.41 E
Araxá	255	19.35 S	46.55 W
Araya	246	10.34 N	64.15 W
Araya, Punta de ≻	246	10.38 N	64.18 W
Arayat	116	15.10 N	120.46 E
Arba	144	9.01 N	40.23 E
Arba ≃	34	41.52 N	1.18 W
Arbagar	88	51.56 N	116.15 E
Ārbālia	126	22.41 N	88.47 E
Arba Minch	144	6.02 N	37.33 E
Arbatax	71	39.56 N	9.42 E
Arbaž	80	57.41 N	48.18 E
Arbedo	58	46.12 N	9.03 E
Arbél	132	32.49 N	35.29 E
Arbesbach	61	48.29 N	14.57 E
Arbia ≃	66	43.08 N	11.28 E
Arboga	40	59.24 N	15.50 E

Symbols in the index entries represent the broad categories identified in the key at the right. Symbols with superior numbers (⋀[1]) identify subcategories (see complete key on page *I · 1)*.

Symbole im Register stellen die rechts im Schlüssel erklärten Kategorien dar. Symbole mit hochgestellten Ziffern (⋀[1]) bezeichnen Unterabteilungen einer Kategorie (vgl. vollständiger Schlüssel auf Seite *I · 1)*.

Los símbolos incluídos en el texto del índice representan las grandes categorias identificadas con la clave a la derecha. Los símbolos con numeros en su parte superior (⋀[1]) identifican las subcategorías (véase la clave completa en la página *I · 1)*.

Les symboles de l'index représentent les catégories indiquées dans la légende à droite. Les symboles suivis d'un indice (⋀[1]) représentent des sous-catégories (voir légende complète à la page *I · 1)*.

Os símbolos incluídos no texto do índice representam as grandes categorias identificadas com a chave à direita. Os símbolos com números em sua parte superior (⋀[1]) identificam as subcategorias (veja-se a chave completa à página *I · 1)*.

Symbol	English	Deutsch	Español	Français	Português
∧	Mountain	Berg	Montaña	Montagne	Montanha
⋀	Mountains	Gebirge	Montañas	Montagnes	Montanhas
)(	Pass	Paß	Paso	Col	Passo
∨	Valley, Canyon	Tal, Cañon	Valle, Cañón	Vallée, Canyon	Vale, Canhão
≚	Plain	Ebene	Llano	Plaine	Planície
≻	Cape	Kap	Cabo	Cap	Cabo
I	Island	Insel	Isla	Île	Ilha
II	Islands	Inseln	Islas	Îles	Ilhas
±	Other Topographic Features	Andere Topographische Objekte	Otros Elementos Topográficos	Autres données topographiques	Outros acidentes topográficos

ESPAÑOL

Nombre	Página	Lat.°'	Long.°' W = Oeste
Arbogaån ≃	40	59.26 N	16.04 E
Arbois	58	46.54 N	5.46 E
Arboledas	252	36.53 S	61.29 W
Arboletes	246	8.51 N	76.26 W
Arbolito, Cerro ∧ [2]	286d	12.10 S	76.57 W
Arbon	58	47.31 N	9.26 E
Arbonne	50	48.25 N	2.34 E
Arborea	71	39.46 N	8.35 E
Arborea -•- [1]	71	39.50 N	8.50 E
Arborfield	184	53.06 N	103.39 W
Arborg	184	50.55 N	97.15 W
Arbrå	26	61.29 N	16.23 E
Arbroath	46	56.34 N	2.35 W
Arbu, Monte ∧	71	39.15 N	9.27 E
Arbuckle	226	39.01 N	122.03 W
Arbuckle, Lake ⊜	220	27.41 N	81.24 W
Arbuckle Creek ≃	220	27.26 N	81.17 W
Arbuckle Mountains ⩘	196	34.25 N	97.20 W
Arbuckles, Lake of the ⊜ [1]	196	34.25 N	97.00 W
Arbury Hills	216	41.33 N	87.51 W
Arbus	71	39.32 N	8.36 E
Arbutus Lake ⊜	276	40.31 N	74.10 W
Arbuzinka	78	47.53 N	31.19 E
Arbuzovo	76	56.21 N	32.27 E
Arc ≃, Fr.	62	43.31 N	5.07 E
Arc ≃, Fr.	62	45.34 N	6.12 E
Arc, Bayou des ≃	194	35.00 N	91.30 W
Arcachon	32	44.37 N	1.12 W
Arcachon, Bassin d' ⊂	32	44.40 N	1.10 W
Arcadas	256	22.42 S	46.52 W
Arcade, It.	64	45.47 N	12.13 E
Arcade, Ca., U.S.	226	34.02 N	118.15 W
Arcade, N.Y., U.S.	210	42.32 N	78.25 W
Arcadia, Ca., U.S.	228	34.08 N	118.02 W
Arcadia, Fl., U.S.	220	27.12 N	81.51 W
Arcadia, In., U.S.	218	40.10 N	86.01 W
Arcadia, Ia., U.S.	198	42.01 N	95.02 W
Arcadia, Ks., U.S.	198	37.38 N	94.37 W
Arcadia, La., U.S.	194	32.32 N	92.55 W
Arcadia, Mi., U.S.	190	44.29 N	86.13 W
Arcadia, Mo., U.S.	194	37.35 N	90.37 W
Arcadia, Ne., U.S.	198	41.25 N	99.07 W
Arcadia, Oh., U.S.	216	41.06 N	83.31 W
Arcadia, Pa., U.S.	214	40.47 N	78.51 W
Arcadia, S.C., U.S.	192	34.57 N	81.59 W
Arcadia, Tx., U.S.	222	29.23 N	95.07 W
Arcadia, Wi., U.S.	190	44.15 N	91.30 W
Arcângelo	256	21.18 S	44.19 W
Arcanum	218	39.59 N	84.33 W
Arcas, Cayos II	232	20.12 N	91.58 W
Arcata	204	40.52 N	124.04 W
Arcatao	236	14.05 N	88.45 W
Arc de Triomphe ⊥	261	48.53 N	2.17 E
Arc Dome ∧	204	38.50 N	117.21 W
Arce	66	41.35 N	13.34 E
Arceburgo	256	21.22 S	46.56 W
Arčeda ≃	80	49.52 N	43.10 E
Arčedinsko-Donskije peski -•- [2]	80	49.33 N	43.15 E
Arcelia	234	18.17 N	100.16 W
Arcen	52	51.29 N	6.11 E
Arc-en-Barrois	58	47.57 N	5.00 E
Arces	50	48.05 N	3.36 E
Arc-et-Senans	58	47.02 N	5.46 E
Arcevia	66	43.30 N	12.56 E
Archambault, Lac ⊜	206	46.18 N	74.15 W
Archangaj □ [8]	88	48.00 N	101.30 E
Archangel → Archangel'sk	24	64.34 N	40.32 E
Archangel'sk	24	64.34 N	40.32 E
Archangel'skaja	78	45.41 N	40.15 E
Archangel'sk Oblast' □ [4]	24	63.00 N	42.00 E
Archangel'skoje, Ross.	76	53.16 N	37.42 E
Archangel'skoje, Ross.	78	51.27 N	40.55 E
Archangel'skoje, Ross.	80	55.13 N	44.05 E
Archangel'skoje, Ross.	80	54.26 N	48.40 E
Archangel'skoje, Ross.	82	55.19 N	35.58 E
Archangel'skoje, Ross.	84	44.37 N	44.05 E
Archangel'skoje, Ross.	265b	55.47 N	37.18 E
Archara	89	49.27 N	130.07 E
Archara ≃	89	49.13 N	129.53 E
Archbald	210	41.29 N	75.32 W
Archbold	216	41.31 N	84.18 W
Archdale	192	35.54 N	79.58 W
Archer	192	29.31 N	82.31 W
Archer ≃	164	13.28 S	141.41 E
Archer, Lake ⊜	283	42.04 N	71.20 W
Archer, Mount ∧	166	23.20 S	150.34 E
Archer Bay ⊂	164	13.25 S	141.43 E
Archer Bend National Park ♠	164	13.30 S	142.20 E
Archer City	196	33.35 N	98.37 W
Archer's Post	154	0.39 N	37.41 E
Arches	58	48.07 N	6.32 E
Arches National Park ♠	200	38.42 N	109.45 W
Archi	66	42.05 N	14.23 E
Archiac	32	45.31 N	0.18 W
Archidona	34	37.05 N	4.23 W
Archipo-Osipovka	78	44.22 N	38.33 E
Archipovka	80	56.38 N	41.14 E
Archipovo	24	66.26 N	45.52 E
Archonskaja	84	43.07 N	44.30 E
Archshofen	56	49.27 N	10.04 E
Archville	276	41.07 N	73.52 W
Arci, Monte ∧	71	39.47 N	8.44 E
Arcidosso	66	42.52 N	11.33 E
Arcille	66	42.48 N	11.15 E
Arcinazzo Romano	66	41.48 N	13.12 E
Arcisate	62	45.54 N	8.52 E
Arcis-sur-Aube	50	48.32 N	4.08 E
Arciz	78	46.00 N	29.26 E
Arckaringa	162	27.56 S	134.45 E
Arckaringa Creek ≃	162	28.10 S	135.22 E
Arc-les-Gray	58	47.27 N	5.35 E
Arco, It.	64	45.55 N	10.53 E
Arco, Id., U.S.	202	43.38 N	113.17 W
Arco de Baúlhe	34	41.29 N	7.58 W
Arcola, Sk., Can.	184	49.37 N	102.30 W
Arcola, It.	64	44.07 N	9.54 E
Arcola, Il., U.S.	194	39.41 N	88.18 W
Arcola, In., U.S.	216	41.06 N	85.17 W
Arcola, Ms., U.S.	194	33.16 N	90.52 W
Arcola, Pa., U.S.	285	40.09 N	75.27 W
Arcola, Tx., U.S.	222	29.31 N	95.27 W
Arconate	266b	45.32 N	8.51 E
Arcore	266b	45.38 N	9.19 E
Arcos	255	20.17 S	45.32 W
Arcos de la Frontera	34	36.45 N	5.48 W
Arcot	122	12.54 N	79.20 E
Arcoverde	250	8.25 S	37.04 W
Arctic Bay	176	73.02 N	85.11 W
Arctic Ocean ╤ [1]	16	85.00 N	170.00 E
Arctic Red ≃	180	67.27 N	133.46 W
Arctic Red River	180	67.27 N	133.46 W
Arctic Village	180	68.08 N	145.19 W
Arctique, Océan Glacial → Arctic Ocean ╤ [1]	16	85.00 N	170.00 E
Arctowski ʊ [3]	9	62.09 S	58.28 W
Arcturus	154	17.47 S	31.20 E
Arcueil	261	48.48 N	2.20 E
Arcuentu, Monte ∧	71	39.35 N	8.33 E
Arcvašen	84	40.38 N	45.32 E
Arcy-sur-Cure	50	47.36 N	3.45 E
Ard, Loch ⊜	46	56.11 N	4.28 W
Arḍ, Ra's al- ≻	128	29.21 N	48.05 E
Arda ≃, Europe	38	41.39 N	26.29 E

FRANÇAIS

Nom	Page	Lat.°'	Long.°' W = Ouest
Arda ≃, It.	64	45.02 N	10.02 E
Ardabīl	128	38.15 N	48.18 E
Ardagger	61	48.11 N	14.50 E
Ardagh	48	52.28 N	9.04 W
Ardahan	130	41.07 N	42.41 E
Ardakān, Īrān	128	32.19 N	53.59 E
Ardakān, Īrān	128	30.16 N	52.01 E
Ardal	128	31.59 N	50.39 E
Ardalanish, Rubh' ≻	46	56.17 N	6.18 W
Årdalsfjorden ⊂ [2]	26	61.12 N	7.30 E
Årdalstangen	26	61.14 N	7.43 E
Ardanuç	130	41.08 N	42.04 E
Ardara, Ire.	48	54.46 N	8.25 W
Árdara, It.	71	40.37 N	8.48 E
Ardara, Pa., U.S.	279b	40.22 N	79.44 W
Ardarroch	46	57.25 N	5.38 W
Ardatov, Ross.	80	55.15 N	43.06 E
Ardatov, Ross.	80	54.51 N	46.13 E
Ardbeg	46	55.39 N	6.05 W
Ardcharnich	46	57.51 N	5.05 W
Ardea	66	41.36 N	12.33 E
Ardèche □ [5]	62	44.40 N	4.20 E
Ardèche ≃	62	44.16 N	4.39 E
Ardee	48	53.52 N	6.33 W
Ardélik	146	12.26 N	21.25 E
Arden, Mb., Can.	184	50.17 N	99.14 W
Arden, Ca., U.S.	226	38.36 N	121.23 W
Arden, De., U.S.	208	39.48 N	75.29 W
Arden, Forest of -•- [3]	42	52.23 N	1.42 W
Arden, Mount ∧	166	32.09 S	137.59 E
Ardenay-sur-Mérize	50	48.00 N	0.25 E
Arden Mines	279b	40.12 N	80.17 W
Ardennes □ [5]	50	49.40 N	4.40 E
Ardennes -•- [1]	56	50.10 N	5.45 E
Ardennes, Canal des ≊	50	49.26 N	4.02 E
Ardenno	58	46.10 N	9.39 E
Ardentinny	46	56.03 N	4.55 W
Ardenza	66	43.31 N	10.19 E
Arderin ∧ [2]	48	53.02 N	7.40 W
Ardersier	46	57.34 N	4.02 W
Ardeşen	130	41.12 N	41.00 E
Ardestān	128	33.22 N	52.23 E
Ardey	263	51.28 N	7.43 E
Ardeygebirge ⩘ [2]	263	51.25 N	7.20 E
Ardez	58	46.46 N	10.11 E
Ardfern	46	56.10 N	5.32 W
Ardglass	48	54.16 N	5.37 W
Ardgroom	48	51.42 N	9.52 W
Ardıçlı	130	40.40 N	37.00 E
Ardila ≃	34	38.12 N	7.28 W
Ardill	184	49.53 N	105.49 W
Ardino	38	41.35 N	25.08 E
Ardlethan	166	34.21 S	146.54 E
Ardlui	46	56.18 N	4.43 W
Ardlussa	46	56.02 N	5.47 W
Ardmolich	46	56.49 N	5.41 W
Ardmore, Ire.	48	51.57 N	7.43 W
Ardmore, Al., U.S.	194	34.59 N	86.50 W
Ardmore, In., U.S.	216	41.41 N	86.19 W
Ardmore, Md., U.S.	284c	38.56 N	76.51 W
Ardmore, Ok., U.S.	196	34.10 N	97.08 W
Ardmore, Pa., U.S.	208	40.01 N	75.18 W
Ardmore Point ≻, Scot., U.K.	46	56.39 N	6.07 W
Ardmore Point ≻, Scot., U.K.	46	55.42 N	6.01 W
Ardnamurchan ≻ [1]	46	56.43 N	6.00 W
Ardnamurchan, Point of ≻	46	56.44 N	6.13 W
Ardnaree	48	54.06 N	9.08 W
Ardnave Point ≻	46	55.54 N	6.20 W
Ardoch	166	27.26 S	144.08 E
Ardon, Ross.	84	43.12 N	44.18 E
Ardon, Schw.	58	46.13 N	7.15 E
Ardon ≃	84	43.17 N	44.18 E
Ardon, Har ∧	132	30.38 N	34.57 E
Ardooie	50	50.59 N	3.12 E
Ardore	68	38.11 N	16.10 E
Ardoux ≃	50	47.42 N	1.35 E
Ardoz, Arroyo de ≃	266a	40.26 N	3.27 W
Ardres	50	50.51 N	1.59 E
Ardres ≃	50	49.18 N	3.40 E
Ardrishaig	46	56.01 N	5.27 W
Ardrossan, Austl.	168b	34.25 S	137.55 E
Ardrossan, Scot., U.K.	46	55.39 N	4.49 W
Ardsley, Eng., U.K.	44	53.32 N	1.28 W
Ardsley, N.Y., U.S.	276	41.00 N	73.50 W
Ardtalnaig	46	56.31 N	4.06 W
Arduan Island I	140	19.55 N	30.22 E
Ardusson ≃	50	48.30 N	3.32 E
Ardvasar	46	57.04 N	5.54 W
Åre	26	63.24 N	13.04 E
Areado	256	21.21 S	46.09 W
Areal	256	22.14 S	43.07 W
Arèches	62	45.41 N	6.34 E
Arecibo	240m	18.28 N	66.43 W
Arecibo, Observatorio de ʊ [3]	240m	18.20 N	66.46 W
Areco ≃	258	33.56 S	59.16 W
Areeiro	266c	38.39 N	9.12 W
Arefjevo	86	57.01 N	90.40 E
Areguá	252	25.18 S	57.25 W
Areia, Bra.	250	6.58 S	35.42 W
Areia, Port.	266c	38.43 N	9.08 W
Areia, Ribeirão da ≃	255	16.07 S	45.52 W
Areia Branca, Bra.	250	4.56 S	37.07 W
Areia Branca, Bra.	287a	22.44 S	43.25 W
Areias	256	22.35 S	44.42 W
Arena	68	38.34 N	16.13 E
Arena, Point ≻	204	38.57 N	123.44 W
Arena, Punta ≻	232	23.33 N	109.28 W
Arena de la Ventana, Punta ≻	232	24.04 N	109.52 W
Arena Island I	116	9.14 N	120.46 E
Arenal, C.R.	236	10.29 N	84.53 W
Arenal, P.R.	240m	17.59 N	66.19 W
Arenal, Laguna de ⊜	236	10.32 N	84.56 W
Arenal, Volcán ∧ [1]	236	10.28 N	84.44 W
Arenápolis	248	14.26 S	56.49 W
Arenas, Cayo I	232	22.08 N	91.24 W
Arenas, Punta ≻	240m	18.07 N	65.35 W
Arenas, Punta de ≻	254	53.09 S	68.13 W
Arenas de San Pedro	34	40.12 N	5.05 W
Arendal	26	58.27 N	8.48 E
Arendonk	56	51.19 N	5.05 E
Arendsee	54	52.53 N	11.30 E
Arendsee ⊜	54	52.53 N	11.30 E
Arendtsville	208	39.55 N	77.18 W
Arenes ≃	266d	41.29 N	2.02 E
Arenig Fawr ∧	42	52.55 N	3.45 W
Arenillas	246	3.33 S	80.04 W
Arenosa Creek ≃	196	28.52 N	96.44 W
Arenys de Mar	34	41.35 N	2.33 E
Arenzano	62	44.24 N	8.41 E
Arenzville	219	39.53 N	90.22 W
Arequipa	248	16.24 S	71.33 W
Arequipa □ [5]	248	16.00 S	72.15 W
Arequito	252	33.09 S	61.28 W
Arero	144	4.45 N	38.49 E
Arês, Bra.	250	6.11 S	35.09 W
Arès, Fr.	32	44.46 N	1.08 W
Arese	266b	45.33 N	9.05 E
Aresing	60	48.32 N	11.18 E
Åreskutan ∧	26	63.26 N	13.06 E
Areuse ≃	58	46.56 N	6.53 E
Arévalo	34	41.04 N	4.43 W
Arezzo	66	43.25 N	11.53 E
Arezzo □ [4]	66	43.32 N	11.50 E
Arfa', Jabal ∧	132	29.51 N	35.27 E
'Arfā', Wādī al- V	132	30.16 N	36.34 E
Arga ≃	34	42.18 N	1.47 W
Argada	88	54.14 N	110.41 E
Argadargada	166	21.40 S	136.40 E
Argajaš	86	55.29 N	60.52 E
Argamasilla de Alba	34	39.07 N	3.06 W
Arganda	34	40.18 N	3.26 W
Argao	116	9.52 N	123.36 E
Arga-Sala ≃	74	68.30 N	112.12 E

PORTUGUÊS

Nome	Página	Lat.°'	Long.°' W = Oeste
Argedeb	144	6.10 N	41.10 E
Argegno	58	45.56 N	9.08 E
Argel → El Djazaïr	148	36.47 N	3.03 E
Argelès-Gazost	32	43.01 N	0.06 E
Argelès-sur-Mer	32	42.33 N	3.01 E
Argelia → Algeria □ [1]	148	28.00 N	3.00 E
Argen ≃	58	47.35 N	9.33 E
Argens ≃	62	43.24 N	6.44 E
Argent	158	26.04 S	28.50 E
Argent, Côte d' ⫯ [2]	32	43.30 N	1.30 W
Argenta, It.	66	44.37 N	11.50 E
Argenta, Il., U.S.	219	39.58 N	88.49 W
Argentan	32	48.45 N	0.01 W
Argentario, Monte ∧	66	42.24 N	11.09 E
Argentat	32	45.06 N	1.56 E
Argentera	62	44.24 N	6.57 E
Argentera ∧	62	44.10 N	7.18 E
Argenteuil	50	48.57 N	2.15 E
Argenteuil □ [6]	206	45.45 N	74.30 W
Argentia	186	47.18 N	53.59 W
Argentiera	71	40.44 N	8.09 E
Argentière	58	45.59 N	6.56 E
Argentières	261	48.39 N	2.52 E
Argentina □ [1]	244	34.00 S	64.00 W
Argentina ≃	62	43.50 N	7.51 E
Argentine	216	42.47 N	83.51 W
Argentine → Argentina □ [1]	244	34.00 S	64.00 W
Argentine Basin ✢ [1]	18	45.00 S	45.00 W
Argentinien → Argentina □ [1]	244	34.00 S	64.00 W
Argentino, Hipódromo ♠	288	34.34 S	58.26 W
Argentino, Lago ⊜	254	50.13 S	72.25 W
Argentona	266d	41.33 N	2.24 E
Argentona, Riera d' ≃	266d	41.31 N	2.26 E
Argenton-Château	32	46.59 N	0.27 W
Argenton-sur-Creuse	32	46.35 N	1.31 E
Argent-sur-Sauldre	50	47.33 N	2.27 E
Argeș □ [6]	38	45.00 N	24.45 E
Argeș ≃	38	44.04 N	26.37 E
Arghandāb ≃	128	31.27 N	64.23 E
Arghastān ≃	120	31.23 N	65.45 E
Argirita	256	21.37 S	42.50 W
Argıthanı	130	38.17 N	31.43 E
Argo	140	19.31 N	30.25 E
Ārgoal	126	21.58 N	87.38 E
Argo Island I	140	19.25 N	30.27 E
Argolikós Kólpos ⊂	38	37.33 N	22.45 E
Argonia	198	37.15 N	97.45 W
Argonne	190	45.39 N	88.52 W
Argonne -•- [1]	56	49.30 N	5.00 E
Argonne National Laboratory ʊ [3]	216	41.43 N	87.58 W
Argopuro, Gunung ∧	115a	7.57 S	113.33 E
Árgos, Ellás	38	37.39 N	22.44 E
Argos, In., U.S.	216	41.14 N	86.15 W
Árgos Orestikón	38	40.28 N	21.16 E
Argostólion	38	38.10 N	20.30 E
Argoules	50	50.21 N	1.50 E
Argueil	50	49.32 N	1.31 E
Arguello, Point ≻	204	34.35 N	120.39 W
Argun	84	43.16 N	45.52 E
Argun ≃	84	43.22 N	45.55 E
Argun' (Ergun) ≃, Asia	74	53.20 N	121.28 E
Argungu	150	12.45 N	4.31 E
Arguni, Teluk ⊂	164	3.06 S	133.42 E
Ārgur	272b	22.48 N	88.13 E
Argut	86	49.51 N	87.03 E
Argut ≃	86	50.16 N	86.43 E
Arguvan	130	38.47 N	38.17 E
Argyle, Austl.	162	33.32 S	115.46 E
Argyle, Mn., U.S.	198	48.19 N	96.49 W
Argyle, Mo., U.S.	219	38.18 N	92.02 W
Argyle, N.Y., U.S.	210	43.14 N	73.30 W
Argyle, Tx., U.S.	222	33.07 N	97.11 W
Argyle, Lake ⊜ [1]	164	16.15 S	128.45 E
'Arhāb, Wādī V	142	28.55 N	31.09 E
Arhavi	130	41.22 N	41.16 E
Arhéa Epídavros ⊥	38	37.37 N	23.02 E
Århus	41	56.09 N	10.13 E
Århus □ [6]	41	56.15 N	10.05 E
Århus Bugt ⊂	41	56.09 N	10.18 E
Aria	172	38.33 S	174.59 E
Aria ≃	164	5.45 S	149.15 E
Ariadnoje	89	45.08 N	134.25 E
Ariah	126	23.33 N	86.20 E
Ariake-kai ⊂	92	33.00 N	130.20 E
Ariāl Khān ≃	126	23.56 N	90.46 E
Ariamácina, Lago di ⊜ [1]	68	39.20 N	16.32 E
Ariamsvlei	156	28.07 S	19.49 E
Ariana	36	36.52 N	10.12 E
Ariano, Isola d' I	64	45.10 N	12.10 E
Ariano Irpino	68	41.09 N	15.05 E
Ariano nel Polesine	64	44.56 N	12.07 E
Ariari ≃	246	2.35 N	72.47 W
Arias	252	33.38 S	62.25 W
Arias, Arroyo de ≃	258	34.17 S	56.06 W
Arias, Cañada ≃	258	34.39 S	58.59 W
Ariaú	250	3.11 S	57.14 W
Aribinda	150	14.14 N	0.52 W
Arica, Chile	248	18.29 S	70.20 W
Arica, Col.	246	2.08 S	71.47 W
Arıcak	130	38.33 N	39.48 E
Aricanduva, Ribeirão ≃	287b	23.32 S	46.33 W
Ariccia	66	41.43 N	12.40 E
Arichat	186	45.31 N	61.01 W
Arichuna	246	7.42 N	67.08 W
Arid, Cape ≻	162	34.00 S	123.09 E
Arida, Nig.	273a	6.34 N	3.16 E
Arida, Nihon	96	34.05 N	135.07 E
Arida ≃	96	34.05 N	135.06 E
Aridal, Sabkhat ⊜	148	26.12 N	14.05 W
Aridhaía	38	40.59 N	22.03 E
Ariège □ [5]	32	43.00 N	1.30 E
Ariège ≃	32	43.31 N	1.25 E
Ari'el, Isr. Occ	132	32.06 N	35.06 E
Ariel, Wa., U.S.	224	45.57 N	122.34 W
Arienzo	68	41.01 N	14.30 E
Arieș ≃	38	46.26 N	23.59 E
'Arif, Har ∧	132	30.26 N	34.44 E
Ārifwāla	123	30.17 N	73.04 E
Ariguanabo, Laguna de ⊜	286b	22.56 N	82.33 W
Ariguaní ≃	246	9.35 N	73.46 W
Arīḥā (Jericho), Isr. Occ	132	31.52 N	35.27 E
Arīḥā, Sūrīy.	130	35.48 N	36.36 E
Arīḥā, Urd.	132	31.25 N	35.47 E
Arikaree ≃	198	40.01 N	101.56 W
Arikaree, North Fork ≃	198	39.39 N	102.57 W
Arikawa	92	32.59 N	129.07 E
Arikha, Har ∧ [2]	132	30.39 N	34.47 E
Arild	41	56.16 N	12.34 E
Arima	241r	10.38 N	61.17 W
Arima -•- [8]	270	34.48 N	135.15 E
Arima ≃	270	34.52 N	135.15 E
Arima-fuji ∧ [2]	270	34.55 N	135.14 E
Arimine-dam -•- [6]	94	36.29 N	137.27 E
Arinagour	46	56.37 N	6.31 W
Aringay	116	16.26 N	120.21 E
Arino -•- [8]	270	34.50 N	135.14 E
Arinos ≃	248	10.25 S	58.20 W
Arinthod	58	46.23 N	5.34 E
Ario de Rosales	234	19.12 N	101.43 W
Ariogala	76	55.16 N	23.30 E
Aripeka	220	28.25 N	82.39 W
Ariporo ≃	246	6.03 N	69.54 W
Aripuanã	248	9.10 S	60.38 W
Aripuanã ≃	248	5.07 S	60.24 W
Ariquemes	248	9.56 S	63.04 W
Arisa ≃	246	7.32 N	64.00 W
Arisaig	46	56.51 N	5.51 W

Arisaig, Sound of ⊂	46	56.51 N	5.51 W
'Arīsh, Wādī al- V	140	31.09 N	33.49 E
Arismendi	246	8.29 N	68.22 W
Aristazabal Island I	182	52.30 N	129.05 W
Aristes	210	40.49 N	76.20 W
Aristizábal, Cabo ≻	254	45.13 S	66.31 W
Aristovo	82	54.37 N	36.40 E
Arıt	130	41.41 N	32.39 E
Aritao	116	16.18 N	121.02 E
Ariton	194	31.36 N	85.43 W
Aritzo	71	39.57 N	9.12 E
Arivonimamo	157b	19.01 S	47.15 E
Ariyalūr	122	11.08 N	79.05 E
Arizaro, Salar de ≚	252	24.42 S	67.45 W
Arizgoiti	34	43.13 N	2.54 W
Arizona	252	35.43 S	65.18 W
Arizona □ [3], U.S.	178	34.00 N	112.00 W
Arizona □ [3], U.S.	200	34.00 N	112.00 W
Arizpe	232	30.20 N	110.10 W
Arja	80	57.30 N	46.00 E
Årjäng	26	59.23 N	12.08 E
Arjasa	112	6.51 S	115.16 E
Arjawinangun	115a	6.39 S	108.24 E
Arjay	192	36.48 N	83.38 W
Arjeplog	24	66.00 N	17.58 E
Arjona, Col.	246	10.15 N	75.21 W
Arjona, Esp.	34	37.56 N	4.03 W
Arka	74	60.03 N	142.12 E
Arkabutla Lake ⊜ [1]	194	34.45 N	90.06 W
Arkadak	80	51.58 N	43.28 E
Arkadelphia	194	34.07 N	93.03 W
Arkaig, Loch ⊜	46	56.58 N	5.08 W
Arkalyk	86	50.13 N	66.50 E
Arkansas □ [3], U.S.	178	34.50 N	92.30 W
Arkansas □ [3], U.S.	194	34.50 N	92.30 W
Arkansas ≃	178	33.48 N	91.04 W
Arkansas, Salt Fork ≃	196	36.36 N	97.03 W
Arkansas City, Ar., U.S.	194	33.36 N	91.12 W
Arkansas City, Ks., U.S.	198	37.03 N	97.02 W
Arkansas Post National Memorial ⊥	194	33.55 N	91.26 W
Arkanū, Jabal ∧	146	22.13 N	24.41 E
Arkatag Shan ⩘	120	36.48 N	89.10 E
Arken-Ahon ∧	146	20.05 N	18.25 E
Arkhangélos	38	36.12 N	28.08 E
Arkhangel'sk → Archangel'sk	24	64.34 N	40.32 E
Arki	123	31.09 N	76.58 E
Árki I	38	37.22 N	26.45 E
Arkit	85	41.47 N	71.58 E
Arklow	48	52.48 N	6.09 W
Arkoma	194	35.21 N	94.26 W
Arkona, Kap ≻	54	54.41 N	13.26 E
Arkösund	26	58.30 N	16.56 E
Arkport	210	42.23 N	77.41 W
Arktičeskij, mys ≻	74	81.15 N	95.45 E
Arktičeskogo Instituta, ostrova II	74	75.20 N	81.55 E
Arkul'	80	57.17 N	50.03 E
Arkville	210	42.08 N	74.37 W
Arkwright	207	41.43 N	71.33 W
Ärla	40	59.17 N	16.40 E
Arlan	80	55.58 N	54.15 E
Arlan, gora ∧	128	39.40 N	54.33 E
Arlanc	62	45.25 N	3.44 E
Arlanda flygplats ⊠	40	59.37 N	17.55 E
Arlanza ≃	34	42.06 N	4.09 W
Arlanzón ≃	34	42.03 N	4.17 W
Arlbergpass)(	64	47.08 N	10.12 E
Arlberg-Tunnel -•- [5]	64	47.08 N	10.12 E
Arlee	202	47.09 N	114.05 W
Arles	62	43.40 N	4.38 E
Arles à Port de Bouc, Canal d' ≊	62	43.40 N	4.37 E
Arlesey	42	52.01 N	0.14 W
Arlesheim	58	47.30 N	7.37 E
Arleta -•- [8]	280	34.15 N	118.26 W
Arleux	50	50.17 N	3.06 E
Arley	262	53.19 N	2.30 W
Arli	150	11.35 N	1.28 E
Arli, Parc National de l' ♠	150	11.35 N	1.30 E
Arlington, S. Afr.	158	28.06 S	27.54 E
Arlington, Ga., U.S.	192	31.26 N	84.43 W
Arlington, In., U.S.	218	39.38 N	85.34 W
Arlington, Ia., U.S.	190	42.44 N	91.40 W
Arlington, Ks., U.S.	198	37.53 N	98.10 W
Arlington, Ky., U.S.	194	36.47 N	89.00 W
Arlington, Ma., U.S.	207	42.24 N	71.09 W
Arlington, Mn., U.S.	190	44.36 N	94.04 W
Arlington, Ne., U.S.	198	41.27 N	96.21 W
Arlington, N.Y., U.S.	210	41.41 N	73.53 W
Arlington, Oh., U.S.	216	40.53 N	83.39 W
Arlington, Or., U.S.	202	45.43 N	120.11 W
Arlington, S.D., U.S.	198	44.21 N	97.07 W
Arlington, Tn., U.S.	194	35.18 N	89.40 W
Arlington, Tx., U.S.	222	32.44 N	97.06 W
Arlington, Vt., U.S.	210	43.04 N	73.09 W
Arlington, Va., U.S.	208	38.52 N	77.06 W
Arlington, Wa., U.S.	224	48.11 N	122.07 W
Arlington □ [6]	284c	38.50 N	77.10 W
Arlington, Lake ⊜ [1]	222	32.42 N	97.13 W
Arlington Heights, Il., U.S.	216	42.05 N	87.58 W
Arlington Heights, Ma., U.S.	283	42.25 N	71.11 W
Arlington International Race Course ♠	278	42.05 N	88.00 W
Arlington Memorial Bridge -•- [5]	284c	38.53 N	77.03 W
Arlington Mill Reservoir ⊜ [1]	283	42.48 N	71.13 W
Arlington National Cemetery -•-	284c	38.53 N	77.04 W
Arlit	150	19.00 N	7.38 E
Arlod	58	46.06 N	5.49 E
Arlon	56	49.41 N	5.49 E
Arlöv	41	55.39 N	13.05 E
Arltunga	162	23.26 S	134.41 E
Arl'uk	86	55.26 N	84.50 E
Arluno	62	45.30 N	8.56 E
Arly ≃	62	45.40 N	6.23 E
Arlyn Oaks	276	40.40 N	73.27 W
Arm ≃	184	50.46 N	105.00 W
Arma	198	37.32 N	94.42 W
Armação, Ponta da ≻	287a	22.53 S	43.08 W
Armada	214	42.50 N	82.53 W
Armadale, Austl.	168a	32.09 S	116.00 E
Armadale, On., Can.	275b	43.50 N	79.15 W
Armadale, S. Afr.	273d	26.17 S	27.57 E
Armadale, Scot., U.K.	46	55.54 N	3.42 W
Arma di Taggia	62	43.50 N	7.51 E
Armageddon → Tel Megiddo ⊥	132	32.35 N	35.11 E
Armagh, N. Ire., U.K.	48	54.21 N	6.39 W
Armagh, Pa., U.S.	214	40.27 N	79.02 W
Armagnac □ [9]	32	43.45 N	0.10 E
Armah, Wādī V	144	18.12 N	51.02 E
Armainvilliers, Étang d' ⊜	261	48.45 N	2.44 E
Armainvilliers, Forêt d' ♠	261	48.45 N	2.45 E
Armance ≃	50	47.26 N	3.33 E
Armançon ≃, Fr.	50	47.57 N	3.30 E
Armançon ≃, Fr.	58	47.33 N	4.17 E
Arm'ansk	78	46.07 N	33.41 E
Armant	140	25.37 N	32.32 E
Armavir	72	45.00 N	41.08 E
Armazém	252	28.16 S	49.01 W
Armbrust	214	40.13 N	79.33 W
Armells Creek ≃	202	47.37 N	108.40 W
Armenia	246	4.31 N	75.41 W
Armenia □ [9]	84	40.30 N	43.30 E
Armenia □ [1], Asia	72	40.00 N	45.00 E
Armenia (Hayastan) □ [1], Asia	84	40.00 N	45.00 E

Armenija → Armenia □ [1]	72	40.00 N	45.00 E
Armeniș	38	45.12 N	22.19 E
Armenistís	38	37.36 N	26.08 E
Armeniya → Armenia □ [1]	72	40.00 N	45.00 E
Armeno	62	45.49 N	8.26 E
Armenonville-les-Gâtineaux	261	48.33 N	1.39 E
Armentières	50	50.41 N	2.53 E
Armento	68	40.18 N	16.04 E
Armería	234	18.56 N	103.58 W
Armería ≃	234	18.52 N	103.59 W
Armero	246	4.58 N	74.54 W
Armidale	166	30.31 S	151.39 E
Armijo	200	35.03 N	106.40 W
Armitage	42	52.44 N	1.53 W
Armit Lake ⊜	176	64.10 N	91.32 W
Armizonskoje	86	55.57 N	67.42 E
Armona	226	36.19 N	119.42 W
Armonk	276	41.07 N	73.42 W
Armor	210	42.44 N	78.48 W
Armori	122	20.28 N	79.59 E
Armour	198	43.19 N	98.20 W
Armoy, Fr.	58	46.21 N	6.31 E
Armoy, N. Ire., U.K.	48	55.07 N	6.20 W
Armstrong, Arg.	252	32.47 S	61.36 W
Armstrong, B.C., Can.	182	50.27 N	119.12 W
Armstrong, Il., U.S.	216	40.18 N	87.53 W
Armstrong, Ia., U.S.	198	43.23 N	94.28 W
Armstrong, Mo., U.S.	194	39.16 N	92.42 W
Armstrong □ [6]	214	40.49 N	79.32 W
Armstrong ≃	164	16.46 S	131.12 E
Armstrong, Mount ∧	180	63.12 N	133.16 W
Armstrong Station	176	50.18 N	89.02 W
Armthorpe	44	53.32 N	1.03 W
Ārmūr	122	18.48 N	78.17 E
Armutlu	130	40.31 N	28.50 E
Arnå ≃	41	54.57 N	8.53 E
Arnaccio	66	43.40 N	10.17 E
Arnaía	38	40.29 N	23.35 E
Arnarfjörður ⊂ [2]	24a	65.45 N	23.40 W
Årnäs	40	58.41 N	13.35 E
Arnaud ≃	176	59.59 N	69.46 W
Arnaudville	194	30.24 N	91.56 W
Arnavad, gora ∧	85	38.33 N	71.31 E
Arnavutköy ≃	267b	41.13 N	29.12 E
Arnay-le-Duc	58	47.08 N	4.29 E
Arnaz	62	45.38 N	7.43 E
Arnborg	41	56.01 N	8.59 E
Arnbruck	60	49.08 N	13.00 E
Arncliffe	274a	33.56 S	151.09 E
Arneburg	54	52.40 N	12.00 E
Arnedo	34	42.13 N	2.06 W
Arneiro dos Marinheiros	266c	38.51 N	9.25 W
Arneiroz	250	6.20 S	40.08 W
Arnejevo	82	54.58 N	37.35 E
Arnemuiden	52	51.30 N	3.41 E
Årnes	26	60.09 N	11.28 E
Arnett	196	36.08 N	99.46 W
Arney ≃	48	54.16 N	7.37 W
Arnhem	52	51.59 N	5.55 E
Arnhem, Cape ≻	164	12.21 S	136.21 E
Arnhem Bay ⊂	164	12.20 S	136.12 E
Arnhem Land -•- [1]	164	13.10 S	134.30 E
Arnhem Land Aboriginal Reserve -•- [4]	164	13.10 S	134.30 E
Arni	64	44.04 N	10.15 E
Arnis	41	54.38 N	9.56 E
Árnissa	38	40.48 N	21.50 E
Arno I [1]	14	7.05 N	171.41 E
Arno ≃	66	43.41 N	10.17 E
Arno, Torrente ≃	266b	45.42 N	8.48 E
Arno Bay	166	33.54 S	136.34 E
Arnold, B.C., Can.	224	49.08 N	122.03 W
Arnold, Eng., U.K.	44	53.00 N	1.08 W
Arnold, Ca., U.S.	204	38.15 N	120.21 W
Arnold, Md., U.S.	208	39.01 N	76.30 W
Arnold, Mn., U.S.	190	46.52 N	92.05 W
Arnold, Mo., U.S.	219	38.25 N	90.22 W
Arnold, Ne., U.S.	198	41.25 N	100.11 W
Arnold, Pa., U.S.	214	40.34 N	79.46 W
Arnold ≃	164	15.19 S	134.06 E
Arnold Arboretum ♠	283	42.18 N	71.08 W
Arnold Mills	283	41.58 N	71.23 W
Arnold Mills Reservoir ⊜ [1]	283	41.59 N	71.25 W
Arnolds Park	198	43.22 N	95.08 W
Arnoldstein	64	46.33 N	13.43 E
Arnon ≃	50	48.16 N	0.38 E
Arnos Vale Airport ⊠	241h	13.09 N	61.13 W
Arnot	210	41.39 N	77.07 W
Arnouville-lès-Gonesse	261	49.00 N	2.25 E
Arnouville-lès-Mantes	261	48.55 N	1.44 E
Arnoya ≃	34	42.15 N	8.09 W
Arnprior	212	45.26 N	76.21 W
Arnsberg	56	51.24 N	8.03 E
Arnsberg □ [5]	52	51.20 N	8.00 E
Arnschwang	60	49.16 N	12.49 E
Arnsdorf	54	51.05 N	13.59 E
Arnside	44	54.12 N	2.50 W
Arnstadt	54	50.50 N	10.57 E
Arnstein	56	49.58 N	9.58 E
Arnstorf	60	48.34 N	12.49 E
Arnum	41	55.15 N	8.59 E
Årø I	41	55.15 N	9.45 E
Aro ≃	246	8.01 N	64.11 W
Aroa	246	10.26 N	68.54 W
Aroa ≃	246	10.40 N	68.19 W
Aroa, Pointe ≻	174s	17.28 S	149.46 W
Aroab	156	26.47 S	19.40 E
Aroali	126	24.03 N	87.56 E
Arochukwu	150	5.23 N	7.55 E
Aroeiras	250	7.31 S	35.41 W
Ar'ofino	80	58.16 N	39.15 E
Arolla	58	46.02 N	7.29 E
Arolsen	56	51.23 N	9.01 E
Aroma	140	15.49 N	36.08 E
Aroma Park	216	41.04 N	87.48 W
Aromas	226	36.53 N	121.39 W
Aromaševo	86	56.52 N	68.39 E
Aron ≃	50	47.15 N	2.02 E
Arona, It.	62	45.46 N	8.34 E
Arona, Pap. N. Gui.	164	6.20 S	146.00 E
Arona, Pa., U.S.	279b	40.16 N	79.39 W
Aroostook ≃	186	46.48 N	67.45 W
Arop Island I	164	5.20 S	147.05 E
Aropuk Lake ⊜	180	61.12 N	163.50 W
Arorae I	14	2.38 S	176.49 E
Arorangi	174k	21.13 S	159.49 W
Aroroy	116	12.31 N	123.24 E
Aros ≃	232	29.09 N	109.40 W
Arosa	58	46.47 N	9.41 E
Arosa, Ría de ⊂ [1]	34	42.28 N	8.57 W
Arosbaya	115a	6.56 S	112.51 E
Årøsund	41	55.16 N	9.45 E
Aro Usu, Tanjung ≻	164	8.20 S	130.45 E
Arowhana ∧	172	38.07 S	177.52 E
Arp	222	32.13 N	95.03 W
Arpa ≃	84	39.28 N	44.57 E
Arpaçay	84	40.52 N	43.20 E
Arpaçay (Achur'an) ≃	84	40.06 N	43.39 E
Arpačin	83	47.14 N	40.11 E
Arpaia	68	41.02 N	14.33 E
Arpajon	50	48.35 N	2.15 E
Ārpāra	126	23.23 N	89.23 E
Arpino	66	41.39 N	13.36 E
Arpoador, Ponta do ≻	287a	22.59 S	43.12 W
Arquà Petrarca	64	45.16 N	11.43 E
Arquà Polesine	64	45.01 N	11.45 E
Arquata del Tronto	66	42.46 N	13.18 E
Arquata Scrivia	62	44.41 N	8.53 E
Arque	248	17.48 S	66.23 W
Arques	50	50.44 N	2.17 E
Arques-la-Bataille	50	49.53 N	1.08 E
Ar-Rabaḍ	128	23.11 N	39.32 E

Ar-Rabbah	132	31.16 N	35.44 E
Arracourt	58	48.44 N	6.32 E
Ar-Radīsīyah Baḥrī	140	24.57 N	32.53 E
Ar-Rafīd	132	32.57 N	35.53 E
Arraga	252	28.04 S	64.14 W
Arrah	150	6.40 N	3.58 W
Ar-Rahad	140	12.43 N	30.39 E
Ar-Raḥāminah	142	31.18 N	31.45 E
Ar-Raḥmānīyah	142	31.06 N	30.38 E
Arraial do Cabo	255	22.58 S	42.01 W
Arraias	255	12.56 S	46.57 W
Arraias ≃, Bra.	250	11.10 S	53.35 W
Arraias ≃, Bra.	255	12.28 S	47.18 W
'Arrām, Wādī V	132	32.55 N	36.10 E
Ar-Ramādī	128	33.25 N	43.17 E
Ar-Ramthā	132	32.34 N	36.00 E
Arran, Island of I	46	55.35 N	5.15 W
Ar-Rank	140	11.45 N	32.48 E
Arran Lake ⊜	212	44.29 N	81.16 W
Ar-Raqqah	130	35.56 N	39.01 E
Ar-Raqqah □ [8]	130	36.00 N	39.00 E
Arras	50	50.17 N	2.47 E
Arras, Nuraghe ⊥	71	39.40 N	9.25 E
Ar-Rāshidah	140	25.35 N	28.56 E
Ar-Rass	128	25.52 N	43.28 E
Ar-Rastan	130	34.55 N	36.44 E
Arrats ≃	32	44.06 N	0.52 E
Ar-Rawḍah, Ar. Su.	128	26.05 N	40.37 E
Ar-Rawḍah, Miṣr	142	27.48 N	30.52 E
Ar-Rawḍah, Miṣr	142	29.27 N	31.00 E
Ar-Rawḍah, Yaman	144	14.28 N	47.17 E
Ar-Rāwuk	144	15.45 N	48.54 E
Ar-Rayramūn	142	27.45 N	30.52 E
Ar-Rayyāḥ ar-Minūfīya ≊	142	30.20 N	31.00 E
Ar-Rayyāḥ at-Tawfīqī ≊	142	30.11 N	31.07 E
Ar-Rayyān	128	25.18 N	51.27 E
Arrecife	148	28.57 N	13.32 W
Arrecifes	252	34.03 S	60.07 W
Arrée, Montagnes d' ⩘	32	48.26 N	3.55 W
Arregui, Laguna ⊜	258	35.05 S	57.33 W
Arrentela	266c	38.38 N	9.06 W
Arresø ⊜	41	55.58 N	12.08 E
Arrey	200	32.50 N	107.19 W
Arriaga	234	16.14 N	93.54 W
Arriba	198	39.17 N	103.16 W
Arrild	41	55.09 N	8.58 E
Ar-Riyāḍ (Riyadh)	128	24.38 N	46.43 E
Arrochar	46	56.12 N	4.44 W
Arroio Grande	252	32.14 S	53.05 W
Arrojado ≃	255	13.24 S	44.20 W
Arronches	34	39.07 N	7.17 W
Arrone ≃, It.	66	41.52 N	12.11 E
Arrone ≃, It.	66	42.18 N	11.38 E
Arros ≃	32	43.40 N	0.02 W
Arroscia ≃	62	44.03 N	8.11 E
Arroux ≃	32	46.29 N	3.58 E
Arrow ≃, Eng., U.K.	42	52.12 N	2.43 W
Arrow ≃, Eng., U.K.	42	52.09 N	1.53 W
Arrow, Lough ⊜	48	54.04 N	8.21 W
Arrow Creek ≃	202	47.43 N	109.50 W
Arrowhead, Lake ⊜ [1], Ca., U.S.	228	34.15 N	117.11 W
Arrowhead, Lake ⊜ [1], Tx., U.S.	196	33.40 N	98.20 W
Arrowhead Peak ∧	228	34.13 N	117.16 W
Arrowhead Provincial Park ♠	212	45.24 N	79.13 W
Arrowhead Village	208	40.04 N	74.07 W
Arrow Lake ⊜	190	48.08 N	90.18 W
Arrowrock Reservoir ⊜ [1]	202	43.36 N	115.51 W
Arrowsmith	216	40.27 N	88.38 W
Arrowsmith, Mount ∧, Austl.	166	30.09 S	141.50 E
Arrowsmith, Mount ∧, B.C., Can.	224	49.13 N	124.36 W
Arrowsmith, Mount ∧, N.Z.	172	43.21 S	170.59 E
Arrowtown	172	44.56 S	168.50 E
Arrowwood	182	50.44 N	113.09 W
Arroyan, Arroyo ≃ [1]	288	34.24 S	58.32 W
Arroyito	252	31.25 S	63.03 W
Arroyo	240m	17.58 N	66.04 W
Arroyo de la Luz	34	39.29 N	6.35 W
Arroyo Grande	204	35.07 N	120.35 W
Arroyo Grande → Ismael Cortinas	258	33.58 S	57.06 W
Arroyo Hondo	200	36.32 N	105.40 W
Arroyo Naranjo -•- [8]	286b	23.02 N	82.23 W
Arroyo Seco	252	33.14 S	60.50 W
Arroyo Seco Park ♠	280	34.06 N	118.12 W
Arroyos y Esteros	252	25.04 S	57.06 W
Arrozal	256	22.37 S	44.03 W
Ar-Ru'at	140	12.21 N	32.17 E
Ar-Rub' al-Khālī -•- [2]	118	20.00 N	51.00 E
Ar-Rubayqī	142	30.10 N	31.46 E
Ar-Ruḥaybah	132	33.45 N	36.42 E
Ar-Rukhaymīyah ╤ [4]	128	29.14 N	45.35 E
Ar-Rumaythah	128	31.32 N	45.12 E
Ar-Rummān	132	32.10 N	35.50 E
Ar-Ruqayyah ⊥	132	32.47 N	37.05 E
Ar-Ruṣāfah ⊥	130	35.37 N	38.45 E
Ar-Ruṣayfah	132	32.01 N	36.03 E
Ar-Ruṣayriṣ	140	11.51 N	34.23 E
Ar-Rushaydah	132	32.40 N	36.50 E
Ar-Ruṭbah	128	33.02 N	40.17 E
Ar-Ru'ūs	142	29.21 N	31.04 E
Ar-Ruways	128	26.08 N	51.13 E
Års	26	56.48 N	9.32 E
Aršan, Ross.	88	51.54 N	102.27 E
Aršan, Ross.	88	53.54 N	99.54 E
Arsanjān	128	29.56 N	53.18 E
Aršan'-Zel'men'	80	47.36 N	44.36 E
Ārsāpota	272b	22.55 N	88.18 E
Arsbeck	56	51.08 N	6.12 E
Arsenal de Marinha ■	266c	38.39 N	9.09 W
Arsenal Football Club ♠	260	51.33 N	0.06 W
Arsenault Lake ⊜	184	55.06 N	108.30 W
Arsenjev	89	44.10 N	133.15 E
Arsenjevka ≃	89	44.54 N	133.35 E
Arsenjevo	76	53.44 N	36.40 E
Ars-en-Ré	32	46.12 N	1.31 W
Arsi □ [4]	144	8.00 N	39.40 E
Arsiè	64	45.59 N	11.45 E
Arsiero	64	45.48 N	11.21 E
Arsikere	122	13.20 N	76.15 E
Arsin	130	40.58 N	39.56 E
Aršincevo	78	45.17 N	36.25 E
Arsk	80	56.06 N	49.54 E
Arslanbob	85	41.21 N	72.56 E
Årslev	41	55.18 N	10.29 E
Arso	164	2.56 S	140.47 E
Arsoli	66	42.02 N	13.01 E
Ársos	130	34.50 N	32.46 E
Ars-sur-Formans	58	45.59 N	4.49 E
Ars-sur-Moselle	56	49.05 N	6.04 E
Årsta havsbad	40	59.05 N	18.10 E
Arsufhsa ≃	84	39.08 N	46.50 E
Ärsunda	40	60.32 N	16.44 E
Art, Île I	175f	19.43 S	163.38 E
Árta, Ellás	38	39.09 N	20.59 E
Artà, Esp.	34	39.42 N	3.21 E
Artarmon	274a	33.49 S	151.11 E
Artašat	84	39.59 N	44.33 E
Arta Terme	64	46.28 N	13.01 E
Arteaga	234	18.28 N	102.25 W
Arteche	116	12.17 N	125.22 E
Arte Contemporânea, Museu de ʊ	287b	23.32 S	46.38 W
Artegna	64	46.14 N	13.09 E
Artemare	62	45.52 N	5.42 E
Artemisa	240p	22.49 N	82.46 W
Artemón	38	36.59 N	24.43 E
Artémou	150	15.31 N	12.16 W
Artemovsk → Art'omovsk	83	48.35 N	38.00 E

≃	River	Fluß	Río	Rivière	Rio
≊	Canal	Kanal	Canal	Canal	Canal
ʟ	Waterfall, Rapids	Wasserfall, Stromschnellen	Cascada, Rápidos	Chute d'eau, Rapides	Cascata, Rápidos
⋈	Strait	Meeresstraße	Estrecho	Détroit	Estreito
⊂	Bay, Gulf	Bucht, Golf	Bahía, Golfo	Baie, Golfe	Baía, Golfo
⊜	Lake, Lakes	See, Seen	Lago, Lagos	Lac, Lacs	Lago, Lagos
≡	Swamp	Sumpf	Pantano	Marais	Pântano
⊠	Ice Features, Glacier	Eis- und Gletscherformen	Accidentes Glaciales	Formes glaciaires	Acidentes glaciares
╤	Other Hydrographic Features	Andere Hydrographische Objekte	Otros Elementos Hidrográficos	Autres données hydrographiques	Outros acidentes hidrográficos

✢	Submarine Features	Untermeerische Objekte	Accidentes Submarinos	Formes de relief sous-marin	Acidentes submarinos
□	Political Unit	Politische Einheit	Unidad Politica	Entité politique	Unidade política
ʊ	Cultural Institution	Kulturelle Institution	Institución Cultural	Institution culturelle	Instituição cultural
⊥	Historical Site	Historische Stätte	Sitio Histórico	Site historique	Sitio histórico
♠	Recreational Site	Erholungs- und Ferienort	Sitio de Recreo	Centre de loisirs	Area de Lazer
⊠	Airport	Flughafen	Aeropuerto	Aéroport	Aeroporto
■	Military Installation	Militäranlage	Instalación Militar	Installation militaire	Instalação militar
-•-	Miscellaneous	Verschiedenes	Misceláneo	Divers	Diversos

Artèn 64 46.00 N 11.50 E
Artenay 50 48.05 N 1.53 E
Artern 54 51.22 N 11.17 E
Artesia, Ca., U.S. 280 33.51 N 118.04 W
Artesia, Ms., U.S. 194 33.24 N 88.38 W
Artesia, N.M., U.S. 196 32.50 N 104.24 W
Artesia Lake ⊜ 226 38.57 N 119.22 W
Artesia → Mosomane 156 24.04 S 26.15 E
Artesian 198 44.00 N 97.55 W
Arth 58 47.04 N 8.31 E
Arthabaska 206 46.02 N 71.55 W
Arthabaska □6 206 46.05 N 72.00 W
Arthal 123 33.16 N 76.11 E
Arthala 272a 28.40 N 77.24 E
Arthies 261 49.06 N 1.48 E
Arthonnay 50 47.56 N 4.13 E
Arthur, On., Can. 212 43.50 N 80.32 W
Arthur, Il., U.S. 194 39.43 N 88.28 W
Arthur, Ne., U.S. 198 41.34 N 101.41 W
Arthur, N.D., U.S. 198 47.06 N 97.13 W
Arthur, Tn., U.S. 192 36.32 N 83.40 W
Arthur ≃, Austl. 166 41.03 S 144.40 E
Arthur ≃, Austl. 168a 33.31 S 116.50 E
Arthur, Lake ⊜1 214 40.57 N 80.05 W
Arthur Creek ≃ 162 22.55 S 136.45 E
Arthur Kill ⊔ 276 40.30 N 74.15 W
Arthurs Pass 172 42.57 S 171.34 E
Arthurs Pass)(172 42.54 S 171.34 E
Arthur's Pass National Park ♠ 172 42.50 S 171.40 E
Arthurs Seat ∧2 169 38.21 S 144.57 E
Arthur's Town 238 24.38 N 75.42 W
Arthurton 168b 34.16 S 137.45 E
Arti 86 56.26 N 58.32 E
Artibonite ≃ 238 19.15 N 72.47 W
Artico, Océano → Arctic Ocean ⊤1 16 85.00 N 170.00 E
Artigas 252 30.24 S 56.28 W
Artigas ⊷8 286c 10.30 N 66.56 W
Artigas, Casa de ⟂ 258 34.39 S 56.03 W
Artik 84 40.37 N 43.59 E
Artilleros 258 34.22 S 57.34 W
Artilleros, Punta > 258 34.28 S 57.32 W
Artillery Lake ⊜ 176 63.09 N 107.52 W
Artlenburg 52 53.22 N 10.29 E
Artney, Glen V 46 56.20 N 4.04 W
Artois □9 50 50.30 N 2.30 E
Artois, Collines de l' ⋏2 50 50.25 N 2.10 E
Art'om 89 43.22 N 132.13 E
Art'om-Ostrov 84 40.28 N 50.20 E
Art'omovka, Ukr. 78 49.46 N 35.04 E
Art'omovka, Ukr. 83 48.29 N 37.23 E
Art'omovka, Ukr. 83 47.53 N 38.38 E
Art'omovo 83 48.22 N 37.53 E
Art'omovsk, Ross. 86 54.21 N 93.26 E
Art'omovsk, Ukr. 83 48.27 N 38.42 E
Art'omovsk, Ukr. 83 48.35 N 38.00 E
Art'omovskij, Ross. 86 57.21 N 61.54 E
Art'omovskij, Ross. 88 58.12 N 114.45 E
Art'omovskij, Ross. 89 43.27 N 132.22 E
Artova 130 40.03 N 36.19 E
Artpark ♠ 284a 43.10 N 79.03 W
Artrutx, Cap d' > 34 39.56 N 3.48 E
Artuby ≃ 62 43.44 N 6.22 E
Artur Nogueira 256 22.35 S 47.09 W
Arturo Merino Benítez, Aeropuerto ⊠ 286e 33.23 S 70.49 W
Arturo Segui ⊷8 258 34.51 S 58.09 W
Artvin 130 41.11 N 41.49 E
Artvin □4 130 41.05 N 42.00 E
Artybaš 86 51.48 N 87.16 E
Artyk 74 64.12 N 145.06 E
Aru, Kepulauan II 164 6.00 S 134.30 E
Aru, Tanjung > 112 2.10 S 116.34 E
Aru, Teluk c 114 4.09 N 98.12 E
Arua 154 3.01 N 30.55 E
Aruã ≃ 250 2.39 S 55.38 W
Aruaddin 144 16.15 N 38.43 E
Aruanã 255 14.54 S 51.05 W
Aruângua (Luangwa) ≃ 154 15.36 S 30.25 E
Aruba □2, N.A. 230 12.30 N 69.58 W
Aruba □2, N.A. 241s 12.30 N 69.58 W
Aru Basin ⊹1 14 5.00 S 134.00 E
Arucas 148 28.07 N 15.31 W
Arue 174s 17.32 S 149.32 W
Arufu 150 7.50 N 9.14 E
Arujá 256 23.24 S 46.20 W
Arujá □7 287b 23.24 S 46.20 W
Arumanduba 250 1.29 S 52.29 W
Arume 174m 26.36 N 128.07 E
Arume-wan c 174m 26.35 N 128.08 E
Aruṇ (Pong) ≃, Asia 124 26.49 N 87.09 E
Arun ≃, Eng., U.K. 42 50.48 N 0.33 W
Arunāchal Pradesh □3 120 28.30 N 95.00 E
Arundel, P.Q., Can. 206 45.58 N 74.37 W
Arundel, Eng., U.K. 42 50.51 N 0.34 W
Arun Qi 89 48.07 N 123.28 E
Årup 41 55.23 N 10.04 E
Aruppukkottai 122 9.31 N 78.06 E
Arurandeua ≃ 250 3.43 S 48.50 W
Arusha 154 3.22 S 36.41 E
Arusha □4 154 4.00 S 36.15 E
Arusha Chini 154 3.35 S 37.20 E
Arusha National Park ♠ 154 3.17 S 36.56 E
Arut ≃ 112 2.42 S 111.34 E
Aruvi ≃ 122 8.49 N 79.55 E
Aruwimi ≃ 138 1.13 N 23.36 E
Arvada 200 39.48 N 105.05 W
Arvagh 48 53.55 N 7.34 W
Arvajcheer 90 46.15 N 102.48 E
Arve ≃ 58 46.12 N 6.08 E
Arverne ⊷8 276 40.35 N 73.48 W
Arves, Les Aiguilles d' ∧ 62 45.08 N 6.21 E
Arvi 120 20.59 N 78.14 E
Arvida 186 48.25 N 71.11 W
Arvidsjaur 24 65.35 N 19.07 E
Arvier 62 45.42 N 7.11 E
Arvieux 62 44.46 N 6.44 E
Arvika 26 59.39 N 12.36 E
Arvillard 62 45.27 N 6.07 E
Arvin 228 35.12 N 118.49 W
Arvo, Lago ⊜ 68 39.14 N 16.29 E
Arvon, Mount ∧ 190 46.45 N 88.09 W
Arvonia 192 37.40 N 78.20 W
Arvorezinha 252 28.53 S 52.10 W
Arwal 124 25.15 N 84.41 E
Arwala 112 7.41 S 126.49 E
Arxan 89 47.11 N 119.57 E
Aryamūn 142 31.11 N 30.54 E
Aryiroúpolis 267c 37.54 N 23.45 E
Arys' 85 42.26 N 68.48 E
Arys' ≃ 85 42.48 N 68.12 E
Arys, ozero ⊜ 86 45.50 N 66.20 E
Arzachena 71 41.05 N 9.23 E
Arzamas 80 55.23 N 43.50 E
Arzana 71 39.55 N 9.31 E
Arzano 68 40.55 N 14.16 E
Arzberg 60 50.04 N 12.12 E
Arzew, Golfe d' c 34 35.50 N 0.10 W
Arzew, Salines d' ⊜ 34 35.40 N 0.15 W
Arzfeld 56 50.05 N 6.16 E
Arzignano 64 45.31 N 11.20 E
Arziw 148 35.51 N 0.19 W
Arz Lubnān ⊷3 130 34.14 N 36.03 E
Arzni 84 40.19 N 44.36 E
Arzon ≃ 62 45.11 N 3.54 E
Arzúa 34 42.56 N 8.09 W
As, Bel. 56 51.01 N 5.35 E
Aš, Česko. 54 50.10 N 12.10 E
Ås, Nor. 26 59.40 N 10.48 E
Asa, Nihon 96 34.33 N 132.26 E
Aša, Ross. 86 55.00 N 57.16 E
Asa ≃, Nihon 94 35.39 N 139.26 E
Asa ≃, Nihon 96 34.01 N 131.09 E
Asa ≃, Ven. 246 6.50 N 63.18 W
Asab 156 25.29 S 17.59 E
Asaba, Nig. 150 6.12 N 6.44 E
Asaba, Nihon 94 34.42 N 137.56 E
Asad, Buḥayrat al- ⊜1 130 36.00 N 38.10 E
Asadābād, Afg. 120 34.52 N 71.09 E
Asadābād, Īrān 128 34.47 N 48.07 E
Asafo 150 6.11 N 0.28 W
Asaga Strait ⊔ 174y 14.11 S 169.40 W
Asagaya ⊷8 268 35.42 N 139.38 E
Aşağıbostancı 130 35.10 N 33.00 E
Aşağıçiğil 130 38.03 N 31.52 E
Aşağı Dağ ∧ 84 40.01 N 43.11 E
Aşağı Kuluşağı 130 38.39 N 38.39 E
Aşağılahan 130 38.50 N 39.59 E
Aşağı Mestikân 130 38.25 N 38.46 E
Ašagy-G'ojn'uk 84 41.18 N 47.00 E
Asahan 114 2.23 N 102.33 E
Asahan ≃ 114 3.02 N 99.52 E
Asahi, Nihon 94 35.14 N 137.22 E
Asahi, Nihon 94 35.59 N 136.07 E
Asahi, Nihon 94 35.43 N 140.39 E
Asahi, Nihon 94 36.05 N 137.21 E
Asahi, Nihon 94 36.14 N 140.31 E
Asahi, Nihon 94 35.02 N 136.40 E
Asahi, Nihon 94 36.07 N 137.52 E
Asahi, Nihon 94 36.57 N 137.34 E
Asahi, Nihon 96 34.59 N 133.50 E
Asahi, Nihon 96 34.51 N 132.16 E
Asahi, Nihon 96 34.17 N 131.28 E
Asahi ⊷8, Nihon 268 35.29 N 139.33 E
Asahi ⊷8, Nihon 270 34.44 N 135.34 E
Asahi ≃ 96 34.36 N 133.58 E
Asahi-dake ∧, Nihon 92a 43.40 N 142.51 E
Asahi-dake ∧, Nihon 94 37.14 N 139.21 E
Asahigawa → Asahikawa 92a 43.46 N 142.22 E
Asahi-gawa-daiichi-dam ⊷6 96 34.53 N 133.22 E
Asahikawa 92a 43.46 N 142.22 E
Asahikawa-chūtonchi, Rikujō-Jieitai- ■ 92a 43.49 N 142.25 E
Asahi-ko ⊜1 96 34.56 N 133.51 E
Asahi-sanchi ⋏ 92 38.25 N 139.50 E
Asaka 94 35.48 N 139.36 E
Asaka, Camp ■ 268 35.47 N 139.36 E
Asakanskij Golec, gora ∧ 88 50.18 N 109.55 E
Asakawa 94 37.05 N 140.25 E
Asake ≃ 94 35.00 N 136.41 E
Asako 96 35.14 N 134.48 E
Asakura 96 33.23 N 130.44 E
Asakusa ⊷8 268 35.43 N 139.49 E
Asālafpur ⊷8 272a 28.38 N 77.05 E
Asale 144 14.22 N 40.32 E
Asale, Lake ⊜ 144 14.19 N 40.18 E
Asamankese 150 5.52 N 0.42 W
Asama-yama ∧ 94 36.24 N 138.31 E
Asanbani, India 126 22.43 N 86.20 E
Asanbāni, India 126 24.07 N 87.27 E
Asani 154 4.25 S 29.05 E
Asankrangwa 150 5.48 N 2.26 W
Asan-man c 98 36.56 N 126.51 E
Āsānsol, India 126 24.14 N 87.17 E
Āsānsol, India 126 23.41 N 86.59 E
Ašap 86 57.07 N 56.30 E
Asar 88 47.56 N 117.38 E
Åsarna 26 62.39 N 14.21 E
Asarum 26 56.12 N 14.50 E
Asashina 94 36.16 N 138.25 E
Āsāsuni 126 22.32 N 89.10 E
Asati 272b 22.29 N 88.14 E
Asa-yama ∧ 96 34.47 N 132.23 E
Asayita 144 11.33 N 41.30 E
Asbach 56 50.40 N 7.25 E
Asbeck 263 51.21 N 7.18 E
Asberg 263 51.26 N 6.40 E
Asbesberg ⋏ 158 28.55 S 23.15 E
Asbest 86 57.00 N 61.30 E
Asbestos 206 45.46 N 71.57 W
Asbestos Range National Park ♠ 166 41.08 S 146.39 E
Asbe Teferi 144 9.02 N 40.58 E
Åsbro 40 59.00 N 15.03 E
Asbury 210 40.41 N 75.00 W
Asbury Park 208 40.13 N 74.01 W
Ascea 68 40.08 N 15.11 E
Ascensión 232 31.06 N 107.59 W
Ascension I 10 7.57 S 14.22 W
Ascent 158 27.12 S 29.03 E
Aščerino 265b 55.36 N 37.46 E
Asch 58 47.57 N 10.49 E
Aschabad (Ashgabat) 128 37.57 N 58.23 E
Aschach an der Donau 61 48.22 N 14.02 E
Aschaffenburg 56 49.59 N 9.09 E
Aschbach Markt 61 48.04 N 14.45 E
Ascheberg, Dtsch. 52 51.47 N 7.37 E
Ascheberg, Dtsch. 54 54.08 N 10.20 E
Aschendorf 52 53.04 N 7.22 E
Aschersleben 54 51.45 N 11.27 E
Asciano 66 43.14 N 11.33 E
Aščikol', ozero ⊜ 86 45.05 N 67.15 E
Aščiozek ≃ 80 49.12 N 48.06 E
Aščitastysor, ozero ⊜ 86 49.19 N 63.59 E
Ascoli Piceno 66 42.51 N 13.34 E
Ascoli Piceno □4 66 43.01 N 13.34 E
Ascoli Satriano 68 41.12 N 15.34 E
Ascona 58 46.09 N 8.46 E
Ascope 248 7.43 S 79.07 W
Ascot, Austl. 171a 27.26 S 153.04 E
Ascot, Eng., U.K. 42 51.25 N 0.41 W
Ascot ≃ 206 45.21 N 71.51 W
Ascotán 252 21.44 S 68.18 W
Ascros 62 43.55 N 7.01 E
Aščykol', ozero ⊜ 85 43.32 N 70.35 E
Aščysu ≃ 86 49.54 N 78.58 E
Aseb 144 13.00 N 42.45 E
Åseda 26 57.10 N 15.20 E
Asedjrad ⋏1 148 24.28 N 1.52 E
Asekejevo 80 53.36 N 52.49 E
Āsela 144 7.59 N 39.08 E
Åsele 26 64.10 N 17.20 E
Asem ≃ 115a 6.14 S 107.42 E
Asembagus 115a 7.45 S 114.14 E
Asembourg 56 49.43 N 6.02 E
Åsen 26 63.36 N 11.03 E
Asendabo 144 9.50 N 37.33 E
Asendorf 52 52.46 N 9.00 E
Asenovgrad 38 42.01 N 24.52 E
Åsensbruk 26 58.48 N 12.25 E
Aseri 76 59.27 N 26.52 E
Aşfar, Jabal al- ∧ 132 32.12 N 36.54 E
Asfordby 42 52.46 N 0.57 W
Aşfūn al-Maţā'inah 140 25.23 N 32.32 E
Åsgårdstrand 26 59.21 N 10.28 E
Ash, Eng., U.K. 42 51.17 N 1.16 E
Ash, Eng., U.K. 42 51.15 N 0.44 W
Ashalim 132 30.58 N 34.40 E
Åshammar 40 60.39 N 16.32 E
Ashanti □4 150 6.45 N 1.30 W
'Asharah, Wādī al- V 142 30.21 N 32.15 E
Asharoken 276 40.56 N 73.22 W
Ashaway 207 41.25 N 71.47 W
Ashbourne, Ire. 48 53.31 N 6.24 W
Ashbourne, Eng., U.K. 44 53.02 N 1.44 W
Ash Brook Swamp Reservation ♠ 276 40.37 N 74.21 W
Ashburn, Ga., U.S. 192 31.42 N 83.39 W
Ashburn, Mo., U.S. 219 39.33 N 91.10 W
Ashburn, Va., U.S. 208 39.02 N 77.29 W
Ashburnham 207 42.38 N 71.54 W
Ashburton, Austl. 274b 37.52 S 145.05 E
Ashburton, N.Z. 172 43.55 S 171.45 E
Ashburton, Eng., U.K. 42 50.31 N 3.45 W
Ashburton ≃, Austl. 162 21.40 S 114.56 E
Ashburton ≃, N.Z. 172 44.04 S 171.48 E
Ashburton, North Branch ≃ 172 43.54 S 171.44 E
Ashburton, South Branch ≃ 172 43.44 S 171.32 E
Ashburton Downs 162 23.24 S 117.04 E
Ashby 207 42.40 N 71.49 W
Ashby, Lake ⊜ 220 28.56 N 81.07 W
Ashby-de-la-Zouch 42 52.46 N 1.28 W
Ashchurch 42 52.00 N 2.07 W
Ash Creek ≃, Ca., U.S. 204 41.05 N 121.08 W
Ash Creek ≃, Ct., U.S. 276 41.08 N 73.14 W
Ashcroft 182 50.43 N 121.17 W
Ashdod, Ma., U.S. 283 42.04 N 70.45 W
Ashdod, Yis. 132 31.49 N 34.40 E
Ashdod, Tel ⟂ 132 31.45 N 34.40 E
Ashdot Ya'aqov 132 32.40 N 35.35 E
Ashdown 194 33.40 N 94.07 W
Asheboro 192 35.42 N 79.48 W
Ashern 184 51.11 N 98.21 W
Asherton 196 28.26 N 99.45 W
Asheville 192 35.36 N 82.33 W
Ashewat Ziārat 120 31.22 N 68.32 E
Asheweig ≃ 176 54.17 N 87.12 W
Ashfield, Austl. 274a 33.53 S 151.08 E
Ashfield, Ma., U.S. 207 42.31 N 72.47 W
Ash Flat 194 36.13 N 91.36 W
Ashford, Austl. 166 29.20 S 151.06 E
Ashford, Eng., U.K. 42 51.08 N 0.53 E
Ashford, Eng., U.K. 260 51.26 N 0.27 W
Ashford, Al., U.S. 194 31.10 N 85.14 W
Ashford, Wa., U.S. 224 46.46 N 122.02 W
Ashford Airport ⊠ 42 51.04 N 1.01 E
Ash Fork 200 35.13 N 112.28 W
Ash Grove 194 37.18 N 93.35 W
Ashhurst 172 40.18 S 175.45 E
Ashibe 92 33.48 N 129.46 E
Ashibetsu 92a 43.31 N 142.11 E
Ashida ≃ 96 34.26 N 133.25 E
Ashikaga 94 36.20 N 139.27 E
Ashikagga-gakkō ⟂ 94 36.22 N 139.30 E
Ashingdon 260 51.36 N 0.42 E
Ashington 44 55.12 N 1.35 W
Ashino-ko ⊜ 94 35.13 N 139.00 E
Ashio 94 36.38 N 139.27 E
Ashio-sanchi ⋏ 94 36.35 N 139.30 E
Ashippun 216 43.14 N 88.31 W
Ashippun ≃ 216 43.10 N 88.33 W
Ashitaka-yama ∧ 94 35.12 N 138.49 E
Ashiya, Nihon 96 33.53 N 130.40 E
Ashiya, Nihon 96 34.43 N 135.17 E
Ashiya ≃ 270 34.43 N 135.18 E
Ashiyasu 94 35.38 N 138.23 E
Ashiyoro 92a 43.15 N 143.30 E
Ashizuri-misaki > 92 32.44 N 133.01 E
Ashizuri-Uwakai-kokuritsu-kōen ♠, Nihon 92 32.45 N 132.45 E
Ashizuri-Uwakai-kokuritsu-kōen ♠, Nihon 96 33.07 N 132.27 E
Ashkhabad → Aschabad 128 37.57 N 58.23 E
Ashkum 216 40.53 N 87.57 W
Ashland, Al., U.S. 194 33.16 N 85.50 W
Ashland, Ca., U.S. 226 37.41 N 122.06 W
Ashland, Il., U.S. 219 39.53 N 90.00 W
Ashland, Ks., U.S. 198 37.11 N 99.45 W
Ashland, Ky., U.S. 188 38.28 N 82.38 W
Ashland, Me., U.S. 186 46.37 N 68.24 W
Ashland, Ma., U.S. 207 42.15 N 71.27 W
Ashland, Ms., U.S. 194 34.49 N 89.10 W
Ashland, Mo., U.S. 219 38.46 N 92.15 W
Ashland, Mt., U.S. 202 45.35 N 106.16 W
Ashland, Ne., U.S. 198 41.02 N 96.22 W
Ashland, N.H., U.S. 188 43.41 N 71.37 W
Ashland, N.J., U.S. 285 39.51 N 75.00 W
Ashland, N.Y., U.S. 210 42.18 N 74.20 W
Ashland, Oh., U.S. 214 40.52 N 82.19 W
Ashland, Or., U.S. 202 42.11 N 122.42 W
Ashland, Pa., U.S. 210 40.46 N 76.20 W
Ashland, Va., U.S. 208 37.45 N 77.28 W
Ashland, Wi., U.S. 190 46.35 N 90.53 W
Ashland □6 214 40.52 N 82.19 W
Ashland, Mount ∧ 202 42.05 N 122.43 W
Ashland City 194 36.16 N 87.03 W
Ashley, Austl. 166 29.19 S 149.49 E
Ashley, Eng., U.K. 262 53.21 N 2.20 W
Ashley, Il., U.S. 219 38.20 N 89.11 W
Ashley, In., U.S. 216 41.32 N 85.04 W
Ashley, Mi., U.S. 190 43.11 N 84.28 W
Ashley, Mo., U.S. 219 39.15 N 91.14 W
Ashley, N.D., U.S. 198 46.01 N 99.22 W
Ashley, Oh., U.S. 214 40.24 N 82.57 W
Ashley, Pa., U.S. 210 41.12 N 75.53 W
Ashley ≃ 172 43.16 S 172.43 E
Ashley Creek ≃ 200 40.21 N 109.22 W
Ashley Falls 207 42.03 N 73.20 W
Ashley Green 260 51.44 N 0.35 W
Ashmore 194 39.32 N 88.01 W
Ashmore Islands II 160 12.14 S 123.05 E
Ashmūn 142 30.18 N 30.58 E
Ashokan Reservoir ⊜1 210 41.58 N 74.10 W
Ashoknagar 120 24.34 N 77.43 E
Ashqelon 132 31.40 N 34.35 E
Ashridge Park ♠ 260 51.48 N 0.34 W
Ash-Shabakah 128 30.49 N 43.39 E
Ash-Shabb ⊤4 140 22.19 N 29.46 E
Ash-Shaddādah 130 36.02 N 40.45 E
Ash-Shāgūr 132 31.50 N 35.39 E
Ash-Shā'ib ∧2 142 29.50 N 30.56 E
Ash-Shajarah 132 32.39 N 35.56 E
Ash-Shallūfah 142 30.07 N 32.34 E
Ash-Shamāl □4 130 34.30 N 36.00 E
Ash-Shamālīyah □4 140 19.15 N 29.00 E
Ash-Shāmīyah 128 31.57 N 44.36 E
Ash-Shanāwīyah 142 29.08 N 31.08 E
Ash-Sharāh ⊷1 132 30.20 N 35.30 E
Ash-Shāriqah 128 25.22 N 55.23 E
Ash-Sharmah 128 28.01 N 35.18 E
Ash-Sharqāṭ 128 35.27 N 43.16 E
Ash-Sharqīyah □4 142 30.48 N 31.48 E
Ash-Sharqīyah ⊷1 128 27.00 N 49.00 E
Ash-Shaṭrah 128 31.25 N 46.10 E
Ash-Shawāshinah 142 29.22 N 30.36 E
Ash-Shawbak 132 30.32 N 35.34 E
Ash-Shawmarah 132 33.07 N 35.08 E
Ash-Shaykh Faḍl 142 28.29 N 30.50 E
Ash-Shaykh 'Ibādah 142 27.48 N 30.52 E
Ash-Shaykh Sa'd 132 32.50 N 36.02 E
Ash-Shaykh Timay 142 27.53 N 30.51 E
Ash-Shiḥr 144 14.44 N 49.35 E
Ash-Shīn 142 31.01 N 30.53 E
Ash-Shināfīyah 128 31.35 N 44.39 E
Ash-Shīyāḥ 132 33.51 N 35.30 E
Ash-Shufayyah 128 23.50 N 39.08 E
Ash-Shuhadā' 142 30.36 N 30.54 E
Ash-Shumlul 128 26.31 N 47.19 E
Ash-Shuqayq 144 17.43 N 42.01 E
Ash-Shurayf 128 25.43 N 39.14 E
Ash-Shurayk 140 18.48 N 33.34 E
Ash-Shuwayfāt 132 33.49 N 35.31 E
Ash Slough ≃ 226 37.02 N 120.32 W
Ashta, India 122 16.57 N 74.24 E
Ashta, India 124 23.01 N 76.43 E
Ashtabula 214 41.51 N 80.47 W
Ashtabula □6 214 41.44 N 80.46 W
Ashtabula ≃ 214 41.55 N 80.47 W
Ashtabula, East Branch ≃ 214 41.48 N 80.37 W
Ashtabula, Lake ⊜1 198 47.11 N 97.58 W
Ashtabula, West Branch ≃ 214 41.48 N 80.37 W
Ashtead 42 51.19 N 0.18 W
Ashton, S. Afr. 158 33.50 S 20.05 E
Ashton, Eng., U.K. 262 53.13 N 2.45 W
Ashton, Id., U.S. 202 44.04 N 111.26 W
Ashton, Il., U.S. 190 41.51 N 89.13 W
Ashton, Ia., U.S. 198 43.18 N 95.47 W
Ashton, Md., U.S. 208 39.08 N 77.00 W
Ashton, Ne., U.S. 198 41.14 N 98.47 W
Ashton, R.I., U.S. 207 41.46 N 71.25 W
Ashton-in-Makerfield 44 53.29 N 2.39 W
Ashton-under-Lyne 44 53.29 N 2.06 W
Ashton upon Mersey 262 53.26 N 2.19 W
Ashuanipi Lake ⊜ 176 52.35 N 66.10 W
Ashuelot ≃ 188 42.46 N 72.29 W
Ashurst's Beacon ∧2 262 53.34 N 2.45 W
Ashville, Al., U.S. 194 33.52 N 86.17 W
Ashville, N.Y., U.S. 214 42.06 N 79.23 W
Ashville, Oh., U.S. 218 39.42 N 82.57 W
Ashville, Pa., U.S. 214 40.34 N 78.33 W
Ashwater 42 50.44 N 4.16 W
Ashwaubenon 190 44.30 N 88.06 W
Ashworth Moor Reservoir ⊜1 262 53.38 N 2.16 W
Asi (Nahr al-'Āṣī) ≃ 130 36.02 N 35.58 E
Asia ⊥1 4 50.00 N 100.00 E
Asia ⊥1 12 50.00 N 100.00 E
Asia, Kepulauan II 108 1.03 N 131.18 E
Asiago 64 45.52 N 11.30 E
Asia Menor → Asia Minor □9 22 39.00 N 32.00 E
Asia Minor □9 22 39.00 N 32.00 E
Asid Gulf c 116 12.07 N 123.30 E
Asie → Asia ⊥1 12 50.00 N 100.00 E
Asie Mineure → Asia Minor □9 22 39.00 N 32.00 E
Asien → Asia ⊥1 12 50.00 N 100.00 E
āsika 120 19.36 N 84.39 E
Asikuma 150 5.35 N 1.00 W
Asilah 148 35.32 N 6.00 W
Asinara, Golfo dell' c 71 41.00 N 8.32 E
Asinara, Isola I 71 41.04 N 8.16 E
Asinaro ≃ 70 36.53 N 15.08 E
Asino 86 57.00 N 86.09 E
Asipoquobah Lake ⊜ 184 53.40 N 91.15 W
'Asīr ⊷1 144 19.00 N 42.00 E
Ašitkovo 82 55.26 N 38.36 E
Aşkale 130 39.55 N 40.42 E
Askam in Furness 44 54.11 N 3.13 W
Askanija-Nova 78 46.27 N 33.52 E
Askanija-nova zapovednik ♠ 78 46.37 N 33.54 E
Askarovo 86 53.21 N 58.30 E
Askeaton 48 52.36 N 8.58 W
Asker 26 59.50 N 10.26 E
Askern 44 53.37 N 1.09 W
Askersund 40 58.53 N 14.54 E
Askham 158 26.59 S 20.47 E
Askim 26 59.35 N 11.10 E
Askino 86 56.05 N 56.34 E
Askira 146 10.39 N 12.55 E
Askival ∧ 46 56.59 N 6.17 W
Askiz 86 53.08 N 90.32 E
Askja ∧1 24a 65.00 N 16.48 W
Askø I 41 54.54 N 11.30 E
Äsköping 40 59.09 N 16.04 E
Askov 41 55.28 N 9.06 E
Askraal 158 34.09 S 20.52 E
Askrigg 44 54.19 N 2.04 W
Askvoll 26 61.21 N 5.04 E
Aslanapa 130 39.13 N 29.52 E
Aslan-Sara 84 39.02 N 48.16 E
Aslantaş Barajı ⊜1 130 37.20 N 36.15 E
Asleigh 284c 39.01 N 77.10 W
Åsljunga 41 56.19 N 13.22 E
Ašlyk 86 57.33 N 68.40 E
Ašlyk ≃ 86 57.50 N 69.12 E
Asmār 120 35.02 N 71.22 E
Asmara → Asmera 144 15.20 N 38.53 E
Asmera 144 15.20 N 38.53 E
Asmundtorp 41 55.53 N 12.56 E
Asnæs 41 55.49 N 11.31 E
Asnæs >1 41 55.40 N 11.00 E
Asnebumskit Hill ∧2 207 42.18 N 71.54 W
Åsnen ⊜ 26 56.38 N 14.42 E
Asni 148 31.14 N 7.55 W
Asnières [-sur-Seine] 50 48.55 N 2.17 E
Asō, Nihon 94 35.59 N 140.29 E
Aso, Nihon 96 32.58 N 131.02 E
Aso ≃ 66 43.06 N 13.51 E
Asoc 152 1.26 N 11.18 E
Aso-kokuritsu-kōen ♠ 92 33.00 N 131.07 E
Asola 64 45.13 N 10.24 E
Asolo 64 45.48 N 11.54 E
Asomante 240m 18.23 N 66.36 W
Ason 273a 6.34 N 3.31 E
Asosa 144 10.03 N 34.32 E
Aso-san ∧ 92 32.53 N 131.06 E
Asoteriba, Jabal ∧ 140 21.51 N 36.30 E
Asotin 202 46.20 N 117.02 W
Asouf, Oued V 148 25.51 N 1.33 E
Asowsches Meer → Azovskoje more ⊤2 78 46.00 N 36.00 E
Asp 34 38.21 N 0.46 W
Aspach 60 48.11 N 13.18 E
Aspach-le-Bas 58 47.46 N 7.09 E
Aspang Markt 61 47.33 N 16.06 E
Aspara ≃ 85 43.17 N 73.28 E
Aspatria 44 54.46 N 3.20 W
Aspe, Gave d' ≃ 32 43.12 N 0.36 W
Aspen 200 39.11 N 106.49 W
Aspen Butte ∧ 202 42.19 N 122.05 W
Aspendale 274b 38.02 S 145.07 E
Aspendos ⟂ 130 37.00 N 31.10 E
Aspen Hill 284c 39.04 N 77.04 W
Aspen Knolls 284c 39.05 N 77.05 W
Aspen Lake ⊜ 202 42.18 N 122.00 W
Asperg 56 48.54 N 9.07 E
Aspermont 196 33.08 N 100.13 W
Aspern ⊷8 264b 48.13 N 16.29 E
Aspers 208 39.59 N 77.13 W
Asperup 41 55.29 N 9.55 E
Aspid, Mount ∧ 180 53.30 N 167.33 W
Aspindza 84 41.36 N 43.15 E
Aspinwall 279b 40.29 N 79.54 W
Aspinwall → Colón 236 9.22 N 79.54 W
Aspiring, Mount ∧ 172 44.23 S 168.44 E
Aspö 40 59.29 N 17.02 E
Aspres-sur-Buëch 62 44.31 N 5.45 E
Aspromonte ⋏ 68 38.10 N 15.55 E
Aspropirgos 267c 38.04 N 23.35 E
Aspull 262 53.34 N 2.35 W
Aspy Bay c 186 46.55 N 60.25 W
Asquins 50 47.29 N 3.45 E
Asquith, Austl. 274a 33.41 S 151.06 E
Asquith, Sk., Can. 184 52.08 N 107.13 W
Asralt chajrchan ∧ 88 48.29 N 107.24 E
Asrāni 123 29.31 N 72.07 E
Assa, Kaz. 85 43.02 N 71.10 E
Assa, Magreb 148 28.34 N 9.27 W
Assa ≃, Kaz. 85 43.55 N 70.25 E
Assa ≃, Ross. 84 43.13 N 45.25 E
As-Sa'ata 140 13.37 N 29.59 E
Assab → Aseb 144 13.00 N 42.45 E
Assabet ≃ 283 42.28 N 71.21 W
As-Sabkhah 130 35.48 N 39.15 E
Aṣ-Ṣadārah 144 14.30 N 48.04 E
As-Sa'dīyah 128 34.11 N 45.07 E
Aṣ-Ṣaff 140 29.34 N 31.17 E
As-Saffānīyah 128 27.58 N 48.47 E
Aṣ-Ṣāfī 132 31.02 N 35.28 E
As-Safīrah 130 36.04 N 37.22 E
Aṣ-Ṣāfiyah 140 15.31 N 30.07 E
Assago 266b 45.24 N 9.08 E
Assai 255 23.22 S 50.49 W
Aṣ-Ṣa'īd □9 140 26.00 N 32.00 E
Assaikwatamo ≃ 184 56.52 N 95.50 W
Assal, Lac ⊜ 144 11.41 N 42.25 E
'Assāl al-Ward 132 33.52 N 36.24 E
Aṣ-Ṣāliḥīyah 142 30.47 N 31.59 E
As-Salīmah 144 14.02 N 45.46 E
As-Sallūm 140 31.34 N 25.09 E
As-Salmān 128 30.30 N 44.32 E
As-Salṭ 132 32.03 N 35.44 E
Assam □3 120 26.00 N 93.00 E
As-Samāwah 128 31.18 N 45.17 E
As-Samū' 132 31.24 N 35.04 E
Assam Valley V 124 26.30 N 90.30 E
'Assān 130 36.05 N 37.14 E
Aṣ-Ṣanāfīn Al-Qiblīyah 142 30.27 N 31.18 E
Aṣ-Ṣanamayn 132 33.05 N 36.10 E
As-Santah 142 30.45 N 31.08 E
Assaq, Oued V 148 25.41 N 14.40 W
Aṣ-Ṣaqlabiyah 130 35.22 N 36.23 E
Aṣ-Ṣarafand 132 33.27 N 35.18 E
Assaré 250 6.52 S 39.52 W
Aṣ-Ṣarīḥ 132 32.30 N 35.54 E
As-Sarīrīyah 142 28.20 N 30.45 E
Assateague Island I 208 38.05 N 75.10 W
Assateague Island National Seashore ♠ 208 38.00 N 75.15 W
Assawoman Bay c 208 38.25 N 75.05 W
Assawoman Canal ≍ 208 38.31 N 75.04 W
Assawompset Pond ⊜ 207 41.50 N 70.55 W
Asse 50 50.55 N 4.12 E
Asse ≃ 62 43.53 N 5.53 E
Assean Lake ⊜ 184 56.13 N 96.30 W
Assebroek 50 51.12 N 3.16 E
Assekaifaf 148 27.08 N 8.50 E
Assel 52 53.41 N 9.25 E
Asseln ⊷8 263 51.32 N 7.35 E
Assembleia Nacional, Palacio da ⊷ 266c 38.43 N 9.09 W
Assemini 71 39.17 N 9.00 E
Assen 52 52.59 N 6.34 E
Assendelft 52 52.27 N 4.45 E
Assenede 50 51.14 N 3.45 E
Assens 41 55.16 N 9.55 E
Asserbo 41 56.01 N 12.01 E
Assergi 66 42.25 N 13.30 E
Asseria ⟂ 36 44.02 N 15.39 E
As-Sīb 128 23.41 N 58.11 E
As-Sidr 128 23.27 N 39.45 E
As-Sijn 132 32.47 N 36.28 E
As-Simākīyah 132 31.18 N 35.48 E
As-Sinbillāwayn 142 30.53 N 31.27 E
Assíni ⟂ 38 37.36 N 22.48 E
Assiniboia 184 49.38 N 105.59 W
Assiniboine ≃ 184 49.53 N 97.08 W
Assiniboine, Mount ∧ 182 50.52 N 115.39 W
Assiniboine Indian Reserve ⊷4 184 50.21 N 103.28 W
Assinika ≃ 184 52.37 N 96.10 W
Assinippi 283 42.09 N 70.51 W
Assis 255 22.40 S 50.25 W
Assis Chataaubriand 252 24.29 S 53.32 W
Assiscunk Creek ≃ 208 40.05 N 74.51 W
Assisi 66 43.04 N 12.37 E
Asslar 56 50.35 N 8.28 E
Assling 60 48.00 N 12.00 E
Asso 62 45.52 N 9.16 E
Assodé ⊤4 150 18.26 N 8.28 E
Assomada 150a 15.06 N 23.41 W
Assonet 207 41.47 N 71.04 W
Assoro 70 37.37 N 14.25 E
As-Subū' ⟂ 140 22.45 N 32.34 E
As-Sūdān → Sudan □1 140 15.00 N 30.00 E
As-Sudd ⊷1 140 8.00 N 31.00 E
As-Sufāl 144 14.06 N 48.42 E
Aṣ-Ṣufayyah 140 15.30 N 34.42 E
Aṣ-Ṣūfīyah 142 30.55 N 31.46 E
As-Sukhnah, Sūrīy. 130 34.52 N 38.52 E
As-Sukhnah, Urd. 132 32.08 N 36.04 E
As-Sulaymānīyah, Ar. Su. 128 24.09 N 47.19 E
As-Sulaymānīyah, 'Irāq 128 35.33 N 45.26 E
As-Sulaymānīyah □4 128 35.30 N 45.25 E
As-Sulaymī 128 26.17 N 41.21 E
As-Sulayyil 144 20.27 N 45.34 E
As-Sulṭān 146 31.07 N 17.10 E
As-Sumayḥ 140 9.49 N 27.39 E
Aṣ-Ṣummān ⊷1 128 25.00 N 47.00 E
As-Summāqīyāt 132 32.26 N 36.24 E
Assumption, Il., U.S. 219 39.31 N 89.02 W
Assumption, Oh., U.S. 216 41.40 N 83.54 W
Assumption Island I 138 9.45 S 46.30 E
Assunpink Creek ≃ 285 40.13 N 74.46 W
As-Su'ūdīyah 142 29.33 N 31.14 E
Aṣ-Ṣuwār 130 35.30 N 40.39 E
As-Suwaydā' 132 32.42 N 36.34 E
As-Suwaydā' □8 132 32.45 N 36.45 E
As-Suways (Suez) 142 29.58 N 32.33 E
As-Suways □4 142 30.12 N 32.30 E
Assynt, Loch ⊜ 46 58.11 N 5.06 W
Ašt 85 40.41 N 70.20 E
Asta, Cima d' ∧ 64 46.10 N 11.36 E
Astachovo 83 47.52 N 39.37 E
Astaffort 32 44.04 N 0.40 E
Astakós 38 38.32 N 21.05 E
Āstāneh, Īrān 128 37.17 N 49.59 E
Āstāneh, Īrān 128 33.53 N 49.22 E
Astara, Azer. 84 38.28 N 48.52 E
Āstārā, Īrān 128 38.26 N 48.52 E
Aštarak 84 40.18 N 44.22 E
Astaškovo 82 55.32 N 38.38 E
Astatula 220 28.43 N 81.44 W
Asten, Ned. 52 51.24 N 5.45 E
Asten, Öst. 61 48.13 N 14.25 E
Asti 62 44.54 N 8.12 E
Asti □4 62 44.55 N 8.10 E
Astica 252 30.56 S 67.23 W
Astico ≃ 64 45.37 N 11.37 E
Astillero 34 43.24 N 3.49 W
Astipálaia 38 36.30 N 26.30 E
Astipálaia I 38 36.35 N 26.25 E
Astley Bridge 262 53.36 N 2.26 W
Astley Green 262 53.29 N 2.27 W
Astley Hall ⟂ 262 53.39 N 2.38 W
Astola Island I 128 25.07 N 63.51 E
Astolfo Dutra 256 21.19 S 42.52 W
Aston, Eng., U.K. 262 53.18 N 2.40 W
Aston, Pa., U.S. 285 39.52 N 75.26 W
Aston Clinton 42 51.48 N 0.44 W
Aston-on-Trent 42 52.52 N 1.23 W
Astor 123 35.22 N 74.51 E
Astor ≃ 123 35.34 N 74.41 E
Astorga, Bra. 255 23.13 S 51.40 W
Astorga, Esp. 34 42.27 N 6.03 W
Astorga, Pil. 116 6.54 N 125.27 E
Astoria, Il., U.S. 219 40.13 N 90.21 W
Astoria, Or., U.S. 224 46.11 N 123.49 W
Astoria ⊷8 276 40.46 N 73.55 W
Astoria Bridge ⊷5 224 46.13 N 123.52 W
Astoria Column ⟂ 224 46.11 N 123.50 W
Åstorp 41 56.08 N 12.57 E
Astove Island I 138 10.06 S 47.45 E
Astra 254 45.44 S 67.30 W
Astrachan' 80 46.21 N 48.03 E
Astrachanka 86 51.33 N 69.47 E
Astrachan' Oblast' □4 80 47.00 N 47.30 E
Astrachanskij 80 46.12 N 47.16 E
Astrachanskij zapovednik ⊷4 80 46.00 N 48.32 E
Astrakhan → Astrachan' 80 46.21 N 48.03 E
Astrodome ♠ 222 29.41 N 95.25 W
Astrolabe, Cape > 175e 8.20 S 160.34 E
Astrolabe Bay c 164 5.20 S 145.50 E
Astrolabe Reefs ⊹2 175f 19.48 S 165.37 E
Astudillo 34 42.12 N 4.18 W
Astura, Torre ⟂ 66 41.24 N 12.46 E
Asturias 116 10.34 N 123.43 E
Asturias □4, Esp. 34 43.20 N 6.00 W
Asturias □4, Esp. 34 43.20 N 6.00 W
Astwood Bank 42 52.15 N 1.56 W
Asubulak 86 49.31 N 83.03 E
Asuisui, Cape > 175a 13.47 S 172.29 W
Asuka 96 34.28 N 135.50 E
Asuka ⊷3 9 71.32 S 24.08 E
Asuke 94 35.08 N 137.19 E
Asunción 252 25.16 S 57.40 W
Asunción, Bahía c 232 27.06 N 114.11 W
Asuncion Island I 108 19.40 N 145.24 E
Asunción Ixtaltepec 234 16.30 N 95.03 W
Asunción Mita 236 14.20 N 89.43 W
Asunción Nochixtlán 234 17.28 N 97.14 W
Åsunden ⊜, Sve. 26 57.58 N 15.50 E
Åsunden ⊜, Sve. 26 57.44 N 13.22 E
Asunga, Wādī V 146 13.21 N 22.17 E
Asuni 71 39.52 N 8.56 E
'Āṣūr, Tall ∧ 132 31.59 N 35.17 E
Asuwa 94 36.01 N 136.16 E
Asuwa ≃ 94 36.04 N 136.11 E
Aswad, Ar-Ra's al- > 144 21.22 N 39.08 E
Aswān 140 24.05 N 32.53 E
Aswān High Dam → 'Āli, As-Sadd al- ⊷6 140 23.58 N 32.52 E
Aswatthaberia 272b 22.26 N 88.32 E
Asy ≃ 85 43.31 N 78.20 E
Asyūṭ 142 27.11 N 31.11 E
Asyūṭ □4 142 27.20 N 30.50 E
Asyūṭī, Wādī al- V 142 27.11 N 31.16 E
Aszód 30 47.39 N 19.31 E
'Ata I, Tonga 14 22.20 S 176.12 W
Ata I, Tonga 174w 21.03 S 175.00 W
Atabaj 85 43.30 N 68.20 E
Atabapo ≃ 246 4.03 N 67.42 W
Atabasca, Lago → Athabasca, Lake ⊜ 176 59.07 N 110.00 W
Atabasca → Athabasca ≃ 176 58.40 N 110.50 W
Atabey 130 37.57 N 30.39 E
Atacama □4 252 27.30 S 70.00 W
Atacama, Desierto de ⊷2 18 24.30 S 69.15 W
Atacama, Puna de ⋏1 252 24.30 S 67.30 W
Atacama, Salar de ≚ 252 23.30 S 68.15 W
Ataco 246 3.35 N 75.23 W
Atacora, Chaîne de l' ⋏ 150 10.45 N 1.30 E
Atacuari ≃ 246 3.47 S 70.44 W
Atafu I1 14 8.33 S 172.30 W
Atagaj 88 55.06 N 99.23 E
Atago-yama ∧, Nihon 94 35.07 N 139.59 E
Atago-yama ∧, Nihon 96 35.03 N 135.37 E
Ātāi ≃1 126 22.51 N 89.33 E
'Aṭā'iṭah, Jabal al- ∧ 132 30.40 N 35.39 E
Atakakup Indian Reserve ⊷4 184 53.24 N 106.55 W
Atakano-seki ⟂ 94 36.24 N 136.25 E
Ataki 78 48.25 N 27.47 E
Atakora □5 150 10.00 N 1.35 E
Atakora, Réserve d' ⊷4 150 11.30 N 2.10 E
Atakpamé 150 7.32 N 1.08 E
Atalaia, Bra. 250 9.31 S 36.02 W
Atalaia, Port. 266c 38.42 N 8.55 W
Atalándi 38 38.39 N 23.00 E
Atalanka 88 54.50 N 103.05 E
Atalaya, Arg. 258 35.02 S 57.32 W
Atalaya, Pan. 236 8.03 N 80.56 W
Atalaya, Perú 248 10.44 S 73.45 W
Atalaya, Cerro ∧, Chile 254 52.45 S 72.42 W
Atalaya, Cerro ∧, Perú 248 12.38 S 71.56 W
Atalaya, Punta > 258 35.01 S 57.31 W
Atamanovka 88 51.56 N 113.37 E
Atamanovo 86 56.24 N 93.36 E
Atambua 112 9.07 S 124.54 E
Atami 94 35.05 N 139.04 E
Atapupu 112 9.00 S 124.51 E
'Atāq 144 14.33 N 46.48 E
'Atāqah, Jabal ⋏ 142 29.58 N 32.20 E
Atâr 150 20.31 N 13.03 W
Ataram, 'Erg n- ⊷2 148 23.46 N 1.44 E
Atarés, Castillo de ⟂ 286b 23.08 N 82.21 W
Atāri 123 31.36 N 74.35 E
Atary 80 57.32 N 49.18 E
Atascadero 226 35.29 N 120.40 W
Atascosa ≃ 196 28.26 N 98.12 W
At'aševo 80 54.36 N 46.06 E
Atasu 86 48.42 N 71.38 E
Atas uul ∧ 102 43.18 N 96.36 E
Atata I 174w 21.03 S 175.15 W
Atatürk Barajı ⊜1 130 37.30 N 38.30 E
Ataturk Tower ⟂ 267b 41.00 N 28.59 E
Ataur 272a 28.43 N 77.24 E
Atauro, Pulau I 112 8.13 S 125.35 E
Atbara ('Aṭbarah) ≃ 140 17.40 N 33.56 E
'Aṭbarah 140 17.42 N 33.59 E
'Aṭbarah (Atbara) ≃ 140 17.40 N 33.56 E
Atbasar 86 51.48 N 68.20 E
At-Baši 85 41.10 N 75.48 E
Atbaši ≃ 85 41.24 N 75.38 E
Atbaši, chrebet ⋏ 85 40.55 N 75.40 E
Atchafalaya ≃ 194 29.53 N 91.28 W
Atchafalaya Bay c 194 29.25 N 91.20 W
Atchison 198 39.33 N 95.07 W
Atco 208 39.46 N 74.53 W
Ate 286d 12.03 S 76.58 W
Atebubu 150 7.45 N 0.59 W
Ateca 34 41.20 N 1.47 W
Atelchu ≃ 255 12.05 S 53.46 W
Ateleta 66 41.51 N 14.12 E
Ateli 124 28.06 N 76.17 E
Atella 68 40.52 N 15.39 E
Atemajac de Brizuela 234 20.11 N 103.42 W
Atemar 80 54.11 N 45.24 E
Atemble 164 5.05 S 144.45 E
Atena Lucana 68 40.27 N 15.33 E
Atenango del Río 234 18.05 N 99.06 W
Atenas → Athínai 38 37.58 N 23.43 E
Atencingo 234 18.30 N 98.36 W
Atengo ≃ 234 21.50 N 104.43 W
Atenguillo 234 20.25 N 104.31 W
Atenguillo ≃ 234 20.55 N 104.38 W
Atenquique 234 19.31 N 103.30 W
Atepcevo 82 55.20 N 36.46 E
Aterau 80 47.07 N 51.56 E
Aterau □4 80 47.30 N 51.00 E
Aterno ≃ 66 42.11 N 13.51 E
Aterrado, Ribeirão do ≃ 256 22.09 S 45.03 W
Atessa 66 42.04 N 14.27 E
Aṭfīḥ 142 29.24 N 31.15 E
Aṭfīḥī, Wādī al- V 142 29.23 N 31.16 E
Ātgharia 126 24.06 N 89.14 E
Atglen 208 39.57 N 75.58 W
Ath 50 50.38 N 3.47 E
Athabasca 182 54.43 N 113.17 W
Athabasca ≃ 176 58.40 N 110.50 W
Athabasca, Lake ⊜ 176 59.07 N 110.00 W
Athalmer 182 50.32 N 116.02 W
Athapapuskow Lake ⊜ 184 54.33 N 101.40 W
Athārabānki ≃1 126 22.49 N 89.39 E
Athārān Hazāri 123 31.11 N 72.06 E
Athboy 48 53.37 N 6.55 W
Athea 48 52.28 N 9.17 W
Athena 202 45.48 N 118.29 W
Athen → Athínai 38 37.58 N 23.43 E
Athènes → Athínai 38 37.58 N 23.43 E
Athenry 48 53.18 N 8.45 W
Athens, On., Can. 212 44.38 N 75.57 W
Athens, Al., U.S. 194 34.48 N 86.58 W
Athens, Ga., U.S. 192 33.57 N 83.22 W
Athens, Il., U.S. 219 39.57 N 89.43 W
Athens, La., U.S. 194 32.39 N 93.01 W
Athens, Mi., U.S. 216 42.05 N 85.14 W
Athens, N.Y., U.S. 210 42.15 N 73.48 W
Athens, Oh., U.S. 188 39.19 N 82.06 W
Athens, Pa., U.S. 210 41.57 N 76.31 W

Symbols in the index entries represent the broad categories identified in the key at the right. Symbols with superior numbers (⋏1) identify subcategories (see complete key on page *I · 1)*.

Symbole im Register stellen die rechts im Schlüssel erklärten Kategorien dar. Symbole mit hochgestellten Ziffern (⋏1) bezeichnen Unterabteilungen einer Kategorie (vgl. vollständiger Schlüssel auf Seite *I · 1)*.

Los símbolos incluídos en el texto del índice representan las grandes categorias identificadas con la clave a la derecha. Los símbolos con numeros en su parte superior (⋏1) identifican las subcategorías (véase la clave completa en la página *I · 1)*.

Les symboles de l'index représentent les catégories indiquées dans la légende à droite. Les symboles suivis d'un indice (⋏1) représentent des sous-catégories (voir légende complète à la page *I · 1)*.

Os símbolos incluídos no texto do índice representam as grandes categorias identificadas com a chave à direita. Os símbolos com números em sua parte superior (⋏1) identificam as subcategorias (veja-se a chave completa à página *I · 1)*.

∧ Mountain	Berg	Montaña	Montagne	Montanha
⋏ Mountains	Gebirge	Montañas	Montagnes	Montanhas
)(Pass	Paß	Paso	Col	Passo
V Valley, Canyon	Tal, Cañon	Valle, Cañón	Vallée, Canyon	Vale, Canhão
≚ Plain	Ebene	Llano	Plaine	Planície
> Cape	Kap	Cabo	Cap	Cabo
I Island	Insel	Isla	Île	Ilha
II Islands	Inseln	Islas	Îles	Ilhas
⊥ Other Topographic Features	Andere Topographische Objekte	Otros Elementos Topográficos	Autres données topographiques	Outros acidentes topográficos

ESPAÑOL
Nombre | Página | Lat. °′ | Long. °′ W = Oeste

Athens, Tn., U.S. 192 35.26 N 84.35 W
Athens, Tx., U.S. 222 32.12 N 95.51 W
Athens, W.V., U.S. 192 37.25 N 81.00 W
Athens, Wi., U.S. 190 45.01 N 90.04 W
Athens
→ Athínai 38 37.58 N 23.43 E
Athenstedt 54 51.56 N 10.55 E
Athens University ⌂[2] 267c 37.59 N 23.44 E
Atherley 212 44.36 N 79.22 W
Atherstone 42 52.35 N 1.31 W
Atherton, Austl. 166 17.16 S 145.29 E
Atherton, Eng., U.K. 44 53.31 N 2.31 W
Atherton, Ca., U.S. 226 37.27 N 122.11 W
Athi ≃ 154 2.59 S 38.31 E
Athiaínou 130 35.04 N 33.32 E
Athiémé 150 6.35 N 1.40 E
Athies-sous-Laon 50 49.34 N 3.41 E
Athínai (Athens), Ellás 38 37.58 N 23.43 E
Athínai (Athens), Ellás 267c 37.58 N 23.43 E
Äthiopien
→ Ethiopia □[1] 144 9.00 N 39.00 E
Athi River 154 1.27 S 36.59 E
Athis-Mons 261 48.43 N 2.24 E
Athlat al-Bāshā ∧[2] 142 27.31 N 32.20 E
Athleague 48 53.34 N 8.15 W
Athlone 48 53.25 N 7.56 W
Athni 122 16.44 N 75.04 E
Athok 110 17.12 N 95.05 E
Athol, N.Z. 172 45.31 S 168.35 E
Athol, Ma., U.S. 207 42.35 N 72.13 W
Athol Bay ⊂ 212 43.53 N 77.15 W
Athol Island I 240b 25.05 N 77.16 W
Atholl, Forest of ⟡[3] 46 56.50 N 4.00 W
Athol Springs 210 42.46 N 78.52 W
Áthos ∧ 38 40.09 N 24.19 E
Ath-Tha'lah 132 32.42 N 36.26 E
Ath-Thamad 140 29.41 N 34.18 E
Ath-Thanīyah 132 31.10 N 35.43 E
Athus 56 49.34 N 5.50 E
Athy 48 53.00 N 7.00 W
Ati 146 13.13 N 18.20 E
Atiak 154 3.15 N 32.07 E
Atibaia 256 23.07 S 46.33 W
Atibainha ≃ 256 22.42 S 47.17 W
Atibainha,
Reservatório ⊜[1] 256 23.10 S 46.20 W
Atico 248 16.14 S 73.39 W
Aticonipi, Lac ⊜ 186 51.52 N 59.22 W
Atienza 34 41.12 N 2.52 W
Atigun Pass)(180 68.08 N 149.29 W
Atik Lake ⊜ 184 55.16 N 96.00 W
Atikokan 190 48.45 N 91.37 W
Atikonak Lake ⊜ 176 52.40 N 64.30 W
Atil 200 30.50 N 111.35 W
Atimari ≃ 248 9.04 S 67.23 W
Atimonan 116 14.00 N 121.55 E
Atina 66 41.37 N 13.48 E
Atiparaná ≃[1] 246 1.51 S 65.37 W
Atiquizaya 236 13.58 N 89.46 W
Atirāmpattinam 122 10.21 N 79.24 E
Atitlán, Lago de ⊜ 236 14.42 N 91.12 W
Atitlán, Volcán ∧[1] 236 14.35 N 91.11 W
Atiu I 14 20.02 S 158.07 W
Atka, Ross. 74 60.50 N 151.48 E
Atka, Ak., U.S. 180 52.12 N 174.12 W
Atka Island I 180 52.15 N 174.30 W
Atkaracalar 130 40.50 N 33.04 E
Atkarsk 80 51.52 N 45.00 E
Atkins 194 35.14 N 92.56 W
Atkinson, Il., U.S. 190 41.25 N 90.00 W
Atkinson, Ne., U.S. 198 42.31 N 98.58 W
Atkinson, N.H., U.S. 207 42.50 N 71.08 W
Atkinson, N.C., U.S. 192 34.31 N 78.10 W
Atkinson Island I 222 29.40 N 94.58 W
Atkinson Lake ⊜ 184 55.59 N 94.48 W
Atkri 164 1.44 S 130.04 E
Atlacomulco 234 19.48 N 99.53 W
Atlanta, Ga., U.S. 192 33.44 N 84.23 W
Atlanta, Il., U.S. 194 40.15 N 89.14 W
Atlanta, Mi., U.S. 190 45.00 N 84.08 W
Atlanta, Mo., U.S. 194 39.53 N 92.28 W
Atlanta, N.Y., U.S. 210 42.33 N 77.28 W
Atlanta, Oh., U.S. 218 39.34 N 83.11 W
Atlanta, Tx., U.S. 194 33.06 N 94.09 W
Atlantic, Ia., U.S. 198 41.24 N 95.00 W
Atlantic, N.C., U.S. 192 34.53 N 76.20 W
Atlantic, Pa., U.S. 214 41.30 N 80.21 W
Atlantic, Va., U.S. 208 37.54 N 75.30 W
Atlantic □[6] 208 39.27 N 74.44 W
Atlantic Beach, Fl., U.S. 192 30.20 N 81.23 W
Atlantic Beach, N.Y., U.S. 276 40.35 N 73.44 W
Atlantic City 208 39.21 N 74.25 W
Atlantic Highlands 208 40.24 N 74.02 W
Atlantic-Indian Basin ✤[1] 6 60.00 S 15.00 E
Atlantic-Indian Ridge ✤[3] 4 53.00 S 15.00 E
Atlántico □[5] 246 10.45 N 75.00 W
Atlántico, Océano
→ Atlantic Ocean ⫪[1] 8 5.00 S 25.00 W
Atlantic Ocean ⫪[1] 4 5.00 S 25.00 W
Atlantic Ocean ⫪[1] 8 5.00 S 25.00 W
Atlantic Peak ∧ 200 42.37 N 109.00 W
Atlántida 252 34.46 S 55.45 W
Atlántida □[5] 236 15.40 N 87.00 W
Atlantique 276 40.39 N 73.10 W
Atlantique □[5] 150 6.35 N 2.15 E
Atlantique, Océan
→ Atlantic Ocean ⫪[1] 8 5.00 S 25.00 W
Atlantischer Ozean
→ Atlantic Ocean ⫪[1] 8 5.00 S 25.00 W
Atlas, Mi., U.S. 216 42.56 N 83.32 W
Atlas, Pa., U.S. 208 40.48 N 76.26 W
Atlasburg 214 40.20 N 80.23 W
Atlas Mountains ⩚ 148 33.00 N 2.00 W
Atlasova, ostrov I 74 50.53 N 155.27 E
Atlasovo 92a 46.01 N 142.09 E
Atlas Saharien ⩚ 148 33.25 N 1.20 E
Atlas Tellien ⩚ 148 36.00 N 3.00 E
Atlin 180 59.35 N 133.42 W
Atlin Lake ⊜ 180 59.20 N 133.45 W
'Atlit 132 32.41 N 34.56 E
Atlixco 234 18.54 N 98.26 W
Ātmakūr 122 15.53 N 78.35 E
Atmanov Ugol 80 53.07 N 41.23 E
Atmis 80 53.28 N 43.57 E
Atmore 194 31.01 N 87.29 W
Åtna ≃ 26 61.44 N 10.49 E
Ätna
→ Etna, Monte ∧[1] 70 37.46 N 15.00 E
Atna Peak ∧ 182 53.57 N 128.03 W
Atnarko ≃ 182 52.22 N 126.04 W
Atnis 86 58.48 N 69.38 E
Atnosen 26 61.44 N 10.49 E
Atō 96 34.24 N 131.43 E
Atocha 248 20.56 S 66.14 W
Atocha, Estación de ⟡[5] 266a 40.24 N 3.41 W
Atocongo 286d 12.08 S 76.56 W
Atocongo ⊥ 286d 12.12 S 76.55 W
Atoka 196 34.23 N 96.07 W
Atotonilco 232 24.15 N 102.45 W
Atotonilco, Cerro ∧ 196 26.08 N 104.43 W
Atotonilco, Lago ⊜ 234 20.22 N 103.39 W
Atotonilco de Tula 234 20.00 N 99.13 W
Atotonilco El Alto 234 20.33 N 102.31 W
Atoui, Khaṭṭ ∨ 150 20.04 N 15.59 W
Atoyac 234 20.01 N 103.32 W
Atoyac ≃, Méx. 234 17.05 N 100.29 W
Atoyac ≃, Méx. 234 19.02 N 96.08 W
Atoyac ≃, Méx. 234 18.10 N 98.31 W
Atoyac ≃, Méx. 234 16.30 N 97.31 W
Atoyac de Álvarez 234 17.12 N 100.26 W
Atoyaquillo ≃ 234 16.37 N 97.41 W
Atpur 272b 22.50 N 88.23 E

FRANÇAIS
Nom | Page | Lat. °′ | Long. °′ W = Ouest

Atrå 26 59.59 N 8.45 E
'Aṭrah, Jabal ∧ 132 29.40 N 35.34 E
Atrai ≃ 124 24.29 N 89.03 E
Atrak (Atrek) ≃ 128 37.28 N 53.57 E
Ätran ≃ 26 56.53 N 12.30 E
Atrato ≃ 246 8.17 N 76.58 W
Atrauli 124 28.02 N 78.17 E
Atrek (Atrak) ≃ 128 37.28 N 53.57 E
Atri 66 42.35 N 13.58 E
Atripalda 68 40.55 N 14.50 E
Atrisco 200 34.59 N 106.41 W
Atrop ⟡[8] 263 51.24 N 6.43 E
Atsion Lake ⊜ 285 39.44 N 74.44 W
Atsugi 94 35.27 N 139.22 E
Atsugi-hikōjō ■ 94 35.28 N 139.27 E
Atsumi, Nihon 92 38.37 N 139.35 E
Atsumi, Nihon 94 34.37 N 137.07 E
Atsumi-hantō ≻[1] 94 34.39 N 137.15 E
Atta 272a 28.34 N 77.20 E
At-Tabbīn 142 29.47 N 31.18 E
Aṭ-Ṭafīlah 132 30.50 N 35.36 E
Aṭ-Ṭafīlah □[8] 132 30.45 N 35.45 E
At-Taḥrīr □[4] 142 30.40 N 30.15 E
Aṭ-Ṭā'if 144 21.16 N 40.24 E
Attainville 261 49.03 N 2.21 E
At-Tāj 146 24.13 N 23.18 E
Aṭ-Ṭalibīyah 273c 30.00 N 31.11 E
At-Tall 132 33.36 N 36.18 E
Attalla 194 34.01 N 86.05 W
At-Tall al-Kabīr 142 30.34 N 31.47 E
At-Ta'mīm □[4] 128 35.25 N 44.20 E
At-Tamīmī 146 32.20 N 23.04 E
Attapu 110 14.48 N 106.50 E
Attar, Oued el ∨ 148 33.27 N 5.26 E
At-Taṭālīyah 142 27.20 N 30.50 E
Attáviros ∧ 38 36.12 N 27.52 E
Attawapiskat 176 52.55 N 82.26 W
Attawapiskat ≃ 176 52.57 N 82.18 W
Attawapiskat Lake ⊜ 176 52.18 N 87.54 W
Attawaugan 207 41.52 N 71.52 W
Aṭ-Ṭawd 142 30.47 N 30.37 E
Aṭ-Ṭawīl ⩚ 128 29.20 N 39.35 E
At-Tayrīyah 142 30.39 N 30.46 E
Aṭ-Ṭaysīyah ≡ 128 28.00 N 44.00 E
Aṭ-Ṭayyibah, Miṣr 142 28.16 N 30.39 E
Aṭ-Ṭayyibah, Sūrīy. 132 32.33 N 36.14 E
Aṭ-Ṭayyibah, Sūrīy. 132 32.48 N 36.46 E
Aṭ-Ṭayyibah, Urd. 132 32.33 N 35.43 E
Attel ≃ 64 48.01 N 12.11 E
Attendorn 56 51.07 N 7.54 E
Attenhausen 58 47.59 N 10.20 E
Attenkirchen 60 48.30 N 11.46 E
Atterbury 219 40.04 N 89.55 W
Attersee 64 47.55 N 13.33 E
Attersee ⊜ 64 47.52 N 13.33 E
Attert ≃ 56 49.52 N 6.05 E
Attica, In., U.S. 216 40.17 N 87.14 W
Attica, Ks., U.S. 198 37.14 N 98.13 W
Attica, N.Y., U.S. 210 42.51 N 78.16 W
Attica, Oh., U.S. 214 41.03 N 82.53 W
Attichy 50 49.25 N 3.03 E
Attigliano 66 42.31 N 12.17 E
Attigny 56 49.29 N 4.35 E
Attikí □[5] 267c 38.00 N 23.40 E
Attikí □[9] 38 38.00 N 23.30 E
'Attīl 132 32.22 N 35.04 E
Attimis 64 46.11 N 13.16 E
Aṭ-Ṭīnah 142 31.03 N 32.18 E
Attingal 122 8.41 N 76.50 E
Attir 140 6.04 N 30.50 E
Attleboro 207 41.56 N 71.17 W
Attleborough 42 52.31 N 1.01 E
Attnang 60 48.01 N 13.43 E
Attock 123 33.54 N 72.15 E
Attoyac ≃ 194 31.29 N 94.18 W
Attu 181a 52.56 N 173.14 E
At-Tubah 144 12.40 N 43.30 E
Attu Island I 181a 52.55 N 173.00 E
Aṭ-Ṭunayb 132 31.48 N 35.57 E
Āttūr, India 122 11.36 N 78.37 E
Aṭ-Ṭūr, Miṣr 140 28.14 N 33.37 E
Aṭ-Ṭuwayshah 140 12.21 N 26.32 E
Aṭ-Ṭuwayyah 128 27.36 N 41.13 E
Attymon 48 53.19 N 8.35 W
Atucatiquini ≃ 248 7.44 S 67.57 W
Atucha 258 33.58 S 59.18 W
Atuel ≃ 252 36.17 S 66.50 W
Atuel, Bañados del ≡ 252 36.30 S 66.55 W
Atuntaqui 246 0.20 N 78.13 W
Atuona 174x 9.48 S 139.02 W
At'urjevo 80 54.21 N 43.19 E
Atushi 85 39.43 N 76.08 E
Åtvidaberg 26 58.12 N 16.00 E
Atwater, Sk., Can. 184 50.47 N 102.10 W
Atwater, Ca., U.S. 226 37.20 N 120.36 W
Atwater, Il., U.S. 219 39.20 N 89.44 W
Atwater, Mn., U.S. 198 45.08 N 94.46 W
Atwater, Oh., U.S. 214 41.01 N 81.10 W
Atwood, On., Can. 212 43.40 N 81.01 W
Atwood, Ca., U.S. 280 33.52 N 117.50 W
Atwood, Il., U.S. 194 39.48 N 88.28 W
Atwood, In., U.S. 216 41.15 N 85.58 W
Atwood, Ks., U.S. 198 39.48 N 101.02 W
Atwood, Tn., U.S. 194 35.58 N 88.40 W
Atwood Lake ⊜[1] 214 40.33 N 81.13 W
Atzalpur 272a 28.43 N 77.21 E
Atzendorf 54 51.55 N 11.35 E
Atzgersdorf ⟡[8] 264b 48.09 N 16.18 E
Au 58 47.19 N 9.59 E
Auagrām 126 23.31 N 87.41 E
Auaiá-Miçu ≃ 250 10.51 S 53.08 W
Aua Island I 164 1.27 S 143.04 E
Aual Edo 144 4.14 N 40.37 E
Auari ≃ 246 3.33 N 63.48 W
Auau Channel ⊍ 229a 20.51 N 156.45 W
Aub 56 49.33 N 10.04 E
Aubá 112 9.02 S 125.22 E
Aubagne 62 43.17 N 5.34 E
Aubange 56 49.35 N 5.48 E
Aube □[5] 50 48.15 N 4.05 E
Aube ≃ 50 48.34 N 3.43 E
Aubenas 62 44.37 N 4.23 E
Aubenton 50 49.50 N 4.12 E
Aubepierre 261 48.38 N 2.53 E
Aubergenville 261 48.58 N 1.51 E
Auberive 58 47.47 N 5.03 E
Auberry 226 37.04 N 119.29 W
Aubervilliers 50 48.55 N 2.23 E
Aubetin ≃ 50 48.49 N 3.01 E
Aubette ≃ 261 49.00 N 1.54 E
Aubigny-en-Artois 50 50.21 N 2.35 E
Aubigny-sur-Nère 50 47.29 N 2.26 E
Aubin 32 44.32 N 2.14 E
Aubinadong ≃ 190 46.51 N 83.22 W
Aubonne 58 46.28 N 6.24 E
Auboué 56 49.13 N 5.59 E
Aubrac ⩚ 32 44.40 N 3.00 E
Aubrey Cliffs ⌓[4] 200 35.45 N 113.00 W
Aubrey Lake ⊜[1] 190 46.54 N 83.11 W
Aubrives 56 50.06 N 4.46 E
Aubry Lake ⊜ 180 67.23 N 126.30 W
Auburn, Austl. 168b 34.01 S 138.41 E
Auburn, Austl. 274a 33.51 S 151.02 E
Auburn, Al., U.S. 194 32.36 N 85.28 W
Auburn, Ca., U.S. 226 38.53 N 121.04 W
Auburn, Il., U.S. 219 39.35 N 89.44 W
Auburn, In., U.S. 216 41.22 N 85.03 W
Auburn, Ky., U.S. 194 37.02 N 86.54 W
Auburn, Me., U.S. 188 44.05 N 70.13 W
Auburn, Ma., U.S. 207 42.11 N 71.50 W
Auburn, Mi., U.S. 190 43.36 N 84.04 W
Auburn, Ne., U.S. 198 40.23 N 95.50 W
Auburn, N.J., U.S. 285 39.42 N 75.22 W
Auburn, N.Y., U.S. 210 42.55 N 76.33 W
Auburn, Pa., U.S. 208 40.35 N 76.05 W
Auburn, Wa., U.S. 224 47.18 N 122.13 W
Auburn ≃ 166 25.38 S 151.12 E
Auburndale, Fl., U.S. 220 28.03 N 81.47 W
Auburndale, Ma., U.S. 283 42.21 N 71.22 W

PORTUGUÊS
Nome | Página | Lat. °′ | Long. °′ W = Oeste

Auburn Heights 216 42.38 N 83.13 W
Auburn Range ⩚ 166 25.10 S 150.30 E
Auburn Ravine ∨ 226 38.51 N 121.31 W
Auburn Southeast 210 42.54 N 76.32 W
Aubusson 32 45.57 N 2.11 E
Auby-sur-Semois 56 49.49 N 5.10 E
Auca Mahuida 252 37.53 S 68.31 W
Auca Mahuida, Cerro ∧ 252 37.45 S 68.56 W
Aucará 248 14.15 S 74.05 W
Auce 76 56.28 N 22.53 E
Auch 32 43.39 N 0.35 E
Auchel 50 50.30 N 2.28 E
Auchenblae 46 56.54 N 2.26 W
Auchencairn 44 54.51 N 3.53 W
Auchi 150 7.02 N 6.14 E
Auchinleck 44 55.28 N 4.17 W
Auchterarder 46 56.18 N 3.43 W
Auchterderran 46 56.09 N 3.16 W
Auchtermuchty 46 56.17 N 3.15 W
Aucilla ≃ 192 30.05 N 83.59 W
Auckland 172 36.52 S 174.46 E
Auckland Islands II 9 50.40 S 166.30 E
Auckland Park ⟡[8] 273d 26.11 S 28.00 E
Auckland Park Race Course ♠ 273d 26.11 S 28.00 E
Aude □[5] 32 43.05 N 2.30 E
Aude ≃ 32 43.13 N 3.14 E
Audenge 32 44.41 N 1.00 W
Audenshaw 262 53.28 N 2.08 W
Audenshaw Reservoirs ⊜[1] 262 53.28 N 2.08 W
Auderghem 50 50.49 N 4.26 E
Audeux 58 47.16 N 5.53 E
Audierne 32 48.01 N 4.32 W
Audincourt 58 47.29 N 6.50 E
Audley 44 53.03 N 2.18 W
Audo Range ⩚ 144 6.30 N 41.30 E
Audrain □[6] 219 39.12 N 91.50 W
Audresselles 50 50.49 N 1.36 E
Audruicq 50 50.53 N 2.05 E
Audubon, Ia., U.S. 198 41.43 N 94.55 W
Audubon, N.J., U.S. 208 39.53 N 75.04 W
Audubon, Pa., U.S. 285 40.07 N 75.27 W
Audubon Lake ⊜[1] 198 47.35 N 101.10 W
Audubon Park, Ky., U.S. 218 38.12 N 85.43 W
Audubon Park, N.J., U.S. 285 39.54 N 75.05 W
Audun-le-Roman 56 49.22 N 5.53 E
Aue 54 50.35 N 12.42 E
Aue ≃ 52 53.11 N 7.41 E
Auerbach, Dtsch. 54 50.41 N 12.54 E
Auerbach, Dtsch. 54 50.30 N 12.23 E
Auerbach, Dtsch. 60 48.48 N 13.06 E
Auerbach in der Oberpfalz 60 49.42 N 11.38 E
Auer
→ Ora 64 46.21 N 11.18 E
Auersberg ∧ 54 50.27 N 12.39 E
Auerswalde 54 50.54 N 12.55 E
Auezov 86 49.46 N 81.38 E
Auf dem Kreinberge 263 51.27 N 7.36 E
Auffargis 261 48.42 N 1.53 E
Auffay 50 49.43 N 1.06 E
Aufsess 60 49.54 N 11.13 E
Augarten ♠ 264b 48.14 N 16.23 E
Augathella 166 25.48 S 146.35 E
Augher 48 54.26 N 7.09 W
Aughnacloy 48 54.25 N 6.58 W
Aughrim 48 52.51 N 6.17 W
Aughton, Eng., U.K. 44 53.22 N 1.18 W
Aughton, Eng., U.K. 262 53.32 N 2.56 W
Aughton Park 262 53.33 N 2.53 W
Aughwick Creek ≃ 214 40.22 N 77.50 W
Auglaize □[6] 216 40.34 N 84.12 W
Auglaize ≃ 216 41.17 N 84.21 W
Augrabies 158 28.37 S 20.20 E
Augrabies Falls National Park ♠ 158 28.35 S 20.19 E
Augrabiesvalle ∟ 158 28.35 S 20.19 E
Au Gres 190 44.02 N 83.41 W
Au Gres ≃ 190 44.02 N 83.40 W
Au Gres, East Branch ≃ 190 44.05 N 83.41 W
Augsburg 58 48.23 N 10.53 E
Augšlīgatne 76 57.14 N 25.02 E
Augusta, Austl. 162 34.19 S 115.10 E
Augusta, It. 70 37.13 N 15.13 E
Augusta, Ar., U.S. 194 35.16 N 91.21 W
Augusta, Ga., U.S. 192 33.28 N 82.01 W
Augusta, Il., U.S. 194 40.13 N 90.57 W
Augusta, Ks., U.S. 198 37.41 N 97.58 W
Augusta, Ky., U.S. 218 38.46 N 84.00 W
Augusta, Me., U.S. 188 44.18 N 69.46 W
Augusta, Mi., U.S. 216 42.20 N 85.21 W
Augusta, Mo., U.S. 219 38.34 N 90.53 W
Augusta, Mt., U.S. 202 47.29 N 112.23 W
Augusta, N.J., U.S. 210 41.07 N 74.43 W
Augusta, Oh., U.S. 214 40.41 N 81.01 W
Augusta, Wi., U.S. 190 44.40 N 91.07 W
Augusta, Golfo di ⊂ 70 37.12 N 15.13 E
Augustdorf 52 51.53 N 8.43 E
Augustenborg 41 54.57 N 9.53 E
Augustine Island I 180 59.22 N 153.28 W
Augusto Severo 250 5.52 S 37.19 W
Augustów 30 53.51 N 22.59 E
Augustowski, Kanał ≚ 76 53.54 N 23.26 E
Augustus, Mount ∧ 162 24.20 S 116.50 E
Augustusburg 54 50.49 N 13.06 E
Augustus Downs 166 18.33 S 139.52 E
Augustus Island I 164 15.20 S 124.30 E
Auila, Ribeirão ≃ 255 12.09 S 53.20 W
Au in der Hallertau 60 48.33 N 11.45 E
Aujon ≃ 58 48.09 N 4.48 E
Auki 175e 8.46 S 160.42 E
Aulander 192 36.13 N 77.06 W
Aulanko 26 61.02 N 24.27 E
Auld, Lake ⊜ 162 22.32 S 123.44 E
Auldearn 46 57.34 N 3.49 W
Aulendorf 58 47.57 N 9.38 E
Aulestad 26 61.13 N 10.17 E
Auletta 68 40.34 N 15.25 E
Aulla 64 44.12 N 9.58 E
Aulnay 32 46.01 N 0.21 W
Aulnay-sous-Bois 50 48.57 N 2.31 E
Aulnay-sur-Mauldre 261 48.56 N 1.51 E
Aulne ≃ 32 48.17 N 4.16 W
Aulneau Peninsula ≻[1] 184 49.23 N 94.29 W
Aulnois-sur-Seille 56 48.52 N 6.19 E
Aulnoye-Aymeries 50 50.12 N 3.50 E
Ault, Fr. 50 50.06 N 1.27 E
Ault, Co., U.S. 200 40.34 N 104.43 W
Ault, Ky., U.S. 218 38.12 N 83.14 W
Aultbea 46 57.50 N 5.35 W
Aultman 214 40.34 N 79.16 W
Aultshire 216 40.13 N 85.19 W
Auma 54 50.42 N 11.54 E
Aumale 50 49.46 N 1.45 E
Auma Point ≻ 164 7.55 S 145.25 E
Aumetz 56 49.25 N 5.56 E
Aumont-Aubrac 32 44.43 N 3.17 E
Aumühle 52 53.31 N 10.19 E
Auna 150 10.12 N 4.45 E
Auneau 50 48.27 N 1.46 E
Auneuil 50 49.22 N 2.00 E
Auning 26 56.26 N 10.23 E
Auno 146 11.50 N 12.53 E
Aunuu I 174u 14.17 S 170.33 W
Auob ≃ 156 26.25 S 20.35 E
Auponhia 112 1.56 S 125.29 E
Aups 62 43.37 N 6.14 E
Aur, Pulau I 112 2.27 N 104.31 E
Aura 26 60.36 N 22.34 E
Aurach 56 49.15 N 10.25 E
Aurach ≃ 56 49.34 N 10.59 E
Aurachmat 85 41.34 N 70.07 E
Auraiya 124 26.28 N 79.31 E
Aurangābād, India 122 19.53 N 75.20 E

Aurangābād, India 124 24.45 N 84.22 E
Auray 32 47.40 N 2.59 W
Aurdal 26 60.56 N 9.24 E
Aure 26 63.16 N 8.32 E
Aurelia 198 42.42 N 95.26 W
Aurelius 216 42.31 N 84.31 W
Aurès, Massif de l' ⩚ 148 35.08 N 6.30 E
Auri, Kepulauan II 164 1.59 S 134.42 E
Aurich 52 53.28 N 7.29 E
Auriesville Shrine ⌂[1] 210 42.54 N 74.19 W
Auriflama 255 20.41 S 50.34 W
Aurigny
→ Alderney I 43b 49.43 N 2.12 W
Aurilândia 255 16.44 S 50.28 W
Aurillac 32 44.56 N 2.26 E
Aurina, Valle ∨ 64 47.00 N 12.00 E
Aurine, Alpi (Zillertaler Alpen) ⩚ 64 47.00 N 11.55 E
Aurino ≃ 64 46.48 N 11.55 E
Auriol 62 43.23 N 5.38 E
Aurisina 64 45.45 N 13.41 E
Aurlandsfjorden ⊂[2] 26 61.05 N 7.02 E
Aurlandsvangen 26 60.54 N 7.11 E
Aurolzmünster 60 48.15 N 13.27 E
Auron 62 44.14 N 6.56 E
Auronzo di Cadore 64 46.33 N 12.26 E
Aurora, Bra. 250 6.57 S 38.58 W
Aurora, Bra. 287a 22.46 S 43.24 W
Aurora, On., Can. 212 44.00 N 79.28 W
Aurora, S. Afr. 158 32.42 S 18.29 E
Aurora, Co., U.S. 200 39.43 N 104.49 W
Aurora, Il., U.S. 216 41.45 N 88.19 W
Aurora, In., U.S. 218 39.03 N 84.54 W
Aurora, Me., U.S. 188 44.51 N 68.19 W
Aurora, Mn., U.S. 190 47.31 N 92.14 W
Aurora, Mo., U.S. 194 36.58 N 93.43 W
Aurora, Ne., U.S. 198 40.52 N 98.00 W
Aurora, N.Y., U.S. 210 42.45 N 76.42 W
Aurora, N.C., U.S. 192 35.18 N 76.47 W
Aurora, Oh., U.S. 214 41.19 N 81.20 W
Aurora, Or., U.S. 224 45.13 N 122.45 W
Aurora, Ut,. U.S. 200 38.55 N 111.56 W
Aurora, W.V., U.S. 188 39.19 N 79.33 W
Aurora □[4] 116 16.00 N 121.40 E
Aurora ⌂ 265a 59.57 N 30.21 E
Aurora do Norte 255 12.43 S 46.24 W
Aurora Pond ⊜ 279a 41.20 N 81.23 W
Auroux 62 44.45 N 3.44 E
Aursunden ⊜ 26 62.40 N 11.40 E
Aurukun 164 13.19 S 141.45 E
Aurukun Aboriginal Land Trust ⟡[4] 164 13.45 S 141.45 E
Aurunci, Monti ⩚ 66 41.22 N 13.40 E
Aus 156 26.40 S 16.15 E
Ausable ≃, On., Can. 190 43.19 N 81.46 W
Au Sable ≃, Mi., U.S. 190 44.25 N 83.20 W
Au Sable, North Branch ≃ 190 44.40 N 84.23 W
Au Sable, South Branch ≃ 190 44.40 N 84.23 W
Au Sable Forks 188 44.26 N 73.40 W
Au Sable Point ≻ 190 44.20 N 83.20 W
Auschwitz
→ Oświęcim 30 50.03 N 19.12 E
Ausevik ⊥ 26 61.32 N 5.16 E
Auskerry I 46 59.02 N 2.34 W
Ausoni, Monti ⩚ 66 41.25 N 13.20 E
Ausserferrera 58 46.33 N 9.26 E
Ausserfragant 64 46.56 N 13.06 E
Aussig
→ Ústí nad Labem 54 50.40 N 14.02 E
Aussois 62 45.14 N 6.45 E
Aust-Agder □[6] 26 58.50 N 8.00 E
Austerlitz, Ned. 52 52.05 N 5.19 E
Austerlitz, N.Y., U.S. 210 42.19 N 73.28 W
Austerlitz, Gare ⟡[5] 261 48.50 N 2.22 E
Austerlitz
→ Slavkov u Brna 61 49.09 N 16.52 E
Austin, Bra. 287a 22.43 S 43.32 W
Austin, Mb., Can. 184 49.57 N 98.56 W
Austin, In., U.S. 218 38.45 N 85.48 W
Austin, Mn., U.S. 190 43.40 N 92.58 W
Austin, Nv., U.S. 204 39.29 N 117.04 W
Austin, Pa., U.S. 214 41.37 N 78.05 W
Austin, Tx., U.S. 222 30.16 N 97.44 W
Austin □[6] 222 29.53 N 96.15 W
Austin ⟡[8] 278 41.54 N 87.45 W
Austin, Lake ⊜ 162 27.40 S 118.00 E
Austin, Lake ⊜[1] 222 30.19 N 97.46 W
Austin Bayou ≃ 222 29.07 N 95.18 W
Austinburg 214 41.46 N 80.51 W
Austin Channel ⊍ 176 75.35 N 103.25 W
Austin Lake ⊜ 216 42.11 N 85.33 W
Austinmer 170 34.18 S 150.56 E
Austin's Post 158 29.32 S 25.49 E
Austintown 214 41.06 N 80.45 W
Austinville 192 36.51 N 80.54 W
Austnes 26 62.38 N 6.16 E
Austonio 222 31.11 N 95.38 W
Austonley 262 53.34 N 1.50 W
Austral 274a 33.56 S 150.48 E
Australes, Îles II 14 23.00 S 150.00 W
Australia □[1] 160 25.00 S 135.00 E
Australia Mountain ∧ 180 63.36 N 138.08 W
Australian Capital Territory □[8] 171b 35.30 S 149.00 E
Australian War Memorial ⊥ 171b 35.17 S 149.09 E
Australia Plains 168b 34.06 S 139.09 E
Australie
→ Australia □[1] 160 25.00 S 135.00 E
Australien
→ Australia □[1] 160 25.00 S 135.00 E
Australind 168a 33.16 S 115.44 E
Austral Seamounts ✤[3] 14 22.40 S 152.45 W
Austråt 26 63.43 N 9.45 E
Austria (Österreich) □[1], Europe 22 47.20 N 13.20 E
Austria (Österreich) □[1], Europe 30 47.20 N 13.20 E
Austvågøya I 24 68.20 N 14.36 E
Autazes 246 3.35 S 59.08 W
Auteuil, Fr. 50 49.21 N 2.05 E
Auteuil, Fr. 261 48.50 N 1.49 E
Autheuil 50 49.06 N 1.17 E
Authie ≃ 50 50.21 N 1.38 E
Authon 62 44.14 N 6.08 E
Authon-du-Perche 50 48.12 N 0.55 E
Authon-la-Plaine 50 48.27 N 1.57 E
Auth Village 284c 38.49 N 76.55 W
Autlán de Navarro 234 19.46 N 104.22 W
Autore, Monte ∧ 66 41.58 N 13.12 E
Autrey-lès-Gray 58 47.29 N 5.30 E
Autriche
→ Austria □[1] 30 47.20 N 13.20 E
Autumn Hill 284b 39.16 N 76.48 W
Autun 32 46.57 N 4.18 E
Auve 56 49.02 N 4.42 E
Auvergne 164 15.41 S 130.01 E
Auvergne □[9] 32 45.25 N 2.30 E
Auvernaux 261 48.32 N 2.30 E
Auvers-sur-Oise 50 49.04 N 2.10 E
Auvézère ≃ 32 45.12 N 0.51 E
Aux Cayes
→ Les Cayes 238 18.12 N 73.45 W
Auxerre 50 47.48 N 3.34 E
Auxier 192 37.44 N 82.45 W
Auxi-le-Château 50 50.14 N 2.07 E
Auxon 50 48.06 N 3.55 E
Auxonne 58 47.12 N 5.23 E
Aux Sable Creek ≃ 216 41.23 N 88.20 W
Auxvasse 219 39.01 N 91.53 W
Auxvasse Creek ≃ 219 38.41 N 91.49 W
Auxy 58 46.57 N 4.24 E
Auyamita, Quebrada ≃ 286c 10.30 N 66.46 W
Auyán Tepuy ∧ 246 5.55 N 62.32 W
Auzances 32 46.02 N 2.30 E
Auzangate, Nevado ∧ 248 13.48 S 71.14 W

Auzon ≃, Fr. 58 48.30 N 4.20 E
Auzon ≃, Fr. 62 44.02 N 4.54 E
Ava, Il., U.S. 194 37.53 N 89.29 W
Ava, Mo., U.S. 194 36.57 N 92.39 W
Avadchara 84 43.31 N 40.39 E
Avadh Plains ≡ 124 26.20 N 82.00 E
Avaí 255 22.08 S 49.22 W
Āvaj 128 35.34 N 49.13 E
Avakubi 154 1.20 N 27.34 E
Aval' 85 40.19 N 71.50 E
Aval, Falaise d' ⌓[4] 50 49.45 N 0.10 E
Avala ⊥ 38 44.45 N 20.35 E
Avaldsnes 26 59.21 N 5.16 E
Avallon 50 47.29 N 3.54 E
Avaloirs, Les ∧[2] 32 48.28 N 0.07 W
Avalon, Ca., U.S. 228 33.20 N 118.19 W
Avalon, N.J., U.S. 208 39.06 N 74.43 W
Avalon, Pa., U.S. 214 40.30 N 80.04 W
Avalon, Tx., U.S. 222 32.12 N 96.48 W
Avalon, Wi., U.S. 216 42.38 N 88.52 W
Avalon Peninsula ≻[1] 186 47.30 N 53.30 W
Ávalos 232 28.35 N 106.00 W
Avana ≃ 174k 21.14 S 159.43 W
Avanos 130 38.43 N 34.51 E
Avant 196 36.29 N 96.03 W
Avaré 255 23.05 S 48.55 W
Avarskoje Kojsu ≃ 84 42.47 N 46.48 E
Avarua 174k 21.12 S 159.46 W
Avarua Harbour ⊂ 174k 21.11 S 159.46 W
Avatanak Island I 180 54.03 N 165.19 W
Avatele 174v 19.06 S 169.55 W
Avatele Bay ⊂ 174v 19.05 S 169.56 W
Avatiu 174k 21.12 S 159.47 W
Avatiu Harbour ⊂ 174k 21.11 S 159.47 W
Avčala 84 41.48 N 44.48 E
Avdejevka 83 48.08 N 37.46 E
Avdotjino 83 47.55 N 37.51 E
Ave ≃ 34 41.20 N 8.45 W
Avebury 42 51.27 N 1.51 W
Avebury Stone Circle ⊥ 42 51.28 N 1.51 W
'Avedat, Ḥorvot ⊥ 132 30.48 N 34.46 E
Avegbadje ∧ 150 7.14 N 0.38 E
Aveiro, Bra. 250 3.15 S 55.10 W
Aveiro, Port. 34 40.38 N 8.39 W
Aveiro, Ria de ≃[1] 34 40.38 N 8.44 W
Avelar 256 22.20 S 43.25 W
Avelengo 64 46.38 N 11.13 E
Aveley 260 51.30 N 0.16 E
Avelgem 50 50.46 N 3.26 E
Avella, It. 68 40.58 N 14.36 E
Avella, Pa., U.S. 214 40.16 N 80.27 W
Avellaneda, Arg. 252 29.07 S 59.40 W
Avellaneda, Arg. 258 34.39 S 58.23 W
Avellaneda □[5] 288 34.40 S 58.20 W
Avellaneda, Estacion ⟡[5] 288 34.41 S 58.22 W
Avelle, Île I 275a 45.24 N 74.00 W
Avellino 68 40.54 N 14.47 E
Avellino □[4], It. 68 41.00 N 15.10 E
Avellino □[4], It. 68 40.57 N 15.00 E
Avenal 226 36.00 N 120.07 W
Avenal Creek ≃ 226 35.47 N 120.04 W
Aven Armand ⌓[5] 32 44.15 N 3.22 E
Avenas 58 46.12 N 4.37 E
Avenches 58 46.53 N 7.02 E
Avenel 276 40.34 N 74.17 W
Aventureiro, Rio do ≃ 256 21.52 S 42.39 W
Avenue 208 38.15 N 76.46 W
Avenwedde 52 51.55 N 8.27 E
Averbode 56 51.02 N 4.59 E
Averbode, Abbaye d' ⌂[1] 56 51.02 N 4.59 E
Averill Lake ⊜ 206 44.59 N 71.44 W
Averill Park 210 42.38 N 73.33 W
Avern ⊜ 40 58.54 N 15.32 E
Avernakø I 41 55.01 N 10.17 E
Avernes 261 49.05 N 1.52 E
Avernes, Ru des ≃ 261 49.04 N 2.51 E
Averøya I 26 63.01 N 7.34 E
Aversa 68 40.58 N 14.12 E
Avery, Ca., U.S. 226 38.13 N 120.22 W
Avery, Id., U.S. 202 47.15 N 115.48 W
Avery, Tx., U.S. 194 33.33 N 94.47 W
Avery Island 194 29.54 N 91.54 W
Avesnelles 50 50.07 N 3.57 E
Avesnes 32 50.07 N 3.56 E
Avesnes-le-Comte 50 50.17 N 2.32 E
Avesnes-lès-Aubert 50 50.12 N 3.23 E
Avesnes-sur-Helpe 50 50.07 N 3.56 E
Avesta 40 60.09 N 16.12 E
Aveto ≃ 62 44.42 N 9.23 E
Avetrana 68 40.21 N 17.43 E
Aveyron □[5] 32 44.15 N 2.40 E
Aveyron ≃ 32 44.05 N 1.16 E
Avezzano 66 42.02 N 13.25 E
Avgustovka 80 52.16 N 50.44 E
Aviano 64 46.04 N 12.36 E
Avich, Loch ⊜ 46 56.16 N 5.20 W
Aviemore 46 57.12 N 3.50 W
Avigliana 62 45.05 N 7.23 E
Avigliano 68 40.44 N 15.44 E
Avignon 62 43.57 N 4.49 E
Ávila 34 40.39 N 4.42 W
Ávila □[4] 34 40.35 N 5.00 W
Ávila, Sierra de ⩚ 34 40.35 N 5.08 W
Avila Beach 226 35.10 N 120.43 W
Avilés 34 43.33 N 5.55 W
Avilla 216 41.22 N 85.14 W
Avilley 58 47.26 N 6.16 E
Avinger 222 32.54 N 94.33 W
Avinurme 76 58.59 N 26.51 E
Avio 64 45.44 N 10.56 E
Avion 50 50.24 N 2.50 E
Avioth 56 49.34 N 5.24 E
Avis 210 41.11 N 77.18 W
Avisio ≃ 64 46.07 N 11.05 E
Avispa, Cerro ∧ 246 1.16 N 65.51 W
Aviston 219 38.36 N 89.36 W
Aviz 34 39.03 N 7.53 W
Avize 50 48.58 N 4.01 E
Avlan Gölü ⊜ 130 36.34 N 29.57 E
Avlum 41 56.16 N 8.48 E
Avnbøl 41 54.58 N 9.39 E
Avnik 130 38.39 N 40.20 E
Avoca, Austl. 169 37.05 S 143.28 E
Avoca, Ia., U.S. 198 41.28 N 95.20 W
Avoca, N.Y., U.S. 210 42.24 N 77.25 W
Avoca, Pa., U.S. 210 41.20 N 75.44 W
Avoca ≃, Austl. 166 35.42 S 143.44 E
Avoca ≃, Ire. 48 52.48 N 6.09 W
Avoca, Mount ∧ 169 37.07 S 143.21 E
Avoca Beach 170 33.29 S 151.29 E
Avocado Heights 280 34.08 N 117.54 W
Avola, B.C., Can. 182 51.47 N 119.19 W
Avola, It. 70 36.54 N 15.08 E
Avon, Austl. 168b 34.17 S 138.20 E
Avon, Fr. 50 48.24 N 2.43 E
Avon, Ct., U.S. 207 41.48 N 72.49 W
Avon, Il., U.S. 190 40.39 N 90.26 W
Avon, Ma., U.S. 207 42.07 N 71.02 W
Avon, Mn., U.S. 190 45.36 N 94.27 W
Avon, Mt., U.S. 202 46.35 N 112.36 W
Avon, N.Y., U.S. 210 42.54 N 77.44 W
Avon, N.C., U.S. 192 35.21 N 75.30 W
Avon, Oh., U.S. 214 41.27 N 82.02 W
Avon, Pa., U.S. 208 40.22 N 76.23 W
Avon, S.D., U.S. 198 43.00 N 98.03 W
Avon □[6] 42 51.30 N 2.40 W
Avon ≃, Austl. 168a 31.40 S 116.07 E
Avon ≃, N.S., Can. 186 45.10 N 64.15 W
Avon ≃, On., Can. 212 43.18 N 81.11 W
Avon ≃, Eng., U.K. 42 50.43 N 1.46 W
Avon ≃, Eng., U.K. 42 52.25 N 1.31 W
Avon ≃, Eng., U.K. 42 51.59 N 2.10 W
Avon ≃, Eng., U.K. 42 51.30 N 2.43 W
Avon ≃, Eng., U.K. 42 50.17 N 3.52 W
Avon ≃, Scot., U.K. 46 56.01 N 3.40 W
Avon ≃, Scot., U.K. 46 57.25 N 3.23 W

Avon, Ben ∧ 46 57.05 N 3.27 W
Avon, Ru d' ≃ 261 48.39 N 2.46 E
Avon Basin ⊂ 279a 41.30 N 82.03 W
Avon by the Sea 208 40.11 N 74.00 W
Avondale, Az., U.S. 200 33.26 N 112.20 W
Avondale, Co., U.S. 198 38.14 N 104.21 W
Avondale, Md., U.S. 284c 38.56 N 76.59 W
Avondale, Oh., U.S. 214 39.47 N 84.08 W
Avondale Heights 274b 37.46 S 144.51 E
Avon Downs 166 20.05 S 137.30 E
Avondrust 158 34.21 S 21.51 E
Avon Lake 214 41.30 N 82.01 W
Avonlea 184 50.00 N 105.04 W
Avonmore, On., Can. 206 45.10 N 74.58 W
Avonmore, Pa., U.S. 214 40.31 N 79.27 W
Avonmore ≃ 48 52.50 N 6.13 W
Avonmouth 42 51.31 N 2.42 W
Avon Park 220 27.35 N 81.30 W
Avon Reservoir ⊜[1] 170 34.24 S 150.40 E
Avontuur 158 33.44 S 23.11 E
Avon Valley National Park ♠ 168a 31.41 S 116.06 E
Avon Water ≃ 46 55.47 N 4.01 W
Avoudrey 58 47.08 N 6.26 E
Avrainville 261 48.34 N 2.15 E
Avranches 32 48.41 N 1.22 W
Avranlo 84 41.39 N 43.52 E
Avre ≃, Fr. 50 49.53 N 2.20 E
Avre ≃, Fr. 50 48.47 N 1.22 E
Avrieux 62 45.13 N 6.43 E
Avroult 50 50.38 N 2.09 E
Avtatkuul' ≃ 180 64.06 N 178.10 E
Avtovo ⟡[8] 265a 59.52 N 30.15 E
Avu Avu 175e 9.50 S 160.23 E
Awa, Nihon 96 34.04 N 134.12 E
Awa, Nihon 174m 26.36 N 127.56 E
Awaba 170 33.01 S 151.33 E
A'waj, Nahr al- ≃ 132 33.20 N 36.34 E
Awaji 96 34.35 N 135.01 E
Awaji-shima I 96 34.21 N 134.51 E
Awakino 172 38.39 S 174.38 E
'Awālī 128 26.05 N 50.33 E
Awang 115b 8.54 S 116.24 E
Awano 94 36.31 N 139.41 E
Awanui 172 35.03 S 173.15 E
Awar 164 4.09 S 144.51 E
Awara 94 36.13 N 136.12 E
Awarawar, Tanjung ≻ 115a 6.45 S 111.56 E
Aware 144 8.15 N 44.10 E
Awarua Point ≻ 172 44.15 S 168.03 E
Awasa 144 6.45 N 38.15 E
Awasa, Lake ⊜ 144 7.05 N 38.25 E
Awasan Bay ⊂ 116 9.56 N 125.36 E
Awash 144 8.59 N 40.10 E
Awash ≃ 144 11.45 N 41.05 E
Awa-shima I, Nihon 92 38.27 N 139.14 E
Awa-shima I, Nihon 96 34.16 N 133.38 E
Awash National Park ♠ 144 9.05 N 40.00 E
Awaso 150 6.14 N 2.16 W
Awatere ≃ 172 41.37 S 174.10 E
Awbārī 146 26.35 N 12.46 E
Awbārī, Ṣaḥrā' ⌓[8] 146 28.00 N 11.30 E
Awdheegle 144 1.59 N 44.50 E
Awe 150 8.09 N 9.07 E
Awe, Loch ⊜ 46 56.15 N 5.17 W
Awegyun 110 12.44 N 98.44 E
Awgu 150 6.04 N 7.29 E
Awīsh al-Ḥajar 142 31.01 N 31.19 E
'Awjā', Wādī al- ∨ 132 31.56 N 35.31 E
Awjilah 146 29.09 N 21.15 E
Awka 150 6.12 N 7.05 E
Awlād Mūsā 142 30.48 N 31.44 E
Awled Djellal 148 34.28 N 5.02 E
Awlef 148 26.58 N 1.05 E
Aworo Kit 140 10.59 N 32.38 E
Aworro 164 7.45 S 143.10 E
Awosting 276 41.09 N 74.20 W
Awsīm 273c 30.07 N 31.08 E
Awul 164 6.00 S 151.00 E
Awuna ≃ 180 69.04 N 155.30 W
Awwal, Ash-Shallāl al- (First Cataract) ∟ 140 24.01 N 32.52 E
Awwalī, Nahr al- ≃ 132 33.35 N 35.23 E
Axamilpa ≃ 234 18.35 N 98.11 W
Axams 64 47.14 N 11.18 E
Axat 32 42.48 N 2.14 E
Axbridge 42 51.18 N 2.49 W
Axe ≃, Eng., U.K. 42 51.19 N 2.59 W
Axe ≃, Eng., U.K. 42 50.42 N 3.03 W
Axe Creek ≃ 169 36.46 S 144.30 E
Axedale 169 36.47 S 144.30 E
Axe Edge ⩚[2] 262 53.14 N 1.57 W
Axel 52 51.16 N 3.55 E
Axel Heiberg Island I 16 79.45 N 91.00 W
Axim 150 4.52 N 2.14 W
Axinim 246 4.02 S 59.22 W
Axiós (Vardar) ≃ 38 40.35 N 22.50 E
Axis 194 30.55 N 88.01 W
Axixá 250 2.51 S 44.04 W
Ax-les-Thermes 32 42.43 N 1.50 E
Axminster 42 50.47 N 3.00 W
Axmouth 42 50.42 N 3.02 W
Axochiapan 234 18.30 N 98.46 W
Axtell, Ks., U.S. 198 39.52 N 96.15 W
Axtell, Ne., U.S. 198 40.28 N 99.07 W
Axtell, Tx., U.S. 222 31.39 N 96.58 W
Aÿ 50 49.03 N 4.00 E
Ayabaca 246 4.38 S 79.43 W
Ayabe 96 35.18 N 135.15 E
Ayachi, Ari n' ∧ 148 32.29 N 4.57 W
Ayacucho, Arg. 252 37.09 S 58.29 W
Ayacucho, Bol. 248 17.51 S 63.20 W
Ayacucho, Perú 248 13.07 S 74.13 W
Ayacucho □[5] 248 14.00 S 74.00 W
Ayakkum Hu ⊜ 120 37.30 N 89.20 E
Ayamé 150 5.37 N 3.11 W
Ayamiken 152 2.07 N 10.01 E
Ayamonte 34 37.13 N 7.24 W
Āyān 272b 22.43 N 88.09 E
Ayancık 130 41.57 N 34.36 E
Ayangba 150 7.30 N 7.08 E
Ayapel 246 8.19 N 75.09 W
Ayarza, Laguna de ⊜ 236 14.25 N 90.08 W
Ayas, It. 62 45.50 N 7.41 E
Ayaş, Tür. 130 40.01 N 32.21 E
Ayase 94 35.26 N 139.26 E
Ayase ≃ 268 35.45 N 139.49 E
Ayauta 96 34.13 N 133.53 E
Ayaviri 248 14.52 S 70.35 W
Ayaviri ≃ 248 15.01 S 70.22 W
'Aybāl, Jabal ∧ 132 32.14 N 35.16 E
Aybastı, Tür. 130 40.41 N 37.24 E
Aybastı, Tür. 130 39.42 N 39.02 E
Ayden 192 35.28 N 77.24 W
Aydere 128 38.24 N 56.45 E
Aydın 130 37.51 N 27.51 E
Aydın □[4] 130 37.45 N 28.00 E
Aydıncık, Tür. 130 36.08 N 33.19 E
Aydıncık, Tür. 130 40.08 N 35.18 E
Aydın Dağları ⩚ 130 38.00 N 28.00 E
Aydınkent 130 37.06 N 31.36 E
Aydıntepe 130 40.24 N 40.09 E
Aydin Ula ∧ 86 42.55 N 87.35 E
Aydosdağı ∧ 267b 40.56 N 29.15 E
Ayelu ∧ 144 10.04 N 40.46 E
Ayer, Schw. 58 46.11 N 7.36 E
Ayer, Ma., U.S. 207 42.33 N 71.35 W
Ayer Baloi 114 1.35 N 103.20 E
Ayer Chawan, Pulau I 271c 1.17 N 103.42 E
Ayer Hitam, Malay. 114 1.55 N 103.11 E
Ayer Hitam, Malay. 114 2.56 N 102.24 E
Ayer Jerneh 114 4.24 N 103.24 E
Ayer Kuning Selatan 114 2.30 N 102.28 E
Ayer Merbau, Pulau I 271c 1.16 N 103.43 E
Ayers Cliff 206 45.10 N 72.03 W
Ayers Rock ∧ 162 25.23 S 131.05 E
Ayersville 216 41.14 N 84.17 W
Ayeyarwady □[8] 110 17.00 N 95.00 E

Symbol	English	Deutsch	Español	Français	Português
≃	River	Fluß	Río	Rivière	Rio
≚	Canal	Kanal	Canal	Canal	Canal
∟	Waterfall, Rapids	Wasserfall, Stromschnellen	Cascada, Rápidos	Chute d'eau, Rapides	Cascata, Rápidos
⊍	Strait	Meeresstraße	Estrecho	Détroit	Estreito
⊂	Bay, Gulf	Bucht, Golf	Bahía, Golfo	Baie, Golfe	Baía, Golfo
⊜	Lake, Lakes	See, Seen	Lago, Lagos	Lac, Lacs	Lago, Lagos
≡	Swamp	Sumpf	Pantano	Marais	Pântano
⊼	Ice Features, Glacier	Eis- und Gletscherformen	Accidentes Glaciales	Formes glaciaires	Acidentes glaciares
⫪	Other Hydrographic Features	Andere Hydrographische Objekte	Otros Elementos Hidrográficos	Autres données hydrographiques	Outros acidentes hidrográficos
✤	Submarine Features	Untermeerische Objekte	Accidentes Submarinos	Formes de relief sous-marin	Acidentes submarinos
□	Political Unit	Politische Einheit	Unidad Politica	Entité politique	Unidade política
⌂	Cultural Institution	Kulturelle Institution	Institución Cultural	Institution culturelle	Instituição cultural
⊥	Historical Site	Historische Stätte	Sitio Histórico	Site historique	Sitio histórico
♠	Recreational Site	Erholungs- und Ferienort	Sitio de Recreo	Centre de loisirs	Area de Lazer
⊠	Airport	Flughafen	Aeropuerto	Aéroport	Aeroporto
■	Military Installation	Militäranlage	Instalación Militar	Installation militaire	Instalação militar
⟡	Miscellaneous	Verschiedenes	Misceláneo	Divers	Diversos

Ayeyarwady (Irrawaddy) ≃ 110 15.50 N 95.06 E
Aygün 130 38.26 N 41.17 E
Ayía Marína 38 37.09 N 26.52 E
Ayía Paraskeví, Ellás 38 39.15 N 26.16 E
Ayía Paraskeví, Ellás 267c 38.01 N 23.50 E
Ayiássos 38 39.05 N 26.23 E
Ayía Varvára 267c 37.59 N 23.39 E
Ayina ≃ 152 1.48 N 13.10 E
Áyioi Anáryiroi 267c 38.02 N 23.43 E
Áyion Óros >[1] 38 40.15 N 24.15 E
Áyios Dhimítrios 267c 37.56 N 23.44 E
Áyios Evstrátios I 38 39.31 N 25.00 E
Áyios Ioánnis Réndis 267c 37.58 N 23.40 E
Áyios Kírikos 38 37.37 N 26.14 E
Áyios Nikólaos 38 35.11 N 25.42 E
Ayiou Nikolaou Monastery ☨[1] 267c 37.53 N 23.27 E
Ayíou Órous, Kólpos c 38 40.12 N 24.03 E
Ayl 132 30.13 N 35.32 E
Aylesbury 42 51.50 N 0.50 W
Aylesford 42 51.18 N 0.29 E
Aylesham 42 51.13 N 1.13 E
Aylmer 188 45.26 N 75.50 W
Aylmer, Lake ⊜ 206 45.50 N 71.22 W
Aylmer, Mount ∧ 182 51.19 N 115.26 W
Aylmer-East 212 45.26 N 75.50 W
Aylmer Lake ⊜ 176 64.05 N 108.30 W
Aylmer West 212 42.46 N 80.59 W
Aylsham, Sk., Can. 184 53.11 N 103.49 W
Aylsham, Eng., U.K. 42 52.49 N 1.15 E
ʻAyn al-ʻArab 130 36.54 N 38.21 E
ʻAyn Dār 128 25.59 N 49.23 E
ʻAyn Dīwār 130 37.17 N 42.11 E
ʻAynīn ⊥[4] 144 20.48 N 41.39 E
Aynor 192 33.59 N 79.11 W
ʻAynūnah 128 28.05 N 35.08 E
Ayo 248 15.41 S 72.16 W
Ayo Ayo 248 17.05 S 68.00 W
Ayod 140 8.07 N 31.26 E
Ayodhya 124 26.48 N 82.12 E
Ayo El Chico 234 20.32 N 102.21 W
Ayom 140 7.52 N 28.23 E
Ayorou 150 14.44 N 0.55 E
Ayos 152 3.54 N 12.31 E
ʻAyoûn el ʻAtroûs 150 16.40 N 9.37 W
Ayr, Austl. 166 19.35 S 147.24 E
Ayr, On., Can. 212 43.17 N 80.27 W
Ayr, Scot., U.K. 44 55.28 N 4.38 W
Ayr ≃ 44 55.29 N 4.28 W
ʻAyrah 132 32.37 N 36.32 E
Ayrancı 130 37.22 N 33.42 E
Ayre, Point of > 44 54.26 N 4.22 W
Aysgarth 44 54.17 N 2.00 W
Aysha 144 10.46 N 42.37 E
ʻAytā al-Fakhkhār 132 33.38 N 35.54 E
ʻAytanīt 132 33.34 N 35.40 E
Ayton, Austl. 164 15.56 S 145.22 E
Ayton, On., Can. 212 44.03 N 80.56 W
Ayton, Eng., U.K. 44 54.14 N 0.29 W
Ayu, Kepulauan II 108 0.28 N 131.03 E
Ayubnagar 126 23.46 N 90.23 E
Ayulhai 102 44.36 N 115.36 E
Ayuñgon 116 9.51 N 123.08 E
Ayuquila ≃ 234 19.23 N 103.51 W
Ayutla 234 20.07 N 104.22 W
Ayutla de los Libres 234 16.54 N 99.13 W
Ayvacık, Tür. 130 39.36 N 26.24 E
Ayvacık, Tür. 130 41.00 N 36.39 E
Ayvalı 130 38.44 N 37.38 E
Ayvalık 130 39.18 N 26.41 E
Aywaille 56 50.28 N 5.40 E
Azabarabān, Ra's > 142 28.51 N 32.43 E
Azacualpa, Hond. 236 14.27 N 86.09 W
Azacualpa, Hond. 236 15.19 N 88.33 W
Azādpur ⊶[8] 272a 28.43 N 77.11 E
Azai 94 35.26 N 136.18 E
Azaila 34 41.17 N 0.29 W
Azalea Park 220 28.32 N 81.18 W
Azama 174m 26.11 N 127.49 E
Azamatovo 80 53.18 N 53.28 E
Azambuja 34 39.04 N 8.52 W
Āzamgarh 124 26.04 N 83.11 E
Azamiga-dake ∧ 96 34.20 N 131.47 E
Azángaro 248 14.55 S 70.13 W
Azángaro ≃ 248 15.17 S 70.10 W
Azanka 86 58.02 N 64.48 E
Azao ∧ 148 25.12 N 8.08 E
Azaouâd ⊶[1] 150 19.00 N 3.00 W
Azaouagh, Vallée de l' V 150 15.30 N 3.18 E
Azapa, Quebrada de ≃ 248 18.30 S 70.17 W
Azar V 150 16.02 N 4.04 E
Azara 150 8.21 N 9.12 E
Āzārbāyjān-e Gharbī □[4] 128 37.40 N 45.00 E
Āzārbāyjān-e Sharqī □[4] 128 38.00 N 47.00 E
Azare 150 11.40 N 10.11 E
Āzar Shahr 128 37.45 N 45.59 E
Azas ≃ 88 52.26 N 96.15 E
Azat, gora ∧[2] 86 46.55 N 69.00 E
Azay-le-Rideau 50 47.16 N 0.28 E
Azay-sur-Cher 50 47.21 N 0.51 E
Azay-sur-Indre 50 47.12 N 0.57 E
Aʻzāz 130 36.35 N 37.03 E
Azazga 148 36.44 N 4.22 E
Azcuénaga 258 34.23 S 59.21 W
Aždaak, gora ∧ 84 40.13 N 44.56 E
Azdavay 130 41.39 N 33.18 E
Azeffâl ⊥[8] 148 21.00 N 14.45 W
Azeffoun 148 36.53 N 4.25 E
Azejevo 80 54.41 N 42.02 E
Azemmour 148 33.20 N 8.25 W
Azenhas do Mar 266c 38.50 N 9.28 W
Azennezal, ʻErg V 148 22.50 N 0.25 E
Azerbaidzhan → Azerbaijan □[1] 22 40.30 N 47.30 E
Azerbaijan □[1], Asia 72 40.30 N 47.30 E
Azerbaijan □[1], Asia 84 40.30 N 47.30 E
Azerbajdžan → Azerbaijan □[1] 72 40.30 N 47.30 E
Azerbaydzan → Azerbaijan □[1] 72 40.30 N 47.30 E
Azergues ≃ 58 45.56 N 4.44 E
Azezo 144 12.35 N 37.28 E
Azgir 80 47.50 N 47.54 E
Azhikode 122 11.59 N 75.21 E
Azilal 148 31.58 N 6.34 W
Azilal □[4] 148 31.55 N 6.30 W
Azile 154 3.32 N 29.52 E
Azincourt 50 50.28 N 2.08 E
Azle 222 32.53 N 97.32 W
Aznakajevo 80 54.53 N 53.04 E
Aznapuquio 286d 11.59 S 77.04 W
Azogues 246 2.44 S 78.50 W
Azoia 266c 38.46 N 9.29 W
Azor 132 32.01 N 34.48 E
Azores → Açores II 148a 38.30 N 28.00 W
Azores-Gibraltar Ridge ⊹[3] 10 37.00 N 16.00 W
Azores Plateau ⊹[3] 10 39.00 N 30.00 W
Azoum, Bahr (Wādī ʻAzūm) V 146 10.53 N 20.15 E
Azov 83 47.07 N 39.25 E
Azov, Sea of → Azovskoje more ⊥[2] 78 46.00 N 36.00 E
Azovo-Sivašskij zapovednik ⊶[4] 78 46.08 N 35.08 E
Azovskij kanal ≅ 83 47.07 N 39.27 E
Azovskoje 78 45.34 N 34.34 E
Azovskoje more (Sea of Azov) ⊥[2] 78 46.00 N 36.00 E
Azoyú 234 16.43 N 98.44 W
Azpeitia 34 43.11 N 2.16 W
Azraq, Al-Bahr al- → Blue Nile ≃ 140 15.38 N 32.31 E
Azraq, Bahr ≃ 146 10.52 N 20.35 E
Azraq, Wādī al- V 140 10.33 N 28.40 E
Azraq ash-Shīshān 132 31.50 N 36.48 E
Azrou 148 33.27 N 5.14 W
Aztalan State Park ♦ 216 43.04 N 88.51 W
Aztec 200 36.49 N 107.59 W
Azteca, Estadio ♦ 286a 19.18 N 99.09 W
Aztec Peak ∧ 200 33.48 N 110.55 W
Aztec Ruins National Monument ♦ 200 36.51 N 108.10 W
Azua 238 18.27 N 70.44 W
Azuaga 34 38.16 N 5.41 W
Azuay □[4] 246 3.00 S 79.00 W
Azucena 252 37.29 S 59.18 W
Azuchi 94 35.09 N 136.08 E
Azuchi-jō ⊥ 94 35.10 N 136.08 E
Azuer ≃ 34 39.08 N 3.36 W
Azuero, Península de >[1] 246 7.40 N 80.35 W
Azufre, Volcán ∧[1] 252 25.11 S 68.31 W
Azuga 38 45.27 N 25.33 E
Azul 252 36.47 S 59.51 W
Azul, Cerro ∧, C.R. 236 9.54 N 85.14 W
Azul, Cerro ∧, Ec. 246a 0.54 S 91.21 W
Azul, Cerro ∧, Hond. 236 14.32 N 88.23 W
Azul, Cordillera ⋀ 248 8.30 S 76.10 W
Azul Casa, Cerro ∧ 252 22.29 S 65.20 W
ʻAzūm, Wādī (Bahr Azoum) V 146 10.53 N 20.15 E
Azuma, Nihon 94 36.31 N 139.19 E
Azuma, Nihon 94 36.33 N 138.54 E
Azuma, Nihon 94 35.56 N 140.28 E
Azuma, Nihon 94 36.36 N 138.20 E
Azumaya-san ∧ 94 36.32 N 138.25 E
Azumazaka 270 34.26 N 135.39 E
Azumi 94 36.11 N 137.47 E
Azur, Côte D' ⊥[2] 62 43.30 N 7.00 E
Azurduy 248 19.59 S 64.29 W
Azure Clouds, Temple of the ☨[1] 271a 40.00 N 116.11 E
Azure Lake ⊜ 182 52.23 N 120.00 W
Azusa 228 34.08 N 117.54 W
Azusa ≃ 94 36.17 N 137.56 E
Ažu-Tajga, gora ∧ 86 51.35 N 88.45 E
Az-Zabābidah 132 32.23 N 35.20 E
Az-Zabadānī 132 33.43 N 36.05 E
Az-Zāb al-Kabīr → Great Zab ≃ 128 36.00 N 43.21 E
Az-Zāb aṣ-Ṣaghīr → Little Zab ≃ 128 35.12 N 43.25 E
Aẓ-Ẓāhirīyah 132 31.25 N 34.58 E
Aẓ-Ẓahrān (Dhahran) 128 26.18 N 50.08 E
Az-Zamālik ⊶[8] 273c 30.04 N 31.13 E
Azzanello 64 45.18 N 9.55 E
Az-Zankalūn 142 30.33 N 31.27 E
Azzano Decimo 64 45.53 N 12.43 E
Az-Zaqāzīq 142 30.35 N 31.31 E
Az-Zarbah 130 36.04 N 36.59 E
Az-Zarqāʼ 132 32.05 N 36.06 E
Az-Zarqāʼ □[8] 132 32.00 N 36.45 E
Az-Zawāmil 142 30.21 N 31.26 E
Az-Zāwiyah 146 32.45 N 12.44 E
Az-Zaydāb 140 17.26 N 33.53 E
Az-Zaydīyah 144 15.18 N 43.04 E
Az-Zaytīyah ⊶[8] 142 29.58 N 32.31 E
Az-Zaytūn ⊶[8] 273c 30.06 N 31.19 E
Azzel Matti, Sebkha ≚ 148 25.55 N 0.56 E
Az-Zilfī 128 26.18 N 44.48 E
Az-Zrārīyah 132 33.21 N 35.20 E
Az-Zubayr 128 30.23 N 47.43 E
ʻAzzūn 132 32.11 N 35.03 E
Azzurra, Grotta (Blue Grotto) ⊥[5] 68 40.35 N 14.14 E

B

Ba ≃, Viet 110 13.02 N 109.03 E
Ba ≃, Zhg. 100 30.25 N 115.02 E
Ba ≃, Zhg. 102 31.03 N 107.08 E
Ba ≃, Zhg. 271a 39.57 N 116.38 E
Ba, Loch ⊜ 46 56.36 N 4.44 W
Baa 112 10.43 S 123.03 E
Baaba, Île I 175f 20.03 S 163.59 E
Baacagaan 102 45.35 N 99.27 E
Baad 58 47.19 N 10.07 E
Baah 112 10.28 S 121.59 E
Baak 263 51.25 N 7.10 E
Baal 56 51.02 N 6.17 E
Baao 116 13.27 N 123.22 E
Baar 58 47.12 N 8.32 E
Baar ⊶[1] 58 48.00 N 8.30 E
Baarbach ≃ 263 51.27 N 7.39 E
Baardheere (Bardera) 144 2.20 N 42.17 E
Baardskeerdersbos 158 34.34 S 19.35 E
Baargaal 144 11.17 N 51.04 E
Baarle-Hertog 56 51.27 N 4.56 E
Baarle-Nassau 52 51.27 N 4.53 E
Baarlo 52 51.20 N 6.05 E
Baarn 52 52.13 N 5.16 E
Baasrode 50 51.02 N 4.10 E
Baba 246 1.47 S 79.40 W
Baba ≃ 152 6.25 N 17.07 E
Baba Burnu >, Tür. 130 41.17 N 31.24 E
Baba Burnu >, Tür. 130 39.29 N 26.04 E
Babaçulândia 250 7.13 S 47.46 W
Babadag, Rom. 38 44.54 N 28.43 E
Babadağ, Tür. 130 37.48 N 28.52 E
Babadag, gora ∧ 84 41.02 N 48.19 E
Babaeski 130 41.26 N 27.06 E
Babahoyo 246 1.49 S 79.31 W
Babaī (Sarju) ≃ 124 27.42 N 81.16 E
Babailiqiao 100 32.26 N 118.57 E
Babajevo 76 59.23 N 35.56 E
Babajkovka 78 49.01 N 34.32 E
Babajurt 84 43.36 N 46.47 E
Babak 112 7.08 N 125.41 E
Babakin 162 32.07 S 118.01 E
Babana 150 10.26 N 3.50 E
Babanango 158 28.30 S 31.00 E
Babanka 78 48.43 N 30.26 E
Babanūsah 140 11.20 N 27.48 E
Babar, Kepulauan II 164 7.50 S 129.45 E
Babar, Pulau I 164 7.55 S 129.45 E
Bābarpur ⊶[8] 272a 28.41 N 77.17 E
Babat, Indon. 112 2.45 S 103.38 E
Babat, Indon. 115a 7.06 S 112.10 E
Babatag, chrebet ⋀ 85 38.15 N 68.20 E
Babati 154 4.13 S 35.45 E
Bābā Valī Ṣāḥeb 120 31.40 N 65.40 E
Babb 182 48.51 N 113.26 W
Babbacombe Bay c 42 50.30 N 3.25 W
Babb Creek ≃ 210 41.33 N 77.23 W
Babbitt, Mn., U.S. 190 47.43 N 91.57 W
Babbitt, Nv., U.S. 204 38.32 N 118.38 W
Bʻabdā 132 33.50 N 35.32 E
Bʻabdāt 132 33.53 N 35.40 E
Babel, Mont de ∧ 186 51.27 N 68.42 W
Babelijamun 164 2.04 S 137.43 E
Bab el Mandeb → Mandeb, Bab el ʊ 144 12.40 N 43.20 E
Babelsberg ⊶[8] 264a 52.24 N 13.05 E
Babelsberg, Schloss ⊥ 264a 52.24 N 13.05 E
Babelthuap I 175b 7.30 N 134.36 E
Babenhausen, Dtsch. 56 49.57 N 8.56 E
Babenhausen, Dtsch. 58 48.09 N 10.15 E
Babenki 82 55.21 N 37.11 E
Babenkovo 83 49.15 N 37.21 E
Babeyru 154 1.52 N 27.27 E
Babi, Pulau I 114 2.05 N 96.39 E
Babia, Arroyo de la ≃ 196 28.25 N 101.45 W
Babian ≃ 102 22.58 N 101.44 E
Babiči 76 52.17 N 30.00 E
Bābil 142 30.41 N 31.00 E
Bābil □[4] 128 32.40 N 44.35 E
Bābil, Aṭlāl (Babylon) ⊥ 128 32.33 N 44.24 E
Babile 144 9.15 N 42.19 E
Babilônia 256 22.33 S 44.28 W
Babimost 30 52.10 N 15.51 E
Babīna 124 25.15 N 78.28 E
Babina Greda 38 45.07 N 18.33 E
Babinda 166 17.20 S 145.55 E
Babine 182 55.19 N 126.37 W
Babine ≃ 182 55.42 N 127.40 W
Babine Lake ⊜ 182 54.45 N 126.00 W
Babine Range ⋀ 182 55.00 N 126.25 W
Babino, Ross. 76 56.44 N 34.17 E
Babino, Ross. 76 59.14 N 31.26 E
Babino, Ross. 76 59.50 N 40.49 E
Babino, Ross. 80 57.22 N 48.45 E
Babiogórski Park Narodowy ♦ 30 49.35 N 19.30 E
Babo 164 2.33 S 133.25 E
Bābol 128 36.34 N 52.42 E
Bābol Sar 128 36.43 N 52.39 E
Baboon Point > 158 32.19 S 18.20 E
Baboquivari Mountains ⋀ 200 31.45 N 111.35 W
Baboquivari Peak ∧ 200 31.46 N 111.35 W
Babor, Djebel ∧ 34 36.30 N 5.28 E
Baborów 30 50.09 N 17.59 E
Babošino 82 54.13 N 37.08 E
Baboua 152 5.48 N 14.49 E
Babrongan Tower ∧[2] 162 18.36 S 123.33 E
Babson Park, Fl., U.S. 220 27.49 N 81.31 W
Babson Park, Ma., U.S. 283 42.18 N 71.23 W
Babson Reservoir ⊜[1] 283 42.38 N 70.40 W
Babstovo 89 48.07 N 132.27 E
Bab-Taza 148 35.03 N 5.14 W
Bābu Bheri 272b 22.51 N 88.14 E
Bābupur, India 126 24.01 N 87.10 E
Bābūpur, India 272a 28.30 N 76.59 E
Babura 150 12.46 N 9.01 E
Bābūsar Pass)(123 35.09 N 74.03 E
Babuškin 88 51.41 N 105.54 E
Babuškin ⊶[8] 265b 55.52 N 37.42 E
Babuyan 116 10.00 N 118.54 E
Babuyan Channel ʊ 116 18.44 N 121.40 E
Babuyan Island I 108 19.32 N 121.57 E
Babuyan Islands II 108 19.15 N 121.40 E
Babylon 210 40.41 N 73.19 W
Babylon → Bābil, Aṭlāl ⊥ 128 32.33 N 44.24 E
Babynino 76 54.23 N 35.43 E
Bača ≃ 64 46.09 N 13.48 E
Bacaadweeyn 144 7.12 N 47.32 E
Bacabal 250 4.14 S 44.47 W
Bacacay 116 13.18 N 123.47 E
Bacadéhuachi 232 29.44 N 109.10 W
Bacajaí ≃ 250 3.27 S 51.53 W
Bacalhau, Canal do ≅ 287a 23.03 S 43.35 W
Bacaligo 84 42.33 N 44.57 E
Bačalino 86 57.46 N 67.17 E
Bacan, Pulau I 164 0.35 S 127.30 E
Bacao 116 10.27 N 119.48 E
Bacarra 116 18.15 N 120.35 E
Bacatuba 250 5.40 S 43.42 W
Bacău 38 46.34 N 26.55 E
Bacău □[6] 38 46.30 N 26.45 E
Baccalieu Island I 186 48.08 N 52.48 W
Bac Can 110 22.08 N 105.50 E
Baccarat 58 48.27 N 6.45 E
Bacchiglione ≃ 64 45.11 N 12.14 E
Bacchus Marsh 169 37.41 S 144.27 E
Baceno 58 46.16 N 8.19 E
Bacerac 232 30.18 N 108.50 W
Bacevičі 76 53.24 N 29.14 E
Bac Giang 110 21.16 N 106.12 E
Bach 58 47.16 N 10.24 E
Bachagou 98 40.36 N 122.54 E
Bachaquero 246 9.56 N 71.08 W
Bacharach 56 50.04 N 7.46 E
Bacharden 128 38.26 N 57.25 E
Bachardok 128 38.46 N 58.30 E
Bachauan 116 12.28 N 122.06 E
Bachčisaraj 78 44.45 N 33.51 E
Bache 106 31.05 N 120.40 E
Bacheng 106 31.27 N 120.52 E
Bachi 100 24.48 N 115.49 E
Bachiniva 232 28.45 N 107.15 W
Bach Ma 110 16.12 N 107.52 E
Bachmač 78 51.13 N 32.46 E
Bachmetjevka 80 51.06 N 44.46 E
Bachmut ≃ 83 48.56 N 38.03 E
Bachmutovka 83 48.52 N 39.03 E
Bachmutovo 76 56.22 N 34.03 E
Bacho 114 6.37 N 101.39 E
Bachok 114 6.04 N 102.24 E
Bacht 85 40.43 N 68.42 E
Bachta, Ross. 74 62.28 N 89.00 E
Bachta, Ross. 86 55.45 N 92.26 E
Bachtemir ≃ 80 45.43 N 47.38 E
Bachten-Berg ∧[2] 264a 52.20 N 12.54 E
Bachty 86 46.39 N 82.42 E
Bachu 90 39.50 N 78.20 E
Bachuma 144 6.48 N 35.53 E
Back ≃, N.T., Can. 176 67.15 N 95.15 W
Back ≃, Va., U.S. 208 37.06 N 76.17 W
Bačka ⊶[1] 38 45.50 N 19.30 E
Bačka Palanka 38 45.15 N 19.24 E
Bačka Topola 38 45.49 N 19.38 E
Back Bay ⊶[8] 283 42.21 N 71.05 W
Back Bay c, India 272c 18.56 N 72.49 E
Back Bay c, Va., U.S. 208 36.35 N 75.57 W
Backberg 40 60.37 N 16.37 E
Backbone Ranges ⋀ 180 63.30 N 129.00 W
Back Branch ≃ 284c 38.50 N 76.48 W
Back Brook ≃ 276 40.26 N 74.39 W
Back Channel ≃[1] 279b 40.30 N 80.05 W
Back Creek ≃ 188 38.02 N 79.54 W
Backe 26 63.49 N 16.24 E
Bäckefors 26 58.48 N 12.10 E
Bäckehagen 40 60.39 N 15.34 E
Backford 262 53.15 N 2.54 W
Bäckhammar 40 59.10 N 14.11 E
Bački Petrovac 38 45.22 N 19.35 E
Backnang 56 48.56 N 9.25 E
Back River c 208 39.16 N 76.27 W
Back River Neck >[1] 284b 39.18 N 76.26 W
Backstairs Passage ʊ 168b 35.42 S 138.05 E
Bac Lieu 110 9.17 N 105.44 E
Bacliff 222 29.31 N 94.59 W
Bac Ninh 110 21.11 N 106.03 E
Baco, Mount ∧ 116 12.49 N 121.10 E
Bacoachi 232 30.38 N 109.56 W
Bacoli 68 40.48 N 14.05 E
Bacolod 116 10.40 N 122.57 E
Bacon 116 13.03 N 124.03 E
Baconga ⊶[8] 273b 4.18 S 15.16 E
Bacon Peak ∧ 224 48.39 N 121.31 W
Bacons Run ≃ 285 40.06 N 74.41 W
Baconton 192 31.22 N 84.09 W
Bacoor 116 14.28 N 120.56 E
Bacoor Bay c 269f 14.28 N 120.54 E
Bac Phan □[9] 110 22.00 N 105.00 E
Bac Quang 110 22.29 N 104.52 E
Bacqueville-en-Caux 50 49.47 N 1.00 E
Bácsalmás 38 46.08 N 19.20 E
Bács-Kiskun □[6] 30 46.30 N 19.25 E
Bacton 42 52.52 N 1.28 E
Bacuag 116 9.37 N 125.38 E
Bacuit Bay c 116 11.07 N 119.23 E
Bácum 232 27.33 N 110.05 W
Bacungan 116 9.56 N 118.42 E
Bacup 44 53.43 N 2.12 W
Bacuranao ≃ 286b 23.10 N 82.14 W
Bacuranao, Presa ⊜[1] 286b 23.07 N 82.13 W
Bacuri, Cachoeira do L 250 5.29 S 54.18 W
Bacuri, Ilha do I 250 2.55 S 49.43 W
Bacuri, Lago do ⊜ 250 3.16 S 42.15 W
Bačurka 24 68.32 N 56.57 E
Bacuyangan 116 9.39 N 122.27 E
Bād 128 33.41 N 52.01 E
Bad ≃, Mi., U.S. 190 43.18 N 84.06 W
Bad ≃, S.D., U.S. 198 44.22 N 100.22 W
Bad ≃, Wi., U.S. 190 46.38 N 90.40 W
Badʻ, Wādī V 142 29.41 N 32.20 E
Bada 88 51.23 N 109.54 E
Bad Abbach 60 48.56 N 12.03 E
Badagara 122 11.36 N 75.35 E
Badagri 150 6.27 N 2.55 E
Badagri □[8] 273a 6.27 N 3.18 E
Badagri Creek c 273a 6.25 N 3.18 E
Badahl 142 28.56 N 30.54 E
Bad Aibling 64 47.52 N 12.00 E
Bada Jāmda 124 22.09 N 85.23 E
Badajia 100 33.57 N 120.17 E
Badajós ≃ 246 3.15 S 63.02 W
Badajós, Lago ⊜ 246 3.15 S 62.47 W
Badajoz 34 38.53 N 6.58 W
Badajoz □[4] 34 38.40 N 6.00 W
Badakani 152 4.46 S 14.52 E
Badakhshān □[4] 120 36.45 N 72.00 E
Badal Khān Goth 120 26.31 N 67.06 E
Badalona 34 41.27 N 2.15 E
Badalucco 62 43.55 N 7.51 E
Badam 85 42.23 N 69.15 E
Bādāmi 122 15.55 N 75.41 E
Bādāmpahār 124 22.06 N 86.06 E
Badana, Lach V 144 0.50 S 42.04 E
Badanah 128 30.59 N 41.02 E
Badanga 146 11.36 N 17.26 E
Badanganj 126 22.54 N 87.33 E
Badaohao 104 41.47 N 121.57 E
Badaohe, Zhg. 98 40.24 N 118.42 E
Badaohe, Zhg. 98 40.02 N 122.17 E
Badarīnāth 124 30.44 N 79.29 E
Badarma 88 57.46 N 102.36 E
Badas 112 4.36 N 114.27 E
Badas, Kepulauan II 112 0.35 N 107.06 E
Badata, gora ∧ 88 51.55 N 111.35 E
Bad Aussee 64 47.36 N 13.47 E
Bad Axe 190 43.48 N 83.00 W
Badaying 98 41.22 N 117.28 E
Badazhou 102 24.36 N 105.04 E
Bad Bentheim 52 52.19 N 7.10 E
Bad Bergzabern 56 49.07 N 8.00 E
Bad Berka 54 50.54 N 11.17 E
Bad Berleburg 52 51.03 N 8.23 E
Bad Berneck 60 50.03 N 11.40 E
Bad Bertrich 56 50.04 N 7.02 E
Bad Bibra 54 51.12 N 11.35 E
Bad Blankenburg 54 50.41 N 11.16 E
Bad Bramstedt 52 53.55 N 9.53 E
Bad Breisig 56 50.31 N 7.18 E
Bad Brückenau 56 50.18 N 9.47 E
Bad Buchau 58 48.03 N 9.36 E
Bad Camberg 56 50.18 N 8.16 E
Bad Creek ≃ 216 41.25 N 83.57 W
Baddā 132 33.41 N 36.26 E
Badda Rogghie ∧ 144 8.43 N 37.41 E
Baddeck 186 46.07 N 60.45 W
Bad Ditzenbach 56 48.35 N 9.41 E
Baddo ≃ 128 27.59 N 64.21 E
Bad Doberan 54 54.06 N 11.53 E
Baddomalhi 123 31.59 N 74.40 E
Bad Dreibergen 52 53.12 N 8.01 E
Bad Driburg 52 51.44 N 9.01 E
Bad Düben 54 51.36 N 12.34 E
Bad Dürkheim 56 49.28 N 8.10 E
Bad Dürrenberg 54 51.18 N 12.04 E
Bad Dürrheim 58 48.01 N 8.32 E
Badé, Centraf. 152 6.41 N 17.07 E
Bade, Indon. 164 7.10 S 139.35 E
Badeggi 150 9.05 N 6.08 E
Badéguichéri 150 14.31 N 5.22 E
Bad Eilsen 52 52.14 N 9.06 E
Badel 54 52.44 N 11.19 E
Bad Elster 54 50.17 N 12.14 E
Bad Ems 56 50.20 N 7.43 E
Baden, On., Can. 212 43.24 N 80.39 W
Baden, Dtsch. 52 53.00 N 9.04 E
Baden, Erit. 144 17.00 N 38.00 E
Baden, Öst. 61 48.00 N 16.14 E
Baden, Schw. 58 47.29 N 8.18 E
Baden, Pa., U.S. 214 40.38 N 80.13 W
Baden-Baden 56 48.46 N 8.14 E
Bad Endbach 56 50.45 N 8.32 E
Badenoch □[9] 46 56.57 N 4.19 W
Baden-Powell, Mount ∧ 228 34.21 N 117.46 W
Badenweiler 58 47.48 N 7.40 E
Baden-Württemberg □[3] 30 48.30 N 9.00 E
Badenyon 46 57.15 N 3.05 W
Baderna 64 45.12 N 13.46 E
Badersleben 54 51.59 N 10.53 E
Bad Essen 52 52.19 N 8.20 E
Bad Feilnbach 64 47.46 N 12.00 E
Badfish Creek ≃ 216 42.50 N 89.10 W
Bad Frankenhausen 54 51.21 N 11.06 E
Bad Freienwalde 54 52.47 N 14.01 E
Bad Friedrichshall 56 49.14 N 9.11 E
Bad Fusch 64 47.12 N 12.51 E
Badgam 123 34.01 N 74.43 E
Bad Gandersheim 52 51.52 N 10.01 E
Badgastein 64 47.07 N 13.08 E
Badger, Nf., Can. 186 48.59 N 56.02 W
Badger, Mn., U.S. 198 48.46 N 96.00 W
Badger Creek ≃, Co., U.S. 198 40.17 N 103.42 W
Badger Creek ≃, Co., U.S. 200 38.28 N 105.52 W
Badger Creek ≃, Or., U.S. 224 45.16 N 121.11 W
Badger Pass)(226 37.40 N 119.39 W
Badger's Mount 260 51.20 N 0.09 E
Badgery's Creek 274a 33.53 S 150.44 E
Badgerys Creek ≃ 274a 33.51 S 150.46 E
Bādghīs □[4] 128 35.00 N 63.45 E
Bad Gleichenberg 61 46.52 N 15.54 E
Bad Godesberg 56 50.41 N 7.10 E
Bad Goisern 64 47.38 N 13.37 E
Bad Gottleuba 54 50.51 N 13.56 E
Bad Griesbach 58 48.27 N 8.14 E
Bad Grund 52 51.48 N 10.14 E
Bad Hall 61 48.02 N 14.13 E
Bad Harzburg 54 51.53 N 10.33 E
Bad Heilbrunn 64 47.45 N 11.28 E
Badhela ⊶[8] 272a 28.38 N 77.04 E
Bad Helmstedt 54 52.14 N 11.03 E
Bad Hersfeld 56 50.52 N 9.42 E
Badhoevedorp 52 52.21 N 4.46 E
Bad Hofgastein 64 47.10 N 13.06 E
Bad Homburg vor der Höhe 56 50.13 N 8.37 E
Bad Honnef 56 50.39 N 7.13 E
Bad Hönningen 56 50.31 N 7.19 E
Bāḍī ≃ 124 27.55 N 83.27 E
Badia (Abtei) 64 46.37 N 11.54 E
Badia, Val V 64 46.40 N 11.53 E
Badia Calavena 64 45.34 N 11.09 E
Badia Polesine 64 45.05 N 11.29 E
Badia Prataglia 66 43.47 N 11.52 E
Badia Tedalda 66 43.42 N 12.11 E
Badile Camuno, Pizzo ∧ 58 46.01 N 10.25 E
Badīn 120 24.39 N 68.50 E
Bādinan 272b 22.54 N 88.14 E
Badinko ≃ 150 13.42 N 9.35 W
Badin Lake ⊜[1] 192 35.27 N 80.06 W
Badiraguato 232 25.22 N 107.31 W
Bad Ischl 64 47.43 N 13.37 E
Bad Kissingen 56 50.12 N 10.04 E
Bad Kleinen 54 53.46 N 11.28 E
Bad Kleinkirchheim 64 46.49 N 13.49 E
Bad Klosterlausnitz 54 50.55 N 11.52 E
Bad Kohlgrub 64 47.40 N 11.03 E
Bad König 56 49.45 N 9.01 E
Bad Königshofen im Grabfeld 56 50.18 N 10.29 E

ENGLISH — Name | Page | Lat.°′ | Long.°′

Bad Kösen 54 51.08 N 11.43 E
Bad Köstritz 54 50.56 N 12.01 E
Bad Kreuznach 56 49.52 N 7.51 E
Bad Krozingen 58 47.55 N 7.43 E
Bādkulla 126 23.17 N 88.32 E
Bad Laasphe 56 50.56 N 8.24 E
Badlands ⋀[2], U.S. 198 46.45 N 103.30 W
Badlands ⋀[2], S.D., U.S. 198 43.30 N 102.20 W
Badlands National Park ♦ 198 43.47 N 102.15 W
Bad Langensalza 56 51.06 N 10.38 E
Bad Lauchstädt 54 51.23 N 11.52 E
Bad Lausick 54 51.08 N 12.38 E
Bad Lauterberg [im Harz] 52 51.38 N 10.28 E
Bad Leonfelden 61 48.33 N 14.19 E
Bādli ⊶[8] 272a 28.45 N 77.09 E
Bad Liebenstein 54 50.49 N 10.21 E
Bad Liebenwerda 54 51.31 N 13.23 E
Bad Liebenzell 56 48.46 N 8.44 E
Bad Lippspringe 52 51.46 N 8.49 E
Bad Meinberg 52 51.53 N 8.58 E
Bad Mergentheim 56 49.30 N 9.46 E
Bad Mitterndorf 60 47.33 N 13.55 E
Bad Mukran 54 54.26 N 13.35 E
Bad Münder 52 52.12 N 9.27 E
Bad Münster am Stein 56 49.49 N 7.51 E
Bad Münstereifel 56 50.33 N 6.46 E
Bad Muskau 54 51.32 N 14.43 E
Bad Nauheim 56 50.22 N 8.44 E
Bad Nenndorf 52 52.20 N 9.22 E
Badnera 122 20.52 N 77.44 E
Badner Lindkogel ∧ 264b 48.01 N 16.11 E
Bad Neuenahr-Ahrweiler 56 50.33 N 7.08 E
Bad Neustadt an der Saale 56 50.19 N 10.13 E
Bad Niedernau 58 48.27 N 8.53 E
Bad Oeynhausen 52 52.12 N 8.48 E
Badogo 150 11.02 N 8.13 W
Badolato 68 38.34 N 16.31 E
Bad Oldesloe 52 53.48 N 10.22 E
Ba Dong, Viet 110 9.40 N 106.34 E
Badong, Zhg. 102 31.02 N 110.20 E
Badonviller 58 48.30 N 6.54 E
Bad Orb 56 50.14 N 9.20 E
Badou, Togo 150 7.35 N 0.36 E
Badou, Zhg. 98 36.27 N 117.55 E
Badouling 100 32.10 N 117.36 E
Badoumbé 150 13.38 N 10.13 W
Bad Peterstal 58 48.26 N 8.12 E
Badplaas 158 25.57 S 30.35 E
Bad Pyrmont 52 51.59 N 9.15 E
Badr 142 30.33 N 30.43 E
Bad Radkersburg 61 46.41 N 15.59 E
Bad Ragaz 58 47.00 N 9.30 E
Bad Rappenau 56 49.14 N 9.06 E
Bad Rehburg 52 52.26 N 9.13 E
Bad Reichenhall 64 47.43 N 12.52 E
Badr Hunayn 128 23.44 N 38.46 E
Bad Rippoldsau 58 48.26 N 8.19 E
Bad River Indian Reservation ⊶[4] 190 46.33 N 90.40 W
Bad Rothenfelde 52 52.06 N 8.09 E
Bad Saarow-Pieskow 54 52.17 N 14.03 E
Bad Sachsa 54 51.36 N 10.32 E
Bad Säckingen 58 47.33 N 7.56 E
Bad Salzdetfurth 52 52.03 N 10.01 E
Bad Salzig 56 50.12 N 7.38 E
Bad Salzschlirf 56 50.37 N 9.29 E
Bad Salzuflen 52 52.05 N 8.44 E
Bad Salzungen 56 50.48 N 10.13 E
Bad Sankt Leonhard im Lavanttal 61 46.58 N 14.48 E
Bad Sassendorf 52 51.35 N 8.10 E
Bad Schandau 54 50.55 N 14.10 E
Bad Schmiedeberg 54 51.41 N 12.44 E
Bad Schwalbach 56 50.08 N 8.04 E
Bad Schwartau 54 53.55 N 10.40 E
Bad Segeberg 52 53.56 N 10.17 E
Bādshāhpur 124 25.47 N 82.49 E
Bad Soden 56 50.08 N 8.30 E
Bad Soden-Salmünster 56 50.17 N 9.22 E
Bad Sooden-Allendorf 56 51.16 N 9.58 E
Bad Steben 54 50.22 N 11.38 E
Bad Stuer 54 53.22 N 12.19 E
Bad Suderode 54 51.44 N 11.07 E
Bad Sulza 54 51.05 N 11.37 E
Bad Sülze 54 54.06 N 12.38 E
Bad Tatzmannsdorf 61 47.20 N 16.13 E
Bad Teinach 56 48.41 N 8.41 E
Bad Tennstedt 54 51.09 N 10.50 E
Bad Tölz 64 47.46 N 11.34 E
Badu, Bra. 287a 22.54 S 43.04 W
Badu, Zhg. 100 26.51 N 119.35 E
Badu, Zhg. 100 28.32 N 117.57 E
Badu, Zhg. 102 24.15 N 105.41 E
Badu Island I 164 10.07 S 142.08 E
Badulla 122 6.59 N 81.03 E
Badung, Selat ʊ 115b 8.40 S 115.22 E
Badupi 120 21.36 N 93.25 E
Bādura 126 22.16 N 90.21 E
Bad Urach 58 48.29 N 9.23 E
Bāduria 126 22.44 N 88.47 E
Badvel 122 14.45 N 79.03 E
Bad Vellach 61 46.26 N 14.33 E
Bad Vilbel 56 50.12 N 8.42 E
Bad Vöslau 61 47.57 N 16.16 E
Bad Waldsee 58 47.55 N 9.45 E
Badwater Creek ≃ 202 43.17 N 108.08 W
Bad Westernkotten 52 51.38 N 8.21 E
Bad Wiessee 64 47.43 N 11.43 E
Bad Wildungen 56 51.07 N 9.07 E
Bad Wilsnack 54 52.57 N 11.57 E
Bad Wimpfen 56 49.14 N 9.09 E
Bad Windsheim 56 49.31 N 10.25 E
Bad Wörishofen 58 48.00 N 10.36 E
Bad Wurzach 58 47.54 N 9.54 E
Badžalskij chrebet ⋀ 89 50.40 N 134.50 E
Bad Zwischenahn 52 53.11 N 8.00 E
Baediam 150 15.03 N 11.51 W
Bække 41 55.34 N 9.09 E
Baena 34 37.37 N 4.19 W
Baependi 256 21.57 S 44.53 W
Baependi ≃ 256 21.52 S 45.04 W
Baer Field ⊠ 216 40.59 N 85.11 W
Baerl ⊶[8] 263 51.29 N 6.41 E
Baesweiler 56 50.54 N 6.11 E
Báez 240p 22.13 N 79.45 W
Baeza, Ec. 246 0.27 S 77.53 W
Baeza, Esp. 34 37.59 N 3.28 W
Baezaeko ≃ 182 53.09 N 123.48 W
Bafang 152 5.09 N 10.11 E
Bafatá 150 12.10 N 14.40 W
Bafelé 150 10.09 N 10.08 W
Baffa 123 34.26 N 73.13 E
Baffin Basin ⊹[1] 16 73.15 N 67.00 W
Baffin Bay c, N.A. 16 73.00 N 66.00 W
Baffin Bay c, Tx., U.S. 196 27.15 N 97.33 W
Baffin Island I 176 68.00 N 70.00 W
Bafia 152 4.44 N 11.16 E
Bafilo 150 9.21 N 1.16 E
Bafing ≃, Afr. 150 13.49 N 10.50 W
Bafing ≃, Mali 150 12.27 N 7.07 W
Bafing Makana 150 12.33 N 10.15 W
Bafoulabé 150 13.48 N 10.50 W
Bafoussam 152 5.29 N 10.24 E
Bāfq 128 31.35 N 55.24 E
Bafra 130 41.34 N 35.56 E
Bafra Burnu > 130 41.44 N 35.58 E
Bāft 128 29.14 N 56.38 E
Bafuku 154 4.15 N 27.54 E
Bafwabaka 154 2.07 N 27.40 E
Bafwabalinga 154 0.51 N 27.04 E
Bafwaboli 154 0.39 N 26.10 E
Bafwangbe 154 1.39 N 26.51 E

DEUTSCH — Name | Seite | Breite°′ | Länge°′ E = Ost

Bafwapada 154 0.56 N 26.57 E
Bafwasende 154 1.05 N 27.16 E
Bafwasomboli 154 1.27 N 27.01 E
Baga 126 22.26 N 90.28 E
Bagabag 116 16.37 N 121.15 E
Bagabag Island I 164 4.50 S 146.15 E
Baga-Burul 80 46.00 N 44.36 E
Bagac 116 14.36 N 120.23 E
Bagacay Point > 116 8.58 N 124.48 E
Bagac Bay c 116 14.36 N 120.22 E
Bagaces 236 10.31 N 85.15 W
Baga Chentej nuruu ⋀ 88 48.30 N 107.30 E
Bagage ∧ 154 3.23 N 40.12 E
Bagagem ≃, Bra. 250 11.37 S 48.12 W
Bagagem ≃, Bra. 255 13.58 S 48.21 W
Bagaha 124 27.06 N 84.05 E
Bagahak ∧ 116 5.03 N 118.44 E
Bagajevskij 78 47.19 N 40.23 E
Bāgalkot 122 16.11 N 75.42 E
Bagamanoc 116 13.57 N 124.17 E
Bagamoyo 154 6.26 S 38.54 E
Bagan 86 54.06 N 77.40 E
Bagana 80 54.22 N 51.25 E
Bagana, Mount ∧ 175e 6.09 S 155.12 E
Bagan Datoh 114 3.59 N 100.47 E
Bagañga 116 7.35 N 126.34 E
Bagan Serai 114 5.01 N 100.32 E
Bagansiapiapi 114 2.09 N 100.49 E
Bagansinembah 114 1.46 N 100.29 E
Bagansitukang 114 2.38 N 100.15 E
Baganza ≃ 64 44.47 N 10.19 E
Bagara 85 40.55 N 68.26 E
Bağarası 130 37.42 N 27.33 E
Bagaroua 150 14.38 N 4.21 E
Bagasra 120 21.29 N 70.57 E
Bagata 152 3.44 S 17.57 E
Bāgātipāra 126 24.18 N 88.57 E
Bagawi 140 12.19 N 34.21 E
Bagband 52 53.21 N 7.36 E
Bagbe ≃ 150 8.42 N 11.15 W
Bagbele 154 4.21 N 29.17 E
Bāgda 126 23.13 N 86.41 E
Bagdad, Az., U.S. 200 34.34 N 113.12 W
Bagdad, Fl., U.S. 194 30.35 N 87.01 W
Bagdad, Ky., U.S. 218 38.15 N 85.03 W
Bagdad → Baghdād 128 33.21 N 44.25 E
Bagdaha 126 23.13 N 88.53 E
Bagdanga 126 24.02 N 88.32 E
Bagdarin 88 54.26 N 113.36 E
Bagdati 84 42.06 N 42.48 E
Bağdere 130 38.07 N 40.44 E
Bagé 252 31.20 S 54.06 W
Bagehadu 120 35.25 N 84.50 E
Bâgé-le-Châtel 58 46.18 N 4.56 E
Bagenkop 41 54.45 N 10.41 E
Bāgerhāt 124 22.40 N 89.48 E
Bagerovo 78 45.23 N 36.17 E
Bages et de Sigean, Étang de c 32 43.05 N 3.03 E
Bāgevādi 122 16.35 N 75.58 E
Baggao 116 17.56 N 121.46 E
Baggeryd 24 57.30 N 14.07 E
Baggetorp 40 59.01 N 16.04 E
Baggio ⊶[8] 266b 45.27 N 9.06 E
Bağgöze 130 37.43 N 41.55 E
Baggs 200 41.02 N 107.39 W
Baggy Point > 42 51.09 N 4.16 W
Bāgh 123 33.59 N 73.47 E
Baghdād 128 33.21 N 44.25 E
Baghdād □[4] 128 33.30 N 44.30 E
Baghdobā 126 22.08 N 87.54 E
Baghelkhand Plateau ⋀[1] 124 23.45 N 82.20 E
Bāgh-e Malek 128 31.32 N 49.55 E
Bagheria 70 38.05 N 13.30 E
Bāgherpāra 126 23.14 N 89.21 E
Bāghia 126 23.27 N 90.29 E
Baghia Bīl ≡ 126 23.07 N 90.03 E
Bāghīn 128 30.12 N 56.48 E
Baghlān 120 36.13 N 68.46 E
Baghlān □[4] 120 35.45 N 69.00 E
Bāghmundi 124 23.12 N 86.03 E
Bāghpat 124 28.57 N 77.13 E
Baghrān Khowleh 120 33.01 N 64.58 E
Bagillt 262 53.16 N 3.10 W
Bağırpaşa Dağı ∧ 130 39.30 N 40.06 E
Bağırsak (Sājūr) ≃ 130 36.40 N 38.05 E
Bağkonak 130 38.12 N 31.17 E
Bagley 198 47.31 N 95.23 W
Bāgli 124 22.39 N 76.21 E
Bağlıca 130 37.53 N 41.46 E
Bağlum 130 40.03 N 32.51 E
Bagmanl'ar 84 40.38 N 46.18 E
Bāgmāri ⊶[8] 272b 22.34 N 88.25 E
Bāgmatī □[8] 124 27.45 N 85.30 E
Bāgmatī ≃ 124 25.31 N 86.44 E
Bagn 26 60.49 N 9.34 E
Bagnacavallo 66 44.25 N 12.00 E
Bagnaia 66 42.25 N 12.09 E
Bāgnān 126 22.28 N 87.59 E
Bagnara Calabra 68 38.18 N 15.49 E
Bagnara di Romagna 66 44.23 N 11.49 E
Bag Narin 102 38.57 N 94.08 E
Bagnasco 62 44.18 N 8.02 E
Bagnell Dam ⊶[6] 194 38.11 N 92.39 W
Bagnères-de-Bigorre 32 43.04 N 0.09 E
Bagnères-de-Luchon 32 42.47 N 0.36 E
Bagnes, Vallée de V 58 46.03 N 7.18 E
Bagneux 261 48.48 N 2.18 E
Bagni Acque Albule, It. 66 41.57 N 12.43 E
Bagni Acque Albule, It. 267a 41.57 N 12.43 E
Bagni del Masino 58 46.15 N 9.36 E
Bagni di Lucca 66 44.01 N 10.35 E
Bagni di Rabbi 64 46.24 N 10.48 E
Bagno a Ripoli 66 43.45 N 11.19 E
Bagno di Romagna 66 43.50 N 11.57 E
Bagnolet 261 48.52 N 2.25 E
Bagnoli del Trigno 66 41.42 N 14.27 E
Bagnoli di Sopra 64 45.11 N 11.53 E
Bagnoli Irpino 68 40.50 N 15.04 E
Bagnolo in Piano 64 44.46 N 10.40 E
Bagnolo Mella 64 45.26 N 10.10 E
Bagnols-en-Forêt 62 43.32 N 6.42 E
Bagnols-sur-Cèze 62 44.10 N 4.37 E
Bagñon 116 13.44 N 122.50 E
Bagnone 64 44.19 N 10.00 E
Bagnoregio 66 42.37 N 12.05 E
Bagno Vignoni 66 43.02 N 11.39 E
Bago (Pegu) 110 17.20 N 96.29 E
Bago □[8] 110 18.00 N 96.00 E
Bågø I 41 55.18 N 9.49 E
Bago ≃ 116 10.33 N 122.50 E
Bagod 61 46.53 N 16.45 E
Bagodar 124 24.05 N 85.52 E
Bagodo 152 6.25 N 13.23 E
Bagoé ≃ 150 12.36 N 6.34 W
Bagolino 64 45.49 N 10.28 E
Bagoni 146 7.53 N 10.43 E
Bagot □[6] 206 45.40 N 72.45 W
Bagotville, Base des Forces canadiennes ■ 186 48.20 N 70.58 W
Bağpınar 130 37.35 N 38.19 E
Bagrationovsk 76 54.23 N 20.39 E
Bagraula ⊶[8] 272a 28.34 N 77.04 E
Bagre 250 1.54 S 50.12 W
Bagrinovcy 78 49.17 N 27.56 E
Bagshot 42 51.22 N 0.42 W
Bag Tal 89 43.20 N 122.16 E
Bāguiati 272b 22.36 N 88.26 E
Baguio 116 16.25 N 120.36 E
Bagula 126 23.19 N 88.39 E
Bagumbayan 269f 14.28 N 121.03 E
Bagyrlaj ≃ 80 48.08 N 51.14 E
Bagzane ∧ 150 17.43 N 8.45 E
Bāh 124 26.53 N 78.36 E
Bāhādurābād Ghāt 124 25.09 N 89.42 E

Symbols in the index entries represent the broad categories identified in the key at the right. Symbols with superior numbers (⋀[1]) identify subcategories (see complete key on page I · 1).

Symbole im Register stellen die rechts im Schlüssel erklärten Kategorien dar. Symbole mit hochgestellten Ziffern (⋀[1]) bezeichnen Unterabteilungen einer Kategorie (vgl. vollständiger Schlüssel auf Seite I · 1).

Los símbolos incluídos en el texto del índice representan las grandes categorias identificadas con la clave a la derecha. Los símbolos con numeros en su parte superior (⋀[1]) identifican las subcategorías (véase la clave completa en la página I · 1).

Les symboles de l'index représentent les catégories indiquées dans la légende à droite. Les symboles suivis d'un indice (⋀[1]) représentent des sous-catégories (voir légende complète à la page I · 1).

Os símbolos incluídos no texto do índice representam as grandes categorias identificadas com a chave à direita. Os símbolos com números em sua parte superior (⋀[1]) identificam as subcategorias (veja-se a chave completa à página I · 1).

Symbol	English	Deutsch	Español	Français	Português
∧	Mountain	Berg	Montaña	Montagne	Montanha
⋀	Mountains	Gebirge	Montañas	Montagnes	Montanhas
)(	Pass	Paß	Paso	Col	Passo
V	Valley, Canyon	Tal, Cañon	Valle, Cañón	Vallée, Canyon	Vale, Canhão
≚	Plain	Ebene	Llano	Plaine	Planície
>	Cape	Kap	Cabo	Cap	Cabo
I	Island	Insel	Isla	Île	Ilha
II	Islands	Inseln	Islas	Îles	Ilhas
⊥	Other Topographic Features	Andere Topographische Objekte	Otros Elementos Topográficos	Autres données topographiques	Outros acidentes topográficos

ESPAÑOL — Nombre · Página · Lat.°′ · Long.°′ W = Oeste
FRANÇAIS — Nom · Page · Lat.°′ · Long.°′ W = Ouest
PORTUGUÊS — Nome · Página · Lat.°′ · Long.°′ W = Oeste

Nombre / Nom / Nome	Página / Page	Lat.°′	Long.°′
Bahādurgarh	124	28.41 N	76.56 E
Bāhādurpur	126	23.25 N	88.28 E
Bahaia, Monte ∧	144	11.20 N	49.45 E
Baha'i Temple ☋[1]	278	42.05 N	87.41 W
Bahamas □[1], N.A.	230	24.15 N	76.00 W
Bahamas □[1], N.A.	238	24.15 N	76.00 W
Bahār	128	34.54 N	48.26 E
Baharāgora	126	22.17 N	86.43 E
Baharampur	126	24.06 N	88.15 E
Baharpur	126	23.41 N	89.34 E
Bahau	114	2.49 N	102.25 E
Bahau ≃	112	2.34 N	116.20 E
Bahāwalnagar	123	29.59 N	73.16 E
Bahāwalpur	123	29.24 N	71.41 E
Bahçe	130	37.14 N	36.34 E
Bahçeköy ◈[8]	267b	41.11 N	28.59 E
Bahçeköy su kemeri ≊[1]	267b	41.03 N	28.59 E
Bahechuan	98	40.59 N	124.49 E
Baheri	124	28.47 N	79.30 E
Bahi, Pil.	116	13.53 N	123.38 E
Bahi, Tan.	154	5.59 S	35.19 E
Bahia □[3]	250	11.00 S	42.00 W
Bahía, Islas de la II	236	16.20 N	86.30 W
Bahía Azul	236	9.11 N	81.54 W
Bahía Blanca	252	38.43 S	62.17 W
Bahía Bustamante	254	45.08 S	66.32 W
Bahía Erasmo, Parque Nacional ♠	254	46.05 S	73.35 W
Bahía Honda	240p	22.54 N	83.10 W
Bahia Honda Key I	220	24.40 N	81.16 W
Bahia Honda Point ›	116	9.24 N	118.07 E
Bahía Kino	232	28.50 N	111.55 W
Bahía Laura	254	48.24 S	66.29 W
Bahía → Salvador	255	12.59 S	38.31 W
Bahīj	142	30.56 N	29.35 E
Bahir Dar	144	11.35 N	37.28 E
Bahi Swamp ☷	154	6.05 S	35.10 E
Bahjoi	124	28.24 N	78.37 E
Bahl	123	28.38 N	75.38 E
Bahlolpur	272a	28.37 N	77.24 E
Bahn	150	7.05 N	8.45 W
Bahnāy	142	30.23 N	31.04 E
Bahnayā	142	30.41 N	31.23 E
Baḥrah	144	21.24 N	39.29 E
Bahraich	124	27.35 N	81.36 E
Bahrain (Al-Baḥrayn) □[1], Asia	118	26.00 N	50.30 E
Bahrain (Al-Baḥrayn) □[1], Asia	128	26.00 N	50.30 E
Baḥr al-Ghazāl □[4]	140	8.30 N	26.00 E
Bahrām Chāh	128	29.26 N	64.03 E
Baḥrānī, Ḥālat al- I	128	24.23 N	54.14 E
Baḥrayn, Khalīj al c	128	25.45 N	50.40 E
Bahrdorf	54	52.23 N	11.00 E
Bahrein → Bahrain □[1]	128	26.00 N	50.30 E
Baḥrīyah, Al-Wāḥāt al- ⍑[4]	140	28.15 N	28.57 E
Bahser	130	37.57 N	39.18 E
Bahtīm	142	30.08 N	31.17 E
Baḥṭīṭ	142	30.29 N	31.38 E
Bāhū Kalāt	128	25.43 N	61.25 E
Bāhū Kalāt ≃	128	25.11 N	61.31 E
Bahulu, Pulau I	112	3.33 S	122.18 E
Bahu-mbelu	112	2.13 S	121.41 E
Bahūt	142	31.10 N	31.19 E
Baï	150	13.38 N	3.22 W
Bai ≃, Zhg.	102	32.10 N	112.20 E
Bai ≃, Zhg.	105	40.43 N	116.33 E
Baia	68	40.49 N	14.04 E
Baia-de-Aramă	38	45.00 N	22.49 E
Baía dos Tigres	152	16.36 S	11.43 E
Baía Farta	152	12.40 S	13.11 E
Baia Mare	38	47.40 N	23.35 E
Baiano	68	40.57 N	14.37 E
Baião	250	2.41 S	49.41 W
Baiardo	62	43.54 N	7.43 E
Baía Rica ≃	248	12.40 S	63.04 W
Baia Sprie	38	47.40 N	23.42 E
Baibao	105	39.04 N	115.31 E
Baibei	100	27.47 N	115.53 E
Baïbokoum	146	7.46 N	15.43 E
Baibuting	106	30.33 N	120.46 E
Baicang	124	30.14 N	90.44 E
Baicao	98	41.13 N	116.07 E
Baicaochang	102	32.08 N	103.59 E
Baicao Ling ⩘	102	26.10 N	101.20 E
Baicha	100	29.11 N	115.37 E
Baicheng, Zhg.	89	45.38 N	122.46 E
Baicheng, Zhg.	90	41.46 N	81.52 E
Baidian	106	30.47 N	119.14 E
Baidiao	102	28.07 N	101.28 E
Baidoa → Baydhabo	144	3.07 N	43.39 E
Baidunzi	102	43.11 N	95.19 E
Baidyabāti	126	22.47 N	88.20 E
Baidyanāth	124	24.29 N	86.42 E
Baidyer Bāzār	126	23.39 N	90.37 E
Baie-Comeau	186	49.13 N	68.10 W
Baie-Comeau-Hauterive, Réserve ♠	186	50.05 N	68.00 W
Baie-des-Ha90 Ha90	186	50.56 N	58.56 W
Baie-de-Shawinigan	206	46.34 N	72.45 W
Baie-des-Moutons	186	50.47 N	59.02 W
Baie-du-Renard	186	49.17 N	61.50 W
Baie-d'Urfé	206	45.25 N	73.55 W
Baie-Johan-Beetz	186	50.17 N	62.48 W
Baie-Mahault	241o	16.16 N	61.35 W
Baienfurt	64	47.49 N	9.38 E
Baiersbronn	58	48.30 N	8.22 E
Baiersdorf	60	49.39 N	11.01 E
Baies, Lac des ⊜	190	47.18 N	77.40 W
Baie-Sainte-Claire	186	49.54 N	64.30 W
Baie-Saint-Paul	186	47.27 N	70.30 W
Baie-Trinité	186	49.25 N	67.18 W
Baie Verte	186	49.56 N	56.11 W
Baieville	206	46.08 N	72.43 W
Baigezhuang	105	39.54 N	118.09 E
Baigneux-les-Juifs	58	47.36 N	4.38 E
Baigong	100	24.18 N	116.14 E
Baigou	105	39.07 N	116.01 E
Baigou ≃	105	39.06 N	116.00 E
Baiguoshu	106	30.45 N	119.07 E
Baigusi	102	33.10 N	103.52 E
Baihāli Jot ∧	123	32.51 N	76.32 E
Baihar	124	22.06 N	80.33 E
Baihe, Zhg.	100	29.12 N	120.55 E
Baihe, Zhg.	102	32.17 N	110.02 E
Baihebu	105	40.39 N	116.10 E
Baihegang	106	31.16 N	121.08 E
Baihekou	102	31.46 N	110.13 E
Baihou	100	24.18 N	116.48 E
Baihua	107	29.07 N	104.37 E
Baihua Shan ∧	105	39.50 N	115.35 E
Baijala	272b	22.51 N	88.16 E
Baijian	105	39.36 N	115.16 E
Baijiang	100	29.51 N	119.20 E
Baijiawu	105	39.30 N	116.28 E
Baijie	107	29.17 N	106.31 E
Baijietan	107	28.44 N	105.30 E
Baijnāth	124	29.55 N	79.37 E
Baiju	100	33.04 N	120.20 E
Baikal, Lago → Bajkal, ozero ⊜	88	53.00 N	107.40 E
Baikal, Lake → Bajkal, ozero ⊜	88	53.00 N	107.40 E
Baikal-See → Bajkal, ozero ⊜	88	53.00 N	107.40 E
Baikeshu	106	30.26 N	118.55 E
Baikonur → Bajkonyr	86	47.50 N	66.03 E
Baikunthapur	272b	22.59 N	88.13 E
Baikunthpur	124	23.15 N	82.33 E
Bailadores	246	8.15 N	71.50 W
Bailaiqiao	100	32.40 N	118.23 E
Bailang	89	46.57 N	120.05 E
Baildon	44	53.52 N	1.46 W
Baile	105	39.55 N	114.51 E
Baile Átha Luain → Athlone	48	53.25 N	7.56 W
Băile Govora	38	45.05 N	24.11 E
Băile Herculane	38	44.54 N	22.25 E
Bailén	34	38.06 N	3.46 W
Băile Olănești	38	45.11 N	24.16 E
Băilești	38	44.02 N	23.21 E
Bailey	192	35.46 N	78.07 W
Bailey Lakes	214	40.57 N	82.21 W
Bailey Run ≃	279b	40.35 N	79.47 W
Baileys Crossroads	284c	38.51 N	77.08 W
Bail Hongal	122	15.49 N	74.52 E
Bailian	102	24.09 N	112.22 E
Bailicun	102	25.45 N	110.33 E
Bailieborough	48	53.54 N	6.59 W
Bailin, Zhg.	100	27.12 N	120.10 E
Bailin, Zhg.	100	26.20 N	113.18 E
Bailin, Zhg.	107	29.11 N	105.57 E
Bailin, Zhg.	107	28.45 N	106.26 E
Bailingmiao → Darhan Muminggan Lianheqi	102	41.50 N	110.27 E
Bailique	250	0.58 N	50.04 W
Bailique, Ilha I	250	1.02 N	49.58 W
Bailleau-sous-Gallardon	261	48.32 N	1.39 E
Bailleul	50	50.44 N	2.44 E
Ba Illi	146	10.30 N	16.34 E
Baillie ≃	176	65.10 N	104.24 W
Baillie Islands II	176	70.33 N	128.10 W
Baillif	241o	16.01 N	61.45 W
Bailly-Romainvilliers	261	48.50 N	2.49 E
Bailong ≃	102	32.18 N	105.42 E
Bailonggang	106	31.15 N	121.44 E
Bailu ≃	100	32.25 N	115.34 E
Bailuchang	107	28.56 N	105.57 E
Bailu Hu ⊜	100	30.03 N	113.06 E
Bailundo	152	12.12 S	15.52 E
Bailuoji	100	29.37 N	113.15 E
Baima, Zhg.	106	31.35 N	119.10 E
Baima, Zhg.	107	30.03 N	103.44 E
Baima, Zhg.	107	29.09 N	104.16 E
Baimachang, Zhg.	102	29.18 N	107.30 E
Baimachang, Zhg.	104	41.59 N	122.30 E
Baimachang, Zhg.	107	29.40 N	103.54 E
Baimaguan	105	40.41 N	116.52 E
Baimakou	102	25.55 N	102.06 E
Baimamiao, Zhg.	102	36.58 N	108.08 E
Baimamiao, Zhg.	107	29.33 N	104.59 E
Baimao, Zhg.	106	31.39 N	120.52 E
Baimao, Zhg.	106	31.35 N	120.54 E
Baima Shan ∧	102	27.12 N	110.32 E
Baimashi	100	29.15 N	118.42 E
Baimazhai	100	28.06 N	115.50 E
Baimiaozi, Zhg.	89	46.18 N	123.35 E
Baimiaozi, Zhg.	98	40.34 N	120.36 E
Baimiaozi, Zhg.	104	41.55 N	122.12 E
Baimiaozi, Zhg.	107	29.47 N	106.29 E
Baimuqiao	106	32.01 N	120.19 E
Baimuru	164	7.30 S	144.49 E
Bain ≃	44	53.05 N	0.12 W
Baïna Bondio	152	5.10 N	16.33 E
Bainang	120	29.11 N	89.12 E
Bainbridge, Ga., U.S.	192	30.54 N	84.34 W
Bainbridge, N.Y., U.S.	210	42.17 N	75.28 W
Bainbridge, Oh., U.S.	218	39.13 N	83.16 W
Bainbridge, Pa., U.S.	208	40.05 N	76.40 W
Bainbridge Island I	224	47.37 N	122.33 W
Bainchi	126	23.07 N	88.14 E
Bainchipota	272b	22.52 N	88.16 E
Bain-de-Bretagne	32	47.50 N	1.41 W
Baing	115b	10.14 S	120.34 E
Bainiqiao	100	29.35 N	114.09 E
Bains-les-Bains, Fr.	58	48.00 N	6.16 E
Bains-les-Bains, Fr.	58	48.20 N	6.20 E
Bainville	198	48.08 N	104.13 W
Bainyik	164	3.40 S	143.00 E
Baipeng	102	24.09 N	109.25 E
Baipu	106	32.15 N	120.46 E
Baiqibao	104	41.48 N	122.30 E
Baiqiu	100	32.44 N	112.38 E
Baiquan, Zhg.	89	47.36 N	126.07 E
Baiquan, Zhg.	100	30.06 N	122.08 E
Baiqueyuan	100	31.48 N	115.05 E
Bair, Pa., U.S.	208	39.54 N	76.50 W
Bā'ir, Urd.	132	30.46 N	36.41 E
Bā'ir, Wādī V	132	30.58 N	37.09 E
Bairab Co ⊜	120	35.00 N	83.03 E
Baird	196	32.23 N	99.23 W
Baird, Mount ∧	202	43.22 N	111.06 W
Bairdford	214	40.37 N	79.52 W
Baird Inlet c	180	60.45 N	164.00 W
Baird Mountains ⩘	180	67.35 N	161.30 W
Baire	240p	20.19 N	76.20 W
Bairiki	174t	1.20 N	173.01 E
Bairin Zuoqi	90	44.00 N	119.00 E
Bair Island I	282	37.32 N	122.13 W
Bairkum	85	42.05 N	68.11 E
Bairnsdale	166	37.50 S	147.38 E
Bairoil	200	42.14 N	107.33 W
Bairrinho	256	22.36 S	47.06 W
Bairro Alto	256	23.29 S	45.21 W
Bairuopu	100	28.12 N	112.46 E
Bais, Fr.	32	48.15 N	0.22 W
Bais, Pil.	116	9.35 N	123.07 E
Baïse ≃	32	44.17 N	0.18 E
Baisha, Zhg.	100	34.20 N	113.14 E
Baisha, Zhg.	100	29.26 N	119.16 E
Baisha, Zhg.	100	25.40 N	118.59 E
Baisha, Zhg.	100	25.24 N	117.16 E
Baisha, Zhg.	100	34.22 N	112.32 E
Baisha, Zhg.	100	26.58 N	115.22 E
Baisha, Zhg.	100	24.39 N	113.31 E
Baisha, Zhg.	107	28.55 N	105.45 E
Baisha, Zhg.	107	29.04 N	106.07 E
Baisha, Zhg.	110	19.17 N	109.27 E
Baishaba	107	30.03 N	106.21 E
Bai Shan I	106	30.35 N	121.43 E
Baishanji	100	33.48 N	116.40 E
Baishantu	104	42.21 N	122.35 E
Baishapu	100	29.58 N	115.04 E
Baishatan	98	36.52 N	121.38 E
Baishe	100	27.02 N	116.20 E
Baishecun	105	40.10 N	116.18 E
Baishi, Zhg.	100	27.18 N	119.45 E
Baishi, Zhg.	100	26.48 N	119.46 E
Baishi, Zhg.	102	22.36 N	110.55 E
Baishidu	100	25.26 N	113.01 E
Baishiyi	107	29.29 N	106.22 E
Baishizhai	104	40.57 N	122.58 E
Baishui, Zhg.	100	28.42 N	113.04 E
Baishui, Zhg.	106	30.34 N	119.39 E
Baishui, Zhg.	107	30.06 N	105.38 E
Baishuifan	100	30.17 N	115.43 E
Baishuijiang	102	33.29 N	106.01 E
Baishun	100	25.12 N	114.01 E
Baishuxia	100	27.22 N	113.41 E
Baisinga	126	21.39 N	86.54 E
Baisley Pond ⊜	276	40.41 N	73.47 W
Baisogala	76	55.38 N	23.43 E
Bāisrasi	126	23.27 N	90.02 E
Baita, India	272b	22.27 N	88.11 E
Baita, Zhg.	106	31.48 N	119.35 E
Baitaḍī	124	29.32 N	80.26 E
Baital	126	22.57 N	87.28 E
Baitazi	98	42.19 N	120.19 E
Baitazibeigou	104	42.17 N	120.48 E
Bai Thuong	110	19.54 N	105.23 E
Baitings Reservoir ⊜[1]	262	53.40 N	1.59 W
Baitou	107	30.37 N	103.36 E
Baitoutan	102	32.30 N	106.56 E
Baitu	106	31.59 N	119.21 E
Baitugang	100	33.28 N	112.22 E
Baiwang	102	24.14 N	108.32 E
Baiwen	102	38.15 N	111.06 E
Baixa da Banheira	266c	38.39 N	9.03 W
Baixa Grande	255	11.57 S	40.11 W
Baixi	107	29.39 N	106.28 E
Baixiang	98	37.32 N	114.34 E
Baixingt	89	43.08 N	121.03 E
Baixio	250	6.44 S	38.43 W
Baixo Longa	152	15.42 S	18.50 E
Baiyan, Zhg.	100	28.04 N	120.02 E
Baiyan, Zhg.	106	31.08 N	119.38 E
Baiyang	100	34.25 N	112.12 E
Baiyang Dian ⊜	98	38.53 N	116.00 E
Baiyanghe	86	43.13 N	88.28 E
Baiyan Shan ∧	100	26.05 N	118.25 E
Baiyer River	164	5.35 S	144.10 E
Baiyin	102	36.47 N	104.07 E
Baiyinheshuo	89	44.31 N	119.51 E
Baiyintaohai	89	43.12 N	120.23 E
Baiyü, Zhg.	102	31.18 N	98.49 E
Baiyu, Zhg.	105	40.01 N	115.37 E
Baiyundu	100	26.10 N	118.47 E
Baiyunguan	271a	39.54 N	116.19 E
Baizhongpu	100	33.22 N	114.50 E
Baizi	107	30.06 N	105.43 E
Baja	30	46.11 N	18.57 E
Baja, Punta ›	232	29.58 N	115.49 W
Baja California	200	32.18 N	115.12 W
Baja California ›[1]	232	28.00 N	113.30 W
Baja California Norte □[3]	232	30.00 N	115.00 W
Baja California Seamount Province ✢	16	26.00 N	124.00 W
Baja California Sur □[3]	232	26.00 N	112.00 W
Bajada del Agrio	252	38.23 S	70.02 W
Bajan, Azer.	84	40.34 N	46.09 E
Baján, Méx.	196	26.32 N	101.15 W
Bajan Adraga	88	48.32 N	111.03 E
Bajan Agt	88	49.02 N	102.05 E
Bajanaul	86	50.47 N	75.42 E
Bajancagaan	102	45.00 N	98.59 E
Bajan Chajrchan	88	49.18 N	96.20 E
Bajanchongor	90	46.08 N	100.43 E
Bajanchongor □[4]	102	45.00 N	99.30 E
Bajancogt	88	45.54 N	106.10 E
Bajandaj	88	53.04 N	105.30 E
Bajandalaj	102	43.28 N	103.28 E
Bajandelger, Mong.	88	47.44 N	108.07 E
Bajandelger, Mong.	102	45.40 N	112.20 E
Bajan Dün	88	49.13 N	113.23 E
Bajandžargalan	102	45.40 N	107.59 E
Bajan Dzürch	88	50.12 N	98.58 E
Bajan-Enger	86	48.25 N	90.50 E
Bajango	88	48.55 N	106.06 E
Bajangol, Ross.	88	50.44 N	103.27 E
Bajan-Gol, Ross.	88	52.49 N	99.54 E
Bajangov'	102	44.44 N	100.24 E
Bajanleg	102	44.33 N	100.50 E
Bajan Nuur	86	48.54 N	91.14 E
Bajanölgij □[4]	86	48.20 N	89.50 E
Bajan-Öndör	102	44.47 N	98.39 E
Bajan-Ovoo, Mong.	88	47.47 N	112.05 E
Bajan-Ovoo, Mong.	102	42.57 N	106.07 E
Bajánsenye	61	46.48 N	16.23 E
Bajan Tümen	88	48.04 N	114.24 E
Bajan Uul, Mong.	88	47.40 N	101.30 E
Bajan Uul, Mong.	88	49.10 N	112.50 E
Bajan Uul, Mong.	88	49.41 N	96.20 E
Bājaur □[9]	123	34.50 N	71.30 E
Baja Verapaz □[5]	236	15.05 N	90.20 W
Bajawa	115b	8.47 S	120.59 E
Bajbičetau ⩘	85	41.12 N	75.15 E
Baj-Chak	88	51.13 N	94.34 E
Bajčunas	80	47.14 N	52.55 E
Bajčurovo	80	51.20 N	42.41 E
Bajdarackaja guba c	72	69.00 N	67.30 E
Bajdonovo	88	54.17 N	104.38 E
Bajdrag ≃	102	45.38 N	99.15 E
Bājegūn, Kūh-e ∧	128	31.28 N	55.51 E
Bājengdoba	124	25.54 N	90.31 E
Bāje Phukura	126	23.09 N	89.45 E
Bajer	88	55.44 N	99.30 E
Bajestān	128	34.31 N	58.10 E
Bajevo	86	53.17 N	80.46 E
Bajgakum	86	44.18 N	66.28 E
Bajganin	86	48.43 N	55.53 E
Bajghera	272a	28.32 N	77.01 E
Bājgīrān	128	37.36 N	58.24 E
Bajgul	80	48.49 N	49.08 E
Bajiaotai	104	41.14 N	121.14 E
Bajiazi, Zhg.	104	42.17 N	122.37 E
Bajiazi, Zhg.	104	42.21 N	121.27 E
Bajiazi, Zhg.	104	41.36 N	123.53 E
Bājil	144	15.04 N	43.16 E
Bajimba, Mount ∧	166	29.18 S	152.07 E
Bajina Bašta	38	43.58 N	19.34 E
Bajkadam	85	43.44 N	69.55 E
Bajkal	88	51.53 N	104.47 E
Bajkal, ozero (Lake Baikal) ⊜	88	53.00 N	107.40 E
Bajkalovo, Ross.	86	57.24 N	63.46 E
Bajkalovo, Ross.	86	57.45 N	67.40 E
Bajkal'sk	88	51.33 N	104.05 E
Bajkal'skij chrebet ⩘	88	55.00 N	108.40 E
Bajkal'skij zapovednik ♠	88	51.25 N	105.10 E
Bajkal'skoje	88	55.21 N	109.12 E
Bajkit	74	61.41 N	96.25 E
Bajkonyr	86	47.50 N	66.03 E
Bajkovo	80	54.47 N	44.51 E
Bajmak	86	52.36 N	58.19 E
Bajmok	38	45.58 N	19.25 E
Bajnazar	86	48.32 N	73.42 E
Bajo, Indon.	112	0.27 N	120.48 E
Bajo, Indon.	115b	8.35 S	119.01 E
Bajo, Canal ≊	266a	40.27 N	3.43 W
Bajo Baudó	246	4.58 N	77.22 W
Bajo Boquete	236	8.47 N	82.26 W
Bajool	166	23.39 S	150.39 E
Bajos de Haina	238	18.25 N	70.02 W
Bajos del Balsamar	234	17.34 N	100.48 W
Bajrački	83	48.22 N	38.32 E
Bajr'aki	80	54.43 N	53.24 E
Bajram-Ali	128	37.37 N	62.10 E
Bajsa	88	53.58 N	113.33 E
Bajseit	85	43.35 N	78.20 E
Baj-Sot	88	51.42 N	95.22 E
Bajsun	85	38.14 N	67.12 E
Bajtajlak	86	45.15 N	75.00 E
Bajulmati	115a	7.56 S	114.23 E
Bajžansaj	85	43.13 N	69.56 E
Bak	61	46.43 N	16.51 E
Bakacak	130	40.12 N	27.06 E
Bakal	86	54.56 N	58.48 E
Bakala	152	6.11 N	20.22 E
Bakaldy	80	55.39 N	44.44 E
Bakali ≃	152	4.34 S	17.06 E
Bakaly	80	55.10 N	53.48 E
Bakambe	152	5.39 S	23.37 E
Bakanas	86	44.50 N	76.15 E
Bakanas ≃	86	47.05 N	79.18 E
Bakap	114	4.26 N	101.04 E
Bakar	116	7.09 N	125.42 E
Bākarganj	124	22.33 N	90.21 E
Bakaruma	124	22.32 N	83.25 E
Bakau, Pulau I	271c	1.16 N	103.43 E
Bakbakty	86	44.35 N	76.40 E
Bakčar	86	57.01 N	82.05 E
Bakčar ≃	86	57.37 N	82.18 E
Bake	112	3.03 S	100.16 E
Bakebe	152	5.35 N	9.33 E
Bakel	150	14.54 N	12.27 W
Bakem	112	1.58 S	105.54 E
Bakenberg ∧[2]	54	54.35 N	13.07 E
Bakenkop	158	28.01 S	23.02 E
Bakeoven Creek ≃	224	45.12 N	121.05 W
Baker, Ca., U.S.	204	35.15 N	116.04 W
Baker, Fl., U.S.	194	30.47 N	86.40 W
Baker, La., U.S.	194	30.35 N	91.10 W
Baker, Mt., U.S.	198	46.22 N	104.17 W
Baker, Or., U.S.	202	44.46 N	117.49 W
Baker ≃, Chile	254	47.49 S	73.37 W
Baker ≃, Wa., U.S.	224	48.38 N	121.41 W
Baker, Canal Ʉ	254	48.00 S	74.00 W
Baker, Mount ∧	224	48.47 N	121.49 W
Baker Butte ∧	200	34.27 N	111.22 W
Baker Canyon V	280	33.47 N	117.38 W
Baker Creek ≃, B.C., Can.	182	52.59 N	122.30 W
Baker Creek ≃, Oh., U.S.	279a	41.21 N	81.54 W
Baker Creek ≃, Or., U.S.	224	45.15 N	123.14 W
Baker Island I, Oc.	14	0.15 N	176.27 W
Baker Island I, Ak., U.S.	182	55.20 N	133.36 W
Baker Lake	176	64.15 N	96.00 W
Baker Lake ⊜, Austl.	162	26.54 S	126.05 E
Baker Lake ⊜, N.T., Can.	176	64.10 N	95.30 W
Baker Lake ⊜, Il., U.S.	278	42.08 N	88.07 W
Baker Lake ⊜[1]	224	48.43 N	121.37 W
Bakersfield	226	35.22 N	119.01 W
Bakersfield South	228	35.20 N	119.03 W
Bakers Hill	168a	31.45 S	116.27 E
Bakers Island I	283	42.32 N	70.47 W
Bakerstown	214	40.39 N	79.56 W
Baker Street	260	51.30 N	0.21 E
Bakersville, N.C., U.S.	192	36.00 N	82.09 W
Bakersville, Oh., U.S.	214	40.21 N	81.39 W
Bakerville	158	26.00 S	26.06 E
Bakeshu	98	42.26 N	124.37 E
Bâ Kêv	110	13.42 N	107.12 E
Bakewell	44	53.13 N	1.40 W
Bakhra	126	22.24 N	88.11 E
Bākhrābād	126	23.43 N	90.53 E
Bakhri	124	25.35 N	86.16 E
Bākhtarān (Kermānshāh)	128	34.19 N	47.04 E
Bākhtarān □[4]	128	34.30 N	47.00 E
Bakhtegān, Daryācheh-ye ⊜	128	29.20 N	54.05 E
Bakhtiyārpur	124	25.28 N	85.31 E
Bakhuis	250	4.42 N	56.49 W
Bakile	154	13.58 S	35.15 E
Bakino	82	56.20 N	38.59 E
Bakinskaja	78	44.46 N	39.18 E
Bakinskij archipelag II	84	39.30 N	49.45 E
Bakır ≃	130	38.55 N	27.00 E
Bakitabu	154	1.29 S	35.34 E
Bakkafjörður	24a	66.04 N	14.45 W
Bakkaflói c	24a	66.10 N	14.45 W
Bakkagerði	24a	65.32 N	13.48 W
Bakkeswar	272b	22.25 N	88.22 E
Bakkeveen	52	53.05 N	6.15 E
Baklan	130	37.58 N	29.36 E
Baklanka	76	58.43 N	40.06 E
Bakloh	123	32.28 N	75.55 E
Bakluši	80	52.07 N	43.22 E
Bako, C. Iv.	150	9.09 N	7.37 W
Bako, Ityo.	144	5.50 N	36.40 E
Bakony ⩘	30	47.15 N	17.50 E
Bakool □[4]	144	4.00 N	44.00 E
Bakoondfontein	158	32.43 S	22.30 E
Bakori	150	11.34 N	7.27 E
Bakou → Baku	84	40.23 N	49.51 E
Bakouma	152	5.42 N	22.47 E
Bakovka	265b	55.41 N	37.20 E
Bakoy ≃	150	13.49 N	10.50 W
Bakruz'ak	86	52.59 N	58.42 E
Baksan	84	43.40 N	43.32 E
Baksan ≃	84	43.42 N	43.32 E
Bakšejevo, Ross.	80	55.44 N	39.53 E
Bakšejevo, Ross.	86	57.26 N	73.00 E
Baksir Chāndpur	126	23.30 N	89.44 E
Bakšty	76	53.56 N	26.11 E
Baksuk ≃	86	51.50 N	69.30 E
Baku (Baky)	84	40.23 N	49.51 E
Bakulin Point ›	116	8.33 N	126.22 E
Bakum	52	52.45 N	8.11 E
Bakumpai	112	1.26 S	113.05 E
Bakun	120	32.32 N	80.26 E
Bakung, Pulau I	112	0.04 N	104.27 E
Bakungan	114	2.56 N	97.30 E
Bakuriani	84	41.46 N	43.32 E
Bakury	80	52.22 N	44.42 E
Bakwa-Kenge	152	4.51 S	22.04 E
Bakwanga → Mbuji-Mayi	152	6.09 S	23.38 E
Bakyrly	86	44.21 N	67.48 E
Bal ≃	126	21.58 N	89.21 E
Bala, On., Can.	212	45.01 N	79.37 W
Bala, Sén.	150	14.02 N	13.10 W
Balâ, Tür.	130	39.34 N	33.08 E
Bala, Wales, U.K.	42	52.54 N	3.35 W
Balabac	116	7.59 N	117.04 E
Balabac Island I	116	7.57 N	117.01 E
Balabac Strait Ʉ	112	7.35 N	117.00 E
Bālā Bāgh	120	34.24 N	70.14 E
Ba'labakk	130	34.00 N	36.12 E
Balabalagan, Kepulauan II	112	2.20 S	117.25 E
Balaban	130	38.28 N	37.36 E
Balabanovo	82	55.11 N	36.40 E
Balabino	78	47.44 N	35.13 E
Balabio, Île I	175f	20.07 S	164.11 E
Balachany	84	40.29 N	49.54 E
Balachčin	86	54.09 N	89.23 E
Balachna	80	56.30 N	43.36 E
Balachta	86	55.24 N	91.37 E
Balachtison, gora ∧	86	54.36 N	93.50 E
Balaci	38	44.21 N	24.55 E
Bala-Cynwyd	285	40.00 N	75.14 W
Balad	128	34.01 N	44.09 E
Baladbandh	272b	22.52 N	88.07 E
Balad'ok	89	53.41 N	133.07 E
Balagansk	88	53.57 N	103.02 E
Bālāghāt	120	21.48 N	80.11 E
Bālāghāt Range ⩘	122	18.45 N	76.30 E
Balagny-sur-Thérain	50	49.18 N	2.20 E
Balaguer	34	41.47 N	0.49 E
Balaikarangan	112	0.50 N	110.26 E
Balaiselasa	112	1.48 S	100.50 E
Balaisepuah	112	0.27 N	111.13 E
Balaj	86	55.52 N	93.59 E
Balaka	152	4.51 S	19.57 E
Balakété	152	6.56 N	19.54 E
Balakirevo	82	56.30 N	38.51 E
Balaklava, Austl.	168b	34.09 S	138.25 E
Balaklava, Ukr.	78	44.30 N	33.36 E
Balakleja, Ukr.	78	49.14 N	31.44 E
Balakleja, Ukr.	78	49.27 N	36.52 E
Bālākot	123	34.33 N	73.21 E
Balakovo	80	52.02 N	47.47 E
Balal, Laga ≃	154	3.25 N	37.15 E
Balallan	46	58.05 N	6.35 W
Balama, Moç.	154	13.20 S	38.30 E
Bal'amā, Urd.	132	32.14 N	36.05 E
Balamban	116	10.30 N	123.42 E
Balambangan, Pulau I	112	7.15 N	116.55 E
Bālā Morghāb	128	35.35 N	63.20 E
Bālandi	272b	22.58 N	88.32 E
Balanga	116	14.41 N	120.32 E
Balangala	152	0.24 N	19.45 E
Ba Lang An, Mui ›	110	15.14 N	108.56 E
Balangero	62	45.16 N	7.31 E
Balangiga	116	11.07 N	125.23 E
Balāngīr	122	20.43 N	83.29 E
Balanguingui Island I	116	6.01 N	121.41 E
Bālān Ṣafar 'Ali	128	38.59 N	47.27 E
Balanṣūrah	142	27.55 N	30.41 E
Balantak, Gunung ∧	112	0.45 S	123.20 E
Balapulang	115a	7.03 S	109.05 E
Bālāpur	122	20.40 N	76.46 E
Balaqs	273c	30.10 N	31.17 E
Balaqṭar	142	31.05 N	30.13 E
Balaraja	115a	6.12 S	106.27 E
Balarāmbāti	272b	22.48 N	88.13 E
Balarāmpota	272b	22.31 N	88.08 E
Balarāmpur	126	23.07 N	86.13 E
Balaruc-le-Vieux	62	43.27 N	3.41 E
Balaši	80	51.24 N	49.55 E
Balašicha	82	55.49 N	37.58 E
Balašov	80	51.32 N	43.08 E
Balassagyarmat	30	48.05 N	19.18 E
Balāṭ	140	25.33 N	29.16 E
Balatan, Indon.	164	6.05 S	134.45 E
Balatan, Pil.	116	13.20 N	123.10 E
Balaton	198	44.14 N	95.52 W
Balaton ⊜	30	46.50 N	17.45 E
Balaurin	112	8.15 S	123.43 E
Balavé	150	12.23 N	4.09 W
Balayan	116	13.57 N	120.44 E
Balayan Bay c	116	13.51 N	120.47 E
Balazote	34	38.53 N	2.08 W
Balbi, Mount ∧[1]	175e	5.55 S	154.59 E
Balbieriškis	76	54.32 N	23.52 E
Balbigny	62	45.49 N	4.11 E
Balbina, Represa ⊜[1]	246	1.20 S	59.40 W
Balboa	236	8.57 N	79.34 W
Balbriggan	48	53.37 N	6.11 W
Balcad	144	2.23 N	45.23 E
Balcanoona	166	30.31 S	139.18 E
Balcarce	252	37.50 S	58.15 W
Balcarres	184	50.48 N	103.33 W
Bălcești	38	44.37 N	23.56 E
Balchaš	86	46.49 N	74.59 E
Balchaš, ozero (Lake Balkhash) ⊜	86	46.00 N	74.00 E
Balch Springs	222	32.43 N	96.37 W
Balcı	130	38.43 N	34.06 E
Balčik	38	43.25 N	28.10 E
Balclutha	172	46.14 S	169.44 E
Balcombe	42	51.04 N	0.08 W
Balcones Escarpment ⩘[4]	196	29.30 N	99.15 W
Balde	252	33.20 S	66.38 W
Baldeador	287a	22.53 S	43.02 W
Bald Eagle	214	40.42 N	78.12 W
Bald Eagle Creek ≃	210	41.08 N	77.24 W
Bald Eagle Mountain ∧	214	41.00 N	77.45 W
Bald Eagle State Park ♠	214	41.00 N	77.40 W
Baldegger See ⊜	58	47.12 N	8.16 E
Baldeneysee ⊜	263	51.24 N	7.03 E
Balderschwang	58	47.28 N	10.06 E
Balderstone	262	53.47 N	2.34 W
Balderton	44	53.03 N	0.47 W
Bald Head ›	162	35.07 S	118.01 E
Bald Hill ∧[2]	166	20.18 S	144.06 E
Bald Hill Branch ≃	284c	18.55 N	76.49 W
Baldhill Creek ≃	198	47.09 N	98.03 W
Bald Hills	171a	27.19 S	153.01 E
Baldichieri d'asti	62	44.54 N	8.07 E
Baldim	255	19.17 S	43.57 W
Bald Island I	162	34.55 S	118.27 E
Bald Knob	194	35.18 N	91.34 W
Bald Knob ∧, Ca., U.S.	282	37.25 N	122.21 W
Bald Knob ∧, Va., U.S.	192	37.56 N	79.51 W
Bald Knoll ∧	200	42.24 N	110.29 W
Bald Mountain ∧, Ct., U.S.	207	41.59 N	72.25 W
Bald Mountain ∧, Nv., U.S.	226	38.33 N	119.07 W
Bald Mountain ∧, Or., U.S.	202	44.48 N	123.33 W
Bald Mountain ∧, Or., U.S.	202	43.16 N	121.21 W
Bald Mountain ∧, Or., U.S.	202	44.36 N	117.53 W
Bald Mountain ∧, Vt., U.S.	210	42.55 N	73.09 W
Bald Mountain State Recreation Area ♠	216	42.46 N	83.14 W
Baldo, Monte ∧	64	45.47 N	10.48 E
Baldock	42	51.59 N	0.12 W
Baldock Lake ⊜	184	56.33 N	97.57 W
Baldone	76	56.45 N	24.24 E
Baldovino, Arroyo ≃	288	34.46 S	58.07 W
Baldoyle	48	53.24 N	6.08 W
Baldpate Pond ⊜	283	42.42 N	71.00 W
Balduinstein	56	50.20 N	7.58 E
Baldur	184	49.23 N	99.15 W
Baldwin, Fl., U.S.	192	30.18 N	81.58 W
Baldwin, La., U.S.	194	29.50 N	91.32 W
Baldwin, Mi., U.S.	190	43.54 N	85.51 W
Baldwin, N.Y., U.S.	210	40.39 N	73.36 W
Baldwin, Pa., U.S.	214	40.23 N	79.57 W
Baldwin, Wi., U.S.	190	44.58 N	92.22 W
Baldwin Bay c	276	40.38 N	73.35 W
Baldwin City	198	38.46 N	95.11 W
Baldwin Creek ≃	279a	41.22 N	81.51 W
Baldwin Hills ⩘[2]	280	34.00 N	118.22 W
Baldwin Lake ⊜	279a	41.21 N	81.51 W
Baldwin Park	228	34.05 N	117.57 W
Baldwin Peninsula ›[1]	180	66.44 N	162.15 W
Baldwinsville	210	43.09 N	76.19 W
Baldwinville	207	42.36 N	72.04 W
Baldwin-Wallace College ☋[2]	279a	41.23 N	81.51 W
Baldwyn	194	34.31 N	88.38 W
Baldy Mountain ∧, B.C., Can.	182	51.28 N	120.02 W
Baldy Mountain ∧, Mb., Can.	184	51.28 N	100.44 W
Baldy Mountain ∧, Mt., U.S.	202	48.09 N	109.39 W
Baldy Mountain ∧, N.M., U.S.	200	36.38 N	105.13 W
Baldy Peak ∧	200	33.55 N	109.35 W
Bale, Hrv.	64	45.02 N	13.48 E
Bale, India	272c	19.08 N	73.06 E
Bale □[4]	144	6.20 N	41.30 E
Bale-Akiosi	273a	6.41 N	3.21 E
Balearen → Balears, Illes II	34	39.30 N	3.00 E
Baléares, Îles → Balears, Illes II	34	39.30 N	3.00 E
Balearic Islands → Balears, Illes II	34	39.30 N	3.00 E
Balears □[4]	34	39.30 N	3.00 E
Balears, Illes (Balearic Islands) II	34	39.30 N	3.00 E
Balease, Gunung ∧	112	2.24 S	120.33 E
Bâle → Basel	58	47.33 N	7.35 E
Balegane	158	26.04 S	31.34 E
Baleh ≃	112	2.01 N	113.01 E
Baleia, Ponta da ›	255	17.40 S	39.07 W
Baleine, Grande rivière de la ≃	176	55.16 N	77.47 W
Baleine, Petite rivière de la ≃	176	56.00 N	76.45 W
Baleine, Rivière à la ≃	176	58.15 N	67.40 W
Balej	88	51.36 N	116.38 E
Balelasberg ⩘	158	27.30 S	30.07 E
Bale Mountains National Park ♠	144	7.00 N	39.40 E
Bâle-Mulhouse, Aéroport ⊠	58	47.35 N	7.32 E
Balen	56	51.10 N	5.09 E
Balena	152	0.55 N	20.00 E
Baleno	116	12.28 N	123.30 E
Baler	116	15.46 N	121.34 E
Baler Bay c	116	15.50 N	121.35 E
Baleshare I	46	57.31 N	7.22 W
Bāleshwar	126	21.30 N	86.56 E
Balesin Island I	116	14.26 N	122.02 E
Balestrand	26	61.12 N	6.32 E
Balestrate	70	38.03 N	13.00 E
Baléya	150	9.15 N	10.29 W
Baléyara	150	13.47 N	2.57 E
Balezino	80	57.58 N	53.00 E
Balfate	236	15.48 N	86.25 W
Balfes Creek	166	20.13 S	145.55 E
Balfour, N.Z.	172	45.50 S	168.35 E
Balfour, S. Afr.	158	26.44 S	28.31 E
Balfour, Scot., U.K.	46	59.01 N	2.55 W
Balfour, N.C., U.S.	192	35.20 N	82.28 W
Balfour Downs	162	22.50 S	120.50 E
Balfour Park ♠	273d	26.08 S	28.06 E
Balfron	46	56.04 N	4.20 W
Balgach	58	47.25 N	9.35 E
Bâlgarija → Bulgaria □[1]	38	43.00 N	25.00 E
Balgazyn	88	51.08 N	95.00 E
Balgo	162	20.09 S	127.48 E
Balgowlah	274a	33.48 S	151.16 E
Balguerie, Cap ›	174x	9.45 S	138.47 W
Balhannah	168b	35.00 S	138.50 E
Bāli	120	25.50 N	74.05 E
Bali □[4]	115b	8.30 S	115.00 E
Bali I	115b	8.20 S	115.00 E
Bali, Laut (Bali Sea) ⍑[2]	112	7.45 S	115.30 E
Bali, Selat Ʉ	112	8.18 S	114.25 E
Bāliākāndi	126	23.38 N	89.33 E
Baliangao	116	8.40 N	123.36 E
Bāliāpāl	126	21.40 N	87.17 E
Bāliāti	126	23.59 N	90.03 E
Balibago	116	13.37 N	121.18 E
Bali Barat National Park ♠	115b	8.15 S	144.40 E
Baliceaux I	241h	12.57 N	61.08 W
Bāli Chak	126	22.22 N	87.33 E
Balicuatro Islands II	116	12.39 N	124.24 E
Balicuatro Point ›	116	12.35 N	124.16 E
Balidianzi	98	41.13 N	124.49 E
Bālidiha	126	21.58 N	86.38 E
Balige	114	2.20 N	99.04 E
Bālighai	126	21.52 N	87.35 E
Balihan	98	41.29 N	118.41 E
Bālihāti	272b	22.44 N	88.19 E
Balıkesir	130	39.39 N	27.53 E
Balıkesir □[4]	130	39.45 N	27.50 E
Balık Gölü ⊜	84	39.47 N	43.34 E
Balīkh ≃	130	35.52 N	39.12 E
Balıklıtohma ≃	130	38.50 N	37.41 E
Balikpapan	112	1.17 S	116.50 E
Balikumbat	152	5.54 N	10.23 E
Balimbing, Indon.	112	5.55 S	104.34 E
Balimbing, Pil.	116	5.05 N	119.58 E
Balimo	164	8.03 S	142.56 E
Balin, Ukr.	78	48.52 N	26.40 E
Balin, Zhg.	89	48.19 N	122.19 E
Balincollig	48	51.53 N	8.35 W
Balindong (Watu)	116	7.55 N	124.12 E
Baling	114	5.40 N	100.55 E
Balingasag	116	8.45 N	124.47 E
Balingen	58	48.16 N	8.51 E
Balingian	112	2.55 N	112.32 E
Balingup	162	33.48 S	115.58 E
Balintang Channel Ʉ	108	19.49 N	121.40 E
Balintore	46	57.45 N	3.54 W
Balipu	105	39.53 N	117.48 E
Balışeyh	130	39.56 N	33.43 E
Baliuag	116	14.57 N	120.54 E
Baliung ≃	115a	6.50 S	105.52 E
Baliungan Island I	116	5.09 N	120.12 E
Baliyingzi	104	41.59 N	121.14 E
Baliza	255	16.15 S	52.25 W
Balizhuang, Zhg.	105	39.16 N	116.28 E
Balizhuang, Zhg.	271a	39.52 N	116.28 E
Balk	52	52.54 N	5.34 E
Balkach, Lago → Balchaš, ozero ⊜	86	46.00 N	74.00 E
Balkan □[8]	128	39.30 N	55.00 E
Balkan Mountains → Stara Planina ⩘	38	42.45 N	25.00 E
Balkan Peninsula ›[1]	10	44.00 N	23.00 E
Balkaria → Kabardino-Balkarija □[3]	84	43.30 N	43.30 E
Balkašino	86	52.31 N	68.46 E
Balkbrug	52	52.36 N	6.24 E
Balkh	120	36.46 N	66.54 E
Balkh □[4]	120	36.30 N	67.00 E
Balkh ≃	120	36.39 N	66.56 E
Balkhash, Lake → Balchaš, ozero ⊜	86	46.00 N	74.00 E
Balkhash → Balchaš	86	46.49 N	74.59 E
Balki	78	47.23 N	34.57 E
Ball	194	31.24 N	92.24 W
Balla	48	53.48 N	9.09 W
Balla Balla	154	20.26 S	29.02 E
Ballabhpur	272b	22.44 N	88.21 E
Ballachulish	46	56.40 N	5.10 W
Balladonia	162	32.27 S	123.51 E
Ballagh	48	52.35 N	7.59 W
Ballaghaderreen	48	53.55 N	8.36 W
Ballālpur	122	19.50 N	79.22 E
Ballan	169	37.36 S	144.14 E
Ballancourt	50	48.31 N	2.23 E
Ballangen	24	68.20 N	16.50 E
Ballantine	202	45.56 N	108.08 W
Ballantrae	44	55.06 N	5.00 W
Ballao	71	39.33 N	9.22 E
Ballarat	169	37.34 S	143.52 E
Ballard, Lake ⊜	162	29.27 S	120.55 E
Ballardvale	207	42.37 N	71.09 W
Ballata	70	37.58 N	12.41 E
Ballater	46	57.03 N	3.03 W
Ballaugh	44	54.20 N	4.32 W
Ball Bay c	174c	29.03 S	167.59 E
Ballé	150	15.20 N	8.35 W
Ballen	41	55.49 N	10.39 E
Ballenas, Bahía de c	232	26.45 N	113.26 W
Ballenato, Punta ›	286b	23.06 N	82.30 W
Ballengeich	158	27.52 S	29.59 E
Ballenita, Punta ›	252	25.46 S	70.44 W
Ballenstedt	54	51.43 N	11.14 E
Balleny Basin ✢[1]	9	67.00 S	170.00 E
Balleny Islands II	9	66.35 S	162.50 E
Balleroy	32	49.11 N	0.50 W
Ballerup	41	55.44 N	12.22 E
Ballesteros, Arg.	252	32.33 S	62.59 W
Ballesteros, Pil.	116	18.25 N	121.31 E
Balleza	232	26.57 N	106.21 W
Balleza ≃	232	27.23 N	106.17 W
Ball Ground	192	34.20 N	84.22 W
Ballı	130	40.50 N	27.03 E
Ballia	124	25.45 N	84.10 E
Ballico	226	37.27 N	120.42 W
Ballidu	162	30.36 S	116.46 E
Ballina, Austl.	166	28.52 S	153.33 E
Ballina, Ire.	48	54.07 N	9.09 W
Ballina, Ire.	48	52.49 N	8.26 W
Ballinakill	48	52.53 N	7.18 W
Ballinalack	48	53.37 N	7.28 W
Ballinascarty	48	51.40 N	8.51 W
Ballinasloe	48	53.20 N	8.13 W
Ballinderry ≃	48	54.40 N	6.31 W
Ballindine	48	53.39 N	8.59 W
Ballineen	48	51.44 N	8.56 W
Ballingarry	48	52.29 N	8.52 W
Ballingeary	48	51.49 N	9.13 W
Ballinger	196	31.44 N	99.56 W
Ballingry	46	56.09 N	3.20 W
Ballingslöv	41	56.13 N	13.51 E
Ballinluig	46	56.38 N	3.39 W
Ballino	64	45.58 N	10.48 E
Ballinrobe	48	53.37 N	9.13 W
Ballinskelligs Bay c	48	51.50 N	10.15 W
Ballintoy	48	55.14 N	6.22 W
Ballintra	48	54.35 N	8.08 W
Balloch	46	57.29 N	4.07 W
Ballon	50	48.10 N	0.14 E
Ballona Creek ≃	280	33.58 N	118.27 W
Ballos, Col d')(	62	44.18 N	6.36 E
Ballouville	207	41.52 N	71.51 W
Ballsh	38	40.36 N	19.44 E
Balls Pyramid I	160	31.45 S	159.15 E

Symbol	English	Deutsch	Español	Français	Português
≃	River	Fluß	Río	Rivière	Rio
≊	Canal	Kanal	Canal	Canal	Canal
L	Waterfall, Rapids	Wasserfall, Stromschnellen	Cascada, Rápidos	Chute d'eau, Rapides	Cascata, Rápidos
Ʉ	Strait	Meeresstraße	Estrecho	Détroit	Estreito
c	Bay, Gulf	Bucht, Golf	Bahía, Golfo	Baie, Golfe	Baía, Golfo
⊜	Lake, Lakes	See, Seen	Lago, Lagos	Lac, Lacs	Lago, Lagos
☷	Swamp	Sumpf	Pantano	Marais	Pântano
⍓	Ice Features, Glacier	Eis- und Gletscherformen	Accidentes Glaciales	Formes glaciaires	Acidentes glaciares
⍑	Other Hydrographic Features	Andere Hydrographische Objekte	Otros Elementos Hidrográficos	Autres données hydrographiques	Outros acidentes hidrográficos
✢	Submarine Features	Untermeerische Objekte	Accidentes Submarinos	Formes de relief sous-marin	Acidentes submarinos
□	Political Unit	Politische Einheit	Unidad Politica	Entité politique	Unidade política
☋	Cultural Institution	Kulturelle Institution	Institución Cultural	Institution culturelle	Instituição cultural
⊥	Historical Site	Historische Stätte	Sitio Histórico	Site historique	Sitio histórico
♠	Recreational Site	Erholungs- und Ferienort	Sitio de Recreo	Centre de loisirs	Area de Lazer
⊠	Airport	Flughafen	Aeropuerto	Aéroport	Aeroporto
■	Military Installation	Militäranlage	Instalación Militar	Installation militaire	Instalação militar
◈	Miscellaneous	Verschiedenes	Misceláneo	Divers	Diversos

Ballston 224 45.04 N 123.19 W
Ballston Lake 210 42.54 N 73.52 W
Ballston Spa 210 43.00 N 73.50 W
Ballville 214 41.20 N 83.09 W
Ballwin 219 38.35 N 90.32 W
Bally, India 272b 22.38 N 88.21 E
Bally, Pa., U.S. 208 40.24 N 75.35 W
Bālly ✈ 8 272b 22.39 N 88.21 E
Ballybay 48 54.08 N 6.54 W
Ballybofey 48 54.48 N 7.47 W
Ballybogy 48 55.07 N 6.34 W
Bālly Bridge ✈ 5 272b 22.39 N 88.21 E
Ballybunnion 48 52.31 N 9.40 W
Ballycanew 48 52.36 N 6.19 W
Ballycastle, Ire. 48 54.16 N 9.23 W
Ballycastle, N. Ire., U.K. 48 55.12 N 6.15 W
Ballyclare 48 54.45 N 6.00 W
Ballyconneely 48 53.26 N 10.02 W
Ballyconnell 48 54.07 N 7.35 W
Ballycotton 48 51.50 N 8.01 W
Ballycroy 48 54.01 N 9.51 W
Ballyduff, Ire. 48 52.27 N 9.40 W
Ballyduff, Ire. 48 52.09 N 8.03 W
Ballyferriter 48 52.09 N 10.26 W
Ballyfinboy ≐ 48 53.02 N 8.15 W
Ballygar 48 53.32 N 8.20 W
Ballygawley 48 54.28 N 7.02 W
Ballygorman 48 55.22 N 7.21 W
Ballygowan 48 54.30 N 5.48 W
Ballygunge ✈ 8 272b 22.31 N 88.21 E
Ballyhaise 48 54.03 N 7.19 W
Ballyhalbert 48 54.30 N 5.28 W
Ballyhaunis 48 53.46 N 8.46 W
Ballyhoura Mountains ʌ 48 52.20 N 8.35 W
Ballyjamesduff 48 53.52 N 7.12 W
Ballylongford 48 52.33 N 9.28 W
Ballymacoda 48 51.57 N 7.54 W
Ballymahon 48 53.34 N 7.45 W
Ballymakeery (Ballyvourney) 48 51.55 N 9.09 W
Ballymena 48 54.52 N 6.17 W
Ballymoe 48 53.42 N 8.29 W
Ballymoney 48 55.04 N 6.31 W
Ballymote 48 54.06 N 8.31 W
Ballymurray 48 53.35 N 8.08 W
Ballynahinch 48 54.24 N 5.54 W
Ballyneety 48 52.35 N 8.33 W
Ballynoe 48 52.03 N 8.05 W
Ballyquintin Point ≻ 48 54.20 N 5.30 W
Ballyragget 48 52.47 N 7.20 W
Ballysadare 48 54.13 N 8.31 W
Ballyshannon 48 54.30 N 8.11 W
Ballyteige Bay ⊂ 48 52.11 N 6.39 W
Ballyvaghan 48 53.07 N 9.07 W
Ballyvoy 48 55.12 N 6.12 W
Ballywalter 48 54.33 N 5.30 W
Balm 220 27.45 N 82.15 W
Balmaceda 254 45.55 S 71.41 W
Balmaceda, Cerro ʌ 254 51.25 S 73.11 W
Balmain 274a 33.51 S 151.11 E
Balme 62 45.18 N 7.13 E
Balmerino 46 56.24 N 3.02 W
Balmertown 184 51.04 N 93.44 W
Balmhorn ʌ 58 46.25 N 7.43 E
Balmoral, Austl. 166 37.15 S 141.51 E
Balmoral, S. Afr. 158 25.52 S 28.59 E
Balmoral Castle ⊥ 46 57.02 N 3.14 W
Balmorhea 196 30.59 N 103.45 W
Balmville 210 41.32 N 74.00 W
Balnacra 46 57.28 N 5.23 W
Balnearia 252 31.00 S 62.40 W
Balobanovo 82 55.51 N 38.14 E
Balobe 154 0.05 N 28.00 E
Baloda Bāzār 120 21.40 N 82.10 E
Balombo 152 12.21 S 14.46 E
Balong, Indon. 115a 7.57 S 111.26 E
Balong, Zhg. 102 36.17 N 97.20 E
Balonne ≐ 166 28.47 S 147.56 E
Balotra 120 25.50 N 72.14 E
Baloži 76 56.53 N 24.06 E
Balpahari Reservoir ⊜ 1 126 24.04 N 86.28 E
Balrāmpur 124 27.26 N 82.11 E
Balranald 166 34.38 S 143.33 E
Balş 38 44.21 N 24.06 E
Balsam Lake 190 45.27 N 92.27 W
Balsam Lake ⊜ 212 44.35 N 78.50 W
Balsamo 255 20.27 S 53.57 W
Balsas 250 7.31 S 46.02 W
Balsas ≐ 234 17.55 N 102.10 W
Balsas, Rio das ≐, Bra. 250 9.58 S 47.52 W
Balsas, Rio das ≐, Bra. 250 7.14 S 44.33 W
Balsas Sur 234 17.59 N 99.47 W
Balseiro ≐ 250 5.51 S 43.44 W
Balsham 42 52.08 N 0.20 E
Balsorano 66 41.49 N 13.34 E
Bålsta 40 59.35 N 17.30 E
Balsthal 58 47.19 N 7.42 E
Balta 78 47.55 N 29.37 E
Baltaj 80 52.28 N 46.38 E
Baltanás 44 41.56 N 4.15 W
Baltasar Brum 252 30.44 S 57.19 W
Baltasi 80 56.21 N 50.12 E
Baltasound 46a 60.45 N 0.52 W
Baltazar, Arroyo de ≐ 258 33.47 S 58.58 W
Bālti — Bel'c' 78 47.46 N 27.56 E
Baltic, Ct., U.S. 207 41.37 N 72.05 W
Baltic, Oh., U.S. 214 40.26 N 81.41 W
Baltic Bay ⊂ 190 48.22 N 83.43 W
Baltico, Mar — Baltic Sea ⚌ 2 24 57.00 N 19.00 E
Baltic Sea ⚌ 2 24 57.00 N 19.00 E
Baltic Station ✈ 5 265a 59.55 N 30.18 E
Baltijsk 76 54.39 N 19.55 E
Baltijskaja kosa ≻ 2 30 54.25 N 19.35 E
Baltim 142 31.33 N 31.05 E
Baltimore, Ire. 48 51.29 N 9.22 W
Baltimore, S. Afr. 156 23.15 S 28.20 E
Baltimore, Md., U.S. 208 39.17 N 76.36 W
Baltimore, Md., U.S. 284b 39.17 N 76.36 W
Baltimore, Oh., U.S. 188 39.50 N 82.36 W
Baltimore, University of ⊕ 2 284b 39.18 N 76.37 W
Baltimore Airpark ⊗ 284b 39.24 N 76.25 W
Baltimore Highlands 284b 39.13 N 76.38 W
Baltimore-Washington International Airport ⊗ 208 39.11 N 76.40 W
Baltinglass 48 52.55 N 6.41 W
Baltique, Mer — Baltic Sea ⚌ 2 24 57.00 N 19.00 E
Baltistān ◆ 1 123 35.18 N 75.37 E
Baltit 123 36.20 N 74.40 E
Baltoji-Vokė 76 54.28 N 25.06 E
Baltoro Glacier ⊓ 123 35.42 N 76.10 E
Baltra, Isla I 246a 0.26 S 90.16 W
Baltrum I 52 53.44 N 7.23 E
Bālu ≐, Bngl. 126 23.44 N 90.30 E
Ba Lu ≐, Viet 110 14.18 N 107.52 E
Baluarte ≐ 234 22.49 N 106.02 W
Baluarte, Arroyo V 196 27.09 N 98.07 W
Baluchistan ◻ 1 120 29.00 N 67.00 E
Baluchistan ◻ 9 128 28.00 N 63.00 E
Balud 116 12.02 N 123.12 E
Bālughāta 126 22.05 N 88.01 E
Bāluhāti 272b 22.39 N 88.16 E
Balui ≐ 112 2.42 N 113.47 E
Balukbaluk Island I 116 6.40 N 121.43 E
Balupe ≐ 76 56.57 N 26.55 E
Balurghāt 124 25.13 N 88.46 E
Balut Island I 116 5.24 N 125.23 E
Balvano 68 40.39 N 15.31 E
Balve 56 51.20 N 7.51 E
Balvi 76 57.08 N 27.17 E
Balvicar 46 56.14 N 5.38 W
Balwina Aboriginal Reserve ✈ 4 162 20.30 S 128.00 E
Balwyn 274b 37.49 S 145.05 E
Balxuca, Arroyo de la ≐ 266d 41.31 N 2.06 E
Balya 130 39.45 N 27.35 E
Balygyčan 74 63.56 N 154.12 E
Balykči 85 40.54 N 71.50 E
Balyksa 86 53.25 N 89.05 E
Balykši 80 47.05 N 51.54 E
Balyktyg-Chem ≐ 88 51.15 N 96.54 E
Balzac 182 51.10 N 114.01 W
Balzar 246 1.22 S 79.54 W
Balzers 58 47.04 N 9.30 E
Bal'zino 88 51.03 N 113.35 E
Balzola 62 45.11 N 8.24 E
Bām, Īrān 128 29.06 N 58.21 E
Bam, Īrān 128 36.58 N 57.59 E
Bama, Nig. 146 11.30 N 13.41 E
Bama, Zhg. 102 24.21 N 107.08 E
Bamaga 164 10.52 S 142.24 E
Bamaji Lake ⊜ 184 51.09 N 91.25 W
Bamako 150 12.39 N 8.00 W
Bāmangāchi 272b 22.46 N 88.31 E
Bāmangawān 126 24.14 N 86.49 E
Bāmanghāra 272b 22.31 N 88.28 E
Bāmanmura 272b 22.42 N 88.31 E
Bamao 100 29.26 N 120.59 E
Bamata 152 1.00 S 21.06 E
Bamba, Mali 150 17.02 N 1.24 W
Bamba, Zaïre 152 5.45 S 18.23 E
Bambamarca 248 6.41 S 78.32 W
Bambana ≐ 236 13.27 N 83.50 W
Bambang 116 16.23 N 121.06 E
Bambannan Island I 116 5.37 N 120.17 E
Bambara Maoundé 150 15.51 N 2.47 W
Bambari 152 5.45 N 20.40 E
Bambaroo 166 18.52 S 146.12 E
Bambāvi 272c 18.58 N 73.03 E
Bamberg, Dtsch. 56 49.53 N 10.53 E
Bamberg, S.C., U.S. 192 33.17 N 81.02 W
Bamber Lake 208 39.54 N 74.19 W
Bamberton 224 48.35 N 123.31 W
Bambesa 154 3.28 N 25.43 E
Bambesi 144 9.45 N 34.38 E
Bambezi 154 20.00 S 28.56 E
Bambili 154 3.39 N 26.07 E
Bambinga 152 3.42 S 18.54 E
Bambio 152 3.54 N 16.59 E
Bamboesberg ʌ 158 31.30 S 26.10 E
Bambool 150 8.10 N 2.02 W
Bamboo Creek 162 20.56 S 120.13 E
Bamboo Springs 162 22.04 S 119.38 E
Bambouti 154 5.24 N 27.12 E
Bambui 255 20.01 S 45.58 W
Bambujka 88 55.47 N 115.48 E
Bambula 154 1.17 S 25.38 E
Bamburgh 44 55.36 N 1.42 W
Bamburral ≐ 248 20.10 S 58.07 W
Bambuto ≐ 200 30.51 N 110.52 W
Bam Co ⊜ 120 31.30 N 91.05 E
Bamenda 105 39.35 N 117.37 E
Bamenda 152 5.56 N 10.10 E
Bamendjou 152 5.24 N 10.19 E
Bamfield 182 48.50 N 125.08 W
Bamhā 142 29.35 N 31.14 E
Bami 128 38.44 N 56.48 E
Bāmiān 120 34.50 N 67.50 E
Bāmiān ◻ 4 120 34.45 N 67.15 E
Bamiancheng 89 43.13 N 124.02 E
Bamingui 152 7.34 N 20.11 E
Bamingui ≐ 146 8.33 N 19.05 E
Bamingui-Bangoran ◻ 5 146 8.15 N 20.15 E
Bamingui-Bangoran, Parc National du ◆ 146 8.00 N 19.40 E
Bam Island I 164 3.35 S 144.50 E
Bāmna 126 22.19 N 90.06 E
Bāmndali ✈ 8 272a 28.33 N 77.03 E
Bamol 164 7.38 S 138.37 E
Bampton, Eng., U.K. 42 51.00 N 3.29 W
Bampton, Eng., U.K. 42 51.44 N 1.33 W
Bampūr 128 27.12 N 60.27 E
Bampūr ≐ 128 27.18 N 59.06 E
Bāmra Hills ʌ 2 120 21.30 N 84.30 E
Bamu ≐ 164 8.01 S 143.33 E
Bamum 120 32.30 N 93.15 E
Ban 150 14.05 N 2.27 W
Bana, Malaŵi 154 12.25 S 34.08 E
Ba Na, Viet 110 15.59 N 107.59 E
Banā, Wādī V 144 13.03 N 45.24 E
Banaba (Ocean Island) I 174d 0.52 S 169.35 E
Banabuiú 250 5.07 S 38.06 W
Banabuiú ≐ 250 5.20 S 39.05 W
Banabuiú, Açude ⊜ 1 250 5.30 S 38.50 W
Ban Aen 110 18.02 N 98.37 E
Banagher 48 53.11 N 7.59 W
Banagi 154 2.16 S 34.51 E
Banago 116 7.30 N 124.07 E
Banagrām 126 22.35 N 89.55 E
Banahao, Mount ʌ 116 14.04 N 121.29 E
Banalia 154 1.33 N 25.20 E
Banamba 150 13.33 N 7.27 W
Banamba, Austl. 166 24.28 S 150.07 E
Banana, Zaïre 152 6.01 S 12.24 E
Banana Creek ≐ 220 28.36 N 80.38 W
Banana Islands II 150 8.07 N 13.13 W
Bananal 250 8.33 S 49.26 W
Bananal ≐, Bra. 256 22.32 S 44.11 W
Bananal ≐, Bra. 255 20.48 S 51.24 W
Bananal, Ilha do I 250 11.30 S 50.30 W
Banana River ⊂ 220 28.25 N 80.38 W
Bananeiras 250 6.45 S 35.37 W
Bananga 110 6.56 N 93.54 E
Banao, Loma de ʌ 240p 21.51 N 79.36 W
Bānār ≐ 124 24.04 N 90.38 E
Banaras — Vārānasi 124 25.20 N 83.00 E
Banari 71 40.34 N 8.42 E
Bānaripāra 126 22.47 N 90.10 E
Banarlı 130 41.04 N 27.20 E
Banās ≐ 120 25.54 N 76.45 E
Banās, Ra's ≻ 140 23.54 N 35.48 E
Banat ◆ 1 38 45.20 N 20.40 E
Banate Bay ⊂ 116 10.58 N 122.48 E
Banaue 116 16.55 N 121.04 E
Banavie 46 56.47 N 5.07 W
Banay, Mount ʌ 116 13.42 N 121.04 E
Banaz 130 38.46 N 29.46 E
Ban Baen Phichit 269a 13.50 N 100.40 E
Ban Ban 110 19.38 N 103.34 E
Ban Bang Chan 269a 13.50 N 100.41 E
Ban Bang O 269a 13.49 N 100.30 E
Ban Bang Phli Yai 269a 13.35 N 100.42 E
Ban Bang Phraek 269a 13.53 N 100.26 E
Ban Bang Pu 269a 13.31 N 100.39 E
Banbar 120 30.49 N 94.59 E
Ban Bat 110 13.25 N 104.01 E
Banbidian 271a 39.54 N 116.32 E
Ban Blech 110 13.12 N 108.13 E
Ban Bonèng 110 17.58 N 104.35 E
Ban Bouang-nom 110 15.47 N 106.47 E
Banbridge 48 54.21 N 6.16 W
Ban Bua Chum 110 15.15 N 101.12 E
Banbuji 100 33.34 N 116.44 E
Ban Bung Fang Nok 269a 13.48 N 100.43 E
Ban Bung Na Rang 110 16.11 N 100.09 E
Ban Bungxai 110 15.42 N 106.42 E
Banbury 42 52.04 N 1.20 W
Bancahsaga 114 0.49 N 101.07 E
Bancalan Island I 116 8.14 N 117.06 E
Banc d'Arguin, Parc National du ◆ 150 20.00 N 16.20 W
Ban Chak 110 14.17 N 105.25 E
Ban Cha La 110 17.11 N 106.05 E
Bānchhārāmpur 126 23.46 N 90.48 E
Banchory 46 57.03 N 2.31 W
Banco, Punta ≻ 236 8.23 N 83.09 W
Bancos, Isla — Banks Island I 176 73.15 N 121.30 W
Bancroft, Ont., Can. 212 45.03 N 77.51 W
Bancroft, Id., U.S. 202 42.43 N 111.53 W
Bancroft, Ia., U.S. 190 43.17 N 94.13 W
Bancroft, Mi., U.S. 216 42.52 N 84.03 W
Bancroft, Ne., U.S. 198 42.00 N 96.34 W
Bancroft — Chililabombwe 154 12.18 S 27.43 E
Bancun 106 30.53 N 118.48 E
Banda, India 124 24.03 N 78.57 E
Bānda, India 124 25.29 N 80.20 E
Banda, Zaïre 154 4.11 N 27.04 E
Banda, Kepulauan II 164 4.35 S 129.55 E
Banda, Laut (Banda Sea) ⚌ 2 108 5.00 S 128.00 E
Banda Aceh (Kutaraja) 114 5.34 N 95.20 E
Bandabe 157b 15.31 S 49.04 E
Banda Besar, Pulau I 164 4.34 S 129.55 E
Bānda Dāūd Shāh 123 33.16 N 71.11 E
Banda del Río Salí 252 26.50 S 65.10 W
Banda Elat 164 5.39 S 132.59 E
Bandahara, Gunung ʌ 114 3.45 N 97.47 E
Bandai-Asahi-kokuritsu-kōen ◆ 92 38.16 N 139.57 E
Bandai-san ʌ 92 37.36 N 140.04 E
Bandak ⊜ 26 59.24 N 8.15 E
Bandama ≐ 150 5.10 N 5.00 W
Bandama Blanc ≐ 150 6.54 N 5.31 W
Bandama Rouge ≐ 150 6.54 N 5.31 W
Bandān, Īrān 128 31.23 N 60.44 E
Ban Dan, Thai 110 15.19 N 105.30 E
Bandanaira 164 4.32 S 129.54 E
Bandan'gou 105 39.08 N 115.11 E
Ban Dangtai 110 17.06 N 104.57 E
Ban Dan Lan Hoi 110 17.00 N 99.35 E
Bandar 115a 7.02 S 109.47 E
Bandar Baharu 114 5.08 N 100.30 E
Bandar Beheshtī 128 25.18 N 60.37 E
Bandardurian 114 2.21 N 99.44 E
Bandar-e 'Abbās 128 27.11 N 56.17 E
Bandar-e Anzalī (Bandar-e Pahlavī) 128 37.28 N 49.27 E
Bandar-e Būshehr 128 28.59 N 50.50 E
Bandar-e Chārak 128 26.43 N 54.16 E
Bandar-e Deylam 128 30.04 N 50.10 E
Bandar-e Gaz 128 36.47 N 53.59 E
Bandar-e Khomeynī (Bandar-e Shāhpūr) 128 30.25 N 49.05 E
Bandar-e Lengeh 128 26.33 N 54.53 E
Bandar-e Māh Shahr 128 30.33 N 49.12 E
Bandar-e Moghūyeh 128 26.35 N 54.31 E
Bandar-e Rīg 128 29.29 N 50.38 E
Bandar-e Torkeman 128 36.56 N 54.06 E
Bandar — Machilīpatnam 122 16.10 N 81.08 E
Bandar Penggaram — Batu Pahat 114 1.51 N 102.56 E
Bandarpulau 114 2.41 N 99.31 E
Bandar Seri Begawan 112 4.56 N 114.55 E
Bandawe 154 11.57 S 34.10 E
Bande 34 42.02 N 7.58 W
Banded Peak ʌ 200 37.06 N 106.38 W
Bandeira, Pico da ʌ 256 20.26 S 41.47 W
Bandeira do Sul 256 21.47 S 46.23 W
Bandeirantes, Bra. 255 13.41 S 50.48 W
Bandeirantes, Bra. 255 19.53 S 54.23 W
Bandeirantes, Bra. 255 23.06 S 50.21 W
Bandeirantes, Palácio dos ⊕ 287b 23.36 S 46.43 W
Bandeirantes, Praia dos ⊥ 2 287a 23.01 S 43.25 W
Bandéko 152 1.56 N 17.28 E
Bandel 272b 22.56 N 88.22 E
Bandeli 157a 12.55 S 45.13 E
Bandelier National Monument ◆ 200 35.45 N 106.20 W
Bandera, Arg. 252 28.54 S 62.16 W
Bandera, Tx., U.S. 196 29.44 N 99.04 W
Bandera, Alto ʌ 238 18.49 N 70.37 W
Banderas 200 31.01 N 105.23 W
Banderas, Bahía de ⊂ 234 20.40 N 105.25 W
Banderilla 234 19.36 N 96.56 W
Bāndhi 120 26.35 N 68.18 E
Bandholm 41 54.50 N 11.29 E
Bandiagara 150 14.21 N 3.37 W
Bandiantaolehai 102 41.41 N 104.06 E
Bāndīkūi 124 27.03 N 76.34 E
Bandipur, India 272b 22.44 N 88.26 E
Bandipur, India 272b 22.51 N 88.10 E
Bandipura 123 34.25 N 74.39 E
Bandirma 130 40.20 N 27.58 E
Bandirma Körfezi ⊂ 130 40.25 N 28.00 E
Bando 152 5.33 S 18.43 E
Bandol 62 43.08 N 5.45 E
Bandon, Ire. 48 51.45 N 8.45 W
Bandon, Or., U.S. 202 43.07 N 124.24 W
Ban Don, Viet 110 12.53 N 107.48 E
Bandon ≐ 48 51.42 N 8.30 W
Ban Don, Ao ⊂ 110 9.20 N 99.25 E
Ban Donhiang 110 18.05 N 101.48 E
Ban Dônko 110 16.12 N 106.17 E
Ban Don Muang 269a 13.55 N 100.36 E
Ban Don — Surat Thani 110 9.08 N 99.19 E
B'andovan 84 39.46 N 49.23 E
Bāndra ✈ 8 272c 19.03 N 72.49 E
Bāndra Point ≻ 272c 19.03 N 72.49 E
Bandrélé 157a 12.54 S 45.12 E
Banduān 126 22.53 N 86.31 E
Bandula 156 19.02 S 33.07 E
Ban Dulad V 144 8.26 N 45.54 E
Bandundu 152 3.18 S 17.20 E
Bandundu ◻ 4 152 4.30 S 18.30 E
Bandung 115a 6.54 S 107.36 E
Bāneasa 38 44.04 N 27.42 E
Baneasa 248 17.09 S 62.50 W
Banes 128 35.59 N 45.53 E
Bāneh 128 35.59 N 45.53 E
Banehra 272a 28.44 N 77.23 E
Banes 240p 20.58 N 75.43 W
Banff, Ab., Can. 182 51.10 N 115.34 W
Banff, Scot., U.K. 46 57.40 N 2.33 W
Banff National Park ◆ 182 51.38 N 116.22 W
Banfield ✈ 8 258 34.44 S 58.23 W
Banfora 150 10.38 N 4.46 W
Banga, India 123 31.11 N 75.59 E
Banga, Pil. 116 11.38 N 122.20 E
Banga, Zaïre 152 5.27 S 20.28 E
Banga ≐ 116 6.44 N 124.34 E
Bangad 116 12.10 N 123.24 E
Bangaduni Island I 126 21.34 N 88.52 E
Bangala Dam ✈ 6 154 20.40 S 31.15 E
Bangalore 122 12.58 N 77.36 E
Bangall 210 41.53 N 73.42 W
Bangalore 122 12.58 N 77.36 E
Bangalur — Bangalore 122 12.58 N 77.36 E
Bangangté 152 5.09 N 10.31 E
Bangaon 126 23.04 N 88.49 E
Bangassou 152 4.50 N 22.07 E
Bangda 102 27.59 N 98.40 E
Bangdag Co ⊜ 120 34.59 N 81.35 E
Bangeluo 120 32.27 N 90.35 E
Bangeswardi 126 23.29 N 89.44 E
Bangeta, Mount ʌ 164 6.15 S 147.04 E
Banggai (Luwuk) 112 1.34 S 123.30 E
Banggai, Kepulauan II 112 1.30 S 123.15 E
Banggai, Pulau I 112 1.37 S 123.33 E
Banggi, Pulau I 116 7.17 N 117.12 E
Banggong Co ⊜ 120 33.45 N 79.30 E
Banghāzī 146 32.07 N 20.04 E
Banghiang ≐ 110 16.03 N 105.15 E
Bangholme 274b 38.02 S 145.11 E
Bangi — Bangui 152 4.22 N 18.35 E
Bangil 115a 7.36 S 112.47 E
Bangjiang 140 11.23 N 32.42 E
Bangjun 105 39.59 N 117.16 E
Bangka, Pulau I, Indon. 112 2.15 S 106.00 E
Bangka, Pulau I, Indon. 112 1.48 N 125.09 E
Bangka, Selat ⊔ 112 2.20 S 105.45 E
Bangkalan 115a 7.02 S 112.44 E
Bang Kapi 269a 13.46 N 100.39 E
Bang Kapi, Khlong ⚌ 269a 13.45 N 100.36 E
Bangkaru, Pulau I 114 2.04 N 97.07 E
Bang Khen 269a 13.52 N 100.36 E
Bang Khun Thian 269a 13.42 N 100.28 E
Bangkinang 112 0.21 N 101.02 E
Bangkir 112 0.48 N 120.14 E
Bangko 112 2.05 S 102.17 E
Bangkog Co ⊜ 120 31.42 N 89.30 E
Bangkok — Krung Thep 110 13.45 N 100.31 E
Bangkok Station ✈ 5 269a 13.44 N 100.32 E
Bangkou 106 31.40 N 121.26 E
Bang Krathum 110 16.34 N 100.18 E
Bang Kruai 269a 13.48 N 100.29 E
Bangkulu, Pulau I 112 1.50 S 123.06 E
Bangkulua 115b 8.41 S 118.13 E
Bangladesch — Bangladesh ◻ 1 120 24.00 N 90.00 E
Bangladesh ◻ 1, Asia 118 24.00 N 90.00 E
Bangladesh ◻ 1, Asia 120 24.00 N 90.00 E
Bang Lamung 110 12.58 N 100.54 E
Bang Mun Nak 110 16.02 N 100.23 E
Ban Gnômmarat Kèo 110 17.36 N 105.10 E
Bangolo 150 7.01 N 7.29 W
Bangor, Ire. 48 54.09 N 9.45 W
Bangor, N. Ire., U.K. 48 54.40 N 5.40 W
Bangor, N. Ire., U.K. 44 54.40 N 5.40 W
Bangor, Wales, U.K. 44 53.13 N 4.08 W
Bangor, Ca., U.S. 226 39.23 N 121.24 W
Bangor, Me., U.S. 188 44.48 N 68.46 W
Bangor, Mi., U.S. 216 42.18 N 86.06 W
Bangor, Pa., U.S. 210 40.51 N 75.12 W
Bangor, Wi., U.S. 190 43.53 N 90.59 W
Bangor, Ja., U.S. 146 8.42 N 19.06 E
Bangoran ≐ 110 14.14 N 100.35 E
Bang Pa In 126 21.48 N 89.43 E
Bāngra ≐ 126 22.10 N 86.32 E
Bangriposi 196 31.43 N 99.08 W
Bangs 200 36.48 N 113.51 W
Bangs, Mount ʌ 110 11.12 N 99.31 E
Bang Saphan 98 40.23 N 122.46 E
Bangshi 278 42.16 N 88.08 W
Bangs Lake ⊜ 115a 6.30 S 110.45 E
Bangsri 256 22.52 S 43.27 W
Bangu ✈ 8 152 3.01 N 15.07 E
Banguè 116 17.36 N 120.37 E
Bangued 152 4.22 N 18.35 E
Bangui, Centraf. 116 18.32 N 120.46 E
Bangui, Pil. 116 18.34 N 120.44 E
Bangui Bay ⊂ 114 3.23 N 98.50 E
Bangunpurba 154 0.27 N 27.17 E
Banguru 102 23.46 N 107.34 E
Bangwei 154 11.05 S 29.45 E
Bangweulu, Lake ⊜ 154 11.30 S 30.15 E
Bangweulu Swamps ⌘ 106 31.39 N 121.29 E
Bangzhen 142 30.28 N 31.11 E
Banhā 110 14.40 N 106.35 E
Ban Hatgnao 110 18.11 N 102.40 E
Ban Hatkiang
Ban Hat Yai — Hat Yai 110 7.01 N 100.28 E
Ban Ha Yaek Pak Kret 269a 13.54 N 100.31 E
Ban Hèt 110 14.44 N 107.29 E
Banhine, Parque Nacional de ◆ 156 22.45 S 32.50 E
Ban Hin Heup 110 18.38 N 102.20 E
Ban Hom 110 15.33 N 98.46 E
Ban Hong 110 18.18 N 98.50 E
Ban Hong Muang 110 17.04 N 105.12 E
Ban Houayxay 110 20.18 N 100.26 E
Ban Huai Yang 110 11.36 N 99.40 E
Ban Hua Lamphu Thong 269a 13.32 N 100.38 E
Bani, Burkina 150 14.02 N 0.02 W
Bani, Centraf. 152 7.07 N 22.49 E
Bani, Pil. 116 16.11 N 119.52 E
Bani, Rep. Dom. 238 18.17 N 70.20 W
Bani ≐ 150 14.30 N 4.12 W
Bani, Jbel ʌ 148 29.30 N 8.00 W
Bania 152 4.00 N 16.07 E
Baniachang 120 24.31 N 91.22 E
Banī 'Adī al-Bahrīyah 142 27.15 N 30.55 E
Banī 'Adī al-Qiblīyah 142 27.15 N 30.56 E
Banī Aḥmad 142 28.03 N 30.46 E
Banī 'Alī 142 28.29 N 30.43 E
Baniara, Indon. 114 2.31 N 98.39 E
Baniara, Pap. N. Gui. 164 9.46 S 149.53 E
Bānibaha 126 23.42 N 89.37 E
Bani Bangou 150 15.03 N 2.42 E
Banie 30 53.08 N 14.38 E
Banié 150 12.43 N 6.25 W
Banifing ≐ 150 12.43 N 6.25 W
Banihāl Pass ✕ 123 33.31 N 75.13 E
Banī Hasan ash-Shurūq 142 27.54 N 30.51 E
Banī Khālid 142 27.50 N 30.44 E
Banikoara 150 11.18 N 2.26 E
Banima 152 5.26 N 23.54 E
Banī Majdūl 273c 30.02 N 31.07 E
Banī Mazār 142 28.30 N 30.48 E
Banī Muḥammadīyāt 142 27.17 N 31.05 E
Banī Mūsā 142 29.08 N 31.03 E
Banīnah 146 32.05 N 20.16 E
Banio, Lagune ⊂ 152 3.35 S 11.00 E
Baniou 34 35.25 N 4.21 E
Banī Rāfi' 142 27.22 N 30.53 E
Banī Salāmah 142 30.19 N 30.51 E
Banī Sha'rān 142 27.19 N 31.03 E
Banī Shuqayr 142 27.23 N 30.59 E
Banister ≐ 192 36.42 N 78.48 W
Banī Suhaylah 132 31.20 N 34.20 E
Banī Suwayf 142 29.05 N 31.05 E
Banī Suwayf ◻ 4 142 29.05 N 31.00 E
Banī 'Ubayd, Miṣr 142 31.01 N 31.39 E
Banī 'Ubayd, Miṣr 142 27.57 N 30.46 E
Banī Walīd 146 31.45 N 14.01 E
Bāniyās, Sūrīy. 130 35.11 N 35.57 E
Bāniyās, Sūrīy. 132 33.15 N 35.41 E
Banī Zayd 132 32.03 N 35.06 E
Banja Luka 38 44.46 N 17.11 E
Banjar 115a 7.22 S 108.32 E
Banjaran 115a 7.03 S 107.35 E
Banjarmasin 112 3.20 S 114.35 E
Banjarnegara 115a 7.23 S 109.41 E
Banjin 106 32.19 N 120.24 E
Banjir Kanal ⚌ 269e 6.07 S 106.45 E
Banjita 126 21.55 N 87.06 E
Banjošče ◆ 1 64 46.00 N 14.20 E
Banjuangou 105 40.44 N 115.11 E
Banjul (Bathurst) 150 13.28 N 16.39 W
Bank 84 39.25 N 49.15 E
Bānka 124 24.53 N 86.55 E
Ban'ka ≐ 265b 55.49 N 37.22 E
Banka Banka 162 18.48 S 134.01 E
Bankābāba 120 22.58 N 87.21 E
Bankana 152 4.25 S 16.11 E
Bankas 150 14.04 N 3.31 W
Ban Katèp 110 16.48 N 105.52 E
Ban Kavak 110 17.05 N 105.33 E
Bankberg ʌ 158 32.22 S 25.26 E
Ban Kèngkabao 110 16.48 N 105.04 E
Ban Kèngkok 110 16.05 N 105.13 E
Ban Kèngtangan 110 16.05 N 105.13 E
Bankeryd 26 57.51 N 14.08 E
Bankfoot 46 56.30 N 3.30 W
Ban Khamphô 110 14.38 N 106.17 E
Ban Khan Na Yao 269a 13.47 N 100.41 E
Bankhari 126 23.44 N 90.03 E
Ban Kheun 110 20.18 N 101.09 E
Ban Khlong Bua Loi 269a 13.51 N 100.41 E
Ban Khlong Kua 269a 13.49 N 100.43 E
Ban Khlong Samrong 269a 13.31 N 100.36 E
Ban Khlong Song 269a 13.55 N 100.37 E
Ban Khok Bao Sao 269a 13.51 N 100.39 E
Ban Khuan Mao 110 7.58 N 99.37 E
Bankilaré 150 14.35 N 0.44 E
Bankim 152 6.05 N 11.30 E
Bankipur 272b 22.48 N 88.14 E
Ban Kota Baru 114 6.27 N 101.21 E
Ban Krang 110 12.52 N 99.48 E
Ban Kruat 110 14.25 N 103.07 E
Banks, Eng., U.K. 44 53.41 N 2.55 W
Banks, Al., U.S. 194 31.48 N 85.50 W
Banks, Or., U.S. 224 45.37 N 123.06 W
Banks, Cape ≻ 274a 34.00 S 151.15 E
Banks, Îles II 175f 13.50 S 167.30 E
Banks, Point ≻ 180 58.36 N 152.18 W
Banksian ≐ 184 53.41 N 94.10 W
Banks Island I, B.C., Can. 182 53.25 N 130.10 W
Banks Island I, N.T., Can. 176 73.15 N 121.30 W
Banks Lake ⊜ 1 202 47.45 N 119.15 W
Banksmeadow 274a 33.58 S 151.13 E
Banks Peninsula ≻ 1 172 43.45 S 173.00 E
Banks Strait ⊔ 166 40.40 S 148.07 E
Banks / Torres ◻ 8 175f 13.50 S 167.20 E
Bankstown 170 33.55 S 151.02 E
Bankstown Aerodrome ⊗ 274a 33.55 S 150.59 E
Banksville 276 41.09 N 73.38 W
Banksville ✈ 8 279b 40.24 N 80.03 W
Ban Kum Daeng 269a 13.53 N 100.36 E
Bankumuna 152 4.28 S 19.57 E
Bānkura 126 23.15 N 87.04 E
Ban Laem Sing 269a 13.30 N 100.34 E
Banlaemen 104 41.51 N 122.27 E
Banlashanzi 104 41.26 N 123.28 E
Ban Lat Phrao 269a 13.47 N 100.36 E
Ban Le Kathe 110 15.49 N 98.53 E
Banliyuan 106 30.50 N 118.58 E
Ban Luk Kho 269a 13.34 N 100.27 E
Ban Mae La Luang 110 18.32 N 97.56 E
Ban Mae Mo 110 18.15 N 99.42 E
Bānmankhi Bazar 124 25.53 N 87.11 E
Banmauk 110 24.24 N 95.51 E
Ban M'diap 110 12.56 N 108.43 E
Ban M'drack 110 12.42 N 108.47 E
Banmian 100 26.02 N 118.06 E
Ban Mit 110 18.51 N 101.55 E
Ban Muangngat 110 19.05 N 104.04 E
Ban Muang Yot 110 19.22 N 100.34 E
Bann ≐ 62 55.10 N 6.46 W
Banna ≐ 62 45.11 N 7.51 E
Ban Nadou 110 15.51 N 105.38 E
Ban Nagnom 110 17.02 N 105.44 E
Ban Nahin 110 18.14 N 104.13 E
Bannaja 88 57.05 N 108.12 E
Ban Nakala 110 16.17 N 105.11 E
Ban Na Kha 110 9.26 N 98.28 E
Ban Nalan 110 15.50 N 106.04 E
Ban Nalè 110 18.42 N 101.34 E
Ban Namcha 110 19.09 N 102.53 E
Ban Nam Chan 110 18.01 N 103.53 E
Ban Namnga 110 20.22 N 102.19 E
Ban Nam Tao 110 17.50 N 101.15 E
Ban Nam Thaeng 110 15.34 N 105.30 E
Ban Naxon 110 18.12 N 103.05 E
Ban Naxouang 110 18.25 N 104.29 E
Bannay 50 47.23 N 2.53 E
Banner Elk 192 36.09 N 81.52 W
Bannerman, Mount ʌ 2 162 19.26 S 127.10 E
Banner Park ◆ 284b 39.19 N 76.42 W
Bannertown 192 36.29 N 80.34 W
Bannesdorf 54 54.28 N 11.13 E
Bannewitz 54 51.00 N 13.43 E
Ban Ngam 110 20.11 N 104.53 E
Bannikovo 86 56.07 N 70.17 E
Banning 228 33.55 N 116.52 W
Banningville — Bandundu 152 3.18 S 17.20 E
Bannister 168a 32.40 S 116.33 E
Bannister ≐ 168a 32.49 S 116.29 E
Bannister Ditch ⚌ 279a 41.18 N 82.01 W
Bannock 214 40.06 N 80.59 W
Bannockburn, Austl. 169 38.03 S 144.10 E
Bannockburn, Scot., U.K. 46 56.06 N 3.55 W
Bannockburn, Il., U.S. 278 42.12 N 87.52 W
Bannockburn, Zimb. 154 20.16 S 29.51 E
Bannockburn Battlesite ⊥ 46 56.06 N 3.54 W
Bannock Creek ≐ 202 42.53 N 112.40 W
Bannock Peak ʌ 202 42.36 N 112.42 W
Ban Nong Lumphuk 110 14.40 N 102.43 E
Ban Nong Takhian 110 13.08 N 101.24 E
Bannovka 86 53.45 N 62.57 E
Bannovskij 83 49.02 N 37.35 E
Bannu 123 32.59 N 70.36 E
Bánokszentgyörgy 30 46.33 N 16.47 E
Banon 62 44.02 N 5.38 E
Ban O Pao 269a 13.50 N 100.38 E
Baños, Ec. 246 1.24 S 78.25 W
Baños, Perú 248 10.05 S 76.45 W
Baños de Cerrato 34 41.55 N 4.28 W
Banow 120 35.38 N 69.15 E
Ban Pak Bong 110 18.28 N 98.49 E
Ban Pak Chan 110 10.32 N 98.51 E
Ban Pakha 110 14.38 N 107.24 E
Ban Pakkhop 110 19.49 N 100.36 E
Ban Pak Nam 110 10.26 N 99.15 E
Ban Pakneun 110 19.14 N 101.50 E
Banpās 126 23.24 N 87.45 E
Ban Phai, Thai 110 16.04 N 102.44 E
Ban Phai, Thai 110 17.33 N 103.00 E
Ban Phak Pang 110 12.38 N 101.26 E
Ban Pho 110 13.36 N 101.05 E
Ban Phon 110 15.25 N 106.42 E
Ban Phông Pho 110 14.36 N 105.52 E
Banphot Phisai 110 15.56 N 99.59 E
Ban Phraek Kasa 269a 13.34 N 100.38 E
Ban Phya 110 13.31 N 102.55 E
Ban Pong 110 13.49 N 99.53 E
Banpu 98 34.28 N 119.18 E
Banpura 126 22.27 N 87.22 E
Banqiao, Zhg. 100 30.06 N 120.27 E
Banqiao, Zhg. 100 33.21 N 116.41 E
Banqiao, Zhg. 105 39.56 N 115.51 E
Banqiao, Zhg. 106 35.56 N 118.39 E
Banqiao, Zhg. 107 29.31 N 105.59 E
Banqiao, Zhg. 107 29.54 N 104.21 E
Banqiaochang 107 32.19 N 16.37 E
Banqiaoji 97 29.41 N 103.47 E
Banqiaozi 98 35.07 N 118.42 E
Banquan 106 32.19 N 120.24 E
Banraeaba 174t 1.20 N 173.02 E
Ban Ron Phibun 110 8.09 N 99.51 E
Ban Sa-ang 110 17.26 N 105.44 E
Ban Saen To 110 16.05 N 99.51 E
Ban Sakhla 269a 13.32 N 100.30 E
Bansalan 116 6.47 N 125.14 E
Ban Salik 110 18.30 N 100.45 E
Ban Samang 110 19.12 N 102.36 E
Ban Sam Phan 110 8.33 N 99.09 E
Ban Sam Pong 110 18.32 N 102.47 E
Ban Samrong 110 14.23 N 102.50 E
Bansang 150 13.26 N 14.39 W
Ban San Xieng La 110 19.27 N 102.26 E
Bansberia 126 22.58 N 88.24 E
Bānsda 120 20.45 N 73.22 E
Bansha 48 52.28 N 8.04 W
Banshadhāra ≐ 122 18.21 N 84.08 E
Banshanpu 100 27.42 N 113.24 E
Banshi 100 25.20 N 115.23 E
Banshigou 104 41.09 N 120.58 E
Bānsi 124 27.11 N 82.56 E
Bānsi ≐ 126 23.50 N 90.15 E
Ban Signo 110 17.51 N 105.04 E
Banská Bystrica 30 48.44 N 19.07 E
Banská Štiavnica 30 48.28 N 18.56 E
Bansko 38 41.50 N 23.29 E
Bānskupi 126 24.10 N 86.41 E
Ban Songkhon 110 17.58 N 105.13 E
Ban Song Kong 269a 13.53 N 100.34 E
Ban Sop Huai Hai 110 19.33 N 98.05 E
Ban Sôpheung 110 18.33 N 104.17 E
Banstala 272b 22.32 N 88.25 E
Banstead 42 51.19 N 0.12 W
Bānswāra 120 23.33 N 74.27 E
Banta 226 37.45 N 121.22 W
Banta, Pulau I 115b 8.25 S 119.14 E
Bantaeng 112 5.32 S 119.56 E
Bantaian 114 1.56 N 100.54 E
Bantaji 100 32.41 N 118.35 E
Ban Takhlo 110 15.27 N 100.48 E
Bantam 207 41.43 N 73.14 W
Bantam Lake ⊜ 207 41.42 N 73.13 W
Ban Tamru 269a 13.31 N 100.41 E
Ban Tao Pun 269a 13.53 N 100.41 E
Bantarkawung 115a 7.13 S 108.55 E
Bantayan 116 11.10 N 123.43 E
Bantayan Island I 116 11.13 N 123.44 E
Banteer 48 52.07 N 8.54 W
Banteln 52 52.04 N 9.44 E
Banten 115a 6.03 S 106.09 E
Banten, Teluk ⊂ 115a 6.00 S 106.10 E
Bantenan, Tanjung ≻ 115a 8.47 S 114.33 E
Ban Teung 110 17.54 N 105.29 E
Ban Thabôk 110 18.22 N 103.12 E
Ban Thanoun 110 19.50 N 101.29 E
Ban Thapayi 110 16.19 N 105.41 E
Bantheville 56 49.21 N 5.05 E
Ban Thieng 110 19.08 N 102.12 E
Ban Tian Sa 110 18.43 N 103.14 E
Bantigui Point ≻ 116 13.41 N 121.28 E
Banting 114 2.49 N 101.30 E
Banton (Jones) 116 12.57 N 122.05 E
Ban Tong Khop 110 17.04 N 104.16 E
Banton Island I 116 12.56 N 122.04 E
Bāntra 272b 22.35 N 88.19 E
Bantry 48 51.41 N 9.27 W
Bantry Bay ⊂ 48 51.38 N 9.48 W
Bantul 115a 7.54 S 110.20 E
Bāntva 120 21.29 N 70.05 E
Banūr 124 30.34 N 76.43 E
Ban Van Hom 110 18.44 N 104.01 E
Ban Vat 110 16.54 N 104.56 E
Banwell 42 51.20 N 2.52 W
Banwy ≐ 42 52.42 N 3.16 W
Ban Xènkhalôk 110 19.42 N 101.54 E
Banxiancun 106 30.33 N 119.42 E
Ban Xot 110 18.11 N 104.05 E
Banya, Punta de la ≻ 34 40.34 N 0.38 E
Banyak, Kepulauan II 114 2.10 N 97.15 E
Ban Ya Plong 110 8.53 N 98.35 E
Banyo 152 6.45 N 11.49 E
Banyoles 34 42.07 N 2.46 E
Banyumas 115a 7.31 S 109.17 E
Banyuwangi 115a 8.12 S 114.21 E
Banyuwedang 115b 8.08 S 114.36 E
Banz 164 5.47 S 144.37 E
Banzare Coast ≻ 2 9 67.00 S 126.00 E
Banzhuyuan 107 28.44 N 106.18 E
Banzi, It. 68 40.52 N 16.01 E
Banzi, Zhg. 100 24.18 N 117.19 E
Bao ≐, Zhg. 100 33.40 N 116.33 E
Bao ≐, Zhg. 105 40.31 N 118.17 E
Bao ≐, Zhg. 105 39.02 N 115.39 E
Bao, Ouadi V 146 16.36 N 23.55 E
Bao'an, Zhg. 100 30.11 N 114.43 E
Bao'an, Zhg. 106 31.46 N 121.21 E
Baoancun 89 48.13 N 125.52 E
Baoan — Zhuolu 105 40.22 N 115.12 E
Baochang 106 32.04 N 121.25 E
Baochang — Taibus Qi 98 41.56 N 115.22 E
Baocheng 102 33.08 N 107.09 E
Baode 102 39.06 N 111.11 E
Baodi 105 39.44 N 117.17 E
Baoding 105 38.52 N 115.29 E
Baofeng 100 33.55 N 113.02 E
Baofu 106 30.31 N 119.29 E
Baoguosi 107 29.35 N 103.25 E
Bao Ha 110 22.11 N 104.21 E
Baohekou 105 40.32 N 118.15 E
Baoji, Zhg. 100 33.08 N 118.19 E
Baoji, Zhg. 102 34.23 N 107.09 E
Baojiagou 105 40.05 N 115.22 E
Baojiapu 104 40.51 N 122.14 E
Baojiatou 106 30.11 N 119.48 E
Baojiawazi 104 41.38 N 123.24 E
Baojing 102 28.43 N 109.25 E
Baokang — Horqin Zuoyi Zhongqi 89 44.07 N 123.18 E
Bao Lac, Viet 110 22.57 N 105.40 E
Bao Lac, Viet 110 11.32 N 107.48 E
Baolin 107 30.24 N 105.02 E
Baolizhen 89 42.56 N 123.46 E
Baolunyuan 102 32.22 N 105.40 E
Baomachang 107 29.58 N 104.12 E
Baon 116 6.47 N 126.05 E
Baonian 116 31.55 N 119.21 E
Baoqiao 102 23.31 N 106.24 E
Baoqing 89 46.21 N 132.14 E
Baoqing 98 36.16 N 119.04 E
Baoquan 152 5.40 N 15.58 E
Baoshan 102 32.39 N 113.54 E
Baoshan, Zhg. 102 26.19 N 104.27 E
Baoshan, Zhg. 102 25.09 N 99.09 E
Baoshan, Zhg. 106 31.25 N 121.29 E
Baoting 110 18.42 N 109.40 E
Baotou (Paotow) 102 40.40 N 109.59 E
Baotun 104 42.29 N 122.52 E
Baoulé ≐ 150 13.33 N 9.54 W
Baowei 102 22.39 N 106.50 E
Baoxikou 100 23.16 N 115.14 E
Baoxingchang 107 29.38 N 105.41 E
Baoxinji 100 32.35 N 115.00 E
Baoyi 100 32.13 N 116.42 E
Baoying 100 33.16 N 119.20 E
Baozhuchang 107 29.48 N 104.15 E
Baozidian 105 40.11 N 117.48 E
Bāp 120 27.23 N 72.21 E
Bapanling 104 40.58 N 123.08 E
Bāpatla 122 15.54 N 80.28 E
Bapaume 50 50.06 N 2.51 E
Bapchule 200 33.08 N 111.52 W
Bapsfontein 158 26.08 S 28.25 E
Baptiste Lake ⊜ 212 45.07 N 78.02 W
Baptistown 208 40.31 N 75.00 W
Bāqa el Gharbīya 132 32.25 N 35.03 E
Baqar, Maṣrif Bahr al- ⚌ 142 31.05 N 32.08 E
Baqar, Wādī al- V 146 27.49 N 18.37 E
Baqēn 120 31.56 N 94.00 E
Baqing 120 32.15 N 93.30 E
B'aqlīn 132 33.41 N 35.33 E
Ba'qūbah 128 33.45 N 44.38 E
Baquedano 252 23.20 S 69.51 W
Baqueiro 269c 10.48 N 106.38 E
Bar, Jugo. 38 42.05 N 19.06 E
Bar, Ross. 88 51.17 N 107.33 E
Bar, Ukr. 78 49.04 N 27.40 E
Bar ≐ 56 49.42 N 4.50 E
Bāra, India 124 25.13 N 87.22 E
Bāra, India 272b 22.43 N 88.31 E
Bāra, India 272b 22.46 N 88.17 E
Bara, Nig. 146 10.22 N 10.44 E
Baraawe 144 1.06 N 44.03 E
Barabai 112 2.35 S 115.23 E
Bara Bāngurda 126 22.57 N 86.24 E
Bāra Banki 124 26.55 N 81.12 E
Barabanovo 82 54.43 N 38.18 E
Barabash 126 23.02 N 86.22 E
Barabinsk 86 55.21 N 78.21 E
Barabinskaja step' ⚌ 86 55.00 N 79.00 E
Baraboo 190 43.28 N 89.44 W
Baraboo ≐ 190 43.29 N 89.26 W
Baraboulé 150 14.13 N 1.51 W
Baracaju ≐ 255 12.21 S 51.00 W
Barachit 34 43.18 N 2.59 W
Baracaldo 144 14.39 N 39.27 E
Barachois Pond Provincial Park ◆ 186 48.30 N 58.14 W
Baracoa, Cuba 240p 20.21 N 74.30 W
Baracoa, Hond. 236 15.43 N 87.52 W
Baradā ≐ 132 33.30 N 36.28 E
Baradero 258 33.48 S 59.30 W
Baradero ≐ 258 33.55 S 59.16 W

Symbols in the index entries represent the broad categories identified in the key at the right. Symbols with superior numbers (ʌ[1]) identify subcategories (see complete key on page I · 1).

Symbole im Register stellen die rechts im Schlüssel erklärten Kategorien dar. Symbole mit hochgestellten Ziffern (ʌ[1]) bezeichnen Unterabteilungen einer Kategorie (vgl. vollständiger Schlüssel auf Seite I · 1).

Los símbolos incluidos en el texto del índice representan las grandes categorías identificadas con la clave a la derecha. Los símbolos con numeros en su parte superior (ʌ[1]) identifican las subcategorías (véase la clave completa en la página I · 1).

Les symboles de l'index représentent les catégories indiquées dans la légende à droite. Les symboles suivis d'un indice (ʌ[1]) représentent des sous-catégories (voir légende complète à la page I · 1).

Os símbolos incluídos no texto do índice representam as grandes categorias identificadas com a chave à direita. Os símbolos com números em sua parte superior (ʌ[1]) identificam as subcategorias (veja-se a chave completa à página I · 1).

ʌ Mountain	Berg	Montaña	Montagne	Montanha
ʌ Mountains	Gebirge	Montañas	Montagnes	Montanhas
✕ Pass	Paß	Paso	Col	Passo
V Valley, Canyon	Tal, Cañon	Valle, Cañón	Vallée, Canyon	Vale, Canhão
⌓ Plain	Ebene	Llano	Plaine	Planície
≻ Cape	Kap	Cabo	Cap	Cabo
I Island	Insel	Isla	Île	Ilha
II Islands	Inseln	Islas	Îles	Ilhas
⊥ Other Topographic Features	Andere Topographische Objekte	Otros Elementos Topográficos	Autres données topographiques	Outros acidentes topográficos

ESPAÑOL — Nombre / Página / Lat.°′ / Long.°′ W = Oeste
FRANÇAIS — Nom / Page / Lat.°′ / Long.°′ W = Ouest
PORTUGUÊS — Nome / Página / Lat.°′ / Long.°′ W = Oeste

Baradili 71 39.43 N 8.54 E
Baradine 166 30.56 S 149.04 E
Bara Doāni 126 22.06 N 89.59 E
Baraga 190 46.46 N 88.29 W
Baragaon
→ Nālanda 124 25.07 N 85.25 E
Baragarh 120 21.20 N 83.37 E
Baragiano 68 40.41 N 15.35 E
Baragoi 154 1.47 N 36.47 E
Baraguá 240p 21.41 N 78.38 W
Baragwanath Aerodrome ⊠ 273d 26.15 S 27.59 E
Baragwanath Military Hospital ♥ 273d 26.16 S 27.56 E
Bārah 140 13.42 N 30.22 E
Barahānuddin 126 22.30 N 90.43 E
Barahona 238 18.12 N 71.06 W
Barāigrām 126 24.19 N 89.10 E
Bara Issa ≃ 150 16.09 N 3.28 W
Barajas, Aeropuerto ⊠ 266a 40.28 N 3.34 W
Barajas de Madrid ◆8 266a 40.28 N 3.35 E
Bara Jorda 126 23.10 N 86.50 E
Barak 130 36.51 N 37.59 E
Barāk ≃ 120 24.52 N 92.30 E
Baraka 154 4.06 S 29.06 E
Baraka (Khawr Barakah) V 144 18.13 N 37.35 E
Barakah 140 10.58 N 27.59 E
Barakah, Khawr (Baraka) V 144 18.13 N 37.35 E
Barākar 126 24.07 N 86.14 E
Barakār ≃ 126 23.42 N 86.48 E
Bara Khunta 126 21.43 N 86.38 E
Baraki 120 33.56 N 68.55 E
Barakkol'skij 86 52.12 N 67.49 E
Bārākpur, Bngl. 126 22.55 N 89.32 E
Bārākpur, India 126 22.46 N 88.21 E
Bārākpur Cantonment 272b 22.46 N 88.22 E
Barakula 166 26.26 S 150.31 E
Barāl 272b 22.27 N 88.22 E
Baral ≃ 126 24.10 N 89.27 E
Baralaba 166 24.11 S 149.49 E
Barām 126 22.57 N 86.18 E
Baram ≃ 112 4.36 N 113.59 E
Baram, Tanjong › 112 4.35 N 113.59 E
Barama ≃ 246 7.40 N 59.15 W
Barāmāria 126 21.42 N 87.04 E
Bārāmati 122 18.09 N 74.35 E
Bārāmūla 123 34.12 N 74.21 E
Baran', Bela. 76 54.29 N 30.18 E
Baran', Bela. 76 54.30 N 28.40 E
Bārān, India 124 25.06 N 76.31 E
Baranagar 126 22.38 N 88.22 E
Baranakovo 86 58.08 N 82.58 E
Barancevo 82 55.04 N 37.38 E
Baranello 66 41.32 N 14.34 E
Barangbarang 112 6.24 S 120.28 E
Barangeon ≃ 50 47.12 N 2.10 E
Barani 150 13.10 N 3.53 W
Baraniki 80 46.31 N 41.50 E
Baranikovka 83 49.10 N 39.50 E
Baranoa 246 10.48 N 74.55 W
Barano d'Ischia 66 40.42 N 13.55 E
Baranof 180 57.05 N 134.50 W
Baranof Island ı 180 57.00 N 135.00 W
Baranoviči 76 53.08 N 26.02 E
Baranovka 78 50.18 N 27.40 E
Baranovskoje 82 55.25 N 38.45 E
Barany, Ross. 76 57.20 N 29.09 E
Barany, Ross. 80 57.38 N 52.16 E
Baranya □6 30 46.05 N 18.15 E
Barão Ataliba Nogueira 256 22.24 S 46.45 W
Barão de Geraldo 256 22.49 S 47.06 W
Barão de Grajaú 250 6.45 S 43.01 W
Barão de Juparanã 256 22.21 S 43.41 W
Barão de Melgaço 248 16.13 S 55.58 W
Barão de Tromai 250 1.29 S 45.36 W
Baraolt 38 46.05 N 25.36 E
Baraque de Fraiture ∧ 56 50.15 N 5.44 E
Baras 116 13.40 N 124.22 E
Barasāhi 126 21.43 N 86.44 E
Bārāsat, India 126 22.43 N 88.29 E
Bārasat, India 272b 22.51 N 88.22 E
Baraševo 80 54.32 N 42.53 E
Baraši 78 50.43 N 28.01 E
Baraški 24 65.40 N 52.10 E
Barat, Lintasan ʊ 115a 7.08 S 112.40 E
Baratã 266c 38.48 N 9.19 W
Baratang Island ı 110 12.13 N 92.45 E
Barataria 194 29.43 N 90.07 W
Barataria Bay c 194 29.22 N 89.57 W
Barat Daya, Kepulauan ıı 108 7.25 S 128.00 E
Barate 112 9.54 S 123.38 E
Bar'atino, Ross. 76 54.19 N 34.31 E
Bar'atino, Ross. 82 54.43 N 36.49 E
Baratolia 126 22.25 N 86.37 E
Baratta 166 31.59 S 139.06 E
Barauana ≃ 246 1.14 N 60.41 W
Baraula 272a 28.34 N 77.22 E
Barauni 124 25.29 N 85.59 E
Baraut 124 29.06 N 77.16 E
Baraya 246 3.10 N 75.04 W
Barbacena 256 21.14 S 43.46 W
Barbacoas 246 1.41 N 78.09 W
Barbades
→ Barbados □1 241g 13.10 N 59.32 W
Barbadillo del Mercado 34 42.02 N 3.21 W
Barbadoes Island ı 285 40.07 N 75.22 W
Barbados □1, N.A. 230 13.10 N 59.32 W
Barbados □1, N.A. 241g 13.10 N 59.32 W
Barbagia ◆1 71 39.55 N 9.12 E
Barbalha 250 7.19 S 39.17 W
Barbar 140 18.01 N 33.59 E
Barbarano Vicentino 64 45.24 N 11.32 E
Barbarasco 64 44.14 N 9.56 E
Barbareta, Isla ı 236 16.26 N 86.09 W
Barbaria, Cap de › 34 38.38 N 1.23 E
Barbaros 130 40.54 N 27.27 E
Barbas, Cap › 148 22.18 N 16.41 W
Barbaši 76 57.42 N 28.24 E
Barbastro 34 42.02 N 0.08 E
Barbate ≃ 34 36.11 N 5.55 W
Barbate de Franco 34 36.12 N 5.55 W
Barbeau Peak ∧ 16 81.54 N 75.01 W
Barbentane 62 43.54 N 4.45 E
Barberà del Vallès 266d 41.31 N 2.08 E
Barber Booth 262 53.22 N 1.50 W
Barberena 236 14.18 N 90.22 W
Barberena ≃ 234 22.34 N 97.52 W
Barberino di Mugello 66 44.00 N 11.15 E
Barberino Val d'Elsa 66 43.32 N 11.10 E
Barbers Point › 229c 21.18 N 158.07 W
Barbers Point Naval Air Station ■ 229c 21.19 N 158.04 W
Barberton, S. Afr. 156 25.48 S 31.03 E
Barberton, Oh., U.S. 214 41.00 N 81.36 W
Barbezieux 32 45.28 N 0.09 W
Bar Bigha 124 25.13 N 85.44 E
Barbil 124 22.06 N 85.20 E
Barbis 54 51.37 N 10.25 E
Barbizon 50 48.27 N 2.36 E
Barbosa, Col. 246 6.26 N 75.20 W
Barbosa, Col. 246 5.57 N 73.37 W
Barboursville 188 38.24 N 82.17 W
Barbourville 192 36.51 N 83.53 W
Barbuda ı 238 17.38 N 61.48 W
Barbuise ≃ 50 48.33 N 3.35 E
Barby 54 51.58 N 11.53 E
Barčadiv 85 38.19 N 72.29 E
Barca Grande ≃ 258 34.09 S 58.23 W
Barcaldine 166 23.33 S 145.17 E
Barcarena 266c 38.44 N 9.17 W
Barcarena, Ribeira de ≃ 266c 38.42 N 9.27 W
Barcarrota 34 38.31 N 6.51 W
Barcău (Berettyó) ≃ 38 46.59 N 21.07 E
Barce
→ Al-Marj 146 32.30 N 20.54 E
Barcellona Pozzo di Gotto 70 38.09 N 15.13 E
Barcelona, Esp. 34 41.23 N 2.11 E
Barcelona, Esp. 266d 41.23 N 2.11 E
Barcelona, Méx. 232 26.12 N 103.25 W
Barcelona, Pil. 116 12.52 N 124.09 E
Barcelona, Ven. 246 10.08 N 64.42 W
Barcelona □4 34 41.40 N 2.00 E
Barcelona ◆8 266a 40.22 N 3.34 E
Barcelona, Aeropuerto Transoceánico de ⊠ 266d 41.18 N 2.05 E
Barcelone
→ Barcelona 34 41.23 N 2.11 E
Barceloneta 240m 18.27 N 66.32 W
Barcelonnette 62 44.23 N 6.39 E
Barcelos, Bra. 246 0.58 S 62.57 W
Barcelos, Port. 34 41.32 N 8.37 W
Barchaticha 80 57.34 N 45.13 E
Barchyn ≃ 88 48.43 N 110.17 E
Barcillonnette 62 44.26 N 5.55 E
Barcin 30 52.52 N 17.57 E
Barcis 64 46.11 N 12.33 E
Barclay 208 39.08 N 75.51 W
Barclay Brook ≃ 276 40.19 N 74.22 W
Barcoo ≃ 166 25.30 S 142.50 E
Barcroft, Lake ⊜1 284c 38.51 N 77.09 W
Barcs 30 45.58 N 17.28 E
Barcy 261 49.01 N 2.53 E
Barczewo 30 53.50 N 20.42 E
Bard 62 45.36 N 7.45 E
Barda, Azer. 84 40.23 N 47.08 E
Barda, Ross. 86 56.54 N 55.38 E
Barda del Medio 252 38.43 S 68.10 W
Bardagué, Enneri V 146 22.06 N 16.28 E
Bardai, Sūd. 140 12.43 N 21.53 E
Bardaï, Tchad 146 21.22 N 16.59 E
Bardawīl, Sabkhat al- ⩩ 140 31.10 N 33.10 E
Barddhamān 126 23.15 N 87.51 E
Bardejov 30 49.18 N 21.16 E
Bardenas Reales ⩕1 34 42.10 N 1.25 W
Bardeskan 128 35.12 N 57.58 E
Bardi 62 44.38 N 9.44 E
Bardīyah 146 31.46 N 25.06 E
Bardız 130 40.26 N 42.20 E
Bardney 44 53.12 N 0.21 W
Bardo 36 36.50 N 10.06 E
Bardoc 162 30.20 S 121.17 E
Bārdoli 120 21.07 N 73.07 E
Bardolino 64 45.33 N 10.43 E
Bardonecchia 62 45.05 N 6.42 E
Bardonia 276 41.07 N 74.00 W
Bardoux, Lac ⊜ 186 51.09 N 67.50 W
Bardowick 52 53.18 N 10.23 E
Bardsey Island ı 42 52.45 N 4.45 W
Bardsey Sound ʊ 42 52.47 N 4.45 W
Bardstown 194 37.48 N 85.28 W
Bardu 24 68.52 N 18.21 E
Bardufoss 24 69.04 N 18.30 E
Bardwell, Ky., U.S. 194 36.52 N 89.00 W
Bardwell, Tx., U.S. 222 32.16 N 96.42 W
Bardwell Lake ⊜1 222 32.16 N 96.39 W
Bare 144 4.42 N 42.47 E
Bareggio 266b 45.29 N 9.00 E
Barei, Wādī V 140 13.27 N 23.57 E
Bareilly 124 28.21 N 79.25 E
Bareli 124 23.00 N 78.14 E
Barenburg 52 52.37 N 8.47 E
Barendrecht 52 51.51 N 4.32 E
Bärenklau 54 51.56 N 14.34 E
Bärenstein, Dtsch. 54 50.30 N 13.02 E
Bärenstein, Dtsch. 54 50.48 N 13.47 E
Barentin 50 49.33 N 0.57 E
Barents Sea ⫧2 12 74.00 N 36.00 E
Barents Trough ✥1 12 75.00 N 29.00 E
Barentu 144 15.04 N 37.37 E
Bareo 112 3.45 N 115.27 E
Baresville 208 39.48 N 76.57 W
Bareta 123 29.52 N 75.42 E
Barfleur 32 49.40 N 1.15 W
Barfleur, Pointe de › 32 49.42 N 1.16 W
Barga 64 44.04 N 10.29 E
Bargāchia, India 126 22.39 N 88.07 E
Bargāchia, India 272b 22.48 N 88.27 E
Bargagli 62 44.27 N 9.05 E
Bargaintown 208 39.22 N 70.35 W
Bargara 166 24.49 S 152.27 E
Bargas 34 39.56 N 4.03 W
Barge, It. 62 44.43 N 7.20 E
Barge, Ityo. 144 6.14 N 36.58 E
Barg-e Matāl 120 35.40 N 71.21 E
Bargemon 62 43.37 N 6.32 E
Bargen 58 47.48 N 8.37 E
Bargersville 218 39.31 N 86.10 W
Barghanak 128 33.56 N 62.26 E
Bargnop 140 9.30 N 28.28 E
Bargo 170 34.18 S 150.35 E
Bargoed 42 51.43 N 3.15 W
Bargteheide 52 53.44 N 10.16 E
Bārguna 126 22.09 N 90.07 E
Barguzin 88 53.37 N 109.37 E
Barguzin ≃ 88 53.27 N 109.00 E
Barguzinskij chrebet ⩕ 88 54.30 N 110.20 E
Barguzinskij zapovednik ♠ 88 54.25 N 109.40 E
Bārh 124 25.29 N 85.43 E
Barhaj 124 26.17 N 83.44 E
Bar Harbor 188 44.23 N 68.12 W
Barharwa 124 24.52 N 87.47 E
Barhau 112 5.19 S 102.10 E
Barhi 124 24.18 N 85.25 E
Bar Hill 42 52.15 N 0.01 E
Barhiya 124 25.17 N 86.02 E
Bāri, India 124 23.03 N 78.05 E
Bāri, India 124 26.39 N 77.36 E
Bari, It. 68 41.07 N 16.52 E
Bari, Zaïre 152 3.19 N 19.23 E
Bari □4, It. 68 40.56 N 16.40 E
Bari □4, Som. 144 10.00 N 50.00 E
Baria ≃ 246 1.56 N 66.35 W
Baricella 64 44.39 N 11.32 E
Barichara 246 6.38 N 73.14 W
Barīdī, Ra's › 128 24.17 N 37.31 E
Bāri Doāb ⩕1 123 30.25 N 73.00 E
Barī Gāv 120 33.52 N 67.49 E
Barigazzo 64 44.16 N 10.39 E
Barigua, Salina de ⩩ 241s 12.08 N 69.59 W
Barika 34 35.23 N 5.22 E
Barika, Oued ≃ 34 35.22 N 5.18 E
Barikiwa 154 9.28 S 37.54 E
Barīkowt 120 35.18 N 71.32 E
Barile 68 40.57 N 15.40 E
Barillas 236 15.48 N 91.18 W
Bariloche
→ San Carlos de Bariloche 254 41.09 S 71.18 W
Barilo-Krepinskaja 83 47.45 N 39.32 E
Barīm (Perim) ı 144 12.39 N 43.25 E
Barima ≃ 246 8.33 N 60.25 W
Barima-Waini □4 246 7.45 N 59.30 W
Barin 84 39.13 N 44.28 E
Barinas, P.R. 240m 18.01 N 66.51 W
Barinas, Ven. 246 8.38 N 70.12 W
Barinas □3 246 8.10 N 69.50 W
Baring 224 47.46 N 121.29 W
Baring, Cape › 176 70.05 N 117.20 W
Baringa, Zaïre 152 6.17 S 16.55 E
Baringa, Zaïre 152 0.45 N 20.52 E
Baringo, Lake ⊜ 154 0.38 N 36.05 E
Båring Vig c 41 55.32 N 9.56 E
Barinitas 246 8.45 N 70.25 W
Bāripada 126 21.56 N 86.43 E
Bariri 255 22.04 S 48.44 W
Bārīs 140 24.40 N 30.36 E
Barisacho 84 42.28 N 44.54 E
Bari Sādri 120 24.25 N 74.28 E
Barisāl 124 22.42 N 90.22 E
Barisan, Pegunungan ⩕ 112 3.00 S 102.15 E
Bari Sardo 71 39.50 N 9.38 E
Barisciano 66 42.19 N 13.35 E
Bariti Bil ⊜ 272b 22.48 N 88.26 E
Barito ≃ 112 3.32 S 114.29 E
Baritú, Parque Nacional ♠ 252 22.30 S 64.35 W
Barjā 132 33.39 N 35.26 E
Barjac 62 44.18 N 4.21 E
Barjols 62 43.33 N 6.00 E
Barjora 126 23.26 N 87.17 E
Barjūj, Wādī V 146 25.57 N 13.12 E
Bark ≃ 216 42.55 N 88.50 W
Barka Kāna 124 23.37 N 85.29 E
Barkal 120 22.44 N 92.23 E
Barkam 102 31.50 N 102.40 E
Barkava 76 56.43 N 26.36 E
Barkelsby 41 54.30 N 9.50 E
Barker, N.Y., U.S. 210 43.19 N 78.33 W
Barker, Ur. 258 34.16 S 57.27 W
Barker Point › 276 40.51 N 73.44 W
Barker Reservoir ⊜1 222 29.44 N 95.44 W
Barkers Brook ≃ 285 40.03 N 74.45 W
Barkerville 182 53.04 N 121.31 W
Barkerville Historic Park ⊥ 182 53.04 N 121.30 W
Barkeyville 214 41.12 N 79.58 W
Barkhamsted Reservoir ⊜1 207 41.57 N 72.57 W
Bārkhān 120 29.54 N 69.31 E
Barkhanpur 126 23.50 N 89.33 E
Barking ◆8 42 51.33 N 0.06 E
Barkingside ◆8 260 51.36 N 0.05 E
Barki Saraiya 124 24.10 N 85.53 E
Barkisland 262 53.41 N 1.55 W
Bark Lake ⊜, On., Can. 190 46.54 N 82.28 W
Bark Lake ⊜, On., Can. 212 45.27 N 77.51 W
Barkley, Lake ⊜1 194 36.40 N 87.55 W
Barkley Sound ʊ 182 48.53 N 125.20 W
Barkly ≃ 169 37.32 S 146.32 E
Barkly, Mount ∧2 162 21.34 S 132.28 E
Barkly East 158 30.58 S 27.33 E
Barkly Tableland ⩕1 162 18.00 S 136.00 E
Barkly West 158 28.05 S 24.31 E
Barkol 90 43.50 N 93.30 E
Barksdale 196 29.44 N 100.02 W
Barkuhi 124 22.13 N 78.42 E
Barla 130 38.01 N 30.47 E
Bârlad
→ Bîrlad 38 46.14 N 27.40 E
Barlassina 266b 45.39 N 9.08 E
Barlaston 42 52.57 N 2.10 W
Barlby 44 53.48 N 1.03 W
Barleben 54 52.12 N 11.37 E
Bar-le-Duc 56 48.47 N 5.10 E
Barlee, Lake ⊜ 162 29.10 S 119.30 E
Barlee, Mount ∧2 162 24.37 S 128.06 E
Barlee Range ⩕ 162 23.35 S 116.00 E
Barles 62 44.16 N 6.16 E
Barletta 68 41.19 N 16.17 E
Barlin 50 50.27 N 2.37 E
Barlinek 30 53.00 N 15.12 E
Barling 194 35.19 N 94.18 W
Barlow 194 37.03 N 89.02 W
Barluk 88 54.32 N 101.43 E
Barma 164 1.54 S 133.00 E
Barmancak, ozero ⊜ 80 48.02 N 44.40 E
Barmašovo 78 47.07 N 32.26 E
Barmedman 166 34.09 S 147.23 E
Barmen ◆8 263 51.17 N 7.13 E
Bārmer 120 25.45 N 71.23 E
Barmera 166 34.15 S 140.28 E
Barmouth 42 52.43 N 4.03 W
Barmouth Bay c 42 52.42 N 4.08 W
Barmstedt 52 53.47 N 9.46 E
Barnaby Manor Oaks 284c 38.50 N 76.58 W
Barnagar 120 23.03 N 75.22 E
Barnāla 123 30.23 N 75.33 E
Barnard Castle 44 54.33 N 1.55 W
Barnasht 142 29.41 N 31.15 E
Bärnau 60 49.49 N 12.26 E
Barnaul 86 53.22 N 83.45 E
Bärnbach 61 47.05 N 15.06 E
Barn Bluff ∧ 166 41.43 S 145.56 E
Barneberg 54 52.08 N 11.03 E
Barnegat 208 39.45 N 74.13 W
Barnegat Bay c 208 39.52 N 74.07 W
Barnegat Light 208 39.45 N 74.06 W
Barne Inlet c 9 80.15 S 160.15 E
Barnes 214 41.40 N 79.01 W
Barnes ◆8 260 51.28 N 0.15 W
Barnesboro 214 40.39 N 78.46 W
Barnes Corners 212 43.49 N 75.49 W
Barnes Ice Cap ⌓ 176 70.00 N 73.15 W
Barnes Lake ⊜ 184 56.23 N 98.06 W
Barnes Sound ʊ 220 25.14 N 80.23 W
Barnesville, Ga., U.S. 192 33.03 N 84.09 W
Barnesville, Mn., U.S. 198 46.39 N 96.25 W
Barnesville, Oh., U.S. 188 39.59 N 81.10 W
Barnet ◆8 42 51.40 N 0.13 W
Barnetby le Wold 44 53.35 N 0.25 W
Barnett 219 39.16 N 89.42 W
Barnetts 208 37.22 N 77.09 W
Barneveld, Ned. 52 52.08 N 5.35 E
Barneveld, N.Y., U.S. 210 43.16 N 75.12 W
Barneville-Carteret 32 49.23 N 1.47 W
Barnhart, Mo., U.S. 219 38.20 N 90.23 W
Barnhart, Tx., U.S. 196 31.08 N 101.10 W
Barnhill 214 40.27 N 81.21 W
Barnim ◆1 54 52.40 N 13.45 E
Barnoldswick 44 53.55 N 2.11 W
Barnówko 54 52.48 N 14.45 E
Barnsboro 285 39.46 N 75.09 W
Barnsdall 196 36.33 N 96.09 W
Barnsley 44 53.34 N 1.28 W
Barnstable 207 41.42 N 70.18 W
Barnstable □6 207 41.42 N 70.18 W
Barnstable Harbor c 207 41.43 N 70.18 W
Barnstaple 42 51.05 N 4.04 W
Barnstaple Bay c 42 51.05 N 4.20 W
Barnston 262 53.21 N 3.05 W
Barnstorf 52 52.42 N 8.30 E
Barnt Green 42 52.22 N 1.59 W
Barnton 262 53.16 N 2.33 W
Barntrup 52 51.59 N 9.06 E
Barnum Island 276 40.36 N 73.39 W
Barnwell, Ab., Can. 182 49.46 N 112.15 W
Barnwell, S.C., U.S. 192 33.14 N 81.21 W
Baro 150 8.37 N 6.25 E
Baro ≃ 144 8.26 N 33.13 E
Barobo 116 8.33 N 126.07 E
Baroda, India 124 25.30 N 76.39 E
Baroda, Mi., U.S. 216 41.57 N 86.29 W
Baroda
→ Vadodara 122 22.18 N 73.12 E
Baroe 158 33.13 S 24.33 E
Barometer ∧ 172 41.50 S 173.39 E
Baron Bluff ⊥4 241n 17.47 N 64.47 W
Baronissi 68 40.44 N 14.45 E
Barons 182 50.00 N 113.05 W
Barora Fa Island ı 175e 7.30 S 158.20 E
Barora Ite Island ı 175e 7.35 S 158.24 E
Barossa Reservoir ⊜1 168b 34.39 S 138.51 E
Barotac Nuevo 116 10.54 N 122.42 E
Barotac Viejo 116 11.03 N 122.51 E
Barouéli 150 13.04 N 6.50 W
Barpathār 120 26.17 N 93.53 E
Barpeta 120 26.19 N 91.00 E
Bar Point › 214 42.03 N 83.06 W
Barqa 120 30.57 N 81.20 E
Barqah (Cyrenaica) □9 146 31.00 N 22.30 E
Barqah, Jabal al- ∧ 132 30.25 N 34.18 E
Barq al-'Izz 142 31.01 N 31.26 E
Barque Canada Reef ✥2 108 8.12 N 113.19 E
Barques, Pointe aux › 190 44.04 N 82.58 W
Barquisimeto 246 10.04 N 69.19 W
Barr 58 48.24 N 7.27 E
Barra, Bra. 250 11.05 S 43.10 W
Barra, Gam. 150 13.20 N 16.36 W
Barra ı 46 56.58 N 7.29 W
Barra, Ponta da › 156 23.47 S 35.32 E
Barra, Sound of ʊ 46 57.05 N 7.25 W
Barraba 166 30.22 S 150.36 E
Barracas ◆8 288 34.38 S 58.22 W
Barrackpore Airport ⊠ 272b 22.47 N 88.22 E
Barrackpore
→ Bārākpur 126 22.46 N 88.21 E
Barrackville 188 39.30 N 80.10 W
Barracouta, Cape › 158 34.26 S 21.22 E
Barra da Estiva 255 13.38 S 41.19 W
Barra de Santo Antônio 250 9.24 S 35.30 W
Barra de São Francisco 256 21.58 S 42.42 W
Barra do Bugres 248 15.05 S 57.11 W
Barra do Corda 250 5.30 S 45.15 W
Barra do Cuanza 152 9.09 S 13.00 E
Barra do Dande 152 8.28 S 13.22 E
Barra do Garças 255 15.53 S 52.15 W
Barra do Mendes 255 11.43 S 42.04 W
Barra do Piraí 256 22.28 S 43.49 W
Barra do Ribeiro 252 30.18 S 51.18 W
Barra dos Coqueiros 250 10.54 S 37.03 W
Barra Falsa, Ponta da › 156 22.55 S 35.37 E
Barrafranca 70 37.22 N 14.12 E
Barra Funda ◆8 287b 23.31 S 46.39 W
Barra Head › 46 56.46 N 7.38 W
Barrali 71 39.28 N 9.06 E
Barra Mansa 256 22.32 S 44.11 W
Barranca, Perú 248 10.45 S 77.46 W
Barranca, Perú 248 4.50 S 76.42 W
Barrancabermeja 246 7.03 N 73.52 W
Barrancas, Col. 246 10.57 N 72.50 W
Barrancas, Ven. 246 8.46 N 70.06 W
Barrancas, Ven. 246 8.42 N 62.11 W
Barrancas ≃ 252 36.52 S 69.45 W
Barranco 286d 12.09 S 77.02 W
Barranco Azul 196 29.21 N 104.17 W
Barranco de Guadalupe 196 30.02 N 104.44 W
Barranco do Velho 34 37.14 N 7.56 W
Barrancos 34 38.08 N 6.59 W
Barrânia 256 21.33 S 46.32 W
Barranqueras 252 27.29 S 58.56 W
Barranquilla 246 10.59 N 74.48 W
Barranquitas 240m 18.11 N 66.18 W
Barras 250 4.15 S 42.18 W
Barrax 34 39.03 N 2.12 W
Barre, Ma., U.S. 207 42.25 N 72.06 W
Barre, Vt., U.S. 188 44.11 N 72.30 W
Barrea 66 41.45 N 13.59 E
Barreal 252 31.38 S 69.28 W
Barree 214 40.35 N 78.06 W
Barre Falls Dam ◆6 207 42.26 N 72.02 W
Barreiras 255 12.08 S 45.00 W
Barreirinha 250 2.47 S 57.03 W
Barreirinhas 250 2.45 S 42.50 W
Barreiro 34 38.40 N 9.05 W
Barreiro ≃, Bra. 255 15.43 S 52.45 W
Barreiro ≃, Bra. 287a 22.52 S 43.34 W
Barreiros 250 8.49 S 35.12 W
Barrême 62 43.57 N 6.22 E
Barren ≃ 194 37.11 N 86.37 W
Barren, Nosy ıı 157b 18.25 S 43.40 E
Barren Island ı 110 12.16 N 93.51 E
Barren Islands ıı 180 58.55 N 152.15 W
Barrenjoey Head › 170 33.34 S 151.20 E
Barren River Lake ⊜1 194 36.45 N 86.02 W
Barren Run ≃ 279b 40.09 N 79.42 W
Barre Plains 207 42.22 N 72.06 W
Barret-le-Bas 62 44.16 N 5.44 E
Barretos 255 20.33 S 48.33 W
Barrett 222 29.53 N 95.04 W
Barrett, Mount ∧ 162 18.10 S 127.33 E
Barrhead, Ab., Can. 182 54.08 N 114.24 W
Barrhead, Scot., U.K. 46 55.48 N 4.24 W
Barrhill 44 55.07 N 4.46 W
Barrie 212 44.24 N 79.40 W
Barriefield 212 44.14 N 76.28 W
Barrie Island ı 190 45.55 N 82.40 W
Barrien 52 52.56 N 8.49 E
Barrier, Cape › 172 36.21 S 175.31 E
Barrier Bay c 9 67.45 S 81.10 E
Barrière 182 51.11 N 120.07 W
Barrier Range ⩕ 166 31.25 S 141.25 E
Barrier Reef ✥2 164 11.36 S 153.00 E
Barrigada 174p 13.28 N 144.48 E
Barrilla Draw V 196 31.21 N 103.23 W
Barr Ilyās 132 33.46 N 35.54 E
Barrington, N.S., Can. 186 43.34 N 65.34 W
Barrington, Il., U.S. 216 42.09 N 88.08 W
Barrington, N.J., U.S. 285 39.51 N 75.03 W
Barrington, R.I., U.S. 207 41.44 N 71.18 W
Barrington Hills 216 42.07 N 88.09 W
Barrington Lake ⊜ 184 56.55 N 100.15 W
Barrington Tops ∧ 166 32.00 S 151.28 E
Barrington Woods 278 42.09 N 88.04 W
Barringun 166 29.01 S 145.43 E
Barrio de la Soledad 234 16.48 N 95.15 W
Barrita Vieja 236 13.55 N 90.54 W
Barrīyat al-Uṣayfir 142 31.18 N 30.40 E
Barro, Bra. 250 7.11 S 38.47 W
Barro, Gui.-B. 150 12.24 N 15.30 W
Barro Alto 255 15.04 S 48.58 W
Barron 190 45.24 N 91.50 W
Barron Creek ≃ 282 37.27 N 122.05 W
Barron Lake 216 41.51 N 86.11 W
Barrouallie 241h 13.14 N 61.17 W
Barrow, Arg. 252 38.18 S 60.14 W
Barrow, Ak., U.S. 180 71.17 N 156.34 W
Barrow ≃ 48 52.15 N 7.00 W
Barrow, Point › 180 71.23 N 156.30 W
Barrow Bay c 212 44.58 N 81.13 W
Barrow Creek 162 21.33 S 133.53 E
Barrowford 44 53.52 N 2.13 W
Barrow-in-Furness 44 54.07 N 3.14 W
Barrow Island ı 162 20.48 S 115.23 E
Barrows 184 52.49 N 101.27 W
Barrow Strait ʊ 176 74.21 N 94.10 W
Barrowsville 207 41.56 N 71.12 W
Barrow upon Humber 44 53.41 N 0.23 W
Barry, Wales, U.K. 42 51.24 N 3.18 W
Barry, Il., U.S. 219 39.41 N 91.02 W
Barry, Tx., U.S. 222 32.06 N 96.38 W
Barry □6 216 42.35 N 85.18 W
Barrydale 158 33.55 S 20.43 E
Barrys Bay 212 45.29 N 77.41 W
Barrys Bay c 212 45.28 N 77.42 W
Barryton 190 43.45 N 85.08 W
Barrytown 210 42.00 N 73.56 W
Barryville 210 41.28 N 74.54 W
Barsakel'mes, ostrov ı 86 45.40 N 59.58 E
Barsalpur 120 28.10 N 72.15 E
Baršatas 86 48.13 N 78.21 E
Bårse 41 55.07 N 11.58 E
Bārsi 122 18.14 N 75.42 E
Baršin 86 49.45 N 69.36 E
Barsinghausen 52 52.18 N 9.27 E
Barskaun 85 42.10 N 77.37 E
Barsø ı 41 55.07 N 9.34 E
Barssel 52 53.10 N 7.44 E
Barst 56 49.04 N 6.50 E
Barstow, Ca., U.S. 228 34.53 N 117.01 W
Barstow, Tx., U.S. 196 31.28 N 103.24 W
Barsuki 82 54.15 N 37.30 E
Bar-sur-Aube 58 48.14 N 4.43 E
Bar-sur-Seine 50 48.07 N 4.22 E
Bart 208 39.56 N 76.05 W
Bārta ≃ 76 56.24 N 21.03 E
Bartala 272b 22.33 N 88.16 E
Bartang ≃ 120 37.56 N 71.34 E
Bartazuga, Jabal ∧ 140 21.44 N 33.33 E
Bartelso 219 38.32 N 89.28 W
Bartenheim 58 47.38 N 7.28 E
Bartenstein 56 49.21 N 9.53 E
Barter Island ı 180 70.08 N 143.35 W
Barth 54 54.22 N 12.43 E
Barthe ≃ 54 54.22 N 12.41 E
Barthélemy, Deo)(110 19.26 N 104.06 E
Bartholomew □6 218 39.13 N 85.55 W
Bartholomew, Bayou ≃ 194 32.43 N 92.04 W
Bartibougou 150 12.52 N 0.48 E
Bartica 246 6.24 N 58.37 W
Bartın 130 41.38 N 32.21 E
Bartle Frere ∧ 166 17.23 S 145.49 E
Bartlesville 196 36.44 N 95.58 W
Bartlett, Il., U.S. 216 41.59 N 88.11 W
Bartlett, Ne., U.S. 198 41.53 N 98.33 W
Bartlett, N.H., U.S. 188 44.04 N 71.17 W
Bartlett, Tn., U.S. 194 35.12 N 89.52 W
Bartlett, Tx., U.S. 222 30.48 N 97.26 W
Bartlett Brook ≃ 283 42.42 N 71.13 W
Bartlett Cove 180 58.27 N 135.55 W
Bartlett Reservoir ⊜1 200 33.52 N 111.37 W
Bartletts ∧2 168a 32.19 S 116.43 E
Bartletts Harbour 186 50.57 N 57.00 W
Bartley 198 40.14 N 100.18 W
Bartolomé Bavio
→ General Mansilla 258 35.05 S 57.45 W
Bartolomé de las Casas 252 25.24 S 59.34 W
Bartolomeu de Gusmão, Aeroporto ⊠ 256 22.56 S 43.43 W
Bartolomeu Dias 156 21.10 S 35.09 E
Barton, Austl. 162 30.31 S 132.39 E
Barton, N.Y., U.S. 210 42.03 N 76.27 W
Barton, Oh., U.S. 214 40.06 N 80.50 W
Barton, Vt., U.S. 188 44.44 N 72.10 W
Barton Aerodrome ⊠ 262 53.28 N 2.23 W
Barton Lake 216 42.06 N 85.35 W
Barton Lake ⊜ 184 52.00 N 94.06 W
Barton-le-Clay 42 51.57 N 0.25 W
Barton Mills 42 52.20 N 0.31 E
Barton Park ♠ 274a 33.57 S 151.09 E
Barton Run ≃ 285 39.53 N 74.51 W
Barton-under-Needwood 42 52.45 N 1.43 W
Barton-upon-Humber 44 53.41 N 0.27 W
Bartonville 190 40.39 N 89.39 W
Barton Water Swing Bridge ◆5 262 53.28 N 2.21 W
Bartoszyce 30 54.16 N 20.49 E
Bartow, Fl., U.S. 220 27.53 N 81.50 W
Bartow, Ga., U.S. 192 32.52 N 82.28 W
Baru, Kali ≍ 269e 6.10 S 106.51 E
Barú, Volcán ∧1 236 8.48 N 82.33 W
Barueri 256 23.31 S 46.53 W
Barugo 116 11.20 N 124.44 E
Bāruipāra 272b 22.46 N 88.14 E
Bāruipur 126 22.21 N 88.27 E
Bārūk, Jabal al- ∧ 132 33.43 N 35.45 E
Barumini 71 39.42 N 9.00 E
Barumun ≃ 114 2.30 N 100.09 E
Barun Bogd uul ∧ 90 44.57 N 100.15 E
Barung, Nusa ı 115a 8.28 S 113.20 E
Barun Su 102 42.27 N 111.01 E
Barun-Torej, ozero ⊜ 88 50.10 N 115.30 E
Baruntse ∧ 124 27.51 N 86.59 E
Barus 114 2.00 N 98.24 E
Baruta 286c 10.26 N 66.53 W
Baruth 54 52.03 N 13.30 E
Baruun Bajan-Ulaan 102 45.10 N 101.24 E
Baruun bogd uul ∧ 102 44.57 N 100.15 E
Baruun-Urt 90 46.42 N 113.15 E
Barva, Volcán ∧1 236 10.08 N 84.06 W
Barvas 46 58.22 N 6.32 W
Barvenkovo 78 48.54 N 37.02 E
Barver 52 52.37 N 8.35 E
Barvicha 265b 55.44 N 37.16 E
Barview 202 43.21 N 124.18 W
Barwa 126 23.51 N 86.26 E
Barwāh 120 22.16 N 76.03 E
Barwāla ◆8 272a 28.46 N 77.04 E
Barwāni 120 22.02 N 74.54 E
Barwa Sāgar 124 25.23 N 78.44 E
Barwell 42 52.32 N 1.21 W
Barwice 30 53.45 N 16.22 E
Barwick 192 30.54 N 83.44 W
Barwidgee 162 27.02 S 120.54 E
Barwon ≃, Austl. 166 30.00 S 148.05 E
Barwon ≃, Austl. 169 38.13 S 144.25 E
Barwon Heads (South Barwon) 169 38.17 S 144.30 E
Barybino, Ross. 82 55.16 N 37.54 E
Barybino, Ross. 82 54.56 N 37.47 E
Barycz ≃ 30 51.42 N 16.15 E
Barykino 83 49.17 N 38.24 E
Barykova, mys › 180 63.02 N 179.29 E
Barykovo 82 54.38 N 38.48 E
Barynino 82 55.47 N 36.21 E
Baryš 80 53.39 N 47.08 E
Baryš ≃ 80 54.35 N 46.48 E
Baryševka 78 50.22 N 31.19 E
Baryševo 86 54.58 N 83.11 E
Baryšniki 80 56.57 N 46.33 E
Barzah 132 33.34 N 36.19 E
Barzas 86 55.43 N 86.19 E
Barzio 58 45.57 N 9.27 E
Bas'a ≃ 76 53.46 N 31.01 E
Basacato del Este 152 3.37 N 8.54 E
Basai Dārāpur ◆8 272a 28.40 N 77.08 E
Bāsa'īdū 128 26.39 N 55.17 E
Basail, Arg. 252 27.52 S 59.18 W
Bāsāil, Bngl. 126 24.14 N 90.04 E
Basakin 80 48.11 N 42.18 E
Basāl 123 33.33 N 72.15 E
Basalt ≃ 166 19.38 S 145.52 E
Basalt Island ı 271d 22.19 N 114.22 E
Basaluzzo 62 44.46 N 8.42 E
Basandīlah 142 31.12 N 31.26 E
Basankusu 152 1.14 N 19.48 E
Bašanta 80 46.05 N 41.56 E
Basanti 126 22.12 N 88.42 E
Basarabi 38 44.10 N 28.24 E
Basatongwula Shan ∧ 120 33.05 N 91.30 E
Basavakalyān 122 17.52 N 76.57 E
Basavilbaso 252 32.22 S 58.53 W
Baščelakskij chrebet ⩕ 86 51.15 N 84.30 E
Baschi 66 42.40 N 12.13 E
Basco 108 20.27 N 121.58 E
Bascom 214 41.07 N 83.17 W
Bascuñán, Cabo › 252 28.51 S 71.30 W
Basdahl 52 53.26 N 8.59 E
Basdorf, Dtsch. 54 52.44 N 13.26 E
Basdorf, Dtsch. 56 51.12 N 8.58 E
Basekpio 154 4.44 N 24.40 E
Basel (Bâle) 58 47.33 N 7.35 E
Baselga di Pinè 64 46.08 N 11.14 E
Baselice 68 41.24 N 14.58 E
Basel-Land □3 58 47.30 N 7.50 E
Basel-Stadt □3 58 47.38 N 7.40 E
Basen ≃ 96 34.48 N 132.51 E
Bas-en-Basset 62 45.18 N 4.06 E
Basentello ≃ 68 40.40 N 16.23 E
Basento ≃ 68 40.21 N 16.50 E
Başeu ≃ 38 47.44 N 27.15 E
Basey 116 11.17 N 125.04 E
Bashaw 182 52.35 N 112.58 W
Basher Kill ≃ 210 41.27 N 74.35 W
Bashi Channel ʊ 108 22.00 N 121.00 E
Bashikejike 120 37.30 N 85.50 E
Bashiqiao 106 31.40 N 120.22 E
Bashkortostan
→ Baškirija □3 86 54.00 N 56.00 E
Bashtīl 273c 30.05 N 31.11 E
Basi, India 123 30.41 N 76.24 E
Basi, India 123 30.36 N 76.50 E
Basiad Bay c 116 14.16 N 122.19 E
Basiano 112 1.16 S 122.50 E
Basibasy 157b 22.10 S 43.40 E
Başıbüyük ◆8 267b 40.57 N 29.08 E
Basicò 70 38.04 N 15.04 E
Basid 85 38.07 N 72.09 E
Basilaki Island ı 164 10.35 S 151.00 E
Basilan □4 116 6.35 N 121.55 E
Basilan Island ı 116 6.34 N 122.03 E
Basilan Peak ∧ 116 6.33 N 122.04 E
Basilan Strait ʊ 116 6.49 N 122.05 E
Basildon 42 51.35 N 0.25 E
Basildon □8 260 51.35 N 0.29 E
Basile 194 30.29 N 92.35 W
Basiliano 64 46.01 N 13.06 E
Basilicata □4 68 40.30 N 16.10 E
Basiluzzo, Isola ı 70 38.39 N 15.07 E
Basin, Mt., U.S. 202 46.16 N 112.15 W
Basin, Wy., U.S. 202 44.22 N 108.02 W
Bäsingen ⊜ 40 60.09 N 16.20 E
Basinger 220 27.24 N 81.01 W
Basingstoke 42 51.15 N 1.05 W
Basingstoke Canal ≍ 260 51.21 N 0.29 W
Basingwerk Abbey ♥1 262 53.17 N 3.12 W
Basin Lake ⊜ 184 52.38 N 105.18 W
Basīrhāt 126 22.40 N 88.53 E
Basīrpur 123 30.35 N 73.50 E
Basīṭ, Ra's al- › 130 35.51 N 35.48 E
Basiyingzi 104 42.05 N 121.37 E
Basjanovskij 86 58.19 N 60.44 E
Baška 36 44.58 N 14.46 E
Baskahegan Lake ⊜ 188 45.30 N 67.48 W
Baskakovka 76 54.36 N 34.19 E
Başkale 128 38.02 N 44.00 E
Baskatong, Réservoir ⊜1 190 46.48 N 75.50 W
Baškaus ≃ 86 51.09 N 87.43 E
Basket Lake ⊜ 184 49.43 N 92.00 W
Basking Ridge 276 40.42 N 74.32 W
Baškino 82 55.18 N 36.41 E
Baškirija □3 86 54.00 N 56.00 E
Baškirskij zapovednik ♠ 86 53.30 N 57.58 E
Baskomutan Milli Parkı ♠ 130 38.50 N 30.05 E
Başköy 84 39.53 N 44.32 E
Baskuduk 86 49.43 N 61.32 E
Baš-Kugandy 85 42.00 N 74.39 E
Baskunčak, ozero ⊜ 80 48.12 N 46.54 E
Baslow 44 53.15 N 1.38 W
Başmakçı 130 37.54 N 30.01 E
Bašmakovo 80 53.12 N 43.02 E
Basmat 122 19.19 N 77.10 E
Bäsna 40 60.32 N 15.12 E
Bāsoda 124 23.51 N 77.56 E
Basoko 152 1.14 N 23.36 E
Basoko ≃ 273b 4.19 S 15.16 E
Basoli 123 32.30 N 75.49 E
Basom 210 43.04 N 78.24 W
Basongo 152 4.20 S 20.24 E
Basora, Punt › 241s 12.25 N 69.52 W
Basovizza 64 45.38 N 13.52 E
Başpınar 130 39.12 N 38.42 E
Basque Lands
→ Euskal Herriko □4 34 43.00 N 2.30 W
Basra
→ Al-Başrah 128 30.30 N 47.47 E
Bas-Rhin □5 32 48.35 N 7.40 E
Bass ≃ 169 38.30 S 145.26 E
Bassano 182 50.47 N 112.28 W
Bassano del Grappa 64 45.46 N 11.44 E
Bassari 150 9.15 N 0.47 E
Bassas da India ✥2 138 21.25 S 39.42 E
Bass Creek ≃ 216 42.37 N 89.04 W
Basse-Califórnie
→ Baja California ›1 232 28.00 N 113.30 W
Bassecourt 58 47.20 N 7.15 E
Bassein ≃1 110 15.56 N 94.18 E
Bassein
→ Pathein 110 16.47 N 94.44 E
Basse-Kotto □5 152 5.00 N 21.30 E
Bassella 34 42.01 N 1.18 E
Bassen 52 53.04 N 9.04 E
Bassendean 168a 31.55 S 115.56 E
Bassenthwaite 44 54.41 N 3.12 W
Bassenthwaite Lake ⊜ 44 54.38 N 3.13 W
Basse-Pointe 240e 14.52 N 61.07 W
Basses, Pointe des › 241o 15.52 N 61.17 W
Basses-Alpes □5 62 44.10 N 6.00 E
Basse Santa Su 150 13.19 N 14.13 W
Basse-Terre, Guad. 241o 16.00 N 61.44 W
Basseterre, St. K.-N. 238 17.18 N 62.43 W
Basse Terre, Trin. 241r 10.08 N 61.18 W
Basse-Terre ı 241o 16.10 N 61.40 W
Bassett, Ne., U.S. 198 42.35 N 99.32 W
Bassett, Va., U.S. 192 36.45 N 79.59 W
Bassett Creek ≃ 194 31.25 N 87.56 W
Bassett Peak ∧ 200 32.30 N 110.17 W
Bassfield 194 31.30 N 89.44 W
Bass Harbor 188 44.14 N 68.20 W
Bass Hill 274a 33.54 S 151.00 E
Bassignana 62 45.00 N 8.44 E
Bassikounou 150 15.52 N 5.57 W
Bassila 150 9.01 N 1.40 E
Bassin des Aghlabites ⊥ 36 35.43 N 10.10 E
Bassingbourn 42 52.04 N 0.03 W
Bass Lake, Ca., U.S. 226 37.19 N 119.33 W
Bass Lake, In., U.S. 216 41.12 N 86.36 W
Bass Lake ⊜, On., Can. 212 44.49 N 76.08 W
Bass Lake ⊜, In., U.S. 216 41.13 N 86.36 W
Bass Lake ⊜1 226 37.19 N 119.34 W
Bass Point › 170 34.36 S 150.54 E
Bass River 186 45.25 N 63.47 W
Bass Strait ʊ 166 39.20 S 145.30 E
Bassum 52 52.51 N 8.43 E
Basswood Lake ⊜, On., Can. 190 46.20 N 83.23 W
Basswood Lake ⊜, N.A. 190 48.06 N 91.40 W
Basta 126 21.41 N 87.03 E
Båstad 26 56.26 N 12.51 E
Basṭah 132 30.14 N 35.32 E
Bastak 128 27.14 N 54.22 E
Basṭām 128 36.29 N 55.04 E
Baštanka 78 47.24 N 32.25 E
Bastei ♠ 54 50.58 N 14.04 E
Bastelica 36 42.00 N 9.02 E
Basti 124 26.48 N 82.43 E
Bastia, Fr. 32 42.42 N 9.27 E
Bastia, It. 66 43.04 N 12.33 E
Bastian 192 37.09 N 81.09 W
Bastiglia 64 44.43 N 11.00 E
Bastimentos 236 9.21 N 82.12 W
Bastimentos, Isla ı 236 9.18 N 82.08 W
Bastogne 56 50.00 N 5.43 E
Bastrop, La., U.S. 194 32.46 N 91.54 W
Bastrop, Tx., U.S. 222 30.06 N 97.18 W
Bastrop □6 222 33.00 N 97.18 W
Bastrop, Lake ⊜1 222 30.09 N 97.18 W
Bastrop Bay c 222 29.06 N 95.11 W
Bastrop State Park ♠ 222 30.07 N 97.17 W
Bastuträsk 26 64.47 N 20.02 E
Basu, Pulau ı 112 0.18 S 103.36 E
Basubāti 272b 22.47 N 88.12 E
Bāsudebpur, India 126 21.49 N 87.38 E
Bāsudebpur, India 272b 22.49 N 88.25 E

≃ River — Fluß — Río — Rivière — Rio
≍ Canal — Kanal — Canal — Canal — Canal
⌞ Waterfall, Rapids — Wasserfall, Stromschnellen — Cascada, Rápidos — Chute d'eau, Rapides — Cascata, Rápidos
ʊ Strait — Meeresstraße — Estrecho — Détroit — Estreito
c Bay, Gulf — Bucht, Golf — Bahía, Golfo — Baie, Golfe — Baía, Golfo
⊜ Lake, Lakes — See, Seen — Lago, Lagos — Lac, Lacs — Lago, Lagos
⩩ Swamp — Sumpf — Pantano — Marais — Pântano
⌓ Ice Features, Glacier — Eis- und Gletscherformen — Accidentes Glaciales — Formes glaciaires — Acidentes glaciares
⫧ Other Hydrographic Features — Andere Hydrographische Objekte — Otros Elementos Hidrográficos — Autres données hydrographiques — Outros acidentes hidrográficos

✥ Submarine Features — Untermeerische Objekte — Accidentes Submarinos — Formes de relief sous-marin — Acidentes submarinos
□ Political Unit — Politische Einheit — Unidad Politica — Entité politique — Unidade política
♥ Cultural Institution — Kulturelle Institution — Institución Cultural — Institution culturelle — Instituição cultural
⊥ Historical Site — Historische Stätte — Sitio Histórico — Site historique — Sitio histórico
♠ Recreational Site — Erholungs- und Ferienort — Sitio de Recreo — Centre de loisirs — Area de Lazer
⊠ Airport — Flughafen — Aeropuerto — Aéroport — Aeroporto
■ Military Installation — Militäranlage — Instalación Militar — Installation militaire — Instalação militar
◆ Miscellaneous — Verschiedenes — Misceláneo — Divers — Diversos

ENGLISH — Name, Page, Lat.°′, Long.°′

DEUTSCH — Name, Seite, Breite°′, Länge°′ E = Ost

Basuo — Dongfang 110 19.05 N 108.39 E
Bāsūs 273c 30.08 N 31.13 E
Baswa 126 24.08 N 87.52 E
Basyūn 142 30.57 N 30.49 E
Bas-Zaïre □[4] 152 5.30 S 14.30 E
Bata 152 1.51 N 9.45 E
Bataan □[4] 116 14.40 N 120.25 E
Bataan, Mount ∧ 116 14.31 N 120.28 E
Bataan Peninsula ›[1] 116 14.40 N 120.25 E
Batabanó 240p 22.43 N 82.17 W
Batabanó, Golfo de ⊂ 240p 22.15 N 82.30 W
Batac 116 18.05 N 120.35 E
Batad 116 11.25 N 123.06 E
Batagaj 74 67.38 N 134.38 E
Batagaj-Alyta 74 67.48 N 130.25 E
Batag Island I 116 12.38 N 125.04 E
Batagol 88 52.22 N 100.45 E
Bataguassu 255 21.42 S 52.22 W
Bataiporã 255 22.20 S 53.17 W
Batajsk 83 47.10 N 39.44 E
Batak 38 41.57 N 24.13 E
Batak, jazovir ⊜[1] 38 41.59 N 24.11 E
Batakan 112 4.05 S 114.38 E
Batala 123 31.48 N 75.12 E
Batalha, Bra. 250 9.41 S 37.08 W
Batalha, Bra. 250 4.01 S 42.05 W
Batalha, Port. 34 39.39 N 8.50 W
Bataly 86 52.52 N 62.00 E
Batam, Pulau I 112 1.05 N 104.03 E
Batama, Ross. 88 53.53 N 101.36 E
Batama, Zaïre 154 0.56 N 26.39 E
Batamaj 74 63.31 N 129.27 E
Batamšinskij 86 50.36 N 58.16 E
Batan, Pil. 116 11.35 N 122.30 E
Batan, Zhg. 98 34.10 N 120.04 E
Batanagar 126 22.31 N 88.15 E
Batang, Indon. 115a 6.55 S 109.45 E
Batang, Zhg. 102 30.02 N 99.02 E
Batangafo 152 7.18 N 18.18 E
Batangas 116 13.45 N 121.03 E
Batangas □[4] 116 13.50 N 121.00 E
Batangas Bay ⊂ 116 13.43 N 121.00 E
Batangbatangdaya 115a 6.56 S 113.59 E
Batang Berjuntai 114 3.23 N 101.25 E
Batang Kali 114 3.28 N 101.38 E
Batangtoru 114 1.29 N 99.03 E
Batan Island I, Pil. 108 20.26 N 121.58 E
Batan Island I, Pil. 116 13.15 N 124.00 E
Batan Islands II 108 20.30 N 121.50 E
Batanta, Pulau I 164 0.50 S 130.40 E
Batas ≃ 287a 22.44 S 43.24 W
Batas Island I 116 11.10 N 119.36 E
Bátaszék 30 46.12 N 18.44 E
Batatais 255 20.53 S 47.37 W
Batatuba 256 23.04 S 46.25 W
Batavia, Arg. 252 34.47 S 65.41 W
Batavia, Il., U.S. 216 41.51 N 88.18 W
Batavia, Ia., U.S. 190 40.59 N 92.10 W
Batavia, Mi., U.S. 216 41.55 N 85.06 W
Batavia, N.Y., U.S. 210 42.59 N 78.11 W
Batavia, Oh., U.S. 218 39.04 N 84.10 W
Batawa 212 44.10 N 77.36 W
Batbatan Island I 116 11.28 N 121.55 E
Batcengel 88 47.47 N 101.58 E
Batchawana ≃ 190 46.55 N 84.32 W
Batchawana Mountain ∧ 190 47.04 N 84.24 W
Batchawanna Island I 190 46.53 N 84.30 W
Batchelor 164 13.04 S 131.01 E
Bătdâmbâng 110 13.06 N 103.12 E
Bate Bay ⊂ 170 34.04 S 151.12 E
Bateckij 76 58.39 N 30.19 E
Bate Heath 262 53.19 N 2.28 W
Batéké, Plateaux ⋀[1] 152 3.30 S 15.45 E
Batemans Bay 166 35.43 S 150.11 E
Batenbrock ◆[8] 263 51.31 N 6.57 E
Batepito ≃ 200 30.48 N 109.11 W
Bates, Mount ∧ 174c 29.01 S 167.56 E
Batesburg 192 33.54 N 81.32 W
Bates Creek ≃ 200 42.41 N 106.37 W
Bates Range ⋀ 162 27.25 S 121.13 E
Batesville, Ar., U.S. 194 35.46 N 91.38 W
Batesville, In., U.S. 218 39.18 N 85.13 W
Batesville, Ms., U.S. 194 34.18 N 89.56 W
Batesville, Tx., U.S. 196 28.57 N 99.37 W
Bath, N.B., Can. 186 46.31 N 67.36 W
Bath, On., Can. 212 44.11 N 76.47 W
Bath, Eng., U.K. 42 51.23 N 2.22 W
Bath, Il., U.S. 219 40.11 N 90.08 W
Bath, Me., U.S. 188 43.54 N 69.49 W
Bath, Mi., U.S. 216 42.49 N 84.26 W
Bath, N.Y., U.S. 210 42.20 N 77.19 W
Bath, Oh., U.S. 214 41.11 N 81.38 W
Bath, Pa., U.S. 208 40.43 N 75.23 W
Bath □[6] 218 38.14 N 83.48 W
Batha □[5] 146 14.00 N 19.00 E
Batha ≃ 146 12.47 N 17.34 E
Bath Addition 285 40.06 N 74.52 W
Bathgate, Scot., U.K. 46 55.55 N 3.39 W
Bathgate, N.D., U.S. 198 48.52 N 97.28 W
Bathinda 123 30.12 N 74.57 E
Bathsheba 241g 13.13 N 59.31 W
Bathurst, Austl. 166 33.25 S 149.35 E
Bathurst, N.B., Can. 186 47.36 N 65.39 W
Bathurst, S. Afr. 158 33.30 S 26.50 E
Bathurst, Cape › 176 70.35 N 128.00 W
Bathurst, Lake ⊜ 170 35.04 S 149.44 E
Bathurst — Banjul 150 13.28 N 16.39 W
Bathurst Inlet 176 66.50 N 108.01 W
Bathurst Inlet ⊂ 176 68.10 N 108.50 W
Bathurst Island I, Austl. 164 11.37 S 130.23 E
Bathurst Island I, N.T., Can. 16 76.00 N 100.30 W
Bathurst Island Aboriginal Reserve ◆[4] 164 11.37 S 130.23 E
Bati 144 11.10 N 40.02 E
Batia 150 10.54 N 1.29 E
Batiāgarh 124 24.07 N 79.21 E
Batié 150 9.53 N 2.55 W
Bāṭin, Wādī al- ∨ 128 29.35 N 47.00 E
Batina 38 45.51 N 18.51 E
Batiquitos Lagoon ⊂ 228 33.05 N 117.18 W
Batīr 132 31.16 N 35.42 E
Batiscan ≃ 206 46.31 N 72.15 W
Batiste Creek ≃ 222 30.04 N 94.28 W
Batkanu 150 9.05 N 12.25 W
Batken 85 40.03 N 70.50 E
Batley 44 53.44 N 1.37 W
Batlow 171b 35.31 S 148.09 E
Batman 130 37.52 N 41.07 E
Batman □[4] 130 38.00 N 41.15 E
Batna 148 35.34 N 6.11 E
Batna □[5] 148 35.30 N 6.10 E
Baṭn al-Ghūl 132 29.44 N 35.52 E
Batnorov 88 47.55 N 111.30 E
Batō, Nihon 94 36.44 N 140.10 E
Bato, Pil. 116 10.20 N 124.47 E
Ba To, Viet 110 14.46 N 108.44 E
Bato, Lake ⊜ 116 13.19 N 123.21 E
Batoala 152 0.48 N 13.27 E
Batoche Rectory National Historic Site ⊥ 184 52.41 N 106.02 W
Batoka 154 16.47 S 27.15 E
Baton Rouge 194 30.27 N 91.09 W
Bator 123 33.06 N 75.19 E
Batorampon Point › 116 7.07 N 121.54 E
Batouri 152 4.26 N 14.22 E
Batovi 255 15.53 S 53.24 W
Batpajsagyr, peski ◆[2] 80 47.20 N 48.40 E
Batrā (Petra) ⊥ 132 30.20 N 35.26 E
Batrā', Jibāl al- ⋀ 132 29.53 N 35.38 E
Baṭrah 142 31.10 N 31.27 E
Ba Tri 110 10.02 N 106.36 E
Batsawul 120 34.15 N 70.52 E
Batson 222 30.15 N 94.37 W
Batsto ≃ 285 39.39 N 74.39 W
Batsto, Skit Branch ≃ 285 39.46 N 74.41 W
Batsto State Historic Site ⊥ 208 39.39 N 74.39 W
Bat Sûmber 88 48.29 N 106.42 E
Battaglia Terme 64 45.17 N 11.47 E
Battambang — Bătdâmbâng 110 13.06 N 103.12 E
Battenberg 56 51.01 N 8.38 E
Batten Kill ≃ 188 43.06 N 73.35 W
Batterie, Pointe de la › 240e 14.44 N 60.54 W
Bätterkinden 58 47.08 N 7.32 E
Battersea ◆[8] 260 51.28 N 0.10 W
Battersea Park ♠ 260 51.29 N 0.09 W
Batticaloa 122 7.43 N 81.42 E
Battice 56 50.39 N 5.49 E
Battin 224 45.29 N 122.34 W
Battipaglia 68 40.37 N 14.58 E
Battle 42 50.55 N 0.29 E
Battle ≃ 176 52.43 N 108.15 W
Battle Creek, Ia., U.S. 198 42.18 N 95.35 W
Battle Creek, Mi., U.S. 216 42.19 N 85.10 W
Battle Creek, Ne., U.S. 198 41.59 N 97.35 W
Battle Creek ≃, N.A. 202 48.36 N 109.11 W
Battle Creek ≃, Ca., U.S. 204 40.21 N 122.11 W
Battle Creek ≃, Id., U.S. 202 42.14 N 116.32 W
Battle Creek ≃, Mi., U.S. 216 42.19 N 85.12 W
Battle Creek ≃, Tx., U.S. 196 32.50 N 98.58 W
Battle Creek, North Fork ≃ 204 40.26 N 122.00 W
Battle Creek, South Fork ≃ 204 40.26 N 122.00 W
Battlefields 154 18.31 S 29.52 E
Battle Green ⊥ 283 42.27 N 71.14 W
Battle Ground, In., U.S. 216 40.30 N 86.50 W
Battle Ground, Wa., U.S. 224 45.46 N 122.31 W
Battle Harbour 176 52.16 N 55.35 W
Battle Lake 198 46.16 N 95.42 W
Battlement Mesa ∧ 200 39.20 N 108.00 W
Battlemount 158 26.57 S 23.46 E
Battle Mountain 204 40.38 N 116.56 W
Battle Mountain ∧ 200 41.02 N 107.16 W
Battlesbridge 260 51.37 N 0.34 E
Battonya 30 46.17 N 21.01 E
Battuello 266b 45.27 N 8.56 E
Batu 115a 7.52 S 112.31 E
Batu ∧ 144 6.55 N 39.46 E
Batu, Bukit ∧ 112 2.16 N 113.43 E
Batu, Kepulauan II 110 0.18 S 98.28 E
Batuan 116 12.25 N 123.47 E
Batu Arang 114 3.19 N 101.28 E
Batuata, Pulau I 112 6.12 S 122.42 E
Batuata, Tanjung › 115b 9.37 S 120.29 E
Batu-Batu 112 4.09 S 119.52 E
Batu Berinchang, Gunong ∧ 114 4.30 N 101.24 E
Batubetumpang 112 2.53 S 106.09 E
Batubrok, Bukit ∧ 112 1.10 N 114.36 E
Batu Caves 114 3.14 N 101.40 E
Batudaka, Pulau I 112 0.28 S 121.48 E
Batu Enam 114 2.35 N 102.43 E
Batu Gajah 114 4.28 N 101.03 E
Batui 112 1.17 S 122.33 E
Batui, Pegunungan ⋀ 112 1.15 S 122.10 E
Batuidu 112 10.38 S 123.25 E
Batukau, Bukit ∧ 115b 8.20 S 115.05 E
Batukelau 112 0.48 N 115.01 E
Batu Laut 114 2.41 N 101.31 E
Batulicin 112 3.27 S 116.00 E
Batumata Point › 164 10.17 S 148.57 E
Batumi 84 41.38 N 41.38 E
Batumundan 114 1.17 N 98.50 E
Batu Pahat (Bandar Penggaram) 114 1.51 N 102.56 E
Batupanjang 114 1.43 N 101.31 E
Batu Puteh, Gunong ∧ 114 4.13 N 101.27 E
Batuputih 112 1.24 N 118.29 E
Baturaja 112 4.08 S 104.10 E
Batu Rakit 114 5.27 N 103.03 E
Baturetno 115a 7.59 S 110.56 E
Baturin 78 51.21 N 32.51 E
Baturino, Ross. 86 57.48 N 85.12 E
Baturino, Ross. 265b 55.35 N 37.31 E
Baturinskaja 78 45.47 N 39.22 E
Baturité 250 4.20 S 38.53 W
Baturotok 115b 8.42 S 117.10 E
Baturusa 112 2.02 S 106.07 E
Batusangkar 112 0.27 S 100.35 E
Batutinggi 112 1.55 S 113.19 E
Bat Yam 132 32.01 N 34.45 E
Batyrevo 80 55.04 N 47.38 E
Batyr-Mala, ozero ⊜ 80 47.35 N 44.45 E
Bau 112 1.25 N 110.08 E
Baú ≃ 250 7.26 S 54.47 W
Bauang 116 16.31 N 120.20 E
Baubašata, gory ⋀ 85 41.20 N 72.45 E
Baubau 112 5.28 S 122.38 E
Bauchi 150 10.19 N 9.50 E
Bauchi □[3] 146 10.30 N 10.15 E
Baucina 70 37.55 N 13.32 E
Baud 32 47.52 N 3.01 W
Bauda 120 20.50 N 84.19 E
Baudette 190 48.42 N 94.35 W
Baudó ≃ 246 4.57 N 77.22 W
Baudouin Stadium ♠ 273b 4.20 S 15.20 E
Baudour 50 50.29 N 3.49 E
Bauernschaft 263 51.34 N 6.33 E
Bauerstown 279b 40.30 N 79.59 W
Baugo Creek ≃ 216 41.40 N 86.04 W
Baukau 112 8.27 S 126.27 E
Bauld, Cape › 186 51.38 N 55.25 W
Baulkham Hills 274a 33.46 S 151.00 E
Baulmes 58 46.48 N 6.32 E
Bauma 58 47.23 N 8.53 E
Baumberg 263 51.07 N 6.54 E
Baume ≃ 62 44.26 N 4.20 E
Baume-les-Dames 58 47.21 N 6.22 E
Baumholder 56 49.37 N 7.20 E
Baumschulenweg ◆[8] 264a 52.28 N 13.29 E
Baun 112 10.18 S 123.43 E
Baunach 56 49.59 N 10.50 E
Baunach ≃ 56 49.59 N 10.51 E
Baunatal 56 51.16 N 9.25 E
Baunei 71 40.02 N 9.40 E
Baunt 88 55.16 N 113.08 E
Baunt, ozero ⊜ 88 55.12 N 113.00 E
Bāuphal 126 22.25 N 90.33 E
Baure 150 12.50 N 8.45 E
Baures 248 13.35 S 63.35 W
Baures ≃ 248 12.30 S 64.18 W
Bauru 255 22.19 S 49.04 W
Baús 255 18.19 S 53.10 W
Bausendorf 56 50.01 N 6.59 E
Bausenhagen 263 51.31 N 7.48 E
Bauska 76 56.24 N 24.14 E
Bauta 240p 22.59 N 82.33 W
Bauta □[7] 286b 22.59 N 82.33 W
Bautino 84 44.33 N 50.15 E
Bautzen 54 51.11 N 14.26 E
Bauxite 194 34.33 N 92.31 W
Bauya 150 8.11 N 12.34 W
Bavans 58 47.29 N 6.44 E
Bavari 62 44.26 N 9.01 E
Bavaria — Bayern □[3] 30 49.00 N 11.30 E
Bavarian Alps — Bayerische Alpen ⋀ 64 47.30 N 11.00 E
Bavay 50 50.18 N 3.47 E
Båven ⊜ 40 59.01 N 16.56 E
Baveno 58 45.55 N 8.30 E
Bavilliers 58 47.37 N 6.50 E
Bavispe 232 30.24 N 108.50 W
Bavispe ≃ 232 29.15 N 109.11 W
Bavleny 80 56.24 N 39.34 E
Bavly 80 54.25 N 53.17 E
Bavnhöj ∧[2] 41 55.55 N 10.07 E
Bavtugaj 84 43.11 N 46.49 E
Baw 110 23.19 N 95.50 E
Bāwal 124 28.05 N 76.35 E
Bawal, Pulau I 112 2.44 S 110.06 E
Bāwāli 272b 22.25 N 88.12 E
Bawang 115a 7.06 S 109.55 E
Baw Baw, Mount ∧ 169 37.50 S 146.17 E
Baw Baw National Park ♠ 169 37.55 S 146.22 E
Baw Beese Lake ⊜ 216 41.54 N 84.36 W
Bawdeswell 42 52.45 N 1.01 E
Bawdwin 110 23.06 N 97.18 E
Bawean, Pulau I 115a 5.46 S 112.40 E
Baweigang 106 31.57 N 120.14 E
Bawku 150 11.05 N 0.14 W
Bawlake 110 19.11 N 97.21 E
Bawmi 110 17.19 N 94.35 E
Bawria 126 22.29 N 88.10 E
Bawtry 44 53.26 N 1.01 W
Baxdo 144 5.46 N 47.15 E
Baxenden 262 53.44 N 2.20 W
Baxian, Zhg. 105 39.06 N 116.23 E
Baxian (Yudongxi), Zhg. 107 29.23 N 106.32 E
Baxley 192 31.46 N 82.20 W
Baxter, Ia., U.S. 190 41.49 N 93.09 W
Baxter, Mn., U.S. 190 46.20 N 94.17 W
Baxter, Tn., U.S. 194 36.09 N 85.38 W
Baxter Estates 276 40.50 N 73.42 W
Baxter Springs 198 37.02 N 94.44 W
Baxter State Park ♠ 188 46.00 N 68.58 W
Baxterville 194 31.05 N 89.35 W
Bay 194 35.44 N 90.33 W
Bay □[4] 144 2.30 N 43.30 E
Bay, Laguna de ⊜ 116 14.23 N 121.15 E
Baya, Zaïre 152 4.57 N 19.43 E
Baya, Zaïre 154 11.52 S 27.27 E
Bayāḍah, Wādī al- ∨ 146 26.08 N 18.35 E
Bayāḍ an-Naṣārā 142 29.04 N 31.08 E
Bayag 116 18.16 N 121.02 E
Bayala 158 27.47 S 32.08 E
Bay al-Kabīr, Wādī ∨ 146 31.15 N 15.57 E
Bayambang 116 15.49 N 120.27 E
Bayamo 240p 20.23 N 76.39 W
Bayamo ≃ 240p 20.34 N 76.44 W
Bayamón 240m 18.24 N 66.09 W
Bayan, Indon. 115b 8.16 S 116.26 E
Bayan, Zhg. 89 46.05 N 127.24 E
Bāyan, Band-e ⋀ 120 34.20 N 65.30 E
Bayāna 124 26.54 N 77.17 E
Bayanbayanan 269f 14.39 N 121.06 E
Bayanchagan 89 47.19 N 124.03 E
Bayang 116 7.48 N 124.12 E
Bayanga 152 2.53 N 16.19 E
Bayange 102 39.19 N 107.31 E
Bayan Har Shan ⋀ 102 33.48 N 98.10 E
Bayanheshuomiao 89 48.51 N 119.46 E
Bayanjie 89 49.36 N 124.37 E
Bayanluke 89 50.52 N 119.33 E
Bayannaobao 102 39.44 N 107.40 E
Bayano, Lago ⊜[1] 246 9.10 N 78.40 W
Bayan Obo 102 41.58 N 110.02 E
Bayan Tal 89 43.44 N 123.16 E
Bayard, Ia., U.S. 198 41.51 N 94.33 W
Bayard, Ne., U.S. 198 41.45 N 103.19 W
Bayard, N.M., U.S. 200 32.45 N 108.07 W
Bayard, Oh., U.S. 214 40.46 N 81.04 W
Bayard, W.V., U.S. 188 39.16 N 79.21 W
Bayard, Col)(62 44.37 N 6.05 E
Bayard Cutting Arboretum State Park ♠ 276 40.45 N 73.10 W
Bayat, Indon. 112 2.06 S 103.38 E
Bayat, Tür. 130 38.59 N 30.56 E
Bayat, Tür. 130 40.39 N 34.15 E
Bayawan 116 9.22 N 122.48 E
Bayawan ≃ 116 9.22 N 122.48 E
Baybay 116 10.41 N 124.48 E
Bayberry 210 43.08 N 76.13 W
Bayble 46 58.12 N 6.13 W
Bayboro 192 35.08 N 76.46 W
Bay Bulls 186 47.19 N 52.49 W
Bayburt 130 40.16 N 40.15 E
Bayburt □[4] 130 40.15 N 40.00 E
Bay Center 224 46.37 N 123.57 W
Bay City, Mi., U.S. 190 43.35 N 83.53 W
Bay City, Or., U.S. 224 45.31 N 123.53 W
Bay City, Tx., U.S. 222 28.58 N 95.58 W
Bay Creek ≃, Il., U.S. 194 37.16 N 88.31 W
Bay Creek ≃, Il., U.S. 219 39.20 N 90.46 W
Baydā', Bi'r ⊤[4] 142 29.45 N 32.13 E
Bay de Verde 186 48.05 N 52.54 W
Baydhabo (Baidoa) 144 3.07 N 43.39 E
Bay du Nord ≃ 186 47.44 N 55.25 W
Baye, Cap › 175f 20.57 S 165.25 E
Bayel 58 48.12 N 4.47 E
Bayerische Alpen ⋀ 64 47.30 N 11.00 E
Bayerisch Eisenstein 60 49.07 N 13.12 E
Bayerischer Wald ⋀ 60 49.00 N 12.40 E
Bayerischer Wald, Nationalpark ♠ 60 48.56 N 13.28 E
Bayern □[3] 30 49.00 N 11.30 E
Bayeuen 114 4.36 N 97.53 E
Bayeux, Bra. 250 7.08 S 34.56 W
Bayeux, Fr. 32 49.16 N 0.42 W
Bay Farm Island I 282 37.43 N 122.14 W
Bayfield, Co., U.S. 200 37.13 N 107.35 W
Bayfield, Wi., U.S. 190 46.48 N 90.49 W
Bayfield, Île I 186 51.13 N 58.23 W
Bayford 260 51.46 N 0.06 W
'Bayh 132 33.44 N 35.31 E
Bayḥān al-Qaṣāḍ 144 14.48 N 45.43 E
Bay Harbor Islands 220 25.53 N 80.08 W
Bayhead, Scot., U.K. 46 57.33 N 7.24 W
Bay Head, N.J., U.S. 208 40.04 N 74.03 W
Bayiji 98 34.18 N 117.41 E
Bayındır 130 38.13 N 27.40 E
Bayingzi 104 41.28 N 120.46 E
Baykan 130 38.09 N 41.47 E
Baykonur — Bajkonyr 86 47.50 N 66.03 E
Bay Kurt 85 39.58 N 75.33 E
Bay L'Argent 186 47.33 N 54.54 W
Bayley Point › 164 16.56 S 139.02 E
Bayley Point Aboriginal Reserve ◆[4] 166 16.57 S 138.55 E
Baylis 219 39.44 N 90.54 W
Bay Meadows Race Track ♠ 282 37.32 N 122.18 W
Bay Minette 194 30.52 N 87.46 W
Baynūnah ◆[1] 128 23.50 N 52.50 E
Bayo 34 43.09 N 8.58 W
Bayombong 116 16.29 N 121.09 E
Bayon 58 48.29 N 6.19 E
Bayona 34 42.07 N 8.51 W
Bayonne, Fr. 32 43.29 N 1.29 W
Bayonne, N.J., U.S. 210 40.40 N 74.06 W
Bayonne ≃ 206 46.05 N 73.10 W
Bayonne Bridge ◆[5] 276 40.38 N 74.09 W
Bayons 62 44.20 N 6.10 E
Bayou Bodcau Reservoir ⊜[1] 194 32.45 N 93.30 W
Bayou Cane 194 29.37 N 90.45 W
Bayou D'Arbonne Lake ⊜[1] 194 32.45 N 92.25 W
Bayou La Batre 194 30.24 N 88.14 W
Bayovar 248 5.50 S 81.03 W
Bay Park 276 40.38 N 73.40 W
Bayport, Fl., U.S. 220 28.33 N 82.39 W
Bay Port, Mi., U.S. 190 43.50 N 83.22 W
Bayport, Mn., U.S. 190 45.01 N 92.46 W
Bayport, N.Y., U.S. 210 40.44 N 73.03 W
Bayramiç 130 39.48 N 26.37 E
Bayramören 130 40.57 N 33.12 E
Bayreuth 60 49.57 N 11.35 E
Bay Ridge 208 38.56 N 76.27 W
Bay Ridge ◆[8] 276 40.37 N 74.02 W
Bay Ridge Channel ⋓ 276 40.39 N 74.02 W
Bayrischzell 64 47.40 N 12.00 E
Bay Roberts 186 47.36 N 53.16 W
Bayrūt (Beirut) 130 33.53 N 35.30 E
Bayrūt □[4] 132 33.56 N 35.30 E
Bays, Lake of ⊜ 212 45.15 N 79.04 W
Bay Saint Louis 194 30.18 N 89.19 W
Bay Shore 210 40.43 N 73.14 W
Bayshore Gardens 220 27.25 N 82.35 W
Bayside, On., Can. 212 44.07 N 77.30 W
Bayside, Ma., U.S. 283 42.18 N 70.53 W
Bayside, Wi., U.S. 216 43.10 N 87.54 W
Bayside ◆[8] 276 40.46 N 73.46 W
Bay Springs 194 31.58 N 89.17 W
Bay Springs Lake ⊜[1] 194 34.35 N 88.20 W
Bayston Hill 42 52.40 N 2.45 W
Bayswater 274b 37.51 S 145.16 E
Bayswater North 274b 37.49 S 145.17 E
Bayt ad-Dīn 132 33.42 N 35.35 E
Bayt al-Faqīh 144 14.32 N 43.20 E
Bayt Ḥānūn 132 31.32 N 34.33 E
Bayt Jālā 132 31.43 N 35.11 E
Bayt Jinn 132 33.19 N 35.53 E
Bayt Laḥm (Bethlehem) 132 31.43 N 35.12 E
Bayt Mirī 132 33.52 N 35.36 E
Baytown 222 29.44 N 94.58 W
Bayt Sāḥūr 132 31.42 N 35.13 E
Bayt Sīrā 132 31.53 N 35.03 E
Bayunglencir 112 2.03 S 103.41 E
Bayview, Austl. 274a 33.40 S 151.18 E
Bay View, N.Z. 172 39.25 S 176.53 E
Bay View, N.Y., U.S. 210 42.47 N 78.51 W
Bay View, Oh., U.S. 214 41.28 N 82.50 W
Bayview ◆[8] 282 37.44 N 122.23 W
Bay Village 214 41.29 N 81.55 W
Bayville, N.J., U.S. 208 39.54 N 74.09 W
Bayville, N.Y., U.S. 210 40.54 N 73.33 W
Baywater 168a 31.55 S 115.56 E
Baywood Park 226 35.20 N 120.50 W
Bayyāḍah, Ra's al- › 132 33.10 N 35.10 E
Bayyā'īyah al-Kabīrah 130 35.42 N 37.09 E
Bayyūḍah ⊤[4] 140 17.32 N 32.07 E
Bayzo 150 13.52 N 4.45 E
Baza 34 37.29 N 2.46 W
Baza, Sierra de ⋀ 34 37.15 N 2.45 W
Bazai 100 24.32 N 114.10 E
Bazainville 261 48.48 N 1.40 E
Bazalija 78 49.43 N 26.27 E
Bazar 88 53.58 N 116.05 E
Bazarčaj 84 39.40 N 45.48 E
Bazard'uz'u, gora ∧ 84 41.13 N 47.51 E
Bāzār-e Panjvā'ī 120 31.32 N 65.28 E
Bazargic — Dobrič 38 43.34 N 27.50 E
Bazar-Kurgan 85 41.02 N 72.45 E
Bazarnyje Mataki 80 54.56 N 49.56 E
Bazarnyj Karabulak 80 52.16 N 46.25 E
Bazarnyj Syzgan 80 53.45 N 46.46 E
Bazarovo 82 54.47 N 38.10 E
Bazaršolan 80 49.04 N 51.56 E
Bazartobe 80 49.23 N 51.50 E
Bazaruto, Ilha do I 156 21.40 S 35.28 E
Bazas 32 44.26 N 0.13 W
Bazavluk ≃ 78 47.34 N 34.04 E
Bazdār 120 26.21 N 65.03 E
Bazeilles 56 49.40 N 4.59 E
Bazemont 261 48.56 N 1.52 E
Bazetta 214 41.20 N 80.47 W
Bazhong 102 31.51 N 106.39 E
Bazi 100 24.46 N 113.10 E
Baziège 32 43.27 N 1.37 E
Bažigan 84 44.33 N 45.41 E
Bazine 198 38.26 N 99.41 W
Baziqiao 106 32.07 N 119.52 E
Bazkovskaja 80 49.36 N 41.43 E
Bazmān 128 27.49 N 60.12 E
Bazmān, Kūh-e ∧ 128 28.04 N 60.00 E
Bazoches-les-Gallerandes 50 48.10 N 2.03 E
Bazoches-sur-Hoëne 50 48.33 N 0.28 E
Bazoj 86 55.45 N 83.22 E
Bazzano 64 44.30 N 11.05 E
Be ≃ 110 11.06 N 106.58 E
Be, Nosy I 157b 13.20 S 48.15 E
Beach, Il., U.S. 216 42.26 N 87.50 W
Beach, N.D., U.S. 198 46.55 N 104.00 W
Beach, Tx., U.S. 222 30.20 N 95.29 W
Beach Channel ⋓ 276 40.35 N 73.50 W
Beach City 214 40.39 N 81.34 W
Beach City Lake ⊜[1] 214 40.41 N 81.36 W
Beach Glen 276 40.56 N 74.29 W
Beach Haven, N.J., U.S. 208 39.33 N 74.14 W
Beach Haven, Pa., U.S. 210 41.04 N 76.11 W
Beach Haven Terrace 208 39.35 N 74.13 W
Beach Lake 210 41.36 N 75.09 W
Beach Lake ⊜ 281 42.33 N 83.43 W
Beach Pond State Park ♠ 207 41.35 N 71.45 W
Beachport 166 37.30 S 140.01 E
Beachville 212 43.05 N 80.49 W
Beachwood, N.J., U.S. 208 39.56 N 74.11 W
Beachwood, Oh., U.S. 214 41.27 N 81.30 W
Beachy Head › 42 50.44 N 0.16 E
Beacon, Austl. 162 30.26 S 117.51 E
Beacon, N.Y., U.S. 210 41.30 N 73.58 W
Beacon Falls 207 41.26 N 73.03 W
Beacon Heights 284c 38.57 N 76.54 W
Beacon Hill, Austl. 274a 33.45 S 151.15 E
Beacon Hill, Wa., U.S. 224 46.08 N 122.57 W
Beacon Hill ∧[2], H.K. 271d 22.21 N 114.09 E
Beacon Hill ∧[2], Wales, U.K. 42 52.23 N 3.12 W
Beacon Rock State Park ♠ 224 45.38 N 122.03 W
Beaconsfield, Austl. 166 41.12 S 146.48 E
Beaconsfield, Austl. 274b 38.03 S 145.22 E
Beaconsfield, P.Q., Can. 206 45.26 N 73.50 W
Beaconsfield, Eng., U.K. 42 51.37 N 0.39 W
Beaconsfield □[8] 260 51.34 N 0.35 W
Beadle Lake 216 42.18 N 85.12 W
Beagh, Slieve ∧[2] 48 54.21 N 7.12 W
Beagle, Canal ⋓ 254 54.53 S 68.10 W
Beagle Bay 162 16.58 S 122.40 E
Beagle Gulf ⊂ 164 12.00 S 130.20 E
Beagle Reef ✣[2] 160 15.20 S 123.29 E
Bealanana 157b 14.33 S 48.44 E
Beale, Cape › 182 48.44 N 125.20 W
Beale, Lake ⊜ 122 19.45 N 73.44 E
Beale Air Force Base ■ 226 39.08 N 121.20 W
Bealiba 169 36.48 S 143.33 E
Bealiba, Mount ∧[2] 169 36.49 S 143.38 E
Beallsville 214 40.04 N 80.01 W
Beals Creek ≃ 196 32.10 N 100.51 W
Beam ≃ 260 51.31 N 0.10 E
Beaminster 42 50.49 N 2.45 W
Bean 260 51.25 N 0.17 E
Beanblossom Creek ≃ 194 39.20 N 86.39 W
Bean Creek ≃ 216 41.35 N 84.19 W
Bear ≃, Sk., Can. 184 54.33 N 103.58 W
Bear ≃, U.S. 200 41.30 N 112.08 W
Bear ≃, Ca., U.S. 226 38.57 N 121.35 W
Bear, Mount ∧ 180 61.17 N 141.09 W
Beara 164 7.30 S 144.50 E
Bear Bay ⊂ 176 75.47 N 87.00 W
Bear Branch 218 38.55 N 85.05 W
Bear Brook ≃, On., Can. 212 45.25 N 75.10 W
Bear Brook ≃, N.J., U.S. 276 41.02 N 74.03 W
Bear Brook State Park ♠ 188 43.05 N 71.26 W
Bear Butte ∧ 198 44.28 N 103.26 W
Bear Canyon ∨ 280 34.14 N 118.07 W
Bear Cove 182 50.44 N 127.27 W
Bear Creek 210 41.11 N 75.45 W
Bear Creek ≃, On., Can. 214 42.44 N 82.23 W
Bear Creek ≃, U.S. 194 34.46 N 88.05 W
Bear Creek ≃, U.S. 196 37.45 N 101.23 W
Bear Creek ≃, U.S. 216 41.17 N 83.57 W
Bear Creek ≃, Al., U.S. 194 33.11 N 88.05 W
Bear Creek ≃, Ca., U.S. 226 38.56 N 122.20 W
Bear Creek ≃, Ca., U.S. 226 38.02 N 121.18 W
Bear Creek ≃, Ca., U.S. 226 37.17 N 120.50 W
Bear Creek ≃, Ca., U.S. 228 34.10 N 117.01 W
Bear Creek ≃, Ca., U.S. 280 34.14 N 117.53 W
Bear Creek ≃, Co., U.S. 200 39.40 N 105.00 W
Bear Creek ≃, Il., U.S. 219 39.33 N 89.23 W
Bear Creek ≃, Il., U.S. 219 40.07 N 91.29 W
Bear Creek ≃, Md., U.S. 284b 39.13 N 76.30 W
Bear Creek ≃, Mo., U.S. 219 39.03 N 91.14 W
Bear Creek ≃, N.D., U.S. 198 46.10 N 98.06 W
Bear Creek ≃, Oh., U.S. 218 39.39 N 84.17 W
Bear Creek ≃, Or., U.S. 202 44.06 N 120.46 W
Bear Creek ≃, Or., U.S. 202 42.26 N 122.58 W
Bear Creek ≃, Pa., U.S. 214 41.23 N 78.50 W
Bear Creek ≃, Wy., U.S. 198 41.41 N 104.13 W
Bear Creek, South Fork ≃ 219 40.09 N 91.18 W
Bear Creek, West Fork ≃ 280 34.16 N 117.53 W
Bearden 194 33.43 N 92.36 W
Beardmore 176 49.36 N 87.57 W
Beardmore Glacier ⊓ 9 83.45 S 171.00 E
Beardsley Lake ⊜[1] 226 38.13 N 120.03 W
Beardstown, Il., U.S. 219 40.01 N 90.25 W
Beardstown, In., U.S. 216 41.08 N 86.36 W
Beardy and Okemasis Indian Reserves ◆[4] 184 52.48 N 106.20 W
Bearfort Mountain ∧ 276 41.09 N 74.23 W
Bear Head Creek ≃ 194 30.18 N 93.35 W
Bear Head Lake ⊜ 184 55.33 N 96.10 W
Bear Head Lake State Park ♠ 190 47.49 N 92.04 W
Bearhead Mountain ∧ 224 47.02 N 121.53 W
Bear Hill ∧[2], Ct., U.S. 207 41.39 N 73.24 W
Bear Hill ∧[2], N.Y., U.S. 210 41.18 N 74.00 W
Bear-in-the-Lodge Creek ≃ 198 43.41 N 101.50 W
Bear Island I, Ant. 9 74.30 S 110.45 W
Bear Island I, Mb., Can. 184 54.53 N 98.04 W
Bear Island I, Ire. 48 51.40 N 9.48 W
Bear Island I, Va., U.S. 284c 38.59 N 77.14 W
Bear Island — Bjørnøya I 12 74.25 N 19.00 E
Bear Lake, B.C., Can. 182 56.11 N 126.51 W
Bear Lake, Pa., U.S. 214 42.00 N 79.30 W
Bear Lake ⊜, Ab., Can. 182 55.16 N 119.00 W
Bear Lake ⊜, B.C., Can. 182 56.06 N 126.45 W
Bear Lake ⊜, Mb., Can. 184 55.08 N 96.00 W
Bear Lake ⊜, On., Can. 212 45.26 N 79.35 W
Bear Lake ⊜, U.S. 200 42.00 N 111.20 W
Bear Mountain ∧, Ca., U.S. 228 35.12 N 118.38 W
Bear Mountain ∧, Ky., U.S. 192 37.32 N 84.16 W
Bear Mountain ∧, Or., U.S. 202 43.51 N 122.53 W
Bear Mountain ∧[2] 210 41.18 N 74.01 W
Bear Mountain State Park ♠ 210 41.17 N 74.00 W
Béarn □[9] 32 43.20 N 0.45 W
Bear Pond ⊜ 276 40.58 N 74.40 W
Bear River 186 44.34 N 65.39 W
Bear River Range ⋀ 200 41.50 N 111.30 W
Bear Run ≃ 279b 40.33 N 80.04 W
Bearsden 46 55.56 N 4.20 W
Bears Paw Mountains ⋀ 202 48.15 N 109.30 W
Bearstead 260 51.16 N 0.35 E
Bearsville 210 42.02 N 74.09 W
Bear Swamp ≃ 285 39.54 N 74.47 W
Bear Swamp ≡ 285 39.53 N 74.45 W
Bear Swamp Brook ≃ 276 41.04 N 74.13 W
Bear Swamp Lake ⊜ 276 41.06 N 74.13 W
Beartooth Mountains ⋀ 202 45.00 N 109.30 W
Beartooth Pass)(202 44.58 N 109.28 W
Bear Town 194 31.13 N 90.27 W
Beās 123 31.31 N 75.17 E
Beās ≃ 123 31.10 N 74.59 E
Beasain 34 43.03 N 2.11 W
Beas de Segura 34 38.15 N 2.53 W
Beasley 222 29.30 N 95.55 W
Beasley Bay ⊂ 208 37.51 N 75.44 W
Beason 219 40.09 N 89.12 W
Beata, Cabo › 238 17.36 N 71.25 W
Beata, Isla I 238 17.35 N 71.31 W
Beatenberg 58 46.42 N 7.48 E
Beato ◆[8] 266c 38.44 N 9.06 W
Beaton 182 50.44 N 117.44 W
Beatrice, Al., U.S. 194 31.44 N 87.12 W
Beatrice, Ne., U.S. 198 40.16 N 96.44 W
Beatrice, Zimb. 154 18.15 S 30.55 E
Beatrice, Cape › 164 14.15 S 136.59 E
Beattie 198 39.51 N 96.25 W
Beattock 44 55.18 N 3.28 W
Beatton ≃ 176 56.10 N 120.25 W
Beatty, Nv., U.S. 204 36.54 N 116.45 W
Beatty, Oh., U.S. 218 39.53 N 83.50 W
Beatty Saugeen ≃ 212 44.08 N 81.02 W
Beattyville 192 37.34 N 83.42 W
Beaubru 56 49.46 N 5.05 E
Beaucaire 62 43.48 N 4.38 E
Beauce ◆[1] 50 48.22 N 1.50 E
Beauceville 188 46.12 N 70.46 W
Beauchamp 261 49.01 N 2.12 E
Beauchamp Roding 260 51.46 N 0.18 E
Beauchêne, Lac ⊜ 190 46.39 N 78.55 W
Beauchêne Island I 254 52.55 S 59.12 W
Beaucoup Creek ≃, Il., U.S. 194 37.47 N 89.17 W
Beaucoup Creek ≃, Il., U.S. 219 38.13 N 89.20 W
Beaucourt 58 47.29 N 6.55 E
Beaudesert 171a 27.59 S 153.00 E
Beaudette ≃ 206 45.12 N 74.19 W
Beaudry, Lac ⊜ 190 47.44 N 78.55 W
Beauduc, Pointe de › 62 43.22 N 4.34 E
Beaufays 56 50.34 N 5.38 E
Beaufort, Austl. 169 37.26 S 143.23 E
Beaufort, Fr. 58 46.34 N 5.26 E
Beaufort, Fr. 62 45.43 N 6.35 E
Beaufort, Lux. 56 49.51 N 6.18 E
Beaufort, Malay. 112 5.20 N 115.45 E
Beaufort, Mo., U.S. 219 38.26 N 91.12 W
Beaufort, N.C., U.S. 192 34.43 N 76.39 W
Beaufort, S.C., U.S. 192 32.25 N 80.40 W
Beaufort, Cape › 162 34.26 S 115.32 E
Beaufort, Massif de ⋀[1] 62 45.44 N 6.35 E
Beaufort Castle — Qal'at ash-Shaqīf ⊥ 132 33.19 N 35.32 E
Beaufort Island I 271d 22.11 N 114.15 E
Beaufort Marine Corps Air Station ■ 192 32.30 N 80.44 W
Beaufort Sea ⊤[2] 16 73.00 N 140.00 W
Beaufort West 158 32.18 S 22.36 E
Beaugency 50 47.47 N 1.38 E
Beauharnois 206 45.19 N 73.52 W
Beauharnois □[6] 206 45.15 N 74.00 W
Beauharnois, Barrage de ◆[6] 275a 45.19 N 73.55 W
Beauharnois, Canal de ⋓ 206 45.19 N 73.54 W
Beaujeu 58 46.09 N 4.36 E
Beaujolais □[9] 32 46.05 N 4.10 E
Beaulieu 42 50.49 N 1.27 W
Beaulieu-lès-Loches 50 47.07 N 1.01 E
Beaulieu-sur-Mer 62 43.42 N 7.20 E
Beauly 46 57.29 N 4.29 W
Beauly ≃ 46 57.28 N 4.28 W
Beauly Firth ⊂[1] 46 57.30 N 4.23 W
Beaumaris, Austl. 274b 37.59 S 145.02 E
Beaumaris, Wales, U.K. 44 53.16 N 4.05 W
Beaumaris Bay ⊂ 274b 38.00 S 145.03 E
Beaumes-de-Venise 62 44.07 N 5.02 E
Beaumesnil 50 49.01 N 0.43 E
Beaumetz-lès-Loges 50 50.14 N 2.39 E
Beaumont, Bel. 50 50.14 N 4.14 E
Beaumont, Nf., Can. 186 49.37 N 55.41 W
Beaumont, Fr. 32 49.40 N 1.51 W
Beaumont, N.Z. 172 45.49 S 169.32 E
Beaumont, Ca., U.S. 228 33.55 N 116.58 W
Beaumont, Ms., U.S. 194 31.10 N 88.55 W
Beaumont, Tx., U.S. 194 30.05 N 94.06 W
Beaumont-du-Gâtinais 50 48.08 N 2.29 E
Beaumont-en-Argonne 56 49.32 N 5.03 E
Beaumont Hill ∧[2] 166 31.33 S 145.13 E
Beaumont-la-Ronce 50 47.34 N 0.40 E
Beaumont-le-Roger 50 49.05 N 0.47 E
Beaumont Place 222 29.50 N 95.14 W
Beaumont-sur-Oise 50 49.08 N 2.17 E
Beaumont-sur-Sarthe 50 48.13 N 0.08 E
Beaune 58 47.02 N 4.50 E
Beaune-la-Rolande 50 48.04 N 2.26 E
Beauport 206 46.52 N 71.11 W
Beaupré 186 47.03 N 70.54 W
Beaupréau 32 47.12 N 1.00 W
Beaupre Island I 212 44.26 N 76.19 W
Beaupré Lake ⊜ 184 54.30 N 107.10 W
Beauraing 56 50.07 N 4.58 E
Beaurepaire 62 45.20 N 5.03 E
Beaurepaire-en-Bresse 58 46.40 N 5.23 E
Beaurières 62 44.35 N 5.33 E
Beaurivage 206 46.25 N 71.14 W
Beaurivage ≃ 206 46.42 N 71.16 W
Beauséjour, Mb., Can. 184 50.04 N 96.33 W
Beauséjour, Guad. 241o 16.18 N 61.04 W
Beausoleil 62 43.45 N 7.26 E
Beausoleil Island I 212 44.51 N 79.52 W
Beautor 50 49.39 N 3.20 E
Beauvais, Fr. 50 49.26 N 2.05 E
Beauvais, Fr. 261 48.32 N 2.03 E
Beauvais Creek ≃ 202 45.29 N 107.45 W
Beauvais-Tillé, Aéroport ⊠ 50 49.28 N 2.07 E
Beauval, Sk., Can. 184 55.09 N 107.37 W
Beauval, Fr. 50 50.06 N 2.20 E
Beauvezer 62 44.09 N 6.36 E
Beauville 32 44.17 N 0.52 E
Beauvoir 261 48.39 N 2.52 E
Beauvoir-sur-Mer 32 46.55 N 2.02 W
Beauvoir-sur-Niort 32 46.11 N 0.28 W
Beaux Arts 224 47.35 N 122.11 W
Beaver, Ak., U.S. 180 66.22 N 147.24 W
Beaver, Ok., U.S. 196 36.48 N 100.31 W
Beaver, Or., U.S. 224 45.16 N 123.49 W
Beaver, Pa., U.S. 214 40.41 N 80.18 W
Beaver, Ut,. U.S. 200 38.16 N 112.38 W
Beaver, Wa., U.S. 224 48.03 N 124.19 W
Beaver, W.V., U.S. 192 37.44 N 81.08 W
Beaver □[6] 214 40.40 N 80.25 W
Beaver ≃, Can. 176 59.43 N 124.16 W
Beaver ≃, Can. 184 55.25 N 107.45 W
Beaver ≃, On., Can. 212 44.34 N 80.27 W
Beaver ≃, U.S. 196 36.35 N 99.30 W
Beaver ≃, N.Y., U.S. 188 43.54 N 75.30 W
Beaver ≃, Pa., U.S. 214 40.40 N 80.18 W
Beaver ≃, Ut,. U.S. 200 39.10 N 112.57 W
Beaver Brook 210 40.55 N 75.59 W
Beaver Brook ≃, U.S. 207 42.40 N 71.19 W
Beaver Brook ≃, Ma., U.S. 283 42.03 N 70.58 W
Beaver Brook ≃, Ma., U.S. 283 42.36 N 71.21 W
Beaver Brook ≃, Ma., U.S. 283 42.23 N 71.14 W
Beaver Brook ≃, N.J., U.S. 276 40.54 N 74.30 W
Beaver Brook ≃, N.J., U.S. 276 40.58 N 74.35 W
Beaver City 198 40.08 N 99.49 W
Beaver Creek, Yk., Can. 180 62.22 N 140.52 W
Beavercreek, Oh., U.S. 218 39.43 N 84.03 W
Beavercreek, Or., U.S. 224 45.17 N 122.32 W
Beaver Creek ≃, On., Can. 212 44.44 N 76.58 W
Beaver Creek ≃, On., Can. 212 44.30 N 77.42 W
Beaver Creek ≃, On., Can. 275b 43.51 N 79.20 W
Beaver Creek ≃, On., Can. 284a 42.58 N 79.01 W
Beaver Creek ≃, U.S. 198 47.20 N 103.39 W
Beaver Creek ≃, U.S. 198 40.04 N 99.20 W
Beaver Creek ≃, U.S. 198 43.25 N 103.59 W
Beaver Creek ≃, U.S. 216 40.58 N 87.49 W
Beaver Creek ≃, Ak., U.S. 180 66.15 N 147.32 W
Beaver Creek ≃, Ca., U.S. 226 38.12 N 120.19 W
Beaver Creek ≃, Co., U.S. 198 40.20 N 103.33 W
Beaver Creek ≃, Co., U.S. 198 38.22 N 104.58 W
Beaver Creek ≃, Il., U.S. 216 42.16 N 88.56 W
Beaver Creek ≃, Il., U.S. 219 38.33 N 89.30 W
Beaver Creek ≃, Ky., U.S. 218 38.31 N 84.11 W
Beaver Creek ≃, Md., U.S. 208 39.32 N 77.42 W

Symbols in the index entries represent the broad categories identified in the key at the right. Symbols with superior numbers (⋀[1]) identify subcategories (see complete key on page *I · 1).*

Symbole im Register stellen die rechts im Schlüssel erklärten Kategorien dar. Symbole mit hochgestellten Ziffern (⋀[1]) bezeichnen Unterabteilungen einer Kategorie (vgl. vollständiger Schlüssel auf Seite *I · 1).*

Los símbolos incluídos en el texto del índice representan las grandes categorías identificadas con la clave a la derecha. Los símbolos con numeros en su parte superior (⋀[1]) identifican las subcategorías (véase la clave completa en la página *I · 1).*

Les symboles de l'index représentent les catégories indiquées dans la légende à droite. Les symboles suivis d'un indice (⋀[1]) représentent des sous-catégories (voir légende complète à la page *I · 1).*

Os símbolos incluídos no texto do índice representam as grandes categorias identificadas com a chave à direita. Os símbolos com números em sua parte superior (⋀[1]) identificam as subcategorias (veja-se a chave completa à página *I · 1).*

∧ Mountain	Berg	Montaña	Montagne	Montanha
⋀ Mountains	Gebirge	Montañas	Montagnes	Montanhas
)(Pass	Paß	Paso	Col	Passo
∨ Valley, Canyon	Tal, Cañon	Valle, Cañón	Vallée, Canyon	Vale, Canhão
≚ Plain	Ebene	Llano	Plaine	Planície
› Cape	Kap	Cabo	Cap	Cabo
I Island	Insel	Isla	Île	Ilha
II Islands	Inseln	Islas	Îles	Ilhas
⊥ Other Topographic Features	Andere Topographische Objekte	Otros Elementos Topográficos	Autres données topographiques	Outros acidentes topográficos

ESPAÑOL · FRANÇAIS · PORTUGUÊS

Nombre / Nom / Nome	Página / Page	Lat.°′	Long.°′ W = Oeste / W = Ouest
Beaver Creek ≃, Mo., U.S.	194	36.38 N	93.02 W
Beaver Creek ≃, Mt., U.S.	202	48.29 N	107.24 W
Beaver Creek ≃, Ne., U.S.	198	40.42 N	97.20 W
Beaver Creek ≃, Ne., U.S.	198	41.26 N	97.42 W
Beaver Creek ≃, N.J., U.S.	285	39.45 N	75.23 W
Beaver Creek ≃, N.Y., U.S.	212	44.36 N	75.22 W
Beaver Creek ≃, N.D., U.S.	198	46.15 N	100.29 W
Beaver Creek ≃, Oh., U.S.	216	41.25 N	83.51 W
Beaver Creek ≃, Oh., U.S.	216	40.34 N	84.45 W
Beaver Creek ≃, Oh., U.S.	218	39.57 N	83.46 W
Beaver Creek ≃, Ok., U.S.	196	34.00 N	97.57 W
Beaver Creek ≃, Or., U.S.	224	44.56 N	121.22 W
Beaver Creek ≃, Pa., U.S.	285	40.00 N	75.42 W
Beaver Creek ≃, Tx., U.S.	196	33.53 N	98.49 W
Beaver Creek ≃, Wy., U.S.	202	42.58 N	108.26 W
Beaver Creek State Park ♠	214	40.44 N	80.35 W
Beaver Crossing	198	40.46 N	97.16 W
Beaverdale	214	40.19 N	78.41 W
Beaver Dam, Ky., U.S.	194	37.24 N	86.52 W
Beaverdam, Oh., U.S.	216	40.50 N	83.59 W
Beaver Dam, Wi., U.S.	190	43.27 N	88.50 W
Beaverdam Brook ≃	276	40.26 N	74.28 W
Beaverdam Creek ≃, U.S.	284c	38.55 N	76.57 W
Beaverdam Creek ≃, Md., U.S.	284c	39.01 N	76.54 W
Beaverdam Creek ≃, N.J., U.S.	285	39.56 N	74.45 W
Beaver Dams	210	42.17 N	76.58 W
Beaver Dams Creek ≃	284a	43.06 N	79.11 W
Beaver Dam Wash ∨	200	36.54 N	114.55 W
Beaverdell	182	49.26 N	119.05 W
Beaver Falls, N.Y., U.S.	212	43.53 N	75.25 W
Beaver Falls, Pa., U.S.	214	40.45 N	80.19 W
Beaverhead ≃	202	45.31 N	112.21 W
Beaverhead Mountains ⩘	202	45.00 N	113.20 W
Beaverhill Lake ⊜, Ab., Can.	182	53.27 N	112.32 W
Beaver Hill Lake ⊜, Mb., Can.	184	54.16 N	94.53 W
Beaverhouse Lake ⊜	190	48.32 N	92.05 W
Beaver Island I	190	45.40 N	85.31 W
Beaver Island State Park ♠	210	42.58 N	78.57 W
Beaver Kill ≃	210	41.59 N	75.08 W
Beaver Lake	210	41.07 N	74.33 W
Beaver Lake ⊜, Ab., Can.	182	54.43 N	111.50 W
Beaver Lake ⊜, On., Can.	212	44.30 N	77.02 W
Beaver Lake ⊜, On., Can.	212	44.44 N	78.17 W
Beaver Lake ⊜, N.J., U.S.	276	41.05 N	74.33 W
Beaver Lake ⊜, N.Y., U.S.	276	40.53 N	73.34 W
Beaver Lake ⊜[1]	194	36.20 N	93.55 W
Beaver Lake Indian Reserve ◆[4]	182	54.39 N	111.54 W
Beaverlodge	182	55.13 N	119.26 W
Beaver Meadow	210	42.40 N	75.41 W
Beaver Meadows	210	40.55 N	75.54 W
Beaver Mountains ⩘	180	62.54 N	156.58 W
Beaver Run ≃, N.J., U.S.	276	41.11 N	74.36 W
Beaver Run ≃, Pa., U.S.	279b	40.34 N	79.33 W
Beaver Run ≃, Pa., U.S.	285	40.10 N	75.40 W
Beaver Run Reservoir ⊜[1]	214	40.29 N	79.33 W
Beavers Bend State Park ♠	194	34.08 N	94.42 W
Beaver Springs	208	40.45 N	77.13 W
Beaver Swamp Brook ≃	276	40.57 N	73.43 W
Beaverton, On., Can.	212	44.26 N	79.09 W
Beaverton, Mi., U.S.	190	43.52 N	84.29 W
Beaverton, Or., U.S.	224	45.29 N	122.48 W
Beaverton ≃	212	44.26 N	79.10 W
Beavertown	210	40.45 N	77.10 W
Beaverville	216	40.57 N	87.39 W
Beāwar	120	26.06 N	74.19 E
Beazley	252	33.45 S	66.39 W
Bebao	157b	17.22 S	44.33 E
Bebar ≃	114	3.07 N	103.27 E
Bebedouro	255	20.56 S	48.28 W
Bebeji	150	11.40 N	8.19 E
Bebek ◆[8]	267b	41.04 N	29.02 E
Bebelevo	82	54.32 N	36.30 E
Bebeli	130	36.41 N	35.27 E
Beberibe	250	4.11 S	38.08 W
Bebertal	54	52.15 N	11.18 E
Bebington	44	53.23 N	3.01 W
Béboto	146	8.16 N	16.56 E
Bebra	56	50.58 N	9.47 E
Becal	232	20.27 N	90.02 W
Bécancour	206	46.20 N	72.26 W
Bécancour ≃	206	46.22 N	72.27 W
Beccar ◆[8]	288	34.28 S	58.31 W
Beccaria	214	40.46 N	78.27 W
Beccles	42	52.28 N	1.34 E
Becconsall	262	53.42 N	2.50 W
Bečej	38	45.37 N	20.03 E
Beceni	38	45.23 N	26.46 E
Becerra Creek ≃	196	28.05 N	98.55 W
Becerreá	34	42.51 N	7.10 W
Becerro, Cayos II	236	15.57 N	83.17 W
Béchar	148	31.37 N	2.13 W
Béchar □[5]	148	29.00 N	3.00 W
Becharof Lake ⊜	180	58.00 N	156.30 W
Bechater	36	37.18 N	9.45 E
Bechem	150	7.05 N	2.02 W
Becher Bay ⊂	224	48.19 N	123.37 W
Becher Point ›	168a	32.23 S	115.44 E
Bechet	38	43.46 N	23.58 E
Bechevin Bay ⊂	180	55.00 N	163.27 W
Bechhofen	56	49.09 N	10.33 E
Bechtelsville	208	40.22 N	75.38 W
Bechuanaland ◆[1]	158	27.10 S	22.10 E
Bechyně	30	49.18 N	14.29 E
Becke	263	51.24 N	7.47 E
Beckemeyer	219	38.36 N	89.26 W
Beckenham ◆[8]	260	51.24 N	0.02 W
Beckenried	58	46.58 N	8.29 E
Becket	207	42.19 N	73.05 W
Beckhausen ◆[8]	263	51.34 N	7.02 E
Beckingen	56	49.24 N	6.42 E
Beckington	42	51.16 N	2.18 W
Beck Lake ⊜	278	42.04 N	87.52 W
Beckler ≃	224	47.43 N	121.21 W
Beckley	188	37.46 N	81.11 W
Beck Pond ⊜	283	42.36 N	70.49 W
Becks Creek ≃	219	39.08 N	88.56 W
Beckum	52	51.45 N	8.02 E
Beckville	222	32.14 N	94.27 W
Beckwith Island I	212	44.52 N	80.08 W
Becky Peak ⋀	204	39.58 N	114.36 W
Beclean	38	47.11 N	24.10 E
Bečov nad Teplou	54	50.02 N	12.19 E
Becsehely	61	46.27 N	16.48 E
Bedale	44	54.17 N	1.35 W
Bédarieux	32	43.37 N	3.09 E
Bédarrides	62	44.02 N	4.54 E
Bédaya	146	8.55 N	17.52 E
Bedburdyck	56	51.07 N	6.34 E
Bedburg, Dtsch.	56	50.59 N	6.35 E
Bedburg, Dtsch.	56	51.03 N	8.23 E
Bedburg-Hau	52	51.45 N	6.10 E
Beddgelert	44	53.01 N	4.06 W
Beddingestrand	41	55.21 N	13.29 E
Beddington ◆[8]	260	51.22 N	0.08 W
Beddome, Mount ⋀	162	25.50 S	134.22 E
Beddouza, Ras ›	148	32.34 N	9.19 W
Bedele	144	8.33 N	36.23 E
Beden Brook ≃	276	40.25 N	74.38 W
Bedeque Bay ⊂	186	46.22 N	63.53 W
Beder	41	56.04 N	10.13 E
Bederkesa	52	53.38 N	8.50 E
Bederwanak	144	9.34 N	44.23 E
Bedesa	144	8.54 N	40.47 E
Bedford, P.Q., Can.	206	45.07 N	72.59 W
Bedford, S. Afr.	158	32.41 S	26.05 E
Bedford, Eng., U.K.	42	52.08 N	0.29 W
Bedford, In., U.S.	218	38.51 N	86.29 W
Bedford, Ia., U.S.	198	40.40 N	94.43 W
Bedford, Ky., U.S.	218	38.35 N	85.19 W
Bedford, Ma., U.S.	207	42.29 N	71.16 W
Bedford, Mi., U.S.	216	42.23 N	85.13 W
Bedford, N.Y., U.S.	210	41.12 N	73.39 W
Bedford, Oh., U.S.	214	41.23 N	81.32 W
Bedford, Pa., U.S.	188	40.01 N	78.30 W
Bedford, Tx., U.S.	222	32.50 N	97.08 W
Bedford, Va., U.S.	192	37.20 N	79.31 W
Bedford □[6]	214	40.09 N	78.30 W
Bedford, Cape ›	164	15.14 S	145.21 E
Bedfordale	168a	32.10 S	116.03 E
Bedford Harbour ⊂	162	33.35 S	120.35 E
Bedford Heights	279a	41.25 N	81.31 W
Bedford Hills	210	41.14 N	73.41 W
Bedford Island I	126	21.51 N	88.05 E
Bedford Level ≅	42	52.27 N	0.02 W
Bedford Park	278	41.46 N	87.49 W
Bedford Park ◆[8]	276	40.52 N	73.53 W
Bedfordshire □[6]	42	52.05 N	0.30 W
Bedford-Stuyvesant ◆[8]	276	40.41 N	73.55 W
Bedi, India	120	22.30 N	70.02 E
Bédi, Tchad	146	11.06 N	18.33 E
Bedias	222	30.46 N	95.57 W
Bedias Creek ≃	222	30.54 N	95.37 W
Bedinggong	112	2.42 S	106.13 E
Bédiondo	146	8.39 N	17.12 E
Bedirli	130	39.35 N	36.38 E
Bedlington	44	55.08 N	1.35 W
Bedminster, N.J., U.S.	276	40.40 N	74.38 W
Bedminster, Pa., U.S.	208	40.26 N	75.11 W
Bedmond	260	51.43 N	0.25 W
Bednodemjanovsk	80	53.56 N	43.10 E
Bedoba	88	58.48 N	97.12 E
Bédoin	62	44.07 N	5.10 E
Bedok	271c	1.19 N	103.57 E
Bedong	114	5.44 N	100.31 E
Bedonia	62	44.30 N	9.38 E
Bedourie	166	24.21 S	139.28 E
Bedum	52	53.17 N	6.36 E
Bedwas	42	51.35 N	3.13 W
Bedworth	42	52.28 N	1.29 W
Beeac	169	38.12 S	143.38 E
Beebe, P.Q., Can.	206	45.01 N	72.09 W
Beebe, Ar., U.S.	194	35.04 N	91.52 W
Beech ≃	194	35.37 N	88.10 W
Beechal Creek ≃	166	27.24 S	145.13 E
Beech Bottom	214	40.13 N	80.39 W
Beech Brook ≃	276	41.08 N	74.18 W
Beech Creek	194	37.10 N	87.03 W
Beech Creek ≃	210	41.04 N	77.34 W
Beechcrest	214	41.05 N	81.20 W
Beecher, Il., U.S.	216	41.20 N	87.37 W
Beecher, Mi., U.S.	216	43.05 N	83.42 W
Beecher City	219	39.11 N	88.47 W
Beecher Falls	206	45.00 N	71.30 W
Beechey Head ›	224	48.19 N	123.39 W
Beech Forest	169	38.38 S	143.34 E
Beech Fork ≃	194	37.46 N	85.41 W
Beech Grove	218	39.43 N	86.05 W
Beechmont	171a	28.07 S	153.11 E
Beechview ◆[8]	279b	40.25 N	80.02 W
Beechwood, Ky., U.S.	218	38.24 N	84.44 W
Beechwood, Ma., U.S.	283	42.12 N	70.49 W
Beechwood, Mi., U.S.	216	46.09 N	88.46 W
Beechworth	166	36.22 S	146.41 E
Beechy	184	50.51 N	107.25 W
Beeck ◆[8]	263	51.29 N	6.44 E
Beeckerwerth ◆[8]	263	51.29 N	6.41 E
Beecroft	274a	33.45 S	151.04 E
Beecroft Head ›	170	35.01 S	150.51 E
Beecroft Peninsula ›[1]	170	35.02 S	150.50 E
Beedenbostel	52	52.38 N	10.16 E
Beef Island I	240m	18.27 N	64.31 W
Beek, Ned.	52	51.51 N	5.54 E
Beek, Ned.	52	51.32 N	5.38 E
Beek, Ned.	56	50.56 N	5.49 E
Beela ≃	44	54.13 N	2.47 W
Beeleigh Abbey ⊍[1]	260	51.44 N	0.40 E
Beelen	52	51.55 N	8.07 E
Beelitz	54	52.14 N	12.58 E
Beemer	198	41.55 N	96.48 W
Beemster ◆[1]	52	52.35 N	4.55 E
Beendorf	54	52.14 N	11.05 E
Beenleigh	171a	27.43 S	153.12 E
Beerburrum	171a	26.58 S	152.58 E
Beerfelden	56	49.34 N	8.58 E
Bee Ridge	220	27.17 N	82.28 W
Beeringgnurding Hill ⋀[2]	162	29.53 S	117.55 E
Beernem	50	51.09 N	3.20 E
Beerse	56	51.19 N	4.52 E
Beersheba → Be'ér Sheva'	132	31.14 N	34.47 E
Beersheba Springs	194	35.28 N	85.39 W
Be'ér Sheva (Beersheba)	132	31.14 N	34.47 E
Be'er Sheva', Naḥal ∨	132	31.11 N	34.35 E
Beerta	52	53.10 N	7.05 E
Be'ér Toviyya	132	31.44 N	34.44 E
Beervlei Brak ≃	158	29.58 S	23.12 E
Beerwah	171a	26.51 S	152.58 E
Beerwah National Park ♠	171a	26.54 S	152.53 E
Be'er Ya'agov	132	31.56 N	34.50 E
Beesenlaublingen	54	51.42 N	11.41 E
Beeskow	54	52.10 N	14.14 E
Beestekraal	156	25.23 S	27.38 E
Beesten	52	52.26 N	7.30 E
Beeston	42	52.56 N	1.12 W
Beet ≃	115a	6.16 S	107.15 E
Beethoven Peninsula ›[1]	9	71.40 S	73.45 W
Beeton	212	44.05 N	79.47 W
Beetsterzwaag	52	53.03 N	6.05 E
Beetz, Lac ⊜	186	50.34 N	62.42 W
Beetzendorf	54	52.42 N	11.05 E
Beeville	196	28.24 N	97.44 W
Beevor, Mount ⋀[2]	168b	34.56 S	139.02 E
Befale	152	0.28 N	20.58 E
Befandriana	157b	15.16 S	48.32 E
Befandriana Atsimo	157b	22.06 S	43.54 E
Befasy	157b	20.33 S	44.23 E
Befori	152	0.06 N	22.17 E
Befotaka, Madag.	157b	13.15 S	48.16 E
Befotaka, Madag.	157b	14.32 S	48.01 E
Befotaka, Madag.	157b	21.29 S	44.44 E
Befotaka, Madag.	157b	23.49 S	46.59 E
Befu ◆[8]	270	34.40 N	135.02 E
Beg, Lough ⊜	48	54.47 N	6.28 W
Bega	166	36.40 S	149.50 E
Bega (Begej) ≃	38	45.13 N	20.19 E
Begamganj, Bngl.	124	22.49 N	91.07 E
Begamganj, India	124	23.36 N	78.20 E
Begampur ◆[8]	272a	28.44 N	77.04 E
Beğdeş	130	37.51 N	39.05 E
Begej (Bega) ≃	38	45.13 N	20.19 E
Beger	102	45.42 N	97.10 E
Beggs	196	35.44 N	96.04 W
Begičevskij	76	53.47 N	38.15 E
Beginsel	158	26.57 S	20.39 E
Beglickaja, kosa ›[2]	83	47.07 N	38.35 E
Begna ≃	26	60.10 N	10.16 E
Begoml'	76	54.44 N	28.04 E
Begonias, Presa ⊜[1]	234	20.55 N	100.50 W
Begoro	150	6.23 N	0.23 W
Begovat → Bekabad	85	40.13 N	69.14 E
Begun'	78	51.24 N	28.17 E
Begunicy	76	59.35 N	29.19 E
Begur, Cap de ›	34	41.57 N	3.14 E
Begusarai	124	25.25 N	86.08 E
Behāla	126	22.31 N	88.19 E
Behauge, Pointe ›	250	4.40 N	51.54 W
Behbahān	128	30.35 N	50.14 E
Behleg	120	36.47 N	91.41 E
Behm Canal ʮ	182	55.41 N	131.35 W
Beho	56	50.13 N	6.00 E
Béhoust	261	48.50 N	1.43 E
Behrāmpur	272a	28.38 N	77.24 E
Behren-lès-Forbach	56	49.10 N	6.57 E
Behring, Détroit de → Bering Strait ʮ	180	65.30 N	169.00 W
Behringen, Dtsch.	52	53.07 N	9.58 E
Behringen, Dtsch.	54	51.01 N	10.31 E
Behshahr	128	36.43 N	53.34 E
Beht, Oued ≃	148	34.25 N	6.26 W
Bei ≃	90	23.09 N	112.48 E
Bei'an	89	48.16 N	126.36 E
Beianhe	105	40.04 N	116.06 E
Beibaihua	105	38.57 N	114.51 E
Beibaozhen	106	31.33 N	121.38 E
Beibei	107	29.49 N	106.26 E
Beicai	106	31.12 N	121.34 E
Beicang	105	39.13 N	117.07 E
Beida ≃	102	40.18 N	99.26 E
Beïda, Chott ⊜	34	35.56 N	5.49 E
Beida → Al-Bayḍā'	146	32.46 N	21.43 E
Beidaihe	98	39.54 N	119.29 E
Beidaoqiao	86	44.12 N	89.38 E
Beidouzhen	107	30.02 N	104.26 E
Beidun	100	26.42 N	118.57 E
Beierfeld	54	50.33 N	12.47 E
Beiersdorf	264a	52.42 N	13.47 E
Beifangcun	105	40.20 N	116.42 E
Beifangzi	104	41.22 N	121.03 E
Beigang	100	29.20 N	113.41 E
Beighton	44	53.20 N	1.20 W
Beigi	144	9.20 N	34.29 E
Beiguan Dao I	100	27.10 N	120.32 E
Beiguo	106	31.47 N	120.33 E
Beihai	102	21.29 N	109.05 E
Bei Hai ⊜	271a	39.56 N	116.22 E
Beihedian	105	39.13 N	115.45 E
Beiheishang'gou	105	39.53 N	118.15 E
Beihuaidian	105	39.16 N	117.33 E
Beijialing	104	41.08 N	124.02 E
Beijiao	100	26.22 N	119.58 E
Beijiean	106	32.15 N	121.12 E
Beijijiazhuang	105	40.01 N	114.51 E
Beijing (Peking), Zhg.	105	39.55 N	116.25 E
Beijing (Peking), Zhg.	271a	39.55 N	116.25 E
Beijing Ji Chang (Capitol Airport) ⊠	105	40.03 N	116.35 E
Beijing Shi (Peking Shih) □[7]	98	40.15 N	116.30 E
Beiji Shan I	100	27.38 N	121.12 E
Beijuma ≃	105	39.30 N	115.56 E
Beikan	100	32.23 N	121.21 E
Beilen	52	52.52 N	6.31 E
Beili	110	19.10 N	108.43 E
Beilifang	104	41.59 N	121.57 E
Beiling	100	24.36 N	115.20 E
Beiliu	102	22.42 N	110.22 E
Beiliuwangshui	105	38.57 N	115.03 E
Beilizigu	105	39.30 N	117.28 E
Beilngries	60	49.02 N	11.29 E
Beilong Shan I	100	27.40 N	120.58 E
Beilrode	54	51.35 N	13.03 E
Beilstein, Dtsch.	56	49.02 N	9.18 E
Beilstein, Dtsch.	56	50.36 N	8.14 E
Beilstein, Dtsch.	56	50.06 N	7.14 E
Beimaizhu	105	39.31 N	117.44 E
Beiminjiatun	104	42.38 N	122.43 E
Beimuzhen	107	29.31 N	105.05 E
Beinamar	146	8.40 N	15.23 E
Beine-Nauroy	50	49.15 N	4.13 E
Beinette	62	44.22 N	7.39 E
Beinwil	58	47.22 N	7.35 E
Beinwil am See	58	47.16 N	8.13 E
Beipa	164	8.30 S	146.35 E
Beipan ≃	102	25.05 N	106.00 E
Beipanxiaozhen	106	31.44 N	121.26 E
Beipiao	104	41.49 N	120.46 E
Beipo	102	21.14 N	109.53 E
Beiqi	98	40.27 N	122.20 E
Beiqiao	106	31.03 N	121.24 E
Beira	156	19.49 S	34.52 E
Beira Baixa □[9]	34	39.45 N	7.30 W
Beira Litoral □[9]	34	40.15 N	8.25 W
Beiru ≃	100	33.43 N	113.35 E
Beirut → Bayrūt	130	33.53 N	35.30 E
Beirut International Airport ⊠	132	33.49 N	35.30 E
Beisanjia	98	42.04 N	124.42 E
Beiseker	182	51.23 N	113.32 W
Beishakou	105	39.08 N	116.07 E
Beishan	102	24.28 N	108.35 E
Bei Shan ⩘	102	41.30 N	96.00 E
Beishangcun	105	39.28 N	116.58 E
Beishipian	105	40.43 N	116.55 E
Beishuangdong	105	40.32 N	117.24 E
Beishuiquan	98	40.05 N	114.40 E
Beisi	102	34.59 N	95.07 E
Beisu	98	38.13 N	114.46 E
Beitaitou	98	37.06 N	118.31 E
Beitang	105	39.07 N	117.42 E
Beitanshiqiao	106	31.05 N	121.38 E
Beitbridge	154	22.13 S	30.00 E
Beith	46	55.45 N	4.38 W
Beitstadfjorden ⊂[2]	26	63.53 N	11.00 E
Beiuș	38	46.40 N	22.21 E
Beiwei	106	32.05 N	121.12 E
Beiwenquan	107	29.51 N	106.24 E
Beiwu	105	40.04 N	116.48 E
Beiwudu	100	33.39 N	113.39 E
Beixiadai	106	32.12 N	120.08 E
Beixiejiadang	105	40.30 N	114.50 E
Beixili	89	51.47 N	125.45 E
Beixin'an	271a	39.55 N	116.08 E
Beixindian	105	39.44 N	116.44 E
Beixing	89	48.29 N	125.40 E
Beixinjing	106	31.13 N	121.22 E
Beixinliu	105	39.16 N	116.31 E
Beixinzhen	106	31.49 N	121.31 E
Beiyan	98	36.33 N	118.42 E
Beiyi ≃	105	39.19 N	115.39 E
Beiyin	106	31.07 N	120.47 E
Beiyindai	104	42.35 N	122.22 E
Beiyuan	105	40.01 N	116.24 E
Beizhaijiawopeng	104	41.14 N	122.41 E
Beizhen, Zhg.	98	37.22 N	118.01 E
Beizhen (Gaoshanzi), Zhg.	104	41.36 N	121.47 E
Beizhouzhuang	106	31.52 N	120.24 E
Beizifu	98	42.09 N	120.29 E
Beja, Bra.	250	1.36 S	48.47 W
Beja, Port.	34	38.01 N	7.52 W
Beja, Ross.	86	53.03 N	90.54 E
Béja, Tun.	148	36.44 N	9.11 E
Beja □[5]	34	37.50 N	8.00 W
Béja □[8]	148	36.35 N	9.20 E
Bejaïa (Bougie)	148	36.45 N	5.05 E
Bejaïa □[5]	148	36.50 N	4.40 E
Bejaïa, Golfe de ⊂	34	36.45 N	5.25 E
Béjar	34	40.23 N	5.46 W
Bejhi ≃	120	29.47 N	67.58 E
Bejlagan	84	39.47 N	47.37 E
Bejneu	86	45.15 N	55.07 E
Bejsug ≃	78	45.54 N	38.56 E
Bejsugskij liman ⊂	78	46.07 N	38.25 E
Bejtonovo	89	53.14 N	124.27 E
Bejucal	240p	22.56 N	82.23 W
Bejucal □[7]	286b	22.56 N	82.23 W
Bejuco	236	8.36 N	79.53 W
Bejucos ≃	234	18.36 N	100.40 W
Bejuma	246	10.11 N	68.16 W
Bek ≃	152	2.29 N	15.15 E
Béka	146	9.04 N	12.53 E
Bekaa Valley → Al-Biqā' ∨	128	33.50 N	36.00 E
Bekabad	85	40.13 N	69.14 E
Bekancan	114	3.18 N	98.24 E
Bekasi	115a	6.14 S	106.59 E
Bekasi ≃	269e	6.10 S	107.02 E
Békásmegyer ◆[8]	264c	47.36 N	19.03 E
Bekasovo	82	55.26 N	36.49 E
Bekdaš	72	41.34 N	52.32 E
Békés	30	46.46 N	21.08 E
Békés □[6]	30	46.46 N	21.08 E
Békéscsaba	30	46.41 N	21.06 E
Beketovo	89	53.13 N	125.01 E
Bekilli	130	38.14 N	29.26 E
Bekily	157b	24.13 S	45.19 E
Bekirhan	130	38.10 N	41.19 E
Bekisopa	157b	21.40 S	45.54 E
Bekitro	157b	24.33 S	45.18 E
Bekkaria	36	35.22 N	8.15 E
Bekkersdal	273d	26.18 S	27.42 E
Bekkevoort	56	50.57 N	4.58 E
Beklemiševo, Ross.	80	53.52 N	47.25 E
Beklemiševo, Ross.	88	52.07 N	112.40 E
Bekodoka	157b	16.58 S	45.07 E
Bekoji	144	7.34 N	39.17 E
Bekok	114	2.18 N	103.08 E
Bekopaka	157b	19.09 S	44.48 E
Bekovo	80	52.28 N	43.43 E
Bektauata, gora ⋀	86	47.30 N	74.50 E
Bektyševo	82	56.34 N	39.14 E
Bekwai	150	6.27 N	1.35 W
Bela, India	124	25.56 N	81.59 E
Bela, Pāk.	120	26.14 N	66.19 E
Bela, Zaïre	154	0.38 N	29.14 E
Bélabo	152	5.00 N	13.20 E
Belabolo	140	8.57 N	25.51 E
Bélâbre	32	46.33 N	1.09 E
Bela Crkva	38	44.54 N	21.26 E
Bela Cruz	250	3.03 S	40.11 W
Belaga	108	2.42 N	113.47 E
Bel'agaš	86	50.48 N	80.44 E
Bel-Air, Fr.	261	48.37 N	2.10 E
Bel Air, Md., U.S.	208	39.32 N	76.20 W
Bel Air, Va., U.S.	284c	38.52 N	77.10 W
Bel Air ◆[8]	280	34.05 N	118.27 W
Bélair, Île I	275a	45.37 N	73.48 W
Bel Aire Estates	207	41.23 N	72.00 W
Belair Recreation Park ♠	168b	35.01 S	138.39 E
Belaja, Ross.	78	51.03 N	35.43 E
Belaja, Ross.	80	57.59 N	51.42 E
Belaja ≃, Ross.	78	45.04 N	39.23 E
Belaja ≃, Ross.	84	44.45 N	39.50 E
Belaja ≃, Ross.	86	55.54 N	53.33 E
Belaja ≃, Ross.	180	65.45 N	173.20 E
Belaja ≃, Ukr.	83	49.18 N	38.52 E
Belaja ≃, Ukr.	83	48.35 N	39.10 E
Belaja, gora ⋀, Ross.	88	53.10 N	119.50 E
Belaja, gora ⋀, Ross.	180	65.50 N	174.40 E
Belaja Ber'ozka	76	52.23 N	33.29 E
Belaja Cerkov'	78	49.49 N	30.07 E
Belaja Cholunica	86	58.50 N	50.48 E
Belaja Gora	76	58.31 N	31.45 E
Belaja Kalitva	78	48.11 N	40.46 E
Belaja Krinica, Ukr.	78	47.21 N	33.10 E
Belaja Krinica, Ukr.	78	50.38 N	29.29 E
Bel'ajevka, Ross.	86	51.24 N	56.26 E
Bel'ajevka, Ross.	86	57.28 N	55.28 E
Bel'ajevka, Ukr.	78	46.29 N	30.12 E
Bel'ajevo	76	55.31 N	31.06 E
Belalcázar	34	38.34 N	5.10 W
Bel Alton	208	38.27 N	76.58 W
Belambanganumpu	112	4.54 S	105.03 E
Belampalli	122	19.02 N	79.30 E
Bělá nad Radbuzou	60	49.36 N	12.44 E
Belang	112	0.57 N	124.47 E
Bélanger ≃	184	53.26 N	97.40 W
Bel'aninovo	265b	55.57 N	37.39 E
Bel'anskij	80	47.45 N	41.33 E
Bela Palanka	38	43.13 N	22.19 E
Bělá pod Bezdězem	54	50.30 N	14.50 E
Belapurpāda	272c	19.01 N	73.02 E
Belarus □[1], Europe	22	53.50 N	28.00 E
Belarus □[1], Europe	76	53.50 N	28.00 E
Belarus Station ◆[5]	265b	55.47 N	37.35 E
Belas	266c	38.47 N	9.16 W
Belau → Palau □[2]	14	5.00 N	137.00 E
Belavenona	157b	24.50 S	47.04 E
Bela Vista, Ang.	152	7.50 S	13.40 E
Bela Vista, Bra.	252	22.06 S	56.31 W
Bela Vista, Moç.	156	26.20 S	32.40 E
Bela Vista ◆[8]	287b	23.33 S	46.38 W
Bela Vista de Goiás	255	16.58 S	48.57 W
Bela Vista do Paraíso	255	23.00 S	51.12 W
Belawan	114	3.47 N	98.41 E
Belaya ⋀	144	11.25 N	36.12 E
Belayan ≃	112	0.14 S	116.36 E
Belaya Tserkov → Belaja Cerkov'	78	49.49 N	30.07 E
Belbo ≃	62	44.54 N	8.31 E
Belbubulo	140	9.57 N	34.04 E
Belbunia	126	23.17 N	87.09 E
Bel'c'	78	47.46 N	27.56 E
Belcamp	208	39.28 N	76.14 W
Belcastro	68	39.02 N	16.47 E
Bełchatów	30	51.22 N	19.21 E
Belchen ⋀	58	47.49 N	7.50 E
Belcher	194	32.44 N	93.49 W
Belcherāgh	120	35.50 N	65.14 E
Belcher Creek ≃	276	41.08 N	74.23 W
Belcher Islands II	176	56.20 N	79.30 W
Belchertown	207	42.16 N	72.24 W
Belchite	34	41.18 N	0.45 W
Bělčice	60	49.30 N	13.53 E
Belcoo	48	54.17 N	7.52 W
Belcourt	198	48.50 N	99.44 W
Belda	126	22.05 N	87.21 E
Beldānga	126	23.56 N	88.15 E
Bel'd'ažki	76	52.39 N	35.42 E
Belding	216	43.05 N	85.13 W
Bele, ozero ⊜	86	54.39 N	90.12 E
Belebej	80	54.07 N	54.07 E
Belebelka	76	57.34 N	30.56 E
Belecke	52	51.29 N	8.20 E
Beled Weyne	144	4.45 N	45.12 E
Bélel, Cam.	152	7.03 N	14.26 E
Belel, Nig.	146	9.38 N	13.12 E
Belém, Bra.	250	1.27 S	48.29 W
Belém, Moç.	154	14.13 S	35.58 E
Belém ◆[8]	266c	38.42 N	9.12 W
Belém, Torre de ⊥	266c	38.42 N	9.13 W
Belém de São Francisco	250	8.46 S	38.58 W
Belén, Arg.	252	27.39 S	67.02 W
Belén, Bol.	248	19.48 S	65.33 W
Belén, Chile	248	18.29 S	69.31 W
Belén, Col.	246	6.00 N	72.55 W
Belén, Nic.	236	11.30 N	85.53 W
Belén, Para.	252	23.30 S	57.06 W
Belen, Tür.	130	36.32 N	36.10 E
Belen, N.M., U.S.	200	34.39 N	106.46 W
Belén, Ur.	252	30.47 S	57.47 W
Belén ≃	252	28.00 S	66.52 W
Belén de Escobar	258	34.21 S	58.47 W
Belén del Refugio	234	21.31 N	102.25 W
Belene	38	43.39 N	25.07 E
Belenichino	78	50.56 N	36.37 E
Belen'kaja ≃	83	48.53 N	38.29 E
Belen'koje, Ukr.	78	47.37 N	35.03 E
Belen'koje, Ukr.	83	48.46 N	37.38 E
Belènzinho ◆[8]	287b	23.32 S	46.35 W
Bélep, Îles II	175f	19.45 S	163.40 E
Beles ≃	144	11.10 N	36.10 E
Belesar, Embalse de ⊜[1]	34	42.45 N	7.40 W
Belet Uen → Beled Weyne	144	4.45 N	45.12 E
Belews Lake ⊜[1]	192	36.17 N	80.03 W
Belfair	224	47.27 N	122.49 W
Belfast, N.Z.	172	43.27 S	172.38 E
Belfast, S. Afr.	156	25.43 S	30.03 E
Belfast, N. Ire., U.K.	48	54.35 N	5.55 W
Belfast, Me., U.S.	188	44.25 N	69.00 W
Belfast, N.Y., U.S.	210	42.20 N	78.06 W
Belfast, Oh., U.S.	218	39.03 N	83.32 W
Belfast (Aldergrove) Airport ⊠	48	54.38 N	6.12 W
Belfast Lough ⊂	48	54.40 N	5.50 W
Belfeld	52	51.19 N	6.06 E
Belfield, Austl.	274a	33.54 S	151.05 E
Belfield, N.D., U.S.	198	46.53 N	103.11 W
Belfiore	64	45.23 N	11.12 E
Belford, Eng., U.K.	44	55.36 N	1.49 W
Belford, N.J., U.S.	276	40.25 N	74.05 W
Belford Roxo	256	22.46 S	43.24 W
Belfort	58	47.38 N	6.52 E
Belfort □[8]	58	47.38 N	6.55 E
Belforte del Chienti	66	43.10 N	13.14 E
Belfry, Ky., U.S.	192	37.37 N	82.16 W
Belfry, Mt., U.S.	202	45.08 N	109.00 W
Belgaum	122	15.52 N	74.31 E
Belgern	54	51.29 N	13.07 E
Bélgica → Belgium □[1]	30	50.50 N	4.00 E
Belgica Mountains ⩘	9	72.35 S	31.10 E
België → Belgium □[1]	30	50.50 N	4.00 E
Belgien → Belgium □[1]	30	50.50 N	4.00 E
Belgioioso	62	45.10 N	9.19 E
Belgique → Belgium □[1]	30	50.50 N	4.00 E
Belgium □[1], Europe	22	50.50 N	4.00 E
Belgium □[1], Europe	30	50.50 N	4.00 E
Belgodère	36	42.35 N	9.01 E
Belgorod	78	50.36 N	36.35 E
Belgorod-Dnestrovskij	78	46.12 N	30.20 E
Belgorod Oblast' □[4]	78	50.45 N	37.30 E
Belgrad → Beograd	38	44.50 N	20.30 E
Belgrade, Mn., U.S.	198	45.27 N	95.00 W
Belgrade, Mt., U.S.	202	45.46 N	111.10 W
Belgrade, Ne., U.S.	198	41.28 N	98.04 W
Belgrade → Beograd	38	44.50 N	20.30 E
Belgrado → Beograd	38	44.50 N	20.30 E
Belgrad Ormanı ◆[3]	267b	41.10 N	28.55 E
Belgrano ◆[8]	288	34.34 S	58.28 W
Belgrano ≃	254	48.15 S	71.14 W
Belgrano, Lago ⊜	254	47.50 S	72.09 W
Belgrano II ⊍[3]	9	77.46 S	38.11 W
Belgrave	274b	37.55 S	145.21 E
Belhar	124	24.55 N	86.36 E
Belhaven	192	35.32 N	76.37 W
Belhus Park ♠	260	51.31 N	0.17 E
Beliābera	126	22.17 N	86.57 E
Beliātor	126	23.20 N	87.13 E
Belica, Hrv.	61	46.26 N	16.27 E
Belica, Ross.	78	51.07 N	35.34 E
Belice ≃	70	37.35 N	12.52 E
Belice → Belize □[1]	232	17.15 N	88.45 W
Belice → Belize City	232	17.30 N	88.12 W
Belichifor	140	6.33 N	33.16 E
Beliči	78	50.29 N	30.19 E
Belici ≃	70	37.31 N	13.50 E
Beličij, ostrov I	89	54.26 N	137.51 E
Belick	76	52.55 N	30.27 E
Belickoje	83	48.25 N	37.13 E
Beli Drim ≃	38	42.06 N	20.25 E
Beliki	78	49.15 N	34.16 E
Beliling, Gunung ⋀	115b	8.37 S	119.59 E
Beli Manastir	38	45.46 N	18.36 E
Belin	32	44.30 N	0.47 W
Belinga	152	1.13 N	13.12 E
Belington	188	39.01 N	79.56 W
Belinskij	80	52.58 N	43.26 E
Belinyu	112	1.38 S	105.46 E
Belitung I	112	2.50 S	107.55 E
Belize □[1], N.A.	230	17.15 N	88.45 W
Belize □[1], N.A.	232	17.15 N	88.45 W
Belize ≃	232	17.32 N	88.14 W
Belize City	232	17.30 N	88.12 W
Belize Inlet ⊂	182	51.08 N	127.15 W
Belka	78	50.49 N	28.11 E
Belknap Crater ⌓[6]	202	44.17 N	121.50 W
Belkofski	180	55.05 N	162.02 W
Bel'kovo	82	56.15 N	38.48 E
Bel'kovskij, Ostrov I	74	75.32 N	135.44 E
Bell, Austl.	274b	37.45 S	145.00 E
Bell, Ciskei	158	33.15 S	27.23 E
Bell, Ca., U.S.	280	33.58 N	118.11 W
Bell □[6]	222	31.03 N	97.27 W
Bell ≃, P.Q., Can.	176	49.48 N	77.38 W
Bell ≃, Yk., Can.	180	67.17 N	137.46 W
Bella	68	40.45 N	15.32 E
Bella Bella	182	52.09 N	128.07 W
Bellac	32	46.07 N	1.02 E
Bella Coola	182	52.22 N	126.46 W
Bella Coola ≃	182	52.22 N	126.43 W
Bell Acres	279b	40.36 N	80.10 W
Bella Flor	248	11.09 S	67.49 W
Bellagio	58	45.59 N	9.15 E
Bellahy	48	53.58 N	8.48 W
Bellair	192	30.10 N	81.44 W
Bellaire, Mi., U.S.	190	44.58 N	85.12 W
Bellaire, Oh., U.S.	188	40.00 N	80.45 W
Bellaire, Tx., U.S.	222	29.42 N	95.27 W
Bella Isla, Estrecho de → Belle Isle, Strait of ʮ	176	51.35 N	56.30 W
Bella Lake ⊜	212	45.27 N	79.02 W
Bellambi	170	34.21 S	150.55 E
Bellamy, Al., U.S.	194	32.26 N	88.08 W
Bellamy, Va., U.S.	208	37.24 N	76.34 W
Bellano	58	46.03 N	9.18 E
Bellaria	66	44.09 N	12.28 E
Bellarine	169	38.08 S	144.37 E
Bellarine Peninsula ›[1]	169	38.13 S	144.35 E
Bellariva	68	41.55 N	15.58 E
Bellary	122	15.09 N	76.56 E
Bellas Artes, Museo de ⊍	286c	10.30 N	66.53 W
Bellas Artes, Palacio de ⊍	286a	19.26 N	99.08 W
Bellata	166	29.55 S	149.47 E
Bella Tola ⋀	58	46.15 N	7.39 E
Bella Unión	252	30.15 S	57.35 W
Bella Vista, Arg.	252	28.30 S	59.03 W
Bella Vista, Arg.	252	27.02 S	65.18 W
Bella Vista, Arg.	258	34.33 S	58.41 W
Bellavista, Chile	286e	33.31 S	70.37 W
Bella Vista, Para.	252	22.08 S	56.31 W
Bellavista, Perú	248	4.54 S	80.42 W
Bellavista, Perú	248	7.04 S	76.35 W
Bellavista, Perú	286d	12.04 S	77.08 W
Bellbird	170	32.51 S	151.21 E
Bellbrook, Austl.	166	30.49 S	152.31 E
Bellbrook, Oh., U.S.	218	39.38 N	84.04 W
Bell Brook ≃	168a	33.01 S	116.15 E
Bell Crags ⋀[2]	44	55.03 N	2.22 W
Bell Creek ≃, Ca., U.S.	280	34.12 N	118.36 W
Bell Creek ≃, In., U.S.	218	40.09 N	85.27 W
Bellé, Sén.	150	14.25 N	12.18 W
Belle, Mo., U.S.	219	38.17 N	91.43 W
Belle, W.V., U.S.	188	38.13 N	81.32 W
Belle ≃, On., Can.	214	42.17 N	82.43 W
Belle ≃, Mi., U.S.	214	42.43 N	82.30 W
Belleair	220	27.55 N	82.48 W
Belleau	50	49.06 N	3.18 E
Belle Ayr Mountain ⋀	210	42.07 N	74.29 W
Belle Bay ⊂	186	47.36 N	55.18 W
Belle Center	216	40.30 N	83.44 W
Belledonne, Chaîne de ⩘	62	45.18 N	6.08 E
Belle-Église	50	49.12 N	2.13 E
Belleek	48	54.28 N	8.06 W
Belle Farm Estates	208	39.23 N	76.45 W
Bellefontaine, Fr.	58	46.33 N	6.04 E
Bellefontaine, Fr.	261	49.06 N	2.28 E
Bellefontaine, Mart.	240e	14.40 N	61.10 W
Bellefontaine, Oh., U.S.	216	40.21 N	83.45 W
Bellefontaine Neighbors	219	38.44 N	90.13 W
Bellefonte, De., U.S.	208	39.45 N	75.30 W
Bellefonte, Md., U.S.	284c	38.47 N	76.52 W
Bellefonte, Pa., U.S.	214	40.54 N	77.46 W
Belle Fourche	198	44.40 N	103.51 W
Belle Fourche ≃	198	44.26 N	102.19 W
Belle Fourche Reservoir ⊜[1]	198	44.44 N	103.42 W
Bellegarde, Fr.	58	46.06 N	5.49 E
Bellegarde, Fr.	62	43.45 N	4.31 E
Bellegarde-du-Loiret	50	47.59 N	2.26 E
Bellegem	50	50.47 N	3.16 E
Belle Glade	220	26.41 N	80.40 W
Belle Glade Camp	220	26.40 N	80.41 W
Bellegrove	208	40.22 N	76.33 W
Belle Haven, Va., U.S.	208	37.33 N	75.49 W
Belle Haven, Va., U.S.	284c	38.47 N	77.04 W
Belleherbe	58	47.16 N	6.40 E
Belle Hôtesse ⋀	241o	16.16 N	61.46 W
Belle-Île I	32	47.20 N	3.10 W
Belle Isle	220	28.27 N	81.21 W
Belle Isle I, Nf., Can.	176	51.55 N	55.20 W
Belle Isle I, Mi., U.S.	281	42.20 N	82.58 W
Belle Isle, Strait of ʮ	176	51.35 N	56.30 W
Belle Isle Park ♠	281	42.20 N	82.59 W
Bellelay	58	47.16 N	7.10 E
Bellême	50	48.22 N	0.34 E
Belle Mead	208	40.28 N	74.39 W
Bellemoor	285	39.43 N	75.35 W
Bellencombre	50	49.42 N	1.14 E
Bellenden Ker National Park ♠	164	17.15 S	145.53 E
Belleoram	186	47.31 N	55.25 W
Belleplain	208	39.16 N	74.52 W
Belle-Plaine, Sk., Can.	184	50.24 N	105.09 W
Belle Plaine, Ia., U.S.	190	41.53 N	92.16 W
Belle Plaine, Ks., U.S.	198	37.23 N	97.16 W
Belle Plaine, Mn., U.S.	190	44.37 N	93.46 W
Belle Rive	219	38.14 N	88.45 W
Belle River	214	42.18 N	82.43 W
Bellerose	276	40.44 N	73.43 W
Bellerose ◆[8]	276	40.45 N	73.43 W
Bellerose Terrace	276	40.43 N	73.43 W
Belle Terre	276	40.58 N	73.04 W
Bellevaux-Ligneuville	56	50.24 N	6.00 E
Belle Vernon	214	40.07 N	79.52 W
Bellevesvre	58	46.50 N	5.22 E
Belleview, Fl., U.S.	192	29.03 N	82.03 W
Belleview, In., U.S.	218	38.53 N	85.23 W
Belle View, Va., U.S.	208	38.46 N	77.03 W
Belleville, On., Can.	212	44.10 N	77.23 W
Belleville, Fr.	56	48.49 N	6.06 E
Belleville, Il., U.S.	219	38.31 N	89.59 W
Belleville, In., U.S.	218	39.41 N	86.29 W
Belleville, Ks., U.S.	198	39.49 N	97.37 W
Belleville, Mi., U.S.	216	42.12 N	83.29 W
Belleville, N.J., U.S.	210	40.47 N	74.09 W
Belleville, N.Y., U.S.	212	43.47 N	76.07 W
Belleville, Pa., U.S.	214	40.36 N	77.43 W
Belleville, R.I., U.S.	207	41.33 N	71.28 W
Belleville, Wi., U.S.	216	42.51 N	89.32 W
Belleville Lake ⊜	281	42.12 N	83.29 W
Belleville-sur-Meuse	56	49.11 N	5.23 E
Belleville-sur-Saône	58	46.06 N	4.45 E
Bellevue, Ab., Can.	182	49.35 N	114.22 W
Bellevue, Fr.	50	49.53 N	4.12 E
Bellevue, Id., U.S.	202	43.27 N	114.15 W
Bellevue, Ia., U.S.	190	42.15 N	90.25 W
Bellevue, Ky., U.S.	218	39.06 N	84.28 W
Bellevue, Md., U.S.	208	38.42 N	76.11 W
Bellevue, Mi., U.S.	216	42.26 N	85.01 W
Bellevue, Ne., U.S.	198	41.08 N	95.53 W
Bellevue, Oh., U.S.	214	41.16 N	82.50 W
Bellevue, Pa., U.S.	214	40.29 N	80.03 W
Bellevue, Tx., U.S.	196	33.38 N	98.01 W
Bellevue, Wa., U.S.	224	47.36 N	122.11 W
Bellevue ◆[8]	273d	26.11 S	28.05 E
Belle Vue Zoological Gardens ♠	262	53.28 N	2.11 W
Bell Ewart	212	44.16 N	79.33 W
Belley	62	45.46 N	5.41 E
Belleydoux	58	46.15 N	5.46 E
Belle Yella	150	7.22 N	10.00 W
Bellflower, Ca., U.S.	228	33.52 N	118.06 W
Bellflower, Il., U.S.	216	40.20 N	88.32 W
Bellflower, Mo., U.S.	219	39.00 N	91.21 W
Bell Gardens	228	33.57 N	118.09 W
Bellheim	56	49.11 N	8.16 E
Bell Hill ⋀[2]	210	43.09 N	75.07 W
Bell Homestead ⊥	212	43.04 N	80.18 W
Bellicourt	50	49.57 N	3.14 E
Bellingdon	260	51.44 N	0.38 W
Bellinge	41	55.20 N	10.20 E
Bellingen	166	30.27 S	152.54 E
Bellingham, Eng., U.K.	44	55.09 N	2.16 W
Bellingham, Ma., U.S.	207	42.05 N	71.28 W
Bellingham, Mn., U.S.	198	45.08 N	96.17 W
Bellingham, Wa., U.S.	224	48.45 N	122.29 W
Bellingham Bay ⊂	224	48.45 N	122.35 W
Bellingshausen ⊍[3]	9	62.12 S	58.58 W
Bellingshausen Sea ⊤[2]	9	71.00 S	85.00 W
Bellingwolde	52	53.07 N	7.09 E
Bellinzago Novarese	62	45.34 N	8.38 E
Bellinzona	58	46.11 N	9.02 E
Bell Island I, Nf., Can.	186	47.36 N	52.58 W
Bell Island I, Nf., Can.	186	50.44 N	55.35 W
Bell Island Hot Springs	182	55.56 N	131.34 W
Bellmawr	208	39.52 N	75.05 W
Bellmead	222	31.35 N	97.06 W
Bellmore	276	40.40 N	73.31 W
Bell Mountain	228	34.35 N	117.15 W
Bellnhausen	56	50.42 N	8.43 E
Bello, Col.	246	6.20 N	75.33 W
Bello, Cuba	286b	23.07 N	82.24 W

Symbol	English	Deutsch	Español	Français	Português
≃	River	Fluß	Río	Rivière	Rio
≅	Canal	Kanal	Canal	Canal	Canal
⌊	Waterfall, Rapids	Wasserfall, Stromschnellen	Cascada, Rápidos	Chute d'eau, Rapides	Cascata, Rápidos
ʮ	Strait	Meeresstraße	Estrecho	Détroit	Estreito
⊂	Bay, Gulf	Bucht, Golf	Bahía, Golfo	Baie, Golfe	Baía, Golfo
⊜	Lake, Lakes	See, Seen	Lago, Lagos	Lac, Lacs	Lago, Lagos
≋	Swamp	Sumpf	Pantano	Marais	Pântano
⊓	Ice Features, Glacier	Eis- und Gletscherformen	Accidentes Glaciales	Formes glaciaires	Acidentes glaciares
⊤	Other Hydrographic Features	Andere Hydrographische Objekte	Otros Elementos Hidrográficos	Autres données hydrographiques	Outros acidentes hidrográficos
✧	Submarine Features	Untermeerische Objekte	Accidentes Submarinos	Formes de relief sous-marin	Acidentes submarinos
□	Political Unit	Politische Einheit	Unidad Politica	Entité politique	Unidade política
⊍	Cultural Institution	Kulturelle Institution	Institución Cultural	Institution culturelle	Instituição cultural
⊥	Historical Site	Historische Stätte	Sitio Histórico	Site historique	Sitio histórico
♠	Recreational Site	Erholungs- und Ferienort	Sitio de Recreo	Centre de loisirs	Area de Lazer
⊠	Airport	Flughafen	Aeropuerto	Aéroport	Aeroporto
■	Military Installation	Militäranlage	Instalación Militar	Installation militaire	Instalação militar
◆	Miscellaneous	Verschiedenes	Misceláneo	Divers	Diversos

ENGLISH Name	Page	Lat.°′	Long.°′	DEUTSCH Name	Seite	Breite°′	Länge°′ E = Ost

Bello Horizonte → Belo Horizonte 255 19.55 S 43.56 W
Bellona 210 42.46 N 77.01 W
Bellona, Récifs ✦[2] 160 21.30 S 159.00 E
Bellona Plateau ✦[3] 14 20.30 S 158.30 E
Bellone, Cap › 157b 16.14 S 49.51 E
Bellosguardo 68 40.25 N 15.19 E
Bellot Strait ⊔ 176 71.58 N 94.45 W
Bellows Falls 188 43.08 N 72.26 W
Belloy-en-France 261 49.05 N 2.22 E
Bellpat 120 28.59 N 68.00 E
Bell Peninsula ›[1] 176 63.50 N 82.00 W
Bell Point 279b 40.33 N 79.33 W
Bells, Tn., U.S. 194 35.43 N 89.05 W
Bells, Tx., U.S. 196 33.37 N 96.25 W
Bellsbank 44 55.18 N 4.23 W
Bells Bay c 212 45.30 N 77.51 W
Bells Corners 212 45.19 N 75.50 W
Bellshill 46 55.49 N 4.01 W
Bells Lake 285 39.44 N 75.02 W
Bells Lake ⊜ 285 39.45 N 75.04 W
Belltown, De., U.S. 208 38.44 N 75.10 W
Belltown, Il., U.S. 219 39.23 N 90.25 W
Belluno 64 46.09 N 12.13 E
Belluno □[4] 64 46.15 N 12.08 E
Bellvale 210 41.15 N 74.18 W
Bell Ville, Arg. 252 32.37 S 62.42 W
Bellville, S. Afr. 158 33.53 S 18.36 E
Bellville, Oh., U.S. 214 40.37 N 82.30 W
Bellville, Tx., U.S. 222 29.57 N 96.15 W
Bellwood, Il., U.S. 278 41.52 N 87.52 W
Bellwood, Ne., U.S. 198 41.20 N 97.14 W
Bellwood, Pa., U.S. 214 40.36 N 78.19 W
Bellwood, Lake ⊜ 212 43.46 N 80.20 W
Belly ≃ 182 49.46 N 113.02 W
Bellyk 86 54.32 N 91.17 E
Belm 52 52.18 N 8.08 E
Belmar, Md., U.S. 284b 39.21 N 76.32 W
Belmar, N.J., U.S. 208 40.10 N 74.01 W
Bélmez 34 38.16 N 5.12 W
Belmiro Braga 256 21.57 S 43.25 W
Belmond 190 42.50 N 93.36 W
Belmont, Austl. 169 38.10 S 144.21 E
Belmont, Austl. 170 33.02 S 151.40 E
Belmont, Mb., Can. 184 49.24 N 99.27 W
Belmont, N.S., Can. 186 45.25 N 63.23 W
Belmont, On., Can. 212 42.53 N 81.05 W
Belmont, S. Afr. 158 29.28 S 24.22 E
Belmont, Eng., U.K. 262 53.38 N 2.30 W
Belmont, Ca., U.S. 226 37.31 N 122.16 W
Belmont, Ma., U.S. 283 42.23 N 71.10 W
Belmont, Mi., U.S. 216 43.05 N 85.37 W
Belmont, Ms., U.S. 194 34.30 N 88.12 W
Belmont, N.H., U.S. 188 43.26 N 71.28 W
Belmont, N.Y., U.S. 210 42.13 N 78.02 W
Belmont, Pa., U.S. 214 40.17 N 78.53 W
Belmont, S.C., U.S. 192 34.02 N 81.01 W
Belmont, Tx., U.S. 222 29.31 N 97.41 W
Belmont, Wi., U.S. 190 42.44 N 90.20 W
Belmont □[6] 214 40.05 N 80.54 W
Belmonte, Bra. 255 15.51 S 38.54 W
Belmonte, Esp. 34 43.17 N 6.14 W
Belmonte, Esp. 34 39.34 N 2.42 W
Belmonte, Port. 34 40.21 N 7.21 W
Belmonte Calabro 68 39.09 N 16.05 E
Belmonte Mezzagno 70 38.02 N 13.23 E
Belmont Harbor c 278 41.57 N 87.38 W
Belmont Lake ⊜, On., Can. 212 44.30 N 77.50 W
Belmont Lake ⊜, N.Y., U.S. 276 40.44 N 73.20 W
Belmont Lake State Park ♦ 276 40.43 N 73.20 W
Belmont Park 214 41.10 N 80.39 W
Belmont Park Race Track ♦ 276 40.43 N 73.43 W
Belmont Reservoir ⊜[1] 262 53.39 N 2.30 W
Belmont Slough ≃ 282 37.33 N 122.14 W
Belmopan 232 17.15 N 88.46 W
Belmore, Austl. 274a 33.55 S 151.05 E
Belmore, Oh., U.S. 216 41.09 N 83.56 W
Belmullet 48 54.14 N 10.00 W
Belmuri 272b 22.57 N 88.09 E
Belo 157b 19.42 S 44.33 E
Belœil, Bel. 50 50.33 N 3.43 E
Beloeil, P.Q., Can. 206 45.34 N 73.12 W
Belœil, Château de ʊ 50 50.35 N 3.44 E
Beloeil, Ruisseau ≃ 275a 45.39 N 73.12 W
Beloglazovo 86 56.05 N 72.40 E
Belogorje, Ross. 78 50.30 N 40.01 E
Belogorje, Ukr. 78 50.01 N 26.25 E
Belogorka 80 50.42 N 53.27 E
Belogornoje 80 52.25 N 47.35 E
Belogorode 82 54.23 N 38.31 E
Belogorodka 78 50.00 N 26.39 E
Belogorovka 83 48.55 N 38.15 E
Belogorsk, Ross. 86 55.05 N 88.28 E
Belogorsk, Ross. 89 50.57 N 128.25 E
Belogorsk, Ukr. 78 45.03 N 34.36 E
Belogorskij 86 49.27 N 83.10 E
Belogorskoje 80 53.35 N 48.12 E
Belogradčik 38 43.38 N 22.41 E
Beloguša 78 51.57 N 26.56 E
Beloha 157b 25.10 S 45.03 E
Belo Horizonte 255 19.55 S 43.56 W
Beloit, Ks., U.S. 198 39.27 N 98.06 W
Beloit, Oh., U.S. 214 40.55 N 80.59 W
Beloit, Wi., U.S. 216 42.30 N 89.01 W
Belo Jardim 250 8.20 S 36.26 W
Belojarsk 86 53.28 N 83.54 E
Beloje, Kaz. 86 48.55 N 82.58 E
Beloje, Ross. 80 58.23 N 39.24 E
Beloje, Ukr. 83 48.31 N 39.04 E
Beloje, ozero ⊜ 76 60.11 N 37.37 E
Beloje more (White Sea) ⊤[2] 24 65.30 N 38.00 E
Belokamenskoje ◆[8] 83 48.41 N 38.06 E
Belokany 84 41.43 N 46.26 E
Belokurakino 83 49.33 N 38.44 E
Belokuricha 86 51.59 N 84.59 E
Beloluck 83 49.41 N 39.02 E
Belomestnaja 76 52.24 N 37.37 E
Belomestnaja Dvojn'a 80 52.42 N 41.03 E
Belomorsk 24 64.32 N 34.48 E
Belomorsko-Baltijskij kanal ≍ 24 62.48 N 34.48 E
Belondo 152 0.16 S 19.31 E
Belonge 152 2.06 S 19.32 E
Belonia 124 23.15 N 91.27 E
Beloomut 76 54.57 N 39.20 E
Beloozersk 76 52.28 N 25.11 E
Belopolje 78 51.09 N 34.18 E
Belorado 34 42.25 N 3.11 W
Belorečensk 78 44.46 N 39.52 E
Beloreck 86 53.58 N 58.24 E
Belören, Tür. 130 40.51 N 33.30 E
Belören, Tür. 130 37.12 N 32.33 E
Belören, Tür. 130 37.39 N 37.34 E
Belorussia → Belarus □[1] 22 53.35 N 28.00 E
Belorussija → Belarus □[1] 72 53.50 N 28.00 E
Belorussiya → Belarus □[1] 72 53.50 N 28.00 E
Belorusskaja gr'ada ∧ 76 53.40 N 27.00 E
Beloščelje 24 64.52 N 46.56 E
Belo-sur-mer 157b 20.44 S 44.00 E
Belot, Lac ⊜ 180 66.55 N 126.18 W
Belousovka, Kaz. 86 50.08 N 82.33 E
Belousovka, Ukr. 78 49.57 N 32.20 E
Belousovo 82 55.05 N 36.40 E
Bel'ov 76 53.48 N 36.08 E
Belo Vale 255 20.25 S 44.01 W
Beloveżskaja Pušča, zapovednik ♦ 76 52.40 N 23.50 E
Belovo, Ross. 86 54.25 N 86.18 E
Belovo, Ross. 86 52.57 N 82.16 E
Belovodsk 83 49.12 N 39.35 E
Belovodskoje 85 42.50 N 74.06 E
Beloz'orje, Ukr. 78 49.29 N 31.35 E
Beloz'orje, Ukr. 78 49.18 N 31.54 E
Beloz'orka 78 46.37 N 32.27 E
Beloz'orsk 76 60.02 N 37.48 E
Beloz'orskoje 78 48.33 N 37.04 E
Belp 58 46.53 N 7.30 E
Belpāda 272c 19.02 N 73.03 E
Belpasso 70 37.35 N 14.58 E
Belper 44 53.01 N 1.29 W
Belpre 188 39.16 N 81.34 W
Belrose 274a 33.44 S 151.13 E
Belsano 214 40.31 N 78.52 W
Belsele 50 51.09 N 4.05 E
Bel'skaja Vol'a 78 51.27 N 25.49 E
Bel'skoje, Ross. 80 54.44 N 40.22 E
Bel'skoje, Ross. 86 57.49 N 92.09 E
Belson Run ≃ 279b 40.12 N 79.37 W
Belspring 192 37.11 N 80.36 W
Belt 202 47.23 N 110.55 W
Beltana 166 30.48 S 138.25 E
Belt Creek ≃ 202 47.36 N 111.02 W
Belted Range ⋏ 204 37.25 N 116.10 W
Belterra 250 2.38 S 54.57 W
Belthorn 262 53.43 N 2.26 W
Beltinci 61 46.36 N 16.15 E
Belton, Eng., U.K. 42 52.34 N 1.41 E
Belton, Eng., U.K. 44 53.33 N 0.49 W
Belton, Mo., U.S. 194 38.48 N 94.31 W
Belton, S.C., U.S. 192 34.31 N 82.29 W
Belton, Tx., U.S. 222 31.03 N 97.27 W
Belton Lake ⊜[1] 222 31.08 N 97.32 W
Beltra 48 54.13 N 8.37 W
Beltrán 252 27.50 S 64.04 W
Beltsville, Md., U.S. 208 39.02 N 76.54 W
Beltsville, Md., U.S. 284c 39.02 N 76.54 W
Bel'tsy → Bel'c' 78 47.46 N 27.56 E
Belturbet 48 54.06 N 7.28 W
Beltway Plaza ◆[9] 284c 39.00 N 76.54 W
Bel'tyrskij 86 53.02 N 90.16 E
Beltzville Lake ⊜[1] 210 40.52 N 75.37 W
Beltzville State Park ♦ 210 40.52 N 75.36 W
Belucha, gora ∧ 86 49.48 N 86.40 E
Belucha, ozero ⊜ 80 49.20 N 46.05 E
Belugino 82 54.47 N 37.54 E
Belumut, Gunong ∧ 114 2.02 N 103.34 E
Belūr, India 122 13.10 N 75.52 E
Belur, India 272b 22.38 N 88.18 E
Beluran 112 5.54 N 117.33 E
Belur Math ʊ[1] 272b 22.38 N 88.22 E
Belušje 24 66.54 N 47.31 E
Belvedere, It. 64 45.44 N 13.23 E
Belvedere, Ca., U.S. 226 37.52 N 122.28 W
Belvedere, Va., U.S. 284c 38.50 N 77.10 W
Belvedere ◆[8] 260 51.29 N 0.09 E
Belvedere ʊ 264b 48.11 N 16.23 E
Belvedere di Spinello 68 39.12 N 16.53 E
Belvedere Homes 220 26.43 N 80.06 W
Belvedere Marittimo 68 39.37 N 15.52 E
Belvedere Ostrense 66 43.34 N 13.09 E
Belvès 32 44.47 N 1.00 E
Belvidere, De., U.S. 208 39.43 N 75.37 W
Belvidere, Il., U.S. 216 42.15 N 88.50 W
Belvidere, N.J., U.S. 210 40.49 N 75.04 W
Belview 198 44.36 N 95.19 W
Belvis 266a 40.33 N 3.33 W
Belvís de la Jara 34 39.45 N 4.57 W
Belvoir, Vale of V 42 52.57 N 0.53 W
Belvoir → Kokhav HaYarden ⊥ 132 32.36 N 35.31 E
Belyando ≃ 166 21.38 S 146.50 E
Belyj 76 55.50 N 32.56 E
Belyj, ostrov I 74 73.10 N 70.45 E
Belyje Berega 76 53.12 N 34.40 E
Belyje Kolodezi 82 54.55 N 38.42 E
Belyje Stolby 82 55.20 N 37.52 E
Belyje Vody 85 42.25 N 69.50 E
Belyj Gorodok 76 56.58 N 37.30 E
Belyj Jar, Ross. 80 53.57 N 48.58 E
Belyj Jar, Ross. 86 53.36 N 91.24 E
Belyj Jar, Ross. 86 58.26 N 85.01 E
Belyj Kalodez' 78 50.02 N 38.40 E
Belyj Kolodez' 78 50.12 N 37.08 E
Belyj Luch ≃ 80 57.43 N 43.42 E
Belyj Rast 82 56.08 N 37.26 E
Belyniči 76 53.59 N 29.42 E
Belynkoviči 76 53.15 N 32.08 E
Belz, Fr. 32 47.41 N 3.10 W
Belz, Ukr. 78 50.23 N 24.01 E
Bełżec 30 50.24 N 23.26 E
Belzig 54 52.08 N 12.35 E
Belzoni 194 33.11 N 90.29 W
Bełżyce 30 51.11 N 22.18 E
Bem 219 38.15 N 91.28 W
Bemaraha, Plateau du ⋏[1] 157b 19.15 S 45.00 E
Bemarivo, Madag. 157b 16.56 S 44.21 E
Bemarivo, Madag. 157b 21.45 S 44.45 E
Bemarivo ≃, Madag. 157b 15.27 S 47.40 E
Bemarivo ≃, Madag. 157b 14.09 S 50.09 E
Bemavo 157b 21.37 S 45.24 E
Bembe 152 7.02 S 14.18 E
Bembéréké 150 10.13 N 2.40 E
Bembézar ≃ 34 37.45 N 5.13 W
Bembezi ≃ 154 18.57 S 27.47 E
Bembou Sambayabé 150 10.55 N 13.44 W
Bembridge 42 50.41 N 1.05 W
Bement 194 39.55 N 88.34 W
Bemidji 190 47.28 N 94.52 W
Bemis 194 35.34 N 88.49 W
Bemmel 52 51.54 N 5.54 E
Bemolanga 157b 17.44 S 45.06 E
Bemposta 256 22.09 S 43.07 W
Bemus Point 214 42.09 N 79.23 W
Bemyž 80 56.08 N 51.44 E
Ben, Kinh ≍ 269c 10.43 N 106.37 E
Bena 150 11.18 N 5.55 E
Benaadir □[4] 144 2.07 N 45.24 E
Benāb 128 37.20 N 46.04 E
Benabarre 34 42.07 N 0.29 E
Bena-Dibele 152 4.07 S 22.50 E
Benagaria 126 24.11 N 87.37 E
Benagerie 166 31.25 S 140.24 E
Benahmed 148 33.07 N 7.17 W
Benain ≃ 112 9.39 S 124.59 E
Ben'akoni 76 54.15 N 25.22 E
Bena-Leka 152 5.08 S 22.10 E
Benalla 166 36.33 S 145.59 E
Benamejí 34 37.16 N 4.32 W
Benares → Vārānasi 124 25.20 N 83.00 E
Bénat, Cap › 62 43.05 N 6.22 E
Benátky nad Jizerou 54 50.17 N 14.51 E
Bena-Tshadi 152 4.40 S 22.49 E
Benavente, Esp. 34 42.00 N 5.41 W
Benavente, Port. 34 38.59 N 8.48 W
Benavides 196 27.35 N 98.24 W
Benavidez 258 34.25 S 58.42 W
Ben Avon 279b 40.31 N 80.05 W
Ben Avon Heights 279b 40.31 N 80.04 W
Ben Badis 34 34.57 N 0.55 W
Benbane Head › 48 55.15 N 6.28 W
Benbecula I 46 57.26 N 7.21 W
Ben Bolt 196 27.39 N 98.05 W
Benbonyathe Hill ∧ 166 30.24 S 139.11 E
Benbrook 222 32.40 N 97.27 W
Benbrook Lake ⊜[1] 222 32.38 N 97.27 W
Ben Cat 110 11.09 N 106.36 E
Ben Cat, Rach ≃ 269c 10.50 N 106.42 E
Bencha, Khao Phanom ∧ 110 8.17 N 98.56 E
Ben-Chicao, Col de)(34 36.12 N 2.45 E
Bencubbin 162 30.48 S 117.52 E
Bend 202 44.03 N 121.18 W
Benda, Tanjung › 115a 6.37 S 111.29 E
Bendaja 150 7.10 N 11.15 W
Bende 150 5.36 N 7.39 E
Bendel □[3] 150 6.00 N 6.00 E
Bendela 152 3.18 S 17.36 E
Bendeleben, Mount ∧ 180 65.10 N 164.03 W
Bendemeer 166 30.53 S 151.10 E
Bender Beyla 144 9.29 N 50.49 E
Benderge ∧ 158 31.06 S 27.58 E
Bendersville 208 39.59 N 77.15 W
Bendery 78 46.48 N 29.29 E
Bendigo 169 36.46 S 144.17 E
Bendimahi ≃ 84 38.56 N 43.38 E
Bendorf 56 50.25 N 7.34 E
Bendugu 150 9.32 N 10.57 W
Bēne 76 56.29 N 23.04 E
Bene Beraq 132 32.05 N 34.50 E
Benedict 208 38.30 N 76.40 W
Benediktenwand ⊥[4] 64 47.39 N 11.28 E
Beneditinos 250 5.27 S 42.22 W
Benedito Leite 250 7.13 S 44.34 W
Bénéna 150 13.07 N 4.22 W
Benenitra 157b 23.27 S 45.05 E
Benepú, Rada ⊤[3] 174z 27.10 S 109.25 W
Beneraird ∧[2] 44 55.04 N 4.57 W
Benešov 30 49.47 N 14.43 E
Benešov nad Ploučnicí 54 50.45 N 14.22 E
Bénestroff 56 48.55 N 6.45 E
Benetutti 71 40.27 N 9.10 E
Beneuvre 58 47.42 N 4.57 E
Bene Vagienna 62 44.33 N 7.50 E
Bénévent-l'Abbaye 32 46.07 N 1.38 E
Benevento 68 41.08 N 14.45 E
Benevento □[4] 68 41.15 N 14.17 E
Benezett 214 41.19 N 78.23 W
Benfeld 58 48.22 N 7.36 E
Benfica ◆[8], Bra. 287a 22.53 S 43.15 W
Benfica ◆[8], Port. 266c 38.45 N 9.12 W
Benfica, Estádio ♦ 266c 38.45 N 9.11 W
Bèng ≃, Lao 110 19.53 N 101.08 E
Beng ≃, Zhg. 98 35.05 N 118.24 E
Benga 154 13.19 S 34.16 E
Bengābād 126 24.18 N 86.21 E
Bengal, Bay of c 12 15.00 N 90.00 E
Bengala, Golfo del → Bengal, Bay of c 12 15.00 N 90.00 E
Bengalen, Golf von → Bengal, Bay of c 12 15.00 N 90.00 E
Bengamisa 154 0.57 N 25.10 E
Bengara 112 3.11 N 117.12 E
Ben Gardane 148 33.08 N 11.13 E
Bengasi → Banghāzī 146 32.07 N 20.04 E
Bengbis 152 3.27 N 12.27 E
Bengbu 100 32.58 N 117.24 E
Benger 168a 33.11 S 115.52 E
Benghazi → Banghāzī 146 32.07 N 20.04 E
Ben Giang 110 15.41 N 107.47 E
Bengkalis 114 1.28 N 102.07 E
Bengkalis, Pulau I 114 1.30 N 102.15 E
Bengkalis, Selat ⊔ 114 1.30 N 102.00 E
Bengkayang 112 0.50 N 109.29 E
Bengkoka ≃ 116 6.50 N 117.03 E
Bengkulu 112 3.48 S 102.16 E
Bengkulu □[4] 112 4.00 S 102.30 E
Bengo □[5] 152 8.30 S 13.20 E
Bengo ≃ 152 8.45 S 13.24 E
Bengo, Baía do c 152 8.43 S 13.21 E
Bengoi 164 3.01 S 130.12 E
Bengough 184 49.24 N 105.08 W
Bengtsfors 26 59.02 N 12.13 E
Benguela 152 12.35 S 13.25 E
Benguela □[5] 152 12.45 S 14.30 E
Benguerir 148 32.14 N 7.57 W
Benguet □[4] 116 16.30 N 120.40 E
Bengut, Cap › 34 36.55 N 3.54 E
Benha → Banhā 142 30.28 N 31.11 E
Benham 192 36.57 N 82.56 W
Ben Hur 222 31.30 N 96.44 W
Beni, Nig. 146 10.27 N 10.24 E
Beni, Zaïre 154 0.30 N 29.28 E
Beni □[5] 248 14.00 S 65.30 W
Beni ≃ 248 10.58 S 66.09 W
Béni Abbas 148 30.08 N 2.10 W
Benicarló 34 40.25 N 0.26 E
Benicia 226 38.02 N 122.09 W
Benicia Capitol State Historic Park ♦ 282 38.03 N 122.09 W
Benicia State Recreation Area ♦ 282 38.05 N 122.13 W
Benicito ≃ 248 11.32 S 65.47 W
Benidorm 34 38.32 N 0.08 W
Beni-Mellal 148 32.22 N 6.29 W
Beni-Mellal □[4] 148 32.22 N 6.27 W
Benin (Bénin) □[1], Afr. 134 9.30 N 2.15 E
Benin (Bénin) □[1], Afr. 150 9.30 N 2.15 E
Benin ≃ 150 5.45 N 5.04 E
Benin, Bight of c[3] 150 5.30 N 3.00 E
Benin City 150 6.19 N 5.41 E
Beni Saf 148 35.19 N 1.23 W
Benisheikh 146 11.49 N 12.29 E
Benissa 34 38.34 N 0.03 E
Beni Suef → Banī Suwayf 142 29.05 N 31.05 E
Benito 184 51.55 N 101.31 W
Benito Juárez, Arg. 252 37.40 S 59.48 W
Benito Juárez, Méx. 234 19.14 N 100.28 W
Benito Juárez, Méx. 234 17.50 N 92.32 W
Benito Juárez, Aeropuerto Internacional ⊠ 286a 19.26 N 99.04 W
Benito Juárez, Presa ⊜[1] 234 16.27 N 95.30 W
Benit Point › 116 9.54 N 125.17 E
Benjamim Constant 256 21.57 S 42.53 W
Benjamin 196 33.35 N 99.48 W
Benjamín, Isla I 254 44.40 S 74.08 W
Benjamín Aceval 252 24.58 S 57.34 W
Benjamin Constant 246 4.22 S 70.02 W
Benjamin Franklin Bridge ◆[5] 285 39.57 N 75.08 W
Benjamín Hill 232 30.10 N 111.10 W
Benjamín Zorrilla 252 39.06 S 65.29 W
Benkelman 198 40.02 N 101.31 W
Benken 54 52.10 N 12.28 E
Benkovac 36 44.02 N 15.37 E
Benld 219 39.05 N 89.48 W
Benllech 44 53.19 N 4.13 W
Ben Lomond 226 37.05 N 122.05 W
Ben Lomond National Park ♦ 166 41.34 S 147.11 E
Ben Mehidi 36 36.46 N 7.54 E
Benmore, Lake ⊜[1] 172 44.25 S 170.15 E
Benndale 194 30.52 N 88.48 W
Benndorf 54 51.34 N 11.29 E
Benneckenstein 54 51.40 N 10.45 E
Bennekom 52 52.00 N 5.40 E
Bennet 198 40.40 N 96.30 W
Bennett, Lake ⊜ 162 22.55 S 130.57 E
Bennetta, ostrov I 74 76.21 N 148.56 E
Bennett Lake ⊜, Can. 180 60.05 N 134.50 W
Bennett Lake ⊜, Mb., Can. 184 53.28 N 96.05 W
Bennett Lake ⊜, On., Can. 212 44.55 N 76.27 W
Bennett Pass)(224 45.18 N 121.39 W
Bennettsbridge 48 52.36 N 7.12 W
Bennetts Creek ≃ 210 42.16 N 77.35 W
Bennettsville 192 34.37 N 79.41 W
Bennettswood 274b 37.51 S 145.07 E
Bennigsen 52 52.14 N 9.40 E
Benninghofen ◆[8] 263 51.29 N 7.31 E
Bennington, In., U.S. 218 38.52 N 85.08 W
Bennington, Ks., U.S. 198 39.01 N 97.35 W
Bennington, Vt., U.S. 210 42.52 N 73.11 W
Bennington □[6] 207 42.50 N 73.08 W
Bennington Battle Monument ⊥ 210 42.53 N 73.13 W
Benniu 106 31.52 N 119.48 E
Bennstedt 54 51.29 N 11.49 E
Beno 152 3.37 S 17.48 E
Benoa 115b 8.46 S 115.13 E
Ben Ohau Range ⋏ 172 44.00 S 170.00 E
Benoit 194 33.39 N 91.00 W
Benom, Gunong ∧ 114 3.49 N 102.04 E
Benoni 158 26.11 S 28.19 E
Benoni □[5] 273d 26.08 S 28.22 E
Benoni-Suid 273d 26.13 S 28.18 E
Bénoué (Benue) ≃ 134 7.48 N 6.46 E
Bénoué, Parc National de la ♦ 146 8.20 N 13.50 E
Benover 260 51.13 N 0.26 E
Bénoy 146 8.59 N 16.19 E
Benque Viejo del Carmen 232 17.05 N 89.08 W
Benrad ◆[8] 263 51.20 N 6.30 E
Benrath ◆[8] 56 51.10 N 6.51 E
Benrath, Schloss ⊥ 263 51.10 N 6.52 E
Bensalem 285 40.04 N 74.56 W
Bensbach ≃ 164 9.08 S 141.00 E
Bensberg 56 50.58 N 7.09 E
Bensdorf 54 52.24 N 12.20 E
Ben Sekka, Rass › 36 37.21 N 9.45 E
Bensenville 278 41.57 N 87.56 W
Bensersiel 52 53.40 N 7.34 E
Benshausen 54 50.38 N 10.35 E
Bensheim 56 49.41 N 8.37 E
Bensley 208 37.26 N 77.26 W
Ben-Slimane 148 33.41 N 7.10 W
Ben-Slimane □[4] 148 33.40 N 7.10 W
Ben Smih 36 36.23 N 7.31 E
Benson, Eng., U.K. 42 51.38 N 1.05 W
Benson, Az., U.S. 200 31.58 N 110.17 W
Benson, Md., U.S. 208 39.30 N 76.23 W
Benson, Mn., U.S. 198 45.18 N 95.35 W
Benson, N.C., U.S. 192 35.22 N 78.32 W
Bensonhurst ◆[8] 276 40.35 N 73.59 W
Benson Point › 174o 1.56 N 157.29 W
Bens Run ≃ 284b 39.19 N 76.48 W
Bent 128 26.17 N 59.31 E
Benta 114 4.01 N 101.58 E
Benteng (Salayar) 112 6.08 S 120.27 E
Bentheim, Dtsch. 52 52.17 N 7.10 E
Bentheim, Mi., U.S. 216 42.42 N 85.55 W
Ben Thuy 110 18.39 N 105.42 E
Bentiaba 152 14.15 S 12.21 E
Bentiaba ≃ 152 14.29 S 12.50 E
Bentinck Island I, Austl. 164 17.04 S 139.30 E
Bentinck Island I, Mya. 110 11.45 N 98.03 E
Bentiu 140 9.14 N 29.50 E
Bentleigh 274b 37.55 S 145.02 E
Bentley, Ab., Can. 182 52.28 N 114.04 W
Bentley, Eng., U.K. 44 53.33 N 1.09 W
Bentley College ʊ[2] 283 42.23 N 71.13 W
Bentleyville, Oh., U.S. 279a 41.25 N 81.26 W
Bentleyville, Pa., U.S. 214 40.07 N 80.00 W
Bento Gomes ≃ 248 16.40 S 57.12 W
Bento Gonçalves 252 29.10 S 51.31 W
Bentol 150 6.26 N 10.36 W
Benton, Ar., U.S. 194 34.33 N 92.35 W
Benton, Il., U.S. 194 37.59 N 88.55 W
Benton, In., U.S. 216 41.30 N 85.45 W
Benton, Ky., U.S. 194 36.51 N 88.21 W
Benton, La., U.S. 194 32.41 N 93.44 W
Benton, Ms., U.S. 194 32.49 N 90.15 W
Benton, Mo., U.S. 194 37.05 N 89.33 W
Benton, Oh., U.S. 214 40.36 N 81.51 W
Benton, Pa., U.S. 210 41.11 N 76.23 W
Benton, Tn., U.S. 192 35.10 N 84.39 W
Benton, Wi., U.S. 190 42.34 N 90.22 W
Benton □[6] 216 40.37 N 87.19 W
Benton City, Mo., U.S. 219 39.08 N 91.45 W
Benton City, Wa., U.S. 202 46.15 N 119.29 W
Bentong 114 3.32 N 101.55 E
Benton Harbor 216 42.07 N 86.26 W
Benton Heights 216 42.07 N 86.24 W
Bentonia 194 32.38 N 90.21 W
Benton Lake ⊜ 202 47.40 N 111.20 W
Benton Ridge 216 41.00 N 83.47 W
Bentonville, Ar., U.S. 194 36.22 N 94.12 W
Bentonville, In., U.S. 218 39.45 N 85.15 W
Bentonville, Oh., U.S. 218 38.45 N 83.37 W
Ben Tre 110 10.14 N 106.23 E
Bent's Old Fort National Historic Site ⊥ 198 38.05 N 103.28 W
Benua, Pulau I 112 0.56 N 107.27 E
Benue □[3] 150 7.15 N 8.00 E
Benue (Bénoué) ≃ 134 7.48 N 6.46 E
Benut 114 1.38 N 103.16 E
Benwee ∧ 48 53.35 N 9.31 W
Benwee Head › 48 54.20 N 9.50 W
Ben Wheeler 222 32.27 N 95.42 W
Benxi (Xiaoshi), Zhg. 104 41.17 N 124.07 E
Benxi (Penhsi), Zhg. 104 41.18 N 123.45 E
Benza 152 6.16 S 12.57 E
Beograd (Belgrade) 38 44.50 N 20.30 E
Beohāri 124 24.03 N 81.23 E
Beonta 272b 22.31 N 88.31 E
Béoumi 150 7.40 N 5.34 W
Beowawe 204 40.35 N 116.28 W
Beppu 96 33.17 N 131.30 E
Beppu-wan c 96 33.18 N 131.35 E
Bequia I 241h 13.01 N 61.13 W
Bequimão 250 2.26 S 44.47 W
Bera 126 24.05 N 89.37 E
Berābāria 272b 22.52 N 88.34 E
Beraberi, India 272b 22.46 N 88.27 E
Berāberi, India 272b 22.51 N 88.12 E
Beraketa, Madag. 157b 24.11 S 45.42 E
Beraketa, Madag. 157b 23.07 S 44.25 E
Beramanja 157b 13.13 S 48.56 E
Bérandjoko 152 3.06 N 17.17 E
Berāsi 124 23.36 N 81.51 E
Berasia 124 23.38 N 77.26 E
Berat 38 40.42 N 19.57 E
Beratzhausen 60 49.06 N 11.48 E
Berau 58 47.42 N 8.15 E
Berau ≃ 112 2.10 N 117.42 E
Berau, Teluk c 164 2.30 S 132.30 E
Beravina 157b 18.10 S 45.14 E
Berazategui 258 34.46 S 58.13 W
Berazategui □[5] 288 34.50 S 58.10 W
Berbenno di Valtellina 64 46.10 N 9.44 E
Berbera 144 10.25 N 45.02 E
Berbérati 152 4.16 N 15.47 E
Berbice ≃ 246 6.17 N 57.32 W
Berceto 64 44.31 N 9.59 E
Berchem, Bel. 50 51.12 N 4.26 E
Berchem, Bel. 50 50.47 N 3.30 E
Berchem-Sainte-Agathe 56 50.52 N 4.17 E
Berchidda 71 40.47 N 9.10 E
Berching 60 49.07 N 11.27 E
Berchtesgaden 64 47.38 N 13.01 E
Berchtesgaden, Nationalpark ♦ 64 47.30 N 13.00 E
Berchum ◆[8] 263 51.23 N 7.32 E
Berck 50 50.24 N 1.34 E
Berclair 196 28.32 N 97.36 W
Berčogur 86 48.25 N 58.44 E
Bercu 50 50.31 N 3.17 E
Berd 84 40.53 N 45.23 E
Berda ≃ 78 46.48 N 36.52 E
Berdaale 144 7.04 N 47.51 E
Berdale 144 4.56 N 45.02 E
Berd'ansk 78 46.45 N 36.49 E
Berd'anskaja kosa ›[2] 78 46.42 N 36.48 E
Berd'anskij zaliv c 78 46.42 N 36.35 E
Berd'auš 86 55.09 N 59.09 E
Berdičev 78 49.54 N 28.36 E
Berdigest'ach 74 62.06 N 126.40 E
Berdniki 80 57.25 N 46.33 E
Berdorf 56 49.50 N 6.21 E
Berdsk 86 54.47 N 83.02 E
Berd'užje 86 55.48 N 68.19 E
Berdyansk → Berd'ansk 78 46.45 N 36.49 E
Béré, Tchad 146 9.20 N 16.09 E
Bere, Turk. 128 39.47 N 58.06 E
Berea, Ky., U.S. 192 37.34 N 84.17 W
Berea, Oh., U.S. 214 41.21 N 81.51 W
Berea, S.C., U.S. 192 34.53 N 82.27 W
Bere Alston 42 50.29 N 4.11 W
Berebei 164 9.31 S 147.27 E
Beregajevo 86 57.10 N 87.32 E
Beregomet 78 48.12 N 25.21 E
Beregovo 78 48.13 N 22.39 E
Beregovoj 86 55.12 N 73.12 E
Bereguardo 62 45.15 N 9.01 E
Bereina 164 8.40 S 146.30 E
Bereka ≃ 78 49.12 N 36.59 E
Bereketli 130 40.31 N 37.18 E
Bereku 154 4.27 S 35.44 E
Berekua 240d 15.14 N 61.19 W
Berekum 150 7.27 N 2.37 W
Bérem 152 7.33 N 13.55 E
Beren, liman ⊜ 80 46.52 N 44.55 E
Berenda Slough ≃ 226 37.00 N 120.29 W
Berendejevo 82 56.36 N 39.01 E
Berens ≃ 184 52.21 N 97.02 W
Berens Island I 184 52.18 N 97.17 W
Berens River 184 52.22 N 97.02 W
Bere Regis 42 50.46 N 2.14 W
Beresford, N.B., Can. 186 47.42 N 65.42 W
Beresford, S.D., U.S. 198 43.04 N 96.46 W
Beresina → Berezina ≃ 76 52.33 N 30.14 E
Berestečko 78 50.23 N 25.07 E
Berești 38 46.06 N 27.53 E
Berettyó (Barcău) ≃ 38 46.59 N 21.07 E
Berettyóújfalu 30 47.14 N 21.32 E
Berevo, Madag. 157b 17.14 S 44.17 E
Berevo, Madag. 157b 19.44 S 44.58 E
Berezajka 76 57.59 N 33.54 E
Berezan' 78 50.19 N 31.30 E
Berezanskaja 78 45.43 N 39.34 E
Berezanskij liman c[1] 78 46.43 N 31.30 E
Berežany 78 49.27 N 24.56 E
Berezdov 78 50.27 N 27.05 E
Berezina ≃, Bela. 76 52.33 N 30.14 E
Berezina ≃, Bela. 76 53.48 N 25.59 E
Berezino, Bela. 76 53.49 N 28.59 E
Berezino, Bela. 76 54.54 N 28.12 E
Berezino, Kaz. 80 50.06 N 48.52 E
Berezino, Ukr. 78 46.14 N 29.12 E
Berezinskij zapovednik ♦ 76 54.40 N 28.15 E
Berezna 78 51.34 N 31.47 E
Berezn'agi 78 49.59 N 41.06 E
Berezn'aki, Ukr. 78 49.09 N 31.57 E
Berezn'aki, Ukr. 78 49.51 N 33.01 E
Bereznegovatoje 78 47.20 N 32.49 E
Berežnica 78 51.27 N 26.27 E
Bereznik 24 62.51 N 42.40 E
Berezniki 86 59.24 N 56.46 E
Berford Lake ⊜ 212 44.48 N 81.11 W
Berg, Dtsch. 64 47.58 N 11.21 E
Berg, Lux. 56 49.49 N 6.05 E
Berg, Nor. 24 69.26 N 17.15 E
Berg, Öst. 64 46.45 N 13.09 E
Berga, Dtsch. 54 50.45 N 12.10 E
Berga, Dtsch. 54 51.27 N 11.00 E
Berga, Esp. 34 42.06 N 1.51 E
Berga, Sve. 40 59.21 N 16.26 E
Bergama 130 39.07 N 27.11 E
Bergambacht 52 51.56 N 4.46 E
Bergamo 62 45.41 N 9.43 E
Bergamo □[4] 64 45.50 N 9.48 E
Bergan Point › 276 40.40 N 73.20 W
Bergantín 246 10.01 N 64.22 W
Bergantino 64 45.05 N 11.15 E
Bergara 34 43.07 N 2.25 W
Bergby 26 60.56 N 17.02 E
Berge, Dtsch. 52 52.37 N 7.44 E
Berge, Dtsch. 54 53.15 N 11.50 E
Berge, Dtsch. 263 51.21 N 7.22 E
Bergedorf ◆[8] 52 53.29 N 10.13 E
Bergei ∧[2] 263 51.13 N 7.46 E
Bergeijk 52 51.19 N 5.22 E
Bergen, Dtsch. 52 52.48 N 9.58 E
Bergen, Dtsch. 54 52.53 N 10.58 E
Bergen, Dtsch. 64 47.48 N 12.35 E
Bergen, Ned. 52 52.40 N 4.41 E
Bergen, Nor. 26 60.23 N 5.20 E
Bergen, N.Y., U.S. 210 43.05 N 77.56 W
Bergen □[6] 210 40.53 N 74.03 W
Bergen aan Zee 52 52.38 N 4.37 E
Bergen [auf Rügen] 54 54.25 N 13.26 E
Bergen Basin c 276 40.39 N 73.49 W
Bergen-Belsen-Denkmal ⊥ 52 52.46 N 9.55 E
Berg en Dal 250 5.09 N 55.04 W
Bergenfield 210 40.55 N 73.59 W
Bergen Mall ◆[9] 276 40.55 N 74.04 W
Bergen → Mons 50 50.27 N 3.56 E
Bergen op Zoom 52 51.30 N 4.17 E
Berger 219 38.40 N 91.20 W
Bergerac 32 44.51 N 0.29 E
Bergères-lès-Vertus 50 48.53 N 4.00 E
Bergerhof 263 51.12 N 7.21 E
Bergfelde 54 52.40 N 13.19 E
Berggiesshübel 54 50.52 N 13.57 E
Berghausen, Dtsch. 263 51.07 N 6.55 E
Berghausen, Dtsch. 263 51.18 N 7.17 E
Bergheim, Dtsch. 56 50.55 N 6.38 E
Bergheim, Fr. 58 48.12 N 7.22 E
Bergheim, Öst. 64 47.50 N 13.02 E
Berghem 52 51.46 N 5.34 E
Berghofen ◆[8] 263 51.29 N 7.32 E
Bergholtz 210 43.06 N 78.53 W
Bergholtz Creek ≃ 284a 43.05 N 78.57 W
Bergholz 214 40.31 N 80.53 W
Bergholz-Rehbrücke 54 52.20 N 13.05 E
Bergisches Land ◆[1] 56 51.00 N 7.10 E
Bergisch Gladbach 56 50.59 N 7.07 E
Bergkamen 52 51.38 N 7.38 E
Bergkvara 26 56.23 N 16.05 E
Bergland 190 46.35 N 89.34 W
Bergneustadt 56 51.01 N 7.39 E
Bergnicourt 50 49.25 N 4.15 E
Bergö I 26 62.58 N 21.11 E
Bergoo 188 38.29 N 80.18 W
Bergplaas 158 33.54 S 22.40 E
Bergrheinfeld 56 50.00 N 10.10 E
Bergsäng 40 60.06 N 13.33 E
Bergsbrunna 40 59.49 N 17.43 E
Bergsche Maas ≃ 52 51.45 N 5.08 E
Bergshamra 40 59.38 N 18.37 E
Bergsjö 26 61.59 N 17.04 E
Bergslagen ◆[1] 40 59.55 N 15.00 E
Bergstrom Air Force Base ■ 222 30.12 N 97.40 W
Bergtheim 56 49.54 N 10.04 E
Berguent 148 34.03 N 2.02 W
Bergues 50 50.58 N 2.26 E
Bergum 52 53.11 N 5.59 E
Bergün 58 46.38 N 9.45 E
Bergville 158 28.52 S 29.18 E
Bergvreten 40 60.31 N 16.26 E
Bergwitz 54 51.48 N 12.35 E
Berhala, Selat ⊔ 112 0.48 S 104.25 E
Beri 124 28.42 N 76.35 E
Berici, Monti ⋏ 64 45.26 N 11.31 E
Berikul'skij 86 55.32 N 88.08 E
Beringa, ostrov I 74 55.00 N 165.15 E
Beringen 56 51.03 N 5.13 E
Bering Glacier ⊓ 180 60.15 N 143.30 W
Beringhausen 56 51.24 N 8.46 E
Beringil 140 12.10 N 25.41 E
Beringin 112 3.41 S 104.18 E
Beringovskij 180 63.03 N 179.19 E
Bering Sea ⊤[2] 16 60.00 N 175.00 W
Bering Strait ⊔ 180 65.30 N 169.00 W
Berinsfield 42 51.40 N 1.11 W
Berislav 78 46.51 N 33.26 E
Berisso 258 34.52 S 57.53 W
Berisso □[5] 288 34.55 S 57.53 W
Berja 34 36.51 N 2.57 W
Berkåk 26 62.50 N 10.00 E
Berkakit 74 56.34 N 124.48 E
Berkane 148 34.59 N 2.20 W
Berkel ≃ 52 52.09 N 6.12 E
Berkeley, Eng., U.K. 42 51.42 N 2.27 W
Berkeley, Ca., U.S. 226 37.52 N 122.16 W
Berkeley, Il., U.S. 278 41.53 N 87.54 W
Berkeley, Mo., U.S. 219 38.45 N 90.19 W
Berkeley, R.I., U.S. 207 41.55 N 71.25 W
Berkeley, Vale of V 42 51.43 N 2.25 W
Berkeley Heights 210 40.41 N 74.26 W
Berkeley Hills 279b 40.32 N 80.00 W
Berkeley Hills ⋏[2] 282 37.54 N 122.16 W
Berkeley Plantation ⊥ 208 37.19 N 77.10 W
Berkeley Springs 188 39.37 N 78.13 W
Berkhamsted 42 51.46 N 0.35 W
Berkheim 58 48.02 N 10.04 E
Berkley, Ma., U.S. 207 41.50 N 71.05 W
Berkley, Mi., U.S. 281 42.30 N 83.11 W
Berkner Island I 9 79.30 S 49.30 W
Berks □[6] 208 40.20 N 75.50 W
Berkshire, Ma., U.S. 207 42.30 N 73.11 W
Berkshire, N.Y., U.S. 210 42.18 N 76.11 W
Berkshire □[6], Eng., U.K. 42 51.30 N 1.20 W
Berkshire □[6], Ma., U.S. 207 42.27 N 73.15 W
Berkshire Downs ⋏[1] 42 51.33 N 1.24 W
Berkshire Hills ⋏[2] 207 42.20 N 73.10 W
Berlaar 56 51.07 N 4.39 E
Berlaimont 50 50.12 N 3.49 E
Berland ≃ 182 54.01 N 116.50 W
Berlanga de Duero 34 41.28 N 2.51 W
Berlenga I 34 39.25 N 9.30 W
Berlengas ≃ 250 5.39 S 42.19 W
Berlevåg 24 70.51 N 29.06 E
Berlicum 52 51.42 N 5.23 E
Berlikum 52 53.15 N 5.39 E
Berlin, Dtsch. 54 52.31 N 13.24 E
Berlin, Dtsch. 264a 52.31 N 13.24 E
Berlin, S. Afr. 158 32.54 S 27.35 E
Berlin, Ct., U.S. 207 41.37 N 72.44 W
Berlin, Md., U.S. 208 38.19 N 75.13 W
Berlin, Ma., U.S. 207 42.22 N 71.38 W
Berlin, N.H., U.S. 188 44.28 N 71.11 W
Berlin, N.J., U.S. 208 39.47 N 74.55 W
Berlin, N.Y., U.S. 210 42.42 N 73.23 W
Berlin, Oh., U.S. 214 40.34 N 81.48 W
Berlin, Pa., U.S. 188 39.55 N 78.57 W
Berlin, Wi., U.S. 190 43.58 N 88.56 W
Berlin □[3] 264a 52.33 N 13.30 E
Berlin, Mount ∧ 9 76.03 S 135.52 W
Berlin Center 214 41.01 N 80.57 W
Berlinchen 54 53.13 N 12.34 E
Berliner Brücke ◆[5] 263 51.27 N 6.47 E
Berlinguet Inlet c 176 71.10 N 85.35 W
Berlin Heights 214 41.20 N 82.30 W
Berlin-Ichthyosaur State Park ♦ 204 38.51 N 117.35 W
Berlin Lake ⊜[1] 214 41.00 N 81.00 W
Berlin Mountain ∧ 210 42.42 N 73.17 W
Berlin Park ♦ 285 39.47 N 74.57 W
Berlin-Schönefeld, Flughafen ⊠ 54 52.23 N 13.31 E
Berlinsville 210 40.47 N 75.35 W
Berlin-Tegel, Flughafen ⊠ 54 52.34 N 13.18 E
Berlin-Tempelhof, Flughafen ⊠ 54 52.29 N 13.25 E
Bermagui 166 36.25 S 150.04 E
Bermamyt, gora ∧ 84 43.41 N 42.27 E
Bermejillo 232 25.53 N 103.37 W
Bermejito ≃ 252 25.39 S 60.11 W
Bermejo 252 31.37 S 67.39 W
Bermejo ≃, Arg. 252 31.52 S 67.22 W
Bermejo ≃, S.A. 252 26.51 S 58.23 W
Bermejo, Paso del)(252 32.50 S 70.05 W
Bermen, Lac ⊜ 176 53.35 N 68.55 W
Bermeo 34 43.26 N 2.43 W
Bermillo de Sayago 34 41.22 N 6.06 W
Bermo 124 23.47 N 85.57 E
Bermondsey ◆[8] 260 51.30 N 0.04 W
Bermuda □[2], N.A. 230 32.20 N 64.45 W
Bermuda □[2], N.A. 240a 32.20 N 64.45 W
Bermuda Rise ✦[3] 16 32.30 N 65.00 W
Bermudes → Bermuda □[2] 240a 32.20 N 64.45 W
Bermudian Creek ≃ 208 40.01 N 76.55 W
Bern (Berne) 58 46.57 N 7.26 E
Bern (Berne) □[3] 58 46.55 N 7.35 E
Bern, Flughafen ⊠ 58 46.55 N 7.30 E
Berna → Bern 58 46.57 N 7.26 E
Bernabéu, Estadio ♦ 266a 40.27 N 3.41 W
Bernal ◆[8] 258 34.42 S 58.17 W
Bernalda 68 40.24 N 16.41 E
Bernalillo 200 35.18 N 106.33 W
Bernam ≃ 114 3.48 N 100.57 E
Bernardo O'Higgins, Parque ♦ 286e 33.28 S 70.40 W
Bernardston 207 42.40 N 72.33 W
Bernardsville 210 40.43 N 74.34 W
Bernasconi 252 37.54 S 63.43 W
Bernate 266b 45.29 N 8.49 E
Bernau am Chiemsee 64 47.48 N 12.22 E
Bernau bei Berlin 54 52.40 N 13.35 E
Bernauer Heide ◆[3] 264a 52.43 N 13.30 E
Bernaville 50 50.08 N 2.10 E
Bernay 50 49.06 N 0.36 E
Bernbeuren 58 47.44 N 10.46 E
Bernburg 54 51.48 N 11.44 E
Berndorf 61 47.57 N 16.08 E
Berne, Dtsch. 52 53.11 N 8.29 E
Berne, In., U.S. 216 40.39 N 84.57 W
Berne, N.Y., U.S. 210 42.38 N 74.08 W
Berne → Bern 58 46.57 N 7.26 E
Berneburg 56 51.04 N 9.53 E
Berner Alpen ⋏ 58 46.30 N 7.30 E
Berneray I, Scot., U.K. 46 56.47 N 7.38 W
Berneray I, Scot., U.K. 46 57.43 N 7.12 W
Berneval-le-Grand 50 49.57 N 1.12 E
Berngardovka 265a 60.01 N 30.36 E
Bernhardina 158 27.53 S 28.40 E
Bernhards Bay 210 43.15 N 75.56 W
Bernhardsthal 61 48.41 N 16.52 E
Bernice 194 32.49 N 92.39 W
Bernie 194 36.40 N 89.58 W
Bernier Bay c 176 71.00 N 87.30 W
Bernier Island I 162 24.52 S 113.08 E
Bernina ⋏ 58 46.22 N 9.50 E
Bernina, Passo del)(58 46.24 N 10.03 E
Bernina, Piz ∧ 58 46.21 N 9.51 E
Bernisdale 46 57.27 N 6.24 W
Bernkastel-Kues 56 49.55 N 7.04 E
Bernried 64 47.52 N 11.17 E
Bernsbach 54 50.34 N 12.46 E
Bernsdorf 54 51.22 N 14.04 E
Bernsfelden 56 49.34 N 9.53 E
Bernstadt 54 51.03 N 14.50 E
Bernville 208 40.26 N 76.07 W
Bero ≃ 152 15.10 S 12.09 E
Beroga 114 2.56 N 101.55 E
Berolzheim 56 49.28 N 9.32 E
Beromünster 58 47.12 N 8.11 E
Berón de Astrada 252 27.33 S 57.32 W
Beror Ḥayil 132 31.33 N 34.38 E
Beroroha 157b 21.41 S 45.10 E
Ber'ostovica 76 53.07 N 23.58 E
Beroun 30 49.58 N 14.04 E
Berounka ≃ 30 50.00 N 14.24 E
Berovo 38 41.42 N 22.51 E
Berowra 170 33.37 S 151.09 E
Ber'oza, Bela. 76 52.32 N 24.59 E
Ber'oza, Ukr. 78 51.44 N 33.52 E
Ber'ozno 78 51.00 N 26.45 E
Ber'ožnoje 76 59.55 N 39.17 E
Ber'ozovaja ≃ 80 48.31 N 41.03 E

Symbols in the index entries represent the broad categories identified in the key at the right. Symbols with superior numbers (⋏[1]) identify subcategories (see complete key on page *I · 1*).

Symbole im Register stellen die rechts im Schlüssel erklärten Kategorien dar. Symbole mit hochgestellten Ziffern (⋏[1]) bezeichnen Unterabteilungen einer Kategorie (vgl. vollständiger Schlüssel auf Seite *I · 1*).

Los símbolos incluídos en el texto del índice representan las grandes categorias identificadas con la clave a la derecha. Los símbolos con numeros en su parte superior (⋏[1]) identifican las subcategorías (véase la clave completa en la página *I · 1*).

Les symboles de l'index représentent les catégories indiquées dans la légende à droite. Les symboles suivis d'un indice (⋏[1]) représentent des sous-catégories (voir légende complète à la page *I · 1*).

Os símbolos incluídos no texto do índice representam as grandes categorias identificadas com a chave à direita. Os símbolos com números em sua parte superior (⋏[1]) identificam as subcategorias (veja-se a chave completa à página *I · 1*).

	English	Deutsch	Español	Français	Português
∧	Mountain	Berg	Montaña	Montagne	Montanha
⋏	Mountains	Gebirge	Montañas	Montagnes	Montanhas
)(	Pass	Paß	Paso	Col	Passo
V	Valley, Canyon	Tal, Cañon	Valle, Cañón	Vallée, Canyon	Vale, Canhão
≚	Plain	Ebene	Llano	Plaine	Planície
›	Cape	Kap	Cabo	Cap	Cabo
I	Island	Insel	Isla	Île	Ilha
II	Islands	Inseln	Islas	Îles	Ilhas
⊥	Other Topographic Features	Andere Topographische Objekte	Otros Elementos Topográficos	Autres données topographiques	Outros acidentes topográficos

ESPAÑOL

Nombre	Página	Lat.°′	Long.°′ W = Oeste
Ber'ozovaja Rudka	78	50.19 N	32.14 E
Ber'ozovka, Bela.	76	53.43 N	25.30 E
Ber'ozovka, Kaz.	80	51.11 N	53.16 E
Ber'ozovka, Ross.	24	65.00 N	56.26 E
Ber'ozovka, Ross.	76	53.26 N	38.53 E
Ber'ozovka, Ross.	80	52.06 N	45.07 E
Ber'ozovka, Ross.	86	59.35 N	56.02 E
Ber'ozovka, Ross.	86	57.37 N	57.18 E
Ber'ozovka, Ross.	86	51.51 N	82.58 E
Ber'ozovka, Ross.	86	56.03 N	93.07 E
Ber'ozovka, Ross.	86	54.02 N	76.35 E
Ber'ozovka, Ross.	86	59.24 N	82.38 E
Ber'ozovka, Ross.	88	57.46 N	116.09 E
Ber'ozovka, Ross.	89	50.35 N	127.52 E
Ber'ozovka, Ross.	265a	59.56 N	30.49 E
Ber'ozovka, Ukr.	78	47.49 N	32.28 E
Ber'ozovka, Ukr.	78	45.35 N	33.20 E
Ber'ozovka, Ukr.	78	47.12 N	30.55 E
Ber'ozovo, Ross.	74	63.56 N	65.02 E
Ber'ozovo, Ross.	80	51.56 N	48.28 E
Ber'ozovo, Ross.	82	54.03 N	36.24 E
Ber'ozovo, Ross.	82	54.19 N	38.17 E
Ber'ozovo, Ukr.	78	51.35 N	27.20 E
Ber'ozovskaja	80	50.16 N	43.59 E
Ber'ozovskij	86	55.39 N	86.16 E
Ber'ozovskij R'adok	76	58.06 N	34.29 E
Ber'ozovskoje	86	55.50 N	89.36 E
Berra	64	44.59 N	11.58 E
Berras, Arroyo los ≃	288	34.34 S	58.40 W
Berre ≃	62	44.24 N	4.40 E
Berre, Étang de ⊂	62	43.27 N	5.08 E
Berrechid	148	33.17 N	7.35 W
Berre-des-Alpes	62	43.50 N	7.19 E
Berre-L'Étang	62	43.28 N	5.11 E
Ber Remad, Oued ∨	148	31.45 N	1.10 E
Berri	166	34.17 S	140.36 E
Berridale	171b	36.22 S	148.50 E
Berriedale	46	58.11 N	3.29 W
Berrien □ [6]	216	41.59 N	86.30 W
Berrien Springs	216	41.56 N	86.20 W
Berrigan	166	35.40 S	145.49 E
Berrima	170	34.30 S	150.20 E
Berriozábal	234	16.48 N	93.16 W
Berriyyane	148	32.50 N	3.46 E
Berrouaghia	34	36.08 N	2.55 E
Berrugosa Point ›	116	10.23 N	125.33 E
Berry, Austl.	170	34.47 S	150.42 E
Berry, Al., U.S.	194	33.39 N	87.36 W
Berry, Ky., U.S.	218	38.31 N	84.23 W
Berry □ [9]	50	47.20 N	2.10 E
Berry, Canal du ≊	50	47.17 N	1.25 E
Berry-au-Bac	50	49.24 N	3.54 E
Berry Creek ≃, Ab., Can.	182	50.50 N	111.36 W
Berry Creek ≃, Tx., U.S.	222	30.40 N	97.36 W
Berryessa, Lake ⊜ [1]	226	38.35 N	122.14 W
Berryessa Creek ≃	282	37.24 N	121.53 W
Berryessa Peak ∧	226	38.40 N	122.11 W
Berry Islands ▮▮	238	25.34 N	77.45 W
Berry Mountain ∧	208	40.31 N	77.02 W
Berrysburg	208	40.36 N	76.49 W
Berrys Creek ≃	276	40.47 N	74.05 W
Berryville	194	36.21 N	93.34 W
Beršad'	78	48.23 N	29.30 E
Berseba	156	26.00 S	17.46 E
Bersenbrück	52	52.33 N	7.56 E
Bersut	80	55.32 N	50.54 E
Berta ≃	130	41.09 N	41.53 E
Bertam	114	5.09 N	102.03 E
Berté, Lac ⊜	186	50.48 N	68.30 W
Bertha	198	46.16 N	95.03 W
Berthåga	40	59.52 N	17.35 E
Berthelsdorf	54	51.05 N	14.13 E
Berthier □ [6]	206	46.30 N	73.45 W
Berthierville	206	46.05 N	73.10 W
Berthold	198	48.18 N	101.44 W
Berthoud	200	40.18 N	105.04 W
Berthoud Pass)(	200	39.45 N	105.45 W
Bertincourt	50	50.05 N	2.59 E
Bertinoro	66	44.09 N	12.08 E
Bertioga	256	23.51 S	46.09 W
Bertioga, Enseada da ⊂	256	23.50 S	46.08 W
Bertkow	54	52.43 N	11.54 E
Bertlich	263	51.37 N	7.04 E
Bertogne	56	50.05 N	5.40 E
Bertolínia	250	7.38 S	43.57 W
Bertoua	152	4.35 N	13.41 E
Bertram	196	30.45 N	98.03 W
Bertrand, Mi., U.S.	216	41.46 N	86.15 W
Bertrand, Ne., U.S.	198	40.31 N	99.38 W
Bertrix	56	49.51 N	5.15 E
Bertry	50	50.05 N	3.27 E
Beru ▮	14	1.20 S	176.00 E
Beruas	114	4.30 N	100.47 E
Beruri	246	3.54 S	61.22 W
Berville	214	42.55 N	82.53 W
Berville-sur-Mer	50	49.26 N	0.22 E
Berwang	58	47.24 N	10.45 E
Berwick, Austl.	169	38.02 S	145.21 E
Berwick, N.S., Can.	186	45.03 N	64.44 W
Berwick, La., U.S.	194	29.41 N	91.13 W
Berwick, Me., U.S.	188	43.15 N	70.51 W
Berwick, Pa., U.S.	210	41.03 N	76.14 W
Berwick-upon-Tweed	44	55.46 N	2.00 W
Berwyn, Il., U.S.	216	41.51 N	87.47 W
Berwyn, Pa., U.S.	208	40.02 N	75.26 W
Berwyn ⋏	42	52.53 N	3.24 W
Berwyn Heights	284c	38.59 N	76.54 W
Bērze ≃	76	56.41 N	23.37 E
Berzé-la-Ville	58	46.22 N	4.42 E
Berz-Macomb Airport ⊠	281	42.40 N	82.58 W
Bès ≃	62	44.08 N	6.14 E
Besalampy	157b	16.45 S	44.30 E
Besana in Brianza	62	45.42 N	9.17 E
Besançon	58	47.15 N	6.02 E
Besani	124	24.08 N	80.17 E
Besar, Gunong ∧, Malay.	114	5.10 N	101.18 E
Besar, Gunong ∧, Malay.	114	2.30 N	103.10 E
Besar, Gunung ∧	112	2.43 S	115.37 E
Besar, Pulau ▮	115b	8.28 S	122.22 E
Besar Hantu, Gunong ∧	114	3.12 N	102.02 E
Besaya ≃	34	43.21 N	4.04 W
Besbes	36	36.42 N	7.51 E
Besed' ≃	76	52.38 N	31.09 E
Besedino	78	51.42 N	36.28 E
Besedy	265b	55.37 N	37.47 E
Besenfeld	56	48.35 N	8.25 E
Bešenkoviči	76	55.03 N	29.27 E
Beserah	114	3.52 N	103.22 E
Besigheim	56	49.00 N	9.08 E
Besikama	112	9.36 S	124.57 E
Beşiktaş ◆ [8]	267b	41.03 N	29.01 E
Beşiri	130	37.55 N	41.18 E
Besitang	114	4.02 N	98.12 E
Beškent	128	38.49 N	65.39 E
Beskid Mountains ⋏	30	49.40 N	20.00 E
Beşkonak	130	37.08 N	31.12 E
Beskra	148	34.51 N	5.44 E
Beskra □ [5]	148	34.00 N	6.00 E
Beškube	85	39.50 N	68.18 E
Beskudnikovo ◆ [8]	265b	55.52 N	37.34 E
Beslan	84	43.12 N	44.33 E
Beslenej	84	44.14 N	41.44 E
Besnard Lake ⊜	184	55.24 N	106.05 W
Besni	130	37.41 N	37.52 E
Besor, Naḥal ∨	132	31.28 N	34.22 E
Besós ≃	266d	41.25 N	2.04 E
Besozzo	62	45.51 N	8.39 E
Besp'atovo	82	54.45 N	38.54 E
Beşpınar, Tür.	130	41.09 N	35.14 E
Beşpınar, Tür.	130	37.51 N	41.36 E
Besputa ≃	82	54.50 N	37.58 E
Bessacarr	44	53.30 N	1.04 W
Bessancourt	261	49.02 N	2.13 E

FRANÇAIS

Nom	Page	Lat.°′	Long.°′ W = Ouest
Bessans	62	45.19 N	7.00 E
Bessarabia □ [9]	78	47.00 N	28.30 E
Bessarabka, Ross.	86	53.37 N	73.17 E
Bessarabka, Ukr.	78	46.20 N	28.58 E
Bessaz, gora ∧	85	43.49 N	68.40 E
Bessbrook	48	54.12 N	6.25 W
Besse, Dtsch.	56	51.13 N	9.23 E
Besse, Nig.	150	11.15 N	4.30 E
Bessèges	62	44.17 N	4.06 E
Bessemer, Al., U.S.	194	33.24 N	86.57 W
Bessemer, Mi., U.S.	190	46.28 N	90.03 W
Bessemer, Pa., U.S.	214	40.58 N	80.29 W
Bessemer City	192	35.17 N	81.17 W
Besser	41	55.52 N	10.39 E
Bessé-sur-Braye	50	47.50 N	0.45 E
Bessheim	26	61.31 N	8.51 E
Besshiyama	96	33.50 N	133.23 E
Bessho	270	34.27 N	135.31 E
Bessonovka	80	53.18 N	45.03 E
Best	52	51.31 N	5.24 E
Best'ach	74	61.52 N	129.55 E
Bestamak, Kaz.	86	49.13 N	78.21 E
Bestamak, Kaz.	86	49.43 N	55.07 E
Beštau, gora ∧	84	44.06 N	43.01 E
Besten	263	51.39 N	6.54 E
Bestensee	54	52.15 N	13.37 E
Bestfield	285	39.43 N	75.36 W
Bestobe	86	52.30 N	73.05 E
Beštor, gora ∧	85	42.03 N	70.50 E
Bestuževo	24	61.37 N	43.58 E
Bestwig	52	51.22 N	8.24 E
Besuki	115a	7.45 S	113.41 E
Besut ≃	114	5.48 N	102.35 E
Beswick Aboriginal Reserve ◆ [4]	164	14.30 S	133.10 E
Betā	272b	22.55 N	88.14 E
Betafo	157b	19.50 S	46.51 E
Betāgi	126	22.25 N	90.11 E
Bet Alfa	132	32.31 N	35.26 E
Beta Main Canal ≊	226	36.34 N	120.11 W
Betamba	152	2.13 S	21.23 E
Betang Melaka	114	2.28 N	102.25 E
Betano	112	9.10 S	125.43 E
Betanzos, Bol.	248	19.34 S	65.27 W
Betanzos, Esp.	34	43.17 N	8.12 W
Betanzos, Ría de ⊂ [1]	34	43.23 N	8.15 W
Betaré Oya	152	5.36 N	14.05 E
Betarsjön ⊜	26	63.44 N	16.52 E
Bet Bet Creek ≃	169	36.52 S	143.52 E
Betbetti	140	15.06 N	24.12 E
Betchworth	260	51.14 N	0.16 W
Bet Dagan	132	32.00 N	34.50 E
Bete Hor	144	11.37 N	39.02 E
Betém	256	22.52 S	44.17 W
Bétera	34	39.35 N	0.27 W
Bétérou	150	9.12 N	2.16 E
Bet Guvrin	132	31.36 N	34.54 E
Bet Ha'arava	132	31.48 N	35.32 E
Bethal	158	26.27 S	29.28 E
Bethalto	219	38.54 N	90.02 W
Bethanien	156	26.32 S	17.11 E
Bethanien □ [5]	156	26.30 S	17.00 E
Bethany, Ct., U.S.	207	41.25 N	72.59 W
Bethany, Il., U.S.	219	39.38 N	88.44 W
Bethany, Mo., U.S.	194	40.16 N	94.01 W
Bethany, N.Y., U.S.	210	42.55 N	78.08 W
Bethany, Ok., U.S.	196	35.31 N	97.37 W
Bethany, Pa., U.S.	210	41.37 N	75.21 W
Bethany, W.V., U.S.	214	40.12 N	80.33 W
Bethany Reservoir ⊜ [1]	226	37.47 N	121.37 W
Bet HaShitta	132	32.33 N	35.26 E
Bethel, Ak., U.S.	180	60.48 N	161.46 W
Bethel, Ct., U.S.	207	41.22 N	73.24 W
Bethel, De., U.S.	208	38.27 N	75.21 W
Bethel, Ky., U.S.	218	38.14 N	83.52 W
Bethel, Me., U.S.	188	44.24 N	70.47 W
Bethel, Mo., U.S.	219	39.52 N	92.01 W
Bethel, N.Y., U.S.	210	41.41 N	74.52 W
Bethel, N.C., U.S.	192	35.48 N	77.22 W
Bethel, Oh., U.S.	218	38.57 N	84.04 W
Bethel, Pa., U.S.	208	40.28 N	76.18 W
Bethel, Wa., U.S.	224	47.32 N	122.38 W
Bethel Acres	196	35.19 N	97.00 W
Bethel Island	226	38.01 N	121.39 W
Bethel Manor	208	37.06 N	76.25 W
Bethel Park	214	40.18 N	80.02 W
Bethelsdorp	158	33.52 S	25.34 E
Bethel Springs	194	35.14 N	88.36 W
Béthencourt-sur-Mer	50	50.05 N	1.30 E
Bethersden	42	51.08 N	0.48 E
Bethesda, Wales, U.K.	44	53.11 N	4.03 W
Bethesda, Md., U.S.	208	38.58 N	77.06 W
Bethesda, Oh., U.S.	188	40.00 N	81.04 W
Bethesdaweg	158	31.55 S	24.45 E
Bethford	284a	42.48 N	78.48 W
Bethgate	284b	39.18 N	76.51 W
Béthisy-Saint-Pierre	50	49.18 N	2.49 E
Bethlehem, S. Afr.	158	28.15 S	28.15 E
Bethlehem, S. Afr.	158	27.10 S	24.00 E
Bethlehem, Ct., U.S.	207	41.38 N	73.12 W
Bethlehem, In., U.S.	218	38.32 N	85.25 W
Bethlehem, Ky., U.S.	218	38.24 N	85.04 W
Bethlehem, Pa., U.S.	210	40.37 N	75.22 W
Bethlehem, W.V., U.S.	188	40.02 N	80.41 W
Bethlehem → Bayt Laḥm	132	31.43 N	35.12 E
Bethlehem Center	210	42.40 N	73.42 W
Bethlehem Steel Corporation ɤ [3], Md., U.S.	284b	39.13 N	76.29 W
Bethlehem Steel Corporation (Lackawanna Plant) ɤ [3], N.Y., U.S.	284a	42.49 N	78.52 W
Bethnal Green ◆ [8]	260	51.32 N	0.03 W
Bethoncourt	58	47.32 N	6.48 E
Bethpage	210	40.44 N	73.28 W
Bethpage State Park ♦	210	40.45 N	73.27 W
Bethulie	158	30.32 S	25.59 E
Bethune, Sk., Can.	184	50.43 N	105.08 W
Béthune, Fr.	50	50.32 N	2.38 E
Bethune, S.C., U.S.	192	34.24 N	80.20 W
Béthune ≃	50	49.53 N	1.09 E
Beticos, Sistemas ⋏	34	37.00 N	4.00 W
Betijoque	246	9.23 N	70.44 W
Betil	126	24.14 N	89.43 E
Betio	174t	1.21 N	172.56 E
Betioky	157b	23.42 S	44.22 E
Betis ≃	114	4.53 N	101.48 E
Betlica	76	54.01 N	33.57 E
Betna ≃	126	22.34 N	89.12 E
Bet Netofa, Biq'at ≍	132	32.49 N	35.19 E
Betnoti	126	21.44 N	86.51 E
Beton-Bazoches	50	48.42 N	3.15 E
Betong, Malay.	112	1.24 N	111.31 E
Betong, Thai	110	5.45 N	101.05 E
Betoota	166	25.42 S	140.44 E
Bétou	152	3.03 N	18.31 E
Betpak-Dala ◆ [2]	86	46.00 N	70.00 E
Betroka	157b	23.16 S	46.06 E
Betsham	260	51.25 N	0.19 E
Bet Sh'ean	132	32.30 N	35.30 E
Bet She'arim, Horbat ⊥	132	32.42 N	35.08 E
Bet Shemesh	132	31.45 N	35.00 E
Betsiamites	186	48.56 N	68.38 W
Betsiamites ≃	186	48.56 N	68.38 W
Betsiamites, Barrage ◆ [6]	186	49.22 N	69.47 W
Betsiamites, Pointe de ›	186	48.55 N	68.37 W
Betsiamites, Réserve indienne de ◆ [4]	186	49.05 N	68.37 W
Betsiboka ≃	157b	16.03 S	46.36 E
Betsie, Point ›	190	44.42 N	86.16 W
Betsioky	157b	21.31 S	44.28 E

PORTUGUÊS

Nome	Página	Lat.°′	Long.°′ W = Oeste
Betsukai	92a	43.23 N	145.17 E
Betsy Layne	192	37.33 N	82.38 W
Betsy Ross Bridge ◆ [5]	285	39.59 N	75.04 W
Bette ∧	146	22.00 N	19.12 E
Bettembourg	56	49.32 N	6.02 E
Bettendorf	190	41.31 N	90.30 W
Betterton	208	39.21 N	76.03 W
Bettiah	124	26.48 N	84.30 E
Bettie	222	32.48 N	94.58 W
Bettles Field	180	66.55 N	151.30 W
Bettola	62	44.47 N	9.36 E
Bettona	66	43.01 N	12.29 E
Bettrath ◆ [8]	263	51.13 N	6.26 E
Bettsville	214	41.14 N	83.14 W
Bettyhill	46	58.32 N	4.14 W
Betty's Bay	158	34.22 S	18.52 E
Betūl	124	21.55 N	77.54 E
Betumbe-Bongo	152	2.11 S	18.46 E
Betung, Indon.	112	1.52 S	103.16 E
Betung, Indon.	112	2.50 S	104.14 E
Betuwe ◆ [1]	52	51.55 N	5.30 E
Betwa ≃	124	25.55 N	80.12 E
Betws-y-Coed	44	53.05 N	3.48 W
Betz	50	49.09 N	2.57 E
Betz ≃	50	48.09 N	2.45 E
Betzdorf	56	50.47 N	7.53 E
Betzenstein	60	49.41 N	11.25 E
Béu	152	6.14 S	15.28 E
Beucha	54	51.19 N	12.34 E
Beugneux	50	49.14 N	3.25 E
Beuil	62	44.06 N	6.59 E
Beulah, Austl.	166	35.56 S	142.26 E
Beulah, Co., U.S.	200	38.04 N	104.59 W
Beulah, Mi., U.S.	190	44.37 N	86.05 W
Beulah, Ms., U.S.	194	33.47 N	90.58 W
Beulah, N.D., U.S.	198	47.15 N	101.46 W
Beulah, Lake ⊜	216	42.49 N	88.23 W
Beulah Beach	214	41.25 N	82.22 W
Beulah Reservoir ⊜ [1]	202	43.56 N	118.09 W
Beulaville	192	34.55 N	77.46 W
Beult ≃	42	51.14 N	0.25 E
Beure	58	47.12 N	6.00 E
Beureunun	114	5.18 N	95.59 E
Beuron	58	48.03 N	8.58 E
Beuthen → Bytom	30	50.22 N	18.54 E
Beuvron ≃, Fr.	50	47.28 N	3.31 E
Beuvron ≃, Fr.	50	47.29 N	1.15 E
Beuvronne ≃	261	48.56 N	2.44 E
Beuvry	50	50.31 N	2.41 E
Beuzeville	50	49.20 N	0.21 E
Bevagna	66	42.56 N	12.36 E
Bevensen	52	53.05 N	10.34 E
Bever ≃	52	52.01 N	7.46 E
Bevera ≃	62	43.49 N	7.34 E
Beveren	50	51.13 N	4.15 E
B. Everett Jordan Lake ⊜ [1]	192	35.45 N	79.00 W
Beverino	62	44.14 N	9.47 E
Beverley, Austl.	168a	32.06 S	116.56 E
Beverley, Eng., U.K.	44	53.52 N	0.26 W
Beverley Minster ɤ [1]	44	53.50 N	0.27 W
Beverley Springs	162	16.43 S	125.28 E
Beverlo	56	51.05 N	5.12 E
Beverly, Ma., U.S.	207	42.33 N	70.52 W
Beverly, N.J., U.S.	208	40.03 N	74.55 W
Beverly, Tx., U.S.	222	31.30 N	97.10 W
Beverly ◆ [8]	278	41.43 N	87.41 W
Beverly Farms, Md., U.S.	284c	39.04 N	77.11 W
Beverly Farms, Ma., U.S.	283	42.34 N	70.49 W
Beverly Harbor ⊂	283	42.32 N	70.53 W
Beverly Hills, Austl.	274a	33.57 S	151.05 E
Beverly Hills, Ca., U.S.	228	34.04 N	118.23 W
Beverly Hills, Fl., U.S.	220	28.56 N	82.28 W
Beverly Hills, Mi., U.S.	216	42.31 N	83.13 W
Beverly Lake ⊜	176	64.36 N	100.30 W
Beverly Municipal Airport ⊠	283	42.35 N	70.55 W
Beverly Run ≃	208	37.55 N	77.11 W
Beverly Shores	216	41.41 N	86.58 W
Bevern	52	51.51 N	9.29 E
Beverstausee ⊜ [1]	263	51.09 N	7.23 E
Beverstedt	52	53.26 N	8.49 E
Beverungen	52	51.39 N	9.22 E
Beverwijk	52	52.28 N	4.40 E
Bevier	194	39.45 N	92.34 W
Bevin, Lac ⊜	206	45.57 N	74.35 W
Bevoalavo	157b	25.13 S	45.26 E
Bewani	164	3.02 S	141.10 E
Bewani Mountains ⋏	164	3.10 S	141.25 E
Bewār	124	27.13 N	79.18 E
Bewdley, On., Can.	212	44.05 N	78.19 W
Bewdley, Eng., U.K.	42	52.22 N	2.19 W
Bewl Water ⊜ [1]	42	51.04 N	0.24 E
Bex	58	46.15 N	7.01 E
Bexhill	42	50.50 N	0.29 E
Bexley, Austl.	274a	33.57 S	151.08 E
Bexley, Oh., U.S.	218	39.58 N	82.56 W
Bexley ◆ [8]	42	51.26 N	0.10 E
Beyazköy	130	41.21 N	27.42 E
Beybach ≃	56	50.13 N	7.23 E
Beyçayırı	130	40.15 N	26.55 E
Beycuma	130	41.19 N	31.59 E
Bey Dağları ⋏	130	36.40 N	30.15 E
Beydagları Olimpos Milli Parkı ♦	130	36.40 N	30.25 E
Beydili	130	40.10 N	31.01 E
Beyenburg ◆ [8]	263	51.15 N	7.18 E
Beykoz ◆ [8]	267b	41.08 N	29.05 E
Beyla	150	8.41 N	8.37 W
Beylerbeyi ◆ [8]	267b	41.03 N	29.03 E
Beylikahır	130	39.42 N	31.13 E
Beylul	144	13.10 N	42.26 E
Beynes	261	48.51 N	1.53 E
Beynes-Thiverval, Aérodrome de ⊠	261	48.51 N	1.54 E
Beyoğlu ◆ [8]	267b	41.02 N	28.59 E
Beypazarı	130	40.10 N	31.56 E
Beypınarı	130	39.31 N	37.44 E
Beypore	122	11.11 N	75.49 E
Beyra	144	6.57 N	47.19 E
Beyrouth → Bayrūt	130	33.53 N	35.30 E
Beyşehir	130	37.41 N	31.43 E
Beyşehir Gölü ⊜	130	37.40 N	31.30 E
Beytüşşebap	128	37.34 N	43.10 E
Bezaha	157b	23.30 S	44.31 E
Bežanickaja vozvyšennost' ⋏ [1]	76	56.54 N	29.20 E
Bežanicy	76	56.58 N	29.53 E
Bezau	58	47.23 N	9.54 E
Bezavona ∧	157b	15.02 S	49.52 E
Bezdež	76	52.19 N	25.18 E
Bezděz ∧	54	50.32 N	14.43 E
Bezděz ⊥	54	50.32 N	14.46 E
Bèze	58	47.28 N	5.16 E
Bežeck	76	57.47 N	36.39 E
Bežeckij Verch ⋏ [1]	76	57.36 N	36.54 E
Bezenčuk	80	52.59 N	49.26 E
Bezerra ≃	255	13.16 S	47.31 W
Bezerros	250	8.14 S	35.45 W
Bezet	132	33.05 N	35.08 E
Béziers	32	43.21 N	3.15 E
Bezmein	128	38.05 N	58.12 E
Bezmenšur	80	56.29 N	51.17 E
Bezno	54	50.22 N	14.48 E
Bezons	261	48.56 N	2.13 E
Bežta	84	42.08 N	46.08 E
Bezwada → Vijayawāda	122	16.31 N	80.37 E
Bezym'anka	80	49.56 N	43.15 E
Bezym'annaja	80	51.20 N	46.26 E
Bezymennoje	83	47.06 N	37.56 E
Bezzecca	64	45.55 N	10.43 E
Bezzubovo	82	55.27 N	38.55 E

Bhabānipur, India	272b	22.57 N	88.27 E
Bhabānipur, India	272b	22.56 N	88.13 E
Bhabhua	124	25.03 N	83.37 E
Bhābta	126	23.59 N	88.15 E
Bhadarwāh	123	32.59 N	75.43 E
Bhadaur	123	30.29 N	75.19 E
Bhādgāon → Bhaktapur	124	27.42 N	85.27 E
Bhadohi	124	25.25 N	82.34 E
Bhādra	123	29.07 N	75.10 E
Bhadra ≃ [1]	126	22.19 N	89.31 E
Bhadrāchalam	122	17.40 N	80.53 E
Bhadrak	120	21.03 N	86.30 E
Bhadrapur	124	26.32 N	88.06 E
Bhadra Reservoir ⊜ [1]	122	13.40 N	75.35 E
Bhadrāvati	122	13.52 N	75.43 E
Bhadreswar	126	22.50 N	88.21 E
Bhādua	272b	22.41 N	88.12 E
Bhāg	120	29.02 N	67.49 E
Bhagaiya	124	25.12 N	87.29 E
Bhāgalpur	124	25.15 N	87.00 E
Bhāgīrathi ≃, India	124	30.08 N	78.35 E
Bhāgīrathi ≃, India	126	23.25 N	88.23 E
Bhagirathpur	126	24.05 N	88.29 E
Bhagwānpur	126	22.07 N	87.45 E
Bhainsa	122	19.06 N	77.58 E
Bhāi Pheru	123	31.12 N	73.57 E
Bhairab ≃ [1]	126	22.51 N	89.34 E
Bhairab Bāzār	120	24.04 N	90.58 E
Bhairhawā	124	27.31 N	83.24 E
Bhaironghāti	120	31.01 N	78.53 E
Bhakkar	123	31.38 N	71.04 E
Bhākra Dam ◆ [6]	123	31.24 N	76.30 E
Bhaktapur	124	27.42 N	85.27 E
Bhal	272c	19.11 N	73.08 E
Bhālki	122	18.02 N	77.13 E
Bhalswa ◆ [8]	272a	28.44 N	77.10 E
Bhalwāl	123	32.16 N	72.54 E
Bhamdūn	132	33.48 N	35.39 E
Bhamo	110	24.16 N	97.14 E
Bhandāra	120	21.10 N	79.39 E
Bhandārdaha	272b	22.37 N	88.13 E
Bhandāria	126	22.29 N	90.04 E
Bhānder	124	25.44 N	78.45 E
Bhānder Plateau ⋏ [1]	124	24.10 N	80.20 E
Bhāndup ◆ [8]	272c	19.09 N	72.57 E
Bhānga	126	23.22 N	89.59 E
Bhāngar	126	22.31 N	88.37 E
Bhāngar Kāta Khāl ≃	272b	22.31 N	88.33 E
Bhanvad	120	21.56 N	69.47 E
Bhārat → India □ [1]	118	20.00 N	77.00 E
Bharatpur, India	124	27.13 N	77.29 E
Bharatpur, India	126	23.53 N	88.05 E
Bharatpur, Nepāl	124	27.14 N	84.21 E
Bharthana	124	26.45 N	79.14 E
Bharūch	120	21.42 N	72.58 E
Bhātai	126	23.36 N	89.11 E
Bhātāpāra	120	21.44 N	81.56 E
Bhātār	126	23.25 N	87.54 E
Bhatgaon → Bhaktapur	124	27.42 N	85.27 E
Bhātghar Lake ⊜ [1]	122	18.12 N	73.49 E
Bhātiāpāra Ghāt	124	23.13 N	89.42 E
Bhatkal	122	13.58 N	74.34 E
Bhātpāra	126	22.52 N	88.24 E
Bhātpur	272b	22.43 N	88.25 E
Bhātsāla	126	22.33 N	90.30 E
Bhattapratāp	126	22.45 N	89.48 E
Bhattiprolu	122	16.06 N	80.47 E
Bhātua	272b	22.57 N	88.22 E
Bhaun	123	32.52 N	72.45 E
Bhaunja	272a	28.40 N	77.25 E
Bhavāni	122	11.27 N	77.41 E
Bhāvnagar	122	21.46 N	72.09 E
Bhawānīgarh	124	30.16 N	76.02 E
Bhawani Mandi	120	24.25 N	75.50 E
Bhawānipatna	122	19.54 N	83.10 E
Bhedia	126	23.36 N	87.42 E
Bheigeir, Beinn ∧ [2]	46	55.44 N	6.05 W
Bhendkhal	272c	18.53 N	72.59 E
Bhera	123	32.29 N	72.55 E
Bheramara	126	24.02 N	88.58 E
Bherī □ [8]	124	28.30 N	81.45 E
Bherī ≃	124	28.44 N	81.16 E
Bheula, Beinn ∧	46	56.08 N	4.58 W
Bhīkampur	272a	28.45 N	77.27 E
Bhīkangaon	120	21.52 N	75.57 E
Bhilai	120	21.13 N	81.26 E
Bhilainagar → Bhilai	120	21.13 N	81.26 E
Bhīlwāra	120	25.21 N	74.38 E
Bhīma ≃	122	16.24 N	77.18 E
Bhīmavaram	122	16.32 N	81.32 E
Bhimbar	123	32.59 N	74.04 E
Bhīmphedī	124	27.32 N	85.07 E
Bhīmpur, India	126	22.37 N	87.08 E
Bhimpur, India	272b	22.46 N	88.08 E
Bhind	124	26.34 N	78.48 E
Bhinga	124	27.43 N	81.56 E
Bhīnmāl	120	25.00 N	72.15 E
Bhiwandi	122	19.18 N	73.04 E
Bhiwāni	124	28.47 N	76.08 E
Bhoāgāchi	272b	22.57 N	88.20 E
Bhojpur	124	27.10 N	87.03 E
Bhojudih	126	23.38 N	86.27 E
Bhokardan	122	20.16 N	75.46 E
Bhola	124	22.41 N	90.39 E
Bhola ≃ [1]	126	22.04 N	89.49 E
Bhongaon	124	27.15 N	79.11 E
Bhongīr	122	17.31 N	78.53 E
Bhonrāsa	124	22.59 N	76.12 E
Bhopāl	124	23.16 N	77.24 E
Bhopar	272c	19.12 N	73.05 E
Bhopura	272a	28.42 N	77.20 E
Bhoutan → Bhutan □ [1]	120	27.30 N	90.30 E
Bhowali	124	29.23 N	79.31 E
Bhuāpur	272a	28.43 N	77.26 E
Bhuban	120	20.53 N	85.50 E
Bhubaneshwar	120	20.14 N	85.50 E
Bhucho	123	30.13 N	75.06 E
Bhuj	120	23.16 N	69.40 E
Bhunarheri	124	30.13 N	76.27 E
Bhunya	158	26.32 S	31.01 E
Bhusāwal	120	21.03 N	75.46 E
Bhūshana	126	23.24 N	89.40 E
Bhutali	272c	19.07 N	73.04 E
Bhutan (Druk-Yul) □ [1], Asia	118	27.30 N	90.30 E
Bhutan (Druk-Yul) □ [1], Asia	120	27.30 N	90.30 E
Bia ≃, Afr.	150	5.21 N	3.11 W
Biá ≃, Bra.	246	3.28 S	67.23 W
Bia, Phou ∧	110	18.59 N	103.09 E
Biābānak	128	32.11 N	64.11 E
Biabo ≃	248	6.58 S	76.23 W
Biacesa	64	45.56 N	10.47 E
Biache-Saint-Vaast	50	50.18 N	2.57 E
Biadene	64	45.47 N	12.04 E
Biafra, Bight of ⊂ [3]	134	4.00 N	8.00 E
Biak ▮	164	1.00 S	136.00 E
Biała	30	50.23 N	17.40 E
Biała ≃	30	50.03 N	20.55 E
Biała Piska	30	53.37 N	22.04 E
Biała Podlaska	30	52.02 N	23.06 E
Biała Podlaska □ [4]	30	52.00 N	23.00 E
Biała Rawska	30	51.49 N	20.29 E
Białobrzegi	30	51.40 N	20.57 E
Białogard	30	54.01 N	16.00 E
Białowieski Park Narodowy ♦	30	52.40 N	23.50 E
Biały Bór	30	53.54 N	16.51 E
Białystok	30	53.09 N	23.09 E
Białystok □ [4]	30	53.00 N	23.00 E
Bian ≃	164	8.07 S	139.56 E
Bian, Bidean nam ∧	46	56.38 N	5.02 W
Biancavilla	70	37.38 N	14.52 E
Bianchi	68	39.06 N	16.24 E
Bianco	68	38.05 N	16.09 E

Bianco, Canale ≊	64	45.02 N	12.05 E
Bianco, Capo ›	70	37.23 N	13.16 E
Bianco, Monte (Mont Blanc) ∧	62	45.50 N	6.52 E
Bian'er	102	31.14 N	101.28 E
Bianga	152	4.51 N	20.25 E
Bian'gezhuang	105	39.28 N	115.53 E
Biankouma	150	7.44 N	7.37 W
Bianlinzhen	98	37.26 N	116.32 E
Bianminchang	107	29.41 N	105.04 E
Bianniulupucun	104	41.30 N	123.42 E
Bianquanwopu	104	41.21 N	120.48 E
Bianzè	62	45.18 N	8.07 E
Biaora	124	23.55 N	76.54 E
Biaro, Pulau ▮	112	2.05 N	125.20 E
Biarritz	32	43.29 N	1.34 W
Biasca	58	46.22 N	8.58 E
Bias Fortes	256	21.36 S	43.46 W
Biassono	62	45.37 N	9.16 E
Biaza	86	56.38 N	78.18 E
Bibā	142	28.55 N	30.59 E
Bibai	92a	43.19 N	141.52 E
Bibala	152	14.46 S	13.21 E
Bībān	142	30.47 N	30.40 E
Bibane, Bahiret el ⊂	148	33.16 N	11.19 E
Bibanga	152	6.15 S	23.56 E
Bibban, Khawr ∨	140	11.00 N	32.41 E
Bibb City	192	32.30 N	84.59 W
Bibbiano	64	44.40 N	10.28 E
Bibbiena	66	43.42 N	11.49 E
Bibbona	66	43.16 N	10.35 E
Bibémi	146	9.19 N	13.53 E
Biberach	58	48.20 N	8.02 E
Biberach an der Riss	58	48.06 N	9.47 E
Biberbach	56	48.31 N	10.48 E
Biberonne ≃	261	48.59 N	2.41 E
Bibert ≃	56	49.27 N	10.59 E
Bibey ≃	34	42.24 N	7.13 W
Bibiani	150	6.28 N	2.20 W
Bībi Chīni	126	22.28 N	90.12 E
Bibione	64	45.38 N	13.00 E
Bibir'ovo	76	54.28 N	33.08 E
Biblián	246	2.42 S	78.52 W
Biblis	56	49.41 N	8.27 E
Bibo	102	29.02 N	99.20 E
Bic	186	48.22 N	68.42 W
Biča	86	57.53 N	70.37 E
Bicas	256	21.43 S	43.04 W
Bicaz	38	46.54 N	26.05 E
Biccari	68	41.24 N	15.11 E
Bicester	42	51.54 N	1.09 W
Bičevinka	76	59.44 N	37.40 E
Biche, Lac la ⊜	182	54.50 N	112.03 W
Bichena	144	10.27 N	38.12 E
Bicheno	166	41.53 S	148.18 E
Bichhia	124	22.27 N	80.42 E
Bichl	64	47.43 N	11.24 E
Bichlbach	58	47.25 N	10.47 E
Bichota Canyon ∨	280	34.16 N	117.48 W
Biči ≃	89	52.10 N	139.50 E
Bičigt	88	47.06 N	95.05 E
Bickerstaffe	262	53.32 N	2.50 W
Bickerton, Cape ›	9	66.20 S	136.56 E
Bickerton Island ▮	164	13.45 S	136.12 E
Bickle Knob ∧	188	38.56 N	79.44 W
Bickley ◆ [8]	260	51.24 N	0.03 E
Bicknacre, Eng., U.K.	42	51.41 N	0.35 E
Bicknacre, Eng., U.K.	260	51.41 N	0.35 E
Bicknell, In., U.S.	194	38.46 N	87.18 W
Bicknell, Ut,. U.S.	200	38.20 N	111.32 W
Bicknor	260	51.18 N	0.40 E
Bicol ≃	116	13.44 N	123.07 E
Bicske	30	47.29 N	18.37 E
Bicudo ≃	255	18.04 S	44.33 W
Bičura	88	50.36 N	107.35 E
Bičurina	86	56.51 N	55.25 E
Bīd	122	18.59 N	75.46 E
Bida, Nig.	146	12.20 N	13.25 E
Bida, Nig.	150	9.05 N	6.01 E
Bīdar	122	17.54 N	77.33 E
Bidde	144	0.58 N	42.37 E
Biddeford	188	43.29 N	70.27 W
Biddenden	42	51.07 N	0.39 E
Biddiyā	132	32.07 N	35.05 E
Biddulph	44	53.08 N	2.10 W
Bideford	42	51.01 N	4.13 W
Bidente ≃	66	44.24 N	12.12 E
Bidford-on-Avon	42	52.10 N	1.51 W
Bidhūna	124	26.49 N	79.31 E
Bidian	100	32.38 N	113.03 E
Bīdokht	128	34.21 N	58.46 E
Bidoni	71	40.07 N	8.56 E
Bidor	114	4.07 N	101.17 E
Bidston	262	53.24 N	3.05 W
Bidwell	188	38.55 N	82.17 W
Bidwell, Mount ∧	204	41.58 N	120.10 W
Bidya ≃ [1]	126	21.56 N	88.42 E
Bidyādhari ≃	272b	22.23 N	88.35 E
Bidyādharpur	272b	22.50 N	88.24 E
Bidžan	89	47.58 N	131.58 E
Bidžan ≃	89	47.44 N	132.19 E
Bie	40	59.05 N	16.12 E
Bié □ [5]	152	12.30 S	17.15 E
Biebelried	56	49.46 N	10.04 E
Bieber, Dtsch.	56	50.09 N	9.19 E
Bieber, Ca., U.S.	204	41.07 N	121.08 W
Biebrza ≃	30	53.13 N	22.25 E
Biecz	30	49.44 N	21.14 E
Biedenkopf	56	50.55 N	8.32 E
Biederitz	54	52.09 N	11.43 E
Biedermannsdorf	264b	48.05 N	16.21 E
Bieguzhuang	105	39.19 N	116.39 E
Biei	92a	43.35 N	142.28 E
Biel (Bienne)	58	47.10 N	7.12 E
Bielawa	30	50.41 N	16.38 E
Bielawski, Mount ∧	226	37.13 N	122.06 W
Bielefeld	52	52.01 N	8.31 E
Bieler Lake ⊜	176	70.20 N	73.00 W
Bielersee ⊜	58	47.05 N	7.10 E
Bielin	54	52.47 N	14.28 E
Biella	62	45.34 N	8.03 E
Bielsk	30	52.40 N	19.49 E
Bielsko-Biała	30	49.49 N	19.02 E
Bielsko-Biała □ [4]	30	49.40 N	19.10 E
Bielsk Podlaski	30	52.47 N	23.12 E
Biemenhorst	52	51.49 N	6.36 E
Bienenbüttel	52	53.08 N	10.29 E
Bienfait	184	49.08 N	102.47 W
Bien Hoa	110	10.57 N	106.49 E
Bienne ≃, Fr.	50	48.15 N	0.04 E
Bienne ≃, Fr.	58	46.20 N	5.38 E
Bienne → Biel	58	47.10 N	7.12 E
Bienno	64	45.56 N	10.18 E
Bientina	66	43.42 N	10.37 E
Bienville	194	32.21 N	92.58 W
Bienville, Lac ⊜	176	55.05 N	72.40 W
Biere, Dtsch.	54	51.58 N	11.39 E
Bière, Schw.	58	46.33 N	6.20 E
Bierné	28	47.49 N	0.32 W
Bieruń Stary	30	50.06 N	19.06 E
Bierutów	30	51.08 N	17.32 E
Bierwart	56	50.34 N	5.01 E
Biesbos ◆ [1]	52	51.45 N	4.50 E
Biesdorf ◆ [8]	264a	52.31 N	13.33 E
Biese ≃	54	52.45 N	11.37 E
Biesel ◆ [8]	263	51.10 N	6.29 E
Biesenthal	54	52.46 N	13.37 E
Bieshan	105	39.58 N	117.29 E
Biesiesvlei	158	26.22 S	25.55 E
Biesles	58	48.05 N	5.18 E
Bieszczadzki Park Narodowy ♦	30	49.05 N	22.45 E
Bieteluobaoluosika	89	48.35 N	119.56 E
Bietigheim	56	48.54 N	8.14 E
Bietigheim-Bissingen	56	48.58 N	9.07 E
Bietschhorn ∧	58	46.24 N	7.51 E
Bièvre	56	49.56 N	5.01 E
Bièvre ≃	261	48.47 N	2.20 E
Bièvres	261	48.45 N	2.13 E

Biferno ≃	66	41.59 N	15.02 E
Bifoun	152	0.22 S	10.23 E
Bifuka	92a	44.29 N	142.21 E
Bifurcación	258	34.19 S	56.48 W
Big ≃, Austl.	169	37.18 S	146.02 E
Big ≃, N.T., Can.	176	72.30 N	125.14 W
Big ≃, Sk., Can.	184	53.50 N	107.02 W
Big ≃, Ak., U.S.	180	63.00 N	154.56 W
Big ≃, Mo., U.S.	219	38.28 N	90.37 W
Biga	130	40.13 N	27.14 E
Bigadiç	130	39.23 N	28.08 E
Big A Mountain ∧	192	37.03 N	82.02 W
Big Annemessex River ⊂	208	38.03 N	75.50 W
Big Antelope Creek ≃	202	42.28 N	117.13 W
Big Bald Mountain ∧, N.B., Can.	186	47.12 N	66.25 W
Big Bald Mountain ∧, Ga., U.S.	192	34.45 N	84.19 W
Big Baldy ∧	202	44.47 N	115.13 W
Big Baldy Mountain ∧	202	46.58 N	110.37 W
Big Bar Creek	182	51.12 N	122.06 W
Big Basin Redwoods State Park ♦	226	37.09 N	122.17 W
Big Bay	190	46.49 N	87.44 W
Big Bay ⊂, N.Z.	172	44.18 S	168.05 E
Big Bay ⊂, Vanuatu	175f	15.06 S	166.54 E
Big Bay De Noc ⊂	190	45.46 N	86.43 W
Big Bay Point ›	212	44.24 N	79.31 W
Big Bear City	228	34.15 N	116.50 W
Big Bear Lake	228	34.15 N	116.53 W
Big Bear Lake ⊜	228	34.15 N	116.55 W
Big Beaver, Sk., Can.	184	49.08 N	105.10 W
Big Beaver, Pa., U.S.	214	40.50 N	80.20 W
Big Beaver Airport ⊠	281	42.33 N	83.06 W
Big Beaver Creek ≃, Mi., U.S.	281	42.32 N	83.01 W
Big Beaver Creek ≃, Oh., U.S.	218	39.01 N	83.03 W
Big Beaver Creek ≃, Wa., U.S.	224	48.40 N	121.08 W
Big Bell	162	27.21 S	117.40 E
Big Belt Mountains ⋏	202	46.40 N	111.25 W
Big Bend, Swaz.	158	26.50 S	31.57 E
Big Bend, Wi., U.S.	216	42.52 N	88.12 W
Big Bend National Park ♦	196	29.12 N	103.12 W
Big Bend Reservoir ⊜ [1]	182	52.57 N	115.37 W
Big Black ≃	194	32.00 N	91.05 W
Big Blue ≃, U.S.	198	39.11 N	96.32 W
Big Blue ≃, In., U.S.	218	39.20 N	85.59 W
Big Blue, West Fork ≃	198	40.42 N	96.59 W
Big Bone Lick State Park ♦	218	38.53 N	84.45 W
Big Bonito Creek ≃	200	33.34 N	109.56 W
Big Brook ≃	276	40.19 N	74.10 W
Big Brushy Creek ≃, Tx., U.S.	222	32.32 N	96.20 W
Big Brushy Creek ≃, Tx., U.S.	222	29.12 N	96.55 W
Big Bureau Creek ≃	194	41.17 N	89.21 W
Bigbury Bay ⊂	42	50.16 N	3.48 W
Big Cabin Creek ≃	194	36.26 N	95.08 W
Big Canyon ∨	196	30.05 N	101.55 W
Big Carlos Pass ⊂	220	26.24 N	81.52 W
Big Cedar Lake ⊜	212	44.37 N	78.10 W
Big Chino Wash ∨	200	34.52 N	112.28 W
Big Clear Lake ⊜	212	44.43 N	76.55 W
Big Clifty	194	37.32 N	86.09 W
Big Coulee Creek ≃	202	46.17 N	108.56 W
Big Cow Creek ≃	194	30.34 N	93.44 W
Big Creek, B.C., Can.	182	51.44 N	123.03 W
Big Creek, Ca., U.S.	226	37.12 N	119.14 W
Big Creek ≃, B.C., Can.	182	51.40 N	122.50 W
Big Creek ≃, On., Can.	214	42.19 N	82.27 W
Big Creek ≃, On., Can.	214	42.36 N	80.27 W
Big Creek ≃, Ar., U.S.	194	34.21 N	91.03 W
Big Creek ≃, Ca., U.S.	226	37.12 N	119.19 W
Big Creek ≃, Ca., U.S.	226	36.53 N	119.15 W
Big Creek ≃, Id., U.S.	202	45.06 N	114.44 W
Big Creek ≃, Il., U.S.	219	39.07 N	88.52 W
Big Creek ≃, In., U.S.	216	40.38 N	86.46 W
Big Creek ≃, In., U.S.	218	38.48 N	85.39 W
Big Creek ≃, Ks., U.S.	198	38.47 N	98.55 W
Big Creek ≃, La., U.S.	194	32.10 N	91.53 W
Big Creek ≃, Mo., U.S.	194	40.02 N	94.07 W
Big Creek ≃, Mo., U.S.	219	38.52 N	90.50 W
Big Creek ≃, Oh., U.S.	279a	41.27 N	81.41 W
Big Creek ≃, Or., U.S.	224	46.11 N	123.35 W
Big Creek ≃, Tx., U.S.	222	31.09 N	96.52 W
Big Creek ≃, Tx., U.S.	222	29.22 N	95.34 W
Big Creek ≃, Wa., U.S.	224	47.15 N	121.10 W
Big Creek, East Fork ≃	194	40.16 N	94.03 W
Big Creek, West Fork ≃	194	40.16 N	94.03 W
Big Creek Parkway ♦	279a	41.24 N	81.45 W
Big Creek Peak ∧	202	44.28 N	113.32 W
Big Crow Island ▮	276	40.37 N	73.33 W
Big Cypress Creek ≃	222	33.00 N	94.51 W
Big Cypress Indian Reservation ◆ [4]	220	26.14 N	80.49 W
Big Cypress National Preserve ♦	220	25.55 N	81.10 W
Big Cypress Swamp ⩨	220	26.10 N	81.38 W
Big Dalton Canyon ∨	280	34.10 N	117.48 W
Big Dalton Wash ∨	280	34.04 N	117.58 W
Big Darby Creek ≃	218	39.37 N	82.58 W
Big Delta	180	64.09 N	145.50 W
Big Desert ◆ [2]	166	35.40 S	141.00 E
Big Diomede Island → Ratmanova, ostrov ▮	180	65.46 N	169.02 W
Big Ditch ≊	216	40.13 N	88.22 W
Big Dry Creek ≃	202	47.30 N	106.19 W
Big Dubbo Hill ∧	171b	35.25 S	148.36 E
Big Eau Pleine ≃	190	44.48 N	90.00 W
Big Elk Creek ≃	208	39.35 N	75.52 W
Big Elkhart Creek ≃	222	31.22 N	95.41 W
Big Elm Creek ≃	222	30.53 N	96.56 W
Bigelow Bight ⊂ [3]	188	43.15 N	70.30 W
Big Escambia Creek ≃	194	30.58 N	87.14 W
Big Falls	190	48.11 N	93.48 W
Big Flat	194	36.00 N	92.24 W
Big Flat Creek ≃	194	31.33 N	87.31 W
Big Flats	210	42.08 N	76.56 W
Bigfork, Mn., U.S.	190	47.44 N	93.39 W
Bigfork, Mt., U.S.	202	48.04 N	114.04 W
Big Fork ≃	190	48.31 N	93.43 W
Big Four Ditch ≊	216	40.27 N	88.10 W
Big Frog Mountain ∧	192	35.00 N	84.32 W
Biggar, Sk., Can.	184	52.04 N	108.00 W
Biggar, Scot., U.K.	46	55.38 N	3.32 W
Biggarsberg ⋏	158	28.12 S	29.48 E
Bigge	56	51.21 N	8.28 E
Bigge Island ▮	164	14.35 S	125.10 E
Biggers	194	36.19 N	90.48 W

≃	River	Fluß	Río	Rivière	Rio
≊	Canal	Kanal	Canal	Canal	Canal
L	Waterfall, Rapids	Wasserfall, Stromschnellen	Cascada, Rápidos	Chute d'eau, Rapides	Cascata, Rápidos
⋈	Strait	Meeresstraße	Estrecho	Détroit	Estreito
⊂	Bay, Gulf	Bucht, Golf	Bahía, Golfo	Baie, Golfe	Baía, Golfo
⊜	Lake, Lakes	See, Seen	Lago, Lagos	Lac, Lacs	Lago, Lagos
⩨	Swamp	Sumpf	Pantano	Marais	Pântano
⍓	Ice Features, Glacier	Eis- und Gletscherformen	Accidentes Glaciales	Formes glaciaires	Acidentes glaciares
⍑	Other Hydrographic Features	Andere Hydrographische Objekte	Otros Elementos Hidrográficos	Autres données hydrographiques	Outros acidentes hidrográficos

✢	Submarine Features	Untermeerische Objekte	Accidentes Submarinos	Formes de relief sous-marin	Acidentes submarinos
□	Political Unit	Politische Einheit	Unidad Politica	Entité politique	Unidade política
ɤ	Cultural Institution	Kulturelle Institution	Institución Cultural	Institution culturelle	Instituição cultural
⊥	Historical Site	Historische Stätte	Sitio Histórico	Site historique	Sitio histórico
♦	Recreational Site	Erholungs- und Ferienort	Sitio de Recreo	Centre de loisirs	Area de Lazer
⊠	Airport	Flughafen	Aeropuerto	Aéroport	Aeroporto
■	Military Installation	Militäranlage	Instalación Militar	Installation militaire	Instalação militar
◆	Miscellaneous	Verschiedenes	Misceláneo	Divers	Diversos

ENGLISH — Name · Page · Lat.°′ · Long.°′
DEUTSCH — Name · Seite · Breite°′ · Länge°′ E = Ost

Biggestausee ⊚[1] 56 51.05 N 7.55 E
Biggin Hill ◆[8] 42 51.18 N 0.04 E
Biggin Hill Aerodrome ⊠ 260 51.19 N 0.03 E
Biggleswade 42 52.05 N 0.17 W
Biggs, Ca., U.S. 226 39.24 N 121.42 W
Biggs, Or., U.S. 224 45.40 N 120.50 W
Big Gull Lake ⊚ 212 44.50 N 76.58 W
Big Gully Creek ≃ 184 53.13 N 109.03 W
Bighāi ≃[1] 126 22.10 N 90.13 E
Big Hawk Lake ⊚ 212 45.10 N 78.44 W
Bighead ≃ 212 44.36 N 80.35 W
Big Hole ≃ 202 45.34 N 112.20 W
Big Hole National Battlefield ⊥ 202 45.35 N 113.35 W
Bighorn ≃ 202 46.09 N 107.28 W
Bighorn Basin ≚[1] 202 44.15 N 108.10 W
Bighorn Canyon National Recreation Area ♦ 202 45.00 N 108.15 W
Big Horn Lake ⊚[1] 202 45.06 N 108.08 W
Bighorn Mountains ⋏ 202 44.00 N 107.30 W
Bight, Head of > 162 31.30 S 131.10 E
Big Huckleberry Mountain ʌ 224 45.51 N 121.47 W
Big Island 192 37.32 N 79.21 W
Big Island I, N.T., Can. 176 62.43 N 70.43 W
Big Island I, On., Can. 184 49.10 N 94.40 W
Big Island I, On., Can. 212 44.33 N 78.30 W
Big Knob ʌ 192 36.40 N 82.31 W
Big Koniuji Island I 180 55.06 N 159.33 W
Big Lake, Ak., U.S. 180 61.33 N 149.52 W
Big Lake, Mn., U.S. 190 45.19 N 93.44 W
Big Lake, Tx., U.S. 196 31.11 N 101.27 W
Big Lake, Wa., U.S. 224 48.24 N 122.14 W
Big Lake ⊚, Me., U.S. 188 45.10 N 67.40 W
Big Lake ⊚, Wa., U.S. 224 48.23 N 122.12 W
Bigler 214 40.59 N 78.19 W
Biglerville 208 39.55 N 77.14 W
Big Lick Creek ≃ 216 40.22 N 85.27 W
Big Lookout Mountain ʌ 202 44.37 N 117.17 W
Big Lost ≃ 202 43.50 N 112.44 W
Big Monon Ditch ≍ 216 40.52 N 86.46 W
Big Mossy Point > 184 53.41 N 97.57 W
Big Mountain ʌ, B.C., Can. 180 56.53 N 131.31 W
Big Mountain ʌ, Nv., U.S. 204 41.17 N 119.04 W
Big Mountain Creek ≃ 182 55.04 N 118.39 W
Big Muddy ≃ 194 37.35 N 89.31 W
Big Muddy, Casey Fork ≃ 194 38.06 N 88.57 W
Big Muddy Creek ≃, Mt., U.S. 198 48.08 N 104.36 W
Big Muddy Creek ≃, N.D., U.S. 198 46.37 N 101.24 W
Big Muddy Lake ⊚ 184 49.08 N 104.54 W
Big Muscamoot Bay c 281 42.33 N 82.40 W
Bignasco 58 46.20 N 8.36 E
Big Nasty Creek ≃ 198 45.41 N 102.51 W
Big Nemaha, North Fork ≃ 198 40.04 N 95.43 W
Bignona 150 12.49 N 16.14 W
Big Oak Flat 226 37.49 N 120.16 W
Bigosovo 76 55.49 N 27.43 E
Bigot, Morne ʌ[2] 240e 14.31 N 61.04 W
Big Otter ≃ 192 37.07 N 79.23 W
Big Otter Creek ≃ 212 42.38 N 80.48 W
Big Ox Creek ≃ 218 38.44 N 85.52 W
Big Pine 204 37.09 N 118.17 W
Big Pine Creek ≃ 216 40.18 N 87.15 W
Big Pine Key 220 24.40 N 81.21 W
Big Pine Key I 220 24.42 N 81.23 W
Big Pine Mountain ʌ 204 34.42 N 119.39 W
Big Piney 200 42.32 N 110.06 W
Big Piney ≃ 194 37.53 N 92.04 W
Big Piney Creek ≃ 194 35.20 N 93.20 W
Big Pipe Creek ≃ 208 39.36 N 77.17 W
Big Plain 218 39.50 N 83.17 W
Big Pocono State Park ♦ 210 41.03 N 75.19 W
Bigpoint 194 30.35 N 88.28 W
Big Pond 210 41.53 N 76.43 W
Big Porcupine Creek ≃ 202 46.16 N 106.43 W
Big Porcupine Lake ⊚ 212 45.27 N 78.36 W
Big Prairie 214 40.40 N 82.06 W
Big Prairie Creek ≃ 194 32.35 N 87.45 W
Big Quilcene ≃ 224 47.49 N 122.52 W
Big Quill Lake ⊚ 184 51.55 N 104.22 W
Big Raccoon Creek ≃ 194 39.46 N 87.22 W
Big Rapids 190 43.41 N 85.29 W
Bigras, Île I 275a 45.31 N 73.51 W
Big Rib ≃ 190 44.56 N 89.41 W
Big Rideau Lake ⊚ 212 44.45 N 76.14 W
Big River 184 53.50 N 107.01 W
Big River Indian Reserve ◆[4] 184 53.33 N 107.10 W
Big Rock 216 41.46 N 88.33 W
Big Rock Creek ≃ 216 41.38 N 88.32 W
Big Rocky Creek ≃ 222 29.34 N 96.50 W
Big Run 214 40.58 N 78.52 W
Big Sable ≃ 190 44.02 N 86.31 W
Big Sable Point > 190 44.03 N 86.31 W
Big Salmon ≃ 180 61.52 N 134.56 W
Big Salmon Range ⋏ 180 61.10 N 133.45 W
Big Sand Lake ⊚ 176 57.45 N 99.42 W
Big Sandy, Mt., U.S. 202 48.10 N 110.06 W
Big Sandy, Tn., U.S. 194 36.14 N 88.05 W
Big Sandy, Tx., U.S. 222 32.35 N 95.07 W
Big Sandy ≃, U.S. 188 38.25 N 82.36 W
Big Sandy ≃, Az., U.S. 200 34.19 N 113.31 W
Big Sandy ≃, Tn., U.S. 194 36.15 N 88.06 W
Big Sandy ≃, Wy., U.S. 202 41.51 N 109.47 W
Big Sandy Creek ≃, Ca., U.S. 226 35.47 N 120.43 W
Big Sandy Creek ≃, Co., U.S. 198 38.06 N 102.29 W
Big Sandy Creek ≃, Ga., U.S. 192 32.42 N 82.57 W
Big Sandy Creek ≃, Mt., U.S. 202 48.34 N 109.48 W
Big Sandy Creek ≃, Ne., U.S. 198 40.13 N 97.18 W
Big Sandy Creek ≃, Tx., U.S. 196 33.11 N 97.40 W
Big Sandy Creek ≃, Tx., U.S. 222 30.31 N 94.28 W
Big Sandy Creek ≃, Tx., U.S. 222 32.33 N 95.05 W
Big Sandy Lake ⊚, Sk., Can. 184 54.26 N 104.04 W
Big Sandy Lake ⊚, Mn., U.S. 190 46.45 N 93.17 W
Big Sandy Reservoir ⊚[1] 200 42.16 N 109.26 W
Big Satilla Creek ≃ 192 31.27 N 82.03 W
Bigsby Island I 184 49.04 N 94.35 W
Big Sewickley Creek ≃ 279b 40.35 N 80.13 W
Big Shawnee Creek ≃ 216 40.15 N 87.18 W
Big Sheep Mountain ʌ 202 47.03 N 105.43 W
Big Signal Peak ʌ 204 39.31 N 123.06 W
Big Sinking Creek ≃ 194 37.55 N 86.31 W
Big Sioux ≃ 198 42.30 N 96.25 W
Big Sixmile Creek ≃ 284a 43.02 N 79.01 W
Big Sky 202 45.17 N 111.17 W
Big Slough ≃ 192 30.56 N 84.33 W
Big Smoky Valley V 204 38.30 N 117.15 W
Big Snowy Mountains ⋏ 202 46.50 N 109.30 W
Big Southern Butte ʌ 202 43.23 N 113.01 W
Big Spanish Channel ꭒ 220 24.44 N 81.20 W
Bigspring, Mo., U.S. 219 38.38 N 91.28 W
Big Spring, Tx., U.S. 196 32.15 N 101.28 W
Big Springs 198 41.03 N 102.04 W
Big Spruce Knob ʌ 188 38.16 N 80.12 W
Big Squaw Mountain ʌ 188 45.30 N 69.45 W
Bigstick Lake ⊚ 184 50.16 N 109.20 W
Bigstone ≃ 184 55.55 N 94.36 W
Big Stone City 198 45.17 N 96.27 W
Big Stone Gap 192 36.52 N 82.44 W
Bigstone Lake ⊚, Mb., Can. 184 53.42 N 95.44 W
Big Stone Lake ⊚, U.S. 198 45.25 N 96.40 W
Big Sunflower ≃ 194 32.40 N 90.40 W
Big Sur 226 36.16 N 121.48 W
Big Sur ≃ 226 36.17 N 121.51 W
Big Sur ◆[1] 226 35.45 N 121.20 W
Big Swamp Creek ≃ 194 32.19 N 86.49 W
Big Swan Creek ≃ 194 35.46 N 87.24 W
Big Thicket National Preserve ♦ 222 32.35 N 94.40 W
Big Thompson ≃ 200 40.21 N 104.45 W
Big Timber 202 45.50 N 109.57 W
Big Timber Creek ≃ 285 39.53 N 75.08 W
Big Timber Creek, North Branch ≃ 285 39.50 N 75.05 W
Big Timber Creek, South Branch ≃ 285 39.50 N 75.05 W
Big Torch Key I 220 24.43 N 81.26 W
Big Tree 210 42.46 N 78.49 W
Big Trout Lake ⊚, On., Can. 176 53.45 N 90.00 W
Big Trout Lake ⊚, On., Can. 212 44.56 N 78.56 W
Big Tujunga Canyon V 228 34.16 N 118.18 W
Big Tujunga Dam ◆[6] 280 34.18 N 118.12 W
Biguaçu 252 27.30 S 48.40 W
Big Valley 182 52.02 N 112.46 W
Bigwa 154 7.13 S 39.09 E
Big Walnut Creek ≃, In., U.S. 194 39.30 N 86.57 W
Big Walnut Creek ≃, Oh., U.S. 218 39.48 N 83.01 W
Big Warrambool ≃ 166 30.05 S 147.33 E
Big Water 200 37.05 N 111.41 W
Big Wells 196 28.34 N 99.34 W
Big White Mountain ʌ 182 49.42 N 118.58 W
Big Wills Creek ≃ 194 33.59 N 86.00 W
Big Wood ≃ 202 42.52 N 114.54 W
Bihać 36 44.49 N 15.52 E
Bīhar 124 25.11 N 85.31 E
Bihār □[3] 124 25.00 N 86.00 E
Biharamulo 154 2.38 S 31.20 E
Bihārīganj 124 25.44 N 86.59 E
Bihor □[6] 38 47.00 N 22.15 E
Bihor, Vîrful ʌ 38 46.27 N 22.42 E
Bihoro 92a 43.49 N 144.07 E
Bihu 100 28.21 N 119.48 E
Bija ≃ 86 52.25 N 85.05 E
Bijagós, Arquipélago dos II 150 11.25 N 16.20 W
Bijainagar 120 25.56 N 74.38 E
Bijaipur 124 26.03 N 77.22 E
Bijaipura 124 24.46 N 77.48 E
Bijāpur 122 16.50 N 75.42 E
Bījār 128 35.52 N 47.36 E
Bijāwar 124 24.38 N 79.30 E
Bijbān Chāh 128 26.54 N 64.42 E
Bījbiāra 123 33.48 N 75.06 E
Bijeljina 38 44.45 N 19.13 E
Bijelo Polje 38 43.02 N 19.44 E
Bijiang 110 26.30 N 98.55 E
Bijia Shan ʌ 105 40.17 N 116.50 E
Bijie 102 27.18 N 105.20 E
Bijlikol', ozero ⊚ 85 43.03 N 70.41 E
Bijna 272b 22.55 N 88.27 E
Bijni 124 26.31 N 90.40 E
Bijnor 124 29.22 N 78.08 E
Bijōki 268 35.49 N 139.39 E
Bijou Creek ≃ 198 40.17 N 103.52 W
Bijpur 126 22.56 N 88.26 E
Bijsk 86 52.34 N 85.15 E
Bijuk-Karasu ≃ 78 45.27 N 34.47 E
Bijwāsan ◆[8] 272a 28.32 N 77.03 E
Bīkāner 120 28.01 N 73.18 E
Bīkaner Canal ≍ 123 30.08 N 73.57 E
Bikar I[1] 14 12.15 N 170.06 E
Bikbulovo 80 55.39 N 53.26 E
Bike 144 9.30 N 41.18 E
Bikeman Island I 174t 1.22 N 173.00 E
Bikenibeu 174t 1.21 N 173.07 E
Bikeqi 102 40.45 N 111.17 E
Bikeru 112 5.15 S 120.07 E
Bikfayyā 132 33.55 N 35.41 E
Bikié 152 3.06 S 13.52 E
Bikin 89 46.48 N 134.16 E
Bikin ≃ 89 46.51 N 134.02 E
Bikini I[1] 14 11.35 N 165.23 E
Bikita 154 20.06 S 31.41 E
Bikl'an' 80 55.37 N 52.10 E
Bikoro 152 0.45 S 18.07 E
Bikuar, Parque Nacional do ♦ 152 15.12 S 14.42 E
Bila ≃ 114 2.30 N 100.08 E
Bilaa Point > 116 9.49 N 125.26 E
Bilac 255 21.24 S 50.28 W
Bilād Zahrān ◆[1] 144 20.16 N 41.14 E
Bílá hora ⊥ 54 50.05 N 14.20 E
Bilang, Teluk c 112 1.15 N 121.25 E
Bilanga 150 12.32 N 0.02 E
Bilāra 120 26.10 N 73.42 E
Bilāri 124 28.38 N 78.48 E
Bil'arsk 80 54.58 N 50.22 E
Bilāsipāra 124 26.14 N 90.14 E
Bilāspur, India 123 31.20 N 76.45 E
Bilāspur, India 124 28.53 N 79.16 E
Bilāspur, India 124 22.05 N 82.09 E
Bil'asuvar 84 39.24 N 48.24 E
Bilatan Island I 116 4.59 N 120.00 E
Bilato 112 0.32 N 122.38 E
Bilauktaung Range ⋏ 110 13.00 N 99.00 E
Bilbao 34 43.15 N 2.58 W
Bilbays 142 30.25 N 31.34 E
Bilbays Military Base ■ 142 30.24 N 31.36 E
Bilbilis ⊥ 34 41.25 N 1.39 W
Bil'čir 88 51.02 N 110.34 E
Bileća 38 42.53 N 18.26 E
Bilecik 130 40.09 N 29.59 E
Bilecik □[4] 130 40.10 N 30.10 E
Biles Island I 285 40.10 N 74.45 W
Biłgoraj 30 50.34 N 22.43 E
Bilgrām 124 27.11 N 80.02 E
Bili 154 4.09 N 25.10 E
Bili ≃ 136 4.09 N 22.29 E
Bilian 100 28.21 N 120.33 E
Bilifyā 142 29.07 N 31.03 E
Bīlīmora 120 20.45 N 72.57 E
Bilin 110 17.14 N 97.15 E
Bilin ≃ 110 17.05 N 97.08 E
Bílina 54 50.35 N 13.45 E
Bílina ≃ 54 50.40 N 14.02 E
Bilioso ≃ 68 40.39 N 16.24 E
Biliran Island I 116 11.35 N 124.28 E
Biliran Strait ꭒ 116 11.30 N 124.28 E
Biliri 146 9.52 N 11.13 E
Biliu ≃ 98 39.30 N 122.36 E
Bilk ◆[8] 263 51.12 N 6.47 E
Billabong Creek ≃ 166 35.06 S 144.02 E
Billeberga 41 55.53 N 13.00 E
Billerbeck 52 51.59 N 7.17 E
Billerica 207 42.33 N 71.16 W
Billericay 42 51.38 N 0.25 E
Billesdon 42 52.37 N 0.55 W
Billesholm 41 56.03 N 13.00 E
Billiat 58 46.04 N 5.47 E
Billigheim 56 49.21 N 9.15 E
Billiluna 162 19.37 S 127.41 E
Billinge, Sve. 41 55.58 N 13.21 E
Billinge, Eng., U.K. 262 53.30 N 2.42 W
Billingen ⋏[2] 26 58.24 N 13.45 E
Billingham 44 54.36 N 1.17 W
Billings, Mo., U.S. 194 37.04 N 93.33 W
Billings, Mt., U.S. 202 45.46 N 108.30 W
Billings, Ok., U.S. 196 36.31 N 97.26 W
Billings, Reprêsa ⊚[1] 256 23.47 S 46.37 W
Billingsfors 26 58.59 N 12.15 E
Billings Heights 202 45.50 N 108.32 W
Billingshurst 42 51.01 N 0.28 W
Billmerich 263 51.30 N 7.47 E
Billolo ≃ 273b 4.07 S 15.19 E
Billom 32 45.44 N 3.21 E
Billund 41 55.44 N 9.07 E
Bill Williams ≃ 200 34.17 N 114.03 W
Bill Williams Mountain ʌ 200 35.12 N 112.12 W
Billy Chinook, Lake ⊚[1] 202 44.33 N 121.20 W
Billy-Montigny 50 50.25 N 2.52 E
Bilma 146 18.41 N 12.56 E
Biloela 166 24.24 S 150.30 E
Bilo Gora ⋏ 36 46.06 N 16.46 E
Biloxi 194 30.23 N 88.53 W
Biloxi ≃ 194 30.26 N 89.00 W
Biloxi Creek ≃ 222 31.05 N 94.37 W
Bilpa Morea Claypan ≚ 166 25.00 S 140.00 E
Bilpin 170 33.30 S 150.31 E
Bilqās Qism Awwal 142 31.13 N 31.21 E
Bilsārā 126 23.05 N 88.10 E
Bilshausen 52 51.37 N 10.10 E
Bilsi 124 28.08 N 78.55 E
Bilston 42 52.34 N 2.04 W
Biltāj 142 31.00 N 30.59 E
Bilthoven 52 52.07 N 5.17 E
Biltine 146 14.32 N 20.55 E
Biltine □[5] 146 15.00 N 21.00 E
Biltmore Forest 192 35.32 N 82.31 W
Bilugyun Island I 110 16.24 N 97.32 E
Bilwaskarma 236 14.45 N 83.53 W
Bilzen 56 50.52 N 5.31 E
Bima 115b 8.28 S 118.43 E
Bimbān 140 24.26 N 32.53 E
Bimbe 152 11.49 S 15.49 E
Bimberi Peak ʌ 171b 35.40 S 148.47 E
Bimbila 150 8.51 N 0.04 E
Bimbo 152 4.18 N 18.33 E
Bimbowrie 166 32.03 S 140.09 E
Bimé 273b 4.09 S 15.11 E
Bimini Islands II 192 25.42 N 79.15 W
Bin ≃ 100 23.40 N 112.58 E
Bina 175e 8.55 S 160.46 E
Bīna-Etāwa 124 24.11 N 78.11 E
Binaiya, Gunung ʌ 164 3.11 S 129.26 E
Binalbagan 116 10.12 N 122.50 E
Binalbagan ≃ 116 10.12 N 122.51 E
Bin'an 89 45.50 N 127.45 E
Binanga 114 1.24 N 99.46 E
Binangonan 116 14.28 N 121.11 E
Binas 50 47.54 N 1.28 E
Binasco 62 45.20 N 9.06 E
Binau 56 49.22 N 9.04 E
Binche 50 50.24 N 4.10 E
Binchuan 102 25.46 N 100.33 E
Bindal 24 65.06 N 12.30 E
Binder, Mong. 88 48.35 N 110.36 E
Binder, Tchad 146 9.58 N 14.28 E
Bindki 124 26.02 N 80.36 E
Bindlach 60 49.59 N 11.37 E
Bindloss 184 50.52 N 110.16 W
Bindo, Mount ʌ 170 33.40 S 150.01 E
Bindow 264a 52.17 N 13.45 E
Bindura 154 17.19 S 31.20 E
Bine-el-Ouidane 148 32.07 N 6.26 W
Binéfar 34 41.51 N 0.18 E
Binford 198 47.33 N 98.20 W
Binga, Pil. 116 10.45 N 119.19 E
Binga, Zaïre 152 2.23 N 20.30 E
Binga, Monte ʌ 156 19.45 S 33.04 E
Bingara 166 29.52 S 150.34 E
Bingaram Island I 122 10.56 N 72.17 E
Bingay Point > 116 13.04 N 124.11 E
Bingcha 100 32.30 N 120.52 E
Bingen, Dtsch. 56 49.57 N 7.54 E
Bingen, Wa., U.S. 224 45.42 N 121.27 W
Binger 196 35.18 N 98.20 W
Bingerbrück 56 49.58 N 7.53 E
Bingerville 150 5.21 N 3.54 W
Bingfang 106 32.15 N 121.20 E
Bingham, Eng., U.K. 42 52.57 N 0.57 W
Bingham, Me., U.S. 188 45.03 N 69.52 W
Bingham ≃ 168a 33.20 S 116.16 E
Bingham Creek ≃ 224 47.09 N 123.24 W
Bingham Farms 281 42.32 N 83.16 W
Binghamton 210 42.05 N 75.55 W
Bin Ghashīr 146 32.41 N 13.11 E
Bin Ghunaymah, Jabal ⋏ 146 25.00 N 15.30 E
Bingi 154 0.24 S 29.05 E
Bingley 44 53.51 N 1.50 W
Bingöl 130 38.53 N 40.29 E
Bingöl □[4] 130 39.00 N 40.40 E
Bingöl Dağları ⋏ 130 39.20 N 41.20 E
Binhai (Dongkan) 100 34.03 N 119.51 E
Binh Ca 110 21.48 N 105.18 E
Binh Chanh 269c 10.40 N 106.34 E
Binh Gia 110 21.59 N 106.21 E
Binh Hung Hoa 269c 10.49 N 106.37 E
Binh Khe 110 13.57 N 108.51 E
Binh Kieu 110 15.35 N 108.04 E
Bin-Houyé 150 6.47 N 8.19 W
Binh Son 110 15.18 N 108.46 E
Binh Trung 269c 10.47 N 106.46 E
Binigsian Point > 116 9.50 N 122.23 E
Bining 56 49.02 N 7.15 E
Binjai, Indon. 112 3.48 N 108.14 E
Binjai, Indon. 114 3.36 N 98.30 E
Binjohara 114 2.12 N 98.12 E
Bīnlūd, Kūh-e ⋏ 128 36.28 N 58.49 E
Binna Burra 171a 28.13 S 153.14 E
Binnah, Ras > 144 11.08 N 51.10 E
Binnaway 166 31.33 S 149.23 E
Binnian, Slieve ʌ 48 54.08 N 5.58 W
Binningen 58 47.32 N 7.34 E
Binodepur 126 23.26 N 89.30 E
Binongko, Pulau I 112 5.57 S 124.02 E
Binpur 126 22.36 N 86.55 E
Binscarth 184 50.37 N 101.16 W
Binsheim ◆[8] 263 51.31 N 6.42 E
Bintan, Pulau I 112 1.05 N 104.30 E
Bintang 150 13.10 N 16.08 W
Bintang, Gunong ʌ 114 5.25 N 100.52 E
Bintauna 112 0.53 N 123.33 E
Bint Goda 140 13.17 N 31.33 E
Bintimani ʌ 150 9.13 N 11.07 W
Bint Jubayl 132 33.07 N 35.26 E
Bintuhan 112 4.48 S 103.22 E
Bintulu 112 3.10 N 113.02 E
Bintuni 164 2.07 S 133.32 E
Bintuni, Teluk c 164 2.20 S 133.30 E
Binxian, Zhg. 89 45.44 N 127.29 E
Binxian, Zhg. 98 37.28 N 117.56 E
Binxian, Zhg. 102 35.00 N 108.08 E
Binyamina 132 32.31 N 34.57 E
Binyang 102 23.18 N 108.46 E
Bin Yauri 150 10.47 N 4.50 E
Binz 54 54.24 N 13.36 E
Binza 273b 4.21 S 15.14 E
Binza ◆[8] 273b 4.20 S 15.14 E
Binza ≃ 273b 4.21 S 15.14 E
Bio Addo 144 8.18 N 49.48 E
Bíobío □[4] 252 37.00 S 72.30 W
Biobío ≃, Chile 252 36.49 S 73.10 W
Bíobío ≃, Chile 252 31.38 S 71.34 W
Biodi 154 3.19 N 28.35 E
Biograd 36 43.56 N 15.27 E
Biogradska Gora Nacionalni Park ♦ 38 42.57 N 19.40 E
Bioko □[4] 152 3.30 N 8.40 E
Bioko I 152 3.30 N 8.40 E
Biola 226 36.48 N 120.00 W
Bionaz 62 45.52 N 7.25 E
Biondo 154 0.23 S 25.13 E
Biondo Monument ⊥ 146 31.25 N 10.15 E
Biot 62 43.38 N 7.06 E
Bipindi 152 3.05 N 10.25 E
Bippus 216 40.56 N 85.37 W
Biqiao 106 31.02 N 119.02 E
Bir, Ras > 144 11.59 N 43.22 E
Bira, India 272b 22.47 N 88.34 E
Bira, Ross. 89 49.15 N 137.16 E
Bira, Ross. 89 49.02 N 132.30 E
Bira ≃ 89 48.07 N 133.21 E
Birab 164 6.12 S 138.25 E
Bīraba 126 23.51 N 90.34 E
Birāk 146 27.32 N 14.16 E
Birakan 89 49.01 N 131.42 E
Bi'r ʿAlī 144 14.01 N 48.19 E
Bi'r al-Uzam 146 31.54 N 23.58 E
Birandža 89 54.35 N 136.18 E
Birao 146 10.17 N 22.47 E
Birati 272b 22.39 N 88.27 E
Birava 154 2.21 S 28.54 E
Bîrca 38 43.58 N 23.37 E
Bircao → Buur Gaabo 144 1.12 S 41.51 E
Birch 262 53.34 N 2.13 W
Birch ≃, Ab., Can. 176 58.30 N 112.15 W
Birch ≃, W.V., U.S. 188 38.35 N 80.53 W
Birch Bay 224 48.55 N 122.45 W
Birch Bay c 224 48.53 N 122.47 W
Birch Bay State Park ♦ 224 49.54 N 123.47 W
Birch Cliff ◆[8] 275b 43.41 N 79.17 W
Birch Creek ≃, Ak., U.S. 180 66.30 N 146.30 W
Birch Creek ≃, Id., U.S. 202 43.51 N 112.43 W
Birch Creek ≃, Mt., U.S. 202 48.26 N 112.15 W
Birch Creek ≃, Mt., U.S. 202 47.45 N 109.34 W
Birch Hill Dam ◆[6] 207 42.38 N 72.09 W
Birch Hills 184 52.59 N 105.25 W
Birchington 42 51.23 N 1.19 E
Birch Island 182 51.36 N 119.55 W
Birch Island I 184 52.25 N 99.55 W
Birch Lake ⊚, Ab., Can. 182 53.19 N 111.35 W
Birch Lake ⊚, On., Can. 184 51.24 N 92.20 W
Birch Lake ⊚, Sk., Can. 184 53.28 N 108.07 W
Birch Mountains ⋏[2] 176 57.30 N 112.30 W
Bir Chouhada 34 35.53 N 6.18 E
Birch Pond ⊚ 283 42.28 N 71.00 W
Birch Reservoir ⊚[1] 196 36.31 N 96.12 W
Birch River 184 52.23 N 101.06 W
Birch Run 190 43.15 N 83.47 W
Birch Run ≃ 285 40.09 N 75.37 W
Birchrunville 285 40.08 N 75.39 W
Birch Tree 194 36.59 N 91.29 W
Birch Vale 262 53.23 N 1.57 W
Birchwood, Eng., U.K. 44 53.13 N 0.36 W
Birchwood, Ak., U.S. 180 61.28 N 149.22 W
Birchwood, Wi., U.S. 190 45.39 N 91.33 W
Birchwood City 284c 38.49 N 76.59 W
Birchwood Park, De., U.S. 285 39.22 N 75.39 W
Birchwood Park, N.J., U.S. 208 40.06 N 74.09 W
Birchy Bay 186 49.21 N 54.44 W
Bird City 198 39.45 N 101.31 W
Bird Creek ≃ 196 36.13 N 95.44 W
Bird Island 198 44.46 N 94.53 W
Bird Island I, S. Afr. 158 33.51 S 26.18 E
Bird Island I, S. Geor. 244 54.00 S 38.05 W
Bird Island ʊ[3] 9 54.00 S 38.03 W
Bird Islet I 160 22.10 S 155.28 E
Bird River c 284b 39.23 N 76.23 W
Birdsall 210 42.23 N 77.55 W
Birdsboro 208 40.15 N 75.48 W
Birds Landing 282 38.08 N 121.52 W
Birdsview 224 48.32 N 121.52 W
Birdsville 166 25.54 S 139.22 E
Birdtail Creek ≃ 184 50.16 N 101.12 W
Birdum 164 15.39 S 133.13 E
Birdum Creek ≃ 164 15.14 S 133.00 E
Birdwood 168b 34.49 S 138.57 E
Birecik 130 37.02 N 37.58 E
Bire Kpatua Game Reserve ◆[4] 154 5.12 N 27.36 E
Bir el Ater 148 34.44 N 8.03 E
Bir Enzaran 148 23.56 N 14.33 W
Bireuen 114 5.12 N 96.41 E
Bir Ghbalou 34 36.16 N 3.35 E
Birgi 126 22.42 N 86.41 E
Birgi Vecchi 70 37.53 N 12.29 E
Biri 116 12.41 N 124.22 E
Birigui 255 21.18 S 50.19 W
Biri Island I 116 12.40 N 124.22 E
Birikčul' 86 53.20 N 89.56 E
Biril'ussy 86 57.07 N 90.32 E
Birimbāl 142 31.21 N 30.30 E
Birimbāl al-Qadīmah 142 31.10 N 31.44 E
Birimşe 130 38.03 N 38.32 E
Biritiba-Mirim 256 23.35 S 46.02 W
Bīrjand 128 32.53 N 59.13 E
Birkat as-Sabʿ 142 30.38 N 31.05 E
Birkat Ghiṭās 142 31.07 N 30.16 E
Birkdale 262 53.37 N 3.02 W
Birkeland 26 58.20 N 8.14 E
Birken 182 50.29 N 122.36 W
Birkenfeld, Dtsch. 56 48.52 N 8.38 E
Birkenfeld, Dtsch. 56 49.51 N 9.42 E
Birkenfeld, Dtsch. 56 49.39 N 7.10 E
Birkenfeld, Or., U.S. 224 45.59 N 123.20 W
Birkenhead 44 53.24 N 3.02 W
Birkenhead Park ♦ 262 53.24 N 3.02 W
Birkenwerder bei Berlin 54 52.41 N 13.16 E
Birkerød 41 55.50 N 12.26 E
Birkesdorf 56 50.49 N 6.28 E
Birket Fatimé 146 12.54 N 19.05 E
Birkfeld 61 47.21 N 15.42 E
Birkholz 264a 52.38 N 13.34 E
Birkkarspitze ʌ 64 47.25 N 11.25 E
Birk-Nack > 41 54.48 N 9.55 E
Birksgate Range ⋏ 162 27.10 S 129.45 E
Bîrlad 38 46.14 N 27.40 E
Bîrlad ≃ 38 45.36 N 27.31 E
Birla Museum ʊ 272b 22.32 N 88.22 E
Birlik, Kaz. 80 47.28 N 50.32 E
Birlik, Kaz. 86 44.05 N 73.31 E
Birling 260 51.19 N 0.25 E
Birling ʌ[2] 274a 33.57 S 150.43 E
Birmā 142 30.51 N 30.54 E
Birmaj 84 39.46 N 47.56 E
Birmania → Burma □[1] 110 22.00 N 98.00 E
Birmanie → Burma □[1] 110 22.00 N 98.00 E
Birmingham, Eng., U.K. 42 52.28 N 1.55 W
Birmingham, Al., U.S. 194 33.31 N 86.48 W
Birmingham, Ia., U.S. 190 40.52 N 91.56 W
Birmingham, Mi., U.S. 216 42.32 N 83.12 W
Birmingham, N.J., U.S. 285 39.58 N 74.42 W
Birmingham, Oh., U.S. 214 41.20 N 82.21 W
Birmingham, Pa., U.S. 214 40.38 N 78.13 W
Birmingham Airport ⊠ 42 52.27 N 1.45 W
Birmitrapur 124 22.24 N 84.46 E
Bîr Mogreïn (Fort-Trinquet) 148 25.14 N 11.35 W
Birnagar 126 23.14 N 88.33 E
Birnamwood 190 44.56 N 89.12 W
Birnbaum 64 46.41 N 12.54 E
Birni 150 10.00 N 1.31 E
Birnie I[1] 14 3.35 S 171.31 W
Birni Ngaouré 150 13.05 N 2.54 E
Birnin Gwari 150 11.01 N 6.48 E
Birnin Kebbi 150 12.32 N 4.12 E
Birni Nkonni 150 13.48 N 5.15 E
Birnin Kudu 150 11.27 N 9.30 E
Birobidžan 89 48.48 N 132.57 E
Birobijan → Jevrej □[3] 89 48.30 N 132.00 E
Birofel'd 89 48.26 N 132.47 E
Birome 222 31.49 N 96.58 W
Birqāsh 142 30.10 N 31.02 E
Birr 48 53.05 N 7.54 W
Birregurra 169 38.20 S 143.48 E
Birrie ≃ 166 29.43 S 146.37 E
Birrindudu 162 18.22 S 129.27 E
Birs (Birse) ≃ 58 47.22 N 7.22 E
Birsk 86 55.25 N 55.32 E
Birstall 42 52.41 N 1.07 W
Birstein 56 50.21 N 9.19 E
Birštonas 76 54.37 N 24.02 E
Birten 263 51.38 N 6.29 E
Birtle 184 50.25 N 101.03 W
Birtley 44 54.54 N 1.34 W
Biru 120 31.30 N 93.51 E
Bir'učij 83 46.53 N 39.33 E
Bir'učij kosa >[2] 78 46.08 N 35.05 E
Bir'učja ≃ 83 47.23 N 39.07 E
Birufu 164 5.52 S 138.24 E
Bir'ukovo 83 47.57 N 39.44 E
Bir'ul'ka 88 53.52 N 106.21 E
Bir'ul'ovo ◆[8] 265b 55.35 N 37.40 E
Birungu, Parc des ♦ 154 1.25 S 29.30 E
Birūr 122 13.37 N 75.58 E
Bir'usa 88 57.10 N 96.30 E
Bir'usa (Ona) ≃ 88 57.43 N 95.24 E
Bir'usinsk 88 55.57 N 97.49 E
Biržai 76 56.12 N 24.45 E
Bîrzava ≃ 38 45.16 N 20.49 E
Birżebbuġa 36 35.49 N 14.32 E
Bisa, Pulau I 164 1.15 S 127.28 E
Bisaccia 68 41.01 N 15.22 E
Bisacquino 70 37.42 N 13.15 E
Bisāi, India 126 22.10 N 86.24 E
Bisai, Nihon 94 35.16 N 136.44 E
Bīsalpur 124 28.18 N 79.48 E
Bisamberg 264b 48.20 N 16.22 E
Bisamberg ʌ[2] 264b 48.19 N 16.22 E
Bisan-shotō II 96 34.24 N 133.50 E
Bisbee, Az., U.S. 200 31.26 N 109.55 W
Bisbee, N.D., U.S. 198 48.37 N 99.22 W
Biscarrosse 32 44.24 N 1.10 W
Biscarrosse et de Parentis, Lac de c 32 44.20 N 1.10 W
Biscay, Bay of c 32 44.00 N 4.00 W
Biscayne, Key I 220 25.42 N 80.10 W
Biscayne Bay c 220 25.33 N 80.15 W
Biscayne National Park ♦ 220 25.25 N 80.12 W
Bisceglie 68 41.14 N 16.31 E
Bischheim 58 48.37 N 7.45 E
Bischofsgrün 60 50.03 N 11.47 E
Bischofsheim, Dtsch. 56 50.24 N 10.01 E
Bischofsheim, Dtsch. 56 49.59 N 8.22 E
Bischofshofen 64 47.25 N 13.13 E
Bischofswerda 54 51.07 N 14.10 E
Bischofswiesen 64 47.39 N 12.57 E
Bischofszell 58 47.29 N 9.15 E
Bischwald, Étang de ⊚ 56 49.00 N 6.42 E
Bischwiller 56 48.46 N 7.52 E
Biscoe, Ar., U.S. 194 34.49 N 91.24 W
Biscoe, N.C., U.S. 192 35.21 N 79.46 W
Biscoe Islands II 9 66.00 S 66.30 W
Biscotasi Lake ⊚ 190 47.19 N 82.07 W
Biscucuy 246 9.22 N 69.59 W
Bise 174m 26.42 N 127.54 E
Bisei 96 34.41 N 133.33 E
Bisentina, Isola I 66 42.35 N 11.54 E
Bisenzio ≃ 66 43.46 N 11.06 E
Biser 86 58.25 N 58.53 E
Biserovo 265b 55.47 N 38.07 E
Biserovskoje, ozero ⊚ 265b 55.46 N 38.07 E
Bisert' ≃ 86 56.39 N 57.55 E
Bise-zaki > 174m 26.43 N 127.53 E
Bisha 144 15.28 N 37.34 E
Bīshah, Wādī V 144 21.24 N 43.26 E
Bishahari 126 23.10 N 89.01 E
Bishan 107 29.37 N 106.13 E
Bishanga 152 4.31 S 21.02 E
Bishaykhāli 126 23.28 N 89.09 E
Bishkek → Biškek 85 42.54 N 74.36 E
Bishkhāli ≃[1] 126 21.59 N 89.59 E
Bishnāh 123 32.37 N 74.52 E
Bishnupur, India 120 24.38 N 93.46 E
Bishnupur, India 126 22.23 N 88.16 E
Bishnupur, India 126 23.05 N 87.19 E
Bishnupur, India 272b 22.37 N 88.31 E
Bisho 158 32.50 S 27.20 E
Bishop, Ca., U.S. 204 37.21 N 118.23 W
Bishop, Pa., U.S. 279b 40.19 N 80.12 W
Bishop, Tx., U.S. 196 27.35 N 97.47 W
Bishop Airport ⊠ 216 42.58 N 83.44 W
Bishop Auckland 44 54.40 N 1.40 W
Bishop Rock I[2] 42a 49.52 N 6.27 W
Bishop's Castle 42 52.29 N 3.00 W
Bishop's Cleeve 42 51.57 N 2.04 W
Bishop's Falls 186 49.01 N 55.30 W
Bishops Frome 42 52.08 N 2.29 W
Bishops Head 208 38.16 N 76.04 W
Bishops Lydeard 42 51.04 N 3.12 W
Bishop's Stortford 42 51.53 N 0.09 E
Bishopsteignton 42 50.34 N 3.31 W
Bishopstoke 42 50.59 N 1.19 W
Bishopston 42 51.35 N 4.03 W
Bishop's Waltham 42 50.58 N 1.12 W
Bishopthorpe 44 53.55 N 1.06 W
Bishopton 206 45.35 N 71.35 W
Bishopville, Md., U.S. 208 38.26 N 75.11 W
Bishopville, S.C., U.S. 192 34.13 N 80.14 W
Bishrah, Maʿṭan ⏚[4] 146 22.58 N 22.39 E
Bishrī, Jabal ʌ 130 35.20 N 39.20 E
Bisignano 68 39.31 N 16.17 E
Bisina, Lake ⊚ 154 1.38 N 33.56 E
Bisinadi Game Reserve ◆[4] 154 0.10 N 38.20 E
Bisingen 58 48.18 N 8.55 E
Biskamža 86 53.30 N 89.30 E
Biskaya, Golf von → Biscay, Bay of c 32 44.00 N 4.00 W
Biškek (Frunze) 85 42.54 N 74.36 E
Biskintā 132 33.57 N 35.48 E
Biškon' ≃ 83 49.15 N 39.35 E
Biskupiec 30 53.52 N 20.58 E
Bisley, Eng., U.K. 42 51.45 N 2.08 W
Bisley, Eng., U.K. 260 51.20 N 0.38 W
Bislich 263 51.41 N 6.29 E
Bislig 116 8.13 N 126.19 E
Bislig Bay c 116 8.14 N 126.22 E
Bismarck, Il., U.S. 216 40.16 N 87.37 W
Bismarck, Mo., U.S. 194 37.46 N 90.37 W
Bismarck, N.D., U.S. 198 46.48 N 100.47 W
Bismarck Archipelago II 164 5.00 S 150.00 E
Bismarck Range ⋏ 164 5.30 S 144.45 E
Bismarck Sea ⏚[2] 164 4.00 S 148.00 E
Bismark 54 52.39 N 11.32 E
Bismil 130 37.51 N 40.40 E
Bismo 26 61.53 N 8.16 E
Bismuna, Laguna c 236 14.45 N 83.20 W
Biso 154 1.46 N 31.25 E
Bison 198 45.31 N 102.27 W
Bison Peak ʌ 200 39.14 N 105.30 W
Bispberg 40 60.22 N 15.47 E
Bispgården 26 63.02 N 16.37 E
Bispingen 52 53.05 N 10.00 E
Bisrakh 272a 28.34 N 77.26 E
Bisrāmpur 124 24.15 N 83.56 E
Bissa, Djebel ʌ 34 36.26 N 1.28 E
Bissau 150 11.51 N 15.35 W
Bissaula 146 7.00 N 10.27 E
Bissegem 50 50.49 N 3.13 E
Bissendorf, Dtsch. 52 52.31 N 9.45 E
Bissendorf, Dtsch. 52 52.14 N 8.10 E
Bissett 184 51.02 N 95.40 W
Bissigh, Lach ≃ 144 0.45 N 41.33 E
Bissikrima 150 10.51 N 10.56 W
Bissingen 56 48.43 N 10.37 E
Bissingheim ◆[8], Dtsch. 263 51.24 N 6.49 E
Bissingheim ◆[8], Dtsch. 263 51.21 N 7.31 E
Bissorã 150 12.14 N 15.31 W
Bistcho Lake ⊚ 176 59.40 N 118.40 W
Bistineau, Lake ⊚[1] 194 32.25 N 93.22 W
Bistra ≃ 38 45.29 N 22.11 E
Bistreț 38 43.54 N 23.30 E
Bistrica 61 46.33 N 16.16 E
Bistrița 38 47.08 N 24.30 E
Bistrița ≃ 38 46.30 N 26.57 E
Bistrița-Năsăud □[6] 38 47.15 N 24.30 E
Biswān 124 27.30 N 81.00 E
Bisztynek 30 54.06 N 20.55 E
Bitadton 116 11.30 N 122.05 E
Bitam 152 2.05 N 11.29 E
Bitam, Oued ≃ 34 35.15 N 5.11 E
Bitatolo ≃ 273b 4.09 S 15.19 E
Bitburg 56 49.58 N 6.31 E
Bitca 265b 55.34 N 37.37 E
Bitca ≃ 265b 55.34 N 37.37 E
Bitche 56 49.03 N 7.26 E
Bitchū 96 34.47 N 133.27 E
Bitéa, Ouadi V 146 13.11 N 20.10 E
Bitetto 68 41.02 N 16.45 E
Bithia ⊥ 71 38.53 N 8.52 E
Bithlo 220 28.33 N 81.06 W
Bithynia □[9] 130 40.10 N 30.15 E
Bitia, Wādī V 140 17.34 N 32.15 E
Bitik 80 50.09 N 50.30 E
Bitkine 146 11.59 N 18.13 E
Bitlis 130 38.22 N 42.06 E
Bitlis □[4] 128 38.30 N 42.10 E
Bitola 38 41.01 N 21.20 E
Bitolj → Bitola 38 41.01 N 21.20 E
Bitonto 68 41.06 N 16.42 E
Bitou 150 11.16 N 0.18 W
Bitra Island I 122 11.33 N 72.09 E
Bitritto 68 41.03 N 16.50 E
Bitschwiller-lès-Thann 58 47.50 N 7.05 E
Bitter Creek ≃, Ut,. U.S. 200 39.58 N 109.25 W
Bitter Creek ≃, Wy., U.S. 200 41.31 N 109.27 W
Bitterfeld 54 51.37 N 12.20 E
Bitterfontein 158 31.00 S 18.32 E
Bitter Lake ⊚ 184 50.08 N 109.48 W
Bittermark ◆[8] 263 51.27 N 7.28 E
Bitterness, Mount ʌ 172 44.45 S 170.18 E
Bittern Lake ⊚ 184 53.55 N 105.50 W
Bitterroot ≃ 202 46.52 N 114.06 W
Bitterroot, East Fork ≃ 202 45.57 N 114.08 W
Bitterroot, West Fork ≃ 202 45.57 N 114.08 W
Bitterroot Range ⋏ 202 47.06 N 115.10 W
Bitterwater Creek ≃ 226 35.41 N 119.58 W
Bitti 71 40.29 N 9.23 E
Bit'ug ≃ 78 50.37 N 39.55 E
Bitung 112 1.27 N 125.11 E
Bitupitá 250 2.54 S 41.16 W
Bituruna 252 26.10 S 51.34 W
Biu 146 10.35 N 12.13 E
Bivalve 208 38.18 N 75.53 W
Bivins 194 33.01 N 94.12 W
Bivio 58 46.28 N 9.38 E
Bivona 70 37.37 N 13.26 E
Bivongi 68 38.28 N 16.27 E
Biwabik 190 47.31 N 92.20 W
Biwa-ko ⊚ 94 35.15 N 136.05 E
Biwa-ko-kokutei-kōen ♦ 94 35.10 N 136.00 E
Biwa-ko-ōhashi ◆[5] 94 35.08 N 135.56 E
Bixby 196 35.56 N 95.52 W
Biyalā 142 31.10 N 31.13 E
Biyang 100 32.44 N 113.20 E
Biysk → Bijsk 86 52.34 N 85.15 E
Bi Yun Si (Temple of the Azure Clouds) ʊ[1] 105 40.00 N 116.11 E
Biz'aki 80 55.56 N 52.28 E
Bizana 158 30.58 S 29.52 E
Biz'ar 86 57.31 N 56.09 E
Bizard, Île I 275a 45.29 N 73.54 W
Bižbul'ak 80 53.43 N 54.16 E
Bizcocho, Cuchilla del ⋏[2] 258 33.45 S 57.30 W
Bizen 96 34.44 N 134.09 E
Bizerte 148 37.17 N 9.52 E
Bizerte □[8] 148 37.10 N 9.50 E
Bizerte, Lac de ⊚ 36 37.12 N 9.52 E
Bīzhanābād 128 27.55 N 58.03 E
Bizkaiko □[4] 34 43.20 N 2.45 W
Bjæverskov 41 55.27 N 12.02 E
Bjala, Blg. 38 43.27 N 25.44 E
Bjala, Blg. 38 42.53 N 27.53 E
Bjala Slatina 38 43.28 N 23.56 E
Bjargtangar > 24a 65.31 N 24.32 W
Bjärnum 41 56.17 N 13.42 E
Bjärred 41 55.43 N 13.01 E
Bjärsjölagård 41 55.44 N 13.41 E
Bjästa 26 63.12 N 18.30 E
Bjelaja → Belaja ≃ 72 55.54 N 53.33 E
Bjelovar 36 45.54 N 16.51 E
Bjernede 41 55.27 N 11.38 E
Bjerre Skov ʌ[2] 41 55.47 N 9.53 E
Bjerringbro 26 56.23 N 9.40 E
Björbo 40 60.28 N 14.42 E
Bjørkelangen 26 59.53 N 11.34 E
Björklinge 40 60.02 N 17.33 E
Björknäs 40 59.19 N 18.14 E
Björkö I 40 59.53 N 19.00 E
Björköby 26 63.21 N 21.19 E
Björköfjärden c 40 59.53 N 18.56 E
Björkvik 40 58.50 N 16.31 E
Björna 26 63.34 N 18.33 E
Bjørnafjorden c[2] 26 60.06 N 5.22 E
Björndammen 40 59.12 N 16.49 E
Björneborg 40 59.15 N 14.15 E
Björneborg → Pori 26 61.29 N 21.47 E
Bjornesfjorden ⊚ 26 60.10 N 7.41 E
Björnlunda 40 59.04 N 17.09 E
Bjørnøya (Bear Island) I 12 74.25 N 19.00 E
Bjurholm 26 63.56 N 19.13 E
Bjuv 41 56.05 N 12.54 E
Bkāsīn 132 33.34 N 35.35 E
Bla 150 12.57 N 5.46 W
Blaby 42 52.34 N 1.09 W
Blace 38 43.17 N 21.18 E
Black (Lixian) (Da) ≃, Asia 110 21.15 N 105.20 E
Black ≃, Mb., Can. 184 50.49 N 96.20 W
Black ≃, On., Can. 190 48.42 N 80.38 W
Black ≃, On., Can. 190 48.36 N 86.16 W

Symbols in the index entries represent the broad categories identified in the key at the right. Symbols with superior numbers (⋏[1]) identify subcategories (see complete key on page *I · 1).*

Symbole im Register stellen die rechts im Schlüssel erklärten Kategorien dar. Symbole mit hochgestellten Ziffern (⋏[1]) bezeichnen Unterabteilungen einer Kategorie (vgl. vollständiger Schlüssel auf Seite *I · 1).*

Los símbolos incluídos en el texto del índice representan las grandes categorias identificadas con la clave a la derecha. Los símbolos con numeros en su parte superior (⋏[1]) identifican las subcategorías (véase la clave completa en la página *I · 1).*

Les symboles de l'index représentent les catégories indiquées dans la légende à droite. Les symboles suivis d'un indice (⋏[1]) représentent des sous-catégories (voir légende complète à la page *I · 1).*

Os símbolos incluídos no texto do índice representam as grandes categorias identificadas com a chave à direita. Os símbolos com números em sua parte superior (⋏[1]) identificam as subcategorias (veja-se a chave completa à página *I · 1).*

ʌ Mountain	Berg	Montaña	Montagne	Montanha
⋏ Mountains	Gebirge	Montañas	Montagnes	Montanhas
)(Pass	Paß	Paso	Col	Passo
V Valley, Canyon	Tal, Cañon	Valle, Cañón	Vallée, Canyon	Vale, Canhão
≚ Plain	Ebene	Llano	Plaine	Planície
> Cape	Kap	Cabo	Cap	Cabo
I Island	Insel	Isla	Île	Ilha
II Islands	Inseln	Islas	Îles	Ilhas
⊥ Other Topographic Features	Andere Topographische Objekte	Otros Elementos Topográficos	Autres données topographiques	Outros acidentes topográficos

ESPAÑOL

Nombre	Página	Lat.°′	Long.°′ W = Oeste
Black ≃, On., Can.	212	44.32 N	77.22 W
Black ≃, On., Can.	212	44.20 N	79.20 W
Black ≃, On., Can.	212	44.42 N	79.19 W
Black ≃, U.S.	194	35.38 N	91.19 W
Black ≃, Ak., U.S.	180	66.39 N	144.50 W
Black ≃, Az., U.S.	200	33.44 N	110.13 W
Black ≃, La., U.S.	194	31.16 N	91.50 W
Black ≃, Mi., U.S.	190	46.40 N	90.03 W
Black ≃, Mi., U.S.	190	43.00 N	82.25 W
Black ≃, Mi., U.S.	190	45.39 N	84.29 W
Black ≃, Mi., U.S.	214	43.00 N	82.25 W
Black ≃, N.M., U.S.	196	32.14 N	104.03 W
Black ≃, N.Y., U.S.	188	43.59 N	76.04 W
Black ≃, N.C., U.S.	192	34.35 N	78.16 W
Black ≃, Oh., U.S.	214	41.28 N	82.11 W
Black ≃, S.C., U.S.	192	33.24 N	79.15 W
Black ≃, Vt., U.S.	188	44.55 N	72.13 W
Black ≃, Vt., U.S.	188	43.16 N	72.27 W
Black ≃, Wa., U.S.	224	46.49 N	123.13 W
Black ≃, Wi., U.S.	190	43.57 N	91.22 W
Black, East Branch ≃	214	41.22 N	82.07 W
Black, East Fork ≃	190	44.26 N	90.42 W
Black, Middle Branch ≃	216	42.25 N	86.14 W
Black, South Branch ≃	216	42.25 N	86.15 W
Black, West Branch ≃	214	41.22 N	82.07 W
Blackadder Water ≃	46	55.46 N	2.15 W
Blackall	166	24.25 S	145.28 E
Black Bay c	190	48.40 N	88.30 W
Black Bay Peninsula ≻[1]	190	48.38 N	88.21 W
Black Bear Creek ≃	196	36.25 N	96.38 W
Black Bear Island Lake ⊜	184	55.38 N	105.40 W
Blackberry Creek ≃	216	41.38 N	88.27 W
Blackberry Heights	216	41.45 N	88.23 W
Black Birch Lake ⊜	184	56.54 N	107.45 W
Black Brook ≃, Ma., U.S.	283	41.59 N	71.03 W
Black Brook ≃, Ma., U.S.	283	42.38 N	71.21 W
Black Brook ≃, N.J., U.S.	276	40.42 N	74.31 W
Black Bullock Hill ∧[2]	168b	35.37 S	138.12 E
Blackburn, Austl.	274b	37.49 S	145.09 E
Blackburn, Eng., U.K.	44	53.45 N	2.29 W
Blackburn, Scot., U.K.	46	55.52 N	3.38 W
Blackburn □[8]	262	53.42 N	2.28 W
Blackburn, Mount ∧	180	61.44 N	143.26 W
Blackbutt	171a	26.53 S	152.06 E
Black Butte ∧, Ca., U.S.	228	34.33 N	117.43 W
Black Butte ∧, Mt., U.S.	202	44.54 N	111.51 W
Black Butte ∧, Mt., U.S.	202	46.47 N	110.56 W
Black Butte Lake ⊜[1]	204	39.45 N	122.20 W
Blackbutt Range ⋏	171a	27.00 S	152.00 E
Black Canyon of the Gunnison National Monument ♦	200	38.32 N	107.42 W
Blackcraig Hill ∧	44	55.20 N	4.08 W
Black Creek, B.C., Can.	182	49.50 N	125.08 W
Black Creek, On., Can.	284a	43.00 N	79.01 W
Black Creek, N.Y., U.S.	210	42.17 N	78.14 W
Black Creek ≃, On., Can.	214	42.43 N	82.21 W
Black Creek ≃, On., Can.	275b	43.41 N	79.32 W
Black Creek ≃, On., Can.	284a	42.59 N	79.01 W
Black Creek ≃, Az., U.S.	200	35.16 N	109.14 W
Black Creek ≃, Mi., U.S.	216	41.49 N	83.54 W
Black Creek ≃, Mi., U.S.	216	43.11 N	86.14 W
Black Creek ≃, Ms., U.S.	194	33.01 N	90.21 W
Black Creek ≃, Ms., U.S.	194	30.39 N	88.39 W
Black Creek ≃, Mo., U.S.	219	39.41 N	91.55 W
Black Creek ≃, N.Y., U.S.	210	43.19 N	75.04 W
Black Creek ≃, N.Y., U.S.	210	43.06 N	77.41 W
Black Creek ≃, N.Y., U.S.	284a	43.05 N	78.57 W
Black Creek ≃, N.Y., U.S.	284a	43.03 N	78.42 W
Black Creek ≃, Pa., U.S.	210	41.00 N	76.10 W
Black Creek ≃, S.C., U.S.	192	34.18 N	79.37 W
Black Creek Park ♦	275b	43.46 N	79.31 W
Black Creek Pioneer Village ⊥	275b	43.47 N	79.32 W
Black Cypress Creek ≃	222	32.53 N	94.26 W
Blackden Heath	262	53.14 N	2.20 W
Black Devon ≃	46	56.06 N	3.47 W
Black Diamond, Ab., Can.	182	50.42 N	114.14 W
Black Diamond, Wa., U.S.	224	47.18 N	122.00 W
Black Donald Lake ⊜[1]	212	45.13 N	76.55 W
Black Down Hills ⋏[2]	42	50.57 N	3.09 W
Blackdown Tableland National Park ♦	166	23.43 S	149.05 E
Blackduck	190	47.43 N	94.32 W
Black Duck ≃	176	56.51 N	89.02 W
Black Eagle	202	47.31 N	111.16 W
Black Esk ≃	44	55.12 N	3.10 W
Blackfalds	182	52.23 N	113.47 W
Blackfeet Indian Reservation ◆[4]	202	48.40 N	113.00 W
Blackfoot, Id., U.S.	202	43.11 N	112.20 W
Blackfoot, Mt., U.S.	182	48.34 N	112.52 W
Blackfoot ≃, Id., U.S.	202	43.08 N	112.30 W
Blackfoot ≃, Mt., U.S.	202	46.52 N	113.53 W
Blackfoot, North Fork ≃	202	46.59 N	113.07 W
Blackfoot Indian Reserve ◆[4]	182	50.45 N	113.00 W
Blackfoot Reservoir ⊜[1]	202	42.55 N	111.35 W
Blackford	46	56.15 N	3.46 W
Blackford □[6]	216	40.27 N	85.22 W
Black Forest → Schwarzwald ⋏	58	48.00 N	8.15 E
Blackhall Colliery	44	54.44 N	1.14 W
Blackhall Mountain ∧	200	41.02 N	106.41 W
Black Hameldon ∧[2]	262	53.44 N	2.08 W
Black Hawk	184	48.48 N	93.59 W
Black Hawk Creek ≃	190	42.30 N	92.21 W
Black Head ≻, Ire.	48	53.08 N	9.17 W
Black Head ≻, Eng., U.K.	42	50.01 N	5.06 W
Blackhead Bay c	186	48.34 N	53.15 W
Blackheath, Austl.	170	33.38 S	150.17 E
Blackheath, S. Afr.	273d	26.08 S	27.58 E
Blackheath, Eng., U.K.	260	51.12 N	0.31 W
Black Hill ∧[2], Eng., U.K.	262	53.20 N	2.01 W
Black Hill ∧[2], Eng., U.K.	262	53.33 N	1.53 W
Black Hills ⋏	198	44.00 N	104.00 W
Black Hills ⋏[2]	282	37.50 N	121.52 W
Blackhope Scar ∧	46	55.44 N	3.05 W

FRANÇAIS

Nom	Page	Lat.°′	Long.°′ W = Ouest
Black Horse, Oh., U.S.	214	41.09 N	81.18 W
Black Horse, Pa., U.S.	285	40.06 N	75.19 W
Black Horse, Pa., U.S.	285	39.55 N	75.25 W
Black Horse Creek ≃	285	40.05 N	75.43 W
Black Island I	184	51.10 N	96.30 W
Black Isle ≻[1]	46	57.35 N	4.15 W
Black Jack	219	38.47 N	90.16 W
Black Jack Mountain ∧	228	33.23 N	118.24 W
Black-Lake	206	46.03 N	71.21 W
Black Lake ⊜, On., Can.	212	44.46 N	76.18 W
Black Lake ⊜, Sk., Can.	176	59.10 N	105.20 W
Black Lake ⊜, Mi., U.S.	190	45.28 N	84.15 W
Black Lake ⊜, N.Y., U.S.	212	44.31 N	75.35 W
Black Lake ⊜, Wa., U.S.	224	47.00 N	122.58 W
Black Lake Bayou ≃	194	32.01 N	93.09 W
Blacklegs Creek ≃	214	40.30 N	79.27 W
Blackley ◆[8]	262	53.31 N	2.13 W
Black Lick	214	40.28 N	79.11 W
Blacklick Creek ≃	214	40.28 N	79.13 W
Blacklick Creek, North Branch ≃	214	40.29 N	78.55 W
Blacklick Estates	218	39.54 N	83.22 W
Blacklog Mountain ∧	214	40.20 N	77.45 W
Blacklunans	46	56.44 N	3.22 W
Black Mesa ∧, U.S.	196	37.05 N	103.10 W
Black Mesa ∧, Az., U.S.	200	36.35 N	110.20 W
Blackmoor ⋏[1]	42	50.24 N	4.46 W
Blackmoorfoot Reservoir ⊜[1]	262	53.37 N	1.51 W
Blackmoor Vale V	42	50.56 N	2.25 W
Blackmore	260	51.41 N	0.19 E
Blackmore, Mount ∧	202	45.27 N	111.01 W
Black Moshannon State Park ♦	214	40.54 N	78.03 W
Black Mountain	192	35.37 N	82.19 W
Black Mountain ∧, D.Y.	124	27.17 N	90.23 E
Black Mountain ∧, Wales, U.K.	42	51.52 N	3.46 W
Black Mountain ∧, U.S.	192	36.54 N	82.54 W
Black Mountain ∧, Az., U.S.	200	32.46 N	110.57 W
Black Mountain ∧, Ca., U.S.	226	35.24 N	120.21 W
Black Mountain ∧, Ca., U.S.	228	35.08 N	117.14 W
Black Mountain ∧, Ca., U.S.	282	37.19 N	122.09 W
Black Mountain ∧, Id., U.S.	202	46.53 N	115.33 W
Black Mountain ∧, Mt., U.S.	202	46.44 N	112.31 W
Black Mountain ∧, Or., U.S.	202	45.13 N	119.17 W
Black Mountain ∧, Wy., U.S.	202	44.45 N	107.22 W
Black Mountain ∧[2], Austl.	166	21.08 S	139.41 E
Black Mountain ∧[2], Ca., U.S.	228	32.59 N	117.07 W
Black Mountain ∧[2], Tx., U.S.	222	31.09 N	97.44 W
Black Mountains ⋏, Wales, U.K.	42	51.57 N	3.08 W
Black Mountains ⋏, Az., U.S.	200	35.30 N	114.30 W
Black Nossob ≃	156	23.05 S	18.45 E
Black Oak	216	41.33 N	87.23 W
Black Peak ∧	200	34.08 N	114.13 W
Black Pine Peak ∧	202	42.08 N	113.08 W
Black Pipe Creek ≃	198	43.47 N	101.14 W
Black Point	226	38.07 N	122.31 W
Black Point ≻, Austl.	168b	34.37 S	137.54 E
Black Point ≻, Austl.	170	34.47 S	150.50 E
Black Point ≻, Ak., U.S.	180	57.00 N	153.18 W
Blackpool	44	53.50 N	3.03 W
Blackpool □[8]	262	53.47 N	3.02 W
Blackpool (Squire's Gate) Airport ⊠	262	53.47 N	3.02 W
Blackpool Football Ground ♦	262	53.49 N	3.03 W
Blackpool Tower ʊ	262	53.49 N	3.03 W
Black Range ⋏	200	33.20 N	107.50 W
Black River, Jam.	241q	18.01 N	77.51 W
Black River, N.Y., U.S.	212	44.00 N	75.47 W
Black River Bay c	212	43.58 N	76.07 W
Black River Falls	190	44.17 N	90.51 W
Black Rock, Austl.	274b	37.59 S	145.01 E
Black Rock, Ar., U.S.	194	36.06 N	91.05 W
Black Rock, Ma., U.S.	283	42.14 N	70.49 W
Black Rock I[2]	48	54.05 N	10.22 W
Black Rock II[1]	244	53.39 S	41.48 W
Black Rock Desert ◆[2]	204	41.10 N	119.00 W
Blackrod	262	53.35 N	2.35 W
Blacksburg, S.C., U.S.	192	35.07 N	81.30 W
Blacksburg, Va., U.S.	192	37.13 N	80.24 W
Blacks Creek ≃	285	40.08 N	74.43 W
Black Sea ⫪[2]	22	43.00 N	35.00 E
Blacks Fork ≃	200	41.24 N	109.38 W
Blacks Harbour	186	45.03 N	66.47 W
Blackshear	192	31.18 N	82.14 W
Blackshear, Lake ⊜[1]	192	31.56 N	83.56 W
Blacksod Bay c	48	54.08 N	10.00 W
Black Springs, Austl.	170	33.52 S	149.42 E
Black Springs, Austl.	274b	37.46 S	145.19 E
Black Springs Hill ∧[2]	274b	37.46 S	145.19 E
Black Star Canyon V	280	33.47 N	117.39 W
Blackstone, Ma., U.S.	207	42.01 N	71.32 W
Blackstone, Va., U.S.	192	37.04 N	77.59 W
Blackstone ≃, Ab., Can.	182	52.50 N	116.07 W
Blackstone ≃, Yk., Can.	180	65.51 N	137.12 W
Blackstone Lake ⊜	212	45.14 N	79.53 W
Black Sugarloaf Mountain ∧	166	31.20 S	151.33 E
Black Thunder Creek ≃	198	43.33 N	104.41 W
Blacktown	170	33.46 S	150.55 E
Blackville	192	33.21 N	81.16 W
Black Volta (Volta Noire) ≃	150	8.41 N	1.33 W
Blackwall Tunnel ◆[5]	260	51.30 N	0.01 E
Blackwalnut Point ≻	208	38.40 N	76.20 W
Black Warrior ≃	194	32.32 N	87.51 W
Blackwatch Hills	210	43.05 N	77.27 W
Blackwater, Austl.	166	23.35 S	148.53 E
Blackwater, Ire.	48	52.26 N	6.21 W
Blackwater ≃, Europe	48	54.31 N	6.34 W
Blackwater ≃, Ire.	48	53.39 N	6.43 W
Blackwater ≃, Ire.	48	51.51 N	7.50 W
Blackwater ≃, Eng., U.K.	42	51.45 N	1.00 E
Blackwater ≃, U.S.	194	30.36 N	87.02 W
Blackwater ≃, Md., U.S.	208	38.21 N	76.01 W
Blackwater ≃, Mo., U.S.	194	38.56 N	92.51 W
Blackwater ≃, Va., U.S.	208	36.33 N	76.55 W
Blackwater Creek ≃, Austl.	166	25.56 S	144.20 E

PORTUGUÊS

Nome	Página	Lat.°′	Long.°′ W = Oeste
Black Water Creek ≃, Fl., U.S.	220	28.51 N	81.24 W
Blackwater Draw V	196	33.35 N	101.50 W
Blackwaterfoot	46	55.30 N	5.19 W
Blackwater Lake ⊜	180	64.00 N	123.05 W
Blackwater Reservoir ⊜[1], Scot., U.K.	46	56.41 N	4.46 W
Blackwater Reservoir ⊜[1], Scot., U.K.	46	56.44 N	3.14 W
Blackwater Sound ʯ	220	25.10 N	80.25 W
Blackwell, Ok., U.S.	196	36.48 N	97.16 W
Blackwell, Tx., U.S.	196	32.05 N	100.19 W
Blackwood, Austl.	168b	35.02 S	138.37 E
Blackwood, Austl.	169	37.29 S	144.19 E
Blackwood, N.J., U.S.	285	39.48 N	75.03 W
Blackwood ≃	162	34.19 S	115.11 E
Blackwood, Cape ≻	164	7.50 S	144.30 E
Blackwood Terrace	285	39.48 N	75.05 W
Bladel	52	51.23 N	5.13 E
Bladenboro	192	34.32 N	78.47 W
Bladensburg, Md., U.S.	284c	38.56 N	76.56 W
Bladensburg, Oh., U.S.	214	40.17 N	82.17 W
Blades	208	38.38 N	75.36 W
Bladgrond	158	28.52 S	19.57 E
Bladnoch ≃	44	54.51 N	4.25 W
Bladworth	184	51.18 N	106.09 W
Blaenau Ffestiniog	42	52.59 N	3.56 W
Blaenavon	42	51.48 N	3.05 W
Bláfell ∧	24a	64.32 N	19.53 W
Blagaj	36	43.15 N	17.50 E
Blagdon	42	51.20 N	2.43 W
Blagodarnoje	86	47.03 N	82.10 E
Blagodarnyj	72	45.06 N	43.27 E
Blagodatnoje, Kaz.	86	51.18 N	72.49 E
Blagodatnoje, Ross.	78	51.32 N	34.54 E
Blagodatnoje, Ukr.	83	47.42 N	37.25 E
Blagodatnoje, Ukr.	83	47.53 N	38.29 E
Blagodatovka	80	52.14 N	50.27 E
Blagoevgrad	38	42.01 N	23.06 E
Blagoveščenka, Kaz.	86	54.22 N	66.58 E
Blagoveščenka, Ross.	80	51.19 N	44.03 E
Blagoveščenka, Ross.	86	52.50 N	79.52 E
Blagoveščensk, Ross.	86	55.01 N	55.59 E
Blagoveščensk, Ross.	89	50.17 N	127.32 E
Blagoveščenskoje, Kaz.	85	43.18 N	74.12 E
Blagoveščenskoje, Ross.	86	58.08 N	62.58 E
Blåhø ∧	26	62.45 N	9.19 E
Blåhøj	41	55.51 N	9.01 E
Blaichach	58	47.34 N	10.15 E
Blaikfjället ∧	26	64.33 N	16.12 E
Blain, Fr.	32	47.29 N	1.46 W
Blain, Pa., U.S.	208	40.20 N	77.31 W
Blaina	42	51.46 N	3.10 W
Blain City	214	40.45 N	78.34 W
Blaine, Mn., U.S.	190	45.09 N	93.14 W
Blaine, Wa., U.S.	224	48.59 N	122.44 W
Blaine Creek ≃	188	38.11 N	82.37 W
Blaine Hill	279b	40.16 N	79.53 W
Blaine Lake	184	52.50 N	106.54 W
Blaineys	224	48.53 N	123.47 W
Blainville	206	45.40 N	73.52 W
Blainville-sur-l'Eau	58	48.33 N	6.24 E
Blair, On., Can.	212	43.23 N	80.23 W
Blair, Ne., U.S.	198	41.32 N	96.07 W
Blair, Ok., U.S.	196	34.46 N	99.20 W
Blair, Wi., U.S.	190	44.18 N	91.14 W
Blair □[6]	214	40.30 N	78.25 W
Blair Athol	166	22.42 S	147.33 E
Blair Atholl	46	56.46 N	3.51 W
Blairgowrie	46	56.36 N	3.21 W
Blairs Mills	214	40.17 N	77.43 W
Blairstown, Ia., U.S.	190	41.54 N	92.05 W
Blairstown, N.J., U.S.	210	40.59 N	74.57 W
Blairsville, Ga., U.S.	192	34.52 N	83.57 W
Blairsville, Pa., U.S.	214	40.25 N	79.15 W
Blaise ≃, Fr.	50	48.46 N	1.25 E
Blaise ≃, Fr.	58	48.38 N	4.43 E
Blaisy-Bas	58	47.22 N	4.44 E
Blaj	38	46.11 N	23.55 E
Blakehurst	274a	33.59 S	151.07 E
Blakeley Canal ≊	226	36.09 N	119.48 W
Blakely, Ga., U.S.	192	31.22 N	84.56 W
Blakely, Pa., U.S.	210	41.28 N	75.35 W
Blakely Island I	224	48.33 N	122.50 W
Blakeney, Eng., U.K.	42	52.58 N	1.00 E
Blakeney, Eng., U.K.	42	51.46 N	2.29 W
Blake Plateau ✢[4]	16	31.00 N	79.00 W
Blake Point ≻	190	48.12 N	88.25 W
Blake Ridge ✢[3]	16	29.00 N	73.30 W
Blakes	208	37.30 N	76.22 W
Blakesburg	190	40.57 N	92.38 W
Blakeslee, Oh., U.S.	216	41.31 N	84.44 W
Blakeslee, Pa., U.S.	210	41.06 N	75.36 W
Blalock Island I	202	45.53 N	119.41 W
Blâmont, Fr.	58	48.35 N	6.51 E
Blamont, Fr.	58	47.23 N	6.51 E
Blanc, Cap ≻	36	37.20 N	9.51 E
Blanc, Cap → Nouâdhibou, Râs ≻	148	20.46 N	17.03 W
Blanc, Mont ∧, P.Q., Can.	186	48.47 N	66.52 W
Blanc, Mont (Monte Bianco) ∧, Europe	62	45.50 N	6.52 E
Blanca	200	37.27 N	105.31 W
Blanca, Bahía c	252	38.55 S	62.10 W
Blanca, Isla I	248	9.06 S	78.38 W
Blanca, Laguna ⊜	254	52.25 S	71.10 W
Blanca, Punta ≻, Arg.	258	34.57 S	57.40 W
Blanca, Punta ≻, Chile	252	25.06 S	70.30 W
Blanca, Sierra ∧	200	31.15 N	105.26 W
Blanca Lake ⊜	224	47.53 N	121.21 W
Blanca Peak ∧	200	37.35 N	105.29 W
Blancas, Peñas ⋏	236	13.15 N	85.41 W
Blanc du Cheilon, Mont ∧	58	45.59 N	7.25 E
Blanchard, Ok., U.S.	196	35.08 N	97.39 W
Blanchard, Pa., U.S.	210	41.04 N	77.36 W
Blanchard, Wa., U.S.	224	48.35 N	122.24 W
Blanchard ≃	216	41.02 N	84.18 W
Blanchardville	190	42.48 N	89.51 W
Blanche ≃, On., Can.	190	47.34 N	79.32 W
Blanche ≃, P.Q., Can.	206	46.40 N	72.08 W
Blanche, Cape ≻	162	33.01 S	134.09 E
Blanche, Dent ∧	58	46.03 N	7.36 E
Blanche, Lake ⊜, Austl.	162	22.25 S	123.17 E
Blanche, Lake ⊜, Austl.	166	29.15 S	139.39 E
Blanche, Mer → Beloje more ⫪[2]	24	65.30 N	38.00 E
Blanche Channel ʯ	175e	8.30 S	157.30 E
Blancheface	261	48.32 N	2.06 E
Blanche Marie Val ∟	250	4.44 N	56.53 W
Blanchester	218	39.17 N	83.59 W
Blanchisseuse	241r	10.47 N	61.18 W
Blanco, S. Afr.	158	33.57 S	22.24 E
Blanco, Tx., U.S.	196	30.06 N	98.25 W
Blanco ≃, Arg.	252	30.12 S	69.05 W
Blanco ≃, Arg.	254	47.22 S	71.12 W
Blanco ≃, Bol.	248	13.09 S	63.46 W
Blanco ≃, Ec.	246	0.28 N	79.25 W
Blanco ≃, Tx., U.S.	196	29.51 N	97.55 W
Blanco, Cabo ≻	236	9.34 N	85.07 W
Blanco, Cabo → Nouâdhibou, Râs ≻	148	20.46 N	17.03 W
Blanco, Cañon V	200	35.20 N	105.05 W
Blanco, Cape ≻	202	42.50 N	124.34 W

Blanco, Lago ⊜	254	54.03 S	69.00 W
Blanco, Mar → Beloje more ⫪[2]	24	65.30 N	38.00 E
Blanco, Monte → Blanc, Mont ∧	62	45.50 N	6.52 E
Blanco, Rio ≃	200	37.07 N	107.03 W
Blanco Creek ≃	196	28.19 N	97.19 W
Blanc-Sablon	186	51.25 N	57.07 W
Bland, Mo., U.S.	219	38.18 N	91.37 W
Bland, Va., U.S.	192	37.06 N	81.06 W
Blanda ≃	24a	65.39 N	20.18 W
Blandburg	214	40.41 N	78.24 W
Blandford	207	42.10 N	72.55 W
Blandford Forum	42	50.52 N	2.11 W
Blanding	200	37.37 N	109.28 W
Blandinsville	190	40.33 N	90.51 W
Blandon	208	40.26 N	75.53 W
Blandy	261	48.34 N	2.47 E
Blanes	34	41.41 N	2.48 E
Blangkejeren	114	3.59 N	97.20 E
Blangpidie	114	3.45 N	96.51 E
Blangy-le-Château	50	49.14 N	0.17 E
Blangy-sur-Bresle	50	49.56 N	1.38 E
Blanice ≃	61	49.05 N	14.03 E
Blankenberg	56	50.45 N	7.22 E
Blankenberge	50	51.19 N	3.08 E
Blankenburg	54	51.48 N	10.58 E
Blankenburg ◆[8]	264a	52.35 N	13.28 E
Blankenese ◆[8]	52	53.33 N	9.48 E
Blankenfelde	54	52.20 N	13.23 E
Blankenfelde ◆[8]	264a	52.37 N	13.23 E
Blankenhain	54	50.51 N	11.21 E
Blankenheim, Dtsch.	54	51.31 N	11.25 E
Blankenheim, Dtsch.	56	50.26 N	6.39 E
Blankensee	54	52.14 N	13.08 E
Blankenstein	263	51.24 N	7.14 E
Blanket	196	31.49 N	98.47 W
Blanquilla, Isla I	246	11.51 N	64.37 W
Blansko	30	49.22 N	16.39 E
Blanský Les ◆[3]	61	48.52 N	14.16 E
Blantyre	154	15.47 S	35.00 E
Blanzac	62	45.07 N	3.51 E
Blanzy	58	46.42 N	4.23 E
Blaricum	52	52.16 N	5.15 E
Blarney	48	51.56 N	8.34 W
Blarney Castle ⊥	48	51.56 N	8.34 W
Blasdell	210	42.47 N	78.49 W
Blasheim	52	52.18 N	8.34 E
Błaszki	30	51.39 N	18.27 E
Blatná	60	49.26 N	13.53 E
Blatnica	38	43.42 N	28.31 E
Blatten	58	46.25 N	7.50 E
Blatzheim	56	50.51 N	6.38 E
Blau ≃	58	48.23 N	9.49 E
Blaubeuren	58	48.24 N	9.47 E
Blauen ∧	58	47.47 N	7.42 E
Blauer Nil → Blue Nile ≃	140	15.38 N	32.31 E
Blaufelden	56	49.18 N	9.58 E
Blaustein	58	48.25 N	9.53 E
Blauvelt	276	41.03 N	73.57 W
Blauvelt State Park ♦	276	41.04 N	73.56 W
Blawenburg	276	40.24 N	74.42 W
Blawnox	279b	40.29 N	79.51 W
Blaxland	170	33.45 S	150.36 E
Blaxland Creek ≃	274a	33.48 S	150.46 E
Blaydon	44	54.58 N	1.42 W
Blaye-et-Sainte-Luce	32	45.08 N	0.39 W
Blayney	166	33.32 S	149.15 E
Blaze, Point ≻	164	12.56 S	130.12 E
Błażowa	30	49.54 N	22.05 E
Bleaker Island I	254	52.13 S	58.53 W
Bleaklow Head ∧	262	53.28 N	1.50 W
Blean	42	51.19 N	1.02 E
Bleckede	54	53.17 N	10.44 E
Bled	36	46.22 N	14.06 E
Bledsoe	196	33.38 N	103.01 W
Bleecker	210	43.07 N	74.22 W
Blefjell ∧	26	59.48 N	9.10 E
Blega	115a	7.08 S	113.03 E
Bleibach	58	48.07 N	8.01 E
Bleiberg ob Villach	64	46.37 N	13.41 E
Bleiburg	61	46.35 N	14.48 E
Bleicherode	54	51.26 N	10.34 E
Blekendorf	54	54.16 N	10.38 E
Blekinge □[9]	26	56.20 N	15.05 E
Blekinge Län □[6]	26	56.20 N	15.20 E
Blendecques	50	50.43 N	2.16 E
Bléneau	50	47.42 N	2.57 E
Blenheim, Austl.	171a	27.39 S	152.20 E
Blenheim, On., Can.	214	42.20 N	82.00 W
Blenheim, N.Z.	172	41.31 S	173.57 E
Blenheim, N.J., U.S.	285	39.48 N	75.05 W
Blenheim Palace ʊ	42	51.47 N	1.21 W
Blenio, Val V	58	46.27 N	8.58 E
Blénod-lès-Pont-à-Mousson	56	48.53 N	6.03 E
Blénod-lès-Toul	58	48.36 N	5.50 E
Bléone ≃	62	44.03 N	6.00 E
Blérancourt	50	49.31 N	3.09 E
Bléré	50	47.20 N	1.00 E
Blerick	52	51.23 N	6.10 E
Blériot-Plage	50	50.57 N	1.50 E
Blesbokspruit ≃	273d	26.14 S	28.29 E
Blessing	222	28.52 N	96.13 W
Blessington	48	53.10 N	6.32 W
Bletchingley	260	51.14 N	0.06 W
Bletchley	42	52.00 N	0.46 W
Bletterans	58	46.45 N	5.27 E
Bleu → Chang ≃	90	31.48 N	121.10 E
Bleue, Mer ≡	212	45.24 N	75.30 W
Bleury	261	48.31 N	1.45 E
Bleus, Monts ⋏	154	1.30 N	30.30 E
Blevio	62	45.50 N	9.05 E
Blewett Falls Lake ⊜[1]	192	35.03 N	79.54 W
Blexen	52	53.32 N	8.32 E
Blidö I	40	59.37 N	18.54 E
Blidworth	44	53.06 N	1.07 W
Bliedinghausen ◆[8]	263	51.09 N	7.12 E
Bliersheim ◆[8]	263	51.23 N	6.43 E
Blies ≃	56	49.07 N	7.04 E
Blieskastel	56	49.14 N	7.16 E
Bligh Sound ʯ	172	44.50 S	167.32 E
Bligh Water ʯ	175g	17.00 S	178.00 E
Bligny	50	49.11 N	3.52 E
Bligny-sur-Ouche	58	47.06 N	4.40 E
Blik, Mount ∧	116	6.58 N	124.15 E
Blina	162	17.46 S	124.32 E
Blind ≃	276	40.57 N	73.42 W
Blind Creek ≃	274b	37.54 S	145.12 E
Blindley Heath	260	51.12 N	0.04 W
Blind River	190	46.10 N	82.58 W
Blinman	166	31.06 S	138.41 E
Blinnenhorn ∧	58	46.26 N	8.19 E
Blinovskij	80	49.23 N	42.19 E
Bliss	210	42.34 N	78.15 W
Blissfield, Mi., U.S.	216	41.49 N	83.51 W
Blissfield, Oh., U.S.	214	40.24 N	81.58 W
Blitar	115a	8.06 S	112.09 E
Blithe ≃	42	52.45 N	1.50 W
Blithfield Reservoir ⊜[1]	42	52.48 N	1.53 W
Blitta	150	8.19 N	0.59 E
Blizn'uki	78	48.52 N	36.33 E
Blocher	218	38.43 N	85.39 W
Block Dam ◆[6]	212	45.12 N	76.54 W
Block Island	207	41.10 N	71.33 W
Block Island I	207	41.11 N	71.35 W
Block Island Sound ʯ	207	41.10 N	71.45 W
Blockley	42	52.01 N	1.45 W
Blockton	198	40.36 N	94.28 W
Blodgett Mills	210	42.34 N	76.08 W
Bloed ≃	158	28.15 S	30.30 E
Bloedel	182	50.07 N	125.23 W
Bloedrivier, S. Afr.	158	28.06 S	30.33 E
Bloedrivier, S. Afr.	158	27.53 S	30.30 E
Bloekomspruit	158	26.45 S	28.21 E
Bloemendaal	52	52.24 N	4.37 E

Bloemfontein	158	29.12 S	26.07 E
Bloemhof	158	27.38 S	25.32 E
Bloemhofdam ⊜[1]	158	27.40 S	25.40 E
Blois	50	47.35 N	1.20 E
Blokhus	26	57.15 N	9.35 E
Blokzijl	52	52.44 N	5.57 E
Blombacher Bach ◆[8]	263	51.15 N	7.14 E
Blombacka	40	59.37 N	13.47 E
Blomberg	52	51.56 N	9.05 E
Blomstermåla	26	56.59 N	16.20 E
Blonay	58	46.28 N	6.54 E
Blönduós	24a	65.39 N	20.15 W
Blongas	115b	8.53 S	116.02 E
Blonville-sur-Mer	50	49.19 N	0.02 E
Blood Indian Creek ≃	184	50.55 N	111.03 W
Blood Indian Reserve ◆[4]	182	49.30 N	113.10 W
Blood Mountain ∧	192	34.44 N	83.56 W
Blood River ⊥	158	28.20 S	30.35 E
Bloodsworth Island I	208	38.10 N	76.03 W
Bloodvein ≃	184	51.45 N	96.44 W
Bloody Foreland ≻	48	55.09 N	8.17 W
Bloomdale	216	41.10 N	83.33 W
Bloomer	190	45.06 N	91.29 W
Bloomfield, On., Can.	212	43.59 N	77.14 W
Bloomfield, Ct., U.S.	207	41.49 N	72.43 W
Bloomfield, In., U.S.	194	39.01 N	86.56 W
Bloomfield, Ia., U.S.	190	40.45 N	92.24 W
Bloomfield, Ky., U.S.	194	37.54 N	85.19 W
Bloomfield, Mo., U.S.	194	36.53 N	89.55 W
Bloomfield, Ne., U.S.	198	42.35 N	97.38 W
Bloomfield, N.J., U.S.	210	40.48 N	74.11 W
Bloomfield, N.M., U.S.	200	36.42 N	107.59 W
Bloomfield, Oh., U.S.	214	40.03 N	81.44 W
Bloomfield ◆[8]	279b	40.27 N	79.56 W
Bloomfield Glens	281	42.33 N	83.20 W
Bloomfield Highlands	281	42.36 N	83.16 W
Bloomfield Hills	216	42.35 N	83.14 W
Bloomfield Village	216	42.33 N	83.15 W
Bloomingburg, N.Y., U.S.	210	41.33 N	74.26 W
Bloomingburg, Oh., U.S.	218	39.36 N	83.23 W
Bloomingdale, Il., U.S.	216	41.57 N	88.04 W
Bloomingdale, Mi., U.S.	216	42.22 N	85.57 W
Bloomingdale, N.J., U.S.	210	41.00 N	74.19 W
Bloomingdale, Oh., U.S.	214	40.21 N	80.49 W
Blooming Glen	208	40.22 N	75.15 W
Blooming Grove, In., U.S.	218	39.30 N	85.04 W
Blooming Grove, N.Y., U.S.	210	41.25 N	74.11 W
Blooming Grove, Pa., U.S.	210	41.21 N	75.09 W
Blooming Grove, Tx., U.S.	222	32.06 N	96.43 W
Blooming Prairie	190	43.52 N	93.03 W
Bloomington, Ca., U.S.	228	34.04 N	117.23 W
Bloomington, Il., U.S.	216	40.29 N	88.59 W
Bloomington, In., U.S.	218	39.09 N	86.31 W
Bloomington, Mn., U.S.	190	44.50 N	93.17 W
Bloomington, N.Y., U.S.	210	41.53 N	74.03 W
Bloomington, Tx., U.S.	196	28.38 N	96.53 W
Bloomington, Wi., U.S.	190	42.53 N	90.55 W
Bloomington, Lake ⊜[1]	216	40.37 N	88.55 W
Blooming Valley	214	41.40 N	80.03 W
Bloomsburg	210	41.00 N	76.27 W
Bloomsbury, Austl.	166	20.43 S	148.35 E
Bloomsbury, N.J., U.S.	210	40.39 N	75.05 W
Bloomsdale Gardens	285	40.07 N	74.52 W
Bloomville, N.Y., U.S.	210	42.20 N	74.48 W
Bloomville, Oh., U.S.	214	41.03 N	83.00 W
Blora	115a	6.57 S	111.25 E
Bloserville	208	40.12 N	77.24 W
Blossburg	210	41.40 N	77.03 W
Blossom	196	33.39 N	95.23 W
Blossom Hill	208	40.05 N	76.19 W
Blötberget	40	60.07 N	15.04 E
Blotzheim	58	47.36 N	7.29 E
Blouberg	156	23.08 S	28.56 E
Blouberg ∧	156	23.01 S	28.59 E
Bloubergstrand	158	33.47 S	18.28 E
Blouin, Lac ⊜	190	48.10 N	77.44 W
Bloumet	148	23.27 N	6.06 E
Blountstown	192	30.26 N	85.02 W
Blountsville	194	34.04 N	86.35 W
Blountville	192	36.31 N	82.19 W
Blovice	60	49.35 N	13.33 E
Blovstrød	41	55.52 N	12.24 E
Blowering Reservoir ⊜[1]	171b	35.30 S	148.15 E
Blowing Rock	192	36.08 N	81.40 W
Bloxham	42	52.02 N	1.22 W
Bloxom	208	37.49 N	75.37 W
Blšanka ≃	54	50.10 N	13.34 E
Blšany	54	50.10 N	13.29 E
Bludenz	58	47.09 N	9.49 E
Bludnaja ≃	88	51.24 N	110.39 E
Blue ≃, Az., U.S.	200	33.13 N	109.11 W
Blue ≃, Co., U.S.	200	40.03 N	106.24 W
Blue ≃, In., U.S.	216	41.07 N	85.30 W
Blue ≃, In., U.S.	218	38.11 N	86.19 W
Blue ≃, Ok., U.S.	196	33.53 N	95.56 W
Blue, Middle Fork ≃	218	38.33 N	86.07 W
Blue, South Fork ≃	218	38.26 N	86.11 W
Blue, West Fork ≃	218	38.33 N	86.07 W
Blue Anchor	285	39.41 N	74.52 W
Blue Anchor Brook ≃	285	39.42 N	74.49 W
Blue Ash	218	39.13 N	84.22 W
Blue Ball	218	39.29 N	84.21 W
Blue Bell	208	40.09 N	75.16 W
Bluebell Hill	260	51.20 N	0.30 E
Blue Bonnets, Champ de Course ♦	275a	45.29 N	73.39 W
Blue Brook ≃	276	40.40 N	74.25 W
Blue Buck Knob ∧[2]	194	36.57 N	92.07 W
Bluebush Swamp ≡	162	20.30 S	137.25 E
Blue Creek, Oh., U.S.	218	38.47 N	83.20 W
Blue Creek, Wa., U.S.	182	48.19 N	117.49 W
Blue Creek, Wa., U.S.	202	48.19 N	117.49 W
Blue Creek ≃, Ca., U.S.	226	38.28 N	120.22 W
Blue Creek ≃, Id., U.S.	202	42.02 N	116.08 W
Blue Creek ≃, Ne., U.S.	198	41.19 N	102.10 W
Blue Creek ≃, Oh., U.S.	216	41.07 N	84.26 W
Blue Creek ≃, Ut,. U.S.	200	41.31 N	112.24 W
Blue Cypress Lake ⊜	220	27.44 N	80.45 W
Blue Earth	190	43.38 N	94.06 W
Blue Earth ≃	190	44.09 N	94.02 W
Bluefield, Va., U.S.	192	37.15 N	81.16 W
Bluefield, W.V., U.S.	192	37.16 N	81.13 W
Bluefields	236	12.00 N	83.45 W
Bluefields, Bahía de c	236	12.02 N	83.44 W
Bluefields Bay c	241q	18.10 N	78.03 W
Blue Grass Airport ⊠	218	38.02 N	84.36 W
Blue Grotto → Azzurra, Grotta •[5]	68	40.35 N	14.14 E

Blue Hill, Me., U.S.	188	44.24 N	68.35 W
Blue Hill, Ne., U.S.	198	40.19 N	98.26 W
Blue Hill Bay c	188	44.15 N	68.30 W
Blue Hills	207	41.40 N	72.56 W
Blue Hills of Couteau ⋏[2]	186	47.59 N	57.43 W
Blue Hills Reservation ♦	283	42.13 N	71.05 W
Blue Island	216	41.39 N	87.40 W
Blue Jay	228	34.15 N	117.13 W
Bluejoint Lake ⊜	202	42.35 N	119.40 W
Blue Knob ∧	214	40.17 N	78.34 W
Blue Knob State Park ♦	214	40.16 N	78.35 W
Blue Lagoon National Park ♦	154	15.30 S	27.25 E
Blue Lake National Park ♦	171a	27.31 S	153.29 E
Blue Licks Battlefield State Park ♦	218	38.26 N	84.00 W
Blue Marsh Lake ⊜[1]	208	40.25 N	76.05 W
Blue Mesa Reservoir ⊜[1]	200	38.27 N	107.10 W
Blue Mosque ʊ[1]	273c	30.02 N	31.15 E
Blue Mound, Il., U.S.	219	39.42 N	89.07 W
Blue Mound, Ks., U.S.	198	38.05 N	95.00 W
Blue Mound, Tx., U.S.	222	32.51 N	97.19 W
Blue Mountain, Ms., U.S.	194	34.40 N	89.01 W
Blue Mountain, N.Y., U.S.	210	42.07 N	74.01 W
Blue Mountain ∧, N.B., Can.	186	47.49 N	66.19 W
Blue Mountain ∧, Nf., Can.	186	50.24 N	57.10 W
Blue Mountain ∧, Ar., U.S.	194	34.41 N	94.03 W
Blue Mountain ∧, Mt., U.S.	198	47.16 N	104.10 W
Blue Mountain ∧, N.H., U.S.	188	44.47 N	71.28 W
Blue Mountain ∧, Pa., U.S.	188	40.15 N	77.30 W
Blue Mountain ∧[2], On., Can.	190	48.15 N	80.07 W
Blue Mountain ∧[2], On., Can.	212	44.40 N	77.58 W
Blue Mountain Peak ∧	241q	18.03 N	76.35 W
Blue Mountains ⋏, Austl.	170	33.37 S	150.17 E
Blue Mountains ⋏, Jam.	241q	18.06 N	76.40 W
Blue Mountains ⋏, U.S.	202	45.30 N	118.15 W
Blue Mountains ⋏, Me., U.S.	188	44.50 N	70.35 W
Blue Mountains National Park ♦	170	33.40 S	150.25 E
Blue Mud Bay c	164	13.26 S	135.56 E
Blue Nile (Al-Bahr al-Azraq) (Abay) ≃	140	15.38 N	32.31 E
Bluenose Lake ⊜	180	68.25 N	119.45 W
Blue Point	276	40.45 N	73.02 W
Blue Point ≻	276	40.44 N	73.02 W
Blue Rapids	198	39.40 N	96.39 W
Blue Ridge, Ab., Can.	182	54.08 N	115.22 W
Blue Ridge, Ga., U.S.	192	34.51 N	84.19 W
Blue Ridge, Il., U.S.	216	40.17 N	88.29 W
Blue Ridge ⋏	178	37.00 N	82.00 W
Blue Ridge Summit	208	39.43 N	77.28 W
Blue River	182	52.05 N	119.17 W
Blue Rock Springs Park ♦	282	38.08 N	122.12 W
Bluesky	182	56.04 N	118.14 W
Blue Springs	198	40.08 N	96.39 W
Blue Stack Mountains ⋏	48	54.45 N	8.05 W
Bluestone ≃	192	37.34 N	80.59 W
Bluestone Dam ◆[6]	192	37.36 N	80.53 W
Bluestone Lake ⊜[1]	192	37.30 N	80.50 W
Bluestone State Park ♦	192	37.37 N	80.56 W
Bluewater	200	35.15 N	107.59 W
Blue Water Bridge ◆[5]	214	43.00 N	82.25 W
Bluff, N.Z.	172	46.36 S	168.20 E
Bluff, Ut,. U.S.	200	37.17 N	109.33 W
Bluff Cape ≻	110	18.00 N	94.26 E
Bluff City, Il., U.S.	219	38.57 N	89.02 W
Bluff City, Tn., U.S.	192	36.28 N	82.15 W
Bluff Cove c	280	33.48 N	118.24 W
Bluff Creek ≃, U.S.	196	36.58 N	97.26 W
Bluff Creek ≃, Ks., U.S.	198	37.02 N	99.29 W
Bluff Dale	196	32.21 N	98.01 W
Bluff Head ≻	271d	22.11 N	114.12 E
Bluff Island I	271d	22.19 N	114.21 E
Bluff Knoll ∧	162	34.23 S	118.20 E
Bluff Park	194	33.24 N	86.51 W
Bluff Point ≻	162	27.50 S	114.06 E
Bluffs	219	39.45 N	90.32 W
Bluff Springs	219	39.59 N	90.21 W
Bluffton, In., U.S.	216	40.44 N	85.10 W
Bluffton, Oh., U.S.	216	40.53 N	83.53 W
Bluffton, S.C., U.S.	192	32.14 N	80.51 W
Bluffy Lake ⊜	184	50.47 N	92.55 W
Bluford	219	38.20 N	88.45 W
Blum	222	32.09 N	97.24 W
Blumberg, Dtsch.	54	52.36 N	13.37 E
Blumberg, Dtsch.	58	47.50 N	8.31 E
Blumenau	252	26.56 S	49.03 W
Blumenhof	184	50.01 N	107.41 W
Blümlisalp ∧	58	46.30 N	7.47 E
Blunt	198	44.30 N	99.59 W
Blup Blup Island I	164	3.30 S	144.37 E
Bly	202	42.23 N	121.02 W
Blying Sound ʯ	180	59.50 N	149.15 W
Blyth, Austl.	168b	33.51 S	138.29 E
Blyth, On., Can.	190	43.44 N	81.26 W
Blyth, Eng., U.K.	44	55.07 N	1.30 W
Blyth ≃, Austl.	164	12.04 S	134.35 E
Blyth ≃, Eng., U.K.	42	52.18 N	1.40 E
Blyth ≃, Eng., U.K.	44	55.08 N	1.31 W
Blyth Bridge	46	55.42 N	3.24 W
Blythe	204	33.36 N	114.35 W
Blythedale	214	40.15 N	79.48 W
Blytheswood	214	42.07 N	82.36 W
Blytheville	194	35.55 N	89.55 W
Blytheville Air Force Base ■	194	35.57 N	89.57 W
Blyth Range ⋏	162	26.50 S	129.00 E
Bnei Braq → Bene Beraq	132	32.05 N	34.50 E
Bø, Nor.	24	68.37 N	14.33 E
Bø, Nor.	26	59.25 N	9.04 E
Bo, S.L.	150	7.56 N	11.21 W
Boa	154	10.32 S	28.06 E
Boac	116	13.27 N	121.50 E
Boaco	236	12.28 N	85.40 W
Boaco □[5]	236	12.30 N	85.30 W
Boadilla del Monte	266a	40.24 N	3.53 W
Boa Esperança, Bra.	255	21.05 S	45.34 W
Boa Esperança, Bra.	256	22.48 S	42.34 W
Boa Esperança, Bra.	256	22.24 S	43.05 W
Boa Esperança, Represa ⊜[1]	250	6.50 S	44.00 W
Bo'ai	102	35.10 N	113.04 E
Boali	152	4.48 N	18.07 E
Boalia	126	23.35 N	88.57 E
Boalsburg	214	40.46 N	77.48 W
Boane	156	26.06 S	32.19 E
Boano, Pulau I	164	2.56 S	127.56 E
Boa Nova	255	14.22 S	40.10 W
Bo'ao	110	19.14 N	110.34 E
Boara Pisani	64	45.08 N	11.47 E
Boara Polesine	64	45.07 N	11.48 E

Symbol	English	Deutsch	Español	Français	Português
≃	River	Fluß	Río	Rivière	Rio
≊	Canal	Kanal	Canal	Canal	Canal
∟	Waterfall, Rapids	Wasserfall, Stromschnellen	Cascada, Rápidos	Chute d'eau, Rapides	Cascata, Rápidos
ʯ	Strait	Meeresstraße	Estrecho	Détroit	Estreito
c	Bay, Gulf	Bucht, Golf	Bahía, Golfo	Baie, Golfe	Baía, Golfo
⊜	Lake, Lakes	See, Seen	Lago, Lagos	Lac, Lacs	Lago, Lagos
≡	Swamp	Sumpf	Pantano	Marais	Pântano
⊓	Ice Features, Glacier	Eis- und Gletscherformen	Accidentes Glaciales	Formes glaciaires	Acidentes glaciares
⫪	Other Hydrographic Features	Andere Hydrographische Objekte	Otros Elementos Hidrográficos	Autres données hydrographiques	Outros acidentes hidrográficos
✢	Submarine Features	Untermeerische Objekte	Accidentes Submarinos	Formes de relief sous-marin	Acidentes submarinos
□	Political Unit	Politische Einheit	Unidad Politica	Entité politique	Unidade política
ʊ	Cultural Institution	Kulturelle Institution	Institución Cultural	Institution culturelle	Instituição cultural
⊥	Historical Site	Historische Stätte	Sitio Histórico	Site historique	Sitio histórico
♦	Recreational Site	Erholungs- und Ferienort	Sitio de Recreo	Centre de loisirs	Area de Lazer
⊠	Airport	Flughafen	Aeropuerto	Aéroport	Aeroporto
■	Military Installation	Militäranlage	Instalación Militar	Installation militaire	Instalação militar
◆	Miscellaneous	Verschiedenes	Misceláneo	Divers	Diversos

Board Camp Mountain ∧ 204 40.42 N 123.43 W
Boardman 214 41.01 N 80.39 W
Boardman ≃ 190 44.46 N 85.38 W
Boarhills 46 56.19 N 2.42 W
Boario Terme 64 45.54 N 10.10 E
Boat Basin 182 49.29 N 126.25 W
Boat Channel ⊔ 212 44.10 N 76.31 W
Boath 46 57.44 N 4.23 W
Boat Lake ⊜ 212 44.44 N 81.13 W
Boatman 166 27.16 S 146.55 E
Boat of Garten 46 57.20 N 3.44 W
Boa Viagem 250 5.07 S 39.44 W
Boa Vista, Bra. 246 2.49 N 60.40 W
Boa Vista, Bra. 256 21.25 S 45.35 W
Boa Vista I 150a 16.05 N 22.50 W
Boa Vista, Morro ∧² 287a 22.53 S 43.06 W
Boavita 246 6.20 N 72.35 W
Boawai 115b 8.46 S 121.10 E
Boayan Island I 116 10.34 N 119.09 E
Boaz 194 34.12 N 86.09 W
Boba 115b 8.57 S 121.04 E
Bobai 102 22.12 N 109.52 E
Bobbau 54 51.41 N 12.16 E
Bobbili 122 18.34 N 83.22 E
Bobbing 260 51.21 N 0.43 E
Bobbingworth 260 51.44 N 0.13 E
Bobbin Head 274a 33.39 S 151.08 E
Bobbio 62 44.46 N 9.23 E
Bobbio Pellice 62 44.48 N 7.07 E
Bobbys Run ≃ 285 39.58 N 74.48 W
Bobcaygeon 212 44.33 N 78.33 W
Bobenheim-Roxheim 56 49.35 N 8.21 E
Bobigny 50 48.54 N 2.27 E
Böbingen, Dtsch. 56 48.49 N 9.54 E
Bobingen, Dtsch. 58 48.16 N 10.50 E
Bobitz 54 53.47 N 11.20 E
Bob Lake ⊜ 212 44.55 N 78.47 W
Böblingen 56 48.41 N 9.01 E
Boblo Island Amusement Park ♦ 281 42.06 N 83.07 W
Bobo Dioulasso 150 11.12 N 4.18 W
Boboiob, gora ∧ 85 40.52 N 70.21 E
Bobo Island I 164 9.08 S 143.14 E
Bobolice 30 53.57 N 16.36 E
Bobonaza ≃ 246 2.36 S 76.38 W
Bobonong 156 21.58 S 28.17 E
Bobos ≃ 234 20.15 N 96.47 W
Bobotsari 115a 7.18 S 109.22 E
Bobr 76 54.20 N 29.16 E
Bobr ≃, Bela. 76 54.03 N 28.51 E
Bóbr ≃, Pol. 30 52.04 N 15.04 E
Bobrik ≃ 76 52.08 N 26.46 E
Bobrikovo 83 47.56 N 39.13 E
Bobrinec 78 48.03 N 32.09 E
Bobrka 78 49.38 N 24.18 E
Bobrov 78 51.06 N 40.02 E
Bobrovica 78 50.44 N 31.22 E
Bobrujsk 76 53.09 N 29.14 E
Bobs Creek ≃ 219 38.57 N 90.42 W
Bobs Lake ⊜ 212 44.40 N 76.35 W
Bobtown 188 39.45 N 79.58 W
Bobuk 140 11.30 N 34.05 E
Bobures 246 9.15 N 71.11 W
Boby, Pic ∧ 157b 22.12 S 46.55 E
Boca ◆⁸ 288 34.38 S 58.21 W
Bôca, Cachoeira da ⌊ 250 5.27 S 54.24 W
Boca Brava, Isla I 236 8.13 N 82.16 W
Boca Chica 240m 17.59 N 66.32 W
Boca Chica Key I 220 24.34 N 81.42 W
Bôca da Mata 250 9.41 S 36.11 W
Boca del Monte 236 8.21 N 82.07 W
Boca del Río 234 19.06 N 96.06 W
Boca del Rosario 258 34.26 S 57.17 W
Boca de Pozo 246 11.00 N 64.23 W
Boca de Quadra ⊔ 182 55.08 N 130.50 W
Boca do Acre 248 8.45 S 67.23 W
Bôca do Jari 250 1.07 S 51.58 W
Bocage, Cap > 175f 21.12 S 165.35 E
Boca Grande 220 26.44 N 82.15 W
Boca Grande Channel ⊔ 220 24.34 N 82.03 W
Boca Grande Key I 220 24.32 N 82.00 W
Bocaina ≃ 256 22.40 S 45.00 W
Bocaina, Parque Nacional de ♦ 256 23.00 S 44.15 W
Bocaina, Serra da ∧∧ 256 22.43 S 44.40 W
Bocaina de Minas 256 22.10 S 44.24 W
Bocaiúva 255 17.07 S 43.49 W
Bocanda 150 7.04 N 4.30 W
Bocanegra 286d 12.01 S 77.07 W
Bocaranga 152 6.59 N 15.39 E
Boca Raton 220 26.21 N 80.05 W
Boca Reservoir ⊜¹ 226 39.24 N 120.06 W
Bocas del Toro 236 9.20 N 82.15 W
Bocas del Toro □⁴ 236 8.50 N 82.10 W
Bocas del Toro, Archipiélago de II 236 9.20 N 82.10 W
Bocaue 116 14.48 N 120.55 E
Bocay 236 14.19 N 85.10 W
Bocay ≃ 236 14.20 N 85.10 W
Boccaleone 66 44.39 N 11.48 E
Boccea ◆⁸ 267a 41.58 N 12.19 E
Bocchigliero 68 39.25 N 16.45 E
Boccon 64 45.19 N 11.39 E
Bocconi 64 44.01 N 11.46 E
Bočejkovo 76 55.01 N 29.09 E
Bochan 88 53.09 N 103.48 E
Bochil 234 16.59 N 92.55 W
Böch Mören 86 49.40 N 90.20 E
Bochnia 30 49.58 N 20.26 E
Bocholt, Bel. 56 51.10 N 5.35 E
Bocholt, Dtsch. 52 51.50 N 6.36 E
Bocholtz 56 50.49 N 6.00 E
Bochov 54 50.06 N 13.02 E
Bochum, Dtsch. 56 51.28 N 7.13 E
Bochum, Dtsch. 263 51.28 N 7.13 E
Bochum, S. Afr. 156 23.17 S 29.07 E
Bockel 52 53.12 N 9.17 E
Böckel ◆⁸ 263 51.13 N 7.12 E
Bockenem 52 52.00 N 10.07 E
Bockhorn 52 53.23 N 8.01 E
Böckstein 64 47.05 N 13.07 E
Bockum ◆⁸, Dtsch. 263 51.21 N 6.38 E
Bockum ◆⁸, Dtsch. 263 51.20 N 6.44 E
Bockum-Hövel 52 51.42 N 7.46 E
Bocognano 36 42.05 N 9.03 E
Bocón, Caño ≃ 246 3.42 N 67.53 W
Boconó 246 9.15 N 70.16 W
Bocq ≃ 56 50.20 N 4.53 E
Bocşa 38 45.23 N 21.47 E
Boczów 54 52.19 N 14.58 E
Boda, Centraf. 152 4.19 N 17.28 E
Böda, Sve. 26 57.15 N 17.03 E
Boda, Sve. 26 61.01 N 15.13 E
Bodafors 26 57.30 N 14.42 E
Boda Glasbruk 26 56.44 N 15.40 E
Bodāi 272b 22.48 N 88.29 E
Bodajbo 88 57.51 N 114.10 E
Bodalangi 152 3.14 N 22.14 E
Bodalla 166 36.05 S 150.03 E
Bodallin 162 31.22 S 118.52 E
Bodåsgruvan 40 60.25 N 16.26 E
Bodcau Creek ≃ 194 33.01 N 93.31 W
Boddam, Scot., U.K. 46 57.28 N 1.47 W
Boddam, Scot., U.K. 46a 59.55 N 1.17 W
Boddington 168a 32.48 S 116.28 E
Bode 198 42.52 N 94.17 W
Bode ≃ 54 51.50 N 11.46 E
Bodega Bay ⊂ 204 38.15 N 123.00 W
Bodegraven 52 52.05 N 4.45 E
Bodélé ◆¹ 146 16.30 N 16.30 E
Bodelschwingh ◆⁸ 263 51.33 N 7.22 E
Boden 26 65.50 N 21.42 E
Bodenburg 52 52.01 N 10.01 E
Bodenfelde 52 51.38 N 9.33 E
Boden → Fleres 64 46.58 N 11.21 E
Bodenheim 56 49.56 N 8.18 E
Bodenmais 60 49.04 N 13.06 E
Bodensee (Lake Constance) ⊜ 58 47.35 N 9.25 E
Bodenteich 54 52.50 N 10.41 E
Bodenwerder 52 51.59 N 9.31 E
Bodenwies ∧ 61 47.45 N 14.34 E
Bodenwöhr 60 49.16 N 12.19 E
Boderg, Lough ⊜ 48 53.52 N 7.58 W
Bode Sadu 150 9.00 N 4.47 E
Bodhan 122 18.40 N 77.54 E
Bodh Gaya 124 24.42 N 84.59 E
Bodiam 42 51.00 N 0.33 E
Bodināyakkanūr 122 10.01 N 77.21 E
Bodine, Mount ∧ 182 55.37 N 125.49 W
Bodjoki 152 2.59 N 22.18 E
Bodjokola 152 3.54 N 20.17 E
Bodmin 42 50.29 N 4.43 W
Bodmin Moor ◆³ 42 50.33 N 4.33 W
Bodø 24 67.17 N 14.23 E
Bodocó 250 7.47 S 39.55 W
Bodoquena, Serra da ∧∧¹ 248 21.00 S 56.50 W
Bodoukpa 152 5.43 N 17.36 E
Bodri ≃ 115a 6.52 S 110.10 E
Bodrog ≃ 30 48.07 N 21.25 E
Bodrum 130 37.02 N 27.26 E
Bodstedt 54 54.22 N 12.37 E
Bo Duc 110 11.58 N 106.48 E
Bodzentyn 30 50.56 N 20.57 E
Boè, Piz ∧ 64 46.31 N 11.48 E
Boëge 58 46.13 N 6.25 E
Boekelo 52 52.13 N 6.47 E
Boele ◆⁸ 263 51.24 N 7.28 E
Boémbé 152 2.54 S 15.39 E
Boende 152 0.13 S 20.52 E
Bœng Lvea 110 12.36 N 105.34 E
Boeni 157a 12.55 S 45.06 E
Boën-sur-Lignon 62 45.44 N 3.59 E
Boeo, Capo > 70 37.48 N 12.25 E
Boerboonfontein 158 33.43 S 20.32 E
Boerne 196 29.47 N 98.43 W
Boeslunde 41 55.18 N 11.17 E
Boesmanland □⁵ 156 19.30 S 20.00 E
Boesmans ≃, S. Afr. 158 28.46 S 30.09 E
Boesmans ≃, S. Afr. 158 33.42 S 26.39 E
Boesmansriviermond 158 33.42 S 26.39 E
Boetsap 158 27.59 S 24.30 E
Boeuf ≃ 194 31.52 N 91.47 W
Boeuf Creek ≃ 219 38.36 N 91.09 W
Boffa 150 10.10 N 14.02 W
Boffalora 266b 45.28 N 8.50 E
Boffzen 52 51.45 N 9.23 E
Bofoku 152 0.57 S 20.53 E
Bofors 40 59.20 N 14.32 E
Bofosso 150 8.40 N 9.42 W
Bōfu → Hōfu 96 34.03 N 131.34 E
Boga 154 1.03 N 29.56 E
Bogachiel ≃ 224 47.55 N 124.28 W
Bogadjim 164 5.25 S 145.45 E
Bogal, Lagh ≃ 154 0.45 N 40.50 E
Bogale 110 16.17 N 95.24 E
Bogalusa 194 30.47 N 89.50 W
Bogan ≃ 166 29.57 S 146.21 E
Bogandé 150 12.59 N 0.08 W
Bog and Vly Meadows ≡ 276 40.56 N 74.19 W
Bogan Gate 166 33.07 S 147.48 E
Bogangolo 152 5.34 N 18.15 E
Bogantungan 166 23.39 S 147.18 E
Bogart, Mount ∧ 182 50.55 N 115.14 W
Bogastow Brook ≃ 283 42.12 N 71.22 W
Bogata 196 33.28 N 95.13 W
Bogataja Černeščina 78 48.59 N 35.35 E
Bogatiščevo-Jepišino 82 54.47 N 38.25 E
Bogatoje 80 53.04 N 51.24 E
Bogatyje Saby 80 56.01 N 50.27 E
Bogatynia 54 50.53 N 15.00 E
Bogatyr' 80 53.25 N 50.02 E
Bogatyrevo 80 50.22 N 48.46 E
Boğazkale 130 40.02 N 34.37 E
Boğazkaya 130 41.27 N 35.54 E
Boğazköy ◆⁸ 267b 41.11 N 28.46 E
Boğazköy ≃ 267b 41.10 N 28.49 E
Boğazlıyan 130 39.12 N 35.15 E
Bogbonga 152 1.35 N 19.25 E
Bogcang ≃ 120 31.56 N 87.24 E
Bogd 102 45.11 N 100.43 E
Bogdanovič 86 56.47 N 62.01 E
Bogdanovka, Ross. 80 52.42 N 50.46 E
Bogdanovka, Ross. 80 52.10 N 52.37 E
Bogda Shan ∧∧ 90 43.30 N 89.45 E
Bogdo Ula ∧ 86 43.50 N 88.20 E
Bogel 56 50.11 N 7.48 E
Bogembaj 86 52.29 N 72.20 E
Bogen 60 48.55 N 12.43 E
Bogense 41 55.34 N 10.06 E
Boger City 192 35.29 N 81.12 W
Boges 56 50.11 N 7.48 E
Bogess Creek ≃ 282 37.18 N 122.19 W
Boget 80 49.40 N 47.59 E
Boggabilla 166 28.37 S 150.21 E
Boggabri 166 30.42 S 150.02 E
Boggeragh Mountains ∧∧ 48 52.03 N 8.55 W
Boggola, Mount ∧ 162 23.48 S 117.40 E
Boggs Run ≃ 279b 40.32 N 80.14 W
Boggstown 218 39.34 N 85.55 W
Boggy Creek ≃ 222 31.07 N 95.46 W
Boggy Peak ∧ 240c 17.03 N 61.51 W
Bogia 164 4.15 S 144.55 E
Bogie Lake ⊜ 281 42.37 N 83.31 W
Bogilima 152 3.34 N 19.16 E
Bogliasco 62 44.23 N 9.04 E
Bognanco Fonti 58 46.07 N 8.12 E
Bognes 24 68.10 N 16.00 E
Bognor Regis 42 50.47 N 0.41 W
Bogny-sur-Meuse 56 49.51 N 4.46 E
Bogo, Cam. 146 10.44 N 14.36 E
Bogo, Pil. 116 11.03 N 124.00 E
Bogø I 41 54.56 N 12.04 E
Bogo Bay ⊂ 116 11.05 N 124.01 E
Bogoduchov 78 50.10 N 35.30 E
Bogol Manyo 144 4.31 N 41.32 E
Bogol'ubovo, Ross. 76 55.32 N 32.57 E
Bogol'ubovo, Ross. 80 56.13 N 40.31 E
Bogomila 38 41.36 N 21.28 E
Bogong, Mount ∧ 166 36.45 S 147.18 E
Bogong Peaks ∧∧ 171b 35.34 S 148.28 E
Bogor 115a 6.35 S 106.47 E
Bogoria, Lake ⊜ 154 0.15 N 36.06 E
Bogoro 154 1.24 N 30.17 E
Bogorodčany 78 48.48 N 24.32 E
Bogorodick 76 53.46 N 38.08 E
Bogorodickoje 80 46.20 N 41.10 E
Bogorodičnoje 83 49.01 N 37.30 E
Bogorodsk, Ross. 24 62.16 N 52.28 E
Bogorodsk, Ross. 80 56.06 N 43.31 E
Bogorodskoje, Ross. 80 57.51 N 50.45 E
Bogorodskoje, Ross. 80 46.20 N 43.53 E
Bogorodskoje, Ross. 82 55.02 N 38.29 E
Bogorodskoje, Ross. 82 55.26 N 36.14 E
Bogorodskoje, Ross. 89 52.22 N 140.30 E
Bogorodskoje ◆⁸ 265b 55.49 N 37.44 E
Bogoso 150 5.34 N 2.01 W
Bogosskij chrebet ∧∧ 84 42.15 N 46.05 E
Bogota 276 40.52 N 74.01 W
Bogotá → Santa Fe de Bogotá 246 4.36 N 74.05 W
Bogotol 86 56.12 N 89.33 E
Bogou 150 10.39 N 0.11 E
Bogovarovo 24 58.59 N 47.01 E
Bogra 124 24.51 N 89.22 E
Bograd 86 54.13 N 90.51 E
Bogrie Hill ∧² 44 55.08 N 3.55 W
Bogučany 88 58.23 N 97.29 E
Bogučar 78 49.57 N 40.33 E
Bogučar ≃ 78 49.57 N 40.39 E
Bogué 150 16.35 N 14.16 W
Bogue Chitto 194 31.26 N 90.27 W
Bogue Chitto ≃ 194 30.35 N 89.49 W
Bogue Chitto Creek ≃ 194 32.10 N 87.14 W
Bogue Phalia ≃ 194 33.15 N 90.44 W
Bogues Bay ⊂ 208 37.52 N 75.29 W
Böğürtlen 130 37.10 N 38.04 E
Boguševsk 76 54.51 N 30.13 E
Boguslav 78 49.33 N 30.53 E
Bogustan 85 41.41 N 70.05 E
Bo Hai (Gulf of Chihli) ⊂ 98 38.30 N 120.00 E
Bohai Haixia ⊔ 98 38.15 N 121.00 E
Bohain-en-Vermandois 50 49.59 N 3.27 E
Bohai Wan ⊂ 98 38.40 N 118.20 E
Bohan 56 49.52 N 4.53 E
Bohannon 208 37.24 N 76.22 W
Böheimkirchen 61 48.12 N 15.46 E
Bohemia 210 40.46 N 73.06 W
Bohemia ≃ 208 39.29 N 75.55 W
Bohemia → Čechy □⁹ 30 49.50 N 14.00 E
Bohemia Downs 162 18.53 S 126.14 E
Bohemian Forest ∧∧ 30 49.15 N 12.45 E
Bohetai 104 42.01 N 123.13 E
Bohicon 150 7.12 N 2.04 E
Bohin 144 11.44 N 51.15 E
Bohinjska Bistrica 36 46.17 N 13.57 E
Böhlen 54 51.12 N 12.23 E
Böhlitz-Ehrenberg ◆⁸ 54 51.21 N 12.17 E
Böhme ≃ 52 52.46 N 9.28 E
Böhmen → Čechy □⁹ 30 49.50 N 14.00 E
Böhmenkirch 56 48.41 N 9.55 E
Böhmerwald → Bohemian Forest ∧∧ 30 49.15 N 12.45 E
Bohmte 52 52.22 N 8.19 E
Bohners Lake 216 42.37 N 88.17 W
Böhnsdorf ◆⁸ 264a 52.24 N 13.33 E
Bohodou 150 9.46 N 9.04 W
Bohol 144 5.45 N 46.09 E
Bohol □⁴ 116 9.50 N 124.10 E
Bohol I 116 9.50 N 124.10 E
Bohol Sea ⩦² 116 9.10 N 124.25 E
Bohon 116 18.30 N 120.35 E
Bohongou 150 12.30 N 0.42 E
Bohorg 152 6.23 N 15.37 E
Bohorok 114 3.30 N 98.12 E
Bohsdorf 54 51.38 N 14.32 E
Bohuslän □⁹ 26 58.15 N 11.50 E
Bohušovice nad Ohří 54 50.29 N 14.07 E
Bohutín 60 49.40 N 13.55 E
Boi 150 9.34 N 9.27 E
Boi, Ponta do > 256 23.58 S 45.15 W
Boiaçu 246 0.27 S 61.46 W
Boiano 66 41.29 N 14.29 E
Boiceville 210 41.59 N 74.15 W
Boiestown 186 46.27 N 66.25 W
Boigu Island I 164 9.16 S 142.12 E
Boila 154 16.10 S 39.50 E
Boiling Springs, N.C., U.S. 192 35.30 N 81.37 W
Boiling Springs, Pa., U.S. 208 40.08 N 77.07 W
Boim 250 2.49 S 55.10 W
Boinville-en-Mantois 261 48.56 N 1.46 E
Boinvilliers 261 48.55 N 1.40 E
Boipeba, Ilha de I 255 13.39 S 38.55 W
Boiro 34 42.39 N 8.54 W
Bois, Lac des ⊜ 180 66.40 N 125.15 W
Bois, Lac des → Woods, Lake of the ⊜ 184 49.15 N 94.45 W
Bois, Rio dos ≃ 255 18.35 S 50.02 W
Bois Blanc Island I 190 45.45 N 84.28 W
Boisbriand 275a 45.37 N 73.51 W
Bois Brule ≃ 190 46.45 N 91.37 W
Boischâtel 206 46.54 N 71.08 W
Bois-Colombes 261 48.55 N 2.16 E
Boisdale, Loch ⊂ 46 57.08 N 7.19 W
Bois d'Arc Creek ≃ 196 33.50 N 95.50 W
Bois-d'Arcy 261 48.48 N 2.01 E
Bois-des-Filion 206 45.40 N 73.45 W
Bois de Sioux ≃ 198 46.16 N 96.36 W
Boise 202 43.36 N 116.12 W
Boise ≃ 202 43.49 N 117.01 W
Boise, Middle Fork ≃ 202 43.42 N 115.38 W
Boise, North Fork ≃ 202 43.42 N 115.38 W
Boise, South Fork ≃ 202 43.36 N 115.51 W
Boise City 196 36.43 N 102.30 W
Boisemont 261 49.01 N 2.00 E
Bois-Guillaume 50 49.28 N 1.08 E
Bois-le-Roi 50 48.28 N 2.42 E
Boissettes 261 48.31 N 2.37 E
Boissevain 184 49.14 N 100.03 W
Boissise-la-Bertrand 261 48.32 N 2.35 E
Boissy-l'Aillerie 261 49.05 N 2.02 E
Boissy-Saint-Léger 50 48.45 N 2.31 E
Boissy-sous-Saint-Yon 261 48.34 N 2.13 E
Boistfort Peak ∧ 224 46.29 N 123.12 W
Boitzenburg 54 53.15 N 13.37 E
Boizenburg 54 53.22 N 10.43 E
Boja 115a 7.06 S 110.16 E
Bojadła 30 51.57 N 15.50 E
Bojarka 78 50.19 N 30.19 E
Bojarkino 82 54.57 N 38.31 E
Bojarsk 88 56.19 N 106.04 E
Bojayá ≃ 246 6.35 N 76.54 W
Bojeador, Cape > 116 18.30 N 120.34 E
Bojelebung 116 6.31 N 122.11 E
Bojevo 78 51.24 N 39.19 E
Boji Plain ≚ 154 1.30 N 39.45 E
Bojizhang 98 41.49 N 117.46 E
Bojnūrd 128 37.28 N 57.19 E
Bojonegoro 115a 7.09 S 111.52 E
Boju 150 7.25 N 7.52 E
Boju Ega 150 7.24 N 8.04 E
B'ojuk-Kirs, gora ∧ 84 39.41 N 46.44 E
Bojuru 252 31.38 S 51.26 W
Bokad 272c 18.53 N 72.58 E
Bokada 152 4.08 N 19.23 E
Bokal 168a 33.29 S 116.54 E
Bokala, Zaïre 152 3.07 S 17.02 E
Bokala, Zaïre 152 2.03 N 18.59 E
Bokani 150 9.26 N 5.13 E
Bokāro Steel City 124 23.45 N 86.07 E
Bokatola 152 0.38 S 18.46 E
Bokchito 196 34.01 N 96.08 W
Boké 150 10.56 N 14.18 W
Bokeelia 220 26.42 N 82.09 W
Bokel 52 53.23 N 8.46 E
Bokela 152 1.08 S 21.56 E
Bokes Creek ≃ 188 40.19 N 83.10 W
Bokfontein 158 32.48 S 19.16 E
Bokhara 158 27.57 S 20.30 E
Bokhara ≃ 166 29.55 S 146.42 E
Boki 146 8.48 N 13.32 E
Bokino 80 52.38 N 41.26 E
Bokkol ∧ 154 1.50 N 37.02 E
Bok Koū 110 10.37 N 104.03 E
Böklund 41 54.36 N 9.34 E
Boknafjorden ⊂² 26 59.10 N 5.35 E
Boko, Congo 152 4.47 S 14.38 E
Boko, Kaz. 86 49.05 N 81.38 E
Bokod 116 16.30 N 120.50 E
Bokode 152 3.58 N 19.29 E
Bokolako 150 13.36 N 12.33 W
Bokonbajevskoje 85 42.07 N 77.00 E
Bokondji 152 2.22 N 18.42 E
Bokondo 152 0.15 N 22.32 E
Bokong 112 9.58 S 124.04 E
Bokoro 146 12.23 N 17.03 E
Boko Songo 152 4.26 S 13.37 E
Bokota 152 0.51 S 22.18 E
Bokote 152 0.05 S 20.08 E
Bokovo-Antratsit → Antracit 83 48.06 N 39.06 E
Bokovo Platovo 83 48.07 N 39.01 E
Bokovskaja 80 49.15 N 41.49 E
Bokpunt > 158 33.34 S 18.19 E
Bokpyin 110 11.16 N 98.46 E
Boksburg 158 26.12 S 28.14 E
Boksburg □⁵ 273d 26.12 S 28.14 E
Boksburg-Noord 273d 26.12 S 28.15 E
Boksburg South 273d 26.14 S 28.15 E
Boksburg-West 273d 26.13 S 28.14 E
Boksitogorsk 76 59.28 N 33.51 E
Bokungu 152 0.41 S 22.19 E
Bol, Hrv. 36 43.16 N 16.40 E
Bol, Tchad 146 13.28 N 14.43 E
Bolaang Mongondow 112 0.56 N 124.10 E
Bolama, Gui.-B. 150 11.35 N 15.28 W
Bolama, Zaïre 152 1.57 N 22.58 E
Bolaman 130 41.03 N 37.37 E
Bolān ≃ 120 28.38 N 67.42 E
Bolanda, Jabal ∧ 140 7.44 N 25.28 E
Bol'andkiik ≃ 85 39.11 N 72.17 E
Bolangum 166 36.46 S 142.53 E
Bolaños 234 21.41 N 103.47 W
Bolaños ≃ 234 21.14 N 104.08 W
Bolaños de Calatrava 34 38.54 N 3.40 W
Bolān Pass)(120 29.45 N 67.35 E
Bolans 240c 17.02 N 61.53 W
Bolay I 152 4.20 N 17.21 E
Bolayır 130 40.31 N 26.45 E
Bolbec 50 49.34 N 0.29 E
Bolčary 86 59.49 N 68.48 E
Bolchov 76 53.27 N 36.01 E
Bolchuny 80 47.59 N 46.25 E
Bolda ≃ 80 46.10 N 48.14 E
Boldasevo 80 54.43 N 45.33 E
Boldekow 54 53.43 N 13.35 E
Bolderslev 41 54.59 N 9.18 E
Bold Heath 262 53.24 N 2.42 W
Boldon 44 54.57 N 1.27 W
Bol'džuan 85 38.19 N 69.40 E
Bole, Ghana 150 9.02 N 2.29 W
Bole, Zhg. 86 44.53 N 82.05 E
Bolechov 78 49.04 N 23.52 E
Boleko 152 1.31 S 19.53 E
Bolero 154 10.59 S 33.45 E
Boles 194 34.46 N 94.02 W
Bolesławiec 30 51.16 N 15.34 E
Boleszkowice 30 52.44 N 14.36 E
Boletice nad Labem 54 50.45 N 14.13 E
Boley 196 35.29 N 96.29 W
Bolgarčaj ≃ 84 39.28 N 48.36 E
Bolgart 162 31.16 S 116.30 E
Bolgatanga 150 10.46 N 0.52 W
Bolgrad 78 45.41 N 28.36 E
Boli, Sūd. 140 6.01 N 28.43 E
Boli, Tchad 146 10.50 N 18.43 E
Boli, Zhg. 89 45.46 N 130.31 E
Bolia 152 1.36 S 18.23 E
Boliden 26 64.52 N 20.23 E
Boligee 194 32.45 N 88.01 W
Boligeqiu 104 42.14 N 121.40 E
Bolíkov 61 49.02 N 15.22 E
Bolinao 116 16.23 N 119.54 E
Bolinas 226 37.54 N 122.42 W
Boling 222 29.15 N 95.56 W
Bolingbrook 216 41.41 N 88.04 W
Bolinger Creek ≃ 282 37.47 N 122.00 W
Bolingo 152 3.30 S 21.43 E
Bolishan 89 43.50 N 123.31 E
Bolivar, Austl. 168b 34.46 S 138.36 E
Bolívar, Col. 246 5.50 N 76.01 W
Bolívar, Col. 246 1.50 N 76.58 W
Bolívar, Col. 246 4.21 N 76.10 W
Bolívar, Perú 248 7.18 S 77.48 W
Bolivar, Mo., U.S. 194 37.36 N 93.24 W
Bolivar, N.Y., U.S. 210 42.04 N 78.10 W
Bolivar, Oh., U.S. 214 40.39 N 81.27 W
Bolivar, Pa., U.S. 214 40.23 N 79.09 W
Bolivar, Tn., U.S. 194 35.15 N 88.59 W
Bolívar □³ 246 6.20 N 63.30 W
Bolívar □⁴ 246 1.35 S 79.00 W
Bolívar □⁵ 246 9.00 N 74.40 W
Bolívar, Cerro ∧ 246 7.28 N 63.25 W
Bolívar, Pico ∧ 246 8.30 N 71.02 W
Bolivar Peninsula >¹ 196 29.27 N 94.39 W
Bolivar Run 214 41.59 N 78.39 W
Bolivia □¹, S.A. 242 17.00 S 65.00 W
Bolivia □¹, S.A. 248 17.00 S 65.00 W
Bolivie → Bolivia □¹ 248 17.00 S 65.00 W
Bolivien → Bolivia □¹ 248 17.00 S 65.00 W
Boljarovo 38 42.09 N 26.49 E
Boljoon 116 9.38 N 123.29 E
Bolkar Dağları ∧∧ 130 37.15 N 34.20 E
Bölkenbusch 263 51.21 N 7.06 E
Boll 56 48.38 N 9.37 E
Bolladello 266b 45.41 N 8.50 E
Bollate 62 45.33 N 9.07 E
Böllberg ∧² 263 51.23 N 7.19 E
Bollendorf 56 49.51 N 6.22 E
Bollène 62 44.17 N 4.45 E
Bollensdorf 264a 52.31 N 13.43 E
Bolles Canal ≊ 220 26.38 N 80.34 W
Bolles Harbor 216 41.51 N 83.24 W
Bollin ≃ 44 53.23 N 2.28 W
Bolling Air Force Base ■ 284c 38.51 N 77.02 W
Bollington, Eng., U.K. 44 53.18 N 2.06 W
Bollington, Eng., U.K. 262 53.22 N 2.25 W
Bollnäs 26 61.21 N 16.25 E
Bollon 166 28.05 S 147.15 E
Bollstabruk 26 63.00 N 17.39 E
Bollstanäs 40 59.30 N 17.56 E
Bollullos par del Condado 34 37.20 N 6.32 W
Bollwerk 263 51.10 N 7.35 E
Bolmen ⊜ 26 56.55 N 13.40 E
Bolnisi 84 41.28 N 44.33 E
Bolo 144 8.50 N 39.22 E
Bolobo 152 2.10 S 16.14 E
Bolochovo 82 54.05 N 37.50 E
Bologna 64 44.29 N 11.20 E
Bologna □⁴ 64 44.28 N 11.26 E
Bologne 58 48.12 N 5.08 E
Bologne → Bologna 64 44.29 N 11.20 E
Bolognesi 248 6.35 S 73.10 W
Bolognetta 70 37.58 N 13.27 E
Bolognola 66 42.59 N 13.14 E
Bologoje 76 57.54 N 34.02 E
Bologovo 76 56.54 N 31.42 E
Bololo 152 3.50 S 21.08 E
Bolomba 152 0.29 N 19.12 E
Bolombo 152 3.59 S 21.22 E
Bolombo ≃ 152 1.32 N 21.14 E
Bolon' 89 49.55 N 136.07 E
Bolon', ozero ⊜ 89 49.51 N 136.22 E
Bolonchén de Rejón 232 20.00 N 89.49 W
Bolondo 152 0.27 N 20.01 E
Bolondrón 240p 22.46 N 81.27 W
Bolong ≃ 170 34.15 S 149.36 E
Bolonia → Bologna 64 44.29 N 11.20 E
Bolótana 71 40.20 N 8.57 E
Bolotino 78 47.42 N 27.21 E
Bolotnoje 86 55.41 N 84.23 E
Boloto 82 54.10 N 36.20 E
Bolotovskoje 86 58.33 N 62.28 E
Bolovens, Plateau des ∧∧¹ 110 15.20 N 106.20 E
Bolpur 126 23.40 N 87.43 E
Bol'šaja 76 59.36 N 41.48 E
Bol'šaja ≃ 80 48.36 N 41.00 E
Bol'šaja Atn'a 80 56.15 N 49.27 E
Bol'šaja Balachn'a ≃ 74 73.37 N 107.05 E
Bol'šaja Ber'ostovica 76 53.11 N 24.01 E
Bol'šaja Blagoveščenka 78 46.51 N 34.03 E
Bol'šaja Brembola 82 56.45 N 38.55 E
Bol'šaja Bukon' 86 48.53 N 82.43 E
Bol'šaja Čalykla ≃ 80 51.51 N 49.34 E
Bol'šaja Černigovka 80 52.07 N 50.52 E
Bol'šaja Chalan' 78 50.56 N 37.26 E

ENGLISH

Name Page Lat.°′ Long.°′

Bol'šaja Cheta ≃ 74 69.33 N 84.15 E
Bol'šaja Chobda ≃ 86 50.56 N 54.34 E
Bol'šaja Chundala 76 60.04 N 34.18 E
Bol'šaja Čuja ≃ 88 58.56 N 112.13 E
Bol'šaja Čurakovka 86 53.03 N 64.20 E
Bol'šaja Damba 80 46.57 N 51.47 E
Bol'šaja Dmitrijevka 80 51.21 N 45.15 E
Bol'šaja Dora 76 59.05 N 37.38 E
Bol'šaja Džalga 80 45.59 N 42.41 E
Bol'šaja Glušica 80 52.24 N 50.28 E
Bol'šaja Ižora 76 59.56 N 29.34 E
Bol'šaja Ižorka ≃ 265a 59.48 N 30.36 E
Bol'šaja Kakša ≃ 80 57.53 N 45.28 E
Bol'šaja Kamenka 80 53.39 N 50.31 E
Bol'šaja Kamenka ≃ 83 48.22 N 40.04 E
Bol'šaja Kandala 80 54.32 N 49.22 E
Bol'šaja Kaskara 86 57.11 N 65.58 E
Bol'šaja Ket' 86 57.39 N 91.45 E
Bol'šaja Kinel' ≃ 80 53.14 N 50.30 E
Bol'šaja Kirsanovka 83 47.40 N 38.54 E
Bol'šaja Kokšaga ≃ 80 56.08 N 47.47 E
Bol'šaja Konkudera ≃ 88 57.34 N 112.30 E
Bol'šaja Kugul'ta ≃ 80 45.45 N 41.57 E
Bol'šaja Kuonamka ≃ 74 70.45 N 113.24 E
Bol'šaja Laba ≃ 84 44.16 N 40.53 E
Bol'šaja Lipovica 80 52.33 N 41.20 E
Bol'šaja Martynovka 80 47.17 N 41.40 E
Bol'šaja Mošanica 76 53.58 N 29.37 E
Bol'šaja Murta 86 56.55 N 93.07 E
Bol'šaja Neva ≃ 265a 59.58 N 30.13 E
Bol'šaja Norja 80 56.41 N 52.43 E
Bol'šaja Ochta ◆⁸ 265a 59.57 N 30.25 E
Bol'šaja Ol'šanka 80 51.32 N 44.17 E
Bol'šaja Orlovka 80 47.20 N 41.16 E
Bol'šaja Osinovaja ≃ 180 66.30 N 174.00 E
Bol'šaja Pas'ma 80 58.38 N 43.53 E
Bol'šaja Rečka 88 51.57 N 104.44 E
Bol'šaja Ržaksa 80 52.08 N 42.13 E
Bol'šaja Sestra ≃ 82 56.16 N 35.56 E
Bol'šaja Smedva ≃ 82 54.50 N 38.34 E
Bol'šaja Sosnova 80 57.40 N 54.36 E
Bol'šaja Talovaja 78 46.58 N 40.37 E
Bol'šaja Tarel' 88 53.45 N 106.40 E
Bol'šaja Tavoložka 80 52.07 N 49.04 E
Bol'šaja Uča 80 56.37 N 52.05 E
Bol'šaja Usa 86 56.44 N 55.06 E
Bol'šaja Ussurka ≃ 89 45.57 N 133.42 E
Bol'šaja Višera 76 58.55 N 32.08 E
Bol'šaja Vladimirovka 86 50.53 N 79.31 E
Bol'šaja Vys' ≃ 78 48.45 N 30.54 E
Bolsa Knolls 226 36.44 N 121.38 W
Bol'šakovo, Ross. 76 54.53 N 21.40 E
Bol'šakovo, Ross. 265b 55.54 N 37.17 E
Bol'šečernigovka 83 48.57 N 39.25 E
Bol'šekrepinskaja 83 47.36 N 39.22 E
Bol'šelig 24 62.07 N 52.25 E
Bolsena 66 42.39 N 11.59 E
Bolsena, Lago di ⊜ 66 42.36 N 11.56 E
Bol'šenarymskoje 86 49.16 N 84.32 E
Bol'šerečje 86 56.06 N 74.38 E
Bol'šereck 74 52.25 N 156.24 E
Bol'šetroickoje 78 50.33 N 37.17 E
Bol'šeustjikinskoje 86 55.57 N 58.16 E
Bol'ševik, Bela. 76 52.34 N 30.53 E
Bol'ševik, Ross. 74 62.44 N 147.30 E
Bol'ševik, Ross. 265a 59.49 N 30.30 E
Bol'ševik, ostrov I 74 78.40 N 102.30 E
Bol'šezemel'skaja Tundra ◆¹ 72 67.30 N 56.00 E
Bolshoi Theatre ⊍ 265b 55.46 N 37.37 E
Bol'šije Algaši 80 55.22 N 46.29 E
Bol'šije Avt'uki 78 52.04 N 29.32 E
Bol'šije Belyniči 82 54.38 N 38.50 E
Bol'šije Berezniki 80 54.11 N 45.58 E
Bol'šije Gorki, Ross. 82 56.28 N 35.51 E
Bol'šije Gorki, Ross. 265a 59.42 N 29.51 E
Bol'šije Kajbicy 80 55.25 N 48.13 E
Bol'šije Kizi, ozero ⊜ 89 51.38 N 140.20 E
Bol'šije Kl'uči 80 55.59 N 48.47 E
Bol'šije Kl'učišči 80 54.08 N 48.14 E
Bol'šije Liachvi ≃ 84 41.58 N 44.06 E
Bol'šije Michalicyny 80 58.29 N 48.14 E
Bol'šije Ozerki 80 52.36 N 46.33 E
Bol'šije Pom'aly 80 56.42 N 46.40 E
Bol'šije Ručji 82 56.36 N 36.58 E
Bol'šije Saly 83 47.24 N 39.41 E
Bol'šije Tarchany 80 54.42 N 48.34 E
Bol'šije Ugli 88 57.47 N 112.51 E
Bol'šije Uki 86 56.57 N 72.37 E
Bol'šije Ždanovy 80 58.40 N 49.05 E
Bol'šoj 80 50.13 N 43.26 E
Bol'šoj An'uj ≃ 74 68.30 N 160.49 E
Bol'šoj Ažbulat, ozero ⊜ 86 53.17 N 77.25 E
Bol'šoj Begičev, ostrov I 74 74.20 N 112.30 E
Bol'šoj Bogdo, gora ∧² 80 48.08 N 46.52 E
Bol'šoj Boktybaj, gora ∧ 86 48.27 N 58.30 E
Bol'šoj Čeremšan ≃ 80 54.11 N 49.39 E
Bol'šoj Civil' ≃ 80 55.54 N 47.28 E
Bol'šoje, ozero ⊜ 265a 60.04 N 30.39 E
Bol'šoje Aksu 86 43.20 N 79.35 E
Bol'šoje Aleksejevskoje 82 55.14 N 38.12 E
Bol'šoje Boldino 80 54.59 N 45.19 E
Bol'šoje Bun'kovo 82 55.51 N 38.37 E
Bol'šoje Goloustnoje 88 52.01 N 105.25 E
Bol'šoje Gorodišče, Ross. 76 57.17 N 30.31 E
Bol'šoje Gorodišče, Ross. 78 50.37 N 37.06 E
Bol'šoje Ignatovo 80 55.02 N 45.34 E
Bol'šoje Jarovoje, ozero ⊜ 86 52.53 N 78.36 E
Bol'šoje Jašaltinskoje, ozero ⊜ 80 46.17 N 42.27 E
Bol'šoje Kibejevo 80 56.55 N 47.05 E
Bol'šoje Korovino 82 54.30 N 39.02 E
Bol'šoje Manuškino 265a 59.53 N 30.49 E
Bol'šoje Michajlovskoje 82 56.47 N 38.04 E
Bol'šoje Mikuškino 80 53.56 N 51.42 E
Bol'šoje Muraškino 80 55.47 N 44.46 E
Bol'šoje Nagatkino 80 54.31 N 47.58 E
Bol'šoje Nurkejevo 80 55.22 N 52.40 E
Bol'šoje Nyrsy 80 55.44 N 50.19 E
Bol'šoje Ogar'ovo 76 53.33 N 37.43 E
Bol'šoje Pikino 80 56.25 N 44.22 E
Bol'šoje Polpino 76 53.14 N 34.30 E
Bol'šoje Ramenje 76 58.21 N 36.40 E
Bol'šoje Rybuškino 80 55.25 N 45.48 E
Bol'šoje Sazonovo 80 58.06 N 53.21 E
Bol'šoje Selo 76 57.43 N 38.56 E
Bol'šoje Šem'akino 80 55.03 N 48.38 E
Bol'šoje Soldatskoje 78 51.21 N 35.31 E
Bol'šoje Sudačje 80 50.49 N 44.05 E
Bol'šoje Topol'noje, ozero ⊜ 86 53.20 N 78.00 E
Bol'šoje Uro 88 53.32 N 109.48 E
Bol'šoje Zagorje 76 57.51 N 28.57 E
Bol'šoje Žokovo 82 54.35 N 38.57 E
Bol'šoj Gašun ≃ 80 47.22 N 42.43 E
Bol'šoj Ginaldag, gora ∧ 84 40.20 N 45.57 E
Bol'šoj Golec, gora ∧ 88 51.52 N 119.24 E
Bol'šoj Irgiz ≃ 80 52.01 N 47.24 E
Bol'šoj Jenisej (Bij-Chem) ≃ 88 51.43 N 94.26 E
Bol'šoj Jugan ≃ 86 60.55 N 73.40 E
Bol'šoj Kamen' 89 43.06 N 132.21 E
Bol'šoj Kandarat' 80 54.25 N 47.00 E
Bol'šoj Kanym, gora ∧ 86 54.13 N 88.20 E
Bol'šoj Karagaj 86 57.57 N 70.15 E
Bol'šoj Karaman ≃ 80 51.40 N 46.38 E

DEUTSCH

Name Seite Breite°′ Länge°′ E = Ost

Bol'šoj Kavkaz (Caucasus) ∧∧ 84 42.30 N 45.00 E
Bol'šoj Ketmen' 86 43.27 N 80.24 E
Bol'šoj Kujal'nik ≃ 78 46.46 N 30.36 E
Bol'šoj Kujaš 86 55.50 N 61.06 E
Bol'šoj Kundyš ≃ 80 56.32 N 47.23 E
Bol'šoj Kuvaj 80 54.37 N 47.05 E
Bol'šoj Kymynej, gora ∧ 180 66.34 N 172.32 W
Bol'šoj L'achovskij, ostrov I 74 73.35 N 142.00 E
Bol'šoj Lug 88 52.07 N 104.10 E
Bol'šoj Matačynaj, gora ∧ 180 66.28 N 179.25 W
Bol'šoj Melik 80 51.38 N 43.18 E
Bol'šoj Nesvetaj ≃ 83 47.27 N 39.54 E
Bol'šoj Onguren 88 53.38 N 107.36 E
Bol'šoj Patom ≃ 88 59.15 N 113.56 E
Bol'šoj Pit ≃ 86 59.01 N 91.44 E
Bol'šoj Porog 86 52.35 N 92.18 E
Bol'šoj Šagan 80 50.57 N 51.08 E
Bol'šoj Sajan ∧∧ 88 52.00 N 99.30 E
Bol'šoj Šalym ≃ 86 60.55 N 70.25 E
Bol'šoj Šantar, ostrov I 89 55.00 N 137.42 E
Bol'šoj Šatan, gora ∧ 86 53.41 N 57.36 E
Bol'šoj Simonogont 265a 59.50 N 29.49 E
Bol'šoj Sorokino 86 56.38 N 69.53 E
Bol'šoj Suchodol 83 48.25 N 39.53 E
Bol'šoj Sundyr' 80 56.07 N 46.46 E
Bol'šoj Tal'cy 76 59.13 N 33.00 E
Bol'šoj Tolkaj 80 53.30 N 51.57 E
Bol'šoj T'uters, ostrov I 76 59.51 N 27.13 E
Bol'šoj Uluj 86 56.39 N 90.36 E
Bol'šoj Uran ≃ 80 52.24 N 53.15 E
Bol'šoj Uvat, ozero ⊜ 86 57.35 N 70.30 E
Bol'šoj Uzen' ≃ 80 48.50 N 49.40 E
Bol'šoj Uzigont 265a 59.48 N 29.53 E
Bol'šoj Vjass 80 53.48 N 45.30 E
Bol'šoj Vlasjevo 89 53.24 N 140.55 E
Bol'šoj Zelenčuk ≃ 84 44.36 N 41.56 E
Bol'šovcy 78 49.12 N 24.44 E
Bolsover 44 53.14 N 1.18 W
Bolsward 52 53.03 N 5.31 E
Boltaña 34 42.27 N 0.04 E
Boltigen 58 46.38 N 7.24 E
Boltino 265b 55.58 N 37.41 E
Bolton, On., Can. 212 43.53 N 79.44 W
Bolton, Eng., U.K. 44 53.35 N 2.26 W
Bolton, Ct., U.S. 207 41.46 N 72.26 W
Bolton, Ms., U.S. 194 32.20 N 90.27 W
Bolton, N.C., U.S. 192 34.19 N 78.24 W
Bolton □⁸ 262 53.34 N 2.28 W
Bolton Abbey 44 53.59 N 1.53 W
Bolton Abbey ⊍¹ 44 53.59 N 1.54 W
Bolton Center 207 41.47 N 72.26 W
Bolton Creek ≃ 212 44.58 N 76.23 W
Bolton Lake ⊜ 184 54.16 N 95.47 W
Bolton-le-Sands 44 54.06 N 2.47 W
Bolton upon Dearne 44 53.31 N 1.19 W
Bolton Wanderers Football Ground ♦ 262 53.34 N 2.25 W
Bolu 130 40.44 N 31.37 E
Bolu □⁴ 130 40.40 N 31.30 E
Bölükyazı 130 38.18 N 42.10 E
Boluntay 120 36.34 N 92.38 E
Boluo, Zhg. 100 23.11 N 114.17 E
Boluo, Zhg. 100 24.27 N 113.03 E
Boluochi 98 41.24 N 119.56 E
Boluokeng 100 24.05 N 113.22 E
Bolus Head > 48 51.46 N 10.21 W
Bolva ≃ 76 53.17 N 34.20 E
Bolvadin 130 38.42 N 31.04 E
Bolwarra 166 17.24 S 144.11 E
Bóly 30 45.58 N 18.32 E
Bolyčevo 82 55.46 N 35.43 E
Bolzaneto 62 44.27 N 8.54 E
Bolzano (Bozen) 64 46.31 N 11.22 E
Bolzano □⁴ 64 46.43 N 11.30 E
Boma 152 5.51 S 13.03 E
Bomaderry 170 34.51 S 150.37 E
Bomal 56 50.23 N 5.32 E
Bomandjokou 152 0.34 N 14.23 E
Bomaneh 152 1.18 N 23.47 E
Bomarsund 26 60.13 N 20.15 E
Bomate 152 1.10 S 19.41 E
Bomba 66 42.02 N 14.22 E
Bombakabo 152 3.04 N 19.42 E
Bombala 166 36.54 S 149.14 E
Bombarral 34 39.16 N 9.09 W
Bombat 130 38.08 N 42.14 E
Bombay, India 122 18.58 N 72.50 E
Bombay, India 272c 18.58 N 72.50 E
Bombay, N.Y., U.S. 206 44.56 N 74.34 W
Bombay, University of ⊍² 272c 18.57 N 72.50 E
Bombay Harbour ⊂ 272c 18.57 N 72.53 E
Bomberai, Semenanjung >¹ 164 3.00 S 133.00 E
Bombetoka, Baie de ⊂ 157b 15.50 S 46.17 E
Bombimba 152 0.31 N 19.24 E
Bombo 154 0.35 N 32.32 E
Bombo ≃ 152 3.58 S 15.59 E
Bombo-Kasanji 152 5.54 S 21.51 E
Bomboma 152 2.25 N 18.54 E
Bombo-Makuka 152 5.26 S 16.19 E
Bombombwa 154 1.21 N 25.30 E
Bombon 261 48.34 N 2.52 E
Bomboyo 146 12.01 N 15.28 E
Bom Conselho 250 9.10 S 36.41 W
Bom Despacho 255 19.43 S 45.15 W
Bomdila 120 27.27 N 92.17 E
Bomei 100 22.57 N 115.46 E
Bömenzien 54 52.59 N 11.31 E
Bom Fim do Bom Jesus 256 23.17 S 47.02 W
Bomhus 40 60.41 N 17.13 E
Bomili 154 1.40 N 27.01 E
Bom Jardim, Ilha do I 287a 23.02 S 43.35 W
Bom Jardim de Goiás 255 16.17 S 52.07 W
Bom Jardim de Minas 256 21.57 S 44.11 W
Bom Jesus, Ang. 152 9.09 S 13.34 E
Bom Jesus, Bra. 250 9.04 S 44.22 W
Bom Jesus da Lapa 255 13.15 S 43.25 W
Bom Jesus de Goiás 255 18.12 S 49.44 W
Bom Jesus dos Perdões 256 23.08 S 46.28 W
Bømlafjorden ⊂² 26 59.39 N 5.20 E
Bomlitz 52 52.54 N 9.37 E
Bømlo I 26 59.46 N 5.12 E
Bommerholz 263 51.23 N 7.18 E
Bommern 263 51.25 N 7.20 E
Bomnak 89 54.46 N 128.51 E
Bomokandi ≃ 154 3.39 N 26.08 E
Bomongiri 152 1.57 S 21.13 E
Bomongo 152 1.22 N 18.21 E
Bompata 150 6.38 N 1.04 W
Bompensiere 70 37.28 N 13.47 E
Bompietro 70 37.44 N 14.06 E
Bomputu 152 0.20 S 20.06 E
Bom Repouso 256 22.28 S 46.09 W
Bom Retiro 252 27.48 S 49.31 W
Bom Retiro ◆⁸ 287b 23.32 S 46.38 W
Bom Sucesso, Bra. 248 15.43 S 56.07 W
Bom Sucesso, Bra. 255 23.42 S 51.45 W
Bom Sucesso, Bra. 256 22.17 S 42.49 W
Bom Sucesso, Bra. 287b 23.25 S 46.24 W
Bomu (Mbomou) ≃ 136 4.08 N 22.26 E
Bon, Cap > 36 37.05 N 11.03 E
Bona 40 58.34 N 15.03 E
Bona Bona Island I 164 10.30 S 149.50 E
Bon Accord 158 25.38 S 28.11 E
Bonaduz 58 46.49 N 9.25 E
Bonaero Park 273d 26.07 S 28.16 E
Bonai 114 1.16 N 100.52 E
Bonaigarh 120 21.50 N 84.57 E
Bon Air 208 37.31 N 77.33 W
Bon Aire 214 40.54 N 79.55 W

Symbols in the index entries represent the broad categories identified in the key at the right. Symbols with superior numbers (∧∧¹) identify subcategories (see complete key on page *I · 1).*

Symbole im Register stellen die rechts im Schlüssel erklärten Kategorien dar. Symbole mit hochgestellten Ziffern (∧∧¹) bezeichnen Unterabteilungen einer Kategorie (vgl. vollständiger Schlüssel auf Seite *I · 1).*

Los símbolos incluídos en el texto del índice representan las grandes categorias identificadas con la clave a la derecha. Los símbolos con numeros en su parte superior (∧∧¹) identifican las subcategorías (véase la clave completa en la página *I · 1).*

Les symboles de l'index représentent les catégories indiquées dans la légende à droite. Les symboles suivis d'un indice (∧∧¹) représentent des sous-catégories (voir légende complète à la page *I · 1).*

Os símbolos incluídos no texto do índice representam as grandes categorias identificadas com a chave à direita. Os símbolos com números em sua parte superior (∧∧¹) identificam as subcategorias (veja-se a chave completa à página *I · 1).*

∧ Mountain	Berg	Montaña	Montagne	Montanha
∧∧ Mountains	Gebirge	Montañas	Montagnes	Montanhas
)(Pass	Paß	Paso	Col	Passo
V Valley, Canyon	Tal, Cañon	Valle, Cañón	Vallée, Canyon	Vale, Canhão
≚ Plain	Ebene	Llano	Plaine	Planície
> Cape	Kap	Cabo	Cap	Cabo
I Island	Insel	Isla	Île	Ilha
II Islands	Inseln	Islas	Îles	Ilhas
± Other Topographic Features	Andere Topographische Objekte	Otros Elementos Topográficos	Autres données topographiques	Outros acidentes topográficos

ESPAÑOL

Nombre	Página	Lat. °′	Long. °′ W = Oeste
Bonaire I	241s	12.10 N	68.15 W
Bonampak ⊥	232	16.44 N	91.05 W
Bönan	40	60.44 N	17.18 E
Bonandolok	114	1.47 N	98.48 E
Bonanza, Nic.	236	14.01 N	84.35 W
Bonanza, Or., U.S.	202	42.11 N	121.24 W
Bonanza, Ut,. U.S.	200	40.01 N	109.10 W
Bonanza Peak ∧	224	48.14 N	120.52 W
Bonao	238	18.56 N	70.25 W
Bonaparte	190	40.41 N	91.48 W
Bonaparte ≃	182	50.46 N	121.17 W
Bonaparte, Lake ⊜	212	44.09 N	75.23 W
Bonaparte, Mount ∧	202	48.45 N	119.08 W
Bonaparte Archipelago II	160	14.17 S	125.18 E
Bonaparte Lake ⊜	182	51.16 N	120.35 W
Bonar Bridge	46	57.53 N	4.21 W
Bonarcado	71	40.04 N	8.38 E
Bonasila Dome ∧	180	62.19 N	160.30 W
Bonasse	241r	10.05 N	61.52 W
Bonassola	62	44.11 N	9.35 E
Bonaventure	186	48.03 N	65.29 W
Bonaventure ≃	186	48.02 N	65.28 W
Bonaventure, Île I	186	48.30 N	64.10 W
Bonavista	186	48.39 N	53.07 W
Bonavista, Cape ›	186	48.42 N	53.05 W
Bonavista Bay ⊂	186	48.45 N	53.20 W
Bonawe	46	56.26 N	5.13 W
Bonawon	116	9.08 N	122.55 E
Bonbeach	274b	38.04 S	145.08 E
Bonboillon	58	47.20 N	5.42 E
Bon Bon	162	30.26 S	135.28 E
Bonbonon Point ›	116	9.03 N	123.08 E
Bonchester Bridge	44	55.24 N	2.40 W
Boncourt	58	47.30 N	6.56 E
Boncuk Dağı ∧	130	36.53 N	29.17 E
Bond	194	30.54 N	89.10 W
Bond □[6]	219	38.53 N	89.25 W
Bondari	80	52.57 N	42.04 E
Bondar'ov	83	49.22 N	39.10 E
Bondar'ovka	83	49.23 N	39.37 E
Bondeno	64	44.53 N	11.25 E
Bondi	274a	33.53 S	151.17 E
Bondo, Zaïre	152	1.22 S	23.53 E
Bondo, Zaïre	152	3.49 N	23.40 E
Bondoc Peninsula ›[1]	116	13.30 N	122.30 E
Bondoc Point ›	116	13.10 N	122.36 E
Bondorf	58	48.31 N	8.49 E
Bondoufle	261	48.37 N	2.23 E
Bondoukou	150	8.02 N	2.48 W
Bondowoso	115a	7.55 S	113.49 E
Bondsville	207	42.12 N	72.20 W
Bonduel	190	44.44 N	88.26 W
Bondues	50	50.42 N	3.06 E
Bondy	261	48.54 N	2.28 E
Bondy, Forêt de ♠	261	48.55 N	2.35 E
Bone, Indon.	112	4.46 S	122.52 E
Bone, Indon.	112	5.09 S	122.37 E
Bone, Teluk ⊂	112	4.00 S	120.40 E
Bône → Annaba	148	36.54 N	7.46 E
Bonebone	112	2.36 S	120.33 E
Bon Echo Provincial Park ♠	212	44.52 N	77.15 W
Bonefro	66	41.42 N	14.56 E
Bone Island I	212	44.56 N	79.51 W
Bonelipu	112	4.50 S	123.11 E
Bonelohe	112	5.48 S	120.27 E
Bönen	52	51.36 N	7.44 E
Boneogeh	112	7.16 S	120.48 E
Bonerate, Pulau I	112	7.22 S	121.08 E
Bon Espérance, Cap de → Good Hope, Cape of ›	158	34.24 S	18.30 E
Bo'ness	46	56.01 N	3.37 W
Bonesteel	198	43.04 N	98.56 W
Bonete, Cerro ∧	252	27.51 S	68.47 W
Bonete Chico, Cerro ∧	252	28.01 S	68.45 W
Bonětice	60	49.41 N	12.49 E
Bone → Watampone	112	4.32 S	120.20 E
Bonfield	216	41.09 N	88.03 W
Bonfinópolis de Minas	255	16.28 S	45.59 W
Bonfol	58	47.29 N	7.09 E
Bonga	144	7.17 N	36.15 E
Bongabon	116	15.38 N	121.08 E
Bongabon ≃	116	12.40 N	121.33 E
Bongabong	116	12.45 N	121.29 E
Bongaigaon	124	26.28 N	90.34 E
Bongak	140	7.27 N	33.14 E
Bongandanga	152	1.30 N	21.03 E
Bongao Island I	116	5.01 N	119.46 E
Bongaree	171a	27.05 S	153.10 E
Bonggaw	116	5.02 N	119.46 E
Bongka	112	0.58 S	121.27 E
Bongka ≃	112	0.59 S	121.05 E
Bong Mieu	110	15.25 N	108.24 E
Bongo, Ang.	152	8.48 S	17.49 E
Bongo, Gabon	152	2.10 S	10.12 E
Bongo, Massif des ⩘	146	8.40 N	22.25 E
Bongo I	152	3.01 N	20.06 E
Bongo II	152	1.47 S	17.41 E
Bongo Island I	116	7.20 N	124.02 E
Bongolu	152	2.48 N	22.29 E
Bongon	112	6.35 N	116.52 E
Bongor	146	10.17 N	15.22 E
Bongou ≃	140	6.42 N	22.04 E
Bongouanou	150	6.39 N	4.12 W
Bong Range ⩘	150	6.50 N	10.00 W
Bong Son	110	14.26 N	109.01 E
Bonham	196	33.34 N	96.10 W
Bonheiden	56	51.02 N	4.32 E
Bonhomme, Col du)(	58	48.10 N	7.06 E
Bonhomme, Morne ∧	238	19.05 N	72.18 W
Bonhomme Island I	219	38.42 N	90.36 W
Bonifacio, Fr.	36	41.23 N	9.10 E
Bonifacio, Pil.	116	8.03 N	123.37 E
Bonifacio, Strait of Ц	36	41.20 N	9.15 E
Bonifacio Monument ⊥	269f	14.39 N	120.59 E
Bonifati	68	39.35 N	15.54 E
Bonifati, Capo ›	68	39.35 N	15.52 E
Bonifay	194	30.47 N	85.40 W
Bonifica del Volturno ≚	68	41.01 N	14.00 E
Bonilla Island I	182	53.29 N	130.36 W
Bonin Islands → Ogasawara-guntō II	14	27.00 N	142.10 E
Bonita	194	32.55 N	91.40 W
Bonita, Point ›	282	37.49 N	122.32 W
Bonita Springs	220	26.20 N	81.46 W
Bonito, Bra.	248	21.08 S	56.28 W
Bonito, Bra.	250	8.29 S	35.44 W
Bonito, It.	68	41.06 N	15.00 E
Bonito ≃, Bra.	255	16.31 S	51.23 W
Bonito ≃, Bra.	256	22.12 S	43.02 W
Bonito ≃, Bra.	256	22.09 S	43.40 W
Bonito, Pico ∧	236	15.38 N	86.55 W
Bonito, Rio ≃	200	33.23 N	105.16 W
Bonito de Santa Fé	250	7.19 S	38.31 W
Bonjol	112	0.01 S	100.13 E
Bonkoukou	150	14.01 N	3.13 E
Bon Meade	279b	40.33 N	80.14 W
Bonn	56	50.44 N	7.05 E
Bonnanaro	71	40.32 N	8.45 E
Bonndorf im Schwarzwald	58	47.49 N	8.20 E
Bonneauville	208	39.46 N	77.10 W
Bonne Bay (Woody Point)	186	49.30 N	57.56 W
Bonne Bay ⊂	186	49.33 N	57.55 W
Bonnebosq	50	49.12 N	0.05 E
Bonnechere ≃	190	45.31 N	76.33 W
Bonneia	144	5.41 N	37.45 E
Bonnelles	261	48.37 N	2.02 E
Bonner	202	46.52 N	113.51 W

FRANÇAIS

Nom	Page	Lat. °′	Long. °′ W = Ouest
Bonners Ferry	202	48.41 N	116.18 W
Bonne-sur-Ménoge	58	46.10 N	6.20 E
Bonnet, Lac du ⊜	184	50.22 N	95.55 W
Bonnétable	50	48.11 N	0.26 E
Bonne Terre	194	37.55 N	90.33 W
Bonnet Plume ≃	180	65.55 N	134.58 W
Bonneuil-sur-Marne	261	48.46 N	2.29 E
Bonneval	50	48.11 N	1.24 E
Bonneval-sur-Arc	62	45.22 N	7.03 E
Bonnevaux	58	46.18 N	6.40 E
Bonneville, Fr.	58	46.05 N	6.25 E
Bonneville, Or., U.S.	224	45.38 N	121.57 W
Bonneville Dam ✦[6]	224	45.39 N	121.56 W
Bonneville Peak ∧	202	42.46 N	112.08 W
Bonneville Salt Flats ≚	200	40.45 N	113.52 W
Bonney, Lake ⊜	166	37.48 S	140.22 E
Bonney Lake	224	47.10 N	122.11 W
Bonnie Doone	192	35.05 N	78.57 W
Bonnières	50	49.02 N	1.35 E
Bonnie Rock	162	30.32 S	118.21 E
Bonnieux	62	43.49 N	5.18 E
Bonnievale	158	33.57 S	20.06 E
Bönninghardt	263	51.35 N	6.28 E
Bönninghardt ⩘[2]	263	51.34 N	6.27 E
Bonnots Mill	219	38.34 N	91.58 W
Bonny	150	4.27 N	7.10 E
Bonny ≃[1]	150	4.20 N	7.10 E
Bonnyrigg, Austl.	274a	33.54 S	150.54 E
Bonnyrigg, Scot., U.K.	46	55.52 N	3.08 W
Bonny-sur-Loire	50	47.34 N	2.50 E
Bonnyville	182	54.16 N	110.44 W
Bono, It.	71	40.25 N	9.02 E
Bono, Ar., U.S.	194	35.54 N	90.48 W
Bono, Oh., U.S.	214	41.38 N	83.16 W
Bonoi	164	1.51 S	137.48 E
Bonorva	71	40.25 N	8.46 E
Bonoua	150	5.16 N	3.36 W
Bonpas Creek ≃	194	38.16 N	87.59 W
Bonriki	174t	1.23 N	173.09 E
Bonriki Airport ⊠	174t	1.22 N	173.10 E
Bons	58	46.16 N	6.23 E
Bonsall	228	33.17 N	117.13 W
Bonsari	272c	19.04 N	73.02 E
Bon Secour	194	30.18 N	87.43 W
Bon-Secours, Bel.	50	50.30 N	3.36 E
Bonsecours, Fr.	50	49.26 N	1.08 E
Bonshaw	186	46.12 N	63.21 W
Bonsucesso ✦[8]	287a	22.52 S	43.15 W
Bontang	112	0.08 N	117.30 E
Bontberg ∧	158	32.21 S	21.04 E
Bontebok National Park ♠	158	34.07 S	20.23 E
Bonthe	150	7.32 N	12.30 W
Bontoc	116	17.05 N	120.58 E
Bon Wier	194	30.44 N	93.39 W
Bonyhád	30	46.19 N	18.32 E
Boo, Kepulauan II	164	1.12 S	129.24 E
Booby Point ›	284b	39.17 N	76.23 W
Boock	54	53.29 N	14.15 E
Boody	219	39.46 N	89.03 W
Boogardie	162	28.02 S	117.47 E
Booischot	56	51.03 N	4.46 E
Bookabie	162	31.50 S	132.41 E
Bookaloo	166	31.55 S	137.22 E
Book Cliffs ≗[4]	200	39.20 N	109.00 W
Booke	152	2.33 S	22.00 E
Booker	196	36.27 N	100.32 W
Booker T. Washington National Monument ♠	192	37.01 N	79.45 W
Bookwalter	218	39.42 N	83.32 W
Boola	150	8.22 N	8.43 W
Boolaloo	162	22.35 S	115.51 E
Booleroo Centre	166	32.53 S	138.21 E
Booligal	166	33.52 S	144.53 E
Boologooro	162	24.21 S	114.02 E
Boom	50	51.05 N	4.22 E
Boomarra	166	19.33 S	140.20 E
Boomer	188	38.09 N	81.17 W
Boomi	166	28.44 S	149.35 E
Boomrivier	158	29.33 S	20.27 E
Boonah	171a	28.00 S	152.41 E
Böön cagaan nuur ⊜	102	45.35 N	99.09 E
Boone, Ia., U.S.	190	42.03 N	93.52 W
Boone, N.C., U.S.	192	36.13 N	81.40 W
Boone □[6], Il., U.S.	216	42.15 N	88.50 W
Boone □[6], In., U.S.	218	40.03 N	86.28 W
Boone □[6], Ky., U.S.	218	38.57 N	84.45 W
Boone □[6], Mo., U.S.	219	38.55 N	92.15 W
Boone ≃	190	42.19 N	93.56 W
Boone Draw V	196	33.51 N	103.42 W
Boone Grove	216	41.21 N	87.08 W
Boone Lake ⊜[1]	192	36.25 N	82.25 W
Boone Reservoir ⊜[1]	279b	40.15 N	80.08 W
Boones Mill	192	37.06 N	79.57 W
Booneville, Ar., U.S.	194	35.08 N	93.55 W
Booneville, Ky., U.S.	192	37.28 N	83.40 W
Booneville, Ms., U.S.	194	34.39 N	88.34 W
Boon Point ›	240c	17.10 N	61.50 W
Boons	158	25.59 S	27.13 E
Boonsboro	208	39.30 N	77.39 W
Boonsville	222	33.04 N	97.52 W
Boonton	210	40.54 N	74.24 W
Boonton Reservoir ⊜[1]	276	40.53 N	74.25 W
Boonville, Ca., U.S.	204	39.00 N	123.21 W
Boonville, In., U.S.	194	38.02 N	87.16 W
Boonville, Mo., U.S.	194	38.58 N	92.44 W
Boonville, N.Y., U.S.	212	43.29 N	75.20 W
Boopi ≃	248	15.41 S	67.15 W
Boorabbin National Park ♠	162	31.13 S	120.10 E
Boorama	144	9.56 N	43.11 E
Boorindal	166	30.21 S	146.08 E
Booroorban	166	34.56 S	144.46 E
Boorowa	166	34.26 S	148.43 E
Boos	50	49.23 N	1.12 E
Boosaaso	144	11.17 N	49.11 E
Boossen	54	52.22 N	14.29 E
Boot	44	54.24 N	3.17 W
Bootahnie Indian Reserve ✦[4]	182	50.24 N	121.31 W
Booth	194	32.30 N	86.34 W
Booth, Lac ⊜	190	46.45 N	78.34 W
Boothbay Harbor	188	43.51 N	69.37 W
Boothby, Cape ›	9	66.34 S	57.16 E
Booth Corner	285	39.51 N	75.29 W
Boothia, Gulf of ⊂	176	71.00 N	91.00 W
Boothia Peninsula ›[1]	176	70.30 N	95.00 W
Boothstown	262	53.30 N	2.25 W
Boothville	194	29.20 N	89.25 W
Booth Wood Reservoir ⊜[1]	262	53.38 N	1.58 W
Boothwyn	285	39.49 N	75.26 W
Bootle	44	53.28 N	3.00 W
Boot Reefs ✢[2]	164	10.00 S	144.40 E
Booué	152	0.06 S	11.56 E
Booysens ✦[8]	273d	26.14 S	28.01 E
Booze Creek ≃	284c	38.59 N	77.07 W
Bopfingen	56	48.51 N	10.21 E
Bo Phloi	110	14.19 N	99.31 E
Bophuthatswana □[1], Afr.	138	26.00 S	25.35 E
Bophuthatswana □[1], Afr.	156	26.00 S	25.35 E
Boping	98	36.36 N	116.07 E
Boping Ling ⩘	100	25.00 N	117.00 E
Bopo	150	7.37 N	7.52 E
Bopolu	150	7.03 N	10.32 W
Boppard	56	50.14 N	7.35 E
Boqér, Har ∧	132	30.52 N	34.43 E
Boqueirão, Ilha do I	287a	22.46 S	43.09 W
Boqueirão, Serra do ⩘[2]	250	11.30 S	43.45 W
Boquerón	236	8.30 N	82.34 W
Boquerón □[5]	252	21.30 S	60.00 W

PORTUGUÊS

Nome	Página	Lat. °′	Long. °′ W = Oeste
Boquerón, Bahía de ⊂	240m	18.01 N	67.12 W
Boquerón, Túnel ✦[5]	286c	10.34 N	67.00 W
Boquet	279b	40.23 N	79.36 W
Boquilla, Presa de la ⊜[1]	232	27.30 N	105.30 W
Boquilla del Refugio	196	25.33 N	102.28 W
Boquillas del Carmen	232	29.17 N	102.53 W
Boquim	250	11.09 S	37.37 W
Bor, Česko.	60	49.43 N	12.47 E
Bor, Jugo.	38	44.05 N	22.07 E
Bor, Ross.	24	63.00 N	42.38 E
Bor, Ross.	80	56.22 N	44.05 E
Bor, Sūd.	140	6.12 N	31.33 E
Bor, Tür.	130	37.54 N	34.34 E
Bor, Lak ≃	154	1.18 N	40.40 E
Bora-Bora I	14	16.30 S	151.45 W
Borabu	110	16.02 N	103.07 E
Boracay Island I	116	11.59 N	121.55 E
Boraha, Nosy I	157b	16.50 S	49.55 E
Borah Peak ∧	202	44.08 N	113.48 W
Boraldaj ≃	85	42.33 N	69.07 E
Borale	144	9.10 N	42.35 E
Borambola	171b	35.12 S	147.41 E
Borang, Tanjung ›	164	5.16 S	133.07 E
Borås	26	57.43 N	12.55 E
Borāzjān	128	29.16 N	51.12 E
Borba, Bra.	246	4.24 S	59.35 W
Borba, Port.	34	38.48 N	7.27 W
Borbeck ✦[8]	263	51.29 N	6.57 E
Borbera ≃	62	44.42 N	8.52 E
Borca di Cadore	64	46.26 N	12.13 E
Borcea, Braţul ≃	38	44.40 N	27.53 E
Borchen	52	51.39 N	8.44 E
Borçka	130	41.22 N	41.40 E
Borculo, Ned.	52	52.07 N	6.31 E
Borculo, Mi., U.S.	216	42.53 N	86.01 W
Borda, Cape ›	166	35.45 S	136.34 E
Borda da Mata	256	22.16 S	46.10 W
Bordeaux, Fr.	32	44.50 N	0.34 W
Bordeaux, S. Afr.	273d	26.06 S	28.01 E
Bordeaux ✦[8]	275a	45.33 N	73.41 W
Bordeaux Mountain ∧[2]	240m	18.20 N	64.44 W
Borden, Austl.	162	34.05 S	118.16 E
Borden, Sk., Can.	184	52.25 N	107.13 W
Borden, Eng., U.K.	260	51.20 N	0.42 E
Borden, In., U.S.	218	38.28 N	85.57 W
Borden, Canadian Forces Base ■	212	44.17 N	79.55 W
Borden Lake ⊜	190	47.50 N	83.18 W
Borden Peninsula ›[1]	176	73.00 N	83.00 W
Bordentown	208	40.08 N	74.42 W
Border Mountains ⩘	164	3.40 S	141.05 E
Borders □[4]	46	55.37 N	3.15 W
Bordertown	166	36.19 S	140.47 E
Bordesholm	30	54.11 N	10.01 E
Borðeyri	24a	65.15 N	21.10 W
Bordighera	62	43.46 N	7.39 E
Bording	41	56.12 N	9.17 E
Bording Kirkeby	41	56.10 N	9.15 E
Bordino, Fiume di ≃	70	37.53 N	12.37 E
Bordj Bou Arreridj	148	36.04 N	4.46 E
Bordj Bounaama	34	35.51 N	1.36 E
Bordj Menaïel	148	36.44 N	3.43 E
Bordj Omar Idriss	148	28.09 N	6.43 E
Bordj Sidi Toui	148	32.44 N	11.22 E
Bordunskij	85	42.40 N	75.37 E
Bore, It.	62	44.43 N	9.47 E
Bore, Ityo.	144	4.40 N	37.40 E
Boré, Mali	150	15.08 N	3.29 W
Boreda	144	6.32 N	37.48 E
Boreham	260	51.46 N	0.33 E
Borehamwood	42	51.40 N	0.16 W
Borel Hill ∧	282	37.19 N	122.12 W
Borello	66	44.03 N	12.11 E
Borensberg	26	58.34 N	15.17 E
Boreray I	46	57.42 N	7.18 W
Boretto	64	44.54 N	10.33 E
Borgallo, Galleria del ✦[5]	62	44.25 N	9.53 E
Borgå → Porvoo	26	60.24 N	25.40 E
Borgarnes	24a	64.35 N	21.53 W
Borgata Costiera	70	37.43 N	12.39 E
Børgefjell Nasjonalpark ♠	24	65.10 N	14.00 E
Borgentreich	52	51.34 N	9.14 E
Börger, Dtsch.	52	52.54 N	7.32 E
Borger, Ned.	52	52.55 N	6.46 E
Borger, Tx., U.S.	196	35.40 N	101.23 W
Borgerhout	50	51.13 N	4.26 E
Borgetto	70	38.03 N	13.08 E
Borggård	40	58.44 N	15.32 E
Borghetto	64	45.41 N	10.56 E
Borghetto di Vara	62	44.13 N	9.43 E
Borghetto Lodigiano	62	45.13 N	9.30 E
Borghetto Santo Spirito	62	44.06 N	8.14 E
Borgholm	26	56.53 N	16.39 E
Borghorst	52	52.07 N	7.23 E
Borgia	68	38.49 N	16.30 E
Borgio-Verezzi	62	44.10 N	8.18 E
Borgloon	56	50.48 N	5.20 E
Borg Mountain ∧	9	72.42 S	3.30 W
Borgne, Lake ⊂	194	30.05 N	89.40 W
Borgnesse, Pointe ›	240e	14.27 N	60.54 W
Borgo	64	46.03 N	11.27 E
Borgo alla Collina	66	43.45 N	11.43 E
Borgo a Mozzano	66	43.59 N	10.33 E
Borgo Cerreto	66	42.49 N	12.54 E
Borgo d'Ale	62	45.21 N	8.03 E
Borgoforte	64	45.03 N	10.45 E
Borgofranco d'Ivrea	62	45.30 N	7.51 E
Borgolavezzaro	62	45.19 N	8.42 E
Borgomanero	62	45.42 N	8.28 E
Borgomaro	62	43.58 N	7.56 E
Borgonovo Val Tidone	62	45.01 N	9.26 E
Borgo Pace	66	43.39 N	12.17 E
Borgoricco	64	45.32 N	11.58 E
Borgorose	66	42.11 N	13.13 E
Borgo San Dalmazzo	62	44.20 N	7.30 E
Borgo San Giacomo	64	45.21 N	9.58 E
Borgo San Lorenzo	66	43.57 N	11.23 E
Borgosatollo	64	45.28 N	10.14 E
Borgosesia	62	45.43 N	8.16 E
Borgo Ticino	266b	45.41 N	8.36 E
Borgo Tossignano	66	44.16 N	11.35 E
Borgou □[5]	150	10.30 N	2.50 E
Borgo Val di Taro	62	44.29 N	9.46 E
Borgo Vercelli	62	45.21 N	8.28 E
Borgsdorf	54	52.42 N	13.14 E
Borgsdorf, Forst ✦[3]	264a	52.42 N	13.19 E
Borgu Game Reserve ✦[4]	150	10.15 N	4.10 E
Borgund ⊍[1]	26	61.03 N	7.49 E
Bori	150	4.42 N	7.21 E
Borig Delijn els ✦[2]	88	50.00 N	94.00 E
Borikhan	110	18.33 N	103.43 E
Borilovo	76	53.22 N	35.58 E
Borinage □[9]	50	50.30 N	4.00 E
Boring, Md., U.S.	208	39.31 N	76.49 W
Boring, Or., U.S.	224	45.25 N	122.22 W
Borinskoje	76	52.27 N	39.22 E
Borislav	78	49.16 N	23.27 E
Borisoglebsk	80	51.23 N	42.06 E
Borisoglebskij	80	57.16 N	39.09 E
Borisov, Bela.	76	54.15 N	28.30 E
Borisov, Ukr.	78	50.11 N	26.31 E
Borisovka, Ross.	76	52.50 N	39.58 E
Borisovka, Ross.	78	50.36 N	36.01 E
Borisovo	82	55.25 N	36.03 E
Borisovo ✦[8]	265b	55.38 N	37.45 E
Borisovo-Sudskoje	76	59.54 N	36.01 E
Borisovskaja	76	60.12 N	39.48 E
Borispol'	78	50.21 N	30.57 E
Borja, Esp.	34	41.50 N	1.32 W
Borja, Perú	246	4.26 S	77.33 W
Bork	52	51.40 N	7.30 E

Borken, Dtsch.	52	51.51 N	6.51 E
Borken, Dtsch.	56	51.03 N	9.16 E
Borkenwirthe	52	51.53 N	6.50 E
Borki, Ross.	86	59.08 N	82.15 E
Borki, Ukr.	78	49.42 N	36.02 E
Borkoldoj, chrebet ⩘	85	41.25 N	77.50 E
Børkop	41	55.39 N	9.39 E
Borkou ✦[1]	146	18.15 N	18.50 E
Borkou-Ennedi-Tibesti □[5]	146	18.15 N	18.50 E
Borkoviči	76	55.40 N	28.20 E
Borkum	52	53.35 N	6.40 E
Borkum I	52	53.35 N	6.41 E
Borland Manor	279b	40.15 N	80.09 W
Borlänge	40	60.29 N	15.25 E
Borle ✦[8]	272c	19.02 N	72.55 E
Borlu	130	38.44 N	28.27 E
Bormes-les-Mimosas	62	43.09 N	6.20 E
Bormida ≃	62	44.23 N	8.13 E
Bormida di Millesimo ≃	62	44.40 N	8.20 E
Bormida di Spigno ≃	62	44.40 N	8.20 E
Bormio	64	46.28 N	10.22 E
Born, Dtsch.	54	52.22 N	11.28 E
Born, Dtsch.	54	54.23 N	12.32 E
Borna, Dtsch.	54	51.19 N	13.11 E
Borna, Dtsch.	54	51.07 N	12.30 E
Borndiep ⊂	52	53.25 N	5.35 E
Borne	52	52.18 N	6.45 E
Borne ≃	62	45.03 N	3.54 E
Borneo (Kalimantan) I	112	0.30 N	114.00 E
Bornheim	56	50.46 N	6.59 E
Bornholm I	26	55.10 N	15.00 E
Bornholte	52	51.52 N	8.29 E
Bornhöved	54	54.04 N	10.16 E
Börnicke, Dtsch.	54	52.41 N	12.56 E
Börnicke, Dtsch.	264a	52.40 N	13.38 E
Börnig ✦[8]	263	51.33 N	7.16 E
Bornim ✦[8]	264a	52.26 N	13.00 E
Borno	64	45.56 N	10.12 E
Bornos, Embalse de ⊜[1]	34	36.50 N	5.30 W
Bornsdorf	54	51.46 N	13.41 E
Bornstedt ✦[8]	264a	52.25 N	13.02 E
Bornu □[3]	146	12.00 N	12.45 E
Boro ≃	140	8.52 N	26.11 E
Borobudur ⊥	115a	7.36 S	110.12 E
Borod'anka	78	50.39 N	29.56 E
Borodarou	150	10.59 N	2.53 E
Borodino, Ross.	82	55.32 N	35.50 E
Borodino, Ross.	82	56.53 N	37.00 E
Borodino, Ross.	88	55.55 N	94.55 E
Borodino, Ukr.	78	46.18 N	29.13 E
Borodulicha	86	50.43 N	80.55 E
Borodulino	80	57.59 N	54.20 E
Borogoncy	74	62.42 N	131.08 E
Borohoro Shan ⩘	86	44.06 N	83.10 E
Boroko	112	0.55 N	123.16 E
Boroml'a	78	50.37 N	34.59 E
Boromo	150	11.45 N	2.56 W
Boron, Mali	150	14.01 N	7.30 W
Boron, Ca., U.S.	228	34.59 N	117.38 W
Boronga Islands II	110	19.58 N	93.06 E
Borongan	116	11.37 N	125.26 E
Boronia	274b	37.52 S	145.17 E
Boron'ki	76	53.09 N	32.08 E
Borore	71	40.13 N	8.48 E
Borotou	150	8.44 N	7.30 W
Boroughbridge	44	54.06 N	1.23 W
Borough Green	42	51.17 N	0.19 E
Borough Park ✦[8]	276	40.38 N	74.00 W
Borovaja, Ukr.	78	50.12 N	30.07 E
Borovaja, Ukr.	83	49.24 N	37.40 E
Borovaja ≃	83	48.58 N	38.24 E
Borovan	38	43.26 N	23.45 E
Borovany	61	48.54 N	14.39 E
Boroviči	76	58.24 N	33.55 E
Borovik ≃	83	49.11 N	38.33 E
Borovka ≃	80	52.54 N	52.00 E
Borovl'anka	86	52.38 N	84.29 E
Borovoj	24	59.55 N	51.38 E
Borovoje, Kaz.	86	53.04 N	70.19 E
Borovoje, Ukr.	78	51.06 N	27.13 E
Borovsk	82	55.12 N	36.30 E
Borovskaja	24	60.46 N	41.06 E
Borovskij	86	57.03 N	65.44 E
Borovskoj	86	53.48 N	64.12 E
Borovskoje, Ross.	86	52.39 N	82.08 E
Borovskoje, Ukr.	83	48.51 N	38.34 E
Borovucha	76	55.36 N	28.37 E
Borovy	60	49.33 N	13.18 E
Borozdino	82	54.07 N	38.22 E
Borraan	144	10.14 N	48.44 E
Borrachudo ≃	255	18.12 S	45.16 W
Borrazópolis	255	23.56 S	51.36 W
Borrby	26	55.27 N	14.10 E
Borre	41	55.00 N	12.28 E
Borre ⊥	26	59.23 N	10.28 E
Borreby	41	55.14 N	11.19 E
Borriana, Esp.	34	39.53 N	0.05 W
Borriana, It.	62	45.30 N	8.02 E
Borris	48	52.35 N	6.55 W
Borrisokane	48	52.59 N	8.07 W
Borrisoleigh	48	52.45 N	7.57 W
Borroloola	164	16.04 S	136.17 E
Borroloola Aboriginal Reserve ✦[4]	164	16.00 S	136.15 E
Borrowdale	44	54.31 N	3.10 W
Börry	52	52.01 N	9.27 E
Borş	38	47.07 N	21.49 E
Borşa, Rom.	38	46.56 N	23.40 E
Borşa, Rom.	38	47.39 N	24.40 E
Borsad	120	22.25 N	72.54 E
Borsano	266b	45.35 N	8.51 E
Borschemich	263	51.04 N	6.25 E
Borščov	78	48.48 N	26.03 E
Borščovo	82	56.30 N	36.51 E
Borščovočnyj chrebet ⩘	88	52.00 N	117.00 E
Borsdorf	54	51.21 N	12.32 E
Borskoje	80	53.02 N	51.43 E
Borsod-Abaúj-Zemplén □[6]	30	48.15 N	21.00 E
Börssum	54	52.04 N	10.35 E
Borstendorf	54	50.46 N	13.10 E
Bortala ≃	86	44.50 N	82.45 E
Borth, Dtsch.	52	51.36 N	6.33 E
Borth, Wales, U.K.	42	52.29 N	4.03 W
Borthwick Water ≃	44	55.24 N	2.50 W
Bortigali	71	40.17 N	8.50 E
Bortigiadas	71	40.53 N	9.02 E
Bort-les-Orgues, Fr.	32	45.24 N	2.30 E
Bort-les-Orgues, Fr.	32	43.49 N	2.53 E
Bortniči	78	50.22 N	30.41 E
Borto	88	53.35 N	111.53 E
Bortondale	285	39.54 N	79.24 W
Boru	164	10.14 S	148.50 E
Boruca	236	9.00 N	83.20 W
Borūjen	128	31.59 N	51.18 E
Borūjerd	128	33.54 N	48.46 E
Bor Ul Shan ⩘	102	41.20 N	98.55 E
Borve	46	56.58 N	7.32 W
Borz'a	88	50.24 N	116.31 E
Borz'a ≃	88	50.38 N	115.38 E
Borzna	78	51.15 N	32.25 E
Boržomi	84	41.50 N	43.21 E
Boržomskij zapovednik ♠	84	41.50 N	43.10 E
Borzonasca	62	44.25 N	9.23 E
Borzyszkowy	30	54.03 N	17.22 E
Bosa	71	40.18 N	8.30 E
Bosaga	86	47.55 N	72.58 E
Bosambi	152	2.24 N	22.39 E
Bosanska Dubica	36	45.11 N	16.49 E
Bosanska Gradiška	36	45.09 N	17.15 E
Bosanska Krupa	36	44.53 N	16.10 E
Bosanski Novi	36	45.03 N	16.23 E
Bosanski Petrovac	36	44.33 N	16.22 E
Bosanski Šamac	38	45.03 N	18.28 E
Bosansko Grahovo	36	44.11 N	16.22 E

Bősárkány	61	47.41 N	17.14 E
Bosau	54	54.06 N	10.25 E
Bosavi, Mount ∧	164	6.35 S	142.50 E
Boscastle	42	50.41 N	4.42 W
Bosco, It.	66	44.53 N	12.14 E
Bosco, It.	66	43.08 N	12.28 E
Boscobel	190	43.08 N	90.42 W
Bosco Chiesanuova	64	45.37 N	11.02 E
Bosco Marengo	62	44.49 N	8.41 E
Boscoreale	68	40.46 N	14.28 E
Bose	102	23.54 N	106.37 E
Bösel	52	53.00 N	7.58 E
Bosencheve, Parque Nacional ♠	234	19.36 N	100.15 W
Bosenge	152	1.18 N	22.19 E
Bósforo, Estrecho del → İstanbul Boğazı Ц	130	41.06 N	29.04 E
Bosham	42	50.49 N	0.52 W
Boshan	98	36.29 N	117.50 E
Boshkung Lake ⊜	212	45.04 N	78.44 W
Boshoek	156	25.30 S	27.09 E
Boshof	158	28.34 S	25.04 E
Boshrūyeh	128	33.53 N	57.26 E
Bosilegrad	38	42.29 N	22.28 E
Bösingen	58	48.14 N	8.34 E
Bosjökloster	41	55.54 N	13.31 E
Boškajnar	85	38.13 N	68.51 E
Boskoop	52	52.04 N	4.35 E
Boskop	158	26.34 S	27.08 E
Boskop ∧	273d	26.05 S	27.57 E
Boskovice	30	49.29 N	16.40 E
Boskuil	158	27.23 S	25.51 E
Bosman	164	4.10 S	144.40 E
Bosna	272b	22.37 N	88.30 E
Bosna ≃	36	45.04 N	18.29 E
Bosna-Hercegovina → Bosnia and Herzegovina □[1]	36	44.15 N	17.30 E
Bošn'akovo	89	49.38 N	142.10 E
Bosnia and Herzegovina □[1], Europe	22	44.15 N	17.30 E
Bosnia and Herzegovina (Bosna-Hercegovina) □[1], Europe	36	44.15 N	17.30 E
Bosnik	164	1.10 S	136.14 E
Boso	272b	22.58 N	88.08 E
Bosobolo	152	4.11 N	19.54 E
Boso-Djafo	152	1.06 N	19.14 E
Bosogo	85	41.09 N	76.25 E
Bōsō-hantō ›[1]	94	35.18 N	140.10 E
Bōsō-kyūryō ⩘[2]	268	35.08 N	139.56 E
Bososama	152	4.18 N	20.00 E
Bösperde	263	51.28 N	7.46 E
Bosphore, Détroit du → İstanbul Boğazı Ц	130	41.06 N	29.04 E
Bosporus → İstanbul Boğazı Ц	130	41.06 N	29.04 E
Bosque □[6]	222	31.55 N	97.35 W
Bosque, Paseo del ♠	288	34.55 S	57.56 W
Bosque Farms	200	34.53 N	106.40 W
Bosques	288	34.49 S	58.14 W
Bosques Petrificados, Monumento Natural ♠	254	47.39 S	68.07 W
Bosqueville	222	31.38 N	97.13 W
Bossangoa	152	6.29 N	17.27 E
Bossdorf	54	51.59 N	12.40 E
Bossé Bangou	150	13.21 N	1.18 E
Bossembélé	152	5.16 N	17.39 E
Bossentele	152	5.41 N	16.38 E
Bossert Estates	285	40.09 N	74.44 W
Bossier City	194	32.30 N	93.43 W
Bossley Park	274a	33.52 S	150.54 E
Bosso	146	13.42 N	13.19 E
Bosso, Dallol V	150	12.25 N	2.50 E
Bossolasco	62	44.32 N	8.02 E
Bossut, Cape ›	162	18.43 S	121.38 E
Bostān, Īrān	128	31.43 N	48.00 E
Bostān, Pāk.	120	30.26 N	67.02 E
Bostancı ✦[8]	267b	40.57 N	29.05 E
Bostandyk	80	49.38 N	48.54 E
Bosten Hu ⊜	90	42.00 N	87.00 E
Bostock Green	262	53.13 N	2.30 W
Boston, Pil.	116	7.52 N	126.22 E
Boston, Eng., U.K.	44	52.59 N	0.01 W
Boston, Ga., U.S.	192	30.47 N	83.47 W
Boston, In., U.S.	218	39.44 N	84.51 W
Boston, Ma., U.S.	207	42.21 N	71.03 W
Boston, Ma., U.S.	283	42.21 N	71.03 W
Boston, N.Y., U.S.	210	42.38 N	78.44 W
Boston, Pa., U.S.	279b	40.18 N	79.49 W
Boston Bar	182	49.52 N	121.26 W
Boston Bay ⊂	283	42.22 N	70.54 W
Boston Brook ≃	283	42.37 N	71.00 W
Boston College ⊍[2]	283	42.20 N	71.10 W
Boston Common ♠	283	42.21 N	71.05 W
Boston Corners	210	42.03 N	73.31 W
Boston Creek ≃	212	43.02 N	79.56 W
Boston Harbor	224	47.08 N	122.54 W
Boston Harbor ⊂	283	42.20 N	70.58 W
Boston Heights	214	41.15 N	81.30 W
Boston Mill	214	41.16 N	81.34 W
Boston Mountains ⩘	194	35.50 N	93.20 W
Boston Spa	44	53.54 N	1.21 W
Boston University ⊍[2]	283	42.21 N	71.07 W
Bosumtwi, Lake ⊜	150	6.30 N	1.25 W
Bosut ≃	38	44.57 N	19.22 E
Boswell, In., U.S.	216	40.31 N	87.22 W
Boswell, Ok., U.S.	196	34.01 N	95.52 W
Boswell, Pa., U.S.	214	40.09 N	79.01 W
Boswell Bay	180	60.24 N	146.08 W
Bosworth	194	39.28 N	93.20 W
Bosworth Airport ⊠	279a	41.26 N	82.00 W
Bosworth Field ⊥	42	52.36 N	1.25 W
Botād	120	22.10 N	71.40 E
Botafogo ✦[8]	287a	22.57 S	43.11 W
Botafogo, Enseada de ⊂	287a	22.57 S	43.10 W
Botany	274a	33.57 S	151.12 E
Botany Bay ✦[8]	260	51.41 N	0.07 W
Botany Bay ⊂	170	33.59 S	151.12 E
Botejevo	78	46.41 N	35.52 E
Botelhos	256	21.39 S	46.24 W
Botera	152	11.37 S	14.17 E
Botersleegte	158	30.35 S	21.22 E
Botesdale	42	52.20 N	1.01 E
Boteti ≃	156	20.08 S	23.23 E
Botev ∧	38	42.43 N	24.55 E
Botevgrad	38	42.54 N	23.47 E
Botha's Hill	158	29.45 S	30.45 E
Bothaville	158	27.27 S	26.36 E
Bothell	224	47.45 N	122.12 W
Bothe-Napa Valley State Park ♠	226	38.32 N	122.32 W
Bothnia, Gulf of ⊂	26	63.00 N	20.00 E
Bothwell, Austl.	166	42.23 S	147.00 E
Bothwell, On., Can.	214	42.38 N	81.52 W
Boticas	34	41.41 N	7.40 W
Botija, Ilha da I	246	3.58 S	62.53 W
Botija, Isla I	258	33.52 S	59.02 W
Botkins	216	40.28 N	84.10 W
Botkul', ozero ⊜	80	48.46 N	46.40 E
Botkyrka	40	59.14 N	17.49 E
Botlich	84	42.39 N	46.14 E
Bot Makak	152	4.00 N	10.55 E
Botna ≃	78	46.45 N	29.34 E
Botnia, Golfo de → Bothnia, Gulf of ⊂	26	63.00 N	20.00 E
Botola	152	1.17 S	18.13 E
Botolan	116	15.17 N	120.01 E
Botoşani	38	47.45 N	26.40 E
Botoşani □[6]	38	48.00 N	26.45 E
Botoşaniţa	38	47.53 N	26.07 E

Botou	150	12.40 N	2.03 E
Botovo	82	56.03 N	38.26 E
Bo Trach	110	17.35 N	106.32 E
Botrange ∧	56	50.30 N	6.08 E
Botricello	68	38.56 N	16.51 E
Botro	150	7.51 N	5.19 W
Botsford	210	41.21 N	73.15 W
Botswana □[1], Afr.	138	22.00 S	24.00 E
Botswana □[1], Afr.	156	22.00 S	24.00 E
Botte Donato, Monte ∧	68	39.17 N	16.26 E
Bottenhavet (Selkämeri) ⊂	26	62.00 N	20.00 E
Bottenviken (Perämeri) ⊂	26	65.00 N	23.00 E
Bottesford	42	52.56 N	0.48 W
Bottineau	198	48.49 N	100.26 W
Bottisham	42	52.13 N	0.16 E
Bottnischer Meerbusen → Bothnia, Gulf of ⊂	26	63.00 N	20.00 E
Bottoms Reservoir ⊜[1]	262	53.28 N	1.58 W
Bottrop	52	51.31 N	6.55 E
Botucatu	255	22.52 S	48.26 W
Botwood	186	49.09 N	55.21 W
Boty	88	52.24 N	118.32 E
Bötzingen	58	48.04 N	7.44 E
Bötzow	54	52.39 N	13.08 E
Bötzsee ⊜	264a	52.34 N	13.50 E
Bouaflé, C. Iv.	150	6.59 N	5.45 W
Bouafle, Fr.	261	48.58 N	1.54 E
Bou Ahmed	148	35.25 N	5.00 W
Bouaké	150	7.41 N	5.02 W
Bou Ali, Oued V	148	31.14 N	4.16 E
Bouânane	148	32.03 N	3.03 W
Bouandougou	150	8.13 N	5.40 W
Bouar	152	5.57 N	15.36 E
Bou Arada	36	36.20 N	9.38 E
Bou Areg, Sebkha ⊂	34	35.10 N	2.45 W
Bouârfa	148	32.30 N	1.59 W
Bouaye	32	47.09 N	1.42 W
Boubandjidah, Parc National de ♠	146	8.45 N	14.45 E
Bou Bernous	148	27.18 N	2.59 W
Boubín ∧	60	48.59 N	13.51 E
Bouca	152	6.30 N	18.17 E
Bouchain	50	50.17 N	3.19 E
Bouchegouf	36	36.28 N	7.44 E
Boucher ≃	186	49.10 N	69.06 W
Boucher, Lac ⊜	186	51.07 N	59.35 W
Boucherville	206	45.36 N	73.27 W
Boucherville, Îles de II	275a	45.37 N	73.28 W
Bouches-du-Rhône □[5]	62	43.30 N	5.00 E
Bouchoir	50	49.45 N	2.41 E
Bouclans	58	47.14 N	6.15 E
Boucle du Baoulé, Parc National de la ♠	150	13.50 N	9.00 W
Bouddi National Park ♠	170	33.31 S	131.24 E
Boudjellil	34	36.20 N	4.21 E
Boudnib	148	31.57 N	4.38 W
Boudouaou	34	36.43 N	3.25 E
Boudry	58	46.57 N	6.50 E
Boué	50	50.01 N	3.42 E
Bouenza □[5]	152	4.00 S	13.45 E
Boufarik	148	36.34 N	2.55 E
Bouffémont	261	49.03 N	2.18 E
Bou Ficha	36	36.18 N	10.29 E
Bougaa	34	36.20 N	5.05 E
Bougainville □[5]	175e	6.00 S	155.00 E
Bougainville I	175e	6.00 S	155.00 E
Bougainville, Cape ›	164	13.54 S	126.06 E
Bougainville, Détroit de Ц	175f	15.50 S	167.10 E
Bougainville Reef ✢[2]	164	15.30 S	147.06 E
Bougainville Strait Ц	175e	6.40 S	156.10 E
Bougar'oûn, Cap ›	34	37.06 N	6.28 E
Bough Beech Reservoir ⊜[1]	260	51.13 N	0.08 E
Boughton	44	53.12 N	1.00 W
Boughton Green	260	51.14 N	0.32 E
Boughton Malherbe	260	51.13 N	0.42 E
Boughton Place ⊍	260	51.13 N	0.32 E
Bougie → Bejaïa	148	36.45 N	5.05 E
Bougou	152	3.45 S	11.12 E
Bougouni	150	11.25 N	7.29 W
Bougouriba ≃	150	10.42 N	2.56 W
Bougzoul	34	35.42 N	2.51 E
Bou Hadjar	36	36.30 N	8.06 E
Bou Hajar	36	35.42 N	10.48 E
Bouillante	241o	16.06 N	61.45 W
Bouillon	56	49.48 N	5.04 E
Bouilly	50	48.12 N	4.00 E
Bouïra	148	36.23 N	3.54 E
Bouïra □[5]	148	36.00 N	4.00 E
Bouisy, Ru de ≃	261	48.34 N	2.45 E
Bou Izakarn	148	29.09 N	9.44 W
Boujad	148	32.48 N	6.26 W
Boujailles	58	46.53 N	6.05 E
Boujdour, Cap ›	148	26.08 N	14.30 W
Bouka ≃	150	11.00 N	10.50 W
Bou Kadir	148	36.04 N	1.07 E
Bou Khadra	36	35.45 N	8.02 E
Boukiéro	273b	4.12 S	15.18 E
Boukiéro, Mont ∧[2]	273b	4.11 S	15.17 E
Boukombé	150	10.11 N	1.06 E
Boula Ibib	146	9.34 N	13.46 E
Boulaide	56	49.54 N	5.49 E
Boularderie Island I	186	46.15 N	60.30 W
Boulay-Moselle	56	49.11 N	6.30 E
Boulbon	62	43.52 N	4.41 E
Boulder, Austl.	162	30.47 S	121.29 E
Boulder, Co., U.S.	200	40.00 N	105.16 W
Boulder, Mt., U.S.	202	46.14 N	112.07 W
Boulder ≃	202	45.52 N	111.57 W
Boulder City	204	35.58 N	114.49 W
Boulder Creek	226	37.07 N	122.07 W
Boulder Creek ≃	200	37.47 N	111.22 W
Boulder Hill	216	41.41 N	88.25 W
Bouleaux, Lac des ⊜	275a	45.33 N	73.19 W
Bouli ≃	150	13.15 N	0.03 E
Boulia	166	22.54 S	139.54 E
Bouligny	56	49.17 N	5.45 E
Boullay-les-Troux	261	48.41 N	2.03 E
Boulmane	148	33.22 N	4.45 W
Boulmane □[4]	148	33.00 N	4.00 W
Boulogne ✦[8]	258	34.31 S	58.34 W
Boulogne, Bois de ♠	261	48.50 N	2.15 E
Boulogne-Billancourt	50	48.50 N	2.15 E
Boulogne-sur-Gesse	32	43.18 N	0.39 E
Boulogne-sur-Mer	50	50.43 N	1.37 E
Bouloire	50	47.58 N	0.33 E
Boulouli	150	15.34 N	9.21 W
Bouloupari	175f	21.52 S	166.04 E
Boulouris-sur-Mer	62	43.25 N	6.48 E
Boulsa	150	12.39 N	0.34 W
Boulsworth Hill ∧	44	53.48 N	2.06 W
Bouly	150	15.19 N	11.48 W
Bou Maad, Djebel ∧	34	36.26 N	2.08 E
Boumalne	148	31.32 N	5.27 W
Boumba ≃	152	2.02 N	15.12 E
Boumbé I ≃	152	4.04 N	15.23 E
Boumbé II ≃	152	4.08 N	15.08 E
Boumboum	150	15.01 N	1.42 W
Boûmdeïd	150	17.26 N	9.50 W
Bou Medfaa	34	36.22 N	2.28 E
Boumentana	152	6.59 N	16.56 E
Boumnyebe	152	3.52 N	10.49 E
Boumou	146	9.02 N	16.26 E
Bouna	150	9.16 N	3.00 W
Boundary	180	64.04 N	141.06 W
Boundary Bay ⊂	224	49.00 N	122.58 W
Boundary Peak ∧	204	37.51 N	118.21 W
Boundary Ranges ⩘	180	59.00 N	134.00 W
Bound Brook	210	40.34 N	74.32 W

≃	River	Fluß	Río	Rivière	Rio
≊	Canal	Kanal	Canal	Canal	Canal
L	Waterfall, Rapids	Wasserfall, Stromschnellen	Cascada, Rápidos	Chute d'eau, Rapides	Cascata, Rápidos
Ц	Strait	Meeresstraße	Estrecho	Détroit	Estreito
⊂	Bay, Gulf	Bucht, Golf	Bahía, Golfo	Baie, Golfe	Baía, Golfo
⊜	Lake, Lakes	See, Seen	Lago, Lagos	Lac, Lacs	Lago, Lagos
≡	Swamp	Sumpf	Pantano	Marais	Pântano
⊓	Ice Features, Glacier	Eis- und Gletscherformen	Accidentes Glaciales	Formes glaciaires	Acidentes glaciares
≚	Other Hydrographic Features	Andere Hydrographische Objekte	Otros Elementos Hidrográficos	Autres données hydrographiques	Outros acidentes hidrográficos

✢	Submarine Features	Untermeerische Objekte	Accidentes Submarinos	Formes de relief sous-marin	Acidentes submarinos
□	Political Unit	Politische Einheit	Unidad Politica	Entité politique	Unidade política
⊍	Cultural Institution	Kulturelle Institution	Institución Cultural	Institution culturelle	Instituição cultural
⊥	Historical Site	Historische Stätte	Sitio Histórico	Site historique	Sitio histórico
♠	Recreational Site	Erholungs- und Ferienort	Sitio de Recreo	Centre de loisirs	Area de Lazer
⊠	Airport	Flughafen	Aeropuerto	Aéroport	Aeroporto
■	Military Installation	Militäranlage	Instalación Militar	Installation militaire	Instalação militar
✦	Miscellaneous	Verschiedenes	Misceláneo	Divers	Diversos

Bound Brook ≃, Ma., U.S. 283 42.13 N 70.47 W
Bound Brook ≃, N.J., U.S. 276 40.35 N 74.30 W
Boundiali 150 9.31 N 6.29 W
Boun Nua 110 21.38 N 101.54 E
Bountiful 200 40.53 N 111.52 W
Bounty Bay c 174e 25.04 S 130.05 W
Bounty Islands II 14 47.42 S 179.04 E
Bounty Trough ✢[1] 14 46.00 S 178.00 E
Bouqteb 148 34.02 N 0.05 E
Bouquet Reservoir ⊜[1] 228 34.35 N 118.24 W
Bouqueval 261 49.01 N 2.26 E
Boura 150 12.25 N 4.33 W
Bouradière 62 43.58 N 5.19 E
Bourail 175f 21.34 S 165.30 E
Bouray-sur-Juine 261 48.31 N 2.18 E
Bourbeuse ≃ 194 38.24 N 90.53 W
Bourbeuse, Dry Fork ≃ 194 38.16 N 91.26 W
Bourbon, In., U.S. 216 41.17 N 86.06 W
Bourbon, Mo., U.S. 194 38.09 N 91.14 W
Bourbon □[6] 218 38.14 N 84.14 W
Bourbon ≃ 206 46.17 N 71.55 W
Bourbon-Lancy 32 46.38 N 3.46 E
Bourbonnais 216 41.08 N 87.52 W
Bourbonnais □[9] 32 46.20 N 3.00 E
Bourbonne-les-Bains 58 47.57 N 5.45 E
Bourbourg 50 50.57 N 2.12 E
Bourbre ≃ 62 45.47 N 5.11 E
Bourdeaux 62 44.35 N 5.08 E
Bourdon, Île I 275a 45.43 N 73.29 W
Bourdon, Réservoir du ⊜[1] 50 47.36 N 3.07 E
Bourdonné 261 48.45 N 1.40 E
Bou Regreg, Oued ≃ 148 34.03 N 6.50 W
Bourem 150 16.57 N 0.21 W
Bourg 194 29.33 N 90.36 W
Bourg-Achard 50 49.21 N 0.49 E
Bourganeuf 32 45.57 N 1.46 E
Bourg-Argental 62 45.18 N 4.33 E
Bourg-de-Péage 62 45.02 N 5.03 E
Bourg-en-Bresse 58 46.12 N 5.13 E
Bourges 32 47.05 N 2.24 E
Bourget 206 45.26 N 75.09 W
Bourget, Lac du ⊜ 62 45.44 N 5.52 E
Bourg-la-Reine 261 48.47 N 2.19 E
Bourg-Lastic 32 45.39 N 2.33 E
Bourg-lés-Valence 62 44.57 N 4.53 E
Bourgneuf 261 48.36 N 2.00 E
Bourgneuf-en-Retz 32 47.02 N 1.57 W
Bourgogne 50 49.21 N 4.04 E
Bourgogne (Burgundy) □[9] 32 47.00 N 4.30 E
Bourgogne, Canal de ≅ 50 47.58 N 3.30 E
Bourgoin-Jallieu 62 45.35 N 5.17 E
Bourg-Saint-Andéol 62 44.22 N 4.39 E
Bourg-Saint-Maurice 62 45.37 N 6.46 E
Bourg-Saint-Pierre 58 45.57 N 7.12 E
Bourgtheroulde 50 49.18 N 0.53 E
Bourgueil 50 47.17 N 0.10 E
Bou Rjeïmât ⊤[4] 150 19.04 N 15.08 W
Bourke 166 30.05 S 145.56 E
Bourmont 58 48.12 N 5.35 E
Bourne 42 52.46 N 0.23 W
Bourne ≃, Fr. 62 45.04 N 5.15 E
Bourne ≃, Eng., U.K. 42 51.02 N 1.47 W
Bournebridge 260 51.38 N 0.11 E
Bourne End 260 51.45 N 0.32 W
Bournemouth 42 50.43 N 1.54 W
Bourneville, Fr. 50 49.23 N 0.37 E
Bourneville, Oh., U.S. 218 39.17 N 83.09 W
Bourn Vincent Memorial Park ♠ 48 52.01 N 9.30 W
Bouroum 150 13.37 N 0.39 W
Bourron-Marlotte 50 48.20 N 2.42 E
Bourscheid 56 49.55 N 6.04 E
Bourtange 52 53.00 N 7.11 E
Bourtanger Moor ◆[3] 52 53.00 N 7.15 E
Bourton-on-the-Water 42 51.53 N 1.45 W
Bourzanga 150 13.41 N 1.33 W
Bou Saâda 148 35.12 N 4.11 E
Bou Salem 36 36.36 N 8.59 E
Bousbecque 50 50.46 N 3.05 E
Bouse 200 33.55 N 114.00 W
Bou Sellam, Oued ≃ 34 36.26 N 4.34 E
Bouse Wash V 200 34.02 N 114.20 W
Bou Smail 148 36.38 N 2.41 E
Boussac 32 46.21 N 2.13 E
Boussé, Burkina 150 12.39 N 1.53 W
Bousse, Fr. 56 49.17 N 6.12 E
Boussières 58 47.09 N 5.54 E
Bousso 146 10.29 N 16.43 E
Boussois 50 50.17 N 4.03 E
Boussouma 150 12.55 N 1.05 W
Boussu 50 50.26 N 3.48 E
Boussy-Saint-Antoine 261 48.41 N 2.32 E
Bout, Pointe du › 240e 14.34 N 61.03 W
Bouteille, Lac de la ⊜ 206 46.42 N 73.41 W
Bouteldja 36 36.47 N 8.12 E
Bou Temezguida ∧ 148 29.21 N 9.55 W
Boutilimit 150 17.33 N 14.42 W
Bouttencourt 50 49.56 N 1.38 E
Bouvard, Cape › 168a 32.41 S 115.37 E
Bouvetøya I 9 54.26 S 3.24 E
Bouvier Bay c 281 42.39 N 82.38 W
Bouvières 62 44.30 N 5.13 E
Bouxières-aux-Dames 56 48.45 N 6.10 E
Bouxwiller 56 48.49 N 7.29 E
Bouyon 62 43.50 N 7.07 E
Bouza 150 14.25 N 6.02 E
Bou Zadjar 34 35.35 N 1.09 W
Bouzonville 56 49.18 N 6.32 E
Bov 41 54.50 N 9.23 E
Bova 68 38.00 N 15.56 E
Bøvågen 26 60.40 N 4.58 E
Bovalino Marina 68 38.10 N 16.11 E
Bova Marina 68 37.56 N 15.55 E
Bovard 279b 40.19 N 79.30 W
Bovec 36 46.20 N 13.33 E
Bovegno 64 45.48 N 10.16 E
Bovenden 52 51.35 N 9.55 E
Bovenkarspel 52 52.42 N 5.15 E
Bøverdal 26 61.43 N 8.21 E
Boves, Fr. 50 49.51 N 2.23 E
Boves, It. 62 44.19 N 7.33 E
Bovey 190 47.17 N 93.25 W
Bovey ≃ 42 50.34 N 3.37 W
Bovey Tracey 42 50.36 N 3.40 W
Bovill 202 46.51 N 116.23 W
Boville Ernica 66 41.38 N 13.28 E
Bovina 196 34.31 N 102.53 W
Bovina Center 210 42.16 N 74.47 W
Bovingdon 42 51.44 N 0.32 W
Bövinghausen ◆[8] 263 51.31 N 7.19 E
Bovington Camp 42 50.42 N 2.14 W
Bovino 68 41.15 N 15.20 E
Bovisio Masciago 266b 45.37 N 9.09 E
Bovolenta 64 45.16 N 11.56 E
Bovolone 64 45.15 N 11.07 E
Bovril 252 31.21 S 59.26 W
Bovrup 41 54.59 N 9.36 E
Bow 224 48.33 N 122.23 W
Bow ≃, Austl. 162 16.32 S 128.39 E
Bow ≃, Ab., Can. 182 49.56 N 111.42 W
Bow ≃, Sk., Can. 184 54.56 N 105.13 W
Bo-Wadrif 158 32.26 S 20.07 E
Bowang 106 31.34 N 118.50 E
Bowbells 198 48.48 N 102.14 W
Bow Brook ≃ 42 52.04 N 2.07 W
Bowburn 44 54.43 N 1.31 W
Bow Creek ≃ 198 39.35 N 99.14 W
Bowden 182 51.55 N 114.02 W
Bowdle 198 45.27 N 99.39 W
Bowdoin, Lake ⊜ 202 48.24 N 107.41 W
Bowdon, Eng., U.K. 262 53.23 N 2.22 W
Bowdon, Ga., U.S. 192 33.32 N 85.15 W
Bowdon, N.D., U.S. 198 47.28 N 99.42 W
Bowelling 168a 33.25 S 116.29 E
Bowen, Arg. 252 35.00 S 67.31 W
Bowen, Austl. 166 20.01 S 148.15 E
Bowen, Il., U.S. 194 40.14 N 91.04 W
Bowen ≃ 166 20.24 S 147.21 E
Bowenfels 170 33.31 S 150.07 E
Bowens Creek ≃ 170 33.21 S 150.35 E
Bowers 208 39.15 N 75.36 W
Bowers Gifford 260 51.34 N 0.32 E
Bowers Mansion ⊥ 226 39.17 N 119.50 W
Bowers Marshes ≡ 260 51.33 N 0.32 E
Bowers Ridge ✢[3] 16 54.00 N 179.00 E
Bowerston 214 40.25 N 81.11 W
Bowersville 218 39.34 N 83.43 W
Bowgreave 44 53.52 N 2.45 W
Bowie, Az., U.S. 200 32.19 N 109.29 W
Bowie, Md., U.S. 208 39.00 N 76.46 W
Bowie, Tx., U.S. 196 33.33 N 97.50 W
Bowie Creek ≃ 194 31.26 N 89.24 W
Bow Island 184 49.52 N 111.22 W
Bowland, Forest of ◆[3] 44 53.58 N 2.32 W
Bowles Creek ≃ 222 32.02 N 94.59 W
Bowley Bar ›[2] 284b 39.18 N 76.23 W
Bowleys Quarters 284b 39.19 N 76.24 W
Bowling Green, Fl., U.S. 220 27.38 N 81.49 W
Bowling Green, Ky., U.S. 194 36.59 N 86.26 W
Bowling Green, Mo., U.S. 219 39.20 N 91.11 W
Bowling Green, Oh., U.S. 216 41.22 N 83.39 W
Bowling Green, Pa., U.S. 285 39.55 N 75.23 W
Bowling Green, Va., U.S. 208 38.02 N 77.20 W
Bowling Green, Cape › 166 19.19 S 147.25 E
Bowling Green Bay National Park ♠ 166 19.28 S 147.14 E
Bowman, Ca., U.S. 226 38.57 N 121.03 W
Bowman, Ga., U.S. 192 34.12 N 83.01 W
Bowman, N.D., U.S. 198 46.10 N 103.23 W
Bowman, S.C., U.S. 192 33.20 N 80.40 W
Bowman, Mount ∧ 182 51.10 N 121.55 W
Bowman Creek ≃, Pa., U.S. 210 41.31 N 75.58 W
Bowman Creek ≃, Wa., U.S. 224 45.50 N 121.03 W
Bowman-Haley Lake ⊜[1] 198 46.00 N 103.20 W
Bowman Island I 9 65.17 S 103.08 E
Bowman Lake ⊜[1] 226 39.27 N 120.38 W
Bowmans 168b 34.09 S 138.16 E
Bowmansdale 208 40.10 N 76.59 W
Bowmanstown 208 40.48 N 75.40 W
Bowmansville, N.Y., U.S. 212 42.56 N 78.41 W
Bowmansville, Pa., U.S. 208 40.10 N 76.04 W
Bowmanville 212 43.55 N 78.41 W
Bowmanville Creek ≃ 212 43.53 N 78.40 W
Bowmont Water ≃ 44 55.34 N 2.09 W
Bowmore 46 55.45 N 6.17 W
Bowness-on-Windermere 44 54.22 N 2.55 W
Bowokan, Kepulauan II 112 2.05 S 123.35 E
Bowral 170 34.28 S 150.25 E
Bowraville 166 30.39 S 152.51 E
Bowron ≃ 182 54.04 N 121.48 W
Bowron Lake Provincial Park ♠ 182 53.10 N 121.06 W
Bowsman 184 52.14 N 101.14 W
Bowwood 154 17.07 S 26.17 E
Box 42 51.26 N 2.15 W
Boxberg 56 49.29 N 9.38 E
Box Butte Creek ≃ 198 42.28 N 102.37 W
Box Creek ≃, Tx., U.S. 222 31.33 N 95.43 W
Box Creek ≃, Tx., U.S. 222 31.35 N 95.10 W
Box Elder 202 48.19 N 110.00 W
Boxelder Creek ≃, U.S. 198 45.59 N 103.57 W
Boxelder Creek ≃, Co., U.S. 198 40.33 N 105.00 W
Box Elder Creek ≃, Co., U.S. 198 40.23 N 104.28 W
Box Elder Creek ≃, Mt., U.S. 202 46.57 N 108.04 W
Boxelder Creek ≃, S.D., U.S. 198 44.01 N 102.27 W
Boxey 186 47.25 N 55.34 W
Boxey Point › 186 47.24 N 55.35 W
Boxford 207 42.39 N 70.59 W
Boxford State Forest ♠ 283 42.39 N 71.02 W
Box Grove 275b 43.51 N 79.14 W
Box Hill 169 37.49 S 145.08 E
Boxholm 26 58.12 N 15.03 E
Boxian 100 33.53 N 115.45 E
Boxing 98 37.08 N 118.07 E
Boxley 260 51.18 N 0.33 E
Boxmeer 52 51.39 N 5.57 E
Boxmoor 260 51.45 N 0.29 W
Boxodoi 98 42.34 N 115.18 E
Boxtel 52 51.35 N 5.20 E
Boyabat 130 41.28 N 34.47 E
Boyabo 152 3.43 N 18.46 E
Boyacá □[5] 246 5.30 N 73.30 W
Boyacıköy ◆[8] 267b 41.06 N 29.02 E
Boyalı 130 41.02 N 33.19 E
Boyalık 130 41.15 N 28.37 E
Boyang 100 28.59 N 116.40 E
Boyanup 168a 33.29 S 115.44 E
Boyasengese 152 3.29 N 20.33 E
Boyce 194 31.23 N 92.40 W
Boyceville 190 45.02 N 92.02 W
Boyd, Mn., U.S. 198 44.50 N 95.54 W
Boyd, Tx., U.S. 222 33.05 N 97.34 W
Boyd ≃ 166 29.51 S 152.35 E
Boyd's Cove 186 49.27 N 54.39 W
Boydton 192 36.40 N 78.23 W
Boyenge 152 0.25 N 18.51 E
Boyer ≃ 198 41.28 N 95.55 W
Boyera 152 0.38 S 19.25 E
Boyer Aḥmadī va Kohkīlūyeh □[4] 128 30.40 N 50.40 E
Boyer Run ≃ 279b 40.13 N 79.32 W
Boyers 214 41.06 N 79.54 W
Boyer's Creek ≃ 284a 43.00 N 79.02 W
Boyertown 208 40.20 N 75.38 W
Boyes Hot Springs 226 38.19 N 122.29 W
Boykins 208 36.34 N 77.12 W
Boyle, Ab., Can. 182 54.35 N 112.49 W
Boyle, Ire. 48 53.58 N 8.18 W
Boyle, Ms., U.S. 194 33.42 N 90.50 W
Boyle Drain ≃ 212 43.42 N 81.06 W
Boyle Heights ◆[8] 280 34.02 N 118.13 W
Boylston, Al., U.S. 194 32.26 N 86.17 W
Boylston, Ma., U.S. 207 42.23 N 71.42 W
Boyne 275b 43.29 N 79.50 W
Boyne ≃, Austl. 166 23.56 S 151.21 E
Boyne ≃, Mb., Can. 184 49.34 N 97.52 W
Boyne ≃, On., Can. 212 44.10 N 79.49 W
Boyne ≃, Ire. 48 53.43 N 6.15 W
Boyne Battlesite ⊥ 48 53.42 N 6.23 W
Boyne City 190 45.12 N 85.00 W
Boynton 196 35.38 N 95.39 W
Boynton Beach 220 26.31 N 80.04 W
Boyo 152 5.43 N 21.33 E
Boyolali 115a 7.32 S 110.35 E
Boysen Reservoir ⊜[1] 202 43.19 N 108.11 W
Boysen State Park ♠ 202 43.23 N 108.07 W
Boys Ranch 196 35.32 N 102.15 W
Boyuibe 248 20.25 S 63.17 W
Boyup Brook 162 33.50 S 116.24 E
Bozburun 130 36.41 N 28.04 E
Boz Burun › 130 40.32 N 28.46 E
Bozburun Yarımadası ›[1] 130 36.40 N 28.10 E
Bozcaada 130 39.50 N 26.04 E
Boz Dağ ∧, Tür. 130 37.18 N 29.12 E
Bozdağ ∧, Tür. 130 36.50 N 36.22 E
Boz Dağ ∧, Tür. 130 38.19 N 28.08 E
Boz Dağlar ⋀ 130 38.20 N 27.45 E
Bozdoğan 130 37.40 N 28.19 E
Bozel 62 45.27 N 6.39 E
Bozeman 202 45.40 N 111.02 W
Bozen → Bolzano 64 46.31 N 11.22 E
Bozene 152 2.56 N 19.12 E
Bozhen 98 38.07 N 116.32 E
Boží Dar 54 50.24 N 12.55 E
Bozkır 130 37.11 N 32.15 E
Bozkurt, Tür. 130 37.49 N 29.37 E
Bozkurt, Tür. 130 41.57 N 34.01 E
Bozman 208 38.46 N 76.16 W
Bozoğlak 130 39.38 N 38.49 E
Bozok 130 37.18 N 40.22 E
Bozoum 152 6.19 N 16.23 E
Bozova, Tür. 130 37.22 N 38.31 E
Bozova, Tür. 130 37.13 N 30.18 E
Bozovici 38 44.55 N 21.59 E
Bozšakol' 86 51.50 N 74.20 E
Bozum 52 53.05 N 5.42 E
Bozüyük 130 39.54 N 30.03 E
Bozzolo 64 45.06 N 10.29 E
Bra 62 44.42 N 7.51 E
Braan ≃ 46 56.33 N 3.35 W
Braås 26 57.04 N 15.03 E
Brabant □[4] 56 50.45 N 4.30 E
Brabante, Isla de → Brabant Island I 9 64.15 S 62.20 W
Brabant Island I 9 64.15 S 62.20 W
Brabant Lake ⊜ 184 56.00 N 103.43 W
Brabrand 41 56.09 N 10.07 E
Brač, Otok I 36 43.20 N 16.40 E
Bracadale, Loch c 46 57.19 N 6.30 W
Bracciano 66 42.06 N 12.10 E
Bracciano, Lago di ⊜ 66 42.07 N 12.14 E
Bracco, Passo del)(62 44.15 N 9.34 E
Bracebridge 212 45.02 N 79.19 W
Bracebridge Heath 44 53.13 N 0.33 W
Braceville, Il., U.S. 216 41.14 N 88.16 W
Braceville, Oh., U.S. 214 41.14 N 80.58 W
Brachfield 222 32.03 N 94.39 W
Bracieux 50 47.33 N 1.33 E
Bracigliano 68 40.49 N 14.42 E
Bracigovo 38 42.01 N 24.22 E
Bräcke 26 62.43 N 15.27 E
Brackel ◆[8] 263 51.32 N 7.33 E
Bracken □[6] 218 38.40 N 84.06 W
Brackendale 182 49.46 N 123.09 W
Brackenheim 56 49.05 N 9.03 E
Brackenhurst 273d 26.19 S 28.06 E
Bracken Lake ⊜ 184 53.37 N 99.50 W
Brackenridge 214 40.36 N 79.44 W
Brackett Field ⊠ 280 34.05 N 117.47 W
Brackettville 196 29.18 N 100.25 W
Brački Kanal ʯ 36 43.24 N 16.40 E
Brackley 42 52.02 N 1.09 W
Bracknell 42 51.26 N 0.45 W
Bracktown 218 38.04 N 84.31 W
Brackwede 52 51.59 N 8.31 E
Braclav 78 48.50 N 28.55 E
Braco 46 56.15 N 3.53 W
Braço do Norte 252 28.17 S 49.11 W
Bracuí ≃ 256 22.57 S 44.24 W
Brad 38 46.08 N 22.47 E
Bradano ≃ 68 40.23 N 16.51 E
Bradbury 280 34.08 N 117.59 W
Bradbury Heights 284c 38.52 N 76.56 W
Braddock, N.J., U.S. 285 39.42 N 74.53 W
Braddock, Pa., U.S. 214 40.24 N 79.52 W
Braddock Acres 284c 38.49 N 77.10 W
Braddock Heights, Md., U.S. 208 39.25 N 77.30 W
Braddock Heights, N.Y., U.S. 210 43.19 N 77.42 W
Braddock Hills 279b 40.25 N 79.51 W
Braddock Point › 210 43.19 N 77.43 W
Braddocks Millpond ⊜ 285 39.49 N 74.51 W
Braden ≃ 220 27.30 N 82.32 W
Bradenton 220 27.29 N 82.34 W
Bradenton Beach 220 27.28 N 82.42 W
Bradenville 214 40.19 N 79.20 W
Braderup 41 54.50 N 8.53 E
Bradford, On., Can. 212 44.07 N 79.34 W
Bradford, Eng., U.K. 44 53.48 N 1.45 W
Bradford, Ar., U.S. 194 35.25 N 91.27 W
Bradford, Il., U.S. 190 41.10 N 89.39 W
Bradford, N.Y., U.S. 210 42.22 N 77.07 W
Bradford, Oh., U.S. 218 40.08 N 84.26 W
Bradford, Pa., U.S. 214 41.57 N 78.38 W
Bradford, R.I., U.S. 207 41.23 N 71.44 W
Bradford, Tn., U.S. 194 36.04 N 88.48 W
Bradford, Vt., U.S. 188 43.59 N 72.09 W
Bradford □[6] 210 41.56 N 78.40 W
Bradford □[8] 262 53.47 N 1.52 W
Bradford Hills 285 40.01 N 75.39 W
Bradford Mountain ∧ 207 41.59 N 73.18 W
Bradford-on-Avon 42 51.20 N 2.15 W
Bradford Regional Airport ⊠ 214 41.48 N 78.38 W
Bradfordwoods 214 40.38 N 80.05 W
Brading 42 50.41 N 1.09 W
Bradley, Ar., U.S. 194 33.05 N 93.39 W
Bradley, Ca., U.S. 226 35.51 N 120.47 W
Bradley, Fl., U.S. 220 27.48 N 81.59 W
Bradley, Il., U.S. 216 41.08 N 87.51 W
Bradley, Mi., U.S. 216 42.38 N 85.39 W
Bradley, S.D., U.S. 198 45.05 N 97.38 W
Bradley Beach 208 40.12 N 74.01 W
Bradley Farms 284c 39.00 N 77.11 W
Bradley Gardens 276 40.34 N 74.39 W
Bradley Institute 154 17.02 S 31.27 E
Bradley International Airport ⊠ 207 41.55 N 72.40 W
Bradley Reefs ✢[2] 175e 6.52 S 160.48 E
Bradley Woods Reservation ♠ 279a 41.25 N 81.58 W
Bradley W. Palmer State Park ♠ 283 42.39 N 70.54 W
Bradner, B.C., Can. 224 49.06 N 122.25 W
Bradner, Oh., U.S. 214 41.19 N 83.26 W
Bradninch 42 50.50 N 3.25 W
Bradore-Bay 186 51.28 N 57.14 W
Bradshaw, Eng., U.K. 262 53.36 N 2.24 W
Bradshaw, Md., U.S. 208 39.25 N 76.22 W
Bradshaw, Ne., U.S. 198 40.53 N 97.44 W
Bradshaw, W.V., U.S. 192 37.21 N 81.47 W
Bradwell-on-Sea 42 51.44 N 0.54 E
Bradworthy 42 50.54 N 4.22 W
Brady, Mt., U.S. 202 48.02 N 111.50 W
Brady, Ne., U.S. 198 41.01 N 100.22 W
Brady, Tx., U.S. 196 31.08 N 99.20 W
Brady Creek ≃ 196 31.07 N 98.59 W
Brady Lake 214 41.09 N 81.19 W
Brady Mountains ⋀[2] 196 31.20 N 99.40 W
Brae 46a 60.23 N 1.21 W
Brædstrup 41 55.58 N 9.37 E
Braemar 46 57.01 N 3.23 W
Braeside, Austl. 162 21.12 S 121.01 E
Braeside, Austl. 274b 37.59 S 145.07 E
Braeside, On., Can. 212 45.28 N 76.24 W
Braga 34 41.33 N 8.26 W
Bragado 252 35.08 S 60.30 W
Bragança, Bra. 250 1.03 S 46.46 W
Bragança, Bra. 256 23.18 S 45.38 W
Bragança, Port. 34 41.49 N 6.45 W
Bragança Paulista 256 22.57 S 46.34 W
Bragar 46 58.24 N 6.40 W
Bragin 78 51.47 N 30.14 E
Braginka ≃ 78 51.22 N 30.24 E
Braginovka 78 48.29 N 36.21 E
Braham 190 45.43 N 93.10 W
Brahetrolleborg ⊥ 41 55.09 N 10.22 E
Brahma Island I 220 27.52 N 81.15 W
Brāhmanbāria 120 23.59 N 91.07 E
Brāhmani ≃, India 120 20.39 N 86.46 E
Brāhmani ≃, India 126 24.09 N 88.01 E
Brahmapur, India 122 19.19 N 84.47 E
Brahmapur, India 272b 22.28 N 88.22 E
Brahmaputra (Yarlung) ≃ 120 24.02 N 90.59 E
Brāhmaur 123 32.27 N 76.32 E
Braich y Pwll › 42 52.48 N 4.36 W
Braidwood, Austl. 166 35.27 S 149.48 E
Braidwood, Il., U.S. 216 41.15 N 88.12 W
Braies (Prags) 64 46.42 N 12.08 E
Brăila 38 45.16 N 27.58 E
Brăila □[6] 38 45.00 N 27.40 E
Brailov 78 49.06 N 28.09 E
Brain ≃ 42 51.48 N 0.39 E
Brainard, Ne., U.S. 198 41.11 N 97.00 W
Brainard, N.Y., U.S. 210 42.30 N 73.31 W
Braine 50 49.20 N 3.32 E
Braine-l'Alleud 50 50.41 N 4.22 E
Braine-le-Château 50 50.41 N 4.16 E
Braine-le-Comte 50 50.36 N 4.08 E
Brainerd 190 46.21 N 94.12 W
Braint ≃ 44 53.08 N 4.19 W
Braintree, Eng., U.K. 42 51.53 N 0.32 E
Braintree, Ma., U.S. 207 42.13 N 71.00 W
Braintree □[8] 260 51.47 N 0.36 E
Brak ≃, S. Afr. 158 31.32 S 21.33 E
Brak ≃, S. Afr. 158 29.35 S 22.55 E
Brake, Dtsch. 52 53.19 N 8.28 E
Brake, Dtsch. 52 52.04 N 8.35 E
Brake, Dtsch. 52 52.01 N 8.55 E
Brakel, Bel. 50 50.48 N 3.46 E
Brakel, Dtsch. 52 51.43 N 9.10 E
Brakna □[4] 150 17.30 N 13.30 W
Brakpan 158 26.14 S 28.22 E
Brakpan □[5] 273d 26.16 S 28.21 E
Brakpoort 158 31.20 S 23.22 E
Brakputs 158 29.29 S 18.24 E
Brakwater 156 22.24 S 17.06 E
Brålanda 26 58.34 N 12.22 E
Bralorne 182 50.47 N 122.49 W
Bramalea 212 43.44 N 79.43 W
Bramall Hall ⊥ 262 53.23 N 2.09 W
Braman 196 36.55 N 97.20 W
Brambauer 263 51.35 N 7.27 E
Bramberg am Wildkogel 64 47.16 N 12.21 E
Bramble Bay c 171a 27.17 S 153.05 E
Bramble Cay I 164 9.08 S 143.52 E
Bramdrupdam 41 55.31 N 9.28 E
Bramey-Lenningsen 263 51.34 N 7.46 E
Bramfeld ◆[8] 52 53.37 N 10.04 E
Bramford 42 52.04 N 1.06 E
Bramhall 262 53.22 N 2.10 W
Bramhope 44 53.53 N 1.37 W
Bramley 260 51.12 N 0.34 W
Bramley ◆[8] 273d 26.08 S 28.05 E
Bramley Mountain ∧ 210 42.18 N 74.49 W
Bramming 41 55.28 N 8.42 E
Brampton, On., Can. 212 43.41 N 79.46 W
Brampton, Eng., U.K. 42 52.19 N 0.14 W
Brampton, Eng., U.K. 44 54.57 N 2.43 W
Brampton Airfield ⊠ 275b 43.40 N 79.47 W
Bramsche 52 52.24 N 7.58 E
Bramsöfjärden ⊜ 40 60.20 N 17.10 E
Bramstedt 52 53.22 N 8.41 E
Brancaleone Marina 68 37.58 N 16.06 E
Brancaster 42 52.58 N 0.39 E
Brancaster Roads ⊤[3] 42 53.00 N 0.41 E
Branch 186 46.53 N 53.57 W
Branch □[6] 216 41.55 N 85.03 W
Branch Brook Park ♠ 276 40.46 N 74.10 W
Branch Dale 208 40.41 N 76.20 W
Branchport 210 42.36 N 77.09 W
Branchville, Ct., U.S. 207 41.16 N 73.26 W
Branchville, N.J., U.S. 210 41.08 N 74.45 W
Branchville, S.C., U.S. 192 33.15 N 80.48 W
Branchville, Va., U.S. 208 36.34 N 77.14 W
Branco 152 12.30 S 20.32 E
Branco ≃, Bra. 246 1.24 S 61.51 W
Branco ≃, Bra. 248 21.00 S 57.48 W
Branco ≃, Bra. 248 10.03 S 67.51 W
Branco ≃, Bra. 248 7.44 S 61.46 W
Branco ≃, Bra. 248 9.37 S 60.33 W
Branco ≃, Bra. 248 9.12 S 64.22 W
Branco ≃, Bra. 250 12.00 S 44.56 W
Branco ≃, Bra. 250 7.01 S 51.42 W
Branco, Ilhéu I 150a 16.39 N 24.41 W
Brand, Dtsch. 56 50.43 N 6.09 E
Brand, Öst. 58 47.06 N 9.44 E
Brandamore 208 40.03 N 75.50 W
Brandaris ∧[2] 241s 12.17 N 68.24 W
Brandberg ∧ 156 21.10 S 14.33 E
Brandbu 26 60.28 N 10.30 E
Brande 41 55.57 N 9.07 E
Brandebourg → Brandenburg 54 52.24 N 12.32 E
Brandeis University ⊕[2] 283 42.22 N 71.16 W
Brandenberg 64 47.29 N 11.53 E
Brandenberg ∧[2] 263 51.20 N 7.37 E
Brandenburg, Dtsch. 54 52.24 N 12.32 E
Brandenburg, Ky., U.S. 194 38.00 N 86.10 W
Brandenburg □[3] 30 52.30 N 13.30 E
Brandenburger Tor ⊥ 264a 52.31 N 13.23 E
Brand-Erbisdorf 54 50.52 N 13.19 E
Brandfort 158 28.47 S 26.30 E
Br'andino 80 54.23 N 49.23 E
Brandis, Dtsch. 54 51.48 N 13.10 E
Brandis, Dtsch. 54 51.20 N 12.36 E
Brandizzo 62 45.11 N 7.51 E
Brandkop 158 31.13 S 19.13 E
Brandon, Mb., Can. 184 49.50 N 99.57 W
Brandon, Eng., U.K. 42 52.27 N 0.37 E
Brandon, Eng., U.K. 44 54.46 N 1.39 W
Brandon, Fl., U.S. 220 27.56 N 82.17 W
Brandon, Ms., U.S. 194 32.16 N 89.59 W
Brandon, S.D., U.S. 198 43.35 N 96.34 W
Brandon, Tx., U.S. 222 32.03 N 96.58 W
Brandon, Vt., U.S. 188 43.47 N 73.05 W
Brandon, Wi., U.S. 190 43.44 N 88.46 W
Brandon Bay c 48 52.15 N 10.05 W
Brandon Head › 48 52.16 N 10.14 W
Brandon Mountain ∧ 48 52.14 N 10.15 W
Brandon Road Lock and Dam ◆[5] 278 41.30 N 88.06 W
Brandonville 210 40.52 N 76.10 W
Brand Park ♠ 280 34.11 N 118.16 W
Brandsen 258 35.10 S 58.14 W
Brands Hatch Motor Race Circuit ♠ 260 51.22 N 0.16 E
Brandsø I 41 55.21 N 9.43 E
Brandt 218 39.54 N 84.05 W
Brandvlei 158 30.25 S 20.30 E
Brandy Camp 214 41.19 N 78.41 W
Brandy Peak ∧ 202 42.36 N 123.53 W
Brandýsek 54 50.10 N 14.10 E
Brandýs nad Labem 54 50.10 N 14.41 E
Brandywine Battlefield ⊥ 208 39.53 N 75.35 W
Brandywine Creek ≃, U.S. 285 39.44 N 75.32 W
Brandywine Creek ≃, In., U.S. 218 39.31 N 85.52 W
Brandywine Creek ≃, Oh., U.S. 279a 41.17 N 81.34 W
Brandywine Creek, East Branch ≃ 208 39.55 N 75.39 W
Brandywine Creek, West Branch ≃ 208 39.55 N 75.39 W
Brandywine Creek State Park ♠ 285 39.48 N 75.35 W
Brandywine Park ♠ 285 39.45 N 75.33 W
Brandywine Springs Park ♠ 285 39.45 N 75.38 W
Branford, Ct., U.S. 207 41.16 N 72.48 W
Branford, Fl., U.S. 192 29.57 N 82.55 W

ENGLISH Name	Page	Lat.°′	Long.°′	DEUTSCH Name	Seite	Breite°′	Länge°′ E = Ost

Brani, Pulau I 271c 1.15 N 103.50 E
Braniewo 30 54.24 N 19.50 E
Branka, Česko. 60 49.50 N 12.33 E
Br'anka, Ross. 86 59.08 N 93.27 E
Br'anka, Ukr. 83 48.29 N 38.39 E
Branlin ≃ 50 47.51 N 3.06 E
Brannenburg 64 47.44 N 12.05 E
Branquinho ≃ 248 5.45 S 71.27 W
Bransby 166 28.14 S 142.04 E
Bransfield Strait ʯ 9 63.00 S 59.00 W
Bransgore 42 50.47 N 1.44 W
Brańsk, Pol. 30 52.45 N 22.51 E
Br'ansk, Ross. 76 53.15 N 34.22 E
Br'anskaja Kosa, mys › 84 44.22 N 47.00 E
Br'ansk Oblast' □[4] 76 53.00 N 34.00 E
Branson 194 36.38 N 93.13 W
Brant 210 42.35 N 79.01 W
Brant □[6] 212 43.10 N 80.20 W
Brant ≃ 44 53.09 N 0.35 W
Br'anta ≃ 89 54.27 N 127.42 E
Brantas ≃ 115a 7.28 S 112.25 E
Brantford 212 43.08 N 80.16 W
Brantingham Lake ⊜ 212 43.42 N 75.17 W
Brant Lake 188 43.40 N 73.45 W
Brantley 194 31.34 N 86.15 W
Brantôme 32 45.22 N 0.39 E
Brant Rock 283 42.05 N 70.38 W
Brantville 186 47.22 N 64.58 W
Branxholme 166 37.51 S 141.47 E
Branxton 170 32.39 S 151.22 E
Branzi 64 46.00 N 9.46 E
Brás ◆[8] 287b 23.32 S 46.36 W
Brás Cubas 256 23.32 S 46.13 W
Bras d'Or Lake ⊜ 186 45.52 N 60.50 W
Brashear 222 33.07 N 95.44 W
Brasilândia ◆[8] 287b 23.28 S 46.41 W
Brasil → Brazil □[1] 242 10.00 S 55.00 W
Brasiléia 248 11.00 S 68.44 W
Brasília 255 15.47 S 47.55 W
Brasília, Parque Nacional de ♠ 255 15.36 S 48.08 W
Brasília de Minas 255 16.12 S 44.26 W
Brasília Legal 250 3.49 S 55.36 W
Brasilien → Brazil □[1] 242 10.00 S 55.00 W
Braslav 76 55.38 N 27.02 E
Brasopolis 256 22.28 S 45.37 W
Brașov 38 45.39 N 25.37 E
Brașov □[6] 38 45.45 N 25.15 E
Brass 150 4.19 N 6.14 E
Brass Castle 210 40.47 N 74.58 W
Brasschaat 50 51.17 N 4.27 E
Brassert 263 51.40 N 7.05 E
Brassey, Banjaran ⋀ 112 4.54 N 117.30 E
Brassey, Mount ∧ 162 23.05 S 134.38 E
Brass Islands II 240m 18.24 N 64.58 W
Brassó → Brașov 38 45.39 N 25.37 E
Brasstown Bald ∧ 192 34.52 N 83.48 W
Brastad 26 58.23 N 11.29 E
Brasted 260 51.16 N 0.06 E
Brasted Chart 260 51.16 N 0.06 E
Břasy 60 49.50 N 13.35 E
Bratca 38 46.56 N 22.37 E
Bratcevo ◆[8] 265b 55.51 N 37.24 E
Bratejevo ◆[8] 265b 55.38 N 37.45 E
Bratenahl 279a 41.32 N 81.37 W
Brateș, Lacul ⊜ 38 45.30 N 28.05 E
Bratislava 30 48.09 N 17.07 E
Bratol'ubovka 86 51.13 N 66.46 E
Bratsk 88 56.05 N 101.48 E
Bratskaja Kada 88 55.02 N 102.06 E
Bratskoje 78 47.52 N 31.34 E
Bratskoje vodochranilišče ⊜[1] 88 56.10 N 102.10 E
Brattfors 40 59.40 N 14.01 E
Brattleboro 207 42.51 N 72.33 W
Bratto 64 45.55 N 10.04 E
Brattvåg 26 62.36 N 6.27 E
Braubach 56 50.16 N 7.40 E
Braulio Carrillo, Parque Nacional ♠ 236 10.10 N 84.00 W
Braúnas 255 19.04 S 42.43 W
Braunau am Inn 60 48.15 N 13.02 E
Braunfels 56 50.31 N 8.23 E
Braunlage 54 51.44 N 10.37 E
Bräunlingen 58 47.55 N 8.26 E
Braunsbedra 54 51.15 N 11.49 E
Braunschweig, Dtsch. 52 52.16 N 10.31 E
Braunschweig, S. Afr. 158 32.48 S 27.22 E
Braunschweig □[5] 54 52.10 N 10.30 E
Braunston 42 52.17 N 1.12 W
Braunton 42 51.07 N 4.10 W
Braunwald 58 46.56 N 9.00 E
Brava I 150a 14.52 N 24.43 W
Brava, Costa ≛[2] 34 41.45 N 3.04 E
Brava, Laguna ⊜ 252 28.22 S 68.50 W
Brava, Punta › 258 34.56 S 56.10 W
Brave 188 39.44 N 80.16 W
Bravića 78 47.22 N 28.26 E
Bråviken c 40 58.38 N 16.32 E
Bravo, Cerro ∧, Bol. 248 17.40 S 64.35 W
Bravo, Cerro ∧, Perú 248 5.32 S 79.15 W
Bravo del Norte (Rio Grande) ≃ 178 25.55 N 97.09 W
Brawley 204 32.58 N 115.31 W
Brawley Peaks ⋀ 204 38.15 N 118.55 W
Brawley Wash V 200 32.34 N 111.26 W
Bray, Bel. 50 50.26 N 4.06 E
Bray, Ire. 48 53.12 N 6.06 W
Bray ≃ 42 50.59 N 3.53 W
Bray, Pays de ◆[1] 50 49.46 N 1.26 E
Braybrook 274b 37.47 S 144.51 E
Bray-Dunes 50 51.05 N 2.31 E
Braye ≃ 50 47.45 N 0.42 E
Bray Head › 48 51.53 N 10.26 W
Bray Island I 176 69.20 N 76.45 W
Braymer 194 39.35 N 93.47 W
Braysur-Seine 50 48.25 N 3.14 E
Bray-sur-Somme 50 49.56 N 2.43 E
Brayton 44 53.46 N 1.05 W
Brazeau ≃ 182 52.55 N 115.15 W
Brazeau, Mount ∧ 182 52.33 N 117.21 W
Brazeau Dam ◆[6] 182 52.45 N 115.30 W
Brazen Head › 158 31.43 S 29.25 E
Brazey-en-Plaine 58 47.08 N 5.13 E
Brazil 194 39.31 N 87.07 W
Brazil (Brasil) □[1] 242 10.00 S 55.00 W
Brazil Basin ✢[1] 8 15.00 S 25.00 W
Brazo Chico, Arroyo ≃ 258 33.45 S 58.32 W
Brazo Largo, Arroyo ≃ 258 33.47 S 58.36 W
Brazoria 222 29.02 N 95.34 W
Brazoria □[6] 222 29.12 N 95.25 W
Brazoria Reservoir ⊜[1] 222 29.05 N 95.01 W
Brazos □[6] 222 30.40 N 96.18 W
Brazos ≃ 196 28.53 N 95.23 W
Brazos, Clear Fork ≃ 196 33.01 N 98.40 W
Brazos, Double Mountain Fork ≃ 196 33.15 N 100.00 W
Brazos, Salt Fork ≃ 196 33.15 N 100.00 W
Brazo Sur [del Rio Coig] ≃ 254 51.32 S 70.04 W
Brazzaville, Congo 152 4.16 S 15.17 E
Brazzaville, Congo 273b 4.16 S 15.17 E
Brazzaville (Maya Maya) Airport ⊠ 273b 4.15 S 15.15 E
Brčko 38 44.53 N 18.48 E
Brda ≃ 30 53.07 N 18.08 E
Brdy ⋀ 60 49.40 N 13.50 E
Brea 228 33.55 N 117.53 W
Brea, Punta › 240m 17.56 N 66.55 W
Brea Canyon V 280 33.55 N 117.55 W
Brea Creek ≃ 280 33.53 N 117.59 W
Breadalbane 166 23.49 S 139.35 E
Brea Dam ◆[6] 280 33.54 N 117.56 W
Breaden Bluff ∧[2] 162 26.56 S 124.32 E
Breadysville 285 40.13 N 75.04 W
Breakenridge, Mount ∧ 182 49.43 N 121.56 W
Breakheart Reservation ♠ 283 42.29 N 71.02 W
Breaksea Sound ʯ 172 45.35 S 166.40 E
Breaks Interstate Park ♠ 192 37.17 N 82.18 W
Bream 42 51.45 N 2.34 W
Bream Bay c 172 35.55 S 174.30 E
Bream Head › 172 35.51 S 174.35 E
Breamish ≃ 44 55.31 N 1.56 W
Bream Tail › 172 36.03 S 174.35 E
Brea Pozo 252 28.15 S 63.57 W
Breaston 44 52.54 N 1.19 W
Bréau 261 48.34 N 2.53 E
Breaux Bridge 194 30.16 N 91.53 W
Breaza 38 45.11 N 25.40 E
Brebes 115a 6.53 S 109.03 E
Bré → Bray 48 53.12 N 6.06 W
Brécey 32 48.44 N 1.10 W
Brechen 56 50.20 N 8.14 E
Brechfa 42 51.57 N 4.09 W
Brechin 46 56.44 N 2.40 W
Brecht 56 51.21 N 4.38 E
Brechten ◆[8] 263 51.35 N 7.28 E
Breckenridge, Co., U.S. 200 39.28 N 106.02 W
Breckenridge, Mi., U.S. 190 43.24 N 84.28 W
Breckenridge, Mn., U.S. 198 46.15 N 96.35 W
Breckenridge, Mo., U.S. 194 39.45 N 93.48 W
Breckenridge, Tx., U.S. 196 32.45 N 98.54 W
Breckerfeld 56 51.16 N 7.28 E
Breckland ◆[1] 42 52.28 N 0.37 E
Brecknock, Península ›[1] 254 54.35 S 71.50 W
Brecknock → Brecon 42 51.57 N 3.24 W
Brecksville 214 41.19 N 81.37 W
Břeclav 30 48.46 N 16.53 E
Brecon 42 51.57 N 3.24 W
Brecon Beacons ∧ 42 51.53 N 3.31 W
Brecon Beacons National Park ♠ 42 51.52 N 3.25 W
Bred 41 55.22 N 10.07 E
Breda, Ned. 52 51.35 N 4.46 E
Breda, Ia., U.S. 198 42.10 N 94.58 W
Bredaryd 26 57.10 N 13.44 E
Bredasdorp 158 34.32 S 20.02 E
Bredbo 171b 35.57 S 149.10 E
Bredbo ≃ 171b 35.58 S 149.08 E
Bredbury 262 53.25 N 2.06 W
Bredbyn 26 63.27 N 18.06 E
Breddin 54 52.52 N 12.13 E
Brede ≃ 41 55.09 N 8.42 E
Bredebro 41 55.03 N 8.49 E
Bredell 273d 26.05 S 28.17 E
Bredenbeck 52 52.15 N 9.37 E
Bredenbruch 263 51.21 N 7.45 E
Bredenbury 184 50.57 N 102.03 W
Bredene 50 51.14 N 2.58 E
Bredeney ◆[8] 263 51.24 N 6.59 E
Bredenscheid-Stüter 263 51.22 N 7.11 E
Bredereiche 54 53.08 N 13.14 E
Bredgar 260 51.18 N 0.42 E
Bredhurst 260 51.20 N 0.35 E
Bredon Hill ∧[2] 42 52.06 N 2.03 W
Bredsjö 40 59.50 N 14.44 E
Bredsjön ⊜ 40 60.13 N 13.55 E
Bredstedt 41 54.37 N 8.59 E
Bredsten 41 55.42 N 9.24 E
Bredy 86 52.26 N 60.21 E
Bree 56 51.08 N 5.36 E
Breë ≃ 158 34.24 S 20.50 E
Breeches, Lac ⊜ 206 45.54 N 71.28 W
Breedoge ≃ 48 53.55 N 8.27 W
Breeds Pond ⊜ 283 42.28 N 70.59 W
Breedsville 216 42.21 N 86.08 W
Breese 219 38.36 N 89.31 W
Breesport 210 42.10 N 76.44 W
Breeza Plains 164 14.50 S 144.07 E
Breezewood 279b 40.34 N 80.03 W
Breg ≃ 58 47.57 N 8.31 E
Bregalnica ≃ 38 41.43 N 22.09 E
Breganze 64 45.42 N 11.34 E
Bregenz 58 47.30 N 9.46 E
Bregenzer Wald ⋀ 58 47.20 N 10.00 E
Bregninge, Dan. 41 55.41 N 11.19 E
Bregninge, Dan. 41 55.01 N 10.37 E
Bregovo 38 44.09 N 22.39 E
Breguzzo 64 46.00 N 10.42 E
Brégy 261 49.05 N 2.52 E
Bréhal 32 48.54 N 1.31 W
Brehna 54 51.33 N 12.12 E
Breiđafjörđur c 24a 65.15 N 23.15 W
Breidbach 158 32.54 S 27.27 E
Breid Bay c 9 70.15 S 24.15 E
Breidenbach 56 49.08 N 7.25 E
Breidenstein 56 50.55 N 8.28 E
Breil-sur-Roya 62 43.56 N 7.30 E
Breinizer 214 40.24 N 79.16 W
Breisach 58 48.01 N 7.40 E
Breisgau □[9] 58 47.45 N 7.45 E
Breitenbrunn 54 50.29 N 12.46 E
Breitenfelde 52 53.36 N 10.38 E
Breitenfurt bei Wien 61 48.08 N 16.08 E
Breitengüssbach 56 49.58 N 10.53 E
Breitenlee ◆[8] 264b 48.15 N 16.30 E
Breitenstein 54 51.37 N 10.56 E
Breitenworbis 54 51.24 N 10.25 E
Breithorn ∧ 58 45.56 N 7.45 E
Breitlingsee ⊜ 54 52.23 N 12.28 E
Breitscheid, Dtsch. 56 50.41 N 8.11 E
Breitscheid, Dtsch. 56 51.22 N 6.52 E
Breitsetten 61 48.12 N 16.42 E
Breitungen 54 50.45 N 10.20 E
Brejinho de Nazaré 250 11.01 S 48.34 W
Brejo 250 3.41 S 42.47 W
Brejões 255 13.06 S 39.48 W
Brejo Grande 250 10.26 S 36.28 W
Brejo Santo 250 7.29 S 39.00 W
Brejtovo 76 58.18 N 37.52 E
Brekken 26 62.39 N 11.53 E
Brekstad 26 63.41 N 9.41 E
Breloh 52 53.01 N 10.04 E
Bremangerlandet I 26 61.51 N 5.02 E
Brembio 62 45.13 N 9.34 E
Brembo ≃ 62 45.35 N 9.32 E
Brême → Bremen 52 53.04 N 8.49 E
Bremelau 58 48.20 N 9.32 E
Bremen, Dtsch. 52 53.04 N 8.49 E
Bremen, Ga., U.S. 192 33.43 N 85.08 W
Bremen, In., U.S. 216 41.26 N 86.08 W
Bremen, Oh., U.S. 188 39.42 N 82.25 W
Bremen □[3] 52 53.05 N 8.50 E
Bremen, Flughafen ⊠ 52 53.03 N 8.46 E
Bremer ≃, Austl. 168b 35.23 S 139.02 E
Bremer ≃, Austl. 171a 27.39 S 152.45 E
Bremer Bay 162 34.24 S 119.22 E
Bremer Bay c 162 34.23 S 119.25 E
Bremerhaven 52 53.33 N 8.34 E
Bremerton 224 47.34 N 122.37 W
Bremerton East 224 47.35 N 122.38 W
Bremervörde 52 53.29 N 9.08 E
Bremgarten 58 47.21 N 8.21 E
Bremke, Dtsch. 52 52.07 N 9.06 E
Bremke, Dtsch. 56 51.15 N 8.12 E
Bremke, Dtsch. 263 51.23 N 7.41 E
Bremner ≃ 190 48.41 N 85.31 W
Bremond 222 31.09 N 96.40 W
Brem River 182 50.26 N 124.39 W
Breña 286d 12.04 S 77.04 W
Brendel Lake ⊜ 281 42.38 N 83.30 W
Brenderup 41 55.29 N 9.59 E

Symbols in the index entries represent the broad categories identified in the key at the right. Symbols with superior numbers (⋀[1]) identify subcategories (see complete key on page *I · 1)*.

Symbole im Register stellen die rechts im Schlüssel erklärten Kategorien dar. Symbole mit hochgestellten Ziffern (⋀[1]) bezeichnen Unterabteilungen einer Kategorie (vgl. vollständiger Schlüssel auf Seite *I · 1)*.

Los símbolos incluídos en el texto del índice representan las grandes categorias identificadas con la clave a la derecha. Los símbolos con numeros en su parte superior (⋀[1]) identifican las subcategorías (véase la clave completa en la página *I · 1)*.

Les symboles de l'index représentent les catégories indiquées dans la légende. Les symboles suivis d'un indice (⋀[1]) représentent des sous-catégories (voir légende complète à la page *I · 1)*.

Os símbolos incluídos no texto do índice representam as grandes categorias identificadas com a chave à direita. Os símbolos com números em sua parte superior (⋀[1]) identificam as subcategorias (veja-se a chave completa à página *I · 1)*.

∧	Mountain	Berg	Montaña	Montagne	Montanha
⋀	Mountains	Gebirge	Montañas	Montagnes	Montanhas
)(	Pass	Paß	Paso	Col	Passo
V	Valley, Canyon	Tal, Cañon	Valle, Cañón	Vallée, Canyon	Vale, Canhão
≚	Plain	Ebene	Llano	Plaine	Planície
›	Cape	Kap	Cabo	Cap	Cabo
I	Island	Insel	Isla	Île	Ilha
II	Islands	Inseln	Islas	Îles	Ilhas
◆	Other Topographic Features	Andere Topographische Objekte	Otros Elementos Topográficos	Autres données topographiques	Outros acidentes topográficos

ESPAÑOL

Nombre	Página	Lat.°′	Long.°′ W = Oeste
Brendlorenzen	56	50.20 N	10.13 E
Brendon Hills ⋌[2]	42	51.07 N	3.25 W
Brenham	222	30.10 N	96.23 W
Brenig, Llyn ◎[1]	44	53.05 N	3.32 W
Brenish	46	58.08 N	7.08 W
Brenish, Aird ≻	46	58.08 N	7.08 W
Bren Mar Park	284c	38.48 N	77.09 W
Brenne ≃	50	47.38 N	4.16 E
Brennero (Brenner)	64	47.00 N	11.30 E
Brennero, Passo del → Brenner Pass ʮ	64	47.00 N	11.30 E
Brenner Pass ʮ	64	47.00 N	11.30 E
Breno, It.	64	45.57 N	10.18 E
Breno, Schw.	58	46.02 N	8.53 E
Brénod	58	46.04 N	5.36 E
Brent, Al., U.S.	194	32.56 N	87.09 W
Brent, Fl., U.S.	194	30.28 N	87.14 W
Brent ◆[8]	42	51.34 N	0.17 W
Brent ≃	260	51.28 N	0.18 W
Brenta ≃	64	45.11 N	12.18 E
Brenta, Gruppo di ⋌	64	46.11 N	10.54 E
Brentford ◆[8]	260	51.29 N	0.18 W
Brenthurst	273d	26.16 S	28.23 E
Brentino	64	45.40 N	10.55 E
Brentonico	64	45.49 N	10.57 E
Brent Reservoir ◎[1]	260	51.35 N	0.15 W
Brentwood, Eng., U.K.	42	51.38 N	0.18 E
Brentwood, Eng., U.K.	260	51.38 N	0.18 E
Brentwood, Ca., U.S.	226	37.55 N	121.41 W
Brentwood, Md., U.S.	208	38.56 N	76.57 W
Brentwood, N.Y., U.S.	210	40.46 N	73.14 W
Brentwood, Oh., U.S.	218	39.13 N	84.31 W
Brentwood, Pa., U.S.	214	40.22 N	79.58 W
Brentwood, Tn., U.S.	194	36.01 N	86.46 W
Brentwood □[8]	260	51.37 N	0.20 E
Brentwood Bay	224	48.35 N	123.28 W
Brentwood Estates	214	40.25 N	80.45 W
Brentwood Heights ◆[8]	280	34.04 N	118.30 W
Brentwood Lake	214	41.19 N	82.05 W
Brentwood Park	273d	26.08 S	28.18 E
Brenz ≃	56	48.34 N	10.24 E
Breo	62	44.23 N	7.49 E
Bréon, Ruisseu du ≃	261	48.40 N	2.49 E
Brera, Palazzo di ▾	266b	45.28 N	9.11 E
Brereton Park	158	26.55 S	30.30 E
Brescello	64	44.54 N	10.31 E
Brescia	64	45.33 N	13.15 E
Brescia □[4]	64	45.38 N	10.18 E
Bresewitz	54	54.24 N	12.40 E
Brésil → Brazil □[1]	242	10.00 S	55.00 W
Breskens	52	51.24 N	3.34 E
Breslau, On., Can.	212	43.28 N	80.25 W
Breslau, Tx., U.S.	222	29.31 N	97.00 W
Breslau → Wrocław	30	51.06 N	17.00 E
Bresle ≃	50	50.04 N	1.22 E
Bresles	50	49.25 N	2.15 E
Bresnahan, Mount ∧	162	23.50 S	117.55 E
Bressanone (Brixen)	64	46.43 N	11.39 E
Bressay I	46a	60.08 N	1.05 W
Bressay Sound ʮ	46a	60.07 N	1.09 W
Bresse ◆[1]	58	46.30 N	5.15 E
Bresso	266b	45.32 N	9.11 E
Bressuire	32	46.51 N	0.30 W
Brest, Blg.	38	43.38 N	24.35 E
Brest, Bela.	76	52.06 N	23.42 E
Brest, Fr.	32	48.24 N	4.29 W
Brest □[8]	76	52.30 N	25.30 E
Brestanica	36	45.59 N	15.29 E
Bretagne (Brittany) □[9]	32	48.00 N	3.00 W
Bretenoux	32	44.55 N	1.50 E
Breteuil	50	49.38 N	2.18 E
Breteuil-sur-Iton	50	48.50 N	0.55 E
Bréthencourt	261	48.30 N	1.55 E
Bretherton	262	53.41 N	2.48 W
Brétigny ■	261	48.35 N	2.20 E
Brétigny-sur-Orge	50	48.37 N	2.19 E
Bretnig	54	51.08 N	14.04 E
Breton	182	53.07 N	114.28 W
Bretón, Canal de ʮ	240p	21.10 N	79.30 W
Breton, Pertuis ʮ	32	46.25 N	1.20 W
Breton Bay ⊂	208	38.16 N	76.39 W
Breton Islands II	194	29.28 N	89.11 W
Breton Sound ʮ	194	29.30 N	89.30 W
Breton Woods	208	40.02 N	74.06 W
Brett ≃	42	51.58 N	0.58 E
Brett, Cape ≻	172	35.10 S	174.20 E
Bretten	56	49.02 N	8.42 E
Breu, Rio do ≃	246	3.29 S	66.20 W
Breueh, Pulau I	110	5.41 N	95.05 E
Breuil-Bois-Robert	261	48.57 N	1.43 E
Breuil-Cervinia	58	45.56 N	7.38 E
Breuillet	261	48.34 N	2.10 E
Breuilpont	50	48.58 N	1.26 E
Breukelen	52	52.10 N	5.00 E
Breux	261	48.34 N	2.11 E
Brevard	192	35.14 N	82.44 W
Brevard □[6]	220	28.18 N	80.42 W
Brévenne ≃	62	45.51 N	4.40 E
Brevens bruk	40	59.01 N	15.35 E
Breves	250	1.40 S	50.29 W
Brevig Mission	180	65.20 N	166.29 W
Brevik, Nor.	26	59.04 N	9.42 E
Brevik, Sve.	40	59.21 N	18.12 E
Brevoort Island I	176	63.30 N	64.20 W
Brewarrina	166	29.57 S	146.52 E
Brewer	188	44.47 N	68.45 W
Brewer Island I	282	37.33 N	122.16 W
Brewersville	218	39.05 N	85.37 W
Brewerton	210	43.14 N	76.08 W
Brewerville	150	6.26 N	10.47 W
Brewongle	170	33.29 S	149.43 E
Brewood	42	52.41 N	2.10 W
Brewster, Ks., U.S.	198	39.22 N	101.22 W
Brewster, Ma., U.S.	207	41.45 N	70.05 W
Brewster, Mn., U.S.	198	43.41 N	95.28 W
Brewster, Ne., U.S.	198	41.56 N	99.51 W
Brewster, N.Y., U.S.	210	41.23 N	73.37 W
Brewster, Oh., U.S.	214	40.42 N	81.35 W
Brewster, Wa., U.S.	202	48.05 N	119.46 W
Brewster, Kap ≻	16	70.19 N	22.05 W
Brewster, Lake ◎	166	33.28 S	146.00 E
Brewster, Mount ∧	172	44.04 S	169.27 E
Brewton	194	31.06 N	87.04 W
Breyten	158	26.16 S	30.00 E
Břežany	61	48.52 N	16.20 E
Brežice	36	45.54 N	15.36 E
Brézina	148	33.04 N	1.14 E
Brézins	62	45.21 N	5.19 E
Březnice	60	49.33 N	13.57 E
Breznik	38	42.44 N	22.54 E
Březno, Česko.	54	50.24 N	13.26 E
Brezno, Slov.	30	48.50 N	19.39 E
Brézolles	50	48.41 N	1.04 E
Březová	54	50.06 N	12.39 E
Březové Hory	60	49.41 N	13.58 E
Bria	152	6.32 N	21.59 E
Brian Boru Peak ∧	182	55.05 N	127.35 W
Briançon	62	44.54 N	6.39 E
Brian Head ∧	200	37.41 N	112.50 W
Brianza □[9]	62	45.40 N	9.10 E
Briar	222	33.00 N	97.34 W
Briarcliff Manor	210	41.08 N	73.49 W
Briar Creek	210	40.10 N	76.46 W
Briar Creek ≃	222	32.06 N	96.22 W
Briare	50	47.38 N	2.44 E
Briare, Canal de ≅	50	48.02 N	2.43 E
Briarres-sur-Essonne	50	48.14 N	2.25 E
Briarwood Beach	214	41.06 N	81.54 W
Briarwood Center ◆[9]	281	42.14 N	83.45 W
Briatico	68	38.43 N	16.02 E
Bribano	64	46.06 N	12.05 E
Bribie Island I	171a	27.00 S	153.07 E

FRANÇAIS

Nom	Page	Lat.°′	Long.°′ W = Ouest
Bričany	78	48.22 N	27.04 E
Bricelyn	190	43.33 N	93.48 W
Brice Run ≃	284b	39.19 N	76.50 W
Brices Cross Roads National Battlefield Site ⊥	194	34.31 N	88.41 W
Briceville	192	36.10 N	84.11 W
Bricherasio	62	44.49 N	7.18 E
Bricht	263	51.41 N	6.51 E
Brickebacken	40	59.15 N	15.15 E
Brick Lake ◎	220	28.10 N	81.12 W
Brick Township	208	40.04 N	74.08 W
Briçonnet, Lac ◎	186	51.27 N	60.11 W
Bricquebec	32	49.28 N	1.38 W
Bridal Veil	224	45.33 N	122.10 W
Bridalveil Fall ∟	226	37.43 N	119.39 W
Bride	44	54.22 N	4.22 W
Bride ≃	48	52.04 N	7.52 W
Bridesburg ◆[8]	285	40.00 N	75.04 W
Bridge	42	51.14 N	1.07 E
Bridge ≃	182	50.45 N	121.55 W
Bridge City	194	30.01 N	93.50 W
Bridge Creek ≃	224	48.26 N	120.52 W
Bridgehampton	207	40.56 N	72.18 W
Bridge Lake	182	51.29 N	120.43 W
Bridgend, Scot., U.K.	46	56.48 N	2.45 W
Bridgend, Scot., U.K.	46	55.48 N	6.16 W
Bridgend, Wales, U.K.	42	51.31 N	3.35 W
Bridgenorth	212	44.23 N	78.23 W
Bridge of Allan	46	56.09 N	3.57 W
Bridge of Gaur	46	56.41 N	4.27 W
Bridge of Orchy	46	56.30 N	4.46 W
Bridge of Weir	46	55.52 N	4.35 W
Bridgeport, On., Can.	212	43.29 N	80.29 W
Bridgeport, Al., U.S.	194	34.56 N	85.42 W
Bridgeport, Ca., U.S.	226	38.10 N	119.13 W
Bridgeport, Ct., U.S.	207	41.10 N	73.12 W
Bridgeport, Il., U.S.	194	38.42 N	87.45 W
Bridgeport, Mi., U.S.	190	43.21 N	83.52 W
Bridgeport, Ne., U.S.	198	41.39 N	103.05 W
Bridgeport, N.J., U.S.	285	39.48 N	75.20 W
Bridgeport, N.Y., U.S.	210	43.09 N	75.58 W
Bridgeport, Oh., U.S.	214	40.04 N	80.44 W
Bridgeport, Pa., U.S.	285	40.06 N	75.21 W
Bridgeport, Tx., U.S.	222	33.12 N	97.45 W
Bridgeport, Wa., U.S.	202	48.00 N	119.40 W
Bridgeport, W.V., U.S.	188	39.17 N	80.15 W
Bridgeport ◆[8]	278	41.51 N	87.39 W
Bridgeport, Lake ◎[1]	222	33.13 N	97.48 W
Bridgeport, University of ▾[2]	276	41.10 N	73.12 W
Bridgeport Airport ⊠	285	39.47 N	75.20 W
Bridgeport Harbor ⊂	276	41.10 N	73.11 W
Bridgeport Municipal Airport ⊠	276	41.10 N	73.08 W
Bridgeport Reservoir ◎[1]	226	38.22 N	119.14 W
Bridger	202	45.17 N	108.54 W
Bridge River Indian Reserve ◆[4]	182	50.45 N	122.00 W
Bridger Peak ∧	200	41.12 N	107.02 W
Bridges Point ≻	174o	1.58 N	157.28 W
Bridgeton, Mo., U.S.	219	38.44 N	90.24 W
Bridgeton, N.J., U.S.	208	39.25 N	75.14 W
Bridgetown, Austl.	162	33.57 S	116.08 E
Bridgetown, Barb.	241g	13.06 N	59.37 W
Bridgetown, N.S., Can.	186	44.51 N	65.18 W
Bridgetown, Oh., U.S.	218	39.09 N	84.38 W
Bridge Trafford	262	53.14 N	2.49 W
Bridgeview	278	41.45 N	87.48 W
Bridgeville, De., U.S.	208	38.44 N	75.36 W
Bridgeville, Pa., U.S.	214	40.21 N	80.06 W
Bridgewater, Austl.	166	42.44 S	147.14 E
Bridgewater, Austl.	168b	35.02 S	138.47 E
Bridgewater, N.S., Can.	186	44.23 N	64.31 W
Bridgewater, Ct., U.S.	210	41.32 N	73.22 W
Bridgewater, Me., U.S.	186	46.25 N	67.50 W
Bridgewater, Ma., U.S.	207	41.59 N	70.58 W
Bridgewater, N.Y., U.S.	210	42.58 N	75.15 W
Bridgewater, Pa., U.S.	285	40.05 N	74.55 W
Bridgewater, S.D., U.S.	198	43.33 N	97.30 W
Bridgewater, Va., U.S.	188	38.22 N	78.58 W
Bridgewater Canal ≅	262	53.20 N	2.45 W
Bridgewater State College ▾[2]	283	41.59 N	70.58 W
Bridgman	216	41.57 N	86.33 W
Bridgnorth	42	52.33 N	2.25 W
Bridgton	188	44.03 N	70.42 W
Bridgwater	42	51.08 N	3.00 W
Bridgwater Bay ⊂	42	51.16 N	3.12 W
Bridlington	44	54.05 N	0.12 W
Bridlington Bay ⊂	44	54.04 N	0.08 W
Bridport	42	50.44 N	2.46 W
Brie ◆[1]	50	48.40 N	3.20 E
Briec	32	48.06 N	4.00 W
Brie-Comte-Robert	50	48.41 N	2.37 E
Brie Française ◆[1]	261	48.40 N	2.50 E
Brieg → Brzeg	30	50.52 N	17.27 E
Brielle, Ned.	52	51.54 N	4.10 E
Brielle, N.J., U.S.	208	40.06 N	74.03 W
Brienne-le-Château	58	48.24 N	4.32 E
Brienne-sur-Aisne	50	49.26 N	4.03 E
Brienno	58	45.55 N	9.07 E
Brienon-sur-Armançon	50	48.00 N	3.37 E
Brien Run ≃	284b	39.20 N	76.28 W
Brienz	58	46.46 N	8.03 E
Brienza	68	40.29 N	15.37 E
Brienzer Rothorn ∧	58	46.48 N	8.04 E
Brienzersee ◎	58	46.43 N	7.57 E
Brier Creek ≃	192	32.47 N	81.26 W
Brierfield	44	53.50 N	2.14 W
Brier Hill	212	44.32 N	75.40 W
Brier Island I	186	44.16 N	66.22 W
Brierley Hill	42	52.29 N	2.07 W
Brier Mountain ∧	210	41.37 N	77.02 W
Briese	264a	52.42 N	13.18 E
Briese ≃	264a	52.41 N	13.15 E
Brieselang	54	52.35 N	13.00 E
Briesen	54	52.20 N	14.16 E
Brieske	54	51.29 N	13.57 E
Brieskow-Finkenheerd	54	52.16 N	14.35 E
Briest	54	52.31 N	12.08 E
Briey	56	49.15 N	5.56 E
Brig	58	46.19 N	8.00 E
Brigach ≃	58	47.58 N	8.30 E
Brigantine	208	39.24 N	74.21 W
Brig Bay	186	51.04 N	56.55 W
Brigden	214	42.49 N	82.17 W
Brigg	44	53.34 N	0.30 W
Briggs	196	30.53 N	97.56 W
Brigham City	200	41.30 N	112.00 W
Brighouse	44	53.42 N	1.47 W
Brighstone	42	50.38 N	1.24 W
Bright	166	36.44 S	146.58 E
Brightlingsea	42	51.49 N	1.02 E
Brightmoor ◆[8]	281	42.24 N	83.14 W
Brighton, Austl.	168b	35.01 S	138.31 E
Brighton, Austl.	169	37.55 S	145.00 E
Brighton, On., Can.	212	44.02 N	77.44 W
Brighton, N.Z.	172	45.57 S	170.20 E
Brighton, Eng., U.K.	42	50.50 N	0.08 W
Brighton, Co., U.S.	200	39.59 N	104.49 W
Brighton, Fl., U.S.	220	27.14 N	81.06 W
Brighton, Il., U.S.	219	39.02 N	90.08 W
Brighton, Ia., U.S.	190	41.10 N	91.49 W

PORTUGUÊS

Nome	Página	Lat.°′	Long.°′ W = Oeste
Brighton, Md., U.S.	284b	39.21 N	76.43 W
Brighton, Mi., U.S.	216	42.31 N	83.46 W
Brighton, N.Y., U.S.	210	43.08 N	77.33 W
Brighton ◆[8]	283	42.21 N	71.08 W
Brighton Airport ⊠	281	42.34 N	83.47 W
Brighton Downs	166	23.22 S	141.34 E
Brighton Indian Reservation ◆[4]	220	27.04 N	81.05 W
Brighton-Le-Sands	274a	33.58 S	151.09 E
Brighton Park ◆[8]	278	41.49 N	87.42 W
Brighton State Recreation Area ♠	216	42.30 N	83.48 W
Brightsand Lake ◎	184	53.36 N	108.52 W
Brightwater	172	41.23 S	173.07 E
Brightwaters	276	40.43 N	73.16 W
Brightwood	224	45.23 N	122.01 W
Brightwood ◆[8]	284c	38.58 N	77.02 W
Brigittenau ◆[8]	264b	48.14 N	16.22 E
Brignoles	62	43.24 N	6.04 E
Brignoud	62	45.15 N	5.54 E
Brig o'Turk	46	56.13 N	4.22 W
Brigstock	42	52.27 N	0.36 W
Brigus	186	47.32 N	53.13 W
Brihuega	34	40.45 N	2.52 W
Briis-sous-Forges	261	48.38 N	2.07 E
Brijuni (Brioni)	64	44.55 N	13.46 E
Brijuni I	64	44.55 N	13.46 E
Brikama	150	13.15 N	16.39 W
Brilhante ≃	255	21.58 S	54.18 W
Brill	42	51.49 N	1.03 W
Brilliant, B.C., Can.	182	49.19 N	117.38 W
Brilliant, Al., U.S.	194	34.01 N	87.45 W
Brilliant, Oh., U.S.	214	40.15 N	80.37 W
Brillion	190	44.10 N	88.03 W
Brilon	56	51.24 N	8.34 E
Brilyn Park	284c	38.54 N	77.10 W
Brimfield, Eng., U.K.	42	52.18 N	2.42 W
Brimfield, In., U.S.	216	41.27 N	85.24 W
Brimfield, Ma., U.S.	207	42.07 N	72.12 W
Brimfield, Oh., U.S.	214	41.06 N	81.21 W
Brimington	44	53.16 N	1.23 W
Brindabella	171b	35.23 S	148.45 E
Brindisi	68	40.38 N	17.56 E
Brindisi □[4]	68	40.35 N	17.40 E
Brindisi Montagna	68	40.37 N	15.57 E
Brindle	262	53.43 N	2.36 W
Bringelly	170	33.56 S	150.44 E
Bringelly Creek ≃	274a	33.58 S	150.38 E
Brinje	36	45.00 N	15.08 E
Brinkerton	279b	40.13 N	79.32 W
Brinkhaven	214	40.28 N	82.12 W
Brinkleigh	284b	39.18 N	76.50 W
Brinkley, Austl.	168b	35.14 S	139.13 E
Brinkley, Ar., U.S.	194	34.53 N	91.11 W
Brinkum	52	53.00 N	8.47 E
Brinkworth	166	33.42 S	138.24 E
Brinnon	224	47.40 N	122.53 W
Brinon-sur-Beuvron	50	47.17 N	3.30 E
Brins, Ābār al- ⊤[4]	142	30.29 N	30.05 E
Brinscall	262	53.41 N	2.34 W
Brinyan	46	59.07 N	2.59 W
Brion, Île I	186	47.48 N	61.28 W
Brione	58	46.18 N	8.47 E
Briones Hills ⋌[2]	282	37.56 N	122.08 W
Briones Regional Park ♠	282	37.56 N	122.08 W
Briones Reservoir ◎[1]	282	37.55 N	122.12 W
Brionne	50	49.12 N	0.43 E
Brion-sur-Ource	58	47.55 N	4.39 E
Brioude	32	45.18 N	3.23 E
Briouze	32	48.42 N	0.22 W
Brisbane, Austl.	171a	27.28 S	153.02 E
Brisbane, Ca., U.S.	226	37.41 N	122.24 W
Brisbane ≃	171a	27.24 S	153.09 E
Brisbane, Mount ∧	171a	27.05 S	152.32 E
Brisbane International Airport ⊠	171a	27.27 S	153.11 E
Brisbane Ranges National Park ♠	169	37.52 S	144.14 E
Brisbane Water ⊂	170	33.28 S	151.20 E
Brisbane Water National Park ♠	170	33.30 S	151.15 E
Brisben	210	42.22 N	75.41 W
Brisbin	214	40.50 N	78.21 W
Briseñas	234	20.16 N	102.33 W
Brisighella	66	44.13 N	11.46 E
Brissac	62	43.52 N	3.42 E
Brissago	58	46.07 N	8.43 E
Bristol, Eng., U.K.	42	51.27 N	2.35 W
Bristol, Ct., U.S.	207	41.41 N	72.57 W
Bristol, Fl., U.S.	192	30.25 N	84.58 W
Bristol, Il., U.S.	216	41.39 N	88.27 W
Bristol, In., U.S.	216	41.43 N	85.49 W
Bristol, N.H., U.S.	188	43.35 N	71.44 W
Bristol, Pa., U.S.	208	40.06 N	74.51 W
Bristol, R.I., U.S.	207	41.40 N	71.16 W
Bristol, S.D., U.S.	198	45.20 N	97.44 W
Bristol, Tn., U.S.	192	36.35 N	82.11 W
Bristol, Vt., U.S.	188	44.08 N	73.04 W
Bristol, Va., U.S.	192	36.35 N	82.11 W
Bristol, Wi., U.S.	216	42.33 N	88.02 W
Bristol □[6], Ma., U.S.	207	41.54 N	71.06 W
Bristol □[6], R.I., U.S.	207	41.42 N	71.18 W
Bristol (Lulsgate) Airport ⊠	42	51.23 N	2.43 W
Bristol Bay ⊂	180	58.00 N	159.00 W
Bristol-Blake Reservation ♠	283	42.06 N	71.19 W
Bristol Center	210	42.49 N	77.23 W
Bristol Channel ʮ	42	51.20 N	4.00 W
Bristol Lake ◎	204	34.28 N	115.41 W
Bristolville	214	41.23 N	80.52 W
Bristow	196	35.49 N	96.23 W
Britânia	255	15.14 S	51.09 W
Británicas, Islas → British Isles II	4	54.00 N	4.00 W
Britannia, On., Can.	275b	43.37 N	79.41 W
Britannia, Eng., U.K.	262	53.41 N	2.11 W
Britannia Beach	182	49.38 N	123.12 W
Britische Jungfern-Inseln → British Virgin Islands □[2]	240m	18.30 N	64.30 W
Britisches Antarktis-Territorium → British Antarctic Territory □[2]	9	60.00 S	45.00 W
British Antarctic Territory □[2]	9	60.00 S	45.00 W
British Columbia □[4], Can.	176	54.00 N	125.00 W
British Columbia □[4], Can.	182	54.00 N	125.00 W
British Honduras → Belize □[1]	232	17.15 N	88.45 W
British Indian Ocean Territory □[2]	12	7.00 S	72.00 E
British Isles II	4	54.00 N	4.00 W
British Mountains ⋌	180	69.00 N	140.20 W
British Museum ▾	260	51.31 N	0.08 W
British Solomon Islands → Solomon Islands □[1]	175e	8.00 S	159.00 E
British Virgin Islands □[2], N.A.	230	18.30 N	64.30 W
British Virgin Islands □[2], N.A.	240m	18.30 N	64.30 W
Britland Edge Hill ∧[2]	262	53.31 N	1.50 W
Briton Ferry	42	51.38 N	3.49 W
Brits	158	25.42 S	27.45 E
Britstown	158	30.37 S	23.30 E
Britt	190	43.05 N	93.48 W
Brittany → Bretagne □[9]	32	48.00 N	3.00 W
Brittas	48	53.14 N	6.27 W
Britten	158	27.42 S	25.17 E
Brittingham	196	25.45 N	103.24 W
Britton, Mi., U.S.	216	41.59 N	83.49 W
Britton, S.D., U.S.	198	45.47 N	97.45 W
Britton, Tx., U.S.	222	32.33 N	97.04 W
Britton, Mount ∧[2]	162	26.31 S	134.43 E
Britz	54	52.53 N	13.49 E
Britz ◆[8]	264a	52.27 N	13.26 E
Brive-la-Gaillarde	32	45.10 N	1.32 E
Brives-Charensac	62	45.03 N	3.56 E
Briviesca	34	42.33 N	3.19 W
Brivio	62	45.44 N	9.27 E
Brixen im Thale	64	47.27 N	12.15 E
Brixham	42	50.24 N	3.30 W
Brixlegg	64	47.25 N	11.53 E
Brixton	166	23.32 S	144.57 E
Brixworth	42	52.20 N	0.54 W
Brlik	85	43.40 N	73.49 E
Brloh	61	48.56 N	14.13 E
Brno	30	49.12 N	16.37 E
Bro	40	59.31 N	17.38 E
Broa, Ensenada de la ⊂	240p	22.35 N	82.00 W
Broad ≃, U.S.	192	34.00 N	81.04 W
Broad ≃, Fl., U.S.	220	25.28 N	81.09 W
Broad ≃, Ga., U.S.	192	33.59 N	82.39 W
Broadalbin	210	43.03 N	74.11 W
Broad Arrow	162	30.20 S	121.27 E
Broad Axe	285	40.10 N	75.15 W
Broadback ≃	176	51.21 N	78.52 W
Broad Bay ⊂	46	58.15 N	6.15 W
Broadbottom	262	53.26 N	2.01 W
Broad Brook	207	41.54 N	72.32 W
Broad Chalke	42	51.02 N	1.57 W
Broadclyst	42	50.46 N	3.26 W
Broad Creek ⊂	208	38.45 N	76.15 W
Broad Creek ≃	208	39.42 N	76.14 W
Broadford, Austl.	169	37.13 S	145.03 E
Broadford, Scot., U.K.	46	57.14 N	5.54 W
Broad Haven ⊂	48	54.18 N	9.55 W
Broadheath	262	53.24 N	2.21 W
Broadhurst Range ⋌	162	22.23 S	122.09 E
Broadkill ≃	208	38.47 N	75.10 W
Broad Law ∧	46	55.30 N	3.22 W
Broadley Common	260	51.45 N	0.04 E
Broadmeadows	169	37.40 S	144.54 E
Broadmoor	226	37.41 N	122.29 W
Broad Neck ≻[1]	208	39.03 N	76.27 W
Broad Oak	42	50.57 N	0.36 E
Broad Pass ʮ	180	63.18 N	149.09 W
Broad Run ≃, Pa., U.S.	285	39.56 N	75.41 W
Broad Run ≃, Pa., U.S.	285	39.59 N	75.40 W
Broad Run ≃, Va., U.S.	208	38.41 N	77.29 W
Broad Sound ʮ, Austl.	166	22.10 S	149.45 E
Broad Sound ʮ, Ma., U.S.	283	42.25 N	70.58 W
Broad Sound Channel ʮ	166	22.05 S	150.20 E
Broadstairs	42	51.22 N	1.27 E
Broad Street	260	51.17 N	0.38 E
Broad Top	214	40.12 N	78.08 W
Broadus	198	45.26 N	105.24 W
Broadview, Sk., Can.	184	50.20 N	102.30 W
Broadview, Il., U.S.	216	41.51 N	87.51 W
Broadview, In., U.S.	218	39.10 N	87.33 W
Broadview Heights	214	41.18 N	81.41 W
Broadwater	198	41.35 N	102.51 W
Broadway, Eng., U.K.	42	52.02 N	1.51 W
Broadway, Oh., U.S.	214	40.20 N	83.24 W
Broadway, Va., U.S.	188	38.38 N	78.46 W
Broadwell	219	40.04 N	89.27 W
Broadwindsor	42	50.49 N	2.48 W
Broadwood	172	35.16 S	173.23 E
Broager	41	54.53 N	9.41 E
Brobo	150	7.43 N	4.42 W
Broby	26	56.15 N	14.05 E
Brobyværk	41	55.14 N	10.15 E
Broc	58	46.36 N	7.06 E
Brocēni	76	56.42 N	22.35 E
Brochel	46	57.26 N	6.01 W
Brochet	176	57.53 N	101.40 W
Brochet, Lac au ◎	186	49.40 N	69.37 W
Brochterbeck	52	52.13 N	7.44 E
Brock	184	51.27 N	108.42 W
Brock ≃	44	53.52 N	2.47 W
Brock Creek ≃	285	40.15 N	74.50 W
Brocken ∧	54	51.48 N	10.36 E
Brockenhurst	42	50.49 N	1.34 W
Brockenscheidt	263	51.38 N	7.25 E
Brockhagen	52	51.59 N	8.20 E
Brockham	260	51.14 N	0.17 W
Brockman ≃	168a	31.41 S	116.07 E
Brockman, Mount ∧	162	22.28 S	117.18 E
Brock Monument ⊥	284a	43.09 N	79.04 W
Brockport, N.Y., U.S.	210	43.12 N	77.56 W
Brockport, Pa., U.S.	214	41.16 N	78.44 W
Brocks Beach	212	44.27 N	80.06 W
Brocks Creek	164	13.28 S	131.25 E
Brockton, Ma., U.S.	207	42.05 N	71.01 W
Brockton, Mt., U.S.	198	48.09 N	104.54 W
Brockton, Pa., U.S.	208	40.45 N	76.04 W
Brockton Reservoir ◎[1]	283	42.07 N	71.03 W
Brock University ▾[2]	284a	43.07 N	79.15 W
Brockville	212	44.35 N	75.41 W
Brockway	214	41.15 N	78.47 W
Brockworth	42	51.51 N	2.09 W
Brocoió, Ilha de I	287a	22.45 S	43.07 W
Brocton	214	42.23 N	79.26 W
Brod, Česko.	60	49.51 N	12.45 E
Brod, Mak.	38	41.31 N	21.12 E
Broddbo	40	59.59 N	16.28 E
Brodenbach	56	50.14 N	7.26 E
Broderick	226	38.35 N	121.30 W
Brodeur Peninsula ≻[1]	176	73.00 N	88.00 W
Brodhead, Ky., U.S.	192	37.24 N	84.24 W
Brodhead, Wi., U.S.	190	42.37 N	89.22 W
Brodhead Creek ≃	210	40.59 N	75.08 W
Brodheadsville	210	40.55 N	75.24 W
Brodick	46	55.35 N	5.09 W
Brodnax	192	36.42 N	78.01 W
Brodnica	30	53.16 N	19.23 E
Brodokalmak	86	55.35 N	62.06 E
Brody, Pol.	30	51.45 N	14.45 E
Brody, Ukr.	78	50.06 N	25.10 E
Broedersput	158	26.49 S	25.08 E
Broek [op Langendijk]	52	52.40 N	4.48 E
Brogan	202	44.14 N	117.30 W
Broglie	50	49.01 N	0.32 E
Brohlbach ≃	56	50.29 N	7.20 E
Broich ◆[8]	263	51.25 N	6.51 E
Broichweiden	56	50.49 N	6.09 E
Brok	30	52.43 N	21.52 E
Brok ∧	123	34.32 N	76.35 E
Brokdorf	52	53.52 N	9.19 E
Broke	170	32.45 S	151.06 E
Broke Inlet ⊂	162	34.55 S	116.25 E
Broken ≃	169	36.41 S	146.00 E
Broken Arrow	196	36.03 N	95.47 W
Broken Bay ⊂	170	33.34 S	151.18 E
Broken Bow, Ne., U.S.	198	41.24 N	99.38 W
Broken Bow, Ok., U.S.	194	34.01 N	94.44 W
Broken Bow Lake ◎[1]	194	34.10 N	94.40 W
Broken Cross, Eng., U.K.	262	53.15 N	2.29 W
Broken Cross, Eng., U.K.	262	53.15 N	2.10 W
Brokenhead ≃	184	50.25 N	96.40 W
Broken Hill	166	31.57 S	141.27 E
Broken Hill → Kabwe	154	14.27 S	28.27 E
Broken Ridge ✣[3]	12	31.30 S	95.00 E
Brokenstraw Creek ≃	214	41.51 N	79.09 W
Broken Sword Creek ≃	214	40.46 N	83.11 W
Brokopondo	250	5.04 N	54.58 W
Brokopondo □[5]	250	4.40 N	55.00 W
Brokopondo Stuwmeer ◎[1]	250	4.45 N	55.00 W
Brölbach ≃	56	50.47 N	7.18 E
Brolo	70	38.09 N	14.50 E
Bromberg → Bydgoszcz	30	53.08 N	18.00 E
Bromborough	262	53.19 N	2.59 W
Brome, P.Q., Can.	206	45.12 N	72.34 W
Brome, Dtsch.	54	52.36 N	10.56 E
Brome □[6]	206	45.10 N	72.30 W
Brome, Lac ◎	206	45.15 N	72.30 W
Brome, Mont ∧	206	45.17 N	72.38 W
Bromham	42	52.09 N	0.31 W
Bromley ◆[8]	42	51.24 N	0.02 E
Bromley Common ◆[8]	260	51.22 N	0.03 E
Bromley Plateau ✣[3]	18	32.00 S	35.00 W
Bromma ◆[8]	40	59.21 N	17.55 E
Bromma flygplats ⊠	40	59.21 N	17.55 E
Brommö I	40	58.50 N	13.41 E
Bromo, Gunung ∧	115a	7.57 S	112.57 E
Bromölla	26	56.04 N	14.28 E
Brompton, Eng., U.K.	44	54.22 N	1.25 W
Brompton, Eng., U.K.	260	51.23 N	0.33 E
Brompton, Lac ◎	206	45.27 N	72.09 W
Bromptonville	206	45.28 N	71.57 W
Bromsgrove	42	52.20 N	2.03 W
Bromyard	42	52.11 N	2.30 W
Bron	62	45.44 N	4.55 E
Bron, Aéroport de ⊠	62	45.43 N	4.56 E
Brønderslev	26	57.16 N	9.58 E
Bronevskaja	24	61.43 N	39.10 E
Brong-Ahafo □[4]	150	7.45 N	1.30 W
Broni	62	45.04 N	9.16 E
Bronickaja Guta	78	50.56 N	27.19 E
Bronkhorstspruit	158	25.48 S	28.44 E
Bronkhorstspruitdam ◎[1]	158	25.55 S	28.42 E
Bronkow	54	51.40 N	13.55 E
Bronllys	42	52.01 N	3.16 W
Bronlund Peak ∧	176	57.26 N	126.38 W
Bronn	60	49.44 N	11.28 E
Bronnicy	82	55.25 N	38.16 E
Bronnikovo	86	58.32 N	68.25 E
Bronnoje	76	52.19 N	30.29 E
Brønnøysund	24	65.30 N	12.10 E
Bronnzell	56	50.31 N	9.41 E
Brøns	41	55.11 N	8.44 E
Bronson, Fl., U.S.	192	29.26 N	82.38 W
Bronson, Ks., U.S.	198	37.54 N	95.04 W
Bronson, Mi., U.S.	216	41.52 N	85.11 W
Bronson, Tx., U.S.	194	31.21 N	94.01 W
Bronson Lake ◎	184	53.52 N	109.43 W
Bronte, It.	70	37.47 N	14.50 E
Bronte, Tx., U.S.	196	31.53 N	100.18 W
Bronte Creek ≃	212	43.23 N	79.43 W
Bronwood	192	31.49 N	84.21 W
Bronx □[6]	210	40.49 N	73.56 W
Bronx ◆[8]	276	40.49 N	73.56 W
Bronx ≃	276	40.49 N	73.52 W
Bronx Park ♠	276	40.52 N	73.53 W
Bronxville	276	40.56 N	73.49 W
Bronx-Whitestone Bridge ◆[5]	276	40.48 N	73.50 W
Bronx Zoo ♠	276	40.51 N	73.53 W
Bronzolo (Branzoll)	64	46.24 N	11.19 E
Brooch, Lac ◎	186	50.44 N	67.58 W
Broodsnyersplaas	158	26.03 S	29.29 E
Brook	216	40.51 N	87.21 W
Brookdale	226	37.06 N	122.06 W
Brooke	208	38.23 N	77.22 W
Brooke □[6]	214	40.18 N	80.33 W
Brookeborough	48	54.19 N	7.24 W
Brookeland	194	31.09 N	94.00 W
Brooker	192	29.53 N	82.19 W
Brooke's Point	116	8.47 N	117.50 E
Brookfield, N.S., Can.	186	45.15 N	63.17 W
Brookfield, Ct., U.S.	207	41.28 N	73.24 W
Brookfield, Il., U.S.	216	41.49 N	87.51 W
Brookfield, Ma., U.S.	207	42.12 N	72.06 W
Brookfield, Mi., U.S.	216	42.27 N	84.47 W
Brookfield, Mo., U.S.	194	39.47 N	93.04 W
Brookfield, N.Y., U.S.	210	42.48 N	75.19 W
Brookfield, Oh., U.S.	214	41.14 N	80.34 W
Brookfield, Wi., U.S.	216	43.03 N	88.06 W
Brookfield Center	207	41.27 N	73.23 W
Brookfield Zoo ♠	278	41.50 N	87.50 W
Brookford	192	35.42 N	81.20 W
Brookhaven, De., U.S.	285	39.42 N	75.41 W
Brookhaven, Ms., U.S.	194	31.34 N	90.26 W
Brookhaven, Pa., U.S.	285	39.52 N	75.22 W
Brookhaven National Laboratory ▾[3]	207	40.54 N	72.52 W
Brookings, Or., U.S.	202	42.03 N	124.16 W
Brookings, S.D., U.S.	198	44.18 N	96.47 W
Brookland, Eng., U.K.	42	50.59 N	0.50 E
Brookland, Ar., U.S.	194	35.54 N	90.34 W
Brookland ◆[8]	284c	38.56 N	76.59 W
Brooklands	214	42.38 N	83.06 W
Brookland Terrace	285	39.44 N	75.37 W
Brooklandville	284b	39.25 N	76.40 W
Brooklawn	285	39.52 N	75.07 W
Brooklet	192	32.22 N	81.39 W
Brooklin	212	43.57 N	78.57 W
Brookline, Ma., U.S.	207	42.21 N	71.07 W
Brookline, N.H., U.S.	207	42.44 N	71.39 W
Brooklyn, N.S., Can.	186	44.03 N	64.42 W
Brooklyn, Ct., U.S.	207	41.47 N	71.57 W
Brooklyn, Il., U.S.	219	40.14 N	90.46 W
Brooklyn, In., U.S.	218	39.32 N	86.22 W
Brooklyn, Ia., U.S.	190	41.44 N	92.26 W
Brooklyn, Mi., U.S.	216	42.06 N	84.14 W
Brooklyn, Ms., U.S.	194	31.03 N	89.11 W
Brooklyn, Oh., U.S.	214	41.26 N	81.44 W
Brooklyn, Pa., U.S.	210	41.45 N	75.48 W
Brooklyn, Wa., U.S.	224	46.47 N	123.31 W
Brooklyn, Wi., U.S.	216	42.51 N	89.22 W
Brooklyn ◆[8], Md., U.S.	284b	39.14 N	76.36 W
Brooklyn ◆[8], N.Y., U.S.	210	40.42 N	74.00 W
Brooklyn Battery Tunnel ◆[5]	276	40.42 N	74.01 W
Brooklyn Bridge ◆[5]	276	40.42 N	74.00 W
Brooklyn Center	190	45.04 N	93.19 W
Brooklyn Heights	279a	41.24 N	81.40 W
Brooklyn Marine Park ♠	276	40.35 N	73.55 W
Brooklyn Museum ▾	276	40.40 N	73.58 W
Brookmans Park	260	51.43 N	0.12 W
Brookmere	182	49.49 N	120.53 W
Brookmont	284c	38.57 N	77.07 W
Brookneal	192	37.03 N	78.56 W
Brook Park	214	41.23 N	81.48 W
Brookport	194	37.07 N	88.37 W
Brooks, Ab., Can.	182	50.35 N	111.53 W
Brooks, Ca., U.S.	226	38.45 N	122.09 W
Brooks, Me., U.S.	188	44.33 N	69.07 W
Brooks, Or., U.S.	224	45.02 N	122.57 W
Brooks, Mount ∧	180	63.11 N	150.40 W
Brooks Air Force Base ■	196	29.21 N	98.25 W
Brooks Bay ⊂	182	50.13 N	127.55 W
Brooksburg	218	38.44 N	85.15 W
Brookshire	222	29.47 N	95.57 W
Brookside, De., U.S.	285	39.40 N	75.43 W
Brookside, N.J., U.S.	276	40.48 N	74.34 W
Brookside, Pa., U.S.	214	42.08 N	80.00 W
Brookside, Tx., U.S.	222	29.35 N	95.18 W
Brookside Park ♠	279a	41.27 N	81.43 W
Brooks Island I	282	37.54 N	122.21 W
Brooks Mountain ∧	180	65.33 N	167.09 W
Brooks Place	283	42.02 N	71.01 W
Brooks Range ⋌	180	68.00 N	154.00 W
Brookston	216	40.36 N	86.52 W
Brook Street	260	51.37 N	0.17 E
Brooksville, Fl., U.S.	220	28.33 N	82.23 W
Brooksville, Ky., U.S.	218	38.40 N	84.03 W
Brooksville, Ms., U.S.	194	33.14 N	88.34 W
Brookton	162	32.22 S	117.01 E
Brooktondale	210	42.23 N	76.24 W
Brookvale	274a	33.46 S	151.17 E
Brookview	210	42.32 N	73.43 W
Brookville, In., U.S.	218	39.25 N	85.00 W
Brookville, Ma., U.S.	207	42.07 N	71.00 W
Brookville, N.Y., U.S.	276	40.48 N	73.34 W
Brookville, Oh., U.S.	218	39.50 N	84.24 W
Brookville, Pa., U.S.	214	41.09 N	79.05 W
Brookville Lake ◎[1]	218	39.30 N	85.00 W
Brookwood	260	51.18 N	0.38 W
Brooloo	166	26.29 S	152.42 E
Broom, Little Loch ⊂	46	57.54 N	5.22 W
Broom, Loch ⊂	46	57.52 N	5.08 W
Broomall	285	39.58 N	75.21 W
Broome	162	17.58 S	122.14 E
Broome □[6]	210	42.08 N	75.54 W
Broome County Airport ⊠	210	42.13 N	75.59 W
Broomes Island	208	38.25 N	76.32 W
Broomfield, Eng., U.K.	260	51.46 N	0.28 E
Broomfield, Eng., U.K.	260	51.14 N	0.38 E
Broomfield, Co., U.S.	200	39.55 N	105.05 W
Broons	32	48.19 N	2.16 W
Brooten	198	45.30 N	95.07 W
Brophy, Mount ∧[2]	162	19.11 S	128.51 E
Brora	46	58.01 N	3.51 W
Brora ≃	46	58.01 N	3.52 W
Brørup	41	55.29 N	9.01 E
Broseley	42	52.37 N	2.29 W
Brosewere Bay ⊂	276	40.37 N	73.42 W
Brosna ≃	48	53.13 N	7.58 W
Brošnev-Osada	78	49.00 N	24.13 E
Brossac	32	45.20 N	0.03 W
Brossard	206	45.26 N	73.29 W
Brossasco	62	44.34 N	7.21 E
Brosso	62	45.30 N	7.48 E
Brotas de Macaúbas	255	12.00 S	42.38 W
Brothers Brook ≃	276	41.02 N	73.36 W
Brötjärna	40	60.30 N	15.01 E
Broto	34	42.36 N	0.06 W
Brotterode	54	50.49 N	10.26 E
Brotton	44	54.34 N	0.56 W
Brou	50	48.13 N	1.11 E
Brough, Eng., U.K.	44	54.32 N	2.19 W
Brough, Eng., U.K.	44	53.44 N	0.35 W
Brough, Scot., U.K.	46	58.39 N	3.20 W
Brougham	212	43.55 N	79.06 W
Brough Head ≻	46	59.08 N	3.17 W
Broughshane	48	54.54 N	6.12 W
Broughton, Eng., U.K.	42	52.23 N	0.46 W
Broughton, Eng., U.K.	44	53.34 N	0.33 W
Broughton, Eng., U.K.	44	53.49 N	2.44 W
Broughton, Eng., U.K.	262	53.49 N	2.44 W
Broughton, Scot., U.K.	46	55.37 N	3.25 W
Broughton, Wales, U.K.	44	53.10 N	2.59 W
Broughton, Pa., U.S.	214	40.21 N	79.59 W
Broughton in Furness	44	54.17 N	3.12 W
Broughton Island I	176	67.35 N	63.50 W
Broughtown	46	59.15 N	2.36 W
Broughty Ferry	46	56.28 N	2.53 W
Broumov	30	50.35 N	16.20 E
Brousseval	58	48.29 N	4.58 E
Brou-sur-Chantereine	261	48.53 N	2.38 E
Brouvelieures	58	48.14 N	6.44 E
Brouwersdam ◆[6]	52	51.46 N	3.51 E
Brouwershaven	52	51.44 N	3.54 E
Brovary	78	50.31 N	30.46 E
Brovst	26	57.06 N	9.32 E
Broward □[6]	220	26.09 N	80.29 W
Browerville	198	46.05 N	94.51 W
Brown □[6], Il., U.S.	219	39.59 N	90.45 W
Brown □[6], In., U.S.	218	39.12 N	86.15 W
Brown □[6], Oh., U.S.	218	38.52 N	83.54 W
Brown, Mount ∧	202	48.52 N	111.09 W
Brown, Point ≻	224	46.56 N	124.10 W
Brownbacks	285	40.11 N	75.37 W
Brown City	190	43.12 N	82.59 W
Brown Clee Hill ∧[2]	42	52.28 N	2.35 W
Brown County State Park ♠	218	39.09 N	86.14 W
Brown Creek ≃	276	40.43 N	73.04 W
Browndale	210	41.40 N	75.27 W
Brown Deer	216	43.09 N	87.57 W
Browne Bay ⊂	176	73.08 N	97.30 W
Brownfield	196	33.10 N	102.16 W
Brown Gelly ∧[2]	42	50.32 N	4.32 W
Brownhills	42	52.39 N	1.55 W
Browning, Il., U.S.	219	40.08 N	90.22 W
Browning, Mo., U.S.	194	40.02 N	93.09 W
Browning, Mt., U.S.	202	48.33 N	113.00 W
Browning Entrance ⊂	182	53.41 N	130.30 W
Browning Island I	212	45.00 N	79.25 W
Brown Lake ◎	176	65.55 N	91.15 W
Brownlee Park	216	42.18 N	85.05 W
Brownlee Reservoir ◎[1]	202	44.40 N	117.05 W
Brown Mountain ∧, Ca., U.S.	204	35.41 N	117.01 W
Brown Mountain ∧, Ca., U.S.	280	34.14 N	118.08 W
Brown Mountain ∧[2]	222	31.51 N	97.39 W
Brown Point ≻	276	40.43 N	73.04 W
Brownsberg, Natuurpark ♠	250	4.50 N	55.10 W
Brownsboro	222	32.18 N	95.37 W
Browns Brook ≃	276	41.09 N	73.17 W
Brownsburg, P.Q., Can.	206	45.41 N	74.25 W
Brownsburg, In., U.S.	218	39.50 N	86.23 W
Browns Canyon V	280	34.18 N	118.35 W
Brownsdale	190	43.44 N	92.52 W
Browns Island I	282	38.02 N	121.52 W
Browns Lake	216	42.42 N	88.14 W
Brownsmead	224	46.13 N	123.32 W
Browns Mills	208	39.58 N	74.35 W
Browns Point	224	47.18 N	122.21 W
Browns Town, Jam.	241q	18.24 N	77.22 W
Brownstown, Il., U.S.	219	38.59 N	88.57 W
Brownstown, In., U.S.	218	38.52 N	86.02 W
Brownstown, Pa., U.S.	208	40.08 N	76.13 W
Brownstown Creek ≃	281	42.06 N	83.13 W
Browns Valley, Ca., U.S.	226	39.15 N	121.23 W
Browns Valley, Mn., U.S.	198	45.35 N	96.49 W
Brownsville, On., Can.	212	42.52 N	80.50 W
Brownsville, Ca., U.S.	226	39.28 N	121.16 W
Brownsville, Fl., U.S.	220	25.50 N	80.17 W
Brownsville, In., U.S.	218	39.39 N	85.00 W
Brownsville, Ky., U.S.	194	37.11 N	86.16 W
Brownsville, La., U.S.	194	32.30 N	92.10 W
Brownsville, Or., U.S.	202	44.23 N	122.59 W
Brownsville, Pa., U.S.	188	40.01 N	79.53 W
Brownsville, Tn., U.S.	194	35.35 N	89.15 W
Brownsville, Tx., U.S.	196	25.54 N	97.29 W
Brownton	190	44.43 N	94.21 W
Browntown	276	40.24 N	74.19 W
Brownvale	182	56.08 N	117.53 W
Brownville, Al., U.S.	194	33.23 N	87.45 W
Brownville, Me., U.S.	188	45.18 N	69.02 W
Brownville, Ne., U.S.	198	40.23 N	95.39 W
Brownville, N.Y., U.S.	212	44.00 N	75.59 W
Brownville Junction	188	45.21 N	69.03 W

Symbol	English	Deutsch	Español	Français	Português
≃	River	Fluß	Río	Rivière	Rio
≅	Canal	Kanal	Canal	Canal	Canal
∟	Waterfall, Rapids	Wasserfall, Stromschnellen	Cascada, Rápidos	Chute d'eau, Rapides	Cascata, Rápidos
ʮ	Strait	Meeresstraße	Estrecho	Détroit	Estreito
⊂	Bay, Gulf	Bucht, Golf	Bahía, Golfo	Baie, Golfe	Baía, Golfo
◎	Lake, Lakes	See, Seen	Lago, Lagos	Lac, Lacs	Lago, Lagos
≣	Swamp	Sumpf	Pantano	Marais	Pântano
⊓	Ice Features, Glacier	Eis- und Gletscherformen	Accidentes Glaciales	Formes glaciaires	Acidentes glaciares
⊤	Other Hydrographic Features	Andere Hydrographische Objekte	Otros Elementos Hidrográficos	Autres données hydrographiques	Outros acidentes hidrográficos
✣	Submarine Features	Untermeerische Objekte	Accidentes Submarinos	Formes de relief sous-marin	Acidentes submarinos
□	Political Unit	Politische Einheit	Unidad Politica	Entité politique	Unidade política
▾	Cultural Institution	Kulturelle Institution	Institución Cultural	Institution culturelle	Instituição cultural
⊥	Historical Site	Historische Stätte	Sitio Histórico	Site historique	Sitio histórico
♠	Recreational Site	Erholungs- und Ferienort	Sitio de Recreo	Centre de loisirs	Area de Lazer
⊠	Airport	Flughafen	Aeropuerto	Aéroport	Aeroporto
■	Military Installation	Militäranlage	Instalación Militar	Installation militaire	Instalação militar
◆	Miscellaneous	Verschiedenes	Misceláneo	Divers	Diversos

Name	Page / Seite	Lat. °′ / Breite °′	Long. °′ / Länge °′ E = Ost
Brown Willy ∧[2]	42	50.35 N	4.36 W
Brownwood	196	31.42 N	98.59 W
Brownwood, Lake ⊜[1]	196	31.51 N	99.02 W
Browse Island I	160	14.07 S	123.33 E
Broxbourne	260	51.45 N	0.01 W
Broxbourne □[8]	260	51.44 N	0.04 W
Broxton	192	31.37 N	82.53 W
Broye ≃	58	46.55 N	7.02 E
Broyhill Park	284c	38.51 N	77.11 W
Broža	76	52.57 N	29.07 E
Brozas	34	39.37 N	6.46 W
Brozzo	64	45.43 N	10.14 E
Brtonigla	64	45.23 N	13.38 E
Brû	58	48.21 N	6.41 E
Bruay-en-Artois	50	50.29 N	2.33 E
Bruay-sur-l'Escaut	50	50.23 N	3.32 E
Bruce, Ms., U.S.	194	33.59 N	89.20 W
Bruce, S.D., U.S.	198	44.26 N	96.53 W
Bruce, Wi., U.S.	190	45.27 N	91.16 W
Bruce □[6]	212	44.30 N	81.15 W
Bruce, Mount ∧	162	22.36 S	118.08 E
Bruce Bay	172	43.35 S	169.41 E
Bruce Creek ≃	275b	43.52 N	79.18 W
Bruce Lake	184	50.48 N	93.24 W
Bruce Lake ⊜	184	50.49 N	93.20 W
Bruce Mines	190	46.18 N	83.48 W
Bruce Museum ʊ	276	41.01 N	73.37 W
Bruce Peninsula ≻[1]	190	44.50 N	81.20 W
Bruce Peninsula National Park ♦	190	45.12 N	81.40 W
Bruce Rock	162	31.53 S	118.09 E
Bruceville	222	31.19 N	97.14 W
Bruchberg ∧	54	51.47 N	10.29 E
Bruchhausen	56	51.26 N	8.01 E
Bruchhausen-Vilsen	52	52.50 N	9.00 E
Bruchmühlbach-Miesau	56	49.24 N	7.26 E
Bruchmühle	264a	52.33 N	13.47 E
Br'uchoveckaja	78	45.48 N	38.59 E
Bruchsal	56	49.07 N	8.35 E
Brück, Dtsch.	54	52.12 N	12.46 E
Bruck, Öst.	64	47.17 N	12.49 E
Bruck an der Leitha	61	48.02 N	16.47 E
Bruck an der Mur	61	47.25 N	15.16 E
Bruckhausen -●-[8]	263	51.29 N	6.44 E
Bruck in der Oberpfalz	60	49.15 N	12.18 E
Brückl	61	46.45 N	14.32 E
Bruckmühl	64	47.53 N	11.54 E
Brucoli -●-[8]	70	37.17 N	15.11 E
Brudager	41	55.07 N	10.41 E
Bruderheim	182	53.47 N	112.56 W
Brue ≃	42	51.13 N	3.00 W
Brue-Auriac	62	43.32 N	5.57 E
Brueil-en-Vexin	261	49.02 N	1.49 E
Brüel	54	53.44 N	11.43 E
Bruff	48	52.29 N	8.33 W
Bruges → Brugge	50	51.13 N	3.14 E
Brugg	58	47.29 N	8.12 E
Brugge (Bruges), Bel.	50	51.13 N	3.14 E
Brügge, Dtsch.	263	51.13 N	7.34 E
Brüggen	56	51.14 N	6.11 E
Brugherio	62	45.33 N	9.18 E
Brugnato	62	44.14 N	9.43 E
Brühl	56	50.48 N	6.54 E
Bruin, Ky., U.S.	218	38.11 N	83.01 W
Bruin, Pa., U.S.	214	41.04 N	79.44 W
Bruinisse	52	51.40 N	4.06 E
Bruin Point ∧	200	39.39 N	110.22 W
Bruit, Pulau I	112	2.35 N	111.20 E
Bruja, Cerro ∧	236	9.29 N	79.34 W
Brule	198	41.05 N	101.53 W
Brule ≃	190	45.57 N	88.12 W
Brûlé, Lac ⊜, Can.	176	52.17 N	63.52 W
Brûlé, Lac ⊜, P.Q., Can.	190	46.57 N	77.12 W
Brule Lake ⊜	212	45.03 N	77.04 W
Brûly	50	49.58 N	4.31 E
Brumadinho	255	20.08 S	44.13 W
Brumado	255	14.13 S	41.40 W
Brumath	56	48.44 N	7.43 E
Brumby Creek ≃	162	24.09 S	118.39 E
Brummen	52	52.05 N	6.09 E
Brumunddal	26	60.53 N	10.56 E
Bruna ≃	66	42.45 N	10.53 E
Brunate	62	45.49 N	9.06 E
Brunau	54	52.45 N	11.28 E
Brundall	42	52.37 N	1.26 E
Brundby	41	55.49 N	10.37 E
Brundidge	194	31.43 N	85.48 W
Brune ≃	50	49.45 N	3.47 E
Bruneau	202	42.52 N	115.47 W
Bruneau ≃	202	42.57 N	115.58 W
Brunei □[1], Asia	108	4.30 N	114.40 E
Brunei □[1], Asia	112	4.30 N	114.40 E
Brunei, Teluk ⊂	112	5.05 N	115.18 E
Brunei → Bandar Seri Begawan	112	4.56 N	114.55 E
Brünen	52	51.43 N	6.39 E
Brunette Creek ≃	162	18.47 S	135.41 E
Brunette Downs	162	18.38 S	135.57 E
Brunette Island I	186	47.16 N	55.54 W
Brunflo	26	63.05 N	14.49 E
Brungle	171b	35.10 S	148.14 E
Brunico (Bruneck)	64	46.48 N	11.56 E
Brünigpass)(	58	46.46 N	8.09 E
Brüninghausen	263	51.13 N	7.41 E
Brunkeberg	26	59.26 N	8.29 E
Brünn, Dtsch.	54	50.27 N	10.51 E
Brunn, Dtsch.	54	53.40 N	13.22 E
Brunna	40	59.51 N	17.26 E
Brunn am Gebirge	61	48.07 N	16.17 E
Brünn → Brno	30	49.12 N	16.37 E
Brunnen, Dtsch.	60	48.38 N	11.18 E
Brunnen, Schw.	58	47.00 N	8.36 E
Brunner, Lake ⊜	172	42.37 S	171.27 E
Brunnerville	208	40.11 N	76.17 W
Brunni	58	47.03 N	8.42 E
Brunnsvik	40	60.12 N	15.08 E
Bruno	184	52.15 N	105.30 W
Brunot Island I	279b	40.28 N	80.03 W
Brunow	264a	52.44 N	13.52 E
Brunoy	50	48.42 N	2.30 E
Brunsbüttel	52	53.54 N	9.07 E
Brunsbüttelkoog	52	53.54 N	9.08 E
Brunson	192	32.55 N	81.11 W
Brunssum	56	50.56 N	5.59 E
Brunswick, Austl.	274b	37.46 S	144.58 E
Brunswick, Ga., U.S.	192	31.08 N	81.29 W
Brunswick, Me., U.S.	188	43.54 N	69.57 W
Brunswick, Md., U.S.	208	39.18 N	77.37 W
Brunswick, Mo., U.S.	194	39.25 N	93.07 W
Brunswick, Oh., U.S.	214	41.14 N	81.50 W
Brunswick ≃	168a	33.15 S	115.45 E
Brunswick, Península ≻[1]	254	53.30 S	71.25 W
Brunswick → Braunschweig	52	52.16 N	10.31 E
Brunswick Junction	168a	33.15 S	115.51 E
Brunswick Lake ⊜	190	49.00 N	83.23 W
Brunswick Naval Air Station ■	188	43.54 N	69.56 W
Brunswick Square -●-[9]	276	40.25 N	74.23 W
Bruntál	30	49.59 N	17.28 E
Bruree	48	52.26 N	8.36 W
Brus, Laguna de ⊂	236	15.50 N	84.35 W
Brus'any	80	53.13 N	49.24 E
Brusasco	62	45.09 N	8.04 E
Bruselas → Bruxelles	50	50.50 N	4.20 E
Brusendorf	264a	52.19 N	13.31 E
Brush	198	40.15 N	103.37 W
Brush Creek ≃, Oh., U.S.	216	41.26 N	84.24 W
Brush Creek ≃, Pa., U.S.	279b	40.23 N	79.46 W
Brush Run ≃, Pa., U.S.	279b	40.18 N	80.07 W
Brush Run ≃, Pa., U.S.	279b	40.16 N	80.10 W
Brush Valley	214	40.32 N	79.04 W
Brushy Creek ≃, Austl.	274b	37.43 S	145.17 E
Brushy Creek ≃, Ok., U.S.	196	34.55 N	95.34 W
Brushy Creek ≃, Tx., U.S.	222	32.59 N	96.12 W
Brushy Creek ≃, Tx., U.S.	222	30.48 N	95.09 W
Brushy Creek ≃, Tx., U.S.	222	31.55 N	95.26 W
Brushy Creek ≃, Tx., U.S.	222	30.43 N	97.03 W
Brushy Creek ≃, Tx., U.S.	222	29.04 N	96.34 W
Brusilov	78	50.17 N	29.32 E
Brusio	58	46.14 N	10.07 E
Brus Laguna	236	15.47 N	84.35 W
Brusovo	76	57.51 N	35.24 E
Brusque	252	27.06 S	48.56 W
Brussel → Bruxelles	50	50.50 N	4.20 E
Brussels, On., Can.	212	43.44 N	81.15 W
Brussels, Il., U.S.	219	38.57 N	90.36 W
Brussels → Bruxelles	50	50.50 N	4.20 E
Brusson	62	45.45 N	7.44 E
Brüssow	54	53.24 N	14.07 E
Brusy	30	53.53 N	17.45 E
Brutelles	50	50.08 N	1.31 E
Bruthen	166	37.43 S	147.48 E
Bruton	42	51.07 N	2.27 W
Bruxelles (Brussels) (Brussel)	56	50.50 N	4.20 E
Bruxelles National, Aéroport ⊠	50	50.54 N	4.30 E
Brüx → Most	54	50.32 N	13.39 E
Bruyères	58	48.12 N	6.43 E
Bruyères-le-Châtel	261	48.36 N	2.11 E
Bruzual	246	8.03 N	69.19 W
Bruzzano Zeffirio	68	38.02 N	16.05 E
Brwinów	30	52.09 N	20.43 E
Bryan, Oh., U.S.	216	41.28 N	84.33 W
Bryan, Tx., U.S.	222	30.40 N	96.22 W
Bryan, Mount ∧	166	33.26 S	138.59 E
Bryan Coast ≗[2]	9	73.45 S	82.00 W
Bryansk → Br'ansk	76	53.15 N	34.22 E
Bryans Road	208	38.37 N	77.04 W
Bryant, Ar., U.S.	194	34.35 N	92.29 W
Bryant, In., U.S.	216	40.32 N	84.58 W
Bryant, S.D., U.S.	198	44.35 N	97.28 W
Bryant Creek ≃	194	36.36 N	92.17 W
Bryant Mountain ∧	207	42.28 N	72.58 W
Bryantville	207	42.02 N	70.50 W
Bryas, Lac ⊜	206	46.44 N	73.05 W
Bryce Canyon National Park ♦	200	37.29 N	112.12 W
Bryher I	42a	49.57 N	6.20 W
Brykalansk	24	65.30 N	54.12 E
Brykovka	80	52.32 N	48.35 E
Bryli	76	53.54 N	30.33 E
Brymbo	44	53.06 N	3.04 W
Bryn	262	53.30 N	2.39 W
Brynamman	42	51.49 N	3.52 W
Bryn Athyn	285	40.08 N	75.04 W
Bryn Brawd ∧[2]	42	52.09 N	3.54 W
Bryncethin	42	51.33 N	3.34 W
Bryne	26	58.44 N	5.39 E
Brynford	262	53.16 N	3.14 W
Bryn Gates	262	53.30 N	2.37 W
Bryn'kovskaja	78	46.02 N	38.35 E
Brynmawr, Wales, U.K.	42	51.49 N	3.11 W
Bryn Mawr, Ca., U.S.	228	34.03 N	117.14 W
Bryn Mawr, Pa., U.S.	208	40.01 N	75.18 W
Bryn Mawr College ʊ[2]	285	40.02 N	75.19 W
Bryrup	41	56.01 N	9.31 E
Bryson, P.Q., Can.	188	45.41 N	76.37 W
Bryson, Tx., U.S.	196	33.10 N	98.23 W
Bryson City	192	35.25 N	83.26 W
Bryte	226	38.36 N	121.33 W
Brza Palanka	38	44.28 N	22.27 E
Brzeg	30	50.52 N	17.27 E
Brześć Kujawski	30	52.37 N	18.55 E
Brześć nad Bugiem → Brest	76	52.06 N	23.42 E
Brzesko	30	49.59 N	20.36 E
Brzeszcze	30	49.59 N	19.08 E
Brzeziny	30	51.48 N	19.46 E
Brzozów	30	49.42 N	22.02 E
Bsharrī	130	34.15 N	36.01 E
Bua ≃	154	12.42 S	34.13 E
Bu'aale	144	1.05 N	42.35 E
Buada Lagoon ⊂	174b	0.31 S	166.55 E
Buad Island I	116	11.40 N	124.51 E
Buagan ≃	269e	6.17 S	106.55 E
Buala	175e	8.08 S	159.35 E
Bū al-Ḥīdān, Wādī V	146	27.25 N	19.22 E
Buangor, Mount ∧	169	37.18 S	143.13 E
Buapinang	112	4.46 S	121.34 E
Buariki	174t	1.36 N	172.58 E
Buatan	114	0.44 N	101.51 E
Bua Yai	110	15.35 N	102.25 E
Buayan ≃	116	6.06 N	125.14 E
Bu'ayrāt al-Ḥasūn	146	31.24 N	15.44 E
Buba	150	11.36 N	14.55 W
Bubai	268	35.40 N	139.29 E
Bū Bānī, Jabal ∧	140	22.38 N	25.00 E
Bubanza	154	3.06 S	29.23 E
Bubaque	150	11.17 N	15.50 W
Bubendorf	58	47.27 N	7.44 E
Bubia	164	6.40 S	146.55 E
Būbiyān I	128	29.45 N	48.15 E
Bubu ≃	154	6.03 S	35.19 E
Bubu, Gunong ∧	114	4.42 N	100.47 E
Bubuan Island I, Pil.	116	6.21 N	121.58 E
Bubuan Island I, Pil.	116	6.11 N	120.58 E
Bubuduo	120	30.06 N	84.38 E
Buburu	152	1.26 N	18.03 E
Bubye ≃	154	22.20 S	31.07 E
Buc	261	48.46 N	2.08 E
Bučač	78	49.04 N	25.23 E
Bucak	130	37.28 N	30.36 E
Bucakkışla	130	36.57 N	33.02 E
Bucaramanga	246	7.08 N	73.09 W
Bucarest → București	38	44.26 N	26.06 E
Bucas Grande Island I	116	9.40 N	125.57 E
Buccaneer Archipelago II	160	16.17 S	123.20 E
Buccheri	70	37.08 N	14.51 E
Bucchianico	66	42.18 N	14.11 E
Buccinasco	266b	45.24 N	9.07 E
Buccino	68	40.37 N	15.23 E
Buccurale	144	4.31 N	42.01 E
Bucelas	266c	38.54 N	9.07 W
Bucelas ∧[2]	266c	38.53 N	9.07 W
Buch -●-[8]	264a	52.38 N	13.30 E
Buchanan, Arg.	258	34.58 S	58.13 W
Buchanan, Sk., Can.	184	51.43 N	102.45 W
Buchanan, Liber.	150	5.57 N	10.02 W
Buchanan, Ga., U.S.	192	33.48 N	85.11 W
Buchanan, Mi., U.S.	216	41.49 N	86.21 W
Buchanan, N.Y., U.S.	210	41.16 N	73.56 W
Buchanan, Va., U.S.	192	37.31 N	79.40 W
Buchanan, Lake ⊜	166	21.28 S	145.52 E
Buchanan, Lake ⊜[1]	196	30.48 N	98.25 W
Buchanan Creek ≃	162	19.11 S	136.16 E
Buchanan Field ⊠	282	37.59 N	122.03 W
Buchanan Hills ⋏[2]	162	18.53 S	131.02 E
Buchan Ness ≻	46	57.28 N	1.45 W
Buchans	186	48.49 N	56.52 W
Buchara	128	39.48 N	64.25 E
Buchara □[8]	128	40.00 N	64.00 E
Bucharest → București	38	44.26 N	26.06 E
Buchbach	60	48.19 N	12.17 E
Buchelay	261	48.59 N	1.40 E
Büchen, Dtsch.	52	53.29 N	10.36 E
Buchen, Dtsch.	56	49.32 N	9.17 E
Buchenberg	58	47.42 N	10.14 E
Büchenbeuren	56	49.55 N	7.16 E
Buchenwald-Denkmal ⊥	54	51.01 N	11.15 E
Buchholz, Dtsch.	54	52.10 N	12.55 E
Buchholz, Dtsch.	56	50.41 N	7.23 E
Buchholz, Dtsch.	263	51.23 N	7.15 E
Buchholz, Dtsch.	264a	52.35 N	13.47 E
Buchholz -●-[8], Dtsch.	263	51.23 N	6.46 E
Buchholz -●-[8], Dtsch.	264a	52.36 N	13.26 E
Buchholz in der Nordheide	52	53.20 N	9.52 E
Büchlberg	60	48.40 N	13.30 E
Buchloe	58	48.02 N	10.44 E
Bucholt	263	51.39 N	6.43 E
Buchon, Point ≻	226	35.15 N	120.54 W
Buchow-Karpzow	264a	52.31 N	12.57 E
Buchs, Schw.	58	47.23 N	8.04 E
Buchs, Schw.	58	47.10 N	9.28 E
Buchufontein	158	30.18 S	19.36 E
Buchy	50	49.35 N	1.22 E
Bučina	60	48.58 N	13.36 E
Bucine	66	43.29 N	11.37 E
Buck, Lake ⊜	162	19.38 S	130.21 E
Buckatunna	194	31.32 N	88.31 W
Buckatunna Creek ≃	194	31.30 N	88.32 W
Buck Branch ≃	284b	39.01 N	77.10 W
Buck Creek	216	40.29 N	86.46 W
Buck Creek ≃, U.S.	196	34.35 N	99.58 W
Buck Creek ≃, In., U.S.	218	39.37 N	85.56 W
Buck Creek ≃, In., U.S.	218	40.11 N	85.30 W
Buck Creek ≃, Ky., U.S.	192	36.59 N	84.29 W
Buck Creek ≃, Oh., U.S.	218	39.56 N	83.51 W
Buck Creek ≃, Pa., U.S.	285	40.15 N	74.50 W
Buckden, Eng., U.K.	42	52.17 N	0.16 W
Buckden, Eng., U.K.	44	54.12 N	2.05 W
Bückeburg	52	52.16 N	9.02 E
Bücken	52	52.46 N	9.07 E
Buckeye	200	33.22 N	112.34 W
Buckeye Creek ≃	226	38.54 N	121.55 W
Buckeye Lake	188	39.56 N	82.28 W
Buckeystown	208	39.20 N	77.25 W
Buckfastleigh	42	50.29 N	3.46 W
Buckhannon	188	38.59 N	80.13 W
Buckhaven	46	56.11 N	3.03 W
Buck Hill Falls	210	41.11 N	75.15 W
Buck Hollow ≃	224	45.10 N	120.50 W
Buckholts	222	30.52 N	97.08 W
Buckhorn ≃	180	66.13 N	161.10 W
Buckhorn Draw V	196	30.39 N	100.52 W
Buckhorn Island State Park ♦	284a	43.03 N	78.59 W
Buckhorn Lake ⊜, On., Can.	212	44.28 N	78.23 W
Buckhorn Lake ⊜, Ca., U.S.	228	34.50 N	117.59 W
Buckie	46	57.40 N	2.58 W
Buckingham, Austl.	168a	33.24 S	116.19 E
Buckingham, P.Q., Can.	188	45.35 N	75.25 W
Buckingham, Eng., U.K.	42	52.00 N	1.00 W
Buckingham, Pa., U.S.	208	40.18 N	75.01 W
Buckingham, Va., U.S.	192	37.32 N	78.37 W
Buckingham Bay ⊂	164	12.10 S	135.46 E
Buckingham Palace ʊ	260	51.30 N	0.08 W
Buckinghamshire □[6]	42	51.45 N	0.48 W
Buck Island I	241n	17.48 N	64.37 W
Buck Island Reef National Monument ♦	241n	17.48 N	64.37 W
Buck Lake ⊜, Ab., Can.	182	53.00 N	114.45 W
Buck Lake ⊜, On., Can.	212	45.25 N	79.24 W
Buckland, Austl.	166	42.37 S	147.43 E
Buckland, Eng., U.K.	260	51.15 N	0.15 W
Buckland, Ak., U.S.	180	65.59 N	161.07 W
Buckland, Ma., U.S.	207	42.35 N	72.47 W
Buckland, Oh., U.S.	216	40.37 N	84.16 W
Buckland Brewer	42	50.57 N	4.14 W
Buckland Common	260	51.45 N	0.39 W
Bucklands	158	29.03 S	23.44 E
Buckleboo	166	32.55 S	136.12 E
Buckley, Wales, U.K.	44	53.09 N	3.04 W
Buckley, Il., U.S.	216	40.36 N	88.02 W
Buckley, Wa., U.S.	224	47.09 N	122.01 W
Buckley ≃	166	20.22 S	137.57 E
Buckley Bay ⊂	9	68.16 S	148.12 E
Bucklin, Ks., U.S.	198	37.32 N	99.38 W
Bucklin, Mo., U.S.	194	39.46 N	92.53 W
Buck Lodge	284c	39.01 N	76.58 W
Buck Mountain ∧, Va., U.S.	192	36.40 N	81.15 W
Buck Mountain ∧, Wa., U.S.	202	48.26 N	119.50 W
Bucknell Heights	284c	38.46 N	77.04 W
Bucknell Manor	208	38.46 N	77.04 W
Buckner	218	38.23 N	85.26 W
Buckner Creek ≃	198	38.11 N	99.34 W
Buckners Creek ≃	222	29.53 N	96.53 W
Buckow	54	52.34 N	14.04 E
Buckow -●-[8]	264a	52.25 N	13.26 E
Bucks □[6]	208	40.19 N	75.08 W
Bucksburn	46	57.12 N	2.18 W
Buckshot Lake ⊜	212	45.00 N	77.04 W
Buckskin Creek ≃	218	39.14 N	83.17 W
Buckskin Gulch V	200	37.01 N	111.52 W
Bucks Knob ∧	224	46.41 N	123.20 W
Bucksport	188	44.34 N	68.47 W
Bucktown	285	40.10 N	75.43 W
Bückwitz	54	52.52 N	12.29 E
Buc-Louis-Blériot, Aérodrome de ⊠	261	48.45 N	2.05 E
Bučmany	78	51.04 N	28.04 E
Bucoda	224	46.47 N	122.52 W
Buco Zau	152	4.46 S	12.33 E
Bucquoy	50	50.08 N	2.42 E
Buctouche	186	46.28 N	64.43 W
Bucun	98	36.37 N	117.27 E
București (Bucharest)	38	44.26 N	26.06 E
Bucutua Island I	116	6.09 N	121.49 E
Bucy-lès-Pierrepont	50	49.39 N	3.54 E
Bucyrus	214	40.48 N	82.58 W
Bud	26	62.55 N	6.55 E
Buda, Il., U.S.	190	41.19 N	89.40 W
Buda, Tx., U.S.	196	30.05 N	97.51 W
Buda -●-[8]	264c	47.30 N	19.02 E
Buda Castle ⊥	264c	47.30 N	19.02 E
Budafok -●-[8]	264c	47.26 N	19.02 E
Budagovo	88	54.38 N	100.08 E
Budai-hegység ⋏	264c	47.31 N	18.58 E
Budakalász	264c	47.37 N	19.03 E
Budakeszi	264c	47.31 N	18.56 E
Buda-Kosel'ovo	76	52.43 N	30.34 E
Budalin	110	22.22 N	95.08 E
Budaörs	264c	47.27 N	18.58 E
Budapest, Magy.	30	47.30 N	19.05 E
Budapest, Magy.	264c	47.30 N	19.05 E
Budapest □[7]	264c	47.30 N	19.05 E
Búđardalur	24a	65.10 N	21.42 W
Budarin	80	47.54 N	42.36 E
Budarino	80	50.31 N	51.04 E
Budatétény -●-[8]	264c	47.25 N	19.01 E
Budaun	124	28.03 N	79.07 E
Budawang National Park ♦	170	35.26 S	150.02 E
Budawang Range ⋏	170	35.20 S	150.03 E
Budayuan	98	40.56 N	125.19 E
Budberg	263	51.32 N	6.38 E
Budbud	144	4.11 N	46.28 E
Budd Coast ≗[2]	9	66.30 S	113.00 E
Buddh Gaya → Bodh Gaya	124	24.42 N	84.59 E
Budd Inlet ⊂	224	47.06 N	122.54 W
Budd Lake	210	40.52 N	74.44 W
Buddtown	285	39.56 N	74.42 W
Buddu	140	11.54 N	24.08 E
Buddusò	71	40.35 N	9.15 E
Bude, Eng., U.K.	42	50.50 N	4.33 W
Bude, Ms., U.S.	194	31.27 N	90.51 W
Bude Bay ⊂	42	50.50 N	4.37 W
Budel	52	51.17 N	5.35 E
Budelli, Isola I	71	41.17 N	9.21 E
Büdelsdorf	41	54.18 N	9.40 E
Büderich	52	51.37 N	6.34 E
Buderus	263	51.33 N	7.38 E
Budești	38	44.14 N	26.28 E
Budge Budge	126	22.27 N	88.10 E
Budhāthum	124	28.04 N	84.50 E
Budhhāta	126	22.36 N	89.10 E
Budhī Gandakī ≃	124	27.48 N	84.45 E
Budhlāda	123	29.56 N	75.34 E
Budi	152	3.04 S	23.56 E
Büdingen	56	50.17 N	9.07 E
Búđir	24a	64.56 N	13.58 W
Budišov nad Budišovkou	30	49.47 N	17.38 E
Budjala	152	2.39 N	19.42 E
Budkov	61	49.03 N	15.39 E
Budleigh Salterton	42	50.38 N	3.20 W
Budogošč'	76	59.17 N	32.27 E
Budogovišči	76	53.36 N	36.18 E
Budoni	71	40.43 N	9.42 E
Bud'onnovka	80	50.52 N	52.48 E
Bud'onnovsk	84	44.46 N	44.09 E
Bud'onnovskaja	80	46.56 N	41.33 E
Bud'onnyj, Kyrg.	85	42.30 N	72.35 E
Bud'onnyj, Ross.	83	47.27 N	39.46 E
Budrio	64	44.32 N	11.32 E
Budslav	76	54.47 N	27.27 E
Budweis → České Budějovice	30	48.59 N	14.28 E
Budworth Mere ⊜	262	53.17 N	2.31 W
Budy	78	49.53 N	36.02 E
Budylka	78	50.30 N	34.26 E
Budyně nad Ohří	54	50.22 N	14.09 E
Budžak ⋏[1]	78	46.10 N	29.00 E
Buea	152	4.09 N	9.14 E
Buëch ≃	62	44.12 N	5.57 E
Buechel	218	38.11 N	85.39 W
Buehl Airport ⊠	285	40.11 N	74.54 W
Bueil	50	48.56 N	1.27 E
Buela	152	5.55 S	14.33 E
Buell	219	39.02 N	91.27 W
Bue Marino, Grotta del ≗[5]	71	40.15 N	9.38 E
Buena	208	39.30 N	74.55 W
Buena Esperanza	252	34.45 S	65.15 W
Buena Esperanza, Cabo de → Good Hope, Cape of ≻	158	34.24 S	18.30 E
Buena Park, Ca., U.S.	228	33.52 N	117.59 W
Buena Park, Wi., U.S.	216	42.48 N	88.14 W
Buenaventura, Col.	246	3.53 N	77.04 W
Buenaventura, Méx.	232	29.51 N	107.29 W
Buena Vista, Bol.	248	17.27 S	63.40 W
Buena Vista, Méx.	204	32.32 N	116.44 W
Buenavista, Méx.	234	22.36 N	100.09 W
Buena Vista, Para.	252	26.08 S	56.03 W
Buenavista, Pil.	116	8.59 N	125.24 E
Buenavista, Pil.	116	13.15 N	121.57 E
Buenavista, Pil.	116	10.04 N	118.49 E
Buenavista, Pil.	116	7.15 N	122.16 E
Buena Vista, Co., U.S.	200	38.50 N	106.07 W
Buena Vista, Fl., U.S.	220	28.11 N	82.44 W
Buena Vista, Ga., U.S.	192	32.19 N	84.31 W
Buena Vista, Md., U.S.	284c	38.57 N	76.50 W
Buena Vista, Ms., U.S.	194	33.53 N	88.50 W
Buena Vista, Pa., U.S.	279b	40.17 N	79.48 W
Buena Vista, Va., U.S.	192	37.44 N	79.21 W
Buena Vista, Bahía de ⊂	240p	22.30 N	79.08 W
Buena Vista Canal ≊	228	35.21 N	119.06 W
Buenavista de Cuéllar	234	18.27 N	99.25 W
Buena Vista Lake Bed ⊜	204	35.11 N	119.17 W
Buenavista Tomatlán	234	19.12 N	102.36 W
Buen Día	196	26.21 N	104.32 W
Buendia, Embalse de ⊜[1]	34	40.25 N	2.43 W
Buenga ≃	152	6.07 S	15.58 E
Bueno ≃	254	40.13 S	73.43 W
Bueno Brandão	256	22.27 S	46.21 W
Buenópolis	255	17.54 S	44.11 W
Buenos Aires, Arg.	258	34.36 S	58.27 W
Buenos Aires, Arg.	288	34.36 S	58.27 W
Buenos Aires, Col.	246	3.02 N	76.38 W
Buenos Aires, C.R.	236	9.10 N	83.20 W
Buenos Aires □[4]	252	36.00 S	60.00 W
Buenos Aires, Lago (Lago General Carrera) ⊜	254	46.35 S	72.00 W
Buen Pasto	254	45.05 S	69.28 W
Buer -●-[8]	263	51.36 N	7.03 E
Buerarema	255	14.57 S	39.19 W
Buerāt, Bi'r Ŧ[4]	142	28.59 N	32.10 E
Buertuokai	85	39.35 N	74.58 E
Buesaco	246	1.23 N	77.09 W
Buescher State Park ♦	222	30.02 N	97.09 W
Buet, Le ∧	58	46.02 N	6.52 E
Buey ≃	240p	20.28 N	77.05 W
Bufalotta, Fosso della ≃	267a	41.59 N	12.30 E
Buffalo, Il., U.S.	219	39.51 N	89.25 W
Buffalo, In., U.S.	216	40.53 N	86.45 W
Buffalo, Ks., U.S.	198	37.42 N	95.41 W
Buffalo, Mn., U.S.	190	45.10 N	93.52 W
Buffalo, Mo., U.S.	194	37.38 N	93.05 W
Buffalo, N.Y., U.S.	210	42.53 N	78.52 W
Buffalo, N.Y., U.S.	284a	42.53 N	78.52 W
Buffalo, Oh., U.S.	188	39.54 N	81.31 W
Buffalo, Ok., U.S.	196	36.50 N	99.37 W
Buffalo, S.C., U.S.	192	34.43 N	81.41 W
Buffalo, S.D., U.S.	198	45.35 N	103.32 W
Buffalo, Tx., U.S.	222	31.28 N	96.04 W
Buffalo, Wy., U.S.	202	44.20 N	106.41 W
Buffalo ≃, Can.	176	60.55 N	115.00 W
Buffalo ≃, S. Afr.	158	28.43 S	30.37 E
Buffalo ≃, Ar., U.S.	194	36.10 N	92.26 W
Buffalo ≃, Mn., U.S.	198	47.06 N	96.49 W
Buffalo ≃, Ms., U.S.	194	31.04 N	91.34 W
Buffalo ≃, N.Y., U.S.	284a	42.53 N	78.53 W
Buffalo ≃, Tn., U.S.	194	36.00 N	87.50 W
Buffalo ≃, Wi., U.S.	190	44.22 N	91.55 W
Buffalo, State University College at ʊ[2]	284a	42.56 N	78.53 W
Buffalo Airpark ⊠	284a	42.52 N	78.43 W
Buffalo Bayou ≃	222	29.46 N	95.05 W
Buffalo Bill Ranch State Historical Park ♦	198	41.10 N	100.48 W
Buffalo Bill Reservoir ⊜[1]	202	44.29 N	109.13 W
Buffalo Bill State Park ♦	202	44.30 N	109.14 W
Buffalo Center	190	43.23 N	93.56 W
Buffalo Coast Guard Base ■	284a	42.52 N	78.54 W
Buffalo Creek ≃, U.S.	198	45.57 N	102.56 W
Buffalo Creek ≃, U.S.	214	40.16 N	80.37 W
Buffalo Creek ≃, Il., U.S.	278	42.08 N	87.55 W
Buffalo Creek ≃, Ia., U.S.	190	42.06 N	91.18 W
Buffalo Creek ≃, Ks., U.S.	198	39.35 N	97.43 W
Buffalo Creek ≃, Ky., U.S.	218	38.28 N	83.03 W
Buffalo Creek ≃, Mn., U.S.	198	44.51 N	94.00 W
Buffalo Creek ≃, N.Y., U.S.	210	42.52 N	78.47 W
Buffalo Creek ≃, Ok., U.S.	196	36.47 N	99.15 W
Buffalo Creek ≃, Pa., U.S.	208	40.29 N	77.08 W
Buffalo Creek ≃, Pa., U.S.	210	40.58 N	76.53 W
Buffalo Creek ≃, Pa., U.S.	214	40.40 N	79.41 W
Buffalo Grove	216	42.09 N	87.57 W
Buffalo Harbor ⊂	284a	42.51 N	78.52 W
Buffalo Lake	198	44.44 N	94.37 W
Buffalo Lake ⊜, Ab., Can.	182	52.27 N	112.54 W
Buffalo Lake ⊜, N.T., Can.	176	60.10 N	115.30 W
Buffalo Lake ⊜[1]	196	34.54 N	102.07 W
Buffalo Museum of Science ʊ	284a	42.54 N	78.51 W
Buffalo Narrows	184	55.51 N	108.30 W
Buffalo National River ♦	194	35.58 N	92.53 W
Buffalo Pound Lake ⊜	184	50.39 N	105.30 W
Buffalo Pound Provincial Park ♦	184	50.36 N	105.30 W
Buffalo Run ≃	279b	40.12 N	79.37 W
Buffalo Zoo ♦	284a	42.56 N	78.51 W
Buffels ≃, S. Afr.	156	29.41 S	17.03 E
Buffels ≃, S. Afr.	158	33.45 S	21.11 E
Buffington Harbor ⊂	278	41.38 N	87.25 W
Buffum, Lake ⊜	220	27.48 N	81.40 W
Buford, Ga., U.S.	192	34.07 N	84.00 W
Buford, Oh., U.S.	218	39.04 N	83.50 W
Buford Dam -●-[6]	192	34.11 N	84.03 W
Buftea	38	44.34 N	25.57 E
Bug ≃	22	52.31 N	21.05 E
Buga, Col.	246	3.54 N	76.17 W
Buga, Nig.	150	8.30 N	7.21 E
Bugajevka, Ross.	83	49.39 N	39.42 E
Bugajevka, Ukr.	83	49.28 N	37.23 E
Bugajevka, Ukr.	83	48.25 N	38.53 E
Bugalagrande	246	4.11 N	76.09 W
Bugala Island I	154	0.40 S	32.20 E
Bugallon	116	15.57 N	120.13 E
Buganga	154	0.03 S	31.59 E
Bugasong	116	11.03 N	122.04 E
Bugat, Mong.	86	48.59 N	90.10 E
Bugat, Mong.	88	47.55 N	101.16 E
Bugbrooke	42	52.12 N	1.01 W
Bug Catooti	144	10.44 N	50.35 E
Buğdaylı	130	40.13 N	27.46 E
Bugeat	32	45.35 N	1.59 E
Bugel, Ujung ≻	115a	6.26 S	111.03 E
Bugene	154	1.35 S	31.08 E
Bugey -●-[1]	58	45.55 N	5.30 E
Buggenhout	50	51.01 N	4.12 E
Buggerru	71	39.24 N	8.24 E
Bugio I	266c	38.39 N	9.18 W
Bugiri	154	0.34 N	33.45 E
Bugle	42	50.24 N	4.47 W
Bug Méridional → Južnyj Bug ≃	78	46.59 N	31.58 E
Bugojno	36	44.03 N	17.27 E
Bugøynes	24	69.58 N	29.39 E
Bugrino	24	68.48 N	49.09 E
Bugry, Ross.	76	58.46 N	35.15 E
Bugry, Ross.	265a	60.04 N	30.24 E
Bugsanga ≃	116	12.26 N	120.59 E
Bugsuk Island I	116	8.15 N	117.18 E
Bugt, Zhg.	89	48.46 N	121.57 E
Bugt, Zhg.	98	42.20 N	120.43 E
Buguba	164	3.41 S	137.30 E
Buguey	116	18.17 N	121.50 E
Bugui Point ≻	116	12.36 N	123.14 E
Bugul'dejka	88	52.33 N	106.05 E
Bugul'ma	80	54.33 N	52.48 E
Bugul'minsko-Belebejevskaja vozvyšennosť ⋏[1]	80	54.54 N	52.42 E
Bugun' ≃	85	42.58 N	68.35 E
Bugun'skoje vodochranilišče ⊜[1]	85	42.45 N	69.05 E
Buguruslan	80	53.39 N	52.26 E
Buh ≃	102	36.58 N	99.48 E
Buhanhua	104	42.39 N	122.46 E
Bū Ḥashīshah, Thamad Ŧ[4]	146	26.23 N	18.47 E
Buḥayrah, Rayyāḥ al- ≊	142	30.43 N	30.45 E
Buḥaythān, Jabal al- ∧	132	30.55 N	35.53 E
Buhera	154	19.18 S	31.29 E
Buhi	116	13.26 N	123.31 E
Buhi, Lake ⊜	116	13.26 N	123.31 E
Bühl, Dtsch.	56	48.42 N	8.08 E
Buhl, Fr.	58	47.56 N	7.11 E
Buhl, Id., U.S.	202	42.35 N	114.45 W
Buhl, Mn., U.S.	190	47.29 N	92.46 W
Buhler	198	38.08 N	97.46 W
Bühler ≃	56	49.10 N	9.47 E
Bühlertal	56	48.41 N	8.10 E
Buhuai	120	33.22 N	80.36 E
Buhuși	38	46.43 N	26.41 E
Bui Dam -●-[6]	150	8.22 N	2.10 W
Buie, Loch ⊂	46	56.20 N	5.52 W
Buile Hill Park ♦	262	53.29 N	2.18 W
Builth Wells	42	52.09 N	3.24 W
Buin, Chile	252	33.44 S	70.45 W
Buin, Pap. N. Gui.	175e	6.50 S	155.44 E
Buin, Piz ∧	58	46.50 N	10.08 E
Buinen	52	52.55 N	6.50 E
Buinsk, Ross.	80	55.12 N	47.03 E
Buinsk, Ross.	80	54.57 N	48.17 E
Buíque	250	8.37 S	37.09 W
Buis-les-Baronnies	62	44.16 N	5.16 E
Buitenpost	52	53.15 N	6.09 E
Buj	80	58.30 N	41.30 E
Buj ≃	80	56.13 N	54.12 E
Bujaki	24	59.03 N	48.40 E
Bujalance	34	37.54 N	4.22 W
Bujant, Mong.	86	48.33 N	89.34 E
Bujant, Mong.	86	48.10 N	91.55 E
Bujant ≃	88	47.08 N	97.38 E
Bujant-Ovoo	102	44.58 N	107.05 E
Bujaraloz	34	41.30 N	0.09 W
Buje	36	45.24 N	13.40 E
Buji	102	33.58 N	95.22 E
Bujnaksk	84	42.49 N	47.07 E
Bujnoviči	78	51.52 N	28.33 E
Bujr nuur ⊜	88	47.48 N	117.42 E
Bujukly	89	49.30 N	142.47 E
Bujumbura	154	3.23 S	29.22 E
Bük, Magy.	61	47.23 N	16.45 E
Buk, Pol.	30	52.22 N	16.31 E
Buka	85	40.48 N	69.11 E
Bukačača	88	52.59 N	116.55 E
Bukačevcy	78	49.15 N	24.29 E
Buka Island I	175e	5.15 S	154.35 E
Bukama	154	9.12 S	25.51 E
Būkān, Īrān	128	36.31 N	46.12 E
Bukan', Ross.	76	53.55 N	34.42 E
Bukanovskaja	80	49.42 N	42.18 E
Buka Passage ʯ	175e	5.25 S	154.41 E
Bukarest → București	38	44.26 N	26.06 E
Bukarevo	82	55.57 N	36.44 E
Bukavu	154	2.30 S	28.52 E
Bukene	154	4.14 S	32.53 E
Bukhara → Buchara	128	39.48 N	64.25 E
Bukhayt, Bi'r Ŧ[4]	142	29.13 N	32.17 E
Bukide, Pulau I	112	3.47 N	125.36 E
Bukidnon □[4]	116	8.00 N	125.00 E
Bukima	154	1.48 S	33.25 E
Bukit Baharu	114	2.13 N	102.16 E
Bukitbatu	114	1.27 N	102.00 E
Bukit Betong	114	4.15 N	101.56 E
Bukit Fraser	114	3.43 N	101.45 E
Bukit Kachi	114	6.24 N	100.32 E
Bukit Mandai	271c	1.25 N	103.45 E
Bukit Mertajam	114	5.22 N	100.28 E
Bukit Panjang	271c	1.23 N	103.46 E
Bukit Serok	114	2.55 N	102.50 E
Bukit Timah	271c	1.20 N	103.47 E
Bukit Timah Race Course ♦	271c	1.20 N	103.48 E
Bukittinggi	112	0.19 S	100.22 E
Bükk ⋏	30	48.05 N	20.30 E
Bukoba	154	1.20 S	31.49 E
Bukombe	154	3.31 S	32.03 E
Bukovica -●-[1]	36	44.10 N	15.40 E
Bukovina □[9]	78	48.00 N	25.30 E
Bukrino	82	54.48 N	36.14 E
Bukuka	88	51.11 N	116.39 E
Bukukun	88	49.27 N	111.08 E
Bukum, Pulau I	271c	1.14 N	103.47 E
Bukumbirwa	154	0.46 S	28.44 E
Bukum Kechil, Pulau I	271c	1.14 N	103.46 E
Bukunga	154	7.41 S	25.56 E
Bukuru	150	9.48 N	8.51 E
Bukuya	154	0.41 N	31.50 E
Bula	164	3.06 S	130.30 E
Bula ≃	80	55.12 N	48.23 E
Bula Atumba	152	8.40 S	14.48 E
Bulacan □[4]	116	15.00 N	121.05 E
Bulacaue Point ≻	116	11.36 N	123.09 E
Bülach	58	47.31 N	8.32 E
Bulajevo	86	54.54 N	70.26 E
Bulak	88	51.02 N	115.21 E
Bulaka ≃	164	8.06 S	139.12 E
Bulak Gölü ⊜	130	38.32 N	32.55 E
Bulalacao	116	12.20 N	121.20 E
Bulalacao Island I	116	11.45 N	120.10 E
Bulalaqui Point ≻	116	11.17 N	124.03 E
Bulan, Pil.	116	12.40 N	123.52 E
Bulan, Pil.	116	6.44 N	124.47 E
Bulan, Ky., U.S.	192	37.18 N	83.09 W
Bulanaš	86	57.16 N	62.00 E
Bulancak	130	40.57 N	38.14 E
Bulandshahr	124	28.24 N	77.51 E
Bulanicha	86	52.48 N	84.57 E
Bulanık	130	39.05 N	42.15 E
Bulan Island I	116	6.08 N	121.50 E
Bulanovo	86	52.27 N	55.10 E
Būlāq	140	25.12 N	30.32 E
Būlāq -●-[8]	273c	30.04 N	31.14 E
Būlāq ad-Dakrūr	273c	30.02 N	31.11 E
Bulava	89	51.55 N	140.25 E
Bulavinovka	83	49.25 N	38.58 E
Bulawa, Gunung ∧	112	0.30 N	123.34 E
Bulawayo	154	20.09 S	28.36 E
Bulbjerg ∧[2]	26	57.09 N	9.02 E
Bulbul	130	36.46 N	36.49 E
Bulbul, Wādī V	140	10.59 N	24.33 E
Bulcherry Island I	126	21.33 N	88.31 E
Buldan	130	38.03 N	28.51 E
Buldāna	122	20.32 N	76.11 E
Buldern	52	51.52 N	7.22 E
Buldibuyo	248	8.07 S	77.22 W
Buldir Island I	181a	52.21 N	175.54 E
Buldon	116	7.33 N	124.25 E
Buldurtinskij	80	50.05 N	53.11 E
Buldyrty ≃	80	49.48 N	52.34 E
Bulembu	158	25.56 S	31.06 E
Bulga	170	32.39 S	151.01 E
Bulgakovka	83	49.11 N	38.33 E
Bulgakovo	76	55.14 N	32.08 E
Bulgan, Mong.	86	46.53 N	91.05 E
Bulgan, Mong.	88	48.45 N	103.34 E
Bulgan, Mong.	102	44.05 N	103.32 E
Bulgan □[4]	88	49.00 N	103.30 E
Bulgar	80	54.57 N	49.05 E
Bulgaria (Bâlgarija) □[1], Europe	22	43.00 N	25.00 E
Bulgaria (Bâlgarija) □[1], Europe	38	43.00 N	25.00 E
Bulgarie → Bulgaria □[1]	38	43.00 N	25.00 E
Bulgarien → Bulgaria □[1]	38	43.00 N	25.00 E
Bulger	214	40.23 N	80.20 W
Bulgnéville	58	48.13 N	5.50 E
Bulgroo	166	25.48 S	143.59 E
Bulhale	144	5.20 N	46.29 E
Buliluyan	116	8.20 N	117.12 E
Buliluyan, Cape ≻	116	8.20 N	117.11 E
Bulim	271c	1.22 N	103.43 E
Bulimba	171a	27.25 S	153.04 E
Bulki	144	6.10 N	36.40 E
Bulkington	42	52.29 N	1.25 W
Bulkley ≃	182	55.13 N	127.40 W
Bulkley Ranges ⋏	182	54.30 N	127.30 W
Bull ≃	182	49.28 N	115.26 W
Bullabulling	162	31.01 S	120.32 E
Bullaque ≃	34	38.59 N	4.17 W
Bullara	162	22.40 S	114.03 E
Bullard	222	32.08 N	95.19 W
Bulla Regia ⊥	36	36.34 N	8.46 E
Bullas	34	38.03 N	1.40 W
Bullaxaar	144	10.23 N	44.25 E
Bullay	56	50.03 N	7.08 E
Bull Creek ≃, Nv., U.S.	204	38.43 N	115.34 W
Bull Creek ≃, N.Y., U.S.	284a	43.03 N	78.50 W
Bull Creek ≃, Oh., U.S.	214	40.42 N	80.32 W
Bull Creek ≃, S.D., U.S.	198	43.41 N	99.28 W
Bull Creek ≃, S.D., U.S.	198	45.40 N	103.18 W
Bull Creek ≃, Tx., U.S.	196	32.36 N	101.10 W
Bulldog	164	7.45 S	146.25 E
Bulle	58	46.37 N	7.04 E
Buller ≃	172	41.44 S	171.35 E
Buller, Mount ∧	169	37.09 S	146.26 E
Bullfinch	162	30.59 S	119.06 E
Bullfrog Creek ≃	200	37.19 N	110.44 W
Bull Harbour	182	50.54 N	127.55 W
Bullhead	198	45.45 N	101.04 W
Bullhead City	204	35.08 N	114.34 W
Bull Hide Creek ≃	222	31.23 N	97.01 W
Bull Hill ∧[2]	262	53.40 N	2.21 W
Bulli	170	34.20 S	150.55 E
Bullicame ♦	66	42.22 N	12.04 E
Büllingen	56	50.25 N	6.16 E
Bullioh	171b	36.12 S	147.20 E
Bullion	261	48.37 N	2.00 E
Bull Lake ⊜[1]	202	43.11 N	109.07 W
Bull Lake Creek ≃	202	43.14 N	109.02 W
Bull Mountain ∧	202	46.05 N	112.04 W
Bullock	192	36.30 N	78.33 W
Bullock Creek	166	17.43 S	144.31 E
Bullock Creek ≃	166	21.40 S	145.09 E
Bulloo ≃	166	28.43 S	142.30 E
Bulloo Downs	166	28.31 S	142.57 E
Bulloo Lake ⊜	166	28.43 S	142.25 E
Bulloo River Overflow ≚	166	28.50 S	142.40 E
Bullpound Creek ≃	182	51.05 N	111.58 W
Bull Run ≃, Or., U.S.	224	45.26 N	122.15 W

Symbols in the index entries represent the broad categories identified in the key at the right. Symbols with superior numbers (⋏[1]) identify subcategories (see complete key on page *I · 1*).

Symbole im Register stellen die rechts im Schlüssel erklärten Kategorien dar. Symbole mit hochgestellten Ziffern (⋏[1]) bezeichnen Unterabteilungen einer Kategorie (vgl. vollständiger Schlüssel auf Seite *I · 1*).

Los símbolos incluídos en el texto del índice representan las grandes categorías identificadas con la clave a la derecha. Los símbolos con numeros en su parte superior (⋏[1]) identifican las subcategorías (véase la clave completa en la página *I · 1*).

Les symboles de l'index représentent les catégories indiquées dans la légende à droite. Les symboles suivis d'un indice (⋏[1]) représentent des sous-catégories (voir légende complète à la page *I · 1*).

Os símbolos incluídos no texto do índice representam as grandes categorias identificadas com a chave à direita. Os símbolos com números em sua parte superior (⋏[1]) identificam as subcategorias (veja-se a chave completa à página *I · 1*).

English	Deutsch	Español	Français	Português
∧ Mountain	Berg	Montaña	Montagne	Montanha
⋏ Mountains	Gebirge	Montañas	Montagnes	Montanhas
)(Pass	Paß	Paso	Col	Passo
V Valley, Canyon	Tal, Cañon	Valle, Cañón	Vallée, Canyon	Vale, Canhão
≚ Plain	Ebene	Llano	Plaine	Planície
≻ Cape	Kap	Cabo	Cap	Cabo
I Island	Insel	Isla	Île	Ilha
II Islands	Inseln	Islas	Îles	Ilhas
≗ Other Topographic Features	Andere Topographische Objekte	Otros Elementos Topográficos	Autres données topographiques	Outros acidentes topográficos

ESPAÑOL — FRANÇAIS — PORTUGUÊS

Nombre / Nom / Nome	Página / Page	Lat.°′	Long.°′ W = Oeste / W = Ouest
Bull Run ≃, Va., U.S.	208	38.43 N	77.23 W
Bull Run Lake ◎	224	45.27 N	121.50 W
Bull Run Reservoir Number 1 ◎[1], Or., U.S.	224	45.30 N	122.04 W
Bull Run Reservoir Number 2 ◎[1], Or., U.S.	224	45.28 N	122.10 W
Bullrun Rock ∧	202	44.21 N	118.17 W
Bulls	172	40.10 S	175.23 E
Bulls Bay ⊂	192	32.59 N	79.33 W
Bullsbrook	168a	31.40 S	116.01 E
Bulls Gap	192	36.15 N	83.05 W
Bull Shoals	194	36.23 N	92.34 W
Bull Shoals Lake ◎[1]	194	36.30 N	92.50 W
Bullskin Creek ≃	218	38.10 N	85.19 W
Bullville	210	41.33 N	74.22 W
Bully Creek ≃	202	43.58 N	117.15 W
Bully Hill	214	41.22 N	79.50 W
Bully-les-Mines	50	50.26 N	2.43 E
Bulmke-Hüllen ◆[8]	263	51.31 N	7.06 E
Bulnaj nuruu ⋏	88	49.05 N	98.30 E
Bulnes	252	36.44 S	72.18 W
Bulo Ghedudo	144	2.52 N	43.01 E
Bulolo	164	7.10 S	146.40 E
Bulpham	260	51.33 N	0.22 E
Bulpitt	219	39.35 N	89.26 W
Bulsār	122	20.38 N	72.56 E
Bulstrode ≃	206	46.02 N	72.15 W
Bultei	71	40.27 N	9.03 E
Bultfontein	158	28.20 S	26.05 E
Buluan	116	6.44 N	124.47 E
Buluan ≃	116	6.47 N	124.47 E
Buluan, Lake ◎	116	6.40 N	124.49 E
Buluduku	114	2.20 N	98.14 E
Bulugansk	88	52.24 N	110.23 E
Bulukumba	112	5.33 S	120.11 E
Bulukuto	152	0.12 S	21.42 E
Bululawang	115a	8.05 S	112.38 E
Bulungu, Zaïre	152	6.04 S	21.54 E
Bulungu, Zaïre	152	4.33 S	18.36 E
Bulupayung	114	1.38 N	99.11 E
Bulusan	116	12.45 N	124.08 E
Bulusan Volcano ∧	116	12.46 N	124.03 E
Bulwater	158	32.29 S	21.48 E
Bulwer	158	29.46 S	29.47 E
Bulyčevo	82	55.06 N	37.15 E
Bulyee	162	32.22 S	117.31 E
Bumba	152	2.11 N	22.28 E
Bumbah, Khalīj al- ⊂	146	32.20 N	23.10 E
Bumbire Island I	154	1.40 S	31.53 E
Bumbles Green	260	51.44 N	0.02 E
Bumbo	152	6.55 S	19.16 E
Bumbu ≃	273b	4.23 S	15.18 E
Bumbulan	112	0.29 N	122.04 E
Bumbun, Pulau I	112	4.27 N	118.40 E
Bumbuna	150	9.03 N	11.44 W
Bumbunga Lake ◎	168b	33.54 S	138.11 E
Bumiayu	115a	7.15 S	109.00 E
Bumijawa	115a	7.10 S	109.07 E
Bumkin Island I	283	42.17 N	70.54 W
Bumping ≃	224	46.59 N	121.06 W
Bumping Lake ◎	224	46.52 N	121.19 W
Bumpus, Mount ∧[2]	176	69.33 N	112.40 W
Bumtang ≃	124	26.56 N	90.51 E
Bumu Hu ◎	120	31.15 N	91.10 E
Buna, Kenya	154	2.47 N	39.31 E
Buna, Pap. N. Gui.	164	8.40 S	148.25 E
Buna, Tx., U.S.	194	30.26 N	93.58 W
Buna, Zaïre	152	3.15 S	18.59 E
Bunagāti	126	23.19 N	89.25 E
Bunai	164	2.11 S	147.14 E
Bunaj	85	38.26 N	71.32 E
Bun'atino	82	56.24 N	37.15 E
Bunavista	196	35.39 N	101.28 W
Bunawan	116	8.12 N	125.57 E
Bunazi	154	1.13 S	31.24 E
Bunbeg	48	55.03 N	8.18 W
Bunbury	168a	33.19 S	115.38 E
Bunceton	194	38.47 N	92.47 W
Bunclody	48	52.38 N	6.40 W
Buncrana	48	55.08 N	7.27 W
Bundaberg	166	24.52 S	152.21 E
Bundanoon	170	34.39 S	150.18 E
Bundarra	166	30.10 S	151.05 E
Bunde, Dtsch.	52	53.11 N	7.16 E
Bünde, Dtsch.	52	52.12 N	8.35 E
Bunde, Ned.	56	50.54 N	5.45 E
Bundeena	274a	34.05 S	151.09 E
Bundenthal	56	49.06 N	7.48 E
Bundey ≃	162	21.46 S	135.37 E
Bündheim	54	51.53 N	10.32 E
Būndi, India	120	25.27 N	75.39 E
Bundi, Pap. N. Gui.	164	5.40 S	145.15 E
Bundick Creek ≃	194	30.36 N	92.57 W
Bundoora	274b	37.42 S	145.04 E
Bundoran	48	54.28 N	8.17 W
Būndu, India	124	23.11 N	85.35 E
Bundu, S. Afr.	158	29.45 S	22.02 E
Bunduqiyah	154	5.06 N	30.53 E
Bund'ur	86	57.32 N	82.01 E
Buner □[9]	123	34.35 N	72.35 E
Bunessan	46	56.19 N	6.14 W
Bunga	150	11.04 N	9.38 E
Bunga ≃	150	11.23 N	9.56 E
Bungamas	112	3.42 S	102.23 E
Bungay	42	52.28 N	1.26 E
Bungbulang	115a	7.27 S	107.35 E
Bunge	26	57.51 N	19.01 E
Bungegep	164	7.48 S	139.52 E
Bungendore	171b	35.15 S	149.27 E
Bunger Hills ⋏[2]	9	66.17 S	100.47 E
Bung Kan	110	18.23 N	103.37 E
Bungku	112	2.33 S	121.58 E
Bungo	152	7.26 S	15.23 E
Bungoma	154	0.34 N	34.34 E
Bungonia	170	34.51 S	149.57 E
Bungo-suidō ʊ	92	33.00 N	132.13 E
Bungo-takada	96	33.33 N	131.27 E
Bungsberg ∧[2]	54	54.12 N	10.43 E
Bungtlang	120	22.20 N	92.46 E
Bungu	154	7.38 S	39.03 E
Buni ≃	115a	7.26 S	106.47 E
Bunia	154	1.34 N	30.15 E
Bunianga	152	3.34 S	20.06 E
Būnīken, Kūh-e ∧	128	26.46 N	58.12 E
Buninyong	169	37.39 S	143.53 E
Buninyong, Mount ∧	169	37.39 S	143.56 E
Bunji	123	35.40 N	74.36 E
Bunkeflo strand	41	55.33 N	12.57 E
Bunker	194	37.27 N	91.12 W
Bunker Group II	166	23.48 S	152.20 E
Bunker Hill, Il., U.S.	219	39.02 N	89.57 W
Bunker Hill, In., U.S.	216	40.40 N	86.06 W
Bunker Hill, Or., U.S.	202	43.21 N	124.12 W
Bunker Hill, Tx., U.S.	222	29.46 N	95.32 W
Bunker Hill ∧	204	39.15 N	117.08 W
Bunker Hill Monument ⊥	283	42.22 N	71.04 W
Bunkeya	154	10.07 S	27.17 E
Bunkie	194	30.57 N	92.10 W
Bunkyō ◆[8]	268	35.43 N	139.45 E
Bunnahowen	48	54.11 N	9.54 W
Bunnell	192	29.27 N	81.15 W
Bunnik	52	52.04 N	5.12 E
Bünningstedt	52	53.41 N	10.13 E
Bunola	214	40.14 N	79.56 W
Bun Plains ⋮	154	0.44 N	40.42 E
Bunratty Castle ⊥	48	52.42 N	8.48 W
Bunschoten	52	52.14 N	5.22 E
Bunsuru ≃	150	13.21 N	6.23 E
Bunta	112	0.48 S	122.10 E
Buntine	162	29.59 S	116.34 E
Buntingford	42	51.57 N	0.01 W
Buntok	112	1.42 S	114.48 E
Bununu Dass	150	10.00 N	9.31 E
Bunut	112	0.46 N	112.30 E
Bunyambili	154	2.21 S	29.25 E
Bünyan	130	38.51 N	35.52 E
Bunyip	169	38.06 S	145.43 E
Bunyip ≃	169	38.13 S	145.27 E
Bunyolo	34	39.25 N	0.47 W
Bunyrevo	82	54.34 N	37.09 E
Bunyu, Pulau I	112	3.30 N	117.50 E
Bunza	150	12.08 N	4.00 E
Buochs	58	46.58 N	8.22 E
Buol	112	1.10 N	121.26 E
Buolkalach	74	72.56 N	119.50 E
Buonalbergo	68	41.13 N	14.59 E
Buona Vista	271c	1.16 N	103.47 E
Buon Bu N'jang	110	12.06 N	107.40 E
Buonconvento	66	43.08 N	11.29 E
Buon Me Thuot	110	12.40 N	108.03 E
Buon Mrong	110	12.48 N	108.28 E
Buon Ngo	110	12.30 N	108.28 E
Buon Thach Hom	110	12.17 N	108.48 E
Buon Ya Soup	110	13.05 N	107.52 E
Buor-Chaja, guba ⊂	74	71.30 N	131.00 E
Buor-Chaja, mys ›	74	71.56 N	132.40 E
Bupul	164	7.31 S	140.52 E
Buqay'āwīyah, Qā' al- ⋮	132	32.03 N	37.07 E
Buqayq	128	25.56 N	49.40 E
Buqda Koosaar	144	4.31 N	44.49 E
Buqde Caqable	144	4.04 N	45.15 E
Buquira ≃	256	23.10 S	45.54 W
Buquirivu ≃	287b	23.28 S	46.28 W
Buqūm, Ḥarrat al- ⊤[9]	144	20.54 N	42.00 E
Bur	88	58.47 N	107.01 E
Bura, Kenya	154	3.30 S	38.18 E
Bura, Kenya	154	1.06 S	39.57 E
Bura Gaurānga ≃[1]	126	22.00 N	90.33 E
Burakin	162	30.31 S	117.10 E
Buraly	80	55.04 N	52.52 E
Buram	140	10.49 N	25.10 E
Buran	86	48.04 N	85.15 E
Burangulovo	86	53.26 N	58.23 E
Buranhém ≃	255	16.27 S	39.04 W
Burankol'	86	46.14 N	54.12 E
Burannoje	86	50.59 N	54.28 E
Burano ≃	66	43.37 N	12.40 E
Burao Kibir	144	8.42 N	45.29 E
Burāq	132	33.10 N	36.29 E
Burāri ◆[8]	272a	28.46 N	77.12 E
Buras	194	29.21 N	89.31 W
Buraševo	82	56.44 N	35.52 E
Burauen	116	10.58 N	124.53 E
Burayd, Bi'r ⊤[4]	142	29.08 N	32.07 E
Buraydah	128	26.20 N	43.59 E
Burayk	146	26.33 N	13.08 E
Buraykah	132	32.50 N	36.34 E
Burbach	56	50.45 N	8.05 E
Burbage, Eng., U.K.	42	51.20 N	1.40 W
Burbage, Eng., U.K.	262	53.15 N	1.56 W
Burbank, Ca., U.S.	226	37.19 N	121.55 W
Burbank, Ca., U.S.	228	34.10 N	118.18 W
Burbank, Il., U.S.	216	41.45 N	87.45 W
Burbank, Il., U.S.	278	41.45 N	87.46 W
Burbank, Oh., U.S.	214	40.59 N	81.59 W
Burbank, Wa., U.S.	202	46.12 N	119.00 W
Burbank Studios ⊍[3]	280	34.09 N	118.21 W
Burbure	50	50.32 N	2.28 E
Burç	130	37.02 N	37.10 E
Burcei	71	39.21 N	9.21 E
Burcevo	82	55.02 N	38.09 E
Burcher	166	33.32 S	147.18 E
Burcin	62	45.26 N	5.26 E
Burco	144	9.31 N	45.34 E
Burda	124	25.50 N	77.35 E
Burdalyk	128	38.25 N	64.20 E
Burdekin ≃	166	19.39 S	147.30 E
Burdekin Falls ʟ	166	20.39 S	147.09 E
Burden	198	37.18 N	96.45 W
Burdeos	116	14.51 N	121.58 E
Burdeos Bay ⊂	116	14.44 N	122.06 E
Burdeos → Bordeaux	32	44.50 N	0.34 W
Burdett, Ab., Can.	182	49.50 N	111.32 W
Burdett, Ks., U.S.	198	38.11 N	99.31 W
Burdett, N.Y., U.S.	210	42.25 N	76.50 W
Burdul	272c	19.07 N	73.07 E
Burdur	130	37.43 N	30.17 E
Burdur □[4]	130	37.30 N	30.00 E
Burdur Gölü ◎	130	37.44 N	30.12 E
Burdwood Bank ✣[3]	18	54.15 S	59.00 W
Bure, Ityo.	144	8.15 N	35.09 E
Bure, Ityo.	144	10.47 N	37.06 E
Bure ≃	42	52.37 N	1.43 E
Bure, Pic de ∧	62	44.38 N	5.56 E
Bureå	26	64.37 N	21.12 E
Bureälven ≃	26	64.37 N	21.13 E
Bureg Changaj	88	48.14 N	103.57 E
Bureinskij chrebet ⋏	89	50.35 N	133.35 E
Bureja	89	49.52 N	129.48 E
Bureja ≃	89	49.25 N	129.35 E
Burekup	168a	33.19 S	115.49 E
Büren, Dtsch.	52	51.33 N	8.33 E
Büren, Mong.	88	47.13 N	95.54 E
Büren an der Aare	58	47.08 N	7.23 E
Büren Chaan	88	49.29 N	99.14 E
Bürengijn nuruu ⋏	88	49.15 N	104.30 E
Bures	261	48.57 N	1.58 E
Bures-sur-Yvette	261	48.42 N	2.10 E
Burey-en-Vaux	58	48.34 N	5.40 E
Burfjord	24	69.56 N	22.00 E
Burford, On., Can.	212	43.06 N	80.26 W
Burford, Eng., U.K.	42	51.49 N	1.38 W
Būr Fu'ād ◆[8]	142	31.15 N	32.19 E
Burg, Dtsch.	54	51.49 N	14.08 E
Burg, Dtsch.	54	52.16 N	11.51 E
Burg, Dtsch.	56	50.42 N	8.19 E
Burg ◆[8]	263	51.08 N	7.09 E
Burg, Schloss ⊥	263	51.08 N	7.10 E
Burga	76	58.45 N	32.29 E
Burgas	38	42.30 N	27.28 E
Burgas □[4]	130	42.10 N	27.00 E
Burgaski zaliv ⊂	38	42.30 N	27.33 E
Burgau	58	48.26 N	10.25 E
Burg [auf Fehmarn]	54	54.26 N	11.12 E
Burgaw	192	34.33 N	77.55 W
Burgaz ◆[8]	267b	40.53 N	29.03 E
Burgaz Adası I	267b	40.53 N	29.04 E
Burgbernheim	56	49.27 N	10.19 E
Burgdorf, Dtsch.	52	52.27 N	10.00 E
Burgdorf, Schw.	58	47.04 N	7.37 E
Burgebrach	56	49.50 N	10.44 E
Bürgel	54	50.56 N	11.45 E
Burgenland □[3]	61	47.30 N	16.20 E
Burgeo	186	47.37 N	57.37 W
Burgersdorp	158	31.00 S	26.20 E
Burger Township	273d	26.05 S	27.46 E
Burges, Mount ∧[2]	162	30.50 S	121.06 E
Burgess	208	37.53 N	76.21 W
Burgess Hill	42	50.57 N	0.07 W
Burgessville	212	43.01 N	80.39 W
Burgettstown	214	40.22 N	80.23 W
Burggrafenberg ∧[2]	263	51.13 N	7.07 E
Burghausen	60	48.09 N	12.49 E
Burghead	46	57.42 N	3.30 W
Burgheim	60	48.42 N	11.01 E
Burgh Heath	260	51.18 N	0.13 W
Burghill	214	41.22 N	80.34 W
Burgh le Marsh	44	53.09 N	0.15 E
Burghūth, Sabkhat al- ◎	130	34.58 N	41.06 E
Burgin	194	37.45 N	84.46 W
Burgio	70	37.36 N	13.17 E
Burgjoss	56	50.12 N	9.29 E
Burgkirchen	60	48.12 N	13.06 E
Burgkunstadt	54	50.08 N	11.14 E
Bürglen, Schw.	58	46.53 N	8.40 E
Bürglen, Schw.	58	47.33 N	9.09 E
Burglengenfeld	60	49.13 N	12.03 E
Burgoon	214	41.16 N	83.15 W
Burgos, Esp.	34	42.21 N	3.42 W
Burgos, It.	71	40.23 N	8.59 E
Burgos, Méx.	232	24.57 N	98.47 W
Burgos, Pil.	116	16.04 N	119.52 E
Burgos, Pil.	116	15.30 N	120.24 E
Burgos □[4]	34	42.20 N	3.40 W
Burgsinn	56	50.09 N	9.38 E
Burgstädt	54	50.55 N	12.49 E
Burgstall	54	52.24 N	11.41 E
Burgstall → Postal	64	46.36 N	11.11 E
Burg Stargard	54	53.29 N	13.18 E
Burgsvik	26	57.03 N	18.16 E
Burgueño, Arroyo ≃	288	34.24 S	58.47 W
Burgund → Bourgogne □[9]	32	47.00 N	4.30 E
Burgundy → Bourgogne □[9]	32	47.00 N	4.30 E
Burgusio (Burgeis)	64	46.42 N	10.31 E
Burgwedel	52	52.29 N	9.51 E
Burgwindheim	56	49.49 N	10.35 E
Burhābalang ≃	126	21.28 N	87.04 E
Burham	260	51.20 N	0.29 E
Burhan Budai Shan ⋏	102	36.00 N	96.00 E
Burhaniye, Tür.	130	37.57 N	28.45 E
Burhaniye, Tür.	130	39.30 N	26.58 E
Burhānpur	120	21.18 N	76.14 E
Burhar	124	23.13 N	81.32 E
Burhave	52	53.34 N	8.21 E
Burholme ◆[8]	285	40.03 N	75.05 W
Buri	255	23.48 S	48.35 W
Burias Island I	116	12.57 N	123.08 E
Burias Pass ʊ	116	13.00 N	123.15 E
Buribaj	86	51.57 N	58.11 E
Būr Ibrāhīm ◆[8]	142	29.57 N	32.34 E
Burica, Punta ›	236	8.03 N	82.53 W
Burien	224	47.28 N	122.20 W
Burigi, Lake ◎	154	2.05 S	31.15 E
Burila Mare	38	44.27 N	22.34 E
Burin	186	47.02 N	55.10 W
Burin Peninsula ›[1]	186	47.00 N	55.40 W
Buri Ram	110	15.00 N	103.07 E
Buriswar ≃[1]	126	21.58 N	90.02 E
Buritama	255	21.03 S	50.08 W
Buriti, Bra.	250	3.55 S	42.57 W
Buriti, Bra.	255	16.27 S	53.27 W
Buriti ≃	248	12.50 S	58.28 W
Buriti Alegre	255	18.09 S	49.03 W
Buriti Bravo	250	5.50 S	43.50 W
Buriticupu ≃	250	4.13 S	46.33 W
Buriti dos Lopes	250	3.10 S	41.52 W
Buritizeiro	255	17.21 S	44.58 W
Būriya	124	30.09 N	77.21 E
Burj al-'Arab	140	30.55 N	29.32 E
Burjassot	34	39.31 N	0.25 W
Burjatija □[3]	88	53.00 N	109.00 E
Burji	144	5.20 N	37.57 E
Burj Islām	130	35.41 N	35.48 E
Burj Mughayzil	142	31.27 N	30.23 E
Burkan ≃	85	41.43 N	76.46 E
Burkau	54	51.10 N	14.10 E
Burkburnett	196	34.05 N	98.34 W
Burke, S.D., U.S.	198	43.10 N	99.17 W
Burke, Tx., U.S.	222	31.14 N	94.46 W
Burke, Va., U.S.	284c	38.47 N	77.16 W
Burke ≃	166	23.12 S	139.33 E
Burke Channel ʊ	182	52.07 N	127.38 W
Burke Island I	9	73.15 S	104.35 W
Burke Lake ◎[1]	284c	38.46 N	77.18 W
Burke Lake County Park ♠	284c	38.45 N	77.18 W
Burke Lakefront Airport ⊠	279a	41.31 N	81.41 W
Burkesville	194	36.47 N	85.22 W
Burket	216	41.09 N	85.58 W
Burketown	166	17.43 S	139.34 E
Burkett Gardens	226	37.57 N	121.15 W
Burkettsville	216	40.21 N	84.39 W
Burkhardtsdorf	54	50.44 N	12.55 E
Burkina Faso □[1], Afr.	134	13.00 N	1.30 W
Burkina Faso □[1], Afr.	150	13.00 N	1.30 W
Burkit	80	47.03 N	50.42 E
Burksville	219	38.16 N	90.09 W
Burla	86	53.19 N	78.21 E
Burla ≃	86	53.20 N	78.02 E
Burladingen	58	48.17 N	9.07 E
Burleigh	208	39.02 N	74.51 W
Burleigh Falls	212	44.34 N	78.13 W
Burleigh Heads	171a	28.06 S	153.27 E
Burleson	222	32.32 N	97.19 W
Burleson □[6]	222	30.30 N	96.43 W
Burley, Id., U.S.	202	42.32 N	113.47 W
Burley, Wa., U.S.	224	47.25 N	122.37 W
Burley Griffin, Lake ◎	171b	35.13 S	149.05 E
Burli, Kaz.	80	51.25 N	52.44 E
Burli, Kaz.	86	53.36 N	61.55 E
Burlingame, Ca., U.S.	226	37.35 N	122.21 W
Burlingame, Ks., U.S.	198	38.45 N	95.00 W
Burlingame State Park ♠	207	41.22 N	71.43 W
Burlington, Nf., Can.	186	49.45 N	56.02 W
Burlington, On., Can.	212	43.19 N	79.47 W
Burlington, Co., U.S.	198	39.18 N	102.16 W
Burlington, Ct., U.S.	207	41.46 N	72.57 W
Burlington, Il., U.S.	216	42.03 N	88.33 W
Burlington, In., U.S.	216	40.29 N	86.24 W
Burlington, Ia., U.S.	190	40.48 N	91.06 W
Burlington, Ks., U.S.	198	38.11 N	95.44 W
Burlington, Ky., U.S.	218	39.01 N	84.43 W
Burlington, Ma., U.S.	207	42.30 N	71.11 W
Burlington, Mi., U.S.	216	42.06 N	85.05 W
Burlington, N.J., U.S.	208	40.04 N	74.51 W
Burlington, N.C., U.S.	192	36.05 N	79.26 W
Burlington, N.D., U.S.	198	48.16 N	101.25 W
Burlington, Pa., U.S.	210	41.47 N	76.37 W
Burlington, Tx., U.S.	222	31.01 N	96.60 W
Burlington, Vt., U.S.	188	44.28 N	73.12 W
Burlington, Wa., U.S.	224	48.28 N	122.19 W
Burlington, Wi., U.S.	216	42.40 N	88.16 W
Burlington, Wy., U.S.	202	44.26 N	108.25 W
Burlington □[6]	208	39.50 N	74.47 W
Burlington Beach	216	41.30 N	87.03 W
Burlington County Airpark ⊠	285	39.56 N	74.50 W
Burlington Island I	285	40.05 N	74.51 W
Burlington Junction	194	40.26 N	95.03 W
Burlington Mall ◆[9]	283	42.29 N	71.13 W
Burlit	89	46.33 N	134.14 E
Burluk	80	50.34 N	44.33 E
Burma (Myanmar) □[1]	110	22.00 N	98.00 E
Burmā, Tall ∧	132	30.38 N	35.50 E
Burmakino	80	57.27 N	40.20 E
Burn ≃	44	54.12 N	1.38 W
Burnaby	224	49.15 N	122.57 W
Burnaby Island I	182	52.24 N	131.20 W
Burnage	262	53.26 N	2.12 W
Burnas, ozero ◎	78	45.52 N	30.08 E
Burnet	196	30.45 N	98.13 W
Burnett ≃	166	24.46 S	152.25 E
Burnett Bay ⊂	176	73.53 N	124.00 W
Burnett Brook ≃	276	40.46 N	74.38 W
Burnett Heads	166	24.46 S	152.25 E
Burnettsville	216	40.46 N	86.36 W
Burney, Ca., U.S.	204	40.52 N	121.39 W
Burney, In., U.S.	218	39.19 N	85.38 W
Burnham, Eng., U.K.	42	51.33 N	0.39 W
Burnham, Il., U.S.	278	41.39 N	87.34 W
Burnham, Pa., U.S.	208	40.38 N	77.34 W
Burnham Beeches ◆[3]	260	51.34 N	0.38 W
Burnham Market	42	52.57 N	0.44 E
Burnham-on-Crouch	42	51.38 N	0.49 E
Burnham-on-Sea	42	51.15 N	3.00 W
Burnhamthorpe	275b	43.37 N	79.36 W
Burnhaven	46	57.29 N	1.47 W
Burnie	166	41.04 S	145.54 E
Burning Tree Estates	284c	39.01 N	77.12 W
Burnips	216	42.44 N	85.50 W
Burniston	44	54.19 N	0.26 W
Burnley	44	53.48 N	2.14 W
Burnley □[8]	262	53.46 N	2.15 W
Burnley Creek ≃	212	44.13 N	77.51 W
Burnley Football Ground ♠	262	53.48 N	2.14 W
Burnmouth	46	55.50 N	2.04 W
Burnoje	85	42.37 N	70.46 E
Burno-Okt'abr'skoje	85	42.42 N	70.49 E
Burnpur	126	23.40 N	86.57 E
Burns, Ks., U.S.	198	38.05 N	96.53 W
Burns, Or., U.S.	202	43.35 N	119.03 W
Burns, Tn., U.S.	194	36.03 N	87.18 W
Burns, Wy., U.S.	198	41.11 N	104.21 W
Burns Creek ≃	198	47.22 N	104.25 W
Burns Flat	196	35.20 N	99.10 W
Burns Harbor	216	41.37 N	87.10 W
Burnside, Austl.	168b	34.57 S	138.40 E
Burnside, Ky., U.S.	192	36.59 N	84.36 W
Burnside, Pa., U.S.	214	40.49 N	78.47 W
Burnside ≃	176	66.51 N	108.04 W
Burnside, Lake ◎	162	25.33 S	123.02 E
Burns Lake	182	54.14 N	125.46 W
Burnsville, Al., U.S.	194	32.28 N	86.53 W
Burnsville, Ms., U.S.	194	34.50 N	88.18 W
Burnsville, N.C., U.S.	192	35.55 N	82.18 W
Burnsville, W.V., U.S.	188	38.51 N	80.39 W
Burnt ≃, On., Can.	212	44.35 N	78.46 W
Burnt ≃, Or., U.S.	202	44.22 N	117.14 W
Burnt Cabins	214	40.05 N	77.54 W
Burnt Corn Creek ≃	194	31.06 N	87.04 W
Burnt Hills	210	42.54 N	73.53 W
Burnt Island, Nf., Can.	186	47.36 N	58.53 W
Burntisland, Scot., U.K.	46	56.03 N	3.15 W
Burnt Meadow Brook ≃	276	41.05 N	74.18 W
Burnt Mills, Lake ◎	208	36.50 N	76.38 W
Burnt Mills Hills	284c	39.02 N	77.00 W
Burnt Mills Manor	284c	39.02 N	77.00 W
Burnt Mountain ∧	228	33.12 N	117.04 W
Burntop	158	26.49 S	30.54 E
Burnt Pine	174c	29.02 S	167.56 E
Burnt Pond ◎	186	48.11 N	57.24 W
Burntwick Island I	260	51.25 N	0.41 E
Burntwood	42	52.41 N	1.56 W
Burntwood ≃	184	56.08 N	96.30 W
Burntwood Lake ◎	184	55.29 N	100.07 W
Burnyj, porog ʟ	86	57.43 N	95.18 E
Buro	144	11.28 N	49.41 E
Buron	84	42.48 N	44.03 E
Buronzo	62	45.29 N	8.16 E
Burow	54	53.46 N	13.16 E
Burpengary	171a	27.10 S	152.57 E
Burpham	260	51.15 N	0.33 W
Burqin	86	47.43 N	86.53 E
Burqin ≃	86	47.40 N	86.55 E
Burra	166	33.40 S	138.56 E
Burra Burra Creek ≃	170	34.10 S	149.38 E
Burracoppin	162	31.23 S	118.29 E
Burra Creek ≃	168b	33.51 S	139.18 E
Burrage	283	42.02 N	70.51 W
Burrage Pond ◎	283	42.01 N	70.52 W
Burragorang, Lake ◎[1]	170	33.57 S	150.26 E
Burramurra	166	20.30 S	137.20 E
Burravoe	46a	60.32 N	1.28 W
Burrawang	170	34.36 S	150.31 E
Burray I	46	58.51 N	2.54 W
Burrel, Shq.	38	41.37 N	20.00 E
Burrel, Ca., U.S.	226	36.30 N	119.59 W
Burrendong Reservoir ◎[1]	166	32.39 S	149.15 E
Burren Junction	166	30.06 S	148.58 E
Burrill Lake ⊂	170	35.23 S	150.27 E
Burrinjuck Reservoir ◎[1]	166	35.00 S	148.45 E
Burro, Serranías del ⋏	196	29.10 N	102.05 W
Burr Oak, In., U.S.	216	41.15 N	86.25 W
Burr Oak, Ks., U.S.	198	39.51 N	98.18 W
Burr Oak, Mi., U.S.	216	41.50 N	85.19 W
Burro Burro ≃	246	4.48 N	58.51 W
Burro Creek ≃	200	34.32 N	113.35 W
Burro Peak ∧	200	32.35 N	108.26 W
Burrowa, Mount ∧	171b	36.05 S	147.42 E
Burrowa-Pine Mountain National Park ♠	171b	36.06 S	147.44 E
Burrow Head ›	44	54.41 N	4.24 W
Burrowhill	260	51.21 N	0.36 W
Burrows	216	40.40 N	86.30 W
Burrows Island I	224	48.29 N	122.42 W
Burr Ridge	278	41.46 N	87.55 W
Burrs Mill Brook ≃	285	39.53 N	74.42 W
Burrton	198	38.01 N	97.40 W
Burrumbeet, Lake ◎	169	37.30 S	143.39 E
Burrundie	164	13.32 S	131.42 E
Burruyacú	252	26.30 S	64.45 W
Burrwood	194	28.58 N	89.22 W
Burry Holms I	42	51.37 N	4.18 W
Burry Port	42	51.42 N	4.15 W
Bürs	58	47.09 N	9.48 E
Bursa	130	40.11 N	29.04 E
Bursa □[4]	130	40.10 N	29.00 E
Būr Safājah	140	26.44 N	33.56 E
Būr Sa'īd (Port Said)	142	31.16 N	32.18 E
Būr Sa'īd □[4]	142	30.36 N	32.15 E
Burscheid	56	51.05 N	7.06 E
Burscough	262	53.35 N	2.51 W
Burscough Bridge	44	53.36 N	2.52 W
Bursey, Mount ∧	9	76.00 S	132.40 W
Bursol'	86	53.11 N	78.27 E
Bürstadt	56	49.38 N	8.27 E
Burstall	184	50.40 N	109.54 W
Burštyn	78	49.17 N	24.37 E
Būr Sūdān (Port Sudan)	140	19.37 N	37.14 E
Burt, Ia., U.S.	190	43.11 N	94.13 W
Burt, N.Y., U.S.	210	43.19 N	78.43 W
Būr Tawfīq ◆[8]	128	29.57 N	32.34 E
Burtenbach	58	48.20 N	10.26 E
Burt Lake ◎	190	45.27 N	84.40 W
Burtnieks ezers ◎	76	57.45 N	25.16 E
Burton, B.C., Can.	182	49.59 N	117.54 W
Burton, Eng., U.K.	42	50.44 N	1.45 W
Burton, Eng., U.K.	262	53.16 N	3.01 W
Burton, Il., U.S.	219	39.55 N	91.15 W
Burton, Mi., U.S.	216	43.01 N	84.16 W
Burton, Mi., U.S.	216	43.02 N	83.36 W
Burton, Oh., U.S.	214	41.28 N	81.08 W
Burton, Tx., U.S.	222	30.11 N	96.36 W
Burton, Wa., U.S.	224	47.23 N	122.27 W
Burton, Lake ◎[1]	192	34.50 N	83.33 W
Burton Fleming	44	54.08 N	0.20 W
Burton Latimer	42	52.23 N	0.41 W
Burtons Bridge	216	42.17 N	88.14 W
Burton Seamount ✣[3]	14	32.00 S	171.45 W
Burtonsville	208	39.07 N	76.56 W
Burton upon Stather	44	53.39 N	0.41 W
Burton upon Trent	42	52.49 N	1.36 W
Burtonwood	262	53.26 N	2.39 W
Burtonwood Airfield ⊠	262	53.24 N	2.39 W
Burträsk	26	64.31 N	20.39 E
Burtundy	166	33.44 S	142.16 E
Burṭus	142	30.09 N	31.08 E
Buru I	108	3.24 S	126.40 E
Buruanga	116	11.51 N	121.53 E
Burukan	89	53.02 N	136.03 E
Buruldaj	85	42.48 N	75.52 E
Burullus, Buḥayrat al- ◎	142	31.30 N	30.50 E
Burūm	144	14.22 N	48.57 E
Burundaj	85	43.23 N	76.51 E
Burundi □[1], Afr.	138	3.15 S	30.00 E
Burundi □[1], Afr.	154	3.15 S	30.00 E
Burundučicha	80	58.21 N	46.07 E
Burun-Šibertuj, gora ∧	88	49.42 N	109.59 E
Bururi	154	3.57 S	29.37 E
Burutu	150	5.21 N	5.31 E
Buruz Bāgān	126	23.03 N	89.00 E
Burwash	190	46.19 N	80.48 W
Burwash Landing	180	61.21 N	139.00 W
Burwell, Eng., U.K.	42	52.16 N	0.19 E
Burwell, Ne., U.S.	198	41.46 N	99.07 W
Burwell Bay ⊂	208	37.04 N	76.38 W
Burwick	46	58.44 N	2.57 W
Burwood, Austl.	274a	33.53 S	151.06 E
Burwood, Austl.	274b	37.51 S	145.06 E
Bury, P.Q., Can.	206	45.28 N	71.30 W
Bury, Eng., U.K.	42	50.54 N	0.34 W
Bury, Eng., U.K.	44	53.36 N	2.17 W
Bury □[8]	262	53.35 N	2.19 W
Buryatia → Burjatija □[3]	88	53.00 N	109.00 E
Buryn'	78	51.13 N	33.49 E
Bury Saint Edmunds	42	52.15 N	0.43 E
Burzaco	258	34.49 S	58.24 W
Burzet	62	44.44 N	4.15 E
Burzil	123	34.52 N	75.07 E
Burzil Pass)(	123	34.54 N	75.06 E
Būṣ, Ghubbat al- ⊂	142	29.36 N	32.22 E
Busa, Mount ∧	116	6.08 N	124.39 E
Busachi	71	40.02 N	8.54 E
Busalla	62	44.34 N	8.57 E
Busambra, Rocca ∧	70	37.51 N	13.24 E
Busana	64	44.22 N	10.19 E
Busanga	152	0.51 S	22.04 E
Busanga Swamp ⋮	154	14.10 S	25.50 E
Busangu	154	8.32 S	25.31 E
Busan → Pusan	98	35.06 N	129.03 E
Buṣayrah	130	35.09 N	40.26 E
Busby, Austl.	274a	33.54 S	150.53 E
Busby, Mt., U.S.	202	45.32 N	106.57 W
Busca	62	44.31 N	7.29 E
Buscate	266b	45.32 N	8.49 E
Buscbusc ≃	144	1.08 S	41.49 E
Buschberg ∧[2]	61	48.34 N	16.23 E
Busche	64	46.02 N	11.59 E
Busch Gardens ♠	280	34.13 N	118.28 W
Buschhausen ◆[8]	263	51.30 N	6.51 E
Busdorf	41	54.29 N	9.32 E
Buseck	56	50.36 N	8.47 E
Buseto Palizzolo	70	38.01 N	12.43 E
Būsh	142	29.09 N	31.08 E
Bush ≃, N. Ire., U.K.	44	55.13 N	6.32 W
Bush ≃, S.C., U.S.	192	34.08 N	81.36 W
Būshehr □[4]	128	28.50 N	51.20 E
Bushenyi	154	0.32 S	30.11 E
Bushey	42	51.39 N	0.22 W
Bushey Heath	260	51.38 N	0.20 W
Bushi	268	35.50 N	139.22 E
Bushimaie ≃	152	6.02 S	23.45 E
Bushiribana	241s	12.33 N	69.58 W
Bushkill	210	41.06 N	75.00 W
Bush Kill ≃	210	41.05 N	74.59 W
Bushkill Falls ʟ	210	41.09 N	75.01 W
Bushland	196	35.11 N	102.04 W
Bush Lot	246	6.12 N	57.16 W
Bushman Land □[9]	158	29.15 S	20.00 E
Bushmills	48	55.12 N	6.32 W
Bushnell, Fl., U.S.	220	28.39 N	82.06 W
Bushnell, Il., U.S.	190	40.33 N	90.30 W
Bush River ≃	208	39.21 N	76.14 W
Bushton	198	38.30 N	98.23 W
Bū Shubayrim, Wādī V	146	27.07 N	19.30 E
Bushwick ◆[8]	276	40.42 N	73.55 W
Bushy Park	166	21.16 S	139.43 E
Bushy Park ♠	260	51.25 N	0.20 W
Bushy Run ≃	279b	40.20 N	79.40 W
Bushy Run Battlefield ⊥	279b	40.21 N	79.38 W
Busia	154	0.28 N	34.05 E
Busigny	50	50.02 N	3.28 E
Busing, Pulau I	271c	1.14 N	103.45 E
Businga	152	3.20 N	20.53 E
Büsingen	58	47.42 N	8.41 E
Busira ≃	152	0.15 S	18.59 E
Busjön ◎, Sve.	40	60.06 N	13.28 E
Busjön ◎, Sve.	40	60.31 N	13.58 E
Busk	78	49.58 N	24.37 E
Buskerud □[6]	26	60.25 N	9.12 E
Buskhyttan	40	58.40 N	16.56 E
Busko Zdrój	30	50.28 N	20.44 E
Buskul'	86	53.45 N	61.12 E
Busle	144	5.28 N	44.25 E
Busoga □[5]	154	0.40 N	33.30 E
Busovača	36	44.06 N	17.53 E
Buṣrā al-Ḥarīrī (Bosor)	132	32.50 N	36.20 E
Buṣrá ash-Shām	132	32.31 N	36.29 E
Bussana	62	43.49 N	7.51 E
Bussang	58	47.53 N	6.51 E
Bussang, Col de)(	58	47.54 N	6.54 E
Busselton	162	33.39 S	115.20 E
Busseri ≃	140	7.41 N	28.03 E
Busseto	64	44.59 N	10.02 E
Bussey	190	41.12 N	92.52 W
Bussières	62	45.50 N	4.16 E
Bussi sul Tirino	66	42.12 N	13.49 E
Busskoje	84	43.50 N	44.37 E
Bussolengo	64	45.28 N	10.51 E
Bussoleno	62	45.08 N	7.09 E
Bussum	52	52.16 N	5.10 E
Bussy-Rabutin, Château de ⊥	58	47.35 N	4.31 E
Bussy-Saint-Georges	261	48.51 N	2.42 E
Bustamante, Méx.	232	26.33 N	100.30 W
Bustamante, Méx.	234	23.26 N	99.47 W
Bustān, Wādī al- V	142	28.24 N	30.49 E
Buštěhrad	54	50.09 N	14.10 E
Buşteni	38	45.25 N	25.32 E
Busti	214	42.02 N	79.17 W
Bustleton ◆[8]	285	40.05 N	75.02 W
Busto Arsizio	62	45.37 N	8.51 E
Busto Garolfo	62	45.33 N	8.53 E
Buston, Taj.	85	40.31 N	69.19 E
Buston, Uzb.	128	40.04 N	64.49 E
Buštyna	78	48.04 N	23.27 E
Busu-Adula	152	2.05 N	21.40 E
Busuanga	116	12.10 N	119.55 E
Busuanga Island I	116	12.05 N	120.05 E
Busu-Djanoa	152	1.43 N	21.23 E
Bušuicha	76	59.02 N	40.26 E
Bušulej	88	52.45 N	117.13 E
Büsum	30	54.08 N	8.51 E
Busu-Melo	152	1.48 N	20.15 E
Bū Sunbul, Jabal ⋏[2]	146	23.10 N	22.21 E
Buta, Ross.	80	55.02 N	51.57 E
Buta, Zaïre	154	2.48 N	24.44 E
Butag	116	12.38 N	123.56 E
Butajira	144	8.07 N	38.22 E
Butala	164	6.42 S	147.37 E
Butan	38	43.39 N	23.45 E
Bután → Bhutan □[1]	120	27.30 N	90.30 E
Butand State Park ♠	226	37.13 N	122.20 W
Butantã ◆[8]	287b	23.34 S	46.43 W
Butantã, Instituto ⊍[3]	287b	23.34 S	46.43 W
Buta Ranquil	252	37.03 S	69.50 W
Butare	154	2.36 S	29.44 E
Butaritari I[1]	14	3.07 N	172.48 E
Butarque, Arroyo de ≃	266a	40.19 N	3.39 W
Butauanan Island I	116	14.07 N	123.17 E
Butchart Gardens ♠	224	48.33 N	123.28 W
Butcher Island (Dia Deva) I	272c	18.58 N	72.54 E
Bute	168b	33.52 S	138.01 E
Bute, Island of I	46	55.50 N	5.06 W
Bute, Kyles of ʊ	46	55.53 N	5.13 W
Bute, Sound of ʊ	46	55.44 N	5.12 W
Büteelijn nuruu ⋏	88	50.00 N	104.50 E
Bute Giarti	144	4.33 N	37.45 E
Bute Inlet ⊂	182	50.37 N	124.53 W
Butemba	154	1.09 N	31.36 E
Butembo	154	0.09 N	29.17 E
Butendorf ◆[8]	263	51.33 N	6.59 E
Butera	70	37.11 N	14.11 E
Butere	154	0.13 N	34.30 E
Bütgenbach	56	50.26 N	6.12 E
Butha Buthe	158	28.45 S	28.15 E
Butha Qi (Zalantun)	89	48.02 N	122.43 E
Buthidaung	110	20.52 N	92.32 E
Buthier ≃	62	45.44 N	7.22 E
Buthroton ⊥	38	39.46 N	20.00 E
Buti	66	43.44 N	10.35 E
Butiá	252	30.07 S	51.58 W
Butiaba	154	1.49 N	31.19 E
Butig Mountains ⋏	116	7.39 N	124.20 E
Butka	86	56.47 N	63.47 E
Butler, Al., U.S.	194	32.05 N	88.13 W
Butler, Ga., U.S.	192	32.33 N	84.14 W
Butler, Il., U.S.	219	39.12 N	89.32 W
Butler, In., U.S.	216	41.25 N	84.52 W
Butler, Ky., U.S.	218	38.47 N	84.22 W
Butler, Mo., U.S.	194	38.15 N	94.19 W
Butler, N.J., U.S.	210	41.00 N	74.20 W
Butler, Oh., U.S.	214	40.35 N	82.25 W
Butler, Ok., U.S.	196	35.38 N	99.11 W
Butler, Pa., U.S.	214	40.51 N	79.53 W
Butler, Tx., U.S.	222	30.19 N	97.18 W
Butler, Wi., U.S.	216	43.06 N	88.04 W
Butler □[6], Oh., U.S.	218	39.26 N	84.30 W
Butler □[6], Pa., U.S.	214	40.52 N	79.54 W
Butler, Lake ◎	220	28.28 N	81.33 W
Butler Lake ◎	278	42.17 N	87.58 W
Butler Point ›	207	41.40 N	70.43 W
Butler Reservoir ◎[1]	276	40.59 N	74.23 W
Butlers Bridge	48	54.02 N	7.22 W
Butlerville	218	39.02 N	85.30 W
Butmīyah	132	32.56 N	35.53 E
Butnau Lake ◎	184	56.13 N	95.20 W
Butner	192	36.07 N	78.45 W
Buto	152	15.46 S	15.09 E
Buton, Pulau I	112	5.00 S	122.55 E
Butong	112	1.06 S	114.50 E
Butru	166	21.30 S	139.43 E
Butsha	154	0.57 N	29.13 E
Buttapietra	64	45.20 N	11.00 E
Butte, Mt., U.S.	202	46.00 N	112.32 W
Butte, Ne., U.S.	198	42.54 N	98.50 W
Butte □[6]	226	39.27 N	121.30 W
Butte City	226	39.28 N	121.59 W
Butte Creek ≃, Ca., U.S.	204	39.12 N	121.56 W
Butte Creek ≃, Or., U.S.	224	45.09 N	122.46 W
Butte du Lion ♠	50	50.40 N	4.24 E
Butte Falls	202	42.32 N	122.33 W
Buttelstedt	54	51.05 N	11.20 E
Butte Mountains ⋏	204	39.50 N	115.05 W
Butten	56	48.58 N	7.13 E
Butter Brook ≃	283	42.31 N	71.24 W
Butter Creek ≃	202	45.52 N	119.19 W
Butterfield, Il., U.S.	278	41.50 N	88.02 W
Butterfield, Mn., U.S.	198	43.57 N	94.47 W
Butterfield Creek ≃	278	41.33 N	87.37 W
Butterfield Lake ◎	212	44.19 N	75.46 W
Butterley Reservoir ◎[1]	262	53.35 N	1.56 W
Buttermere	44	54.33 N	3.17 W
Butternut	190	46.00 N	90.29 W
Butternut Creek ≃, N.Y., U.S.	210	42.25 N	75.22 W
Butternut Creek ≃, N.Y., U.S.	210	43.06 N	76.00 W
Butterwick	44	52.59 N	0.05 E
Butterworth, Malay.	114	5.25 N	100.24 E
Butterworth, Transkei	158	32.23 S	28.04 E
Buttevant	48	52.14 N	8.40 W
Büttgen	56	51.12 N	6.36 E
Buttlar	56	50.45 N	9.57 E
Buttle Lake ◎	182	49.46 N	125.36 W
Button Islands II	176	60.35 N	64.45 W
Buttonville	275b	43.52 N	79.22 W
Buttonville Airfield ⊠	275b	43.52 N	79.23 W
Buttonwillow	226	35.24 N	119.28 W
Buttrio	64	46.01 N	13.20 E
Buttstädt	54	51.07 N	11.25 E
Butty Head ›	162	33.54 S	121.38 E
Buttzville	210	40.49 N	75.00 W
Butuan	116	8.57 N	125.33 E
Butuan Bay ⊂	116	9.06 N	125.20 E
Butuj	88	53.27 N	112.22 E
Bū Tumayyim, Wādī V	146	26.56 N	19.13 E
Buṭūris	142	31.00 N	30.15 E
Buturlino, Ross.	80	55.34 N	44.55 E
Buturlino, Ross.	82	54.55 N	37.29 E
Buturlinovka	78	50.50 N	40.36 E
Buṭwal	124	27.42 N	83.27 E
Butylicy	80	55.32 N	41.31 E
Butzbach	56	50.26 N	8.40 E
Bützfleth	52	53.39 N	9.28 E
Bützow	54	53.50 N	11.59 E
Bützsee ◎	54	52.49 N	12.53 E
Butztown	208	40.39 N	75.22 W
Buuhoodle	144	8.15 N	46.20 E
Buulo Berde	144	3.51 N	45.34 E
Buur Gaabo	144	1.12 S	41.51 E
Buurgplaatz ∧	56	50.10 N	6.01 E
Buur Hakaba	144	2.47 N	44.05 E
Buur Haybe	144	3.57 N	45.07 E
Buwarah, Sabkhat al- ⋮	130	35.09 N	41.12 E
Buwaydān	132	33.12 N	36.26 E
Buxar	124	25.35 N	83.59 E
Buxtehude	52	53.28 N	9.41 E
Buxton, Boph.	158	27.38 S	24.42 E
Buxton, Guy.	246	6.47 N	58.02 W
Buxton, Eng., U.K.	44	53.15 N	1.55 W
Buxton, N.C., U.S.	192	35.16 N	75.32 W
Buxton, N.D., U.S.	198	47.36 N	97.05 W
Buxton, Or., U.S.	224	45.41 N	123.11 W
Buxton, Mount ∧	182	51.35 N	127.55 W
Buxy	58	46.43 N	4.41 E
Buye	154	4.38 N	27.30 E
Buyiqiao	106	31.47 N	119.48 E
Buyo	150	6.16 N	7.03 W
Buyo, Barrage de ◆[6]	150	6.15 N	7.05 W
Buyuan ≃	102	21.51 N	101.13 E
Büyükada	130	40.52 N	29.07 E
Büyükada I	267b	40.52 N	29.07 E
Büyükarmutlu	130	39.35 N	38.26 E
Büyükbakkal ◆[8]	267b	40.59 N	29.11 E
Büyükçeçeli	130	39.43 N	33.52 E
Büyükçekmece	130	41.01 N	28.34 E
Büyükdere ◆[8]	267b	41.09 N	29.02 E
Büyükeceli	130	36.11 N	33.40 E
Büyükkale	130	38.01 N	27.34 E
Büyükkarıştıran	130	41.18 N	27.32 E
Büyükkemikli Burnu ›	130	40.18 N	26.14 E
Büyükmenderes ≃	130	37.28 N	27.11 E
Büyükzap → Great Zab ≃	128	36.00 N	43.21 E
Buyun Shan ∧	98	40.06 N	122.42 E
Buyun Uzun	128	39.13 N	63.19 E
Buzan ≃	80	46.18 N	49.06 E
Buzanaj, peski ◆[2]	80	47.30 N	49.50 E
Buzançais	32	46.53 N	1.25 E
Buzancy	56	49.25 N	4.57 E
Bužaninovo	82	56.23 N	38.18 E
Bužarovo	82	55.59 N	36.47 E
Buzău	38	45.09 N	26.49 E
Buzău □[6]	38	45.15 N	26.45 E
Buzău ≃	38	45.26 N	27.44 E
Buzen	96	33.37 N	131.08 E
Búzi ≃	156	19.50 S	34.43 E
Buziaş	38	45.39 N	21.36 E
Buziji	100	33.49 N	118.14 E
Buzinovka	80	48.32 N	43.53 E
Búzios, Ilha dos I	256	23.48 S	45.08 W
Búzios, Ponta dos ›	255	22.44 S	41.53 W
Buzlanovo	265b	55.46 N	37.13 E
Buzovna	84	40.31 N	50.04 E
Buzuluk, Kaz.	86	51.55 N	66.16 E
Buzuluk, Ross.	80	52.47 N	52.15 E
Buzuluk ≃, Ross.	80	50.13 N	42.12 E
Buzuluk ≃, Ross.	80	52.47 N	52.16 E
Buzzards Bay	207	41.44 N	70.37 W
Buzzards Bay ⊂	207	41.33 N	70.47 W
Bwana Mkubwa	154	13.01 S	28.42 E

Symbol	English	Deutsch	Español	Français	Português
≃	River	Fluß	Río	Rivière	Rio
≅	Canal	Kanal	Canal	Canal	Canal
ʟ	Waterfall, Rapids	Wasserfall, Stromschnellen	Cascada, Rápidos	Chute d'eau, Rapides	Cascata, Rápidos
ʊ	Strait	Meeresstraße	Estrecho	Détroit	Estreito
⊂	Bay, Gulf	Bucht, Golf	Bahía, Golfo	Baie, Golfe	Baía, Golfo
◎	Lake, Lakes	See, Seen	Lago, Lagos	Lac, Lacs	Lago, Lagos
⋮	Swamp	Sumpf	Pantano	Marais	Pântano
⌂	Ice Features, Glacier	Eis- und Gletscherformen	Accidentes Glaciales	Formes glaciaires	Acidentes glaciares
⊤	Other Hydrographic Features	Andere Hydrographische Objekte	Otros Elementos Hidrográficos	Autres données hydrographiques	Outros acidentes hidrográficos
✣	Submarine Features	Untermeerische Objekte	Accidentes Submarinos	Formes de relief sous-marin	Acidentes submarinos
□	Political Unit	Politische Einheit	Unidad Politica	Entité politique	Unidade política
⊍	Cultural Institution	Kulturelle Institution	Institución Cultural	Institution culturelle	Institução cultural
⊥	Historical Site	Historische Stätte	Sitio Histórico	Site historique	Sitio histórico
♠	Recreational Site	Erholungs- und Ferienort	Sitio de Recreo	Centre de loisirs	Area de Lazer
⊠	Airport	Flughafen	Aeropuerto	Aéroport	Aeroporto
■	Military Installation	Militäranlage	Instalación Militar	Installation militaire	Instalação militar
◆	Miscellaneous	Verschiedenes	Misceláneo	Divers	Diversos

ENGLISH — Name, Page, Lat.°′, Long.°′
DEUTSCH — Name, Seite, Breite°′, Länge°′ E = Ost

Name	Page	Lat.	Long.
Bwasa	152	3.53 S	18.25 E
Bwendi	154	4.01 N	26.41 E
Bwlch	42	51.54 N	3.15 W
By	40	60.12 N	16.28 E
Byādgi	122	14.41 N	75.29 E
Byam Channel ⋃	176	75.20 N	105.20 W
Byam Martin Channel ⋃	176	75.45 N	104.00 W
Byam Martin Island I	176	75.15 N	104.00 W
Byberry Creek ≃	285	40.04 N	74.59 W
Byblos → Jubayl	130	34.07 N	35.39 E
Byček ≃	83	48.26 N	37.47 E
Bychawa	30	51.01 N	22.32 E
Bychov	76	53.32 N	30.12 E
Byčicha	76	55.41 N	29.58 E
Byčki, Ross.	76	54.15 N	34.39 E
Byčki, Ross.	80	53.38 N	40.54 E
Byculla ⇾[8]	272c	18.58 N	72.49 E
Byczyna	30	51.07 N	18.11 E
Bydalen	26	63.06 N	13.47 E
Bydgoszcz	30	53.08 N	18.00 E
Bydgoszcz □[4]	30	53.15 N	18.00 E
Byelorussia → Belarus □[1]	72	53.50 N	28.00 E
Byers, Pa., U.S.	285	40.05 N	75.41 W
Byers, Tx., U.S.	196	34.04 N	98.11 W
Byersdale	279b	40.37 N	80.13 W
Byers Run ≃	279b	40.24 N	79.42 W
Byesville	188	39.58 N	81.32 W
Byfang ⇾[8]	263	51.24 N	7.06 E
Byfield, Eng., U.K.	42	52.11 N	1.14 W
Byfield, Ma., U.S.	207	42.45 N	70.56 W
Byfleet	42	51.20 N	0.29 W
Byford	168a	32.13 S	116.00 E
Byforde	284c	39.01 N	77.05 W
Bygdeå	26	64.04 N	20.51 E
Bygdeträsket ⊜	26	64.26 N	20.32 E
Bygdin	26	61.20 N	8.48 E
Bygdin ⊜	26	61.21 N	8.36 E
Bygi	80	57.13 N	53.44 E
Byglandsfjord	26	58.41 N	7.48 E
Byglandsfjorden ⊜	26	58.48 N	7.50 E
Byhalia	194	34.52 N	89.41 W
Byk ≃	78	46.55 N	29.28 E
Bykle	26	59.21 N	7.20 E
Bykov	89	47.21 N	142.32 E
Bykovec	78	47.13 N	28.27 E
Bykovka, Ross.	82	55.29 N	37.40 E
Bykovka, Ukr.	78	50.17 N	27.58 E
Bykovo, Ross.	80	49.47 N	45.22 E
Bykovo, Ross.	82	54.01 N	37.54 E
Bykovo, Ross.	82	55.37 N	38.04 E
Bykovo Airport ⊠	265b	55.36 N	38.05 E
Bylas	200	33.08 N	110.07 W
Bylbasovka	83	48.51 N	37.30 E
Bylderup	41	54.57 N	9.07 E
Byley	262	53.13 N	2.25 W
Bylkyldak	86	48.38 N	75.16 E
Bylnice	30	49.04 N	18.01 E
Bylot Island I	176	73.13 N	78.34 W
Byng Inlet	190	45.46 N	80.33 W
Bynum, Mt., U.S.	182	47.58 N	112.18 W
Bynum, N.C., U.S.	192	35.46 N	79.08 W
Bynum, Tx., U.S.	222	31.58 N	97.00 W
Byōdōin Temple ✪[1]	270	34.53 N	135.48 E
Byram ≃	276	40.59 N	73.39 W
Byramgore Reef ✦[2]	122	11.54 N	71.49 E
Byram Lake Reservoir ⊜[1]	276	41.10 N	73.41 W
Byrd, Lac ⊜	190	47.01 N	76.56 W
Byrdstown	194	36.34 N	85.07 W
Byrka	88	50.39 N	118.31 E
Byrnedale	214	41.17 N	78.30 W
Byro	162	26.05 S	116.09 E
Byrock	166	30.40 S	146.24 E
Byron, Ca., U.S.	226	37.52 N	121.38 W
Byron, Ga., U.S.	192	32.39 N	83.45 W
Byron, Il., U.S.	190	42.07 N	89.15 W
Byron, Mi., U.S.	216	42.49 N	83.57 W
Byron, N.Y., U.S.	210	43.04 N	78.03 W
Byron, Wy., U.S.	202	44.47 N	108.30 W
Byron, Cape ›	166	28.39 S	153.38 E
Byron, Isla I	254	47.47 S	75.12 W
Byron Bay	166	28.39 S	153.37 E
Byron Center	216	42.49 N	85.42 W
Byrranga, gory ⩘	74	75.00 N	104.00 E
Byšice-Liblice	54	50.19 N	14.38 E
Bysjön ⊜	40	60.23 N	14.30 E
Byske	26	64.57 N	21.12 E
Byskeälven ≃	26	64.57 N	21.13 E
Bystraja ≃	80	47.58 N	41.00 E
Bystřany	54	50.38 N	13.51 E
Bystrica ≃	80	58.38 N	49.05 E
Bystřice	30	49.45 N	14.41 E
Bystřice pod Hostýnem	30	49.24 N	17.40 E
Bystrij Tanyp ≃	86	55.46 N	54.35 E
Bystrovka	85	42.47 N	75.43 E
Bystryj	86	57.50 N	73.58 E
Bystryj Istok	86	52.23 N	84.24 E
Bystrzyca Kłodzka	30	50.18 N	16.38 E
Bytantaj ≃	74	68.46 N	134.20 E
Bytča, Bela.	76	54.18 N	28.24 E
Bytča, Slov.	30	49.14 N	18.36 E
Byten'	76	52.54 N	25.29 E
Bytkov	78	48.38 N	24.26 E
Bytom (Beuthen)	30	50.22 N	18.54 E
Bytoš'	76	53.50 N	34.06 E
Bytów	30	54.11 N	17.30 E
Byumba	154	1.35 S	30.04 E
Byvalki	78	51.51 N	30.37 E
Byxelkrok	26	57.20 N	17.00 E
Bzyb' ≃	84	43.12 N	40.18 E
Bzybskij chrebet ⩘	84	43.18 N	40.41 E
C			
Ca ≃	110	18.46 N	105.47 E
Čaa-Chol'	86	51.32 N	92.23 E
Caacupé	252	25.23 S	57.09 W
Čaadajevka	80	53.09 N	45.56 E
Čaadajevo	80	55.40 N	42.02 E
Caaguazú	252	25.26 S	56.02 W
Caaguazú □[5]	252	25.00 S	55.45 W
Caála	152	12.51 S	15.33 E
Caamaño Sound ⋃	182	52.49 N	129.28 W
Caapiranga	246	3.18 S	61.13 W
Caapucú	252	26.13 S	57.12 W
Caarapó	255	22.38 S	54.48 W
Caatinga	255	17.10 S	45.53 W
Caazapá	252	26.09 S	56.24 W
Caazapá □[5]	252	26.10 S	56.00 W
Cabaçal ≃	248	16.00 S	57.42 W
Cabadbaran	116	9.10 N	125.38 E
Cabadiangan Plateau ⩘[1]	116	9.50 N	122.36 E
Cabagan	116	17.26 N	121.46 E
Cabaiguán	240p	22.05 N	79.30 W
Cabalete Island I	116	14.17 N	121.50 E
Cabalian	116	10.16 N	125.10 E
Cabaliana, Lago ⊜	246	3.20 S	60.50 W
Cabalian Bay ⊂	116	10.13 N	125.10 E
Cabalian Point ›	116	12.06 N	122.01 E
Caballero Creek ≃	280	34.11 N	118.32 W
Caballito ⇾[8]	288	34.37 S	58.27 W
Caballones, Cayo I	240p	20.52 N	79.00 W
Caballo Reservoir ⊜[1]	200	32.58 N	107.18 W
Cabana	248	8.24 S	78.02 W
Cabanaconde	248	15.37 S	71.59 W
Cabañas	240p	22.58 N	82.55 W
Cabanatuan	116	15.29 N	120.58 E
Cabangan	116	15.10 N	120.03 E
Cabano	186	47.41 N	68.53 W
Čabanovka	83	49.02 N	38.46 E
Cabarroguis	116	16.33 N	121.32 E
Cabarruyan Island I	116	16.18 N	119.59 E
Cabaun Island I	116	12.34 N	124.30 E
Cabeceiras	255	15.48 S	46.59 W
Cabeço de Montachique	266c	38.54 N	9.11 W
Cabellera, Sierra de la ⩘	200	30.55 N	109.07 W
Cabery	216	41.00 N	88.12 W
Cabeza del Buey	34	38.43 N	5.13 W
Cabeza de Tigre	286c	10.28 N	66.46 W
Cabezas	248	18.46 S	63.24 W
Cabiao	116	15.15 N	120.51 E
Cabiate	266b	45.40 N	9.10 E
Cabildo, Arg.	252	38.29 S	61.54 W
Cabildo, Chile	252	32.26 S	71.05 W
Cabimas	246	10.23 N	71.28 W
Cabin Branch ≃, Md., U.S.	284b	39.13 N	76.35 W
Cabin Branch ≃, Md., U.S.	284c	38.51 N	76.48 W
Cabin Creek ≃	198	46.55 N	104.52 W
Cabinda	152	5.33 S	12.12 E
Cabinda □[5]	152	5.00 S	12.30 E
Cabinet Mountains ⩘	202	48.20 N	116.00 W
Cabingaan Island I	116	5.41 N	121.03 E
Cabin John	208	38.58 N	77.09 W
Cabin John Creek ≃	284b	38.58 N	77.09 W
Cabin John Creek Park ♦	284c	38.59 N	77.09 W
Cabin John Regional Park ♦	284c	39.02 N	77.09 W
Cabiri	152	8.52 S	13.39 E
Cabixi ≃	248	13.41 S	60.44 W
Cable	190	46.12 N	91.17 W
Cable Airport ⊠	280	34.08 N	117.41 W
Cables	162	27.59 S	123.23 E
Cabo	250	8.17 S	35.02 W
Cabo Blanco	254	47.12 S	65.45 W
Cabo de Hornos, Parque Nacional ♦	250	55.45 S	67.25 W
Cabo Delgado □[5]	154	12.35 S	39.00 E
Cabo Frio	255	22.53 S	42.01 W
Cabo Gracias a Dios	236	14.59 N	83.10 W
Cabo Ledo	152	9.39 S	13.17 E
Cabonga, Réservoir ⊜[1]	190	47.20 N	76.35 W
Cabool	194	37.07 N	92.06 W
Caboolture	166	27.05 S	152.57 E
Cabo Orange, Parque Nacional do ♦	250	3.00 N	51.00 W
Cabora Bassa	154	15.35 S	32.48 E
Cabora Bassa Dam ⇾[6]	154	15.35 S	32.42 E
Cabo Raso	254	44.21 S	65.14 W
Caborca	232	30.37 N	112.06 W
Cabo Rojo	240m	18.05 N	67.09 W
Cabot, Ar., U.S.	194	34.58 N	92.00 W
Cabot, Pa., U.S.	214	40.46 N	79.46 W
Cabot, Mount ∧	188	44.31 N	71.24 W
Cabot Head ›	212	45.14 N	81.17 W
Cabot Strait ⋃	186	47.20 N	59.30 W
Cabo Verde	256	21.28 S	46.24 W
Cabo Verde ≃	256	21.28 S	46.17 W
Cabo Verde → Cape Verde □[1]	150a	16.00 N	24.00 W
Cabra	34	37.28 N	4.27 W
Cabra Corral, Embalse ⊜[1]	252	25.15 S	65.25 W
Cabra Island I	116	13.53 N	120.02 E
Cabramatta	274a	33.54 S	150.56 E
Cabramatta Creek ≃	274a	33.54 S	150.57 E
Cabramurra	171b	35.58 S	148.23 E
Cabras	71	39.56 N	8.32 E
Cabras, Stagno di ⊜	71	39.57 N	8.29 E
Cabras Island I	174p	13.27 N	144.40 E
Cabrel	234	20.06 N	105.14 W
Cabrera ≃, Col.	246	3.26 N	75.07 W
Cabrera ≃, Esp.	34	42.25 N	6.49 W
Cabrera, Illa de I	34	39.09 N	2.56 E
Cabrera, Sierra de la ⩘	34	42.12 N	6.40 W
Cabrera de Mar	266d	41.32 N	2.24 E
Cabreúva	256	23.18 S	47.08 W
Cabri	184	50.37 N	108.28 W
Cabriel ≃	34	39.14 N	1.03 W
Cabrillo National Monument ♦	228	32.41 N	117.15 W
Cabrils	266d	41.32 N	2.22 E
Cabrobó	250	8.31 S	39.19 W
Cabruta	246	7.38 N	66.15 W
Cabucgayan	116	11.29 N	124.34 E
Cabuçu	256	22.50 S	42.55 W
Cabuçu ≃, Bra.	287a	22.59 S	43.37 W
Cabuçu ≃, Bra.	287a	22.48 S	43.37 W
Cabuçu de Cima ≃	287b	23.31 S	46.33 W
Cabugao	116	17.48 N	120.27 E
Cabulauan Island I	116	11.23 N	120.06 E
Cabullónes, Punta ›	240m	17.58 N	66.35 W
Cabulo	152	10.15 S	16.40 E
Cabure	246	11.08 N	69.38 W
Cabuta	152	9.50 S	14.48 E
Cabuya	236	9.36 N	85.06 W
Cabuyal	236	10.40 N	85.40 W
Cabuyaro	246	4.18 N	72.49 W
Caca	80	48.11 N	44.40 E
Caçador	252	26.47 S	51.00 W
Čačak	38	43.53 N	20.21 E
Cacaohatán	236	14.59 N	92.10 W
Cacaoui, Lac ⊜	186	50.53 N	66.58 W
Caçapava	256	23.06 S	45.42 W
Caçapava do Sul	252	30.30 S	53.30 W
Caçapava Velha	256	23.07 S	45.39 W
Cacapon ≃	188	39.37 N	78.16 W
Cacapon State Park ♦	188	39.32 N	78.23 W
Cacas	130	38.23 N	41.17 E
Caccamo	70	37.56 N	13.40 E
Caccia, Capo ›	71	40.34 N	8.09 E
Caccuri	68	39.14 N	16.47 E
Čačenka ≃	265b	55.46 N	37.18 E
Cacequi	252	29.53 S	54.49 W
Cáceres, Bra.	248	16.04 S	57.41 W
Cáceres, Col.	246	7.35 N	75.20 W
Cáceres, Esp.	34	39.29 N	6.22 W
Cáceres □[4]	34	39.40 N	6.05 E
Cachan	261	48.48 N	2.20 E
Cacharí	252	36.24 S	59.32 W
Cache	196	34.37 N	98.37 W
Cache ≃, Ar., U.S.	194	34.42 N	91.20 W
Cache ≃, Il., U.S.	194	37.04 N	89.10 W
Caché, Lac ⊜	206	46.21 N	74.39 W
Cache Creek	182	50.48 N	121.19 W
Cache Creek ≃, Ca., U.S.	226	38.42 N	121.42 W
Cache Creek ≃, Ca., U.S.	228	35.06 N	117.58 W
Cache Creek, North Fork ≃	226	38.59 N	122.30 W
Cache la Poudre ≃	200	40.25 N	104.36 W
Cache la Poudre, North Fork ≃	198	40.54 N	105.22 W
Cache Mountain ∧	180	65.31 N	147.20 W
Cache Peak ∧, Ca., U.S.	228	35.13 N	118.15 W
Cache Peak ∧, Id., U.S.	202	42.11 N	113.40 W
Cache Slough ≃	226	38.11 N	121.40 W
Cacheu	150	12.16 N	16.10 W
Cacheu ⊂[1]	150	12.10 N	16.21 W
Cachí	252	25.06 S	66.11 W
Cachimbo	250	9.24 S	54.56 W
Cachimbo, Serra do ⩘	250	8.30 S	55.50 W
Cachimo	152	8.21 S	21.20 E
Cachingues	152	13.05 S	16.43 E
Cachir	88	48.06 N	98.52 E
Cachkadzor	84	40.33 N	44.43 E
Cachoeira ≃	256	23.06 S	46.29 W
Cachoeira, Reservatório ⊜[1]	256	23.03 S	46.15 W
Cachoeira, Rio da ≃	287a	23.00 S	43.18 W
Cachoeira Alta	255	18.48 S	50.58 W
Cachoeira de Goiás	255	16.44 S	50.38 W
Cachoeira de Manteiga	255	16.39 S	45.16 W
Cachoeira de Minas	256	22.21 S	45.47 W
Cachoeira do Arari	250	1.01 S	48.58 W
Cachoeira do Sul	252	30.02 S	52.54 W
Cachoeira Grande, Alto da ∧	256	21.54 S	44.06 W
Cachoeira Paulista	256	22.40 S	45.01 W
Cachoeiras	287a	22.39 S	43.28 W
Cachoeiras de Macacu	256	22.28 S	42.39 W
Cachoeirinha	250	8.29 S	36.14 W
Cachoeiro de Itapemirim	255	20.51 S	41.06 W
Cachos, Punta ›	252	27.39 S	71.02 W
Cachos, Rio dos ≃	287b	23.36 S	46.26 W
Čachrov	60	49.16 N	13.18 E
Cachuela Esperanza	248	10.32 S	65.38 W
Cachuma, Lake ⊜[1]	204	34.35 N	119.55 W
Cacilhas	266c	38.41 N	9.09 W
Cacine	150	11.08 N	14.57 W
Caciporé ≃	250	3.51 N	51.08 W
Caciporé, Cabo ›	250	3.55 N	51.07 W
Căciulaţi	38	44.38 N	26.10 E
Cacnipa Island I	116	10.30 N	119.04 E
Cacocum	240p	20.44 N	76.23 W
Cacólo	152	10.07 S	19.17 E
Caconda	152	13.43 S	15.06 E
Caconde	256	21.33 S	46.38 W
Cacra	248	12.48 S	75.48 W
Cactus	196	36.04 N	102.00 W
Cactus Flat ≚	204	37.45 N	116.45 W
Cactus Peak ∧	204	37.47 N	116.53 W
Caçu	255	18.37 S	51.04 W
Cacuaco	152	8.47 S	13.22 E
Cacula	152	14.29 S	14.10 E
Caculé	255	14.30 S	42.13 W
Caculuvar ≃	152	16.46 S	14.36 E
Cacuri, Ang.	152	8.14 S	18.20 E
Cacuri, Ven.	246	4.48 N	65.21 W
Cacuso	152	9.26 S	15.43 E
Cadale	144	2.45 N	46.19 E
Čadan	86	51.17 N	91.35 E
Cadaqués	34	42.17 N	3.17 E
Cadariri ≃	248	6.20 S	57.46 W
Čadca	30	49.26 N	18.48 E
Caddington	42	51.51 N	0.27 W
Caddo, Ok., U.S.	196	34.07 N	96.15 W
Caddo, Tx., U.S.	196	32.38 N	98.40 W
Caddo ≃	194	34.10 N	93.03 W
Caddo Creek ≃	196	34.14 N	96.59 W
Caddo Lake ⊜[1]	194	32.42 N	94.01 W
Caddo Mills	222	33.04 N	96.14 W
Caddo Peak ∧	222	32.29 N	97.24 W
Caddy Vista	216	42.50 N	87.54 W
Cadell ≃	166	22.51 S	141.55 E
Cadena, Arroyo de la ≃	196	26.17 N	104.00 W
Cadena, Cerro ∧	196	25.50 N	104.04 W
Cadena, Punta ›	240m	18.18 N	67.14 W
Cadenberge	52	53.46 N	9.04 E
Cadenet	62	43.44 N	5.22 E
Cadeo	62	44.58 N	9.48 E
Cadereyta de Jiménez	232	25.36 N	100.00 W
Cader Idris ∧	42	52.42 N	3.54 W
Cadibarrawirracanna, Lake ⊜	162	28.52 S	135.27 E
Cadig, Mount ∧	116	14.09 N	122.27 E
Cadillac, Sk., Can.	184	49.44 N	107.43 W
Cadillac, Fr.	32	44.38 N	0.19 W
Cadillac, Mi., U.S.	190	44.15 N	85.24 W
Cadipietra (Steinhaus)	64	46.59 N	11.59 E
Cadishead	262	53.25 N	2.26 W
Cadix → Cádiz	34	36.32 N	6.18 W
Cádiz, Esp.	34	36.32 N	6.18 W
Cadiz, Pil.	116	10.57 N	123.18 E
Cadiz, In., U.S.	218	39.57 N	85.30 W
Cadiz, Ky., U.S.	194	36.51 N	87.50 W
Cadiz, Oh., U.S.	214	40.16 N	80.59 W
Cádiz □[4]	34	36.35 N	5.50 W
Cádiz, Bahía de ⊂	34	36.32 N	6.16 W
Cádiz, Golfo de ⊂	34	36.50 N	7.10 W
Cadiz Lake ⊜	204	34.18 N	115.24 W
Cadlao Island I	116	11.13 N	119.21 E
Cadnam	42	50.55 N	1.35 W
Čadobec	88	58.40 N	98.51 E
Čadobec ≃	88	58.40 N	98.50 E
Cadogan	214	40.45 N	79.34 W
Cadomin	182	53.02 N	117.20 W
Cadoneghe	64	45.26 N	11.55 E
Cadore ⇾[1]	64	46.30 N	12.20 E
Cadosia	210	41.58 N	75.16 W
Cadott	190	44.56 N	91.09 W
Cadoux	162	30.47 S	117.08 E
Caduruan Point ›	116	11.45 N	124.05 E
Caduta, Fosso delle ≃	267a	41.56 N	12.12 E
Cadwell	192	32.20 N	83.02 W
Cady Marsh Ditch ≊	278	41.33 N	87.29 W
Cady Mountain ∧[2]	224	48.33 N	123.07 W
Čadyr-Lunga	78	46.03 N	28.47 E
Cadzand	52	51.22 N	3.25 E
Caen	32	49.11 N	0.21 W
Caengo (Kwenge) ≃	152	4.50 S	18.42 E
Caerano di San Marco	64	45.47 N	12.00 E
Caere ⊥	66	42.02 N	12.07 E
Caergwrle	44	53.07 N	3.03 W
Caerleon	42	51.37 N	2.57 W
Caernarfon	44	53.08 N	4.16 W
Caernarfon Bay ⊂	44	53.05 N	4.30 W
Caernarfon Castle ⊥	44	53.08 N	4.16 W
Caerphilly	42	51.35 N	3.14 W
Caerphilly Castle ⊥	42	51.34 N	3.14 W
Caersws	42	52.31 N	3.25 W
Caesar Creek ≃	218	39.29 N	84.06 W
Caesar Creek, Anderson Fork ≃	218	39.33 N	83.58 W
Caesar Creek Lake ⊜[1]	218	39.30 N	84.00 W
Cæsarea → Qesari, Horbat ⊥	132	32.30 N	34.53 E
Caetanópolis	255	19.18 S	44.24 W
Caeté	255	19.54 S	43.40 W
Caeté ≃	248	9.03 S	68.39 W
Caeté, Morro ∧[2]	287a	23.03 S	43.31 W
Caetité	255	14.04 S	42.29 W
Cafayate	252	26.05 S	65.58 W
Cafelândia do Leste	255	16.40 S	53.25 W
Cafima	152	16.39 S	16.27 E
Cafu	152	16.27 S	15.14 E
Cafuini ≃	246	1.17 N	57.11 W
Cagaan Chajrchan	88	49.25 N	94.15 E
Cagaan Gol	86	48.57 N	89.07 E
Cagaan Nuur, Mong.	86	49.32 N	89.42 E
Cagaannuur, Mong.	88	50.20 N	105.03 E
Cagaan-Ovoo	102	45.51 N	105.17 E
Cagaan Uul	88	49.28 N	98.30 E
Cagaan-Üür	88	50.32 N	101.30 E
Cágado ≃	256	22.02 S	43.09 W
Čagan ≃	80	51.12 N	51.20 E
Cagan-Aman	80	47.34 N	46.43 E
Cagan-Churtej, chrebet ⩘	88	51.32 N	110.00 E
Cagarras, Ilhas II	287a	23.02 S	43.12 W
Cagayan □[4]	116	18.00 N	121.50 E
Cagayan ≃	116	18.22 N	121.37 E
Cagayancillo	116	9.34 N	121.12 E
Cagayan de Oro	116	8.29 N	124.39 E
Cagayan de Tawi-Tawi	116	7.01 N	118.30 E
Cagayan Island I	116	9.36 N	121.14 E
Cagayan Islands II	116	9.40 N	121.16 E
Cagayan Sulu Island I	116	7.01 N	118.30 E
Čagda	74	58.45 N	130.37 E
Cageri	84	42.39 N	42.45 E
Caggiano	68	40.34 N	15.29 E
Çağış	130	39.30 N	28.01 E
Çağlarca	130	39.05 N	39.10 E
Cagli	66	43.33 N	12.39 E
Cagliari	71	39.13 N	9.07 E
Cagliari □[4]	71	39.30 N	8.45 E
Cagliari, Golfo di ⊂	71	39.08 N	9.11 E
Cagliari, Stagno di ⊜	71	39.13 N	9.02 E
Čaglinka ≃	86	53.59 N	69.47 E
Cagnano Varano	68	41.49 N	15.47 E
Cagnes-sur-Mer	62	43.40 N	7.09 E
Čagoda	76	59.10 N	35.17 E
Čagoda ≃	76	59.05 N	35.18 E
Čagodošča ≃	76	58.57 N	36.35 E
Čagojan	89	52.08 N	128.15 E
Čagra ≃	80	52.37 N	48.15 E
Cagraray Island I	116	13.18 N	123.52 E
Cagua	246	10.11 N	67.27 W
Caguán ≃	246	0.08 S	74.18 W
Caguas	240m	18.14 N	66.02 W
Cagveri	84	41.48 N	43.29 E
Cagwait	116	8.55 N	126.18 E
Cahaba ≃	194	32.20 N	87.05 W
Cahabón	236	15.34 N	89.49 W
Cahabón ≃	236	15.25 N	89.36 W
Cahama	152	16.17 S	14.19 E
Caha Mountains ⩘	48	51.45 N	9.45 W
Caher	48	52.21 N	7.56 W
Caherdaniel	48	51.45 N	10.05 W
Cahersiveen	48	51.57 N	10.13 W
Cahokia	219	38.34 N	90.11 W
Cahokia Creek ≃	219	38.47 N	90.01 W
Cahokia Mounds State Park ♦	219	38.39 N	90.03 W
Cahoon Creek ≃	279a	41.29 N	81.55 W
Cahoon Park ♦	279a	41.29 N	81.56 W
Cahoonzie	210	41.26 N	74.43 W
Cahore Point ›	48	52.34 N	6.11 W
Cahors	32	44.27 N	1.26 E
Cahto Peak ∧	204	39.41 N	123.35 W
Cahuilla Indian Reservation ⇾[4]	204	33.30 N	116.43 W
Cahuinari ≃	246	1.21 S	70.44 W
Cahuita, Punta ›	236	9.45 N	82.49 W
Caí ≃	252	29.56 S	51.16 W
Caia ≃	34	38.50 N	7.05 W
Caianda	152	11.02 S	23.31 E
Caiapó ≃, Bra.	250	8.52 S	49.36 W
Caiapó ≃, Bra.	255	15.49 S	51.53 W
Caiapó, Serra do ⩘	255	17.00 S	52.00 W
Caiapônia	255	16.57 S	51.49 W
Caiazzo	68	41.11 N	14.22 E
Caibarién	240p	22.31 N	79.28 W
Cai Bau, Dao I	110	21.10 N	107.27 E
Caibiran	116	11.34 N	124.35 E
Caiçara, Bra.	250	6.36 S	35.29 W
Caiçara, Bra.	255	15.34 S	50.12 W
Caicara, Caño ≃	246	7.44 N	69.04 W
Caicara de Maturín	246	9.49 N	63.36 W
Caicara de Orinoco	246	7.37 N	66.10 W
Caicedonia	246	4.20 N	75.50 W
Caicó	250	6.27 S	37.06 W
Caicos Bank ✦[4]	238	21.35 N	71.55 W
Caicos Islands II	238	21.56 N	71.58 W
Caicos Passage ⋃	238	22.00 N	72.30 W
Caieiras	256	23.22 S	46.44 W
Caieiras □[7]	287b	23.23 S	46.41 W
Caigou	100	33.16 N	114.32 E
Caiguna	162	32.17 S	125.25 E
Caihuaping	100	26.54 N	113.23 E
Caijiachang	107	29.44 N	106.29 E
Caijiagang	107	28.55 N	106.21 E
Caijialou	104	41.24 N	121.06 E
Caijiapo	102	34.17 N	107.39 E
Caijiazhuang	105	40.48 N	114.44 E
Caille	62	43.46 N	6.44 E
Cailloma	248	15.12 S	71.46 W
Caillou Bay ⊂	194	29.06 N	90.56 W
Caima Bay ⊂	116	13.42 N	122.48 E
Caimán, Islas → Cayman Islands □[2]	238	19.30 N	80.40 W
Caimanera	240p	19.59 N	75.09 W
Caïmanes → Cayman Islands □[2]	238	19.30 N	80.40 W
Caiman Point ›	116	15.55 N	119.46 E
Caimbambo	152	12.58 S	14.01 E
Cain ≃	42	52.46 N	3.08 W
Cain Creek ≃	198	44.17 N	98.10 W
Cainde	152	15.42 S	13.12 E
Caine ≃	248	18.23 S	65.21 W
Caino	64	45.38 N	10.18 E
Cains ≃	186	46.40 N	65.47 W
Cainsdorf	54	50.41 N	12.29 E
Cainsville	194	40.28 N	93.59 W
Cainta	269f	14.35 N	121.07 E
Cai Nuoc	110	8.56 N	105.01 E
Cairano	68	40.54 N	15.22 E
Cairari	250	2.33 S	49.07 W
Caird Coast ±[2]	9	76.00 S	24.30 W
Caire, Le → Al-Qāhirah	142	30.03 N	31.15 E
Cairnbrook	214	40.07 N	78.49 W
Cairn Curran Reservoir ⊜[1]	169	37.04 S	143.59 E
Cairndow	46	56.15 N	4.56 W
Cairngorm Mountains ⩘	46	57.04 N	3.50 W
Cairn Mountain ∧	180	61.10 N	155.20 W
Cairnryan	44	54.58 N	5.02 W
Cairns	166	16.55 S	145.46 E
Cairns Lake ⊜	184	51.42 N	94.30 W
Cairnsmore of Carsphairn ∧	44	55.15 N	4.12 W
Cairnsmore of Fleet ∧	44	54.59 N	4.20 W
Cairn Table ∧	44	55.29 N	4.02 W
Cairn Water ≃	44	55.07 N	3.45 W
Cairo, Ga., U.S.	192	30.52 N	84.12 W
Cairo, Il., U.S.	194	37.00 N	89.10 W
Cairo, Ne., U.S.	198	41.00 N	98.36 W
Cairo, N.Y., U.S.	210	42.17 N	73.59 W
Cairo, Oh., U.S.	216	40.49 N	84.05 W
Cairo, W.V., U.S.	188	39.12 N	81.09 W
Cairo (Almaza) Airport ⊠, Mişr	273c	30.06 N	31.22 E
Cairo (Imbābah) Airport ⊠, Mişr	273c	30.04 N	31.12 E
Cairo, University of ✪[2]	273c	30.02 N	31.12 E
Cairo → Al-Qāhirah	142	30.03 N	31.15 E
Cairoçu, Pico do ∧	256	23.18 S	44.36 W
Cairofa	152	14.05 S	12.54 E
Cairo International Airport ⊠	142	30.08 N	31.24 E
Cairo Main Station ⇾[5]	273c	30.04 N	31.15 E
Cairo Montenotte	62	44.24 N	8.16 E
Cairu	255	13.30 S	39.03 W
Caister-on-Sea	42	52.39 N	1.44 E
Caistor	44	53.30 N	0.20 W
Caitingqiao	105	39.54 N	117.39 E
Caitou	152	14.28 S	13.06 E
Caiundo	152	15.46 S	17.28 E
Caivano	68	40.57 N	14.18 E
Caiwan	102	25.50 N	110.50 E
Caixi	100	25.15 N	116.28 E
Caiyu	105	39.39 N	116.37 E
Caizhuang	98	34.17 N	114.08 E
Caizi Hu ⊜	100	30.48 N	117.05 E
Čaja ≃, Ross.	86	58.08 N	82.57 E
Čaja ≃, Ross.	88	58.15 N	109.35 E
Cajabamba, Ec.	246	1.42 S	78.45 W
Cajabamba, Perú	248	7.37 S	78.03 W
Cajacay	248	10.10 S	77.26 W
Caja de Muertos, Isla I	240m	17.54 N	66.32 W
Cajamar	256	23.21 S	46.53 W
Cajamarca	248	7.10 S	78.31 W
Cajamarca □[5]	248	6.15 S	78.50 W
Čajan	85	43.02 N	69.23 E
Čajan ≃	85	42.52 N	68.56 E
Cajapió	250	2.58 S	44.48 W
Cajarc	32	44.29 N	1.50 E
Cajari	250	3.20 S	45.01 W
Cajari ≃	250	0.48 S	51.43 W
Cajatambo	248	10.29 S	77.02 W
Čajatyn, chrebet ⩘	89	52.25 N	138.25 E
Cajàzeiras	250	6.54 S	38.34 W
Čajek	85	41.56 N	74.30 E
Čajkovskij	80	56.47 N	54.09 E
Čajniče	38	43.33 N	19.04 E
Cajones ≃	234	17.45 N	95.55 W
Cajones, Cayos ✦[2]	236	16.05 N	83.12 W
Cajon Mountain ∧	228	34.16 N	117.25 W
Cajon Pass)(	228	34.19 N	117.26 W
Cajon Summit)(	228	34.21 N	117.27 W
Caju ⇾[8]	287a	22.53 S	43.13 W
Cajuru	255	21.17 S	47.18 W
Caka	102	36.48 N	99.19 E
Caka Yanhu ⊜	102	36.40 N	99.20 E
Čakčar, chrebet ⩘	85	38.35 N	67.28 E
Cakeni	152	17.48 S	19.27 E
Cakir	88	50.27 N	103.35 E
Çakıralan	130	41.10 N	35.47 E
Çakırgöl Dağı ∧	130	40.34 N	39.42 E
Çakırhüyük	130	37.34 N	37.50 E
Çakmak	130	37.37 N	34.19 E
Çakmak Dağı ∧	130	39.46 N	42.12 E
Čakovec	61	46.23 N	16.26 E
Čakovice ⇾[8]	54	50.08 N	14.31 E
Cakung ≃	269e	6.06 S	106.56 E
Çal	130	38.05 N	29.24 E
Cala, Transkei	158	31.30 S	27.37 E
Cala, Tür.	84	41.05 N	43.21 E
Cala, Embalse de ⊜[1]	34	37.50 N	6.00 W
Calabacillas	234	23.13 N	99.45 W
Calabanga	116	13.42 N	123.12 E
Calabar	150	4.57 N	8.19 E
Calabasas, Arroyo ≃	280	34.12 N	118.36 W
Calabazar ⇾[8]	286b	23.01 N	82.22 W
Calabazas Creek ≃	282	37.25 N	121.58 W
Calabernardo	70	36.52 N	15.08 E
Calabogie	212	45.18 N	76.43 W
Calabogie Lake ⊜	212	45.16 N	76.45 W
Calabozo	246	8.56 N	67.26 W
Calabozo, Ensenada de ⊂	246	11.30 N	71.45 W
Calabria □[4]	68	39.00 N	16.30 E
Calabria, Parco Nazionale di ♦	68	38.09 N	15.54 E
Calabritto	68	40.47 N	15.13 E
Calabro ≃	70	37.53 N	14.11 E
Calabugdong Island I	116	11.06 N	119.41 E
Calaca	116	13.56 N	120.49 E
Calacuccia	36	42.20 N	9.03 E
Caladang, Mount ∧	116	14.49 N	121.21 E
Caladesi Island I	220	28.02 N	82.49 W
Caladesi Island State Park ♦	220	28.02 N	82.48 W
Cala d'Oliva	71	41.05 N	8.20 E
Calafat	38	43.59 N	22.56 E
Calafquén, Lago ⊜	254	39.31 S	72.10 W
Calagnaan Island I	116	11.29 N	123.13 E
Cala Gonone	71	40.18 N	9.38 E
Calagua Islands II	116	14.27 N	122.55 E
Calahorra	34	42.18 N	1.58 W
Calais, Fr.	50	50.57 N	1.50 E
Calais, Me., U.S.	188	45.11 N	67.16 W
Calais, Canal de ≊	50	50.57 N	1.51 E
Calais, Pas de (Strait of Dover) ⋃	50	51.00 N	1.30 E
Calala	152	12.59 S	23.30 E
Calalaste, Sierra de ⩘	252	25.30 S	67.30 W
Calalzo di Cadore	64	46.27 N	12.23 E
Calama	252	22.28 S	68.56 W
Calamar, Col.	246	10.15 N	74.55 W
Calamar, Col.	246	1.58 N	72.41 W
Calamarca	248	16.55 S	68.09 W
Calamba, Pil.	116	14.13 N	121.10 E
Calamba, Pil.	116	8.35 N	123.39 E
Calamian Group II	116	12.00 N	120.00 E
Calamity Creek ≃	196	29.41 N	103.42 W
Calamocha	34	40.55 N	1.18 W
Calamonaci	70	37.31 N	13.17 E
Calamus ≃	198	41.48 N	99.09 W
Calañas	34	37.39 N	6.53 W
Calanca, Val V	58	46.22 N	9.07 E
Calanda	34	40.56 N	0.14 W
Calandagan Island I	116	10.39 N	120.15 E
Calang	114	4.38 N	95.34 E
Calangianus	71	40.56 N	9.11 E
Calanna	68	38.11 N	15.43 E
Calapan	116	13.25 N	121.10 E
Calape	116	9.54 N	123.52 E
Calapooia ≃	202	44.38 N	123.08 W
Calapooya Mountains ⩘	202	43.30 N	122.50 W
Călăraşi	38	44.11 N	27.20 E
Călăraşi □[6]	38	44.20 N	27.10 E
Calarcá	246	4.31 N	75.38 W
Calascibetta	70	37.35 N	14.16 E
Calasetta	71	39.07 N	8.22 E
Calatabiano	70	37.49 N	15.14 E
Calatafimi	70	37.55 N	12.52 E
Calatagan	116	13.50 N	120.38 E
Calatayud	34	41.21 N	1.38 W
Calau	54	51.45 N	13.56 E
Calauag Bay ≃	116	14.02 N	122.13 E
Calavá, Capo ›	70	38.11 N	14.55 E
Calaveras □[6]	226	38.12 N	120.41 W
Calaveras ≃	226	37.58 N	121.22 W
Calaveras, North Fork ≃	226	38.12 N	120.43 W
Calaveras Big Trees State Park ♦	226	38.16 N	120.19 W
Calaveras Point ›	282	37.28 N	122.03 W
Calaveras Reservoir ⊜[1]	226	37.28 N	121.49 W
Calaveritas Creek ≃	226	38.10 N	120.40 W
Calavino	64	46.03 N	10.59 E
Calavite, Cape ›	116	13.27 N	120.18 E
Calavite, Mount ∧	116	13.29 N	120.24 E
Calavite Passage ⋃	116	13.36 N	120.25 E
Calavon ≃	62	43.51 N	5.00 E
Calawah ≃	224	47.56 N	124.27 W
Calawah, North Fork ≃	224	47.58 N	124.20 W
Calawah, South Fork ≃	224	47.58 N	124.20 W
Calayan	116	19.16 N	121.28 E
Calayan Island I	116	19.20 N	121.27 E
Čalba	89	52.43 N	131.27 E
Calbayog	116	12.04 N	124.36 E
Calbe	54	51.54 N	11.46 E
Calbiga	116	11.38 N	125.01 E
Calbuco	254	41.46 S	73.08 W
Calca	248	13.20 S	71.57 W
Calçado ≃	256	22.05 S	43.04 W
Calcasieu ≃	194	30.05 N	93.20 W
Calcasieu Lake ⊜	194	29.50 N	93.17 W
Calceta	246	0.51 S	80.10 W
Calcha	248	21.06 S	67.31 W
Calchaquí	252	29.54 S	60.18 W
Calchaquí ≃	252	26.03 S	65.50 W
Calciano	68	40.35 N	16.11 E
Calcinaia	66	43.41 N	10.37 E
Calcinato	64	45.27 N	10.24 E
Calcio	62	45.30 N	9.50 E
Calcium	212	44.01 N	75.51 W
Calçoene	250	2.30 N	50.57 W
Calçoene ≃	250	2.30 N	50.50 W
Calcutta, India	126	22.32 N	88.22 E
Calcutta, India	272b	22.32 N	88.22 E
Calcutta, Oh., U.S.	214	40.40 N	80.34 W
Calcutta University ✪[2]	272b	22.35 N	88.22 E
Caldaro (Kaltern)	64	46.25 N	11.14 E
Caldarola	66	43.08 N	13.13 E
Caldas, Bra.	256	21.56 S	46.23 W
Caldas, Col.	246	6.05 N	75.38 W
Caldas □[5]	246	5.15 N	75.30 W
Caldas da Rainha	34	39.24 N	9.08 W
Caldas de Reyes	34	42.36 N	8.38 W
Caldas Novas	255	17.45 S	48.38 W
Caldè	58	45.57 N	8.38 E
Caldecott Tunnel ⇾[5]	282	37.52 N	122.12 W
Calder ≃, Eng., U.K.	44	53.44 N	1.21 W
Calder ≃, Eng., U.K.	262	53.49 N	2.24 W
Calder, Loch ⊜	46	58.31 N	3.36 W
Caldera	252	27.04 S	70.50 W
Caldera de Taburiente, Parque Nacional de la ♦	148	28.48 N	17.52 W
Calder and Hebble Navigation Canal ≊	262	53.43 N	1.54 W
Calder Bridge	44	54.27 N	3.29 W
Calderbrook	262	53.39 N	2.05 W
Calderdale □[8]	262	53.44 N	2.00 W
Calderstones Park ♦	262	53.23 N	2.54 W
Caldes	64	46.22 N	10.56 E
Caldes ≃	266d	41.31 N	2.13 E
Caldew ≃	44	54.54 N	2.56 W
Caldey Island I	42	51.38 N	4.41 W
Caldicot	42	51.36 N	2.45 W
Caldiero	64	45.22 N	11.11 E
Çaldıran	84	39.09 N	43.55 E
Čaldonazzo	64	45.59 N	11.16 E
Caldonazzo, Lago di ⊜	64	46.01 N	11.15 E
Čaldonka	88	53.47 N	119.12 E
Caldwell, Id., U.S.	202	43.39 N	116.41 W
Caldwell, Ks., U.S.	198	37.01 N	97.36 W
Caldwell, N.J., U.S.	276	40.51 N	74.17 W
Caldwell, Oh., U.S.	188	39.44 N	81.31 W
Caldwell, Tx., U.S.	222	30.31 N	96.41 W
Caldwell □[6]	222	29.50 N	97.40 W
Caldwell Creek ≃	214	41.37 N	79.37 W
Caldwell-Wright Airport ⊠	276	40.53 N	74.17 W
Caldy	262	53.21 N	3.10 W
Cale ≃	42	50.59 N	2.20 W
Caledon, On., Can.	212	43.52 N	80.00 W
Caledon, S. Afr.	158	34.12 S	19.23 E
Caledon (Mohokare) ≃	158	30.31 S	26.05 E
Caledon East	212	43.52 N	79.52 W
Caledonia, Belize	232	18.14 N	88.29 W
Caledonia, N.S., Can.	186	44.22 N	65.02 W
Caledonia, On., Can.	212	43.04 N	79.56 W
Caledonia, Il., U.S.	216	42.22 N	88.53 W
Caledonia, Mi., U.S.	216	42.47 N	85.31 W
Caledonia, Mn., U.S.	190	43.38 N	91.29 W
Caledonia, Ms., U.S.	194	33.40 N	88.19 W
Caledonia, N.Y., U.S.	210	42.58 N	77.51 W
Caledonia, Oh., U.S.	214	40.38 N	82.58 W
Caledonia, Pa., U.S.	214	41.17 N	78.27 W
Caledonian Canal ≊	46	56.50 N	5.06 W
Caledonia State Park ♦	208	39.56 N	77.29 W
Calego	152	12.10 S	23.36 E
Calella	34	41.37 N	2.40 E
Calemba	152	16.04 S	15.44 E
Calen	166	20.54 S	148.46 E
Calendžicha	84	42.37 N	42.04 E
Calenzano	66	43.51 N	11.09 E
Calera, Al., U.S.	194	33.06 N	86.45 W
Calera, Ok., U.S.	196	33.56 N	96.25 W
Calera Creek ≃	282	37.27 N	121.54 W
Caleta, Punta ›	240p	20.04 N	74.18 W
Caleta Olivia	254	46.26 S	67.32 W
Caleufú	252	35.35 S	64.33 W
Calexico	204	32.40 N	115.29 W
Calf Island I	283	42.20 N	70.54 W
Calf Islands II	276	40.59 N	73.38 W
Calfkiller ≃	194	35.49 N	85.29 W
Calf of Man I	44	54.03 N	4.48 W
Calfpasture ≃	188	37.58 N	79.28 W
Calf Pasture Point ›	276	41.05 N	73.24 W
Calgary	182	51.03 N	114.05 W
Calhan	198	39.02 N	104.17 W
Calhariz ⇾[8]	266c	38.44 N	9.12 W
Calhoun, Al., U.S.	194	32.03 N	86.32 W
Calhoun, Ga., U.S.	192	34.30 N	84.57 W
Calhoun, Ky., U.S.	194	37.32 N	87.15 W
Calhoun, Mo., U.S.	194	38.28 N	93.37 W
Calhoun, Tn., U.S.	192	35.17 N	84.44 W
Calhoun □[6], Il., U.S.	219	39.09 N	90.37 W
Calhoun □[6], Mi., U.S.	216	42.14 N	85.00 W
Calhoun City	194	33.51 N	89.18 W
Calhoun Falls	192	34.05 N	82.35 W
Cali, Col.	246	3.27 N	76.31 W
Çalı, Tür.	130	40.10 N	28.54 E
Čalian Point ›	116	6.07 N	125.42 E
Calicoan Island I	116	10.59 N	125.48 E
Calico Ghost Town ⊥	228	34.57 N	116.52 W
Calico Rock	194	36.07 N	92.08 W
Calicut	122	11.15 N	75.46 E
Caliente, Ca., U.S.	228	35.17 N	118.37 W
Caliente, Nv., U.S.	204	37.36 N	114.30 W
Caliente Creek ≃	228	35.17 N	118.48 W
Califon	210	40.43 N	74.50 W
California, Mo., U.S.	194	38.37 N	92.33 W
California, Pa., U.S.	214	40.03 N	79.53 W
California □[3], U.S.	178	37.30 N	119.30 W
California □[3], U.S.	204	37.30 N	119.30 W
California, Golfo de ⊂	232	28.00 N	112.00 W
California, University of ✪[2]	282	37.52 N	122.15 W
California Aqueduct ≊[1]	204	33.52 N	117.12 W
California City	228	35.08 N	117.58 W
California Creek ≃	196	33.05 N	99.33 W
California Institute of Technology ✪[2]	280	34.08 N	118.08 W
California Institution for Men ✪	280	33.59 N	117.40 W
California Institution for Women ✪	280	33.57 N	117.38 W
California-Los Angeles, University of (U.C.L.A.) ✪[2]	280	34.04 N	118.26 W
California State Polytechnic University ✪[2]	280	34.04 N	117.49 W
California State University (Dominguez Hills) ✪[2], Ca., U.S.	280	33.52 N	118.17 W
California State University (Los Angeles) ✪[2], Ca., U.S.	280	34.04 N	118.10 W
California State University (Northridge) ✪[2], Ca., U.S.	280	34.14 N	118.32 W
California State University (Fullerton) ✪[2], Ca., U.S.	280	33.53 N	117.53 W
California State University (Long Beach) ✪[2], Ca., U.S.	280	33.47 N	118.06 W
California State University (Hayward) ✪[2], Ca., U.S.	282	37.39 N	122.04 W
Calihualá	234	17.35 N	98.10 W
Calilegua	252	23.47 S	64.47 W
Calilegua, Parque Nacional ♦	252	23.40 S	64.50 W
Călimăneşti	38	45.14 N	24.20 E
Călimani, Munţii ⩘	38	47.07 N	25.03 E
Calimera	68	40.15 N	18.17 E
Calimere, Point ›	122	10.18 N	79.52 E
Calimesa	228	34.00 N	117.03 W
Calindó ≃	255	14.26 S	43.51 W
Calingasta	252	31.19 S	69.25 W
Calingiri	162	31.06 S	116.27 E
Calinog	116	11.07 N	122.32 E

Symbols in the index entries represent the broad categories identified in the key at the right. Symbols with superior numbers (⩘[1]) identify subcategories (see complete key on page *I · 1*).

Symbole im Register stellen die rechts im Schlüssel erklärten Kategorien dar. Symbole mit hochgestellten Ziffern (⩘[1]) bezeichnen Unterabteilungen einer Kategorie (vgl. vollständiger Schlüssel auf Seite *I · 1*).

Los símbolos incluídos en el texto del índice representan las grandes categorias identificadas con la clave a la derecha. Los símbolos con numeros en su parte superior (⩘[1]) identifican las subcategorías (véase la clave completa en la página *I · 1*).

Les symboles de l'index représentent les catégories indiquées dans la légende à droite. Les symboles suivis d'un indice (⩘[1]) représentent des sous-catégories (voir légende complète à la page *I · 1*).

Os símbolos incluídos no texto do índice representam as grandes categorias identificadas com a chave à direita. Os símbolos com números em sua parte superior (⩘[1]) identificam as subcategorias (veja-se a chave completa à página *I · 1*).

English	Deutsch	Español	Français	Português
∧ Mountain	Berg	Montaña	Montagne	Montanha
⩘ Mountains	Gebirge	Montañas	Montagnes	Montanhas
)(Pass	Paß	Paso	Col	Passo
V Valley, Canyon	Tal, Cañon	Valle, Cañón	Vallée, Canyon	Vale, Canhão
≚ Plain	Ebene	Llano	Plaine	Planície
› Cape	Kap	Cabo	Cap	Cabo
I Island	Insel	Isla	Île	Ilha
II Islands	Inseln	Islas	Îles	Ilhas
± Other Topographic Features	Andere Topographische Objekte	Otros Elementos Topográficos	Autres données topographiques	Outros acidentes topográficos

Calintaan 116 12.35 N 120.56 E
Calion 194 33.19 N 92.32 W
Calipatria 204 33.07 N 115.30 W
Calispell Peak ∧ 202 48.26 N 117.30 W
Calistoga 226 38.34 N 122.34 W
Calitri 68 40.54 N 15.27 E
Calitzdorp 158 33.33 S 21.42 E
Calizzano 62 44.14 N 8.07 E
Calka 84 41.37 N 44.05 E
Calkinskoje vodochranilišče ⊜1 84 41.38 N 44.03 E
Čalkojdy 85 40.44 N 73.39 E
Calla 226 37.46 N 121.11 W
Callabonna, Lake ⊜ 166 29.45 S 140.04 E
Callabonna Creek ≃ 166 29.38 S 140.08 E
Callac 32 48.24 N 3.26 W
Callaghan, Mount ∧ 204 39.42 N 116.57 W
Callahan 192 30.33 N 81.49 W
Callahan, Mount ∧ 200 39.26 N 108.07 W
Callahans 276 40.58 N 74.37 W
Callan 48 52.33 N 7.23 W
Callander, On., Can. 190 46.13 N 79.23 W
Callander, Scot., U.K. 46 56.15 N 4.14 W
Callang 116 17.02 N 121.38 E
Callanish 46 58.12 N 6.43 W
Callanmarca 248 12.52 S 74.38 W
Callanna 166 29.38 S 137.55 E
Callantsoog 52 52.49 N 4.41 E
Callao, Perú 248 12.04 S 77.09 W
Callao, Va., U.S. 208 37.58 N 76.33 W
Callao □4 286d 12.04 S 77.09 W
Callaquén, Volcán ∧1 252 37.54 S 71.26 W
Callas 62 43.35 N 6.32 E
Callaway 198 41.17 N 99.55 W
Callaway □6 219 38.50 N 91.52 W
Callaway Gardens ♦ 192 32.51 N 84.52 W
Calle 56 51.20 N 8.13 E
Callensburg 214 41.08 N 79.33 W
Callery 214 40.45 N 80.02 W
Call Hill ∧2 210 42.13 N 77.40 W
Calliano, It. 62 45.00 N 8.15 E
Calliano, It. 64 45.56 N 11.05 E
Calliaqua 241h 13.08 N 61.12 W
Callicoon 210 41.46 N 75.03 W
Callicoon Center 210 41.50 N 74.57 W
Callinam 196 28.29 N 98.21 W
Calling Lake 182 55.15 N 113.12 W
Calling Lake ⊜ 182 55.13 N 113.15 W
Callington, Austl. 168b 35.07 S 139.02 E
Callington, Eng., U.K. 42 50.30 N 4.18 W
Calliope 166 24.00 S 151.12 E
Callosa d'En Sarrià 34 38.39 N 0.07 W
Callosa de Segura 34 38.08 N 0.52 W
Calloway Canal ≅ 226 35.24 N 119.01 W
Calmar, Ab., Can. 182 53.16 N 113.49 W
Calmar, Ia., U.S. 190 43.11 N 91.51 W
Calmar → Kalmar 26 56.40 N 16.22 E
Călmățui ≃ 38 44.50 N 27.50 E
Calmazzo 66 43.40 N 12.46 E
Calmbach 56 48.46 N 8.35 E
Calm Lake ⊜ 190 48.46 N 92.04 W
Čal'mny-Varre 24 67.10 N 37.33 E
Čalna 24 61.55 N 34.01 E
Calnali 234 20.55 N 98.35 W
Calne 42 51.27 N 2.00 W
Calobre 236 8.19 N 80.51 W
Calola 152 16.30 S 17.51 E
Calolbon 116 13.36 N 124.06 E
Calólo 152 10.00 S 14.53 E
Calolziocorte 62 45.48 N 9.26 E
Calonne-Ricouart 50 50.29 N 2.29 E
Caloocan 116 14.39 N 120.58 E
Caloosahatchee ≃ 220 26.31 N 82.01 W
Caloosahatchee Canal ≅ 220 26.46 N 81.27 W
Caloote 168b 34.58 S 139.16 E
Calore ≃, It. 68 41.11 N 14.28 E
Calore ≃, It. 68 40.31 N 15.01 E
Caloundra 166 26.48 S 153.09 E
Calouste-Gulbenkian, Museu de ⊕ 266c 38.44 N 9.08 W
Caloveto 68 39.30 N 16.45 E
Calp 34 38.39 N 0.03 E
Calpulalpan 234 19.35 N 98.35 W
Čalpy 80 55.05 N 53.06 E
Calshot 42 50.49 N 1.19 W
Calstock 42 50.30 N 4.12 W
Caltabellotta 70 37.34 N 13.13 E
Caltagirone 70 37.14 N 14.31 E
Caltagirone ≃ 70 37.21 N 14.42 E
Caltanissetta 70 37.29 N 14.04 E
Caltanissetta □4 70 37.29 N 14.04 E
Caltavuturo 70 37.49 N 13.53 E
Çaltılıbük 130 39.57 N 28.36 E
Caltra 48 53.26 N 8.25 W
Čaltyr' 83 47.17 N 39.30 E
Caluango 152 8.21 S 19.40 E
Calubian 116 11.27 N 124.26 E
Calucinga 152 11.18 S 16.12 E
Călugăreni 38 44.07 N 26.01 E
Caluire-et-Cuire 62 45.48 N 4.51 E
Calumbolaca 152 9.09 S 13.48 E
Calumet, Mi., U.S. 190 47.14 N 88.27 W
Calumet, Mn., U.S. 190 47.19 N 93.16 W
Calumet, Pa., U.S. 214 40.13 N 79.28 W
Calumet ≃ 278 41.44 N 87.32 W
Calumet, Lake ⊜ 216 41.41 N 87.35 W
Calumet City 216 41.36 N 87.31 W
Calumet Harbor c 278 41.44 N 87.32 W
Calumet Park 278 41.39 N 87.39 W
Calumet Park ♦ 278 41.43 N 87.32 W
Calumet Sag Channel ≅ 278 41.42 N 87.57 W
Calumpit 116 14.55 N 120.46 E
Calunda 152 12.06 S 23.23 E
Caluquembe 152 13.47 S 14.44 E
Calusa Island I 116 9.37 N 121.01 E
Caluso 62 45.18 N 7.53 E
Caluula 144 11.58 N 50.45 E
Caluula, Raasiga ≻ 144 11.59 N 50.47 E
Caluya Island I 116 11.55 N 121.34 E
Calvados □5 32 49.10 N 0.30 W
Calvello 68 40.28 N 15.51 E
Calver 44 53.16 N 1.38 W
Calvera 68 40.09 N 16.09 E
Calvert, Al., U.S. 194 31.09 N 88.01 W
Calvert, Tx., U.S. 222 30.58 N 96.40 W
Calvert □6 208 38.33 N 76.35 W
Calvert ≃ 164 16.17 S 137.44 E
Calvert, Lough ⊜ 169 38.11 S 143.42 E
Calvert City 194 37.02 N 88.21 W
Calvert Hills 166 17.15 S 137.20 E
Calvert Island I 182 51.35 N 128.00 W
Calverton, Eng., U.K. 44 53.02 N 1.05 W
Calverton, Md., U.S. 284c 39.03 N 76.56 W
Calverton, N.Y., U.S. 207 40.55 N 72.45 W
Calvi 32 42.34 N 8.45 E
Calvi, Monte ∧ 66 43.05 N 10.37 E
Calvia 34 39.34 N 2.31 E
Calvi dell'Umbria 66 42.24 N 12.34 E
Calvillo 234 21.51 N 102.43 W
Calvin, Ok., U.S. 196 34.58 N 96.14 W
Calvin, Pa., U.S. 214 40.20 N 78.02 W
Calvinia 158 31.25 S 19.45 E
Calvisano 64 45.20 N 10.20 E
Calvo, Monte ∧ 68 41.44 N 15.46 E
Calvörde 54 52.23 N 11.17 E
Calw 56 48.43 N 8.44 E
Calwa 226 36.42 N 119.45 W
Calypso 192 35.09 N 78.06 W
Calzada 248 6.02 S 77.02 W
Cam ≃ 42 52.21 N 0.15 E
Camabatela 152 8.11 S 15.22 E
Camaçã ≃ 248 6.35 S 66.27 W
Camaçari 255 12.41 S 38.18 W
Camachigama, Lac ⊜ 190 47.50 N 76.19 W
Camacupa 152 12.03 S 17.30 E
Camaguán 246 8.06 N 67.36 W
Camagüey 240p 21.23 N 77.55 W
Camagüey □4 240p 21.30 N 78.00 W
Camagüey, Archipiélago de II 240p 22.30 N 78.10 W
Camaiore 64 43.56 N 10.18 E
Camaiú ≃ 248 5.30 S 59.42 W
Camajuaní 240p 22.28 N 79.44 W
Camaldoli, Eremo di ⊕1 66 43.46 N 11.47 E
Camamu 255 13.57 S 39.07 W
Camaná 248 16.37 S 72.42 W
Camaná ≃ 248 16.39 S 72.46 W
Camanaú ≃ 246 1.51 S 61.14 W
Camanche 190 41.47 N 90.15 W
Camanche Reservoir ⊜1 226 38.13 N 120.58 W
Camandag Island I 116 11.59 N 124.25 E
Camanducaia 256 22.46 S 46.09 W
Camanducaia ≃, Bra. 256 22.39 S 46.58 W
Camanducaia ≃, Bra. 256 22.55 S 46.25 W
Camano Island I 224 48.10 N 122.30 W
Camaoí ≃ 250 3.12 S 48.04 W
Camapuã 255 19.30 S 54.05 W
Camaquã 252 30.51 S 51.49 W
Camaquã ≃ 252 31.17 S 51.47 W
Camará 246 3.55 S 62.44 W
Camarajibe 250 8.01 S 34.58 W
Camararé ≃ 248 12.15 S 58.55 W
Camarat, Cap ≻ 62 43.12 N 6.41 E
Camarda 66 42.23 N 13.29 E
Çamardı 130 37.50 N 35.00 E
Camarès 32 43.49 N 2.53 E
Camargo, Bol. 248 20.39 S 65.13 W
Camargo, Méx. 232 27.40 N 105.10 W
Camargos, Reprêsa de ⊜1 256 21.25 S 44.30 W
Camargue ✦1 62 43.34 N 4.34 E
Camargue, Parc Naturel Régional de ♦ 62 43.30 N 4.28 E
Camarillo 228 34.12 N 119.02 W
Camarillo Heights 228 34.14 N 119.02 W
Camarina ⊥ 70 36.52 N 14.27 E
Camariñas 34 43.07 N 9.10 W
Camarines Norte □4 116 14.10 N 122.40 E
Camarines Sur □4 116 13.35 N 123.20 E
Camarón, Arroyo ≃ 196 27.08 N 100.00 W
Camarón, Cabo ≻ 236 16.00 N 85.05 W
Camarones 254 44.48 S 65.42 W
Camarones, Bahía c 254 44.45 S 65.34 W
Camas, Esp. 34 37.24 N 6.02 W
Camas, Tür. 130 40.55 N 37.32 E
Camas, Wa., U.S. 224 45.35 N 122.23 W
Camas Creek ≃, Id., U.S. 202 43.20 N 114.24 W
Camas Creek ≃, Id., U.S. 202 44.53 N 114.44 W
Camas Creek ≃, Id., U.S. 202 43.53 N 112.21 W
Camas Creek ≃, Or., U.S. 202 45.01 N 118.59 W
Camastra 70 37.15 N 13.47 E
Camatagua, Embalse de ⊜1 246 9.50 N 67.00 W
Camatambo 152 6.30 S 15.18 E
Ca Mau 110 9.11 N 105.08 E
Ca Mau, Mui ≻ 110 8.38 N 104.44 E
Camaxilo 152 8.21 S 18.56 E
Camba 112 4.54 S 119.50 E
Camba Cassai 152 9.40 S 19.18 E
Cambados 34 42.30 N 8.48 W
Cambará 255 23.03 S 50.05 W
Čambarak 84 40.36 N 45.21 E
Camberley 42 51.21 N 0.45 W
Camberwell 169 37.50 S 145.04 E
Camberwell ✦8 260 51.28 N 0.05 W
Cambiano 62 44.58 N 7.47 E
Cambo 44 55.10 N 1.57 W
Cambo ≃ 152 7.40 S 17.17 E
Cambodia (Kâmpuchéa) □1, Asia 108 13.00 N 105.00 E
Cambodia (Kâmpuchéa) □1, Asia 110 13.00 N 105.00 E
Cambois 44 55.10 N 1.31 W
Cambonda, Serra ∧ 152 12.06 S 14.00 E
Camboon 166 25.03 S 150.26 E
Cambooya 171a 27.42 S 151.52 E
Camboriú 252 27.01 S 48.38 W
Camborne 42 50.12 N 5.19 W
Cambra 210 41.11 N 76.18 W
Cambrai, Austl. 168b 34.39 S 139.17 E
Cambrai, Fr. 50 50.10 N 3.14 E
Cambremer 50 49.09 N 0.03 E
Cambria, Ca., U.S. 226 35.33 N 121.04 W
Cambria, In., U.S. 216 40.22 N 86.33 W
Cambria, Mi., U.S. 216 41.49 N 84.39 W
Cambria, Wi., U.S. 190 43.32 N 89.06 W
Cambria □6 214 40.29 N 79.16 W
Cambria Ice Field ⊠ 182 55.55 N 129.30 W
Cambrian Mountains ∧ 28 52.35 N 3.35 W
Cambrian Park 226 37.15 N 121.55 W
Cambridge (Galt), On., Can. 212 43.22 N 80.19 W
Cambridge, N.Z. 172 37.53 S 175.28 E
Cambridge, Eng., U.K. 42 52.13 N 0.08 E
Cambridge, Id., U.S. 202 44.34 N 116.41 W
Cambridge, Il., U.S. 190 41.18 N 90.11 W
Cambridge, Ia., U.S. 190 41.53 N 93.31 W
Cambridge, Md., U.S. 208 38.33 N 76.04 W
Cambridge, Ma., U.S. 207 42.22 N 71.06 W
Cambridge, Mn., U.S. 190 45.34 N 93.13 W
Cambridge, Ne., U.S. 198 40.16 N 100.09 W
Cambridge, N.Y., U.S. 210 43.01 N 73.22 W
Cambridge, Oh., U.S. 188 40.02 N 81.35 W
Cambridge, Wi., U.S. 216 43.00 N 89.01 W
Cambridge Bay 176 69.03 N 105.05 W
Cambridge City 218 39.48 N 85.10 W
Cambridge Fiord c2 176 71.20 N 74.44 W
Cambridge Gulf c 164 14.55 S 128.15 E
Cambridge Park 274a 33.45 S 150.43 E
Cambridge Reservoir ⊜1 283 42.24 N 71.16 W
Cambridgeshire □6 42 52.20 N 0.05 E
Cambridge Springs 214 41.48 N 80.03 W
Cambrils 34 41.04 N 1.03 E
Cambriú, Ponta de ≻ 252 25.10 S 47.55 W
Cambuci ✦8 287b 23.34 S 46.37 W
Cambuí 256 22.37 S 46.04 W
Cambulo 152 7.48 S 21.14 E
Cambundi-Catembo 152 10.09 S 17.31 E
Cambuquira 256 21.51 S 45.18 W
Cambural 286c 10.26 N 66.59 W
Camburg 54 51.03 N 11.42 E
Camburi ≃ 256 23.41 S 45.28 W
Camby 218 39.40 N 86.19 W
Čamčakly 128 37.56 N 63.46 E
Camden, Austl. 170 34.03 S 150.42 E
Camden, S. Afr. 158 26.38 S 30.07 E
Camden, Al., U.S. 194 31.59 N 87.17 W
Camden, Ar., U.S. 194 33.35 N 92.50 W
Camden, De., U.S. 208 39.06 N 75.32 W
Camden, Il., U.S. 219 40.09 N 90.46 W
Camden, In., U.S. 216 40.36 N 86.32 W
Camden, Me., U.S. 188 44.12 N 69.03 W
Camden, Mi., U.S. 216 41.45 N 84.45 W
Camden, Ms., U.S. 194 32.46 N 89.50 W
Camden, N.J., U.S. 208 39.55 N 75.07 W
Camden, N.Y., U.S. 210 43.20 N 75.44 W
Camden, N.C., U.S. 192 36.19 N 76.10 W
Camden, Oh., U.S. 218 39.37 N 84.38 W
Camden, S.C., U.S. 192 34.14 N 80.36 W
Camden, Tn., U.S. 194 36.03 N 88.05 W
Camden, Tx., U.S. 222 30.55 N 94.44 W
Camden □6, N.J., U.S. 208 39.57 N 75.07 W
Camden □6, N.C., U.S. 208 36.28 N 76.21 W
Camden ✦8 260 51.33 N 0.10 W
Camden, Grupo II 254 54.40 S 71.58 W
Camden Aerodrome ⊠ 274a 34.03 S 150.41 E
Camden Bay c 180 70.00 N 145.00 W
Camden Hills State Park ♦ 188 44.17 N 69.05 W
Camden Lake ⊜ 212 44.25 N 76.52 W
Camden Station ✦5 284b 39.17 N 76.37 W
Camdenton 194 38.00 N 92.44 W
Camedo 58 46.09 N 8.37 E
Cameia, Parque Nacional da ♦ 152 11.45 S 21.20 E
Camel ≃ 42 50.33 N 4.55 W
Camel, Mount ∧2 169 36.45 S 144.43 E
Camelback Mountain ∧, Ak., U.S. 180 62.33 N 157.20 W
Camelback Mountain ∧, Pa., U.S. 210 41.03 N 75.21 W
Camelford 42 50.37 N 4.41 W
Çameli 130 37.05 N 29.20 E
Camels Hump ∧ 188 44.19 N 72.53 W
Cameo Acres 282 37.51 N 121.58 W
Camerano 66 43.32 N 13.33 E
Cameri 62 45.30 N 8.39 E
Cameri, Aeroporto di ⊠ 266b 45.32 N 8.40 E
Camerino 66 43.08 N 13.04 E
Cameron, Ca., U.S. 226 38.39 N 120.56 W
Cameron, La., U.S. 194 29.47 N 93.19 W
Cameron, Mo., U.S. 194 39.44 N 94.14 W
Cameron, N.Y., U.S. 210 42.12 N 77.24 W
Cameron, Pa., U.S. 214 41.27 N 78.10 W
Cameron, S.C., U.S. 192 33.33 N 80.42 W
Cameron, Tx., U.S. 222 30.51 N 96.58 W
Cameron, W.V., U.S. 188 39.49 N 80.34 W
Cameron, Wi., U.S. 190 45.24 N 91.44 W
Cameron □6 214 41.31 N 78.14 W
Cameron ≃ 224 49.17 N 124.38 W
Cameron, Lac ⊜ 206 46.06 N 74.50 W
Cameron Highlands 114 4.29 N 101.27 E
Cameron Hills ∧2 176 59.48 N 118.00 W
Cameron Lake ⊜, B.C., Can. 224 49.17 N 124.37 W
Cameron Lake ⊜, On., Can. 212 44.34 N 78.45 W
Cameron Mills 210 42.11 N 77.22 W
Cameron Mountains ∧ 172 46.00 S 167.00 E
Cameron Run ≃ 284c 38.48 N 77.04 W
Cameroon (Cameroun) □1 134 6.00 N 12.00 E
Cameroon Mountain ∧ 152 4.12 N 9.11 E
Camerota 68 40.02 N 15.23 E
Cameroun → Cameroon □1 134 6.00 N 12.00 E
Camerún → Cameroon □1 134 6.00 N 12.00 E
Cametá 250 2.15 S 49.30 W
Camfield 164 17.09 S 131.21 E
Çamiçi Gölü ⊜ 130 37.30 N 27.25 E
Camiguin □4 116 9.15 N 124.40 E
Camiguin Island I, Pil. 116 18.56 N 121.55 E
Camiguin Island I, Pil. 116 9.11 N 124.42 E
Camiling 116 15.42 N 120.24 E
Camilla 192 31.13 N 84.12 W
Camillus 210 43.02 N 76.19 W
Camin 54 53.27 N 10.58 E
Camiña 248 19.18 S 69.26 W
Caminha 34 41.52 N 8.50 W
Camino 226 38.44 N 120.40 W
Camiranga 250 1.48 S 46.17 W
Camiri 248 20.03 S 63.31 W
Camisano Vicentino 64 45.31 N 11.43 E
Camisea ≃ 248 11.35 S 72.58 W
Camissombo 152 8.10 S 20.39 E
Camlad ≃ 42 52.36 N 3.10 W
Çamlıbel 130 40.05 N 36.29 E
Çamlıdere, Tür. 130 40.30 N 32.29 E
Çamlıdere, Tür. 130 37.08 N 39.03 E
Çamlıyayla 130 37.09 N 34.36 E
Cam Lo 110 16.49 N 106.59 E
Čamlyk ≃ 84 44.45 N 40.45 E
Cammal 214 41.24 N 77.28 W
Cammarata 70 37.38 N 13.38 E
Cammarta, Monte ∧ 70 37.37 N 13.36 E
Camoapa 236 12.23 N 85.31 W
Camocim 250 2.54 S 40.50 W
Camogli 62 44.21 N 9.09 E
Çamoluk 130 40.08 N 38.45 E
Camonica, Val ∨ 64 46.00 N 10.20 E
Camooweal 166 19.55 S 138.07 E
Camopi ≃ 250 3.11 N 52.20 W
Camorim ≃ 287a 22.59 S 43.25 W
Camorim, Represa do ⊜1 287a 22.58 S 43.27 W
Camorta Island I 110 8.08 N 93.30 E
Camote, Cerro ∧ 286d 11.57 S 77.06 W
Camotes Islands II 116 10.40 N 124.24 E
Camotes Sea ⊤2 116 10.30 N 124.15 E
Camotlán ≃ 234 22.01 N 104.15 W
Camowen ≃ 48 54.36 N 7.18 W
Camp □6 222 33.00 N 94.58 W
Campagna 68 40.40 N 15.08 E
Campagna di Roma ✦1 66 41.50 N 12.35 E
Campagna Lupia 64 45.21 N 12.06 E
Campagnano di Roma 66 42.08 N 12.23 E
Campagnatico 66 42.53 N 11.16 E
Campagne-lès-Hesdin 50 50.24 N 1.52 E
Campaign 194 35.46 N 85.37 W
Campamento 236 14.33 N 86.42 W
Campana, Arg. 258 34.10 S 58.57 W
Campana, It. 68 39.24 N 16.50 E
Campana, Isla I 254 48.20 S 75.15 W
Campanario 34 38.52 N 5.37 W
Campanario, Cerro de ∧ 248 5.57 S 77.31 W
Campanella, Punta ≻ 68 40.34 N 14.19 E
Campanero, Cerro ∧ 246 5.54 N 65.12 W
Campanha 256 21.50 S 45.24 W
Campania □4 68 40.55 N 14.50 E
Campania Island I 182 53.05 N 129.30 W
Camparada 266b 45.39 N 9.19 E
Campaspe ≃, Austl. 166 21.00 S 146.24 E
Campaspe ≃, Austl. 169 36.41 S 144.31 E
Campbell, S. Afr. 158 28.48 S 23.44 E
Campbell, Ca., U.S. 226 37.17 N 121.56 W
Campbell, Mn., U.S. 198 46.05 N 96.24 W
Campbell, Mo., U.S. 194 36.29 N 90.04 W
Campbell, Ne., U.S. 198 40.18 N 98.44 W
Campbell, N.Y., U.S. 210 42.13 N 77.11 W
Campbell, Oh., U.S. 214 41.04 N 80.35 W
Campbell, Tx., U.S. 222 33.09 N 95.57 W
Campbell □6 218 38.55 N 84.20 W
Campbell, Cape ≻ 172 41.44 S 174.17 E
Campbell Airport ⊠ 279b 40.21 N 80.11 W
Campbellfield 274b 37.41 S 144.57 E
Campbellford 212 44.18 N 77.48 W
Campbell Hall 210 41.27 N 74.16 W
Campbell Hill ∧2 216 40.22 N 83.43 W
Campbell Island 182 52.10 N 128.09 W
Campbell Island I 9 52.30 S 169.05 E
Campbell Lake ⊜ 182 50.01 N 125.27 W
Campbell Plateau ✦3 9 51.00 S 170.00 E
Campbell Point ≻ 171a 27.22 S 153.55 E
Campbellpore 123 33.46 N 72.22 E
Campbell Range ∧ 180 61.08 N 129.45 W
Campbell River 182 50.01 N 125.15 W
Campbells ≃ 170 33.42 S 149.37 E
Campbell's Airport ⊠ 278 42.20 N 88.04 W
Campbell's-Bay 188 45.44 N 76.36 W
Campbellsburg, In., U.S. 218 38.39 N 86.15 W
Campbellsburg, Ky., U.S. 218 38.31 N 85.12 W
Campbell Slough ≃ 226 39.22 N 121.51 W
Campbellsport 190 43.35 N 88.16 W
Campbells River ≃ 170 33.54 S 149.37 E
Campbells Run ≃ 279b 40.24 N 80.05 W
Campbellsville 194 37.20 N 85.20 W
Campbellton, N.B., Can. 186 48.00 N 66.40 W
Campbellton, Nf., Can. 186 49.17 N 54.56 W
Campbellton, P.E., Can. 186 46.47 N 64.18 W
Campbellton, Fl., U.S. 192 30.56 N 85.24 W
Campbell Town, Austl. 166 41.56 S 147.29 E
Campbelltown, Austl. 168b 34.53 S 138.40 E
Campbelltown, Austl. 170 34.04 S 150.49 E
Campbelltown, Pa., U.S. 208 40.17 N 76.35 W
Campbellville 212 43.29 N 79.59 W
Campbeltown 46 55.26 N 5.36 W
Camp Creek ≃, Ca., U.S. 226 38.38 N 120.40 W
Camp Creek ≃, Mo., U.S. 219 39.02 N 91.12 W
Camp Creek Lake ⊜1 222 31.03 N 96.19 W
Camp David ⊕ 208 39.38 N 77.28 W
Camp de Frileuse ■ 261 48.52 N 1.55 E
Camp de Satory ■ 261 48.47 N 2.06 E
Camp Dix 218 38.29 N 83.17 W
Camp Douglas 190 43.55 N 90.16 W
Campeche 232 19.51 N 90.32 W
Campeche □3 232 19.00 N 90.30 W
Campeche, Bahía de c 232 20.00 N 94.00 W
Campeche Bank ✦4 16 22.00 N 90.00 W
Campechuela 240p 20.14 N 77.17 W
Campegine 64 44.45 N 10.32 E
Campello Monti 58 45.56 N 8.15 E
Camperdown, Austl. 169 38.14 S 143.09 E
Camperdown, S. Afr. 158 29.42 S 30.33 E
Camperville 184 51.59 N 100.09 W
Campestre 256 21.43 S 46.15 W
Cam Pha 110 21.01 N 107.19 E
Camp Hill, Al., U.S. 194 32.48 N 85.39 W
Camp Hill, Pa., U.S. 208 40.14 N 76.55 W
Campi Bisenzio 66 43.49 N 11.08 E
Campidano ✦1 71 39.30 N 8.47 E
Campiglia dei Fosci 66 43.27 N 11.03 E
Campiglia Marittima 66 43.03 N 10.37 E
Campillo de Llerena 34 38.30 N 5.50 W
Campillos 34 37.03 N 4.51 W
Campina ✦1 34 37.45 N 4.45 W
Campina Grande 250 7.13 S 35.53 W
Campinas 256 22.54 S 47.05 W
Campina Verde 255 19.31 S 49.28 W
Campinho, Rio do ≃ 287a 22.52 S 43.37 W
Campione del Garda 64 45.45 N 10.45 E
Campi Salentina 68 40.24 N 18.01 E
Campitello 64 46.28 N 11.44 E
Camp King 150 4.55 N 7.58 W
Camp Lake 216 42.32 N 88.09 W
Camp Lake ⊜ 212 45.27 N 78.54 W
Camp Leger ■ 261 48.34 N 2.34 E
Camp Lejeune Marine Corps Base ■ 192 34.40 N 77.21 W
Campli 66 42.43 N 13.41 E
Camplong 112 10.02 S 123.55 E
Campo, Cam. 152 2.22 N 9.49 E
Campo, Moç. 156 17.44 S 36.21 E
Campo, Co., U.S. 198 37.06 N 102.34 W
Campo, Réserve de ✦4 152 2.35 N 9.57 E
Campoalegre 246 2.41 N 75.20 W
Campo Alegre ≃ 250 9.19 S 50.06 W
Campo Alegre de Goiás 255 17.39 S 47.45 W
Campobasso 66 41.34 N 14.39 E
Campobasso □4 68 41.38 N 14.35 E
Campobello di Licata 70 37.15 N 13.55 E
Campobello di Mazara 70 37.38 N 12.45 E
Campobello Island I 186 44.53 N 66.55 W
Campo Belo 255 20.53 S 45.16 W
Campo Blenio 58 46.34 N 8.56 E
Campo Catino 66 41.48 N 13.20 E
Campocologno 58 46.13 N 10.08 E
Campodarsego 64 45.30 N 11.54 E
Campo de Criptana 34 39.24 N 3.07 W
Campo de la Cruz 246 10.23 N 74.53 W
Campo de Marte ♦ 286d 12.04 S 77.03 W
Campo de Marte ■ 287b 23.30 S 46.37 W
Campo de Mayo ■ 288 34.32 S 58.38 W
Campo di Giove 66 42.01 N 14.03 E
Campo di Trens (Trens) 64 46.52 N 11.29 E
Campo do Coelho 256 22.15 S 42.39 W
Campodolcino 58 46.24 N 9.21 E
Campo Erê 252 26.23 S 53.03 W
Campofelice di Fitalia 70 37.50 N 13.29 E
Campofelice di Roccella 70 37.59 N 13.53 E
Campofiorito 70 37.45 N 13.16 E
Campo Florido 255 19.47 S 48.35 W
Campoformido 64 46.01 N 13.09 E
Campo Formoso 250 10.31 S 40.20 W
Campofranco 70 37.30 N 13.43 E
Campogalliano 64 44.41 N 10.50 E
Campo Gallo 252 26.35 S 62.51 W
Campo Grande, Arg. 252 27.13 S 54.58 W
Campo Grande, Bra. 255 20.27 S 54.37 W
Campo Grande ✦8, Bra. 256 22.54 S 43.34 W
Campo Grande ✦8, Port. 266c 38.45 N 9.09 W
Campo Indian Reservation ✦4 204 32.40 N 116.20 W
Campo Largo, Arg. 252 26.48 S 60.50 W
Campo Largo, Bra. 252 25.26 S 49.32 W
Campolaro 64 45.55 N 10.20 E
Campolasta (Astfeld) 64 46.40 N 11.22 E
Campolato, Capo ≻ 70 37.17 N 15.12 E
Campo Libertad ■ 286b 23.05 N 82.26 W
Campolide 256 21.36 S 43.53 W
Campolieto 66 41.38 N 14.46 E
Campo Ligure 62 44.32 N 8.42 E
Campo Limpo Paulista 256 23.12 S 46.48 W
Campo Maior, Bra. 250 4.49 S 42.10 W
Campo Maior, Port. 34 39.01 N 7.04 W
Campomarino 66 41.57 N 15.02 E
Campo Militar Número Uno ■ 286a 19.27 N 99.14 W
Campomorone 62 44.30 N 8.53 E
Campo Mourão 255 24.03 S 52.22 W
Campo Novo 252 27.42 S 53.48 W
Campo Pequeno ♦ 266c 38.44 N 9.08 W
Campo Quijano 252 24.55 S 65.39 W
Campora 68 40.19 N 15.17 E
Camporeale 70 37.54 N 13.06 E
Camporgiano 64 44.09 N 10.20 E
Camporredondo 248 6.07 S 78.21 W
Campos 255 21.45 S 41.18 W
Campos Altos 255 19.41 S 46.10 W
Camposampiero 64 45.34 N 11.56 E
Campo Santo, Arg. 252 24.40 S 65.06 W
Camposanto, It. 64 44.47 N 11.08 E
Campos Belos 255 13.03 S 46.53 W
Campos de Cunha 256 22.55 S 44.49 W
Campos do Jordão 256 22.44 S 45.35 W
Campos Elísios 256 22.42 S 43.17 W
Campos Gerais 256 21.14 S 45.46 W
Campos Novos 252 27.24 S 51.12 W
Campos Sales 250 7.04 S 40.23 W
Campo Tencia, Pizzo ∧ 58 46.26 N 8.43 E
Campotosto 66 42.33 N 13.22 E
Campotosto, Lago di ⊜1 66 42.32 N 13.22 E
Campo Tures (Sand in Taufers) 64 46.55 N 11.57 E
Campovalano 66 42.44 N 13.40 E
Camp Parks Communications Annex ■ 282 37.44 N 121.54 W
Camp Pendleton Marine Corps Base ■ 228 33.19 N 117.18 W
Camp Point 219 40.02 N 91.04 W
Camp Ruby 222 30.42 N 94.45 W
Campsie 274a 33.55 S 151.06 E
Campsie Fells ∧2 46 56.02 N 4.12 W
Camp Springs 208 38.48 N 76.54 W
Campti 194 31.53 N 93.07 W
Campton 192 37.44 N 83.32 W
Camptonville 226 39.27 N 121.03 W
Camptown 210 41.43 N 76.14 W
Campus 216 41.01 N 88.18 W
Campuya ≃ 246 1.43 S 73.30 W
Camp Verde 200 34.33 N 111.51 W
Campville 210 42.06 N 76.09 W
Camp Wood 196 29.40 N 100.01 W
Cam Ranh 110 11.54 N 109.09 E
Cam Ranh, Vinh c 110 11.53 N 109.10 E
Camrose, Ab., Can. 182 53.01 N 112.50 W
Camrose, Wales, U.K. 42 51.51 N 5.01 W
Camsell ≃ 176 65.40 N 118.07 W
Camu ≃ 250 1.15 N 57.09 W
Camucia 66 43.16 N 11.58 E
Camucuio 152 14.12 S 13.20 E
Camurí Chiquito, Quebrada ≃ 286c 10.37 N 66.52 W
Çamurlu Dağ ∧ 130 40.21 N 42.26 E
Camuy 240m 18.29 N 66.51 W
Cam Xuyen 110 18.15 N 106.00 E
Čamyndy 85 41.37 N 74.20 E
Čamzinka 80 54.24 N 45.47 E
Çan, Tür. 130 40.02 N 27.03 E
Çan, Tür. 130 39.09 N 40.13 E
Can ≃ 42 51.44 N 0.28 E
Canaan, Ct., U.S. 207 42.01 N 73.19 W
Canaan, Fl., U.S. 220 28.48 N 81.14 W
Canaan, In., U.S. 218 38.52 N 85.25 W
Canaan, N.Y., U.S. 210 42.25 N 73.27 W
Canaan, Vt., U.S. 206 44.59 N 71.32 W
Canaan ≃ 186 45.55 N 65.47 W
Canaan Lake ⊜ 276 40.47 N 73.01 W
Canaan Valley State Park ♦ 188 39.02 N 79.32 W
Cana-brava ≃, Bra. 255 13.11 S 48.11 W
Cana-brava ≃, Bra. 255 12.12 S 48.40 W
Cañacao Bay c 269f 14.29 N 120.55 E
Canaçari, Lago ⊜ 250 2.57 S 58.15 W
Canada □1 176 60.00 N 95.00 W
Cañada, Loma la ∧2 240p 21.41 N 82.57 W
Canada Bay c 186 50.43 N 56.10 W
Cañada de Caracheo 234 20.22 N 100.57 W
Cañada de Gómez 252 32.49 S 61.24 W
Cañada Honda 252 31.59 S 68.33 W
Canada Lake ⊜ 210 43.10 N 74.32 W
Cañada Nieto 258 33.43 S 58.05 W
Canadarago Lake ⊜ 210 42.48 N 75.01 W
Canada's Wonderland ♦ 275b 43.51 N 79.33 W
Cañada Verde → Villa Huidobro 252 34.50 S 64.35 W
Canadaway Creek ≃ 214 42.28 N 79.22 W
Canadensis 210 41.11 N 75.15 W
Canadian 196 35.54 N 100.22 W
Canadian ≃, U.S. 196 35.27 N 95.03 W
Canadian ≃, Co., U.S. 200 40.53 N 106.20 W
Canadian, Deep Fork ≃ 196 35.28 N 95.50 W
Canadian Forces Base Trenton ■ 212 44.07 N 77.33 W
Canadice Lake ⊜ 210 42.43 N 77.34 W
Cañadón Seco 254 46.33 S 67.35 W
Canaguá ≃ 246 7.57 N 69.36 W
Canaima 246 6.14 N 62.52 W
Canaima, Parque Nacional ♦ 246 4.27 N 62.00 W
Canajoharie 210 42.54 N 74.34 W
Çanakkale 130 40.09 N 26.24 E
Çanakkale □4 130 40.10 N 26.45 E
Çanakkale Boğazı (Dardanelles) ⊍ 130 40.15 N 26.25 E
Canal, Islas del → Channel Islands II 28 49.20 N 2.20 W
Canala 175f 21.32 S 165.57 E
Canale 62 44.48 N 8.00 E
Canale, Val ∨ 64 46.29 N 13.30 E
Canalejas 234 19.55 N 99.39 W
Canal Flats 182 50.09 N 115.48 W
Canal Fulton 214 40.53 N 81.35 W
Canal Lake ⊜ 212 44.34 N 79.03 W
Canal Lewisville 214 40.18 N 81.50 W
Canal Point 220 26.51 N 80.38 W
Canals 252 33.33 S 62.53 W
Canal Winchester 188 39.51 N 82.48 W
Canamã ≃ 248 8.45 S 59.15 W
Canandaigua 210 42.52 N 77.20 W
Canandaigua Lake ⊜ 210 42.49 N 77.16 W
Canandaigua Outlet ≃ 210 43.04 N 77.00 W
Cananea 232 30.57 N 110.18 W
Cananéia 252 25.01 S 47.57 W
Canan Station 214 40.28 N 78.26 W
Canapine, Forca ✕ 66 42.45 N 13.12 E
Canápolis 255 18.44 S 49.13 W
Canapville 50 49.19 N 0.08 E
Cañar 246 2.33 S 78.56 W
Cañar □4 246 2.30 S 79.00 W
Canard ≃ 214 42.09 N 83.06 W
Canard, Lac au ⊜ 206 45.48 N 71.31 W
Canarias, Islas (Canary Islands) II 148 28.00 N 15.30 W
Canaries 241f 13.55 N 61.04 W
Canaro 64 44.56 N 11.40 E
Canarreos, Archipiélago de los II 240p 21.50 N 82.30 W
Canarsie ✦8 276 40.38 N 73.53 W
Canarsie Park ♦ 276 40.38 N 73.53 W
Canarsie Pol I 276 40.37 N 73.52 W
Canary Basin ✦1 10 30.00 N 25.00 W
Canary Islands → Canarias, Islas II 148 28.00 N 15.30 W
Cañas 236 10.25 N 85.07 W
Canaseraga 210 42.27 N 77.46 W
Canaseraga Creek ≃ 210 42.45 N 77.50 W
Cañasgordas 246 6.45 N 76.01 W
Canastota 210 43.04 N 75.45 W
Canatlán 232 24.31 N 104.47 W
Canaveral, Cape ≻ 220 28.27 N 80.32 W
Canaveral Bight c3 220 28.26 N 80.33 W
Canaveral National Seashore ♦ 220 28.45 N 80.45 W
Canaveral Peninsula ≻1 220 28.28 N 80.34 W
Cañaveras 34 40.22 N 2.24 W
Canavese □9 62 45.20 N 7.40 E
Canavieiras 255 15.39 S 38.57 W
Cañazas 236 8.19 N 81.13 W
Canazei 64 46.28 N 11.46 E
Canbelego 166 31.33 S 146.19 E
Canberra 171b 35.17 S 149.08 E
Canberra Wildlife Gardens ♦ 171b 35.20 S 149.09 E
Canby, Ca., U.S. 204 41.26 N 120.52 W
Canby, Mn., U.S. 198 44.42 N 96.16 W
Canby, Or., U.S. 224 45.15 N 122.41 W
Cancajanang, Mount ∧ 116 11.04 N 124.47 E
Cancale 32 48.41 N 1.51 W
Cancano, Lago di ⊜1 64 46.31 N 10.18 E
Cance ≃ 62 45.12 N 4.48 E
Cancellara 68 40.44 N 15.56 E
Cancello e Arnone 68 41.04 N 14.03 E
Canchaque 248 5.24 S 79.36 W
Canche ≃ 50 50.31 N 1.39 E
Cancon 32 44.32 N 0.38 E
Cancún 232 21.05 N 86.46 W
Čančur 88 53.49 N 106.59 E
Canda 64 45.03 N 11.30 E
Candala → Qandala 144 11.28 N 49.52 E
Candarave 248 17.16 S 70.15 W
Çandarlı 130 38.56 N 26.56 E
Çandarlı Körfezi c 130 38.52 N 26.55 E
Candás 34 43.35 N 5.46 W
Candé 32 47.34 N 1.02 W
Candeias, Bra. 255 12.40 S 38.33 W
Candeias, Bra. 255 20.47 S 45.16 W
Candeias ≃ 248 8.39 S 63.31 W
Candela, It. 68 41.08 N 15.31 E
Candela, Méx. 232 26.50 N 100.40 W
Candela, Río de ≃ 196 27.16 N 100.18 W
Candelaria, Arg. 252 27.28 S 55.44 W
Candelaria, Arg. 252 32.04 S 65.49 W
Candelária, Bra. 252 29.40 S 52.48 W
Candelaria, Col. 246 3.25 N 76.20 W
Candelaria, Cuba 240p 22.44 N 82.58 W
Candelaria, Pil. 116 15.38 N 119.56 E
Candelaria ≃ 232 18.37 N 91.14 W
Candelaria Loxicha 234 15.54 N 96.31 W
Candelaro ≃ 68 41.34 N 15.53 E
Candeleda 34 40.09 N 5.14 W
Candelo, Austl. 166 36.46 S 149.42 E
Candelo, It. 62 45.33 N 8.07 E
Candiac 206 45.23 N 73.31 W
Candia Canavese 62 45.20 N 7.53 E
Candia → Iráklion 38 35.20 N 25.09 E
Candia Lomellina 62 45.11 N 8.36 E
Cândido Aguilar 232 25.30 N 98.02 W
Cândido de Abreu 252 24.35 S 51.20 W
Cândido Mendes 250 1.27 S 45.43 W
Candies Creek ≃ 192 35.18 N 84.51 W
Candijay 116 9.49 N 124.30 E
Çandır, Tür. 130 40.16 N 33.29 E
Çandır, Tür. 130 39.15 N 35.32 E
Candle 180 65.55 N 161.56 W
Candle Lake ⊜ 184 53.50 N 105.18 W
Candlemas Islands II 18 57.03 S 26.40 W
Candlestick 194 32.15 N 90.20 W
Candlestick Park ♦ 282 37.43 N 122.23 W
Candlewood, Lake ⊜1 207 41.32 N 73.27 W
Candlewood Isle 207 41.28 N 73.27 W
Candlewood Knolls 207 41.28 N 73.27 W
Candlewood Shores 207 41.28 N 73.26 W
Čandman', Mong. 86 50.02 N 92.03 E
Čandman', Mong. 102 45.20 N 97.58 E
Cando, Ang. 152 16.30 S 18.19 E
Cando, Sk., Can. 184 52.23 N 108.14 W
Cando, N.D., U.S. 198 48.29 N 99.12 W
Candombé ≃ 152 16.54 S 21.52 E
Candon 116 17.12 N 120.27 E
Candon Point ≻ 116 17.13 N 120.24 E
Candor, N.Y., U.S. 210 42.13 N 76.20 W
Candor, N.C., U.S. 192 35.17 N 79.44 W
Candover 158 27.28 S 31.57 E
Cane ≃, Austl. 162 21.33 S 115.23 E
Cane ≃, La., U.S. 194 31.31 N 92.43 W
Cane ≃, N.C., U.S. 192 36.00 N 82.16 W
Caneadea 210 42.23 N 78.09 W
Canea → Khaniá 38 35.31 N 24.02 E
Caneças 266c 38.49 N 9.14 W
Cane Creek ≃ 194 36.29 N 90.28 W
Canegrate 266b 45.34 N 8.56 E
Canela 252 29.22 S 50.50 W
Canelas 232 25.06 N 106.34 W
Canelles, Embalse de ⊜1 34 42.10 N 0.30 E
Canelli 62 44.43 N 8.17 E
Canelones 258 34.32 S 56.17 W
Canelones □5 258 34.35 S 56.15 W
Canelón Grande, Arroyo ≃ 258 34.30 S 56.24 W
Cane Run ≃ 218 38.13 N 84.37 W
Cañete, Chile 252 37.48 S 73.24 W
Cañete, Esp. 34 40.03 N 1.35 W
Caneva 64 45.58 N 12.26 E
Caney 198 37.00 N 95.56 W
Caney ≃ 196 36.20 N 95.42 W
Caney Brook ≃ 276 41.07 N 73.50 W
Caney Creek ≃, Ar., U.S. 194 33.46 N 93.07 W
Caney Creek ≃, Tx., U.S. 196 28.46 N 95.39 W
Caney Creek ≃, Tx., U.S. 222 32.48 N 95.33 W
Caney Creek ≃, Tx., U.S. 222 30.28 N 95.38 W
Caney Creek ≃, Tx., U.S. 222 30.04 N 96.08 W
Caney Creek ≃, Tx., U.S. 222 31.52 N 96.13 W
Caney Creek ≃, Tx., U.S. 222 31.03 N 94.33 W
Caney Creek ≃, Tx., U.S. 222 30.53 N 95.48 W
Caney Creek ≃, Tx., U.S. 222 30.07 N 95.10 W
Canfield 214 41.01 N 80.45 W
Canfield Island I 276 41.06 N 73.23 W
Canfranc 34 42.43 N 0.31 W
Cangaíba ✦8 287b 23.30 S 46.31 W
Cangallo 248 13.33 S 74.12 W
Cangamba 152 13.40 S 19.54 E
Cangandala 152 9.45 S 16.33 E
Cangandala, Parque Nacional da ♦ 152 9.45 S 16.50 E
Cangas, Bra. 248 16.05 S 56.33 W
Cangas, Esp. 34 42.16 N 8.47 W
Cangas de Narcea 34 43.11 N 6.33 W
Cangas de Onís 34 43.21 N 5.07 W
Cangbu 100 30.49 N 114.35 E
Can Gioc ≃ 269c 10.42 N 106.37 E
Cangkuang, Tanjung ≻ 115a 6.51 S 105.15 E
Cangniutun 105 39.23 N 115.54 E
Cango Caves ⊥5 158 33.23 S 22.14 E
Cangola 152 7.58 S 15.52 E
Cangombe 152 14.24 S 19.59 E
Cangongo 152 9.24 S 17.30 E
Cangqian, Zhg. 106 30.17 N 120.25 E
Cangqian, Zhg. 106 30.17 N 119.52 E
Cangshangtun 105 40.03 N 117.32 E
Canguaretama 250 6.24 S 35.08 W
Canguçu 252 31.24 S 52.41 W
Canguera 256 23.36 S 47.09 W
Cangumbe 152 12.00 S 19.17 E
Cangwu 102 23.22 N 111.13 E
Cangxi 102 31.48 N 105.59 E
Čangyrtaš 85 40.53 N 72.50 E
Cangyuan 102 23.12 N 99.16 E
Cangzhou 98 38.19 N 116.51 E
Canhoca 152 9.15 S 14.41 E
Canhotinho 250 8.53 S 36.12 W
Caniapiscau ≃ 176 57.40 N 69.30 W
Caniapiscau, Lac ⊜ 176 54.10 N 69.55 W
Canicanian 116 14.46 N 122.01 E
Canicattì 70 37.21 N 13.51 E
Canicattini Bagni 70 37.02 N 15.04 E
Canigao Channel ⊍ 116 10.15 N 124.42 E
Canigou, Pic du ∧ 32 42.31 N 2.27 E
Canillas ✦8 266a 40.28 N 3.38 W
Canillejas ✦8 266a 40.27 N 3.37 W
Canim Lake 182 51.46 N 120.54 W
Canim Lake ⊜ 182 51.52 N 120.45 W
Canim Lake Indian Reserve ✦4 182 51.47 N 121.00 W
Canindé 250 4.22 S 39.19 W
Canindé ≃ 250 6.15 S 42.52 W
Canindeyú □5 252 24.15 S 55.15 W

Symbol	English	Deutsch	Español	Français	Português
≃	River	Fluß	Río	Rivière	Rio
≅	Canal	Kanal	Canal	Canal	Canal
⌊	Waterfall, Rapids	Wasserfall, Stromschnellen	Cascada, Rápidos	Chute d'eau, Rapides	Cascata, Rápidos
⊍	Strait	Meeresstraße	Estrecho	Détroit	Estreito
c	Bay, Gulf	Bucht, Golf	Bahía, Golfo	Baie, Golfe	Baía, Golfo
⊜	Lake, Lakes	See, Seen	Lago, Lagos	Lac, Lacs	Lago, Lagos
⩰	Swamp	Sumpf	Pantano	Marais	Pântano
⊠	Ice Features, Glacier	Eis- und Gletscherformen	Accidentes Glaciales	Formes glaciaires	Acidentes glaciares
⊤	Other Hydrographic Features	Andere Hydrographische Objekte	Otros Elementos Hidrográficos	Autres données hydrographiques	Outros acidentes hidrográficos
✦	Submarine Features	Untermeerische Objekte	Accidentes Submarinos	Formes de relief sous-marin	Acidentes submarinos
□	Political Unit	Politische Einheit	Unidad Política	Entité politique	Unidade política
⊕	Cultural Institution	Kulturelle Institution	Institución Cultural	Institution culturelle	Instituição cultural
⊥	Historical Site	Historische Stätte	Sitio Histórico	Site historique	Sítio histórico
♦	Recreational Site	Erholungs- und Ferienort	Sitio de Recreo	Centre de loisirs	Área de Lazer
⊠	Airport	Flughafen	Aeropuerto	Aéroport	Aeroporto
■	Military Installation	Militäranlage	Instalación Militar	Installation militaire	Instalação militar
✦	Miscellaneous	Verschiedenes	Misceláneo	Divers	Diversos

Canino 66 42.28 N 11.45 E
Canipaan 116 8.35 N 117.16 E
Canipo Island I 116 10.59 N 120.57 E
Canisius College ✦[2] 284a 42.55 N 78.52 W
Canisp ʌ 46 58.07 N 5.03 W
Canistear Reservoir ◎[1] 276 41.08 N 74.29 W
Canisteo 210 42.16 N 77.36 W
Canisteo ≃ 210 42.07 N 77.08 W
Canistota 198 43.35 N 97.17 W
Cañitas de Felipe Pescador 234 23.36 N 102.43 W
Canjáyar 34 37.00 N 2.44 W
Canjinge 152 10.12 S 21.17 E
Cankhor 144 10.46 N 46.13 E
Çankırı 130 40.36 N 33.37 E
Çankırı □[4] 130 40.45 N 33.25 E
Canlaon 116 10.22 N 123.12 E
Canlaon Volcano ʌ[1] 116 10.25 N 123.08 E
Canley Vale 274a 33.53 S 150.57 E
Canmore 182 51.05 N 115.21 W
Canna 68 44.25 N 7.30 E
Canna I 46 57.04 N 6.34 W
Canna, Sound of ⊻ 46 57.03 N 6.25 W
Cannanore 122 11.51 N 75.22 E
Cannara 66 43.00 N 12.35 E
Canne ⊥ 68 41.18 N 16.09 E
Cannel City 192 37.47 N 83.16 W
Cannelton 194 37.54 N 86.44 W
Canner ≃ 56 49.24 N 6.16 E
Cannero-Riviera 58 46.01 N 8.41 E
Cannes 62 43.33 N 7.01 E
Cannes, Bayou des ≃ 194 30.12 N 92.35 W
Canneto, It. 66 43.12 N 10.44 E
Canneto, It. 70 38.29 N 14.58 E
Canneto sull'Oglio 64 45.09 N 10.25 E
Cannich 46 57.21 N 4.46 W
Cannich ≃ 46 57.21 N 4.44 W
Cannifton 212 44.12 N 77.23 W
Canning, Arg. 288 34.53 S 58.30 W
Canning, Austl. 168a 32.02 S 115.56 E
Canning, N.S., Can. 186 45.09 N 64.25 W
Canning ≃, Austl. 168a 32.01 S 115.51 E
Canning ≃, Ak., U.S. 180 70.05 N 145.30 W
Canning Hill ʌ[2] 162 28.50 S 117.49 E
Canning Lake ◎ 212 44.56 N 78.38 W
Canning Reservoir ◎[1] 168a 32.10 S 116.09 E
Cannington, On., Can. 212 44.21 N 79.02 W
Cannington, Eng., U.K. 42 51.09 N 3.04 W
Cannobio 58 46.04 N 8.42 E
Cannock 42 52.42 N 2.09 W
Cannock Chase ✦[1] 42 52.43 N 2.00 W
Cannon ≃ 190 44.35 N 92.33 W
Cannon Air Force Base ■ 196 34.23 N 103.18 W
Cannon Ball 198 46.23 N 100.35 W
Cannonball ≃ 198 46.26 N 100.38 W
Cannon Beach 224 45.53 N 123.57 W
Cannondale 207 41.12 N 73.25 W
Cannon Falls 190 44.30 N 92.54 W
Cannonsburg 216 43.03 N 85.28 W
Cannonsville Reservoir ◎[1] 210 42.08 N 75.19 W
Cannonvale 166 20.17 S 148.42 E
Cann River 166 37.34 S 149.10 E
Caño, Isla del I 236 8.44 N 83.53 W
Canoas 252 29.56 S 51.11 W
Canoas ≃, Bra. 252 27.36 S 51.25 W
Canoas ≃, Bra. 256 21.30 S 47.09 W
Canobie Lake 283 42.48 N 71.14 W
Canobie Lake ◎ 283 42.49 N 71.15 W
Canobie Lake Park ◆ 283 42.48 N 71.15 W
Canoe 182 50.45 N 119.13 W
Canoe ≃, B.C., Can. 182 52.09 N 118.27 W
Canoe ≃, Ma., U.S. 283 41.58 N 71.08 W
Canoe Brook ≃ 276 40.45 N 74.22 W
Canoe Brook Reservoirs ◎[1] 276 40.45 N 74.21 W
Canoe Creek Indian Reserve ✦[4] 182 51.32 N 122.15 W
Canoe Lake ◎ 184 55.11 N 108.15 W
Canoe Lake Indian Reserve ✦[4] 184 55.08 N 108.12 W
Canoga Park ✦[8] 280 34.12 N 118.35 W
Canoinhas 252 26.10 S 50.24 W
Canol 180 65.14 N 126.56 W
Canon 192 34.21 N 83.07 W
Canon ≃ 224 46.36 N 123.53 W
Canonbie 44 55.05 N 2.57 W
Canon City 200 38.24 N 105.13 W
Cañón del Sumidero, Parque Nacional ◆ 234 16.45 N 93.05 W
Caño Negro 236 10.54 N 84.44 W
Canonsburg 214 40.15 N 80.11 W
Canonsburg Lake ◎ 279b 40.16 N 80.07 W
Canoochee ≃ 192 31.59 N 81.18 W
Canoole Cise 144 2.02 N 42.19 E
Canopus ⊥ 142 31.18 N 30.03 E
Canora 184 51.37 N 102.26 W
Canosa di Puglia 68 41.13 N 16.04 E
Canossa ⊥ 64 44.35 N 10.27 E
Canot, Pointe › 241o 16.12 N 61.28 W
Canouan I 238 12.43 N 61.20 W
Canova 198 43.52 N 97.30 W
Canova Beach 220 28.08 N 80.34 W
Cañovanas 240m 18.23 N 65.54 W
Cánoves ≃ 266d 41.37 N 2.22 E
Canow 54 53.12 N 12.54 E
Canowindra 166 33.34 S 148.38 E
Can Quer, Torrente de ≃ 266d 41.31 N 2.11 E
Cansado 148 20.51 N 17.02 W
Cansanção 250 10.41 S 39.31 W
Canso 186 45.20 N 61.00 W
Canso, Strait of ⊻ 186 45.37 N 61.25 W
Canta 248 11.25 S 76.38 W
Cantabria 234 19.50 N 101.44 W
Cantabria (Santander) □[4], Esp. 34 43.15 N 4.00 W
Cantabria □[4], Esp. 34 43.15 N 4.00 W
Cantábrica, Cordillera ⋏ 34 43.00 N 5.00 W
Cantabriques — Cantábrica, Cordillera ⋏ 34 43.00 N 5.00 W
Cantagalo 255 21.58 S 42.22 W
Cantagalo, Cachoeira ⌊ 250 7.18 S 54.52 W
Cantal □[5] 32 45.05 N 2.45 E
Cantalejo 34 41.15 N 3.55 W
Cantalupo in Sabina 66 42.18 N 12.39 E
Cantalupo nel Sannio 66 41.31 N 14.24 E
Čantal'vejergyn ≃ 180 67.38 N 179.22 W
Cantanhede, Bra. 250 3.39 S 44.24 W
Cantanhede, Port. 34 40.21 N 8.36 W
Cantareira ✦[8] 287b 23.27 S 46.37 W
Cantareira, Serra da ⋏ 287b 23.25 S 46.39 W
Cantaura 246 9.19 N 64.21 W
Cant Clough Reservoir ◎[1] 262 53.46 N 2.09 W
Canteleu 50 49.27 N 1.02 E
Canterbury, Austl. 274a 33.55 S 151.07 E
Canterbury, Austl. 274b 37.49 S 145.05 E
Canterbury, N.B., Can. 186 45.53 N 67.29 W
Canterbury, Eng., U.K. 42 51.17 N 1.05 E
Canterbury Bight ⊂[3] 172 44.15 S 171.38 E
Canterbury Cathedral ✝[1] 42 51.17 N 1.05 E
Canterbury Park Racecourse ◆ 274a 33.54 S 151.07 E
Canterbury Plains ≚ 172 44.00 S 171.45 E
Canterbury Woods 284c 38.49 N 77.15 W
Can Tho 110 10.02 N 105.47 E
Cantiano 66 43.28 N 12.38 E
Cantil 228 35.18 N 117.58 W
Cantiles, Cayo I 240p 21.36 N 82.02 W
Cantin Lake ◎ 184 53.27 N 95.10 W
Canto do Buriti 250 8.07 S 42.58 W
Canto do Pontes 287a 22.58 S 43.04 W
Canto Grande, Quebrada V 286d 11.59 S 77.01 W
Cantoira 62 45.21 N 7.23 E
Canton, Ct., U.S. 207 41.49 N 72.53 W
Canton, Ga., U.S. 192 34.14 N 84.29 W
Canton, Il., U.S. 190 40.33 N 90.02 W
Canton, Ks., U.S. 198 38.23 N 97.25 W
Canton, Ma., U.S. 207 42.09 N 71.08 W
Canton, Mn., U.S. 190 43.31 N 91.55 W
Canton, Ms., U.S. 194 32.36 N 90.02 W
Canton, Mo., U.S. 219 40.07 N 91.37 W
Canton, N.J., U.S. 208 39.28 N 75.24 W
Canton, N.Y., U.S. 188 44.35 N 75.10 W
Canton, N.C., U.S. 192 35.31 N 82.50 W
Canton, Oh., U.S. 214 40.47 N 81.22 W
Canton, Ok., U.S. 196 36.03 N 98.35 W
Canton, Pa., U.S. 210 41.39 N 76.51 W
Canton, S.D., U.S. 198 43.18 N 96.35 W
Canton, Tx., U.S. 222 32.33 N 95.51 W
Canton Airport ✈ 174h 2.46 S 171.43 W
Canton — Guangzhou 100 23.06 N 113.16 E
Canton — Kanton I 174h 2.50 S 171.40 W
Canton Lake ◎[1] 196 36.08 N 98.36 W
Canton Lake State Recreational Area ◆ 196 36.08 N 98.39 W
Cantonment 194 30.36 N 87.20 W
Cantorbéry — Canterbury 42 51.17 N 1.05 E
Cantrall 219 39.56 N 89.41 W
Cantribana 266c 38.53 N 9.25 W
Cantù 62 45.44 N 9.08 E
Cantu ≃ 252 24.46 S 52.54 W
Cantua Creek 226 36.30 N 120.19 W
Cantua Creek ≃ 226 36.28 N 120.17 W
Cantwell 180 63.23 N 148.57 W
Cañuelas 258 35.03 S 58.44 W
Cañuelas □[5] 288 34.56 S 58.41 W
Cañuelas, Arroyo ≃ 288 34.55 S 58.38 W
Canumã 246 4.02 S 59.04 W
Canumã ≃ 246 3.55 S 59.10 W
Canungra 171a 28.01 S 153.10 E
Canungra Creek ≃ 171a 27.55 S 153.06 E
Canungra Jungle Training Ground ■ 171a 28.02 S 153.10 E
Canutama 248 6.32 S 64.20 W
Canutillo 200 31.54 N 106.35 W
Canvastown 172 41.18 S 173.40 E
Canvey Island 42 51.32 N 0.36 E
Canvey Island I 42 51.33 N 0.34 E
Čany 86 55.19 N 76.46 E
Čany, ozero ◎ 86 54.50 N 77.30 E
Cany-Barville 50 49.47 N 0.38 E
Canyon, Yk., Can. 180 60.52 N 137.02 W
Canyon, Ca., U.S. 282 37.49 N 122.09 W
Canyon, Tx., U.S. 196 34.58 N 101.55 W
Canyon City 202 44.23 N 118.56 W
Canyon Country 228 34.25 N 118.28 W
Canyon Creek 182 55.22 N 115.05 W
Canyon Creek ≃, Az., U.S. 200 33.49 N 110.40 W
Canyon Creek ≃, Ca., U.S. 226 39.22 N 120.45 W
Canyon Creek ≃, Id., U.S. 202 42.59 N 115.59 W
Canyon Creek ≃, Wa., U.S. 224 45.57 N 122.22 W
Canyon Creek ≃, Wa., U.S. 224 48.43 N 120.55 W
Canyon de Chelly National Monument ◆ 200 36.01 N 109.26 W
Canyon Ferry Lake ◎[1] 202 46.33 N 111.37 W
Canyon Lake ◎[1] 196 29.52 N 98.16 W
Canyonlands National Park ◆ 200 38.10 N 110.00 W
Canyonville 202 42.55 N 123.16 W
Canzar 152 7.38 S 21.32 E
Canzo 62 45.51 N 9.16 E
Cao ≃, Zhg. 98 40.29 N 124.08 E
Cao ≃, Zhg. 105 38.52 N 115.46 E
Cao Bang 110 22.40 N 106.15 E
Caochi 107 30.19 N 104.24 E
Caocun 106 31.42 N 118.56 E
Caodian, Zhg. 106 28.39 N 120.23 E
Caodian, Zhg. 100 33.21 N 112.39 E
Caodian, Zhg. 102 32.32 N 111.11 E
Cao'e 100 30.01 N 120.52 E
Cao'e ≃ 100 30.06 N 120.46 E
Caofang 100 26.04 N 116.35 E
Caogezhai 105 40.09 N 117.50 E
Caohe, Zhg. 105 38.57 N 115.32 E
Caohe, Zhg. 269b 31.09 N 121.25 E
Caohecheng 104 40.46 N 124.02 E
Caohekou 104 40.54 N 123.53 E
Caohezhang 104 41.04 N 124.03 E
Caojian 102 25.38 N 99.07 E
Caojiawopeng 104 42.00 N 122.20 E
Caojiawopu 104 42.37 N 122.19 E
Caojiawu 105 39.24 N 116.31 E
Caojiazhen 106 31.55 N 121.38 E
Caojiezi 107 29.53 N 106.24 E
Caojing 106 30.47 N 121.24 E
Caojun 100 29.41 N 116.17 E
Cao Lanh 110 10.27 N 105.38 E
Caolaoji 100 33.06 N 117.22 E
Caolisport, Loch ⊂ 46 55.54 N 5.37 W
Caomaji 98 34.52 N 116.17 E
Caombo 152 8.43 S 16.51 E
Caonao ≃ 240p 22.05 N 78.05 W
Caoniao 106 32.56 N 120.20 E
Caonillas, Lago ◎ 240m 18.16 N 66.39 W
Caopeng 106 31.44 N 121.17 E
Caoping 100 28.48 N 118.22 E
Caopu 98 34.34 N 118.52 E
Caoqiao 106 31.32 N 119.59 E
Caorle 64 45.36 N 12.53 E
Caorso 62 45.03 N 9.52 E
Caoshi, Zhg. 98 42.17 N 125.16 E
Caoshi, Zhg. 100 33.32 N 116.29 E
Caota 100 29.42 N 120.08 E
Caotang 100 31.16 N 118.59 E
Caoxi 100 28.42 N 117.18 E
Caoxian 98 34.53 N 115.33 E
Caoyangxi 100 26.34 N 118.47 E
Cap, Le — Cape Town 158 33.55 S 18.22 E
Cap, Pointe du › 241f 14.07 N 60.57 W
Capac 190 43.00 N 82.55 W
Capaccio 68 40.25 N 15.05 E
Capacciotti, Lago di ◎[1] 68 41.10 N 15.47 E
Capaci 70 38.10 N 13.14 E
Capage 152 13.21 S 21.05 E
Čapajev 80 50.12 N 51.10 E
Čapajevka, Ross. 82 54.38 N 35.50 E
Čapajevka, Ukr. 78 49.33 N 32.06 E
Čapajevka, Ukr. 78 49.23 N 30.26 E
Čapajevka, Ukr. 78 47.29 N 36.20 E
Čapajevo 80 53.08 N 49.37 E
Čapajevo 78 49.21 N 35.54 E
Čapajevsk 80 52.58 N 49.41 E
Capala 152 13.37 S 14.45 E
Capalbio 66 42.27 N 11.25 E
Capalonga 116 14.20 N 122.30 E
Capanaparo ≃ 246 7.01 N 67.07 W
Capanema, Bra. 250 1.12 S 47.11 W
Capanema, Bra. 252 25.40 S 53.48 W
Capangombe 152 15.05 S 13.08 E
Capanne, Monte ʌ 66 42.46 N 10.10 E
Capannoli 66 43.35 N 10.41 E
Capannori 66 43.50 N 10.34 E
Capão Bonito 255 24.01 S 48.20 W
Capão Doce, Morro do ʌ 252 26.43 S 51.25 W
Capão Redondo ✦[8] 287b 23.40 S 46.46 W
Capaotigamau, Lac ◎ 186 50.18 N 68.14 W
Caparaó, Parque Nacional do ◆ 255 20.33 S 41.45 W
Caparica 266c 38.40 N 9.12 W
Caparo Viejo ≃ 246 7.46 N 70.23 W
Capas 116 15.20 N 120.35 E
Capatárida 246 11.11 N 70.37 W
Cap-aux-Meules (Grindstone Island) 186 47.23 N 61.52 W
Cap aux Meules, Île du I 186 47.23 N 61.54 W
Capay 226 38.32 N 122.03 W
Cap-Chat 186 49.06 N 66.42 W
Cap-de-la-Madeleine 206 46.22 N 72.31 W
Cape (Kaap) □[4] 156 31.00 S 23.00 E
Cape ≃ 166 20.49 S 146.51 E
Cape Arid National Park ◆ 162 33.40 S 123.25 E
Cape Barren Island I 166 40.25 S 148.12 E
Cape Basin ✦[1] 8 37.00 S 7.00 E
Cape Bougainville Aboriginal Reserve ✦[4] 164 14.10 S 126.30 E
Cape Breton Highlands National Park ◆ 186 46.45 N 60.45 W
Cape Breton Island I 186 46.00 N 60.30 W
Cape Broyle 186 47.06 N 52.57 W
Cape Canaveral 220 28.24 N 80.36 W
Cape Canaveral Air Force Station ■ 220 28.29 N 80.35 W
Cape Charles 208 37.16 N 76.01 W
Cape Coast 150 5.05 N 1.15 W
Cape Cod Bay ⊂ 207 41.52 N 70.22 W
Cape Cod Canal ≃ 207 41.47 N 70.30 W
Cape Cod National Seashore ◆ 207 41.56 N 70.00 W
Cape Comorin — Kanniyākumari 122 8.05 N 77.34 E
Cape Coral 220 26.33 N 81.56 W
Cape Croker Indian Reserve ✦[4] 212 44.55 N 81.01 W
Cape Dorset 176 64.14 N 76.32 W
Cape Elizabeth 188 43.33 N 70.12 W
Cape Fear ≃ 192 33.53 N 78.00 W
Cape Girardeau 194 37.18 N 89.31 W
Cape Hatteras National Seashore ◆ 192 35.30 N 76.35 W
Cape Henlopen State Park ◆ 208 38.45 N 75.06 W
Cape Jervis 168b 35.36 S 138.06 E
Cape Johnson Tablemount ✦[3] 14 17.08 N 177.15 W
Cape Krusenstern National Monument ◆ 180 67.30 N 163.40 W
Capela 250 10.30 S 37.04 W
Cape LaHave Island I 186 44.12 N 64.22 W
Capela la Hune 186 47.33 N 56.52 W
Capel Curig 44 53.06 N 3.54 W
Capelengue 152 9.12 S 19.43 E
Capelinha 255 17.42 S 42.31 W
Capelinha do Embirazal 256 22.02 S 45.26 W
Cape Lisburne 180 68.52 N 166.05 W
Capel'ka 76 58.03 N 28.59 E
Capella 166 23.05 S 148.02 E
Capella ʌ 164 5.00 S 141.05 E
Capelle [aan de IJssel] 52 51.55 N 4.35 E
Capellen 56 49.38 N 5.59 E
Capelongo 152 14.54 S 15.08 E
Cape Lookout National Seashore ◆ 192 34.40 N 76.23 W
Cape Lookout State Park ◆ 224 45.21 N 123.59 W
Capel Saint Mary 42 52.00 N 1.04 E
Cape May 208 38.56 N 74.54 W
Cape May □[6] 208 38.56 N 74.55 W
Cape May Coast Guard Air Station ■ 208 38.57 N 74.53 W
Cape May Court House 208 39.04 N 74.49 W
Cape May Point 208 38.56 N 74.56 W
Capembe ≃ 152 16.10 S 21.00 E
Cape Melville National Park ◆ 164 14.20 S 144.30 E
Capenda Camulemba 152 9.24 S 18.27 E
Capenga ≃ 287a 22.49 S 43.37 W
Capenhurst 262 53.15 N 2.57 W
Cape of Good Hope Nature Reserve ◆ 158 34.18 S 18.26 E
Cape Pole 180 55.58 N 133.48 W
Cape Pond ◎ 283 42.38 N 70.38 W
Cape Porpoise 188 43.22 N 70.26 W
Cape Range National Park ◆ 162 22.10 S 113.55 E
Cape Rise ✦[3] 8 42.00 S 15.00 E
Capernaum — Kefar Naḥum ⊥ 132 32.53 N 35.34 E
Cape Romanzof 180 61.49 N 165.56 W
Capertee 170 33.09 S 149.59 E
Capertee ≃ 170 33.12 S 150.28 E
Cape Sable Island I 186 43.25 N 65.37 W
Cape Scott Provincial Park ◆ 182 50.45 N 128.20 W
Capesterre 241o 15.54 N 61.13 W
Capesterre, Pointe de la › 241o 16.03 N 61.33 W
Capesterre-Belle-Eau 241o 16.03 N 61.34 W
Capesthorne Hall ⊥ 262 53.15 N 2.14 W
Capestrano 66 42.16 N 13.46 E
Capetinga ≃ 256 22.04 S 47.14 W
Cape Tormentine 186 46.08 N 63.47 W
Cape Town (Kaapstad) 158 33.55 S 18.22 E
Cape Verde (Cabo Verde) □[1] 134 16.00 N 24.00 W
Cape Verde (Cabo Verde) □[1], Afr. 150a 16.00 N 24.00 W
Cape Verde Basin ✦[1] 8 15.00 N 30.00 W
Cape Verde Islands — Cape Verde □[1] 150a 16.00 N 24.00 W
Cape Verde Terrace ✦[3] 10 18.00 N 20.00 W
Capeville 208 37.12 N 75.57 W
Cape Vincent 212 44.07 N 76.19 W
Cape Yakataga 180 60.04 N 142.26 W
Cape York Peninsula ›[1] 164 14.00 S 142.30 E
Cap-Haïtien 238 19.45 N 72.12 W
Capilla de Farruco 252 32.53 S 55.25 W
Capilla del Monte 252 30.51 S 64.31 W
Capilla del Señor 258 34.18 S 59.06 W
Capim ≃ 250 1.40 S 47.47 W
Capim Melado, Morro do ʌ 287a 22.50 S 43.29 W
Capinas Point › 116 11.05 N 125.14 E
Capinópolis 255 18.41 S 49.35 W
Capinota 248 17.43 S 66.14 W
Capinzal 252 27.20 S 51.36 W
Capira 236 8.45 N 79.53 W
Cap Island I 116 5.57 N 120.06 E
Capistrano, Bra. 250 4.28 S 38.55 W
Capistrano, It. 68 38.41 N 16.17 E
Capistrano Beach 228 33.27 N 117.40 W
Capistrello 66 41.57 N 13.23 E
Capitachouane ≃ 190 47.36 N 76.54 W
Capitachouane, Lac ◎ 190 48.05 N 75.55 W
Capital Airport ✈ 219 39.51 N 89.41 W
Capital Centre ✦ 284c 38.54 N 76.51 W
Capital City Airport ✈ 216 42.47 N 84.35 W
Capitan 200 33.32 N 105.34 W
Capitán Aracena, Isla I 254 54.10 S 71.20 W
Capitán Arturo Prat ✝[3] 9 62.30 S 59.41 W
Capitán Bado 255 23.16 S 55.32 W
Capitán Bermúdez 252 32.49 S 60.43 W
Capitán Meza 252 26.55 S 55.15 W
Capitan Peak ʌ 200 33.36 N 105.16 W
Capitán Sarmiento 252 34.10 S 59.48 W
Capitão de Campos 250 4.28 S 41.57 W
Capitão Enéas 255 16.21 S 43.43 W
Capitola 226 36.58 N 121.57 W
Capitol Heights 208 38.53 N 76.54 W
Capitol Park 208 39.08 N 75.30 W
Capitol Peak ʌ 204 41.50 N 117.18 W
Capitol Reef National Park ◆ 200 38.11 N 111.20 W
Capitol View 192 33.57 N 80.56 W
Capivari 255 23.00 S 47.31 W
Capivari ≃, Bra. 248 19.16 S 57.10 W
Capivari ≃, Bra. 255 12.30 S 39.55 W
Capivari ≃, Bra. 256 22.14 S 44.57 W
Capivari ≃, Bra. 256 21.53 S 46.15 W
Capivari ≃, Bra. 256 22.26 S 45.47 W
Capivari ≃, Bra. 256 24.09 S 46.48 W
Capivari ≃, Bra. 256 22.56 S 47.16 W
Capivari ≃, Bra. 256 21.30 S 44.20 W
Capivari ≃, Bra. 256 21.12 S 44.52 W
Capivari, Canal ≃ 287a 22.42 S 43.21 W
Capiz □[4] 116 11.30 N 122.30 E
Capiz — Roxas 116 11.35 N 122.45 E
Capizzi 70 37.51 N 14.29 E
Caplan 186 48.06 N 65.41 W
Čaplejevka 78 51.43 N 33.12 E
Caplen 222 29.29 N 94.33 W
Caples Lake ◎[1] 226 38.42 N 120.03 W
Caplina ≃ 248 18.14 S 70.33 W
Čaplinka 78 46.23 N 33.32 E
Čaplino, Ross. 180 64.25 N 172.15 W
Čaplino, Ukr. 78 48.09 N 36.14 E
Čapljina 36 43.07 N 17.42 E
Caplone, Monte ʌ 64 45.48 N 10.38 E
Čaplygin 76 53.14 N 39.58 E
Cap Mountain ʌ 180 63.25 N 123.29 W
Capnoyan Island I 116 10.44 N 120.54 E
Capoche ≃ 154 15.23 S 32.53 E
Capodichino, Aeroporto di ✈ 68 40.50 N 14.17 E
Capodimonte 66 42.33 N 11.55 E
Capo di Ponte 64 46.02 N 10.21 E
Capo d'Orlando 70 38.10 N 14.53 E
Capoeira, Corredeira ⌊ 250 6.48 S 58.21 W
Capolago 58 45.55 N 8.59 E
Capoliveri 66 42.45 N 10.22 E
Caporolo ≃ 152 12.56 S 13.00 E
Caposele 68 40.49 N 15.13 E
Capostrada 66 43.57 N 10.54 E
Capot ≃ 240e 14.51 N 61.05 W
Capoterra 71 39.11 N 8.58 E
Capoti-an, Mount ʌ 116 11.45 N 125.15 E
Capotoan, Mount ʌ 116 12.09 N 124.57 E
Cappadocia □[9] 130 38.30 N 36.00 E
Cappamore 48 52.37 N 8.20 W
Cap-Pelé 186 46.13 N 64.18 W
Cappella Islands II 240m 18.17 N 64.54 W
Cappelle 66 42.03 N 13.22 E
Cappelle sul Tavo 66 42.28 N 14.06 E
Cappeln 52 52.48 N 8.07 E
Cappenberg 263 51.39 N 7.32 E
Cappenberg, Schloss ⊥ 263 51.39 N 7.32 E
Cappercleuch 44 55.29 N 3.12 W
Cappoquin 48 52.08 N 7.50 W
Capracotta 66 41.50 N 14.16 E
Capraia 66 43.03 N 9.50 E
Capraia, Isola I 66 42.08 N 15.31 E
Capraia, Isola di I 66 43.02 N 9.49 E
Capranica 66 42.15 N 12.11 E
Caprara, Punta › 71 41.07 N 8.19 E
Caprarola 66 42.19 N 12.14 E
Capreol 190 46.43 N 80.56 W
Caprera, Isola I 71 41.12 N 9.28 E
Caprese Michelangelo 66 43.39 N 11.59 E
Capri 68 40.33 N 14.14 E
Capri, Isola di I 68 40.33 N 14.13 E
Capriati a Volturno 68 41.28 N 14.08 E
Capricorn, Cape › 166 23.30 S 151.13 E
Capricorn Channel ⊻ 166 23.00 S 152.20 E
Capricorn Group II 166 23.28 S 152.00 E
Capri Leone 70 38.05 N 14.44 E
Caprino Veronese 64 45.36 N 10.47 E
Caprivi Oss □[5] 156 17.45 S 24.00 E
Caprivi Zipfel (Caprivi Strip) □[9] 156 17.59 S 23.00 E
Caprolace, Lago di ◎ 66 41.21 N 12.58 E
Capron, Il., U.S. 216 42.24 N 88.44 W
Capron, Va., U.S. 208 36.42 N 77.12 W
Cap Saint Jacques — Vung Tau 110 10.21 N 107.04 E
Cap-Santé 206 46.40 N 71.47 W
Capstone 260 51.21 N 0.34 E
Captain Anthony Meldahl Dam ✦[6] 218 38.48 N 84.11 W
Captain Cook 229d 19.29 N 155.55 W
Captain Cook Bridge ✦[5] 274a 34.00 S 151.08 E
Captain Cook Landing Place Park ⊥ 274a 34.00 S 151.14 E
Captain Cook Monument ⊥ 174c 29.00 S 167.56 E
Captain Daniel Wright Woods ◆ 278 42.13 N 87.56 W
Captain Harbor ⊂ 276 41.00 N 73.36 W
Captain Pond ◎ 283 42.48 N 71.10 W
Captains Flat 171b 35.35 S 149.27 E
Captieux 32 44.18 N 0.16 W
Captina Creek ≃ 188 39.52 N 80.48 W
Captiva 220 26.31 N 82.11 W
Captiva Island I 220 26.31 N 82.11 W
Captree Island I 276 40.39 N 73.16 W
Captree State Park ◆ 276 40.39 N 73.16 W
Capua 68 41.06 N 14.12 E
Capual Island I 116 6.02 N 121.24 E
Capuáva 287b 23.39 S 46.29 W
Capuça 152 17.22 S 21.18 E
Capucapu ≃ 246 1.45 S 58.35 W
Capucin › 240d 15.38 N 61.28 W
Capul 116 12.25 N 124.11 E
Capulín, Río del ≃ 196 27.31 N 101.33 W
Capulin Mountain National Monument ◆ 196 36.48 N 103.55 W
Capul Island I 116 12.26 N 124.10 E
Capuna 152 15.38 S 19.43 E
Capunda 152 14.57 S 14.03 E
Capurro 258 34.25 S 56.28 W
Capurso 68 41.03 N 16.55 E
Caputh 54 52.21 N 13.00 E
Cap-Vert — Cape Verde □[1] 150a 16.00 N 24.00 W
Caquende 256 21.20 S 44.33 W
Caquetá □[5] 246 1.00 N 74.00 W
Caquetá (Japurá) ≃ 246 3.08 S 64.46 W
Caquiaviri 248 17.03 S 68.38 W
Čar ≃ 86 50.22 N 80.55 E
Čara, Ityo. 144 5.52 N 37.12 E
Čara, Ross. 88 56.54 N 118.12 E
Čara ≃ 74 60.22 N 120.50 E
Cará, Ilha do I 250 0.01 S 50.50 W
Caraballeda 286c 10.37 N 66.50 W
Caraballeda, Punta › 286c 10.37 N 66.51 W
Carabanchel Alto ✦[8] 266a 40.22 N 3.45 W
Carabanchel Bajo ✦[8] 266a 40.23 N 3.47 W
Carabao Island I 116 12.04 N 121.56 E
Carabaya ≃ 248 14.43 S 70.17 W
Carabaya, Cordillera de ⋏ 248 13.50 S 70.45 W

ENGLISH — Name, Page, Lat.°′, Long.°′ · DEUTSCH — Name, Seite, Breite°′, Länge°′ E = Ost

Carabayllo 286d 11.52 S 77.02 W
Carabelas Grande ≃ 258 34.15 S 58.43 W
Carabinani ≃ 246 1.58 S 61.31 W
Carabobo □[3] 246 10.10 N 68.05 W
Carabost 171b 35.36 S 147.44 E
Caracal 38 44.07 N 24.21 E
Caracalla, Terme di ⊥ 267a 41.53 N 12.29 E
Caracaraí 246 1.50 N 61.08 W
Caracas, Ven. 246 10.30 N 66.56 W
Caracas, Ven. 286c 10.30 N 66.56 W
Čarach 86 59.03 N 62.15 E
Carache 246 9.38 N 70.14 W
Caracol, Bra. 250 9.17 S 43.20 W
Caracol, Bra. 252 22.01 S 57.02 W
Caracollo 248 17.39 S 67.10 W
Caracorum — Karakoram Range ⋏ 120 35.30 N 77.00 E
Carácuaro de Morelos 234 18.46 N 101.02 W
Caradoc Indian Reserve ✦[4] 214 42.48 N 81.29 W
Caraffa di Catanzaro 68 38.53 N 16.29 E
Caraga 116 7.20 N 126.34 E
Caraga ≃ 116 7.20 N 126.34 E
Caragh, Lough ◎ 48 52.03 N 9.52 W
Caraghnan Mountain ʌ 166 31.20 S 149.03 E
Caraglio 62 44.25 N 7.26 E
Caraguata, Arroyo ≃ 288 34.24 S 58.38 W
Caraguatatuba 256 23.37 S 45.25 W
Caraguatatuba, Enseada de ⊂ 256 23.40 S 45.20 W
Caraguatay 252 25.14 S 56.52 W
Caraí 255 17.12 S 41.42 W
Caraibamba 248 14.24 S 73.09 W
Caraïbes, Îles des — West Indies II 230 19.00 N 70.00 W
Caraïbes, Mer des — Caribbean Sea ✦[2] 230 15.00 N 73.00 W
Caraigres, Cerro ʌ 236 9.43 N 84.05 W
Caraíva ≃ 255 16.48 S 39.08 W
Carajari ≃ 250 4.45 S 54.20 W
Carajás 250 6.06 S 50.23 W
Carajás, Serra dos ⋏ 250 5.50 S 51.20 W
Caralue Bluff ʌ[2] 166 33.26 S 136.16 E
Caramagna-Piemonte 62 44.46 N 7.44 E
Caramanico Terme 66 42.09 N 14.00 E
Caramay 116 10.11 N 119.14 E
Caramoan 116 13.46 N 123.52 E
Caramoan Peninsula ›[1] 116 13.48 N 123.40 E
Caramoran 116 13.59 N 124.08 E
Caramy ≃ 62 43.26 N 6.12 E
Caranavi 248 15.46 S 67.36 W
Carandaí 255 20.57 S 43.48 W
Carandayti 248 20.45 S 63.04 W
Carangola 255 20.44 S 42.02 W
Carano 64 46.16 N 11.27 E
Caransebeş 38 45.25 N 22.13 E
Carapá ≃ 252 24.30 S 54.20 W
Carapachay ✦[1] 288 34.25 S 58.35 W
Carapajó 250 2.16 S 49.22 W
Cara-Paraná ≃ 246 1.45 S 73.13 W
Carapeguá 252 25.48 S 57.14 W
Carapelle ≃ 68 41.30 N 15.55 E
Carapicuíba 256 23.31 S 46.50 W
Carapicuíba □[7] 287b 23.31 S 46.53 W
Carapo ≃ 246 7.30 N 64.02 W
Caraquet 186 47.48 N 64.57 W
Caráquez ⊂ 246 0.36 S 80.25 W
Carare ≃ 246 6.48 N 74.06 W
Carasco 62 44.21 N 9.21 E
Caraş-Severin □[6] 38 45.00 N 22.00 E
Caratasca, Laguna de ⊂ 236 15.23 N 83.55 W
Carate Brianza 62 45.41 N 9.14 E
Caratinga 255 19.47 S 42.08 W
Carauari 246 4.52 S 66.54 W
Caraúbas 250 5.47 S 37.34 W
Caravaca 34 38.06 N 1.51 W
Caravaggio 62 45.30 N 9.38 E
Caravela, Ilha I 150 11.30 N 16.20 W
Caravelas 255 17.45 S 39.15 W
Caraveli 248 15.46 S 73.22 W
Caravelle, Presqu'île de la ›[1] 240e 14.45 N 60.55 W
Caravius, Monte is ʌ 71 39.09 N 8.49 E
Caraway 194 35.45 N 90.19 W
Carayaó 252 25.10 S 56.26 W
Caraz 248 9.03 S 77.45 W
Caraza ✦[8] 288 34.42 S 58.26 W
Carazinho 252 28.18 S 52.48 W
Carazo □[5] 236 11.45 N 86.15 W
Carballiño 34 42.26 N 8.04 W
Carballo 34 43.13 N 8.41 W
Carberry 184 49.52 N 99.20 W
Carbet, Pitons du ⋏ 240e 14.42 N 61.07 W
Carbo 232 29.42 N 110.58 W
Carbol ≃ 70 37.32 N 12.59 E
Carbon, Ab., Can. 182 51.29 N 113.09 W
Carbon, Pa., U.S. 279b 40.17 N 79.34 W
Carbon, Tx., U.S. 196 32.16 N 98.50 W
Carbon □[6] 210 40.52 N 75.45 W
Carbon ≃ 224 47.07 N 122.13 W
Carbon, Cap › 34 36.47 N 5.06 E
Carbonado 224 47.04 N 122.03 W
Carbonara, Capo › 71 39.06 N 9.31 E
Carbonara, Pizzo ʌ 70 37.54 N 14.02 E
Carbonare 64 45.56 N 11.13 E
Carbonate 266b 45.41 N 8.56 E
Carbon-Blanc 32 44.53 N 0.31 W
Carbon Canyon Dam ✦[6] 280 33.55 N 117.50 W
Carbon Creek ≃ 280 33.49 N 118.04 W
Carbondale, Co., U.S. 200 39.24 N 107.12 W
Carbondale, Il., U.S. 194 37.43 N 89.13 W
Carbondale, Ks., U.S. 198 38.49 N 95.41 W
Carbondale, Pa., U.S. 210 41.34 N 75.30 W
Carbone 68 40.09 N 16.05 E
Carbonear 186 47.45 N 53.14 W
Carboneras de Guadazaon 34 39.53 N 1.48 W
Carbon Hill 194 33.53 N 87.31 W
Carbonia 71 39.10 N 8.31 E
Carbonin 64 46.37 N 12.13 E
Carbost 46 57.18 N 6.22 W
Carcaixent 34 39.08 N 0.27 W
Carcajou ≃ 180 65.37 N 128.43 W
Carcalgong Hill ʌ 170 32.52 S 149.41 E
Carcans, Lac de ⊂ 32 45.08 N 1.08 W
Carcar 116 10.06 N 123.38 E
Carcarañá 252 32.51 S 61.09 W
Carcarañá ≃ 252 32.27 S 60.48 W
Carcare 62 44.21 N 8.18 E
Carcar Point › 116 10.05 N 123.41 E
Carcassonne 32 43.13 N 2.21 E
Carcastillo 34 42.23 N 1.26 W
Carcavelos, Port. 266c 38.41 N 9.20 W
Carcavelos, Port. 266c 38.53 N 9.14 W
Carceri, Eremo delle ✝[1] 66 43.05 N 12.42 E
Carcès 62 43.28 N 6.11 E
Carchi □[4] 246 0.45 N 78.00 W
Carcroft 44 53.34 N 1.11 W
Carcross 180 60.10 N 134.42 W
Cardabia 162 23.06 S 113.48 E
Čardak, Tür. 130 38.06 N 36.49 E
Čardak, Uzb. 85 41.37 N 69.56 E
Cardal 258 34.18 S 56.24 W
Cardano al Campo 266b 45.39 N 8.47 E
Čardara 85 41.17 N 67.55 E
Čardara, step' ✦[1] 85 41.20 N 68.00 E
Čardarinskoje vodochranilišče ◎[1] 85 41.10 N 68.15 E
Cardeña 34 38.13 N 4.19 W
Cárdenas, Cuba 240p 23.02 N 81.12 W
Cárdenas, Méx. 234 22.00 N 99.40 W
Cárdenas, Méx. 234 17.59 N 93.22 W
Cárdenas, Nic. 236 11.12 N 85.31 W
Cárdenas, Bahía de ⊂ 240p 23.05 N 81.10 W
Cardener ≃ 34 41.41 N 1.51 E
Carderock Springs 284c 38.59 N 77.10 W
Cardiel, Lago ◎ 254 48.55 S 71.15 W
Cardiff, Austl. 170 32.57 S 151.41 E
Cardiff, Wales, U.K. 42 51.29 N 3.13 W
Cardiff, Md., U.S. 208 39.43 N 76.20 W
Cardiff, N.J., U.S. 208 39.24 N 74.35 W
Cardiff by the Sea 228 33.01 N 117.16 W
Cardigan, P.E., Can. 186 46.14 N 62.37 W
Cardigan, Wales, U.K. 42 52.06 N 4.40 W
Cardigan Bay ⊂, P.E., Can. 186 46.10 N 62.30 W
Cardigan Bay ⊂, Wales, U.K. 42 52.30 N 4.20 W
Cardigan Island I 42 52.08 N 4.41 W
Cardigan State Park ◆ 188 43.38 N 71.54 W
Cardinal 212 44.47 N 75.23 W
Cardinale 68 38.38 N 16.23 E
Cardinal Heights 212 45.27 N 75.37 W
Cardinal Lake ◎ 182 56.14 N 117.44 W
Cardington, Boph. 158 27.11 S 23.30 E
Cardington, Oh., U.S. 214 40.30 N 82.53 W
Cardinia Creek ≃ 274b 38.12 S 145.23 E
Cardinia Reservoir ◎[1] 169 37.58 S 145.25 E
Cardona 258 33.53 S 57.23 W
Cardonal, Punta › 232 28.28 N 111.45 W
Cardoso 255 20.04 S 49.54 W
Cardozo 252 32.38 S 56.21 W
Card Sound ⊻ 220 25.20 N 80.18 W
Cardston 182 49.12 N 113.18 W
Cardwell, Austl. 166 18.16 S 146.02 E
Cardwell, Mo., U.S. 194 36.02 N 90.17 W
Cardwell Mountain ʌ 194 35.41 N 85.41 W
Čardžou 128 39.06 N 63.34 E
Čardžou □[8] 128 38.51 N 63.34 E
Careaçu 256 22.02 S 45.42 W
Careen Lake ◎ 184 57.00 N 108.10 W
Carega, Cima ʌ 64 45.44 N 11.08 E
Carei 38 47.42 N 22.28 E
Careiro 246 3.12 S 59.45 W
Careiro, Ilha do I 246 3.10 S 59.44 W
Carén 252 30.51 S 70.47 W
Čarencavan 84 40.24 N 44.38 E
Carencro 194 30.19 N 92.02 W
Carentan 32 49.18 N 1.14 W
Careri 68 38.10 N 16.07 E
Cares ≃ 34 43.19 N 4.36 W
Caresana 62 45.13 N 8.30 E
Caretta 192 37.20 N 81.40 W
Carevščina 80 52.27 N 46.43 E
Carey 214 40.57 N 83.22 W
Carey, Lake ◎ 162 29.05 S 122.15 E
Carey Downs 162 25.38 S 115.27 E
Careysburg 150 6.30 N 10.32 W
Cargados Carajos Shoals II 12 16.38 S 59.38 E
Cargill 46 56.30 N 3.22 W
Carhaix-Plouguer 32 48.17 N 3.35 W
Carhuamayo 248 10.55 S 76.02 W
Carhuanca 248 13.45 S 73.48 W
Carhuaz 248 9.16 S 77.38 W
Carhué 252 37.11 S 62.44 W
Caria □[9] 130 37.30 N 28.00 E
Cariacica 255 20.16 S 40.25 W
Cariaco 246 10.29 N 63.33 W
Cariaco, Golfo de ⊂ 246 10.30 N 64.00 W
Cariamanga 246 4.20 S 79.35 W
Cariango 152 10.37 S 15.20 E
Cariati 68 39.30 N 16.56 E
Caribana, Punta › 246 8.37 N 76.52 W
Caribbean Sea ✦[2] 230 15.00 N 73.00 W
Caribe, Mar — Caribbean Sea ✦[2] 230 15.00 N 73.00 W
Cariboo ≃ 182 52.40 N 121.40 W
Cariboo Mountains ⋏ 182 53.00 N 121.00 W
Caribou, N.S., Can. 186 45.44 N 62.42 W
Caribou, Me., U.S. 188 46.51 N 68.00 W
Caribou ≃ 176 59.20 N 94.44 W
Caribou, Lac du ◎ 206 46.56 N 72.50 W
Caribou Island I 190 47.22 N 85.49 W
Caribou Mountain ʌ, Id., U.S. 202 43.06 N 111.18 W
Caribou Mountain ʌ, Me., U.S. 188 45.26 N 70.38 W
Caribou Mountains ⋏ 176 59.12 N 115.40 W
Caribou Range ⋏ 202 43.05 N 111.15 W
Caričanka 78 48.57 N 34.29 E
Carichic 232 27.56 N 107.03 W
Caricuao 286c 10.27 N 66.59 W
Caricuao, Quebrada ≃ 286c 10.26 N 66.59 W
Caricyn — Volgograd 80 48.44 N 44.25 E
Caridad, Pil. 116 10.50 N 124.45 E
Caridad, Pil. 269f 14.29 N 120.53 E
Caridade 250 4.13 S 39.12 W
Carife 68 41.01 N 15.12 E
Carigara 116 11.18 N 124.41 E
Carigara Bay ⊂ 116 11.24 N 124.40 E
Carignan, P.Q., Can. 275a 45.27 N 73.18 W
Carignan, Fr. 56 49.38 N 5.10 E
Carignano, It. 62 44.55 N 7.40 E
Carignano, It. 66 43.49 N 12.56 E
Cari Laufquen Grande, Lago ◎ 254 41.07 S 69.30 W
Carinda 166 30.28 S 147.41 E
Cariñena 34 41.20 N 1.13 W
Caringbah 274a 34.03 S 151.08 E
Carinhanha 255 14.18 S 43.47 W
Carinhanha ≃ 255 14.20 S 43.47 W
Carini 70 38.08 N 13.11 E
Carini, Golfo di ⊂ 70 38.12 N 13.22 E
Carinish 46 57.31 N 7.18 W
Carinola 68 41.11 N 13.58 E
Carioca, Serra da ⋏ 256 22.47 S 44.18 W
Caripe 246 10.12 N 63.29 W
Caripi ≃ 250 3.56 N 51.27 W
Caripito 246 10.08 N 63.06 W
Carira 250 10.21 S 37.42 W
Cariré 250 3.57 S 40.27 W
Caririaçu 250 7.02 S 39.17 W
Carisbrook 169 37.02 S 143.49 E
Carisbrooke 42 50.41 N 1.19 W
Carisolo 64 46.10 N 10.45 E
Carite 286c 10.24 N 67.01 W
Carite, Lago ◎[1] 240m 18.04 N 66.06 W
Cariús 250 6.32 S 39.30 W
Cariús ≃ 250 6.24 S 39.30 W
Carkesar 85 41.02 N 70.53 E
Carlentini 70 37.16 N 15.01 E
Carle Place 276 40.45 N 73.36 W
Carles 116 11.34 N 123.08 E
Carlet 34 39.14 N 0.31 W
Carleton, Mi., U.S. 216 42.03 N 83.23 W
Carleton, Ne., U.S. 198 40.18 N 97.40 W
Carleton, Mount ʌ 186 47.23 N 66.53 W
Carleton Place 212 45.08 N 76.09 W
Carletonville 158 26.23 S 27.22 E
Carlin 204 40.42 N 116.06 W
Carling 56 49.10 N 6.43 E
Carlingford 274a 33.47 S 151.03 E
Carlingford Lough ⊂ 48 54.04 N 6.10 W
Carlinville 219 39.16 N 89.52 W
Carlinville, Lake ◎[1] 219 39.14 N 89.51 W
Carlisle, On., Can. 212 43.23 N 79.59 W
Carlisle, Eng., U.K. 44 54.54 N 2.55 W
Carlisle, Ar., U.S. 194 34.46 N 91.44 W
Carlisle, In., U.S. 194 38.58 N 87.24 W
Carlisle, Ia., U.S. 190 41.30 N 93.29 W
Carlisle, Ky., U.S. 218 38.18 N 84.01 W
Carlisle, Ma., U.S. 283 42.31 N .0 W
Carlisle, N.Y., U.S. 210 42.45 N 74.27 W
Carlisle, Oh., U.S. 218 39.35 N 84.20 W
Carlisle, Pa., U.S. 208 40.12 N 77.11 W
Carlisle Barracks ■ 208 40.13 N 77.11 W

Symbols in the index entries represent the broad categories identified in the key at the right. Symbols with superior numbers (⋏[1]) identify subcategories (see complete key on page *I · 1*).

Symbole im Register stellen die rechts im Schlüssel erklärten Kategorien dar. Symbole mit hochgestellten Ziffern (⋏[1]) bezeichnen Unterabteilungen einer Kategorie (vgl. vollständiger Schlüssel auf Seite *I · 1*).

Los símbolos incluídos en el texto del índice representan las grandes categorías identificadas con la clave a la derecha. Los símbolos con numeros en su parte superior (⋏[1]) identifican las subcategorías (véase la clave completa en la página *I · 1*).

Les symboles de l'index représentent les catégories indiquées dans la légende à droite. Les symboles suivis d'un indice (⋏[1]) représentent des sous-catégories (voir légende complète à la page *I · 1*).

Os símbolos incluídos no texto do índice representam as grandes categorias identificadas com a chave à direita. Os símbolos com números em sua parte superior (⋏[1]) identificam as subcategorias (veja-se a chave completa à página *I · 1*).

	English	Deutsch	Español	Français	Português
ʌ	Mountain	Berg	Montaña	Montagne	Montanha
⋏	Mountains	Gebirge	Montañas	Montagnes	Montanhas
)(	Pass	Paß	Paso	Col	Passo
V	Valley, Canyon	Tal, Cañon	Valle, Cañón	Vallée, Canyon	Vale, Canhão
≚	Plain	Ebene	Llano	Plaine	Planície
›	Cape	Kap	Cabo	Cap	Cabo
I	Island	Insel	Isla	Île	Ilha
II	Islands	Inseln	Islas	Îles	Ilhas
⊥	Other Topographic Features	Andere Topographische Objekte	Otros Elementos Topográficos	Autres données topographiques	Outros acidentes topográficos

ESPAÑOL — Nombre | Página | Lat. °′ | Long. °′ W = Oeste
FRANÇAIS — Nom | Page | Lat. °′ | Long. °′ W = Ouest
PORTUGUÊS — Nome | Página | Lat. °′ | Long. °′ W = Oeste

Nombre / Nom / Nome	Página / Page	Lat. °′	Long. °′
Carlisle Bay ⊂	241g	13.05 N	59.37 W
Carlisle Gardens	210	43.11 N	78.39 W
Carlisle Island I	180	52.52 N	170.02 W
Carlisle Springs	208	40.16 N	77.10 W
Carl Junction	194	37.10 N	94.33 W
Carlls ≃	276	40.41 N	73.20 W
Carloforte	71	39.08 N	8.18 E
Carlopoli	68	39.03 N	16.27 E
Carlópolis	255	23.25 S	49.41 W
Carlos, Isla I	254	54.03 S	73.20 W
Carlos Alves	256	21.37 S	43.07 W
Carlos Barbosa	252	29.18 S	51.30 W
Carlos Beguerie	258	35.29 S	59.06 W
Carlos Casares	252	35.38 S	61.21 W
Carlos Chagas	255	17.43 S	40.45 W
Carlos City	218	40.02 N	85.02 W
Carlos Forseca Amador	236	11.59 N	86.31 W
Carlos Keen	258	34.29 S	59.14 W
Carlos Manuel de Céspedes	240p	21.35 N	78.17 W
Carlos Pellegrini	252	32.03 S	61.48 W
Carlos Reyles	252	33.03 S	56.29 W
Carlos Sampaio	287a	22.42 S	43.31 W
Carlos Tejedor	252	35.23 S	62.25 W
Carlow	48	52.50 N	6.55 W
Carlow □6	48	52.40 N	6.50 W
Carloway	46	58.17 N	6.48 W
Carl Sandburg Home National Historic Site ⊥	192	35.16 N	82.27 W
Carlsbad, Ca., U.S.	228	33.09 N	117.20 W
Carlsbad, N.M., U.S.	196	32.25 N	104.13 W
Carlsbad, Tx., U.S.	196	31.36 N	100.38 W
Carlsbad Caverns National Park ♦	196	32.08 N	104.35 W
Carlsbad → Karlovy Vary	54	50.11 N	12.52 E
Carlsberg Ridge ✢3	12	6.00 N	61.00 E
Carlsborg	224	48.05 N	123.10 W
Carlsfeld	54	50.26 N	12.35 E
Carlstadt	276	40.50 N	74.05 W
Carlton, Austl.	274a	33.58 S	151.08 E
Carlton, Eng., U.K.	42	52.58 N	1.05 W
Carlton, Eng., U.K.	44	53.42 N	1.01 W
Carlton, Mn., U.S.	190	46.39 N	92.25 W
Carlton, Or., U.S.	224	45.18 N	123.11 W
Carlton, Tx., U.S.	196	31.55 N	98.10 W
Carlton Gardens ♦	274b	37.48 S	144.59 E
Carlton Lake ◎	224	45.18 N	123.11 W
Carluke	46	55.45 N	3.51 W
Carlyle, Sk., Can.	184	49.38 N	102.16 W
Carlyle, Il., U.S.	219	38.36 N	89.22 W
Carlyle Lake ◎1	219	38.40 N	89.18 W
Carmacks	180	62.05 N	136.18 W
Carmagnola	62	44.51 N	7.43 E
Carman	184	49.32 N	98.00 W
Carmanah Creek ≃	224	48.37 N	124.44 W
Carmangay	182	50.08 N	113.07 W
Carmanville	186	49.24 N	54.17 W
Carmarthen	42	51.52 N	4.19 W
Carmarthen Bay ⊂	42	51.40 N	4.30 W
Carmaux	32	44.03 N	2.09 E
Carmel, Wales, U.K.	262	53.17 N	3.15 W
Carmel, Ca., U.S.	226	36.33 N	121.55 W
Carmel, In., U.S.	218	39.58 N	86.07 W
Carmel, N.J., U.S.	208	39.26 N	75.07 W
Carmel, N.Y., U.S.	210	41.26 N	73.41 W
Carmel ≃	226	36.32 N	121.56 W
Carmel, Mount ∧	226	36.23 N	121.47 W
Carmel, Mount → Karmel, Har ∧	132	32.44 N	35.02 E
Carmel Bay ⊂	226	36.33 N	121.57 W
Carmel Head ›	44	53.24 N	4.34 W
Carmel Highlands	226	36.30 N	121.56 W
Carmel Hills	226	36.32 N	121.53 W
Carmel Mountain ∧2	228	32.55 N	117.13 W
Carmelo	258	34.00 S	58.17 W
Carmel Point	226	36.31 N	122.55 W
Carmel Valley	226	36.29 N	121.43 W
Carmel Woods	226	36.34 N	121.54 W
Carmen, Pil.	116	8.59 N	125.17 E
Carmen, Pil.	116	9.50 N	124.12 E
Carmen, Pil.	116	10.35 N	124.01 E
Carmen, Pil.	116	12.37 N	122.07 E
Carmen, Ok., U.S.	196	36.34 N	98.27 W
Carmen, Ur.	252	33.15 S	56.01 W
Carmen, Isla I	232	25.57 N	111.12 W
Carmen, Isla del I	232	18.42 N	91.40 W
Carmen, Río del ≃	252	28.45 S	70.30 W
Carmen Alto	252	23.11 S	69.40 W
Carmen → Ciudad del Carmen	232	18.38 N	91.50 W
Carmen de Apicalá	246	4.09 N	74.44 W
Carmen de Areco	252	34.22 S	59.49 W
Carmen de Huechuraba	286e	33.21 S	70.40 W
Carmen de Patagones	254	40.48 S	62.59 W
Carmer Hill ∧2	214	41.54 N	77.58 W
Carmi	194	38.05 N	88.09 W
Carmi, Lake ◎	206	44.58 N	72.53 W
Carmiano	68	40.21 N	18.03 E
Carmichael	226	38.37 N	121.19 W
Carmignano di Brenta	64	45.38 N	11.42 E
Carmila	166	21.55 S	149.25 E
Carmine	222	30.09 N	96.41 W
Carmo	256	21.56 S	42.37 W
Carmo, Monte ∧	62	44.11 N	8.11 E
Carmo, Ribeirão do ≃	256	21.20 S	45.10 W
Carmo, Rio do ≃	250	5.02 S	37.12 W
Carmo da Cachoeira	256	21.28 S	45.13 W
Carmo de Minas	256	22.07 S	45.08 W
Carmo do Paranaíba	255	18.59 S	46.21 W
Carmo do Rio Verde	255	15.21 S	49.42 W
Carmody Hills	284c	38.54 N	76.54 W
Carmona, Esp.	34	37.28 N	5.38 W
Carmona, Pil.	116	14.19 N	121.03 E
Carmópolis de Minas	255	20.33 S	44.38 W
Carmzow	54	53.23 N	14.02 E
Carnaíba	250	7.48 S	37.49 W
Carnamah	162	29.42 S	115.53 E
Carnarvon, Austl.	162	24.53 S	113.40 E
Carnarvon, S. Afr.	158	30.56 S	22.08 E
Carnarvon → Caernarfon	44	53.08 N	4.16 W
Carnarvon National Park ♦	166	25.00 S	148.00 E
Carnatic □9	118	12.30 N	78.15 E
Carnation	224	47.38 N	121.54 W
Carnaval, Arroyo ≃	288	34.52 S	58.02 W
Carnaxide	266c	38.43 N	9.15 W
Carncastle	48	54.54 N	5.53 W
Carndonagh	48	55.15 N	7.15 W
Carnduff	184	49.10 N	101.50 W
Carnedd Llewelyn ∧	44	53.10 N	3.58 W
Carnedd Wen ∧	42	52.41 N	3.35 W
Carnegie, Austl.	162	25.43 S	122.59 E
Carnegie, N.Y., U.S.	210	42.45 N	78.51 W
Carnegie, Ok., U.S.	196	35.06 N	98.36 W
Carnegie, Pa., U.S.	214	40.24 N	80.05 W
Carnegie, Lake ◎	162	26.10 S	122.30 E
Carnegie Institute ψ2	279b	40.27 N	79.57 W
Carnegie-Mellon University ψ2	279b	40.27 N	79.57 W
Carnegie Ridge ✢3	18	1.00 S	85.00 W
Carnelian Bay	226	39.14 N	120.05 W
Carnetin	261	48.54 N	2.42 E
Carnew	48	52.43 N	6.30 W
Carneys Point	208	39.42 N	75.28 W
Carnforth	44	54.08 N	2.46 W
Carnia	64	46.22 N	13.08 E
Carnia ✦1	64	46.25 N	13.00 E
Carniche, Alpi (Karnische Alpen) ⋏	64	46.40 N	13.00 E
Car Nicobar Island I	110	9.10 N	92.47 E
Carnide ✦8	266c	38.46 N	9.11 W
Carnières	50	50.10 N	3.21 E
Carniques → Karnische Alpen ⋏	64	46.40 N	13.00 E
Carnlough	48	54.59 N	6.00 W
Carno	42	52.33 N	3.31 W
Carnon-Plage	62	43.32 N	3.59 E
Carnot, Centraf.	152	4.56 N	15.52 E
Carnot, Pa., U.S.	214	40.31 N	80.13 W
Carnot, Cape ›	166	34.57 S	135.38 E
Carnoules	62	43.18 N	6.11 E
Carnoustie	46	56.30 N	2.44 W
Carnsore Point ›	48	52.10 N	6.22 W
Carnwath	46	55.43 N	3.38 W
Carnwath ≃	180	68.26 N	128.50 W
Caro	190	43.29 N	83.23 W
Caroga Creek ≃	210	42.58 N	74.38 W
Caroga Lake	210	43.08 N	74.29 W
Carol Beach Estates	216	42.31 N	87.49 W
Carol City	220	25.56 N	80.14 W
Carole Acres	284c	39.04 N	77.00 W
Caroleen	192	35.16 N	81.47 W
Carole Highlands	284c	38.58 N	76.59 W
Carolei	68	39.15 N	16.13 E
Carolina, Bra.	250	7.20 S	47.28 W
Carolina, Col.	246	6.43 N	75.17 W
Carolina, El Sal.	236	13.51 N	88.19 W
Carolina, P.R.	240m	18.23 N	65.57 W
Carolina, S. Afr.	158	26.05 S	30.06 E
Carolina, R.I., U.S.	207	41.27 N	71.39 W
Carolina Beach	192	34.02 N	77.53 W
Carolinas, Puntan ›	174n	14.55 N	145.38 E
Caroline □6, Md., U.S.	208	38.53 N	75.50 W
Caroline □6, Va., U.S.	208	38.00 N	77.20 W
Caroline I1	14	9.58 S	150.13 W
Caroline du Nord → North Carolina □3	192	35.30 N	80.00 W
Caroline du Sud → South Carolina □3	192	34.00 N	81.00 W
Caroline Islands II	14	8.00 N	147.00 E
Caroline Livermore, Mount ∧2	282	37.52 N	122.26 W
Caroline Peak ∧	172	45.56 S	167.13 E
Carol Stream	278	41.54 N	88.08 W
Caron	184	50.28 N	105.52 W
Caron, Lac ◎	190	48.00 N	78.53 W
Çarona	64	46.01 N	9.47 E
Čaronda	76	60.34 N	38.59 E
Caroní ≃	246	8.21 N	62.43 W
Caronia	70	38.01 N	14.26 E
Caronia ≃	70	38.03 N	14.26 E
Caronno Pertusella	266b	45.36 N	9.03 E
Carora	246	10.11 N	70.05 W
Carosino	68	40.27 N	17.23 E
Carouge	58	46.11 N	6.09 E
Car'ov	80	48.40 N	45.22 E
Carovigno	68	40.42 N	17.39 E
Carovilli	66	41.43 N	14.17 E
Car'ovščina	80	53.37 N	44.45 E
Čarozero	76	60.28 N	38.39 E
Carp	212	45.21 N	76.02 W
Carp ≃, On., Can.	212	45.29 N	76.14 W
Carp ≃, Mi., U.S.	190	46.02 N	84.42 W
Carpaneto Piacentino	62	44.55 N	9.47 E
Carpanzano	68	39.09 N	16.18 E
Carpates → Carpathian Mountains ⋏	22	48.00 N	24.00 E
Carpathian Mountains ⋏	22	48.00 N	24.00 E
Carpații Meridionali ⋏	38	45.30 N	24.15 E
Cárpatos → Carpathian Mountains ⋏	22	48.00 N	24.00 E
Carpegna	66	43.47 N	12.20 E
Carpenedolo	64	45.22 N	10.26 E
Carpentaria, Gulf of ⊂	164	14.00 S	139.00 E
Carpenter	198	41.02 N	104.21 W
Carpenter Creek ≃	216	40.54 N	87.12 W
Carpenter Lake ◎	182	50.50 N	122.30 W
Carpentersville	216	42.07 N	88.15 W
Carpentertown	279b	40.11 N	79.31 W
Carpentras	62	44.03 N	5.03 E
Carpet Museum ψ	267d	35.43 N	51.24 E
Carpi	64	44.47 N	10.53 E
Carpignano Sesia	62	45.32 N	8.25 E
Carpina	250	7.51 S	35.15 W
Carpineti	64	44.28 N	10.31 E
Carpineto Romano	66	41.36 N	13.05 E
Carpino	68	41.51 N	15.51 E
Carpinone	66	41.35 N	14.19 E
Carpinteria	204	34.23 N	119.31 W
Carpio	198	48.26 N	101.42 W
Carp Lake ◎	182	54.45 N	123.20 W
Carpolac	166	36.44 S	141.19 E
Carquefou	32	47.18 N	1.30 W
Carqueiranne	62	43.05 N	6.05 E
Carquinez Bridge ✦5	282	38.04 N	122.14 W
Carquinez Strait ꟸ	282	38.02 N	122.12 W
Carra, Lough ◎	48	53.42 N	9.16 W
Carrabelle	192	29.51 N	84.39 W
Carradale	46	55.35 N	5.28 W
Carramar	274a	33.53 S	150.58 E
Carrancas	256	21.30 S	44.39 W
Carr and Craggs Moor ✦3	262	53.43 N	2.09 W
Carranglan	116	15.58 N	121.04 E
Carranza, Cabo ›	252	35.36 S	72.38 W
Carrao ≃	246	6.17 N	62.51 W
Carrara	64	44.05 N	10.06 E
Carrascal	116	9.22 N	125.56 E
Carrasco ✦8	258	34.54 S	56.05 W
Carrasco, Aeropuerto Nacional de ⊠	258	34.52 S	56.02 W
Carrathool	166	34.24 S	145.26 E
Carrauntoohil ∧	48	51.59 N	9.45 W
Carrazedo	250	1.36 S	51.54 W
Carrboro	192	35.54 N	79.04 W
Carr Bridge	46	57.17 N	3.49 W
Carrcroft	285	39.47 N	75.30 W
Carrcroft Crest	285	39.47 N	75.30 W
Carrefour Pompadour ♦	261	48.46 N	2.26 E
Carregueira, Serra da ⋏2	266c	38.48 N	9.15 W
Carreria	252	21.59 S	58.35 W
Carreta, Punta ›	248	14.13 S	76.18 W
Carreta Quemada, Arroyo ≃	258	34.21 S	56.41 W
Carriacou I	238	12.30 N	61.27 W
Carrick ✦8	279b	40.23 N	79.59 W
Carrick ✦1	44	55.12 N	4.38 W
Carrickart	48	55.10 N	7.47 W
Carrickfergus	48	54.43 N	5.49 W
Carrickmacross	48	53.58 N	6.43 W
Carrick on Shannon	48	53.57 N	8.05 W
Carrick on Suir	48	52.21 N	7.25 W
Carrie, Mount ∧	224	47.53 N	123.39 W
Carriere	194	30.37 N	89.39 W
Carrière, Lac ◎	190	47.14 N	77.12 W
Carrières, Pointe aux ›	275a	45.31 N	73.54 W
Carrières-sous-Bois	261	48.57 N	2.07 E
Carrières-sous-Poissy	261	48.57 N	2.03 E
Carrières-sur-Seine	261	48.55 N	2.11 E
Carriers Mills	194	37.41 N	88.38 W
Carrieton	166	32.26 S	138.32 E
Carrigahorig	48	53.04 N	8.09 W
Carrigaline	48	51.48 N	8.24 W
Carrigallen	48	53.59 N	7.39 W
Carrillo, C.R.	236	9.52 N	85.30 W
Carrillo, Méx.	232	26.54 N	103.55 W
Carrington, Eng., U.K.	262	53.26 N	2.24 W
Carrington, N.D., U.S.	198	47.26 N	99.07 W
Carrington Island I	202	41.00 N	112.37 W
Carrington Moss ✦3	262	53.25 N	2.23 W
Carr Inlet ⊂	224	47.17 N	122.42 W
Carrión ≃	34	41.53 N	4.32 W
Carrión de los Condes	34	42.20 N	4.36 W
Carrizal ≃	234	23.03 N	97.46 W
Carrizal, Cerro ∧	196	26.43 N	100.36 W
Carrizal Bajo	252	28.05 S	71.10 W
Carrizo	34	42.35 N	5.50 W
Carrizo Creek ≃, U.S.	196	36.05 N	102.36 W
Carrizo Creek ≃, N.M., U.S.	196	35.40 N	103.43 W
Carrizo Mountain ∧	200	33.41 N	105.42 W
Carrizo Mountains ⋏	200	36.45 N	109.10 W
Carrizo Plain ≚	226	35.25 N	120.00 W
Carrizo Springs	196	28.31 N	99.51 W
Carrizo Wash ∨, U.S.	200	34.36 N	109.26 W
Carrizo Wash ∨, Ca., U.S.	204	33.05 N	115.56 W
Carrizozo	200	33.38 N	105.52 W
Carro	62	43.20 N	5.02 E
Carrodano	62	44.14 N	9.39 E
Carroll, Ia., U.S.	198	42.03 N	94.52 W
Carroll, Ne., U.S.	198	42.16 N	97.11 W
Carroll □6, In., U.S.	216	40.36 N	86.41 W
Carroll □6, Ky., U.S.	218	38.39 N	85.06 W
Carroll □6, Md., U.S.	208	39.35 N	77.00 W
Carroll □6, Oh., U.S.	214	40.34 N	81.05 W
Carroll Lake ◎	184	51.07 N	95.05 W
Carroll Park ♦	284b	39.17 N	76.39 W
Carrolls	224	46.05 N	122.52 W
Carrollton, Al., U.S.	194	33.10 N	88.06 W
Carrollton, Ga., U.S.	192	33.35 N	85.05 W
Carrollton, Il., U.S.	219	39.18 N	90.24 W
Carrollton, Ky., U.S.	218	38.40 N	85.10 W
Carrollton, Mi., U.S.	190	43.27 N	83.55 W
Carrollton, Ms., U.S.	194	33.30 N	89.55 W
Carrollton, Mo., U.S.	194	39.21 N	93.29 W
Carrollton, Oh., U.S.	214	40.34 N	81.05 W
Carrollton, Tx., U.S.	222	32.57 N	96.53 W
Carrollton Manor	208	39.05 N	76.35 W
Carrolltown	214	40.36 N	78.43 W
Carrollwood	284b	39.20 N	76.23 W
Carron ≃, Austl.	166	17.42 S	141.06 E
Carron ≃, Scot., U.K.	46	57.25 N	5.27 W
Carron ≃, Scot., U.K.	46	56.02 N	3.44 W
Carron ≃, Scot., U.K.	46	57.53 N	4.21 W
Carron, Loch ⊂	46	57.22 N	5.31 W
Carronbridge	44	55.16 N	3.48 W
Carron Valley Reservoir ◎1	46	56.02 N	4.05 W
Carros	62	43.48 N	7.11 E
Carrot ≃	184	53.50 N	101.17 W
Carrot River	184	53.17 N	103.35 W
Carrouges	28	48.34 N	0.09 W
Carrowmore Lake ◎	48	54.12 N	9.47 W
Carrsville	208	36.43 N	76.50 W
Carrù	62	44.29 N	7.52 E
Carrum	169	38.05 S	145.08 E
Carrum Downs	274b	38.06 S	145.11 E
Carrum North	274b	38.03 S	145.09 E
Carrville	194	32.32 N	85.52 W
Carryduff	48	54.31 N	5.53 W
Carry Falls Reservoir ◎1	188	44.25 N	74.45 W
Carry-le-Rouet	62	43.20 N	5.09 E
Carsaig	46	56.17 N	6.00 W
Çarşamba	130	41.12 N	36.44 E
Čaršanga	128	37.30 N	66.01 E
Carseland	182	50.51 N	113.28 W
Carshalton ✦8	260	51.22 N	0.10 W
Čarsk	86	49.35 N	81.05 E
Carsoli	66	42.06 N	13.05 E
Carson, Ca., U.S.	228	33.49 N	118.16 W
Carson, N.D., U.S.	198	46.25 N	101.33 W
Carson, Va., U.S.	208	37.02 N	77.23 W
Carson, Wa., U.S.	224	45.43 N	121.49 W
Carson ≃	204	39.45 N	118.40 W
Carson, East Fork ≃	226	38.59 N	119.49 W
Carson, West Fork ≃	226	38.59 N	119.49 W
Carson City, Mi., U.S.	190	43.10 N	84.50 W
Carson City, Nv., U.S.	226	39.10 N	119.46 W
Carsondale	284c	38.57 N	76.50 W
Carson Lake ◎, On., Can.	212	45.31 N	77.46 W
Carson Lake ◎, Nv., U.S.	204	39.19 N	118.43 W
Carson Range ⋏	226	39.15 N	119.50 W
Carson Sink ◎	204	39.45 N	118.30 W
Carson Valley ∨	226	39.00 N	119.48 W
Carstairs, Ab., Can.	182	51.34 N	114.06 W
Carstairs, Scot., U.K.	46	55.42 N	3.42 W
Carstensz-Toppen → Jaya, Puncak ∧	164	4.05 S	137.11 E
Carswell Air Force Base ■	222	32.47 N	97.26 W
Cartagena, Chile	252	33.33 S	71.37 W
Cartagena, Col.	246	10.25 N	75.32 W
Cartagena, Esp.	34	37.36 N	0.59 W
Cartago, Col.	246	4.45 N	75.55 W
Cartago, C.R.	236	9.52 N	83.55 W
Çartago □4	236	9.50 N	83.45 W
Čartak	85	41.05 N	71.50 E
Cartaxo	34	39.09 N	8.47 W
Cartaxos ∧2	266c	38.54 N	9.20 W
Cartaya	34	37.17 N	7.09 W
Carter	196	35.13 N	99.30 W
Carter □6	218	38.20 N	83.05 W
Carter Bridge ✦5	273a	6.28 N	3.23 E
Carter Caves State Resort Park ♦	218	38.22 N	83.10 W
Carteret	210	40.34 N	74.13 W
Carter Lake	198	41.17 N	95.55 W
Carter Mountain ∧	202	44.12 N	109.25 W
Carters Lake ◎1	192	34.35 N	84.35 W
Cartersville	192	34.09 N	84.48 W
Carterton, N.Z.	172	41.02 S	175.31 E
Carterton, Eng., U.K.	42	51.45 N	1.35 W
Carterville	194	37.45 N	89.04 W
Carthage, Tun.	148	36.51 N	10.21 E
Carthage, Ar., U.S.	194	34.04 N	92.33 W
Carthage, Il., U.S.	190	40.24 N	91.08 W
Carthage, In., U.S.	218	39.44 N	85.34 W
Carthage, Ms., U.S.	194	32.43 N	89.32 W
Carthage, Mo., U.S.	194	37.10 N	94.18 W
Carthage, N.Y., U.S.	212	43.58 N	75.36 W
Carthage, N.C., U.S.	192	35.20 N	79.25 W
Carthage, S.D., U.S.	198	44.10 N	97.42 W
Carthage, Tn., U.S.	194	36.15 N	85.57 W
Carthage, Tx., U.S.	194	32.09 N	94.20 W
Carthage ⊥	36	36.52 N	10.20 E
Cartier Islands II	160	12.32 S	123.32 E
Cartierville ✦8	275a	45.32 N	73.42 W
Cartierville, Aéroport de ⊠	275a	45.31 N	73.43 W
Cartridge Hill ∧2	262	53.41 N	2.30 W
Cartura	64	45.16 N	11.50 E
Cartwright, Mb., Can.	184	49.06 N	99.20 W
Cartwright, Nf., Can.	176	53.42 N	57.01 W
Caruaru	250	8.17 S	35.58 W
Caruban	115a	7.33 S	111.39 E
Çarumas	248	16.49 S	70.43 W
Čarüngol	88	49.14 N	106.29 E
Carunjamba ≃	152	13.57 S	12.25 E
Carúpano	246	10.40 N	63.14 W
Caruray	116	10.20 N	119.00 E
Carutapera	250	1.13 S	46.01 W
Caruthers	226	36.32 N	119.50 W
Caruthersville	194	36.11 N	89.39 W
Carutu ≃	246	5.05 N	63.28 W
Carvalhopolis	256	21.47 S	46.51 W
Carvalhos	256	22.00 S	44.28 W
Carver	207	41.53 N	70.45 W
Carversville	208	40.23 N	75.04 W
Carvin	50	50.29 N	2.58 E
Carvoeiro	246	1.24 S	61.59 W
Carvoeiro, Cabo ›	34	39.21 N	9.24 W
Cary, Il., U.S.	216	42.12 N	88.14 W
Cary, Ms., U.S.	194	32.48 N	90.55 W
Cary, N.C., U.S.	192	35.47 N	78.46 W
Cary ≃	42	51.09 N	2.59 W
Caryčelekskij zapovednik ♦	85	41.50 N	71.55 E
Çaryk, ozero ◎	80	46.13 N	42.43 E
Čarymovo	86	58.31 N	77.42 E
Čaryn	86	43.46 N	79.24 E
Čaryš ≃	86	52.22 N	83.45 E
Čaryšskoje	86	51.24 N	83.35 E
Caryville, Fl., U.S.	194	30.46 N	85.48 W
Caryville, Tn., U.S.	192	36.17 N	84.13 W
Casablanca (Dar-el-Beida)	148	33.39 N	7.35 W
Casablanca □4	148	33.35 N	7.30 W
Casablanca ✦8	286b	23.09 N	82.20 W
Casabona	68	39.15 N	16.57 E
Casa Branca	256	21.46 S	47.04 W
Casacalenda	66	41.44 N	14.51 E
Casa de la Torrecilla	266a	40.19 N	3.37 W
Casa del Campo ♦	266a	40.32 N	3.47 W
Casa de Piedra, Embalse ◎1	252	38.15 S	67.20 W
Casa Grande	200	32.52 N	111.45 W
Casa Grande National Monument ♦	200	32.59 N	111.32 W
Casainhos	266c	38.53 N	9.10 W
Casalanguida	66	42.03 N	14.30 E
Casalattico	66	41.37 N	13.43 E
Casalbordino	66	42.09 N	14.35 E
Casalbuono	68	40.13 N	15.41 E
Casalbuttano	64	45.15 N	9.58 E
Casal di Principe	68	41.00 N	14.08 E
Casale Abbruciato ✦8	267a	41.44 N	12.33 E
Casalecchio di Reno	64	44.28 N	11.16 E
Casale Monferrato	62	45.08 N	8.27 E
Casale sul Sile	64	45.36 N	12.19 E
Casaletto Spartano	68	40.09 N	15.37 E
Casalmaggiore	64	44.59 N	10.26 E
Casalmorano	62	45.17 N	9.54 E
Casalnuovo Monterotaro	68	41.37 N	15.06 E
Casa Loma ψ	275b	43.41 N	79.25 W
Casalone ✦8	267a	41.56 N	12.41 E
Casalotti ✦8	267a	41.55 N	12.22 E
Casalpusterlengo	62	45.11 N	9.39 E
Casal Velino	68	40.11 N	15.06 E
Casalvieri	66	41.38 N	13.43 E
Casamance ≃	150	12.33 N	16.46 W
Casamari, Abbazia di ψ1	66	41.41 N	13.29 E
Casamassima	68	40.57 N	16.55 E
Casamicciola Terme	68	40.45 N	13.54 E
Casanare □3	246	5.45 N	72.00 W
Casanare ≃	246	6.02 N	69.51 W
Casanay	246	10.30 N	63.25 W
Casa Nova	250	9.07 S	40.58 W
Casarano	68	40.00 N	18.10 E
Casar de Cáceres	34	39.34 N	6.25 W
Casarsa della Delizia	64	45.57 N	12.50 E
Casas	234	23.44 N	98.45 W
Casas Adobes	200	32.19 N	110.59 W
Casas Grandes ≃	232	31.22 N	107.31 W
Casas Ibáñez	34	39.17 N	1.28 W
Casasimarro	34	39.22 N	2.02 W
Casauman ≃	116	7.16 N	126.31 E
Casa Verde ✦8	287b	23.30 S	46.39 W
Casavieja	34	40.17 N	4.46 W
Casbas	252	36.45 S	62.30 W
Casca	252	28.34 S	51.59 W
Casca, Rio da ≃	248	14.52 S	55.52 W
Cascadas Basaseachic, Parque Nacional ♦	232	28.10 N	108.22 W
Cascade, B.C., Can.	182	49.01 N	118.13 W
Cascade, Id., U.S.	202	44.30 N	116.02 W
Cascade, Ia., U.S.	190	42.17 N	91.00 W
Cascade, Mi., U.S.	216	42.55 N	85.30 W
Cascade, Mt., U.S.	202	47.16 N	111.41 W
Cascade, Wi., U.S.	190	43.39 N	88.00 W
Cascade ≃, N.Z.	172	44.02 S	168.22 E
Cascade ≃, Wa., U.S.	224	48.32 N	121.26 W
Cascade Bay ⊂	174c	29.01 S	167.58 E
Cascade Locks	224	45.40 N	121.53 W
Cascade Mountains (Cascade Range) ⋏	202	45.00 N	121.30 W
Cascade Park ♦	279a	41.23 N	82.06 W
Cascade Point ›	172	44.00 S	168.22 E
Cascade Range ⋏	178	45.00 N	121.30 W
Cascade Reservoir ◎1	202	44.35 N	116.06 W
Cascade Tunnel ✦5	224	47.40 N	121.03 W
Cascadura ✦8	287a	22.53 S	43.20 W
Cascais	34	38.42 N	9.25 W
Cascalho Rico	255	18.34 S	47.52 W
Cascapédia ≃	186	48.11 N	65.54 W
Cascatinha	256	22.29 S	43.09 W
Cascavel, Bra.	250	4.07 S	38.14 W
Cascavel, Bra.	252	24.57 S	53.28 W
Cascia	66	42.43 N	13.01 E
Casciana Terme	66	43.31 N	10.32 E
Cascina	66	43.41 N	10.33 E
Casco Bay ⊂	188	43.40 N	70.00 W
Çascumpec Bay ⊂	186	46.45 N	64.03 W
Čascy	82	55.37 N	36.52 E
Casei Gerola	62	45.00 N	8.55 E
Case Inlet ⊂	224	47.19 N	122.53 W
Casekow	54	53.12 N	14.12 E
Casella	62	44.32 N	9.00 E
Caselle, Aeroporto di ⊠	62	45.13 N	7.40 E
Caselle in Pittari	68	40.10 N	15.33 E
Caselle Torinese	62	45.10 N	7.39 E
Cà Selva, Lago di ◎1	64	46.16 N	12.40 E
Casenove	66	42.58 N	12.50 E
Casentino ∨	66	43.40 N	11.50 E
Casenuove	266b	45.38 N	8.42 E
Case-Pilote	240e	14.38 N	61.08 W
Caseros	258	34.36 S	58.33 W
Caserta	68	41.04 N	14.20 E
Caserta □4	68	41.14 N	14.10 E
Caseville	190	43.56 N	83.16 W
Case Western Reserve University ψ2	279a	41.30 N	81.36 W
Casey, Il., U.S.	194	39.17 N	87.59 W
Casey, Ia., U.S.	198	41.30 N	94.31 W
Casey ψ3	9	66.17 S	110.32 E
Casey, Mount ∧	202	48.26 N	116.42 W
Casey Bay ⊂	9	67.20 S	48.00 E
Casey Key I	220	27.10 N	82.29 W
Caseyr ›	144	11.49 N	51.15 E
Caseyville	219	38.38 N	90.02 W
Cash	222	32.59 N	96.07 W
Cashel, Ire.	48	53.25 N	9.48 W
Cashel, Ire.	48	52.31 N	7.53 W
Cashie ≃	192	35.53 N	76.49 W
Cashiers	192	35.06 N	83.05 W
Cashmere	202	47.31 N	120.28 W
Cashmere Downs	162	28.58 S	119.35 E
Cashton	190	43.44 N	90.46 W
Cashtown	208	39.53 N	77.22 W
Casigua	246	8.46 N	72.30 W
Casiguran, Pil.	116	16.17 N	122.07 E
Casiguran, Pil.	116	12.52 N	124.00 E
Casiguran Sound ꟸ	116	16.06 N	121.58 E
Casilda, Arg.	252	33.03 S	61.10 W
Casilda, Cuba	240p	21.46 N	79.59 W
Casimcea	38	44.43 N	28.23 E
Casimiro Castillo	234	19.38 N	104.28 W
Casina	64	44.30 N	10.30 E
Casino	166	28.52 S	153.03 E
Casiquiare ≃	246	2.01 N	67.07 W
Casita	200	31.00 N	110.53 W
Casitas Springs	228	34.22 N	119.18 W
Čáslav	30	49.54 N	15.23 E
Casma	248	9.28 S	78.19 W
Čašniki	76	54.52 N	29.08 E
Čašnikovo	265b	55.59 N	37.25 E
Časnočor, gora ∧	24	67.45 N	33.25 E
Casola in Lunigiana	64	44.14 N	10.10 E
Casola Valsenio	66	44.13 N	11.37 E
Casole d'Elsa	66	43.20 N	11.02 E
Casoli	66	42.07 N	14.18 E
Cason	222	33.02 N	94.49 W
Casorate Primo	62	45.19 N	9.01 E
Casorate Sempione	62	45.40 N	8.44 E
Casorezzo	266b	45.31 N	8.54 E
Çasoria	68	40.54 N	14.17 E
Časov Jar	83	48.35 N	37.50 E
Časovo	24	62.01 N	50.36 E
Caspe	34	41.14 N	0.02 W
Casper	200	42.52 N	106.18 W
Casper Creek, Middle Fork ≃	200	43.01 N	106.29 W
Caspian	190	46.03 N	88.37 W
Caspian Sea ⊤2	72	42.00 N	50.30 E
Caspienne, Mer → Caspian Sea ⊤2	72	42.00 N	50.30 E
Caspio, Depresión del → Prikaspijskaja nizmennost' ≚	80	48.00 N	52.00 E
Caspio, Mar → Caspian Sea ⊤2	72	42.00 N	50.30 E
Caspoggio	64	46.16 N	9.52 E
Cass □6, Il., U.S.	219	39.57 N	90.13 W
Cass □6, In., U.S.	216	40.45 N	86.21 W
Cass □6, Mi., U.S.	216	41.55 N	86.01 W
Cass □6, Tx., U.S.	222	33.05 N	94.32 W
Cass ≃	190	43.23 N	83.59 W
Cassadaga	214	42.20 N	79.18 W
Cassadaga Creek ≃	214	42.05 N	79.08 W
Cassadaga Lakes ◎	214	42.21 N	79.19 W
Cassaday Point ›	284a	42.52 N	79.13 W
Cassagnas	62	44.16 N	3.45 E
Cassai	152	10.33 S	21.59 E
Cassai (Kasai) ≃	152	3.02 S	16.57 E
Cassamba	152	13.06 S	20.18 E
Cassandra	214	40.24 N	78.38 W
Cassanje ≃	248	17.06 S	57.23 W
Cassano allo Ionio	68	39.47 N	16.20 E
Cassano d'Adda	62	45.32 N	9.31 E
Cassano delle Murge	68	40.53 N	16.46 E
Cassano Magnago	62	45.41 N	8.50 E
Cassaro	70	37.07 N	14.56 E
Cass Benton Parkway ♦	281	42.25 N	83.28 W
Cass City	190	43.36 N	83.10 W
Cassel	50	50.48 N	2.29 E
Casselberry	220	28.40 N	81.19 W
Cassella	216	40.25 N	84.34 W
Casselman	206	45.19 N	75.05 W
Casselton	198	46.54 N	97.12 W
Cássia, Bra.	255	20.36 S	46.56 W
Cassia, Fl., U.S.	220	28.53 N	81.28 W
Cássia dos Coqueiros	256	21.17 S	47.10 W
Cassiar	180	59.16 N	129.40 W
Cassiar Mountains ⋏	176	59.00 N	129.00 W
Cassibile ≃	70	36.57 N	15.11 E
Cassidy	224	49.04 N	123.53 W
Cassidy Airfield ⊠	174o	1.57 N	157.18 W
Cassilândia	255	19.09 S	51.45 W
Cassimbazar	126	24.07 N	88.16 E
Cassine	62	44.45 N	8.31 E
Cassinetta di Lugagnano	266b	45.25 N	8.54 E
Cassinga	152	15.08 S	16.05 E
Cassino, Bra.	252	32.11 S	52.10 W
Cassino, It.	66	41.30 N	13.49 E
Cassio	64	44.35 N	10.02 E
Cassipore ✦8	272b	22.37 N	88.22 E
Cassis	62	43.13 N	5.32 E
Cass Lake	190	47.22 N	94.36 W
Cass Lake ◎, Mi., U.S.	281	42.36 N	83.22 W
Cass Lake ◎, Mn., U.S.	190	47.25 N	94.32 W
Cassley ≃	46	57.58 N	4.35 W
Cassoalala	152	9.30 S	14.22 E
Cassoango	152	13.42 S	20.56 E
Cassolnovo	62	45.22 N	8.48 E
Cassone	64	45.44 N	10.46 E
Cassongue	152	11.51 S	15.03 E
Cassopolis	216	41.54 N	86.00 W
Casstown	218	40.03 N	84.07 W
Cassumba, Ilha I	255	17.46 S	39.17 W
Cassunda	152	10.57 S	21.03 E
Cassununga	255	16.03 S	53.38 W
Cassville, In., U.S.	216	40.33 N	86.08 W
Cassville, Mo., U.S.	194	36.40 N	93.52 W
Cassville, N.Y., U.S.	210	42.57 N	75.15 W
Cassville, Pa., U.S.	214	40.18 N	78.02 W
Cassville, Wi., U.S.	190	42.42 N	90.59 W
Castac Lake ◎	228	34.50 N	118.51 W
Castagnaro	64	45.07 N	11.24 E
Castagneto Carducci	66	43.10 N	10.36 E
Castaic	228	34.30 N	118.37 W
Castaic Creek ≃	228	34.25 N	118.37 W
Castaic Lake ◎1	228	34.32 N	118.37 W
Castalia	214	41.24 N	82.48 W
Castanea	210	41.07 N	77.25 W
Castanhal	250	1.18 S	47.55 W
Castanheira de Pêra	34	40.00 N	8.13 W
Castaños	196	26.47 N	101.25 W
Castañones, Punta ›	236	12.28 N	87.11 W
Castano Primo	62	45.33 N	8.47 E
Casteggio	62	45.00 N	9.07 E
Castel	43b	49.28 N	2.34 W
Castelar	258	34.40 S	58.40 W
Castel Baronia	68	41.03 N	15.11 E
Castel Bolognese	66	44.19 N	11.48 E
Castelbuono	70	37.56 N	14.05 E
Castelcivita	68	40.30 N	15.15 E
Casteldaccia	70	38.03 N	13.32 E
Castel d'Ario	64	45.11 N	10.58 E
Casteldarne (Ehrenburg)	64	46.48 N	11.50 E
Casteldelfino	62	44.35 N	7.04 E
Castel del Monte	66	42.22 N	13.43 E
Castel del Piano	66	42.53 N	11.32 E
Castel del Rio	66	44.12 N	11.30 E
Castel di Decima ✦8	267a	41.45 N	12.26 E
Castel di Guido ✦8	267a	41.54 N	12.17 E
Castel di Ieri	66	42.06 N	13.44 E
Castel di Iudica	70	37.30 N	14.38 E
Castel di Leva ✦8	267a	41.47 N	12.32 E
Castel di Lucio	70	37.53 N	14.19 E
Castel di Sangro	66	41.47 N	14.06 E
Castel di Tora	66	42.13 N	12.58 E
Castelfidardo	66	43.28 N	13.33 E
Castelfiorentino	66	43.36 N	10.58 E
Castelfondo	64	46.27 N	11.07 E
Castelforte	66	41.18 N	13.49 E
Castelfranco Emilia	64	44.37 N	11.03 E
Castelfranco in Miscano	68	41.18 N	15.05 E
Castelfranco Veneto	64	45.40 N	11.55 E
Castel Frentano	66	42.12 N	14.22 E
Castel Fusano ✦8	267a	41.44 N	12.19 E
Castel Gandolfo	66	41.45 N	12.39 E
Castel Giorgio	66	42.42 N	11.59 E
Castelgrande	68	40.47 N	15.26 E
Castelhanos, Baía de ⊂	256	23.51 S	45.15 W
Castelhanos, Ponta dos ›	256	23.10 S	44.06 W
Casteljaloux	32	44.19 N	0.05 E
Castellabate	68	40.17 N	14.57 E
Castell'Alfero	62	44.59 N	8.13 E
Castellalto	66	42.40 N	13.49 E
Castellammare, Golfo di ⊂	70	38.08 N	12.54 E
Castellammare del Golfo	70	38.01 N	12.53 E
Castellammare di Stabia	68	40.42 N	14.29 E
Castellamonte	62	45.23 N	7.42 E
Castellana, Grotte di ±5	68	40.53 N	17.07 E
Castellana Grotte	68	40.53 N	17.11 E
Castellana Sicula	70	37.47 N	14.02 E
Castellane	62	43.51 N	6.31 E
Castellaneta	68	40.37 N	16.57 E
Castellanza	62	45.37 N	8.54 E
Castellarano	64	44.30 N	10.44 E
Castell'Arquato	62	44.51 N	9.52 E
Castell'Azzara	66	42.46 N	11.42 E
Castellazzo Bormida	62	44.51 N	8.34 E
Castellbisbal	266d	41.29 N	1.59 E
Castelldefels	266d	41.17 N	1.59 E
Castelleone	62	45.18 N	9.46 E
Castelletto	266b	45.30 N	8.48 E
Castelletto di Brenzone	64	45.41 N	10.45 E
Castelli, Arg.	252	36.06 S	57.47 W
Castelli, It.	66	42.29 N	13.43 E
Castellina in Chianti	66	43.28 N	11.17 E
Castellina Marittima	66	43.25 N	10.35 E
Castelli Romani ✦1	267a	41.46 N	12.42 E
Castelló □4	34	40.10 N	0.10 W
Castello, Monte ∧	66	43.03 N	9.49 E
Castello d'Annone	62	44.53 N	8.19 E
Castelló de la Plana	34	39.59 N	0.02 W
Castello di Fiemme	64	46.17 N	11.26 E
Castello Lavazzo	64	46.17 N	12.18 E
Castellote	34	40.48 N	0.19 W
Castello Tesino	64	46.04 N	11.38 E
Castellucchio	64	45.09 N	10.39 E
Castelluccio	68	40.00 N	15.58 E
Castell'Umberto	70	38.05 N	14.48 E
Castelluzzo	70	38.06 N	12.44 E
Castel Madama	66	41.58 N	12.52 E
Castel Maggiore	64	44.34 N	11.22 E
Castelmagno	62	44.24 N	7.13 E
Castelmassa	64	45.01 N	11.18 E
Castelmauro	66	41.50 N	14.43 E
Castelmezzano	68	40.32 N	16.03 E
Castelmoron-sur-Lot	32	44.24 N	0.30 E
Castelnaudary	32	43.19 N	1.57 E
Castelnau-Montratier	32	44.16 N	1.21 E
Castelnovo di Sotto	64	44.49 N	10.34 E
Castelnovo ne'Monti	64	44.26 N	10.24 E
Castelnuovo	64	45.26 N	10.47 E
Castelnuovo Berardenga	66	43.21 N	11.30 E
Castelnuovo dell'Abate	66	43.00 N	11.31 E
Castelnuovo della Daunia	68	41.35 N	15.07 E
Castelnuovo di Garfagnana	64	44.06 N	10.24 E
Castelnuovo di Porto	66	42.07 N	12.30 E
Castelnuovo di Val di Cecina	66	43.12 N	10.59 E
Castelnuovo Don Bosco	62	45.03 N	7.58 E
Castelnuovo Nigra	62	45.26 N	7.41 E
Castelnuovo Rangone	64	44.33 N	10.56 E
Castelnuovo Scrivia	62	44.59 N	8.53 E
Castelo	255	20.36 S	41.12 W
Castelo Branco	34	39.49 N	7.30 W
Castelo do Piauí	250	5.20 S	41.33 W
Castel Pagano	68	41.24 N	14.48 E
Castel Porziano ✦8	267a	41.44 N	12.24 E
Castelraimondo	66	43.12 N	13.04 E
Castel Romano ✦8	267a	41.44 N	12.27 E
Castel San Gimignano	66	43.24 N	11.00 E
Castel San Giorgio	68	40.47 N	14.42 E
Castel San Giovanni	62	45.04 N	9.26 E
Castel San Lorenzo	68	40.25 N	15.14 E
Castel San Pietro Terme	66	44.24 N	11.35 E
Castel Sant'Elia	66	42.15 N	12.22 E
Castelsaraceno	68	40.10 N	16.00 E
Castelsardo	71	40.55 N	8.43 E
Castelsarrasin	32	44.02 N	1.06 E
Castelsilano	68	39.16 N	16.46 E
Casteltermini	70	37.32 N	13.39 E
Castelvecchio Subequo	66	42.08 N	13.44 E
Castelvetere in Val Fortore	68	41.27 N	14.56 E
Castelvetrano	70	37.41 N	12.47 E
Castelvetro di Modena	64	44.30 N	10.57 E
Castelvetro Piacentino	64	45.05 N	9.59 E
Castel Viscardo	66	42.45 N	12.00 E
Castel Volturno, It.	66	44.13 N	11.37 E
Castel Volturno, It.	68	41.02 N	13.56 E
Castenaso	64	44.30 N	11.28 E
Castenedolo	64	45.28 N	10.18 E
Casterton	166	37.35 S	141.24 E
Castets	32	43.53 N	1.09 W
Castiglioncello	66	43.24 N	10.24 E
Castiglione Chiavarese	62	44.16 N	9.31 E
Castiglione d'Adda	62	45.13 N	9.41 E
Castiglione dei Pepoli	64	44.08 N	11.09 E
Castiglione del Lago	66	43.07 N	12.03 E
Castiglione della Pescaia	66	42.46 N	10.53 E
Castiglione delle Stiviere	64	45.23 N	10.29 E
Castiglione del Pepoli	66	44.08 N	11.09 E
Castiglione di Sicilia	70	37.53 N	15.07 E
Castiglione d'Orcia	66	43.00 N	11.37 E
Castiglione d'Ossola	58	46.03 N	8.13 E
Castiglione Messer Marino	66	41.52 N	14.27 E
Castiglione Olona	62	45.46 N	8.52 E
Castiglion Fibocchi	66	43.32 N	11.46 E
Castiglion Fiorentino	66	43.20 N	11.55 E
Castile	210	42.37 N	78.03 W
Castilho	255	20.52 S	51.29 W
Castilla	248	5.12 S	80.38 W
Castilla, Playa de ±2	34	37.00 N	6.33 W
Castilla-La Mancha □4	34	39.30 N	3.00 W
Castilla la Nueva □9	34	40.00 N	3.45 W
Castilla la Vieja □9	34	41.30 N	4.00 W
Castilla-León □4	34	41.30 N	5.00 W
Castillo	258	33.53 S	57.40 W
Castillo, Cerro ∧	254	43.03 S	71.57 W
Castillo, Pampa del ≚	254	45.58 S	68.24 W
Castillo de San Marcos National Monument ♦	192	29.44 N	81.20 W
Castillo Incaico de Ingapirca ⊥	246	2.34 S	78.50 W
Castillon-la-Bataille	32	44.51 N	0.03 W
Castillos	252	34.12 S	53.50 W
Castillos, Laguna de ◎	252	34.20 S	53.54 W
Castine	188	44.23 N	68.48 W
Castione della Presolana	64	45.54 N	10.04 E
Castions di Strada	64	45.54 N	13.11 E
Castle Acre	42	52.42 N	0.41 E
Castle Air Force Base ■	226	37.22 N	120.34 W
Castlebar	48	53.52 N	9.17 W
Castlebay	46	56.57 N	7.28 W
Castlebellingham	48	53.54 N	6.23 W
Castleberry	194	31.17 N	87.01 W
Castleblayney	48	54.07 N	6.44 W
Castle Bruce	240d	15.26 N	61.16 W
Castle Cape ›	180	56.15 N	158.06 W
Castle Cary	42	51.06 N	2.31 W
Castlecliff	172	39.57 S	174.59 E

Symbol	English	Deutsch	Español	Français	Português
≃	River	Fluß	Río	Rivière	Rio
≋	Canal	Kanal	Canal	Canal	Canal
ᒪ	Waterfall, Rapids	Wasserfall, Stromschnellen	Cascada, Rápidos	Chute d'eau, Rapides	Cascata, Rápidos
ꟸ	Strait	Meeresstraße	Estrecho	Détroit	Estreito
⊂	Bay, Gulf	Bucht, Golf	Bahía, Golfo	Baie, Golfe	Baía, Golfo
◎	Lake, Lakes	See, Seen	Lago, Lagos	Lac, Lacs	Lago, Lagos
☷	Swamp	Sumpf	Pantano	Marais	Pântano
⊓	Ice Features, Glacier	Eis- und Gletscherformen	Accidentes Glaciales	Formes glaciaires	Acidentes glaciares
⊤	Other Hydrographic Features	Andere Hydrographische Objekte	Otros Elementos Hidrográficos	Autres données hydrographiques	Outros acidentes hidrográficos

Symbol	English	Deutsch	Español	Français	Português
✢	Submarine Features	Untermeerische Objekte	Accidentes Submarinos	Formes de relief sous-marin	Acidentes submarinos
□	Political Unit	Politische Einheit	Unidad Politica	Entité politique	Unidade política
ψ	Cultural Institution	Kulturelle Institution	Institución Cultural	Institution culturelle	Instituição cultural
⊥	Historical Site	Historische Stätte	Sitio Histórico	Site historique	Sitio histórico
♦	Recreational Site	Erholungs- und Ferienort	Sitio de Recreo	Centre de loisirs	Area de Lazer
⊠	Airport	Flughafen	Aeropuerto	Aéroport	Aeroporto
■	Military Installation	Militäranlage	Instalación Militar	Installation militaire	Instalação militar
✦	Miscellaneous	Verschiedenes	Misceláneo	Divers	Diversos

Castlecomer 48 52.48 N 7.12 W
Castleconnell 48 52.43 N 8.30 W
Castlecrag 274a 33.48 S 151.13 E
Castle Crags State Park ♦ 204 41.10 N 122.20 W
Castle Creek 210 42.14 N 75.55 W
Castle Creek ≃, Austl. 169 36.41 S 145.29 E
Castle Creek ≃, Id., U.S. 202 43.06 N 116.16 W
Castle Dale 200 39.23 N 110.27 W
Castledawson 48 54.47 N 6.33 W
Castlederg 48 54.42 N 7.36 W
Castledermot 48 52.55 N 6.50 W
Castle Dome Peak ∧ 200 33.05 N 114.08 W
Castle Donington 42 52.51 N 1.19 W
Castle Douglas 44 54.57 N 3.56 W
Castlefinn 48 54.47 N 7.35 W
Castleford 44 53.44 N 1.21 W
Castlegar 182 49.19 N 117.40 W
Castle Harbour ⊂ 240a 32.21 N 64.40 W
Castle Hill 274a 33.44 S 151.00 E
Castle Hills, De., U.S. 208 39.41 N 75.33 W
Castle Hills, Tx., U.S. 196 29.32 N 98.31 W
Castleisland 48 52.14 N 9.27 W
Castlemaine, Austl. 169 37.04 S 144.13 E
Castlemaine, Ire. 48 52.09 N 9.43 W
Castlemartyr 48 51.55 N 8.03 W
Castlemore 275b 43.47 N 79.41 W
Castle Mountain ∧, Ab., Can. 182 51.18 N 115.55 W
Castle Mountain ∧, Yk., Can. 180 64.32 N 135.25 W
Castle Mountain ∧, Ca., U.S. 226 35.56 N 120.20 W
Castle Neck ▸¹ 283 42.41 N 70.45 W
Castle Neck ≃ 283 42.40 N 70.44 W
Castle Park 228 32.36 N 117.04 W
Castle Peak ∧, Co., U.S. 200 39.01 N 106.52 W
Castle Peak ∧, Id., U.S. 202 44.02 N 114.35 W
Castle Peak ∧, Wa., U.S. 224 48.58 N 120.51 W
Castlepoint 172 40.54 S 176.13 E
Castle Point ⊡⁸ 260 51.33 N 0.35 E
Castlepollard 48 53.40 N 7.17 W
Castlerea 48 53.46 N 8.29 W
Castlereagh ≃ 166 30.12 S 147.32 E
Castle Rock, Co., U.S. 200 39.22 N 104.51 W
Castle Rock, Pa., U.S. 285 39.58 N 75.26 W
Castle Rock, Wa., U.S. 224 46.16 N 122.54 W
Castle Rock ∧, Or., U.S. 202 44.02 N 118.11 W
Castle Rock ∧, Va., U.S. 192 37.57 N 78.44 W
Castle Rock Butte ∧ 198 45.00 N 103.27 W
Castle Rock Lake ⊜¹ 190 43.56 N 89.58 W
Castle Shannon 279b 40.21 N 80.01 W
Castleshaw Moor ✢³ 262 53.36 N 2.00 W
Castleside 44 54.50 N 1.52 W
Castleton, Eng., U.K. 44 53.21 N 1.46 W
Castleton, Eng., U.K. 44 54.28 N 0.56 W
Castleton, Eng., U.K. 262 53.35 N 2.11 W
Castleton, In., U.S. 218 39.54 N 86.03 W
Castleton, Vt., U.S. 188 43.36 N 73.10 W
Castleton on Hudson 210 42.32 N 73.45 W
Castletown, I. of Man 44 54.04 N 4.40 W
Castletown, Scot., U.K. 46 58.35 N 3.23 W
Castletown Bearhaven (Castletown Bere) 48 51.39 N 9.55 W
Castletown Bere → Castletown Bearhaven 48 51.39 N 9.55 W
Castletown Geoghegan 48 53.26 N 7.38 W
Castletownroche 48 52.10 N 8.28 W
Castletownshend 48 51.32 N 9.11 W
Castlewellan 48 54.16 N 5.57 W
Castlewood, Ky., U.S. 218 38.04 N 84.27 W
Castlewood, S.D., U.S. 198 44.43 N 97.01 W
Castlewood, Va., U.S. 192 36.53 N 82.16 W
Častoje 82 54.11 N 37.47 E
Častooz'ornoje 86 55.34 N 67.53 E
Castor 182 52.13 N 111.53 W
Castor ≃, On., Can. 212 45.18 N 75.10 W
Castor ≃, Mo., U.S. 194 36.51 N 89.44 W
Castorano 66 42.54 N 13.43 E
Castor Creek ≃ 194 31.47 N 92.22 W
Castorland 212 43.53 N 75.30 W
Castra Vetera ⊥ 263 51.39 N 6.28 E
Castres 32 43.36 N 2.15 E
Castricum 52 52.33 N 4.39 E
Castries, Fr. 62 43.40 N 3.59 E
Castries, St. Luc. 241f 14.01 N 61.00 W
Castries, Port ⊂ 241f 14.01 N 61.01 W
Castro, Bra. 252 24.47 S 50.00 W
Castro, Chile 254 42.29 S 73.46 W
Castro, It. 64 45.48 N 10.04 E
Castro, Arroyo de ≃ 258 33.37 S 56.10 W
Castro, Punta ▸ 254 43.22 S 65.03 W
Castro Barros 252 30.35 S 65.44 W
Castrocaro Terme 66 44.10 N 11.57 E
Castrocielo 66 41.32 N 13.42 E
Castro Daire 34 40.54 N 7.56 W
Castro dei Volsci 66 41.30 N 13.24 E
Castro del Río 34 37.41 N 4.28 W
Castrofilippo 70 37.21 N 13.46 E
Castrojeriz 34 42.17 N 4.08 W
Castro Marim 34 37.13 N 7.26 W
Castronuño 34 41.23 N 5.16 W
Castronuovo di Sant'Andrea 68 40.11 N 16.11 E
Castronuovo di Sicilia 70 37.41 N 13.36 E
Castropignano 66 41.37 N 14.33 E
Castropol 34 43.32 N 7.02 W
Castrop-Rauxel 52 51.34 N 7.18 E
Castroreale 70 38.06 N 15.12 E
Castro-Urdiales 34 43.23 N 3.13 W
Castro Valley 226 37.41 N 122.05 W
Castro Verde 34 37.42 N 8.05 W
Castrovillari 68 39.49 N 16.13 E
Castroville, Ca., U.S. 226 36.45 N 121.45 W
Castroville, Tx., U.S. 196 29.21 N 98.52 W
Castrovirreyna 248 13.16 S 75.19 W
Castuera 34 38.43 N 5.33 W
Çast uul ∧ 86 48.40 N 90.45 E
Častyje 80 57.19 N 54.59 E
Casummit Lake 184 51.28 N 92.24 W
Casupá 252 34.07 S 55.39 W
Caswell Sound ⊔ 172 45.00 S 167.10 E
Çat 130 39.40 N 41.00 E
Čat ≃ 184 51.07 N 91.25 W
Catabola 152 12.09 S 17.16 E
Cataby 162 30.43 S 115.31 E
Catacamas 236 14.48 N 85.54 W
Catacaos 248 5.16 S 80.41 W
Catacocha 246 4.04 S 79.38 W
Cataguarino 256 21.18 S 42.43 W
Cataguases 256 21.24 S 42.41 W
Catahoula Lake ⊜ 194 31.30 N 92.06 W
Çatak 128 38.01 N 43.07 E
Çatakköprü 130 38.09 N 41.12 E
Catalaban Island I 116 11.51 N 125.28 E
Çatalan 130 37.14 N 35.16 E
Catalão 255 18.10 S 47.57 W
Catalão, Ponta do ▸ 287a 22.51 S 43.13 W
Çatalca 130 41.09 N 28.27 E
Çatalçam 130 40.00 N 38.51 E
Catalfaro ≃ 70 37.22 N 14.43 E
Catalina, Nf., Can. 186 48.31 N 53.05 W
Catalina, Chile 252 25.13 S 69.43 W
Catalina, Punta ▸ 254 52.32 S 68.47 W
Catalina → Santa Catalina Island I 228 33.23 N 118.24 W
Catalonia → Catalunya ⊡⁴ 34 41.40 N 1.30 E
Catalunya ⊡⁴ 34 41.40 N 1.30 E
Catalzeytin 130 41.57 N 34.13 E
Catamarca ⊡⁴ 252 27.00 S 67.00 W
Catamare 286c 10.36 N 67.02 W
Catamayo 246 3.59 S 79.21 W
Catamayo ≃ 246 4.18 S 80.09 W
Catanauan 116 13.36 N 122.19 E
Catanduanes ⊡⁴ 116 13.47 N 124.16 E
Catanduanes Island I 116 13.45 N 124.15 E
Catanduva 255 21.08 S 48.58 W
Catane → Catania 70 37.30 N 15.06 E
Catania 70 37.30 N 15.06 E
Catania ⊡⁴ 70 37.23 N 14.40 E
Catania, Golfo di ⊂ 70 37.24 N 15.09 E
Catania, Piana di ≍ 70 37.25 N 14.51 E
Cataño 240m 18.27 N 66.07 W
Catanzaro 68 38.54 N 16.36 E
Catanzaro ⊡⁴ 68 38.54 N 16.36 E
Catanzaro Lido 68 38.49 N 16.36 E
Cataonia ⊡⁹ 130 38.00 N 35.00 E
Catára ≃ 152 13.34 S 12.35 E
Cataract Canyon ∨ 200 36.03 N 112.35 W
Cataract Reservoir ⊜¹ 170 34.16 S 150.48 E
Catarama 246 1.35 S 79.28 W
Cataraqui 212 44.16 N 76.32 W
Cataraqui ≃ 212 44.13 N 76.28 W
Catarina 250 6.12 S 39.54 W
Catarman, Pil. 116 9.08 N 124.40 E
Catarman, Pil. 116 12.30 N 124.38 E
Catarroja 34 39.24 N 0.24 W
Catasauqua 208 40.39 N 75.29 W
Catatumbo ≃ 246 9.22 N 71.45 W
Catawba 218 40.00 N 83.37 W
Catawba ≃ 192 34.36 N 80.54 W
Catawba Island 214 41.35 N 82.50 W
Catawissa, Mo., U.S. 219 38.25 N 90.47 W
Catawissa, Pa., U.S. 210 40.57 N 76.27 W
Catawissa Creek ≃ 210 40.57 N 76.28 W
Cataxa 154 15.58 S 33.12 E
Cat Ba, Dao I 110 20.50 N 107.00 E
Catbalogan 116 11.46 N 124.53 E
Catchabutan, Punta ▸ 236 15.50 N 86.32 W
Catchacoma Lake ⊜ 212 44.45 N 78.20 W
Cateco Cangola 152 8.27 S 15.48 E
Catedral, Cerro ∧² 252 34.23 S 54.40 W
Cateel 116 7.48 N 126.27 E
Cateel ≃ 116 7.47 N 126.27 E
Cateel Bay ⊂ 116 7.54 N 126.25 E
Catemaco 234 18.25 N 95.07 W
Catemaco, Laguna ⊜ 234 18.25 N 95.05 W
Catembe 156 26.00 S 32.33 E
Catenanuova 70 37.34 N 14.41 E
Caterham 42 51.17 N 0.04 W
Caterino Rodriguez 232 24.51 N 100.19 W
Catete 152 9.06 S 13.43 E
Catete ✢⁸ 287a 22.55 S 43.10 W
Catete ≃ 250 6.04 S 54.09 W
Catfish Creek ≃, On., Can. 212 42.39 N 81.01 W
Catfish Creek ≃, N.Y., U.S. 212 43.31 N 76.19 W
Catfish Creek ≃, Tx., U.S. 222 31.47 N 95.56 W
Catford ✢⁸ 260 51.27 N 0.01 W
Catharine Creek ≃ 210 42.21 N 76.51 W
Cathcart 158 32.18 S 27.09 E
Cathead Mountain ∧ 210 43.17 N 74.17 W
Cathedral City 204 33.46 N 116.27 W
Cathedral Gorge State Park ♦ 204 37.50 N 114.30 W
Cathedral Mountain ∧ 196 30.10 N 103.40 W
Cathedral of the Pines ☗¹ 207 42.47 N 71.58 W
Cathedral Provincial Park ♦ 202 49.05 N 120.10 W
Cathedral Range ⋏ 226 37.47 N 119.21 W
Catherines Peak ∧ 241q 18.04 N 76.42 W
Catheys Valley 226 37.25 N 120.06 W
Cathlamet 224 46.12 N 123.22 W
Catholic University ☗² 284c 38.56 N 77.00 W
Catia ✢⁸ 286c 10.31 N 66.57 W
Catia La Mar 286c 10.36 N 67.02 W
Ca' Tiepolo 66 44.56 N 12.22 E
Catignano 66 42.21 N 13.57 E
Catió 150 11.13 N 15.10 W
Catirina, Punta ▸ 71 40.29 N 9.32 E
Cat Island I, Ba. 238 24.27 N 75.30 W
Cat Island I, Ma., U.S. 283 42.31 N 70.49 W
Cat Island I, Ms., U.S. 194 30.13 N 89.06 W
Čatkal ≃ 85 41.38 N 70.01 E
Čatkal'skij chrebet ⋏ 85 41.40 N 71.05 E
Cat Lake ⊜ 184 51.40 N 91.50 W
Catlettsburg 188 38.24 N 82.36 W
Catlin 194 40.03 N 87.42 W
Catlins ≃ 172 46.29 S 169.43 E
Catlodge 46 57.00 N 4.15 W
Catnip Mountain ∧ 204 41.52 N 119.23 W
Cato 210 43.10 N 76.34 W
Catoche, Cabo ▸ 232 21.35 N 87.05 W
Catoctin Creek ≃ 208 39.18 N 77.33 W
Catoctin Mountain ∧ 208 39.26 N 77.31 W
Cato Island I 166 23.15 S 155.32 E
Catolé do Rocha 250 6.21 S 37.45 W
Católica, Universidad ☗², Chile 286e 33.27 S 70.39 W
Católica, Universidad ☗², Perú 286d 12.04 S 77.05 W
Caton 44 54.04 N 2.43 W
Catonsville 208 39.16 N 76.43 W
Catonsville Manor 284b 39.18 N 76.44 W
Catoosa 196 36.11 N 95.44 W
Catorce 234 23.42 N 100.54 W
Catorce, Sierra de ⋏ 234 23.36 N 100.52 W
Catota 152 13.52 S 17.15 E
Catria, Monte ∧ 66 43.28 N 12.42 E
Catriló 252 36.26 S 63.24 W
Catrimani ≃ 246 0.28 N 61.44 W
Catrine 46 55.30 N 4.20 W
Cats, Mont des ∧² 50 50.47 N 2.40 E
Catshill 42 52.22 N 2.03 W
Catskill 210 42.13 N 73.51 W
Catskill Aqueduct ≃ 276 41.11 N 73.48 W
Catskill Creek ≃ 210 42.12 N 73.51 W
Catskill Game Farm ♦ 210 42.15 N 74.01 W
Catskill Mountains ⋏ 210 42.10 N 74.30 W
Catskill Park ♦ 210 42.00 N 74.30 W
Cat Spring 222 29.51 N 96.20 W
Catt, Mount ∧ 182 54.21 N 128.47 W
Cattai Creek ≃ 274a 33.40 S 150.56 E
Cattaraugus 210 42.19 N 78.52 W
Cattaraugus ⊡⁶ 214 42.15 N 78.45 W
Cattaraugus Creek ≃ 214 42.35 N 79.10 W
Cattaraugus Creek, South Branch ≃ 214 42.26 N 78.53 W
Cattaraugus Indian Reservation ✢⁴ 210 42.33 N 78.56 W
Cattenom 56 49.25 N 6.15 E
Catterick 44 54.22 N 1.38 W
Catterick Garrison 44 54.22 N 1.43 W
Cattle Canyon ∨ 280 34.14 N 117.46 W
Cattolica 66 43.58 N 12.44 E
Cattolica del Sacro Cuore, Università ☗² 266b 45.27 N 9.11 E
Cattolica Eraclea 70 37.26 N 13.24 E
Catton 44 54.55 N 2.15 W
Catu 255 12.21 S 38.23 W
Catuala 152 16.29 S 19.03 E
Catuane 156 26.48 S 32.18 E
Catubig 116 12.24 N 125.03 E
Catubig ≃ 116 12.34 N 125.01 E
Catuçaba 256 23.15 S 45.12 W
Catumbela 152 12.25 S 13.34 E
Catumbela ≃ 152 12.27 S 13.29 E
Catur 154 13.45 S 35.30 E
Catus 32 44.34 N 1.20 E
Catwick, Îles II 110 10.00 N 109.00 E
Čatyrk'ol', ozero ⊜ 85 40.38 N 75.17 E
Čatyrtaš 85 40.55 N 76.26 E
Cau ≃ 110 21.07 N 106.18 E
Cau, Rach ≃ 269c 10.51 N 106.49 E
Cauaburi ≃ 246 0.17 S 65.56 W
Cauayan, Pil. 116 16.56 N 121.46 E
Cauayan, Pil. 116 9.58 N 122.37 E
Caubvick, Mount (Mont d'Iberville) ∧ 176 58.53 N 63.43 W
Cauca ⊡⁵ 246 2.30 N 76.50 W
Cauca ≃ 246 8.54 N 74.28 W
Caucaia 250 3.42 S 38.39 W
Caucaia do Alto 256 23.41 S 47.02 W
Caucase, Monts du → Bol'šoj Kavkaz ⋏ 84 42.30 N 45.00 E
Caucasia 246 8.00 N 75.12 W
Caucaso → Bol'šoj Kavkaz ⋏ 84 42.30 N 45.00 E
Caucasus → Bol'šoj Kavkaz ⋏ 84 42.30 N 45.00 E
Caucete 252 31.39 S 68.17 W
Cauchari, Salar de ≍ 252 23.50 S 66.50 W
Cauchon Lake ⊜ 184 55.25 N 96.30 W
Caudebec-en-Caux 50 49.32 N 0.44 E
Caudebec-lès-Elbeuf 50 49.17 N 1.02 E
Caudry 50 50.08 N 3.25 E
Caughdenoy 210 43.16 N 76.12 W
Caughnawaga 275a 45.25 N 73.41 W
Caughnawaga Indian Reserve ✢⁴ 206 45.23 N 73.41 W
Cauitan, Mount ∧ 116 17.16 N 121.00 E
Cauit Point ▸, Pil. 116 12.16 N 122.38 E
Cauit Point ▸, Pil. 116 9.18 N 126.12 E
Cauldcleuch Head ∧ 44 55.18 N 2.51 W
Caulfield 169 37.53 S 145.03 E
Caulfield Racecourse ♦ 274b 37.53 S 145.02 E
Caulkerbush 44 54.54 N 3.40 W
Caulonia 68 38.23 N 16.25 E
Caumont-sur-Durance 62 43.54 N 4.57 E
Caumsett State Park ♦ 276 40.55 N 73.28 W
Caúngula 152 8.25 S 18.40 E
Čaunskaja guba ⊂ 74 69.20 N 170.00 E
Cauquenes 252 35.58 S 72.21 W
Caura ≃ 246 7.38 N 64.53 W
Caurés ≃ 246 1.21 S 62.20 W
Caurimare ≃ 286c 10.28 N 66.48 W
Causapscal 186 48.22 N 67.14 W
Čausovo 82 54.49 N 36.55 E
Caussade 32 44.10 N 1.32 E
Čausy 76 53.48 N 30.58 E
Cautário ≃ 248 12.13 S 64.34 W
Caution, Cape ▸ 182 51.10 N 127.47 W
Cauto ≃ 240p 20.33 N 77.14 W
Čauvaj 85 40.08 N 72.13 E
Caux, Pays de ✢¹ 50 49.40 N 0.40 E
Cava 256 22.41 S 43.26 W
Cava de' Tirreni 68 40.42 N 14.42 E
Cávado ≃ 34 41.32 N 8.48 W
Cavaglià 62 45.24 N 8.05 E
Cavaillon 62 43.50 N 5.02 E
Cavalaire-sur-Mer 62 43.10 N 6.32 E
Cavalcante 255 13.48 S 47.30 W
Cavalese 64 46.17 N 11.27 E
Cavalheiro 255 17.15 S 48.02 W
Cavalier 198 48.47 N 97.37 W
Cavalière 62 43.09 N 6.26 E
Cavalla (Cavally) ≃ 150 4.22 N 7.32 W
Cavalleria, Cap de ▸ 34 40.05 N 4.05 E
Cavallermaggiore 62 44.43 N 7.41 E
Cavalli Islands II 172 35.02 S 173.58 E
Cavallino, Litorale di ⊥² 64 45.27 N 12.30 E
Cavallo, Île I 71 41.21 N 9.16 E
Cavallo, Monte ∧ 64 46.08 N 12.30 E
Cavally (Cavalla) ≃ 150 4.22 N 7.32 W
Cavalos, Ribeirão dos ≃ 256 21.29 S 44.13 W
Cava Manara 62 45.08 N 9.07 E
Cavan 48 54.00 N 7.21 W
Cavan ⊡⁶ 48 53.55 N 7.15 W
Cavanaugh, Lake ⊜ 224 48.23 N 122.00 W
Čavan'ga 24 66.06 N 37.47 E
Cavarzere 64 45.08 N 12.05 E
Cavaso del Tomba 64 45.51 N 11.52 E
Çavdır 130 37.09 N 29.42 E
Cave, It. 66 41.49 N 12.56 E
Cave, N.Z. 172 44.19 S 170.57 E
Cave City, Ar., U.S. 194 35.56 N 91.32 W
Cave City, Ky., U.S. 194 37.08 N 85.57 W
Cave Creek ≃ 200 33.34 N 112.07 W
Cave del Predil 64 46.26 N 13.34 E
Cavedine 64 45.59 N 10.59 E
Cave In Rock 194 37.29 N 88.10 W
Caveiras ≃ 252 27.35 S 50.56 W
Cavelo 152 17.33 S 19.21 E
Cavendish 166 37.31 S 142.02 E
Cavernago 62 45.38 N 9.46 E
Cavertitz 54 51.23 N 13.08 E
Cave Run Lake ⊜¹ 188 38.03 N 83.30 W
Cave Spring 192 34.14 N 85.20 W
Cavettsville 279b 40.22 N 79.46 W
Cavezzo 64 44.50 N 11.02 E
Cavi 62 44.17 N 9.22 E
Caviana de Fora, Ilha I 250 0.10 N 50.10 W
Cavili Island I 116 9.17 N 120.50 E
Cavinzas, Isla I 286d 12.07 S 77.13 W
Cavite 116 14.29 N 120.55 E
Cavite ⊡⁴ 116 14.15 N 120.50 E
Čavka 84 41.44 N 41.45 E
Čavlisaj 85 41.08 N 69.44 E
Cavo, Monte ∧ 267a 41.45 N 12.42 E
Cavoli, Isola dei I 71 39.05 N 9.33 E
Cavonne ≃ 68 40.17 N 16.47 E
Cavour 62 44.47 N 7.22 E
Cavour, Canale ≡ 62 45.11 N 7.54 E
Cavriago 64 44.42 N 10.31 E
Cavriana 64 45.21 N 10.36 E
Cavtat 38 42.35 N 18.13 E
Çavuş 130 37.36 N 31.56 E
Çavuşbaşı ≃ 267b 40.58 N 28.51 E
Çavuşçu Gölü ⊜ 130 38.25 N 31.53 E
Cawatose, Lac ⊜ 190 47.20 N 77.07 W
Cawayan 116 11.56 N 123.46 E
Cawdor 46 57.31 N 3.56 W
Cawker City 198 39.30 N 98.26 W
Cawnpore → Kānpur 124 26.28 N 80.21 E
Cawood, Eng., U.K. 44 53.50 N 1.07 W
Cawood, Ky., U.S. 192 36.47 N 83.13 W
Cawston, B.C., Can. 182 49.11 N 119.45 W
Cawston, Eng., U.K. 42 52.46 N 1.10 E
Cawthon 222 30.25 N 96.14 W
Caxambu 256 21.59 S 44.56 W
Caxias, Bra. 250 4.50 S 43.21 W
Caxias, Port. 266c 38.42 N 9.16 W
Caxias do Sul 252 29.10 S 51.11 W
Caxinas, Punta ▸ 236 16.01 N 86.02 W
Caxito 152 8.33 S 13.36 E
Caxiuana, Baía de ⊂ 250 1.45 S 51.20 W
Caxopa 152 11.52 S 20.52 E
Çay 130 38.35 N 31.02 E
Cayacal, Punta ▸ 234 17.56 N 102.11 W
Çayağzı ✢⁸ 267b 41.13 N 29.12 E
Çayağzı ≃ 267b 41.14 N 29.12 E
Cayambe 246 0.03 N 78.08 W
Cayambe ∧¹ 246 0.00 77.59 W
Cayapoñga 116 5.48 N 125.33 E
Çaybaşı 130 41.02 N 37.06 E
Cayce 192 33.57 N 81.04 W
Çaycuma 130 41.25 N 32.05 E
Caycuse 224 48.53 N 124.22 W
Caycuse ≃ 224 48.48 N 124.41 W
Cay Duong, Vinh ⊂ 110 10.10 N 104.45 E
Cayenne 250 4.56 N 52.20 W
Cayenne ⊡⁸ 250 4.00 N 52.30 W
Cayes → Les Cayes 238 18.12 N 73.45 W
Cayeux-sur-Mer 50 50.11 N 1.29 E
Cayey 240m 18.07 N 66.10 W
Cayey, Sierra de ⋏ 240m 18.07 N 66.02 W
Çayıralan 130 39.18 N 35.40 E
Çayırbaşı 130 40.53 N 42.36 E
Çayırhan 130 40.06 N 31.37 E
Çayırlı 130 39.48 N 40.01 E
Çaylarbaşı 130 37.41 N 39.00 E
Caylus 32 44.14 N 1.46 E
Cayman Brac I 238 19.43 N 79.49 W
Cayman Islands ⊡², N.A. 230 19.30 N 80.40 W
Cayman Islands ⊡², N.A. 238 19.30 N 80.40 W
Cayman Trench ✣¹ 16 19.00 N 80.00 W
Cayna 248 10.11 S 76.20 W
Caynabo 144 8.57 N 46.26 E
Cayo Agua, Isla I 236 9.09 N 82.02 W
Çayözü 130 39.36 N 38.11 E
Cay Point ▸ 240b 24.59 N 77.25 W
Çayra 130 40.41 N 39.06 E
Cayres 62 44.55 N 3.48 E
Cay Sal Bank ✣² 238 23.45 N 80.00 W
Çaytepe 130 38.48 N 40.41 E
Cayucos 226 35.27 N 120.54 W
Cayuga, In., U.S. 194 39.56 N 87.27 W
Cayuga, N.Y., U.S. 210 42.55 N 76.44 W
Cayuga, N.D., U.S. 198 46.04 N 97.23 W
Cayuga, Tx., U.S. 222 31.57 N 95.57 W
Cayuga ⊡⁶ 210 42.56 N 76.34 W
Cayuga and Seneca Canal ≡ 210 42.56 N 76.44 W
Cayuga Creek ≃, N.Y., U.S. 210 42.52 N 78.47 W
Cayuga Creek ≃, N.Y., U.S. 284a 43.04 N 78.57 W
Cayuga Heights 210 42.27 N 76.29 W
Cayuga Lake ⊜ 210 42.45 N 76.45 W
Cayuta 210 42.17 N 76.42 W
Cayuta Creek ≃ 210 41.59 N 76.30 W
Cazage 152 11.02 S 20.45 E
Cazalla de la Sierra 34 37.56 N 5.45 W
Căzănești 38 44.37 N 27.01 E
Cazaux et de Sanguinet, Lac de ⊂ 32 44.30 N 1.10 W
Cazenovia 210 42.55 N 75.51 W
Cazenovia Creek ≃ 210 42.52 N 78.50 W
Cazenovia Creek, East Branch ≃ 210 42.46 N 78.38 W
Cazenovia Creek, West Branch ≃ 210 42.46 N 78.39 W
Cazenovia Lake ⊜ 210 42.57 N 75.53 W
Cazenovia Park ♦ 284a 42.51 N 78.48 W
Cazères 32 43.13 N 1.05 E
Cazhai 269b 31.12 N 121.34 E
Cazin 36 44.58 N 15.57 E
Cazis 58 46.43 N 9.25 E
Čazma 36 45.45 N 16.37 E
Cazombo 152 11.54 S 22.52 E
Cazones ≃ 234 20.44 N 97.12 W
Cazones, Golfo de ⊂ 240p 21.55 N 81.20 W
Cazorla, Esp. 34 37.55 N 3.00 W
Cazorla, Ven. 246 8.01 N 67.00 W
Cazula 154 15.25 S 33.40 E
Ccapi 248 13.52 S 72.05 W
Cchaltubo 84 42.20 N 42.35 E
Cchenisckali ≃ 84 42.07 N 42.18 E
Cchinvali 84 42.13 N 43.56 E
Čchorocku 84 42.32 N 42.07 E
Cchunkuri 84 42.23 N 42.34 E
Cea ≃ 34 42.00 N 5.36 W
Ceanannus Mór (Kells) 48 53.44 N 6.53 W
Ceará ⊡³ 250 5.00 S 40.00 W
Ceará → Fortaleza 250 3.43 S 38.30 W
Ceará-Mirim 250 5.38 S 35.26 W
Ceará-Mirim ≃ 250 5.40 S 35.13 W
Ceatharlach → Carlow 48 52.50 N 6.55 W
Cebaco, Isla De I 246 7.32 N 81.09 W
Ceballos 232 26.32 N 104.09 W
Čebarkul' 86 54.58 N 60.25 E
Çebeci ✢⁸ 267b 41.07 N 28.52 E
Čeboksarskoje vodochranilišče ⊜¹ 24 56.10 N 46.00 E
Čeboksary 80 56.09 N 47.15 E
Cebolla Creek ≃ 200 38.29 N 107.13 W
Cebollar 252 29.06 S 66.33 W
Cebollas 234 23.23 N 104.50 W
Cebollatí 252 33.16 S 53.47 W
Cebollatí ≃ 252 33.09 S 53.38 W
Cebollita Peak ∧ 200 34.43 N 107.51 W
Céboruco, Volcán ∧¹ 234 21.09 N 104.30 W
Čebotovka, Ross. 83 48.41 N 40.00 E
Čebotovka, Ross. 83 48.42 N 39.51 E
Cebreros 34 40.27 N 4.28 W
Čebrikovo 78 47.09 N 30.06 E
Čebsara 76 59.12 N 38.50 E
Cebu 116 10.18 N 123.54 E
Cebu ⊡⁴ 116 10.20 N 123.45 E
Cebu I 116 10.20 N 123.45 E
Čeburgol' 78 45.34 N 38.07 E
Cebu Strait ⊔ 116 9.45 N 123.40 E
Ceccano 66 41.34 N 13.20 E
Cecchignola ✢⁸ 267a 41.49 N 12.29 E
Çeceda 196 26.04 N 103.25 W
Čečel'nik 78 48.14 N 29.21 E
Čečen', ostrov I 84 43.58 N 47.45 E
Cecer Chaan → Öndörchaan 88 47.19 N 110.39 E
Cecerleg, Mong. 88 48.52 N 101.14 E
Cecerleg, Mong. 88 47.30 N 101.27 E
Cecerleg, Mong. 88 49.30 N 97.36 E
Čečersk 76 52.55 N 30.55 E
Čečeviči 76 53.31 N 29.51 E
Cecheng 105 39.06 N 116.48 E
Čechov, Ross. 82 55.09 N 37.27 E
Čechov, Ross. 89 47.28 N 141.59 E
Čechova, gora ∧ 89 47.03 N 142.50 E
Čechtice 30 49.37 N 15.03 E
Čechy ⊡⁹ 30 49.50 N 14.00 E
Cecil, Ga., U.S. 192 31.02 N 83.23 W
Cecil, Oh., U.S. 216 41.13 N 84.35 W
Cecil, Pa., U.S. 214 40.19 N 80.10 W
Cecil ⊡⁶ 208 39.36 N 75.50 W
Cecil Field Naval Air Station ■ 192 30.12 N 81.52 W
Cecilia 194 37.39 N 85.57 W
Cecilia, Mount ∧² 162 20.45 S 120.55 E
Cecil Park 274a 33.52 S 150.51 E
Cecil Plains 166 27.32 S 151.12 E
Cecil Rhodes, Mount ∧ 162 25.26 S 121.26 E
Cecilton 208 39.24 N 75.52 W
Cecina 66 43.19 N 10.31 E
Cecina ≃ 66 43.18 N 10.29 E
Cecita, Lago di ⊜ 68 39.24 N 16.30 E
Čečnja-Ingušetija ⊡³ 84 43.15 N 45.40 E
Čečuj ≃ 88 58.12 N 109.18 E
Čečujsk 88 58.05 N 108.42 E
Cedar ≃, U.S. 190 41.17 N 91.21 W
Cedar ≃, Mi., U.S. 190 43.53 N 84.29 W
Cedar ≃, Mi., U.S. 190 45.25 N 87.21 W
Cedar ≃, Ne., U.S. 198 41.22 N 97.57 W
Cedar ≃, N.Y., U.S. 188 43.51 N 74.11 W
Cedar ≃, Wa., U.S. 224 47.30 N 122.12 W
Cedar, Middle Branch ≃ 216 42.38 N 84.05 W
Cedar, West Branch ≃ 216 42.41 N 84.09 W
Cedar, West Fork ≃ 190 42.37 N 92.29 W

ENGLISH Name	Page	Lat.°′	Long.°′

Cedar Bayou ≃ 222 29.41 N 94.56 W
Cedar Beach 284b 39.17 N 76.25 W
Cedar Bluff Reservoir ⊜¹ 198 38.47 N 99.47 W
Cedar Bluffs 198 41.23 N 96.36 W
Cedar Breaks National Monument ♦ 200 37.29 N 112.53 W
Cedar Brook 208 39.42 N 74.54 W
Cedar Brook ≃, N.J., U.S. 276 40.19 N 74.33 W
Cedar Brook ≃, N.J., U.S. 276 40.23 N 74.23 W
Cedar Brook ≃, N.J., U.S. 285 39.40 N 74.43 W
Cedar Brook Park ♦ 275b 43.45 N 79.14 W
Cedarburg 190 43.17 N 87.59 W
Cedar City, Mo., U.S. 219 38.35 N 92.10 W
Cedar City, Ut., U.S. 200 37.40 N 113.03 W
Cedar Creek 222 30.05 N 97.30 W
Cedar Creek ≃, Al., U.S. 194 32.13 N 87.06 W
Cedar Creek ≃, Az., U.S. 200 33.48 N 110.18 W
Cedar Creek ≃, Ct., U.S. 276 41.09 N 73.13 W
Cedar Creek ≃, De., U.S. 208 38.55 N 75.20 W
Cedar Creek ≃, Ga., U.S. 194 34.08 N 85.19 W
Cedar Creek ≃, Id., U.S. 202 42.24 N 114.49 W
Cedar Creek ≃, In., U.S. 216 41.12 N 85.02 W
Cedar Creek ≃, Ia., U.S. 190 40.58 N 91.40 W
Cedar Creek ≃, Ia., U.S. 198 42.24 N 94.59 W
Cedar Creek ≃, Ky., U.S. 218 38.25 N 84.53 W
Cedar Creek ≃, Mo., U.S. 219 38.38 N 92.13 W
Cedar Creek ≃, N.D., U.S. 198 46.07 N 101.18 W
Cedar Creek ≃, Oh., U.S. 214 41.38 N 83.17 W
Cedar Creek ≃, Pa., U.S. 279b 40.10 N 79.47 W
Cedar Creek ≃, Tx., U.S. 196 32.53 N 98.37 W
Cedar Creek ≃, Tx., U.S. 222 30.51 N 96.12 W
Cedar Creek ≃, Tx., U.S. 222 32.04 N 96.05 W
Cedar Creek ≃, Tx., U.S. 222 30.02 N 97.17 W
Cedar Creek ≃, Wa., U.S. 224 45.56 N 122.37 W
Cedar Creek Reservoir ⊜¹ 222 32.20 N 96.10 W
Cedar Crest Manor 285 39.41 N 75.28 W
Cedaredge 200 38.54 N 107.55 W
Cedar Falls 190 42.31 N 92.26 W
Cedar Grove, On., Can. 275b 43.52 N 79.12 W
Cedar Grove, In., U.S. 218 39.21 N 84.56 W
Cedar Grove, N.J., U.S. 276 40.51 N 74.13 W
Cedar Grove, W.V., U.S. 188 38.13 N 81.25 W
Cedar Grove, Wi., U.S. 190 43.34 N 87.49 W
Cedar Grove Reservoir ⊜¹ 276 40.52 N 74.13 W
Cedar Heights, Md., U.S. 284c 38.54 N 76.54 W
Cedar Heights, Pa., U.S. 285 40.05 N 75.17 W
Cedar Hill, Mo., U.S. 219 38.21 N 90.39 W
Cedar Hill, N.Y., U.S. 210 42.33 N 73.47 W
Cedar Hill, Tn., U.S. 194 36.33 N 86.59 W
Cedar Hill, Tx., U.S. 222 32.35 N 96.57 W
Cedar Hills 224 45.30 N 122.47 W
Cedar Hollow 285 40.04 N 75.31 W
Cedarhurst, Md., U.S. 208 39.07 N 76.41 W
Cedarhurst, N.Y., U.S. 276 40.37 N 73.43 W
Cedar Island I, Md., U.S. 208 37.56 N 75.52 W
Cedar Island I, N.Y., U.S. 276 40.38 N 73.21 W
Cedar Island I, Va., U.S. 208 37.39 N 75.36 W
Cedar Island Lake ⊜ 281 42.38 N 83.28 W
Cedar Key 192 29.08 N 83.02 W
Cedar Knolls 276 40.49 N 74.26 W
Cedar Lake, In., U.S. 216 41.21 N 87.26 W
Cedar Lake, Tx., U.S. 222 28.54 N 95.35 W
Cedar Lake ⊜, On., Can. 190 46.02 N 78.30 W
Cedar Lake ⊜, In., U.S. 216 41.22 N 87.26 W
Cedar Lake ⊜, N.J., U.S. 276 40.55 N 74.28 W
Cedar Lake ⊜, Tx., U.S. 196 32.49 N 102.17 W
Cedar Lake ⊜¹ 184 53.15 N 100.10 W
Cedar Lake Creek ≃ 222 28.50 N 95.35 W
Cedar Lane 222 28.54 N 95.38 W
Cedar Mill 224 45.32 N 122.51 W
Cedarmont 158 26.50 S 29.01 E
Cedar Mountain ∧ 204 41.36 N 120.16 W
Cedar Point 216 41.16 N 89.08 W
Cedar Point ▸, Ct., U.S. 276 41.06 N 73.22 W
Cedar Point ▸, Oh., U.S. 214 41.42 N 83.20 W
Cedar Point ▸, Oh., U.S. 214 41.30 N 82.41 W
Cedar Pond ⊜ 276 41.07 N 74.06 W
Cedar Rapids, Ia., U.S. 190 41.59 N 91.40 W
Cedar Rapids, Ne., U.S. 198 41.34 N 98.09 W
Cedar Ridge 226 39.12 N 121.01 W
Cedar Run ≃ 208 38.41 N 77.29 W
Cedars 285 40.13 N 75.22 W
Cedars of Lebanon → Arz Lubnān ✢³ 130 34.14 N 36.03 E
Cedar Springs, On., Can. 214 42.17 N 82.02 W
Cedar Springs, Mi., U.S. 190 43.13 N 85.33 W
Cedar Swamp ≋, Ma., U.S. 283 42.33 N 71.05 W
Cedar Swamp ≋, N.J., U.S. 285 39.48 N 75.20 W
Cedartown 192 34.03 N 85.15 W
Cedarvale, B.C., Can. 182 55.01 N 128.20 W
Cedar Vale, Ks., U.S. 198 37.06 N 96.30 W
Cedarville, S. Afr. 158 30.23 S 29.03 E
Cedarville, Ca., U.S. 204 41.31 N 120.10 W
Cedarville, In., U.S. 216 41.12 N 85.01 W
Cedarville, Ma., U.S. 207 41.48 N 70.33 W
Cedarville, Mi., U.S. 190 46.00 N 84.22 W
Cedarville, N.J., U.S. 208 39.19 N 75.12 W
Cedarville, N.Y., U.S. 210 42.56 N 75.07 W
Cedarville, Oh., U.S. 218 39.44 N 83.48 W
Cedarville, Pa., U.S. 285 40.14 N 75.40 W
Cedarville Reservoir ⊜¹ 216 41.12 N 85.01 W
Cedar Wash ∨ 200 35.53 N 111.25 W
Cedarwood Park 208 40.03 N 74.08 W
Cedegolo 64 46.05 N 10.21 E
Cedeira 34 43.39 N 8.03 W
Čeder 88 51.25 N 94.45 E
Cedillo, Embalse de ⊜¹ 34 39.40 N 7.25 W

DEUTSCH Name	Seite	Breite°′	Länge°′ E = Ost

Cedral 234 23.48 N 100.44 W
Cedrino ≃ 71 40.23 N 9.44 E
Cedro 250 6.36 S 39.03 W
Cedro, Cerro ∧ 234 18.35 N 99.42 W
Cedros, Hond. 236 14.35 N 87.08 W
Cedros, Méx. 232 24.41 N 101.47 W
Cedros, Isla I 232 28.12 N 115.15 W
Ceduna 162 32.07 S 133.40 E
Cedynia 30 52.50 N 14.14 E
Ceel 102 45.36 N 95.51 E
Ceelaayo 144 11.15 N 48.54 E
Ceel Afweyne 144 9.55 N 47.15 E
Ceel Berdaale 144 3.14 N 43.11 E
Ceel Berde 144 4.50 N 43.39 E
Ceel Buur 144 4.40 N 46.37 E
Ceel Dhaab 144 8.56 N 46.30 E
Ceeldheere, Som. 144 5.22 N 46.11 E
Ceel Dheere, Som. 144 3.51 N 47.12 E
Ceel Doofaar 144 10.38 N 49.02 E
Ceel Waaq 144 2.44 N 41.01 E
Ceel Xamurre 144 7.13 N 48.54 E
Ceemadle 144 5.14 N 46.56 E
Ceepeecee 182 49.52 N 126.43 W
Ceerigaabo 144 10.37 N 47.22 E
Cefalà Diana 70 37.54 N 13.28 E
Cefalonia → Kefallinía I 38 38.15 N 20.35 E
Cefalù 70 38.02 N 14.01 E
Cefni ≃ 44 53.12 N 4.23 W
Cefn-mawr 42 52.58 N 3.04 W
Ceg 144 8.58 N 45.20 E
Cega ≃ 34 41.33 N 4.46 W
Čeganly 80 53.54 N 53.34 E
Čegdomyn 89 51.07 N 133.05 E
Čegem ≃ 84 43.38 N 43.48 E
Čegem Pervyj 84 43.34 N 43.35 E
Čegitun' 180 66.34 N 171.06 W
Cegléd 30 47.10 N 19.48 E
Ceglie Messapico 68 40.39 N 17.31 E
Cehegín 34 38.06 N 1.48 W
Ceheng 102 25.10 N 105.48 E
Cehnice 60 49.12 N 14.02 E
Cehu-Silvaniei 38 47.25 N 23.11 E
Ceiba 240m 18.16 N 65.39 W
Ceibo ≃ 258 33.57 S 58.27 W
Ceilán → Sri Lanka ⊡¹ 122 7.00 N 81.00 E
Čeil'dag 84 40.17 N 49.18 E
Ceiriog ≃ 42 52.57 N 3.02 W
Ceirw ≃ 44 52.59 N 3.27 W
Čejč 61 48.57 N 16.57 E
Čekalin 82 54.06 N 36.15 E
Čekan 80 54.51 N 53.34 E
Čekanovskij 88 56.13 N 101.25 E
Çekerek 130 40.04 N 35.31 E
Çekerek ≃ 130 40.34 N 35.46 E
Čekmaguš 86 55.08 N 54.40 E
Çekme ✢⁸ 267b 41.03 N 29.10 E
Čekšino 76 59.39 N 40.33 E
Čekujevo 24 63.34 N 38.56 E
Čekunda 89 50.48 N 132.10 E
Čel'abinsk 86 55.10 N 61.24 E
Čel'abinsk Oblast' ⊡⁴ 86 54.30 N 60.30 E
Čelákovice 54 50.10 N 14.46 E
Celâlli 130 39.42 N 37.26 E
Celano 66 42.05 N 13.33 E
Celanova 34 42.09 N 7.58 W
Celaya 234 20.31 N 100.49 W
Čelbas ≃ 78 46.06 N 38.59 E
Čelbasskaja 78 45.59 N 39.22 E
Celbridge 48 53.20 N 6.33 W
Celebes Basin ✣¹ 14 4.00 N 122.00 E
Celebes Sea ⊤² 112 3.00 N 122.00 E
Celebes → Sulawesi I 112 2.00 S 121.00 E
Čeleken 128 39.26 N 53.07 E
Celendín 248 6.52 S 78.09 W
Celenza sul Trigno 66 41.52 N 14.35 E
Celenza Valfortore 68 41.34 N 14.58 E
Celerina 58 46.31 N 9.51 E
Celeryville 214 41.02 N 82.45 W
Celeste 196 33.18 N 96.12 W
Celestún 232 20.52 N 90.24 W
Celica 246 4.07 S 79.59 W
Celico 68 39.19 N 16.20 E
Çelikhan 130 38.02 N 38.15 E
Čelina, Ross. 80 46.32 N 41.02 E
Celina, Oh., U.S. 216 40.32 N 84.34 W
Celina, Tn., U.S. 194 36.33 N 85.30 W
Celina, Tx., U.S. 196 33.19 N 96.47 W
Celinnoje, Ross. 86 53.04 N 85.40 E
Celinnoje, Ross. 86 54.31 N 63.39 E
Celinnyj 80 46.40 N 44.32 E
Celinograd 86 51.10 N 71.30 E
Celinograd ⊡⁸ 86 51.00 N 70.00 E
Celje 36 46.14 N 15.16 E
Čelkar 86 47.50 N 59.36 E
Cellar Head ▸ 46 58.26 N 6.10 W
Celldömölk 30 47.16 N 17.09 E
Celle 52 52.37 N 10.05 E
Celle, Ruisseau la ≃ 261 48.35 N 2.01 E
Celle Ligure 62 44.20 N 8.33 E
Celles 56 50.14 N 5.01 E
Celles-sur-Plaine 58 48.28 N 6.57 E
Cellettes 50 47.32 N 1.23 E
Cellina ≃ 64 46.02 N 12.47 E
Cellino Attanasio 66 42.36 N 13.52 E
Cellino San Marco 68 40.28 N 17.58 E
Čelmozero 24 64.18 N 31.48 E
Čelno-Veršiny 80 54.26 N 51.06 E
Čelobitjevo 265b 55.55 N 37.40 E
Celone ≃ 68 41.36 N 15.41 E
Celorico da Beira 34 40.38 N 7.23 W
Celoron 214 42.06 N 79.17 W
Celtic Sea ⊤² 28 51.00 N 6.30 W
Celtic Shelf ✣⁴ 10 49.15 N 7.00 W
Çeltikçi, Tür. 130 40.20 N 32.28 E
Çeltikçi, Tür. 130 37.32 N 30.29 E
Čel'uš 86 51.32 N 87.46 E
Čel'uskin, mys ▸ 74 77.45 N 104.20 E
Čel'uskincev park ♦ 265a 60.01 N 30.19 E
Cemaes Head ▸ 42 52.07 N 4.44 W
Čemal 86 51.25 N 86.01 E
Čembilej 80 55.19 N 45.43 E
Cembra 64 46.10 N 11.13 E
Cembra, Val di ∨ 64 46.10 N 11.13 E
Cement 196 34.55 N 98.08 W
Cement City 216 42.04 N 84.19 W
Cementon, N.Y., U.S. 210 42.09 N 73.55 W
Cementon, Pa., U.S. 208 40.41 N 75.30 W
Čemer 78 51.07 N 31.13 E
Čemerisy 78 51.42 N 30.24 E
Čemerno 36 43.11 N 18.37 E
Čemerovcy 78 49.01 N 26.21 E
Čemesskaja buchta ⊂ 78 44.40 N 37.50 E
Cemilbey 130 40.21 N 35.04 E
Çemişkezek 130 39.04 N 38.55 E
Cemmaes 42 52.37 N 3.42 W
Čemolgan 85 43.23 N 76.37 E
Cempi, Teluk ⊂ 115b 8.44 S 118.25 E
Čenča 88 55.57 N 110.59 E
Cencenighe 64 46.21 N 11.58 E
Čenchermandal 88 47.37 N 109.05 E
Čency 82 56.03 N 36.01 E
Cenderawasih, Teluk ⊂ 164 2.30 S 135.20 E
Cendras 62 44.09 N 4.04 E
Cene 62 45.47 N 9.49 E
Cenepa ≃ 246 4.35 S 78.12 W
Ceneri, Monte)(58 46.08 N 8.55 E
Cengel 86 48.56 N 89.10 E
Čengel'dy, Kaz. 85 41.51 N 68.59 E
Čengel'dy, Kaz. 85 43.59 N 77.26 E
Çengelköy ✢⁸ 267b 41.03 N 29.03 E
Çengerli 130 39.48 N 38.52 E
Cengles, Croda di ∧ 64 46.34 N 10.38 E
Ceno ≃ 36 44.41 N 10.05 E
Cenovo 38 43.32 N 25.39 E
Cenrana 112 3.18 S 118.50 E
Censeau 58 46.49 N 6.04 E
Centallo 62 44.30 N 7.35 E

Symbols in the index entries represent the broad categories identified in the key at the right. Symbols with superior numbers (⋏¹) identify subcategories (see complete key on page I · 1).

Symbole im Register stellen die rechts im Schlüssel erklärten Kategorien dar. Symbole mit hochgestellten Ziffern (⋏¹) bezeichnen Unterabteilungen einer Kategorie (vgl. vollständiger Schlüssel auf Seite I · 1).

Los símbolos incluídos en el texto del índice representan las grandes categorias identificadas con la clave a la derecha. Los símbolos con numeros en su parte superior (⋏¹) identifican las subcategorías (véase la clave completa en la página I · 1).

Les symboles de l'index représentent les catégories indiquées dans la légende à droite. Les symboles suivis d'un indice (⋏¹) représentent des sous-catégories (voir légende complète à la page I · 1).

Os símbolos incluídos no texto do índice representam as grandes categorias identificadas com a chave à direita. Os símbolos com números em sua parte superior (⋏¹) identificam as subcategorias (veja-se a chave completa à página I · 1).

∧ Mountain	Berg	Montaña	Montagne	Montanha
⋏ Mountains	Gebirge	Montañas	Montagnes	Montanhas
)(Pass	Paß	Paso	Col	Passo
∨ Valley, Canyon	Tal, Cañon	Valle, Cañón	Vallée, Canyon	Vale, Canhão
≍ Plain	Ebene	Llano	Plaine	Planície
▸ Cape	Kap	Cabo	Cap	Cabo
I Island	Insel	Isla	Île	Ilha
II Islands	Inseln	Islas	Îles	Ilhas
⊥ Other Topographic Features	Andere Topographische Objekte	Otros Elementos Topográficos	Autres données topographiques	Outros acidentes topográficos

ESPAÑOL — Nombre | Página | Lat.°′ | Long.°′ W = Oeste
FRANÇAIS — Nom | Page | Lat.°′ | Long.°′ W = Ouest
PORTUGUÊS — Nome | Página | Lat.°′ | Long.°′ W = Oeste

Centenario 252 38.48 S 68.08 W
Centenário do Sul 255 22.48 S 51.37 W
Centennial Lake ⊜ 285 39.50 N 74.51 W
Centennial Lake ⊜¹ 212 45.10 N 72.05 W
Centennial Mountains ⋏ 202 44.35 N 111.55 W
Centennial Park ♠, Austl. 274a 33.54 S 151.14 E
Centennial Park ♠, On., Can. 275b 43.39 N 79.35 W
Centennial Wash V 200 33.14 N 112.46 W
Centeno 66 42.48 N 11.49 E
Center, Co., U.S. 200 37.45 N 106.06 W
Center, In., U.S. 216 40.26 N 86.04 W
Center, Mo., U.S. 219 39.30 N 91.31 W
Center, Ne., U.S. 198 42.36 N 97.52 W
Center, N.D., U.S. 198 47.06 N 101.17 W
Center, Tx., U.S. 194 31.47 N 94.10 W
Centerbrook 207 41.21 N 72.24 W
Center Brunswick 210 42.45 N 73.37 W
Centerburg 214 40.18 N 82.41 W
Center City 190 45.23 N 92.48 W
Center Cross 208 37.48 N 76.46 W
Centereach 210 40.51 N 73.06 W
Centerfield 218 38.21 N 83.24 W
Center Hill 220 28.38 N 81.59 W
Center Hill Lake ⊜¹ 194 36.00 N 85.45 W
Center Line 214 42.29 N 83.01 W
Center Moriches 188 40.48 N 72.47 W
Center Mountain ∧ 202 45.06 N 115.13 W
Center Point, Al., U.S. 194 33.37 N 86.41 W
Center Point, Ia., U.S. 190 42.11 N 91.47 W
Center Point, Tx., U.S. 196 29.57 N 99.02 W
Centerport, N.Y., U.S. 210 40.54 N 73.22 W
Centerport, Pa., U.S. 208 40.29 N 76.01 W
Center Square, N.J., U.S. 285 39.46 N 75.23 W
Center Square, Pa., U.S. 208 40.10 N 75.18 W
Centerton, In., U.S. 218 39.30 N 86.23 W
Centerton, N.J., U.S. 285 39.31 N 75.10 W
Center Valley 208 40.32 N 75.24 W
Centerville, De., U.S. 285 39.49 N 75.37 W
Centerville, In., U.S. 218 39.49 N 84.59 W
Centerville, Ia., U.S. 190 40.43 N 92.52 W
Centerville, Ma., U.S. 207 41.38 N 70.20 W
Centerville, Mo., U.S. 194 37.26 N 90.57 W
Centerville, N.Y., U.S. 210 42.29 N 78.15 W
Centerville, Oh., U.S. 218 39.37 N 84.09 W
Centerville, Pa., U.S. 188 40.02 N 79.58 W
Centerville, S.D., U.S. 198 43.07 N 96.57 W
Centerville, Tn., U.S. 194 35.46 N 87.28 W
Centerville, Tx., U.S. 222 31.15 N 95.58 W
Centerville, Ut,. U.S. 200 40.55 N 111.52 W
Centerville, Wa., U.S. 224 45.45 N 120.54 W
Centinela 196 28.47 N 100.34 W
Cento 64 44.43 N 11.17 E
Centocelle ◆⁸ 267a 41.53 N 12.34 E
Cento Croci, Passo di)(62 44.25 N 9.37 E
Centola 68 40.04 N 15.19 E
Central, Bra. 250 11.08 S 42.08 W
Central, Ak., U.S. 180 65.34 N 144.48 W
Central, Az., U.S. 200 32.52 N 109.47 W
Central, N.M., U.S. 200 32.46 N 108.08 W
Central, S.C., U.S. 192 34.43 N 82.46 W
Central, Tx., U.S. 222 31.26 N 94.49 W
Central □⁴, Ghana 150 5.30 N 1.00 W
Central □⁴, Kenya 154 0.45 S 37.00 E
Central □⁴, Malaŵi 154 13.00 S 34.00 E
Central □⁴, Sol.Is. 175e 9.10 S 159.50 E
Central □⁴, Scot., U.K. 46 56.05 N 4.20 W
Central □⁴, Zam. 154 14.30 S 29.00 E
Central □⁵, Bots. 156 21.30 S 26.00 E
Central □⁵, Pap. N. Gui. 164 9.00 S 147.00 E
Central □⁵, Para. 252 25.30 S 57.30 W
Central □⁵, Ug. 154 0.10 N 32.00 E
Central, Cordillera ⋏, Col. 246 5.00 N 75.00 W
Central, Cordillera ⋏, C.R. 236 10.10 N 84.05 W
Central, Cordillera ⋏, Pan. 236 8.30 N 81.30 W
Central, Cordillera ⋏, Perú 248 8.00 S 77.00 W
Central, Cordillera ⋏, Pil. 116 17.20 N 120.57 E
Central, Cordillera ⋏, P.R. 240m 18.10 N 66.35 W
Central, Macizo → Central, Massif ⋏ 32 45.00 N 3.10 E
Central, Massif ⋏ 32 45.00 N 3.10 E
Central, Planalto ⋏¹ 242 18.00 S 47.00 W
Central, Sistema ⋏ 34 40.30 N 5.00 W
Central African Republic □¹ 136 7.00 N 21.00 E
Central Aguirre 240m 17.57 N 66.13 W
Central Barren 218 38.22 N 86.06 W
Central Brāhui Range ⋏ 120 29.20 N 66.55 E
Central Bridge 210 42.42 N 74.20 W
Central Butte 184 50.47 N 106.30 W
Central City, Il., U.S. 219 38.32 N 89.07 W
Central City, Ia., U.S. 190 42.12 N 91.31 W
Central City, Ky., U.S. 194 37.17 N 87.07 W
Central City, Ne., U.S. 198 41.06 N 98.00 W
Central City, Pa., U.S. 214 40.06 N 78.48 W
Central Division □⁵ 175g 18.05 S 178.30 E
Central Falls 207 41.53 N 71.23 W
Central Heights 200 33.24 N 110.48 W
Central Highlands 279b 40.16 N 79.50 W
Centralia, Il., U.S. 219 38.31 N 89.08 W
Centralia, Ks., U.S. 198 39.43 N 96.07 W
Centralia, Mo., U.S. 219 39.12 N 92.08 W
Centralia, Tx., U.S. 222 31.16 N 95.02 W
Centralia, Wa., U.S. 224 46.42 N 122.57 W
Centralia, Lake ⊜ 219 38.32 N 88.59 W
Centralia Draw V 196 31.27 N 101.16 W
Centralia Reservoir ⊜¹ 219 38.32 N 89.08 W
Centralina 255 18.34 S 49.13 W
Central Intelligence Agency ⚑ 284c 38.57 N 77.09 W
Central Island I 154 3.30 N 36.03 E
Central Islip 210 40.47 N 73.12 W
Central Kalahari Game Reserve ◆⁴ 156 22.15 S 23.45 E
Central Lake 190 45.04 N 85.15 W
Central Makrān Range ⋏ 128 26.40 N 64.30 E
Central'no-Bokovskoj ◆⁸ 83 48.11 N 39.03 E
Central'nolesnoj Zapovednik ◆⁴ 76 56.32 N 32.50 E
Central Nyack 276 41.06 N 73.57 W
Central'nyj, Ross. 76 53.41 N 39.38 E
Central'nyj, Ross. 86 57.41 N 80.57 E
Central'nyj, Ross. 86 58.45 N 84.28 E
Central'nyj, Ross. 86 55.12 N 87.40 E
Central'nyj, Ross. 265b 55.53 N 37.52 E
Central'nyje Karakumy ◆² 128 39.00 N 60.00 E
Central Pacific Basin ✢¹ 14 5.00 N 175.00 W
Central Park, N.J., U.S. 276 40.26 N 74.18 W
Central Park, Wa., U.S. 224 46.58 N 123.41 W
Central Park ♠ 276 40.47 N 73.58 W
Central Point 202 42.22 N 122.54 W
Central Railroad Station ◆⁵ 272c 18.58 N 72.50 E
Central Range ⋏, Leso. 158 29.35 S 28.35 E
Central Range ⋏, Pap. N. Gui. 164 5.00 S 142.30 E
Central Square 210 43.17 N 76.08 W
Central Utah Canal ≍ 200 39.35 N 112.12 W
Central Valley, Ca., U.S. 204 40.40 N 122.22 W
Central Valley, N.Y., U.S. 210 41.19 N 74.07 W
Central Village 207 41.43 N 71.54 W
Centre 194 34.09 N 85.40 W
Centre □⁶ 210 40.55 N 77.47 W
Centre, Canal du ≍ 32 46.27 N 4.07 E
Centre Atomique de Marcoule ⚑³ 62 44.08 N 4.42 E
Centre City 285 39.46 N 75.10 W
Centre d'Énergie de Pierrelatte ⚑³ 62 44.21 N 4.44 E
Centre Hall 214 40.50 N 77.41 W
Centre Island 276 40.54 N 73.32 W
Centre Island I 172 46.28 S 167.51 E
Centre Island Park ♠ 275b 43.37 N 79.23 W
Centre Lake ⊜ 212 44.36 N 75.51 W
Centre Peak ∧ 182 55.41 N 126.26 W
Centre-Sud □⁴ 152 4.10 N 12.00 E
Centreville, Al., U.S. 194 32.56 N 87.08 W
Centreville, Il., U.S. 219 38.35 N 90.07 W
Centreville, Ky., U.S. 218 38.13 N 84.24 W
Centreville, Md., U.S. 208 39.02 N 76.04 W
Centreville, Mi., U.S. 216 41.55 N 85.31 W
Centreville, Ms., U.S. 194 31.05 N 91.04 W
Centreville, Va., U.S. 208 38.50 N 77.25 W
Centro Puntas 240m 18.22 N 67.16 W
Centro Simón Bolívar ◆⁹ 286c 10.30 N 66.55 W
Centuripe 70 37.37 N 14.44 E
Century, Fl., U.S. 194 30.58 N 87.15 W
Century, W.V., U.S. 188 39.05 N 80.11 W
Century City ◆⁸ 280 34.03 N 118.26 W
Century III Mall ◆⁹ 279b 40.21 N 79.57 W
Century Village 220 26.42 N 80.05 W
Cenxi 102 22.59 N 111.00 E
Čepca 80 57.54 N 53.25 E
Čepca ≃ 80 58.36 N 50.04 E
Čepeckij 80 58.29 N 51.12 E
Čepel' 78 49.19 N 36.55 E
Čepelare 38 41.44 N 24.41 E
Čepel'ovo 82 55.11 N 37.30 E
Čepovan 64 46.03 N 13.47 E
Cepoy 50 48.03 N 2.44 E
Ceprano 66 41.33 N 13.31 E
Čepřovice 60 49.10 N 13.59 E
Ceptia 152 12.56 S 17.35 E
Cepu 115a 7.09 S 111.35 E
Ceraino 64 45.35 N 10.50 E
Cerami 70 37.49 N 14.30 E
Cerami ≃ 70 37.42 N 14.29 E
Ceram Sea → Seram, Laut ⊤² 108 2.30 S 128.00 E
Ceram → Seram I 164 3.00 S 129.00 E
Cerano, It. 62 45.25 N 8.47 E
Cerano, Méx. 234 20.07 N 101.23 W
Ceraso 68 40.11 N 15.15 E
Cerbicale, Îles II 71 41.34 N 9.24 E
Čerčany 30 49.51 N 14.43 E
Cerchiara di Calabria 68 39.51 N 16.23 E
Čerchov ∧ 60 49.23 N 12.47 E
Cercié 58 46.07 N 4.40 E
Cerco, Alto do ∧ 256 22.38 S 45.22 W
Cercola 66 40.51 N 14.21 E
Cerda 70 37.54 N 13.49 E
Čerdakly 80 54.23 N 48.51 E
Cerdanyola del Vallès 266d 41.30 N 2.09 E
Cerdas 248 20.48 S 66.29 W
Cerdeña, Isla de → Sardegna I 71 40.00 N 9.00 E
Čerdojak 86 48.48 N 84.00 E
Cerdon, Fr. 50 47.38 N 2.22 E
Cerdon, Fr. 58 46.05 N 5.28 E
Čerdyn' 24 60.23 N 56.24 E
Cère ≃ 32 44.55 N 1.53 E
Cerea 64 45.12 N 11.13 E
Cereal 184 51.25 N 110.48 W
Cereales 252 36.49 S 63.51 W
Čerecha ≃ 76 57.46 N 28.21 E
Cereglio 64 44.18 N 11.04 E
Čereja 76 54.37 N 29.17 E
Čerek ≃ 84 43.42 N 44.03 E
Čeremchovo 88 53.09 N 103.05 E
Čeremisinovo 78 51.54 N 37.15 E
Čeremoš ≃ 78 48.23 N 25.37 E
Čeremšan, Ross. 80 55.15 N 48.07 E
Čeremšan, Ross. 80 54.40 N 51.30 E
Čeremšanka, Ross. 86 59.10 N 76.51 E
Čeremšanka, Ross. 86 56.07 N 60.19 E
Čeremšany 89 44.42 N 135.43 E
Cerenti 112 0.30 S 101.52 E
Čerepanovka 80 57.07 N 54.10 E
Čerepanovo 86 54.13 N 83.22 E
Čerepaška, ostrov I 83 47.11 N 38.59 E
Čerepet' 82 54.07 N 36.23 E
Čerepkovo ◆⁸ 265b 55.46 N 37.23 E
Čerepovec 76 59.08 N 37.54 E
Ceres, Arg. 252 29.53 S 61.57 W
Ceres, Bra. 255 15.17 S 49.35 W
Ceres, It. 62 45.19 N 7.23 E
Ceres, S. Afr. 158 33.21 S 19.18 E
Ceres, Ca., U.S. 226 37.35 N 120.57 W
Ceres, N.Y., U.S. 210 42.00 N 78.16 W
Ceresco, Mi., U.S. 216 42.16 N 85.04 W
Ceresco, Ne., U.S. 198 41.03 N 96.38 W
Ceresole Reale 62 45.26 N 7.15 E
Céreste 62 43.51 N 5.35 E
Céret 32 42.29 N 2.45 E
Cereté 246 8.53 N 75.48 W
Čerevkovka 78 48.50 N 37.40 E
Čerevkovka ◆⁸ 83 48.50 N 37.40 E
Čerevkovo 24 61.46 N 45.12 E
Cereweh 115b 8.52 S 116.51 E
Cerf Island I 138 9.32 S 50.59 E
Čerga 86 51.35 N 85.38 E
Cergy 261 49.02 N 2.04 E
Ceri ≃ 42 52.03 N 4.29 W
Ceriale 62 44.06 N 8.14 E
Ceriana 62 43.53 N 7.46 E
Ceriano 266b 45.38 N 9.05 E
Cerignola 68 41.16 N 15.54 E
Čerikov 76 53.34 N 31.23 E
Cérilly 32 46.37 N 2.49 E
Cerisano 68 39.16 N 16.11 E
Cerisiers 50 48.08 N 3.29 E
Čerkašina 88 58.37 N 108.30 E
Čerkasovo 82 54.33 N 36.48 E
Čerkasskoje, Ross. 80 52.26 N 47.13 E
Čerkasskoje, Ukr. 78 48.44 N 35.22 E
Čerkasskoje, Ukr. 83 48.50 N 37.23 E
Čerkassy, Ross. 76 52.41 N 38.43 E
Čerkassy, Ukr. 78 49.26 N 32.04 E
Čerkassy □⁴ 78 49.30 N 31.30 E
Çerkeş 130 40.50 N 32.54 E
Čerkesovskij 80 50.41 N 42.34 E
Čerkessk 84 44.14 N 42.04 E
Çerkezköy 130 41.17 N 28.00 E
Čerkizovo, Ross. 82 55.12 N 38.45 E
Čerkizovo, Ross. 265b 55.58 N 37.48 E
Čerkizovo, Ross. 265b 55.57 N 37.22 E
Cerknica 36 45.48 N 14.22 E
Čerkovišče 76 55.54 N 30.51 E
Čerlak 86 54.09 N 74.48 E
Čerlakskij 86 53.47 N 74.31 E
Cermei 38 46.33 N 21.51 E
Čermen 84 43.11 N 44.42 E
Cermignano 66 42.35 N 13.47 E
Çermik 130 38.09 N 39.27 E
Čermoz 86 58.53 N 56.08 E
Čern' 76 53.27 N 36.55 E
Cerna, Hrv. 38 45.11 N 18.42 E
Cerna, Rom. 38 45.04 N 28.18 E
Čern'achov 78 50.27 N 28.39 E
Čern'achovsk (Insterburg) 76 54.38 N 21.49 E
Černá hora ∧ 60 48.58 N 13.48 E
Čern'ajevo 89 52.45 N 126.00 E
Černak 85 43.24 N 68.02 E
Čern'anka 78 50.55 N 37.49 E
Cernăuţi → Černovcy 78 48.18 N 25.56 E
Černava 76 53.37 N 39.09 E
Černavčicy 76 52.13 N 23.44 E
Černavka, Ross. 80 52.18 N 47.14 E
Černavka, Ross. 80 52.11 N 42.25 E
Cernavodă 38 44.21 N 28.01 E
Černá v Pošumaví 61 48.44 N 14.07 E
Cernay 58 47.49 N 7.10 E
Cernay-la-Ville 50 48.40 N 1.58 E
Cerne Abbas 42 50.49 N 2.29 W
Černeckoje 82 55.15 N 37.20 E
Cernei, Munţii ⋏ 38 45.02 N 22.31 E
Černelica 78 48.48 N 25.26 E
Černevcy 78 48.33 N 28.09 E
Černigov 78 51.30 N 31.18 E
Černigov □⁴ 78 51.15 N 32.00 E
Černigovka, Kaz. 86 50.28 N 71.27 E
Černigovka, Ross. 89 49.37 N 129.57 E
Černigovka, Ross. 89 44.21 N 132.33 E
Černigovka, Ukr. 78 47.13 N 36.14 E
Černigovskaja 78 44.41 N 39.40 E
Černi vrâh ∧ 38 42.34 N 23.17 E
Černobaj 78 49.41 N 32.19 E
Cernobbio 62 45.50 N 9.04 E
Černobyl' 78 51.16 N 30.14 E
Černogolovka 82 56.00 N 38.22 E
Černogorsk 86 53.49 N 91.18 E
Černokol'skaja 86 56.42 N 72.49 E
Černomorskij zapovednik ◆⁴ 78 46.10 N 32.00 E
Černorečenskoje 85 43.00 N 74.55 E
Černorečje 84 43.15 N 45.41 E
Černošín 60 49.49 N 12.53 E
Černovcy 78 48.18 N 25.56 E
Černovcy □⁸ 78 43.30 N 26.00 E
Čerňovice 60 49.49 N 13.06 E
Černovka, Ross. 86 56.47 N 76.28 E
Černovka, Ross. 89 51.43 N 128.12 E
Čern'ovo, Ross. 76 58.39 N 28.14 E
Čern'ovo, Ross. 82 54.43 N 38.36 E
Čern'ovo, Ross. 265b 55.50 N 37.18 E
Černovskije Kopi 88 52.00 N 113.15 E
Černovskoje, Ross. 80 58.42 N 47.23 E
Černovskoje, Ross. 80 57.29 N 54.36 E
Černucha 80 55.36 N 43.46 E
Černuchi 78 50.16 N 32.57 E
Černuchino 83 48.19 N 38.30 E
Cernusco sul Naviglio 62 45.31 N 9.19 E
Černuška, Ross. 86 56.29 N 56.03 E
Černuška, Ross. 88 52.58 N 101.55 E
Cerny-en-Laonnois 50 49.27 N 3.40 E
Černyševsk 88 52.35 N 117.00 E
Černyševskij 74 63.00 N 112.15 E
Černyškovskij 80 48.27 N 42.14 E
Černyšova, gr'ada ⋏ 24 66.30 N 59.00 E
Čer'omuchova 80 54.57 N 51.09 E
Čer'omuski ◆⁸ 265b 55.41 N 37.35 E
Cerralvo 232 26.06 N 99.37 W
Cerralvo, Isla I 232 24.15 N 109.55 W
Cerreto, Passo del)(64 44.18 N 10.13 E
Cerreto d'Esi 66 43.19 N 12.59 E
Cerreto Guidi 66 43.45 N 10.53 E
Cerreto Sannita 68 41.17 N 14.33 E
Cerrigydrudion 44 53.02 N 3.33 W
Cërrik 38 41.02 N 19.57 E
Cerrillos, Arg. 252 24.54 S 65.29 W
Cerrillos, Chile 286e 33.30 S 70.43 W
Cerrillos, N.M., U.S. 200 35.26 N 106.07 W
Cerrina 62 45.07 N 8.13 E
Cerritos, Méx. 234 22.26 N 100.17 W
Cerritos, Ca., U.S. 280 33.52 N 118.05 W
Cerro 58 45.54 N 8.36 E
Cerro, Forca di)(66 42.45 N 12.47 E
Cerro Azul, Arg. 252 27.38 S 55.29 W
Cerro Azul, Bra. 252 24.50 S 49.15 W
Cerro Azul, Méx. 234 21.12 N 97.44 W
Cerro Azul, Perú 248 13.02 S 76.30 W
Cerro Chato 252 33.06 S 55.08 W
Cerro Colorado 252 33.52 S 55.33 W
Cerro Corá 250 6.03 S 36.21 W
Cerro de las Mesas ⊥ 234 18.47 N 96.05 W
Cerro de los Angeles ⚑¹ 266a 40.19 N 3.41 W
Cerro de Pasco 248 10.41 S 76.16 W
Cerro Gordo 219 39.53 N 88.43 W
Cerro Grande ≃ 286c 10.37 N 66.49 W
Cerro Largo 252 28.09 S 54.45 W
Cerro Maggiore 266b 45.36 N 8.58 E
Cerro Moreno 252 23.28 S 70.25 W
Cerrón, Cerro ∧ 246 10.19 N 70.39 W
Cerro Navia 286e 33.25 S 70.43 W
Cerrón Grande, Embalse ⊜¹ 236 14.00 N 89.00 W
Cerro Prieto 204 32.27 N 115.17 W
Cerros Colorados, Embalse ⊜¹ 252 38.35 S 68.40 W
Cerros de Amotape, Parque Nacional ♠ 246 4.10 S 80.30 W
Cerro Vera 252 33.11 S 57.28 W
Čerskij 74 68.45 N 161.45 E
Čerskogo, chrebet ⋏, Ross. 74 65.00 N 144.00 E
Čerskogo, chrebet ⋏, Ross. 88 52.00 N 114.00 E
Čerskogo, gora ∧ 88 55.05 N 108.40 E
Cersosimo 68 40.03 N 16.21 E
Certaldo 66 43.33 N 11.02 E
Čertanovka ≃ 265b 55.38 N 37.47 E
Čertanovo ◆⁸ 265b 55.38 N 37.37 E
Čertkovo 83 49.23 N 40.10 E
Čertolino 76 56.12 N 33.54 E
Čertomlyk 78 47.37 N 34.09 E
Certosa (Karthaus) 64 46.42 N 10.54 E
Certosa di Pavia 62 45.15 N 9.09 E
Čerusti 76 55.33 N 40.01 E
Červ'anka 88 57.41 N 99.33 E
Cervantes, Austl. 162 30.30 S 115.04 E
Cervantes, Pil. 116 16.59 N 120.44 E
Cervarezza 64 44.23 N 10.20 E
Cervaro 66 41.29 N 13.54 E
Cervaro ≃ 68 41.30 N 15.52 E
Cervati, Monte ∧ 68 40.17 N 15.29 E
Cervelló 266d 41.24 N 1.57 E
Cervello, Cozzo ∧ 68 39.24 N 16.05 E
Cervelló, Riera de ≃ 266d 41.24 N 2.01 E
Červen' 76 53.42 N 28.26 E
Červen Brjag 38 43.16 N 24.06 E
Červený Kostelec 30 50.29 N 16.06 E
Cervera 34 41.40 N 1.17 E
Cervera del Río Alhama 34 42.01 N 1.57 W
Cervera de Pisuerga 34 42.52 N 4.30 W
Cerveteri 66 42.00 N 12.06 E
Cervi, Monte dei ∧ 70 37.53 N 13.58 E
Cervia 66 44.15 N 12.22 E
Cervialto, Monte ∧ 68 40.47 N 15.08 E
Cervignano del Friuli 64 45.49 N 13.20 E
Cervin, Mont → Matterhorn ∧ 58 45.59 N 7.43 E
Cervinara 68 41.01 N 14.37 E
Cervino (Matterhorn) ∧ 58 45.59 N 7.43 E
Cervione 36 42.20 N 9.31 E
Červl'onnaja 84 43.30 N 45.54 E
Cervo, Esp. 34 43.40 N 7.25 W
Cervo, It. 62 43.55 N 8.07 E
Cervo ≃ 62 45.22 N 8.24 E
Cervo, Capo > 62 43.55 N 8.08 E
Cervo, Rio do ≃, Bra. 256 21.12 S 45.10 W
Cervo, Rio do ≃, Bra. 256 22.07 S 45.49 W
Cervo, Serra do ∧ 256 22.06 S 46.07 W
Červonaja Kamenka 78 48.38 N 33.26 E
Červonoarmejsk, Ukr. 78 50.28 N 28.14 E
Červonoarmejsk, Ukr. 78 50.08 N 25.16 E
Červonoarmejskoje, Ukr. 78 45.47 N 28.44 E
Červonoarmejskoje, Ukr. 78 47.57 N 35.27 E
Červonograd 78 50.24 N 24.14 E
Červonogranitnoje 78 50.34 N 28.33 E
Červonoje, Ukr. 78 51.46 N 34.04 E
Červonoje, Ukr. 78 49.57 N 28.53 E
Červonoje, ozero ⊜ 76 52.24 N 27.57 E
Červonopartizansk 83 48.04 N 39.50 E
Červonyj Donec 78 49.29 N 36.34 E
Cesana Torinese 62 44.57 N 6.47 E
Cesano, It. 66 43.45 N 13.10 E
Cesano, It. 66 42.07 N 12.21 E
Cesano ≃ 66 43.45 N 13.10 E
Cesano Boscone 266b 45.27 N 9.06 E
Cesano Maderno 62 45.38 N 9.08 E
Cesar □⁵ 246 9.20 N 73.30 W
Cesar ≃ 246 9.00 N 73.58 W
Cesaró 70 37.50 N 14.43 E
Cesate 266b 45.36 N 9.05 E
Cesena 66 44.08 N 12.15 E
Cesenatico 66 44.12 N 12.24 E
Cesi, Poggio ∧² 267a 42.02 N 12.44 E
Cesiomaggiore 64 46.05 N 11.59 E
Cēsis 76 57.18 N 25.15 E
Česká Kamenice 54 50.47 N 14.26 E
Česká Kublice 60 49.22 N 12.52 E
Česká Lípa 54 50.42 N 14.32 E
Česká Třebová 30 49.54 N 16.27 E
České Budějovice 61 48.59 N 14.28 E
České středohoří ⋏ 54 50.35 N 14.09 E
Českomoravská vrchovina ⋏¹ 30 49.20 N 15.30 E
Český Brod 54 50.02 N 14.58 E
Český Krumlov 61 48.49 N 14.19 E
Česma 86 53.50 N 60.40 E
Çeşme 130 38.18 N 26.19 E
Cessalto 64 45.42 N 12.36 E
Češskaja guba ⊂ 24 67.30 N 46.30 E
Cessnock 170 32.50 S 151.21 E
Cesson 261 48.34 N 2.36 E
Cestos ≃ 150 5.40 N 9.10 W
Cesvaine 76 56.58 N 26.19 E
Čet' ≃ 86 56.51 N 86.48 E
Cetara 68 40.39 N 14.42 E
Cetate 38 44.06 N 23.03 E
Cetatea Albă → Belgorod-Dnestrovskij 78 46.12 N 30.20 E
Četbulak 85 41.17 N 73.58 E
Cetian 100 25.44 N 116.22 E
Cetina ≃ 36 43.26 N 16.42 E
Cetinje 38 42.23 N 18.55 E
Çetinkaya 130 39.15 N 37.38 E
Cetona 66 42.58 N 11.54 E
Cetona, Monte ∧ 66 42.56 N 11.52 E
Cetraro 68 39.31 N 15.56 E
Cetronia 208 40.35 N 75.31 W
Četyrboki 78 50.02 N 27.01 E
Céüse, Montagne de ∧ 62 44.31 N 5.57 E
Ceuta 34 35.53 N 5.19 W
Ceva 62 44.23 N 8.02 E
Cevedale, Monte (Zufallspitze) ∧ 64 46.27 N 10.37 E
Cevennen → Cévennes ◆¹ 32 44.00 N 3.30 E
Cévennes ◆¹ 32 44.00 N 3.30 E
Cévennes, Parc National des ♠ 32 44.15 N 3.40 E
Cevins 62 45.35 N 6.28 E
Cevio 58 46.19 N 8.36 E
Cevizli 130 37.12 N 31.45 E
Ceyhan 130 37.04 N 35.47 E
Ceyhan ≃ 130 36.45 N 35.41 E
Ceylanpınar 130 36.51 N 40.02 E
Ceylon, Sk., Can. 184 49.28 N 104.36 W
Ceylon, Mn., U.S. 198 43.32 N 94.37 W
Ceylon → Sri Lanka □¹ 122 7.00 N 81.00 E
Ceyzériat 58 46.10 N 5.19 E
Cèze ≃ 62 44.06 N 4.42 E
Chaam, Ned. 52 51.31 N 4.52 E
Cha-am, Thai 110 12.48 N 99.58 E
Chaanling 100 29.39 N 113.49 E
Chaatl Island I 182 53.00 N 132.25 W
Chabanais 32 45.52 N 0.43 E
Chabang Tiga 114 5.19 N 103.08 E
Chabaricha 24 65.50 N 52.16 E
Chabařovice 54 50.40 N 13.56 E
Chabarovo 72 69.39 N 60.24 E
Chabarovsk 89 48.27 N 135.06 E
Chabarovsk Kraj □⁸ 89 52.00 N 138.00 E
Chabarowsk → Chabarovsk 89 48.27 N 135.06 E
Chabary 86 53.37 N 79.33 E
Chabás 252 33.15 S 61.22 W
Chabeuil 62 44.54 N 5.01 E
Chabez 84 44.02 N 41.47 E
Chābi 124 22.49 N 80.41 E
Chabjuwardoo Bay ⊂ 162 22.57 S 113.48 E
Chablais ◆¹ 58 46.18 N 6.39 E
Chablis 50 47.49 N 3.48 E
Chabogongba 120 31.47 N 81.14 E
Chaboje 265a 59.53 N 30.46 E
Chabot, Lake ⊜, Ca., U.S. 282 37.43 N 122.07 W
Chabot, Lake ⊜, Ca., U.S. 282 38.08 N 122.14 W
Chabris 50 47.15 N 1.39 E
Chabuchaer 86 43.42 N 81.04 E
Chabu-Rabot, pereval)(85 38.40 N 70.43 E
Chacabuco 252 34.38 S 60.29 W
Chacaito, Quebrada ≃ 286c 10.29 N 66.52 W
Chacaltianguis 234 18.20 N 95.50 W
Chacao 286c 10.30 N 66.51 W
Chácara 256 21.41 S 43.13 W
Chacarita, Cementerio de la ◆ 288 34.33 S 58.28 W
Chacarrão, Cachoeira do ⌞ 250 6.32 S 58.12 W
Chacayán 248 10.24 S 76.25 W
Chachani, Nevado ∧ 248 16.12 S 71.33 W
Chachapoyas, Perú 242 6.13 S 77.51 W
Chachapoyas, Perú 248 6.13 S 77.51 W
Chachas 248 15.30 S 72.16 W
Chachoengsao 110 13.42 N 101.05 E
Chāchora 124 24.10 N 76.59 E
Chāchro 120 25.07 N 70.15 E
Chachu 120 33.16 N 81.41 E
Chačinčaj ≃ 84 40.13 N 47.18 E
Chaclacyo 248 11.59 S 76.46 W
Chačmas 84 41.28 N 48.48 E
Chaco □⁴ 252 26.25 S 60.30 W
Chaco □⁵ 248 20.00 S 60.30 W
Chaco ≃ 200 36.46 N 108.39 W
Chaco Austral ◆¹ 252 26.30 S 61.30 W
Chaco Boreal ◆¹ 252 23.00 S 60.00 W
Chaco Central ◆¹ 252 25.00 S 59.45 W
Chaco Culture National Historical Park ♠ 200 36.06 N 108.00 W
Chaco Mesa ∧ 200 35.47 N 107.35 W
Chacón, Arroyo ≃ 288 34.53 S 58.39 W
Chacon, Cape > 182 54.42 N 132.00 W
Chacra Cerro 286d 11.55 S 77.04 W
Chacuaco Creek ≃ 196 37.34 N 103.38 W
Chad (Tchad) □¹, Afr. 136 15.00 N 19.00 E
Chad (Tchad) □¹, Afr. 146 15.00 N 19.00 E
Chad, Lake (Lac Tchad) ⊜ 146 13.20 N 14.00 E
Chada-Bulak 88 50.38 N 116.18 E
Chadbourn 192 34.19 N 78.49 W
Chadderton 44 53.33 N 2.08 W
Chadds Ford 285 39.52 N 75.35 W
Chādegān 128 32.46 N 50.39 E
Chadian, Zhg. 102 26.48 N 105.48 E
Chadian, Zhg. 105 39.14 N 117.45 E
Chadian, Zhg. 107 30.14 N 105.56 E
Chadianzi 107 30.31 N 104.22 E
Chadiza 154 14.05 S 32.28 E
Chadron 198 42.49 N 103.00 W
Chadstone 274b 37.53 S 145.05 E
Chadwell Saint Mary 260 51.29 N 0.22 E
Chadwick 190 42.01 N 89.53 W
Chadwick Manor 284b 39.19 N 76.46 W
Chadwick Pond ⊜ 283 42.44 N 71.05 W
Chadwicks 210 43.01 N 75.16 W
Chadyženks 78 44.25 N 39.33 E
Chadžalmachi 84 42.26 N 47.13 E
Chadžibejskij liman ⊜ 78 46.39 N 30.33 E
Chae Hom 110 18.43 N 99.35 E
Chaem ≃ 110 18.11 N 98.38 E
Chaersen 89 46.19 N 121.54 E
Chaeryŏng 98 38.24 N 125.36 E
Chafarinas, Islas II 34 35.11 N 2.26 W
Chafe 150 11.56 N 6.55 E
Chaffee 194 37.10 N 89.39 W
Chaffins 207 42.21 N 71.51 W
Chāgai 128 29.18 N 64.42 E
Chāgai Hills ⋏² 128 29.30 N 64.15 E
Chagandianlisu 102 41.47 N 103.29 E
Chagang Do □⁴ 98 40.50 N 126.30 E
'Chaghcharān 120 34.32 N 65.15 E
Chagny 58 46.55 N 4.45 E
Chagos Archipelago II 12 6.00 S 72.00 E
Chagos-Laccadive Plateau ✢³ 12 3.00 N 73.00 E
Chagrin ≃ 214 41.40 N 81.27 W
Chagrin, Aurora Branch ≃ 279a 41.25 N 81.25 W
Chagrin Falls 214 41.26 N 81.24 W
Chagrin Falls Park 214 41.21 N 81.32 W
Chagrin Valley Parkway ♠ 279a 41.26 N 81.25 W
Chaguanas 241r 10.31 N 61.25 W
Chaguaramas 246 9.20 N 66.16 W
Chahaignes 50 47.44 N 0.31 E
Chāhak 128 33.17 N 58.54 E
Chahal 236 15.45 N 89.34 W
Chahancheluo 98 41.39 N 114.22 E
Chahanwusu → Dulan 102 36.16 N 98.28 E
Chahār Borjak 128 30.17 N 62.03 E
Chahār Deh-ye Ghowrband 120 34.59 N 68.44 E
Chahār Maḩāl va Bakhtīārī □⁴ 128 32.00 N 51.00 E
Chahayang 89 48.24 N 124.15 E
Chahe, Zhg. 100 33.16 N 119.02 E
Chahe, Zhg. 102 33.48 N 97.22 E
Chahe, Zhg. 105 39.50 N 115.21 E
Chāh Gheybī, Hāmūn-e ≋ 128 28.06 N 60.50 E
Chahuamiao 100 33.00 N 115.56 E
Chahuites 234 16.17 N 94.11 W
Chai ≃ 104 42.20 N 123.52 E
Chai Badan 110 15.04 N 101.05 E
Chāībāsa 124 22.34 N 85.49 E
Chaigou 98 36.15 N 119.36 E
Chaihe 89 44.47 N 129.42 E
Chaijiawan 100 29.10 N 113.06 E
Chaillé-les-Marais 32 46.24 N 1.01 W
Chailley 50 48.05 N 3.42 E
Chailly-en-Bière 50 48.28 N 2.35 E
Chai Nat 110 15.11 N 100.08 E
Chainhurst 260 51.12 N 0.29 E
Chain O'Lakes State Park ♠, Il., U.S. 216 42.27 N 88.11 W
Chain O'Lakes State Park ♠, In., U.S. 216 41.20 N 85.26 W
Chainpur 124 23.08 N 84.15 E
Chaipudyrskaja guba ⊂ 24 68.30 N 59.30 E
Chaiqiao 100 29.51 N 121.56 E
Chairel, Laguna de ⊂ 234 22.17 N 97.57 W
Chaishudian 105 40.46 N 116.30 E
Chaiši 84 42.57 N 42.12 E
Chait 85 39.11 N 70.53 E
Chaital 126 22.31 N 88.47 E
Chaitén 254 42.55 S 72.43 W
Chaiwopu 86 43.33 N 87.59 E
Chaiya 110 9.23 N 99.14 E
Chaiyaphum 110 15.48 N 102.02 E
Chajarí 252 30.46 S 57.59 W
Chajdarken 85 39.57 N 71.21 E
Chajia 107 29.37 N 104.27 E
Chajian 100 32.40 N 118.46 E
Chajianling 98 39.14 N 114.36 E
Chajiaqiao 100 34.00 N 120.07 E
Chajrchan 88 48.35 N 101.56 E
Chajrchandulaan 102 45.57 N 102.03 E
Chajul 236 15.30 N 91.02 W
Chaka 154 4.49 N 31.14 E
Chakachamna Lake ⊜ 180 61.13 N 152.35 W
Chakāltor 126 23.14 N 86.22 E
Chak Amru 123 32.22 N 75.11 E
Chakari 154 18.05 S 29.51 E
Chakaria 120 21.45 N 92.05 E
Chakarnaba 146 14.13 N 20.51 E
Chakasija □³ 86 53.00 N 90.00 E
Chākdaha, India 126 23.05 N 88.31 E
Chakdaha, India 272b 22.20 N 88.20 E
Chake Chake 154 5.15 S 39.46 E
Chakhānsūr 128 31.10 N 62.04 E
Chākia 124 26.25 N 85.03 E
Chakkarat 110 15.00 N 102.16 E
Chakou, Zhg. 98 38.03 N 113.36 E
Chakou, Zhg. 105 38.53 N 116.41 E
Chakradharpur 124 22.42 N 85.38 E
Chakrāta 120 30.42 N 77.51 E
Chāksu 120 26.36 N 75.57 E
Chākulia 126 22.29 N 86.43 E
Chakwadām 102 27.29 N 98.31 E
Chakwāl 123 32.56 N 72.52 E
Chal 272c 19.06 N 73.08 E
Chala 248 15.52 S 74.16 W
Chalabesa 154 11.22 S 31.01 E
Chalais 32 45.16 N 0.02 E
Chālakuda 122 10.18 N 76.20 E
Chalamont 58 46.00 N 5.10 E
Chalampé 58 47.49 N 7.33 E
Chalan Kanoa 174n 15.08 N 145.43 E
Chalatenango 236 14.03 N 88.56 W
Chalaua 154 16.06 S 39.11 E
Chalaux ≃ 50 47.23 N 3.54 E
Chalaxung 102 34.10 N 97.44 E
Chalbi Desert ◆² 154 3.00 N 37.20 E
Chalchgol 88 48.11 N 114.54 E
Chalchihuites 234 23.29 N 103.53 W
Chalchis Terara ∧ 144 9.08 N 36.44 E
Chalchuapa 236 13.59 N 89.41 W
Chalchyn ≃ 88 47.55 N 117.47 E
Chalcis → Khalkís 38 38.28 N 23.36 E
Chalco ≃ 286a 19.19 N 99.08 W
Chaldan 84 40.43 N 47.15 E
Chaldon 260 51.17 N 0.07 W
Chaleine 261 48.36 N 1.43 E
Chalengkou 120 38.02 N 93.54 E
Châlette-sur-Loing 50 48.01 N 2.44 E
Chaleur Bay ⊂ 186 48.00 N 65.45 W
Chalfant 279b 40.25 N 79.52 W
Chalfant Run ≃ 279b 40.25 N 79.48 W
Chalfont 208 40.17 N 75.13 W
Chalfont Common 260 51.38 N 0.33 W
Chalfonte 285 39.49 N 75.32 W
Chalfont Saint Giles 260 51.38 N 0.34 W
Chalfont Saint Peter 42 51.37 N 0.33 W
Chalford 42 51.45 N 2.09 W
Chalhuanca 248 14.17 S 73.15 W
Chalía ≃ 254 49.35 S 69.34 W
Chalifert 261 48.53 N 2.46 E
Chalilovo 86 51.24 N 58.04 E
Chalindrey 58 47.48 N 5.26 E
Chaling 100 26.47 N 113.33 E
Chālisgaon 122 20.28 N 75.01 E
Chalisi 102 32.55 N 102.04 E
Chaliun 88 48.50 N 103.59 E
Chalk 260 51.26 N 0.25 E
Chalkabad 86 42.42 N 59.43 E
Chalk Draw V 196 29.36 N 103.15 W
Chalk River 190 46.01 N 77.27 W
Chalkyitsik 180 66.39 N 143.43 W
Challakere 122 14.19 N 76.39 E
Challans 32 46.51 N 1.53 W
Challapata 248 18.54 S 66.47 W
Challenge 226 39.29 N 121.13 W
Challenger, Mount ∧ 224 48.50 N 121.20 W
Challenger Deep ✢¹ 14 11.21 N 142.12 E
Challes-les-Eaux 62 45.33 N 5.59 E
Challis 202 44.30 N 114.13 W
Challviri, Salar de ≋ 248 22.32 S 67.34 W
Chal'mer-Ju 24 67.58 N 64.50 E
Chalmers 216 40.39 N 86.52 W
Chalmette 194 29.56 N 89.57 W
Chalone Creek ≃ 226 36.21 N 121.14 W
Chalonnes-sur-Loire 32 47.21 N 0.46 W
Châlons-sur-Marne 50 48.57 N 4.22 E
Chalon-sur-Saône 58 46.47 N 4.51 E
Chalosse ◆¹ 32 43.45 N 0.30 W
Chalt 123 36.15 N 74.20 E
Chaltel, Cerro (Monte Fitzroy) ∧ 254 49.17 S 73.05 W
Chalturino 78 49.31 N 35.17 E
Chaluhe 89 43.43 N 126.00 E
Châlus, Fr. 32 45.39 N 0.59 E
Chālūs, Īrān 128 36.38 N 51.26 E
Cham, Dtsch. 60 49.13 N 12.41 E
Cham, Schw. 58 47.11 N 8.28 E
Chama 200 36.54 N 106.34 W
Chama ≃ 246 9.03 N 71.40 W
Chama, Rio ≃ 200 36.03 N 106.05 W
Chamah, Gunong ∧ 114 5.13 N 101.33 E
Chamaicó 252 35.03 S 64.58 W
Chamama 154 12.55 S 33.43 E
Chamamat'urt 84 43.36 N 46.30 E
Chaman 120 30.55 N 66.27 E
Chamangonge 152 11.16 S 20.24 E
Chamao, Khao ∧ 110 12.57 N 101.45 E
Chamarande 261 48.31 N 2.13 E
Chamar-Daban, chrebet ⋏ 88 51.15 N 105.00 E
Chāmārpāra 272b 22.35 N 88.08 E
Chamaya ≃ 248 5.44 S 78.39 W
Chamb ≃ 60 49.13 N 12.42 E
Chamba, India 123 32.34 N 76.08 E
Chamba, Moç. 154 12.07 S 36.57 E
Chamba, Tan. 154 11.35 S 36.58 E
Chambal ≃ 120 26.30 N 79.15 E
Chambaran, Plateau de ⋏¹ 62 45.15 N 5.15 E
Chambas 240p 22.12 N 78.55 W
Chamberlain, Sk., Can. 184 50.50 N 105.34 W
Chamberlain, S.D., U.S. 198 43.48 N 99.19 W
Chamberlain ≃ 164 15.08 S 128.06 E
Chamberlain Lake ⊜ 186 46.17 N 69.20 W
Chamberlin, Mount ∧ 180 69.16 N 144.55 W
Chamberry, Ruisseau ≃ 275a 45.20 N 73.58 W
Chambers, Az., U.S. 200 35.11 N 109.25 W
Chambers, Ne., U.S. 198 42.12 N 98.44 W
Chambers, N.Y., U.S. 210 42.16 N 76.57 W
Chambers □⁶ 222 29.42 N 94.40 W
Chambers Brook ≃ 276 40.35 N 74.41 W
Chambersburg, Il., U.S. 219 39.49 N 90.39 W
Chambersburg, In., U.S. 218 38.31 N 86.24 W
Chambersburg, Pa., U.S. 208 39.56 N 77.39 W
Chambers Corner 285 40.01 N 74.44 W
Chambers Creek ≃ 222 31.58 N 96.10 W
Chambers Creek, North Fork ≃ 222 32.16 N 96.58 W
Chambers Creek, South Fork ≃ 222 32.16 N 96.58 W
Chambers Island I 190 45.11 N 87.21 W
Chambéry 62 45.34 N 5.56 E
Chambeshi ≃ 154 11.21 S 30.37 E
Chambi, Jebel ∧ 148 35.11 N 8.42 E
Chambira ≃, Perú 246 4.28 S 74.50 W
Chambira ≃, Perú 246 3.55 S 73.45 W
Chamblee 192 33.53 N 84.17 W
Chambley-Bussières 56 49.03 N 5.54 E
Chambly, P.Q., Can. 206 45.27 N 73.17 W
Chambly, Fr. 50 49.10 N 2.15 E
Chambly □⁶ 206 45.30 N 73.20 W
Chambly, Bassin de ⊜ 206 45.27 N 73.17 W
Chambly, Canal de ≍ 275a 45.25 N 73.15 W
Chambois 50 48.48 N 0.07 E
Chambon-sur-Dolore 62 45.30 N 3.37 E
Chambon-sur-Voueize 32 46.11 N 2.25 E
Chambord, Château de ⊥ 50 47.37 N 1.31 E
Chambourcy 261 48.54 N 2.03 E
Chambri Lake ⊜ 164 4.16 S 143.08 E
Chambry 261 49.00 N 2.54 E
Chamburi Kalāt 128 26.09 N 64.43 E
Chamdo → Qamdo 102 31.11 N 97.15 E
Chāme, Nepāl 124 28.33 N 84.15 E
Chame, Pan. 236 8.35 N 79.53 W
Chame, Punta > 236 8.39 N 79.42 W
Chamela 234 19.32 N 105.05 W
Chamelecón 236 15.24 N 88.01 W
Chamelecón ≃ 236 15.51 N 87.49 W
Chamical 252 30.21 S 66.19 W
Chamizo 258 34.10 S 56.41 W
Chamizo, Arroyo ≃ 258 34.15 S 56.44 W
Chamkanī 120 33.48 N 69.49 E
Chāmlūjā ≃ 124 29.38 N 80.24 E
Chamo, Lake ⊜ 144 5.50 N 37.33 E
Chamois, It. 62 45.50 N 7.37 E
Chamois, Mo., U.S. 219 38.40 N 91.46 W
Chamojie 89 49.25 N 124.45 E
Chamoli 124 30.24 N 79.21 E
Chamonix-Mont-Blanc 58 45.55 N 6.52 E
Chamousset 62 45.33 N 6.12 E
Chamoux-sur-Gelon 62 45.32 N 6.13 E
Chāmpa 124 22.03 N 82.39 E
Champagne, Yk., Can. 180 60.47 N 136.29 W
Champagne, Fr. 62 45.16 N 4.48 E
Champagne □⁹ 32 49.00 N 4.30 E
Champagne Castle ∧ 158 29.06 S 29.20 E
Champagne-en-Valromay 58 45.54 N 5.41 E
Champagner-Berg ∧² 264a 52.31 N 13.05 E
Champagne-sur-Seine 50 48.24 N 2.48 E
Champagney 58 47.42 N 6.41 E
Champagnole 58 46.45 N 5.55 E
Champagny 62 45.27 N 6.42 E
Chāmpāhāti 126 22.23 N 88.29 E
Champaign 194 40.06 N 88.14 W
Champaign □⁶, Il., U.S. 216 40.07 N 88.12 W
Champaign □⁶, Oh., U.S. 218 40.07 N 83.45 W
Champapur 126 24.02 N 86.31 E
Champaquí, Cerro ∧ 252 31.59 S 64.56 W

≃ River	Fluß	Río	Rivière	Rio
≍ Canal	Kanal	Canal	Canal	Canal
⌞ Waterfall, Rapids	Wasserfall, Stromschnellen	Cascada, Rápidos	Chute d'eau, Rapides	Cascata, Rápidos
)(Strait	Meeresstraße	Estrecho	Détroit	Estreito
⊂ Bay, Gulf	Bucht, Golf	Bahía, Golfo	Baie, Golfe	Baía, Golfo
⊜ Lake, Lakes	See, Seen	Lago, Lagos	Lac, Lacs	Lago, Lagos
≋ Swamp	Sumpf	Pantano	Marais	Pântano
Ice Features, Glacier	Eis- und Gletscherformen	Accidentes Glaciales	Formes glaciaires	Acidentes glaciares
⊤ Other Hydrographic Features	Andere Hydrographische Objekte	Otros Elementos Hidrográficos	Autres données hydrographiques	Outros acidentes hidrográficos
✢ Submarine Features	Untermeerische Objekte	Accidentes Submarinos	Formes de relief sous-marin	Acidentes submarinos
□ Political Unit	Politische Einheit	Unidad Politica	Entité politique	Unidade política
⚑ Cultural Institution	Kulturelle Institution	Institución Cultural	Institution culturelle	Institução cultural
⊥ Historical Site	Historische Stätte	Sitio Histórico	Site historique	Sitio histórico
♠ Recreational Site	Erholungs- und Ferienort	Sitio de Recreo	Centre de loisirs	Area de Lazer
⊠ Airport	Flughafen	Aeropuerto	Aéroport	Aeroporto
■ Military Installation	Militäranlage	Instalación Militar	Installation militaire	Instalação militar
◆ Miscellaneous	Verschiedenes	Misceláneo	Divers	Diversos

Champasak 110 14.53 N 105.52 E
Champāwat 124 29.20 N 80.06 E
Champcueil 261 48.31 N 2.27 E
Champdāni 126 22.48 N 88.21 E
Champdeniers 32 46.29 N 0.24 W
Champdepraz 62 45.41 N 7.39 E
Champdeuil 261 48.37 N 2.44 E
Champdor 58 46.01 N 5.36 E
Champdoré, Lac ⊜ 176 55.55 N 65.49 W
Champeaux 50 48.35 N 2.48 E
Champeix 32 45.36 N 3.08 E
Champerico 236 14.18 N 91.55 W
Champéry 58 46.10 N 6.52 E
Champex 58 46.02 N 7.07 E
Champier 62 45.27 N 5.17 E
Champigneulles 56 48.44 N 6.10 E
Champigny-sur-Marne 261 48.49 N 2.31 E
Champion, Ab., Can. 182 50.14 N 113.09 W
Champion, Mi., U.S. 190 46.30 N 87.57 W
Champion, Oh., U.S. 214 41.17 N 80.51 W
Champion, Pa., U.S. 214 40.05 N 79.21 W
Champions 222 29.59 N 95.31 W
Champlain 206 44.59 N 73.26 W
Champlain □[6] 206 46.45 N 72.35 W
Champlain ≃ 206 46.27 N 72.17 W
Champlain, Lake ⊜ 188 44.45 N 73.15 W
Champlain, Pont ◆[5] 206 45.28 N 73.32 W
Champlain Canal ≅ 210 43.20 N 73.34 W
Champlan 261 48.43 N 2.16 E
Champlin Creek ≃ 276 40.43 N 73.12 W
Champlitte-et-le-Prélot 58 47.37 N 5.31 E
Champlon 56 50.07 N 5.28 E
Champoluc 62 45.50 N 7.44 E
Champotón 232 19.21 N 90.43 W
Champrond-en-Gâtine 50 48.24 N 1.05 E
Champs 50 47.44 N 3.36 E
Champs-sur-Marne 261 48.51 N 2.36 E
Chāmpua 124 22.05 N 85.40 E
Champvans 58 47.06 N 5.26 E
Chāmrāil 272b 22.38 N 88.18 E
Chāmrājnagar Rāmasamudram 122 11.55 N 76.57 E
Chamrousse 62 45.08 N 5.52 E
Chamsara ≃ 88 52.42 N 95.46 E
Chamusca 34 39.21 N 8.29 W
Chamza Chakimzada 85 40.26 N 71.30 E
Chana 110 6.55 N 100.44 E
Chanabadskij 85 40.49 N 72.58 E
Chanakyapuri □[9] 272a 28.36 N 77.11 E
Chañar 252 30.32 S 65.58 W
Chañaral 252 26.21 S 70.37 W
Chañaral, Isla I 252 29.02 S 71.35 W
Chanas 62 45.18 N 4.49 E
Chānasma 120 23.43 N 72.07 E
Chanbogd 102 43.12 N 107.10 E
Chancay 248 11.35 S 77.16 W
Chancay ≃ 248 11.37 S 77.15 W
Chance 208 38.10 N 75.56 W
Chanceaux 58 47.31 N 4.42 E
Chanceaux-sur-Choisille 50 47.28 N 0.42 E
Chanch 88 51.30 N 100.40 E
Chanchelulla Peak ∧ 204 40.28 N 122.59 W
Chanchiang → Zhanjiang 102 21.16 N 110.28 E
Chanchöchij uul ⋌ 88 49.30 N 94.30 E
Chanchongor 102 43.50 N 104.25 E
Chanco 252 35.44 S 72.32 W
Chancy 58 46.08 N 6.00 E
Chanda 88 55.00 N 107.14 E
Chanda ≃ 88 55.00 N 107.14 E
Chāndābila 126 22.05 N 87.00 E
Chanda → Chandrapur 122 19.57 N 79.18 E
Chandagajty 86 50.44 N 92.03 E
Chandalar 180 67.30 N 148.30 W
Chandalar ≃ 180 66.36 N 145.48 W
Chandalar, East Fork ≃ 180 67.05 N 147.16 W
Chandalar, Middle Fork ≃ 180 67.10 N 148.19 W
Chandalar, North Fork ≃ 180 67.10 N 148.19 W
Chandan Chauki 124 28.33 N 80.47 E
Chandankiāri 126 23.34 N 86.22 E
Chandannagar 126 22.51 N 88.21 E
Chandanpratāp 126 23.33 N 89.24 E
Chāndar 126 23.54 N 89.58 E
Chandausi 124 28.27 N 78.46 E
Chāndbāli 120 20.47 N 86.46 E
Chandeleur Islands II 194 29.48 N 88.51 W
Chandeleur Sound ⊍ 194 29.55 N 89.10 W
Chanderi 124 24.43 N 78.08 E
Chandernagore → Chandannagar 126 22.51 N 88.21 E
Chandīgarh 123 30.44 N 76.55 E
Chandīgarh □[8] 123 30.45 N 76.50 E
Chāndil 124 22.58 N 86.03 E
Chandīpur 126 23.59 N 89.01 E
Chanditala 272b 22.41 N 88.16 E
Chandla 124 25.05 N 80.12 E
Chandler, P.Q., Can. 186 48.21 N 64.41 W
Chandler, Az., U.S. 200 33.18 N 111.50 W
Chandler, In., U.S. 194 38.02 N 87.22 W
Chandler, Ok., U.S. 196 35.42 N 96.52 W
Chandler, Tx., U.S. 222 32.18 N 95.29 W
Chandler ≃ 180 69.27 N 151.30 W
Chandler, Mount ∧[2] 162 27.00 S 133.20 E
Chandler Lake ⊜ 180 68.15 N 152.43 W
Chandler Park ♦ 281 42.24 N 82.58 W
Chandler's Cross 260 51.40 N 0.27 W
Chandler's Ford 42 50.59 N 1.23 W
Chandlers Valley 214 41.56 N 79.18 W
Chandlerville 219 40.02 N 90.09 W
Chandless ≃ 248 9.08 S 69.51 W
Chāndor Hills ⋌[2] 122 20.30 N 74.00 E
Chandos Lake ⊜ 212 44.49 N 78.00 W
Chāndpara 126 22.58 N 88.47 E
Chāndpur, Bngl. 120 22.08 N 91.55 E
Chāndpur, Bngl. 124 23.13 N 90.39 E
Chāndpur, India 124 29.09 N 78.16 E
Chāndpur ◆[8] 272a 28.45 N 77.01 E
Chāndra 126 22.28 N 87.09 E
Chandrabhāga ≃ 123 32.59 N 76.25 E
Chandra Dighalia 126 23.04 N 89.46 E
Chandrakona 126 22.44 N 87.31 E
Chandrakona Road 126 22.44 N 87.21 E
Chandrapur 122 19.57 N 79.18 E
Chāndvad 122 20.20 N 74.15 E
Chandyga 74 62.40 N 135.36 E
Chanfang 105 39.56 N 115.55 E
Chang (Yangtze) ≃, Zhg. 90 31.48 N 121.10 E
Chang ≃, Zhg. 100 28.59 N 116.42 E
Chang ≃, Zhg. 100 26.53 N 119.41 E
Chang, Ko I 110 12.05 N 102.20 E
Changa 84 44.27 N 50.36 E
Changaj 88 47.52 N 99.28 E
Changajn nuruu ⋌ 90 47.30 N 100.00 E
Changal 88 49.19 N 104.24 E
Changalane 156 26.17 S 32.11 E
Chang'an 102 26.00 N 109.34 E
Changanācheri 122 9.28 N 76.33 E
Changane ≃ 156 24.43 S 33.32 E
Changan → Xi'an 102 34.15 N 108.52 E
Chang'anzhen 106 30.28 N 120.27 E
Changara 154 16.54 S 33.14 E
Changarul'skij chrebet ⋌ 88 51.10 N 103.00 E
Changbai 98 41.26 N 128.11 E
Changbai Shan ⋌ 98 41.40 N 128.00 E
Changbu 100 23.48 N 115.26 E
Changcaocun 105 39.49 N 115.47 E
Changchaoling 106 31.00 N 119.40 E
Changcheng, Zhg. 100 31.49 N 116.54 E
Changcheng, Zhg. 110 19.24 N 108.42 E
Chang Cheng (Great Wall) ⊥ 98 40.30 N 116.30 E
Chang Chenmo ≃ 120 34.17 N 78.19 E
Changchiak'ou → Zhangjiakou 105 40.50 N 114.53 E
Ch'angchih → Changzhi 102 36.11 N 113.08 E
Changchou → Zhangzhou 100 24.33 N 117.39 E
Changchow → Changzhou 106 31.47 N 119.57 E
Changchun 89 43.53 N 125.19 E
Changchunling 89 45.22 N 125.28 E
Changdan 98 37.56 N 126.45 E
Changdang Hu ⊜ 106 31.35 N 119.35 E
Changdao (Sihou) 98 37.56 N 120.42 E
Changde 102 29.02 N 111.41 E
Changdian 105 40.01 N 116.32 E
Ch'angdo 98 38.30 N 127.40 E
Ch'ang-dong 98 39.03 N 126.34 E
Change Islands 186 49.40 N 54.25 W
Changeon ≃ 50 47.16 N 0.05 E
Changfeng 100 32.27 N 117.09 E
Changgang 100 24.38 N 113.05 E
Changgangzi 104 41.26 N 122.41 E
Changge 100 34.15 N 113.50 E
Changgi-ap ≻ 98 36.05 N 129.34 E
Changgi-li 271b 37.35 N 126.44 E
Changgi-ri 271b 37.38 N 126.41 E
Changgou 105 39.34 N 115.53 E
Changgouyu 105 39.44 N 115.52 E
Changguandian 100 32.58 N 115.16 E
Changguowei 100 29.15 N 121.56 E
Changgye-ri 98 34.33 N 126.49 E
Changgyong Palace ◍ 271b 37.36 N 127.00 E
Changhai 98 39.18 N 122.35 E
Chang-hai → Shanghai 106 31.14 N 121.28 E
Changhang 98 36.01 N 126.40 E
Changhe 106 30.11 N 120.11 E
Changhowŏn 98 37.08 N 127.39 E
Chang Hu ⊜ 100 30.15 N 112.35 E
Changhua, T'aiwan 100 24.05 N 120.32 E
Changhua, Zhg. 100 30.11 N 119.13 E
Changhŭng 98 34.41 N 126.52 E
Changhŭng-ni 98 40.24 N 128.19 E
Changi 271c 1.23 N 103.59 E
Changi, Tanjong ≻ 271c 1.23 N 104.00 E
Changi International Airport ⊠ 271c 1.22 N 103.59 E
Changi Prison ◍ 271c 1.22 N 103.58 E
Changji 86 44.01 N 87.19 E
Changjiang, Zhg. 100 25.19 N 113.56 E
Changjiang, Zhg. 110 19.17 N 109.02 E
Changjiangbu 100 30.52 N 113.43 E
Changjiapuzi 104 40.51 N 123.43 E
Changjiazhuang 105 40.35 N 115.24 E
Changjie 100 29.16 N 121.40 E
Changjing 106 31.45 N 120.29 E
Changjin-gang ≃ 98 41.24 N 127.45 E
Changjin-ŭp 98 40.23 N 127.15 E
Changkai 100 28.04 N 116.18 E
Changkalajier 85 40.09 N 76.59 E
Changkeng 106 30.19 N 121.57 E
Changkiakow → Zhangjiakou 105 40.50 N 114.53 E
Changlapod Pass)(124 30.08 N 87.06 E
Changle, Zhg. 98 36.42 N 118.49 E
Changle, Zhg. 100 29.25 N 120.37 E
Changle, Zhg. 100 26.00 N 119.31 E
Changlejie 100 28.52 N 113.19 E
Changleqiao 106 30.21 N 119.51 E
Changlezhen 106 31.56 N 121.15 E
Changli, Zhg. 98 36.57 N 119.45 E
Changli, Zhg. 98 39.43 N 119.11 E
Changling 89 44.15 N 123.58 E
Changlingfeng 105 40.11 N 118.24 E
Changlingji 100 32.30 N 114.54 E
Changlingzi, Zhg. 98 39.47 N 122.43 E
Changlingzi, Zhg. 98 39.33 N 121.19 E
Changlinhe 100 31.40 N 117.29 E
Changlun 114 6.26 N 100.26 E
Changmar 120 34.15 N 79.45 E
Changmong-ni 98 34.58 N 128.41 E
Changning, Zhg. 102 26.19 N 112.21 E
Changning, Zhg. 102 24.55 N 99.35 E
Changning (Anningqiao), Zhg. 102 28.21 N 104.53 E
Changning, Zhg. 105 39.59 N 114.55 E
Ch'angnyŏng 98 35.33 N 128.29 E
Changnyŏn-ni 98 38.37 N 125.16 E
Changokurt 72 61.58 N 64.18 E
Ch'angpin 100 23.19 N 121.27 E
Changping 105 40.14 N 116.14 E
Changputong 102 28.05 N 98.29 E
Ch'angp'yŏng-dong 98 41.27 N 127.31 E
Changqiao, Zhg. 100 24.15 N 117.39 E
Changqiao, Zhg. 100 26.49 N 118.50 E
Changqing 98 36.34 N 116.43 E
Changsa 102 19.51 N 110.53 E
Changsan-got ≻ 98 38.08 N 124.39 E
Changsha, Zhg. 100 28.12 N 112.58 E
Changsha, Zhg. 100 24.13 N 116.07 E
Changshaba Shuiku ⊜[1] 107 29.42 N 104.40 E
Changshageng 107 30.00 N 104.35 E
Changshan, Zhg. 98 36.54 N 117.50 E
Changshan, Zhg. 100 28.55 N 118.30 E
Changshan, Zhg. 107 29.30 N 104.13 E
Changshan ≃ 100 28.57 N 118.50 E
Changshan Qundao II 98 39.00 N 122.45 E
Changsheng 100 26.16 N 116.01 E
Changshengqiao 107 29.31 N 106.39 E
Changshitai 104 42.33 N 120.43 E
Changshitou 102 35.03 N 99.11 E
Changshou 102 29.51 N 107.06 E
Changshoudian 100 31.26 N 112.35 E
Changshoujie 100 28.44 N 113.57 E
Changshu 106 31.39 N 120.45 E
Changshui 102 34.21 N 111.29 E
Changsŏng 98 35.20 N 126.49 E
Changsŏng-ni 98 40.58 N 127.04 E
Changsu 98 35.40 N 127.32 E
Changtai, Zhg. 100 24.40 N 117.46 E
Changtai, Zhg. 100 28.34 N 118.37 E
Changtai, Zhg. 104 41.34 N 122.00 E
Changtancun 104 41.33 N 123.02 E
Ch'angte → Changde 102 29.02 N 111.41 E
Changteh → Anyang 98 36.06 N 114.21 E
Changting, Zhg. 89 44.32 N 128.47 E
Changting, Zhg. 100 25.52 N 116.20 E
Changtumiao 102 43.30 N 114.34 E
Changuinola 236 9.25 N 82.32 W
Changuinola ≃ 236 9.28 N 82.27 W
Changwu, Zhg. 89 46.00 N 125.36 E
Changwu, Zhg. 102 35.09 N 107.42 E
Changxindianzhen 105 39.49 N 116.12 E
Changxing 106 31.01 N 119.54 E
Changxing Dao I, Zhg. 98 39.34 N 121.23 E
Changxing Dao I, Zhg. 106 31.24 N 121.42 E
Changxingdian, Zhg. 104 41.33 N 123.23 E
Changxingdian, Zhg. 104 41.27 N 121.44 E
Changxingzhen 104 41.40 N 122.14 E
Changxuanling 100 31.08 N 114.20 E
Changyi 98 36.51 N 119.23 E
Changyŏn 98 38.15 N 125.06 E
Changyuan 98 35.13 N 114.39 E
Changyukou 105 40.46 N 115.08 E
Changzhi 102 36.11 N 113.08 E
Changzhou (Changchow) 106 31.47 N 119.57 E
Chanhanga 152 16.04 S 14.07 E
Chanh Hung 269c 10.44 N 106.41 E
Chani 88 57.05 N 120.58 E
Chani ≃ 88 57.02 N 120.59 E
Chanino 76 54.13 N 36.37 E
Chanka, ozero (Xingkai Hu) ⊜ 89 45.00 N 132.24 E
Chankiang → Zhanjiang 102 21.16 N 110.28 E
Chankou 102 35.52 N 104.27 E
Chanlar 84 40.34 N 46.20 E
Channagiri 122 14.02 N 75.56 E
Channahon 216 41.26 N 88.14 W
Channapatna 122 12.39 N 77.13 E
Channel Country ◆[1] 166 24.45 S 141.00 E
Channel Islands II, Europe 43b 49.20 N 2.20 W
Channel Islands II, Ca., U.S. 204 33.30 N 119.15 W
Channel Islands National Park ♦ 204 33.28 N 119.02 W
Channel Lake 216 42.29 N 88.08 W
Channel-Port-aux-Basques 186 47.34 N 59.09 W
Channel Tunnel ◆[5] 50 51.00 N 1.35 E
Channelview 222 29.46 N 95.06 W
Channing, Mi., U.S. 190 46.08 N 88.05 W
Channing, Tx., U.S. 196 35.41 N 102.20 W
Chānpādānga 126 22.50 N 87.58 E
Chantada 34 42.37 N 7.46 W
Chantajskoje, ozero ⊜ 74 68.20 N 91.00 E
Chantajskoje vodochranilišče ⊜[1] 72 68.00 N 88.00 E
Chantang 100 33.41 N 117.37 E
Chantau 86 44.13 N 73.51 E
Chanteloup 261 48.51 N 2.44 E
Chanteloup-les-Vignes 261 48.59 N 2.02 E
Chanthaburi 110 12.36 N 102.09 E
Chantilly 50 49.12 N 2.28 E
Chantonnay 32 46.41 N 1.03 W
Chantraine 58 48.10 N 6.26 E
Chantrans 58 47.03 N 6.09 E
Chantrey Inlet ⊂ 176 67.48 N 96.20 W
Chanty-Mansijsk 74 61.00 N 69.06 E
Chanty-Mansijskij Avtonomnyj Okrug □[8] 86 60.15 N 70.45 E
Chanujn ≃ 88 49.22 N 102.22 E
Chanumla 110 8.19 N 93.05 E
Chanute 198 37.40 N 95.27 W
Chanute Air Force Base ■ 216 40.18 N 88.09 W
Chanuwāla 123 32.44 N 73.08 E
Chanžonkovo 83 48.06 N 38.06 E
Chao ≃ 105 40.36 N 117.08 E
Chao, Isla I 248 8.45 S 78.47 W
Chao'an 100 23.41 N 116.38 E
Chaobai ≃ 105 39.48 N 117.08 E
Chaobai Xinhe ≃ 105 39.37 N 117.26 E
Chaocheng 98 36.05 N 115.35 E
Ch'aochou 100 22.33 N 120.32 E
Ch'aochou → Chao'an 100 23.41 N 116.38 E
Chao Hu ⊜ 100 31.31 N 117.33 E
Chaomidian 105 39.04 N 117.01 E
Chao Phraya ≃ 110 13.32 N 100.36 E
Chaor ≃ 89 46.48 N 123.37 E
Chaoshui, Zhg. 89 49.44 N 127.21 E
Chaoshui, Zhg. 98 37.42 N 120.55 E
Chaouen 148 35.10 N 5.16 W
Chaouen □[4] 148 35.15 N 5.00 W
Chaource 50 48.04 N 4.08 E
Chaoxian 100 31.36 N 117.52 E
Chaoyang, Zhg. 89 44.34 N 126.20 E
Chaoyang, Zhg. 100 23.17 N 116.37 E
Chaoyang, Zhg. 104 41.35 N 120.28 E
Chaoyangchuan 98 42.54 N 129.21 E
Chaoyangcun 89 50.02 N 124.16 E
Chaoyanggou 104 42.07 N 121.04 E
Chaoyangpo 89 43.37 N 124.42 E
Chaoyangshan 89 43.02 N 125.40 E
Chaozhuang 98 34.18 N 114.56 E
Chapada dos Guimarães 248 15.26 S 55.45 W
Chapada dos Veadeiros, Parque Nacional da ♦ 255 13.58 S 47.30 W
Chapadinha 250 3.44 S 43.21 W
Chapala 234 20.18 N 103.12 W
Chapala, Laguna de ⊜ 234 20.15 N 103.00 W
Chapare ≃, Bol. 248 15.58 S 64.42 W
Chapare ≃, Bol. 248 16.25 S 64.35 W
Chapareillan 62 45.28 N 5.58 E
Chāparmukh 120 26.12 N 92.32 E
Chaparra, Bahía de ⊂ 240p 21.13 N 76.31 W
Chaparral 246 3.43 N 75.28 W
Chapčeranga 88 49.42 N 112.24 E
Chapeauroux 62 44.50 N 3.44 E
Chapecó 252 27.06 S 52.36 W
Chapel-en-le-Frith 44 53.20 N 1.54 W
Chapelfell Top ∧ 44 54.41 N 2.13 W
Chapelhall 46 55.50 N 3.56 W
Chapel Hill, De., U.S. 285 39.42 N 75.44 W
Chapel Hill, N.C., U.S. 192 35.54 N 79.03 W
Chapel Hill, Tn., U.S. 194 35.37 N 86.41 W
Chapel Hill Channel ⊍ 276 40.32 N 74.02 W
Chapelle Creek ≃ 198 44.16 N 99.55 W
Chapellerie 261 49.02 N 2.26 E
Chapel Oaks 284c 38.54 N 76.55 W
Chapel Point ≻ 42 50.16 N 4.46 W
Chapel Saint Leonards 44 53.13 N 0.19 E
Chapelton 241q 18.05 N 77.16 W
Chapeltown, Eng., U.K. 44 53.28 N 1.28 W
Chapeltown, Eng., U.K. 262 53.38 N 2.24 W
Chapet 261 48.58 N 1.56 E
Chapéu, Morro do ∧ 255 14.55 S 42.31 W
Chapéu, Ribeirão do ≃ 256 23.14 S 45.18 W
Chapicuy 252 31.39 S 57.54 W
Chapimarca 248 13.58 S 73.04 W
Chapin 219 39.46 N 90.24 W
Chapin, Lake ⊜ 216 41.56 N 86.21 W
Chaplain, Lake ⊜[1] 224 47.57 N 121.51 W
Chapleau 190 47.50 N 83.24 W
Chapleau ≃ 190 48.29 N 82.57 W
Chapleau, Lac ⊜ 206 46.14 N 74.57 W
Chaplin, Sk., Can. 184 50.28 N 106.40 W
Chaplin, Ct., U.S. 207 41.47 N 72.07 W
Chaplin ≃ 194 37.50 N 85.11 W
Chaplin Lake ⊜ 184 50.18 N 106.35 W
Chapman, Ks., U.S. 198 38.58 N 97.01 W
Chapman, Ne., U.S. 198 41.01 N 98.09 W
Chapman, Pa., U.S. 208 40.46 N 75.24 W
Chapman, Cape ≻ 176 69.12 N 88.59 W
Chapman, Mount ∧ 182 51.50 N 118.20 W
Chapman College ◍[2] 280 33.47 N 117.51 W
Chapman Creek ≃ 198 38.58 N 97.00 W
Chapman Lake ⊜ 184 56.58 N 98.12 W
Chapman's (Okwa) ≃ 156 22.30 S 23.00 E
Chapmanville 188 37.58 N 82.01 W
Chapman Woods 280 34.08 N 118.05 W
Chapo 196 29.17 N 104.20 W
Chaponval 261 49.04 N 2.09 E
Chappaqua 210 41.09 N 73.45 W
Chappell 198 41.05 N 102.28 W
Chappell Hill 222 30.09 N 96.16 W
Chāpra 126 23.32 N 88.33 E
Chapry 83 47.14 N 39.31 E
Chaptico Bay ⊂ 208 38.21 N 76.49 W
Chapultepec, Méx. 204 31.50 N 116.38 W
Chapultepec, Méx. 204 32.22 N 115.05 W
Chapultepec, Bosque de ♦ 286a 19.25 N 99.12 W
Chapultepec, Castillo de ⊥ 286a 19.25 N 99.11 W
Chá Pungana 152 13.44 S 18.39 E
Chaqui 248 19.36 S 65.32 W
Chaquiago 252 27.32 S 66.21 W
Char ≃ 42 50.44 N 2.53 W
Char ⫪[4] 148 21.31 N 12.51 W
Charaa ≃ 88 49.38 N 105.49 E
Charabali 80 47.24 N 47.16 E
Chara-Chužar 88 52.30 N 99.39 E
Charadai 252 27.38 S 59.54 W
Charagauli 84 42.01 N 43.12 E
Charagua 248 19.48 S 63.13 W
Charagun 88 51.36 N 111.05 E
Char-Ajrag 102 45.49 N 109.17 E
Charal 88 51.58 N 96.39 E
Charalá 246 6.17 N 73.10 W
Charām 128 30.45 N 50.44 E
Charaña 248 17.36 S 69.28 W
Charanor 88 50.05 N 116.40 E
Charanpur 126 23.45 N 87.02 E
Charapán 234 19.41 N 102.06 W
Charapucu, Ilha I 250 0.18 S 50.48 W
Charata 252 27.13 S 61.12 W
Charauz 88 52.16 N 106.17 E
Charavines-les-Bains 62 45.26 N 5.31 E
Charazani → Amarete 248 15.14 S 68.58 W
Charazargaj 88 52.57 N 104.41 E
Charbala 74 64.07 N 120.19 E
Char Bansi 126 22.59 N 90.43 E
Charbatovo 88 53.46 N 106.00 E
Charbon 170 32.54 S 149.58 E
Charcana 248 15.15 S 73.04 W
Charcas 234 23.08 N 101.07 W
Charco Azul, Bahía de ⊂ 236 8.15 N 82.45 W
Charco Hondo 240m 18.25 N 66.43 W
Charcos de Figueroa 232 27.45 N 102.11 W
Charcos de Risa 232 26.15 N 103.10 W
Charcot Island I 9 69.45 S 75.15 W
Charcyzsk 83 48.02 N 38.09 E
Chard 42 50.53 N 2.58 W
Chardon 214 41.36 N 81.08 W
Charduār 120 26.52 N 92.46 E
Chardzhou → Čardžou 128 39.06 N 63.34 E
Charef, Oued V 148 34.07 N 2.05 W
Charente □[5] 32 45.40 N 0.10 E
Charente ≃ 32 45.57 N 1.05 W
Charente-Maritime □[5] 32 45.30 N 0.45 W
Charenton-du-Cher 32 46.44 N 2.38 E
Charenton-le-Pont 261 48.49 N 2.25 E
Charentonne ≃ 50 49.07 N 0.44 E
Charest ≃ 206 46.36 N 72.14 W
Chārghāt 126 24.17 N 88.45 E
Char Hāim 126 23.04 N 90.38 E
Chari ≃ 146 12.58 N 14.31 E
Chariāl Canal ≅ 272b 22.28 N 88.11 E
Chari-Baguirmi □[5] 146 11.30 N 16.30 E
Charik 88 54.15 N 101.39 E
Chārīkār 120 35.01 N 69.11 E
Charing 42 51.13 N 0.48 E
Charing Cross 214 42.20 N 82.06 W
Charino, Ross. 76 59.57 N 43.44 E
Charino, Ross. 82 54.33 N 37.52 E
Charistvala 84 42.26 N 43.02 E
Chariton 190 41.00 N 93.18 W
Chariton ≃ 194 39.19 N 92.57 W
Chariton, Mussel Fork ≃ 194 39.24 N 92.55 W
Charitonovo, Ross. 24 61.27 N 47.28 E
Charitonovo, Ross. 82 56.52 N 36.44 E
Charity 246 7.24 N 58.36 W
Charkhāri 124 25.24 N 79.45 E
Charkhi Dādri 124 28.37 N 76.16 E
Char'kin 80 48.46 N 51.49 E
Charkop ◆[8] 272c 19.13 N 72.49 E
Char'kov (Kharkov) 78 50.00 N 36.15 E
Char'kov □[4] 78 49.30 N 36.30 E
Charkow → Char'kov 78 50.00 N 36.15 E
Char Lākhpur 126 24.04 N 90.40 E
Charland, Lac ⊜ 206 46.52 N 74.11 W
Charlbury 42 51.53 N 1.29 W
Charl Cilliers 158 26.39 S 29.12 E
Charlemagne 206 45.43 N 73.29 W
Charlemont 207 42.37 N 72.52 W
Charleroi, Bel. 50 50.25 N 4.26 E
Charleroi, Pa., U.S. 214 40.08 N 79.53 W
Charleroi à Bruxelles, Canal de ≅ 50 50.51 N 4.19 E
Charles □[6] 208 38.32 N 76.59 W
Charles ≃ 207 42.22 N 71.03 W
Charles, Cape ≻ 208 37.08 N 75.58 W
Charles, Lake ⊜ 278 42.15 N 87.58 W
Charles, Peak ∧ 162 32.52 S 121.11 E
Charlesbourg 206 46.51 N 71.16 W
Charles Branch ≃ 284c 38.47 N 76.48 W
Charles City, Ia., U.S. 190 43.03 N 92.40 W
Charles City, Va., U.S. 208 37.20 N 77.04 W
Charles City □[6] 208 37.20 N 77.02 W
Charles de Gaulle, Aéroport ⊠ 50 49.01 N 2.33 E
Charles Island I 176 62.40 N 74.15 W
Charles Lee Tilden Regional Park ♦ 282 37.54 N 122.15 W
Charles Mill Lake ⊜[1] 214 40.45 N 82.22 W
Charles Mound ∧[2] 190 42.30 N 90.14 W
Charles Point ≻ 164 12.23 S 130.36 E
Charles Sound ⊍ 172 45.02 S 167.04 E
Charleston, Austl. 168b 34.55 S 138.54 E
Charleston, N.Z. 172 41.54 S 171.26 E
Charleston, Ar., U.S. 194 35.17 N 94.02 W
Charleston, Il., U.S. 194 39.29 N 88.10 W
Charleston, Ms., U.S. 194 34.00 N 90.03 W
Charleston, Mo., U.S. 194 36.55 N 89.21 W
Charleston, S.C., U.S. 192 32.46 N 79.55 W
Charleston, W.V., U.S. 188 38.20 N 81.37 W
Charleston Air Force Base ■ 192 32.55 N 80.03 W
Charleston Lake ⊜ 212 44.32 N 76.00 W
Charleston Peak ∧ 204 36.16 N 115.42 W
Charlestown, Austl. 170 32.58 S 151.42 E
Charlestown, Ire. 48 53.57 N 8.49 W
Charlestown, St. K.-N. 238 17.08 N 62.37 W
Charlestown, S. Afr. 158 27.30 S 29.55 E
Charlestown, In., U.S. 218 38.27 N 85.40 W
Charlestown, Md., U.S. 208 39.34 N 75.58 W
Charlestown, N.H., U.S. 188 43.14 N 72.25 W
Charlestown, Pa., U.S. 285 40.06 N 75.33 W
Charlestown, R.I., U.S. 207 41.22 N 71.38 W
Charles Town, W.V., U.S. 188 39.17 N 77.51 W
Charlestown ◆[8] 283 42.23 N 71.04 W
Charlestown of Aberlour 46 57.28 N 3.14 W
Charlesworth 262 53.26 N 1.59 W
Charleville 166 26.24 S 146.15 E
Charleville-Mézières 56 49.46 N 4.43 E
Charleville → Ráth Luirc 48 52.21 N 8.41 W
Charlevoix 190 45.19 N 85.15 W
Charlevoix, Lake ⊜ 190 45.15 N 85.08 W
Charley ≃ 180 65.20 N 142.49 W
Charlie Bluff 216 42.50 N 88.58 W
Charlie Creek ≃ 220 27.21 N 81.49 W
Charlie Lake 182 56.16 N 120.57 W
Charlieu 32 46.10 N 4.10 E
Charlotte, Mi., U.S. 216 42.33 N 84.50 W
Charlotte, N.C., U.S. 192 35.13 N 80.50 W
Charlotte, Tn., U.S. 194 36.10 N 87.20 W
Charlotte, Tx., U.S. 196 28.51 N 98.42 W
Charlotte □[6] 220 26.54 N 81.58 W
Charlotte Amalie 240m 18.21 N 64.56 W
Charlotte Court House 192 37.03 N 78.39 W
Charlotte Creek ≃ 210 42.27 N 75.01 W
Charlotte Harbor 220 26.57 N 82.04 W
Charlotte Harbor ⊂ 220 26.45 N 82.12 W
Charlotte Lake ⊜ 182 52.11 N 125.20 W
Charlottenberg 26 59.53 N 12.17 E
Charlottenburg ◆[8] 264a 52.31 N 13.16 E
Charlottenburg, Schloss ⊥ 264a 52.31 N 13.14 E
Charlottesburg Reservoir ⊜[1] 276 41.02 N 74.26 W
Charlottes Pass ♦ 171b 36.25 S 145.20 E
Charlottesville, In., U.S. 218 39.47 N 85.36 W
Charlottesville, Va., U.S. 192 38.01 N 78.28 W
Charlottetown 186 46.14 N 63.08 W
Charlotteville 210 42.33 N 74.40 W
Charlovka 24 68.47 N 37.15 E
Charlton, Austl. 166 36.16 S 143.21 E
Charlton, Ma., U.S. 207 42.08 N 71.58 W
Charlton ◆[8] 260 51.29 N 0.02 E
Charlton City 207 42.08 N 71.59 W
Charlton Island I 176 52.00 N 79.30 W
Charlton Kings 42 51.53 N 2.03 W
Charlu 24 61.48 N 30.52 E
Charly-sur-Marne 50 48.58 N 3.17 E
Charm 214 40.30 N 81.47 W
Charmentray 261 48.57 N 2.47 E
Charmes 58 48.22 N 6.17 E
Charmes-sur-Rhône 62 44.52 N 4.50 E
Charmey 58 46.38 N 7.10 E
Charminster 42 50.43 N 2.28 W
Charmois-l'Orgueilleux 58 48.06 N 6.16 E
Charmont-en-Beauce 50 48.14 N 2.06 E
Charmouth 42 50.45 N 2.55 W
Charnay-lès-Mâcon 58 46.18 N 4.47 E
Charneca 266c 38.44 N 9.27 W
Charneca ◆[8] 266c 38.47 N 9.08 W
Charnley ≃ 164 16.25 S 124.57 E
Charnock Richard 262 53.38 N 2.41 W
Char nuur ⊜, Mong. 88 48.20 N 96.05 E
Char nuur ⊜, Mong. 88 48.06 N 93.12 E
Charnwood Forest ◆[3] 42 52.43 N 1.15 W
Charny, P.Q., Can. 206 46.43 N 71.16 W
Charny, Fr. 50 47.53 N 3.06 E
Charny, Fr. 261 48.58 N 2.46 E
Charny-sur-Meuse 56 49.12 N 5.22 E
Charo 234 19.45 N 101.03 W
Charolles 32 46.26 N 4.17 E
Charouine 148 29.01 N 0.16 W
Charovsk 76 59.59 N 40.11 E
Charpi ≃ 89 49.40 N 136.10 E
Charquemont 58 47.13 N 6.49 E
Charred Oak Estates 284c 39.00 N 77.10 W
Charrette Creek ≃ 219 38.37 N 91.03 W
Charron Lake ⊜ 184 52.45 N 95.15 W
Charroux 32 46.09 N 0.24 E
Chars 50 49.10 N 1.56 E
Chārsadda 123 34.09 N 71.44 E
Charter Oak, Ca., U.S. 280 34.06 N 117.52 W
Charter Oak, Ia., U.S. 198 42.04 N 95.35 W
Charters Towers 166 20.05 S 146.16 E
Charterwood 279b 40.33 N 80.00 W
Chartiers Creek ≃ 214 40.28 N 80.03 W
Chartiers Run ≃, Pa., U.S. 279b 40.36 N 79.43 W
Chartiers Run ≃, Pa., U.S. 279b 40.15 N 80.12 W
Chartley 207 41.56 N 71.13 W
Chartres 50 48.27 N 1.30 E
Chartrettes 50 48.29 N 2.42 E
Chartridge 260 51.44 N 0.39 W
Chart Sutton 260 51.13 N 0.35 E
Chartwell ⊥ 260 51.14 N 0.05 E
Char Us nuur ⊜ 90 48.00 N 92.10 E
Charutajuvom 24 66.49 N 59.30 E
Chās 126 23.38 N 86.10 E
Chasav'urt 84 43.15 N 46.37 E
Chascomús 258 35.34 S 58.01 W
Chascomús, Laguna ⊜ 258 35.36 S 58.01 W
Chašdala 85 39.42 N 67.07 E
Chase, B.C., Can. 182 50.49 N 119.41 W
Chase, Ak., U.S. 180 62.27 N 150.07 W
Chase, Ks., U.S. 198 38.21 N 98.20 W
Chase, Md., U.S. 208 39.21 N 76.22 W
Chase, Mount ∧ 188 46.07 N 68.29 W
Chase Brook ≃ 283 42.48 N 71.27 W
Chase City 192 36.47 N 78.27 W
Chase Field Naval Air Station ■ 196 28.21 N 97.40 W
Chasefu 154 11.55 S 33.08 E
Chase Lake 212 43.46 N 75.19 W
Chase River 224 49.08 N 123.55 W
Chashma Barrage ◆[6] 123 32.26 N 71.23 E
Chasicó 254 40.18 S 68.58 W
Chasidaba 104 42.19 N 121.19 E
Chaska 190 44.47 N 93.36 W
Chaslands Mistake ≻ 172 46.38 S 169.22 E
Chasŏng 98 41.27 N 126.37 E
Chasŏngganggu 98 41.34 N 126.36 E
Chassahowitzka 220 28.43 N 82.34 W
Chassahowitzka Bay ⊂ 220 28.41 N 82.40 W
Chassahowitzka Swamp ≡ 220 28.38 N 82.37 W
Chasseron, Mont ∧ 58 46.51 N 6.33 E
Chasse-sur-Rhône 62 45.34 N 4.49 E
Chassezac ≃ 62 44.26 N 4.19 E
Chašuri 84 42.00 N 43.36 E
Chasurta 88 52.17 N 108.52 E
Chasuta 248 6.35 S 76.11 W
Chāt 128 37.59 N 55.16 E
Chatanbulag 102 43.09 N 109.08 E
Chatanga 74 71.58 N 102.30 E
Chatanga ≃ 74 72.55 N 106.00 E
Chatangskij zaliv ⊂ 74 73.30 N 109.00 E
Chatanika 180 65.07 N 147.31 W
Chatanika ≃ 180 65.04 N 149.18 W
Château-Arnoux 62 44.06 N 6.00 E
Chateaubelair 241h 13.17 N 61.15 W
Châteaubriant 32 47.43 N 1.23 W
Château-Chinon 32 47.04 N 3.56 E
Château d'Oex 58 46.28 N 7.08 E
Château-du-Loir 50 47.42 N 0.25 E
Châteaudun 50 48.05 N 1.20 E
Châteaufort 261 48.44 N 2.06 E
Chateaugay 206 44.55 N 74.04 W
Château-Gontier 32 47.50 N 0.42 W
Châteauguay 206 45.23 N 73.45 W
Châteauguay □[6] 206 45.15 N 73.45 W
Châteauguay ≃ 188 45.24 N 73.45 W
Châteauguay-Centre 206 45.21 N 73.45 W
Châteauguay Heights 275a 45.23 N 73.44 W
Château-Landon 50 48.09 N 2.42 E
Château-la-Vallière 50 47.33 N 0.19 E
Châteaulin 32 48.12 N 4.05 W
Châteaumeillant 32 46.34 N 2.12 E
Châteauneuf 62 43.23 N 5.10 E
Châteauneuf-de-Randon 62 44.39 N 3.40 E
Châteauneuf-du-Pape 62 44.03 N 4.50 E
Châteauneuf-du-Rhône 62 44.29 N 4.43 E
Châteauneuf-en-Thymerais 50 48.35 N 1.15 E
Châteauneuf-sur-Charente 32 45.36 N 0.03 W
Châteauneuf-sur-Loire 50 47.52 N 2.14 E
Châteauneuf-sur-Sarthe 32 47.41 N 0.30 W
Châteauneuf-Val-de-Bargis 50 47.17 N 3.14 E
Château-Porcien 50 49.32 N 4.15 E
Château-Queyras 62 44.45 N 6.47 E
Châteauredon 62 44.01 N 6.13 E
Châteaurenard, Fr. 50 47.56 N 2.56 E
Châteaurenard, Fr. 62 43.53 N 4.51 E
Château-Renault 50 47.35 N 0.55 E
Château-Richer 186 46.58 N 71.01 W
Châteauroux 32 46.49 N 1.42 E
Château-Salins 56 48.49 N 6.30 E
Château-Thierry 50 49.03 N 3.24 E
Châteauvillain 58 48.02 N 4.55 E
Châtel 58 46.17 N 6.50 E
Châtel-Censoir 50 47.31 N 3.38 E
Châtelet 50 50.24 N 4.31 E
Châtelineau 56 50.25 N 4.31 E
Châtellerault 32 46.49 N 0.33 E
Châtel-Saint-Denis 58 46.32 N 6.54 E
Châtel-sur-Moselle 58 48.18 N 6.24 E
Châtelus-Malvaleix 32 46.18 N 2.01 E
Châtenay-en-France 261 49.04 N 2.27 E
Châtenay-Malabry 261 48.46 N 2.17 E
Châtenois, Fr. 58 48.16 N 7.24 E
Châtenois, Fr. 58 48.18 N 5.50 E
Châtenois-les-Forges 58 47.34 N 6.51 E
Chater ≃ 42 52.38 N 0.32 W
Chatfield, Mn., U.S. 190 43.50 N 92.11 W
Chatfield, Oh., U.S. 214 40.57 N 82.56 W
Chatgal 88 50.26 N 100.09 E
Chatham, N.B., Can. 186 47.02 N 65.28 W
Chatham, On., Can. 214 42.24 N 82.11 W
Chatham, Eng., U.K. 42 51.23 N 0.32 E
Chatham, Il., U.S. 219 39.40 N 89.42 W
Chatham, La., U.S. 194 32.18 N 92.27 W
Chatham, Ma., U.S. 207 41.40 N 69.57 W
Chatham, N.J., U.S. 210 40.44 N 74.23 W
Chatham, N.Y., U.S. 210 42.21 N 73.35 W
Chatham, Oh., U.S. 214 41.06 N 82.01 W
Chatham, Pa., U.S. 208 39.51 N 75.49 W
Chatham, Va., U.S. 192 36.49 N 79.23 W
Chatham ◆[8] 278 41.45 N 87.37 W
Chatham ≃ 220 25.42 N 81.17 W
Chatham, Isla I 254 50.40 S 74.20 W
Chatham Head 186 47.00 N 65.33 W
Chatham Islands II 14 43.55 S 176.30 W
Chatham Rise ◆[3] 14 43.30 S 178.00 W
Chatham Sound ⊍ 182 54.32 N 130.35 W
Chatham Strait ⊍ 180 57.30 N 134.45 W
Chatian 100 27.54 N 118.58 E
Châtillon, Fr. 261 48.48 N 2.17 E
Châtillon, It. 62 45.45 N 7.37 E
Châtillon-Coligny 50 47.50 N 2.51 E
Châtillon-en-Bazois 32 47.03 N 3.40 E
Châtillon-en-Diois 62 44.41 N 5.28 E
Châtillon-la-Borde 261 48.33 N 2.49 E
Châtillon-sur-Chalaronne 58 46.07 N 4.58 E
Châtillon-sur-Indre 32 46.59 N 1.11 E
Châtillon-sur-Loire 50 47.35 N 2.45 E
Châtillon-sur-Marne 50 49.06 N 3.45 E
Châtillon-sur-Seine 58 47.51 N 4.33 E
Chating 106 31.21 N 119.25 E
Chātmohar 126 24.13 N 89.15 E
Chat Moss ◆[3] 262 53.27 N 2.27 W
Chato, Cerro ∧ 254 42.29 S 72.01 W
Chatom 194 31.27 N 88.15 W
Chatonville 261 48.33 N 1.52 E
Chatou 261 48.54 N 2.09 E
Chatpur ◆[8] 272b 22.36 N 88.22 E
Chatra, India 124 24.13 N 84.52 E
Chatra, India 272b 22.46 N 88.20 E
Châtres 261 48.43 N 2.49 E
Chats, Lac des ⊜ 212 45.28 N 76.23 W
Chatsquot Mountain ∧ 182 53.08 N 127.30 W
Chatswood 274a 33.48 S 151.12 E
Chatsworth, Austl. 166 21.58 S 140.19 E
Chatsworth, On., Can. 212 44.27 N 80.54 W
Chatsworth, Ga., U.S. 192 34.45 N 84.46 W
Chatsworth, Il., U.S. 216 40.45 N 88.17 W
Chatsworth, N.J., U.S. 208 39.49 N 74.32 W
Chatsworth, Zimb. 154 19.38 S 31.13 E
Chatsworth ◆[8] 280 34.15 N 118.36 W
Chatsworth House ◍ 44 53.13 N 1.36 W
Chatsworth Reservoir ⊜[1] 228 34.14 N 118.37 W
Chattahoochee 192 30.42 N 84.50 W
Chattahoochee ≃ 192 30.52 N 84.57 W
Chattanooga, Oh., U.S. 216 40.38 N 84.47 W
Chattanooga, Tn., U.S. 194 35.02 N 85.18 W
Chattaroy 192 37.42 N 82.16 W
Chattenden 260 51.25 N 0.32 E
Chatteris 42 52.27 N 0.03 E
Châttillon-de-Michaille 58 46.08 N 5.47 E
Chattolanee 284b 39.24 N 76.45 W
Chatton 44 55.33 N 1.55 W
Chatun' 82 55.00 N 37.50 E
Chaturat 110 15.34 N 101.51 E
Chatwood 208 39.58 N 75.35 W
Chatyrka 74 62.03 N 175.15 E
Chaubaria 126 22.59 N 88.40 E
Chaubourg, Mount ∧[2] 241f 14.02 N 60.57 W
Chauconin 261 48.58 N 2.51 E
Chaudes-Aigues 32 44.51 N 3.00 E
Chaudfontaine 56 50.35 N 5.38 E
Chaudière ≃ 186 46.45 N 71.17 W
Chau Doc 110 10.42 N 105.07 E
Chauekuktuli, Lake ⊜ 180 60.03 N 158.45 W
Chauffayer 62 44.45 N 6.01 E
Chaugācha, Bngl. 126 23.16 N 89.01 E
Chaugācha, Bngl. 126 23.16 N 89.01 E
Chauhtan 120 25.29 N 71.04 E
Chauk 110 20.54 N 94.50 E
Chaukhandi 272a 28.37 N 77.24 E
Chaullay 248 12.57 S 72.39 W
Chaulnes 50 49.49 N 2.48 E
Chaumergy 58 46.51 N 5.29 E
Chaumes-en-Brie 261 48.40 N 2.51 E
Chaumont, Fr. 58 48.07 N 5.08 E
Chaumont, N.Y., U.S. 212 44.04 N 76.07 W
Chaumont ≃ 212 44.04 N 76.08 W
Chaumont Bay ⊂ 212 44.02 N 76.13 W
Chaumont-en-Vexin 50 49.16 N 1.53 E
Chaumont-Porcien 50 49.39 N 4.15 E
Chaumont-sur-Aire 56 48.56 N 5.15 E
Chaumont-sur-Loire 50 47.29 N 1.11 E
Chaumont-sur-Tharonne 50 47.37 N 1.54 E
Chaumua 272b 22.39 N 88.33 E
Chauncey 188 39.23 N 82.07 W
Chaŭn-do I 98 34.53 N 126.03 E
Chaungwabyin 110 13.41 N 98.22 E
Chaungzon 110 16.22 N 97.32 E
Chauny 50 49.37 N 3.13 E
Chaupāran 124 24.23 N 85.15 E
Chaussin 58 46.58 N 5.25 E
Chausu-yama ∧ 94 35.14 N 137.39 E
Chausuyama-kofun ⊥ 94 36.25 N 139.50 E
Chautārā 124 27.46 N 85.42 E
Chautauqua 214 42.12 N 79.28 W
Chautauqua □[6] 214 42.15 N 79.30 W
Chautauqua Creek ≃ 214 42.20 N 79.36 W
Chautauqua Lake ⊜ 214 42.12 N 79.27 W
Chautengo, Laguna ⊂ 234 16.37 N 99.07 W
Chauvigny 32 46.34 N 0.39 E
Chauvin, Ab., Can. 184 52.42 N 110.07 W
Chauvin, La., U.S. 194 29.26 N 90.35 W
Chauvirey-le-Châtel 58 47.47 N 5.45 E
Chauvry 261 49.03 N 2.16 E
Chavakkad 122 10.32 N 76.06 E
Chaval 250 3.02 S 41.15 W
Chavanges 58 48.31 N 4.34 E
Chavannes, Lac ⊜ 190 46.51 N 77.10 W
Chavarría, Arg. 252 28.57 S 58.35 W
Chavarría, Perú 286d 12.01 S 77.05 W
Chavast 85 40.13 N 68.50 E
Chavenay 261 48.51 N 1.59 E
Chavenay-Villepreux, Aérodrome de ⊠ 261 48.51 N 1.58 E
Chavertovo 82 54.17 N 39.12 E
Chaves, Bra. 250 0.10 S 49.55 W
Chaves, Port. 34 41.44 N 7.28 W

Symbols in the index entries represent the broad categories identified in the key at the right. Symbols with superior numbers (⋌[1]) identify subcategories (see complete key on page *I · 1)*.

Symbole im Register stellen die rechts im Schlüssel erklärten Kategorien dar. Symbole mit hochgestellten Ziffern (⋌[1]) bezeichnen Unterabteilungen einer Kategorie (vgl. vollständiger Schlüssel auf Seite *I · 1)*.

Los símbolos incluídos en el texto del índice representan las grandes categorías identificadas con la clave a la derecha. Los símbolos con numeros en su parte superior (⋌[1]) identifican las subcategorías (véase la clave completa en la página *I · 1)*.

Les symboles de l'index représentent les catégories indiquées dans la légende à droite. Les symboles suivis d'un indice (⋌[1]) représentent des sous-catégories (voir légende complète à la page *I · 1)*.

Os símbolos incluídos no texto do índice representam as grandes categorias identificadas com a chave à direita. Os símbolos com números em sua parte superior (⋌[1]) identificam as subcategorias (veja-se a chave completa à página *I · 1)*.

∧ Mountain	Berg	Montaña	Montagne	Montanha
⋌ Mountains	Gebirge	Montañas	Montagnes	Montanhas
)(Pass	Paß	Paso	Col	Passo
V Valley, Canyon	Tal, Cañon	Valle, Cañón	Vallée, Canyon	Vale, Canhão
≚ Plain	Ebene	Llano	Plaine	Planície
≻ Cape	Kap	Cabo	Cap	Cabo
I Island	Insel	Isla	Île	Ilha
II Islands	Inseln	Islas	Îles	Ilhas
⊥ Other Topographic Features	Andere Topographische Objekte	Otros Elementos Topográficos	Autres données topographiques	Outros acidentes topográficos

ESPAÑOL Nombre	Página	Lat.°′	Long.°′ W = Oeste

FRANÇAIS Nom	Page	Lat.°′	Long.°′ W = Ouest

PORTUGUÊS Nome	Página	Lat.°′	Long.°′ W = Oeste

Chaville 261 48.48 N 2.10 E
Chaviña 248 14.59 S 73.50 W
Cháviva 246 4.22 N 72.20 W
Chavki 82 54.20 N 38.13 E
Chavornay 58 46.43 N 6.34 E
Chavuma 152 13.05 S 22.40 E
Chawa'nanake 120 31.36 N 89.41 E
Chawang 110 8.25 N 99.30 E
Chawinda 123 32.21 N 74.42 E
Chay ≃ 110 21.39 N 105.12 E
Chayanta 248 18.27 S 66.30 W
Chayuan, Zhg. 100 29.20 N 121.34 E
Chayuan, Zhg. 100 27.40 N 112.57 E
Chayue 106 30.49 N 119.21 E
Chazay-d'Azergues 62 45.53 N 4.37 E
Chazelles-sur-Lyon 62 45.38 N 4.23 E
Chazratišoch, chrebet ᴧ 85 38.30 N 70.15 E
Chazy 188 44.53 N 73.26 W
Chbar ≃ 110 13.19 N 107.05 E
Cheadle, Eng., U.K. 42 52.59 N 1.59 W
Cheadle, Eng., U.K. 44 53.24 N 2.13 W
Cheadle Hulme 262 53.22 N 2.12 W
Cheaha Mountain ᴧ 194 33.30 N 85.47 W
Cheakamus Indian Reserve ◆4 182 49.48 N 123.11 W
Cheam ◆8 260 51.21 N 0.13 W
Cheam View 224 49.15 N 121.41 W
Cheapside 222 29.17 N 97.24 W
Cheat ≃ 188 39.45 N 79.54 W
Cheat, Shavers Fork ≃ 188 39.06 N 79.33 W
Cheb 54 50.01 N 12.25 E
Chebacco Lake ⊜ 283 42.37 N 70.48 W
Chebanse 216 41.00 N 87.54 W
Chebba 148 35.14 N 10.02 E
Chebeigou 89 43.28 N 127.04 E
Chebogue Point ≻ 186 43.45 N 66.07 W
Cheboksary → Čeboksary 80 56.09 N 47.15 E
Cheboygan 190 45.38 N 84.28 W
Chech, Erg ◆2 148 25.00 N 2.15 W
Ch'ech'eng 100 22.05 N 120.42 E
Chechnia → Čečnja-Ingušetija □3 84 43.15 N 45.40 E
Chech'ŏn 98 37.08 N 128.12 E
Checiny 30 50.48 N 20.28 E
Checleset Bay ⊂ 182 50.03 N 127.40 W
Checotah 196 35.28 N 95.31 W
Chedabucto Bay ⊂ 186 45.23 N 61.10 W
Chedaoyu 105 40.22 N 117.57 E
Cheddar 42 51.17 N 2.46 W
Cheddleton 44 53.04 N 2.02 W
Cheduba Island I 110 18.48 N 93.38 E
Cheduba Strait ⋓ 110 18.56 N 93.45 E
Chedun 100 24.09 N 117.19 E
Chée ≃ 56 48.45 N 4.39 E
Cheektowaga 210 42.55 N 78.46 W
Cheepie 166 26.39 S 145.01 E
Cheesequake 276 40.25 N 74.17 W
Cheesequake Creek ≃ 276 40.28 N 74.16 W
Cheesequake State Park ♠ 276 40.26 N 74.16 W
Cheetham Hill ◆8 262 53.31 N 2.15 W
Chefang, Zhg. 104 41.35 N 121.26 E
Chefang, Zhg. 106 31.15 N 120.45 E
Chef-Boutonne 32 46.07 N 0.04 W
Chefoo → Yantai 98 37.33 N 121.20 E
Chefornak 180 60.13 N 164.12 W
Chefumage ≃ 152 12.15 S 22.19 E
Chefuzwe 156 17.38 S 24.30 E
Chegar Prerah 114 4.25 N 101.56 E
Chegga ⊤4 148 25.30 N 5.46 W
Chegutu 154 18.10 S 30.14 E
Chehalis 224 46.39 N 122.57 W
Chehalis ≃ 224 46.57 N 123.50 W
Chehalis, South Fork ≃ 224 46.40 N 123.15 W
Chehalis Indian Reservation ◆4 224 46.49 N 123.13 W
Chehe 102 25.00 N 107.38 E
Chehel Dokhtarān 128 35.06 N 62.19 E
Chehegiao 105 40.21 N 118.16 E
Cheil, Ras el ≻ 144 7.44 N 49.50 E
Cheine 54 52.52 N 11.04 E
Cheiron, Cime du ᴧ 62 43.49 N 6.58 E
Chejiatun 104 41.57 N 123.01 E
Chejiawopeng 104 42.29 N 123.07 E
Cheju 90 33.31 N 126.32 E
Cheju-do I 90 33.20 N 126.30 E
Chekiang → Zhejiang □4 100 29.00 N 120.00 E
Chek Jawa, Tanjong ≻ 271c 1.24 N 104.00 E
Chek Kang 271d 22.26 N 114.21 E
Chela, Serra da ᴧ 152 16.00 S 13.10 E
Chelan 202 47.50 N 120.00 W
Chelan □6 224 47.56 N 120.52 W
Chelan, Lake ⊜ 202 48.05 N 120.30 W
Chelas ◆8 266c 38.45 N 9.07 W
Cheleiros 266c 38.53 N 9.20 W
Cheleiros, Ribeira de ≃ 266c 38.54 N 9.22 W
Chelelektu 144 6.00 N 38.09 E
Chelford 262 53.16 N 2.16 W
Chelforó 252 39.04 S 66.32 W
Chelghoum el Aïd 148 36.10 N 6.10 E
Chéliff, Oued ≃ 148 36.01 N 0.07 E
Chelīk-e Yās Khān 120 37.05 N 66.14 E
Chellaston 42 52.53 N 1.27 W
Chelles 50 48.53 N 2.36 E
Chelles-le-Pin, Aérodrome de ⊠ 261 48.55 N 2.35 E
Chełm 30 51.10 N 23.28 E
Chełm □4 30 51.20 N 23.20 E
Chelmer ≃ 42 51.44 N 0.42 E
Chelmer and Blackwater Navigation ≅ 260 51.44 N 0.43 E
Chełmno 30 53.22 N 18.26 E
Chelmorton 262 53.13 N 1.50 W
Chelmsford, On., Can. 190 46.35 N 81.12 W
Chelmsford, Eng., U.K. 42 51.44 N 0.28 E
Chelmsford, Ma., U.S. 207 42.35 N 71.21 W
Chelmsford □8 260 51.44 N 0.30 E
Chelmsford Dam ⊜1 158 28.02 S 29.52 E
Chełmża 30 53.12 N 18.37 E
Chelsea, Austl. 169 38.03 S 145.07 E
Chelsea, Ia., U.S. 190 41.55 N 92.23 W
Chelsea, Ma., U.S. 207 42.23 N 71.02 W
Chelsea, Mi., U.S. 216 42.19 N 84.01 W
Chelsea, Ok., U.S. 196 36.32 N 95.25 W
Chelsea, Pa., U.S. 285 39.52 N 75.28 W
Chelsea, Vt., U.S. 188 43.59 N 72.26 W
Chelsea Estates 208 39.41 N 75.36 W
Chelsea Park 224 47.28 N 122.21 W
Chelsfield ◆8 260 51.21 N 0.08 E
Cheltenham, Austl. 274a 33.46 S 151.05 E
Cheltenham, Austl. 274b 37.58 S 145.03 E
Cheltenham, Eng., U.K. 42 51.54 N 2.04 W
Cheltenham, Md., U.S. 208 38.44 N 76.49 W
Cheltenham, Pa., U.S. 208 40.03 N 75.05 W
Chel'ul'ja 26 61.44 N 30.41 E
Chelvand 128 38.18 N 48.50 E
Chelyabinsk → Čel'abinsk 86 55.10 N 61.24 E
Chelyāma 126 23.37 N 86.33 E
Chelyan 188 38.11 N 81.29 W
Chelyuskintsy Ice Tongue ⊓ 9 66.20 S 82.00 E
Chemaïa 148 32.05 N 8.37 W
Chemainus 224 48.55 N 123.43 W
Chemainus ≃ 224 48.53 N 123.41 W
Chemaogang 106 31.33 N 121.52 E
Chemax 232 20.39 N 87.56 W
Chemba 154 17.08 S 34.52 E
Chembūr ◆8 272c 19.04 N 72.54 E
Chemchām, Sebkhet ⊜ 148 21.05 N 12.05 W
Chemčik ≃ 86 51.47 N 92.00 E
Chemehuevi Indian Reservation ◆4 204 34.30 N 114.23 W
Chemillé 32 47.13 N 0.44 W
Chemin 58 46.59 N 5.19 E
Cheminis, Colline ᴧ2 190 48.08 N 79.31 W
Chemnitz 54 50.50 N 12.55 E
Chemnitz ≃ 54 50.59 N 12.47 E
Chemor 114 4.43 N 101.07 E
Chemulpo → Inch'ŏn 98 37.28 N 126.38 E
Chemult 202 43.13 N 121.46 W
Chemung, Il., U.S. 216 42.25 N 88.40 W
Chemung, N.Y., U.S. 210 42.01 N 76.37 W
Chemung □6 210 42.06 N 76.49 W
Chemung ≃ 210 41.55 N 76.31 W
Chemung County Airport ⊠ 210 42.10 N 76.53 W
Chemung Lake ⊜ 212 44.25 N 78.22 W
Chena, Cerro ᴧ 286e 33.36 N 70.45 W
Chenāb ≃ 123 29.23 N 71.02 E
Chenachane 148 26.00 N 4.15 W
Chenail Ecarté ≃1 214 42.28 N 82.29 W
Chenango □6 210 42.32 N 75.31 W
Chenango ≃ 210 42.05 N 75.55 W
Chenango Bridge 210 42.10 N 75.51 W
Chenango Forks 210 42.14 N 75.50 W
Chenango Valley State Park ♠ 210 42.14 N 75.50 W
Chenārān 128 36.39 N 59.06 E
Chenaut 258 34.15 S 59.13 W
Chen Barag Qi 89 49.21 N 119.31 E
Chenbofang 98 37.27 N 115.18 E
Chencai 100 29.37 N 120.22 E
Chenchiang → Zhenjiang 106 32.13 N 119.26 E
Chencun 100 22.58 N 113.13 E
Chendai 100 23.48 N 117.24 E
Chendauli ◆8 272c 19.07 N 72.54 E
Chenderiang 114 4.16 N 101.14 E
Chenderoh, Tasek ⊜1 114 4.58 N 100.57 E
Chêne, Rivière du ≃, P.Q., Can. 206 46.34 N 72.00 W
Chêne, Rivière du ≃, P.Q., Can. 206 45.33 N 73.54 W
Chenele 152 12.54 S 23.54 E
Chenequa 216 43.06 N 88.23 W
Chénéville 206 45.53 N 75.03 W
Cheney, Ks., U.S. 198 37.37 N 97.46 W
Cheney, Wa., U.S. 202 47.29 N 117.34 W
Cheney Reservoir ⊜1 198 37.45 N 97.50 W
Cheneys Point 214 42.08 N 79.24 W
Cheneyville 194 31.00 N 92.17 W
Chenfang 100 28.01 N 117.32 E
Cheng'an 98 36.27 N 114.41 E
Chengannūr 122 9.20 N 76.38 E
Chengbu 102 26.18 N 110.13 E
Chengchow → Zhengzhou 102 34.48 N 113.39 E
Chengde (Xiabancheng), Zhg. 105 40.47 N 118.08 E
Chengde, Zhg. 105 40.58 N 117.53 E
Chengdu (Chengtu) 107 30.39 N 104.04 E
Chengele 120 28.47 N 96.16 E
Chenggang 100 26.32 N 115.26 E
Chenggu 102 33.10 N 107.22 E
Chenghai 100 23.30 N 116.46 E
Cheng Hu ⊜ 106 31.13 N 120.49 E
Chenghuang 102 22.32 N 109.39 E
Chengjia 100 24.50 N 112.50 E
Chengjiahe 100 32.18 N 112.27 E
Chengjiang 102 24.45 N 102.54 E
Chengjiangzhen 107 29.57 N 106.37 E
Chengjiazhen 107 29.24 N 104.36 E
Chengkou 102 31.54 N 108.41 E
Chenglingji 100 29.26 N 113.09 E
Chenglong 100 24.51 N 114.41 E
Chengmai 110 19.48 N 110.02 E
Chengnao 106 31.10 N 120.53 E
Chengpu 100 25.46 N 118.48 E
Chengqian 98 35.21 N 117.21 E
Chengqianwei 100 28.09 N 116.13 E
Chengshan Jiao ≻ 98 37.24 N 122.42 E
Chengteh → Chengde 105 40.58 N 117.53 E
Chengtu → Chengdu 107 30.39 N 104.04 E
Ch'engtzuliao 269d 25.06 N 121.27 E
Chengwu 98 34.58 N 115.52 E
Chengxian 102 33.43 N 105.41 E
Chengxi Hu ⊜ 100 32.24 N 116.15 E
Chengyang, Zhg. 98 36.18 N 120.22 E
Chengyang, Zhg. 100 29.59 N 119.42 E
Chengzi, Zhg. 98 41.57 N 116.14 E
Chengzi, Zhg. 98 39.58 N 116.02 E
Chengzitan 98 39.30 N 122.30 E
Ch'enhsien → Chenxian 100 25.48 N 112.59 E
Chen Hu ⊜ 100 30.29 N 113.22 E
Chenies 260 51.41 N 0.32 W
Chenil, Lac ⊜ 186 51.51 N 59.41 W
Cheniménil 58 48.08 N 6.36 E
Chenji 100 33.50 N 119.11 E
Chenjiachang, Zhg. 107 29.35 N 104.52 E
Chenjiachang, Zhg. 107 30.04 N 105.15 E
Chenjiagang 98 34.25 N 119.49 E
Chenjiahe 102 29.28 N 109.59 E
Chenjiaji 100 30.42 N 114.21 E
Chenjiapang 106 31.14 N 121.20 E
Chenjiapu 105 40.31 N 115.37 E
Chenjiaqiao 106 31.27 N 121.16 E
Chenjiatun, Zhg. 104 42.20 N 124.06 E
Chenjiatun, Zhg. 104 40.57 N 121.01 E
Chenjiawan 106 31.02 N 120.35 E
Chenjiaxiang 100 31.29 N 113.42 E
Chenjiazhen 106 31.30 N 121.48 E
Chenjiazui 105 39.17 N 116.59 E
Chenkeng 100 25.06 N 116.15 E
Chenlingjiao 106 30.23 N 118.47 E
Chenliu 98 34.43 N 114.31 E
Chenlung 269b 31.17 N 121.25 E
Chennevières 261 49.00 N 2.07 E
Chennevières-lès-Louvres 261 49.03 N 2.33 E
Chenoa 216 40.44 N 88.43 W
Chenonceaux 50 47.20 N 1.04 E
Chenonceaux, Château de ⊥ 50 47.20 N 1.04 E
Chenôve 58 47.17 N 5.00 E
Chenoweth 224 45.37 N 121.13 W
Chenqiao 98 34.58 N 114.32 E
Chenqingqiao 89 49.08 N 127.16 E
Chenshanzhuang 105 39.43 N 117.30 E
Chenshichang 107 29.17 N 106.00 E
Chens-sur-Léman 58 46.20 N 6.16 E
Chentang 102 23.54 N 110.33 E
Chentejn nuruu ᴧ 88 48.30 N 108.30 E
Chentij 88 48.00 N 109.45 E
Chentij □4 88 48.00 N 110.30 E
Chenxi 102 27.51 N 109.59 E
Chenxian 100 25.48 N 112.59 E
Chenxiangtun 104 41.36 N 123.30 E
Chenyang 100 33.47 N 120.10 E
Chenyang → Shenyang 104 41.48 N 123.27 E
Cheonan → Ch'ŏnan 98 36.48 N 127.09 E
Cheongju → Ch'ŏngju 98 36.39 N 127.31 E
Cheo Reo 110 13.24 N 108.27 E
Chepachet 207 41.54 N 71.40 W
Chepaúa 152 12.58 S 22.43 E
Chepén 248 7.13 S 79.27 W
Chépénéhé 175f 20.47 S 167.09 E
Chepes 252 31.21 S 66.36 W
Chepkotet ᴧ 154 1.15 N 35.26 E
Chepo 246 9.10 N 79.06 W
Chepstow 42 51.39 N 2.41 W
Cheptainville 261 48.33 N 2.16 E
Cher □5 32 47.05 N 2.30 E
Cher ≃ 32 47.21 N 0.29 E
Cheradi, Isole II 68 40.27 N 17.10 E
Cherain 56 50.11 N 5.52 E
Cherán 234 19.41 N 101.57 W
Chéran ≃ 62 45.53 N 5.56 E
Cheranchi 150 12.40 N 7.42 E
Cherangany Hills ᴧ2 154 1.15 N 35.27 E
Cherasco 62 44.39 N 7.51 E
Cherāt 123 33.49 N 71.53 E
Cheraw 192 34.41 N 79.53 W
Cheraw State Park ♠ 192 34.36 N 79.55 W
Cherbaniani Reef ✢2 122 12.18 N 71.53 E
Cherbourg 32 49.39 N 1.39 W
Cherchell 148 36.36 N 2.12 E
Cheremkhovo → Čeremchovo 88 53.09 N 103.05 E
Chérence 261 49.05 N 1.41 E
Chereponi 150 10.09 N 0.17 E
Cherepovets → Čerepovec 76 59.08 N 37.54 E
Chergui, Chott ech ⊜ 148 34.21 N 0.30 E
Chergui, Île I 148 34.44 N 11.14 E
Chergui, Zahrez ⊜ 148 35.12 N 3.32 E
Cheribon → Cirebon 115a 6.44 S 108.34 E
Cherio ≃ 64 45.46 N 9.55 E
Cherita, Sebkhet ⊜ 36 35.21 N 10.19 E
Cheriton 208 37.17 N 75.58 W
Cheriyam Island I 122 10.09 N 73.40 E
Cherkassy → Čerkassy 78 49.26 N 32.04 E
Cherkessia → Karačajevo-Čerkesija □3 84 44.00 N 42.00 E
Cherkessk → Čerkessk 84 44.14 N 42.04 E
Cherlen → Kerulen ≃ 90 48.48 N 117.00 E
Chermside 171a 27.23 S 153.02 E
Chernigov → Černigov 78 51.30 N 31.18 E
Chernobyl → Černobyl' 78 51.16 N 30.14 E
Chernofski 180 53.24 N 167.33 W
Chernogorsk → Černogorsk 86 53.49 N 91.18 E
Chernovtsy → Černovcy 78 48.18 N 25.56 E
Chero ≃ 62 44.58 N 9.51 E
Cherokee, Al., U.S. 194 34.45 N 87.58 W
Cherokee, Ia., U.S. 198 42.44 N 95.33 W
Cherokee, Ks., U.S. 198 37.20 N 94.48 W
Cherokee, Ok., U.S. 196 36.45 N 98.21 W
Cherokee, Tx., U.S. 196 30.59 N 98.43 W
Cherokee □6 222 31.48 N 95.10 W
Cherokee, Lake ⊜1 222 32.21 N 94.39 W
Cherokee Canal ≅ 226 39.18 N 121.55 W
Cherokee Lake ⊜1 192 36.16 N 83.20 W
Cherokee Point ≻ 192 26.16 N 77.03 W
Cherokee Ranch 208 40.25 N 75.55 W
Cherokees, Lake O' The ⊜1 194 36.39 N 94.49 W
Cherokee Village 194 36.17 N 91.30 W
Chéroy 50 48.12 N 3.00 E
Cherpuči 86 53.01 N 138.52 E
Cherquenco 252 38.41 S 72.00 W
Cherrabun 162 18.29 S 125.19 E
Cherrapunji 120 25.18 N 91.42 E
Cherry Brook ≃, Ma., U.S. 283 42.23 N 71.17 W
Cherry Brook ≃, N.J., U.S. 276 41.01 N 74.00 W
Cherry City 279b 40.29 N 79.58 W
Cherry Creek, B.C., Can. 224 49.17 N 124.47 W
Cherry Creek, N.Y., U.S. 214 42.17 N 79.06 W
Cherry Creek ≃, Az., U.S. 200 33.41 N 110.49 W
Cherry Creek ≃, Ca., U.S. 226 37.53 N 119.58 W
Cherry Creek ≃, Co., U.S. 198 39.45 N 105.01 W
Cherry Creek ≃, Mt., U.S. 198 46.48 N 105.15 W
Cherry Creek ≃, N.D., U.S. 198 47.41 N 103.02 W
Cherry Creek ≃, S.D., U.S. 198 44.36 N 101.30 W
Cherry Creek ≃, Tx., U.S. 196 31.13 N 103.34 W
Cherry Creek, East Fork ≃ 226 38.06 N 119.47 W
Cherry Creek, West Fork ≃ 226 38.04 N 119.54 W
Cherry Fork 218 38.53 N 83.37 W
Cherry Grove, N.Y., U.S. 210 40.39 N 73.06 W
Cherry Grove, Or., U.S. 224 45.26 N 123.14 W
Cherry Hill, Il., U.S. 278 41.32 N 88.02 W
Cherry Hill, N.J., U.S. 208 39.56 N 75.01 W
Cherry Hill ◆8 284b 39.15 N 76.38 W
Cherry Hill Mall ◆9 285 39.56 N 75.02 W
Cherry Island I 285 39.43 N 75.31 W
Cherry Lake ⊜1 226 38.00 N 119.54 W
Cherryland 226 37.41 N 122.06 W
Cherry Lane 279b 40.34 N 79.33 W
Cherryplain 210 42.38 N 73.22 W
Cherry Point Marine Corps Air Station ■ 192 34.54 N 76.54 W
Cherryvale 198 37.16 N 95.33 W
Cherry Valley, Ar., U.S. 194 35.24 N 90.45 W
Cherry Valley, Ca., U.S. 228 33.57 N 116.53 W
Cherry Valley, Il., U.S. 216 42.14 N 88.56 W
Cherry Valley, Ma., U.S. 207 42.14 N 71.52 W
Cherry Valley, N.Y., U.S. 210 42.47 N 74.45 W
Cherry Valley, Pa., U.S. 214 41.10 N 79.48 W
Cherry Valley Creek ≃ 210 42.35 N 74.56 W
Cherryville, N.C., U.S. 192 35.22 N 81.22 W
Cherryville, Pa., U.S. 208 40.45 N 75.33 W
Cherrywood 275b 43.52 N 79.08 W
Cherson 78 46.38 N 32.35 E
Cherson □4 78 46.45 N 33.30 E
Chersonesskij, mys ≻ 78 44.35 N 33.23 E
Chertsey 42 51.24 N 0.30 W
Cherwell ≃ 42 51.44 N 1.15 W
Chesaning 190 43.11 N 84.06 W
Chesapeake 208 36.49 N 76.16 W
Chesapeake and Delaware Canal ≅ 208 39.32 N 75.51 W
Chesapeake and Ohio Canal National Historical Park ♠ 208 39.03 N 77.16 W
Chesapeake Bay ⊂ 208 38.40 N 76.25 W
Chesapeake Bay Bridge-Tunnel ◆5 208 37.00 N 76.02 W
Chesapeake Beach 208 38.41 N 76.32 W
Chesaw 182 48.56 N 119.03 W
Chesdin, Lake ⊜1 208 37.15 N 77.33 W
Cheseaux 58 46.35 N 6.36 E
Chesham 42 51.43 N 0.38 W
Chesham Bois 260 51.41 N 0.37 W
Cheshire, Ct., U.S. 207 41.29 N 72.54 W
Cheshire, Ma., U.S. 207 42.33 N 73.09 W
Cheshire, N.Y., U.S. 210 42.49 N 77.20 W
Cheshire □6, Eng., U.K. 44 53.23 N 2.30 W
Cheshire □6, N.H., U.S. 207 42.50 N 72.15 W
Cheshire Plain ≡ 44 53.17 N 2.40 W
Cheshire Reservoir ⊜1 207 42.32 N 73.11 W
Chesht-e Sharīf 128 34.21 N 63.44 E
Cheshunt 42 51.43 N 0.02 W
Chesil Beach ◆2 42 50.38 N 2.33 W
Chesilhurst 285 39.43 N 74.52 W
Cheslatta Lake ⊜ 182 53.44 N 125.18 W
Chesley 212 44.17 N 81.05 W
Chesnee 192 35.08 N 81.51 W
Chess ≃ 260 51.38 N 0.27 W
Chessington ◆8 260 51.21 N 0.18 W
Chessy 261 48.53 N 2.46 E
Chest Creek ≃ 214 40.53 N 78.44 W
Chester, Eng., U.K. 44 53.12 N 2.54 W
Chester, Ca., U.S. 204 40.18 N 121.13 W
Chester, Ct., U.S. 207 41.24 N 72.27 W
Chester, Il., U.S. 194 37.54 N 89.49 W
Chester, Md., U.S. 208 38.58 N 76.17 W
Chester, Ma., U.S. 207 42.16 N 72.58 W
Chester, Mt., U.S. 202 48.30 N 110.58 W
Chester, Ne., U.S. 198 40.00 N 97.37 W
Chester, N.J., U.S. 210 40.47 N 74.41 W
Chester, Ok., U.S. 196 36.12 N 98.55 W
Chester, Pa., U.S. 208 39.50 N 75.21 W
Chester, S.C., U.S. 192 34.42 N 81.12 W
Chester, Tx., U.S. 222 30.55 N 94.36 W
Chester, Vt., U.S. 188 43.15 N 72.35 W
Chester, Va., U.S. 208 37.21 N 77.26 W
Chester, W.V., U.S. 214 40.36 N 80.33 W
Chester □6 208 39.58 N 75.36 W
Chester □8 262 53.16 N 2.52 W
Chester ≃ 208 39.00 N 76.10 W
Chester Basin 186 44.34 N 64.19 W
Chesterbrook 284c 38.55 N 77.09 W
Chester Brook ≃ 283 42.23 N 71.14 W
Chesterbrook Woods 284c 38.56 N 77.08 W
Chester Creek ≃ 208 39.50 N 75.22 W
Chester Creek, East Branch ≃ 285 39.56 N 75.32 W
Chester Creek, West Branch ≃ 285 39.54 N 75.27 W
Chesterfield, Eng., U.K. 44 53.15 N 1.25 W
Chesterfield, Ct., U.S. 207 41.24 N 72.11 W
Chesterfield, Il., U.S. 219 39.15 N 90.04 W
Chesterfield, In., U.S. 218 40.06 N 85.35 W
Chesterfield, Ma., U.S. 207 42.23 N 72.50 W
Chesterfield, S.C., U.S. 192 34.44 N 80.05 W
Chesterfield, Va., U.S. 192 37.22 N 77.30 W
Chesterfield □6 208 37.20 N 77.25 W
Chesterfield, Île I 157b 16.20 S 43.58 E
Chesterfield, Îles II 160 19.30 S 158.00 E
Chesterfield Inlet 176 63.21 N 90.42 W
Chesterfield Inlet ⊂ 176 63.25 N 90.45 W
Chester Heights 285 39.53 N 75.28 W
Chester Hill, Austl. 274a 33.53 S 151.00 E
Chesterhill, Oh., U.S. 188 39.29 N 81.51 W
Chester Hill, Pa., U.S. 214 40.53 N 78.14 W
Chester Island I 285 39.50 N 75.21 W
Chesterland 214 41.31 N 81.21 W
Chester-le-Street 44 54.52 N 1.34 W
Chester Morse Lake ⊜1 224 47.23 N 121.42 W
Chesters 44 55.23 N 2.36 W
Chester Springs 285 40.06 N 75.37 W
Chesterton 216 41.36 N 87.03 W
Chesterton Range ᴧ 166 25.30 S 147.27 E
Chestertown 208 39.12 N 76.04 W
Chesterville, On., Can. 212 45.06 N 75.14 W
Chesterville, Oh., U.S. 214 40.29 N 82.41 W
Chestnut 219 40.03 N 89.11 W
Chestnut Hill, Ma., U.S. 283 42.20 N 71.10 W
Chestnut Hill, Pa., U.S. 210 40.04 N 75.12 W
Chestnut Hill ◆8 285 40.04 N 75.13 W
Chestnut Hill ᴧ2 285 40.13 N 75.43 W
Chestnut Hill Estates 285 39.41 N 75.42 W
Chestnut Hill Reservoir ⊜1 283 42.20 N 71.10 W
Chestnut Ridge ᴧ 214 40.09 N 79.24 W
Chestnut Ridge Park ♠ 284a 42.43 N 78.46 W
Chest Peak ᴧ 172 43.06 S 172.01 E
Chesuncook Lake ⊜ 188 46.00 N 69.20 W
Cheswick 214 40.32 N 79.47 W
Cheswold 208 39.13 N 75.35 W
Chet ≃ 42 52.33 N 1.32 E
Cheta ≃ 74 71.54 N 102.06 E
Chetaïbi 36 37.04 N 7.23 E
Chetco ≃ 202 42.03 N 124.16 W
Chetek 190 45.18 N 91.39 W
Chéticamp 186 46.38 N 61.01 W
Chet Iter, Oued V 148 21.39 N 2.30 E
Chetopa 198 37.02 N 95.05 W
Chettlatt Island I 122 11.42 N 72.42 E
Chetumal 232 18.30 N 88.18 W
Chetumal, Bahía ⊂ 232 18.20 N 88.05 W
Chetwynd 182 55.42 N 121.40 W
Cheung Chau I 271d 22.12 N 114.01 E
Cheung Shue Tan 271d 22.26 N 114.12 E
Chevak 180 61.39 N 165.17 W
Cheval-Blanc, Montagne du ᴧ 62 44.07 N 6.26 E
Chevannes 261 48.32 N 2.27 E
Chevelon Creek ≃ 200 34.57 N 110.31 W
Chevening 260 51.18 N 0.08 E
Chevenoz 58 46.20 N 6.39 E
Cheverly 284c 38.55 N 76.54 W
Chevigny 50 47.30 N 1.28 E
Chevillon 58 48.32 N 5.08 E
Chevilly-Larue 261 48.46 N 2.21 E
Cheviot, N.Z. 172 42.49 S 173.16 E
Cheviot, Oh., U.S. 218 39.09 N 84.36 W
Cheviot Hills ᴧ2 44 55.22 N 2.22 W
Chevreuse 261 48.42 N 2.03 E
Chevreville 261 49.07 N 2.51 E
Chevril, Lac du ⊜ 62 45.29 N 6.56 E
Chevry-Cossigny 261 48.43 N 2.40 E
Chevy Chase 284c 38.58 N 77.04 W
Chevy Chase Heights 214 40.36 N 79.08 W
Chevy Chase View 284c 39.01 N 77.05 W
Chewacan ≃ 202 42.30 N 120.18 W
Chew Bahir (Lake Stefanie) ⊜ 144 4.40 N 36.50 E
Chewelah 202 48.16 N 117.42 W
Chew Magna 42 51.22 N 2.35 W
Chew Reservoir ⊜1 262 53.31 N 1.56 W
Chews Landing 285 39.50 N 75.04 W
Chewton, Austl. 169 37.05 S 144.16 E
Chewton, Pa., U.S. 214 40.53 N 80.20 W
Chexbres 58 46.29 N 6.47 E
Cheyenne, Ok., U.S. 196 35.36 N 99.40 W
Cheyenne, Wy., U.S. 200 41.08 N 104.49 W
Cheyenne ≃ 198 44.40 N 101.15 W
Cheyenne, Dry Fork ≃ 198 43.25 N 105.23 W
Cheyenne River Indian Reservation ◆4 198 45.00 N 100.40 W
Cheyenne Wells 198 38.49 N 102.21 W
Cheyne Bay ⊂ 162 34.35 S 118.50 E
Cheyne Point ≻ 162 33.58 S 122.34 E
Cheyney 285 39.56 N 75.31 W
Cheyney University of Pennsylvania ⊻2 285 39.56 N 75.32 W
Chezhen 98 37.54 N 117.37 E
Chhabra 124 24.40 N 76.50 E
Chhachhrauli 124 30.15 N 77.22 E
Chhajārsi 272a 28.38 N 77.23 E
Chhalera Bāngar 272a 28.33 N 77.20 E
Chhanka 126 23.59 N 89.55 E
Chhapra 124 25.46 N 84.45 E
Chhātak 120 25.02 N 91.40 E
Chhatarpur, India 124 24.23 N 84.11 E
Chhatarpur, India 124 24.55 N 79.36 E
Chhātna 126 23.18 N 86.58 E
Chhatrapur 122 19.21 N 84.59 E
Chhattīsgarh ◆1 122 21.15 N 82.00 E
Chhay Arêng ≃ 110 11.31 N 103.25 E
Chhêb Kândal 110 13.45 N 105.24 E
Chhibrāmau 124 27.09 N 79.31 E
Chhinămor 272b 22.48 N 88.18 E
Chhindwāra 124 22.04 N 78.56 E
Chhiruti 126 24.01 N 88.11 E
Chhitauni 124 27.09 N 83.58 E
Chhlong ≃ 110 12.15 N 105.58 E
Chhota Bāisdia 126 22.00 N 90.27 E
Chhota-Chhindwāra 124 23.03 N 79.29 E
Chhota Udepur 120 22.19 N 74.01 E
Chhukha Dzong 124 27.09 N 89.36 E
Chi ≃, Thai 110 15.11 N 104.43 E
Chi ≃, Thai 110 15.18 N 103.31 E
Chi ≃, Zhg. 100 32.51 N 117.59 E
Chia 246 4.52 N 74.04 W
Chia, Laguna ⊜ 234 22.10 N 98.02 W
Chiador 256 22.01 S 43.03 W
Chiahsien 100 23.05 N 120.35 E
Chiahsing → Jiaxing 106 30.46 N 120.45 E
Chiai 100 23.29 N 120.27 E
Chialamberto 62 45.22 N 7.21 E
Chiali 100 23.10 N 120.10 E
Chiambala ≃ 152 16.22 S 11.49 E
Chiampo 64 45.33 N 11.17 E
Chiampo ≃ 64 45.20 N 11.16 E
Chiamussu → Jiamusi 89 46.50 N 130.21 E
Chiana, Val di V 66 43.15 N 11.50 E
Chianciano Terme 66 43.03 N 11.50 E
Chiang Dao 110 19.22 N 98.58 E
Chiange 152 15.45 S 13.48 E
Chiang Kham 110 19.32 N 100.18 E
Chiang Khan 110 17.52 N 101.36 E
Chiang Khian 110 19.37 N 100.00 E
Chiang Mai 110 18.47 N 98.59 E
Chiangmen → Jiangmen 100 22.35 N 113.05 E
Chiang Rai 110 19.54 N 99.50 E
Chiang Saen 110 20.16 N 100.05 E
Chiangtu → Yangzhou 100 32.24 N 119.26 E
Chiangyin → Jiangyin 106 31.55 N 120.16 E
Chiani ≃ 66 42.52 N 12.14 E
Chian → Ji'an 100 27.07 N 114.58 E
Chianni 66 43.29 N 10.38 E
Chianti □4 66 43.22 N 11.23 E
Chianti ᴧ1 66 43.25 N 11.20 E
Chianti, Monti del ᴧ 66 43.32 N 11.25 E
Chiaohsi 100 24.49 N 121.46 E
Chiaohsien → Jiaoxian 98 36.18 N 119.58 E
Chiaopan 100 24.50 N 121.21 E
Chiaotso → Jiaozuo 102 35.15 N 113.13 E
Chiao-Tung Normal University ⊻2 269b 31.14 N 121.24 E
Chiapa 248 19.32 S 69.13 W
Chiapa de Corzo 234 16.42 N 93.00 W
Chiapaot'ai 100 24.11 N 121.00 E
Chiapas □3 232 16.30 N 92.30 W
Chiaramonte Gulfi 70 37.02 N 14.42 E
Chiaramonti 71 40.45 N 8.49 E
Chiaravalle 66 43.36 N 13.19 E
Chiaravalle Centrale 68 38.41 N 16.25 E
Chiareggio 64 46.19 N 9.47 E
Chiari 62 45.32 N 9.56 E
Chiaromonte 68 40.07 N 16.13 E
Chiasso 58 45.50 N 9.01 E
Chiautla de Tapia 234 18.17 N 98.36 W
Chiautzingo 234 19.12 N 98.28 W
Chiavari 62 44.19 N 9.19 E
Chiavenna 58 46.19 N 9.24 E
Chiawelo 273d 26.17 S 27.52 E
Chiba 94 35.36 N 140.07 E
Chiba □5 94 35.30 N 140.20 E
Chibabava 156 20.19 S 33.39 E
Chiba-kō ⊂ 268 35.35 N 140.06 E
Chibakou 100 29.36 N 113.01 E
Chibango 152 13.38 S 21.56 E
Chiba University ⊻2 268 35.38 N 140.06 E
Chibemba 152 15.45 S 14.05 E
Chibi 154 20.19 S 30.29 E
Chibia 152 15.11 S 13.41 E
Chibouet ≃ 206 45.47 N 72.52 W
Chibougamau 176 49.55 N 74.22 W
Chibuto 156 24.44 S 33.33 E
Chibuzhangchu Hu ⊜ 120 33.25 N 90.15 E
Chibwe 154 14.12 S 28.31 E
Chicago, Il., U.S. 216 41.51 N 87.39 W
Chicago, Il., U.S. 278 41.51 N 87.39 W
Chicago, North Branch ≃ 216 41.53 N 87.38 W
Chicago, North Branch, West Fork ≃ 278 42.03 N 87.54 W
Chicago, South Branch ≃ 278 41.53 N 87.38 W
Chicago, University of ⊻2 278 41.47 N 87.36 W
Chicago Botanic Garden ♠ 278 42.09 N 87.47 W
Chicago Harbor ⊂ 278 41.53 N 87.37 W
Chicago Heights 216 41.30 N 87.38 W
Chicago-Hinsdale Airport ⊠ 278 41.46 N 87.56 W
Chicago Lawn ◆8 278 41.47 N 87.41 W
Chicago-Midway Airport ⊠ 216 41.47 N 87.45 W
Chicago-O'Hare International Airport ⊠ 278 41.59 N 87.54 W
Chicago Park 226 39.09 N 120.58 W
Chicago Portage National Historic Site ⊥ 278 41.48 N 87.49 W
Chicago Ridge 216 41.42 N 87.46 W
Chicago Sanitary and Ship Canal ≅ 278 41.32 N 88.05 W
Chicago Stadium ♠ 278 41.53 N 87.40 W
Chicama ≃ 248 7.56 S 79.17 W
Chicamacomico ≃ 208 38.26 N 75.59 W
Chicamba, Barragem de ◆6 156 19.08 S 33.00 E
Chicapa ≃ 152 6.25 S 20.47 E
Chicayán ≃ 234 21.59 N 94.06 W
Chic-Chocs, Monts ᴧ 186 48.55 N 66.00 W
Chichagof Island I 180 57.30 N 135.30 W
Chichas, Cordillera de ᴧ 248 21.00 S 66.20 W
Chīchāwatni 123 30.32 N 72.42 E
Chiché ≃ 250 8.15 S 53.30 W
Chicheng 98 40.54 N 115.46 E
Chichén Itzá ⊥ 232 20.40 N 88.35 W
Chichester, Eng., U.K. 42 50.50 N 0.48 W
Chichester, N.Y., U.S. 210 42.06 N 74.19 W
Chichester Range ᴧ 162 22.00 S 118.50 E
Chichi 100 23.50 N 120.47 E
Chichibu 94 35.59 N 139.05 E
Chichibu-Tama-kokuritsu-kōen ♠ 94 35.52 N 139.00 E
Chichica 236 8.22 N 81.40 W
Chichicastenango 236 14.56 N 91.07 W
Chichigalpa 236 12.34 N 87.02 W
Chichigapa 234 17.47 N 94.25 W
Ch'ich'ihaerh → Qiqihar 89 47.19 N 123.55 E
Chichihualco 234 17.41 N 99.39 W
Chichijima-rettō II 14 27.06 N 142.12 E
Chichimilá 232 20.37 N 88.13 W
Chichiriviche 246 10.56 N 68.16 W
Chicholi 124 22.01 N 77.40 E
Chichra 126 22.19 N 86.53 E
Chickahominy ≃ 208 37.14 N 76.53 W
Chickaloon 180 61.48 N 148.28 W
Chickamauga 192 34.52 N 85.17 W
Chickamauga Lake ⊜1 192 35.22 N 85.02 W
Chickamin ≃ 182 55.47 N 130.58 W
Chickasaw, Al., U.S. 194 30.45 N 88.04 W
Chickasaw, Oh., U.S. 216 40.26 N 84.30 W
Chickasaw Bogue ≃ 194 32.17 N 87.55 W
Chickasawhatchie Creek ≃ 192 31.19 N 84.29 W
Chickasawhay ≃ 194 31.00 N 88.45 W
Chickasaw National Recreation Area ♠ 196 34.25 N 96.59 W
Chickasha 196 35.03 N 97.56 W
Chicken 180 64.04 N 141.56 W
Chicken Brook ≃ 283 42.08 N 71.25 W
Chickerell 42 50.37 N 2.30 W
Chickies Creek ≃ 208 40.03 N 76.32 W
Chiclana de la Frontera 34 36.25 N 6.08 W
Chiclayo 248 6.46 S 79.51 W
Chico, Ca., U.S. 204 39.43 N 121.50 W
Chico, Tx., U.S. 196 33.17 N 97.47 W
Chico, Wa., U.S. 224 47.36 N 122.42 W
Chico ≃, Arg. 254 43.48 S 66.25 W
Chico ≃, Arg. 254 42.25 S 70.30 W
Chico ≃, Arg. 254 49.56 S 68.32 W
Chico ≃, Cuba 286b 23.02 N 82.17 W
Chico ≃, Pan. 236 8.20 N 80.28 W
Chico ≃, Pil. 116 17.58 N 121.36 E
Chico ≃, S.A. 254 51.40 S 69.09 W
Chicoasén, Presa ⊜1 234 16.55 N 93.05 W
Chicobi, Lac ⊜ 190 48.53 N 78.30 W
Chico Creek ≃ 198 38.15 N 104.20 W
Chicolete Creek ≃ 222 29.05 N 96.49 W
Chicomba 152 14.09 S 14.57 E
Chicomo 156 24.31 S 34.17 E
Chicomuselo 232 15.46 N 92.16 W
Chiconautla, Cerro ᴧ 286a 19.39 N 98.58 W
Chicono 154 12.56 S 35.43 E
Chicontepec de Tejeda 234 20.58 N 98.10 W
Chicopee, Ga., U.S. 192 34.15 N 83.50 W
Chicopee, Ma., U.S. 207 42.08 N 72.36 W
Chicopee ≃ 207 42.09 N 72.37 W
Chicora 214 40.56 N 79.44 W
Chicot, Lake ⊜ 194 33.20 N 91.14 W
Chicot, Rivière du ≃ 275a 45.35 N 73.51 W
Chicot State Park ♠ 194 30.47 N 92.19 W
Chicoutimi 186 48.26 N 71.04 W
Chicoutimi ≃ 186 48.26 N 71.05 W
Chicoutimi, Réserve ♠ 186 48.30 N 70.15 W
Chicú, Cerro ᴧ 236 8.35 N 80.51 W
Chicualoque 234 20.23 N 97.39 W
Chicuma 152 13.23 S 14.51 E
Chicxulub 232 21.08 N 89.31 W
Chidambaram 122 11.24 N 79.42 E
Chiddingfold 42 51.06 N 0.37 W
Chiddingstone Causeway 260 51.12 N 0.10 E
Chidenguele 156 24.54 S 34.13 E
Chidlow 168a 31.52 S 116.14 E
Chi-do I 98 35.04 N 126.13 E
Chidralada Palace ⊻ 269a 13.46 N 100.32 E
Chief 222 32.33 N 96.10 W
Chief Justice William Cushing Memorial State Park ♠ 283 42.10 N 70.45 W
Chiefland 192 29.28 N 82.51 W
Chiefs Point ≻ 212 44.42 N 81.18 W
Chief's Point Indian Reserve ◆4 212 44.41 N 81.17 W
Chiehyang → Jieyang 100 23.35 N 116.21 E
Chiemgauer Alpen ᴧ 64 47.40 N 12.30 E
Chiemsee ⊜ 64 47.54 N 12.29 E
Chien, Bayou de ≃ 194 36.35 N 89.11 W
Chienes (Kiens) 64 46.48 N 11.50 E
Chiengi 154 8.39 S 29.10 E
Chiengo 152 13.20 S 21.55 E
Chiens, Rivière aux ≃ 275a 45.39 N 73.46 W
Chienti ≃ 66 43.18 N 13.45 E
Chieo Lan Reservoir ⊜1 110 9.00 N 98.45 E
Chieri 62 45.01 N 7.49 E
Chiers ≃ 56 49.39 N 5.00 E
Chiesa in Valmalenco 64 46.16 N 9.51 E
Chiese ≃ 64 45.08 N 10.25 E
Chieti 66 42.21 N 14.10 E
Chieti □4 66 42.07 N 14.21 E
Chietla 234 18.31 N 98.35 W
Chieuti 68 41.51 N 15.10 E
Chieveley 42 51.27 N 1.19 W
Chièvres 56 50.35 N 3.48 E
Chifeng (Ulanhad) 98 42.18 N 119.00 E
Chigasaki 94 35.19 N 139.24 E
Chiginagak, Mount ᴧ 180 57.08 N 156.59 W
Chigmit Mountains ᴧ 180 60.00 N 153.00 W
Chignahuapan 234 19.50 N 98.02 W
Chignall Saint James 260 51.46 N 0.25 E
Chignall Smealy 260 51.47 N 0.25 E
Chignecto, Cape ≻ 186 45.20 N 64.57 W
Chignecto Bay ⊂ 186 45.35 N 64.45 W
Chignik 180 56.18 N 158.23 W
Chignik Bay ⊂ 180 56.22 N 158.15 W
Chignik Lagoon 180 56.21 N 158.31 W
Chignik Lake 180 56.15 N 158.45 W
Chignolo Po 62 45.09 N 9.29 E
Chigombe ≃ 156 23.26 S 33.19 E
Chigorodó 246 7.41 N 76.42 W
Chigu 100 27.34 N 114.40 E
Chigubo 156 22.50 S 33.34 E
Chigu Co ⊜ 120 28.40 N 91.45 E
Chigwell 42 51.38 N 0.05 E
Chigwell Row 260 51.37 N 0.07 E
Chigyŏng 98 39.51 N 127.26 E
Chihaya-akasaka 270 34.24 N 135.38 E
Chihaya Castle ⊥ 270 34.24 N 135.40 E
Chihe 100 32.32 N 117.58 E
Ch'ihfeng → Chifeng 98 42.18 N 119.00 E
Chihli, Gulf of → Bo Hai ⊂ 100 38.30 N 120.00 E
Chihpen 100 22.42 N 121.02 E
Ch'ihshang 100 23.07 N 121.12 E
Chihsi → Jixi 89 45.17 N 130.59 E
Ch'ihsing Shan ᴧ, T'aiwan 100 25.10 N 121.33 E
Ch'ihsing Shan ᴧ, T'aiwan 269d 25.10 N 121.33 E
Ch'ihsing Yen I 100 21.46 N 120.49 E
Chihtungtsun 100 22.44 N 120.14 E
Chihu 100 24.07 N 117.51 E
Chihuahua 232 28.38 N 106.05 W
Chihuahua □3 232 28.30 N 106.00 W
Chihuahuan Desert ◆2 16 35.00 N 106.00 W
Chii-san ᴧ 98 35.20 N 127.44 E
Chii-san Kukrip Kongwŏn ♠ 98 35.20 N 127.39 E
Chiitola 26 61.16 N 29.38 E
Chikaskia ≃ 196 36.37 N 97.15 W
Chik Ballāpur 122 13.28 N 77.44 E

Symbol	English	Deutsch	Español	Français	Português
≃	River	Fluß	Río	Rivière	Rio
≅	Canal	Kanal	Canal	Canal	Canal
⌊	Waterfall, Rapids	Wasserfall, Stromschnellen	Cascada, Rápidos	Chute d'eau, Rapides	Cascata, Rápidos
⋓	Strait	Meeresstraße	Estrecho	Détroit	Estreito
⊂	Bay, Gulf	Bucht, Golf	Bahía, Golfo	Baie, Golfe	Baía, Golfo
⊜	Lake, Lakes	See, Seen	Lago, Lagos	Lac, Lacs	Lago, Lagos
⩩	Swamp	Sumpf	Pantano	Marais	Pântano
⊓	Ice Features, Glacier	Eis- und Gletscherformen	Accidentes Glaciales	Formes glaciaires	Acidentes glaciares
⊤	Other Hydrographic Features	Andere Hydrographische Objekte	Otros Elementos Hidrográficos	Autres données hydrographiques	Outros acidentes hidrográficos
✢	Submarine Features	Untermeerische Objekte	Accidentes Submarinos	Formes de relief sous-marin	Acidentes submarinos
□	Political Unit	Politische Einheit	Unidad Politica	Entité politique	Unidade política
⊻	Cultural Institution	Kulturelle Institution	Institución Cultural	Institution culturelle	Instituição cultural
⊥	Historical Site	Historische Stätte	Sitio Histórico	Site historique	Sitio histórico
♠	Recreational Site	Erholungs- und Ferienort	Sitio de Recreo	Centre de loisirs	Area de Lazer
⊠	Airport	Flughafen	Aeropuerto	Aéroport	Aeroporto
■	Military Installation	Militäranlage	Instalación Militar	Installation militaire	Instalação militar
◆	Miscellaneous	Verschiedenes	Misceláneo	Divers	Diversos

Chikhli 122 20.21 N 76.15 E
Chikindzonot 232 20.20 N 88.29 W
Chikmagalūr 122 13.19 N 75.47 E
Chiknai ≈ 126 24.06 N 89.17 E
Chiknāyakanhalli 122 13.26 N 76.37 E
Chikoa 154 13.24 S 32.07 E
Chikodi 122 16.26 N 74.36 E
Chikou 100 30.44 N 117.32 E
Chikrêng ≈ 110 12.51 N 104.14 E
Ch'iku 100 23.08 N 120.07 E
Chikugo 96 33.12 N 130.30 E
Chikugo ≈ 92 33.09 N 130.21 E
Chikujō-kichi, Kōkū-jieitai- ■ 96 33.41 N 131.03 E
Chikuma ≈ 94 36.59 N 138.35 E
Chikuminuk Lake ⊜ 180 60.14 N 159.00 W
Chikura 94 34.57 N 139.57 E
Chikusa 96 35.09 N 134.26 E
Chikusa ≈ 96 34.44 N 134.24 E
Chikushino 96 33.29 N 130.31 E
Chikwawa 154 16.03 S 34.48 E
Chi-kyaw 110 20.17 N 93.54 E
Chikyu-misaki > 92a 42.18 N 141.00 E
Chila 152 12.04 S 14.29 E
Chilacachapa 234 18.17 N 99.43 W
Chilakalūrupet 122 16.05 N 80.10 E
Chilako ≈ 182 53.54 N 122.59 W
Chilam Chauki 123 35.03 N 75.07 E
Chilanga 154 15.34 S 28.17 E
Chilanko Forks 182 52.06 N 124.10 W
Chilapa de Álvarez 234 17.36 N 99.10 W
Chilās 123 35.26 N 74.05 E
Chilaw 122 7.34 N 79.47 E
Chilca, Perú 248 12.32 S 76.44 W
Chilca, Perú 248 12.09 S 75.11 W
Chilca, Punta > 248 12.27 S 76.48 W
Chilchota 234 19.51 N 102.08 W
Chilcotin ≈ 182 51.45 N 122.24 W
Chilcott Island I 166 16.58 S 149.58 E
Childers 166 25.14 S 152.17 E
Childersburg 194 33.16 N 86.21 W
Childer Thornton 262 53.17 N 2.57 W
Childress 196 34.25 N 100.12 W
Childs 210 41.34 N 75.32 W
Chile □¹ 244 30.00 S 71.00 W
Chile, Hipódromo ◆ 286e 33.24 S 70.41 W
Chile, Universidad de ⋓² 286e 33.27 S 70.40 W
Chile Basin ⟡¹ 18 33.00 S 80.00 W
Chile Chico 254 46.33 S 71.44 W
Chilecito, Arg. 252 29.10 S 67.30 W
Chilecito, Arg. 252 33.53 S 69.03 W
Chilengue, Serra do ⋏ 152 13.10 S 15.18 E
Chileno, Arroyo ≈, Ur. 258 33.55 S 58.08 W
Chileno, Arroyo ≈, Ur. 288 34.22 S 57.54 W
Chile Rise ⟡³ 18 40.00 S 90.00 W
Chilete 248 7.14 S 78.51 W
Chilham 42 51.15 N 0.57 E
Chilhowie 192 36.47 N 81.40 W
Chili 216 40.52 N 86.02 W
Chili ≈ 248 16.23 S 71.46 W
Chili, Ouadi V 146 16.44 N 20.53 E
Chilia, Braţul ≈¹ 78 45.18 N 29.40 E
Chili Center 210 43.06 N 77.44 W
Chili
 → Chile □¹ 244 30.00 S 71.00 W
Chilika Lake ⊜ 122 19.45 N 85.25 E
Chililabombwe (Bancroft) 154 12.18 S 27.43 E
Chilingchang 107 28.58 N 105.31 E
Chilin
 → Jilin 89 43.51 N 126.33 E
Chilivani 71 40.36 N 8.56 E
Chilkat Pass)(180 59.43 N 136.35 W
Chilko ≈ 182 52.08 N 123.30 W
Chilko Lake ⊜ 182 51.20 N 124.05 W
Chilko Lake Indian Reserve ⟿⁴ 182 51.25 N 124.07 W
Chillagoe 166 17.09 S 144.32 E
Chillán 252 36.36 S 72.07 W
Chillar 252 37.18 S 59.59 W
Chilla Saroda ⟿⁸ 272a 28.36 N 77.18 E
Chillicothe, Il., U.S. 190 40.55 N 89.29 W
Chillicothe, Mo., U.S. 194 39.47 N 93.33 W
Chillicothe, Oh., U.S. 218 39.19 N 82.58 W
Chillicothe, Tx., U.S. 196 34.15 N 99.30 W
Chilliwack 224 49.10 N 121.57 W
Chilliwack ≈ 224 49.05 N 121.57 W
Chilliwack Lake ⊜ 224 49.03 N 121.25 W
Chillón 286d 11.55 S 77.05 W
Chillón ≈ 248 11.57 S 77.09 W
Chillon, Château de ⊥ 58 46.25 N 6.56 E
Chillum 284c 38.58 N 76.59 W
Chilly 84 39.25 N 49.05 E
Chilly-Mazarin 261 48.42 N 2.19 E
Chilmāri 124 25.33 N 89.43 E
Chilmark 207 41.20 N 70.44 W
Chilo 218 38.48 N 84.08 W
Chiloane, Ilha I 156 20.40 S 34.55 E
Chiloé, Isla Grande de I 254 42.30 S 73.55 W
Chilok 88 51.21 N 110.28 E
Chilok ≈ 88 51.19 N 106.59 E
Chilón 232 17.14 N 92.25 W
Chilonga 154 12.03 S 31.21 E
Chilongo 152 13.55 S 16.35 E
Chiloquin 202 42.34 N 121.51 W
Chilovo 76 57.46 N 29.23 E
Chilpancingo de los Bravo 234 17.33 N 99.30 W
Chilpi 124 22.15 N 81.33 E
Chilston Park ◆ 260 51.12 N 0.42 E
Chiltern □⁸ 260 51.40 N 0.37 W
Chiltern Hills ⋏² 42 51.42 N 0.48 W
Chilton, Eng., U.K. 44 54.39 N 1.33 W
Chilton, Tx., U.S. 222 31.16 N 97.03 W
Chilton, Wi., U.S. 190 44.01 N 88.09 W
Chiluage 152 9.30 S 21.47 E
Chilubula Mission 154 10.09 S 31.00 E
Chilumba 154 10.28 S 34.12 E
Chilung 100 25.08 N 121.44 E
Chilung ≈ 269d 25.07 N 121.27 E
Chilung Kang C 269d 25.09 N 121.45 E
Chilung Shih □⁷ 269d 25.08 N 121.45 E
Chiluvya 154 12.18 S 34.01 E
Chilwa, Lake ⊜ 154 15.12 S 35.50 E
Chilwell 169 38.10 S 144.21 E
Chimaco 152 15.12 S 21.56 E
Chimacum 224 48.00 N 122.46 W
Chimacum Creek ≈ 224 48.03 N 122.45 W
Chimakela 152 15.24 S 16.58 E
Chimaltenango 236 14.40 N 90.49 W
Chimaltenango □⁵ 236 14.40 N 90.55 W
Chimaltitán 234 21.46 N 103.50 W
Chimán 246 8.42 N 78.37 W
Chimanimani National Park ◆ 154 19.48 S 33.56 E
Chimay 50 50.03 N 4.19 E
Chimayo 200 36.00 N 105.55 W
Chimbarongo 252 34.42 S 71.03 W
Chimbas 252 31.29 S 68.32 W
Chimborazo □⁴ 246 2.00 S 78.40 W
Chimborazo ⋀ 236 13.05 N 85.58 W
Chimborazo ⋀¹ 246 1.28 S 78.48 W
Chimbote 248 9.05 S 78.36 W
Chimbu □⁵ 164 6.05 S 145.00 E
Chimbua 152 16.32 S 15.08 E
Ch'imei Yü I 100 23.13 N 119.26 E
Chimichagua 246 9.15 N 73.49 W
Chimkent
 → Čimkent 85 42.18 N 69.36 E
Chimki 82 55.54 N 37.26 E
Chimki-Chovrino ⟿⁸ 265b 55.51 N 37.30 E
Chimkinskoje vodochranilišče ⊜¹ 265b 55.51 N 37.28 E
Chimney Reservoir ⊜¹ 204 41.25 N 117.10 W
Chimney Rock National Historic Site ◆ 198 41.39 N 103.20 W
Chimoio 156 19.08 S 33.29 E
Chimon Island I 276 41.04 N 73.23 W
Chimpay 252 39.10 S 66.09 W
Chimpembe 154 9.31 S 29.33 E
Chimpôro ≈ 152 17.20 S 17.17 E
Chin □⁸ 110 22.00 N 93.30 E
China, Méx. 232 25.42 N 99.14 W
Chinā, Nihon 174m 26.24 N 127.46 E
China (Zhongguo) □¹ 90 35.00 N 105.00 E
China, Tanjong > 271c 1.14 N 103.51 E
Chinácota 246 7.37 N 72.36 W
China Grove 192 35.34 N 80.34 W
China Lake ⊜ 204 35.46 N 117.39 W
China Lake Naval Weapons Center ■ 204 35.35 N 117.10 W
Chinameca 236 13.30 N 88.21 W
China Meridional, Mar de
 → South China Sea ⊤² 108 10.00 N 113.00 E
Chinan 98 35.48 N 127.25 E
Chinandega 236 12.37 N 87.09 W
Chinandega □⁵ 236 12.45 N 87.05 W
Chinan
 → Jinan 98 36.40 N 116.57 E
China Spring 222 31.39 N 97.18 W
Chinati Peak ⋀ 196 29.57 N 104.29 W
Chinatown ⟿⁸ 282 37.48 N 122.26 W
Chincha Alta 248 13.27 S 76.08 W
Chinchaga ≈ 176 58.50 N 118.20 W
Chincheros 248 13.27 S 73.44 W
Chinchiang
 → Quanzhou 100 24.54 N 118.35 E
Chinchilla, Austl. 166 26.45 S 150.38 E
Chinchilla, Pa., U.S. 210 41.28 N 75.41 W
Chinchiná 246 4.58 N 75.36 W
Chincholi 272c 19.10 N 73.08 E
Chinchón, Esp. 34 40.08 N 3.25 W
Chinch'ŏn, Taehan 98 36.52 N 127.26 E
Chinchorro, Banco ⟡⁴ 232 18.35 N 87.22 W
Chinchou
 → Jinzhou 104 41.07 N 121.08 E
Chincilla de Monte Aragón 34 38.55 N 1.43 W
Chincolco 252 32.13 S 70.50 W
Chincoteague 208 37.55 N 75.22 W
Chincoteague Bay C 208 38.06 N 75.15 W
Chincoteague Inlet C 208 37.53 N 75.25 W
Chinde 156 18.37 S 36.24 E
Chindo 98 34.28 N 126.15 E
Chin-do I 98 34.25 N 126.15 E
Chindong 98 35.07 N 128.29 E
Chindwinn ≈ 110 21.26 N 95.15 E
Chine (la République populaire de)
 → China □¹, Asia 90 35.00 N 105.00 E
Chine (nationaliste)
 → Taiwan □¹, Asia 100 23.30 N 121.00 E
Chinen 174m 26.09 N 127.49 E
Chineni 123 33.02 N 75.17 E
Chine Orientale, Mer de
 → East China Sea ⊤² 90 30.00 N 126.00 E
Chinese Camp 226 37.52 N 120.26 W
Chinese Cemetery ⟿ 269f 14.38 N 120.59 E
Chinese University ⋓² 271d 22.26 N 114.12 E
Chingamba 152 12.49 S 18.20 E
Chingansk 89 49.07 N 131.11 E
Chingarora Creek ≈ 276 40.27 N 74.12 W
Ch'ingchiang
 → Qingjiang 100 33.35 N 119.02 E
Chingford ⟿⁸ 260 51.38 N 0.01 E
Chingleput 122 12.42 N 79.59 E
Chingmei ⟿⁸ 269d 24.59 N 121.32 E
Chingola 154 12.32 S 27.52 E
Chingoni 157a 12.48 S 45.08 E
Chingoroi 152 13.37 S 14.01 E
Chingshih
 → Jinshi 102 29.39 N 111.52 E
Ch'ingtao
 → Qingdao 98 36.06 N 120.19 E
Chingtechen
 → Jingdezhen 100 29.16 N 117.11 E
Ch'ingt'ung 269d 25.02 N 121.43 E
Chinguar 152 12.36 S 16.20 E
Chinguetti 150 20.27 N 12.22 W
Chingune 156 20.38 S 34.55 E
Chinhae 98 35.09 N 128.40 E
Chinhae-man C 98 35.01 N 128.34 E
Chin Hills ⋏² 110 22.30 N 93.30 E
Chinhoyi 154 17.22 S 30.12 E
Chinhsien
 → Jinxian 98 39.04 N 121.40 E
Chinhua
 → Jinhua 100 29.07 N 119.39 E
Ch'inhuangtao
 → Qinhuangdao 98 39.56 N 119.36 E
Chīni 120 31.32 N 78.15 E
Chiniak, Cape > 180 57.36 N 152.08 W
Chining
 → Jining, Zhg. 98 35.25 N 116.36 E
Chining
 → Jining, Zhg. 102 40.57 N 113.02 E
Chiniot 123 31.43 N 72.59 E
Chinīt ≈ 110 12.55 N 105.35 E
Chinitna Point > 180 59.43 N 153.02 W
Chiniziua 156 19.00 S 35.09 E
Chinjan 120 30.34 N 67.58 E
Chinju 98 35.11 N 128.05 E
Chinkiang
 → Zhenjiang 106 32.13 N 119.26 E
Chinko ≈ 136 4.50 N 23.53 E
Chinkuashih 100 25.07 N 121.51 E
Chin Lakes ⊜ 182 49.37 N 112.13 W
Chinle 200 36.09 N 109.33 W
Chinle Creek ≈ 200 37.12 N 109.43 W
Chinle Wash V 200 36.54 N 109.45 W
Chinley 262 53.20 N 1.56 W
Chinley Churn ⋀² 262 53.21 N 1.57 W
Chinmen 100 24.27 N 118.21 E
Chinmen Tao I 100 24.27 N 118.23 E
Chinnampo
 → Namp'o 98 38.45 N 125.23 E
Chinnor 42 51.43 N 0.56 W
Chino, Nihon 94 35.59 N 138.09 E
Chino, Ca., U.S. 228 34.00 N 117.41 W
Chino Airport ⊠ 280 33.59 N 117.38 W
Chino Creek ≈ 280 33.53 N 117.38 W
Chino Hills ⋏² 280 33.56 N 117.45 W
Chinon 50 47.10 N 0.15 E
Chinook, Ab., Can. 184 51.27 N 110.56 W
Chinook, Mt., U.S. 202 48.35 N 109.13 W
Chinook, Wa., U.S. 224 46.16 N 123.56 W
Chinook Cove 182 51.14 N 120.10 W
Chino Valley 200 34.45 N 112.27 W
Chinowths Corner 226 36.20 N 119.19 W
Chinpāi 126 23.50 N 87.28 E
Chinquapin 192 34.49 N 77.49 W
Chinsali 154 10.34 S 32.03 E
Chinshan 100 25.13 N 121.38 E
Chinshui 100 24.36 N 120.53 E
Chintāmani 122 13.24 N 78.04 E
Chintembwe 154 13.25 S 33.59 E
Chintheche 154 11.52 S 34.09 E
Chinú 246 9.06 N 75.24 W
Chinunje 154 11.19 S 37.19 E
Chinwangtao
 → Qinhuangdao 98 39.56 N 119.36 E
Chiny 56 49.44 N 5.20 E
Chinyama Litapi 152 13.31 S 22.21 E
Chioco 154 16.25 S 32.50 E
Chioggia 64 45.13 N 12.17 E
Chiomonte 62 45.07 N 6.59 E
Chios
 → Khíos 38 38.22 N 26.08 E
Chios
 → Khíos I 38 38.22 N 26.00 E
Chipamanu (Xipamanu) ≈ 248 10.43 S 67.50 W
Chipao 248 14.15 S 73.57 W
Chipata (Fort Jameson) 154 13.39 S 32.40 E
Chipei Tao I 100 23.45 N 119.37 E
Chipera 154 15.28 S 32.30 E
Chiperone ⋀ 154 16.28 S 35.12 E
Chipili 154 10.44 S 29.04 E
Chiping 98 36.37 N 116.16 E
Chipinge 154 20.12 S 32.38 E
Chip Lake ⊜ 182 53.40 N 115.20 W
Chipley 194 30.46 N 85.32 W
Chiplūn 122 17.32 N 73.31 E
Chipman 186 46.11 N 65.53 W
Chipogolo 154 6.52 S 36.02 E
Chipoka 154 14.00 S 34.31 E
Chipola ≈ 192 30.01 N 85.05 W
Chippawa ⟿⁸ 284a 43.04 N 79.03 W
Chippawa Channel ≈¹ 284a 43.04 N 79.01 W
Chippego Lake ⊜ 212 44.34 N 76.49 W
Chippenham 42 51.28 N 2.07 W
Chipperfield 260 51.42 N 0.29 W
Chippewa ≈, Mi., U.S. 190 43.35 N 84.17 W
Chippewa ≈, Mn., U.S. 198 44.56 N 95.44 W
Chippewa ≈, Wi., U.S. 190 44.25 N 92.10 W
Chippewa, East Branch ≈ 198 45.20 N 95.36 W
Chippewa, East Fork ≈ 190 45.53 N 91.05 W
Chippewa, Lake ⊜ 190 45.56 N 91.13 W
Chippewa Bay C 212 44.27 N 75.47 W
Chippewa Creek ≈ 212 44.27 N 75.46 W
Chippewa Falls 190 44.56 N 91.23 W
Chippewa Lake 214 41.04 N 81.54 W
Chippewanuck Creek ≈ 216 41.07 N 86.12 W
Chipping Campden 42 52.03 N 1.46 W
Chipping Norton 42 51.56 N 1.32 W
Chipping Ongar 42 51.43 N 0.15 E
Chipping Sodbury 42 51.33 N 2.24 W
Chippis 58 46.17 N 7.33 E
Chippokes Plantation State Park ◆ 208 37.08 N 76.44 W
Chipps Island I 282 38.03 N 121.55 W
Chipre
 → Cyprus □¹ 130 35.00 N 33.00 E
Chipstead, Eng., U.K. 260 51.17 N 0.09 E
Chipstead, Eng., U.K. 260 51.18 N 0.10 W
Chipuriro 154 16.39 S 30.42 E
Chiquelequele 152 16.40 S 19.06 E
Chiquián 248 10.09 S 77.11 W
Chiquihuitlán 234 17.59 N 96.48 W
Chiquimula 236 14.48 N 89.33 W
Chiquimula □⁵ 236 14.40 N 89.25 W
Chiquimulilla 236 14.05 N 90.23 W
Chiquinquirá 246 5.37 N 73.50 W
Chiquintirca 248 13.09 S 73.41 W
Chiquita 152 8.38 S 17.05 E
Chiquito ≈ 234 18.29 N 101.07 W
Chiquito Creek ≈ 226 37.20 N 119.20 W
Chira ≈ 246 4.54 S 81.08 W
Chira, Isla I 236 10.06 N 85.09 W
Chirad 272c 19.09 N 73.07 E
Chiradzulu 154 15.42 S 35.10 E
Chirāgh Delhi ⟿⁸ 272a 28.32 N 77.14 E
Chīrāla 122 15.49 N 80.21 E
Chiramba 154 16.55 S 34.39 E
Chirape 156 21.18 S 33.33 E
Chirāwa 120 28.15 N 75.38 E
Chirchik
 → Čirčik 85 41.29 N 69.35 E
Chire (Shire) ≈ 154 17.42 S 35.19 E
Chiredzi 154 21.03 S 31.45 E
Chireno 194 31.30 N 94.21 W
Chirens 62 45.25 N 5.33 E
Chirfa 146 20.57 N 12.21 E
Chīrgaon 124 25.35 N 78.49 E
Chiriaco ≈ 248 5.05 S 78.19 W
Chiricahua Mountains ⋏ 200 31.50 N 109.15 W
Chiricahua National Monument ◆ 200 32.02 N 109.19 W
Chiricahua Peak ⋀ 200 31.52 N 109.20 W
Chiriguaná 246 9.22 N 73.36 W
Chirikof Island I 180 55.50 N 155.35 W
Chirilagua 236 13.13 N 88.08 W
Chirinos 248 5.16 S 78.52 W
Chiriquí 236 8.24 N 82.19 W
Chiriquí □⁴ 236 8.30 N 82.00 W
Chiriquí, Golfo de C 246 8.00 N 82.20 W
Chiriquí, Laguna de C 236 9.03 N 82.00 W
Chiriquí Grande 236 8.57 N 82.07 W
Chiriquí Viejo ≈ 236 8.20 N 82.41 W
Chirk 42 52.56 N 3.03 W
Chirki 126 24.03 N 86.09 E
Chirle 272c 18.56 N 73.02 E
Chirmiri 124 23.12 N 82.21 E
Chirnside 46 55.48 N 2.13 W
Chiromo 154 16.33 S 35.08 E
Chirovo 76 58.56 N 33.24 E
Chirripó ≈ 236 10.41 N 83.41 W
Chirripó, Cerro ⋀ 236 9.29 N 83.30 W
Chirripó, Parque Nacional ◆ 236 9.30 N 83.30 W
Chirsa 84 41.31 N 46.06 E
Chirundu 154 15.59 S 28.54 E
Chirvosti 265a 59.57 N 30.37 E
Chiryū 94 35.00 N 137.02 E
Chisago City 190 45.22 N 92.53 W
Chisamba 154 14.58 S 28.23 E
Chisana 180 62.09 N 142.10 W
Chisasibi 176 53.50 N 79.00 W
Chiscas 246 6.33 N 72.29 W
Chisec 236 15.49 N 90.17 W
Chiseldon 42 51.31 N 1.44 W
Chisenga 154 9.56 S 33.26 E
Chisep'o 98 34.50 N 128.42 E
Ch'ishan 100 22.53 N 120.28 E
Chishanji 98 36.56 N 122.23 E
Chishi 100 27.42 N 117.58 E
Chishisi 100 25.32 N 113.11 E
Chisholm, Al., U.S. 194 32.25 N 86.15 W
Chisholm, Me., U.S. 188 44.28 N 70.12 W
Chisholm, Mn., U.S. 190 47.29 N 92.53 W
Chisholm, Tx., U.S. 222 32.51 N 96.22 W
Chisholm Mills 182 54.55 N 114.08 W
Chishtiān Mandi 123 29.48 N 72.52 E
Chishui 102 28.29 N 105.38 E
Chishui ≈, Zhg. 102 28.53 N 105.48 E
Chishui ≈, Zhg. 107 28.49 N 105.50 E
Chishuihe 102 27.50 N 105.32 E
Chišig-Öndör 88 48.19 N 103.25 E
Chisimaio
 → Kismaayo 144 0.22 N 42.32 E
Chişinău
 → Kišin'ov 78 47.00 N 28.50 E
Chişineu-Criş 38 46.31 N 21.31 E
Chislaviči 76 54.11 N 32.10 E
Chislehurst ⟿⁸ 260 51.25 N 0.04 E
Chisone ≈ 62 44.49 N 7.25 E
Chisone, Valle del V 62 45.01 N 7.07 E
Chisos Mountains ⋏ 196 29.15 N 103.20 W
Chisseaux 50 47.20 N 1.05 E
Chissengue 152 9.14 S 20.42 E
Chissilo 152 13.34 S 16.30 E
Chistochina 180 62.34 N 144.40 W
Chistopol
 → Čistopol' 80 55.21 N 50.37 E
Chiswellgreen 260 51.44 N 0.22 W
Chiswick ⟿⁸ 260 51.29 N 0.16 W
Chita, Bol. 248 20.06 S 66.57 W
Chita, Col. 246 6.11 N 72.28 W
Chita, Nihon 94 35.00 N 136.51 E
Chita
 → Čita 88 52.03 N 113.30 E
Chitado 152 17.20 S 13.54 E
Chitagá 246 7.09 N 72.40 W
Chita-hantō >¹ 94 34.50 N 136.53 E
Chitambo 154 12.55 S 30.39 E
Chitanda ≈ 152 16.01 S 15.12 E
Chitarda 126 21.50 N 86.57 E
Chitata 152 13.47 S 15.43 E
Chitato 152 7.20 S 20.47 E
Chita-wan C 94 34.47 N 136.58 E
Chitek ≈ 184 54.06 N 108.16 W
Chitek Lake ⊜, Mb., Can. 184 52.26 N 99.25 W
Chitek Lake ⊜, Sk., Can. 184 53.44 N 107.47 W
Chitembo 152 13.34 S 16.40 E
Chitina 180 61.31 N 144.27 W
Chitina ≈ 180 61.30 N 144.28 W
Chitipa 154 9.43 S 33.16 E
Chitokoloki 152 13.50 S 23.13 E
Chitose 92a 42.49 N 141.39 E
Chitose-chūtonchi, Rikujō-jieitai- ■ 92a 42.46 N 141.40 E
Chitou Shan I 100 27.40 N 120.50 E
Chitra ≈¹ 126 22.53 N 89.40 E
Chitradurga 122 14.14 N 76.24 E
Chitrakūt Dham 124 25.11 N 80.52 E
Chitrāl 123 35.51 N 71.47 E
Chitrasāli 272b 22.52 N 88.09 E
Chitrāvati ≈ 122 14.48 N 78.14 E
Chitré 236 7.58 N 80.26 W
Chittagong 120 22.20 N 91.50 E
Chittagong □⁵ 120 23.00 N 91.00 E
Chīttāpur 122 17.07 N 77.05 E
Chittaranjan 126 23.52 N 86.52 E
Chittaurgarh 120 24.53 N 74.38 E
Chittenango 210 43.02 N 75.52 W
Chittenango Creek ≈ 210 43.11 N 76.00 W
Chittenango Falls 210 42.59 N 75.50 W
Chittering 162 31.29 S 116.06 E
Chittoor 122 13.12 N 79.07 E
Chittūr 122 10.42 N 76.45 E
Chitu, Ityo. 144 8.36 N 37.59 E
Ch'itu, T'aiwan 269d 25.06 N 121.43 E
Chitungwiza 154 17.45 S 31.16 E
Chiuchiang
 → Jiujiang 100 29.44 N 115.59 E
Chíuchíu 252 22.21 S 68.39 W
Chiuduno 62 45.40 N 9.51 E
Chiumbe 152 12.29 S 16.08 E
Chiumbe ≈ 152 7.00 S 21.12 E
Chiúme 152 15.03 S 21.14 E
Chiuppano 64 45.46 N 11.28 E
Chiuro 64 46.10 N 9.59 E
Chiusa (Klausen) 64 46.38 N 11.34 E
Chiusa di Pesio 62 44.19 N 7.40 E
Chiusa di San Michele 62 45.06 N 7.19 E
Chiusaforte 64 46.24 N 13.18 E
Chiusa Sclafani 70 37.41 N 13.16 E
Chiusella ≈ 62 45.24 N 7.55 E
Chiusi 66 43.01 N 11.57 E
Chiusi, Lago di ⊜ 66 43.03 N 11.58 E
Chiúta 154 15.34 S 33.17 E
Chiuta, Lake ⊜ 154 14.55 S 35.50 E
Chiv 84 41.46 N 47.54 E
Chiva 72 41.24 N 60.22 E
Chivacoa 246 10.10 N 68.54 W
Chivasso 62 45.11 N 7.53 E
Chivato, Punta > 232 27.05 N 111.59 W
Chivay 248 15.40 S 71.35 W
Chivhu 154 19.01 S 30.53 E
Chivilcoy 252 34.53 S 60.01 W
Chivirira Falls ⌊ 154 21.14 S 32.20 E
Chiwanda 154 11.22 S 34.54 E
Chiwawa ≈ 224 47.47 N 120.40 W
Chixi 100 28.22 N 116.22 E
Chixoy (Salinas) ≈ 232 16.28 N 90.33 W
Chixoy, Embalse ⊜¹ 236 15.15 N 90.30 W
Chiyoda, Nihon 94 36.12 N 139.26 E
Chiyoda, Nihon 94 36.11 N 140.14 E
Chiyoda, Nihon 96 34.41 N 132.32 E
Chiyoda ⟿⁸ 268 35.41 N 139.44 E
Chizarira National Park ◆ 154 17.45 S 28.00 E
Chizhen 100 31.55 N 118.12 E
Chizizhen 100 32.22 N 115.11 E
Chizu 96 35.16 N 134.14 E
Chjargas 88 49.32 N 93.48 E
Chjargas nuur ⊜ 88 49.12 N 93.24 E
Chkalov
 → Orenburg 86 51.54 N 55.06 E
Chlebnikovo, Ross. 80 56.38 N 49.56 E
Chlebnikovo, Ross. 265b 55.58 N 37.31 E
Chlebodarnyj 80 46.41 N 40.50 E
Chlebodarovka 83 47.29 N 37.23 E
Chlevnoje 76 52.12 N 39.05 E
Chloride 200 35.24 N 114.11 W
Chlum 60 48.52 N 13.55 E
Chlum ⋀ 61 48.42 N 14.04 E
Chmelevicy 80 57.45 N 46.22 E
Chmelevo 82 56.09 N 39.08 E
Chmelevoje 78 48.34 N 31.24 E
Chmelita 76 55.25 N 33.53 E
Chmel'nickij 78 49.25 N 27.00 E
Chmel'nickij □⁴ 78 49.30 N 27.00 E
Chmel'nik 78 49.33 N 27.57 E
Chmel'niki, Ross. 82 56.52 N 38.13 E
Chmel'niki, Ross. 82 56.53 N 38.39 E
Chmielnik 30 50.37 N 20.46 E
Chmost' ≈ 76 54.45 N 32.34 E
Choa Chu Kang 271c 1.22 N 103.41 E
Choāli 272b 22.24 N 88.24 E
Chŏâm Khsant 110 14.13 N 104.56 E
Choba 154 2.26 N 38.03 E
Chobe □⁵ 156 18.30 S 25.00 E
Chobe ≈ 156 17.50 S 25.05 E
Chobeju 24 64.53 N 60.10 E
Chobe National Park ◆ 156 18.45 S 24.15 E
Chobham 260 51.21 N 0.36 W
Chobham Common ◆ 260 51.23 N 0.37 W
Chobi 84 42.21 N 41.53 E
Chocamán 234 18.59 N 97.01 W
Choccolocco Creek ≈ 194 33.33 N 86.11 W
Choceň 30 50.00 N 16.13 E
Chocenice 60 49.33 N 13.31 E
Chochis, Cerro ⋀ 248 18.04 S 60.03 W
Choch'iwŏn 98 36.37 N 127.18 E
Chochloma 80 56.58 N 43.54 E
Chöchmor't 88 47.21 N 94.33 E
Chochol'skij 78 51.34 N 38.45 E
Cho Chu 110 21.54 N 105.39 E
Chocianów 30 51.25 N 15.55 E
Chociwel 30 53.28 N 15.19 E
Chocó □⁵ 246 6.00 N 77.00 W
Chocolate Bay C 222 29.11 N 95.09 W
Chocolate Bayou ≈ 222 29.13 N 95.13 W
Chocolate Mountains ⋏ 204 33.20 N 115.15 W
Chocontá 246 5.09 N 73.41 W
Chocope 248 7.47 S 79.13 W
Choctawhatchee, East Fork ≈ 194 31.21 N 85.33 W
Choctawhatchee, West Fork ≈ 194 31.21 N 85.33 W
Choctawhatchee Bay C 194 30.25 N 86.21 W
Choctaw Lake ⊜¹ 218 39.58 N 83.29 W
Chodarus 88 52.36 N 99.19 E
Chodavaram 122 17.50 N 82.57 E
Chodecz 30 52.24 N 19.01 E
Ch'o-do I, C.M.I.K. 98 38.32 N 124.50 E
Ch'o-do I, Taehan 98 34.14 N 127.15 E
Chodoi 114 2.50 N 101.27 E
Chodorov 78 49.24 N 24.17 E
Chodosy 76 53.56 N 31.29 E
Chodov 54 50.11 N 12.43 E
Chodovaja Griva 80 57.08 N 50.16 E
Chodovaricha 24 68.57 N 53.40 E
Chodz' ≈ 84 44.43 N 40.45 E
Chodžaimetk 85 39.37 N 69.14 E
Chodžakala 128 38.43 N 56.20 E
Chodžejli 72 42.48 N 59.25 E
Chodzież 30 52.59 N 16.56 E
Choele-Choel 252 39.16 S 65.41 W
Chofombo 154 14.35 S 31.50 E
Chōfu 94 35.39 N 139.33 E
Chofu Airport ⊠ 268 35.40 N 139.32 E
Chogo Lungma Glacier ⊓ 123 35.52 N 75.19 E
Chogot 88 53.15 N 105.52 E
Choiceland 184 53.27 N 104.25 W
Choichuff, Laga ≈ 154 1.34 N 39.24 E
Choire, Loch ⊜ 46 58.13 N 4.21 W
Choisel 261 48.41 N 2.01 E
Choiseul 241f 13.47 N 61.03 W
Choiseul I 175e 7.05 S 157.00 E
Choiseul Sound ⌒ 254 51.57 S 58.35 W
Choisy 58 45.59 N 6.03 E
Choisy-le-Roi 261 48.46 N 2.25 E
Choix 232 26.43 N 108.17 W
Chojna 30 52.58 N 14.28 E
Chojnice 30 53.42 N 17.34 E
Chojniki 78 51.53 N 29.56 E
Chojnów 30 51.17 N 15.56 E
Chōkai-san ⋀ 92 39.06 N 140.03 E
Choke ⋏ 144 10.45 N 37.35 E
Choke Canyon Lake ⊜¹ 196 28.30 N 98.20 W
Chokio 198 45.34 N 96.10 W
Chokoloskee 220 25.48 N 81.21 W
Chokwé 156 24.36 S 33.00 E
Cholame 226 35.43 N 120.17 W
Cholame Creek ≈ 226 35.39 N 120.22 W
Cholame Hills ⋏² 226 35.45 N 120.30 W
Cholbon 88 51.53 N 116.15 E
Choldarkipčak 85 39.51 N 68.52 E
Cholet 32 47.04 N 0.53 W
Cholila 254 42.31 S 71.27 W
Chŏlla Namdo □⁴ 98 34.45 N 127.00 E
Chŏlla Pukdo □⁴ 98 35.45 N 127.15 E
Cholm 76 57.09 N 31.11 E
Cholmeč', Bela. 78 52.09 N 30.37 E
Cholmec, Ross. 76 56.21 N 33.21 E
Cholmogorovka 86 44.25 N 78.31 E
Cholmogorskaja 24 63.49 N 40.39 E
Cholmogory 24 64.15 N 41.40 E
Cholmsk 89 47.03 N 142.03 E
Cholmskij 78 44.52 N 38.24 E
Cholmy, Ross. 82 54.56 N 38.33 E
Cholmy, Ukr. 78 51.52 N 32.36 E
Cholm-Žirkovskij 76 55.31 N 33.29 E
Cholodnaja Balka 83 48.02 N 38.04 E
Choloj ≈ 88 53.12 N 112.47 E
Choloma 236 15.34 N 87.56 W
Chölönbujr 88 47.55 N 112.57 E
Cholopeniči 76 54.31 N 28.58 E
Ch'ŏlsan 98 39.46 N 124.40 E
Cholsey 42 51.34 N 1.10 W
Choltobino 82 54.11 N 38.28 E
Choltoson 88 50.20 N 103.20 E
Choluj, Ross. 80 56.34 N 41.53 E
Choluj, Ross. 80 56.04 N 42.08 E
Cholula [de Rivadabia] 234 19.04 N 98.18 W
Choluteca 236 13.18 N 87.12 W
Choluteca □⁵ 236 13.20 N 87.10 W
Choluteca ≈ 236 13.07 N 87.19 W
Choma 154 16.48 S 26.59 E
Chomedey ⟿⁸ 275a 45.32 N 73.44 W
Chomen Swamp ≡ 144 9.25 N 37.20 E
Chomérac 62 44.42 N 4.39 E
Chomičev 80 48.11 N 45.01 E
Chomiomo ⋀ 124 28.01 N 88.31 E
Cho Moi, Viet 110 10.33 N 105.24 E
Cho Moi, Viet 269c 10.51 N 106.38 E
Chomo Lhāri ⋀ 124 27.50 N 89.15 E
Chom Thong 110 18.25 N 98.41 E
Chomūm 120 27.10 N 75.44 E
Chomutec 78 50.06 N 33.44 E
Chomutov 54 50.28 N 13.26 E
Chomutovka 78 51.56 N 34.33 E
Chomutovka ≈ 54 50.11 N 13.37 E
Chomutovo, Ross. 76 52.51 N 37.27 E
Chomutovo, Ross. 88 52.28 N 104.25 E
Chomutovskaja 83 47.03 N 40.04 E
Chomutovskaja Step', zapovednik ◆ 83 47.17 N 38.11 E
Chōnan, Nihon 94 35.24 N 140.14 E
Ch'ŏnan, Taehan 98 36.48 N 127.09 E
Chon'atino 82 55.11 N 38.07 E
Chon Buri 110 13.22 N 100.59 E
Chonchi 254 42.38 S 73.47 W
Choncholoj 88 51.08 N 108.14 E
Chon Daen 110 16.11 N 100.51 E
Chone 246 0.41 S 80.06 W
Chone ≈ 246 0.35 S 80.25 W
Chong'an 100 27.45 N 118.02 E
Ch'ŏngch'ŏn-gang ≈ 98 39.35 N 125.28 E
Ch'ŏngdan 98 37.58 N 125.56 E
Chongde 106 30.32 N 120.26 E
Ch'ŏngdo 98 35.38 N 128.43 E
Chonggu 106 31.12 N 121.10 E
Ch'ŏngha 98 36.13 N 129.20 E
Ch'onghak-ni 271b 37.43 N 127.05 E
Chonghe 89 44.43 N 127.45 E
Ch'ŏngjin 98 41.47 N 129.50 E
Chŏngju, C.M.I.K. 98 39.41 N 125.13 E
Ch'ŏngju, Taehan 98 36.39 N 127.31 E
Chŏng Kal 110 13.57 N 103.35 E
Chongkanzhen 107 30.09 N 105.37 E
Chongli (Xiwanzi) 98 40.54 N 115.16 E
Chongming 106 31.37 N 121.24 E
Chongming Dao I 106 31.36 N 121.33 E
Chongoene 156 25.00 S 33.47 E
Chongor 102 45.59 N 112.45 E
Chongos Bajo 248 12.07 S 75.16 W
Chongoyape 248 6.39 S 79.24 W
Chong Pang 271c 1.26 N 103.50 E
Chŏngp'yŏng-chŏsuji ⊜¹ 98 37.40 N 127.30 E
Chongqing, Zhg. 107 30.39 N 103.41 E
Chongqing (Chungking), Zhg. 107 29.34 N 106.35 E
Chongren, Zhg. 100 29.37 N 120.43 E
Chongren, Zhg. 100 27.46 N 116.01 E
Chongru 100 27.01 N 120.10 E
Ch'ŏngsan 98 36.22 N 127.46 E
Ch'ŏngsan-do I 98 34.11 N 126.54 E
Chongshi 100 25.24 N 115.28 E
Chŏngsŏn 98 37.22 N 128.38 E
Ch'ŏngsong 98 41.47 N 129.48 E
Chŏngŭp 98 35.36 N 126.51 E
Chongwe ≈ 154 15.43 S 29.20 E
Chongwu 100 24.53 N 118.55 E
Chongxi 98 42.07 N 128.59 E
Chongxin 102 35.13 N 107.29 E
Ch'ŏngyang, Taehan 98 36.27 N 126.48 E
Chongyang, Zhg. 100 29.33 N 114.00 E
Chongyang ≈ 100 27.18 N 118.08 E
Chongyi 100 25.44 N 114.18 E
Chongzuo 102 22.21 N 107.26 E
Choni 84 42.20 N 42.25 E
Chŏnju 98 35.49 N 127.08 E
Chonkham 120 27.48 N 96.02 E
Ch'ŏnma 98 40.03 N 125.01 E
Chonobad 85 40.48 N 72.58 E
Chonos, Archipiélago de los II 254 45.00 S 74.00 W
Ch'ŏnsu-ri 98 41.43 N 128.45 E
Chontaleña, Cordillera ⋏ 236 11.50 N 84.50 W
Chontales □⁵ 236 12.05 N 85.10 W
Chon Thanh 110 11.24 N 106.36 E
Chŏnŭi 98 36.42 N 127.11 E
Chonuu 74 66.27 N 143.06 E
Chonzie, Ben ⋀ 46 56.27 N 3.59 W
Cho Oyu
 → Chopu ⋀ 124 28.06 N 86.39 E
Chopda 120 21.15 N 75.18 E
Cho Phuoc Hai 110 10.26 N 107.18 E
Chopim ≈ 252 25.35 S 53.05 W
Chopinzinho 252 25.51 S 52.30 W
Chopon 124 24.31 N 83.02 E
Chop'or ≈ 80 49.36 N 42.19 E
Chop'orskij zapovednik ⟿⁴ 80 51.15 N 41.48 E
Choptank ≈ 208 38.38 N 76.13 W
Chopu ⋀ 124 28.06 N 86.39 E
Chopwell 44 54.55 N 1.49 W
Chor 89 47.53 N 134.58 E
Chor ≈ 89 47.48 N 134.43 E
Chora Saādatpur 272a 28.36 N 77.21 E
Chordil sar'dag ⋏ 88 50.50 N 99.40 E
Chorejver 24 67.25 N 58.03 E
Chorges 62 44.33 N 6.17 E
Chorin ⊥ 54 52.54 N 13.52 E
Chorina ≈ 83 49.23 N 38.13 E
Chorinsk 88 52.10 N 109.46 E
Chorley 44 53.39 N 2.39 W
Chorley □⁸ 262 53.38 N 2.38 W
Chorleywood 260 51.39 N 0.31 W
Chorlovo 82 55.20 N 38.49 E
Chorlton-cum-Hardy ⟿⁸ 262 53.27 N 2.17 W
Chorog 120 37.31 N 71.33 E
Chorol', Ross. 89 44.25 N 132.04 E
Chorol, Ukr. 78 49.47 N 33.17 E
Chorol ≈ 78 49.28 N 33.47 E
Chorolque, Cerro ⋀ 248 20.56 S 66.01 W
Choros, Isla I 252 29.16 S 71.33 W
Chorošovo 82 55.08 N 38.47 E
Chorošovo ⟿⁸ 265b 55.47 N 37.28 E
Chorostkov 78 49.13 N 25.55 E
Choroszcz 30 53.09 N 22.59 E
Chorreras 232 28.50 N 105.18 W
Chorrillos 286d 12.10 S 77.02 W
Chorrochó 250 8.59 S 39.06 W
Chorro Creek ≈ 226 35.20 N 120.50 W
Chort'ak, gora ⋀ 88 53.15 N 110.45 E
Ch'ŏrwŏn 98 38.16 N 127.12 E
Chorzele 30 53.16 N 20.55 E
Ch'osan 98 40.50 N 125.47 E
Chosanch'am 98 40.22 N 126.11 E
Chosedachard 24 67.02 N 59.22 E
Chosen 220 26.42 N 80.41 W
Chošeutovo 80 47.02 N 47.50 E
Chōshi 94 35.44 N 140.50 E
Choshi-ōhashi ⟿⁵ 94 35.44 N 140.50 E
Chōshi-zuka-kofun ⊥ 94 34.42 N 137.50 E
Choshui ≈ 100 24.03 N 120.24 E
Chosica 248 11.54 S 76.42 W
Chos Malal 252 37.23 S 70.16 W
Chosŏn Minjujuŭi In'min Konghwaguk
 → Korea, North □¹ 98 40.00 N 127.00 E
Chosrech 84 41.59 N 47.18 E
Chosta 84 43.33 N 39.53 E
Choszczno 30 53.10 N 15.26 E
Chota 248 6.33 S 78.39 W
Chotanāgpur Plateau ⋏¹ 124 23.30 N 84.30 E
Chotča ≈ 82 56.54 N 37.35 E
Choteau 202 47.48 N 112.10 W
Choteau Creek ≈ 198 42.51 N 98.09 W
Chotěboř 30 49.43 N 15.40 E
Choten' 78 51.07 N 34.46 E
Chotěšov, Česko. 60 49.39 N 13.12 E
Chotešov, Ukr. 78 51.43 N 24.47 E
Chotila 120 22.25 N 71.11 E
Chotilovo 76 57.44 N 34.05 E
Chotimsk 76 53.26 N 32.35 E
Chotin 78 48.29 N 26.30 E
Chotisino 82 54.24 N 36.33 E
Chot'kovo, Ross. 76 52.56 N 35.23 E
Chot'kovo, Ross. 76 53.46 N 35.14 E
Chot'kovo, Ross. 82 56.15 N 38.00 E
Chotovn'a 76 53.17 N 30.32 E
Chotuš' 82 54.32 N 37.44 E
Chotynec 76 53.08 N 35.24 E
Chotyniči 76 52.38 N 26.18 E
Chouchiak'ou
 → Shangshui 100 33.33 N 114.34 E
Chouk'ou
 → Shangshui 100 33.33 N 114.34 E
Choûm 148 21.18 N 13.01 W
Chouteau 196 36.11 N 95.20 W
Chovaling 85 38.21 N 69.58 E
Chovd, Mong. 86 49.16 N 90.55 E
Chovd, Mong. 86 48.08 N 91.23 E
Chovd, Mong. 86 48.01 N 91.38 E
Chovd, Mong. 102 44.42 N 102.24 E
Chovd □⁴ 86 48.00 N 91.30 E
Chovd ≈ 90 48.06 N 92.11 E
Chövsgöl 102 43.36 N 109.39 E
Chövsgöl □⁴ 88 50.00 N 100.00 E
Chövsgöl nuur ⊜ 88 51.00 N 100.30 E
Chovu-Aksy 88 51.11 N 93.53 E
Chowan ≈ 192 36.00 N 76.40 W
Chowchilla 226 37.07 N 120.15 W
Chowchilla ≈ 226 37.07 N 120.32 W
Chowchilla, East Fork ≈ 226 37.20 N 119.50 W
Chowchilla, West Fork ≈ 226 37.20 N 119.50 W
Chowkay 123 34.41 N 70.56 E
Chown, Mount ⋀ 182 53.24 N 119.22 W
Ch'owŏn-ni 98 39.40 N 127.17 E
Choya 252 28.30 S 64.52 W
Choyak-to I 98 34.22 N 126.54 E
Chrapun' 78 51.42 N 27.29 E
Chr'aščevka 80 53.48 N 49.06 E
Chrást 60 49.48 N 13.29 E
Chrebtovo 82 56.35 N 38.16 E
Chrenovoje 80 51.07 N 40.17 E
Chreščatij 83 49.37 N 39.42 E
Chřibská 54 50.50 N 14.29 E
Chříč 60 49.57 N 13.39 E
Chriesman 222 30.36 N 96.46 W
Chrisman 194 39.48 N 87.40 W
Chrissiesmeer 158 26.16 S 30.13 E
Chrissiesmeer ⊜ 158 26.19 S 30.13 E
Christanshåb (Qasigiannguit) 176 68.50 N 51.12 W
Christchurch, N.Z. 172 43.32 S 172.38 E
Christchurch, Eng., U.K. 42 50.44 N 1.45 W
Christ Church Cathedral ⋓¹ 273a 6.27 N 3.23 E
Christian □⁶ 219 39.33 N 89.18 W
Christian ≈ 180 66.36 N 145.49 W
Christian, Cape > 176 70.31 N 68.18 W
Christian, Point > 174e 25.04 S 130.07 W
Christiana, Jam. 241q 18.10 N 77.29 W
Christiana, S. Afr. 158 27.52 S 25.08 E
Christiana, De., U.S. 285 39.39 N 75.39 W
Christiana, Pa., U.S. 208 39.57 N 75.59 W
Christiana Creek ≈ 216 41.41 N 85.59 W
Christianburg 218 38.17 N 85.06 W
Christian Channel ⌒ 212 44.47 N 80.08 W
Christian Island I 212 44.50 N 80.13 W
Christian Island Indian Reserve ⟿⁴ 212 44.50 N 80.10 W
Christiansburg, Oh., U.S. 218 40.03 N 84.01 W
Christiansburg, Va., U.S. 192 37.07 N 80.24 W
Christiansfeld 41 55.21 N 9.29 E
Christiansø I 26 55.19 N 15.12 E
Christian Sound ⌒ 180 55.56 N 134.40 W
Christiansted 241n 17.45 N 64.42 W
Christie, Mount ⋀ 180 63.01 N 129.40 W
Christie, Mount ⋀² 216 42.53 N 83.20 W
Christie Bay C 176 62.32 N 111.10 W
Christie Lake ⊜, Mb., Can. 184 56.54 N 96.56 W

Symbols in the index entries represent the broad categories identified in the key at the right. Symbols with superior numbers (⋏¹) identify subcategories (see complete key on page *I · 1)*.

Symbole im Register stellen die rechts im Schlüssel erklärten Kategorien dar. Symbole mit hochgestellten Ziffern (⋏¹) bezeichnen Unterabteilungen einer Kategorie (vgl. vollständiger Schlüssel auf Seite *I · 1)*.

Los símbolos incluídos en el texto del índice representan las grandes categorias identificadas con la clave a la derecha. Los símbolos con numeros en su parte superior (⋏¹) identifican las subcategorías (véase la clave completa en la página *I · 1)*.

Les symboles de l'index représentent les catégories indiquées dans la légende à droite. Les symboles suivis d'un indice (⋏¹) représentent des sous-catégories (voir légende complète à la page *I · 1)*.

Os símbolos incluídos no texto do índice representam as grandes categorias identificadas com a chave à direita. Os símbolos com números em sua parte superior (⋏¹) identificam as subcategorias (veja-se a chave completa à página *I · 1)*.

	English	Deutsch	Español	Français	Português
⋀	Mountain	Berg	Montaña	Montagne	Montanha
⋏	Mountains	Gebirge	Montañas	Montagnes	Montanhas
)(	Pass	Paß	Paso	Col	Passo
V	Valley, Canyon	Tal, Cañon	Valle, Cañón	Vallée, Canyon	Vale, Canhão
≡	Plain	Ebene	Llano	Plaine	Planície
>	Cape	Kap	Cabo	Cap	Cabo
I	Island	Insel	Isla	Île	Ilha
II	Islands	Inseln	Islas	Îles	Ilhas
≐	Other Topographic Features	Andere Topographische Objekte	Otros Elementos Topográficos	Autres données topographiques	Outros acidentes topográficos

ESPAÑOL Nombre	Página	Lat.°′	Long.°′ W = Oeste
FRANÇAIS Nom	Page	Lat.°′	Long.°′ W = Ouest
PORTUGUÊS Nome	Página	Lat.°′	Long.°′ W = Oeste

Christie Lake ⊜, On., Can.	212	44.48 N	76.26 W
Christina ≃, Ab., Can.	184	56.40 N	111.03 W
Christina ≃, De., U.S.	285	39.43 N	75.31 W
Christina Lake ⊜, Ab., Can.	182	55.38 N	110.55 W
Christina Lake ⊜, B.C., Can.	182	49.05 N	118.14 W
Christinovka	78	48.49 N	29.58 E
Christišče	83	48.55 N	37.30 E
Christmas	220	28.32 N	81.01 W
Christmas Bay ⊂	222	29.03 N	95.11 W
Christmas Creek	162	18.53 S	125.55 E
Christmas Creek ≃	162	18.29 S	125.23 E
Christmas Island ▫², Oc.	108	10.30 S	105.40 E
Christmas Island ▫², Oc.	112	10.30 S	105.40 E
Christmas Island → Kiritimati I¹	174o	1.52 N	157.20 W
Christmas Mountain ∧	180	64.34 N	160.34 W
Christmas Ridge ✣³	14	5.00 N	160.00 W
Christoforovka	78	47.59 N	33.05 E
Christoforovo	24	60.53 N	47.13 E
Christ of the Andes → Cristo Redentor ⊥	252	32.50 S	70.05 W
Christoph Columbus-Spitze → Cristóbal Colón, Pico ∧	246	10.50 N	73.41 W
Christopher	194	37.58 N	89.03 W
Christopher, Lake ⊜	162	24.49 S	127.42 E
Christoval	196	31.12 N	100.30 W
Chroma ≃	74	71.36 N	144.49 E
Chromtau	86	50.17 N	58.27 E
Chrudim	30	49.57 N	15.48 E
Chrustal'nyj	89	44.24 N	135.06 E
Chrzanów	30	50.09 N	19.24 E
Chu (Xam) ≃, Asia	110	19.53 N	105.45 E
Chu ≃, Zhg.	100	32.08 N	118.43 E
Chu ≃, Zhg.	106	32.15 N	119.03 E
Chuādanga	124	23.38 N	88.51 E
Chualar	226	36.34 N	121.31 W
Chuanbu	106	31.17 N	119.49 E
Chuanchang ≃	106	33.46 N	119.51 E
Chuanergu	105	39.20 N	117.43 E
Chuan'gang	106	31.57 N	120.30 E
Chuangjiapuzi	104	40.50 N	124.06 E
Chuanliao	100	28.17 N	120.13 E
Chuansha	106	31.12 N	121.42 E
Chuanshan	100	29.53 N	121.57 E
Chuanxindian	104	41.25 N	120.30 E
Chuanyao Gang ⊂	106	32.12 N	121.25 E
Chuathbaluk	180	61.40 N	159.15 W
Chubbuck	202	42.55 N	112.27 W
Chūbu-Sangaku-kokuritsu-kōen ♦	94	36.30 N	137.41 E
Chubut ▫⁴	254	44.00 S	69.00 W
Chubut ≃	254	43.20 S	65.03 W
Ch'üchiang → Shaoguan	100	24.50 N	113.37 E
Chuchi Lake ⊜	182	55.10 N	124.33 W
Chuchou → Zhuzhou	100	27.50 N	113.09 E
Chuchra	78	50.13 N	34.49 E
Chu Chua	182	51.21 N	120.10 W
Chuchuwayha Indian Reserve ✦⁴	182	49.21 N	120.06 W
Chuckatuck	208	36.52 N	76.35 W
Chučni	84	41.57 N	47.55 E
Chucuito	248	15.53 S	69.53 W
Chucun	100	33.04 N	116.32 E
Chucunaque ≃	246	8.09 N	77.44 W
Chudan ≃	88	52.08 N	109.40 E
Chudanskij chrebet ↗	88	52.00 N	110.00 E
Chudat	84	41.38 N	48.42 E
Chudeč	60	49.58 N	13.05 E
Chudleigh	42	50.36 N	3.38 W
Chudojelan'	88	54.42 N	99.37 E
Chudžand (Leninabad)	85	40.17 N	69.37 E
Chudžand ▫⁴	85	39.15 N	69.30 E
Chudzirt	86	47.05 N	91.10 E
Chuen Lung	271d	22.24 N	114.06 E
Chugach Islands II	180	59.06 N	151.42 W
Chugach Mountains ↗	180	61.00 N	145.00 W
Chuginadak Island I	180	52.49 N	169.50 W
Chūgoku-sanchi ↗	96	34.58 N	132.57 E
Chugwater	200	41.45 N	104.49 W
Chugwater Creek ≃	198	42.07 N	104.51 W
Chugyn-ri	271b	37.39 N	126.50 E
Chūhar Kāna	123	31.45 N	73.48 E
Chuhe	100	34.03 N	113.35 E
Chuhuichupa	232	29.38 N	108.22 W
Chui	252	33.41 S	53.27 W
Chuius Mountain ∧	182	54.51 N	124.40 W
Chukai	114	4.15 N	103.25 E
Chukchi Sea ⊤²	16	69.00 N	171.00 W
Chuke Hu ⊜	120	31.40 N	88.00 E
Chukou	100	25.44 N	113.22 E
Chulalongkorn University ✪²	269a	13.44 N	100.33 E
Chula Vista	228	32.38 N	117.05 W
Chuld	102	45.04 N	105.35 E
Chulga ≃	24	64.20 N	61.00 E
Chullora	274a	33.54 S	151.04 E
Chulmleigh	42	50.55 N	3.52 W
Chulo	84	41.41 N	42.18 E
Chulp'o	98	35.37 N	126.40 E
Chulucanas	248	5.06 S	80.10 W
Chulumani	248	16.24 S	67.31 W
Chuluota	220	28.38 N	81.10 W
Chuma	248	15.24 S	68.56 W
Chumalag	84	43.14 N	44.28 E
Chumbicha	252	28.52 S	66.14 W
Chummi, ozero ⊜	89	50.18 N	137.17 E
Chum Phae	110	16.32 N	102.06 E
Chumphon	110	10.30 N	99.10 E
Chumphon Buri	110	15.21 N	103.24 E
Chumpi	248	15.06 S	73.46 W
Chum Saeng	110	15.54 N	100.19 E
Chumunjin	98	37.54 N	128.49 E
Chunal	262	53.25 N	1.57 W
Chunan, T'aiwan	100	24.41 N	120.52 E
Chun'an, Zhg.	100	29.35 N	118.58 E
Chunār	124	25.08 N	82.54 E
Chuncheon → Ch'unch'ŏn	98	37.52 N	127.43 E
Chunchi, Ec.	246	2.17 S	78.55 W
Chunchi, Zhg.	100	27.22 N	119.20 E
Ch'unch'ŏn	98	37.52 N	127.43 E
Chunchula	194	30.55 N	88.12 W
Chŭnd	123	31.26 N	72.16 E
Chung-ang University ✪²	271b	37.30 N	126.58 E
Chungari ≃	89	50.04 N	136.55 E
Ch'ungch'ŏng Namdo ▫⁴	98	36.30 N	127.00 E
Ch'ungch'ŏng Pukdo ▫⁴	98	36.45 N	128.00 E
Chunggang-ni	98	40.52 N	127.20 E
Chung Hau	271d	22.16 N	114.00 E
Chunghom	269d	25.00 N	121.30 E
Chung Hsing Bridge ✦⁵	269d	25.03 N	121.29 E
Chunghwa	98	38.52 N	125.47 E
Ch'ungju	98	36.58 N	127.58 E
Chungking → Chongqing	107	29.34 N	106.35 E
Chungli	100	24.57 N	121.13 E
Chungliao	100	23.52 N	120.46 E
Ch'ungmu	98	34.51 N	128.25 E
Chungp'u	100	23.25 N	120.31 E
Chungp'yŏngjang	98	41.11 N	128.03 E
Chungsam-ni	98	38.34 N	127.09 E
Chŭngsan	98	39.06 N	125.22 E
Chŭngsanha-ri ✦⁸	271b	37.35 N	126.54 E
Chungshan Bridge ✦⁵	269d	25.05 N	121.31 E
Chungshan → Zhongshan	100	22.31 N	113.22 E
Chunguj ≃	88	48.51 N	93.32 E
Chungyang Shanmo ↗	100	23.30 N	121.00 E
Chunheji	100	32.12 N	115.22 E
Chunhua, Zhg.	102	34.50 N	108.31 E
Chunhua, Zhg.	106	31.56 N	118.56 E
Chunhuhux	232	19.12 N	88.55 W
Chūniān	123	30.58 N	73.59 E
Chuntuqui	232	17.31 N	90.09 W
Chünüj ≃	88	48.48 N	102.00 E
Chunya	154	8.32 S	33.25 E
Ch'unyang, Taehan	98	36.56 N	128.54 E
Chunyang, Zhg.	89	43.43 N	129.28 E
Chunzach	84	42.33 N	46.43 E
Chūō	96	35.00 N	133.58 E
Chūō ✦⁸, Nihon	268	35.40 N	139.47 E
Chūō ✦⁸, Nihon	270	34.42 N	135.11 E
Chuŏr Phnum Krâvanh ↗	110	12.00 N	103.15 E
Chuosijia	102	31.53 N	101.59 E
Chupaca	248	12.04 S	75.19 W
Chupadera Arroyo V	200	33.47 N	106.37 W
Chupadero, Cerro ∧	200	31.01 N	111.37 W
Chupara Point ⟩	241r	10.48 N	61.22 W
Chuquibamba	248	15.50 S	72.39 W
Chuquibambilla	248	14.07 S	72.43 W
Chuquicamata	252	22.19 S	68.56 W
Chuquisaca ▫⁵	248	20.00 S	64.20 W
Chur	58	46.51 N	9.32 E
Churāchāndpur	120	24.20 N	93.40 E
Churāmankāti	126	23.14 N	89.09 E
Churcampa	248	12.42 S	74.24 W
Church	262	53.45 N	2.24 W
Churchdown	42	51.53 N	2.10 W
Church Hill	192	36.31 N	82.42 W
Churchill, Mb., Can.	176	58.46 N	94.10 W
Churchill, Oh., U.S.	214	41.09 N	80.39 W
Churchill, Pa., U.S.	279b	40.27 N	79.51 W
Churchill, Va., U.S.	284c	38.54 N	77.10 W
Churchill ≃, Can.	176	58.47 N	94.12 W
Churchill ≃, Nf., Can.	176	53.30 N	60.10 W
Churchill, Cape ⟩	176	58.46 N	93.12 W
Churchill, Mount ∧, B.C., Can.	182	49.58 N	123.51 W
Churchill, Mount ∧, Ak., U.S.	180	61.25 N	141.43 W
Churchill Downs ♦	218	38.12 N	85.46 W
Churchill Falls ⌞	176	53.35 N	64.27 W
Churchill Lake ⊜	184	55.55 N	108.20 W
Churchill National Park ♦	169	37.58 S	145.17 E
Church Point	194	30.24 N	92.12 W
Church Rock	200	35.32 N	108.35 W
Church Street	260	51.26 N	0.28 E
Church Stretton	42	52.32 N	2.49 W
Churchton	208	38.48 N	76.32 W
Churchtown, Eng., U.K.	262	53.40 N	2.58 W
Churchtown, Pa., U.S.	208	40.08 N	75.58 W
Church View	208	37.41 N	76.41 W
Churchville, On., Can.	275b	43.38 N	79.45 W
Churchville, Md., U.S.	208	39.33 N	76.14 W
Churchville, N.Y., U.S.	210	43.06 N	77.53 W
Churchville, Pa., U.S.	285	40.11 N	75.01 W
Churdan	198	42.09 N	94.28 W
Churen Himāl ∧	124	28.44 N	83.12 E
Chure Śringklā ↗	124	27.40 N	83.40 E
Churfirsten ↗	58	47.08 N	9.17 E
Chürmen	102	43.20 N	104.05 E
Churmuli	89	51.00 N	136.50 E
Churn ≃	42	51.38 N	1.53 W
Churn Creek ≃	182	51.30 N	122.17 W
Churnet ≃	44	52.55 N	1.50 W
Churni ≃¹	126	23.08 N	88.30 E
Chursdorf	54	50.46 N	12.15 E
Chūru	120	28.18 N	74.57 E
Churubusco, In., U.S.	216	41.13 N	85.19 W
Churubusco, N.Y., U.S.	206	44.57 N	73.56 W
Churuguara	246	10.49 N	69.32 W
Churumuco de Morelos	234	18.37 N	101.38 W
Churwalden	58	46.47 N	9.33 E
Chušenga	88	51.27 N	110.55 E
Chushan	100	23.45 N	120.40 E
Chushul	120	33.36 N	78.39 E
Chuska Mountains ↗	200	36.15 N	108.50 W
Chuska Peak ∧	200	35.53 N	108.50 W
Chusovoy → Čusovoj	86	58.17 N	57.49 E
Chust	78	48.10 N	23.18 E
Chusuut uul ↗	88	47.45 N	105.45 E
Chūta	174m	26.32 N	127.58 E
Chutag	88	49.23 N	102.43 E
Chutag Uul	102	43.23 N	110.13 E
Chute-à-Blondeau	206	45.35 N	74.29 W
Chute-Panet	206	46.51 N	71.51 W
Chutorskoj	80	46.52 N	42.59 E
Chutor Smyčka	89	49.27 N	140.02 E
Chutung	100	24.44 N	121.05 E
Chuúl	98	41.33 N	129.34 E
Chuvashia → Čuvašija ▫³	80	55.30 N	47.00 E
Chuwang	98	36.02 N	114.52 E
Chuwang-san Kukrip Kongwŏn ♦	98	36.26 N	129.10 E
Chuwei	269d	25.08 N	121.27 E
Chuxian	100	32.19 N	118.17 E
Chuxiong	102	25.02 N	101.30 E
Chuy	252	33.41 S	53.27 W
Chuzenji-ko ⊜	94	36.44 N	139.29 E
Chuzhai	100	33.22 N	113.17 E
Chužir	88	53.11 N	107.20 E
Chūzu	94	35.06 N	136.00 E
Chvalynsk	80	52.30 N	48.07 E
Chvančkara	84	42.34 N	43.01 E
Chvastoviči	76	53.28 N	35.06 E
Chvatovka	80	52.21 N	46.34 E
Chvojnaja	76	58.54 N	34.32 E
Chvorost'anka	80	52.36 N	48.59 E
Chvostovo	92a	46.08 N	142.14 E
Chwefru ≃	42	52.09 N	3.25 W
Ch'wiya-ri	98	38.03 N	125.32 E
Chyńčešt'	78	46.49 N	28.34 E
Chypre → Cyprus ▫¹	130	35.00 N	33.00 E
Chyrov	78	49.33 N	22.49 E
Ci ≃, Zhg.	98	38.19 N	115.23 E
Ci ≃, Zhg.	100	33.27 N	115.31 E
Ciagola, Monte ∧	64	39.54 N	15.53 E
Ciales	240m	18.20 N	66.28 W
Ciamis	115a	7.20 S	108.21 E
Ciampino	66	41.48 N	12.36 E
Ciampino, Aeroporto di ✈	267a	41.48 N	12.36 E
Cianciana	70	37.31 N	13.26 E
Ciandur	115a	6.24 S	105.59 E
Cianjur	115a	6.49 S	107.08 E
Ciano d'Enza	64	44.36 N	10.24 E
Cianorte	255	23.37 S	52.37 W
Cians, Gorges du V	62	43.57 N	6.59 E
Čiatura	84	42.17 N	43.17 E
Ciavolo	70	37.46 N	12.33 E
Ciawi, Indon.	115a	7.10 S	108.09 E
Ciawi, Indon.	115a	6.40 S	106.50 E
Ciawigebang	115a	6.58 S	108.34 E
Ciba	107	29.07 N	105.55 E
Cibadak	115a	6.53 S	106.46 E
Cibaliung	115a	6.46 S	105.51 E
Čibargata	85	41.08 N	69.48 E
Cibatu	115a	7.06 S	107.59 E
Cibeber	115a	6.56 S	107.07 E
Cibecue	200	34.02 N	110.29 W
Cibiana	64	46.23 N	12.17 E
Cibinong	115a	6.27 S	106.51 E
Čibisovka	78	50.47 N	40.05 E
Čibižek	86	54.27 N	93.40 E
Cibolo Creek ≃, Tx., U.S.	196	28.57 N	97.53 W
Cibolo Creek ≃, Tx., U.S.	196	29.34 N	104.24 W
Cibolo Creek ≃, Tx., U.S.	196	28.27 N	98.54 W
Cibuta	200	31.04 N	110.54 W
Cicagna	62	44.25 N	9.14 E
Čičagova, zaliv ⊂	68	39.01 N	16.29 E
Cicalengka	115a	6.59 S	107.50 E
Čičarija ↗	36	45.30 N	13.54 E
Čičatka	89	54.03 N	121.18 E
Cicciano	68	40.58 N	14.32 E
Cicero, Il., U.S.	216	41.50 N	87.45 W
Cicero, In., U.S.	218	40.07 N	86.00 W
Cicero, N.Y., U.S.	210	43.10 N	76.07 W
Cicero Creek ≃	194	40.01 N	86.01 W
Cicero Dantas	250	10.36 S	38.23 W
Čičhačovo, Ross.	76	57.17 N	29.54 E
Čichačovo, Ross.	89	51.50 N	141.07 E
Čichareši	84	42.48 N	43.03 E
Ciche, Sgurr na ∧	46	57.01 N	5.27 W
Cicheng	100	30.00 N	121.22 E
Čičikleja ≃	78	47.23 N	31.34 E
Čičkajul ≃	86	57.34 N	85.44 E
Ciclados, Islas → Kikládhes II	38	37.30 N	25.00 E
Cicolano ✦¹	66	42.12 N	13.12 E
Cicurug	115a	6.47 S	106.47 E
Cidacos ≃	34	42.19 N	1.55 W
Cidade, Rio da ≃	256	22.25 S	43.09 W
Cidade Universitária ✪², Bra.	287a	22.52 S	43.14 W
Cidade Universitária ✪², Bra.	287b	23.33 S	46.43 W
Cide	130	41.54 N	33.00 E
Cidra	240m	18.11 N	66.10 W
Cidra, Lago de ⊜¹	240m	18.12 N	66.08 W
Ciechanów	30	52.53 N	20.38 E
Ciechanów ▫⁴	30	53.00 N	20.20 E
Ciechanowiec	30	52.42 N	22.31 E
Ciechocinek	30	52.52 N	18.49 E
Ciego de Ávila	240p	21.51 N	78.46 W
Ciego de Ávila ▫⁴	240p	22.00 N	78.40 W
Ciempozuelos	34	40.10 N	3.37 W
Ciénaga	246	11.01 N	74.15 W
Ciénaga de Oro	246	8.53 N	75.37 W
Ciénega de Flores	196	25.57 N	100.11 W
Cienfuegos	240p	22.09 N	80.27 W
Cienfuegos ▫⁴	240p	22.10 N	80.25 W
Cienfuegos, Bahía de ⊂	240p	22.07 N	80.29 W
Čierna [nad Tisou]	30	48.25 N	22.05 E
Čierny Balog	30	48.45 N	19.40 E
Cies, Islas II	34	42.13 N	8.54 W
Cieszanów	30	50.16 N	23.08 E
Cieszyn	30	49.45 N	18.38 E
Cieza	34	38.14 N	1.25 W
Çiftalan ✦⁸	267b	41.15 N	28.54 E
Çiftehan	130	37.31 N	34.46 E
Çifteler	130	39.22 N	31.03 E
Çiftlik	130	38.11 N	34.30 E
Cifuentes, Cuba	240p	22.39 N	80.03 W
Cifuentes, Esp.	34	40.47 N	2.37 W
Čiganak, Kaz.	86	45.06 N	73.58 E
Čiganak, Ross.	80	51.47 N	43.18 E
Čiganaki	80	47.57 N	43.05 E
Čigirin	78	49.04 N	32.40 E
Cigliano	62	45.18 N	8.01 E
Čigorak	80	51.26 N	42.09 E
Cigou	100	33.51 N	113.35 E
Cigüela ≃	34	39.08 N	3.44 W
Cihanbeyli	130	38.40 N	32.56 E
Cihara	115a	6.52 S	106.06 E
Cihuatlán	234	19.14 N	104.35 W
Čiili	86	44.10 N	66.45 E
Cijara, Embalse de ⊜¹	34	39.18 N	4.52 W
Čijen	85	43.08 N	75.55 E
Cijiawu	105	39.48 N	115.59 E
Čijirčik, pereval ✕	85	40.15 N	73.20 E
Čijli ≃	85	40.17 N	72.08 E
Cijulang	115a	7.44 S	108.27 E
Čik	86	55.01 N	82.27 E
Cikajang	115a	7.22 S	107.47 E
Cikalong-kulon	115a	6.42 S	107.12 E
Cikampek	115a	6.24 S	107.27 E
Čikan	88	54.54 N	105.39 E
Čikarang	115a	6.15 S	107.09 E
Cikatomas	115a	7.37 S	108.15 E
Čikišl'ar	128	37.34 N	53.55 E
Čikoj	88	50.16 N	106.54 E
Čikoj ≃	88	51.02 N	106.39 E
Čikola	84	43.12 N	43.55 E
Cikou	100	29.42 N	114.46 E
Cikssi	100	38.30 N	115.50 E
Cilacap	115a	7.44 S	109.00 E
Cilamaya	115a	6.15 S	107.35 E
Cilavegna	62	45.19 N	8.44 E
Çıldır	84	41.08 N	43.07 E
Çıldır Gölü ⊜	84	41.04 N	43.15 E
Ciledug	115a	6.54 S	108.44 E
Cilegon	115a	6.01 S	106.03 E
Čilekovo	80	47.50 N	43.30 E
Cilento ✦	68	40.17 N	15.19 E
Cilento ✦¹	68	40.15 N	15.10 E
Čil'gazi	85	40.10 N	70.39 E
Cilicia ✦⁹	130	36.40 N	34.20 E
Čilik, Kaz.	85	43.36 N	78.15 E
Čilik, Kaz.	86	51.07 N	54.07 E
Čilik ≃	85	43.05 N	78.28 E
Cililin	115a	6.56 S	107.26 E
Cilimus	115a	6.52 S	108.29 E
Cilincing ✦⁸	269e	6.06 S	106.56 E
Cill Airne → Killarney	48	52.03 N	9.30 W
Cill Chainnigh → Kilkenny	48	52.39 N	7.15 W
Cilleruelo de Bezana	34	42.58 N	3.51 W
Čil'ma ≃	24	65.27 N	52.06 E
Cima Banche (Schluderbach)	64	46.37 N	12.11 E
Cima Gogna	64	46.31 N	12.28 E
Cimahi	115a	6.53 S	107.32 E
Cimalaka	115a	6.49 S	107.56 E
Cimalmotto	58	46.17 N	8.29 E
Cimarron, Ks., U.S.	198	37.48 N	100.20 W
Cimarron, N.M., U.S.	200	36.30 N	104.54 W
Cimarron ≃, U.S.	196	36.10 N	96.17 W
Cimarron ≃, N.M., U.S.	196	36.20 N	104.31 W
Cimarron, North Fork ≃	196	37.25 N	101.13 W
Čimbaj	86	42.57 N	59.47 E
Čimčinej, gora ∧²	180	63.37 N	178.04 E
Cimini, Monti ↗	66	42.20 N	12.10 E
Ciminna	70	37.54 N	13.34 E
Cimino, Monte ∧	66	42.24 N	12.12 E
Čimion	85	40.16 N	71.31 E
Cimišlija	78	46.32 N	28.44 E
Cimitile	68	40.56 N	14.31 E
Čimkent	85	42.18 N	69.36 E
Čimkent ▫⁴	85	43.00 N	69.00 E
Čimkorgon	85	42.50 N	75.30 E
Cimla ≃	80	48.01 N	42.24 E
Ciml'ansk	80	47.38 N	42.04 E
Ciml'anskoje vodochranilišče ⊜¹	80	48.00 N	43.00 E
Cimolais	64	46.17 N	12.26 E
Cimone, Monte ∧	64	44.12 N	10.42 E
Cîmpeni	38	46.22 N	23.03 E
Cîmpia Turzii	38	46.33 N	23.54 E
Cîmpina	38	45.08 N	25.44 E
Cimpu	112	3.25 S	120.22 E
Cîmpulung	38	45.16 N	25.03 E
Cîmpulung Moldovenesc	38	47.31 N	25.34 E
Čimtarga, gora ∧	85	39.12 N	68.10 E
Čina ≃	88	54.20 N	112.24 E
Čina, Tanjung ⟩	112	5.56 S	104.45 E
Činabad	85	40.52 N	71.58 E
Činadijevo	78	48.30 N	22.50 E
Činandali	84	41.53 N	45.34 E
Činar	130	37.44 N	40.25 E
Činarcik	130	40.39 N	29.06 E
Cinaruco ≃	246	6.41 N	67.07 W
Činaz	85	40.56 N	68.45 E
Cinca ≃	34	41.26 N	0.21 E
Cincar ∧	36	43.54 N	17.04 E
Cincinnati, Ia., U.S.	190	40.37 N	92.55 W
Cincinnati, Oh., U.S.	218	39.09 N	84.27 W
Cincinnatus	210	42.32 N	75.53 W
Cinco, Canal Numero ≃	252	37.35 S	57.20 W
Cinco Balas, Cayos II	240p	21.06 N	79.20 W
Cinco de Mayo	196	25.46 N	104.19 W
Cinco Pinos	236	13.14 N	86.52 W
Cinco Saltos	252	38.49 S	68.04 W
Cinderella	273d	26.15 S	28.16 E
Cinderella Dam ⊜¹	273d	26.15 S	28.14 E
Cinderford	42	51.50 N	2.29 W
Cinder Island I	276	40.36 N	73.36 W
Cine	130	37.36 N	28.04 E
Cinebar	224	46.36 N	122.32 W
Cinecittà ✪³	267a	41.51 N	12.34 E
Cinema	182	53.14 N	122.27 W
Ciney	56	50.18 N	5.06 E
Cinfães	34	41.04 N	8.05 W
Čingaly	86	60.13 N	69.45 E
Čingis	86	54.08 N	81.41 E
Čingistaj	86	49.13 N	85.55 E
Cingoli	66	43.22 N	13.13 E
Cingolino	66	42.53 N	11.24 E
Cinisello Balsamo	62	45.33 N	9.13 E
Činišeucy	78	47.42 N	28.52 E
Cinisi	70	38.09 N	13.06 E
Cinja-Voryk	24	63.13 N	52.38 E
Cinkota ✦⁸	264c	47.31 N	19.14 E
Cinnaminson	285	40.00 N	74.59 W
Cinovec	54	50.43 N	13.45 E
Cinq, Lac des ⊜	206	46.51 N	72.59 W
Cinq Doigts, Lac ⊜	206	46.36 N	74.32 W
Cinquefrondi	68	38.25 N	16.06 E
Cinquemiglia, Piano delle ≃	66	41.50 N	14.00 E
Cinqueterre ▫⁹	62	44.10 N	9.45 E
Cintalapa	234	16.44 N	93.43 W
Cinto, Monte ∧	36	42.23 N	8.56 E
Cinto Euganeo	64	45.16 N	11.40 E
Cintra, Golfe de ⊂	148	23.00 N	16.20 W
Cintra → Sintra	34	38.48 N	9.23 W
Ciocănești	38	44.12 N	27.04 E
Ciociaria ✦¹	66	41.45 N	13.15 E
Čiomas	115a	6.12 S	106.01 E
Čiovo, Otok I	36	43.30 N	16.20 E
Čipa ≃	88	55.23 N	115.55 E
Ciparay	115a	7.03 S	107.43 E
Cipatujah	115a	7.45 S	108.00 E
Cipikan	88	54.55 N	113.21 E
Cipikan ≃	88	55.14 N	113.05 E
Cipó	250	11.06 S	38.31 W
Cipó ≃	255	18.40 S	43.59 W
Cipolândia	255	20.08 S	55.24 W
Cipolletti	252	38.56 S	67.59 W
Čiqikou	107	29.35 N	106.26 E
Čir	80	48.29 N	43.10 E
Čir ≃	80	48.35 N	42.51 E
Ciraadhame	144	10.30 N	49.22 E
Čirachčaj ≃	84	41.40 N	48.11 E
Čiragidzor	84	40.27 N	46.19 E
Ciranjang	115a	6.49 S	107.14 E
Circeo, Monte ∧	66	41.14 N	13.03 E
Circeo, Parco Nazionale del ♦	66	41.17 N	13.05 E
Čirčik	85	41.29 N	69.35 E
Čirčik ≃	85	40.54 N	68.41 E
Çirçir	130	40.04 N	36.48 E
Circle, Ak., U.S.	180	65.50 N	144.04 W
Circle, Mt., U.S.	202	47.20 N	105.35 W
Circle Hot Springs	180	65.28 N	144.39 W
Circleville, N.Y., U.S.	210	41.31 N	75.23 W
Circleville, Oh., U.S.	218	39.36 N	82.56 W
Circleville, Pa., U.S.	279b	40.20 N	79.44 W
Circleville, Ut., U.S.	200	38.10 N	112.16 W
Circleville Mountain ∧	200	38.12 N	112.24 W
Circular Reef ✣²	164	3.25 S	147.47 E
Circus World ♦	220	28.14 N	81.38 W
Cirebon	115a	6.44 S	108.34 E
Cireglio	66	43.59 N	10.51 E
Ciremay, Gunung ∧	115a	6.54 S	108.24 E
Cirencester	42	51.44 N	1.59 W
Cirey-sur-Vezouze	58	48.35 N	6.57 E
Cirgalandy	88	50.36 N	97.20 E
Ciriè	62	45.14 N	7.36 E
Cirigliano	68	40.24 N	16.10 E
Čirikovo	82	55.23 N	37.14 E
Ciriquiri ≃	248	8.05 S	65.18 W
Čirinda	180	64.33 N	175.25 E
Cirk, gora ∧	38	47.35 N	25.07 E
Cirò	38	39.23 N	17.04 E
Cirò Marina	68	39.22 N	17.08 E
Ciro Redondo	240p	22.01 N	78.43 W
Čirpan	38	42.12 N	25.20 E
Ciruas	115a	6.06 S	106.13 E
Cisa, Passo della ✕	64	44.28 N	9.55 E
Cisano	64	45.32 N	10.43 E
Cisarua	115a	6.40 S	106.59 E
Cisco, Il., U.S.	219	40.01 N	88.43 W
Cisco, Tx., U.S.	196	32.23 N	98.58 W
Cishan	100	36.37 N	114.07 E
Cishangang	106	30.55 N	119.31 E
Ciskei ▫¹, Afr.	138	32.50 S	27.00 E
Ciskei ▫¹, Afr.	158	32.50 S	27.00 E
Čiškovo	62	45.39 N	8.58 E
Cisliano	266b	45.27 N	8.59 E
Čišmar	54	54.11 N	10.59 E
Čismena	82	56.02 N	36.13 E
Cismon ≃	64	45.55 N	11.43 E
Cismon del Grappa	64	45.55 N	11.44 E
Čišmy	86	54.35 N	55.20 E
Cisnădie	38	45.43 N	24.09 E
Cisne	194	38.31 N	88.26 W
Cisneros	246	6.33 N	75.04 W
Cisnes ≃	254	44.45 S	72.42 W
Cisolok	115a	6.57 S	106.26 E
Cison di Valmarino	64	45.58 N	12.10 E
Cispus ≃	224	46.25 N	122.10 W
Cisse ≃	50	47.25 N	0.47 E
Cissna Park	216	40.33 N	87.53 W
Čistá, Česko.	54	50.06 N	12.44 E
Čistá, Česko.	60	50.02 N	13.35 E
Cisterna di Latina	66	41.35 N	12.49 E
Cisternino	68	40.44 N	17.25 E
Cistern Point ⟩	238	23.43 N	77.35 W
Cistierna	34	42.48 N	5.07 W
Čistoje	80	53.05 N	48.26 E
Čistooz'ornoje	86	54.43 N	76.33 E
Čistopol'	80	55.21 N	50.37 E
Čistopolje, Kaz.	86	52.34 N	67.15 E
Čistopolje, Ross.	83	47.31 N	39.27 E
Čistovodovka	83	49.24 N	37.20 E
Čita	88	52.03 N	113.30 E
Čita ≃	88	52.03 N	113.30 E
Citac, Nevado ∧	248	12.48 S	75.14 W
Čita Oblast' ▫⁴	88	52.00 N	117.00 E
Citaré ≃	250	1.11 N	54.41 W
Cité Universitaire ✪²	261	48.49 N	2.20 E
Citra	192	29.24 N	82.06 W
Citronelle	194	31.05 N	88.13 W
Citrus ▫⁶	220	28.52 N	82.28 W
Citrusdal	158	32.36 S	19.00 E
Citrus Heights	226	38.42 N	121.16 W
Citrus Springs	220	29.00 N	82.27 W
Citrus Tower ✪	220	28.33 N	81.44 W
Cittadella	64	45.39 N	11.47 E
Città della Pieve	66	42.57 N	12.00 E
Città del Vaticano → Vatican City ▫¹	66	41.54 N	12.27 E
Città di Castello	66	43.27 N	12.14 E
Cittaducale	66	42.23 N	12.57 E
Cittanova	68	38.21 N	16.05 E
Cittareale	66	42.37 N	13.10 E
Città Sant'Angelo	66	42.31 N	14.03 E
Città Universitaria ✪²	267a	41.55 N	12.31 E
City Beach	168a	31.56 S	115.45 E
City Bell ✦⁸	258	34.52 S	58.05 W
City Island ✦⁸	276	40.51 N	73.47 W
City Mills	283	42.06 N	71.21 W
City of Hope National Medical Center ✪	280	34.08 N	117.58 W
City Of Industry	280	34.01 N	117.57 W
City of London ✦⁸	260	51.31 N	0.05 W
City of Refuge → Pu'uhonua o Honaunau National Historic Site ♦	229d	19.25 N	155.54 W
City of Sunrise	220	26.08 N	80.14 W
City Point	220	28.24 N	80.45 W
City University of New York Brooklyn College ✪²	276	40.38 N	73.57 W
City University of New York City College ✪²	276	40.49 N	73.57 W
City University of New York Queens College ✪²	276	40.44 N	73.49 W
City University of New York York College ✪²	276	40.42 N	73.48 W
Ciucaș, Vîrful ∧	38	45.31 N	25.55 E
Ciudad Acuña	232	29.18 N	100.55 W
Ciudad Altamirano	234	18.20 N	100.40 W
Ciudad Barrios	236	13.46 N	88.16 W
Ciudad Bolívar	246	8.08 N	63.33 W
Ciudad Bolivia	246	8.21 N	70.34 W
Ciudad Camargo	232	26.19 N	98.50 W
Ciudad Constitución	232	24.59 N	111.39 W
Ciudad Cortés	236	8.58 N	83.32 W
Ciudad Cuauhtémoc	234	22.28 N	102.20 W
Ciudad Darío	236	12.43 N	86.08 W
Ciudad de Carangas	248	17.53 S	66.11 W
Ciudad de Guayana → Ciudad Guayana	246	8.22 N	62.40 W
Ciudad de la Habana ▫⁴	240p	23.08 N	82.22 W
Ciudad del Cabo → Cape Town	158	33.55 S	18.22 E
Ciudad del Carmen	232	18.38 N	91.50 W
Ciudad del Este	252	25.30 S	54.36 W
Ciudad del Maíz	234	22.24 N	99.36 W
Ciudad de los Deportes ♦	286a	19.23 N	99.11 W
Ciudad del Vaticano → Vatican City ▫¹	66	41.54 N	12.27 E
Ciudad de México (Mexico City), Méx.	234	19.24 N	99.09 W
Ciudad de México (Mexico City), Méx.	286a	19.24 N	99.09 W
Ciudad de Nutrias	246	8.05 N	69.18 W
Ciudad Deportiva ♦, Cuba	286b	23.07 N	82.22 W
Ciudad Deportiva ♦, Méx.	286a	19.24 N	99.06 W
Ciudadela, Parque de la ♦	266d	41.23 N	2.11 E
Ciudad General Belgrano	288	34.43 S	58.32 W
Ciudad Guayana	246	8.22 N	62.40 W
Ciudad Guzmán	234	19.41 N	103.29 W
Ciudad Hidalgo, Méx.	234	19.41 N	100.34 W
Ciudad Hidalgo, Méx.	236	14.41 N	92.09 W
Ciudad Juárez	232	31.44 N	106.29 W
Ciudad Lerdo	196	25.32 N	103.32 W
Ciudad Lerdo de Tejada	234	18.37 N	95.31 W
Ciudad Lineal ✦⁸	266a	40.27 N	3.40 W
Ciudad López Mateos	286a	19.33 N	99.15 W
Ciudad Madero	234	22.16 N	97.50 W
Ciudad Mante	234	22.44 N	98.57 W
Ciudad Manuel Doblado	234	20.44 N	101.56 W
Ciudad Mendoza	234	18.48 N	97.11 W
Ciudad Miguel Alemán	232	26.23 N	99.01 W
Ciudad Morelos	232	32.38 N	114.52 W
Ciudad Obregón	232	27.29 N	109.56 W
Ciudad Ojeda (Lagunillas)	246	10.12 N	71.19 W
Ciudad Piar	246	7.27 N	63.19 W
Ciudad Real	34	38.59 N	3.56 W
Ciudad Real ▫⁴	34	38.50 N	3.45 W
Ciudad Rodrigo	34	40.36 N	6.32 W
Ciudad Sahagún	234	19.47 N	98.33 W
Ciudad Sandino	236	13.43 N	86.08 W
Ciudad Serdán	234	18.59 N	97.27 W
Ciudad Tecún Umán	236	14.40 N	92.09 W
Ciudad Trujillo → Santo Domingo	238	18.28 N	69.54 W
Ciudad Universitaria ✪⁸	266a	40.27 N	3.44 W
Ciudad Universitaria ✪², Esp.	266a	40.27 N	3.43 W
Ciudad Universitaria ✪², Méx.	286a	19.20 N	99.11 W
Ciudad Universitaria ✪², Ven.	286c	10.29 N	66.53 W
Ciudad Valles	234	21.59 N	99.01 W
Ciudad Victoria, Méx.	204	32.20 N	115.06 W
Ciudad Victoria, Méx.	234	23.44 N	99.08 W
Ciudad Vieja	236	14.31 N	90.46 W
Ciuma	152	13.14 S	15.40 E
Ciutadella	34	40.02 N	3.50 E
Civa Burnu ⟩	130	41.22 N	36.35 E
Civate	62	45.50 N	9.21 E
Civenna	62	45.56 N	9.16 E
Civetta, Monte ∧	64	46.23 N	12.03 E
Civezzano	64	46.05 N	11.11 E
Cividale del Friuli	64	46.06 N	13.25 E
Cividate al Piano	62	45.33 N	9.50 E
Cividate Camuno	64	45.57 N	10.17 E
Civil' ≃	80	56.08 N	47.35 E
Civil'sk	80	55.53 N	47.29 E
Civita	68	39.49 N	16.18 E
Civitacampomarano	66	41.47 N	14.41 E
Civita Castellana	66	42.17 N	12.25 E
Civita di Bagno	66	42.18 N	13.26 E
Civitanova Alta	66	43.19 N	13.40 E
Civitanova Marche	66	41.40 N	14.24 E
Civitanova del Sannio	66	43.18 N	13.44 E
Civitaquana	66	42.19 N	13.54 E
Civitavecchia	66	42.06 N	11.48 E
Civitella del Tronto	66	42.46 N	13.40 E
Civitella di Romagna	64	44.00 N	11.56 E
Civitella in Val di Chiana	66	43.25 N	11.43 E
Civitella Marittima	66	43.00 N	11.17 E
Civitella Roveto	66	41.54 N	13.25 E
Civray	32	46.09 N	0.18 E
Čivril	130	38.18 N	29.45 E
Ciwidey	115a	7.06 S	107.27 E
Cixerri ≃	71	39.17 N	8.59 E
Cixi	100	30.11 N	121.15 E
Cixian	98	36.22 N	114.23 E
Cixiqiao	106	31.38 N	120.03 E
Ciyutuo	104	41.31 N	122.53 E
Čiža	24	67.06 N	44.19 E
Čižapka ≃	86	59.01 N	79.36 E
Čiža Vtoraja	80	50.52 N	49.40 E
Cize	58	46.12 N	5.26 E
Cizhuping	107	29.11 N	103.36 E
Čižinskije razlivy ⊞	80	50.25 N	49.40 E
Cizre	130	37.20 N	42.12 E
C.J. Strike Reservoir ⊜¹	202	42.57 N	115.53 W
Čkalovo, Kaz.	86	53.38 N	70.24 E
Čkalovo, Ukr.	78	46.28 N	34.11 E
Čkalov → Orenburg	86	51.54 N	55.06 E
Čkalovsk, Kaz.	85	41.15 N	68.00 E
Čkalovsk, Ross.	80	56.46 N	43.16 E
Čkalovsk, Taj.	85	40.13 N	69.50 E
Čkalovskij	265b	55.54 N	38.04 E
C K Creek ≃	202	47.36 N	108.29 W
Čkyně	60	49.07 N	13.49 E
Čl'a, ozero ⊜	89	53.27 N	140.03 E
Clachan	46	55.45 N	5.34 W
Clackamas	224	45.24 N	122.34 W
Clackamas ▫⁶	224	45.10 N	122.16 W
Clackamas ≃	224	45.22 N	122.36 W
Clackamas, Oak Grove Fork ≃	224	45.05 N	122.03 W
Clackamas Heights	224	45.23 N	122.34 W
Clackline	168a	31.43 S	116.31 E
Clackmannan	46	56.06 N	3.46 W
Clacton-on-Sea	42	51.48 N	1.09 E
Cladich	46	56.21 N	5.05 W
Claerwen ≃	42	52.16 N	3.35 W
Claerwen Reservoir ⊜¹	42	52.17 N	3.43 W
Claflin	198	38.31 N	98.32 W
Claiborne	194	31.32 N	87.31 W
Clain ≃	32	46.47 N	0.32 E
Claire, Lake ⊜	176	58.35 N	112.05 W
Claire, Pointe ⟩	275a	45.25 N	73.50 W
Clairefontaine-en-Yvelines	50	48.37 N	1.55 E
Clair Engle Lake ⊜¹	204	40.52 N	122.43 W
Claireville	275b	43.45 N	79.38 W
Claireville Reservoir ⊜¹	275b	43.44 N	79.39 W
Clairis ≃	50	48.07 N	2.45 E
Clairmarais	50	50.46 N	2.18 E
Clairmont	182	55.16 N	118.47 W
Clairton	214	40.17 N	79.52 W
Clairvaux-les-Lacs	58	46.34 N	5.45 E
Claix	62	45.07 N	5.40 E
Clallam ▫⁶	224	48.10 N	123.49 W
Clallam Bay	224	48.15 N	124.15 W
Clam ≃, Mi., U.S.	190	44.05 N	85.00 W
Clam ≃, Wi., U.S.	190	45.57 N	92.33 W
Clam, North Fork ≃	190	45.46 N	92.18 W
Clamart	261	48.48 N	2.16 E
Clamecy	50	47.27 N	3.31 E
Clam Gulch	180	60.15 N	151.22 W
Clam Lake ⊜	184	55.19 N	105.43 W
Clamp Island	162	29.56 S	119.06 E
Clampton	204	39.40 N	117.55 W
Clan Alpine Mountains ↗	182	53.34 N	110.44 W
Clandonald	260	51.15 N	0.30 W
Clandon Park ♦	170	32.55 S	149.57 E
Clandulla	48	53.18 N	6.41 W
Clane	62	44.00 N	7.09 E
Clans	194	32.50 N	86.37 W
Clanton	158	32.11 S	18.54 E
Clanwilliam	46	55.46 N	5.22 W
Claonaig	42	52.09 N	0.31 W
Clapham	62	44.07 N	7.25 E
Clapier, Mont ∧	190	46.02 N	82.13 W
Clapperton Island I	214	41.24 N	79.32 W
Clapp Farm	46	58.17 N	4.08 W
Clàr, Loch nan ⊜	252	31.50 S	58.49 W
Clara, Arg.	48	53.20 N	7.36 W
Clara, Ire.	194	31.34 N	88.41 W
Clara, Ms., U.S.	166	18.30 S	141.18 E
Clara ≃	198	44.57 N	95.21 W
Clara City	110	10.54 N	97.55 E
Clara Island I	252	37.54 S	59.17 W
Claraz	166	33.25 S	143.55 E
Clare, Austl.	168b	33.50 S	138.36 E
Clare, Austl.	42	52.05 N	0.35 E
Clare, Eng., U.K.	190	43.49 N	84.46 W
Clare, Mi., U.S.	48	52.50 N	9.00 W
Clare ▫⁶	212	44.28 N	77.17 W
Clare ≃, On., Can.	48	53.20 N	9.03 W
Clare ≃, Ire.	48	52.49 N	8.57 W
Clarecastle	48	53.21 N	8.57 W
Claregalway	48	53.48 N	10.00 W
Clare Island I	214	43.58 N	79.07 W
Claremont, On., Can.	260	51.21 N	0.22 W
Claremont, Eng., U.K.	228	34.05 N	117.43 W
Claremont, Ca., U.S.	188	43.22 N	72.20 W
Claremont, N.H., U.S.	198	45.40 N	98.00 W
Claremont, S.D., U.S.	208	37.13 N	76.57 W
Claremont, Va., U.S.	204	39.53 N	120.57 W
Claremont ∧	196	36.18 N	95.36 W
Claremore	48	53.44 N	9.00 W
Claremorris	172	42.10 S	173.56 E
Clarence, N.Z.	216	40.28 N	87.58 W
Clarence, Il., U.S.	190	41.53 N	91.03 W
Clarence, Ia., U.S.	219	39.44 N	92.15 W
Clarence, Mo., U.S.	210	42.59 N	78.35 W
Clarence, N.Y., U.S.	214	41.03 N	77.56 W
Clarence, Pa., U.S.	166	29.25 S	153.22 E
Clarence ≃, Austl.	172	42.10 S	173.57 E
Clarence ≃, N.Z.	254	54.10 S	71.50 W
Clarence, Isla I	180	65.15 N	166.40 W
Clarence, Port ⊂			
Clarence Cannon Dam ✦⁶	219	39.31 N	91.39 W
Clarence Center	210	43.00 N	78.35 W
Clarence Creek	206	45.30 N	75.13 W
Clarence Fahnestock Memorial State Park ♦	210	41.26 N	73.50 W
Clarence Island I	9	61.09 S	54.06 W
Clarence J. Brown Reservoir ⊜¹	218	39.58 N	83.44 W
Clarence Strait ꓤ, Austl.	164	12.00 S	131.00 E
Clarence Strait ꓤ, Ak., U.S.	180	55.25 N	132.00 W
Clarence Town, Austl.	170	32.35 S	151.47 E
Clarence Town, Ba.	238	23.06 N	74.59 W
Clarenceville, P.Q., Can.	206	45.04 N	73.15 W
Clarenceville, Mi., U.S.	281	42.27 N	83.19 W
Clarendon, Austl.	168b	35.07 S	138.38 E
Clarendon, Ar., U.S.	194	34.41 N	91.18 W
Clarendon, N.Y., U.S.	210	43.11 N	78.04 W
Clarendon, Pa., U.S.	214	41.46 N	79.05 W
Clarendon, Tx., U.S.	196	34.56 N	100.53 W
Clarendon Hills	278	41.47 N	87.57 W
Clarens	158	28.30 S	28.29 E
Clarenville	186	48.10 N	53.58 W
Claresholm	182	50.02 N	113.35 W
Claret	62	43.52 N	3.54 E
Clarholz	52	51.54 N	8.11 E
Claridge	214	40.21 N	79.37 W
Clarie Coast ⸗²	9	66.30 S	133.00 E
Clarin	116	9.58 N	124.01 E
Clarinda	198	40.44 N	95.02 W
Clarines	246	9.56 N	65.10 W
Clarington	214	41.20 N	79.07 W
Clarion, Ia., U.S.	190	42.43 N	93.43 W
Clarion, Pa., U.S.	214	41.12 N	79.23 W
Clarion ▫⁶	214	41.13 N	79.24 W
Clarion ≃	214	41.07 N	79.41 W
Clarión, Isla I	232	18.22 N	114.44 W
Clarion, West Branch ≃	214	41.29 N	78.41 W
Clarion Fracture Zone ✣	14	18.00 N	122.00 W
Clarissa	198	46.07 N	94.56 W
Clark, N.J., U.S.	276	40.38 N	74.18 W
Clark, Oh., U.S.	214	40.27 N	81.54 W
Clark, S.D., U.S.	198	44.52 N	97.43 W
Clark, Tx., U.S.	222	30.23 N	94.56 W
Clark ▫⁶, In., U.S.	218	38.17 N	85.44 W

≃ River	Fluß	Río	Rivière	Rio	✣ Submarine Features	Untermeerische Objekte	Accidentes Submarinos	Formes de relief sous-marin	Acidentes submarinos
≃ Canal	Kanal	Canal	Canal	Canal	▫ Political Unit	Politische Einheit	Unidad Política	Entité politique	Unidade política
⌞ Waterfall, Rapids	Wasserfall, Stromschnellen	Cascada, Rápidos	Chute d'eau, Rapides	Cascata, Rápidos	✪ Cultural Institution	Kulturelle Institution	Institución Cultural	Institution culturelle	Instituição cultural
ꓤ Strait	Meeresstraße	Estrecho	Détroit	Estreito	⊥ Historical Site	Historische Stätte	Sitio Histórico	Site historique	Sitio histórico
⊂ Bay, Gulf	Bucht, Golf	Bahía, Golfo	Baie, Golfe	Baía, Golfo	♦ Recreational Site	Erholungs- und Ferienort	Sitio de Recreo	Centre de loisirs	Area de Lazer
⊜ Lake, Lakes	See, Seen	Lago, Lagos	Lac, Lacs	Lago, Lagos	✈ Airport	Flughafen	Aeropuerto	Aéroport	Aeroporto
⊞ Swamp	Sumpf	Pantano	Marais	Pântano	■ Military Installation	Militäranlage	Instalación Militar	Installation militaire	Instalação militar
⊞ Ice Features, Glacier	Eis- und Gletscherformen	Accidentes Glaciales	Formes glaciaires	Acidentes glaciares	✦ Miscellaneous	Verschiedenes	Misceláneo	Divers	Diversos
⊤ Other Hydrographic Features	Andere Hydrographische Objekte	Otros Elementos Hidrográficos	Autres données hydrographiques	Outros acidentes hidrográficos					

Clark □[6], Oh., U.S. 218 39.56 N 83.49 W
Clark □[6], Wa., U.S. 224 45.48 N 122.31 W
Clark, Lake ⊜ 180 60.15 N 154.15 W
Clark, Mount ∧ 180 64.25 N 124.12 W
Clark, Point ≻ 190 44.04 N 81.45 W
Clark Air Base (U.S.) ■ 116 15.11 N 120.32 E
Clark Branch ≐ 285 39.43 N 74.45 W
Clark Canyon Reservoir ⊜[1] 202 44.58 N 112.51 W
Clark Creek ≐ 208 40.22 N 76.58 W
Clarkdale 200 34.46 N 112.03 W
Clarke ≐ 166 19.12 S 145.30 E
Clarke City 186 50.12 N 66.38 W
Clarke Island I 166 40.33 S 148.10 E
Clarke Lake ⊜ 184 54.25 N 106.51 W
Clarke Range ⩘ 166 20.50 S 148.33 E
Clarkesville 192 34.36 N 83.31 W
Clarkfield 198 44.47 N 95.48 W
Clark Fork 202 48.08 N 116.10 W
Clark Fork ≐ 202 48.09 N 116.15 W
Clark Hill 218 38.18 N 83.12 W
Clarklake 216 42.04 N 84.21 W
Clark Lake ⊜ 216 42.07 N 84.19 W
Clark Mills 210 43.06 N 75.22 W
Clark Mountain ∧, Ca., U.S. 204 35.32 N 115.35 W
Clark Mountain ∧, Wa., U.S. 224 48.03 N 120.57 W
Clarks, La., U.S. 194 32.01 N 92.08 W
Clarks, Ne., U.S. 198 41.12 N 97.50 W
Clarks ≐ 194 37.03 N 88.33 W
Clarks, West Fork ≐ 194 36.59 N 88.31 W
Clarksboro 285 39.47 N 75.13 W
Clarksburg, On., Can. 212 44.43 N 80.27 W
Clarksburg, Ca., U.S. 226 38.25 N 121.32 W
Clarksburg, Il., U.S. 219 39.20 N 88.44 W
Clarksburg, In., U.S. 218 39.26 N 85.20 W
Clarksburg, Md., U.S. 208 39.14 N 77.16 W
Clarksburg, N.J., U.S. 208 40.11 N 74.26 W
Clarksburg, Oh., U.S. 218 39.30 N 83.09 W
Clarksburg, W.V., U.S. 188 39.16 N 80.20 W
Clarksburg State Park ♦ 207 42.43 N 73.06 W
Clarks Creek ≐, Ks., U.S. 198 39.05 N 96.42 W
Clarks Creek ≐, Ky., U.S. 218 38.40 N 84.44 W
Clarksdale 194 34.12 N 90.34 W
Clarks Green 210 41.30 N 75.42 W
Clark's Harbour 186 43.26 N 65.38 W
Clarks Hill 216 40.14 N 86.43 W
Clarks Hill Lake ⊜[1] 192 33.50 N 82.20 W
Clarks Island I 283 42.01 N 70.38 W
Clarks Mills 214 41.24 N 80.11 W
Clarkson, On., Can. 275b 43.31 N 79.37 W
Clarkson, Ky., U.S. 194 37.29 N 86.13 W
Clarkson, Ne., U.S. 198 41.43 N 97.07 W
Clarkson, N.Y., U.S. 210 43.14 N 77.56 W
Clarks Point 180 58.51 N 158.30 W
Clarks Summit 210 41.29 N 75.42 W
Clarkston, Mi., U.S. 216 42.44 N 83.25 W
Clarkston, Wa., U.S. 202 46.24 N 117.02 W
Clark's Town 241q 18.25 N 77.34 W
Clarksville, Ar., U.S. 194 35.28 N 93.27 W
Clarksville, De., U.S. 208 38.32 N 75.08 W
Clarksville, In., U.S. 218 38.15 N 85.47 W
Clarksville, Ia., U.S. 190 42.47 N 92.40 W
Clarksville, Md., U.S. 208 39.12 N 76.56 W
Clarksville, Mi., U.S. 216 42.50 N 85.14 W
Clarksville, Mo., U.S. 219 39.22 N 90.54 W
Clarksville, N.Y., U.S. 210 42.35 N 73.58 W
Clarksville, Oh., U.S. 218 39.24 N 83.58 W
Clarksville, Tn., U.S. 194 36.31 N 87.21 W
Clarksville, Tx., U.S. 196 33.36 N 95.03 W
Clarksville, Va., U.S. 192 36.37 N 78.33 W
Clarksville City 222 32.32 N 94.34 W
Clarkton, Mo., U.S. 194 36.27 N 89.58 W
Clarkton, N.C., U.S. 192 34.29 N 78.39 W
Claro ≐, Bra. 248 13.25 S 56.35 W
Claro ≐, Bra. 255 15.28 S 51.43 W
Claro ≐, Bra. 255 19.06 S 47.52 W
Claro ≐, Bra. 255 19.08 S 50.40 W
Claro, Arroyo ≐ 288 34.25 S 58.41 W
Claro, Ribeirão ≐ 287b 23.40 S 46.17 W
Clary 50 50.05 N 3.24 E
Claryville 210 41.55 N 74.34 W
Clashmore 48 52.00 N 7.48 W
Clatskanie 224 46.06 N 123.12 W
Clatskanie ≐ 224 46.08 N 123.14 W
Clatsop □[6] 224 46.01 N 123.41 W
Clatsop Spit ≻[2] 224 46.13 N 124.01 W
Clatteringshaws Lake ⊜ 44 55.05 N 4.17 W
Claude 196 35.07 N 101.22 W
Claudy 48 54.54 N 7.09 W
Claughton 44 54.06 N 2.40 W
Claussnitz 54 50.56 N 12.53 E
Clausthal-Zellerfeld 52 51.48 N 10.20 E
Claver 116 9.35 N 125.44 E
Claverack 210 42.13 N 73.44 W
Claveria, Pil. 116 18.37 N 121.05 E
Claveria, Pil. 116 8.38 N 124.55 E
Clavet 184 52.00 N 106.23 W
Clavey ≐ 226 37.52 N 120.07 W
Clawit, Mount ∧ 116 16.58 N 120.58 E
Clawson, Mi., U.S. 281 42.32 N 83.08 W
Clawson, Tx., U.S. 222 31.24 N 94.47 W
Claxton 192 32.09 N 81.54 W
Clay, Ky., U.S. 194 37.28 N 87.49 W
Clay, Tx., U.S. 222 30.23 N 96.21 W
Clay, W.V., U.S. 188 38.27 N 81.05 W
Clay □[6] 219 38.45 N 88.40 W
Claybank Creek ≐ 194 31.10 N 85.44 W
Clay Center, Ks., U.S. 198 39.22 N 97.07 W
Clay Center, Ne., U.S. 198 40.31 N 98.03 W
Clay Center, Oh., U.S. 214 41.33 N 83.21 W
Clay City, Il., U.S. 194 38.41 N 88.21 W
Clay City, In., U.S. 194 39.16 N 87.06 W
Clay City, Ky., U.S. 192 37.51 N 83.55 W
Clay Creek ≐ 198 38.06 N 102.31 W
Clay Cross 44 53.10 N 1.24 W
Claydon 42 52.06 N 1.07 E
Claye-Souilly 50 48.57 N 2.42 E
Claygate 260 51.22 N 0.20 W
Claygate Cross 260 51.16 N 0.19 E
Clayhole Wash V 200 36.59 N 113.17 W
Clayhurst 182 56.15 N 120.01 W
Claymont 208 39.48 N 75.27 W
Clayoquot Sound 𝔲 182 49.11 N 126.08 W
Claypole 288 34.48 S 58.20 W
Claypool, Az., U.S. 200 33.24 N 110.50 W
Claypool, In., U.S. 216 41.07 N 85.52 W
Claysburg 214 40.17 N 78.27 W
Clay Springs 200 34.21 N 110.17 W
Claysville 214 40.07 N 80.24 W
Clayton, Austl. 274b 37.56 S 145.07 E
Clayton, Eng., U.K. 262 53.47 N 1.50 W
Clayton, Al., U.S. 194 31.52 N 85.26 W
Clayton, Ca., U.S. 282 37.57 N 121.56 W
Clayton, De., U.S. 208 39.17 N 75.38 W
Clayton, Ga., U.S. 192 34.52 N 83.24 W
Clayton, Il., U.S. 219 40.01 N 90.57 W
Clayton, In., U.S. 218 39.41 N 86.31 W
Clayton, La., U.S. 194 31.43 N 91.32 W
Clayton, Mi., U.S. 216 41.52 N 84.14 W
Clayton, Mo., U.S. 219 38.38 N 90.19 W
Clayton, N.J., U.S. 208 39.39 N 75.05 W
Clayton, N.M., U.S. 196 36.27 N 103.11 W
Clayton, N.Y., U.S. 212 44.14 N 76.05 W
Clayton, N.C., U.S. 192 35.39 N 78.27 W
Clayton, Ok., U.S. 196 34.35 N 95.21 W
Clayton, Tx., U.S. 222 32.06 N 94.28 W
Clayton, Wa., U.S. 182 48.00 N 117.33 W
Clayton ≐ 166 29.06 S 138.05 E
Claytonia 214 41.00 N 79.58 W
Clayton-le-Moors 262 53.47 N 2.23 W
Clayton-le-Woods 262 53.41 N 2.38 W
Clayton Park ♦ 285 39.52 N 75.29 W
Clayton Valley V 282 37.58 N 121.58 W
Claytonville 216 40.34 N 87.49 W
Clay Village 218 38.11 N 85.07 W
Clayville 210 42.59 N 75.15 W
Clear ≐ 182 56.11 N 119.42 W
Clear, Cape ≻, Ire. 48 51.24 N 9.30 W
Clear, Cape ≻, Ak., U.S. 180 59.48 N 147.54 W
Clear, Lake ⊜ 212 45.26 N 77.12 W
Clear, Mount ∧ 171b 35.52 S 149.04 E
Clear Boggy Creek ≐ 196 34.03 N 95.47 W
Clearbrook, B.C., Can. 224 49.08 N 122.26 W
Clearbrook, Mn., U.S. 198 47.41 N 95.25 W
Clear Creek 218 39.07 N 86.32 W
Clear Creek ≐, Al., U.S. 194 34.00 N 87.19 W
Clear Creek ≐, Az., U.S. 200 34.59 N 110.38 W
Clear Creek ≐, Ca., U.S. 204 40.31 N 122.22 W
Clear Creek ≐, Ca., U.S. 280 34.17 N 118.12 W
Clear Creek ≐, Ca., U.S. 282 37.20 N 122.21 W
Clear Creek ≐, Ky., U.S. 218 38.10 N 85.17 W
Clear Creek ≐, Mo., U.S. 194 38.00 N 93.56 W
Clear Creek ≐, Mt., U.S. 202 48.46 N 109.25 W
Clear Creek ≐, Ne., U.S. 198 41.08 N 99.06 W
Clear Creek ≐, Oh., U.S. 218 39.33 N 84.20 W
Clear Creek ≐, Or., U.S. 224 45.23 N 122.29 W
Clear Creek ≐, Or., U.S. 224 45.09 N 121.31 W
Clear Creek ≐, Tn., U.S. 192 36.05 N 84.42 W
Clear Creek ≐, Tx., U.S. 196 33.16 N 97.03 W
Clear Creek ≐, Tx., U.S. 222 29.09 N 97.23 W
Clear Creek ≐, Tx., U.S. 222 29.33 N 95.05 W
Clear Creek ≐, Wa., U.S. 224 46.07 N 122.00 W
Clear Creek ≐, Wy., U.S. 202 44.53 N 106.04 W
Clear Creek State Park ♦ 214 41.20 N 79.05 W
Clearfield, Ia., U.S. 198 40.48 N 94.28 W
Clearfield, Ky., U.S. 218 38.09 N 83.25 W
Clearfield, Pa., U.S. 214 41.01 N 78.26 W
Clearfield, Ut,. U.S. 200 41.06 N 112.01 W
Clearfield □[6] 214 41.02 N 78.27 W
Clearfield Creek ≐ 214 41.02 N 78.24 W
Clear Fork Reservoir ⊜[1] 214 40.42 N 82.38 W
Clearing ◆[8] 278 41.47 N 87.47 W
Clear Island I 48 51.26 N 9.30 W
Clearlake, Ca., U.S. 226 38.57 N 122.38 W
Clear Lake, Ia., U.S. 190 43.08 N 93.22 W
Clear Lake, S.D., U.S. 198 44.44 N 96.40 W
Clearlake, Wa., U.S. 224 48.28 N 122.14 W
Clear Lake, Wi., U.S. 190 45.15 N 92.16 W
Clear Lake ⊜, Mb., Can. 184 50.42 N 100.00 W
Clear Lake ⊜, On., Can. 212 44.59 N 79.33 W
Clear Lake ⊜, On., Can. 212 45.14 N 79.57 W
Clear Lake ⊜, On., Can. 212 44.30 N 78.13 W
Clear Lake ⊜, In., U.S. 216 41.44 N 84.50 W
Clear Lake ⊜[1], Ca., U.S. 204 39.02 N 122.50 W
Clear Lake ⊜[1], La., U.S. 194 31.55 N 93.05 W
Clearlake Oaks 226 39.07 N 122.40 W
Clearlake Park 226 38.58 N 122.39 W
Clear Lake Reservoir ⊜[1] 204 41.52 N 121.08 W
Clear Lake Shores 222 29.33 N 95.02 W
Clearmont 202 44.38 N 106.22 W
Clear Run 214 41.08 N 78.45 W
Clear Site 180 64.19 N 149.11 W
Clearview, Oh., U.S. 214 41.25 N 82.10 W
Clearview, Wa., U.S. 224 47.45 N 122.06 W
Clearview, W.V., U.S. 214 40.09 N 80.41 W
Clearview Estates 279b 40.34 N 80.16 W
Clearwater, B.C., Can. 182 51.38 N 120.02 W
Clearwater, Mb., Can. 184 49.08 N 99.01 W
Clearwater, Fl., U.S. 220 27.57 N 82.48 W
Clearwater, Ks., U.S. 198 37.30 N 97.30 W
Clearwater, Ne., U.S. 198 42.10 N 98.11 W
Clearwater, S.C., U.S. 192 33.29 N 81.53 W
Clearwater, Wa., U.S. 224 47.34 N 124.17 W
Clearwater ≐, Can. 184 56.44 N 111.23 W
Clearwater ≐, Ab., Can. 182 52.23 N 114.50 W
Clearwater ≐, B.C., Can. 182 51.42 N 120.00 W
Clearwater ≐, Id., U.S. 202 46.25 N 117.02 W
Clearwater ≐, Mn., U.S. 198 47.54 N 96.16 W
Clearwater ≐, Mt., U.S. 202 46.58 N 113.23 W
Clearwater ≐, Wa., U.S. 224 47.33 N 124.21 W
Clearwater, Middle Fork ≐ 202 46.09 N 115.59 W
Clearwater, North Fork ≐ 202 46.30 N 116.19 W
Clearwater, South Fork ≐ 202 46.09 N 115.59 W
Clear Water Bay c 271d 22.17 N 114.18 E
Clearwater Beach Island I 220 27.59 N 82.49 W
Clearwater Lake ⊜, B.C., Can. 182 52.15 N 120.13 W
Clearwater Lake ⊜, Mb., Can. 184 54.05 N 101.00 W
Clearwater Lake Provincial Park ♦ 184 54.03 N 101.10 W
Clearwater Mountains ⩘ 202 46.00 N 115.30 W
Cleator Moor 44 54.31 N 3.30 W
Clebit 196 34.21 N 94.52 W
Cleburne 222 32.20 N 97.23 W
Cleckheaton 44 53.43 N 1.43 W
Cle Elum 224 47.11 N 120.56 W
Cle Elum ≐ 224 47.11 N 121.01 W
Cle Elum Lake ⊜[1] 224 47.18 N 121.06 W
Cleethorpes 44 53.34 N 0.02 W
Cleeve Cloud ∧[2] 42 51.54 N 2.00 W
Clefmont 58 48.06 N 5.31 E
Cleggan 48 53.33 N 10.09 W
Cleland Conservation Park ♦ 168b 34.59 S 138.44 E
Cleland Heights 285 39.44 N 75.34 W
Clelles 62 44.50 N 5.37 E
Clementon 285 39.48 N 74.59 W
Clementsport 186 44.40 N 65.37 W
Clemson 192 34.41 N 82.50 W
Clemville 222 29.00 N 96.08 W
Clendenin 188 38.29 N 81.20 W
Clendening Lake ⊜[1] 214 40.16 N 81.13 W
Clenze 54 52.56 N 10.58 E
Cleobury Mortimer 42 52.23 N 2.29 W
Cleona 208 40.20 N 76.28 W
Cléon-d'Andran 62 44.37 N 4.56 E
Cleopatra Needle ∧ 116 10.07 N 118.58 E
Clères 50 49.36 N 1.07 E
Clerke Rocks II[1] 244 55.01 S 34.41 W
Clermont, Austl. 166 22.49 S 147.39 E
Clermont, P.Q., Can. 186 47.41 N 70.14 W
Clermont, Fr. 50 49.23 N 2.24 E
Clermont, Fl., U.S. 220 28.32 N 81.46 W
Clermont, N.J., U.S. 285 39.59 N 74.48 W
Clermont, Pa., U.S. 214 41.41 N 78.29 W
Clermont □[6] 218 39.05 N 84.11 W
Clermont-en-Argonne 56 49.06 N 5.04 E
Clermont-Ferrand 32 45.47 N 3.05 E
Clermont State Park ♦ 210 42.05 N 73.55 W
Clerval 58 47.24 N 6.30 E
Clervaux 56 50.04 N 6.01 E
Cléry-Saint-André 50 47.49 N 1.45 E
Cles 64 46.22 N 11.02 E
Cleve 166 33.42 S 136.30 E
Clevedon 42 51.27 N 2.51 W
Cleveland, Austl. 171a 27.32 S 153.17 E
Cleveland, Al., U.S. 194 33.59 N 86.34 W
Cleveland, Fl., U.S. 220 26.57 N 82.00 W
Cleveland, Ga., U.S. 192 34.35 N 83.45 W
Cleveland, Ms., U.S. 194 33.44 N 90.43 W
Cleveland, N.Y., U.S. 210 43.14 N 75.53 W
Cleveland, N.C., U.S. 192 35.43 N 80.40 W
Cleveland, Oh., U.S. 214 41.29 N 81.41 W
Cleveland, Oh., U.S. 279a 41.29 N 81.41 W
Cleveland, Ok., U.S. 196 36.18 N 96.27 W
Cleveland, Tn., U.S. 194 35.09 N 84.52 W
Cleveland, Tx., U.S. 222 30.20 N 95.05 W
Cleveland, Va., U.S. 192 36.56 N 82.09 W
Cleveland □[6] 44 54.35 N 1.15 W
Cleveland, Cape ≻ 166 19.11 S 147.01 E
Cleveland, Mount ∧, Austl. 166 41.25 S 145.23 E
Cleveland, Mount ∧, Mt., U.S. 202 48.56 N 113.51 W
Cleveland Heights 214 41.31 N 81.33 W
Cleveland Hills ⩘[2] 44 54.23 N 1.05 W
Cleveland-Hopkins International Airport ⊠ 279a 41.25 N 81.51 W
Clevelândia 252 26.24 S 52.21 W
Clevelândia do Norte 250 3.49 N 51.52 W
Cleveland Museum of Art ♦ 279a 41.31 N 81.37 W
Cleveland National Forest ♦ 280 33.47 N 117.38 W
Cleveland Park ◆[8] 284c 38.56 N 77.04 W
Cleveland Peninsula ≻[1] 182 55.45 N 132.00 W
Cleveland Pond ⊜ 283 42.07 N 70.58 W
Cleveland State University ♦[2] 279a 41.30 N 81.40 W
Cleveland Zoo ♦ 279a 41.27 N 81.43 W
Cleveleys 44 53.53 N 3.03 W
Cleversburg 208 40.02 N 77.28 W
Cleves 218 39.10 N 84.45 W
Cleves → Kleve 52 51.48 N 6.09 E
Clew Bay c 48 53.50 N 9.50 W
Clewer 158 25.55 S 29.07 E
Clewiston 220 26.45 N 80.56 W
Cley next the Sea 42 52.58 N 1.03 E
Clichy 50 48.54 N 2.18 E
Clichy-sous-Bois 261 48.55 N 2.33 E
Clifden 48 53.29 N 10.01 W
Clifden Bay c 48 53.28 N 10.05 W
Cliffdale Creek ≐ 166 16.56 S 138.48 E
Cliffdell 224 46.44 N 120.42 W
Cliffe 42 51.28 N 0.30 E
Cliffe Marshes ⩸ 260 51.28 N 0.30 E
Cliffe Woods 260 51.26 N 0.30 E
Clifford, On., Can. 212 43.58 N 80.58 W
Clifford, S. Afr. 158 31.04 S 27.28 E
Clifford, In., U.S. 218 39.16 N 85.52 W
Clifford, Pa., U.S. 210 41.39 N 75.36 W
Clifford Park ♦ 274b 37.43 S 145.16 E
Cliffside 210 42.31 N 74.59 W
Cliffside Park 276 40.58 N 73.57 W
Cliffwood 276 40.26 N 74.14 W
Cliffwood Beach 276 40.26 N 74.13 W
Clifton, Austl. 171a 27.56 S 151.54 E
Clifton, Eng., U.K. 262 53.46 N 2.49 W
Clifton, Az., U.S. 200 33.03 N 109.17 W
Clifton, Il., U.S. 216 40.56 N 87.56 W
Clifton, Ks., U.S. 198 39.34 N 97.16 W
Clifton, N.J., U.S. 210 40.51 N 74.09 W
Clifton, N.Y., U.S. 210 43.03 N 77.49 W
Clifton, Or., U.S. 224 46.12 N 123.27 W
Clifton, Tn., U.S. 194 35.23 N 87.59 W
Clifton, Tx., U.S. 222 31.46 N 97.34 W
Clifton, Lake ⊜ 168a 32.49 S 115.41 E
Clifton Court Forebay ⊜[1] 226 37.50 N 121.35 W
Clifton Forge 192 37.48 N 79.49 W
Clifton Gorge V 42 51.28 N 2.37 W
Clifton Heights, N.Y., U.S. 284a 42.44 N 78.56 W
Clifton Heights, Pa., U.S. 285 39.55 N 75.17 W
Clifton Hills 166 26.52 S 138.50 E
Clifton Knolls 210 42.52 N 73.46 W
Clifton Park ♦ 284b 39.19 N 76.35 W
Clifton Point ≻ 240b 25.01 N 77.34 W
Clifton Springs 210 42.57 N 77.08 W
Clifty, Mount ∧ 224 47.07 N 121.10 W
Clifty Creek ≐ 218 39.09 N 85.54 W
Clifty Falls State Park ♦ 218 38.45 N 85.26 W
Clignon ≐ 50 49.07 N 3.04 E
Climax, Sk., Can. 184 49.13 N 108.23 W
Climax, Co., U.S. 200 39.22 N 106.10 W
Climax, Ga., U.S. 192 30.52 N 84.25 W
Climax, Mi., U.S. 216 42.14 N 85.20 W
Climax, Pa., U.S. 214 40.59 N 79.23 W
Clinch ≐ 192 35.53 N 84.29 W
Clinchco 192 37.09 N 82.21 W
Clingen 54 51.14 N 10.55 E
Clingmans Dome ∧ 192 35.35 N 83.30 W
Clinton, B.C., Can. 182 51.05 N 121.35 W
Clinton, On., Can. 190 43.37 N 81.32 W
Clinton, N.Z. 172 46.12 S 169.22 E
Clinton, Al., U.S. 194 32.55 N 88.00 W
Clinton, Ar., U.S. 194 35.35 N 92.27 W
Clinton, Ct., U.S. 207 41.16 N 72.31 W
Clinton, Il., U.S. 219 40.09 N 88.57 W
Clinton, In., U.S. 194 39.39 N 87.23 W
Clinton, Ia., U.S. 190 41.50 N 90.11 W
Clinton, Ky., U.S. 194 36.40 N 88.59 W
Clinton, La., U.S. 194 30.51 N 91.00 W
Clinton, Me., U.S. 188 44.38 N 69.30 W
Clinton, Md., U.S. 208 38.45 N 76.53 W
Clinton, Ma., U.S. 207 42.25 N 71.41 W
Clinton, Mi., U.S. 216 42.04 N 83.58 W
Clinton, Mn., U.S. 198 45.27 N 96.26 W
Clinton, Ms., U.S. 194 32.20 N 90.19 W
Clinton, Mo., U.S. 194 38.22 N 93.46 W
Clinton, N.J., U.S. 210 40.38 N 74.54 W
Clinton, N.Y., U.S. 210 43.02 N 75.22 W
Clinton, N.C., U.S. 192 34.59 N 78.19 W
Clinton, Oh., U.S. 214 40.56 N 81.42 W
Clinton, Ok., U.S. 196 35.30 N 98.58 W
Clinton, Pa., U.S. 214 40.29 N 80.18 W
Clinton, S.C., U.S. 192 34.28 N 81.52 W
Clinton, Tn., U.S. 192 36.06 N 84.07 W
Clinton, Tx., U.S. 222 33.06 N 96.14 W
Clinton, Wa., U.S. 224 47.58 N 122.21 W
Clinton, Wi., U.S. 216 42.33 N 88.51 W
Clinton □[6], Il., U.S. 219 38.37 N 89.22 W
Clinton □[6], In., U.S. 216 40.17 N 86.31 W
Clinton □[6], Mi., U.S. 216 42.56 N 84.36 W
Clinton □[6], N.Y., U.S. 206 44.57 N 73.42 W
Clinton □[6], Oh., U.S. 218 39.27 N 83.50 W
Clinton □[6], Pa., U.S. 210 41.08 N 71.26 W
Clinton ≐ 214 42.36 N 82.48 W
Clinton, Cape ≻ 166 22.32 S 150.47 E
Clinton, Lake ⊜[1] 194 40.10 N 88.50 W
Clinton, Middle Branch ≐ 281 42.36 N 82.54 W
Clinton, North Branch ≐ 214 42.36 N 82.54 W
Clinton-Colden Lake ⊜ 176 63.58 N 107.27 W
Clintondale 210 41.01 N 77.29 W
Clinton Lake ⊜[1] 198 38.55 N 95.25 W
Clinton Park 210 42.36 N 73.43 W
Clinton Reservoir ⊜[1] 276 41.05 N 74.27 W
Clinton Township 214 42.33 N 82.53 W
Clintonville, Mi., U.S. 281 42.43 N 83.22 W
Clintonville, Pa., U.S. 214 41.12 N 79.53 W
Clintonville, Wi., U.S. 190 44.37 N 88.45 W
Clintwood 192 37.09 N 82.27 W
Clio, Al., U.S. 194 31.42 N 85.36 W
Clio, Mi., U.S. 190 43.10 N 83.44 W
Clio, S.C., U.S. 192 34.34 N 79.32 W
Clipperton, Île I[1] 230 10.17 N 109.13 W
Clipperton Fracture Zone ✢ 16 10.00 N 115.00 W
Clisham ∧ 46 57.57 N 6.49 W
Clisson 32 47.05 N 1.17 W
Clitheroe 44 53.53 N 2.23 W
Clitunno ≐ 66 42.56 N 12.37 E
Clive 172 39.35 S 176.55 E
Cloates, Point ≻ 162 22.43 S 113.40 E
Clock Face 262 53.25 N 2.43 W
Clocolan 158 29.00 S 27.30 E
Clodomira 252 27.35 S 64.08 W
Cloe 214 40.56 N 78.56 W
Cloete 196 27.55 N 101.10 W
Cloghan, Ire. 48 53.13 N 7.53 W
Cloghan, Ire. 48 54.51 N 7.56 W
Cloghane 48 52.13 N 10.12 W
Clogheen 48 52.16 N 8.00 W
Clogher 48 54.25 N 7.12 W
Clogher Head ≻ 48 53.48 N 6.12 W
Cloghjordan 48 52.57 N 8.02 W
Clonakilty 48 51.37 N 8.54 W
Clonakilty Bay c 48 51.35 N 8.50 W
Cloncurry 166 20.42 S 140.30 E
Cloncurry ≐ 166 18.37 S 140.40 E
Clondalkin 48 53.19 N 6.24 W
Clonee 48 53.25 N 6.26 W
Clones 48 54.11 N 7.15 W
Clonfert 48 53.14 N 8.05 W
Clonmacnois ⊥ 48 53.20 N 7.59 W
Clonmany 48 55.14 N 7.25 W
Clonmel 48 52.21 N 7.42 W
Clonroche 48 52.27 N 6.43 W
Clontarf 274a 33.48 S 151.16 E
Cloone 48 53.57 N 7.46 W
Clo-oose 224 48.40 N 124.49 W
Cloppenburg 52 52.50 N 8.02 E
Cloquallum Creek ≐ 224 46.58 N 123.24 W
Cloquet 190 46.43 N 92.27 W
Cloquet ≐ 190 46.52 N 92.35 W
Clorinda 252 25.17 S 57.43 W
Closter 276 40.58 N 73.57 W
Cloudcroft 200 32.57 N 105.44 W
Cloud Peak ∧, Ak., U.S. 180 68.24 N 148.26 W
Cloud Peak ∧, Wy., U.S. 202 44.25 N 107.10 W
Cloudy Bay c 172 41.27 S 174.10 E
Cloudy Mountain ∧ 180 63.11 N 156.05 W
Clough 48 54.18 N 5.50 W
Clough Foot 262 53.43 N 2.08 W
Clova 46 56.50 N 3.06 W
Clova, Glen V 46 56.49 N 3.04 W
Clove Lakes Park ♦ 276 40.37 N 74.07 W
Clovelly, Austl. 274a 33.55 S 151.16 E
Clovelly, Eng., U.K. 42 51.00 N 4.24 W
Clover 192 35.06 N 81.13 W
Clover Bank 210 42.45 N 78.53 W
Clover Creek ≐, Id., U.S. 202 42.34 N 115.38 W
Clover Creek ≐, Id., U.S. 202 43.00 N 115.11 W
Cloverdale, B.C., Can. 224 49.06 N 122.44 W
Cloverdale, Al., U.S. 194 34.56 N 87.46 W
Cloverdale, Ca., U.S. 204 38.48 N 123.00 W
Cloverdale, Il., U.S. 278 41.56 N 88.07 W
Cloverdale, In., U.S. 194 39.30 N 86.47 W
Cloverdale, Ky., U.S. 218 38.10 N 84.53 W
Cloverdale, Mi., U.S. 216 42.32 N 85.23 W
Cloverdale, Oh., U.S. 216 41.01 N 84.18 W
Cloverdale, Or., U.S. 224 45.12 N 123.53 W
Cloverdale Mall ◆[9] 275b 43.38 N 79.34 W
Cloverdene 273d 26.09 S 28.22 E
Cloverleaf 222 29.46 N 95.10 W
Clover Pass 182 55.28 N 131.47 W
Cloverport 194 37.50 N 86.37 W
Cloverville 216 43.11 N 86.10 W
Clovis, Ca., U.S. 226 36.49 N 119.42 W
Clovis, N.M., U.S. 196 34.24 N 103.12 W
Clowbridge Reservoir ⊜[1] 262 53.45 N 2.16 W
Clowne 44 53.18 N 1.16 W
Cloyes-sur-le-Loir 50 48.00 N 1.14 E
Cloyne 48 51.51 N 8.08 W
Cluain Meala → Clonmel 48 52.21 N 7.42 W
Cluanie, Loch ⊜ 46 57.07 N 5.05 W
Cluj-Napoca 38 46.47 N 23.36 E
Cluj-Napoca □[6] 38 46.45 N 23.45 E
Clun 42 52.26 N 3.00 W
Clun ≐ 42 52.22 N 2.53 W
Clune 214 40.34 N 79.18 W
Clunes 169 37.18 S 143.47 E
Clun Forest ◆[3] 42 52.28 N 3.07 W
Clunie Water ≐ 46 57.00 N 3.24 W
Cluny, Austl. 166 24.31 S 139.35 E
Cluny, Fr. 58 46.26 N 4.39 E
Cluses 58 46.04 N 6.36 E
Clusone 64 45.53 N 9.57 E
Clute 222 29.01 N 95.23 W
Clutha ≐ 172 46.21 S 169.48 E
Clwyd □[6] 44 53.05 N 3.20 W
Clwyd ≐ 44 53.20 N 3.30 W
Clwyd, Vale of V 44 53.12 N 3.24 W
Clwydian Range ⩘ 44 53.10 N 3.20 W
Clydach 42 51.43 N 3.50 W
Clyde, Austl. 274a 33.50 S 151.00 E
Clyde, Ab., Can. 182 54.09 N 113.39 W
Clyde, N.Z. 172 45.11 S 169.19 E
Clyde, Ca., U.S. 226 38.02 N 122.02 W
Clyde, Ks., U.S. 198 39.35 N 97.23 W
Clyde, Mi., U.S. 281 42.41 N 83.37 W
Clyde, N.Y., U.S. 210 43.05 N 76.52 W
Clyde, N.C., U.S. 192 35.32 N 82.54 W
Clyde, Oh., U.S. 214 41.18 N 82.58 W
Clyde, Tx., U.S. 196 32.24 N 99.30 W
Clyde ≐, Austl. 170 35.23 S 150.15 E
Clyde ≐, N.S., Can. 186 43.35 N 65.25 W
Clyde ≐, On., Can. 212 44.58 N 76.22 W
Clyde ≐, Scot., U.K. 46 55.44 N 4.55 W
Clyde ≐, N.Y., U.S. 210 43.04 N 77.00 W
Clyde ≐, Vt., U.S. 188 44.56 N 72.12 W
Clyde, Firth of c[1] 46 55.42 N 5.00 W
Clydebank 46 55.54 N 4.24 W
Clydegale Lake ⊜ 212 45.25 N 78.23 W
Clyde Lake ⊜ 182 55.18 N 111.28 W
Clyde No.03 214 39.59 N 80.03 W
Clyde Park 202 45.53 N 110.36 W
Clyde Potts Reservoir ⊜[1] 276 40.48 N 74.35 W
Clyde River 176 70.25 N 68.30 W
Clydesdale 158 26.54 S 27.55 E
Clydesdale V 46 55.42 N 3.50 W
Clymer, N.Y., U.S. 214 42.01 N 79.37 W
Clymer, Pa., U.S. 214 40.40 N 79.00 W
Clynnog-fawr 44 53.01 N 4.23 W
Clywedog ≐ 42 52.27 N 3.32 W
Ćmielów 30 50.53 N 21.31 E
Cna ≐, Bela. 76 52.10 N 27.03 E
Cna ≐, Ross. 76 57.33 N 34.36 E
Cna ≐, Ross. 80 54.32 N 42.05 E

ENGLISH

Name | Page | Lat.°′ | Long.°′

Cna ≐, Ross. 82 55.03 N 39.09 E
Cnori 84 41.37 N 45.59 E
Côa ≐ 34 41.05 N 7.06 W
Coacalco 286a 19.37 N 99.05 W
Coachella 204 33.40 N 116.10 W
Coachella Canal ≖ 204 33.34 N 116.00 W
Coachford 48 51.53 N 8.48 W
Coacoyole 232 24.31 N 106.34 W
Coacuilco 234 21.07 N 98.35 W
Coahoma 196 32.18 N 101.18 W
Coahuayana 234 18.44 N 103.41 W
Coahuayutla de Guerrero 234 18.19 N 101.49 W
Coahuila 200 32.12 N 114.59 W
Coahuila □[3] 232 27.20 N 102.00 W
Coal ≐ 180 59.39 N 126.57 W
Coalbrook 158 26.51 S 27.53 E
Coalbrookdale 42 52.38 N 2.30 W
Coalburg 214 41.11 N 80.36 W
Coalburn 46 55.36 N 3.54 W
Coal City 216 41.17 N 88.17 W
Coalcomán ≐ 234 18.11 N 103.08 W
Coalcomán de Matamoros 234 18.47 N 103.09 W
Coal Creek 180 65.22 N 143.10 W
Coal Creek ≐, Co., U.S. 198 40.30 N 104.26 W
Coal Creek ≐, In., U.S. 194 39.57 N 87.25 W
Coal Creek ≐, Wa., U.S. 202 47.19 N 118.36 W
Coal Creek Flat 172 45.29 S 169.18 E
Coaldale, Ab., Can. 182 49.43 N 112.37 W
Coaldale, Pa., U.S. 210 40.49 N 75.54 W
Coal Fire Creek ≐ 194 33.15 N 88.18 W
Coal Fork 188 38.19 N 81.32 W
Coalgate, N.Z. 172 43.29 S 171.58 E
Coalgate, Ok., U.S. 196 34.32 N 96.13 W
Coal Grove 188 38.30 N 82.38 W
Coal Harbour 182 50.36 N 127.35 W
Coal Hill 194 35.26 N 93.40 W
Coal Hill Park ♦ 271a 39.56 N 116.23 E
Coalhurst 182 49.45 N 112.56 W
Coalinga 226 36.08 N 120.21 W
Coalisland 48 54.33 N 6.42 W
Coal Island I 172 46.07 S 166.38 E
Coalmont 182 49.31 N 120.41 W
Coalpit Heath 42 51.32 N 2.28 W
Coalport 214 40.44 N 78.32 W
Coal River 180 59.45 N 126.55 W
Coal Run ≐ 279b 40.21 N 80.07 W
Coalspur 182 53.11 N 117.01 W
Coalton 219 39.17 N 89.19 W
Coaltown 214 41.02 N 80.20 W
Coal Valley V 204 38.00 N 115.05 W
Coalville, S. Afr. 158 26.01 S 29.10 E
Coalville, Eng., U.K. 42 52.44 N 1.20 W
Coalville, Ut,. U.S. 200 40.55 N 111.23 W
Coamo 240m 18.05 N 66.22 W
Coamo, Lago ⊜[1] 240m 18.01 N 66.23 W
Coapilla 234 17.08 N 93.10 W
Coaraci 255 14.38 S 39.32 W
Coari 246 4.05 S 63.08 W
Coari ≐ 246 4.30 S 63.33 W
Coari, Lago de ⊜ 246 4.15 S 63.22 W
Coarsegold 226 37.16 N 119.42 W
Coast □[4] 154 3.00 S 39.30 E
Coast Mountains ⩘ 176 55.00 N 129.00 W
Coast Ranges ⩘ 178 41.00 N 123.30 W
Coatán ≐ 236 14.48 N 92.31 W
Coatbridge 46 55.52 N 4.01 W
Coatepec 234 19.27 N 96.58 W
Coatepec Harinas 234 18.54 N 99.43 W
Coatepeque 236 14.42 N 91.52 W
Coatepeque, Lago de ⊜ 236 13.52 N 89.33 W
Coates Creek ≐ 212 44.24 N 79.54 W
Coatesville 208 39.58 N 75.49 W
Coaticook 206 45.08 N 71.48 W
Coaticook ≐ 206 45.20 N 71.53 W
Coatsburg 219 40.02 N 91.10 W
Coats Island I 176 62.30 N 83.00 W
Coats Land ◆[1] 9 77.00 S 28.00 W
Coatzacoalcos 234 18.09 N 94.25 W
Coatzacoalcos ≐ 234 18.10 N 94.27 W
Coatzintla 234 20.29 N 97.27 W
Coayllo 248 12.44 S 76.28 W
Coazze 62 45.03 N 7.18 E
Cobá ⊥ 232 20.36 N 87.35 W
Cobadin 38 44.04 N 28.13 E
Coballo Cocha 246 3.54 S 70.32 W
Cobalt, On., Can. 190 47.24 N 79.41 W
Cobalt, Ct., U.S. 207 41.33 N 72.33 W
Cobán 236 15.29 N 90.19 W
Çobanlar 130 38.41 N 30.47 E
Čobar 166 31.30 S 145.49 E
Cobargo 166 36.23 S 149.53 E
Cobb 226 38.49 N 122.43 W
Cobb Creek ≐ 196 35.05 N 98.25 W
Cobberas, Mount ∧ 166 36.52 S 148.10 E
Cobbetts Pond ⊜ 283 42.48 N 71.17 W
Cobbin's Brook ≐ 260 51.41 N 0.01 W
Cobb Island 208 38.16 N 76.51 W
Cobb Island I, Md., U.S. 208 38.16 N 76.51 W
Cobb Island I, Va., U.S. 208 37.20 N 75.44 W
Cobbitty 274a 34.01 S 150.41 E
Cobbitty ∧[2] 274a 33.59 S 150.42 E
Cobble Hill 224 48.41 N 123.36 W
Cobble Mountain Reservoir ⊜[1] 207 42.08 N 72.55 W
Cobblestone Mountain ∧ 228 34.37 N 118.52 W
Cobb Neck ≻[1] 208 38.20 N 76.55 W
Cobbs Creek ≐ 285 39.54 N 75.15 W
Cobbs Creek Park ♦ 285 39.58 N 75.16 W
Cobb Seamount ✢[3] 16 46.46 N 130.49 W
Cobden, Austl. 169 38.20 S 143.05 E
Cobden, On., Can. 190 45.38 N 76.53 W
Cobden, Il., U.S. 194 37.31 N 89.15 W
Cobeña 266a 40.34 N 3.30 W
Cobequid Bay c 186 45.21 N 63.45 W
Cobequid Mountains ⩘ 186 45.31 N 64.05 W
Cobh 48 51.51 N 8.17 W
Cobham, Eng., U.K. 42 51.20 N 0.25 W
Cobham, Eng., U.K. 260 51.23 N 0.24 E
Cobham ≐ 184 53.15 N 93.58 W
Cobham Hall ⊥ 260 51.23 N 0.25 E
Cobija, Bol. 248 11.02 S 68.44 W
Cobija, Chile 252 22.33 S 70.16 W
Coblenz → Koblenz 56 50.21 N 7.35 E
Cobleskill 210 42.40 N 74.29 W
Cobleskill Creek ≐ 210 42.43 N 74.20 W
Coboconk 212 44.39 N 78.48 W
Cobo Hall ♦ 281 42.19 N 83.03 W
Cobolgo, gora ∧ 84 42.50 N 46.23 E
Çoboto, Cerro ∧ 200 31.29 N 112.05 W
Čoboty 265b 55.39 N 37.21 E
Cobourg 212 43.58 N 78.10 W
Cobourg Peninsula ≻[1] 164 11.20 S 132.15 E
Cobquecura 252 36.08 S 72.47 W
Cobram 166 35.55 S 145.39 E
Cobras, Ilha das I 287a 22.54 S 43.10 W
Cobras, Ribeirão das ≐ 256 23.08 S 46.05 W
Cobre ≐ 236 8.01 N 81.18 W
Cobre, Barranca del V 232 27.28 N 107.50 W
Cóbuè 154 12.04 S 34.50 E
Coburg, Austl. 169 37.45 S 144.58 E
Coburg, Dtsch. 56 50.15 N 10.58 E
Coburg Island I 176 76.00 N 79.25 W
Coburn 210 40.52 N 77.28 W
Coburn Mountain ∧ 188 45.28 N 70.06 W
Coca ≐ 246 0.29 S 76.58 W
Coca, Laguna ⊜ 286b 22.57 N 82.27 W
Coca, Pizzo di ∧ 64 46.04 N 10.01 E

DEUTSCH

Name | Seite | Breite°′ | Länge°′ E = Ost

Cocachacra 248 17.06 S 71.46 W
Cocais, Ribeirão dos ≐ 256 21.59 S 47.15 W
Cocal 250 3.28 S 41.34 W
Cocalico Creek ≐ 208 40.07 N 76.14 W
Coccaglio 64 45.34 N 9.58 E
Cocconato 62 45.05 N 8.02 E
Cocentaina 34 38.45 N 0.26 W
Cochabamba 248 17.24 S 66.09 W
Cochabamba □[5] 248 17.30 S 65.40 W
Čochatauri 84 42.01 N 42.15 E
Cochato ≐ 283 42.10 N 71.01 W
Coche, Isla I 246 10.45 N 63.55 W
Cochem 56 50.11 N 7.09 E
Cochesett 283 42.01 N 71.02 W
Cochetopa Creek ≐ 200 38.31 N 106.47 W
Cochichewick, Lake ⊜ 283 42.42 N 71.06 W
Cochin 122 9.58 N 76.14 E
Cochin China → Nam Phan □[9] 110 11.00 N 107.00 E
Cochinos, Bahía de (Bay of Pigs) c 240p 22.07 N 81.10 W
Cochinos, Cayos II 236 15.57 N 86.33 W
Cochise Head ∧ 200 32.03 N 109.18 W
Cochiti Indian Reservation ◆[4] 200 35.37 N 106.20 W
Cochituate 207 42.19 N 71.21 W
Cochituate, Lake ⊜ 283 42.17 N 71.22 W
Cochituate State Park ♦ 207 42.20 N 71.22 W
Cochran 192 32.23 N 83.21 W
Cochrane, Ab., Can. 182 51.11 N 114.28 W
Cochrane, On., Can. 176 49.04 N 81.01 W
Cochrane, Chile 254 47.16 S 72.33 W
Cochrane, Wi., U.S. 190 44.13 N 91.50 W
Cochrane ≐ 176 57.52 N 101.38 W
Cochrane, Cerro (Monte San Lorenzo) ∧ 254 47.37 S 72.19 W
Cochrane, Lago (Lago Pueyrredón) ⊜ 254 47.20 S 72.00 W
Cochranton 214 41.31 N 80.02 W
Cochranville 208 39.53 N 75.55 W
Cochstedt 54 51.53 N 11.24 E
Cockatoo-Inseln → Buccaneer Archipelago II 160 16.17 S 123.20 E
Cock Bridge 46 57.09 N 3.14 W
Cockburn 166 32.05 S 141.00 E
Cockburn, Canal 𝔲 254 54.20 S 71.30 W
Cockburn, Cape ≻ 164 11.20 S 132.52 E
Cockburn, Mount ∧ 162 22.46 S 130.36 E
Cockburn Island I 190 45.55 N 83.22 W
Cockburn Sound 𝔲 168a 32.12 S 115.42 E
Cockburnspath 46 55.56 N 2.21 W
Cock Clarks 260 51.42 N 0.37 E
Cockenoe Island I 276 41.05 N 73.21 W
Cockenzie 46 55.58 N 2.58 W
Cocker ≐ 44 54.39 N 3.22 W
Cockerham 44 53.59 N 2.50 W
Cockermouth 44 54.40 N 3.21 W
Cockeysville 208 39.28 N 76.38 W
Cockfield 44 54.37 N 1.48 W
Cockfosters ◆[8] 260 51.39 N 0.09 W
Cocklebiddy 162 32.02 S 126.06 E
Cockpit Country ◆[1] 241q 18.18 N 77.43 W
Cockrell Hill 222 32.44 N 96.53 W
Cockroach Island I 240m 18.24 N 65.04 W
Cockscomb Point ≻ 174u 14.14 S 170.40 W
Coclé □[4] 236 8.30 N 80.15 W
Coclé del Norte ≐ 236 9.05 N 80.35 W
Coclois 50 48.28 N 4.20 E
Coco ≐ 236 15.00 N 83.10 W
Coco, Cayo I 240p 22.30 N 78.28 W
Coco, Isla del I 230 5.32 N 87.04 W
Côco, Rio do ≐ 250 9.27 S 50.02 W
Cocoa 220 28.23 N 80.44 W
Cocoa Beach 220 28.19 N 80.36 W
Cocobeach 152 0.59 N 9.36 E
Coco Channel 𝔲 110 13.45 N 93.00 E
Cococi 250 6.25 S 40.30 W
Cocodrie Lake ⊜[1] 194 30.58 N 92.25 W
Coco Islands II 110 14.05 N 93.18 E
Coconino Plateau ⩘[1] 200 35.50 N 112.30 W
Cocorocuma, Cayos ✢[2] 236 15.45 N 83.00 W
Cocos 255 14.10 S 44.33 W
Cocos (Keeling) Islands □[2] 14 12.10 S 96.55 E
Cocos Bay c 241r 10.27 N 61.00 W
Cocos Island I 174p 13.14 N 144.39 E
Cocos Lagoon c 174p 13.14 N 144.38 E
Cocos Ridge ✢[3] 16 5.30 N 86.00 W
Cocotá ◆[8] 287a 22.49 S 43.11 W
Cocuiza ≐ 246 10.59 N 71.17 W
Cocula, Méx. 234 18.14 N 99.40 W
Cocula, Méx. 234 20.23 N 103.50 W
Cod ≐ 44 54.10 N 1.22 W
Cod, Cape ≻[1] 207 41.42 N 70.15 W
Codăești 38 46.52 N 27.46 E
Codajás 246 3.50 S 62.05 W
Codaruina 71 40.56 N 8.49 E
Coddenham 42 52.09 N 1.07 E
Codera, Cabo ≻ 246 10.35 N 66.05 W
Coderre 184 50.10 N 106.23 W
Coderre, Ruisseau ≐ 275a 45.43 N 73.19 W
Codesa 182 55.45 N 118.04 W
Codfish Island I 172 46.47 S 167.38 E
Codigoro 66 44.49 N 12.08 E
Cod Island I 176 57.45 N 61.50 W
Codlea 38 45.42 N 25.27 E
Codnor 44 53.03 N 1.23 W
Codó 250 4.29 S 43.53 W
Codogno 62 45.09 N 9.42 E
Codorus 208 39.48 N 76.52 W
Codorus Creek ≐ 208 40.03 N 76.38 W
Codorus State Park ♦ 208 39.48 N 76.54 W
Codòzinho 250 4.46 S 44.10 W
Çodpa 248 18.50 S 69.44 W
Čodro 86 50.50 N 88.34 E
Codroipo 64 45.58 N 12.59 E
Codrongianos 71 40.39 N 8.41 E
Codroy 186 47.53 N 59.24 W
Codroy Pond 186 48.04 N 58.52 W
Codru-Moma, Munții ⩘ 38 46.30 N 22.20 E
Codsall 42 52.38 N 2.12 W
Cody, Ne., U.S. 198 42.56 N 101.14 W
Cody, Wy., U.S. 202 44.31 N 109.03 W
Coeburn 192 36.56 N 82.27 W
Coelemu 252 36.29 S 72.42 W
Coelho da Rocha 256 22.47 S 43.23 W
Coelho Neto 250 4.15 S 43.00 W
Coemba 152 12.08 S 18.05 E
Coen 164 13.56 S 143.12 E
Coen ≐, Austl. 164 13.56 S 142.02 E
Coén ≐, C.R. 236 9.34 N 82.58 W
Coeneo [de la Libertad] 234 19.49 N 101.35 W
Coeroeni ≐ 250 3.21 N 57.31 W
Coesfeld 52 51.56 N 7.10 E
Coetivy Island I 138 7.08 S 56.16 E
Coeur d'Alene 202 47.40 N 116.46 W
Coeur d'Alene ≐ 202 47.28 N 116.48 W
Coeur d'Alene Indian Reservation ◆[4] 202 47.18 N 116.45 W
Coeur d'Alene Lake ⊜ 202 47.32 N 116.48 W
Coeur d'Alene Mountains ⩘ 202 47.50 N 116.05 W
Coevorden 52 52.40 N 6.45 E
Coeymans 210 42.28 N 73.48 W
Coffeen 219 39.05 N 89.24 W
Coffeen Lake ⊜[1] 219 39.03 N 89.20 W
Coffeeville 194 33.58 N 89.40 W
Coffeyville 198 37.02 N 95.36 W
Coffin Bay 162 34.37 S 135.29 E
Coffin Bay c 162 34.27 S 135.19 E

Symbols in the index entries represent the broad categories identified in the key at the right. Symbols with superior numbers (⩘[1]) identify subcategories (see complete key on page I · 1).

Symbole im Register stellen die rechts im Schlüssel erklärten Kategorien dar. Symbole mit hochgestellten Ziffern (⩘[1]) bezeichnen Unterabteilungen einer Kategorie (vgl. vollständiger Schlüssel auf Seite I · 1).

Los símbolos incluídos en el texto del índice representan las grandes categorias identificadas con la clave a la derecha. Los símbolos con numeros en su parte superior (⩘[1]) identifican las subcategorías (véase la clave completa en la página I · 1).

Les symboles de l'index représentent les catégories indiquées dans la légende à droite. Les symboles suivis d'un indice (⩘[1]) représentent des sous-catégories (voir légende complète à la page I · 1).

Os símbolos incluídos no texto do índice representam as grandes categorias identificadas com a chave à direita. Os símbolos com números em sua parte superior (⩘[1]) identificam as subcategorias (vejase a chave completa à página I · 1).

∧	Mountain	Berg	Montaña	Montagne	Montanha
⩘	Mountains	Gebirge	Montañas	Montagnes	Montanhas
)(	Pass	Paß	Paso	Col	Passo
V	Valley, Canyon	Tal, Cañon	Valle, Cañón	Vallée, Canyon	Vale, Canhão
≃	Plain	Ebene	Llano	Plaine	Planície
≻	Cape	Kap	Cabo	Cap	Cabo
I	Island	Insel	Isla	Île	Ilha
II	Islands	Inseln	Islas	Îles	Ilhas
✢	Other Topographic Features	Andere Topographische Objekte	Otros Elementos Topográficos	Autres données topographiques	Outros acidentes topográficos

ESPAÑOL — Nombre | Página | Lat.°′ | Long.°′ W = Oeste
FRANÇAIS — Nom | Page | Lat.°′ | Long.°′ W = Ouest
PORTUGUÊS — Nome | Página | Lat.°′ | Long.°′ W = Oeste

Coffin Bay Peninsula ≻1 162 34.32 S 135.15 E
Coffs Harbour 166 30.18 S 153.08 E
Cofimvaba 158 32.00 S 27.35 E
Cofradía 236 15.24 N 88.09 W
Cofre de Perote, Cerro ∧ 234 19.29 N 97.08 W
Cofre de Perote, Parque Nacional ♠ 234 19.32 N 97.10 W
Cofrents 34 39.14 N 1.04 W
Coggeshall 42 51.52 N 0.41 E
Coggiola 62 45.41 N 8.11 E
Coggon 190 42.16 N 91.31 W
Coghill, Mount ∧ 170 35.10 S 149.44 E
Coghinas ≃ 71 40.56 N 8.48 E
Coghinas, Lago del ⊜ 71 40.45 N 9.02 E
Coglians, Monte (Hohe Warte) ∧ 64 46.37 N 12.53 E
Cogliate 266b 45.39 N 9.05 E
Cognac 32 45.42 N 0.20 W
Cogne 62 45.37 N 7.21 E
Cognin 62 45.34 N 5.54 E
Cogo 152 1.05 N 9.42 E
Cogoleto 62 44.23 N 8.39 E
Cogolin 62 43.15 N 6.32 E
Cogollo del Cengio 64 45.47 N 11.25 E
Cogolludo 34 40.57 N 3.05 W
Cogolo 64 46.21 N 10.41 E
Cogoon ≃ 166 27.19 S 148.50 E
Čograjskoje vodochranilišče ⊜1 80 45.30 N 44.25 E
Cogswell 198 46.06 N 97.46 W
Cogswell Reservoir ⊜1 280 34.14 N 117.58 W
Cogt 102 45.20 N 96.38 E
Cogtoandman' 102 45.50 N 104.28 E
Cogton Bay c 116 9.51 N 124.33 E
Cogt-Ovoo 102 44.25 N 105.20 E
Çoğun 130 39.20 N 34.08 E
Cohansey ≃ 208 39.21 N 75.22 W
Cohasset 207 42.14 N 70.48 W
Cohasset Harbor c 283 42.15 N 70.47 W
Cohengu ≃ 248 10.17 S 73.57 W
Cohoctah 216 42.46 N 83.57 W
Cohocton 210 42.30 N 77.30 W
Cohocton ≃ 210 42.09 N 77.05 W
Cohoe 180 60.23 N 151.18 W
Cohoes 210 42.46 N 73.42 W
Cohoon, Lake ⊜1 208 36.45 N 76.38 W
Cohuna 166 35.49 S 144.13 E
Coiba, Isla de I 246 7.27 N 81.45 W
Coig ≃ 254 50.58 S 69.11 W
Coigeach, Rubha ≻ 46 58.06 N 5.26 W
Coignières 261 48.45 N 1.55 E
Coihaique 254 45.34 S 72.04 W
Coils Creek ≃ 204 39.32 N 116.16 W
Coimbatore 122 11.00 N 76.58 E
Coimbra, Bra. 248 19.55 S 57.47 W
Coimbra, Bra. 255 20.52 S 42.48 W
Coimbra, Port. 34 40.12 N 8.25 W
Coín, Esp. 34 36.40 N 4.45 W
Coin, Ia., U.S. 198 40.39 N 95.13 W
Coina ≃ 266c 38.38 N 9.03 W
Coipasa, Lago ⊜ 248 19.12 S 68.07 W
Coipasa, Salar de ≡ 248 19.26 S 68.09 W
Coire → Chur 58 46.51 N 9.32 E
Čojbalsan, Mong. 88 48.25 N 114.52 E
Čojbalsan, Mong. 88 48.04 N 114.30 E
Čojbalsan uul ∧ 88 47.49 N 107.00 E
Cojedes 246 9.37 N 68.55 W
Cojedes □3 246 9.20 N 68.20 W
Cojímar ◆8 286b 23.10 N 82.18 W
Cojímar ≃ 286b 23.10 N 82.17 W
Cojudo Blanco, Cerro ∧ 254 47.05 S 69.20 W
Cojumatlán de Régules 234 20.07 N 102.50 W
Cojutepeque 236 13.43 N 88.56 W
Çokak 130 37.45 N 36.19 E
Cokato 190 45.04 N 94.11 W
Cokeburg 214 40.06 N 80.04 W
Coker 273a 6.29 N 3.20 E
Cokeville 200 42.04 N 110.57 W
Čoktal 85 42.36 N 76.44 E
Čokurdach 74 70.38 N 147.55 E
Colāba ◆8 272c 18.54 N 72.48 E
Colāba Point ≻ 272c 18.53 N 72.48 E
Colac 169 38.20 S 143.35 E
Colac, Lake ⊜ 169 38.18 S 143.35 E
Çolaklı 130 38.22 N 38.33 E
Colalao del Valle 252 26.22 S 65.57 W
Colapsin Point ≻ 116 6.38 N 125.25 E
Colares, Bra. 250 0.56 S 48.17 W
Colares, Port. 266c 38.48 N 9.27 W
Colares, Ribeira de ≃ 266c 38.49 N 9.28 W
Colatina 255 19.32 S 40.37 W
Cölbe 56 50.51 N 8.48 E
Colbeck, Cape ≻ 9 77.06 S 157.48 W
Colberry Park 281 42.36 N 83.16 W
Colbert 196 33.51 N 96.30 W
Colbinabbin 166 36.35 S 144.49 E
Colbitz 54 52.19 N 11.36 E
Colbitz-Letzlinger Heide ◆3 54 52.27 N 11.35 E
Colborne, On., Can. 212 42.51 N 80.19 W
Colborne, On., Can. 212 44.00 N 77.53 W
Colbún 252 35.42 S 71.25 W
Colbún, Embalse ⊜1 252 35.40 S 71.20 W
Colburn, Eng., U.K. 44 54.23 N 1.41 W
Colburn, In., U.S. 216 40.31 N 86.42 W
Colby, Ks., U.S. 198 39.23 N 101.03 W
Colby, Wi., U.S. 190 44.54 N 90.18 W
Colca 248 12.18 S 75.13 W
Colca ≃ 248 15.51 S 72.26 W
Colcamar 248 6.16 S 77.55 W
Colchester, On., Can. 214 41.59 N 82.56 W
Colchester, Eng., U.K. 42 51.54 N 0.54 E
Colchester, Ct., U.S. 207 41.34 N 72.19 W
Colchester, Il., U.S. 190 40.25 N 90.47 W
Coldbackie 46 58.31 N 4.23 W
Cold Bay 180 55.11 N 162.30 W
Cold Bay c 180 55.13 N 162.33 W
Coldblow ◆8 260 51.26 N 0.10 E
Cold Brook 210 43.15 N 75.03 W
Cold Creek ≃ 212 44.12 N 77.36 W
Colden 210 42.39 N 78.41 W
Cold Fell ∧ 44 54.54 N 2.36 W
Cold Harbor Battlefield ⊥ 208 37.36 N 77.20 W
Coldingham 46 55.53 N 2.10 W
Colditz 54 51.07 N 12.48 E
Cold Lake 184 54.27 N 110.10 W
Cold Lake ⊜ 184 54.33 N 110.05 W
Cold Lake, Canadian Forces Base ■ 184 54.25 N 110.17 W
Cold Lake Indian Reserve ◆4 184 54.33 N 110.10 W
Cold Norton 260 51.40 N 0.40 E
Coldrano 64 46.38 N 10.50 E
Cold Spring, Ky., U.S. 218 39.01 N 84.26 W
Cold Spring, Mn., U.S. 190 45.27 N 94.25 W
Cold Spring, N.J., U.S. 208 38.58 N 74.55 W
Cold Spring, N.Y., U.S. 210 41.25 N 73.57 W
Coldspring, Tx., U.S. 222 30.36 N 95.08 W
Cold Spring Harbor 276 40.52 N 73.27 W
Cold Spring Harbor c 276 40.53 N 73.28 W
Coldsprings, On., Can. 212 44.17 N 78.18 W
Cold Springs, N.Y., U.S. 210 43.08 N 76.15 W
Cold Spring Terrace 276 40.50 N 73.26 W
Coldstream, Austl. 169 37.44 S 145.23 E
Coldstream, Scot., U.K. 46 55.39 N 2.15 W
Cold Stream ≃ 226 39.35 N 120.22 W
Coldwater, On., Can. 212 44.42 N 79.40 W
Coldwater, Ks., U.S. 198 37.16 N 99.19 W
Coldwater, Mi., U.S. 216 41.56 N 85.00 W
Coldwater, Ms., U.S. 194 34.41 N 89.58 W
Coldwater, Oh., U.S. 216 40.28 N 84.37 W
Coldwater ≃, On., Can. 212 44.44 N 79.39 W
Coldwater ≃, Mi., U.S. 216 42.04 N 85.08 W
Coldwater ≃, Ms., U.S. 194 34.11 N 90.13 W
Coldwater Canyon V 280 34.14 N 117.44 W
Coldwater Creek ≃ 196 36.40 N 101.08 W
Coldwater Indian Reserve ◆4 182 50.04 N 120.48 W
Coldwater Lake ⊜ 216 41.49 N 84.58 W
Cole □6 219 38.30 N 92.13 W
Cole ≃, Ang. 152 9.07 S 15.50 E
Cole ≃, Eng., U.K. 42 51.42 N 1.42 W
Coleambally 166 34.49 S 145.52 E
Colebrook, N.H., U.S. 188 44.53 N 71.29 W
Colebrook, Oh., U.S. 214 41.32 N 80.46 W
Colebrook River Lake ⊜1 207 42.03 N 73.04 W
Cole Camp 194 38.27 N 93.12 W
Coledale 170 34.17 S 150.57 E
Coleen ≃ 180 67.05 N 142.31 W
Coleford, Eng., U.K. 42 51.48 N 2.36 W
Coleford, Eng., U.K. 42 51.14 N 2.27 W
Colégio, Morro do ∧ 287b 23.38 S 46.21 W
Coleman, Ab., Can. 182 49.38 N 114.30 W
Coleman, Fl., U.S. 220 28.47 N 82.04 W
Coleman, Md., U.S. 208 39.20 N 76.04 W
Coleman, Mi., U.S. 190 43.45 N 84.35 W
Coleman, Tx., U.S. 196 31.49 N 99.25 W
Coleman, Wi., U.S. 190 45.03 N 88.02 W
Coleman ≃ 164 15.06 S 141.38 E
Coleman, Lake ⊜1 196 32.02 N 99.30 W
Colembert 50 50.45 N 1.50 E
Colen Lakes ⊜ 184 54.33 N 95.25 W
Colenso 158 28.50 S 29.44 E
Colerain 214 40.07 N 80.49 W
Coleraine, Austl. 166 37.36 S 141.42 E
Coleraine, N. Ire., U.K. 48 55.08 N 6.40 W
Coleraine, Mn., U.S. 190 47.17 N 93.25 W
Coleridge 198 42.30 N 97.12 W
Coleridge, Lake ⊜ 172 43.17 S 171.30 E
Coles 194 31.16 N 91.01 W
Coles, Punta ≻ 248 17.42 S 71.23 W
Colesberg 158 30.45 S 25.05 E
Coles Brook ≃ 276 40.55 N 74.02 W
Coleshill, Eng., U.K. 42 52.30 N 1.42 W
Coleshill, Eng., U.K. 260 51.39 N 0.38 W
Coles Point 208 38.09 N 76.38 W
Colesville, Md., U.S. 284c 39.05 N 77.00 W
Colesville, N.J., U.S. 210 41.15 N 74.39 W
Coleto Creek ≃ 196 28.41 N 97.01 W
Coleville, Sk., Can. 184 51.43 N 109.16 W
Coleville, Ca., U.S. 226 38.33 N 119.30 W
Colfax, Ca., U.S. 226 39.06 N 120.57 W
Colfax, Il., U.S. 216 40.34 N 88.36 W
Colfax, In., U.S. 194 40.11 N 86.40 W
Colfax, Ia., U.S. 190 41.40 N 93.14 W
Colfax, La., U.S. 194 31.31 N 92.42 W
Colfax, Wa., U.S. 202 46.52 N 117.21 W
Colfax, Wi., U.S. 190 44.59 N 91.43 W
Colfiorito 66 43.02 N 12.55 E
Colgate 216 43.12 N 88.12 W
Colgate Creek ≃ 284b 39.15 N 76.32 W
Colgong 124 25.16 N 87.13 E
Colgrave Sound ⊔ 46a 60.37 N 0.58 W
Colhué Huapi, Lago ⊜ 254 45.30 S 68.48 W
Coliban ≃ 169 36.56 S 144.33 E
Colibris, Pointe des ≻, Guad. 241o 16.17 N 61.06 W
Colibris, Pointe des ≻, Guad. 241o 16.15 N 61.11 W
Colico 58 46.08 N 9.22 E
Coligny, Fr. 58 46.23 N 5.21 E
Coligny, S. Afr. 158 26.17 S 26.15 E
Colijnsplaat 52 51.46 N 3.51 E
Colima, Méx. 200 32.25 N 115.05 W
Colima, Méx. 234 19.14 N 103.43 W
Colima □3 234 19.10 N 104.00 W
Colima, Nevado de ∧ 234 19.33 N 103.38 W
Colimes ≃ 246 1.32 S 80.00 W
Colin ≃ 50 47.08 N 2.32 E
Colina 252 33.12 S 70.41 W
Colinas, Bra. 250 6.02 S 44.14 W
Colinas, Bra. 255 14.12 S 48.03 W
Colinet 186 47.13 N 53.33 W
Colinton, Austl. 171b 35.51 S 149.09 E
Colinton, Ab., Can. 182 54.37 N 113.15 W
Coll I 46 56.38 N 6.34 W
Colla 258 34.04 S 57.21 W
Colla, Arroyo ≃ 258 34.19 S 57.20 W
Collagna 64 44.21 N 10.16 E
Collalbo (Klobenstein) 64 46.32 N 11.28 E
Collalto Sabino 66 42.08 N 13.02 E
Collamer 210 43.06 N 76.04 W
Collarenebri 166 29.33 S 148.35 E
Collarmele 66 42.03 N 13.38 E
Collaroy 274a 33.44 S 151.18 E
Collazzone 66 42.54 N 12.26 E
Collbran 200 39.14 N 107.57 W
Collecchio 64 44.45 N 10.13 E
Collecorvino 66 42.27 N 14.01 E
Colle di Tora 66 42.13 N 12.57 E
Colle di Val d'Elsa 66 43.25 N 11.07 E
Colleen Bawn 154 21.00 S 29.13 E
Colleferro 66 41.44 N 12.59 E
College 180 64.51 N 147.47 W
College City 226 39.00 N 122.00 W
College Corner 218 39.30 N 84.36 W
Collegedale 194 35.04 N 85.03 W
College Meadows 218 39.56 N 86.07 W
College Park, Ga., U.S. 192 33.39 N 84.26 W
College Park, Md., U.S. 208 38.58 N 76.56 W
College Park Airport ⊠ 284c 38.58 N 76.55 W
College Place 202 46.02 N 118.23 W
College Point ◆8 276 40.47 N 73.51 W
College Station, Ar., U.S. 194 34.43 N 92.13 W
College Station, Tx., U.S. 222 30.37 N 96.20 W
Collegeville, In., U.S. 216 40.54 N 87.09 W
Collegeville, Pa., U.S. 208 40.11 N 75.27 W
Collégien 261 48.50 N 2.40 E
Collegno 62 45.05 N 7.34 E
Colle Isarco (Gossensass) 64 46.56 N 11.26 E
Collepardo 66 41.46 N 13.22 E
Collepasso 68 40.04 N 18.10 E
Collepietro 66 42.13 N 13.46 E
Collerina 166 29.41 S 146.38 E
Collesalvetti 66 43.35 N 10.28 E
Colle Sannita 68 41.22 N 14.50 E
Collesano 70 37.55 N 13.56 E
Colletorto 66 41.40 N 14.58 E
Colleymount 182 54.01 N 126.09 W
Colleyville 222 32.52 N 97.09 W
Colliano 68 40.43 N 15.17 E
Colli a Volturno 66 41.36 N 14.06 E
Colli del Tronto 66 42.52 N 13.44 E
Colli di Monte Bove 66 42.06 N 13.09 E
Collie 168a 33.21 S 116.09 E
Collie ≃ 168a 33.18 S 115.44 E
Collie East ≃ 168a 33.18 S 116.10 E
Collier □6 220 26.10 N 81.22 W
Collier Bay c 160 16.10 S 124.15 E
Collier Bridge ◆5 220 26.57 N 82.04 W
Collier City 220 26.14 N 80.09 W
Collier Law ∧2 44 54.46 N 1.58 W
Collier Range ⋏ 162 24.43 S 119.12 E
Collier Range National Park ♠ 162 24.40 S 119.15 E
Collier Row ◆8 260 51.36 N 0.10 E
Colliers 214 40.22 N 80.32 W
Collier-Seminole State Park ♠ 220 25.59 N 81.36 W
Colliersville 210 42.29 N 74.59 W
Collierville 194 35.02 N 89.39 W
Collie South ≃ 168a 33.18 S 116.10 E
Collieston 46 57.21 N 1.56 W
Colliford Lake Reservoir ⊜1 42 50.32 N 4.33 W
Colligan ≃ 48 52.06 N 7.38 W
Collin □6 222 33.07 N 96.35 W
Collina, Passo della)(66 44.01 N 10.56 E
Collingbourne Kingston 42 51.18 N 1.40 W
Collingdale 208 39.54 N 75.16 W
Collingham 44 53.54 N 1.24 W
Collingswood 285 39.55 N 75.04 W
Collingwood, Austl. 274b 37.48 S 145.00 E
Collingwood, On., Can. 212 44.29 N 80.13 W
Collingwood, N.Z. 172 40.40 S 172.41 E
Collingwood Bay c 164 9.20 S 149.30 E
Collins, Ga., U.S. 192 32.10 N 82.06 W
Collins, Ia., U.S. 190 41.54 N 93.18 W
Collins, Ms., U.S. 194 31.38 N 89.33 W
Collins, N.Y., U.S. 210 42.30 N 78.55 W
Collins, Oh., U.S. 214 41.16 N 82.30 W
Collins ≃ 194 35.48 N 85.37 W
Collins, Mount ∧2 190 47.51 N 80.59 W
Collins Bay 212 44.15 N 76.36 W
Collinsburg 214 40.13 N 79.46 W
Collins Center 210 42.30 N 78.51 W
Collins Lake ⊜ 212 44.22 N 76.27 W
Collins Park 208 39.41 N 75.33 W
Collinston 194 32.41 N 91.52 W
Collinsville, Austl. 166 20.34 S 147.51 E
Collinsville, Al., U.S. 194 34.15 N 85.51 W
Collinsville, Ca., U.S. 282 38.05 N 121.51 W
Collinsville, Ct., U.S. 207 41.48 N 72.55 W
Collinsville, Il., U.S. 219 38.40 N 89.59 W
Collinsville, Ms., U.S. 194 32.29 N 88.50 W
Collinsville, N.J., U.S. 276 40.49 N 74.28 W
Collinsville, Ok., U.S. 196 36.21 N 95.50 W
Collinsville, Tx., U.S. 196 33.32 N 96.54 W
Collinwood 194 35.10 N 87.44 W
Collio 64 45.48 N 10.20 E
Collipulli 252 37.57 S 72.26 W
Collister 202 43.38 N 116.15 W
Collobrières 62 43.14 N 6.18 E
Collombey 58 46.16 N 6.57 E
Collomsville 210 41.09 N 77.09 W
Collon 48 53.47 N 6.29 W
Collonges 58 46.08 N 5.54 E
Collooney 48 54.11 N 8.29 W
Collserola, Serra de ⋏ 266d 41.26 N 2.07 E
Colma 226 37.41 N 122.28 W
Colma Creek ≃ 282 37.38 N 122.23 W
Colman 198 43.58 N 96.48 W
Colmar 58 48.05 N 7.22 E
Colmar Manor 284c 38.55 N 76.56 W
Colmars 62 44.11 N 6.38 E
Colmenar 34 36.54 N 4.20 W
Colmenar de Oreja 34 40.06 N 3.23 W
Colmenar Viejo 34 40.40 N 3.46 W
Colmeneros 234 18.06 N 101.40 W
Colmesneil 194 30.54 N 94.25 W
Colmnitz 54 50.54 N 13.31 E
Colmonell 44 55.08 N 4.55 W
Coln ≃ 42 51.42 N 1.42 W
Colnbrook 260 51.29 N 0.31 W
Colne 44 53.52 N 2.09 W
Colne ≃, Eng., U.K. 42 51.48 N 1.01 E
Colne ≃, Eng., U.K. 260 51.26 N 0.30 W
Colney Heath 260 51.44 N 0.15 W
Colney Street 260 51.42 N 0.20 W
Colo 190 42.01 N 93.18 W
Colo ≃ 170 33.26 S 150.53 E
Colobraro 68 40.11 N 16.25 E
Cologna Veneta 64 45.18 N 11.23 E
Cologne, Mn., U.S. 190 44.46 N 93.46 W
Cologne, N.J., U.S. 208 39.30 N 74.36 W
Cologne → Köln 56 50.56 N 6.59 E
Cologno al Serio 62 45.37 N 9.42 E
Cologno Monzese 266b 45.32 N 9.17 E
Cololo, Nevado ∧ 248 14.53 S 69.06 W
Coloma, Ca., U.S. 226 38.48 N 120.53 W
Coloma, Mi., U.S. 216 42.11 N 86.18 W
Coloma, Wi., U.S. 190 44.02 N 89.31 W
Colomb-Béchar → Béchar 148 31.37 N 2.13 W
Colombes 50 48.55 N 2.15 E
Colombey-les-Belles 58 48.32 N 5.54 E
Colombey-les-Deux-Eglises 58 48.13 N 4.53 E
Colômbia, Bra. 255 20.30 S 48.37 W
Colombia, Col. 246 3.24 N 74.49 W
Colombia, Cuba 240p 20.59 N 77.25 W
Colombia, Méx. 196 27.42 N 99.45 W
Colombia □1, S.A. 242 4.00 N 72.00 W
Colombia □1, S.A. 246 4.00 N 72.00 W
Colombian Basin ✦1 16 13.00 N 76.00 W
Colombie-Britannique → British Columbia □4 182 54.00 N 125.00 W
Colombie → Colombia □1 246 4.00 N 72.00 W
Colombier 58 46.58 N 6.52 E
Colombo, Bra. 252 25.17 S 49.14 W
Colombo, S. Lan. 122 6.56 N 79.51 E
Colome 198 43.15 N 99.42 W
Colomiers 32 43.37 N 1.20 E
Colón, Arg. 252 33.53 S 61.07 W
Colón, Arg. 252 32.13 S 58.08 W
Colón, Cuba 240p 22.43 N 80.54 W
Colón, Méx. 234 20.48 N 100.03 W
Colón, Pan. 236 9.22 N 79.54 W
Colon, Mi., U.S. 216 41.57 N 85.19 W
Colón, Ur. 252 33.53 S 54.43 W
Colón, Ur. 258 34.48 S 56.14 W
Colón □4 236 9.00 N 80.20 W
Colón □5 236 15.40 N 85.30 W
Colón, Archipiélago de (Galapagos Islands) II 246a 0.30 S 90.30 W
Colón, Cementerio ◆ 286b 23.08 N 82.23 W
Colón, Isla I 236 9.24 N 82.17 W
Colón, Montañas de ⋏ 236 14.55 N 84.45 W
Colón, Teatro ♠ 288 34.36 S 58.23 W
Colona 162 31.38 S 132.05 E
Colonard-Corubert 50 48.25 N 0.39 E
Colonarie ≃ 241h 13.14 N 61.06 W
Colonel Danforth Park ♠ 275b 43.47 N 79.10 W
Colonelganj 124 27.08 N 81.42 E
Coloneşti 38 46.34 N 27.18 E
Colonet 204 31.05 N 116.10 W
Colonet, Cabo ≻ 204 30.58 N 116.19 W
Colongulac, Lake ⊜ 169 38.10 S 143.11 E
Colonia, Micron. 174q 9.31 N 138.08 E
Colonia, N.J., U.S. 210 40.34 N 74.18 W
Colonia □5 258 34.10 S 57.30 W
Colônia ≃ 255 15.11 S 39.45 W
Colonia, Aeropuerto ⊠ 258 34.28 S 57.49 W
Colonia, Cuchilla de la ⋏2 258 34.15 S 57.35 W
Colonia Alvear 252 35.00 S 67.40 W
Colonia Caroya 252 31.02 S 64.05 W
Colonia del Sacramento 258 34.28 S 57.51 W
Colonia Dora 252 28.36 S 62.57 W
Colonia Elisa 252 26.56 S 59.32 W
Colonia Guadalupe 204 32.04 N 116.37 W
Colonia Hogar Ricardo Gutiérrez 288 34.51 S 58.51 W
Colonia José Mármol 252 26.59 S 60.44 W
Colonia → Köln 56 50.56 N 6.59 E
Colonial Acres 208 39.31 N 76.20 W
Colonia Lavalleja 252 31.06 S 57.01 W
Colonial Beach 208 38.15 N 76.57 W
Colonial Crest 208 40.20 N 76.50 W
Colônia Leopoldina 250 8.57 S 35.39 W
Colonial Heights 208 37.14 N 77.24 W
Colonial Manor 285 39.51 N 75.09 W
Colonial National Historical Park ♠ 208 37.12 N 76.45 W
Colonial Park 208 40.18 N 76.48 W
Colonial Village, N.Y., U.S. 210 43.08 N 78.58 W
Colonial Village, Pa., U.S. 285 40.04 N 75.24 W
Colonial Village Airport ⊠ 284a 43.08 N 78.58 W
Colonial Williamsburg ⊥ 208 37.16 N 76.42 W
Colonia Morelos 200 30.50 N 109.10 W
Colonia Nicolich 258 34.50 S 56.02 W
Colonia Progreso 204 32.35 N 115.37 W
Colonia Providencia 240m 17.59 N 66.00 W
Colonias Unidas 252 26.42 S 59.38 W
Colonia Valdense 258 34.20 S 57.14 W
Colonia Vicente Guerrero 232 30.45 N 116.00 W
Colonia Villafañe 252 26.12 S 59.05 W
Colonie 210 42.43 N 73.50 W
Colon Koret 152 0.34 N 23.28 E
Colonna 267a 41.50 N 12.45 E
Colonna, Capo ≻ 68 39.02 N 17.11 E
Colonnata 64 44.05 N 10.10 E
Colón Ridge ✦3 18 2.00 N 96.00 W
Colonsay 184 51.59 N 105.53 W
Colonsay I 46 56.04 N 6.13 W
Colony 198 38.04 N 95.21 W
Colora 208 39.40 N 76.06 W
Colorada, Laguna ≡ 254 44.50 S 68.15 W
Colorada, Punta ≻ 288 34.45 S 58.06 W
Coloradas, Lomas ⋏2 254 43.24 S 67.24 W
Colorado, C.R. 236 10.46 N 83.35 W
Colorado, Hond. 236 15.47 N 87.19 W
Colorado, Ak., U.S. 180 63.09 N 149.26 W
Colorado □6 222 29.40 N 96.30 W
Colorado □3 178 39.00 N 105.30 W
Colorado ≃, Arg. 244 39.50 S 62.08 W
Colorado ≃, Bra. 248 13.03 S 62.20 W
Colorado ≃, Méx. 234 16.30 N 97.31 W
Colorado ≃, N.A. 200 31.54 N 114.57 W
Colorado ≃, Tx., U.S. 196 28.36 N 95.58 W
Colorado, Canal do ≅ 287a 23.00 S 43.25 W
Colorado, Cerro ∧, Arg. 254 45.02 S 69.38 W
Colorado, Cerro ∧, Chile 286e 33.24 S 70.45 W
Colorado, Cerro ∧, Perú 286d 12.07 S 76.55 W
Colorado, Williams Fork ≃ 200 40.03 N 106.11 W
Colorado City, Az., U.S. 200 36.59 N 112.58 W
Colorado City, Co., U.S. 200 37.56 N 104.50 W
Colorado City, Tx., U.S. 196 32.23 N 100.51 W
Colorado de Abajo 196 26.28 N 99.54 W
Colorado Grande, Salina ≡ 252 38.15 S 63.47 W
Colorado National Monument ♠ 200 39.04 N 108.25 W
Colorado Plateau ⋏1 200 36.30 N 108.00 W
Colorado River Aqueduct ≅1 204 33.50 N 117.23 W
Colorado River Indian Reservation ◆4 200 34.00 N 114.25 W
Colorados, Archipiélago de los II 240p 22.36 N 84.20 W
Colorado Springs 200 38.50 N 104.49 W
Colorines 234 19.07 N 100.12 W
Colorno 64 44.56 N 10.23 E
Colosimi 68 39.07 N 16.24 E
Colosseo ⊥ 267a 41.54 N 12.29 E
Colotepec ≃ 234 15.47 N 97.03 W
Colotlán 234 22.06 N 103.16 W
Colotlán ≃ 234 22.06 N 103.42 W
Colotlipa 234 17.25 N 99.09 W
Colo Vale 170 34.24 S 150.29 E
Čolpon 85 42.12 N 75.28 E
Čolpon-Ata 85 42.40 N 77.06 E
Colpoys Bay c 212 44.47 N 81.05 W
Colquechaca 248 18.40 S 66.01 W
Colquencha 248 17.00 S 68.17 W
Colquiri 248 17.25 S 67.08 W
Colquitt 192 31.10 N 84.44 W
Colsterworth 42 52.48 N 0.37 W
Colstrip 202 45.53 N 106.37 W
Colt 194 35.07 N 90.48 W
Colta 248 15.10 S 73.18 W
Coltauco 252 34.18 S 71.06 W
Coltishall 42 52.44 N 1.22 E
Colton, Austl. 162 33.29 S 134.56 E
Colton, Ca., U.S. 228 34.04 N 117.18 W
Colton, Oh., U.S. 216 41.28 N 83.57 W
Colton, Or., U.S. 224 45.10 N 122.26 W
Colton, S.D., U.S. 198 43.47 N 96.55 W
Coltons Point 208 38.13 N 76.45 W
Colts Neck 208 40.17 N 74.10 W
Coltsville Center 214 41.05 N 80.34 W
Columbia, Al., U.S. 192 31.17 N 85.06 W
Columbia, Ca., U.S. 226 38.02 N 120.24 W
Columbia, Ct., U.S. 207 41.42 N 72.18 W
Columbia, Il., U.S. 219 38.26 N 90.12 W
Columbia, In., U.S. 218 39.35 N 85.12 W
Columbia, Ky., U.S. 194 37.06 N 85.18 W
Columbia, La., U.S. 194 32.06 N 92.04 W
Columbia, Md., U.S. 208 39.14 N 76.50 W
Columbia, Ms., U.S. 194 31.15 N 89.50 W
Columbia, Mo., U.S. 219 38.57 N 92.20 W
Columbia, N.J., U.S. 210 40.55 N 75.05 W
Columbia, N.C., U.S. 192 35.55 N 76.15 W
Columbia, Pa., U.S. 208 40.02 N 76.30 W
Columbia, S.C., U.S. 192 34.00 N 81.02 W
Columbia, Tn., U.S. 194 35.36 N 87.02 W
Columbia □6, N.Y., U.S. 210 42.15 N 73.47 W
Columbia □6, Or., U.S. 224 45.57 N 123.03 W
Columbia □6, Pa., U.S. 210 41.00 N 76.28 W
Columbia ≃ 176 46.15 N 124.05 W
Columbia, Cape ≻ 16 83.08 N 70.35 W
Columbia, Lake ⊜1 216 42.05 N 84.18 W
Columbia, Mount ∧ 182 52.09 N 117.25 W
Columbia Airport ⊠ 279a 41.19 N 81.58 W
Columbia Basin ≡1 202 46.45 N 119.05 W
Columbia Center 279a 41.19 N 81.56 W
Columbia City, In., U.S. 216 41.09 N 85.29 W
Columbia City, Or., U.S. 224 45.53 N 122.48 W
Columbia Cross Roads 210 41.50 N 76.48 W
Columbia Falls, Me., U.S. 188 44.39 N 67.43 W
Columbia Falls, Mt., U.S. 202 48.22 N 114.10 W
Columbia Heights 224 46.09 N 122.58 W
Columbia Hills 284b 39.15 N 76.50 W
Columbia Icefield ⊓ 182 52.10 N 117.30 W
Columbia Lake ⊜ 182 50.15 N 115.57 W
Columbia Lake Indian Reserve ◆4 182 50.25 N 115.57 W
Columbia Mountains ⋏ 182 52.00 N 119.00 W
Columbiana, Al., U.S. 194 33.10 N 86.36 W
Columbiana, Oh., U.S. 214 40.53 N 80.41 W
Columbiana □6 214 40.47 N 80.46 W
Columbia Plateau ⋏1 202 44.00 N 117.30 W
Columbia Regional Airport ⊠ 219 38.50 N 92.13 W
Columbia Road Reservoir ⊜1 198 45.45 N 98.15 W
Columbia State Historical Park ♠ 226 38.02 N 120.25 W
Columbia Station 214 41.20 N 81.57 W
Columbia University ✿2 276 40.48 N 73.58 W
Columbiaville, Mi., U.S. 190 43.09 N 83.24 W
Columbiaville, N.Y., U.S. 210 42.19 N 73.45 W
Columbine, Cape ≻ 158 32.47 S 17.52 E
Columbrets, Illes II 34 39.52 N 0.40 E
Columbus, Ga., U.S. 192 32.29 N 84.59 W
Columbus, In., U.S. 218 39.12 N 85.55 W
Columbus, Ks., U.S. 198 37.10 N 94.50 W
Columbus, Ms., U.S. 194 33.29 N 88.25 W
Columbus, Mt., U.S. 202 45.38 N 109.15 W
Columbus, Ne., U.S. 198 41.25 N 97.22 W
Columbus, N.J., U.S. 208 40.04 N 74.43 W
Columbus, N.M., U.S. 200 31.49 N 107.38 W
Columbus, N.C., U.S. 192 35.15 N 82.11 W
Columbus, N.D., U.S. 198 48.54 N 102.46 W
Columbus, Oh., U.S. 214 39.57 N 82.59 W
Columbus, Pa., U.S. 214 41.56 N 79.35 W
Columbus, Tx., U.S. 222 29.42 N 96.32 W
Columbus, Wi., U.S. 190 43.20 N 89.00 W
Columbus Air Force Base ■ 194 33.38 N 88.26 W
Columbus Grove 216 40.55 N 84.03 W
Columbus Junction 190 41.16 N 91.21 W
Columbus Lake ⊜1 194 33.35 N 88.30 W
Columbus Park ♠ 278 41.53 N 87.47 W
Columbus Point ≻, Ba. 238 24.08 N 75.16 W
Columbus Point ≻, Trin. 241r 11.08 N 60.48 W
Columbus Salt Marsh ≡ 204 38.04 N 117.58 W
Coluna 255 18.14 S 42.50 W
Colusa 226 39.12 N 122.00 W
Colusa □6 226 39.13 N 122.01 W
Colusa Trough ≅ 226 39.02 N 121.59 W
Colver 214 40.32 N 78.47 W
Colville, N.Z. 172 36.38 S 175.28 E
Colville, Wa., U.S. 202 48.32 N 117.54 W
Colville ≃, Ak., U.S. 180 70.25 N 150.30 W
Colville ≃, Wa., U.S. 202 48.37 N 118.05 W
Colville, Cape ≻ 172 36.28 S 175.21 E
Colville Channel ⊔ 172 36.23 S 175.24 E
Colville Indian Reservation ◆4 202 48.15 N 119.00 W
Colville Lake ⊜ 180 67.10 N 126.00 W
Colvin Run 284c 38.58 N 77.18 W
Colwell 44 55.04 N 2.04 W
Colwood 224 48.26 N 123.29 W
Colwyn 285 39.55 N 75.15 W
Colwyn Bay 44 53.18 N 3.43 W
Colyton, Austl. 274a 33.47 S 150.48 E
Colyton, Eng., U.K. 42 50.44 N 3.04 W
Comacchio 66 44.42 N 12.11 E
Comacchio, Valli di c 66 44.38 N 12.06 E
Comal 115a 6.55 S 109.31 E
Comala 234 19.19 N 103.45 W
Comalapa, Guat. 236 14.44 N 90.53 W
Comalapa, Nic. 236 12.17 N 85.31 W
Comalcalco 234 18.16 N 93.13 W
Comallo, Arroyo ≃ 254 40.29 S 70.12 W
Coman, Mount ∧ 9 74.02 S 65.04 W
Comana 38 43.54 N 28.19 E
Comanche, Ok., U.S. 196 34.22 N 97.57 W
Comanche, Tx., U.S. 196 31.53 N 98.36 W
Comanche Creek ≃, Co., U.S. 198 39.53 N 104.19 W
Comanche Creek ≃, Tx., U.S. 196 31.06 N 102.24 W
Comandante Ferraz ✿3 9 62.05 S 58.23 W
Comandante Fontana 252 25.20 S 59.41 W
Comandante Leal 252 30.53 S 65.47 W
Comandante Luis Piedrabuena 254 49.59 S 68.54 W
Comandante Nicanor Otamendi 252 38.07 S 57.51 W
Comănești 38 46.25 N 26.26 E
Comanjá de Corona 234 21.19 N 101.42 W
Comarapa 248 17.54 S 64.29 W
Comar Gambon 144 3.10 N 45.47 E
Comas, Perú 248 11.46 S 75.02 W
Comas, Perú 286d 11.57 S 77.04 W
Comayagua 236 14.25 N 87.37 W
Comayagua □5 236 14.30 N 87.40 W
Comayagua, Montañas de ⋏ 236 14.23 N 87.26 W
Combahee ≃ 192 32.30 N 80.31 W
Combarbalá 252 31.11 S 71.02 W
Combeaufontaine 58 47.43 N 5.53 E
Combe Martin 42 51.13 N 4.02 W
Comber, On., Can. 214 42.14 N 82.33 W
Comber, N. Ire., U.K. 48 54.33 N 5.45 W
Comberbach 262 53.17 N 2.32 W
Combermere Bay c 110 19.37 N 93.34 E
Comberton 42 52.11 N 0.02 E
Combe Seamount ✦3 14 12.32 S 177.35 W
Combie, Lake ⊜1 226 39.01 N 121.02 W
Comblain-au-Pont 56 50.28 N 5.35 E
Combles 50 50.01 N 2.52 E
Combloux 62 45.54 N 6.39 E
Combourg 32 48.25 N 1.45 W
Comboyne 166 31.36 S 152.29 E
Comboyuro Point ≻ 171a 27.04 S 153.24 E
Combres 50 48.19 N 1.04 E
Combronde 32 45.59 N 3.05 E
Combs 262 53.18 N 1.57 W
Combs-la-Ville 50 48.40 N 2.34 E
Combs Reservoir ⊜1 262 53.19 N 1.57 W
Comburg ✿1 56 49.06 N 9.44 E
Comb Wash V 200 37.13 N 109.42 W
Come by Chance 186 47.51 N 53.58 W
Comeglians 64 46.31 N 12.52 E
Comelico Superiore 64 46.35 N 12.30 E
Comendado Levy Gasparain 256 22.01 S 43.12 W
Comendador 238 18.53 N 71.42 W
Comendador Gomes 255 19.41 S 49.05 W
Comer 192 34.03 N 83.07 W
Comercinho 255 16.19 S 41.47 W
Comerío 240m 18.13 N 66.14 W
Comet 166 23.37 S 148.33 E
Comet ≃ 166 23.34 S 148.32 E
Cometela 156 21.51 S 34.29 E
Comfort, N.C., U.S. 192 35.00 N 77.30 W
Comfort, Tx., U.S. 196 29.58 N 98.54 W
Comfort, Cape ≻ 176 65.08 N 83.21 W
Comfort, Point ≻ 276 40.27 N 74.08 W
Comfrey 198 44.06 N 94.54 W
Comilla 124 23.27 N 91.12 E
Comines 50 50.46 N 3.01 E
Comino, Capo ≻ 71 40.32 N 9.49 E
Comino → Kemmuna I 36 36.00 N 14.20 E
Comiskey Park ♠ 278 41.50 N 87.38 W
Comiso 70 36.56 N 14.36 E
Comitan de Dominguez 232 16.15 N 92.08 W
Comitini 70 37.24 N 13.39 E
Comloșu Mare 38 45.54 N 20.38 E
Commack 210 40.50 N 73.17 W
Commagene □9 130 37.50 N 38.00 E
Commencement Bay c 224 47.17 N 122.28 W
Commentry 32 46.17 N 2.44 E
Commerce, Ca., U.S. 280 34.00 N 118.09 W
Commerce, Ga., U.S. 192 34.12 N 83.27 W
Commerce, Mi., U.S. 216 42.34 N 83.30 W
Commerce, Ok., U.S. 196 36.56 N 94.52 W
Commerce, Tx., U.S. 196 33.14 N 95.53 W
Commerce City 198 39.49 N 104.56 W
Commerciale Luigi Bocconi, Università ✿2 266b 45.26 N 9.11 E
Commercial Point 218 39.46 N 83.04 W
Commercy 56 48.45 N 5.35 E
Commewijne □5 250 5.50 N 55.00 W
Comminges ◆1 32 43.15 N 0.45 E
Committee Bay c 176 68.30 N 86.30 W
Commodore 214 40.43 N 78.57 W
Commodore Barry Bridge ◆5 285 39.49 N 75.22 W
Commondale 158 27.20 S 30.56 E
Common Edge 262 53.47 N 3.02 W
Commonwealth Bay c 9 66.54 S 142.40 E
Commonwealth Range ⋏ 9 84.15 S 172.20 E
Commoron Creek ≃ 166 28.22 S 150.08 E
Community Center 228 34.16 N 118.44 W
Como, Austl. 274a 34.00 S 151.04 E
Como, It. 62 45.47 N 9.05 E
Como, Ms., U.S. 194 34.30 N 89.56 W
Como, N.C., U.S. 208 36.30 N 77.00 W
Como, Tx., U.S. 222 33.03 N 95.28 W
Como, Wi., U.S. 216 42.37 N 88.28 W
Como □4 58 45.59 N 9.13 E
Como, Lago di ⊜ 58 46.00 N 9.20 E
Como, Lake ⊜ 216 42.36 N 88.29 W
Como, Mount ∧ 226 39.02 N 119.28 W
Comodoro Rivadavia 254 45.52 S 67.30 W
Como Lake ⊜ 190 47.55 N 83.30 W
Comologno 58 46.12 N 8.34 E
Comonfort 234 20.43 N 100.46 W
Comoras → Comoros □1 157a 12.10 S 44.15 E
Comores, Archipel des II 157a 12.10 S 44.15 E
Comores → Comoros □1 157a 12.10 S 44.15 E
Comorin, Cape ≻ 122 8.06 N 77.33 E
Comoros (Comores) □1, Afr. 138 12.10 S 44.15 E
Comoros (Comores) □1, Afr. 157a 12.10 S 44.15 E
Comox 182 49.40 N 124.55 W
Comox, Canadian Forces Base ■ 182 49.43 N 124.54 W
Companhia Siderúrgica Nacional ✿3 256 22.31 S 44.07 W
Compans 261 49.00 N 2.40 E
Compatsch 58 46.58 N 10.25 E
Compiègne 50 49.25 N 2.50 E
Compo Cove c 276 41.07 N 73.21 W
Compostela, Méx. 234 21.15 N 104.53 W
Compostela, Pil. 116 7.40 N 126.02 E
Comprida, Ilha I, Bra. 252 24.50 S 47.42 W
Comprida, Ilha I, Bra. 287a 23.02 S 43.12 W
Comps-sur-Artuby 62 43.43 N 6.30 E
Compstall 262 53.25 N 2.03 W
Compton, Eng., U.K. 260 51.13 N 0.38 W
Compton, Ca., U.S. 228 33.53 N 118.13 W
Compton, Il., U.S. 216 41.42 N 89.05 W
Compton □6 206 45.20 N 71.25 W
Compton Airport ⊠ 280 33.53 N 118.15 W
Compton Creek ≃, Ca., U.S. 280 33.50 N 118.12 W
Compton Creek ≃, N.J., U.S. 276 40.26 N 74.05 W
Comptonville 273d 26.17 S 27.58 E
Comrie 46 56.22 N 4.00 W
Comstock, Mi., U.S. 216 42.17 N 85.30 W
Comstock, Ne., U.S. 198 41.33 N 99.15 W
Comstock, Tx., U.S. 196 29.41 N 101.11 W
Comstock Park 216 43.02 N 85.40 W
Comunanza 66 42.57 N 13.25 E
Con ≃, Ross. 76 52.54 N 36.00 E
Çon ≃, Viet 110 19.02 N 104.58 E
Čona ≃, Ross. 74 62.54 N 111.06 E
Cona ≃, Scot., U.K. 46 56.46 N 5.14 W
Co Nag ⊜ 120 32.00 N 91.15 E
Conakry 150 9.31 N 13.43 W
Conambo ≃ 246 2.07 S 76.03 W
Conanicut Island I 207 41.32 N 71.21 W
Cona Niyeo 254 41.53 S 67.00 W
Conara Junction 166 41.50 S 147.26 E
Conasauga ≃ 192 34.33 N 84.55 W
Conaskonk Point ≻ 276 40.27 N 74.11 W
Conca ≃ 66 43.58 N 12.43 E
Concarán 252 32.34 S 65.15 W
Concarneau 32 47.52 N 3.55 W
Conceição, Bra. 248 7.24 S 58.05 W
Conceição, Bra. 250 7.33 S 38.31 W
Conceição, Moç. 156 18.45 S 36.10 E
Conceição, Cachoeira ʟ 248 9.34 S 64.22 W
Conceição, Ilha da I 287a 22.52 S 43.07 W
Conceição da Barra 255 18.35 S 39.45 W
Conceição da Pedra 256 22.09 S 45.27 W
Conceição das Alagoas 255 19.55 S 48.23 W
Conceição de Ipanema 255 19.55 S 41.41 W
Conceição de Jacareí 256 23.02 S 44.09 W
Conceição do Almeida 255 12.48 S 39.12 W
Conceição do Araguaia 250 8.15 S 49.17 W
Conceição do Canindé 250 7.54 S 41.34 W
Conceição do Coité 250 11.33 S 39.16 W
Conceição do Formoso 256 21.25 S 43.21 W
Conceição do Mato Dentro 255 19.01 S 43.25 W
Conceição do Maú 246 3.35 N 59.53 W
Conceição do Norte 255 12.13 S 47.18 W
Conceição do Rio Verde 256 21.53 S 45.05 W
Conceição dos Ouros 256 22.25 S 45.47 W
Concepción, Arg. 252 28.23 S 57.53 W
Concepción, Arg. 252 27.20 S 65.35 W
Concepción, Bol. 248 11.29 S 66.31 W
Concepción, Bol. 248 16.15 S 62.04 W
Concepción, Chile 252 36.50 S 73.03 W
Concepción, Col. 246 6.46 N 72.42 W
Concepción, Para. 252 23.25 S 57.17 W
Concepción, Perú 248 11.55 S 75.17 W
Concepcion, Pil. 116 12.24 N 122.06 E
Concepcion, Pil. 116 11.13 N 123.06 E
Concepcion, Pil. 116 10.42 N 123.03 E
Concepcion, Pil. 116 15.19 N 120.39 E
Concepción □5 252 23.00 S 57.00 W
Concepción, Bahía c 232 26.39 N 111.48 W
Concepción, Canal ⊔ 254 50.30 S 74.55 W
Concepción, Laguna ⊜ 248 17.29 S 61.25 W
Concepción, Volcán ∧1 236 11.34 N 85.37 W
Concepcion Bay c 116 11.15 N 123.07 E
Concepción de Ataco 236 13.52 N 89.51 W
Concepción de Buenos Aires 234 19.58 N 103.16 W
Concepción de la Sierra 252 27.59 S 55.31 W
Concepcíon del Oro 232 24.38 N 101.25 W
Concepción del Uruguay 252 32.29 S 58.14 W
Concepción Huista 236 15.37 N 91.41 W
Concepción Quezaltepeque 236 14.06 N 88.58 W
Conception, Point ≻ 204 34.27 N 120.27 W
Conception Bay c, Nf., Can. 186 47.45 N 53.00 W

Symbol	English	Deutsch	Español	Français	Português
≃	River	Fluß	Río	Rivière	Rio
≅	Canal	Kanal	Canal	Canal	Canal
ʟ	Waterfall, Rapids	Wasserfall, Stromschnellen	Cascada, Rápidos	Chute d'eau, Rapides	Cascata, Rápidos
⊔	Strait	Meeresstraße	Estrecho	Détroit	Estreito
c	Bay, Gulf	Bucht, Golf	Bahía, Golfo	Baie, Golfe	Baía, Golfo
⊜	Lake, Lakes	See, Seen	Lago, Lagos	Lac, Lacs	Lago, Lagos
≡	Swamp	Sumpf	Pantano	Marais	Pântano
⊓	Ice Features, Glacier	Eis- und Gletscherformen	Accidentes Glaciales	Formes glaciaires	Acidentes glaciares
⫪	Other Hydrographic Features	Andere Hydrographische Objekte	Otros Elementos Hidrográficos	Autres données hydrographiques	Outros acidentes hidrográficos
✦	Submarine Features	Untermeerische Objekte	Accidentes Submarinos	Formes de relief sous-marin	Acidentes submarinos
□	Political Unit	Politische Einheit	Unidad Politica	Entité politique	Unidade política
✿	Cultural Institution	Kulturelle Institution	Institución Cultural	Institution culturelle	Institução cultural
⊥	Historical Site	Historische Stätte	Sitio Histórico	Site historique	Sitio histórico
♠	Recreational Site	Erholungs- und Ferienort	Sitio de Recreo	Centre de loisirs	Area de Lazer
⊠	Airport	Flughafen	Aeropuerto	Aéroport	Aeroporto
■	Military Installation	Militäranlage	Instalación Militar	Installation militaire	Instalação militar
◆	Miscellaneous	Verschiedenes	Misceláneo	Divers	Diversos

Conception Bay c, Namibia 156 23.53 S 14.28 E
Concession 154 17.22 S 30.57 E
Conchagua 236 13.19 N 87.52 W
Conchagua, Volcán ∧[1] 236 13.14 N 87.46 W
Conchal 256 22.20 S 47.10 W
Conchalí 286e 33.24 S 70.39 W
Conchalí, Cerros de ⋀ 286e 33.20 S 70.38 W
Conchas ≃ 196 35.23 N 104.18 W
Conchas Dam 196 35.22 N 104.11 W
Conchas Lake ⊜[1] 196 35.25 N 104.14 W
Conche 186 50.53 N 55.54 W
Conches-en-Ouche 50 48.58 N 0.56 E
Conchi 252 22.02 S 68.38 W
Conchillas 258 34.15 S 58.04 W
Conchitas, Arroyo ≃ 288 34.45 S 58.09 W
Concho 200 34.28 N 109.36 W
Concho ≃ 196 31.34 N 99.43 W
Conchos ≃, Méx. 232 29.35 N 104.25 W
Conchos ≃, Méx. 232 24.55 N 97.40 W
Concise 58 46.51 N 6.43 E
Conco 64 45.48 N 11.36 E
Concón 252 32.55 S 71.31 W
Concononogon Point ≻ 116 12.14 N 120.13 E
Conconully 182 48.33 N 119.44 W
Concord, Austl. 274a 33.52 S 151.06 E
Concord, On., Can. 275b 43.48 N 79.29 W
Concord, Ca., U.S. 226 37.58 N 122.01 W
Concord, Ga., U.S. 192 33.05 N 84.26 W
Concord, Il., U.S. 219 39.49 N 90.22 W
Concord, Ky., U.S. 218 38.41 N 83.29 W
Concord, Ma., U.S. 207 42.27 N 71.20 W
Concord, Mi., U.S. 216 42.10 N 84.38 W
Concord, Mo., U.S. 219 38.31 N 90.23 W
Concord, N.H., U.S. 188 43.12 N 71.32 W
Concord, N.C., U.S. 192 35.24 N 80.34 W
Concord, Pa., U.S. 214 40.15 N 77.42 W
Concord, Tx., U.S. 222 31.16 N 96.09 W
Concord ≃ 283 42.39 N 71.18 W
Concord Battleground ⊥ 283 42.28 N 71.21 W
Concordia, Arg. 252 31.24 S 58.02 W
Concórdia, Bra. 246 4.35 S 66.35 W
Concórdia, Bra. 252 27.14 S 52.01 W
Concordia, Méx. 234 23.17 N 106.04 W
Concordia, Perú 246 4.30 S 74.55 W
Concordia, Ks., U.S. 198 39.34 N 97.39 W
Concordia, Mo., U.S. 194 38.59 N 93.34 W
Concordia Gardens 216 41.09 N 85.08 W
Concordia Sagittaria ⊥ 64 45.45 N 12.51 E
Concordia sulla Secchia 64 44.55 N 10.59 E
Concord Naval Weapons Station ■ 282 38.03 N 122.02 W
Concordville 285 39.53 N 75.31 W
Concord West 274a 33.51 S 151.05 E
Concorezzo 62 45.35 N 9.20 E
Concrete 224 48.32 N 121.44 W
Con Cuong 110 19.02 N 104.54 E
Conda 152 11.06 S 14.20 E
Condamine 166 26.56 S 150.08 E
Condamine ≃ 166 27.07 S 149.48 E
Condat-en-Féniers 32 45.21 N 2.46 E
Condé, Ang. 152 10.50 S 14.37 E
Conde, Bra. 255 11.49 S 37.37 W
Condé, Fr. 32 48.51 N 0.33 W
Conde, S.D., U.S. 198 45.09 N 98.05 W
Condécourt 261 49.02 N 1.57 E
Condé-en-Brie 50 49.00 N 3.33 E
Condega 236 13.21 N 86.24 W
Condeixa 250 0.54 S 48.36 W
Condé-sur-l'Escaut 50 50.27 N 3.35 E
Condè-sur-Vesgre 261 48.45 N 1.40 E
Condeúba 255 14.53 S 41.59 W
Condevilla 286d 12.02 S 77.05 W
Condino 64 45.53 N 10.36 E
Condobolin 166 33.05 S 147.09 E
Condom 32 43.58 N 0.22 E
Condon 202 45.14 N 120.11 W
Condoto 246 5.06 N 76.37 W
Condove 62 45.07 N 7.18 E
Condrieu 62 45.27 N 4.46 E
Condroz □[9] 56 50.25 N 5.00 E
Cone 196 33.48 N 101.23 W
Conecuh ≃ 194 30.58 N 87.14 W
Conegliano 64 45.53 N 12.18 E
Conejos 200 37.05 N 106.01 W
Conejos ≃ 200 37.18 N 105.44 W
Conemaugh 214 40.24 N 78.52 W
Conemaugh ≃ 214 40.28 N 79.27 W
Conemaugh River Lake ⊜[1] 214 40.28 N 79.17 W
Conembaro, Cerro ∧ 234 18.40 N 102.06 W
Cone Mountain ∧ 180 66.12 N 156.03 W
Conero, Monte ∧ 66 43.33 N 13.36 E
Conestoga 208 39.57 N 76.21 W
Conestoga Creek ≃ 208 39.56 N 76.23 W
Conestogo 212 43.32 N 80.30 W
Conestogo ≃ 212 43.32 N 80.29 W
Conestogo Lake ⊜ 212 43.44 N 80.44 W
Conesus 210 42.43 N 77.41 W
Conesus Lake ⊜ 210 42.47 N 77.43 W
Conesville 214 40.11 N 81.53 W
Conewago Creek ≃ 208 40.07 N 76.42 W
Conewago Lake ⊜ 208 40.06 N 76.52 W
Conewango Creek ≃ 214 41.50 N 79.09 W
Coney Island ◆[8] 276 40.34 N 74.00 W
Confederation Lake ⊜ 184 51.05 N 92.44 W
Configni 66 42.25 N 12.38 E
Conflans-en-Jarnisy 56 49.10 N 5.51 E
Conflans-Sainte-Honorine 50 48.59 N 2.06 E
Conflenti 68 39.04 N 16.17 E
Conflict Group II 164 10.45 S 151.45 E
Confluence 188 39.48 N 79.21 W
Confolens 32 46.01 N 0.41 E
Confraternidad, Parque ♦ 286d 12.09 S 77.02 W
Confusion Bay c 186 49.58 N 55.47 W
Confuso ≃ 252 25.09 S 57.34 W
Cong 48 53.32 N 9.19 W
Congamond 207 42.01 N 72.46 W
Congaree ≃ 192 33.45 N 80.37 W
Congelin 168a 32.50 S 116.54 E
Congers 210 41.09 N 73.56 W
Congers Lake ⊜ 276 41.09 N 73.57 W
Cong Hoa Stadium ♦ 269c 10.45 N 106.40 E
Conghua 100 23.32 N 113.32 E
Congjiang 102 25.41 N 108.47 E
Congleton 44 53.10 N 2.13 W
Congo □[1], Afr. 138 1.00 S 15.00 E
Congo □[1], Afr. 152 1.00 S 15.00 E
Congo (Zaire) (Zaïre) ≃ 138 6.04 S 12.24 E
Congo, Democratic Republic of the → Zaire □[1] 138 4.00 S 25.00 E
Congo, République démocratique du → Zaire □[1] 138 4.00 S 25.00 E
Congo, république du → Congo □[1] 152 1.00 S 15.00 E
Congo, Serra do ⋀ 152 6.30 S 13.43 E
Congo Basin =[1] 10 0.00 20.00 E
Congonhal 256 22.09 S 46.02 W
Congonhas, Aeroporto de ⊠ 256 23.38 S 46.38 W
Congost ≃ 266d 41.33 N 2.15 E
Congresbury 42 51.23 N 2.48 W
Congress, Sk., Can. 184 49.46 N 106.00 W
Congress, Oh., U.S. 214 40.55 N 82.03 W
Conie ≃ 50 48.06 N 1.30 E
Conigli, Isola dei I 70a 35.30 N 12.33 E
Coningsby 44 53.07 N 0.10 W
Conisbrough 44 53.29 N 1.13 W
Coniston, On., Can. 190 46.29 N 80.51 W
Coniston, Eng., U.K. 44 54.22 N 3.05 W
Coniston Water ⊜ 44 54.20 N 3.04 W
Conitaca 232 24.10 N 106.43 W
Conjeeveram → Kānchipuram 122 12.50 N 79.43 E
Conjola 170 35.13 S 150.27 E
Çonjola Lake c 170 35.16 S 150.27 E
Čon-Kemin ≃ 85 42.42 N 75.54 E
Conklin, Ab., Can. 182 55.38 N 111.05 W
Conklin, N.Y., U.S. 210 42.02 N 75.48 W
Conklingville Dam ◆[6] 210 43.17 N 74.02 W
Conklin Point ≻ 276 40.41 N 73.17 W
Conkouati 152 4.00 S 11.13 E
Conliège 58 46.39 N 5.36 E
Conlin, Lake ⊜ 220 28.14 N 81.07 W
Conn, Lough ⊜ 48 54.04 N 9.20 W
Connah's Quay 44 53.13 N 3.03 W
Connaught □[9] 48 53.45 N 9.00 W
Connaughton 285 40.05 N 75.19 W
Connaughton, Mount ∧[2] 162 22.42 S 122.40 E
Connaught Place ♦ 272a 28.38 N 77.12 E
Connaux 62 44.05 N 4.36 E
Conneaut 214 41.56 N 80.33 W
Conneaut Creek ≃ 214 41.58 N 80.33 W
Conneaut Lake 214 41.36 N 80.19 W
Conneaut Lake ⊜ 214 41.37 N 80.18 W
Conneaut Outlet ≃ 214 41.33 N 80.06 W
Conneautville 214 41.45 N 80.22 W
Connecticut □[3], U.S. 178 41.45 N 72.45 W
Connecticut □[3], U.S. 207 41.45 N 72.45 W
Connecticut ≃ 188 41.17 N 72.21 W
Connell 202 46.39 N 118.51 W
Connell, Mount ∧ 182 49.18 N 115.38 W
Connellsville 188 40.01 N 79.35 W
Connelly 210 41.55 N 73.59 W
Connel Park 44 55.23 N 4.12 W
Connemara 166 24.13 S 142.17 E
Connemara ◆[1] 48 53.25 N 9.45 W
Conner 116 17.48 N 121.19 E
Conner, Mount ∧ 162 25.23 S 131.54 E
Connerré 50 48.03 N 0.30 E
Connersville, Fl., U.S. 220 27.54 N 81.47 W
Connersville, In., U.S. 218 39.38 N 85.08 W
Connetquot ≃ 276 40.43 N 73.08 W
Connetquot Brook ≃ 276 40.45 N 73.09 W
Connetquot River State Park ♦ 210 40.46 N 73.09 W
Connewarre, Lake ⊜ 169 38.14 S 144.27 E
Conn Island I 284c 39.00 N 77.16 W
Conn Lake ⊜ 176 70.34 N 73.30 W
Connoquenessing 214 40.49 N 80.59 W
Connoquenessing Creek ≃ 214 40.51 N 80.19 W
Connors Range ⋀ 166 21.40 S 149.10 E
Conodoguinet Creek ≃ 208 40.17 N 76.55 W
Conon ≃ 46 57.34 N 4.26 W
Cononaco ≃ 246 1.32 S 75.35 W
Cononbridge 46 57.34 N 4.26 W
Conorochite ≃ 246 2.41 N 67.29 W
Conotton Creek ≃ 214 40.34 N 81.23 W
Conover 192 35.42 N 81.13 W
Conowingo 208 39.40 N 76.09 W
Conowingo ◆[6] 208 39.33 N 76.04 W
Conowingo Creek ≃ 208 39.41 N 76.12 W
Conowingo Dam ◆[6] 208 39.39 N 76.10 W
Conquest 184 51.32 N 107.17 W
Conquista 255 19.56 S 47.33 W
Conrad, Ia., U.S. 190 42.13 N 92.52 W
Conrad, Mt., U.S. 202 48.10 N 111.56 W
Conrado 256 22.32 S 43.33 W
Conroe 222 30.18 N 95.27 W
Conroe, Lake ⊜[1] 222 30.25 N 95.37 W
Çonsandolo 66 44.39 N 11.46 E
Čon-Saryoj 85 42.37 N 76.53 E
Conscience Bay c 276 40.57 N 73.07 W
Consdorf 56 49.46 N 6.20 E
Consecon 212 44.00 N 77.31 W
Conselheiro Lafaiete 255 20.40 S 43.48 W
Conselheiro Paulino 256 22.13 S 42.31 W
Conselheiro Pena 255 19.10 S 41.30 W
Conselice 66 44.31 N 11.49 E
Conselve 64 45.14 N 11.52 E
Conservatória 256 22.18 S 43.57 W
Consett 44 54.51 N 1.49 W
Conshohocken 208 40.04 N 75.18 W
Consolação 256 22.33 S 45.55 W
Consolação ◆[8] 287b 23.33 S 46.39 W
Consolación del Sur 240p 22.30 N 83.31 W
Consolidated Main Reef Mines ◆[7] 273d 26.11 S 27.56 E
Con Son II 110 8.43 N 106.36 E
Consort 184 52.01 N 110.46 W
Constable 206 44.56 N 74.18 W
Constableville 212 43.34 N 75.25 W
Constance, Lake → Bodensee ⊜ 58 47.35 N 9.25 E
Constance → Konstanz 58 47.40 N 9.10 E
Constance Lake ⊜ 212 45.25 N 75.58 W
Constância 34 39.28 N 8.20 W
Constanța 38 44.11 N 28.39 E
Constanța □[6] 38 44.20 N 28.20 E
Constant Creek ≃ 212 45.17 N 76.46 W
Constantia 210 43.14 N 76.00 W
Constantina 34 37.52 N 5.37 W
Constantine 216 41.50 N 85.40 W
Constantine, Cape ≻ 180 58.25 N 158.50 W
Constantine → Qacentina 148 36.22 N 6.37 E
Constantinople → İstanbul 130 41.01 N 28.58 E
Constant Lake ⊜ 212 45.24 N 77.00 W
Constitución, Chile 252 35.20 S 72.25 W
Constitución, Ur. 252 31.05 S 57.50 W
Constitución ◆[8] 288 34.37 S 58.23 W
Constitución de 01080507, Parque Nacional ♦ 204 32.05 N 115.55 W
Constitution, Mount ∧ 224 48.40 N 122.50 W
Consuegra 34 39.28 N 3.36 W
Consul 184 49.21 N 109.30 W
Consuma 66 43.47 N 11.35 E
Consuma, Passo della)(66 43.47 N 11.36 E
Contai 126 21.47 N 87.45 E
Contamana 248 7.15 S 74.54 W
Contarina 64 45.00 N 12.13 E
Contas, Rio de ≃ 255 14.17 S 39.01 W
Contee 208 39.05 N 76.52 W
Contendas do Sincorá 255 13.45 S 41.02 W
Contentnea Creek ≃ 192 35.21 N 77.23 W
Contes 62 43.49 N 7.19 E
Contessa Entellina 70 37.44 N 13.11 E
Contigliano 66 42.24 N 12.46 E
Continental 216 41.06 N 84.15 W
Continental Peak ∧ 200 42.16 N 108.43 W
Contoocook Lake ⊜ 207 42.47 N 72.01 W
Contraalmirante Cordero 252 38.44 S 68.10 W
Contra Costa □[6] 226 37.55 N 121.55 W
Contra Costa Canal ≡ 282 38.02 N 121.58 W
Contra Loma Reservoir ⊜[1] 282 37.58 N 121.49 W
Contramaestre 240p 20.18 N 76.15 W
Contramaestre ≃ 240p 20.31 N 76.18 W
Contratación 246 6.18 N 73.29 W
Contrecoeur 206 45.51 N 73.14 W
Contre Island ≻[1] 276 40.54 N 73.32 W
Contreras, Embalse de ⊜[1] 34 39.32 N 1.30 W
Contreras, Isla I 254 51.55 S 74.55 W
Contres 50 47.25 N 1.26 E
Contrexéville 58 48.11 N 5.54 E
Contrisson 56 48.48 N 4.57 E
Controller Bay c 180 60.07 N 144.15 W
Contumazá 248 7.22 S 78.49 W
Contursi 68 40.39 N 15.14 E
Contwoyto Lake ⊜ 176 65.42 N 110.50 W
Conty 50 49.44 N 2.09 E
Contz-les-Bains 56 49.27 N 6.21 E
Convención 246 8.28 N 73.21 W
Convent 194 30.01 N 90.49 W
Convento 236 9.21 N 83.30 W
Convent Station 276 40.47 N 74.26 W
Conversano 68 40.58 N 17.08 E
Converse 216 40.34 N 85.52 W
Converse Lake ⊜ 276 41.08 N 73.39 W
Converse Pond Brook ≃ 276 41.03 N 73.40 W
Convoy 216 40.55 N 84.42 W
Conway, P.E., Can. 186 46.40 N 63.59 W
Conway, S. Afr. 158 31.43 S 25.16 E
Conway, Ar., U.S. 194 35.05 N 92.26 W
Conway, Fl., U.S. 220 28.30 N 81.19 W
Conway, Ma., U.S. 207 42.30 N 72.42 W
Conway, Mo., U.S. 194 37.30 N 92.49 W
Conway, N.H., U.S. 188 43.58 N 71.07 W
Conway, N.C., U.S. 192 36.26 N 77.13 W
Conway, Pa., U.S. 214 40.39 N 80.14 W
Conway, S.C., U.S. 192 33.50 N 79.02 W
Conway, Wa., U.S. 224 48.21 N 122.21 W
Conway, Cape ≻ 166 20.32 S 148.56 E
Conway, Lake ⊜ 162 28.17 S 135.35 E
Conway, Lake ⊜[1] 194 35.00 N 92.25 W
Conway, Mount ∧ 162 23.45 S 133.25 E
Conway National Park ♦ 166 20.22 S 148.51 E
Conway Springs 198 37.23 N 97.38 W
Conwy 44 53.17 N 3.50 W
Conwy ≃ 44 53.17 N 3.50 W
Conwy, Vale of V 44 53.12 N 3.48 W
Conwy Bay c 44 53.18 N 3.55 W
Conyers 192 33.40 N 84.01 W
Conyngham 210 40.59 N 76.03 W
Coo 56 50.24 N 5.52 E
Coober Pedy 162 29.01 S 134.43 E
Coogee, Austl. 168a 32.07 S 115.46 E
Coogee, Austl. 274a 33.55 S 151.16 E
Coogee Bay c 274a 33.55 S 151.16 E
Cook, Austl. 162 30.37 S 130.25 E
Cook, In., U.S. 216 41.22 N 87.26 W
Cook, Mn., U.S. 190 47.51 N 92.41 W
Cook, Ne., U.S. 198 40.30 N 96.09 W
Cook, Wa., U.S. 224 45.43 N 121.40 W
Cook □[6] 216 41.53 N 87.45 W
Cook, Bahía c 254 55.10 S 70.10 W
Cook, Baie de c 174s 17.29 S 149.49 W
Cook, Cape ≻ 182 50.08 N 127.55 W
Cook, Mount ∧ 172 43.36 S 170.10 E
Cook, Point ≻ 274b 37.55 S 144.48 E
Cook, Récif de ✦[2] 175f 19.25 S 163.50 E
Cookardinia 171b 35.34 S 147.14 E
Cook Bay c 212 44.15 N 79.30 W
Cook Creek ≃ 224 47.17 N 124.05 W
Cooke, Mount ∧ 168a 32.25 S 116.18 E
Cookernup 168a 33.00 S 115.54 E
Cookes Peak ∧ 200 32.32 N 107.44 W
Cookeville 194 36.09 N 85.30 W
Cook Forest State Park ♦ 214 41.22 N 79.12 W
Cookham 42 51.34 N 0.43 W
Cookhouse 158 32.45 S 25.49 E
Cook Ice Shelf ⊓ 9 68.40 S 152.30 E
Cooking Lake ⊜ 182 53.25 N 113.02 W
Cook Inlet c 180 60.30 N 152.00 W
Cook-Inseln → Cook Islands □[2] 14 20.00 S 158.00 W
Cook Island I 174o 1.57 N 157.28 W
Cook Islands □[2] 14 20.00 S 158.00 W
Cooks ≃ 274a 33.56 S 151.10 E
Cooksburg 214 41.20 N 79.12 W
Cooks Falls 210 41.57 N 74.59 W
Cook's Harbour 186 51.36 N 55.52 W
Cookshire 206 45.25 N 71.38 W
Cooksmill Green 260 51.44 N 0.22 E
Cooks Mills 284a 43.00 N 79.11 W
Cookstown, On., Can. 212 44.11 N 79.42 W
Cookstown, N. Ire., U.K. 48 54.39 N 6.45 W
Cook Strait ⊻ 172 41.15 S 174.30 E
Cooksville, Il., U.S. 216 40.33 N 88.43 W
Cooksville, Md., U.S. 208 39.19 N 77.01 W
Cooksville, Wi., U.S. 216 42.50 N 89.14 W
Cooksville Creek ≃ 275b 43.34 N 79.34 W
Cooktown 164 15.28 S 145.15 E
Cookville 222 33.11 N 94.51 W
Coolabah 166 31.02 S 146.43 E
Cooladdi 166 26.39 S 145.28 E
Coolah 166 31.50 S 149.42 E
Coolamon 166 34.49 S 147.12 E
Coolaney 48 54.10 N 8.36 W
Coolangatta 171a 28.10 S 153.32 E
Coolawanyah 162 21.47 S 117.48 E
Coole ≃ 50 48.56 N 4.21 E
Cooleemee 192 35.48 N 80.33 W
Cooley Lake ⊜ 281 42.37 N 83.27 W
Coolgardie 162 30.57 S 121.10 E
Coolidge, Az., U.S. 200 32.58 N 111.31 W
Coolidge, Ga., U.S. 192 31.00 N 83.51 W
Coolidge, Tx., U.S. 222 31.45 N 96.38 W
Coolidge, Mount ∧ 198 43.44 N 103.29 W
Coolidge Dam ◆[6] 200 33.00 N 110.20 W
Coolidge Point ≻ 283 42.34 N 70.44 W
Coolin 202 48.28 N 116.50 W
Cooling 260 51.27 N 0.32 E
Cooloola National Park ♦ 166 26.05 S 153.00 E
Cooloongup, Lake ⊜ 168a 32.18 S 115.47 E
Coolspring 214 41.02 N 79.05 W
Coolumburra Hill ∧ 170 35.01 S 150.10 E
Coolup 168a 32.44 S 115.53 E
Cooma 171b 36.14 S 149.08 E
Cooma Creek ≃ 171b 36.07 S 149.11 E
Coombe Cottage ⊥ 274b 37.43 S 145.23 E
Coomberdale 162 30.28 S 116.02 E
Coomera 171a 27.52 S 153.19 E
Coomera ≃ 171a 27.53 S 153.24 E
Coominya 171a 27.23 S 152.30 E
Coonabarabran 166 31.16 S 149.17 E
Coonalpyn 166 35.42 S 139.51 E
Coonamble 166 30.57 S 148.23 E
Coonana 162 31.01 S 123.07 E
Coon Creek ≃, Ca., U.S. 226 38.51 N 121.34 W
Coon Creek ≃, Il., U.S. 216 42.15 N 88.48 W
Coon Creek ≃, Tx., U.S. 222 31.59 N 95.52 W
Coon Creek Lake ⊜[1] 222 32.04 N 95.52 W
Coondambo 166 31.04 S 135.52 E
Coongan ≃ 162 20.53 S 119.47 E
Coonoor 122 11.21 N 76.49 E
Coon Rapids, Ia., U.S. 198 41.52 N 94.41 W
Coon Rapids, Mn., U.S. 190 45.10 N 93.19 W
Coontown 276 40.37 N 74.31 W
Coon Valley 190 43.42 N 91.00 W
Cooper 196 33.22 N 95.41 W
Cooper ≃, N.J., U.S. 285 39.57 N 75.07 W
Cooper ≃, Wa., U.S. 224 47.23 N 121.23 W
Cooper, Mount ∧, Austl. 162 26.11 S 127.56 E
Cooper, Mount ∧, B.C., Can. 182 50.11 N 117.12 W
Cooper, North Branch ≃ 285 39.55 N 75.02 W
Cooper Center 216 42.23 N 85.37 W
Cooper Creek ≃ 166 28.29 S 137.46 E
Cooper Island I 240m 18.22 N 64.30 W
Cooper Landing 180 60.29 N 149.51 W
Cooper Mountain ∧ 180 60.23 N 149.51 W
Cooper River Parkway ♦ 285 39.55 N 75.03 W
Cooper Road 194 32.26 N 93.48 W
Coopers 194 32.46 N 86.33 W
Coopersale Common 260 51.42 N 0.08 E
Coopersburg 208 40.30 N 75.23 W
Coopers Plains, Austl. 171a 27.34 S 153.02 E
Coopers Plains, N.Y., U.S. 210 42.11 N 77.08 W
Cooperstown, N.Y., U.S. 210 42.42 N 74.55 W
Cooperstown, N.D., U.S. 198 47.26 N 98.07 W
Cooperstown, Pa., U.S. 214 41.30 N 79.52 W
Cooperstown, Pa., U.S. 214 40.43 N 79.57 W
Coopersville 216 43.03 N 85.56 W
Coorabie 162 31.54 S 132.18 E
Cooranbong 170 33.04 S 151.27 E
Coorong National Park ♦ 166 36.01 S 139.32 E
Coorow 162 29.53 S 116.01 E
Cooroy 166 26.25 S 152.55 E
Coorparoo 171a 27.30 S 153.03 E
Coos □[6] 206 45.04 N 71.20 W
Coosa ≃ 194 32.30 N 86.16 W
Coosawhatchie ≃ 192 32.32 N 80.52 W
Coos Bay 202 43.22 N 124.12 W
Coos Bay c 202 43.23 N 124.16 W
Cootamundra 166 34.39 S 148.02 E
Cootehill 48 54.04 N 7.05 W
Cooyar 171a 26.59 S 151.50 E
Cooyar Creek ≃ 171a 26.50 S 152.04 E
Çooyar Mountain ∧ 171a 26.57 S 151.47 E
Čop 78 48.26 N 22.10 E
Copacabana, Arg. 252 28.12 S 67.29 W
Copacabana, Bol. 248 16.10 S 69.05 W
Copacabana, Col. 246 6.20 N 75.30 W
Copacabana ◆[8] 287a 22.58 S 43.11 W
Copacabana, Forte de ⊥ 287a 22.59 S 43.11 W
Copainalá 234 17.05 N 93.12 W
Copake 210 42.06 N 73.33 W
Copake Falls 210 42.07 N 73.31 W
Copala 234 16.37 N 98.58 W
Copalillo 234 18.02 N 99.07 W
Copalis ≃ 224 47.07 N 124.13 W
Copalis Beach 224 47.06 N 124.10 W
Copalita ≃ 234 15.46 N 96.03 W
Copán, Hond. 236 14.50 N 89.09 W
Copan, Ok., U.S. 196 36.53 N 95.55 W
Copán □[5] 236 14.50 N 89.00 W
Copán ⊥ 236 14.50 N 89.09 W
Copanatoyac 234 17.15 N 98.45 W
Copándaro 234 19.53 N 101.13 W
Copan Lake ⊜[1] 196 36.55 N 95.56 W
Copano Bay c 196 28.05 N 97.05 W
Copatana 246 2.48 S 67.04 W
Cope 198 39.39 N 102.51 W
Copeá, Paraná ≃[1] 246 3.52 S 63.20 W
Copeau ≃ 184 52.45 N 103.00 W
Copeland 220 25.57 N 81.21 W
Copeland Island I 48 54.41 N 5.32 W
Copenhagen 212 43.53 N 75.40 W
Copenhagen → København 41 55.40 N 12.35 E
Copenhague → København 41 55.40 N 12.35 E
Copenhaver 284c 39.04 N 77.11 W
Copertino 68 40.16 N 18.03 E
Copetonas 252 38.43 S 60.27 W
Copeville 222 33.05 N 96.25 W
Copiague 210 40.40 N 73.24 W
Copiague Neck ≻[1] 276 40.40 N 73.22 W
Copiapó 252 27.22 S 70.20 W
Copiapó ≃ 252 27.19 S 70.56 W
Copinsay I 46 58.54 N 2.40 W
Coplay 208 40.40 N 75.29 W
Copley, Austl. 166 30.32 S 138.25 E
Copley, Oh., U.S. 214 41.06 N 81.39 W
Copmanthorpe 44 53.55 N 1.08 W
Copoas, Mount ∧ 116 10.48 N 119.17 E
Çopolo 152 10.22 S 14.07 E
Čopoviči 78 50.49 N 27.58 E
Copparo 64 44.54 N 11.49 E
Coppell 222 32.57 N 97.01 W
Coppename ≃ 250 5.48 N 55.55 W
Coppenbrügge 52 52.07 N 9.32 E
Copper ≃ 180 60.30 N 144.50 W
Copperas Cove 196 31.07 N 97.54 W
Copperas Mountain ∧ 276 41.02 N 74.28 W
Copperbelt □[4] 154 13.00 S 28.00 E
Copper Butte ∧ 202 48.42 N 118.28 W
Copper Canyon → Cobre, Barranca del V 232 27.28 N 107.50 W
Copper Center 180 61.58 N 145.19 W
Copper Cliff 190 46.28 N 81.04 W
Copper Creek ≃ 192 36.40 N 82.45 W
Copper Harbor 190 47.27 N 87.53 W
Coppermine 176 67.50 N 115.05 W
Coppermine ≃ 176 67.49 N 115.04 W
Copper Mine Point ≻, Br. Vir. Is. 240m 18.26 N 64.25 W
Coppermine Point ≻, On., Can. 190 46.59 N 84.47 W
Copper Mountain 182 49.20 N 120.33 W
Copper Mountain ∧, Ak., U.S. 182 55.14 N 132.36 W
Copper Mountain ∧, Wy., U.S. 200 43.27 N 107.57 W
Copperopolis 226 37.59 N 120.38 W
Coppet 58 46.19 N 6.12 E
Coppin State College ⚬[2] 284b 39.19 N 76.40 W
Copplestone 42 50.49 N 3.45 W
Coppull 262 53.37 N 2.40 W
Copster Green 262 53.48 N 2.30 W
Coptic Museum ⚬ 273c 30.00 N 31.13 E
Copton Creek ≃ 182 54.16 N 119.15 W
Copton Point ≻ 116 10.00 N 123.22 E
Coqên 120 31.20 N 85.25 E
Coquet ≃ 44 55.22 N 1.37 W
Coquet Dale V 44 55.16 N 1.50 W
Coquí 240m 17.59 N 66.14 W
Coquilhatville → Mbandaka 152 0.04 N 18.16 E
Coquille 202 43.10 N 124.11 W
Coquille ≃ 202 43.07 N 124.26 W
Coquille, East Fork ≃ 202 43.06 N 124.04 W
Coquille, Middle Fork ≃ 202 43.05 N 124.09 W
Coquille, South Fork ≃ 202 43.02 N 124.07 W
Coquimatlán 234 19.12 N 103.48 W
Coquimbo 252 29.58 S 71.21 W
Coquimbo □[4] 252 30.45 S 71.00 W
Coquina Key I 220 27.44 N 82.38 W
Corabia 38 43.46 N 24.30 E
Coração de Jesus 255 16.42 S 44.22 W
Coração de Maria 255 12.14 S 38.45 W
Corace ≃ 68 38.49 N 16.37 E
Coracora 248 15.02 S 73.47 W
Corail, Mer de → Coral Sea ⊤[2] 14 20.00 S 158.00 E
Coral 214 40.29 N 79.10 W
Coral Bay c, Pil. 116 8.25 N 117.20 E
Coral Bay c, Vir. Is., U.S. 240m 18.20 N 64.41 W
Coral Gables 220 25.43 N 80.16 W
Coral Harbour 176 64.08 N 83.10 W
Coral Hills 284c 38.52 N 76.55 W
Coralque ≃ 248 16.26 S 70.45 W
Coral Sea ⊤[2] 14 20.00 S 158.00 E
Coral Sea Basin ✦[1] 14 14.00 S 152.00 E
Coral Sea Islands Territory □[8] 166 18.30 S 152.00 E
Coral Springs 220 26.16 N 80.13 W
Coralville 190 41.40 N 91.34 W
Coralville Lake ⊜[1] 190 41.47 N 91.48 W
Coram, Mt., U.S. 202 48.25 N 114.02 W
Coram, N.Y., U.S. 210 40.52 N 73.00 W
Corangamite, Lake ⊜ 169 38.10 S 143.25 E

ENGLISH				DEUTSCH			
Name	Page	Lat.°′	Long.°′	Name	Seite	Breite°′	Länge°′ E = Ost

Corantijn (Corentyne) ≃ 250 5.55 N 57.05 W
Coraopolis 214 40.31 N 80.10 W
Coraopolis Heights 279b 40.29 N 80.10 W
Corato 68 41.09 N 16.25 E
Corbara, Lago di ⊜[1] 66 42.43 N 12.15 E
Corbeil-Essonnes 50 48.36 N 2.29 E
Corbenay 58 47.54 N 6.20 E
Corbeny 50 49.28 N 3.49 E
Corbeolona 62 45.10 N 9.22 E
Corbera, Riera de ≃ 266d 41.27 N 1.59 E
Corberon 58 47.01 N 4.59 E
Corbett 210 42.03 N 75.02 W
Corbetta 62 45.28 N 8.55 E
Corbett National Park ♦ 124 29.40 N 78.45 E
Corbettsville 210 42.01 N 75.48 W
Corbie 50 49.55 N 2.30 E
Corbière Point ≻ 43b 49.11 N 2.15 W
Corbières ⋀ 32 42.55 N 2.38 E
Corbigny 50 47.15 N 3.40 E
Corbin 192 36.56 N 84.05 W
Corbion 56 49.48 N 5.00 E
Corbola 64 45.00 N 12.05 E
Corbones ≃ 34 37.36 N 5.39 W
Corbridge 44 54.58 N 2.01 W
Corbu 38 44.29 N 24.43 E
Corby 42 52.29 N 0.40 W
Corcaigh → Cork 48 51.54 N 8.28 W
Córcega 240m 18.19 N 67.15 W
Córcega, Isla de → Corse I 36 42.00 N 9.00 E
Corciano 66 43.08 N 12.17 E
Corcieux 58 48.10 N 6.53 E
Corcolle ◆[8] 267a 41.55 N 12.46 E
Corcoran 226 36.05 N 119.33 W
Corcovado, Golfo c 254 43.30 S 73.30 W
Corcovado, Morro do ∧ 287a 22.57 S 43.13 W
Corcovado, Parque Nacional ♦ 236 8.35 N 83.40 W
Corcovado, Volcán ∧[1] 254 43.12 S 72.48 W
Corcubión 34 42.57 N 9.11 W
Cordeaux Reservoir ⊜[1] 170 34.22 S 150.45 E
Cordeiro 255 22.02 S 42.22 W
Cordele, Ga., U.S. 192 31.57 N 83.46 W
Cordele, Tx., U.S. 222 29.08 N 96.38 W
Cordell 196 35.17 N 98.59 W
Cordell Hull Reservoir ⊜[1] 194 36.25 N 85.40 W
Cordenons 64 45.59 N 12.42 E
Corder 194 39.05 N 93.38 W
Cordes 32 44.04 N 1.57 E
Cordignano 64 45.57 N 12.25 E
Cordillera □[5] 252 25.15 S 57.00 W
Cordillera de los Picachos, Parque Nacional ♦ 246 3.00 N 74.30 W
Cordillo Downs 166 26.43 S 140.38 E
Cordisburgo 255 19.07 S 44.21 W
Cordislândia 256 21.48 S 45.43 W
Córdoba, Arg. 252 31.24 S 64.11 W
Córdoba, Esp. 34 37.53 N 4.46 W
Córdoba, Méx. 234 18.53 N 96.56 W
Córdoba □[4], Arg. 252 32.00 S 64.00 W
Córdoba □[4], Esp. 34 38.00 N 4.50 W
Córdoba □[5] 246 8.20 N 75.40 W
Córdoba, Península ≻[1] 254 53.20 S 72.50 W
Cordon 116 16.40 N 121.28 E
Córdova, Perú 248 14.04 S 75.03 W
Cordova, Al., U.S. 194 33.45 N 87.11 W
Cordova, Ak., U.S. 180 60.33 N 145.46 W
Cordova, Il., U.S. 190 41.41 N 90.19 W
Cordova, Md., U.S. 208 38.52 N 75.59 W
Cordova Bay c 182 54.55 N 132.35 W
Cordova → Córdoba 34 37.53 N 4.46 W
Cordova Lake ⊜ 212 44.35 N 77.49 W
Cordova Peak ∧ 180 60.51 N 145.16 W
Corea, Estrecho de → Korea Strait ⊻ 90 34.00 N 129.00 E
Corea del Norte → Korea, North □[1] 98 40.00 N 127.00 E
Corea del Sur → Korea, South □[1] 98 36.30 N 128.00 E
Coreaú 250 3.33 S 40.39 W
Coreaú ≃ 250 2.54 S 40.50 W
Core Creek ≃ 285 40.11 N 74.55 W
Corée, Détroit de → Korea Strait ⊻ 90 34.00 N 129.00 E
Coree, Mount ∧ 171b 35.18 S 148.48 E
Corée du Nord → Korea, North □[1] 98 40.00 N 127.00 E
Corée du Sud → Korea, South □[1] 98 36.30 N 128.00 E
Coreglia Antelminelli 64 44.04 N 10.31 E
Coreinbob 171b 35.13 S 147.38 E
Coremas 250 7.01 S 37.58 W
Corentyne (Corantijn) ≃ 250 5.55 N 57.05 W
Corerepe 232 25.40 N 108.40 W
Corese Terra 66 42.10 N 12.42 E
Corey Lake ⊜ 216 41.55 N 85.45 W
Corfe Castle 42 50.38 N 2.04 W
Corfield 166 21.43 S 143.22 E
Corfu 210 42.57 N 78.24 W
Corfu → Kérkira 38 39.36 N 19.56 E
Corfu → Kérkira I 38 39.40 N 19.42 E
Corhanwarrabul Creek ≃ 274b 37.55 S 145.12 E
Cori 66 41.39 N 12.55 E
Coria 34 39.59 N 6.32 W
Coria del Río 34 37.16 N 6.03 W
Coribe 255 13.50 S 44.28 W
Coricudgy, Mount ∧ 170 32.50 S 150.22 E
Corigliano Calabro 68 39.36 N 16.31 E
Corigliano d'Otranto 68 40.09 N 18.15 E
Corinaldo 66 43.39 N 13.03 E
Corinda 166 17.53 S 138.35 E
Corinne, Pa., U.S. 285 39.54 N 75.40 W
Corinne, Ut,. U.S. 200 41.33 N 112.06 W
Corinne, W.V., U.S. 192 37.34 N 81.21 W
Corinth, Ky., U.S. 218 38.29 N 84.33 W
Corinth, Ms., U.S. 194 34.56 N 88.31 W
Corinth, N.Y., U.S. 210 43.14 N 73.49 W
Corinth, Gulf of → Korinthiakós Kólpos c 38 38.19 N 22.04 E
Corinth Canal → Korínthou, Dhiórix ≡ 38 37.57 N 22.56 E
Corinth → Kórinthos 38 37.56 N 22.56 E
Corinto, Bra. 255 18.21 S 44.27 W
Corinto, El Sal. 236 13.49 N 87.58 W
Corinto, Nic. 236 12.29 N 87.10 W
Corio 169 38.04 S 144.23 E
Corio Bay c 169 38.07 S 144.24 E
Coripata 248 16.18 S 67.36 W
Corire 248 16.14 S 72.28 W
Coris 248 9.50 S 77.45 W
Corisco, Isla de I 152 0.53 N 9.20 E
Corixo Grande (Curiche Grande) ≃ 248 17.43 S 57.43 W
Cork (Corcaigh) 48 51.54 N 8.28 W
Cork □[6] 48 51.58 N 8.35 W
Cork Airport ⊠ 48 51.51 N 8.29 W
Cork Harbour c 48 51.45 N 8.15 W
Corkscrew 220 26.28 N 81.33 W
Çorkscrew Swamp ≣ 220 26.25 N 81.34 W
Čorku 85 39.58 N 70.33 E
Corlay 32 48.19 N 3.03 W
Corleone 70 37.49 N 13.18 E
Corleto Perticara 68 40.23 N 16.03 E
Çorlu 130 41.09 N 27.48 E
Cormainville 50 48.08 N 1.36 E
Cormano 266b 45.33 N 9.10 E
Cormatin 58 46.33 N 4.41 E
Cormeilles 50 49.15 N 0.23 E
Cormeilles-en-Parisis 50 48.59 N 2.12 E
Cormery 50 47.16 N 0.51 E
Cormons 64 45.58 N 13.28 E
Cormoran Reef ✦[2] 175b 7.50 N 134.32 E
Cormorant 184 54.14 N 100.35 W
Cormorant Lake ⊜ 184 54.13 N 100.47 W
Çorna 64 45.53 N 10.10 E
Čornaja, Ross. 24 68.35 N 56.30 E
Čornaja, Ross. 82 55.45 N 38.04 E
Čornaja, Ukr. 78 47.37 N 29.20 E
Čornaja ≃, Ross. 265a 59.47 N 30.10 E
Čornaja ≃, Ross. 265a 59.50 N 30.00 E
Čornaja ≃, Ross. 265a 60.01 N 30.10 E
Čornaja ≃, Ross. 265a 59.55 N 30.59 E
Čornaja ≃, Ross. 265b 55.41 N 37.58 E
Čornaja Cholunica 86 58.51 N 51.42 E
Čornaja Gr'az', Ross. 82 54.31 N 35.52 E
Čornaja Gr'az', Ross. 82 54.58 N 36.48 E
Čornaja Gr'az', Ross. 265b 55.58 N 37.19 E
Čornaja Rečka 265a 59.56 N 30.58 E
Čornaja rečka ≃, Ross. 265a 59.46 N 30.45 E
Čornaja rečka ≃, Ross. 265a 59.55 N 30.22 E
Čornaja Sloboda 24 60.48 N 37.46 E
Cornaredo 266b 45.30 N 9.02 E
Cornas 62 44.58 N 4.51 E
Cornedo Vicentino 64 45.37 N 11.20 E
Cornelia, S. Afr. 158 27.13 S 28.52 E
Cornelia, Ga., U.S. 192 34.30 N 83.31 W
Cornélio Procópio 255 23.08 S 50.39 W
Cornelius, N.C., U.S. 192 35.29 N 80.51 W
Cornelius, Or., U.S. 224 45.31 N 123.03 W
Cornelius Grinnell Bay c 176 63.20 N 64.50 W
Cornell, Il., U.S. 216 41.00 N 88.44 W
Cornell, Wi., U.S. 190 45.10 N 91.08 W
Cornellà de Llobregat 266d 41.21 N 2.05 E
Corner Brook 186 48.57 N 57.57 W
Corner Inlet c 169 38.43 S 146.20 E
Corner Store 285 40.07 N 75.30 W
Cornersville 194 35.21 N 86.50 W
Cornes, Lac des ⊜ 206 46.43 N 75.09 W
Corneta, Punta ≻ 234 15.39 N 96.34 W
Cornforth 44 54.42 N 1.31 W
Cornhill 46 57.36 N 2.42 W
Cornholme 262 53.44 N 2.08 W
Cornia ≃ 66 42.57 N 10.33 E
Corniglia 62 44.07 N 9.42 E
Corniglio 64 44.28 N 10.05 E
Corning, Ar., U.S. 194 36.24 N 90.34 W
Corning, Ca., U.S. 204 39.55 N 122.10 W
Corning, Ia., U.S. 198 40.59 N 94.44 W
Corning, Ks., U.S. 198 39.39 N 96.01 W
Corning, N.Y., U.S. 210 42.08 N 77.03 W
Corning, Oh., U.S. 188 39.36 N 82.05 W
Cornish 188 43.48 N 70.48 W
Cornish, Mount ∧ 162 20.13 S 126.28 E
Cornland 219 39.56 N 89.24 W
Çorno ≃ 66 42.49 N 12.55 E
Čornobajevka 78 46.42 N 32.32 E
Çorno Grande ∧ 66 42.28 N 13.34 E
Čornoje, Kaz. 86 51.44 N 77.34 E
Čornoje, Ross. 80 57.32 N 46.25 E
Čornolesskoje 84 44.42 N 43.42 E
Čornomorskij 78 44.51 N 38.29 E
Čornomorskoje, Ukr. 78 45.03 N 35.58 E
Čornomorskoje, Ukr. 78 45.30 N 32.42 E
Čornoreck 86 52.45 N 76.40 E
Cornuda 64 45.50 N 12.00 E
Cornwall, On., Can. 206 45.02 N 74.44 W
Cornwall, N.Y., U.S. 210 41.26 N 74.01 W
Cornwall, Pa., U.S. 208 40.16 N 76.24 W
Cornwall □[6] 42 50.30 N 4.40 W
Cornwall Bridge 207 41.49 N 73.22 W
Cornwallis Island I 176 75.15 N 94.30 W
Cornwall on Hudson 210 41.27 N 74.00 W
Çornwell 220 27.23 N 81.05 W
Čornyj Jar 80 48.04 N 46.08 E
Čornyj Mys, Ross. 24 68.20 N 38.37 E
Čornyj Mys, Ross. 86 55.33 N 80.04 E
Čornyj Ostrov 78 49.32 N 26.46 E
Čornyj Otrog 86 51.55 N 55.59 E
Čornyj Tašlyk ≃ 78 48.11 N 30.51 E
Corny Point 166 34.55 S 137.03 E
Coro 246 11.25 N 69.41 W
Coro, Golfete de c 241s 11.30 N 69.55 W
Coroaci 255 18.35 S 42.17 W
Coroa Grande 256 22.54 S 43.52 W
Coroatá 250 4.08 S 44.08 W
Çoroca ≃ 152 15.43 S 11.55 E
Čoroch (Çoruh) ≃ 130 41.36 N 41.35 E
Corocoro 248 17.12 S 68.29 W
Corocoro Island I 246 8.30 N 60.10 W
Coroico 248 16.10 S 67.44 W
Coroico ≃ 248 15.27 S 67.50 W
Coromandel, Bra. 255 18.28 S 47.13 W
Coromandel, N.Z. 172 36.46 S 175.30 E
Coromandel Coast •[2] 122 13.30 N 80.30 E
Coromandel Peninsula ≻[1] 172 36.50 S 175.35 E
Coromandel Range ⋀ 172 37.00 S 175.40 E
Coron 116 12.00 N 120.12 E
Corona, Ca., U.S. 228 33.52 N 117.33 W
Corona, N.M., U.S. 200 34.15 N 105.36 W
Corona ◆[8] 276 40.45 N 73.52 W
Coronación, Golfo de la → Coronation Gulf c 176 68.25 N 110.00 W
Coronación, Isla de la → Coronation Island I 9 60.37 S 45.30 W
Corona del Mar ◆[8] 228 33.36 N 117.52 W
Coronado, Méx. 234 22.55 N 100.56 W
Coronado, Ca., U.S. 228 32.41 N 117.10 W
Coronado, Bahía de c 236 9.00 N 83.50 W
Coronado National Memorial ♦ 200 31.10 N 110.29 W
Coronado Naval Amphibious Base ■ 228 32.40 N 117.10 W
Coronados, Golfo c 254 41.40 S 74.00 W
Coronation 182 52.05 N 111.27 W
Coronation Gardens ♦ 275b 43.41 N 79.29 W
Coronation Gulf c 176 68.25 N 110.00 W
Coronation Island I, Ant. 9 60.37 S 45.30 W
Coronation Island I, Ak., U.S. 180 55.52 N 134.15 W
Coronation Park ♦ 273d 26.06 S 27.47 E
Coron Bay c 116 11.54 N 120.08 E
Coronda 252 31.58 S 60.55 W
Coronel 252 37.01 S 73.08 W
Coronel Bogado 252 27.11 S 56.18 W
Coronel Dorrego 252 38.42 S 61.17 W
Coronel Du Graty 252 27.40 S 60.56 W
Coronel Eugenio del Busto 252 38.57 S 64.15 W
Coronel Fabriciano 255 19.31 S 42.38 W
Coronel Moldes, Arg. 252 25.16 S 65.29 W
Coronel Moldes, Arg. 252 33.38 S 64.36 W
Coronel Murta 255 16.37 S 42.11 W
Coronel Oviedo 252 25.25 S 56.27 W
Coronel Pacheco 256 21.35 S 43.16 W
Coronel Ponce 255 15.34 S 55.01 W
Coronel Pringles 252 37.58 S 61.22 W
Coronel Sapucaia 255 23.15 S 55.31 W
Coronel Suárez 252 37.28 S 61.55 W
Coronel Vidal 252 37.27 S 57.43 W
Coronel Vivida 252 25.58 S 52.34 W
Corongo 248 8.35 S 77.55 W
Corongoros 234 19.17 N 102.48 W
Coronie □[5] 250 5.50 N 56.20 W
Coron Island I 116 11.55 N 120.14 E

Symbols in the index entries represent the broad categories identified in the key at the right. Symbols with superior numbers (⋀[1]) identify subcategories (see complete key on page *I · 1).*

Symbole im Register stellen die rechts im Schlüssel erklärten Kategorien dar. Symbole mit hochgestellten Ziffern (⋀[1]) bezeichnen Unterabteilungen einer Kategorie (vgl. vollständiger Schlüssel auf Seite *I · 1).*

Los símbolos incluídos en el texto del índice representan las grandes categorias identificadas con la clave a la derecha. Los símbolos con numeros en su parte superior (⋀[1]) identifican las subcategorías (véase la clave completa en la página *I · 1).*

Les symboles de l'index représentent les catégories indiquées dans la légende à droite. Les symboles suivis d'un indice (⋀[1]) représentent des sous-catégories (voir légende complète à la page *I · 1).*

Os símbolos incluídos no texto do índice representam as grandes categorias identificadas com a chave à direita. Os símbolos com números em sua parte superior (⋀[1]) identificam as subcategorias (veja-se a chave completa à página *I · 1).*

	English	Deutsch	Español	Français	Português
∧	Mountain	Berg	Montaña	Montagne	Montanha
⋀	Mountains	Gebirge	Montañas	Montagnes	Montanhas
)(	Pass	Paß	Paso	Col	Passo
V	Valley, Canyon	Tal, Cañon	Valle, Cañón	Vallée, Canyon	Vale, Canhão
=	Plain	Ebene	Llano	Plaine	Planície
≻	Cape	Kap	Cabo	Cap	Cabo
I	Island	Insel	Isla	Île	Ilha
II	Islands	Inseln	Islas	Îles	Ilhas
•	Other Topographic Features	Andere Topographische Objekte	Otros Elementos Topográficos	Autres données topographiques	Outros acidentes topográficos

ESPAÑOL

Nombre	Página	Lat.°′	Long.°′ W = Oeste
Coronita	228	33.52 N	117.36 W
Coropuna, Nevado ∧	248	15.31 S	72.42 W
Çorovodë	38	40.30 N	20.13 E
Corowa	166	36.02 S	146.23 E
Corozal, Belize	232	18.24 N	88.24 W
Corozal, Col.	246	9.19 N	75.18 W
Corozal, Hond.	236	15.48 N	86.43 W
Corozal, P.R.	240m	18.21 N	66.17 W
Corps	62	44.49 N	5.57 E
Corpus	252	27.07 S	55.31 W
Corpus Christi	196	27.48 N	97.23 W
Corpus Christi, Lake ⊜[1]	196	28.10 N	97.53 W
Corpus Christi Bay ⊂	196	27.48 N	97.20 W
Corpus Christi Naval Air Station ■	196	27.42 N	97.16 W
Corque	248	18.21 S	67.42 W
Corquín	236	14.34 N	88.52 W
Corral	254	39.52 S	73.26 W
Corral de Almaguer	34	39.46 N	3.11 W
Corral de Bustos	252	33.17 S	62.12 W
Corralero, Laguna ⊂	234	16.12 N	98.07 W
Corralillo	240p	22.59 N	80.35 W
Corralito	252	32.03 S	64.12 W
Corralito, Arroyo del ≃	258	33.39 S	58.03 W
Corralito, Cuchilla del ⋏[2]	258	33.40 S	57.44 W
Corralitos, Méx.	196	26.57 N	104.39 W
Corralitos, Ca., U.S.	226	36.59 N	121.48 W
Corran	46	56.43 N	5.14 W
Corraun Peninsula ≻[1]	48	53.54 N	9.53 W
Correas, Arroyo ≃	288	34.24 S	58.32 W
Correboi, Arcu)(	71	40.05 N	9.21 E
Correctionville	198	42.28 N	95.47 W
Corredor	287b	23.27 S	46.19 W
Correggio	64	44.46 N	10.47 E
Corregidor Island I	116	14.23 N	120.35 E
Correго do Bom Jesus	256	22.38 S	46.02 W
Córrego do Ouro	256	21.22 S	45.47 W
Córrego Rico	255	15.14 S	47.48 W
Correia de Almeida	256	21.17 S	43.38 W
Corrente	250	10.27 S	45.10 W
Corrente ≃, Bra.	255	19.19 S	50.50 W
Corrente ≃, Bra.	255	13.08 S	43.28 W
Correntes	250	9.08 S	36.19 W
Correntes ≃	248	17.21 S	55.37 W
Correntes, Cabo das ≻	156	24.11 S	35.34 E
Correnti, Isola delle I	70	36.38 N	15.05 E
Correntina	255	13.20 S	44.39 W
Corrèze □[5]	32	45.20 N	1.50 E
Correzzana	266b	45.40 N	9.18 E
Corrib, Lough ⊜	48	53.26 N	9.14 W
Corridonia	66	43.15 N	13.30 E
Corrientes	252	27.28 S	58.50 W
Corrientes □[4]	252	29.00 S	58.00 W
Corrientes ≃, Arg.	252	30.21 S	59.33 W
Corrientes ≃, S.A.	246	3.43 S	74.35 W
Corrientes, Bahía de ⊂	240p	21.51 N	84.36 W
Corrientes, Cabo ≻, Arg.	252	38.01 S	57.32 W
Corrientes, Cabo ≻, Col.	246	5.30 N	77.34 W
Corrientes, Cabo ≻, Cuba	240p	21.45 N	84.31 W
Corrientes, Cabo ≻, Méx.	234	20.25 N	105.42 W
Corrigan	222	30.59 N	94.49 W
Corrigin	162	32.21 S	117.52 E
Corrimal	170	34.22 S	150.54 E
Corringham	260	51.31 N	0.28 E
Corriverton	246	5.53 N	57.08 W
Corrofin	48	52.56 N	9.03 W
Corroios	266c	38.38 N	9.09 W
Corropoli	66	42.49 N	13.50 E
Corrumpa Creek ≃	196	36.36 N	102.52 W
Corry	214	41.55 N	79.38 W
Corryong	171b	36.12 S	147.54 E
Corryong Creek ≃	171b	36.06 S	147.59 E
Corryvreckan, Gulf of Ʉ	46	56.09 N	5.44 W
Corsano	68	39.53 N	18.22 E
Corse (Corsica) I	36	42.00 N	9.00 E
Corse, Cap ≻	62	43.00 N	9.25 E
Corse-du-Sud □[5]	36	41.50 N	9.00 E
Corserine ∧	44	55.09 N	4.22 W
Corsham	42	51.26 N	2.11 W
Corsica, Pa., U.S.	214	41.10 N	79.12 W
Corsica, S.D., U.S.	198	43.25 N	98.24 W
Corsica → Corse I	36	42.00 N	9.00 E
Corsicana	222	32.05 N	96.28 W
Corsica River ⊂	208	39.05 N	76.08 W
Corsico	62	45.26 N	9.07 E
Corsock	44	55.04 N	3.57 W
Corson Inlet ⊂	208	39.12 N	74.39 W
Cortaccia (Kurtatsch)	64	46.19 N	11.13 E
Cortachy	46	56.43 N	2.58 W
Cort Adelaer, Kap ≻	176	62.00 N	42.00 W
Cortale	68	38.50 N	16.25 E
Cortazar	234	20.29 N	100.56 W
Corte	36	42.18 N	9.08 E
Corte Alto	254	40.57 S	73.10 W
Cortegana	34	37.55 N	6.49 W
Corte Madera	226	37.55 N	122.31 W
Corte Madera Creek ≃	282	37.23 N	122.14 W
Cortemaggiore	64	44.59 N	9.56 E
Cortemilia	62	44.35 N	8.12 E
Corteno Golgi	64	46.10 N	10.15 E
Cortes	116	9.17 N	126.11 E
Cortés □[5]	236	15.30 N	88.00 W
Cortes ʊ	266a	40.25 N	3.41 W
Cortés, Bahía de ⊂	240p	22.05 N	83.52 W
Cortez, Co., U.S.	200	37.20 N	108.35 W
Cortez, Fl., U.S.	220	27.28 N	82.41 W
Cortez, Sea of → California, Golfo de ⊂	232	28.00 N	112.00 W
Cortez Mountains ⋏	204	40.20 N	116.20 W
Cortina Creek ≃	226	39.06 N	122.02 W
Cortina d'Ampezzo	64	46.32 N	12.08 E
Cortines	258	34.34 S	59.13 W
Čortkov	78	49.01 N	25.48 E
Cortland, Il., U.S.	216	41.55 N	88.41 W
Cortland, In., U.S.	218	38.58 N	85.58 W
Cortland, Ne., U.S.	198	40.30 N	96.42 W
Cortland, N.Y., U.S.	210	42.36 N	76.10 W
Cortland, Oh., U.S.	214	41.19 N	80.43 W
Cortland □[6]	210	42.36 N	76.11 W
Corton	42	52.32 N	1.44 E
Cortona	66	43.16 N	11.59 E
Çorubal (Koliba) ≃	150	11.57 N	15.06 W
Čoruch-Dajron	85	40.24 N	69.40 E
Coruche	34	38.57 N	8.31 W
Çoruh (Čoroch) ≃	130	41.36 N	41.35 E
Çorum, Tür.	130	39.14 N	28.27 E
Çorum, Tür.	130	40.33 N	34.58 E
Çorum □[4]	130	40.30 N	34.40 E
Corumbá	248	19.01 S	57.39 W
Corumbá ≃	255	18.19 S	48.55 W
Corumbá de Goiás	255	15.55 S	48.48 W
Corumbaíba	255	18.09 S	48.34 W
Corumbataí ≃	252	23.55 S	51.57 W
Corumbaú, Ponta do ≻	255	16.53 S	39.06 W
Corumbiara ≃	248	13.13 S	62.06 W
Corumo ≃	246	6.49 N	60.52 W
Corund	38	46.28 N	25.11 E
Corunna, On., Can.	214	42.53 N	82.26 W
Corunna, In., U.S.	216	41.26 N	85.08 W
Corunna, Mi., U.S.	216	42.58 N	84.07 W
Corunna Downs	162	21.28 S	119.51 E
Corunna → La Coruña	34	43.22 N	8.23 W
Coruripe	250	10.08 S	36.10 W
Corvallis, Mt., U.S.	202	46.18 N	114.06 W

FRANÇAIS

Nom	Page	Lat.°′	Long.°′ W = Ouest
Corvallis, Or., U.S.	202	44.33 N	123.15 W
Corvara in Badia	64	46.33 N	11.52 E
Corve Dale V	42	52.30 N	2.40 W
Corvey, Kloster ʊ[1]	52	51.46 N	9.25 E
Corviale ◆[8]	267a	41.52 N	12.25 E
Corvo I	148a	39.42 N	31.06 W
Corwen	42	52.59 N	3.22 W
Corwin, Cape ≻	180	59.54 N	165.41 W
Corwith	190	42.59 N	93.57 W
Corydon, In., U.S.	218	38.12 N	86.07 W
Corydon, Ia., U.S.	190	40.45 N	93.19 W
Corydon, Ky., U.S.	194	37.44 N	87.42 W
Coryell	222	31.33 N	97.37 W
Coryell □[6]	222	31.25 N	97.40 W
Coryell Creek ≃	222	31.23 N	97.35 W
Coryton	260	51.31 N	0.31 E
Coryville	214	41.53 N	78.24 W
Corzu	38	44.28 N	23.10 E
Corzuela	252	26.57 S	60.58 W
Cosa (Ansedonia) ⊥	66	42.25 N	11.18 E
Cosamaloapan [de Carpio]	232	18.22 N	95.48 W
Cosapa	248	18.11 S	68.40 W
Coscile ≃	68	39.42 N	16.28 E
Cos Cob	276	41.02 N	73.36 W
Cos Cob Harbor ⊂	276	41.01 N	73.36 W
Coscomatepec [de Bravo]	234	19.04 N	97.02 W
Coseley	42	52.33 N	2.06 W
Cosenza	68	39.17 N	16.15 E
Cosenza □[4]	68	39.28 N	16.25 E
Cosgroves Creek ≃	274a	33.50 S	150.46 E
Coshocton	214	40.16 N	81.51 W
Coshocton □[6]	214	40.16 N	81.51 W
Cosigüina, Punta ≻	236	12.54 N	87.41 W
Cosigüina, Volcán ∧[1]	236	12.59 N	87.34 W
Cos → Kos I	38	36.50 N	27.10 E
Coslada	266a	40.26 N	3.34 W
Cosmo ◆[8]	256	22.54 S	43.37 W
Cosmoledo Island I	138	9.43 S	47.35 E
Cosmópolis, Bra.	256	22.38 S	47.12 W
Cosmopolis, Wa., U.S.	224	46.57 N	123.46 W
Cosmos	198	44.56 N	94.41 W
Cosmos ◆[8]	287a	22.55 S	44.37 W
Cosne-Cours-sur-Loire	50	47.24 N	2.55 E
Cosoleacaque	234	18.00 N	94.37 W
Cospán	248	7.26 S	78.33 W
Cosquín	252	31.15 S	64.29 W
Cossato	62	45.34 N	8.10 E
Cossatot ≃	194	33.48 N	94.09 W
Cossayuna	210	43.11 N	73.26 W
Cossayuna Lake ⊜	210	43.12 N	73.25 W
Cossebaude	54	51.05 N	13.38 E
Cossé-le-Vivien	28	47.57 N	0.55 W
Cossoine	71	40.27 N	8.43 E
Cosson ≃	50	47.30 N	1.15 E
Cossonay	58	46.37 N	6.31 E
Cost	222	29.26 N	97.32 W
Costa, Cayo I	220	26.41 N	82.15 W
Costa, Cordillera de la ⋏	286c	10.33 N	66.52 W
Costa, Sierra de la → Coast Ranges ⋏	178	41.00 N	123.30 W
Costacciaro	66	43.21 N	12.42 E
Costa de Caparica	266c	38.38 N	9.14 W
Costa del Marfil → Ivory Coast □[1]	150	8.00 N	5.00 W
Costa de San José	258	33.51 S	56.53 W
Costa di Rovigo	64	45.03 N	11.42 E
Costa Mesa	228	33.38 N	117.55 W
Costanera, Cadena → Coast Mountains ⋏	176	55.00 N	129.00 W
Costanera Sur, Parque Natural ♦	288	34.37 S	58.21 W
Costanero, Canal de ≊	288	34.28 S	58.28 W
Costa Rica	232	24.32 N	107.18 W
Costa Rica □[1], N.A.	230	10.00 N	84.00 W
Costa Rica □[1], N.A.	236	10.00 N	84.00 W
Costaros	62	44.54 N	3.50 E
Costas	256	22.39 S	45.56 W
Costello	214	41.36 N	78.03 W
Costelloe	48	53.17 N	9.32 W
Costermansville → Bukavu	154	2.30 S	28.52 E
Costessey	42	52.40 N	1.11 E
Costești	38	44.40 N	24.53 E
Costiera, Catena ⋏	68	39.20 N	16.05 E
Costigan Lake ⊜	184	56.56 N	105.55 W
Costigliole d'Asti	62	44.47 N	8.11 E
Costigliole Saluzzo	62	44.34 N	7.29 E
Costilla	200	36.58 N	105.31 W
Costilla Creek ≃	200	36.59 N	105.43 W
Cosumnes ≃	226	38.16 N	121.26 W
Cosumnes, Middle Fork ≃	226	38.33 N	120.51 W
Cosumnes, North Fork ≃	226	38.33 N	120.51 W
Cosumnes, South Fork ≃	226	38.33 N	120.49 W
Coswig, Dtsch.	54	51.07 N	13.34 E
Coswig, Dtsch.	54	51.53 N	12.26 E
Cotabambas	248	13.45 S	72.21 W
Cotabato	116	7.13 N	124.15 E
Cotacajes ≃	248	16.00 S	67.01 W
Cotagaita	248	20.50 S	65.41 W
Cotagaita ≃	248	21.01 S	65.23 W
Cotahuasi	248	15.12 S	72.56 W
Cotão ∧[2]	266c	38.45 N	9.18 W
Cotati	226	38.20 N	122.42 W
Coteau-Landing	206	45.15 N	74.13 W
Coteau-Station	206	45.17 N	74.14 W
Coteaux	238	18.12 N	74.02 W
Côte d'Ivoire → Ivory Coast □[1]	150	8.00 N	5.00 W
Côte-d'Or □[5]	50	47.30 N	4.50 E
Cotegipe	255	12.02 S	44.15 W
Cote Indian Reserve ◆[4]	184	51.38 N	101.53 W
Cotentin ≻[1]	32	49.30 N	1.30 W
Côte-Saint-Luc	275a	45.28 N	73.40 W
Côtes-d'Armor □[5]	32	48.25 N	2.40 W
Côte Visitation ◆[8]	275a	45.33 N	73.36 W
Cothi ≃	42	51.52 N	4.10 W
Coti ≃	248	8.36 S	65.33 W
Cotia	256	23.37 S	46.56 W
Cotia □[7]	287b	23.38 S	46.56 W
Cotia ≃	256	23.31 S	46.51 W
Cotia, Reprêsa de ⊜[1]	287b	23.44 S	46.57 W
Cotignac	62	43.32 N	6.09 E
Cotignola	66	44.23 N	11.56 E
Cotija de la Paz	234	19.49 N	102.43 W
Cotingo ≃	246	3.55 N	60.30 W
Cotis, Laguna ⊜	258	35.11 S	59.16 W
Cotmeana ≃	38	44.24 N	24.45 E
Cotoca	248	17.49 S	63.03 W
Cotonou	150	6.21 N	2.26 E
Cotopaxi □[4]	246	0.55 S	78.55 W
Cotopaxi ∧[1]	246	0.40 S	78.26 W
Cotopaxi, Parque Nacional ♦	246	0.15 S	78.25 W
Cotorra, Isla I	241r	10.02 N	62.16 W
Cotorro ◆[8]	286b	23.03 N	82.16 W
Cotronei	68	39.09 N	16.47 E
Cotswold Hills ⋏[2]	42	51.45 N	2.10 W
Cottage Grove, In., U.S.	218	39.36 N	84.52 W
Cottage Grove, Or., U.S.	202	43.47 N	123.03 W
Cottage Grove, Wi., U.S.	216	43.05 N	89.12 W
Cottage Hills	219	38.55 N	90.04 W
Cottageville	192	32.56 N	80.28 W
Cottam, On., Can.	214	42.08 N	82.45 W
Cottam, Eng., U.K.	262	53.47 N	2.46 W
Cottanello	66	42.24 N	12.41 E

PORTUGUÊS

Nome	Página	Lat.°′	Long.°′ W = Oeste
Cottbus	54	51.45 N	14.19 E
Cottekill	210	41.51 N	74.06 W
Cottel Island I	186	48.51 N	53.42 W
Cottenham	42	52.18 N	0.09 E
Cotter	194	36.16 N	92.32 W
Cotter ≃	171b	35.19 S	148.57 E
Cottesloe	168a	31.59 S	115.45 E
Cottiennes, Alpes (Alpi Cozie) ⋏	62	44.45 N	7.00 E
Cottingham	44	53.47 N	0.24 W
Cottleville	219	38.44 N	90.39 W
Cottondale, Al., U.S.	194	33.11 N	87.27 W
Cottondale, Fl., U.S.	192	30.47 N	85.22 W
Cotton Lake ⊜, Mb., Can.	184	55.05 N	96.50 W
Cotton Lake ⊜, Tx., U.S.	222	29.48 N	94.48 W
Cotton Plant	194	35.00 N	91.15 W
Cottonport	194	30.59 N	92.03 W
Cotton Valley	194	32.49 N	93.25 W
Cottonwood, Az., U.S.	200	34.44 N	112.00 W
Cottonwood, Ca., U.S.	204	40.23 N	122.16 W
Cottonwood, Id., U.S.	202	46.02 N	116.20 W
Cottonwood, Mn., U.S.	198	44.36 N	95.40 W
Cottonwood ≃, Ks., U.S.	198	38.23 N	96.03 W
Cottonwood ≃, Mn., U.S.	198	44.17 N	94.25 W
Cottonwood Creek ≃, Ca., U.S.	226	36.52 N	120.12 W
Cottonwood Creek ≃, Ca., U.S.	226	36.27 N	119.20 W
Cottonwood Creek ≃, Mt., U.S.	202	48.33 N	107.45 W
Cottonwood Creek ≃, N.D., U.S.	198	46.16 N	98.15 W
Cottonwood Creek ≃, Ok., U.S.	196	35.54 N	97.27 W
Cottonwood Creek ≃, Or., U.S.	202	43.53 N	117.43 W
Cottonwood Creek ≃, Tx., U.S.	196	31.23 N	103.46 W
Cottonwood Creek ≃, Tx., U.S.	196	32.48 N	100.21 W
Cottonwood Creek ≃, Ut,. U.S.	200	39.09 N	110.55 W
Cottonwood Creek ≃, Wy., U.S.	202	43.51 N	108.09 W
Cottonwood Creek, Middle Fork ≃	204	40.23 N	122.20 W
Cottonwood Creek, South Fork ≃	204	40.23 N	122.20 W
Cottonwood Falls	198	38.22 N	96.32 W
Cottonwood Wash V, Az., U.S.	200	36.19 N	113.59 W
Cottonwood Wash V, Az., U.S.	200	35.00 N	110.39 W
Cotubandê	287a	22.51 S	43.01 W
Cotuhé ≃	246	2.53 S	69.44 W
Cotui	238	19.03 N	70.09 W
Cotuit	207	41.37 N	70.26 W
Cotulla	196	28.26 N	99.14 W
Cotunduba, Ilha de I	287a	22.58 S	43.09 W
Coubert	261	48.40 N	2.42 E
Coubre, Pointe de la ≻	32	45.41 N	1.13 W
Coubron	261	48.55 N	2.35 E
Couches-les-Mines	58	46.52 N	4.34 E
Couchiching, Lake ⊜	212	44.40 N	79.23 W
Coucouron	62	44.48 N	3.58 E
Coucy-le-Château-Auffrique	50	49.31 N	3.19 E
Coudekerque-Branche	50	51.02 N	2.24 E
Coudersport	214	41.46 N	78.01 W
Coudres, Île aux I	186	47.24 N	70.23 W
Couesnon ≃	32	48.37 N	1.31 W
Cougar	224	46.03 N	122.17 W
Cougar Reservoir ⊜[1]	202	44.06 N	122.12 W
Couhé	32	46.18 N	0.11 E
Couillet	50	50.23 N	4.27 E
Couilly-Pont-aux-Dames	261	48.53 N	2.52 E
Coulanges-la-Vineuse	50	47.42 N	3.35 E
Coulanges-sur-Yonne	50	47.31 N	3.32 E
Coulee City	202	47.36 N	119.17 W
Coulee Dam	202	47.57 N	118.58 W
Coulee Dam National Recreation Area ♦	202	48.10 N	118.15 W
Coulihaut	240d	15.30 N	61.29 W
Coulman Island I	9	73.27 S	169.40 E
Coulmier-le-Sec	58	47.45 N	4.29 E
Coulogne	50	50.55 N	1.53 E
Coulomby	50	50.42 N	2.00 E
Coulommiers	50	48.49 N	3.05 E
Coulon ≃	62	43.51 N	5.00 E
Coulonge ≃	190	45.51 N	76.46 W
Coulonge Est ≃	190	46.06 N	76.44 W
Coulsdon ◆[8]	260	51.19 N	0.08 W
Coulta	166	34.23 S	135.29 E
Coulters	279b	40.18 N	79.48 W
Coulterville, Ca., U.S.	226	37.42 N	120.11 W
Coulterville, Il., U.S.	194	38.11 N	89.36 W
Counce	194	35.02 N	88.16 W
Council	202	44.44 N	116.26 W
Council Bluffs	198	41.15 N	95.51 W
Council Grove	198	38.39 N	96.29 W
Council Grove Lake ⊜[1]	198	38.42 N	96.31 W
Coundon	44	54.40 N	1.39 W
Countegany	171b	36.11 S	149.27 E
Countesthorpe	42	52.33 N	1.08 W
Country Campus	222	30.49 N	95.26 W
Country Club Estates	220	28.03 N	81.57 W
Country Club Hills	278	41.34 N	87.43 W
Country Club View	284c	38.49 N	77.19 W
Country Hills	279b	40.19 N	79.42 W
Country Homes	202	47.44 N	117.24 W
Country Ridge Estates	276	41.02 N	73.41 W
Countryside	278	41.46 N	87.52 W
Countryside Lake ⊜	278	42.15 N	88.03 W
Countryside Manor	278	42.18 N	87.56 W
Coupar Angus	46	56.33 N	3.17 W
Coupeville	224	48.13 N	122.41 W
Coupland	222	30.28 N	97.24 W
Coupon	214	40.32 N	78.31 W
Coupvray	261	48.54 N	2.48 E
Courbevoie	50	48.54 N	2.15 E
Courbons	62	44.06 N	6.12 E
Courçay	50	47.15 N	0.52 E
Courcelle	261	48.42 N	2.06 E
Courcelles, Bel.	50	50.28 N	4.22 E
Courcelles, Fr.	261	49.07 N	2.18 E
Courcelles-Chaussy	56	49.07 N	6.24 E
Courcelles-sur-Nied	56	49.04 N	6.18 E
Courchevel	62	45.25 N	6.38 E
Cour-Cheverny	50	47.30 N	1.27 E
Courcibo ≃	250	4.53 N	53.00 W
Courçon	32	46.15 N	0.49 W
Courcouronnes	261	48.37 N	2.24 E
Courdimanche	261	49.02 N	2.00 E
Cour-et-Buis	62	45.26 N	5.00 E
Courgent	261	48.54 N	1.40 E
Courland → Kurzeme □[9]	76	56.50 N	22.30 E
Courmayeur	62	45.47 N	6.58 E
Couronne, Cap ≻	62	43.19 N	5.03 E
Couronnement, Île du → Coronation Island I	9	60.37 S	45.30 W
Courpière	62	45.45 N	3.33 E
Courquetaine	261	48.41 N	2.45 E
Course Brook ≃	283	42.17 N	71.22 W
Courseulles	28	49.20 N	0.27 W
Courson-les-Carrières	50	47.36 N	3.30 E
Court	58	47.14 N	7.20 E
Courtacon	50	48.42 N	3.17 E
Courtalain	50	48.05 N	1.09 E
Courtenay, B.C., Can.	182	49.41 N	125.00 W
Courtenay, Fr.	50	48.02 N	3.03 E
Courthézon	62	44.05 N	4.53 E
Courtice	212	43.55 N	78.46 W
Courtisols	56	48.59 N	4.31 E
Courtland, On., Can.	212	42.51 N	80.38 W
Courtland, Al., U.S.	194	34.40 N	87.18 W
Courtland, Ca., U.S.	226	38.20 N	121.34 W
Courtland, Va., U.S.	208	36.42 N	77.04 W
Courtleigh	284b	39.22 N	76.46 W
Courtmacsherry	48	51.38 N	8.43 W
Courtmacsherry Bay ⊂	48	51.35 N	8.40 W
Courtney, Pa., U.S.	279b	40.13 N	79.58 W
Courtney, Tx., U.S.	222	30.16 N	96.04 W
Courtney Creek ≃	196	31.16 N	102.50 W
Courtomer, Fr.	50	48.38 N	0.22 E
Courtomer, Fr.	261	48.39 N	2.54 E
Courtown	48	52.38 N	6.13 W
Courtrai → Kortrijk	50	50.50 N	3.16 E
Courtright	214	42.49 N	82.28 W
Courtry, Fr.	261	48.33 N	2.46 E
Courtry, Fr.	261	48.55 N	2.36 E
Court-Saint-Étienne	50	50.39 N	4.34 E
Courville-sur-Eure	50	48.27 N	1.15 E
Coushatta	194	32.00 N	93.20 W
Cousin ≃	50	47.15 N	4.04 E
Cousiño Macul, Parque ♦	286e	33.30 S	70.35 W
Cousolre	50	50.15 N	4.09 E
Coussegrey	50	47.57 N	4.01 E
Coussey	58	48.25 N	5.41 E
Coustellet	62	43.53 N	5.11 E
Coutances	32	49.03 N	1.26 W
Coutevroult	261	48.52 N	2.51 E
Couto do Magalhães	250	8.17 S	49.16 W
Couto Magalhães ≃	255	13.37 S	53.09 W
Coutras	32	45.02 N	0.08 W
Coutts	182	49.00 N	111.57 W
Couture, Lac ⊜	176	60.07 N	75.20 W
Couture-sur-Loir	50	47.45 N	0.41 E
Couves, Ilha das I	256	23.25 S	44.52 W
Couvet	58	46.56 N	6.38 E
Couvin	50	50.03 N	4.29 E
Cova da Piedade	266c	38.40 N	9.10 W
Covane	156	21.22 S	33.56 E
Covasna	38	45.51 N	26.11 E
Covasna □[6]	38	46.00 N	26.00 E
Cove, Scot., U.K.	46	57.51 N	5.42 W
Cove, Or., U.S.	202	45.17 N	117.48 W
Cove Bay	46	57.06 N	2.04 W
Covedale	218	39.07 N	84.36 W
Cove Harbor ⊂	276	41.03 N	73.30 W
Cove Island I	190	45.17 N	81.44 W
Covelo, Ang.	152	12.06 S	13.55 E
Covelo, Ca., U.S.	204	39.47 N	123.14 W
Cove Neck	276	40.53 N	73.31 W
Cove Neck ≻[1]	276	40.53 N	73.30 W
Coventry, Eng., U.K.	42	52.25 N	1.30 W
Coventry, Ct., U.S.	207	41.46 N	72.18 W
Coventry, De., U.S.	285	39.40 N	75.38 W
Coventry, R.I., U.S.	207	41.41 N	71.34 W
Coventry Cathedral ʊ[1]	42	52.25 N	1.30 W
Coventryville	285	40.10 N	75.41 W
Cove Palisades State Park ♦	202	44.34 N	121.15 W
Cove Point	208	38.22 N	76.23 W
Cove Point ≻	208	38.23 N	76.23 W
Cover ≃	44	54.17 N	1.46 W
Covered Wells	200	31.48 N	111.59 W
Covert	216	42.17 N	86.15 W
Covigliaio	66	44.08 N	11.18 E
Covilhã	34	40.17 N	7.30 W
Covina	228	34.05 N	117.53 W
Covington, Ga., U.S.	192	33.35 N	83.51 W
Covington, In., U.S.	194	40.08 N	87.23 W
Covington, Ky., U.S.	218	39.05 N	84.30 W
Covington, La., U.S.	194	30.28 N	90.06 W
Covington, Oh., U.S.	218	40.07 N	84.21 W
Covington, Ok., U.S.	196	36.18 N	97.35 W
Covington, Pa., U.S.	210	41.45 N	77.05 W
Covington, Tn., U.S.	194	35.33 N	89.38 W
Covington, Tx., U.S.	222	32.11 N	97.16 W
Covington, Va., U.S.	192	37.47 N	79.59 W
Covões	266c	38.50 N	9.20 W
Covunco, Arroyo ≃	252	38.29 S	69.32 W
Cow ≃	190	47.23 N	83.59 W
Cowal ≻[1]	46	56.05 N	5.08 W
Cowal, Lake ⊜	166	33.35 S	147.25 E
Cowan, Ky., U.S.	218	38.24 N	83.54 W
Cowan, Tn., U.S.	194	35.09 N	86.00 W
Cowan, Lake ⊜	162	31.50 S	121.50 E
Cowan Creek ≃	274a	33.40 S	151.10 E
Cowanesque	210	41.56 N	77.30 W
Cowanesque ≃	210	42.00 N	77.07 W
Cowan Heights	280	33.47 N	117.47 W
Cowan Lake ⊜, Sk., Can.	184	54.00 N	107.15 W
Cowan Lake ⊜, Oh., U.S.	218	39.23 N	83.54 W
Cowan Lake State Park ♦	218	39.23 N	83.53 W
Cowansburg	279b	40.15 N	79.46 W
Cowanshannock Creek ≃	214	40.51 N	79.30 W
Cowansville, P.Q., Can.	206	45.12 N	72.45 W
Cowansville, Pa., U.S.	214	40.53 N	79.36 W
Cowaramup	162	33.52 S	115.05 E
Coward	192	33.58 N	79.44 W
Coward Springs	166	29.24 S	136.49 E
Cowarie	166	27.43 S	138.20 E
Cow Bayou ≃	222	31.19 N	97.00 W
Cowbridge	42	51.28 N	3.27 W
Cowburn Tunnel ◆[5]	262	53.21 N	1.52 W
Cow Canyon V	280	34.01 N	120.06 W
Cowcowing Lakes ⊜	162	31.01 S	117.18 E
Cow Creek ≃, Ks., U.S.	198	38.02 N	97.56 W
Cow Creek ≃, Mt., U.S.	202	47.47 N	108.56 W
Cow Creek ≃, Ok., U.S.	196	34.10 N	98.00 W
Cow Creek ≃, Or., U.S.	202	42.57 N	123.20 W
Cow Creek ≃, Wa., U.S.	202	46.45 N	118.09 W
Cowden, Il., U.S.	219	39.15 N	88.52 W
Cowden, Pa., U.S.	279b	40.19 N	80.13 W
Cowdenbeath	46	56.07 N	3.21 W
Coweeman ≃	224	46.06 N	122.52 W
Cowell	166	33.41 S	136.55 E
Cowen	188	38.24 N	80.33 W
Cowen, Mount ∧	202	45.23 N	110.29 W
Cowes, Austl.	169	38.27 S	145.14 E
Cowes, Eng., U.K.	42	50.45 N	1.18 W
Cowessess Indian Reserve ◆[4]	184	50.31 N	102.42 W
Coweta	196	35.57 N	95.39 W
Cow Green Reservoir ⊜[1]	44	54.40 N	2.18 W
Cow Gulch ≃	202	46.02 N	107.52 W
Cow Head	186	49.55 N	57.48 W
Cowhouse Creek ≃	222	31.10 N	97.35 W
Cowichan ≃	224	48.46 N	123.38 W
Cowichan Bay	224	48.44 N	123.40 W
Cowichan Lake ⊜	224	48.54 N	124.20 W
Cowiche Creek, North Fork ≃	224	46.38 N	120.41 W
Cowiche Creek, South Fork ≃	224	46.38 N	120.41 W
Cowie Water ≃	46	56.58 N	2.12 W
Cowles Dam ⊜[1]	273d	26.13 S	28.28 E
Cowlesville	210	42.51 N	78.28 W
Cowley, Austl.	166	26.54 S	144.49 E
Cowley, Ab., Can.	182	49.34 N	114.05 W
Cowley, Eng., U.K.	42	51.43 N	1.12 W
Cowley, Wy., U.S.	202	44.53 N	108.28 W
Cowley ◆[8]	260	51.32 N	0.29 W
Cowley, Mount ∧	169	38.33 S	143.52 E
Cowlitz □[6]	224	46.07 N	122.43 W
Cowlitz ≃	224	46.05 N	122.53 W
Cowm Reservoir ⊜[1]	262	53.40 N	2.11 W
Cow Palace ʊ	282	37.42 N	122.25 W
Cowpasture ≃	188	37.48 N	79.45 W
Cowpens	192	35.01 N	81.48 W
Cowpens National Battlefield ♦	192	35.06 N	81.46 W
Cowra	166	33.50 S	148.41 E
Cox ≃	164	15.19 S	135.25 E
Cox, Mount ∧[2]	162	24.55 S	125.36 E
Coxá ≃	255	14.16 S	44.11 W
Cox Creek ≃	212	43.35 N	80.29 W
Coxheath	42	51.14 N	0.30 E
Coxim	255	18.30 S	54.45 W
Coxim ≃	255	18.34 S	54.46 W
Coxipi, Lac ⊜	186	51.33 N	58.25 W
Coxquihui	234	20.11 N	97.35 W
Cox River Aboriginal Reserve ◆[4]	164	15.40 S	134.45 E
Coxs ≃	170	33.57 S	150.25 E
Coxsackie	210	42.21 N	73.48 W
Cox's Bāzār	120	21.26 N	91.59 E
Cox's Cove	186	49.07 N	58.05 W
Coyaguaima, Cerro ∧	252	22.55 S	66.35 W
Coyah	150	9.43 N	13.23 W
Coyame	232	29.28 N	105.06 W
Coyanosa Draw V	196	31.18 N	103.06 W
Coya Sur	252	22.25 S	69.38 W
Coyle, Water of ≃	44	55.28 N	4.32 W
Coyoacán ◆[8]	286a	19.20 N	99.10 W
Coyote	226	37.13 N	121.44 W
Coyote Creek ≃, Ca., U.S.	204	33.13 N	116.13 W
Coyote Creek ≃, Ca., U.S.	226	37.28 N	122.03 W
Coyote Creek ≃, Ca., U.S.	280	33.47 N	118.05 W
Coyote Creek, East Fork ≃	226	37.10 N	121.30 W
Coyote Creek, Middle Fork ≃	226	37.10 N	121.30 W
Coyote Hills ⋏[2]	282	37.33 N	122.05 W
Coyote Hills Regional Park ♦	282	37.33 N	122.06 W
Coyote Lake ⊜	204	35.04 N	116.45 W
Coyote Lake ⊜[1]	226	37.06 N	121.32 W
Coyotepec	234	19.46 N	99.12 W
Coyote Point ≻	282	37.35 N	122.19 W
Coyote Wash V, Az., U.S.	200	32.40 N	114.08 W
Coyote Wash V, N.M., U.S.	200	36.11 N	108.33 W
Coy Pond ⊜	283	42.36 N	70.49 W
Coyuca de Benítez	234	17.02 N	100.04 W
Coyuca de Catalán	234	18.20 N	100.39 W
Coyutla	234	20.15 N	97.39 W
Cozad	198	40.51 N	99.59 W
Cozes	32	45.35 N	0.50 W
Cozie, Alpi (Alpes Cottiennes) ⋏	62	44.45 N	7.00 E
Cozoyoapan	234	16.46 N	98.15 W
Cozumel	232	20.31 N	86.55 W
Cozumel, Isla I	232	20.25 N	86.55 W
Cozy Lake	276	41.01 N	74.30 W
Crab Alley Bay ⊂	208	38.55 N	76.17 W
Crab Creek ≃	202	46.49 N	119.55 W
Crab Meadow ≡	276	40.55 N	73.20 W
Crab Orchard, Ky., U.S.	192	37.27 N	84.30 W
Crab Orchard, Tn., U.S.	192	35.54 N	84.52 W
Crab Orchard Lake ⊜[1]	194	37.43 N	89.05 W
Crabtree	214	40.21 N	79.28 W
Crabtree Creek ≃	279b	40.21 N	79.30 W
Crabtree Mills	206	45.58 N	73.28 W
Craches	261	48.34 N	1.49 E
Crackenback ≃	171b	36.21 S	148.36 E
Craco	68	40.23 N	16.26 E
Cracovie → Kraków	30	50.03 N	19.58 E
Cradle Mountain-Lake Saint Clair National Park ♦	166	42.00 S	146.00 E
Cradock, Austl.	166	32.04 S	138.30 E
Cradock, S. Afr.	158	32.08 S	25.36 E
Cradock Channel Ʉ	172	36.11 S	175.15 E
Crafers	168b	35.01 S	138.47 E
Crafton	214	40.26 N	80.03 W
Crafts Creek ≃	285	40.07 N	74.46 W
Cragg Vale	262	53.42 N	2.00 W
Cragsmoor	210	41.40 N	74.23 W
Crai	42	51.55 N	3.36 W
Craig, B.C., Can.	224	49.18 N	124.15 W
Craig, Ak., U.S.	182	55.29 N	133.09 W
Craig, Co., U.S.	200	40.30 N	107.32 W
Craig, Mo., U.S.	194	40.11 N	95.22 W
Craig, Ne., U.S.	198	41.47 N	96.21 W
Craig, Point ∧	162	26.51 S	126.19 E
Craigavon	48	54.27 N	6.24 W
Craig Beach	214	41.07 N	81.01 W
Craig Creek ≃	192	37.39 N	79.49 W
Craigellachie	182	50.59 N	118.43 W
Craighall ◆[8]	273d	26.07 S	28.02 E
Craighall Park ◆[8]	273d	26.08 S	28.01 E
Craighouse	46	55.51 N	5.57 W
Craigmont	202	46.14 N	116.27 W
Craigmyle	182	51.40 N	112.15 W
Craignish Point ≻	46	56.07 N	5.37 W
Craignure	46	56.28 N	5.42 W
Craigsville, Pa., U.S.	214	40.51 N	79.39 W
Craigsville, Va., U.S.	192	38.04 N	79.23 W
Craigville	216	40.47 N	85.06 W
Craik	184	51.03 N	105.49 W
Crail	46	56.16 N	2.38 W
Crailsheim	56	49.08 N	10.04 E
Craiova	38	44.19 N	23.48 E
Crake ≃	44	54.14 N	3.03 W
Craley	208	39.57 N	76.31 W
Cramant	50	48.59 N	3.59 E
Cramlington	44	55.05 N	1.36 W
Cranage	262	53.12 N	2.22 W
Cranberry	214	41.21 N	79.43 W
Cranberry Brook ≃	283	42.11 N	71.01 W
Cranberry Creek	210	43.09 N	74.14 W
Cranberry Island I	212	44.44 N	81.18 W
Cranberry Lake	210	40.57 N	74.44 W
Cranberry Lake ⊜, On., Can.	212	44.26 N	76.19 W
Cranberry Lake ⊜, On., Can.	212	44.47 N	75.50 W
Cranberry Lake ⊜, N.Y., U.S.	188	44.10 N	74.50 W
Cranberry Lake ⊜, Wa., U.S.	224	47.17 N	123.05 W
Cranberry Mountain ∧	182	50.42 N	118.12 W
Cranberry Pond ⊜	276	41.08 N	74.12 W
Cranberry Portage	184	54.35 N	101.23 W
Cranborne Chase ◆[3]	42	50.55 N	2.05 W
Cranbourne	169	38.06 S	145.17 E
Cranbrook, Austl.	162	34.18 S	117.32 E
Cranbrook, B.C., Can.	182	49.31 N	115.46 W
Cranbrook, Eng., U.K.	42	51.06 N	0.33 E
Cranbrook Academy of Art ʊ	281	42.34 N	83.14 W
Cranbury	276	40.18 N	74.30 W
Cranbury Brook ≃	276	40.19 N	74.37 W
Crandall	222	32.37 N	96.27 W
Crandon	190	45.34 N	88.54 W
Crandon Lakes	210	41.07 N	74.50 W
Crane, Az., U.S.	204	32.42 N	114.40 W
Crane, In., U.S.	194	38.53 N	86.54 W
Crane, Mo., U.S.	194	36.54 N	93.34 W
Crane, Tx., U.S.	196	31.23 N	102.20 W
Crane Beach ♦[2]	283	42.41 N	70.46 W
Cranebrook	274a	33.43 S	150.42 E
Crane Creek ≃	190	43.01 N	91.58 W
Crane Lake ⊜, On., Can.	212	45.13 N	79.57 W
Crane Lake ⊜, Sk., Can.	184	50.06 N	109.06 W
Crane Mountain ∧	202	42.04 N	120.13 W
Crane Neck Point ≻	210	40.58 N	73.10 W
Crane River Indian Reserve ◆[4]	184	51.30 N	99.14 W
Cranesville	214	41.54 N	80.21 W
Cranfield	42	52.05 N	0.35 W
Cranfills Gap	222	31.46 N	97.50 W
Cranford	210	40.39 N	74.19 W
Crange ◆[8]	263	51.32 N	7.11 E
Cran-Gévrier	58	45.54 N	6.06 E
Crank	262	53.29 N	2.45 W
Cranleigh	42	51.09 N	0.30 W
Crans	58	46.19 N	7.28 E
Cranston	207	41.46 N	71.26 W
Cranston Heights	285	39.38 N	75.38 W
Craon	32	47.51 N	0.57 W
Craonne	50	49.26 N	3.47 E
Craponne, Fr.	62	45.44 N	4.43 E
Craponne, Fr.	62	45.20 N	3.51 E
Craponne, Canal de ≊	62	43.40 N	4.39 E
Craryville	210	42.11 N	73.35 W
Crasna, Rom.	38	45.36 N	26.08 E
Crasna, Rom.	38	46.31 N	27.51 E
Crasna (Kraszna) ≃	38	48.09 N	22.20 E
Crassier	58	46.22 N	6.11 E
Crater Lake ⊜	202	42.56 N	122.06 W
Crater Lake National Park ♦	202	42.49 N	122.08 W
Crater Mount ∧	164	6.30 S	145.10 E
Crater Point ≻	164	5.22 S	152.09 E
Craters of the Moon National Monument ♦	202	43.20 N	113.35 W
Crateús	250	5.10 S	40.40 W
Crathie	46	57.02 N	3.12 W
Crati ⋏	68	39.43 N	16.31 E
Crato	250	7.14 S	39.23 W
Crau ◆[1]	62	43.36 N	4.50 E
Crauford, Cape ≻	176	73.43 N	84.50 W
Craughwell	48	53.13 N	8.43 W
Cravant	50	47.41 N	3.41 E
Cravari ≃	248	12.06 S	58.03 W
Cravat	219	38.25 N	89.06 W
Craven	184	50.39 N	104.50 W
Craven Arms	42	52.26 N	2.50 W
Cravensville	171b	36.24 S	147.34 E
Cravo Norte	246	6.18 N	70.12 W
Cravo Norte ≃	246	6.18 N	70.12 W
Cravo Sur ≃	246	4.42 N	71.36 W
Crawfish ≃	216	43.00 N	88.49 W
Crawford, Scot., U.K.	44	55.28 N	3.40 W
Crawford, Co., U.S.	200	38.42 N	107.36 W
Crawford, Ms., U.S.	194	33.18 N	88.36 W
Crawford, Ne., U.S.	198	42.40 N	103.24 W
Crawford, Tx., U.S.	222	31.32 N	97.27 W
Crawford □[6], In., U.S.	218	38.20 N	86.28 W
Crawford □[6], Oh., U.S.	214	40.48 N	82.58 W
Crawford □[6], Pa., U.S.	214	41.39 N	80.10 W
Crawford Bay	182	49.42 N	116.48 W
Crawford Countryside	278	41.32 N	87.43 W
Crawford Notch State Park ♦	188	44.13 N	71.25 W
Crawfordsville, Ar., U.S.	194	35.13 N	90.19 W
Crawfordsville, In., U.S.	194	40.02 N	86.52 W
Crawfordville, Fl., U.S.	192	30.10 N	84.22 W
Crawfordville, Ga., U.S.	192	33.33 N	82.53 W
Crawinkel	54	50.47 N	10.47 E
Crawley	42	51.07 N	0.12 W
Crawshawbooth	262	53.43 N	2.17 W
Crayford ◆[8]	260	51.27 N	0.11 E
Crays Hill	260	51.36 N	0.28 E
Crazy Mountains ⋏	202	46.08 N	110.20 W
Crazy Peak ∧	202	46.01 N	110.16 W
Crazy Woman Creek ≃	202	44.29 N	106.08 W
Creagan	46	56.33 N	5.17 W
Creagorry	46	57.26 N	7.19 W
Creal Springs	194	37.37 N	88.50 W
Creamery	285	40.13 N	75.25 W
Crean Lake ⊜	184	54.05 N	106.10 W
Crêches-sur-Saône	58	46.15 N	4.47 E
Crécy, Forêt de ♦	261	48.48 N	2.53 E
Crécy-en-Brie	50	48.51 N	2.55 E
Crécy-en-Ponthieu	50	50.15 N	1.53 E
Crécy-sur-Serre	50	49.42 N	3.37 E
Credenhill	42	52.06 N	2.48 W
Credit ≃	212	43.33 N	79.35 W
Crediton	42	50.47 N	3.39 W
Cree ≃, Sk., Can.	176	59.00 N	105.47 W
Cree ≃, Scot., U.K.	44	54.52 N	4.20 W
Creede	200	37.50 N	106.55 W
Creedmoor	192	36.07 N	78.41 W
Creedmore	222	30.12 N	97.43 W
Creegh	48	52.44 N	9.26 W
Creek Brook ≃	283	42.47 N	71.08 W
Creek Locks	210	41.52 N	74.03 W
Creekmouth ◆[8]	260	51.31 N	0.06 E
Creekside	214	40.40 N	79.11 W
Creekwood	278	41.39 N	87.59 W
Creel	232	27.45 N	107.38 W
Cree Lake ⊜	176	57.30 N	106.30 W
Creemore	212	44.19 N	80.06 W
Creetown	44	54.54 N	4.23 W
Cregganbaun	48	53.42 N	9.51 W
Creglingen	56	49.28 N	10.01 E
Crégy-lès-Meaux	261	48.58 N	2.52 E
Créhange	56	49.03 N	6.35 E
Creighton, Sk., Can.	184	54.45 N	101.54 W
Creighton, S. Afr.	158	30.01 S	29.51 E
Creighton, Ne., U.S.	198	42.28 N	97.54 W
Creighton, Pa., U.S.	214	40.35 N	79.46 W
Creighton Mine	190	46.28 N	81.11 W
Creightons Creek ≃	169	36.43 S	145.22 E
Creil, Fr.	50	49.16 N	2.29 E
Creil, Ned.	52	52.45 N	5.40 E
Crema	62	45.22 N	9.41 E
Cremia	58	46.05 N	9.16 E
Crémieu	62	45.43 N	5.15 E
Cremlingen	54	52.15 N	10.39 E
Cremona, Ab., Can.	182	51.33 N	114.29 W
Cremona, It.	64	45.07 N	10.02 E
Cremona □[4]	64	45.12 N	10.00 E
Crenshaw, Ms., U.S.	194	34.30 N	90.12 W
Crenshaw, Pa., U.S.	214	41.15 N	78.46 W
Crep Nudo ∧	64	46.13 N	12.24 E
Crepori ≃	250	5.42 S	57.08 W
Crépy-en-Laonnois	50	49.36 N	3.31 E
Crépy-en-Valois	50	49.14 N	2.54 E
Créquy	50	50.29 N	2.03 E
Creran, Loch ⊜	46	56.31 N	5.20 W
Cres	36	44.58 N	14.25 E
Cres, Otok I	36	44.50 N	14.25 E
Cresaptown	188	39.35 N	78.50 W
Crescent, N.Y., U.S.	210	42.49 N	73.43 W
Crescent, Ok., U.S.	196	35.57 N	97.35 W
Crescent, Or., U.S.	202	43.27 N	121.41 W
Crescent, Lake ⊜	224	48.05 N	123.50 W
Crescent Beach, B.C., Can.	224	49.04 N	122.53 W

≃	River	Fluß	Río	Rivière	Rio
≊	Canal	Kanal	Canal	Canal	Canal
⌞	Waterfall, Rapids	Wasserfall, Stromschnellen	Cascada, Rápidos	Chute d'eau, Rapides	Cascata, Rápidos
Ʉ	Strait	Meeresstraße	Estrecho	Détroit	Estreito
⊂	Bay, Gulf	Bucht, Golf	Bahía, Golfo	Baie, Golfe	Baía, Golfo
⊜	Lake, Lakes	See, Seen	Lago, Lagos	Lac, Lacs	Lago, Lagos
≡	Swamp	Sumpf	Pantano	Marais	Pântano
⊡	Ice Features, Glacier	Eis- und Gletscherformen	Accidentes Glaciales	Formes glaciaires	Acidentes glaciares
⊤	Other Hydrographic Features	Andere Hydrographische Objekte	Otros Elementos Hidrográficos	Autres données hydrographiques	Outros acidentes hidrográficos

✢	Submarine Features	Untermeerische Objekte	Accidentes Submarinos	Formes de relief sous-marin	Acidentes submarinos
□	Political Unit	Politische Einheit	Unidad Politica	Entité politique	Unidade política
ʊ	Cultural Institution	Kulturelle Institution	Institución Cultural	Institution culturelle	Instituçāo cultural
⊥	Historical Site	Historische Stätte	Sitio Histórico	Site historique	Sitio histórico
♦	Recreational Site	Erholungs- und Ferienort	Sitio de Recreo	Centre de loisirs	Area de Lazer
⊠	Airport	Flughafen	Aeropuerto	Aéroport	Aeroporto
■	Military Installation	Militäranlage	Instalación Militar	Installation militaire	Instalação militar
◆	Miscellaneous	Verschiedenes	Misceláneo	Divers	Diversos

Crescent Beach, Fl., U.S. 220 27.15 N 82.32 W
Crescent City, Ca., U.S. 204 41.45 N 124.12 W
Crescent City, Fl., U.S. 192 29.25 N 81.30 W
Crescent City, Il., U.S. 216 40.46 N 87.51 W
Crescent Ditch ≚ 226 36.29 N 120.07 W
Crescent Heights, N.J., U.S. 285 39.58 N 74.43 W
Crescent Heights, Tx., U.S. 222 32.11 N 95.56 W
Crescentino 62 45.11 N 8.06 E
Crescent Lake ⊜, Fl., U.S. 192 29.28 N 81.30 W
Crescent Lake ⊜, Or., U.S. 202 43.29 N 121.59 W
Crescent Lake Estates 281 42.38 N 83.25 W
Crescent Spur 182 53.35 N 120.41 W
Crescentville ◆8 285 40.02 N 75.05 W
Crescenzago ◆8 266b 45.30 N 9.15 E
Cresco, Ia., U.S. 190 43.22 N 92.06 W
Cresco, Pa., U.S. 210 41.09 N 75.17 W
Crespano del Grappa 64 45.49 N 11.50 E
Crespian 62 43.53 N 4.06 E
Crespières 261 48.53 N 1.55 E
Crespin 50 50.25 N 3.39 E
Crespino 64 44.59 N 11.53 E
Crespo 252 32.02 S 60.19 W
Cressbrook Creek ≃ 171a 27.05 S 152.27 E
Cressely 261 48.43 N 2.05 E
Cressey 226 37.25 N 120.40 W
Cresskill 276 40.56 N 73.57 W
Cresskill Brook ≃ 276 40.57 N 73.58 W
Cresson, Pa., U.S. 214 40.27 N 78.35 W
Cresson, Tx., U.S. 222 32.32 N 97.37 W
Cressona 208 40.37 N 76.11 W
Cressy 169 38.02 S 143.38 E
Crest 62 44.44 N 5.02 E
Cresta 58 46.28 N 9.31 E
Crested Butte 200 38.52 N 106.59 W
Cresthaven 220 26.03 N 80.08 W
Crest Hill 216 41.33 N 88.05 W
Crestline, Ca., U.S. 228 34.14 N 117.17 W
Crestline, Oh., U.S. 214 40.47 N 82.44 W
Creston, B.C., Can. 182 49.06 N 116.31 W
Creston, Nf., Can. 186 47.09 N 55.11 W
Creston, Ca., U.S. 226 35.31 N 120.31 W
Creston, Il., U.S. 216 41.56 N 88.58 W
Creston, Ia., U.S. 198 41.03 N 94.21 W
Creston, Oh., U.S. 214 40.59 N 81.53 W
Crestone Peak ∧ 200 37.58 N 105.36 W
Crestview, Fl., U.S. 194 30.45 N 86.34 W
Crestview, Wi., U.S. 216 42.49 N 87.49 W
Crestview Heights 210 42.05 N 76.07 W
Crestwood, Il., U.S. 278 41.39 N 87.45 W
Crestwood, Ky., U.S. 218 38.19 N 85.28 W
Crestwood, Mo., U.S. 219 38.33 N 90.22 W
Crestwood Hills 192 35.56 N 84.05 W
Creswell, Eng., U.K. 44 53.16 N 1.12 W
Creswell, Or., U.S. 202 43.55 N 123.01 W
Creswell Bay c 176 72.35 N 93.25 W
Creswell Creek ≃ 162 18.10 S 135.11 E
Creswell Downs 162 17.57 S 135.55 E
Creswick 169 37.26 S 143.54 E
Creta
— Kríti I 38 35.29 N 24.42 E
Crete, Il., U.S. 216 41.27 N 87.38 W
Crete, Ne., U.S. 198 40.37 N 96.57 W
Crete, Sea of
— Kritikón Pélagos ⊤2 38 35.46 N 23.54 E
Créteil 50 48.48 N 2.28 E
Crete
— Kríti I 38 35.29 N 24.42 E
Crétéville 36 36.40 N 10.20 E
Cretin, Cape › 164 6.40 S 147.52 E
Creus, Cap de › 34 42.19 N 3.19 E
Creuse □5 32 46.05 N 2.00 E
Creuse ≃ 32 47.00 N 0.34 E
Creussen 60 49.51 N 11.37 E
Creutzwald 56 49.12 N 6.41 E
Creuzburg 56 51.03 N 10.15 E
Crevacuore 62 45.41 N 8.15 E
Crevalcore 64 44.43 N 11.09 E
Creve Coeur, Il., U.S. 190 40.38 N 89.35 W
Creve Coeur, Mo., U.S. 219 38.39 N 90.25 W
Crèvecœur-en-Auge 50 49.07 N 0.01 E
Crèvecœur-en-Brie 261 48.45 N 2.55 E
Crèvecœur-le-Grand 50 49.36 N 2.05 E
Crevillent 34 38.15 N 0.48 W
Crevoladossola 58 46.09 N 8.18 E
Crewe, Eng., U.K. 44 53.05 N 2.27 W
Crewe, Va., U.S. 192 37.10 N 78.07 W
Crewkerne 42 50.53 N 2.48 W
Crews Lake ⊜ 220 28.23 N 82.31 W
Crewsville 220 27.16 N 81.36 W
Crianlarich 46 56.23 N 4.36 W
Crib Point 169 38.22 S 145.12 E
Cricamola ≃ 236 8.59 N 81.54 W
Cricaré ≃ 255 18.37 S 40.05 W
Criccieth 42 52.55 N 4.14 W
Crichi 68 38.57 N 16.38 E
Criciúma 252 28.40 S 49.23 W
Crick 42 52.21 N 1.07 W
Cricket 192 36.10 N 81.11 W
Crickhowell 42 51.53 N 3.07 W
Cricklade 42 51.39 N 1.51 W
Cridersville 216 40.39 N 84.09 W
Crieff 46 56.23 N 3.52 W
Criel-sur-Mer 50 50.01 N 1.19 E
Criffell ∧ 44 54.57 N 3.38 W
Crikvenica 36 45.11 N 14.42 E
Crillon, Mount ∧ 180 58.40 N 137.10 W
Crimea
— Krymskij poluostrov ›1 78 45.00 N 34.00 E
Crimmitschau 54 50.49 N 12.23 E
Crimond 46 57.36 N 1.54 W
Crinan 46 56.05 N 5.35 W
Crîngeni 38 44.01 N 24.47 E
Cringila 170 34.28 S 150.53 E
Cripple Creek 200 38.44 N 105.10 W
Criquetot l'Esneval 50 49.39 N 0.16 E
Crirninoso, Monte ∧ 256 21.32 S 43.25 W
Crisenoy 261 48.36 N 2.45 E
Crisfield 208 37.59 N 75.51 W
Crisólia 256 22.15 S 46.25 W
Crisóstomo, Ribeirão ≃ 250 10.19 S 50.26 W
Crispiano 68 40.36 N 17.14 E
Criss Creek 182 51.03 N 120.44 W
Crissiumal 252 27.30 S 54.07 W
Cristal, Monts de ⋀ 152 0.30 N 10.30 E
Cristal, Sierra del ⋀ 240p 20.33 N 75.31 W
Cristalândia 250 10.36 S 49.11 W
Cristália 255 16.43 S 42.52 W
Cristalina 255 16.45 S 47.36 W
Cristalino ≃ 255 12.38 S 50.40 W
Cristallo ∧ 64 46.34 N 12.12 E
Cristianópolis 255 17.13 S 48.45 W
Cristina 256 22.13 S 45.16 W
Cristinápolis 250 11.29 S 37.46 W
Cristino Castro 250 8.49 S 44.13 W
Cristóbal 236 9.21 N 79.55 W
Cristóbal Colón, Pico ∧ 246 10.50 N 73.41 W
Cristóbal Obregón 234 16.20 N 93.30 W
Cristoforo Colombo, Aeroporto di ⊠ 62 44.25 N 8.49 E
Cristo Redentor ⊥ 252 32.50 S 70.05 W
Cristo Redentor, Estatua do ✝1 287a 22.57 S 43.13 W
Cristuru-Secuiesc 38 46.17 N 25.02 E
Crişul Alb ≃ 38 46.42 N 21.17 E
Crişul Negru ≃ 38 46.42 N 21.16 E
Crişul Repede (Sebes Körös) ≃ 38 46.55 N 20.59 E
Crittenden 218 38.46 N 84.36 W
Crivitz, Dtsch. 54 53.35 N 11.38 E
Crivitz, Wi., U.S. 190 45.13 N 88.00 W
Crixalândia 255 15.18 S 47.15 W
Crixás 255 14.27 S 49.58 W
Crixás ≃ 250 11.02 S 48.34 W
Crixás-Açu ≃ 255 13.19 S 50.36 W
Crixás-Mirim ≃ 255 13.30 S 50.30 W
Črna 61 46.28 N 14.51 E
Crna ≃ 38 41.35 N 21.59 E
Crna Gora □3 38 42.30 N 19.18 E
Črni vrh ∧ 61 46.29 N 15.14 E
Črnomelj 36 45.34 N 15.11 E
Croachy 46 57.19 N 4.14 W
Croagh Patrick ∧ 48 53.46 N 9.40 W
Croajingolong National Park ♦ 166 37.40 S 149.30 E
Croal ≃ 262 53.33 N 2.23 W
Croatia □1, Europe 22 45.10 N 15.30 E
Croatia (Hrvatska) □1, Europe 36 45.10 N 15.30 E
Croce dello Scrivano, Passo)(68 40.34 N 15.50 E
Croce Domini, Passo di)(64 45.54 N 10.24 E
Crocefieschi 62 44.35 N 9.01 E
Crocetta del Montello 64 45.50 N 12.02 E
Crocheron 208 38.14 N 76.03 W
Crockenhill 260 51.23 N 0.10 E
Crocker 194 37.56 N 92.15 W
Crocker, Banjaran ⋀ 112 5.40 N 116.14 E
Crockery Creek ≃ 216 43.02 N 86.05 W
Crocketford 44 55.02 N 3.50 W
Crockett, Ca., U.S. 226 38.03 N 122.12 W
Crockett, Tx., U.S. 222 31.19 N 95.27 W
Crockham Hill 260 51.14 N 0.04 E
Crocus Hill
— The Valley 238 18.13 N 63.04 W
Croft 262 53.26 N 2.33 W
Crofton, B.C., Can. 224 48.52 N 123.38 W
Crofton, Ky., U.S. 194 37.02 N 87.29 W
Crofton, Md., U.S. 208 39.00 N 76.41 W
Crofton, Ne., U.S. 198 42.43 N 97.29 W
Croft State Park ♦ 192 34.49 N 81.52 W
Croggan 46 56.22 N 5.42 W
Croghan 212 43.53 N 75.23 W
Croglin 44 54.49 N 2.39 W
Croick 46 57.53 N 4.35 W
Croil Islands II 206 44.58 N 74.58 W
Croisette, Cap › 62 43.13 N 5.20 E
Croisilles 50 50.12 N 2.53 E
Croissy-Beaubourg 261 48.50 N 2.40 E
Croissy-sur-Seine 261 48.53 N 2.09 E
Croix 50 50.40 N 3.09 E
Croix, Lac à la ⊜ 186 51.16 N 70.13 W
Croix, Lac la ⊜ 190 48.21 N 92.05 W
Croker, Cape ›, Austl. 164 10.58 S 132.35 E
Croker, Cape ›, On., Can. 212 44.58 N 80.59 W
Croker Island I 164 11.12 S 132.32 E
Crolles 62 45.17 N 5.53 E
Cromarty 46 57.40 N 4.02 W
Cromarty Firth c1 46 57.41 N 4.07 W
Cromby 285 40.09 N 75.32 W
Cromer, Austl. 274a 33.44 S 151.17 E
Cromer, Eng., U.K. 42 52.56 N 1.18 E
Cromford 44 53.06 N 1.34 W
Cromínia 255 17.17 S 49.21 W
Cromore 46 58.09 N 6.29 W
Crompton Point › 240d 15.35 N 61.19 W
Cromwell, N.Z. 172 45.03 S 169.12 E
Cromwell, Al., U.S. 194 32.13 N 88.16 W
Cromwell, Ct., U.S. 207 41.35 N 72.38 W
Cromwell, In., U.S. 216 41.24 N 85.36 W
Cromwell Park ♦ 279a 41.28 N 82.08 W
Cronadun 172 42.02 S 171.52 E
Cronenberg ◆8 263 51.12 N 7.08 E
Cronin, Mount ∧ 182 54.54 N 126.52 W
Cronton 262 53.23 N 2.46 W
Cronulla 170 34.03 S 151.09 E
Cronulla Beach ⊥2 274a 34.02 S 151.11 E
Croob, Slieve ∧2 48 54.20 N 5.58 W
Crook, Eng., U.K. 44 54.43 N 1.44 W
Crook, Co., U.S. 198 40.51 N 102.48 W
Crooked ≃, B.C., Can. 182 54.50 N 122.54 W
Crooked ≃, Mo., U.S. 194 39.13 N 93.49 W
Crooked ≃, Or., U.S. 202 44.34 N 121.16 W
Crooked Creek 180 61.52 N 158.08 W
Crooked Creek ≃, U.S. 196 36.57 N 100.06 W
Crooked Creek ≃, Ar., U.S. 194 36.14 N 92.29 W
Crooked Creek ≃, Il., U.S. 219 38.30 N 89.25 W
Crooked Creek ≃, In., U.S. 216 40.45 N 86.30 W
Crooked Creek ≃, Mo., U.S. 219 39.34 N 91.55 W
Crooked Creek ≃, Pa., U.S. 210 41.55 N 77.08 W
Crooked Creek ≃, Pa., U.S. 214 40.45 N 79.33 W
Crooked Creek Lake ⊜1 214 40.42 N 79.30 W
Crooked Island I 238 22.45 N 74.13 W
Crooked Island Passage ⊔ 238 22.55 N 74.35 W
Crooked Lake, In., U.S. 216 41.41 N 85.02 W
Crooked Lake, Mi., U.S. 216 42.29 N 85.25 W
Crooked Lake ⊜, Nf., Can. 186 48.24 N 56.17 W
Crooked Lake ⊜, Sk., Can. 184 50.36 N 102.45 W
Crooked Lake ⊜, N.A. 190 48.13 N 91.50 W
Crooked Lake ⊜, Fl., U.S. 220 27.48 N 81.35 W
Crooked Lake ⊜, In., U.S. 216 41.40 N 85.03 W
Crooked River 184 52.51 N 103.44 W
Crookes Point › 276 40.32 N 74.08 W
Crookham 279b 40.12 N 79.59 W
Crookston 198 47.46 N 96.36 W
Crookstown 48 51.50 N 8.50 W
Crooksville 188 39.46 N 82.05 W
Crookwell 166 34.28 S 149.28 E
Croom 48 52.31 N 8.42 W
Cropalati 68 39.31 N 16.43 E
Cropani 68 38.58 N 16.47 E
Cropper 218 38.18 N 85.06 W
Crosby, Eng., U.K. 44 53.30 N 3.02 W
Crosby, Mn., U.S. 190 46.28 N 93.57 W
Crosby, Ms., U.S. 194 31.17 N 91.03 W
Crosby, N.D., U.S. 198 48.54 N 103.17 W
Crosby, Pa., U.S. 214 41.45 N 78.24 W
Crosby, Tx., U.S. 222 29.55 N 95.04 W
Crosby, Mount ∧ 202 43.53 N 109.20 W
Crosby Lake ⊜ 212 44.45 N 76.26 W
Crosbyton 196 33.39 N 101.14 W
Crosia 68 39.34 N 16.46 E
Crosne 261 48.43 N 2.28 E
Cross ≃ 152 4.42 N 8.21 E
Cross Banks II 283 42.43 N 70.49 W
Cross Bay c 184 53.15 N 99.25 W
Cross Bay Bridge ◆5 276 40.35 N 73.49 W
Crossbost 46 58.08 N 6.23 W
Cross City 192 29.38 N 83.07 W
Cross County Center ◆9 276 40.56 N 73.51 W
Cross Creek ≃, Ca., U.S. 226 36.08 N 119.38 W
Cross Creek ≃, Oh., U.S. 214 40.18 N 80.36 W
Crossen 54 50.45 N 12.29 E
Crossens 262 53.41 N 2.57 W
Crossett 194 33.07 N 91.57 W
Cross Fell ∧ 44 54.42 N 2.29 W
Crossfield 182 51.26 N 114.02 W
Crossgar 48 54.24 N 5.45 W
Cross Hands 42 51.48 N 4.04 W
Crosshaven 48 51.48 N 8.17 W
Crosshill 44 55.19 N 4.39 W
Crossinsee ⊜ 264a 52.22 N 13.41 E
Cross Island I 272c 18.57 N 72.51 E
Cross Keys 285 39.42 N 75.01 W
Cross Keys Airfield ⊠ 285 39.42 N 75.02 W
Cross Lake 184 54.37 N 97.47 W
Cross Lake ⊜, Mb., Can. 184 54.45 N 97.30 W
Cross Lake ⊜, On., Can. 190 46.53 N 79.57 W
Cross Lake ⊜, N.Y., U.S. 210 43.08 N 76.29 W
Crossley, Mount ∧ 172 42.50 S 172.04 E
Crossmaglen 48 54.05 N 6.37 W
Crossman 168a 32.47 S 116.36 E
Crossman ≃ 168a 32.47 S 116.32 E
Crossman Peak ∧ 200 34.32 N 114.07 W
Crossmolina 48 54.06 N 9.20 W
Cross Plains, In., U.S. 218 38.57 N 85.12 W
Cross Plains, Tx., U.S. 196 32.08 N 99.11 W
Cross Plains, Wi., U.S. 190 43.06 N 89.39 W
Cross River □3 150 5.50 N 8.30 E
Cross Roads 222 32.03 N 95.58 W
Cross Sound ⊔ 180 58.10 N 136.30 W
Crossville, Il., U.S. 194 38.09 N 88.03 W
Crossville, Tn., U.S. 194 35.56 N 85.01 W
Crosswicks 285 40.09 N 74.38 W
Crosswicks Creek ≃ 208 40.09 N 74.43 W
Crostolo ≃ 64 44.55 N 10.38 E
Croston 44 53.39 N 2.46 W
Croswell 190 43.16 N 82.37 W
Crotch Lake ⊜ 212 44.55 N 76.48 W
Crotenay 58 46.45 N 5.49 E
Crothersville 218 38.48 N 85.50 W
Croton 214 40.14 N 82.41 W
Crotona Park ♦ 276 40.50 N 73.54 W
Croton Creek ≃ 196 33.18 N 100.25 W
Crotone 68 39.05 N 17.07 E
Croton Falls 210 41.21 N 73.40 W
Croton-on-Hudson 210 41.12 N 73.53 W
Croton Point › 276 41.10 N 73.54 W
Crottendorf 54 50.30 N 12.56 E
Crouch ≃ 42 51.37 N 0.57 E
Crouse Run ≃ 279b 40.35 N 79.58 W
Crouy 50 49.24 N 3.22 E
Crow ≃ 190 45.15 N 93.31 W
Crow, North Fork ≃ 190 45.05 N 93.45 W
Crow, South Fork ≃ 190 45.05 N 93.45 W
Crow Agency 202 45.36 N 107.27 W
Crowborough 42 51.03 N 0.09 E
Crow Creek ≃, U.S. 198 40.23 N 104.29 W
Crow Creek ≃, Ca., U.S. 282 37.42 N 122.03 W
Crow Creek ≃, Il., U.S. 194 40.56 N 89.27 W
Crow Creek ≃, Mt., U.S. 198 45.45 N 105.06 W
Crow Creek ≃, Mt., U.S. 202 46.11 N 111.29 W
Crow Creek ≃, S.D., U.S. 198 43.57 N 99.15 W
Crow Creek ≃, Wy., U.S. 202 43.19 N 109.09 W
Crow Creek Indian Reservation ◆4 198 44.11 N 99.30 W
Crowder, Ms., U.S. 194 34.10 N 90.08 W
Crowder, Ok., U.S. 196 35.07 N 95.40 W
Crowduck Lake ⊜ 184 50.08 N 95.15 W
Crowdy Head › 166 31.50 S 152.45 E
Crowe ≃ 212 44.22 N 77.46 W
Crowe Lake ⊜ 212 44.29 N 77.46 W
Crowell 196 33.59 N 99.43 W
Crowfoot, Mount ∧ 172 45.33 S 167.03 E
Crow Hill ∧2 262 53.42 N 1.58 W
Crowhurst 260 51.12 N 0.01 W
Crow Indian Reservation ◆4 202 45.27 N 108.00 W
Crow Lake 184 49.12 N 93.57 W
Crow Lake ⊜ 212 44.43 N 76.37 W
Crowland 42 52.41 N 0.11 W
Crowle 44 53.37 N 0.49 W
Crowley, Ca., U.S. 226 36.21 N 119.17 W
Crowley, La., U.S. 194 30.12 N 92.22 W
Crowley, Tx., U.S. 222 32.34 N 97.21 W
Crowley, Lake ⊜1 204 37.37 N 118.44 W
Crowleys Ridge ∧ 194 35.45 N 90.45 W
Crowlin Islands II 46 57.20 N 5.44 W
Crown 214 41.23 N 79.16 W
Crown Hill 212 44.26 N 79.39 W
Crown Island I 164 5.05 S 146.55 E
Crown Memorial Beach ♦ 282 37.46 N 122.16 W
Crown Mines ◆7 273d 26.13 S 28.00 E
Crown Mountain ∧ 240m 18.21 N 64.58 W
Crown Point, In., U.S. 216 41.25 N 87.21 W
Crownpoint, N.M., U.S. 200 35.40 N 108.09 W
Crown Point, N.Y., U.S. 188 43.57 N 73.26 W
Crown Point State Park ♦ 224 45.32 N 122.15 W
Crown Prince Frederik Island I 176 70.02 N 86.50 W
Crown Village 276 40.40 N 73.27 W
Crow Peak ∧ 202 46.18 N 111.54 W
Crow Rock Creek ≃ 202 47.06 N 106.15 W
Crows Fork Creek ≃ 219 38.47 N 91.52 W
Crows Landing 226 37.24 N 121.04 W
Crows Nest, Austl. 171a 27.16 S 152.03 E
Crows Nest, Austl. 274a 33.50 S 151.12 E
Crowsnest, Ab., Can. 182 49.38 N 114.41 W
Crows Nest Falls National Park ♦ 171a 27.16 S 152.08 E
Crowsnest Pass 182 49.36 N 114.26 W
Crowsnest Pass)(182 49.39 N 114.45 W
Crows Nest Peak ∧ 198 44.03 N 103.58 W
Crowthorne 42 51.23 N 0.49 W
Crowton 262 53.16 N 2.38 W
Crow Wing ≃ 198 46.19 N 94.20 W
Croxley Green 42 51.39 N 0.27 W
Croxteth Park ♦ 262 53.26 N 2.53 W
Croy 46 57.31 N 4.02 W
Croyde 42 51.07 N 4.13 W
Croydon, Austl. 166 18.12 S 142.14 E
Croydon, Austl. 169 37.48 S 145.17 E
Croydon, Austl. 274a 33.53 S 151.07 E
Croydon, Pa., U.S. 208 40.05 N 74.54 W
Croydon ◆8 42 51.23 N 0.06 W
Croydon Park 274a 33.54 S 151.07 E
Croydon Peak ∧ 188 43.28 N 72.13 W
Croydon Station 182 53.05 N 119.44 W
Crozet 192 38.04 N 78.42 W
Crozet, Îles II 6 46.00 S 52.00 E
Crozet Basin ⊥1 6 39.00 S 60.00 E
Crozon 32 48.15 N 4.29 W
Cruachan, Ben ∧ 46 56.25 N 5.08 W
Cruas 62 44.39 N 4.46 E
Crucea 38 44.32 N 28.14 E
Crucero 248 14.21 S 70.00 W
Cruces, Cuba 240p 22.21 N 80.16 W
Cruces, Méx. 232 29.26 N 107.24 W
Crucoli 68 39.25 N 17.00 E
Cruden Bay 46 57.25 N 1.50 W
Crudgington 42 52.46 N 2.33 W
Crudine Creek ≃ 170 33.05 S 149.40 E
Cruger 194 33.19 N 90.13 W
Cruillas 232 24.45 N 98.31 W
Crum Creek ≃ 285 39.51 N 75.19 W
Crumhorn Mountain ∧ 210 42.33 N 74.55 W
Crumlin, On., Can. 212 43.01 N 81.09 W
Crumlin, N. Ire., U.K. 48 54.37 N 6.14 W
Crum Lynne 285 39.52 N 75.20 W
Crummock Water ⊜ 44 54.34 N 3.18 W
Crump Lake ⊜ 202 42.17 N 119.50 W
Crumpton 208 39.14 N 75.55 W
Crumstown 216 41.38 N 86.25 W
Crupet 56 50.21 N 4.48 E
Cruseilles 58 46.02 N 6.07 E
Cruser Brook ≃ 276 40.27 N 74.39 W
Crusheen 48 52.58 N 8.53 W
Crusnes 56 49.26 N 5.55 E
Crusnes ≃ 56 49.27 N 5.36 E
Crustepec, Cerro ∧ 234 21.15 N 97.53 W
Cruz, Arroyo de la ≃, Ca., U.S. 226 35.42 N 121.09 W
Cruz, Arroyo de la ≃, Ur. 258 34.00 S 56.08 W
Cruz, Cabo › 240p 19.51 N 77.44 W
Cruz, Cañada de la ≃ 258 34.09 S 58.58 W
Cruz, Cayo I 240p 22.15 N 77.49 W
Cruz, Pico de la ∧ 148 28.44 N 17.52 W
Cruz Alta, Arg. 252 33.01 S 61.49 W
Cruz Alta, Bra. 252 28.39 S 53.36 W
Cruz Bay 240m 18.20 N 64.48 W
Cruz de Elorza 234 23.49 N 100.29 W
Cruz del Eje 252 30.44 S 64.48 W
Cruz del Marquez, Cerro ∧ 286a 19.12 N 99.15 W
Cruzeiro 256 22.34 S 44.58 W
Cruzeiro do Oeste 255 23.46 S 53.04 W
Cruzeiro do Sul 248 7.38 S 72.36 W
Cruzeta 250 6.25 S 36.47 W
Cruz Grande, Chile 252 29.25 S 71.18 W
Cruz Grande, Méx. 234 16.44 N 99.08 W
Cruzília 256 21.50 S 44.48 W
Cruz Machado 252 26.01 S 51.21 W
Cruzy-le-Châtel 50 47.51 N 4.12 E
Crvenka 38 45.39 N 19.28 E
Crymych 42 51.59 N 4.40 W
Crynant 42 51.43 N 3.45 W
Crysler 188 45.13 N 75.09 W
Crystal, Mn., U.S. 190 45.01 N 93.21 W
Crystal, N.D., U.S. 198 48.35 N 97.40 W
Crystal ≃ 200 39.25 N 107.14 W
Crystal Bay 226 39.13 N 120.00 W
Crystal Bay c 220 28.55 N 82.43 W
Crystal Beach, On., Can. 284a 42.52 N 79.04 W
Crystal Beach, Fl., U.S. 220 28.05 N 82.46 W
Crystal Beach, Tx., U.S. 222 29.27 N 94.38 W
Crystal Brook 166 33.21 S 138.13 E
Crystal Cave ⊥5 208 40.32 N 75.51 W
Crystal City, Mb., Can. 184 49.09 N 98.56 W
Crystal City, Mo., U.S. 219 38.13 N 90.22 W
Crystal City, Tx., U.S. 196 28.40 N 99.49 W
Crystal Creek ≃ 278 41.58 N 87.51 W
Crystal Falls 190 46.05 N 88.20 W
Crystal Gardens 216 42.14 N 88.23 W
Crystal Lake, Il., U.S. 216 42.14 N 88.18 W
Crystal Lake, N.Y., U.S. 210 42.31 N 74.12 W
Crystal Lake, N.Y., U.S. 210 42.28 N 78.20 W
Crystal Lake ⊜, On., Can. 212 44.45 N 78.30 W
Crystal Lake ⊜, Ma., U.S. 283 42.29 N 71.05 W
Crystal Lake ⊜, Ma., U.S. 283 42.48 N 71.09 W
Crystal Lake ⊜, Mi., U.S. 190 44.40 N 86.10 W
Crystal Lake ⊜, N.J., U.S. 276 41.02 N 74.15 W
Crystal Lakes 218 39.52 N 84.04 W
Crystal Lawns 216 41.34 N 88.09 W
Crystal Manor 216 42.14 N 88.17 W
Crystal Palace Stadium and Motor Race Track ♦ 260 51.25 N 0.04 W
Crystal River 192 28.54 N 82.35 W
Crystal Spring Lake ⊜ 285 39.43 N 75.01 W
Crystal Springs, Fl., U.S. 220 28.10 N 82.09 W
Crystal Springs, Ms., U.S. 194 31.59 N 90.21 W
Crystal Springs Dam ◆6 282 37.32 N 122.22 W
Crystal Vista 216 42.14 N 88.24 W
Csepel ◆8 264c 47.24 N 19.14 E
Csepel-sziget I 30 47.15 N 18.57 E
Csepreg 61 47.24 N 16.43 E
Cserhát ⋀ 30 47.55 N 19.30 E
Cserta ≃ 61 46.35 N 16.36 E
Csesznek ⊥ 30 47.16 N 17.53 E
Csesztreg 61 46.43 N 16.31 E
Csobánka 264c 47.38 N 18.58 E
Csomád 264c 47.40 N 19.15 E
Csömodér 61 46.37 N 16.39 E
Csömör 264c 47.33 N 19.14 E
Csömöri-patak ≃ 264c 47.36 N 19.07 E
Csongrád 30 46.43 N 20.09 E
Csongrád □6 30 46.25 N 20.15 E
Csorna 30 47.37 N 17.16 E
Csurgó 30 46.16 N 17.06 E
Ču 85 43.36 N 73.45 E
Ču □4 85 42.30 N 74.30 E
Ču ≃ 86 45.00 N 67.44 E
Cúa 246 10.10 N 66.54 W
Cuacnopalan 234 18.49 N 97.30 W
Cuácua ≃ 154 17.54 S 36.48 E
Cuajimalpa ◆8 286a 19.21 N 99.18 W
Cuajinicuilapa 234 16.28 N 98.25 W
Cuajone 248 17.00 S 70.43 W
Cuále 152 8.06 S 16.03 E
Cua Lo 110 18.49 N 105.43 E
Cuamato 152 17.05 S 15.09 E
Cuamba 154 14.49 S 36.33 E
Cuambog 116 7.20 N 125.52 E
Cuanavale ≃ 152 15.07 S 19.14 E
Cuando 152 16.32 S 22.07 E
Cuando (Kwando) ≃ 152 18.27 S 23.32 E
Cuando Cubango □5 152 16.00 S 20.00 E
Cuangar 152 17.36 S 18.39 E
Cuango, Ang. 152 14.30 S 18.59 E
Cuango, Ang. 152 9.10 S 17.58 E
Cuango, Ang. 152 6.17 S 16.41 E
Cuango (Kwango) ≃ 152 3.14 S 17.23 E
Cuanza ≃ 152 9.19 S 13.08 E
Cuanza Norte □5 152 8.50 S 14.30 E
Cuanza Sul □5 152 10.50 S 14.50 E
Cuao ≃ 246 4.55 N 67.40 W
Cuapiaxtla 234 19.18 N 97.46 W
Cuareim (Quaraí) ≃ 252 30.12 S 57.36 W
Cuaró 252 30.37 S 56.54 W
Cuartillo, Arroyo ≃ 258 33.45 S 59.06 W
Cuarto ≃ 252 33.25 S 62.56 W
Cuatir ≃ 152 17.01 S 18.09 E
Cuatro Caminos 286b 22.54 N 82.23 W
Cuatro Ciénegas [de Carranza] 196 26.59 N 102.05 W
Cuatro Islands II 116 10.31 N 124.39 E
Cuauhtémoc, Méx. 232 28.25 N 106.52 W
Cuauhtémoc, Méx. 234 19.20 N 103.36 W
Cuauhtémoc, Méx. 234 22.38 N 98.08 W
Cuautepec el Alto ◆8 286a 19.34 N 99.08 W
Cuautitlán 234 19.26 N 104.23 W
Cuautitlán ≃ 286a 19.41 N 99.13 W
Cuautitlán [de Romero Rubio] 234 19.40 N 99.11 W
Cuautitlán Izcalli 286a 19.39 N 99.13 W
Cuautla, Méx. 234 20.11 N 104.21 W
Cuautla, Méx. 234 18.48 N 98.57 W
Cuautzin, Volcán ∧1 286a 19.09 N 99.06 W

ENGLISH — Name | Page | Lat.°′ | Long.°′

Cuba, Port. 34 38.10 N 7.53 W
Cuba, Al., U.S. 194 32.25 N 88.22 W
Cuba, Il., U.S. 190 40.29 N 90.11 W
Cuba, Ks., U.S. 198 39.48 N 97.27 W
Cuba, Mo., U.S. 194 38.03 N 91.24 W
Cuba, N.M., U.S. 200 36.01 N 106.57 W
Cuba, N.Y., U.S. 210 42.13 N 78.16 W
Cuba □1, N.A. 230 21.30 N 80.00 W
Cuba □1, N.A. 240p 21.30 N 80.00 W
Cubabi, Cerro ∧ 200 31.42 N 112.46 W
Cubadak 112 0.19 N 100.00 E
Cubagua, Isla I 246 10.48 N 64.10 W
Cuba Island I 276 40.38 N 73.32 W
Cubal 152 13.02 S 14.19 E
Cubal ≃, Ang. 152 15.22 S 12.39 E
Cubal ≃, Ang. 152 12.42 S 13.56 E
Cubal ≃, Ang. 152 11.19 S 13.48 E
Cuba Lake ⊜ 210 42.15 N 78.18 W
Cubanea 254 41.02 S 70.16 W
Cubango (Okavango) ≃ 138 18.50 S 22.25 E
Çubangui ≃ 152 14.22 S 19.58 E
Čubaricha 86 57.37 N 68.22 E
Čubarovo 82 55.12 N 36.56 E
Cubatão 256 23.53 S 46.25 W
Cubatão, Serra do ⊥4 256 23.52 S 46.28 W
Cubati 250 6.51 S 36.21 W
Cub Hills ⋀2 184 54.20 N 104.30 W
Çubia ≃ 152 16.01 S 21.50 E
Čublas 24 64.44 N 45.00 E
Cub Run ≃ 208 38.48 N 77.28 W
Çubuk 130 40.15 N 33.02 E
Čuc ≃ 250 1.22 N 53.33 W
Cucamonga 228 34.06 N 117.35 W
Cucamonga Creek ≃ 280 33.57 N 117.37 W
Cucamonga Peak ∧ 228 34.14 N 117.36 W
Cuccaro Vetere 68 40.09 N 15.18 E
Çucco, Monte ∧ 66 43.22 N 12.45 E
Čučeviči 76 52.35 N 26.52 E
Cucharas ≃ 198 37.55 N 104.32 W
Cucharas, Sierra ⋀ 234 22.20 N 98.55 W
Cuchi 152 14.36 S 16.58 E
Cuchi ≃ 152 15.28 S 17.21 E
Cuchibi ≃ 152 15.00 S 20.45 E
Cuchilla Alta, Cerro ∧ 236 15.10 N 88.12 W
Cuchillo-Có 252 38.20 S 64.37 W
Cuchillo Negro Creek ≃ 200 33.08 N 107.14 W
Çuchivero ≃ 246 7.40 N 65.57 W
Čuchloma 76 58.45 N 42.41 E
Čuchlomskoje, ozero ⊜ 76 58.46 N 42.35 E
Cuchumatanes, Sierra los ⋀ 236 15.35 N 91.25 W
Cuckels Brook ≃ 276 40.33 N 74.33 W
Cuckfield 42 51.00 N 0.09 W
Cuckney 44 53.15 N 1.08 W
Çuckold Point › 284b 39.14 N 76.24 W
Čučkovo, Ross. 76 59.36 N 41.14 E
Čučkovo, Ross. 80 54.17 N 41.26 E
Çucuí 246 1.12 N 66.50 W
Čučuleny 78 47.02 N 28.22 E
Cucumbi 152 10.17 S 19.05 E
Cucuron 62 43.47 N 5.26 E
Cucurpe 232 30.20 N 110.43 W
Cúcuta 246 7.54 N 72.31 W
Cudachar 84 42.21 N 47.11 E
Cudahy, Ca., U.S. 280 33.57 N 118.11 W
Cudahy, Wi., U.S. 216 42.57 N 87.51 W
Cuddalore 122 11.45 N 79.45 E
Cuddapah 122 14.28 N 78.49 E
Cuddeback Lake ⊜ 228 35.18 N 117.28 W
Cuddebackville 210 41.28 N 74.36 W
Cuddia ≃ 70 37.53 N 12.37 E
Cuddington 44 53.14 N 2.36 W
Cuddle Lake ⊜ 184 55.25 N 95.47 W
Cuddy 279b 40.21 N 80.09 W
Cuddy Mountain ∧ 202 44.46 N 116.47 W
Cudgegong 170 32.48 S 149.49 E
Cudgegong ≃ 170 32.37 S 149.43 E
Cudgewa 171b 36.12 S 147.46 E
Cudgewa Creek ≃ 171b 36.03 S 147.55 E
Cudham ◆8 260 51.19 N 0.05 E
Çudia Park ♦ 275b 43.43 N 79.13 W
Čudin 76 52.44 N 26.59 E
Cudjoe Key I 220 24.40 N 81.30 W
Čudnov 78 50.04 N 28.06 E
Čudovo 76 59.07 N 31.41 E
Čudskoje ozero (Peipsi järv) ⊜ 76 58.45 N 27.30 E
Cudworth, Sk., Can. 184 52.30 N 105.45 W
Cudworth, Eng., U.K. 44 53.35 N 1.25 W
Cue 162 27.25 S 117.54 E
Cuebe ≃ 152 15.48 S 17.30 E
Cueio ≃, Ang. 152 15.27 S 21.21 E
Cueio ≃, Ang. 152 16.17 S 17.46 E
Cuelei ≃ 152 15.33 S 17.21 E
Cuéllar 34 41.24 N 4.19 W
Cuenca, Ec. 246 2.53 S 78.59 W
Cuenca, Esp. 34 40.04 N 2.08 W
Cuenca □4 34 39.55 N 2.10 W
Cuencamé [de Ceniceros] 232 24.53 N 103.42 W
Cuerámaro 234 20.37 N 101.43 W
Cuernavaca 234 18.55 N 99.15 W
Cuero 222 29.05 N 97.17 W
Cuers 62 43.14 N 6.04 E
Cuervos 204 32.38 N 114.52 W
Cuesmes 50 50.26 N 3.55 E
Cuesta Pass)(226 35.21 N 120.38 W
Cueto 240p 20.39 N 75.56 W
Cuetzala del Progreso 234 18.07 N 99.50 W
Cuetzalan del Progreso 234 20.02 N 97.31 W
Cuevas del Almanzora 34 37.18 N 1.53 W
Çuevo 248 20.27 S 63.32 W
Čufarovo 80 54.06 N 47.19 E
Cuffley 42 51.42 N 0.07 W
Cufra
— Al-Kufrah ⊤4 146 24.20 N 23.15 E
Cufré 258 34.12 S 57.06 W
Cufré, Arroyo ≃ 258 34.27 S 57.09 W
Cuggiono 62 45.31 N 8.49 E
Cugir 38 45.50 N 23.22 E
Cuglieri 71 40.11 N 8.34 E
Çugo ≃ 152 7.18 S 16.39 E
Čugujev 78 49.50 N 36.41 E
Čugujevka 89 44.08 N 133.53 E
Čugunaš 86 52.52 N 87.46 E
Čuguš, gora ∧ 84 43.47 N 40.16 E
Cuiabá 248 15.35 S 56.05 W
Cuiabá ≃ 248 17.53 S 57.27 W
Cuiari 246 1.30 N 68.11 W
Cuiari ≃ 246 1.30 N 68.11 W
Cuicatlán 234 17.48 N 96.58 W
Cuichapa 234 17.59 N 94.15 W
Cuieiras ≃ 246 2.50 S 60.31 W
Cuigezhuang, Zhg. 105 40.01 N 116.28 E
Cuigezhuang, Zhg. 105 40.02 N 117.54 E
Cuihuangkou 105 39.32 N 117.11 E
Cuijiatun 104 40.57 N 121.09 E
Cuijiazhuang 104 40.57 N 122.44 E
Cuilapa 236 14.17 N 90.18 W
Cuilcagh ∧ 48 54.10 N 7.48 W
Cuilco 236 15.24 N 91.58 W
Cuillin Hills ⋀2 46 57.15 N 6.15 W
Cuilo (Kwilu) ≃, Afr. 152 3.22 S 17.22 E
Cuilo ≃, Afr. 152 5.52 S 16.35 E
Cuilo Futa 152 6.25 S 15.44 E
Cuimba 152 6.08 S 14.38 E
Cuio 152 12.58 S 12.58 E
Cuiqiao 98 34.12 N 114.36 E
Cuiseaux 58 46.30 N 5.24 E
Cuisery 58 46.33 N 5.00 E
Cuisy 261 49.01 N 2.46 E
Cuité 250 6.29 S 36.09 W
Cuitláhuac 234 18.49 N 96.43 W
Cuíto ≃ 152 18.01 S 20.48 E

DEUTSCH — Name | Seite | Breite°′ | Länge°′ E = Ost

Cuíto-Cuanavale 152 15.10 S 19.10 E
Cuitzeo, Laguna de ⊜ 234 19.55 N 101.05 W
Cuitzeo del Porvenir 234 19.59 N 101.09 W
Cuiuni ≃ 246 0.45 S 63.07 W
Cuivre ≃ 219 38.56 N 90.42 W
Cuivre, North Fork ≃ 219 39.02 N 90.59 W
Cuivre, West Fork ≃ 219 39.02 N 90.59 W
Cuivre River State Park ♦ 219 39.02 N 90.57 W
Čuja 88 59.12 N 112.25 E
Čuja ≃, Ross. 86 50.24 N 86.39 E
Čuja ≃, Ross. 88 59.17 N 112.24 E
Cují 286c 10.28 N 67.02 W
Çukas 112 0.25 S 104.18 E
Čukčagirskoje ozero ⊜ 89 52.00 N 136.36 E
Čukotskaja Avtonomnaja Oblast' □8 180 66.00 N 178.00 E
Čukotskij, mys › 180 64.14 N 173.10 W
Čukotskij poluostrov ›1 180 66.00 N 175.00 W
Çukurca 128 37.15 N 43.37 E
Čukurčak 85 41.47 N 71.07 E
Cukurino 83 48.05 N 37.18 E
Çulaba 116 11.40 N 124.32 E
Čulak-Kurgan 85 43.46 N 69.12 E
Culaman 116 5.58 N 125.40 E
Culari ≃ 250 1.27 N 53.42 W
Culasi, Pil. 116 11.26 N 122.03 E
Culasi, Pil. 116 10.43 N 125.43 E
Culasian 116 8.51 N 117.29 E
Culasi Point › 116 11.37 N 122.42 E
Culbertson, Mt., U.S. 198 48.08 N 104.30 W
Culbertson, Ne., U.S. 198 40.13 N 100.50 W
Culbertson Run ≃ 285 40.03 N 75.45 W
Culbin 168a 33.10 S 116.50 E
Culburra 170 34.57 S 150.47 E
Culcairn 166 35.40 S 147.03 E
Culcheth 262 53.27 N 2.32 W
Culdaff 48 55.18 N 7.11 W
Culdaff Bay c 48 55.17 N 7.10 W
Culebra 240m 18.18 N 65.18 W
Culebra, Isla de I 240m 18.19 N 65.17 W
Culebra, Sierra de la ⋀ 34 41.54 N 6.20 W
Culebra Peak ∧ 200 37.07 N 105.11 W
Culebrinas ≃ 240m 18.24 N 67.11 W
Culebrita, Isla I 240m 18.19 N 65.14 W
Culebro, Arroyo del ≃ 266a 40.19 N 3.34 W
Culemborg 52 51.56 N 5.13 E
Culgoa ≃ 166 29.56 S 146.20 E
Culham Inlet c 162 33.55 S 120.04 E
Culiacán, Méx. 232 24.04 N 107.05 W
Culiacán, Méx. 232 24.48 N 107.24 W
Culiacán, Cerro ∧ 234 20.20 N 100.58 W
Culiacancito 232 24.50 N 107.32 W
Culijón, Nevado ∧ 248 14.38 S 69.14 W
Culion 116 11.53 N 120.01 E
Culion Island I 116 11.50 N 119.55 E
Cúllar de Baza 34 37.35 N 2.34 W
Cull Creek ≃ 282 37.42 N 122.03 W
Cullen, Scot., U.K. 46 57.41 N 2.49 W
Cullen, La., U.S. 194 32.58 N 93.27 W
Cullen Bullen 170 33.18 S 150.01 E
Cullen Point › 164 11.57 S 141.54 E
Culleoka, Tn., U.S. 194 35.28 N 86.58 W
Culleoka, Tx., U.S. 222 33.08 N 96.29 W
Cullera 34 39.10 N 0.15 W
Cullicudden 46 57.39 N 4.13 W
Cullin, Lough ⊜ 48 53.57 N 9.12 W
Cullinan 158 25.40 S 28.31 E
Cullman 194 34.10 N 86.50 W
Culloden Battlesite ⊥ 46 57.28 N 4.05 W
Cullom 216 40.53 N 88.16 W
Cullompton 42 50.52 N 3.24 W
Cullowhee 192 35.18 N 83.10 W
Cully 58 46.29 N 6.44 E
Cullybackey 48 54.53 N 6.21 W
Çulm ≃ 42 50.46 N 3.31 W
Čul'man 74 56.52 N 124.52 E
Cülmen 130 37.19 N 38.48 E
Culmore 284c 38.51 N 77.08 W
Culoz 62 45.51 N 5.47 E
Culpeper 188 38.28 N 77.59 W
Culpina 248 20.50 S 64.58 W
Culrain 46 57.55 N 4.24 W
Cults 46 57.07 N 2.10 W
Cultus Lake 224 49.04 N 121.58 W
Cultus Lake ⊜ 224 49.03 N 121.58 W
Cultus Lake Provincial Park ♦ 224 49.03 N 121.58 W
Culú-Culú, Arroyo ≃ 258 35.19 S 58.57 W
Culú-Culú, Laguna ⊜ 258 35.20 S 58.59 W
Çuluene ≃ 255 12.56 S 52.51 W
Čuluunchoroot 88 49.41 N 114.15 E
Čuluut 102 45.48 N 107.05 E
Čuluutyn ≃ 88 49.11 N 100.41 E
Culvain ∧ 46 56.56 N 5.17 W
Culver, In., U.S. 216 41.13 N 86.25 W
Culver, Or., U.S. 202 44.31 N 121.12 W
Culver, Point › 162 32.54 S 124.43 E
Culver City 228 34.01 N 118.23 W
Culverden 172 42.46 S 172.51 E
Culvers Lake 210 41.10 N 74.48 W
Çulverstone Green 260 51.20 N 0.21 E
Čulym 86 55.06 N 80.58 E
Čulym ≃, Ross. 86 57.43 N 83.51 E
Čulym ≃, Ross. 86 54.38 N 78.16 E
Čulyšman ≃ 86 51.20 N 87.45 E
Čum 24 67.06 N 63.07 E
Cuma 152 12.52 S 15.05 E
Çuma (Cumae) ⊥ 68 40.50 N 14.06 E
Čumakovo 86 55.41 N 79.02 E
Cumalı 130 36.42 N 27.27 E
Cuman' 78 50.49 N 25.53 E
Cumaná 246 10.28 N 64.10 W
Cumanacoa 246 10.15 N 63.55 W
Cumanayagua 240p 22.09 N 80.12 W
Cumaovası 130 38.15 N 27.09 E
Cumare, Cerro ∧2 246 0.28 N 73.52 W
Cumari 255 18.16 S 48.11 W
Cumbal 246 0.54 N 77.47 W
Cumbal, Nevado ∧ 246 0.57 N 77.52 W
Cumbe 250 10.21 S 37.14 W
Cumbee 220 28.04 N 81.55 W
Cumberland, B.C., Can. 182 49.37 N 125.01 W
Cumberland, Ia., U.S. 198 41.16 N 94.52 W
Cumberland, Ky., U.S. 192 36.58 N 82.59 W
Cumberland, Md., U.S. 188 39.39 N 78.45 W
Cumberland, Va., U.S. 192 37.29 N 78.14 W
Cumberland, Wa., U.S. 224 47.16 N 121.55 W
Cumberland, Wi., U.S. 190 45.31 N 92.01 W
Cumberland □6, N.J., U.S. 208 39.26 N 75.14 W
Cumberland □6, Pa., U.S. 208 40.12 N 77.12 W
Cumberland ≃ 178 37.09 N 88.25 W
Cumberland, Lake ⊜1 194 36.57 N 84.55 W
Cumberland, South Fork ≃ 192 36.58 N 84.36 W
Cumberland City 194 36.23 N 87.38 W
Cumberland Falls State Resort Park ♦ 192 36.50 N 84.20 W
Cumberland Gap)(192 36.36 N 83.41 W
Cumberland Gap National Historical Park ♦ 192 36.36 N 83.40 W
Cumberland Hill 207 41.58 N 71.27 W
Cumberland House 184 53.58 N 102.16 W
Cumberland Indian Reserve ◆4 184 53.04 N 104.50 W

Symbols in the index entries represent the broad categories identified in the key at the right. Symbols with superior numbers (⋀1) identify subcategories (see complete key on page *I · 1).*

Symbole im Register stellen die rechts im Schlüssel erklärten Kategorien dar. Symbole mit hochgestellten Ziffern (⋀1) bezeichnen Unterabteilungen einer Kategorie (vgl. vollständiger Schlüssel auf Seite *I · 1).*

Los símbolos incluídos en el texto del índice representan las grandes categorias identificadas con la clave a la derecha. Los símbolos con numeros en su parte superior (⋀1) identifican las subcategorías (véase la clave completa en la página *I · 1).*

Les symboles de l'index représentent les catégories indiquées dans la légende à droite. Les symboles suivis d'un indice (⋀1) représentent des sous-catégories (voir légende complète à la page *I · 1).*

Os símbolos incluídos no texto do índice representam as grandes categorias identificadas com a chave à direita. Os símbolos com números em sua parte superior (⋀1) identificam as subcategorias (veja-se a chave completa à página *I · 1).*

∧ Mountain	Berg	Montaña	Montagne	Montanha
⋀ Mountains	Gebirge	Montañas	Montagnes	Montanhas
)(Pass	Paß	Paso	Col	Passo
V Valley, Canyon	Tal, Cañon	Valle, Cañón	Vallée, Canyon	Vale, Canhão
≚ Plain	Ebene	Llano	Plaine	Planície
› Cape	Kap	Cabo	Cap	Cabo
I Island	Insel	Isla	Île	Ilha
II Islands	Inseln	Islas	Îles	Ilhas
⊥ Other Topographic Features	Andere Topographische Objekte	Otros Elementos Topográficos	Autres données topographiques	Outros acidentes topográficos

ESPAÑOL

Nombre	Página	Lat.°′	Long.°′ W = Oeste
Cumberland Island National Seashore ♠	192	30.50 N	81.27 W
Cumberland Islands II	166	20.40 S	149.09 E
Cumberland Lake ⊜	184	54.02 N	102.17 W
Cumberland Peninsula ≻ [1]	176	66.50 N	64.00 W
Cumberland Plateau ⋏ [1]	192	36.20 N	84.30 W
Cumberland Sound ⋓	176	65.10 N	65.30 W
Cumbernauld	46	55.58 N	3.59 W
Cumborah	166	29.44 S	147.46 E
Cumbria □ [6]	44	54.30 N	3.00 W
Cumbrian Mountains ⋏	44	54.30 N	3.05 W
Čumbur-Kosa	83	46.57 N	38.53 E
Cumby	222	33.08 N	95.50 W
Cumeral Nuevo	200	30.54 N	110.51 W
Çumiana	62	44.59 N	7.22 E
Čumikan	89	54.42 N	135.19 E
Cuminapanema ≃	250	1.09 S	54.54 W
Cuminá → Paru de Oeste ≃	250	1.30 S	56.00 W
Cuminestown	46	57.32 N	2.20 W
Cumming	192	34.12 N	84.08 W
Cummings Mountain ∧	228	35.03 N	118.34 W
Cummington	207	42.27 N	72.53 W
Cummins	166	34.16 S	135.44 E
Cummins, Mount ∧	182	52.03 N	118.15 W
Cummins Creek ≃	222	29.43 N	96.31 W
Cummins Range ⋏	162	19.05 S	127.10 E
Cumnock	44	55.27 N	4.16 W
Cumnor	42	51.44 N	1.20 W
Cumpas	232	30.02 N	109.48 W
Çumra	130	37.34 N	32.48 E
Cumshewa Inlet ⊂	182	53.03 N	131.45 W
Cumuripa	232	28.08 N	109.53 W
Cumwhinton	44	54.52 N	2.51 W
Čumyš ≃	86	53.31 N	83.10 E
Čun'a ≃, Ross.	74	61.36 N	96.30 E
Čuna ≃, Ross.	88	57.47 N	95.26 E
Cunani	250	2.52 N	51.06 W
Cunauaru ≃	246	3.10 S	63.01 W
Cunaviche	246	7.22 N	67.25 W
Cunco	252	38.55 S	72.02 W
Cuncumén	252	31.53 S	70.38 W
Cundeelee Reserve ✦ [4]	162	30.30 S	123.25 E
Cunderdin	162	31.39 S	117.15 E
Cundinamarca □ [5]	246	5.00 N	74.00 W
Cunduacán	234	18.04 N	93.10 W
Čundža	86	43.32 N	79.28 E
Cunene □ [5]	152	16.30 S	15.30 E
Cunene (Kunene) ≃	152	17.20 S	11.50 E
Cuneo	62	44.23 N	7.32 E
Cuneo □ [4]	62	44.31 N	7.34 E
Cunewalde	54	51.06 N	14.30 E
Cuney	222	32.02 N	95.25 W
Cung Hau, Cua ≃ [1]	110	9.46 N	106.34 E
Cung Son	110	13.02 N	108.58 E
Çüngüş	130	38.13 N	39.17 E
Cunha	256	23.05 S	44.58 W
Cunhambebe	256	23.00 S	44.20 W
Cunha Porã	252	26.54 S	53.09 W
Cunhinga	152	12.11 S	16.47 E
Cunhinga ≃	152	10.38 S	16.48 E
Cunhuã, Igarapé ≃	248	5.46 S	64.36 W
Cunlhat	62	45.38 N	3.35 E
Cunliffe	168b	34.05 S	137.45 E
Cunnamulla	166	28.04 S	145.41 E
Cunningham, Austl.	171a	28.09 S	151.51 E
Cunningham, Ks., U.S.	198	37.38 N	98.25 W
Cunningham, Lake ⊜	240b	25.04 N	77.26 W
Cunninghame □ [9]	46	55.40 N	4.30 W
Cunningham Falls State Park ♠	208	39.35 N	77.27 W
Cunningham Park ♠, Ma., U.S.	283	42.15 N	71.03 W
Cunningham Park ♠, N.Y., U.S.	276	40.44 N	73.46 W
Čunojar	88	57.27 N	97.18 E
Cunqian	100	28.30 N	115.10 E
Čunskij, Ross.	88	56.05 N	99.41 E
Čunskij, Ross.	88	57.26 N	97.31 E
Cuntan	107	29.37 N	106.36 E
Cunucunuma ≃	246	3.13 N	65.58 W
Čuny	76	59.39 N	36.04 E
Čuokkaraš'ša ∧	24	69.57 N	24.32 E
Cuorgnè	62	45.23 N	7.39 E
Čupa	24	66.16 N	33.00 E
Čupachovka	78	50.23 N	34.36 E
Čupalejka	80	55.11 N	42.33 E
Cupar, Sk., Can.	184	50.57 N	104.12 W
Cupar, Scot., U.K.	46	56.19 N	3.01 W
Cupecê, Ribeirão ≃	287b	23.37 S	46.42 W
Cupello	66	42.04 N	14.40 E
Cuperly	50	49.04 N	4.26 E
Cupertino	226	37.19 N	122.01 W
Cupica, Golfo de ⊂	246	6.35 N	77.25 W
Cupins	255	19.51 S	51.03 W
Cupra Marittima	66	43.01 N	13.51 E
Cupramontana	66	43.27 N	13.07 E
Ćuprija	38	43.56 N	21.23 E
Čuprovo	24	64.14 N	46.36 E
Cupsaw Lake ⊜	276	41.07 N	74.15 W
Cuqiao	107	30.36 N	103.59 E
Cuquema ≃	152	12.03 S	17.40 E
Cuquenán ≃	246	4.45 N	61.30 W
Cuquío	234	20.55 N	103.02 W
Čur	80	57.07 N	52.58 E
Curaçá	250	8.59 S	39.54 W
Curaçao I	241s	12.11 N	69.00 W
Curacautín	252	38.26 S	71.53 W
Curacaví	252	33.24 S	71.09 W
Čuračiki	80	55.44 N	47.26 E
Curaglia	58	46.41 N	8.51 E
Cural Novo, Ribeirão ≃	256	21.17 S	43.51 W
Curanilahue	252	37.28 S	73.21 W
Curanipe	252	35.50 S	72.38 W
Curanja ≃	248	9.58 S	70.58 W
Čurapča	74	62.00 N	132.24 E
Curapi ≃	250	1.25 N	53.49 W
Curaray ≃	246	2.20 S	74.05 W
Čurbek	85	39.59 N	69.56 E
Curcani	38	44.12 N	26.35 E
Curdies ≃	169	38.30 S	142.55 E
Cure ≃	50	47.40 N	3.41 E
Curecanti National Recreation Area ♠	200	38.24 N	107.25 W
Curepipe	157c	20.19 S	57.31 E
Curepto	252	35.05 S	72.01 W
Curequetê ≃	248	8.20 S	65.40 W
Čureški prohod)(	38	42.47 N	23.49 E
Curiapo	246	8.33 N	61.00 W
Curib	84	42.14 N	46.49 E
Curiche Grande (Corixo Grande) ≃	248	17.43 S	57.43 W
Curicó	252	34.59 S	71.14 W
Curicuriari ≃	246	0.14 S	66.48 W
Curières, Lac ⊜	206	46.41 N	74.51 W
Curimatá	250	10.02 S	44.17 W
Curimeo	234	20.01 N	101.42 W
Curinga	68	38.49 N	16.19 E
Curious, Mount ∧	162	27.28 S	114.20 E
Curisevo ≃	255	12.14 S	53.17 W
Curitiba	252	25.25 S	49.15 W
Curitibanos	252	27.18 S	50.36 W
Curiuaú ≃	246	1.51 S	61.14 W
Curiúva	255	24.02 S	50.27 W
Curl Curl	274a	33.46 S	151.18 E
Curlew	182	48.53 N	118.35 W
Curlewis	166	31.07 S	150.16 E
Curnamona	166	31.39 S	139.32 E
Curoca Norte	152	16.18 S	12.58 E
Curone ≃	62	45.03 N	8.54 E

FRANÇAIS

Nom	Page	Lat.°′	Long.°′ W = Ouest
Curon Venosta (Graun)	64	46.49 N	10.32 E
Čurovići	78	52.10 N	32.01 E
Currais Novos	250	6.15 S	36.31 W
Curralinho	250	1.48 S	49.47 W
Curramulka	168b	34.42 S	137.42 E
Curran	219	39.44 N	89.46 W
Currant Creek ≃, Co., U.S.	200	38.29 N	105.24 W
Currant Creek ≃, Mt., U.S.	202	46.22 N	108.39 W
Currant Mountain ∧	204	38.55 N	115.25 W
Currarong	170	35.01 S	150.49 E
Currency Creek	168b	35.28 S	138.46 E
Current ≃, On., Can.	190	48.27 N	89.11 W
Current ≃, U.S.	194	36.16 N	90.57 W
Current Islands II	192	25.22 N	76.49 W
Currie, Austl.	166	39.56 S	143.52 E
Currie, Scot., U.K.	46	55.54 N	3.20 W
Currie, Mn., U.S.	198	44.04 N	95.39 W
Currituck	192	36.26 N	76.00 W
Currituck □ [6]	208	36.28 N	76.03 W
Currituck Seamount ✣ [3]	14	30.00 S	173.30 W
Currituck Sound ⋓	192	36.20 N	75.52 W
Curry	180	62.37 N	150.01 W
Curry, Lake ⊜ [1]	226	38.22 N	122.08 W
Curry Rivel	42	51.02 N	2.52 W
Curryville, Mo., U.S.	219	39.20 N	91.20 W
Curryville, Pa., U.S.	214	40.17 N	78.20 W
Cursi	68	40.09 N	18.18 E
Curslack ✦ [8]	52	53.27 N	10.13 E
Curtarolo	64	45.31 N	11.50 E
Curtea de Argeș	38	45.08 N	24.41 E
Curtice	214	41.29 N	82.49 W
Curtina	252	32.09 S	56.07 W
Curtin Springs	162	25.20 S	131.45 E
Curtis, Esp.	34	43.07 N	8.03 W
Curtis, Ar., U.S.	194	33.59 N	93.06 W
Curtis, Ne., U.S.	198	40.37 N	100.30 W
Curtis, Port ⊤ [3]	166	24.00 S	151.30 E
Curtis Bay ⊂	284b	39.13 N	76.35 W
Curtis Channel ⋓	166	23.30 S	151.45 E
Curtis Creek ⊂	284b	39.12 N	76.35 W
Curtis Island I, Austl.	166	23.38 S	151.09 E
Curtis Island I, N.Z.	14	30.30 S	178.34 W
Curtis Lake ⊜	176	66.38 N	89.02 W
Curtisville	214	40.38 N	79.51 W
Curu ≃	250	3.22 S	39.04 W
Curuá ≃, Bra.	250	5.23 S	54.22 W
Curuá ≃, Bra.	250	1.55 S	55.07 W
Curuá ≃, Bra.	255	13.51 S	51.38 W
Curuá, Ilha do I	250	0.48 N	50.10 W
Curuaés ≃	250	7.30 S	54.45 W
Curuan	116	7.13 N	122.14 E
Curuá-Una ≃	250	2.24 S	54.05 W
Curubandé	236	10.43 N	85.26 W
Curuçá	250	0.43 S	47.50 W
Curuçá ✦ [8]	287b	23.30 S	46.25 W
Curuçá ≃	246	4.27 S	71.23 W
Curuçambaba	250	2.08 S	49.18 W
Curug, Indon.	115a	6.15 S	106.33 E
Čurug, Jugo.	38	45.29 N	20.04 E
Curuguaty	252	24.31 S	55.42 W
Curumo	286c	10.27 N	66.52 W
Curumu	250	1.01 S	51.03 W
Curunga	152	12.51 S	21.12 E
Curup	112	3.28 S	102.32 E
Curupá	250	9.54 S	45.54 W
Curupayty, Riacho ≃	248	22.03 S	58.00 W
C'urupinsk	78	46.37 N	32.43 E
Cururu ≃, Bra.	248	7.12 S	58.03 W
Cururu ≃, Bra.	250	0.39 S	50.11 W
Cururu-Açu ≃	250	8.58 S	57.13 W
Cururupu	250	1.50 S	44.52 W
Curuzú Cuatiá	252	29.47 S	58.03 W
Curva Grande	250	2.37 S	45.27 W
Curvelo	255	18.45 S	44.25 W
Curwensville	214	40.58 N	78.31 W
Curwensville Lake ⊜ [1]	214	40.55 N	78.37 W
Curwensville State Park ♠	214	40.55 N	78.34 W
Cusago	266b	45.27 N	9.02 E
Cusano Milanino	62	45.33 N	9.11 E
Cusano Mutri	68	41.20 N	14.30 E
Cusco	248	13.31 S	71.59 W
Cusco □ [5]	248	12.30 S	72.30 W
Cuscuzeiro, Pico do ∧	256	23.18 S	44.47 W
Cushabatay ≃	248	7.09 S	75.08 W
Cushendall	48	55.06 N	6.04 W
Cushendun	48	55.07 N	6.03 W
Cushina ≃	48	53.11 N	7.05 W
Cushing, Ok., U.S.	196	35.59 N	96.46 W
Cushing, Tx., U.S.	222	31.43 N	94.50 W
Cushing Memorial State Park ♠	283	42.10 N	70.45 W
Cushman	194	35.52 N	91.45 W
Cushman, Lake ⊜ [1]	224	47.28 N	123.14 W
Cusiana ≃	246	4.33 N	71.51 W
Cusick	202	48.20 N	117.17 W
Cusihuiriáchic	232	28.14 N	106.50 W
Cusna, Monte ∧	64	44.17 N	10.23 E
Čusovaja ≃	86	58.13 N	56.22 E
Čusovoj	86	58.17 N	57.49 E
Cusset	32	46.08 N	3.28 E
Cusseta	192	32.18 N	84.46 W
Cussewago Creek ≃	214	41.38 N	80.11 W
Cussey-sur-l'Ognon	58	47.20 N	5.56 E
Cusso ≃	152	14.16 S	15.36 E
Çust, N.Z.	172	43.19 S	172.22 E
Čust, Uzb.	85	41.00 N	71.15 E
Custar	216	41.17 N	83.51 W
Custer, Mi., U.S.	190	43.57 N	86.13 W
Custer, Mt., U.S.	202	46.07 N	107.33 W
Custer, Ok., U.S.	196	35.40 N	98.53 W
Custer, S.D., U.S.	198	43.46 N	103.35 W
Custer, Wa., U.S.	224	48.55 N	122.38 W
Custer Battlefield National Monument ♠	202	45.32 N	107.20 W
Custer City	214	41.54 N	78.39 W
Custer Creek ≃	198	46.42 N	105.29 W
Custer State Park ♠	198	43.43 N	103.23 W
Custines	56	48.48 N	6.09 E
Custódia	250	8.07 S	37.39 W
Custonaci	70	38.04 N	12.41 E
Cut, Nuhu I	164	5.35 S	133.00 E
Cut and Shoot	222	30.19 N	95.25 W
Cutato ≃	152	10.33 S	16.48 E
Cut Bank	202	48.37 N	112.19 W
Cutbank ≃	182	54.44 N	118.31 W
Cut Bank Creek ≃, N.A.	198	48.35 N	100.52 W
Cut Bank Creek ≃, Mt., U.S.	202	48.29 N	112.14 W
Cut Beaver Lake ⊜	184	53.47 N	102.38 W
Čutejevo	80	55.16 N	47.47 E
Cutervo	248	6.22 S	78.51 W
Cutervo, Parque Nacional ♠	248	6.10 S	78.45 W
Cuthand Creek ≃	194	33.23 N	94.57 W
Cuthbert	192	31.46 N	84.47 W
Cut Knife	184	52.44 N	109.01 W
Cutler, Ca., U.S.	226	36.31 N	119.17 W
Cutler, Me., U.S.	188	44.39 N	67.12 W
Cutler Ridge	220	25.34 N	80.20 W
Cutlerville	216	42.50 N	85.39 W
Čutovo	78	49.43 N	35.10 E
Cutral-Có	252	38.56 S	69.14 W
Cutro	68	39.02 N	16.59 E
Cutrofiano	68	40.07 N	18.12 E
Cuttack	120	20.30 N	85.50 E
Cuttyhunk Island I	207	41.25 N	70.56 W
Čutyr'	80	57.24 N	53.17 E
Cutzamala ≃	234	18.22 N	100.39 W
Cutzamala de Pinzón	234	18.28 N	100.34 W
Cutzio	234	18.39 N	100.54 W
Čuvašija □ [3]	80	55.30 N	47.00 E
Cuvette □ [5]	152	0.30 S	16.00 E

PORTUGUÊS

Nome	Página	Lat.°′	Long.°′ W = Oeste
Cuvier, Cape ≻	162	24.05 S	113.22 E
Cuvilly	50	49.33 N	2.42 E
Cuvo ≃	152	10.50 S	13.47 E
Cuxhaven	52	53.52 N	8.42 E
Cuxton	260	51.22 N	0.27 E
Cuyabá → Cuiabá	248	15.35 S	56.05 W
Cuyaguateje ≃	240p	22.05 N	83.58 W
Cuyahoga □ [6]	214	41.30 N	81.41 W
Cuyahoga ≃	214	41.30 N	81.42 W
Cuyahoga County Airport ⊠	279a	41.34 N	81.29 W
Cuyahoga Falls	214	41.08 N	81.29 W
Cuyahoga Heights	279a	41.26 N	81.39 W
Cuyahoga Valley National Recreation Area ♠	214	41.20 N	81.35 W
Cuyama ≃	204	34.54 N	120.18 W
Cuyamaca Peak ∧	204	32.57 N	116.36 W
Cuyamaca Rancho State Park ♠	204	32.58 N	116.32 W
Cuyamel	236	15.38 N	88.12 W
Cuyapo	116	15.46 N	120.40 E
Cuyk	52	51.44 N	5.52 E
Cuyler	210	42.44 N	75.57 W
Cuylerville	210	42.47 N	77.52 W
Cuyo	116	10.51 N	121.00 E
Cuyo East Pass ⋓	116	11.00 N	121.28 E
Cuyo Island I	116	10.51 N	121.02 E
Cuyo Islands II	116	11.04 N	120.57 E
Cuyo West Pass ⋓	116	11.00 N	120.30 E
Cuyubini ≃	246	8.20 N	60.20 W
Cuyuni ≃	246	6.23 N	58.41 W
Cuyuni-Mazaruni □ [4]	246	6.00 N	60.00 W
Cuyutlán, Laguna ⊂	234	19.00 N	104.10 W
Cuzco → Cusco	248	13.31 S	71.59 W
Čuzik ≃	86	58.03 N	80.37 E
Cuzna ≃	34	38.04 N	4.41 W
Cuzzago	58	46.00 N	8.22 E
Cvetkovo	78	49.11 N	31.33 E
Cvetnogorsk	86	54.14 N	90.27 E
Cvetnoje	78	48.57 N	32.29 E
Cvikov	54	50.48 N	14.40 E
Cwmbran	42	51.39 N	3.00 W
Cyangugu	154	2.29 S	28.54 E
Cybinka	30	52.12 N	14.48 E
Cybulev	78	49.06 N	29.50 E
Cyclades → Kikládhes II	38	37.30 N	25.00 E
Cyclone	214	41.50 N	78.35 W
Cygnet	216	41.14 N	83.38 W
Cygnet Bay ⊂	162	16.35 S	123.05 E
Cygnet Lake ⊜	184	56.47 N	94.54 W
Cygnet River	168b	35.42 S	137.31 E
Cylburn Park ♠	284b	39.21 N	76.39 W
Cynin ≃	42	51.48 N	4.29 W
Cynthiana, Ky., U.S.	218	38.23 N	84.17 W
Cynthiana, Oh., U.S.	218	39.10 N	83.21 W
Cynwyl Elfed	42	51.55 N	4.22 W
Cypern → Cyprus □ [1]	130	35.00 N	33.00 E
Cypress, Ca., U.S.	280	33.49 N	118.02 W
Cypress, La., U.S.	194	31.36 N	93.02 W
Cypress, Tx., U.S.	222	29.58 N	95.42 W
Cypress Bayou ≃	194	35.03 N	91.42 W
Cypress Creek ≃, Fl., U.S.	220	28.05 N	82.24 W
Cypress Creek ≃, Tx., U.S.	194	30.19 N	93.45 W
Cypress Creek ≃, Tx., U.S.	222	30.02 N	95.19 W
Cypress Gardens ♠	220	28.00 N	81.42 W
Cypress Hills ⋏ [2]	184	49.40 N	109.30 W
Cypress Hills Provincial Park ♠, Ab., Can.	184	49.39 N	110.10 W
Cypress Hills Provincial Park ♠, Sk., Can.	184	49.39 N	109.30 W
Cypress Island I	224	48.35 N	122.42 W
Cypress Lake ⊜, Sk., Can.	184	49.28 N	109.29 W
Cypress Lake ⊜, Fl., U.S.	220	28.05 N	81.19 W
Cypress Point ≻	226	36.35 N	121.59 W
Cypress Quarters	220	27.15 N	80.48 W
Cypress River	184	49.34 N	99.05 W
Cypress Swamp ≃	208	37.02 N	76.53 W
Cypress Swamp ≡	208	38.30 N	75.17 W
Cyprus □ [1], Asia	22	35.00 N	33.00 E
Cyprus □ [1], Asia	130	35.00 N	33.00 E
Cyprus, North (Kuzey Kıbrıs) □ [1], Asia	22	35.15 N	33.40 E
Cyprus, North (Kuzey Kıbrıs) □ [1], Asia	130	35.15 N	33.40 E
Cyrenaica → Barqah □ [9]	146	31.00 N	22.30 E
Cyrene	219	39.17 N	91.06 W
Cyrene ⊥	146	32.49 N	21.52 E
Cyril	196	34.53 N	98.12 W
Cyrildene ✦ [8]	273d	26.11 S	28.06 E
Cyrus Field Bay ⊂	176	62.50 N	64.55 W
Cysoing	50	50.34 N	3.13 E
Cythera → Kíthira I	38	36.20 N	22.58 E
Czaplinek	30	53.34 N	16.14 E
Czarna Białostocka	30	53.19 N	23.16 E
Czarna Woda	30	53.51 N	18.06 E
Czarne	30	53.42 N	16.57 E
Czarnków	30	52.55 N	16.34 E
Czech Republic (Česká Republika) □ [1], Europe	22	49.30 N	15.30 E
Czech Republic (Česká Republika) □ [1], Europe	30	49.40 N	15.10 E
Czempiń	30	52.10 N	16.47 E
Czerniejewo	30	52.26 N	17.30 E
Czernowitz → Černovcy	78	48.18 N	25.56 E
Czersk	30	53.48 N	18.00 E
Czerwieńsk	30	52.01 N	15.25 E
Częstochowa	30	50.49 N	19.06 E
Częstochowa □ [4]	30	50.40 N	19.15 E
Człopa	30	53.06 N	16.08 E
Człuchów	30	53.41 N	17.21 E
Czudec	30	49.57 N	21.50 E

D

Da ≃	100	28.10 N	120.14 E
Daaden	56	50.44 N	7.58 E
Da'an, Zhg.	89	45.28 N	124.18 E
Da'an, Zhg.	100	23.05 N	115.37 E
Da'an, Zhg.	107	29.23 N	106.01 E
Da'an, Zhg.	110	23.19 N	110.34 E
Daanbantayan	116	11.14 N	124.00 E
Daba	104	42.06 N	122.00 E
Ḍabāb, Jabal aḍ- ∧	132	31.02 N	35.38 E
Dabagou	104	42.27 N	122.00 E
Ḍab'ah, Ra's aḍ- ≻	140	31.05 N	28.26 E
Dabai	150	11.31 N	5.11 E
Dabaizhuang	105	39.27 N	117.23 E
Dabajuro	246	11.02 N	70.40 W
Dabakala	150	8.22 N	4.26 W
Dabali	104	41.51 N	120.37 E
Daba Ling ∧	100	24.28 N	113.17 E
Dabancheng	86	43.21 N	88.19 E
Dabangdian	100	31.37 N	113.41 E
Dabaojiagangzi	104	42.09 N	123.33 E
Dabaozhuang	105	40.18 N	116.58 E
Dabaozi	105	40.11 N	115.10 E
Daba Shan ⋏	102	31.55 N	109.05 E
Dabasi	107	28.55 N	105.09 E
Dabat	144	12.58 N	37.48 E
Dabayingzi	104	42.11 N	121.35 E
Dabbāgh, Jabal ∧	128	27.52 N	35.45 E
Dabbūriya	132	32.41 N	35.22 E
Dabegabis	158	28.07 S	18.36 E
Dabeiba	246	7.01 N	76.16 W
Dabeiwa	105	40.48 N	117.31 E
Dabeiyingzi	104	42.05 N	122.08 E
Dabendorf	54	52.14 N	13.26 E
Daberas	156	25.38 S	18.29 E
Daberg ✦ [8]	263	51.40 N	7.47 E
Dabhoi	120	22.11 N	73.26 E
Dābhol	122	17.36 N	73.10 E
Dab'ī, Wādī aḍ- V	132	31.42 N	36.42 E
Dąbie	30	52.06 N	18.49 E
Dąbie ✦ [8]	54	53.24 N	14.40 E
Dąbie, Jezioro ⊜	54	53.27 N	14.40 E
Dabie Shan ⋏	100	31.00 N	115.40 E
Dabilda	146	12.46 N	14.34 E
Da → Black ≃	110	21.15 N	105.20 E
Dablān	130	34.52 N	40.34 E
Ďáblice ✦ [8]	54	50.08 N	14.29 E
Dabnou	150	14.09 N	5.22 E
Dabo	58	48.39 N	7.14 E
Dabob Bay ⊂	224	47.47 N	122.50 W
Dabobeizhuang	105	39.18 N	117.59 E
Dabola	150	10.45 N	11.07 W
Dabong	114	5.23 N	102.01 E
Daborow	144	6.21 N	48.43 E
Dabou	150	5.19 N	4.23 W
Daboya	150	9.32 N	1.23 W
Dabra	124	25.54 N	78.20 E
Dābri ✦ [8]	272a	28.37 N	77.05 E
Dąbrowa Białostocka	30	53.39 N	23.20 E
Dąbrowa Tarnowska	30	50.11 N	21.00 E
Dabsan Hu ⊜	102	36.58 N	94.55 E
Dabu, Zhg.	100	23.52 N	116.54 E
Dabu, Zhg.	100	24.19 N	116.43 E
Dabu, Zhg.	100	24.20 N	114.35 E
Dabus ≃	144	10.48 N	35.10 E
Dabusutu-Ula, gora ∧	86	50.44 N	92.40 E
Dacaitun	104	41.38 N	121.18 E
Dacangzigou	104	40.59 N	121.01 E
Dacaocun	105	40.34 N	117.07 E
Dacca → Dhaka	126	23.43 N	90.25 E
Dachakou	100	29.38 N	118.18 E
Dachang, Zhg.	105	39.53 N	116.59 E
Dachang, Zhg.	106	32.12 N	118.45 E
Dachang, Zhg.	106	31.18 N	121.25 E
Dachang Airport ⊠	269b	31.18 N	121.25 E
Dachangshan Dao I	98	39.10 N	122.34 E
Dachau	60	48.15 N	11.27 E
Dachauer Moos ≡	60	48.12 N	11.25 E
Dacheng	100	28.34 N	115.31 E
Dachengji	100	33.52 N	119.26 E
Dachenjiabao	106	32.11 N	120.22 E
Dachen Shan I	106	30.21 N	121.52 E
Dachixu	100	25.10 N	116.46 E
Dachongyu	105	40.23 N	117.41 E
Dachsberg ∧ [2]	263	51.30 N	6.30 E
Dachsteinhöhlen ⊥ [5]	64	47.32 N	13.43 E
Dačice	61	49.05 N	15.26 E
Dac Lac, Cao Nguyen ⋏ [1]	110	12.50 N	108.05 E
Dačnoje ✦ [8]	265a	59.50 N	30.16 E
Dacoma	196	36.39 N	98.33 W
Dacorum □ [8]	260	51.45 N	0.30 W
Dac To	110	14.42 N	107.51 E
Dacun, Zhg.	102	27.55 N	101.08 E
Dacun, Zhg.	106	31.12 N	119.40 E
Dadal	88	49.01 N	111.37 E
Dadanawa	246	2.50 N	59.30 W
Dadaolizhuang	105	39.59 N	116.59 E
Dadaotun	104	41.46 N	122.13 E
Dadar ✦ [8]	272c	19.01 N	72.50 E
Daday	130	41.28 N	33.28 E
Dadayungou	104	41.23 N	123.25 E
Daddys Creek ≃	192	36.05 N	84.47 W
Dade □ [6]	220	25.33 N	80.32 W
Dade Battlefield Historic Memorial ⊥	220	28.38 N	82.09 W
Dade City	220	28.21 N	82.11 W
Dadeldhurā	124	29.18 N	80.35 E
Dadès, Oued ≃	148	30.55 N	6.47 W
Dadeville	194	32.49 N	85.45 W
Dādhar	120	29.28 N	67.39 E
Dadian	100	33.36 N	117.16 E
Dadiangas → General Santos	116	6.07 N	125.11 E
Dadianzi	104	42.11 N	124.02 E
Dadingjiawopu	104	41.13 N	122.16 E
D'adino	88	55.44 N	105.45 E
Dadiya	146	9.37 N	11.26 E
Dadle	144	5.20 N	46.58 E
Ḍadnah	128	25.33 N	56.21 E
Dadonggejiang	105	39.51 N	116.48 E
Dadongzhou	104	41.44 N	124.00 E
Dadou ≃	32	43.44 N	1.49 E
Dādpur, India	272b	22.42 N	88.33 E
Dādpur, India	272b	22.54 N	88.31 E
Dādra and Nagar Haveli □ [8]	122	20.05 N	73.00 E
Dādu	120	26.44 N	67.47 E
Dadu ≃	102	29.33 N	103.45 E
Dadugang	102	22.23 N	100.55 E
Dadukou, Zhg.	100	25.44 N	119.05 E
Dadukou, Zhg.	107	28.45 N	105.13 E
Dadukou, Zhg.	107	29.28 N	106.29 E
Daegu → Taegu	98	35.52 N	128.35 E
Daejeon → Taejŏn	98	36.20 N	127.26 E
Daerhanwangfu	89	44.19 N	122.15 E
Da'erhao	98	41.45 N	116.01 E
Daet	116	14.05 N	122.55 E
Daf'	146	28.03 N	19.57 E
Dafan, Zhg.	100	29.41 N	114.40 E
Dafan, Zhg.	104	42.38 N	122.11 E
Dafang	102	27.04 N	105.31 E
Dafangshen, Zhg.	104	42.25 N	123.14 E
Dafangshen, Zhg.	104	42.34 N	123.28 E
Dafangshen, Zhg.	104	42.36 N	123.04 E
Dafanhe	104	42.13 N	123.43 E
Dafanpuzi	104	41.37 N	122.50 E
Dafeng	100	33.12 N	120.30 E
Dafna	132	33.14 N	35.38 E
Dafoe	184	51.46 N	104.32 W
Dafoe ≃	184	55.55 N	94.48 W
Dafoe Lake ⊜	184	55.43 N	96.15 W
Da Fo Si (Great Buddha Temple) ⌂ [1]	106	30.16 N	120.09 E
Dafoutuo	105	40.24 N	115.58 E
Dafu	100	29.55 N	118.35 E
Dafu ≃	100	30.52 N	113.32 E
Dāfūr al-Janūbīyah □ [4]	140	11.45 N	25.25 E
Dagā ≃	110	16.56 N	94.45 E
Daga Medo	144	7.59 N	43.01 E
Dagana	150	16.31 N	15.30 W
Dagang, Zhg.	100	33.12 N	120.07 E
Dagang, Zhg.	100	22.49 N	113.23 E
Dagang, Zhg.	106	32.12 N	119.39 E
Dagangtou	100	28.18 N	119.44 E
Daganwangzhai	104	40.49 N	122.33 E
Daganzo de Arriba	266a	40.33 N	3.27 W
Dagaokan	104	40.46 N	122.22 E
Dagaolifangcun	104	41.10 N	122.28 E
Dagaolitun	104	42.26 N	123.53 E
Dagaoyang	106	30.35 N	120.26 E
Daga Post	140	9.12 N	33.58 E
Dağardı	130	39.26 N	29.00 E
Dagash	140	19.22 N	33.24 E
Dağbeli	130	37.12 N	30.31 E
Dagcanglhamo	102	34.02 N	102.30 E
Dagda	76	56.06 N	27.32 E
Dageløkke	41	55.04 N	10.53 E
Dagenham ✦ [8]	260	51.32 N	0.10 E
Dagestan □ [3]	72	43.00 N	47.00 E
Dagestan → Altaj □ [3]	86	51.00 N	86.00 E
Dagestanskije Ogni	84	42.07 N	48.12 E
Daggafontein	273d	26.18 S	28.28 E
Daggafontein Mines ✦ [7]	273d	26.18 S	28.29 E
Daggett	228	34.51 N	116.53 W
Dagg Sound ⋓	172	45.23 S	166.46 E
Daghfalī	140	19.17 N	32.30 E
Dağkızılca	130	38.18 N	27.24 E
Daglung	120	28.54 N	90.33 E
Dagmersellen	58	47.13 N	7.59 E
Dagö → Hiiumaa I	76	58.52 N	22.40 E
Dagomys	84	43.40 N	39.41 E
Dagongtun	89	42.48 N	121.58 E
Dagoretti	154	1.18 S	36.46 E
Dagsboro	208	38.32 N	75.14 W
Dagshai	123	30.53 N	77.03 E
Dagu	105	38.59 N	117.41 E
Dagu ≃	98	36.15 N	120.06 E
Dagua	164	3.25 S	143.20 E
Daguan, Zhg.	100	31.14 N	117.01 E
Daguan, Zhg.	102	27.44 N	104.16 E
Daguan Hu ⊜	100	30.00 N	116.24 E
Daguao	240m	18.14 N	65.41 W
Dagufen'gou	105	40.41 N	116.20 E
D'Aguilar, Cape ≻	271d	22.14 N	114.15 E
D'Aguilar, Mount ∧	171a	27.19 S	152.47 E
D'Aguilar Range ⋏	171a	27.10 S	152.45 E
Dagujia	98	42.22 N	124.52 E
Dagujiazi	104	42.20 N	123.20 E
Da Guokui Shan ∧	89	45.17 N	129.30 E
Dagupan	116	16.03 N	120.20 E
Daguragu Aboriginal Reserve ✦ [4]	162	17.35 S	130.30 E
Dagushan	104	41.03 N	123.02 E
Dagus Mines	214	41.21 N	78.36 W
Dagutang	100	29.38 N	116.06 E
Dagwin	110	18.04 N	97.41 E
Dagzê Co ⊜	120	31.55 N	87.35 E
Dahabān	144	21.55 N	39.04 E
Dahalac National Park ♠	144	15.40 N	40.05 E
Dahanchang	105	39.29 N	117.05 E
Dahaneh-ye Ghowrī	120	35.54 N	68.30 E
Dahaneh-ye Kāshār	120	35.09 N	66.14 E
Dahan-e Qowmghī	120	34.28 N	66.31 E
Dahantun	104	42.10 N	122.41 E
Dahasah, Wādī V	142	28.08 N	31.00 E
Dahḍāḥ, Tall ∧ [2]	132	32.36 N	36.03 E
Dahe	106	31.42 N	120.37 E
Dahebei	105	39.10 N	117.39 E
Dahei	120	21.42 N	72.35 E
Daheiding Shan ∧	89	47.58 N	129.07 E
Daheiyugou	104	41.21 N	121.55 E
Dahekou	106	32.16 N	119.05 E
Dahengdu	100	29.03 N	121.30 E
Dahenqin Dao I	100	22.06 N	113.30 E
Daheqiao	100	29.25 N	115.16 E
Dahijuri	126	22.31 N	86.59 E
Da Hinggan Ling ⋏	90	49.00 N	122.00 E
Dahīrpur ✦ [8]	272a	28.43 N	77.12 E
Dahl	56	51.18 N	7.31 E
Dahl ✦ [8]	263	51.11 N	6.26 E
Dahlak Archipelago II	144	15.45 N	40.30 E
Dahle	263	51.18 N	7.45 E
Dahlem	56	50.23 N	6.33 E
Dahlem ✦ [8]	264a	52.28 N	13.17 E
Dahlem, Museum ⌂	264a	52.27 N	13.18 E
Dahlen	54	51.22 N	12.59 E
Dahlenburg	54	53.11 N	10.44 E
Dahlerau	263	51.13 N	7.19 E
Dahlewitz	54	52.19 N	13.26 E
Dahlgren, Il., U.S.	194	38.12 N	88.41 W
Dahlgren, Va., U.S.	208	38.19 N	77.03 W
Dahlhausen	54	53.03 N	12.20 E
Dahlia	154	18.35 S	27.08 E
Dahlonega	192	34.31 N	83.59 W
Dahlonega Plateau ⋏ [1]	192	34.10 N	84.20 W
Dahlwitz	264a	52.30 N	13.38 E
Dahlwitz-Hoppegarten	54	52.30 N	13.38 E
Dahmani	36	35.57 N	8.50 E
Dahmarū	142	28.41 N	30.49 E
Dahme, Dtsch.	54	51.52 N	13.25 E
Dahme, Dtsch.	54	54.13 N	11.04 E
Dahme ≃	54	52.25 N	13.35 E
Dahn	56	49.09 N	7.47 E
Dāhod	120	22.50 N	74.16 E
Dahomey → Benin □ [1]	150	9.30 N	2.15 E
Dahong	106	31.53 N	121.17 E
Dahongmen	105	39.50 N	116.25 E
Dahongqi	104	41.52 N	122.36 E
Dahong Shan ⋏	100	31.30 N	113.00 E
Dahongtaizi	104	41.41 N	121.23 E
Dahoucun	105	38.51 N	115.37 E
Dahra	146	29.34 N	17.50 E
Dahra ⋏	34	36.25 N	1.00 E
Dähre	54	52.48 N	10.54 E
Dahsah, Wādī ad- V	142	27.19 N	31.26 E
Dahshūr	142	29.45 N	31.14 E
Dahu, Zhg.	100	26.22 N	119.06 E
Dahu, Zhg.	100	26.04 N	117.19 E
Dahua	102	23.44 N	107.59 E
Dahuan	100	22.33 N	113.29 E
Dahuangdi	104	42.08 N	122.27 E
Dahuangji	98	35.06 N	115.15 E
Dahuangpu	105	39.26 N	117.16 E
Dahuangshanpu	104	41.16 N	121.23 E
Dahuashan	105	40.17 N	117.04 E
Dahuasi	107	30.05 N	104.08 E
Dahujiang	100	26.10 N	114.57 E
Dahūk	128	36.52 N	43.00 E
Dahūk □ [4]	128	37.00 N	43.00 E
Dahuni	164	10.31 S	149.55 E
Dahuofang Shuiku ⊜ [1]	98	41.55 N	124.15 E
Dahushan	104	41.37 N	122.09 E
Dahy, Nafūd ad- ✦ [2]	118	22.20 N	45.35 E
Dai I	175e	7.57 S	160.37 E
Dai ≃	100	26.14 N	119.40 E
Dai, Pulau I	164	7.33 S	129.41 E
Daia	38	44.00 N	25.59 E
Daian	94	35.05 N	136.33 E
Daibosatsu-rei ∧	94	35.45 N	138.51 E
Daibu, Zhg.	100	32.19 N	117.12 E
Daibu, Zhg.	106	31.18 N	119.30 E
Daibutsu ⌂ [1]	94	35.19 N	139.32 E
Daiei	96	35.29 N	133.45 E
Daifang	100	27.32 N	115.41 E
Daigo	94	36.46 N	140.21 E
Daigo ✦ [8]	270	34.57 N	135.50 E
Daiguantun	105	39.57 N	117.50 E
Dai Hai ⊜	102	40.31 N	112.43 E
Daihaiyingzi	104	42.30 N	121.26 E
Daiji	100	33.48 N	115.03 E
Daijiagou	107	30.00 N	106.33 E
Daijiayao	100	32.56 N	120.19 E
Daikanbō ∧	96	33.00 N	131.04 E
Daik-u	110	17.47 N	96.40 E
Dā'il	132	32.45 N	36.08 E
Dailekh	124	28.50 N	81.44 E
Dailing	89	47.01 N	129.02 E
Dailly	44	55.16 N	4.43 W
Daimanji-san ∧	92	36.15 N	133.19 E
Daimiel	34	39.04 N	3.37 W
Daimon, Nihon	94	36.44 N	137.03 E
Daimon, Nihon	268	35.53 N	139.44 E
Daimuken-zan ∧	94	35.15 N	138.10 E
Dainan	100	32.43 N	120.06 E
Daingean	48	53.18 N	7.17 W
Daingerfield	222	33.01 N	94.43 W
Dainhāt	126	23.37 N	88.04 E
Dainichiga-take ∧	94	36.00 N	136.50 E
Dainkog	102	32.31 N	97.59 E
Daintree	164	16.15 S	145.19 E
Daintree National Park ♠	164	16.15 S	145.10 E
Daiō-zaki ≻	92	34.17 N	136.54 E
Dāira Dīn Panāh	123	30.34 N	70.56 E
Dairago	266b	45.34 N	8.52 E
Daireaux	252	36.36 S	61.45 W
Dairen → Dalian	98	38.53 N	121.35 E
Dairsie	46	56.20 N	2.56 W
Dairy City → Cypress	280	33.50 N	118.01 W
Dairy Creek, East Fork ≃	224	45.34 N	123.09 W
Dairy Creek, West Fork ≃	224	45.34 N	123.09 W
Dairyland	210	41.45 N	74.33 W
Dairyland → La Palma	280	33.51 N	118.02 W
Dairyland Reservoir ⊜ [1]	190	45.30 N	91.00 W
Dairy Valley → Cerritos	280	33.51 N	118.05 W
Dai-sen ∧	96	35.22 N	133.33 E
Daisen-oki-kokuritsu-kōen ♠	96	35.20 N	133.35 E
Daisen-zan ∧	96	34.07 N	133.56 E
Daisetsu-zan-kokuritsu-kōen ♠	92a	43.30 N	142.57 E
Daisetta	222	30.06 N	94.38 W
Daishan	100	30.14 N	122.12 E
Daishin	94	37.12 N	140.15 E
Daishōji ≃	94	36.18 N	136.15 E
Daisizhen	107	29.14 N	105.09 E
Daitō, Nihon	96	34.42 N	135.38 E
Daitō, Nihon	96	35.19 N	132.58 E
Daiwa, Nihon	96	34.32 N	132.57 E
Daiwa, Nihon	96	34.57 N	132.39 E
Daixi	106	30.40 N	120.01 E
Daixian	102	39.08 N	113.01 E
Daixiqiao	106	31.36 N	120.04 E
Daiya ≃	94	36.45 N	139.46 E
Daiyun Shan ⋏	100	25.46 N	118.16 E
Dajabón	238	19.33 N	71.42 W
Dājal	120	29.33 N	70.23 E
Da'jānīyah, Jabal ad- ∧	132	30.34 N	35.43 E
Dajarra	166	21.41 S	139.31 E
Dajian Shan ∧	102	26.42 N	103.34 E
Dajidian	105	38.50 N	115.26 E
Dajindian	100	34.24 N	112.58 E
Dajing, Zhg.	100	28.24 N	121.07 E
Dajing, Zhg.	100	28.59 N	113.19 E
Dajin Shan II	106	30.41 N	121.26 E
Dajishan	100	24.38 N	114.26 E
Dajitai	104	42.20 N	121.11 E
Dajiuba	120	36.50 N	89.35 E
Daji Yang ⋓	100	30.54 N	122.18 E
Daju	105	39.12 N	115.31 E
Da Juh	102	36.36 N	94.04 E
Dak ⊜	128	32.48 N	61.14 E
Daka ≃	150	8.19 N	0.13 W
Dakangpu	104	41.32 N	121.06 E
Dakanzi	104	40.52 N	122.53 E
Dakar	150	14.40 N	17.26 W
Dakar □ [4]	150	14.45 N	17.25 W
Dākātia ≃ [1]	126	22.57 N	90.42 E
Dakeng	100	26.18 N	115.32 E
Dakengkou	100	24.33 N	113.37 E
Daketa ≃	144	7.16 N	42.13 E
Dak Gle	110	15.11 N	107.48 E
Dakhal, Bi'r ad- ⊤ [4]	142	28.40 N	32.24 E
Dakhal, Wādī ad- V	142	28.49 N	32.45 E
Dākhilah, Al-Wāḥāt ad- ⊤ [4]	140	25.30 N	29.05 E
Dakhin Shāhbāzpur Island I	126	22.30 N	90.45 E
Dakhla	148	23.43 N	15.57 W
Dakhlet Nouâdhibou □ [4]	148	20.40 N	16.00 W
Dakingari	150	11.37 N	4.01 E
Dakka → Dhaka	124	23.43 N	90.25 E
Dākoānk	110	7.02 N	93.43 E
Dakongcheng	105	39.30 N	117.09 E
Dakongwan	104	40.51 N	122.19 E
Dakoro	150	14.31 N	6.46 E
Dakota City, Ia., U.S.	190	42.43 N	94.12 W
Dakota City, Ne., U.S.	198	42.24 N	96.25 W
Dakou	100	34.27 N	112.44 E
Dakoutun	105	39.35 N	117.14 E
Đakovica	38	42.23 N	20.25 E
Đakovo	38	45.19 N	18.25 E
Dakshin Gangotri ⌂ [3]	9	70.05 S	12.00 E
Dakshingram	126	24.03 N	87.48 E
Dakumu	89	48.51 N	124.18 E
Dakunlun	98	36.34 N	117.52 E
Dakwa	154	4.00 N	26.26 E
Dakwah, Tall ad- ∧ [2]	132	33.25 N	36.56 E
Dala, Ang.	152	11.03 S	20.17 E
Dala, Ang.	152	8.05 S	15.50 E
Dala, Sol.Is.	175e	8.35 S	160.40 E
Dalaas	58	47.07 N	10.00 E
Dalaba	150	10.42 N	12.15 W
Dalabani	150	10.28 N	9.27 W
Dala Cachibo	152	10.28 S	14.39 E
Dalad Qi	102	40.28 N	110.02 E
Dala-Floda	40	60.31 N	14.47 E
Dalaguete	116	9.46 N	123.32 E
Dalahan (Shiqizhan)	89	52.06 N	125.46 E
Dala-Husby	40	60.21 N	16.00 E
Dala-Järna	26	60.33 N	14.21 E
Dalajchöl	86	47.59 N	90.47 E
Dalaji	89	51.38 N	120.06 E
Dalälven ≃	40	60.38 N	17.27 E
Dalama	130	37.47 N	28.04 E
Dalaman ≃	130	36.40 N	28.45 E
Dalāmī	140	11.52 N	30.28 E
Dalan	100	23.19 N	114.47 E
Dalan Dzadgad	102	43.37 N	104.29 E
Dalandžargalan	102	45.55 N	109.05 E
Dalane ✦ [1]	26	58.35 N	6.20 E
Dalang	100	22.57 N	113.56 E
Dalantuozi	104	41.28 N	122.47 E
Dalao	150	11.29 N	13.40 W
Dalarna □ [9]	26	61.01 N	14.04 E
Dalarö	40	59.08 N	18.24 E
Dalat, Malay.	112	2.44 N	111.56 E
Da Lat, Viet	110	11.56 N	108.25 E
Dalayaozi	105	40.49 N	117.41 E
Dālbandin	128	28.53 N	64.25 E
Dalbeattie	44	54.56 N	3.49 W
D'Albertis Dome ∧	164	5.00 S	142.05 E
Dalbosjön ⊂	26	58.45 N	12.48 E
Dalby, Austl.	166	27.11 S	151.16 E
Dalby, Sve.	41	55.40 N	13.20 E
Dalby Söderskogs Nationalpark ♠	41	55.43 N	13.17 E
Dalcahue	254	42.23 S	73.40 W
Dalch ≃	42	50.52 N	3.47 W
Dale, Nor.	26	60.35 N	5.49 E
Dale, Nor.	26	61.22 N	5.25 E
Dale, Wales, U.K.	42	51.43 N	5.11 W
Dale, In., U.S.	194	38.10 N	86.59 W
Dale, Pa., U.S.	214	40.18 N	78.54 W
Dale, Tx., U.S.	222	29.56 N	97.34 W
Dale ≃	168a	32.10 S	116.49 E
Dale, Mount ∧	168a	32.08 S	116.18 E
Dale Bridge	168a	32.05 S	116.49 E
Dalecarlia → Dalarna □ [9]	26	61.01 N	14.04 E
Dale City	208	38.38 N	77.18 W
Dale Hollow Lake ⊜ [1]	192	36.36 N	85.19 W
Dale Lake ⊜	204	34.08 N	115.42 W
Dalen	26	59.27 N	8.00 E
Dalengtu	98	41.11 N	113.45 E
Dalešice, údolní nádrž ⊜ [1]	61	49.09 N	16.05 E
Daleside	158	26.30 S	28.04 E
Dale South ≃	168a	32.16 S	116.47 E
Dalesville	206	45.42 N	74.24 W
Dalesville ≃	206	45.40 N	74.24 W
Daleszyce	30	50.48 N	20.48 E
Dalet	110	19.59 N	93.51 E

≃ River	Fluß	Río	Rivière	Rio
≅ Canal	Kanal	Canal	Canal	Canal
∟ Waterfall, Rapids	Wasserfall, Stromschnellen	Cascada, Rápidos	Chute d'eau, Rapides	Cascata, Rápidos
⋓ Strait	Meeresstraße	Estrecho	Détroit	Estreito
⊂ Bay, Gulf	Bucht, Golf	Bahía, Golfo	Baie, Golfe	Baía, Golfo
⊜ Lake, Lakes	See, Seen	Lago, Lagos	Lac, Lacs	Lago, Lagos
≡ Swamp	Sumpf	Pantano	Marais	Pântano
⍓ Ice Features, Glacier	Eis- und Gletscherformen	Accidentes Glaciales	Formes glaciaires	Acidentes glaciares
⊤ Other Hydrographic Features	Andere Hydrographische Objekte	Otros Elementos Hidrográficos	Autres données hydrographiques	Outros acidentes hidrográficos

✣ Submarine Features	Untermeerische Objekte	Accidentes Submarinos	Formes de relief sous-marin	Acidentes submarinos
□ Political Unit	Politische Einheit	Unidad Politica	Entité politique	Unidade política
⌂ Cultural Institution	Kulturelle Institution	Institución Cultural	Institution culturelle	Instituição cultural
⊥ Historical Site	Historische Stätte	Sitio Histórico	Site historique	Sitio histórico
♠ Recreational Site	Erholungs- und Ferienort	Sitio de Recreo	Centre de loisirs	Area de Lazer
⊠ Airport	Flughafen	Aeropuerto	Aéroport	Aeroporto
■ Military Installation	Militäranlage	Instalación Militar	Installation militaire	Instalação militar
✦ Miscellaneous	Verschiedenes	Misceláneo	Divers	Diversos

Daleville, Al., U.S. 194 31.18 N 85.42 W
Daleville, In., U.S. 218 40.07 N 85.33 W
Daleville, Pa., U.S. 210 41.18 N 75.31 W
Dalfsen 52 52.30 N 6.16 E
Dalgaranga 162 27.46 S 117.02 E
Dalgaranger ∧ 162 27.51 S 117.06 E
Dalgety 171b 36.30 S 148.50 E
Dalgety Bay 46 56.02 N 3.20 W
Dalgety Brook ≐ 162 25.07 S 115.47 E
Dalgety Downs 162 25.17 S 116.15 E
Dalgomai 124 26.06 N 90.47 E
Dalhalvaig 46 58.28 N 3.54 W
Dalhart 196 36.03 N 102.30 W
Dalhausen 52 51.37 N 9.17 E
Dalhousie, N.B., Can. 186 48.04 N 66.23 W
Dalhousie, India 123 32.32 N 75.59 E
Dalhousie, Cape > 180 70.14 N 129.42 W
Dalhousie Island I 126 21.35 N 88.45 E
Dalhousie Lake ⊜ 212 44.58 N 76.35 W
Dalhousie Square ♦ 272b 22.33 N 88.22 E
Dali, Zhg. 102 34.47 N 109.57 E
Dali, Zhg. 102 25.38 N 100.09 E
Dalian (Dairen) 98 38.53 N 121.35 E
Dalian Dao I 100 25.40 N 119.42 E
Daliangdi 98 41.54 N 115.45 E
Daliang Shan ⋏ 102 28.00 N 103.00 E
Dalianhe 104 40.57 N 123.15 E
Daliankeng 105 40.54 N 117.45 E
Dalian Wan c 98 38.57 N 121.45 E
Dalianwukou 106 30.17 N 119.00 E
Daliao ≐ 104 40.42 N 122.08 E
Dalías 34 36.49 N 2.52 W
Dalikou 100 26.52 N 118.00 E
Dalin, Zhg. 89 43.43 N 122.45 E
Dalin, Zhg. 107 30.17 N 104.07 E
Daling 104 41.27 N 121.15 E
Daling ≐ 98 40.56 N 121.43 E
Dalingbeigou 104 40.42 N 123.08 E
Dalipe Point > 116 10.46 N 121.55 E
Daliushugou 104 40.46 N 122.14 E
Daliutai 104 41.25 N 121.55 E
Daliutun 104 42.14 N 122.46 E
Daliuzhen 105 38.51 N 116.19 E
Daliuzhuang 100 33.04 N 114.03 E
Daliyat et Karmil 132 32.42 N 35.03 E
Daliyya 132 32.35 N 35.04 E
Dalizi 98 41.45 N 126.49 E
Dalj 38 45.29 N 18.59 E
Daljā' 142 27.39 N 30.42 E
Dalkarlsberg 40 59.26 N 14.51 E
Dalkeith 46 55.54 N 3.04 W
Dālkola 124 25.52 N 87.51 E
Dall, Mount ∧ 180 62.35 N 152.18 W
Dallāh, 'Ayn ⊹[4] 140 27.19 N 27.20 E
Dallardsville 222 30.38 N 94.38 W
Dallas, Scot., U.K. 46 57.33 N 3.28 W
Dallas, Al., U.S. 194 33.50 N 86.39 W
Dallas, Ga., U.S. 192 33.55 N 84.50 W
Dallas, N.C., U.S. 192 35.18 N 81.10 W
Dallas, Or., U.S. 202 44.55 N 123.18 W
Dallas, Pa., U.S. 210 41.20 N 75.57 W
Dallas, Tx., U.S. 222 32.46 N 96.47 W
Dallas, Wi., U.S. 190 45.15 N 91.48 W
Dallas □[6] 222 32.17 N 96.47 W
Dallas Center 190 41.41 N 93.57 W
Dallas City 190 40.38 N 91.10 W
Dallas-Fort Worth Regional Airport ⊠ 222 32.54 N 97.01 W
Dallas Naval Air Station ■ 222 32.44 N 96.59 W
Dallastown 208 39.53 N 76.38 W
Dallgow 54 52.32 N 13.05 E
Dallıbahçe 130 39.09 N 39.53 E
Dalli Rājhara 122 20.35 N 81.04 E
Dall Island I 182 54.50 N 132.55 W
Dall Lake ⊜ 180 60.18 N 163.35 W
Dalmā I 128 24.30 N 52.20 E
Dalmacija □[9] 36 43.00 N 17.00 E
Dalmacio Vélez Sarsfield 252 32.36 S 63.35 W
Dalmally 46 56.24 N 4.58 W
Dal'mamedli 84 40.42 N 46.34 E
Dalmatia 208 40.39 N 76.54 W
Dalmatia → Dalmacija □[9] 36 43.00 N 17.00 E
Dalmatovo 86 56.16 N 62.56 E
Dalmau 124 26.04 N 81.02 E
Dalmellington 44 55.19 N 4.24 W
Dalmeny 184 52.20 N 106.46 W
Dalmine 62 45.39 N 9.36 E
Dalmose 41 55.18 N 11.26 E
Dal'n'aja 89 45.56 N 142.04 E
Dal'n'aja Muja 88 54.21 N 103.37 E
Dalnaspidal 46 56.50 N 4.14 W
Dal'negorsk 89 44.35 N 135.35 E
Dal'neje-Konstantinovo 80 55.49 N 44.06 E
Dal'nerečensk 89 45.55 N 133.43 E
Dal'ne-Rusanovo 82 54.15 N 85.45 E
Dal'nik 78 46.28 N 30.34 E
Daloa 150 6.53 N 6.27 W
Dalongchang 105 39.50 N 116.06 E
Dalonghua 105 39.18 N 115.18 E
Dalongtian 100 24.14 N 115.44 E
Dalovice 54 50.11 N 12.55 E
Dalqū 140 20.07 N 30.37 E
Dalroy 182 51.07 N 113.39 W
Dalry, Scot., U.K. 44 55.07 N 4.10 W
Dalry, Scot., U.K. 46 55.43 N 4.44 W
Dalrymple 44 55.23 N 4.35 W
Dalrymple, Mount ∧ 166 21.02 S 148.38 E
Dalrymple Creek ≐ 171a 27.59 S 151.46 E
Dalrymple Lake ⊜ 212 44.38 N 79.07 W
Dalsbruk (Taalintehdas) 26 60.02 N 22.31 E
Dalsingpara 124 26.47 N 89.22 E
Dalsing Sarai 124 25.40 N 85.50 E
Dalsjöfors 26 57.43 N 13.05 E
Dalsland □[9] 26 58.30 N 12.50 E
Dals-Långed 26 58.55 N 12.18 E
Dal'stroja 88 68.19 N 177.39 W
Dāltenganj 124 24.02 N 84.04 E
Dalton, S. Afr. 158 29.20 S 30.40 E
Dalton, Eng., U.K. 262 53.34 N 1.24 W
Dalton, Ga., U.S. 192 34.47 N 84.58 W
Dalton, Ma., U.S. 207 42.28 N 73.10 W
Dalton, Ne., U.S. 198 41.24 N 102.58 W
Dalton, N.Y., U.S. 210 42.32 N 77.57 W
Dalton, Oh., U.S. 214 40.47 N 81.41 W
Dalton, Pa., U.S. 210 41.32 N 75.44 W
Dalton City 219 39.43 N 88.48 W
Dalton Gardens 202 47.43 N 116.46 W
Dalton Iceberg Tongue ⊓ 9 66.15 S 121.30 E
Dalton-in-Furness 44 54.09 N 3.11 W
Dalu 104 41.27 N 123.19 E
Dalubeikou 105 38.59 N 117.12 E
Daludalu 114 1.05 N 100.15 E
Dalu Dao I 98 39.44 N 123.45 E
Daluis, Gorges de V 62 44.04 N 6.49 E
Dalum, Dan. 41 55.22 N 10.22 E
Dalum, Dtsch. 52 52.35 N 7.14 E
Daluojiazhuang 104 40.31 N 122.09 E
Daluotaozi 104 41.17 N 122.52 E
Daluoxi 100 25.14 N 118.36 E
Daluping 100 26.11 N 114.30 E
Dalupiri Island I, Pil. 116 19.05 N 121.14 E
Dalupiri Island I, Pil. 116 12.25 N 124.16 E
Daluxi 100 24.28 N 117.01 E
Dalview 273d 26.15 S 28.21 E
Dalvík 24a 65.59 N 18.32 W
Dalwallinu 162 30.17 S 116.40 E
Dalwhinnie 46 56.56 N 4.14 W
Dalworthington Gardens 222 32.42 N 97.10 W
Daly ≐ 164 13.20 S 130.19 E
Daly Bay c 176 64.00 N 89.40 W
Daly City 226 37.43 N 122.31 W
Daly Lake ⊜ 184 56.33 N 105.40 W
Daly Point > 212 44.53 N 80.14 W
Daly River 164 13.45 S 130.50 E
Daly River Aboriginal Reserve ◆[4] 164 14.20 S 130.00 E
Daly Waters 164 16.15 S 133.22 E
Dam ≐ 120 33.56 N 92.41 E
Dāmā, Sūrīy. 132 32.57 N 36.25 E
Dama, Zhg. 100 32.03 N 118.02 E
Damagum 146 11.41 N 11.20 E
Damān 122 20.25 N 72.51 E
Damān □[8] 122 20.10 N 73.00 E
Damanhūr Shubra 273c 30.07 N 31.14 E
Damanhūr 142 31.02 N 30.28 E
Damanling 105 40.36 N 115.08 E
Damaopu 104 41.16 N 121.07 E
Damar 130 41.15 N 41.34 E
Damar, Pulau I, Indon. 164 1.00 S 128.24 E
Damar, Pulau I, Indon. 164 7.09 S 128.40 E
Damara 152 4.58 N 18.42 E
Damaraland □[5] 156 21.00 S 14.20 E
Damaraland □[9] 156 22.34 S 17.06 E
Damās 142 30.48 N 31.20 E
Damasco — Dimashq 132 33.30 N 36.18 E
Damascus, Ar., U.S. 194 35.22 N 92.24 W
Damascus, Ga., U.S. 192 34.33 N 84.56 W
Damascus, Md., U.S. 208 39.17 N 77.12 W
Damascus, Oh., U.S. 214 40.54 N 80.58 W
Damascus, Pa., U.S. 210 41.42 N 75.04 W
Damascus, Va., U.S. 192 36.38 N 81.47 W
Damascus — Dimashq 132 33.30 N 36.18 E
Damascus International Airport ⊠ 132 33.29 N 36.13 E
Damas — Dimashq 132 33.30 N 36.18 E
Damaskus — Dimashq 132 33.30 N 36.18 E
Damāt 142 30.57 N 30.57 E
Damaturu 146 11.45 N 11.58 E
Damāvand 128 35.43 N 52.04 E
Damāvand, Qolleh-ye ∧ 128 35.56 N 52.08 E
Damba 152 6.41 S 15.08 E
Dambach-la-Ville 58 48.20 N 7.26 E
Dambarta 150 12.26 N 8.31 E
Dambeck 54 52.48 N 11.09 E
Dambuki 89 54.21 N 127.38 E
Dam Doi 110 8.50 N 105.15 E
Damelevières 58 48.33 N 6.23 E
Damen Dao I 100 27.58 N 121.06 E
Damengjialazi 104 41.04 N 120.53 E
Damengzhuang 105 39.32 N 116.59 E
Damergou ◆[1] 150 15.00 N 8.55 E
Damerham 42 50.57 N 1.52 W
Dämeritzsee ⊜ 264a 52.25 N 13.45 E
Damery 50 49.04 N 3.53 E
Dames Quarter 208 38.11 N 75.53 W
Dam Gamad 140 13.17 N 27.28 E
Dāmghān 128 36.09 N 54.22 E
Damianópolis 255 14.33 S 46.10 W
Damianzhen 107 30.36 N 104.10 E
Damiao, Zhg. 98 42.26 N 118.22 E
Damiao, Zhg. 98 34.20 N 117.23 E
Damiao, Zhg. 102 37.18 N 104.39 E
Damiao, Zhg. 104 42.33 N 122.18 E
Damiaochang 107 29.39 N 106.05 E
Damiaogou 104 41.06 N 123.52 E
Damiaojiang 106 31.00 N 120.28 E
Damiaoshang 105 39.56 N 115.12 E
Dămienești 38 46.44 N 26.59 E
Damietta Branch → Dumyāṭ, Far' ≐ 142 31.32 N 31.51 E
Damietta → Dumyāṭ 142 31.25 N 31.48 E
Damietta Mouth → Dumyāṭ, Maṣabb ≐[1] 142 31.32 N 31.51 E
Damin 100 28.56 N 120.29 E
Daming 98 36.19 N 115.06 E
Damingzhen 104 42.34 N 123.36 E
Damintun 104 41.52 N 122.56 E
Dāmiyā 132 32.06 N 35.33 E
Damlacık 130 37.56 N 38.39 E
Damm 263 51.40 N 6.48 E
Dammai Island I 116 5.47 N 120.25 E
Dammarie 50 48.21 N 1.30 E
Dammarie-lès-Lys 50 48.31 N 2.39 E
Dammartin-en-Goële 50 49.03 N 2.41 E
Dammartin-en-Serve 50 48.54 N 1.37 E
Dammastock ∧ 58 46.39 N 8.25 E
Damme, Bel. 50 51.15 N 3.17 E
Damme, Dtsch. 52 52.30 N 8.08 E
Damme, Dtsch. 54 53.17 N 14.01 E
Dammer Berge ⋏[2] 52 52.32 N 8.10 E
Dāmodar ≐ 124 22.17 N 88.05 E
Dāmodar Main Canal ≐ 126 23.01 N 87.53 E
Damoh, India 118 23.50 N 79.27 E
Damoh, India 124 23.50 N 79.27 E
Damon 222 29.17 N 95.45 W
Damongo 150 9.05 N 1.49 W
Damotapāda 272c 19.03 N 73.04 E
Damous 34 36.33 N 1.42 E
Damozhuang 105 39.53 N 115.40 E
Dampar, Tasek ⊜ 114 3.02 N 102.43 E
Dampelas — Sabang 112 0.11 N 119.51 E
Dampier 162 20.39 S 116.45 E
Dampier, Cape > 164 6.02 S 151.02 E
Dampier, Selat ꭒ 164 0.40 S 130.40 E
Dampier Archipelago II 162 20.35 S 116.35 E
Dampier Land >[1] 162 17.30 S 122.55 E
Dampierre, Fr. 50 48.42 N 1.59 E
Dampierre, Fr. 58 47.09 N 5.45 E
Dampierre, Château de ⊥ 261 48.42 N 1.59 E
Dampierre-en-Burly 50 47.46 N 2.31 E
Dampierre-sur-Linotte 58 47.31 N 6.14 E
Dampierre-sur-Salon 58 47.33 N 5.41 E
Dampier Strait ꭒ 164 5.36 S 148.12 E
Dampit 115a 8.13 S 112.45 E
Dampmart 261 48.53 N 2.44 E
Damprichard 58 47.15 N 6.53 E
Dâmrei, Chuŏr Phnum ⋏ 110 11.00 N 104.05 E
Damujī ≐ 240p 22.11 N 80.33 W
Damüls 58 47.17 N 9.53 E
Dāmurhuda 126 23.36 N 88.47 E
Damutougou 98 42.28 N 118.56 E
Damville 50 48.52 N 1.04 E
Damvillers 56 49.20 N 5.24 E
Damxung 120 30.31 N 91.08 E
Dan 132 33.14 N 35.39 E
Dan ≐, U.S. 192 36.42 N 78.45 W
Dan ≐, Zhg. 102 33.02 N 111.20 E
Dana, Cam. 146 10.14 N 15.18 E
Dana, In., U.S. 194 39.48 N 87.29 W
Dana, Mount ∧ 226 37.54 N 119.13 W
Dana, Pulau I 112 10.50 S 121.16 E
Danabao 102 22.08 N 103.22 E
Danai 112 0.29 N 103.26 E
Danajon Bank ⋆[4] 116 10.16 N 124.17 E
Danakil — Denakil ◆[1] 144 13.00 N 41.00 E
Danakil National Park ♦ 144 10.50 N 40.45 E
Danané 150 7.16 N 8.09 W
Da Nang 110 16.04 N 108.13 E
Danan'gou 105 40.32 N 117.49 E
Danao, Pil. 116 10.32 N 124.02 E
Danao, Pil. 116 12.29 N 122.39 E
Dana Point 228 33.29 N 117.44 W
Dana Point > 228 33.28 N 117.43 W
Dānāpur 124 25.38 N 85.03 E
Danba 102 31.00 N 101.50 E
Danboro 208 40.21 N 75.08 W
Danbury, Eng., U.K. 42 51.44 N 0.33 E
Danbury, Ct., U.S. 207 41.23 N 73.27 W
Danbury, Ia., U.S. 198 42.14 N 95.43 W
Danbury, Ne., U.S. 198 40.02 N 100.24 W
Danbury, N.C., U.S. 192 36.24 N 80.12 W
Danbury, Tx., U.S. 222 29.14 N 95.21 W
Danby Lake ⊜ 204 34.14 N 115.07 W
Dancheng 100 33.39 N 115.11 E
Danchengji 100 33.47 N 116.17 E
Dancug 144 10.58 N 49.04 E
Dand 120 31.37 N 65.41 E
Dandaragan 162 30.40 S 115.42 E
Dande ≐ 152 8.28 S 13.21 E
Dandeli 122 15.15 N 74.37 E
Dandenong 169 37.59 S 145.12 E
Dandenong, Mount ∧ 274b 37.50 S 145.21 E
Dandenong Creek ≐ 274b 38.01 S 145.05 E
Dandenong Ranges National Park ♦ 169 37.53 S 145.20 E
Danderyd 40 59.25 N 18.01 E
Dandīl 142 29.10 N 31.02 E
Dandong 98 40.08 N 124.20 E
Dandot 123 32.39 N 72.58 E
Dandridge 192 36.00 N 83.24 W
Dan Dume 150 11.27 N 7.10 E
Dane □[6] 216 43.04 N 89.15 W
Dane ≐ 44 53.15 N 2.31 W
Dane County Regional Airport-Truax Field ⊠ 216 43.08 N 89.20 W
Dänemark — Denmark □[1] 26 56.00 N 10.00 E
Dänemark-Strasse — Denmark Strait ꭒ 10 67.00 N 25.00 W
Danevang 222 29.03 N 96.13 W
Danewitz 264a 52.44 N 13.40 E
Danfeng 102 33.40 N 110.17 E
Danfengzhen 102 24.50 N 103.56 E
Danforth, Il., U.S. 216 40.49 N 87.59 W
Danforth, Me., U.S. 188 45.39 N 67.52 W
Danforth Hills ⋏ 200 40.15 N 108.00 W
Dang ≐ 102 40.30 N 94.42 E
Dānga, Bngl. 126 23.54 N 90.36 E
Dānga, India 272b 22.47 N 88.28 E
Danga ≐ 271c 1.27 N 103.43 E
Dangadiha 126 21.30 N 86.19 E
Dangan Liedao II 100 22.00 N 114.14 E
Dangara, Taj. 85 38.06 N 69.22 E
Dangara, Uzb. 85 40.35 N 70.54 E
Dangba 98 40.46 N 118.32 E
Dangchang 102 34.03 N 104.23 E
Dangcheng 98 38.46 N 114.34 E
Dange, Ang. 152 7.56 S 15.02 E
Dange, Ang. 152 8.09 S 14.46 E
Dange, Nig. 150 12.52 N 5.21 E
Dange-Iâ-Menha 152 9.32 S 14.39 E
Danger, Point > 171a 28.10 S 153.33 E
Danger Point > 158 34.40 S 19.17 E
Danggali Conservation Park ♦ 166 33.20 S 140.40 E
Danghe Nanshan ⋏ 102 38.53 N 96.11 E
Danghui 105 40.03 N 117.04 E
Dangila 144 11.16 N 36.50 E
Dangkou 106 31.32 N 120.34 E
Dango 140 10.00 N 24.45 E
Dan Gora 150 11.30 N 8.09 E
Dangori 120 27.40 N 95.35 E
Dangriga 232 16.58 N 88.13 W
Dangshan 98 34.26 N 116.21 E
Dangtu 100 31.34 N 118.30 E
Dan Gulbi 150 11.38 N 6.16 E
Dangyang 102 30.50 N 111.38 E
Dangyu 105 40.30 N 116.40 E
Dani 150 13.43 N 0.10 W
Dania 220 26.03 N 80.08 W
Daniel 200 42.51 N 110.04 W
Daniel, Mount ∧ 224 47.34 N 121.11 W
Daniel Boone Home ⊥ 219 38.39 N 90.52 W
Daniel Boone Homestead State Historic Site ⊥ 208 40.21 N 75.49 W
Daniel-Johnson, Barrage ◆[6] 186 50.39 N 68.44 W
Daniels 284b 39.26 N 77.03 W
Daniel's Harbour 186 50.14 N 57.35 W
Danielskuil 158 28.11 S 23.33 E
Danielson 207 41.48 N 71.53 W
Daniels Pass)(200 40.18 N 111.15 W
Daniels Run ≐ 284c 38.51 N 77.17 W
Danielsville, Ga., U.S. 192 34.07 N 83.13 W
Danielsville, Pa., U.S. 208 40.48 N 75.32 W
Danilov 80 58.12 N 40.12 E
Danilovka, Kaz. 86 52.23 N 70.39 E
Danilovka, Ross. 80 52.33 N 45.23 E
Danilovka, Ross. 80 50.21 N 44.06 E
Danilovo 82 55.40 N 38.46 E
Danilovskaja vozvyšennost' ⋏[1] 80 58.12 N 40.16 E
Danilovskoje 82 56.48 N 35.45 E
Daning, Zhg. 102 36.33 N 110.38 E
Daning, Zhg. 102 24.39 N 111.51 E
Daningbashi 85 38.45 N 75.04 E
Dänisch Nienhof 54 54.28 N 10.07 E
Daniupucun 104 41.23 N 122.37 E
Danja 150 11.21 N 7.31 E
Danjiangkou Shuiku ⊜[1] 102 32.37 N 111.30 E
Danjo-guntō II 92 32.02 N 128.23 E
Danjoutin 58 47.37 N 6.52 E
Dank 128 23.33 N 56.17 E
Dankama 150 13.20 N 7.44 E
Dankersen 52 52.17 N 8.58 E
Danki 82 54.55 N 37.34 E
Dankov 76 53.15 N 39.08 E
Dankova, Pik ∧ 85 41.05 N 77.38 E
Danleng, Zhg. 102 29.18 N 103.10 E
Danleng, Zhg. 102 29.58 N 103.31 E
Danleng, Zhg. 107 30.01 N 103.30 E
Danlí 236 14.00 N 86.35 W
Danmark → Denmark □[1] 26 56.00 N 10.00 E
Dannebrog 198 41.07 N 98.32 W
Dannemare 41 54.45 N 11.12 E
Dannemarie 58 47.38 N 7.08 E
Dannemora, Sve. 40 60.11 N 17.49 E
Dannemora, N.Y., U.S. 188 44.43 N 73.43 W
Dannenberg 54 53.06 N 11.05 E
Dannenreich 264a 52.19 N 13.45 E
Dannenwalde 54 53.04 N 13.11 E
Dannevirke 172 40.12 S 176.07 E
Dannewerk 41 54.29 N 9.31 E
Dannhauser 158 28.04 S 30.04 E
Dano 150 11.09 N 3.04 W
Danompari 112 0.09 N 115.02 E
Dañoso, Cabo > 254 48.50 S 67.13 W
Dan Ryan Woods ♦ 278 41.45 N 87.39 W
Dan Sai 110 17.17 N 101.09 E
Danshan 107 30.06 N 104.54 E
Danshui 100 22.49 N 114.27 E
Dansville, Mi., U.S. 216 42.34 N 84.18 W
Dansville, N.Y., U.S. 210 42.33 N 77.41 W
Dāntan 126 21.57 N 87.16 E
Dante 192 36.58 N 82.17 W
Dantewāra 122 18.54 N 81.21 E
Dantuzhen 106 32.12 N 119.31 E
Danube ≐ 22 45.20 N 29.40 E
Danube, Mouths of the ≐[1] 38 45.10 N 29.50 E
Danubio → Danube ≐ 22 45.20 N 29.40 E
Danubyu 110 17.15 N 95.35 E
Danvers, Il., U.S. 190 40.31 N 89.10 W
Danvers, Ma., U.S. 207 42.34 N 70.55 W
Danvers ≐ 283 42.32 N 70.53 W
Danville, P.Q., Can. 206 45.47 N 72.01 W
Danville, Ar., U.S. 194 35.03 N 93.23 W
Danville, Ca., U.S. 226 37.49 N 121.59 W
Danville, Ga., U.S. 192 32.36 N 83.14 W
Danville, Il., U.S. 194 40.07 N 87.37 W
Danville, In., U.S. 218 39.45 N 86.31 W
Danville, Ky., U.S. 194 37.42 N 84.46 W
Danville, Mo., U.S. 219 38.54 N 91.32 W
Danville, Oh., U.S. 214 40.26 N 82.15 W
Danville, Pa., U.S. 210 40.57 N 76.36 W
Danville, Vt., U.S. 188 44.25 N 72.07 W
Danville, Va., U.S. 192 36.35 N 79.23 W
Danville, Wa., U.S. 182 48.59 N 118.30 W
Danxian (Nada) 110 19.35 N 109.17 E
Danyang, Zhg. 100 26.22 N 119.30 E
Danyang, Zhg. 106 32.00 N 119.35 E
Danzig → Gdańsk 30 54.23 N 18.40 E
Dao 116 10.31 N 121.57 E
Dâo ≐, Port. 34 40.20 N 8.11 W
Dao ≐, Zhg. 100 30.44 N 114.39 E
Daocheng 102 29.06 N 100.38 E
Daodemiao 89 43.41 N 120.19 E
Daodi 105 39.32 N 118.11 E
Daoguanhe 100 30.54 N 114.57 E
Daohu 100 29.42 N 117.29 E
Daolazui 105 40.06 N 115.06 E
Daoliban 104 41.52 N 121.37 E
Daolin 100 27.59 N 112.42 E
Daolinggang 98 34.02 N 114.34 E
Daoliupu 107 30.12 N 105.09 E
Daomaguan 98 39.07 N 114.38 E
Daosa 124 26.53 N 76.20 E
Daoshiwu 106 30.18 N 118.57 E
Daoshuqiao 106 31.51 N 119.41 E
Daotiandi 89 48.53 N 130.03 E
Dao Timmi 146 20.32 N 13.33 E
Daotou 98 37.14 N 120.20 E
Daoukro 150 7.03 N 3.58 W
Daoulas 32 48.22 N 4.15 W
Daoura, Oued V 148 28.15 N 3.30 W
Daoxian 102 25.35 N 111.27 E
Daozhen 102 28.42 N 107.56 E
Daozi 89 45.00 N 123.43 E
Dapa 116 9.46 N 126.03 E
Dapango 150 10.52 N 0.12 E
Dapanzhuang 98 37.20 N 115.28 E
Dapaozi 89 45.27 N 122.07 E
Dapchi 146 12.28 N 11.32 E
Dapdap 116 14.14 N 122.15 E
Dapeng 100 22.34 N 114.29 E
Daphne 194 30.36 N 87.54 W
Dapiak, Mount ∧ 116 8.15 N 123.28 E
Daping, Zhg. 100 23.11 N 115.49 E
Daping, Zhg. 100 24.24 N 115.58 E
Dapingshan 102 25.30 N 109.39 E
Dapishi 100 26.30 N 112.54 E
Dapitan 116 8.39 N 123.25 E
Dapitan ≐ 116 8.38 N 123.25 E
Dapitan Bay c 116 8.40 N 123.23 E
Dapto 170 34.30 S 150.47 E
Dapu, Zhg. 98 40.34 N 124.12 E
Dapu, Zhg. 100 23.16 N 113.32 E
Dapu, Zhg. 106 31.19 N 119.56 E
Dapujie 100 27.01 N 112.46 E
Da Qaidam 102 37.53 N 95.07 E
Da Qaidam Hu ⊜ 102 37.50 N 95.00 E
Daqian 106 30.55 N 120.11 E
Daqiangmen 106 31.29 N 120.27 E
Daqiangzi 104 42.21 N 120.29 E
Daqiao, Zhg. 100 29.39 N 121.26 E
Daqiao, Zhg. 100 26.38 N 118.54 E
Daqiao, Zhg. 100 28.11 N 114.16 E
Daqiao, Zhg. 100 32.21 N 119.41 E
Daqiao, Zhg. 100 24.56 N 113.09 E
Daqiao, Zhg. 106 30.59 N 121.14 E
Daqiao, Zhg. 107 28.52 N 105.40 E
Daqiaojie 106 30.46 N 119.14 E
Daqiaokou 100 27.06 N 113.38 E
Daqiaotou 106 30.47 N 120.52 E
Daqiaozhai 102 25.21 N 106.15 E
Daqing 98 39.13 N 118.51 E
Daqing ≐ 105 39.04 N 116.55 E
Daqinggou, Zhg. 98 41.12 N 125.07 E
Daqinggou, Zhg. 98 41.16 N 114.10 E
Daqing Shan ∧, Zhg. 89 45.35 N 127.51 E
Daqing Shan ∧, Zhg. 104 42.03 N 123.45 E
Daqing Shan ∧, Zhg. 104 41.47 N 121.15 E
Daqiu 100 25.24 N 119.39 E
Daqqāq 140 12.56 N 26.58 E
Daquan 102 41.21 N 95.17 E
Daquanshan 98 40.14 N 113.47 E
Daquantou 105 39.31 N 114.46 E
Daquanyan 104 42.37 N 123.32 E
Dāqūf 142 28.24 N 30.38 E
Daqu Shan I 100 30.27 N 122.20 E
Dara, Sén. 150 15.21 N 15.29 W
Dar'ā, Sūrīy. 132 32.37 N 36.06 E
Dar'ā □[8] 132 33.00 N 36.10 E
Dārāb 128 28.45 N 54.34 E
Darāban 120 31.44 N 70.20 E
Darabani 38 48.11 N 26.35 E
Darāfisah 140 13.23 N 31.59 E
Daraga 116 11.54 N 123.52 E
Daragodleh 144 10.10 N 44.51 E
Daraina 157b 13.12 S 49.40 E
Darājīl 142 30.39 N 30.52 E
Daram Island I 116 11.38 N 124.47 E
Dārān 128 32.59 N 50.24 E
Daraoli ◆[8] 272c 19.11 N 72.48 E
Darap 112 1.13 S 112.03 E
Dār as-Salām 273c 29.59 N 31.13 E
Darasun 88 51.40 N 114.00 E
Daraut-Kurgan 85 39.33 N 72.13 E
Darave 272c 19.02 N 73.01 E
Darāw 140 24.25 N 32.56 E
Darawah 142 30.13 N 31.06 E
Dārayyā 132 33.27 N 36.15 E
Darazo 146 11.00 N 10.24 E
Darb Al-Ḥājj 142 30.10 N 31.33 E
Darb al-Ḥajj, Jabal ∧ 132 30.05 N 35.26 E
Darband 123 34.20 N 72.52 E
Darbāsīyah 130 37.04 N 40.39 E
Darbaza 85 41.35 N 69.02 E
Darbėnai 76 56.01 N 21.15 E
Dar-Beni-Kriche-Bahri 34 35.30 N 5.20 W
Darbhanga 124 26.10 N 85.54 E
Darbod (Taikang) 89 46.52 N 124.27 E
D'Arbonne, Bayou ≐ 194 32.34 N 92.09 W
Darburruk 144 9.44 N 44.31 E
Darby, Mt., U.S. 202 46.01 N 114.10 W
Darby, Pa., U.S. 208 39.55 N 75.15 W
Darby, Cape > 180 64.20 N 162.22 W
Darby Creek ≐ 285 39.52 N 75.18 W
Darbydale 218 39.51 N 83.11 W
Darčeli 84 42.27 N 41.42 E
Darchan 88 49.29 N 105.55 E
D'Archiac, Mount ∧ 172 43.28 S 170.35 E
D'Arcy 182 50.33 N 122.29 W
D'Arcy Island I 224 48.34 N 123.17 W
Darda 38 45.37 N 18.41 E
Dardadine 168a 33.14 S 116.50 E
Dardanelle, Ar., U.S. 194 35.13 N 93.09 W
Dardanelle, Ca., U.S. 226 38.20 N 119.50 W
Dardanelle Lake ⊜[1] 194 35.25 N 93.20 W
Dardanelles → Çanakkale Boğazı ꭒ 130 40.15 N 26.25 E
Dardanup 168a 33.24 S 115.45 E
Dardara 34 35.08 N 5.15 W
Dardenelles Cone ∧ 226 38.25 N 119.53 W
Dardenne Creek ≐ 219 38.52 N 90.32 W
Dardesheim 54 51.59 N 10.49 E
Dardistān □[9] 123 35.30 N 74.00 E
Dare 208 37.10 N 76.26 W
Darebin Creek ≐ 274b 37.47 S 145.02 E
Dareda 154 4.13 S 35.33 E
Dar-el-Beida → Casablanca 148 33.39 N 7.35 W
Darende 130 38.34 N 37.30 E
Darent ≐ 42 51.28 N 0.13 E
Daresbury 262 53.21 N 2.38 W
Dar es Salaam 154 6.48 S 39.17 E
Dar es Salaam □[4] 154 6.30 S 39.25 E
Daressalam → Dar es Salaam 154 6.48 S 39.17 E
Darfeld 52 52.01 N 7.16 E
Darfo 64 45.53 N 10.11 E
Dārfūr ash-Shamālīyah □[4] 140 16.00 N 25.25 E
Dargai 123 34.30 N 71.54 E
Dargan-Ata 72 40.29 N 62.10 E
Dargaville 172 35.56 S 173.53 E
Dargeçit 130 37.33 N 41.44 E
Dargol 150 13.55 N 1.15 E
Dargol ≐ 150 13.53 N 1.33 E
Dargun 54 53.54 N 12.51 E
Darhan Muminggan Lianheqi 102 41.50 N 110.27 E
Dari 140 5.48 N 30.21 E
Dāriāpur 126 23.36 N 89.27 E
Darıca 130 40.45 N 29.23 E
Darie Hills ⋏ 144 8.21 N 47.16 E
Darién, Col. 246 3.56 N 76.31 W
Darien, Ct., U.S. 207 41.04 N 73.28 W
Darien, Ga., U.S. 192 31.22 N 81.26 W
Darien, Il., U.S. 278 41.45 N 87.58 W
Darien, N.Y., U.S. 210 42.54 N 78.21 W
Darien, Wi., U.S. 216 42.36 N 88.42 W
Darien, Parque Nacional ♦ 246 7.40 N 77.40 W
Darién, Serranía del ⋏ 246 8.20 N 77.22 W
Darien Center 210 42.54 N 78.23 W
Darien Lakes State Park ♦ 210 42.55 N 78.25 W
Dariense, Cordillera ⋏ 236 12.55 N 85.30 W
Dariganga 102 45.18 N 113.52 E
Darigayos Point > 116 16.50 N 120.20 E
Dariv 88 46.57 N 93.38 E
Darjevka 83 47.42 N 39.41 E
Dārjiling 124 27.02 N 88.16 E
Darjinskij 86 49.04 N 72.56 E
Darjinskoje 80 51.20 N 51.44 E
Darkan 168a 33.20 S 116.44 E
Darke □[6] 218 40.06 N 84.38 W
Darke Peak 166 33.28 S 136.12 E
Darkhāna 123 30.39 N 72.11 E
Dar Khazīneh 128 31.54 N 48.59 E
Dark Head > 241h 13.17 N 61.16 W
Darkin ≐ 168a 32.00 S 116.14 E
Darkūsh 130 35.59 N 36.23 E
Darlag 102 33.48 N 99.52 E
Darley Woods 285 39.49 N 75.28 W
Darling, S. Afr. 158 33.23 S 18.23 E
Darling, Ms., U.S. 194 34.21 N 90.16 W
Darling ≐ 166 34.07 S 141.55 E
Darling, Lake ⊜[1] 198 48.35 N 101.40 W
Darling Downs ◆[1] 166 27.30 S 150.30 E
Darlingford 184 49.12 N 98.22 W
Darling Range ⋏ 162 31.25 S 116.00 E
Darlington, Austl. 169 38.00 S 143.03 E
Darlington, Eng., U.K. 44 54.31 N 1.34 W
Darlington, Md., U.S. 208 39.38 N 76.12 W
Darlington, Pa., U.S. 214 40.49 N 80.26 W
Darlington, Pa., U.S. 285 39.54 N 75.28 W
Darlington, S.C., U.S. 192 34.17 N 79.52 W
Darlington, Wi., U.S. 190 42.40 N 90.07 W
Darlington Brook ≐ 276 41.05 N 74.11 W
Darlington Corners 285 39.55 N 75.34 W
Darlington Range ⋏ 171a 27.50 S 153.15 E
Darlot, Lake ⊜ 162 27.48 S 121.35 E
Darłowo 30 54.26 N 16.23 E
Darmagī, Kūh-e ∧ 128 26.35 N 58.54 E
Darmstadt 56 49.53 N 8.40 E
Darmstadt □[5] 56 49.45 N 8.40 E
Darnah 146 32.46 N 22.39 E
Darnall 158 29.23 S 31.18 E
Darnétal 50 49.27 N 1.09 E
Darney 58 48.05 N 6.03 E
Darnick 166 32.51 S 143.37 E
Darnley, Cape > 9 67.43 S 69.30 E
Darnley Bay c 176 69.35 N 123.30 W
Daroca 34 41.07 N 1.25 W
Darodih 126 23.14 N 86.27 E
Daror 144 8.14 N 44.42 E
Dar-Ould-Zidouh 148 32.22 N 6.49 W
Darou Mousti 150 15.03 N 16.03 W
Darovoje 82 54.34 N 38.22 E
Darr ≐ 166 23.39 S 143.50 E
Darra 171a 27.34 S 152.58 E
Darragh 279b 40.16 N 79.41 W
Darrah, Mount ∧ 182 49.28 N 114.35 W
Darregueira 252 37.42 S 63.10 W
Darreh Gaz 128 37.27 N 59.07 E
Darrington 224 48.15 N 121.36 W
Darrouzett 196 36.27 N 100.20 W
Darryl Gardens 284b 39.25 N 76.25 W
Dārsana 126 23.32 N 88.52 E
Darscheid 56 50.12 N 6.53 E
Darss >[1] 54 54.25 N 12.31 E
Darsser Ort > 54 54.29 N 12.31 E
Dart ≐ 42 50.20 N 3.33 W
Dart, Cape > 9 73.06 S 126.20 W
Dār Ta'izzah 130 36.17 N 36.51 E
Dartford 42 51.27 N 0.14 E
Dartford □[8] 260 51.26 N 0.15 E
Dartford Tunnel ◆[5] 260 51.28 N 0.16 E
Dartmoor 166 37.55 S 141.17 E
Dartmoor ◆[3] 42 50.35 N 3.55 W
Dartmoor National Park ♦ 42 50.37 N 3.52 W
Dartmouth, N.S., Can. 186 44.40 N 63.34 W
Dartmouth, Eng., U.K. 42 50.21 N 3.35 W
Dartmouth ≐ 186 48.53 N 64.34 W
Dartmouth, Lake ⊜ 166 26.04 S 145.18 E
Dartmouth Woods 285 39.50 N 75.31 W
Darton 44 53.36 N 1.32 W
Daru, Pap. N. Gui. 164 9.04 S 143.21 E
Daru, S.L. 150 7.59 N 10.50 W
Daruvar 36 45.36 N 17.13 E
Darvaza 128 40.11 N 58.24 E
Darvazskij chrebet ⋏ 85 38.30 N 71.15 E
Darvel 46 55.37 N 4.18 W
Darvinskij Zapovednik ◆[4] 76 58.50 N 37.40 E
Darwāzahgêy 120 31.48 N 67.44 E
Darwen 44 53.42 N 2.28 W
Darwen ≐ 262 53.45 N 2.41 W
Darwendale 154 17.43 S 30.33 E
Dārwha 122 20.19 N 77.46 E
Darwin, Arg. 254 39.12 S 65.46 W
Darwin, Austl. 164 12.28 S 130.50 E
Darwin, Bahía c 254 45.27 S 74.40 W
Darwin, Cordillera ⋏ 254 54.40 S 70.00 W
Darwin, Isla I 246a 1.39 N 92.00 W
Darwin, Volcán ∧[1] 246a 0.10 S 91.18 W
Darwin River 164 12.49 S 130.58 E
Daryābād 124 26.53 N 81.33 E
Darya Khān 123 31.48 N 71.06 E
Daryāpur 120 20.56 N 77.20 E
Darzāb 120 35.58 N 65.22 E
Darzo 64 45.51 N 10.33 E
Dār Zubi 140 13.07 N 23.40 E
Dās 123 35.09 N 75.05 E
Dās I 128 25.09 N 52.53 E
Dasanjiazi 104 42.31 N 122.54 E
Dašava 78 49.16 N 24.01 E
Daš Balbar 88 49.31 N 114.21 E
Dasburg 56 50.03 N 6.07 E
Dase → Dese 144 11.05 N 39.41 E
Dašev 78 49.00 N 29.26 E
Dasha ≐ 98 38.20 N 115.22 E
Dashafa 105 39.19 N 116.19 E
Dashalitu 104 42.31 N 122.30 E
Dashan 98 38.02 N 117.39 E
Dashankou 105 40.17 N 115.49 E
Dashanpu 107 29.25 N 104.49 E
Dashaping 100 29.24 N 113.51 E
Dashengfenchang 106 31.53 N 121.34 E
Dashengpu 104 41.13 N 121.02 E
Dashentang 105 39.13 N 117.56 E
Dashetai 102 40.58 N 109.19 E
Dashi 107 30.39 N 105.37 E
Dashi ≐ 105 39.35 N 116.05 E
Dashields Dam ◆[6] 214 40.33 N 80.12 W
Dashiqiao, Zhg. 100 33.57 N 113.53 E
Dashiqiao, Zhg. 104 41.52 N 123.17 E
Dashiqiao, Zhg. 107 30.07 N 106.12 E
Dashiqiao, Zhg. 107 30.28 N 106.29 E
Dashitou, Zhg. 89 43.19 N 128.28 E
Dashitou, Zhg. 102 42.49 N 95.19 E
Dashizhai 89 46.16 N 121.25 E
Dashlūṭ 142 27.34 N 30.42 E
Dash Point 224 47.19 N 122.26 W
Dasht ≐ 128 25.10 N 61.40 E
Dashu 106 31.13 N 120.56 E
Dashun 100 28.06 N 119.52 E
Dashutang 102 23.00 N 103.55 E
Dashuwan 105 40.37 N 117.19 E
Dasi (Huangfansi) 102 38.15 N 100.22 E
Dasiji 100 33.48 N 115.55 E
Dašinčilen 88 47.51 N 104.03 E
Dasing 60 48.23 N 11.03 E
Dasizhan 89 45.53 N 130.24 E
Daska 123 32.20 N 74.21 E
Daškesan 84 40.30 N 46.04 E
Daskop 158 33.44 S 22.43 E
Daškovka 76 53.44 N 30.13 E
Dasmina 126 22.17 N 90.35 E
Dasol 116 15.59 N 119.52 E
Dasol Bay c 116 15.53 N 119.51 E
Dassalan Island I 116 6.45 N 121.28 E
Dassel, Dtsch. 52 51.48 N 9.41 E
Dassel, Mn., U.S. 190 45.04 N 94.18 W
Dasseneiland I 158 33.26 S 18.04 E
Dasserat, Lac ⊜ 190 48.16 N 79.25 W
Dassiefontein 158 31.35 S 24.25 E
Dassow 54 53.50 N 10.59 E
Dasswang 60 49.09 N 11.40 E
Dastakert 84 39.23 N 46.02 E
Dastgardān 128 34.19 N 56.51 E
Daštidžum 85 38.01 N 70.12 E
Daštioburdon 85 39.24 N 69.04 E
Dastjerd 128 34.33 N 50.15 E
Dasūa 123 31.49 N 75.38 E
Dāsuria 126 24.07 N 89.08 E
Datachang 107 28.55 N 104.21 E
Datagenoyang 112 2.03 N 115.10 E
Datai 105 39.58 N 115.54 E
Dataizi 104 41.17 N 121.46 E
Datan, Zhg. 98 41.35 N 116.00 E
Datan, Zhg. 98 39.31 N 122.11 E
Datang, Zhg. 100 24.47 N 113.43 E
Datang, Zhg. 100 25.17 N 114.56 E
Datang, Zhg. 102 22.23 N 108.23 E
Datang, Zhg. 102 24.11 N 109.00 E
Datça 130 36.45 N 27.40 E
Datchet 260 51.29 N 0.34 W
Datchet Reservoir ⊜[1] 260 51.29 N 0.33 W
Date 92a 42.27 N 140.51 E
Date Creek ≐ 200 34.13 N 113.29 W
Datia 124 25.40 N 78.28 E
Datian, Zhg. 100 25.42 N 117.49 E
Datian, Zhg. 100 24.06 N 116.19 E
Datian Ding ∧ 102 22.17 N 111.13 E
Datianwei 100 25.54 N 115.10 E
Dativli 272c 19.11 N 73.03 E
D'at'kovo 76 53.36 N 34.20 E
D'atlovіči 76 52.20 N 26.50 E
D'atlovo, Bela. 76 53.28 N 25.24 E
D'atlovo, Ross. 82 56.14 N 36.16 E
Datong, Zhg. 89 46.03 N 124.50 E
Datong, Zhg. 100 30.48 N 117.45 E
Datong, Zhg. 100 32.50 N 118.52 E
Datong, Zhg. 102 37.03 N 101.45 E
Datong, Zhg. 102 40.05 N 113.18 E
Datong ≐ 102 36.20 N 102.55 E
Datong Shan ⋏ 102 38.00 N 99.30 E
Datongzhen 106 32.12 N 121.19 E
Datoushan 98 41.50 N 117.08 E
Dātra 272b 22.58 N 88.16 E
Datta 89 49.18 N 140.22 E
Dattapāra 126 23.01 N 90.53 E
Dattapukur 126 22.45 N 88.33 E
Dattapulia 126 23.14 N 88.43 E
Datteln 52 51.40 N 7.23 E
Datteln-Hamm-Kanal ≍ 263 51.39 N 7.21 E
Dattilo 70 37.58 N 12.39 E
Datu, Tanjung > 112 2.05 N 109.39 E
Datuan 106 30.58 N 121.44 E
Datumakuta 112 2.32 N 117.51 E
Datun, Zhg. 89 43.49 N 125.12 E
Datun, Zhg. 98 40.37 N 119.57 E
Datun, Zhg. 104 40.59 N 122.55 E
Datuopu 100 28.03 N 112.58 E
Datu Piang 116 7.01 N 124.30 E
Daua (Dawa) ≐ 144 4.11 N 42.06 E
Daudkāndi 126 23.32 N 90.43 E
Dāud Khel 123 32.53 N 71.34 E
Daudnagar 124 25.02 N 84.24 E
Daugai 76 54.22 N 24.20 E
Daugård 41 55.44 N 9.43 E
Daugava (Zapadnaja Dvina) ≐ 76 57.04 N 24.03 E
Daugavpils 76 55.53 N 26.32 E
Dauin 116 9.12 N 123.16 E
Daulatabad 126 24.08 N 88.22 E
Daulatkhān 126 22.38 N 90.49 E
Daulatpur, Bngl. 126 24.00 N 88.52 E
Daulatpur, Bngl. 126 22.53 N 89.31 E
Daulatpur, Bngl. 126 23.58 N 89.50 E
Daulatpur, India 272b 22.26 N 88.18 E
Daulatpur, Pāk. 120 26.30 N 67.58 E
Daulatpur ◆[8] 272a 28.44 N 77.06 E
Daule, Ec. 246 0.24 N 80.00 W
Daule, Ec. 246 1.50 S 79.56 W
Daule, India 272c 19.10 N 73.03 E
Daule ≐ 246 2.10 S 79.52 W
Daultāla 123 33.12 N 73.09 E
Daulton Creek ≐ 226 37.04 N 119.59 W
Daun 56 50.11 N 6.50 E
Daund 122 18.28 N 74.36 E
Daung Kyun I 110 12.14 N 98.05 E
Daunia, Monti della ⋏ 68 41.27 N 15.06 E
Dauphin, Mb., Can. 184 51.09 N 100.03 W
Dauphin, Pa., U.S. 208 40.22 N 76.55 W
Dauphin □[6] 208 40.15 N 76.52 W
Dauphin ≐ 184 51.58 N 98.04 W
Dauphiné □[9] 62 44.50 N 6.00 E
Dauphin Island 194 30.15 N 88.07 W
Dauphin Island I 194 30.14 N 88.12 W
Dauphin Lake ⊜ 184 51.17 N 99.48 W
Daura 150 13.02 N 8.21 E
Daurija 88 49.56 N 116.52 E
Daurskoje 86 55.14 N 92.05 E
Dausenau 56 50.20 N 7.45 E
D'Auteuil, Lac ⊜ 186 50.38 N 61.17 W
Dautphetal 56 50.51 N 8.32 E
Dāvangere 122 14.28 N 75.55 E
Davant 194 29.37 N 89.51 W
Davao 116 7.04 N 125.36 E
Davao □[4] 116 7.40 N 125.50 E
Davao ≐ 116 7.04 N 125.37 E
Davao del Sur □[4] 116 6.50 N 125.20 E
Davao Gulf c 116 6.40 N 125.55 E
Davao Oriental □[4] 116 7.30 N 126.30 E
Dāvar Panāh 128 27.21 N 62.21 E
Dāvarzan 128 36.23 N 56.50 E
Davegoriale 144 8.45 N 44.50 E
Davel 158 26.24 S 29.40 E
Daveluyville 206 46.12 N 72.08 W
Davenda 88 53.33 N 119.18 E
Davenham 262 53.14 N 2.31 W
Davenport, Ca., U.S. 226 37.00 N 122.11 W
Davenport, Fl., U.S. 220 28.09 N 81.36 W
Davenport, Ia., U.S. 190 41.31 N 90.34 W
Davenport, Ne., U.S. 198 40.18 N 97.48 W
Davenport, N.Y., U.S. 210 42.28 N 74.51 W
Davenport, Ok., U.S. 196 35.42 N 96.45 W
Davenport, Wa., U.S. 202 47.39 N 118.08 W
Davenport, Mount ∧ 162 22.23 S 130.51 E
Davenport Downs 166 24.08 S 141.07 E
Davenport Range ⋏ 162 20.47 S 134.48 E
Daventry 42 52.16 N 1.09 W

Symbols in the index entries represent the broad categories identified in the key at the right. Symbols with superior numbers (⋏[1]) identify subcategories (see complete key on page *I · 1*).

Symbole im Register stellen die rechts im Schlüssel erklärten Kategorien dar. Symbole mit hochgestellten Ziffern (⋏[1]) bezeichnen Unterabteilungen einer Kategorie (vgl. vollständiger Schlüssel auf Seite *I · 1*).

Los símbolos incluidos en el texto del índice representan las grandes categorías identificadas con la clave a la derecha. Los símbolos con numeros en su parte superior (⋏[1]) identifican las subcategorías (véase la clave completa en la página *I · 1*).

Les symboles de l'index représentent les catégories indiquées dans la légende à droite. Les symboles suivis d'un indice (⋏[1]) représentent des sous-catégories (voir légende complète à la page *I · 1*).

Os símbolos incluídos no texto do índice representam as grandes categorias identificadas com a chave à direita. Os símbolos com números em sua parte superior (⋏[1]) identificam as subcategorias (veja-se a chave completa à página *I · 1*).

∧ Mountain	Berg	Montaña	Montagne	Montanha
⋏ Mountains	Gebirge	Montañas	Montagnes	Montanhas
)(Pass	Paß	Paso	Col	Passo
V Valley, Canyon	Tal, Cañon	Valle, Cañón	Vallée, Canyon	Vale, Canhão
⩡ Plain	Ebene	Llano	Plaine	Planície
> Cape	Kap	Cabo	Cap	Cabo
I Island	Insel	Isla	Île	Ilha
II Islands	Inseln	Islas	Îles	Ilhas
≐ Other Topographic Features	Andere Topographische Objekte	Otros Elementos Topográficos	Autres données topographiques	Outros acidentes topográficos

ESPAÑOL Nombre	Página	Lat.°′	Long.°′ W = Oeste

FRANÇAIS Nom	Page	Lat.°′	Long.°′ W = Ouest

PORTUGUÊS Nome	Página	Lat.°′	Long.°′ W = Oeste

Davey, Port ⊂ 166 43.19 S 145.55 E
Daveyton 273d 26.09 S 28.25 E
David 236 8.26 N 82.26 W
David City 198 41.15 N 97.07 W
David-Gorodok 78 52.03 N 27.14 E
Davido-Nikol'skoje 83 48.30 N 39.50 E
Davids Island I 276 40.53 N 73.46 W
Davidson, Sk., Can. 184 51.16 N 105.59 W
Davidson, N.C., U.S. 192 35.29 N 80.50 W
Davidson, Ok., U.S. 196 34.14 N 99.04 W
Davidson, Mount ∧ 170 33.09 S 150.07 E
Davidson Creek ≃ 222 30.21 N 96.27 W
Davidson Heights 214 40.35 N 80.15 W
Davidson Lake ◎ 184 53.47 N 99.37 W
Davidson Mountains ✗ 180 68.45 N 142.10 W
Davidson Park ♦ 274a 33.45 S 151.12 E
Davidsville 214 40.14 N 78.56 W
Davie 220 26.03 N 80.13 W
Davies, Mount ∧ 162 26.14 S 129.16 E
Davignab 158 27.32 S 19.48 E
Davila 116 18.29 N 120.35 E
Davilla 222 30.47 N 97.17 W
Davington 44 55.18 N 3.12 W
Davin Lake ◎ 184 56.50 N 103.40 W
Davinópolis 255 15.58 S 50.08 W
Daviot 46 57.25 N 4.08 W
Davis, Ca., U.S. 226 38.32 N 121.44 W
Davis, N.C., U.S. 192 34.47 N 76.27 W
Davis, Ok., U.S. 196 34.30 N 97.07 W
Davis, W.V., U.S. 188 39.07 N 79.27 W
Davis ≃ 162 21.42 S 121.05 E
Davis ᴜ³ 9 68.35 S 77.58 E
Davis, Mount ∧ 188 39.47 N 79.10 W
Davis Bay ⊂ 9 66.08 S 134.05 E
Davisboro 192 32.58 N 82.36 W
Davisburg 216 42.45 N 83.33 W
Davis City 190 40.38 N 93.48 W
Davis Cove 186 47.40 N 54.18 W
Davis Creek ≃, Mi., U.S. 281 42.27 N 83.43 W
Davis Creek ≃, Mo., U.S. 219 39.12 N 91.53 W
Davis Dam 200 35.10 N 114.33 W
Davis Dam -◆-⁶ 200 35.11 N 114.21 W
Davis Island I 279b 40.29 N 80.05 W
Davis Lake ◎ 278 42.16 N 88.05 W
Davis-Monthan Air Force Base ■ 200 32.11 N 110.53 W
Davis Mountains ✗ 196 30.35 N 104.00 W
Davison 216 43.02 N 83.31 W
Davis Park 210 40.42 N 72.59 W
Davis Point ≻ 282 38.03 N 122.15 W
Davis Sea ≉² 9 66.00 S 92.00 E
Davis Strait ꓤ 176 67.00 N 57.00 W
Davlekanovo 86 54.13 N 55.03 E
Davo ≃ 150 5.00 N 6.08 W
Davoli 68 38.39 N 16.29 E
Davos 58 46.48 N 9.50 E
Davron 261 48.52 N 1.57 E
Davst 86 50.36 N 92.28 E
Davulga 130 38.58 N 31.23 E
Davutlar 130 37.43 N 27.17 E
Davy 192 37.28 N 81.39 W
Davydkovo, Ross. 82 56.17 N 36.49 E
Davydkovo, Ross. 265b 55.35 N 37.12 E
Davydov, gora ∧ 88 52.34 N 107.25 E
Davydov Brod 78 47.14 N 33.12 E
Davydovka 78 51.10 N 39.25 E
Davydovo 82 55.37 N 38.52 E
Davydovskoje 82 55.52 N 36.48 E
Davyhulme 262 53.27 N 2.22 W
Dawa, Zhg. 104 41.00 N 122.03 E
Dawa, Zhg. 104 41.54 N 123.32 E
Dawa (Daua) ≃ 144 4.11 N 42.06 E
Dawan 100 22.47 N 114.05 E
Dawaki 150 12.06 N 8.20 E
Dawan 102 23.52 N 109.29 E
Dawang 98 36.58 N 118.31 E
Dawangcun 106 30.45 N 118.59 E
Dawangdian 105 39.04 N 115.26 E
Dawangdong 105 38.53 N 116.21 E
Dawangjia Dao I 98 39.27 N 123.07 E
Dawangsangou 104 41.43 N 121.36 E
Dawangzhuang 269b 31.22 N 121.25 E
Dawangzhuang, Zhg. 105 39.23 N 116.28 E
Dawangzhuang, Zhg. 105 38.59 N 115.56 E
Dawāsir, Wādī ad- ᐯ 144 20.24 N 46.29 E
Dawatun 104 41.05 N 121.01 E
Dawei (Tavoy) 110 14.05 N 98.12 E
Daweizhuang 105 39.34 N 116.53 E
Daweiziqou 104 42.38 N 123.09 E
Dawen ≃ 98 35.38 N 116.24 E
Dawenkou 98 35.59 N 117.07 E
Dawera, Pulau I 164 7.44 S 130.00 E
Dawes Park ♦ 278 42.03 N 87.40 W
Dawlan 110 16.44 N 98.01 E
Dawlish 42 50.35 N 3.28 W
Dawn 208 37.50 N 77.22 W
Dawna Range ✗ 110 16.50 N 98.15 E
Dawqah 144 19.36 N 40.54 E
Dawrah 140 12.22 N 24.19 E
Daws Heath 260 51.34 N 0.37 E
Dawson, Yk., Can. 180 64.04 N 139.25 W
Dawson, Ga., U.S. 192 31.46 N 84.26 W
Dawson, Il., U.S. 219 39.51 N 89.28 W
Dawson, Mn., U.S. 198 44.55 N 96.03 W
Dawson, Ne., U.S. 198 40.07 N 95.49 W
Dawson, Tx., U.S. 222 31.53 N 96.42 W
Dawson ≃ 166 23.38 S 149.46 E
Dawson, Isla I 254 53.55 S 70.45 W
Dawson, Mount ∧ 182 51.09 N 117.25 W
Dawson Bay ⊂ 184 52.55 N 100.50 W
Dawson Creek 182 55.46 N 120.14 W
Dawson Inlet ⊂ 176 61.50 N 93.25 W
Dawson-Lambton Glacier ≉ 9 76.15 S 27.30 W
Dawson Range ✗, Austl. 166 24.20 S 149.45 E
Dawson Range ✗, Yk., Can. 180 62.40 N 139.00 W
Dawson Ridge 214 40.42 N 80.22 W
Dawson Springs 194 37.10 N 87.41 W
Dawsonville 192 34.25 N 84.07 W
Dawu, Zhg. 100 31.34 N 114.06 E
Dawu, Zhg. 102 31.07 N 101.08 E
Dawudapu 104 41.36 N 123.03 E
Dawuji 271a 39.51 N 116.30 E
Dawujiawopeng 104 41.55 N 122.29 E
Dawujiazi 104 42.16 N 121.52 E
Dawulaba 104 42.13 N 122.23 E
Dawulah 104 41.56 N 121.05 E
Dax 32 43.43 N 1.03 W
Daxian 102 31.18 N 107.30 E
Daxin, Zhg. 100 33.54 N 118.30 E
Daxin, Zhg. 102 22.50 N 107.26 E
Daxing, Zhg. 98 39.44 N 116.20 E
Daxing (Huangcun), Zhg. 105 39.44 N 116.20 E
Daxing, Zhg. 106 31.50 N 121.40 E
Daxingchang 107 30.17 N 103.26 E
Daxingcun 106 31.45 N 121.40 E
Daxingzhai 102 23.13 N 102.21 E
Daxinji 100 34.03 N 119.28 E
Daxinzhuang, Zhg. 105 40.23 N 116.44 E
Daxinzhuang, Zhg. 105 39.26 N 118.20 E
Daxiyang 106 30.21 N 121.58 E
Daxu, Zhg. 100 29.32 N 121.52 E
Daxu, Zhg. 102 25.09 N 110.21 E
Daxue Shan ✗ 102 30.10 N 101.50 E
Daxujia 98 34.18 N 117.34 E
Dayakou 102 22.46 N 100.18 E
Dayanchi 102 27.41 N 101.55 E
Dayang, Zhg. 98 36.04 N 116.31 E
Dayang, Zhg. 100 25.56 N 118.48 E
Dayang ≃ 98 39.54 N 123.40 E
Dayang Bunting, Pulau I 114 6.14 N 99.48 E
Dayangcha 98 42.04 N 126.43 E
Dayanggou 104 41.14 N 123.51 E
Dayang Shan I 106 30.35 N 122.00 E
Dayangshu 89 49.45 N 124.35 E
Dayao, Zhg. 100 27.59 N 113.42 E
Dayao, Zhg. 102 25.43 N 101.13 E
Dayaoshan 102 24.05 N 110.17 E
Daya Wan ⊂ 100 22.37 N 114.40 E
Dayboro 171a 27.11 S 152.50 E
Daye 100 30.06 N 114.57 E
Dayghar 272c 19.09 N 73.03 E
Day Heights 218 39.11 N 84.14 W
Dayi 107 30.37 N 103.31 E
Dayiji 100 32.32 N 119.14 E
Daying, Zhg. 98 34.27 N 113.59 E
Daying, Zhg. 98 39.53 N 123.07 E
Daying, Zhg. 98 39.19 N 113.46 E
Daying, Zhg. 98 37.19 N 115.43 E
Daying, Zhg. 100 33.59 N 112.51 E
Daying, Zhg. 105 39.05 N 116.08 E
Daying (Taping) ≃ 102 24.17 N 97.14 E
Dayingzi, Zhg. 98 41.19 N 118.19 E
Dayingzi, Zhg. 98 41.28 N 120.21 E
Dayingzi, Zhg. 104 41.08 N 122.50 E
Dayiqiao 106 31.44 N 120.45 E
Day Island 224 47.15 N 122.33 W
Day Lake ◎ 224 48.23 N 121.58 W
Daylesford 169 37.21 S 144.09 E
Daymán ≃ 252 31.30 S 58.02 W
Daym Zubayr 140 7.43 N 26.13 E
Dayong, Zhg. 100 22.28 N 113.16 E
Dayong, Zhg. 102 29.06 N 110.29 E
Dayou 98 34.12 N 119.52 E
Dayr, Jabal ad- ∧ 140 12.27 N 30.42 E
Dayr Abū Sa'īd 132 32.30 N 35.41 E
Dayr al-Balah 132 31.25 N 34.21 E
Dayr al-Ghuṣūn 132 32.21 N 35.05 E
Dayr 'Alī 132 33.17 N 36.18 E
Dayr 'Allā 132 32.12 N 35.37 E
Dayr 'Aṭīyah 130 34.06 N 36.46 E
Dayr az-Zawr 130 35.20 N 40.09 E
Dayr az-Zawr □⁸ 130 35.00 N 40.30 E
Dayr Dibwān 132 31.55 N 35.16 E
Dayr Ḥāfir 130 36.09 N 37.42 E
Dayr Jabal At-Tayr 142 28.17 N 30.45 E
Dayr Mawās 142 27.38 N 30.51 E
Dayr Qānūn 132 33.36 N 36.08 E
Dayr Sharaf 132 32.15 N 35.11 E
Dayrūt, Miṣr 142 27.33 N 30.49 E
Dayrūt, Miṣr 142 31.13 N 30.30 E
Dayrūt ash-Sharīf 142 27.35 N 30.49 E
Days Island I 284b 39.24 N 76.22 W
Daysland 182 52.52 N 112.15 W
Day Star Indian Reserve -◆-⁴ 184 51.43 N 104.14 W
Dayton, Il., U.S. 216 41.23 N 88.47 W
Dayton, In., U.S. 216 40.22 N 86.46 W
Dayton, Ia., U.S. 190 42.15 N 94.04 W
Dayton, Ky., U.S. 218 39.06 N 84.28 W
Dayton, Mi., U.S. 216 41.48 N 86.26 W
Dayton, Nv., U.S. 226 39.14 N 119.35 W
Dayton, N.J., U.S. 276 40.22 N 74.30 W
Dayton, N.Y., U.S. 210 42.25 N 78.58 W
Dayton, Oh., U.S. 218 39.45 N 84.11 W
Dayton, Or., U.S. 224 45.13 N 123.04 W
Dayton, Pa., U.S. 214 40.52 N 79.14 W
Dayton, Tn., U.S. 194 35.29 N 85.00 W
Dayton, Tx., U.S. 222 30.02 N 94.53 W
Dayton, Va., U.S. 188 38.24 N 78.56 W
Dayton, Wa., U.S. 202 46.19 N 117.58 W
Dayton, Wy., U.S. 202 44.52 N 107.15 W
Daytona Beach 192 29.12 N 81.01 W
Dayton Municipal Airport ≍ 218 39.54 N 84.13 W
Dayu, Indon. 112 1.59 S 115.04 E
Dayu, Zhg. 100 25.24 N 114.22 E
Dayuba 107 29.15 N 103.34 E
Dayu Ling ✗ 100 25.20 N 114.16 E
Da Yunhe (Grand Canal) ≋ 90 32.12 N 119.31 E
Dayu Shan I, Zhg. 100 26.57 N 120.21 E
Dayu Shan I, Zhg. 106 30.19 N 121.58 E
Dayushupu 104 41.32 N 121.24 E
Dayville, Ct., U.S. 207 41.50 N 71.53 W
Dayville, Or., U.S. 202 44.28 N 119.32 W
Dazaifu ⊥ 96 33.31 N 130.31 E
Dazaoliyingzi 104 42.07 N 121.20 E
Dazaomiao 106 32.06 N 121.29 E
Dazhang ≃ 100 25.56 N 119.12 E
Dazhangzi 98 40.38 N 118.07 E
Dazhaotai 104 41.14 N 123.03 E
Dazhengjiatun 98 39.37 N 122.52 E
Dazhengzhuangzi 105 40.29 N 117.08 E
Dazhi 100 34.29 N 113.17 E
Dazhiba 102 27.09 N 99.52 E
Dazhifang 104 41.21 N 123.12 E
Dazhou 100 28.53 N 118.58 E
Dazhu 102 30.48 N 107.12 E
Dazhuangke 105 40.32 N 115.42 E
Dazhubao 107 28.59 N 103.38 E
Dazhuyuan 100 23.43 N 115.57 E
Dazifangshen 104 42.27 N 124.12 E
Dazilling 104 41.21 N 123.16 E
Daziying 104 41.42 N 123.36 E
Dazkırı 130 37.55 N 29.52 E
Dazu 107 29.43 N 105.42 E
Dazui 100 30.16 N 114.02 E
De Aar 158 30.39 S 24.00 E
Dead ≃, Me., U.S. 188 45.20 N 69.58 W
Dead ≃, Mi., U.S. 190 46.34 N 87.24 W
Dead ≃, N.J., U.S. 276 40.39 N 74.31 W
Deadhorse 180 70.11 N 148.27 W
Dead Horse Point State Park ♦ 200 38.28 N 109.44 W
Deadman 182 50.45 N 120.55 W
Deadman Brook ≃ 276 41.08 N 73.22 W
Deadman Creek ≃ 226 37.12 N 120.42 W
Deadman Hill ∧ 162 23.48 S 119.25 E
Deadman's Cay 238 23.14 N 75.14 W
Deadmans Creek ≃ 274a 33.58 S 151.00 E
Deadman's Creek Indian Reserve -◆-⁴ 182 50.49 N 121.00 W
Dead Run ≃ 284c 38.57 N 77.11 W
Dead Sea (Al-Bahr al-Mayyit) (Yam HaMelah) ◎ 132 31.30 N 35.30 E
Deadwood 198 44.22 N 103.43 W
Deadwood Lake ◎ 202 44.05 N 115.40 W
Deagan Island I 116 12.15 N 123.51 E
Deakin 162 30.46 S 128.58 E
Deakin, Mount ∧² 162 17.38 S 130.48 E
Deakin Bay ⊂ 162 68.23 S 150.10 E
Deal, Eng., U.K. 42 51.14 N 1.24 E
Deal, N.J., U.S. 208 40.15 N 74.00 W
Deale 208 38.46 N 76.33 W
Dealesville 158 28.40 S 25.37 E
Deal Island 208 38.09 N 75.56 W
Deal Island I 208 38.09 N 75.56 W
Deam Lake ◎¹ 218 38.28 N 85.51 W
De'an 100 29.20 N 115.46 E
Dean ≃, B.C., Can. 182 52.50 N 126.57 W
Dean ≃, Eng., U.K. 262 53.20 N 2.15 W
Dean, Forest of ♦³ 42 51.48 N 2.30 W
Dean Channel ꓤ 182 52.33 N 127.13 W
Deane 262 53.34 N 2.28 W
Deán Funes 252 30.26 S 64.21 W
Dean Row 262 53.20 N 2.11 W
Deans 276 40.24 N 74.30 W
Deansboro 210 43.00 N 75.26 W
Deans Dundas Bay ⊂ 176 72.15 N 118.25 W
Deanville 222 30.26 N 96.46 W
Dearborn 216 42.18 N 83.10 W
Dearborn □⁶ 218 39.06 N 84.51 W
Dearborn ≃ 202 47.07 N 111.55 W
Dearborn Heights 216 42.19 N 83.16 W
Dearg, Beinn ∧ 46 57.47 N 4.56 W
Dearham 44 54.43 N 3.26 W
Dearne ≃ 44 53.30 N 1.16 W
Dear Reservoir ◎¹ 44 55.20 N 3.37 W
Dease ≃ 180 59.54 N 128.30 W
Dease Arm ⊂ 180 66.52 N 119.37 W
Dease Lake ◎ 180 58.35 N 130.02 W
Dease Strait ꓤ 176 68.40 N 108.00 W
Death Valley 204 36.18 N 116.25 W
Death Valley ᐯ 204 36.30 N 117.00 W
Death Valley National Monument ♦ 204 36.30 N 117.00 W
Deatsville 194 32.36 N 86.23 W
Deauville 50 49.22 N 0.04 E
Deba 146 10.20 N 11.54 E
Debagrām 126 23.41 N 88.18 E
Debal'cevo 83 48.20 N 38.24 E
Debāndapur 272b 22.52 N 88.22 E
Debao 102 23.21 N 106.31 E
Debar 38 41.31 N 20.30 E
De Bary 220 28.52 N 81.18 W
Debauch Mountain ∧ 180 64.31 N 159.52 W
Débé 241r 10.12 N 61.27 W
Debed ≃ 84 41.22 N 44.58 E
Deben ≃ 42 51.58 N 1.24 E
Debenham 42 52.13 N 1.11 E
De Beque 200 39.20 N 108.12 W
De Berry 194 32.18 N 94.10 W
Debesy 80 57.39 N 53.49 E
Debhāta 124 22.33 N 88.58 E
Dębica 30 50.04 N 21.24 E
De Bilt 52 52.06 N 5.10 E
Debipur 126 24.14 N 88.38 E
Debīr Char 126 22.24 N 90.41 E
Dęblin 30 51.35 N 21.50 E
Dębno 30 52.45 N 14.40 E
Débo, Lac ◎ 150 15.18 N 4.09 W
Deborah, Mount ∧ 180 63.38 N 147.15 W
Deborah West, Lake ◎ 162 30.45 S 119.07 E
Deboyne Islands II 164 10.45 S 152.25 E
Debra 126 22.24 N 87.33 E
Debra Sina 144 9.51 N 39.50 E
Debre Birhan 144 9.40 N 39.33 E
Debrecen 30 47.32 N 21.38 E
Debre Markos 144 10.20 N 37.45 E
Debre May 144 11.19 N 37.30 E
Debre Tabor 144 11.50 N 38.05 E
Debre Zebit 144 11.50 N 38.40 E
Debre Zeyit 144 8.45 N 38.59 E
Debrzno 30 53.33 N 17.14 E
Debstedt 52 53.37 N 8.38 E
Decatur, Al., U.S. 194 34.36 N 86.59 W
Decatur, Ga., U.S. 192 33.46 N 84.17 W
Decatur, Il., U.S. 219 39.50 N 88.57 W
Decatur, In., U.S. 216 40.50 N 84.56 W
Decatur, Mi., U.S. 216 42.06 N 85.58 W
Decatur, Ms., U.S. 194 32.26 N 89.06 W
Decatur, Ne., U.S. 198 42.00 N 96.14 W
Decatur, Oh., U.S. 218 38.49 N 83.42 W
Decatur, Tn., U.S. 192 35.30 N 84.47 W
Decatur, Tx., U.S. 222 33.14 N 97.35 W
Decatur □⁶ 219 39.20 N 85.29 W
Decatur, Lake ◎¹ 219 39.51 N 88.52 W
Decatur Island I 224 48.31 N 122.50 W
Decatur Municipal Airport ≍ 219 39.50 N 88.52 W
Decaturville 194 35.35 N 88.07 W
Decazeville 32 44.34 N 2.15 E
Deccan ✗¹ 122 17.00 N 78.00 E
Decelles, Réservoir ◎¹ 190 47.42 N 78.08 W
Deception ≃ 156 21.04 S 24.25 E
Deception, Mount ∧ 224 47.49 N 123.14 W
Deception Bay ⊂ 171a 27.07 S 153.05 E
Deception Island I 9 62.57 S 60.38 W
Deception Lake ◎ 184 56.33 N 104.15 W
Deception Pass ≍ 224 48.24 N 122.38 W
Deception Pass State Park ♦ 224 48.24 N 122.39 W
Dechang 102 27.24 N 102.10 E
Dechêne, Lac ◎ 186 51.15 N 67.51 W
Dechenhöhle ⊥⁵ 263 51.22 N 7.39 E
Decherd 194 35.12 N 86.04 W
Dechhu 120 26.47 N 72.20 E
Déchy 50 50.21 N 3.07 E
Decimomannu 71 39.19 N 8.58 E
Decimoputzu 71 39.20 N 8.55 E
Děčín 54 50.48 N 14.13 E
Děčínské stěny ✗ 54 50.50 N 14.12 E
Decize 32 46.50 N 3.28 E
Decker Lake 182 54.17 N 125.50 W
Decker Lake ◎¹ 222 30.18 N 97.36 W
Deckers Point 214 40.46 N 78.59 W
Deckerville 190 43.31 N 82.44 W
De Cocksdorp 52 53.08 N 4.52 E
Decollatura 68 39.03 N 16.21 E
Decorah 190 43.18 N 91.47 W
Decs 30 46.17 N 18.46 E
Deda 38 46.57 N 24.53 E
Dedaye 110 16.24 N 95.53 E
Deddington 42 51.59 N 1.19 W
Dededo 174p 13.31 N 144.49 E
Dedegöl Dağları ✗ 130 37.47 N 31.13 E
Dedegöl Tepesi ∧ 130 37.39 N 31.17 E
Dedeleben 54 52.03 N 10.25 E
Dedeli 84 39.11 N 43.05 E
Dedelow 54 53.22 N 13.48 E
Dedemsvaart 52 52.36 N 6.28 E
Dedenevo 82 56.15 N 37.31 E
Deder 144 9.22 N 41.26 E
Dedersdorf 52 53.27 N 8.30 E
Dedham 207 42.14 N 71.10 W
Dedilovskije Vyselki 82 54.20 N 38.03 E
Dedinovo 82 55.03 N 39.07 E
Dedo, Cerro ∧ 254 44.49 S 71.52 W
Dedo de Deus, Pico ∧ 256 22.30 S 43.03 W
De Doorns 158 33.28 S 19.41 E
Dedoplis-Ckaro 84 41.28 N 46.07 E
Dédougou 150 12.28 N 3.28 W
Dedoviči 76 57.32 N 29.56 E
Dedovsk 82 55.52 N 37.07 E
Dedu 89 48.31 N 126.14 E
Deduru ≃ 122 7.36 N 79.48 E
Dedza 154 14.22 S 34.20 E
Dee ≃, Ire. 48 53.52 N 6.21 W
Dee ≃, U.K. 44 53.20 N 3.12 W
Dee ≃, Eng., U.K. 44 54.18 N 2.32 W
Dee ≃, Scot., U.K. 44 54.50 N 4.03 W
Dee ≃, Scot., U.K. 46 57.09 N 2.07 W
Dee, Loch ◎ 44 55.05 N 4.24 W
Deedsville 216 40.55 N 86.06 W
De Efteling ♦ 52 51.39 N 5.02 E
Deeg 124 27.28 N 77.20 E
Deelfontein 158 30.59 S 23.48 E
Deelpan 158 26.19 S 25.36 E
Deenwood 192 31.14 N 82.23 W
Deep ≃, In., U.S. 216 41.37 N 87.16 W
Deep ≃, N.C., U.S. 192 35.36 N 79.03 W
Deepavaal Brook ≃ 276 40.53 N 74.16 W
Deep Bay ⊂ 184 56.25 N 103.00 W
Deep Brook ≃, Ma., U.S. 283 42.38 N 71.22 W
Deep Brook ≃, N.J., U.S. 276 40.58 N 74.09 W
Deep Creek ≃, Austl. 169 37.37 S 144.48 E
Deep Creek ≃, Ca., U.S. 228 34.20 N 117.14 W
Deep Creek ≃, De., U.S. 208 38.38 N 75.37 W
Deep Creek ≃, Id., U.S. 202 42.15 N 116.40 W
Deep Creek ≃, Md., U.S. 284b 39.17 N 76.28 W
Deep Creek ≃, Tx., U.S. 196 32.45 N 99.10 W
Deep Creek ≃, Tx., U.S. 196 32.31 N 100.55 W
Deep Creek ≃, Ut., U.S. 200 40.10 N 113.50 W
Deep Creek Conservation Park ♦ 168b 35.39 S 138.12 E
Deep Creek Indian Reserve -◆-⁴ 182 52.16 N 122.07 W
Deeping Fen ≛ 42 52.44 N 0.13 W
Deep Red Creek ≃ 196 34.17 N 98.39 W
Deep River, On., Can. 190 46.06 N 77.30 W
Deep River, Ct., U.S. 207 41.23 N 72.26 W
Deep River, Ia., U.S. 190 41.34 N 92.22 W
Deep River, Wa., U.S. 224 46.21 N 123.41 W
Deep Run ≃, Md., U.S. 284b 39.13 N 76.42 W
Deep Run ≃, Md., U.S. 284b 39.25 N 76.40 W
Deep Run ≃, N.J., U.S. 276 40.26 N 74.22 W
Deep Run ≃, N.J., U.S. 285 39.44 N 74.41 W
Deepwater, Austl. 166 29.27 S 151.51 E
Deepwater, Mo., U.S. 194 38.15 N 93.46 W
Deep Water, N.J., U.S. 208 39.41 N 75.29 W
Deep Well 162 24.25 S 134.05 E
Deer ≃, N.Y., U.S. 188 44.55 N 74.43 W
Deer ≃, N.Y., U.S. 212 43.45 N 75.34 W
Deer Creek, In., U.S. 216 40.37 N 86.23 W
Deer Creek, Mn., U.S. 198 46.23 N 95.19 W
Deer Creek ≃, U.S. 208 39.37 N 76.09 W
Deer Creek ≃, Ca., U.S. 204 39.56 N 122.04 W
Deer Creek ≃, Ca., U.S. 226 35.56 N 119.28 W
Deer Creek ≃, Ca., U.S. 226 38.22 N 121.21 W
Deer Creek ≃, Ca., U.S. 226 39.13 N 121.17 W
Deer Creek ≃, Ca., U.S. 282 37.24 N 122.09 W
Deer Creek ≃, Il., U.S. 278 41.32 N 87.37 W
Deer Creek ≃, In., U.S. 216 40.34 N 86.41 W
Deer Creek ≃, Ks., U.S. 198 39.40 N 99.06 W
Deer Creek ≃, Ms., U.S. 194 32.33 N 90.47 W
Deer Creek ≃, Ne., U.S. 198 40.28 N 100.00 W
Deer Creek ≃, Oh., U.S. 218 39.27 N 83.00 W
Deer Creek ≃, Ok., U.S. 196 35.38 N 98.28 W
Deer Creek ≃, Or., U.S. 224 45.08 N 123.15 W
Deer Creek ≃, Pa., U.S. 279b 40.32 N 79.51 W
Deer Creek ≃, Wa., U.S. 224 48.16 N 121.55 W
Deer Creek ≃, Wy., U.S. 200 42.52 N 105.52 W
Deer Creek ≃, Wy., U.S. 202 43.09 N 107.42 W
Deer Creek Indian Reservation -◆-⁴ 190 47.50 N 93.25 W
Deer Creek Lake ◎¹ 218 39.40 N 83.15 W
Deerfield, Il., U.S. 216 42.10 N 87.50 W
Deerfield, In., U.S. 216 40.17 N 84.59 W
Deerfield, Ks., U.S. 198 37.58 N 101.07 W
Deerfield, Ma., U.S. 207 42.32 N 72.36 W
Deerfield, Mi., U.S. 216 41.53 N 83.46 W
Deerfield, Oh., U.S. 214 41.01 N 81.03 W
Deerfield, Wi., U.S. 216 43.03 N 89.04 W
Deerfield ≃ 207 42.35 N 72.35 W
Deerfield Beach 220 26.19 N 80.06 W
Deerfield Street 208 39.31 N 75.14 W
Deer Grove ♦ 278 42.09 N 88.04 W
Deer Harbor 224 48.37 N 123.00 W
Deering 180 66.05 N 162.43 W
Deering, Mount ∧² 162 24.53 S 129.04 E
Deer Island ≻¹ 283 42.21 N 70.58 W
Deer Island I, N.B., Can. 186 45.00 N 66.57 W
Deer Island I, Ak., U.S. 180 54.53 N 162.15 W
Deer Island I, Or., U.S. 224 45.58 N 122.50 W
Deer Isle 188 44.13 N 68.40 W
Deer Lake, Nf., Can. 186 49.10 N 57.26 W
Deer Lake, Pa., U.S. 208 40.37 N 76.03 W
Deer Lake ◎, Nf., Can. 186 49.07 N 57.35 W
Deer Lake ◎, On., Can. 184 52.40 N 94.30 W
Deer Lakes Regional Park ♦ 279b 40.38 N 79.49 W
Deerlijk 50 50.51 N 3.21 E
Deer Lodge 202 46.23 N 112.44 W
Deer Mountain ∧ 188 45.01 N 70.56 W
Deer Park, Austl. 274b 37.47 S 144.47 E
Deer Park, Al., U.S. 194 31.13 N 88.19 W
Deer Park, Ca., U.S. 226 38.32 N 122.28 W
Deer Park, Il., U.S. 278 42.09 N 88.04 W
Deer Park, N.Y., U.S. 210 40.45 N 73.19 W
Deer Park, Oh., U.S. 218 39.12 N 84.23 W
Deer Park, Tx., U.S. 222 29.42 N 95.07 W
Deer Park, Wa., U.S. 202 47.57 N 117.28 W
Deer Park ♦ 272a 28.33 N 77.11 E
Deer Park Airport ≍ 276 40.46 N 73.19 W
Deerpass Bay ⊂ 180 65.56 N 122.25 W
Deer Pond ◎, Nf., Can. 186 48.30 N 54.45 W
Deer Pond ◎, N.J., U.S. 276 40.57 N 74.24 W
Deer River, Mn., U.S. 190 47.19 N 93.47 W
Deer River, N.Y., U.S. 212 43.56 N 75.36 W
Deer Sound ꓤ 46 58.58 N 2.48 W
Deersville 214 40.18 N 81.11 W
Deer Trail 198 39.36 N 104.02 W
Deerwood 190 46.28 N 93.53 W
Dee Why 170 33.45 S 151.17 E
Dee Why Head ≻ 274a 33.46 S 151.19 E
Dee Why Lagoon ⊂ 274a 33.45 S 151.18 E
Deex Nugaaleed ᐯ 144 7.58 N 49.51 E
Defengzhuang 98 41.02 N 113.16 E
Defereggen ᐯ 64 46.55 N 12.25 E
Defereggen Alpen ✗ 64 46.52 N 12.20 E
Deferiet 212 44.02 N 75.41 W
Defiance, Ia., U.S. 198 41.49 N 95.20 W
Defiance, Oh., U.S. 216 41.17 N 84.21 W
Defiance, Pa., U.S. 214 40.10 N 78.14 W
Defiance □⁶ 216 41.19 N 84.30 W
Defiance, Mount ∧ 224 45.38 N 121.43 W
Defiance Plateau ✗¹ 200 36.00 N 109.15 W
De Forest 190 43.14 N 89.20 W
De Forest Lake ◎¹ 276 41.08 N 73.58 W
Defu 271c 1.21 N 103.54 E
De Funiak Springs 194 30.43 N 86.06 W
Deganga 126 22.40 N 88.39 E
Deganwy 44 53.17 N 3.50 W
Deganya 132 32.42 N 35.35 E
Dêgê 102 31.50 N 98.40 E
Degeberga 26 55.50 N 14.05 E
Degeh Bur 144 8.13 N 43.34 E
Dégelis (Sainte-Rose-du-Dégelis) 186 47.33 N 68.39 W
Degema 150 4.45 N 6.47 E
Degerby 26 60.02 N 20.23 E
Degeres 85 43.14 N 75.49 E
Degerfors 40 59.14 N 14.26 E
Degerhamn 26 56.21 N 16.24 E
Degerndorf 64 47.44 N 12.06 E
Deggendorf 60 48.51 N 12.59 E
Deggingen 58 48.36 N 9.43 E
Degh ≃ 123 31.36 N 74.09 E
Değirmendere 130 38.07 N 27.09 E
Değirmenlik 130 35.15 N 33.29 E
Deglunden ◎ 40 60.05 N 13.49 E
Dego 62 44.27 N 8.19 E
Degollado 234 20.28 N 102.09 W
Degoma 144 12.28 N 37.37 E
Degong 114 4.05 N 101.08 E
De Graafschap -◆-¹ 52 52.00 N 6.30 E
De Graff 216 40.18 N 83.54 W
De Gray Lake ◎¹ 194 34.15 N 93.15 W
De Grey 162 20.10 S 119.12 E
De Grey ≃ 162 20.12 S 119.11 E
Degt'ari 78 50.35 N 32.45 E
Degt'arka ≃ 265a 59.57 N 30.52 E
Degunino -◆-⁸ 265b 55.52 N 37.33 E
De Haan 50 51.16 N 3.02 E
Dehak ≃ 128 32.01 N 58.35 E
Dehalak Deset I 144 15.40 N 40.05 E
Deharda 126 21.40 N 87.25 E
De Hart Reservoir ◎¹ 208 40.28 N 76.45 W
Deh Bālā 123 34.04 N 70.29 E
Deh Bīd 128 30.38 N 53.13 E
Dehdez 128 31.43 N 50.17 E
Deh-e Salm 128 31.12 N 59.19 E
Dehgolān 128 35.17 N 47.25 E
Dehibat 148 32.01 N 10.42 E
Dehiwala-Mount Lavinia 122 6.51 N 79.52 E
Deh Kord 128 33.49 N 48.53 E
Dehlorān 128 32.41 N 47.16 E
De Hoek 158 32.57 S 18.46 E
Dehpehk I 174r 6.57 N 158.18 E
Dehra Dūn 124 30.19 N 78.02 E
Dehri 124 24.52 N 84.11 E
Dehrn 56 50.25 N 8.05 E
Dehu 122 18.35 N 73.51 E
Dehua 100 25.32 N 118.15 E
Dehuang 98 35.12 N 114.25 E
Dehui 89 44.34 N 125.43 E
Deidesheim 56 49.24 N 8.54 E
Deilbach ≃ 263 51.23 N 7.05 E
Deilinghofen 56 51.22 N 7.47 E
Deining 60 49.13 N 11.32 E
Deinze 50 50.59 N 3.32 E
Deir el Asad 132 32.56 N 35.16 E
Deister ✗ 52 52.15 N 9.30 E
Deiva Marina 62 44.13 N 9.31 E
Dej 38 47.09 N 23.52 E
Deje 40 59.36 N 13.28 E
Dejima 94 36.05 N 140.20 E
Dejnau 128 39.15 N 63.11 E
De Jongs, Tanjong ≻ 164 6.56 S 138.32 E
Deka ≃ 154 18.04 S 26.42 E
De Kalb, Il., U.S. 216 41.55 N 88.45 W
De Kalb, Ms., U.S. 194 32.46 N 88.39 W
De Kalb, Tx., U.S. 194 33.30 N 94.36 W
De Kalb □⁶, Il., U.S. 216 41.59 N 88.41 W
De Kalb □⁶, In., U.S. 216 41.22 N 85.04 W
De Kalb Junction 212 44.30 N 75.16 W
Dekan, Hochland von — Deccan ✗¹ 122 17.00 N 78.00 E
De-Kastri 89 51.28 N 140.47 E
Dekehtik I 174r 7.00 N 158.12 E
Dekemhare 144 15.05 N 39.02 E
Dekese 152 3.27 S 21.24 E
Deke Sokehs I 174r 6.59 N 158.11 E
Dekhgila Military Base ■ 142 31.08 N 29.48 E
Dekina 150 7.39 N 7.02 E
Dékoa 152 6.19 N 19.04 E
De Koog 52 53.05 N 4.45 E
De Krim 52 52.38 N 6.38 E
De La Blanche, Lac ◎ 186 50.05 N 69.29 W
Delabole 42 50.37 N 4.42 W
Delafield 216 43.03 N 88.24 W
Del Aire 280 33.55 N 118.21 W
Delamere, Austl. 164 15.45 S 131.33 E
Delamere, Austl. 168b 35.35 S 138.11 E
Delamere, Eng., U.K. 262 53.13 N 2.39 W
Delamere Forest ♦³ 44 53.14 N 2.38 W
Delami Mayal, Jabal ∧ 140 11.38 N 30.23 E
Del Amo Fashion Center ♦⁹ 280 33.50 N 118.21 W
De Lancey, N.Y., U.S. 210 42.12 N 74.58 W
De Lancey, Pa., U.S. 214 40.59 N 78.58 W
Delanco 208 40.03 N 74.57 W
De Land 220 29.01 N 81.18 W
Delanggu 115a 7.37 S 110.41 E
Delano, Ca., U.S. 226 35.46 N 119.14 W
Delano, Mn., U.S. 190 45.02 N 93.47 W
Delano, Pa., U.S. 210 40.50 N 76.04 W
Delano Peak ∧ 200 38.22 N 112.23 W
Delanson 210 42.44 N 74.11 W
Delaport Point ≻ 240b 25.05 N 77.27 W
Delapu 120 31.35 N 90.35 E
Delārām 128 32.11 N 63.25 E
Delareyville 158 26.44 S 25.29 E
Delarof Islands II 181a 51.30 N 178.45 W
Delaronde Lake ◎ 184 54.05 N 107.05 W
Del'atiči 76 53.47 N 25.59 E
Delatite ≃ 169 37.10 S 146.00 E
Delavan, Il., U.S. 190 40.22 N 89.32 W
Delavan, Wi., U.S. 216 42.37 N 88.38 W
Delavan Lake 216 42.35 N 88.37 W
Delavan Lake ◎ 216 42.37 N 88.38 W
Delaware, On., Can. 214 42.55 N 81.25 W
Delaware, N.J., U.S. 210 40.53 N 75.03 W
Delaware, Oh., U.S. 214 40.17 N 83.04 W
Delaware, Ok., U.S. 196 36.46 N 95.38 W
Delaware □⁶, In., U.S. 216 40.18 N 85.23 W
Delaware □⁶, N.Y., U.S. 210 42.17 N 74.55 W
Delaware □⁶, Oh., U.S. 214 40.18 N 83.04 W
Delaware □⁶, Pa., U.S. 208 39.55 N 75.23 W
Delaware □³, U.S. 178 39.10 N 75.30 W
Delaware □³, U.S. 208 39.10 N 75.30 W
Delaware ≃, U.S. 188 39.20 N 75.25 W
Delaware ≃, Ks., U.S. 198 39.03 N 95.24 W
Delaware, East Branch ≃ 210 41.55 N 75.17 W
Delaware, University of ᴜ² 285 39.41 N 75.45 W
Delaware, West Branch ≃ 210 41.56 N 75.17 W
Delaware and Raritan Canal ≋ 208 40.29 N 74.26 W
Delaware Aqueduct ≋¹ 210 42.05 N 74.54 W
Delaware Bay ⊂ 208 39.05 N 75.15 W
Delaware City 208 39.34 N 75.35 W
Delaware Lake ◎¹ 214 40.20 N 83.00 W
Delaware Memorial Bridge ♦⁵ 285 39.41 N 74.50 W
Delaware Memorial Bridges ♦⁵ 208 39.41 N 75.31 W
Delaware Mountains ✗ 196 31.35 N 104.40 W
Delaware Museum of Natural History ᴜ 285 39.47 N 75.36 W
Delaware Park 210 40.43 N 75.11 W
Delaware Park ♦ 284a 42.56 N 78.52 W
Delaware Park Race Track ♦ 285 39.42 N 75.40 W
Delaware Seashore State Park ♦ 208 38.38 N 75.04 W
Delaware State Park ♦ 214 40.23 N 83.04 W
Delaware Water Gap 210 40.59 N 75.09 W
Delaware Water Gap National Recreation Area ♦ 210 41.08 N 74.55 W
Delbrück 52 51.46 N 8.33 E
Delburne 182 52.12 N 113.14 W
Delcambre 194 29.57 N 91.59 W
Del Campillo 252 34.22 S 64.29 W
Del Carril 258 35.31 S 59.30 W
Del City 196 35.26 N 97.26 W
Delcommune, Lac ◎¹ 154 10.45 S 25.45 E
Del Dios 228 33.04 N 117.08 W
Delegate 166 37.03 S 148.58 E
Délembé 146 9.53 N 22.37 E
Delémont 58 47.22 N 7.21 E
De Leon 196 32.06 N 98.32 W
De Leon Springs 192 29.07 N 81.21 W
Delet ꓤ 26 60.15 N 20.35 E
Delevan 210 42.29 N 78.28 W
Delfim Moreira 256 22.30 S 45.17 W
Delfinópolis 255 20.20 S 46.51 W
Delft 52 52.00 N 4.21 E
Delft Island I 122 9.30 N 79.42 E
Delfzijl 52 53.19 N 6.46 E
Delgada, Punta ≻ 254 42.46 S 63.38 W
Delgado 236 13.43 N 89.10 W
Delgado, Cabo ≻ 154 10.40 S 40.35 E
Del Gallego 116 13.56 N 122.36 E
Delgany 48 53.08 N 6.05 W
Delger ≃ 88 49.17 N 100.40 E
Delger chaan uul ∧ 88 50.00 N 106.22 E
Delgerchangaj 102 45.15 N 104.50 E
Delgerchet 102 45.52 N 110.26 E
Delgercogt 102 46.08 N 106.23 E
Delgerech 102 45.48 N 111.12 E
Del Haven 208 39.03 N 74.56 W
Delhi, On., Can. 212 42.51 N 80.30 W
Delhi, India 124 28.40 N 77.13 E
Delhi, India 272a 28.40 N 77.13 E
Delhi, Ca., U.S. 226 37.26 N 120.46 W
Delhi, Il., U.S. 219 39.03 N 90.15 W
Delhi, Ia., U.S. 190 42.25 N 91.19 W
Delhi, La., U.S. 194 32.27 N 91.29 W
Delhi, N.Y., U.S. 210 42.16 N 74.54 W
Delhi □⁸ 124 28.37 N 77.10 E
Delhi Cantonment 272a 28.36 N 77.08 E
Delhi Hills 218 39.05 N 84.36 W
Delhi Railroad Station ♦⁵ 272a 28.40 N 77.13 E
Delhi Tail Distributary ≋ 272a 28.41 N 77.10 E
Delhi University ᴜ² 272a 28.42 N 77.13 E
Deli, Pulau I 115a 7.00 S 105.32 E
Delia, Ab., Can. 182 51.38 N 112.23 W
Delia, It. 70 37.21 N 13.55 E
Delia ≃ 70 37.19 N 13.58 E
Delianuova 68 38.14 N 15.55 E
Deliblato 38 44.50 N 21.03 E
Delice 130 39.58 N 34.02 E
Delice ≃ 130 40.28 N 34.10 E
Delices 240d 15.17 N 61.16 W
Deliceto 68 41.13 N 15.23 E
Delicias, Cuba 240p 21.11 N 76.34 W
Delicias, Méx. 232 28.13 N 105.28 W
De Lier 52 51.57 N 4.15 E
Delight 194 34.01 N 93.30 W
Delightful 214 41.18 N 80.57 W
Delījān 128 33.59 N 50.40 E
Deliilyas 130 39.20 N 36.48 E
Deliktaş 130 39.21 N 37.13 E
Delingde 74 70.08 N 114.00 E
Delingha 102 37.14 N 97.12 E
Dělinkalns ∧² 76 57.30 N 26.58 E
Déli Pályaudvar ♦⁵ 264c 47.30 N 19.01 E
Delisle 184 51.55 N 107.08 W
Delisle ≃ 206 45.17 N 74.11 W
Delitua 114 3.30 N 98.41 E
Delitzsch 54 51.31 N 12.20 E
Delkern 228 35.21 N 119.01 W
Dell 46 58.30 N 6.20 W
Dellach 64 46.40 N 13.05 E
Dell City 200 31.56 N 105.12 W
Delle 58 47.30 N 7.00 E
Dellenbaugh, Mount ∧ 200 36.07 N 113.32 W
Dellensjöarna ◎ 26 61.54 N 16.41 E
Delles 148 36.55 N 3.55 E
Delligsen 52 51.57 N 9.48 E
Dello 64 45.25 N 10.04 E
Dell Rapids 198 43.50 N 96.43 W
Dellroy 214 40.33 N 81.11 W
Dellwig 263 51.29 N 7.41 E
Dellwig -◆-⁸ 263 51.29 N 6.56 E
Dellwood 219 38.44 N 90.17 W
Dellwood Highlands 278 41.34 N 88.03 W
Del Mar, Ca., U.S. 228 32.57 N 117.15 W
Delmar, De., U.S. 208 38.27 N 75.34 W
Delmar, Ia., U.S. 190 42.00 N 90.36 W
Delmar, Md., U.S. 208 38.27 N 75.34 W
Delmar, N.Y., U.S. 210 42.37 N 73.49 W
Del Mar Hills 196 27.37 N 99.26 W
Delmarva Peninsula ≻¹ 208 38.30 N 75.30 W
Del Mar Woods 278 42.12 N 87.51 W
Delmas, Sk., Can. 184 52.55 N 108.36 W
Delmas, S. Afr. 158 26.08 S 28.43 E
Delmas □⁵ 273d 26.10 S 28.33 E
Delme 56 48.53 N 6.24 E
Delme ≃ 52 53.05 N 8.40 E
Delmenhorst 52 53.03 N 8.38 E
Delmiro Gouveia 250 9.23 S 37.59 W
Delmont, N.J., U.S. 208 39.12 N 74.57 W
Delmont, Pa., U.S. 214 40.25 N 79.34 W
Delmont, S.D., U.S. 198 43.16 N 98.09 W
Del Monte Heights 226 36.36 N 121.50 W
Del Monte Park 226 36.36 N 121.56 W
Delnice 64 45.24 N 14.48 E
Del Norte 200 37.40 N 106.21 W
Del Norte Coast Redwood State Park ♦ 204 41.38 N 124.05 W
De-Longa, ostrova II 74 76.30 N 153.00 E
De Long Mountains ✗ 180 68.20 N 162.00 W
De-Long-Strasse — Longa, proliv ꓤ 74 70.20 N 178.00 E
Deloraine, Austl. 166 41.31 S 146.39 E
Deloraine, Mb., Can. 184 49.12 N 100.29 W
Delorme, Lac ◎ 176 54.31 N 69.52 W
Deloro 212 44.31 N 77.37 W
Delos — Dhílos ⊥ 38 37.26 N 25.16 E
Delph 44 53.34 N 2.01 W
Delphi 216 40.35 N 86.40 W
Delphi — Delfoí ⊥ 38 38.30 N 22.29 E
Delphi Falls 210 42.53 N 75.55 W
Delphos, Ks., U.S. 198 39.16 N 97.46 W
Delphos, Oh., U.S. 216 40.50 N 84.20 W
Delph Reservoir ◎¹ 262 53.38 N 2.27 W
Delportshoop 158 28.22 S 24.20 E
Del Puerto Creek ≃ 226 37.32 N 121.07 W
Delran 285 40.01 N 74.57 W
Delrath 263 51.08 N 6.47 E
Delray ♦⁸ 281 42.18 N 83.08 W
Delray Beach 220 26.27 N 80.04 W
Del Rey 226 36.40 N 119.36 W
Del Rey Oaks 226 36.36 N 121.50 W
Del Rio, Fl., U.S. 220 28.03 N 82.26 W
Del Rio, Tx., U.S. 196 29.21 N 100.53 W
Del Rosa 228 34.08 N 117.15 W
Delsbo 26 61.48 N 16.35 E
Delson 206 45.22 N 73.33 W
Delstern ♦⁸ 263 51.20 N 7.31 E
Delta, On., Can. 212 44.37 N 76.08 W
Delta, Méx. 200 32.22 N 115.12 W
Delta, Co., U.S. 200 38.44 N 108.04 W
Delta, Mo., U.S. 194 37.11 N 89.44 W
Delta, Oh., U.S. 216 41.34 N 84.00 W
Delta, Pa., U.S. 208 39.43 N 76.19 W
Delta, Ut., U.S. 200 39.21 N 112.34 W
Delta □⁹ 150 5.30 N 6.00 E
Delta ≃ 180 64.09 N 146.18 W
Delta Amacuro □⁸ 246 8.30 N 61.30 W
Delta Barrage ♦⁶ 142 30.11 N 31.07 E
Delta Beach 184 50.11 N 98.19 W
Delta City 194 33.04 N 90.47 W
Delta Downs 166 17.00 S 141.18 E
Delta Junction 180 64.02 N 145.41 W
Delta Mendota Canal ≋ 226 37.49 N 121.34 W
Delta Peak ∧ 180 56.39 N 129.34 W

Symbol	English	Deutsch	Español	Français	Português
≃	River	Fluß	Río	Rivière	Rio
≋	Canal	Kanal	Canal	Canal	Canal
⌊	Waterfall, Rapids	Wasserfall, Stromschnellen	Cascada, Rápidos	Chute d'eau, Rapides	Cascata, Rápidos
ꓤ	Strait	Meeresstraße	Estrecho	Détroit	Estreito
⊂	Bay, Gulf	Bucht, Golf	Bahía, Golfo	Baie, Golfe	Baía, Golfo
◎	Lake, Lakes	See, Seen	Lago, Lagos	Lac, Lacs	Lago, Lagos
≛	Swamp	Sumpf	Pantano	Marais	Pântano
≉	Ice Features, Glacier	Eis- und Gletscherformen	Accidentes glaciares	Formes glaciaires	Acidentes glaciares
✶	Other Hydrographic Features	Andere Hydrographische Objekte	Otros Elementos Hidrográficos	Autres données hydrographiques	Outros acidentes hidrográficos

Symbol	English	Deutsch	Español	Français	Português
-◆-	Submarine Features	Untermeerische Objekte	Accidentes Submarinos	Formes de relief sous-marin	Acidentes submarinos
□	Political Unit	Politische Einheit	Unidad Política	Entité politique	Unidade política
ᴜ	Cultural Institution	Kulturelle Institution	Institución Cultural	Institution culturelle	Instituição cultural
⊥	Historical Site	Historische Stätte	Sitio Histórico	Site historique	Sítio histórico
♦	Recreational Site	Erholungs- und Ferienort	Sitio de Recreo	Centre de loisirs	Área de Lazer
≍	Airport	Flughafen	Aeropuerto	Aéroport	Aeroporto
■	Military Installation	Militäranlage	Instalación Militar	Installation militaire	Instalação militar
♦	Miscellaneous	Verschiedenes	Misceláneo	Divers	Diversos

Delta Reservoir ⊜1 210 43.17 N 75.26 W
Deltaville 208 37.33 N 76.20 W
Delton 216 42.29 N 85.24 W
Deltona 220 28.54 N 81.15 W
Delungra 166 29.39 S 150.50 E
Del'un-Uranskij chrebet ⋏ 88 56.30 N 114.00 E
Delüün 86 47.42 N 90.59 E
De Luz Creek ≃ 228 33.22 N 117.19 W
Del Valle 222 30.12 N 97.40 W
Del Valle, Lake ⊜1 226 37.35 N 121.43 W
Del Verme Falls ⌞ 144 5.27 N 40.17 E
Delvin 48 53.36 N 7.05 W
Delvinë 38 39.57 N 20.06 E
Del Viso 258 34.27 S 58.48 W
Delyn □8 262 53.16 N 3.11 W
Demak 115a 6.53 S 110.38 E
Demaki 80 58.26 N 51.43 E
Dem'ansk 76 57.38 N 32.28 E
Demarcation Point > 180 69.40 N 141.15 W
Demarest 276 40.57 N 73.57 W
Demarest Brook ≃ 276 40.57 N 73.58 W
Demavend, Mount → Damāvand, Qolleh-ye ∧ 128 35.56 N 52.08 E
Demba 152 5.30 S 22.16 E
Demba Chio 152 9.41 S 13.41 E
Dembecha 144 10.35 N 37.30 E
Dembéni 157a 11.50 S 43.24 E
Dembi 144 8.05 N 36.27 E
Dembia, Centraf. 154 5.07 N 24.25 E
Dembia, Zaïre 154 3.31 N 25.50 E
Dembi Dolo 144 8.32 N 34.48 E
Dembo 152 3.56 S 12.35 E
Dême ≃ 50 47.43 N 0.29 E
Demer ≃ 56 50.58 N 4.42 E
Demerara ≃ 246 6.48 N 58.10 W
Demerara-Mahaica □4 246 6.40 N 58.00 W
Demerthin 54 52.58 N 12.17 E
Demidov 76 55.16 N 31.31 E
Demidovka 78 50.25 N 25.20 E
Demidovo 76 59.17 N 38.17 E
Deming, N.M., U.S. 200 32.16 N 107.45 W
Deming, Wa., U.S. 224 48.49 N 122.12 W
Demini ≃ 246 0.46 S 62.56 W
Demirci 130 39.03 N 28.40 E
Demir Kapija V 38 41.24 N 22.15 E
Demirköprü Barajı ⊜1 130 38.40 N 28.20 E
Demirköy 130 41.49 N 27.45 E
Demirtaş 130 40.16 N 29.06 E
Demitz-Thumitz 54 51.09 N 14.14 E
Demjanka ≃ 86 59.34 N 69.20 E
Demjanovo 24 60.22 N 47.03 E
Demjanskoje 86 59.36 N 69.18 E
Demjas 80 51.13 N 49.08 E
Demmeltrath ◆8 263 51.11 N 7.03 E
Demmin 54 53.54 N 13.02 E
Demmitt 182 55.26 N 119.54 W
Demnate 148 31.44 N 6.59 W
Democracy Monument ⊥ 269a 13.45 N 100.30 E
Democrat Point > 276 40.37 N 73.18 W
Demoiselles, Grotte des ±5 62 43.55 N 3.45 E
Demone, Val ◆1 70 37.58 N 14.35 E
Demonte 62 44.19 N 7.17 E
De Montigny, Lac ⊜ 190 48.08 N 77.54 W
Demopolis 194 32.31 N 87.50 W
Demorest 192 34.33 N 83.32 W
De Mossville 218 38.48 N 84.25 W
Demotte 216 41.12 N 87.12 W
Dempo, Gunung ∧ 112 4.02 S 103.09 E
Dempster, Point > 162 33.39 S 123.52 E
Demsa 146 9.32 N 13.14 E
Demta 164 2.20 S 140.08 E
Demurino 78 48.10 N 36.29 E
De Naauwte 158 30.08 S 21.42 E
Denain 50 50.20 N 3.23 E
Denair 226 37.32 N 120.47 W
Denakil ◆1 144 13.00 N 41.00 E
Denali 180 63.11 N 147.28 W
Denali National Park 180 63.44 N 148.54 W
Denali National Park ♦ 180 63.15 N 150.30 W
Denan 144 6.30 N 43.30 E
Denare Beach 184 54.40 N 102.05 W
Denau 85 38.16 N 67.54 E
Denbigh, On., Can. 212 45.08 N 77.16 W
Denbigh, Wales, U.K. 44 53.11 N 3.25 W
Denbigh, Cape > 180 64.23 N 161.31 W
Den Burg 52 53.03 N 4.48 E
Denby Dale 44 53.35 N 1.38 W
Den Chai 110 17.59 N 100.04 E
Dendang 112 3.05 S 107.54 E
Dender (Dendre) ≃ 50 51.02 N 4.06 E
Denderleeuw 50 50.53 N 4.04 E
Dendermonde 50 51.02 N 4.07 E
Dendre (Dender) ≃ 50 51.02 N 4.06 E
Dendron, S. Afr. 156 23.25 S 29.11 E
Dendron, Va., U.S. 208 37.02 N 76.56 W
Dendy Park ♦ 274b 37.56 S 145.00 E
Deneba 144 9.50 N 39.09 E
Denekamp 52 52.23 N 7.00 E
Denenchōfu ◆8 268 35.35 N 139.41 E
Deneysville 158 26.53 S 28.06 E
Denežnikovo, Ross. 82 55.26 N 38.07 E
Denežnikovo, Ukr. 83 49.02 N 38.57 E
Dengcheng 100 33.41 N 114.27 E
Deng Deng 152 5.12 N 13.31 E
Denge 154 3.34 N 28.14 E
Denge Marsh ≋ 42 50.57 N 0.55 E
Dengfeng 100 34.29 N 113.04 E
Denggongchang 107 30.24 N 103.49 E
Dengguanzhen 107 29.10 N 104.56 E
Dengkou 102 40.20 N 106.59 E
Denglongshu 98 41.20 N 115.15 E
Dengmingsi 98 37.53 N 116.42 E
Dêngqên 102 31.32 N 95.27 E
Dengshahe 98 39.13 N 122.04 E
Dengta 100 24.01 N 114.49 E
Denguiro 152 5.38 N 23.02 E
Dengxian 102 32.42 N 112.01 E
Dengyoufang 98 41.34 N 114.32 E
Den Haag → 's-Gravenhage 52 52.06 N 4.18 E
Denham, Austl. 162 25.55 S 113.32 E
Denham, Eng., U.K. 260 51.34 N 0.30 W
Denham, In., U.S. 216 41.09 N 86.43 W
Denham, Mount ∧ 241q 18.13 N 77.32 W
Denham Aerodrome ⊠ 260 51.36 N 0.31 W
Denham Island I 166 16.43 S 139.09 E
Denham Place ᵾ 260 51.34 N 0.30 W
Denham Range ⋏ 166 21.55 S 147.46 E
Denham Sound ꓘ 162 25.40 S 113.15 E
Denham Springs 194 30.29 N 90.57 W
Den Helder 52 52.54 N 4.45 E
Denholme 262 53.48 N 1.54 W
Dénia 34 38.51 N 0.07 E
Denial Bay 162 32.06 S 133.32 E
Dénié 150 11.14 N 7.29 W
Deniliquin 166 35.32 S 144.58 E
Deniskoviči, Bela. 76 52.44 N 26.41 E
Deniskoviči, Ross. 76 52.19 N 31.43 E
Denison, Ia., U.S. 198 42.01 N 95.21 W
Denison, Tx., U.S. 196 33.45 N 96.32 W
Denison, Mount ∧ 180 58.25 N 154.27 W
Denison Dam ◆6 196 33.50 N 96.34 W
Denisovka 24 66.14 N 55.20 E
Denisovo 82 54.28 N 37.51 E
Denisy 261 48.33 N 1.56 E
Denizli 130 37.46 N 29.06 E
Denizli □4 130 37.40 N 29.15 E
Denkanikota 122 12.32 N 77.48 E
Denkendorf 60 48.56 N 11.27 E
Denkingen 58 47.53 N 9.19 E
Denklingen, Dtsch. 56 50.55 N 7.39 E
Denklingen, Dtsch. 58 47.55 N 10.51 E
Den'kovo 82 56.01 N 36.21 E
Denmark, Austl. 162 34.57 S 117.21 E
Denmark, S.C., U.S. 192 33.19 N 81.08 W
Denmark, Wi., U.S. 190 44.20 N 87.49 W
Denmark (Danmark) □1, Europe 22 56.00 N 10.00 E
Denmark (Danmark) □1, Europe 26 56.00 N 10.00 E
Denmark, Lake ⊜ 276 40.58 N 74.31 W
Denmark Bay c 176 70.33 N 103.20 W
Denmark Strait ꓘ 10 67.00 N 25.00 W
Denmead 42 50.54 N 1.04 W
Dennemont 261 49.01 N 1.42 E
Dennery 241f 13.55 N 60.54 W
Dennis 207 41.44 N 70.11 W
Dennis Head > 46 59.23 N 2.23 W
Dennison 214 40.23 N 81.20 W
Dennis Port 207 41.39 N 70.07 W
Denniston 172 41.44 S 171.48 E
Denniston Creek ≃ 282 37.30 N 122.28 W
Dennisville 208 39.11 N 74.49 W
Denny 46 56.02 N 3.55 W
Den Oever 52 52.56 N 5.02 E
Denouval 261 48.58 N 2.03 E
Denpasar 115b 8.39 S 115.13 E
Denshaw 262 53.35 N 2.02 W
Dent Ditch ≌ 279a 41.18 N 82.08 W
Denton, Eng., U.K. 44 53.27 N 2.07 W
Denton, Md., U.S. 208 38.53 N 75.49 W
Denton, Mi., U.S. 281 42.20 N 83.03 W
Denton, Mt., U.S. 202 47.19 N 109.56 W
Denton, N.C., U.S. 192 35.38 N 80.06 W
Denton, Tx., U.S. 222 33.12 N 97.07 W
Denton □6 222 33.07 N 97.10 W
Denton Creek ≃ 196 32.58 N 96.57 W
Dentonia Park ♦ 275b 43.42 N 79.17 W
D'Entrecasteaux, Point > 162 34.50 S 116.00 E
D'Entrecasteaux Islands II 164 9.30 S 150.40 E
D'Entrecasteaux National Park ♦ 162 34.41 S 115.58 E
Dents du Midi ⋏ 58 46.10 N 6.56 E
Denver, Co., U.S. 200 39.44 N 104.59 W
Denver, In., U.S. 216 40.51 N 86.04 W
Denver, Ia., U.S. 190 42.40 N 92.20 W
Denver, Pa., U.S. 208 40.13 N 76.08 W
Denver City 196 32.57 N 102.49 W
Denville 210 40.53 N 74.28 W
Denzlingen 58 48.04 N 7.52 E
Deoband 124 29.42 N 77.41 E
Deocha 126 24.03 N 87.35 E
Deodoro ◆8 287a 22.51 S 43.23 W
Deogarh, India 120 25.32 N 73.54 E
Deogarh, India 122 21.32 N 84.44 E
Deogarh, India 124 24.33 N 78.15 E
Deogarh ∧ 124 23.32 N 82.16 E
Deogarh Hills ⋏2 124 23.35 N 82.30 E
Deoghar 124 24.29 N 86.42 E
Deogsu Palace ᵾ 271b 37.35 N 126.58 E
Deolāli 122 19.57 N 73.50 E
Deoli 126 22.03 N 86.49 E
Deoli ◆8 272a 28.30 N 77.14 E
Deongwar, Mount ∧ 171a 27.12 S 152.16 E
Deopāra 126 22.55 N 90.15 E
Deori, India 124 23.08 N 78.41 E
Deori, India 124 23.24 N 79.01 E
Deoria 124 26.31 N 83.47 E
Deosai Mountains ⋏ 123 35.20 N 75.12 E
Deosil 124 23.42 N 82.15 E
Dep ≃ 89 52.54 N 127.45 E
Depāl 126 21.44 N 87.33 E
De Panne 50 51.06 N 2.35 E
Depāra 272b 22.53 N 88.34 E
Departure Bay 224 49.12 N 123.58 W
DePaul University ᵾ2 278 41.56 N 87.39 W
Depauville 212 44.08 N 76.04 W
Depauw 218 38.20 N 86.13 W
De Peel ≋ 52 51.25 N 6.00 E
De Pere 190 44.26 N 88.03 W
Depew, N.Y., U.S. 210 42.54 N 78.41 W
Depew, Ok., U.S. 196 35.48 N 96.30 W
Deping 98 37.28 N 116.57 E
De Pinte 50 51.00 N 3.39 E
Depoe Bay 202 44.48 N 124.03 W
Depok 115a 6.24 S 106.50 E
Deport 196 33.32 N 95.19 W
Deposit 210 42.03 N 75.25 W
Deptford 285 39.50 N 75.07 W
Deptford ◆8 260 51.28 N 0.02 W
Deptford Mall ◆9 285 39.50 N 75.06 W
Deptford Terrace 285 39.48 N 75.09 W
Depuch Island I 162 20.38 S 117.43 E
Depue 190 41.19 N 89.18 W
Deputy 218 38.48 N 85.39 W
Dêqên 102 28.38 N 98.52 E
Deqing, Zhg. 102 23.09 N 111.45 E
Deqing, Zhg. 106 30.33 N 120.05 E
De Queen 194 34.02 N 94.20 W
De Quincy 194 30.27 N 93.25 W
Dera ≃ 264c 47.39 N 19.05 E
Dera, Lach (Lak Dera) V 144 0.35 N 41.50 E
Dera Bugti 120 29.02 N 69.09 E
Dera Ghāzi Khān 123 30.03 N 70.38 E
Dera Gopipur 123 31.54 N 76.13 E
Dera Ismāīl Khān 123 31.50 N 70.54 E
Derakht-e Yaḥyá 120 31.50 N 68.08 E
Dera Nānak 123 32.02 N 75.01 E
Dera Nawāb 123 29.06 N 71.16 E
Derāwar Fort 123 28.46 N 71.20 E
Deražn'a 78 49.16 N 27.26 E
Derbent 84 42.03 N 48.18 E
Derbeškinskij 80 55.52 N 53.30 E
Derbetovka 80 45.48 N 43.05 E
Der Bodden ꓘ 54 54.16 N 13.12 E
Derby, Austl. 162 17.18 S 123.38 E
Derby, Austl. 166 41.09 S 147.47 E
Derby, S. Afr. 158 25.55 S 27.02 E
Derby, Eng., U.K. 42 52.55 N 1.29 W
Derby, Ct., U.S. 207 41.19 N 73.05 W
Derby, Ks., U.S. 198 37.32 N 97.16 W
Derby, Me., U.S. 188 45.14 N 68.58 W
Derby, N.Y., U.S. 210 42.40 N 78.58 W
Derby, Oh., U.S. 218 39.46 N 83.12 W
Derby, Vt., U.S. 206 44.57 N 72.08 W
Derby Acres 226 35.15 N 119.35 W
Derby Line 206 45.00 N 72.05 W
Derbyshire □6 44 53.00 N 1.33 W
Der-Chantecoq, Lac du ⊜1 58 48.35 N 4.46 E
Derdepoort 156 24.42 S 26.20 E
Dere 130 39.00 N 39.18 E
Derečin 76 53.15 N 24.55 E
Derecske 30 47.21 N 21.34 E
Dereköy, Tür. 130 40.08 N 37.47 E
Dereköy, Tür. 130 41.56 N 27.21 E
Dereköy, Tür. 130 39.16 N 27.19 E
Dereli 130 40.45 N 38.27 E
Derenburg 54 51.52 N 10.54 E
Derendorf ◆8 263 51.15 N 6.48 E
Derenwu 105 39.40 N 116.46 E
Dereseki ◆8 267b 41.08 N 29.08 E
Derev'anka 24 61.34 N 34.27 E
Derg ≃ 48 54.44 N 7.25 W
Derg, Lough ⊜, Ire. 48 54.36 N 7.53 W
Derg, Lough ⊜, Ire. 48 52.57 N 8.19 W
Dergači, Ross. 80 51.14 N 48.46 E
Dergači, Ukr. 78 50.07 N 36.07 E
Dergaon 120 26.42 N 93.58 E
Der Grabow c 54 54.23 N 12.50 E
De Ridder 194 30.50 N 93.17 W
De Rijp 52 52.34 N 4.50 E
Derik 130 37.22 N 40.17 E
Derinkuyu 130 38.23 N 34.45 E
Der Kanal → English Channel ꓘ 28 50.20 N 1.00 W
Derkul 80 51.16 N 51.18 E
Derkul ≃ 83 48.35 N 39.41 E
Dermbach 56 50.43 N 10.06 E
Dermott 194 33.31 N 91.26 W
Dermulo 64 46.20 N 11.04 E
Derne 263 51.35 N 7.41 E
Derne ◆8 263 51.34 N 7.31 E
Dernieres, Isles II 194 29.02 N 90.47 W
Dernoviči 78 51.36 N 29.43 E
Deroche 224 49.11 N 122.04 W
Dero Eri 144 9.01 N 46.43 E
Dêrong 102 28.47 N 99.14 E
Déroute, Passage de la ꓘ 32 49.25 N 2.00 W
Derrame 196 26.19 N 104.23 W
Derravaragh, Lough ⊜ 48 53.40 N 7.24 W
Derre 154 16.56 S 36.11 E
Derrick City 214 41.58 N 78.34 W
Derrinallum 169 37.57 S 143.13 E
Derry, N.H., U.S. 188 42.52 N 71.19 W
Derry, Pa., U.S. 214 40.20 N 79.18 W
Derrybrien 48 53.04 N 8.36 W
Derrykeighan 48 55.08 N 6.29 W
Derry → Londonderry 48 54.59 N 7.20 W
Derryveagh Mountains ⋏ 48 55.00 N 8.05 W
Derry West 275b 43.39 N 79.42 W
Der Sārāi ◆8 272a 28.33 N 77.11 E
Dersau 54 54.07 N 10.20 E
Dersingham 42 52.51 N 0.30 E
Derudeb 140 17.32 N 36.06 E
De Rust 158 33.30 S 22.32 E
Deruta 66 42.59 N 12.25 E
De Ruyter 210 42.45 N 75.53 W
DeRuyter Reservoir ⊜1 210 42.49 N 75.53 W
Der'uzino 82 56.18 N 38.16 E
Derval 32 47.40 N 1.40 W
Derventa 38 44.58 N 17.55 E
Derwent 182 53.39 N 110.58 W
Derwent ≃, Austl. 166 43.03 S 147.22 E
Derwent ≃, Eng., U.K. 44 53.45 N 0.57 W
Derwent ≃, Eng., U.K. 44 54.57 N 1.41 W
Derwent ≃, Eng., U.K. 44 54.38 N 3.34 W
Derwent ≃, Eng., U.K. 44 52.53 N 1.17 W
Derwent Bridge 166 42.08 S 146.13 E
Derwent Reservoir ⊜1 44 54.50 N 2.00 W
Derwent Water ⊜ 44 54.34 N 3.08 W
Deržavino 80 53.13 N 52.22 E
Deržavinsk 86 51.03 N 66.19 E
Desaguadero ≃, Arg. 252 34.13 S 66.47 W
Desaguadero ≃, Bol. 248 18.24 S 67.05 W
Desagüe, Canal de ≌ 286a 19.29 N 99.05 W
Des Allemands 194 29.49 N 90.28 W
Desamparados 236 9.54 N 84.04 W
Désappointement, Îles du II 14 14.10 S 141.20 W
Des Arc 194 34.58 N 91.29 W
Desborough 42 52.27 N 0.49 W
Descabezado Grande, Volcán ∧1 252 35.36 S 70.45 W
Descanso, Bra. 252 26.50 S 53.35 W
Descanso, Ca., U.S. 204 32.51 N 116.37 W
Descanso, Punta > 204 32.16 N 117.03 W
Descanso Gardens ♦ 280 34.12 N 118.13 W
Descartes 32 46.58 N 0.42 E
Deschaillons 206 46.32 N 72.07 W
Deschambault 206 46.39 N 71.56 W
Deschambault Lake 184 54.55 N 103.22 W
Deschambault Lake ⊜ 184 54.40 N 103.35 W
Descharme Lake ⊜ 184 57.05 N 109.13 W
Deschênes 212 45.23 N 75.48 W
Deschênes, Lac ⊜ 212 45.22 N 75.51 W
Deschutes ≃, Or., U.S. 202 45.38 N 120.54 W
Deschutes ≃, Wa., U.S. 224 47.02 N 122.54 W
Descoberto 256 21.27 S 42.58 W
Desdunes 238 19.17 N 72.39 W
Dese 144 11.05 N 39.41 E
Deseado ≃ 254 47.45 S 65.54 W
Deseado, Cabo > 254 52.44 S 74.44 W
Desembarco de los 0303 Orientales, Monumento ⊥ 258 33.48 S 58.25 W
Desengaño, Punta > 254 49.15 S 67.37 W
Desenzano del Garda 64 45.28 N 10.32 E
Deseret Peak ∧ 200 40.28 N 112.38 W
Deseronto 212 44.12 N 77.03 W
Désert ≃ 190 46.23 N 75.58 W
Désert, Lac ⊜ 190 46.35 N 76.19 W
Desertas, Ilhas II 148 32.30 N 16.30 W
Desert Creek ≃ 226 38.48 N 119.19 W
Desert Hot Springs 204 33.57 N 116.30 W
Desert Lake ⊜, On., Can. 212 44.32 N 76.35 W
Desert Lake ⊜, Nv., U.S. 204 36.58 N 115.05 W
Desert Mountains ⋏ 226 39.16 N 119.00 W
Desert Peak ∧ 200 41.11 N 113.22 W
Desert Valley V 204 41.15 N 118.20 W
Desert View Highlands 228 34.37 N 118.13 W
Desford 42 52.39 N 1.17 W
Desha 194 35.44 N 91.40 W
Deshaies 241o 16.18 N 61.48 W
Desheng 102 24.45 N 108.28 E
Deshengchang 107 29.06 N 105.25 E
Deshengpo 102 26.58 N 103.59 E
Deshengtai 104 42.14 N 123.45 E
Deshengyingzi 104 41.44 N 123.14 E
Deshler, Ne., U.S. 198 40.08 N 97.43 W
Deshler, Oh., U.S. 216 41.12 N 83.53 W
Deshnok 120 27.48 N 73.21 E
Deshon Manor 214 40.52 N 79.57 W
Deshu 128 30.26 N 63.19 E
Deshun 106 31.58 N 120.29 E
Desiderio Tello 252 31.13 S 66.19 W
Desio 62 45.37 N 9.13 E
Des Lacs ≃ 198 48.17 N 101.25 W
Deslinde, Arroyo ≃ 258 33.44 S 58.52 W
Desloge 194 37.52 N 90.31 W
Desmarais 182 55.56 N 113.49 W
De Smet 198 44.23 N 97.33 W
De Smet, Lake ⊜1 202 44.29 N 106.45 W
Des Moines, Ia., U.S. 190 41.36 N 93.36 W
Des Moines, N.M., U.S. 196 36.45 N 103.50 W
Des Moines, Wa., U.S. 224 47.24 N 122.19 W
Des Moines ≃ 178 40.22 N 91.26 W
Des Moines, East Fork ≃ 198 42.41 N 94.12 W
Dešná, Česko. 61 48.58 N 15.33 E
Desna, Ukr. 78 50.56 N 30.46 E
Desna ≃, Europe 78 50.33 N 30.32 E
Desna ≃, Ross. 82 55.26 N 37.30 E
Desolación, Isla I 254 53.00 S 74.10 W
Désolation, Cap de la → Disappointment, Cape > 244 54.53 S 36.07 W
Desolation Point > 116 10.28 N 125.39 E
Desor, Mount ∧2 190 47.58 N 89.01 W
De Soto, Il., U.S. 194 37.49 N 89.13 W
De Soto, In., U.S. 216 40.15 N 85.17 W
De Soto, Mo., U.S. 194 38.08 N 90.33 W
De Soto, Tx., U.S. 222 32.35 N 96.51 W
De Soto □6 220 27.11 N 81.48 W
De Soto City 220 27.26 N 81.24 W
De Soto National Memorial ⊥ 220 27.31 N 82.40 W
De Soto State Park ♦ 194 34.28 N 85.36 W
Despatch 158 33.46 S 25.30 E
Despeñaperros, Desfiladero de)(34 38.24 N 3.30 W
Des Plaines 216 42.02 N 87.53 W
Des Plaines ≃ 216 41.24 N 88.16 W
Despotovac 38 44.05 N 21.33 E
Despujols 116 12.31 N 122.01 E
Desroches, Île I 138 5.41 S 53.41 E
Desruisseaux 241f 13.47 N 60.56 W
Dessau 54 51.50 N 12.14 E
Dessel 56 51.14 N 5.07 E
Deşt 130 39.10 N 39.22 E
Destacado Island I 116 12.16 N 124.06 E
De Steeg 52 52.02 N 6.04 E
Destek 130 40.51 N 36.12 E
Destelbergen 50 51.03 N 3.48 E
Desterro 250 7.17 S 37.06 W
Destin 194 30.23 N 86.29 W
Destruction, Mount ∧2 162 24.35 S 127.59 E
Destruction Bay 180 61.15 N 138.48 W
Destruction Island I 224 47.40 N 124.30 W
Desulo 71 40.01 N 9.14 E
Desvres 50 50.40 N 1.50 E
Deta 38 45.24 N 21.13 E
Detčino 82 54.49 N 36.19 E
Dete 154 18.38 S 26.50 E
Dethlingen 52 52.57 N 10.07 E
Detling 260 51.18 N 0.34 E
Detmold 52 51.56 N 8.52 E
Detmold □5 52 52.00 N 8.45 E
Detour, Point > 190 45.36 N 86.37 W
De Tour Village 190 46.00 N 83.54 W
Detrital Wash V 200 36.02 N 114.28 W
Detroit, Il., U.S. 219 39.37 N 90.40 W
Detroit, Mi., U.S. 216 42.20 N 83.03 W
Detroit, Mi., U.S. 281 42.20 N 83.03 W
Detroit, Or., U.S. 202 44.44 N 122.08 W
Detroit, Tx., U.S. 196 33.40 N 95.16 W
Detroit ≃ 214 42.06 N 83.08 W
Detroit Beach 216 41.55 N 83.20 W
Detroit City Airport ⊠ 281 42.25 N 83.01 W
Detroit Institute of Arts ᵾ 281 42.22 N 83.04 W
Detroit Lake ⊜1 202 44.42 N 122.10 W
Detroit Lakes 198 46.48 N 95.50 W
Detroit Mercy, University Of ᵾ2 281 42.25 N 83.08 W
Detroit Metropolitan-Wayne County Airport ⊠ 281 42.13 N 83.22 W
Detroit Race Course ♦ 281 42.23 N 83.19 W
Detroit-Windsor Tunnel ◆5 281 42.20 N 83.02 W
Detroit Zoological Park ♦ 281 42.29 N 83.09 W
Detskosel'skij 265a 59.44 N 30.28 E
Dettelbach 56 49.48 N 10.09 E
Dettifoss ⌞ 24a 65.50 N 16.20 W
Dettingen an der Erms 56 48.32 N 9.20 E
Dettwiller 56 48.45 N 7.28 E
Det Udom 110 14.54 N 105.05 E
Detva 30 48.31 N 19.28 E
Deua National Park ♦ 166 36.00 S 149.45 E
Deuben 54 51.06 N 12.04 E
Deuels Corners 284a 42.45 N 78.45 W
Deuil-la-Barre 261 48.59 N 2.20 E
Deūlgaon Rāja 122 20.01 N 76.02 E
Deulpur 272b 22.36 N 88.10 E
Deulti 126 22.26 N 87.56 E
Deurne, Bel. 50 51.13 N 4.28 E
Deurne, Ned. 52 51.28 N 5.47 E
Deusen ◆8 263 51.33 N 7.26 E
Deutsche Bucht c 30 54.30 N 7.30 E
Deutsch Eylau → Iława 30 53.37 N 19.33 E
Deutschfeistritz 61 47.11 N 15.20 E
Deutschkreutz 61 47.36 N 16.38 E
Deutsch Krone → Wałcz 30 53.17 N 16.28 E
Deutschland → Germany □1 30 51.00 N 10.00 E
Deutschlandsberg 61 46.49 N 15.13 E
Deutsch-Neudorf 54 50.38 N 13.27 E
Deutsch Wagram 61 48.18 N 16.34 E
Deutsch Wusterhausen 264a 52.18 N 13.35 E
Deutzen 54 51.06 N 12.26 E
Deux-Montagnes 206 45.32 N 73.53 W
Deux-Montagnes □6 206 45.35 N 74.05 W
Deux Montagnes, Lac des ⊜ 206 45.28 N 73.59 W
Deux-Sèvres □5 32 46.30 N 0.20 W
Deva 38 45.53 N 22.55 E
Devakottai 122 9.57 N 78.49 E
De Valls Bluff 194 34.47 N 91.27 W
Devaprayāg 124 30.09 N 78.37 E
Dev'atern'a 80 56.12 N 53.24 E
Dev'atiny 24 60.56 N 36.46 E
Devault 285 40.05 N 75.32 W
Dévaványa 30 47.02 N 20.58 E
Devecikonağı 130 39.55 N 28.34 E
Devecser 30 47.06 N 17.26 E
Devedağı Tepesi ∧ 130 40.34 N 41.21 E
Devegeçidi Barajı ⊜1 130 38.05 N 39.55 E
Develi 130 38.23 N 35.30 E
Deventer 52 52.15 N 6.10 E
Deveron ≃ 46 57.40 N 2.31 W
Devers 222 30.02 N 94.36 W
Devers Canal, West Branch ≌ 222 29.57 N 94.46 W
Deversoir Military Base ■ 142 30.25 N 32.20 E
Devès, Monts du ⋏ 32 45.00 N 3.45 E
Devgadh Bāriva 120 22.42 N 73.54 E
De View, Bayou ≃ 194 34.48 N 91.18 W
Devīkot 120 26.42 N 71.12 E
Devil Lake ⊜ 212 44.35 N 76.27 W
Deville 56 49.53 N 4.42 E
Déville-lès-Rouen 50 49.28 N 1.02 E
Devil Peak ∧ 226 37.32 N 119.44 W
Devil River Peak ∧ 172 40.58 S 172.39 E
Devils ≃ 196 29.39 N 100.58 W
Devil's Bridge 42 52.23 N 3.51 W
Devils Brook ≃ 276 40.20 N 74.37 W
Devils Canyon V 280 34.16 N 117.58 W
Devil's Den State Park ♦ 194 35.46 N 94.16 W
Devils Hole Rapids ⌞ 284a 43.08 N 79.03 W
Devils Hopyard State Park ♦ 207 41.28 N 72.22 W
Devils Island → Diable, Île du I 250 5.17 N 52.35 W
Devils Lake 198 48.06 N 98.51 W
Devils Lake ⊜, Mi., U.S. 216 41.58 N 84.17 W
Devils Lake ⊜, N.D., U.S. 198 48.01 N 98.52 W
Devils Lake State Park ♦ 190 43.24 N 89.44 W
Devils Marbles ♦ 162 20.30 S 134.14 E
Devils Paw ∧ 180 58.44 N 133.50 W
Devils Postpile National Monument ♦ 226 37.37 N 119.05 W
Devils Tower ∧ 198 44.31 N 104.57 W
Devils Tower National Monument ♦ 198 44.31 N 104.57 W
Devil's Water ≃ 44 54.58 N 2.02 W
Devin 38 41.45 N 24.24 E
Devine, B.C., Can. 182 50.32 N 122.30 W
Devine, Tx., U.S. 196 29.08 N 98.54 W
Devizes 42 51.22 N 1.59 W
Devladovo 78 48.07 N 33.45 E
Devli 120 25.45 N 75.23 E
De Voe Lake ⊜ 276 40.23 N 74.23 W
Devoll ≃ 38 40.49 N 19.51 E
Dévoluy ⋏ 62 44.39 N 5.53 E
Devon, Ab., Can. 182 53.22 N 113.44 W
Devon, S. Afr. 158 26.21 S 28.48 E
Devon, Pa., U.S. 285 40.02 N 75.25 W
Devon □6 42 50.45 N 3.50 W
Devon ≃, Eng., U.K. 42 53.04 N 0.43 W
Devon ≃, Scot., U.K. 46 56.07 N 3.51 W
Devon Island I 16 75.00 N 87.00 W
Devonport, Austl. 166 41.11 S 146.21 E
Devonport, N.Z. 172 36.49 S 174.48 E
Devonport, Eng., U.K. 42 50.22 N 4.10 W
Devonshire 285 39.49 N 75.32 W
Devonshire Plaza ◆9 281 42.17 N 83.00 W
Devore 228 34.13 N 117.25 W
Devoto 252 31.24 S 62.19 W
Devrek 130 41.13 N 31.57 E
Devrekâni 130 41.36 N 33.51 E
Devres ≃ 130 41.06 N 34.25 E
Devure ≃ 154 20.00 S 32.20 E
Dewa, Ujung > 114 2.55 N 95.48 E
Dewakang-lompo, Pulau I 112 5.24 S 118.25 E
Dewar 196 35.27 N 95.56 W
Dewart 210 41.07 N 76.53 W
Dewart Lake ⊜ 216 41.22 N 85.47 W
Dewās 120 22.58 N 76.04 E
Dewa-sanchi ⋏2 92 39.05 N 140.10 E
Dewdney 224 49.10 N 122.12 W
Dewetsdorp 158 29.33 S 26.34 E
Dewey, Il., U.S. 216 40.19 N 88.17 W
Dewey, Ok., U.S. 196 36.47 N 95.56 W
Dewey, Wa., U.S. 224 48.25 N 122.37 W
Dewey Beach 208 38.41 N 75.04 W
Deweyville 194 30.18 N 93.45 W
De Witt, Ar., U.S. 194 34.17 N 91.20 W
Dewitt, Il., U.S. 219 40.11 N 88.47 W
De Witt, Ia., U.S. 190 41.49 N 90.32 W
De Witt, Mi., U.S. 216 42.50 N 84.34 W
De Witt, Ne., U.S. 198 40.23 N 96.55 W
De Witt, N.Y., U.S. 210 43.02 N 76.03 W
De Witt □6, Il., U.S. 216 40.12 N 88.55 W
De Witt □6, Tx., U.S. 222 29.07 N 97.20 W
Dewittville 214 42.14 N 79.27 W
Dewsbury 44 53.42 N 1.37 W
Dexing 100 28.54 N 117.36 E
Dexingjie 98 39.54 N 122.50 E
Dexter, Me., U.S. 188 45.01 N 69.17 W
Dexter, Mi., U.S. 216 42.20 N 83.53 W
Dexter, Mo., U.S. 194 36.47 N 89.57 W
Dexter, N.M., U.S. 196 33.11 N 104.22 W
Dexter, N.Y., U.S. 212 44.00 N 76.02 W
Dexterity Fiord c2 176 71.11 N 73.03 W
Deyang 102 31.14 N 104.22 E
Dey-Dey, Lake ⊜ 162 29.12 S 131.04 E
Deyhūk 128 33.17 N 57.30 E
Deyyer 128 27.50 N 51.55 E
Dez ≃ 128 31.39 N 48.52 E
Dezfūl 128 32.23 N 48.24 E
Dez Gerd 128 30.45 N 51.57 E
Dezhou 98 37.27 N 116.18 E
Dežneva, mys > 180 66.06 N 169.45 W
Dezong 120 32.09 N 90.20 E
Dezzo di Scalve 64 45.59 N 10.05 E
Dgâmcha, Sebkhet te-n- ⊜ 150 18.45 N 15.48 W
Dhabān Singh 123 31.44 N 73.34 E
Dhāding 124 27.52 N 84.55 E
Dhādkā 126 22.47 N 86.30 E
Dháfna ∧ 267c 38.07 N 23.38 E
Dháfni 38 37.48 N 22.01 E
Dhafnion Monastery ᵾ1 267c 38.01 N 23.38 E
Dhahab 140 28.29 N 34.32 E
Dhahab, Wādī adh- V 132 32.44 N 35.54 E
Dhahran → Aẓ-Ẓahrān 128 26.18 N 50.08 E
Dhaka (Dacca), Bngl. 126 23.43 N 90.25 E
Dhāka, India 124 26.41 N 85.10 E
Dhaka □5 120 24.15 N 90.15 E
Dhākauli 124 24.45 N 77.51 E
Dhakuria Lake ⊜ 272b 22.31 N 88.22 E
Dhaleswari ≃ 126 23.32 N 90.34 E
Dháli 130 35.01 N 33.25 E
Dhamār 144 14.46 N 44.23 E
Dhāmpur 124 29.19 N 78.31 E
Dhāmrai 126 23.55 N 90.13 E
Dhamtari 122 20.41 N 81.34 E
Dhāmura 126 22.53 N 90.12 E
Dhanaula 123 30.17 N 75.35 E
Dhanaura 124 28.58 N 78.15 E
Dhanbād 126 23.48 N 86.27 E
Dhandhuka 120 22.22 N 71.59 E
Dhanera 126 23.25 N 86.39 E
Dhaneswargāti 126 23.25 N 89.20 E
Dhangadhī 124 28.41 N 80.36 E
Dhaniakhāli 126 22.58 N 88.06 E
D'Hanis 196 29.20 N 99.17 W
Dhankuṭa 124 26.59 N 87.20 E
Dhansar 272c 19.07 N 73.05 E
Dhānyahānā 272b 22.48 N 88.11 E
Dhār 120 22.36 N 75.18 E
Dharampur 122 20.32 N 73.11 E
Dharān 124 26.49 N 87.17 E
Dharangaon 120 21.01 N 75.16 E
Dhārāpuram 122 10.44 N 77.31 E
Dhāri 120 21.20 N 71.01 E
Dhārīwāl 123 31.57 N 75.19 E
Dharmābād 122 18.54 N 77.51 E
Dharmapuri 122 12.08 N 78.10 E
Dharmavaram 122 14.26 N 77.43 E
Dharmjaygarh 124 22.28 N 83.13 E
Dharmkot 123 30.57 N 75.14 E
Dharmshāla 123 32.13 N 76.19 E
Dharoor, Tog V 144 10.20 N 50.30 E
Dharug National Park ♦ 170 33.25 S 151.05 E
Dhasān ≃ 124 25.48 N 79.24 E
Dhātrigrām 126 23.15 N 88.20 E
Dhaulpur 124 26.42 N 77.54 E
Dhawalāgiri □8 124 28.30 N 83.30 E
Dhawalāgiri ∧ 124 28.42 N 83.30 E
Dhebar Lake ⊜ 120 24.16 N 74.00 E
Dhelfoí ⊥ 38 38.30 N 22.29 E
Dhenkānāl 120 20.40 N 85.36 E
Dherínia 130 35.03 N 33.57 E
Dhërmiu ᵾ1 38 40.08 N 19.42 E
Dherue, Loch an ⊜ 46 58.25 N 4.27 W
Dheskáti 38 39.55 N 21.49 E
Dheune ≃ 58 46.54 N 5.00 E
Dhiavolítsion 38 37.18 N 21.58 E
Dhībān 132 31.30 N 35.47 E
Dhidhimótikhon 38 41.21 N 26.30 E
Dhiinsoor 144 2.24 N 42.59 E
Dhíkti ∧ 38 35.08 N 25.22 E
Dhílos ⊥ 38 37.26 N 25.16 E
Dhimitsána 38 37.37 N 22.03 E
Dhiónisos 267c 38.06 N 23.53 E
Dhī Qār □4 128 31.00 N 46.15 E
Dhirāsrām 126 23.57 N 90.25 E
Dhirwah, Wādī adh- V 132 31.18 N 36.56 E
Dhodhekánisos (Dodecanese) II 38 36.30 N 27.00 E
Dhodhóni ⊥ 38 39.34 N 20.47 E
Dhofar → Ẓufār ◆1 118 17.00 N 54.10 E
Dhokra 272b 22.40 N 88.34 E
Dholka 120 22.43 N 72.28 E
Dhomhnuill, Sgurr ∧ 46 56.45 N 5.27 W
Dhone 122 15.25 N 77.53 E
Dhopākhola 126 23.08 N 89.10 E
Dhorāji 120 21.44 N 70.27 E
Dhosha 126 22.15 N 88.33 E
Dhowa 126 24.03 N 86.54 E
Dhoxáton 38 41.05 N 24.14 E
Dhrāngadhra 120 22.59 N 71.28 E
Dhrapetsóna 267c 37.57 N 23.37 E
Dhrol 120 22.34 N 70.25 E
Dhron ≃ 56 49.52 N 6.54 E
Dhubāb 144 12.56 N 43.25 E
Dhuburi 124 26.01 N 89.59 E
Dhudiāl 123 33.04 N 72.58 E
Dhulāgarh 272b 22.35 N 88.11 E
Dhule 120 20.54 N 74.47 E
Dhulia → Dhule 120 20.54 N 74.47 E
Dhuliān 124 24.41 N 87.58 E
Dhulikhel 124 27.37 N 85.33 E
Dhūlsīrās ◆8 272a 28.33 N 77.02 E
Dhünn 56 51.06 N 7.16 E
Dhünn-Stausee ⊜1 263 51.05 N 7.16 E
Dhupgāri 124 26.36 N 89.01 E
Dhurbo 144 11.37 N 50.20 E
Dhūri 124 30.22 N 75.52 E
Dhutumkhar ≃ 272c 18.54 N 73.00 E
Dhuudo 144 9.20 N 50.12 E
Dhuudo V 144 9.14 N 50.39 E
Dhuusa Mareeb 144 5.31 N 46.24 E
Día I 38 35.27 N 25.13 E
Diabaig 46 57.34 N 5.40 W
Diabakania 150 10.38 N 10.58 W
Diable, Île du (Devils Island) I 250 5.17 N 52.35 W
Diable, Lac du ⊜ 206 46.31 N 74.20 W
Diable, Pointe du > 240e 14.47 N 60.54 W
Diable, Rivière du ≃ 206 46.03 N 74.38 W
Diables, Morne aux ∧ 240d 15.37 N 61.27 W
Diablo, Ca., U.S. 226 37.50 N 121.58 W
Diablo, Wa., U.S. 224 48.43 N 121.09 W
Diablo, Canyon V 200 35.18 N 110.59 W
Diablo, Isla del → Diable, Île du I 250 5.17 N 52.35 W
Diablo, Mount ∧ 226 37.53 N 121.55 W
Diablo, Pico del ∧ 232 30.59 N 115.45 W
Diablo, Sierra del ⋏ 196 27.20 N 104.05 W
Diablo Lake ⊜1 224 48.43 N 121.08 W
Diablo Plateau ⋏1 200 31.30 N 105.30 W
Diablo Range ⋏ 226 37.00 N 121.20 W
Diablotins, Morne ∧ 240d 15.30 N 61.24 W
Diabo 150 7.47 N 5.11 W
Diaca 154 11.30 S 39.59 E
Diadema 256 23.42 S 46.37 W
Diadema □7 287b 23.42 S 46.36 W
Diafarabé 150 14.09 N 5.01 W
Diagonal 198 40.48 N 94.20 W
Diaka ≃1 150 15.13 N 4.14 W
Dialakoto 150 13.19 N 13.18 W
Dialassagou 150 13.45 N 3.37 W
Diamant, Pointe du > 240e 14.27 N 61.03 W
Diamante, Arg. 252 32.04 S 60.39 W
Diamante, It. 68 39.41 N 15.49 E
Diamante ≃ 252 34.31 S 66.56 W
Diamante, Punta > 234 16.47 N 99.52 W
Diamante de Ubá 256 21.12 S 42.55 W
Diamantina 255 18.15 S 43.36 W
Diamantina ≃ 166 26.45 S 139.10 E
Diamantina Fracture Zone ✢ 14 36.00 S 105.00 E
Diamantina Lakes 166 23.46 S 141.09 E
Diamantino 248 14.25 S 56.27 W
Diamantino ≃ 255 16.08 S 52.28 W
Diamond, Il., U.S. 216 41.17 N 88.15 W
Diamond, Mo., U.S. 194 37.00 N 94.19 W
Diamond, Oh., U.S. 214 41.06 N 81.01 W
Diamond Bar 228 34.01 N 117.48 W
Diamond Brook ≃ 276 40.56 N 74.08 W
Diamond Creek 274b 37.41 S 145.09 E
Diamond Creek ≃ 169 37.44 S 145.09 E
Diamond Harbour 126 22.12 N 88.12 E
Diamond Head ±6 229c 21.16 N 157.49 W
Diamond Hill 207 41.59 N 71.24 W
Diamond Hill Reservoir ⊜1 283 42.00 N 71.24 W
Diamond Hill State Park ♦ 283 42.00 N 71.26 W
Diamond Islets II 166 17.25 S 150.58 E
Diamond Lake 216 42.15 N 88.00 W
Diamond Lake ⊜, On., Can. 212 45.04 N 78.02 W
Diamond Lake ⊜, Il., U.S. 278 42.15 N 88.00 W
Diamond Lake ⊜, Mi., U.S. 216 41.54 N 85.59 W
Diamond Lake ⊜, Or., U.S. 202 43.10 N 122.09 W
Diamond Peak ∧, Id., U.S. 202 44.09 N 113.05 W
Diamond Peak ∧, Or., U.S. 202 43.33 N 122.09 W
Diamond Peak ∧, Wa., U.S. 202 46.07 N 117.32 W
Diamond Springs 226 38.41 N 120.48 W
Diamondville 200 41.46 N 110.32 W
Diana 222 32.43 N 94.45 W
Diana Bay c 176 60.50 N 69.50 W
Dianalund 41 55.32 N 11.30 E
Dianbai 102 21.30 N 111.01 E
Dian Chi ⊜ 102 24.50 N 102.42 E
Diancun 105 39.55 N 116.14 E
Dianfangba 102 32.54 N 103.35 E
Diangounté Kamara 150 14.33 N 9.31 W
Dianhu 100 33.58 N 119.38 E
Dianji 98 36.32 N 120.27 E
Dianjiang 102 30.21 N 107.23 E
Diano, Vallo di V 68 40.21 N 15.36 E
Diano Marina 62 43.54 N 8.05 E
Dianópolis 250 11.38 S 46.50 W
Dianqianhe 100 30.44 N 116.02 E
Dianra 150 8.45 N 6.14 W
Dianshang 106 31.10 N 118.51 E
Dianshan Hu ⊜ 106 31.08 N 120.55 E
Diantou 100 27.18 N 120.11 E
Dianzi 104 41.37 N 122.05 E
Diaobingshan 104 42.28 N 123.33 E
Diao'ecun 105 40.43 N 115.49 E
Diaohetou 105 39.17 N 116.41 E
Diaopu 100 32.22 N 119.54 E
Diaoshuilouzi 104 40.59 N 122.22 E
Diaotai 100 29.40 N 119.39 E
Diaowo 105 39.30 N 116.04 E
Diapaga 150 12.04 N 1.47 E
Diapangou 150 12.07 N 0.11 E
Diapblo, Puntan > 174n 15.00 N 145.35 E
Dias 256 22.28 S 45.34 W
Diascund Creek Reservoir ⊜1 208 37.27 N 76.54 W
Diawala 150 10.07 N 5.28 W
Diaz 194 35.38 N 91.15 W
Diaz Point > 156 26.38 S 15.05 E
Dibai 124 28.13 N 78.15 E
Dibāng ≃ 120 27.50 N 95.32 E
Dibaya 152 6.30 S 22.57 E
Dibay → Dubayy 128 25.18 N 55.18 E
Dibbīn 132 32.26 N 36.34 E
Dibble Iceberg Tongue ⊓ 9 65.40 S 135.10 E
Dibeng 158 27.35 S 22.54 E
D'Iberville 194 30.25 N 88.53 W
Dibete 156 23.45 S 26.26 E
Dibi 144 4.13 N 41.56 E
Dibo 144 6.31 N 41.52 E
Diboll 222 31.11 N 94.46 W
Dibrugarh 120 27.29 N 94.54 E
Dibs 140 12.34 N 24.14 E
Dibs, Bi'r ⊤4 140 22.12 N 29.32 E
Dichāon Kalān ◆8 272a 28.39 N 76.59 E
Dick, Mount ∧2 168a 31.35 S 116.42 E
Dickelsbach ≃ 263 51.24 N 6.45 E
Dickens 196 33.37 N 100.50 W
Dickerson 208 39.13 N 77.25 W
Dickey ≃ 224 47.55 N 124.37 W
Dickey Lake ⊜, On., Can. 212 44.47 N 77.44 W
Dickey Lake ⊜, Wa., U.S. 224 48.06 N 124.31 W
Dickinson, N.D., U.S. 198 46.52 N 102.47 W
Dickinson, Pa., U.S. 208 40.07 N 77.20 W
Dickinson, Tx., U.S. 222 29.27 N 95.03 W
Dickinson Bayou ≃ 222 29.28 N 94.58 W
Dickinson Island I 281 42.37 N 82.38 W
Dickins Seamount ✢3 16 54.30 N 137.00 W
Dicks 158 27.43 S 30.10 E
Dickson, Ok., U.S. 196 34.11 N 96.59 W
Dickson, Tn., U.S. 194 36.04 N 87.23 W
Dickson City 210 41.28 N 75.36 W
Dicle, Tür. 130 37.18 N 42.04 E
Dicle, Tür. 130 38.22 N 40.04 E

Symbols in the index entries represent the broad categories identified in the key at the right. Symbols with superior numbers (⋏1) identify subcategories (see complete key on page *I* · 1).

Symbole im Register stellen die rechts im Schlüssel erklärten Kategorien dar. Symbole mit hochgestellten Ziffern (⋏1) bezeichnen Unterabteilungen einer Kategorie (vgl. vollständiger Schlüssel auf Seite *I* · 1).

Los símbolos incluídos en el texto del índice representan las grandes categorias identificadas con la clave a la derecha. Los símbolos con numeros en su parte superior (⋏1) identifican las subcategorías (véase la clave completa en la página *I* · 1).

Les symboles de l'index représentent les catégories indiquées dans la légende à droite. Les symboles suivis d'un indice (⋏1) représentent des sous-catégories (voir légende complète à la page *I* · 1).

Os símbolos incluídos no texto do índice representam as grandes categorias identificadas com a chave à direita. Os símbolos com números em sua parte superior (⋏1) identificam as subcategorias (veja-se a chave completa à página *I* · 1).

∧ Mountain	Berg	Montaña	Montagne	Montanha
⋏ Mountains	Gebirge	Montañas	Montagnes	Montanhas
)(Pass	Paß	Paso	Col	Passo
V Valley, Canyon	Tal, Cañon	Valle, Cañón	Vallée, Canyon	Vale, Canhão
≃ Plain	Ebene	Llano	Plaine	Planície
> Cape	Kap	Cabo	Cap	Cabo
I Island	Insel	Isla	Île	Ilha
II Islands	Inseln	Islas	Îles	Ilhas
± Other Topographic Features	Andere Topographische Objekte	Otros Elementos Topográficos	Autres données topographiques	Outros acidentes topográficos

ESPAÑOL · FRANÇAIS · PORTUGUÊS

Nombre / Nom / Nome	Página / Page	Lat.°′	Long.°′ W = Oeste / W = Ouest
Dicle → Tigris ≏	128	31.00 N	47.25 E
Dicomano	66	43.53 N	11.31 E
Diculom	116	7.54 N	122.14 E
Dicun	100	33.46 N	117.32 E
Didam	52	51.56 N	6.08 E
Didao	89	45.22 N	130.51 E
Didbiran	89	51.58 N	139.20 E
Didcot	42	51.37 N	1.15 W
Didesa ≏	144	9.56 N	35.45 E
Didiéni	150	13.53 N	8.06 W
Didimbo	152	17.30 S	21.45 E
Didinga Hills ⋏	154	4.20 N	33.35 E
Didsbury	182	51.40 N	114.08 W
Didsbury ⊕ [8]	262	53.25 N	2.14 W
Diduyon ≏	116	16.36 N	121.42 E
Dīdwāna	120	27.24 N	74.34 E
Didy	157b	18.07 S	48.32 E
Die	62	44.45 N	5.22 E
Die Aue ⊕ [1]	263	51.40 N	6.35 E
Die Berg ∧	156	25.12 S	30.09 E
Die Boss	158	31.59 S	19.44 E
Diébougou	150	10.58 N	3.15 W
Dieburg	56	49.54 N	8.50 E
Dieciocho de Julio	252	33.41 S	53.33 W
Diecke	150	7.21 N	8.58 W
Diedenhofen → Thionville	56	49.22 N	6.10 E
Diedersdorf	264a	52.20 N	13.21 E
Die Erpe ≏	264a	52.27 N	13.38 E
Diefenbaker, Lake ⊜ [1]	184	51.00 N	106.55 W
Diego de Almagro	252	26.23 S	70.03 W
Diego de Almagro, Isla I	254	51.25 S	75.10 W
Diego de Ocampo, Pico ∧	238	19.35 N	70.45 W
Diego Garcia I	12	7.20 S	72.25 E
Diego Gaynor	258	34.17 S	59.14 W
Diego Pérez, Cayería de II	240p	22.05 N	81.40 W
Diego Ramírez, Islas II	244	56.30 S	68.44 W
Die Haard ⊕ [1]	263	51.41 N	7.15 E
Diekirch	56	49.53 N	6.10 E
Dieksee ⊜	54	54.10 N	10.30 E
Dieleemu	86	46.22 N	88.43 E
Dielingen	52	52.26 N	8.20 E
Dielsdorf	58	47.29 N	8.27 E
Diéma	150	14.32 N	9.12 W
Diemansputs	158	29.54 S	21.33 E
Diembéring	150	12.28 N	16.47 W
Diemel ≏	52	51.39 N	9.27 E
Diemel-Talsperre ⊕ [6]	56	51.22 N	8.43 E
Diemen	52	52.20 N	4.58 E
Diemuchuoke	120	32.42 N	79.29 E
Dien Bien Phu	110	21.23 N	103.01 E
Dien Khanh	110	12.15 N	109.06 E
Diepenau	52	52.25 N	8.44 E
Diepenbeek	56	50.54 N	5.24 E
Diepenheim	52	52.12 N	6.33 E
Diepensee	264a	52.22 N	13.31 E
Diepenveen	52	52.18 N	6.08 E
Diepholz	52	52.35 N	8.21 E
Diepoldsau	58	47.23 N	9.38 E
Dieppe, N.B., Can.	186	46.06 N	64.45 W
Dieppe, Fr.	50	49.56 N	1.05 E
Dierbao	98	40.20 N	114.32 E
Dierdorf	56	50.33 N	7.39 E
Dieren	52	52.03 N	6.06 E
Dierks	194	34.07 N	94.00 W
Diersbach	60	48.25 N	13.34 E
Diersfordt	263	51.42 N	6.33 E
Di'er Songhua ≏	89	45.26 N	124.39 E
Diesdorf	54	52.45 N	10.52 E
Dieskau	54	51.26 N	12.02 E
Diessem ⊕ [8]	263	51.20 N	6.35 E
Diessen	64	47.56 N	11.06 E
Diessenhofen	58	47.41 N	8.45 E
Diest	56	50.59 N	5.03 E
Dietenheim	58	48.12 N	10.04 E
Dietersburg	60	48.30 N	12.55 E
Dietersdorf	56	50.13 N	10.49 E
Dietfurt	56	48.57 N	10.56 E
Dietfurt an der Altmühl	60	49.02 N	11.35 E
Dietikon	58	47.24 N	8.24 E
Dietmannsried	58	47.49 N	10.17 E
Dietrich	202	42.54 N	114.15 W
Dietzenbach	56	50.01 N	8.47 E
Dietzhölztal	56	50.50 N	8.19 E
Dieue-sur-Meuse	56	49.04 N	5.25 E
Dieulefit	62	44.31 N	5.04 E
Dieulouard	56	48.51 N	6.04 E
Dieuze	56	48.49 N	6.43 E
Dieveniškės	76	54.12 N	25.37 E
Diever	52	52.52 N	6.19 E
Die Ville ⋏ [2]	56	50.40 N	6.55 E
Die Wurzen (Koren))(	64	46.31 N	13.45 E
Diez	56	50.22 N	8.01 E
Diez de Octubre	232	24.44 N	104.39 W
Dif	144	0.59 N	40.57 E
Difang	98	35.23 N	117.52 E
Diffa	146	13.19 N	12.37 E
Diffa □ [5]	146	16.00 N	13.30 E
Differdange	56	49.32 N	5.52 E
Difficult Run ≏	284c	38.58 N	77.14 W
Diffun	116	16.34 N	121.33 E
Difuri I	122	5.24 N	73.38 E
Digambar Jain Temple ʋ [1]	272b	22.36 N	88.23 E
Digambarpur	126	21.57 N	88.22 E
Digba	154	4.24 N	25.47 E
Digboi	120	27.23 N	95.38 E
Digby	186	44.37 N	65.46 W
Digby Neck ≻ [1]	186	44.30 N	66.10 W
Dige	98	34.22 N	114.28 E
Digerberget ∧ [2]	40	60.35 N	13.25 E
Digges Islands II	176	62.35 N	77.50 W
Diggle	262	53.34 N	1.59 W
Dighalia	126	23.07 N	89.39 E
Dighipāra	126	21.58 N	88.17 E
Dighode	272c	18.54 N	73.02 E
Dighra	272b	22.47 N	88.32 E
Dighton, Ks., U.S.	198	38.28 N	100.28 W
Dighton, Ma., U.S.	207	41.48 N	71.07 W
Di Giorgio	228	35.15 N	118.51 W
Dīglūr	122	18.33 N	77.36 E
Digmoor	262	53.32 N	2.45 W
Dīgnagar	126	23.27 N	87.41 E
Dignano	64	46.05 N	12.56 E
Digne	62	44.06 N	6.14 E
Digoin	32	46.29 N	3.59 E
Digomi	84	41.47 N	44.44 E
Digong	104	42.11 N	122.03 E
Digor	84	40.23 N	43.24 E
Digora	84	43.10 N	44.09 E
Digos	116	6.45 N	125.20 E
Digra	272b	22.50 N	88.20 E
Digras	122	20.07 N	77.43 E
Digri	120	25.10 N	69.07 E
Digui	152	5.28 N	20.50 E
Digul ≏	164	7.07 S	138.42 E
Dihaer	86	42.35 N	89.49 E
Dihun	144	7.18 N	42.42 E
Diirmentobe	86	45.44 N	63.37 E
Dijag	24	65.48 N	57.39 E
Dijlah, Wādī V	142	29.58 N	31.18 E
Dijlah → Tigris ≏	128	31.00 N	47.25 E
Dijle (Dyle) ≏	56	51.04 N	4.25 E
Dijohan Point ≻	116	16.19 N	122.14 E
Dijon	58	47.19 N	5.01 E
Dik	146	9.58 N	17.31 E
Dikaja	76	59.15 N	39.30 E
Dikala	154	4.41 N	31.23 E
Dikan'ka	78	49.49 N	34.32 E
Dikbıyık	130	41.13 N	36.38 E
Dike	190	42.27 N	92.37 W
Dikhil	144	11.06 N	42.22 E
Dikili	130	39.04 N	26.53 E
Dikirnis	142	31.05 N	31.35 E
Dikli	76	57.35 N	25.06 E
Diklosmta, gora ∧	84	42.29 N	45.47 E
Dikmen	130	39.53 N	32.50 E
Dikodougou	150	9.04 N	5.46 W
Diksmuide (Dixmude)	50	51.02 N	2.52 E
Dikson	74	73.30 N	80.35 E
Dikwa	146	12.02 N	13.56 E
Dila	144	6.21 N	38.17 E
Dilektepe	130	38.04 N	41.49 E
Dile Point ≻	116	17.34 N	120.20 E
Dilerpur	272b	22.51 N	88.10 E
Dili	112	8.33 S	125.35 E
Dilia V	146	16.53 N	11.00 E
Diligent Strait ʮ	110	12.11 N	92.57 E
Di Linh	110	11.35 N	108.04 E
Diližan	84	40.45 N	44.52 E
Diližanskij zapovednik ♦	84	40.40 N	45.00 E
Dill ≏	56	50.33 N	8.29 E
Dill City	196	35.16 N	99.08 W
Dillenburg	56	50.44 N	8.17 E
Diller	198	40.06 N	96.56 W
Dilley, Or., U.S.	224	45.29 N	123.07 W
Dilley, Tx., U.S.	196	28.40 N	99.10 W
Dilling	140	12.03 N	29.39 E
Dillingen	56	49.21 N	6.44 E
Dillingen an der Donau	56	48.34 N	10.29 E
Dillingham	180	59.02 N	158.29 W
Dillon, Co., U.S.	200	39.37 N	106.02 W
Dillon, Mt., U.S.	202	45.12 N	112.38 W
Dillon, S.C., U.S.	192	34.24 N	79.22 W
Dillon ≏	184	55.56 N	108.57 W
Dillon Cone ∧	172	42.16 S	173.13 E
Dillon Lake ⊜	184	55.45 N	109.30 W
Dillon Lake ⊜ [1]	188	40.02 N	82.10 W
Dillon Mountain ∧	200	33.51 N	108.48 W
Dillon Reservoir ⊜ [1]	200	39.35 N	106.02 W
Dillon State Park ♦	188	40.03 N	82.08 W
Dillonvale	214	40.11 N	80.46 W
Dillsboro	218	39.01 N	85.03 W
Dillsburg	208	40.06 N	77.02 W
Dilltown	214	40.29 N	79.00 W
Dillwyn	192	37.32 N	78.27 W
Dilly	150	15.01 N	7.40 W
Dilolo	152	10.42 S	22.20 E
Dilsen	56	51.02 N	5.44 E
Dilworth	198	46.52 N	96.42 W
Dilworthtown	285	39.54 N	75.34 W
Dima, Ang.	152	15.27 S	20.10 E
Dima, Indon.	114	1.20 N	97.20 E
Dimāpur	120	25.54 N	93.44 E
Dimaro	64	46.20 N	10.52 E
Dimasalang	116	12.12 N	123.51 E
Dimashq (Damascus)	132	33.30 N	36.18 E
Dimashq □ [8]	132	33.30 N	37.00 E
Dimass, Rass ≻	36	35.37 N	11.03 E
Dimataling	116	7.32 N	123.22 E
Dimbelenge	152	5.33 S	23.07 E
Dimbokro	150	6.39 N	4.42 W
Dimboola	166	36.27 S	142.02 E
Dîmbovița □ [6]	38	45.00 N	25.30 E
Dimbovița ≏	38	44.14 N	26.27 E
Dimbulah	166	17.09 S	145.07 E
Dime	144	6.16 N	36.20 E
Dime Box	222	30.21 N	96.50 W
Dimitrov	83	48.15 N	37.18 E
Dimitrovgrad, Blg.	38	42.03 N	25.36 E
Dimitrovgrad, Jugo.	38	43.01 N	22.47 E
Dimitrovgrad, Ross.	80	54.14 N	49.39 E
Dimitrovo	78	48.36 N	33.01 E
Dimitrovo → Pernik	38	42.36 N	23.02 E
Dimitrovskoje	85	40.16 N	69.03 E
Dimlang ∧	146	8.24 N	11.47 E
Dimmitt	196	34.33 N	102.18 W
Dimo	154	5.19 N	29.10 E
Dimock	210	41.45 N	75.32 W
Dimona	132	31.04 N	35.02 E
Dimondale	216	42.38 N	84.38 W
Dina	123	33.02 N	73.36 E
Dinach	144	9.15 N	50.37 E
Dinagat	116	9.59 N	125.35 E
Dinagat Island I	116	10.12 N	125.35 E
Dinagat Sound ʮ	116	9.59 N	125.50 E
Dinahican Point ≻	116	14.42 N	121.44 E
Dinājpur	124	25.38 N	88.38 E
Dinalupihan	116	14.52 N	120.28 E
Dinamarca, Estrecho de → Denmark Strait ʮ	10	67.00 N	25.00 W
Dinamarca → Denmark □ [1]	26	56.00 N	10.00 E
Dinami	68	38.31 N	16.09 E
Dinamita	196	25.43 N	103.38 W
Dinamo	80	50.15 N	41.38 E
Dinan	32	48.27 N	2.02 W
Dīnānagar	123	32.09 N	75.28 E
Dinant	56	50.16 N	4.55 E
Dinar	130	38.04 N	30.10 E
Dinara (Dinaric Alps) ⋏	36	43.50 N	16.35 E
Dinard	32	48.38 N	2.04 W
Dinaric Alps → Dinara ⋏	36	43.50 N	16.35 E
Dinarische Alpen → Dinara ⋏	36	43.50 N	16.35 E
Dinas, Pil.	116	7.38 N	123.20 E
Dinas, Wales, U.K.	42	52.00 N	4.54 W
Dinas Head ≻	42	52.02 N	4.55 W
Dinas Powys	42	51.26 N	3.14 W
Dindanko	150	14.08 N	9.30 W
Dindar, Nahr ad- (Dinder) ≏	140	14.06 N	33.40 E
Dīndārpur ⊕ [8]	272a	28.36 N	76.59 E
Dinde	152	14.12 S	13.44 E
Dinder (Nahr ad-Dindar) ≏	140	14.06 N	33.40 E
Dinder National Park ♦	140	12.40 N	35.20 E
Dindi ≏	122	16.21 N	79.13 E
Dindigul	122	10.21 N	77.57 E
Dindima	150	10.18 N	10.12 E
Dindori	124	22.57 N	81.05 E
Dineksaray	130	37.23 N	32.37 E
Dinga, Pāk.	120	25.26 N	67.10 E
Dinga, Pāk.	123	32.38 N	73.43 E
Dinga, Zaïre	152	5.19 S	16.34 E
Dingalan Bay c	116	15.18 N	121.25 E
Ding'an	110	19.44 N	110.21 E
Dingba	154	3.24 N	27.55 E
Dingbian	102	37.40 N	107.41 E
Dingbianji	102	36.37 N	108.41 E
Dingbu	106	31.18 N	119.10 E
Dingden	52	51.46 N	6.37 E
Dinge	152	4.58 S	12.22 E
Dingelsdorf	58	47.44 N	9.09 E
Dingelstädt	54	51.18 N	10.19 E
Dingelstedt	54	51.58 N	10.58 E
Dingeryu	105	39.37 N	114.55 E
Dingfeng	106	31.20 N	121.45 E
Dinggou	100	32.34 N	119.39 E
Dinggyê	124	28.29 N	88.06 E
Dinghai	100	30.02 N	122.06 E
Dingila	154	3.39 N	26.22 E
Dingjia	107	29.24 N	106.09 E
Dingjiagou	104	40.40 N	122.35 E
Dingjiandian	106	32.06 N	120.52 E
Dingjiasuo	100	32.32 N	120.40 E
Dingjiazhuang	106	32.11 N	120.16 E
Dingkouzhen	102	39.55 N	106.40 E
Dingle	48	52.08 N	10.15 W
Dingle ⊕ [8]	262	53.23 N	2.57 W
Dingle Bay c	48	52.05 N	10.15 W
Dingley	274b	37.58 S	145.07 E
Dinglingen	58	48.20 N	7.50 E
Dingman Creek ≏	212	42.55 N	81.25 W
Dingmans Ferry	210	41.14 N	74.53 W
Dingnan	100	24.48 N	114.59 E
Dingnan ≏	100	24.28 N	115.26 E
Dingo	166	23.39 S	149.20 E
Dingolfing	60	48.38 N	12.31 E
Dingras	116	18.06 N	120.42 E
Dingshuzhen	106	31.17 N	119.50 E
Dingtao	98	35.04 N	115.34 E
Dingtuna	40	59.34 N	16.22 E
Dinguira	150	14.11 N	11.16 W
Dinguiraye	150	11.18 N	10.43 W
Dingwall, N.S., Can.	186	46.54 N	60.28 W
Dingwall, Scot., U.K.	46	57.35 N	4.29 W
Dingxi	102	35.33 N	104.32 E
Dingxian	98	38.32 N	114.59 E
Dingxiang	102	38.30 N	113.00 E
Dingxiao	102	25.13 N	105.07 E
Dingxing	105	39.17 N	115.46 E
Dingyan	100	32.23 N	120.45 E
Dingyuan	100	32.32 N	117.40 E
Dingzhouying	105	40.20 N	115.43 E
Dingzichang	107	28.54 N	106.08 E
Dingzi Gang c	98	36.37 N	120.50 E
Dinh, Mui ≻	110	11.22 N	109.01 E
Dinhāta	124	26.08 N	89.28 E
Dinh Ca	110	21.45 N	106.03 E
Dinh Lap	110	21.33 N	107.06 E
Dinin ≏	48	52.43 N	7.18 W
Dinkel ≏	52	52.30 N	6.58 E
Dinkelsbühl	56	49.04 N	10.19 E
Dinkelscherben	58	48.21 N	10.35 E
Dinkey Creek ≏	226	36.54 N	119.07 W
Dinklage	52	52.40 N	8.07 E
Dinnebito Wash V	200	35.29 N	111.14 W
Dinner Point ≻	220	28.28 N	82.41 W
Dinnet	46	57.03 N	2.54 W
Dinnington	44	53.22 N	1.12 W
Dinokwe	156	23.24 S	26.40 E
Dinorwic	184	49.41 N	92.30 W
Dinorwic Lake ⊜	184	49.37 N	92.33 W
Dinosaur	200	40.14 N	109.00 W
Dinosaur Lake ⊜ [1]	182	55.57 N	122.07 W
Dinosaur National Monument ♦	200	40.32 N	108.58 W
Dinosaur Provincial Park ♦	182	50.45 N	111.30 W
Dinskaja	78	45.13 N	39.14 E
Dinslaken	52	51.34 N	6.44 E
Dinslakener Bruch	263	51.35 N	6.43 E
Dinslaken-Schwarze Heide, Flughafen ⊠	263	51.37 N	6.51 E
Dinsmore	184	51.20 N	107.26 W
Dintel ≏	52	51.39 N	4.22 E
Dinteloord	52	51.37 N	4.22 E
Dinuba	226	36.32 N	119.23 W
Dinwiddie, S. Afr.	273d	26.16 S	28.10 E
Dinwiddie, Va., U.S.	208	37.04 N	77.35 W
Dinwiddie □ [6]	208	37.10 N	77.20 W
Dinxperlo	52	51.52 N	6.29 E
Diö	26	56.38 N	14.13 E
Diobo	152	2.16 N	20.29 E
Dioïla	150	12.29 N	6.48 W
Diois □ [9]	62	44.40 N	5.20 E
Diomede	180	65.47 N	169.00 W
Dion ≏	150	10.12 N	8.39 W
Dionísio	255	19.49 S	42.45 W
Dionísio Cerqueira	252	26.15 S	53.38 W
Dionne, Lac ⊜	186	49.26 N	67.55 W
Dions	62	43.56 N	4.19 E
Diorama	255	16.21 S	51.14 W
Dios	175e	5.33 S	154.58 E
Dios, Cayos de II	240p	21.39 N	81.09 W
Diósd	264c	47.25 N	18.57 E
Diouloulou	150	13.03 N	16.36 W
Dioumanténé	150	10.32 N	5.55 W
Dioundiou	150	12.37 N	3.33 E
Dioungani	150	14.19 N	2.44 W
Dioura	150	14.50 N	5.15 W
Diourbel	150	14.40 N	16.15 W
Diourbel □ [4]	150	14.45 N	16.30 W
Dipaculao	116	15.51 N	121.32 E
Dipai	100	23.50 N	114.06 E
Dīpālpur	123	30.40 N	73.39 E
Dipignano	68	39.15 N	16.15 E
Dipilo, Pizzo ∧	70	37.57 N	13.59 E
Dipkarpaz	130	35.36 N	34.23 E
Diplo	120	24.28 N	69.35 E
Dipolog	116	8.35 N	123.20 E
Dippoldiswalde	54	50.54 N	13.40 E
Dipton	172	45.54 S	168.22 E
Dipu	106	30.38 N	119.41 E
Diqiyingzi	104	42.11 N	121.29 E
Dique Florentino Ameghino	254	43.40 S	66.25 W
Dīr	123	35.12 N	71.53 E
Dira, Djebel ∧	34	36.05 N	3.38 E
Diré	150	16.16 N	3.24 W
Direction, Cape ≻	164	12.51 S	143.32 E
Dire Dawa	144	9.37 N	41.52 E
Direkli	130	39.43 N	36.40 E
Diriamba	236	11.51 N	86.14 W
Dirico	152	17.58 S	20.47 E
Dirillo, Lago ⊜	70	37.08 N	14.42 E
Diriomo	236	11.52 N	86.03 W
Dirj	146	30.09 N	10.26 E
Dirk Hartog Island I	162	25.48 S	113.00 E
Dirkiesdorp	158	27.10 S	30.25 E
Dirkou	146	19.01 N	12.53 E
Dirkshorn	52	52.45 N	4.45 E
Dirksland	52	51.44 N	4.06 E
Dirnaich	60	48.27 N	12.30 E
Dirrah	140	13.37 N	26.06 E
Dirranbandi	166	28.35 S	148.14 E
Dirri	144	4.20 N	46.37 E
Dirs	144	18.32 N	42.05 E
Dirschau → Tczew	30	54.06 N	18.47 E
Dirty Devil ≏	200	37.53 N	110.24 W
Dīsa	120	24.15 N	72.10 E
Dīsah	140	12.02 N	34.19 E
Disappointment, Cape ≻, S. Geor.	244	54.53 S	36.07 W
Disappointment, Cape ≻, Wa., U.S.	224	46.18 N	124.03 W
Disappointment, Lake ⊜	162	23.30 S	122.50 E
Disappointment, Mount ∧	169	37.25 S	145.18 E
Disappointment Creek ≏	200	38.01 N	108.51 W
Disaster Bay c	166	37.17 S	150.00 E
Disautel	182	48.22 N	119.14 W
Disbrow Drain ≍	281	42.06 N	83.27 W
Disco	214	42.41 N	83.02 W
Discovery	273d	26.10 S	27.54 E
Discovery Bay c, Austl.	166	38.12 S	141.07 E
Discovery Bay c, H.K.	271d	22.18 N	114.01 E
Discovery Bay c, Wa., U.S.	224	48.05 N	122.52 W
Discovery Island I	224	48.25 N	123.15 W
Discovery Passage ʮ	182	50.00 N	125.15 W
Discovery Tablemount ⊕ [3]	8	42.00 S	0.10 E
Disentis	58	46.43 N	8.51 E
Dishāshah	142	28.59 N	30.51 E
Dishergarh	126	23.41 N	86.50 E
Dishman	202	47.39 N	117.16 W
Dishnā	140	26.07 N	32.28 E
Dishna ≏	180	63.37 N	157.18 W
Disihao	89	50.28 N	124.35 E
Disko	216	41.00 N	85.57 W
Disko I	176	69.50 N	53.30 W
Disko Bugt c	176	69.15 N	52.00 W
Disley	262	53.21 N	2.02 W
Disley Tunnel ⊕ [5]	262	53.22 N	2.03 W
Dismal ≏	198	41.50 N	100.05 W
Dismal Lakes ⊜	176	67.26 N	117.07 W
Dismal Swamp Canal ≍	208	36.45 N	76.20 W
Disna	76	55.33 N	28.10 E
Disna ≏	76	55.34 N	28.12 E
Disney	196	36.28 N	95.00 W
Disneyland ♦	228	33.48 N	117.55 W
Disneyworld ♦	220	28.27 N	81.28 W
Diso	68	40.00 N	18.23 E
Dispur	120	26.08 N	91.47 E
Disputanta	208	37.07 N	77.13 W
Disraeli	206	45.54 N	71.21 W
Diss	42	52.23 N	1.07 E
Dissen	52	52.07 N	8.12 E
Dissimieux, Lac ⊜	186	49.51 N	69.48 W
Distant	214	40.58 N	79.21 W
Disteghil Sār ∧	123	36.19 N	75.12 E
Disteln	263	51.36 N	7.09 E
Distington	44	54.36 N	3.32 W
District Heights	284c	38.51 N	76.53 W
District of Columbia □ [3]	208	38.54 N	77.01 W
Distrito Especial □ [5]	246	4.15 N	74.15 W
Distrito Federal □ [5], Arg.	258	34.36 S	58.26 W
Distrito Federal □ [5], Bra.	255	15.45 S	47.45 W
Distrito Federal □ [5], Méx.	234	19.15 N	99.10 W
Distrito Federal □ [5], Ven.	246	10.30 N	66.55 W
Distroff	56	49.20 N	6.16 E
Disūq	142	31.08 N	30.39 E
Ditfurt	54	51.50 N	11.11 E
Dithmarschen ⊕ [1]	30	54.05 N	9.00 E
Dit Island I	116	11.15 N	120.56 E
Dittáino ≏	70	37.25 N	15.00 E
Ditton, Eng., U.K.	260	51.18 N	0.27 E
Ditton, Eng., U.K.	262	53.22 N	2.45 W
Ditton ≏	206	45.23 N	71.12 W
Ditton Priors	42	52.30 N	2.35 W
Ditzingen	56	48.49 N	9.03 E
Ditzum	52	53.18 N	7.16 E
Diu	120	20.42 N	70.59 E
Diu □ [8]	120	20.42 N	70.59 E
Diuata Mountains ⋏	116	9.10 N	125.47 E
Diuata Point ≻	116	9.05 N	125.12 E
Dīva	272c	19.09 N	72.59 E
Divalá	236	8.25 N	82.43 W
Dīvāndarreh	128	35.55 N	47.02 E
Dívčice	61	49.06 N	14.19 E
Dive	272c	19.11 N	73.02 E
Divejevo	80	55.03 N	43.15 E
Divenié	152	2.41 S	12.05 E
Divenskaja	76	59.12 N	30.01 E
Diveria ≏	58	46.09 N	8.19 E
Divernon	219	39.33 N	89.39 W
Dives ≏	32	49.19 N	0.05 W
Diviči	84	41.12 N	48.59 E
Dividing Creek	208	39.16 N	75.06 W
Dividing Creek ≏	208	38.05 N	75.32 W
Dividing Ridge ∧	219	39.07 N	90.39 W
Divignano	266b	45.40 N	8.36 E
Divilacan Bay c	116	17.25 N	122.19 E
Divin	76	51.58 N	24.35 E
Divine Corners	210	41.48 N	74.40 W
Divinhe	156	20.40 S	34.49 E
Divino	255	20.37 S	42.09 W
Divinolândia	256	21.40 S	46.45 W
Divinópolis	255	20.09 S	44.54 W
Divion	50	50.28 N	2.30 E
Divi Point ≻	122	15.58 N	81.09 E
Divis ∧ [2]	48	54.37 N	6.01 W
Divisa Nova	256	21.31 S	46.12 W
Divisor, Serra do (Cordillera Ultraoriental) ⋏ [1]	248	8.20 S	73.30 W
Divizija	78	45.57 N	29.59 E
Divnogorsk	86	55.58 N	92.22 E
Divnoje	80	45.55 N	43.22 E
Divo	150	5.50 N	5.22 W
Divodar	120	24.06 N	71.47 E
Divonne-les-Bains	58	46.22 N	6.08 E
Divriği	130	39.23 N	38.07 E
Dīwāl Qol	120	34.19 N	67.54 E
Dix, Il., U.S.	219	38.27 N	88.56 W
Dix, Ne., U.S.	198	41.14 N	103.29 W
Dix ≏	192	37.49 N	84.43 W
Dix, Lac des ⊜	58	46.03 N	7.24 E
Dixboro	216	42.19 N	83.39 W
Dixfield	188	44.32 N	70.27 W
Dix Hills	276	40.49 N	73.22 W
Dixie	275b	43.36 N	79.36 W
Dixie Valley V	204	39.50 N	117.55 W
Dix Milles, Lac ⊜	190	46.46 N	77.45 W
Dixmoor	278	41.38 N	87.40 W
Dixmude → Diksmuide	50	51.02 N	2.52 E
Dixon, Ca., U.S.	226	38.19 N	121.49 W
Dixon, Il., U.S.	190	41.50 N	89.28 W
Dixon, Ky., U.S.	194	37.31 N	87.41 W
Dixon, Mo., U.S.	194	37.59 N	92.05 W
Dixon, N.M., U.S.	200	36.11 N	105.53 W
Dixon, Oh., U.S.	216	40.57 N	84.48 W
Dixon Entrance ʮ	182	54.25 N	132.30 W
Dixons Mills	194	32.04 N	87.47 W
Dixons Pond ⊜	276	40.56 N	74.27 W
Dixonville	214	40.42 N	79.00 W
Dixville	206	45.04 N	71.46 W
Diyā al-Kawm	142	30.38 N	31.05 E
Diyadin	84	39.33 N	43.41 E
Diyālā □ [4]	128	34.00 N	45.00 E
Diyālā (Sīrvān) ≏	128	33.14 N	44.31 E
Diyanga	152	1.29 S	11.52 E
Diyarbakır	130	37.55 N	40.14 E
Diyarbakır □ [4]	130	38.05 N	40.15 E
Diyarb Najm	142	30.45 N	31.26 E
Diyu al-Wasta	142	30.54 N	31.30 E
Dizangsi	104	41.26 N	120.57 E
Dizhou	102	23.00 N	106.20 E
Dizy	50	49.04 N	3.58 E
Dizzard Point ≻	42	50.45 N	4.38 W
Dja ≏	152	2.02 N	15.12 E
Dja, Réserve du ⊕ [4]	152	3.05 N	13.00 E
Djabalpur → Jabalpur	124	23.10 N	79.57 E
Djabir	152	0.32 N	24.05 E
Djadié ≏	152	0.46 N	12.58 E
Djado	146	21.01 N	12.18 E
Djado, Plateau du ⋏ [1]	146	21.45 N	12.50 E
Djaipur → Jaipur	120	26.55 N	75.49 E
Djakarta → Jakarta	269e	6.10 S	106.48 E
Djakonovo	82	54.34 N	38.20 E
Djakovka	80	50.43 N	46.46 E
Djakovo	83	47.57 N	39.09 E
Djakovo ⊕ [8]	265b	55.39 N	37.40 E
Djamâa	148	33.32 N	6.00 E
Djamba, Ang.	152	16.46 S	13.59 E
Djamba, Zaïre	152	9.49 S	22.07 E
Djambala	152	2.33 S	14.45 E
Djamschedpur → Jamshedpur	126	22.48 N	86.11 E
Djanet	148	24.34 N	9.29 E
Djaouro Mbali	152	5.52 N	13.29 E
Djaret, Oued V	148	26.32 N	1.30 E
Djebobo ∧	150	8.20 N	0.35 E
Djébrène	146	11.14 N	19.01 E
Djédaa	146	13.31 N	18.34 E
Djedda → Jiddah	144	21.30 N	39.12 E
Djedi, Oued V	148	34.28 N	6.05 E
Djéké Djéké	146	8.25 N	18.12 E
Djelo-Binza	273b	4.23 S	15.16 E
Djema	140	6.03 N	25.19 E
Djember	146	10.25 N	17.50 E
Djember → Jember	115a	8.10 S	113.42 E
Djemila ⊥	34	36.25 N	5.44 E
Djénné	150	13.54 N	4.33 W
Djenoun, Garet el ∧	148	25.05 N	5.25 E
Djérem ≏	152	5.20 N	13.24 E
Djibasso	150	13.07 N	4.10 W
Djibo	150	14.06 N	1.38 W
Djibouti	144	11.36 N	43.09 E
Djibouti □ [1], Afr.	136	11.30 N	43.00 E
Djibouti □ [1], Afr.	144	11.30 N	43.00 E
Djibrouïa	150	13.13 N	11.14 W
Djiri	273b	4.08 S	15.19 E
Djiri ≏	273b	4.11 S	15.20 E
Djohong	152	6.50 N	14.42 E
Djokjakarta → Yogyakarta	115a	7.48 S	110.22 E
Djokoumatombi	152	0.47 N	15.22 E
Djokupunda	152	5.27 S	20.58 E
Djolu	152	0.37 N	22.21 E
Djombo	152	1.21 N	20.22 E
Djoua ≏	152	1.13 N	13.12 E
Djouari ≏	273b	4.13 S	15.08 E
Djoubissi	152	6.12 N	20.45 E
Djoué ≏	273b	4.19 S	15.14 E
Djougou	150	9.42 N	1.40 E
Djoum	152	2.40 N	12.40 E
Djouna	146	10.27 N	20.04 E
Djourab, Erg du • [8]	146	16.40 N	18.50 E
Djugu	154	1.55 N	30.30 E
Djúpivogur	24a	64.40 N	14.10 W
Djura	40	60.37 N	15.00 E
Djurås	40	60.33 N	15.08 E
Djurmo	40	60.33 N	15.10 E
Djurö	40	59.19 N	18.41 E
Djurö I	26	58.52 N	13.28 E
Djursholm	40	59.24 N	18.05 E
Dlouhá Ves	60	49.12 N	13.31 E
Dmanisi	84	41.22 N	44.12 E
Dmitr'ašovka	76	52.09 N	39.04 E
Dmitrija Lapteva, proliv ʮ	74	73.00 N	142.00 E
Dmitrijevka, Kaz.	85	43.30 N	77.02 E
Dmitrijevka, Ross.	76	52.53 N	40.47 E
Dmitrijevka, Ross.	86	55.10 N	75.36 E
Dmitrijevka, Ukr.	78	50.56 N	32.58 E
Dmitrijevka, Ukr.	83	47.56 N	38.56 E
Dmitrijevka, Ukr.	83	48.55 N	39.10 E
Dmitrijev-L'govskij	78	52.08 N	35.05 E
Dmitrijevskij	86	49.08 N	57.50 E
Dmitrijevskoje, Ross.	80	45.48 N	41.54 E
Dmitrijevskoje, Ross.	82	54.40 N	37.38 E
Dmitrijev Usad, Ross.	76	54.08 N	43.08 E
Dmitrijev Usad, Ross.	80	54.14 N	43.18 E
Dmitrijevy Gory	80	55.12 N	41.47 E
Dmitrov	82	56.21 N	37.31 E
Dmitrovcy	82	55.16 N	38.55 E
Dmitroviči	76	53.59 N	29.06 E
Dmitrovka, Ukr.	78	45.29 N	35.04 E
Dmitrovka, Ukr.	78	48.48 N	32.44 E
Dmitrovka, Ukr.	78	46.51 N	36.35 E
Dmitrovskij Pogost	76	55.19 N	39.49 E
Dmitrovsk-Orlovskij	76	52.30 N	35.09 E
Dmuchajlovka	78	49.03 N	34.46 E
Dnepr ≏	78	46.30 N	32.18 E
Dnepr'any	78	46.44 N	33.16 E
Dneprodzeržinsk	78	48.30 N	34.37 E
Dneprodzeržinskoje vodochranilšče ⊜ [1]	78	48.45 N	34.00 E
Dnepropetrovsk	78	48.27 N	34.59 E
Dnepropetrovsk □ [4]	78	48.30 N	35.00 E
Dneprovka	78	47.26 N	34.38 E
Dneprovskij liman c [1]	78	46.35 N	31.55 E
Dneprovsko-Bugskij kanal ≍	76	52.03 N	25.35 E
Dneprovskoje	76	55.40 N	33.55 E
Dnestr ≏	78	46.18 N	30.17 E
Dnestrovskij liman ⊜	78	46.15 N	30.17 E
Dnieper → Dnepr ≏	78	46.30 N	32.18 E
Dniepropetrovsk → Dnepropetrovsk	78	48.27 N	34.59 E
Dniester → Dnestr ≏	78	46.18 N	30.17 E
Dno	76	57.50 N	29.59 E
Do, Lac ⊜	150	15.54 N	2.45 W
Doa	154	16.44 S	34.32 E
Do Āb-e Mīkh-e Zarrīn	120	35.16 N	68.00 E
Doaktown	186	46.33 N	66.08 W
Doangdoangan-Besar, Pulau I	112	5.24 S	117.55 E
Doany	157b	14.22 S	49.31 E
Doba	146	8.39 N	16.51 E
Dobane	140	6.24 N	24.42 E
Dobbertin	54	53.37 N	12.04 E
Dobbiaco (Toblach)	64	46.44 N	12.14 E
Dobbin	222	30.22 N	95.46 W
Dobbins	226	39.22 N	121.12 W
Dobbins Air Force Base ■	192	33.54 N	84.31 W
Dobbs Ferry	210	41.00 N	73.52 W
Dobczyce	30	49.54 N	20.06 E
Dobel	56	48.48 N	8.29 E
Dobele	76	56.37 N	23.16 E
Döbeln	54	51.07 N	13.07 E
Doberai, Jazirah (Vogelkop) ≻ [1]	164	1.30 S	132.30 E
Döberitz	264a	52.33 N	13.03 E
Doberlug-Kirchhain	54	51.38 N	13.34 E
Döbern	54	51.37 N	14.36 E
Dobiegniew	30	52.59 N	15.47 E
Döbling ⊕ [8]	264b	48.15 N	16.22 E
Dobo	164	5.46 S	134.13 E
Doboj	38	44.44 N	18.06 E
Dobra, Pol.	30	51.54 N	18.37 E
Dobra, Pol.	30	53.35 N	15.18 E
Dobra ≏	36	45.33 N	15.31 E
Dobr'anka, Ross.	86	58.27 N	56.24 E
Dobr'anka, Ukr.	78	52.04 N	31.11 E
Dobr'ankka	78	48.21 N	30.54 E
Dobřany	60	49.40 N	13.18 E
Dobra Stausee ⊜ [1]	61	48.35 N	15.20 E
Dobre Miasto	30	53.59 N	20.25 E
Döbriach	64	46.47 N	13.39 E
Dobrič	38	43.34 N	27.50 E
Dobrich → Dobrič	38	43.34 N	27.50 E
Dobrinka, Ross.	80	52.09 N	40.29 E
Dobrinka, Ross.	80	48.49 N	42.58 E
Dobrinka, Ross.	80	50.49 N	41.51 E
Dobříš	30	49.47 N	14.11 E
Dobritz	54	52.01 N	12.13 E
Dobrodzień	30	50.44 N	18.27 E
Dobroje, Ross.	76	57.06 N	32.02 E
Dobroje, Ross.	76	52.52 N	39.48 E
Dobroměřice	54	50.23 N	13.46 E
Dobromil'	78	49.34 N	22.47 E
Dobropolje	78	48.28 N	37.05 E
Dobroslavka	76	52.24 N	26.15 E
Dobroteasa	38	44.47 N	24.23 E
Dobrotvor	78	50.14 N	24.22 E
Dobroveličkovka	78	48.23 N	31.11 E
Dobrovolje	78	48.41 N	36.37 E
Dobrovol'sk	76	54.46 N	22.31 E
Dobrudžansko plato ⋏ [1]	38	43.32 N	27.50 E
Dobruja ⊕ [1]	38	44.00 N	28.00 E
Dobruš	76	52.25 N	31.19 E
Dobruška	30	50.17 N	16.10 E
Dobryn'	78	51.46 N	29.12 E
Dobrzany	30	53.22 N	15.25 E
Dobrzyń nad Wisłą	30	52.38 N	19.20 E
Dobšiná	30	48.49 N	20.23 E
Dobson	192	36.23 N	80.43 W
Dobzha	120	28.28 N	88.14 E
Doce ≏, Bra.	255	19.37 S	39.49 W
Doce ≏, Bra.	255	18.28 S	51.05 W
Doce de Octubre	196	25.38 N	97.47 W
Dochart ≏	46	56.28 N	4.20 W
Döčin ≏	88	49.39 N	114.48 E
Docker River	162	24.52 S	129.05 E
Docking	42	52.55 N	0.38 E
Dock Junction	192	31.11 N	81.31 W
Dockton	224	47.22 N	122.27 W
Dockweiler	56	50.15 N	6.46 E
Dockweiler Beach State Park ♦	280	33.55 N	118.26 W
Doctor Arroyo	234	23.40 N	100.11 W
Doctor Cecilio Báez	252	25.03 S	56.19 W
Doctor Coss	196	25.55 N	99.11 W
Doctor Edmund A. Babler Memorial State Park ♦	219	38.36 N	90.43 W
Doctor Hicks Range ⋏	162	28.40 S	124.20 E
Doctor Pedro P. Peña	252	22.26 S	62.22 W
Doctors Creek ≏	208	40.11 N	74.41 W
Doda	123	33.08 N	75.34 E
Dod Ballāpur	122	13.18 N	77.32 E
Doddinghurst	42	51.40 N	0.18 E
Doddridge	194	33.05 N	93.54 W
Dodds Island I	219	38.35 N	91.59 W
Doddsville	194	33.39 N	90.31 W
Dodecanese → Dhodhekánisos II	38	36.30 N	27.00 E
Dodéo	152	7.29 N	12.04 E
Dodge, Ne., U.S.	198	41.43 N	96.52 W
Dodge, Tx., U.S.	222	30.45 N	95.24 W
Dodge □ [6]	216	43.14 N	88.40 W
Dodge Brothers State Park Number 4 ♦, Mi., U.S.	281	42.37 N	83.22 W
Dodge Brothers State Park Number 8 ♦, Mi., U.S.	281	42.36 N	83.01 W
Dodge Center	190	44.01 N	92.51 W
Dodge City	198	37.45 N	100.01 W
Dodge Park	284c	38.56 N	76.53 W
Dodger Stadium ♦	280	34.04 N	118.14 W
Dodgeville	190	42.57 N	90.07 W
Dodman Point ≻	42	50.13 N	4.48 W
Dodo Goei	140	5.57 N	29.26 E
Dodola	144	7.02 N	39.07 E
Dodoma	154	6.11 S	35.45 E
Dodoma □ [4]	154	6.00 S	36.00 E
Dodori ≏	154	1.52 S	41.02 E
Dodsland	184	51.48 N	108.49 W
Dodson, La., U.S.	194	32.04 N	92.39 W
Dodson, Mt., U.S.	202	48.23 N	108.14 W
Dodson, Tx., U.S.	196	34.46 N	100.02 W
Dodson Peninsula ≻ [1]	9	75.46 S	62.50 W
Dodurga	130	39.48 N	29.55 E
Doe Lake ⊜	212	45.32 N	79.25 W
Doe River	182	56.00 N	120.05 W
Doerun	192	31.19 N	83.55 W
Doesburg	52	52.01 N	6.09 E
Doetinchem	52	51.58 N	6.17 E
Dog ≏	190	48.51 N	89.37 W
Dogāchia	272b	22.58 N	88.31 E
Dogai Coring ⊜	120	34.30 N	89.15 E
Dōga-mori ∧	96	33.09 N	132.53 E
Doğanbey, Tür.	130	37.37 N	27.11 E
Doğanbey, Tür.	130	38.04 N	26.53 E
Doğanbey, Tür.	130	37.48 N	31.54 E
Doğanca	130	37.49 N	42.20 E
Doğançay	130	40.37 N	30.20 E
Doganella	66	41.34 N	12.56 E
Doğanhisar	130	38.09 N	31.41 E
Doğankent, Tür.	130	36.52 N	35.18 E
Doğankent, Tür.	130	40.48 N	38.56 E
Doğanşehir	130	38.06 N	37.53 E
Doğanyol	130	38.19 N	39.03 E
Doğanyurt, Tür.	130	42.00 N	33.27 E
Doğanyurt, Tür.	130	40.41 N	36.43 E
Dog Creek	182	51.35 N	122.15 W
Dog Creek ≏, B.C., Can.	182	51.35 N	122.17 W
Dog Creek ≏, Mt., U.S.	202	47.44 N	109.36 W
Dog Creek ≏, Oh., U.S.	216	41.03 N	84.23 W
Dog Ear Creek ≏	198	43.42 N	99.59 W
Dog Island I, Anguilla	238	18.17 N	63.16 W
Dog Island I, Fl., U.S.	192	29.48 N	84.35 W
Dog Islands II	240m	18.29 N	64.28 W
Dog Lake ⊜, Mb., Can.	184	51.02 N	98.30 W
Dog Lake ⊜, On., Can.	190	48.46 N	89.32 W
Dog Lake ⊜, On., Can.	190	48.18 N	84.10 W
Dog Lake ⊜, On., Can.	212	44.27 N	76.20 W
Dogliani	62	44.32 N	7.56 E
Dogna	64	46.27 N	13.19 E
Dōgo I	92	36.15 N	133.16 E
Do Gonbadān	128	30.21 N	50.48 E
Dogondoutchi	150	13.38 N	4.02 E
Doğonşar	130	40.14 N	37.33 E
Dōgo-yama ∧	96	35.04 N	133.14 E
Dogpound Creek ≏	182	51.50 N	114.24 W
Dogs, Isle of I	260	51.29 N	0.01 W
D'ogtevo, Ross.	78	49.10 N	40.39 E
D'ogtevo, Ross.	80	49.11 N	40.39 E
Doğubayazıt	84	39.32 N	44.08 E
Doguéraoua	150	13.58 N	5.35 E
Doğu Karadeniz Dağları ⋏	130	40.30 N	40.30 E
Dogura	164	10.05 S	150.05 E
Doha → Ad-Dawḥah	128	25.17 N	51.32 E
Dohār	126	23.35 N	90.09 E
Dohhi	124	24.32 N	84.54 E
Dohna	54	50.57 N	13.51 E
Dohrgaul	263	51.06 N	7.27 E
Dohrīghāt	124	26.16 N	83.31 E
Doi	96	33.57 N	133.26 E
Doi, Kinh ≍	269c	10.43 N	106.37 E
Doilungdêqên	124	29.48 N	90.47 E
Doiran, Lake ⊜	38	41.13 N	22.44 E
Doiras, Embalse de ⊜ [1]	34	43.10 N	6.45 W
Dois de Novembro, Cachoeira ᒪ	248	8.52 S	62.16 W
Dois Irmãos, Pico ∧	287a	22.59 S	43.14 W
Dois Irmãos de Goiás	250	9.16 S	49.05 W
Doi Suthep-Pui National Park ♦	110	18.50 N	98.50 E
Dōjō	268	35.51 N	139.37 E
Dōjō ⊕ [8]	270	34.52 N	135.14 E
Doka, Indon.	164	6.39 S	134.15 E
Doka, Sūd.	140	13.31 N	35.46 E
Doki ≏	96	34.18 N	133.48 E
Dokka	26	60.50 N	10.05 E
Dokkum	52	53.19 N	6.00 E
Dökmetepe	130	40.19 N	36.18 E
Dokri	120	27.23 N	68.06 E
Dokšicy	76	54.54 N	27.46 E
Dokská pahorkatina ⋏ [2]	54	50.30 N	14.45 E
Doksy	54	50.35 N	14.38 E
Dokučajevsk	83	47.44 N	37.40 E
Dol'a, Ukr.	83	47.53 N	37.41 E
Dola, Oh., U.S.	216	40.47 N	83.42 W
Dolak ≏	164	7.48 S	139.00 E
Doland	198	44.53 N	98.06 W
Dolany	60	49.27 N	13.15 E
Dolavon	254	43.18 S	65.42 W
Dolayoba	267b	40.54 N	29.15 E
Dolbeau	176	48.53 N	72.14 W
Dolberg	52	51.42 N	7.55 E
Dolceacqua	62	43.51 N	7.37 E
Dolcedorme, Serra ∧	68	39.53 N	16.13 E
Dol-de-Bretagne	32	48.33 N	1.45 W
Dole	58	47.06 N	5.30 E
Dolega	236	8.34 N	82.25 W
Dolen	222	30.26 N	94.54 W
Dolgaja	86	55.49 N	64.15 E
Dolgaja, kosa ≻ [2]	78	46.43 N	37.41 E
Dolgarrog	44	53.11 N	3.51 W
Dolgelin	54	52.29 N	14.24 E
Dolgellau	42	52.44 N	3.53 W
Dolgen'koje	83	49.01 N	37.19 E

	English	Deutsch	Español	Français	Português
≏	River	Fluß	Río	Rivière	Rio
≍	Canal	Kanal	Canal	Canal	Canal
ᒪ	Waterfall, Rapids	Wasserfall, Stromschnellen	Cascada, Rápidos	Chute d'eau, Rapides	Cascata, Rápidos
ʮ	Strait	Meeresstraße	Estrecho	Détroit	Estreito
c	Bay, Gulf	Bucht, Golf	Bahía, Golfo	Baie, Golfe	Baía, Golfo
⊜	Lake, Lakes	See, Seen	Lago, Lagos	Lac, Lacs	Lago, Lagos
≋	Swamp	Sumpf	Pantano	Marais	Pântano
⊼	Ice Features, Glacier	Eis- und Gletscherformen	Accidentes Glaciales	Formes glaciaires	Acidentes glaciares
ᵼ	Other Hydrographic Features	Andere Hydrographische Objekte	Otros Elementos Hidrográficos	Autres données hydrographiques	Outros acidentes hidrográficos
⊕	Submarine Features	Untermeerische Objekte	Accidentes Submarinos	Formes de relief sous-marin	Acidentes submarinos
□	Political Unit	Politische Einheit	Unidad Politica	Entité politique	Unidade política
ʋ	Cultural Institution	Kulturelle Institution	Institución Cultural	Institution culturelle	Instituição cultural
⊥	Historical Site	Historische Stätte	Sitio Histórico	Site historique	Sitio histórico
♦	Recreational Site	Erholungs- und Ferienort	Sitio de Recreo	Centre de loisirs	Area de Lazer
⊠	Airport	Flughafen	Aeropuerto	Aéroport	Aeroporto
■	Military Installation	Militäranlage	Instalación Militar	Installation militaire	Instalação militar
◆	Miscellaneous	Verschiedenes	Misceláneo	Divers	Diversos

ENGLISH / DEUTSCH

Name | Page (Seite) | Lat.°′ (Breite°′) | Long.°′ (Länge°′ E = Ost)

Dolgeville 210 43.06 N 74.46 W
Dolgij, ostrov I 24 69.15 N 59.04 E
Dolgij Most 88 56.45 N 96.48 E
Dolginovo 76 54.39 N 27.29 E
Dolgoi Island I 180 55.10 N 161.45 W
Dolgoje 78 52.04 N 37.34 E
Dolgoprudnyj 82 55.56 N 37.31 E
Dolgorukovo 76 52.19 N 38.21 E
Dolgoščelje 24 66.03 N 43.24 E
Dolianova 71 39.22 N 9.10 E
Dolina, Ukr. 78 48.58 N 24.01 E
Dolina, Ukr. 83 48.59 N 37.27 E
Dolinnyj 80 51.16 N 52.11 E
Dolinovskoje 83 48.36 N 38.33 E
Dolinsk 89 47.21 N 142.48 E
Dolinskaja 78 48.07 N 32.44 E
Dolisie 152 4.12 S 12.41 E
Dolj □[6] 38 44.15 N 23.45 E
Döllach 64 46.58 N 12.54 E
Dollar 46 56.09 N 3.40 W
Dollard ⊂ 52 53.17 N 7.10 E
Dollard-des-Ormeaux 206 45.29 N 73.49 W
Dollar Law ∧ 46 55.33 N 3.17 W
Döllbach 56 50.26 N 9.44 E
Dolle 54 52.25 N 11.37 E
Dollern 52 53.32 N 9.32 E
Dollerup 41 54.46 N 9.40 E
Döllnitz 54 51.24 N 12.01 E
Dollnstein 60 48.52 N 11.04 E
Döllstädt 54 51.05 N 10.49 E
Dolmabahce Palace ✪ 267b 41.02 N 29.00 E
Dolmatovka 78 46.13 N 32.26 E
Dolmatovskij 80 57.29 N 42.18 E
Dolni Dâbnik 38 43.24 N 24.26 E
Dolní Dvořiště 61 48.39 N 14.27 E
Dolní Jiřetín 54 50.35 N 13.33 E
Dolni Lom 38 43.31 N 22.47 E
Dolni Žandov 60 50.02 N 12.34 E
Dolný Kubín 30 49.12 N 19.17 E
Dolo 64 45.25 N 12.05 E
Dolohmwar ∧ 174r 6.52 N 158.14 E
Dolokmerawan 114 3.10 N 99.08 E
Dolokparibuan 114 3.01 N 98.39 E
Dolomites
— Dolomiti ⋏ 64 46.25 N 11.50 E
Dolomiti (Dolomiten) ⋏ 64 46.25 N 11.50 E
Dolon′ 86 50.40 N 79.18 E
Dolon ≃ 62 45.18 N 4.46 E
Dolon, pereval)(85 41.52 N 75.45 E
Dolores, Arg. 252 36.20 S 57.40 W
Dolores, Col. 246 3.33 N 74.54 W
Dolores, Guat. 232 16.31 N 89.25 W
Dolores, Méx. 196 26.20 N 101.29 W
Dolores, Co., U.S. 200 37.28 N 108.30 W
Dolores, Ur. 252 33.33 S 58.13 W
Dolores, Ven. 246 8.18 N 69.34 W
Dolores ≃, Pil. 116 12.02 N 125.29 E
Dolores ≃, U.S. 200 38.49 N 109.17 W
Dolores, Mission ✪[1] 282 37.46 N 122.26 W
Dolores Hidalgo 234 21.10 N 100.56 W
Dolphin, Cape > 254 51.15 S 58.57 W
Dolphin and Union Strait ʊ 176 69.05 N 114.45 W
Dolphin Head ∧ 241q 18.22 N 78.10 W
Dölsach 64 46.49 N 12.51 E
Dolsk 30 52.00 N 17.03 E
Dol′skoje 82 54.47 N 36.26 E
Dolton, Eng., U.K. 42 50.53 N 4.01 W
Dolton, Il., U.S. 216 41.38 N 87.36 W
Dolwyddelan 44 53.03 N 3.53 W
Dolžak 78 48.41 N 26.32 E
Dolžanskaja, Ross. 78 46.37 N 37.48 E
Dolžanskaja, Ukr. 83 48.03 N 39.39 E
Dolžicy, Ross. 76 58.00 N 29.51 E
Dolžicy, Ross. 76 58.31 N 29.08 E
Dolžik 78 50.13 N 35.55 E
Dom ∧ 58 46.06 N 7.50 E
Dom, Gunung ∧ 164 2.40 S 136.53 E
D′oma ≃ 86 54.42 N 55.57 E
Domacha 76 52.28 N 34.58 E
Domačovo 78 51.44 N 23.37 E
Domadare 144 1.50 N 41.13 E
Domaine, Pointe du > 275a 45.23 N 73.54 W
Domanevka 78 47.37 N 30.58 E
Domaniči 76 53.02 N 33.25 E
Domanico 68 39.13 N 16.12 E
Dom Aquino 255 15.48 S 54.53 W
Domar, Enneri V 146 18.11 N 18.04 E
Domariāganj 124 27.13 N 82.40 E
Domart-en-Ponthieu 50 50.04 N 2.07 E
Domasi 154 15.18 S 35.20 E
Domaška 80 53.00 N 50.47 E
Domaso 58 46.09 N 9.19 E
Domat/Ems 58 46.50 N 9.28 E
Domažlice 60 49.27 N 12.56 E
Dombaj 84 43.17 N 41.37 E
Dombaj-Ul′gen, gora ∧ 84 43.14 N 41.41 E
Dombarovskij 86 50.46 N 59.32 E
Dombås 26 62.05 N 9.08 E
Dombasle-sur-Meurthe 58 48.38 N 6.21 E
Dombe 156 19.59 S 33.25 E
Dombe Grande 152 12.58 S 13.11 E
Dombes ◆[1] 58 46.00 N 5.03 E
Dombóvár 30 46.23 N 18.08 E
Dombrád 30 48.14 N 21.56 E
Dombresson 58 47.04 N 6.58 E
Domburg 52 51.34 N 3.30 E
Dom Cavati 255 19.23 S 42.06 W
Dôme, Puy de ∧ 32 45.47 N 2.58 E
Dome Creek 182 53.44 N 121.01 W
Domegge di Cadore 64 46.27 N 12.25 E
Domène 62 45.12 N 5.50 E
Dome Peak ∧, Pil. 116 5.37 N 125.20 E
Dome Peak ∧, Wa., U.S. 224 48.18 N 121.02 W
Domett 172 42.51 S 173.13 E
Domèvre-en-Haye 56 48.49 N 5.55 E
Domeyko 252 28.57 S 70.54 W
Domeyko, Cordillera ⋏ 252 24.30 S 69.00 W
Domfront 32 48.36 N 0.39 W
Domiciano Ribeiro 255 16.56 S 47.46 W
Dominal, Parc ♦ 62 44.52 N 6.32 E
Domíngo M. Irala 252 25.54 S 54.43 W
Domingos Martins 255 20.22 S 40.40 W
Dominguez 280 33.50 N 118.13 W
Dominguez Channel ʊ 280 38.47 N 118.15 W
Dominguez Hills ⋏[2] 280 33.52 N 118.14 W
Dominica □[1], N.A. 230 15.30 N 61.20 W
Dominica □[1], N.A. 240d 15.30 N 61.20 W
Dominicain (république)
— Dominican Republic □[1] 238 19.00 N 70.40 W
Dominical 236 9.13 N 83.51 W
Dominicana, República
— Dominican Republic □[1] 238 19.00 N 70.40 W
Dominican Republic (República Dominicana) □[1], N.A. 230 19.00 N 70.40 W
Dominican Republic (República Dominicana) □[1], N.A. 238 19.00 N 70.40 W
Dominica Passage ʊ 238 15.45 N 61.30 W
Dominikanische Republik
— Dominican Republic □[1] 238 19.00 N 70.40 W
Dominion 186 46.13 N 60.01 W
Dominion, Cape > 176 66.13 N 74.28 W
Dominion Astrophysical Observatory ✪[3] 224 48.31 N 123.25 W
Dominion City 184 49.08 N 97.09 W
Dominique
— Dominica □[1] 240d 15.30 N 61.20 W
Domiongo 152 4.37 S 21.15 E
Domitilla, Catacombe di ⊥ 267a 41.52 N 12.31 E
Dömitz 54 53.08 N 11.14 E
Dom Joaquim 255 18.57 S 43.16 W
Domleschg V 58 46.44 N 9.28 E
Dommartin-lès-Toul 58 48.40 N 5.54 E
Dommartin-Varimont 56 48.58 N 4.46 E
Dommary-Baroncourt 56 49.17 N 5.42 E
Dommel ≃ 52 51.40 N 5.20 E
Dommitzsch 54 51.38 N 12.53 E
Domnarvet 40 60.30 N 15.27 E
Domneşti 38 44.25 N 25.56 E
Domnino 82 54.10 N 38.11 E
Dom Noi ≃ 110 15.17 N 105.28 E
Domo 144 7.54 N 46.52 E
Domodedovo 82 55.26 N 37.46 E
Domodossola 58 46.07 N 8.17 E
Domohani 124 26.35 N 88.48 E
Domoni 157a 12.15 S 44.32 E
Domont 261 49.02 N 2.20 E
Dompaire 58 48.13 N 6.13 E
Dom Pedrito 252 30.59 S 54.40 W
Dom Pedro 250 4.29 S 44.27 W
Dom Pedro II, Estação ◆[5] 287a 23.54 S 43.12 W
Dompu 115b 8.32 S 118.28 E
Domremy 184 52.47 N 105.44 W
Domrémy-la-Pucelle 58 48.27 N 5.41 E
Domselaar 258 35.04 S 58.18 W
Dom Silvério 255 20.09 S 42.58 W
Domsjö 26 63.15 N 18.43 E
Domus de Maria 71 38.57 N 8.52 E
Domusnovas 71 39.19 N 8.39 E
Domuyo, Volcán ∧[1] 252 36.38 S 70.26 W
Domvast 50 50.12 N 1.55 E
Dom Viçoso 256 22.13 S 45.09 W
Dom Yai ≃ 110 15.18 N 105.10 E
Domžale 36 46.08 N 14.36 E
Don ≃, On., Can. 212 43.39 N 79.21 W
Don ≃, India 122 16.17 N 76.27 E
Don ≃, Lao 110 15.07 N 105.48 E
Don ≃, Ross. 72 47.04 N 39.18 E
Don ≃, Eng., U.K. 44 53.39 N 0.59 W
Don ≃, Eng., U.K. 262 53.47 N 2.14 W
Don ≃, Scot., U.K. 46 57.08 N 2.05 W
Don, East Branch ≃, On., Can. 212 43.42 N 79.20 W
Don, East Branch ≃, On., Can. 275b 43.43 N 79.20 W
Don, West Branch ≃ 275b 43.43 N 79.20 W
Dona Ana, Moç. 154 17.25 S 35.07 E
Dona Ana, N.M., U.S. 200 32.23 N 106.48 W
Donada 64 45.02 N 12.12 E
Donadeu 252 26.43 S 62.44 W
Dona Euzébia 256 21.18 S 42.48 W
Donaghadee 48 54.39 N 5.33 W
Donaghmore 48 54.32 N 6.49 W
Donahoe Creek ≃ 222 30.49 N 97.12 W
Donald 166 36.22 S 143.00 E
Donalda 182 52.35 N 112.34 W
Donaldson, Ar., U.S. 194 34.14 N 92.55 W
Donaldson, In., U.S. 216 41.22 N 86.27 W
Donaldson, Pa., U.S. 208 40.38 N 76.24 W
Donaldson Crossroads 279b 40.16 N 80.07 W
Donaldson Dam ⊜[1] 273d 26.17 S 27.41 E
Donaldsonville 194 30.06 N 90.59 W
Donalsonville 192 31.02 N 84.52 W
Doñana, Parque Nacional de ♦ 34 37.00 N 6.30 W
Donard, Slieve ∧ 48 54.11 N 5.55 W
Donau
— Danube ≃ 22 45.20 N 29.40 E
Donaueschingen 58 47.57 N 8.29 E
Donaufeld ◆[8] 264b 48.15 N 16.25 E
Donaukanal ≊ 264b 48.10 N 16.30 E
Donaumoos ≋, Dtsch. 58 48.30 N 10.15 E
Donaumoos ≋, Dtsch. 60 48.40 N 11.15 E
Donaupark ♦ 264b 48.14 N 16.25 E
Donauried ◆[1] 56 48.35 N 10.40 E
Donaustadt ◆[8] 264b 48.13 N 16.30 E
Donaustauf 60 49.02 N 12.13 E
Donauturm ✪ 264b 48.14 N 16.25 E
Donauwörth 56 48.43 N 10.46 E
Don Benito 34 38.57 N 5.52 W
Dönberg ◆[8] 263 51.18 N 7.10 E
Don Bosco ◆[8] 258 34.42 S 58.18 W
Doncaster, Austl. 274b 37.47 S 145.08 E
Doncaster, On., Can. 275b 43.48 N 79.25 W
Doncaster, Eng., U.K. 44 53.32 N 1.07 W
Doncaster ≃ 206 45.58 N 74.06 W
Doncaster East 274b 37.47 S 145.10 E
Doncaster Indian Reserve ◆[4] 206 46.09 N 74.07 W
Donchêry 56 49.42 N 4.52 E
Doncovka 83 49.35 N 39.16 E
Dondaicha 120 21.20 N 74.34 E
Dondo, Ang. 152 9.38 S 14.25 E
Dondo, Moç. 156 19.36 S 34.44 E
Dondo, Teluk ⊂ 112 0.55 N 120.30 E
Dondra Head > 122 5.55 N 80.35 E
Dond′ušany 78 48.15 N 27.37 E
Doneck, Ross. 83 48.21 N 40.02 E
Doneck, Ukr. 83 48.00 N 37.48 E
Doneck □[4] 78 48.00 N 37.30 E
Doneckij kr′až ∧ 83 48.15 N 38.45 E
Donegal, Ire. 48 54.39 N 8.07 W
Donegal, S. Afr. 158 26.10 S 23.58 E
Donegal, Pa., U.S. 214 40.07 N 79.23 W
Donegal □[6] 48 54.50 N 8.00 W
Donegal Bay ⊂ 48 54.30 N 8.30 W
Doneraile, Ire. 48 52.13 N 8.35 W
Doneraile, S.C., U.S. 192 34.19 N 79.53 W
Donetsk
— Doneck 83 48.00 N 37.48 E
Dong ≃, Zhg. 100 23.06 N 114.00 E
Dong ≃, Zhg. 100 23.42 N 117.13 E
Dong ≃, Zhg. 100 25.00 N 118.27 E
Dong ≃, Zhg. 102 42.10 N 101.00 E
Donga ≃ 146 8.19 N 9.58 E
Dong′an, Zhg. 89 47.20 N 134.10 E
Dong′an, Zhg. 100 33.24 N 114.24 E
Dong′an, Zhg. 102 26.17 N 111.07 E
Dong′an, Zhg. 106 30.30 N 118.48 E
Dong′an, Zhg. 106 31.35 N 119.44 E
Dongan
— Mishan 89 45.33 N 131.52 E
Dongao 100 29.12 N 121.25 E
Dongara 162 29.15 S 114.56 E
Dongargarh 120 21.12 N 80.44 E
Dongba, Zhg. 105 39.58 N 116.32 E
Dongba, Zhg. 106 31.18 N 119.03 E
Dongbahe 105 39.58 N 116.27 E
Dongbaimiao 105 40.34 N 116.05 E
Dongbei 100 27.15 N 116.06 E
Dongbeicha 98 41.43 N 127.23 E
Dongbeijipo 98 36.06 N 117.08 E
Dongchan 107 30.20 N 105.20 E
Dongchang 106 31.52 N 121.38 E
Dongchangjie 106 32.04 N 119.18 E
Dongcheng 100 28.56 N 121.16 E
Dongchong 100 26.35 N 119.52 E
Dongchuan (Xincun) 102 26.10 N 103.01 E
Dongcun 106 30.57 N 121.46 E
Dongdaoan 98 38.21 N 117.12 E
Dong Dian ≋ 105 39.03 N 116.35 E
Dongduluo 105 39.04 N 115.15 E
Dong′e (Tongcheng) 98 36.14 N 116.16 E
Dongen 52 51.37 N 4.56 E
Dong′ezhen 98 36.11 N 116.16 E
Dongfang (Basuo) 110 19.05 N 108.39 E
Dongfeng, Zhg. 98 42.40 N 125.28 E
Dongfeng, Zhg. 100 27.20 N 118.53 E
Dongfengtai 105 39.34 N 117.45 E
Donggala 112 0.40 S 119.44 E
Donggang 100 22.58 N 115.57 E
Donggangzi 89 45.53 N 129.49 E
Donggi 112 1.33 S 122.15 E
Donggi Cona ⊜ 102 37.10 N 96.55 E
Donggong Shan ⋏ 100 27.36 N 119.26 E
Donggongsuo 106 32.07 N 121.25 E
Donggou, Zhg. 98 39.54 N 124.09 E
Donggou, Zhg. 100 33.38 N 119.40 E
Donggou, Zhg. 106 32.17 N 118.59 E
Donggu 100 26.46 N 115.22 E
Dongguan, Zhg. 100 27.49 N 116.25 E
Dongguan, Zhg. 100 23.03 N 113.46 E
Dongguan, Zhg. 106 30.22 N 119.28 E
Dongguan, Zhg. 107 30.47 N 106.16 E
Dongguang 98 37.53 N 116.30 E
Dongguanpu 106 31.13 N 120.43 E
Dongguanyingzi 104 41.55 N 120.38 E
Donggugang 105 39.10 N 116.49 E
Dong Hai, Viet 110 12.34 N 109.14 E
Donghai (Niushan), Zhg. 98 34.30 N 118.47 E
Donghai Dao I 102 21.02 N 110.25 E
Dong Hai
— East China Sea ⊤[2] 90 30.00 N 126.00 E
Dongheng ≊ 106 31.54 N 120.17 E
Donghezhen 106 31.08 N 120.17 E
Dong Hoi 110 17.29 N 106.36 E
Donghu 100 26.28 N 113.07 E
Dong Hu ⊜ 120 32.10 N 84.40 E
Donghuanggou 104 40.43 N 123.29 E
Dongi 112 2.02 S 121.28 E
Dongio 58 46.27 N 8.58 E
Dongjia 98 37.18 N 118.24 E
Dongjiangkou 102 33.37 N 108.49 E
Dongjie 100 25.53 N 116.22 E
Dongjielang 100 31.03 N 115.57 E
Dongjingcheng 89 44.07 N 129.09 E
Dongjingji 98 40.02 N 114.01 E
Dongjingling 104 41.18 N 123.15 E
Dongjug 120 29.58 N 94.53 E
Dongkaihecheng 104 41.04 N 122.38 E
Dongkalang 112 0.10 N 120.06 E
Dongkeng, Zhg. 100 24.59 N 114.54 E
Dongkeng, Zhg. 100 27.48 N 119.42 E
Dong Khe 110 22.26 N 106.27 E
Dongkou 98 35.29 N 115.20 E
Donglan 102 24.40 N 107.18 E
Donglaohuyu 104 42.28 N 124.17 E
Donglaojunpu 104 41.24 N 121.22 E
Dongli 102 20.50 N 110.20 E
Dongliang 104 42.00 N 121.25 E
Dongliangjia 105 40.52 N 118.17 E
Donglidian 98 36.02 N 118.23 E
Donglinchang 107 29.39 N 104.07 E
Dongling 104 41.50 N 123.35 E
Dongliu, Zhg. 100 30.14 N 116.53 E
Dongliu, Zhg. 106 32.06 N 118.58 E
Dongliujiazi 104 42.21 N 122.44 E
Donglizhuang 105 39.21 N 116.47 E
Donglong 100 23.36 N 116.50 E
Donglucun 89 49.28 N 128.50 E
Dongmen 100 28.29 N 114.02 E
Dongming 98 35.18 N 115.08 E
Dong Nai ≃ 110 10.45 N 106.46 E
Dongnangou 104 41.25 N 122.02 E
Dong Nhien, Rach ≃ 269c 10.49 N 106.46 E
Dongning 89 44.04 N 131.07 E
Dongo, Ang. 152 14.36 S 15.48 E
Dongo, It. 58 46.07 N 9.17 E
Dongo, Zaïre 152 2.43 N 18.24 E
Dongobe 152 4.37 N 23.12 E
Dongobesh 154 4.04 S 35.23 E
Dongola
— Dunqulah 140 19.10 N 30.29 E
Dongon Point > 116 12.44 N 120.48 E
Dongou 152 2.02 N 18.04 E
Dongping, Zhg. 98 35.55 N 116.18 E
Dongping, Zhg. 100 27.24 N 118.39 E
Dongping, Zhg. 102 21.43 N 112.15 E
Dongping Hu ⊜ 98 36.00 N 116.12 E
Dongpu 100 30.03 N 120.34 E
Dongqian 106 30.52 N 120.23 E
Dongqiao 100 31.12 N 112.48 E
Dongqing 106 31.49 N 120.03 E
Dongqingduizi 104 41.02 N 122.08 E
Dongsanjiazi 104 41.54 N 122.48 E
Dongsanlintang 106 31.09 N 121.31 E
Dongsanpu 100 33.38 N 117.09 E
Dongsha ≃ 104 41.07 N 121.50 E
Dongshaer 120 28.41 N 89.09 E
Dongshajiao 100 30.19 N 122.09 E
Dongshan, Zhg. 100 23.42 N 117.24 E
Dongshan, Zhg. 102 19.50 N 110.14 E
Dongshan, Zhg. 106 31.04 N 120.24 E
Dongshan Dao I 100 23.40 N 117.25 E
Dongshanqiao 106 31.52 N 118.46 E
Dongshe 106 32.07 N 121.12 E
Dongsheng 102 39.49 N 109.59 E
Dongsheshanzi 104 42.15 N 123.09 E
Dongshi, Zhg. 100 24.43 N 115.59 E
Dongshi, Zhg. 100 24.42 N 118.27 E
Dongshi, Zhg. 271a 39.49 N 116.34 E
Dongshuiyan 105 39.15 N 115.23 E
Dongtai 100 32.51 N 120.20 E
Dongtai Hu ⊂ 106 31.05 N 120.30 E
Dongtaipingzhen 89 45.18 N 122.05 E
Dongtangou 105 39.23 N 118.22 E
Dongtianmu Shan ∧ 106 30.22 N 119.31 E
Dongtiao ≃ 106 30.51 N 120.06 E
Dongting 98 38.29 N 115.08 E
Dongtinghu 106 30.53 N 119.30 E
Dongting Hu ⊜ 102 29.20 N 112.54 E
Dongtingxi 102 28.34 N 110.36 E
Dongtou 100 27.50 N 121.09 E
Dongtou Shan I 100 27.50 N 121.08 E
Dong Trieu 110 21.05 N 106.31 E
Dongtuhulu 104 41.55 N 121.33 E
Dongtuoshanzi 104 42.10 N 123.08 E
Dongtuozi 104 41.17 N 121.53 E
Dong Van 110 23.16 N 105.22 E
Dongwangfu 89 44.47 N 120.53 E
Dongwangzhuang 106 32.16 N 120.32 E
Dongwe ≃ 152 13.58 S 23.53 E
Dongwuquan 105 39.20 N 115.43 E
Dongxi, Zhg. 100 28.35 N 120.02 E
Dongxi, Zhg. 102 28.47 N 106.39 E
Dongxi, Zhg. 107 30.24 N 104.33 E
Dongxia 106 31.11 N 119.05 E
Dongxiagaogao 104 42.36 N 122.30 E
Dongxiang 100 28.13 N 116.35 E
Dongxiang Dao I 100 25.36 N 119.48 E
Dongxing 89 46.23 N 127.52 E
Dongxingchang, Zhg. 107 29.16 N 103.55 E
Dongxingchang, Zhg. 107 29.36 N 105.04 E
Dongxinghe 105 39.46 N 114.49 E
Dongxinpu 104 41.00 N 123.18 E
Dongxinzhen 106 31.57 N 121.42 E
Dongyang, Zhg. 89 48.03 N 124.17 E
Dongyang, Zhg. 100 29.16 N 120.14 E
Dongyangqiao 106 30.52 N 120.34 E
Dongyao 98 35.56 N 113.58 E
Dongyian 105 39.22 N 115.46 E
Dongyin ≃ 105 39.09 N 117.43 E
Dongyou 100 27.10 N 118.37 E
Dongyuemiao 106 31.36 N 119.14 E
Dongyuezhen 107 30.24 N 103.32 E
Dongzhang 100 25.44 N 119.17 E
Dongzhaocun 105 40.02 N 116.46 E
Dongzhaozhuang 105 39.57 N 118.24 E
Dongzhenbeng 106 30.59 N 121.01 E
Dongzhi 100 30.07 N 116.59 E
Dongzhizhuang 105 40.25 N 116.50 E
Dongzhuangpu 105 40.34 N 115.42 E
Dongziya 105 38.50 N 116.44 E
Donie 222 31.29 N 96.13 W
Doninga 150 10.37 N 1.26 W
Donington 42 52.55 N 0.12 W
Doniphan, Mo., U.S. 194 36.37 N 90.49 W
Doniphan, Ne., U.S. 198 40.46 N 98.22 W
Don Islands II 116 11.05 N 123.38 E
Donja Stubica 36 45.59 N 15.58 E
Donjek ≃ 180 62.35 N 140.00 W
Donjezk
— Doneck 83 48.00 N 37.48 E
Donji Vakuf 36 44.09 N 17.25 E
Donk 52 51.33 N 5.37 E
Donkerpoort 158 30.32 S 25.30 E
Donkey Creek ≃ 198 44.12 N 104.58 W
Donkey Town 260 51.20 N 0.39 W
Donmãnick Islands II 126 22.00 N 90.37 E
Don Martín 196 27.32 N 100.37 W
Don Matías 246 6.30 N 75.22 W
Don Mills ◆[8] 275b 43.44 N 79.20 W
Don Mills Centre ◆[9] 275b 43.44 N 79.21 W
Don Muang Airport ⊠ 269a 13.56 N 100.37 E
Donna 196 26.10 N 98.03 W
Donna, Punta sa ∧ 71 40.35 N 9.25 E
Donna Buang, Mount ∧ 169 37.43 S 145.40 E
Donnacona 206 46.40 N 71.47 W
Donnalucata 70 36.45 N 14.38 E
Donnaz 62 45.36 N 7.46 E
Donnell Lake ⊜[1] 226 38.20 N 119.56 W
Donnellson 219 39.02 N 89.29 W
Donnelly, Ab., Can. 182 55.44 N 117.06 W
Donnelly, Ak., U.S. 180 63.41 N 145.53 W
Donnelly, Id., U.S. 202 44.43 N 116.04 W
Donnellys Crossing 172 35.43 S 173.37 E
Donnemarie-Dontilly 50 48.29 N 3.08 E
Donner 194 29.41 N 90.56 W
Donner Lake ⊜[1] 226 39.20 N 120.16 W
Donner Memorial State Park ♦ 226 39.18 N 120.16 W
Donner Pass)(226 39.19 N 120.20 W
Donnersberg ∧ 56 50.23 N 8.32 E
Donner und Blitzen ≃ 202 43.17 N 118.49 W
Donnybrook, Austl. 162 33.35 S 115.49 E
Donnybrook, S. Afr. 158 30.00 S 29.48 E
Donora 214 40.10 N 79.51 W
Donostia (San Sebastián) 34 43.19 N 1.59 W
Donovan 216 40.53 N 87.37 W
Don Pedro Reservoir ⊜[1] 226 37.43 N 120.23 W
Don Peninsula >[1] 182 52.30 N 128.10 W
Donque 152 15.28 S 14.06 E
Donskaja gr′ada ⋏[2] 80 49.30 N 42.00 E
Donskoj, Ross. 76 53.58 N 38.20 E
Donskoj, Ross. 83 47.25 N 40.14 E
Donskoj, Ross. 83 48.49 N 40.06 E
Donskoje, Ross. 76 52.37 N 39.00 E
Donskoje, Ross. 80 45.21 N 41.59 E
Donskoje, Ukr. 83 47.31 N 37.33 E
Donskoje belogorje ⋏[1] 78 50.30 N 39.45 E
Donsol 116 12.54 N 123.36 E
Don Torcuato 288 34.30 S 58.38 W
Don Torcuato, Aeródromo ⊠ 288 34.30 S 58.36 W
Donuzlav, ozero ⊜ 78 45.23 N 33.05 E
Donyztau ⋏ 86 46.25 N 57.00 E
Donzdorf 56 48.41 N 9.48 E
Donzère 62 44.27 N 4.43 E
Donzy 50 47.22 N 3.08 E
Dooagh 48 53.59 N 10.09 W
Dood nuur ⊜ 88 51.20 N 99.20 E
Doogort 48 54.01 N 10.01 W
Doolow 144 4.10 N 42.05 E
Doomadgee 166 17.56 S 138.49 E
Doomadgee Aboriginal Reserve ◆[4] 166 17.43 S 138.36 E
Doon, On., Can. 212 43.23 N 80.26 W
Doon, Ia., U.S. 198 43.16 N 96.13 W
Doon ≃ 44 55.26 N 4.38 W
Doon, Loch ⊜ 44 55.15 N 4.22 W
Doonbeg 48 52.44 N 9.32 W
Doonbeg ≃ 48 52.44 N 9.34 W
Doon Doon Aboriginal Reserve ◆[4] 164 16.15 S 128.15 E
Doonerak, Mount ∧ 180 67.56 N 150.37 W
Doonside 274a 33.46 S 150.52 E
Dooralong 170 33.12 S 151.22 E
Doorn 52 52.03 N 5.21 E
Doorndam 158 28.03 S 21.03 E
Doornik
— Tournai 50 50.36 N 3.23 E
Door Peninsula >[1] 190 44.55 N 87.20 W
Dopping Brook ≃ 283 42.12 N 71.23 W
Do Qal′eh 128 32.18 N 61.31 E
Dor 132 32.37 N 34.55 E
Dora 194 33.43 N 87.05 W
Dora, Lake ⊜, Austl. 162 22.05 S 122.55 E
Dora, Lake ⊜, Fl., U.S. 220 29.00 N 81.37 W
Dora Baltea ≃ 62 45.11 N 8.05 E
Dora di Rhêmes ≃ 62 45.42 N 7.11 E
Dorado 240m 18.28 N 66.15 W
Dorāha 123 30.49 N 76.01 E
Dorāh Ān)(123 36.07 N 71.15 E
Dorain, Beinn ∧ 46 56.30 N 4.42 W
Dorândia 256 22.27 S 43.57 W
Dora Riparia ≃ 62 45.05 N 7.44 E
Doraville 192 33.53 N 84.17 W
Dorback Burn ≃ 46 57.31 N 3.40 W
Dorcheat, Bayou ≃ 194 32.30 N 93.21 W
Dorchester, N.B., Can. 186 45.54 N 64.31 W
Dorchester, On., Can. 212 42.59 N 81.04 W
Dorchester, Eng., U.K. 42 50.43 N 2.26 W
Dorchester, Eng., U.K. 42 51.39 N 1.10 W
Dorchester, Il., U.S. 219 39.05 N 89.53 W
Dorchester, Ne., U.S. 198 40.38 N 97.06 W
Dorchester, N.J., U.S. 208 39.16 N 74.58 W
Dorchester, Wi., U.S. 190 45.00 N 90.20 W
Dorchester □[6] 208 38.34 N 76.04 W
Dorchester ◆[8] 283 42.17 N 71.04 W
Dorchester, Cape > 176 65.29 N 77.30 W
Dorchester Bay ⊂ 283 42.19 N 71.02 W
Dorchester Crossing 186 46.10 N 64.34 W
Dorchester Estates 284c 38.47 N 76.55 W
Dorchester Heights National Historic Site ⊥ 283 42.20 N 71.03 W
Dorchheim 56 50.30 N 8.04 E
Dordabis 156 22.52 S 17.38 E
Dordives 50 48.09 N 2.46 E
Dordogne □[5] 32 45.10 N 0.45 E
Dordogne ≃ 32 45.02 N 0.35 W
Dordon 42 52.36 N 1.37 W
Dordrecht, Ned. 52 51.49 N 4.40 E
Dordrecht, S. Afr. 158 31.20 S 27.03 E
Doré ≃, Sk., Can. 184 54.56 N 107.45 W
Dore ≃, Fr. 62 45.50 N 3.35 E
Dore ≃, Eng., U.K. 42 51.57 N 2.52 W
Dore, Monts ⋏ 32 45.30 N 2.45 E
Doreissou 146 10.33 N 15.08 E
Doré Lake 184 54.38 N 107.24 W
Doré Lake ⊜ 184 54.46 N 107.17 W
Dorena 202 43.43 N 122.51 W
Dörentrup 52 52.03 N 8.59 E
Dores 46 57.22 N 4.15 W
Dores do Indaiá 255 19.27 S 45.36 W
Dores do Paraibuna 256 21.31 S 43.39 W
Dorfen 60 48.17 N 12.08 E
Dorfgastein 64 47.15 N 13.06 E
Dorfmark 52 52.54 N 9.46 E
Dorgali 71 40.17 N 9.35 E
Dörgön nuur ⊜ 88 47.40 N 93.30 E
Doring ≃ 158 31.54 S 18.39 E
Doringbaai 158 31.48 S 18.15 E
Doringkop ∧ 273d 26.15 S 27.50 E
Dorino 82 56.28 N 36.09 E
Dorion-Vaudreuil 206 45.23 N 74.01 W
Dorje Lāpka ∧ 124 28.11 N 85.47 E
Dorking 42 51.14 N 0.20 W
Dorloo 210 42.43 N 74.37 W
Dormaa Ahenkro 150 7.17 N 2.53 W
Dormagen 56 51.05 N 6.50 E
Dormans 50 49.04 N 3.38 E
Dormidontovka 89 47.45 N 134.57 E
Dormont 279b 40.23 N 80.02 W
Dornach 58 47.29 N 7.37 E
Dornap ◆[8] 263 51.15 N 7.04 E
Dornbach ◆[8] 264b 48.14 N 16.18 E
Dornbirn 58 47.25 N 9.44 E
Dornburg 56 50.30 N 8.07 E
Dorndorf, Dtsch. 54 51.00 N 11.40 E
Dorndorf, Dtsch. 56 50.50 N 10.05 E
Dornecy 50 47.26 N 3.35 E
Dorney 260 51.30 N 0.40 W
Dornhan 58 48.21 N 8.30 E
Dornie 46 57.17 N 5.31 W
Dorno 62 45.09 N 8.57 E
Dornoch 46 57.52 N 4.02 W
Dornoch Firth ⊂[1] 46 57.53 N 4.00 W
Dornod □[4] 88 48.00 N 115.00 E
Dornogov′ □[4] 102 44.30 N 110.00 E
Dornsife 208 40.45 N 76.47 W
Dornstadt 58 48.28 N 9.56 E
Dornstetten 58 48.28 N 8.30 E
Dornumersiel 52 53.40 N 7.28 E
Doro, Indon. 115a 7.02 S 109.41 E
Doro, Mali 150 16.09 N 0.51 W
Dorochovo 82 55.33 N 36.23 E
Dorog 30 47.43 N 18.44 E
Dorogobuž 76 54.55 N 33.18 E
Doroḥ 128 32.17 N 60.30 E
Dorohoi 38 47.57 N 26.24 E
Dorokempo 115b 8.33 S 118.15 E
Doromata 115b 8.46 S 118.13 E
Doromo 154 3.49 N 26.17 E
Dorošata 80 57.21 N 51.08 E
Dorošicha 82 56.52 N 35.50 E
Dorotea 26 64.16 N 16.24 E
Dorothy 208 39.24 N 74.49 W
Dorothy, Lake ⊜ 224 47.34 N 121.22 W
Dorotockeys Run ≃ 276 40.59 N 73.58 W
Dorpat
— Tartu 76 58.23 N 26.43 E
Dörpen 52 52.57 N 7.20 E
Dorr 216 42.43 N 85.43 W
Dorrance 198 38.50 N 98.35 W
Dorre Island I 162 25.09 S 113.07 E
Dorrigo 166 30.21 S 152.43 E
Dorris 204 41.58 N 121.55 W
Dorsale ⋏ 36 36.00 N 9.50 E
Dorset, Oh., U.S. 214 41.41 N 80.40 W
Dorset, Vt., U.S. 210 43.15 N 73.05 W
Dorset □[6] 42 50.47 N 2.20 W
Dorset Peak ∧ 188 43.19 N 73.02 W
Dorsey Run ≃ 284b 39.11 N 76.48 W
Dorseyville 279b 40.35 N 79.53 W
Dorsten 52 51.39 N 6.58 E
Dorstfeld ◆[8] 263 51.31 N 7.25 E
Dortan 58 46.19 N 5.40 E
Dörtdivan 130 40.43 N 32.04 E
Dort
— Dordrecht 52 51.49 N 4.40 E
Dortmund, Dtsch. 52 51.31 N 7.28 E
Dortmund, Dtsch. 263 51.31 N 7.28 E
Dortmund-Ems-Kanal ≊ 52 51.32 N 7.27 E
Dortmunder Rieselfelder ◆[1] 263 51.39 N 7.25 E
Dortmund-Wickede, Flughafen ⊠ 263 51.32 N 7.35 E
Dorton 192 37.16 N 82.34 W
Dörtyol 130 36.52 N 36.12 E
Do Rūd 128 33.28 N 49.04 E
Dorum 52 53.41 N 8.34 E
Doruma 154 4.44 N 27.42 E
Dorval 206 45.27 N 73.44 W
Dorval, Île I 275a 45.26 N 73.45 W
Dorval Gardens Centre ◆[9] 275a 45.27 N 73.44 W
Dörverden 52 52.51 N 9.13 E
Dörvöldžin 88 48.08 N 93.58 E
Dörzbach 56 49.23 N 9.42 E
Dos, Canal Numero ≊ 252 36.21 S 56.54 W
Dosara 150 12.32 N 6.09 E
Do Sārī 128 28.25 N 57.59 E
Dos Arroyos 234 17.02 N 99.40 W
Dosatuj 88 50.23 N 118.38 E
Dos Bahías, Cabo > 254 44.55 S 65.32 W
Dos Bocas 240m 18.20 N 66.40 W
Dos Bocas, Lago ⊜[1] 240m 18.19 N 66.40 W
Doščatoje 80 55.23 N 42.07 E
Döşemealtı 130 37.04 N 30.36 E
Dosewallips ≃ 224 47.42 N 122.53 W
Dos Hermanas 34 37.17 N 5.55 W
Dos Hermanas, Islas II 258 34.05 S 58.17 W
Dōshi 94 35.32 N 139.02 E
Dōshi ≃ 94 35.36 N 139.14 E
Doshisha University ✪[2] 270 35.02 N 135.46 E
Dosi 164 5.56 S 134.34 E
Dösjebro 41 55.49 N 13.01 E
Do Son 110 20.42 N 106.47 E
Dosoris Island >[1] 276 40.53 N 73.38 W
Dosoris Pond ⊜ 276 40.54 N 73.38 W
Dos Palos 226 36.59 N 120.37 W
Dos Pos 241s 12.15 N 68.20 W
Dos Quebradas 246 4.51 N 75.40 W
Dos Reyes, Punta > 252 24.33 S 70.35 W
Dosse ≃ 54 53.13 N 12.20 E
Dosséo, Bahr ≃ 146 9.01 N 19.38 E
Dossin Great Lakes Museum ✪ 281 42.20 N 82.59 W
Dosso 150 13.03 N 3.12 E
Dosso □[5] 150 13.00 N 3.00 E
Dossor 80 47.32 N 53.01 E
Doster 216 42.27 N 85.33 W
Doswell 208 37.51 N 77.27 W
Dothan 194 31.13 N 85.23 W
Doting Cove 186 49.27 N 53.57 W
Dot Lake 180 63.40 N 144.04 W
Dotnuva 76 55.21 N 23.54 E
Dotson 222 32.01 N 94.31 W
Döttingen 58 47.34 N 8.16 E
Doty 224 46.38 N 123.16 W
Dou ≃ 105 39.13 N 118.03 E
Douai 50 50.22 N 3.04 E
Douala 152 4.03 N 9.42 E
Douala-Edéa, Réserve de ◆[4] 152 4.30 S 9.50 E
Douarnenez 32 48.06 N 4.20 W
Doubabougou 150 14.13 N 7.59 W
Double, Lac ⊜ 186 50.46 N 70.23 W
Doublé, Pointe > 241o 16.20 N 61.00 W
Double Bayou 222 29.41 N 94.39 W
Double Cone ∧ 172 45.04 S 168.48 E
Double Island Point > 166 25.56 S 153.11 E
Double Mountain ∧ 228 35.02 N 118.29 W
Double Point > 166 17.39 S 146.09 E
Double Springs 194 34.08 N 87.24 W
Doubletop Peak ∧ 200 43.21 N 110.17 W
Doubs 58 46.56 N 6.21 E
Doubs □[5] 58 47.10 N 6.25 E
Doubs ≃ 58 46.54 N 5.02 E
Doubs, Saut de ʟ 58 47.05 N 6.43 E
Doubtful Sound ʊ 172 45.17 S 166.51 E
Doubtless Bay ⊂ 172 34.55 S 173.25 E
Douchy 50 47.57 N 3.03 E
Douchy-les-Mines 50 50.18 N 3.23 E
Doudeville 50 49.43 N 0.48 E
Doudian 105 39.39 N 116.03 E
Doué ≃[1] 150 16.38 N 15.02 W
Douentza 150 15.00 N 2.57 W
Dougga ⊥ 36 36.25 N 9.13 E
Doughboy 170 35.15 S 149.39 E
Doughboy Bay ⊂ 172 47.02 S 167.41 E
Douglas, Austl. 164 16.29 S 145.28 E
Douglas, Mb., Can. 184 49.53 N 99.42 W
Douglas, On., Can. 212 45.31 N 76.56 W
Douglas, I. of Man 44 54.09 N 4.28 W
Douglas, S. Afr. 158 29.04 S 23.46 E
Douglas, Scot., U.K. 46 55.33 N 3.51 W
Douglas, Ak., U.S. 180 58.16 N 134.22 W
Douglas, Az., U.S. 200 31.20 N 109.32 W
Douglas, Ga., U.S. 192 31.30 N 82.51 W
Douglas, Mi., U.S. 216 42.38 N 86.12 W
Douglas, N.D., U.S. 198 47.51 N 101.30 W
Douglas, Wy., U.S. 200 42.45 N 105.22 W
Douglas □[6] 226 38.55 N 119.39 W
Douglas ≃ 44 53.43 N 2.50 W
Douglas, Cape > 180 58.52 N 153.18 W
Douglas, Mount ∧ 180 58.52 N 153.31 W
Douglas, Mount ∧[2] 162 28.39 S 123.53 E
Douglas Aircraft Company ✪[3] 280 33.50 N 118.09 W
Douglas Channel ʊ 182 53.30 N 129.12 W
Douglas Creek ≃ 200 40.06 N 108.46 W
Douglas Lake 182 50.10 N 120.12 W
Douglas Lake ⊜[1] 192 36.00 N 83.22 W
Douglas Lake Indian Reserve ◆[4] 182 50.10 N 120.49 W
Douglas Park 170 34.11 S 150.43 E
Douglas Park ♦ 278 41.52 N 87.42 W
Douglass, Ks., U.S. 198 37.31 N 97.01 W
Douglass, Tx., U.S. 222 31.40 N 94.53 W
Douglass Run ≃ 279b 40.15 N 79.48 W
Douglassville 208 40.15 N 75.44 W
Douglasville 192 33.45 N 84.44 W
Douglas Water ≃ 46 55.38 N 3.46 W
Dougouzi, Zhg. 89 49.57 N 127.01 E
Dougouzi, Zhg. 104 41.16 N 122.34 E
Douhutun 98 42.06 N 124.50 E
Douigny 152 3.11 S 10.45 E
Doujiapu 104 41.05 N 122.12 E
Doujiazhuang 105 40.22 N 116.59 E
Doukkane, Djebel ∧ 36 35.23 N 8.00 E
Doulaincourt 58 48.19 N 5.12 E
Doulevant-le-Château 58 48.23 N 4.55 E
Doullens 50 50.09 N 2.21 E
Doumanaba 150 11.40 N 5.56 W
Doumanga 152 2.41 S 12.40 E
Doumba Bélo 152 5.05 N 14.18 E
Doumdégué 152 7.29 N 18.58 E
Doumé, Cam. 152 5.32 N 12.19 E
Doumé, Cam. 152 4.14 N 13.27 E
Doumé ≃ 152 4.06 N 14.34 E
Doumen, Zhg. 100 22.12 N 113.16 E
Doumen, Zhg. 105 39.18 N 115.53 E
Douna 150 14.39 N 1.44 W
Doune 46 56.12 N 4.05 W
Doune Castle ⊥ 46 56.11 N 4.03 W
Dounguila 152 2.53 S 11.58 E
Doupov 54 50.10 N 13.08 E
Doupovské hory ⋏ 54 50.13 N 13.08 E
Dour 50 50.24 N 3.47 E
Doura 150 13.14 N 5.55 W
Dourada, Serra ⋏[1] 255 13.10 S 48.45 W
Douradinho 256 21.45 S 45.46 W
Dourado ≃ 256 21.43 S 45.44 W
Dourados 255 22.13 S 54.48 W
Dourados ≃ 255 21.58 S 54.18 W
Dourbali 146 11.49 N 15.52 E
Dourdan 50 48.32 N 2.01 E
Dourdou ≃ 32 44.00 N 2.41 E
Dourges 50 50.26 N 2.59 E
Dourkoulé 146 14.27 N 22.13 E
Douro ≃, Bra. 287a 22.42 S 43.35 W
Douro (Duero) ≃, Europe 34 41.08 N 8.40 W
Doushanhe 100 31.38 N 114.42 E
Dousman 216 43.00 N 88.28 W
Douthat State Park ♦ 192 37.55 N 79.50 W
Douvaine 58 46.19 N 6.18 E
Douvres, Falaises de ±[4] 273b 4.06 S 15.25 E
Douvres
— Dover 42 51.08 N 1.19 E
Douvrin 50 50.31 N 2.50 E
Doux ≃ 62 45.04 N 4.50 E
Douy-la-Ramée 261 49.04 N 2.53 E
Douyu 98 37.53 N 114.30 E
Douz 148 33.28 N 9.01 E
Douze ≃ 32 43.54 N 0.30 W
Douzhangzhuang 105 39.23 N 116.55 E
Douzishan 107 29.04 N 104.57 E
Douziyu 105 40.18 N 117.19 E
Douzy 56 49.40 N 5.03 E
Dovadola 66 44.07 N 11.53 E
Dovbyš 78 50.22 N 27.59 E
Dove ≃, Eng., U.K. 44 52.50 N 1.35 W
Dove ≃, Eng., U.K. 44 54.12 N 0.54 W
Dove Creek 200 37.45 N 108.54 W
Dove Creek ≃, Tx., U.S. 196 31.20 N 100.36 W
Dove Creek ≃, Ut., U.S. 200 41.37 N 113.15 W
Dove Holes 262 53.18 N 1.53 W
Dove Holes Tunnel ◆[5] 262 53.18 N 1.53 W
Dover, Austl. 166 43.19 S 147.01 E
Dover, S. Afr. 158 27.02 S 27.46 E
Dover, Eng., U.K. 42 51.08 N 1.19 E
Dover, Ar., U.S. 194 35.24 N 93.06 W
Dover, De., U.S. 208 39.09 N 75.31 W
Dover, Fl., U.S. 220 27.59 N 82.13 W
Dover, Id., U.S. 202 48.15 N 116.36 W
Dover, Ky., U.S. 218 38.45 N 83.52 W
Dover, Ma., U.S. 283 42.14 N 71.17 W
Dover, N.H., U.S. 188 43.11 N 70.52 W
Dover, N.J., U.S. 210 40.53 N 74.34 W
Dover, N.C., U.S. 192 35.12 N 77.26 W
Dover, Oh., U.S. 214 40.31 N 81.28 W
Dover, Ok., U.S. 196 35.58 N 97.54 W
Dover, Pa., U.S. 208 40.00 N 76.51 W
Dover, Tn., U.S. 194 36.29 N 87.50 W
Dover, Point > 162 32.32 S 125.32 E
Dover, Strait of (Pas de Calais) ʊ 50 51.00 N 1.30 E
Dover Air Force Base ■ 208 39.08 N 75.28 W
Dover-Foxcroft 188 45.11 N 69.13 W
Dover Heights 274a 33.53 S 151.17 E
Dover Hills 276 40.52 N 74.33 W
Dover Plains 210 41.44 N 73.35 W
Dovers Hills ⋏[2] 162 23.10 S 128.45 E
Dove Stone Reservoir ⊜[1] 262 53.32 N 1.58 W
Doveton 274b 38.00 S 145.14 E
Dovey Valley V 42 52.35 N 3.50 W
Dovol′noje 86 54.30 N 79.40 E
Dovre 26 61.59 N 9.15 E
Dovrefjell ⋏ 26 62.06 N 9.25 E
Dovrefjell Nasjonalpark ♦ 26 62.18 N 9.36 E
Dovsk 76 53.09 N 30.28 E
Dowa 154 13.40 S 33.58 E
Dowagiac 216 41.59 N 86.06 W
Dowagiac ≃ 216 41.51 N 86.16 W
Dowagiac Creek ≃ 216 41.49 N 86.10 W
Dowally 46 56.36 N 3.37 W
Dow City 198 41.55 N 95.29 W
Dowden Terrace 284c 38.50 N 77.08 W
Dowell 208 38.20 N 76.27 W
Dowerin 162 31.12 S 117.02 E
Dowi, Tanjung > 114 1.31 N 97.25 E
Dowker, Île I 275a 45.24 N 73.54 W
Dowlatābād, Afg. 120 36.26 N 64.55 E
Dowlatābād, Afg. 120 36.59 N 66.50 E
Dowlatābād, Īrān 128 28.18 N 56.40 E
Dowlat Yār 120 34.33 N 65.47 E
Dowling Lake ⊜ 182 51.44 N 112.00 W
Downderry 42 50.22 N 4.22 W
Downe ◆[8] 260 51.20 N 0.03 E
Down East 285 40.03 N 75.32 W
Downers Grove 216 41.48 N 88.00 W
Downey, Ca., U.S. 228 33.56 N 118.07 W
Downey, Id., U.S. 202 42.25 N 112.07 W
Downey Creek ≃ 224 48.16 N 121.14 W
Downham, Eng., U.K. 42 52.26 N 0.15 E
Downham, Eng., U.K. 260 51.38 N 0.30 E
Downham Market 42 52.36 N 0.23 E
Down House ⊥ 260 51.20 N 0.03 E

Symbols in the index entries represent the broad categories identified in the key at the right. Symbols with superior numbers (⋏[1]) identify subcategories (see complete key on page *I · 1).*

Symbole im Register stellen die rechts im Schlüssel erklärten Kategorien dar. Symbole mit hochgestellten Ziffern (⋏[1]) bezeichnen Unterabteilungen einer Kategorie (vgl. vollständiger Schlüssel auf Seite *I · 1).*

Los símbolos incluídos en el texto del índice representan las grandes categorias identificadas con la clave a la derecha. Los símbolos con numeros en su parte superior (⋏[1]) identifican las subcategorías (véase la clave completa en la página *I · 1).*

Les symboles de l'index représentent les catégories indiquées dans la légende à droite. Les symboles suivis d'un indice (⋏[1]) représentent des sous-catégories (voir légende complète à la page *I · 1).*

Os símbolos incluídos no texto do índice representam as grandes categorias identificadas com a chave à direita. Os símbolos com números em sua parte superior (⋏[1]) identificam as subcategorias (veja-se a chave completa à página *I · 1).*

∧ Mountain	Berg	Montaña	Montagne	Montanha
⋏ Mountains	Gebirge	Montañas	Montagnes	Montanhas
)(Pass	Paß	Paso	Col	Passo
V Valley, Canyon	Tal, Cañon	Valle, Cañón	Vallée, Canyon	Vale, Canhão
≚ Plain	Ebene	Llano	Plaine	Planície
> Cape	Kap	Cabo	Cap	Cabo
I Island	Insel	Isla	Île	Ilha
II Islands	Inseln	Islas	Îles	Ilhas
± Other Topographic Features	Andere Topographische Objekte	Otros Elementos Topográficos	Autres données topographiques	Outros acidentes topográficos

ESPAÑOL

Nombre	Página	Lat.°′	Long.°′ W = Oeste
Downieville	226	39.33 N	120.49 W
Downing	194	40.29 N	92.22 W
Downingtown	208	40.00 N	75.42 W
Downingtown Airport ⊠	285	39.59 N	75.45 W
Downpatrick	48	54.20 N	5.43 W
Downpatrick Head ›	48	54.20 N	9.20 W
Downs, Il., U.S.	216	40.24 N	88.52 W
Downs, Ks., U.S.	198	39.30 N	98.32 W
Downs Mountain ∧	200	43.18 N	109.40 W
Downsview Dells Park ♠	275b	43.44 N	79.30 W
Downsville	210	42.04 N	74.59 W
Downsville Dam ◈[6]	210	42.05 N	74.58 W
Downton	42	51.00 N	1.44 W
Downton, Mount ∧	182	52.42 N	124.51 W
Downton Lake ⊜	182	50.51 N	123.00 W
Downwind Acres Airfield ⊠	281	42.09 N	83.34 W
Dows	190	42.39 N	93.30 W
Dowshī	120	35.37 N	68.41 E
Doygaab	144	0.59 N	43.32 E
Doyle	204	40.01 N	120.06 W
Doyles	186	47.50 N	59.12 W
Doylesburg	214	40.13 N	77.42 W
Doylestown, Oh., U.S.	214	40.58 N	81.41 W
Doylestown, Pa., U.S.	208	40.18 N	75.07 W
Doyline	194	32.32 N	93.25 W
Dōzan ≃	96	33.58 N	133.47 E
Dōzen II	92	36.05 N	133.05 E
Dozier	194	31.29 N	86.21 W
Dozois, Réservoir ⊜[1]	190	47.30 N	77.05 W
Dozza	66	44.22 N	11.37 E
Drâa, Cap ›	148	28.44 N	11.08 W
Dra'a, Hamada du ◈[2]	148	29.00 N	6.45 W
Drâa, Oued V	148	28.43 N	11.09 W
Draa el Mizan	34	36.32 N	3.50 E
Drabble → José Enrique Rodó	258	33.41 S	57.34 W
Drabenderhöhe	56	50.57 N	7.27 E
Drabov	78	49.58 N	32.08 E
Drac ≃	62	45.13 N	5.41 E
Dracena	255	21.32 S	51.29 W
Drachenfels ⊥	56	50.40 N	7.12 E
Drachten	52	53.06 N	6.05 E
Dracut	207	42.40 N	71.18 W
Dragalina	38	44.26 N	27.20 E
Drăgănești-Olt	38	44.10 N	24.32 E
Drăgănești-Vlașca	38	44.06 N	25.36 E
Drăgășani	38	44.40 N	24.16 E
Drag Lake ⊜	212	45.05 N	78.24 W
Dragone ≃	64	44.23 N	10.37 E
Dragonera I	34	39.35 N	2.19 E
Dragoni	68	41.16 N	14.18 E
Dragonja ≃	64	45.28 N	13.37 E
Dragons Mouths ⩌	241r	10.45 N	61.46 W
Dragon Swamp ≃	208	37.33 N	76.34 W
Dragoon	200	32.01 N	110.02 W
Dragør	41	55.36 N	12.41 E
Draguignan	62	43.32 N	6.28 E
Drain	202	43.39 N	123.19 W
Drake, Mo., U.S.	219	38.28 N	91.28 W
Drake, N.D., U.S.	198	47.55 N	100.22 W
Drakenburg	52	52.41 N	9.13 E
Drakensberg ⋀	156	27.00 S	30.00 E
Drake Passage ⩌	18	58.00 S	70.00 W
Drake Peak ∧	202	42.19 N	120.07 W
Drakesboro	194	37.13 N	87.02 W
Drakes Branch	192	36.59 N	78.36 W
Drakes Brook ≃	276	40.49 N	74.43 W
Drake Well Museum ♁	214	41.36 N	79.39 W
Drakino	82	54.52 N	37.17 E
Dráma	38	41.09 N	24.08 E
Drammen	26	59.44 N	10.15 E
Dran	110	11.51 N	108.35 E
Drancy	50	48.56 N	2.27 E
Dranda	84	42.53 N	41.09 E
Drang ≃	110	13.19 N	107.21 E
Drangajökull ⊓	24a	66.11 N	22.15 W
Drangstedt	52	53.36 N	8.44 E
Dranov, Ostrovul I	38	44.52 N	29.15 E
Dransfeld	52	51.30 N	9.45 E
Dranske	54	54.38 N	13.14 E
Drap	62	43.45 N	7.19 E
Draper, N.C., U.S.	192	36.31 N	79.41 W
Draper, Ut,. U.S.	200	40.31 N	111.51 W
Draperstown	48	54.48 N	6.47 W
Drās	123	34.27 N	75.46 E
Drās ≃	123	34.37 N	75.59 E
Drau (Drava) (Dráva) ≃	36	45.33 N	18.55 E
Drava (Drau) (Dráva) ≃	36	45.33 N	18.55 E
Draveil	50	48.41 N	2.25 E
Dravinja ≃	36	46.22 N	15.57 E
Dravograd	61	46.35 N	15.02 E
Dravosburg	279b	40.21 N	79.51 W
Drawno	30	53.13 N	15.45 E
Drawsko Pomorskie	30	53.32 N	15.48 E
Drayton, On., Can.	212	43.46 N	80.40 W
Drayton, Eng., U.K.	42	51.38 N	1.18 W
Drayton, N.D., U.S.	198	48.34 N	97.10 W
Drayton, S.C., U.S.	192	34.58 N	81.54 W
Drayton Plains	216	42.41 N	83.22 W
Drayton Valley	182	53.13 N	114.59 W
Draženov	60	49.28 N	12.52 E
Drean	36	36.41 N	7.46 E
Drebkau	54	51.39 N	14.13 E
Dreieich	56	50.01 N	8.41 E
Dreifelder Weiher ⊜	56	50.36 N	7.49 E
Dreihausen	56	50.43 N	8.50 E
Dreiherrnspitze (Picco dei Tre Signori) ∧	64	47.04 N	12.15 E
Dreikikir	164	3.35 S	142.45 E
Drejø I	41	54.58 N	10.25 E
Dremsel, Mount ∧	164	2.10 S	146.55 E
Drena	64	45.58 N	10.56 E
Drenovec	38	43.42 N	22.59 E
Drensteinfurt	52	51.48 N	7.44 E
Drenthe □[4]	52	52.45 N	6.30 E
Dresde → Dresden	54	51.03 N	13.44 E
Dresden, On., Can.	214	42.35 N	82.11 W
Dresden, Dtsch.	54	51.03 N	13.44 E
Dresden, N.Y., U.S.	210	42.41 N	76.58 W
Dresden, Oh., U.S.	214	40.07 N	82.00 W
Dresden, Tn., U.S.	194	36.17 N	88.42 W
Dresher	285	40.08 N	75.10 W
Dretun	76	55.41 N	29.13 E
Dreux	50	48.44 N	1.22 E
Drevenack	263	51.40 N	6.45 E
Drew	194	33.48 N	90.31 W
Drewer	263	51.40 N	7.07 E
Drewitz, Dtsch.	54	52.22 N	13.07 E
Drewitz, Dtsch.	54	52.12 N	12.10 E
Drewitz ◈[8]	264a	52.22 N	13.08 E
Drewryville	208	36.42 N	77.18 W
Drews Reservoir ⊜[1]	202	42.10 N	120.40 W
Drew University ♁[2]	276	40.46 N	74.25 W
Drexel	218	39.44 N	84.17 W
Drexel Gardens	218	39.44 N	86.15 W
Drexel Hill	285	39.56 N	75.17 W
Drexel University ♁[2]	285	39.57 N	75.11 W
Drezdenko	30	52.51 N	15.50 E
Drezna	82	55.44 N	38.51 E
Dribin	76	54.08 N	31.06 E
Driebergen	52	52.03 N	5.16 E
Drienov	30	48.53 N	21.17 E
Drifton	210	41.00 N	75.54 W
Driftpile ≃	182	55.23 N	115.40 W
Drift Pile River Indian Reserve ◈[4]	182	55.18 N	115.45 W
Driftwood, B.C., Can.	182	55.49 N	126.25 W
Driftwood, Pa., U.S.	214	41.20 N	78.08 W

FRANÇAIS

Nom	Page	Lat.°′	Long.°′ W = Ouest
Driftwood ≃, B.C., Can.	182	55.43 N	126.15 W
Driftwood ≃, In., U.S.	218	39.12 N	85.56 W
Driftwood Creek ≃	198	40.11 N	100.39 W
Driggs	202	43.43 N	111.06 W
Drimnin	46	56.36 N	6.00 W
Drimoleague	48	51.38 N	9.14 W
Drin ≃	38	41.45 N	19.34 E
Drina ≃	38	44.53 N	19.21 E
Dringenberg	52	51.40 N	9.02 E
Drinit, Gjiri i ⊂	38	41.45 N	19.28 E
Driorejo	115a	7.21 S	112.37 E
Driscoll	196	27.40 N	97.45 W
Driskill Mountain ∧[2]	194	32.25 N	92.54 W
Drissa ≃	76	55.47 N	27.55 E
Drisv'aty, ozero ⊜	76	55.38 N	26.35 E
Driver	208	36.49 N	76.30 W
Drizzle Lake ⊜	212	45.20 N	78.10 W
Drjanovo	38	42.58 N	25.27 E
Drnholec	61	48.52 N	16.29 E
Drniš	36	43.51 N	16.09 E
Dro	64	45.58 N	10.54 E
Drøbak	26	59.39 N	10.39 E
Drobeta-Turnu Severin	38	44.38 N	22.39 E
Drobylevo	82	55.44 N	35.53 E
Drobyšovo, Ross.	86	53.58 N	74.40 E
Drobyš'ovo, Ukr.	83	49.02 N	37.44 E
Drochtersen	52	53.42 N	9.23 E
Drocourt	261	49.03 N	1.46 E
Droë Harts ≃	158	27.35 S	24.41 E
Drogheda (Droichead Átha)	48	53.43 N	6.21 W
Drogičin	76	52.11 N	25.09 E
Drogobyč	78	49.21 N	23.30 E
Drohiczyn	30	52.24 N	22.41 E
Drohobycz → Drogobyč	78	49.21 N	23.30 E
Droichead Átha → Drogheda	48	53.43 N	6.21 W
Droichead Nua	48	53.11 N	6.48 W
Droitwich	42	52.16 N	2.09 W
Drokija	78	48.03 N	27.48 E
Drolshagen	56	51.01 N	7.46 E
Dromahair	48	54.14 N	8.19 W
Dromana	169	38.21 S	144.58 E
Dromara	48	54.23 N	6.01 W
Dromcolliher	48	52.20 N	8.54 W
Drôme □[5]	62	44.35 N	5.10 E
Drôme ≃	62	44.46 N	4.46 E
Drömling ◈[1]	54	52.29 N	11.04 E
Dromod	48	53.51 N	7.55 W
Dromore, N. Ire., U.K.	48	54.25 N	6.09 W
Dromore, N. Ire., U.K.	48	54.31 N	7.28 W
Dromore West	48	54.15 N	8.53 W
Dronero	62	44.28 N	7.22 E
Dronfield	44	53.19 N	1.27 W
Drongan	44	55.26 N	4.27 W
Drongen	50	51.03 N	3.40 E
Dronne ≃	32	45.02 N	0.09 W
Dronninglund	26	57.09 N	10.18 E
Dronrijp	52	53.11 N	5.38 E
Dröschede	263	51.22 N	7.39 E
Drosendorf Stadt	61	48.52 N	15.37 E
Drosiá	267c	38.07 N	23.52 E
Drösing	61	48.32 N	16.54 E
Droskovo	76	52.31 N	37.05 E
Drottningholm slott ⊥	40	59.19 N	17.53 E
Droué	50	48.02 N	1.05 E
Droue-sur-Drouette	261	48.36 N	1.42 E
Drouette ≃	261	48.37 N	1.37 E
Drouin	169	38.08 S	145.51 E
Drov'anaja	88	51.35 N	113.02 E
Droylsden	262	53.29 N	2.10 W
Droyssig	54	51.02 N	12.01 E
Dr. Petru Groza	38	46.32 N	22.28 E
Druid Hill Park ♠	284b	39.19 N	76.39 W
Druja	76	55.47 N	27.27 E
Druk-Yul → Bhutan □[1]	120	27.30 N	90.30 E
Drulingen	56	48.52 N	7.11 E
Drum, Mount ∧	180	62.07 N	144.35 W
Drumbeg	46	58.14 N	5.12 W
Drumbo	212	43.14 N	80.33 W
Drumcliff	48	54.20 N	8.30 W
Drumheller	182	51.28 N	112.42 W
Drumlish	48	53.48 N	7.46 W
Drummond, N.Z.	172	46.09 S	168.09 E
Drummond, Mt., U.S.	202	46.40 N	113.08 W
Drummond, Wi., U.S.	190	46.20 N	91.15 W
Drummond □[6]	206	45.50 N	72.20 W
Drummond, Lake ⊜	208	36.36 N	76.28 W
Drummond Island I	190	46.00 N	83.40 W
Drummond Range ⋀	166	23.30 S	147.15 E
Drummondville	206	45.53 N	72.29 W
Drummore	44	54.42 N	4.54 W
Drummoyne	274a	33.51 S	151.09 E
Drumquin	48	54.37 N	7.30 W
Drumright	196	35.59 N	96.36 W
Drumshanbo	48	54.02 N	8.02 W
Drunen	52	51.42 N	5.08 E
Drusenheim	56	48.46 N	7.57 E
Druskininkai	76	54.01 N	23.58 E
Drut' ≃	76	53.03 N	30.42 E
Druten	52	51.54 N	5.36 E
Druyes-les-Belles-Fontaines	50	47.33 N	3.25 E
Družba, Kaz.	86	45.15 N	82.26 E
Družba, Ross.	265b	55.53 N	37.45 E
Družba, Ukr.	78	52.03 N	33.56 E
Družina	74	68.14 N	145.18 E
Družkovka	83	48.37 N	37.33 E
Družnaja Gorka	76	59.17 N	30.08 E
Drvar	36	44.22 N	16.24 E
Drwęca ≃	30	53.00 N	18.42 E
Dry ≃	164	14.54 S	132.24 E
Dry Arm ⊂	202	47.45 N	106.20 W
Dry Bay ⊂	180	59.08 N	138.25 W
Dryberry Lake ⊜	184	49.33 N	93.53 W
Dryburgh Abbey ♁[1]	46	55.34 N	2.40 W
Dry Cimarron ≃	196	36.54 N	102.59 W
Dry Creek ≃, Ca., U.S.	204	38.35 N	122.51 W
Dry Creek ≃, Ca., U.S.	226	37.27 N	120.37 W
Dry Creek ≃, Ca., U.S.	226	38.39 N	121.28 W
Dry Creek ≃, Ca., U.S.	226	38.22 N	122.18 W
Dry Creek ≃, Ca., U.S.	226	38.58 N	121.32 W
Dry Creek ≃, Ca., U.S.	226	39.13 N	121.25 W
Dry Creek ≃, Ca., U.S.	226	38.14 N	121.24 W
Dry Creek ≃, Ca., U.S.	226	36.58 N	120.13 W
Dry Creek ≃, Ca., U.S.	226	36.47 N	119.46 W
Dry Creek ≃, Ca., U.S.	282	37.22 N	122.23 W
Dry Creek ≃, Or., U.S.	202	43.34 N	117.21 W
Dry Creek ≃, Or., U.S.	224	45.30 N	121.03 W
Dry Creek ≃, Tx., U.S.	222	32.46 N	95.28 W
Dry Creek ≃, Wy., U.S.	202	43.13 N	108.54 W
Dry Creek ≃, Wy., U.S.	202	44.30 N	108.03 W
Dry Creek Mountain ∧	204	41.22 N	116.22 W
Dryden, On., Can.	184	49.47 N	92.50 W
Dryden, N.Y., U.S.	210	42.29 N	76.17 W
Dryden, Wa., U.S.	224	47.32 N	120.33 W

PORTUGUÊS

Nome	Página	Lat.°′	Long.°′ W = Oeste
Dry Devils ≃, Tx., U.S.	196	29.47 N	100.59 W
Dry Devils ≃, Tx., U.S.	196	30.20 N	100.57 W
Dryfe Water ≃	44	55.08 N	3.26 W
Dry Fork ≃	194	37.58 N	91.31 W
Dry Frio ≃	196	29.17 N	99.39 W
Drygalski Island I	9	65.45 S	92.30 E
Dry Lake ⊜	198	48.15 N	98.58 W
Drymen	46	56.04 N	4.27 W
Dry Prong	194	31.34 N	92.31 W
Dry Ridge	218	38.40 N	84.35 W
Dry Run	214	40.10 N	77.45 W
Drysdale	169	38.11 S	144.34 E
Drysdale ≃	164	13.59 S	126.51 E
Drysdale River National Park ♠	164	15.00 S	127.00 E
Dry Tortugas II	220	24.38 N	82.55 W
Drzewica	30	51.27 N	20.28 E
Drzewice	54	52.38 N	14.38 E
Dschang	152	5.27 N	10.04 E
Dschidda → Jiddah	144	21.30 N	39.12 E
Dschuba → Jubba ≃	144	0.15 S	42.38 E
Du	150	10.30 N	0.59 W
Du ≃	102	32.48 N	110.38 E
Dua ≃	152	3.20 N	20.53 E
Duabo	150	5.40 N	8.05 W
Duāigaon	126	24.14 N	90.51 E
Duala → Douala	152	4.03 N	9.42 E
Dualchi	71	40.13 N	8.54 E
Du'an	102	24.06 N	108.10 E
Duancun	105	38.52 N	115.56 E
Duane L. Bliss State Park ♠	226	38.59 N	120.06 W
Duanesburg	210	42.46 N	74.08 W
Duanjialing	105	39.59 N	117.09 E
Duaringa	166	23.43 S	149.40 E
Duarte	228	34.08 N	117.58 W
Duarte, Pico ∧	238	19.02 N	70.59 W
Duartina	255	22.24 S	49.25 W
Duas Barras	256	22.02 S	42.32 W
Duayaw Nkwanta	150	7.10 N	2.06 W
Dubā, Ar. Su.	128	27.21 N	35.40 E
Dubá, Česko.	54	50.34 N	14.33 E
Dubach	194	32.41 N	92.39 W
Dubai → Dubayy	128	25.18 N	55.18 E
Dubawnt ≃	176	64.33 N	100.06 W
Dubawnt Lake ⊜	176	63.08 N	101.30 W
Dubayy	128	25.18 N	55.18 E
Dubbeldam	52	51.47 N	4.42 E
Dubbo	166	32.15 S	148.36 E
Dube ≃	150	5.45 N	8.00 W
Dubele	154	2.54 N	29.33 E
Dübendorf	58	47.25 N	8.38 E
Dübener Heide ◈[3]	54	51.40 N	12.40 E
Dubenskij	86	51.27 N	56.38 E
Dubesar'	78	47.16 N	29.08 E
Dubh Artach II[1]	46	56.08 N	6.40 W
Dubí	54	50.42 N	13.45 E
Dubi Bheri	272b	22.53 N	88.17 E
Dubica	36	45.11 N	16.48 E
Dubie	154	8.33 S	28.32 E
Dubinino	82	56.09 N	37.01 E
Dubino	58	46.09 N	9.27 E
Dubjazy	80	56.08 N	49.13 E
Dubki, Ross.	265a	60.00 N	30.00 E
Dubki, Ross.	265b	55.41 N	37.14 E
Dublin, Austl.	168b	34.27 S	138.21 E
Dublin, On., Can.	212	43.31 N	81.17 W
Dublin (Baile Átha Cliath), Ire.	48	53.20 N	6.15 W
Dublin, Ca., U.S.	226	37.42 N	121.56 W
Dublin, Ga., U.S.	192	32.32 N	82.54 W
Dublin, In., U.S.	218	39.48 N	85.12 W
Dublin, Md., U.S.	208	39.39 N	76.16 W
Dublin, Oh., U.S.	214	40.06 N	83.07 W
Dublin, Pa., U.S.	208	40.22 N	75.12 W
Dublin, Tx., U.S.	196	32.05 N	98.20 W
Dublin, Va., U.S.	192	37.06 N	80.41 W
Dublin □[6]	48	53.20 N	6.15 W
Dublin (Collinstown) Airport ⊠	48	53.26 N	6.15 W
Dublin Bay ⊂	48	53.20 N	6.06 W
Dublin Canyon V	282	37.42 N	121.59 W
Dublon I	175c	7.23 N	151.53 E
Dubna, Ross.	82	54.09 N	36.58 E
Dubna, Ross.	82	56.44 N	37.10 E
Dubna ≃, Lat.	76	56.22 N	26.10 E
Dubna ≃, Ross.	82	56.47 N	37.15 E
Dubňany	30	48.55 N	17.06 E
Dubnevo	82	55.06 N	38.08 E
Dubnica nad Váhom	30	48.58 N	18.09 E
Dubno	78	50.26 N	25.44 E
Dubois, Id., U.S.	202	44.10 N	112.13 W
Dubois, Il., U.S.	219	38.13 N	89.13 W
Dubois, In., U.S.	194	38.26 N	86.48 W
Du Bois, Ne., U.S.	198	40.02 N	96.02 W
Du Bois, Pa., U.S.	214	41.07 N	78.45 W
Dubois, Wy., U.S.	200	43.32 N	109.37 W
Du Bois Reservoir ⊜[1]	214	41.06 N	78.38 W
Duboistown	210	41.13 N	77.02 W
Dub'onki	80	54.27 N	46.18 E
Dubossarskoje vodochranilišče ⊜[1]	78	47.35 N	29.00 E
Dubovaja Rošča	76	53.11 N	36.04 E
Dubov'azovka	78	51.08 N	33.22 E
Dubovići	78	51.38 N	33.35 E
Dubovka, Ross.	78	51.26 N	41.25 E
Dubovka, Ross.	80	49.03 N	44.50 E
Dubovoje	76	53.08 N	40.05 E
Dubovskij	80	56.21 N	46.48 E
Dubovskoje	80	47.25 N	42.46 E
Dubovyj Ovrag	80	48.20 N	44.37 E
Dubovyj Umet	80	52.59 N	50.17 E
Duboweitun	89	50.42 N	120.14 E
Dubra	126	23.32 N	86.31 E
Dubrājpur	126	23.48 N	87.23 E
Dubréka	150	9.48 N	13.31 W
Dubrova, Bela.	76	52.25 N	29.58 E
Dubrova, Bela.	78	51.47 N	28.13 E
Dubrova, Ross.	80	56.59 N	54.33 E
Dubrova, Ross.	80	57.42 N	55.01 E
Dubrovica	78	51.34 N	26.34 E
Dubroviči	80	54.39 N	39.56 E
Dubrovicy	82	56.46 N	39.10 E
Dubrovino	86	55.28 N	83.17 E
Dubrovka, Ross.	76	53.42 N	33.30 E
Dubrovka, Ross.	76	59.13 N	36.13 E
Dubrovka, Ross.	76	59.51 N	30.56 E
Dubrovka, Ross.	82	54.44 N	36.21 E
Dubrovka, Ukr.	83	47.54 N	39.02 E
Dubrovki	80	53.49 N	43.19 E
Dubrovnik	38	42.38 N	18.07 E
Dubrovno	76	54.35 N	30.41 E
Dubrovnoje, Kaz.	86	54.49 N	68.06 E
Dubrovnoje, Ross.	86	57.58 N	69.25 E
Dubrovo	76	59.51 N	33.34 E
Dubrovskoje	88	58.45 N	111.10 E
Dubunskaja	86	43.46 N	80.13 E
Dubuque	190	42.30 N	90.39 W
Dubysa ≃	76	55.05 N	23.26 E
Duchana	85	38.02 N	68.13 E
Duchang	100	29.15 N	116.13 E
Duchcov	54	50.37 N	13.45 E
Ducherow	54	53.46 N	13.46 E
Duchesne	200	40.09 N	110.24 W
Duchesne ≃	200	40.05 N	109.41 W
Duchess	166	21.22 S	139.52 E
Duchovnickoje	80	52.28 N	48.15 E
Duchovščina	76	55.12 N	32.25 E
Duck ≃, Austl.	274a	33.50 S	151.02 E
Duck ≃, Tn., U.S.	194	36.02 N	87.52 W
Duckabush ≃	224	47.38 N	122.56 W
Duck Bay	184	52.10 N	100.09 W
Duck Creek ≃, On., Can.	281	42.18 N	82.41 W

Duck Creek ≃, Ca., U.S.	226	37.55 N	121.16 W
Duck Creek ≃, In., U.S.	218	40.08 N	85.57 W
Duck Creek ≃, Nv., U.S.	204	40.06 N	114.43 W
Duck Creek ≃, N.D., U.S.	198	46.03 N	102.14 W
Duck Creek ≃, Tx., U.S.	196	33.14 N	100.42 W
Duck Creek ≃, Tx., U.S.	222	32.48 N	96.31 W
Duck Creek ≃, Tx., U.S.	222	31.06 N	96.17 W
Duck Creek ≃, Wi., U.S.	190	44.33 N	88.02 W
Duck Hill	194	33.37 N	89.42 W
Duck Island Harbor ⊂	276	40.55 N	73.23 W
Duck Key I	220	24.46 N	80.56 W
Duck Lake, Sk., Can.	184	52.47 N	106.13 W
Duck Lake, Mi., U.S.	216	42.24 N	84.47 W
Duck Lake ⊜, Mb., Can.	184	54.52 N	98.11 W
Duck Lake ⊜, Mi., U.S.	216	42.23 N	84.47 W
Duck Lake ⊜, Mi., U.S.	281	42.40 N	83.35 W
Duck Mountain ∧	184	51.35 N	101.00 W
Duck Mountain Provincial Park ♠, Mb., Can.	184	51.36 N	100.55 W
Duck Mountain Provincial Park ♠, Sk., Can.	184	51.38 N	101.53 W
Duck Valley Indian Reservation ◈[4]	204	42.00 N	116.10 W
Duckwall Mountain ∧	226	37.58 N	120.07 W
Duclair	50	49.29 N	0.53 E
Ducos	240e	14.34 N	60.58 W
Du Couedic, Cape ›	166	36.04 S	136.42 E
Ducun	106	31.07 N	120.27 E
Duda ≃	246	2.33 N	74.02 W
Dudačkino	76	59.57 N	32.53 E
Dudčany	78	47.12 N	33.46 E
Duddington	42	52.36 N	0.32 W
Duddon ≃	44	54.15 N	3.13 W
Dudelange	56	49.28 N	6.05 E
Dudergofka ≃	265a	59.52 N	30.12 E
Duderstadt	52	51.31 N	10.16 E
Dūdhi	124	24.13 N	83.15 E
Dudhkośī ≃	124	27.08 N	86.26 E
Dudhnai	124	25.59 N	90.44 E
Dudinka	74	69.25 N	86.15 E
Dudkin	78	47.53 N	40.32 E
Dudley, Eng., U.K.	42	52.30 N	2.05 W
Dudley, Eng., U.K.	44	55.03 N	1.35 W
Dudley, Ma., U.S.	207	42.02 N	71.55 W
Dudley, Pa., U.S.	214	40.12 N	78.10 W
Dudley Pond ⊜	283	42.20 N	71.22 W
Dudleyville	200	32.58 N	110.47 W
Dudna ≃	122	19.07 N	76.54 E
Dudorovskij	76	53.40 N	35.22 E
Ḍūḍuwā Śṛingklā ⋀	124	27.45 N	82.30 E
Dudwa National Park ♠	124	28.30 N	80.40 E
Dudweiler	56	49.17 N	7.02 E
Dudzele	50	51.17 N	3.14 E
Due	89	50.50 N	142.06 E
Duékoué	150	6.45 N	7.21 W
Dueré	250	11.20 S	49.17 W
Dueré ≃	250	10.59 S	49.48 W
Duerji	89	45.39 N	121.49 E
Duerna ≃	34	42.19 N	5.54 W
Duero (Douro) ≃	34	41.08 N	8.40 W
Dueville	64	45.38 N	11.32 E
Due West	192	34.20 N	82.23 W
Dufault, Lac ⊜	190	48.19 N	79.00 W
Duff Dunbar	123	32.15 N	77.12 E
Duffel	50	51.06 N	4.31 E
Dufferin □[6]	212	44.05 N	80.15 W
Duffer Peak ∧	204	41.40 N	118.44 W
Duffield, Austl.	162	25.50 S	134.40 E
Duffield, Eng., U.K.	44	52.58 N	1.29 W
Duffins Creek ≃	212	43.49 N	79.02 W
Dufftown	46	57.26 N	3.08 W
Dufourspitze ∧	58	45.55 N	7.52 E
Dufresne ≃	206	46.16 N	73.59 W
Dufur	224	45.27 N	121.07 W
Dugadda	124	29.48 N	78.37 E
Duga Resa	36	45.27 N	15.30 E
Duga-Zapadnaja, mys ›	74	59.09 N	145.59 E
Dugdemona ≃	194	31.47 N	92.22 W
Dugede	120	30.54 N	90.48 E
Dugger	194	39.04 N	87.16 W
Dugino	83	47.09 N	39.27 E
Dugi Otok I	36	44.00 N	15.04 E
Dugna	82	54.25 N	36.51 E
Dugny-sur-Meuse	56	49.06 N	5.23 E
Dug Pond ⊜	283	42.17 N	71.22 W
Du Gué ≃	176	57.21 N	70.45 W
Dugui Qarag	102	39.38 N	108.40 E
Dugway Proving Ground ■	200	40.10 N	113.15 W
Duhernal Lake ⊜	276	40.24 N	74.22 W
Duhi	140	7.07 N	28.45 E
Duhnen	52	53.53 N	8.38 E
Duhu	100	22.04 N	112.56 E
Ḍuhūr ash-Shuwayr	132	33.55 N	35.43 E
Duich, Loch ⊂	46	57.14 N	5.30 W
Duida, Cerro ∧	246	3.25 N	65.40 W
Duifken Point ›	164	12.33 S	141.38 E
Duingen	52	52.00 N	9.42 E
Duingt	62	45.50 N	6.12 E
Duino	64	45.46 N	13.36 E
Duirinish	46	57.19 N	5.41 W
Duisburg, Dtsch.	56	51.25 N	6.46 E
Duisburg, Dtsch.	263	51.25 N	6.46 E
Duissern ◈[8]	263	51.26 N	6.47 E
Duitama	246	5.50 N	73.02 W
Duitsland → Germany □[1]	30	51.00 N	10.00 E
Duiveland I	52	51.38 N	4.00 E
Duiwelskloof	156	23.42 S	30.06 E
Duji, Zhg.	98	34.11 N	115.48 E
Duji, Zhg.	98	37.44 N	116.50 E
Dujiahang	106	31.03 N	121.29 E
Dujuuma	144	1.15 N	42.34 E
Dukambiya	144	14.47 N	37.28 E
Dukana ⍑[4]	154	3.59 N	37.16 E
Dukazi	120	30.54 N	92.52 E
Duke	196	34.39 N	99.34 W
Duke Center	214	41.57 N	78.28 W
Duke Island I	182	54.56 N	131.20 W
Duke of York Bay ⊂	176	65.25 N	84.50 W
Duke of York Island I	164	4.10 S	152.26 E
Dukes □[6]	207	41.23 N	70.31 W
Dukes Brook ≃	276	40.33 N	74.37 W
Duk Fadiat	140	7.45 N	31.25 E
Duk Faiwil	140	7.30 N	31.29 E
Dukhān	128	25.25 N	50.48 E
Dukhmays	142	31.07 N	31.04 E
Duki	120	30.09 N	68.34 E
Dukinfield	262	53.29 N	2.05 W
Dukla	30	49.34 N	21.41 E
Dukla Pass)(	30	49.25 N	21.43 E
Dukou	102	26.40 N	101.39 E
Dūkštas	76	55.32 N	26.20 E
Duku, Nig.	146	10.49 N	10.46 E
Duku, Nig.	150	11.10 N	4.55 E
Dula	152	4.41 N	20.22 E
Dūlāb ◈[8]	267d	35.39 N	51.27 E
Dulag	116	10.57 N	125.02 E
Dulāi	124	23.57 N	89.31 E
Dulais ≃	42	51.41 N	3.47 W
Dulan (Chahanwusu)	102	36.16 N	98.28 E
Dul'apino	80	57.15 N	40.49 E
Dulas ≃	42	52.36 N	3.50 W
Dulas Bay ⊂	44	53.23 N	4.15 W
Dulata	86	43.26 N	80.50 E

Dulayb, Khawr V	140	11.45 N	32.47 E
Dulaym	146	25.58 N	14.03 E
Dulce	200	36.56 N	106.59 W
Dulce ≃	252	30.31 S	62.32 W
Dulce, Arroyo ≃	258	35.28 S	57.41 W
Dulce, Golfo ⊂	236	8.32 N	83.14 W
Dulce Grande	234	22.59 N	102.14 W
Dulce Nombre de Culmí	236	15.09 N	85.37 W
Dul'durga	88	50.41 N	113.36 E
Duleek	48	53.39 N	6.25 W
Dulgalach ≃	74	67.44 N	133.12 E
Dulin	98	38.22 N	116.43 E
Duliu, Zhg.	105	39.13 N	116.16 E
Duliu, Zhg.	105	39.01 N	116.54 E
Duliu Jianhe ≃	105	38.51 N	117.20 E
Duljo Point ›	116	9.35 N	123.43 E
Dulkaninna	166	29.01 S	138.27 E
Dülken	56	51.15 N	6.20 E
Dulles International Airport ⊠	208	38.58 N	77.28 W
Dullstroom	156	25.27 S	30.07 E
Dülmen	52	51.51 N	7.16 E
Dulnain Bridge	46	57.16 N	3.41 W
Dulnan ≃	46	57.18 N	3.40 W
Dulovka	76	57.32 N	28.20 E
Dulovo	38	43.49 N	27.09 E
Dulq Maghār	130	36.22 N	38.39 E
D'ul'tydag, gora ∧	84	41.58 N	46.56 E
Dulung ≃	126	22.08 N	87.05 E
Dulunguin Point ›	116	7.45 N	122.05 E
Duluth, Ga., U.S.	192	34.00 N	84.08 W
Duluth, Mn., U.S.	190	46.45 N	92.07 W
Dulverton	42	51.03 N	3.33 W
Dulwich ◈[8]	260	51.26 N	0.05 W
Duma, Bots.	156	18.45 S	22.46 E
Dūmā, Lubnān	130	34.12 N	35.50 E
Dūmā, Sūrīy.	132	33.35 N	36.24 E
Duma, Zaïre	154	4.57 N	27.19 E
Dumaguete	116	9.18 N	123.18 E
Dumai	114	1.41 N	101.27 E
Dumalag	116	11.18 N	122.37 E
Dumalinao	116	7.49 N	123.23 E
Dumali Point ›	116	13.07 N	121.33 E
Dumanjug	116	10.04 N	123.26 E
Dumanlıdağ ∧	84	40.31 N	43.25 E
Dumanquilas Bay ⊂	116	7.34 N	123.04 E
Dumaran Channel ⩌	116	10.25 N	119.45 E
Dumaran Island I	116	10.33 N	119.51 E
Dumaresq ≃	166	28.40 S	150.28 E
Dumaring	112	1.36 N	118.12 E
Dumas, Ar., U.S.	194	33.53 N	91.29 W
Dumas, Tx., U.S.	196	35.51 N	101.58 W
Ḍumayr	132	33.38 N	36.40 E
Dumbarton	46	55.57 N	4.35 W
Dumbarton Bridge ◈[5]	282	37.31 N	122.07 W
Dumbarton Point ›	282	37.30 N	122.06 W
Ďumbier ∧	30	48.57 N	19.37 E
Dumbleyung	162	33.19 S	117.44 E
Dumbo	152	14.06 S	17.24 E
Dumboa	146	11.10 N	12.45 E
Dumbrăveni	38	46.14 N	24.35 E
Dum Dum	126	22.35 N	88.24 E
Dum Dum International Airport ⊠	126	22.38 N	88.25 E
Dume, Point ›	228	34.00 N	118.48 W
Dumei	100	24.47 N	117.21 E
Dumfries, Scot., U.K.	44	55.04 N	3.37 W
Dumfries, Va., U.S.	208	38.34 N	77.19 W
Dumfries and Galloway □[4]	44	55.00 N	4.00 W
Duminiči	76	53.55 N	35.06 E
Dumjor	272b	22.38 N	88.13 E
Dumka	126	24.16 N	87.15 E
Dumlupınar	130	38.52 N	30.00 E
Dummar	132	33.32 N	36.14 E
Dümmer ⊜	52	52.31 N	8.19 E
Dummer Range ⋀	162	20.11 S	125.59 E
Dumoga-Bone National Park ♠	112	0.30 N	123.25 E
Dumoga Kecil	112	0.31 N	123.55 E
Dumoine ≃	190	46.13 N	77.51 W
Dumoine, Lac ⊜	190	46.53 N	77.54 W
Dumont, Ia., U.S.	190	42.45 N	92.58 W
Dumont, N.J., U.S.	210	40.56 N	73.59 W
Dumont, Lac ⊜	190	46.04 N	76.27 W
Dumont d'Urville ♁[3]	9	66.35 S	140.00 E
Dümpelfeld	56	50.27 N	6.56 E
Dümpten ◈[8]	263	51.27 N	6.54 E
Dumpu	164	5.50 S	145.45 E
Dumra	124	26.34 N	85.31 E
Dumraon	124	25.33 N	84.09 E
Dumuria, Bngl.	126	22.47 N	89.26 E
Dumuriā, India	126	22.11 N	86.20 E
Dumyāṭ (Damietta)	142	31.25 N	31.48 E
Dumyāṭ □[4]	142	31.20 N	31.45 E
Dumyāṭ, Far' (Damietta Branch) ≃	142	31.32 N	31.51 E
Dumyāṭ, Maṣabb (Damietta Mouth) ≃[1]	142	31.32 N	31.51 E
Dün ∧	54	51.21 N	10.30 E
Dünaburg → Daugavpils	76	55.53 N	26.32 E
Duna → Danube ≃	22	45.20 N	29.40 E
Dunaff Head ›	48	55.17 N	7.33 W
Dunaföldvár	30	46.48 N	18.55 E
Dunaharaszti	30	47.21 N	19.05 E
Dunaj, Ross.	89	42.52 N	132.22 E
Dunaj, Ross.	265a	59.58 N	30.56 E
Dunaj, ostrova II	74	73.52 N	124.29 E
Dunaj → Danube ≃	22	45.20 N	29.40 E
Dunajec ≃	30	50.14 N	20.44 E
Dunajevcy	78	48.54 N	26.51 E
Dunajevo	88	52.05 N	117.02 E
Dunajská Streda	30	48.01 N	17.35 E
Dunakeszi	30	47.38 N	19.08 E
Dunany Point ›	48	53.52 N	6.14 W
Dunărea → Danube ≃	22	45.20 N	29.40 E
Dunărea Veche, Brațul ≃	38	45.17 N	28.02 E
Duna-Tisza-csatorna ≊	264c	47.21 N	19.05 E
Dunaújváros	30	46.58 N	18.57 E
Dunavățu-de-Sus	38	44.59 N	29.13 E
Dunav → Danube ≃	22	45.20 N	29.40 E
Duna-Völgyi-főcsatorna ≊	30	46.12 N	18.56 E
Dunback	172	45.23 S	170.38 E
Dunbar, Scot., U.K.	46	56.00 N	2.31 W
Dunbar, W.V., U.S.	188	38.21 N	81.44 W
Dunbarton	275b	43.49 N	79.06 W
Dunbeath	46	58.15 N	3.25 W
Dunblane, Sk., Can.	184	51.11 N	106.52 W
Dunblane, Scot., U.K.	46	56.12 N	3.59 W
Dunboyne	48	53.24 N	6.28 W
Duncan, B.C., Can.	224	48.47 N	123.42 W
Duncan, Az., U.S.	200	32.43 N	109.06 W
Duncan, Ms., U.S.	194	34.02 N	90.44 W
Duncan, Ok., U.S.	196	34.30 N	97.57 W
Duncan ≃	182	50.11 N	116.57 W
Duncan Lake ⊜[1]	182	50.20 N	117.00 W
Duncannon	208	40.23 N	77.01 W
Duncan Passage ⩌	110	11.00 N	92.30 E
Duncans	241q	18.28 N	77.32 W
Duncansby Head ›	46	58.39 N	3.02 W
Duncans Creek ≃	274a	33.53 S	150.39 E
Duncansville	214	40.25 N	78.26 W
Duncanville	222	32.39 N	96.54 W
Dunchurch	42	52.20 N	1.16 W
Duncormick	48	52.14 N	6.39 W
Dundaga	76	57.31 N	22.21 E
Dundāhera	272a	28.38 N	77.26 E

Dundalk, On., Can.	212	44.10 N	80.24 W
Dundalk (Dún Dealgan), Ire.	48	54.01 N	6.25 W
Dundalk, Md., U.S.	208	39.15 N	76.31 W
Dundalk Bay ⊂	48	53.57 N	6.17 W
Dundas, Austl.	274a	33.48 S	151.02 E
Dundas, On., Can.	212	43.16 N	79.58 W
Dundas, Mn., U.S.	190	44.25 N	93.12 W
Dundas, Cape ›	212	44.57 N	81.07 W
Dundas, Lake ⊜	162	32.35 S	121.50 E
Dundas Island I	182	54.33 N	130.55 W
Dundas Peninsula ›[1]	176	74.50 N	111.30 W
Dundas Strait ⩌	164	11.20 S	131.35 E
Dún Dealgan → Dundalk	48	54.01 N	6.25 W
Dundee, S. Afr.	158	28.12 S	30.16 E
Dundee, Scot., U.K.	46	56.28 N	2.58 W
Dundee, Fl., U.S.	220	28.01 N	81.37 W
Dundee, Il., U.S.	216	42.06 N	88.17 W
Dundee, Mi., U.S.	216	41.57 N	83.39 W
Dundee, Ms., U.S.	194	34.31 N	90.27 W
Dundee, N.Y., U.S.	210	42.31 N	76.58 W
Dundee, Oh., U.S.	214	40.35 N	81.37 W
Dundee, Or., U.S.	224	45.16 N	123.00 W
Dundee Creek ⊂	284b	39.21 N	76.22 W
Dundgov' □[4]	102	45.30 N	106.30 E
Dundīṭ	142	30.41 N	31.18 E
Dundonald	46	55.34 N	4.35 W
Dundoo	166	27.39 S	144.39 E
Dundrum, Ire.	48	52.33 N	8.03 W
Dundrum, N. Ire., U.K.	48	54.16 N	5.51 W
Dundrum Bay ⊂	48	54.13 N	5.45 W
Dundurn	184	51.49 N	106.30 W
Duneaton Water ≃	46	55.32 N	3.42 W
Dunedin, N.Z.	172	45.52 S	170.30 E
Dunedin, Fl., U.S.	220	28.01 N	82.46 W
Dunedoo	166	32.01 S	149.24 E
Duneland Beach	216	41.35 N	86.50 W
Dunellen	276	40.35 N	74.28 W
Dunewood	276	40.38 N	73.11 W
Dunfanaghy	48	55.11 N	7.59 W
Dunfermline	46	56.04 N	3.29 W
Du Ngae, Khao ∧	110	15.10 N	98.47 E
Dungannon, N. Ire., U.K.	48	54.31 N	6.46 W
Dungannon, Va., U.S.	192	36.49 N	82.28 W
Dūngarpur	120	23.50 N	73.43 E
Dungarvan	48	52.05 N	7.37 W
Dungarvan Harbour ⊂	48	52.10 N	7.35 W
Dungas	150	13.04 N	9.20 E
Dungau ◈[1]	60	48.50 N	12.40 E
Dungeness ›	42	50.55 N	0.58 E
Dungeness ≃	224	48.08 N	123.06 W
Dungeness, Punta ›	254	52.23 S	68.25 W
Dungeness Bay ⊂	224	48.10 N	123.07 W
Dungeness Spit ›[2]	224	48.10 N	123.09 W
Dungiven	48	54.55 N	6.55 W
Dunglow	48	54.57 N	8.22 W
Dungo, Lagoa do ⊜	152	17.20 S	18.58 E
Dungog	166	32.24 S	151.46 E
Dungu	154	3.37 N	28.34 E
Dungu ≃	154	3.37 N	28.34 E
Dungun	114	4.47 N	103.26 E
Dungun ≃	114	4.47 N	103.23 E
Dunham	206	45.08 N	72.48 W
Dunham Lake ⊜	281	42.39 N	83.41 W
Dunham-on-the-Hill	262	53.15 N	2.47 W
Dunham Park ♠	262	53.23 N	2.24 W
Dunham Town	262	53.23 N	2.24 W
Dunheved	274a	33.45 S	150.47 E
Dunheved → Launceston	42	50.38 N	4.21 W
Dunholme	44	53.18 N	0.28 W
Dunhou	100	27.02 N	114.58 E
Dunhua	89	43.21 N	128.13 E
Dunhuang	102	40.12 N	94.41 E
Dunières	62	45.13 N	4.20 E
Dunilovo, Ross.	76	57.46 N	38.55 E
Dunilovo, Ross.	80	57.00 N	41.27 E
Dunkeld	46	56.34 N	3.35 W
Dunkeld ◈[8]	273d	26.09 S	28.03 E
Dunkellin ≃	48	53.12 N	8.54 W
Dunkelsteinerwald ◈[3]	61	48.15 N	15.29 E
Dunkern ⊜	40	59.09 N	16.52 E
Dunker Pond ⊜	276	41.05 N	74.28 W
Dunkerque	50	51.03 N	2.22 E
Dunkerrin	48	52.55 N	7.55 W
Dunkery Hill ∧[2]	42	51.11 N	3.35 W
Dunkineely	48	54.38 N	8.23 W
Dunkinsville	218	38.51 N	83.30 W
Dunkirk, Eng., U.K.	42	51.17 N	0.59 E
Dunkirk, In., U.S.	216	40.22 N	85.12 W
Dunkirk, N.Y., U.S.	214	42.28 N	79.20 W
Dunkirk, Oh., U.S.	216	40.47 N	83.38 W
Dunkirk → Dunkerque	50	51.03 N	2.22 E
Dunk's Green	260	51.15 N	0.19 E
Dunkuj	140	12.50 N	32.49 E
Dunkwa, Ghana	150	5.22 N	1.12 W
Dunkwa, Ghana	150	5.58 N	1.46 W
Dún Laoghaire	48	53.17 N	6.08 W
Dunlap, In., U.S.	216	41.38 N	85.55 W
Dunlap, Ia., U.S.	198	41.51 N	95.36 W
Dunlap, Tn., U.S.	194	35.22 N	85.23 W
Dunlap Acres	228	34.03 N	117.06 W
Dunlavin	48	53.02 N	6.41 W
Dunleary → Dún Laoghaire	48	53.17 N	6.08 W
Dunleer	48	53.50 N	6.24 W
Dunleith	285	39.42 N	75.33 W
Dun-le-Palestel	32	46.18 N	1.40 E
Dunlo	214	40.17 N	78.43 W
Dunlop	46	55.43 N	4.32 W
Dunloy	48	55.01 N	6.25 W
Dunmanus Bay ⊂	48	51.35 N	9.45 W
Dunmanway	48	51.43 N	9.06 W
Dunmarra	164	16.42 S	133.25 E
Dunmore, Ire.	48	53.36 N	8.46 W
Dunmore, Pa., U.S.	210	41.25 N	75.37 W
Dunmore Cave ⏊[5]	48	52.44 N	7.15 W
Dunmore East	48	52.09 N	7.00 W
Dunmore Town	238	25.30 N	76.39 W
Dunmurry	48	54.33 N	6.01 W
Dunn	192	35.18 N	78.36 W
Dunnamanagh	48	54.52 N	7.18 W
Dünnbach ≃	56	50.10 N	7.18 E
Dunnellon	220	29.02 N	82.27 W
Dunnet	46	58.37 N	3.20 W
Dunnet Bay ⊂	46	58.37 N	3.24 W
Dunnet Head ›	46	58.40 N	3.24 W
Dunnigan	226	38.53 N	121.58 W
Dunning	198	41.49 N	100.06 W
Dunning Creek ≃	214	40.02 N	78.28 W
Dunnington	44	53.57 N	0.59 W
Dunningtown	279b	40.25 N	79.35 W
Dunn Loring	284c	38.53 N	77.14 W
Dunn Loring Woods	284c	38.52 N	77.14 W
Dunnockshaw	262	53.45 N	2.17 W
Dunnottar Castle ⊥	46	56.57 N	2.11 W
Dunns Bridge	216	41.13 N	86.59 W
Dunnville	212	42.54 N	79.36 W
Dunolly	169	36.52 S	143.44 E
Dunoon	46	55.57 N	4.56 W
Dunqul ⍑[4]	140	23.26 N	31.37 E
Dunqulah	140	19.10 N	30.29 E
Dunqulah al-Qadīmah	140	18.13 N	30.45 E
Dunqunāb	140	21.06 N	37.05 E
Dunqunāb, Khalīj ⊂	140	21.05 N	37.08 E
Dunrea	184	49.25 N	99.44 W
Dun Rig ∧	46	55.34 N	3.10 W
Duns	46	55.47 N	2.20 W
Dunsandel	172	43.40 S	172.11 E
Dunsborough	162	33.36 S	115.06 E
Dunseith	198	48.48 N	100.03 W
Dunsford	42	50.41 N	3.40 W
Dunsmuir	204	41.13 N	122.16 W
Dunstable, Eng., U.K.	42	51.53 N	0.32 W
Dunstable, Ma., U.S.	207	42.40 N	71.29 W

≃	River	Fluß	Río	Rivière	Rio
≊	Canal	Kanal	Canal	Canal	Canal
⌞	Waterfall, Rapids	Wasserfall, Stromschnellen	Cascada, Rápidos	Chute d'eau, Rapides	Cascata, Rápidos
⩌	Strait	Meeresstraße	Estrecho	Détroit	Estreito
⊂	Bay, Gulf	Bucht, Golf	Bahía, Golfo	Baie, Golfe	Baía, Golfo
⊜	Lake, Lakes	See, Seen	Lago, Lagos	Lac, Lacs	Lago, Lagos
⁞	Swamp	Sumpf	Pantano	Marais	Pântano
⊓	Ice Features, Glacier	Eis- und Gletscherformen	Accidentes Glaciales	Formes glaciaires	Acidentes glaciares
⍑	Other Hydrographic Features	Andere Hydrographische Objekte	Otros Elementos Hidrográficos	Autres données hydrographiques	Outros acidentes hidrográficos

✧	Submarine Features	Untermeerische Objekte	Accidentes Submarinos	Formes de relief sous-marin	Acidentes submarinos
□	Political Unit	Politische Einheit	Unidad Politica	Entité politique	Unidade política
♁	Cultural Institution	Kulturelle Institution	Institución Cultural	Institution culturelle	Instituição cultural
⊥	Historical Site	Historische Stätte	Sitio Histórico	Site historique	Sitio histórico
♠	Recreational Site	Erholungs- und Ferienort	Sitio de Recreo	Centre de loisirs	Area de Lazer
⊠	Airport	Flughafen	Aeropuerto	Aéroport	Aeroporto
■	Military Installation	Militäranlage	Instalación Militar	Installation militaire	Instalação militar
◈	Miscellaneous	Verschiedenes	Misceláneo	Divers	Diversos

ENGLISH — Name / Page / Lat.°′ / Long.°′
DEUTSCH — Name / Seite / Breite°′ / Länge°′ E = Ost

Dunstaffnage Castle ⊥ 46 56.26 N 5.32 W
Dunstan Mountains ⩚ 172 44.57 S 169.32 E
Dunster, B.C., Can. 182 53.08 N 119.50 W
Dunster, Eng., U.K. 42 51.12 N 3.27 W
Dun-sur-Auron 32 46.53 N 2.34 E
Dun-sur-Meuse 56 49.23 N 5.11 E
Duntelchaig, Loch ⊜ 46 57.20 N 4.18 W
Dunton Green 42 51.18 N 0.11 E
Dunton Wayletts 260 51.35 N 0.24 E
Duntou 100 29.21 N 119.46 E
Duntroon 172 44.52 S 170.41 E
Dunvegan, S. Afr. 273d 26.09 S 28.09 E
Dunvegan, Scot., U.K. 46 57.26 N 6.35 W
Dunvegan, Loch c 46 57.28 N 6.40 W
Dunvegan Castle ⊥ 46 57.26 N 6.35 W
Dunvegan Head ≻ 46 57.31 N 6.43 W
Dunville 186 47.16 N 53.54 W
Dunwich 171a 27.31 S 153.23 E
Dunyāpur 123 29.48 N 71.44 E
Duobukur ≃ 89 49.56 N 125.12 E
Duogu'nao 102 31.32 N 103.14 E
Duojundian 105 39.22 N 117.31 E
Duolun (Dolonnur) 98 42.15 N 116.18 E
Duolundabohuer 120 33.25 N 93.54 E
Duomo ᵾ[1] 266b 45.27 N 9.11 E
Duomula 120 34.07 N 82.30 E
Duoyuezhen 107 30.11 N 103.42 E
Duozhu 100 22.59 N 114.43 E
Duozhuang 98 35.35 N 118.12 E
Du Page ≃[6] 216 41.52 N 88.06 W
Du Page ≃ 216 41.25 N 88.14 W
Du Page, East Branch ≃ 278 41.42 N 88.09 W
Dupang Ling ⩚ 102 25.32 N 111.11 E
Duparquet, Lac ⊜ 190 48.28 N 79.16 W
Dupax 116 16.17 N 121.05 E
Duping 102 27.11 N 108.20 E
Dupl'atka 80 51.07 N 42.20 E
Dupli 82 54.21 N 36.54 E
Dupo 219 38.31 N 90.13 W
Dupont, In., U.S. 218 38.53 N 85.31 W
Dupont, Oh., U.S. 216 41.03 N 84.18 W
Dupont, Pa., U.S. 210 41.19 N 75.44 W
Du Pont, Wa., U.S. 224 47.05 N 122.37 W
Dupont Research Center ᵾ[3] 285 39.46 N 75.34 W
Düppel, Berliner Forst ◆[3] 264a 52.25 N 13.08 E
Dupree 198 45.02 N 101.36 W
Duque Bacelar 250 4.09 S 42.57 W
Duque de Caxias 256 22.47 S 43.18 W
Duque de Caxias □[7] 287a 22.45 S 43.16 W
Duque de York, Isla I 254 50.40 S 75.20 W
Duquesne 214 40.22 N 79.51 W
Duquesne University ᵾ[2] 279b 40.26 N 79.59 W
DuQuoin 194 37.59 N 89.15 W
Dūrā 132 31.30 N 35.02 E
Durack ≃ 164 15.33 S 127.52 E
Durack Ranges ⩚ 160 17.00 S 128.00 E
Durağan 130 41.25 N 35.04 E
Durak 130 39.42 N 28.17 E
Durak Dağı ∧ 84 39.47 N 43.42 E
Dural 170 33.41 S 151.02 E
Duran 200 34.28 N 105.23 W
Durance ≃ 62 43.55 N 4.44 E
Durand, Il., U.S. 190 42.26 N 89.19 W
Durand, Mi., U.S. 216 42.54 N 83.59 W
Durand, Wi., U.S. 190 44.37 N 91.57 W
Durand Reef ✦[2] 175f 22.03 S 168.39 E
Duran Durat I 271c 1.15 N 103.51 E
Durango, Esp. 34 43.10 N 2.37 W
Durango, Méx. 234 24.02 N 104.40 W
Durango, Co., U.S. 200 37.16 N 107.52 W
Durango □[3] 232 24.50 N 104.50 W
Duranillin 168a 33.31 S 116.48 E
Durant, Ia., U.S. 190 41.35 N 90.54 W
Durant, Ms., U.S. 194 33.04 N 89.51 W
Durant, Ok., U.S. 196 33.59 N 96.22 W
Duras 32 44.41 N 0.11 E
Duratón ≃ 34 41.37 N 4.07 W
Duraur V 144 10.33 N 49.07 E
Durazno 252 33.22 S 56.31 W
Durazzo → Durrës 38 41.19 N 19.26 E
Durbādānga 126 22.57 N 89.15 E
Durban 158 29.55 S 30.56 E
Durban Roodepoort Deep Gold Mines ✦[7] 273d 26.10 S 27.51 E
Durbanville 158 33.50 S 18.39 E
Durbe 76 56.35 N 21.21 E
D'urbel'džin 85 41.16 N 74.57 E
Durbet-Daba, pereval)(86 49.37 N 89.25 E
Durbin 188 38.32 N 79.49 W
Durbuy 56 50.21 N 5.28 E
Durchholz 263 51.23 N 7.17 E
Durdent ≃ 50 49.51 N 0.36 E
Đurđevac 36 46.03 N 17.04 E
Durdur V 144 10.34 N 43.58 E
Dureji 120 25.53 N 67.18 E
Düren 56 50.48 N 6.28 E
Durg 120 21.11 N 81.17 E
Durgāpur 126 23.29 N 87.20 E
Durham, On., Can. 212 44.10 N 80.49 W
Durham, Eng., U.K. 44 54.47 N 1.34 W
Durham, Ca., U.S. 204 39.38 N 121.47 W
Durham, Ct., U.S. 207 41.28 N 72.40 W
Durham, Mo., U.S. 219 39.58 N 91.40 W
Durham, N.H., U.S. 188 43.08 N 70.55 W
Durham, N.C., U.S. 192 35.59 N 78.53 W
Durham, Or., U.S. 224 45.25 N 122.46 W
Durham □[6], On., Can. 212 43.56 N 78.53 W
Durham □[6], Eng., U.K. 44 54.45 N 1.45 W
Durham Cathedral ᵾ[1] 44 54.46 N 1.36 W
Durham Downs 166 27.05 S 141.54 E
Durham Heights ∧ 176 71.08 N 122.56 W
Durham Pond ⊜ 276 41.00 N 74.27 W
Durhamville 210 43.07 N 75.40 W
Durian ≃ 115a 6.01 S 106.24 E
Durian, Selat ⊻ 114 0.42 N 103.42 E
Duriansebatang 112 0.47 S 109.56 E
Durian Tipus 114 3.07 N 102.13 E
D'urinskije razlivy ⊞ 80 50.25 N 50.20 E
Durlabhpur 272b 22.47 N 88.29 E
Durlach ◆[8] 56 49.00 N 8.28 E
Durlešty 78 47.02 N 28.45 E
Durmersheim 56 48.56 N 8.16 E
Durmitor ∧ 38 43.08 N 19.01 E
Durness 46 58.33 N 4.45 W
Durness, Kyle of c 46 58.34 N 4.49 W
Durneva, ostrova II 80 45.25 N 52.50 E
Durnikino 80 51.39 N 42.49 E
Dürnkrut 61 48.28 N 16.51 E
Dürnstein ⊥ 61 48.24 N 15.32 E
Duro ⩚ 144 5.31 N 37.12 E
Durón 34 40.38 N 2.43 W
Duross Heights 285 39.40 N 75.37 W
Dürre Liesing ≃ 264b 48.08 N 16.16 E
Durrell 186 49.40 N 54.44 W
Dürrenboden 58 46.57 N 8.50 E
Durrës 38 41.19 N 19.26 E
Durrie 166 25.38 S 140.16 E
Durrington 42 51.13 N 1.45 W
Dürröhrsdorf 54 51.01 N 14.00 E
Durrow 48 52.50 N 7.22 W
Durrus 48 51.36 N 9.31 W
Dursey Head ≻ 48 51.35 N 10.14 W
Dursey Island I 48 51.36 N 10.12 W
Dursley 42 51.42 N 2.21 W
Dursunbey 130 39.35 N 28.38 E
D'urt'uli 86 55.29 N 54.52 E
Duru 154 4.14 N 28.45 E
Duru Gölü ⊜ 130 41.20 N 28.35 E
Durulova 130 38.17 N 38.01 E
Durunkah 142 27.08 N 31.10 E
Durūz, Jabal ad- ⩚ 132 32.40 N 36.44 E
D'Urville, Tanjung ≻ 164 1.28 S 137.54 E
D'Urville Island I 172 40.50 S 173.52 E
Duryea 210 41.20 N 75.44 W
Dury Voe c 46a 60.20 N 1.08 W
Dušak 128 37.13 N 60.02 E
Dušanbe 85 38.35 N 68.48 E
Dušekan 88 60.39 N 109.03 E
Dušeti 84 42.06 N 44.42 E
Dusetos 76 55.45 N 25.51 E
Dushan, Zhg. 100 31.36 N 116.14 E
Dushan, Zhg. 102 25.53 N 107.30 E
Du Shan ∧ 98 40.30 N 118.45 E
Dushanbe → Dušanbe 85 38.35 N 68.48 E
Dushan Hu ⊜ 98 35.06 N 116.52 E
Dushantou 106 30.46 N 119.47 E
Dushanzi 86 44.20 N 84.51 E
Dusheng 98 38.23 N 116.33 E
Dushichang 107 29.10 N 106.31 E
Dushikou 98 41.17 N 115.38 E
Dushore 210 41.31 N 76.24 W
Düshorn 52 52.49 N 9.37 E
Dushu 100 33.21 N 113.09 E
Dushu Hu ⊜ 106 31.17 N 120.42 E
Dusios ežeras ⊜ 76 54.18 N 23.42 E
Dusky Sound ⊻ 172 45.47 S 166.28 E
Dušocha, gora ∧ 85 39.10 N 70.01 E
Duson 194 30.14 N 92.11 W
Dušonovo 82 56.04 N 38.18 E
Düssel 263 51.16 N 7.03 E
Düssel ≃ 263 51.13 N 6.45 E
Düsseldorf, Dtsch. 56 51.12 N 6.47 E
Düsseldorf, Dtsch. 263 51.12 N 6.47 E
Düsseldorf □[5] 52 51.15 N 7.00 E
Düsseldorf, Flughafen ⊠ 56 51.17 N 6.47 E
Düsseldorf, Universität ᵾ[2] 263 51.12 N 6.48 E
Dusslingen 58 48.27 N 9.03 E
Dussnang 58 47.26 N 8.58 E
Dustin 196 35.16 N 96.01 W
Dutch Creek ≃, B.C., Can. 182 50.20 N 115.52 W
Dutch Creek ≃, Ar., U.S. 194 35.03 N 93.24 W
Dutchess □[6] 210 41.42 N 73.56 W
Dutch Harbor 180 53.53 N 166.32 W
Dutch John 200 40.55 N 109.23 W
Dutchman Creek ≃ 226 37.11 N 120.28 W
Dutianjie 102 24.38 N 101.31 E
Dutluca 130 39.09 N 38.37 E
Dutlwe 156 23.55 S 23.47 E
Dutoitspiek ∧ 158 33.46 S 19.12 E
Dutou, Zhg. 100 22.54 N 115.12 E
Dutou, Zhg. 106 31.19 N 120.54 E
Dutovlje 64 45.46 N 13.50 E
Dutovo 24 63.47 N 56.35 E
Dutsen Wai 150 10.50 N 8.12 E
Dutton, Austl. 168b 34.22 S 139.08 E
Dutton, On., Can. 214 42.39 N 81.30 W
Dutton, Eng., U.K. 262 53.19 N 2.38 W
Dutton, Mi., U.S. 216 42.50 N 85.35 W
Dutton, Mt., U.S. 202 47.50 N 111.42 W
Dutton ≃ 166 20.45 S 143.12 E
Dutton, Mount ∧, Ak., U.S. 180 55.10 N 162.15 W
Dutton, Mount ∧, Ut., U.S. 200 38.01 N 112.13 W
Dutun 105 39.46 N 117.02 E
Dutzow 219 38.37 N 90.59 W
Duut 86 47.30 N 91.40 E
Duval, Lac ⊜ 190 46.19 N 76.55 W
Duvall 224 47.44 N 121.59 W
Duvan 86 55.42 N 57.54 E
Duvanka ≃ 83 49.35 N 38.10 E
Duved 26 63.24 N 12.52 E
Duvernay ◆[8] 275a 45.35 N 73.40 W
Duvno 36 43.43 N 17.14 E
Duwamish 224 47.32 N 122.19 W
Duwaydār, Bi'r ad- ᵶ[4] 142 30.55 N 32.31 E
Duxbury 207 42.02 N 70.40 W
Duxbury Bay c 207 42.02 N 70.39 W
Duxbury Beach ⊥[2] 283 42.03 N 70.38 W
Duxun 100 23.55 N 117.37 E
Duyagan Point ≻ 116 12.36 N 121.33 E
Duyun 102 26.12 N 107.31 E
Düzce 130 40.50 N 31.10 E
Duze 100 29.07 N 118.56 E
Dve Mogili 38 43.36 N 25.52 E
Dvina Occidental → Zapadnaja Dvina ≃ 76 57.04 N 24.03 E
Dvina Septentrional → Severnaja Dvina ≃ 24 64.32 N 40.30 E
Dvinje, ozero ⊜ 76 56.08 N 31.12 E
Dvinskaja guba c 24 65.00 N 39.45 E
Dvinsk → Daugavpils 76 55.53 N 26.32 E
Dvojnovskij 80 51.03 N 42.27 E
Dvorcy 82 54.37 N 36.00 E
Dvorec 88 58.23 N 99.56 E
Dvoriši 76 58.12 N 35.13 E
Dvornikovo 82 55.30 N 38.38 E
Dvuch Cirkov, gora ∧ 74 67.35 N 168.07 E
Dvugorbaja, gora ∧ 180 68.30 N 179.20 E
Dvulučnoje 78 50.02 N 38.02 E
Dvurečnaja 78 49.52 N 37.40 E
Dvůr Králové [nad Labem] 30 50.26 N 15.48 E
Dwangwa ≃ 154 12.33 S 34.12 E
Dwarbasini 272b 22.59 N 88.14 E
Dwārka 120 22.14 N 68.58 E
Dwārka ≃ 126 23.44 N 88.11 E
Dwārkeswar ≃ 126 23.06 N 87.21 E
Dwarli 272c 19.12 N 73.08 E
Dwars Kill ≃ 276 40.58 N 73.58 W
Dwellingup 168a 32.43 S 116.02 E
D.W. Field Park ◆ 283 42.06 N 71.03 W
Dwight 216 41.05 N 88.25 W
Dwight D. Eisenhower Lock ≡ 206 45.00 N 74.45 W
Dwina-Bucht → Dvinskaja guba c 24 65.00 N 39.45 E
Dwingeloo 52 52.50 N 6.21 E
Dworshak Reservoir ⊜[1] 202 46.40 N 116.00 W
Dwyfor ≃ 44 52.55 N 4.17 W
Dwyka 158 33.02 S 21.30 E
Dwyka ≃ 158 33.18 S 21.39 E
Dyaul Island I 164 2.56 S 150.55 E
Dybbøl 41 54.55 N 9.45 E
Dyberry Creek ≃ 210 41.35 N 75.15 W
Dyce 46 57.12 N 2.11 W
Dyche Stadium ◆ 278 42.04 N 87.41 W
Dychtau, gora ∧ 84 43.03 N 43.08 E
Dyck, Schloss ⊥ 263 51.09 N 6.34 E
Dyer, In., U.S. 216 41.29 N 87.31 W
Dyer, Tn., U.S. 194 36.04 N 88.59 W
Dyer, Cape ≻ 176 66.37 N 61.18 W
Dyer Bay c 212 45.10 N 81.18 W
Dyer Island I 158 34.41 S 19.25 E
Dyero 150 12.52 N 6.28 W
Dyersburg 194 36.02 N 89.23 W
Dyersville 190 42.29 N 91.07 W
Dyess Air Force Base ■ 196 32.25 N 99.51 W
Dyfed □[6] 42 52.00 N 4.30 W
Dyfi ≃ 42 52.32 N 4.03 W
Dyje (Thaya) ≃ 30 48.37 N 16.56 E
Dyke 46 57.36 N 3.41 W
Dyke Ackland Bay c 164 9.00 S 148.45 E
Dyken Pond ⊜ 210 42.43 N 73.26 W
Dykes Pond ⊜ 283 42.36 N 70.44 W
Dyle (Dijle) ≃ 56 51.04 N 4.25 E
Dyleň ∧ 60 49.58 N 12.30 E
Dylym 84 43.04 N 46.38 E
Dymchurch 42 51.02 N 1.00 E
Dyment 184 49.37 N 92.19 W
Dymer 78 50.47 N 30.18 E
Dymock 42 51.59 N 2.26 W
Dynamo Stadium ◆ 265b 55.48 N 37.34 E
Dynów 30 49.49 N 22.14 E
Dyreborg 41 55.04 N 10.13 E
Dyrnesvågen 26 63.26 N 7.51 E
Dyrotz 264a 52.33 N 12.58 E
Dysart, Austl. 166 22.27 S 148.20 E
Dysart, Sk., Can. 184 50.56 N 104.02 W
Dysart, Scot., U.K. 46 56.08 N 3.08 W
Dysart, Ia., U.S. 190 42.10 N 92.18 W
Dysart, Pa., U.S. 214 40.36 N 78.31 W
Dýšina 60 49.46 N 13.29 E
Dysnų ežeras ⊜ 76 55.29 N 26.20 E
Dysselsdorp 158 33.34 S 22.28 E
Dysynni ≃ 42 52.36 N 4.05 W
Dzaamar 88 48.10 N 104.50 E
Dzaamaryn uul ∧ 88 48.10 N 104.30 E
Džabžur 84 40.54 N 43.58 E
Dzachuj 102 44.59 N 96.37 E
Džagdy, chrebet ⩚ 89 53.40 N 131.00 E
Džalagaš 85 45.05 N 64.40 E
Džalal-Abad 86 40.56 N 73.00 E
Džalal-Abad □[4] 85 41.30 N 72.30 E
Džalinda 89 53.29 N 123.54 E
Džamantau, gory ⩚ 85 40.55 N 74.40 E
Džamašuj 85 40.52 N 71.28 E
Džambejty 80 50.16 N 52.35 E
Džambul, Kaz. 80 47.34 N 50.12 E
Džambul, Kaz. 85 42.54 N 71.22 E
Džambul, Kaz. 86 47.12 N 71.42 E
Džambul □[4] 85 43.30 N 72.30 E
Džambul, gora ∧ 86 44.46 N 73.08 E
Džanga 128 40.00 N 53.03 E
Džangi-Džol 85 41.36 N 72.08 E
Džankoj 78 45.43 N 34.24 E
Džansugurov 86 45.24 N 79.29 E
Džanybek 80 49.25 N 46.51 E
Dzaoudzi 157a 12.47 S 45.17 E
Džardžan 74 68.43 N 124.02 E
Džargalant, Mong. 88 48.40 N 100.43 E
Džargalant, Mong. 88 46.57 N 115.15 E
Džargalant, Mong. 88 48.33 N 99.20 E
Džargalant → Chovd 86 48.01 N 91.39 E
Džargaltchaan 88 47.28 N 109.30 E
Džarylgačskij, ostrov I 78 46.02 N 32.55 E
Džarylgačskij zaliv c 78 46.05 N 32.50 E
Dzaudzhikau → Vladikavkaz 84 43.03 N 44.40 E
Džaur 89 50.02 N 138.30 E
Džava 84 42.24 N 43.54 E
Dzavchan 88 48.48 N 93.07 E
Dzavchan □[4] 88 48.00 N 96.00 E
Dzavchan ≃ 88 48.54 N 93.23 E
Dzavchan Mandal 88 48.19 N 95.07 E
Džavchlant → Uliastaj 88 47.45 N 96.49 E
Džazator 86 49.43 N 87.23 E
Džbán ∧ 54 50.12 N 13.45 E
Džebel 128 39.38 N 54.13 E
Džebrail 84 39.23 N 47.02 E
Dzegamčaj ≃ 84 41.00 N 45.53 E
Dzelter ≃ 88 50.30 N 105.06 E
Dzemul 232 21.12 N 89.18 W
Dzeng 152 3.45 N 12.00 E
Dženretlen, mys ≻ 180 67.07 N 173.45 W
Džergetal 85 41.30 N 75.47 E
Džermuk 84 39.51 N 45.41 E
Dzerzhinsk → Dzeržinsk 80 56.15 N 43.24 E
Dzeržinsk, Bela. 76 53.41 N 27.08 E
Dzeržinsk, Ross. 80 56.15 N 43.24 E
Dzeržinsk, Ukr. 78 50.09 N 27.56 E
Dzeržinsk, Ukr. 83 48.26 N 37.50 E
Dzeržinskaja, gora ∧[2] 76 53.51 N 27.03 E
Dzeržinskij, Ross. 82 55.38 N 37.50 E
Dzeržinskij, Ukr. 78 48.02 N 39.26 E
Dzeržinskij ◆[8] 83 48.02 N 37.48 E
Dzeržinskoje, Kaz. 86 45.50 N 81.07 E
Dzeržinskoje, Ross. 86 56.49 N 95.18 E
Džetim, chrebet ⩚ 85 41.35 N 77.05 E
Džetygara 86 52.11 N 61.12 E
Džetyoguz 85 42.27 N 78.14 E
Džetyoguzskij zapovednik ◆ 85 42.15 N 78.20 E
Džetysaj 85 40.47 N 68.16 E
Dzezdy 86 48.04 N 67.05 E
Džezkazgan, Kaz. 86 47.53 N 67.27 E
Džezkazgan, Kaz. 86 47.47 N 67.46 E
Džezkazgan □[8] 86 47.30 N 70.00 E
Dzhalilabad 84 39.14 N 48.31 E
Dzhambul → Džambul 85 42.54 N 71.22 E
Działdowo 30 53.15 N 20.10 E
Działoszyce 30 50.22 N 20.21 E
Dzibalchén 232 19.31 N 89.45 W
Dzibilchaltun ⊥ 232 21.05 N 89.36 W
Džida ≃ 88 50.37 N 106.14 E
Džidinskij chrebet ⩚ 88 50.10 N 102.00 E
Dzierzgoń 30 53.56 N 19.21 E
Dzierżoniów (Reichenbach) 30 50.44 N 16.39 E
Dzilam González 232 21.17 N 88.56 W
Džilav 85 39.19 N 67.45 E
Džilga 85 41.43 N 69.01 E
Džinst 102 45.24 N 100.35 E
Dzioua 148 33.14 N 5.14 E
Džirgatal' 85 39.13 N 71.12 E
Dzitás 232 20.51 N 88.31 W
Dzitbalché 232 20.19 N 90.03 W
Dziwna ≃[1] 54 54.01 N 14.44 E
Dziwnów 30 54.03 N 14.45 E
Džizak 85 40.06 N 67.50 E
Džizak □[4] 85 40.30 N 67.30 E
Dzodze 150 6.14 N 1.00 E
Džubga 78 44.20 N 38.43 E
Džugdžur, chrebet ⩚ 74 58.00 N 136.00 E
Džūkste 76 56.47 N 23.15 E
Džul'fa 84 38.58 N 45.38 E
Džumabazar 85 39.31 N 67.13 E
Džumgoltau, chrebet ⩚ 85 42.18 N 74.32 E
Dzungarian Basin → Junggar Pendi ≡[1] 86 45.00 N 88.00 E
Dzungarian Gate (Džungarskije vorota))(86 45.25 N 82.25 E
Džungarskij Alatau, chrebet ⩚ 86 45.00 N 81.00 E
Džungarskije vorota → Dzungarian Gate)(86 45.25 N 82.25 E
Džurak-Sal ≃ 80 47.18 N 43.36 E
Dzürch 88 48.55 N 100.10 E
Džurin 78 48.41 N 28.18 E
Džurun 86 49.15 N 57.37 E
Džusaly 86 45.28 N 64.05 E
Dzüün Changaj 88 49.17 N 95.14 E
Dzüün Charaa 88 48.52 N 106.28 E
Dzüün Gov' 88 49.55 N 93.47 E
Dzuunmod 88 47.45 N 106.55 E
Džvari 84 42.43 N 42.04 E
Dzygovka 78 48.22 N 28.19 E

E

Eads 198 38.28 N 102.46 W
Eagar 200 34.06 N 109.17 W
Eagle, Ak., U.S. 180 64.46 N 141.16 W
Eagle, Co., U.S. 200 39.39 N 106.49 W
Eagle, N.Y., U.S. 210 42.33 N 78.18 W
Eagle, Wi., U.S. 216 42.52 N 88.28 W
Eagle ≃, Nf., Can. 176 53.35 N 57.25 W
Eagle ≃, Yk., Can. 180 67.20 N 137.10 W
Eagle ≃, Co., U.S. 200 39.39 N 107.04 W
Eagle, Mount ∧[2] 241n 17.46 N 64.49 W
Eagle Bay 182 50.56 N 119.12 W
Eagle Bend 198 46.09 N 95.02 W
Eagle Bridge 210 42.57 N 73.24 W
Eagle Butte 198 45.00 N 101.14 W
Eagle Chief Creek ≃ 196 36.22 N 98.27 W
Eagle Creek 224 45.21 N 122.21 W
Eagle Creek ≃, Sk., Can. 184 52.22 N 107.24 W
Eagle Creek ≃, Az., U.S. 200 32.58 N 109.25 W
Eagle Creek ≃, In., U.S. 218 39.43 N 86.12 W
Eagle Creek ≃, Ky., U.S. 218 38.36 N 85.04 W
Eagle Creek ≃, Mt., U.S. 202 48.12 N 111.11 W
Eagle Creek ≃, N.M., U.S. 196 32.47 N 104.20 W
Eagle Creek ≃, Oh., U.S. 214 41.18 N 80.53 W
Eagle Creek ≃, Oh., U.S. 218 38.43 N 83.51 W
Eagle Creek ≃, Or., U.S. 202 44.45 N 117.10 W
Eagle Creek ≃, Or., U.S. 224 45.21 N 122.23 W
Eagle Creek, East Fork ≃ 218 38.47 N 83.43 W
Eagle Creek, West Fork ≃ 218 38.47 N 83.43 W
Eagle Creek Reservoir ⊜[1] 218 39.50 N 86.18 W
Eagledale 224 47.37 N 122.32 W
Eagle Grove 190 42.39 N 93.54 W
Eagle Harbor 210 43.15 N 78.15 W
Eaglehawk 169 36.43 S 144.15 E
Eagle Hill ≃ 283 42.42 N 70.49 W
Eagle Key I 220 25.09 N 80.36 W
Eagle Lake, Fl., U.S. 220 27.59 N 81.45 W
Eagle Lake, Me., U.S. 186 47.02 N 68.35 W
Eagle Lake, Mi., U.S. 216 41.48 N 86.02 W
Eagle Lake, Tx., U.S. 222 29.35 N 96.20 W
Eagle Lake ⊜, B.C., Can. 182 51.55 N 124.25 W
Eagle Lake ⊜, On., Can. 184 49.42 N 93.13 W
Eagle Lake ⊜, On., Can. 184 50.39 N 94.54 W
Eagle Lake ⊜, On., Can. 212 44.41 N 76.43 W
Eagle Lake ⊜, On., Can. 212 45.08 N 78.29 W
Eagle Lake ⊜, Ca., U.S. 204 40.39 N 120.44 W
Eagle Lake ⊜, Me., U.S. 186 46.20 N 69.20 W
Eagle Lake ⊜, Mi., U.S. 216 41.48 N 86.02 W
Eagle Lake ⊜, Tx., U.S. 222 29.34 N 96.21 W
Eagle Lake ⊜, Wi., U.S. 216 42.42 N 88.07 W
Eagle Mountain, Ca., U.S. 204 33.49 N 115.27 W
Eagle Mountain, Tx., U.S. 222 32.52 N 97.30 W
Eagle Mountain ∧ 202 46.20 N 115.07 W
Eagle Mountain ∧[2] 190 47.54 N 90.33 W
Eagle Mountain Lake ⊜[1] 222 32.55 N 97.30 W
Eagle Nest Butte ∧ 198 43.27 N 101.39 W
Eagle Nest Lake ⊜ 222 29.13 N 95.37 W
Eagle Pass 196 28.42 N 100.29 W
Eagle Peak ∧, Ca., U.S. 204 41.17 N 120.12 W
Eagle Peak ∧, Ca., U.S. 228 35.15 N 118.28 W
Eagle Peak ∧, Ca., U.S. 282 37.54 N 121.54 W
Eagle River, Mi., U.S. 190 47.24 N 88.18 W
Eagle River, Wi., U.S. 190 45.55 N 89.14 W
Eagle Rock 192 37.38 N 79.48 W
Eagle Rock ◆[8] 280 34.09 N 118.12 W
Eagle Rock Reservation ◆ 276 40.49 N 74.14 W
Eaglesfield 44 55.03 N 3.12 W
Eaglesham, Ab., Can. 182 55.47 N 117.53 W
Eaglesham, Scot., U.K. 46 55.44 N 4.18 W
Eagles Mere 210 41.25 N 76.35 W
Eagleton Village 192 35.48 N 83.56 W
Eagletown 194 34.02 N 94.34 W
Eagle Village 180 64.47 N 141.07 W
Eagleville, Ct., U.S. 207 41.47 N 72.16 W
Eagleville, Pa., U.S. 285 40.10 N 75.24 W
Eagleville, Wi., U.S. 216 42.52 N 88.26 W
Ealing ◆[8] 42 51.31 N 0.20 W
Eamont ≃ 44 54.40 N 2.39 W
Earaheedy 162 25.34 S 121.39 E
Earby 44 53.56 N 2.08 W
Earcroft 262 53.43 N 2.29 W
Eardisley 42 52.08 N 2.59 W
Eardley Lake ⊜ 184 52.32 N 96.05 W
Ear Falls 184 50.38 N 93.13 W
Earle 194 35.16 N 90.28 W
Earlestown 262 53.27 N 2.39 W
Earl Grey 184 50.56 N 104.45 W
Earlham 194 41.29 N 94.07 W
Earlimart 226 35.53 N 119.16 W
Earlington 194 37.16 N 87.30 W
Earlish 46 57.34 N 6.23 W
Earl Park 216 40.40 N 87.24 W
Earl Rowe Provincial Park ◆ 212 44.10 N 79.54 W
Earls Barton 42 52.15 N 0.45 W
Earls Colne 42 51.56 N 0.42 E
Earlsferry 46 56.11 N 2.50 W
Earl Shilton 42 52.35 N 1.20 W
Earl Soham 42 52.14 N 1.16 E
Earlston 46 55.39 N 2.40 W
Earlton 210 42.21 N 73.54 W
Earlville, Il., U.S. 216 41.35 N 88.55 W
Earlville, N.Y., U.S. 210 42.44 N 75.33 W
Earlville, Pa., U.S. 208 40.19 N 75.44 W
Earlwood 274a 33.56 S 151.08 E
Early, Ia., U.S. 198 42.27 N 95.09 W
Early, Tx., U.S. 196 31.45 N 98.54 W
Early Winters Creek ≃ 224 48.35 N 120.35 W
Earn ≃ 46 56.21 N 3.19 W
Earn, Loch ⊜ 46 56.23 N 4.14 W
Earnslaw, Mount ∧ 172 44.37 S 168.24 E
Earth 196 34.14 N 102.24 W
Eas 175f 16.22 S 168.12 E
Easington, Eng., U.K. 44 53.40 N 0.07 E
Easington, Eng., U.K. 44 54.47 N 1.19 W
Easingwold 44 54.07 N 1.11 W
Easky 48 54.18 N 8.58 W
Easley 192 34.49 N 82.36 W
East ≃, On., Can. 190 45.20 N 79.17 W
East ≃, Co., U.S. 200 38.40 N 106.51 W
East ≃, N.Y., U.S. 276 40.48 N 73.48 W
East, University of the ᵾ[2] 269f 14.36 N 120.59 E
East Acton 283 42.28 N 71.24 W
East Allen ≃ 216 41.05 N 84.52 W
East Alliance 214 40.55 N 81.04 W
East Alligator ≃ 164 12.08 S 132.42 E
East Alton 219 38.52 N 90.06 W
East Amherst 210 43.01 N 78.42 W
East-Angus 206 45.29 N 71.40 W
East Arlington 210 43.03 N 73.08 W
East Atlantic Beach 276 40.35 N 73.43 W
East Aurora 210 42.46 N 78.36 W
East Avon 210 42.55 N 77.42 W
East Baines ≃ 164 15.38 S 129.58 E
East Bangor 210 40.52 N 75.11 W
East Barming 260 51.16 N 0.28 E
East Barnet ◆[8] 260 51.38 N 0.09 W
East Basin c 279a 41.32 N 81.40 W
East Bay c, Fl., U.S. 194 30.05 N 85.32 W
East Bay c, N.Y., U.S. 210 40.38 N 73.32 W
East Bay c, Tx., U.S. 222 29.30 N 94.35 W
East Bedfont ◆[8] 260 51.27 N 0.26 W
East Bend 192 36.12 N 80.30 W
East Berbice-Corentyne □[4] 246 4.00 N 58.15 W
East Berkshire 206 44.56 N 72.42 W
East Berlin, Ct., U.S. 207 41.37 N 72.42 W
East Berlin, N.J., U.S. 285 39.48 N 74.55 W
East Berlin, Pa., U.S. 208 39.56 N 76.58 W
East Bernard 222 29.32 N 96.04 W
East Bernstadt 192 37.11 N 84.07 W
East Berwick 210 41.03 N 76.13 W
East Bethany 210 42.56 N 78.06 W
East Bhāgīrath Plain ⊻ 126 23.30 N 88.30 E
East Bijou Creek ≃ 198 39.51 N 104.08 W
East Billerica 283 42.34 N 71.14 W
East Blackstone 207 42.02 N 71.31 W
East Bloomfield 210 42.54 N 77.26 W
East Boston ◆[8] 283 42.23 N 71.02 W
Eastbourne, N.Z. 172 41.18 S 174.54 E
Eastbourne, Eng., U.K. 42 50.46 N 0.17 E
East Brady 214 40.59 N 79.36 W
East Braintree 184 49.37 N 95.38 W
East Branch 210 41.59 N 75.08 W
East Branch Lake ⊜[1] 214 41.35 N 78.35 W
East Brewster 207 41.46 N 70.03 W
East Brewton 194 31.05 N 87.03 W
East Bridgewater 207 42.02 N 70.58 W
East Brimfield Lake ⊜[1] 207 42.06 N 72.10 W
East Brookfield 207 42.13 N 72.02 W
East Brooklyn 207 41.47 N 71.53 W
East Brother I 271d 22.20 N 113.58 E
East Brunswick 208 40.25 N 74.23 W
East Bucas Island I 116 9.43 N 126.02 E
East Burwood 274b 37.51 S 145.09 E
Eastbury 260 51.37 N 0.25 W
East Butler 214 40.53 N 79.51 W
East Cache Creek ≃ 196 34.08 N 98.16 W
East Caicos I 238 21.41 N 71.30 W
East Calder 46 55.54 N 3.27 W
East Canaan 207 42.00 N 73.17 W
East Canada Creek ≃ 210 43.00 N 74.45 W
East Canton 214 40.47 N 81.17 W
East Cape ≻, N.Z. 172 37.41 S 178.33 E
East Cape ≻, Ak., U.S. 181a 51.21 N 179.29 E
East Cape ≻, Fl., U.S. 220 25.07 N 81.05 W
East Carancahua Creek ≃ 222 28.51 N 96.19 W
East Carbon 200 39.32 N 110.24 W
East Carlisle 214 41.19 N 82.05 W
East Caroline Basin ✦[1] 14 4.00 N 146.45 E
East Castor ≃ 212 45.16 N 75.17 W
East Catfish Creek ≃ 214 42.47 N 81.04 W
East Channel ≃[1] 180 69.20 N 134.00 W
East Chatham 210 42.25 N 73.32 W
East Chelmsford 207 42.36 N 71.18 W
Eastchester 207 40.57 N 73.49 W
Eastchester Bay c 276 40.51 N 73.48 W
East Chicago 216 41.38 N 87.27 W
East Chicago Heights 278 41.30 N 87.35 W
East China Sea ᵶ[2] 90 30.00 N 126.00 E
Eastchurch 42 51.25 N 0.52 E
East Clandon 260 51.15 N 0.29 W
East Claridon 214 41.32 N 81.07 W
East Cleddau ≃ 42 51.46 N 4.52 W
East Cleveland 214 41.32 N 81.34 W
East Coast Bays 172 36.45 S 174.46 E
East Concord 210 42.33 N 78.38 W
Eastcote ◆[8] 260 51.35 N 0.24 W
East Cote Blanche Bay c 194 29.35 N 91.40 W
East Coulee 182 51.20 N 112.29 W
East Creek ≃ 276 40.27 N 74.09 W
East Cross Creek ≃ 212 44.17 N 78.44 W
East Dean 42 50.45 N 0.12 E
East Delaware Aqueduct ≡[1] 210 41.52 N 74.31 W
East Dennis 207 41.44 N 70.09 W
East Dereham 42 52.41 N 0.56 E
East Detroit 214 42.28 N 82.57 W
East Dismal Swamp ≡ 192 35.45 N 76.35 W
East Ditch ≡ 276 40.56 N 74.19 W
East Douglas 207 42.04 N 71.42 W
East Dublin 192 32.32 N 82.52 W
East Dubuque 190 42.29 N 90.38 W
East Dundee 216 42.06 N 88.16 W
East Durham 210 42.22 N 74.06 W
East Ely 204 39.15 N 114.53 W
Eastend, Sk., Can. 184 49.31 N 108.48 W
East End, Vir. Is., U.S. 240m 18.21 N 64.40 W
East End Point ≻ 240b 25.03 N 77.16 W
East Enterprise 218 38.52 N 84.59 W
Easter Island → Pascua, Isla de I 174z 27.07 S 109.22 W
Easterly 222 31.06 N 96.23 W
Eastern □[4], Ghana 150 6.30 N 0.30 W
Eastern □[4], Kenya 154 0.05 N 38.00 E
Eastern □[4], S.L. 150 8.15 N 11.00 W
Eastern □[4], Zam. 154 13.00 S 32.15 E
Eastern □[5] 154 1.25 N 33.50 E
Eastern Bay c 208 38.51 N 76.19 W
Eastern Channel → Tsushima-kaikyō ⊻ 92 34.00 N 129.00 E
Eastern Cherokee Indian Reservation ✦[4] 192 35.25 N 83.24 W
Eastern Cove c 168b 35.46 S 137.50 E
Eastern Creek ≃, Austl. 166 20.10 S 141.08 E
Eastern Creek ≃, Austl. 274a 33.39 S 150.51 E
Eastern Division □[5] 175g 19.00 S 180.00 E
Eastern Fields ✦[2] 164 10.20 S 145.45 E
Eastern Ghāts ⩚ 122 14.00 N 78.50 E
Eastern Highlands □[5] 164 6.30 S 145.15 E
Eastern Island I 174g 28.12 N 177.20 W
Eastern Isles II 42a 49.57 N 6.15 W
Eastern Michigan University ᵾ[2] 281 42.15 N 83.37 W
Eastern Neck Island I 208 39.02 N 76.13 W
Eastern Point ≻ 283 42.35 N 70.40 W
Eastern Samar □[4] 116 12.00 N 125.00 E
Eastern Sayans → Vostočnyj Sajan ⩚ 88 53.00 N 97.00 E
Eastern Shore ✦[1] 208 38.40 N 75.50 W
Eastern Yamuna Canal ≡ 272a 28.40 N 77.15 E
East Falkland I 254 51.55 S 59.00 W
East Falls ◆[8] 285 40.01 N 75.11 W
East Falmouth 207 41.34 N 70.33 W
East Farleigh 260 51.15 N 0.29 E
East Farmingdale 276 40.44 N 73.26 W
East Faxon 210 41.15 N 76.58 W
East Fayetteville 192 35.05 N 78.51 W
Eastfield 44 54.14 N 0.24 W
East Flat Rock 192 35.16 N 82.25 W
Eastford 207 41.54 N 72.04 W
East Foxboro 283 42.03 N 71.12 W
East Freedom 214 40.21 N 78.26 W
East Freetown 207 41.46 N 70.57 W
East Frisian Islands → Ostfriesische Inseln II 52 53.44 N 7.25 E
East Gaffney 192 35.04 N 81.37 W
East Gallatin ≃ 202 45.53 N 111.20 W
Eastgate 224 47.34 N 122.09 W
East Ghor Canal → Ghawr ash-Sharqīyah, Qanāt al- ≡ 132 32.41 N 35.38 E
East Glacier Park 202 48.26 N 113.13 W
East Glenville 210 42.53 N 73.55 W
East Granby 207 41.56 N 72.43 W
East Grand Forks 198 47.55 N 97.01 W
East Grand Rapids 216 42.56 N 85.36 W
East Greenbush 210 42.35 N 73.42 W
East Greenville, Oh., U.S. 214 40.48 N 81.36 W
East Greenville, Pa., U.S. 208 40.24 N 75.30 W
East Greenwich, N.Y., U.S. 210 43.09 N 73.24 W
East Greenwich, R.I., U.S. 207 41.39 N 71.27 W
East Grinstead 42 51.08 N 0.01 W
East Gwillimbury 212 44.08 N 79.25 W
East Haddam 207 41.27 N 72.27 W
East Half Hollow Hills 276 40.57 N 72.11 W
Eastham, Eng., U.K. 262 53.19 N 2.58 W
Eastham, Ma., U.S. 207 41.49 N 69.58 W
East Ham ◆[8] 260 51.32 N 0.03 E
East Hampton, Ct., U.S. 207 41.34 N 72.30 W
Easthampton, Ma., U.S. 207 42.16 N 72.40 W
East Hampton, N.Y., U.S. 207 40.57 N 72.11 W
East Hanningfield 260 51.41 N 0.34 E
East Hanover 276 40.48 N 74.22 W
East Harbor State Park ◆ 214 41.32 N 82.49 W
East Harling 42 52.26 N 0.55 E
East Hartford 207 41.46 N 72.36 W
East Hartland 207 41.59 N 72.54 W
East Harwich 207 41.43 N 70.02 W
East Haven 207 41.16 N 72.52 W
East Hazel Crest 278 41.35 N 87.39 W
East Helena 202 46.35 N 111.54 W
East Hemet 228 33.45 N 116.57 W
East Herkimer 210 43.02 N 74.58 W
East Hertfordshire □[8] 260 51.46 N 0.02 W
East Hickory 214 41.35 N 79.24 W
East Highland Park 208 37.36 N 77.25 W
East Hills, Austl. 274a 33.58 S 150.59 E
East Hills, N.Y., U.S. 276 40.47 N 73.37 W
East Hoathly 42 50.55 N 0.10 E
East Horsley 42 51.15 N 0.26 W
East Humber ≃ 212 43.47 N 79.35 W
East Huntington 276 40.52 N 73.24 W
East Ilsley 42 51.32 N 1.17 W
East Irvington 276 41.03 N 73.51 W
East Island ≻[1] 276 40.54 N 73.38 W
East Islip 276 40.43 N 73.11 W
East Jewett 210 42.14 N 74.09 W
East Jordan 190 45.09 N 85.07 W
East Keansburg 276 40.26 N 74.07 W
East Kelowna 182 49.51 N 119.25 W
East Kilbride 46 55.46 N 4.10 W
East Killingly 207 41.50 N 71.49 W
East Kingston 210 41.57 N 73.58 W
Eastlake, Mi., U.S. 190 44.15 N 86.18 W
Eastlake, Oh., U.S. 214 41.39 N 81.27 W
East Lake ⊜, On., Can. 184 53.42 N 93.10 W
East Lake ⊜, On., Can. 212 43.55 N 77.12 W
East Lake ⊜, N.J., U.S. 276 40.58 N 74.21 W
East Lake Tohopekaliga ⊜ 220 28.18 N 81.17 W
East Lamma Channel ⊻ 271d 22.14 N 114.09 E
Eastland 196 32.24 N 98.49 W
Eastland Center ◆[9] 281 42.27 N 82.56 W
Eastland Shopping Plaza ◆[9] 279b 40.22 N 79.50 W
East Lansdowne 285 39.56 N 75.16 W
East Lansing 216 42.44 N 84.29 W
East Laurinburg 192 34.46 N 79.26 W
East Leake 42 52.49 N 1.10 W
Eastleigh 42 50.58 N 1.22 W
East Lewistown 214 40.57 N 80.42 W
East Liberty 216 40.19 N 83.34 W
East Liberty ◆[8] 279b 40.27 N 79.55 W
East Licking Creek ≃ 208 40.32 N 77.24 W
East Lindfield 274a 33.46 S 151.11 E
East Linton 46 55.59 N 2.39 W
East Liverpool 214 40.37 N 80.34 W
East London (Oos-Londen) 158 33.00 S 27.55 E
East Longmeadow 207 42.03 N 72.30 W
East Los Angeles 228 34.01 N 118.10 W
East Lyme 207 41.22 N 72.13 W
East Lynn 216 40.28 N 87.48 W
East Lynn Lake ⊜[1] 188 38.05 N 82.20 W
Eastmain 176 52.15 N 78.30 W
Eastmain ≃ 176 52.15 N 78.35 W
Eastmain-Opinaca, Réservoir ⊜[1] 176 52.25 N 76.35 W
East Malling 260 51.17 N 0.26 E
Eastman, P.Q., Can. 206 45.18 N 72.19 W
Eastman, Ga., U.S. 192 32.11 N 83.10 W
Eastman Lake ⊜[1] 226 37.14 N 119.58 W
East Mansfield 283 42.01 N 71.10 W
East Mariana Basin ✦[1] 14 12.00 N 153.00 E
East Marin Island I 282 37.58 N 122.27 W
East Markham 44 53.15 N 0.54 W
East McKeesport 279b 40.23 N 79.48 W
East Meadow 210 40.43 N 73.33 W
East Meadow ≃ 283 42.47 N 71.02 W
East Meadow Brook ≃ 276 40.39 N 73.34 W
East Meadowview 216 41.08 N 87.52 W
East Mecca 214 41.24 N 80.45 W
East Meredith 210 42.25 N 74.53 W
East Midlands Airport ⊠ 42 52.50 N 1.20 W
East Millbury 207 42.13 N 71.44 W
East Mill Creek ≃ 222 29.55 N 96.17 W
East Millinocket 188 45.37 N 68.34 W
East Millstone 276 40.30 N 74.35 W
East Missoula 202 46.52 N 113.58 W
East Molesey 260 51.24 N 0.21 W
East Moline 190 41.30 N 90.26 W
East Monongahela 279b 40.12 N 79.55 W
East Mountain 222 32.35 N 94.51 W
East Mustang Creek ≃ 222 29.03 N 96.27 W
East Naples 220 26.06 N 81.44 W
East Nassau 210 42.30 N 73.30 W
East Newark 276 40.48 N 73.59 W
East New Britain □[5] 164 6.00 S 152.00 E
East New Market 208 38.35 N 75.55 W
East New York ◆[8] 276 40.40 N 73.53 W
East Nishnabotna ≃ 198 40.39 N 95.37 W
East Nodaway ≃ 194 40.38 N 95.01 W
East Norriton 208 40.09 N 75.18 W
East Northfield 207 42.43 N 72.27 W
East Northport 210 40.52 N 73.19 W
East Norwich 210 40.50 N 73.32 W
East Novaya Zemlya Trough ✦[1] 12 73.30 N 61.00 E
East Olympia 224 46.58 N 122.50 W
Easton, Eng., U.K. 42 50.32 N 2.26 W
Easton, Ca., U.S. 226 36.39 N 119.47 W
Easton, Ct., U.S. 207 41.15 N 73.17 W
Easton, Il., U.S. 219 40.14 N 89.50 W
Easton, Md., U.S. 208 38.46 N 76.04 W
Easton, Ma., U.S. 283 42.02 N 71.06 W
Easton, Pa., U.S. 208 40.41 N 75.13 W
Easton, Tx., U.S. 222 32.23 N 94.35 W
Easton, Wa., U.S. 224 47.14 N 121.10 W
Eastondale 283 42.02 N 71.04 W
Easton Reservoir ⊜[1] 207 41.16 N 73.16 W

Symbols in the index entries represent the broad categories identified in the key at the right. Symbols with superior numbers (⩚[1]) identify subcategories (see complete key on page *I · 1).*

Symbole im Register stellen die rechts im Schlüssel erklärten Kategorien dar. Symbole mit hochgestellten Ziffern (⩚[1]) bezeichnen Unterabteilungen einer Kategorie (vgl. vollständiger Schlüssel auf Seite *I · 1).*

Los símbolos incluídos en el texto del índice representan las grandes categorias identificadas con la clave a la derecha. Los símbolos con numeros en su parte superior (⩚[1]) identifican las subcategorías (véase la clave completa en la página *I · 1).*

Les symboles de l'index représentent les catégories indiquées dans la légende à droite. Les symboles suivis d'un indice (⩚[1]) représentent des sous-catégories (voir légende complète à la page *I · 1).*

Os símbolos incluídos no texto do índice representam as grandes categorias identificadas com a chave à direita. Os símbolos com números em sua parte superior (⩚[1]) identificam as subcategorias (veja-se a chave completa à página *I · 1).*

	English	Deutsch	Español	Français	Português
∧	Mountain	Berg	Montaña	Montagne	Montanha
⩚	Mountains	Gebirge	Montañas	Montagnes	Montanhas
)(	Pass	Paß	Paso	Col	Passo
V	Valley, Canyon	Tal, Cañon	Valle, Cañón	Vallée, Canyon	Vale, Canhão
⊻	Plain	Ebene	Llano	Plaine	Planície
≻	Cape	Kap	Cabo	Cap	Cabo
I	Island	Insel	Isla	Île	Ilha
II	Islands	Inseln	Islas	Îles	Ilhas
⊥	Other Topographic Features	Andere Topographische Objekte	Otros Elementos Topográficos	Autres données topographiques	Outros acidentes topográficos

ESPAÑOL — Nombre · Página · Lat.°′ · Long.°′ W = Oeste
FRANÇAIS — Nom · Page · Lat.°′ · Long.°′ W = Ouest
PORTUGUÊS — Nome · Página · Lat.°′ · Long.°′ W = Oeste

Nombre / Nom / Nome	Página / Page	Lat.°′	Long.°′
East Orange	210	40.46 N	74.12 W
East Orleans	207	41.47 N	69.58 W
East Otto	210	42.23 N	78.45 W
Eastover	192	33.52 N	80.41 W
East Pacific Rise ✦[3]	6	20.00 S	115.00 W
East Pakistan → Bangladesh □[1]	118	24.00 N	90.00 E
East Palatka	192	29.39 N	81.35 W
East Palestine	214	40.50 N	80.32 W
East Palo Alto	226	37.28 N	122.08 W
East Park Reservoir ⊜[1]	226	39.21 N	122.30 W
East Parkrose	224	45.33 N	122.32 W
East Peak ∧	116	11.13 N	119.29 E
East Peckham	42	51.15 N	0.23 E
East Pecos	200	35.34 N	105.39 W
East Pembroke, Ma., U.S.	283	42.05 N	70.46 W
East Pembroke, N.Y., U.S.	210	42.59 N	78.18 W
East Peoria	190	40.39 N	89.34 W
East Pepperell	207	42.39 N	71.34 W
East Petersburg	208	40.06 N	76.21 W
East Pharsalia	210	42.34 N	75.43 W
East Pine	182	55.43 N	121.13 W
East Pines	284c	38.57 N	76.55 W
East Pittsburgh	279b	40.23 N	79.50 W
Eastpoint, Fl., U.S.	192	29.44 N	84.52 W
East Point, Ga., U.S.	192	33.40 N	84.26 W
East Point ›, P.E., Can.	186	46.27 N	61.58 W
East Point ›, Ma., U.S.	207	42.25 N	70.54 W
East Point ›, Vir. Is., U.S.	241n	17.45 N	64.34 W
Eastpoint ◆[9]	284b	39.18 N	76.31 W
Eastport, Nf., Can.	186	48.39 N	53.45 W
Eastport, Id., U.S.	202	49.00 N	116.10 W
Eastport, Me., U.S.	188	44.54 N	66.59 W
Eastport, N.Y., U.S.	207	40.49 N	72.44 W
East Porterville	204	36.04 N	118.56 W
East Potomac Park ♠	284c	38.52 N	77.01 W
East Prairie	194	36.46 N	89.23 W
East Prairie ≃	182	55.34 N	116.25 W
East Prospect	208	39.58 N	76.31 W
East Providence	207	41.48 N	71.22 W
East Pryor Mountain ∧	202	45.11 N	108.20 W
East Quogue	207	40.51 N	72.35 W
East Rājasthān Uplands ⋀[1]	124	26.40 N	76.35 E
East Randolph	210	42.10 N	78.56 W
East Retford	44	53.19 N	0.56 W
East Richmond	226	37.57 N	122.19 W
Eastridge Center ◆[9]	282	37.20 N	121.49 W
East Rigaud ≃	206	45.27 N	74.22 W
Eastriggs	44	54.59 N	3.10 W
East River ⊂	208	37.24 N	76.21 W
East Rochester, N.Y., U.S.	210	43.06 N	77.29 W
East Rochester, Oh., U.S.	214	40.45 N	81.02 W
East Rockaway	276	40.38 N	73.40 W
East Rockingham	192	34.55 N	79.45 W
East Rockwood	216	42.03 N	83.13 W
East Rosebud Creek ≃	202	45.29 N	109.27 W
East Rudolf National Park ♠	154	3.55 N	36.20 E
East Rutherford	276	40.50 N	74.05 W
Eastry	42	51.15 N	1.18 E
East Saint Louis	219	38.38 N	90.09 W
East Salem	208	40.37 N	77.14 W
East Salt Creek ≃	200	39.13 N	108.54 W
East Sandwich	207	41.44 N	70.27 W
East Sandy Creek ≃	214	41.22 N	79.51 W
East Schodack	210	42.34 N	73.38 W
East Scotia Basin ✦[1]	9	57.00 S	35.00 W
East Sepik □[5]	164	4.00 S	143.30 E
East Setauket	210	40.57 N	73.06 W
East Shoal Lake ⊜	184	50.23 N	97.37 W
East Siberian Sea → Vostočno-Sibirskoje more ▾[2]	12	74.00 N	166.00 E
East Side	210	41.04 N	75.46 W
Eastside Bypass ≊	226	37.05 N	120.28 W
East Side Canal ≊, Ca., U.S.	226	37.21 N	120.55 W
East Side Canal ≊, Ca., U.S.	226	35.33 N	119.33 W
East Sixteen Mile Creek ≃	275b	43.28 N	79.48 W
East Smethport	214	41.49 N	78.26 W
East Smithfield	210	41.52 N	76.38 W
East Sooke	224	48.22 N	123.43 W
Eastsound	224	48.41 N	122.54 W
East Sound ɥ	224	48.39 N	122.53 W
East Sparta	214	40.40 N	81.21 W
East Spencer	192	35.40 N	80.25 W
East Springbrook	284c	39.04 N	77.00 W
East Springfield, Oh., U.S.	214	40.27 N	80.52 W
East Springfield, Pa., U.S.	214	41.57 N	80.28 W
East Stony Creek ≃	210	43.15 N	74.12 W
East Stour ≃	42	51.08 N	0.53 E
East Stroudsburg	210	40.59 N	75.10 W
East Sudbury	283	42.24 N	71.24 W
East Sussex □[6]	42	50.55 N	0.15 E
East Syracuse	210	43.04 N	76.05 W
East Tawas	190	44.16 N	83.29 W
East Templeton	207	42.33 N	72.02 W
East Texas	210	40.33 N	75.33 W
East Thompson	207	42.00 N	71.48 W
East Tilbury	260	51.28 N	0.26 E
East Troy	216	42.47 N	88.24 W
East Tustin	280	33.46 N	117.49 W
Eastvale	214	40.46 N	80.19 W
East Vandergrift	214	40.36 N	79.34 W
Eastview	218	40.19 N	80.38 W
Eastville	208	37.21 N	75.56 W
East Walker ≃	204	38.53 N	119.10 W
East Walpole	207	42.09 N	71.12 W
East Wareham	207	41.45 N	70.40 W
East Washington	214	40.10 N	80.14 W
East Waterford	208	40.22 N	77.36 W
East Wemyss	46	56.09 N	3.04 W
East Wenatchee	202	47.24 N	120.17 W
East Wenonah	285	39.47 N	75.08 W
East White Plains	276	41.03 N	73.47 W
Eastwick ◆[8]	285	39.55 N	75.14 W
East Wickham ◆[8]	260	51.28 N	0.07 E
East Williamson	210	43.14 N	77.09 W
East Williston	276	40.46 N	73.38 W
East Wilmington	192	34.13 N	77.53 W
East Wittering	42	50.41 N	0.53 W
Eastwood, Austl.	274a	33.48 S	151.05 E
Eastwood, Eng., U.K.	44	53.01 N	1.18 W
Eastwood, Eng., U.K.	260	51.34 N	0.40 E
Eastwood, Eng., U.K.	262	53.43 N	2.03 W
Eastwood, Mi., U.S.	216	42.18 N	85.33 W
Eastwood, Pa., U.S.	279b	40.17 N	79.31 W
East Worcester	210	42.37 N	74.40 W
East Yegua Creek ≃	222	30.19 N	96.45 W
East Yellow Creek ≃	194	39.38 N	93.04 W
East York, On., Can.	212	43.41 N	79.20 W
East York, Pa., U.S.	208	39.58 N	76.43 W
Eaton, Austl.	168a	33.19 S	115.43 E
Eaton, Co., U.S.	200	40.31 N	104.42 W
Eaton, In., U.S.	216	40.20 N	85.21 W
Eaton, N.Y., U.S.	210	42.51 N	75.37 W
Eaton, Oh., U.S.	218	39.44 N	84.38 W
Eaton ≃	206	45.28 N	71.39 W
Eaton Estates	214	41.19 N	82.01 W
Eatonia	184	51.13 N	109.23 W
Eaton Nord ≃	206	45.24 N	71.35 W
Eaton Park	220	28.00 N	81.54 W
Eaton Rapids	216	42.30 N	84.39 W
Eatons Neck	276	40.56 N	73.24 W
Eatons Neck ›[1]	276	40.57 N	73.23 W
Eatons Neck Point ›	210	40.57 N	73.24 W
Eaton Socon	42	52.13 N	0.18 W
Eatonton	192	33.19 N	83.23 W
Eatontown	208	40.17 N	74.03 W
Eatonville	224	46.52 N	122.15 W
Eaton Wash V	280	34.04 N	118.03 W
Eaton Wash Dam ◆[6]	280	34.10 N	118.06 W
Eau ≃	44	53.31 N	0.44 W
Eaubonne	261	49.00 N	2.17 E
Eau Claire, Mi., U.S.	216	41.59 N	86.17 W
Eau Claire, Pa., U.S.	214	41.08 N	79.48 W
Eau Claire, Wi., U.S.	190	44.48 N	91.29 W
Eau Claire ≃, Wi., U.S.	190	44.49 N	91.31 W
Eau Claire ≃, Wi., U.S.	190	44.55 N	89.37 W
Eau Claire, Lac à l' ⊜, P.Q., Can.	176	56.10 N	74.25 W
Eau Claire, Lac à l' ⊜, P.Q., Can.	206	46.33 N	73.04 W
Eau d'Heure ≃	56	50.18 N	4.24 E
Eau Galle ≃	190	44.37 N	92.00 W
Eau Gallie	220	28.08 N	80.38 W
Eaulne ≃	50	49.54 N	1.07 E
Eauripik I[1]	108	6.42 N	143.03 E
Eauripik Rise ✦[3]	14	3.00 N	142.00 E
Eauze	32	43.52 N	0.06 E
Ebabaka	152	2.30 S	18.19 E
Eban	150	9.44 N	4.56 E
Ebanga	152	12.44 S	14.44 E
Ebangalakata	152	0.29 S	21.29 E
Ebano	234	22.13 N	98.22 W
Ebb and Flow Indian Reserve ◆[4]	184	51.05 N	99.05 W
Ebb and Flow Lake ⊜	184	51.05 N	98.56 W
Ebbegebirge ⋀	56	51.08 N	7.46 E
Ebben Creek ≃	283	42.38 N	70.45 W
Ebberup	41	55.15 N	9.59 E
Ebbetts Pass)(	226	38.33 N	119.48 W
Ebbs	64	47.38 N	12.13 E
Ebbw ≃	42	51.33 N	2.59 W
Ebbw Vale	42	51.47 N	3.12 W
Ebebiyín	152	2.09 N	11.20 E
Ebeji (El Beïd) ≃	146	12.32 N	14.11 E
Ebejty, ozero ⊜	86	54.38 N	71.44 E
Ebeleben	54	51.17 N	10.43 E
Ebeltoft	41	56.12 N	10.41 E
Ebeltoft Vig ⊂	41	56.10 N	10.36 E
Ebenau	64	47.47 N	13.11 E
Ebendorf	54	52.11 N	11.34 E
Ebene Reichenau	64	46.51 N	13.54 E
Ebenezer	275b	43.46 N	79.40 W
Ebenezer Ridge ∧	218	39.06 N	84.55 W
Eben Junction	190	46.21 N	86.58 W
Ebensburg	214	40.29 N	78.43 W
Ebensee	64	47.48 N	13.46 E
Ebensfeld	56	50.04 N	10.58 E
Eberbach	56	49.28 N	8.59 E
Ebergassing	264b	48.03 N	16.31 E
Eber Gölü ⊜	130	38.38 N	31.12 E
Ebergötzen	52	51.34 N	10.06 E
Ebermannstadt	60	49.43 N	11.13 E
Ebern	56	50.05 N	10.47 E
Eberndorf	61	46.35 N	14.38 E
Ebersbach, Dtsch.	54	51.00 N	14.35 E
Ebersbach, Dtsch.	56	48.43 N	9.31 E
Ebersberg	60	48.05 N	11.58 E
Eberschwang	60	48.09 N	13.34 E
Ebersdorf	52	53.31 N	9.03 E
Ebersdorf bei Coburg	56	50.13 N	11.04 E
Eberstein	61	46.48 N	14.34 E
Eberswalde	54	52.50 N	13.49 E
Ebetsu	92a	43.07 N	141.34 E
Ebian	102	29.10 N	103.20 E
Ebina	94	35.26 N	139.25 E
Ebingen	58	48.13 N	9.01 E
Ebino	92	32.03 N	130.50 E
Ebinur Hu ⊜	86	44.55 N	82.55 E
Ebi-Sekigahara-Yōrō-kokutei-kōen ♠	94	35.30 N	136.30 E
Ebnat	58	47.15 N	9.08 E
Ebo	152	11.02 S	14.41 E
Ebola ≃	152	3.20 N	20.57 E
Eboli	68	40.37 N	15.04 E
Ebolowa	152	2.54 N	11.09 E
Ebon I[1]	14	4.35 N	168.44 E
Ebonda	152	2.12 N	22.21 E
Ebony	156	22.05 S	15.15 E
Eboshi-yama ∧	96	35.04 N	133.04 E
Eboué Stadium ♠	273b	4.17 S	15.18 E
Ebrach	56	49.50 N	10.29 E
Ebre, Delta de l' ⩡[2]	34	40.43 N	0.54 E
Ebreichsdorf	61	47.58 N	16.24 E
Ébrié, Lagune ⊂	150	5.14 N	4.26 W
Ebro (Ebre) ≃	34	40.43 N	0.54 E
Ebro, Embalse del ⊜[1]	34	43.00 N	3.58 W
Ebstorf	52	53.01 N	10.25 E
Ebute-Ikorodu	273a	6.37 N	3.30 E
Ebute-Metta ◆[8]	273a	6.29 N	3.23 E
Ecatepec	286a	19.35 N	99.04 W
Écaussinnes-d'Enghen	50	50.34 N	4.10 E
Ecclefechan	44	55.03 N	3.17 W
Eccles, Eng., U.K.	44	53.29 N	2.21 W
Eccles, Eng., U.K.	260	51.19 N	0.29 E
Eccles, W.V., U.S.	192	37.46 N	81.15 W
Eccleshall	42	52.52 N	2.15 W
Eccleston, Eng., U.K.	44	53.38 N	2.43 W
Eccleston, Eng., U.K.	262	53.27 N	2.47 W
Eccleston, Md., U.S.	284b	39.24 N	76.44 W
Eceabat	130	40.11 N	26.21 E
Echabi	89	53.30 N	142.59 E
Echague	116	16.42 N	121.40 E
Echallens	58	46.38 N	6.38 E
Echaporã	255	22.26 S	50.12 W
Echarcon	261	48.34 N	2.24 E
Échauffour	50	48.44 N	0.23 E
Ech Cheliff (Orléansville)	148	36.10 N	1.20 E
Ech Cheliff □[5]	148	36.20 N	1.50 E
Echeconnee Creek ≃	192	32.39 N	83.36 W
Echelon Mall ◆[9]	285	39.51 N	75.00 W
Echeng	100	30.24 N	114.51 E
Échenoz-la-Méline	58	47.36 N	6.08 E
Echi ≃	94	35.13 N	136.07 E
Echigawa	94	35.10 N	136.12 E
Echigo-sammyaku ⋀	92	37.50 N	139.50 E
Echimamish ≃	184	54.20 N	97.27 W
Eching	60	48.18 N	11.37 E
Echizen	94	35.54 N	136.00 E
Echizen-Kaga-kaigan-kokutei-kōen ♠	94	36.08 N	136.05 E
Echizen-misaki ›	94	35.59 N	135.57 E
Echo	198	44.37 N	95.25 W
Echo Bay	176	66.05 N	118.02 W
Echo Bay ⊂	276	40.54 N	73.46 W
Echoing ≃	184	55.51 N	92.05 W
Echoing Lake ⊜	184	54.31 N	92.15 W
Echo Lake ⊜, Il., U.S.	278	42.13 N	88.05 W
Echo Lake ⊜, N.J., U.S.	276	41.04 N	74.25 W
Echo Summit ∧	226	38.50 N	120.02 W
Echouani, Lac ⊜	190	47.46 N	75.42 W
Echt, Ned.	52	51.06 N	5.52 E
Echt, Scot., U.K.	46	57.08 N	2.26 W
Echternach	56	49.48 N	6.26 E
Echternacherbrück	56	49.49 N	6.25 E
Echuca	166	36.08 S	144.46 E
Echunga	168b	35.07 S	138.48 E
Écija	34	37.32 N	5.05 W
Ecilda Paullier	258	34.22 S	57.04 W
Eck, Loch ⊜	46	56.05 N	5.00 W
Eckartsberga	54	51.07 N	11.34 E
Eckbolsheim	58	48.35 N	7.41 E
Eckernförde	41	54.28 N	9.50 E
Eckernförder Bucht ⊂	41	54.30 N	10.02 E
Eckerö I	26	60.14 N	19.35 E
Eckington	44	53.19 N	1.21 W
Eckley	210	40.59 N	75.51 W
Eckville	182	52.21 N	114.22 W
Eckwarderhörne	52	53.31 N	8.14 E
Eclectic	194	32.38 N	86.02 W
Ecleto	222	29.03 N	97.45 W
Ecleto Creek ≃	196	28.52 N	97.45 W
Eclipse Sound ɥ	176	72.38 N	79.00 W
Ečmiadzin	84	40.10 N	44.18 E
Ecola State Park ♠	224	45.57 N	123.58 W
Ècole ≃	261	48.32 N	2.33 E
Écommoy	50	47.50 N	0.16 E
Econfina ≃	192	30.02 N	83.55 W
Econlockhatchee ≃	220	28.42 N	81.02 W
Economy, In., U.S.	218	39.58 N	85.05 W
Economy, Pa., U.S.	214	40.39 N	80.14 W
Economy Park ♠	279b	40.37 N	80.12 W
Ecoporanga	255	18.23 S	40.50 W
Écorce, Lac de l' ⊜[1]	190	47.05 N	76.24 W
Écorces, Lac des ⊜	206	46.00 N	74.32 W
Ecorse	216	42.14 N	83.08 W
Ecorse ≃	281	42.14 N	83.09 W
Ecorse, South Branch ≃	281	42.14 N	83.09 W
Écos	50	49.10 N	1.39 E
Écosse → Scotland □[8]	28	57.00 N	4.00 W
Écouen	50	49.01 N	2.23 E
Écouen, Château d' ⊥	261	49.01 N	2.23 E
Écouis	50	49.19 N	1.26 E
Ecoute, Ru d' ≃	261	48.39 N	2.26 E
Ecquevilly	261	48.57 N	1.55 E
Écrins, Barre des ∧	62	44.55 N	6.22 E
Écrins, Massif des ⋀[1]	62	44.55 N	6.20 E
Écrins, Parc National des ♠	62	44.50 N	6.15 E
Écrosnes	261	48.33 N	1.44 E
Ecru	194	34.21 N	89.01 W
Ecser	264c	47.27 N	19.20 E
Ecstall ≃	182	54.09 N	129.56 W
Ecuador □[1], S.A.	242	2.00 S	77.30 W
Ecuador □[1], S.A.	246	2.00 S	77.30 W
Ecuandureo	234	20.10 N	102.11 W
Écueillé	32	47.05 N	1.21 E
Écuisses	58	46.45 N	4.32 E
Ecum Secum	186	44.58 N	62.08 W
Écury-sur-Coole	50	48.54 N	4.20 E
Ed, Erit.	144	13.52 N	41.40 E
Ed, Sve.	26	58.55 N	11.55 E
Eda ◆[8]	268	35.34 N	139.34 E
Edah	162	28.17 S	117.10 E
Edam, Sk., Can.	184	53.12 N	108.46 W
Edam, Ned.	52	52.31 N	5.03 E
Eday I	46	59.11 N	2.47 W
Edderton	46	57.50 N	4.10 W
Eddington Gardens	285	40.06 N	74.57 W
Eddleston	46	55.43 N	3.13 W
Eddrachillis Bay ⊂	46	58.18 N	5.15 W
Eddy	222	31.18 N	97.15 W
Eddystone	208	39.51 N	75.20 W
Eddystone Point ›	166	41.00 S	148.21 E
Eddystone Rocks II[1]	42	50.12 N	4.15 W
Eddyville, Ia., U.S.	190	41.09 N	92.38 W
Eddyville, Ky., U.S.	194	37.05 N	88.04 W
Eddyville, N.Y., U.S.	210	41.54 N	74.02 W
Ede, Ned.	52	52.03 N	5.40 E
Ede, Nig.	150	7.44 N	4.27 E
Edéa	152	3.48 N	10.08 E
Edebäck	40	60.04 N	13.33 E
Edebo	40	60.01 N	18.34 E
Edegem	52	51.09 N	4.27 E
Edehon Lake ⊜	176	60.25 N	97.15 W
Edéia	255	17.18 S	49.55 W
Edelény	30	48.18 N	20.44 E
Edelsfeld	60	49.34 N	11.42 E
Edelshausen	60	48.37 N	11.17 E
Edelweiss	273d	26.16 S	28.28 E
Edelweiss Spitze ∧	64	47.07 N	12.50 E
Edemissen	52	52.23 N	10.16 E
Eden, Austl.	166	37.04 S	149.54 E
Éden, Bra.	287a	22.48 S	43.24 W
Eden, N. Ire., U.K.	48	54.44 N	5.47 W
Eden, Mi., U.S.	216	42.32 N	84.26 W
Eden, Ms., U.S.	194	32.59 N	90.19 W
Eden, N.Y., U.S.	210	42.39 N	78.53 W
Eden, Tx., U.S.	196	31.12 N	99.50 W
Eden, Wy., U.S.	200	42.03 N	109.26 W
Eden ≃, Eng., U.K.	42	51.10 N	0.11 E
Eden ≃, Eng., U.K.	44	54.57 N	3.01 W
Eden ≃, Scot., U.K.	46	56.22 N	2.50 W
Eden ≃, Wales, U.K.	42	52.48 N	3.53 W
Edenbridge	42	51.12 N	0.04 E
Edenburg	158	29.45 S	25.56 E
Eden Canyon V	282	37.42 N	122.01 W
Edendale, N.Z.	172	46.19 S	168.47 E
Edendale, S. Afr.	158	29.39 S	30.18 E
Edendale, S. Afr.	273d	26.09 S	28.09 E
Edenderry	48	53.20 N	7.03 W
Edenfield	262	53.40 N	2.18 W
Eden Hill ∧[2]	207	41.20 N	73.19 W
Edenkoben	56	49.17 N	8.07 E
Eden Lake ⊜	184	56.38 N	100.15 W
Eden Mills	212	43.35 N	80.09 W
Eden Park ◆[8]	260	51.23 N	0.02 W
Edenside V	44	54.40 N	2.35 W
Edenton	192	36.03 N	76.36 W
Edenvale	273d	26.08 S	28.09 E
Eden Valley, Austl.	168b	34.39 S	139.06 E
Eden Valley, Mn., U.S.	190	45.19 N	94.32 W
Edenville	158	27.37 S	27.34 E
Edeowie	166	31.27 S	138.27 E
Eder ≃	56	51.13 N	9.27 E
Ederkopf ∧	56	50.56 N	8.12 E
Ederny	48	54.32 N	7.39 W
Edersee ⊜[1]	56	51.11 N	9.00 E
Eder-Talsperre ◆[6]	56	51.11 N	9.02 E
Edesheim	56	49.16 N	8.08 E
Edessa → Édhessa	38	40.48 N	22.03 E
Edewecht	52	53.07 N	8.02 E
Edfu → Idfū	140	24.58 N	32.52 E
Edgar, Ne., U.S.	198	40.22 N	97.58 W
Edgar, Wi., U.S.	190	44.55 N	89.57 W
Edgard	194	30.03 N	90.34 W
Edgar Ranges ⋀	162	18.43 S	123.25 E
Edgars Creek ≃	274b	37.44 S	144.58 E
Edgartown	207	41.23 N	70.30 W
Edgartown Harbor ⊂	207	41.24 N	70.30 W
Edgecliff	222	32.39 N	97.22 W
Edgecumbe	172	37.59 S	176.50 E
Edgefield	192	33.47 N	81.55 W
Edge Hill ◆[8]	262	53.24 N	2.57 W
Edge Hill ∧	42	52.08 N	1.27 W
Edgeley, On., Can.	275b	43.48 N	79.31 W
Edgeley, N.D., U.S.	198	46.21 N	98.42 W
Edgely	285	40.07 N	74.50 W
Edgemere	208	39.14 N	76.26 W
Edgemont, Ca., U.S.	228	33.53 N	117.18 W
Edgemont, Pa., U.S.	285	39.57 N	75.27 W
Edgemont, S.D., U.S.	198	43.18 N	103.49 W
Edgemont Park	216	42.44 N	84.36 W
Edgemoor	285	39.45 N	75.30 W
Edge Mountain ∧	180	58.12 N	152.06 W
Edgeøya I	12	77.45 N	22.30 E
Edgeroi	166	30.07 S	149.48 E
Edgerton, Ab., Can.	184	52.45 N	110.27 W
Edgerton, In., U.S.	216	41.05 N	84.49 W
Edgerton, Mn., U.S.	198	43.52 N	96.07 W
Edgerton, Oh., U.S.	216	41.26 N	84.44 W
Edgerton, Wi., U.S.	216	42.50 N	89.04 W
Edgerton, Wy., U.S.	200	43.24 N	106.14 W
Edgewater, Al., U.S.	194	33.31 N	86.57 W
Edgewater, Fl., U.S.	220	28.59 N	80.54 W
Edgewater, N.J., U.S.	276	40.50 N	73.58 W
Edgewater Park	285	40.04 N	74.54 W
Edgewater Park ♠	279a	41.29 N	81.43 W
Edgewater Point ›	276	40.55 N	73.44 W
Edgewood, B.C., Can.	182	49.47 N	118.08 W
Edgewood, Fl., U.S.	220	28.29 N	81.22 W
Edgewood, Il., U.S.	219	38.55 N	88.40 W
Edgewood, In., U.S.	218	40.06 N	85.44 W
Edgewood, Ia., U.S.	190	42.38 N	91.24 W
Edgewood, Md., U.S.	208	39.25 N	76.17 W
Edgewood, Oh., U.S.	214	41.52 N	80.46 W
Edgewood, Pa., U.S.	279b	40.25 N	79.52 W
Edgewood, Tx., U.S.	222	32.42 N	95.53 W
Edgeworth	214	40.33 N	80.11 W
Edgeworthstown → Mostrim	48	53.42 N	7.36 W
Edgware ◆[8]	260	51.37 N	0.17 W
Edgworth	262	53.39 N	2.24 W
Édhessa	38	40.48 N	22.03 E
Ediger	56	50.06 N	7.09 E
Edimbourg → Edinburgh	46	55.57 N	3.13 W
Edimburgo → Edinburgh	46	55.57 N	3.13 W
Edina, Liber.	150	6.01 N	10.10 W
Edina, Mn., U.S.	190	44.53 N	93.20 W
Edina, Mo., U.S.	219	40.10 N	92.10 W
Edinboro	214	41.52 N	80.07 W
Edinboro Lake ⊜	214	41.53 N	80.08 W
Edinburg, Il., U.S.	219	39.39 N	89.23 W
Edinburg, In., U.S.	218	39.21 N	85.58 W
Edinburg, Ms., U.S.	194	32.47 N	89.20 W
Edinburg, N.Y., U.S.	210	43.13 N	74.07 W
Edinburg, N.D., U.S.	198	48.29 N	97.51 W
Edinburg, Oh., U.S.	214	41.06 N	81.09 W
Edinburg, Tx., U.S.	196	26.18 N	98.09 W
Edinburg, Va., U.S.	188	38.49 N	78.33 W
Edinburgh	46	55.57 N	3.13 W
Edinburgh (Turnhouse) Airport ⊠	46	55.57 N	3.21 W
Edinburgh, Arrecife ✦[2]	236	14.50 N	82.39 W
Edinburgh Castle ⊥	46	55.56 N	3.14 W
Edinburgh Channel ɥ	236	14.45 N	82.40 W
Edinburgh Mountain ∧	224	48.38 N	124.24 W
Edincik	130	40.20 N	27.51 E
Edingen → Enghien	50	50.42 N	4.02 E
Edirne	130	41.40 N	26.34 E
Edirne □[4]	130	41.20 N	26.40 E
Edison, Ga., U.S.	192	31.33 N	84.44 W
Edison, N.J., U.S.	210	40.27 N	74.18 W
Edison, Oh., U.S.	214	40.33 N	82.51 W
Edison, Pa., U.S.	208	40.17 N	75.07 W
Edison Bridge ◆[5]	214	41.27 N	82.49 W
Edison National Historic Site ⊥	276	40.47 N	74.14 W
Edison Park ◆[8]	278	42.01 N	87.49 W
Edisseja	84	44.03 N	44.33 E
Edisto ≃	192	32.39 N	80.24 W
Edisto, North Fork ≃	192	33.16 N	80.53 W
Edisto, South Fork ≃	192	33.16 N	80.53 W
Edisto Island I	192	32.35 N	80.20 W
Edith	170	33.48 S	149.55 E
Edith, Mount ∧	202	46.26 N	111.11 W
Edithburgh	168b	35.06 S	137.44 E
Edith Cavell, Mount ∧	182	52.40 N	118.03 W
Edith River	164	14.11 S	132.02 E
Edithvale	274b	38.02 S	145.07 E
Edith Weston	42	52.37 N	0.37 W
Edjejou, Oued i-n- V	148	22.46 N	4.05 E
Edjeleh	148	27.38 N	9.50 E
Edjerir ≃	150	18.06 N	0.50 E
Edjudina	162	29.48 S	122.23 E
Edmeston	210	42.41 N	75.14 W
Edmond	196	35.39 N	97.28 W
Edmondbyers	44	54.51 N	1.58 W
Edmonds	224	47.48 N	122.22 W
Edmondson Heights	284b	39.18 N	76.43 W
Edmonston	284c	38.57 N	76.56 W
Edmonton, Austl.	166	17.01 S	145.45 E
Edmonton, Ab., Can.	182	53.33 N	113.28 W
Edmonton, Ky., U.S.	194	36.58 N	85.36 W
Edmonton ◆[8]	260	51.37 N	0.04 W
Edmore, Mi., U.S.	190	43.24 N	85.02 W
Edmore, N.D., U.S.	198	48.24 N	98.27 W
Edmund	162	23.46 S	116.02 E
Edmund Lake ⊜	184	54.45 N	93.15 W
Edmundson Acres	228	35.14 N	118.49 W
Edmundston	186	47.22 N	68.20 W
Edna, Ks., U.S.	198	37.03 N	95.21 W
Edna, Pa., U.S.	279b	40.19 N	79.39 W
Edna, Tx., U.S.	222	28.58 N	96.38 W
Edna Bay	180	55.57 N	133.40 W
Ednor	208	39.09 N	76.59 W
Edo ≃	94	35.37 N	139.53 E
Edogawa ◆[8]	268	35.42 N	139.52 E
Edolo	64	46.11 N	10.20 E
Edom	222	32.22 N	95.37 W
Edon	216	41.33 N	84.46 W
Edosaki	94	35.57 N	140.19 E
Edremit	130	39.35 N	27.01 E
Edremit Körfezi ⊂	130	39.30 N	26.45 E
Edrengijn nuruu ⋀	102	44.15 N	97.45 E
Edsall Park	284c	38.48 N	77.11 W
Edsbro	40	59.54 N	18.29 E
Edsbruk	26	58.02 N	16.28 E
Edsbyn	26	61.23 N	15.49 E
Edsgatan	40	59.26 N	13.33 E
Edson	182	53.35 N	116.26 W
Edson Butte ∧	202	42.52 N	124.20 W
Eduardo Castex	252	35.54 S	64.18 W
Eduardo VII, Península → Edward VII Peninsula ›[1]	9	77.40 S	155.00 W
Eduni, Mount ∧	180	64.15 N	128.04 W
Edward ≃, Austl.	164	14.44 S	141.35 E
Edward ≃, Austl.	166	35.33 S	144.58 E
Edward, Lake ⊜	154	0.25 S	29.30 E
Edward, Mount ∧	162	23.22 S	131.55 E
Edwardes Park ♠	274b	37.43 S	145.00 E
Edward Island I	190	48.24 N	88.36 W
Edward River Aboriginal Reserve ◆[4]	164	14.30 S	141.45 E
Edwards, Ca., U.S.	228	34.54 N	117.53 W
Edwards, Ms., U.S.	194	32.19 N	90.36 W
Edwards, N.Y., U.S.	212	44.19 N	75.15 W
Edwards ≃	190	41.09 N	90.59 W
Edwards Air Force Base ■	228	34.54 N	117.52 W
Edwards Airport ⊠	276	40.45 N	73.03 W
Edwardsburg	216	41.47 N	86.04 W
Edwards Butte ∧	224	45.23 N	123.41 W
Edwards Gardens ♠	275b	43.44 N	79.22 W
Edwards Plateau ⋀[1]	196	31.20 N	101.00 W
Edwards Point ›	169	38.13 S	144.42 E
Edwards Run ≃	285	39.48 N	75.12 W
Edwardsville, Il., U.S.	219	38.48 N	89.57 W
Edwardsville, In., U.S.	218	38.16 N	85.55 W
Edwardsville, Pa., U.S.	210	41.16 N	75.55 W
Edward VIII Bay ⊂	9	66.50 S	57.00 E
Edward VII Peninsula ›[1]	9	77.40 S	155.00 W
Edwinstowe	44	53.12 N	1.04 W
Edzell	46	56.48 N	2.39 W
Edziza, Mount ∧	180	57.40 N	130.36 W
Eede	52	51.15 N	3.28 E
Eefde	52	52.10 N	6.14 E
Eek	180	60.12 N	162.15 W
Eek ≃	180	60.12 N	162.15 W
Eeklo	50	51.11 N	3.34 E
Eel ≃, Ca., U.S.	204	40.40 N	124.20 W
Eel ≃, In., U.S.	194	39.07 N	86.57 W
Eel ≃, In., U.S.	216	40.45 N	86.22 W
Eel, Middle Fork ≃	204	39.42 N	123.21 W
Eel, North Fork ≃	204	39.57 N	123.26 W
Eel, South Fork ≃	204	40.22 N	123.55 W
Eel Bay ⊂	212	44.19 N	76.02 W
Eelde	52	53.07 N	6.35 E
Eels Creek ≃	212	44.35 N	78.03 W
Eels Lake ⊜	212	44.54 N	78.08 W
Eemskanaal ≊	52	53.15 N	6.45 E
Eerbeek	52	52.07 N	6.04 E
Eersel	52	51.22 N	5.19 E
Eesti → Estonia □[1]	22	59.00 N	26.00 E
Eexta	52	53.10 N	6.59 E
Efate □[8]	175f	17.45 S	168.20 E
Éfaté I	175f	17.40 S	168.25 E
Eferding	61	48.18 N	14.02 E
Efes (Ephesus) ⊥	130	37.55 N	27.17 E
Effigy Mounds National Monument ♠	190	43.06 N	91.13 W
Effingham, Eng., U.K.	260	51.16 N	0.24 W
Effingham, Il., U.S.	194	39.07 N	88.32 W
Effingham, Ks., U.S.	198	39.31 N	95.24 W
Effingham □[6]	219	39.07 N	88.33 W
Effingham Lake ⊜	212	44.59 N	77.22 W
Effort	210	40.56 N	75.26 W
Efiduasi	150	6.51 N	1.24 W
Efkere	130	38.47 N	35.40 E
Eflâni	130	41.26 N	32.57 E
Eforie Nord	38	44.06 N	28.38 E
Eforie Sud	38	44.03 N	28.38 E
Efringen-Kirchen	58	47.49 N	7.35 E
Ega ≃	34	42.19 N	1.55 W
Egadi, Isole II	70	37.58 N	12.16 E
Egan	222	32.28 N	97.17 W
Egaña	252	36.59 S	59.06 W
Egan Range ⋀	204	39.10 N	114.55 W
Eganville	190	45.32 N	77.06 W
Egau ≃	58	48.36 N	10.34 E
Egba □[8]	273a	6.41 N	3.23 E
Egbe, Nig.	150	8.16 N	5.31 E
Egbe, Nig.	273a	6.33 N	3.17 E
Egbunda	154	2.44 N	27.12 E
Egedesminde (Aasiaat)	176	68.42 N	52.45 W
Égée, Mer → Aegean Sea ▾[2]	38	38.30 N	25.00 E
Egegik	180	58.13 N	157.22 W
Egeln	54	51.56 N	11.25 E
Egeo, Mar → Aegean Sea ▾[2]	38	38.30 N	25.00 E
Eger	30	47.54 N	20.23 E
Eger ≃, Dtsch.	56	48.50 N	10.37 E
Eger (Ohře) ≃, Europe	54	50.32 N	14.08 E
Eger → Cheb	54	50.01 N	12.25 E
Egeria Mountain ∧	182	53.55 N	130.22 W
Egernsund	41	54.54 N	9.37 E
Egerpohl	263	51.07 N	7.27 E
Egersund	26	58.27 N	6.00 E
Egerton	262	53.38 N	2.26 W
Egerton, Mount ∧	9	80.50 S	158.50 E
Egeskov ⊥	41	55.10 N	10.30 E
Egestorf	52	53.11 N	10.04 E
Egestorf [am Süntel]	52	52.17 N	9.31 E
Egg	58	47.26 N	9.54 E
Egg Creek ≃	198	48.22 N	100.47 W
Egge ⋀	52	51.40 N	8.55 E
Eggebek	41	54.37 N	9.22 E
Eggelsberg	60	48.05 N	13.00 E
Eggenberg, Schloss ⊥	61	47.05 N	15.25 E
Eggenburg	61	48.39 N	15.50 E
Eggenfelden	60	48.25 N	12.46 E
Eggenstein-Leopoldshafen	56	49.04 N	8.23 E
Eggerscheid	263	51.19 N	6.53 E
Eggersdorf	54	52.32 N	13.49 E
Eggesin	54	53.41 N	14.05 E
Egg Harbor City	208	39.31 N	74.38 W
Egg Island Point ›	208	39.11 N	75.08 W
Egg Lagoon	166	39.39 S	143.58 E
Egg Lake ⊜, Mb., Can.	184	54.21 N	101.26 W
Egg Lake ⊜, Sk., Can.	184	55.05 N	105.30 W
Egglestone Abbey ʋ[1]	44	54.32 N	1.54 W
Egglham	60	48.32 N	13.04 E
Egglkofen	60	48.24 N	12.27 E
Eggmühl	60	48.51 N	12.11 E
Egham	42	51.26 N	0.34 W
Egherta	144	2.04 N	43.11 E
Éghezée	56	50.36 N	4.54 E
Egijn ≃	88	49.24 N	103.36 E
Eğil	130	38.15 N	40.05 E
Egilsay I	46	59.09 N	2.56 W
Egilsstaðir	24a	65.16 N	14.18 W
Eging	60	48.43 N	13.16 E
Egipto → Egypt □[1]	140	27.00 N	30.00 E
Égletons	32	45.24 N	2.03 E
Eglin Air Force Base ■	194	30.29 N	86.30 W
Eglinton	48	55.02 N	7.11 W
Eglisau	58	47.34 N	8.32 E
Egloskerry	42	50.39 N	4.27 W
Égly	261	48.35 N	2.13 E
Egmond aan Zee	52	52.36 N	4.37 E
Egmond-Binnen	52	52.35 N	4.39 E
Egmont, Cape ›	172	39.17 S	173.45 E
Egmont, Mount → Taranaki, Mount ∧	172	39.18 S	174.04 E
Egmont Bay ⊂	186	46.35 N	64.12 W
Egmont Channel ɥ	220	27.36 N	82.45 W
Egmont Key I	220	27.35 N	82.46 W
Egmont National Park ♠	172	39.15 S	174.05 E
Egna (Neumarkt)	64	46.19 N	11.16 E
Egnach	58	47.33 N	9.23 E
Egnazia ⊥	68	40.53 N	17.24 E
Egoryevsk → Jegorjevsk	82	55.23 N	39.02 E
Egota ◆[8]	268	35.43 N	139.40 E
Egra	126	21.54 N	87.32 E
Egremont, Ab., Can.	182	54.02 N	113.08 W
Egremont, Eng., U.K.	44	54.29 N	3.33 W
Égreville	50	48.10 N	2.52 E
Eğridir	130	37.52 N	30.51 E
Eğridir Gölü ⊜	130	38.02 N	30.53 E
Eğriköy	130	38.44 N	27.21 E
Egrisskij chrebet ⋀	84	42.49 N	42.24 E
Egton	44	54.26 N	0.45 W
Egtved	41	55.37 N	9.18 E
Éguas, Rio das ≃	255	13.26 S	44.14 W
Éguilles	62	43.34 N	5.22 E
Eguisheim	58	48.03 N	7.18 E
Egum Atoll I[1]	164	9.25 S	151.55 E
Egvekinot	180	66.19 N	179.10 W
Egyházasrádóc	61	47.05 N	16.37 E
Egypt, Ma., U.S.	207	42.12 N	70.45 W
Egypt, Pa., U.S.	208	40.41 N	75.32 W
Egypt, Tx., U.S.	222	29.24 N	96.14 W
Egypt (Mişr) □[1], Afr.	136	27.00 N	30.00 E
Egypt (Mişr) □[1], Afr.	140	27.00 N	30.00 E
Egypt, Lake of ⊜[1]	194	37.35 N	88.55 W
Égypte → Egypt □[1]	140	27.00 N	30.00 E
Egyptian Museum ʋ	273c	30.03 N	31.14 E
Eha-Amufu	150	6.40 N	7.46 E
Ehekirchen	60	48.38 N	11.06 E
Ehen ≃	44	54.25 N	3.30 W
Ehime □[5]	96	33.40 N	132.50 E
Ehingen	58	48.17 N	9.43 E
Ehingen ◆[8]	263	51.22 N	6.42 E
Ehle ≃	54	52.12 N	11.44 E
Ehmen	54	52.24 N	10.41 E
Ehra-Lessien	54	52.34 N	10.46 E
Ehrang	56	49.49 N	6.41 E
Ehrenberg	200	33.36 N	114.31 W
Ehrenberg Range ⋀	162	23.18 S	130.20 E
Ehrenbreitstein, Feste ⊥	56	50.21 N	7.37 E
Ehrenburg ⊥	56	50.12 N	7.27 E
Ehrenfeld	214	40.22 N	78.46 W
Ehrenfriedersdorf	54	50.38 N	12.58 E
Ehrenhausen	61	46.43 N	15.35 E
Ehreshoven	56	50.58 N	7.20 E
Ehrhardt	192	33.05 N	81.00 W
Ehrhorn	52	53.10 N	9.53 E
Ehringhausen	263	51.11 N	7.33 E
Ehringhausen ◆[8]	263	51.09 N	7.11 E
Ehrwald	64	47.24 N	10.55 E
Ehwa Women's University ʋ[2]	271b	37.34 N	126.56 E
Ei	92	31.12 N	130.30 E
Eibar	34	43.11 N	2.28 W
Eibau	54	50.58 N	14.40 E
Eibelstadt	56	49.43 N	10.00 E
Eibenstock	54	50.29 N	12.35 E
Eibergen	52	52.06 N	6.39 E
Eibiswald	61	46.41 N	15.15 E
Eibsee ⊜	64	47.27 N	10.58 E
Eicha	54	50.21 N	10.34 E
Eich-Berg ∧[2]	264a	52.39 N	13.50 E
Eiche, Dtsch.	264a	52.34 N	13.36 E
Eiche, Dtsch.	264a	52.25 N	12.58 E
Eichenbarleben	54	52.10 N	11.24 E
Eichenbrandt	264a	52.38 N	13.51 E
Eichendorf	60	48.38 N	12.51 E
Eichgraben	61	48.10 N	15.59 E
Eichlinghofen ◆[8]	263	51.29 N	7.24 E
Eichsfeld ◆[1]	56	51.25 N	10.20 E
Eichstädt	264a	52.42 N	13.07 E
Eichstätt	60	48.54 N	11.12 E
Eichstetten	58	48.05 N	7.44 E
Eichtersheim	56	49.14 N	8.46 E
Eichwalde	54	52.22 N	13.37 E
Eickelborn	52	51.39 N	8.13 E
Eicken ◆[8]	263	51.13 N	6.26 E
Eickerend	263	51.13 N	6.34 E
Eickerkopf ∧[2]	263	51.21 N	7.42 E
Eicklingen	52	52.33 N	10.10 E
Eide	26	62.55 N	7.26 E
Eidelstedt ◆[8]	52	53.36 N	9.53 E
Eider ≃	41	54.19 N	8.58 E
Eiderstedt ›[1]	41	54.22 N	8.50 E
Eidfjord	26	60.28 N	7.05 E
Eidsvåg, Nor.	26	60.27 N	5.21 E
Eidsvåg, Nor.	26	62.47 N	8.03 E
Eidsvold	166	25.22 S	151.07 E
Eidsvoll	26	60.19 N	11.14 E
Eifa	56	50.58 N	8.34 E
Eifel ⋀	56	50.15 N	6.45 E
Eiffel, Tour ⊥	261	48.51 N	2.18 E
Eiffel Flats	154	18.15 S	29.59 E
Eifgenbach ≃	263	51.05 N	7.09 E
Eige, Carn ∧	46	57.17 N	5.07 W
Eigen ◆[8]	263	51.33 N	6.57 E
Eigenji	94	35.04 N	136.18 E
Eigenrieden	54	51.11 N	10.22 E
Eiger ∧	58	46.35 N	8.00 E
Eigg I	46	56.54 N	6.10 W
Eigg, Sound of ɥ	46	56.51 N	6.13 W
Eight Degree Channel ɥ	122	8.00 N	73.00 E
Eighteenmile Creek ≃, N.Y., U.S.	210	42.43 N	78.58 W
Eighteenmile Creek ≃, N.Y., U.S.	210	43.21 N	78.43 W
Eight Mile Creek ≃, On., Can.	284a	43.14 N	79.11 W
Eightmile Creek ≃, In., U.S.	216	40.57 N	85.22 W
Eightmile Creek ≃, Or., U.S.	224	45.36 N	121.05 W
Eights Coast ⩡[2]	9	73.30 S	93.00 W
Eighty Four	279b	40.11 N	80.08 W
Eighty Mile Beach ⩡[2]	162	19.45 S	121.00 E
Eiheiji	94	36.05 N	136.20 E
Eijerlandsche Gat ⊂	52	53.12 N	4.50 E
Eijsden	56	50.47 N	5.43 E
Eikeren ⊜	26	59.38 N	9.58 E
Eikisdalsvatnet ⊜	26	62.34 N	8.11 E
Eildon	169	37.14 S	145.56 E
Eildon, Lake ⊜[1]	169	37.11 S	145.55 E
Eilean Gowan Island I	212	45.02 N	79.25 W
Eileen	216	41.17 N	88.15 W
Eilenburg	54	51.27 N	12.37 E
Eil Malk I	175b	7.09 N	134.22 E
Eilpe ◆[8]	263	51.21 N	7.29 E
Eilsleben	54	52.09 N	11.13 E
Eimbeckhausen	52	52.14 N	9.25 E
Eimke	52	52.58 N	10.19 E
Eina	26	60.38 N	10.36 E
Einasleigh	166	18.31 S	144.05 E
Einasleigh ≃	166	17.30 S	142.17 E
Einbeck	52	51.49 N	9.52 E
Eindhoven	52	51.26 N	5.28 E
Eine	50	50.52 N	3.37 E
Einme	110	16.54 N	95.11 E
Einöd	56	49.16 N	7.19 E
Einödriegel ∧	60	48.56 N	13.02 E
Einruhr	56	50.35 N	6.22 E
Einsiedel	54	50.46 N	12.58 E
Einsiedeln	58	47.08 N	8.45 E
Einville-au-Jard	58	48.39 N	6.30 E
Eirauli	272c	19.10 N	72.59 E
Éire → Ireland □[1]	48	53.00 N	8.00 W
Eiru ≃	248	6.42 S	69.52 W
Eirunepé	248	6.40 S	69.52 W
Eisbach ≃	56	49.38 N	8.22 E
Eisch ≃	56	49.45 N	6.07 E
Eiseb ≃	156	20.33 S	20.59 E
Eisenach	54	50.59 N	10.19 E
Eisenberg, Dtsch.	54	50.58 N	11.53 E
Eisenberg, Dtsch.	56	49.38 N	8.05 E
Eisenberg ∧[2]	61	47.12 N	16.24 E
Eisenerz	61	47.33 N	14.53 E
Eisenerzer Alpen ⋀	61	47.28 N	14.45 E
Eisenhower Center ʋ	198	38.54 N	97.12 W
Eisenhower Memorial Park ♠	276	40.44 N	73.34 W
Eisenhüttenstadt	54	52.10 N	14.39 E
Eisenkappel	61	46.29 N	14.35 E
Eisenschmitt	56	50.03 N	6.43 E
Eisenstadt	61	47.51 N	16.32 E
Eisfeld	54	50.26 N	10.54 E
Eisgarn	61	48.54 N	15.06 E
Eishken	46	58.01 N	6.32 W
Eishort, Loch ⊂	46	57.10 N	5.59 W
Eišiškės	76	54.10 N	25.00 E
Eisk → Jejsk	78	46.42 N	38.16 E
Eisleben	54	51.31 N	11.32 E
Eislingen	56	48.42 N	9.42 E
Eisriesenwelt ⩡[5]	64	47.32 N	13.10 E
Eita	174t	1.21 N	173.05 E
Eitorf	56	50.46 N	7.26 E
Eivissa	34	38.54 N	1.26 E
Eivissa (Ibiza) I	34	39.00 N	1.25 E
Ejasi → Eyasi, Lake ⊜	154	3.40 S	35.05 E
Ejby, Dan.	41	55.30 N	12.07 E
Ejby, Dan.	41	55.26 N	9.57 E
Ejea de los Caballeros	34	42.08 N	1.08 W
Ejeda	157b	24.20 S	44.31 E
Ejército Rebelde, Presa ⊜[1]	286b	23.01 N	82.20 W
Ejido	246	8.33 N	71.14 W
Ejido Jaboncillos	232	28.57 N	102.39 W
Ejigbo	273a	6.33 N	3.18 E
Ejin Horo Qi	102	39.27 N	109.40 E
Ejin Qi	102	41.50 N	100.50 E
Ejstrup	41	55.59 N	9.17 E
Ejura	150	7.23 N	1.22 W
Ejutla de Crespo	234	16.34 N	96.44 W
Ekalaka	198	45.53 N	104.33 W
Ekáli	267c	38.07 N	23.50 E
Ekanga	152	2.23 S	23.14 E
Ekas	115b	8.53 S	116.27 E
Ekaterinburg → Jekaterinburg	86	56.51 N	60.36 E

Symbol	English	Deutsch	Español	Français	Português
≃	River	Fluß	Río	Rivière	Rio
≊	Canal	Kanal	Canal	Canal	Canal
V	Waterfall, Rapids	Wasserfall, Stromschnellen	Cascada, Rápidos	Chute d'eau, Rapides	Cascata, Rápidos
ɥ	Strait	Meeresstraße	Estrecho	Détroit	Estreito
⊂	Bay, Gulf	Bucht, Golf	Bahía, Golfo	Baie, Golfe	Baía, Golfo
⊜	Lake, Lakes	See, Seen	Lago, Lagos	Lac, Lacs	Lago, Lagos
⩫	Swamp	Sumpf	Pantano	Marais	Pântano
⩩	Ice Features, Glacier	Eis- und Gletscherformen	Accidentes Glaciales	Formes glaciaires	Acidentes glaciares
▾	Other Hydrographic Features	Andere Hydrographische Objekte	Otros Elementos Hidrográficos	Autres données hydrographiques	Outros acidentes hidrográficos
✦	Submarine Features	Untermeerische Objekte	Accidentes Submarinos	Formes de relief sous-marin	Acidentes submarinos
□	Political Unit	Politische Einheit	Unidad Politica	Entité politique	Unidade política
ʋ	Cultural Institution	Kulturelle Institution	Institución Cultural	Institution culturelle	Instituição cultural
⊥	Historical Site	Historische Stätte	Sitio Histórico	Site historique	Sitio histórico
♠	Recreational Site	Erholungs- und Ferienort	Sitio de Recreo	Centre de loisirs	Area de Lazer
⊠	Airport	Flughafen	Aeropuerto	Aéroport	Aeroporto
■	Military Installation	Militäranlage	Instalación Militar	Installation militaire	Instalação militar
◆	Miscellaneous	Verschiedenes	Misceláneo	Divers	Diversos

ENGLISH: Name — Page — Lat.°′ — Long.°′
DEUTSCH: Name — Seite — Breite°′ — Länge°′ E = Ost

Name	Page	Lat.°′	Long.°′
Ekaterinodar			
→ Krasnodar	78	45.02 N	39.00 E
Ekaterinoslav			
→ Dnepropetrovsk	78	48.27 N	34.59 E
Ekeby	41	56.00 N	12.58 E
Ekenäs (Taamisaari)	26	59.58 N	23.26 E
Ekenässjön	26	57.30 N	15.00 E
Ekerö I	40	59.18 N	17.43 E
Eket, Nig.	150	4.39 N	7.56 E
Eket, Sve.	41	56.15 N	13.11 E
Eketahuna	172	40.39 S	175.42 E
Ekhínos	38	41.17 N	24.59 E
Ekiatapskij chrebet ⋏	74	68.30 N	179.00 E
Ekibastuz	86	51.42 N	75.22 E
Ekimčan	89	53.04 N	132.58 E
Ekitykskij chrebet ⋏	180	67.45 N	179.00 E
Eko			
→ Lagos	150	6.27 N	3.24 E
Ekoli	152	0.23 S	24.16 E
Ekoln ◎	40	59.45 N	17.37 E
Ekolsund	40	59.37 N	17.22 E
Ekolsundsviken ⊂	40	59.35 N	17.24 E
Ekombe	152	1.16 N	21.36 E
Ekonda	74	65.47 N	105.17 E
Ekoungounou	152	0.33 S	15.38 E
Ekovamou	152	0.07 N	16.31 E
Ekpoma	150	6.46 N	6.08 E
Eksāra	272b	22.38 N	88.17 E
Eksel	56	51.09 N	5.23 E
Eksjö	26	57.40 N	14.57 E
Ekuk	180	58.49 N	158.34 W
Ekuku	152	0.42 S	21.38 E
Ekuta	152	2.59 N	18.42 E
Ekwan ≃	176	53.14 N	82.13 W
Ekwata	152	0.13 S	9.18 E
Ekwendeni	154	11.23 S	33.50 E
Ekwok	180	59.22 N	157.30 W
Ela	110	19.37 N	96.13 E
El Aaiún (La'youn)	148	27.09 N	13.12 W
El Abiadh Sidi Cheikh	148	32.56 N	0.42 E
El 'Açâba □4	150	16.10 N	11.30 W
El 'Açâba ⋏1	150	16.00 N	12.00 W
El-			
→ Ad-, Al-, An-, Ar-, As-, Ash-, At-, Az-			
El Adde	144	2.35 N	46.09 E
El Adeb Larache	148	27.22 N	8.52 E
El Adelanto	236	14.10 N	89.50 W
El Affroun	34	36.30 N	2.38 E
El Agreb	148	30.48 N	5.30 E
El Aguacate	286c	10.28 N	66.59 W
El Aguacate ≃	234	18.16 N	100.40 W
El Aguilar	252	23.12 S	65.42 W
El Agustino	286d	12.03 S	76.59 W
El Agustino, Cerro ∧2	286d	12.04 S	77.00 W
Elaía	38	39.35 N	20.20 E
Elaine	194	34.18 N	90.51 W
El Alamein			
→ Al-'Alamayn	140	30.49 N	28.57 E
El Álamo, Méx.	196	27.32 N	100.52 W
El Álamo, Méx.	196	26.29 N	99.46 W
El Álamo, Méx.	204	31.34 N	116.02 W
El Alia	36	37.10 N	10.03 E
El Alto, Arg.	252	28.18 S	65.22 W
El Alto, Perú	246	4.18 S	81.07 W
Elam	285	39.51 N	75.32 W
Elamanchili	122	17.33 N	82.52 E
El Amparo de Apure	246	7.06 N	70.45 W
Elan ≃, Rom.	38	46.07 N	28.04 E
Elan ≃, Wales, U.K.	42	52.17 N	3.31 W
Élancourt	261	48.47 N	1.58 E
Elands ≃, S. Afr.	156	25.10 S	29.10 E
Elands ≃, S. Afr.	158	25.31 S	26.39 E
Elandsbaai	158	32.19 S	18.21 E
Elandsfontein	273d	26.10 S	28.12 E
Elandsvlei	158	32.19 S	19.33 E
El Angel	246	0.37 N	77.56 W
Elanora Heights	274a	33.42 S	151.17 E
El Aouinet	36	35.52 N	7.54 E
El Arahal	34	37.16 N	5.33 W
El Arba	34	36.37 N	3.13 E
El Arco	232	28.00 N	113.25 W
El Arenal	234	20.47 N	103.42 W
El Aricha	148	34.09 N	1.10 W
El Aroussa	36	36.22 N	9.28 E
El Arrayán	286e	33.21 S	70.28 W
Elassón	38	39.54 N	22.11 E
Elat	132	29.33 N	34.57 E
Elat, Gulf of			
→ Aqaba, Gulf of ⊂	128	29.00 N	34.40 E
Elat, Sede Te'ufa ⊠	132	29.34 N	34.55 E
El Avagi	144	3.36 N	46.57 E
El Ávila, Cerro ∧	286c	10.33 N	66.52 W
El Ávila, Parque Nacional ♦	246	10.35 N	66.48 W
Elazığ	130	38.41 N	39.14 E
Elazığ □4	130	38.35 N	39.30 E
El Azúcar, Presa de ◎1	196	26.10 N	99.00 W
El Azul, Sierra ⋏	234	23.25 N	100.30 W
Elba, Al., U.S.	194	31.24 N	86.04 W
Elba, Mi., U.S.	216	43.02 N	83.26 W
Elba, N.Y., U.S.	210	43.04 N	78.11 W
Elba, Isola d' I	66	42.46 N	10.17 E
Elba			
→ Elbe ≃	30	53.50 N	9.00 E
El'ban	89	50.06 N	136.31 E
El Banco	246	9.00 N	73.58 W
El Barco de Avila	34	40.21 N	5.31 W
El Barco de Valdeorras	34	42.25 N	6.59 W
El Barreal	200	31.17 N	107.10 W
El Barril	234	23.02 N	102.08 W
Elbasan	38	41.06 N	20.05 E
Elbaşı	130	38.41 N	35.59 E
El Baúl	246	8.57 N	68.17 W
El Baúl, Cerro ∧, Méx.	234	17.38 N	100.19 W
El Baúl, Cerro ∧, Méx.	234	16.36 N	94.13 W
Elbe	224	46.45 N	121.49 W
Elbe (Labe) ≃	30	53.50 N	9.00 E
Elbe, Île d'			
→ Elba, Isola di I	66	42.46 N	10.17 E
Elbe-Havel-Kanal ≍	54	52.24 N	12.23 E
El Beïd (Ebeji) ≃	146	12.32 N	14.11 E
El-Beida			
→ Al-Baydā'	146	32.46 N	21.43 E
Elbe-Lübeck-Kanal ≍	54	53.50 N	10.36 E
Elberfeld ◆8	263	51.16 N	7.08 E
Elbert	198	39.13 N	104.32 W
Elbert, Mount ∧	200	39.07 N	106.27 W
Elberta	190	44.37 N	86.13 W
Elberton	192	34.06 N	82.52 W
Elbeuf	50	49.17 N	1.00 E
Elbeyli	130	36.41 N	37.26 E
El Beyyadh	148	33.40 N	1.01 E
Elbing			
→ Elbląg	30	54.10 N	19.25 E
Elbingerode	54	51.45 N	10.46 E
Elbistan	130	38.13 N	37.12 E
Elbląg (Elbing)	30	54.10 N	19.25 E
Elbląg □4	30	54.00 N	19.30 E
El Bluff	236	11.59 N	83.40 W
El Bolsón	254	41.58 S	71.31 W
El Bonillo	34	38.57 N	2.32 W
El-Borj	34	35.43 N	5.40 W
El-Borouj	148	32.30 N	7.10 W
El Bosque, Chile	286e	33.34 S	70.41 W
El Bosque, Méx.	234	17.04 N	92.44 W
El Boulaïda	148	36.28 N	2.50 E
El Boulaïda □5	148	36.20 N	2.20 E
Elbow	184	51.07 N	106.35 W
Elbow ≃	182	51.03 N	114.02 W
Elbow Cay I	238	23.57 N	80.29 W
Elbow Lake	198	45.59 N	95.58 W
Elbow Lake ◎	184	54.50 N	100.53 W
Elbridge	210	43.02 N	76.27 W
El'brus, gora (Mount Elbrus) ∧	84	43.21 N	42.26 E
Elbrus, Mount			
→ El'brus, gora ∧	84	43.21 N	42.26 E
El'brusskij	84	43.38 N	42.10 E
Elbsandsteingebirge ⋏	54	50.50 N	14.20 E
Elburg	52	52.26 N	5.50 E
El Burgo de Osma	34	41.35 N	3.04 W
Elburn	216	41.53 N	88.28 W
Elburz Mountains			
→ Alborz, Reshteh-ye Kūhhā-ye ⋏	128	36.00 N	53.00 E
El'buzd	83	46.53 N	39.41 E
El'buzd ≃	83	46.53 N	39.43 E
El Cabezo, Arrecife ✤2	234	19.04 N	95.51 W
El Caburé	252	26.01 S	62.22 W
El Caimanero, Laguna ⊂	234	23.00 N	106.07 W
El Cajon	228	32.47 N	116.57 W
El Cajón, Embalse ◎1	236	15.00 N	87.35 W
El Calafate	254	50.20 S	72.18 W
El Callao	246	7.21 N	61.49 W
El Calvario, Col.	246	4.22 N	73.40 W
El Calvario, Ven.	246	8.59 N	67.00 W
El Calvario ◆8	286b	23.05 N	82.20 W
El Campamento	240m	18.22 N	66.28 W
El Campamento ◆8	266a	40.24 N	3.46 W
El Campo	222	29.11 N	96.16 W
El Capitan ∧, Ca., U.S.	226	37.43 N	119.38 W
El Capitan ∧, Mt., U.S.	202	46.01 N	114.23 W
El Caracol Depósito de Evaporación Solar ✦3	286a	19.35 N	99.00 W
El Caribe	286c	10.37 N	66.50 W
El Carmen, Arg.	252	24.23 S	65.16 W
El Cármen, Bol.	248	18.49 S	58.33 W
El Carmen, Chile	286e	33.21 S	70.43 W
El Carmen, Col.	246	8.30 N	73.27 W
El Carmen, Méx.	234	15.35 N	93.05 W
El Carmen, Perú	248	13.30 S	76.04 W
El Carmen, Ven.	286c	10.24 N	67.01 W
El Carmen, Ven.	286c	10.24 N	66.50 W
El Carmen ≃	232	30.42 N	106.29 W
El Carmen, Canal ≍	286e	33.18 S	70.41 W
El Carmen, Laguna ⊂	234	18.17 N	93.48 W
El Carmen de Bolívar	246	9.43 N	75.08 W
El Carricito	232	28.24 N	103.23 W
El Carril	252	25.05 S	65.28 W
El Casco	196	25.34 N	104.35 W
El Castillo de La Concepción	236	11.01 N	84.24 W
El Cedral	236	16.26 N	90.03 W
El Cedrito	232	29.11 N	101.59 W
El Cenajo, Embalse de ◎1	34	38.25 N	2.00 W
El Centinela	204	32.38 N	115.40 W
El Centinela, Cerro ∧	234	19.13 N	104.17 W
El Centro	204	32.47 N	115.33 W
El Cerrito, Col.	246	3.42 N	76.19 W
El Cerrito, Ca., U.S.	226	37.54 N	122.18 W
El Cerrito, Ca., U.S.	228	37.54 N	122.18 W
El Cerro, Bol.	248	17.31 S	61.34 W
El Cerro, Ur.	258	34.00 S	58.15 W
El Cerro Del Aripo ∧	241r	10.43 N	61.15 W
El Chamal	234	23.56 N	97.54 W
El Chante	234	19.41 N	104.10 W
Elche de la Sierra	34	38.27 N	2.03 W
Elche			
→ Elx	34	38.15 N	0.42 W
El Chichonal, Volcán ∧1	234	17.22 N	93.14 W
El Chile, Montaña ∧	236	14.22 N	86.51 W
El'chkakvun ≃	180	68.42 N	171.00 E
Elcho	190	45.26 N	89.11 W
Elcho Island I	164	11.55 S	135.45 E
El Chorrillo	252	33.18 S	66.16 W
El Ciprés	204	31.50 N	116.38 W
El Cobre	240p	20.03 N	75.57 W
El Cocuy	246	6.25 N	72.27 W
El Cojo	286c	10.37 N	66.53 W
El Cojo, Quebrada ≃	286c	10.37 N	66.53 W
El Colorado	252	26.18 S	59.22 W
El Cóndor, Cerro ∧	252	26.38 S	68.22 W
El Congo	236	13.54 N	89.30 W
El Corazón	246	1.12 S	79.06 W
El Corcovado	254	43.32 S	71.36 W
El Corozo	286c	10.35 N	66.58 W
El Corpus	236	13.16 N	87.03 W
El Corte ≃	234	17.03 N	94.54 W
El Corte de Madera Creek ≃	282	37.19 N	122.20 W
El Cortijo	286e	33.22 S	70.42 W
El Coto	240m	18.28 N	66.44 W
El Coyote	200	30.50 N	112.40 W
El Coyote ≃	232	30.32 N	113.02 W
El Coyote, Laguna ◎	196	27.14 N	103.18 W
El Cozón	232	31.18 N	112.29 W
El Cristo	240p	20.07 N	75.45 W
El Cubo			
→ Casigua	246	8.46 N	72.30 W
El Cuco	236	13.10 N	88.07 W
El Cuervo, Laguna ◎	232	29.17 N	105.57 W
El Cuidado	234	22.20 N	103.07 W
El Cuy	254	39.56 S	68.20 W
Elda	34	38.29 N	0.47 W
Eldagsen	52	52.10 N	9.40 E
El Dambahaddo	144	3.17 N	46.40 E
El Dátil	232	30.07 N	112.15 W
Elde ≃	54	53.14 N	11.27 E
Eldekanal ≍	54	53.24 N	11.36 E
Eldena, Dtsch.	54	53.13 N	11.25 E
Eldena, Dtsch.	54	54.05 N	13.26 E
El Der ∨	144	8.49 N	47.28 E
El Dere	144	5.07 N	43.10 E
Elder Island I	276	40.38 N	73.23 W
Elder Mills	275b	43.49 N	79.38 W
Eldersville	214	40.21 N	80.29 W
Elderton	214	40.42 N	79.21 W
El Descanso	204	32.12 N	116.55 W
El Desemboque, Méx.	232	29.30 N	112.27 W
El Desemboque, Méx.	232	30.30 N	112.59 W
Eldforsen	40	60.26 N	14.13 E
El'dikan	74	60.48 N	135.11 E
Eldingen	52	52.41 N	10.21 E
Eld Inlet ⊂	224	47.04 N	123.01 W
Eldivan	130	40.32 N	33.31 E
El Diviso	246	1.22 N	78.14 W
El Djazaïr (Algiers)	148	36.47 N	3.03 E
El Djazaïr □5	148	36.50 N	3.00 E
El Djelfa	148	34.40 N	3.15 E
El Djelfa □5	148	35.20 N	3.50 E
El Doce	234	17.13 N	94.03 W
Eldon, Ia., U.S.	190	40.55 N	92.13 W
Eldon, Mo., U.S.	194	38.20 N	92.34 W
Eldon Hazlet State Park ♦	219	38.39 N	89.22 W
Eldora, Ia., U.S.	190	42.21 N	93.05 W
Eldora, Pa., U.S.	279b	40.10 N	79.53 W
Eldorado, Arg.	252	26.24 S	54.38 W
Eldorado, Bra.	252	24.32 S	48.06 W
El Dorado, Méx.	232	24.17 N	107.21 W
El Dorado, Ar., U.S.	194	33.12 N	92.39 W
El Dorado, Ca., U.S.	226	38.41 N	120.51 W
Eldorado, Il., U.S.	194	37.48 N	88.26 W
El Dorado, Ks., U.S.	198	37.49 N	96.51 W
Eldorado, Oh., U.S.	218	39.54 N	84.40 W
Eldorado, Ok., U.S.	196	34.28 N	99.38 W
Eldorado, Tx., U.S.	196	30.51 N	100.36 W
El Dorado, Ven.	246	6.44 N	61.38 W
El Dorado □6	226	38.43 N	120.48 W
Eldorado Hills	226	38.37 N	120.27 W
Eldoradopark	273d	26.18 S	27.53 E
El Dorado Park ♦	280	33.49 N	118.05 W
Eldorado Peak ∧	224	48.32 N	121.08 W
El Dorado Springs	194	37.52 N	94.01 W
Eldoret	154	0.31 N	35.17 E
Eldred, Il., U.S.	219	39.17 N	90.33 W
Eldred, N.Y., U.S.	210	41.32 N	74.53 W
Eldred, Pa., U.S.	214	41.57 N	78.23 W
Eldridge	190	41.39 N	90.35 W
Eldridge, Mount ∧	180	64.46 N	141.48 W
Eldridges Hill	285	39.40 N	75.18 W
El Dudu	144	2.37 N	41.46 E
El Durazno, Arroyo ≃	258	34.41 S	58.52 W
Eleanor	188	38.32 N	81.55 W
Eleanor, Lake ◎1	226	37.59 N	119.51 W
Eleasar	158	26.40 S	26.53 E
Electra	196	34.01 N	98.55 W
Electric City	202	47.56 N	119.02 W
Eleele	229b	21.55 N	159.35 W
Elefante, Isla del			
→ Elephant Island I	9	61.10 S	55.14 W
Elefantes, Estero ⊂2	254	46.10 S	73.41 W
Elefantes, Rio dos (Olifants) ≃	156	24.10 S	32.40 E
Elegest ≃	88	51.32 N	94.05 E
El Eglab ◆2	148	26.25 N	5.00 W
Elei, Wādī ∨	140	22.04 N	34.27 E
Eleja	76	56.26 N	23.42 E
Elektrogorsk	82	55.53 N	38.47 E
Elektrostal'	82	55.47 N	38.28 E
Elektrougli	82	55.43 N	38.13 E
Elektrozavod	80	52.34 N	54.01 E
Elele	150	5.07 N	6.48 E
Elena	38	42.56 N	25.53 E
El Encantado	286c	10.27 N	66.47 W
El Encanto, Col.	246	1.37 S	73.14 W
El Encanto, Guat.	232	17.17 N	89.34 W
Elend	54	51.44 N	10.41 E
Elepete	273a	6.41 N	3.28 E
Elephant, Mount ∧2	169	37.58 S	143.12 E
Elephanta Caves ⊥5	272c	18.58 N	72.56 E
Elephanta Island (Ghārāpuri) I	272c	18.57 N	72.55 E
Elephant Butte Lake State Park ♦	200	33.11 N	107.14 W
Elephant Butte Reservoir ◎1	200	33.19 N	107.10 W
Elephant Island I	9	61.10 S	55.14 W
Elephant Lake ◎	212	45.08 N	78.07 W
Elephant Mountain ∧	188	44.46 N	70.46 W
Elesbão Veloso	250	6.13 S	42.08 W
Eleşkirt	130	39.48 N	42.42 E
El Espinal	234	16.29 N	95.03 W
El Estor	236	15.32 N	89.21 W
Elets			
→ Jelec	76	52.37 N	38.30 E
El Eulma	148	36.08 N	5.40 E
Eleusis			
→ Elevsís	38	38.02 N	23.32 E
Eleutério	256	22.19 S	46.43 W
Eleutero ≃	70	38.06 N	13.29 E
Eleuthera I	238	25.10 N	76.14 W
Eleuthera Point ➤	238	24.40 N	76.11 W
Eleva	190	44.34 N	91.28 W
Eleven Point ≃	194	36.09 N	91.05 W
Elevsínos, Kólpos ⊂	267c	38.02 N	23.34 E
Elevsís	38	38.02 N	23.32 E
Elevtheroúpolis	38	40.55 N	24.16 E
El Fahs	36	36.22 N	9.55 E
El Faro, It.	71	40.36 N	8.13 E
El Faro, P.R.	240m	18.00 N	66.47 W
Elfenbeinküste			
→ Ivory Coast □1	150	8.00 N	5.00 W
El Ferrol del Caudillo	34	43.29 N	8.14 W
Elfers	220	28.13 N	82.43 W
Elfgen	263	51.05 N	6.32 E
Elfin Cove	180	58.12 N	136.20 W
Elfrida	200	31.41 N	109.41 W
Elfros	184	51.43 N	103.52 W
El Fud	144	7.20 N	42.50 E
El Fuerte	232	26.25 N	108.39 W
El Galpón	252	25.23 S	64.38 W
Elgershausen	56	51.16 N	9.22 E
El Ghazawet	148	35.06 N	1.51 W
Elgin, Austl.	168a	33.31 S	115.37 E
Elgin, On., Can.	212	44.36 N	76.13 W
Elgin, Scot., U.K.	46	57.39 N	3.20 W
Elgin, Il., U.S.	216	42.02 N	88.16 W
Elgin, Ia., U.S.	190	42.57 N	91.37 W
Elgin, Mn., U.S.	190	44.07 N	92.15 W
Elgin, Ne., U.S.	198	41.59 N	98.05 W
Elgin, N.D., U.S.	198	46.24 N	101.50 W
Elgin, Oh., U.S.	216	40.44 N	84.28 W
Elgin, Ok., U.S.	196	34.46 N	98.17 W
Elgin, Or., U.S.	202	45.33 N	117.54 W
Elgin, Pa., U.S.	214	41.54 N	79.45 W
Elgin, Tx., U.S.	222	30.20 N	97.22 W
Elgin □6	214	42.42 N	81.15 W
Elgin, Lake ◎	206	45.45 N	71.20 W
Elgol	46	57.09 N	6.06 W
El Golfete ◎	236	15.44 N	88.53 W
El Goloso ◆8	266a	40.33 N	3.42 W
Elgon, Mount ∧	154	1.08 N	34.33 E
Elgoras, gora ∧	24	68.06 N	31.30 E
El Granada	226	37.30 N	122.28 W
El Grara	148	32.46 N	4.34 E
El Grove	34	42.30 N	8.52 W
El Grullo	234	19.48 N	104.13 W
El Guaje	232	27.52 N	103.18 W
El Guaje, Laguna ◎	232	28.00 N	103.13 W
El Guamo	246	10.02 N	74.59 W
El Guanábano	286c	10.24 N	67.01 W
El Guapo	246	10.09 N	65.58 W
El Guarapo	286c	10.36 N	66.58 W
El Guayabo de Abajo	232	26.00 N	107.26 W
El Guayaneco, Parque Nacional ♦	254	48.15 S	75.30 W
El'gygytgyn, ozero ◎	180	67.30 N	172.00 E
El Hadjar	36	36.48 N	7.45 E
Elham	42	51.10 N	1.07 E
El Hammâmi ◆1	148	23.03 N	11.30 W
El Hank ⊥4	148	24.30 N	7.00 W
El Haouaria	36	37.03 N	11.02 E
El Hatillo	286c	10.26 N	66.49 W
El Hatillo, Quebrada ≃	286c	10.27 N	66.47 W
El Havre			
→ Le Havre	50	49.30 N	0.08 E
El Higo	234	21.46 N	98.28 W
Elhovo	38	42.10 N	26.34 E
El Huecú	252	37.37 S	70.36 W
El Huisache	234	22.55 N	100.25 W
Eliase	164	8.21 S	130.47 E
Elías Romero	258	34.46 S	58.52 W
Eliasville	196	32.57 N	98.46 W
Elida, N.M., U.S.	196	33.56 N	103.39 W
Elida, Oh., U.S.	216	40.47 N	84.12 W
El Ídolo, Isla I	234	21.25 N	97.27 W
El Idrissia	148	34.30 N	2.37 E
Elila	154	2.43 S	25.53 E
Elila ≃	154	2.45 S	25.53 E
Elim, Namibia	156	17.48 S	15.31 E
Elim, S. Afr.	158	34.35 S	19.45 E
Elim, Ak., U.S.	180	64.37 N	162.15 W
Elimsport	210	41.08 N	77.02 W
El Infiernillo, Canal ≍	232	29.09 N	112.15 W
Elingampangu	152	2.03 S	24.02 E
Elin Pelin	38	42.40 N	23.36 E
Eliot	188	43.09 N	70.48 W
Elipa	152	0.53 S	24.34 E
Elisabeth-Sophien-Koog	41	54.30 N	8.53 E
Élisabethville	261	48.58 N	1.51 E
Élisabethville			
→ Lubumbashi	154	11.40 S	27.28 E
Elisenvaara	24	61.25 N	29.46 E
Eliseu Martins	250	8.13 S	43.42 W
Elista	80	46.16 N	44.14 E
Elizabeth, Austl.	168b	34.43 S	138.40 E
Elizabeth, Co., U.S.	200	39.21 N	104.35 W
Elizabeth, Il., U.S.	190	42.19 N	90.13 W
Elizabeth, La., U.S.	194	30.52 N	92.47 W
Elizabeth, N.J., U.S.	210	40.39 N	74.12 W
Elizabeth, Pa., U.S.	214	40.16 N	79.53 W
Elizabeth, W.V., U.S.	188	39.03 N	81.23 W
Elizabeth ≃, N.J., U.S.	276	40.38 N	74.12 W
Elizabeth ≃, Va., U.S.	208	36.54 N	76.20 W
Elizabeth, Bahía ⊂	246a	0.38 S	91.27 W
Elizabeth, Cape ➤	224	47.22 N	124.22 W
Elizabeth, Lake ◎1	282	37.33 N	121.58 W
Elizabeth, West Branch ≃	276	40.42 N	74.14 W
Elizabeth Bay ⊂	156	27.04 S	15.11 E
Elizabeth City	192	36.18 N	76.13 W
Elizabeth Creek ≃	222	33.02 N	97.14 W
Elizabeth Islands II	207	41.27 N	70.47 W
Elizabeth Lake ◎	281	42.38 N	83.23 W
Elizabeth Lake Estates	281	42.38 N	83.22 W
Elizabeth Park ♦	281	42.07 N	83.11 W
Elizabeth Reef I1	160	29.56 S	159.04 E
Elizabethton	192	36.20 N	82.12 W
Elizabethtown, Il., U.S.	194	37.26 N	88.18 W
Elizabethtown, In., U.S.	218	39.08 N	85.48 W
Elizabethtown, Ky., U.S.	194	37.41 N	85.51 W
Elizabethtown, N.Y., U.S.	188	44.12 N	73.35 W
Elizabethtown, N.C., U.S.	192	34.37 N	78.36 W
Elizabethtown, Pa., U.S.	208	40.09 N	76.36 W
Elizabethville	208	40.32 N	76.48 W
Eliza Howell Park ♦	281	42.24 N	83.16 W
Elizaville, In., U.S.	218	40.08 N	86.24 W
Elizaville, N.Y., U.S.	210	42.03 N	73.48 W
El-Jadida (Mazagan)	148	33.16 N	8.30 W
El-Jadida □4	148	33.00 N	8.40 W
El Jaralito	232	26.07 N	104.10 W
El Jebel	200	39.23 N	107.05 W
El-Jebha	34	35.13 N	4.38 W
El Jem	148	35.18 N	10.43 E
El Jícaro ≃	236	13.31 N	86.00 W
El Jobean	220	26.58 N	82.13 W
El Juile	234	17.45 N	94.59 W
Ełk	30	53.50 N	22.22 E
Elk □6	214	41.26 N	78.43 W
Elk ≃, Ab., Can.	182	52.55 N	115.40 W
Elk ≃, B.C., Can.	182	49.10 N	115.14 W
Ełk ≃, Pol.	30	53.31 N	22.47 E
Elk ≃, U.S.	194	34.46 N	87.16 W
Elk ≃, Co., U.S.	200	40.29 N	106.58 W
Elk ≃, Ks., U.S.	198	37.15 N	95.41 W
Elk ≃, Mn., U.S.	190	45.18 N	93.34 W
Elk ≃, Mo., U.S.	194	36.38 N	94.38 W
Elk ≃, W.V., U.S.	188	38.21 N	81.38 W
Elk ≃, Wi., U.S.	190	45.42 N	90.37 W
Elkader	190	42.51 N	91.24 W
El Kantara	148	33.41 N	10.55 E
El-Karafab	140	18.10 N	31.36 E
Elk Bayou ≃	226	36.06 N	119.24 W
Elk City	196	35.24 N	99.24 W
Elk City Lake ◎1	198	37.15 N	95.55 W
Elk Creek	204	39.36 N	122.32 W
Elk Creek ≃, Ok., U.S.	196	34.48 N	99.09 W
Elk Creek ≃, Or., U.S.	202	43.38 N	123.34 W
Elk Creek ≃, Pa., U.S.	214	42.01 N	80.22 W
Elk Creek ≃, S.D., U.S.	198	44.15 N	102.22 W
Elk Creek ≃, Wa., U.S.	224	46.38 N	123.17 W
Elkedra ≃	162	21.08 S	136.22 E
El Kef	148	36.11 N	8.43 E
El Kef □8	148	36.00 N	9.00 E
El-Kelâa-des-Srarhna	148	32.02 N	7.23 W
El-Kelâa-des-Srarhna □4	148	32.05 N	7.30 W
El Kere	144	5.51 N	42.06 E
El Kerma	34	35.36 N	0.35 W
Elk Grove	226	38.24 N	121.22 W
Elk Grove Village	278	42.00 N	87.58 W
Elkhart, Il., U.S.	219	40.01 N	89.29 W
Elkhart, In., U.S.	216	41.40 N	85.58 W
Elkhart, Ks., U.S.	198	37.00 N	101.53 W
Elkhart, Tx., U.S.	222	31.38 N	95.35 W
Elkhart □6	216	41.35 N	85.50 W
Elkhart ≃	216	41.41 N	85.58 W
Elkhart Lake	190	43.50 N	88.01 W
El Khaṭṭ ⊥4	148	22.40 N	10.05 W
Elkhead Creek ≃	200	40.31 N	107.26 W
Elkhead Mountains ⋏	200	40.50 N	107.05 W
Elk Hills ⋏2	226	35.15 N	119.25 W
El Khnâchîch ⊥4	148	21.50 N	3.45 W
Elkhorn, Mb., Can.	184	49.58 N	101.14 W
Elk Horn, Ia., U.S.	198	41.35 N	95.03 W
Elkhorn, Wi., U.S.	216	42.40 N	88.32 W
Elkhorn ≃	198	41.07 N	96.19 W
Elkhorn City	192	37.18 N	82.21 W
Elkhorn Creek ≃, Ky., U.S.	218	38.19 N	84.52 W
Elkhorn Creek ≃, Mo., U.S.	219	39.05 N	91.20 W
Elkhorn Mountain ∧	182	49.48 N	125.50 W
Elkin	192	36.14 N	80.50 W
Elkins	188	38.55 N	79.50 W
Elkins Park	208	40.04 N	75.07 W
Elk Island I	184	50.45 N	96.32 W
Elk Island National Park ♦	182	53.37 N	112.45 W
Elkland	210	41.59 N	77.18 W
Elk Mills	208	39.39 N	75.49 W
Elk Mountain	200	41.41 N	106.24 W
Elk Mountain ∧, Wa., U.S.	224	46.08 N	122.28 W
Elk Mountain ∧, Wy., U.S.	200	41.38 N	106.32 W
Elk Neck ➤1	208	39.35 N	75.55 W
Elk Neck State Park ♦	208	39.30 N	75.58 W
Elko, B.C., Can.	182	49.18 N	115.07 W
Elko, Nv., U.S.	204	40.49 N	115.45 W
El Kouif	36	35.29 N	8.19 E
Elk Peak ∧	202	46.27 N	110.46 W
Elk Plain	224	47.04 N	122.24 W
Elk Point, Ab., Can.	182	53.54 N	110.54 W
Elk Point, S.D., U.S.	198	42.41 N	96.41 W
Elk Rapids	190	44.53 N	85.24 W
El Krib	36	36.19 N	9.09 E
Elkridge	284b	39.12 N	76.42 W
Elk River, Id., U.S.	202	46.47 N	116.10 W
Elk River, Mn., U.S.	190	45.18 N	93.35 W
Elk River ⊂	208	39.31 N	75.55 W
El Kseur	34	36.46 N	4.49 E
Elk State Park ♦	214	41.38 N	78.34 W
Elkton, Ky., U.S.	194	36.48 N	87.09 W
Elkton, Md., U.S.	208	39.36 N	75.50 W
Elkton, Mi., U.S.	190	43.49 N	83.10 W
Elkton, Oh., U.S.	214	40.46 N	80.42 W
Elkton, S.D., U.S.	198	44.14 N	96.28 W
Elkton, Va., U.S.	188	38.24 N	78.37 W
El Kure	144	5.41 N	42.21 E
Elkville	194	37.54 N	89.14 W
Ell, Lake ◎	162	29.13 S	127.46 E
Ellamar	180	60.54 N	146.42 W
Elland	44	53.41 N	1.50 W
Ellard Lake ◎	184	54.33 N	91.55 W
Ellás			
→ Greece □1	38	39.00 N	22.00 E
Ellavalla	162	25.05 S	114.22 E
Ellaville	192	32.14 N	84.18 W
Ellefeld	54	50.29 N	12.23 E
Ellef Ringnes Island I	16	78.30 N	104.00 W
El Leh	144	3.48 N	39.48 E
Elleker	162	35.00 S	117.43 E
Ellemandsbjerg ∧2	41	56.07 N	10.32 E
Ellen ≃	44	54.43 N	3.30 W
Ellen, Mount ∧	200	38.07 N	110.49 W
Ellen Brook ≃	168a	31.48 S	116.00 E
Ellendale, Austl.	162	17.56 S	124.48 E
Ellendale, De., U.S.	208	38.48 N	75.25 W
Ellendale, Mn., U.S.	190	43.52 N	93.18 W
Ellendale, N.D., U.S.	198	46.00 N	98.31 W
Ellensburg	202	46.59 N	120.32 W
Ellenton, Fl., U.S.	220	27.31 N	82.31 W
Ellenton, Ga., U.S.	192	31.10 N	83.35 W
Ellenville	210	41.43 N	74.23 W
Eller ◆8	263	51.12 N	6.51 E
Ellerbe	192	35.04 N	79.46 W
Ellero ≃	62	44.27 N	7.54 E
Ellerspring ∧2	56	49.55 N	7.37 E
Ellès	36	35.57 N	9.06 E
Ellesmere	42	52.54 N	2.54 W
Ellesmere, Lake ⊂	172	43.48 S	172.25 E
Ellesmere Island I	16	81.00 N	80.00 W
Ellesmere Park	262	53.29 N	2.20 W
Ellesmere Port	44	53.17 N	2.54 W
Ellesmere Port □8	262	53.18 N	2.47 W
Ellettsville	194	39.14 N	86.37 W
Ellewoutsdijk	52	51.24 N	3.49 E
Ellezelles	50	50.44 N	3.41 E
Ellice ≃	176	68.02 N	103.26 W
Ellice Islands			
→ Tuvalu □1	14	8.00 S	178.00 E
Ellichpur			
→ Achalpur	120	21.16 N	77.31 E
Ellicott City	208	39.16 N	76.47 W
Ellicott Creek ≃	210	43.01 N	78.53 W
Ellicott Creek Park ♦	284a	43.01 N	78.50 W
Ellicottville	210	42.16 N	78.40 W
Ellijay	192	34.41 N	84.28 W
El Limón, Méx.	234	18.05 N	101.59 W
El Limón, Méx.	234	19.49 N	104.11 W
El Limoncito	286c	10.29 N	66.47 W
El Limón de Teachi	232	24.43 N	107.08 W
Ellingen	56	49.04 N	10.58 E
Ellinger	222	29.50 N	96.44 W
Ellinghorst ◆8	263	51.34 N	6.57 E
Ellington, Eng., U.K.	44	55.13 N	1.34 W
Ellington, Ct., U.S.	207	41.54 N	72.28 W
Ellington, Mo., U.S.	194	37.14 N	90.58 W
Ellington, N.Y., U.S.	214	42.13 N	79.07 W
Elliniko International Airport ⊠	267c	37.54 N	23.44 E
Ellinikón	267c	37.53 N	23.44 E
Ellinwood	198	38.21 N	98.34 W
Elliot	158	31.18 S	27.50 E
Elliot, Mount ∧	166	19.29 S	146.58 E
Elliotdale	158	31.55 S	28.38 E
Elliotganj	126	23.31 N	90.52 E
Elliot Lake	190	46.23 N	82.39 W
Elliot Lake ◎	184	52.55 N	95.20 W
Elliott, Austl.	162	17.33 S	133.32 E
Elliott, Il., U.S.	216	40.28 N	88.16 W
Elliott, Ia., U.S.	198	41.09 N	95.10 W
Elliott, Ms., U.S.	194	33.36 N	89.45 W
Elliott □6	218	38.13 N	83.10 W
Elliott, Mount ∧	162	20.29 S	126.37 E
Elliott Bay ⊂	224	47.36 N	122.22 W
Elliott Key I	220	25.27 N	80.11 W
Elliottville	218	38.11 N	83.16 W
Ellis	198	38.56 N	99.33 W
Ellis □6	222	32.20 N	96.48 W
Ellisburg	212	43.44 N	76.08 W
Ellis Island I	276	40.42 N	74.02 W
Ellis Mountain ∧	224	48.10 N	124.19 W
Ellison Creek Reservoir ◎1	222	32.56 N	94.43 W
Ellisport	224	47.25 N	122.26 W
Ellisras	156	23.40 S	27.46 E
Elliston, Austl.	162	33.39 S	134.55 E
Elliston, Nf., Can.	186	48.38 N	53.03 W
Elliston, Mt., U.S.	202	46.33 N	112.25 W
Ellisville, Ms., U.S.	194	31.36 N	89.11 W
Ellisville, Mo., U.S.	219	38.35 N	90.35 W
Ellmau	64	47.31 N	12.18 E
Ellmauer Halt ∧	64	47.34 N	12.18 E
Ellon	46	57.22 N	2.05 W
Ellora	122	20.01 N	75.10 E
Elloree	192	33.31 N	80.34 W
Ellore			
→ Elūru	122	16.42 N	81.06 E
Ellport	214	40.51 N	80.15 W
Ellrich	54	51.35 N	10.40 E
Ellsworth, Il., U.S.	216	40.27 N	88.43 W
Ellsworth, Ks., U.S.	198	38.43 N	98.13 W
Ellsworth, Me., U.S.	188	44.32 N	68.25 W
Ellsworth, Mi., U.S.	190	45.09 N	85.14 W
Ellsworth, Mn., U.S.	198	43.31 N	96.01 W
Ellsworth, Oh., U.S.	214	41.01 N	80.52 W
Ellsworth, Pa., U.S.	214	40.06 N	80.01 W
Ellsworth, Wa., U.S.	224	45.37 N	122.36 W
Ellsworth, Wi., U.S.	190	44.43 N	92.29 W
Ellsworth Air Force Base ■	198	44.08 N	103.05 W
Ellsworth Land ◆1	9	75.30 S	80.00 W
Ellsworth Mountains ⋏	9	79.00 S	85.00 W
El Lucero	196	25.53 N	103.25 W
Ellwangen	56	48.57 N	10.07 E
Ellwanger Berge ⋏2	56	49.00 N	10.15 E
Ellwood City	214	40.51 N	80.17 W
Elm, Dtsch.	52	53.31 N	9.12 E
Elm, Schw.	58	46.55 N	9.11 E
Elm, Eng., U.K.	42	52.38 N	0.10 E
Elm ∧	64	47.40 N	13.57 E
Elm ⋏2	54	52.09 N	10.53 E
Elm ≃, U.S.	198	45.36 N	98.19 W
Elm ≃, Il., U.S.	194	38.24 N	88.14 W
Elm ≃, N.D., U.S.	198	47.15 N	96.50 W
Elma, Ia., U.S.	190	43.14 N	92.26 W
Elma, N.Y., U.S.	210	42.51 N	78.38 W
Elma, Wa., U.S.	224	47.00 N	123.24 W
El Macero	226	38.33 N	121.41 W
El Machorro, Punta ➤	200	31.03 N	114.51 W
Elmadağ (Küçükyozgat)	130	39.55 N	33.15 E
Elmadağ ∧	130	39.49 N	33.00 E
El Mahia ◆1	148	22.30 N	2.30 W
El Maitén	254	42.03 S	71.10 W
El Malah	34	35.24 N	1.05 W
Elmalı	130	36.44 N	29.56 E
Elmalı Bendi ◆6	267b	41.04 N	29.06 E
El Maneadero	232	31.45 N	116.35 W
El Manteco	246	7.27 N	62.32 W
El Marsa el Kebir	148	35.45 N	0.43 W
Elmas	71	39.16 N	9.03 E
Elmas, Aeroporto di ⊠	71	39.14 N	9.03 E
Elmas Burnu ➤	267b	41.13 N	29.13 E
El Masnou	266d	41.29 N	2.19 E
Elmaton	222	28.53 N	96.09 W
El Mayoco	254	42.39 S	70.59 W
Elmbridge □8	260	51.22 N	0.23 W
Elm Brook ≃	283	42.29 N	71.16 W
Elm City	192	35.48 N	77.51 W
Elm Creek, Mb., Can.	184	49.41 N	98.00 W
Elm Creek, Ne., U.S.	198	40.43 N	99.22 W
Elm Creek ≃, Mn., U.S.	198	43.45 N	94.11 W
Elm Creek ≃, S.D., U.S.	198	44.21 N	102.42 W
Elm Creek ≃, Tx., U.S.	196	28.54 N	100.12 W
Elm Creek ≃, Tx., U.S.	196	32.40 N	99.41 W
Elm Creek ≃, Tx., U.S.	196	33.12 N	98.50 W
Elm Creek ≃, Tx., U.S.	222	29.15 N	97.32 W
El Meco	234	22.35 N	99.20 W
El Médano	232	24.25 N	111.30 W
Elmen	58	47.20 N	10.32 E
El Menia	148	30.30 N	2.50 E
Elmer	208	39.35 N	75.10 W
El Mghayyar	148	33.55 N	5.58 E
Elm Grove	216	43.02 N	88.04 W
Elmhurst, Austl.	169	37.11 S	143.15 E
Elmhurst, Il., U.S.	216	41.53 N	87.56 W
Elmhurst, Pa., U.S.	210	41.22 N	75.32 W
Elmhurst ◆8	276	40.44 N	73.53 W
El Mijao	286c	10.23 N	66.48 W
El Milagro	252	31.01 S	65.59 W
El Miliyya	148	36.48 N	6.14 E
El Mimbre	196	25.40 N	102.20 W
Elmina	150	5.05 N	1.21 W
El Minao	240m	18.22 N	66.05 W
Elmira, On., Can.	212	43.36 N	80.33 W
Elmira, P.E., Can.	186	46.27 N	62.04 W
Elmira, Ca., U.S.	226	38.21 N	121.55 W
Elmira, N.Y., U.S.	210	42.05 N	76.48 W
El Mirador ∧	234	19.25 N	98.42 W
El Mirage	200	33.36 N	112.19 W
El Mirage Lake ◎	228	34.38 N	117.35 W
Elmira Heights	210	42.07 N	76.49 W
Elm Mott	222	31.40 N	97.06 W
Elmo, Mt., U.S.	182	47.49 N	114.20 W
Elmo, Tx., U.S.	222	32.43 N	96.10 W
El Mochito	236	14.49 N	88.06 W
El Mohammadia	148	35.33 N	0.03 E
El Molinillo	34	39.28 N	4.13 W
Elmont, N.Y., U.S.	276	40.42 N	73.42 W
Elmont, Va., U.S.	208	37.42 N	77.29 W
El Monte, Chile	252	33.41 S	71.01 W
El Monte, Ca., U.S.	228	34.04 N	118.01 W
El Monte Airport ⊠	280	34.06 N	118.02 W
Elmora	214	40.36 N	78.45 W
El Moral	196	28.51 N	100.39 W
Elmore, Austl.	166	36.30 S	144.37 E
Elmore, Mn., U.S.	190	43.30 N	94.05 W
Elmore, Oh., U.S.	214	41.28 N	83.17 W
Elmore City	196	34.37 N	97.23 W
El Morro ⊥	240m	18.28 N	66.07 W
El Morro National Monument ♦	200	35.05 N	108.22 W
Elm Point ➤	276	40.49 N	73.46 W
Elmpt	56	51.13 N	6.10 E
El Mreiti ╤4	148	23.29 N	7.52 W
El Mreyyé ◆1	150	19.30 N	7.00 W
Elmschenhagen ◆8	54	54.18 N	10.12 E
Elmsdale	186	44.58 N	63.30 W
Elmsford	210	41.03 N	73.49 W
Elmshorn	52	53.45 N	9.39 E
Elm Springs	194	36.12 N	94.14 W
Elmsta	26	59.58 N	18.48 E
Elmstein	56	49.21 N	7.56 E
Elmswell	42	52.15 N	0.53 E
El Mulato	196	29.22 N	104.10 W
El Multe	232	17.41 N	91.24 W
Elmvale	212	44.35 N	79.52 W
Elmville	218	38.20 N	84.46 W
Elmwood, On., Can.	212	44.14 N	81.03 W
Elmwood, Il., U.S.	190	40.46 N	89.57 W
Elmwood, Md., U.S.	284b	39.21 N	76.32 W
Elmwood, Ma., U.S.	283	42.00 N	70.57 W
Elmwood, Ne., U.S.	198	40.50 N	96.17 W
Elmwood, Wi., U.S.	190	44.46 N	92.08 W
Elmwood ◆8	285	39.56 N	75.14 W
Elmwood Park, Il., U.S.	216	41.55 N	87.48 W
Elmwood Park, N.J., U.S.	276	40.54 N	74.07 W
Elmwood Park, Wi., U.S.	216	42.41 N	87.50 W
Elmwood Park ♦	285	40.08 N	75.21 W
El Naranjo ≃	234	18.41 N	103.45 W
El Naranjo de Chila	234	18.55 N	102.28 W
Elne	32	42.36 N	2.58 E
El Negralejo	266a	40.24 N	3.31 W
El Negrito	236	15.16 N	87.41 W
El Nido, Pil.	116	11.11 N	119.23 E
El Nido, Ca., U.S.	226	37.08 N	120.29 W
El Nihuil	252	35.02 S	68.40 W
El Niybo	144	4.32 N	39.59 E
El Nopal, Cerro ∧	232	28.15 N	107.36 W
Elnora, Ab., Can.	182	51.59 N	113.12 W
Elnora, In., U.S.	194	38.52 N	87.05 W
El Oasis	286c	10.35 N	66.59 W
El-Obeid			
→ Al-Ubayyiḍ	140	13.11 N	30.13 E
Elobey, Islas II	152	0.59 N	9.30 E
El Ocote, Cerro ∧	232	25.58 N	106.08 W
Elogbatindi	152	3.27 N	10.08 E
Eloida, Lake ◎	212	44.40 N	75.58 W
Elói Mendes	256	21.37 S	45.34 W
Eloise	220	27.59 N	81.44 W
Elora, On., Can.	212	43.41 N	80.26 W
Elora, Tn., U.S.	194	35.00 N	86.21 W
El Oro □4	246	3.30 S	79.50 W
Elortondo	252	33.42 S	61.37 W
Elorza	246	7.03 N	69.31 W
El Otro Lado	286c	10.24 N	66.49 W
Eloy	200	32.45 N	111.33 W
Eloy Alfaro	246	2.12 S	79.50 W
Éloyes	58	48.06 N	6.37 E
El Pacayal	232	15.37 N	92.02 W
El Palmar, Bol.	248	21.54 S	63.39 W
El Palmar, Ven.	246	7.58 N	61.53 W
El Palmar, Ven.	286c	10.38 N	66.52 W
El Palomar	288	34.36 S	58.36 W
El Palomar, Base Aérea Militar ■	288	34.37 S	58.37 W
El Palqui	252	30.45 S	70.59 W
El Pantanoso, Arroyo ≃	288	34.47 S	58.40 W
El Pao, Ven.	246	8.01 N	62.38 W
El Pao, Ven.	246	9.38 N	68.08 W
El Papiol	266d	41.26 N	2.01 E
El Paraíso, Hond.	236	13.51 N	86.34 W
El Paraíso, Méx.	234	17.25 N	100.15 W
El Paraíso □5	236	14.10 N	86.30 W
El Pardo ◆8	266a	40.31 N	3.47 W
El Pardo, Embalse de ◎1	266a	40.33 N	3.48 W
El Pardo, Monte de ⋏2	266a	40.33 N	3.48 W
El Paso, Il., U.S.	216	40.44 N	89.00 W
El Paso, Tx., U.S.	200	31.45 N	106.29 W
El Paso Creek ≃	228	35.02 N	118.51 W
El Paso de Robles			
→ Paso Robles	226	35.38 N	120.41 W
El Paso Peaks ⋏	204	35.28 N	117.43 W
El Paují	286c	10.26 N	66.49 W
El Pedregal ◆8	286c	10.30 N	66.51 W
El Peñón Blanco, Cerro ∧	234	22.31 N	101.40 W
El Peñuelo	232	24.34 N	100.46 W
El Peral	286e	33.35 S	70.34 W
El Perú	246	7.19 N	61.49 W
El Pescadero, Laguna ⊂	234	22.12 N	105.20 W
El Pescado, Arroyo ≃	258	34.54 S	57.47 W
Elphin	48	53.51 N	8.12 W
Elphinstone	184	50.33 N	100.19 W
El Picacho, Cerro ∧	234	20.40 N	100.43 W
El Pilar	246	10.32 N	63.09 W
El Pinar, Parque Nacional ♦	286c	10.29 N	66.56 W
El Piñón	246	10.24 N	74.50 W
El Pintado	252	24.38 S	61.27 W
El Piojo, Arroyo ≃	288	34.50 S	58.45 W
El Piquete	252	24.13 S	64.39 W
El Pital, Cerro ∧	236	14.23 N	89.08 W
El Placer	234	23.33 N	106.10 W
El Planchón, Volcán ∧1	252	35.13 S	70.34 W
El Plantío ◆8	266a	40.28 N	3.49 W
El Plomo	200	31.15 N	112.04 W
El Polvorín	240m	18.26 N	66.17 W
El Pont de Segur	34	42.24 N	0.45 E
El Porcal	266a	40.18 N	3.32 W
El Portal, Ca., U.S.	226	37.40 N	119.46 W
El Portal, Fl., U.S.	220	25.51 N	80.11 W
El Port de Pollença	34	39.55 N	3.05 E
El Porvenir, Méx.	196	27.33 N	104.57 W
El Porvenir, Méx.	234	15.44 N	93.22 W
El Porvenir, Perú	248	8.05 S	79.00 W
El Potosí, Punta ➤	234	17.32 N	101.28 W
El Potrero	196	26.23 N	100.27 W
El Prat de Llobregat	34	41.20 N	2.06 E

Symbols in the index entries represent the broad categories identified in the key at the right. Symbols with superior numbers (⋏1) identify subcategories (see complete key on page *I* · *1*).

Symbole im Register stellen die rechts im Schlüssel erklärten Kategorien dar. Symbole mit hochgestellten Ziffern (⋏1) bezeichnen Unterabteilungen einer Kategorie (vgl. vollständiger Schlüssel auf Seite *I* · *1*).

Los símbolos incluídos en el texto del índice representan las grandes categorias identificadas con la clave a la derecha. Los símbolos con numeros en su parte superior (⋏1) identifican las subcategorías (véase la clave completa en la página *I* · *1*).

Les symboles de l'index représentent les catégories indiquées dans la légende à droite. Les symboles suivis d'un indice (⋏1) représentent des sous-catégories (voir légende complète à la page *I* · *1*).

Os símbolos incluídos no texto do índice representam as grandes categorias identificadas com a chave à direita. Os símbolos com números em sua parte superior (⋏1) identificam as subcategorias (veja-se a chave completa à página *I* · *1*).

English	Deutsch	Español	Français	Português
∧ Mountain	Berg	Montaña	Montagne	Montanha
⋏ Mountains	Gebirge	Montañas	Montagnes	Montanhas
)(Pass	Paß	Paso	Col	Passo
∨ Valley, Canyon	Tal, Cañon	Valle, Cañón	Vallée, Canyon	Vale, Canhão
≚ Plain	Ebene	Llano	Plaine	Planície
➤ Cape	Kap	Cabo	Cap	Cabo
I Island	Insel	Isla	Île	Ilha
II Islands	Inseln	Islas	Îles	Ilhas
◆ Other Topographic Features	Andere Topographische Objekte	Otros Elementos Topográficos	Autres données topographiques	Outros acidentes topográficos

ESPAÑOL — Nombre, Página, Lat.°′, Long.°′ W = Oeste
FRANÇAIS — Nom, Page, Lat.°′, Long.°′ W = Ouest
PORTUGUÊS — Nome, Página, Lat.°′, Long.°′ W = Oeste

Nombre / Nom / Nome	Página / Page	Lat.°′	Long.°′
El Progreso, Ec.	246a	0.54 S	89.33 W
El Progreso, Guat.	236	14.21 N	89.51 W
El Progreso, Hond.	236	15.21 N	87.49 W
El Progreso □[5]	236	14.50 N	90.00 W
El Puente del Arzobispo	34	39.48 N	5.10 W
El Puerto de Santa María	34	36.36 N	6.13 W
El Puesto	252	27.57 S	67.38 W
El Qala	148	36.50 N	8.30 E
El Qoll	148	37.00 N	6.34 E
El Quebrachal	252	25.17 S	64.04 W
El Quelite	234	23.32 N	106.28 W
Elquera Bushland ♦	274a	33.42 S	151.04 E
Elqui ≃	252	29.54 S	71.17 W
Elrama	214	40.15 N	79.55 W
El Ranchito	234	18.40 N	103.41 W
El Rastro	246	9.03 N	67.27 W
El Real de Santa María	246	8.08 N	77.43 W
El Recreo ✈[8]	286c	10.30 N	66.53 W
El Refugio	234	21.57 N	100.02 W
El Remolino	196	28.44 N	101.07 W
El Reno	196	35.31 N	97.57 W
El Rey, Parque Nacional ♦	252	25.00 S	64.40 W
El Rio	228	34.13 N	119.10 W
El Rito	200	36.20 N	106.11 W
El Rito ≃	200	36.12 N	106.14 W
El Roba	154	3.57 N	40.01 E
El Roble, Mesa ∧	232	31.31 N	115.31 W
El Rom	132	33.11 N	35.46 E
El Rosario, Laguna ⊜	234	17.52 N	93.48 W
El Rosarito	232	28.38 N	114.04 W
Elrose	184	51.13 N	108.01 W
Elroy	190	43.44 N	90.16 W
El Rucio	234	23.23 N	102.05 W
Elsa, Yk., Can.	180	63.55 N	135.28 W
Elsa, Tx., U.S.	196	26.17 N	97.59 W
Elsa ≃	66	43.43 N	10.52 E
Elsah	219	38.57 N	90.22 W
El Sahuaro	200	31.05 N	112.55 W
El Salado	252	26.25 S	70.19 W
El Salado, Parque Nacional ♦	246	2.12 S	80.00 W
El Salitre	246	1.50 S	79.48 W
El Salto, Méx.	234	23.47 N	105.22 W
El Salto, Méx.	234	20.32 N	103.11 W
El Salvador, Chile	252	26.17 S	69.43 W
El Salvador, Pil.	116	8.34 N	124.32 E
El Salvador □[1], N.A.	230	13.50 N	88.55 W
El Salvador □[1], N.A.	236	13.50 N	88.55 W
El Samán de Apure	246	7.55 N	68.44 W
El Santo	240p	22.42 N	79.41 W
Elsass → Alsace □[9]	32	48.30 N	7.30 E
El Sauce, Laguna ⊜	258	35.20 S	58.16 W
El Sauz	232	29.02 N	106.16 W
El Sauzal	232	31.54 N	116.41 W
Elsberry	219	39.10 N	90.46 W
Elsbethen	64	47.45 N	13.05 E
Elsburg	273d	26.15 S	28.12 E
Elsdorf, Dtsch.	52	53.14 N	9.20 E
Elsdorf, Dtsch.	56	50.54 N	6.34 E
El Seco, Laguna ⊜	258	35.31 S	58.42 W
El Segundo	228	33.55 N	118.24 W
El Seibo	238	18.46 N	69.02 W
Elsen	52	51.44 N	8.39 E
Elsenham	42	51.55 N	0.14 E
Elsen Nur ⊜	120	35.11 N	92.15 E
Elsenz ≃	56	49.24 N	8.48 E
Elsey	263	51.22 N	7.34 E
Elsfleth	52	53.14 N	8.28 E
El Siasgo, Arroyo ≃	258	35.33 S	58.33 W
Elsie, Mi., U.S.	216	43.05 N	84.23 W
Elsie, Or., U.S.	224	45.52 N	123.35 W
Elsinore	200	38.40 N	112.08 W
Elsinore, Lake ⊜[1]	228	33.39 N	117.21 W
Elsinore → Helsingør	41	56.02 N	12.37 E
El Sitio	286c	10.28 N	66.46 W
Elsmere, De., U.S.	208	39.44 N	75.35 W
Elsmere, Ky., U.S.	218	39.00 N	84.36 W
Elsmere, N.Y., U.S.	210	42.37 N	73.49 W
El Sobrante	226	37.58 N	122.17 W
El Socorro	246	8.59 N	65.44 W
El Sombrero	246	9.23 N	67.03 W
Elspark	273d	26.16 S	28.14 E
Elspeet	52	52.17 N	5.46 E
Elst	52	51.55 N	5.50 E
Elstal	54	52.32 N	12.59 E
Elstead	42	51.11 N	0.43 W
Elster	54	51.50 N	12.49 E
Elsterberg	54	50.36 N	12.10 E
Elstergebirge ⋀	54	50.15 N	12.20 E
Elsterwerda	54	51.28 N	13.31 E
Elston, In., U.S.	216	40.22 N	86.55 W
Elston, Mo., U.S.	219	38.37 N	92.19 W
Elstra	54	51.13 N	14.08 E
Elstree	42	51.39 N	0.16 W
Elstree Aerodrome ⊠	260	51.39 N	0.19 W
El Sueco	232	29.54 N	106.24 W
El Tagarete, Cerro ∧	232	26.31 N	105.56 W
El Tajín ⊥	234	20.27 N	97.23 W
El Tala	252	26.07 S	65.17 W
El Talar	258	34.27 S	58.39 W
El Tamarindo	236	13.11 N	87.54 W
El Tambo, Col.	246	1.26 N	77.23 W
El Tambo, Perú	248	12.04 S	75.13 W
El Tanque	196	26.28 N	99.38 W
El Tapextle	234	23.52 N	105.33 W
El Tarf	36	36.45 N	8.20 E
El Tecuán	232	25.29 N	107.00 W
El Tejocote, Cerro ∧	234	18.48 N	103.03 W
Elten	52	51.52 N	6.10 E
El Terrero	234	18.58 N	102.28 W
Eltham, Austl.	169	37.44 S	145.09 E
Eltham, N.Z.	172	39.26 S	174.18 E
Eltham ✈[8]	260	51.27 N	0.04 E
Eltham Palace ⊍	260	51.27 N	0.03 E
El Tigre	246	8.55 N	64.15 W
El Tigre, Isla I	236	13.16 N	87.38 W
El Tigrito → San José de Guanipa	246	8.54 N	64.09 W
El Timbiriche	234	18.38 N	101.31 W
Eltmann	56	49.58 N	10.40 E
El Tocuyo	246	9.47 N	69.48 W
El Tofo	252	29.27 S	71.15 W
El'ton, Ross.	80	49.08 N	46.50 E
Elton, Eng., U.K.	262	53.16 N	2.49 W
Elton, La., U.S.	194	30.28 N	92.41 W
Elton, Pa., U.S.	214	40.17 N	78.48 W
El'ton, ozero ⊜	80	49.16 N	46.35 E
El Toreo ♦	286a	19.27 N	99.13 W
El Toro	228	33.37 N	117.41 W
El Toro ∧	240m	18.16 N	65.49 W
El Toro, Isla I	234	21.26 N	97.31 W
El Toro Marine Corps Air Station ■	228	33.41 N	117.44 W
El Tranco, Embalse de ⊜[1]	34	38.10 N	2.45 W
El Tránsito, Chile	252	28.52 S	70.17 W
El Tránsito, El Sal.	236	13.22 N	88.21 W
El Trébol	252	32.12 S	61.42 W
El Triunfo, Hond.	236	13.06 N	87.00 W
El Triunfo, Méx.	232	23.47 N	110.08 W
El Triunfo, Cerro ∧	234	15.40 N	92.49 W
El Triunfo de la Cruz	236	15.46 N	87.26 W
El Tuito	234	20.19 N	105.22 W
El Tulillo	234	22.30 N	104.05 W
El Tunal	252	25.15 S	64.27 W
El Turbio	254	51.41 S	72.05 W
Eltville	56	50.02 N	8.07 E
Eltz, Burg ⊥	56	50.12 N	7.20 E
El-Uarre	144	3.41 N	45.20 E
Elura → Ellora	122	20.01 N	75.10 E
Elūru	122	16.42 N	81.06 E
Elva	76	58.13 N	26.25 E
El Valle	236	8.36 N	80.08 W
El Valle ✈[8]	286c	10.27 N	66.55 W
Elvas	34	38.53 N	7.10 W
Elvas ≃	256	21.12 S	44.08 W
Elven	32	47.44 N	2.35 W
El Vendrell	34	41.13 N	1.32 E
El Verano	226	38.18 N	122.29 W
El Verde	234	23.21 N	106.09 W
Elverdissen	52	52.05 N	8.38 E
Elverlingsen	263	51.17 N	7.42 E
Elverta	226	38.43 N	121.28 W
Elverum	26	60.53 N	11.34 E
El Viejo	236	12.40 N	87.10 W
El Vigía	246	8.38 N	71.39 W
El Vigía, Cerro ∧	234	21.19 N	104.03 W
Elvins	194	37.50 N	90.31 W
Elvira	258	35.14 S	59.29 W
Elvo ≃	62	45.23 N	8.21 E
El Volcán	252	33.49 S	70.11 W
El Wad	148	33.20 N	6.58 E
El Wak	154	2.49 N	40.56 E
El Walamo	234	23.07 N	106.15 W
El Wanza	148	35.57 N	8.04 E
Elwell, Lake ⊜[1]	202	48.22 N	111.17 W
Elwha ≃	224	48.10 N	123.35 W
Elwood, Austl.	274b	37.53 S	144.59 E
Elwood, Il., U.S.	216	41.24 N	88.07 W
Elwood, In., U.S.	216	40.16 N	85.50 W
Elwood, Ks., U.S.	198	39.45 N	94.52 W
Elwood, Ne., U.S.	198	40.35 N	99.51 W
Elwood, N.J., U.S.	208	39.35 N	74.43 W
Elwood, N.Y., U.S.	207	40.50 N	73.20 W
Elwood Park, Fl., U.S.	220	27.28 N	82.30 W
Elwood Park, Pa., U.S.	279b	40.10 N	80.17 W
Elwy ≃	44	53.16 N	3.26 W
Elwyn	285	39.54 N	75.24 W
Elx	34	38.15 N	0.42 W
Elxleben	54	51.02 N	10.56 E
Ely, Eng., U.K.	42	52.24 N	0.16 E
Ely, Mn., U.S.	190	47.54 N	91.52 W
Ely, Mo., U.S.	219	39.41 N	91.39 W
Ely, Nv., U.S.	204	39.14 N	114.53 W
Ely, Isle of ✈[1]	42	52.24 N	0.10 E
El Yagual	246	7.29 N	68.25 W
Ely Cathedral ⊍[1]	42	52.24 N	0.16 E
Elyria	214	41.22 N	82.06 W
Elyria Airport ⊠	279a	41.20 N	82.06 W
Elysburg	210	40.51 N	76.33 W
Elysian Park ♦	280	34.05 N	118.14 W
El Yunque ∧	240m	18.19 N	65.48 W
Elywood Park ♦	279a	41.23 N	82.06 W
Elz	56	50.25 N	8.02 E
Elz ≃	58	48.21 N	7.45 E
Elzach	58	48.10 N	8.04 E
El Zamural	286c	10.27 N	67.00 W
El Zapotal	234	15.27 N	93.10 W
Elzbach ≃	56	50.12 N	7.22 E
Elze, Dtsch.	52	52.35 N	9.44 E
Elze, Dtsch.	52	52.07 N	9.44 E
El Zig-Zag	286c	10.33 N	66.58 W
Émaé I	175f	17.04 S	168.24 E
Emajõgi ≃	76	58.26 N	27.15 E
Emali	154	2.05 S	37.38 E
Emam Khomeyni Mosque ⊍[1]	267d	35.40 N	51.25 E
Emāmshahr (Shāhrūd)	128	36.25 N	55.01 E
Emån ≃	26	57.08 N	16.30 E
Émancé	261	48.35 N	1.44 E
Emas, Parque Nacional das ♦	255	18.08 S	52.48 W
Emba	86	48.50 N	58.08 E
Emba ≃	80	46.38 N	53.14 E
Embarcación	252	23.13 S	64.06 W
Embarras ≃, Ab., Can.	182	53.27 N	116.37 W
Embarras ≃, Il., U.S.	194	38.39 N	87.37 W
Embarras, North Fork ≃	194	38.55 N	87.59 W
Embarrass	190	44.39 N	88.42 W
Embarrass ≃, Mn., U.S.	190	47.24 N	92.25 W
Embarrass ≃, Wi., U.S.	190	44.23 N	88.45 W
Embetsu	92a	44.44 N	141.47 E
Embid	34	40.58 N	1.43 W
Embleton	44	55.30 N	1.37 W
Embo	46	57.54 N	3.59 W
Emboabas	256	21.18 S	44.08 W
Embondo	152	0.15 N	19.38 E
Emborcação, Represa ⊜[1]	255	18.30 S	47.50 W
Embrach	58	47.30 N	8.36 E
Embreeville, Pa., U.S.	285	39.56 N	75.44 W
Embreeville, Tn., U.S.	192	36.10 N	82.27 W
Embro	212	43.09 N	80.54 W
Embrun, On., Can.	212	45.16 N	75.17 W
Embrun, Fr.	62	44.34 N	6.30 E
Embry	50	50.29 N	1.58 E
Embsay	44	53.58 N	1.59 W
Embu, Bra.	256	23.39 S	46.51 W
Embu, Kenya	154	0.32 S	37.27 E
Embu □[7]	287b	23.40 S	46.50 W
Embu-Guaçu	256	23.49 S	46.48 W
Embu-Guaçu □[7]	287b	23.48 S	46.48 W
Embu-mirim ≃	287b	23.39 S	46.51 W
Emden, Dtsch.	52	53.22 N	7.12 E
Emden, Il., U.S.	194	40.18 N	89.29 W
Emden, Mo., U.S.	219	39.48 N	91.52 W
Emei	107	29.36 N	103.31 E
Emeigh	214	40.42 N	78.47 W
Emel' (Emin) ≃	86	46.20 N	81.46 E
Emelle	194	32.43 N	88.18 W
Emerado	198	47.55 N	97.21 W
Émerainville	261	48.49 N	2.37 E
Emerald, Austl.	166	23.32 S	148.10 E
Emerald, Austl.	169	37.56 S	145.26 E
Emerald Bay State Park ♦	226	38.57 N	120.05 W
Emerald Lake	226	37.28 N	122.16 W
Emerson, Mb., Can.	184	49.00 N	97.12 W
Emerson, Ar., U.S.	194	33.05 N	93.11 W
Emerson, Ga., U.S.	192	34.07 N	84.45 W
Emerson, Ia., U.S.	198	41.01 N	95.24 W
Emerson, Mo., U.S.	219	39.53 N	91.42 W
Emerson, Ne., U.S.	198	42.17 N	96.44 W
Emerson, N.J., U.S.	276	40.58 N	74.01 W
Emery, S.D., U.S.	198	43.36 N	97.37 W
Emery, Ut,. U.S.	200	38.55 N	111.14 W
Emeryville, On., Can.	214	42.18 N	82.45 W
Emeryville, Ca., U.S.	226	37.50 N	122.17 W
Emet	130	39.20 N	29.15 E
Emgayet	146	29.04 N	12.58 E
Emhouse	222	32.09 N	96.35 W
Emi	88	50.36 N	97.49 E
Emigrant Gap	226	39.17 N	120.40 W
Emigrant Gap)(	226	39.18 N	120.40 W
Emigsville	208	40.01 N	76.44 W
Emiliano Mitre, Canal ⊻	288	34.36 S	58.18 W
Emiliano Zapata, Méx.	232	17.45 N	91.46 W
Emiliano Zapata, Méx.	234	16.10 N	94.01 W
Emiliano Zapata, Bahía ⊂	232	19.40 N	87.30 W
Emilia-Romagna □[4]	66	44.35 N	11.00 E
Emílio de Carvalho	152	5.55 S	12.57 E
Emily Provincial Park ♦	212	44.21 N	78.31 W
Emin	86	46.32 N	83.39 E
Emin (Emel') ≃	86	46.20 N	81.46 E
Eminābād	123	32.02 N	74.16 E
Emine, nos ›	38	42.42 N	27.51 E
Eminence, Ky., U.S.	218	38.22 N	85.10 W
Eminence, Mo., U.S.	194	37.09 N	91.21 W
Emiralem	130	38.36 N	27.09 E
Emiratos Arabes Unidos → United Arab Emirates □[1]	128	24.00 N	54.00 E
Emirau Island I	164	1.40 S	150.00 E
Emirdağ	130	39.01 N	31.10 E
Emır Dağları ⋀	130	38.50 N	31.15 E
Emirhan	130	39.42 N	37.46 E
Emir Pasha Gulf ⊂	154	2.32 S	31.52 E
Emissi, Tarso ∧	146	21.13 N	18.32 E
Emita	166	40.00 S	147.54 E
Emlembe ∧	158	25.57 S	31.11 E
Emlenton	214	41.11 N	79.43 W
Emlichheim	52	52.36 N	6.50 E
Emmaån ≃	40	58.44 N	15.35 E
Emmaboda	26	56.38 N	15.32 E
Emmaste	76	58.42 N	22.36 E
Emmaus, Ross.	82	56.47 N	36.07 E
Emmaus, Pa., U.S.	208	40.32 N	75.29 W
Emmaville	166	29.26 S	151.36 E
Emme ≃	58	47.13 N	7.34 E
Emmeline Lake ⊜	184	55.00 N	106.22 W
Emmeloord	52	52.43 N	5.45 E
Emmen	52	52.47 N	6.54 E
Emmenbrücke	58	47.04 N	8.17 E
Emmendingen	58	48.07 N	7.50 E
Emmental V	58	46.56 N	7.45 E
Emmer ≃	52	52.03 N	9.23 E
Emmer-Compascuum	52	52.48 N	7.02 E
Emmer-Erfscheidenveen	52	52.48 N	7.01 E
Emmerich	52	51.50 N	6.15 E
Emmerstedt	54	52.15 N	10.58 E
Emmerthal	52	52.03 N	9.23 E
Emmet, Austl.	166	24.40 S	144.28 E
Emmet, Ar., U.S.	194	33.43 N	93.28 W
Emmetsburg	198	43.06 N	94.40 W
Emmett, Id., U.S.	202	43.52 N	116.29 W
Emmett, Mi., U.S.	214	42.59 N	82.45 W
Emmiganūru	122	15.44 N	77.29 E
Emmitsburg	208	39.42 N	77.20 W
Emmonak	180	62.46 N	164.30 W
Emneth	42	52.38 N	0.11 E
Emo	190	48.38 N	93.50 W
Emőd	30	47.56 N	20.49 E
Emory	222	32.52 N	95.46 W
Emory ≃	192	35.56 N	84.29 W
Emory Peak ∧	196	29.13 N	103.17 W
Empalme	232	27.58 N	110.51 W
Empalme Escobedo	234	20.41 N	100.44 W
Empalme Purísima	234	23.55 N	105.05 W
Empalme San Vicente	258	34.58 S	58.22 W
Empangeni	158	28.50 S	31.48 E
Empedrado, Arg.	252	27.57 S	58.48 W
Empedrado, Chile	252	35.36 S	72.17 W
Emperor Jimmu, Tomb of ⊥	270	34.29 N	135.47 E
Emperor Nintoku, Tomb of ⊥	270	34.34 N	135.29 E
Emperor Range ⋀	175e	5.45 S	154.55 E
Emperor Seamounts ✦[3]	6	42.00 N	170.00 E
Emperor Tenchi, Tomb of ⊥	270	34.59 N	135.48 E
Empfingen	58	48.24 N	8.42 E
Empire, Ca., U.S.	226	37.38 N	120.54 W
Empire, La., U.S.	194	29.23 N	89.35 W
Empire, Nv., U.S.	204	40.34 N	119.20 W
Empire, Oh., U.S.	214	40.30 N	80.37 W
Empoli	66	43.43 N	10.57 E
Emporia, Ks., U.S.	198	38.24 N	96.10 W
Emporia, Va., U.S.	208	36.41 N	77.32 W
Emporium	214	41.30 N	78.14 W
Empress	184	50.57 N	110.00 W
Empress Augusta Bay ⊂	175e	6.25 S	155.05 E
Emptinne	56	50.19 N	5.07 E
Empty Quarter → Ar-Rub' al-Khālī ✈[2]	118	20.00 N	51.00 E
Ems ≃	52	53.20 N	7.06 E
Emscher ≃	263	51.34 N	6.42 E
Emscherbruch ✈[1]	263	51.34 N	7.09 E
Emsdetten	52	52.10 N	7.31 E
Ems-Jade-Kanal ≍	52	53.19 N	7.10 E
Emskirchen	56	49.33 N	10.43 E
Emsland ✈[1]	52	52.50 N	7.20 E
Emst ✈[8]	263	51.21 N	7.30 E
Emstek	52	52.50 N	8.09 E
Emsworth, Eng., U.K.	42	50.51 N	0.56 W
Emsworth, Pa., U.S.	214	40.30 N	80.05 W
Emu	89	43.45 N	128.10 E
Emu, Mount ∧[2]	169	37.35 S	143.27 E
Emu Creek ≃	171a	26.56 S	152.19 E
Emu Downs	168b	33.54 S	138.59 E
Emukae	92	33.18 N	129.38 E
Emu Park	166	23.15 S	150.50 E
Emu Plains	274a	33.45 S	150.41 E
Emur ≃	89	53.24 N	124.00 E
Emuren	273a	6.40 N	3.31 E
Emyvale	48	54.20 N	6.59 W
En (Inn) ≃, Europe	32	48.35 N	13.28 E
En ≃, Zhg.	100	27.12 N	115.08 E
Ena	94	35.27 N	137.25 E
Enana	156	17.29 S	16.19 E
Enånger	26	61.32 N	17.00 E
Enard Bay ⊂	46	58.05 N	5.20 W
Enarotali	164	3.55 S	136.21 E
Ena-san ∧	94	35.26 N	137.36 E
Ena-san Tunnel ✈[5]	94	35.30 N	137.40 E
Enbacka	40	60.25 N	15.36 E
Enborne ≃	42	51.24 N	1.06 W
Encampment	200	41.12 N	106.47 W
Encampment ≃	200	41.18 N	106.43 W
Encantado	252	29.15 S	51.53 W
Encantado ✈[8]	287a	22.54 S	43.18 W
Encanto, Cape ›	116	15.44 N	121.37 E
Encarnação ✈[8]	266c	38.47 N	9.06 W
Encarnación	252	27.20 S	55.54 W
Encarnación de Díaz	234	21.31 N	102.14 W
Encha	98	37.25 N	115.42 E
Enchenberg	56	49.01 N	7.20 E
Enchi	150	5.49 N	2.49 W
Enchilayas	200	30.50 N	112.50 W
Enchovas, Enseada das ⊂	256	23.57 S	45.18 W
Enciastraia, Monte ∧	62	44.22 N	6.53 E
Encinal	196	28.02 N	99.21 W
Encinitas	228	33.02 N	117.17 W
Encino, N.M., U.S.	200	34.39 N	105.27 W
Encino, Tx., U.S.	196	26.57 N	98.08 W
Encino ✈[8]	280	34.09 N	118.30 W
Encino Reservoir ⊜[1]	280	34.05 N	118.31 W
Encontrados	246	9.03 N	72.14 W
Encounter Bay ⊂	168b	35.35 S	138.44 E
Encrucijada, Cuba	240p	22.37 N	79.52 W
Encrucijada, Méx.	234	18.18 N	93.29 W
Encruzilhada	255	15.31 S	40.54 W
Encruzilhada do Sul	252	30.32 S	52.31 W
Encs	30	48.20 N	21.08 E
Endako	182	54.05 N	125.02 W
Endako ≃	182	54.05 N	124.55 W
Endau ≃	114	2.39 N	103.38 E
Ende	115b	8.50 S	121.39 E
Ende, Pulau I	115b	8.53 S	121.32 E
Ende, Teluk ⊂	115b	8.52 S	121.30 E
Endeavor, Pa., U.S.	214	41.35 N	79.23 W
Endeavor, Wi., U.S.	190	43.42 N	89.27 W
Endeavour	184	52.08 N	102.40 W
Endeavour Strait ⊻	164	10.50 S	142.15 E
Endelave I	41	55.46 N	10.17 E
Enderbury I[1]	14	3.08 S	171.05 W
Enderby, B.C., Can.	182	50.33 N	119.08 W
Enderby, Eng., U.K.	42	52.36 N	1.12 W
Enderby Land ✈[1]	9	67.30 S	53.00 E
Enderlin	198	46.37 N	97.36 W
Endicott, N.Y., U.S.	210	42.05 N	76.02 W
Endicott, Wa., U.S.	202	46.55 N	117.40 W
Endicott Mountains ⋀	180	67.50 N	152.00 W
Endimari ≃	248	8.46 S	66.07 W
Endine	64	45.46 N	9.59 E
Endine Gaiano	64	45.48 N	9.59 E
Endingen	58	48.09 N	7.42 E
Endja, Oued ≃	34	36.31 N	6.15 E
Endō	268	35.23 N	139.27 E
Endola	156	17.37 S	15.50 E
'En Dor	132	32.39 N	35.25 E
Endorf in Oberbayern	64	47.54 N	12.18 E
Endre ≃	62	43.28 N	6.36 E
Endrick ∧	170	35.12 S	150.12 E
Endrick ≃	170	35.01 S	150.03 E
Endwell	210	42.06 N	76.01 W
Ene ≃	248	11.09 S	74.19 W
Eneabba	162	29.50 S	115.20 E
Enemonzo	64	46.25 N	12.53 E
Enewetak I[1]	14	11.30 N	162.15 E
Enez	130	40.44 N	26.04 E
Enfida	36	36.07 N	10.23 E
Enfield, Austl.	168b	34.53 S	138.35 E
Enfield, Austl.	274a	33.53 S	151.06 E
Enfield, N.Z.	172	45.03 S	170.52 E
Enfield, Ct., U.S.	207	41.58 N	72.35 W
Enfield, N.H., U.S.	188	43.38 N	72.08 W
Enfield, N.C., U.S.	192	36.10 N	77.40 W
Enfield, Va., U.S.	208	37.43 N	77.12 W
Enfield ✈[8]	42	51.40 N	0.05 W
Enga □[5]	164	5.30 S	143.30 E
Engadine	170	34.04 S	151.01 E
Engaño, Cabo ›	238	18.37 N	68.20 W
Engaru	92a	44.03 N	143.31 E
Engažimo	88	57.51 N	114.56 E
Engcobo	158	31.37 S	28.00 E
'En Gedi	132	31.27 N	35.23 E
Engelberg	58	46.49 N	8.25 E
Engelhard	192	35.30 N	75.59 W
Engelhartszell	60	48.31 N	13.44 E
Engel's	80	51.30 N	46.07 E
Engelsdorf	54	51.20 N	12.29 E
Engelskirchen	56	50.59 N	7.24 E
Engelsmanplaat I	52	53.28 N	6.02 E
Engel's'ovo	83	48.22 N	39.23 E
Engen, B.C., Can.	182	54.02 N	124.18 W
Engen, Dtsch.	58	47.51 N	8.46 E
Engenheiro Navarro	255	17.17 S	43.57 W
Engenheiro Passos	256	22.30 S	44.41 W
Engenheiro Paulo de Frontin	256	22.33 S	43.41 W
Engenho	248	15.10 S	56.25 W
Engenho, Ilha do I	287a	22.50 S	43.07 W
Engenho de Dentro ✈[8]	287a	22.54 S	43.18 W
Engenho do Mato	287a	22.52 S	43.01 W
Éngenho Novo	256	21.49 S	43.00 W
Engenho Nôvo ✈[8]	287a	22.55 S	43.17 W
Enger	52	52.08 N	8.34 E
Engestofte	41	54.46 N	11.34 E
Engesvang	41	56.10 N	9.21 E
'En Gev	132	32.47 N	35.38 E
Enggano, Pulau I	112	5.24 S	102.16 E
Enghershatu ∧	144	16.40 N	38.20 E
Enghien (Edingen)	50	50.42 N	4.02 E
Enghien-les-Bains	261	48.58 N	2.19 E
Enghien-Moisselles, Aéroport d' ⊠	261	49.02 N	2.21 E
Engiadina Bassa V	58	46.50 N	10.20 E
Engis	56	50.35 N	5.25 E
Engizek Dağı ∧	130	37.50 N	37.10 E
Engjan	26	63.09 N	8.32 E
England	194	34.32 N	91.58 W
England □[8]	28	52.30 N	1.30 W
England Air Force Base ■	194	31.20 N	92.33 W
Englebright Lake ⊜[1]	226	39.15 N	121.15 W
Englee	186	50.44 N	56.06 W
Englefield, Cape ›	176	69.51 N	85.39 W
Englefield Green	260	51.26 N	0.35 W
Englefontaine	50	50.11 N	3.39 E
Englehart	190	47.49 N	79.52 W
Englehart ≃	190	47.51 N	79.50 W
Engleside	208	38.43 N	77.05 W
Englewood, B.C., Can.	182	50.33 N	126.53 W
Englewood, Co., U.S.	200	39.38 N	104.59 W
Englewood, Fl., U.S.	220	26.57 N	82.21 W
Englewood, In., U.S.	218	38.50 N	86.31 W
Englewood, Ks., U.S.	198	37.02 N	99.58 W
Englewood, N.J., U.S.	210	40.53 N	73.58 W
Englewood, Oh., U.S.	218	39.52 N	84.18 W
Englewood, Tn., U.S.	192	35.25 N	84.29 W
Englewood ✈[8]	278	41.47 N	87.39 W
Englewood Cliffs	276	40.53 N	73.57 W
Englewood Dam ✈[6]	218	39.52 N	84.17 W
English, In., U.S.	218	38.20 N	86.27 W
English, Ky., U.S.	218	38.37 N	85.08 W
English ≃, On., Can.	176	50.12 N	95.00 W
English (Rivière des Anglais) ≃, N.A.	206	45.13 N	73.50 W
English ≃, Ia., U.S.	190	41.29 N	91.30 W
English Bay	180	59.22 N	151.55 W
English Bāzār → Ingrāj Bāzār	124	25.00 N	88.09 E
English Center	210	41.26 N	77.17 W
English Channel (La Manche) ⊻	28	50.20 N	1.00 W
English Coast ≗[2]	9	73.45 S	73.00 W
English Harbour West	186	47.28 N	55.29 W
Englishman ≃	224	49.22 N	124.18 W
Englishtown	208	40.17 N	74.21 W
Engong	152	0.36 N	10.06 E
Engter	52	52.23 N	8.04 E
Énguera	34	38.59 N	0.41 W
Engum	41	55.44 N	9.40 E
Engure	76	57.10 N	23.13 E
Engures ezers ⊜	76	57.16 N	23.06 E
Engwilen	58	47.37 N	9.05 E
'En Harod	132	32.33 N	35.23 E
'En HaShofét	132	32.35 N	35.06 E
Enid	196	36.23 N	97.52 W
Enid Lake ⊜[1]	194	34.10 N	89.50 W
Enilda	182	55.25 N	116.18 W
Eningen unter Achalm	58	48.29 N	9.16 E
Eniwa	92a	42.45 N	141.33 E
Eniwetok → Enewetak I[1]	14	11.30 N	162.15 E
eNjesuthi ∧	158	29.09 S	29.23 E
Enka	192	35.32 N	82.39 W
Enkenbach	56	49.29 N	7.54 E
Enkhuizen	52	52.42 N	5.17 E
Enkirch	56	49.59 N	7.07 E
Enköping	40	59.38 N	17.04 E
Enle	102	24.00 N	101.07 E
Enmedio	196	29.04 N	103.29 W
Enmedio, Cerro de ∧	234	19.48 N	100.36 W
Enmelen	180	65.01 N	175.54 W
Enna	70	37.34 N	14.16 E
Enna □[4]	70	37.35 N	14.26 E
Ennadai Lake ⊜	176	60.53 N	101.15 W
Enné, Ouadi V	146	14.24 N	18.45 E
Ennedi ⋀[1]	146	17.15 N	22.00 E
Ennell, Lough ⊜	48	53.28 N	7.24 W
Ennenda	58	47.01 N	9.05 E
Ennepe ≃	263	51.22 N	7.27 E
Ennepestausee ⊜[1]	263	51.14 N	7.25 E
Ennepetal	56	51.18 N	7.22 E
Ennerdale Water ⊜	44	54.31 N	3.23 W
Ennery	261	49.05 N	2.06 E
Enngonia	166	29.19 S	145.51 E
Enniger	52	51.50 N	7.56 E
Ennigerloh	52	51.50 N	8.02 E
Ennigloh	52	52.12 N	8.34 E
Ennis, Ire.	48	52.50 N	8.59 W
Ennis, Mt., U.S.	202	45.20 N	111.43 W
Ennis, Tx., U.S.	222	32.19 N	96.37 W
Enniscorthy	48	52.30 N	6.34 W
Enniskillen	48	54.21 N	7.38 W
Ennis Lake ⊜[1]	202	45.26 N	111.41 W
Ennistimon	48	52.57 N	9.15 W
Enns	61	48.13 N	14.29 E
Enns ≃	30	48.14 N	14.32 E
Ennstaler Alpen ⋀	61	47.37 N	14.35 E
Eno	26	62.48 N	30.09 E
Enø I	41	55.10 N	11.40 E
Eno ≃	96	34.53 N	132.41 E
Enochs	196	33.52 N	102.46 W
Enogera Military Camp ■	171a	27.25 S	152.58 E
Enola	208	40.17 N	76.56 W
Enon	218	39.53 N	83.56 W
Enontekiö	24	68.23 N	23.38 E
Enon Valley	214	40.51 N	80.28 W
Enoree ≃	192	34.26 N	81.25 W
Enosburg Falls	188	44.54 N	72.48 W
Eno-shima I	94	35.18 N	139.29 E
Enping	102	22.11 N	112.17 E
Enrekang	112	3.34 S	119.47 E
Enrile	116	17.34 N	121.42 E
Enrique Fynn	258	34.50 S	59.08 W
Enrique Urien	252	27.34 S	60.32 W
Enriquillo	238	17.54 N	71.14 W
Enriquillo, Lago ⊜	238	18.27 N	71.39 W
Ens	52	52.38 N	5.50 E
Ensay I	46	57.46 N	7.05 W
Enschede	52	52.12 N	6.53 E
Ensdorf	60	49.21 N	11.56 E
Ensenada, Arg.	258	34.51 S	57.55 W
Ensenada, Méx.	232	31.52 N	116.37 W
Ensenada, P.R.	240m	17.58 N	66.56 W
Ensenada □[5]	288	34.50 S	58.00 W
Enshi	102	30.17 N	109.19 E
Enshū-nada ⊤[2]	92	34.27 N	137.38 E
Ensisheim	58	47.52 N	7.21 E
Enstaberga	40	58.45 N	16.51 E
Entebbe	154	0.04 N	32.28 E
Entenbühl ∧	60	49.46 N	12.24 E
Enter	52	52.18 N	6.34 E
Enterprise, Guy.	246	6.56 N	58.24 W
Enterprise, Al., U.S.	194	31.18 N	85.51 W
Enterprise, Ca., U.S.	204	39.32 N	121.22 W
Enterprise, Ks., U.S.	198	38.54 N	97.07 W
Enterprise, Ms., U.S.	194	32.10 N	88.49 W
Enterprise, Or., U.S.	202	45.25 N	117.16 W
Enterprise, Ut,. U.S.	200	37.34 N	113.43 W
Entiat ≃	202	47.40 N	120.14 W
Entiat, Lake ⊜[1]	202	47.40 N	120.12 W
Entiat Mountains ⋀	224	48.00 N	120.42 W
Entinas, Punta de las ›	34	36.41 N	2.46 W
Entlebuch	58	47.00 N	8.04 E
Entlebuch V	58	46.58 N	8.00 E
Entracque	62	44.14 N	7.24 E
Entraigues-sur-Sorgue	62	44.00 N	4.55 E
Entrains-sur-Nohain	50	47.27 N	3.15 E
Entrance, Cape ›	164	2.21 S	150.12 E
Entraunes	62	44.11 N	6.45 E
Entraygues	32	44.39 N	2.34 E
Entrechaux	62	44.13 N	5.08 E
Entrée, Île d' I	186	47.17 N	61.42 W
Entremont-le-Vieux	62	45.26 N	5.53 E
Entrepeñas, Embalse de ⊜[1]	34	40.34 N	2.42 W
Entre Rios, Bol.	248	21.32 S	64.12 W
Entre Rios, Bra.	255	11.56 S	38.05 W
Entre Ríos □[4]	252	32.00 S	59.00 W
Entre Ríos, Cordillera ⋀	236	14.05 N	85.37 W
Entre-Rios de Minas	255	20.41 S	44.04 W
Entrevaux	62	43.57 N	6.49 E
Entrèves	62	45.49 N	6.57 E
Entriken	214	40.20 N	78.12 W
Entroncamento	34	39.28 N	8.28 W
Entupido	256	22.30 S	44.51 W
Entwistle	182	53.36 N	115.00 W
Enu, Pulau I	164	7.05 S	134.30 E
Enugu	150	6.27 N	7.27 E
Enumclaw	224	47.12 N	121.59 W
Enurmino	180	66.57 N	171.49 W
Envalira, Port d')(	34	42.35 N	1.45 E
Envermeu	50	49.54 N	1.16 E
Envies, Rivière des ≃	206	46.37 N	72.24 W
Envigado	246	6.10 N	75.35 W
Envira	248	7.18 S	70.13 W
Envira ≃	248	6.42 S	69.46 W
'En Yahav	132	30.38 N	35.11 E
Enyamba	154	3.40 S	24.58 E
Enyang	102	31.48 N	106.31 E
Enyellé	152	2.49 N	18.06 E
Enys, Mount ∧	172	43.14 S	171.38 E
Enz ≃	56	49.01 N	9.07 E
Enza ≃	64	44.54 N	10.31 E
Enzan	94	35.42 N	138.44 E
Enzbach ≃	56	49.54 N	6.25 E
Enzenkirchen	60	48.23 N	13.39 E
Enzesfeld	61	47.55 N	16.10 E
Enzklösterle	56	48.40 N	8.28 E
Eo ≃	34	43.28 N	7.03 W
Eolia	219	39.14 N	91.00 W
Eolie o Lipari, Isole II	70	38.30 N	14.50 E
Epanomí	38	40.26 N	22.56 E
Épars, Bois de l' ♦	261	48.45 N	1.45 E
Epe, Dtsch.	52	52.11 N	7.02 E
Epe, Ned.	52	52.21 N	6.00 E
Epe, Nig.	150	6.37 N	3.59 E
Epecuén, Lago ⊜	252	37.10 S	62.54 W
Épéhy	50	50.02 N	3.10 E
Epéna	152	1.22 N	17.29 E
Épernay	50	49.03 N	3.57 E
Épernon	50	48.37 N	1.41 E
Epes	194	32.41 N	88.07 W
Ephesus → Efes ⊥	130	37.55 N	27.17 E
Ephraim	200	39.21 N	111.35 W
Ephrata, Pa., U.S.	208	40.10 N	76.10 W
Ephrata, Wa., U.S.	202	47.19 N	119.33 W
Ephrata Cloister ⊥	208	40.12 N	76.09 W
Ephratah	210	43.00 N	74.32 W
Epi □[8]	175f	16.42 S	168.15 E
Épi I	175f	16.43 S	168.15 E
Épiais-lès-Louvres	261	49.02 N	2.33 E
Épila	34	41.36 N	1.17 W
Épinac-Les-Mines	58	46.59 N	4.31 E
Épinal	58	48.11 N	6.27 E
Épinay-sous-Sénart	261	48.42 N	2.31 E
Épinay-sur-Orge	261	48.40 N	2.20 E
Épinay-sur-Seine	261	48.57 N	2.19 E
Epirus → Ípeiros □[9]	38	39.40 N	20.50 E
Episcopia	68	40.04 N	16.06 E
Episkopí	130	34.40 N	32.54 E
Époisses	50	47.30 N	4.10 E
Epokiro	156	21.41 S	19.08 E
Epomeo, Monte ∧	68	40.44 N	13.54 E
Épône	261	48.57 N	1.49 E
Eport, Loch ⊂	46	57.33 N	7.11 W
Eppalock, Lake ⊜[1]	169	36.52 S	144.31 E
Eppelborn	56	49.24 N	6.58 E
Eppendorf ✈[8]	263	51.27 N	7.11 E
Eppenhausen ✈[8]	263	51.21 N	7.31 E
Eppeville	50	49.44 N	3.03 E
Epping, Austl.	169	37.39 S	145.02 E
Epping, Austl.	274a	33.46 S	151.05 E
Epping, Eng., U.K.	42	51.43 N	0.07 E
Epping, N.H., U.S.	188	43.02 N	71.04 W
Eppingen	56	49.08 N	8.54 E
Epping Forest □[8]	260	51.43 N	0.10 E
Epping Forest ✈[3]	42	51.40 N	0.03 E
Epping Green, Eng., U.K.	260	51.44 N	0.05 E
Epping Green, Eng., U.K.	260	51.45 N	0.07 W
Epping Upland	260	51.43 N	0.06 E
Epsom	42	51.20 N	0.16 W
Epsom and Ewell □[8]	260	51.20 N	0.16 W
Epsom Downs Race Course ♦	260	51.19 N	0.15 W
Epte ≃	50	49.04 N	1.37 E
Épuisay	50	47.54 N	0.56 E
Epukiro ≃	156	20.45 S	21.05 E
Epupa Falls ⌊	152	16.55 S	13.10 E
Epuyén	254	42.14 S	71.21 W
Epworth	44	53.32 N	0.49 W
Eqlīd	128	30.55 N	52.39 E
Equality	194	37.44 N	88.20 W
Équateur □[4]	152	1.00 N	20.30 E
Équateur → Ecuador □[1]	246	2.00 S	77.30 W
Equatorial Guinea (Guinea Ecuatorial) □[1]	152	2.00 N	9.00 E
Équihen-Plage	50	50.41 N	1.34 E
Equimina ≃	152	13.11 S	12.47 E
Equinox Mountain ∧	210	43.10 N	73.08 W
Equinunk	210	41.51 N	75.14 W
Equi Terme	64	44.09 N	10.10 E
Era ≃, It.	66	43.40 N	10.38 E
Era ≃, Pap. N. Gui.	164	7.35 S	144.41 E
Erac Creek ≃	166	26.56 S	145.48 E
Eraclea	64	45.35 N	12.40 E
Eraclea ⊥	68	40.13 N	16.40 E
Eraclea Minoa ⊥	70	37.23 N	13.17 E
Eradu	162	28.41 S	115.02 E
Éragny	261	49.01 N	2.06 E
Eramosa ≃	212	43.32 N	80.14 W
Eran Bay ⊂	116	9.06 N	117.43 E
Eranga	152	1.52 S	18.56 E
Erangal ✈[8]	272c	19.10 N	72.47 E
Erap	164	6.35 S	146.40 E
Erath	194	29.57 N	92.02 W
Erave	164	6.40 S	143.50 E
Erave ≃	164	6.40 S	143.55 E
Erba	62	45.48 N	9.15 E
Erba, Jabal ∧, Sūd.	140	19.04 N	36.46 E
Erba, Jabal ∧, Sūd.	140	20.45 N	36.50 E
Erbaa	130	40.42 N	36.36 E
Erbach, Dtsch.	56	49.40 N	8.59 E
Erbach, Dtsch.	58	48.20 N	9.53 E
Erbendorf	60	49.50 N	12.03 E
Erbeskopf ∧	56	49.44 N	7.05 E
Erchie	68	40.26 N	17.44 E
Erciş	84	39.02 N	43.22 E
Erciyes Dağı ∧	130	38.32 N	35.28 E
Ercolano	68	40.48 N	14.21 E
Ercolano (Herculaneum) ⊥	68	40.46 N	14.20 E
Érd	30	47.23 N	18.56 E
Erdao ≃, Zhg.	98	42.39 N	127.35 E
Erdao ≃, Zhg.	104	42.16 N	122.20 E
Erdao Bai ≃	98	42.34 N	128.08 E
Erdaobaihe	98	42.22 N	128.07 E
Erdaofang, Zhg.	104	41.54 N	123.57 E
Erdaofang, Zhg.	104	41.37 N	122.34 E
Erdaofangshen	104	42.09 N	123.17 E
Erdaogangzi, Zhg.	104	41.57 N	122.09 E
Erdaogangzi, Zhg.	104	42.04 N	123.06 E
Erdaohe	89	43.37 N	127.35 E
Erdaohezi, Zhg.	89	45.07 N	127.16 E
Erdaohezi, Zhg.	89	45.08 N	129.39 E
Erdaojingzi	104	41.49 N	122.20 E
Erdaoliangzi, Zhg.	98	40.50 N	119.04 E
Erdaoliangzi, Zhg.	105	40.31 N	118.03 E
Erdaowan	89	47.58 N	124.33 E
Erdek	130	40.24 N	27.48 E
Erdemli	130	36.37 N	34.18 E
Erdene, Mong.	88	47.48 N	107.55 E
Erdene, Mong.	102	44.15 N	111.14 E
Erdene, Mong.	102	45.08 N	97.45 E
Erdene Bulgan	88	50.07 N	101.35 E
Erdene-Büren	86	48.26 N	91.27 E
Erdenedalaj	102	46.02 N	104.55 E
Erdene Mandal	88	48.30 N	101.21 E
Erdenheim	285	40.05 N	75.12 W
Erdevik	38	45.07 N	19.25 E
Erdiao	106	32.12 N	121.12 E
Erding	60	48.18 N	11.54 E
Erdinger Moos ☷	60	48.22 N	11.52 E
Erdnijevskij	80	46.52 N	46.17 E
Erebato ≃	246	5.54 N	64.16 W
Erebus, Mount ∧	9	77.32 S	167.09 E
Ereğli, Tür.	130	37.31 N	34.04 E
Ereğli, Tür.	130	41.17 N	31.25 E
Eregun	273a	6.36 N	3.22 E
Erei, Monti ⋀	70	37.27 N	14.19 E
Erenas	116	12.25 N	124.19 E
Erenhot	102	43.46 N	112.05 E
Erenköy ✈[8]	267b	40.58 N	29.04 E
Erepecuru, Lago do ⊜	250	1.20 S	56.35 W
Eresma ≃	34	41.26 N	4.45 W
Eressós	38	39.18 N	25.51 E
Erétria	38	38.24 N	23.48 E
Erexim	252	27.38 S	52.17 W
Erez	132	31.34 N	34.34 E
Érezée	56	50.18 N	5.33 E
Erfa ≃	56	49.40 N	9.23 E
Erfde	41	54.19 N	9.19 E
Erfelek	130	41.53 N	34.55 E
Erfenisdam ⊜[1]	158	28.33 S	26.50 E
Erfoud	148	31.28 N	4.10 W
Erft ≃	56	51.11 N	6.44 E
Erftstadt	56	50.48 N	6.46 E
Erfurt	54	50.58 N	11.01 E
Ergak-Targak-Tajga, chrebet ⋀	88	53.25 N	95.30 E
Ergani	130	38.17 N	39.46 E
Ergene ≃	130	41.01 N	26.22 E
Ergenzingen	58	48.29 N	8.48 E
Erges (Erjas) ≃	34	39.40 N	7.01 W
Ērgļi	76	56.54 N	25.38 E
Ergolding	60	48.35 N	12.10 E
Ergoldsbach	60	48.41 N	12.12 E
Ergste	56	51.25 N	7.34 E
Erguig, Bahr ≃	146	11.22 N	15.24 E
Ergun (Argun') ≃	74	53.20 N	121.28 E
Ergun Youqi	89	50.14 N	120.10 E
Ergun Zuoqi	89	50.47 N	121.31 E
Erguvejem ≃	180	65.20 N	176.00 W
Er Hai ⊜	102	25.48 N	100.11 E
Erhlin	100	23.54 N	120.22 E
Erhshui	100	23.49 N	120.36 E
Erhulai	98	41.23 N	125.08 E
Eria ≃	34	42.03 N	5.44 W
Erial	208	39.46 N	75.00 W
Eriba	140	16.37 N	36.04 E
Eriboll	46	58.28 N	4.41 W
Eriboll, Loch ⊂	46	58.31 N	4.41 W
Erica, Austl.	169	37.59 S	146.22 E
Erica, Ned.	52	52.43 N	6.55 E
Erice	70	38.02 N	12.35 E
Ericeira	34	38.59 N	9.25 W
Erichsen Lake ⊜	176	70.38 N	80.21 W
Erichshagen	52	52.40 N	9.14 E
Ericht, Loch ⊜	46	56.48 N	4.24 W
Erick	196	35.12 N	99.51 W
Erickson, B.C., Can.	182	49.05 N	116.28 W
Erickson, Mb., Can.	184	50.30 N	99.55 W
Ericson	198	41.46 N	98.40 W
Erie, Co., U.S.	200	40.03 N	105.03 W
Erie, Il., U.S.	190	41.39 N	90.04 W
Erie, Ks., U.S.	198	37.34 N	95.14 W
Erie, Mi., U.S.	216	41.47 N	83.29 W
Erie, Pa., U.S.	214	42.07 N	80.05 W
Erie □[6], N.Y., U.S.	210	42.54 N	78.53 W
Erie □[6], Oh., U.S.	214	41.27 N	82.42 W
Erie □[6], Pa., U.S.	214	42.08 N	80.04 W
Erie, Lake ⊜	214	42.15 N	81.00 W
Erieau	214	42.16 N	81.56 W
Erie Basin ⊂	276	40.40 N	74.01 W
Erie Beach, On., Can.	214	42.16 N	82.00 W
Erie Beach, On., Can.	284a	42.53 N	78.57 W
Erie Canal → New York State Barge Canal ≍	210	43.05 N	78.43 W
Erie County Fairgrounds ♦	284a	42.45 N	78.49 W
Erie International Airport ⊠	214	42.05 N	80.11 W

	English	Deutsch	Español	Français	Português
≃	River	Fluß	Río	Rivière	Rio
≍	Canal	Kanal	Canal	Canal	Canal
⌊	Waterfall, Rapids	Wasserfall, Stromschnellen	Cascada, Rápidos	Chute d'eau, Rapides	Cascata, Rápidos
⊻	Strait	Meeresstraße	Estrecho	Détroit	Estreito
⊂	Bay, Gulf	Bucht, Golf	Bahía, Golfo	Baie, Golfe	Baía, Golfo
⊜	Lake, Lakes	See, Seen	Lago, Lagos	Lac, Lacs	Lago, Lagos
☷	Swamp	Sumpf	Pantano	Marais	Pântano
⊓	Ice Features, Glacier	Eis- und Gletscherformen	Accidentes Glaciales	Formes glaciaires	Acidentes glaciares
⊤	Other Hydrographic Features	Andere Hydrographische Objekte	Otros Elementos Hidrográficos	Autres données hydrographiques	Outros acidentes hidrográficos
✦	Submarine Features	Untermeerische Objekte	Accidentes Submarinos	Formes de relief sous-marin	Acidentes submarinos
□	Political Unit	Politische Einheit	Unidad Politica	Entité politique	Unidade política
⊍	Cultural Institution	Kulturelle Institution	Institución Cultural	Institution culturelle	Instituição cultural
⊥	Historical Site	Historische Stätte	Sitio Histórico	Site historique	Sitio histórico
♦	Recreational Site	Erholungs- und Ferienort	Sitio de Recreo	Centre de loisirs	Area de Lazer
⊠	Airport	Flughafen	Aeropuerto	Aéroport	Aeroporto
■	Military Installation	Militäranlage	Instalación Militar	Installation militaire	Instalação militar
✈	Miscellaneous	Verschiedenes	Misceláneo	Divers	Diversos

Name	Page	Lat.°′	Long.°′
Eriksberg ⊥	40	58.56 N	16.22 E
Eriksdale	184	50.52 N	98.06 W
Erímanthos ∧	38	37.59 N	21.51 E
Erimo	92a	42.01 N	143.09 E
Erimo-misaki >	92a	41.55 N	143.15 E
Erin, On., Can.	212	43.45 N	80.07 W
Erin, N.Y., U.S.	210	42.11 N	76.40 W
Erin, Tn., U.S.	194	36.19 N	87.41 W
Erindale	275b	43.32 N	79.39 W
Ering	60	48.18 N	13.09 E
Eriskay I	46	57.04 N	7.18 W
Erisort, Loch c	46	58.07 N	6.24 W
Eriswil	58	47.05 N	7.51 E
Erith ◆[8]	260	51.29 N	0.10 E
Erithraí	38	38.13 N	23.19 E
Eritrea □[1], Afr.	144	15.20 N	39.00 E
Eritrea □[1], Afr.	144	15.20 N	39.00 E
Erivan — Jerevan	84	40.11 N	44.30 E
Erjas (Erges) ≃	34	39.40 N	7.01 W
Erjiazhen	106	32.02 N	121.13 E
Erkelenz	56	51.05 N	6.19 E
Erken ⊜	40	59.51 N	18.34 E
Erken-Jurt	84	44.27 N	41.54 E
Erkheim	58	48.02 N	10.20 E
Erkilet	130	38.49 N	35.27 E
Erkina ≃	48	52.51 N	7.23 W
Erkner	54	52.25 N	13.45 E
Erkner, Forst ◆[3]	264a	52.22 N	13.47 E
Erkowit	140	18.46 N	37.07 E
Erkrath	56	51.13 N	6.55 E
Erl	64	47.41 N	12.11 E
Erlach, Öst.	61	47.43 N	16.13 E
Erlach, Schw.	58	47.03 N	7.06 E
Erlands Point	224	47.36 N	122.42 W
Erlangen	60	49.36 N	11.01 E
Erlanger	218	39.01 N	84.36 W
Erlanghe	100	30.19 N	116.04 E
Erlangmiao	100	33.46 N	112.23 E
Erlau ≃	60	48.34 N	13.36 E
Erlauf ≃	61	48.12 N	15.11 E
Erlbach	54	50.18 N	12.22 E
Erldunda	162	25.14 S	133.12 E
Erle ◆[8]	263	51.33 N	7.05 E
Erli	62	44.08 N	8.06 E
Erling	106	31.53 N	119.36 E
Erling, Lake ⊜[1]	194	33.05 N	93.35 W
Erlistoun	162	28.20 S	122.08 E
Erlongshan, Zhg.	89	50.04 N	126.47 E
Erlongshan, Zhg.	89	47.20 N	132.28 E
Erlongshantun	89	48.28 N	126.31 E
Erlsbach	64	46.55 N	12.15 E
Erma	208	38.58 N	74.54 W
Ermana, chrebet ∧∧	88	50.00 N	113.30 E
Ermatingen	58	47.41 N	9.06 E
Erme ≃	42	50.18 N	3.56 W
Ermelindo Matarazzo ◆[8]	287b	23.29 S	46.29 W
Ermelo, Ned.	52	52.17 N	5.37 E
Ermelo, S. Afr.	158	26.34 S	29.58 E
Ermendegou	104	42.02 N	121.56 E
Ermenek	130	36.38 N	32.54 E
Ermenek ≃	130	36.35 N	33.23 E
Ermenonville	50	49.08 N	2.42 E
Ermidas	34	38.00 N	8.23 W
Ermil Post	140	13.37 N	27.36 E
Ermineskin Indian Reserve ◆[4]	182	52.52 N	113.30 W
Ermington	274a	33.48 S	151.04 E
Ermita de Guadalupe	234	22.36 N	103.03 W
Ermita de los Correas	234	22.54 N	103.01 W
Ermont	50	48.59 N	2.16 E
Ermoúpolis	38	37.26 N	24.56 E
Ermsleben	54	51.44 N	11.21 E
Ernaballa	162	26.17 S	132.07 E
Erndtebrück	56	50.59 N	8.15 E
Erne ≃	48	54.30 N	8.16 W
Erne, Lower Lough ⊜	48	54.26 N	7.46 W
Erne, Upper Lough ⊜	48	54.14 N	7.32 W
Ernée	32	48.18 N	0.56 W
Ernest	214	40.41 N	79.10 W
Ernestina	258	35.16 S	59.34 W
Ernest Sound ʮ	182	55.52 N	132.10 W
Ernici, Monti ∧∧	66	41.48 N	13.22 E
Ernstbrunn	61	48.32 N	16.22 E
Ernst Thälmann, Pioneerpark ♠	264a	52.28 N	13.33 E
Ernst-Thälmann-Stadion ♠	264a	52.23 N	13.05 E
Erode	122	11.21 N	77.44 E
Eromanga	166	26.40 S	143.16 E
Erongo	156	21.44 S	15.53 E
Erongo ∧∧	156	21.45 S	15.37 E
Erota	144	16.14 N	37.55 E
Erp	56	50.46 N	6.43 E
Erpuzi	105	40.29 N	115.33 E
Erquelinnes	50	50.18 N	4.07 E
Err, Piz d' ∧	58	46.33 N	9.41 E
Errabiddy	162	25.28 S	117.07 E
Er-Rachidia	148	31.58 N	4.25 W
Er-Rachidia □[4]	148	31.15 N	4.05 W
Errego	154	16.02 S	37.14 E
Errer ≃	144	7.32 N	42.05 E
Er-Riad — Ar-Riyāḍ	128	24.38 N	46.43 E
Errigal Mountain ∧	48	55.02 N	8.07 W
Errington	224	49.17 N	124.22 W
Erris Head >	48	54.19 N	10.00 W
Errochty, Loch ⊜	46	56.45 N	4.12 W
Errogie	46	57.16 N	4.22 W
Errol Heights	224	45.28 N	122.36 W
Erromango I	175f	18.45 S	169.05 E
Ersekë	38	40.20 N	20.41 E
Ershijiazi	104	41.17 N	120.32 E
Ershilipu	105	40.07 N	117.24 E
Ershiqizhan	89	53.23 N	123.16 E
Ershiwuzhan	89	53.22 N	123.55 E
Erskine	198	47.40 N	96.00 W
Erskine, Lake ⊜	276	41.06 N	74.15 W
Erskine Inlet c	176	76.15 N	102.20 W
Erskine Park	274a	33.49 S	150.47 E
Erstein	58	48.26 N	7.40 E
Erste Wiener Hochquellenleitung ≌[1]	61	48.10 N	16.17 E
Erstfeld	58	46.49 N	8.39 E
Ertai, Zhg.	86	46.07 N	90.06 E
Ertai, Zhg.	86	44.14 N	80.52 E
Ertaizi, Zhg.	104	41.52 N	121.56 E
Ertaizi, Zhg.	104	42.05 N	123.35 E
Ertaizi, Zhg.	104	42.35 N	124.00 E
Ertaizi, Zhg.	104	40.47 N	120.54 E
Ertil'	78	51.51 N	40.49 E
Ertingen	58	48.06 N	9.28 E
Ertix (Irtyš) ≃	74	61.04 N	68.52 E
Erto	64	46.16 N	12.22 E
Ertuğrul	130	39.34 N	27.43 E
Ertvelde	50	51.11 N	3.45 E
Eruar	126	23.28 N	87.52 E
Erudina	166	31.28 S	139.23 E
Eruh	130	37.46 N	42.11 E
Erundu	156	20.36 S	16.25 E
Erunkan	273a	6.37 N	3.24 E
Erva, Ponta da >	266c	38.50 N	8.58 W
Erval	252	32.02 S	53.24 W
Erval d'Oeste	252	27.13 S	51.34 W
Ervalla	40	59.22 N	15.15 E
Erving	207	42.36 N	72.23 W
Ervy-le-Châtel	50	48.02 N	3.55 E
Erwin, N.C., U.S.	192	35.19 N	78.40 W
Erwin, Tn., U.S.	192	36.08 N	82.25 W
Erwitte	52	51.37 N	8.20 E
Erwood	184	52.50 N	102.10 W
Erxleben	54	52.13 N	11.14 E
Érythrée — Eritrea □[1]	144	15.20 N	39.00 E
Eryuan	102	26.06 N	99.55 E
Erzaohang	106	31.05 N	121.49 E
Erzberg ◆[7]	61	47.32 N	14.54 E
Erzgebirge (Krušné hory) ∧∧	54	50.30 N	13.10 E
Erzhan	89	43.58 N	128.44 E
Erzhuang	105	39.24 N	117.22 E
Erzin	88	50.15 N	95.10 E
Erzincan	130	39.44 N	39.29 E
Erzincan □[4]	130	39.40 N	39.30 E
Erzingen	58	47.39 N	8.25 E
Erzurum	130	39.55 N	41.17 E
Erzurum □[4]	130	40.00 N	41.30 E
Esa'ala	164	9.44 S	150.49 E
Esambo	152	3.40 S	23.24 E
Esan-misaki >	92a	41.49 N	141.11 E
Esashi, Nihon	92	41.52 N	140.07 E
Esashi, Nihon	92	39.12 N	141.09 E
Esashi, Nihon	92a	44.56 N	142.35 E
Esbiye	130	40.57 N	38.44 E
Esbjerg	26	55.28 N	8.27 E
Esbly	261	48.54 N	2.49 E
Esbo — Espoo	26	60.13 N	24.40 E
Esborn	263	51.23 N	7.20 E
Esca ≃	34	42.37 N	1.03 W
Escada	250	8.22 S	35.14 W
Escalada	258	34.10 S	59.07 W
Escalante, Pil.	116	10.50 N	123.33 E
Escalante, Ut,. U.S.	200	37.46 N	111.36 W
Escalante ≃, Ut,. U.S.	200	37.17 N	110.53 W
Escalante ≃, Ven.	246	9.15 N	71.50 W
Escalante Desert ◆[2]	200	37.50 N	113.30 W
Escalaplano	71	39.37 N	9.21 E
Escalón, Méx.	232	26.45 N	104.20 W
Escalon, Ca., U.S.	226	37.47 N	120.59 W
Escalona	34	40.10 N	4.24 W
Escambia ≃	194	30.32 N	87.11 W
Escanaba	190	45.44 N	87.04 W
Escanaba ≃	190	45.47 N	87.04 W
Escandón, Puerto)(	34	40.17 N	1.00 W
Escárcega	232	18.37 N	90.43 W
Escarpada Point >	116	18.31 N	122.13 E
Escarpado Peak ∧	116	8.36 N	117.22 E
Escarpment	284a	43.10 N	79.00 W
Escatawpa ≃	194	30.25 N	88.35 W
Escaudain	50	50.20 N	3.21 E
Escaut (Schelde) ≃	50	51.22 N	4.15 E
Eschach	58	47.44 N	9.36 E
Eschau	58	48.29 N	7.43 E
Esche ≃	56	48.54 N	6.04 E
Eschebrügge	52	52.37 N	6.46 E
Eschede	52	52.44 N	10.14 E
Eschen	58	47.13 N	9.31 E
Eschenau	60	49.34 N	11.12 E
Eschenbach	60	49.45 N	11.49 E
Eschenburg	56	50.49 N	8.20 E
Eschenlohe	64	47.36 N	11.11 E
Eschershausen	52	51.56 N	9.38 E
Eschlkam	60	49.18 N	12.55 E
Escholzmatt	58	46.55 N	7.56 E
Eschscholtz Bay c	180	66.18 N	161.25 W
Esch-sur-Alzette	56	49.30 N	5.59 E
Esch-sur-Sûre	56	49.55 N	5.55 E
Eschwege	56	51.11 N	10.04 E
Eschweiler	56	50.49 N	6.16 E
Esclave, Grand Lac de l' — Great Slave Lake ⊜	176	61.30 N	114.00 W
Esclavo, Gran Lago del — Great Slave Lake ⊜	176	61.30 N	114.00 W
Escobal	236	9.09 N	79.58 W
Escobar □[5]	288	34.23 S	58.46 W
Escobar, Arroyo ≃	288	34.21 S	58.44 W
Escobedo, Méx.	196	27.13 N	101.21 W
Escobedo, Méx.	232	29.05 N	102.19 W
Escocesa, Bahía c	238	19.25 N	69.45 W
Escoheag	207	41.36 N	71.45 W
Escondido	228	33.07 N	117.05 W
Escondido ≃, Méx.	196	28.39 N	100.34 W
Escondido ≃, Nic.	236	12.04 N	83.45 W
Escondido Creek ≃	228	33.01 N	117.15 W
Escorial — San Lorenzo de El Escorial	34	40.35 N	4.09 W
Escoutay ≃	62	44.29 N	4.42 E
Escravos ≃[1]	150	5.35 N	5.10 E
Escrick	44	53.53 N	1.02 W
Escuadrón 201 ◆[8]	286a	19.22 N	99.06 W
Escudero, Arroyo ≃	258	34.20 S	57.05 W
Escudo de Veraguas, Isla I	236	9.06 N	81.33 W
Escuinapa de Hidalgo	234	22.51 N	105.48 W
Escuintla, Guat.	236	14.18 N	90.47 W
Escuintla, Méx.	232	15.20 N	92.38 W
Escuintla □[5]	236	14.10 N	91.00 W
Escuminac, Point >	186	47.04 N	64.46 W
Esebi	154	2.57 N	30.39 E
Eséka	152	3.39 N	10.46 E
Eşen	130	36.27 N	29.16 E
Eşen ≃	130	36.16 N	29.15 E
Esenler ◆[8]	267b	41.02 N	28.51 E
Esens	52	53.39 N	7.37 E
Esera ≃	34	42.06 N	0.15 E
Esesi	130	39.49 N	39.19 E
Eşfahān (Isfahan)	128	32.40 N	51.38 E
Eşfahān □[4]	128	33.00 N	52.00 E
Esfandaqeh	128	28.38 N	57.12 E
Esfarāyen	128	37.02 N	57.27 E
Esgueva ≃	34	41.40 N	4.43 W
Eshan	102	24.11 N	102.22 E
Esher ◆[8]	42	51.23 N	0.22 W
Eshkāshem	123	36.42 N	71.34 E
Eshowe	158	28.58 S	31.29 E
Esh-Sham — Dimashq	132	33.30 N	36.18 E
Eshta'ol	132	31.47 N	35.00 E
Esh Winning	44	54.47 N	1.43 W
Esiama	150	4.56 N	2.21 W
Esigodini	154	20.18 S	28.56 E
Esine	64	45.55 N	10.15 E
Esino ≃	66	43.39 N	13.22 E
Esira	157b	24.20 S	46.42 E
Esk	171a	27.15 S	152.25 E
Esk ≃, N.Z.	172	43.06 S	171.57 E
Esk ≃, U.K.	44	54.58 N	3.04 W
Esk ≃, Eng., U.K.	44	54.29 N	0.37 W
Esk ≃, Eng., U.K.	44	54.21 N	3.23 W
Esk ≃, Scot., U.K.	46	55.57 N	3.03 W
Eskdale, N.Z.	172	39.24 S	176.50 E
Eskdale, W.V., U.S.	188	38.05 N	81.26 W
Eskdale V	44	55.10 N	3.00 W
Eske, Lough ⊜	48	54.41 N	8.03 W
Eski Dzhumaya — Tărgovište	38	43.15 N	26.34 E
Eskifjördur	24a	65.04 N	13.59 W
Eskiikan	85	43.12 N	68.31 E
Eskilstrup	41	54.51 N	11.54 E
Eskilstuna	40	59.22 N	16.30 E
Eskimalatya	130	38.26 N	38.23 E
Eskimo Lakes ⊜	180	69.15 N	132.17 W
Eskimo Point	176	61.07 N	94.03 W
Eskipazar	130	40.58 N	32.33 E
Eskişehir	130	39.46 N	30.32 E
Eskişehir □[4]	130	39.35 N	31.10 E
Eskridge	198	38.51 N	96.06 W
Esla ≃	34	41.29 N	6.03 W
Eslāmābād	128	34.06 N	46.31 E
Eslām Qal'eh	128	34.40 N	61.04 E
Eslāmshahr	128	35.40 N	51.10 E
Eslarn	60	49.35 N	12.32 E
Eslohe	56	51.15 N	8.09 E
Eslöv	41	55.50 N	13.20 E
Eşme	130	38.24 N	28.59 E
Esmeralda, Austl.	166	18.50 S	142.34 E
Esmeralda, Cuba	240p	21.51 N	78.07 W
Esmeralda, Méx.	196	25.40 N	103.30 W
Esmeralda, Isla I	254	48.57 S	75.25 W
Esmeraldas	246	0.59 N	79.42 W
Esmeraldas □[4]	246	0.40 N	79.30 W
Esmeraldas ≃	246	0.58 N	79.38 W
Esmirna — İzmir	130	38.25 N	27.09 E
Esmond, N.D., U.S.	198	48.02 N	99.45 W
Esmond, R.I., U.S.	207	41.52 N	71.29 W
Esnagi Lake ⊜	190	48.38 N	84.32 W
Esneux	56	50.32 N	5.34 E
Esong	152	2.09 N	10.58 E
Esopus Creek ≃	210	42.04 N	73.56 W
Espada, Punta >	246	12.05 N	71.07 W
Espagne — Spain □[1]	34	40.00 N	4.00 W
Espalion	32	44.31 N	2.46 E
Espaly-Saint-Marcel	62	45.03 N	3.52 E
España — Spain □[1]	34	40.00 N	4.00 W
Espanola, On., Can.	190	46.15 N	81.46 W
Espanola, N.M., U.S.	200	35.59 N	106.04 W
Española, Isla I	246a	1.25 S	89.42 W
Esparto	226	38.41 N	122.00 W
Esparza	236	9.59 N	84.40 W
Espasingen	58	47.49 N	9.00 E
Espe, Dan.	41	55.12 N	10.25 E
Espe, Kaz.	85	43.52 N	74.10 E
Espejo	34	37.41 N	4.33 W
Espelkamp	52	52.25 N	8.36 E
Espenberg, Cape >	180	66.33 N	163.36 W
Espenhain	54	51.11 N	12.29 E
Espera, Arroyo ≃[1]	288	34.24 S	58.36 W
Espera Feliz	255	20.39 S	41.55 W
Esperança, Bra.	246	4.24 S	69.52 W
Esperança, Bra.	250	7.01 S	35.51 W
Esperance, Austl.	162	33.51 S	121.53 E
Esperance, N.Y., U.S.	210	42.46 N	74.15 W
Esperance Bay c	162	33.51 S	121.53 E
Esperantina	250	3.54 S	42.14 W
Esperantinópolis	250	4.53 S	44.53 W
Esperanza, Arg.	252	31.27 S	60.56 W
Esperanza, Cuba	240p	22.27 N	80.06 W
Esperanza, Méx.	232	27.35 N	109.56 W
Esperanza, Méx.	234	18.52 N	97.24 W
Esperanza, Pil.	116	8.43 N	125.36 E
Esperanza, Pil.	116	11.44 N	124.03 E
Esperanza, P.R.	240m	18.06 N	65.28 W
Esperanza, S. Afr.	158	30.21 S	30.40 E
Esperanza ʊ[3]	9	63.24 S	56.59 W
Esperanza Inlet c	182	49.48 N	126.50 W
Espergærde	41	56.00 N	12.34 E
Esperia	66	41.23 N	13.41 E
Esperito, Arroyo ≃[1]	288	34.23 S	58.36 W
Espevær	26	59.36 N	5.10 E
Espichel, Cabo >	34	38.25 N	9.13 W
Espinal	246	4.09 N	74.53 W
Espinazo	196	26.16 N	101.06 W
Espinazo, Sierra del — Espinhaço, Serra do ∧∧	255	17.30 S	43.30 W
Espingarda ≃	250	10.03 S	47.13 W
Espinhaço, Serra do ∧∧	255	17.30 S	43.30 W
Espinho	34	41.00 N	8.39 W
Espinillo	252	24.58 S	58.34 W
Espinillo, Arroyo ≃	258	34.59 S	57.36 W
Espinillo, Punta del >	258	34.50 S	56.26 W
Espino	246	8.34 N	66.01 W
Espinosa	255	14.56 S	42.50 W
Espírito Santo □[3]	255	19.30 S	40.30 W
Espírito Santo do Dourado	256	22.03 S	45.58 W
Espírito Santo — Vila Velha	250	3.13 N	51.13 W
Espiritu Santo I	175f	15.15 S	166.50 E
Espíritu Santo, Isla I	232	24.30 N	110.22 W
Espita	232	21.01 N	88.19 W
Espoir, Bay d' c	186	47.50 N	55.51 W
Espoo (Esbo)	26	60.13 N	24.40 E
Esposende	34	41.32 N	8.47 W
Esposizione Universale di Roma ♠	267a	41.50 N	12.28 E
Espugues de Llobregat	266d	41.22 N	2.05 E
Espumoso	252	28.44 S	52.51 W
Espungabera	156	20.29 S	32.48 E
Espy	210	41.00 N	76.24 W
Espyville Station	214	41.36 N	80.29 W
Esquatzel Coulee V	202	46.17 N	119.07 W
Esquel	254	42.54 S	71.19 W
Esquimalt	224	48.26 N	123.24 W
Esquina	252	30.01 S	59.32 W
Esquina Negra	258	35.02 S	58.03 W
Esquipulas, Guat.	236	14.34 N	89.21 W
Esquipulas, Nic.	236	12.40 N	85.47 W
Esquiú	252	29.23 S	65.17 W
Esrum Sø ⊜	41	56.00 N	12.24 E
Essa ≃	76	54.53 N	28.40 E
Essaoui Mellene, Oued V	148	27.26 N	6.40 E
Essaouira (Mogador)	148	31.30 N	9.47 W
Essaouira □[4]	148	31.25 N	9.30 W
Essarts	261	48.30 N	1.46 E
Essé	152	4.05 N	11.53 E
Esse ≃	66	43.16 N	11.54 E
Esseg — Osijek	38	45.33 N	18.41 E
Es-Sekhira	148	34.17 N	10.06 E
Essen, Bel.	50	51.28 N	4.28 E
Essen, Dtsch.	52	52.43 N	7.57 E
Essen, Dtsch.	56	51.28 N	7.01 E
Essen, Dtsch.	263	51.28 N	7.01 E
Essenbach	60	48.37 N	12.13 E
Essenberg ◆[8]	263	51.26 N	6.42 E
Essendon, Austl.	169	37.46 S	144.55 E
Essendon, Eng., U.K.	260	51.46 N	0.09 W
Essendon, Mount ∧	162	24.59 S	120.28 E
Essendon Airport ⊠	169	37.43 S	144.53 E
Essen-Mülheim, Flughafen ⊠	263	51.24 N	6.58 E
Essentuki — Jessentuki	84	44.03 N	42.51 E
Essequibo ≃	246	6.59 N	58.23 W
Essequibo Islands-West Demerara □[4]	246	6.40 N	58.30 W
Es Sers	36	36.04 N	9.02 E
Essex, On., Can.	214	42.10 N	82.49 W
Essex, Ct., U.S.	207	41.21 N	72.23 W
Essex, Il., U.S.	216	41.11 N	88.11 W
Essex, Ia., U.S.	198	40.50 N	95.18 W
Essex, Md., U.S.	208	39.18 N	76.28 W
Essex, Ma., U.S.	207	42.37 N	70.47 W
Essex, Mo., U.S.	194	36.48 N	89.51 W
Essex, Mt., U.S.	182	48.16 N	113.36 W
Essex □[6], On., Can.	214	42.10 N	82.50 W
Essex □[6], Eng., U.K.	42	51.48 N	0.40 E
Essex □[6], Ma., U.S.	207	42.40 N	70.55 W
Essex □[6], N.J., U.S.	210	40.48 N	74.12 W
Essex □[6], Vt., U.S.	206	44.57 N	71.43 W
Essex □[6], Va., U.S.	208	37.55 N	76.55 W
Essex ≃	283	42.39 N	70.46 W
Essex Bay c	283	42.39 N	70.44 W
Essex Fells	276	40.49 N	74.17 W
Essex Junction	188	44.29 N	73.06 W
Essex Skypark ⊠	284b	39.18 N	76.28 W
Essexville	190	43.36 N	83.50 W
Essing	60	48.56 N	11.47 E
Essington	285	39.52 N	75.18 W
Essling ◆[8]	264b	48.13 N	16.32 E
Esslingen	56	48.45 N	9.16 E
Es Smala es Souassi	36	35.21 N	10.33 E
Esson Lake ⊜	212	45.02 N	78.16 W
Essonne □[5]	50	48.36 N	2.20 E
Essonne ≃	50	48.37 N	2.29 E
Essoyes	58	48.04 N	4.32 E
Es-Suki	140	13.20 N	33.54 E
Essvik	26	62.19 N	17.24 E
Est □[4]	152	4.00 N	14.00 E
Est, Canal de l' ≌	56	48.45 N	5.35 E
Est, Cap >	157b	15.16 S	50.29 E
Est, Gare ◆[5]	261	48.53 N	2.22 E
Est, Île de l' I	186	47.37 N	61.26 W
Est, Pointe de l' >	186	49.08 N	61.41 W
Estacada	224	45.17 N	122.19 W
Estaca de Bares, Punta de la >	34	43.46 N	7.42 W
Estacado, Llano ≚	196	33.30 N	102.40 W
Estación La Colorado	234	23.52 N	102.26 W
Estado, Parque do ♠	287b	23.39 S	46.37 W
Estados, Isla de los (Staten Island) I	254	54.47 S	64.15 W
Estados Unidos — United States □[1]	178	38.00 N	97.00 W
Eşţahbān	128	29.08 N	54.04 E
Estaires	50	50.38 N	2.43 E
Estambul — İstanbul	130	41.01 N	28.58 E
Estância, Bra.	250	11.16 S	37.26 W
Estancia, Pil.	116	11.28 N	123.09 E
Estancia, S. Afr.	158	26.17 S	29.52 E
Estancia, N.M., U.S.	200	34.45 N	106.03 W
Estancia Los López	234	20.53 N	104.31 W
Estanislao del Campo	252	25.03 S	60.06 W
Estanzuelas	236	13.38 N	88.30 W
Estarreja	34	40.45 N	8.34 W
Estats, Pique d' ∧	34	42.40 N	1.24 E
Estavayer-le-Lac	58	46.51 N	6.50 E
Estcourt	158	29.01 S	29.52 E
Este	64	45.14 N	11.39 E
Este ≃	52	53.32 N	9.47 E
Este, Parque Nacional del ♠	286c	10.30 N	66.50 W
Este, Punta >	240m	18.08 N	65.16 W
Esteban Echeverría	258	34.50 S	58.28 W
Esteban Echeverría □[5]	288	34.51 S	58.32 W
Estefanía, Lago — Stefanie, Lake ⊜	144	4.40 N	36.50 E
Esteio	252	29.51 S	51.10 W
Estelí	236	13.05 N	86.23 W
Estelí □[5]	236	13.10 N	86.20 W
Estella	34	42.40 N	2.02 W
Estelline, S.D., U.S.	198	44.34 N	96.54 W
Estelline, Tx., U.S.	196	34.33 N	100.26 W
Estell Manor	208	39.24 N	74.44 W
Estèng	62	44.14 N	6.45 E
Estepa	34	37.18 N	4.54 W
Estepas de Kirguises — Kirgizskij chrebet ∧∧	85	42.30 N	74.00 E
Estepona	34	36.26 N	5.08 W
Ester	180	64.51 N	148.01 W
Esterel ∧∧	62	43.30 N	6.50 E
Esterhazy	184	50.40 N	102.08 W
Esterhazy, Schloss ⊥	61	47.51 N	16.32 E
Estérias, Cap >	152	0.37 N	9.20 E
Esternay	50	48.44 N	3.34 E
Estero	220	26.26 N	81.49 W
Estero Bay c, Ca., U.S.	226	35.24 N	120.53 W
Estero Bay c, Fl., U.S.	220	26.25 N	81.52 W
Estero Island I	220	26.26 N	81.56 W
Estéron ≃	62	43.49 N	7.11 E
Esteros	252	26.37 S	63.39 W
Esterwegen	52	52.59 N	7.38 E
Estes Park	200	40.22 N	105.31 W
Este Sudeste, Cayos del II	236	12.26 N	81.27 W
Estevan	184	49.08 N	102.59 W
Estevan Group II	182	53.05 N	129.40 W
Estevan Point	182	49.23 N	126.33 W
Esther Island I	180	60.50 N	148.05 W
Estherville	198	43.24 N	94.49 W
Estill	192	32.45 N	81.14 W
Estissac	50	48.16 N	3.49 E
Estiva	256	22.28 S	46.02 W
Estiva, Ribeirão da ≃	287b	23.44 S	46.23 W
Estiva, Rio da ≃	255	12.23 S	45.05 W
Estling, Lake ⊜	276	40.53 N	74.30 W
Estocolmo — Stockholm	40	59.20 N	18.03 E
Eston, Sk., Can.	184	51.10 N	108.46 W
Eston, Eng., U.K.	44	54.34 N	1.07 W
Estonia (Eesti) □[1], Europe	22	59.00 N	26.00 E
Estonia (Eesti) □[1], Europe	76	59.00 N	26.00 E
Estoril	34	38.42 N	9.23 W
Estrasburgo — Strasbourg	58	48.35 N	7.45 E
Estrées-Saint-Denis	50	49.26 N	2.39 E
Estrela	252	29.29 S	51.58 W
Estrela ∧	34	40.19 N	7.37 W
Estrela ≃	287a	22.43 S	43.13 W
Estrela, Serra da ∧∧	34	40.20 N	7.38 W
Estrela do Norte	255	13.49 S	49.04 W
Estrela do Sul	255	18.46 S	47.42 W
Estrella ≃	226	35.45 N	120.41 W
Estremadura □[9]	34	39.15 N	9.10 W
Estremoz	34	38.51 N	7.35 W
Estribo	234	22.26 N	99.17 W
Estrondo, Serra do ∧∧[1]	250	9.00 S	48.45 W
Estuaire □[4]	152	0.15 N	10.00 E
Estuary	184	50.56 N	109.46 W
Esumba, Île I	152	2.00 N	21.12 E
Eszék — Osijek	38	45.33 N	18.41 E
Esztergom	30	47.48 N	18.45 E
Étables	32	48.38 N	2.50 W
Etadunna	166	28.43 S	138.38 E
Etah, India	124	27.38 N	78.40 E
Etah, Kal. Nun.	16	78.19 N	72.38 W
Étain	56	49.13 N	5.38 E
Etajima	96	34.15 N	132.30 E
Eta-jima I	96	34.15 N	132.28 E
Étalle	56	49.41 N	5.36 E
Étamaniou ≃	186	50.17 N	59.58 W
Étampes	50	48.26 N	2.09 E
Etamunbanie, Lake ⊜	166	26.15 S	139.44 E
Étaples	50	50.31 N	1.39 E
États-Unis — United States □[1]	178	38.00 N	97.00 W
Etāwah	124	26.46 N	79.02 E
Etchemin ≃	186	46.46 N	71.14 W
Etchojoa	232	26.55 N	109.38 W
Etéké	152	1.29 S	11.35 E
Etembue	152	1.17 N	9.25 E
Etendard, Pic de l' ∧	62	45.09 N	6.09 E
Ethan	198	43.32 N	97.59 W
Ethel	194	33.07 N	89.27 W
Ethel ≃	162	24.09 S	118.26 E
Ethel, Mount ∧	200	40.39 N	106.41 W
Ethelbert	184	51.31 N	100.22 W
Ethel Creek	162	22.54 S	120.09 E
Ethel Lake ⊜	180	63.21 N	136.00 W
Etherow ≃	262	53.24 N	2.03 W
Ethiopia (Ityopiya) □[1], Afr.	136	9.00 N	39.00 E
Ethiopia (Ityopiya) □[1], Afr.	144	9.00 N	39.00 E
Ethiopian Plateau ∧∧[1]	144	9.00 N	38.00 E
Ethiopie — Ethiopia □[1]	144	9.00 N	39.00 E
Ethridge, Mt., U.S.	202	48.33 N	112.07 W
Ethridge, Tn., U.S.	194	35.19 N	87.18 W
Eticoga	150	11.09 N	16.08 W
Eticuera Creek ≃	226	38.41 N	122.16 W
Etigo-heiya ≚	92	37.45 N	139.00 E
Etili	130	39.59 N	26.54 E
Étiolles	261	48.38 N	2.29 E
Etiopía — Ethiopia □[1]	144	9.00 N	39.00 E
Etive, Loch ⊜	46	56.29 N	5.09 W
Etiwanda	228	34.08 N	117.31 W
Etjo ∧	156	21.09 S	16.30 E
Etna, Ca., U.S.	204	41.27 N	122.53 W
Etna, N.Y., U.S.	210	42.29 N	76.23 W
Etna, Pa., U.S.	214	40.30 N	79.56 W
Etna, Wy., U.S.	200	43.02 N	111.00 W
Etna, Monte (Mongibello) ∧[1]	70	37.46 N	15.00 E
Etna Green	216	41.17 N	86.03 W
Etne	26	59.40 N	5.56 E
Etobicoke	212	43.42 N	79.32 W
Etobicoke Creek ≃	212	43.35 N	79.32 W
Etoile	154	11.38 S	27.34 E
Étoile, Chaîne de l' ∧∧	62	43.22 N	5.30 E
Etoka	152	0.10 N	23.23 E
Etolin Island I	180	56.08 N	132.26 W
Etolin Strait ʮ	180	60.20 N	165.15 W
Etomami ≃	184	52.48 N	102.33 W
Eton, Austl.	166	21.16 S	148.58 E
Eton, Eng., U.K.	42	51.30 N	0.36 W
Eton College ʊ[2]	260	51.30 N	0.36 W
Etondo	152	7.46 S	23.36 E
Etorofu-tō — Iturup, ostrov I	92a	44.54 N	147.30 E
Etosha National Park ♠	156	19.00 S	15.50 E
Etosha Pan ≚	156	18.45 S	16.15 E
Etoumbi	152	0.01 S	14.57 E
Etowah	192	35.19 N	84.31 W
Etowah ≃	192	34.15 N	85.11 W
Étréchy	50	48.30 N	2.12 E
Étrépagny	50	49.18 N	1.37 E
Étretat	50	49.42 N	0.12 E
Etrotroka	157b	22.53 S	47.36 E
Etroubles	62	45.49 N	7.14 E
Etrusca, Necropoli ⊥	66	42.15 N	11.47 E
Etsch — Adige ≃	64	45.10 N	12.20 E
Ettal	64	47.34 N	11.05 E
Ettalong	170	33.31 S	151.21 E
Ettelbruck	56	49.52 N	6.05 E
Ettenheim	58	48.15 N	7.49 E
Etten-Leur	52	51.34 N	4.38 E
Etterbeek	56	50.50 N	4.23 E
Etters	208	40.09 N	76.45 W
Et Tîdra I	150	19.44 N	16.24 W
Ettington	42	52.09 N	1.36 W
Ettlingen	56	48.56 N	8.24 E
Ettrema Creek ≃	170	34.50 S	150.22 E
Ettrick	208	37.14 N	77.25 W
Ettrick Forest ◆[3]	46	55.30 N	3.00 W
Ettrick Pen ∧	44	55.22 N	3.16 W
Ettrick Water ≃	46	55.31 N	2.55 W
Ettringen, Dtsch.	56	50.21 N	7.13 E
Ettringen, Dtsch.	58	48.06 N	10.39 E
Etuku	154	3.43 S	25.44 E
Etyka	88	51.00 N	116.50 E
Etzatlán	234	20.46 N	104.05 W
Etzikom Coulee ≃	184	49.25 N	111.10 W
Etzná ⊥	232	19.35 N	90.15 W
Eu	50	50.03 N	1.25 E
Eua I	14	21.22 S	174.56 W
Eua Iki I	174w	21.07 S	174.59 W
Eubank Acres	222	30.23 N	97.42 W
Euboea — Évvoia I	38	38.34 N	23.50 E
Eucalyptus Hills	228	32.56 N	116.56 W
Euchiniko ≃	182	53.14 N	123.30 W
Eucla	162	31.43 S	128.52 E
Euclid, Oh., U.S.	214	41.35 N	81.31 W
Euclid, Pa., U.S.	214	41.00 N	79.56 W
Euclid Center	216	42.08 N	86.24 W
Euclid Creek ≃	279a	41.35 N	81.35 W
Euclid Creek Reservation ♠	279a	41.33 N	81.32 W
Euclides da Cunha	250	10.31 S	39.01 W
Eucumbene	171b	36.07 S	148.38 E
Eucumbene ≃	171b	36.21 S	148.38 E
Eucumbene, Lake ⊜[1]	171b	36.05 S	148.45 E
Eudistes, Lac des ⊜	186	50.30 N	65.15 W
Eudora, Ar., U.S.	194	33.06 N	91.15 W
Eudora, Ks., U.S.	198	38.56 N	95.05 W
Eudunda	168b	34.11 S	139.04 E
Eufaula, Al., U.S.	194	31.53 N	85.08 W
Eufaula, Ok., U.S.	196	35.17 N	95.34 W
Eufaula Lake ⊜[1]	196	35.17 N	95.31 W
Eufrates — Euphrates ≃	128	31.00 N	47.25 E
Euganei, Colli ∧∧[2]	64	45.19 N	11.40 E
Eugendorf	64	47.52 N	13.07 E
Eugene	202	44.03 N	123.05 W
Eugenia, Punta >	232	27.50 N	115.05 W
Eugenia Lake ⊜	212	44.20 N	80.30 W
Eugenio Bustos	252	33.46 S	69.04 W
Eugênio de Melo	256	23.09 S	45.47 W
Eugmo I	26	63.49 N	22.45 E
Eugowra	166	33.26 S	148.23 E
Euijeongbu — Ŭijŏngbu	98	37.44 N	127.03 E
Euless	222	32.50 N	97.04 W
Eulo	166	28.10 S	145.03 E
Eume ≃	34	43.25 N	8.08 W
Eumemmerring Creek ≃	274b	38.03 S	145.10 E
Eumungerie	166	31.57 S	148.37 E
Eunápolis	255	16.22 S	39.35 W
Eungella National Park ♠	166	21.00 S	148.30 E
Eunice, La., U.S.	194	30.29 N	92.25 W
Eunice, N.M., U.S.	196	32.26 N	103.09 W
Eupen	56	50.38 N	6.02 E
Euphrates (Firat) (Nahr al-Furāt) ≃	128	31.00 N	47.25 E
Euphrat — Euphrates ≃	128	31.00 N	47.25 E
Eupora	194	33.32 N	89.16 W
Eure	208	36.25 N	76.51 W
Eure □[5]	50	49.10 N	1.00 E
Eure ≃	50	49.18 N	1.12 E
Eure-et-Loir □[5]	50	48.30 N	1.30 E
Eureka, Ak., U.S.	180	61.56 N	147.10 W
Eureka, Ca., U.S.	204	40.48 N	124.09 W
Eureka, Il., U.S.	190	40.43 N	89.16 W
Eureka, Ks., U.S.	198	37.49 N	96.17 W
Eureka, Mo., U.S.	219	38.30 N	90.37 W
Eureka, Mt., U.S.	202	48.52 N	115.03 W
Eureka, Nv., U.S.	204	39.30 N	115.57 W
Eureka, Pa., U.S.	214	40.15 N	78.46 W
Eureka, S.C., U.S.	192	34.42 N	81.11 W
Eureka, S.D., U.S.	198	45.46 N	99.37 W
Eureka, Tx., U.S.	222	32.01 N	96.18 W
Eureka, Ut,. U.S.	200	39.57 N	112.07 W
Eureka, Mount ∧	162	26.34 S	121.32 E
Eureka Springs	194	36.24 N	93.44 W
Eurialo, Castello ⊥	70	37.06 N	15.14 E
Eurinilla Creek ≃	166	30.50 S	140.01 E
Euroa	169	36.45 S	145.35 E
Euro Disney, Parc ♠	261	48.51 N	2.47 E
Europa, Île I	138	22.20 S	40.22 E
Europa, Picos de ∧∧	34	43.12 N	4.48 W
Europabrücke ◆[5]	64	47.11 N	11.23 E
Europa Point >	34	36.10 N	5.22 W
Europe ⊥[1]	4	50.00 N	28.00 E
Europe ⊥[1]	10	50.00 N	28.00 E
Europoort ◆[5]	52	51.57 N	4.07 E
Eursinge	52	52.46 N	6.28 E
Eurville	58	48.35 N	5.02 E
Euseigne	58	46.10 N	7.25 E
Euskal Herriko □[4]	34	43.00 N	2.30 W
Euskirchen	56	50.39 N	6.47 E
Eustace	222	32.18 N	96.01 W
Eustis, Fl., U.S.	220	28.51 N	81.41 W
Eustis, Ne., U.S.	198	40.39 N	100.09 W
Eustis, Lake ⊜	220	28.50 N	81.44 W
Euston	166	34.35 S	142.44 E
Euston Station ◆[5]	260	51.32 N	0.08 W
Eutaw	194	32.50 N	87.53 W
Eutin	54	54.08 N	10.37 E
Eutingen	56	48.55 N	8.45 E
Eutsuk Lake ⊜	182	53.20 N	126.44 W
Eutzsch	54	51.49 N	12.38 E
Euxton	44	53.39 N	2.40 W
Euzet-les-Bains	62	44.04 N	4.14 E
Eva	194	34.20 N	86.46 W
Evadale	194	30.21 N	94.04 W
Eva Downs	162	18.01 S	134.52 E
Evale	152	16.33 S	15.44 E
Evällen ⊜	40	60.03 N	18.20 E
Evançon ≃	62	45.40 N	7.41 E
Evandale	166	41.34 S	147.14 E
Evans	200	40.22 N	104.41 W
Evans, Lac ⊜	176	50.55 N	77.00 W
Evans, Mount ∧	200	39.35 N	105.38 W
Evansburg, Ab., Can.	182	53.36 N	115.01 W
Evansburg, Pa., U.S.	285	40.11 N	75.26 W
Evans Center	210	42.39 N	79.02 W
Evans City	214	40.46 N	80.03 W
Evans Creek ≃	202	42.25 N	123.11 W
Evansdale	190	42.28 N	92.16 W
Evans Head >	166	29.07 S	153.26 E
Evans Mills	212	44.05 N	75.48 W
Evansport	216	41.25 N	84.24 W
Evans Strait ʮ	176	63.15 N	82.00 W
Evanston, Il., U.S.	216	42.02 N	87.41 W
Evanston, Pa., U.S.	279b	40.16 N	79.41 W
Evanston, Wy., U.S.	200	41.16 N	110.57 W
Evansville, Il., U.S.	194	38.05 N	89.56 W
Evansville, In., U.S.	194	37.58 N	87.33 W
Evansville, Mn., U.S.	198	46.00 N	95.40 W
Evansville, Wi., U.S.	216	42.46 N	89.17 W
Evansville, Wy., U.S.	200	42.51 N	106.16 W
Evant	196	31.29 N	98.09 W
Evanton	46	57.40 N	4.20 W
Eva Perón — La Plata	258	34.55 S	57.57 W
Evart	190	43.54 N	85.15 W
Evarts	192	36.51 N	83.11 W
Evaz	128	27.46 N	53.59 E
Ève	261	49.05 N	2.42 E
Evecquemont	261	49.02 N	1.57 E
Eveking	263	51.14 N	7.44 E
Eveleth	190	47.27 N	92.32 W
Evelyn, Mount ∧[2]	164	13.36 S	132.53 E
Evening Shade	194	36.04 N	91.37 W
Evenkamp	263	51.40 N	7.39 E
Evenlode ≃	42	51.47 N	1.21 W
Evensk	74	61.57 N	159.14 E
Evenwood	44	54.37 N	1.46 W
Even Yehuda	132	32.16 N	34.53 E
Everard, Lake ⊜	162	31.25 S	135.05 E
Everard, Mount ∧, Austl.	162	26.16 S	132.04 E
Everard, Mount ∧, B.C., Can.	182	51.05 N	125.45 W
Everard Ranges ∧∧	162	27.05 S	132.28 E
Evercreech	42	51.09 N	2.30 W
Evere	56	50.52 N	4.24 E
Everest	198	39.40 N	95.25 W
Everest, Mount (Qomolangma Feng) ∧	124	27.59 N	86.56 E
Everett, On., Can.	212	44.11 N	79.57 W
Everett, Ma., U.S.	207	42.24 N	71.03 W
Everett, N.J., U.S.	276	40.21 N	74.09 W
Everett, Pa., U.S.	188	40.00 N	78.22 W
Everett, Wa., U.S.	224	47.58 N	122.12 W
Everett, Mount ∧	207	42.06 N	73.25 W
Evergem	50	51.07 N	3.42 E
Everglades City	220	25.52 N	81.23 W
Everglades National Park ♠	220	25.27 N	80.53 W
Evergreen, Al., U.S.	194	31.26 N	86.57 W
Evergreen, Ca., U.S.	204	35.54 N	120.26 W
Evergreen, Mt., U.S.	202	48.13 N	114.18 W
Evergreen, Tx., U.S.	222	30.33 N	95.14 W
Evergreen Lake ⊜[1]	216	40.40 N	89.02 W
Evergreen Park	216	41.43 N	87.42 W
Evergreen Plaza ◆[9]	278	41.43 N	87.41 W
Everly	198	43.09 N	95.19 W
Everman	222	32.37 N	97.17 W
Everman, Volcán ∧[1]	232	18.48 N	110.59 W
Everöd	26	55.54 N	14.06 E
Eversael	263	51.33 N	6.39 E
Eversberg	56	51.21 N	8.20 E
Eversen	52	52.45 N	10.02 E
Everson, Pa., U.S.	214	40.05 N	79.35 W
Everson, Wa., U.S.	224	48.55 N	122.20 W
Everswinkel	52	51.55 N	7.50 E
Everton	218	39.34 N	85.05 W
Everton ◆[8]	262	53.25 N	2.58 W
Everton Football Ground ♠	262	53.26 N	2.58 W
Evesen	52	52.17 N	8.59 E
Evesham, Sk., Can.	184	52.24 N	109.50 W
Evesham, Eng., U.K.	42	52.06 N	1.56 W
Evesham, Vale of V	42	52.06 N	1.50 W
Évian-les-Bains	58	46.23 N	6.35 E
Evijärvi	26	63.22 N	23.29 E
Evinayong	152	1.27 N	10.34 E
Eving ◆[8]	263	51.33 N	7.29 E
Evingsen	263	51.18 N	7.44 E
Evionnaz	58	46.11 N	7.01 E
Evisa	36	42.15 N	8.47 E
Evje	26	58.36 N	7.51 E
Evolène	58	46.07 N	7.30 E
Évora	34	38.34 N	7.54 W
Evoron, ozero ⊜	89	51.28 N	136.30 E
Evpatoria — Jevpatorija	78	45.12 N	33.22 E
Évrange	56	49.30 N	6.12 E
Évreux	50	49.01 N	1.09 E
Evrieu	62	45.35 N	5.34 E
'Evron	132	32.59 N	35.06 E
Évros (Marica) (Meriç) ≃	38	40.52 N	26.12 E
Evrótas ≃	38	36.48 N	22.40 E
Évry	50	48.38 N	2.27 E
Évry-les-Châteaux	261	48.39 N	2.38 E
E. V. Spence Reservoir ⊜[1]	196	31.55 N	100.35 W
Evungu	154	4.27 S	25.12 E
Évvoia I	38	38.34 N	23.50 E
Évzonos ∧	267c	37.57 N	23.49 E
Ewa	229c	21.20 N	158.02 W
Ewa Beach	229c	21.18 N	158.00 W
Ewan	285	39.42 N	75.11 W
Ewaninga	162	23.58 S	133.58 E
Ewan Lake ⊜	285	39.42 N	75.11 W
Ewansville	285	39.59 N	74.44 W
Ewbank	158	26.14 S	23.35 E
Ewbank da Câmara	256	21.31 S	43.33 W
Ewe, Loch c	46	57.48 N	5.40 W
Ewell, Eng., U.K.	260	51.21 N	0.15 W
Ewell, Md., U.S.	208	37.59 N	76.02 W
Ewen	190	46.32 N	89.16 W
Ewenkiku Zizhiqi	89	49.07 N	119.40 E
Ewes Water ≃	44	55.08 N	3.00 W
Ewing, Ky., U.S.	218	38.25 N	83.51 W
Ewing, Mo., U.S.	219	40.00 N	91.42 W
Ewing, Ne., U.S.	198	42.15 N	98.20 W
Ewing, Va., U.S.	192	36.38 N	83.25 W
Ewingsville	279b	40.24 N	80.06 W
Ewing Township	208	40.16 N	74.46 W
Ewo	152	0.53 S	14.49 E
Ewu	273a	6.33 N	3.19 E
Exaltación	248	13.16 S	65.15 W
Excelda	158	32.16 S	22.08 E
Excello	218	39.29 N	84.25 W
Excelsior	158	28.56 S	27.06 E
Excelsior Mountain ∧	226	38.02 N	119.18 W
Excelsior Park ♠	274a	33.45 S	151.01 E
Excelsior Springs	194	39.20 N	94.13 W
Excenevex	58	46.21 N	6.21 E
Exchange	210	41.07 N	76.41 W
Exchange Station ◆[5]	262	53.25 N	2.59 W
Excursion Inlet	180	58.25 N	135.27 W
Exe ≃	42	50.37 N	3.25 W
Executive Committee Range ∧∧	9	76.50 S	126.00 W
Exeter, Austl.	170	34.38 S	150.19 E
Exeter, On., Can.	190	43.21 N	81.29 W
Exeter, Eng., U.K.	42	50.43 N	3.31 W
Exeter, Ca., U.S.	226	36.17 N	119.08 W
Exeter, Ne., U.S.	198	40.38 N	97.27 W
Exeter, N.H., U.S.	188	42.58 N	70.56 W
Exeter, Pa., U.S.	210	41.19 N	75.49 W
Exeter, R.I., U.S.	207	41.34 N	71.32 W

Symbols in the index entries represent the broad categories identified in the key at the right. Symbols with superior numbers (∧∧[1]) identify subcategories (see complete key on page *I · 1).*

Symbole im Register stellen die rechts im Schlüssel erklärten Kategorien dar. Symbole mit hochgestellten Ziffern (∧∧[1]) bezeichnen Unterabteilungen einer Kategorie (vgl. vollständiger Schlüssel auf Seite *I · 1).*

Los símbolos incluídos en el texto del índice representan las grandes categorias identificadas con la clave a la derecha. Los símbolos con numeros en su parte superior (∧∧[1]) identifican las subcategorías (véase la clave completa en la página *I · 1).*

Les symboles de l'index représentent les catégories indiquées dans la légende à droite. Les symboles suivis d'un indice (∧∧[1]) représentent des sous-catégories (voir légende complète à la page *I · 1).*

Os símbolos incluídos no texto do índice representam as grandes categorias identificadas com a chave à direita. Os símbolos com números em sua parte superior (∧∧[1]) identificam as subcategorias (veja-se a chave completa à página *I · 1).*

	English	Deutsch	Español	Français	Português
∧	Mountain	Berg	Montaña	Montagne	Montanha
∧∧	Mountains	Gebirge	Montañas	Montagnes	Montanhas
)(	Pass	Paß	Paso	Col	Passo
V	Valley, Canyon	Tal, Cañon	Valle, Cañón	Vallée, Canyon	Vale, Canhão
≚	Plain	Ebene	Llano	Plaine	Planície
>	Cape	Kap	Cabo	Cap	Cabo
I	Island	Insel	Isla	Île	Ilha
II	Islands	Inseln	Islas	Îles	Ilhas
⊥	Other Topographic Features	Andere Topographische Objekte	Otros Elementos Topográficos	Autres données topographiques	Outros acidentes topográficos

ESPAÑOL · FRANÇAIS · PORTUGUÊS

Nombre / Nom / Nome	Página / Page / Página	Lat.°′	Long.°′ W = Oeste / W = Ouest / W = Oeste
Exeter ≃	188	43.02 N	70.55 W
Exeter Sound ⊔	176	66.14 N	62.00 W
Exford	42	51.08 N	3.38 W
Exhibition of Economic Achievements ⊛	265b	55.50 N	37.37 E
Exhibition Park ♠	275b	43.38 N	79.25 W
Exhibition Stadium ♠	275b	43.38 N	79.25 W
Exincourt	58	47.30 N	6.50 E
Exira	198	41.35 N	94.52 W
Exline Slough ≃	216	41.05 N	87.47 W
Exloërmond	52	52.54 N	6.57 E
Exmes	50	48.46 N	0.11 E
Exminster	42	50.41 N	3.29 W
Exmoor ⋏[1]	42	51.10 N	3.45 W
Exmoor National Park ♠	42	51.12 N	3.46 W
Exmore	208	37.31 N	75.49 W
Exmouth, Austl.	162	21.56 S	114.07 E
Exmouth, Eng., U.K.	42	50.37 N	3.25 W
Exmouth Gulf ⊂	162	22.00 S	114.20 E
Exmouth Plateau ✣[3]	14	19.00 S	114.00 E
Exning	42	52.16 N	0.21 E
Expedition Range ⋏	166	24.30 S	149.05 E
Experiment	192	33.15 N	84.16 W
Exploits ≃	186	49.05 N	55.20 W
Exploits, Bay of ⊂	186	49.24 N	55.00 W
Exploits Dam ◆[6]	186	48.45 N	56.30 W
Expo Memorial Park ♠	270	34.48 N	135.32 E
Export	214	40.25 N	79.37 W
Exposition Park ♠	280	34.01 N	118.17 W
Exshaw	182	51.03 N	115.09 W
Extension	224	49.06 N	123.57 W
Exter	52	52.08 N	8.46 E
Externsteine ⊥	52	51.52 N	8.55 E
Extertal	52	52.04 N	9.07 E
Exton	208	40.02 N	75.37 W
Extoraz ≃	234	21.06 N	99.23 W
Extrema	256	22.51 S	46.19 W
Extremadura □[4]	34	39.15 N	6.15 W
Exu	250	7.31 S	39.43 W
Exuma Cays II	238	24.15 N	76.30 W
Exuma Sound ⊔	238	24.15 N	76.00 W
Eyak	180	60.32 N	145.36 W
Eyam	44	53.17 N	1.41 W
Eyasi, Lake ◎	154	3.40 S	35.05 E
Eydehavn	26	58.31 N	8.53 E
Eye, Eng., U.K.	42	52.19 N	1.09 E
Eye, Eng., U.K.	42	52.35 N	0.10 W
Eyebrow	184	50.47 N	106.09 W
Eyehill Creek ≃	184	52.40 N	109.39 W
Eyemouth	46	55.52 N	2.06 W
Eye Peninsula >[1]	46	58.13 N	6.13 W
Eyers Grove	210	41.05 N	76.31 W
Eye Water ≃	46	55.53 N	2.06 W
Eygalières	62	43.45 N	4.57 E
Eyguières	62	43.42 N	5.02 E
Eyhorne Street	260	51.16 N	0.38 E
Eyjafjörđur ⊂[2]	24a	65.54 N	18.15 W
Eyl	144	7.59 N	49.49 E
Eylar Mountain ∧	204	37.28 N	121.33 W
Eymet	32	44.40 N	0.24 E
Eymir	130	40.02 N	35.14 E
Eymoutiers	32	45.44 N	1.44 E
Eynesil	130	41.03 N	39.08 E
Eynhallow Sound ⊔	46	59.08 N	3.06 W
Eynort, Loch ⊂	46	57.13 N	7.18 W
Eynsford	260	51.22 N	0.13 E
Eynsham	42	51.48 N	1.22 W
Eyota	190	43.59 N	92.13 W
Eyrarbakki	24a	63.53 N	21.05 W
Eyre	162	32.15 S	126.18 E
Eyrecourt	48	53.11 N	8.07 W
Eyre Creek ≃	166	26.40 S	139.00 E
Eyre Mountains ⋏	172	45.20 S	168.30 E
Eyre North, Lake ◎	166	28.40 S	137.10 E
Eyre Peninsula >[1]	162	34.00 S	135.45 E
Eyre South, Lake ◎	166	29.30 S	137.20 E
Eyrieux ≃	62	44.48 N	4.48 E
Eystrup	52	52.46 N	9.13 E
Eythorne	42	51.11 N	1.17 E
Eythra	54	51.14 N	12.17 E
Eyüp ◆[8]	267b	41.03 N	28.55 E
Eyvānekey	128	35.20 N	52.04 E
Eyzaguirre, Canal ≊	286e	33.36 S	70.41 W
Ézanville	261	49.02 N	2.22 E
Ezbekīyah ◆[8]	273c	30.03 N	31.15 E
Ezeiza, Aeropuerto Internacional de ⊠	288	34.49 S	58.32 W
Ezequiel Ramos Mexía, Embalse ◎[1]	254	39.30 S	69.00 W
Ezere	76	56.26 N	22.22 E
Ežerėlis	76	54.53 N	23.37 E
Ezeriș	38	45.24 N	21.53 E
Ezine	130	39.47 N	26.20 E
Ezinepazarı	130	40.34 N	36.09 E
Ezop, chrebet ⋏	89	52.36 N	133.37 E
Ežva	24	61.47 N	50.40 E
Ézy-sur-Eure	50	48.52 N	1.25 E
Ezzell	222	29.17 N	96.58 W
F			
Faaa Airport ⊠	174s	17.33 S	149.36 W
Faafaxdhuun	144	2.13 N	41.37 E
Faal	174q	9.37 N	138.10 E
Faaone	174s	17.40 S	149.18 W
Fabala	150	9.44 N	9.05 W
Fabbrico	64	44.52 N	10.50 E
Fabens	200	31.30 N	106.09 W
Fåberg	26	61.10 N	10.24 E
Faber Lake ◎	176	63.56 N	117.15 W
Fabert Seamount ✣[3]	14	24.07 S	158.33 W
Fabius	210	42.50 N	75.59 W
Fåborg	41	55.06 N	10.15 E
Fábrega, Cerro ∧	236	9.07 N	82.52 W
Fabrègues	62	43.33 N	3.46 E
Fabreville ◆[8]	275a	45.34 N	73.50 W
Fabriano	66	43.20 N	12.54 E
Fabrica di Roma	66	42.20 N	12.18 E
Fabričnyj	85	43.11 N	76.24 E
Fabrizia	68	38.29 N	16.18 E
Facatativá	246	4.49 N	74.22 W
Facha	146	29.27 N	17.18 E
Faches-Thumesnil	50	50.35 N	3.04 E
Fachi	146	18.06 N	11.34 E
Facpi Point >	174p	13.20 N	144.38 E
Factoryville	210	41.34 N	75.47 W
Facundo	254	45.18 S	69.58 W
Fada	146	17.14 N	21.33 E
Fada, Lochan ◎	46	57.41 N	5.18 W
Fadalto	64	46.05 N	12.20 E
Fada Ngourma	150	12.04 N	0.21 E
Fadd	30	46.28 N	18.50 E
Faddeja, zaliv ⊂	74	76.40 N	107.20 E
Faddejevskij, ostrov I	74	75.30 N	144.00 E
Faddoi	140	8.07 N	32.07 E
Fadian Point >	174p	13.26 N	144.49 E
Fadiffolu Atoll I[1]	122	5.25 N	73.30 E
Fadit	140	9.58 N	32.13 E
Faedis	64	46.10 N	13.20 E
Fænø I	41	55.29 N	9.42 E
Faenza	66	44.17 N	11.53 E
Faeroe Islands □[2]	22	62.00 N	7.00 W
Faeröerne → Faeroe Islands □[2]	22	62.00 N	7.00 W
Faete, Monte ∧	267a	41.45 N	12.44 E
Fafa	150	15.20 N	0.43 E
Fafa ≃	152	7.18 N	18.16 E
Fafakourou	150	13.04 N	14.34 W
Fafe	34	41.27 N	8.10 W
Fafen ≃	144	5.59 N	44.25 E
Faga ≃	150	13.15 N	0.55 E
Fagaitua	174u	14.16 S	170.37 W
Fagamalo	175a	13.25 S	172.21 W
Făgăraș	38	45.51 N	24.58 E
Făgărașului, Munții ⋏	38	45.35 N	25.00 E
Fagasa	174u	14.17 S	170.43 W
Fagatogo	174u	14.17 S	170.41 W
Fagel	41	54.27 N	9.31 E
Fagernes	26	60.59 N	9.15 E
Fagersta	40	60.00 N	15.47 E
Fagertärn ◆[4]	40	58.46 N	14.42 E
Fagerviken	40	60.33 N	17.45 E
Făget	38	45.51 N	22.10 E
Faggen Bach ≃	64	47.05 N	10.40 E
Faggo	150	11.23 N	9.57 E
Fagnano, Lago ◎	254	54.35 S	68.00 W
Fagnano Castello	68	39.34 N	16.03 E
Fagnano Olona	62	45.40 N	8.52 E
Fagnières	50	48.58 N	4.19 E
Faguibine, Lac ◎	150	16.45 N	3.54 W
Fagundes, Rio do ≃	256	22.12 S	43.11 W
Fagurhólsmýri	24a	63.54 N	16.38 W
Fagwir	140	9.33 N	30.25 E
Fahan	48	55.05 N	7.28 W
Fahl, Oued el V	148	31.15 N	4.41 E
Fahraj	128	28.58 N	58.52 E
Fährdorf	54	53.58 N	11.28 E
Fahrland	54	52.28 N	13.01 E
Fahrlander See ◎	264a	52.27 N	13.01 E
Fahrnau	58	47.39 N	7.50 E
Fahrn → Varna	64	46.44 N	11.38 E
Fahuaqiao	106	30.52 N	121.25 E
Faial I	148a	38.34 N	28.42 W
Faichuk II	175c	7.23 N	151.40 E
Fā'id	142	30.19 N	32.19 E
Fā'id Military Base ■	142	30.20 N	32.16 E
Faido	58	46.29 N	8.48 E
Faillon, Lac ◎	190	48.21 N	76.38 W
Failsworth	44	53.31 N	2.09 W
Fains-les-Sources	56	48.47 N	5.08 E
Fairbairn Airport ⊠	171b	35.18 S	149.15 E
Fairbairn Park ♠	274b	37.47 S	144.55 E
Fairbairn Reservoir ◎[1]	166	23.45 S	148.00 E
Fairbank	190	42.38 N	92.02 W
Fairbanks, Ak., U.S.	180	64.51 N	147.43 W
Fairbanks, La., U.S.	194	30.00 N	92.02 W
Fair Bluff	192	34.18 N	79.02 W
Fairborn	218	39.49 N	84.01 W
Fairbourne	42	52.41 N	4.03 W
Fairburn	192	33.34 N	84.34 W
Fairbury, Il., U.S.	216	40.44 N	88.30 W
Fairbury, Ne., U.S.	198	40.08 N	97.10 W
Fairchance	188	39.49 N	79.45 W
Fairchild	190	44.36 N	90.57 W
Fairchild Air Force Base ■	202	47.38 N	117.38 W
Fairchild Creek ≃	212	43.07 N	80.07 W
Fairdale	216	42.06 N	88.56 W
Faire	116	17.53 N	121.34 E
Fairfax, Al., U.S.	194	32.47 N	85.11 W
Fairfax, Ca., U.S.	226	37.59 N	122.35 W
Fairfax, De., U.S.	285	39.47 N	75.32 W
Fairfax, Mn., U.S.	198	44.31 N	94.43 W
Fairfax, Mo., U.S.	194	40.20 N	95.23 W
Fairfax, Ok., U.S.	196	36.34 N	96.42 W
Fairfax, S.C., U.S.	192	32.57 N	81.14 W
Fairfax, S.D., U.S.	198	43.01 N	98.53 W
Fairfax, Vt., U.S.	188	44.39 N	73.00 W
Fairfax, Va., U.S.	208	38.50 N	77.18 W
Fairfax □[6]	208	38.45 N	77.15 W
Fairfax Forest	284c	38.52 N	77.15 W
Fairfax Park	284c	38.47 N	77.14 W
Fairfax State Recreation Area ♠	218	39.02 N	86.29 W
Fairfax Station	284c	38.48 N	77.19 W
Fairfield, Austl.	170	33.52 S	150.57 E
Fairfield, Al., U.S.	194	33.33 N	86.47 W
Fairfield, Ca., U.S.	226	38.14 N	122.02 W
Fairfield, Ct., U.S.	210	41.08 N	73.15 W
Fairfield, Id., U.S.	202	43.20 N	114.47 W
Fairfield, Il., U.S.	194	38.22 N	88.21 W
Fairfield, Ia., U.S.	190	41.00 N	91.57 W
Fairfield, Me., U.S.	188	44.35 N	69.35 W
Fairfield, Mt., U.S.	202	47.36 N	111.58 W
Fairfield, Ne., U.S.	198	40.25 N	98.06 W
Fairfield, N.J., U.S.	276	40.53 N	74.16 W
Fairfield, N.Y., U.S.	210	43.08 N	74.55 W
Fairfield, Oh., U.S.	218	39.20 N	84.33 W
Fairfield, Pa., U.S.	214	39.47 N	77.22 W
Fairfield, Tx., U.S.	222	31.43 N	96.09 W
Fairfield □[6]	207	41.15 N	73.20 W
Fairfield Lake ◎[1]	222	31.50 N	96.05 W
Fairfield University ⊛[2]	276	41.09 N	73.15 W
Fairford	42	51.44 N	1.47 W
Fairgrove	190	43.31 N	83.32 W
Fair Harbor	210	40.38 N	73.11 W
Fairhaven, Ma., U.S.	207	41.38 N	70.54 W
Fair Haven, Mi., U.S.	214	42.40 N	82.39 W
Fair Haven, N.J., U.S.	208	40.21 N	74.02 W
Fair Haven, N.Y., U.S.	210	43.18 N	76.42 W
Fairhaven, Oh., U.S.	218	39.38 N	84.47 W
Fair Haven, Vt., U.S.	188	43.35 N	73.15 W
Fair Haven, Va., U.S.	284c	38.47 N	77.05 W
Fairhaven Bay ◎	283	42.26 N	71.21 W
Fair Haven Beach State Park ♠, N.Y., U.S.	210	43.21 N	76.41 W
Fair Haven Beach State Park ♠, N.Y., U.S.	212	43.21 N	76.41 W
Fair Head >	48	55.13 N	6.09 W
Fairhope, Al., U.S.	194	30.31 N	87.54 W
Fairhope, Oh., U.S.	214	40.51 N	81.19 W
Fairhope, Pa., U.S.	214	40.07 N	79.50 W
Fair Isle I	46	59.32 N	1.39 W
Fairknoll	284c	39.05 N	76.59 W
Fairland, In., U.S.	218	39.35 N	85.51 W
Fairland, Md., U.S.	284c	39.05 N	76.58 W
Fairland, Ok., U.S.	196	36.45 N	94.50 W
Fairlane Town Center ◆[9]	281	42.19 N	83.13 W
Fair Lawn, N.J., U.S.	210	40.56 N	74.07 W
Fairlawn, Oh., U.S.	214	41.07 N	81.36 W
Fairlee	284c	38.52 N	77.16 W
Fairleigh Dickinson University ⊛[2], N.J., U.S.	276	40.50 N	74.07 W
Fairleigh Dickinson University (Florham-Madison) ⊛[2], N.J., U.S.	276	40.46 N	74.26 W
Fairleigh Dickinson University (Teaneck) ⊛[2], N.J., U.S.	276	40.53 N	74.02 W
Fairless Hills	208	40.10 N	74.51 W
Fairlie, N.Z.	172	44.06 S	170.50 E
Fairlie, Scot., U.K.	46	55.46 N	4.51 W
Fairlight	42	50.53 N	0.40 E
Fairmont, Il., U.S.	216	41.33 N	88.03 W
Fairmont, Mn., U.S.	198	43.39 N	94.27 W
Fairmont, Ne., U.S.	198	40.38 N	97.35 W
Fairmont, N.C., U.S.	192	34.29 N	79.06 W
Fairmont, Pa., U.S.	279b	40.19 N	79.43 W
Fairmont, Wa., U.S.	224	48.54 N	122.16 W
Fairmont, W.V., U.S.	188	39.29 N	80.08 W
Fairmont City	219	38.40 N	90.06 W
Fairmont Hot Springs	182	50.19 N	115.53 W
Fairmont Reservoir ◎[1]	228	34.43 N	118.26 W
Fairmont Terrace	282	37.43 N	122.07 W
Fairmount, Ga., U.S.	192	34.26 N	84.42 W
Fairmount, Il., U.S.	194	40.03 N	87.56 W
Fairmount, In., U.S.	216	40.24 N	85.39 W
Fairmount, N.Y., U.S.	210	43.02 N	76.14 W
Fairmount, N.D., U.S.	198	46.03 N	96.36 W
Fairmount City	214	41.01 N	79.19 W
Fairmount Heights	208	38.54 N	76.54 W
Fairmount Park ♠	285	40.00 N	75.12 W
Fair Ness >	176	63.24 N	72.05 W
Fair Oaks, Ca., U.S.	226	38.38 N	121.16 W
Fair Oaks, Ga., U.S.	192	33.54 N	84.32 W
Fair Oaks, In., U.S.	216	41.05 N	87.16 W
Fairoaks, Pa., U.S.	279b	40.34 N	80.13 W
Fairoaks Airport ⊠	260	51.21 N	0.32 W
Fair Plain	216	42.05 N	86.27 W
Fairplains	192	36.13 N	81.10 W
Fairplay	200	39.13 N	106.00 W
Fairpoint	214	40.07 N	80.55 W
Fairport, On., Can.	275b	43.49 N	79.05 W
Fairport, N.Y., U.S.	210	43.05 N	77.26 W
Fairport Beach	275b	43.48 N	79.06 W
Fairport Harbor	214	41.44 N	81.16 W
Fairseat	260	51.20 N	0.20 E
Fairton	208	39.22 N	75.13 W
Fairview, Austl.	164	15.33 S	144.19 E
Fairview, Ab., Can.	182	56.04 N	118.23 W
Fairview, Ga., U.S.	192	34.56 N	85.17 W
Fairview, Il., U.S.	190	40.38 N	90.10 W
Fairview, In., U.S.	216	40.18 N	85.11 W
Fairview, Ks., U.S.	198	39.50 N	95.43 W
Fairview, Md., U.S.	208	39.09 N	76.29 W
Fairview, Mi., U.S.	190	44.43 N	84.03 W
Fairview, Mt., U.S.	198	47.51 N	104.02 W
Fairview, N.J., U.S.	276	40.51 N	73.58 W
Fairview, N.Y., U.S.	210	41.43 N	73.55 W
Fairview, Oh., U.S.	214	40.03 N	81.14 W
Fairview, Ok., U.S.	196	36.16 N	98.28 W
Fairview, Pa., U.S.	214	42.01 N	80.15 W
Fairview, Tn., U.S.	194	35.58 N	87.07 W
Fairview, Ut,. U.S.	200	39.37 N	111.26 W
Fairview, W.V., U.S.	188	39.35 N	80.14 W
Fairview Heights	219	38.10 N	90.00 W
Fairview Lanes	214	41.23 N	82.40 W
Fairview Mall ◆[9]	275b	43.47 N	79.21 W
Fairview Park, In., U.S.	194	39.40 N	87.25 W
Fairview Park, Oh., U.S.	214	41.26 N	81.51 W
Fairview Park, Pa., U.S.	210	41.10 N	75.53 W
Fairview Peak ∧, Nv., U.S.	204	39.14 N	118.08 W
Fairview Peak ∧, Or., U.S.	202	43.35 N	122.39 W
Fairview Pointe Claire Centre ◆[9]	275a	45.28 N	73.50 W
Fairview Shores	220	28.35 N	81.23 W
Fairview Village	285	40.10 N	75.23 W
Fairvilla	220	28.35 N	81.24 W
Fairville	285	39.51 N	75.38 W
Fairweather Mountain ∧	180	58.54 N	137.32 W
Fairy Lake ◎	212	45.20 N	79.11 W
Fairy Meadow	170	34.23 S	150.54 E
Fairy Stone State Park ♠	192	36.48 N	80.06 W
Fairy Water ≃	48	54.37 N	7.20 W
Fais I	108	9.46 N	140.31 E
Faisalabad (Lyallpur)	123	31.25 N	73.05 E
Faison	192	35.06 N	78.08 W
Faistós ⊥	38	35.01 N	24.48 E
Faith	198	45.01 N	102.02 W
Faiyum → Al-Fayyūm	142	29.19 N	30.50 E
Faizābād	124	26.47 N	82.08 E
Fajansovyj	76	54.04 N	34.24 E
Fajardo	240m	18.20 N	65.39 W
Fajou, Îlet à I	241o	16.21 N	61.35 W
Fajr, Wādī V	128	30.06 N	38.18 E
Fajzabad	85	38.34 N	69.19 E
Fakahatchee Strand ⁂	220	39.35 N	89.25 W
Fakaofo I[1]	14	9.22 S	171.14 W
Fakarava I[1]	14	16.20 S	145.37 W
Fakejev	80	48.57 N	49.56 E
Fakel	80	57.38 N	53.02 E
Fakenham	42	52.50 N	0.51 E
Fakfak	164	2.55 S	132.18 E
Fakılı	130	39.13 N	35.00 E
Fakīrganj	124	25.58 N	90.02 E
Fakī Ṣādiq	140	12.08 N	23.55 E
Fakrinkotti	140	18.01 N	31.20 E
Fakse	41	55.15 N	12.08 E
Fakse Bugt ⊂	41	55.10 N	12.15 E
Fakse Ladeplads	41	55.13 N	12.11 E
Faku	104	42.30 N	123.24 E
Fal ≃	42	50.08 N	5.02 W
Falaba	150	9.51 N	11.19 W
Faladyé	150	13.08 N	8.20 W
Falaise	32	48.54 N	0.12 W
Fālākāta	124	26.32 N	89.12 E
Falam	110	22.55 N	93.40 E
Falāvarjān	128	32.33 N	51.30 E
Falcade	64	46.21 N	11.51 E
Falcão	256	22.17 S	44.16 W
Fălciu	38	46.18 N	28.08 E
Falck	56	49.14 N	6.38 E
Falcognana di Sotto ◆[8]	267a	41.45 N	12.33 E
Falcón □[3]	246	11.00 N	69.50 W
Falcon, Cap >	34	35.46 N	0.48 W
Falcon, Cape >	224	45.46 N	123.59 W
Falcón, Presa (Falcon Reservoir) ◎[1]	196	26.37 N	99.11 W
Falconara Albanese	68	39.16 N	16.05 E
Falconara Alta	66	43.37 N	13.24 E
Falconara Marittima	66	43.37 N	13.24 E
Falconbridge	190	46.35 N	80.48 W
Falconcrest	285	39.58 N	75.33 W
Falcone	70	38.07 N	15.05 E
Falcone, Capo del >	71	40.58 N	8.12 E
Falconer	214	42.07 N	79.11 W
Falcon Heights	202	42.08 N	121.45 W
Falcon Reservoir (Presa Falcón) ◎[1]	196	26.37 N	99.11 W
Falconwood	210	43.00 N	78.57 W
Faldsled	41	55.09 N	10.09 E
Faléa	150	12.16 N	11.17 W
Faleasao	174y	14.13 S	169.32 W
Falelatai	175a	13.55 S	171.59 W
Falelima	175a	13.32 S	172.41 W
Falémé ≃	150	14.46 N	12.14 W
Falenki	80	58.22 N	51.35 E
Falerii Novi ⊥	66	42.16 N	12.20 E
Falerna	68	39.00 N	16.10 E
Falerone	66	43.06 N	13.28 E
Falešty	78	47.34 N	27.43 E
Falfurrias	196	27.13 N	98.08 W
Falher	182	55.44 N	117.12 W
Falicon	62	43.45 N	7.17 E
Fálirou, Órmos ⊂	267c	37.56 N	23.40 E
Falkenberg, Dtsch.	54	52.48 N	13.58 E
Falkenberg, Dtsch.	54	51.35 N	13.14 E
Falkenberg, Dtsch.	60	49.52 N	12.14 E
Falkenberg, Dtsch.	60	48.28 N	12.43 E
Falkenberg, Sve.	26	56.54 N	12.28 E
Falkenberg ◆[8]	264a	52.34 N	13.33 E
Falkenhagen, Dtsch.	54	53.12 N	12.12 E
Falkenhagen, Dtsch.	54	52.26 N	14.19 E
Falkenhagener See ◎	264a	52.34 N	13.08 E
Falkenrehde	264a	52.30 N	12.56 E
Falkensee	54	52.33 N	13.04 E
Falkenstein	54	50.29 N	12.22 E
Falkenthal	54	52.54 N	13.17 E
Falkirk	46	56.00 N	3.48 W
Falkland, B.C., Can.	182	50.30 N	119.33 W
Falkland, Scot., U.K.	46	56.15 N	3.12 W
Falkland-Inseln → Falkland Islands □[2]	254	51.45 S	59.00 W
Falkland Islands □[2], S.A.	244	51.45 S	59.00 W
Falkland Islands □[2], S.A.	254	51.45 S	59.00 W
Falkland Plateau ✣[3]	18	51.00 S	50.00 W
Falkland Sound ⊔	254	51.45 S	59.25 W
Falköping	26	58.10 N	13.31 E
Falkville	194	34.22 N	86.54 W
Fall ≃, On., Can.	212	44.59 N	76.22 W
Fall ≃, Ks., U.S.	198	37.24 N	95.40 W
Fall ≃, Wa., U.S.	224	46.47 N	123.30 W
Falla	40	58.41 N	15.45 E
Fallais	56	50.37 N	5.10 E
Fallbach	61	48.39 N	16.25 E
Fallbrook	228	33.22 N	117.15 W
Fallbrook Square ◆[9]	280	34.12 N	118.38 W
Fall City	224	47.34 N	121.53 W
Fall Creek	190	44.45 N	91.16 W
Fall Creek ≃, In., U.S.	218	39.47 N	86.11 W
Fall Creek ≃, N.Y., U.S.	210	42.28 N	76.31 W
Fall Creek Falls State Park ♠, Tn., U.S.	192	35.39 N	85.25 W
Fall Creek Falls State Park ♠, Tn., U.S.	194	35.39 N	85.25 W
Fallen Jerusalem I	240m	18.25 N	64.27 W
Fallen Leaf	226	38.53 N	120.04 W
Fallen Leaf Reservoir ◎[1]	226	38.54 N	120.03 W
Fallentimber	214	40.41 N	78.30 W
Fallentimber Creek ≃	182	51.45 N	114.39 W
Fallen Timbers State Memorial ⊥	216	41.33 N	83.42 W
Fallersleben	54	52.25 N	10.43 E
Fallin	46	56.06 N	3.52 W
Falling ≃	192	37.01 N	78.55 W
Fallingbostel	52	52.52 N	9.41 E
Falling Creek ≃	208	37.26 N	77.26 W
Fallon, Mt., U.S.	198	46.50 N	105.07 W
Fallon, Nv., U.S.	204	39.28 N	118.46 W
Fall River, Ks., U.S.	198	37.36 N	96.01 W
Fall River, Ma., U.S.	207	41.42 N	71.09 W
Fall River, Wi., U.S.	190	43.23 N	89.02 W
Fall River Lake ◎[1]	198	37.42 N	96.08 W
Fall River Mills	204	41.00 N	121.26 W
Falls	210	41.28 N	75.51 W
Falls □[6]	222	31.17 N	96.55 W
Fallsburg	210	41.44 N	74.36 W
Falls Church	208	38.53 N	77.11 W
Falls City, Ne., U.S.	198	40.03 N	95.36 W
Falls City, Or., U.S.	202	44.51 N	123.26 W
Falls Creek, Austl.	170	34.59 S	150.36 E
Falls Creek, Pa., U.S.	214	41.09 N	78.48 W
Falls Creek ≃	226	37.57 N	119.46 W
Fallsington	208	40.12 N	74.48 W
Falls Lake ◎[1]	192	36.00 N	78.45 W
Falls Pond ◎	283	41.58 N	71.20 W
Falls Run ≃	284b	39.22 N	76.52 W
Fallston	208	39.31 N	76.25 W
Falls Village	207	41.57 N	73.21 W
Falmer	42	50.51 N	0.04 W
Falmey	150	12.36 N	2.51 E
Falmouth, Jam.	241q	18.30 N	77.39 W
Falmouth, Eng., U.K.	42	50.08 N	5.04 W
Falmouth, Ky., U.S.	218	38.40 N	84.19 W
Falmouth, Me., U.S.	188	43.43 N	70.14 W
Falmouth, Ma., U.S.	207	41.33 N	70.36 W
Falmouth, Va., U.S.	208	38.19 N	77.28 W
Falmouth Bay ⊂	42	50.05 N	5.01 W
Falmouth Heights	207	41.33 N	70.36 W
False Cape >, Fl., U.S.	220	28.35 N	80.34 W
False Cape >, Va., U.S.	208	36.39 N	76.51 W
False Divi Point >	122	15.43 N	80.49 E
False Ducks Islands II	212	43.57 N	76.49 W
False Pass	180	54.52 N	163.24 W
Falset	34	41.08 N	0.49 E
Falsino ≃	250	0.56 N	51.35 W
Fal'šivyj Gelendžik	78	44.31 N	38.09 E
Falso, Cabo >, Hond.	236	15.12 N	83.20 W
Falso, Cabo >, Rep. Dom.	238	17.47 N	71.41 W
Falso Cabo de Hornos >	254	55.43 S	68.05 W
Falster I	41	54.48 N	11.58 E
Falsterbo	41	55.24 N	12.50 E
Falstone	44	55.11 N	2.25 W
Falterona, Monte ∧	66	43.52 N	11.42 E
Fălticeni	38	47.28 N	26.18 E
Falun, Sve.	40	60.36 N	15.38 E
Falun, Zhg.	107	29.58 N	104.29 E
Falzarego, Passo di)(	64	46.31 N	12.00 E
Fam, Kepulauan II	164	0.40 S	130.15 E
Fama	256	21.25 S	46.51 W
Fama, Ouadi V	146	15.22 N	20.34 E
Famagusta → Gazimağusa	130	35.07 N	33.57 E
Famaillá	252	27.03 S	65.24 W
Famatina	252	28.55 S	67.31 W
Famatina, Sierra de ⋏	252	29.00 S	67.51 W
Fambach	54	50.44 N	10.22 E
Fameck	56	49.18 N	6.07 E
Famenne ◆[1]	56	50.10 N	5.15 E
Familleureux	50	50.31 N	4.12 E
Family Lake ◎	184	51.54 N	95.30 W
Fan ≃	104	42.16 N	123.40 E
Fana	150	12.47 N	6.57 W
Fanaco, Lago ◎	70	37.39 N	13.33 E
Fanad Head >	48	55.16 N	7.38 W
Fanado ≃	255	17.10 S	42.40 W
Fanambana	157b	13.34 S	50.00 E
Fanan I	175c	7.11 N	151.59 E
Fanano	64	44.12 N	10.47 E
Fanārah	142	30.17 N	32.21 E
Fanchang	100	31.07 N	118.12 E
Fanch'eng → Xiangfan	102	32.03 N	112.01 E
Fancher, Il., U.S.	219	39.16 N	88.47 W
Fancher, N.Y., U.S.	210	43.15 N	66.06 W
Fanchon, Pointe >	238	18.26 N	74.29 W
Fanchuan	100	32.40 N	119.42 E
Fancy	241h	13.22 N	61.11 W
Fancy Creek ≃	198	39.28 N	96.45 W
Fancy Prairie	219	39.59 N	89.36 W
Fandriana	157b	20.14 S	47.23 E
Fane ≃	48	53.57 N	6.22 W
Fanepura	123	31.29 N	72.54 E
Faneromenis Monastery ⊛[1]	267c	37.59 N	23.26 E
Fang	110	19.55 N	99.13 E
Fangaga ∧	144	17.30 N	38.01 E
Fangak	140	9.04 N	30.53 E
Fangbian	106	31.42 N	119.06 E
Fangcheng, Zhg.	100	33.16 N	112.59 E
Fangcheng, Zhg.	102	21.49 N	108.22 E
Fangcheng, Zhg.	105	39.16 N	115.28 E
Fangcun, Zhg.	100	29.04 N	118.36 E
Fangcun, Zhg.	100	26.50 N	118.15 E
Fangdao	100	27.01 N	118.06 E
Fängersee ◎	264a	52.35 N	13.50 E
Fangguan	105	39.20 N	115.58 E
Fangji	100	31.54 N	115.35 E
Fangjiachang	107	30.05 N	104.16 E
Fangjiazhuang	106	30.45 N	119.53 E
Fangliao	100	22.22 N	120.35 E
Fangmutun	98	42.34 N	124.34 E
Fangniu	102	27.40 N	100.25 E
Fangshan, T'aiwan	100	22.16 N	120.39 E
Fangshan, Zhg.	98	39.42 N	115.58 E
Fang Shan ∧	106	31.40 N	119.16 E
Fang Shan ∧[2]	106	31.29 N	119.09 E
Fangshanzhen	104	41.54 N	122.05 E
Fangshen	104	42.02 N	124.04 E
Fangshengpu	107	30.20 N	104.54 E
Fangsi	98	36.56 N	116.29 E
Fangtai	106	31.19 N	121.12 E
Fangxi	100	28.23 N	114.38 E
Fangxian	102	32.02 N	110.45 E
Fangxianzhen	106	32.00 N	119.44 E
Fangzheng	89	45.50 N	128.50 E
Fangzi	98	36.36 N	119.07 E
Fanhões	266c	38.53 N	9.09 W
Fanipol'	76	53.45 N	27.20 E
Fanjakana	157b	21.10 S	46.53 E
Fanjiadai	106	32.04 N	120.15 E
Fanjiadian	104	41.41 N	121.50 E
Fanjiatun	89	43.43 N	125.06 E
Fanjiazhuang	105	39.12 N	117.20 E
Fannaråki ∧	26	61.31 N	7.55 E
Fannettsburg	214	40.04 N	77.50 W
Fannich, Loch ◎	46	57.38 N	5.00 W
Fannrem	26	63.16 N	9.50 E
Fanny, Mount ∧	202	45.20 N	117.41 W
Fanny Bay	182	49.30 N	124.50 W
Fano	66	43.50 N	13.01 E
Fanø I	26	55.25 N	8.25 E
Fanqiao	100	28.48 N	121.10 E
Fans, Col des)(	62	44.56 N	4.47 E
Fanshan, Zhg.	100	27.21 N	120.24 E
Fanshan, Zhg.	105	40.13 N	115.25 E
Fanshang	106	31.40 N	120.01 E
Fanshawe Lake ◎	212	43.05 N	81.10 W
Fansher Creek ≃	214	42.37 N	82.01 W
Fanshui	100	33.07 N	119.25 E
Fan Si Pan ∧	110	22.15 N	103.46 E
Fantasy Island ♠	284a	43.02 N	78.58 W
Fanthyttan	40	59.40 N	15.06 E
Fanwood	276	40.38 N	74.23 W
Fanxian	98	35.57 N	115.38 E
Fanzhen	98	36.14 N	117.21 E
Faoileann, Bàgh nam ⊂	46	57.23 N	7.17 W
Faqīrah, Wādī V	142	28.52 N	30.57 E
Faqqū'ah	132	32.30 N	35.24 E
Fāqūs	142	30.44 N	31.48 E
Farab	85	39.14 N	67.28 E
Faraday ⊛[3]	9	65.15 S	64.16 W
Faraday, Mount ∧	172	42.02 S	171.34 E
Faradje	154	3.44 N	29.43 E
Faradofay	157b	25.02 S	47.00 E
Farafangana	157b	22.49 S	47.50 E
Farāfirah, Al-Wāḥat al- ⊤[4]	140	27.15 N	28.10 E
Farāh	128	32.22 N	62.07 E
Farāh □[4]	128	33.00 N	62.30 E
Farāh ≃	128	31.29 N	61.24 E
Faraḥābād	267d	35.42 N	51.30 E
Farahalana	157b	14.26 S	50.10 E
Farā'id, Jabal al- ∧	140	23.31 N	35.20 E
Fara in Sabina	66	42.12 N	12.43 E
Farallón, Paso del ⊔	288	34.41 S	57.57 W
Farallon de Medinilla I	108	16.01 N	146.04 E
Farallon de Pajaros I	108	20.32 N	144.54 E
Farallon Islands II	204	37.43 N	123.03 W
Faramana	150	12.03 N	4.40 W
Faranah	150	10.02 N	10.44 W
Farángi Samariás (Samaria Gorge) V	38	35.18 N	24.00 E
Fara Novarese	62	45.33 N	8.27 E
Farasān, Jazā'ir II	144	16.48 N	41.54 E
Farasān al-Kabīr I	144	16.42 N	42.00 E
Faratsiho	157b	19.24 S	46.57 E
Faraulep I[1]	108	8.36 N	144.33 E
Farber	219	39.16 N	91.34 W
Farbovano	78	50.09 N	31.51 E
Farcău, Vîrful ∧	38	47.56 N	24.27 E
Farchant	64	47.32 N	11.06 E
Farcy	261	48.31 N	2.37 E
Fardes ≃	34	37.35 N	3.00 W
Fare ≃	50	47.39 N	0.14 E
Fareara, Pointe >	174s	17.52 S	149.39 W
Fareham	42	50.51 N	1.10 W
Fårevejle	41	55.48 N	11.27 E
Farewell	180	62.31 N	153.53 W
Farewell, Cape >	172	40.30 S	172.41 E
Farewell Spit >[2]	172	40.31 S	172.52 E
Färgelanda	26	58.34 N	11.59 E
Fargniers	50	49.39 N	3.19 E
Fargo	198	46.52 N	96.47 W
Far Hills	276	40.41 N	74.38 W
Faria ≃	287a	22.53 S	43.15 W
Fāri'ah, Wādī al- V	132	32.06 N	35.31 E
Faribault	190	44.17 N	93.16 W
Faribault, Lac ◎	176	59.00 N	72.00 W
Farīdābad	124	28.26 N	77.19 E
Farīdganj	126	23.08 N	90.45 E
Farīdkot	123	30.40 N	74.45 E
Farīdnagar	124	28.46 N	77.37 E
Farīdpur, Bngl.	126	24.10 N	89.26 E
Farīdpur, Bngl.	126	23.36 N	89.50 E
Farīdpur, India	124	28.13 N	79.33 E
Farié Haoussa	150	13.48 N	1.38 E
Fārigh, Wādī al- V	146	29.59 N	19.25 E
Färila	26	61.48 N	15.51 E
Farilhões II	34	39.28 N	9.34 W
Farim	150	12.27 N	15.17 W
Farīmān	128	35.43 N	59.53 E
Farina	219	38.50 N	88.46 W
Faringdon	42	51.40 N	1.35 W
Farington	262	53.43 N	2.42 W
Farinha ≃	250	6.51 S	47.30 W
Farini d'Olmo	62	44.43 N	9.34 E
Fariš	85	40.35 N	66.52 E
Fariske	130	36.37 N	32.38 E
Fāriskūr	142	31.20 N	31.43 E
Farit, Amba ∧	144	10.56 N	38.58 E
Färjestaden	26	56.39 N	16.27 E
Farkwa	154	5.24 S	35.36 E
Farleigh	260	51.19 N	0.02 W
Farley	190	42.26 N	91.00 W
Farley Green	260	51.12 N	0.29 W
Farmahīn	128	34.30 N	49.41 E
Farmer City	216	40.14 N	88.38 W
Farmers Branch	222	32.55 N	96.53 W
Farmersburg	194	39.14 N	87.22 W
Farmers Fork	208	38.02 N	76.45 W
Farmer's Museum ⊛	210	42.42 N	74.57 W
Farmers Retreat	218	38.58 N	85.06 W
Farmersville, Ca., U.S.	226	36.17 N	119.12 W
Farmersville, Il., U.S.	219	39.26 N	89.39 W
Farmersville, Pa., U.S.	208	40.08 N	76.10 W
Farmersville, Tx., U.S.	222	33.09 N	96.21 W
Farmersville Station	210	42.26 N	78.22 W
Farmerville	194	32.46 N	92.24 W
Farmingdale, N.J., U.S.	208	40.11 N	74.10 W
Farmingdale, N.Y., U.S.	276	40.43 N	73.26 W
Farmington, Ca., U.S.	226	37.56 N	120.59 W
Farmington, Ct., U.S.	207	41.43 N	72.49 W
Farmington, De., U.S.	208	38.52 N	75.34 W
Farmington, Il., U.S.	190	40.41 N	90.00 W
Farmington, Ia., U.S.	190	40.38 N	91.44 W
Farmington, Me., U.S.	188	44.40 N	70.09 W
Farmington, Mi., U.S.	216	42.27 N	83.22 W
Farmington, Mn., U.S.	190	44.38 N	93.08 W
Farmington, Mo., U.S.	194	37.47 N	90.25 W
Farmington, Mt., U.S.	182	47.54 N	112.11 W
Farmington, N.H., U.S.	188	43.23 N	71.03 W
Farmington, N.M., U.S.	200	36.43 N	108.13 W
Farmington, Ut,. U.S.	200	40.58 N	111.53 W
Farmington ≃	207	41.51 N	72.38 W
Farmington, West Branch ≃	207	41.52 N	72.57 W
Farmington Flood Control Basin ◎[1]	226	37.55 N	120.55 W
Farmington Hills	281	42.28 N	83.23 W
Farmingville	210	40.49 N	73.01 W
Farmland	218	40.11 N	85.07 W
Far Mountain ∧	182	52.46 N	125.17 W
Farm Pond ◎, Ma., U.S.	283	42.17 N	71.26 W
Farm Pond ◎, Ma., U.S.	283	42.14 N	71.21 W
Farmville, N.C., U.S.	192	35.35 N	77.35 W
Farmville, Va., U.S.	192	37.18 N	78.23 W
Färna	40	59.47 N	15.51 E
Farnam	198	40.42 N	100.12 W
Farnawā	142	30.59 N	30.39 E
Farnborough	42	51.17 N	0.46 W
Farnborough ◆[8]	260	51.21 N	0.04 E
Farncombe	260	51.12 N	0.36 W
Farndon	44	53.05 N	0.51 W
Färnebofjärden ◎	40	60.14 N	16.47 E
Farne Islands II	44	55.38 N	1.38 W
Farnham, P.Q., Can.	206	45.17 N	72.59 W
Farnham, Eng., U.K.	42	51.13 N	0.49 W
Farnham, N.Y., U.S.	214	42.36 N	79.05 W
Farnham, Va., U.S.	208	37.53 N	76.37 W
Farnham, Mount ∧	182	50.29 N	116.30 W
Farnham Common	260	51.33 N	0.37 W
Farnham Royal	260	51.32 N	0.37 W
Farnhamville	198	42.16 N	94.24 W
Farningham	260	51.23 N	0.13 E
Farnroda	54	50.56 N	10.23 E
Farnworth, Eng., U.K.	44	53.33 N	2.24 W
Farnworth, Eng., U.K.	262	53.23 N	2.44 W
Faro, Bra.	250	2.11 S	56.44 W
Faro, Port.	34	37.01 N	7.56 W
Faro □[5]	34	37.15 N	8.00 W
Faro ≃	146	9.21 N	12.55 E
Faro, Punta del >	70	38.16 N	15.39 E
Faro, Réserve du ◆[4]	146	8.10 N	12.35 E
Färöer → Faeroe Islands □[2]	22	62.00 N	7.00 W
Fårön I	26	57.56 N	19.08 E
Fårösund	26	57.52 N	19.03 E
Farquhar, Cape >	162	23.37 S	113.37 E
Farquhar Group II	138	10.10 S	51.10 E
Farr	46	57.21 N	4.12 W
Farra d'Isonzo	64	45.56 N	12.31 E
Farragut	198	40.43 N	95.28 W
Farragut State Recreation Area ♠	202	47.55 N	116.35 W
Farrandsville	210	41.10 N	77.31 W
Farrar ≃	46	57.24 N	4.50 W
Farrar Pond ◎	283	42.25 N	71.21 W
Farrars Creek ≃	166	25.35 S	140.43 E
Farrāshband	128	28.53 N	52.06 E
Farrell	214	41.12 N	80.29 W
Farrell Flat	168b	33.50 S	138.47 E
Farrer Park ♠	271c	1.19 N	103.51 E
Farrington Lake ◎	276	40.26 N	74.28 W
Farrington Lake Heights	276	40.26 N	74.27 W
Far Rockaway ◆[8]	276	40.36 N	73.45 W
Farrukhābād	124	27.24 N	79.34 E
Farrukhnagar, India	124	28.27 N	76.49 E
Farrukhnagar, India	272a	28.43 N	77.23 E
Fārs □[4]	128	29.00 N	53.00 E
Fársala	38	39.18 N	22.23 E
Farschviller	56	49.06 N	6.54 E
Fārsī	128	33.47 N	63.15 E
Fārsī, Jazīreh-ye I	128	27.58 N	50.11 E
Farsīs	142	30.40 N	31.14 E
Farsø	26	56.47 N	9.21 E
Farsta	40	59.14 N	18.04 E
Farsund	26	58.05 N	6.48 E
Fartak, Ra's >	118	15.38 N	52.15 E
Farukolu I	122	6.12 N	73.16 E
Farum	41	55.48 N	12.22 E
Fårvang	41	56.16 N	9.44 E
Farvel, Kap >	176	59.45 N	44.00 W
Farwell, Mi., U.S.	190	43.50 N	84.52 W
Farwell, Tx., U.S.	196	30.15 N	103.15 W
Fāryāb □[4]	128	36.00 N	65.00 E
Fasā	128	28.56 N	53.42 E
Fasano	68	40.50 N	17.22 E
Faščovka	83	48.16 N	38.37 E
Fashkhah, 'Ayn ⊤[4]	132	31.43 N	35.27 E
Fåsjön ◎	40	59.36 N	14.58 E
Fasmund >[1]	41	54.32 N	13.35 E
Fassa	150	13.26 N	8.15 W
Fassberg	52	52.54 N	10.10 E
Fasterholt	41	56.01 N	9.07 E
Fastnet Rock I[2]	48	51.24 N	9.35 W
Fastov	78	50.06 N	29.55 E
Fastoveckaja	78	45.56 N	40.09 E
Fatagar Tuting, Tanjung >	164	2.46 S	131.57 E
Fataki	154	4.46 S	28.11 E
Fatala ≃	150	10.13 N	14.00 W
Fat Deer Key I	220	24.44 N	81.00 W
Fate	222	32.56 N	96.23 W
Fatehābād, India	123	29.31 N	75.27 E
Fatehābād, India	124	27.01 N	78.19 E
Fatehgarh, India	124	27.22 N	79.38 E
Fatehgarh, India	124	24.48 N	76.58 E
Fatehgarh Chūriān	123	31.52 N	74.58 E
Fatehjang	123	33.34 N	72.39 E
Fatehpur, India	120	27.59 N	74.57 E
Fatehpur, India	124	25.56 N	80.48 E
Fatehpur, India	124	27.10 N	81.13 E
Fatehpur, India	126	24.05 N	87.44 E
Fatehpur, India	126	22.17 N	88.14 E
Fatehpur, Pāk.	123	31.09 N	71.13 E
Fatehpur Sīkri	124	27.06 N	77.40 E
Fathai	140	8.05 N	31.48 E
Fathom Five National Marine Park ♠	190	45.15 N	81.40 W
Fatick	150	14.20 N	16.25 W
Fatick □[4]	150	14.00 N	16.30 W
Fatigue, Mount ∧	169	38.34 S	146.18 E
Fatima, Arg.	258	34.26 S	59.00 W
Fátima, Port.	34	39.37 N	8.39 W
Fatima do Sol	255	22.16 S	54.25 W
Fatima do Sul	252	22.16 S	54.22 W
Fāṭimah, Wādī V	144	21.27 N	39.09 E
Fatoto	150	13.26 N	13.52 W
Fat'ož	78	52.07 N	35.52 E
Fatsa	130	41.02 N	37.31 E
Fatshan → Foshan	100	23.03 N	113.09 E
Fat Tong Point >	271d	22.16 N	114.15 E
Fatu-Berlio	112	8.56 S	125.52 E
Fatulla	126	23.38 N	90.29 E
Fatumu	174w	21.13 S	175.07 W
Fatunda	152	4.08 S	17.13 E
Fatwā	124	25.31 N	85.19 E
Fauabu	175e	8.34 S	160.43 E
Faucigny	58	46.07 N	6.22 E
Faucille, Col de la)(	58	46.22 N	6.02 E
Faucilles, Monts ⋏	58	48.07 N	6.16 E
Faucogney	58	47.51 N	6.34 E
Faucon-de-Barcelonnette	62	44.24 N	6.41 E
Fauglia	66	43.34 N	10.31 E
Fauldhouse	46	55.50 N	3.37 W
Faulkton	198	45.02 N	99.07 W
Faulquemont	56	49.03 N	6.36 E
Fauquembergues	50	50.36 N	2.05 E
Fauquier	182	49.53 N	118.05 W
Fauquier □[6]	208	38.35 N	77.35 W
Făurei	38	45.06 N	27.14 E
Faure Island I	162	25.51 S	113.52 E
Fauresmith	158	29.42 S	25.21 E
Fauro Island I	175e	6.55 S	156.04 E
Fauske	24	67.15 N	15.24 E
Faust	182	55.19 N	115.38 W
Faustovo	82	55.26 N	38.29 E
Fauville-en-Caux	50	49.39 N	0.35 E
Fauvillers	56	49.51 N	5.40 E
Faux-Cap	157b	25.33 S	45.32 E
Fåvang	26	61.27 N	10.11 E
Favara	70	37.19 N	13.39 E
Faverges	62	45.45 N	6.18 E
Faverney	58	47.46 N	6.06 E
Faversham	42	51.20 N	0.53 E
Favières	261	48.46 N	2.47 E
Favignana	70	37.56 N	12.20 E
Favignana, Isola I	70	37.56 N	12.19 E
Favoriten ◆[8]	264b	48.11 N	16.23 E
Favourable Lake ◎	184	52.53 N	93.56 W
Favrieux	261	48.57 N	1.39 E
Fawcett	182	54.32 N	114.05 W
Fawcett Lake ◎	182	55.19 N	113.57 W
Fawkham Green	260	51.22 N	0.17 E

≃	River	Fluß	Río	Rivière	Rio
≊	Canal	Kanal	Canal	Canal	Canal
⌞	Waterfall, Rapids	Wasserfall, Stromschnellen	Cascada, Rápidos	Chute d'eau, Rapides	Cascata, Rápidos
⊔	Strait	Meeresstraße	Estrecho	Détroit	Estreito
⊂	Bay, Gulf	Bucht, Golf	Bahía, Golfo	Baie, Golfe	Baía, Golfo
◎	Lake, Lakes	See, Seen	Lago, Lagos	Lac, Lacs	Lago, Lagos
⁂	Swamp	Sumpf	Pantano	Marais	Pântano
⊓	Ice Features, Glacier	Eis- und Gletscherformen	Accidentes Glaciales	Formes glaciaires	Acidentes glaciares
⊤	Other Hydrographic Features	Andere Hydrographische Objekte	Otros Elementos Hidrográficos	Autres données hydrographiques	Outros acidentes hidrográficos
✣	Submarine Features	Untermeerische Objekte	Accidentes Submarinos	Formes de relief sous-marin	Acidentes submarinos
□	Political Unit	Politische Einheit	Unidad Politica	Entité politique	Unidade política
⊛	Cultural Institution	Kulturelle Institution	Institución Cultural	Institution culturelle	Institução cultural
⊥	Historical Site	Historische Stätte	Sitio Histórico	Site historique	Sitio histórico
♠	Recreational Site	Erholungs- und Ferienort	Sitio de Recreo	Centre de loisirs	Area de Lazer
⊠	Airport	Flughafen	Aeropuerto	Aéroport	Aeroporto
■	Military Installation	Militäranlage	Instalación Militar	Installation militaire	Instalação militar
◆	Miscellaneous	Verschiedenes	Misceláneo	Divers	Diversos

ENGLISH | DEUTSCH

Name	Page	Lat.°′	Long.°′
Fawkner	274b	37.43 S	144.58 E
Fawkner Park ♠	274b	37.50 S	144.59 E
Fawley	42	50.49 N	1.20 W
Fawn ≃, On., Can.	176	55.22 N	88.20 W
Fawn ≃, U.S.	216	41.51 N	85.40 W
Fawn Grove	208	39.44 N	76.27 W
Fawnie Nose ʌ	182	53.16 N	125.08 W
Fawnie Range ⋏	182	53.10 N	125.00 W
Fawsett Farms	284c	38.59 N	77.14 W
Faxaflói ⊂	24a	64.25 N	23.00 W
Faxälven ≃	26	63.13 N	17.13 E
Faxinal	255	23.59 S	51.22 W
Faxinal do Soturno	252	29.37 S	53.26 W
Faxon	210	41.15 N	76.58 W
Faya	146	17.55 N	19.07 E
Fayd	128	27.07 N	42.27 E
Fayence	62	43.37 N	6.41 E
Fayerweather Island I	276	41.08 N	73.13 W
Fayette, Al., U.S.	194	33.41 N	87.49 W
Fayette, Ia., U.S.	190	42.50 N	91.48 W
Fayette, Ms., U.S.	194	31.42 N	91.03 W
Fayette, Mo., U.S.	194	39.08 N	92.41 W
Fayette, N.Y., U.S.	210	42.49 N	76.49 W
Fayette, Oh., U.S.	216	41.40 N	84.19 W
Fayette □[6], Il., U.S.	219	38.58 N	89.06 W
Fayette □[6], In., U.S.	218	39.39 N	85.08 W
Fayette □[6], Ky., U.S.	218	38.07 N	84.30 W
Fayette □[6], Oh., U.S.	218	39.32 N	83.26 W
Fayette □[6], Pa., U.S.	214	40.05 N	79.39 W
Fayette □[6], Tx., U.S.	222	29.50 N	96.57 W
Fayette, Lake ⊜[1]	222	29.56 N	96.44 W
Fayette City	214	40.06 N	79.50 W
Fayetteville, Ar., U.S.	194	36.03 N	94.09 W
Fayetteville, Ga., U.S.	192	33.26 N	84.27 W
Fayetteville, Il., U.S.	219	38.22 N	89.48 W
Fayetteville, N.Y., U.S.	210	43.02 N	76.00 W
Fayetteville, N.C., U.S.	192	35.03 N	78.52 W
Fayetteville, Oh., U.S.	218	39.11 N	83.55 W
Fayetteville, Pa., U.S.	208	39.54 N	77.33 W
Fayetteville, Tn., U.S.	194	35.09 N	86.34 W
Fayetteville, Tx., U.S.	222	29.54 N	96.41 W
Fayetteville, W.V., U.S.	188	38.03 N	81.06 W
Faylakah I	128	29.27 N	48.20 E
Fayl-Billot	58	47.47 N	5.36 E
Fayrā	144	13.17 N	43.25 E
Fay-sur-Lignon	62	44.59 N	4.14 E
Fayville	207	42.17 N	71.30 W
Fayyum → Al-Fayyūm	142	29.19 N	30.50 E
Fažana	64	44.55 N	13.49 E
Fazao	150	8.42 N	0.46 E
Fazao, Parc National du ♠	150	8.40 N	0.42 E
Fazeley	42	52.37 N	1.42 W
Fazenda de Cima	248	15.56 S	56.37 W
Fazenda Libongo	152	8.24 S	13.24 E
Fazenda Nova	255	16.11 S	50.48 W
Fāzilka	123	30.24 N	74.02 E
Fāzilpur	120	29.18 N	70.27 E
Fazzān (Fezzan) □[9]	146	26.00 N	14.00 E
Fdérik	148	22.41 N	12.43 W
Feale ≃	48	52.28 N	9.40 W
Fear, Cape ≻	192	33.50 N	77.58 W
Fearnhead	262	53.25 N	2.33 W
Feasterville	208	40.08 N	75.00 W
Feather ≃	204	38.47 N	121.36 W
Feather, Middle Fork ≃	204	39.34 N	121.26 W
Feather, North Fork ≃	204	39.34 N	121.28 W
Feather, North Fork, East Branch ≃	204	40.01 N	121.13 W
Feather, South Fork ≃	204	39.33 N	121.28 W
Featherbed Top ʌ	262	53.26 N	1.52 W
Featherly Regional Park ♠	280	33.52 N	117.42 W
Featherston	172	41.07 S	175.20 E
Featherstone, Eng., U.K.	44	53.41 N	1.21 W
Featherstone, Zimb.	154	18.42 S	30.49 E
Feathertop, Mount ʌ	166	36.54 S	147.08 E
Fécamp	50	49.45 N	0.22 E
Fedala → Mohammedia	148	33.44 N	7.24 W
Fedderwardergroden	52	53.35 N	8.05 E
Feddet ≻[1]	41	55.09 N	12.07 E
Federación	252	31.00 S	57.54 W
Federal, Arg.	252	30.57 S	58.48 W
Federal, Pa., U.S.	279b	40.23 N	80.09 W
Federal Capital Territory □[3]	150	9.00 N	7.15 E
Federalsburg	208	38.41 N	75.46 W
Federal Territory □[8]	273a	6.29 N	3.25 E
Federal Way	224	47.19 N	122.18 W
Federation Forest State Park ♠	224	47.09 N	121.40 W
Federsee ⊜	58	48.05 N	9.38 E
Fedeshk	128	32.45 N	58.50 E
Fedje	26	60.47 N	4.42 E
Fedorino	82	55.08 N	36.06 E
Fedosejevka	80	46.53 N	44.00 E
Fedosejevskaja	24	62.07 N	40.42 E
Fedosicha	86	54.47 N	81.54 E
Fedosjino	82	55.08 N	38.30 E
Fedotovo	82	55.41 N	39.12 E
Feeagh, Lough ⊜	48	53.55 N	9.36 W
Feeding Hills	207	42.04 N	72.40 W
Feerfeer	144	8.30 N	47.55 E
Feesburg	218	38.52 N	83.58 W
Fefan I	175c	7.21 N	151.51 E
Fehérgyarmat	30	47.58 N	22.32 E
Fehmarn I	54	54.28 N	11.08 E
Fehmarnbelt (Femer Bælt) ʯ	41	54.35 N	11.15 E
Fehmarnsund ʯ	54	54.24 N	11.07 E
Fehrbellin	54	52.49 N	12.46 E
Fehring	61	46.56 N	16.01 E
Feia, Lagoa ⊂	255	22.00 S	41.20 W
Feicheng	98	36.15 N	116.46 E
Feichten	58	47.02 N	10.44 E
Feidong	100	31.52 N	117.29 E
Feignies	50	50.18 N	3.55 E
Feigumfossen ʟ	26	61.23 N	7.26 E
Feiheji	100	33.36 N	115.36 E
Fei Huang ≃	100	33.35 N	119.02 E
Feijó	248	8.09 S	70.21 W
Feiketu	89	45.46 N	127.09 E
Feilding	172	40.13 S	175.34 E
Feiler ʌ	64	47.07 N	10.52 E
Feiliqiao	106	31.05 N	119.05 E
Feilitzsch	54	50.22 N	11.56 E
Feilong, Zhg.	107	30.25 N	106.20 E
Feilong, Zhg.	107	30.36 N	105.54 E
Feilongguan	107	28.57 N	105.05 E
Feiluan	100	26.35 N	119.35 E
Feira	154	15.37 S	30.25 E
Feira de Santana	255	12.15 S	38.57 W
Feistritz ≃	61	47.01 N	16.08 E
Feistritz an der Gail	64	46.34 N	13.36 E
Feistritzer Spitze ʌ	61	46.31 N	14.45 E
Feixi	100	31.42 N	117.10 E
Feixian	98	35.18 N	117.57 E
Feixiang	98	36.34 N	114.49 E
Feiyun ≃	100	27.48 N	120.36 E
Fejaj, Chott ≡	148	33.55 N	9.10 E
Fejér □[6]	30	47.10 N	18.35 E
Fejø I	41	54.57 N	11.26 E
Feke	130	37.53 N	35.58 E
Feklistova, ostrov I	89	55.02 N	136.55 E
Felâhiye	130	39.06 N	35.35 E
Felanitx	34	39.28 N	3.08 E
Felbertauerntunnel ◆[5]	64	47.08 N	12.31 E
Felda	220	26.33 N	81.26 W
Felda ≃, Dtsch.	56	50.51 N	10.05 E
Felda ≃, Dtsch.	56	50.42 N	9.03 E
Feldafing	64	47.57 N	11.17 E
Feldaist ≃	61	48.19 N	14.34 E
Feld am See	64	46.47 N	13.45 E
Feldbach	61	46.57 N	15.54 E
Feldberg, Dtsch.	54	53.20 N	13.26 E
Feldberg, Dtsch.	58	47.51 N	8.02 E
Feldberg ʌ	58	47.52 N	8.00 E
Felderbach ≃	263	51.22 N	7.08 E
Feldhausen ◆[8]	263	51.37 N	6.59 E
Feldis	58	46.48 N	9.26 E
Feldkirch	58	47.14 N	9.36 E
Feldkirchen an der Donau	61	48.21 N	14.03 E
Feldkirchen bei Graz	61	47.01 N	15.27 E
Feldkirchen in Kärnten	61	46.43 N	14.05 E
Feldmark	263	51.41 N	6.38 E
Feldstetten	58	48.28 N	9.37 E
Felhit	144	16.43 N	38.02 E
Feliciano, Méx.	234	18.01 N	101.58 W
Feliciano, P.R.	240m	18.28 N	67.08 W
Feliciano, Arroyo ≃	252	31.06 S	59.54 W
Felicity	218	38.50 N	84.05 W
Felino	64	44.42 N	10.15 E
Felipe Carrillo Puerto, Méx.	234	19.08 N	102.42 W
Felipe Carrillo Puerto, Méx.	234	21.09 N	104.52 W
Felix, Cape ≻	176	69.54 N	97.50 W
Felix, Rio ≃	196	33.08 N	104.19 W
Felixburg	154	19.29 S	30.51 E
Felixdorf	61	47.53 N	16.15 E
Felixlândia	255	18.47 S	44.55 W
Felixstowe	42	51.58 N	1.20 E
Felixton	158	28.50 S	31.53 E
Félix U. Gómez	232	29.50 N	111.30 W
Felizzano	62	44.54 N	8.26 E
Fella ≃	64	46.21 N	13.07 E
Fellbach	56	48.48 N	9.15 E
Felletin	32	45.53 N	2.10 E
Felling	44	54.57 N	1.33 W
Fellingsbro	40	59.26 N	15.35 E
Fellows	226	35.11 N	119.32 W
Fellows Creek ≃	281	42.17 N	83.26 W
Fellowship	285	39.55 N	74.58 W
Fellsburg	214	40.11 N	79.49 W
Fellsmere	220	27.46 N	80.36 W
Fellwick	285	40.08 N	75.11 W
Felpham	42	50.47 N	0.39 W
Felsberg	56	51.08 N	9.25 E
Felső-Válicka ≃	61	46.52 N	16.53 E
Feltham ◆[8]	260	51.27 N	0.24 W
Felt Lake ⊜	282	37.23 N	122.11 W
Felton, Ca., U.S.	226	37.03 N	122.04 W
Felton, De., U.S.	208	39.00 N	75.34 W
Felton, Pa., U.S.	208	39.51 N	76.34 W
Feltre	64	46.01 N	11.54 E
Felts Mills	212	44.01 N	75.46 W
Feltwell	42	52.29 N	0.32 E
Femer Bælt (Fehmarnbelt) ʯ	41	54.35 N	11.15 E
Femme Osage Creek ≃	219	38.39 N	90.44 W
Femmøller	41	56.14 N	10.35 E
Femø I	41	54.58 N	11.33 E
Femund ⊜	26	62.12 N	11.52 E
Femundsenden	26	61.55 N	11.55 E
Femundsmarka Nasjonalpark ♠	26	62.20 N	12.07 E
Fen ≃	102	35.36 N	110.42 E
Fena Valley Reservoir ⊜[1]	174p	13.21 N	144.42 E
Fendaozi	104	41.35 N	120.51 E
Fenelon Falls	212	44.32 N	78.45 W
Fenelton	214	40.52 N	79.44 W
Fener ◆[8]	267b	41.02 N	28.56 E
Fenerbahce Stadium ♠	267b	40.59 N	29.02 E
Fener Burnu ≻	130	41.07 N	39.25 E
Fener Tepesi ʌ[2]	267b	41.09 N	28.47 E
Fenestrelle	62	45.02 N	7.03 E
Fénétrange	56	48.51 N	7.01 E
Feng ≃	105	39.25 N	116.57 E
Fengcheng, Zhg.	98	40.27 N	124.02 E
Fengcheng, Zhg.	100	28.10 N	115.46 E
Fengcheng, Zhg.	102	38.32 N	101.50 E
Fengcheng, Zhg.	106	30.55 N	121.38 E
Fengdengwu	105	39.42 N	117.55 E
Fengdian	107	30.41 N	104.51 E
Fengdu	102	29.58 N	107.41 E
Fengfeng	98	36.28 N	114.14 E
Fenggang, Zhg.	100	28.34 N	116.34 E
Fenggang, Zhg.	102	27.58 N	107.47 E
Fenggaopu	107	29.24 N	105.41 E
Fenghua	100	29.40 N	121.24 E
Fenghuang, Zhg.	100	23.58 N	116.44 E
Fenghuang, Zhg.	102	24.25 N	107.17 E
Fenghuang, Zhg.	102	27.58 N	109.19 E
Fenghuang, Zhg.	106	31.21 N	121.44 E
Fenghuangchang	107	29.44 N	106.19 E
Fenghuang Shan ʌ	107	28.54 N	106.35 E
Fenghuanjing	100	31.11 N	117.49 E
Fenghui	100	29.56 N	120.58 E
Fengjia, Zhg.	98	37.03 N	121.42 E
Fengjia, Zhg.	104	42.35 N	122.30 E
Fengjiabao	102	36.12 N	104.49 E
Fengjiakou	98	38.11 N	116.44 E
Fengjianjiao	106	30.41 N	120.51 E
Fengjiatun	104	41.14 N	122.00 E
Fengjiawopeng	104	42.19 N	123.40 E
Fengjiaxiang	106	30.56 N	121.06 E
Fengjie	102	31.03 N	109.31 E
Fengjing	106	30.53 N	121.01 E
Fengkou	100	30.05 N	113.18 E
Fengle, Zhg.	89	45.47 N	125.26 E
Fengle, Zhg.	100	27.13 N	118.11 E
Fenglezhen	98	36.14 N	114.18 E
Fengliang	100	23.59 N	116.14 E
Fenglin, T'aiwan	100	23.45 N	121.26 E
Fenglin, Zhg.	100	28.19 N	120.46 E
Fengling Guan)(	100	28.14 N	118.29 E
Fenglingtou	100	28.26 N	117.50 E
Fengman	89	43.46 N	126.41 E
Fengnan (Xugezhuang)	105	39.34 N	118.06 E
Fengning (Dagezhen)	98	41.12 N	116.32 E
Fengpin	100	23.36 N	121.31 E
Fengpingzi	102	32.46 N	105.12 E
Fengqiao, Zhg.	100	29.46 N	120.26 E
Fengqiao, Zhg.	106	31.19 N	120.33 E
Fengqing	102	24.46 N	99.52 E
Fengqiu	98	35.05 N	114.25 E
Fengrun	105	39.50 N	118.07 E
Fengshan, Zhg.	89	46.22 N	128.30 E
Fengshan, Zhg.	98	41.14 N	117.05 E
Fengshan, Zhg.	102	22.01 N	109.59 E
Fengshi	100	24.42 N	116.34 E
Fengshun	100	23.48 N	116.11 E
Fengtai, Zhg.	100	32.44 N	116.43 E
Fengtai, Zhg.	105	39.51 N	116.16 E
Fengtian, Zhg.	100	27.24 N	114.43 E
Fengtian, Zhg.	100	25.46 N	115.30 E
Fengtien → Shenyang	104	41.48 N	123.27 E
Fengting	100	25.16 N	118.54 E
Fengwan	100	24.48 N	113.50 E
Fengxi	102	31.48 N	109.50 E
Fengxian, Zhg.	98	34.42 N	116.34 E
Fengxian, Zhg.	102	33.57 N	106.44 E
Fengxian, Zhg.	106	30.55 N	121.27 E
Fengxiang	102	34.29 N	107.29 E
Fengxin	100	28.43 N	115.23 E
Fengyang, Zhg.	100	32.52 N	117.34 E
Fengyang, Zhg.	100	24.49 N	117.53 E
Fengyi	102	31.44 N	103.53 E
Fengyu	100	26.31 N	119.18 E
Fengyüan	100	24.15 N	120.43 E
Fengzhen	102	40.24 N	113.09 E
Fengzhou	100	25.41 N	113.52 E
Fengzhuangtou	106	31.00 N	118.39 E
Fenholloway ≃	192	29.59 N	83.47 W
Fen Hu ⊜	106	31.00 N	120.47 E
Feni	124	23.00 N	91.24 E
Fenicia Moncata ⊥	70	37.33 N	14.57 E
Feni Islands II	14	4.05 S	153.42 E
Fenimore Pass ʯ	180	52.00 N	175.35 W
Fenino	265b	55.44 N	37.57 E
Fenis	62	45.44 N	7.29 E
Feniscowles	262	53.43 N	2.32 W
Fenjie	106	32.17 N	120.20 E
Fennimore	190	42.59 N	90.39 W
Fennville	216	42.35 N	86.06 W
Fenny Compton	42	52.09 N	1.20 W
Fenny Stratford	42	52.00 N	0.43 W
Feno, Capo di ≻, Fr.	36	41.57 N	8.36 E
Feno, Capo di ≻, Fr.	71	41.23 N	9.06 E
Fenoarivo, Madag.	157b	18.26 S	46.34 E
Fenoarivo, Madag.	157b	21.43 S	46.24 E
Fenoarivo, Madag.	157b	20.52 S	46.53 E
Fenoarivo Atsinanana	157b	17.22 S	49.25 E
Fensfjorden ⊂[2]	26	60.51 N	4.50 E
Fenshui	104	40.41 N	122.32 E
Fenshui ≃	100	29.49 N	119.41 E
Fenshui'ao	100	25.20 N	114.43 E
Fenshuidunshen	106	31.30 N	120.01 E
Fenshuiling, Zhg.	107	28.51 N	105.35 E
Fenshuiling, Zhg.	107	30.20 N	105.15 E
Fenshuipu	107	30.05 N	104.05 E
Fenshuizhen	107	29.44 N	103.55 E
Fenshuizui	100	30.35 N	113.38 E
Fensmark	41	55.17 N	11.49 E
Fenstanton	42	52.18 N	0.04 W
Fenton, Mi., U.S.	216	42.47 N	83.42 W
Fenton, Mo., U.S.	219	38.32 N	90.22 W
Fenton, Lake ⊜	216	42.50 N	83.43 W
Fentou	105	38.53 N	116.32 E
Fentress	222	29.45 N	97.47 W
Fenway Park ♠	283	42.21 N	71.06 W
Fenwick	188	38.13 N	80.34 W
Fenwick Island ≻[1]	208	38.25 N	75.03 W
Fenyang	102	37.17 N	111.48 E
Fenyi	100	27.47 N	114.42 E
Feodosija	78	45.02 N	35.23 E
Feodosijskij zaliv ⊂	78	45.05 N	35.35 E
Fépin	56	50.01 N	4.44 E
Fer, Cap de ≻	148	37.05 N	7.10 E
Ferbane	48	53.15 N	7.49 W
Ferbitz	264a	52.30 N	13.01 E
Ferch	264a	52.19 N	12.56 E
Fercher Berge ʌ[2]	264a	52.19 N	12.57 E
Ferchland	54	52.26 N	12.00 E
Ferdig	182	48.45 N	111.46 W
Ferdinand	194	38.13 N	86.51 W
Ferdinandshof	54	53.39 N	13.53 E
Ferdows	128	34.00 N	58.09 E
Fère-Champenoise	50	48.45 N	3.59 E
Fère-en-Tardenois	50	49.12 N	3.31 E
Ferencváros ◆[8]	264c	47.28 N	19.06 E
Ferentillo	66	42.37 N	12.47 E
Ferentino	66	41.42 N	13.15 E
Fergana	85	40.23 N	71.46 E
Fergana □[4]	85	40.30 N	71.20 E
Ferganskaja dolina V	85	40.50 N	71.30 E
Ferganskij chrebet ⋏	85	41.00 N	74.00 E
Fergus	212	43.42 N	80.22 W
Fergus Falls	198	46.16 N	96.04 W
Ferguson, Austl.	168a	33.26 S	115.51 E
Ferguson, B.C., Can.	182	50.41 N	117.28 W
Ferguson, Ky., U.S.	192	37.04 N	84.36 W
Ferguson, Mo., U.S.	219	38.44 N	90.18 W
Ferguson ≃	168a	33.21 S	115.40 E
Fergusonville	285	40.07 N	74.54 W
Fergusson Island I	164	9.30 S	150.40 E
Fériana	148	34.57 N	8.34 E
Ferihegyi Airport ⊠	264c	47.26 N	19.15 E
Ferkéssédougou	150	9.36 N	5.12 W
Ferla	70	37.07 N	14.56 E
Ferlach	61	46.31 N	14.18 E
Ferleiten	64	47.10 N	12.49 E
Ferlo ◆[1]	150	0.15 N	0.14 W
Ferlo, Vallée du V	150	15.42 N	15.30 W
Fermiers, Île aux I	275a	45.40 N	73.27 W
Fermignano	66	43.40 N	12.39 E
Fermin, Point ≻	228	33.42 N	118.18 W
Fermi National Accelerator Laboratory ʊ[3]	216	41.50 N	88.15 W
Fermo	66	43.09 N	13.43 E
Fermont	176	52.47 N	67.05 W
Fermoselle	34	41.19 N	6.23 W
Fermoy	48	52.08 N	8.16 W
Fernández	252	27.55 S	63.54 W
Fernández Leal	200	30.51 N	108.17 W
Fernandina, Isla I	246a	0.25 S	91.30 W
Fernandina Beach	192	30.40 N	81.27 W
Fernando de la Mora	252	25.19 S	57.36 W
Fernando de Noronha, Ilha I	250	3.51 S	32.25 W
Fernandópolis	255	20.16 S	50.14 W
Fernando Póo → Bioko I	152	3.30 N	8.40 E
Fernán-Núñez	34	37.40 N	4.43 W
Fernão Veloso, Baía de ⊂	154	14.20 S	40.45 E
Ferndale, S. Afr.	273d	26.05 S	27.59 E
Ferndale, Ca., U.S.	204	40.34 N	124.15 W
Ferndale, Fl., U.S.	220	28.37 N	81.42 W
Ferndale, Md., U.S.	208	39.10 N	76.38 W
Ferndale, Mi., U.S.	216	42.27 N	83.08 W
Ferndale, N.Y., U.S.	210	41.46 N	74.44 W
Ferndale, Pa., U.S.	214	40.17 N	78.54 W
Ferndale, Wa., U.S.	202	48.50 N	122.35 W
Ferndale Lake ⊜	222	32.57 N	95.05 W
Ferndown	42	50.48 N	1.55 W
Ferney-Voltaire	58	46.15 N	6.07 E
Fern Glen	210	40.57 N	76.10 W
Fernhill Heath	42	52.14 N	2.12 W
Fernie	182	49.30 N	115.03 W
Fernilee	262	53.18 N	1.58 W
Fernilee Reservoir ⊜[1]	262	53.17 N	1.59 W
Fernley	204	39.36 N	119.15 W
Ferno	62	45.37 N	8.45 E
Fernow, Mount ʌ	224	47.45 N	121.14 W
Fern Park	220	28.41 N	81.20 W
Fernpass)(	58	47.22 N	10.50 E
Fern Ridge Lake ⊜[1]	202	44.05 N	123.18 W
Ferns	48	52.35 N	6.31 W
Fernvale	171a	27.27 S	152.39 E
Fernway	214	40.41 N	80.07 W
Fernwood, Id., U.S.	202	47.06 N	116.23 W
Fernwood, N.Y., U.S.	210	43.16 N	73.40 W
Fernwood, Pa., U.S.	285	39.57 N	75.15 W
Ferny Creek	274b	37.53 S	145.21 E
Feroé, Islas → Faeroe Islands □[2]	22	62.00 N	7.00 W
Feroës → Faeroe Islands □[2]	22	62.00 N	7.00 W
Ferokh	122	11.11 N	75.51 E
Feroleto Antico	68	38.58 N	16.23 E
Feroleto della Chiesa	68	38.28 N	16.04 E
Ferolle Point ≻	186	51.05 N	57.07 W
Ferozepore → Fīrozpur	123	30.55 N	74.36 E
Ferrandina	68	40.29 N	16.28 E
Ferrara	64	44.50 N	11.35 E
Ferrara □[4]	64	44.48 N	11.50 E
Ferrat, Cap ≻	34	35.54 N	0.23 W
Ferrato, Capo ≻	71	39.18 N	9.38 E
Ferraz de Vasconcelos	256	23.32 S	46.22 W
Ferraz de Vasconcelos □[7]	287b	23.33 S	46.21 W
Ferrazzano	66	41.32 N	14.40 E
Ferré, Cap ≻	240e	14.28 N	60.49 W
Ferreira, Ang.	152	12.53 S	22.48 E
Ferreira, S. Afr.	158	29.13 S	26.10 E
Ferreira do Alentejo	34	38.03 N	8.07 W
Ferreira Gomes	250	0.48 N	51.08 W
Ferreiros	256	22.25 S	43.34 W
Ferrell	285	39.41 N	75.12 W
Ferrell's Bridge Dam ◆[6]	222	32.45 N	94.30 W
Ferreñafe	248	6.38 S	79.45 W
Ferrera Erbognone	62	45.07 N	8.52 E
Ferret	58	45.55 N	7.06 E
Ferret, Cap ≻	32	44.37 N	1.15 W
Ferreyra	252	31.28 S	64.08 W
Ferriday	194	31.37 N	91.33 W
Ferriere	62	44.38 N	9.30 E
Ferrière-la-Grande	50	50.15 N	4.00 E
Ferrières	50	48.05 N	2.47 E
Ferrières-en-Brie	50	48.49 N	2.43 E
Ferris	222	32.32 N	96.39 W
Ferritslev	41	55.18 N	10.36 E
Ferro ≃	255	12.27 S	54.31 W
Ferro, Canale del V	64	46.21 N	13.07 E
Ferrol, Península de ≻[1]	248	9.10 S	78.37 W
Ferrol → El Ferrol del Caudillo	34	43.29 N	8.14 W
Ferron	200	39.05 N	111.08 W
Ferron Creek ≃	200	39.09 N	110.55 W
Ferros	255	19.14 S	43.02 W
Ferru, Monte ʌ	71	39.44 N	9.38 E
Ferruzzano	68	38.02 N	16.05 E
Ferry, Pointe ≻	241o	16.17 N	61.49 W
Ferryhill	44	54.41 N	1.33 W
Ferryland	186	47.02 N	52.53 W
Ferry Point Park ♠	276	40.49 N	73.50 W
Ferrysburg	216	43.05 N	86.13 W
Ferry Village	284a	43.58 N	78.57 W
Ferryville → Menzel Bourguiba	148	37.10 N	9.48 E
Feršampenuaz	86	53.32 N	59.51 E
Fertile	198	47.32 N	96.16 W
Fertilia, Aeroporto di ⊠	71	40.37 N	8.15 E
Fertő (Neusiedler See) ⊜	61	47.50 N	16.45 E
Fertőd ⊥	61	47.37 N	16.53 E
Fertőrákos	61	47.43 N	16.39 E
Fertőújlak	61	47.40 N	16.51 E
Ferulargiu, Monte ʌ	71	40.31 N	9.34 E
Ferzikovo	82	54.32 N	36.45 E
Fès	148	34.05 N	4.57 W
Fès □[4]	148	33.55 N	4.57 W
Feshi	152	6.07 S	18.10 E
Feshie ≃	46	57.08 N	3.55 W
Fessenden	198	47.38 N	99.37 W
Festus	219	38.13 N	90.23 W
Fetcham	42	51.17 N	0.22 W
Fet Dom, Tanjung ≻	164	1.53 S	129.43 E
Fété Bowé	150	14.56 N	13.30 W
Fetești	38	44.23 N	27.50 E
Fethaland, Point of ≻	46a	60.38 N	1.18 W
Fethard	48	52.27 N	7.41 W
Fethiye	130	36.37 N	29.07 E
Fethiye Körfezi ⊂	130	36.40 N	29.00 E
Fetisovo	72	42.46 N	52.38 E
Fetlar I	46a	60.37 N	0.52 W
Fetsund	26	59.56 N	11.10 E
Fetterangus	46	57.33 N	2.01 W
Fettercairn	46	56.51 N	2.34 W
Feucherolles	261	48.52 N	1.58 E
Feucht	60	49.22 N	11.13 E
Feuchtwangen	56	49.10 N	10.20 E
Feudingen	56	50.56 N	8.19 E
Feuerland → Tierra del Fuego, Isla Grande de I	254	54.00 S	69.00 W
Feuet	146	24.57 N	10.04 E
Feuilles, Baie aux ⊂	176	58.55 N	69.20 W
Feuilles, Rivière aux ≃	176	58.47 N	70.04 W
Feuquières-en-Vimeu	50	50.04 N	1.36 E
Feura Bush	210	42.35 N	73.53 W
Feurs	62	45.45 N	4.14 E
Fevik	26	58.23 N	8.42 E
Fevzipaşa	130	37.07 N	36.37 E
Féy	56	49.02 N	6.06 E
Feyẕābād, Afg.	120	37.06 N	70.34 E
Feyẕābād, Īrān	128	35.01 N	58.46 E
Feyzin	62	45.40 N	4.51 E
Fez → Fès	148	34.05 N	4.57 W
Fezzan → Fazzān □[9]	146	26.00 N	14.00 E
Ffestiniog	42	52.58 N	3.55 W
Fforest Fawr ◆[1]	42	51.52 N	3.36 W
F. Gilbert Hills State Forest ♠	283	42.03 N	71.17 W
Fhada, Beinn ʌ	46	57.13 N	5.18 W
Fiambalá	252	27.41 S	67.38 W
Fiamignano	66	42.16 N	13.07 E
Fian	150	10.23 N	2.29 W
Fianarantsoa	157b	21.26 S	47.05 E
Fianarantsoa □[4]	157b	22.00 S	47.00 E
Fianga	146	9.55 N	15.09 E
Fiano	62	45.13 N	7.31 E
Fiantsonana	157b	19.09 S	46.12 E
Fiastra, Abbazia di ʊ[1]	66	43.13 N	13.25 E
Fiavè	64	46.00 N	10.50 E
Ficarazzi	70	38.05 N	13.28 E
Ficarolo	64	44.57 N	11.26 E
Ficarra	70	38.06 N	14.50 E
Fiche	144	9.52 N	38.46 E
Fichtelberg	60	50.01 N	11.51 E
Fichtelberg ʌ	54	50.26 N	12.57 E
Fichtelgebirge ⋏	30	50.00 N	11.55 E
Fichtenau	264a	52.27 N	13.42 E
Ficksburg	158	28.57 S	27.50 E
Ficulle	66	42.50 N	12.04 E
Ficuzza ≃	70	37.00 N	14.20 E
Fidalgo ≃	250	7.28 S	42.32 W
Fidalgo Island I	224	48.25 N	122.35 W
Fidān, Wādī al- V	132	30.46 N	35.18 E
Fiddlers Hamlet	260	51.41 N	0.08 E
Fiddletown	226	38.30 N	120.46 W
Fiddyment Creek ≃	278	41.36 N	88.03 W
Fidelity	219	39.09 N	90.10 W
Fidenza	64	44.52 N	10.03 E
Fidīmīn	142	29.23 N	30.46 E
Fiditi	150	7.45 N	3.53 E
Fidji → Fiji □[1]	175g	18.00 S	178.00 E
Fidler Lake ⊜	184	57.11 N	96.57 W
Fidschi → Fiji □[1]	175g	18.00 S	178.00 E
Fiè (Völs)	64	46.31 N	11.30 E
Fieberbrunn	64	47.29 N	12.33 E
Field	182	51.24 N	116.29 W
Fieldale	192	36.42 N	79.56 W
Field Museum ʊ	278	41.53 N	87.37 W
Fieldon	219	39.07 N	90.30 W
Fieldsboro	285	40.08 N	74.43 W
Fieldstone	276	40.44 N	74.33 W
Fiemme, Val di V	64	46.24 N	11.25 E
Fiener Bruch ≡	54	52.19 N	12.10 E
Fienvillers	50	50.07 N	2.14 E
Fier	38	40.43 N	19.34 E
Fier ≃	58	45.56 N	5.50 E
Fiéra Campionaria ♠	266b	45.28 N	9.09 E
Fiera di Primiero	64	46.10 N	11.49 E
Fierenana	157b	18.29 S	48.24 E
Fiery Creek ≃, Austl.	166	18.23 S	139.52 E
Fiery Creek ≃, Austl.	169	37.44 S	142.56 E
Fiery Range ⋏	171b	35.30 S	148.40 E
Fierzës, Liqeni i ⊜[1]	38	42.10 N	20.15 E
Fiesch	58	46.20 N	8.10 E
Fiesole	66	43.48 N	11.17 E
Fiesso d'Artico	64	45.24 N	12.02 E
Fiesso Umbertiano	64	44.56 N	11.36 E
Fife	224	47.14 N	122.22 W
Fife □[4]	46	56.13 N	3.02 W
Fife Lake, Sk., Can.	184	49.12 N	105.43 W
Fife Lake, Mi., U.S.	190	44.34 N	85.21 W
Fife Lake ⊜	184	49.14 N	105.53 W
Fife Ness ≻	46	56.17 N	2.36 W
Fifield	190	45.52 N	90.25 W
Fifteenmile Creek ≃, Or., U.S.	224	45.37 N	121.07 W
Fifteenmile Creek ≃, Wy., U.S.	202	44.01 N	108.01 W
Fifth Cataract → Khāmis, Ash-Shallāl al- ʟ	140	18.23 N	33.47 E
Fifth Depot Lake ⊜	212	44.36 N	76.52 W
Figeac	32	44.37 N	2.02 E
Figeholm	26	57.22 N	16.33 E
Fig Garden	226	36.48 N	119.47 W
Fighting Island I	281	42.13 N	83.07 W
Figline Valdarno	66	43.37 N	11.28 E
Figtree	154	20.24 S	28.21 E
Figueira	287a	22.42 S	43.27 W
Figueira, Cachoeira ʟ	250	9.49 S	58.13 W
Figueira da Foz	34	40.09 N	8.52 W
Figueira → Governador Valadares	255	18.51 S	41.56 W
Figueres	34	42.16 N	2.58 E
Figuig	148	32.10 N	1.15 W
Figuig □[4]	148	32.40 N	2.15 W
Fihaonana	157b	18.36 S	47.12 E
Fiherenana ≃	157b	23.19 S	43.37 E
Fiji □[1], Oc.	14	18.00 S	178.00 E
Fiji □[1], Oc.	175g	18.00 S	178.00 E
Fiji Islands II	14	18.00 S	178.00 E
Fijnaart	52	51.37 N	4.31 E
Fik	144	8.10 N	42.18 E
Fika	146	11.17 N	11.18 E
Fiktūriyā, Bi'r ⊤[4]	142	30.24 N	30.36 E
Filabusi	154	20.34 S	29.20 E
Filadélfia, Bra.	250	7.21 S	47.30 W
Filadelfia, C.R.	236	10.26 N	85.34 W
Filadelfia, It.	68	38.48 N	16.18 E
Filadelfia → Philadelphia	208	39.57 N	75.07 W
Fil'akovo	30	48.17 N	19.51 E
Filandari	68	38.37 N	16.02 E
Filatova Gora	76	57.40 N	28.10 E
Filchner Ice Shelf ⊓	9	79.00 S	40.00 W
Filderstadt	56	48.41 N	9.13 E
File Lake ⊜	184	54.53 N	100.20 W
Filettino	66	41.53 N	13.19 E
Filey	44	54.12 N	0.17 W
Filey Bay ⊂	44	54.12 N	0.16 W
Fili ◆[8]	265b	55.45 N	37.31 E
Filí ⊥	38	38.10 N	23.40 E
Filiano	68	40.49 N	15.42 E
Filiași	38	44.33 N	23.31 E
Filiatrá	38	37.10 N	21.35 E
Filicudi, Isola I	70	38.34 N	14.34 E
Filimonovo	86	56.12 N	95.28 E
Filingué	150	14.21 N	3.19 E
Filipinas, Mar de → Philippine Sea ⊤[2]	14	20.00 N	135.00 E
Filipinas → Philippines □[1]	116	13.00 N	122.00 E
Filipino Cemetery and Memorial ◆	269f	14.31 N	121.02 E
Fílippoi ⊥	38	41.00 N	24.16 E
Filippovka	80	53.59 N	49.46 E
Filippovo	80	58.18 N	50.30 E
Filippovskoje, Ross.	82	56.06 N	38.37 E
Filippovskoje, Ross.	82	56.48 N	39.07 E
Filipstad	40	59.43 N	14.10 E
Filisola	234	17.50 N	94.19 W
Fillmore, Sk., Can.	184	49.50 N	103.25 W
Fillmore, Ca., U.S.	228	34.23 N	118.55 W
Fillmore, Il., U.S.	219	39.07 N	89.17 W
Fillmore, N.Y., U.S.	210	42.27 N	78.06 W
Fillmore, Ut,. U.S.	200	38.58 N	112.19 W
Fillmore Glen State Park ♠	210	42.42 N	76.20 W
Filogaso	68	38.41 N	16.14 E
Filomeno Mata	234	20.12 N	97.42 W
Filonovskaja	80	50.34 N	42.46 E
Filottrano	66	43.26 N	13.21 E
Fils ≃	56	48.42 N	9.25 E
Filskov	41	55.48 N	9.02 E
Filton	42	51.31 N	2.35 W
Filtu	144	5.07 N	40.39 E
Filzbach	58	47.07 N	9.08 E
Fimi ≃	152	3.01 S	16.58 E
Fina, Réserve de ◆[4]	150	12.50 N	8.30 W
Finale Emilia	64	44.50 N	11.17 E
Finale Ligure	62	44.10 N	8.20 E
Finarwa	144	13.06 N	39.01 E
Fincastle	192	37.29 N	79.52 W
Finch	206	45.11 N	75.07 W
Fincham	42	52.37 N	0.30 E
Finchley ◆[8]	260	51.36 N	0.10 W
Finderne	276	40.34 N	74.35 W
Findhorn	46	57.39 N	3.36 W
Findhorn ≃	46	57.38 N	3.38 W
Fındık	130	37.31 N	41.58 E
Findlay, Il., U.S.	219	39.31 N	88.45 W
Findlay, Oh., U.S.	216	41.02 N	83.39 W
Findlay, Mount ʌ	182	50.04 N	116.28 W
Findley Lake	214	42.07 N	79.44 W
Findley Lake ⊜	214	42.06 N	79.43 W
Findochty	46	57.41 N	2.54 W
Fine Arts, Museum of ʊ	283	42.20 N	71.06 W
Finedon	42	52.20 N	0.39 W
Finejevo	82	56.02 N	38.53 E
Finesville	210	40.36 N	75.10 W
Fingal, On., Can.	214	42.43 N	81.19 W
Fingal, N.D., U.S.	198	46.45 N	97.47 W
Finger Lake ⊜	184	53.09 N	93.30 W
Fíngoè	154	15.12 S	31.50 E
Finike	130	36.18 N	30.09 E
Finike Körfezi ⊂	130	36.17 N	30.16 E
Finisk ≃	48	52.07 N	7.50 W
Finistère □[5]	32	48.20 N	4.00 W
Finisterre	196	25.59 N	103.15 W
Finisterre, Cabo de ≻	34	42.53 N	9.16 W
Finisterre → Land's End ≻	42	50.03 N	5.44 W
Finisterre Range ⋏	164	5.50 S	146.05 E
Finja	41	56.10 N	13.41 E
Finjasjön ⊜	41	56.08 N	13.42 E
Finke	162	25.34 S	134.35 E
Finke ≃	162	26.20 S	136.00 E
Finke, Mount ʌ[2]	162	30.55 S	134.02 E
Finke Gorge National Park ♠	162	24.15 S	132.50 E
Finkenkrug	264a	52.34 N	13.03 E
Finkenwerder ◆[8]	52	53.31 N	9.52 E
Finksburg	208	39.29 N	76.53 W
Finland (Suomi) □[1], Europe	22	64.00 N	26.00 E
Finland (Suomi) □[1], Europe	24	64.00 N	26.00 E
Finland, Gulf of (Suomenlahti) (Finskij zaliv) ⊂	26	60.00 N	27.00 E
Finlande → Finland □[1]	24	64.00 N	26.00 E
Finlandia, Golfo de → Finland, Gulf of ⊂	26	60.00 N	27.00 E
Finlandia → Finland □[1]	24	64.00 N	26.00 E
Finland Station ◆[5]	265a	59.57 N	30.22 E
Finlas, Loch ⊜	44	55.15 N	4.25 W
Finlay ≃	176	56.54 N	124.57 W
Finley, Austl.	166	35.39 S	145.35 E
Finley, N.D., U.S.	198	47.30 N	97.50 W
Finley Creek ≃	194	36.58 N	93.22 W
Finleyville, Pa., U.S.	214	40.09 N	78.11 W
Finleyville, Pa., U.S.	214	40.15 N	80.00 W
Finleyville Airport ⊠	279b	40.15 N	80.01 W
Finmoore	182	53.59 N	123.37 W
Finn ≃	48	54.50 N	7.29 W
Finne ◆[1]	54	51.13 N	11.19 E
Finnegan	182	51.07 N	112.04 W

Name	Seite	Breite°′	Länge°′ E = Ost
Finnentrop	56	51.09 N	7.58 E
Finnerödja	40	58.56 N	14.26 E
Finney Creek ≃	224	48.31 N	121.51 W
Finnhamn	40	59.28 N	18.50 E
Finnigan, Mount ʌ	164	15.49 S	145.17 E
Finnis, Cape ≻	162	33.38 S	134.51 E
Finnischer Meerbusen → Finland, Gulf of ⊂	26	60.00 N	27.00 E
Finniss	168b	35.24 S	138.49 E
Finniss ≃	168b	35.30 S	138.53 E
Finnland → Finland □[1]	24	64.00 N	26.00 E
Finnmark □[6]	24	70.00 N	25.00 E
Finn Mountain ʌ	180	60.37 N	157.11 W
Finno ʌ[2]	154	3.27 N	41.32 E
Finnskogen ◆[3]	26	60.40 N	12.40 E
Finnsnes	24	69.14 N	17.59 E
Finocchio ◆[8]	267a	41.53 N	12.41 E
Finow	54	52.50 N	13.43 E
Finowfurt	54	52.51 N	13.41 E
Finowkanal ≅	54	52.51 N	13.24 E
Fins, Fr.	50	50.02 N	3.03 E
Fins, 'Umān	128	22.56 N	59.13 E
Finsbury	273d	26.13 S	27.39 E
Finschhafen	164	6.35 S	147.50 E
Finse	26	60.36 N	7.30 E
Finskij zaliv → Finland, Gulf of ⊂	26	60.00 N	27.00 E
Finspång	40	58.43 N	15.47 E
Finsta	40	59.44 N	18.30 E
Finsteraarhorn ʌ	58	46.32 N	8.08 E
Finsterwalde	54	51.38 N	13.42 E
Finsterwolde	52	53.12 N	7.04 E
Fintel	52	53.10 N	9.40 E
Fintona	48	54.30 N	7.19 W
Fintown	48	54.52 N	8.08 W
Finvoy	48	55.00 N	6.30 W
Fionn Loch ⊜	46	57.46 N	5.29 W
Fiora ≃	66	42.20 N	11.34 E
Fiorano Modenese	64	44.32 N	10.49 E
Fiordland National Park ♠	172	45.30 S	167.20 E
Fiorenzuola d'Arda	62	44.56 N	9.55 E
Fiorenzuola di Focara	66	43.57 N	12.48 E
Fiorito ◆[8]	288	34.42 S	58.27 W
Fīq	132	32.47 N	35.42 E
Fırat → Euphrates ≃	128	31.00 N	47.25 E
Firavitoba	246	5.40 N	73.00 W
Fircrest	224	47.14 N	122.30 W
Fire ≃	190	48.52 N	83.21 W
Firebaugh	226	36.51 N	120.27 W
Firebrick	218	38.41 N	83.03 W
Fire Island I	210	40.42 N	73.00 W
Fire Island Inlet ⊂	276	40.38 N	73.16 W
Fire Island National Seashore ♠	188	40.38 N	73.08 W
Fire Island Pines	276	40.40 N	73.04 W
Fire Islands II	276	40.40 N	73.11 W
Firenze (Florence)	66	43.46 N	11.15 E
Firenze □[4]	66	43.50 N	11.20 E
Firenzuola	66	44.07 N	11.23 E
Firesteel Creek ≃	198	43.43 N	97.58 W
Firgrove	262	53.37 N	2.08 W
Firmat	252	33.27 S	61.29 W
Firminópolis	255	16.40 S	50.19 W
Firminy	62	45.23 N	4.18 E
Firmo	68	39.43 N	16.10 E
Firovo	76	57.29 N	33.40 E
Fīrozābād	124	27.09 N	78.25 E
Fīrozpur	123	30.55 N	74.36 E
Firozpur Jhirka	124	27.48 N	76.57 E
Firsanovka	265b	55.57 N	37.15 E
Firsovo	88	52.20 N	118.06 E
First Broad ≃	192	35.11 N	81.37 W
First Cataract → Awwal, Ash-Shallāl al- ʟ	140	24.01 N	32.52 E
First Cliff ⊥[4]	283	42.12 N	70.43 W
First Connecticut Lake ⊜	206	45.05 N	71.15 W
First Han-gang Bridge ◆[5]	271b	37.32 N	126.56 E
First Herring Brook ≃	283	42.11 N	70.45 W
First Watchung Mountain ʌ	276	40.55 N	74.10 W
Firth	198	40.31 N	96.36 W
Firth ≃	180	69.32 N	139.22 W
Fir'uza	128	37.56 N	58.04 E
Fīrūzābād	128	28.50 N	52.36 E
Fīrūz Kūh	128	35.45 N	52.47 E
Fischa ≃	61	48.07 N	16.41 E
Fischamend	61	48.07 N	16.37 E
Fischbach, Dtsch.	56	49.44 N	7.23 E
Fischbach, Dtsch.	60	49.25 N	11.12 E
Fischbachau	64	47.43 N	11.57 E
Fischbacher Alpen ⋏	61	47.28 N	15.30 E
Fischbeck, Dtsch.	52	52.09 N	9.17 E
Fischbeck, Dtsch.	54	52.32 N	12.01 E
Fischeln ◆[8]	263	51.18 N	6.35 E
Fischen	58	47.28 N	10.16 E
Fischhausen → Primorsk	76	54.44 N	20.01 E
Fischland ⊥[2]	54	54.22 N	12.25 E
Fish ≃, Austl.	170	33.29 S	149.37 E
Fish (Vis) ≃, Namibia	156	28.07 S	17.45 E
Fish ≃, Al., U.S.	194	30.25 N	87.50 W
Fish ≃, Me., U.S.	186	47.15 N	68.36 W
Fishbourne	42	50.44 N	1.12 W
Fish Brook ≃, Ma., U.S.	283	42.38 N	70.58 W
Fish Brook ≃, Ma., U.S.	283	42.42 N	71.13 W
Fish Camp	226	37.29 N	119.38 W
Fish Canyon V	280	34.11 N	117.55 W
Fish Creek ≃, On., Can.	212	43.13 N	81.13 W
Fish Creek ≃, U.S.	216	41.28 N	84.45 W
Fish Creek ≃, Mi., U.S.	190	43.04 N	84.51 W
Fish Creek ≃, Mt., U.S.	202	46.17 N	109.13 W
Fish Creek ≃, N.Y., U.S.	212	43.12 N	75.43 W
Fish Creek ≃, Or., U.S.	224	45.09 N	122.09 W
Fish Creek, East Branch ≃	212	43.16 N	75.38 W
Fish Creek, West Branch ≃	212	43.16 N	75.38 W
Fish Creek Mountain ʌ	224	45.05 N	122.08 W
Fisheating Creek ≃	220	26.57 N	81.07 W
Fisher, Austl.	162	30.33 S	130.58 E
Fisher, Ar., U.S.	194	35.29 N	90.58 W
Fisher, Il., U.S.	216	40.18 N	88.21 W
Fisher, La., U.S.	194	31.29 N	93.27 W
Fisher, Pa., U.S.	214	41.16 N	79.15 W
Fisher ≃, Mb., Can.	184	51.26 N	97.18 W
Fisher ≃, Mt., U.S.	202	48.22 N	115.19 W
Fisher Bay ⊂, Mb., Can.	184	51.30 N	97.16 W
Fisher Bay ⊂, Mi., U.S.	281	42.36 N	82.39 W
Fisher Branch	184	51.05 N	97.37 W
Fisher Channel ʯ	182	52.10 N	127.42 W
Fisher Heights	279b	40.10 N	79.54 W
Fishermans Island I	208	37.06 N	75.58 W
Fisherman's Wharf ◆	282	37.48 N	122.25 W
Fisher Peak ʌ	192	36.33 N	80.50 W
Fisher River Indian Reserve ◆[4]	184	51.26 N	97.20 W
Fishers, In., U.S.	218	39.57 N	86.00 W
Fishers, N.Y., U.S.	210	43.00 N	77.28 W
Fishers Island I	207	41.16 N	72.02 W
Fishers Peak ʌ	196	37.06 N	104.28 W
Fisher Strait ʯ	176	63.15 N	83.30 W
Fishertown	214	40.08 N	78.35 W

Symbols in the index entries represent the broad categories identified in the key at the right. Symbols with superior numbers (⋏[1]) identify subcategories (see complete key on page *I · 1).*

Symbole im Register stellen die rechts im Schlüssel erklärten Kategorien dar. Symbole mit hochgestellten Ziffern (⋏[1]) bezeichnen Unterabteilungen einer Kategorie (vgl. vollständiger Schlüssel auf Seite *I · 1).*

Los símbolos incluídos en el texto del índice representan las grandes categorias identificadas con la clave a la derecha. Los símbolos con numeros en su parte superior (⋏[1]) identifican las subcategorias (véase la clave completa en la página *I · 1).*

Les symboles de l'index représentent les catégories indiquées dans la légende à droite. Les symboles suivis d'un indice (⋏[1]) représentent des sous-catégories (voir légende complète à la page *I · 1).*

Os símbolos incluídos no texto do índice representam as grandes categorias identificadas com a chave à direita. Os símbolos com números em sua parte superior (⋏[1]) identificam as subcategorias (veja-se a chave completa à página *I · 1).*

ʌ Mountain	Berg	Montaña	Montagne	Montanha
⋏ Mountains	Gebirge	Montañas	Montagnes	Montanhas
)(Pass	Paß	Paso	Col	Passo
V Valley, Canyon	Tal, Cañon	Valle, Cañón	Vallée, Canyon	Vale, Canhão
≚ Plain	Ebene	Llano	Plaine	Planície
≻ Cape	Kap	Cabo	Cap	Cabo
I Island	Insel	Isla	Île	Ilha
II Islands	Inseln	Islas	Îles	Ilhas
⊥ Other Topographic Features	Andere Topographische Objekte	Otros Elementos Topográficos	Autres données topographiques	Outros acidentes topográficos

ESPAÑOL · FRANÇAIS · PORTUGUÊS

Nombre / Nom / Nome	Página / Page / Página	Lat.°′	Long.°′ W = Oeste / W = Ouest / W = Oeste
Fisherville	275b	43.47 N	79.28 W
Fishguard	42	51.59 N	4.59 W
Fishhook	219	39.48 N	90.53 W
Fish House	210	43.08 N	74.08 W
Fishing Bay ⊂	208	38.18 N	76.01 W
Fishing Creek	208	38.20 N	76.14 W
Fishing Creek ≃, Ky., U.S.	192	37.06 N	84.41 W
Fishing Creek ≃, N.C., U.S.	192	35.57 N	77.31 W
Fishing Creek ≃, Pa., U.S.	210	40.58 N	76.28 W
Fishing Creek ≃, Pa., U.S.	210	41.07 N	77.29 W
Fishing Creek ≃, S.C., U.S.	192	34.36 N	80.54 W
Fishing Islands II	212	44.45 N	81.20 W
Fishing Lake ⊜, Mb., Can.	184	52.07 N	95.25 W
Fishing Lake ⊜, Sk., Can.	184	51.50 N	103.32 W
Fishkill	210	41.32 N	73.53 W
Fishkill Creek ≃	210	41.29 N	73.59 W
Fish Lake	216	41.34 N	86.33 W
Fish Lake ⊜, On., Can.	212	44.06 N	77.11 W
Fish Lake ⊜, Mi., U.S.	216	42.03 N	85.52 W
Fish Lake ⊜, Wa., U.S.	224	47.50 N	120.42 W
Fishmoor Reservoir ⊜[1]	262	53.44 N	2.28 W
Fish Point ›	214	41.43 N	82.40 W
Fishpool	262	53.35 N	2.17 W
Fish River	166	17.55 S	137.45 E
Fishs Eddy	210	41.58 N	75.10 W
Fisk	194	36.46 N	90.12 W
Fiskárdhon	38	38.27 N	20.35 E
Fiskdale	207	42.06 N	72.06 W
Fiskebäckskil	26	58.15 N	11.27 E
Fismes	50	49.18 N	3.41 E
Fišt, gora ∧	84	43.58 N	39.54 E
Fitchburg, Ma., U.S.	207	42.35 N	71.48 W
Fitchburg, Wi., U.S.	216	42.57 N	89.28 W
Fitchville, Ct., U.S.	207	41.33 N	72.09 W
Fitchville, Oh., U.S.	214	41.06 N	82.29 W
Fitful Head ›	46a	59.54 N	1.23 W
Fitiuta	174y	14.13 S	169.27 W
Fito, Mount ∧	175a	13.55 S	171.44 W
Fitri, Lac ⊜	146	12.50 N	17.28 E
Fittja	40	59.15 N	17.52 E
Fittleworth	42	50.58 N	0.35 W
Fitzgerald	192	31.42 N	83.15 W
Fitzgerald River National Park ♦	162	34.00 S	119.30 E
Fitz Henry	279b	40.10 N	79.45 W
Fitz Hugh Sound Ʉ	182	51.40 N	127.57 W
Fitzmaurice ≃	164	14.50 S	129.44 E
Fitz Roy, Arg.	254	47.02 S	67.15 W
Fitzroy, Austl.	274b	37.48 S	144.59 E
Fitzroy ≃, Austl.	162	17.31 S	123.35 E
Fitzroy ≃, Austl.	166	23.32 S	150.52 E
Fitzroy, Monte (Cerro Chaltel) ∧	254	49.17 S	73.05 W
Fitzroy Crossing	162	18.11 S	125.35 E
Fitzroy Falls Reservoir ⊜[1]	170	34.38 S	150.30 E
Fitzwilliam	207	42.46 N	72.08 W
Fitzwilliam Island I	190	45.30 N	81.45 W
Fiuggi	66	41.48 N	13.13 E
Fiumalbo	64	44.11 N	10.39 E
Fiumedinisi	70	38.02 N	15.23 E
Fiumefreddo Bruzio	68	39.14 N	16.04 E
Fiumefreddo di Sicilia	70	37.47 N	15.12 E
Fiume → Rijeka	36	45.20 N	14.27 E
Fiumesino	66	43.38 N	13.22 E
Fiume Veneto	64	45.56 N	12.44 E
Fiumicino	36	41.46 N	12.14 E
Fiumicino ✦[8]	66	41.46 N	12.14 E
Five Corners	283	42.01 N	71.07 W
Five Cowrie Creek ≃[1]	273a	6.27 N	3.27 E
Five Dock	274a	33.52 S	151.08 E
Five Forks	284c	38.47 N	77.16 W
Five Islands	186	45.25 N	64.02 W
Five Islands Harbour ⊂	240c	17.06 N	61.54 W
Fivemile ≃	276	41.03 N	73.27 W
Fivemile Creek ≃, N.Y., U.S.	210	42.22 N	77.22 W
Fivemile Creek ≃, Or., U.S.	224	45.36 N	121.05 W
Fivemile Creek ≃, Wy., U.S.	202	43.14 N	108.12 W
Fivemile Point	210	42.06 N	75.48 W
Fivemiletown	48	54.23 N	7.18 W
Five Penny Borve	46	58.25 N	6.25 W
Five Points, Ca., U.S.	226	36.26 N	120.06 W
Five Points, In., U.S.	218	39.35 N	86.20 W
Five Points, N.M., U.S.	200	35.03 N	106.39 W
Five Points, Oh., U.S.	218	39.41 N	83.12 W
Five Points, Pa., U.S.	214	40.34 N	80.15 W
Five Points, Pa., U.S.	285	39.50 N	75.42 W
Fivizzano	64	44.14 N	10.08 E
Fiwila Mission	154	13.58 S	29.36 E
Fixin	58	47.15 N	4.58 E
Fix-Saint-Geneys	62	45.08 N	3.40 E
Fizi	154	4.18 S	28.57 E
Fizuli	84	39.37 N	47.08 E
Fjællebroen	41	55.03 N	10.24 E
Fjærlandsfjorden ⊂[2]	26	61.17 N	6.40 E
Fjällåsen	24	67.29 N	20.10 E
Fjällbacka	26	58.36 N	11.17 E
Fjällsjöälven ≃	26	63.29 N	16.50 E
Fjärdhundra	40	59.47 N	16.56 E
Fjärdhundra □[9]	40	59.47 N	16.55 E
Fjenneslev	41	55.26 N	11.40 E
Fjerritslev	26	57.05 N	9.16 E
Fjugesta	40	59.10 N	14.52 E
Fkih-Ben-Salah	148	32.32 N	6.40 W
Flacksta	40	59.23 N	16.27 E
Fladnitz im Raabtal	61	46.59 N	15.47 E
Fladså ≃	41	55.19 N	8.54 E
Fladungen	56	50.31 N	10.08 E
Flag Creek ≃	278	41.43 N	87.55 W
Flagler	198	39.17 N	103.04 W
Flagler Beach	192	29.28 N	81.07 W
Flagstaff, Transkei	158	31.05 S	29.29 E
Flagstaff, Az., U.S.	200	35.11 N	111.39 W
Flagstaff Lake ⊜[1]	188	45.10 N	70.15 W
Flagtown	276	40.31 N	74.41 W
Flaken-See ⊜	264a	52.25 N	13.46 E
Flåm	26	60.50 N	7.07 E
Flambeau ≃	190	45.18 N	91.15 W
Flambeau, South Fork ≃	190	45.39 N	90.48 W
Flamborough, On., Can.	212	43.20 N	79.53 W
Flamborough, Eng., U.K.	44	54.06 N	0.07 W
Flamborough Head ›	44	54.07 N	0.04 W
Fläming ✦[1]	54	52.00 N	12.30 E
Flaming Gorge National Recreation Area ♦	200	41.30 N	109.30 W
Flaming Gorge Reservoir ⊜[1]	200	41.15 N	109.30 W
Flamingo	220	25.09 N	80.56 W
Flamingo, Teluk ⊂	164	5.33 S	138.00 E
Flanagan	216	40.52 N	88.51 W
Flanagan ≃	184	52.50 N	93.28 W
Flanagan Passage Ʉ	240m	18.18 N	64.39 W
Flanders, On., Can.	190	48.44 N	92.05 W
Flanders, N.J., U.S.	276	40.50 N	74.41 W
Flanders, N.Y., U.S.	207	40.49 N	72.36 W
Flanders (Flandre) □[9]	50	51.00 N	3.00 E
Flanders Airport ⊠	276	40.50 N	74.41 W
Flandes	246	4.18 N	74.49 W
Flandorf	264b	48.21 N	16.23 E
Flandreau	198	44.02 N	96.35 W
Flandre → Flanders □[9]	50	51.00 N	3.00 E
Flannan Islands II	46	58.18 N	7.36 W
Flåren ⊜	26	57.02 N	14.06 E
Flasher	198	46.27 N	101.13 W
Flåsjön ⊜	26	64.06 N	15.51 E
Flat, Ak., U.S.	180	62.27 N	158.01 W
Flat, Tx., U.S.	222	31.19 N	97.38 W
Flat ≃, N.T., Can.	180	61.33 N	125.18 W
Flat ≃, Mi., U.S.	190	42.56 N	85.20 W
Flat ≃, N.C., U.S.	192	36.05 N	78.49 W
Flat Bay	186	48.24 N	58.36 W
Flat Branch ≃	219	39.33 N	89.16 W
Flatbush ✦[8]	276	40.39 N	73.56 W
Flat Creek ≃, Ky., U.S.	218	38.17 N	83.48 W
Flat Creek ≃, Mo., U.S.	194	36.45 N	93.31 W
Flat Creek ≃, Mt., U.S.	202	47.43 N	109.50 W
Flat Creek ≃, N.J., U.S.	276	40.27 N	74.10 W
Flat Creek Reservoir ⊜[1]	222	32.14 N	95.45 W
Flatey	24a	65.19 N	23.07 W
Flateyri	24a	65.59 N	23.42 W
Flathead ≃	202	47.22 N	114.47 W
Flathead, Middle Fork ≃	202	48.28 N	114.04 W
Flathead, North Fork ≃	202	48.28 N	114.04 W
Flathead, South Fork ≃	202	48.23 N	114.04 W
Flathead Indian Reservation ✦[4]	202	47.30 N	114.25 W
Flathead Lake ⊜	202	47.52 N	114.08 W
Flat Holm I	42	51.23 N	3.08 W
Flat Lake ⊜	182	54.39 N	112.55 W
Flat Lick	192	36.49 N	83.46 W
Flatonia	222	29.41 N	97.06 W
Flatow	264a	52.44 N	12.57 E
Flat River, P.E., Can.	186	46.01 N	62.52 W
Flat River, Mo., U.S.	194	37.51 N	90.31 W
Flat River Reservoir ⊜[1]	207	41.42 N	71.37 W
Flat Rock, Al., U.S.	194	34.46 N	85.42 W
Flat Rock, Il., U.S.	194	38.54 N	87.40 W
Flat Rock, In., U.S.	218	39.22 N	85.50 W
Flat Rock, Mi., U.S.	216	42.05 N	83.17 W
Flat Rock, Oh., U.S.	214	41.14 N	82.51 W
Flatrock ≃	218	39.12 N	85.56 W
Flatrock Creek ≃	216	41.10 N	84.27 W
Flatrock Lake ⊜	184	55.37 N	100.47 W
Flatruet ⋏[2]	26	62.45 N	12.50 E
Flats	222	32.50 N	95.53 W
Flattery, Cape ›, Austl.	164	14.58 S	145.21 E
Flattery, Cape ›, Wa., U.S.	224	48.23 N	124.43 W
Flatts	240a	32.19 N	64.44 W
Flatwillow Creek ≃	202	46.56 N	107.55 W
Flatwood	194	32.27 N	86.15 W
Flatwoods	188	38.31 N	82.43 W
Flaugherty Run ≃	279b	40.33 N	80.13 W
Flaunden	260	51.42 N	0.32 W
Flavigny-sur-Moselle	58	48.34 N	6.11 E
Flavigny-sur-Ozerain	58	47.30 N	4.32 E
Flavy-le-Martel	50	49.43 N	3.12 E
Flawil	58	47.24 N	9.12 E
Flaxcombe	184	51.29 N	109.36 W
Flaxman Island I	180	70.13 N	146.00 W
Flax Pond ⊜, Ma., U.S.	283	42.29 N	70.57 W
Flax Pond ⊜, N.Y., U.S.	276	40.58 N	73.08 W
Flaxton	198	48.53 N	102.23 W
Flaxville	198	48.48 N	105.10 W
Flechas Point ›	116	10.22 N	119.34 E
Flechtingen	54	52.20 N	11.14 E
Fleckeby	41	54.29 N	9.41 E
Flecken Zechlin	54	53.09 N	12.46 E
Fleesensee ⊜	54	53.30 N	12.29 E
Fleet	42	51.16 N	0.50 W
Fleet ≃	46	57.57 N	4.05 W
Fleets Bay ⊂	208	37.40 N	76.19 W
Fleetville	210	41.36 N	75.43 W
Fleetwing Estates	285	40.07 N	74.51 W
Fleetwood, Eng., U.K.	44	53.56 N	3.01 W
Fleetwood, Pa., U.S.	208	40.27 N	75.49 W
Flehe ✦[8]	263	51.12 N	6.47 E
Flehingen	56	49.05 N	8.46 E
Fleischmanns	210	42.09 N	74.31 W
Fleischman Village	284c	38.51 N	76.57 W
Flekkefjord	26	58.17 N	6.41 E
Fleming, Co., U.S.	198	40.40 N	102.50 W
Fleming, Pa., U.S.	214	40.55 N	77.52 W
Fleming □[6]	218	38.21 N	83.42 W
Fleming Creek ≃, On., Can.	214	42.38 N	81.47 W
Fleming Creek ≃, Ky., U.S.	218	38.22 N	83.57 W
Fleming Creek ≃, Mi., U.S.	281	42.16 N	83.40 W
Fleming-Neon	192	37.11 N	82.42 W
Flemingsburg	218	38.25 N	83.44 W
Flemington, N.J., U.S.	210	40.30 N	74.51 W
Flemington, Pa., U.S.	210	41.07 N	77.28 W
Flemington Racecourse ♦	274b	37.47 S	144.55 E
Flemish Cap ✣[4]	16	47.00 N	45.00 W
Flemsdorf	54	53.02 N	14.10 E
Flen	40	59.04 N	16.35 E
Flensburg	41	54.47 N	9.26 E
Flensburger Förde ⊂	41	54.49 N	9.45 E
Fleres (Boden)	64	46.58 N	11.21 E
Flers	32	48.45 N	0.34 W
Flers-sur-Noye	50	49.44 N	2.15 E
Flesherton	212	44.16 N	80.33 W
Flesko, Tanjung ›	112	0.29 N	124.30 E
Fletcher, On., Can.	214	42.18 N	82.18 W
Fletcher, N.C., U.S.	192	35.25 N	82.30 W
Fletcher, Oh., U.S.	218	40.08 N	84.06 W
Fletcher, Ok., U.S.	196	34.49 N	98.14 W
Fletcher Islands II	9	72.40 S	94.10 W
Fletcher Moss Museum ʋ	262	53.25 N	2.14 W
Fletcher Pond ⊜[1]	190	44.58 N	83.52 W
Fletchers Creek ≃	275b	43.38 N	79.42 W
Fleurance	32	43.50 N	0.40 E
Fleur-de-Lys	186	50.07 N	56.08 W
Fleurier	58	46.54 N	6.35 E
Fleurieu Peninsula ›[1]	168b	35.30 S	138.30 E
Fleurus	56	50.29 N	4.33 E
Fleurville	58	46.27 N	4.53 E
Fleury-les-Aubrais	50	47.56 N	1.55 E
Fleury-Mérogis	261	48.38 N	2.22 E
Fleury-sur-Andelle	50	49.22 N	1.22 E
Fleuth ≃	263	51.32 N	6.26 E
Flevoland □[4]	52	52.30 N	5.30 E
Flexanville	261	48.51 N	1.44 E
Flexenpass)(	58	47.09 N	10.10 E
Fley ✦[8]	263	51.23 N	7.30 E
Flieden	56	50.25 N	9.33 E
Flierich	263	51.35 N	7.48 E
Flight Locks ʋ[3]	284a	43.08 N	79.12 W
Flimby	44	54.41 N	3.31 W
Flims	58	46.50 N	9.17 E
Flinders	169	38.28 S	145.01 E
Flinders ≃	166	17.36 S	140.36 E
Flinders Bay ⊂	162	34.23 S	115.19 E
Flinders Chase National Park ♦	166	36.00 S	136.45 E
Flinders Island I, Austl.	162	33.44 S	134.31 E
Flinders Island I, Austl.	166	40.00 S	148.00 E
Flinders Peak ∧	171a	27.49 S	152.49 E
Flinders Peak ∧[2]	169	37.51 S	144.24 E
Flinders Ranges National Park ♦	166	31.20 S	138.45 E
Flinders Reefs ✣[2]	166	17.37 S	148.31 E
Flinders Street Station ✦[5]	274b	37.49 S	144.58 E
Flinesjön ⊜	40	60.23 N	16.06 E
Flines-lèz-Râches	50	50.25 N	3.11 E
Flin Flon	184	54.46 N	101.53 W
Flingern ✦[8]	263	51.14 N	6.49 E
Flins-sur-Seine	261	48.58 N	1.52 E
Flint, Wales, U.K.	44	53.15 N	3.07 W
Flint, Mi., U.S.	216	43.00 N	83.41 W
Flint, Tx., U.S.	222	32.12 N	95.21 W
Flint I	14	11.26 S	151.48 W
Flint ≃, U.S.	194	34.30 N	86.31 W
Flint ≃, Ga., U.S.	192	30.52 N	84.38 W
Flint ≃, Mi., U.S.	190	43.21 N	84.03 W
Flint, South Branch ≃	216	43.10 N	83.23 W
Flint Castle ⊥	262	53.16 N	3.07 W
Flint Creek ≃, Al., U.S.	194	34.30 N	86.57 W
Flint Creek ≃, Mt., U.S.	202	46.39 N	113.08 W
Flint Creek ≃, N.Y., U.S.	210	42.57 N	77.03 W
Flint Creek Range ⋏	202	46.20 N	113.05 W
Flinthill	219	38.53 N	90.52 W
Flint Hills ⋏[2]	198	37.50 N	96.40 W
Flint Lake ⊜, N.T., Can.	176	69.10 N	74.20 W
Flint Lake ⊜, In., U.S.	216	41.31 N	87.03 W
Flinton, Austl.	166	27.54 S	149.34 E
Flinton, Pa., U.S.	214	40.43 N	78.31 W
Flint Peak ∧	280	34.10 N	118.12 W
Flint Pond ⊜	283	42.40 N	71.26 W
Flintrännan Ʉ	41	55.34 N	12.50 E
Flintridge	228	34.11 N	118.11 W
Flintville	194	35.03 N	86.25 W
Flipper Point ›	174a	19.18 N	166.35 E
Flippin	194	36.16 N	92.35 W
Flirey	56	48.53 N	5.50 E
Flirsch	58	47.09 N	10.24 E
Flisa	26	60.34 N	12.06 E
Flitwick	42	52.00 N	0.29 W
Flix, Pantà de ⊜[1]	34	41.15 N	0.25 E
Flixecourt	50	50.01 N	2.05 E
Flize	56	49.42 N	4.46 E
Flobecq (Vloesberg)	50	50.44 N	3.44 E
Floby	26	58.08 N	13.20 E
Floda, Sve.	26	57.48 N	12.22 E
Floda, Sve.	40	59.04 N	16.21 E
Flodden	44	55.38 N	2.10 W
Flodden Field Battlesite ⊥	44	55.38 N	2.13 W
Flogny	50	47.57 N	3.52 E
Flöha	54	50.51 N	13.04 E
Flöha ≃	54	50.51 N	13.04 E
Floing	56	49.43 N	4.56 E
Flomaton	194	31.00 N	87.15 W
Flomborn	56	49.41 N	8.08 E
Flomot	196	34.14 N	100.59 W
Floodwood	190	46.55 N	92.55 W
Flora, Il., U.S.	194	38.40 N	88.29 W
Flora, In., U.S.	216	40.32 N	86.31 W
Flora, Ms., U.S.	194	32.32 N	90.18 W
Florac	32	44.19 N	3.36 E
Florala	194	31.00 N	86.19 W
Floral City	220	28.45 N	82.17 W
Floral Park, Mt., U.S.	202	45.57 N	112.26 W
Floral Park, N.Y., U.S.	210	40.43 N	73.42 W
Florange	56	49.20 N	6.07 E
Florânia	250	6.08 S	36.49 W
Flora Vista	200	36.47 N	108.04 W
Flore, Piton ∧	241f	13.58 N	60.57 W
Floreffe	56	50.26 N	4.45 E
Florence, Al., U.S.	194	34.47 N	87.40 W
Florence, Az., U.S.	200	33.02 N	111.23 W
Florence, Ca., U.S.	228	33.58 N	118.14 W
Florence, Co., U.S.	200	38.23 N	105.07 W
Florence, Ks., U.S.	198	38.14 N	96.55 W
Florence, Ky., U.S.	218	38.59 N	84.37 W
Florence, N.J., U.S.	285	40.07 N	74.49 W
Florence, Or., U.S.	202	43.58 N	124.05 W
Florence, Pa., U.S.	214	40.26 N	80.26 W
Florence, S.C., U.S.	192	34.11 N	79.45 W
Florence, Tx., U.S.	222	30.51 N	97.48 W
Florence, Wi., U.S.	190	45.55 N	88.15 W
Florence → Firenze	66	43.46 N	11.15 E
Florencia	246	1.36 N	75.36 W
Florencia → Firenze	66	43.46 N	11.15 E
Florencio Sánchez	258	33.53 S	57.24 W
Florencio Varela	258	34.49 S	58.17 W
Florencio Varela □[5]	288	34.52 S	58.15 W
Florennes	56	50.15 N	4.37 E
Florentia	273d	26.16 S	28.08 E
Florentino Ameghino, Embalse ⊜[1]	254	43.55 S	66.20 W
Florenville	56	49.42 N	5.18 E
Florenz → Firenze	66	43.46 N	11.15 E
Flores	250	7.51 S	37.59 W
Flores □[5]	258	33.48 S	56.50 W
Flores ✦[8]	288	34.38 S	58.28 W
Flores I, Indon.	115b	8.30 S	121.00 E
Flores I, Port.	148a	39.26 N	31.13 W
Flores, Laut (Flores Sea) ⊤[2]	112	8.00 S	120.00 E
Flores, Rio das ≃	256	22.05 S	43.34 W
Flores, Selat Ʉ	115b	8.25 S	122.55 E
Flores da Cunha	252	29.02 S	51.11 W
Flores de Goiás	255	14.34 S	47.04 W
Flores Island I	182	49.20 N	126.10 W
Flores Sea → Flores, Laut ⊤[2]	112	8.00 S	120.00 E
Floresta, Bra.	250	8.36 S	38.34 W
Floresta, It.	70	37.59 N	14.55 E
Floresta ✦[8]	288	34.38 S	58.29 W
Floresta Azul	255	14.51 S	39.41 W
Florestal de Monsanto, Parque ♦	266c	38.43 N	9.11 W
Floreşty	78	47.53 N	28.17 E
Floresville	196	29.08 N	98.09 W
Florham Park	210	40.47 N	74.23 W
Floriano, Bra.	250	6.47 S	43.01 W
Floriano, Bra.	256	22.27 S	44.18 W
Floriano Peixoto	248	9.03 S	67.24 W
Florianópolis	252	27.35 S	48.34 W
Florida, Col.	246	3.21 N	76.15 W
Florida, Cuba	240p	21.32 N	78.14 W
Florida, Hond.	236	15.01 N	88.50 W
Florida, Perú	248	5.50 S	77.55 W
Florida, P.R.	240m	18.22 N	66.34 W
Florida, P.R.	240m	18.14 N	65.47 W
Florida, S. Afr.	273d	26.11 S	27.55 E
Florida, In., U.S.	218	40.10 N	85.42 W
Florida, N.Y., U.S.	210	41.19 N	74.21 W
Florida, Oh., U.S.	216	41.20 N	84.12 W
Florida, Ur.	258	34.06 S	56.13 W
Florida □[5]	258	34.00 S	56.15 W
Florida ✦[8]	288	34.31 S	58.30 W
Florida □[3], U.S.	178	28.00 N	82.00 W
Florida □[3], U.S.	192	28.00 N	82.00 W
Florida ≃	200	37.03 N	107.52 W
Florida, Cape ›	220	25.40 N	80.09 W
Florida, Straits of Ʉ	238	25.00 N	79.45 W
Florida Bay ⊂	220	25.00 N	80.45 W
Floridablanca	246	7.04 N	73.06 W
Florida Caverns State Park ♦	192	30.50 N	85.18 W
Florida City	220	25.26 N	80.28 W
Florida Islands II	175e	9.00 S	160.10 E
Florida Keys II	220	24.45 N	81.00 W
Florida Lake ⊜[1]	273d	26.11 S	27.54 E
Florida Ridge	220	27.35 N	80.23 W
Floridia	70	37.05 N	15.09 E
Florido ≃	232	27.43 N	105.10 W
Floridsdorf ✦[8]	264b	48.16 N	16.24 E
Floridsdorfer Brücke ✦[5]	264b	48.14 N	16.23 E
Florien	194	31.26 N	93.27 W
Florin	226	38.29 N	121.24 W
Flórina	38	40.47 N	21.24 E
Florisbad	158	28.46 S	26.06 E
Florissant	219	38.47 N	90.19 W
Florissant Fossil Beds National Monument ♦	200	38.54 N	105.16 W
Floriston	226	39.24 N	120.01 W
Florø	26	61.36 N	5.00 E
Flörsheim	56	50.01 N	8.26 E
Florvåg	26	60.25 N	5.14 E
Flosaille	62	45.39 N	5.18 E
Floss	60	49.44 N	12.17 E
Flossach ≃, Dtsch.	58	48.24 N	10.25 E
Flossach ≃, Dtsch.	64	48.13 N	10.30 E
Flossenbürg	60	49.44 N	12.21 E
Flossmoor	216	41.32 N	87.41 W
Flotantes, Jardínes ♦	286a	19.16 N	99.06 W
Flöthbach ≃	263	51.17 N	6.26 E
Flotta I	46	58.50 N	3.07 W
Flotte, Cap de ›	175f	21.10 S	167.25 E
Flotten Lake ⊜	184	54.38 N	108.30 W
Flourtown	285	40.06 N	75.12 W
Flower Hill	276	40.48 N	73.40 W
Flower Mound	222	33.02 N	97.04 W
Flower's Cove	186	51.18 N	56.44 W
Flowery Branch	192	34.11 N	83.55 W
Floyd, N.M., U.S.	196	34.13 N	103.35 W
Floyd, Tx., U.S.	222	33.09 N	96.15 W
Floyd, Va., U.S.	192	36.54 N	80.19 W
Floyd □[6]	218	38.18 N	85.49 W
Floyd ≃	198	42.29 N	96.23 W
Floydada	196	33.59 N	101.20 W
Floyds Fork ≃	194	38.00 N	85.41 W
Fluchthorn ∧	58	46.53 N	10.13 E
Flüela Pass)(	58	46.45 N	9.57 E
Flüelen	58	46.54 N	8.38 E
Fluessen ⊜	52	52.57 N	5.30 E
Flühli	58	46.53 N	8.01 E
Flumen ≃	34	41.43 N	0.09 W
Flumendosa ≃	71	39.26 N	9.37 E
Flumendosa, Lago Alto del ⊜	71	39.56 N	9.26 E
Flumeri	68	41.05 N	15.09 E
Flumet	62	45.49 N	6.30 E
Fluminimaggiore	71	39.26 N	8.30 E
Flums	58	47.05 N	9.20 E
Flüren	263	51.41 N	6.33 E
Flushing, Mi., U.S.	216	43.03 N	83.51 W
Flushing, Oh., U.S.	214	40.08 N	81.03 W
Flushing ✦[8]	276	40.45 N	73.49 W
Flushing Airport ⊠	276	40.47 N	73.50 W
Flushing Bay ⊂	276	40.47 N	73.51 W
Flushing Meadow-Corona Park ♦	276	40.45 N	73.51 W
Flushing → Vlissingen	52	51.26 N	3.35 E
Fluvanna, N.Y., U.S.	214	42.07 N	79.18 W
Fluvanna, Tx., U.S.	196	32.53 N	101.09 W
Fluvià ≃	34	42.12 N	3.07 E
Fly ≃	164	8.30 S	143.41 E
Fly Creek	210	42.43 N	74.59 W
Fly Creek ≃	202	45.59 N	107.59 W
Flyinge	41	55.45 N	13.21 E
Flying Fish Cove	112	10.25 S	105.43 E
Flynn	222	31.09 N	96.08 W
Foam Lake	184	51.39 N	103.33 W
Fobbing	260	51.32 N	0.29 E
Fobello	62	45.53 N	8.10 E
Foča, Bos.	38	43.31 N	18.46 E
Foça, Tür.	130	38.39 N	26.46 E
Focene ✦[8]	267a	41.48 N	12.14 E
Fochabers	46	57.37 N	3.05 W
Fochville	158	26.30 S	27.30 E
Fockbek	41	54.18 N	9.36 E
Focşani	38	45.41 N	27.11 E
Fodda, Oued ≃	34	35.14 N	1.28 E
Fodé	152	5.29 N	23.18 E
Fodécontea	150	10.50 N	14.22 W
Foding Shan ∧	102	27.08 N	108.02 E
F'odorovka, Kaz.	80	51.09 N	51.59 E
F'odorovka, Kaz.	86	53.22 N	76.18 E
F'odorovka, Kaz.	86	53.38 N	62.42 E
F'odorovka, Ross.	80	53.28 N	49.38 E
F'odorovka, Ross.	80	52.21 N	52.55 E
F'odorovka, Ross.	82	56.15 N	37.14 E
F'odorovka, Ross.	83	47.20 N	38.23 E
F'odorovka, Ross.	86	56.05 N	78.49 E
F'odorovka, Ross.	86	53.11 N	55.11 E
F'odorovka, Ukr.	78	49.23 N	35.07 E
F'odorovka, Ukr.	78	47.33 N	36.33 E
F'odorovskoje, Ross.	82	56.44 N	36.58 E
F'odorovskoje, Ross.	82	56.08 N	38.04 E
F'odorovskoje, Ross.	82	56.07 N	38.52 E
Foëcy	50	47.10 N	2.10 E
Foelsche ≃	164	16.03 S	136.50 E
Foeni	38	45.30 N	20.53 E
Fogang (Shijiao)	100	23.52 N	113.32 E
Fogdön ›[1]	40	59.25 N	16.52 E
Fogelevo	85	42.03 N	69.32 E
Fogelsville	208	40.35 N	75.38 W
Foggaret el Arab	148	27.03 N	2.59 E
Foggaret ez Zoua	148	27.20 N	3.00 E
Foggia	68	41.27 N	15.34 E
Foggia □[4]	68	41.30 N	15.30 E
Foggy Island Bay ⊂	180	70.15 N	147.30 W
Foglia ≃	66	43.55 N	12.54 E
Foglianise	68	41.10 N	14.40 E
Fogliano, Lago di ⊂	66	41.24 N	12.54 E
Foglizzo	62	45.16 N	7.49 E
Fogo	186	49.43 N	54.17 W
Fogo I	150a	14.55 N	24.25 W
Fogo, Cape ›	186	49.39 N	54.00 W
Fogo Island I	186	49.40 N	54.13 W
Fogolawa	150	12.19 N	8.41 E
Fogueteiro	266c	38.37 N	9.07 W
Fohnsdorf	61	47.13 N	14.41 E
Föhr I	30	54.43 N	8.30 E
Foia ∧	34	37.19 N	8.36 W
Foiano della Chiana	66	43.15 N	11.49 E
Foiano di Val Fortore	68	41.21 N	14.59 E
Foinaven ∧	46	58.25 N	4.53 W
Foins, Lac aux ⊜	190	47.05 N	78.11 W
Foivre ≃	56	49.30 N	4.32 E
Foix	32	42.58 N	1.36 E
Foix □[9]	32	43.00 N	1.40 E
Fojnica	36	43.58 N	17.54 E
Foki	80	56.42 N	54.21 E
Fokino	76	53.27 N	34.24 E
Fokku	150	11.40 N	4.31 E
Folakara	157b	18.20 S	45.02 E
Folamasi	104	41.56 N	121.27 E
Folarskardnuten ∧	26	60.37 N	7.45 E
Folcroft	208	39.53 N	75.17 W
Folda ⊂[2]	24	67.36 N	14.50 E
Foldingbro	41	55.26 N	9.01 E
Folembray	50	49.33 N	3.17 E
Foley, Al., U.S.	194	30.24 N	87.41 W
Foley, Mn., U.S.	190	45.39 N	93.54 W
Foley, Mo., U.S.	219	39.02 N	90.44 W
Foleyet	190	48.15 N	82.27 W
Foley Island I	176	68.35 N	75.10 W
Folgaria	64	45.55 N	11.10 E
Folgefonni ⍓	26	60.00 N	6.20 E
Folger Hill ∧[2]	207	41.17 N	70.01 W
Foligno	66	42.57 N	12.42 E
Folk	219	38.26 N	92.06 W
Folkärna	40	60.09 N	16.19 E
Folkestone	42	51.05 N	1.11 E
Folkingham	42	52.54 N	0.24 W
Folkston	192	30.49 N	82.00 W
Folkwangmuseum ʋ	263	51.27 N	7.00 E
Follafoss	26	63.59 N	11.06 E
Follainville-Dennemont	261	49.01 N	1.43 E
Follansbee	214	40.19 N	80.35 W
Folldal	26	62.08 N	10.03 E
Folle Anse, Pointe de ›	241o	15.57 N	61.20 W
Follebu	26	61.14 N	10.17 E
Follets Island I	222	29.02 N	95.10 W
Follett	196	36.26 N	100.08 W
Follina	64	45.57 N	12.07 E
Föllinge	26	63.40 N	14.37 E
Follonica	66	42.55 N	10.45 E
Follonica, Golfo di ⊂	66	42.54 N	10.43 E
Folly Branch ≃	284b	38.56 N	76.49 W
Folmhusen	52	53.10 N	7.28 E
Folschviller	56	49.04 N	6.41 E
Folsom, Ca., U.S.	226	38.40 N	121.10 W
Folsom, N.J., U.S.	208	39.36 N	74.50 W
Folsom, Pa., U.S.	285	39.53 N	75.19 W
Folsom Lake ⊜[1]	226	38.43 N	121.08 W
Folsom Lake State Recreation Area ♦	226	38.46 N	121.06 W
Fomboni	157a	12.16 S	43.45 E
Fomento, Cuba	240p	22.06 N	79.43 W
Fomento, Ur.	258	34.26 S	57.14 W
Fomin	80	46.58 N	43.38 E
Fominiči	76	54.07 N	34.41 E
Fominki	80	55.57 N	42.22 E
Fominskaja	24	61.17 N	48.40 E
Fominskoje, Ross.	24	59.43 N	42.05 E
Fominskoje, Ross.	76	58.59 N	39.06 E
Fomkino	80	54.25 N	50.30 E
Foncine-le-Bas	58	46.38 N	6.03 E
Fonda, Ia., U.S.	198	42.34 N	94.50 W
Fonda, N.Y., U.S.	210	42.57 N	74.22 W
Fondachelli	70	37.58 N	15.11 E
Fond du Lac, Sk., Can.	176	59.19 N	107.10 W
Fond du Lac, Wi., U.S.	190	43.46 N	88.26 W
Fond du Lac ≃	176	59.17 N	106.00 W
Fond du Lac Indian Reservation ✦[4]	190	46.45 N	92.37 W
Fondi	66	41.21 N	13.25 E
Fondi, Lago di ⊂	66	41.19 N	13.20 E
Fondo	64	46.26 N	11.08 E
Fondouk el Aouareb	36	35.34 N	9.46 E
Fongfong	140	12.56 N	23.14 E
Fonni	71	40.07 N	9.15 E
Fonsagrada	34	43.08 N	7.04 W
Fonseca	246	10.54 N	72.51 W
Fonseca, Golfo de ⊂	236	13.10 N	87.40 W
Fons-Outre-Gardon	62	43.54 N	4.11 E
Font ≃	44	55.10 N	1.44 W
Fontaine, Fr.	58	47.40 N	7.00 E
Fontaine, Fr.	62	45.11 N	5.40 E
Fontainebleau, Fr.	50	48.24 N	2.42 E
Fontainebleau, S. Afr.	273d	26.07 S	27.59 E
Fontaine-Française	58	47.31 N	5.22 E
Fontaine-le-Dun	50	49.49 N	0.51 E
Fontaine-lès-Dijon	58	47.21 N	5.01 E
Fontaine-lès-Grès	50	48.25 N	3.54 E
Fontaine-lès-Luxeuil	58	47.51 N	6.20 E
Fontaines	58	46.51 N	4.46 E
Fontaines-sur-Saône	62	45.50 N	4.51 E
Fontan	62	44.00 N	7.33 E
Fontana, Arg.	252	27.25 S	59.02 W
Fontana, Ca., U.S.	228	34.05 N	117.26 W
Fontana, Wi., U.S.	216	42.33 N	88.34 W
Fontana, Lago ⊜	254	44.56 S	71.30 W
Fontanafredda	64	45.58 N	12.34 E
Fontana Lake ⊜[1]	192	35.26 N	83.38 W
Fontanarosa	68	41.01 N	15.01 E
Fontanarossa, Aeroporto di ⊠	70	37.29 N	15.03 E
Fontanelas	266c	38.51 N	9.26 W
Fontanelice	66	44.15 N	11.33 E
Fontanella	64	45.27 N	9.48 E
Fontanellato	64	44.53 N	10.10 E
Fontanelle	198	41.17 N	94.33 W
Fontanetto Po	62	45.12 N	8.11 E
Fontanigorda	62	44.33 N	9.19 E
Fontarabie, Lac ⊜	186	51.10 N	66.25 W
Fontas ≃	176	58.20 N	121.50 W
Fonte, Bra.	287b	23.25 S	46.21 W
Fonte, It.	64	45.47 N	11.53 E
Fonte, It.	66	41.46 N	13.13 E
Fonte Avellana, Monastero di ʋ[1]	66	43.29 N	12.45 E
Fonte Blanda	66	42.34 N	11.10 E
Fonte Boa	246	2.32 S	66.01 W
Fonte Colombo, Convento di ʋ[1]	66	42.23 N	12.50 E
Fontenay, Abbaye de ʋ[1]	50	47.39 N	4.24 E
Fontenay-aux-Roses	261	48.47 N	2.17 E
Fontenay-en-Parisis	261	49.03 N	2.27 E
Fontenay-le-Comte	32	46.28 N	0.48 W
Fontenay-le-Fleury	261	48.49 N	2.03 E
Fontenay-lès-Briis	261	48.37 N	2.09 E
Fontenay-le-Vicomte	261	48.33 N	2.24 E
Fontenay-Saint-Père	261	49.02 N	1.45 E
Fontenay-sous-Bois	261	48.51 N	2.29 E
Fontenay-Trésigny	50	48.42 N	2.52 E
Fonteneau, Lac ⊜	186	51.55 N	61.30 W
Fontenelle	186	48.53 N	64.33 W
Fontenelle Creek ≃	200	42.05 N	110.08 W
Fontenelle Reservoir ⊜[1]	200	42.05 N	110.06 W
Fontespina	66	43.17 N	13.45 E
Fontevivo	64	44.51 N	10.10 E
Font Hill Manor	284b	39.17 N	76.52 W
Fonti del Clitunno ⊤[4]	66	42.49 N	12.46 E
Fontoy	56	49.21 N	6.00 E
Fontur ›	24a	66.23 N	14.30 W
Fontvieille	62	43.43 N	4.43 E
Fonyód	30	46.44 N	17.34 E
Fonzaso	64	46.01 N	11.48 E
Foochow → Fuzhou	100	26.06 N	119.17 E
Foot Creek ≃	198	45.26 N	98.29 W
Foothill Farms	226	38.40 N	121.20 W
Foothills	182	53.04 N	116.48 W
Footprint Lake ⊜	184	55.47 N	98.53 W
Footscray	169	37.48 S	144.54 E
Footville	216	42.40 N	89.12 W
Foping	102	33.21 N	107.59 E
Foppolo	64	46.03 N	9.45 E
Fora, Ponta de ›	287a	22.57 S	43.07 W
Foraker, Mount ∧	180	62.56 N	151.26 W
Forari	175f	17.39 S	168.32 E
Forbach, Dtsch.	56	48.41 N	8.21 E
Forbach, Fr.	56	49.11 N	6.54 E
Forbes	166	33.23 S	148.01 E
Forbes, Lac ⊜	206	46.31 N	74.12 W
Forbes, Mount ∧	182	51.52 N	116.56 W
Forbes Field ♦	279b	40.27 N	79.57 W
Forbesganj	124	26.18 N	87.15 E
Forbes Reef	158	26.10 S	31.05 E
Forbes Road	214	40.21 N	79.32 W
Forbestown	226	39.31 N	121.16 W
Forcados	150	5.22 N	5.24 E
Forcados ≃[1]	150	5.25 N	5.19 E
Forcalquier	62	43.58 N	5.47 E
Force	214	41.15 N	78.30 W
Forchheim, Dtsch.	54	50.43 N	13.16 E
Forchheim, Dtsch.	60	49.43 N	11.04 E
Forclaz, Col de la)(	58	46.04 N	7.00 E
Ford, Scot., U.K.	46	56.10 N	5.26 W
Ford, Ks., U.S.	198	37.38 N	99.45 W
Ford □[6]	216	40.27 N	88.06 W
Ford ≃	190	45.40 N	87.09 W
Ford, Cape ›	164	13.26 S	129.52 E
Ford City, Ca., U.S.	226	35.09 N	119.27 W
Ford City, Pa., U.S.	214	40.46 N	79.31 W
Ford City ✦[9]	278	41.46 N	87.44 W
Ford Cliff	214	40.45 N	79.32 W
Ford Dam ✦[6]	281	42.13 N	83.33 W
Ford Dry Lake ⊜	204	33.38 N	115.00 W
Førde, Nor.	26	59.36 N	5.29 E
Førde, Nor.	26	61.27 N	5.52 E
Førdefjorden ⊂[2]	26	61.28 N	5.39 E
Forden	42	52.36 N	3.08 W
Förderstedt	54	51.54 N	11.38 E
Fordham University ʋ[2]	276	40.51 N	73.53 W
Fordingbridge	42	50.56 N	1.47 W
Ford Lake ⊜	281	42.13 N	83.36 W
Ford Mansion ⊥	276	40.48 N	74.28 W
Ford Motor Company (River Rouge Plant) ʋ[3]	281	42.18 N	83.10 W
Ford Museum ʋ	281	42.18 N	83.14 W
Fordongianus	71	39.59 N	8.48 E
Ford Ranges ⋏	9	77.00 S	145.00 W
Fords	276	40.31 N	74.18 W
Fords Bridge	166	29.45 S	145.26 E
Fordsburg ✦[8]	273d	26.13 S	28.02 E
Fords Prairie	224	46.44 N	122.59 W
Fordsville	194	37.38 N	86.43 W
Fordville	198	48.13 N	97.47 W
Fordyce	194	33.48 N	92.24 W
Fordyce Lake ⊜[1]	226	39.23 N	120.28 W
Foré	150	13.08 N	10.42 W
Forécariah	150	9.26 N	13.06 W
Forel, Mont ∧	176	67.00 N	37.00 W
Foreland Point ›	42	51.16 N	3.47 W
Foreman	194	33.43 N	94.23 W
Foremost	184	49.29 N	111.25 W
Forenza	68	40.51 N	15.51 E
Forepaugh Airport ⊠	279a	41.21 N	81.30 W
Foresman	216	40.52 N	87.18 W
Forest, Bel.	50	50.48 N	4.19 E
Forest, On., Can.	190	43.06 N	82.00 W
Forest, In., U.S.	216	40.22 N	86.19 W
Forest, Ms., U.S.	194	32.21 N	89.28 W
Forest, Oh., U.S.	216	40.48 N	83.30 W
Forest □[6]	214	41.29 N	79.27 W
Forest, Middle Branch ≃	198	48.13 N	97.48 W
Forest Acres	192	34.01 N	80.59 W
Forestburg	182	52.35 N	112.04 W
Forest City, Ia., U.S.	190	43.15 N	93.38 W
Forest City, N.C., U.S.	192	35.20 N	81.51 W
Forest City, Pa., U.S.	210	41.39 N	75.28 W
Forest Creek ≃	226	38.23 N	120.28 W
Forest Gate ✦[8]	260	51.33 N	0.02 E
Forest Glade	222	31.39 N	96.31 W
Forest Grove, B.C., Can.	182	51.46 N	121.06 W
Forest Grove, Or., U.S.	224	45.31 N	123.06 W
Forest Grove, Pa., U.S.	279b	40.18 N	75.04 W
Forest Heights	284c	38.49 N	77.00 W
Forest Hill, Austl.	171a	27.35 S	152.22 E
Forest Hill, Austl.	171b	35.09 S	147.27 E
Forest Hill, Austl.	274b	37.50 S	145.11 E
Foresthill, Ca., U.S.	226	39.01 N	120.49 W
Forest Hill, Md., U.S.	208	39.35 N	76.23 W
Forest Hill, Tx., U.S.	222	32.40 N	97.16 W
Forest Hill ✦[8]	275b	43.42 N	79.24 W
Forest Hill Park ♦	279a	41.31 N	81.35 W
Forest Hill Parkway ♦	279a	41.33 N	81.36 W
Forest Hills	279b	40.25 N	79.51 W
Forest Hills ✦[8]	276	40.42 N	73.51 W
Forest Home	194	31.52 N	86.50 W
Forestier Peninsula ›[1]	166	42.57 S	147.55 E
Forest Knolls	284c	39.02 N	77.01 W
Forest Lake, Il., U.S.	216	42.13 N	88.03 W
Forest Lake, Mn., U.S.	190	45.16 N	92.59 W
Forest Lake ⊜, Il., U.S.	278	42.13 N	88.03 W
Forest Lake ⊜, Ma., U.S.	283	42.43 N	71.15 W
Forest Lawn Memorial Park ✦	280	34.09 N	118.19 W
Forest Manor	284c	38.50 N	76.53 W
Forest Park, Ga., U.S.	192	33.37 N	84.22 W
Forest Park, Il., U.S.	278	41.52 N	87.48 W
Forest Park, Oh., U.S.	218	39.16 N	84.34 W
Forest Park ✦[8]	284b	39.19 N	76.41 W
Forest Park ♦	276	40.42 N	73.51 W
Forest River	278	42.05 N	87.54 W
Forest Row	42	51.06 N	0.02 E
Forest View	278	41.49 N	87.47 W
Forestville, Austl.	274a	33.46 S	151.13 E
Forestville, P.Q., Can.	186	48.45 N	69.06 W
Forestville, Md., U.S.	284c	38.50 N	76.52 W
Forestville, N.Y., U.S.	214	42.28 N	79.10 W
Forestville, Pa., U.S.	214	41.06 N	80.00 W
Forestville, Wi., U.S.	190	44.41 N	87.28 W
Forêt l'Orient, Lac de la ⊜[1]	50	48.17 N	4.20 E
Forêt-Noire → Schwarzwald ⋏	58	48.00 N	8.15 E
Forez, Monts du ⋏	32	45.35 N	3.48 E
Forfar	46	56.38 N	2.54 W
Forfry	261	49.03 N	2.51 E
Forgan	196	36.54 N	100.32 W
Forgaria	64	46.13 N	12.58 E
Forge Acres	284b	39.25 N	76.27 W
Forge Heights	284b	39.25 N	76.25 W
Forges-les-Bains	261	48.38 N	2.06 E
Forges-les-Eaux	50	49.37 N	1.33 E
Forget, Pointe ›	275a	45.27 N	73.58 W
Forge Village	207	42.34 N	71.29 W
Forggensee ⊜	58	47.36 N	10.44 E
Forillon, Parc National de ♦	186	48.55 N	64.12 W
Forino	68	40.52 N	14.44 E
Foristell	219	38.49 N	90.57 W
Fork	208	39.28 N	76.27 W
Forked Creek ≃	216	41.19 N	88.09 W
Forked Deer ≃	194	35.56 N	89.35 W
Forked Deer, Middle Fork ≃	194	36.01 N	89.13 W
Forked Deer, North Fork ≃	194	36.00 N	89.26 W
Forked Deer, South Fork ≃	194	36.00 N	89.26 W
Forked River	208	39.50 N	74.11 W
Forks	224	47.57 N	124.23 W
Forkston	210	41.31 N	76.07 W
Forksville	210	41.29 N	76.36 W
Forleti, Arroyo ≃	288	34.35 S	58.41 W
Forlì	66	44.13 N	12.03 E
Forlì □[4]	64	44.05 N	12.02 E
Forlimpopoli	66	44.11 N	12.07 E
Forman	198	46.06 N	97.38 W
Formazza	58	46.22 N	8.26 E
Formby	44	53.34 N	3.05 W
Formby Hills ⋏[2]	262	53.34 N	3.06 W
Formby Point ›	44	53.33 N	3.06 W
Formentera I	34	38.42 N	1.28 E
Formentor, Cap de ›	34	39.58 N	3.12 E
Formerie	50	49.39 N	1.44 E
Formia	66	41.15 N	13.37 E
Formiga	255	20.27 S	45.25 W
Formiga ≃	250	11.15 S	48.27 W
Formigine	64	44.34 N	10.51 E
Formignana	64	44.50 N	11.51 E
Formosa, Arg.	252	26.11 S	58.11 W
Formosa, Bra.	255	15.32 S	47.20 W
Formosa □[4]	252	25.00 S	60.00 W
Formosa, Ilha I	150	11.29 N	15.58 W
Formosa, Serra ⋏[1]	250	12.00 S	55.00 W
Formosa Strait → Taiwan Strait Ʉ	100	24.00 N	119.00 E
Formosa → Taiwan □[1]	100	23.30 N	121.00 E
Formoso ≃, Bra.	250	10.34 S	49.56 W
Formoso ≃, Bra.	255	13.26 S	44.14 W
Formoso ≃, Bra.	255	18.25 S	52.28 W
Formoso ≃, Bra.	256	21.20 S	43.10 W

≃	River	Fluß	Río	Rivière	Rio
≚	Canal	Kanal	Canal	Canal	Canal
ʟ	Waterfall, Rapids	Wasserfall, Stromschnellen	Cascada, Rápidos	Chute d'eau, Rapides	Cascata, Rápidos
Ʉ	Strait	Meeresstraße	Estrecho	Détroit	Estreito
⊂	Bay, Gulf	Bucht, Golf	Bahía, Golfo	Baie, Golfe	Baía, Golfo
⊜	Lake, Lakes	See, Seen	Lago, Lagos	Lac, Lacs	Lago, Lagos
⩩	Swamp	Sumpf	Pantano	Marais	Pântano
⍓	Ice Features, Glacier	Eis- und Gletscherformen	Accidentes Glaciales	Formes glaciaires	Acidentes glaciares
⊤	Other Hydrographic Features	Andere Hydrographische Objekte	Otros Elementos Hidrográficos	Autres données hydrographiques	Outros acidentes hidrográficos
✣	Submarine Features	Untermeerische Objekte	Accidentes Submarinos	Formes de relief sous-marin	Acidentes submarinos
□	Political Unit	Politische Einheit	Unidad Politica	Entité politique	Unidade política
ʋ	Cultural Institution	Kulturelle Institution	Institución Cultural	Institution culturelle	Institução cultural
⊥	Historical Site	Historische Stätte	Sitio Histórico	Site historique	Sitio histórico
♦	Recreational Site	Erholungs- und Ferienort	Sitio de Recreo	Centre de loisirs	Area de Lazer
⊠	Airport	Flughafen	Aeropuerto	Aéroport	Aeroporto
■	Military Installation	Militäranlage	Instalación Militar	Installation militaire	Instalação militar
✦	Miscellaneous	Verschiedenes	Misceláneo	Divers	Diversos

Fornæs › 26 56.27 N 9.36 E
Forncelle 66 43.55 N 11.06 E
Fornelli 71 41.00 N 8.14 E
Forney 222 32.44 N 96.28 W
Forni Avoltri 64 46.35 N 12.46 E
Forni di sopra 64 46.25 N 12.35 E
Forni di sotto 64 46.23 N 12.40 E
Forni di Val d'Astico 64 45.51 N 11.22 E
Forno 64 46.21 N 11.37 E
Forno Alpi Graie 62 45.22 N 7.13 E
Forno di Zoldo 64 46.21 N 12.11 E
Fornosovo 76 59.35 N 30.35 E
Fornovo di Taro 64 44.42 N 10.06 E
Foro Romano ⊥ 267a 41.54 N 12.29 E
Føroyar
— Faeroe Islands □2 22 62.00 N 7.00 W
Forpost 86 56.47 N 72.10 E
Forres, Arg. 252 27.53 S 63.58 W
Forres, Scot., U.K. 46 57.37 N 3.38 W
Forrest, Austl. 162 30.51 S 128.06 E
Forrest, Austl. 169 38.31 S 143.43 E
Forrest, Il., U.S. 216 40.45 N 88.24 W
Forrest ≐ 164 15.18 S 128.04 E
Forrest, Mount ∧ 162 24.48 S 127.45 E
Forrestal Research Center ✦3 276 40.21 N 74.37 W
Forrest City 194 35.00 N 90.47 W
Forrester Island I 182 54.48 N 133.32 W
Forrest Lakes ◎ 162 29.12 S 128.46 E
Forreston, Il., U.S. 190 42.07 N 89.34 W
Forreston, Tx., U.S. 222 32.16 N 96.52 W
Forrest River Aboriginal Reserve ✦4 164 15.00 S 127.40 E
Fors 40 60.13 N 16.18 E
Forsan 196 32.07 N 101.22 W
Forsayth 166 18.35 S 143.36 E
Forsbacka 40 60.37 N 16.53 E
Forsby 26 60.30 N 25.56 E
Forserum 26 57.42 N 14.28 E
Forshaga 40 59.32 N 13.28 E
Forsmark 40 60.22 N 18.09 E
Forssa 26 60.49 N 23.38 E
Forst 54 51.44 N 14.39 E
Förste 52 51.44 N 10.12 E
Forster 166 32.11 S 152.31 E
Forstwald ✦8 263 51.18 N 6.30 E
Forsyth, Ga., U.S. 192 33.02 N 83.56 W
Forsyth, Il., U.S. 219 39.56 N 88.57 W
Forsyth, Mo., U.S. 194 36.41 N 93.07 W
Forsyth, Mt., U.S. 202 46.15 N 106.40 W
Forsyth Island I 164 16.50 S 139.06 E
Forsyth Range ∧ 166 22.45 S 143.15 E
Fort ✦8 272c 18.56 N 72.50 E
Fort Abbās 123 29.12 N 72.52 E
Fort Adams 194 31.05 N 91.32 W
Fort Albany 176 52.15 N 81.37 W
Fort Alexander Indian Reserve ✦4 184 50.27 N 96.15 W
Fortaleza 250 3.43 S 38.30 W
Fortaleza ≐ 248 10.40 S 77.52 W
Fortaleza de Santa Teresa ◆ 252 33.59 S 53.32 W
Fortaleza do Ituxi 248 7.29 S 66.20 W
Fortaleza dos Nogueiras 250 6.54 S 46.09 W
Fort Amherst National Historic Park ◆ 186 46.12 N 63.09 W
Fort Ancient State Memorial ⊥ 218 39.24 N 84.06 W
Fort Anne National Historic Park ◆ 186 44.44 N 65.26 W
Fort Apache Indian Reservation ✦4 200 34.01 N 110.28 W
Fort-Archambault
— Sarh 146 9.09 N 18.23 E
Fort Assiniboine 182 54.20 N 114.46 W
Fort Atkinson 216 42.55 N 88.50 W
Fort Augusta ⊥ 210 40.53 N 76.46 W
Fort Augustus 46 57.09 N 4.41 W
Fort Baker ■ 282 37.50 N 122.29 W
Fort Battleford National Historic Park ◆ 184 52.42 N 108.15 W
Fort Bayard
— Zhanjiang 102 21.16 N 110.28 E
Fort Beaufort 158 32.46 S 26.40 E
Fort Beauséjour National Historic Park ◆ 186 45.51 N 64.18 W
Fort Belknap Agency 202 48.28 N 108.45 W
Fort Belknap Indian Reservation ✦4 202 48.16 N 108.38 W
Fort Belvoir ■ 208 38.44 N 77.10 W
Fort Bend □6 222 29.32 N 95.47 W
Fort Benjamin Harrison ■ 218 39.52 N 86.01 W
Fort Benning ■ 192 32.22 N 84.50 W
Fort Benton 202 47.49 N 110.40 W
Fort Berthold Indian Reservation ✦4 198 47.40 N 102.25 W
Fort Bidwell 204 41.51 N 120.09 W
Fort Bliss ■ 200 32.15 N 106.00 W
Fort Bowie National Historic Site ⊥ 200 32.09 N 109.24 W
Fort Bragg 204 39.26 N 123.48 W
Fort Bragg ■ 192 35.09 N 78.59 W
Fort Branch 194 38.15 N 87.34 W
Fort Bridger 200 41.19 N 110.23 W
Fort Calhoun 198 41.27 N 96.01 W
Fort Campbell ■ 194 36.39 N 87.29 W
Fort Canby State Park ◆ 224 46.17 N 124.04 W
Fort-Carnot 157b 21.53 S 47.28 E
Fort Caroline National Memorial ⊥ 192 30.20 N 81.30 W
Fort Carson ■ 200 38.44 N 104.48 W
Fort Casey Historical State Park ◆ 224 48.10 N 122.40 W
Fort Chambly National Historic Park ◆ 206 45.27 N 73.17 W
Fort Chipewyan 176 58.42 N 111.08 W
Fort Churchill Historic State Monument ⊥ 226 39.18 N 119.17 W
Fort Clatsop National Memorial ⊥ 224 46.08 N 123.54 W
Fort Cobb 196 35.05 N 98.26 W
Fort Cobb Reservoir ◎1 196 35.12 N 98.29 W
Fort Collins 200 40.35 N 105.05 W
Fort Columbia Historical State Park ◆ 224 46.15 N 123.56 W
Fort Constantine 166 20.28 S 140.37 E
Fort-Coulonge 186 45.51 N 76.44 W
Fort Covington 206 44.59 N 74.29 W
Fort Custer State Recreation Area ◆ 216 42.18 N 85.20 W
Fort Davis, Al., U.S. 192 32.14 N 85.42 W
Fort Davis, Tx., U.S. 196 30.35 N 103.53 W
Fort Davis National Historic Site ⊥ 196 30.33 N 103.53 W
Fort de Douaumont ⊥ 56 49.13 N 5.25 E
Fort Defiance 200 35.44 N 109.04 W
Fort-de-France 240e 14.36 N 61.05 W
Fort-de-France, Baie de ⊂ 240e 14.34 N 61.04 W
Fort-de-France-Lamentin, Aérodrome de ✈ 240e 14.35 N 61.00 W
Fort Deposit 194 31.59 N 86.34 W
Fort Detrick ■ 208 39.27 N 77.26 W
Fort de Vaux ⊥ 56 49.12 N 5.28 E
Fort Devens ■ 207 42.32 N 71.37 W
Fort Dix ■ 208 40.00 N 74.33 W
Fort Dodge 190 42.29 N 94.10 W
Fort Donelson National Military Park ◆ 194 36.26 N 87.49 W
Fort Duchesne 200 40.17 N 109.51 W
Fort Dupont Park ◆ 284c 38.53 N 76.57 W
Forte, Monte ∧ 71 40.43 N 8.15 E
Forteau 186 51.28 N 56.58 W
Forte dei Marmi 64 43.57 N 10.10 E
Forte de Magoito 266c 38.52 N 9.27 W
Fort Edward 210 43.16 N 73.35 W
Forte República 152 7.45 S 16.23 E
Fort Erie 212 42.54 N 78.56 W
Fort Erie Race Track ◆ 284a 42.55 N 78.56 W
Fortescue ≐ 162 21.00 S 116.06 E
Fort Eustis ■ 208 37.09 N 76.35 W
Fortevoit 46 56.20 N 3.32 W
Fortezza (Franzensfeste) 64 46.47 N 11.37 E
Fort Fairfield 186 46.46 N 67.50 W
Fort Fitzgerald 176 59.53 N 111.37 W
Fort Foote Village 284c 38.46 N 77.01 W
Fort-Foureau 146 12.05 N 15.02 E
Fort Frances 190 48.36 N 93.24 W
Fort Franklin 180 65.11 N 123.46 W
Fort Fraser 182 54.04 N 124.33 W
Fort Frederica National Monument ⊥ 192 31.12 N 81.26 W
Fort Gaines 192 31.36 N 85.02 W
Fort Garland 200 37.25 N 105.26 W
Fort Gay 188 38.06 N 82.35 W
Fort George ⊥ 284a 43.15 N 79.04 W
Fort George G. Meade ■ 208 39.05 N 76.50 W
Fort Gibson 196 35.47 N 95.15 W
Fort Gibson Lake ◎1 196 36.00 N 95.18 W
Fort Good Hope 180 66.15 N 128.38 W
Fort Gordon ■ 192 33.25 N 82.11 W
Fort-Gouraud
— Fdérik 148 22.41 N 12.43 W
Fort Green 220 27.36 N 81.56 W
Forth 46 55.47 N 3.41 W
Forth ≐ 46 56.03 N 3.44 W
Forth, Carse of ∨ 46 56.08 N 4.05 W
Forth, Firth of ⊂ 46 56.10 N 2.45 W
Fortha 50 50.56 N 10.14 E
Fort Hall 202 43.02 N 112.26 W
Fort Hall Indian Reservation ✦4 202 43.10 N 112.10 W
Fort Hamilton ■ 276 40.37 N 74.02 W
Forth Bridge ✦5 46 56.00 N 3.25 W
Fort Hertz
— Putao 102 27.21 N 97.24 E
Fort Hill ■ 188 38.04 N 77.19 W
Fort Hill
— Chitipa 154 9.43 S 33.16 E
Fort Hill State Memorial ⊥ 218 39.07 N 83.25 W
Fort Hood ■ 222 31.08 N 97.46 W
Fort Howard 208 39.12 N 76.27 W
Fort Huachuca ■ 200 31.33 N 110.20 W
Fort Hunter 210 42.57 N 74.17 W
Fort Hunter Liggett ■ 226 35.55 N 121.15 W
Fortierville 206 46.29 N 72.02 W
Fortin 234 18.54 N 97.00 W
Fortin, Lac ◎ 186 50.50 N 67.46 W
Fortín Ayacucho 248 19.58 S 59.47 W
Fortín Coroneles Sanchez 248 19.20 S 59.58 W
Fortine 182 48.45 N 114.54 W
Fortín Florida 248 20.45 S 59.17 W
Fortín Garrapatal 248 21.27 S 61.30 W
Fortín Teniente Montanía 252 22.04 S 59.57 W
Fortín Uno 252 38.51 S 65.17 W
Fort Jackson ■ 192 34.01 N 80.57 W
Fort Jameson
— Chipata 154 13.39 S 32.40 E
Fort Jefferson National Monument ◆ 220 24.37 N 82.54 W
Fort Jennings 216 40.54 N 84.17 W
Fort Jeudy, Point of › 241k 12.00 N 61.42 W
Fort Johnson 210 42.57 N 74.14 W
Fort Johnston
— Mangochi 154 14.28 S 35.16 E
Fort Jones 204 41.36 N 122.50 W
Fort Kent 186 47.15 N 68.35 W
Fort Klamath 202 42.42 N 121.59 W
Fort Knox ■ 194 37.54 N 85.57 W
Fort-Lamy
— N'Djamena 146 12.07 N 15.03 E
Fort Langley 224 49.10 N 122.35 W
Fort Langley National Historic Park ◆ 224 49.10 N 122.35 W
Fort Laramie 200 42.12 N 104.31 W
Fort Laramie National Historic Site ⊥ 198 42.09 N 104.41 W
Fort Larned National Historic Site ⊥ 198 38.10 N 99.12 W
Fort Lauderdale 220 26.07 N 80.08 W
Fort Lauderdale-Hollywood International Airport ✈ 220 26.04 N 80.09 W
Fort Laurens State Memorial ⊥ 214 40.38 N 81.27 W
Fort Leavenworth ■ 198 39.21 N 94.55 W
Fort Le Boeuf ⊥ 214 41.56 N 79.59 W
Fort Lee 210 40.51 N 73.58 W
Fort Lee ■ 208 37.14 N 77.20 W
Fort Lennox National Historic Park ◆ 206 45.06 N 73.16 W
Fort Leonard Wood ■ 194 37.45 N 92.07 W
Fort Lewis ■ 224 47.05 N 122.35 W
Fort Liard 176 60.15 N 123.28 W
Fort-Liberté 238 19.39 N 71.49 W
Fort Lincoln State Park ◆ 198 46.45 N 100.52 W
Fort Littleton 214 40.04 N 77.58 W
Fort Loramie 216 40.21 N 84.22 W
Fort Loudoun Lake ◎1 192 35.45 N 84.10 W
Fort Lupton 200 40.05 N 104.48 W
Fort Lyon Canal ≡ 198 38.11 N 102.31 W
Fort Macleod 182 49.43 N 113.25 W
Fort Madison 190 40.37 N 91.18 W
Fort-Mahon-Plage 50 50.21 N 1.34 E
Fort Malden National Historic Park ◆ 281 42.06 N 83.07 W
Fort Matanzas National Monument ⊥ 192 29.40 N 81.18 W
Fort McClellan ■ 194 33.43 N 85.47 W
Fort McDermitt Indian Reservation ✦4 202 42.00 N 117.32 W
Fort McDowell Indian Reservation ✦4 200 33.38 N 111.41 W
Fort McHenry National Monument and Historic Shrine ◆ 208 39.16 N 76.35 W
Fort McKinley 218 39.47 N 84.15 W
Fort McMurray 184 56.44 N 111.23 W
Fort McNair ■ 284c 38.52 N 77.01 W
Fort McPherson 180 67.27 N 134.53 W
Fort Meade 220 27.45 N 81.48 W
Fort Mill 192 35.00 N 80.56 W
Fort Miller 210 43.10 N 73.35 W
Fort Mitchell, Al., U.S. 192 32.21 N 85.01 W
Fort Mitchell, Ky., U.S. 218 39.03 N 84.32 W
Fort Mojave Indian Reservation ✦4 200 34.55 N 114.35 W
Fort Monmouth ■ 208 40.19 N 74.02 W
Fort Monroe ■ 208 37.00 N 76.18 W
Fort Montgomery 210 41.20 N 73.59 W
Fort Morgan 198 40.15 N 103.47 W
Fort Myer ■ 284c 38.53 N 77.05 W
Fort Myers 220 26.38 N 81.52 W
Fort Myers Beach 220 26.27 N 81.56 W
Fort Myers Shores 220 26.43 N 81.45 W
Fort Myers Villas 220 26.34 N 81.52 W
Fort Necessity National Battlefield ⊥ 188 39.47 N 79.39 W
Fort Neck ›1 276 40.39 N 73.28 W
Fort Nelson 176 58.49 N 122.43 W
Fort Nelson ≐ 176 59.30 N 124.00 W
Fort Niagara Beach 284a 43.16 N 79.03 W
Fort Niagara State Park ◆, N.Y., U.S. 210 43.16 N 79.03 W
Fort Niagara State Park ◆, N.Y., U.S. 284a 43.16 N 79.03 W
Fort Nonsense ⊥ 276 40.48 N 74.29 W
Fort Norman 180 64.54 N 125.34 W
Fort Nottingham 158 29.25 S 29.55 E
Fort Ogden 220 27.05 N 81.57 W
Fort Ord ■ 226 36.40 N 121.48 W
Fortore ≐ 68 41.55 N 15.17 E
Fort Parker State Park ◆ 222 31.36 N 96.33 W
Fort Payne 194 34.26 N 85.43 W
Fort Peck 202 48.00 N 106.26 W
Fort Peck Dam ✦6 202 47.52 N 106.38 W
Fort Peck Indian Reservation ✦4 202 48.22 N 105.40 W
Fort Peck Lake ◎1 202 47.45 N 106.50 W
Fort Pierce 220 27.26 N 80.19 W
Fort Pierce Inlet ⊂ 220 27.28 N 80.18 W
Fort Pierre 198 44.21 N 100.22 W
Fort Pitt Tunnels ✦5 279b 40.25 N 80.00 W
Fort Plain 210 42.55 N 74.37 W
Fort Point National Historic Site ⊥ 282 37.48 N 122.28 W
Fort Polk ■ 194 31.04 N 93.11 W
Fort Portal 154 0.40 N 30.17 E
Fort Providence 176 61.21 N 117.39 W
Fort Pulaski National Monument ◆ 192 32.01 N 80.59 W
Fort Qu'Appelle 184 50.46 N 103.48 W
Fort Raleigh National Historic Site ⊥ 192 35.55 N 75.40 W
Fort Randall Dam ✦6 198 42.48 N 98.35 W
Fort Recovery 216 40.24 N 84.46 W
Fort Resolution 176 61.10 N 113.40 W
Fortress Mountain ∧ 202 44.20 N 109.47 W
Fortress of Louisbourg National Historic Park ◆ 186 45.56 N 59.57 W
Fort Riley ■ 198 39.04 N 96.47 W
Fort Ritchie ■ 208 39.43 N 77.30 W
Fort Rixon 154 20.01 S 29.18 E
Fort Robinson State Park ◆ 198 42.41 N 103.30 W
Fort Rodd Hill National Historic Park ◆ 224 48.26 N 123.28 W
Fortrose, N.Z. 172 46.34 S 168.48 E
Fortrose, Scot., U.K. 46 57.34 N 4.09 W
Fort Rosebery
— Mansa 154 11.12 S 28.53 E
Fort Rucker ■ 194 31.20 N 85.42 W
Fort Saint James 182 54.26 N 124.15 W
Fort Saint John 182 56.15 N 120.51 W
Fort Salonga 276 40.55 N 73.18 W
Fort Sam Houston ■ 196 29.27 N 98.27 W
Fort Saskatchewan 182 53.43 N 113.13 W
Fort Scott 198 37.50 N 94.42 W
Fort Seneca 214 41.13 N 83.10 W
Fort-Ševčenko 84 44.31 N 50.16 E
Fort Severn 176 56.00 N 87.38 W
Fort Shawnee 216 40.41 N 84.08 W
Fort Sheridan ■ 216 42.13 N 87.48 W
Fort Sill ■ 196 34.40 N 98.25 W
Fort Simcoe Historical State Park ◆ 224 46.21 N 120.50 W
Fort Simpson 176 61.52 N 121.23 W
Fort Sisseton State Park ◆ 198 45.39 N 97.32 W
Fort Smith, N.T., Can. 176 60.00 N 111.53 W
Fort Smith, Ar., U.S. 194 35.23 N 94.23 W
Fort Steele 182 49.37 N 115.38 W
Fort Stevens State Park ◆ 224 46.10 N 124.00 W
Fort Stewart ■ 192 31.52 N 81.37 W
Fort Stockton 196 30.53 N 102.52 W
Fort Sumner 196 34.28 N 104.14 W
Fort Sumter National Monument ◆ 192 32.44 N 79.46 W
Fort Supply 196 36.34 N 99.34 W
Fort Tejon State Historical Park ◆ 228 34.52 N 118.53 W
Fort Thomas, Az., U.S. 200 33.02 N 109.57 W
Fort Thomas, Ky., U.S. 218 39.04 N 84.26 W
Fort Thompson 198 44.04 N 99.26 W
Fort Tilden ■ 276 40.33 N 73.53 W
Fort Totten 198 47.58 N 98.59 W
Fort Totten Indian Reservation ✦4 198 47.53 N 98.50 W
Fort Totten Park ◆ 284c 38.57 N 77.00 W
Fort Towson 196 34.01 N 95.15 W
Fort-Trinquet
— Bîr Mogreïn 148 25.14 N 11.35 W
Fortuna, Arg. 252 35.07 S 65.23 W
Fortuna, C.R. 236 10.30 N 84.35 W
Fortuna, Ca., U.S. 204 40.35 N 124.09 W
Fortuna, Río de la ≐ 248 16.36 S 58.46 W
Fortuna Ledge (Marshall) 180 61.53 N 162.05 W
Fortune 186 47.04 N 55.50 W
Fortune Bay ⊂ 186 47.25 N 55.25 W
Fortune Ditch ≡ 279a 41.20 N 82.03 W
Fortune Harbour 186 49.31 N 55.15 W
Fortuneswell 42 50.34 N 2.27 W
Fort Union National Monument ◆ 200 35.55 N 105.01 W
Fort Union Trading Post National Historical Site ⊥ 198 48.00 N 104.03 W
Fort Valley 192 32.33 N 83.53 W
Fort Vancouver National Historic Site ⊥ 224 45.38 N 122.37 W
Fort Vermilion 176 58.24 N 116.00 W
Fort Victoria 218 39.55 N 85.50 W
Fortville 218 39.55 N 85.50 W
Fort Wadsworth ■ 276 40.36 N 74.04 W
Fort Walton Beach 194 30.24 N 86.37 W
Fort Washakie 200 43.00 N 108.52 W
Fort Washington 208 40.08 N 75.12 W
Fort Washington Forest 208 38.43 N 76.59 W
Fort Washington State Park ◆ 285 40.07 N 75.14 W
Fort Wayne 216 41.07 N 85.07 W
Fort Wayne Military Museum ◆ 281 42.18 N 83.06 W
Fort Wellington 246 6.24 N 57.36 W
Fort Wellington National Historic Park ◆ 212 44.44 N 75.31 W
Fort White 192 29.55 N 82.42 W
Fort William 46 56.49 N 5.07 W
Fort William
— Thunder Bay 190 48.23 N 89.15 W
Fort Worth 222 32.43 N 97.19 W
Fort Yates 198 46.05 N 100.37 W
Forty Foot Drain ≡ 42 52.28 N 0.05 W
Forty Fort 210 41.16 N 75.52 W
Fortymile ≐ 180 64.26 N 140.32 W
Fort Yukon 180 66.34 N 145.17 W
Fort Yuma Indian Reservation ✦4 204 32.48 N 114.34 W
Forum ⊥ 275a 45.29 N 73.35 W
Forūr, Jazīreh-ye I 128 26.17 N 54.32 E
Forza d'Agrò 70 37.55 N 15.20 E
Foscagno, Passo di ⋊ 64 46.30 N 10.08 E
Fosdinovo 64 44.08 N 10.01 E
Fosforescente, Bahía ⊂ 240m 17.59 N 67.01 W
Fosforitnyj 82 55.19 N 38.54 E
Foshan 100 23.03 N 113.09 E
Fosna ›1, Nor. 24 64.00 N 10.30 E
Fosna ›1, Nor. 26 63.45 N 10.25 E
Fosnavåg 26 62.21 N 5.39 E
Foso 150 5.42 N 1.17 W
Foss 46 56.41 N 3.58 W
Foss ≐, Eng., U.K. 44 53.57 N 1.06 W
Foss ≐, Wa., U.S. 224 47.43 N 121.18 W
Fossacesia 66 42.15 N 14.29 E
Fossacesia Marina 66 42.15 N 14.30 E
Fossa Eugeniana ≡ 263 51.33 N 6.36 E
Fossano 62 44.33 N 7.43 E
Fossanova, Abbazia di ✦1 66 41.29 N 13.13 E
Fossato, Colle di ⋊ 66 43.19 N 12.47 E
Fossato di Vico 66 43.18 N 12.46 E
Fossé 56 49.27 N 5.00 E
Fosse-Martin 261 49.05 N 2.54 E
Fosses 261 49.06 N 2.29 E
Fosses-la-Ville 56 50.24 N 4.42 E
Fossil 202 44.59 N 120.12 W
Fossil Butte National Monument ◆ 202 41.50 N 110.40 W
Fossil Downs 162 18.08 S 125.38 E
Fossil Lake ◎ 202 43.18 N 120.15 W
Fossombrone 66 43.41 N 12.48 E
Fosston 198 47.34 N 95.45 W
Fos-sur-Mer 62 43.26 N 4.57 E
Foster, Austl. 169 38.39 S 146.12 E
Foster, Ky., U.S. 218 38.47 N 84.12 W
Foster, R.I., U.S. 207 41.51 N 71.45 W
Foster ≐ 184 55.47 N 105.49 W
Foster, Mount ∧ 180 59.48 N 135.29 W
Foster Brook 214 41.59 N 78.37 W
Foster City 226 37.33 N 122.16 W
Foster Creek ≐ 198 44.34 N 98.12 W
Fosterdale 210 41.42 N 74.58 W
Foster Joseph Sayers Reservoir ◎1 214 41.02 N 77.40 W
Foster Park 228 34.21 N 119.18 W
Fosters 194 33.05 N 87.41 W
Fosters Pond ◎ 283 42.37 N 71.08 W
Foster Street 260 51.46 N 0.09 E
Foster Village 229c 21.21 N 157.55 W
Fostoria 214 41.09 N 83.25 W
Föt 264c 47.37 N 19.12 E
Fotadrevo 157b 24.03 S 45.01 E
Fotan 100 24.12 N 117.53 E
Fóti-Somlyó ∧2 264c 47.38 N 19.13 E
Foucarmont 50 49.51 N 1.34 E
Fou-Chouen
— Fushun 104 41.52 N 123.53 E
Fouesnant 32 47.54 N 4.01 W
Foug 56 48.41 N 5.47 E
Fougamou 152 1.13 S 10.36 E
Fougères 32 48.21 N 1.12 W
Fougères-sur-Bièvre 50 47.27 N 1.21 E
Fougerolles 58 47.53 N 6.24 E
Fouhsin
— Fuxin 104 42.03 N 121.46 E
Foujiu 261 48.35 N 2.47 E
Fouke 194 33.16 N 93.53 W
Foula I 46a 60.08 N 2.05 W
Foulain 58 48.02 N 5.13 E
Foulalaba 150 10.41 N 7.22 W
Foula Mori 150 12.10 N 13.51 W
Foulatari 146 13.41 N 12.03 E
Foul Bay ⊂ 140 23.30 N 35.39 E
Fouling
— Fuling 102 29.42 N 107.21 E
Foulness ≐ 44 53.47 N 0.43 W
Foulness Island I 42 51.36 N 0.55 E
Foulness Point › 42 51.38 N 0.57 E
Foulpointe 157b 17.41 S 49.31 E
Foulsham 42 52.48 N 1.01 E
Foulwind, Cape › 172 41.45 S 171.28 E
Foumban 152 5.43 N 10.55 E
Foumbot 152 5.30 N 10.38 E
Foumbouni 157a 11.50 S 43.30 E
Foum-el-Hisn 148 28.59 N 8.53 W
Foum-Zguid 148 30.04 N 6.54 W
Foundiougne 150 14.08 N 16.28 W
Fountain, Co., U.S. 198 38.40 N 104.42 W
Fountain, Fl., U.S. 192 30.09 N 85.38 W
Fountain □6 216 40.17 N 87.13 W
Fountain City, In., U.S. 218 39.57 N 84.55 W
Fountain City, Wi., U.S. 190 44.07 N 91.43 W
Fountain Creek ≐, Co., U.S. 198 38.15 N 104.35 W
Fountain Creek ≐, Il., U.S. 219 38.20 N 90.22 W
Fountain Green 200 39.37 N 111.38 W
Fountain Hill 208 40.36 N 75.23 W
Fountain Inn 192 34.41 N 82.11 W
Fountain Park 216 41.50 N 84.32 W
Fountain Peak ∧ 204 34.57 N 115.32 W
Fountain Place 194 30.31 N 91.09 W
Fountains Abbey ✦1 44 54.07 N 1.34 W
Fountains Creek ≐ 208 36.33 N 77.21 W
Fountaintown 218 39.41 N 85.46 W
Fountain Valley 228 33.42 N 117.57 W
Fourche LaFave ≐ 194 34.58 N 92.35 W
Fourche Maline ≐ 194 34.55 N 94.55 W
Fourchu 186 45.43 N 60.15 W
Four Corners 202 44.55 N 122.58 W
Four Elms 260 51.13 N 0.06 E
Four Hole Swamp ≐ 192 33.03 N 80.24 W
Fouriesburg 158 28.38 S 28.14 E
Fourmies 50 50.00 N 4.03 E
Four Mile Creek ≐, On., Can. 284a 43.15 N 79.08 W
Fourmile Creek ≐, N.Y., U.S. 284a 43.17 N 79.00 W
Four Mile Creek ≐, Oh., U.S. 218 39.26 N 84.32 W
Four Mile Creek State Park ◆ 284a 43.16 N 79.00 W
Fourmile Draw ∨ 196 32.40 N 104.18 W
Four Mile Lake ◎ 212 44.40 N 78.44 W
Four Mile Run ≐ 284c 38.50 N 77.02 W
Four Mountains, Islands of II 180 52.50 N 170.00 W
Fournaise, Piton de la ∧ 157c 21.14 S 55.43 E
Fourneau, Pointe à › 275a 45.22 N 73.51 W
Fourneaux, Fr. 50 45.41 N 3.48 E
Fourneaux, Fr. 62 45.11 N 6.39 E
Fournier, Lac ◎ 186 51.33 N 65.25 W
Fournière, Lac ◎ 190 48.04 N 78.03 W
Fournoi I 38 37.34 N 26.30 E
Four Oaks 192 35.26 N 78.25 W
Fourqueux 261 48.53 N 2.04 E
Fours 32 46.49 N 3.43 E
Fourteenmile Creek ≐ 218 38.26 N 85.37 W
Fourth Cataract
— Rābi', Ash-Shallāl ar- ↳ 140 18.47 N 32.03 E
Fourth Cliff ✦4 283 42.09 N 70.42 W
Four Towns 281 42.37 N 83.25 W
Fous, Pointe des › 240d 15.12 N 61.20 W
Foussard ≐ 50 48.16 N 1.17 E
Fouta Djalon ✦1 150 11.30 N 12.30 W
Fou-Tcheou
— Fuzhou 100 26.06 N 119.17 E
Foux, Cap à › 238 19.41 N 73.27 W
Fouyang
— Fuyang 100 32.54 N 115.49 E
Fouzon ≐ 50 47.16 N 1.27 E
Foveaux Strait ⊔ 172 46.35 S 168.00 E
Foveran 46 57.18 N 2.02 W

ENGLISH | DEUTSCH
Name Page Lat.°′ Long.°′ | Name Seite Breite°′ Länge°′ E = Öst

Fowey 42 50.20 N 4.38 W
Fowler, Ca., U.S. 226 36.37 N 119.40 W
Fowler, Co., U.S. 198 38.07 N 104.01 W
Fowler, In., U.S. 216 40.37 N 87.19 W
Fowler, Ks., U.S. 198 37.23 N 100.11 W
Fowler, Mi., U.S. 216 43.00 N 84.44 W
Fowler, Oh., U.S. 214 41.19 N 80.40 W
Fowler, Lake ◎ 168b 35.06 S 137.37 E
Fowler, Point › 162 32.02 S 132.29 E
Fowler Creek ≐ 281 42.17 N 83.30 W
Fowlers Bay 162 31.59 S 132.27 E
Fowlerton 196 28.28 N 98.48 W
Fowlerville 216 42.39 N 84.04 W
Fowling
— Jingdezhen 100 29.16 N 117.11 E
Fowman 128 37.13 N 49.19 E
Fox 180 64.51 N 147.46 W
Fox ≐, Mb., Can. 184 56.03 N 93.18 W
Fox ≐, U.S. 194 40.18 N 91.30 W
Fox ≐, U.S. 216 41.21 N 88.50 W
Fox ≐, Il., U.S. 194 38.32 N 88.08 W
Fox ≐, Wi., U.S. 190 44.32 N 88.01 W
Fox, Cape › 182 54.47 N 130.51 W
Foxboro, On., Can. 212 44.15 N 77.26 W
Foxboro, Ma., U.S. 207 42.03 N 71.15 W
Foxborough Raceway ◆ 283 42.06 N 71.16 W
Fox Burg 214 41.03 N 74.13 W
Foxburg 214 41.09 N 79.41 W
Fox Chapel 279b 40.30 N 79.55 W
Fox Chase ✦8 285 40.04 N 75.05 W
Fox Chase Manor 285 40.05 N 75.06 W
Fox Creek ≐, Ky., U.S. 218 38.16 N 83.41 W
Fox Creek ≐, N.Y., U.S. 210 42.41 N 74.18 W
Foxe Basin ⊂ 176 68.25 N 77.00 W
Foxe-Becken
— Foxe Basin ⊂ 176 68.25 N 77.00 W
Foxe Channel ⊔ 176 64.30 N 80.00 W
Foxen ◎ 26 59.23 N 11.52 E
Foxe Peninsula ›1 176 65.00 N 76.00 W
Foxford 48 53.58 N 9.08 W
Fox Glacier 172 43.28 S 170.01 E
Foxhall 284c 39.04 N 77.03 W
Fox Harbour 186 47.19 N 53.55 W
Fox Hills 284c 39.02 N 77.11 W
Foxhole 42 50.21 N 4.52 W
Foxholes 44 54.08 N 0.28 W
Fox Hollow Lake ◎ 276 41.02 N 74.40 W
Fox Island I, On., Can. 212 44.28 N 78.24 W
Fox Island I, Wa., U.S. 224 47.16 N 122.37 W
Fox Islands II 180 53.30 N 168.00 W
Fox Lake, Il., U.S. 216 42.23 N 88.11 W
Fox Lake, Wi., U.S. 190 43.33 N 88.54 W
Fox Lake ◎ 216 42.25 N 88.09 W
Fox Mountain ∧ 180 61.55 N 133.22 W
Foxpark 200 41.05 N 106.09 W
Fox Point 216 43.09 N 87.54 W
Fox Point › 276 40.54 N 73.35 W
Fox River Estates 216 41.58 N 88.20 W
Fox River Grove 216 42.12 N 88.12 W
Foxton 172 40.28 S 175.18 E
Foxton Beach 172 40.28 S 175.13 E
Foxvale 283 42.02 N 71.14 W
Fox Valley, Austl. 274a 33.45 S 151.06 E
Fox Valley, Sk., Can. 184 50.29 N 109.28 W
Foxwells 208 37.38 N 76.18 W
Foxwist Green 262 53.12 N 2.34 W
Foxworth 194 31.14 N 89.52 W
Foyedong 150 8.41 N 11.12 W
Foyers 46 57.14 N 4.29 W
Foyle ≐ 48 54.59 N 7.18 W
Foyle, Lough ⊂ 48 55.06 N 7.08 W
Foynes 48 52.37 N 9.06 W
Foza 64 45.54 N 11.38 E
Foz de Areia, Represa de ◎1 252 26.00 S 51.35 W
Foz do Cunene 152 17.16 S 11.50 E
Foz do Iguaçu 252 25.33 S 54.35 W
Foz do Jordão 248 9.23 S 71.56 W
Foz Giraldo 34 40.00 N 7.43 W
Fozilinġ 100 31.20 N 116.17 E
Frabosa Soprana 62 44.17 N 7.48 E
Frackville 208 40.47 N 76.13 W
Fraction Run ≐ 278 41.34 N 88.04 W
Fraga, Arg. 252 33.30 S 65.48 W
Fraga, Esp. 34 41.31 N 0.21 E
Fragagnano 68 40.26 N 17.28 E
Fragneto Monforte 68 41.15 N 14.46 E
Fragoso, Cayo I 240p 22.44 N 79.30 W
Fragrant Hills Park ◆ 271a 39.59 N 116.11 E
Fragua, Sierra de la ∧ 196 26.41 N 102.13 W
Fraile Muerto 252 32.31 S 54.32 W
Fraïn, Chott el ◎ 34 35.57 N 5.38 E
Fraire 50 50.16 N 4.30 E
Fraisans 58 47.09 N 5.46 E
Fraisse 62 45.23 N 4.15 E
Fraize 58 48.11 N 7.00 E
Fram 61 46.27 N 15.38 E
Frameries 50 50.24 N 3.54 E
Framingham 207 42.16 N 71.25 W
Framingham State College ✦2 283 42.18 N 71.26 W
Framlingham 42 52.13 N 1.21 E
Frammersbach 56 50.04 N 9.28 E
Frammes Mountains ∧ 9 67.50 S 62.35 E
Frampol 30 50.41 N 22.40 E
Frampton Cotterell 42 51.32 N 2.29 W
Frampton on Severn 42 51.46 N 2.22 W
França, Bra. 250 11.34 S 40.36 W
Franca, Bra. 255 20.32 S 47.24 W
Franca-Iosifa, Zemľa (Franz Josef Land) II 12 81.00 N 55.00 E
Français, Récif des ✦2 175f 19.40 S 163.20 E
Francavilla al Mare 66 42.25 N 14.17 E
Francavilla Angitola 68 38.46 N 16.16 E
Francavilla d'Ete 66 43.11 N 13.32 E
Francavilla di Sicilia 70 37.54 N 15.08 E
Francavilla Fontana 68 40.31 N 17.35 E
Francavilla in Sinni 68 40.05 N 16.12 E
Francavilla Marittima 68 39.49 N 16.23 E
France □1, Europe 22 46.00 N 2.00 E
France □1, Europe 32 46.00 N 2.00 E
Frances ≐ 180 60.12 N 129.02 W
Francés, Cabo ›, Cuba 240p 21.38 N 83.12 W
Francés, Cabo ›, Cuba 240p 21.54 N 84.02 W
Frances Creek 164 13.35 S 131.52 E
Francês dos Carvalhos 256 22.05 S 44.29 W
Frances Lake ◎ 180 61.25 N 129.30 W
Francés Viejo, Cabo › 238 19.39 N 69.55 W
Francesville 216 40.59 N 86.52 W
Franceville 152 1.38 S 13.35 E
Francfort-sur-Main
— Frankfurt am Main 56 50.07 N 8.40 E
Franche-Comté □9 58 47.00 N 6.00 E
Franchère, Lac ◎ 206 46.47 N 74.58 W
Franches-Montagnes ✦1 58 47.12 N 7.00 E
Francia 252 32.33 S 56.37 W
Francia, Estación de ✦5 266d 41.23 N 2.11 E
Francia, Peña de ∧ 34 42.35 N 8.02 W
Francia
— France □1 32 46.00 N 2.00 E
Francis 184 50.05 N 103.55 W
Francis, Lake ◎ 206 45.02 N 71.20 W
Francis Case, Lake ◎1 198 43.15 N 99.00 W
Francisco A. Berra 258 35.23 S 58.51 W
Francisco Álvarez 258 34.38 S 58.52 W
Francisco Beltrão 252 26.05 S 53.04 W
Francisco I. Madero, Méx. 232 25.45 N 103.21 W
Francisco I. Madero, Méx. 232 24.32 N 104.22 W
Francisco I. Madero, Méx. 234 21.36 N 104.49 W
Francisco José, Tierra
— Franca-Iosifa, Zemľa II 12 81.00 N 55.00 E
Francisco Morato 256 23.16 S 46.45 W
Francisco Morazán □5 236 14.15 N 87.15 W
Francisco Murguía 234 24.00 N 103.01 W
Francisco Perito Moreno, Parque Nacional ◆ 254 47.50 S 72.08 W
Francisco Sá 255 16.28 S 43.30 W
Francisco Zarco 204 32.06 N 116.30 W
Francis E. Warren Air Force Base ■ 198 41.09 N 104.52 W
Francistown 156 21.11 S 27.32 E
Francitas 222 28.52 N 96.20 W
Franco da Rocha 256 23.20 S 46.43 W
Francofonte 70 37.14 N 14.53 E
François 186 47.35 N 56.45 W
François, Lacs à ◎ 186 51.40 N 65.49 W
François-Joseph, Îles du
— Franca-Iosifa, Zemľa II 12 81.00 N 55.00 E
François Lake 182 54.04 N 125.44 W
François Lake ◎ 182 54.00 N 125.40 W
Francolise 68 41.11 N 14.03 E
Franconia Notch State Park ◆ 188 44.06 N 71.43 W
Franconville 261 48.59 N 2.14 E
Francs Peak ∧ 202 43.58 N 109.20 W
Francueil 50 47.19 N 1.05 E
Franeker 52 53.11 N 5.32 E
Frangy 58 46.01 N 5.56 E
Frank 279b 40.16 N 79.48 W
Frank and Poet Drain ≡ 281 42.06 N 83.12 W
Frankby 262 53.22 N 3.08 W
Frankel City 196 32.23 N 102.47 W
Franken □9 30 50.00 N 10.00 E
Frankenau 56 51.05 N 8.56 E
Frankenbach 56 50.40 N 8.34 E
Frankenberg 54 50.54 N 13.01 E
Frankenberg-Eder 56 51.03 N 8.48 E
Frankenburg 60 48.05 N 13.30 E
Frankenheim 56 50.32 N 10.04 E
Frankenhöhe ∧ 56 49.15 N 10.15 E
Frankenmarkt 64 47.59 N 13.25 E
Frankenmuth 190 43.19 N 83.44 W
Frankenstein 56 49.26 N 7.58 E
Frankenthal 56 49.32 N 8.21 E
Frankenwald ∧ 54 50.18 N 11.36 E
Frankfield 241q 18.09 N 77.22 W
Frankford, On., Can. 212 44.12 N 77.36 W
Frankford, De., U.S. 208 38.31 N 75.14 W
Frankford, Mo., U.S. 219 39.29 N 91.19 W
Frankford ✦8 285 40.01 N 75.05 W
Frankford Arsenal ■ 285 40.00 N 75.04 W
Frankfort, S. Afr. 158 32.44 S 27.28 E
Frankfort, S. Afr. 158 27.17 S 28.30 E
Frankfort, Il., U.S. 216 41.29 N 87.50 W
Frankfort, In., U.S. 216 40.16 N 86.30 W
Frankfort, Ks., U.S. 198 39.42 N 96.25 W
Frankfort, Ky., U.S. 218 38.12 N 84.52 W
Frankfort, Mi., U.S. 190 44.38 N 86.14 W
Frankfort, N.Y., U.S. 210 43.02 N 75.04 W
Frankfort, Oh., U.S. 218 39.24 N 83.10 W
Frankfort, S.D., U.S. 198 44.52 N 98.18 W
Frankfort Springs 214 40.30 N 80.25 W
Frankfurt am Main 56 50.07 N 8.40 E
Frankfurt am Main, Flughafen ✈ 56 50.02 N 8.33 E
Frankfurt an der Oder 54 52.20 N 14.33 E
Frank G. Bonelli Regional County Park ◆ 280 34.05 N 117.49 W
Frank Hann National Park ◆ 162 32.50 S 120.25 E
Fränkische Alb ∧2 60 49.20 N 11.30 E
Fränkische Rezat ≐ 56 49.11 N 10.41 E
Fränkische Saale ≐ 56 50.03 N 9.42 E
Fränkische Schweiz ✦1 60 49.45 N 11.25 E
Frank Key I 220 25.07 N 80.54 W
Frankland ≐ 162 34.58 S 116.49 E
Frankleben 54 51.18 N 11.56 E
Franklin, S. Afr. 158 30.18 S 29.30 E
Franklin, Az., U.S. 200 32.40 N 109.04 W
Franklin, Ga., U.S. 192 33.16 N 85.05 W
Franklin, Id., U.S. 202 42.00 N 111.48 W
Franklin, Il., U.S. 219 39.37 N 90.03 W
Franklin, In., U.S. 218 39.28 N 86.03 W
Franklin, Ky., U.S. 194 36.43 N 86.34 W
Franklin, La., U.S. 194 29.47 N 91.30 W
Franklin, Me., U.S. 188 44.35 N 68.13 W
Franklin, Ma., U.S. 207 42.05 N 71.23 W
Franklin, Mi., U.S. 281 42.31 N 83.18 W
Franklin, Mn., U.S. 198 44.31 N 94.52 W
Franklin, Ne., U.S. 198 40.05 N 98.57 W
Franklin, N.H., U.S. 188 43.26 N 71.38 W
Franklin, N.J., U.S. 210 41.07 N 74.34 W
Franklin, N.Y., U.S. 210 42.20 N 75.09 W
Franklin, N.C., U.S. 192 35.10 N 83.22 W
Franklin, Oh., U.S. 218 39.33 N 84.18 W
Franklin, Pa., U.S. 214 41.24 N 79.50 W
Franklin, Tn., U.S. 194 35.55 N 86.52 W
Franklin, Tx., U.S. 222 31.01 N 96.29 W
Franklin, Vt., U.S. 206 44.58 N 72.55 W
Franklin, Va., U.S. 208 36.40 N 76.55 W
Franklin, W.V., U.S. 188 38.39 N 79.20 W
Franklin, Wi., U.S. 216 42.54 N 88.03 W
Franklin □6, Il., U.S. 219 38.00 N 89.00 W
Franklin □6, In., U.S. 218 39.25 N 85.01 W
Franklin □6, Ky., U.S. 218 38.14 N 84.52 W
Franklin □6, Ma., U.S. 207 42.36 N 72.36 W
Franklin □6, Mo., U.S. 219 38.25 N 91.03 W
Franklin □6, N.Y., U.S. 206 44.57 N 74.18 W
Franklin □6, Oh., U.S. 218 39.57 N 83.00 W
Franklin □6, Pa., U.S. 208 39.56 N 77.40 W
Franklin □6, Tx., U.S. 222 33.07 N 95.13 W
Franklin □6, Vt., U.S. 206 44.57 N 72.52 W
Franklin, Mount ∧ 171b 35.29 S 148.47 E
Franklin, Point › 180 70.54 N 158.48 W
Franklin Bay ⊂ 176 69.45 N 126.00 W
Franklin Canyon Reservoir ◎1 280 34.06 N 118.25 W
Franklin Delano Roosevelt National Historic Site ⊥ 210 41.46 N 73.56 W
Franklin Delano Roosevelt Park ◆ 285 39.54 N 75.11 W
Franklin D. Roosevelt Lake ◎1 202 48.20 N 118.10 W
Franklin Farms 279b 40.10 N 80.16 W
Franklin Grove 190 41.50 N 89.18 W
Franklin Harbor ⊂ 166 33.42 S 136.56 E
Franklin Institute ◆ 285 39.57 N 75.11 W
Franklin Island I 212 45.25 N 80.20 W
Franklin Lake ◎, N.T., Can. 176 66.56 N 96.03 W
Franklin Lake ◎, Nv., U.S. 204 40.24 N 115.12 W
Franklin Lake ◎, N.J., U.S. 276 40.59 N 74.13 W
Franklin Lakes 276 41.01 N 74.12 W
Franklin-Lower Gordon Wild Rivers National Park ◆ 166 42.46 S 145.45 E
Franklin Mountains ∧, N.T., Can. 180 63.00 N 123.50 W
Franklin Mountains ∧, N.Z. 172 44.55 S 167.45 E
Franklin Park, Il., U.S. 216 41.56 N 87.51 W

Symbols in the index entries represent the broad categories identified in the key at the right. Symbols with superior numbers (∧1) identify subcategories (see complete key on page I · 1).

Symbole im Register stellen die rechts im Schlüssel erklärten Kategorien dar. Symbole mit hochgestellten Ziffern (∧1) bezeichnen Unterabteilungen einer Kategorie (vgl. vollständiger Schlüssel auf Seite I · 1).

Los símbolos incluídos en el texto del índice representan las grandes categorías identificadas con la clave a la derecha. Los símbolos con numeros en su parte superior (∧1) identifican las subcategorías (véase la clave completa en la página I · 1).

Les symboles de l'index représentent les catégories indiquées dans la légende à droite. Les symboles suivis d'un indice (∧1) représentent des sous-catégories (voir légende complète à la page I · 1).

Os símbolos incluídos no texto do índice representam as grandes categorias identificadas com a chave à direita. Os símbolos com números em sua parte superior (∧1) identificam as subcategorias (veja-se a chave completa à página I · 1).

English	Deutsch	Español	Français	Português
∧ Mountain	Berg	Montaña	Montagne	Montanha
∧ Mountains	Gebirge	Montañas	Montagnes	Montanhas
⋊ Pass	Paß	Paso	Col	Passo
∨ Valley, Canyon	Tal, Cañon	Valle, Cañón	Vallée, Canyon	Vale, Canhão
≐ Plain	Ebene	Llano	Plaine	Planície
› Cape	Kap	Cabo	Cap	Cabo
I Island	Insel	Isla	Île	Ilha
II Islands	Inseln	Islas	Îles	Ilhas
✦ Other Topographic Features	Andere Topographische Objekte	Otros Elementos Topográficos	Autres données topographiques	Outros acidentes topográficos

ESPAÑOL — Nombre · Página · Lat.°′ · Long.°′ W = Oeste
FRANÇAIS — Nom · Page · Lat.°′ · Long.°′ W = Ouest
PORTUGUÊS — Nome · Página · Lat.°′ · Long.°′ W = Oeste

Franklin Park, Md., U.S. 284c 39.03 N 77.06 W
Franklin Park, N.J., U.S. 276 40.26 N 74.32 W
Franklin Park, N.Y., U.S. 210 43.05 N 76.05 W
Franklin Park, Pa., U.S. 279b 40.35 N 80.06 W
Franklin Park, Va., U.S. 284c 38.55 N 77.09 W
Franklin Park ♦ 283 42.18 N 71.06 W
Franklin Pond ⊜ 276 41.06 N 74.35 W
Franklin Ridge ∧ 282 38.00 N 122.10 W
Franklin River 224 49.06 N 124.49 W
Franklin Roosevelt Park -◆-8 273d 26.09 S 27.59 E
Franklin Springs 210 43.02 N 75.24 W
Franklin Square 210 40.42 N 73.40 W
Franklin State Forest ♦ 283 42.04 N 71.26 W
Franklin Strait ꒰ 176 72.00 N 96.00 W
Franklinton, La., U.S. 194 30.50 N 90.09 W
Franklinton, N.C., U.S. 192 36.06 N 78.27 W
Franklintown 208 40.05 N 77.02 W
Franklinville, N.J., U.S. 208 39.37 N 75.04 W
Franklinville, N.Y., U.S. 210 42.20 N 78.27 W
Frankreich
→ France □1 32 46.00 N 2.00 E
Frankston, Austl. 169 38.08 S 145.07 E
Frankston, Tx., U.S. 222 32.03 N 95.30 W
Franksville 216 42.45 N 87.54 W
Frankton 216 40.13 N 85.46 W
Frankville 194 31.38 N 88.08 W
Frånö 26 62.54 N 17.50 E
Fr'anovo 82 56.08 N 38.27 E
Franschhoek 158 33.55 S 19.09 E
Fransfontein 156 20.12 S 15.01 E
Frånsta 26 62.30 N 16.09 E
Františkovy Lázně 54 50.04 N 12.21 E
Franvillers 50 49.58 N 2.30 E
Franzburg 54 54.11 N 12.52 E
Franzensburg ⊥ 264b 48.04 N 16.22 E
Franzensfeste
→ Fortezza 64 46.47 N 11.37 E
Franz Josef 172 43.24 S 170.11 E
Franz Josef Land
→ Franca Iosifa, Zeml'a II 12 81.00 N 55.00 E
Franz-Josefs-Bahnhof -◆-5 264b 48.13 N 16.21 E
Franz-Josefs-Höhe -◆- 64 47.04 N 12.45 E
Französische Süd- und Antarktis-Gebiete
→ French Southern and Antarctic Territories □2 6 49.30 S 69.30 E
Französisch-Polynesien
→ French Polynesia □2 14 15.00 S 140.00 W
Frasca, Capo della ⟩ 71 39.46 N 8.27 E
Frascati 66 41.48 N 12.41 E
Frascineto 68 39.50 N 16.16 E
Frasdorf 64 47.48 N 12.16 E
Fraser, Co., U.S. 200 39.56 N 105.49 W
Fraser, Mi., U.S. 281 42.32 N 82.56 W
Fraser ≃, B.C., Can. 182 49.09 N 123.12 W
Fraser ≃, Nf., Can. 176 56.35 N 61.55 W
Fraser ≃, Co., U.S. 200 40.06 N 105.58 W
Fraser, Mount ∧ 162 25.39 S 118.23 E
Fraserburg 158 31.55 S 21.30 E
Fraserburgh 46 57.42 N 2.00 W
Fraser Island I 166 25.15 S 153.10 E
Fraser Lake 182 54.04 N 124.51 W
Fraser Lake ⊜ 182 54.05 N 124.35 W
Fraser Mills 224 49.14 N 122.52 W
Fraser National Park ♦ 169 37.10 S 145.50 E
Fraser Plateau ∧1 182 52.00 N 123.00 W
Fraser Range 162 32.03 S 122.48 E
Frasertown 172 38.58 S 177.24 E
Frasne 58 46.51 N 6.10 E
Frasnes-lez-Anvaing 50 50.40 N 3.36 E
Frassine ≃ 64 45.18 N 11.37 E
Frassinoro 64 44.18 N 10.34 E
Frati, Monte dei ∧ 66 43.40 N 12.10 E
Fratres 54 48.59 N 15.21 E
Frattamaggiore 68 40.57 N 14.16 E
Frattócchie 267a 41.46 N 12.37 E
Frauenfeld 58 47.34 N 8.54 E
Frauenkirchen 61 47.50 N 16.56 E
Frauenstein 54 50.48 N 13.32 E
Frauental an der Lassnitz 61 46.48 N 15.14 E
Frauenwald 54 50.35 N 10.51 E
Fray Bentos 252 33.08 S 58.18 W
Fray Jorge, Parque Nacional ♦ 252 30.40 S 71.45 W
Fray Luis Beltrán 252 39.19 S 65.46 W
Fray Marcos 252 34.11 S 55.44 W
Frazee 198 46.43 N 95.42 W
Frazer, Mt., U.S. 202 48.03 N 106.02 W
Frazer, Pa., U.S. 208 40.02 N 75.33 W
Frazeysburg 214 40.07 N 82.07 W
Frazier Mountain ∧ 228 34.47 N 118.58 W
Frazier Park 228 34.49 N 118.56 W
Fr'azino 82 55.58 N 38.04 E
Frazzanò 70 38.04 N 14.44 E
Frechen 56 50.54 N 6.49 E
Frechilla 34 42.08 N 4.50 W
Freckenhorst 52 51.55 N 7.58 E
Freckleton 262 53.45 N 2.52 W
Freddo ≃ 70 38.01 N 12.54 E
Fredeburg 56 51.11 N 8.18 E
Freden 52 51.56 N 9.54 E
Fredensborg 41 55.58 N 12.24 E
Fredensborg ⊥ 41 55.58 N 12.23 E
Frederic 190 45.39 N 92.28 W
Frederica 208 39.00 N 75.27 W
Fredericia 41 55.35 N 9.46 E
Frederick, Il., U.S. 219 40.04 N 90.26 W
Frederick, Md., U.S. 208 39.24 N 77.24 W
Frederick, Ok., U.S. 196 34.23 N 99.01 W
Frederick, S.D., U.S. 198 45.49 N 98.30 W
Frederick □6 208 39.25 N 77.25 W
Frederick Hills ∧2 164 12.41 S 136.00 E
Frederick House ≃ 190 49.06 N 81.10 W
Frederick House Lake ⊜ 190 48.40 N 80.55 W
Frederick Island I 162 34.04 S 122.00 E
Frederick Reef ✢2 166 20.58 S 154.23 E
Fredericksburg, In., U.S. 218 38.26 N 86.11 W
Fredericksburg, Ia., U.S. 190 42.57 N 92.11 W
Fredericksburg, Oh., U.S. 214 40.40 N 81.52 W
Fredericksburg, Pa., U.S. 214 40.27 N 76.26 W
Fredericksburg, Tx., U.S. 196 30.16 N 98.52 W
Fredericksburg, Va., U.S. 208 38.18 N 77.27 W
Fredericksburg Battlefield ⊥ 208 38.17 N 77.28 W
Frederick Sound ꒰ 180 57.00 N 133.00 W
Fredericktown, Mo., U.S. 194 37.33 N 90.17 W
Fredericktown, Oh., U.S. 214 40.28 N 82.32 W
Frederico Westphalen 252 27.22 S 53.24 W
Fredericton 186 45.58 N 66.39 W
Fredericton Junction 186 45.40 N 66.37 W
Frederik Hendrikeiland
→ Yos Sudarso, Pulau I 164 7.50 S 138.30 E
Frederiksberg, Dan. 41 55.25 N 11.34 E
Frederiksberg, Dan. 41 55.41 N 12.32 E
Frederiksborg □6 41 55.56 N 12.18 E
Frederiksborg ⊥ 41 55.56 N 12.19 E
Frederikshåb (Paamiut) 176 62.00 N 49.43 W
Frederikshavn 26 57.26 N 10.32 E
Frederikssund 41 55.50 N 12.04 E
Frederiksted 241n 17.43 N 64.53 W
Frederiksværk 41 55.58 N 12.02 E
Frederik Willem IV Vallen ⌞ 250 3.28 N 57.37 W
Fredersdorf bei Berlin 54 52.31 N 13.44 E
Fredonia, Col. 246 5.55 N 75.41 W
Fredonia, Az., U.S. 200 36.03 N 112.08 W
Fredonia, Ks., U.S. 198 37.32 N 95.49 W
Fredonia, N.Y., U.S. 214 42.26 N 79.19 W
Fredonia, N.D., U.S. 198 46.19 N 99.05 W
Fredonia, Pa., U.S. 214 41.20 N 80.14 W
Fredrika 26 64.05 N 18.24 E
Fredriksberg 40 60.08 N 14.23 E
Fredrikstad 26 59.13 N 10.57 E
Freeburg, Il., U.S. 219 38.25 N 89.54 W
Freeburg, Mo., U.S. 219 38.18 N 91.55 W
Freeburg, Pa., U.S. 208 40.46 N 76.57 W
Freedom, Ca., U.S. 226 36.56 N 121.46 W
Freedom, Pa., U.S. 214 40.40 N 80.14 W
Freehold, N.J., U.S. 208 40.15 N 74.16 W
Freehold, N.Y., U.S. 210 42.22 N 74.03 W
Freeland, Mi., U.S. 190 43.31 N 84.07 W
Freeland, Pa., U.S. 210 41.01 N 75.53 W
Freeland, Wa., U.S. 224 48.01 N 122.32 W
Freeland Park 216 40.37 N 87.30 W
Freeling, Mount ∧ 162 22.35 S 133.06 E
Freel Peak ∧ 226 38.52 N 119.54 W
Freels, Cape ⟩, Nf., Can. 186 49.15 N 53.28 W
Freels, Cape ⟩, Nf., Can. 186 46.37 N 53.33 W
Freeman 198 43.21 N 97.26 W
Freeman ≃ 182 54.20 N 114.47 W
Freeman, Lake ⊜ 216 40.42 N 86.45 W
Freemansburg 210 40.37 N 75.20 W
Freemount 48 52.16 N 8.53 W
Freeport, Ba. 238 26.30 N 78.45 W
Freeport, N.S., Can. 186 44.17 N 66.19 W
Freeport, On., Can. 212 43.25 N 80.25 W
Freeport, Fl., U.S. 194 30.29 N 86.08 W
Freeport, Il., U.S. 190 42.17 N 89.37 W
Freeport, Me., U.S. 188 43.51 N 70.06 W
Freeport, Mi., U.S. 216 42.45 N 85.18 W
Freeport, N.Y., U.S. 210 40.39 N 73.35 W
Freeport, Oh., U.S. 214 40.12 N 81.15 W
Freeport, Pa., U.S. 214 40.40 N 79.41 W
Freeport, Tx., U.S. 222 28.57 N 95.21 W
Freer 196 27.52 N 98.37 W
Freest 54 54.08 N 13.43 E
Freeston 222 31.32 N 96.15 W
Freestone 171a 28.08 S 152.08 E
Freestone □6 222 31.44 N 96.10 W
Freetown, Antig. 240c 17.03 N 61.42 W
Freetown, S.L. 150 8.30 N 13.15 W
Freetown, In., U.S. 218 38.58 N 86.07 W
Freetown, N.Y., U.S. 207 40.58 N 72.11 W
Freeville 210 42.30 N 76.20 W
Freewood Acres 208 40.10 N 74.15 W
Freezeout Lake ⊜ 202 47.40 N 112.03 W
Fregenal de la Sierra 34 38.10 N 6.39 W
Fregene -◆-8 66 41.51 N 12.12 E
Freiberg 54 50.54 N 13.20 E
Freiberger Mulde ≃ 54 51.10 N 12.48 E
Freiburg □5 58 48.00 N 8.25 E
Freiburg an der Elbe 52 53.49 N 9.17 E
Freiburg
→ Fribourg 58 46.48 N 7.09 E
Freiburg im Breisgau 58 47.59 N 7.51 E
Freienbach 58 47.12 N 8.45 E
Freienhufen 54 51.35 N 13.58 E
Freie Universität ᵾ2 264a 52.26 N 13.16 E
Freigericht 56 50.08 N 9.07 E
Freihung 60 49.37 N 11.55 E
Freiland 61 47.58 N 15.34 E
Freilassing 64 47.50 N 12.59 E
Freilingen 56 50.33 N 7.50 E
Freinberg 60 48.34 N 13.31 E
Freinsheim 56 49.30 N 8.13 E
Freirina 252 28.30 S 71.06 W
Freisen 56 49.33 N 7.14 E
Freisenbruch -◆-8 263 51.27 N 7.06 E
Freising 60 48.23 N 11.44 E
Freistadt 61 48.31 N 14.31 E
Freital 54 51.00 N 13.39 E
Freiwalde 54 51.58 N 13.44 E
Freixial 266c 38.54 N 9.09 W
Fréjus 62 43.26 N 6.44 E
Fréjus, Tunnel du -◆-5 62 45.08 N 6.40 E
Frémainville 261 49.04 N 1.52 E
Fremantle 168a 32.03 S 115.45 E
Fremdingen 56 48.58 N 10.27 E
Fremington 42 51.04 N 4.07 W
Fremont, Ca., U.S. 226 37.32 N 121.59 W
Fremont, In., U.S. 216 41.43 N 84.55 W
Fremont, Ia., U.S. 190 41.12 N 92.26 W
Fremont, Mi., U.S. 190 43.28 N 85.56 W
Fremont, Ne., U.S. 198 41.26 N 96.29 W
Fremont, N.C., U.S. 192 35.32 N 77.58 W
Fremont, Oh., U.S. 214 41.21 N 83.07 W
Fremont, Wi., U.S. 190 44.15 N 88.51 W
Fremont ≃ 200 38.24 N 110.42 W
Fremont Canyon V 200 33.48 N 117.42 W
Fremont Island I 200 41.09 N 112.20 W
Fremont Lake ⊜ 202 42.57 N 109.49 W
Fremont Peak ∧, Ca., U.S. 226 36.46 N 121.30 W
Fremont Peak ∧, Ca., U.S. 228 35.12 N 117.27 W
Fremont Valley V 228 35.10 N 118.00 W
French ≃ 190 45.56 N 80.54 W
French Broad ≃ 192 35.57 N 83.51 W
Frenchburg 192 37.57 N 83.37 W
French Camp 226 37.53 N 121.16 W
Frenchcap Cay I 240m 18.14 N 64.51 W
French Creek ≃, Mb., Can. 184 57.02 N 92.12 W
French Creek ≃, U.S. 214 41.25 N 79.50 W
French Creek ≃, Oh., U.S. 279a 41.27 N 82.07 W
French Creek ≃, Pa., U.S. 208 40.08 N 75.31 W
French Creek ≃, S.D., U.S. 198 43.38 N 102.55 W
French Creek, South Branch ≃, Pa., U.S. 214 41.54 N 79.54 W
French Creek, South Branch ≃, Pa., U.S. 285 40.10 N 75.42 W
French Creek, West Branch ≃ 214 41.58 N 79.52 W
French Creek State Park ♦ 208 40.13 N 75.47 W
French Frigate Shoals ✢2 14 23.45 N 166.10 W
French Guiana (Guyane français) □2, S.A. 242 4.00 N 53.00 W
French Guiana (Guyane français) □2, S.A. 250 4.00 N 53.00 W
French Island I 169 38.21 S 145.21 E
French Lick 194 38.32 N 86.37 W
Frenchman (Frenchman Creek) ≃ 202 48.24 N 107.05 W
Frenchman Bay c 188 44.25 N 68.10 W
Frenchman Butte 184 53.35 N 109.38 W
Frenchman Creek (Frenchman) ≃, N.A. 202 48.24 N 107.05 W
Frenchman Creek ≃, U.S. 198 40.13 N 100.50 W
Frenchman Lake ⊜ 204 36.48 N 116.56 W
Frenchman Point ⟩ 212 44.35 N 81.18 W
Frenchman's Bay c 275b 43.49 N 79.05 W
Frenchmans Cap ∧ 166 42.16 S 145.50 E
Frenchman's Creek ≃, On., Can. 284a 42.56 N 78.56 W
Frenchmans Creek ≃, Ca., U.S. 282 37.29 N 122.27 W
French Meadows Reservoir ⊜1 226 39.07 N 120.25 W
Frenchpark 48 53.52 N 8.26 W
French Pass 172 40.56 S 173.50 E
French Polynesia □2 14 15.00 S 140.00 W
Frenchs Forest 274a 33.45 S 151.14 E
French Southern and Antarctic Territories □2 6 49.30 S 69.30 E
French Stream ≃ 283 42.07 N 70.53 W
Frenchtown 210 40.31 N 75.03 W
Frenda 148 35.02 N 1.01 E
Freneuse 261 49.03 N 1.36 E
Frensdorferhaar 52 52.25 N 7.03 E
Frenštát pod Radhoštěm 30 49.33 N 18.14 E
Frentani, Monti dei ∧ 66 41.54 N 14.37 E
Frépillon 261 49.03 N 2.12 E
Frere 158 28.52 S 29.47 E
Freren 52 52.29 N 7.32 E
Fresco 150 5.05 N 5.34 W
Fresco ≃ 250 6.39 S 51.59 W
Freshfield 262 53.34 N 3.04 W
Freshfield, Mount ∧ 182 51.44 N 116.57 W
Freshford 48 52.43 N 7.24 W
Fresh Meadows -◆-8 276 40.44 N 73.48 W
Fresh Pond ⊜, Ma., U.S. 283 42.23 N 71.09 W
Fresh Pond ⊜, N.Y., U.S. 276 40.55 N 73.18 W
Freshwater 42 50.40 N 1.30 W
Freshwater Creek ≃ 226 39.12 N 122.04 W
Fresia 254 41.09 S 73.27 W
Fresnes 261 48.45 N 2.19 E
Fresne-Saint-Mamès 58 47.33 N 5.52 E
Fresnes-en-Woëvre 56 49.08 N 5.39 E
Fresnes-sur-Escaut 50 50.26 N 3.35 E
Fresnes-sur-Marne 261 48.56 N 2.45 E
Fresnillo 234 23.10 N 102.53 W
Fresno, Col. 246 5.09 N 75.01 W
Fresno, Ca., U.S. 226 36.44 N 119.46 W
Fresno, Oh., U.S. 214 40.20 N 81.44 W
Fresno, Tx., U.S. 222 29.32 N 95.27 W
Fresno □6 226 36.38 N 119.45 W
Fresno ≃ 226 37.05 N 120.33 W
Fresno, Lewis Fork ≃ 226 37.20 N 119.39 W
Fresno Air Terminal ⊠ 226 36.46 N 119.43 W
Fresno Reservoir ⊜1 202 48.41 N 109.57 W
Fresno Slough ≃ 226 36.47 N 120.22 W
Fresnoy-Folny 50 49.53 N 1.26 E
Fresnoy-le-Grand 50 49.57 N 3.25 E
Fressenneville 50 50.04 N 1.34 E
Fressin 50 50.27 N 2.03 E
Freswick 46 58.35 N 3.05 W
Frétéval 50 47.53 N 1.13 E
Frétigney-et-Velloreille 58 47.29 N 5.56 E
Fretin 50 50.33 N 3.08 E
Frettes 58 47.41 N 5.34 E
Freu, Cap des ⟩ 34 39.45 N 3.27 E
Freudenberg, Dtsch. 56 49.44 N 9.19 E
Freudenberg, Dtsch. 56 50.54 N 7.52 E
Freudenberg, Dtsch. 264a 52.42 N 13.49 E
Freudenstadt 58 48.28 N 8.25 E
Frévent 50 50.16 N 2.17 E
Frew ≃ 162 20.00 S 135.38 E
Frewena 162 19.25 S 135.25 E
Frewsburg 214 42.03 N 79.09 W
Freyburg 54 51.13 N 11.46 E
Freycinet, Cape ⟩ 162 34.06 S 114.59 E
Freycinet Estuary c1 162 26.25 S 113.45 E
Freycinet National Park ♦ 166 42.10 S 148.20 E
Freycinet Peninsula ⟩1 166 42.13 S 148.18 E
Freyenstein 54 53.17 N 12.20 E
Freyming-Merlebach 56 49.09 N 6.48 E
Freyre 252 31.10 S 62.06 W
Freystadt 60 49.12 N 11.20 E
Freyung 60 48.48 N 13.33 E
Fria 150 10.05 N 13.32 W
Fria, Cape ⟩ 152 18.30 S 12.01 E
Friant 226 36.59 N 119.42 W
Friant Dam -◆-6 226 37.00 N 119.43 W
Friant-Kern Canal ≋ 226 35.22 N 119.06 W
Friars Point 194 34.22 N 90.38 W
Frías, Arg. 252 28.39 S 65.09 W
Frías, Perú 248 4.52 S 79.57 W
Fribourg (Freiburg) 58 46.48 N 7.09 E
Fribourg (Freiburg) □3 58 46.45 N 7.05 E
Frick 58 47.31 N 8.01 E
Frick Park ♦ 279b 40.26 N 79.54 W
Friday 222 31.07 N 95.15 W
Friday Harbor 224 48.32 N 123.00 W
Fridaythorpe 44 54.01 N 0.40 W
Fridingen an der Donau 58 48.01 N 8.56 E
Fridley 190 45.05 N 93.15 W
Fridolfing 60 48.00 N 12.49 E
Fridtjof Nansen, Mount ∧ 9 85.21 S 167.33 W
Friedberg, Dtsch. 56 50.20 N 8.45 E
Friedberg, Dtsch. 58 48.21 N 10.58 E
Friedberg, Öst. 61 47.27 N 16.03 E
Friedeburg [/Saale] 54 51.37 N 11.44 E
Friedenau -◆-8 264a 52.28 N 13.20 E
Friedens 214 40.03 N 79.00 W
Friedensburg 208 40.36 N 76.14 W
Friedersdorf, Dtsch. 54 52.17 N 13.47 E
Friedersdorf, Dtsch. 54 51.01 N 14.34 E
Friedersdorf, Dtsch. 54 51.39 N 12.21 E
Friedesheim 158 27.55 S 26.43 E
Friedland, Dtsch. 54 52.06 N 14.16 E
Friedland, Dtsch. 54 53.40 N 13.33 E
Friedland, Dtsch. 56 51.25 N 9.55 E
Friedrich-Ebert-Brücke -◆-5 263 51.28 N 6.43 E
Friedrich Krupp-Aktiengesellschaft ᵾ3 263 51.28 N 7.00 E
Friedrichroda 54 50.52 N 10.34 E
Friedrichsbrunn 54 51.41 N 11.02 E
Friedrichsdorf 56 50.15 N 8.38 E
Friedrichsfeld 263 51.38 N 6.39 E
Friedrichsfelde -◆-8 264a 52.31 N 13.31 E
Friedrichshafen 58 47.39 N 9.28 E
Friedrichshagen -◆-8 264a 52.27 N 13.38 E
Friedrichshof 264a 52.19 N 13.46 E
Friedrichsort -◆-8 54 54.24 N 10.11 E
Friedrichsruh, Schloss ⊥ 52 53.32 N 10.20 E
Friedrichsruhe 54 53.31 N 11.45 E
Friedrichstadt 41 54.22 N 9.05 E
Friedrichsthal, Dtsch. 54 52.48 N 13.16 E
Friedrichsthal, Dtsch. 56 49.19 N 7.06 E
Friedrichstrasse, Bahnhof -◆-5 264a 52.31 N 13.24 E
Friedrichswalde 54 53.02 N 13.42 E
Frielas 266c 38.49 N 9.09 W
Frielendorf 56 50.58 N 9.19 E
Friemersheim -◆-8 263 51.23 N 6.42 E
Friend, Ne., U.S. 198 40.39 N 97.17 W
Friend, Or., U.S. 224 45.21 N 121.16 W
Friends Colony -◆-8 272a 28.34 N 77.16 E
Friendship, N.Y., U.S. 210 42.12 N 78.08 W
Friendship, Tn., U.S. 194 35.54 N 89.14 W
Friendship, Wi., U.S. 190 43.58 N 89.49 W
Friendship Creek ≃ 285 39.55 N 74.43 W
Friendship Shoal ✢2 112 5.58 N 112.31 E
Friends Meeting House State Memorial ⊥ 214 40.09 N 80.47 W
Friendswood 222 29.31 N 95.12 W
Friern Barnet -◆-8 260 51.37 N 0.10 W
Fries 192 36.42 N 80.58 W
Friesach 61 46.57 N 14.24 E
Friesack 54 52.44 N 12.34 E
Friesenheim 58 48.22 N 7.53 E
Friesenhofen 58 47.45 N 10.04 E
Friesenried 58 47.52 N 10.31 E
Friesland □4 52 53.03 N 5.45 E
Friesland □9 30 53.00 N 5.40 E
Fries Mills 285 39.39 N 75.03 W
Friesoythe 52 53.01 N 7.51 E
Frigate Point ⟩ 174g 28.11 N 177.24 W
Frigento 68 41.01 N 15.06 E
Frignano 68 41.00 N 14.10 E
Frignano -◆-1 64 44.20 N 10.51 E
Friguia 150 12.03 N 10.56 W
Fritala 26 61.26 N 21.52 E
Frillendorf -◆-8 263 51.28 N 7.05 E
Frindsbury 260 51.24 N 0.30 E
Frinsted 260 51.17 N 0.43 E
Frinton-on-Sea 42 51.50 N 1.14 E
Frintrop -◆-8 263 51.29 N 6.55 E
Frío ≃, N.A. 236 11.08 N 84.46 W
Frio ≃, Tx., U.S. 196 28.30 N 98.10 W
Frio, Cabo ⟩ 255 22.53 S 42.00 W
Friockheim 46 56.38 N 2.38 W
Frio Draw V 196 34.50 N 102.19 W
Friona 196 34.38 N 102.43 W
Frisa, Loch ⊜ 46 56.34 N 6.05 W
Frisange 56 49.32 N 6.12 E
Frisches Haff
→ Vislinskij zaliv c 30 54.27 N 19.40 E
Frisco, Pa., U.S. 214 40.51 N 80.16 W
Frisco, Tx., U.S. 222 33.09 N 96.49 W
Frisco City 194 31.26 N 87.24 W
Frisco Creek ≃ 196 36.34 N 101.23 W
Frisian Islands II 30 53.35 N 6.40 E
Friskney 44 53.04 N 0.11 E
Fristad 26 57.50 N 13.01 E
Fritch 196 35.38 N 101.36 W
Fritsla 26 57.33 N 12.47 E
Fritzlar 56 51.08 N 9.16 E
Friuli □9 64 46.00 N 13.00 E
Friuli-Venezia Giulia □4 64 46.00 N 13.00 E
Friza, proliv ꒰ 74 45.30 N 149.10 E
Frizington 44 54.32 N 3.30 W
Frobisher 184 49.12 N 102.26 W
Frobisher Bay c 176 62.30 N 66.00 W
Frobisher Lake ⊜ 184 56.25 N 108.20 W
Frodsham, Eng., U.K. 44 53.18 N 2.44 W
Frodsham, Eng., U.K. 262 53.18 N 2.44 W
Frog Lake ⊜ 184 53.55 N 110.18 W
Frohavet ꒰ 24 63.52 N 9.26 E
Frohburg 54 51.03 N 12.33 E
Frohlinde -◆-8 263 51.32 N 7.21 E
Frohnau -◆-8 264a 52.38 N 13.18 E
Frohnhausen 263 51.29 N 7.48 E
Frohnhausen -◆-8 263 51.27 N 6.58 E
Frohnleiten 61 47.16 N 15.20 E
Frohse 52 52.02 N 11.43 E
Froid 198 48.20 N 104.30 W
Froid, Lac ⊜ 206 46.40 N 74.32 W
Froid, Ruisseau ≃ 206 46.23 N 74.46 W
Froidmont-Cohartille 50 49.41 N 3.42 E
Froidos 56 49.03 N 5.07 E
Froissy 50 49.34 N 2.13 E
Froitzheim 56 50.42 N 6.34 E
Frolišči, Ross. 80 56.25 N 42.39 E
Frolišči, Ross. 82 56.18 N 39.13 E
Frolovo 80 49.47 N 43.39 E
Froman Run ≃ 279b 40.12 N 80.00 W
Fromberg 202 45.23 N 108.54 W
Frombork 30 54.22 N 19.41 E
Frome 42 51.14 N 2.20 W
Frome ≃, Austl. 166 29.06 S 137.52 E
Frome ≃, Eng., U.K. 42 52.03 N 2.38 W
Frome ≃, Eng., U.K. 42 50.41 N 2.05 W
Frome, Lake ⊜ 166 30.48 S 139.48 E
Frome Downs 166 31.13 S 139.46 E
Fromelennes 56 50.08 N 4.52 E
Fromentières 50 48.54 N 3.43 E
Frömern 263 51.30 N 7.44 E
Fromhorn 58 48.15 N 8.52 E
Fröndenberg 56 51.28 N 7.46 E
Frönsberg 263 51.21 N 7.46 E
Fronteiras 250 7.05 S 40.37 W
Frontenac, Fl., U.S. 220 28.27 N 80.46 W
Frontenac, Ks., U.S. 198 37.27 N 94.41 W
Frontenac □6, On., Can. 212 44.40 N 76.45 W
Frontenac □6, P.Q., Can. 206 45.42 N 71.15 W
Frontenard 58 46.55 N 5.10 E
Frontenex-Villard-Rosset 62 45.38 N 6.19 E
Frontera, Méx. 232 26.56 N 101.27 W
Frontera, Méx. 234 18.32 N 92.38 W
Fronteras 200 30.56 N 109.31 W
Frontier, Sk., Can. 184 49.12 N 108.34 W
Frontier, Mi., U.S. 216 41.47 N 84.36 W
Frontier, Wy., U.S. 200 41.48 N 110.32 W
Frontignan 62 43.27 N 3.45 E
Frontino 246 6.46 N 76.08 W
Frontino, Páramo ∧ 246 6.28 N 76.04 W
Frontón, Isla I 286d 12.07 S 77.11 W
Front Range ∧, Leso. 158 29.05 S 28.20 E
Front Range ∧, Co., U.S. 200 39.45 N 105.45 W
Front Royal 188 38.55 N 78.11 W
Frose 54 51.48 N 11.23 E
Frosinone 66 41.38 N 13.19 E
Frosinone □4 66 41.37 N 13.27 E
Frosolone 66 41.36 N 14.27 E
Frösön 26 63.11 N 14.32 E
Frost 222 32.05 N 96.48 W
Frostavallen 41 55.58 N 13.30 E
Frostburg 188 39.39 N 78.55 W
Frost Creek ≃ 276 40.54 N 73.37 W
Frostproof 220 27.44 N 81.31 W
Frotheim 52 52.21 N 8.40 E
Frouard 56 48.46 N 6.08 E
Frövi 40 59.28 N 15.22 E
Frøya I 24 63.43 N 8.42 E
Fruges 50 50.31 N 2.08 E
Fruita 200 39.09 N 108.43 W
Fruitdale, Al., U.S. 194 31.20 N 88.24 W
Fruitdale, Or., U.S. 202 42.24 N 123.20 W
Fruithurst 194 33.43 N 85.26 W
Fruitland, Id., U.S. 202 44.00 N 116.54 W
Fruitland, Md., U.S. 208 38.19 N 75.37 W
Fruitland Park 220 28.51 N 81.54 W
Fruitport 216 43.07 N 86.09 W
Fruitvale, B.C., Can. 182 49.07 N 117.33 W
Fruitvale, Tx., U.S. 222 32.41 N 95.48 W
Fruitvale, Wa., U.S. 202 46.37 N 120.33 W
Fruitville 192 27.19 N 82.27 W
Frumușita 38 45.40 N 28.04 E
Frunze, Kyrg. 85 40.07 N 71.44 E
Frunze, Ukr. 78 46.16 N 34.52 E
Frunze, Ukr. 83 48.40 N 38.45 E
Frunze
→ Biškek 85 42.54 N 74.36 E
Frunzovka 78 47.20 N 29.44 E
Frutal 255 20.02 S 48.55 W
Frutigen 58 46.35 N 7.39 E
Frutillar 254 41.07 S 73.03 W
Fryburg 214 41.21 N 79.26 W
Frýdek-Místek 30 49.41 N 18.22 E
Frydlant 30 50.56 N 15.05 E
Frye 279b 40.11 N 79.56 W
Fryeburg 188 44.00 N 70.58 W
Fryerning 260 51.41 N 0.22 E
Fryingpan ≃ 200 39.22 N 107.02 W
Fu ≃, Zhg. 100 28.36 N 116.04 E
Fu ≃, Zhg. 100 29.52 N 115.28 E
Fu ≃, Zhg. 102 29.59 N 106.16 E
Fua'amotu 174w 21.16 S 175.08 W
Fua'amotu International Airport ⊠ 174w 21.17 S 175.08 W
Fu'an, Zhg. 100 27.08 N 119.40 E
Fu'an, Zhg. 100 32.41 N 120.41 E
Fuanjie 100 25.29 N 117.53 E
Fubao 107 28.47 N 106.05 E
Fubine 62 44.58 N 8.26 E
Fucecchio 66 43.44 N 10.48 E
Fuchang 100 30.06 N 113.08 E
Fucheng 98 37.52 N 116.07 E
Fuchikou 100 29.51 N 115.27 E
Fuchow
→ Fuzhou 100 28.01 N 116.20 E
Fuchs-Berg ∧2 264a 52.27 N 13.51 E
Fuchskaute ∧ 56 50.27 N 7.52 E
Füchtorf 52 52.03 N 8.02 E
Fuchū, Nihon 94 35.40 N 139.29 E
Fuchū, Nihon 94 36.39 N 137.10 E
Fuchū, Nihon 96 34.24 N 132.30 E
Fuchū, Nihon 96 34.34 N 133.14 E
Fuchun ≃ 106 30.10 N 120.09 E
Fucine 64 46.18 N 10.44 E
Fucino, Conca del ≡ 66 42.01 N 13.31 E
Fudan University ᵾ2 269b 31.17 N 121.29 E
Fuday I 46 57.03 N 7.23 W
Fuding 100 27.21 N 120.12 E
Fudu ≃ 107 29.52 N 106.10 E
Fuefuki ≃ 94 35.33 N 138.28 E
Fuego, Volcán de ∧1 236 14.29 N 90.53 W
Fuelbeckestausee ⊜1 263 51.15 N 7.40 E
Fuencaliente 34 38.24 N 4.18 W
Fuencarral -◆-8 266a 40.30 N 3.41 W
Fuenlabrada 266a 40.17 N 3.48 W
Fuensalida 34 40.03 N 4.12 W
Fuensanta, Embalse de ⊜1 34 38.23 N 2.13 W
Fuente 196 28.40 N 100.32 W
Fuente de Cantos 34 38.15 N 6.18 W
Fuente de Oro 246 3.28 N 73.37 W
Fuenteobejuna 34 38.16 N 5.25 W
Fuentesaúco 34 41.14 N 5.30 W
Fuentes de Ebro 34 41.31 N 0.38 W
Fuerli 105 39.40 N 116.41 E
Fuerte ≃ 232 25.54 N 109.22 W
Fuerte Olimpo 248 21.02 S 57.54 W
Fuerteventura I 148 28.20 N 14.00 W
Fuerza, Castillo de la ⊥ 286b 23.09 N 82.21 W
Fufeng 102 34.20 N 107.51 E
Fuga Island I 116 18.52 N 121.22 E
Fugama, Wādī V 140 14.43 N 24.36 E
Fügen 64 47.21 N 11.51 E
Fuglebjerg 41 55.18 N 11.34 E
Fugløysund ꒰ 24 70.12 N 20.20 E
Fugong 102 27.09 N 98.52 E
Fugou 98 34.04 N 114.24 E
Fuhai 86 47.06 N 87.23 E
Fuhe 100 23.22 N 113.37 E
Fuhlenbrock -◆-8 263 51.32 N 6.54 E
Fuhrberg 52 52.34 N 9.50 E
Fuhse ≃ 52 52.37 N 10.03 E
Fuhsien
→ Fuxian 98 39.37 N 122.01 E
Fuhu 100 29.11 N 118.04 E
Fuji, Nihon 94 35.09 N 138.39 E
Fuji, Zhg. 94 34.24 N 114.48 E
Fuji, Zhg. 107 29.09 N 105.23 E
Fuji ≃ 94 35.07 N 138.39 E
Fuji, Mount
→ Fuji-san ∧1 94 35.22 N 138.44 E
Fujiafeng 105 39.11 N 117.32 E
Fujian (Fukien) □4 100 26.00 N 118.00 E
Fujiatun 104 41.42 N 123.44 E
Fujiawopu 104 40.58 N 122.14 E
Fujiazhen 107 29.57 N 104.18 E
Fujiazhuangcun 104 41.15 N 122.20 E
Fujie 106 31.09 N 119.27 E
Fujieda 94 34.52 N 138.16 E
Fuji-Hakone-Izu-kokuritsu-kōen ♦ 94 35.21 N 138.44 E
Fujiidera 96 34.34 N 135.36 E
Fujikawa 94 35.08 N 138.37 E
Fujikubo 268 35.50 N 139.32 E
Fujimi, Nihon 94 36.27 N 139.05 E
Fujimi, Nihon 94 35.55 N 138.15 E
Fujimi, Nihon 94 35.51 N 139.33 E
Fujin 89 47.14 N 132.00 E
Fujino 94 35.37 N 139.10 E
Fujinomiya 94 35.12 N 138.38 E
Fujioka, Nihon 94 35.12 N 137.12 E
Fujioka, Nihon 94 36.15 N 139.05 E
Fujioka, Nihon 94 36.15 N 139.39 E
Fuji-san ∧1 94 35.22 N 138.44 E
Fujisawa 94 35.21 N 139.29 E
Fujishiro 94 35.55 N 140.07 E
Fujiwara, Nihon 94 35.09 N 136.30 E
Fujiwara, Nihon 94 36.51 N 139.44 E
Fujiwara-dam -◆-6 94 36.49 N 139.02 E
Fujiyama
→ Fuji-san ∧1 94 35.22 N 138.44 E
Fuji-yoshida 94 35.29 N 138.48 E
Fukagawa 92a 43.43 N 142.03 E
Fukagawa -◆-8 268 35.40 N 139.48 E
Fukami 268 35.28 N 139.28 E
Fukane I 174w 21.05 S 175.02 W
Fukang 86 44.10 N 87.59 E
Fukasaka-tunnel -◆-5 94 35.35 N 136.10 E
Fuka Shan ∧ 89 47.55 N 120.53 E
Fukaya 94 36.12 N 139.17 E
Fukiage 94 36.06 N 139.27 E
Fukiai -◆-8 270 34.42 N 135.12 E
Fukien
→ Fujian □4 100 26.00 N 118.00 E
Fukou, Zhg. 100 26.28 N 117.40 E
Fukou, Zhg. 100 25.45 N 118.28 E
Fukube 96 35.33 N 134.18 E
Fukuchiyama 96 35.18 N 135.07 E
Fukude 94 34.40 N 137.53 E
Fukue 92 32.41 N 128.50 E
Fukuei Chiao ⟩ 100 25.18 N 121.32 E
Fukue-jima I 92 32.40 N 128.45 E
Fukui, Nihon 96 36.04 N 136.13 E
Fukui, Nihon 270 34.51 N 135.34 E
Fukui □5 92 36.00 N 136.15 E
Fukuma 96 33.46 N 130.28 E
Fukumitsu 94 36.33 N 136.52 E
Fukuno 94 36.35 N 136.55 E
Fukuoka, Nihon 94 35.34 N 137.27 E
Fukuoka, Nihon 94 36.42 N 136.56 E
Fukuoka, Nihon 96 33.35 N 130.24 E
Fukuoka □5 96 33.45 N 130.30 E
Fukuoka-chūtonchi, Rikujō-jieitai- ▪ 96 33.32 N 130.28 E
Fukuroda-no-taki ⌞ 94 36.46 N 140.25 E
Fukuroi 94 34.45 N 137.55 E
Fukushima, Nihon 92 37.45 N 140.28 E
Fukushima, Nihon 92a 41.29 N 140.15 E
Fukushima □5 94 37.08 N 140.00 E
Fukushima -◆-8 270 34.42 N 135.29 E
Fukusumi 270 34.37 N 135.56 E
Fukutani -◆-8 270 34.43 N 135.02 E
Fukuyama 96 34.29 N 133.22 E
Fukuzaki 96 34.57 N 134.45 E
Fulacunda 150 11.44 N 15.03 W
Fūlādī, Kūh-e ∧ 120 34.38 N 67.32 E
Fūlād Maḥalleh 128 36.02 N 53.44 E
Fulanga Island I 175g 19.08 S 178.34 W
Fulanga Passage ꒰ 175g 19.00 S 178.40 W
Fulbourn 42 52.11 N 0.13 E
Fulda, Dtsch. 56 50.33 N 9.41 E
Fulda, Mn., U.S. 198 43.52 N 95.36 W
Fulda ≃ 30 51.25 N 9.39 E
Fuldatal 56 51.22 N 9.31 E
Fuldera 58 46.37 N 10.22 E
Fule 102 25.27 N 104.19 E
Fulerum -◆-8 263 51.26 N 6.57 E
Fulford Harbour 224 48.46 N 123.27 W
Fulgatore 70 37.57 N 12.42 E
Fulham -◆-8 260 51.29 N 0.12 W
Fuli 100 23.11 N 121.14 E
Fuliji 100 33.46 N 116.58 E
Fuling 102 29.42 N 107.21 E
Fulitun 89 46.42 N 131.10 E
Fullarton ≃ 166 20.15 S 141.10 E
Fullen ⊜ 40 60.31 N 16.09 E
Fuller Springs 222 31.18 N 94.41 W
Fullerton, Ca., U.S. 228 33.52 N 117.55 W
Fullerton, Ky., U.S. 218 38.43 N 82.58 W
Fullerton, Md., U.S. 284b 39.22 N 76.31 W
Fullerton, Ne., U.S. 198 41.21 N 97.58 W
Fullerton, Pa., U.S. 208 40.38 N 75.28 W
Fullerton Municipal Airport ⊠ 280 33.52 N 117.59 W
Fullerton Point ⟩ 240c 17.06 N 61.54 W
Fulmer 260 51.33 N 0.34 W
Fulong 102 22.57 N 107.41 E
Fulongchang 107 30.03 N 103.38 E
Fulongquan 89 44.22 N 124.36 E
Fulpmes 64 47.10 N 11.21 E
Fulshear 222 29.41 N 95.54 W
Fulton, Al., U.S. 194 31.47 N 87.43 W
Fulton, Ar., U.S. 194 33.36 N 93.48 W
Fulton, Il., U.S. 190 41.52 N 90.09 W
Fulton, In., U.S. 216 40.56 N 86.15 W
Fulton, Ks., U.S. 198 38.00 N 94.43 W
Fulton, Ky., U.S. 194 36.30 N 88.52 W
Fulton, Md., U.S. 208 39.09 N 76.55 W
Fulton, Mi., U.S. 216 47.17 N 88.21 W
Fulton, Ms., U.S. 194 34.16 N 88.24 W
Fulton, Mo., U.S. 219 38.50 N 91.56 W
Fulton, N.Y., U.S. 210 43.19 N 76.25 W
Fulton, Oh., U.S. 214 40.27 N 82.49 W
Fulton, Tx., U.S. 196 28.04 N 97.02 W
Fulton □6, Il., U.S. 219 40.13 N 90.17 W
Fulton □6, In., U.S. 216 41.04 N 86.13 W
Fulton □6, N.Y., U.S. 210 43.00 N 74.22 W
Fulton □6, Oh., U.S. 216 41.33 N 84.09 W
Fulton □6, Pa., U.S. 214 40.06 N 78.04 W
Fulton ≃ 182 54.48 N 126.07 W
Fultondale 194 33.36 N 86.47 W
Fultonham 210 42.31 N 75.03 W
Fultonville 210 42.57 N 74.22 W
Fuluchang 107 29.38 N 106.08 E
Fulufjället ∧ 26 61.33 N 12.43 E
Fuluzhen 107 29.18 N 103.40 E
Fulwood 44 53.47 N 2.41 W
Fumaça 256 22.17 S 44.19 W
Fumahashi 94 36.42 N 137.19 E
Fumane 156 24.29 S 33.58 E
Fumay 56 49.59 N 4.42 E
Fumel 32 44.29 N 0.57 E
Fumin, Zhg. 102 25.16 N 102.26 E
Fumin, Zhg. 106 31.54 N 121.10 E
Fumintun 98 42.29 N 126.22 E
Fuminzhen 106 31.37 N 121.39 E
Funa ≃ 273b 4.23 S 15.19 E
Funabashi 94 35.42 N 139.59 E
Funafuti I 14 8.31 S 179.13 E
Funagawa
→ Oga 92 39.53 N 139.51 E
Funakuyā 175d 24.30 N 124.17 E
Funan 100 32.39 N 115.32 E
Funan Gaba 144 4.25 N 37.57 E
Funaoka 96 35.23 N 134.14 E
Funasaka 270 34.48 N 135.17 E
Funäsdalen 26 62.32 N 12.33 E
Funchal 148 32.38 N 16.54 W
Funchal □5 148 32.40 N 16.55 W
Fundación 246 10.31 N 74.11 W
Fundão 34 40.08 N 7.30 W
Fundão, Ilha do I 287a 22.51 S 43.14 W
Funde 272c 18.54 N 72.58 E
Fundo ≃ 250 10.12 S 44.39 W
Fundo, Arroio ≃ 287a 22.58 S 43.22 W
Fundy, Bay of c 186 45.00 N 66.00 W
Fundy National Park ♦ 186 45.38 N 65.00 W
Fünfkirchen
→ Pécs 30 46.05 N 18.13 E
Funhalouro 156 23.03 S 34.25 E
Funil, Represa do ⊜1 256 22.33 S 44.35 W
Funil, Ribeirão do ≃ 256 22.02 S 43.46 W
Funil, Rio do ≃ 256 22.58 S 44.34 W
Funing, Zhg. 98 39.54 N 119.14 E
Funing, Zhg. 100 33.47 N 119.48 E
Funing, Zhg. 102 23.33 N 105.35 E
Funiuchang 107 29.03 N 106.33 E
Funiu Shan ∧ 100 33.40 N 112.30 E
Funk Island I 186 49.46 N 53.10 W
Funks Creek ≃ 226 39.19 N 122.11 W
Funkturm ᵾ 264a 52.31 N 13.16 E
Funne ≃ 263 51.42 N 7.36 E
Funnel Creek ≃ 166 22.18 S 148.57 E
Funnel Hill ∧2 272c 18.54 N 73.07 E
Funo 96 34.53 N 132.47 E
Funshinagh, Lough ⊜ 48 53.31 N 8.07 W
Funsi 150 10.17 N 1.58 W
Funtana Coberta ⊥ 71 39.34 N 9.21 E
Funtua 150 11.31 N 7.17 E
Funza 246 4.40 N 74.09 W
Fuorn, Pass dal (Ofenpass))(58 46.37 N 10.15 E
Fuping 102 34.47 N 109.07 E
Fuqiao 106 31.36 N 121.12 E
Fuqikou 100 29.44 N 117.48 E
Fuqing 100 25.44 N 119.22 E
Fuquay-Varina 192 35.35 N 78.48 W
Füramoos 58 48.00 N 9.53 E
Furancungo 154 14.55 S 33.35 E
Furano 92a 43.21 N 142.24 E
Furāt, Nahr al-
→ Euphrates ≃ 128 31.00 N 47.25 E
Furci Siculo 70 37.57 N 15.23 E
Furculești 38 43.52 N 25.09 E
Fures 62 45.19 N 5.30 E
Fūrg 128 28.18 N 55.13 E
Furkapass)(58 46.34 N 8.25 E
Furka-Tunnel -◆-5 58 46.33 N 8.26 E
Furlong 208 40.18 N 75.05 W
Furmanov 80 57.15 N 41.07 E
Furmanovka 86 44.17 N 72.57 E
Furmanovo 80 49.42 N 49.28 E
Furn, Wādī al- V 142 30.13 N 31.40 E
Furnace 46 56.09 N 5.10 W
Furnace Brook ≃ 283 42.06 N 70.43 W
Furnace Creek ≃ 284b 39.11 N 76.35 W
Furnace Pond ⊜ 283 42.03 N 70.49 W
Furnari 70 38.07 N 15.08 E
Furnas, Represa de ⊜1 255 20.45 S 46.00 W
Furn ash-Shubbāk 132 33.52 N 35.31 E
Furneaux Group II 166 40.10 S 148.05 E
Furness Abbey ᵾ1 44 54.07 N 3.12 W
Furness Fells ∧2 44 54.18 N 3.07 W
Furnes
→ Veurne 50 51.04 N 2.40 E
Furong Shan ∧ 100 27.30 N 115.52 E
Furqlus 130 34.36 N 37.05 E
Fürstenau, Dtsch. 52 51.50 N 9.19 E
Fürstenau, Dtsch. 52 52.31 N 7.40 E
Fürstenberg, Dtsch. 52 51.44 N 9.24 E
Fürstenberg, Dtsch. 54 52.09 N 14.40 E
Fürstenberg/Havel 54 53.11 N 13.08 E
Fürstenfeld 61 47.03 N 16.05 E
Fürstenfeldbruck 60 48.10 N 11.15 E
Fürstenhagen 56 51.12 N 9.41 E
Fürstenstein 60 48.43 N 13.20 E
Fürstenwalde 54 52.21 N 14.04 E
Fürstenwerder 54 53.24 N 13.34 E
Fürstenzell 60 48.32 N 13.19 E
Furtei 71 39.34 N 8.57 E
Fürth, Dtsch. 56 49.28 N 10.59 E
Fürth, Dtsch. 56 49.39 N 8.47 E
Furth im Wald 60 49.18 N 12.51 E

≃	River	Fluß	Río	Rivière	Rio
≋	Canal	Kanal	Canal	Canal	Canal
⌞	Waterfall, Rapids	Wasserfall, Stromschnellen	Cascada, Rápidos	Chute d'eau, Rapides	Cascata, Rápidos
꒰	Strait	Meeresstraße	Estrecho	Détroit	Estreito
c	Bay, Gulf	Bucht, Golf	Bahía, Golfo	Baie, Golfe	Baia, Golfo
⊜	Lake, Lakes	See, Seen	Lago, Lagos	Lac, Lacs	Lago, Lagos
≡	Swamp	Sumpf	Pantano	Marais	Pântano
▣	Ice Features, Glacier	Eis- und Gletscherformen	Accidentes Glaciales	Formes glaciaires	Acidentes glaciares
≄	Other Hydrographic Features	Andere Hydrographische Objekte	Otros Elementos Hidrográficos	Autres données hydrographiques	Outros acidentes hidrográficos

✢	Submarine Features	Untermeerische Objekte	Accidentes Submarinos	Formes de relief sous-marin	Acidentes submarinos
□	Political Unit	Politische Einheit	Unidad Politica	Entité politique	Unidade política
ᵾ	Cultural Institution	Kulturelle Institution	Institución Cultural	Institution culturelle	Institução cultural
⊥	Historical Site	Historische Stätte	Sitio Histórico	Site historique	Sitio histórico
♦	Recreational Site	Erholungs- und Ferienort	Sitio de Recreo	Centre de loisirs	Area de Lazer
⊠	Airport	Flughafen	Aeropuerto	Aéroport	Aeroporto
▪	Military Installation	Militäranlage	Instalación Militar	Installation militaire	Instalação militar
-◆-	Miscellaneous	Verschiedenes	Misceláneo	Divers	Diversos

Name	Page	Lat.	Long.
Furtwangen	58	48.03 N	8.12 E
Furuba ≃	256	23.21 S	44.57 W
Furubō-san ∧[2]	270	34.53 N	135.19 E
Furudal	26	61.10 N	15.08 E
Furudono	94	37.05 N	140.34 E
Furukawa, Nihon	92	38.34 N	140.58 E
Furukawa, Nihon	94	36.14 N	137.11 E
Furulund	41	55.46 N	13.04 E
Furusund	40	59.40 N	18.55 E
Furu-tone ≃	94	35.48 N	139.51 E
Furuvik	40	60.39 N	17.20 E
Furuyakami	268	35.55 N	139.32 E
Fürwiggestausee ⊜[1]	263	51.09 N	7.41 E
Fury and Hecla Strait ʉ	176	69.56 N	84.00 W
Fusagasugá	246	4.21 N	74.22 W
Fusain ≃	50	48.09 N	2.45 E
Fusan → Pusan	98	35.06 N	129.03 E
Fuscaldo	68	39.25 N	16.02 E
Fusch	64	47.13 N	12.49 E
Fuschl am See	64	47.48 N	13.18 E
Fuschun → Fushun	104	41.52 N	123.53 E
Fuse	268	35.53 N	140.00 E
Fuse → Higashiōsaka	96	34.39 N	135.35 E
Fushan, Zhg.	98	37.29 N	121.16 E
Fushan, Zhg.	102	35.58 N	111.51 E
Fushan, Zhg.	106	31.49 N	120.46 E
Fushimi ◆[8]	270	34.55 N	135.46 E
Fushino ≃	96	34.03 N	131.24 E
Fushuigang	100	31.21 N	113.40 E
Fushun (Funan), Zhg.	104	41.52 N	123.53 E
Fushun, Zhg.	107	29.11 N	105.00 E
Fushuncheng	104	41.53 N	123.51 E
Fusignano	66	44.28 N	11.57 E
Fusilier	184	51.51 N	109.46 W
Fusine in Valromana	64	46.30 N	13.39 E
Fusin → Fuxin	104	42.03 N	121.46 E
Fusio	58	46.27 N	8.40 E
Fusō	94	35.21 N	136.55 E
Fusong	98	42.18 N	127.20 E
Fussa	94	35.45 N	139.20 E
Füssen	64	47.34 N	10.42 E
Fuste, Picacho del ∧	196	27.35 N	102.47 W
Fusui	102	22.32 N	107.56 E
Futa, Passo della)(	66	44.05 N	11.17 E
Futaba	94	35.41 N	138.30 E
Futago-san ∧	96	33.35 N	131.36 E
Futamatagawa ◆[8]	268	35.28 N	139.33 E
Futamata → Tenryū	94	34.52 N	137.49 E
Futami, Nihon	94	34.30 N	136.47 E
Futami, Nihon	96	33.41 N	132.38 E
Futang, Zhg.	102	24.26 N	112.09 E
Futang, Zhg.	106	30.40 N	119.35 E
Futaoi-jima I	96	34.06 N	130.47 E
Futatabi-yama ∧	270	34.43 N	135.11 E
Futatsubashi ◆[8]	268	35.28 N	139.30 E
Futatsu-ne I[2]	174f	24.46 N	141.18 E
Fu Tau Pun Chau I	271d	22.21 N	114.22 E
Futian	100	27.26 N	114.56 E
Futianhe	100	31.30 N	115.05 E
Futianpu	100	27.22 N	112.47 E
Futjāni ≃	126	24.06 N	90.09 E
Futschou → Fuzhou	100	26.06 N	119.17 E
Futtsu, Nihon	94	35.19 N	139.49 E
Futtsu, Nihon	94	35.13 N	139.52 E
Futtsu-misaki >	268	35.19 N	139.46 E
Futun ≃	100	26.51 N	117.46 E
Futuna I	175f	19.32 S	170.14 E
Futuna, Île I	14	14.15 S	178.09 W
Futuyu	105	39.18 N	114.50 E
Fuveau	62	43.27 N	5.34 E
Fuwah	142	31.12 N	30.33 E
Fuwen	86	47.13 N	89.39 E
Fuxi, Zhg.	100	27.14 N	119.50 E
Fuxi, Zhg.	100	25.14 N	113.52 E
Fuxi ≃	107	29.09 N	104.57 E
Fuxian (Wafangdian), Zhg.	98	39.37 N	122.01 E
Fuxian, Zhg.	102	36.02 N	109.13 E
Fuxian Hu ⊜	102	24.30 N	102.55 E
Fuxin, Zhg.	104	42.03 N	121.46 E
Fuxin, Zhg.	104	42.08 N	121.45 E
Fuxing, Zhg.	107	30.27 N	106.04 E
Fuxing, Zhg.	107	30.24 N	104.53 E
Fuxing, Zhg.	107	29.54 N	105.43 E
Fuxingchang	107	29.40 N	105.13 E
Fuxing Dao I	269b	31.17 N	121.23 E
Fuxinghao	104	42.35 N	120.32 E
Fuyang, Zhg.	100	32.54 N	115.49 E
Fuyang, Zhg.	100	30.03 N	119.57 E
Fuyang, Zhg.	100	23.36 N	116.37 E
Fuyang ≃	98	38.14 N	116.05 E
Fuyouertuo Shan ∧	89	45.52 N	119.48 E
Fuyu, Zhg.	89	47.49 N	124.27 E
Fuyu, Zhg.	89	45.10 N	124.50 E
Fuyuan, Zhg.	89	48.21 N	134.18 E
Fuyuan, Zhg.	102	25.39 N	104.12 E
Fuzhai	100	29.32 N	120.02 E
Fuzhong	102	24.28 N	111.22 E
Fuzhou, Zhg.	100	28.01 N	116.20 E
Fuzhou (Foochow), Zhg.	100	26.06 N	119.17 E
Fuzhoucheng	98	39.45 N	121.47 E
Fuzhuang	98	34.57 N	118.17 E
Fuzhuangyi	98	38.02 N	116.08 E
Fyfield	42	51.45 N	0.16 W
Fylde □[8]	262	53.46 N	2.53 W
Fylde >[1]	44	53.47 N	2.56 W
Fyn □[6]	41	55.20 N	10.25 E
Fyn I	41	55.20 N	10.30 E
Fyne, Loch C	46	56.00 N	5.24 W
Fyns Hoved >	41	55.37 N	10.36 E
Fyresvatn ⊜	26	59.06 N	8.12 E
Fyrisån ≃	40	59.47 N	17.39 E
Fysingen ⊜	40	59.34 N	17.55 E
Fyvie	46	57.25 N	2.23 W
Fzâra, Gara'et ⊜	36	36.47 N	7.30 E
G			
Ga	150	9.47 N	2.30 W
Gaaden	264b	48.03 N	16.12 E
Gaalkacyo	144	6.47 N	47.26 E
Gaanderen	52	51.56 N	6.21 E
Gabah	144	8.08 N	50.02 E
Gabai	146	11.05 N	11.39 E
Gabaldon	116	15.28 N	121.19 E
Gabare	38	43.19 N	23.55 E
Gabarus	186	45.50 N	60.09 W
Gabarus Bay C	186	45.51 N	60.07 W
Gabas ≃	32	43.46 N	0.42 W
Gabbs	204	38.52 N	117.55 W
Gabby Heights	214	40.09 N	80.15 W
Gabela, Ang.	152	10.48 S	14.20 E
Gabel'a, Azer.	84	40.59 N	47.50 E
Gaberones → Gaborone	156	24.45 S	25.55 E
Gabès	148	33.53 N	10.07 E
Gabès □[8]	148	33.15 N	9.00 E
Gabès, Golfe de C	148	34.00 N	10.25 E
Gabia	152	4.34 S	17.07 E
Gabiarra	255	16.15 S	39.41 W
Gabicce Mare	66	43.58 N	12.46 E
Gabii ⊥	267a	41.54 N	12.43 E
Gabil	146	11.09 N	18.12 E
Gabilan Creek ≃	226	36.41 N	121.38 W
Gabilan Range ⋏	226	36.30 N	121.15 W
Gąbin	30	52.25 N	19.44 E
Gabir	140	8.35 N	24.40 E
Gable Mountain ∧	182	54.30 N	121.40 W
Gablenz	54	51.41 N	14.31 E
Gablingen	58	48.27 N	10.49 E
Gablitz	61	48.14 N	16.09 E
Gablonz → Jablonec nad Nisou	30	50.44 N	15.10 E
Gabon □[1], Afr.	138	1.00 S	11.45 E
Gabon □[1], Afr.	152	1.00 S	11.45 E
Gabon, Estuaire du C[1]	152	0.25 N	9.20 E
Gaborone	156	24.45 S	25.55 E
Gabras	140	10.16 N	26.14 E
Gabria	64	45.52 N	13.34 E
Gabriel	250	11.14 S	41.53 W
Gabriel Strait ʉ	176	61.45 N	65.30 W
Gabriel y Galan, Embalse de ⊜[1]	34	40.15 N	6.15 W
Gabriel Zamora	234	19.05 N	102.05 W
Gābrīk	128	25.44 N	58.28 E
Gabriola	224	49.12 N	123.50 W
Gabriola Island I	224	49.10 N	123.47 W
Gabrovo	38	42.52 N	25.19 E
Gabun → Gabon □[1]	152	1.00 S	11.45 E
Gaby	62	45.43 N	7.53 E
Gacé	50	48.48 N	0.18 E
Gachetá	246	4.49 N	73.36 W
Gachpar	174q	9.33 N	138.10 E
Gachsārān	128	30.12 N	50.47 E
Gackle	198	46.37 N	99.08 W
Gacko	38	43.10 N	18.32 E
Gad'ač	78	50.22 N	34.00 E
Gadag	122	15.25 N	75.37 E
Gadamai	140	17.09 N	36.06 E
Gādarwāra	124	22.55 N	78.47 E
Gadbjerg	41	55.46 N	9.20 E
Gäddede	26	64.30 N	14.09 E
Gadderbaum	52	52.00 N	8.31 E
Gade ≃	260	51.38 N	0.28 W
Gadebusch	54	53.42 N	11.07 E
Gadein	140	8.11 N	28.44 E
Gadera ≃	64	46.47 N	11.54 E
Gadevang	41	55.58 N	12.18 E
Gadilovići	76	53.05 N	30.16 E
Gadis ≃	114	1.03 N	98.55 E
Gadmen	58	46.44 N	8.21 E
Gado Bravo, Ilha do I	250	10.54 S	42.52 W
Gádor	34	36.57 N	2.29 W
Gadra	120	25.40 N	70.37 E
Gadrut	84	39.32 N	47.02 E
Gadsden, Al., U.S.	194	34.00 N	86.00 W
Gadsden, Az., U.S.	200	32.33 N	114.47 W
Gadwāl	122	16.14 N	77.48 E
Gadzi	152	4.47 N	16.42 E
Gaerwen	44	53.13 N	4.16 W
Găeşti	38	44.43 N	25.19 E
Gaeta	66	41.12 N	13.35 E
Gaeta, Golfo di C	66	41.06 N	13.30 E
Gaferut I	108	9.14 N	145.23 E
Gaffney	192	35.04 N	81.39 W
Gafour	36	36.18 N	9.19 E
Gafsa	148	34.25 N	8.48 E
Gafsa □[8]	148	34.15 N	8.25 E
Gafurov	85	40.14 N	69.44 E
Gag, Pulau I	164	0.27 S	129.52 E
Gagal	146	9.01 N	15.08 E
Gagarawa	150	12.25 N	9.32 E
Gagarin	76	55.33 N	35.00 E
Gage	196	36.18 N	99.45 W
Gagere ≃	150	13.21 N	6.23 E
Gages Lake	278	42.21 N	87.59 W
Gages Lake ⊜	278	42.21 N	88.00 W
Gagetown	186	45.47 N	66.09 W
Gagetown, Canadian Forces Base ■	186	45.43 N	66.15 W
Gaggenau	56	48.48 N	8.19 E
Gaggi	70	37.51 N	15.13 E
Gaggiano	62	45.24 N	9.02 E
Gaghamni	140	11.41 N	28.19 E
Gagil Tamil I	174q	9.32 N	138.10 E
Gagino	80	55.14 N	45.02 E
Gagliano Castelferrato	70	37.43 N	14.32 E
Gagliano del Capo	68	39.50 N	18.22 E
Gagnef	40	60.35 N	15.04 E
Gagnia	152	1.28 S	16.02 E
Gagnoa	150	6.08 N	5.56 W
Gagnon	176	51.53 N	68.10 W
Gagnon, Lac ⊜	206	46.07 N	75.07 W
Gagny	261	48.53 N	2.32 E
Gagra	84	43.20 N	40.15 E
Gagret	123	31.40 N	76.04 E
Gahanna	218	40.01 N	82.52 W
Gahlen	52	51.40 N	6.52 E
Gaiarine	64	45.52 N	12.29 E
Gaibandha	124	25.19 N	89.33 E
Gaichtpass)(	58	47.27 N	10.37 E
Gaigalava	76	56.40 N	27.18 E
Gaighāta	126	22.56 N	88.44 E
Gaijiatun	104	40.50 N	122.37 E
Gail	196	32.46 N	101.27 W
Gail ≃	64	46.36 N	13.53 E
Gailberg Sattel)(	64	46.43 N	12.58 E
Gail Creek ≃	222	31.07 N	95.23 W
Gaildorf	56	49.00 N	9.46 E
Gaillac	32	43.54 N	1.55 E
Gaillard, Château ⊥	50	48.09 N	1.54 E
Gaillard, Lac ⊜	186	50.06 N	68.47 W
Gaillard, Lake ⊜	207	41.21 N	72.46 W
Gaillefontaine	50	49.39 N	1.37 E
Gaillimh → Galway	48	53.16 N	9.03 W
Gaillon, Fr.	50	49.10 N	1.20 E
Gaillon, Fr.	261	49.02 N	1.54 E
Gailtaler Alpen ⋏	64	46.42 N	13.00 E
Gaima	164	8.20 S	142.55 E
Gaimán	254	43.17 S	65.29 W
Gaimersheim	60	48.49 N	11.22 E
Gaines, Mi., U.S.	216	42.52 N	83.54 W
Gaines, Pa., U.S.	210	41.45 N	77.34 W
Gainesboro	194	36.21 N	85.39 W
Gainesville, Fl., U.S.	192	29.39 N	82.19 W
Gainesville, Ga., U.S.	192	34.17 N	83.49 W
Gainesville, Mo., U.S.	194	36.36 N	92.25 W
Gainesville, N.Y., U.S.	210	42.38 N	78.08 W
Gainesville, Tx., U.S.	196	33.37 N	97.07 W
Gainford	44	54.32 N	1.44 W
Gainsborough, Sk., Can.	184	49.10 N	101.26 W
Gainsborough, Eng., U.K.	44	53.24 N	0.46 W
Gainsborough Creek ≃	184	49.10 N	101.02 W
Gaiole in Chianti	66	43.28 N	11.26 E
Gairatganj	124	23.24 N	78.13 E
Gairdner ≃	162	34.17 S	119.28 E
Gairdner, Lake ⊜	162	31.35 S	136.00 E
Gairloch	46	57.42 N	5.40 W
Gairloch, Loch C	46	57.44 N	5.44 W
Gairn ≃	46	57.03 N	3.05 W
Gais, It.	64	46.50 N	11.57 E
Gais, Schw.	58	47.22 N	9.27 E
Gaisberg ∧	64	47.48 N	13.07 E
Gaisbeuren	58	47.54 N	9.43 E
Gaital, Cerro ∧	236	8.37 N	80.07 W
Gaither	208	39.21 N	76.59 W
Gaithersburg	208	39.08 N	77.12 W
Gaixian	98	40.24 N	122.22 E
Gaizina Kalns ∧[2]	76	56.52 N	25.57 E
Gaj, Hrv.	36	45.29 N	17.02 E
Gaj, Ross.	86	51.27 N	58.27 E
Gajā	272b	22.52 N	88.10 E
Gajahmungkur, Waduk ⊜[1]	115a	7.55 S	110.55 E
Gajčur ≃	78	47.57 N	36.11 E
Gajendragarh	122	15.44 N	75.59 E
Gajiram	146	12.30 N	13.12 E
Gajny	24	60.15 N	54.15 E
Gājol	124	25.13 N	88.12 E
Gajsin	78	48.48 N	29.24 E
Gajsinghpur	123	29.40 N	73.27 E
Gajuapara ≃	250	4.17 S	47.25 W
Gajutino	76	58.42 N	38.32 E
Gajvoron	78	48.22 N	29.52 E
Gakarosa ∧	158	27.54 S	23.33 E
Gakona	180	62.18 N	145.18 W
Gākuch	123	36.10 N	73.45 E
Gakugsa	24	61.34 N	36.26 E
Gāla, Bngl.	126	24.18 N	89.54 E
Gala, Zhg.	124	28.16 N	89.23 E
Galaassija	128	39.52 N	64.27 E
Galāchipa	126	22.10 N	90.25 E
Galahad	182	52.31 N	111.56 W
Galamares	266c	38.48 N	9.25 W
Galán, Cerro ∧	252	25.55 S	66.52 W
Galana ≃	154	3.09 S	40.08 E
Galangue	152	13.48 S	16.09 E
Galanovo	80	56.09 N	54.07 E
Galanta	30	48.12 N	17.43 E
Galápagos □[4]	246a	0.30 S	90.30 W
Galápagos, Parque Nacional de ♠	246a	0.15 S	90.15 W
Galapagos Islands → Colón, Archipiélago de II	246a	0.30 S	90.30 W
Galaroza	34	37.55 N	6.42 W
Galas ≃	114	5.31 N	102.12 E
Galashiels	46	55.37 N	2.49 W
Galata ◆[8]	267b	41.01 N	28.58 E
Galata Köprüsü ◆[5]	267b	41.00 N	28.57 E
Galata Tower ʊ	267b	41.01 N	28.58 E
Galatea	172	38.25 S	176.45 E
Galați	38	45.26 N	28.03 E
Galați □[6]	38	45.45 N	27.45 E
Galatia	194	37.50 N	88.36 W
Galatia □[9]	130	39.30 N	32.40 E
Galatina	68	40.10 N	18.10 E
Galatone	68	40.09 N	18.04 E
Galatro	68	38.28 N	16.06 E
Galátsion	267c	38.01 N	23.45 E
Galatz → Galați	38	45.26 N	28.03 E
Galaure ≃	62	45.11 N	4.49 E
Gala Water ≃	46	55.37 N	2.48 W
Galax	192	36.39 N	80.55 W
Galaxídhion	38	38.22 N	22.23 E
Galbyn gov' ◆[2]	102	42.30 N	107.00 E
Galdhøpiggen ∧	26	61.37 N	8.17 E
Gale, Lac ⊜	190	46.46 N	76.51 W
Galeairy Lake ⊜	212	45.29 N	78.17 W
Galeana, Méx.	232	30.07 N	107.38 W
Galeana, Méx.	232	24.50 N	100.04 W
Galeão, Aeroporto do ⊠	256	22.50 S	43.15 W
Galeata	66	44.00 N	11.55 E
Galegu	140	12.36 N	35.02 E
Galeh Dār	128	27.38 N	52.42 E
Galela	108	1.50 N	127.50 E
Galena, Austl.	162	27.50 S	114.41 E
Galena, Ak., U.S.	180	64.44 N	156.57 W
Galena, Il., U.S.	190	42.25 N	90.25 W
Galena, In., U.S.	218	38.21 N	85.56 W
Galena, Ks., U.S.	198	37.04 N	94.38 W
Galena, Md., U.S.	208	39.20 N	75.52 W
Galena, Mo., U.S.	194	36.48 N	93.27 W
Galena, Oh., U.S.	214	40.12 N	82.52 W
Galena Park	222	29.43 N	95.13 W
Galenbecker See ⊜	54	53.38 N	13.43 E
Galeota Point >	241r	10.08 N	60.59 W
Galera ≃	248	14.25 S	60.07 W
Galera, Punta >, Chile	254	39.59 S	73.43 W
Galera, Punta >, Ec.	246	0.49 N	80.03 W
Galera, Punta de >	34	39.10 N	1.05 E
Galera Point >	241r	10.49 N	60.55 W
Galeras, Volcán ∧[1]	246	1.13 N	77.22 W
Galeria ⊥	267a	42.02 N	12.18 E
Galeria, Fosso la ≃	267a	41.48 N	12.21 E
Galesburg, Il., U.S.	190	40.56 N	90.22 W
Galesburg, Mi., U.S.	216	42.17 N	85.25 W
Gales Creek	224	45.35 N	123.12 W
Gales Creek ≃	224	45.29 N	123.06 W
Gales Ferry	207	41.25 N	72.04 W
Gales Point >	283	42.33 N	70.47 W
Galesville, Md., U.S.	208	38.50 N	76.32 W
Galesville, Wi., U.S.	190	44.04 N	91.20 W
Galeton	214	41.43 N	77.38 W
Galeville	210	43.05 N	76.10 W
Galgasc	144	0.11 N	41.38 E
Galgate	44	54.00 N	2.47 W
Galguduud □[4]	144	5.00 N	46.30 E
Galheiros	255	13.18 S	46.25 W
Gali	84	42.38 N	41.44 E
Gali, Torrente de ≃	266d	41.28 N	2.00 E
Galiano	224	48.52 N	123.21 W
Galiano Island I	224	48.56 N	123.29 W
Galibier, Col du)(	62	45.04 N	6.24 E
Galič, Ross.	80	58.23 N	42.21 E
Galič, Ukr.	78	49.08 N	24.43 E
Galicia □[4]	34	42.45 N	8.00 W
Galicia □[9]	22	49.00 N	22.00 E
Galičskaja vozvyšennost' ⋏[2]	24	58.25 N	42.20 E
Galičskoje, ozero ⊜	80	58.24 N	42.18 E
Galien	216	41.47 N	86.29 W
Galien ≃	216	41.48 N	86.45 W
Galilee	207	41.22 N	71.30 W
Galilee, Lake ⊜	166	22.21 S	145.48 E
Galilee, Sea of → Kinneret, Yam ⊜	132	32.48 N	35.35 E
Galilee → HaGalil □[9]	132	32.54 N	35.20 E
Galiléia	255	19.00 S	41.33 W
Galim	152	7.06 N	12.29 E
Galina Point >	241q	18.24 N	76.53 W
Galindo Creek ≃	282	37.58 N	122.02 W
Galion	214	40.44 N	82.47 W
Galion, Baie du C	240e	14.44 N	60.57 W
Galis	115a	7.08 S	113.33 E
Galisteo Creek ≃	200	35.31 N	106.22 W
Galite, Canal de la ʉ	36	37.20 N	9.00 E
Galiuro Mountains ⋏	200	32.40 N	110.20 W
Galiwinku	164	12.02 S	135.34 E
Galižana	64	44.56 N	13.52 E
Galka'yo	144	6.47 N	47.26 E
Galkhausen	263	51.05 N	6.58 E
Galkino, Kaz.	86	52.14 N	78.20 E
Galkino, Ross.	82	54.46 N	35.49 E
Galkino, Ross.	86	55.36 N	62.55 E
Gall'aaral	85	40.02 N	67.35 E
Gallan Head >	46	58.14 N	7.03 W
Gallarate	62	45.40 N	8.47 E
Gallardon	50	48.32 N	1.42 E
Gallatin, Mo., U.S.	194	39.54 N	93.57 W
Gallatin, Pa., U.S.	279b	40.12 N	79.53 W
Gallatin, Tn., U.S.	194	36.23 N	86.26 W
Gallatin, Tx., U.S.	222	31.54 N	95.09 W
Gallatin □[6]	218	38.45 N	84.51 W
Gallatin ≃	202	45.56 N	111.29 W
Gallatin Range ⋏	202	45.15 N	111.05 W
Galle	122	6.02 N	80.13 E
Gállego ≃	34	41.39 N	0.51 W
Gallegos ≃	254	51.36 S	68.59 W
Galles → Wales □[8]	28	52.30 N	3.30 W
Galleyend	260	51.42 N	0.29 E
Galley Head >	48	51.30 N	8.57 W
Galleywood	260	51.42 N	0.28 E
Galliano	194	29.26 N	90.17 W
Galliate	62	45.29 N	8.42 E
Gallicano	64	44.04 N	10.26 E
Gallicano nel Lazio	267a	41.52 N	12.49 E
Gallicchio	68	40.17 N	16.08 E
Gallico	68	38.10 N	15.41 E
Galliera Veneta	64	45.39 N	11.49 E
Gallinara I	62	44.02 N	8.14 E
Gallinas ≃	196	35.10 N	104.55 W
Gallinas, Punta >	246	12.28 N	71.40 W
Gallinas Creek ≃	282	38.01 N	122.30 W
Gallinas Peak ∧	200	34.13 N	105.45 W
Gallio	64	45.53 N	11.33 E
Gallipoli, Austl.	166	19.10 S	137.55 E
Gallipoli, It.	68	40.03 N	17.58 E
Gallipoli → Gelibolu	130	40.24 N	26.40 E
Gallipoli Peninsula → Gelibolu Yarımadası >[1]	130	40.20 N	26.30 E
Gallipolis	188	38.48 N	82.12 W
Gallitzin	214	40.28 N	78.33 W
Gallivaggio	58	46.21 N	9.21 E
Gällivare	24	67.07 N	20.45 E
Gallneukirchen	61	48.21 N	14.25 E
Gällö	26	62.55 N	15.14 E
Gallo, Capo >	70	38.13 N	13.19 E
Gallo, Lago del ⊜[1]	64	46.37 N	10.10 E
Gallo, Lago di ⊜[1]	58	46.37 N	10.10 E
Gallo, Laguna ⊜	258	35.30 S	58.28 W
Gallo Arroyo V	200	33.55 N	105.00 W
Galloo Island I	212	43.54 N	76.25 W
Galloupes Point >	283	42.28 N	70.53 W
Galloway □[9]	44	55.00 N	4.25 W
Galloway, Mull of >	44	54.38 N	4.50 W
Galloway Creek ≃, Md., U.S.	284b	39.18 N	76.23 W
Galloway Creek ≃, Mi., U.S.	281	42.39 N	83.12 W
Galluis	261	48.48 N	1.48 E
Gallup	200	35.31 N	108.44 W
Gallupville	210	42.40 N	74.14 W
Gallur	34	41.52 N	1.19 W
Gallura ◆[1]	71	41.00 N	9.13 E
Gally, Ru de ≃	261	48.53 N	1.53 E
Gälnan ʉ	40	59.31 N	18.45 E
Gålö I	40	59.05 N	18.17 E
Galop Island I	212	44.46 N	75.24 W
Galoppo, Ippodromo del ♠	266b	45.28 N	9.07 E
Galougo	150	13.50 N	11.04 W
Galsi	126	23.20 N	87.42 E
Galston	46	55.36 N	4.24 W
Galt, Mong.	88	48.46 N	99.53 E
Galt, Ca., U.S.	226	38.15 N	121.17 W
Gal Tardo	144	3.34 N	45.58 E
Galtat Zemmour	148	25.15 N	12.20 W
Galtelli	71	40.23 N	9.37 E
Galten	41	56.09 N	9.55 E
Galten C	40	59.27 N	16.09 E
Galtür	58	46.58 N	10.11 E
Galtymore Mountain ∧	48	52.22 N	8.10 W
Galty Mountains ⋏	48	52.25 N	8.10 W
Galūgāh-e Āsīyeh	128	34.01 N	59.55 E
Galugur	114	2.34 N	99.39 E
Galula	154	8.36 S	33.02 E
Galunggung, Gunung ∧	115a	7.15 S	108.03 E
Galuut	88	48.33 N	113.12 E
Galva, Il., U.S.	190	41.10 N	90.02 W
Galva, Ia., U.S.	198	42.30 N	95.25 W
Galva, Ks., U.S.	198	38.22 N	97.32 W
Galvarino	252	38.24 S	72.47 W
Galveston, In., U.S.	216	40.34 N	86.11 W
Galveston, Tx., U.S.	222	29.17 N	94.47 W
Galveston □[6]	222	29.20 N	94.53 W
Galveston Bay C	222	29.36 N	94.57 W
Galveston Island I	222	29.13 N	94.55 W
Gálvez	252	32.02 S	61.13 W
Gálvez ≃	248	5.12 S	72.53 W
Galvin, Austl.	274b	37.51 S	144.49 E
Galvin, Wa., U.S.	224	46.44 N	123.01 W
Galway (Gaillimh), Ire.	48	53.16 N	9.03 W
Galway, N.Y., U.S.	210	43.01 N	74.02 W
Galway □[6]	48	53.20 N	9.00 W
Galway Bay C	48	53.10 N	9.15 W
Gam (Jin) ≃	110	21.55 N	105.12 E
Gam, Pulau I	164	0.27 S	130.36 E
Gama, Isla I	254	40.29 S	62.12 W
Gamaches	50	49.59 N	1.33 E
Gamagōri	94	34.50 N	137.14 E
Gamalejevka	80	52.16 N	53.26 E
Gamaliel	194	36.38 N	85.47 W
Ga-Mankoeng	156	23.57 S	29.42 E
Gamare, Lake ⊜	144	11.30 N	41.40 E
Gamarra	246	8.20 N	73.45 W
Gamawa	146	12.08 N	10.32 E
Gamay	116	12.23 N	125.18 E
Gamay Bay C	116	12.21 N	125.21 E
Gamba	120	28.17 N	88.32 E
Gambach	56	50.28 N	8.44 E
Gambaga	150	10.32 N	0.26 W
Gambais	261	48.46 N	1.40 E
Gambaiseuil	261	48.45 N	1.44 E
Gambang	114	3.43 N	103.06 E
Gambara, It.	64	45.15 N	10.18 E
Gámbara, Méx.	234	18.55 N	102.05 W
Gambarie	68	38.10 N	15.50 E
Gambassi	66	43.32 N	10.57 E
Gambatesa	66	41.30 N	14.54 E
Gambela	144	8.18 N	34.37 E
Gambell	180	63.46 N	171.46 W
Gambellara	64	45.28 N	11.20 E
Gamber	208	39.27 N	76.56 W
Gambia □[1], Afr.	134	13.30 N	15.30 W
Gambia □[1], Afr.	150	13.30 N	15.30 W
Gambia (Gambie) ≃	150	13.28 N	16.34 W
Gambi Atrash	140	10.03 N	33.47 E
Gambie (Gambia) ≃	150	13.28 N	16.34 W
Gambie → Gambia □[1]	150	13.30 N	15.30 W
Gambier	214	40.22 N	82.23 W
Gambier, Îles II	6	21.20 S	136.30 W
Gamble Mansion State Historic Site ⊥	220	27.32 N	82.32 W
Gambo, Nf., Can.	186	48.46 N	54.14 W
Gambo, Centraf.	152	4.39 N	22.16 E
Gamboa	236	9.07 N	79.42 W
Gamboli	120	29.50 N	68.26 E
Gambolò	62	45.15 N	8.51 E
Gamboma	152	1.53 S	15.51 E
Gamboula	152	4.08 N	15.09 E
Gambrill State Park ♠	208	39.30 N	77.30 W
Gamchab ≃	156	28.15 S	17.26 E
Gamé	150	6.44 N	1.11 E
Game Creek ≃	285	39.41 N	75.28 W
Gamen-See ⊜	264a	52.40 N	13.51 E
Gaming	61	47.56 N	15.06 E
Gamka ≃	158	33.18 S	21.39 E
Gamlakarleby → Kokkola	26	63.50 N	23.07 E
Gamla Uppsala	40	59.54 N	17.38 E
Gamleby	26	57.54 N	16.24 E
Gamlitz	61	46.43 N	15.33 E
Gammel Estrup ⊥	26	56.26 N	10.21 E
Gammelstad ʊ[1]	26	65.38 N	22.01 E
Gammertingen	58	48.15 N	9.13 E
Gammon ≃	184	51.07 N	95.09 W
Gammon, Point >	207	41.36 N	70.16 W
Gammon Ranges National Park ♠	166	30.29 S	139.10 E
Gamō, Nihon	94	35.03 N	136.11 E
Gamō, Nihon	268	35.52 N	139.48 E
Gamoep	158	29.55 S	18.25 E
Ga-Mogara ≃	158	27.07 S	22.57 E
Gamo Gofa □[4]	144	5.45 N	37.00 E
Gamon	150	13.20 N	12.55 W
Gamova, mys >	89	42.35 N	131.12 E
Gamph, Slieve ⋏	48	54.05 N	9.00 W
Gampoko	273b	4.16 S	15.10 E
Gampola	122	7.10 N	80.34 E
Gampongbatak	114	4.48 N	97.39 E
Gampoui	273b	4.08 S	15.22 E
Gams	58	47.12 N	9.28 E
Gamsfeld ∧	64	47.37 N	13.29 E
Gamtoos ≃	158	33.58 S	25.01 E
Gamud ∧	144	4.05 N	38.03 E
G'amyš, gora ∧	84	40.18 N	46.23 E
Gan ≃, Zhg.	89	49.12 N	125.14 E
Gan ≃, Zhg.	100	29.12 N	116.00 E
Ganado, Az., U.S.	200	35.42 N	109.32 W
Ganado, Tx., U.S.	222	29.02 N	96.31 W
Ganano ≃	116	16.45 N	121.44 E
Gananoque	212	44.20 N	76.10 W

Symbols	ENGLISH	DEUTSCH			
∧	Mountain	Berg	Montaña	Montagne	Montanha
⋏	Mountains	Gebirge	Montañas	Montagnes	Montanhas
)(	Pass	Paß	Paso	Col	Passo
V	Valley, Canyon	Tal, Cañon	Valle, Cañón	Vallée, Canyon	Vale, Canhão
≚	Plain	Ebene	Llano	Plaine	Planície
>	Cape	Kap	Cabo	Cap	Cabo
I	Island	Insel	Isla	Île	Ilha
II	Islands	Inseln	Islas	Îles	Ilhas
⊥	Other Topographic Features	Andere Topographische Objekte	Otros Elementos Topográficos	Autres données topographiques	Outros acidentes topográficos

ENGLISH

Name	Page	Lat.°′	Long.°′
Gananoque ≃	212	44.19 N	76.09 W
Gananoque Lake ⊜	212	44.27 N	76.09 W
Ganaraska ≃	212	43.57 N	78.18 W
Ganargua Creek ≃	210	43.04 N	77.00 W
Ganassi	116	7.49 N	124.06 E
Ganāveh	128	29.34 N	50.31 E
Gancevići	76	52.45 N	26.26 E
Ganchangba	107	28.52 N	103.41 E
Ganči	85	39.58 N	69.08 E
Ganda, Ang.	152	13.02 S	14.40 E
Ganda, Zaïre	152	4.05 N	23.32 E
Gandadiwata, Bulu ∧	112	2.42 S	119.27 E
Gandajika	152	6.45 S	23.57 E
Gandak (Nārāyani) ≃	124	25.39 N	85.13 E
Gaṇḍakī □[8]	124	28.15 N	84.15 E
Gandara	258	35.26 S	58.06 W
Ganda Singhwāla	123	31.02 N	74.31 E
Gandāva	120	28.37 N	67.29 E
Gandavaroyi Falls ↳	154	17.17 S	29.07 E
Gānde	126	24.10 N	86.26 E
Gander	186	48.57 N	54.37 W
Gander ≃	186	49.15 N	54.30 W
Gander Bay	186	49.18 N	54.29 W
Gander Bay C	186	49.25 N	54.28 W
Ganderkesee	52	53.02 N	8.32 E
Gander Lake ⊜	186	48.55 N	54.40 W
Gandesa	34	41.03 N	0.26 E
Gandevi	120	20.49 N	72.59 E
Gand → Gent	50	51.03 N	3.43 E
Gāndhinagar	120	23.12 N	72.40 E
Gāndhi Sāgar ⊜[1]	120	24.18 N	75.21 E
Gandi	150	12.55 N	5.49 E
Gandi, Wādī V	140	11.23 N	24.31 E
Gandia	34	38.58 N	0.11 W
Gandino	62	45.49 N	9.54 E
Gando	152	12.30 S	17.25 E
Gandole	146	8.26 N	11.34 E
Gandou	152	2.24 N	17.27 E
Gandrange	56	49.16 N	6.08 E
Gandria	58	46.01 N	9.00 E
Gandu	255	13.45 S	39.30 W
Gandy Bridge ◆[5]	220	27.53 N	82.34 W
G'andžačaj ≃	84	40.54 N	46.28 E
Ganfang	100	28.40 N	114.51 E
Ganfosi	107	29.36 N	104.03 E
Gangādharpur	272b	22.36 N	88.11 E
Gangafani	150	14.23 N	2.24 W
Ganga → Ganges ≃	124	23.22 N	90.32 E
Gangājalghāti	126	23.25 N	87.07 E
Gangala-Na-Bodio	154	3.41 N	29.08 E
Gangalingolo	273b	4.20 S	15.09 E
Gan Gan	254	42.30 S	68.16 W
Gangānagar	123	29.55 N	73.53 E
Gangāpur, India	120	25.13 N	74.16 E
Gangāpur, India	122	19.41 N	75.01 E
Gangāpur, India	124	26.29 N	76.43 E
Gangara, Niger	150	14.36 N	8.30 E
Gangara, Niger	150	13.33 N	7.14 E
Gāngārāmpur	124	25.24 N	88.31 E
Ganga Sāgar	126	21.38 N	88.05 E
Gangaw	110	22.11 N	94.07 E
Gangāwati	122	15.26 N	76.32 E
Gangaw Range ⋏	110	24.50 N	96.40 E
Ganga-Yamuna Doāb ⋏[1]	124	26.40 N	79.30 E
Gangcheng	98	35.52 N	116.52 E
Gangdaba, Tchabal ∧	152	7.44 N	12.45 E
Gangdhār	120	23.57 N	75.37 E
Gangdisê Shan ⋏	120	31.00 N	82.00 E
Gangelt	56	50.59 N	5.59 E
Ganges, B.C., Can.	224	48.51 N	123.30 W
Ganges, Fr.	62	43.56 N	3.42 E
Ganges (Ganga) (Padma) ≃	124	23.22 N	90.32 E
Ganges, Mouths of the ≃[1]	120	22.00 N	89.00 E
Ganges Delta ≚[2]	124	23.00 N	89.00 E
Ganghu	120	32.05 N	86.45 E
Gangi	70	37.49 N	14.13 E
Gangkofen	60	48.26 N	12.34 E
Gangkou, Zhg.	100	29.45 N	115.44 E
Gangkou, Zhg.	100	29.12 N	113.19 E
Gangkou, Zhg.	100	29.21 N	117.58 E
Gangkou, Zhg.	100	22.38 N	113.22 E
Gangkou, Zhg.	100	22.36 N	114.54 E
Gangkou, Zhg.	106	30.44 N	118.54 E
Gangkouzhen	106	31.45 N	120.40 E
Gangmar Co ⊜	120	33.46 N	84.15 E
Gang Mills	210	42.08 N	77.06 W
Gāngnāpur	126	23.09 N	88.38 E
Gangneung → Kangnŭng	98	37.45 N	128.54 E
Gango ≃	152	9.48 S	15.40 E
Gangoa	102	37.15 N	100.28 E
Gangoh	124	29.46 N	77.15 E
Gangotri, India	120	31.01 N	78.27 E
Gangotri, India	120	30.56 N	79.02 E
Gangou	98	40.30 N	119.27 E
Gangoumen	98	41.40 N	116.35 E
Gangouyi	102	36.01 N	105.03 E
Gangqiao	107	30.13 N	105.22 E
Gang Ranch	182	51.33 N	122.20 W
Gangshangji	100	28.06 N	116.30 E
Gangtok	124	27.20 N	88.37 E
Gangtou	98	38.04 N	113.56 E
Gangtouli	106	31.42 N	119.02 E
Gangu	102	34.45 N	105.20 E
Gangwa, Zaïre	152	3.30 S	20.55 E
Gangwa, Zhg.	105	39.48 N	116.10 E
Gangwei	100	24.20 N	118.01 E
Ganhezi	86	44.08 N	88.32 E
Ganhu	102	44.33 N	94.09 E
Gani	164	0.47 S	128.13 E
Ganišob	85	39.03 N	70.47 E
Ganj Dundwara	124	27.44 N	78.57 E
Ganjiang	107	29.42 N	103.38 E
Ganlan Shan ∧	124	29.54 N	90.02 E
Ganlu	106	31.32 N	120.35 E
Ganluchang	107	29.54 N	104.47 E
Ganluo	102	29.03 N	102.59 E
Gannahoek	158	26.44 S	24.08 E
Gannan	89	47.54 N	123.30 E
Gannano, Lago di ⊜	68	40.19 N	16.26 E
Gannapan	158	30.23 S	22.12 E
Gannat	32	46.06 N	3.12 E
Gannett Peak ∧	200	43.11 N	109.39 W
Gannovka	83	48.33 N	38.35 E
Gannvalley	198	44.02 N	98.59 W
Ganpingsi	102	35.13 N	102.30 E
Ganpu	106	30.24 N	120.53 E
Ganq	120	37.25 N	92.15 E
Ganquan	102	36.25 N	109.16 E
Gansbaai	158	34.35 S	19.22 E
Gänsbrunnen	58	47.16 N	7.28 E
Gänserndorf	61	48.20 N	16.43 E
Gansevoort	210	43.12 N	73.39 W
Ganshoren	56	50.52 N	4.18 E
Ganspan	158	27.57 S	24.47 E
Gansu (Kansu) □[4]	102	37.00 N	103.00 E
Ganta	150	7.15 N	8.59 W
Gantan	100	29.37 N	119.34 E
Gantang, Zhg.	100	26.56 N	119.40 E
Gantang, Zhg.	102	22.58 N	109.00 E
Gantao ≃	98	38.01 N	114.07 E
Gante → Gent	50	51.03 N	3.43 E
Gantheaume, Cape >	166	36.05 S	137.27 E
Gantheaume Bay C	162	27.44 S	114.07 E
Gantheaume Point >	162	17.59 S	122.10 E
Gantiadi	84	43.24 N	40.06 E
Gantian	100	27.30 N	113.10 E
Gantt	194	31.24 N	86.29 W
Gantung	112	2.58 S	108.09 E
Gantung, Mount ∧	116	8.57 N	117.48 E
Gan'uškino	80	46.36 N	49.16 E
Ganwo	150	11.13 N	4.42 E
Ganxi, Zhg.	100	28.08 N	118.06 E
Ganxi, Zhg.	102	29.02 N	109.32 E
Ganyanchi	102	36.39 N	105.18 E

DEUTSCH

Name	Seite	Breite°′	Länge°′ E = Ost
Ganyesa	158	26.35 S	24.10 E
Ganyu (Qing Kou)	98	34.52 N	119.10 E
Ganzê	102	31.40 N	100.01 E
Ganzhenyi	100	30.33 N	113.21 E
Ganzhou, Zhg.	100	25.54 N	114.55 E
Ganzhou, Zhg.	100	28.49 N	115.25 E
Ganzhou → Zhangye	102	38.56 N	100.27 E
Ganzhuermiao	88	48.24 N	118.08 E
Ganzlin	54	53.23 N	12.15 E
Ganzo Azul	248	8.51 S	74.44 W
Gao	150	16.16 N	0.03 W
Gao □[4]	150	18.00 N	1.30 E
Gao'an	100	28.25 N	115.22 E
Gaobaita	271a	39.53 N	116.30 E
Gaobei	100	26.37 N	114.38 E
Gaobeidian	271a	39.54 N	116.33 E
Gaobu	100	27.48 N	117.01 E
Gaochang	107	28.49 N	104.24 E
Gaocheng, Zhg.	98	38.04 N	114.49 E
Gaocheng, Zhg.	100	31.57 N	113.25 E
Gaocheng, Zhg.	106	31.28 N	119.48 E
Gaochengzhai	104	41.24 N	123.43 E
Gaochun	106	31.20 N	118.52 E
Gaocun	98	37.05 N	122.12 E
Gaodianzi	102	30.40 N	110.01 E
Gao Feng ∧	106	30.34 N	118.40 E
Gaogongmiao	100	33.25 N	115.53 E
Gaogou	100	34.03 N	119.15 E
Gaohe	100	22.47 N	112.57 E
Gaohebu	100	30.44 N	116.50 E
Gaoil, Sliabh ∧	46	55.55 N	5.28 W
Gaojiabu	102	38.30 N	110.11 E
Gaojiadi	98	41.33 N	114.58 E
Gaojiadian	98	42.40 N	124.28 E
Gaojian	100	29.04 N	121.14 E
Gaojiapuzi	104	41.22 N	123.36 E
Gaojiaqiao	106	30.43 N	120.38 E
Gaojiatun	104	41.06 N	121.19 E
Gaojiawopeng	104	41.28 N	122.10 E
Gaojiawopu	104	41.50 N	122.47 E
Gaojiazhai	269b	31.23 N	121.33 E
Gaojiazhen	102	30.05 N	107.51 E
Gaokan	104	40.46 N	122.23 E
Gaokeng	100	27.40 N	113.58 E
Gaolan	102	36.25 N	103.56 E
Gaolan Dao I	100	21.55 N	113.15 E
Gaolao	104	41.54 N	120.59 E
Gaoli	105	39.17 N	115.38 E
Gaoliang	107	29.45 N	105.15 E
Gaoliban	104	41.39 N	121.58 E
Gaolifangshen	104	42.27 N	123.21 E
Gaolimen	98	40.22 N	124.02 E
Gaoling	105	40.32 N	117.01 E
Gaolinying	105	39.06 N	115.38 E
Gaoliying	105	40.10 N	116.29 E
Gaoliyingzi	104	41.56 N	124.17 E
Gaolong	100	26.56 N	113.45 E
Gaolou	105	39.59 N	116.50 E
Gaolouchang, Zhg.	107	29.51 N	104.41 E
Gaolouchang, Zhg.	107	30.03 N	105.58 E
Gaoluo	98	37.27 N	113.55 E
Gaomi	98	36.23 N	119.44 E
Gaona	252	25.12 S	64.05 W
Gaopi	100	24.14 N	116.39 E
Gaoping, Zhg.	102	35.48 N	112.52 E
Gaoping, Zhg.	107	30.28 N	105.45 E
Gaopingba	107	30.47 N	106.06 E
Gaoqiao, Zhg.	100	30.08 N	119.56 E
Gaoqiao, Zhg.	100	26.36 N	117.46 E
Gaoqiao, Zhg.	102	28.06 N	106.36 E
Gaoqiao, Zhg.	106	32.14 N	119.38 E
Gaoqiao, Zhg.	106	31.21 N	121.34 E
Gaoqiaomen	106	32.01 N	118.51 E
Gaoqiaozhen	104	40.55 N	121.00 E
Gaoqing (Tianzhen)	98	37.11 N	117.47 E
Gaoqipu	104	41.32 N	121.40 E
Gaosha	100	26.27 N	117.56 E
Gaoshaling	105	38.51 N	117.36 E
Gaoshan, Zhg.	100	25.29 N	119.34 E
Gaoshan, Zhg.	107	29.26 N	104.28 E
Gaoshanbao	105	40.40 N	117.29 E
Gaoshangbao	98	39.11 N	118.30 E
Gaoshanpu	102	27.10 N	105.14 E
Gaoshantai	104	42.22 N	122.28 E
Gaoshanzi	104	41.34 N	122.02 E
Gaoshengchang	107	29.59 N	105.31 E
Gaoshengzhen	104	41.20 N	122.12 E
Gaoshi	107	29.36 N	104.44 E
Gaoshikan	107	29.12 N	105.04 E
Gaosichang	107	30.17 N	104.52 E
Gaotai	102	39.20 N	99.58 E
Gaotaishan	104	42.02 N	122.52 E
Gaotan, Zhg.	100	30.23 N	117.23 E
Gaotan, Zhg.	100	23.12 N	115.22 E
Gaotan, Zhg.	102	32.22 N	108.36 E
Gaotang	98	36.54 N	116.14 E
Gaotangji	100	32.24 N	116.01 E
Gaotingsi	100	26.05 N	112.53 E
Gaotuozi	104	41.08 N	122.40 E
Gaoua	150	10.20 N	3.11 W
Gaoual	150	11.45 N	13.12 W
Gaoxian	102	28.20 N	104.38 E
Gaoxingru	100	26.28 N	115.14 E
Gaoxinji	98	34.11 N	115.33 E
Gaoya	98	36.22 N	118.49 E
Gaoyang	98	34.30 N	114.40 E
Gaoyapu	107	29.14 N	106.19 E
Gaoyi	98	37.36 N	114.36 E
Gaoyou, Zhg.	100	32.47 N	119.27 E
Gaoyou, Zhg.	100	28.25 N	115.31 E
Gaoyou Hu ⊜	100	32.50 N	119.20 E
Gaozhangjia	102	36.06 N	107.18 E
Gaozhou	102	21.55 N	110.50 E
Gaozi	106	32.11 N	119.18 E
Gaoziba	107	29.01 N	106.00 E
Gaozuo	100	33.57 N	118.03 E
Gap, Fr.	62	44.34 N	6.05 E
Gap, Pa., U.S.	208	39.59 N	76.01 W
Gapālnagar	272b	22.49 N	88.08 E
Gapan	116	15.19 N	120.57 E
Gapeau ≃	62	43.07 N	6.11 E
Gapern ⊜	40	59.31 N	13.40 E
Gar	120	32.11 N	79.59 E
Gar ≃	120	32.28 N	79.44 E
Gara, Lough ⊜	48	53.55 N	8.25 W
Garacad	144	6.57 N	49.19 E
Garachiné	246	8.04 N	78.22 W
Garadag	144	9.26 N	46.52 E
Gārādāha	126	24.14 N	89.34 E
Garagoa	246	5.05 N	73.21 W
Garaguso	68	40.33 N	16.14 E
Garah	166	29.04 S	149.38 E
Garai ≃[1]	126	23.32 N	89.31 E
Garaina	164	7.50 S	147.10 E
Gārākhola Madhukhāli	126	23.33 N	89.38 E
Garamba ≃	154	3.53 N	29.12 E
Garamba, Parc National de la ♠	154	4.10 N	29.30 E
Gara Muleta ∧	144	9.17 N	41.47 E
Garānberia	272b	22.24 N	88.34 E
Garancières	261	48.49 N	1.46 E
Garango	150	11.48 N	0.34 W
Garanhuns	250	8.54 S	36.29 W
Garapan	174n	15.12 N	145.43 E
Garara	164	8.37 S	148.17 E
Garautha	124	25.34 N	79.18 E
Garba	146	9.12 N	20.30 E
Garbagna	266b	45.23 N	8.39 E
Garbagnate Milanese	266b	45.35 N	9.05 E
Garbahaarrey	144	3.19 N	42.13 E
Garbatella ◆[8]	267a	41.52 N	12.29 E
Garba Tula	154	0.32 N	38.31 E
Garber	196	36.26 N	97.35 W
Garberville	204	40.06 N	123.47 W
Garbokaraj	88	54.09 N	99.52 E
Garboldisham	42	52.24 N	0.56 E
Garbsen	52	52.25 N	9.34 E
Garça	255	22.14 S	49.37 W
Garças, Rio das ≃	255	15.54 S	52.16 W

Symbols in the index entries represent the broad categories identified in the key at the right. Symbols with superior numbers (⋏[1]) identify subcategories (see complete key on page *I · 1*).

Symbole im Register stellen die rechts im Schlüssel erklärten Kategorien dar. Symbole mit hochgestellten Ziffern (⋏[1]) bezeichnen Unterabteilungen einer Kategorie (vgl. vollständiger Schlüssel auf Seite *I · 1*).

Los símbolos incluídos en el texto del índice representan las grandes categorias identificadas con la clave a la derecha. Los símbolos con numeros en su parte superior (⋏[1]) identifican las subcategorías (véase la clave completa en la página *I · 1*).

Les symboles de l'index représentent les catégories indiquées dans la légende à droite. Les symboles suivis d'un indice (⋏[1]) représentent des souscatégories (voir légende complète à la page *I · 1*).

Os símbolos incluídos no texto do índice representam as grandes categorias identificadas com a chave à direita. Os símbolos com números em sua parte superior (⋏[1]) identificam as subcategorias (veja-se a chave completa à página *I · 1*).

ESPAÑOL / FRANÇAIS / PORTUGUÊS

Nombre / Nom / Nome	Página / Page / Página	Lat.°′	Long.°′ W = Oeste / W = Ouest / W = Oeste
Garcevo	76	52.45 N	32.59 E
Garches	261	48.51 N	2.11 E
Garching	60	48.15 N	11.39 E
Garching an der Alz	60	48.08 N	12.34 E
Garchitorena	116	13.52 N	123.40 E
García	232	29.59 N	108.20 W
García, Laguna ⊜	288	34.58 S	58.09 W
García de la Cadena	234	21.09 N	103.28 W
García de Sola, Embalse de ⊜[1]	34	39.15 N	5.05 W
Garcia Hernandez	116	9.37 N	124.18 E
Garcias	255	20.34 S	52.13 W
Garcitas Creek ≃	222	28.51 N	96.46 W
Gard □[5]	62	44.00 N	4.00 E
Gard ≃	62	43.51 N	4.37 E
Gard, Pont du ◆[5]	62	43.56 N	4.36 E
Garda	64	45.34 N	10.42 E
Garda, Lago di ⊜	64	45.40 N	10.41 E
Gardabani	84	41.28 N	45.06 E
Gardanne	62	43.27 N	5.28 E
Garde, Lac la ⊜	190	46.46 N	78.14 W
Gardelegen	54	52.31 N	11.23 E
Garden ≃	190	46.32 N	84.09 W
Gardena	228	33.53 N	118.18 W
Gardena, Val ∨	64	46.35 N	11.35 E
Garden Acres	226	37.58 N	121.13 W
Garden City, Ga., U.S.	192	32.06 N	81.09 W
Garden City, Ks., U.S.	198	37.58 N	100.52 W
Garden City, Mi., U.S.	216	42.19 N	83.19 W
Garden City, Mo., U.S.	194	38.33 N	94.11 W
Garden City, N.Y., U.S.	210	40.43 N	73.38 W
Garden City, Tx., U.S.	196	31.52 N	101.29 W
Garden City Park	276	40.44 N	73.39 W
Garden City → Qasr al-Dubārā ◆[8]	273c	30.02 N	31.14 E
Garden City Raceway ♠	284a	43.09 N	79.11 W
Gardendale	194	33.39 N	86.48 W
Garden Farms	226	35.24 N	120.07 W
Garden Gate Village	282	37.20 N	122.02 W
Garden Grove, Ca., U.S.	228	33.46 N	117.56 W
Garden Grove, Ia., U.S.	190	40.50 N	93.36 W
Garden Home	224	45.27 N	122.45 W
Garden Island ❙, Austl.	168a	32.13 S	115.41 E
Garden Island ❙, Mi., U.S.	190	45.49 N	85.30 W
Garden Lakes	192	34.17 N	85.16 W
Garden Peninsula ≻[1]	190	45.45 N	86.35 W
Garden Plain	198	37.39 N	97.41 W
Garden Prairie	216	42.15 N	88.44 W
Garden Reach	126	22.33 N	88.17 E
Gardenside	218	38.03 N	84.33 W
Garden State Arts Center ⊍	276	40.24 N	74.11 W
Garden State Park Race Track ♠	285	39.55 N	75.02 W
Garden State Plaza ◆[9]	276	40.55 N	74.05 W
Gardenton	184	49.05 N	96.40 W
Garden Valley	226	38.51 N	120.51 W
Garden View	210	41.16 N	77.03 W
Gardenville	208	40.22 N	75.07 W
Gardermoen	26	60.13 N	11.06 E
Gardey	252	37.17 S	59.21 W
Gardeyz	120	33.37 N	69.07 E
Gardinas → Grodno	76	53.41 N	23.50 E
Gardiner, Me., U.S.	188	44.13 N	69.46 W
Gardiner, Mt., U.S.	202	45.01 N	110.42 W
Gardiner, N.Y., U.S.	210	41.41 N	74.09 W
Gardiner, Or., U.S.	202	43.43 N	124.06 W
Gardiner, Wa., U.S.	224	48.03 N	122.55 W
Gardiner Dam ◆[6]	184	51.17 N	106.51 W
Gardiner Range ⩕	162	23.50 S	131.46 E
Gardiners Bay ⊂	207	41.08 N	72.10 W
Gardiners Creek ≃	274b	37.50 S	145.02 E
Gardiners Island ❙	207	41.05 N	72.07 W
Garding	41	54.20 N	8.46 E
Gardner, Il., U.S.	216	41.11 N	88.18 W
Gardner, Ks., U.S.	198	38.48 N	94.55 W
Gardner, Ma., U.S.	207	42.34 N	71.59 W
Gardner Canal ⊂	182	53.28 N	128.15 W
Gardner Lake ⊜	207	41.31 N	72.13 W
Gardner Pinnacles ❙❙[1]	14	25.00 N	167.55 W
Gardnersville	218	38.46 N	84.30 W
Gardnertown	210	41.32 N	74.04 W
Gardnerville	226	38.56 N	119.44 W
Gardno	54	53.15 N	14.38 E
Gardolo	64	46.07 N	11.05 E
Gardon d'Alès ≃	62	44.02 N	4.08 E
Gardon d'Anduze ≃	62	44.02 N	4.08 E
Gardone Riviera	64	45.37 N	10.34 E
Gardone Val Trompia	64	45.41 N	10.11 E
Gårdsjö	40	58.52 N	14.19 E
Gårdskär	40	60.37 N	17.35 E
Gare Loch ⊂	46	56.01 N	4.48 W
Garelochhead	46	56.05 N	4.50 W
Gareloi Island ❙	181a	51.47 N	178.48 W
Garenfeld ◆[8]	263	51.24 N	7.31 E
Garenin	46	58.21 N	6.50 W
Gare Simon	273b	4.15 S	15.11 E
Garešnica	36	45.35 N	16.56 E
Garessio	62	44.12 N	8.02 E
Garet, Mont ∧[1]	175f	14.16 S	167.30 E
Garfield, Ks., U.S.	198	38.04 N	99.14 W
Garfield, N.J., U.S.	210	40.52 N	74.06 W
Garfield, N.M., U.S.	200	32.45 N	107.15 W
Garfield, Wa., U.S.	202	47.00 N	117.08 W
Garfield Heights	214	41.25 N	81.36 W
Garfield Mountain ∧	202	44.31 N	112.37 W
Garfield Park	285	39.42 N	75.33 W
Garfield Park ♠, Il., U.S.	278	41.53 N	87.43 W
Garfield Park ♠, Oh., U.S.	279a	41.26 N	81.36 W
Garfield Peak ∧	200	42.47 N	107.18 W
Garforth	44	53.48 N	1.22 W
Garga	88	54.26 N	110.33 E
Gargaliánoi	38	37.04 N	21.39 E
Gargano, Promontorio del ≻	68	41.50 N	16.00 E
Gargano, Testa del ≻	68	41.49 N	16.12 E
Gargantua, Cape ≻	190	47.36 N	85.02 W
Garga Sarali	152	5.11 N	14.00 E
Gargazzone (Gargazon)	64	46.35 N	11.12 E
Gargellen	58	46.58 N	9.56 E
Gargenville	261	49.00 N	1.49 E
Garges-lès-Gonesse	261	48.58 N	2.25 E
Gargnano	64	45.41 N	10.40 E
Gargouna	150	15.56 N	0.13 E
Gargrave	44	53.59 N	2.06 W
Gargždai	76	55.43 N	21.24 E
Garhākota	124	23.46 N	79.09 E
Garhbeta	126	22.51 N	87.19 E
Garhdīwāla	123	31.44 N	75.45 E
Garhi Habībullāh Khān	123	34.24 N	73.23 E
Garhi Jasaya	272a	28.46 N	77.16 E
Garhi Katiya	272a	28.45 N	77.16 E
Garhi Khairo	120	28.04 N	67.59 E
Garhi Malehra	124	25.02 N	79.40 E
Garhjāt Hills ⩕[2]	126	21.47 N	86.20 E
Garhmuktesar	124	28.48 N	78.06 E
Garhshankar	123	31.13 N	76.08 E
Garhwa	124	24.11 N	83.49 E
Gari	86	59.26 N	62.21 E
Garibaldi, Bra.	252	29.15 S	51.32 W
Garibaldi, B.C., Can.	182	49.58 N	123.09 W
Garibaldi, Or., U.S.	224	45.34 N	123.55 W
Garibaldi, Casa di ⊥	71	41.13 N	9.27 E
Garibaldi, Mount ∧	182	49.51 N	123.01 W
Garibaldi Provincial Park ♠	182	50.00 N	122.50 W
Garies	158	30.30 S	18.00 E
Garigliano ≃	68	41.13 N	13.45 E
Gariglione, Monte ∧	68	39.09 N	16.41 E
Garín	258	34.26 S	58.44 W
Garín, Arroyo ≃	288	34.23 S	58.43 W
Garin Regional Park ♠	282	37.38 N	122.03 W
Garipçe Burnu ≻	267b	41.13 N	29.07 E
Garissa	154	0.28 S	39.38 E
Garita Palmera	236	13.44 N	90.05 W
Gariya	272b	22.28 N	88.23 E
Gārji	272b	22.51 N	88.19 E
Garkida	146	10.25 N	12.36 E
Garko	150	11.38 N	8.48 E
Garland, Al., U.S.	194	31.33 N	86.49 W
Garland, Md., U.S.	284b	39.11 N	76.39 W
Garland, Pa., U.S.	214	41.49 N	79.27 W
Garland, Tx., U.S.	222	32.54 N	96.38 W
Garland, Ut,. U.S.	200	41.44 N	112.09 W
Garland Park ♠	275b	43.44 N	79.35 W
Garland Peak ∧	224	48.01 N	120.43 W
Garlasco	62	45.12 N	8.55 E
Garlate	62	45.49 N	9.23 E
Garlate, Lago di ⊜	58	45.49 N	9.24 E
Garliava	76	54.49 N	23.52 E
Garlieston	44	54.48 N	4.22 W
Garlin	32	43.34 N	0.15 W
Garm	85	39.02 N	70.22 E
Garm Āb	120	32.14 N	65.01 E
Garmal	144	8.35 N	50.19 E
Gärmersdorf	60	49.26 N	11.54 E
Garmī	128	39.01 N	48.03 E
Garmisch-Partenkirchen	64	47.29 N	11.05 E
Garmouth	46	57.40 N	3.07 W
Garmsār	128	35.20 N	52.13 E
Garnavillo	190	42.52 N	91.14 W
Garne	261	48.41 N	1.58 E
Garner, Ia., U.S.	190	43.06 N	93.36 W
Garner, N.C., U.S.	192	35.42 N	78.36 W
Garnet Range ⩕	202	46.45 N	113.15 W
Garnett	198	38.16 N	95.14 W
Garnijskij zapovednik ♠	84	40.00 N	44.55 E
Garnish	186	47.14 N	55.22 W
Garnock ≃	46	55.38 N	4.42 W
Garnpung, Lake ⊜	166	33.30 S	143.12 E
Gāro Hills ⩕[2]	124	25.30 N	90.30 E
Garona → Garonne ≃	32	45.02 N	0.36 W
Garonne ≃	32	45.02 N	0.36 W
Garoowe	144	8.24 N	48.29 E
Garou, Lac ⊜	150	16.04 N	2.45 W
Garoua, Cam.	146	9.18 N	13.24 E
Garoua, Niger	146	13.53 N	13.11 E
Garoua Boulaï	152	5.53 N	14.33 E
Garove Island ❙	164	4.40 S	149.30 E
Garpenberg	40	60.19 N	16.12 E
Garphyttan	40	59.19 N	14.56 E
Garphyttans Nationalpark ♠	40	59.17 N	14.51 E
Garqu Yan, Zhg.	118	34.29 N	92.35 E
Garqu Yan, Zhg.	120	33.50 N	92.28 E
Garraf, Costa de ⊥[2]	266d	41.16 N	2.02 E
Garrattsville	210	42.39 N	75.10 W
Garrel	52	52.57 N	8.01 E
Garret Mountain Reservation ♠	276	40.54 N	74.11 W
Garretson	198	43.43 N	96.30 W
Garrett, In., U.S.	216	41.20 N	85.08 W
Garrett, Ky., U.S.	192	37.28 N	82.49 W
Garrett Creek ≃	222	32.57 N	95.44 W
Garrett Park	208	39.02 N	77.05 W
Garrett Park Estates	284c	39.02 N	77.06 W
Garrettsville	214	41.17 N	81.06 W
Garrison, N. Ire., U.K.	48	54.25 N	8.05 W
Garrison, Ky., U.S.	218	38.36 N	83.10 W
Garrison, Md., U.S.	208	39.24 N	76.45 W
Garrison, Mt., U.S.	202	46.31 N	112.48 W
Garrison, N.Y., U.S.	210	41.23 N	73.56 W
Garrison, N.D., U.S.	198	47.39 N	101.24 W
Garrison, Tx., U.S.	222	31.49 N	94.30 W
Garrison Dam ◆[6]	198	47.22 N	101.25 W
Garron Point ≻	48	55.03 N	5.57 W
Garros	46	57.37 N	6.11 W
Garrovillas	34	39.43 N	6.33 W
Garry ≃	46	56.43 N	3.47 W
Garry, Loch ⊜	206	45.15 N	74.43 W
Garry Bay ⊂	176	68.55 N	85.05 W
Garry Lake ⊜	176	66.00 N	100.00 W
Gars am Kamp	61	48.36 N	15.40 E
Garsdale Head	44	54.19 N	2.20 W
Garsen	154	2.16 S	40.07 E
Garskolk	158	30.41 S	22.02 E
Gårslev	41	55.38 N	9.43 E
Garson	190	46.34 N	80.52 W
Garson Lake ⊜	184	56.19 N	110.02 W
Garstang	44	53.55 N	2.47 W
Garstedt	52	53.41 N	9.58 E
Garsten	61	48.01 N	14.24 E
Garston	260	51.41 N	0.23 W
Garston ◆[8]	262	53.21 N	2.53 W
Garswood	262	53.29 N	2.40 W
Gartempe ≃	32	46.48 N	0.50 E
Gartenstadt ◆[8]	263	51.30 N	7.26 E
Garthby Station (Beaulac)	206	45.50 N	71.23 W
Gartow	54	53.02 N	11.29 E
Gartrop-Bühl	263	51.40 N	6.49 E
Gartz	54	53.12 N	14.23 E
Garu	150	10.51 N	0.11 W
Garub	156	26.33 S	16.00 E
Garubhāsa	124	26.33 N	90.22 E
Gārulia	126	22.49 N	88.22 E
Garut	115a	7.13 S	107.54 E
Garve	46	57.37 N	4.42 W
Garvellachs ❙❙	46	56.14 N	5.47 W
Garvey Reservoir ⊜[1]	280	34.13 N	118.07 W
Garvie Mountains ⩕	172	45.30 S	168.50 E
Garwin	190	42.05 N	92.40 W
Garwolin	30	51.54 N	21.37 E
Garwood, N.J., U.S.	276	40.39 N	74.19 W
Garwood, Tx., U.S.	222	29.27 N	96.24 W
Gary, In., U.S.	216	41.35 N	87.20 W
Gary, S.D., U.S.	198	44.47 N	96.27 W
Gary, Tx., U.S.	194	32.07 N	94.22 W
Gary, W.V., U.S.	192	37.21 N	81.33 W
Garyarsa	120	31.44 N	80.21 E
Gary Harbor ⊂	278	41.38 N	87.20 W
Garyi	102	30.54 N	98.56 E
Gary Municipal Airport ⊠	278	41.37 N	87.25 W
Garysburg	208	36.27 N	77.33 W
Garz	54	54.19 N	13.20 E
Garza	252	28.09 S	63.32 W
Garza Ayala	196	26.29 N	100.02 W
Garza García	196	25.40 N	100.24 W
Garzas Creek ≃	226	37.13 N	120.57 W
Garzeno	58	46.08 N	9.15 E
Garzón, Col.	246	2.12 N	75.38 W
Garzón, Ur.	252	34.36 S	54.33 W
Gas	261	48.34 N	1.40 E
Gasan	116	13.19 N	121.51 E
Gasan-Kuli	128	37.27 N	53.59 E
Gas City	216	40.29 N	85.36 W
Gascogne □[9]	32	44.00 N	0.05 E
Gascogne, Golfe de → Biscay, Bay of ⊂	32	44.00 N	4.00 W
Gasconade	219	38.40 N	91.33 W
Gasconade □[6]	219	38.27 N	91.30 W
Gasconade ≃	194	38.40 N	91.33 W
Gasconade, Osage Fork ≃	194	37.45 N	92.26 W
Gascoyne ≃	162	24.52 S	113.37 E
Gascoyne, Mount ∧	162	24.58 S	116.38 E
Gascoyne Junction	162	25.03 S	115.12 E
Gash (Nahr al-Qāsh) ≃	140	16.48 N	35.51 E
Gashaka	146	7.21 N	11.27 E
Gasherbrum I ∧	123	35.43 N	76.43 E
Gas Hu ⊜	120	38.10 N	90.42 E
Gashua	146	12.54 N	11.00 E
Gasline	284a	42.53 N	79.11 W
Gasny	50	49.05 N	1.36 E
Gaspar	252	26.56 S	48.58 W
Gaspard Creek ≃	182	51.34 N	122.17 W
Gasparilla Island ❙	220	26.46 N	82.16 W
Gasparilla Sound ɥ	220	26.48 N	82.15 W
Gaspé	186	48.50 N	64.29 W
Gaspé, Baie de ⊂	186	48.46 N	64.17 W
Gaspé, Cap ≻	186	48.45 N	64.10 W
Gaspé Peninsula → Gaspésie, Péninsule de la ≻[1]	186	48.30 N	65.00 W
Gaspereau Lake ⊜	186	44.57 N	64.34 W
Gasperina	68	38.44 N	16.30 E
Gaspésie, Parc Provincial de la ♠	186	48.55 N	66.00 W
Gaspésie, Péninsule de la ≻[1]	186	48.30 N	65.00 W
Gaspoltshofen	60	48.08 N	13.46 E
Gasport	210	43.11 N	78.34 W
Gaspra	78	44.27 N	34.07 E
Gassan	150	12.49 N	3.12 W
Gas-san ∧	92	38.32 N	140.01 E
Gassaway	188	38.40 N	80.46 W
Gasse	64	47.23 N	11.09 E
Gasselte	52	52.57 N	6.46 E
Gassin	62	43.13 N	6.35 E
Gassino Torinese	62	45.08 N	7.49 E
Gassol	146	8.32 N	10.28 E
Gastein → Badgastein	64	47.07 N	13.08 E
Gasteiner Tal ∨	64	47.11 N	13.06 E
Gasteiz → Vitoria	34	42.51 N	2.40 W
Gastello	89	49.07 N	142.58 E
Gaston, In., U.S.	216	40.18 N	85.30 W
Gaston, N.C., U.S.	192	36.30 N	77.38 W
Gaston, Or., U.S.	224	45.26 N	123.08 W
Gaston, Lake ⊜[1]	192	36.35 N	78.00 W
Gastonia, N.C., U.S.	192	35.15 N	81.11 W
Gastonia, Tx., U.S.	222	32.37 N	96.24 W
Gastonville	279b	40.15 N	79.59 W
Gastoúni	38	37.51 N	21.16 E
Gastre	254	42.17 S	69.14 W
Gästrikland □[9]	40	60.30 N	16.27 E
Gat	132	31.37 N	34.47 E
Gata, Cabo de ≻	34	36.43 N	2.12 W
Gata, Sierra de ⩕	34	40.14 N	6.45 W
Gătaia	38	45.26 N	21.26 E
Gátas, Akrotírion ≻	130	34.34 N	33.02 E
Gatčina	76	59.34 N	30.08 E
Gate	196	36.51 N	100.03 W
Gateacre ◆[8]	262	53.23 N	2.51 W
Gate City	192	36.38 N	82.34 W
Gatehouse of Fleet	44	54.53 N	4.11 W
Gatersleben	54	51.49 N	11.17 E
Gates, N.Y., U.S.	210	43.09 N	77.41 W
Gates, N.C., U.S.	208	36.30 N	76.46 W
Gates □[6]	208	36.28 N	76.43 W
Gateshead	44	54.58 N	1.37 W
Gateshead Island ❙	176	70.22 N	100.27 W
Gates Mills	279a	41.31 N	81.24 W
Gates of the Arctic National Park ♠	180	67.45 N	153.30 W
Gatesville, N.C., U.S.	192	36.24 N	76.45 W
Gatesville, Tx., U.S.	222	31.26 N	97.44 W
Gateway	200	38.40 N	108.58 W
Gateway Arch ⊍	219	38.37 N	90.12 W
Gateway National Recreation Area ♠	276	40.34 N	74.06 W
Gateway of India ⊥	272c	18.55 N	72.50 E
Gaths Mine	154	20.00 S	30.31 E
Gathurst	262	53.34 N	2.42 W
Gatié Loumo	150	15.28 N	4.37 W
Gâtine, Hauteurs de ⩕[2]	32	46.40 N	0.50 W
Gatineau	212	45.29 N	75.38 W
Gatineau □[6]	212	45.25 N	75.45 W
Gatineau ≃	176	45.27 N	75.40 W
Gatineau, Parc de la ♠	188	45.30 N	76.05 W
Gatley	262	53.23 N	2.14 W
Gatlinburg	192	35.42 N	83.30 W
Gato, Arroyo del ≃, Arg.	288	34.51 S	57.56 W
Gato, Arroyo del ≃, Arg.	288	34.55 S	58.37 W
Ga'ton	132	33.00 N	35.13 E
Gato Negro	286c	10.33 N	66.57 W
Gatow ◆[8]	264a	52.29 N	13.11 E
Gatow, Flugplatz ⊠	264a	52.28 N	13.08 E
Gattendorf	61	48.01 N	16.59 E
Gattières	62	43.46 N	7.11 E
Gattinara	62	45.37 N	8.22 E
Gatton	171a	27.33 S	152.17 E
Gattorna	62	44.26 N	9.11 E
Gatún, Esclusas de ◆[5]	236	9.16 N	79.55 W
Gatún, Lago ⊜[1]	236	9.12 N	79.55 W
Gatvand	128	32.15 N	48.50 E
Gau-Algesheim	56	49.57 N	8.01 E
Gauchy	50	49.49 N	3.16 E
Gaucín	34	36.31 N	5.19 W
Gauer Lake ⊜	184	57.00 N	97.50 W
Gauguin, Musée ⊍	174s	17.45 S	149.23 W
Gauja ≃	76	57.09 N	24.16 E
Gaujiena	76	57.30 N	26.40 E
Gaukler Point ≻	281	42.27 N	82.52 W
Gaula ≃	26	63.21 N	10.14 E
Gauley ≃	188	38.10 N	81.12 W
Gauley Bridge	188	38.10 N	81.11 W
Gaultois	186	47.36 N	55.54 W
Gaunless ≃	44	54.40 N	1.41 W
Gau-Odernheim	56	49.47 N	8.11 E
Gaur	124	26.46 N	85.17 E
Gaurain-Ramecroix	50	50.35 N	3.29 E
Gaurambha	126	22.39 N	89.34 E
Gaurela	124	22.45 N	81.54 E
Gaurhāti	126	22.46 N	87.48 E
Gauribaradia	126	23.45 N	89.52 E
Gauribidanūr	122	13.37 N	77.31 E
Gauri Phānta	124	28.41 N	80.33 E
Gauripur	124	26.05 N	89.58 E
Gaurīśaṅgkar ∧	124	27.57 N	86.21 E
Gaurnadi	126	22.58 N	90.14 E
Gause	222	30.47 N	96.43 W
Gausta ∧	26	59.50 N	8.35 E
Gauthiot, Chutes ⌞	146	9.43 N	14.34 E
Gauting	60	48.04 N	11.23 E
Gavà	34	41.18 N	2.01 E
Gāvanpāda	272c	18.57 N	73.01 E
Gavardo	64	45.35 N	10.26 E
Gávdhos ❙	38	34.50 N	24.06 E
Gávea ◆[8]	287a	22.58 S	43.14 W
Gávea, Hipódromo da ♠	287a	22.58 S	43.13 W
Gávea, Pedra da ∧	287a	23.00 S	43.17 W
Gavel-Långsjön ⊜	40	59.50 N	18.18 E
Gavello	64	45.01 N	11.55 E
Gavet	62	45.04 N	5.52 E
Gavi	62	44.41 N	8.49 E
Gavia, Arroyo de la ≃	266a	40.21 N	3.40 W
Gavião ≃	255	14.06 S	41.01 W
Gavião, Pico do ∧	256	21.37 S	44.50 W
Gavien	164	3.54 S	144.07 E
Gavilán	286c	10.24 N	66.51 W
Gavinana	66	44.05 N	10.45 E
Gavins Point Dam ◆[6]	198	42.48 N	97.40 W
Gaviões	256	22.34 S	42.33 W
Gavirate	62	45.50 N	8.43 E
Gavja ≃	76	53.49 N	25.35 E
Gāv Khūnī, Bāṭlāq-e ⩦	128	32.10 N	52.50 E
Gävle	40	60.40 N	17.10 E
Gävleborgs Län □[6]	26	61.30 N	16.15 E
Gävlebukten ⊂	40	60.42 N	17.20 E
Gavnø	41	55.11 N	11.44 E
Gavoi	71	40.10 N	9.12 E
Gavorrano	66	42.55 N	10.54 E
Gavrilov-Jam	80	57.18 N	39.51 E
Gavrilovka	83	48.37 N	37.31 E
Gavrilovka Vtoraja	80	52.53 N	42.46 E
Gavrilov Posad	80	56.33 N	40.07 E
Gávrion	38	37.52 N	24.46 E
Gavry	76	56.55 N	27.53 E
Gawachab	156	27.03 S	17.50 E
Gāwān	124	24.37 N	85.55 E
Gaweinstal	61	48.28 N	16.35 E
Gāwīlgarh Hills ⩕[2]	122	21.20 N	77.00 E
Gawler	168b	34.37 S	138.44 E
Gawler ≃	168b	34.41 S	138.27 E
Gawler Ranges ⩕	162	32.30 S	136.00 E
Gawso	150	6.48 N	2.31 W
Gawsworth	262	53.13 N	2.10 W
Gawthorpe Hall ⊥	262	53.48 N	2.18 W
Gaxun Nur (Juyanhai) ⊜	102	42.22 N	100.34 E
Gaya, India	124	24.47 N	85.00 E
Gaya, Niger	150	11.53 N	3.27 E
Gaya, Nig.	150	11.53 N	9.02 E
Gay City State Park ♠	207	41.42 N	72.28 W
Gayéri	150	12.39 N	0.29 E
Gay Head	207	41.20 N	70.48 W
Gay Hill	222	30.16 N	96.30 W
Gaylord, Mi., U.S.	190	45.01 N	84.40 W
Gaylord, Mn., U.S.	190	44.33 N	94.13 W
Gaylordsville	207	41.38 N	73.29 W
Gayndah	166	25.37 S	151.36 E
Gays Mills	190	43.19 N	90.50 W
Gayton, Eng., U.K.	42	52.45 N	0.34 E
Gayton, Eng., U.K.	262	53.19 N	3.06 W
Gaza □[5]	156	23.30 S	32.45 E
Gaza → Ghazzah	132	31.30 N	34.28 E
Gazalkent	85	41.33 N	69.47 E
Gazaoua	150	13.32 N	7.55 E
Gaza Strip □[9]	132	31.25 N	34.20 E
Gazelle Channel ɥ	164	2.50 S	150.55 E
Gazelle Peninsula ≻[1]	164	4.40 S	152.00 E
Gazeran	261	48.38 N	1.46 E
Gazeran, Bois de ♠	261	48.40 N	1.45 E
Gazi, Kenya	154	4.25 S	39.30 E
Gazi, Zaïre	154	1.04 N	24.31 E
Gaziantep	130	37.05 N	37.22 E
Gaziantep □[4]	130	37.00 N	37.20 E
Gazimağusa (Famagusta)	130	35.07 N	33.57 E
Gazimağusa Körfezi ⊂	130	35.15 N	34.10 E
Gazimur ≃	88	52.57 N	120.22 E
Gazimurskij Zavod	88	51.33 N	118.22 E
Gazipaşa	130	36.17 N	32.20 E
Gazira Sporting Club ♠	273c	30.04 N	31.13 E
Gazivoda Jezero ⊜[1]	38	42.55 N	20.40 E
Gaznau	85	40.10 N	71.02 E
Gazoldo degli Ippoliti	64	45.12 N	10.35 E
Gazos Creek ≃	226	37.10 N	122.22 W
Gazzada	62	45.47 N	8.51 E
Gazzaniga	62	45.48 N	9.50 E
Gazzuolo	64	45.04 N	10.35 E
Gbangbatok	150	7.48 N	12.23 W
Gbanhala ≃	150	10.14 N	8.38 W
Gbaoui Bodanga	152	5.33 N	16.45 E
Gbarnga	150	7.00 N	9.29 W
Gbogbo	273a	6.36 N	3.31 E
Gboko	150	7.20 N	8.57 E
Gbon	150	9.50 N	6.27 W
Gbwado	152	3.54 N	20.46 E
Gcoverega	156	19.08 S	24.15 E
Gdańsk (Danzig)	30	54.23 N	18.40 E
Gdańsk □[4]	30	54.15 N	18.25 E
Gdansk, Gulf of ⊂	30	54.40 N	19.15 E
Gden'	78	51.20 N	30.25 E
Gdov	76	58.44 N	27.48 E
Gdyel	34	35.48 N	0.26 W
Gdynia	30	54.32 N	18.33 E
Gearhart	224	46.01 N	123.54 W
Gearhart Mountain ∧	202	42.30 N	120.53 W
Gearhartville	214	40.53 N	78.15 W
Geary, N.B., Can.	186	45.46 N	66.29 W
Geary, Ok., U.S.	196	35.43 N	98.22 W
Geauga □[6]	214	41.35 N	81.12 W
Geauga Lake Park ♠	279a	41.21 N	81.23 W
Geba ≃	150	11.46 N	15.36 W
Gebaberg ∧	56	50.36 N	10.16 E
Gebe, Pulau ❙	164	0.05 S	129.20 E
Gebeit Mine	140	21.03 N	36.19 E
Gebenbach	60	49.32 N	11.53 E
Gebesee	54	51.07 N	10.56 E
Gebi	84	42.46 N	43.30 E
Gebilu	144	10.35 N	41.28 E
Gebiz	130	37.06 N	30.56 E
Gebra	54	51.24 N	10.35 E
Gebweiler → Guebwiller	58	47.55 N	7.12 E
Gebze	130	40.48 N	29.25 E
Gecha	144	7.31 N	35.22 E
Gechang	106	31.05 N	119.27 E
Geçitkale	130	35.15 N	33.45 E
Gecun	106	32.10 N	119.37 E
Geddes, Mi., U.S.	281	42.16 N	83.40 W
Geddes, S.D., U.S.	198	43.15 N	98.41 W
Gede, Gunung ∧	115a	6.47 S	106.59 E
Gedera	132	31.49 N	34.46 E
Gedern	56	50.25 N	9.12 E
Gedian	100	30.32 N	114.38 E
Gedikler	130	39.06 N	38.49 E
Gediksaray	130	40.27 N	35.38 E
Gedi National Monument ♠	154	3.19 S	40.03 E
Gedinne	56	49.59 N	4.56 E
Gediz	130	39.02 N	29.25 E
Gediz ≃	130	38.35 N	26.48 E
Gedlegube	144	6.52 N	45.02 E
Gedo	144	8.58 N	37.27 E
Gedo □[4]	144	3.00 N	42.00 E
Gedongdalem	112	5.04 S	105.25 E
Gedongtataan	115a	5.23 S	105.05 E
Gedser	41	54.35 N	11.57 E
Gedser Odde ≻	41	54.34 N	11.59 E
Geduld	273d	26.15 S	28.25 E
Gedun	100	27.39 N	118.26 E
Geebung	171a	27.22 S	153.03 E
Gee Cross	262	53.26 N	2.04 W
Geehi	171b	36.24 S	148.11 E
Geehi ≃	171b	36.11 S	148.02 E
Geel	56	51.10 N	5.00 E
Geelong	169	38.08 S	144.21 E
Geelong West	169	38.08 S	144.20 E
Geelvink Channel ɥ	162	28.30 S	114.10 E
Geer ≃	56	50.51 N	5.42 E
Geeste ≃	52	53.32 N	8.35 E
Geesthacht	52	53.26 N	10.22 E
Geeveston	166	43.10 S	146.55 E
Gefell	54	50.26 N	11.52 E
Gefle → Gävle	40	60.40 N	17.10 E
Gefrees	54	50.06 N	11.44 E
Gegang	100	30.04 N	117.38 E
Gegenmiao	89	45.58 N	122.15 E
Gegong	100	30.05 N	117.11 E
Gegou	98	35.24 N	118.32 E
Gegu	105	38.59 N	117.30 E
Gehackte Berge ⩕[2]	264a	52.41 N	13.30 E
Gehrden	52	52.18 N	9.36 E
Gehren	54	50.39 N	10.59 E
Gehu	100	27.46 N	119.16 E
Ge Hu ⊜	106	31.36 N	119.51 E
Gehua	164	10.20 S	150.25 E
Geidam	146	12.57 N	11.57 E
Geiger	194	32.52 N	88.18 W
Geigertown	208	40.13 N	75.50 W
Geihoku	96	34.44 N	132.17 E
Geikie ≃	176	57.45 N	103.52 W
Geilenkirchen	56	50.57 N	6.07 E
Geilo	26	60.31 N	8.12 E
Geinō	94	34.48 N	136.25 E
Geiranger	26	62.06 N	7.12 E
Geisa	56	50.43 N	9.57 E
Geisberg ∧	60	49.53 N	11.03 E
Geisecke	263	51.27 N	7.37 E
Geisei	96	33.31 N	133.49 E
Geiselhöring	60	48.50 N	12.23 E
Geisenfeld	60	48.41 N	11.37 E
Geisenhausen	60	48.28 N	12.15 E
Geisenheim	56	49.59 N	7.58 E
Geisingen	58	47.55 N	8.38 E
Geislingen an der Steige	56	48.36 N	9.50 E
Geismar	52	51.31 N	9.57 E
Geispolsheim	58	48.31 N	7.39 E
Geisstein ∧	64	47.20 N	12.30 E
Geistenbeck ◆[8]	263	51.09 N	6.27 E
Geistown	214	40.17 N	78.52 W
Geist Reservoir ⊜[1], In., U.S.	218	39.56 N	85.56 W
Geist Reservoir ⊜[1], Pa., U.S.	285	39.57 N	75.24 W
Geisweid	56	50.55 N	8.01 E
Geita	154	2.52 S	32.10 E
Geithain	54	51.03 N	12.41 E
Geiyō-shotō ❙❙	96	34.10 N	132.45 E
Gejah	272a	28.31 N	77.23 E
Gejiatun	98	40.27 N	119.55 E
Gejiu (Kokiu)	102	23.22 N	103.06 E
Geka, mys ≻	180	64.26 N	178.10 E
Gela	70	37.04 N	14.15 E
Gela ≃	70	37.03 N	14.15 E
Gela, Golfo di ⊂	70	37.03 N	14.10 E
Geladandong ∧	120	33.16 N	91.27 E
Geladi	144	6.57 N	46.25 E
Gelai ∧[1]	154	2.33 S	36.05 E
Gelan	102	30.03 N	107.04 E
Gelang, Tanjong ≻	114	3.58 N	103.26 E
Gelaochang	107	29.36 N	103.39 E
Gelasa, Selat ɥ	112	2.40 S	107.15 E
Gelber Fluss → Huang ≃	90	37.32 N	118.19 E
Gelbes Meer → Yellow Sea ⊤[2]	90	36.00 N	123.00 E
Gelderland □[4]	52	52.10 N	5.50 E
Geldermalsen	52	51.53 N	5.17 E
Geldern	52	51.31 N	6.20 E
Geldrop	52	51.25 N	5.33 E
Geleen	56	50.58 N	5.52 E
Gelembe	130	39.10 N	27.50 E
Gelemso	144	8.48 N	40.35 E
Gelenau	54	50.42 N	12.58 E
Gelendost	130	38.07 N	31.01 E
Gelendžik	78	44.33 N	38.06 E
Gelfingen	58	47.13 N	8.16 E
Gelgaudiškis	76	55.05 N	23.00 E
Gelib → Jilib	144	0.29 N	42.46 E
Gelibolu	130	40.24 N	26.40 E
Gelibolu Yarımadası (Gallipoli Peninsula) ≻[1]	130	40.20 N	26.30 E
Gelibolu Yarımadası Milli Parkı ♠	130	40.05 N	26.10 E
Gelinden	56	50.46 N	5.15 E
Gélise ≃	32	44.11 N	0.17 E
Geliting	115b	8.39 S	122.18 E
Geliting, Teluk ⊂	115b	8.36 S	122.17 E
Gellénháza	61	46.46 N	16.47 E
Gellenstrom ɥ	54	54.28 N	13.03 E
Gellep-Stratum ◆[8]	263	51.20 N	6.41 E
Gellibrand ≃	169	38.41 S	143.09 E
Gellibrand, Mount ∧[2]	169	38.14 S	143.48 E
Gellibrand, Point ≻	274b	37.52 S	144.54 E
Gellibrand River	169	38.32 S	143.32 E
Gellingen → Ghislenghien	50	50.39 N	3.52 E
Gellinsoor	144	6.26 N	46.42 E
Gel'm'azov	78	49.49 N	31.49 E
Gelnhausen	56	50.11 N	9.11 E
Gelså ≃	41	55.19 N	8.54 E
Gelsdorf	56	50.35 N	7.02 E
Gelsenkirchen	52	51.31 N	7.07 E
Gelsenkirchen-Horst, Galopprennbahn ♠	263	51.32 N	7.02 E
Gelsted	41	55.24 N	9.59 E
Gelt ≃	44	54.56 N	2.47 W
Geltendorf	60	48.07 N	11.01 E
Gelterkinden	58	47.28 N	7.51 E
Gelting	41	54.45 N	9.53 E
Geltow	54	52.22 N	12.58 E
Geltsa	144	6.14 N	37.05 E
Geluji	98	37.08 N	121.50 E
Geluksburg	158	28.30 S	29.33 E
Geluwe	50	50.48 N	3.04 E
Gemas	114	2.35 N	102.37 E
Gembloux	56	50.34 N	4.41 E
Gembrook	169	37.57 S	145.33 E
Gemen	52	51.51 N	6.52 E
Gemena	152	3.15 N	19.46 E
Gémenos	62	43.18 N	5.38 E
Gemerek	130	39.11 N	36.05 E
Gemert	52	51.34 N	5.40 E
Gemla	26	56.52 N	14.38 E
Gemlik	130	40.26 N	29.09 E
Gemlik Körfezi ⊂	130	40.25 N	28.55 E
Gemolong	115a	7.24 S	110.50 E
Gemona del Friuli	64	46.16 N	13.09 E
Gemonio	62	45.53 N	8.40 E
Gemsbok National Park ♠	156	25.15 S	21.10 E
Gemünd	56	50.34 N	6.30 E
Gemünden, Dtsch.	56	50.03 N	9.41 E
Gemünden, Dtsch.	56	50.58 N	8.58 E
Gemünden, Dtsch.	56	49.54 N	7.28 E
Gen ≃	89	50.16 N	119.22 E
Genadendal	158	34.02 S	19.33 E
Genaibashi	268	35.21 N	140.04 E
Genale (Jubba) ≃	144	0.15 S	42.38 E
Genappe	50	50.36 N	4.27 E
Genarp	41	55.36 N	13.23 E
Genazzano	66	41.50 N	12.58 E
Genç	130	38.46 N	40.35 E
Gençay	32	46.23 N	0.24 E
Gencek	130	37.27 N	31.33 E
Gencsapáti	61	47.17 N	16.36 E
Gending	115a	7.48 S	113.18 E
Gendrey	58	47.12 N	5.41 E
Gendringen	52	51.52 N	6.22 E
Gendt	52	51.53 N	5.59 E
Genegantslet Creek ≃	210	42.18 N	75.48 W
Genemuiden	52	52.37 N	6.07 E
General ≃	236	8.59 N	83.11 W
General Acha	252	37.23 S	64.36 W
General Alvear, Arg.	252	36.03 S	60.01 W
General Alvear, Arg.	252	34.58 S	67.42 W
General Aquino	252	24.26 S	56.42 W
General Arenales	252	34.18 S	61.18 W
General Belgrano	252	35.46 S	58.30 W
General Bernardo O'Higgins ⊍[3]	9	63.19 S	57.54 W
General Bravo	232	25.48 N	99.10 W
General Butler State Resort Park ♠	218	38.40 N	85.10 W
General Cabrera	252	32.48 S	63.52 W
General Campos	252	31.32 S	58.24 W
General Carneiro	255	15.42 S	52.45 W
General Carrera, Lago (Lago Buenos Aires) ⊜	254	46.35 S	72.00 W
General Cepeda	232	25.23 N	101.27 W
General Conesa, Arg.	252	36.30 S	57.20 W
General Conesa, Arg.	254	40.06 S	64.26 W
General Daniel Cerri	252	38.42 S	62.24 W
General del Sur, Cementerio ◆	286c	10.28 N	66.55 W
General Elizardo Aquino	252	26.53 S	56.17 W
General Enrique Martínez	252	33.12 S	53.48 W
General Enrique Mosconi	252	22.36 S	63.49 W
General Escobedo, Méx.	196	25.49 N	100.20 W
General Escobedo, Méx.	232	25.30 N	105.15 W
General Eugenio A. Garay, Para.	248	20.31 S	62.08 W
General Eugenio A. Garay, Para.	252	25.55 S	56.11 W
General Galarza	252	32.43 S	59.24 W
General Güemes	252	24.40 S	65.03 W
General Guido	252	36.40 S	57.46 W
General Hornos	258	34.53 S	58.56 W
General Island ❙	116	9.25 N	126.00 E
General José de San Martín	252	26.33 S	59.21 W
General Juan José Ríos	232	25.40 N	108.40 W
General Juan Madariaga	252	37.00 S	57.09 W
General La Madrid	252	37.16 S	61.17 W
General Las Heras	258	34.56 S	58.57 W
General Las Heras □[5]	288	34.56 S	58.51 W
General Lavalle	252	36.24 S	56.58 W
General Leonidas Plaza Gutiérrez	246	2.58 S	78.25 W
General Levalle	252	34.01 S	63.56 W
General Lorenzo Vintter	254	40.44 S	64.29 W
General Luna	116	9.47 N	126.09 E
General MacArthur (Pambuhan Sur)	116	11.15 N	125.32 E
General Mansilla (Bartolomé Bavio)	258	35.05 S	57.45 W
General Manuel Belgrano, Cerro ∧	252	29.01 S	67.49 W
General Mitchell Field ⊠	216	42.57 N	87.54 W
General Motors Corporation (Pontiac Division) ⊍[3]	281	42.49 N	83.17 W
General Motors Proving Grounds ⊍[3]	281	42.35 N	83.41 W
General Motors Technical Center ⊍[3]	281	42.31 N	83.02 W
General'nyj ≃	265a	60.00 N	30.32 E
General O'Brien	252	34.54 S	60.45 W
General Pacheco	288	34.28 S	58.38 W
General Pánfilo Natera	234	22.40 N	102.06 W
General Paz	258	35.31 S	58.19 W
General Pico	252	35.40 S	63.44 W
General Pinedo	252	27.19 S	61.17 W
General Pinto	252	34.46 S	61.53 W
General Pizarro	252	24.13 S	64.01 W
General Roca	252	39.02 S	67.35 W
General Rodríguez	258	34.36 S	58.57 W
General San Martín, Arg.	252	37.59 S	63.34 W
General San Martín, Arg.	258	34.34 S	58.32 W
General San Martín □[5]	288	34.34 S	58.34 W
General Santos (Dadiangas)	116	6.07 N	125.11 E
General Sarmiento	258	34.33 S	58.43 W
General Sarmiento □[5]	288	34.32 S	58.43 W
General'skoje	83	47.28 N	39.35 E
General Terán	232	25.16 N	99.41 W
General Tinio	116	15.21 N	121.03 E
General Toševo	38	43.42 N	28.02 E
General Treviño	196	26.14 N	99.29 W
General Viamonte (Los Toldos)	252	35.01 S	61.01 W
General Villegas	252	35.02 S	63.01 W
General Vintter, Lago (Lago Palena) ⊜	254	43.55 S	71.40 W
General Warren Village	285	40.02 N	75.32 W
General Zuazua	196	25.54 N	100.07 W
Genesee, Id., U.S.	202	46.33 N	116.55 W
Genesee, Pa., U.S.	214	41.59 N	77.52 W
Genesee, Wi., U.S.	216	42.58 N	88.21 W
Genesee □[6], Mi., U.S.	216	42.56 N	83.41 W
Genesee □[6], N.Y., U.S.	210	43.00 N	78.11 W
Genesee ≃	210	43.16 N	77.36 W
Geneseo, Il., U.S.	190	41.26 N	90.09 W
Geneseo, Ks., U.S.	198	38.30 N	98.09 W
Geneseo, N.Y., U.S.	210	42.47 N	77.49 W
Gênes → Genova	62	44.25 N	8.57 E
Geneva, S. Afr.	158	27.50 S	27.08 E
Geneva, Al., U.S.	194	31.01 N	85.51 W
Geneva, Fl., U.S.	220	28.44 N	81.07 W
Geneva, Il., U.S.	216	41.53 N	88.18 W
Geneva, In., U.S.	216	40.35 N	84.57 W
Geneva, Ne., U.S.	198	40.31 N	97.35 W
Geneva, N.Y., U.S.	210	42.52 N	77.00 W
Geneva, Oh., U.S.	214	41.48 N	80.56 W
Geneva, Pa., U.S.	214	41.35 N	80.14 W
Geneva, Wa., U.S.	224	48.45 N	122.24 W
Geneva, Lake (Lac Léman) (Lac de Gèneve) ⊜, Europe	58	46.25 N	6.30 E
Geneva, Lake ⊜, Wi., U.S.	216	42.34 N	88.30 W
Geneva → Genève	58	46.12 N	6.09 E
Geneva-on-the-Lake	214	41.52 N	80.57 W
Genève (Geneva)	58	46.12 N	6.09 E
Genève □[3]	58	46.15 N	6.10 E
Genève, Lac de → Geneva, Lake ⊜	58	46.25 N	6.30 E
Genève-Cointrin, Aéroport ⊠	58	46.14 N	6.06 E
Genevois ◆[1]	58	46.03 N	6.14 E
Genévriers, Île des ❙	186	51.15 N	58.26 W
Genf → Genève	58	46.12 N	6.09 E
Genga	66	43.26 N	12.56 E
Gengenbach	58	48.24 N	8.01 E
Genghis Khan, Wall of ⊥, Asia	88	49.00 N	115.00 E
Genghis Khan, Wall of ⊥, Mong.	88	49.00 N	116.00 E
Gengji	100	33.47 N	112.47 E
Gengma	102	23.34 N	99.06 E
Gengputou	106	31.12 N	119.55 E
Gengzhuang	104	40.59 N	122.42 E
Geničesk	78	46.11 N	34.48 E
Génicourt	261	49.05 N	2.04 E
Génicourt-sur-Meuse	56	49.02 N	5.26 E
Genil ≃	34	37.42 N	5.19 W
Génissiat	58	46.03 N	5.47 E
Genk	56	50.58 N	5.30 E
Genkai	96	33.51 N	130.30 E
Genkai-kokutei-kōen ♠	96	33.54 N	130.31 E
Genkai-nada ⊤[2]	92	34.00 N	130.00 E
Genkanyj, chrebet ⩕	180	66.15 N	172.20 W
Genlis	58	47.14 N	5.13 E
Gennach ≃	58	48.10 N	10.43 E
Gennargentu, Monti del ⩕	71	40.01 N	9.19 E
Gennebreck	263	51.19 N	7.12 E
Gennep	52	51.42 N	5.58 E

Symbol	English	Deutsch	Español	Français	Português
≃	River	Fluß	Río	Rivière	Rio
≡	Canal	Kanal	Canal	Canal	Canal
⌞	Waterfall, Rapids	Wasserfall, Stromschnellen	Cascada, Rápidos	Chute d'eau, Rapides	Cascata, Rápidos
ɥ	Strait	Meeresstraße	Estrecho	Détroit	Estreito
⊂	Bay, Gulf	Bucht, Golf	Bahía, Golfo	Baie, Golfe	Baía, Golfo
⊜	Lake, Lakes	See, Seen	Lago, Lagos	Lac, Lacs	Lago, Lagos
⩦	Swamp	Sumpf	Pantano	Marais	Pântano
⊓	Ice Features, Glacier	Eis- und Gletscherformen	Accidentes Glaciales	Formes glaciaires	Acidentes glaciares
⊤	Other Hydrographic Features	Andere Hydrographische Objekte	Otros Elementos Hidrográficos	Autres données hydrographiques	Outros acidentes hidrográficos
✦	Submarine Features	Untermeerische Objekte	Accidentes Submarinos	Formes de relief sous-marin	Acidentes submarinos
□	Political Unit	Politische Einheit	Unidad Politica	Entité politique	Unidade política
⊍	Cultural Institution	Kulturelle Institution	Institución Cultural	Institution culturelle	Institução cultural
⊥	Historical Site	Historische Stätte	Sitio Histórico	Site historique	Sitio histórico
♠	Recreational Site	Erholungs- und Ferienort	Sitio de Recreo	Centre de loisirs	Area de Lazer
⊠	Airport	Flughafen	Aeropuerto	Aéroport	Aeroporto
■	Military Installation	Militäranlage	Instalación Militar	Installation militaire	Instalação militar
◆	Miscellaneous	Verschiedenes	Misceláneo	Divers	Diversos

ENGLISH | DEUTSCH

Name / Name	Page / Seite	Lat.°′ / Breite°′	Long.°′ / Länge°′ E = Ost
Genner	41	55.07 N	9.26 E
Gennes	32	47.20 N	0.14 W
Gennevilliers	261	48.56 N	2.18 E
Genoa, Austl.	166	37.29 S	149.35 E
Genoa, Il., U.S.	216	42.05 N	88.41 W
Genoa, Ne., U.S.	198	41.26 N	97.43 W
Genoa, Nv., U.S.	226	39.00 N	119.50 W
Genoa, N.Y., U.S.	210	42.40 N	76.32 W
Genoa, Oh., U.S.	214	41.31 N	83.21 W
Genoa, Wi., U.S.	190	43.34 N	91.13 W
Genoa, Arroyo ≃	254	44.58 S	70.06 W
Genoa City	216	42.29 N	88.19 W
Genoa → Genova	62	44.25 N	8.57 E
Genoa Peak ∧	226	39.03 N	119.53 W
Genola	62	44.35 N	7.39 E
Génolhac	62	44.21 N	3.57 E
Genova (Genoa)	62	44.25 N	8.57 E
Genova □ 4	62	44.30 N	9.04 E
Genova, Golfo di c	62	44.10 N	8.55 E
Genova, Val V	64	46.11 N	10.40 E
Genovesa, Isla I	246a	0.20 N	89.58 W
Genrijetty, ostrov I	74	77.06 N	156.30 E
Gensan → Wŏnsan	98	39.09 N	127.25 E
Gens de Terre ≃	190	46.53 N	76.00 W
Genshagen	264a	52.19 N	13.19 E
Genshagener Heide ◆ 3	264a	52.20 N	13.18 E
Genshiryoku-kenkyūsho ʊ 3	94	36.27 N	140.36 E
Gensingen	56	49.53 N	7.55 E
Gensungen	56	51.08 N	9.26 E
Gent (Gand)	50	51.03 N	3.43 E
Gentbrugge	50	51.03 N	3.45 E
Gent-Brugge, Kanaal ≍	50	51.03 N	3.43 E
Genteng	115a	8.22 S	114.09 E
Genteng, Gili I	115a	7.12 S	113.54 E
Genteng, Tanjung ≻	115a	7.23 S	106.24 E
Genthin	54	52.24 N	12.09 E
Gentilly	261	48.49 N	2.21 E
Gentilly ≃	206	46.24 N	72.21 W
Genting	114	3.42 N	98.10 E
Gentio do Ouro	250	11.25 S	42.30 W
Gentioux	32	45.47 N	1.59 E
Gentofte	41	55.45 N	12.33 E
Gentry	194	36.16 N	94.29 W
Gentry, Lake ⊜	220	28.08 N	81.15 W
Genua → Genova	62	44.25 N	8.57 E
Genuang	114	2.29 N	102.53 E
Genval	50	50.43 N	4.29 E
Genyem	164	2.46 S	140.12 E
Genzano di Lucania	68	40.51 N	16.02 E
Genzano di Roma	66	41.42 N	12.41 E
Geographe Bay c	162	33.35 S	115.15 E
Geographe Channel ꓤ	162	24.40 S	113.20 E
Geokčaj	84	40.39 N	47.44 E
Geokčaj ≃	84	40.39 N	47.45 E
Geok-Tepe	128	38.09 N	57.58 E
Geonkhāli	126	22.12 N	88.03 E
George, S. Afr.	158	33.58 S	22.24 E
George, Ia., U.S.	198	43.20 N	96.00 W
George, Tx., U.S.	222	30.59 N	96.07 W
George ≃, Austl.	162	20.50 S	117.28 E
George ≃, P.Q., Can.	176	58.49 N	66.10 W
George, Cape ≻	186	45.53 N	61.53 W
George, Lake ⊜, Austl.	162	22.37 S	123.38 E
George, Lake ⊜, Austl.	166	35.05 S	149.25 E
George, Lake ⊜, N.A.	190	46.28 N	84.10 W
George, Lake ⊜, Ug.	154	0.02 N	30.12 E
George, Lake ⊜, U.S.	216	41.45 N	85.00 W
George, Lake ⊜, Fl., U.S.	192	29.17 N	81.36 W
George, Lake ⊜, In., U.S.	216	41.40 N	87.30 W
George, Lake ⊜, N.Y., U.S.	188	43.35 N	73.35 W
George Air Force Base ■	228	34.35 N	117.22 W
George B. Stevenson Dam ◆ 6	214	41.25 N	78.01 W
George Gill Range ⋏	162	24.15 S	131.36 E
George H. Crosby Manitou State Park ♠	190	47.29 N	91.10 W
George Island I	254	52.19 S	59.45 W
George Mason University ʊ 2	284c	38.50 N	77.17 W
Georgensgmünd	56	49.11 N	11.00 E
Georgenthal	54	50.49 N	10.40 E
Georges ≃	170	33.57 S	150.58 E
Georges Bank ✣ 4	16	41.15 N	67.30 W
Georges Island I	283	42.19 N	70.56 W
George Sound ꓤ	172	44.50 S	167.23 E
Georges River Bridge ◆ 5	274a	34.00 S	151.07 E
Georges Run	214	40.21 N	80.37 W
Georges Run ≃	279b	40.23 N	80.06 W
Georgetown, Austl.	166	18.18 S	143.33 E
George Town, Austl.	166	41.06 S	146.50 E
Georgetown, P.E., Can.	186	46.11 N	62.32 W
George Town, Cay. Is.	238	19.18 N	81.23 W
Georgetown, Gam.	150	13.30 N	14.47 W
Georgetown, Guy.	246	6.48 N	58.10 W
George Town (Pinang), Malay.	114	5.25 N	100.20 E
Georgetown, St. Vin.	241h	13.16 N	61.08 W
Georgetown, Ca., U.S.	226	38.54 N	120.50 W
Georgetown, Co., U.S.	200	39.42 N	105.41 W
Georgetown, Ct., U.S.	207	41.15 N	73.26 W
Georgetown, De., U.S.	208	38.41 N	75.23 W
Georgetown, Fl., U.S.	192	29.23 N	81.38 W
Georgetown, Ga., U.S.	192	31.53 N	85.06 W
Georgetown, Id., U.S.	202	42.29 N	111.22 W
Georgetown, Il., U.S.	194	39.58 N	87.38 W
Georgetown, In., U.S.	218	38.17 N	85.58 W
Georgetown, Ky., U.S.	218	38.12 N	84.33 W
Georgetown, Ma., U.S.	207	42.43 N	70.59 W
Georgetown, Ms., U.S.	194	31.52 N	90.09 W
Georgetown, N.J., U.S.	285	40.04 N	74.39 W
Georgetown, N.Y., U.S.	210	42.46 N	75.44 W
Georgetown, Oh., U.S.	218	38.51 N	83.54 W
Georgetown, Pa., U.S.	214	40.39 N	80.30 W
Georgetown, S.C., U.S.	192	33.22 N	79.17 W
Georgetown, Tx., U.S.	222	30.37 N	97.40 W
Georgetown ◆ 8	284c	38.54 N	77.03 W
Georgetown, Lake ⊜ 1	222	30.40 N	97.45 W
Georgetown → Halton Hills	190	43.37 N	79.56 W
Georgetown Lake ⊜	202	46.11 N	113.17 W
Georgetown Rowley State Forest ♠	283	42.42 N	70.58 W
Georgetown University ʊ 2	284c	38.54 N	77.04 W
George V Coast ⩡ 2	9	68.30 S	147.30 E
George VI Sound ꓤ	9	71.00 S	68.00 W
George Washington Birthplace National Monument ♠	208	38.11 N	76.56 W
George Washington Bridge ◆ 5	276	40.51 N	73.57 W
George Washington Carver National Monument ♠	194	37.00 N	94.19 W
George West	196	28.19 N	98.07 W
Georg Forster ʊ 3	9	70.47 S	11.51 E
Georgia □ 1, Asia	72	42.00 N	44.00 E
Georgia □ 1, Asia	84	42.00 N	44.00 E
Georgia □ 3, U.S.	178	32.50 N	83.15 W
Georgia □ 3, U.S.	192	32.50 N	83.15 W
Georgia, Strait of ꓤ	182	49.20 N	124.00 W
Georgia del Sur, Isla de → South Georgia I	244	54.15 S	36.45 W
Georgiana	194	31.38 N	86.44 W
Georgian Bay c	190	45.15 N	80.50 W
Georgian Bay Islands National Park ♠	190	44.54 N	79.52 W
Géorgie du Sud → South Georgia I	244	54.15 S	36.45 W
Georgijevka, Kaz.	85	43.03 N	74.43 E
Georgijevka, Kaz.	85	42.11 N	70.00 E
Georgijevka, Kaz.	86	49.19 N	81.35 E
Georgijevka, Ross.	80	53.18 N	51.01 E
Georgijevka, Ukr.	83	48.26 N	39.17 E
Georgijevsk	84	44.09 N	43.28 E
Georgina ≃	166	23.30 S	139.47 E
Georgina Island I	212	44.23 N	79.17 W
Georgina Island Indian Reserve ◆ 4	212	44.22 N	79.19 W
Georgsmarienhütte	52	52.12 N	8.02 E
Georg von Neumayer ʊ 3	9	70.37 S	8.22 W
Gera	54	50.52 N	12.04 E
Gera ≃	54	51.08 N	10.56 E
Geraardsbergen	50	50.46 N	3.52 E
Geraberg	54	50.43 N	10.50 E
Gerabronn	56	49.15 N	9.55 E
Gerace	68	38.16 N	16.13 E
Geraci Siculo	70	37.51 N	14.09 E
Geral, Serra ⩡ 4, Bra.	250	11.15 S	46.30 W
Geral, Serra ⩡ 4, Bra.	252	26.30 S	50.30 W
Gerald	219	38.23 N	91.19 W
Geral de Goiás, Serra ⩡ 4	242	13.00 S	46.15 W
Geraldine, N.Z.	172	44.05 S	171.14 E
Geraldine, Mt., U.S.	202	47.36 N	110.15 W
Geraldton, Austl.	162	28.46 S	114.36 E
Geraldton, On., Can.	176	49.44 N	86.57 W
Gerar, Naḥal V	132	31.24 N	34.26 E
Gerard, Lake ⊜	276	41.06 N	74.33 W
Gerard, Mount ∧	162	27.13 S	122.41 E
Gérardmer	58	48.04 N	6.53 E
Geras	61	48.48 N	15.40 E
Gerasa ⊥	132	32.17 N	35.53 E
Gerasdorf	61	48.18 N	16.28 E
Gerasimovka	86	58.37 N	71.53 E
Gerber	204	40.03 N	122.08 W
Gerber Reservoir ⊜ 1	202	42.12 N	121.06 W
Gerbéviller	58	48.30 N	6.31 E
Gerblingerode	52	51.29 N	10.15 E
Gerbstedt	54	51.38 N	11.37 E
Gerca	78	48.09 N	26.16 E
Gerchsheim	56	49.42 N	9.47 E
Gercüş	130	37.34 N	41.23 E
Gerdau	158	26.28 S	26.06 E
Gerdine, Mount ∧	180	61.35 N	152.26 W
Gerdview	273d	26.10 S	28.11 E
Gère ≃	62	45.32 N	4.54 E
Gerede	130	40.48 N	32.12 E
Gereja Cathedral ʊ 1	269e	6.10 S	106.49 E
Gerenzano	266b	45.38 N	9.00 E
Gereshk	120	31.48 N	64.34 E
Geretsried	64	47.51 N	11.28 E
Gérgal	34	37.07 N	2.33 W
Gerge'bil	84	42.31 N	47.05 E
Gerger	130	37.57 N	39.01 E
Geria Nij	126	23.56 N	86.55 E
Gerik	114	5.25 N	101.08 E
Gering	198	41.49 N	103.39 W
Geringswalde	54	51.04 N	12.54 E
Geriş	130	36.58 N	31.44 E
Gerlachovský štít ∧	30	49.12 N	20.08 E
Gerlafingen	58	47.10 N	7.34 E
Gerli ◆ 8	288	34.41 S	58.23 W
Gerlingen	56	48.48 N	9.03 E
Gerlos	64	47.14 N	12.02 E
Gerlospass)(	64	47.14 N	12.08 E
Gerlova Hut'	60	49.10 N	13.17 E
Germa (Jarmah) ⊥	146	26.33 N	13.04 E
Germagnano	62	45.15 N	7.28 E
Germain, Grand lac ⊜	186	51.12 N	66.41 W
Germania	214	41.39 N	77.40 W
Germano	214	40.25 N	80.57 W
Germanoviči	76	55.25 N	27.44 E
Germansen, Mount ∧	182	55.37 N	124.50 W
Germansen Lake ⊜	182	55.41 N	124.53 W
Germansen Landing	182	55.47 N	124.43 W
Germansville	208	40.42 N	75.42 W
Germantown, Il., U.S.	219	38.33 N	89.32 W
Germantown, Ky., U.S.	218	38.39 N	83.57 W
Germantown, N.Y., U.S.	210	42.08 N	73.54 W
Germantown, Oh., U.S.	218	39.37 N	84.22 W
Germantown, Tn., U.S.	194	35.05 N	89.48 W
Germantown, Wi., U.S.	216	43.13 N	88.06 W
Germantown ◆ 8	285	40.03 N	75.11 W
Germantown Dam ◆ 6	218	39.38 N	84.24 W
Germany (Deutschland) □ 1, Europe	22	51.00 N	10.00 E
Germany (Deutschland) □ 1, Europe	30	51.00 N	10.00 E
Germany Flats ⩡	276	41.05 N	74.39 W
Germay	58	48.25 N	5.21 E
Germencik	130	37.51 N	27.37 E
Germendorf	54	52.45 N	13.10 E
Germering	60	48.08 N	11.22 E
Germersheim	56	49.13 N	8.22 E
Germfask	190	46.14 N	85.55 W
Germiston	158	26.13 S	28.11 E
Germiston □ 5	273d	26.15 S	28.10 E
Germiston South	273d	26.15 S	28.10 E
Gernika-Lumo (Guernica y Luno)	34	43.19 N	2.41 W
Gernrode	54	51.43 N	11.08 E
Gernsbach	56	48.46 N	8.19 E
Gernsheim	56	49.44 N	8.29 E
Gero	94	35.48 N	137.14 E
Geroda	56	50.17 N	9.53 E
Gerola Alta	58	46.03 N	9.32 E
Geroldsgrün	54	50.20 N	11.35 E
Geroldstein	56	50.06 N	7.56 E
Gerolsbach	60	48.30 N	11.22 E
Gerolstein	56	50.13 N	6.40 E
Gerolzhofen	56	49.54 N	10.21 E
Gerona	116	15.36 N	120.36 E
Gerona → Girona	34	41.59 N	2.49 E
Geronimo	196	34.28 N	98.22 W
Gerpinnes	50	50.20 N	4.31 E
Gerrards Cross	260	51.35 N	0.34 W
Gerrei ◆ 1	71	39.28 N	9.17 E
Gerresheim ◆ 8	263	51.14 N	6.52 E
Gerringong	170	34.45 S	150.50 E
Gerry	214	42.12 N	79.15 W
Gers □ 5	32	43.40 N	0.30 E
Gers ≃	32	44.09 N	0.39 E
Gersau	58	47.00 N	8.32 E
Gersdorf	54	50.45 N	12.42 E
Gersfeld	56	50.27 N	9.55 E
Gershøj	41	55.43 N	11.59 E
Gersprenz ≃	56	49.59 N	9.04 E
Gerstetten	56	48.37 N	10.01 E
Gersthofen	58	48.25 N	10.53 E
Gerstungen	56	50.58 N	10.04 E
Gertak Sanggul, Tanjong ≻	114	5.15 N	100.11 E
Gerthe ◆ 8	263	51.31 N	7.17 E
Gerufa	156	19.17 S	26.02 E
Gervais	224	45.06 N	122.53 W
Gerwisch	54	52.10 N	11.44 E
Gerza	142	29.26 N	31.11 E
Gerze, Tür.	130	41.48 N	35.12 E
Gêrzê, Zhg.	120	32.16 N	84.12 E
Gerzen	60	48.31 N	12.25 E
Gerzensee	58	46.51 N	7.33 E
Gescher	52	51.57 N	6.59 E
Geschriebenstein (Írottkő) ∧	61	47.21 N	16.26 E
Geschwenda	54	50.44 N	10.49 E
Gesees	60	49.54 N	11.32 E
Geseke	52	51.38 N	8.31 E
Geser	164	3.53 S	130.54 E
Gesher HaZiw	132	33.02 N	35.06 E
Gesi	115a	7.20 S	111.01 E
Gesoa	164	8.25 S	143.35 E
Gespunsart	56	49.49 N	4.50 E
Gessertshausen	58	48.20 N	10.44 E
Gesso ≃	62	44.24 N	7.33 E
Gessopalena	66	42.03 N	14.16 E
Gesten	41	55.31 N	9.12 E
Gesualdo	68	41.00 N	15.04 E
Geta	26	60.23 N	19.50 E
Getafe	34	40.18 N	3.43 W
Getafe, Aeropuerto ⊠	266a	40.18 N	3.43 W
Gete ≃	56	50.57 N	5.07 E
Gethaoli	272c	19.08 N	73.01 E
Geti	154	1.13 N	30.12 E
Getinge	26	56.49 N	12.44 E
Gettorf	41	54.24 N	9.58 E
Gettysburg, Oh., U.S.	218	40.06 N	84.29 W
Gettysburg, Pa., U.S.	208	39.49 N	77.13 W
Gettysburg, S.D., U.S.	198	45.00 N	99.57 W
Gettysburg National Military Park ♠	208	39.49 N	77.15 W
Getulândia	256	22.40 S	44.06 W
Getulina	255	21.49 S	49.55 W
Getulio	116	10.45 N	122.40 E
Getúlio Vargas	252	27.50 S	52.16 W
Getz Ice Shelf ⊓	9	75.00 S	129.00 W
Getzville	210	43.01 N	78.46 W
Geumpang	114	4.48 N	96.09 E
Geureudong, Gunung ∧	114	4.48 N	96.48 E
Gevān	128	26.03 N	57.17 E
Gevaş	128	38.16 N	43.07 E
Gevelsberg	56	51.19 N	7.20 E
Gevgelija	38	41.08 N	22.30 E
Gévora ≃	34	38.53 N	6.57 W
Gevrey-Chambertin	58	47.14 N	4.57 E
Gewane	144	10.10 N	40.39 E
Geweke ◆ 8	263	51.22 N	7.25 E
Gex	58	46.20 N	6.04 E
Geyer	54	50.37 N	12.55 E
Geyer Ditch ≍	216	41.36 N	86.25 W
Geyikli	130	39.48 N	26.12 E
Geysdorp	158	26.32 S	25.18 E
Geyser	202	47.15 N	110.29 W
Geyserville	204	38.42 N	122.54 W
Geyshtasar, Kūh-e ∧	84	38.51 N	47.14 E
Geyuan	100	28.31 N	117.44 E
Geyve	130	40.30 N	30.18 E
Gézenti	146	21.41 N	18.18 E
Gezer	132	31.52 N	34.55 E
Gföhl	61	48.31 N	15.30 E
Ghaapplato ⋏ 1	158	27.30 S	24.00 E
Ghabāghib	132	33.10 N	36.13 E
Ghābat al-'Arab	140	9.02 N	29.29 E
Ghadaf, Wādī al- V	132	31.46 N	36.50 E
Ghadāmis	146	30.08 N	9.30 E
Ghaddūwah	146	26.26 N	14.18 E
Ghafe	272c	19.05 N	73.07 E
Ghagghar ≃	123	29.30 N	74.53 E
Ghāghara ≃	124	25.47 N	84.37 E
Ghaghar Reservoir ⊜ 1	124	24.38 N	83.11 E
Ghāghra	124	23.17 N	84.33 E
Ghakhar	123	32.18 N	74.09 E
Ghallah, Wādī al- V	140	10.25 N	27.32 E
Ghammāzah al-Kubrā	142	29.43 N	31.18 E
Ghamrīn	142	30.30 N	30.55 E
Ghana □ 1, Afr.	134	8.00 N	1.00 W
Ghana □ 1, Afr.	150	8.00 N	1.00 W
Ghansoli	272c	19.08 N	72.59 E
Ghanzi	156	21.38 S	21.45 E
Ghanzi □ 5	156	22.00 S	23.00 E
Ghārāpuri	272c	18.54 N	72.56 E
Gharaunda	124	29.33 N	76.58 E
Gharbah, Wādī V	142	29.40 N	31.58 E
Gharbi, Chott ⊜	148	33.50 N	1.30 W
Gharbi, Oued el V	148	31.50 N	0.51 E
Gharbīyah, Aṣ-Ṣaḥrā' al- (Western Desert) ◆ 2	140	27.00 N	27.00 E
Ghardaïa	148	32.31 N	3.37 E
Ghardimaou	36	36.26 N	8.27 E
Gharghoda	124	22.10 N	83.21 E
Gharībwāl	123	32.41 N	73.10 E
Gharīfah	132	33.38 N	35.33 E
Gharig	140	10.47 N	27.33 E
Ghārīyat al-Gharbīyah	132	32.41 N	36.13 E
Ghārīyat ash-Sharqīyah	132	32.40 N	36.16 E
Gharo	120	24.44 N	67.35 E
Gharrāf, Shaṭṭ al- ≃	128	32.30 N	45.48 E
Gharroli ◆ 8	272a	28.37 N	77.20 E
Gharsa, Chott el ⊜	148	34.06 N	7.50 E
Gharw, Jazīrat I	142	31.21 N	30.06 E
Gharyān	146	32.10 N	13.01 E
Ghaṣm	132	32.33 N	36.22 E
Ghāt	146	24.58 N	10.11 E
Ghātāl	126	22.40 N	87.43 E
Ghatampur	272b	22.54 N	88.10 E
Ghatere, Mount ∧	175e	7.49 S	158.54 E
Ghates Occidentales → Western Ghāts ⋏	122	14.00 N	75.00 E
Ghates Orientales → Eastern Ghāts ⋏	122	14.00 N	78.50 E
Ghātkopar ◆ 8	272c	19.05 N	72.54 E
Ghātprabha ≃	122	16.20 N	75.48 E
Ghātsīla	126	22.36 N	86.29 E
Għawdex (Gozo) I	36	36.03 N	14.15 E
Ghawr ash-Sharqīyah, Qanāt al- (East Ghor Canal) ≍	132	32.41 N	35.38 E
Ghaylah ∧ 1	132	33.11 N	37.05 E
Ghayl Bā Wazīr	144	14.48 N	49.21 E
Ghayl Bin Yumayn ⩒ 4	144	15.33 N	49.23 E
Ghayth, Wādī V	132	30.59 N	36.00 E
Ghazāl, Baḥr al- ≃	140	9.31 N	30.25 E
Ghazal, Bahr el V	146	13.01 N	15.28 E
Ghazālat al-Khīs	142	30.34 N	31.34 E
Ghāziābād	123	28.40 N	77.26 E
Ghāzīpur, India	124	25.35 N	83.34 E
Ghazipur, India	272b	22.36 N	88.34 E
Ghāzipur ◆ 8	272a	28.38 N	77.19 E
Ghazīr	130	34.01 N	35.40 E
Ghazlūna	120	31.24 N	67.49 E
Ghaznī	120	33.33 N	68.26 E
Ghaznī □ 4	120	33.15 N	67.45 E
Ghaznī ≃	120	32.35 N	67.58 E
Ghazni Khel	123	32.33 N	70.44 E
Ghazzah (Gaza), Isr. Occ	132	31.30 N	34.28 E
Ghazzah, Lubnān	132	33.40 N	35.49 E
Gheā ≃	272b	22.52 N	88.19 E
Ghedi	64	45.24 N	10.16 E
Ghemme	62	45.37 N	8.25 E
Ghennes Heights	279b	40.09 N	79.56 W
Ghent, Ky., U.S.	218	38.44 N	85.03 W
Ghent, N.Y., U.S.	210	42.19 N	73.36 W
Ghent, Oh., U.S.	214	41.09 N	81.38 W
Ghent → Gent	50	51.03 N	3.43 E
Gheora ◆ 8	272a	28.42 N	77.01 E
Gheorghe Gheorghiu-Dej	38	46.14 N	26.44 E
Gheorgheni	38	46.43 N	25.36 E
Gherla	38	47.02 N	23.55 E
Ghesar	272c	19.09 N	73.05 E
Ghigo	62	44.53 N	7.03 E
Ghilarza	71	40.07 N	8.50 E
Ghilizane	148	35.44 N	0.30 E
Ghīn, Tall ∧	132	32.39 N	36.43 E
Ghior	126	23.54 N	89.53 E
Ghislenghien (Gellingen)	50	50.39 N	3.52 E
Ghisonaccia	36	42.00 N	9.25 E
Ghizar ≃	123	36.15 N	73.25 E
Ghizunabeana Islands II	175e	7.31 S	158.42 E
Ghlin	50	50.28 N	3.53 E
Ghlò, Beinn a' ∧	46	56.50 N	3.43 W
Ghogha	120	21.41 N	72.17 E
Gholson	222	31.43 N	97.12 W
Ghonda ◆ 8	272a	28.41 N	77.16 E
Ghondi ◆ 8	272a	28.42 N	77.16 E
Ghorāsahan	124	26.50 N	85.08 E
Ghoshpur, Bngl.	126	23.27 N	89.39 E
Ghoshpur, India	272b	22.23 N	88.29 E
Ghotki	120	28.01 N	69.19 E
Ghowr □ 4	128	34.00 N	65.00 E
Ghubaysh	140	12.09 N	27.21 E
Ghudāf, Wādī al- V	128	32.56 N	43.30 E
Ghulayfiqah	144	14.27 N	43.02 E
Ghunthur	130	34.23 N	37.09 E
Ghurāb, Jabal ∧ 2	142	28.58 N	31.16 E
Ghurayrah	144	18.37 N	42.41 E
Ghūriān	128	34.21 N	61.30 E
Ghushuri	272b	22.37 N	88.22 E
Ghuwaybah, Wādī V	142	29.36 N	32.20 E
Ghuwayr, 'Ayn al- ⩒ 4	132	31.37 N	35.25 E
Ghuzzayil, Sabkhat ⊜	146	29.50 N	19.35 E
Giaginskaja	78	44.53 N	40.05 E
Gianh ≃	110	17.40 N	106.30 E
Giannutri, Isola di I	66	42.15 N	11.06 E
Giano, Monte ∧	66	42.25 N	13.06 E
Giano dell'Umbria	66	42.50 N	12.35 E
Giant City State Park ♠	194	37.39 N	89.12 W
Giant Mountain ∧	188	44.10 N	73.44 W
Giant's Castle ∧	158	29.21 S	29.27 E
Giant's Castle Game Reserve ◆ 4	158	29.16 S	29.30 E
Giant's Causeway ♠	48	55.14 N	6.30 W
Giants Neck	207	41.18 N	72.13 W
Giants Tomb Island I	212	44.55 N	80.00 W
Gianyar	115b	8.32 S	115.20 E
Gia Rai	110	9.14 N	105.28 E
Giardinello	70	38.05 N	13.09 E
Giardinetto	68	41.19 N	15.24 E
Giardini	70	37.50 N	15.17 E
Giarratana	70	37.03 N	14.48 E
Giarre	70	37.43 N	15.11 E
Giaveno	62	45.02 N	7.21 E
Giazza	64	45.39 N	11.07 E
Giba	71	39.04 N	8.38 E
Gibara	240p	21.07 N	76.08 W
Gibbon, Mn., U.S.	190	44.32 N	94.31 W
Gibbon, Ne., U.S.	198	40.44 N	98.50 W
Gibbons	182	53.50 N	113.20 W
Gibbonsville	202	45.33 N	113.55 W
Gibb River	164	16.25 S	126.22 E
Gibbs, Mount ∧	162	32.55 S	120.00 E
Gibbsboro	285	39.50 N	74.58 W
Gibbstown	208	39.49 N	75.17 W
Gibellina	70	37.47 N	12.58 E
Gibeon	156	25.09 S	17.43 E
Gibilmanna, Santuario di ʊ 1	70	37.59 N	14.02 E
Gibraleón	34	37.23 N	6.58 W
Gibraltar, Gib.	34	36.08 N	5.21 W
Gibraltar, Mi., U.S.	216	42.06 N	83.12 W
Gibraltar, Pa., U.S.	208	40.17 N	75.52 W
Gibraltar □ 2, Europe	22	36.08 N	5.21 W
Gibraltar □ 2, Europe	34	36.08 N	5.21 W
Gibraltar, Strait of (Estrecho de Gibraltar) ꓤ	34	35.57 N	5.36 W
Gibraltar Point ≻, On., Can.	275b	43.36 N	79.23 W
Gibraltar Point ≻, Eng., U.K.	44	53.05 N	0.19 E
Gibsland	194	32.32 N	93.03 W
Gibson, Austl.	162	33.39 S	121.48 E
Gibson, Ga., U.S.	192	33.14 N	82.35 W
Gibson, N.Y., U.S.	210	42.08 N	76.59 W
Gibson, Pa., U.S.	210	41.44 N	75.38 W
Gibson ≃	212	44.58 N	79.51 W
Gibson, Lake ⊜ 1	284a	43.06 N	79.14 W
Gibsonburg	214	41.23 N	83.19 W
Gibson City	216	40.27 N	88.22 W
Gibson Desert ◆ 2	162	24.30 S	126.00 E
Gibson Hill ∧ 2	214	41.51 N	80.10 W
Gibsonia, Fl., U.S.	220	28.06 N	81.58 W
Gibsonia, Pa., U.S.	214	40.38 N	79.59 W
Gibson Indian Reserve ◆ 4	212	45.01 N	79.44 W
Gibson Island I	208	39.05 N	76.26 W
Gibsons	182	49.24 N	123.30 W
Gibsonton	220	27.51 N	82.22 W
Gidajevo	24	59.57 N	52.22 E
Gidami	144	9.58 N	34.37 E
Gidda	144	9.34 N	35.23 E
Giddalūr	122	15.21 N	78.55 E
Giddarbāha	123	30.12 N	74.40 E
Giddings	222	30.10 N	96.56 W
Gideälven ≃	26	63.20 N	19.08 E
Gidea Park ◆ 8	260	51.35 N	0.12 E
Gideåvallen	26	63.29 N	18.58 E
Gideon	194	36.27 N	89.55 W
Gidgee	162	27.16 S	119.22 E
Gidgi, Lake ⊜	162	29.16 S	126.03 E
Gidhni	126	22.29 N	86.51 E
Gidole	144	5.38 N	37.30 E
Gidrotorf	80	56.28 N	43.33 E
Gidžaki, gora ∧	84	40.25 N	49.01 E
Giebelstadt	56	49.39 N	9.56 E
Gieboldehausen	52	51.36 N	10.13 E
Giedraičiai	76	55.05 N	25.15 E
Gielow	54	53.42 N	12.44 E
Gielsdorf	264a	52.36 N	13.52 E
Gien	50	47.42 N	2.38 E
Giengen	56	48.37 N	10.14 E
Giens	62	43.02 N	6.08 E
Gier ≃	62	45.35 N	4.46 E
Gierath	263	51.07 N	6.33 E
Gierle	56	51.16 N	4.51 E
Gieselwerder	52	51.36 N	9.33 E
Giesenkirchen ◆ 8	263	51.09 N	6.30 E
Giessbachfälle ⌞	58	46.42 N	8.03 E
Giessen	56	50.35 N	8.40 E
Giessen □ 5	56	50.40 N	8.40 E
Gieten	52	53.00 N	6.46 E
Giethoorn	52	52.43 N	6.05 E
Gièvres	50	47.16 N	1.40 E
Giez	62	45.45 N	6.15 E
Giffone	68	38.27 N	16.10 E
Giffoni Valle Piana	68	40.44 N	14.56 E
Gifford, Scot., U.K.	46	55.54 N	2.45 W
Gifford, Fl., U.S.	220	27.40 N	80.24 W
Gifford, Il., U.S.	216	40.18 N	88.01 W
Gifford, In., U.S.	216	41.06 N	87.01 W
Gifford, Pa., U.S.	214	41.51 N	78.36 W
Gifford ≃	176	70.21 N	83.05 W
Gifford Creek	162	24.05 S	116.11 E
Gifford Pinchot State Park ♠	208	40.04 N	76.53 W
Giffre ≃	58	46.05 N	6.30 E
Gifhorn	52	52.29 N	10.33 E
Giflitz	56	51.09 N	9.07 E
Gif-sur-Yvette	261	48.42 N	2.08 E
Gifu	94	35.25 N	136.45 E
Gifu □ 5	94	35.45 N	137.00 E
Gigant	80	46.30 N	41.20 E
Giganta, Sierra de la ⋏	232	26.00 N	111.30 W
Gigante	246	2.23 N	75.33 W
Gigante Islands II	116	11.36 N	123.20 E
Gigen	38	43.42 N	24.29 E
Gigena → Alcira	252	32.45 S	64.20 W
Giggleswick	44	54.04 N	2.17 W
Gigha, Sound of ꓤ	46	55.41 N	5.42 W
Gigha Island I	46	55.41 N	5.46 W
Gig Harbor	224	47.19 N	122.34 W
Giglio, Isola del I	66	42.21 N	10.54 E
Giglio Castello	66	42.22 N	10.54 E
Gigliola	66	44.51 N	12.14 E
Giglio Porto	66	42.22 N	10.55 E
Gigmoto	116	13.47 N	124.23 E
Gignod	62	45.46 N	7.17 E
Gihu → Gifu	94	35.25 N	136.45 E
Gijón	34	43.32 N	5.40 W
Gikongoro	154	2.29 S	29.34 E
Gila ≃	200	32.43 N	114.33 W
Gila, Middle Fork ≃	200	33.14 N	108.14 W
Gila Bend	200	32.56 N	112.42 W
Gila Bend Indian Reservation ◆ 4	200	33.00 N	112.46 W
Gila Bend Mountains ⋏	200	33.10 N	113.10 W
Gila Cliff Dwellings National Monument ♠	200	33.02 N	108.16 W
Gila Mountains ⋏	200	33.05 N	109.50 W
Gīlān □ 4	128	37.15 N	49.30 E
Gīlān-e Gharb	128	34.08 N	45.55 E
Gila River Indian Reservation ◆ 4	200	33.12 N	112.00 W
Gilātala	126	22.36 N	89.41 E
Gilberdyke	44	53.45 N	0.44 W
Gilbert, La., U.S.	194	32.02 N	91.39 W
Gilbert, Mn., U.S.	190	47.29 N	92.27 W
Gilbert ≃, Austl.	166	16.35 S	141.15 E
Gilbert ≃, Austl.	168b	34.22 S	138.40 E
Gilbert, Mount ∧	182	50.51 N	124.20 W
Gilbert Airport ⊠	279a	41.22 N	81.58 W
Gilbert Island I	219	39.35 N	91.11 W
Gilbert Islands → Kiribati □ 1	14	5.00 S	170.00 W
Gilbert Lake ⊜	281	42.34 N	83.17 W
Gilbert Lake State Park ♠	210	42.36 N	75.08 W
Gilberton	210	40.48 N	76.13 W
Gilbertown	194	31.52 N	88.19 W
Gilbert Peak ∧	224	46.30 N	121.25 W
Gilbert Plains	184	51.09 N	100.29 W
Gilbert River	166	18.09 S	142.52 E
Gilberts	216	42.06 N	88.23 W
Gilbert Seamount ✣ 3	16	52.50 N	150.10 W
Gilbertsville, N.Y., U.S.	210	42.28 N	75.19 W
Gilbertsville, Pa., U.S.	208	40.19 N	75.37 W
Gilbertville	207	42.18 N	72.12 W
Gilbjerg Hoved ≻	41	56.08 N	12.17 E
Gilboa	216	41.01 N	83.55 W
Gilboa', Haré ⋏ 2	132	32.30 N	35.23 E
Gilbués	250	9.50 S	45.21 W
Gilching	60	48.07 N	11.17 E
Gildehaus	52	52.18 N	7.06 E
Gildford	202	48.34 N	110.17 W
Gilead	216	41.48 N	85.09 W
Giles, Arroyo de ≃	258	34.20 S	59.23 W
Giles Meteorological Station ʊ 3	162	25.02 S	128.18 E
Giles Point ≻	168b	35.03 S	137.45 E
Gilette	62	43.51 N	7.10 E
Gilford	48	54.23 N	6.22 W
Gilford Island I	182	50.45 N	126.25 W
Gilford Park	208	39.58 N	74.08 W
Gilgai	162	31.15 S	119.56 E
Gilgandra	166	31.42 S	148.39 E
Gilgil	154	0.30 S	36.19 E
Gil Gil Creek ≃	166	29.10 S	148.51 E
Gilgit	123	35.55 N	74.18 E
Gilgit ≃	123	35.44 N	74.38 E
Gilgo Island I	276	40.38 N	73.25 W
Gilgo State Park ♠	276	40.38 N	73.22 W
Gilima	154	3.55 N	28.22 E
Gilimanuk	115a	8.10 S	114.26 E
Gilirang	112	3.55 S	120.09 E
Gil Island I	182	53.13 N	129.15 W
Gill, Lough ⊜	48	54.16 N	8.24 W
Gillam	184	56.21 N	94.43 W
Gilleland Creek ≃	222	30.13 N	97.32 W
Gilleleje	41	56.07 N	12.19 E
Gillen, Lake ⊜	162	26.11 S	124.38 E
Gilles, Lake ⊜	166	32.50 S	136.45 E
Gillespie	219	39.07 N	89.49 W
Gillespies Point ≻	172	43.24 S	169.50 E
Gillett, Ar., U.S.	194	34.07 N	91.22 W
Gillett, Pa., U.S.	210	41.57 N	76.48 W
Gillett, Wi., U.S.	190	44.53 N	88.18 W
Gillette, N.J., U.S.	276	40.41 N	74.28 W
Gillette, Wy., U.S.	198	44.17 N	105.30 W
Gillette Castle State Park ♠	207	41.26 N	72.25 W
Gillian, Lake ⊜	176	69.32 N	75.23 W
Gillingham, Eng., U.K.	42	51.24 N	0.33 E
Gillingham, Eng., U.K.	42	51.02 N	2.17 W
Gillingham □ 8	260	51.22 N	0.35 E
Gills Rock	190	45.17 N	87.01 W
Gilman, Ct., U.S.	207	41.34 N	72.11 W
Gilman, Il., U.S.	216	40.46 N	87.59 W
Gilman, Ia., U.S.	190	41.52 N	92.47 W
Gilman, Wi., U.S.	190	45.10 N	90.48 W
Gilman Hot Springs	228	33.50 N	116.59 W
Gilman Lake	285	39.41 N	75.11 W
Gilmer, Il., U.S.	278	42.14 N	88.02 W
Gilmer, Tx., U.S.	222	32.43 N	94.56 W
Gilmer Park	216	41.36 N	86.15 W
Gilmore	171b	35.20 S	148.11 E
Gilmore City	198	42.44 N	94.27 W
Gilmore Creek ≃	171b	35.18 S	148.13 E
Gilo ≃	144	8.10 N	33.15 E
Gilroy	226	37.00 N	121.34 W
Gilserberg	56	50.57 N	9.04 E
Gilsizer Slough ≃	226	38.58 N	121.44 W
Gilston Park ♠	260	51.48 N	0.04 E
Giltner	198	40.46 N	98.09 W
Gil'uj ≃	89	53.58 N	127.30 E
Giluwe, Mount ∧	164	6.05 S	143.50 E
Gilwern	42	51.51 N	3.06 W
Gilze	52	51.33 N	4.57 E
Gimån ≃	26	62.28 N	16.20 E
Gimbi	144	9.10 N	35.42 E
Gimcheon → Kimch'ŏn	98	36.07 N	128.05 E
Gimie, Mount ∧	241f	13.52 N	61.01 W
Gimigliano	68	38.58 N	16.32 E
Gimlet	218	38.13 N	83.09 W
Gimli	184	50.38 N	96.59 W
Gimo	40	60.11 N	18.11 E
Gimoly	24	63.03 N	32.19 E
Gimone ≃	32	44.00 N	1.06 E
Gimont	32	43.38 N	0.53 E
Gimpu	112	1.36 S	120.02 E
Ginderich	263	51.39 N	6.32 E
Ginebra → Genève	58	46.12 N	6.09 E
Gineste, Col de la)(	62	43.15 N	5.27 E
Gingell	216	42.43 N	83.17 W
Gingera, Mount ∧	171b	35.35 S	148.47 E
Ginger Hill	279b	40.12 N	80.00 W
Ginger Island I	240m	18.24 N	64.28 W
Gingin, Austl.	162	31.21 S	115.42 E
Gin Gin, Austl.	166	25.00 S	151.58 E
Gingindlovu	158	29.02 S	31.30 E
Gingoog	116	8.50 N	125.07 E
Gingoog Bay c	116	8.59 N	125.05 E
Gingst	54	54.27 N	13.16 E
Ginir	144	7.07 N	40.46 E
Ginkakuji Temple ʊ 1	270	35.03 N	135.47 E
Ginkgo State Park ♠	202	46.59 N	120.01 W
Ginnosar	132	32.51 N	35.31 E
Ginosa	68	40.35 N	16.46 E
Ginostra	70	38.47 N	15.11 E
Ginowan	174m	26.17 N	127.46 E
Ginoza	174m	26.28 N	127.57 E
Ginter	214	40.46 N	78.23 W
Ginza ◆ 8	268	35.40 N	139.47 E
Gioi	68	40.17 N	15.13 E
Gioia, Golfo di c	68	38.30 N	15.45 E
Gioia dei Marsi	66	41.57 N	13.42 E
Gioia del Colle	68	40.48 N	16.56 E
Gioia Tauro	68	38.26 N	15.54 E
Gioia Vecchio	66	41.54 N	13.44 E
Gioiosa Ionica	68	38.20 N	16.18 E
Gioiosa Marea	70	38.10 N	14.54 E
Giong Rieng	110	9.55 N	105.19 E
Giornico	58	46.24 N	8.52 E
Giovi, Passo dei)(	62	44.33 N	8.57 E
Giovinazzo	68	41.11 N	16.40 E
Giporlos	116	11.07 N	125.27 E
Gipping ≃	42	52.04 N	1.10 E
Gipsy	214	40.48 N	78.53 W
Gipuzkoako □ 4	34	43.10 N	2.10 W
Giraglia, Île de la I	62	43.02 N	9.24 E
Giralia	162	22.41 S	114.21 E
Giraltovce	30	49.07 N	21.31 E
Girard, Il., U.S.	219	39.26 N	89.46 W
Girard, Ks., U.S.	198	37.30 N	94.50 W
Girard, Mi., U.S.	216	42.02 N	85.00 W
Girard, Oh., U.S.	214	41.09 N	80.42 W
Girard, Pa., U.S.	214	42.00 N	80.19 W
Girard, Tx., U.S.	196	33.22 N	100.40 W
Girardot	246	4.18 N	74.48 W
Girardville	208	40.47 N	76.17 W
Giraud, Pointe ≻	240d	15.19 N	61.15 W
Giraul ≃	152	15.04 S	12.08 E
Giraumont	56	49.10 N	5.55 E
Girbovu	38	44.44 N	23.21 E
Girdletree	208	38.05 N	75.23 W
Giresun	130	40.55 N	38.24 E
Giresun □ 4	130	40.30 N	38.30 E
Giresun Dağları ⋏	130	40.30 N	39.00 E
Girgarre	166	36.24 S	144.59 E
Girgaum ◆ 8	272c	18.57 N	72.48 E
Girgenti → Agrigento	70	37.18 N	13.35 E
Girgir, Cape ≻	164	3.50 S	144.34 E
Giri ≃	152	0.28 N	17.59 E
Girīdīh	126	24.11 N	86.18 E
Girifalco	68	38.49 N	16.25 E
Girilambone	166	31.15 S	146.54 E
Girmeli	130	37.07 N	41.26 E
Girna ≃	122	21.08 N	75.19 E
Gir National Park ♠	120	21.00 N	70.50 E
Girne (Kyrenia)	130	35.20 N	33.19 E
Giro, Nig.	150	11.06 N	4.46 E
Giro, Zaïre	154	3.08 N	29.15 E
Giromagny	58	47.45 N	6.50 E
Girón, Ec.	246	3.10 S	79.08 W
Giron, Fr.	58	46.14 N	5.46 E
Girona	34	41.59 N	2.49 E
Girona □ 4	34	42.00 N	2.40 E
Gironde □ 5	32	44.45 N	0.35 W
Gironde c 1	32	45.20 N	0.45 W
Gironville-sous-les-Côtes	56	48.48 N	5.40 E
Girou ≃	32	43.46 N	1.23 E
Girouxville	182	55.45 N	117.20 W
Gīr Range ⋏	120	21.18 N	71.00 E
Girton	42	52.14 N	0.05 E
Girtys Run ≃	279b	40.28 N	79.58 W
Giru	166	19.31 S	147.06 E
Giruá	252	28.02 S	54.21 W
Girvan	44	55.15 N	4.51 W
Girvan, Water of ≃	44	55.15 N	4.51 W
Girvas	24	62.30 N	33.40 E
Gisborne, Austl.	169	37.29 S	144.35 E
Gisborne, N.Z.	172	38.40 S	178.01 E
Gisborne Lake ⊜	186	47.48 N	54.50 W
Giscome	182	54.04 N	122.22 W
Gisenyi	154	1.42 S	29.15 E
Gishyita	154	2.11 S	29.18 E
Gislaved	26	57.18 N	13.32 E
Gislev	41	55.13 N	10.37 E
Gislinge	41	55.44 N	11.33 E
Gislövs läge	41	55.21 N	13.14 E
Gisors	50	49.17 N	1.47 E
Gissar	85	38.33 N	68.35 E
Gissarskij chrebet ⋏	85	39.00 N	68.40 E
Gisselfeld	41	55.18 N	11.59 E
Gissi	66	42.01 N	14.33 E
Gisslarbo	40	59.38 N	15.49 E
Gistel	50	51.10 N	2.57 E
Giswil	58	46.50 N	8.11 E
Gitambo	154	4.21 N	24.45 E
Gitarama	154	2.07 S	29.45 E
Gitega	154	3.26 S	29.56 E
Gittelde	52	51.48 N	10.10 E
Giuba, Isole II	144	0.45 S	42.19 E
Giudicarie, Valli V	64	45.58 N	10.45 E
Giugliano in Campania	68	40.56 N	14.12 E
Giuliana	70	37.40 N	13.14 E
Giulianova	66	42.45 N	13.57 E
Giulie, Alpi → Julian Alps ⋏	36	46.00 N	14.00 E
Giumbo → Jumboo	144	0.15 S	42.38 E
Giurgiu	38	43.53 N	25.57 E
Giurgiu □ 6	38	44.10 N	26.00 E
Giussano	62	45.42 N	9.14 E
Giuvala, Pasul)(	38	45.26 N	25.17 E
Giv'atayim	132	32.04 N	34.48 E
Giv'at Brenner	132	31.52 N	34.48 E
Give	41	55.51 N	9.15 E
Giverny	50	49.04 N	1.32 E
Givet	56	50.08 N	4.50 E
Givors	62	45.35 N	4.46 E
Givrine, Col de la)(	58	46.27 N	6.05 E
Givry	58	46.47 N	4.45 E
Givry-en-Argonne	56	48.57 N	4.53 E
Givry Island I	175c	7.07 N	151.53 E
Giyon	144	8.30 N	38.00 E
Giza → Al-Jīzah	142	30.01 N	31.13 E
Gīzāb	120	33.23 N	66.16 E
Giždunan	128	40.06 N	64.41 E
Gizen	140	10.49 N	34.48 E
Gizeux	50	47.24 N	0.12 E
Gižiga	74	62.03 N	160.30 E
Gižiginskaja guba c	74	61.30 N	158.00 E
Gizo	175e	8.06 S	156.51 E
Gizo Island I	175e	8.04 S	156.48 E
Giżycko	30	54.03 N	21.47 E
Gizzeria	68	38.59 N	16.12 E
Gjandža	84	40.40 N	46.22 E
Gjedved	41	55.56 N	9.51 E
Gjern	41	56.14 N	9.45 E
Gjirokastër	38	40.05 N	20.10 E
Gjoa Haven	176	68.38 N	95.57 W
Gjøvik	26	60.48 N	10.42 E
Gjuesevo	38	42.14 N	22.28 E
Gjuhëzës, Kep i ≻	38	40.25 N	19.18 E
Glace Bay	186	46.12 N	59.57 W
Glacier, B.C., Can.	182	51.16 N	117.31 W
Glacier, Wa., U.S.	224	48.53 N	121.56 W
Glacier Bay c	180	58.40 N	136.00 W
Glacier Bay National Park ♠	180	58.45 N	136.30 W
Glacier Hills	276	40.51 N	74.28 W
Glacier National Park ♠, B.C., Can.	182	51.15 N	117.35 W
Glacier National Park ♠, Mt., U.S.	202	48.35 N	113.40 W
Glacier Peak ∧	224	48.07 N	121.07 W
Glad'	76	59.07 N	32.06 E

Symbols in the index entries represent the broad categories identified in the key at the right. Symbols with superior numbers (⋏ 1) identify subcategories (see complete key on page *I · 1).*

Symbole im Register stellen die rechts im Schlüssel erklärten Kategorien dar. Symbole mit hochgestellten Ziffern (⋏ 1) bezeichnen Unterabteilungen einer Kategorie (vgl. vollständiger Schlüssel auf Seite *I · 1).*

Los símbolos incluídos en el texto del índice representan las grandes categorias identificadas con la clave a la derecha. Los símbolos con numeros en su parte superior (⋏ 1) identifican las subcategorías (véase la clave completa en la página *I · 1).*

Les symboles de l'index représentent les catégories indiquées dans la légende à droite. Les symboles suivis d'un indice (⋏ 1) représentent des sous-catégories (voir légende complète à la page *I · 1).*

Os símbolos incluídos no texto do índice representam as grandes categorias identificadas com a chave à direita. Os símbolos com números em sua parte superior (⋏ 1) identificam as subcategorias (veja-se a chave completa à página *I · 1).*

Symbol	English	Deutsch	Español	Français	Português
∧	Mountain	Berg	Montaña	Montagne	Montanha
⋏	Mountains	Gebirge	Montañas	Montagnes	Montanhas
)(	Pass	Paß	Paso	Col	Passo
V	Valley, Canyon	Tal, Cañon	Valle, Cañón	Vallée, Canyon	Vale, Canhão
⩡	Plain	Ebene	Llano	Plaine	Planície
≻	Cape	Kap	Cabo	Cap	Cabo
I	Island	Insel	Isla	Île	Ilha
II	Islands	Inseln	Islas	Îles	Ilhas
⩡	Other Topographic Features	Andere Topographische Objekte	Otros Elementos Topográficos	Autres données topographiques	Outros acidentes topográficos

ESPAÑOL Nombre / FRANÇAIS Nom / PORTUGUÊS Nome	Página / Page / Página	Lat.°′	Long.°′ W = Oeste / W = Ouest / W = Oeste
Gl'ad'anskoje	86	54.54 N	65.06 E
Gladbach → Mönchengladbach	56	51.12 N	6.28 E
Gladbeck	52	51.34 N	6.59 E
Gladbrook	190	42.11 N	92.42 W
Gladden	279b	40.21 N	80.11 W
Gladden Heights	279b	40.22 N	80.15 W
Glade Creek ≃	202	45.54 N	119.42 W
Gladenbach	56	50.46 N	8.34 E
Glades □ 6	220	26.59 N	81.12 W
Glade Spring	192	36.47 N	81.46 W
Gladesville	274a	33.50 S	151.08 E
Gladewater	222	32.32 N	94.56 W
Gladewater, Lake ⊜ 1	222	32.35 N	94.57 W
Gladkovka	78	46.23 N	32.36 E
Gladsakse	41	55.44 N	12.29 E
Gladstone, Austl.	166	23.51 S	151.16 E
Gladstone, Austl.	166	33.17 S	138.22 E
Gladstone, Mb., Can.	184	50.13 N	98.57 W
Gladstone, Mi., U.S.	190	45.51 N	87.01 W
Gladstone, Mo., U.S.	194	39.12 N	94.33 W
Gladstone, N.J., U.S.	210	40.43 N	74.39 W
Gladstone, Or., U.S.	224	45.22 N	122.35 W
Gladstone Brook ≃	276	40.43 N	74.40 W
Gladwin	190	43.58 N	84.29 W
Gladwyne	285	40.02 N	75.17 W
Gladys Lake ⊜	180	59.55 N	132.55 W
Glænø I	41	55.12 N	11.28 E
Glafsfjorden ⊜	26	59.34 N	12.37 E
Glåma ≃	26	59.12 N	10.57 E
Glamis	46	56.36 N	3.00 W
Glamis Castle ⊥	46	56.37 N	3.00 W
Glamoč	36	44.03 N	16.51 E
Glamor Lake ⊜	212	44.58 N	78.23 W
Glamsbjerg	41	55.16 N	10.07 E
Glan	116	5.49 N	125.10 E
Glan ⊜	40	58.37 N	15.58 E
Glan ≃, Dtsch.	56	49.47 N	7.43 E
Glan ≃, Öst.	61	46.36 N	14.25 E
Glan ≃, Pil.	116	5.50 N	125.12 E
Glanamman	42	51.48 N	3.54 W
Gland	58	46.26 N	6.16 E
Gland ≃	50	49.55 N	4.05 E
Glandon, Col du)(	62	45.14 N	6.11 E
Glandorf, Dtsch.	52	52.05 N	7.59 E
Glandorf, Oh., U.S.	216	41.01 N	84.04 W
Glâne ≃	58	46.47 N	7.08 E
Glanegg	61	46.44 N	14.11 E
Glanerbrug	52	52.13 N	6.58 E
Glanmire	48	51.55 N	8.24 W
Glanshammar	40	59.19 N	15.24 E
Glanum ⊥	62	43.49 N	4.47 E
Glan-y-Don	262	53.19 N	3.15 W
Glaris → Glarus	58	47.02 N	9.04 E
Glarner Alpen ⋌	58	46.55 N	9.00 E
Glärnisch ⋌	58	47.00 N	9.00 E
Glarus	58	47.02 N	9.04 E
Glarus □ 3	58	47.00 N	9.03 E
Glascarnoch, Loch ⊜	46	57.40 N	4.50 W
Glasco, Ks., U.S.	198	39.21 N	97.50 W
Glasco, N.Y., U.S.	210	42.02 N	73.56 W
Glasgow, Scot., U.K.	46	55.53 N	4.15 W
Glasgow, Il., U.S.	219	39.33 N	90.29 W
Glasgow, Ky., U.S.	194	36.59 N	85.54 W
Glasgow, Mo., U.S.	194	39.13 N	92.50 W
Glasgow, Mt., U.S.	202	48.11 N	106.38 W
Glasgow, Pa., U.S.	214	40.42 N	78.27 W
Glasgow, Va., U.S.	192	37.38 N	79.27 W
Glasgow (Abbotsinch) Airport ⊠	46	55.52 N	4.26 W
Glashütte, Dtsch.	52	53.41 N	10.02 E
Glashütte, Dtsch.	54	50.51 N	13.47 E
Glashütte ⊸ 8	263	51.13 N	6.52 E
Glaslyn	184	53.21 N	108.22 W
Glaslyn ≃	44	52.56 N	4.06 W
Glas Maol ∧	46	56.52 N	3.22 W
Glasow	54	52.20 N	13.28 E
Glass, Loch ⊜	46	57.43 N	4.30 W
Glassan	48	53.28 N	7.52 W
Glassboro	208	39.42 N	75.06 W
Glassboro State College ⊎ 2	285	39.42 N	75.07 W
Glass House Mountains	171a	26.53 S	152.58 E
Glassmanor	284c	38.49 N	76.59 W
Glass Mountains ⋌	196	30.25 N	103.15 W
Glassport	214	40.19 N	79.53 W
Glastonbury, Eng., U.K.	42	51.06 N	2.43 W
Glastonbury, Ct., U.S.	207	41.42 N	72.36 W
Glatt ≃	58	47.34 N	8.28 E
Glatten	58	48.26 N	8.31 E
Glattfelden	58	47.33 N	8.30 E
Glatz → Kłodzko	30	50.27 N	16.39 E
Glaubitz	54	51.19 N	13.22 E
Glauchau	54	50.49 N	12.32 E
Glaven ≃	42	52.58 N	1.03 E
Glaze Brook ≃	262	53.25 N	2.27 W
Glazebury	262	53.28 N	2.30 W
Glaževo	76	59.41 N	32.05 E
Glazok	80	53.06 N	40.42 E
Glazov	80	58.09 N	52.40 E
Glazovo, Ross.	82	54.57 N	37.22 E
Glazovo, Ross.	82	54.47 N	37.34 E
Glazovo, Ross.	82	55.38 N	35.46 E
Glazunovka	76	52.30 N	36.19 E
Glazunovskaja	80	49.50 N	42.51 E
Gleason	194	36.12 N	88.36 W
Glebovka	78	46.38 N	39.59 E
Glebovo, Ross.	82	56.54 N	37.43 E
Glebovo, Ross.	82	56.39 N	38.42 E
Gleed	224	46.40 N	120.37 W
Glehn	263	51.10 N	6.35 E
Gleichen	182	50.52 N	113.03 W
Gleidingen	52	52.16 N	9.50 E
Gleinalpe ⋌	61	47.15 N	15.03 E
Gleisdorf	61	47.06 N	15.44 E
Gleiwitz → Gliwice	30	50.17 N	18.40 E
Glejbjerg	41	55.33 N	8.50 E
Glemsford	42	52.06 N	0.41 E
Glen ≃, Ire.	48	54.38 N	8.40 W
Glen ≃, Eng., U.K.	42	52.51 N	0.06 W
Glen Acres	285	39.58 N	75.34 W
Glen Afton	172	37.37 S	175.02 E
Glen Alice	170	33.02 S	150.13 E
Glen Allen	208	37.39 N	77.30 W
Glen Alpine	192	35.43 N	81.46 W
Glenamoy	48	54.14 N	9.42 W
Glenarchy	275b	43.29 N	79.46 W
Glenarden	208	38.56 N	76.52 W
Glenarm, N. Ire., U.K.	48	54.58 N	5.57 W
Glen Arm, Md., U.S.	284b	39.27 N	76.30 W
Glen Ashton Farms	285	40.06 N	74.55 W
Glen Aubrey	210	42.15 N	76.01 W
Glenavon, Sk., Can.	184	50.10 N	103.10 W
Glen Avon, S. Afr.	158	31.43 S	26.12 E
Glen Avon, Ca., U.S.	228	34.01 N	117.29 W
Glenavy, N.Z.	172	44.55 S	171.06 E
Glenavy, N. Ire., U.K.	48	54.36 N	6.13 W
Glenboro	184	49.32 N	99.15 W
Glenbrook	170	33.46 S	150.37 E
Glenbrook Heights	226	39.15 N	121.02 W
Glenburn, N.D., U.S.	198	48.30 N	101.13 W
Glenburn, Pa., U.S.	210	41.31 N	75.44 W
Glen Burnie	208	39.09 N	76.37 W
Glen Burnie Park	208	39.09 N	76.38 W
Glen Campbell	214	40.49 N	78.50 W
Glen Canyon V	200	37.10 N	110.50 W
Glen Canyon Dam ⊸ 6	200	36.48 N	111.13 W
Glen Canyon National Recreation Area ♠	200	37.00 N	111.20 W
Glen Carbon	219	38.44 N	89.58 W
Glencoe, Austl.	166	37.42 S	140.37 E
Glencoe, On., Can.	214	42.45 N	81.43 W
Glencoe, S. Afr.	158	28.12 S	30.07 E
Glencoe, Al., U.S.	194	33.57 N	85.55 W
Glencoe, Il., U.S.	216	42.08 N	87.45 W
Glencoe, Ky., U.S.	218	38.42 N	84.49 W
Glencoe, Md., U.S.	208	39.32 N	76.38 W
Glencoe, Mn., U.S.	190	44.46 N	94.09 W
Glencolumbkille	48	54.43 N	8.45 W
Glencoul, Loch ⊂	46	58.14 N	4.58 W
Glencova	154	19.59 S	31.26 E
Glen Cove	210	40.51 N	73.38 W
Glendale, Az., U.S.	200	33.32 N	112.11 W
Glendale, Ca., U.S.	228	34.08 N	118.15 W
Glendale, Ma., U.S.	207	42.17 N	73.20 W
Glendale, Ms., U.S.	194	31.21 N	89.18 W
Glendale, Mo., U.S.	219	38.35 N	90.22 W
Glendale, Or., U.S.	202	42.44 N	123.25 W
Glendale, R.I., U.S.	207	41.58 N	71.37 W
Glendale, Tx., U.S.	222	31.01 N	95.18 W
Glendale, Ut., U.S.	200	37.19 N	112.35 W
Glendale, Wi., U.S.	216	43.08 N	87.56 W
Glendale, Zimb.	154	17.21 S	31.04 E
Glendale Heights, Il., U.S.	278	41.54 N	88.04 W
Glendale Heights, Md., U.S.	284c	38.59 N	76.49 W
Glendale Lake ⊜	214	40.41 N	78.32 W
Glendalough ⊥	48	53.01 N	6.26 W
Glen Davis	170	33.08 S	150.17 E
Glendive	198	47.06 N	104.42 W
Glendo	200	42.30 N	105.01 W
Glendoe Forest ⊸ 3	46	57.06 N	4.37 W
Glendon, Ab., Can.	182	54.15 N	111.10 W
Glendon, Pa., U.S.	208	40.40 N	75.14 W
Glendora, Ca., U.S.	228	34.08 N	117.51 W
Glendora, N.J., U.S.	285	39.50 N	75.04 W
Glendo Reservoir ⊜ 1	198	42.31 N	104.58 W
Glendo State Park ♠	198	42.33 N	104.58 W
Glendowan	48	54.58 N	7.57 W
Glen Eagle, Austl.	168a	32.17 S	116.11 E
Gleneagle, Austl.	171a	27.57 S	152.59 E
Glen Echo	284c	38.58 N	77.08 W
Glen Echo Amusement Park ♠	284c	38.58 N	77.08 W
Glen Echo Heights	284c	38.58 N	77.08 W
Gleneden Beach	202	44.53 N	124.02 W
Glen Elder	198	39.29 N	98.18 W
Glenelg, Austl.	168b	34.59 S	138.31 E
Glenelg, Scot., U.K.	46	57.13 N	5.38 W
Glenelg ≃	166	38.03 S	141.00 E
Glen Ellen	226	38.22 N	122.31 W
Glenelly ≃	48	54.44 N	7.18 W
Glen Ellyn	278	41.52 N	88.04 W
Glen Ellyn Countryside	278	41.55 N	88.04 W
Glenfarg	46	56.16 N	3.24 W
Glenfarne	48	54.17 N	7.59 W
Glenfield, Austl.	274a	33.58 S	150.54 E
Glenfield, Eng., U.K.	42	52.39 N	1.12 W
Glenfield, N.Y., U.S.	212	43.43 N	75.24 W
Glenfield, Pa., U.S.	279b	40.31 N	80.08 W
Glenfinnan	46	56.52 N	5.27 W
Glen Flora	222	29.21 N	96.12 W
Glen Florrie	162	22.55 S	115.59 E
Glenford	210	42.00 N	74.07 W
Glen Forest	168a	31.54 S	116.06 E
Glengallan Creek ≃	171a	28.09 S	151.53 E
Glen Gardner	210	40.41 N	74.56 W
Glengarriff	48	51.45 N	9.33 W
Glengarry Range ⋌	162	26.13 S	118.59 E
Glengyle	166	24.48 S	139.37 E
Glenham	210	41.31 N	73.55 W
Glenhaven	274a	33.42 S	151.00 E
Glen Head	276	40.50 N	73.37 W
Glen Helen	162	23.43 S	132.40 E
Glen Hills	208	39.04 N	77.12 W
Glenhope	172	41.39 S	172.39 E
Glenhuntly	274b	37.54 S	145.03 E
Glen Innes	166	29.44 S	151.44 E
Glen Island I	276	40.53 N	73.47 W
Glen Lake	224	48.26 N	123.31 W
Glenluce	44	54.53 N	4.49 W
Glenluce Abbey ⊎ 1	44	54.53 N	4.50 W
Glen Lyon	210	41.10 N	76.04 W
Glen Miller	212	44.08 N	77.35 W
Glen Mills	285	39.55 N	75.30 W
Glenmont, N.Y., U.S.	210	42.36 N	73.46 W
Glenmont, Oh., U.S.	214	40.31 N	82.06 W
Glenmoor	214	40.40 N	80.37 W
Glenmoore, Pa., U.S.	208	40.05 N	75.46 W
Glen Moore, Pa., U.S.	208	40.03 N	76.18 W
Glenmora	194	30.58 N	92.35 W
Glenmore	284b	39.11 N	76.36 W
Glenmorgan	166	27.15 S	149.41 E
Glenn, Ca., U.S.	226	39.31 N	122.01 W
Glenn, Mi., U.S.	216	42.31 N	86.13 W
Glenn □ 6	226	39.29 N	122.18 W
Glennallen	180	62.07 N	145.33 W
Glennamaddy	48	53.37 N	8.35 W
Glenn-Colusa Canal ≍	226	39.07 N	122.08 W
Glenn Dale	284c	38.59 N	76.49 W
Glenns Creek ≃	218	38.09 N	84.52 W
Glenns Ferry	202	42.57 N	115.18 W
Glenn Shoals, Lake ⊜ 1	219	39.13 N	89.28 W
Glennville	192	31.56 N	81.55 W
Glen Oak	278	41.53 N	88.02 W
Glenolden	285	39.54 N	75.17 W
Glenoma	224	46.30 N	122.09 W
Glenorchy	172	44.51 S	168.23 E
Glenore Grove	171a	27.32 S	152.24 E
Glenorie	170	33.33 S	151.00 E
Glenormiston	166	22.55 S	138.48 E
Glen Park	212	44.00 N	75.57 W
Glenreagh	166	30.03 S	152.59 E
Glen Richey	214	40.57 N	78.29 W
Glen Riddle	285	39.54 N	75.26 W
Glenridge, Ma., U.S.	283	42.14 N	71.19 W
Glen Ridge, N.J., U.S.	276	40.48 N	74.12 W
Glen Robertson	206	45.21 N	74.30 W
Glen Rock, N.J., U.S.	276	40.57 N	74.08 W
Glen Rock, Pa., U.S.	208	39.47 N	76.43 W
Glenrock, Wy., U.S.	200	42.52 N	105.52 W
Glen Rose	222	32.14 N	97.45 W
Glen Ross	212	44.16 N	77.36 W
Glenrothes	46	56.12 N	3.10 W
Glenroy, Austl.	162	21.46 S	114.49 E
Glenroy, Austl.	162	17.22 S	126.06 E
Glenroy, Austl.	274b	37.42 S	144.55 E
Glenroy ≃	172	42.00 S	172.20 E
Glens Falls	210	43.18 N	73.38 W
Glenshaw	214	40.31 N	79.58 W
Glenshee V	46	56.48 N	3.30 W
Glenside, S. Afr.	158	29.25 S	30.47 E
Glenside, N.J., U.S.	208	39.40 N	75.29 W
Glenside, Pa., U.S.	208	40.06 N	75.09 W
Glen Spey	210	41.29 N	74.49 W
Glen Stewart Park ♠	275b	43.41 N	79.18 W
Glenties	48	54.47 N	8.17 W
Glen Ullin	198	46.48 N	101.49 W
Glenview	216	42.04 N	87.47 W
Glenview Countryside	278	42.04 N	87.50 W
Glenview Naval Air Station ■	216	42.05 N	87.50 W
Glenville, Ire.	48	52.03 N	8.26 W
Glenville, Mn., U.S.	190	43.34 N	93.16 W
Glenville, N.Y., U.S.	276	41.04 N	73.50 W
Glenville, W.V., U.S.	188	38.56 N	80.50 W
Glenvista	273d	26.17 S	28.13 E
Glen Waverley	274b	37.53 S	145.10 E
Glen White	192	37.43 N	81.16 W
Glen Wild	210	41.29 N	74.49 W
Glen Wild Lake ⊜	276	41.02 N	74.20 W
Glenwillard	214	40.34 N	80.13 W
Glen Williams	212	43.40 N	79.55 W
Glenwillow	214	41.22 N	81.28 W
Glenwood, Ab., Can.	182	49.22 N	113.31 W
Glenwood, Nf., Can.	186	48.59 N	54.52 W
Glenwood, Al., U.S.	194	31.39 N	86.10 W
Glenwood, Ar., U.S.	194	34.19 N	93.33 W
Glenwood, Ga., U.S.	192	32.10 N	82.40 W
Glenwood, Il., U.S.	278	41.32 N	87.36 W
Glenwood, In., U.S.	218	39.37 N	85.18 W
Glenwood, Ia., U.S.	198	41.02 N	95.44 W
Glenwood, Mn., U.S.	198	45.39 N	95.23 W
Glenwood, N.J., U.S.	210	41.15 N	74.29 W
Glenwood, N.M., U.S.	200	33.19 N	108.52 W
Glenwood, N.Y., U.S.	210	42.37 N	78.39 W
Glenwood, Or., U.S.	224	45.38 N	123.16 W
Glenwood, Tx., U.S.	222	32.39 N	94.51 W
Glenwood, Ut., U.S.	200	38.45 N	111.59 W
Glenwood, Va., U.S.	192	36.35 N	79.21 W
Glenwood, Wa., U.S.	224	46.01 N	121.17 W
Glenwood City	190	45.03 N	92.10 W
Glenwood Landing	276	40.50 N	73.39 W
Glenwood Park	284c	38.58 N	76.50 W
Glenwood Springs	200	39.33 N	107.19 W
Gleschendorf	54	54.02 N	10.40 E
Glesien	54	51.27 N	12.13 E
Gletsch	58	46.34 N	8.22 E
Glew	258	34.53 S	58.23 W
Glidden, Ia., U.S.	198	42.03 N	94.43 W
Glidden, Tx., U.S.	222	29.42 N	96.35 W
Glidden, Wi., U.S.	190	46.08 N	90.34 W
Glide	202	43.18 N	123.06 W
Gliener Berg ∧ 2	264a	52.42 N	13.00 E
Glienicke, Dtsch.	54	52.13 N	14.05 E
Glienicke, Dtsch.	54	52.37 N	13.19 E
Glífa	38	38.57 N	22.58 E
Glifádha	267c	37.52 N	23.45 E
Glimåkra	26	56.18 N	14.08 E
Glimmingehus	26	55.30 N	14.13 E
Glin	48	52.34 N	9.17 W
Glina	36	45.20 N	16.06 E
Glina ≃	36	45.26 N	16.07 E
Glin'any	78	49.49 N	24.30 E
Glinde	52	53.32 N	10.13 E
Glindow	54	52.21 N	12.54 E
Glindowsee ⊜	264a	52.21 N	12.56 E
Glinka	76	54.39 N	32.52 E
Glinkovo	85	42.55 N	69.40 E
Glittertinden ∧	26	61.39 N	8.33 E
Gliwice (Gleiwitz)	30	50.17 N	18.40 E
G. L. Martin State Airport ⊠	284b	39.20 N	76.25 W
Globe, Az., U.S.	200	33.23 N	110.47 W
Globe, Ky., U.S.	218	38.17 N	83.14 W
Globino	78	49.23 N	33.17 E
Glod'any	78	47.47 N	27.31 E
Glodeanu-Siliștea	38	44.50 N	26.48 E
Glodok ⊸ 8	269e	6.08 S	106.48 E
Glogau → Głogów	30	51.40 N	16.05 E
Gloggnitz	61	47.40 N	15.57 E
Glogn ≃	58	46.46 N	9.12 E
Głogów, Pol.	30	51.40 N	16.05 E
Głogów, Pol.	30	50.10 N	21.58 E
Głogówek	30	50.22 N	17.51 E
Glommersträsk	26	65.16 N	19.38 E
Glonn	64	47.59 N	11.52 E
Glonn ≃	60	48.26 N	11.36 E
Glorenza (Glurns)	64	46.40 N	10.33 E
Glória	250	9.11 S	38.18 W
Gloria, Bahía de la ⊂	240p	21.50 N	77.40 W
Glória de Dourados	255	22.21 S	54.13 W
Gloria Glens Park	214	41.03 N	81.54 W
Glorieta	200	35.34 N	105.46 W
Glorieuses, Îles II	138	11.30 S	47.20 E
Glörstausee ⊜ 1	263	51.14 N	7.29 E
Glos-la-Ferrière	50	48.51 N	0.36 E
Glossop	44	53.27 N	1.57 W
Glossopteris, Mount ∧	9	84.44 S	113.51 W
Gloster	194	31.11 N	91.01 W
Glostrup	41	55.40 N	12.24 E
Glotovka	80	53.57 N	46.42 E
Glotovo	24	63.30 N	49.23 E
Gloucester, Austl.	166	31.59 S	151.58 E
Gloucester, On., Can.	212	45.22 N	75.35 W
Gloucester, Eng., U.K.	42	51.53 N	2.14 W
Gloucester, Ma., U.S.	207	42.36 N	70.39 W
Gloucester, Va., U.S.	208	37.24 N	76.31 W
Gloucester □ 6, N.J., U.S.	208	39.50 N	75.10 W
Gloucester □ 6, Va., U.S.	208	37.25 N	76.30 W
Gloucester, Cape >	164	5.27 S	148.25 E
Gloucester, Vale of V	42	51.55 N	2.10 W
Gloucester City	285	39.53 N	75.07 W
Gloucester Fisherman ⊥	283	42.36 N	70.40 W
Gloucester Harbor ⊂	207	42.36 N	70.40 W
Gloucester Island I	166	20.01 S	148.27 E
Gloucester Point	208	37.15 N	76.29 W
Gloucester Pool ⊜	212	44.51 N	79.43 W
Gloucestershire □ 6	42	51.47 N	2.15 W
Glouster	188	39.30 N	82.05 W
Glover-Archbold Park ♠	284c	38.55 N	77.05 W
Glover Creek ≃	194	34.02 N	94.56 W
Glover Island I	186	48.44 N	57.45 W
Glovers Reef ✦ 2	232	16.49 N	87.48 W
Gloversville	210	43.03 N	74.20 W
Glovertown	186	48.41 N	54.02 W
Glowe	54	54.35 N	13.28 E
Glöwen	54	52.55 N	12.05 E
Głowno	30	51.58 N	19.44 E
Głubczyce	30	50.13 N	17.49 E
Glubokij, Ross.	78	48.31 N	40.19 E
Glubokij, Ross.	80	47.01 N	42.47 E
Glubokij, Ross.	89	52.53 N	129.44 E
Glubokoje, Bela.	76	55.08 N	27.41 E
Glubokoje, Kaz.	86	50.06 N	82.19 E
Glubokoje, Ross.	82	54.32 N	38.32 E
Głuchołazy	30	50.20 N	17.22 E
Gluchov	78	51.41 N	33.53 E
Gluchovo	265b	55.46 N	37.16 E
Glückauf-Kampfbahn ♠	263	51.32 N	7.05 E
Glücksburg	41	54.50 N	9.33 E
Glückstadt, Dtsch.	52	53.47 N	9.25 E
Gluckstadt, S. Afr.	158	27.57 S	31.02 E
Glucomanka, gora ∧	89	45.10 N	135.48 E
Glud	41	55.49 N	10.00 E
Glumslöv	41	55.56 N	12.48 E
Glumsø	41	55.21 N	11.42 E
Gluša	76	53.05 N	28.52 E
Glusburn	44	53.54 N	1.59 W
Glusk	76	52.54 N	28.41 E
Gluškeviči	78	51.34 N	27.47 E
Gluškovo	78	51.22 N	34.38 E
Glybokaja	78	48.07 N	25.56 E
Glyde ≃, Austl.	164	12.15 S	135.03 E
Glyde ≃, Ire.	48	53.52 N	6.21 W
Glyder Fawr ∧	44	53.06 N	4.01 W
Glyme ≃	42	51.49 N	1.22 W
Glyndebourne	42	50.52 N	0.04 E
Glyndon, Md., U.S.	208	39.28 N	76.48 W
Glyndon, Mn., U.S.	198	46.52 N	96.34 W
Glyngøre	26	56.46 N	8.52 E
Glyn-Neath	42	51.46 N	3.38 W
Gmelinka	80	50.24 N	46.54 E
Gmünd, Öst.	61	48.47 N	15.00 E
Gmünd, Öst.	64	46.54 N	13.32 E
Gmund am Tegernsee	64	47.45 N	11.44 E
Gmunden	64	47.55 N	13.48 E
Gnadenhutten	214	40.21 N	81.26 W
Gnadenhutten Monument ⊥	214	40.21 N	81.25 W
Gnalta	166	31.03 S	142.20 E
Gnaraloo	162	23.51 S	113.31 E
Gnarp	26	62.03 N	17.16 E
Gnarpurt, Lake ⊜	169	38.03 S	143.24 E
Gnarrenburg	52	53.22 N	9.00 E
Gnaw Bone	218	39.12 N	86.09 W
Gnesen → Gniezno	30	52.31 N	17.37 E
Gnesta	40	59.03 N	17.18 E
Gnezdovo	76	54.47 N	31.47 E
Gniben >	41	56.01 N	11.18 E
Gniew	30	53.51 N	18.49 E
Gniewkowo	30	52.54 N	18.25 E
Gniezno	30	52.31 N	17.37 E
Gnilaja Lipa ≃	78	49.07 N	24.44 E
Gnilec	76	52.22 N	36.01 E
Gniloj Jelanec ≃	78	47.20 N	31.44 E
Gniloj Tikič ≃	78	48.47 N	30.53 E
Gnivan'	78	49.06 N	28.20 E
Gnjilane	38	42.28 N	21.29 E
Gnoien	54	53.58 N	12.42 E
Gnosall	42	52.47 N	2.15 W
Gnosjö	26	57.22 N	13.44 E
Gnowangerup	162	33.56 S	117.59 E
Gō ≃	96	35.02 N	132.13 E
Goa	116	13.42 N	123.29 E
Goa □ 3	122	15.20 N	74.00 E
Goageb	156	26.44 S	17.15 E
Goalen Head >	166	36.40 S	150.05 E
Goāliar ≃	126	24.07 N	90.18 E
Goālpāra	124	26.11 N	90.37 E
Goāltor	126	22.43 N	87.10 E
Goan	150	13.14 N	5.09 W
Goascorán	236	13.36 N	87.45 W
Goascorán ≃	236	13.25 N	87.48 W
Goat Fell ∧	46	55.38 N	5.12 W
Goathland	44	54.23 N	0.44 W
Goat Island I	284a	43.05 N	79.04 W
Goat Mountain ∧	202	47.21 N	113.21 W
Goat Peak ∧	224	46.56 N	121.16 W
Goba, Ityo.	144	7.02 N	40.00 E
Goba, Moç.	156	26.12 S	32.08 E
Gobabis	156	22.30 S	18.58 E
Gobabis □ 5	156	22.30 S	19.00 E
Gobai ≃	126	23.37 N	86.28 E
Gobardānga	126	22.53 N	88.45 E
Göbel	130	40.00 N	28.09 E
Gobernador Andonaegui	258	34.10 S	59.19 W
Gobernador Costa	254	44.04 S	70.35 W
Gobernador Gregores	254	48.46 S	70.15 W
Gobernador Ingeniero Valentín Virasoro	252	28.03 S	56.02 W
Gobernador Juan E. Martínez	252	28.55 S	58.56 W
Gobernador Monteverde	288	34.48 S	58.16 W
Gobernador Racedo	252	31.34 S	60.04 W
Gobernador Udaondo	258	35.18 S	58.36 W
Gobi ⊸ 2	102	43.00 N	105.00 E
Gobindapur, India	126	23.16 N	87.58 E
Gobindapur, India	272b	22.23 N	88.25 E
Gobindapur, India	272b	22.55 N	88.12 E
Gobindgarh	123	30.41 N	76.18 E
Gobindpur	126	23.50 N	86.31 E
Göblberg ∧	60	48.06 N	13.32 E
Gobles	216	42.21 N	85.52 W
Gobō	96	33.53 N	135.10 E
Gobowen	42	52.53 N	3.02 W
Gobra	126	23.45 N	89.12 E
Gobur	154	4.20 N	31.04 E
Gobustan	84	40.06 N	49.24 E
Gobza ≃	76	55.16 N	31.31 E
Göçbeyli	130	39.13 N	27.25 E
Goceano, Catena del ⋌	71	40.28 N	9.02 E
Goce Delčev	38	41.34 N	23.44 E
Goch	52	51.41 N	6.10 E
Gochas	156	24.55 S	18.55 E
Gochsheim	56	50.01 N	10.16 E
Go Cong	269c	10.50 N	106.50 E
Göcsej ⋌ 2	61	46.43 N	16.42 E
Goðafoss ∟	24a	65.40 N	17.30 W
Godalming	42	51.11 N	0.37 W
Godalo	144	4.28 N	43.24 E
Godar	128	28.10 N	63.14 E
Godāvari ≃	122	17.00 N	81.45 E
Godāvari, Mouths of the ≃ 1	122	16.25 N	82.00 E
Godbout	186	49.19 N	67.37 W
Godbout ≃	186	49.19 N	67.36 W
Godda	124	24.50 N	87.13 E
Goddard	218	38.22 N	83.37 W
Goddard Space Flight Center ⊎	284c	39.00 N	76.52 W
Godeffroy	210	41.27 N	74.37 W
Godega di Sant'Urbano	64	45.56 N	12.24 E
Godegård	40	58.44 N	15.09 E
Godelheim	52	51.44 N	9.22 E
Godere	144	5.05 N	43.50 E
Goderich	190	43.45 N	81.43 W
Goderville	50	49.39 N	0.22 E
Godfrey	219	38.57 N	90.11 W
Godhavn (Qeqertarsuaq)	176	69.15 N	53.33 W
Godhra	120	22.45 N	73.38 E
Godinlabe	144	5.54 N	46.38 E
Godinne	56	50.21 N	4.52 E
Godley	222	32.27 N	97.32 W
Godmanchester	42	52.19 N	0.11 W
Godo, Indon.	115b	8.33 S	118.40 E
Gōdo, Nihon	94	35.25 N	136.36 E
Gōdo, Nihon	268	35.51 N	139.44 E
Gödöllő	264c	47.36 N	19.22 E
Gödöllői Dombság ⋌ 2	264c	47.37 N	19.16 E
Godong	115a	7.02 S	110.46 E
Godoy Cruz	252	32.55 S	68.50 W
Godramstein	56	49.12 N	8.05 E
Godrano	70	37.54 N	13.26 E
Gods ≃	184	56.22 N	92.51 W
Godshill	42	50.38 N	1.14 W
Godshorn	52	52.26 N	9.43 E
Gods Lake	184	54.40 N	94.09 W
Gods Lake ⊜	184	54.40 N	94.20 W
Gods Mercy, Bay of ⊂	176	63.30 N	86.10 W
Godstone	42	51.15 N	0.04 W
Godthåb (Nuuk)	176	64.11 N	51.44 W
Godunovo	82	56.29 N	39.02 E
Godwin Austen → K2 ∧	123	35.53 N	76.30 E
Goéland, Lac au ⊜	176	49.47 N	76.48 W
Goélands, Lac aux ⊜	176	55.27 N	64.17 W
Goeree I	52	51.50 N	3.55 E
Goes	52	51.30 N	3.54 E
Goetzenbruck	56	48.59 N	7.23 E
Goff, Som.	144	2.39 N	41.00 E
Goff, Ks., U.S.	198	39.39 N	95.55 W
Goff Creek ≃	196	36.43 N	101.29 W
Goffle Brook ≃	276	40.56 N	74.08 W
Goff's Oak	260	51.43 N	0.05 W
Goffstown	188	43.01 N	71.36 W
Gogama	190	47.40 N	81.43 W
Gogebic, Lake ⊜	190	46.30 N	89.35 W
Gogebic Range ⋌ 2	190	46.30 N	90.10 W
Göggingen	58	48.20 N	10.52 E
Gogland, ostrov I	76	60.04 N	27.00 E
Goglio	58	46.18 N	8.16 E
Gogoi	156	20.17 S	33.08 E
Gogolevo	78	49.56 N	33.48 E
Gogonou	150	10.50 N	2.50 E
Gogo-shima I	96	33.54 N	132.41 E
Gogrial	140	8.32 N	28.07 E
Gohad	124	26.26 N	78.27 E
Gohāla	126	23.15 N	89.59 E
Gohāla ≃	126	24.08 N	89.35 E
Gohāna	124	29.08 N	76.42 E
Gohfeld	52	52.12 N	8.45 E
Gohitafla	150	7.30 N	5.53 W
Göhl	54	54.17 N	10.56 E
Gohoku	96	33.39 N	133.21 E
Go Home Lake ⊜	212	45.00 N	79.51 W
Gohpur	120	26.53 N	93.38 E
Gohr	263	51.06 N	6.43 E
Göhrde	54	53.08 N	10.52 E
Göhren	54	54.20 N	13.44 E
Goiana, Bra.	250	7.33 S	34.59 W
Goianá, Bra.	256	21.32 S	43.12 W
Goianápolis	255	16.30 S	49.01 W
Goiandira	255	18.08 S	48.06 W
Goianésia	255	15.18 S	49.07 W
Goiânia	255	16.40 S	49.16 W
Goianinha	250	6.16 S	35.12 W
Goiás	255	15.56 S	50.08 W
Goiás □ 3	255	16.00 S	50.00 W
Goiatuba	255	18.01 S	49.22 W
Goichran	120	31.04 N	78.07 E
Goil, Loch ⊂	46	56.08 N	4.52 W
Goio-Erê	252	24.12 S	53.01 W
Gôio-Erê ≃	252	24.14 S	53.21 W
Goirle	52	51.32 N	5.04 E
Góis	34	40.09 N	8.07 W
Goito	64	45.15 N	10.40 E
Gojam □ 4	144	11.00 N	37.00 E
Gojeb ≃	144	7.20 N	37.21 E
Gojō	96	34.21 N	135.42 E
Gojōme	92	39.56 N	140.07 E
Gojra	123	31.09 N	72.41 E
Gojtchskij, pereval)(	84	44.18 N	39.18 E
Gök ≃	130	41.24 N	35.08 E
Gokāk	122	16.10 N	74.50 E
Gokarna	126	24.03 N	88.07 E
Gokase ≃	92	32.35 N	131.42 E
Gökçeada I	130	40.10 N	25.50 E
Gökçebey	130	41.19 N	32.08 E
Gökçedağ	130	39.33 N	28.56 E
Gökçekent	130	40.19 N	38.07 E
Gökçeli	130	40.35 N	36.44 E
Gökçen	130	38.07 N	27.53 E
Gökçesu	130	40.54 N	31.58 E
Gökdere, Tür.	130	38.44 N	40.13 E
Gökdere, Tür.	130	40.29 N	36.47 E
Gōkōmutsumi	268	35.48 N	139.59 E
Gökova Körfezi ⊂	130	36.50 N	28.00 E
Göksholm	40	59.16 N	15.33 E
Göksu ≃, Tür.	84	39.19 N	42.17 E
Göksu ≃, Tür.	130	36.19 N	34.02 E
Göksu ≃, Tür.	130	37.37 N	35.35 E
Göksu ≃, Tür.	267b	41.06 N	29.03 E
Göksun	130	38.03 N	36.30 E
Göktaş	130	41.17 N	41.46 E
Göktepe	130	37.15 N	28.36 E
Göktürk ⊸ 8	267b	41.11 N	28.53 E
Gokwe	154	18.07 S	28.58 E
Gol	26	60.42 N	8.57 E
Gol, Khawr V	140	6.55 N	30.16 E
Golabāri	272b	22.36 N	88.20 E
Golāghāt	120	26.31 N	93.58 E
Gola Gokarannāth	124	28.05 N	80.28 E
Gola Island I	48	55.05 N	8.22 W
Golaja Pristan'	78	46.31 N	32.31 E
Gołańcz	30	52.57 N	17.18 E
Golan Heights ▴ 4	132	32.55 N	35.42 E
Golāshkerd	128	27.59 N	57.16 E
Golbāf	128	29.51 N	57.44 E
Gölbası, Tür.	130	37.50 N	37.40 E
Gölbaşı, Tür.	130	39.48 N	32.49 E
Golborne	262	53.29 N	2.36 W
Golcar	262	53.39 N	1.51 W
Gol'čicha	74	71.43 N	83.36 E
Golconda, Il., U.S.	194	37.22 N	88.29 W
Golconda, Nv., U.S.	204	40.57 N	117.29 W
Gölcük, Tür.	130	39.18 N	27.59 E
Gölcük, Tür.	130	40.44 N	29.48 E
Golczewo	54	53.49 N	14.59 E
Gołdap	30	54.19 N	22.19 E
Goldau	58	47.03 N	8.33 E
Gold Bar	224	47.51 N	121.41 W
Gold Beach	202	42.24 N	124.25 W
Goldbeck	54	52.43 N	11.52 E
Goldberg	54	53.35 N	12.05 E
Goldberger See ⊜	54	53.36 N	12.07 E
Goldbergtunnel ⊸ 5	263	51.01 N	7.28 E
Goldbey	58	48.12 N	6.26 E
Goldboro	186	45.11 N	61.39 W
Gold Bridge	182	50.51 N	122.50 W
Gold Coast ▴ 2	150	5.20 N	0.45 W
Gold Coast → Southport	171a	27.58 S	153.25 E
Gold Creek	180	62.46 N	149.41 W
Gold Creek ≃	182	49.04 N	115.12 W
Golden, B.C., Can.	182	51.18 N	116.58 W
Golden, Ire.	48	52.29 N	7.58 W
Golden, Co., U.S.	200	39.45 N	105.13 W
Golden, Il., U.S.	219	40.07 N	91.01 W
Golden Bay ⊂	172	40.40 S	172.50 E
Golden Beach	220	25.57 N	80.07 W
Golden Brook ≃	283	42.44 N	71.19 W
Golden City	194	37.23 N	94.05 W
Goldendale	224	45.49 N	120.49 W
Golden Ears Provincial Park ♠	182	49.30 N	122.25 W
Goldene Aue V	54	51.25 N	11.00 E
Golden Gate	220	26.09 N	81.43 W
Golden Gate)(	226	37.49 N	122.29 W
Golden Gate Bridge ⊸ 5	282	37.49 N	122.28 W
Golden Gate Fields Race Track ♠	282	37.53 N	122.19 W
Golden Gate Highlands National Park ♠	158	28.30 S	28.40 E
Golden Gate National Recreation Area ♠	282	37.49 N	122.31 W
Golden Gate Park ♠	282	37.46 N	122.28 W
Golden Green	260	51.12 N	0.21 E
Golden Hill Creek ≃	210	43.22 N	78.28 W
Golden Hinde ∧	182	49.40 N	125.45 W
Golden Horn → Haliç ⊂	267b	41.02 N	28.58 E
Golden Lake ⊜	190	45.35 N	77.20 W
Golden Meadow	194	29.22 N	90.15 W
Golden Prairie	184	50.14 N	109.38 W
Golden Ring Mall ⊸ 9	284b	39.20 N	76.29 W
Golden Rock	122	10.48 N	78.44 E
Goldenrod	220	28.37 N	81.18 W
Golden Spike National Historic Site ⊥	202	41.38 N	112.35 W
Goldenstedt	52	52.48 N	8.25 E
Golden Valley V	42	52.02 N	2.56 W
Golders Green ⊸ 8	260	51.35 N	0.12 W
Goldfield, Ia., U.S.	190	42.44 N	93.55 W
Goldfield, Nv., U.S.	204	37.42 N	117.14 W
Gold Lake ⊜	212	44.43 N	78.17 W
Goldlauter	54	50.38 N	10.44 E
Gold Mountain ∧	204	37.15 N	117.18 W
Goldney	258	34.37 S	59.18 W
Goldonna	194	32.01 N	92.54 W
Goldpan Peak ∧	180	61.12 N	153.22 W
Gold River	182	49.41 N	126.08 W
Gold Rock	184	49.27 N	92.43 W
Gold Run	226	39.10 N	120.52 W
Goldsand Lake ⊜	184	57.02 N	101.08 W
Goldsboro, Md., U.S.	208	39.02 N	75.47 W
Goldsboro, N.C., U.S.	192	35.23 N	77.59 W
Goldsmith, In., U.S.	216	40.17 N	86.08 W
Goldsmith, Tx., U.S.	196	31.58 N	102.36 W
Goldsmith, Lake ⊜	169	37.32 S	143.21 E
Goldston	192	35.35 N	79.19 W
Goldstone Lake ⊜	228	35.22 N	116.54 W
Goldstream Provincial Park ♠	224	48.29 N	123.33 W
Goldsworthy	162	20.20 S	119.30 E
Goldsworthy, Mount ∧ 2	162	20.21 S	119.32 E
Goldthwaite	196	31.26 N	98.34 W
Göle	130	40.48 N	42.36 E
Golec, gora ∧	88	58.39 N	94.10 E
Goleen	48	51.28 N	9.43 W
Golela	158	27.20 S	31.55 E
Goleniów	30	53.36 N	14.50 E
Golestan Palace ⊎	267d	35.41 N	51.25 E
Goleta	204	34.26 N	119.49 W
Golf, Fl., U.S.	220	26.31 N	80.06 W
Golf, Il., U.S.	278	42.03 N	87.48 W
Golfcrest	216	41.57 N	83.22 W
Golfe-Juan	62	43.34 N	7.05 E
Golfito	236	8.38 N	83.11 W
Golf Manor	285	39.42 N	75.28 W
Golf Mill ⊸ 9	278	42.03 N	87.50 W
Golfo Aranci	71	40.59 N	9.38 E
Golfo de Santa Clara	232	31.42 N	114.30 W
Golfside	281	42.15 N	83.41 W
Golf View	208	39.43 N	75.28 W
Golfview Hills	278	41.47 N	87.56 W
Gölhisar	130	37.10 N	29.30 E
Goliad	196	28.40 N	97.23 W
Goliad □ 6	222	28.52 N	97.22 W
Golicyno, Ross.	80	53.38 N	44.07 E
Golicyno, Ross.	80	55.58 N	40.26 E
Golicyno, Ross.	82	55.37 N	36.59 E
Golina	30	52.16 N	18.05 E
Golin Baixing	89	44.53 N	121.58 E
Golinda	222	31.25 N	97.05 W
Goljama Kamčija ≃	38	43.03 N	27.29 E
Goljam Perelik ∧	38	41.36 N	24.34 E
Goljanovo ⊸ 8	265b	55.49 N	37.48 E
Goljevo	265b	55.48 N	37.19 E
Gölköy	130	40.42 N	37.38 E
Gollach ≃	56	49.31 N	10.00 E
Göllersbach ≃	61	48.22 N	16.11 E
Göllet	130	40.45 N	42.18 E
Golling an der Salzach	64	47.36 N	13.10 E
Golm	264a	52.24 N	12.57 E
Gölmarmara	130	38.42 N	27.56 E
Golmberg ∧ 2	54	52.01 N	13.21 E
Gol'movskij	83	48.25 N	38.05 E
Golmud	102	36.22 N	94.55 E
Golmud ≃	102	36.54 N	95.11 E
Golo ≃	32	42.31 N	9.32 E
Goloby	78	51.06 N	24.59 E
Golodnaja Guba, ozero ⊜	24	67.52 N	52.48 E
Gologory ⋌	78	49.45 N	24.35 E
Golo Island I	116	13.40 N	120.22 E
Golok (Kolok) ≃	114	6.15 N	102.05 E
Golongoso	146	9.00 N	19.09 E
Gölören	130	37.48 N	33.52 E
Gölova	130	40.04 N	38.37 E
Golovačovka	85	42.52 N	71.13 E
Golovanevsk	78	48.23 N	30.28 E
Golovanovo	80	54.55 N	40.27 E
Golovčin	76	54.04 N	29.55 E
Golovčino	78	50.32 N	35.47 E
Golovin	180	64.33 N	163.02 W
Golovinka	84	43.48 N	39.28 E
Golovino, Ross.	76	55.58 N	40.26 E
Golovino, Ross.	82	56.01 N	39.11 E
Golovinščino	80	53.18 N	43.59 E
Golovinskaja	88	53.26 N	102.43 E
Golovnino	82	54.23 N	36.10 E
Golovno	78	51.21 N	24.04 E
Golovskoje	88	55.30 N	105.32 E
Golpāyegān	128	33.27 N	50.18 E
Gölpazarı	130	40.15 N	30.19 E
Golra	123	33.42 N	72.58 E
Golrān	128	35.06 N	61.41 E
Gols	61	47.54 N	16.55 E
Gol'šany	76	54.15 N	26.01 E
Gölsdorf	54	51.59 N	12.39 E
Golspie, Austl.	170	34.17 S	149.40 E
Golspie, Scot., U.K.	46	57.58 N	3.58 W
Golssen	54	51.58 N	13.36 E
Gol't'ajevo	82	55.13 N	36.02 E
Gol't'avino	88	58.26 N	98.27 E
Golub-Dobrzyń	30	53.08 N	19.02 E
Golubi	76	59.28 N	41.39 E
Golubinskij	80	48.52 N	43.34 E
Golubovka, Kaz.	86	53.09 N	74.12 E
Golubovka, Ukr.	78	48.53 N	35.19 E
Golubovka ⊸ 8	83	48.38 N	38.39 E
Golumet'	88	53.03 N	102.21 E
Golungo Alto	152	9.08 S	14.46 E
Golva	198	46.44 N	103.59 W
Golweyn	144	1.40 N	44.35 E
Gölyaka	130	40.47 N	30.59 E
Golynki	76	54.52 N	31.23 E
Golyšmanovo, Ross.	86	56.28 N	68.38 E
Golyšmanovo, Ross.	86	56.23 N	68.23 E
Golzheim ⊸ 8	263	51.15 N	6.46 E
Golzow, Dtsch.	54	52.34 N	14.29 E
Golzow, Dtsch.	54	52.16 N	12.36 E
Goma	154	1.41 S	29.14 E
Gomadan-zan ∧	96	34.03 N	135.34 E
Gomagoi	64	46.35 N	10.32 E
Gomang Co ⊜	120	31.15 N	89.15 E
Gomaringen	58	48.27 N	9.05 E
Gomas, Sierra de ⋌	196	26.23 N	100.32 W
Gomati ≃	124	25.32 N	83.10 E
Gomati Plain ≚	124	26.30 N	81.10 E
Goma Tsétsé	273b	4.14 S	15.08 E
Gombari	154	2.43 N	29.04 E
Gombe, Nig.	146	10.19 N	11.02 E
Gombe, Zaïre	152	0.42 S	17.35 E
Gombe Stream National Park ♠	154	4.30 S	29.42 E
Gombi	146	10.10 N	12.45 E
Gomboro	150	13.29 N	2.46 W
Gomel'	76	52.25 N	31.00 E
Gomel' □ 8	76	52.30 N	30.00 E
Gomer	216	40.51 N	84.11 W
Gomera I	148	28.06 N	17.08 W
Gometra I	46	56.29 N	6.17 W
Gometz-la-Ville	261	48.40 N	2.08 E
Gometz-le-Châtel	261	48.41 N	2.08 E
Gomez	220	27.06 N	80.09 W
Gómez Farías, Méx.	232	29.18 N	107.40 W
Gómez Farías, Méx.	234	19.47 N	103.29 W
Gómez Palacio	232	25.34 N	103.30 W
Gómez Plata	246	6.41 N	75.12 W
Gomīshān	128	37.04 N	54.06 E
Gommécourt	261	49.05 N	1.36 E
Gommern	54	52.04 N	11.50 E
Gomo Co ⊜	120	33.47 N	85.30 E
Gomogomo	164	6.40 S	134.43 E
Gomoh	126	23.52 N	86.10 E
Gompa	123	35.02 N	77.20 E
Goms V	58	46.27 N	8.15 E
Gomshall	260	51.13 N	0.27 W
Gomumu, Pulau I	164	1.49 S	127.38 E
Gonābād	128	34.20 N	58.42 E
Gonaïves	238	19.27 N	72.41 W
Gonaka	152	2.56 S	13.14 E
Gonam	74	57.21 N	131.12 E
Gonam ≃	74	57.21 N	131.14 E
Gonarezhou National Park ♠	154	21.30 S	32.00 E
Gonars	64	45.53 N	13.13 E
Gonäs	40	60.09 N	15.06 E
Gonâve, Golfe de la ⊂	238	19.00 N	73.30 W
Gonâve, Île de la I	238	18.51 N	73.03 W
Gonbad-e Qābūs	128	37.17 N	55.17 E
Gonçalves	256	22.40 S	45.51 W
Gonçalves Dias	250	4.57 S	44.14 W
Gončarovka	78	50.32 N	39.28 E
Goncelin	62	45.20 N	5.59 E
Gonda	124	27.08 N	81.56 E
Gondal	120	21.58 N	70.48 E
Gondang	115a	7.24 S	111.06 E
Gondarbal	123	34.14 N	74.47 E
Gondar → Gonder	144	12.40 N	37.30 E
Gonder	144	12.40 N	37.30 E
Gonder □ 4	144	13.10 N	37.00 E
Gondey	146	9.09 N	19.19 E
Gondia	120	21.27 N	80.12 E
Gondola	156	19.10 S	33.40 E
Gondomar	34	41.09 N	8.32 W
Gondrecourt-le-Château	58	48.31 N	5.30 E
Gondreville	58	48.42 N	5.58 E

Symbol	English	Deutsch	Español	Français	Português
≃	River	Fluß	Río	Rivière	Rio
≍	Canal	Kanal	Canal	Canal	Canal
∟	Waterfall, Rapids	Wasserfall, Stromschnellen	Cascada, Rápidos	Chute d'eau, Rapides	Cascata, Rápidos
)(	Strait	Meeresstraße	Estrecho	Détroit	Estreito
⊂	Bay, Gulf	Bucht, Golf	Bahía, Golfo	Baie, Golfe	Baía, Golfo
⊜	Lake, Lakes	See, Seen	Lago, Lagos	Lac, Lacs	Lago, Lagos
⩶	Swamp	Sumpf	Pantano	Marais	Pântano
⊼	Ice Features, Glacier	Eis- und Gletscherformen	Accidentes Glaciales	Formes glaciaires	Acidentes glaciares
≃	Other Hydrographic Features	Andere Hydrographische Objekte	Otros Elementos Hidrográficos	Autres données hydrographiques	Outros acidentes hidrográficos
✦	Submarine Features	Untermeerische Objekte	Accidentes Submarinos	Formes de relief sous-marin	Acidentes submarinos
□	Political Unit	Politische Einheit	Unidad Politica	Entité politique	Unidade política
⊎	Cultural Institution	Kulturelle Institution	Institución Cultural	Institution culturelle	Instituição cultural
⊥	Historical Site	Historische Stätte	Sitio Histórico	Site historique	Sitio histórico
♠	Recreational Site	Erholungs- und Ferienort	Sitio de Recreo	Centre de loisirs	Area de Lazer
⊠	Airport	Flughafen	Aeropuerto	Aéroport	Aeroporto
■	Military Installation	Militäranlage	Instalación Militar	Installation militaire	Instalação militar
⊸	Miscellaneous	Verschiedenes	Misceláneo	Divers	Diversos

Gondrexange, Étang de ⊜ 58 48.42 N 6.54 E
Goneãna 123 30.19 N 74.54 E
Gönen, Tür. 130 40.06 N 27.39 E
Gonén, Yis. 132 33.08 N 35.39 E
Gonesse 50 48.59 N 2.27 E
Gonfaron 62 43.19 N 6.17 E
Gong ≃ 100 26.00 N 115.22 E
Gong'an 102 30.02 N 112.04 E
Gonganbao 86 44.59 N 86.18 E
Gonganpucun 104 41.19 N 123.27 E
Gongbuchang 105 40.17 N 116.15 E
Gongchangling 104 41.06 N 123.30 E
Gongcheng 102 24.49 N 110.46 E
Gongchenqiao 106 30.20 N 120.08 E
Gongchuan, Zhg. 100 26.06 N 117.24 E
Gongchuan, Zhg. 102 23.40 N 107.50 E
Gongcun 105 39.28 N 116.10 E
Gongdaoqiao 100 32.36 N 119.22 E
Gongdian 100 28.06 N 116.56 E
Gongen-yama ∧ 94 35.40 N 139.01 E
Gongfang 100 27.36 N 115.34 E
Gonggar 120 29.17 N 90.46 E
Gongga Shan (Minya Konka) ∧ 102 29.35 N 101.51 E
Gonghe 102 36.20 N 100.48 E
Gonghui 98 41.12 N 114.37 E
Gongjialu 106 31.17 N 121.40 E
Gongjiatun 104 40.55 N 120.37 E
Gongjiazhai 104 41.57 N 124.01 E
Gongjing 107 29.21 N 104.43 E
Gongjingying 105 39.12 N 116.11 E
Gongkou 98 35.38 N 119.47 E
Gongli 98 35.55 N 117.24 E
Gongling 100 26.18 N 119.40 E
Gongliu 86 43.30 N 82.15 E
Gonglu Shan ∧ 106 30.39 N 119.18 E
Gongo 146 9.00 N 18.56 E
Gongola □3 146 9.00 N 11.40 E
Gongola ≃ 146 9.30 N 12.04 E
Gongoué 152 0.32 S 9.12 E
Gongo-Yembe 152 1.58 S 18.40 E
Gongpengzi 89 45.09 N 125.39 E
Gongping 100 23.05 N 115.24 E
Gongpingxu 100 26.12 N 112.51 E
Gongshan 102 25.50 N 103.13 E
Gongshiya 120 31.25 N 84.37 E
Gongsizhen 106 31.41 N 121.48 E
Gongtangtou 106 31.48 N 118.42 E
Gongxi 100 27.38 N 115.52 E
Gongxian 102 34.48 N 113.03 E
Gongyefu 98 42.16 N 118.32 E
Gongyemiao 89 43.40 N 121.06 E
Gongyingzi 98 40.54 N 119.41 E
Gongzhutun 104 42.10 N 123.00 E
Gongzui 107 29.19 N 103.28 E
Goni, It. 71 39.34 N 9.17 E
Goñi, Ur. 252 33.31 S 56.24 W
Goniądz 30 53.30 N 22.45 E
Gonini ≃ 250 4.10 N 54.24 W
Goniri 146 11.30 N 12.20 E
Gonjo 102 30.43 N 98.19 E
Gonnesa 71 39.16 N 8.28 E
Gonnesa, Golfo di c 71 39.17 N 8.23 E
Gonnosfanadiga 71 39.29 N 8.39 E
Gonnostramatza 71 39.41 N 8.50 E
Gonochovo 86 52.57 N 81.20 E
Gōnoura 92 33.45 N 129.41 E
Gonubie Mouth 158 32.57 S 28.01 E
Gonža 89 53.36 N 125.19 E
Gonzaga, It. 64 44.57 N 10.49 E
Gonzaga, Pil. 116 18.16 N 122.00 E
Gonzales, Ca., U.S. 226 36.30 N 121.26 W
Gonzales, La., U.S. 194 30.14 N 90.55 W
Gonzales, Tx., U.S. 222 29.30 N 97.27 W
Gonzales □6 222 29.28 N 97.30 W
González, Méx. 234 22.50 N 98.27 W
González, Ur. 258 34.14 S 56.52 W
González, Riacho ≃ 252 22.48 S 57.54 W
González Catán 258 34.46 S 58.39 W
González Chaves 252 38.02 S 60.06 W
González Moreno 252 35.33 S 63.22 W
González Ortega, Méx. 204 32.40 N 115.23 W
González Ortega, Méx. 234 23.11 N 102.29 W
González Ortega, Méx. 234 23.59 N 103.27 W
González Risos 258 34.52 S 59.13 W
Gonzanamá 246 4.15 S 79.27 W
Goobarragandra ≃ 171b 35.20 S 148.15 E
Goochland 192 37.41 N 77.53 W
Good Easter 260 51.47 N 0.21 E
Goodells 214 42.59 N 82.40 W
Goode Mountain ∧ 224 48.29 N 120.55 W
Goodenough, Mount ∧ 180 67.56 N 135.31 W
Goodenough Bay c 164 9.55 S 150.00 E
Goodenough Island I 164 9.20 S 150.15 E
Gooderham 212 44.54 N 78.23 W
Goodeve 184 51.04 N 103.10 W
Goodfellow Air Force Base ■ 196 31.26 N 100.25 W
Good Hope, S. Afr. 158 31.51 S 21.55 E
Good Hope, Oh., U.S. 218 39.26 N 83.21 W
Good Hope, Cape of (Kaap die Gooie Hoop) ≻ 158 34.24 S 18.30 E
Goodhope Bay c 180 66.10 N 163.45 W
Good Hope Mountain ∧ 182 51.09 N 124.10 W
Goodhouse 158 28.57 S 18.13 E
Goodhue 190 44.24 N 92.37 W
Gooding 202 42.56 N 114.42 W
Goodison 214 42.44 N 83.10 W
Goodland, Fl., U.S. 220 25.55 N 81.38 W
Goodland, In., U.S. 216 40.45 N 87.17 W
Goodland, Ks., U.S. 198 39.21 N 101.42 W
Goodlands 184 49.05 N 100.35 W
Goodlow Park 222 32.07 N 96.14 W
Goodman, Ms., U.S. 194 32.58 N 89.54 W
Goodman, Wi., U.S. 190 45.37 N 88.21 W
Goodna 171a 27.37 S 152.54 E
Goodnews Bay 180 59.07 N 161.35 W
Goodnight 200 38.14 N 104.43 W
Goodooga 166 29.07 S 147.27 E
Goodradigbee ≃ 171b 35.08 S 148.41 E
Goodrich, Mi., U.S. 216 42.55 N 83.30 W
Goodrich, N.D., U.S. 198 47.28 N 100.07 W
Goodrich, Tx., U.S. 222 30.36 N 94.57 W
Good Spirit Lake ⊜ 184 51.34 N 102.40 W
Good Spirit Lake Provincial Park ♦ 184 51.36 N 102.45 W
Good Thunder 190 44.00 N 94.03 W
Goodview 190 44.03 N 91.41 W
Goodville 208 40.08 N 76.00 W
Goodwater 194 33.03 N 86.03 W
Goodwell 196 36.35 N 101.38 W
Goodwick 42 52.00 N 5.00 W
Goodwin, Lake ⊜ 224 48.08 N 122.18 W
Goodwives ≃ 276 41.04 N 73.28 W
Goodwood 212 44.02 N 79.12 W
Goodyear 200 33.26 N 112.21 W
Goof, Webi ≃ 144 1.10 N 43.43 E
Googong Reservoir ⊜1 171b 35.27 S 149.16 E
Gooie Hoop, Kaap die — Good Hope, Cape of ≻ 158 34.24 S 18.30 E
Goole 44 53.42 N 0.52 W
Goolgowi 166 33.59 S 145.42 E
Goolwa 168b 35.31 S 138.47 E
Goomalling 162 31.19 S 116.49 E
Goombalie 166 29.59 S 145.23 E
Goombungee 171a 27.18 S 151.51 E
Goomburra 171a 28.03 S 152.07 E
Goonda 156 19.51 S 34.00 E
Goondiwindi 166 28.32 S 150.19 E
Goongarrie 162 30.03 S 121.09 E
Goongarrie National Park ♦ 162 29.58 S 121.34 E
Goonyella 166 21.45 S 147.55 E
Goor 52 52.14 N 6.35 E
Goose ≃, Ab., Can. 182 54.58 N 117.11 W
Goose ≃, N.D., U.S. 198 47.28 N 96.52 W
Goose Bay c 281 42.35 N 82.41 W
Goose Bay — Happy Valley-Goose Bay 176 53.20 N 60.25 W
Gooseberry Creek ≃ 202 43.55 N 108.04 W
Goose Creek 192 32.58 N 80.01 W
Goose Creek ≃, U.S. 202 42.33 N 113.46 W
Goose Creek ≃, Ne., U.S. 198 42.02 N 100.03 W
Goose Creek ≃, N.Y., U.S. 214 42.06 N 79.22 W
Goose Creek ≃, Va., U.S. 208 39.06 N 77.29 W
Goose Island I 182 51.55 N 128.25 W
Goose Lake ⊜, Mb., Can. 184 54.26 N 101.30 W
Goose Lake ⊜, On., Can. 184 51.46 N 93.00 W
Goose Lake ⊜, On., Can. 212 44.25 N 78.52 W
Goose Lake ⊜, On., Can. 214 42.31 N 82.31 W
Goose Lake ⊜, Sk., Can. 184 51.45 N 107.23 W
Goose Lake ⊜, U.S. 204 41.57 N 120.25 W
Goose Lake Canal ≅ 226 35.50 N 119.37 W
Goose Lake Prairie State Park ♦ 216 41.21 N 88.18 W
Gooseprairie 224 46.54 N 121.15 W
Goostrey 262 53.13 N 2.20 W
Gooty 122 15.07 N 77.38 E
Gopālganj, Bngl. 124 23.01 N 89.50 E
Gopālganj, India 124 26.28 N 84.26 E
Gopālnagar, India 126 23.03 N 88.45 E
Gopālnagar, India 272b 22.50 N 88.14 E
Gopālpur, Bngl. 124 24.33 N 89.56 E
Gopālpur, India 272b 22.38 N 88.27 E
Gopeng 114 4.28 N 101.10 E
Göpfritz an der Wild 61 48.43 N 15.24 E
Gopiballabhpur 126 22.13 N 86.54 E
Gopichettipālaiyam 122 11.28 N 77.27 E
Gopinagar 272b 22.50 N 88.07 E
Goppenstein 58 46.22 N 7.45 E
Göppingen 56 48.42 N 9.40 E
Goqên 102 29.15 N 96.59 E
Go Quao 110 9.43 N 105.17 E
Gor 123 35.32 N 74.31 E
Góra, Pol. 30 51.40 N 16.33 E
Gora, Ross. 76 60.02 N 41.43 E
Gor'ačegorsk 86 55.24 N 88.55 E
Gor'ačij Kl'uč 84 44.37 N 39.07 E
Gor'ačinsk 88 52.59 N 108.18 E
Goradit 144 11.25 N 38.25 E
Goradiz 84 39.27 N 47.20 E
Góra Kalwaria 30 51.59 N 21.12 E
Gorakhpur 124 26.45 N 83.22 E
Gor'any 76 55.25 N 29.02 E
Goras 124 25.32 N 76.56 E
Goražde 38 43.40 N 18.56 E
Gorbačevo Michajlovka 83 47.50 N 38.00 E
Gorbatov 80 56.08 N 43.04 E
Gorbatovka 80 56.15 N 43.45 E
Gorbica 88 53.06 N 119.13 E
Gorboviči 76 53.49 N 30.41 E
Gorčucha 80 57.43 N 43.43 E
Gorda, Punta ≻, Chile 248 19.18 S 70.18 W
Gorda, Punta ≻, Cuba 240p 22.24 N 82.10 W
Gorda, Punta ≻, Nic. 236 14.21 N 83.12 W
Gorda, Punta ≻, Nic. 236 11.26 N 83.48 W
Gordejevka 76 52.59 N 31.58 E
Gordes, Fr. 62 43.54 N 5.12 E
Gördes, Tür. 130 38.54 N 28.18 E
Gordil 146 9.44 N 21.35 E
Gørding 41 55.29 N 8.48 E
Gordion ⊥ 130 39.41 N 32.01 E
Gordo 194 33.19 N 87.54 W
Gordo, Cerro ∧ 234 20.46 N 102.35 W
Gordola 58 46.11 N 8.52 E
Gordon, Scot., U.K. 46 55.41 N 2.34 W
Gordon, Ga., U.S. 192 32.52 N 83.19 W
Gordon, Ne., U.S. 198 42.48 N 102.12 W
Gordon, Oh., U.S. 218 39.56 N 84.31 W
Gordon, Pa., U.S. 208 40.45 N 76.21 W
Gordon, Wi., U.S. 190 46.14 N 91.47 W
Gordon ≃ 224 48.35 N 124.24 W
Gordon, Isla I 254 54.58 S 69.35 W
Gordon, Lake ⊜1 166 42.42 S 146.12 E
Gordon Creek ≃ 198 42.49 N 100.40 W
Gordon Downs 162 18.44 S 128.35 E
Gordon Heights 207 40.51 N 72.58 W
Gordon Horne Peak ∧ 182 51.46 N 118.50 W
Gordon Indian Reserve ◆4 184 51.16 N 104.16 W
Gordon Lake ⊜, Ab., Can. 184 56.30 N 110.25 W
Gordon Lake ⊜, Sk., Can. 184 55.50 N 106.26 W
Gordon Lakes 276 41.03 N 74.22 W
Gordon Pass c 220 26.06 N 81.48 W
Gordon River 224 48.47 N 124.21 W
Gordon's Bay 158 34.10 S 18.52 E
Gordonsville 188 38.08 N 78.11 W
Gordonton 172 37.40 S 175.18 E
Gordonvale 166 17.05 S 145.47 E
Gordonville 220 27.57 N 81.49 W
Gore, Austl. 166 28.17 S 151.29 E
Gore, N.S., Can. 186 45.07 N 63.43 W
Gore, Ityo. 144 8.08 N 35.33 E
Gore, N.Z. 172 46.06 S 168.58 E
Goré, Tchad 146 7.53 N 16.40 E
Gore Bay 190 45.55 N 82.28 W
Gorebridge 46 55.51 N 3.02 W
Goreda 164 3.39 S 134.58 E
Goree 196 33.28 N 99.31 W
Gore Hill 274a 33.49 S 151.11 E
Görele 130 41.02 N 39.00 E
Gorelki 82 54.15 N 37.37 E
Goreloje 80 52.57 N 41.28 E
Gorelovo 265a 59.47 N 30.08 E
Gorelovo Airport ✈ 265a 59.47 N 30.05 E
Gorelyj ≃ 265a 59.58 N 30.28 E
Göreme Milli Parkı ♦ 130 38.26 N 34.54 E
Gore Mountain ∧ 188 44.55 N 71.48 W
Gorenki 265b 55.48 N 37.55 E
Gore Point ≻, Austl. 166 17.38 S 139.56 E
Gore Point ≻, Ak., U.S. 180 59.12 N 151.00 W
Gore Range ⋏ 200 40.00 N 106.30 W
Goretovka ≃ 265b 55.56 N 37.20 E
Goreville 194 37.33 N 88.58 W
Gorey, Ire. 48 52.40 N 6.18 W
Gorey, Jersey 43b 49.12 N 2.02 W
Gorfoundurei 144 4.30 N 46.41 E
Gorgān 128 36.50 N 54.29 E
Gorgān ≃ 128 36.59 N 54.04 E
Gorgany ⋏ 78 48.30 N 24.00 E
Gorge Lake ⊜1 224 48.42 N 121.13 W
Görgeshausen 56 50.24 N 7.56 E
Gorgoglione 68 40.23 N 16.09 E
Gorgol □4 150 16.00 N 13.00 W
Gorgol el Abiod ≃ 150 16.14 N 12.58 W
Gorgol el Akhdar ≃ 150 16.13 N 12.58 W
Gorgona, Isla I 246 2.59 N 78.12 W
Gorgonzola 64 45.32 N 9.24 E
Gorgor 248 10.35 S 77.02 W
Gorgora 144 12.13 N 37.16 E
Gorgoram 146 12.38 N 10.43 E
Gorgota 38 44.47 N 26.05 E
Gorgova 38 45.11 N 29.10 E
Gorham, Me., U.S. 188 43.40 N 70.26 W
Gorham, N.H., U.S. 188 44.23 N 71.10 W
Gorham, N.Y., U.S. 210 42.47 N 77.07 W
Gorhambury House ⊥ 260 51.47 N 0.24 W
Gori 84 41.58 N 44.07 E
Goria 272b 22.24 N 88.29 E
Gorica — Gorizia 64 45.57 N 13.38 E
Goričan 61 46.23 N 16.41 E
Goricy 76 57.09 N 36.44 E
Gorinchem 52 51.50 N 5.00 E
Goring 42 51.32 N 1.09 W
Goring-by-Sea 42 50.49 N 0.25 W
Goring Gap V 42 51.32 N 1.08 W
Goris 84 39.31 N 46.23 E
Göritz 54 53.24 N 13.54 E
Göritzhain 54 50.58 N 12.47 E
Gorizia 64 45.57 N 13.38 E
Gorizia □4 64 45.55 N 13.30 E
Gorj □6 38 45.00 N 23.20 E
Gorjani 38 45.24 N 18.21 E
Gor'kaja Balka 84 44.17 N 43.59 E
Gor'kaja balka ≃ 84 44.38 N 45.00 E
Görke 54 53.51 N 13.38 E
Gorkhā 124 28.00 N 84.37 E
Gorki, Bela. 76 54.17 N 30.59 E
Gorki, Ross. 80 57.38 N 45.05 E
Gorki, Ross. 82 54.18 N 36.08 E
Gorki, Ross. 82 55.32 N 37.45 E
Gorki, Ross. 82 56.54 N 38.51 E
Gorki, Ross. 265b 55.57 N 37.55 E
Gor'kij — Nižnij Novgorod 80 56.20 N 44.00 E
Gorki — Nižnij Novgorod 80 56.20 N 44.00 E
Gorki Vtoryje 265b 55.44 N 37.11 E
Gor'koje, ozero ⊜ 86 52.30 N 81.20 E
Gor'kovskoje 86 55.22 N 74.24 E
Gor'kovskoje vodochranilišče ⊜1 80 57.00 N 43.10 E
Gorky — Nižnij Novgorod 80 56.20 N 44.00 E
Gorky Park ♦ 265b 55.44 N 37.36 E
Gorlago 62 45.40 N 9.49 E
Gorla Maggiore 266b 45.40 N 8.53 E
Gorla Minore 266b 45.39 N 8.54 E
Gorleston on Sea 42 52.36 N 1.43 E
Gørlev 41 55.32 N 11.14 E
Gorlice 30 49.40 N 21.10 E
Görlitz 54 51.09 N 14.59 E
Gorlosen 54 53.11 N 11.27 E
Gorlovka, Sak. 84 41.14 N 43.42 E
Gorlovka, Ukr. 83 48.18 N 38.03 E
Gorlovo 76 53.50 N 39.02 E
Gorm, Loch ⊜ 46 55.48 N 6.25 W
Gorman, Ca., U.S. 228 34.48 N 118.51 W
Gorman, Tx., U.S. 196 32.12 N 98.40 W
Gorman Creek ≃ 228 34.38 N 118.45 W
Görmin 54 53.59 N 13.16 E
Gorn'ackij, Ross. 24 67.32 N 64.03 E
Gorn'ackij, Ross. 78 48.17 N 40.55 E
Gorn'ackoje 78 47.42 N 34.08 E
Gorna Dzhumaya — Blagoevgrad 38 42.01 N 23.06 E
Gornaja Prolejka 80 49.24 N 44.59 E
Gorn'ak, Ross. 76 53.36 N 39.29 E
Gorn'ak, Ross. 86 51.00 N 81.29 E
Gorn'ak, Ukr. 78 50.20 N 24.10 E
Gorn'ak, Ukr. 83 48.04 N 37.24 E
Gornalunga ≃ 70 37.24 N 15.03 E
Gorna Orjahovica 38 43.07 N 25.41 E
Gornergrat ♦ 58 45.59 N 7.47 E
Gornja Radgona 61 46.41 N 16.00 E
Gornji Grad 36 46.18 N 14.49 E
Gornji Milanovac 38 44.01 N 20.27 E
Gornji Vakuf 36 43.56 N 17.35 E
Gorno-Altajsk 86 51.58 N 85.58 E
Gorno-Altay — Altaj □3 86 51.00 N 86.00 E
Gorno-Badachšanskaja Avtonomnaja Respublika □3 85 38.30 N 73.00 E
Gornoje 86 48.29 N 85.00 E
Gorno-Lesnoj zapovednik ♦ 85 41.10 N 69.55 E
Gornopravdinsk 86 60.07 N 69.54 E
Gornostajevka 78 47.01 N 33.44 E
Gorno-Vod'anoje 80 49.16 N 44.56 E
Gornovodnoje 89 43.42 N 134.44 E
Gornozavodsk, Ross. 86 58.20 N 58.32 E
Gornozavodsk, Ross. 89 46.34 N 141.49 E
Gornyj, Ross. 80 51.46 N 48.34 E
Gornyj, Ross. 89 44.57 N 133.59 E
Gornyj, Ross. 89 50.48 N 136.29 E
Gornyj Balyklej 80 49.34 N 45.04 E
Gornyje Kl'uči 89 45.12 N 133.31 E
Gornyj Tikič ≃ 78 48.47 N 30.53 E
Goro, Ityo. 144 6.56 N 40.32 E
Goro, N. Cal. 175f 22.16 S 167.02 E
Gorochan ∧ 144 9.22 N 37.04 E
Gorochov 78 50.30 N 24.45 E
Gorochovatka 83 49.21 N 37.31 E
Gorochovec 80 56.12 N 42.40 E
Gorochovje 76 56.31 N 30.29 E
Gorodec, Bela. 76 52.12 N 24.40 E
Gorodec, Bela. 76 52.58 N 30.21 E
Gorodec, Bela. 76 53.33 N 30.02 E
Gorodec, Ross. 76 58.32 N 29.47 E
Gorodec, Ross. 80 56.38 N 43.30 E
Gorodec, Ukr. 78 51.17 N 26.19 E
Gorodeja 76 53.19 N 26.32 E
Gorodenka 38 48.41 N 25.29 E
Gorodišče, Bela. 76 53.19 N 26.00 E
Gorodišče, Bela. 76 53.44 N 29.48 E
Gorodišče, Ross. 76 59.38 N 32.08 E
Gorodišče, Ross. 78 51.09 S 38.04 E
Gorodišče, Ross. 80 53.17 N 45.42 E
Gorodišče, Ross. 80 48.48 N 44.29 E
Gorodišče, Ross. 82 54.53 N 38.13 E
Gorodišče, Ross. 82 56.47 N 38.52 E
Gorodišče, Ukr. 78 49.17 N 31.27 E
Gorodišče, Ukr. 83 48.19 N 38.39 E
Gorodišče, Ukr. 83 49.03 N 39.38 E
Gorodišči 82 55.52 N 39.05 E
Gorodkovka 78 48.23 N 28.42 E
Gorodn'a, Ross. 82 54.57 N 38.49 E
Gorodn'a, Ross. 82 56.43 N 36.19 E
Gorodn'a, Ukr. 78 51.53 N 31.36 E
Gorodn'a ≃ 265b 55.38 N 37.48 E
Gorodnica 78 50.48 N 27.20 E
Gorodno 76 57.32 N 29.35 E
Gorodok, Bela. 76 55.28 N 29.59 E
Gorodok, Ukr. 78 49.47 N 23.39 E
Gorodok, Ukr. 78 49.10 N 26.34 E
Gorod'onka 78 48.41 N 25.29 E
Goroka 164 6.05 S 145.25 E
Gorokan 170 33.16 S 151.30 E
Gorom-Gorom 150 14.26 N 0.14 W
Gorong, Pulau I 164 3.59 S 131.25 E
Gorongosa, Parque Nacional da ♦ 156 18.45 S 34.15 E
Gorongosa, Serra da ∧ 154 18.30 S 34.03 E
Gorongose ≃ 156 20.30 S 34.40 E
Gorontalo 112 0.33 N 123.03 E
Goronyo 150 13.29 N 5.39 E
Goroubi ≃ 150 12.54 N 2.23 E
Gorouol ≃ 150 14.42 N 0.53 E
Górowo Iławeckie 30 54.17 N 20.30 E
Gorple Reservoirs ⊜1 262 53.47 N 2.06 W
Gorran ⊜ [illegible]
Gorredijk 52 53.00 N 6.05 E
Gorron 28 48.25 N 0.49 W
Görsdorf 54 51.54 N 13.29 E
Goršečnoje 78 51.32 N 38.02 E
Gorsedd 262 53.17 N 3.16 W
Gorseinon 42 51.40 N 4.02 W
Gorskaja 265a 60.03 N 29.59 E
Gorskoje 83 48.46 N 38.30 E
Gorškovo 82 54.26 N 37.59 E
Gorst 224 47.32 N 122.42 W
Gort 48 53.04 N 8.50 W
Gortahork 48 55.08 N 8.09 W
Gorton ◆8 262 53.27 N 2.10 W
Görtschitz ≃ 61 46.45 N 14.32 E
Goru, Vîrful ∧ 38 45.48 N 26.25 E
Görükle 130 40.14 N 28.50 E
Gorumna Island I 48 53.14 N 9.40 W
Gor'un ≃ 89 50.45 N 137.50 E
Gorutuba ≃ 255 14.57 S 43.33 W
Görwihl 58 47.39 N 8.04 E
Gory, Bela. 76 54.16 N 31.13 E
Gory, Kaz. 80 48.38 N 51.46 E
Goryn' ≃ 78 52.08 N 27.17 E
Gorzano, Monte ∧ 66 42.37 N 13.24 E
Gorze 56 49.03 N 6.00 E
Görz — Gorizia 64 45.57 N 13.38 E
Görzig 54 51.40 N 12.00 E
Görzke 54 52.10 N 12.22 E
Górzno 30 53.13 N 19.38 E
Gorzów Śląski 30 51.02 N 18.24 E
Gorzów Wielkopolski (Landsberg an der Warthe) 30 52.44 N 15.15 E
Gorzów Wielkopolski □4 30 52.45 N 15.20 E
Górzyca 54 52.29 N 14.40 E
Gosāba 126 22.10 N 88.48 E
Gosairhāt 126 23.05 N 90.26 E
Gosaldo 64 46.13 N 11.58 E
Gosau 64 47.34 N 13.31 E
Gosauseen ⊜ 64 47.32 N 13.31 E
Gosberton 42 52.51 N 0.09 W
Gošča 78 50.36 N 26.41 E
Göschenen 58 46.40 N 8.35 E
Goschen Strait ⊔ 164 10.09 S 150.56 E
Gose 96 34.27 N 135.44 E
Gosen, Dtsch. 264a 52.24 N 13.43 E
Gosen, Nihon 92 37.44 N 139.11 E
Gosford 170 33.26 S 151.21 E
Gosforth, Eng., U.K. 44 55.01 N 1.37 W
Gosforth, Eng., U.K. 44 54.26 N 3.27 W
Gosforth Park ♦ 273d 26.14 S 28.10 E
Gosforth Park Race Course ♦ 273d 26.14 S 28.08 E
Goshabi 140 17.58 N 31.06 E
Goshen, N.S., Can. 186 45.23 N 61.59 W
Goshen, Ca., U.S. 226 36.21 N 119.25 W
Goshen, Ct., U.S. 207 41.49 N 73.13 W
Goshen, In., U.S. 216 41.34 N 85.50 W
Goshen, Ma., U.S. 207 42.26 N 72.48 W
Goshen, N.J., U.S. 208 39.08 N 74.51 W
Goshen, N.Y., U.S. 210 41.24 N 74.19 W
Goshen, Oh., U.S. 218 39.14 N 84.10 W
Goshiki 96 34.24 N 134.47 E
Goshogawara 92 40.48 N 140.27 E
Goshute Indian Reservation ◆4 200 39.53 N 114.08 W
Goshute Lake ⊜ 204 40.08 N 114.38 W
Goshute Valley V 204 40.40 N 114.30 W
Goslar 52 51.54 N 10.25 E
Gosnells 168a 32.04 S 116.00 E
Gospić 36 44.33 N 15.23 E
Gosport, Eng., U.K. 42 50.48 N 1.08 W
Gosport, In., U.S. 194 39.21 N 86.40 W
Gossa 54 51.40 N 12.26 E
Gossas 150 14.30 N 16.04 W
Gossau 58 47.25 N 9.15 E
Gosse ◆8 263 51.08 N 7.01 E
Gosse Bluff ∧ 162 23.49 S 132.19 E
Gosselies 56 50.28 N 4.25 E
Gössenheim 56 50.01 N 9.46 E
Gossensass — Colle Isarco 64 46.56 N 11.26 E
Gosser Hill 279b 40.37 N 79.37 W
Gossi 150 15.49 N 1.17 W
Gossinga 140 8.39 N 25.59 E
Gössnitz 54 50.53 N 12.26 E
Gossolengo 62 44.59 N 9.37 E
Gössweinstein 60 49.46 N 11.20 E
Gostagajevskaja 78 45.01 N 37.30 E
Gostilovo 82 55.18 N 38.36 E
Gostiščevo 78 50.47 N 36.39 E
Gostivar 38 41.47 N 20.54 E
Göstling an der Ybbs 61 47.48 N 14.55 E
Gostyń 30 51.53 N 17.00 E
Gostynin 30 52.26 N 19.29 E
Gosudarev Bajrak 83 48.21 N 38.08 E
Göta älv ≃ 26 57.42 N 11.52 E
Göta kanal ≅ 40 58.50 N 13.58 E
Gotchen Creek ≃ 224 46.00 N 121.30 W
Got Creek ≃ 284a 43.03 N 78.42 W
Gotebo 196 35.04 N 98.52 W
Göteborg (Gothenburg) 26 57.43 N 11.58 E
Göteborgs och Bohus län □6 26 58.30 N 11.30 E
Gotel Mountains ⋏ 152 6.55 N 11.15 E
Gotemba 94 35.18 N 138.56 E
Götene 26 58.32 N 13.29 E
Goteštу 78 46.09 N 28.10 E
Gotha, Dtsch. 54 50.57 N 10.41 E
Gotha, Fl., U.S. 220 28.32 N 81.31 W
Gothem 26 57.35 N 18.43 E
Gothenburg 198 40.55 N 100.09 W
Gothenburg — Göteborg 26 57.43 N 11.58 E
Gothèye 150 13.52 N 1.34 E
Gotland I 26 57.30 N 18.33 E
Gotlands Län □6 26 57.30 N 18.30 E
Gotoputovo 86 56.46 N 70.10 E
Gotō-rettō II 92 32.50 N 129.00 E
Gotska Sandön I 26 58.23 N 19.16 E
Gōtsu 96 35.00 N 132.14 E
Gottenheim 58 48.03 N 7.44 E
Götterswickerhamm 263 51.35 N 6.40 E
Gottesbrücke 264a 52.25 N 13.49 E
Gotthard Tunnel ◆5 58 46.35 N 8.35 E
Göttin 264a 52.27 N 12.54 E
Göttingen, Dtsch. 52 51.32 N 9.55 E
Göttingen, Dtsch. 56 50.52 N 8.46 E
Göttin See ⊜ 264a 52.28 N 12.54 E
Gottmadingen 58 47.44 N 8.47 E
Gottolengo 64 45.17 N 10.16 E
Gottorf, Schloss ⊥ 41 54.30 N 9.32 E
Gottsbüren 52 51.35 N 9.30 E
Gottvaterkapelle ɷ1 60 49.42 N 11.41 E
Götzendorf 264b 48.01 N 16.35 E
Götzis 58 47.20 N 9.38 E
Gouarec 32 48.13 N 3.11 W
Goubangzi 104 41.22 N 121.46 E
Goubone 146 20.43 N 17.08 E
Gouda, Ned. 52 52.01 N 4.43 E
Gouda, S. Afr. 158 33.19 S 19.04 E
Goudet 62 44.53 N 3.55 E
Goudge 252 34.40 S 68.08 W
Goudhurst 42 51.07 N 0.28 E
Goudiry 150 14.11 N 12.43 W
Goudoumaria 146 13.42 N 11.10 E
Goudswaard 52 51.47 N 4.16 E
Gouéké 150 8.02 N 8.43 W
Goûfi, Djebel el ∧ 34 36.57 N 6.27 E
Gougezhuang 105 38.53 N 116.11 E
Gough Island I 10 40.20 S 10.00 W
Gough Lake ⊜ 182 52.02 N 112.28 W
Gouin, Réservoir ⊜1 176 48.38 N 74.54 W
Goujiaozhen 107 30.36 N 106.33 E
Goukou 89 48.39 N 122.06 E
Goulais ≃ 190 46.43 N 84.27 W
Goulburn 170 34.45 S 149.43 E
Goulburn ≃ 169 36.41 S 145.12 E
Goulburn Islands II 164 11.33 S 133.26 E
Goulburn Weir ⊜1 169 36.45 S 145.08 E
Gould 194 33.59 N 91.33 W
Gould City 190 46.05 N 85.41 W
Gould Park 210 42.04 N 73.55 W
Goulds 220 25.33 N 80.22 W
Gouldsboro 210 41.44 N 75.28 W
Gouldsboro State Park ♦ 210 41.13 N 75.28 W
Goulet Lake ⊜ 184 55.23 N 96.18 W
Goulia 150 10.01 N 7.11 W
Goulicun 106 31.40 N 120.00 E
Goulimime 148 28.56 N 10.04 W

ENGLISH — Name | Page | Lat.°′ | Long.°′

DEUTSCH — Name | Seite | Breite°′ | Länge°′ E = Ost

Goulimine □4 148 28.30 N 9.45 W
Goulmima 148 31.02 N 5.00 W
Goumbati ∧2 150 13.08 N 12.06 W
Goumbou 150 14.59 N 7.27 W
Gouménissa 38 40.57 N 22.27 E
Goumois 58 47.16 N 6.57 E
Gouna 146 8.32 N 13.34 E
Gounda ≃ 146 9.25 N 20.57 E
Goundam 150 16.25 N 3.40 W
Goundi 146 9.22 N 17.22 E
Gounou-Gaya 146 9.38 N 15.31 E
Gouougang, Mount ∧ 170 33.53 S 150.07 E
Goupillières 261 48.53 N 1.46 E
Gouraya 34 36.34 N 1.55 E
Gourbassi 150 13.24 N 11.38 W
Gourbeyre 241o 16.00 N 61.42 W
Gourcy 150 13.13 N 2.21 W
Gourdhead Run ≃ 279b 40.33 N 79.57 W
Gourdon, Fr. 32 44.44 N 1.23 E
Gourdon, Fr. 62 43.43 N 6.59 E
Gouré 150 13.58 N 10.18 E
Gouri ⊥ 124 24.53 N 88.07 E
Gourin 32 48.08 N 3.36 W
Gouripur 124 24.46 N 90.34 E
Gourits ≃ 158 34.21 S 21.52 E
Gourlay Lake ⊜ 190 48.52 N 84.54 W
Gourma Rharous 150 16.53 N 1.55 W
Gournay-en-Bray 50 49.29 N 1.44 E
Gournay-sur-Marne 261 48.52 N 2.34 E
Gouro 146 19.33 N 19.33 E
Gourock 46 55.58 N 4.49 W
Goussainville 50 49.01 N 2.28 E
Goussonville 261 48.55 N 1.46 E
Goutou 105 39.49 N 117.11 E
Gouveia, Bra. 255 18.27 S 43.44 W
Gouveia, Port. 266c 38.50 N 9.26 W
Gouverneur 212 44.20 N 75.27 W
Gouyadong 100 25.10 N 112.55 E
Gouyave 241k 12.10 N 61.44 W
Gov'altaj □4 102 45.30 N 96.00 E
Govan 184 51.18 N 105.00 W
Go Vap 269c 10.49 N 106.41 E
Govardhan 124 27.30 N 77.28 E
Gove 198 38.57 N 100.29 W
Govea ≃ 286b 22.56 N 82.30 W
Govena, mys ≻ 74 59.48 N 166.06 E
Govenlock 184 49.15 N 109.48 W
Gove Peninsula ≻1 164 12.20 S 136.50 E
Goverla, gora ∧ 78 48.10 N 24.32 E
Governador, Ilha do I 287a 22.48 S 43.12 W
Governador Portela 256 22.29 S 43.30 W
Governador Valadares 255 18.51 S 41.56 W
Government Camp 224 45.18 N 121.45 W
Governor Bond Lake ⊜1 219 38.56 N 89.23 W
Governor Dodge State Park ♦ 190 43.00 N 90.07 W
Governor Generoso 116 6.39 N 126.05 E
Governor Head ≻ 170 35.07 S 150.46 E
Governor Nice Memorial Bridge ◆5 208 38.22 N 77.00 W
Governor Printz Park ♦ 285 39.52 N 75.18 W
Governor's Harbour 238 25.10 N 76.14 W
Governors Island I 276 40.41 N 74.01 W
Govind Ballabh Pant Sāgar ⊜1 124 24.05 N 82.50 E
Govindgarh 124 24.23 N 81.18 E
Govind Sāgar ⊜1 123 31.20 N 76.45 E
Gov'-Ugtaal 102 46.04 N 107.30 E
Gowan ≃ 184 55.49 N 94.08 W
Gowanda 210 42.27 N 78.56 W
Gowan Range ⋏ 166 25.00 S 145.00 E
Gowen City 208 40.45 N 76.32 W
Gower 194 39.36 N 94.35 W
Gower ≻1 42 51.36 N 4.10 W
Gowerton 42 51.39 N 4.01 W
Gowienica ≃ 54 53.40 N 14.38 E
Gowmal (Gumal) ≃ 120 31.56 N 70.22 E
Gowmal Kalay 120 32.29 N 68.55 E
Gowna, Lough ⊜ 48 53.51 N 7.34 W
Gowrie 198 42.16 N 94.17 W
Gowy ≃ 44 53.17 N 2.51 W
Goya 252 29.08 S 59.16 W
Goyania — Goiânia 255 16.40 S 49.16 W
Goyatz 54 52.01 N 14.09 E
Goyave 241o 16.08 N 61.34 W
Goyaves, Grande Rivière à ≃ 241o 16.18 N 61.37 W
Goyaves, Îlets à II 241o 16.10 N 61.48 W
Goyder ≃ 164 12.38 S 135.11 E
Goyder Creek ≃ 162 25.39 S 134.47 E
Goyelle, Lac ⊜ 186 50.47 N 60.45 W
Goyeneche 258 35.20 S 58.43 W
Goyer, Île I 275a 45.29 N 73.17 W
Goyerkāta 124 26.42 N 89.02 E
Göynücek 130 40.24 N 35.32 E
Göynük, Tür. 130 39.08 N 40.53 E
Göynük, Tür. 130 40.24 N 30.47 E
Göynük ≃, Tür. 130 38.53 N 40.34 E
Göynük ≃, Tür. 130 40.20 N 30.05 E
Goyt ≃ 262 53.24 N 2.09 W
Goz-Beïda 146 12.13 N 21.25 E
Gozdnica 30 51.26 N 15.06 E
Gozdowice 54 52.45 N 14.18 E
Göze Dağı ∧ 130 41.24 N 42.30 E
Gözeli 130 38.25 N 39.04 E
Gozen-yama 94 36.32 N 140.20 E
Gozha Co ⊜ 120 34.59 N 81.06 E
Gözne 130 36.59 N 34.34 E
Gozo — Għawdex I 36 36.03 N 14.15 E
Göz Tepe ∧2 267b 41.06 N 29.06 E
Gozzano 62 45.45 N 8.26 E
Graaff-Reinet 158 32.14 S 24.32 E
Graafwater 158 32.00 S 18.37 E
Graauw 52 51.20 N 4.05 E
Grabc'ovo 82 54.34 N 36.22 E
Graben-Neudorf 56 49.09 N 8.29 E
Grabenstätt 64 47.51 N 12.32 E
Grabill 216 41.12 N 84.58 W
Grabo 150 4.55 N 7.30 W
Grabouw 158 34.09 S 19.02 E
Grabovaja Balka, les ♦ 83 48.09 N 38.37 E
Grabovo 86 53.07 N 74.52 E
Grabow 54 53.16 N 11.34 E
Grabowiec 30 50.50 N 23.33 E
Grabów nad Prosną 30 51.31 N 18.06 E
Gračac 36 44.18 N 15.51 E
Gračanica 38 44.42 N 18.19 E
Gračanica, Manastir ɷ1 38 42.36 N 21.09 E
Graçay 50 47.08 N 1.51 E
Grace 202 42.34 N 111.43 W
Gracefield 188 46.06 N 76.03 W
Graceham 208 39.36 N 77.22 W
Graceton 214 40.40 N 79.10 W
Graceville, Fl., U.S. 192 30.57 N 85.31 W
Graceville, Mn., U.S. 198 45.34 N 96.26 W
Gračevka 80 55.06 N 36.49 E
Grächen 58 46.12 N 7.50 E
Grachovo 80 56.04 N 51.58 E
Grači 80 49.49 N 43.33 E
Gracia ◆8 266d 41.23 N 2.09 E
Gracias 236 14.35 N 88.35 W
Gracias a Dios □5 236 15.10 N 84.20 W
Gracias a Dios, Cabo ≻ 236 15.00 N 83.10 W
Gračiki ≃ 83 48.30 N 39.52 E
Graciosa 148a 39.04 N 28.00 W
Graciosa, Isla I 148 29.15 N 13.30 W
Gračov 80 49.26 N 41.32 E
Gračovka, Ross. 80 52.07 N 40.01 E
Gračovka, Ross. 80 52.57 N 52.52 E
Gračov Kust 80 51.59 N 49.50 E
Gradačac 38 44.53 N 18.26 E
Gradara 66 43.57 N 12.46 E
Gradaús 250 7.43 S 51.11 W
Gr'adcy 76 56.24 N 31.55 E
Gräddö 40 59.46 N 19.02 E
Gradisca d'Isonzo 64 45.53 N 13.30 E
Gradižsk 78 49.13 N 33.07 E
Grado, Esp. 34 43.23 N 6.04 W
Grado, It. 64 45.40 N 13.23 E
Grado, Laguna di c 64 45.43 N 13.20 E
Gradoli 66 42.39 N 11.51 E
Grady, Ar., U.S. 194 34.04 N 91.42 W
Grady, N.M., U.S. 196 34.49 N 103.19 W
Gradyville 285 39.57 N 75.28 W
Graemsay I 46 58.56 N 3.17 W
Græsted 41 56.04 N 12.17 E
Graettinger 198 43.14 N 94.45 W
Gräfelfing 60 48.07 N 11.25 E
Grafenau 60 48.52 N 13.25 E
Gräfenberg 60 49.39 N 11.15 E
Grafenberg ◆8 263 51.14 N 6.50 E
Gräfenhainichen 54 51.44 N 12.27 E
Gräfenroda 54 50.45 N 10.48 E
Gräfenthal 54 50.31 N 11.18 E
Gräfentonna 54 51.05 N 10.44 E
Grafenwöhr 60 49.43 N 11.54 E
Graffignano 66 42.34 N 12.12 E
Grafham Water ⊜ 42 52.17 N 0.20 W
Gräfinau-Angstedt 54 50.42 N 11.01 E
Grafing bei München 60 48.02 N 11.59 E
Gråfjell ∧ 26 60.16 N 9.29 E
Graford 196 32.56 N 98.14 W
Gräfrath ◆8 263 51.13 N 7.04 E
Grafschaft Bentheim □9 52 52.30 N 7.00 E
Grafton, Austl. 166 29.41 S 152.56 E
Grafton, On., Can. 212 44.00 N 78.01 W
Grafton, Il., U.S. 219 38.58 N 90.25 W
Grafton, Ma., U.S. 207 42.12 N 71.41 W
Grafton, N.Y., U.S. 210 42.46 N 73.27 W
Grafton, N.D., U.S. 198 48.24 N 97.24 W
Grafton, Oh., U.S. 214 41.16 N 82.03 W
Grafton, W.V., U.S. 188 39.20 N 80.01 W
Grafton, Wi., U.S. 190 43.19 N 87.57 W
Grafton, Cape ≻ 164 16.52 S 145.55 E
Grafton Lakes State Park ♦ 210 42.48 N 73.28 W
Grafty Green 260 51.12 N 0.41 E
Graglia 62 45.33 N 7.59 E
Gragnano 68 40.41 N 14.31 E
Gragnano Trebbiense 62 45.01 N 9.34 E
Graham, Ca., U.S. 280 34.15 N 118.31 W
Graham, N.C., U.S. 192 36.04 N 79.24 W
Graham, Tx., U.S. 196 33.06 N 98.35 W
Graham, Wa., U.S. 224 47.03 N 122.17 W
Graham, Mount ∧ 200 32.42 N 109.52 W
Graham Cave State Park ♦ 219 38.55 N 91.32 W
Graham Creek ≃ 218 38.49 N 85.39 W
Graham Island I 182 53.40 N 132.30 W
Graham Lake ⊜, On., Can. 212 44.34 N 75.53 W
Graham Lake ⊜, Me., U.S. 188 44.40 N 68.25 W
Graham Land ◆1 9 66.00 S 63.30 W
Graham Memorial Park ♦ 284b 39.25 N 76.30 W
Graham Moore, Cape ≻ 176 72.52 N 76.04 W
Graham Moore Bay c 176 75.26 N 101.25 W
Grahamstad — Grahamstown 158 33.19 S 26.31 E
Grahamstown 158 33.19 S 26.31 E
Grahamsville 210 41.51 N 74.33 W
Grahn 218 38.17 N 83.04 W
Graie, Alpi (Alpes Grées) ⋏ 62 45.30 N 7.10 E
Graiguenarmanagh 48 52.32 N 6.57 W
Grain 42 51.28 N 0.43 E
Grain, Isle of I 42 51.27 N 0.41 E
Grain Coast ⊥2 150 5.00 N 9.00 W
Grainfield 198 39.06 N 100.27 W
Grajagan 115a 8.35 S 114.13 E
Grajagan, Teluk c 115a 8.40 S 114.18 E
Grajaú 250 5.49 S 46.08 W
Grajaú ≃ 250 3.41 S 44.48 W
Grajewo 30 53.39 N 22.27 E
Grajvoron 78 50.28 N 35.39 E
Gram 41 55.17 N 9.04 E
Gramacho 287a 22.44 S 43.18 W
Gramada 38 43.50 N 22.39 E
Gramado 252 29.24 S 50.54 W
Gramalote 246 7.53 N 72.48 W
Gramastetten 61 48.23 N 14.12 E
Gramat 32 44.47 N 1.43 E
Gramatneusiedl 264b 48.02 N 16.29 E
Grambling 194 32.31 N 92.42 W
Gramilla 252 27.18 S 64.37 W
Gramínea 256 22.10 S 46.38 W
Graminha, Reprêsa ⊜1 256 21.40 S 46.35 W
Grammer 218 39.09 N 85.43 W
Grammichele 70 37.13 N 14.38 E
Grammont — Geraardsbergen 50 50.46 N 3.52 E
Gramoteino 86 54.31 N 86.22 E
Grampian 214 40.57 N 78.36 W
Grampian □4 46 57.15 N 2.45 W
Grampian Mountains ⋏ 46 56.55 N 4.00 W
Grampians National Park ♦ 166 37.20 S 142.30 E
Gramschatz 56 49.56 N 9.58 E
Gramsh 38 40.52 N 20.11 E
Gramzow 54 53.12 N 14.00 E
Grana ≃ 62 44.25 N 7.27 E
Granaatboskolk 158 30.02 S 19.51 E
Granada, Col. 246 3.34 N 73.45 W
Granada, Esp. 34 37.13 N 3.41 W
Granada, Nic. 236 11.56 N 85.57 W
Granada, Pil. 116 10.40 N 123.02 E
Granada, Co., U.S. 198 38.03 N 102.18 W
Granada, Mn., U.S. 190 43.41 N 94.20 W
Granada □4 34 37.15 N 3.15 W
Granada □5 236 11.50 N 86.00 W
Granada — Grenada □1 241k 12.07 N 61.40 W
Granada Hills ◆8 280 34.16 N 118.31 W
Granado 286d 12.04 S 76.57 W
Granaglione 66 44.07 N 10.58 E
Gran Altiplanicie Central ⋏1 254 48.55 S 69.45 W
Granard 48 53.47 N 7.30 W
Granarolo dell'Emilia 64 44.33 N 11.27 E
Granatello 70 37.53 N 12.32 E
Gran Bahía Australiana — Great Australian Bight c3 162 35.00 S 135.00 E
Gran Bajo de San Julián V 254 49.30 S 68.30 W
Gran Barrera de Arrecifes — Great Barrier Reef ◆2 160 18.00 S 145.50 E
Granbergsdal 40 59.24 N 14.35 E
Granbury 222 32.26 N 97.47 W
Granbury, Lake ⊜1 222 32.25 N 97.45 W
Granby, P.Q., Can. 206 45.24 N 72.44 W
Granby, Co., U.S. 200 40.05 N 105.56 W
Granby, Ct., U.S. 207 41.57 N 72.47 W
Granby, Ma., U.S. 207 42.15 N 72.31 W
Granby, Mo., U.S. 194 36.55 N 94.15 W
Granby ≃ 182 49.03 N 118.25 W
Granby, Lake ⊜1 200 40.09 N 105.50 W
Gran Canaria I 148 28.00 N 15.36 W
Grancey-le-Château 58 47.40 N 5.02 E
Gran Chaco ⊆ 252 23.00 S 60.00 W
Grand 58 48.23 N 5.29 E
Grand ≃, On., Can. 212 42.51 N 79.34 W
Grand ≃, U.S. 194 39.23 N 93.06 W
Grand ≃, Mi., U.S. 216 43.04 N 86.15 W
Grand ≃, Oh., U.S. 214 41.46 N 81.17 W

Symbols in the index entries represent the broad categories identified in the key at the right. Symbols with superior numbers (⋏1) identify subcategories (see complete key on page I · 1).

Symbole im Register stellen die rechts im Schlüssel erklärten Kategorien dar. Symbole mit hochgestellten Ziffern (⋏1) bezeichnen Unterabteilungen einer Kategorie (vgl. vollständiger Schlüssel auf Seite I · 1).

Los símbolos incluídos en el texto del índice representan las grandes categorías identificadas con la clave a la derecha. Los símbolos con numeros en su parte superior (⋏1) identifican las subcategorías (véase la clave completa en la página I · 1).

Les symboles de l'index représentent les catégories indiquées dans la légende à droite. Les symboles suivis d'un indice (⋏1) représentent des sous-catégories (voir légende complète à la page I · 1).

Os símbolos incluídos no texto do índice representam as grandes categorias identificadas com a chave à direita. Os símbolos com números em sua parte superior (⋏1) identificam as subcategorias (veja-se a chave completa à página I · 1).

∧ Mountain	Berg	Montaña	Montagne	Montanha
⋏ Mountains	Gebirge	Montañas	Montagnes	Montanhas
≍ Pass	Paß	Paso	Col	Passo
V Valley, Canyon	Tal, Cañon	Valle, Cañón	Vallée, Canyon	Vale, Canhão
⊆ Plain	Ebene	Llano	Plaine	Planície
≻ Cape	Kap	Cabo	Cap	Cabo
I Island	Insel	Isla	Île	Ilha
II Islands	Inseln	Islas	Îles	Ilhas
⊥ Other Topographic Features	Andere Topographische Objekte	Otros Elementos Topográficos	Autres données topographiques	Outros acidentes topográficos

ESPAÑOL — Nombre, Página, Lat.°′, Long.°′ W = Oeste
FRANÇAIS — Nom, Page, Lat.°′, Long.°′ W = Ouest
PORTUGUÊS — Nome, Página, Lat.°′, Long.°′ W = Oeste

Grand ≃, S.D., U.S. 198 45.40 N 100.32 W
Grand ≃, Wi., U.S. 190 43.45 N 89.16 W
Grand, East Fork ≃ 194 40.12 N 94.21 W
Grand, Lac ⊜ 190 47.10 N 76.57 W
Grand, North Fork ≃ 198 45.47 N 102.16 W
Grand, South Fork ≃ 198 45.43 N 102.17 W
Grandas 34 43.13 N 6.52 W
Grand Bahama I 238 26.38 N 78.25 W
Grand Ballon ʌ 58 47.55 N 7.08 E
Grand Bank 186 47.06 N 55.46 W
Grand Banks of Newfoundland ✢4 16 45.00 N 53.00 W
Grand-Bassam 150 5.12 N 3.44 W
Grand Bay, N.B., Can. 186 45.18 N 66.12 W
Grand Bay, Al., U.S. 194 30.28 N 88.20 W
Grand Beach 184 50.35 N 96.40 W
Grand Bend 190 43.15 N 81.45 W
Grand Béréby 150 4.38 N 6.55 W
Grand Blanc 216 42.55 N 83.37 W
Grand-Bourg 241o 15.53 N 61.19 W
Grand Bruit 186 47.41 N 58.13 W
Grand Caille Point › 241f 13.52 N 61.05 W
Grand Calumet ≃ 278 41.38 N 87.34 W
Grand Calumet, Île du I 190 45.44 N 76.41 W
Grand Canal ≊ 48 53.21 N 6.14 W
Grand Canal → Da Yunhe ≊ 90 32.12 N 119.31 E
Grand Cane 194 32.05 N 93.48 W
Grand Cañon du Verdon ♠ 62 43.47 N 6.27 E
Grand Canyon 200 36.03 N 112.08 W
Grand Canyon V 200 36.10 N 112.45 W
Grand Canyon National Park ♠ 200 36.15 N 112.58 W
Grand Canyon of Pennsylvania ♠ 210 41.43 N 77.28 W
Grand Cayman I 238 19.20 N 81.15 W
Grand Central Terminal ✦5 276 40.45 N 73.59 W
Grand Centre 184 54.25 N 110.13 W
Grand Cess 150 4.36 N 8.10 W
Grandchamp, Fr. 58 47.43 N 5.27 E
Grandchamp, Fr. 261 48.43 N 1.37 E
Grand-Charmont 58 47.32 N 6.50 E
Grand Chenier 194 29.46 N 92.58 W
Grand Combin ʌ 58 45.56 N 7.18 E
Grand Coulee 202 47.56 N 119.00 W
Grand Coulee V 202 47.45 N 119.15 W
Grand Coulee Dam ✦6 202 47.57 N 118.59 W
Grand-Couronne 50 49.21 N 1.00 E
Grand Cul-de-Sac Marin ⊂ 241o 16.20 N 61.35 W
Grande ≃, Arg. 252 36.52 S 69.45 W
Grande ≃, Arg. 252 24.12 S 64.42 W
Grande ≃, Bol. 248 15.51 S 64.39 W
Grande ≃, Bra. 242 11.05 S 43.09 W
Grande ≃, Bra. 255 20.06 S 51.04 W
Grande ≃, Bra. 287a 22.55 S 43.25 W
Grande ≃, Bra. 287b 23.45 S 46.22 W
Grande ≃, Chile 252 30.35 S 71.11 W
Grande ≃, Esp. 34 39.07 N 0.44 W
Grande ≃, It. 70 37.55 N 13.13 E
Grande ≃, Méx. 234 18.50 N 102.05 W
Grande ≃, Méx. 234 17.43 N 96.56 W
Grande ≃, Nic. 236 12.28 N 86.21 W
Grande ≃, Pan. 236 8.18 N 80.24 W
Grande ≃, Perú 248 14.59 S 75.29 W
Grande ≃, S.A. 254 53.48 S 67.40 W
Grande ≃, Ven. 246 8.39 N 60.59 W
Grande, Arroyo ≃, Arg. 258 34.37 S 59.25 W
Grande, Arroyo ≃, Arg. 288 34.45 S 58.08 W
Grande, Arroyo ≃, Méx. 234 23.55 N 98.44 W
Grande, Arroyo ≃, Ur. 252 33.08 S 57.09 W
Grande, Arroyo ≃, Ur. 258 33.37 S 57.09 W
Grande, Bahía ⊂3 254 50.45 S 68.45 W
Grande, Boca ⊂ 220 26.43 N 82.16 W
Grande, Boca ≃1 246 8.38 N 60.30 W
Grande, Cañada ≃, Arg. 258 35.15 S 59.23 W
Grande, Cañada ≃, Arg. 258 35.19 S 57.48 W
Grande, Cayo I 240p 20.59 N 79.09 W
Grande, Cerro ʌ, Méx. 232 28.46 N 107.32 W
Grande, Cerro ʌ, Méx. 234 23.39 N 100.51 W
Grande, Cerro ʌ, Méx. 234 21.45 N 103.05 W
Grande, Cerro ʌ, Méx. 234 20.43 N 101.12 W
Grande, Cerro ʌ, Méx. 234 23.22 N 103.35 W
Grande, Corixa (Curiche Grande) ≋ 248 17.10 S 58.20 W
Grande, Cuchilla ʌ 252 33.15 S 55.07 W
Grande, Curiche (Corixa Grande) ≋ 248 17.10 S 58.20 W
Grande, Igarapé ≃ 250 3.37 S 48.53 W
Grande, Ilha I, Bra. 252 23.45 S 54.03 W
Grande, Ilha I, Bra. 256 23.09 S 44.14 W
Grande, Isola I 70 37.53 N 12.26 E
Grande, Lago ⊜, Arg. 254 47.44 S 68.04 W
Grande, Lago ⊜, Bra. 250 2.16 S 54.17 W
Grande, Laguna ⊜, Arg. 258 34.14 S 58.53 W
Grande, Laguna ⊜, Méx. 234 20.06 N 96.40 W
Grande, Mare (Taranto) ⊂ 68 40.27 N 17.12 E
Grande, Naviglio ≊ 266b 45.35 N 8.42 E
Grande, Ponta › 255 16.22 S 39.01 W
Grande, Praia ⩡2 256 24.05 S 46.30 W
Grande, Punta › 252 21.54 S 70.12 W
Grande, Ribeirão ≃ 256 21.24 S 44.29 W
Grande, Rio (Bravo del Norte) ≃ 178 25.55 N 97.09 W
Grande, Salina ≋ 68 40.26 N 17.18 E
Grande, Serra ʌʌ 250 6.00 S 40.52 W
Grande, Sierra ʌʌ 196 29.40 N 104.55 W
Grande-Anse 186 47.48 N 65.11 W
Grande Anse, La ⊂ 275a 45.23 N 73.53 W
Grande Anse Bay ⊂ 241k 12.02 N 61.45 W
Grande Baie, La ⊂ 275a 45.29 N 74.00 W
Grande Cache 182 53.53 N 119.08 W
Grande Casse, Pointe de la ʌ 62 45.24 N 6.50 E
Grande Cayemite I 238 18.37 N 73.45 W
Grande Chartreuse, Couvent de la ♰1 62 45.22 N 5.50 E
Grande de Añasco ≃ 240m 18.16 N 67.11 W
Grande de Arecibo ≃ 240m 18.29 N 66.42 W
Grande de Jutaí, Ilha I 250 3.15 S 49.37 W
Grande de Lipez ≃ 248 20.47 S 67.14 W
Grande de Loíza ≃ 240m 18.27 N 65.53 W
Grande de Manacapuru, Lago ⊜ 246 3.04 S 61.25 W
Grande de Manatí ≃ 240m 18.29 N 66.32 W
Grande de Matagalpa ≃ 236 12.54 N 83.32 W
Grande de Santiago ≃ 234 21.36 N 105.26 W
Grande de Tarija ≃ 248 22.53 S 64.21 W
Grande de Térraba ≃ 236 8.59 N 83.37 W
Grande do Curuaí, Lago ⊜ 250 2.15 S 55.20 W
Grande do Gurupá, Ilha I 250 1.00 S 51.30 W
Grande do Tapará, Ilha I 250 2.14 S 54.39 W
Grande Île de Criques I 273b 4.20 S 15.25 E
Grande Inferior, Cuchilla ʌʌ2 258 33.50 S 56.27 W
Grande-Entrée 186 47.33 N 61.34 W
Grande-Prairie 182 55.10 N 118.48 W
Grand Erg de Bilma ✦2 146 18.30 N 14.00 E
Grand Erg Occidental ✦2 148 30.30 N 0.30 E
Grand Erg Oriental ✦2 148 30.30 N 7.00 E
Grande-Rivière 186 48.24 N 64.30 W
Grande Rivière, La ≃ 176 53.50 N 79.00 W
Grande Ronde ≃ 202 46.05 N 116.59 W
Grandes, Salinas ≚, Arg. 252 23.43 S 66.00 W
Grandes, Salinas ≚, Arg. 252 30.05 S 65.05 W
Grandes Antillas, Islas → Greater Antilles II 238 20.00 N 74.00 W
Grandes Antilles, Îles → Greater Antilles II 238 20.00 N 74.00 W
Grande Sassière, Aiguille de la ʌ 62 45.30 N 7.00 E
Grande Sauldre ≃ 50 47.22 N 1.55 E
Gran Desierto de Arena → Great Sandy Desert ✦2 162 21.30 S 125.00 E
Gran Desierto Victoria → Great Victoria Desert ✦2 162 28.30 S 127.45 E
Grandes-Piles 206 46.41 N 72.44 W
Grande-Synthe 50 51.01 N 2.19 E
Grand-Étang 186 46.33 N 61.02 W
Grande-Terre I 241o 16.20 N 61.25 W
Grande Vigie, Pointe de la › 241o 16.31 N 61.28 W
Grand Eyvia ≃ 62 45.42 N 7.14 E
Grand Falls, N.B., Can. 186 47.03 N 67.44 W
Grand Falls, Nf., Can. 186 48.56 N 55.40 W
Grandfalls, Tx., U.S. 196 31.20 N 102.51 W
Grandfather Mountain ʌ 192 36.07 N 81.48 W
Grandfield 196 34.13 N 98.41 W
Grand Forks, B.C., Can. 182 49.02 N 118.27 W
Grand Forks, N.D., U.S. 198 47.55 N 97.01 W
Grand Forks Air Force Base ■ 198 47.57 N 97.25 W
Grand-Fort-Philippe 50 51.00 N 2.06 E
Grand-Fougeray 32 47.44 N 1.44 W
Grand-Gallargues 62 43.43 N 4.10 E
Grand Gorge 210 42.21 N 74.29 W
Grand-Halleux 56 50.19 N 5.54 E
Grand Haven 216 43.03 N 86.13 W
Grand Haven State Park ♠ 216 43.02 N 86.13 W
Grand Hers ≃ 32 43.47 N 1.20 E
Grandiči 76 53.43 N 23.49 E
Grandin, Lac ⊜ 176 63.59 N 119.00 W
Grandioznyj, pik ʌ 88 53.50 N 96.11 E
Grand Island, Fl., U.S. 220 28.53 N 81.44 W
Grand Island, Ne., U.S. 198 40.55 N 98.20 W
Grand Island, N.Y., U.S. 212 43.01 N 78.58 W
Grand Island I, On., Can. 212 44.34 N 78.50 W
Grand Island I, Mi., U.S. 190 46.30 N 86.40 W
Grand Island I, N.Y., U.S. 210 43.02 N 78.58 W
Grand Isle 194 29.14 N 89.59 W
Grand Isle □6 206 44.57 N 73.17 W
Grand Junction, Co., U.S. 200 39.03 N 108.33 W
Grand Junction, Ia., U.S. 198 42.01 N 94.14 W
Grand Junction, Mi., U.S. 216 42.24 N 86.04 W
Grand Junction, Tn., U.S. 194 35.02 N 89.11 W
Grand Lac Salé → Great Salt Lake ⊜ 200 41.10 N 112.30 W
Grand lac Victoria ⊜ 190 47.31 N 77.30 W
Grand-Lahou 150 5.08 N 5.01 W
Grand Lake 200 40.15 N 105.49 W
Grand Lake ⊜, N.B., Can. 186 45.55 N 66.05 W
Grand Lake ⊜, Nf., Can. 186 49.00 N 57.25 W
Grand Lake ⊜, N.A. 186 45.43 N 67.50 W
Grand Lake ⊜, La., U.S. 194 29.55 N 92.47 W
Grand Lake ⊜, La., U.S. 194 29.55 N 91.25 W
Grand Lake ⊜, Mi., U.S. 190 45.18 N 83.30 W
Grand Lake ⊜, Oh., U.S. 216 40.30 N 84.32 W
Grand Lake Saint Marys State Park ♠ 216 40.33 N 84.27 W
Grand Ledge 216 42.45 N 84.44 W
Grand Lieu, Lac de ⊜ 32 47.06 N 1.40 W
Grand'Maison, Barrage de ✦6 62 45.12 N 6.07 E
Grand Manan Channel ⅄ 186 44.45 N 66.52 W
Grand Manan Island I 186 44.40 N 66.50 W
Grand Marais, Mi., U.S. 190 46.40 N 85.59 W
Grand Marais, Mn., U.S. 190 47.45 N 90.20 W
Grand Meadow 190 43.42 N 92.34 W
Grand-Mère 206 46.37 N 72.41 W
Grand Mesa ʌ 200 39.00 N 108.00 W
Grandmesnil, Lac ⊜ 186 51.19 N 67.33 W
Grand Morin ≃ 50 48.54 N 2.50 E
Grand Muveran ʌ 58 46.14 N 7.08 E
Grandola, It. 58 46.02 N 9.13 E
Grândola, Port. 34 38.10 N 8.34 W
Grand Pabos, Rivière du ≃ 186 48.21 N 64.43 W
Grand Palace ♰ 269a 13.45 N 100.30 E
Grand Passage ⅄ 175f 18.45 S 163.10 E
Grand-Popo 150 6.17 N 1.50 E
Grand Portage 190 47.57 N 89.41 W
Grand Portage Indian Reservation ✦4 190 47.55 N 89.45 W
Grand Portage National Monument ♠ 190 48.02 N 89.38 W
Grand Prairie 222 32.44 N 96.59 W
Grandpré 56 49.20 N 4.52 E
Grand Pré National Historic Park ♠ 186 45.08 N 64.18 W
Grand Prix Airport ⊠ 281 42.33 N 83.11 W
Grand Rapids, Mb., Can. 184 53.08 N 99.20 W
Grand Rapids, Mi., U.S. 216 42.58 N 85.40 W
Grand Rapids, Mn., U.S. 190 47.14 N 93.31 W
Grand Rapids, Oh., U.S. 216 41.24 N 83.51 W
Grand Rhône ≃ 62 43.20 N 4.50 E
Grand Ridge 216 41.14 N 88.50 W
Grandrieu, Bel. 50 50.12 N 4.10 E
Grandrieu, Fr. 62 44.47 N 3.38 E
Grand River 214 41.44 N 81.17 W
Grand' Rivière 240e 14.52 N 61.11 W
Grand Ronde 224 45.03 N 123.36 W
Grand Roy 241k 12.08 N 61.45 W
Grand Ruisseau, Le ≃ 275a 45.39 N 73.12 W
Grand-Saint-Bernard, Col du)(58 45.50 N 7.10 E
Grand-Saint-Bernard, Tunnel du ✦5 58 45.51 N 7.11 E
Grand Saline 222 32.40 N 95.42 W
Grand Saline Creek ≃ 222 32.41 N 95.36 W
Grand-Santi 250 4.19 N 54.24 W
Grandson 58 46.49 N 6.38 E
Grand Terrace 228 34.02 N 117.18 W
Grand Teton ʌ 202 43.44 N 110.48 W
Grand Teton National Park ♠ 202 43.30 N 110.45 W
Grand Tower 194 37.37 N 89.29 W
Grand Traverse Bay ⊂ 190 45.02 N 85.30 W
Grand Traverse Bay, East Arm ⊂ 190 44.52 N 85.28 W
Grand Traverse Bay, West Arm ⊂ 190 44.52 N 85.35 W
Grandtully 46 56.39 N 3.46 W
Grand Turk 238 21.28 N 71.08 W
Grand Union Canal ≊ 260 51.30 N 0.02 W
Grand Valley, On., Can. 212 43.54 N 80.19 W
Grand Valley, Pa., U.S. 214 41.43 N 79.32 W
Grandview, Mb., Can. 184 51.10 N 100.42 W
Grandview, Il., U.S. 219 42.06 N 89.50 W
Grandview, Mo., U.S. 194 38.53 N 94.31 W
Grandview, Pa., U.S. 279b 40.10 N 79.52 W
Grandview, Tx., U.S. 222 32.16 N 97.11 W
Grandview, Wa., U.S. 202 46.15 N 119.54 W
Grand View, Wi., U.S. 190 46.22 N 91.06 W
Grandview Beach 216 41.50 N 83.24 W
Grandview Heights, Oh., U.S. 218 39.58 N 83.02 W
Grandview Heights, Pa., U.S. 208 40.03 N 76.17 W
Grandview Homes 216 40.44 N 84.04 W
Grand View-on-Hudson 276 41.44 N 73.55 W
Grandvillars 58 47.33 N 6.58 E
Grandville 216 42.54 N 85.45 W
Grandvilliers 50 49.40 N 1.56 E
Grand Wash Cliffs ⩡4 200 35.40 N 113.50 W
Grand Winterberg ʌ 56 48.59 N 7.37 E
Grandyle Village 210 43.00 N 78.57 W
Grâne 62 44.44 N 4.55 E
Grañén 34 41.56 N 0.22 W
Graneros 252 34.04 S 70.44 W
Gran → Esztergom 30 47.48 N 18.45 E
Granetalsperre ✦6 52 51.48 N 10.27 E
Graney, Lough ⊜ 48 52.59 N 8.40 W
Grangärde 40 60.16 N 14.59 E
Grange, Austl. 168b 34.54 S 138.30 E
Grange, Eng., U.K. 262 53.23 N 3.09 W
Grange, Bois de la ♠ 261 48.45 N 2.30 E
Grange-Bléneau, Château de la ⊥ 50 48.41 N 2.55 E
Grange Hill 260 51.37 N 0.05 E
Grangemouth 46 56.02 N 3.45 W
Grängen ⊜ 40 59.45 N 14.47 E
Grangent, Lac de ⊜1 62 45.25 N 4.15 E
Grange-over-Sands 44 54.12 N 2.55 W
Granger, Tx., U.S. 222 30.43 N 97.26 W
Granger, Wa., U.S. 202 46.20 N 120.11 W
Granger, Wy., U.S. 200 41.35 N 109.58 W
Granger Draw V 196 30.20 N 100.57 W
Granger Lake ⊜1 222 30.42 N 97.22 W
Grängesberg 40 60.05 N 14.59 E
Granges → Grenchen 58 47.11 N 7.24 E
Granges-sur-Vologne 58 48.09 N 6.47 E
Grangeville, Id., U.S. 202 45.55 N 116.07 W
Grangeville, Pa., U.S. 208 39.47 N 76.58 W
Grangousier Hill ʌ2 190 47.35 N 84.56 W
Gran Guardia 252 25.52 S 58.53 W
Granite, Md., U.S. 284b 39.21 N 76.51 W
Granite, Ok., U.S. 196 34.57 N 99.22 W
Granite City 219 38.42 N 90.08 W
Granite Creek ≃ 224 48.43 N 120.55 W
Granite Dome ʌ 226 38.13 N 119.44 W
Granite Downs 162 26.57 S 133.30 E
Granite Falls, Mn., U.S. 198 44.48 N 95.32 W
Granite Falls, N.C., U.S. 192 35.47 N 81.25 W
Granite Falls, Wa., U.S. 224 48.05 N 121.58 W
Granite Lake ⊜1 186 48.08 N 57.05 W
Granite Mountain ʌ, Austl. 171b 35.44 S 148.13 E
Granite Mountain ʌ, Ak., U.S. 180 65.26 N 161.14 W
Granite Mountain ʌ, Ak., U.S. 182 55.30 N 132.35 W
Granite Mountains ʌʌ 202 42.35 N 107.30 W
Granite Pass)(202 44.38 N 107.30 W
Granite Peak 162 25.38 S 121.21 E
Granite Peak ʌ, Mt., U.S. 202 45.10 N 109.48 W
Granite Peak ʌ, Mt., U.S. 202 45.34 N 112.02 W
Granite Peak ʌ, Nv., U.S. 204 41.40 N 117.35 W
Granite Peak ʌ, Nv., U.S. 204 40.48 N 119.25 W
Granite Range ʌʌ 204 41.00 N 119.35 W
Graniteville, Ma., U.S. 207 42.35 N 71.27 W
Graniteville, S.C., U.S. 192 33.33 N 81.48 W
Graniteville, Vt., U.S. 188 44.09 N 72.29 W
Graniti 70 37.53 N 15.14 E
Granitnoje 83 47.27 N 37.52 E
Granitogorsk 85 42.44 N 73.27 E
Granitola, Capo › 70 37.34 N 12.41 E
Granitola Torretta 70 37.34 N 12.40 E
Granity 172 41.38 S 171.51 E
Granitzenbach ≃ 61 47.11 N 14.46 E
Granja, Bra. 250 3.06 S 40.50 W
Granja, Port. 266c 38.51 N 9.06 W
Gran Khingan → Da Hinggan Ling ʌʌ 90 49.00 N 122.00 E
Granki 76 54.51 N 31.27 E
Grankulla (Kauniainen) 26 60.13 N 24.45 E
Gran Lago Salado → Great Salt Lake ⊜ 200 41.10 N 112.30 W
Gran Laguna Salada ⊜ 254 44.24 S 67.23 W
Granma □4 240p 21.20 N 76.50 W
Gränna 26 58.01 N 14.28 E
Grannoch, Loch ⊜ 44 55.00 N 4.17 W
Granollers 34 41.37 N 2.18 E
Granön 26 64.15 N 19.19 E
Granov 78 48.52 N 29.34 E
Gran Pajonal ʌʌ 248 10.45 S 74.30 W
Gran Paradiso ʌ 62 45.32 N 7.16 E
Gran Paradiso, Parco Nazionale del ♠ 62 45.34 N 7.18 E
Gran Pilastro (Hochfeiler) ʌ 64 46.58 N 11.44 E
Gran Rio ≃ 250 4.01 N 55.31 W
Gran Sasso d'Italia ʌʌ 66 42.27 N 13.42 E
Gransee 54 53.00 N 13.09 E
Grant, Fl., U.S. 220 27.55 N 80.31 W
Grant, Mi., U.S. 190 43.20 N 85.48 W
Grant, Ne., U.S. 198 40.50 N 101.43 W
Grant □6, In., U.S. 216 40.33 N 85.40 W
Grant □6, Ky., U.S. 218 38.39 N 84.39 W
Grant ≃ 190 42.40 N 90.45 W
Grant, Lake ⊜ 218 39.00 N 83.53 W
Grant, Mount ʌ 204 38.34 N 118.48 W
Grant, Point › 169 38.31 S 145.07 E
Granta ≃ 42 52.10 N 0.06 E
Grant Birthplace ⊥ 218 38.54 N 84.14 W
Grant City 194 40.29 N 94.24 W
Grantham, Austl. 171a 27.34 S 152.12 E
Grantham, Eng., U.K. 42 52.55 N 0.39 W
Grantham, Pa., U.S. 208 40.09 N 77.00 W
Grant-Kohrs Ranch National Historic Site ⊥ 202 46.25 N 112.40 W
Grant Lake ⊜1 226 37.50 N 119.07 W
Grantley Adams International Airport ⊠ 241g 13.04 N 59.29 W
Grant Mills 283 41.57 N 71.26 W
Granton 46 55.59 N 3.14 W
Grantorto 64 45.36 N 11.43 E
Grantown-on-Spey 46 57.19 N 3.37 W
Grant Park 216 41.14 N 87.39 W
Grant Park ♠ 278 41.52 N 87.37 W
Grant Point › 176 68.19 N 98.53 W
Grant Range ʌʌ 204 38.25 N 115.30 W
Grants 200 35.09 N 107.50 W
Grantsburg, In., U.S. 218 38.17 N 86.28 W
Grantsburg, Wi., U.S. 190 45.46 N 92.40 W
Grantshouse 46 55.53 N 2.19 W
Grants Pass 202 42.26 N 123.19 W
Grants Patch 162 30.27 S 121.07 E
Grant-Suttie Bay ⊂ 176 69.47 N 77.15 W
Grantsville, Ut., U.S. 200 40.36 N 112.27 W
Grantsville, W.V., U.S. 188 38.55 N 81.05 W
Grantville, Ga., U.S. 192 33.14 N 84.50 W
Grantville, Pa., U.S. 208 40.23 N 76.39 W
Granum 182 49.52 N 113.30 W
Granville, Austl. 274a 33.50 S 151.01 E
Granville, Fr. 32 48.50 N 1.36 W
Granville, Il., U.S. 190 41.15 N 89.13 W
Granville, Ma., U.S. 207 42.04 N 72.51 W
Granville, Mo., U.S. 219 39.34 N 92.06 W
Granville, N.Y., U.S. 188 43.24 N 73.15 W
Granville, N.D., U.S. 198 48.16 N 100.50 W
Granville, Oh., U.S. 214 40.04 N 82.31 W
Granville, Pa., U.S. 208 40.33 N 77.38 W
Granville, W.V., U.S. 188 39.38 N 79.59 W
Granville Lake ⊜ 184 56.18 N 100.30 W
Granvin 26 60.33 N 6.43 E
Granzin, Dtsch. 54 53.25 N 12.53 E
Granzin, Dtsch. 54 53.30 N 11.56 E
Grão Mogol 255 16.34 S 42.54 W
Grão-Mogol ≃ 256 21.46 S 43.40 W
Grape Creek ≃ 200 38.26 N 105.16 W
Grape Island I 283 42.16 N 70.55 W
Grapeland 222 31.29 N 95.28 W
Grapeview 224 47.19 N 122.50 W
Grapeville 214 40.19 N 79.36 W
Grapevine 222 32.56 N 97.04 W
Grapevine Lake ⊜1 222 32.59 N 97.06 W
Grapevine Peak ʌ 204 36.57 N 117.09 W
Grappa, Monte ʌ 64 45.52 N 11.48 E
Grappenhall 262 53.22 N 2.32 W
Grarem 34 36.31 N 6.19 E
Gras, Lac de ⊜ 176 64.30 N 110.30 W
Grasbult 158 30.52 S 21.47 E
Grasdorf 52 52.06 N 10.09 E
Graskop 156 24.58 S 30.49 E
Grasleben 54 52.18 N 11.01 E
Grasmere, S. Afr. 158 26.26 S 27.52 E
Grasmere, Eng., U.K. 44 54.28 N 3.02 W
Grasmere Lake ⊜ 276 40.36 N 74.05 W
Gräsö 40 60.21 N 18.28 E
Gräsö I 40 60.24 N 18.25 E
Grasonville 208 38.57 N 76.12 W
Grass ≃, Mb., Can. 184 56.03 N 96.33 W
Grass ≃, N.Y., U.S. 188 44.59 N 74.46 W
Grass, North Branch ≃ 188 44.25 N 75.06 W
Grass, South Branch ≃ 188 44.22 N 75.05 W
Grassano 68 40.38 N 16.18 E
Grassau 64 47.47 N 12.27 E
Grass Creek 202 43.56 N 108.39 W
Grass Creek ≃ 202 43.52 N 108.22 W
Grasscroft 262 53.32 N 2.02 W
Grasse 62 43.40 N 6.55 E
Grassendale ✦8 262 53.21 N 2.54 W
Grassflat 214 41.00 N 78.07 W
Grass Hassock Channel ⅄ 276 40.36 N 73.48 W
Grasshopper Creek ≃ 202 45.06 N 112.47 W
Grassington 44 54.04 N 2.00 W
Grass Island I 276 40.39 N 73.18 W
Grässjön ⊜ 40 59.52 N 13.43 E
Grass Lake 216 42.15 N 84.13 W
Grass Lake ⊜ 216 42.27 N 88.10 W
Grassmere, Lake ⊜ 172 41.44 S 174.10 E
Grass Patch 162 33.14 S 121.43 E
Grass Range 202 47.01 N 108.48 W
Grassridge Dam ⊜1 158 31.45 S 25.29 E
Grass River Provincial Park ♠ 184 54.40 N 100.50 W
Grass Valley, Austl. 168a 31.38 S 116.48 E
Grass Valley, Ca., U.S. 226 39.13 N 121.03 W
Grass Valley, Or., U.S. 224 45.21 N 120.47 W
Grassy 166 40.03 S 144.04 E
Grassy ≃ 190 48.22 N 81.27 W
Grassy Bay ⊂ 276 40.38 N 73.48 W
Grassy Brook ≃ 284a 43.03 N 79.07 W
Grassy Creek ≃, In., U.S. 216 40.55 N 86.30 W
Grassy Creek ≃, Mo., U.S. 219 39.54 N 91.37 W
Grassy Hill ʌ 271d 22.25 N 114.09 E
Grassy Island I 276 41.04 N 73.23 W
Grassy Island Lake ⊜ 184 51.50 N 110.20 W
Grassy Key I 220 24.46 N 80.57 W
Grassy Lake 182 49.49 N 111.43 W
Grassy Lake ⊜ 220 27.13 N 81.20 W
Grassy Plains 182 53.57 N 125.54 W
Grassy Sprain Reservoir ⊜1 276 40.58 N 73.51 W
Gråsten 41 54.55 N 9.36 E
Grästorp 26 58.20 N 12.40 E
Graterford 285 40.13 N 75.27 W
Graterford State Correctional Institution ♰ 285 40.14 N 75.26 W
Grates Point › 186 48.10 N 52.57 W
Gratis 218 39.38 N 84.31 W
Gratitunon 115a 7.43 S 113.00 E
Gratkorn 61 47.08 N 15.21 E
Gratwein 61 47.07 N 15.19 E
Gratz, Ky., U.S. 218 38.28 N 84.57 W
Gratz, Pa., U.S. 208 40.37 N 76.43 W
Gratztown 279b 40.14 N 79.47 W
Graubünden (Grischun) □3 58 46.45 N 9.30 E
Graudenz → Grudziądz 30 53.29 N 18.45 E
Graue Hörner ʌ 58 46.57 N 9.23 E
Graukogel ʌ 64 47.06 N 13.10 E
Graulhet 32 43.46 N 2.00 E
Graulinster 56 49.45 N 6.18 E
Graun → Curon Venosta 64 46.49 N 10.32 E
Graupa 54 51.00 N 13.54 E
Gravatá 250 8.12 S 35.34 W
Gravatá ≃ 255 16.53 S 42.10 W
Grave 52 51.45 N 5.44 E
Grave Creek ≃ 202 42.39 N 123.35 W
Gravedona 58 46.09 N 9.18 E
Gravelbourg 184 49.53 N 106.34 W
Gravelines 50 50.59 N 2.07 E
Gravellona-Toce 58 45.55 N 8.26 E
Gravell Point › 176 67.10 N 76.43 W
Gravelly Bay ⊂ 284a 42.52 N 79.15 W
Gravelly Brook ≃ 276 40.25 N 74.13 W
Gravelly Pond ⊜ 283 42.36 N 70.48 W
Gravelotte, Fr. 56 49.07 N 6.01 E
Gravelotte, S. Afr. 156 23.56 S 30.34 E
Gravenhurst 212 44.55 N 79.22 W
Grävenwiesbach 56 50.23 N 8.27 E
Grave Peak ʌ 202 46.24 N 114.44 W
Gravesend, Austl. 166 29.35 S 150.19 E
Gravesend, Eng., U.K. 42 51.27 N 0.24 E
Gravesend Bay ⊂ 276 40.36 N 74.01 W
Gravesham □8 260 51.25 N 0.24 E
Gravette 194 36.25 N 94.27 W
Gravigny 50 49.03 N 1.10 E
Gravina 70 37.34 N 15.03 E
Gravina di Matera ≃ 68 40.37 N 16.49 E
Gravina in Puglia 68 40.49 N 16.25 E
Gravina Island I 182 55.17 N 131.45 W
Gray, Fr. 58 47.27 N 5.35 E
Gray, Ga., U.S. 192 33.00 N 83.32 W
Gray, Ky., U.S. 192 36.56 N 84.00 W
Gray, Pa., U.S. 214 40.08 N 79.05 W
Grayback Mountain ʌ, Ak., U.S. 180 57.08 N 153.54 W
Grayback Mountain ʌ, Or., U.S. 202 42.07 N 123.18 W
Grayland 224 46.48 N 124.05 W
Grayling, Ak., U.S. 180 62.57 N 160.03 W
Grayling, Mi., U.S. 190 44.39 N 84.42 W
Graylyn Crest 285 39.48 N 75.31 W
Grays 42 51.29 N 0.20 E
Grays ≃ 224 46.18 N 123.41 W
Grays Harbor □6 224 47.09 N 123.45 W
Grays Harbor ⊂ 224 46.56 N 124.05 W
Grayshott 42 51.11 N 0.45 W
Grayslake 216 42.21 N 88.03 W
Grays Lake ⊜ 278 42.21 N 88.03 W
Grays Lake ≋ 202 43.04 N 111.26 W
Grays Lake Outlet ≃ 202 43.22 N 111.46 W
Grayson, Sk., Can. 184 50.44 N 102.40 W
Grayson, Al., U.S. 194 34.16 N 87.19 W
Grayson, Ca., U.S. 226 37.33 N 121.10 W
Grayson, Ky., U.S. 218 38.19 N 82.56 W
Grayson, La., U.S. 194 32.02 N 92.06 W
Grayson Lake ⊜1 218 38.13 N 83.00 W
Grayson Lake State Park ♠ 218 38.13 N 83.02 W
Grays Peak ʌ 200 39.37 N 105.45 W
Grays Point 274a 34.04 S 151.05 E
Grays River 224 46.21 N 123.36 W
Gray Summit 219 38.29 N 90.49 W
Graysville 194 35.26 N 85.05 W
Graytown 214 41.33 N 83.16 W
Grayville 194 37.57 N 88.10 W
Gray Wolf ≃ 224 47.55 N 123.07 W
Graz 61 47.05 N 15.27 E
Grazalema 34 36.46 N 5.22 W
Graždanka ✦8 265a 60.00 N 30.24 E
Gr'azeva ≃ 265b 55.51 N 37.08 E
Gr'azi 80 52.29 N 39.57 E
Grazierville 214 40.40 N 78.16 W
Gr'aznoje 82 54.02 N 39.07 E
Gr'aznovo, Ross. 82 54.18 N 36.49 E
Gr'aznovo, Ross. 265b 55.57 N 37.34 E
Gr'aznyj Irtek 80 51.56 N 53.11 E
Gr'azovec 76 58.53 N 40.14 E
Grdelica 38 42.54 N 22.04 E
Greåker 26 59.16 N 11.02 E
Greasby 262 53.23 N 3.07 W
Great ≃ 241k 12.08 N 61.36 W
Great Adventure ♠ 208 40.09 N 74.27 W
Great Altcar 262 53.33 N 3.01 W
Great America ♠ 282 37.24 N 121.59 W
Great Amwell 260 51.48 N 0.01 W
Great Artesian Basin ≚1 166 25.00 S 143.00 E
Great Australian Bight ⊂3 162 35.00 S 130.00 E
Great Ayton 44 54.30 N 1.08 W
Great Baddow 42 51.43 N 0.29 E
Great Bahama Bank ✢4 238 23.15 N 78.00 W
Great Barford 42 52.09 N 0.21 W
Great Barrier Island I 172 36.10 S 175.25 E
Great Barrier Reef ✢2 160 18.00 S 146.50 E
Great Barrier Reef Marine Park ♠ 166 21.00 S 151.00 E
Great Barrington 207 42.11 N 73.21 W
Great Barrow 262 53.12 N 2.48 W
Great Basin ≚1 178 40.00 N 117.00 W
Great Basin National Park ♠ 204 38.55 N 114.14 W
Great Bay ⊂ 208 39.30 N 74.23 W
Great Bear ≃ 180 64.54 N 125.35 W
Great Bear Lake ⊜ 176 66.00 N 120.00 W
Great Beaver Lake ⊜ 182 54.25 N 123.45 W
Great Belt → Storebælt ⅄ 41 55.30 N 11.00 E
Great Bend, Ks., U.S. 198 38.21 N 98.45 W
Great Bend, N.Y., U.S. 212 44.02 N 75.43 W
Great Bend, Pa., U.S. 210 41.58 N 75.44 W
Great Bernera I 46 58.13 N 6.49 W
Great Bitter Lake → Murrah al-Kubrā, Al-Buḥayrah al- ⊜ 142 30.20 N 32.23 E
Great Blasket Island I 48 52.05 N 10.32 W
Great Blue Hill ʌ2 207 42.13 N 71.07 W
Great Bookham 260 51.16 N 0.22 W
Great Braxted 260 51.48 N 0.42 E
Great Brewster Island I 283 42.20 N 70.53 W
Great Britain I 22 54.00 N 2.00 W
Great Brook ≃ 276 40.42 N 74.31 W
Great Buddha ♰1 268 35.19 N 139.32 E
Great Budworth 262 53.18 N 2.30 W
Great Burnt Lake ⊜ 186 48.20 N 56.13 W
Great Burstead 260 51.36 N 0.25 E
Great Camanoe I 240m 18.29 N 64.32 W
Great Captain Island I 276 40.59 N 73.38 W
Great Central 182 49.19 N 124.59 W
Great Central Lake ⊜ 182 49.27 N 125.12 W
Great Channel ⅄ 110 6.25 N 94.20 E
Great Chazy ≃ 188 44.56 N 73.23 W
Great Clifton 44 54.39 N 3.29 W
Great Coco Island I 110 14.05 N 93.24 E
Great Coharie Creek ≃ 192 34.50 N 78.22 W
Great Cove ⊂ 276 40.43 N 73.14 W
Great Crosby 262 53.29 N 3.01 W
Great Crossing 218 38.08 N 84.38 W
Great Cumbrae Island I 46 55.46 N 4.55 W
Great Dismal Swamp ≋ 192 36.30 N 76.30 W
Great Ditch ≊ 276 40.24 N 74.31 W
Great Divide Basin ≚1 202 42.00 N 108.10 W
Great Dividing Range ʌʌ 160 25.00 S 147.00 E
Great Driffield 44 54.00 N 0.27 W
Great Duck Island I 190 45.40 N 82.58 W
Great Dunmow 42 51.53 N 0.22 E
Great Eau ≃ 44 53.25 N 0.13 E
Great Egg Harbor ≃ 208 39.18 N 74.40 W
Great Egg Harbor Bay ⊂ 208 39.18 N 74.37 W
Great Egg Harbor Inlet ⊂ 208 39.20 N 74.34 W
Greater Antilles II 238 20.00 N 74.00 W
Greater Buffalo International Airport ⊠ 210 42.56 N 78.44 W
Greater Cincinnati Airport ⊠ 218 39.03 N 84.40 W
Greater Khingan Range → Da Hinggan Ling ʌʌ 90 49.00 N 122.00 E
Greater London □6 42 51.30 N 0.10 W
Greater Manchester □6 44 53.30 N 2.20 W
Greater Pittsburgh International Airport ⊠ 214 40.29 N 80.14 W
Greater Sunda Islands II 108 2.00 S 110.00 E
Greater Wilmington Airport ⊠ 208 39.41 N 75.36 W
Greater Wollongong → Wollongong 170 34.25 S 150.54 E
Great Escape ♠ 210 43.22 N 73.42 W
Great Exuma I 238 23.32 N 75.50 W
Great Falls, Mb., Can. 184 50.27 N 96.02 W
Great Falls, Mt., U.S. 202 47.30 N 111.17 W
Great Falls, S.C., U.S. 192 34.34 N 80.54 W
Great Falls, Va., U.S. 284c 39.00 N 77.17 W
Great Falls ∟ 284c 39.00 N 77.16 W
Great Falls Park ♠ 284c 39.00 N 77.15 W
Great Fish Point › 158 33.30 S 27.10 E
Great Gable ʌ 44 54.28 N 3.12 W
Great Gaddesden 260 51.47 N 0.30 W
Great Grimsby → Grimsby 44 53.35 N 0.05 W
Great Guana Cay I 238 24.00 N 76.20 W
Great Hameldon ʌ2 262 53.45 N 2.19 W
Great Harwood 44 53.48 N 2.24 W
Great Haywood 42 52.48 N 2.00 W
Great Himalaya Range ʌʌ 120 29.00 N 83.00 E
Greathouse Peak ʌ 202 46.46 N 109.21 W
Great Inagua I 238 21.05 N 73.18 W
Great Indian Desert (Thar Desert) ✦2 120 27.00 N 71.00 E
Great Island I, Ire. 48 51.52 N 8.17 W
Great Island I, N.Y., U.S. 276 40.38 N 73.30 W
Great Island I, N.Y., U.S. 276 41.05 N 73.44 W
Great Karroo (Groot Karroo) ʌʌ1 158 32.25 S 22.40 E
Great Kills ✦8 276 40.33 N 74.10 W
Great Kills Harbor ⊂ 276 40.32 N 74.08 W
Great Kills Park ♠ 276 40.33 N 74.08 W
Great La Cloche Island I 190 46.01 N 81.52 W
Great Lake ⊜ 166 41.52 S 146.45 E
Great Lakes Naval Training Center ■ 216 42.18 N 87.50 W
Great Lakes Steel Works ♰3 281 42.15 N 83.08 W
Great Machipongo Inlet ⊂ 208 37.22 N 75.43 W
Great Malvern 42 52.07 N 2.19 W
Great Marsh ≋ 208 36.32 N 75.57 W
Great Marton 262 53.48 N 3.02 W
Great Massingham 42 52.46 N 0.40 E
Great Meadows 210 40.52 N 74.54 W
Great Meadows National Wildlife Refuge ✦4 283 42.29 N 71.20 W
Great Mercury Island I 172 36.37 S 175.48 E
Great Meteor Tablemount ✢3 18 30.00 N 28.30 W
Great Miami ≃ 188 39.06 N 84.49 W
Great Mills 208 38.14 N 76.30 W
Great Misery Island I 283 42.33 N 70.48 W
Great Missenden 42 51.43 N 0.43 W
Great Mis Tor ʌ 42 50.34 N 4.01 W
Great Mosque ♰1 146 32.46 N 22.40 E
Great Namaqualand □9 156 25.00 S 17.00 E
Great Neck 276 40.48 N 73.43 W
Great Neck ›1, Ma., U.S. 283 42.42 N 70.48 W
Great Neck ›1, N.Y., U.S. 276 40.50 N 73.45 W
Great Neck Estates 276 40.47 N 73.44 W
Great Nicobar I 110 7.00 N 93.50 E
Great North East Channel ⅄ 164 9.30 S 143.25 E
Great Notch Reservoir ⊜1 276 40.53 N 74.12 W
Great Ormes Head › 44 53.21 N 3.52 W
Great Ouse ≃ 42 52.47 N 0.22 E
Great Oxney Green 260 51.44 N 0.25 E
Great Palm Island I 166 18.43 S 146.37 E
Great Parndon 260 51.45 N 0.05 E
Great Patchogue Lake ⊜ 276 40.46 N 73.01 W
Great Peconic Bay ⊂ 207 40.56 N 72.30 W
Great Pee Dee ≃ 192 33.21 N 79.16 W
Great Piece Meadows ≋ 276 40.54 N 74.19 W
Great Plain of the Koukdjuak ≚ 176 66.00 N 73.00 W
Great Plains ≚ 16 42.00 N 100.00 W
Great Point › 207 41.23 N 70.03 W
Great Pubnico Lake ⊜ 186 43.42 N 65.43 W
Great Quittacas Pond ⊜ 207 41.48 N 70.54 W
Great River 276 40.45 N 73.10 W
Great Ruaha ≃ 154 7.56 S 37.52 E
Great Sacandaga Lake ⊜ 210 43.08 N 74.10 W
Great Saint Bernard Pass → Grand-Saint-Bernard, Col du)(58 45.50 N 7.10 E
Great Sale Cay I 192 27.00 N 78.12 W
Great Salt Lake ⊜ 200 41.10 N 112.30 W
Great Salt Lake Desert ✦2 200 40.40 N 113.30 W
Great Salt Plains Lake ⊜1 196 36.44 N 98.12 W
Great Sand Dunes National Monument ♠ 200 37.43 N 105.36 W
Great Sand Hills ʌʌ2 184 50.35 N 109.05 W
Great Sandy Desert ✦2 162 21.30 S 125.00 E
Great Sandy National Park ♠ 166 24.59 S 153.17 E
Great Sankey 44 53.23 N 2.37 W
Great Santa Cruz Island I 116 6.52 N 122.03 E
Great Scarcies (Kolenté) ≃ 150 8.55 N 13.08 W
Great Sea Reef ✢2 175g 16.15 S 179.00 E
Great Seneca Creek ≃ 208 39.08 N 77.20 W
Great Shelford 42 52.09 N 0.09 E
Great Sitkin Island I 180 52.03 N 176.07 W
Great Slave Lake ⊜ 176 61.30 N 114.00 W
Great Smoky Mountains ʌʌ 192 35.35 N 83.30 W
Great Smoky Mountains National Park ♠ 192 35.39 N 83.30 W
Great Sound ⅄, Ber. 240a 32.17 N 64.51 W
Great Sound ⅄, N.J., U.S. 208 39.06 N 74.47 W
Great South Bay ⊂ 210 40.40 N 73.17 W
Great Stour ≃ 42 51.19 N 1.15 E
Great Sutton 262 53.17 N 2.56 W
Great Swamp National Wildlife Refuge ✦4 276 40.43 N 74.28 W
Great Tenasserim ≃ 110 12.24 N 98.37 E
Great Tobago I 240m 18.27 N 64.48 W
Great Torrington 42 50.57 N 4.08 W

≃	River	Fluß	Río	Rivière	Rio
≊	Canal	Kanal	Canal	Canal	Canal
∟	Waterfall, Rapids	Wasserfall, Stromschnellen	Cascada, Rápidos	Chute d'eau, Rapides	Cascata, Rápidos
⅄	Strait	Meeresstraße	Estrecho	Détroit	Estreito
⊂	Bay, Gulf	Bucht, Golf	Bahía, Golfo	Baie, Golfe	Baía, Golfo
⊜	Lake, Lakes	See, Seen	Lago, Lagos	Lac, Lacs	Lago, Lagos
≋	Swamp	Sumpf	Pantano	Marais	Pântano
⊓	Ice Features, Glacier	Eis- und Gletscherformen	Accidentes Glaciales	Formes glaciaires	Acidentes glaciares
≚	Other Hydrographic Features	Andere Hydrographische Objekte	Otros Elementos Hidrográficos	Autres données hydrographiques	Outros acidentes hidrográficos

✢	Submarine Features	Untermeerische Objekte	Accidentes Submarinos	Formes de relief sous-marin	Acidentes submarinos
□	Political Unit	Politische Einheit	Unidad Política	Entité politique	Unidade política
♰	Cultural Institution	Kulturelle Institution	Institución Cultural	Institution culturelle	Institução cultural
⊥	Historical Site	Historische Stätte	Sitio Histórico	Site historique	Sítio histórico
♠	Recreational Site	Erholungs- und Ferienort	Sitio de Recreo	Centre de loisirs	Área de Lazer
⊠	Airport	Flughafen	Aeropuerto	Aéroport	Aeroporto
■	Military Installation	Militäranlage	Instalación Militar	Installation militaire	Instalação militar
✦	Miscellaneous	Verschiedenes	Misceláneo	Divers	Diversos

ENGLISH — Name / Page / Lat.°′ / Long.°′
DEUTSCH — Name / Seite / Breite°′ / Länge°′ E = Ost

Great Totham 260 51.47 N 0.43 E
Great Usutu (Maputo) (Lusutfu) ≃ 158 26.11 S 32.42 E
Great Valley 210 42.13 N 78.38 W
Great Victoria Desert ◆[2] 162 28.30 S 127.45 E
Great Wall ʊ[3] 9 62.13 S 58.58 W
Great Wall → Chang Cheng ⊥ 98 40.30 N 116.30 E
Great Waltham 260 51.48 N 0.28 E
Great Warley 260 51.35 N 0.17 E
Great Western Forum ♦ 280 33.57 N 118.20 W
Great Whernside ∧ 44 54.09 N 1.59 W
Great Wicomico ≃ 208 37.48 N 76.18 W
Great Wyrley 42 52.41 N 2.01 W
Great Yarmouth 42 52.37 N 1.44 E
Great Zab (Büyükzap) (Az-Zāb al-Kabīr) ≃ 128 36.00 N 43.21 E
Great Zimbabwe Ruins National Park ♦ 154 20.17 S 30.57 E
Grebbestad 26 58.42 N 11.15 E
Grebenhain 56 50.29 N 9.19 E
Grebenka 78 50.07 N 32.25 E
Grebenstein 56 51.26 N 9.24 E
Grebnevo 265b 55.58 N 38.05 E
Greb'onki 78 49.57 N 30.12 E
Gréboun ∧ 150 20.00 N 8.35 E
Grèce → Greece □[1] 38 39.00 N 22.00 E
Grecia 236 10.05 N 84.18 W
Grecia → Greece □[1] 38 39.00 N 22.00 E
Grečiškino 83 48.52 N 38.54 E
Grecken ⊜ 40 59.35 N 14.44 E
Greco 252 32.48 S 57.03 W
Greco ◆[8] 266b 45.30 N 9.13 E
Greco, Monte ∧ 66 41.48 N 14.00 E
Greco Island I 282 37.31 N 122.11 W
Greding 60 49.03 N 11.21 E
Gredos, Sierra de ⋏ 34 40.18 N 5.05 W
Gredstedbro 41 55.24 N 8.45 E
Greece 210 43.12 N 77.41 W
Greece (Ellás) □[1], Europe 22 39.00 N 22.00 E
Greece (Ellás) □[1], Europe 38 39.00 N 22.00 E
Greeley, Co., U.S. 200 40.25 N 104.42 W
Greeley, Ks., U.S. 198 38.19 N 95.26 W
Greeley, Ne., U.S. 198 41.33 N 98.32 W
Greeley, Pa., U.S. 210 41.25 N 75.00 W
Greeleyville 192 33.34 N 79.59 W
Green □[6] 216 42.48 N 89.25 W
Green ≃, N.B., Can. 186 47.18 N 68.09 W
Green ≃, U.S. 200 38.11 N 109.53 W
Green ≃, U.S. 207 42.35 N 72.36 W
Green ≃, U.S. 207 42.10 N 73.22 W
Green ≃, Il., U.S. 190 41.28 N 90.23 W
Green ≃, Il., U.S. 216 41.46 N 89.10 W
Green ≃, Ky., U.S. 194 37.55 N 87.30 W
Green ≃, N.D., U.S. 198 46.52 N 102.35 W
Green ≃, Vt., U.S. 210 43.06 N 73.13 W
Green ≃, Wa., U.S. 224 47.33 N 122.20 W
Green ≃, Wa., U.S. 224 46.20 N 122.34 W
Greenacres, Ca., U.S. 226 35.23 N 119.07 W
Green Acres, De., U.S. 285 39.47 N 75.30 W
Greenacres, Wa., U.S. 202 47.39 N 117.06 W
Green Acres ◆[9] 276 40.40 N 73.43 W
Greenacres City 220 26.37 N 80.07 W
Greenbackville 208 38.00 N 75.23 W
Greenbank 224 48.06 N 122.34 W
Green Bay 190 44.31 N 88.01 W
Green Bay ⊂, Nf., Can. 186 49.43 N 55.58 W
Green Bay ⊂, On., Can. 212 44.38 N 76.36 W
Green Bay ⊂, U.S. 190 45.00 N 87.30 W
Greenbelt 284c 39.00 N 76.52 W
Greenbelt Park ♦ 284c 38.59 N 76.54 W
Greenbo Lake ⊜ 218 38.29 N 82.54 W
Greenbo Lake State Resort Park ♦ 218 38.29 N 82.54 W
Greenbooth Reservoir ⊜[1] 262 53.38 N 2.13 W
Greenbrae 226 37.57 N 122.31 W
Greenbrier, Ar., U.S. 194 35.14 N 92.23 W
Green Brier, Tn., U.S. 194 36.25 N 86.48 W
Greenbrier ≃ 192 37.39 N 80.53 W
Greenbrier State Park ♦ 208 39.33 N 77.38 W
Green Brook 276 40.36 N 74.27 W
Green Brook ≃ 276 40.33 N 74.32 W
Greenburg 194 30.51 N 90.40 W
Greenbush, Ma., U.S. 207 42.11 N 70.45 W
Greenbush, Mn., U.S. 198 48.42 N 96.10 W
Greenbush, Va., U.S. 208 37.45 N 75.41 W
Greenbushes 162 33.51 S 116.03 E
Green Camp 214 40.31 N 83.12 W
Green Cape › 166 37.15 S 150.03 E
Greencastle, Ire. 48 55.12 N 6.59 W
Greencastle, In., U.S. 194 39.38 N 86.51 W
Greencastle, Pa., U.S. 188 39.47 N 77.43 W
Green City 194 40.16 N 92.57 W
Green Cove Springs 192 29.59 N 81.40 W
Green Creek 208 39.02 N 74.54 W
Green Creek ≃, Oh., U.S. 214 41.26 N 83.01 W
Green Creek ≃, Pa., U.S. 285 39.53 N 75.28 W
Greencrest Park 214 41.23 N 80.24 W
Greendale, Austl. 274a 33.55 S 150.39 E
Greendale, In., U.S. 218 39.06 N 84.51 W
Greendale, Wi., U.S. 216 42.56 N 87.59 W
Greene, Dtsch. 52 51.52 N 9.56 E
Greene, Ia., U.S. 190 42.53 N 92.48 W
Greene, N.Y., U.S. 210 42.19 N 75.46 W
Greene, R.I., U.S. 207 41.41 N 71.44 W
Greene □[6], Il., U.S. 219 39.18 N 90.24 W
Greene □[6], N.Y., U.S. 210 42.13 N 73.52 W
Greene □[6], Oh., U.S. 218 39.41 N 83.56 W
Greeneville 192 36.06 N 82.42 W
Greenfield, Eng., U.K. 262 53.32 N 2.01 W
Greenfield, Wales, U.K. 44 53.18 N 3.13 W
Greenfield, Ca., U.S. 226 36.19 N 121.14 W
Greenfield, Il., U.S. 219 39.20 N 90.12 W
Greenfield, In., U.S. 218 39.47 N 85.46 W
Greenfield, Ia., U.S. 198 41.18 N 94.27 W
Greenfield, Ma., U.S. 207 42.35 N 72.36 W
Greenfield, Mo., U.S. 194 37.24 N 93.50 W
Greenfield, Oh., U.S. 218 39.21 N 83.22 W
Greenfield, Tn., U.S. 194 36.09 N 88.48 W
Greenfield, Wi., U.S. 216 42.58 N 88.02 W
Greenfield-Park, P.Q., Can. 275a 45.29 N 73.29 W
Greenfield Park, N.Y., U.S. 210 41.44 N 74.29 W
Greenfields Village 285 75.10 N 39.49 W
Greenfield Village ⊥ 281 42.18 N 83.14 W
Greenford ◆[8] 260 51.32 N 0.21 W
Green Forest 194 36.20 N 93.26 W
Green Harbor 207 42.04 N 70.39 W
Green Harbor ≃ 283 42.05 N 70.39 W
Green Head › 162 30.05 S 114.58 E
Green Hill 285 39.59 N 75.36 W
Greenhill ◆[8] 260 51.35 N 0.20 W
Greenhills, S. Afr. 273d 26.10 S 27.40 E
Greenhills, Oh., U.S. 218 39.16 N 84.31 W
Greenhithe 260 51.27 N 0.17 E
Greenhorn Creek ≃ 198 38.08 N 104.38 W
Greenhurst 214 42.07 N 79.19 W
Green Hut Park 276 40.50 N 74.39 W
Green Island, N.Z. 172 45.54 S 170.26 E
Greenisland, N. Ire., U.K. 48 54.42 N 5.52 W
Green Island, N.Y., U.S. 210 42.44 N 73.41 W
Green Island I 241k 12.14 N 61.35 W
Green Island Bay ⊂ 116 10.12 N 119.22 E
Green Islands II 14 4.30 S 154.10 E
Green Knoll 276 40.36 N 74.36 W
Green Lake, Sk., Can. 184 54.17 N 107.47 W
Green Lake, Wi., U.S. 190 43.50 N 88.57 W
Green Lake ⊜, B.C., Can. 182 51.24 N 121.15 W
Green Lake ⊜, Sk., Can. 184 54.10 N 107.43 W
Green Lake ⊜, Mi., U.S. 281 42.36 N 83.25 W
Green Lake ⊜, N.Y., U.S. 284a 42.45 N 78.45 W
Green Lake ⊜, Wi., U.S. 190 43.41 N 88.57 W
Green Lakes State Park ♦ 212 43.03 N 75.58 W
Greenlal (Saint-Grégoire-de-Greenlay) 206 45.34 N 72.01 W
Greenland, Ar., U.S. 194 35.59 N 94.10 W
Greenland, Mi., U.S. 190 46.46 N 89.06 W
Greenland (Kalaallit Nunaat) □[2] 16 70.00 N 40.00 W
Greenland Basin ✦[1] 16 73.30 N 5.00 W
Greenland-Iceland Rise ✦[3] 10 67.00 N 27.00 W
Greenlands 158 27.07 S 27.40 E
Greenland Sea ⊤[2] 16 77.00 N 1.00 W
Green Lane 208 40.20 N 75.28 W
Green Lane Reservoir ⊜[1] 208 40.22 N 75.29 W
Greenlaw 46 55.43 N 2.28 W
Greenlawn 276 40.52 N 73.21 W
Greenlawn Park 285 40.07 N 74.51 W
Greenleaf 198 39.43 N 96.58 W
Green Lookout Mountain ∧ 224 45.52 N 122.08 W
Green Manorville 207 42.00 N 72.32 W
Green Meadows 284c 38.58 N 76.57 W
Greenmount, Austl. 171a 27.47 S 151.54 E
Greenmount, Eng., U.K. 262 53.37 N 2.20 W
Greenmount, Md., U.S. 208 39.37 N 76.51 W
Green Mountains ⋏ 188 43.45 N 72.45 W
Green Oak Lake ⊜ 281 42.27 N 83.43 W
Green Oaks 278 42.18 N 87.55 W
Greenock, Austl. 168b 34.27 S 138.55 E
Greenock, Scot., U.K. 46 55.57 N 4.45 W
Greenock, Pa., U.S. 279b 40.19 N 79.48 W
Greenodd 44 54.14 N 3.04 W
Greenore Point › 48 52.15 N 6.18 W
Greenough 162 28.57 S 114.44 E
Greenough ≃ 162 28.51 S 114.38 E
Greenough, Mount ∧ 180 69.10 N 141.35 W
Green Park 208 40.23 N 77.19 W
Green Peter Lake ⊜[1] 202 44.28 N 122.30 W
Green Point › 276 40.43 N 73.06 W
Green Pond, Al., U.S. 194 33.13 N 87.07 W
Green Pond, N.J., U.S. 276 41.01 N 74.29 W
Green Pond ⊜ 276 41.00 N 74.30 W
Green Pond Brook ≃ 276 40.53 N 74.34 W
Greenport 207 41.06 N 72.21 W
Green Ridge 285 39.51 N 75.25 W
Green River, Pap. N. Gui. 164 3.55 S 141.10 E
Green River, Ut,. U.S. 200 38.59 N 110.09 W
Green River, Wy., U.S. 200 41.31 N 109.27 W
Green River Lake ⊜[1] 194 37.15 N 85.15 W
Greensboro, Al., U.S. 194 32.42 N 87.35 W
Greensboro, Fl., U.S. 192 30.34 N 84.44 W
Greensboro, Ga., U.S. 192 33.34 N 83.10 W
Greensboro, Md., U.S. 208 38.58 N 75.48 W
Greensboro, N.C., U.S. 192 36.04 N 79.47 W
Greensborough 274b 37.42 S 145.06 E
Greensburg, In., U.S. 218 39.20 N 85.29 W
Greensburg, Ks., U.S. 198 37.36 N 99.17 W
Greensburg, Ky., U.S. 194 37.15 N 85.29 W
Greensburg, Oh., U.S. 214 40.56 N 81.28 W
Greensburg, Pa., U.S. 214 40.18 N 79.32 W
Greens Farms 276 41.07 N 73.19 W
Greens Fork 218 39.53 N 85.02 W
Greens Fork ≃ 218 39.45 N 85.07 W
Greenside ◆[8] 273d 26.09 S 28.01 E
Greens Lake ⊂ 222 29.16 N 94.59 W
Greens Peak ∧ 200 34.07 N 109.35 W
Greenspond 186 49.04 N 53.34 W
Green Springs 214 41.15 N 83.03 W
Greenstead 260 51.42 N 0.14 E
Greenstone 208 39.45 N 77.27 W
Greenstone Point › 46 57.55 N 5.38 W
Green Street 260 51.40 N 0.16 W
Green Street Green ◆[8] 260 51.21 N 0.04 E
Greensville □[6] 208 36.40 N 77.30 W
Green Swamp ≡, Fl., U.S. 220 28.20 N 81.48 W
Green Swamp ≡, N.C., U.S. 192 34.10 N 78.20 W
Greentown, In., U.S. 216 40.28 N 85.58 W
Greentown, Oh., U.S. 214 40.56 N 81.28 W
Greentown, Pa., U.S. 210 41.19 N 75.18 W
Green Tree 279b 40.24 N 80.02 W
Greenup, Il., U.S. 194 39.14 N 88.09 W
Greenup, Ky., U.S. 218 38.34 N 82.49 W
Greenup □[6] 218 38.33 N 83.00 W
Greenup Dam ◆[6] 218 38.39 N 82.52 W
Greenvale, Austl. 166 18.59 S 145.07 E
Greenvale, N.Y., U.S. 276 40.49 N 73.38 W
Green Valley, On., Can. 206 45.16 N 74.36 W
Green Valley, Az., U.S. 200 31.52 N 110.59 W
Green Valley, Il., U.S. 190 40.24 N 89.38 W
Green Valley Creek ≃ 226 38.13 N 122.08 W
Greenview 219 40.04 N 89.44 W
Green Village, N.J., U.S. 276 40.44 N 74.27 W
Greenvillage, Pa., U.S. 208 40.00 N 77.36 W
Greenville, Liber. 150 5.01 N 9.03 W
Greenville, Al., U.S. 194 31.49 N 86.37 W
Greenville, Ca., U.S. 204 40.08 N 120.57 W
Greenville, Fl., U.S. 192 30.28 N 83.37 W
Greenville, Ga., U.S. 192 33.01 N 84.42 W
Greenville, Il., U.S. 219 38.53 N 89.24 W
Greenville, In., U.S. 218 38.22 N 85.59 W
Greenville, Ky., U.S. 194 37.12 N 87.10 W
Greenville, Me., U.S. 188 45.28 N 69.35 W
Greenville, Mi., U.S. 190 43.10 N 85.15 W
Greenville, Ms., U.S. 194 33.24 N 91.03 W
Greenville, Mo., U.S. 194 37.08 N 90.27 W
Greenville, N.H., U.S. 207 42.46 N 71.48 W
Greenville, N.Y., U.S. 210 40.59 N 73.49 W
Greenville, N.Y., U.S. 276 40.59 N 73.49 W
Greenville, N.C., U.S. 192 35.36 N 77.22 W
Greenville, Oh., U.S. 218 40.06 N 84.37 W
Greenville, Pa., U.S. 214 41.24 N 80.23 W
Greenville, R.I., U.S. 207 41.52 N 71.33 W
Greenville, S.C., U.S. 192 34.51 N 82.23 W
Greenville, Tx., U.S. 222 33.08 N 96.06 W
Greenville Creek ≃ 218 40.07 N 84.22 W
Greenville Place 285 39.46 N 75.36 W
Greenwater ≃ 224 47.09 N 121.39 W
Greenwater Lake ⊜ 190 48.34 N 90.26 W
Greenwater Lake Provincial Park ♦ 184 52.33 N 103.33 W
Greenwell Point 170 34.55 S 150.44 E
Greenwich, Austl. 274a 33.50 S 151.11 E
Greenwich, Ct., U.S. 207 41.01 N 73.37 W
Greenwich, N.J., U.S. 208 39.23 N 75.20 W
Greenwich, N.Y., U.S. 210 43.05 N 73.29 W
Greenwich, Oh., U.S. 214 41.01 N 82.30 W
Greenwich ◆[8] 42 51.28 N 0.02 E
Greenwich Cove ⊂ 276 41.01 N 73.35 W
Greenwich Creek ≃ 276 41.02 N 73.37 W
Greenwich Observatory ʊ[3] 260 51.28 N 0.00
Greenwich Point › 276 41.00 N 73.34 W
Greenwich Village ◆[8] 276 40.44 N 74.00 W
Greenwood, B.C., Can. 182 49.05 N 118.41 W
Greenwood, Ar., U.S. 194 35.12 N 94.15 W
Greenwood, Ca., U.S. 226 38.54 N 120.55 W
Greenwood, De., U.S. 208 38.48 N 75.35 W
Greenwood, In., U.S. 218 39.36 N 86.06 W
Greenwood, Ma., U.S. 283 42.29 N 71.04 W
Greenwood, Ms., U.S. 194 33.30 N 90.10 W
Greenwood, Ne., U.S. 198 40.57 N 96.26 W
Greenwood, N.Y., U.S. 210 42.08 N 77.38 W
Greenwood, Pa., U.S. 214 40.32 N 78.21 W
Greenwood, S.C., U.S. 192 34.11 N 82.09 W
Greenwood, Wi., U.S. 190 44.46 N 90.35 W
Greenwood, Lake ⊜[1] 192 34.15 N 82.02 W
Greenwood Cemetery ◆ 276 40.39 N 73.59 W
Greenwood Lake 210 41.13 N 74.17 W
Greenwood Lake ⊜, U.S. 210 41.11 N 74.19 W
Greenwood Lake ⊜, Ma., U.S. 283 42.00 N 71.17 W
Greenwood Race Track ♦ 275b 43.40 N 79.19 W
Greer, Oh., U.S. 214 40.31 N 82.13 W
Greer, S.C., U.S. 192 34.56 N 82.13 W
Greers Ferry Lake ⊜[1] 194 35.30 N 92.10 W
Greerton 172 37.43 S 176.08 E
Grées, Alpes (Alpi Graie) ⋏ 62 45.30 N 7.10 E
Greeson, Lake ⊜[1] 194 34.10 N 93.45 W
Greet ≃ 44 53.03 N 0.53 W
Greetland 262 53.41 N 1.52 W
Greetsiel 52 53.30 N 7.05 E
Greffiers 261 48.37 N 1.51 E
Grefrath, Dtsch. 56 51.20 N 6.20 E
Grefrath, Dtsch. 263 51.10 N 6.38 E
Gregadoo 171b 35.14 S 147.27 E
Gregbe 150 6.48 N 6.43 W
Gregg 279b 40.24 N 80.10 W
Gregg □[6] 222 32.30 N 94.50 W
Greggio 62 45.27 N 8.23 E
Greg Greg 171b 36.03 S 148.02 E
Gregoire Lake Indian Reserve ◆[4] 184 56.28 N 111.10 W
Gregório ≃ 248 6.50 S 70.46 W
Gregory, Mi., U.S. 216 42.27 N 84.05 W
Gregory, S.D., U.S. 198 43.13 N 99.25 W
Gregory, Tx., U.S. 196 27.55 N 97.17 W
Gregory ≃ 166 17.53 S 139.17 E
Gregory, Lake ⊜, Austl. 162 20.10 S 127.20 E
Gregory, Lake ⊜, Austl. 162 25.38 S 119.58 E
Gregory, Lake ⊜, Austl. 166 28.55 S 139.00 E
Gregory National Park ♦ 164 16.30 S 130.30 E
Gregory Range ⋏ 166 19.00 S 143.05 E
Grégy-sur-Yerre 261 48.40 N 2.37 E
Greifenburg 64 46.45 N 13.11 E
Greifendorf 54 51.01 N 13.06 E
Greifensee 58 47.22 N 8.41 E
Greifensee ⊜ 58 47.21 N 8.41 E
Greifenstein 264b 48.21 N 16.15 E
Greiffenberg 54 53.05 N 13.58 E
Greiffenburg ⊥ 263 51.20 N 6.38 E
Greifswald 54 54.05 N 13.23 E
Greifswalder Bodden ⊂ 54 54.15 N 13.35 E
Greifswalder Oie I 54 54.14 N 13.55 E
Greim ∧ 61 47.15 N 14.09 E
Grein 61 48.14 N 14.51 E
Greiz 54 50.39 N 12.12 E
Grejdernoje 80 46.53 N 45.01 E
Grejsdal 41 55.45 N 9.32 E
Grekov 80 47.24 N 43.41 E
Grekovo 83 48.54 N 40.14 E
Grem'ačevo 82 54.14 N 36.15 E
Grem'ačij 88 57.01 N 108.12 E
Grem'ačinsk, Ross. 86 58.34 N 57.51 E
Grem'ačinsk, Ross. 88 52.48 N 107.57 E
Grem'ačje 78 51.29 N 39.00 E
Gremersdorf 54 54.20 N 10.55 E
Gremicha 24 68.03 N 39.27 E
Grenå 26 56.25 N 10.53 E
Grenada 194 33.46 N 89.48 W
Grenada □[1], N.A. 230 12.07 N 61.40 W
Grenada □[1], N.A. 241k 12.07 N 61.40 W
Grenada Lake ⊜[1] 194 33.50 N 89.40 W
Grenade → Grenada □[1] 241k 12.07 N 61.40 W
Grenadier Island I 212 44.03 N 76.22 W
Grenadier Pond ⊜ 275b 43.38 N 79.28 W
Grenadines II 238 12.40 N 61.15 W
Grenagh 48 52.00 N 8.37 W
Grenay 50 50.27 N 2.44 E
Grenchen 58 47.11 N 7.24 E
Grenell 212 44.16 N 76.04 W
Grenen ›[2] 26 57.44 N 10.40 E
Grenfell, Austl. 166 33.54 S 148.10 E
Grenfell, Sk., Can. 184 50.25 N 102.56 W
Grenloch 285 39.47 N 75.03 W
Grenoble 62 45.10 N 5.43 E
Grenola 198 37.20 N 96.27 W
Grenora 198 48.37 N 103.56 W
Grenville, P.Q., Can. 206 45.37 N 74.36 W
Grenville, Gren. 241k 12.07 N 61.37 W
Grenville, Cape › 164 11.58 S 143.14 E
Grenville Bay 206 45.38 N 74.36 W
Grenville Bay ⊂ 241k 12.07 N 61.36 W
Grenville Channel ⊔ 182 53.40 N 129.40 W
Grenzaa ≃ 52 52.39 N 6.45 E
Grenz-Berge ∧[2] 264a 52.27 N 13.44 E
Grenzlandring ♦ 56 51.11 N 6.17 E
Gréolières 62 43.48 N 6.57 E
Gréoux-les-Bains 62 43.45 N 5.53 E
Greppin 54 51.39 N 12.18 E
Gresenhorst 54 54.09 N 12.26 E
Gresham 224 45.29 N 122.25 W
Gresham Park 192 33.42 N 84.19 W
Gresik, Indon. 112 2.18 S 103.57 E
Gresik, Indon. 115a 7.09 S 112.38 E
Gressåmoen Nasjonalpark ♦ 26 64.15 N 13.08 E
Gresse-en-Vercors 62 44.54 N 5.34 E
Gressey 261 48.50 N 1.37 E
Gressitt 208 37.29 N 76.43 W
Gressk 76 53.10 N 27.29 E
Gressoney, Val di V 62 45.47 N 7.49 E
Gressoney-la-Trinité 62 45.50 N 7.49 E
Gressoney-Saint-Jean 62 45.47 N 7.49 E
Gressy 261 48.58 N 2.41 E
Gresten 61 48.00 N 15.02 E
Grésy-sur-Aix 62 45.43 N 5.57 E
Grésy-sur-Isère 62 45.36 N 6.15 E
Greta 170 32.41 S 151.24 E
Greta ≃, Eng., U.K. 44 54.32 N 1.53 W
Greta ≃, Eng., U.K. 44 54.36 N 3.10 W
Greta ≃, Eng., U.K. 44 54.09 N 2.36 W
Gretna, Mb., Can. 184 49.02 N 97.35 W
Gretna, Scot., U.K. 44 54.59 N 3.04 W
Gretna, La., U.S. 194 29.54 N 90.03 W
Gretna, Va., U.S. 192 36.57 N 79.21 W
Gretz-Armainvilliers 50 48.44 N 2.44 E
Greussen 54 51.14 N 10.57 E
Greve, Dan. 41 55.36 N 12.15 E
Greve, It. 66 43.35 N 11.19 E
Greve ≃ 66 43.46 N 11.13 E
Grevel ◆[8] 263 51.34 N 7.33 E
Grevelingen ⊔ 52 51.45 N 4.00 E
Grevelingendam ◆[5] 52 51.40 N 4.10 E
Greven 52 52.05 N 7.36 E
Grevená 38 40.05 N 21.25 E
Grevenbroich 56 51.05 N 6.35 E
Greven-Granzin 54 53.29 N 10.48 E
Grevenmacher 56 49.42 N 6.20 E
Grevesmühlen 54 53.51 N 11.10 E
Greve Strand 41 55.35 N 12.14 E
Greville Bay ⊂ 186 45.22 N 64.38 W
Grevinge 41 55.48 N 11.34 E
Grey □[6] 212 44.20 N 80.45 W
Grey ≃, Nf., Can. 186 47.38 N 57.05 W
Grey ≃, N.Z. 172 42.27 S 171.12 E
Grey, Cape › 164 13.00 S 136.40 E
Grey, Point ›, Austl. 169 38.34 S 143.59 E
Grey, Point ›, B.C., Can. 224 49.16 N 123.16 W
Greyabbey 48 54.32 N 5.33 W
Greybull 202 44.29 N 108.03 W
Greybull ≃ 202 44.28 N 108.03 W
Grey Eagle 190 45.49 N 94.44 W
Grey Islands II 186 50.50 N 55.37 W
Greylingstad 158 26.44 S 28.45 E
Greylock, Mount ∧ 207 42.38 N 73.10 W
Greymouth 172 42.28 S 171.12 E
Grey Range ⋏ 166 27.00 S 143.35 E
Grey River 186 47.35 N 57.06 W
Greys ≃ 202 43.10 N 111.00 W
Greystanes 274a 33.49 S 150.55 E
Greystoke 44 54.40 N 2.52 W
Greystones 48 53.09 N 6.04 W
Greyton 158 34.04 S 19.38 E
Greytown, N.Z. 172 41.05 S 175.27 E
Greytown, S. Afr. 158 29.07 S 30.30 E
Greytown → San Juan del Norte 236 10.55 N 83.42 W
Grez-Doiceau 56 50.44 N 4.42 E
Grez-sur-Loing 50 48.19 N 2.42 E
Grezzana 64 45.31 N 11.01 E
Gribanovskij 80 51.27 N 41.58 E
Gribbel Island I 182 53.25 N 129.00 W
Gribbin Head › 42 50.19 N 4.40 W
Gribingui □[5] 152 7.00 N 19.15 E
Gribingui ≃ 146 8.33 N 19.05 E
Gribingui-Bamingui, Réserve de Faune du ◆[4] 146 8.00 N 19.10 E
Gribovka 82 54.19 N 38.27 E
Gricev 78 49.58 N 27.14 E
Gridley, Ca., U.S. 226 39.21 N 121.41 W
Gridley, Il., U.S. 216 40.44 N 88.52 W
Griebnitz See ⊜ 264a 52.24 N 13.06 E
Griechenland → Greece □[1] 38 39.00 N 22.00 E
Griekwastad 158 28.49 S 23.15 E
Grier City 210 40.50 N 76.04 W
Gries am Brenner 64 47.03 N 11.29 E
Griesbach im Rottal 60 48.28 N 13.11 E
Griesen 64 47.29 N 10.56 E
Griesheim 56 49.50 N 8.34 E
Gries im Sellrain 64 47.12 N 11.09 E
Grieskirchen 60 48.14 N 13.50 E
Griessem 52 52.00 N 9.12 E
Griesspitzen ∧ 64 47.22 N 10.58 E
Griffen 61 46.42 N 14.44 E
Griffin, Sk., Can. 184 49.40 N 103.26 W
Griffin, Ga., U.S. 192 33.14 N 84.15 W
Griffin, Lake ⊜ 220 28.52 N 81.51 W
Griffin Bay ⊂ 224 48.30 N 122.58 W
Griffiss Air Force Base ■ 210 43.14 N 75.26 W
Griffith, Austl. 166 34.17 S 146.03 E
Griffith, In., U.S. 216 41.31 N 87.25 W
Griffith Airport ⊠ 278 41.31 N 87.23 W
Griffith Island I, N.T., Can. 176 74.35 N 95.30 W
Griffith Island I, On., Can. 212 44.51 N 80.54 W
Griffith Park ♦ 280 34.09 N 118.17 W
Grifton 192 35.22 N 77.26 W
Griggs Drain ≊ 281 42.11 N 83.26 W
Griggs Reservoir ⊜[1] 214 40.03 N 83.06 W
Griggstown 276 40.26 N 74.36 W
Griggsville 219 39.42 N 90.43 W
Grignan 62 44.25 N 4.54 E
Grignano 64 45.42 N 13.43 E
Grignasco 62 45.41 N 8.20 E
Grigno 64 46.01 N 11.38 E
Grignols 32 44.23 N 0.03 W
Grignon 261 48.51 N 1.57 E
Grigny, Fr. 62 45.37 N 4.47 E
Grigny, Fr. 261 48.40 N 2.24 E
Grigoriopol' 78 47.10 N 29.18 E
Grigorjevka, Kyrg. 85 42.43 N 77.30 E
Grigorjevka, Ross. 83 47.27 N 38.23 E
Grigorjevka, Ukr. 78 46.17 N 33.44 E
Grigorjevskoje, Ross. 82 54.49 N 37.59 E
Grigorjevskoje, Ross. 82 54.48 N 39.15 E
Grigorovka, Ross. 82 54.38 N 36.20 E
Grigorovka, Ukr. 78 51.03 N 32.51 E
Grigorovka, Ukr. 78 50.05 N 30.39 E
Grigorovo 82 56.42 N 37.35 E
Grigorovskoje 82 54.17 N 36.21 E
Grijalva ≃, Méx. 232 18.36 N 92.39 W
Grijalva (Cuilco) ≃, N.A. 232 17.01 N 93.22 W
Grijpskerk 52 53.15 N 6.18 E
Grillbach ≃ 263 51.11 N 6.44 E
Grillby 40 59.37 N 17.15 E
Grillenburg 54 50.57 N 13.31 E
Grim, Cape › 166 40.41 S 144.41 E
Grima 152 3.59 N 17.06 E
Grimajlov 78 49.20 N 26.01 E
Grimaldi 68 39.08 N 16.14 E
Grimari 152 5.44 N 20.03 E
Grimaud 62 43.16 N 6.31 E
Grimbergen 50 50.56 N 4.23 E
Grimeford Village 262 53.36 N 2.34 W
Grimes 226 39.04 N 121.54 W
Grimes □[6] 222 30.35 N 96.00 W
Grimlinghausen 263 51.10 N 6.44 E
Grimma 54 51.14 N 12.43 E
Grimmen 54 54.07 N 13.02 E
Grimmenstein 61 47.38 N 16.06 E
Grimmialp 58 46.34 N 7.29 E
Grimnitzsee ⊜ 54 52.58 N 13.47 E
Grimsargh 262 53.48 N 2.38 W
Grimsby, On., Can. 212 43.12 N 79.34 W
Grimsby, Eng., U.K. 44 53.35 N 0.05 W
Grimselpass)(58 46.34 N 8.21 E
Grimselsee ⊜ 58 46.34 N 8.18 E
Grímsey I 24a 66.34 N 18.00 W
Grimshaw 182 56.11 N 117.36 W
Grímsstaðir 24a 65.40 N 16.01 W
Grimstad 26 58.20 N 8.36 E
Grimstead 208 37.30 N 76.18 W
Grímsvötn ∧ 24a 64.24 N 17.22 W
Grin'ava 78 47.59 N 24.49 E
Grindavík 24a 63.52 N 22.27 W
Grindelwald 58 46.37 N 8.02 E
Grindsted 41 55.45 N 8.56 E
Grindstone Island I 212 44.16 N 76.07 W
Grindstone Island → Cap-aux-Meules 186 47.23 N 61.52 W
Grinnell 190 41.44 N 92.43 W
Grinnell, Lake ⊜ 276 41.06 N 74.38 W
Grinnell Peninsula ›[1] 176 76.40 N 95.00 W
Grin'ovo 76 52.35 N 33.04 E
Grintavec ∧ 61 46.21 N 14.32 E
Grinzing ◆[8] 264b 48.15 N 16.21 E
Grip 26 63.14 N 7.37 E
Gripsholm slott ⊥ 40 59.15 N 17.13 E
Gripsholmsviken ⊂ 40 59.17 N 17.20 E
Griqualand East □[9] 158 30.30 S 29.00 E
Griqualand West □[9] 158 28.20 S 23.30 E
Grisdale 224 47.22 N 123.37 W
Grisee → Gresik 115a 7.09 S 112.38 E
Grišino 82 56.13 N 37.40 E
Griškovcy 78 49.56 N 28.36 E
Gris-Nez, Cap › 50 50.52 N 1.35 E
Grisolia 68 39.43 N 15.51 E
Grisons → Graubünden □[3] 58 46.45 N 9.30 E
Grisslehamn 40 60.06 N 18.50 E
Grissom Air Force Base ■ 216 40.40 N 86.08 W
Gristow 54 54.10 N 13.20 E
Griswold, Mb., Can. 184 49.45 N 100.25 W
Griswold, Ia., U.S. 198 41.14 N 95.08 W
Griswold Creek ≃ 279a 41.27 N 81.23 W
Griswoldville 207 42.39 N 72.42 W
Grisy-Suisnes 261 48.41 N 2.40 E
Grivaï Pamia 152 7.03 N 19.26 E
Grivenskaja 78 45.38 N 38.09 E
Grizzana 64 44.15 N 11.09 E
Grizzly Bay ⊂ 226 38.07 N 122.01 W
Grizzly Bear Mountain ∧ 176 65.22 N 121.00 W
Grizzly Bear's Head and Lead Man Indian Reserve ◆[4] 184 52.33 N 108.16 W
Grizzly Creek ≃ 282 37.52 N 122.06 W
Grizzly Flats 226 38.38 N 120.31 W
Grizzly Island I 282 38.08 N 121.58 W
Grizzly Mountain ∧, Id., U.S. 202 47.43 N 116.06 W
Grizzly Mountain ∧, Or., U.S. 202 44.26 N 120.57 W
Grizzly Mountain ∧, Wa., U.S. 202 48.25 N 118.30 W
Grizzly Slough ≃ 282 38.06 N 121.53 W
Grmeč ⋏ 36 44.40 N 16.30 E
Groaíras 250 3.53 S 40.23 W
Groais Island I 186 50.57 N 55.35 W
Grobbendonk 56 51.12 N 4.43 E
Gröben 264a 52.17 N 13.10 E
Gröbener-See ⊜ 264a 52.17 N 13.11 E
Gröbenzell 60 48.11 N 11.22 E
Grobiņa 76 56.33 N 21.10 E
Groblersdal 156 25.15 S 29.25 E
Groblershoop 158 28.55 S 20.59 E
Gröbming 64 47.26 N 13.54 E
Grobogan 115a 7.01 S 110.55 E
Gröbzig 54 51.41 N 11.52 E
Grodekovo 85 42.49 N 71.29 E
Grödig 64 47.44 N 13.02 E
Gröditsch 54 52.03 N 13.59 E
Gröditz 54 51.24 N 13.27 E
Grodków 30 50.43 N 17.22 E
Grodno 76 53.41 N 23.50 E
Grodno □[8] 76 53.30 N 25.00 E
Grodovka 83 48.15 N 37.23 E
Grodz'anka 76 53.33 N 28.45 E
Grodzisk Mazowiecki 30 52.07 N 20.37 E
Grodzisk [Wielkopolski] 30 52.14 N 16.22 E
Groede 52 51.23 N 3.30 E
Groen ≃, S. Afr. 158 30.40 S 23.17 E
Groen ≃, S. Afr. 158 29.00 S 22.10 E
Groënland → Greenland □[2] 16 70.00 N 40.00 W
Groenlandia → Greenland □[2] 16 70.00 N 40.00 W
Groenlo 52 52.03 N 6.38 E
Groenvlei 158 27.27 S 30.13 E
Groesbeck, Oh., U.S. 218 39.13 N 84.35 W
Groesbeck, Tx., U.S. 222 31.31 N 96.32 W
Groesbeek 52 51.47 N 5.55 E
Grofa, gora ∧ 78 48.37 N 23.56 E
Grogol, Kali ≃ 269e 6.10 S 106.47 E
Grogol-hilir ◆[8] 269e 6.13 S 106.47 E
Grohnde 52 52.01 N 9.25 E
Groitzsch 54 51.09 N 12.16 E
Groix 32 47.38 N 3.28 W
Groix, Île de I 32 47.38 N 3.27 W
Grójec 30 51.52 N 20.52 E
Grokgak 115a 8.11 S 114.47 E
Grolley 58 46.50 N 7.05 E
Grombalia 148 36.36 N 10.30 E
Grömitz 54 54.09 N 10.58 E
Gromo 64 45.58 N 9.56 E
Gromokleja ≃ 78 47.21 N 32.14 E
Gromoslavka 80 48.12 N 43.37 E
Gromovka 78 46.19 N 34.06 E
Gronau, Dtsch. 52 52.13 N 7.00 E
Gronau, Dtsch. 52 52.05 N 9.46 E
Grondines (Saint-Charles-des-Grondines) 206 46.36 N 72.03 W
Grondneus 158 28.06 S 20.48 E
Grone 52 51.32 N 9.53 E
Grönenbach 58 47.52 N 10.13 E
Grong 24 64.28 N 12.18 E
Gröningen, Dtsch. 54 51.56 N 11.13 E
Groningen, Ned. 52 53.13 N 6.33 E
Groningen, Sur. 250 5.48 N 55.28 W
Groningen □[4] 52 53.15 N 6.45 E
Grønland → Greenland □[2] 16 70.00 N 40.00 W
Gronlid 184 53.06 N 104.28 W
Grønsund ⊔ 41 54.53 N 12.08 E
Grönwohld 52 53.39 N 10.25 E
Groom 196 35.12 N 101.06 W
Groom Lake ⊜ 204 37.15 N 115.48 W
Groot ≃, S. Afr. 158 33.54 S 21.39 E
Groot ≃, S. Afr. 158 33.45 S 24.36 E
Groot-Berg ≃ 158 32.47 S 18.08 E
Groot-Brakrivier 158 34.02 S 22.14 E
Grootdraaidam ⊜[1] 158 26.56 S 29.20 E
Grootebroek 52 52.43 N 5.13 E
Groote Eylandt I 164 14.00 S 136.40 E
Groote Eylandt Aboriginal Reserve ◆[4] 164 14.00 S 136.40 E
Grootfontein 156 19.32 S 18.05 E
Groot Karasberge ⋏ 158 27.20 S 18.40 E
Groot Karroo → Great Karroo ⋏[1] 158 32.25 S 22.40 E
Groot-Kei ≃ 158 32.41 S 28.22 E
Groot Laagte ≃ 156 20.37 S 21.37 E
Groot-Letaba ≃ 156 23.58 S 31.50 E
Groot-Marico 156 25.37 S 26.26 E
Grootpan 158 25.58 S 26.33 E
Groot-Swartberge ⋏ 158 33.22 S 22.20 E
Groot-Vis ≃ 158 33.30 S 27.08 E
Grootvlei 158 26.44 S 28.32 E
Grootvloer ≚ 158 30.00 S 20.40 E
Gröpelingen ◆[8] 52 53.07 N 8.46 E
Gropello Cairoli 62 45.11 N 9.00 E
Gropeni 38 45.04 N 27.53 E
Grosbliederstroff 56 49.09 N 7.01 E
Gros Bois, Parc de ♦ 261 48.44 N 2.32 E
Groscavallo 62 45.22 N 7.15 E
Grose ≃ 170 33.36 S 150.41 E
Grosio 64 46.18 N 10.16 E
Gros Islet 241f 14.05 N 60.58 W
Groslay 261 48.59 N 2.21 E
Gros Mécatina, Cap du › 186 50.45 N 59.00 W
Gros-Morne 240e 14.43 N 61.01 W
Gros Morne ∧ 186 49.36 N 57.48 W
Gros Morne National Park ♦ 186 49.40 N 57.45 W
Grosne ≃ 58 46.42 N 4.56 E
Grosnez Point › 43b 49.16 N 2.15 W
Grosotto 64 46.17 N 10.15 E
Gros Piton ∧ 241f 13.49 N 61.04 W
Grosrouvre 261 48.47 N 1.46 E
Grossa, Ponta ›, Bra. 256 23.35 S 45.13 W
Grossa, Ponta ›, Bra. 287a 22.47 S 43.11 W
Grossache (Tiroler Ache) ≃ 60 47.51 N 12.30 E
Grossaitingen 58 48.14 N 10.47 E
Grossalmerode 56 51.15 N 9.46 E
Grossalsleben 54 51.59 N 11.13 E
Gross Ammensleben 54 52.14 N 11.31 E
Grossarl 64 47.14 N 13.12 E
Gross-Beeren 54 52.21 N 13.18 E
Gross Berkel 52 52.04 N 9.19 E
Grossbodungen 54 51.28 N 10.28 E
Gross Börnecke 54 51.50 N 11.29 E
Grossbothen 54 51.11 N 12.44 E
Grossbottwar 56 49.00 N 9.17 E
Grossbreitenbach 54 50.35 N 11.02 E
Grossdeuben 54 51.14 N 12.23 E
Grossdubrau 54 51.15 N 14.28 E
Gross Düngen 52 52.06 N 10.01 E
Grosse Antillen → Greater Antilles II 238 20.00 N 74.00 W
Grosse Aue ≃ 52 52.37 N 9.10 E
Grosse Australische Bucht → Great Australian Bight ⊂[3] 162 35.00 S 135.00 E
Grossebersdorf 54 50.47 N 11.57 E
Grosse Ebene → Great Plains ≚ 16 42.00 N 100.00 W
Grossefehn 52 53.24 N 7.36 E
Grosse Herrenwiese ≡ 264a 52.17 N 13.20 E
Grosse Ile 216 42.08 N 83.09 W
Grosse Ile I 216 42.08 N 83.09 W
Grosse Île, La I 186 47.37 N 61.31 W
Grosse Laber ≃ 60 48.56 N 12.30 E
Grosse Mühl ≃ 61 48.25 N 13.59 E
Grossenbaum ◆[8] 263 51.22 N 6.47 E
Grossenbrode 54 54.22 N 11.05 E
Grossengottern 54 51.09 N 10.34 E
Grossengstingen 58 48.23 N 9.17 E
Grossenhain 54 51.17 N 13.31 E
Grossenkneten 52 52.56 N 8.16 E
Grossen-Linden 56 50.31 N 8.39 E
Grossenlüder 56 50.35 N 9.32 E
Grossenritte 56 51.15 N 9.23 E
Grossenwiehe 41 54.43 N 9.15 E
Gross-Enzersdorf 61 48.12 N 16.33 E
Grosse Pointe 214 42.23 N 82.54 W
Grosse Pointe › 241o 16.01 N 61.16 W
Grosse Pointe Farms 214 42.25 N 82.53 W
Grosse Pointe Park 214 42.22 N 82.56 W
Grosse Pointe Shores 214 42.26 N 82.53 W
Grosse Pointe Woods 214 42.26 N 82.54 W
Grosser Arber ∧ 60 49.07 N 13.07 E
Grosser Bären-See → Great Bear Lake ⊜ 176 66.00 N 120.00 W
Grosser Beerberg ∧ 54 50.37 N 10.44 E
Grosser Bösenstein ∧ 61 47.26 N 14.24 E
Grosser Buchstein ∧ 61 47.36 N 14.35 E
Grosser Chingan → Da Hinggan Ling ⋏ 90 49.00 N 122.00 E
Grosser Feldberg ∧ 56 50.14 N 8.26 E
Grosser Galtenberg ∧ 64 47.20 N 11.58 E
Grosser Gleichberg ∧ 54 50.23 N 10.35 E
Grosser Heuberg ⋏[1] 58 48.06 N 8.55 E
Grosser Inselsberg ∧ 54 50.52 N 10.28 E
Grosser Jasmunder Bodden ⊂ 54 54.31 N 13.29 E
Grosser Knallstein ∧ 61 47.19 N 13.58 E
Grosser Königstuhl ∧ 64 46.57 N 13.47 E
Grosser Müggelsee ⊜ 54 52.26 N 13.39 E
Grosse Röder ≃ 54 51.30 N 13.25 E
Grosser oder Kaiser-Kanal → Da Yunhe ≊ 90 32.12 N 119.31 E
Grosse Rodl ≃ 61 48.20 N 14.09 E
Grosser Peilstein ∧ 61 48.18 N 15.06 E
Grosser Plessower See ⊜ 264a 52.23 N 12.54 E
Grosser Plöner See ⊜ 54 54.06 N 10.25 E
Grosser Priel ∧ 61 47.43 N 14.04 E
Grosser Rachel ∧ 60 48.59 N 13.24 E
Grosser Ravens-Berg ∧[2] 264a 52.21 N 13.04 E
Grosser Salz-See → Great Salt Lake ⊜ 200 41.10 N 112.30 W
Grosser Seddiner See ⊜ 264a 52.17 N 13.02 E
Grosser Selchower See ⊜ 54 52.14 N 13.53 E
Grosser Sklaven-See → Great Slave Lake ⊜ 176 61.30 N 114.00 W
Grosser Speikkogel ∧ 61 46.47 N 14.58 E
Grosser Walfisch-Fluss → Baleine, Grande rivière de la ≃ 176 55.16 N 77.47 W
Grosser Wannsee ⊜ 264a 52.26 N 13.11 E
Grosser Winterberg ∧[2] 54 50.54 N 14.16 E
Grosser Zern-See ⊜ 264a 52.24 N 12.56 E
Grosse Sandspitze ∧ 64 46.46 N 12.49 E
Grosse Sandwüste → Great Sandy Desert ◆[2] 162 21.30 S 125.00 E
Grosses Barrier-Riff → Great Barrier Reef ✦[2] 160 18.00 S 145.50 E
Grosses Meer ⊜ 52 53.25 N 7.17 E
Grosses Moor ◆[3], Dtsch. 52 52.35 N 8.45 E
Grosses Moor ◆[3], Dtsch. 52 52.40 N 8.20 E
Grosses Schulerloch ♦ 60 48.55 N 11.48 E
Grosse Sundainseln → Greater Sunda Islands II 108 2.00 S 110.00 E
Grosses Walsertal V 58 47.14 N 9.56 E
Grosse Syrte → Surt, Khalīj ⊂ 146 31.30 N 18.00 E
Grosseto 66 42.46 N 11.08 E
Grosseto □[4] 66 42.50 N 11.15 E
Grosse Tulln ≃ 61 48.20 N 16.02 E
Grossevići 89 47.59 N 139.30 E
Grosse Windgällen ∧ 58 46.49 N 8.44 E
Gross-Gerau 56 49.55 N 8.29 E
Gross-Gerungs 61 48.34 N 14.57 E
Gross Gleidingen 54 52.14 N 10.25 E
Gross Glienicke 264a 52.28 N 13.07 E
Gross-Glienicker See ⊜ 264a 52.28 N 13.06 E
Grossglockner ∧ 64 47.04 N 12.42 E
Grossgmain 64 47.43 N 12.55 E
Grossgörschen 54 51.13 N 12.11 E
Gross Grönau 54 53.46 N 10.44 E
Grosshansdorf 52 53.40 N 10.17 E
Grosshartmannsdorf 54 50.48 N 13.19 E
Gross-Hehlen 52 52.39 N 10.03 E
Grossheide 52 53.35 N 7.20 E
Grosshennersdorf 54 50.59 N 14.47 E
Grosshöchstetten 58 46.55 N 7.38 E
Grossholzleute 58 47.41 N 10.05 E
Grossjedlersdorf ◆[8] 264b 48.17 N 16.25 E
Grosskayna 54 51.17 N 11.56 E
Gross Kienitz 264a 52.19 N 13.28 E
Gross-Kollmar 52 53.44 N 9.30 E
Grosskorbetha 54 51.16 N 12.01 E
Gross Kreutz 54 52.24 N 12.46 E

Symbols in the index entries represent the broad categories identified in the key at the right. Symbols with superior numbers (⋏[1]) identify subcategories (see complete key on page *I · 1*).

Symbole im Register stellen die rechts im Schlüssel erklärten Kategorien dar. Symbole mit hochgestellten Ziffern (⋏[1]) bezeichnen Unterabteilungen einer Kategorie (vgl. vollständiger Schlüssel auf Seite *I · 1*).

Los símbolos incluídos en el texto del índice representan las grandes categorias identificadas con la clave a la derecha. Los símbolos con numeros en su parte superior (⋏[1]) identifican las subcategorías (véase la clave completa en la página *I · 1*).

Les symboles de l'index représentent les catégories indiquées dans la légende à droite. Les symboles suivis d'un indice (⋏[1]) représentent des sous-catégories (voir légende complète à la page *I · 1*).

Os símbolos incluídos no texto do índice representam as grandes categorias identificadas com a chave à direita. Os símbolos com números em sua parte superior (⋏[1]) identificam as subcategorias (veja-se a chave completa à página *I · 1*).

∧ Mountain	Berg	Montaña	Montagne	Montanha
⋏ Mountains	Gebirge	Montañas	Montagnes	Montanhas
)(Pass	Paß	Paso	Col	Passo
V Valley, Canyon	Tal, Cañon	Valle, Cañón	Vallée, Canyon	Vale, Canhão
≚ Plain	Ebene	Llano	Plaine	Planície
› Cape	Kap	Cabo	Cap	Cabo
I Island	Insel	Isla	Île	Ilha
II Islands	Inseln	Islas	Îles	Ilhas
⏏ Other Topographic Features	Andere Topographische Objekte	Otros Elementos Topográficos	Autres données topographiques	Outros acidentes topográficos

ESPAÑOL: Nombre · Página · Lat.°′ · Long.°′ W = Oeste
FRANÇAIS: Nom · Page · Lat.°′ · Long.°′ W = Ouest
PORTUGUÊS: Nome · Página · Lat.°′ · Long.°′ W = Oeste

Grosskrut 61 48.38 N 16.43 E
Grosslehna 54 51.18 N 12.10 E
Gross Leine 54 52.00 N 14.03 E
Grosslittgen 56 50.02 N 6.47 E
Gross-Machnow 264a 52.16 N 13.28 E
Grossmehring 60 48.46 N 11.32 E
Grossmont 228 32.47 N 116.59 W
Gross Muckrow 54 52.04 N 14.26 E
Grössnöbach 60 48.21 N 11.35 E
Gross Oesingen 52 52.38 N 10.29 E
Grossörner 54 51.37 N 11.29 E
Grossos 250 4.59 S 37.09 W
Grossostheim 56 49.55 N 9.04 E
Grosspetersdorf 61 47.14 N 16.19 E
Grosspostwitz 54 51.07 N 14.26 E
Grossquenstedt 54 51.56 N 11.07 E
Grossraming 61 47.53 N 14.33 E
Grossräschen 54 51.35 N 14.00 E
Gross Rhüden 52 51.56 N 10.07 E
Grossrinderfeld 56 49.39 N 9.44 E
Gross Rodensleben 54 52.08 N 11.25 E
Grossröhrsdorf 54 51.08 N 14.01 E
Gross Rosenburg 54 51.55 N 11.53 E
Grossrückerswalde 54 50.38 N 13.07 E
Grossrudestedt 54 51.05 N 11.06 E
Gross Sankt Florian 61 46.49 N 15.19 E
Gross-Sarau 54 53.45 N 10.44 E
Grossschirma 54 50.58 N 13.17 E
Grossschönau 54 50.54 N 14.40 E
Gross Schönebeck 54 52.54 N 13.32 E
Gross-Schulzendorf 264a 52.16 N 13.21 E
Gross-Siegharts 61 48.48 N 15.24 E
Grosssölk 64 47.25 N 13.58 E
Gross-Umstadt 56 49.52 N 8.55 E
Grossvenediger ∧ 64 47.06 N 12.21 E
Grosswardein → Oradea 38 47.03 N 21.57 E
Grossweil 64 47.41 N 11.18 E
Grossweissenbach 61 48.33 N 15.10 E
Gross Wittensee 41 54.24 N 9.46 E
Gross Ziethen, Dtsch. 264a 52.24 N 13.27 E
Gross Ziethen, Dtsch. 264a 52.44 N 13.01 E
Gross-Zimmern 56 49.52 N 8.50 E
Grostenquin 56 48.59 N 6.44 E
Grosvenor, Lake ⊜ 180 58.40 N 155.15 W
Grosvenor Dale 207 41.58 N 71.53 W
Gros Ventre ≃ 202 43.33 N 110.46 W
Groswater Bay ⊂ 176 54.20 N 57.30 W
Grote Nete ≃ 56 51.07 N 4.34 E
Groton, Ct., U.S. 207 41.21 N 72.04 W
Groton, Ma., U.S. 207 42.36 N 71.34 W
Groton, N.Y., U.S. 210 42.35 N 76.22 W
Groton, S.D., U.S. 198 45.26 N 98.05 W
Grottaferrata 66 41.47 N 12.40 E
Grottaglie 68 40.32 N 17.26 E
Grottaminarda 68 41.04 N 15.02 E
Grottammare 66 42.59 N 13.52 E
Grotte 70 37.24 N 13.42 E
Grotte di Castro 66 42.40 N 11.52 E
Grotteria 68 38.22 N 16.17 E
Grottoes 188 38.16 N 78.49 W
Grottole 68 40.36 N 16.23 E
Grou, Oued V 148 33.56 N 6.45 W
Grouard Mission 182 55.31 N 116.09 W
Groundbirch 182 55.47 N 120.55 W
Groundhog ≃ 176 49.43 N 81.58 W
Grouse Creek ≃, Ks., U.S. 198 37.00 N 96.55 W
Grouse Creek ≃, Ut,. U.S. 200 41.22 N 113.55 W
Grouse Creek Mountain ∧ 202 44.22 N 113.54 W
Grouw 52 53.05 N 5.45 E
Grove, Eng., U.K. 42 51.36 N 1.25 W
Grove, Ok., U.S. 196 36.35 N 94.46 W
Grove, Pa., U.S. 285 40.01 N 75.38 W
Grove City, Fl., U.S. 220 26.54 N 82.19 W
Grove City, Mn., U.S. 198 45.09 N 94.40 W
Grove City, Oh., U.S. 218 39.52 N 83.05 W
Grove City, Pa., U.S. 214 41.09 N 80.05 W
Grove Hill 194 31.42 N 87.46 W
Groveland, Ca., U.S. 226 37.50 N 120.13 W
Groveland, Fl., U.S. 220 28.33 N 81.51 W
Groveland, Ma., U.S. 207 42.45 N 71.01 W
Groveland, N.Y., U.S. 210 42.39 N 77.46 W
Grovely Ridge ∧ 42 51.08 N 2.04 W
Grove Mountains ⩘ 9 72.53 S 74.53 E
Grove Park ◆[8] 260 51.26 N 0.01 E
Groveport 218 39.52 N 82.53 W
Grover 210 41.37 N 76.52 W
Grover City 204 35.07 N 120.37 W
Grover Cleveland Birthplace ⊥ 276 40.50 N 74.16 W
Grover Cleveland Park ♠ 284a 42.57 N 78.49 W
Grover Hill 216 41.01 N 84.28 W
Grovers Mills 276 40.19 N 74.37 W
Groves 194 29.56 N 93.55 W
Groveton, N.H., U.S. 188 44.35 N 71.30 W
Groveton, Pa., U.S. 279b 40.30 N 80.06 W
Groveton, Tx., U.S. 222 31.03 N 95.07 W
Groveton, Va., U.S. 284c 38.46 N 77.05 W
Grovetown 192 33.27 N 82.11 W
Groveville 208 40.10 N 74.40 W
Growa Point > 150 4.21 N 7.37 W
Growler Peak ∧ 200 32.24 N 113.07 W
Growler Wash V 200 32.35 N 113.30 W
Groznoje 85 42.36 N 71.12 E
Groznyj 84 43.20 N 45.42 E
Groznyy → Groznyj 84 43.20 N 45.42 E
Grube, Dtsch. 54 54.14 N 11.01 E
Grube, Dtsch. 264a 52.26 N 12.57 E
Grubišno Polje 36 45.42 N 17.10 E
Grubweg 60 48.35 N 13.29 E
Grudovo 38 42.21 N 27.10 E
Grudziądz 30 53.29 N 18.45 E
Gruesa, Punta > 248 20.22 S 70.11 W
Gruetli-Laager 194 35.22 N 85.40 W
Grugapark ♠ 263 51.26 N 7.00 E
Grugliasco 62 45.04 N 7.35 E
Gruia 38 44.16 N 22.42 E
Gruinard Bay ⊂ 46 57.53 N 5.31 W
Gruinart, Loch ⊂ 46 55.52 N 6.20 W
Gruiten 56 51.14 N 7.01 E
Gruitrode 56 51.05 N 5.35 E
Grulla 196 26.16 N 98.39 W
Grumello del Monte 62 45.38 N 9.52 E
Grumento Nova 68 40.17 N 15.53 E
Grumentum ⊥ 68 40.17 N 15.55 E
Grumman-Bethpage Airport ⊠ 276 40.45 N 73.29 W
Grumman Corporation ⛫[3] 276 40.45 N 73.30 W
Grumme ◆[8] 263 51.30 N 7.14 E
Grumo Appula 68 41.01 N 16.42 E
Grums 26 59.21 N 13.06 E
Grun' 78 50.16 N 34.36 E
Grüna 54 50.49 N 12.47 E
Grünau 156 27.44 S 18.23 E
Grünau ◆[8] 264a 52.25 N 13.34 E
Grünau im Almtal 64 47.51 N 13.57 E
Grunavat, Loch ⊜ 46 58.10 N 6.55 W
Grünbach 54 50.26 N 12.22 E
Grünberg 56 50.35 N 8.58 E
Grünberg → Zielona Góra 30 51.56 N 15.31 E
Grünburg 61 47.57 N 14.15 E
Grundlsee ⊜ 64 47.38 N 13.52 E
Grundy 192 37.16 N 82.05 W
Grundy □[6] 216 41.22 N 88.26 W
Grundy Center 190 42.21 N 92.46 W
Grundy Lake Provincial Park ♠ 190 45.48 N 80.34 W
Grünefeld 264a 52.41 N 12.58 E
Grünenplan 52 51.57 N 9.44 E
Grünewald, Dtsch. 54 51.24 N 14.00 E
Grünewald, Dtsch. 263 51.13 N 7.37 E
Grunewald ◆[8] 264a 52.30 N 13.17 E
Grunewald, Berliner Forst ◆[3] 264a 52.28 N 13.13 E
Grunewald, Jagdschloss ⊥ 264a 52.28 N 13.16 E
Grünhain 54 50.35 N 12.48 E
Grünhainichen 54 50.46 N 13.08 E
Grünheide 54 52.25 N 13.49 E
Grünsfeld 56 49.36 N 9.44 E
Grünstadt 56 49.34 N 8.10 E
Grüntal 264a 52.45 N 13.44 E
Grunthal 184 49.25 N 96.52 W
Grünwald 60 48.02 N 11.31 E
Gruševka 78 47.55 N 40.40 E
Gruševka ≃ 83 47.26 N 40.00 E
Gruševskaja 83 47.26 N 39.57 E
Grušino 76 59.27 N 44.09 E
Gruting 46a 60.14 N 1.30 W
Gruver 196 36.16 N 101.24 W
Gruyère, Lac de la ⊜ 58 46.38 N 7.06 E
Gruyères 58 46.35 N 7.05 E
Gruzdžiai 76 56.06 N 23.16 E
Gruzija → Georgia □[1] 72 42.00 N 44.00 E
Gruziya → Georgia □[1] 72 42.00 N 44.00 E
Gruznovka 88 55.09 N 105.12 E
Gruzskaja Balka 78 46.25 N 40.19 E
Gruzskij Jelančik ≃ 83 47.07 N 38.04 E
Gruzskoje 83 48.33 N 37.18 E
Gruzsko-Zor'anskoje 83 47.56 N 38.06 E
Grybów 30 49.38 N 20.56 E
Grycken ⊜ 40 60.27 N 16.13 E
Gryfice 30 53.56 N 15.12 E
Gryfino 30 53.12 N 14.30 E
Grytgöl 40 58.48 N 15.33 E
Grythyttan 40 59.42 N 14.32 E
Gschnitz 64 47.03 N 11.22 E
Gschütt, Pass)(64 47.35 N 13.30 E
Gschwend 56 48.56 N 9.44 E
Gstaad 58 46.28 N 7.17 E
Gsteig 58 46.23 N 7.16 E
Gu ≃ 100 27.02 N 115.03 E
Gua 124 22.12 N 85.23 E
Guabaria ≃[1] 126 22.10 N 90.30 E
Guabito 236 9.30 N 82.37 W
Guabu 106 32.16 N 118.53 E
Guacanayabo, Golfo de ⊂ 240p 20.28 N 77.30 W
Guacara 246 10.14 N 67.53 W
Guacarí 246 3.46 N 76.20 W
Gu Achi 200 32.19 N 112.02 W
Guachinango 234 20.32 N 104.24 W
Guachiría ≃ 246 5.27 N 70.36 W
Guachochi 232 26.51 N 107.05 W
Guaçuí 255 20.46 S 41.41 W
Guadajira ≃ 34 38.52 N 6.41 W
Guadajoz ≃ 34 37.50 N 4.51 W
Guadalajara, Esp. 34 40.38 N 3.10 W
Guadalajara, Méx. 234 20.40 N 103.20 W
Guadalajara □[4] 34 40.50 N 2.30 W
Guadalaviar ≃ 34 40.21 N 1.08 W
Guadalcanal 34 38.06 N 5.49 W
Guadalcanal □[4] 175e 9.50 S 160.00 E
Guadalcanal I 175e 9.32 S 160.12 E
Guadalcázar 234 22.37 N 100.24 W
Guadalén ≃ 34 38.05 N 3.32 W
Guadalén, Embalse de ⊜[1] 34 38.25 N 3.15 W
Guadalentin ≃ 34 37.59 N 1.04 W
Guadalete ≃ 34 36.35 N 6.13 W
Guadalhorce ≃ 34 36.41 N 4.27 W
Guadalimar ≃ 34 38.05 N 3.06 W
Guadalmena ≃ 34 38.19 N 2.56 W
Guadalmez ≃ 34 38.46 N 5.04 W
Guadalope ≃ 34 41.15 N 0.03 W
Guadalquivir ≃ 34 36.47 N 6.22 W
Guadalupe, Bol. 248 18.33 S 64.05 W
Guadalupe, Col. 246 2.01 N 75.45 W
Guadalupe, C.R. 236 9.57 N 84.03 W
Guadalupe, Méx. 196 28.09 N 100.36 W
Guadalupe, Méx. 232 25.41 N 100.15 W
Guadalupe, Méx. 234 22.45 N 102.31 W
Guadalupe, Perú 248 7.15 S 79.29 W
Guadalupe, Ca., U.S. 204 34.58 N 120.34 W
Guadalupe □[6] 222 29.37 N 97.45 W
Guadalupe ◆[8] 287a 22.50 S 43.23 W
Guadalupe ≃, Méx. 204 32.05 N 116.53 W
Guadalupe ≃, Ca., U.S. 282 37.25 N 121.58 W
Guadalupe ≃, Tx., U.S. 196 28.30 N 96.53 W
Guadalupe, Basílica de ⛫[1] 286a 19.29 N 99.07 W
Guadalupe, Isla I 178 29.00 N 118.16 W
Guadalupe, Presa de ⊜[1] 286a 19.37 N 99.16 W
Guadalupe, Sierra de ⩘, Esp. 34 39.26 N 5.25 W
Guadalupe, Sierra de ⩘, Méx. 286a 19.35 N 99.08 W
Guadalupe [Bravos] 232 31.23 N 106.07 W
Guadalupe del Norte ≅ 286a 19.34 N 99.01 W
Guadalupe de Ramírez 234 17.45 N 98.10 W
Guadalupe → Guadeloupe □[2] 241o 16.15 N 61.35 W
Guadalupe Mountains ⩘ 196 32.20 N 105.00 W
Guadalupe Mountains National Park ♠ 196 31.55 N 104.55 W
Guadalupe Peak ∧ 196 31.50 N 104.52 W
Guadalupe Seamount ✣[3] 14 27.50 N 168.45 E
Guadalupe Slough ≃ 282 37.27 N 122.02 W
Guadalupe Victoria, Méx. 196 27.47 N 101.04 W
Guadalupe Victoria, Méx. 232 24.27 N 104.07 W
Guadalupe Victoria, Méx. 234 19.17 N 97.21 W
Guadalupe Victoria, Presa ⊜[1] 234 23.50 N 104.46 W
Guadalupita 200 36.08 N 105.14 W
Guadarrama, Puerto de)(34 40.43 N 4.10 W
Guadarrama, Sierra de ⩘ 34 40.55 N 4.00 W
Guadazaón ≃ 34 39.42 N 1.36 W
Guadeloupe □[2], N.A. 230 16.15 N 61.35 W
Guadeloupe □[2], N.A. 241o 16.15 N 61.35 W
Guadeloupe Passage ⊔ 238 16.45 N 61.30 W
Guadiana ≃ 34 37.14 N 7.22 W
Guadiana, Bahía de ⊂ 240p 22.05 N 84.24 W
Guadiana Menor ≃ 34 37.56 N 3.15 W
Guadiaro ≃ 34 36.17 N 5.17 W
Guadiato ≃ 34 38.20 N 5.22 W
Guadiela ≃ 34 40.22 N 2.49 W
Guadix 34 37.18 N 3.08 W
Guafo, Isla I 254 43.36 S 74.43 W
Guagnano 68 40.24 N 17.57 E
Guagua 116 14.58 N 120.38 E
Guahe 105 39.12 N 115.00 E
Guaianases ◆[8] 287b 23.33 S 46.25 W
Guaíba 252 30.06 S 51.19 W
Guaíba ⊂[1] 252 30.15 S 51.12 W
Guaicaipuro □[5] 286c 10.25 N 66.57 W
Guaihe 100 33.28 N 112.59 E
Guaimaca 236 14.32 N 86.51 W
Guáimaro 240p 21.03 N 77.21 W
Guaimoreto, Laguna de ⊂ 236 15.58 N 85.55 W
Guaimozi 98 41.31 N 125.26 E
Guainía □[5] 246 2.30 N 69.00 W
Guainía ≃ 246 2.01 N 67.07 W
Guaió ≃ 287b 23.31 S 46.19 W
Guaipava 256 21.40 S 45.43 W
Guaiquinima, Cerro ∧ 246 5.49 N 63.40 W
Guaíra, Bra. 252 24.04 S 54.15 W
Guaíra, Bra. 255 20.19 S 48.18 W
Guairá □[5] 252 25.45 S 56.30 W
Guaire ≃ 286c 10.25 N 66.46 W
Guáitara ≃ 246 1.34 N 77.27 W
Guaitecas, Archipiélago de las II 254 43.57 S 73.50 W
Guajaba, Cayo I 240p 21.50 N 77.30 W
Guajará ≃ 250 1.48 S 53.02 W
Guajará-Açu 250 1.38 S 48.07 W
Guajará-Miri 250 1.29 S 48.17 W
Guajará-Mirim 248 10.48 S 65.22 W
Guajataca ≃ 240m 18.29 N 66.57 W
Guajataca, Lago de ⊜[1] 240m 18.23 N 66.55 W
Guajiasi 104 41.15 N 120.54 E
Gualaca 236 8.32 N 82.18 W
Gualaceo 246 2.54 S 78.47 W
Gualala 204 38.45 N 123.31 W
Gualán 236 15.08 N 89.22 W
Gualaquiza 246 3.24 S 78.33 W
Gualdo Tadino 66 43.14 N 12.47 E
Gualeguay 252 33.09 S 59.20 W
Gualeguay ≃ 252 33.19 S 59.39 W
Gualeguaychú 252 33.01 S 58.31 W
Gualicho, Salina del ≚ 254 40.24 S 65.15 W
Gualjaina 254 42.42 S 70.30 W
Gualtieri 64 44.54 N 10.38 E
Guam □[2], Oc. 14 13.28 N 144.47 E
Guam □[2], Oc. 174p 13.28 N 144.47 E
Guamá ≃, Bra. 250 1.29 S 48.30 W
Guamá ≃, Cuba 240p 22.11 N 83.41 W
Guamal, Col. 246 9.09 N 74.14 W
Guamal, Col. 246 3.52 N 73.44 W
Guamal, Quebrada ≃ 286c 10.31 N 66.59 W
Guamblín, Isla I 254 44.51 S 75.05 W
Guaminí 252 37.02 S 62.25 W
Guam International Airport ⊠ 174p 13.29 N 144.48 E
Guamo 246 4.02 N 74.58 W
Guamo Embarcadero 240p 20.37 N 76.58 W
Guamote 246 1.56 S 78.43 W
Guamúchil, Méx. 232 25.28 N 108.06 W
Guamúchil, Méx. 234 25.28 N 108.06 W
Guamués ≃ 246 0.32 N 76.33 W
Gua Musang 114 4.53 N 101.58 E
Gu'an 105 39.26 N 116.18 E
Guan ≃, Zhg. 100 32.16 N 115.42 E
Guan ≃, Zhg. 100 34.29 N 119.49 E
Guanábana 240m 18.01 N 67.07 W
Guanabara, Baía de ⊂ 287a 22.50 S 43.10 W
Guanabara, Palácio ⛫ 287a 22.56 S 43.11 W
Guanacaste □[4] 236 10.30 N 85.15 W
Guanacaste, Cordillera de ⩘ 236 10.45 N 85.05 W
Guanacaste, Parque Nacional ♠ 236 10.50 N 85.30 W
Guanacaure, Cerro ∧ 236 13.14 N 87.07 W
Guanaceví 232 25.56 N 105.57 W
Guanache ≃ 248 5.53 S 74.21 W
Guanahacabibes, Golfo de ⊂ 240p 22.08 N 84.35 W
Guanahacabibes, Península de >[1] 240p 21.57 N 84.35 W
Guana Island I 240m 18.29 N 64.34 W
Guanaja 236 16.27 N 85.54 W
Guanaja, Isla de I 236 16.30 N 85.55 W
Guanajay 240p 22.55 N 82.42 W
Guanajibo ≃ 240m 18.10 N 67.11 W
Guanajibo, Punta > 240m 18.10 N 67.11 W
Guanajuato 234 21.01 N 101.15 W
Guanajuato □[3] 234 21.00 N 101.00 W
Guanambi 255 14.13 S 42.47 W
Guanaparo, Caño ≃ 246 8.19 N 68.10 W
Guañape, Islas II 248 8.33 S 78.57 W
Guanare 246 9.03 N 69.45 W
Guanare ≃ 246 8.13 N 67.46 W
Guanarito 246 8.42 N 69.12 W
Guanay 248 15.28 S 67.52 W
Guanay, Cerro ∧ 246 5.51 N 66.18 W
Guanay, Cerro ∧[2] 286d 12.07 S 77.13 W
Guanbuqiao 100 29.56 N 114.21 E
Guanchao 100 26.41 N 114.58 E
Guancheng, Zhg. 100 30.11 N 121.25 E
Guancheng, Zhg. 107 30.01 N 103.54 E
Guancun 106 31.30 N 119.43 E
Guandacol 252 29.31 S 68.32 W
Guandanghu 100 30.06 N 113.37 E
Guandi, Zhg. 98 41.48 N 116.52 E
Guandi, Zhg. 98 42.37 N 118.27 E
Guandian 100 32.40 N 118.04 E
Guandu, Zhg. 100 24.17 N 113.53 E
Guandu, Zhg. 107 30.04 N 106.25 E
Guane 240p 22.12 N 84.05 W
Guang'an 107 30.28 N 106.39 E
Guang'anmen Station ◆[5] 271a 39.53 N 116.20 E
Guangchang 100 26.50 N 116.14 E
Guangde 106 30.54 N 119.26 E
Guangdong (Kwangtung) □[4] 90 23.00 N 113.00 E
Guangfeng 100 28.25 N 118.11 E
Guangfu, Zhg. 106 31.18 N 120.23 E
Guangfu, Zhg. 107 30.13 N 104.41 E
Guangfu, Zhg. 269b 31.21 N 121.19 E
Guangfuyingzi 104 42.14 N 120.58 E
Guanghua 102 32.25 N 111.36 E
Guangji 100 29.52 N 115.34 E
Guangling, Zhg. 98 39.47 N 114.17 E
Guangling, Zhg. 106 32.06 N 120.13 E
Guanglu Dao I 98 39.09 N 122.21 E
Guangmao Shan ∧ 102 27.02 N 100.58 E
Guangming Ding ∧ 100 30.07 N 118.10 E
Guangnan 102 24.10 N 105.06 E
Guangningsi, Zhg. 98 39.08 N 121.45 E
Guangningsi, Zhg. 98 40.27 N 118.31 E
Guangping 98 36.30 N 114.57 E
Guangrao 98 37.02 N 118.25 E
Guangsbunchang 107 29.22 N 105.31 E
Guangshan 100 32.02 N 114.52 E
Guangshui 100 31.40 N 114.00 E
Guangxing 107 29.04 N 106.33 E
Guangxi Zhuangzu Zizhiqu (Kwangsi Chuang) □[4] 102 24.00 N 109.00 E
Guangyuan 102 32.26 N 105.52 E
Guangyuanzhen 107 30.37 N 104.47 E
Guangze 100 27.32 N 117.20 E
Guangzhen 106 30.45 N 121.07 E
Guangzhou (Canton) 100 23.06 N 113.16 E
Guangzong 98 37.06 N 115.08 E
Guanhães 255 18.46 S 42.53 W
Guanhu 98 34.26 N 117.59 E
Guánica 240m 17.58 N 66.55 W
Guánica, Laguna de ⊜ 240m 18.00 N 66.56 W
Guaniguanico, Cordillera de ⩘ 240p 22.35 N 83.45 W
Guanipa ≃ 246 9.56 N 62.26 W
Guanjian 107 29.59 N 105.59 E
Guanjian ≃ 107 30.00 N 106.01 E
Guankou, Zhg. 100 30.35 N 115.20 E
Guankou, Zhg. 107 30.39 N 103.26 E
Guanlin 106 31.32 N 119.42 E
Guanling 102 25.57 N 105.29 E
Guanlipu 104 41.37 N 123.18 E
Guanmenshan 89 47.23 N 122.20 E
Guannan (Xin'anzhen) 98 34.07 N 119.23 E
Guano 246 1.35 S 78.38 W
Guano Creek ≃ 202 42.12 N 119.31 W
Guanputou 105 38.58 N 117.04 E
Guanqian, Zhg. 100 30.42 N 117.39 E
Guanqian, Zhg. 100 27.48 N 118.31 E
Guanqian, Zhg. 100 25.57 N 116.33 E
Guanqian, Zhg. 100 26.12 N 117.57 E
Guanqiao, Zhg. 98 34.58 N 117.14 E
Guanqiao, Zhg. 100 25.03 N 118.06 E
Guanqiaopu 100 31.08 N 112.54 E
Guanshanchang 107 28.46 N 103.42 E
Guanshi 100 26.43 N 112.53 E
Guanshui 98 40.55 N 124.33 E
Guanta 246 10.14 N 64.36 W
Guantánamo 240p 20.08 N 75.12 W
Guantánamo □[4] 240p 20.20 N 75.00 W
Guantánamo ≃ 240p 19.55 N 75.12 W
Guantánamo, Bahía de ⊂ 240p 20.00 N 75.08 W
Guantanamo Bay Naval Station ■ 240p 19.55 N 75.10 W
Guantang 106 31.37 N 119.06 E
Guantangqiao 106 32.09 N 119.27 E
Guantao (Nanguantao) 98 36.35 N 115.19 E
Guanting, Zhg. 100 34.19 N 113.47 E
Guanting, Zhg. 105 40.13 N 115.37 E
Guanting Shuiku ⊜[1] 105 40.20 N 115.38 E
Guantou, Zhg. 100 28.03 N 120.41 E
Guantou, Zhg. 100 26.08 N 119.33 E
Guantunpu 98 40.28 N 113.24 E
Guanxian, Zhg. 98 36.30 N 115.27 E
Guanxian, Zhg. 102 31.00 N 103.40 E
Guanxun 100 24.19 N 117.45 E
Guanyin 107 30.16 N 103.51 E
Guanyinchang, Zhg. 107 30.28 N 105.16 E
Guanyinchang, Zhg. 107 29.15 N 104.02 E
Guanyingzicun 104 41.52 N 121.53 E
Guanyinpu 107 28.58 N 104.53 E
Guanyinqiao, Zhg. 107 29.05 N 104.46 E
Guanyinqiao, Zhg. 107 29.46 N 104.12 E
Guanyinshan 106 32.01 N 120.58 E
Guanyinsi 106 31.48 N 118.57 E
Guanyintan 107 29.35 N 105.14 E
Guanyintang, Zhg. 100 31.01 N 112.35 E
Guanyintang, Zhg. 105 39.52 N 116.31 E
Guanyintang, Zhg. 106 32.09 N 121.09 E
Guanyinzhen 107 29.06 N 104.24 E
Guanyinzhou 100 29.30 N 113.09 E
Guanyun (Dayishan) 98 34.20 N 119.17 E
Guanzhuang, Zhg. 98 37.12 N 114.30 E
Guanzhuang, Zhg. 100 32.49 N 114.16 E
Guanzhuang, Zhg. 100 28.58 N 117.24 E
Guapí 246 2.36 N 77.54 W
Guapiaçu ≃ 256 22.40 S 42.55 W
Guapiara 255 24.10 S 48.32 W
Guápiles 236 10.13 N 83.46 W
Guapimirim 256 22.32 S 42.59 W
Guapimirim ≃ 256 22.40 S 42.58 W
Guapo Bay ⊂ 241r 10.12 N 61.40 W
Guaporé 252 28.51 S 51.54 W
Guaporé (Itenes) ≃ 248 11.54 S 65.01 W
Guaqui 248 16.35 S 68.51 W
Guará ≃ 255 12.59 S 44.49 W
Guara, Sierra de ⩘ 34 42.17 N 0.10 W
Guarabira 250 6.51 S 35.29 W
Guaraçaí 255 21.02 S 51.11 W
Guaracarumbo 286c 10.34 N 66.59 W
Guaraci 255 20.29 S 48.57 W
Guaraciaba do Norte 250 4.10 S 40.46 W
Guaraciana 255 17.03 S 43.41 W
Guaraguara, Punta > 241r 10.31 N 62.19 W
Guaraí ≃ 287a 22.42 S 43.02 W
Guaramirim 252 26.27 S 49.00 W
Guaranda 246 1.36 S 79.00 W
Guaranésia 256 21.18 S 46.48 W
Guarani 256 21.22 S 43.03 W
Guaraniaçu 252 25.06 S 52.52 W
Guarani das Missões 252 28.08 S 54.34 W
Guarani de Goiás 255 13.59 S 46.31 W
Guarapari 255 20.40 S 40.30 W
Guarapiranga, Reprêsa ⊜[1] 256 23.44 S 46.44 W
Guarapuava 252 25.23 S 51.27 W
Guaraqueçaba 252 25.17 S 48.21 W
Guarará 256 21.43 S 43.02 W
Guarará ≃ 287b 23.39 S 46.30 W
Guararé 246 7.49 N 80.17 W
Guararema 256 23.25 S 46.02 W
Guaratiba, Morro de ∧ 287a 23.04 S 43.33 W
Guaratinga 255 16.34 S 39.34 W
Guaratinguetá 256 22.49 S 45.13 W
Guaratinguetá ≃ 256 22.49 S 45.13 W
Guaratuba 252 25.54 S 48.34 W
Guar Chempedak 114 5.52 N 100.28 E
Guarcino 66 41.48 N 13.19 E
Guarda 34 40.32 N 7.16 W
Guardado de Abajo 196 26.22 N 98.57 W
Guardafui, Cape → Caseyr > 144 11.49 N 51.15 E
Guardavalle 68 38.30 N 16.30 E
Guardea 66 42.37 N 12.18 E
Guardia Escolta 252 28.59 S 62.08 W
Guardiagrele 66 42.11 N 14.13 E
Guardia Lombardi 68 40.57 N 15.12 E
Guardia Mitre 254 40.26 S 63.41 W
Guardia Sanframondi 68 41.15 N 14.36 E
Guardo 34 42.47 N 4.50 W
Guareña 34 38.51 N 6.06 W
Guareña ≃ 34 41.29 N 5.23 W
Guarenas 246 10.28 N 66.37 W
Guarenas ≃ 286c 10.30 N 66.45 W
Guariba ≃ 248 7.41 S 60.18 W
Guarico 246 9.32 N 69.48 W
Guárico □[3] 246 8.40 N 66.35 W
Guárico ≃ 246 7.55 N 67.23 W
Guárico, Embalse del ⊜[1] 246 9.05 N 67.25 W
Guarico, Punta > 240p 20.37 N 74.44 W
Guariquito ≃ 246 7.40 N 66.18 W
Guarizama 236 14.55 N 86.20 W
Guarujá 256 24.00 S 46.16 W
Guarulhos 256 23.28 S 46.32 W
Guarulhos □[7] 287b 23.26 S 46.29 W
Guasare ≃ 246 11.03 N 72.02 W
Guasave 232 25.34 N 108.27 W
Guasdualito 246 7.15 N 70.44 W
Guasila 71 39.34 N 9.03 E
Guasipati 246 7.28 N 61.54 W
Guastalla 64 44.55 N 10.39 E
Guastatoya 236 14.51 N 90.04 W
Guāsuba ≃[1] 126 21.38 N 88.53 E
Guatajiagua 236 13.40 N 88.13 W
Guatemala, Cuba 240p 20.46 N 75.39 W
Guatemala, Guat. 236 14.38 N 90.31 W
Guatemala □[5] 236 14.40 N 90.30 W
Guatemala □[1], N.A. 230 15.30 N 90.15 W
Guatemala □[1], N.A. 236 15.30 N 90.15 W
Guatemala Basin ✣[1] 16 11.00 N 95.00 W
Guateque 246 5.00 N 73.28 W
Guatimozín 252 33.27 S 62.27 W
Guatopo, Parque Nacional ♠ 246 10.05 N 66.25 W
Guatraché 252 37.40 S 63.32 W
Guatuaro Point > 241r 10.20 N 60.59 W
Guaugurina 164 10.37 S 150.28 E
Guavi ≃ 164 7.49 S 143.15 E
Guaviare □[8] 246 2.00 N 72.00 W
Guaviare ≃ 246 4.03 N 67.44 W
Guaxindiba ≃ 287a 22.44 S 43.02 W
Guaxupé 256 21.18 S 46.42 W
Guayabal, Cuba 240p 20.42 N 77.36 W
Guayabal, Ven. 246 8.00 N 67.24 W
Guayabal, Lago ⊜[1] 240m 18.06 N 66.30 W
Guayabero ≃ 246 2.36 N 72.47 W
Guayacán 252 29.58 S 71.22 W
Guayaguayare 241r 10.08 N 61.02 W
Guayalejo ≃ 234 22.27 N 98.29 W
Guayama 240m 17.59 N 66.07 W
Guayambre ≃ 236 14.26 N 86.02 W
Guayameo 234 18.12 N 101.19 W
Guayana → Ciudad Guayana 246 8.22 N 62.40 W
Guayana → Guyana □[1] 246 5.00 N 59.00 W
Guayaneco, Archipiélago II 254 47.45 S 75.10 W
Guayanés, Punta > 240m 18.04 N 65.48 W
Guayanilla 240m 18.01 N 66.47 W
Guayanilla, Bahía de ⊂ 240m 18.00 N 66.46 W
Guayape 236 14.45 N 86.52 W
Guayape ≃ 236 14.26 N 85.58 W
Guayapo ≃ 246 4.30 N 67.35 W
Guayaquil 246 2.10 S 79.50 W
Guayaquil, Golfo de ⊂ 246 3.00 S 80.30 W
Guayaramerín 248 10.48 S 65.23 W
Guayas □[4] 246 2.00 S 80.00 W
Guayas ≃, Col. 246 1.23 N 74.50 W
Guayas ≃, Ec. 246 2.36 S 79.52 W
Guayatayoc, Laguna de ⊜ 252 23.25 S 65.51 W
Guaycora 232 28.50 N 109.21 W
Guaycurú, Arroyo ≃ 258 34.00 S 56.50 W
Guaymas 232 27.56 N 110.54 W
Guaynabo 240m 18.22 N 66.07 W
Guayquiraró ≃ 252 30.10 S 58.34 W
Guayuriba ≃ 246 3.55 N 73.05 W
Guazacapán 236 14.04 N 90.25 W
Guazapares 232 27.22 N 108.15 W
Guazárachi 232 26.57 N 106.43 W
Guazhou 106 32.15 N 119.23 E
Guazunamby, Arroyo ≃ 288 34.24 S 58.38 W
Guba, Ityo. 144 10.16 N 35.17 E
Guba, Zaïre 154 10.40 S 26.26 E
Gubacha 86 58.52 N 57.36 E
Gubam 164 8.40 S 141.55 E
Gubany 76 56.37 N 30.40 E
Gubari 80 51.32 N 42.33 E
Gubat 116 12.55 N 124.07 E
Gubavica ⌞ 36 43.26 N 16.54 E
Gubbi 122 13.19 N 76.56 E
Gubbio 66 43.21 N 12.35 E
Gubeikou 105 40.42 N 117.09 E
Guben 54 51.57 N 14.43 E
Gubentaoligai 104 42.16 N 122.13 E
Gubin 30 51.56 N 14.45 E
Gubinicha 78 48.48 N 35.15 E
Gubino, Ross. 80 53.19 N 48.44 E
Gubino, Ross. 82 55.42 N 39.07 E
Gubio 146 12.29 N 12.48 E
Gubkin 78 51.18 N 37.32 E
Gubug 115a 7.03 S 110.40 E
Gucheng (Zhengjiakou), Zhg. 98 37.22 N 115.56 E
Gucheng, Zhg. 100 33.59 N 117.29 E
Gucheng, Zhg. 100 32.46 N 118.32 E
Gucheng, Zhg. 100 25.53 N 116.11 E
Gucheng, Zhg. 102 32.18 N 111.35 E
Gucheng, Zhg. 105 40.32 N 116.02 E
Gucheng, Zhg. 105 39.08 N 115.42 E
Gucheng, Zhg. 106 30.29 N 119.46 E
Guchengcang 100 32.34 N 115.20 E
Gucheng Hu ⊜ 106 31.17 N 118.54 E
Guchengzi, Zhg. 104 42.33 N 123.45 E
Guchengzi, Zhg. 104 40.58 N 122.36 E
Guchengzi, Zhg. 104 40.40 N 120.31 E
Guchengzi, Zhg. 104 41.44 N 123.35 E
Gučin-Us 102 45.27 N 102.25 E
Gücük 130 38.12 N 37.29 E
Gūdalūr 122 9.41 N 77.16 E
Gúdar, Sierra de ⩘ 34 40.27 N 0.42 W
Gudauta 84 43.06 N 40.37 E
Gudbrandsdalen V 26 61.30 N 10.00 E
Gudenå ≃ 26 56.29 N 10.13 E
Gudensberg 56 51.10 N 9.22 E
Gudermes 84 43.20 N 46.08 E
Guderup 41 54.59 N 9.53 E
Gudgenby ≃ 171b 35.39 S 149.04 E
Gudhjem 26 55.13 N 14.59 E
Gudianzi 100 31.49 N 116.05 E
Gudivāda 122 16.27 N 80.59 E
Gudiyāttam 122 12.57 N 78.52 E
Gudme 41 55.09 N 10.43 E
Gudow 54 53.33 N 10.46 E
Güdül 130 40.13 N 32.15 E
Gūdūr 122 14.08 N 79.51 E
Gudvangen 26 60.52 N 6.50 E
Guebwiller (Gebweiler) 58 47.55 N 7.12 E
Guéckédou 150 8.33 N 10.09 W
Gué-de-Longroi 261 48.30 N 1.43 E
Gué-d'Hossus 50 49.57 N 4.32 E
Guédi, Mont ∧ 146 12.14 N 18.58 E
Guéguen, Lac ⊜ 190 48.06 N 77.13 W
Guéherville 261 48.32 N 1.53 E
Güejar ≃ 246 2.55 N 73.14 W
Guélendeng 146 10.56 N 15.32 E
Guelma 148 36.28 N 7.26 E
Guelma □[5] 148 36.10 N 7.50 E
Guelph 212 43.33 N 80.15 W
Guémené-sur-Scorff 32 48.04 N 3.12 W
Güemes 234 23.56 N 99.00 W
Guemes Island I 224 48.33 N 122.37 W
Guené 150 11.44 N 3.13 E
Guenguel ≃ 254 45.41 S 70.20 W
Guer 32 47.54 N 2.07 W
Guéra □[5] 146 11.30 N 18.30 E
Guéra, Massif de ∧ 146 11.55 N 18.12 E
Guérande 32 47.20 N 2.26 W
Guercif 148 34.15 N 3.21 W
Guerdjoumane, Djebel ∧ 34 36.25 N 2.51 E
Güere ≃ 246 9.50 N 65.08 W
Guéréda 146 14.31 N 22.05 E
Guéret 32 46.10 N 1.52 E
Guérin Kouka 150 9.41 N 0.37 E
Guerla Mandata Shan ∧ 120 30.26 N 81.20 E
Guermantes 261 48.51 N 2.42 E
Guerne 214 40.46 N 81.54 W
Guernes 261 49.01 N 1.38 E
Guerneville 204 38.30 N 123.00 W
Guernica 258 34.56 S 58.25 W
Guernica → Gernika-Lumo 34 43.19 N 2.41 W
Guernsey 200 42.16 N 104.44 W
Guernsey □[6] 214 40.08 N 81.30 W
Guernsey □[2], Europe 22 49.28 N 2.35 W
Guernsey □[2], Europe 43b 49.28 N 2.35 W
Guernsey Reservoir ⊜[1] 198 42.19 N 104.48 W
Guernsey State Park ♠ 198 42.20 N 104.50 W
Guerrero, Méx. 196 28.20 N 100.23 W
Guerrero, Méx. 232 28.33 N 107.30 W
Guerrero □[3] 234 17.40 N 100.00 W
Guerrero Negro 232 27.56 N 114.08 W
Guerville 261 48.57 N 1.44 E
Guerzim 148 29.45 N 1.47 W
Guesle ≃ 261 48.36 N 1.40 E
Guessou-Sud 150 10.03 N 2.38 E
Guest Peninsula >[1] 9 76.18 S 148.00 W
Gueydan 194 30.01 N 92.30 W
Guéyo 150 5.49 N 6.36 W
Gufang 100 29.04 N 119.32 E
Guffin Bay ⊂ 212 44.01 N 76.09 W
Guga 89 52.43 N 137.35 E
Gugang 100 28.17 N 113.46 E
Guge ∧ 144 6.10 N 37.26 E
Gugera 123 30.58 N 73.19 E
Gugging 264b 48.19 N 16.15 E
Güglia, Pass dal)(58 46.28 N 9.44 E
Güglingen 56 49.04 N 9.00 E
Guglionesi 66 41.55 N 14.55 E
Gugu ∧ 144 8.12 N 39.58 E
Guguan 102 40.27 N 99.13 E
Guguan I 108 17.19 N 145.51 E
Guhe 100 31.54 N 117.58 E
Gui ≃ 102 23.28 N 111.18 E
Guia 248 15.22 S 56.14 W
Guia de Pacobaíba 256 22.43 S 43.10 W
Guia Lopes da Laguna 248 21.26 S 56.07 W
Guiana Basin ✣[1] 18 11.00 N 52.00 W
Guiana Island I 240c 17.07 N 61.44 W
Guibéroua 150 6.14 N 6.10 W
Guibes 156 26.41 S 16.42 E
Güicán 246 6.28 N 72.25 W
Guichen 32 47.58 N 1.48 W
Guichi 100 30.40 N 117.28 E
Guichón 252 32.21 S 57.12 W
Guicun 100 33.37 N 114.11 E
Guidan Roumji 150 13.40 N 6.42 E
Guidari 146 9.17 N 16.40 E
Guide 102 36.03 N 101.28 E
Guide, Mount ∧[2] 162 22.36 S 136.54 E
Guide Post 44 55.10 N 1.35 W
Guider 146 9.56 N 13.57 E
Guide Rock 198 40.04 N 98.19 W
Guidexiang 107 29.51 N 104.47 E
Guidigri 146 13.40 N 9.51 E
Guidimaka □[4] 150 15.30 N 12.10 W
Guidimouni 150 13.42 N 9.30 E
Guiding 102 26.34 N 107.14 E
Guidizzolo 64 45.19 N 10.35 E
Guidong 100 26.05 N 113.57 E
Guidonia 66 42.01 N 12.45 E
Guidouma 152 1.37 S 10.41 E
Guiers ≃ 62 45.37 N 5.37 E
Guiers, Lac de ⊜ 150 16.12 N 15.50 W
Guifujie 100 27.20 N 120.01 E
Guiglia 64 44.26 N 10.58 E
Guiglo 150 6.33 N 7.29 W
Guignes-Rabutin 50 48.38 N 2.48 E
Guihuayuan 107 30.37 N 105.25 E
Guihulngan 116 10.07 N 123.16 E
Güija, Lago de ⊜ 236 14.17 N 89.31 W
Guijalo 116 13.44 N 123.52 E
Guiji 100 32.51 N 116.33 E
Guijingqiao 106 31.21 N 119.40 E
Guijuelo 34 40.33 N 5.40 W
Guil ≃ 62 44.40 N 6.36 E
Guilarte, Monte ∧ 240m 18.09 N 66.46 W
Guilderland 210 42.42 N 73.54 W
Guildford, Austl. 274a 33.51 S 150.59 E
Guildford, Eng., U.K. 42 51.14 N 0.35 W
Guildford □[8] 260 51.16 N 0.32 W
Guildford Cathedral ⛫[1] 260 51.14 N 0.35 W
Guildhall 188 44.33 N 71.33 W
Guildtown 46 56.28 N 3.24 W
Guiler 89 46.11 N 121.45 E
Guilford, Ct., U.S. 207 41.17 N 72.40 W
Guilford, In., U.S. 218 39.10 N 84.55 W
Guilford, Me., U.S. 188 45.10 N 69.23 W
Guilford, N.Y., U.S. 210 42.24 N 75.29 W
Guilford Courthouse National Military Park ♠ 192 36.01 N 79.45 W
Guilherand 62 44.56 N 4.52 E
Guilin (Kweilin) 102 25.17 N 110.17 E
Guilinchang 107 30.13 N 105.50 E
Guilinzhen 107 30.15 N 104.53 E
Guillaume-Delisle, Lac ⊜ 176 56.15 N 76.17 W
Guillaumes 62 44.05 N 6.51 E
Guillermo E. Hudson 288 34.47 S 58.10 W
Guillestre 62 44.40 N 6.39 E
Guillon 50 47.31 N 4.06 E
Guilsfield 42 52.42 N 3.09 W
Guilvinec 32 47.47 N 4.17 W
Guimarães, Bra. 250 2.08 S 44.36 W
Guimarães, Port. 34 41.27 N 8.18 W
Guimaras Island I 116 10.35 N 122.37 E
Guimaras Strait ⊔ 116 10.30 N 122.44 E
Guimba 116 15.40 N 120.46 E
Guimbal 116 10.40 N 122.19 E
Guimeishan 100 24.44 N 114.52 E
Guimu Zhang ∧ 100 24.40 N 116.48 E
Guin 194 33.57 N 87.54 W
Guinan 102 35.24 N 100.57 E
Guinayang 269f 14.42 N 121.08 E
Guinayangan 116 13.54 N 122.27 E
Guinda 226 38.50 N 122.12 W
Guindulman 116 9.46 N 124.29 E
Guindulman Bay ⊂ 116 9.44 N 124.29 E
Guinea 208 38.08 N 77.26 W
Guinea (Guinée) □[1], Afr. 134 11.00 N 10.00 W
Guinea (Guinée) □[1], Afr. 150 11.00 N 10.00 W
Guinea, Gulf of ⊂ 10 2.00 N 2.30 E
Guinea Basin ✣[1] 10 0.00 5.00 W
Guinea-Bissau (Guiné-Bissau) □[1], Afr. 134 12.00 N 15.00 W
Guinea-Bissau (Guiné-Bissau) □[1], Afr. 150 12.00 N 15.00 W
Guineacor Creek ≃ 170 34.21 S 150.05 E
Guinea Ecuatorial → Equatorial Guinea □[1] 152 2.00 N 9.00 E
Guinea Rise ✣[3] 10 8.00 S 0.00
Guiné-Bissau → Guinea-Bissau □[1] 150 12.00 N 15.00 W
Guinecourt, Lac ⊜ 186 50.55 N 69.16 W
Guinée-Bissau → Guinea-Bissau □[1] 150 12.00 N 15.00 W
Guinée équitoriale → Equatorial Guinea □[1] 152 2.00 N 9.00 E
Guinée → Guinea □[1] 150 11.00 N 10.00 W
Guiné → Guinea-Bissau □[1] 150 12.00 N 15.00 W
Güines, Cuba 240p 22.50 N 82.02 W
Guînes, Fr. 50 50.52 N 1.52 E
Guingamp 32 48.33 N 3.11 W
Guinguinéo 150 14.16 N 15.57 W
Guinobatan 116 13.11 N 123.36 E
Güinope 236 13.51 N 86.55 W
Guintacan Island I 116 11.19 N 123.54 E
Guintinguintin, Mount ∧ 116 12.25 N 122.24 E
Guintinua Island I 116 14.26 N 122.51 E
Guiones, Punta > 236 9.54 N 85.41 W
Guiong 116 6.25 N 122.01 E
Guiperreux 261 48.40 N 1.42 E
Guiperreux, Étang de ⊜ 261 48.40 N 1.43 E
Guiping 102 23.20 N 110.09 E
Guir, Hammada du ◆[2] 148 30.45 N 3.15 W
Guir, Oued V 148 30.29 N 2.17 W
Güira de Melena 240p 22.48 N 82.30 W
Guiraí ≃ 255 22.40 S 53.34 W
Guiratinga 255 16.21 S 53.45 W
Guiren 100 33.42 N 118.12 E
Güiria 246 10.34 N 62.18 W
Guiricema 255 21.00 S 42.43 W
Guisachan Forest ◆[3] 46 57.17 N 4.55 W
Guisanbourg 250 4.25 N 51.56 W
Guisborough 44 54.32 N 1.04 W
Guiscard 50 49.39 N 3.03 E
Guise 50 49.54 N 3.38 E
Guiseley 44 53.53 N 1.42 W
Guisijan 116 11.05 N 122.03 E
Güisisil ∧ 236 12.37 N 86.13 W
Guist Creek ≃ 218 38.09 N 85.13 W
Guitiriz 34 43.11 N 7.54 W
Guitou 100 24.58 N 113.25 E
Guitrancourt 261 49.01 N 1.47 E
Guîtres 32 45.03 N 0.11 W
Guitry 150 5.31 N 5.14 W
Guiuan 116 11.02 N 125.43 E
Guixi 100 28.16 N 117.10 E
Guixian 102 23.06 N 109.39 E
Guiyang, Zhg. 100 25.46 N 112.43 E
Guiyang (Kweiyang), Zhg. 102 26.35 N 106.43 E
Güiza ≃ 246 1.22 N 78.36 W

≃ River	Fluß	Río	Rivière	Rio
≅ Canal	Kanal	Canal	Canal	Canal
⌞ Waterfall, Rapids	Wasserfall, Stromschnellen	Cascada, Rápidos	Chute d'eau, Rapides	Cascata, Rápidos
⊔ Strait	Meeresstraße	Estrecho	Détroit	Estreito
⊂ Bay, Gulf	Bucht, Golf	Bahía, Golfo	Baie, Golfe	Baía, Golfo
⊜ Lake, Lakes	See, Seen	Lago, Lagos	Lac, Lacs	Lago, Lagos
≚ Swamp	Sumpf	Pantano	Marais	Pântano
⍝ Ice Features, Glacier	Eis- und Gletscherformen	Accidentes Glaciales	Formes glaciaires	Acidentes glaciares
⇟ Other Hydrographic Features	Andere Hydrographische Objekte	Otros Elementos Hidrográficos	Autres données hydrographiques	Outros acidentes hidrográficos
✣ Submarine Features	Untermeerische Objekte	Accidentes Submarinos	Formes de relief sous-marin	Acidentes submarinos
□ Political Unit	Politische Einheit	Unidad Politica	Entité politique	Unidade política
⛫ Cultural Institution	Kulturelle Institution	Institución Cultural	Institution culturelle	Institução cultural
⊥ Historical Site	Historische Stätte	Sitio Histórico	Site historique	Sitio histórico
♠ Recreational Site	Erholungs- und Ferienort	Sitio de Recreo	Centre de loisirs	Area de Lazer
⊠ Airport	Flughafen	Aeropuerto	Aéroport	Aeroporto
■ Military Installation	Militäranlage	Instalación Militar	Installation militaire	Instalação militar
◆ Miscellaneous	Verschiedenes	Misceláneo	Divers	Diversos

ENGLISH — Name Page Lat.°′ Long.°′
DEUTSCH — Name Seite Breite°′ Länge°′ E = Ost

Guizhou (Kweichow) □[4] 102 27.00 N 107.00 E
Gujarāt □[3] 118 22.00 N 72.00 E
Gūjar Khān 123 33.16 N 73.19 E
Gujba 146 11.30 N 11.55 E
Gujiabeng 106 30.45 N 120.59 E
Gujiang 100 27.11 N 114.49 E
Gujiatun 104 40.39 N 124.08 E
Gujiatuo 107 29.14 N 106.12 E
Gujiazhai 269b 31.22 N 121.28 E
Gujiazi, Zhg. 104 42.02 N 123.01 E
Gujiazi, Zhg. 104 41.44 N 124.11 E
Gujrānwāla 123 32.09 N 74.11 E
Gujrāt 123 32.34 N 74.05 E
Gukas'an 84 41.03 N 43.52 E
Gukou 100 26.27 N 118.38 E
Gukovo 83 48.03 N 39.56 E
Gul, Tanjong › 271c 1.17 N 103.39 E
Gul'a 88 54.41 N 121.01 E
Gul'aj-Borisovka 78 46.38 N 40.13 E
Gul'ajevskije Koški, ostrova II 24 68.55 N 55.10 E
Gul'ajpole 78 47.38 N 36.16 E
Gulang 102 37.36 N 102.58 E
Gulaothi 124 28.36 N 77.47 E
Gulargambone 166 31.20 S 148.28 E
Gulbarga 122 17.20 N 76.50 E
Gulbene 76 57.11 N 26.45 E
Gul'ča 85 40.19 N 73.26 E
Gul'ča ≃ 85 40.20 N 73.26 E
Guldasteh 267d 35.36 N 51.16 E
Guldborg 41 54.52 N 11.45 E
Guldborg Sund ⊔ 41 54.48 N 11.48 E
Guldsmedshyttan 40 59.42 N 15.06 E
Güldüzü 130 36.52 N 37.07 E
Gülebağdı 130 39.52 N 39.50 E
Guledagudda 122 16.03 N 75.48 E
Guleitou 100 23.47 N 117.36 E
Gülek Boğazı)(130 37.16 N 34.48 E
Gulf □[5] 164 7.00 S 145.00 E
Gulf Gate Estates 220 27.15 N 82.31 W
Gulf Hammock 192 29.15 N 82.43 W
Gulf Harbors 220 28.14 N 82.45 W
Gulf Islands National Seashore ♠ 194 30.14 N 88.42 W
Gulf of Alaska Seamount Province ⊹ 16 56.00 N 147.00 W
Gulfport, Fl., U.S. 220 27.45 N 82.40 W
Gulfport, Ms., U.S. 194 30.22 N 89.05 W
Gulf Shores 194 30.14 N 87.42 W
Gulf State Park ♠ 194 30.16 N 87.40 W
Gulf Stream ≃ 212 43.51 N 75.56 W
Gulgong 166 32.22 S 149.32 E
Guli 106 31.38 N 120.50 E
Gulian 89 52.55 N 122.19 E
Gulicun 106 31.52 N 118.41 E
Gul Imām 123 32.16 N 70.32 E
Gulistān, Pāk. 120 30.36 N 66.35 E
Gulistan, Uzb. 85 40.30 N 68.46 E
Guliya Shan ∧ 89 49.48 N 122.25 E
Guljanci 38 43.38 N 24.42 E
Gulkana 180 62.16 N 145.23 W
Gull ≃ 212 44.37 N 78.49 W
Gulland Rock II[1] 42 50.34 N 4.59 W
Gullane 46 56.02 N 2.50 W
Gullfoss L 24a 64.24 N 20.08 W
Gullholmen 26 58.11 N 11.24 E
Gullion, Slieve ∧[2] 48 54.08 N 6.27 W
Gull Island I 281 42.32 N 82.41 W
Gullivan Bay c 220 25.52 N 81.38 W
Gull Lake 184 50.08 N 108.27 W
Gull Lake ⊜, Ab., Can. 182 52.35 N 114.00 W
Gull Lake ⊜, On., Can. 184 51.18 N 91.58 W
Gull Lake ⊜, On., Can. 212 44.51 N 78.47 W
Gull Lake ⊜, Mi., U.S. 216 42.24 N 85.25 W
Gull Lake ⊜, Mn., U.S. 190 46.25 N 94.20 W
Gullrock Lake ⊜ 184 50.58 N 93.40 W
Gullspång 40 58.59 N 14.06 E
Güllük 130 37.14 N 27.36 E
Güllük Körfezi c 130 37.12 N 27.20 E
Gulmarg 123 34.03 N 74.23 E
Gulnam 140 6.55 N 29.30 E
Gülnar 130 36.20 N 33.25 E
Gulong 89 45.51 N 124.14 E
Gulpen 56 50.48 N 5.54 E
Gülper See ⊜ 54 52.44 N 12.14 E
Gulph Mills 285 40.04 N 75.21 W
Gülpınar 130 39.32 N 26.07 E
Gul'ripš 84 42.57 N 41.06 E
Gul'šad 86 46.39 N 74.24 E
Gülşehir 130 38.45 N 34.38 E
Gulshan 126 23.49 N 90.27 E
Gulsvik 26 60.23 N 9.35 E
Gulu, Ug. 154 2.47 N 32.18 E
Gulu, Zhg. 120 28.06 N 89.17 E
Gulukguluk 115a 7.04 S 113.40 E
Guluogongba 120 34.20 N 84.50 E
Guluy 144 14.44 N 36.43 E
Gulwe 154 6.30 S 36.29 E
Gumaca 116 13.55 N 122.06 E
Gumahang 116 12.35 N 123.16 E
Gumal (Gowmal) ≃ 120 31.56 N 70.22 E
Gumare 156 19.21 S 22.12 E
Gumba, Ang. 152 11.40 S 16.34 E
Gumba, Zaïre 152 2.57 N 21.26 E
Gumbinnen → Gusev 76 54.36 N 22.12 E
Gumbiro 154 10.16 S 35.39 E
Gumel 150 12.39 N 9.22 E
Gumeracha 168b 34.49 S 138.53 E
Gumiao 100 32.26 N 113.16 E
Gumieńce ✦[8] 54 53.25 N 14.30 E
Gumistskij zapovednik ♠ 84 43.15 N 41.05 E
Gumla 124 23.03 N 84.33 E
Gumma □[5] 94 36.30 N 139.00 E
Gummersbach 56 51.02 N 7.34 E
Gummi 150 12.09 N 5.09 E
Gumpas Pond ⊜ 283 42.44 N 71.22 W
Gumpas Pond Brook ≃ 283 42.42 N 71.21 W
Gumpoldskirchen 264b 48.03 N 16.17 E
Gum Swamp Creek ≃ 192 32.08 N 82.55 W
Gumti ≃ 126 23.32 N 90.43 E
Gümüşçay 130 40.16 N 27.17 E
Gümüşhacıköy 130 40.53 N 35.14 E
Gümüşhane 130 40.27 N 39.29 E
Gümüşhane □[4] 130 40.15 N 39.45 E
Gümüşkent 130 38.50 N 34.32 E
Gümüşköy ✦[8] 267b 41.14 N 28.58 E
Gümüşova 130 40.51 N 30.57 E
Gümüşsü 130 38.14 N 30.01 E
Gun ≃ 216 42.28 N 85.40 W
Guna, India 124 24.39 N 77.19 E
Guna, Ityo. 144 8.19 N 39.51 E
Guna ∧ 144 11.42 N 38.12 E
Gunbar 166 34.01 S 145.25 E
Gun Barrel City 222 32.20 N 96.10 W
Gun Creek ≃ 284a 43.03 N 78.55 W
Gunda 88 52.47 N 111.44 E
Gundagai 166 35.04 S 148.07 E
Gundelfingen, Dtsch. 56 48.33 N 10.22 E
Gundelfingen, Dtsch. 58 48.03 N 7.52 E
Gundelsheim 56 49.17 N 9.09 E
Gundik 115a 7.12 S 110.54 E
Gundji 152 2.05 N 21.27 E
Gundlakamma ≃ 122 15.32 N 80.14 E
Gundlupet 122 11.48 N 76.41 E
Gündoğdu 130 40.15 N 27.07 E
Gündoğmuş 130 36.48 N 32.01 E
Guneh Ghar ∧ 123 35.19 N 71.47 E
Güney 130 38.09 N 29.05 E
Gungartan ∧ 171b 36.18 S 148.24 E
Gungi 152 6.21 S 19.15 E
Gungo 152 11.48 S 14.08 E
Güngören ✦[8] 267b 41.01 N 28.53 E
Gungu 152 5.44 S 19.19 E
Gunib 84 42.25 N 46.57 E
Gunisao ≃ 184 53.54 N 97.58 W
Gunisao Lake ⊜ 184 53.33 N 96.15 W
Gunjrauliya 124 26.35 N 84.34 E
Gun Lake ⊜ 216 42.37 N 85.32 W
Gunma 94 36.24 N 139.00 E
Gunnar 176 59.23 N 108.53 W
Günnarijn 102 45.38 N 102.01 E
Gunnarn 26 65.00 N 17.40 E
Gunnbjørn Fjeld ∧ 16 68.55 N 29.53 W
Gunnebo 26 57.43 N 16.32 E
Gunnedah 166 30.59 S 150.15 E
Gunning Island I 276 40.22 N 73.59 W
Gunnislake 42 50.31 N 4.12 W
Gunnison, Co., U.S. 200 38.32 N 106.55 W
Gunnison, Ut,. U.S. 200 39.09 N 111.49 W
Gunnison ≃ 200 39.03 N 108.35 W
Gunnison, Lake Fork ≃ 200 38.28 N 107.19 W
Gunnison, North Fork ≃ 200 38.47 N 107.50 W
Gunn Peak ∧ 224 47.49 N 121.27 W
Gunong Mulu National Park ♠ 112 4.10 N 114.55 E
Gunpowder Creek ≃, Austl. 166 19.14 S 139.58 E
Gunpowder Creek ≃, Ky., U.S. 218 38.53 N 84.47 W
Gunpowder Falls ≃ 208 39.24 N 76.22 W
Gunpowder Falls State Park ♠ 208 39.37 N 76.40 W
Gunpowder River c 208 39.22 N 76.22 W
Gunsan → Kunsan 98 35.58 N 126.41 E
Gunskirchen 60 48.08 N 13.57 E
Gunston Cove c 208 38.40 N 77.09 W
Guntakal 122 15.10 N 77.23 E
Güntersberge 54 51.38 N 10.59 E
Guntersblum 56 49.47 N 8.21 E
Guntersdorf 61 48.39 N 16.03 E
Guntersville 194 34.21 N 86.17 W
Guntersville Dam ✦[6] 194 34.13 N 86.23 W
Guntersville Lake ⊜[1] 194 34.45 N 86.03 W
Guntingsaga 114 2.33 N 99.39 E
Guntramsdorf 61 48.03 N 16.19 E
Guntung 114 1.38 N 101.34 E
Guntūr 122 16.18 N 80.27 E
Gunungkencana 115a 6.34 S 106.04 E
Gunungmegang 112 3.27 S 103.52 E
Gunungsahilan 112 0.06 N 101.18 E
Gunungsitoli 114 1.17 N 97.37 E
Gunungtua 114 1.30 N 99.37 E
Gunupur 122 19.05 N 83.49 E
Gunyidi 162 30.08 S 116.04 E
Günyüzü 130 39.24 N 31.50 E
Günz ≃ 58 48.27 N 10.16 E
Gunza ≃ 152 11.10 S 13.50 E
Günzburg 58 48.27 N 10.16 E
Gunzenhausen 56 49.07 N 10.45 E
Gunzigou 104 41.31 N 123.58 E
Guo ≃ 100 32.57 N 117.14 E
Guobei 107 29.33 N 105.08 E
Guodian 106 30.27 N 120.33 E
Guoji 100 32.59 N 113.06 E
Guojiadian 104 41.51 N 121.30 E
Guojiajiang 106 32.17 N 120.50 E
Guojiatun, Zhg. 98 41.31 N 117.02 E
Guojiatun, Zhg. 104 42.00 N 122.51 E
Guojiatun, Zhg. 104 40.52 N 122.04 E
Guojiawopeng 104 42.03 N 122.46 E
Guojiayao 105 40.37 N 115.39 E
Guojiayuan 106 32.10 N 120.35 E
Guojiga 86 43.47 N 80.48 E
Guoleizhuang 98 40.44 N 114.36 E
Guolutan 100 32.04 N 115.40 E
Guosu 98 38.24 N 114.00 E
Guoyang 100 33.32 N 116.12 E
Guoyangzhen 102 38.54 N 112.50 E
Guozhuang 98 35.25 N 117.10 E
Guozhuangmiao 106 31.49 N 119.01 E
Gupei 98 34.09 N 117.54 E
Gupis 123 36.14 N 73.26 E
Gura 80 57.18 N 51.25 E
Gura, Wādī V 140 17.28 N 35.10 E
Gurabo 240m 18.16 N 65.58 W
Guraferda 144 6.51 N 35.04 E
Gura-Galbena 78 46.43 N 28.42 E
Gurage ∧ 144 8.24 N 38.24 E
Gurahonț 38 46.16 N 22.21 E
Gura Humorului 38 47.33 N 25.54 E
Gurais 123 34.38 N 74.50 E
Guran 88 54.46 N 100.38 E
Gurara ≃ 150 8.12 N 6.41 E
Gurban Anggir 102 37.45 N 97.30 E
Gurban Obo 102 43.14 N 112.28 E
Gurdāspur 123 32.02 N 75.31 E
Gurdon 194 33.55 N 93.09 W
Gurdžaani 84 41.43 N 45.48 E
Güre 130 38.39 N 29.10 E
Gurejev 80 47.21 N 43.16 E
G'urg'an 84 40.23 N 50.19 E
Gurgaon 124 28.28 N 77.02 E
Gurgei, Jabal ∧ 140 13.50 N 24.19 E
Gurghiului, Munții ⩘ 38 46.41 N 25.12 E
Gurgó ∧[2] 61 46.31 N 16.50 E
Gurgueia ≃ 250 6.50 S 43.24 W
Gurgur 144 7.48 N 41.32 E
Gurha 120 25.11 N 71.40 E
Guri 144 7.27 N 40.36 E
Guri, Embalse de ⊜[1] 246 7.30 N 62.50 W
Gurig National Park ♠ 164 11.25 S 132.15 E
Gurjevo 82 54.42 N 36.28 E
Gurjevsk, Ross. 76 54.47 N 20.38 E
Gurjevsk, Ross. 86 54.17 N 85.56 E
Gurk 61 46.52 N 14.18 E
Gurk ≃ 61 46.36 N 14.31 E
Gurk ʊ[1] 61 46.52 N 14.15 E
Gurktaler Alpen ⩘ 64 46.55 N 14.00 E
Gūr Kūh ∧ 128 26.06 N 58.28 E
Gurla Mandhata → Guerla Mandata Shan ∧ 120 30.26 N 81.20 E
Gurlevo 76 59.28 N 28.54 E
Gurnee 216 42.22 N 87.54 W
Gurnet Point › 283 42.01 N 70.34 W
Gürpınar 128 38.18 N 43.25 E
Gurror 174q 9.27 N 138.04 E
Gursarai 124 25.37 N 79.11 E
Gurskoje 89 50.21 N 138.12 E
Gurskøy I 26 62.15 N 5.41 E
Gürsu 130 40.13 N 29.12 E
Gurué 154 15.25 S 36.58 E
Guru Har Sahāi 123 30.43 N 74.25 E
Gurumeti ≃ 154 2.05 S 33.57 E
Gurun, Malay. 114 5.49 N 100.29 E
Gürün, Tür. 130 38.43 N 37.17 E
Gurupá 250 1.25 S 51.39 W
Gurupi 250 11.43 S 49.04 W
Gurupi ≃ 250 1.13 S 46.06 W
Guru Sikhar ∧ 120 24.39 N 72.46 E
Gurvanbulag 88 47.38 N 103.31 E
Gurvansajchan 102 45.32 N 107.00 E
Gurvan Sajchan uul ⩘ 102 43.50 N 103.30 E
Gurvantes 102 43.26 N 101.36 E
Gurzuf 78 44.33 N 34.17 E
Gus' ≃ 80 55.00 N 41.11 E
Gusar 85 39.28 N 67.50 E
Gušari 85 38.55 N 68.51 E
Gusarka 78 47.23 N 36.31 E
Gus'atin 78 49.05 N 26.11 E
Gusau 150 12.12 N 6.40 E
Gus'-Chrustal'nyj 80 55.37 N 40.40 E
Guselka 80 50.27 N 45.09 E
Güsen 54 52.21 N 11.59 E
Gusen ≃ 61 48.15 N 14.30 E
Gusev, Ross. 76 54.36 N 22.12 E
Gusev, Ross. 78 48.27 N 40.32 E
Gusevo 76 56.06 N 33.21 E
Gusevskij 80 55.40 N 40.34 E
Gushan, Zhg. 98 39.53 N 123.36 E
Gushan, Zhg. 98 36.30 N 116.53 E
Gushan, Zhg. 106 31.44 N 120.33 E
Gu Shan ∧, Zhg. 100 26.05 N 119.22 E
Gu Shan ∧, Zhg. 104 41.18 N 120.35 E
Gushanbeizifu 104 42.10 N 120.30 E
Gushankou 105 39.38 N 115.49 E
Gushantun 89 48.18 N 123.47 E
Gushanzi, Zhg. 98 40.22 N 120.03 E
Gushanzi, Zhg. 104 41.03 N 123.03 E
Gushi, Zhg. 100 28.34 N 119.24 E
Gushi, Zhg. 100 32.12 N 115.41 E
Gushiago 150 9.55 N 0.12 W
Gushikami 174m 26.07 N 127.45 E
Gushikawa 174m 26.21 N 127.52 E
Gushu, Zhg. 104 42.36 N 123.26 E
Gushu, Zhg. 105 39.55 N 117.35 E
Gushuji 98 34.15 N 115.48 E
Gusi 112 6.07 N 117.08 E
Gusino 76 54.44 N 31.22 E
Gusinoje, ozero ⊜ 88 51.12 N 106.24 E
Gusinoje Ozero 88 51.09 N 106.10 E
Gusinoozersk 88 51.17 N 106.30 E
Guskef 85 39.02 N 69.20 E
Guskhara 126 23.30 N 87.45 E
Gus'-Khrustal'nyy → Gus'-Chrustal'nyj 80 55.37 N 40.40 E
Guskube 175d 24.45 N 125.26 E
Gusong 102 28.18 N 105.14 E
Guspini 71 39.32 N 8.37 E
Gussago 64 45.35 N 10.09 E
Gusselby 40 59.39 N 15.14 E
Güssing 61 47.04 N 16.20 E
Gussola 64 45.00 N 10.20 E
Gusswerk 61 47.45 N 15.18 E
Gustav Holm, Kap › 176 67.00 N 34.00 W
Gustavo A. Madero ✦[8] 286a 19.29 N 99.07 W
Gustavo Díaz Ordaz 234 17.44 N 94.23 W
Gustavsberg 40 59.19 N 18.23 E
Gustavus 180 58.25 N 135.44 W
Güsten 54 51.49 N 11.35 E
Gustia 272b 22.59 N 88.26 E
Gustine, Ca., U.S. 226 37.15 N 120.59 W
Gustine, Tx., U.S. 196 31.51 N 98.24 W
Gustorf 56 51.04 N 6.34 E
Güstrow 54 53.48 N 12.10 E
Gusum 26 58.16 N 16.29 E
Gus'-Železnyj 80 55.03 N 41.10 E
Gutach 58 48.15 N 8.13 E
Gutaj 88 49.59 N 108.12 E
Gutanggou 104 42.02 N 124.10 E
Gutara ≃ 88 54.50 N 97.23 E
Gutarskij chrebet ⩘ 88 54.30 N 97.40 E
Gutau 61 48.25 N 14.37 E
Gutcher 46a 60.40 N 1.00 W
Gutenfels, Burg ⊥ 56 50.07 N 7.46 E
Guten Hoffnung, Kap der → Good Hope, Cape of › 158 34.24 S 18.30 E
Güterfelde 264a 52.22 N 13.12 E
Gütersloh 52 51.54 N 8.23 E
Guthrie, In., U.S. 218 38.59 N 86.31 W
Guthrie, Ky., U.S. 194 36.38 N 87.09 W
Guthrie, Ok., U.S. 196 35.52 N 97.25 W
Guthrie, Tx., U.S. 196 33.37 N 100.19 W
Guthrie Center 198 41.40 N 94.30 W
Guthrie Lake ⊜ 184 55.17 N 100.38 W
Gutian, Zhg. 100 26.36 N 118.46 E
Gutian, Zhg. 100 25.15 N 116.46 E
Gutian, Zhg. 100 25.43 N 116.57 E
Gutian ≃ 100 26.22 N 118.42 E
Gutierrez 248 19.25 S 63.34 W
Gutiérrez Zamora 234 20.27 N 97.05 W
Gutland ✦[1] 56 49.40 N 6.10 E
Gutob Bay c 116 12.09 N 119.54 E
Guton, gora ∧ 84 41.51 N 46.45 E
Gutorfölde 61 46.39 N 16.44 E
Guttannen 58 46.39 N 8.18 E
Guttau 54 51.15 N 14.34 E
Guttenberg, Ia., U.S. 190 42.47 N 91.05 W
Guttenberg, N.J., U.S. 276 40.47 N 74.00 W
Gutu 154 19.38 S 31.10 E
Gutujevskij, ostrov I 265a 59.54 N 30.14 E
Gutulia Nasjonalpark ♠ 26 62.02 N 12.12 E
Guty 78 50.08 N 35.21 E
Gützkow 54 53.56 N 13.24 E
Güvem 130 40.36 N 32.40 E
Guwāhāti 120 26.10 N 91.45 E
Guxhagen 56 51.12 N 9.28 E
Guxi 107 30.18 N 105.52 E
Guxian, Zhg. 98 37.35 N 121.09 E
Guxian, Zhg. 100 32.26 N 113.37 E
Guxian, Zhg. 100 27.09 N 115.31 E
Guxiandu 100 29.06 N 116.50 E
Guxiansi 100 32.01 N 116.20 E
Guxiong 106 31.55 N 118.38 E
Guy 222 29.21 N 95.47 W
Guyana □[1], S.A. 242 5.00 N 59.00 W
Guyana □[1], S.A. 246 5.00 N 59.00 W
Guyancourt 261 48.46 N 2.04 E
Guyancourt, Aéroport de ⊠ 261 48.45 N 2.05 E
Guyandotte ≃ 188 38.26 N 82.23 W
Guyane française → French Guiana □[2] 250 4.00 N 53.00 W
Guyane → Guyana □[1] 246 5.00 N 59.00 W
Guyang, Zhg. 98 34.58 N 114.58 E
Guyang, Zhg. 102 41.03 N 110.03 E
Guye 105 39.44 N 118.25 E
Guy Fawkes River National Park ♠ 166 30.02 S 152.18 E
Guyi, Zhg. 100 25.38 N 118.47 E
Guyi, Zhg. 107 30.22 N 103.33 E
Guyin 102 23.58 N 105.47 E
Guymon 196 36.40 N 101.28 W
Guyonne, Ruisseau la ≃ 261 48.49 N 1.52 E
Guyot, Mount ∧ 192 35.42 N 83.15 W
Guyra 166 30.14 S 151.40 E
Guysborough 186 45.23 N 61.30 W
Guys Mills 214 41.38 N 79.59 W
Guyton 192 32.20 N 81.23 W
Guyuan (Pingdingbu), Zhg. 98 41.40 N 115.41 E
Guyuan, Zhg. 102 36.01 N 106.17 E
Guzar 72 38.36 N 66.15 E
Güzel ≃ 84 39.44 N 43.01 E
Güzelbahçe 130 38.21 N 26.54 E
Güzelsu 130 36.54 N 31.53 E
Güzelyurt, Kıbrıs 130 35.12 N 32.59 E
Güzelyurt, Tür. 130 38.17 N 34.23 E
Güzelyurt Körfezi c 130 35.10 N 32.50 E
Guzhang 102 28.31 N 109.57 E
Guzhen, Zhg. 100 33.19 N 117.21 E
Guzhen, Zhg. 100 22.37 N 113.11 E
Guzhu 100 26.58 N 116.16 E
Guzmán 232 31.13 N 107.27 W
Guzmán, Laguna de ⊜ 200 31.20 N 107.30 W
Guzmán → Ciudad Guzmán 234 19.41 N 103.29 W
Gvardejsk 76 54.39 N 21.05 E
Gvardejskoje, Ukr. 78 48.44 N 35.19 E
Gvardejskoje, Ukr. 78 49.20 N 26.42 E
Gvardejskoje, Ukr. 78 45.07 N 34.01 E
Gvazda 78 50.44 N 40.30 E
Gvozdec 78 48.34 N 25.17 E
Gwa 110 17.36 N 94.35 E
Gwabegar 166 30.36 S 148.58 E
Gwadabawa 150 13.20 N 5.15 E
Gwādar 128 25.07 N 62.19 E
Gwagwada 150 10.14 N 7.14 E
Gwai 154 19.15 S 27.42 E
Gwai ≃ 154 17.59 S 26.52 E
Gwalangu 152 2.19 N 18.11 E
Gwalchmai 44 53.15 N 4.25 W
Gwāl Haidarzai 120 30.44 N 68.48 E
Gwalia 162 28.55 S 121.20 E
Gwalior 124 26.13 N 78.10 E
Gwambygine 168a 31.59 S 116.48 E
Gwanda 154 20.57 S 29.01 E
Gwandu 150 12.30 N 4.41 E
Gwane 154 4.43 N 25.50 E
Gwangjang Bridge ✦[5] 271b 37.33 N 127.05 E
Gwangju → Kwangju 98 35.09 N 126.54 E
Gwarzo 150 11.56 N 7.56 E
Gwasero 150 9.29 N 3.30 E
Gwash ≃ 42 52.39 N 0.27 W
Gwātar Bay c 128 25.04 N 61.36 E
Gwatt 58 46.43 N 7.38 E
Gwaun ≃ 42 52.00 N 4.58 W
Gwda ≃ 30 53.04 N 16.44 E
Gweebarra ≃ 48 54.50 N 8.20 W
Gweebarra Bay c 48 54.52 N 8.20 W
Gweedore 48 55.03 N 8.14 W
Gweesalia 48 54.07 N 9.54 W
Gwelo ≃ 154 18.45 S 28.36 E
Gwembe 154 16.30 S 27.35 E
Gwendraeth Fâch ≃ 42 51.44 N 4.18 W
Gwendraeth Fawr ≃ 42 51.43 N 4.18 W
Gwent □[6] 42 51.43 N 2.57 W
Gweru 154 19.27 S 29.49 E
Gweta 156 20.10 S 25.18 E
Gwinhurst 285 39.47 N 75.29 W
Gwinn 190 46.16 N 87.26 W
Gwinner 198 46.13 N 97.39 W
Gwobu 154 2.37 N 26.13 E
Gwongorella National Park ♠ 171a 28.10 S 153.17 E
Gwydir ≃ 166 29.27 S 149.48 E
Gwynedd 285 40.12 N 75.15 W
Gwynedd □[6] 28 53.00 N 4.00 W
Gwynedd Square 285 40.13 N 75.18 W
Gwynedd Valley 285 40.11 N 75.15 W
Gwynn 208 37.30 N 76.17 W
Gwynneville 218 39.39 N 85.38 W
Gwynn Island I 208 37.30 N 76.17 W
Gwynn Oak Amusement Park ♠ 284b 39.20 N 76.43 W
Gwynns Falls ≃ 284b 39.16 N 76.37 W
Gwynns Falls Park ♠ 284b 39.18 N 76.41 W
Gy 58 47.24 N 5.49 E
Gyál 264c 47.23 N 19.14 E
Gya La)(124 28.44 N 84.40 E
Gyáli-patak ≃ 264c 47.24 N 19.07 E
Gyangtse → Gyangzê 120 28.57 N 89.35 E
Gyangzê 120 28.57 N 89.35 E
Gyaring Co ⊜ 120 31.10 N 88.15 E
Gyaring Hu ⊜ 102 34.53 N 97.58 E
Gybdan 80 56.33 N 51.39 E
Gyda 74 70.52 N 78.30 E
Gydanskaja guba c 74 71.20 N 76.30 E
Gydanskij poluostrov ›[1] 74 70.50 N 79.00 E
Gyebu 164 3.03 S 133.51 E
Gyemo Chen ∧ 124 27.20 N 88.52 E
Gyeongbog Palace ʊ 271b 37.36 N 126.57 E
Gyeongju → Kyŏngju 98 35.51 N 129.14 E
Gyirong, Zhg. 120 28.29 N 85.20 E
Gyirong, Zhg. 120 28.57 N 85.15 E
Gyldenløves Fjord c[2] 176 64.30 N 41.30 W
Gyldenløveshøj ∧[2] 41 55.33 N 11.52 E
Gylling 41 55.53 N 10.11 E
Gymea Bay 274a 34.02 S 151.05 E
Gym Peak ∧ 200 32.04 N 107.35 W
Gympie 166 26.11 S 152.40 E
Gyobingauk 110 18.13 N 95.39 E
Gyōda 94 36.08 N 139.28 E
Gyoma 30 46.56 N 20.50 E
Gyöngyös 30 47.47 N 19.56 E
Gyöngyös ≃ 61 47.14 N 16.55 E
Győr 30 47.42 N 17.38 E
Győr-Moson-Sopron □[6] 30 47.35 N 17.15 E
Gypsey Race ≃ 44 54.05 N 0.12 W
Gypsum, Co., U.S. 200 39.38 N 106.57 W
Gypsum, Ks., U.S. 198 38.42 N 97.25 W
Gypsum, Oh., U.S. 214 41.29 N 82.52 W
Gypsum Creek ≃, U.S. 200 37.09 N 109.52 W
Gypsum Creek ≃, Ks., U.S. 198 38.51 N 97.25 W
Gypsum Hills ⩘[2] 196 36.25 N 99.20 W
Gypsum Point › 176 61.53 N 114.35 W
Gypsumville 184 51.45 N 98.35 W
Gyrbovec 78 46.50 N 29.21 E
Gysinge 40 60.17 N 16.53 E
Gyttorp 40 59.31 N 14.58 E
Gyula 30 46.39 N 21.17 E
Gyulafehérvár → Alba-Iulia 38 46.04 N 23.35 E
Gžat' ≃ 76 55.56 N 34.33 E
Gžatsk 86 55.42 N 78.11 E
Gžel' 82 55.36 N 38.24 E
Gzhatsk → Gagarin 76 55.33 N 35.00 E

H

Haag 61 48.07 N 14.34 E
Haag am Hausruck 60 48.11 N 13.38 E
Haagen 58 47.38 N 7.40 E
Haag in Oberbayern 60 48.10 N 12.11 E
Haag → 's-Gravenhage 52 52.06 N 4.18 E
Haaksbergen 52 52.09 N 6.44 E
Haalenberg 156 26.52 S 15.30 E
Haaltert 50 50.54 N 4.00 E
Haamstede 52 51.43 N 3.45 E
Haan 56 51.11 N 7.00 E
Haapajärvi 26 63.45 N 25.20 E
Haapajärvi ⊜ 26 63.33 N 27.00 E
Haapamäki 26 62.15 N 24.28 E
Haapavesi 26 64.08 N 25.22 E
Haapiti 174s 17.34 S 149.52 W
Haapsalu 76 58.56 N 23.33 E
Haar 60 48.06 N 11.44 E
Haar ✦[8] 263 51.26 N 7.13 E
Ha'Arava (Wādī al-'Arabah) V, Asia 132 30.10 N 35.10 E
Ha'Arava (Wādī al-Jayb) V, Asia 132 30.58 N 35.24 E
Haardt ⩘ 56 49.15 N 8.00 E
Haaren, Dtsch. 52 51.34 N 8.44 E
Haaren, Ned. 52 51.36 N 5.12 E
Haarlem, Ned. 52 52.23 N 4.38 E
Haarlem, S. Afr. 158 33.44 S 23.20 E
Haarlemmermeer ✦[1] 52 52.15 N 4.38 E
Haarstrang ∧ 52 51.35 N 8.10 E
Haarzopf ✦[8] 263 51.25 N 6.58 E
Haast 172 43.53 S 169.03 E
Haast ≃ 172 43.50 S 169.02 E
Haast Bluff 162 23.30 S 131.50 E
Haast Pass)(172 44.06 S 169.21 E
Haasts Bluff Reserve ✦[4] 162 23.30 S 130.30 E
Haatinao, Pointe › 174x 9.47 S 138.51 W
Haava, Canal ⊔ 174x 9.53 S 139.04 W
Hab ≃ 120 24.53 N 66.41 E
Habahe 86 47.53 N 86.12 E
Habana, Bahía de la c 286b 23.08 N 82.20 W
Habaqi, Zhg. 104 42.38 N 122.02 E
Habaqi, Zhg. 104 42.36 N 122.52 E
Habaqila 102 42.01 N 106.02 E
Habartov 54 50.08 N 12.33 E
Ḥabashīyah, Jabal ⩘ 144 16.40 N 49.40 E
Habaswein 154 1.01 N 39.29 E
Ḥabawnah, Wādī V 144 17.51 N 44.59 E
Habay-la-Neuve 56 49.44 N 5.39 E
Ḥabbān 144 14.21 N 47.05 E
Ḥabbānīyah, Hawr al- ⊜ 128 33.17 N 43.29 E
Ḥabbūsh 132 33.24 N 35.29 E
Hab Chauki 120 25.01 N 66.53 E
Habère-Poche 58 46.15 N 6.29 E
Haberfield 274a 33.53 S 151.08 E
Haberli 130 37.19 N 41.38 E
Habermehl Peak ∧ 9 71.49 S 6.38 E
Ḥabīb, Wādī V 142 27.20 N 31.30 E
Habiganj 120 24.23 N 91.25 E
Habikino 96 34.33 N 135.37 E
Habīlah 140 12.41 N 22.33 E
Habinghorst 263 51.35 N 7.18 E
Habo 26 57.55 N 14.04 E
Habob, Wādī V 140 18.07 N 35.01 E
Habomai-shotō → Malaja Kuril'skaja Gr'ada II 92a 43.30 N 146.10 E
Haboro 92a 44.22 N 141.42 E
Hābra 126 22.50 N 88.38 E
Habsburg ⊥ 58 47.28 N 8.13 E
Habsheim 58 47.44 N 7.25 E
Habu 270 34.27 N 135.24 E
Habur (Nahr al-Khābūr) ≃ 130 35.08 N 40.26 E
Habutaki 270 34.25 N 135.26 E
Hache, Lac la ⊜ 182 51.50 N 121.30 W
Hachen 56 51.22 N 7.59 E
Hachenburg 56 50.39 N 7.50 E
Hachi 120 27.46 N 94.01 E
Hachijō 270 34.37 N 135.48 E
Hachijō-jima I 90 33.05 N 139.48 E
Hachiman 94 35.45 N 136.57 E
Hachiman-misaki › 94 35.08 N 140.19 E
Hachiman → Ōmi-hachiman 94 35.08 N 136.06 E
Hachinohe 92 40.30 N 141.29 E
Hachiōji 94 35.39 N 139.20 E
Hachmühlen 52 52.10 N 9.28 E
Hacıbektaş 130 38.57 N 34.35 E
Hacienda Heights 228 34.00 N 117.57 W
Hacienda Miravalles 236 10.41 N 85.14 W
Hacienda Murciélago 236 10.55 N 85.44 W
Hacıhamza 130 41.05 N 34.28 E
Hacılar 130 38.39 N 35.27 E
Hack, Mount ∧ 166 30.46 S 138.48 E
Hackås 26 62.55 N 14.31 E
Hackberry, Az., U.S. 200 35.22 N 113.43 W
Hackberry, La., U.S. 194 29.59 N 93.20 W
Hackberry Creek ≃, Ks., U.S. 198 38.48 N 100.03 W
Hackberry Creek ≃, Tx., U.S. 222 31.53 N 97.12 W
Hackensack 210 40.53 N 74.02 W
Hackensack ≃ 276 40.43 N 74.06 W
Hacketstown 48 52.52 N 6.33 W
Hackett, Ar., U.S. 194 35.11 N 94.24 W
Hackett, Pa., U.S. 279b 40.15 N 80.01 W
Hacketts 260 51.45 N 0.05 W
Hackettstown 210 40.52 N 74.48 W
Hacking ≃ 274a 34.04 S 151.06 E
Hacking, Port c 274a 34.05 S 151.09 E
Hackleburg 194 34.16 N 87.49 W
Hackney ✦[8] 260 51.33 N 0.03 W
Hack Point 208 39.27 N 75.52 W
Håckren ⊜ 26 63.11 N 13.35 E
Haco 152 10.12 S 15.44 E
Hacreş Dağları ⩘ 130 38.38 N 41.37 E
Hadāli 123 32.18 N 72.12 E
Hadalīya 140 16.10 N 36.06 E
Hadamar 56 50.27 N 8.02 E
Ḥaḍan, Ḥarrat ≐[9] 144 21.30 N 41.23 E
Hadano 94 35.22 N 139.14 E
Ḥadāribah, Ra's al- › 140 22.04 N 36.54 E
HaDarom □[5] 132 30.40 N 34.50 E
Hadat 89 49.40 N 119.40 E
Hadayingzi 104 42.22 N 121.40 E
Ḥadd, Ra's al- › 118 22.32 N 59.48 E
Haddad, Ouadi V 146 14.40 N 18.46 E
Ḥaddādīn, Qārat al- ∧[2] 142 30.04 N 30.58 E
Haddam, Ct., U.S. 207 41.28 N 72.30 W
Haddam, Ks., U.S. 198 39.51 N 97.18 W
Haddenham, Eng., U.K. 42 51.46 N 0.56 W
Haddenham, Eng., U.K. 42 52.22 N 0.09 E
Haddington 46 55.58 N 2.47 W
Haddock 192 33.01 N 83.25 W
Haddon Downs 166 26.21 S 140.50 E
Haddonfield 208 39.53 N 75.02 W
Haddon Heights 208 39.52 N 75.03 W
Haddon Hills 285 39.54 N 75.03 W
Hadejia 150 12.30 N 9.59 E
Hadejia ≃ 134 12.50 N 10.51 E
Hadeln, Land ✦[1] 52 53.45 N 8.45 E
Haden 171a 27.14 S 151.53 E
Ḥadera 132 32.26 N 34.55 E
Ḥadera ≃ 132 32.27 N 34.53 E
Hadersdorf ✦[8] 264b 48.13 N 16.14 E
Hadersfeld 264b 48.20 N 16.15 E
Haderslev 41 55.15 N 9.30 E
Haderslev Fjord c 41 55.17 N 9.40 E
Hadfield, Austl. 274b 37.42 S 144.56 E
Hadfield, Eng., U.K. 262 53.28 N 1.58 W
Hadībū 118 12.38 N 54.02 E
Ḥadīd, Jabal ∧[2] 142 30.20 N 30.06 E
Ḥadīd, Jabal al- ∧[2] 142 28.47 N 31.04 E
Hadım 130 36.59 N 32.28 E
Hadjout 34 36.31 N 2.25 E
Hadleigh, Eng., U.K. 42 52.03 N 0.58 E
Hadleigh, Eng., U.K. 260 51.33 N 0.37 E
Hadleigh Castle ⊥ 260 51.33 N 0.36 E
Hadley, Eng., U.K. 42 52.42 N 2.29 W
Hadley, Ma., U.S. 207 42.20 N 72.35 W
Hadley, Mi., U.S. 216 42.57 N 83.24 W
Hadley, N.Y., U.S. 210 43.19 N 73.50 W
Hadley, Pa., U.S. 214 41.25 N 80.14 W
Hadley Bay c 176 72.30 N 107.45 W
Hadley Creek ≃ 219 39.37 N 91.12 W
Hadlock 224 48.01 N 122.45 W
Hadlow 42 51.14 N 0.20 E
Hadlyme 207 41.25 N 72.24 W
Hadmersleben 54 51.59 N 11.18 E
Hadong, Taehan 98 35.05 N 127.44 E
Ha Dong, Viet 110 20.58 N 105.46 E
Ḥaḍramawt ✦[1] 144 15.00 N 50.00 E
Hadrian's Wall ⊥ 44 54.59 N 2.26 W
Hadsten 41 56.20 N 10.03 E
Hadsund 26 56.43 N 10.07 E
Hadyai → Hat Yai 110 7.01 N 100.28 E
Haeju 98 38.02 N 125.42 E
Haemgon-ni ✦[8] 271b 37.35 N 126.49 E
Haena 229b 22.14 N 159.34 W
Haenam 98 34.34 N 126.35 E
Haena Point › 229b 22.14 N 159.34 W
Haenertsburg 156 24.00 S 29.50 E
Haengyŏng-ni 98 42.33 N 129.56 E
Haernao 104 41.46 N 120.28 E
Hafeïra, Oued el V 148 25.18 N 10.48 W
Hafelekarspitze ∧ 64 47.19 N 11.23 E
Haffen-Mehr 52 51.44 N 6.28 E
Hafford 184 52.43 N 107.21 W
Haffouz 36 35.38 N 9.41 E
Hafik 130 39.52 N 37.24 E
Ḥafīra, Qā' al- ≚ 132 31.06 N 36.14 E
Ḥafīrat al-'Ayda 128 26.26 N 39.10 E
Ḥafīt, Jabal ∧ 128 24.03 N 55.46 E
Ḥāfiẓ, Bi'r ⊤[4] 142 30.51 N 29.40 E
Hāfizābād 123 32.04 N 73.41 E
Hāflong 120 25.11 N 93.02 E
Hafnarfjördur 24a 64.03 N 21.56 W
Haft Gel 128 31.27 N 49.27 E
Hafun, Ras › 144 10.27 N 51.24 E
Haga, Nihon 94 36.32 N 140.04 E
Haga, Nihon 96 35.09 N 134.33 E
Hagachi-zaki › 94 34.41 N 138.45 E
HaGadol, HaMakhtésh ≐[7] 132 30.56 N 34.59 E
Haga-Haga 158 32.46 S 28.14 E
Hagal 98 40.23 N 127.15 E
HaGalil (Galilee) □[9] 132 32.54 N 35.20 E
Hagaman 210 42.59 N 74.09 W
Hagan 192 32.09 N 81.56 W
Hagari ≃ 122 15.45 N 76.56 E
Hagar Shores 216 42.13 N 86.22 W
Hagarstown 219 38.57 N 89.10 W
Hage 52 53.36 N 7.17 E
Hagelberg ∧[2] 54 52.08 N 12.32 E
Hagemeister Island I 180 58.40 N 161.00 W
Hagen, Dtsch. 52 52.34 N 9.26 E
Hagen, Dtsch. 52 52.12 N 7.59 E
Hagen, Dtsch. 56 51.22 N 7.28 E
Hagenbrunn 264b 48.20 N 16.25 E
Hagengebirge ⩘ 64 47.32 N 13.07 E
Hagenow 54 53.26 N 11.11 E
Hagensborg 182 52.23 N 126.33 W
Hagenwerder 54 51.04 N 14.58 E
Hagere Hiywet 144 8.59 N 37.51 E
Hagere Selam 144 6.29 N 38.31 E
Hagerman, Id., U.S. 202 42.48 N 114.53 W
Hagerman, N.M., U.S. 196 33.06 N 104.19 W
Hagerman Corners 275b 43.50 N 79.18 W
Hagerstown, In., U.S. 218 39.54 N 85.09 W
Hagerstown, Md., U.S. 188 39.38 N 77.43 W
Hagersville 212 42.58 N 80.03 W
Hagetmau 32 43.40 N 0.35 W
Hagfors 40 60.02 N 13.42 E
Haggen ⊜ 40 60.06 N 15.13 E
Haggetts Pond ⊜ 283 42.39 N 71.12 W
Haggin, Mount ∧ 202 46.05 N 113.05 W
Hagi 96 34.24 N 131.25 E
Ha Giang 110 22.50 N 104.59 E
Hagitani 270 34.54 N 135.35 E
Hagiwara 94 35.52 N 137.12 E
Hagley 42 52.26 N 2.08 W
Hagley Museum ʊ 285 39.46 N 75.35 W
Hagondange 56 49.15 N 6.10 E
HaGosherim 132 33.13 N 35.37 E
Hags Head › 48 52.57 N 9.30 W
Hague, Sk., Can. 184 52.30 N 106.25 W
Hague, N.D., U.S. 198 46.01 N 99.59 W
Hague, Cap de la › 32 49.43 N 1.57 W
Haguenau 56 48.49 N 7.47 E
Hagues Peak ∧ 200 40.29 N 105.38 W
Hahaïa 157a 11.33 S 43.17 E
Hahajima-rettō II 14 26.37 N 142.10 E
Haharro, Uebi ≃ 144 1.37 N 44.13 E
Hāhipur 272b 22.47 N 88.10 E
Hahira 192 30.59 N 83.22 W
Hahlen 52 52.18 N 8.50 E
Hahn am See 56 50.31 N 7.53 E
Hahnbach 60 49.32 N 11.48 E
Hahndorf 168b 35.03 S 138.49 E
Hahnenberg 263 51.12 N 7.24 E
Hahnenkamm ∧ 64 47.25 N 12.22 E
Hahnenklee-Bockswiese 52 51.51 N 10.20 E
Hahnerberg ✦[8] 263 51.13 N 7.09 E
Hahnstätten 56 50.18 N 8.04 E
Hahntown 279b 40.19 N 79.44 W
Haho ≃ 150 6.17 N 1.23 E
Hahyŏn-ni 98 38.33 N 127.57 E
Hai ≃ 105 39.00 N 117.43 E
Hai'an 100 32.34 N 120.28 E
Haian Shanmo ⩘ 100 23.25 N 121.25 E
Haibara, Nihon 94 34.32 N 135.57 E
Haibara, Nihon 94 34.44 N 138.13 E
Haibatpur 272a 28.37 N 77.26 E
Haibei 89 47.39 N 126.51 E
Haicheng, Zhg. 100 24.25 N 117.51 E
Haicheng, Zhg. 104 40.52 N 122.45 E
Haicheng ≃ 104 40.56 N 122.21 E
Haidargarh 124 26.37 N 81.22 E
Haidārpur ✦[8] 272a 28.43 N 77.09 E
Haidenaab ≃ 60 49.36 N 12.08 E
Haiderabad → Hyderābād, India 122 17.23 N 78.29 E
Haiderabad → Hyderābād, Pāk. 120 25.22 N 68.22 E
Haidershofen 61 48.05 N 14.28 E
Haidian 105 39.59 N 116.18 E
Haiding 60 48.13 N 13.58 E
Haidmühle 60 48.50 N 13.46 E
Haïdra 36 35.34 N 8.27 E
Haidstein ∧ 60 49.13 N 12.48 E
Haidun 100 29.36 N 121.49 E
Hai Duong 110 20.56 N 106.19 E
Haifa, Bay of → Ḥefa, Mifraz c 132 32.52 N 35.03 E
Haifa → Ḥefa 132 32.50 N 35.00 E
Haifeng 100 22.59 N 115.21 E
Haifengzheng 106 31.53 N 121.46 E
Haifuzhen 106 31.59 N 121.42 E
Haig 162 31.01 S 126.05 E
Haig, Mount ∧ 182 49.17 N 114.29 W
Haiger 56 50.44 N 8.13 E
Haigerloch 58 48.22 N 8.48 E
Haigh 262 53.35 N 2.36 W
Haigler 198 40.00 N 101.56 W
Haihezhen 100 33.44 N 120.02 E
Haijima 268 35.42 N 139.21 E
Haikang 102 20.56 N 110.04 E
Haikou, Zhg. 100 28.20 N 120.06 E
Haikou, Zhg. 100 25.43 N 119.28 E
Haikou, Zhg. 100 29.04 N 117.46 E
Haikou, Zhg. 102 20.03 N 110.19 E
Haiku 229a 20.55 N 156.19 W
Ḥā'il 128 27.33 N 41.42 E
Hailākāndi 120 24.41 N 92.34 E
Hailar 89 49.12 N 119.42 E
Hailar ≃ 90 49.35 N 117.55 E
Hailasen 89 46.13 N 121.00 E
Hailesboro 212 44.18 N 75.27 W
Hailey, Eng., U.K. 260 51.46 N 0.01 W
Hailey, Id., U.S. 202 43.31 N 114.18 W
Haileybury 190 47.27 N 79.38 W
Haileyville 196 34.51 N 95.34 W
Hailin 89 44.35 N 129.22 E
Hailing Dao I 102 21.37 N 111.55 E
Haillicourt 50 50.28 N 2.35 E
Hailong (Meihekou) 98 42.32 N 125.38 E
Hailsham 42 50.52 N 0.16 E
Hailun 89 47.28 N 126.58 E
Hailuoto 26 65.00 N 24.43 E
Hailuoto I 26 65.02 N 24.42 E
Haiman Tepesi ∧[2] 267b 41.12 N 29.15 E
Haimen, Zhg. 100 28.41 N 121.27 E
Haimen, Zhg. 100 23.14 N 116.38 E
Haimen, Zhg. 106 31.55 N 121.10 E
Haimen Wan c 100 23.09 N 116.34 E
Haimhausen 60 48.19 N 11.34 E
Haimiao 98 37.13 N 119.51 E
Haiming 64 47.15 N 10.53 E
Haina 56 51.02 N 8.58 E
Hainan □[4] 110 19.00 N 109.30 E
Hainan Dao I 110 19.00 N 109.30 E
Hainan → Hainan Dao I 110 19.00 N 109.30 E
Hainault ✦[8] 260 51.36 N 0.06 E
Hainaut □[4] 50 50.30 N 3.50 E
Hainaut □[9] 50 50.30 N 3.50 E
Hainburg an der Donau 61 48.09 N 16.57 E
Hainchen 56 50.51 N 8.12 E
Haines, Ak., U.S. 180 59.14 N 135.27 W
Haines, Or., U.S. 202 44.54 N 117.56 W
Haines City 220 28.06 N 81.37 W
Haines Falls 210 42.11 N 74.05 W
Haines Junction 180 60.45 N 137.30 W
Hainesport 208 39.59 N 74.49 W
Hainesville 278 42.21 N 88.04 W
Hainewalde 54 50.54 N 14.41 E

Symbols in the index entries represent the broad categories identified in the key at the right. Symbols with superior numbers (⩘[1]) identify subcategories (see complete key on page *I · 1*).

Symbole im Register stellen die rechts im Schlüssel erklärten Kategorien dar. Symbole mit hochgestellten Ziffern (⩘[1]) bezeichnen Unterabteilungen einer Kategorie (vgl. vollständiger Schlüssel auf Seite *I · 1*).

Los símbolos incluídos en el texto del índice representan las grandes categorias identificadas con la clave a la derecha. Los símbolos con numeros en su parte superior (⩘[1]) identifican las subcategorías (véase la clave completa en la página *I · 1*).

Les symboles de l'index représentent les catégories indiquées dans la légende à droite. Les symboles suivis d'un indice (⩘[1]) représentent des sous-catégories (voir légende complète à la page *I · 1*).

Os símbolos incluídos no texto do índice representam as grandes categorias identificadas com a chave à direita. Os símbolos com números em sua parte superior (⩘[1]) identificam as subcategorias (veja-se a chave completa à página *I · 1*).

∧	Mountain	Berg	Montaña	Montagne	Montanha
⩘	Mountains	Gebirge	Montañas	Montagnes	Montanhas
)(	Pass	Paß	Paso	Col	Passo
V	Valley, Canyon	Tal, Cañon	Valle, Cañón	Vallée, Canyon	Vale, Canhão
≚	Plain	Ebene	Llano	Plaine	Planície
›	Cape	Kap	Cabo	Cap	Cabo
I	Island	Insel	Isla	Île	Ilha
II	Islands	Inseln	Islas	Îles	Ilhas
≐	Other Topographic Features	Andere Topographische Objekte	Otros Elementos Topográficos	Autres données topographiques	Outros acidentes topográficos

ESPAÑOL — Nombre / Página / Lat. °′ / Long. °′ W = Oeste

Hainfeld 61 48.02 N 15.46 E
Hainich ⩘ 54 51.05 N 10.27 E
Hainichen 54 50.58 N 13.07 E
Haining (Xiashi) 106 30.32 N 120.41 E
Hainleite ⩘ 54 51.20 N 10.48 E
Hainsberg 54 50.59 N 13.38 E
Hainzenberg 64 47.13 N 11.54 E
Hai Phong 110 20.52 N 106.41 E
Haiqiao 106 31.47 N 121.19 E
Haiqing 89 47.53 N 134.40 E
Haitangxi 107 29.33 N 106.35 E
Haitan Xia ⩂ 100 25.27 N 119.38 E
Haiti (Haïti) □1, N.A. 230 19.00 N 72.25 W
Haiti (Haïti) □1, N.A. 238 19.00 N 72.25 W
Haitou, Zhg. 98 34.56 N 119.10 E
Haitou, Zhg. 110 19.34 N 108.58 E
Haitouji 98 35.23 N 115.19 E
Haitun 102 38.50 N 96.41 E
Haiwee Reservoirs ⊜1 204 36.10 N 117.57 W
Haiyan, Zhg. 102 36.54 N 101.12 E
Haiyan, Zhg. 106 30.31 N 120.57 E
Haiyang (Dongcun) 98 36.46 N 121.10 E
Haiyang Dao I 98 39.02 N 123.14 E
Haiyuan 102 36.35 N 105.40 E
Haizhou, Zhg. 98 34.34 N 119.11 E
Haizhou, Zhg. 100 22.40 N 113.10 E
Haizhoumiao 104 42.00 N 121.39 E
Haizhou Wan ⊂ 98 35.00 N 119.30 E
Haizhouyingzi 104 42.07 N 121.46 E
Ḩajar, Tall al- ∧2 132 33.21 N 37.03 E
Ḩajar Banga 140 11.30 N 23.00 E
Hajdú-Bihar □6 30 47.25 N 21.30 E
Hajdúböszörmény 30 47.41 N 21.30 E
Hajdúnánás 30 47.51 N 21.26 E
Hajdúszoboszló 30 47.27 N 21.24 E
Hajeb el Ayoun 36 35.24 N 9.33 E
Hajiadian 98 41.32 N 117.10 E
Hājīganj 126 23.15 N 90.50 E
Hajiki-saki ≻ 92 38.19 N 138.31 E
Haji Langar 120 35.52 N 79.21 E
Hājīpur, India 124 25.41 N 85.13 E
Hājīpur, India 126 22.49 N 87.38 E
Hajipur, India 272b 22.57 N 88.19 E
Ḩājj, Wādī al- V 142 30.03 N 32.45 E
Hajnówka 30 52.45 N 23.36 E
Hajo-do I 98 34.17 N 126.03 E
Ḩajr, Wādī V 144 14.04 N 48.40 E
Ḩajūl, Wādī V 142 29.42 N 32.22 E
Hakata 96 34.12 N 133.07 E
Hakata-jima I 96 34.13 N 133.05 E
Hakataramea ≃ 172 44.44 S 170.29 E
Hakendover 56 50.48 N 4.59 E
Hakha 110 22.39 N 93.37 E
Haki 96 33.20 N 130.50 E
Ḩakīm, Abyār al- ⇁4 146 31.36 N 23.29 E
Hakkâri 128 37.34 N 43.45 E
Hakkâri □4 128 37.20 N 43.45 E
Hakken-san ∧ 92 34.10 N 135.54 E
Hakkōda-san ∧ 92 40.40 N 140.53 E
Hako-dake ∧ 92a 44.40 N 142.25 E
Hakodate 92a 41.45 N 140.43 E
Hakone 94 35.12 N 139.06 E
Hakone-no-seki-ato ⊥ 94 35.10 N 139.02 E
Hakone-tōge ⋊ 94 35.11 N 139.01 E
Hakone-yama ∧ 94 35.14 N 139.02 E
Håksberg 40 60.11 N 15.12 E
Hakskeenpan ≍ 158 26.48 S 20.12 E
Haktanır 130 36.51 N 38.50 E
Hakuba 94 36.42 N 137.52 E
Hakui 94 36.53 N 136.47 E
Hakupu 174v 19.06 S 169.50 W
Hakusan 94 34.38 N 136.21 E
Haku-san ∧ 94 36.09 N 136.46 E
Haku-san-kokuritsu-kōen ♦ 94 36.12 N 136.47 E
Hakushū 94 35.48 N 138.20 E
Hakuta 96 35.21 N 133.17 E
Hakuta ≃ 96 35.26 N 133.15 E
Hāla 120 25.49 N 68.25 E
Halaaobao 102 42.11 N 107.20 E
Ḩalab (Aleppo) 130 36.12 N 37.10 E
Ḩalab □8 130 36.00 N 37.30 E
Halabjah 128 35.10 N 45.59 E
Halachó 232 20.29 N 90.05 W
Halaerjige 104 42.24 N 122.11 E
Halagetu 104 42.34 N 122.40 E
Halahai 89 44.39 N 125.07 E
Halahushao 104 42.11 N 121.44 E
Ḩalā'ib 140 22.13 N 36.38 E
Halalii Lake ⊜ 229b 21.52 N 160.11 W
Halamutai 86 46.10 N 84.52 E
Halangingie Point ≻ 174v 19.03 S 169.57 W
Halasa 140 14.26 N 30.39 E
Halas-patak ≃ 264c 47.24 N 19.20 E
Halataojie 104 42.30 N 122.06 E
Halatieke Shan ⩘ 85 40.30 N 77.05 E
Halaula 229d 20.14 N 155.48 W
Hålaveden ⩘2 26 58.05 N 14.45 E
Halawa, Cape ≻ 229a 21.10 N 156.43 W
Halawa Bay ⊂ 229a 21.10 N 156.44 W
Halawa Heights 229c 21.22 N 157.55 W
Halawotelake 120 37.17 N 90.20 E
Halbach ✦8 263 51.12 N 7.12 E
Halba Deset I 144 12.56 N 42.55 E
Halbe 52 52.06 N 13.42 E
Halberstadt 54 51.54 N 11.02 E
Halbert, Lake ⊜1 222 32.04 N 96.25 W
Halberton 42 50.55 N 3.25 W
Halbrite 184 49.30 N 103.33 W
Ḩalbūn 132 33.40 N 36.15 E
Halbury 168b 34.05 S 138.31 E
Halcombe 172 40.09 S 175.30 E
Halcon, Mount ∧ 116 13.16 N 121.00 E
Halcottsville 210 42.12 N 74.36 W
Haldeman 218 38.15 N 83.19 W
Halden 26 59.09 N 11.23 E
Halden ✦8 263 51.23 N 7.31 E
Haldensleben 54 52.18 N 11.26 E
Haldern 52 51.46 N 6.27 E
Haldī 126 22.03 N 88.05 E
Haldī ≃ 126 22.01 N 88.03 E
Haldībāri 124 26.20 N 88.46 E
Haldībunia 126 22.26 N 89.38 E
Haldimand-Norfolk □6 212 42.48 N 80.10 W
Haldwāni 124 29.13 N 79.31 E
Hale, Eng., U.K. 44 53.23 N 2.21 W
Hale, Eng., U.K. 262 53.20 N 2.48 W
Hale, Mo., U.S. 194 39.36 N 93.20 W
Hale ≃ 162 24.56 S 135.53 E
Haleakala Crater ≛6 229a 20.43 N 156.13 W
Haleakala National Park ♦ 229a 20.44 N 156.13 W
Halebarns 262 53.22 N 2.19 W
Haleb → Ḩalab 130 36.12 N 37.10 E
Hale Center 196 34.03 N 101.50 W
Hale Creek ≃ 282 37.23 N 122.06 W
Haledon 276 40.56 N 74.11 W
Haledon Reservoir ⊜1 276 40.59 N 74.12 W
Hale Eddy 210 42.00 N 75.23 W
Hale Head ≻ 262 53.19 N 2.48 W
Haleiwa 229c 21.35 N 158.06 W
Halekii-Pihana Heiaus State Monument ⊥ 229a 20.54 N 156.29 W
Halenkov 30 49.19 N 18.08 E
Hales Corners 216 42.56 N 88.02 W
Halesite 207 40.52 N 73.25 W
Halesowen 42 52.26 N 2.05 W
Hale Street 260 51.13 N 0.24 E
Halesworth 42 52.21 N 1.30 E
Halewood 262 53.22 N 2.49 W
Haleyville 194 34.13 N 87.37 W
Half Assini 150 5.03 N 2.53 W
Ḩalfāyah, Naqb al- (Halfaya Pass) ⋊ 140 31.30 N 25.11 E
Halfaya Pass → Ḩalfāyah, Naqb al- ⋊ 140 31.30 N 25.11 E

FRANÇAIS — Nom / Page / Lat. °′ / Long. °′ W = Ouest

Half Day 278 42.12 N 87.56 W
Halfeti 130 37.15 N 37.52 E
Half Hollow Hills 276 40.48 N 73.21 W
Halfing 64 47.57 N 12.16 E
Halfmoon Bay, B.C., Can. 182 49.31 N 123.54 W
Halfmoon Bay, N.Z. 172 46.54 S 168.08 E
Half Moon Bay, Ca., U.S. 226 37.27 N 122.25 W
Halfmoon Bay ⊂, Austl. 274b 37.58 S 145.00 E
Half Moon Bay ⊂, Ca., U.S. 282 37.29 N 122.28 W
Half Moon Bay Airport ⊠ 282 37.31 N 122.30 W
Half Moon Bay State Beach ♦ 282 37.29 N 122.27 W
Halfway, Md., U.S. 188 39.37 N 77.45 W
Halfway, Or., U.S. 202 44.52 N 117.06 W
Halfway ≃ 176 56.10 N 121.35 W
Halfway Lake ⊜ 184 55.03 N 98.24 W
Halgån ≃ 40 60.16 N 13.27 E
Ḩalḩūl 132 31.35 N 35.07 E
Ḩalī ⇁4 144 18.42 N 41.20 E
Haliburton 212 45.03 N 78.31 W
Haliburton □6 212 44.10 N 78.30 W
Haliburton Lake ⊜ 212 45.12 N 78.24 W
Halibut Point ≻ 283 42.42 N 70.38 W
Haliç (Golden Horn) ⊂ 267b 41.02 N 28.58 E
Halicarnassus ⊥ 130 37.03 N 27.23 E
Halidmand 212 42.56 N 79.51 W
Halifax, Austl. 166 18.35 S 146.18 E
Halifax, N.S., Can. 186 44.39 N 63.36 W
Halifax, Eng., U.K. 44 53.44 N 1.52 W
Halifax, Ma., U.S. 207 41.59 N 70.51 W
Halifax, N.C., U.S. 192 36.19 N 77.35 W
Halifax, Pa., U.S. 208 40.28 N 76.55 W
Halifax, Va., U.S. 192 36.45 N 78.55 W
Halifax, Canadian Forces Base ■ 186 44.43 N 63.38 W
Halifax Bay ⊂ 166 18.50 S 146.30 E
Halifax Citadel National Historic Park ♦ 186 44.36 N 63.39 W
Halifax Harbour ⊂ 186 44.35 N 63.31 W
Haliimaile 229a 20.52 N 156.20 W
Halīl ≃ 128 27.28 N 58.44 E
Halimatazi 104 42.37 N 122.35 E
Halim Perdanakusuma Airport ■ 269e 6.16 S 106.54 E
Halimun, Gunung ∧ 115a 6.42 S 106.26 E
Halingen 263 51.27 N 7.44 E
Hālisahar 126 22.56 N 88.25 E
Haliyāl 122 15.20 N 74.46 E
Haljala 76 59.26 N 26.16 E
Halkalı ✦8 267b 41.02 N 28.47 E
Halkapınar 130 37.25 N 34.13 E
Halkett, Cape ≻ 180 70.49 N 152.12 W
Halkirk 46 58.30 N 3.30 W
Halkyn 262 53.14 N 3.11 W
Halkyn Mountain ∧ 262 53.14 N 3.13 W
Hall, Austl. 171b 35.10 S 149.04 E
Hall, In., U.S. 218 39.33 N 86.32 W
Hall, N.Y., U.S. 210 42.48 N 77.04 W
Hällabrottet 40 59.07 N 15.12 E
Halladale ≃ 46 58.33 N 3.55 W
Hallam 274b 38.01 S 145.06 E
Hallam Peak ∧ 182 52.11 N 118.46 W
Halland □9 26 57.00 N 12.40 E
Hallandale 220 25.58 N 80.08 W
Hallands Län □6 26 56.45 N 13.00 E
Hallands Väderö I 26 56.26 N 12.33 E
Halla-san ∧ 90 33.22 N 126.32 E
Hallau 58 47.42 N 8.27 E
Hällberga 40 59.19 N 16.36 E
Hällbybrunn 40 59.24 N 16.25 E
Hällbymagasinet ⊜1 26 63.56 N 17.13 E
Halle, Bel. 50 50.44 N 4.13 E
Halle, Dtsch. 52 52.04 N 8.22 E
Halle, Dtsch. 52 51.59 N 9.33 E
Halle, Dtsch. 54 51.29 N 11.58 E
Halleberg ∧2 26 58.23 N 12.27 E
Hällefors 40 59.47 N 14.30 E
Hälleforsnäs 40 59.10 N 16.30 E
Hallein 64 47.41 N 13.06 E
Hällekis 26 58.38 N 13.25 E
Hallen 26 63.11 N 14.05 E
Hallenberg 56 51.06 N 8.37 E
Hallencourt 50 49.59 N 1.53 E
Halle-Neustadt 54 51.29 N 11.56 E
Hallertau ✦1 60 48.35 N 11.45 E
Hällestad 40 58.44 N 15.34 E
Hallett, Cape ≻ 9 72.19 S 170.18 E
Hallettsville 222 29.26 N 96.56 W
Halley ⊛3 9 75.36 S 26.46 W
Halliday 198 47.21 N 102.20 W
Halligen II 30 54.35 N 8.35 E
Halling 260 51.21 N 0.27 E
Hallingdalselvi ≃ 26 60.24 N 9.35 E
Hällingsåfallet ⌞ 26 64.20 N 14.20 E
Hall in Tirol 64 47.17 N 11.31 E
Hall Island I 180 60.40 N 173.05 W
Hall Islands II 14 8.37 N 152.00 E
Halliste ≃ 76 58.31 N 25.03 E
Hall-i'-th'-Wood ♦ 262 53.36 N 2.26 W
Hall Lake ⊜ 176 68.41 N 82.17 W
Hall Meadow Brook Reservoir ⊜1 207 41.52 N 73.10 W
Hall Mountain ∧ 202 48.49 N 117.15 W
Hällnäs 26 64.19 N 19.38 E
Hallock 198 48.46 N 96.56 W
Hallowell 188 44.17 N 69.47 W
Hall Peninsula ≻1 176 63.30 N 66.00 W
Halls 194 35.52 N 89.23 W
Halls Bayou ≃ 222 29.12 N 95.07 W
Hallsberg 40 59.04 N 15.07 E
Halls Brook ≃ 283 42.00 N 70.43 W
Halls Creek 162 18.16 S 127.46 E
Halls Creek ≃ 200 37.18 N 110.45 W
Halls Gap 166 37.08 S 142.31 E
Halls Lake ⊜ 212 45.07 N 78.45 W
Halls Stream ≃ 206 45.01 N 71.30 W
Hållsta 40 59.18 N 16.27 E
Hallstadt 56 49.55 N 10.52 E
Hallstahammar 40 59.37 N 16.13 E
Hallstatt 64 47.33 N 13.39 E
Hallstätter See ⊜ 64 47.35 N 13.39 E
Hallstavik 40 60.03 N 18.36 E
Hallstead 210 41.57 N 75.44 W
Hallsville, Mo., U.S. 219 39.07 N 92.13 W
Hallsville, Tx., U.S. 222 32.30 N 94.34 W
Halluin 50 50.47 N 3.08 E
Hallwiler See ⊜ 58 47.18 N 8.13 E
Hallwood 208 37.52 N 75.35 W
Halma 56 50.05 N 5.08 E
Halmahera I 108 1.00 N 128.00 E
Halmahera, Laut (Halmahera Sea) ⇁2 108 1.00 S 129.00 E
Halmstad 26 56.39 N 12.50 E
Halpine Village 284c 39.04 N 77.07 W
Hals 26 57.00 N 10.19 E
Halsafjorden ⊂2 26 63.03 N 8.11 E
Halsall 262 53.35 N 2.57 W
Halsbrücke 54 50.57 N 13.21 E
Halsey, Ne., U.S. 198 41.54 N 100.16 W
Halsey, Or., U.S. 202 44.23 N 123.06 W
Halsey Harbor ⊂ 116 11.45 N 119.56 E
Halsey Valley 210 42.08 N 76.27 W
Hälsingborg → Helsingborg 41 56.03 N 12.42 E
Hälsingland □9 26 61.30 N 17.00 E
Halstad 198 47.21 N 96.49 W
Halstead, Eng., U.K. 42 51.57 N 0.38 E
Halstead, Eng., U.K. 260 51.20 N 0.08 E
Halstead, Ks., U.S. 198 38.00 N 97.30 W
Halstenbek 52 53.38 N 9.50 E
Halsteren 52 51.32 N 4.16 E
Halstow Marshes ≍ 260 51.29 N 0.33 E

PORTUGUÊS — Nome / Página / Lat. °′ / Long. °′ W = Oeste

Haltang ≃ 102 39.00 N 94.40 E
Haltern 52 51.46 N 7.10 E
Haltiatunturi ∧ 24 69.18 N 21.16 E
Haltom City 222 32.47 N 97.16 W
Halton, Eng., U.K. 44 54.05 N 2.46 W
Halton, Eng., U.K. 262 53.20 N 2.42 W
Halton □6 212 43.30 N 79.53 W
Halton □8 262 53.20 N 2.44 W
Halton Hills 212 43.39 N 79.55 W
Haltwhistle 44 54.58 N 2.27 W
Halura, Pulau I 115b 10.19 S 120.11 E
Ḩaluẓa, Ḩolot ≛8 132 31.05 N 34.28 E
Halūzonī, Wādī al- V 273c 30.05 N 31.24 E
Halvarsgårdarna 40 60.24 N 15.23 E
Halvarsnoren ⊜ 40 59.35 N 14.36 E
Halver 56 51.11 N 7.30 E
Halvorson, Mount ∧ 182 53.15 N 120.33 W
Halwell 42 50.22 N 3.43 W
Ham, Fr. 50 49.45 N 3.04 E
Ham, Tchad 146 10.00 N 15.41 E
Ham ✦8 260 51.26 N 0.19 W
Ham ≃ 158 28.32 S 19.34 E
Ham, Oued el ≃ 34 35.42 N 4.52 E
Ḩamad 140 15.19 N 33.43 E
Hamada 96 34.53 N 132.05 E
Hamadān 128 34.48 N 48.30 E
Hamadān □4 128 35.00 N 48.40 E
Ḩamāh 130 35.08 N 36.45 E
Ḩamāh □8 130 35.10 N 37.00 E
Hamahika-jima I 174m 26.19 N 127.57 E
Hamakeza 89 47.05 N 120.52 E
Hamakita 94 34.48 N 137.47 E
Hamale 150 10.59 N 2.44 W
Hamamatsu 94 34.42 N 137.44 E
Hamamatsukita-kichi, Kōkū-jieitai- ■ 94 34.45 N 137.42 E
Hamamözü 130 40.48 N 35.02 E
Haman 98 35.15 N 128.24 E
Hamanaka 92a 43.05 N 145.10 E
Hamana-ko ⊜ 94 34.45 N 137.34 E
Hamano 268 35.33 N 140.08 E
Hamaoka 94 34.39 N 138.08 E
Hamar 26 60.48 N 11.06 E
Hamasaka 96 35.37 N 134.27 E
Ḩamāṭah, Jabal ∧ 140 24.12 N 35.00 E
Hamatang 98 40.12 N 124.20 E
Hama-tombetsu 92a 45.07 N 142.23 E
Hambach 56 49.04 N 7.02 E
Hambaek-san ∧ 98 37.09 N 128.55 E
Hambantota 122 6.07 N 81.07 E
Hambergen 52 53.18 N 8.49 E
Hamber Provincial Park ♦ 182 52.25 N 117.40 W
Hamble 42 50.52 N 1.19 W
Hambledon 42 50.56 N 1.04 W
Hambleton 44 53.52 N 2.57 W
Hambleton Hills ⩘2 44 54.16 N 1.12 W
Hamborn ✦8 263 51.29 N 6.46 E
Hambourg → Hamburg 52 53.33 N 9.59 E
Hamburg, Ciskei 158 33.17 S 27.28 E
Hamburg, Dtsch. 52 53.33 N 9.59 E
Hamburg, Ar., U.S. 194 33.13 N 91.47 W
Hamburg, Ct., U.S. 207 41.23 N 72.21 W
Hamburg, Il., U.S. 219 39.14 N 90.43 W
Hamburg, Ia., U.S. 198 40.36 N 95.39 W
Hamburg, Mi., U.S. 216 42.27 N 83.48 W
Hamburg, N.J., U.S. 210 41.09 N 74.34 W
Hamburg, N.Y., U.S. 210 42.42 N 78.49 W
Hamburg, Pa., U.S. 208 40.33 N 75.58 W
Hamburg □3 52 53.35 N 10.00 E
Hamburg, Flughafen ⊠ 52 53.38 N 10.00 E
Hamburg Airport ⊠ 284a 42.42 N 78.55 W
Hamburg Ditch ≍ 208 36.31 N 76.33 W
Hamburger Hallig ≻1 41 54.36 N 8.49 E
Hamburg Mountains ⩘ 276 41.08 N 74.32 W
Hamburgo → Hamburg 52 53.33 N 9.59 E
Hamburgsund 26 58.33 N 11.16 E
Ḩamḑ, Wādī al- V 128 25.54 N 36.38 E
Ḩamdah 144 19.02 N 43.36 E
Hamdallay Timbou 150 12.03 N 10.37 W
Hamdam Āb, Dasht-e ≍ 128 34.45 N 61.30 E
Ḩamdānah 144 19.58 N 40.35 E
Hamden, Ct., U.S. 207 41.23 N 72.53 W
Hamden, N.Y., U.S. 210 42.12 N 75.00 W
Hamden, Oh., U.S. 188 39.09 N 82.31 W
Hamdibey 130 39.50 N 27.15 E
Häme ✦1 26 61.45 N 25.10 E
Hämeenkangas ✦3 26 61.45 N 22.40 E
Hämeenkylä 26 60.16 N 24.47 E
Hämeen lääni □4 26 61.30 N 24.30 E
Hämeenlinna 26 61.00 N 24.27 E
Hamel 168a 32.52 S 115.55 E
HaMelah, Yam → Dead Sea ⊜ 132 31.30 N 35.30 E
Hämelerwald 52 52.22 N 10.05 E
Hamelin 162 26.26 S 114.11 E
Hamelin Pool ⊂ 162 26.15 S 114.05 E
Hameln 52 52.06 N 9.21 E
HaMerkaz □5 132 32.05 N 34.55 E
Hamer Koke 144 5.12 N 36.45 E
Hamero Hadad 144 7.34 N 42.18 E
Hamersleben 54 52.04 N 11.05 E
Hamersley Range ⩘ 162 21.53 S 116.46 E
Hamersley Range National Park ♦ 162 22.40 S 118.15 E
Hamersville 218 38.55 N 83.59 W
Hames Creek ≃ 226 35.53 N 120.50 W
Hamgyŏng Namdo □4 98 40.00 N 127.30 E
Hamgyŏng Pukdo □4 98 41.45 N 129.50 E
Hamgyŏng-sanmaek ⩘ 98 41.00 N 128.30 E
Ham House ⊥ 260 51.27 N 0.19 W
Hamhŭng 98 39.54 N 127.32 E
Hami (Kumul) 102 42.48 N 93.27 E
Hamidiye 130 41.09 N 26.40 E
Hamiguitan, Mount ∧ 116 6.44 N 126.11 E
Hamilton, Austl. 166 37.45 S 142.02 E
Hamilton, Ber. 240a 32.17 N 64.46 W
Hamilton, On., Can. 212 43.15 N 79.51 W
Hamilton, N.Z. 172 37.47 S 175.17 E
Hamilton, Scot., U.K. 46 55.47 N 4.03 W
Hamilton, Al., U.S. 194 34.08 N 87.59 W
Hamilton, Ak., U.S. 180 62.54 N 163.53 W
Hamilton, Ga., U.S. 192 32.45 N 84.52 W
Hamilton, Il., U.S. 190 40.23 N 91.20 W
Hamilton, In., U.S. 216 41.32 N 84.54 W
Hamilton, Ks., U.S. 198 37.58 N 96.09 W
Hamilton, Ma., U.S. 207 42.37 N 70.52 W
Hamilton, Mi., U.S. 216 42.40 N 86.00 W
Hamilton, Mo., U.S. 194 39.44 N 93.59 W
Hamilton, Mt., U.S. 202 46.14 N 114.09 W
Hamilton, N.Y., U.S. 210 42.49 N 75.32 W
Hamilton, N.C., U.S. 192 35.56 N 77.12 W
Hamilton, Oh., U.S. 218 39.23 N 84.33 W
Hamilton, R.I., U.S. 207 41.32 N 71.26 W
Hamilton, Tx., U.S. 196 31.42 N 98.07 W
Hamilton, Wa., U.S. 224 48.31 N 121.59 W
Hamilton □6, In., U.S. 218 40.03 N 86.01 W
Hamilton □6, N.Y., U.S. 210 43.24 N 74.25 W
Hamilton □6, Oh., U.S. 218 39.06 N 84.31 W
Hamilton ✦8 284b 39.21 N 76.33 W
Hamilton ≃ 166 23.30 S 139.47 E
Hamilton, Lake ⊜ 220 28.03 N 81.39 W
Hamilton, Lake ⊜1 194 34.30 N 93.05 W
Hamilton, Mount ∧, Ak., U.S. 180 61.10 N 159.46 W
Hamilton, Mount ∧, Ca., U.S. 226 37.21 N 121.38 W
Hamilton, Mount ∧, Nv., U.S. 204 39.14 N 115.32 W
Hamilton Acres 180 64.51 N 147.40 W
Hamilton Air Force Base ■ 282 38.03 N 122.31 W

Hamilton City 204 39.44 N 122.00 W
Hamilton Creek ≃ 162 26.40 S 135.19 E
Hamilton Creek Indian Reserve ✦4 182 50.11 N 120.30 W
Hamilton Dome 200 43.46 N 108.34 W
Hamilton Harbour ⊂ 212 43.17 N 79.50 W
Hamilton Hill 168a 32.05 S 115.46 E
Hamilton Hotel 166 22.50 S 140.35 E
Hamilton Inlet ⊂ 176 54.00 N 57.30 W
Hamilton Lake ⊜ 216 41.33 N 84.55 W
Hamilton Mountain ∧ 188 43.25 N 74.22 W
Hamilton Park, In., U.S. 216 40.17 N 85.19 W
Hamilton Park, Pa., U.S. 208 40.02 N 76.20 W
Hamilton Sound ⩂ 186 49.30 N 54.30 W
Hamilton Square 285 40.13 N 74.39 W
Hamilton-Wentworth □6 212 43.15 N 80.00 W
Ḩamīm, Wādī al- V 146 30.10 N 21.32 E
Hamina 26 60.34 N 27.12 E
Hamiota 184 50.11 N 100.36 W
Ḩāmir, Wādī V 128 31.37 N 42.12 E
Hamīrpur, India 123 31.41 N 76.31 E
Hamīrpur, India 124 25.57 N 80.09 E
Hamjong-ni 98 38.59 N 125.17 E
Hamler 216 41.13 N 84.02 W
Hamlet, In., U.S. 216 41.32 N 86.34 W
Hamlet, N.C., U.S. 192 34.53 N 79.41 W
Hamlet, Oh., U.S. 218 39.01 N 84.12 W
Hamlet, Mount ∧ 180 68.47 N 165.57 W
Hamley Bridge 168b 34.21 S 138.41 E
Hamlin, N.Y., U.S. 210 43.18 N 77.55 W
Hamlin, Pa., U.S. 210 41.24 N 75.24 W
Hamlin, Tx., U.S. 196 32.53 N 100.08 W
Hamlin, W.V., U.S. 188 38.16 N 82.06 W
Hamlin Beach State Park ♦ 210 43.22 N 77.58 W
Hamlin Lake ⊜ 190 44.03 N 86.27 W
Hamlin Valley Wash V 200 38.53 N 114.01 W
Hamm 52 51.41 N 7.49 E
Hamm ✦8, Dtsch. 263 51.15 N 6.25 E
Hamm ✦8, Dtsch. 263 51.12 N 6.44 E
Hamm ✦8, Dtsch. 263 51.23 N 7.03 E
Ḩammād, Wādī V 142 29.45 N 32.24 E
Hamma Hamma ≃ 224 47.33 N 123.03 W
Håmmålfjell ∧ 26 62.27 N 11.17 E
Ḩammām at-Turkumān 130 36.32 N 39.03 E
Hammamet, Alg. 36 35.27 N 7.58 E
Hammamet, Tun. 148 36.24 N 10.37 E
Hammamet, Golfe de ⊂ 36 36.05 N 10.40 E
Hammam Lif 148 36.44 N 10.20 E
Ḩammānā 132 33.49 N 35.44 E
Hammar 40 58.49 N 14.57 E
Ḩammār, Hawr al- ⊜ 128 30.50 N 47.10 E
Hammarby 40 60.33 N 16.34 E
Hammarn 40 59.45 N 14.30 E
Hammarö 40 59.20 N 13.31 E
Hammarön I 40 59.19 N 13.31 E
Hammarstrand 26 63.06 N 16.21 E
Hamme 50 51.06 N 4.08 E
Hamme ≃ 52 53.10 N 8.44 E
Hammel 41 56.15 N 9.52 E
Hammelburg 56 50.07 N 9.53 E
Hamme-Mille 56 50.47 N 4.43 E
Hammerdal 26 63.36 N 15.21 E
Hammerfest 24 70.40 N 23.42 E
Hämmern 263 51.08 N 7.21 E
Hammershus ⊥ 26 55.16 N 14.45 E
Hammersley Inlet ⊂ 224 47.12 N 123.00 W
Hammersmith ✦8 260 51.30 N 0.14 W
Hammerum 41 56.08 N 9.04 E
Hamminkeln 52 51.44 N 6.35 E
Hammon 196 35.37 N 99.22 W
Hammonasset ≃ 207 41.16 N 72.33 W
Hammond, In., U.S. 216 41.35 N 87.30 W
Hammond, La., U.S. 194 30.30 N 90.27 W
Hammond, N.Y., U.S. 212 44.26 N 75.41 W
Hammond, Or., U.S. 224 46.12 N 123.57 W
Hammond, Wi., U.S. 190 44.58 N 92.26 W
Hammond Island I, Austl. 164 10.35 S 142.13 E
Hammond Island I, Ca., U.S. 282 38.06 N 121.57 W
Hammond Pond Park ♦ 283 42.19 N 71.11 W
Hammondsport 210 42.24 N 77.13 W
Hammondsville 214 40.33 N 80.43 W
Hammondville 274a 33.57 S 150.57 E
Hammonia 158 28.43 S 27.49 E
Hammonton 208 39.38 N 74.48 W
Hamningberg 24 70.31 N 30.37 E
Ham-Nord 206 45.54 N 71.39 W
Hamoir 56 50.26 N 5.32 E
Hamont 56 51.15 N 5.33 E
HaMore, Giv'at ∧ 132 32.37 N 35.21 E
Hamorton 285 39.52 N 75.39 W
Hamoyet, Jabal ∧ 144 17.33 N 38.02 E
Hampden, Austl. 168b 34.09 S 139.03 E
Hampden, Nf., Can. 186 49.33 N 56.51 W
Hampden, N.Z. 172 45.19 S 170.49 E
Hampden, Me., U.S. 188 44.44 N 68.50 W
Hampden, Ma., U.S. 207 42.03 N 72.24 W
Hampden, N.D., U.S. 198 48.32 N 98.39 W
Hampden □6 207 42.07 N 72.36 W
Hampden Sydney 192 37.15 N 78.29 W
Hampetorp 40 59.09 N 15.40 E
Hampi 122 15.24 N 76.37 E
Hampshire 216 42.05 N 88.31 W
Hampshire □6, Eng., U.K. 42 51.05 N 1.15 W
Hampshire □6, Ma., U.S. 207 42.19 N 72.38 W
Hampshire Downs ⩘1 42 51.15 N 1.17 W
Hampshire Heights 279b 40.20 N 79.33 W
Hampstead, P.Q., Can. 275a 45.29 N 73.38 W
Hampstead, Md., U.S. 208 39.36 N 76.51 W
Hampstead, N.C., U.S. 192 34.22 N 77.42 W
Hampstead ✦8 260 51.33 N 0.11 W
Hampstead Heath ♦ 260 51.34 N 0.10 W
Hampton, Austl. 274b 37.56 S 145.00 E
Hampton, N.B., Can. 186 45.32 N 65.51 W
Hampton, On., Can. 212 43.58 N 78.45 W
Hampton, Ar., U.S. 194 33.32 N 92.28 W
Hampton, Ct., U.S. 207 41.47 N 72.03 W
Hampton, Fl., U.S. 192 29.51 N 82.07 W
Hampton, Ga., U.S. 192 33.23 N 84.16 W
Hampton, Ia., U.S. 190 42.44 N 93.12 W
Hampton, Ne., U.S. 198 40.52 N 97.53 W
Hampton, N.H., U.S. 188 42.56 N 70.50 W
Hampton, N.J., U.S. 210 40.42 N 74.57 W
Hampton, Pa., U.S. 208 39.56 N 77.04 W
Hampton, S.C., U.S. 192 32.52 N 81.06 W
Hampton, Tn., U.S. 192 36.17 N 82.10 W
Hampton, Va., U.S. 208 37.01 N 76.20 W
Hampton ✦8 260 51.25 N 0.22 W
Hampton, Mount ∧ 9 76.29 S 125.48 W
Hampton Bays 207 40.52 N 72.31 W
Hampton Butte ∧ 202 43.46 N 120.17 W
Hampton Court Palace ⊛ 42 51.24 N 0.20 W
Hampton Harbour ⊂ 162 20.40 S 116.30 E
Hampton National Historic Site ⊥ 284b 39.25 N 76.35 W
Hampton Park 274b 38.02 S 145.15 E
Hampton Roads ⇁3 208 36.58 N 76.20 W
Hampton Roads Bridge-Tunnel ✦5 208 37.00 N 76.18 W
Hampton Tableland ⩘1 162 32.10 S 126.10 E
Hamp'yŏng 98 35.05 N 126.30 E
Hamr 54 50.35 N 13.35 E
Hamra 26 61.39 N 15.00 E

Ḩamrā', Al-Ḩamādah al- ✦2 146 30.00 N 12.00 E
Hamra, As Saquia al V 148 27.15 N 13.21 W
Hamra, Ouadi V 146 12.52 N 21.15 E
Ḩamrah, Jabal al- ∧ 132 29.39 N 34.47 E
Ḩamran, Har ∧ 132 30.41 N 34.34 E
Hamra Nationalpark ♦ 26 61.45 N 14.55 E
Ḩamrat ash-Shaykh 140 14.35 N 27.58 E
Hams Bluff ≛4 241n 17.46 N 64.52 W
Hams Fork ≃ 200 41.35 N 109.59 W
Hamstreet 42 51.04 N 0.51 E
Ham-Sud 206 45.46 N 71.36 W
Ham Tan 110 10.40 N 107.46 E
Hamtramck 216 42.23 N 83.02 W
Hāmūn, Daryācheh-ye ⊜ 128 30.50 N 61.07 E
Hamur 84 39.36 N 42.59 E
Hamura 94 35.45 N 139.19 E
Hamyang 98 35.32 N 127.42 E
Hamzalı 130 38.19 N 41.09 E
Han 150 10.41 N 2.27 W
Han ≃, Zhg. 100 23.41 N 116.38 E
Han ≃, Zhg. 102 30.35 N 114.17 E
Han, Grottes de ≛5 56 50.08 N 5.15 E
Han, Nong ⊜ 110 17.12 N 104.11 E
Hana 229a 20.45 N 155.59 W
Hanábana ≃ 240p 22.23 N 80.58 W
Hanahan 192 32.55 N 80.01 W
Hanailike 85 39.16 N 76.26 E
Ḩanak 128 25.33 N 36.56 E
Hanakaoo Point ≻ 229a 20.55 N 156.42 W
Hanalei 229b 22.12 N 159.30 W
Hanalei Bay ⊂ 229b 22.13 N 159.31 W
Hanamaki 92 39.23 N 141.07 E
Hanamaulu 229b 21.59 N 159.21 W
Hanamenu, Baie ⊂ 174x 9.46 S 139.08 W
Hanam-ni 98 38.23 N 126.43 E
Hanang ∧ 154 4.26 S 35.24 E
Hanapepe 229b 21.54 N 159.35 W
Hānār Char 126 23.08 N 90.38 E
Hanataka-sen ∧ 96 35.24 N 132.45 E
Hanateio 174x 9.59 S 139.06 W
Hanatetena 174x 9.58 S 139.04 W
Hanau 56 50.08 N 8.55 E
Hanaui 174x 9.45 S 139.05 W
Hanawa, Nihon 94 36.57 N 140.25 E
Hanawa, Nihon 268 35.13 N 139.53 E
Hanbury ≃ 176 63.37 N 104.33 W
Hanceville, B.C., Can. 182 51.55 N 123.03 W
Hanceville, Al., U.S. 194 34.03 N 86.46 W
Hanchang 107 30.26 N 103.43 E
Hancheng, Zhg. 102 35.28 N 110.29 E
Hancheng, Zhg. 105 39.39 N 118.02 E
Hanches 261 48.36 N 1.39 E
Hanchō 270 34.49 N 135.27 E
Han-ch'ŏn ≃ 271b 37.33 N 127.02 E
Hanchuan 100 30.39 N 113.48 E
Hanchung → Hanzhong 102 33.08 N 107.02 E
Hancock, Md., U.S. 188 39.41 N 78.10 W
Hancock, Mi., U.S. 190 47.07 N 88.34 W
Hancock, Mn., U.S. 198 45.29 N 95.47 W
Hancock, N.Y., U.S. 210 41.57 N 75.17 W
Hancock, Wi., U.S. 190 44.08 N 89.31 W
Hancock □6, Il., U.S. 219 40.13 N 91.15 W
Hancock □6, In., U.S. 218 39.47 N 85.46 W
Hancock □6, Oh., U.S. 216 41.02 N 83.39 W
Hancock □6, W.V., U.S. 214 40.30 N 80.33 W
Hancock, Lake ⊜ 220 27.58 N 81.50 W
Hancocks Bridge 208 39.30 N 75.27 W
Hancun 105 39.24 N 116.36 E
Handa, Nihon 94 34.53 N 136.56 E
Handa, Nihon 96 34.02 N 134.02 E
Handa, Som. 144 10.40 N 51.07 E
Handa I 46 58.22 N 5.12 W
Handan 98 36.37 N 114.29 E
Handaokou 98 34.16 N 116.24 E
Handawor 123 34.24 N 74.17 E
Handen 40 59.10 N 18.08 E
Handeni 154 5.26 S 38.01 E
Handforth 262 53.21 N 2.13 W
Handlová 30 48.44 N 18.46 E
Handöl 26 63.16 N 12.26 E
Handorf 52 51.59 N 7.41 E
Handsworth 184 49.48 N 103.00 W
Handub 140 19.14 N 37.16 E
Handzame 50 51.02 N 3.00 E
Haneda Airport ⊠ 268 35.33 N 139.46 E
HaNegev (Negev Desert) ✦1 132 30.30 N 34.55 E
Haney 224 49.13 N 122.36 W
Hane-yama ∧ 96 33.14 N 131.08 E
Hane-zaki ≻ 96 33.22 N 134.02 E
Hanford 226 36.19 N 119.38 W
Hanford Site ⊛3 202 46.35 N 119.30 W
Han'gang 98 34.39 N 114.38 E
Han-gang ≃ 98 37.45 N 126.11 E
Hanga Roa 174z 27.09 S 109.26 W
Hangatiki 172 38.15 S 175.10 E
Hangbu 100 28.53 N 118.49 E
Hangchow Bay → Hangzhou Wan ⊂ 100 30.25 N 121.00 E
Hangchow → Hangzhou 106 30.15 N 120.10 E
Hanger ≃ 144 9.35 N 36.02 E
Hanggai 106 30.35 N 119.23 E
Hanggin Houqi 102 40.55 N 107.15 E
Hanggin Qi 102 39.56 N 108.54 E
Hang Hau Town 271d 22.19 N 114.16 E
Hanging Gardens ♦ 272c 18.58 N 72.48 E
Hanging Rock State Park ♦ 192 36.25 N 80.15 W
Hangingstone Hill ∧2 42 50.39 N 3.57 W
Hanging Woman Creek ≃ 202 45.19 N 106.31 W
Hangklip, Kaap ≻ 158 34.26 S 18.48 E
Hangkou 100 29.03 N 114.27 E
Hangman Creek ≃ 202 47.38 N 117.27 W
Hangö (Hanko) 26 59.50 N 22.57 E
Hangou 105 39.18 N 117.07 E
Hang-Tcheou → Hangzhou 106 30.15 N 120.10 E
Hangtou 106 31.01 N 121.35 E
Hangtschou → Hangzhou 106 30.15 N 120.10 E
Hangu, Pak. 123 33.32 N 71.04 E
Hangu, Zhg. 105 39.15 N 117.47 E
Hangu, Zhg. 107 28.58 N 104.30 E
Hanguang 100 24.16 N 113.08 E
Hanguchang 107 29.32 N 106.21 E
Hangugang 105 39.15 N 116.56 E
Hangzhou (Hangchow) 106 30.15 N 120.10 E
Hangzhou Wan (Hangchow Bay) ⊂ 100 30.25 N 121.00 E
Hani 130 38.24 N 40.24 E
Hänigsen 52 52.29 N 10.05 E
Hanimadu I 122 6.45 N 73.09 E
Ḩanīsh II 144 13.45 N 42.45 E
Ḩanīsh al-Kabīr, Jazīrat al- I 144 13.43 N 42.45 E
Ḩanita 132 33.05 N 35.10 E
Hanjalipan 112 2.15 S 112.47 E
Hanjiagou 104 40.42 N 120.47 E
Hanjiang 100 25.30 N 119.06 E
Hanjiapuzi 104 40.48 N 123.14 E
Hanjiashu 105 39.11 N 117.04 E
Hanjiawa 106 31.16 N 119.18 E
Hankamer 222 29.51 N 94.38 W
Hankasalmi 26 62.23 N 26.26 E
Hanke 26 59.12 N 10.47 E
Hankendi 130 38.35 N 39.04 E
Hankensbüttel 54 52.44 N 10.36 E
Hankey 158 33.50 S 24.53 E
Hankins 210 41.49 N 75.05 W
Hankinson 198 46.04 N 96.54 W

Hanko → Hangö 26 59.50 N 22.57 E
Hankow → Wuhan 100 30.36 N 114.17 E
Hanks Pond ⊜ 276 41.05 N 74.26 W
Hanku → Hangu 105 39.15 N 117.47 E
Hānle 120 32.48 N 79.00 E
Hanley 184 51.37 N 106.27 W
Hanmer 190 46.39 N 80.56 W
Hanmer Springs 172 42.31 S 172.49 E
Hanmiao 89 44.33 N 119.59 E
Hann ≃ 164 17.10 S 126.10 E
Hann, Mount ∧ 164 15.51 S 125.48 E
Hanna, Ab., Can. 182 51.38 N 111.54 W
Hanna, In., U.S. 216 41.24 N 86.46 W
Hanna, Ok., U.S. 196 35.12 N 95.53 W
Hanna, Wy., U.S. 200 41.52 N 106.33 W
Hanna City 190 40.41 N 89.47 W
Hannaford 198 47.18 N 98.11 W
Hannah 198 48.58 N 98.41 W
Hannah Bay ⊂ 176 51.05 N 79.45 W
Hannastown 214 40.21 N 79.30 W
Hannibal, Mo., U.S. 219 39.42 N 91.21 W
Hannibal, N.Y., U.S. 210 43.19 N 76.34 W
Hanningfield Reservoir ⊜1 260 51.39 N 0.31 E
Hannō 94 35.51 N 139.19 E
Hannover 52 52.24 N 9.44 E
Hannover □5 52 52.30 N 9.15 E
Hannover, Flughafen ⊠ 52 52.27 N 9.42 E
Hannut 56 50.40 N 5.05 E
Hanö I 26 56.00 N 14.50 E
Hanobası 130 38.35 N 33.50 E
Hanöbukten ⊂ 26 55.45 N 14.30 E
Ha Noi 110 21.02 N 105.51 E
Hanönü 130 41.38 N 34.28 E
Hanoura 96 33.57 N 134.38 E
Hanover, On., Can. 212 44.09 N 81.02 W
Hanover, S. Afr. 158 31.04 S 24.29 E
Hanover, Ct., U.S. 207 41.38 N 72.03 W
Hanover, Il., U.S. 190 42.15 N 90.16 W
Hanover, In., U.S. 218 38.42 N 85.28 W
Hanover, Ks., U.S. 198 39.53 N 96.52 W
Hanover, Ma., U.S. 207 42.06 N 70.48 W
Hanover, Mi., U.S. 216 42.06 N 84.33 W
Hanover, N.H., U.S. 188 43.42 N 72.17 W
Hanover, N.M., U.S. 200 32.48 N 108.05 W
Hanover, Oh., U.S. 214 40.04 N 82.15 W
Hanover, Pa., U.S. 208 39.48 N 76.59 W
Hanover, Va., U.S. 208 37.45 N 77.22 W
Hanover, Wi., U.S. 216 42.38 N 89.10 W
Hanover □6 208 37.42 N 77.20 W
Hanover, Isla I 254 51.00 S 74.40 W
Hanover Airport ⊠ 276 40.50 N 74.21 W
Hanover Center 283 42.07 N 70.50 W
Hanover → Hannover 52 52.24 N 9.44 E
Hanover Park 216 42.00 N 88.09 W
Hanover Road 158 30.58 S 24.33 E
Hanoverton 214 40.45 N 80.56 W
Hanovre → Hannover 52 52.24 N 9.44 E
Hanpan, Cape ≻ 175e 5.01 S 154.37 E
Hanryeosudo Kukrip Kongwŏn ♦ 98 34.46 N 128.30 E
Hansanjiazi 104 41.44 N 122.57 E
Hansard 182 54.05 N 121.52 W
Hanscom Air Force Base ■ 207 42.28 N 71.17 W
Hans Creek ≃ 210 43.06 N 74.08 W
Hansdiha 124 24.36 N 87.05 E
Hansen Dam ✦6 280 34.16 N 118.23 W
Hansen Flood Control Basin ≍1 228 34.16 N 118.23 W
Hanshan 100 31.44 N 118.08 E
Hansharo ⊥ 94 35.02 N 138.56 E
Hansi, India 120 32.27 N 77.50 E
Hānsi, India 123 29.06 N 75.58 E
Hansia 272b 22.48 N 88.24 E
Hanska 198 44.08 N 94.29 W
Hānskhāli 126 23.21 N 88.37 E
Hans Lollik Island I 240m 18.24 N 64.55 W
Hanslope 42 52.06 N 0.49 W
Hans Meyer Range ⩘ 164 4.20 S 152.55 E
Hanson 207 42.04 N 70.52 W
Hanson ≃ 162 20.15 S 133.25 E
Hanson Lake ⊜ 184 54.42 N 102.49 W
Hanstholm 26 57.07 N 8.38 E
Han-sur-Lesse 56 50.08 N 5.11 E
Han-sur-Nied 56 48.59 N 6.26 E
Hansville 224 47.55 N 122.33 W
Hansweert 52 51.26 N 4.00 E
Hantaj 88 49.31 N 103.13 E
Hāntālbunia 126 22.44 N 89.31 E
Hantamsberg ⩘ 158 31.22 S 19.45 E
Hantan → Handan 98 36.37 N 114.29 E
Hantes ≃ 50 50.19 N 4.11 E
Hant's Harbour 186 48.01 N 53.16 W
Hantsport 186 45.04 N 64.11 W
Hantu, Pulau I 271c 1.14 N 103.45 E
Hantu, Tanjong ≻ 114 4.18 N 100.34 E
Hantzsch ≃ 176 67.32 N 72.25 W
Hanumangarh 123 29.35 N 74.19 E
Hanumān Nagar 124 26.30 N 86.51 E
Hanušovce nad Topľou 30 49.02 N 21.30 E
Hanušovice 30 50.05 N 16.55 E
Hanveden ⩘2 40 59.07 N 18.00 E
Hanwood 166 34.20 S 146.03 E
Hanworth ✦8 260 51.26 N 0.23 W
Hanxinzhuang 105 40.16 N 116.44 E
Hanyang 107 29.44 N 103.44 E
Hanyangping 102 32.41 N 108.34 E
Hanyin 102 32.42 N 108.50 E
Hanyū 94 36.10 N 139.32 E
Hanyuan 102 29.22 N 102.38 E
Hanyuangai 102 29.30 N 102.31 E
Hanzan 96 34.16 N 133.51 E
Hanzhong 102 33.08 N 107.02 E
Hanzhuang 98 34.38 N 117.24 E
Hao I1 14 18.15 S 140.54 W
Hao ≃ 100 28.27 N 119.56 E
Haohekou 100 28.38 N 112.49 E
Haojiadian 100 31.47 N 113.44 E
Haoli → Hegang 89 47.24 N 130.17 E
Haoluqi 106 30.38 N 119.34 E
HaOn 132 32.43 N 35.38 E
Hāora 126 22.35 N 88.20 E
Hāora Bridge ✦5 272b 22.35 N 88.21 E
Hāora Railroad Station ✦5 272b 22.35 N 88.21 E
Haouach, Ouadi V 146 16.45 N 19.35 E
Haoxue 102 30.00 N 112.20 E
Haozhikou 107 29.36 N 105.02 E
Haparanda 26 65.50 N 24.10 E
Hapatoni, Baie ⊂ 174x 9.58 S 139.07 W
Hapert 52 51.23 N 5.15 E
Hapeville 192 33.39 N 84.24 W
Happ'o-ri 98 40.12 N 127.49 E
Happy 196 34.45 N 101.52 W
Happy Camp 204 41.47 N 123.22 W
Happy Jack 200 34.45 N 111.11 W
Happy Valley-Goose Bay 176 53.20 N 60.25 W
Happy Valley Race Course ♦ 271d 22.16 N 114.10 E
Hapsford 262 53.16 N 2.48 W
Hapsu 98 41.13 N 128.51 E
Hapton 262 53.47 N 2.19 W
Hāpur 124 28.43 N 77.47 E
Ḩaql 128 29.18 N 34.57 E
Haquira 248 14.13 S 72.11 W
Har 164 5.20 S 133.10 E
Har, Laga ≃ 154 1.40 N 39.36 E
Hara, Nihon 94 35.58 N 138.14 E
Hara, Nihon 268 35.50 N 139.46 E

≃ River / Fluß / Río / Rivière / Rio
⌒ Canal / Kanal / Canal / Canal / Canal
⌞ Waterfall, Rapids / Wasserfall, Stromschnellen / Cascada, Rápidos / Chute d'eau, Rapides / Cascata, Rápidos
⩂ Strait / Meeresstraße / Estrecho / Détroit / Estreito
⊂ Bay, Gulf / Bucht, Golf / Bahía, Golfo / Baie, Golfe / Baía, Golfo
⊜ Lake, Lakes / See, Seen / Lago, Lagos / Lac, Lacs / Lago, Lagos
≍ Swamp / Sumpf / Pantano / Marais / Pântano
⊓ Ice Features, Glacier / Eis- und Gletscherformen / Accidentes Glaciales / Formes glaciaires / Acidentes glaciares
⇁ Other Hydrographic Features / Andere Hydrographische Objekte / Otros Elementos Hidrográficos / Autres données hydrographiques / Outros acidentes hidrográficos

✦ Submarine Features / Untermeerische Objekte / Accidentes Submarinos / Formes de relief sous-marin / Acidentes submarinos
□ Political Unit / Politische Einheit / Unidad Política / Entité politique / Unidade política
⊛ Cultural Institution / Kulturelle Institution / Institución Cultural / Institution culturelle / Instituição cultural
⊥ Historical Site / Historische Stätte / Sitio Histórico / Site historique / Sítio histórico
♦ Recreational Site / Erholungs- und Ferienort / Sitio de Recreo / Centre de loisirs / Área de Lazer
⊠ Airport / Flughafen / Aeropuerto / Aéroport / Aeroporto
■ Military Installation / Militäranlage / Instalación Militar / Installation militaire / Instalação militar
✦ Miscellaneous / Verschiedenes / Misceláneo / Divers / Diversos

ENGLISH — Name | Page | Lat.°' | Long.°'

DEUTSCH — Name | Seite | Breite°' | Länge°' E = Ost

Name	Page	Lat.°'	Long.°'
Ḥaraḍ, Ar. Su.	128	24.08 N	49.05 E
Härad, Sve.	40	59.23 N	16.55 E
Ḥaraḍ, Yaman	144	16.28 N	43.04 E
Ḥaraḍ, Jabal al- ∧	132	29.40 N	35.49 E
Haraiki I[1]	14	17.28 S	143.27 W
Harajuku	268	35.54 N	139.21 E
Haraldsted	41	55.30 N	11.47 E
Haramachi	92	37.38 N	140.58 E
Haramachida	268	35.33 N	139.27 E
Haramosh ∧	123	35.50 N	74.54 E
Haramosh Range ⩚	123	35.40 N	75.22 E
Harappa	123	30.38 N	72.52 E
Harappa Road	123	30.36 N	72.55 E
Harare (Salisbury)	154	17.50 S	31.03 E
Harar → Harer	144	9.18 N	42.08 E
Ḥarash, Bi'r al- ⊽[4]	146	25.30 N	22.12 E
Ḥarastā al-Baṣal	132	33.34 N	36.22 E
Hārāt	272b	22.53 N	88.11 E
Haraz-Djombo	146	13.57 N	19.26 E
Haraze-Mangueigne	146	9.55 N	20.48 E
Harbāti	272b	22.55 N	88.33 E
Harbert	216	41.52 N	86.38 W
Harbeson	208	38.43 N	75.17 W
Harbin	89	45.45 N	126.41 E
Harbiye	130	36.11 N	36.05 E
Harbke	54	52.12 N	11.03 E
Harbo	40	60.06 N	17.12 E
Harbonnières	50	49.51 N	2.40 E
Harboør	26	56.37 N	8.12 E
Harbor	202	42.03 N	124.15 W
Harbor Beach	190	43.50 N	82.39 W
Harbor City ⊶[8]	280	33.48 N	118.17 W
Harborcreek	214	42.10 N	79.57 W
Harbord	170	33.47 S	151.17 E
Harbor Isle	276	40.36 N	73.40 W
Harbor Side	228	32.37 N	117.05 W
Harbor Springs	190	45.25 N	84.59 W
Harborton	208	37.39 N	75.49 W
Harbor Tunnel ⊶[5]	284b	39.15 N	76.34 W
Harbor View	214	41.42 N	83.27 W
Harbour Breton	186	47.29 N	55.48 W
Harbour Buffett	186	47.31 N	54.05 W
Harbour Deep	186	50.22 N	56.31 W
Harbour Grace	186	47.42 N	53.13 W
Harbours, Bay of ⊂	254	52.15 S	59.15 W
Harbourville	186	45.09 N	64.49 W
Harburg	56	48.47 N	10.41 E
Harburg ⊶[8]	52	53.28 N	9.59 E
Hårby	41	55.13 N	10.07 E
Harchies	50	50.29 N	3.41 E
Harcourt, Austl.	169	37.00 S	144.15 E
Harcourt, Fr.	50	49.10 N	0.48 E
Harcuvar Mountains ⩚	200	34.00 N	113.30 W
Hard	58	47.29 N	9.41 E
Harda	124	22.20 N	77.06 E
Hardangerfjorden ⊂[2]	26	60.10 N	6.00 E
Hardangerjøkulen ⍓	26	60.33 N	7.26 E
Hardangervidda ⩚[1]	26	60.20 N	7.30 E
Hardangervidda Nasjonalpark ♦	26	60.15 N	7.05 E
Hardapdam ⊜[1]	156	24.28 S	17.48 E
Hardee □[6]	220	27.29 N	81.48 W
Hardeeville	192	32.17 N	81.04 W
Hardegarijp	52	53.13 N	5.56 E
Hardegsen	52	51.39 N	9.49 E
Hardelot-Plage	50	50.38 N	1.35 E
Hardenberg	52	52.34 N	6.37 E
Harderwijk	52	52.21 N	5.36 E
Hardesty	196	36.36 N	101.11 W
Hardey ≃	162	22.45 S	116.07 E
Hardgrave, Mount ∧[2]	171a	27.30 S	153.29 E
Hardheim	56	49.36 N	9.28 E
Hardin, Il., U.S.	219	39.09 N	90.37 W
Hardin, Mt., U.S.	202	45.43 N	107.36 W
Hardin, Tx., U.S.	222	30.09 N	94.44 W
Hardin □[6], Oh., U.S.	216	40.39 N	83.36 W
Hardin □[6], Tx., U.S.	222	30.20 N	94.35 W
Harding, S. Afr.	158	30.34 S	29.58 E
Harding, Il., U.S.	216	41.31 N	88.51 W
Harding, Ma., U.S.	283	42.12 N	71.27 W
Harding, Lake ⊜[1]	192	32.40 N	85.06 W
Harding Lake ⊜	184	56.13 N	98.23 W
Harding Lakes	208	39.27 N	74.45 W
Hardinsburg, In., U.S.	218	38.27 N	86.16 W
Hardinsburg, Ky., U.S.	194	37.46 N	86.27 W
Hardisty	182	52.40 N	111.18 W
Hardisty Lake ⊜	176	64.30 N	117.45 W
Hardoi	124	27.25 N	80.07 E
Hardoi Branch ≍	124	28.41 N	80.08 E
Hardricourt	261	49.01 N	1.54 E
Hardscrabble Wash V	200	34.39 N	109.28 W
Hardt	263	51.07 N	6.58 E
Hardtner	198	37.00 N	98.38 W
Hardwick, Ga., U.S.	192	33.04 N	83.13 W
Hardwick, Ma., U.S.	207	42.21 N	72.12 W
Hardwick, Vt., U.S.	188	44.30 N	72.22 W
Hardwood	194	30.49 N	91.23 W
Hardwood Ridge ∧	210	41.15 N	75.23 W
Hardy, Ar., U.S.	194	36.18 N	91.28 W
Hardy, Ne., U.S.	198	40.00 N	97.55 W
Hardy, Península >[1]	254	55.25 S	68.30 W
Hardy Bay ⊂	176	75.02 N	115.16 W
Hardy Creek ≃	214	42.52 N	81.52 W
Hardy Lake ⊜[1]	218	38.47 N	85.42 W
Hardy Lake State Recreation Area ♦	218	38.44 N	86.26 W
Hardys Pond ⊜	283	42.25 N	71.15 W
Hare, Mount ∧	180	66.38 N	136.12 W
Hare Bay	186	48.51 N	54.01 W
Hare Bay ⊂	186	51.18 N	55.50 W
Harefield ⊶[8]	260	51.36 N	0.29 W
Hareid	26	62.22 N	6.02 E
Hare Indian ≃	180	66.18 N	128.38 W
Harelbeke	50	50.51 N	3.18 E
Haren, Dtsch.	52	52.47 N	7.14 E
Haren, Ned.	52	53.10 N	6.35 E
Hareøen I	176	70.25 N	54.50 W
Harer	144	9.18 N	42.08 E
Harerge □[4]	144	8.00 N	43.00 E
Hareskov	41	55.46 N	12.25 E
Hareto	144	9.20 N	37.06 E
Harewa	144	9.55 N	41.59 E
Harewood	172	43.29 S	172.35 E
Harewood Park	284b	39.23 N	76.22 W
Harfaz	130	38.01 N	41.19 E
Harfleur	50	49.30 N	0.12 E
Harford, N.Y., U.S.	210	42.26 N	76.14 W
Harford, Pa., U.S.	210	41.47 N	75.42 W
Harford □[6]	208	39.32 N	76.21 W
Harford Heights	279b	40.22 N	79.46 W
Harford Mills	210	42.25 N	76.12 W
Harg, Sve.	40	59.49 N	18.57 E
Harg, Sve.	40	60.11 N	18.24 E
Hargele	144	5.20 N	42.05 E
Hargeville	261	48.53 N	1.45 E
Hargeysa	144	9.35 N	44.04 E
Harghita □[6]	38	46.35 N	25.30 E
Harghita, Munții ⩚	38	46.15 N	25.45 E
Hargrave ≃	184	54.24 N	98.48 W
Hargrave Lake ⊜	184	54.29 N	99.40 W
Hargshamn	40	60.10 N	18.28 E
Har Hu (Heihai) ⊜	102	38.15 N	97.40 E
Hāriabhānga ≃[1]	126	21.43 N	89.05 E
Hariāna	123	31.38 N	75.51 E
Hariarapitu	114	2.33 N	98.35 E
Ḥarīb	144	14.57 N	45.30 E
Haribes	156	24.20 S	17.40 E
Ḥaricha, Ḥamâda el ⊶[2]	148	22.36 N	3.31 W
Haridwār	124	29.58 N	78.10 E
Harigabessho	270	34.37 N	135.58 E
Harihar	122	14.31 N	75.48 E
Harihari	172	43.09 S	170.33 E
Hariharpāra	126	24.02 N	88.27 E
Harīke	123	31.10 N	74.57 E
Ḥārim	130	36.12 N	36.31 E
Ḥarim, Jabal al- ∧	128	25.58 N	56.14 E
Harima	96	34.42 N	134.53 E
Harima-nada ⊽[2]	96	34.29 N	134.35 E
Harinagar	124	27.09 N	84.19 E
Harinākunda	126	23.39 N	89.03 E
Haringey ⊶[8]	42	51.35 N	0.07 W
Hāringhāta ≃[1]	126	21.54 N	89.57 E
Haringvliet ⩊	52	51.47 N	4.10 E
Haringvlietbrug ⊶[5]	52	51.43 N	4.20 E
Haringvlietdam ⊶[5]	52	51.50 N	4.03 E
Haripāl	272b	22.49 N	88.07 E
Haripur, India	126	24.18 N	87.05 E
Haripur, India	272b	22.56 N	88.14 E
Harīpur, Pāk.	123	33.59 N	72.56 E
Harirāmpur	126	23.42 N	89.57 E
Harīrūd (Tedžen) ≃	128	37.24 N	60.38 E
Harischandra Range ⩚	122	19.15 N	74.05 E
Ḥārithān	130	36.16 N	37.05 E
Hariyo	144	5.00 N	47.23 E
Harjavalta	26	61.19 N	22.08 E
Härjedalen □[9]	26	62.20 N	13.00 E
Harkaway	274b	38.00 S	145.21 E
Härkeberga	40	59.42 N	17.11 E
Harkema-Opeinde	52	53.11 N	6.08 E
Harker Heights	222	31.05 N	97.40 W
Harkers Island	192	34.41 N	76.33 W
Harker Village	285	39.51 N	75.09 W
Harkness Memorial State Park ♦	207	41.18 N	72.07 W
Harkortsee ⊜	263	51.24 N	7.25 E
Harlaching ⊶[8]	60	48.06 N	11.33 E
Harlan, In., U.S.	216	41.11 N	84.55 W
Harlan, Ia., U.S.	198	41.39 N	95.19 W
Harlan, Ky., U.S.	192	36.50 N	83.19 W
Harlan County Lake ⊜[1]	198	40.04 N	99.16 W
Harlech	42	52.52 N	4.07 W
Harlem, Fl., U.S.	220	26.44 N	80.57 W
Harlem, Ga., U.S.	192	33.24 N	82.18 W
Harlem, Mt., U.S.	202	48.32 N	108.47 W
Harlem ⊶[8]	276	40.49 N	73.56 W
Harlem River ⩊	276	40.48 N	73.54 W
Harlem Springs	214	40.31 N	81.02 W
Harlesden ⊶[8]	260	51.32 N	0.15 W
Harlesiel	52	53.43 N	7.49 E
Harleston	42	52.24 N	1.18 E
Harleton	222	32.41 N	94.35 W
Hårlev	41	55.21 N	12.15 E
Harleysville	208	40.17 N	75.23 W
Harlin	171a	26.59 S	152.22 E
Harlingen, Ned.	52	53.10 N	5.24 E
Harlingen, Tx., U.S.	196	26.11 N	97.41 W
Harlinger Land ⊶[1]	52	53.40 N	7.30 E
Harlingerode	54	51.54 N	10.31 E
Harlington ⊶[8]	260	51.29 N	0.26 W
Harlösa	41	55.43 N	13.32 E
Harlow	42	51.47 N	0.08 E
Harlow □[8]	260	51.44 N	0.07 E
Harlowton	202	46.26 N	109.50 W
Harlpur	272b	22.42 N	88.10 E
Harman	188	38.55 N	79.31 W
Harmancık	130	39.41 N	29.10 E
Harmånger	26	61.56 N	17.13 E
Harmanli, Blg.	38	41.56 N	25.54 E
Harmanlı, Tür.	130	37.51 N	37.45 E
Harmanschlag	61	48.39 N	14.47 E
Harmar Heights	279b	40.33 N	79.49 W
Harmarville	279b	40.32 N	79.51 W
Hármashatár-hegy ∧	264c	47.33 N	19.00 E
Harmelen	52	52.05 N	4.58 E
Harmil I	144	16.31 N	40.09 E
Harmonsburg	214	41.40 N	80.19 W
Harmonville	285	40.06 N	75.17 W
Harmony, Ca., U.S.	226	35.35 N	121.01 W
Harmony, In., U.S.	194	39.32 N	87.06 W
Harmony, Mn., U.S.	190	43.33 N	92.00 W
Harmony, N.J., U.S.	210	40.44 N	75.08 W
Harmony, Pa., U.S.	214	40.48 N	80.07 W
Harmony, R.I., U.S.	207	41.53 N	71.35 W
Harmony Brook ≃	276	40.48 N	74.34 W
Harmony Heights	220	27.29 N	80.21 W
Harmony Hills	285	39.42 N	75.41 W
Harmonyville	285	40.11 N	75.43 W
Harnai, India	122	17.48 N	73.06 E
Harnai, Pāk.	120	30.06 N	67.56 E
Harnäs	40	60.39 N	17.22 E
Harnātānr	124	27.19 N	84.01 E
Harndrup	41	55.28 N	10.02 E
Harnes	50	50.27 N	2.54 E
Härnevi	40	59.44 N	17.05 E
Harney ≃	220	25.25 N	81.10 W
Harney, Lake ⊜	220	28.45 N	81.03 W
Harney Basin ≚[1]	202	43.15 N	119.00 W
Harney Lake ⊜	202	43.14 N	119.07 W
Harney Peak ∧	198	43.51 N	103.31 W
Harney Pond Canal ≍	220	27.00 N	81.04 W
Härnösand	26	62.38 N	17.56 E
Haro, Esp.	34	42.35 N	2.51 W
Haro, Ityo.	144	8.28 N	38.37 E
Haro, Cabo >	232	27.52 N	110.54 W
Ḥarod ≃	132	32.31 N	35.33 E
Harola	272a	28.36 N	77.19 E
Harold Hill ⊶[8]	260	51.36 N	0.13 E
Harold Parker State Forest ♦	283	42.37 N	71.05 W
Haroldswick	46a	60.41 N	0.50 W
Harold Wood ⊶[8]	260	51.36 N	0.14 E
Haro Strait ⩊	224	48.30 N	123.15 W
Harouè	58	48.28 N	6.11 E
Harpālpur	124	25.17 N	79.20 E
Harpanahalli	122	14.48 N	75.59 E
Harpen ⊶[8]	263	51.29 N	7.16 E
Harpenden	42	51.49 N	0.22 W
Harper, Liber.	150	4.25 N	7.43 W
Harper, Ks., U.S.	198	37.17 N	98.01 W
Harper, Tx., U.S.	196	30.18 N	99.15 W
Harper, Wa., U.S.	224	47.31 N	122.31 W
Harper, Mount ∧	180	64.14 N	143.50 W
Harper Lake ⊜	228	35.02 N	117.17 W
Harpers Ferry National Historical Park ♦	188	39.13 N	77.45 W
Harpersfield	210	42.26 N	74.41 W
Harper Town	44	54.55 N	2.31 W
Harper Woods	214	42.25 N	82.55 W
Harpille ∧	62	43.50 N	6.48 E
Harpstedt	52	52.54 N	8.35 E
Harpster	214	40.44 N	83.15 W
Harpsund ⚑	40	59.06 N	16.29 E
Harpurhey ⊶[8]	262	53.31 N	2.13 W
Harpur Hill	262	53.14 N	1.54 W
Harpursville	210	42.11 N	75.38 W
Harqin	98	41.08 N	119.38 E
Harqin Qi (Jinshan)	98	41.56 N	118.36 E
Harquahala Mountain ∧	200	33.49 N	113.21 W
Ḥarrah	144	14.57 N	50.19 E
Ḥārrah, Jabal al- ∧	132	33.04 N	35.59 E
Harrai	124	22.37 N	79.13 E
Harran	130	36.51 N	39.00 E
Ḥarrān al-ʻAwāmīd	132	33.27 N	36.34 E
Harray, Loch of ⊜	46	59.01 N	3.13 W
Harrell	194	33.30 N	92.23 W
Harricana ≃	176	51.15 N	79.45 W
Harrietfield	46	56.25 N	3.39 W
Harrietsham	42	51.15 N	0.41 E
Harriman, N.Y., U.S.	210	41.18 N	74.09 W
Harriman, Tn., U.S.	192	35.56 N	84.33 W
Harriman Reservoir ⊜[1]	207	42.50 N	72.53 W
Harriman State Park ♦	210	41.14 N	74.09 W
Harrington, Eng., U.K.	44	54.37 N	3.34 W
Harrington, De., U.S.	208	38.55 N	75.34 W
Harrington, Me., U.S.	188	44.37 N	67.48 W
Harrington, Wa., U.S.	202	47.28 N	118.15 W
Harrington Creek ≃	282	37.19 N	122.18 W
Harrington Drain ≍	281	42.36 N	82.54 W
Harrington Park	276	40.59 N	73.58 W
Harris, Sk., Can.	184	51.44 N	107.35 W
Harris, Scot., U.K.	46	56.59 N	6.20 W
Harris, Mn., U.S.	190	45.35 N	92.58 W
Harris, N.Y., U.S.	210	41.43 N	74.44 W
Harris, R.I., U.S.	207	41.43 N	71.31 W
Harris □[6]	222	29.50 N	95.22 W
Harris ≃	168a	33.18 S	116.09 E
Harris ⊶[1]	46	57.55 N	6.50 W
Harris, Lake ⊜, Austl.	162	31.08 S	135.14 E
Harris, Lake ⊜, Fl., U.S.	220	28.46 N	81.49 W
Harris, Sound of ⩊	46	57.45 N	7.10 W
Harris Bay ⊂	212	45.23 N	77.50 W
Harris Brook ≃	283	42.44 N	71.13 W
Harrisburg, Ar., U.S.	194	35.33 N	90.43 W
Harrisburg, Il., U.S.	194	37.44 N	88.32 W
Harrisburg, In., U.S.	218	39.41 N	85.11 W
Harrisburg, Ne., U.S.	198	41.33 N	103.44 W
Harrisburg, Oh., U.S.	214	40.53 N	81.13 W
Harrisburg, Or., U.S.	202	44.16 N	123.10 W
Harrisburg, Pa., U.S.	208	40.16 N	76.53 W
Harrisburg International Airport ⊗	208	40.12 N	76.45 W
Harris Creek ⊂	208	38.45 N	76.18 W
Harris Creek ≃, Austl.	274a	33.57 S	150.57 E
Harris Creek ≃, Tx., U.S.	222	32.33 N	95.08 W
Harrisfield	274b	37.57 S	145.11 E
Harris Hill	210	42.58 N	78.40 W
Harrislee	41	54.48 N	9.22 E
Harrismith, Austl.	162	32.56 S	117.52 E
Harrismith, S. Afr.	158	28.18 S	29.03 E
Harrison, Ar., U.S.	194	36.13 N	93.06 W
Harrison, Id., U.S.	202	47.27 N	116.47 W
Harrison, Il., U.S.	216	42.25 N	89.11 W
Harrison, Mi., U.S.	190	44.01 N	84.47 W
Harrison, Ne., U.S.	198	42.41 N	103.53 W
Harrison, N.J., U.S.	276	40.44 N	74.09 W
Harrison, N.Y., U.S.	210	40.58 N	73.43 W
Harrison, Oh., U.S.	218	39.15 N	84.49 W
Harrison □[6], In., U.S.	218	38.17 N	86.07 W
Harrison □[6], Ky., U.S.	218	38.25 N	84.19 W
Harrison □[6], Oh., U.S.	214	40.16 N	81.05 W
Harrison □[6], Tx., U.S.	222	32.35 N	94.35 W
Harrison ≃	224	49.14 N	121.57 W
Harrison, Cape >	176	54.55 N	57.55 W
Harrison Bay ⊂	180	70.30 N	151.30 W
Harrisonburg, La., U.S.	194	31.46 N	91.49 W
Harrisonburg, Va., U.S.	188	38.26 N	78.52 W
Harrison City	279b	40.21 N	79.39 W
Harrison Hot Springs	224	49.18 N	121.47 W
Harrison Islands II	176	69.13 N	90.30 W
Harrison Lake ⊜	182	49.30 N	121.50 W
Harrison Mills	224	49.14 N	121.57 W
Harrisons Brook ≃	276	40.38 N	74.34 W
Harrison Tomb State Memorial ⊥	218	39.09 N	84.46 W
Harrison Valley	214	41.57 N	77.39 W
Harrisonville, Md., U.S.	284b	39.23 N	77.50 W
Harrisonville, Mo., U.S.	194	38.39 N	94.20 W
Harrisonville, N.J., U.S.	285	39.41 N	75.15 W
Harris Park	274a	33.49 S	151.01 E
Harris Pond ⊜	283	42.45 N	71.16 W
Harris Reservoir ⊜[1]	222	29.14 N	95.33 W
Harriston, On., Can.	212	43.54 N	80.53 W
Harriston, Ms., U.S.	194	31.43 N	91.01 W
Harristown	219	39.51 N	89.05 W
Harrisville, Austl.	171a	27.49 S	152.40 E
Harrisville, Mi., U.S.	190	44.39 N	83.17 W
Harrisville, N.Y., U.S.	212	44.09 N	75.19 W
Harrisville, Oh., U.S.	214	40.11 N	80.53 W
Harrisville, Pa., U.S.	214	41.08 N	80.00 W
Harrisville, R.I., U.S.	207	41.57 N	71.40 W
Harrisville, W.V., U.S.	188	39.12 N	81.03 W
Harrod	216	40.42 N	83.55 W
Harrodsburg	194	37.45 N	84.50 W
Harrods Creek ≃	218	38.20 N	85.38 W
Harrogate	44	54.00 N	1.33 W
Harrold	196	34.05 N	99.02 W
Harrop Lake ⊜	184	52.38 N	95.58 W
Harrow	214	42.02 N	82.55 W
Harrow ⊶[8]	42	51.35 N	0.21 W
Harrow on the Hill ⊶[8]	260	51.34 N	0.20 W
Harrow School ⚑[2]	260	51.34 N	0.20 W
Harrowsmith	212	44.24 N	76.40 W
Harry S. Truman Airport ⊗	240m	18.21 N	64.59 W
Harry S. Truman Reservoir ⊜[1]	194	38.10 N	93.45 W
Har Sai Shan ∧	102	35.28 N	97.55 E
Harsefeld	52	53.27 N	9.30 E
Harsens Island	214	42.34 N	82.34 W
Harsens Island I	281	42.35 N	82.38 W
Harsewinkel	52	51.58 N	8.13 E
Harsīn	128	34.16 N	47.35 E
Harşit ≃	130	41.01 N	38.52 E
Harskamp	52	52.07 N	5.45 E
Harsleben	54	51.52 N	11.05 E
Harstad	24	68.46 N	16.30 E
Harstena	26	58.16 N	17.01 E
Har Su	89	48.09 N	122.25 E
Harsūd	124	22.06 N	76.44 E
Harsum	52	52.12 N	9.57 E
Hart, Mi., U.S.	190	43.41 N	86.21 W
Hart, Tx., U.S.	196	34.23 N	102.07 W
Hart ≃	180	65.51 N	136.22 W
Hart, Lake ⊜, Austl.	166	31.08 S	136.24 E
Hart, Lake ⊜, Fl., U.S.	220	28.22 N	81.13 W
Ḥartā	132	32.42 N	35.51 E
Hartbees ≃	158	28.45 S	20.32 E
Hartbeesfontein	158	26.42 S	26.26 E
Hartbeespoort	158	25.44 S	27.52 E
Hartberg	61	47.17 N	15.59 E
Hartenholm	52	53.54 N	10.03 E
Hartenstein	54	50.39 N	12.40 E
Hart Fell ∧	44	55.25 N	3.25 W
Hartfield	208	37.34 N	76.30 W
Hartford, Eng., U.K.	262	53.15 N	2.33 W
Hartford, Al., U.S.	194	31.06 N	85.41 W
Hartford, Ar., U.S.	194	35.01 N	94.22 W
Hartford, Ct., U.S.	207	41.46 N	72.41 W
Hartford, Il., U.S.	219	38.50 N	90.05 W
Hartford, In., U.S.	218	38.59 N	84.57 W
Hartford, Ks., U.S.	198	38.18 N	95.57 W
Hartford, Ky., U.S.	194	37.27 N	86.54 W
Hartford, Mi., U.S.	216	42.12 N	86.10 W
Hartford, N.J., U.S.	285	39.58 N	74.53 W
Hartford, N.Y., U.S.	210	43.21 N	73.22 W
Hartford, Oh., U.S.	214	41.19 N	80.34 W
Hartford, S.D., U.S.	198	43.37 N	96.56 W
Hartford, Wi., U.S.	190	43.19 N	88.22 W
Hartford □[6]	207	41.46 N	72.41 W
Hartford City	216	40.27 N	85.22 W
Hartha	54	51.05 N	12.58 E
Hartington	198	42.37 N	97.15 W
Hart Island I	276	40.51 N	73.46 W
Hart Lake ⊜	202	42.24 N	119.51 W
Hartland, N.B., Can.	186	46.18 N	67.32 W
Hartland, Eng., U.K.	42	50.59 N	4.29 W
Hartland, Il., U.S.	216	42.22 N	88.31 W
Hartland, Me., U.S.	188	44.53 N	69.26 W
Hartland, Mi., U.S.	216	42.39 N	83.45 W
Hartland, N.Y., U.S.	210	43.14 N	78.35 W
Hartland, Wi., U.S.	216	43.06 N	88.20 W
Hartland Point >	42	51.02 N	4.31 W
Hartlepool	44	54.42 N	1.11 W
Hartleton	210	40.54 N	77.10 W
Hartley, Austl.	170	33.33 S	150.11 E
Hartley, Eng., U.K.	260	51.23 N	0.19 E
Hartley, Ia., U.S.	198	43.10 N	95.28 W
Hartley, Tx., U.S.	196	35.53 N	102.24 W
Hartley Bay	182	53.25 N	129.15 W
Hartlip	260	51.21 N	0.39 E
Hart Lot	210	43.01 N	76.28 W
Hartly	208	39.10 N	75.42 W
Hartmannsdorf	54	50.53 N	12.48 E
Hartmannshain	56	50.28 N	9.16 E
Hart-Miller Island I	208	39.15 N	76.23 W
Hart Mountain ∧	184	52.29 N	101.25 W
Hartney	184	49.28 N	100.30 W
Hartola	26	61.35 N	26.01 E
Harts ≃	158	28.24 S	24.17 E
Hartsburg	219	38.41 N	92.18 W
Hartsdale	210	41.01 N	73.47 W
Hartselle	194	34.26 N	86.56 W
Härtsfeld ⊶[1]	56	48.50 N	10.15 E
Hartshill	42	52.32 N	1.32 W
Hartshorne	196	34.50 N	95.33 W
Harts Range	162	23.00 S	134.55 E
Hartstene Island I	224	47.14 N	122.53 W
Hartstown	214	41.33 N	80.23 W
Hartsville, In., U.S.	218	39.16 N	85.41 W
Hartsville, Pa., U.S.	285	40.14 N	75.05 W
Hartsville, S.C., U.S.	192	34.22 N	80.04 W
Hartsville, Tn., U.S.	194	36.23 N	86.10 W
Hartswater	158	27.34 S	24.43 E
Hartville, Mo., U.S.	194	37.15 N	92.30 W
Hartville, Oh., U.S.	214	40.57 N	81.19 W
Hartwell	192	34.21 N	82.55 W
Hartwell Lake ⊜[1]	192	34.30 N	82.55 W
Hartwick	210	42.39 N	75.02 W
Hartwick Pines State Park ♦	190	44.47 N	84.41 W
Hartz Mountains National Park ♦	166	43.15 S	146.50 E
Harue	94	36.08 N	136.14 E
Haruki	270	34.29 N	135.23 E
Haruku, Pulau I	164	3.34 S	128.29 E
Hārūn	140	11.20 N	25.43 E
Haruna	94	36.23 N	138.53 E
Hārūnābād	123	29.37 N	73.08 E
Haruna-san ∧	94	36.28 N	138.52 E
Haruniye	130	37.17 N	36.27 E
Haruno, Nihon	94	34.57 N	137.53 E
Haruno, Nihon	96	33.30 N	133.30 E
Harūr	122	12.04 N	78.30 E
Hārūt ≃	128	31.35 N	61.18 E
Harvard, Il., U.S.	216	42.25 N	88.36 W
Harvard, Ma., U.S.	207	42.30 N	71.35 W
Harvard, Ne., U.S.	198	40.37 N	98.05 W
Harvard University ⚑[2]	283	42.22 N	71.07 W
Harvel, Eng., U.K.	260	51.21 N	0.22 E
Harvel, Il., U.S.	219	39.21 N	89.32 W
Harvest, Mount ∧[2]	162	25.54 S	126.28 E
Harvey, Austl.	168a	33.05 S	115.54 E
Harvey, N.B., Can.	186	45.43 N	64.43 W
Harvey, Il., U.S.	216	41.36 N	87.38 W
Harvey, N.D., U.S.	198	47.46 N	99.56 W
Harvey ≃	168a	32.46 S	115.43 E
Harvey Estuary ⊂[1]	168a	32.43 S	115.42 E
Harvey Mountain ∧	207	42.18 N	73.25 W
Harvey Reservoir ⊜[1]	168a	33.05 S	115.58 E
Harveysburg	218	39.30 N	84.00 W
Harveys Lake	210	41.23 N	76.02 W
Harwell	42	51.37 N	1.18 W
Harwich, Eng., U.K.	42	51.57 N	1.17 E
Harwich, Ma., U.S.	207	41.41 N	70.04 W
Harwich Port	207	41.40 N	70.04 W
Harwick	279b	40.34 N	79.48 W
Harwinton	207	41.46 N	73.03 W
Harwood, Eng., U.K.	262	53.35 N	2.23 W
Harwood, Tx., U.S.	222	29.40 N	97.30 W
Harwood Heights	278	41.58 N	87.48 W
Harwood Mines	210	40.57 N	76.01 W
Harwood Park	284b	39.12 N	76.44 W
Haryāna □[3]	120	29.20 N	76.20 E
Harz ⩚	54	51.45 N	10.30 E
Harzgerode	54	51.38 N	11.08 E
Ḥaṣā, Bi'r al- ⊽[4]	140	22.58 N	35.40 E
Ḥasā, Wādī al- V	132	31.05 N	35.27 E
Hasafen	86	45.14 N	90.20 E
Ḥaṣāh, Wādī al- V	132	30.38 N	37.09 E
Hasaki	94	35.44 N	140.50 E
Hasalbag	120	37.54 N	76.44 E
Ḥasanābād	267d	35.44 N	51.19 E
Ḥasanābād-e Khāleṣeh	267d	35.37 N	51.12 E
Hasan Abdāl	123	33.49 N	72.41 E
Hasançelebi	130	38.58 N	37.54 E
Hasan Dağı ∧	130	38.08 N	34.12 E
Hasankale → Pasinler	130	39.59 N	41.41 E
Hasankeyf	130	37.43 N	41.25 E
Ḥasan Kīādeh	128	37.24 N	49.58 E
Hasanpur	124	28.43 N	78.17 E
Hasayaz	130	40.15 N	33.20 E
Ḥāṣbānī, Nahr al- ≃	132	33.11 N	35.37 E
Ḥāṣbayyā	132	33.24 N	35.41 E
Hasbek	130	39.33 N	35.33 E
Hasbergen, Dtsch.	52	52.14 N	7.57 E
Hasbergen, Dtsch.	52	53.05 N	8.40 E
Hasbrouck Heights	276	40.51 N	74.04 W
Hascosay I	46a	60.37 N	0.59 W
Hasdo ≃	120	21.44 N	82.44 E
Hasdo-Rāmpur Basin ≚[1]	124	22.50 N	82.35 E
Hase, Nihon	94	35.47 N	138.06 E
Hase, Nihon	270	34.32 N	135.54 E
Hase ≃, Dtsch.	52	52.41 N	7.18 E
Hase ≃, Nihon	270	34.34 N	135.38 E
Hasel ≃	54	50.32 N	10.27 E
Häselgehr	58	47.19 N	10.30 E
Haselhorst ⊶[8]	264a	52.33 N	13.15 E
Haselünne	52	52.40 N	7.29 E
Hasenkamp	252	31.31 S	59.51 W
Hashā', Jabal al- ∧	144	13.45 N	44.30 E
HaShefela ⊶[1]	132	31.40 N	34.55 E
Hashima	94	35.19 N	136.42 E
Hashimoto, Nihon	96	34.19 N	135.37 E
Hashimoto, Nihon	270	34.26 N	135.23 E
Hashira-jima I	96	34.01 N	132.25 E
Hashiri-jima I	96	34.21 N	133.27 E
Hashitai	89	49.24 N	125.18 E
Hasht Sāl ⊶[8]	272a	28.38 N	77.03 E
Hasil, Pulau I	164	1.06 S	128.24 E
Hāsilpur	123	29.43 N	72.33 E
Ḥāsīn-e Bozorg	84	39.23 N	44.42 E
Haskayne	262	53.34 N	2.58 W
Haskeir Islands II	46	57.42 N	7.41 W
Haskell, Ok., U.S.	196	35.49 N	95.40 W
Haskell, Tx., U.S.	196	33.09 N	99.44 W
Haskell Pond ⊜	283	42.37 N	70.44 W
Hasketh Bank	262	53.43 N	2.51 W
Haskins	216	41.27 N	83.42 W
Haskovo	38	41.56 N	25.33 E
Haskovo □[4]	130	41.50 N	25.50 E
Hasköy, Tür.	130	41.38 N	26.41 E
Hasköy, Tür.	130	40.59 N	42.52 E
Hasköy ⊶[8]	267b	41.02 N	28.58 E
Haslach im Kinzigtal	58	48.16 N	8.06 E
Hasle, Dan.	41	55.10 N	10.10 E
Hasle, Schw.	58	47.01 N	7.39 E
Haslemere	42	51.06 N	0.43 W
Haslett	216	42.44 N	84.24 W
Haslev	41	55.20 N	11.58 E
Haslingden	44	53.43 N	2.18 W
Haslingden Grane	262	53.42 N	2.21 W
Haslington	44	53.06 N	2.24 W
Haslital V	58	46.42 N	8.10 E
Haslum	26	59.50 N	10.22 E
Hasmark	41	55.33 N	10.28 E
Ḥasmat ʻUmar, Bi'r ⊽[4]	140	21.46 N	34.00 E
Hāsnābād	126	22.35 N	88.55 E
Hasnācha	272b	22.26 N	88.09 E
Haspe ⊶[8]	263	51.21 N	7.26 E
Hasperos Canyon V	200	33.50 N	105.02 W
Hasper-Stausee ⊜[1]	263	51.18 N	7.25 E
Haspres	50	50.15 N	3.25 E
Ḥaṣṣ, Jabal al- ∧[2]	130	35.52 N	37.22 E
Hassa	130	36.50 N	36.29 E
Hassan	122	13.00 N	76.05 E
Hassard	219	39.39 N	91.40 W
Hassayampa ≃	200	33.20 N	112.43 W
Hassberge ⩚[2]	56	50.12 N	10.29 E
Hassbergen	52	52.44 N	9.13 E
Hassel, Dtsch.	52	52.48 N	9.11 E
Hassel, Dtsch.	263	51.39 N	7.30 E
Hassel ⊶[8]	263	51.36 N	7.03 E
Hasselbeck-Schwarzbach	263	51.16 N	6.53 E
Hasselfelde	54	51.41 N	10.51 E
Hasselfors	40	59.05 N	14.39 E
Hassels ⊶[8]	263	51.10 N	6.53 E
Hasselt, Bel.	56	50.56 N	5.20 E
Hasselt, Ned.	52	52.35 N	6.05 E
Hassfurt	56	50.02 N	10.31 E
Hassi Bel Guebbour	148	28.46 N	6.27 E
Hassi el Ghella	34	35.28 N	1.03 W
Hassi Mameche	34	35.52 N	0.04 E
Hassi Messaoud	148	31.43 N	5.59 E
Hassi Zehana	34	35.01 N	0.53 W
Hassleben	54	53.13 N	13.41 E
Hässleholm	41	56.09 N	13.46 E
Hasslinghausen	56	51.20 N	7.17 E
Hassloch	56	49.22 N	8.16 E
Hasson Heights	214	41.26 N	79.41 W
Hästbo	40	60.27 N	16.27 E
Hasten ⊶[8], Dtsch.	263	51.12 N	7.09 E
Hästen ⊶[8], Dtsch.	263	51.09 N	7.06 E
Hastière-Lavaux	56	50.13 N	4.50 E
Hastings, Austl.	169	38.18 S	145.11 E
Hastings, Barb.	241g	13.04 N	59.35 W
Hastings, On., Can.	212	44.18 N	77.57 W
Hastings, N.Z.	172	39.38 S	176.51 E
Hastings, Eng., U.K.	42	50.51 N	0.36 E
Hastings, Fl., U.S.	192	29.43 N	81.30 W
Hastings, Il., U.S.	278	41.41 N	87.58 W
Hastings, Mi., U.S.	216	42.39 N	85.17 W
Hastings, Mn., U.S.	190	44.44 N	92.51 W
Hastings, Ne., U.S.	198	40.35 N	98.23 W
Hastings, N.Y., U.S.	210	43.22 N	76.09 W
Hastings, Pa., U.S.	214	40.39 N	78.42 W
Hastings □[6]	212	44.45 N	77.40 W
Hastings Battlesite ⊥	42	50.53 N	0.31 E
Hastings-on-Hudson	276	40.59 N	73.52 W
Hastingwood	260	51.45 N	0.09 E
Hastrup	41	55.26 N	12.11 E
Hasty	198	38.06 N	102.57 W
Hasuda	94	35.59 N	139.40 E
Hasumi	96	34.52 N	132.37 E
Haswell	198	38.27 N	103.09 W
Hata	94	36.11 N	137.51 E
Hat'ae-do I	98	34.32 N	126.03 E
Ha Tan	110	18.30 N	105.20 E
Hatanagi-dam ⊶[6]	94	35.18 N	138.12 E
Hatashō	94	35.10 N	136.15 E
Hatay □[4]	130	36.30 N	36.15 E
Hatboro	208	40.10 N	75.06 W
Hatch, N.M., U.S.	200	32.39 N	107.09 W
Hatch, Ut,. U.S.	200	37.38 N	112.26 W
Hat Chao Mai National Park ♦	110	7.40 N	99.35 E
Hatches Creek	162	20.56 S	135.12 E
Hatchet Creek ≃	194	32.52 N	86.20 W
Hatchet Lake	186	44.35 N	63.40 W
Hatchie ≃	194	35.35 N	89.53 W
Hatchineha, Lake ⊜	220	28.02 N	81.25 W
Hatchlands ⊥	260	51.15 N	0.28 W
Hatchmere	262	53.15 N	2.40 W
Hatchville	207	41.37 N	70.33 W
Hatch Wash V	200	38.32 N	109.36 W
Hat Creek ≃, U.S.	198	43.16 N	103.36 W
Hat Creek ≃, Ca., U.S.	204	40.59 N	121.33 W
Haţeg	38	45.37 N	22.57 E
Hateruma-shima I	175d	24.03 N	123.47 E
Hatfield, Austl.	166	33.52 S	143.45 E
Hatfield, Eng., U.K.	42	51.46 N	0.13 W
Hatfield, Eng., U.K.	44	53.34 N	1.00 W
Hatfield, Ar., U.S.	194	34.29 N	94.22 W
Hatfield, Ma., U.S.	207	42.22 N	72.35 W
Hatfield Aerodrome ⊗	260	51.46 N	0.16 W
Hatfield House ⊥	260	51.46 N	0.13 W
Hatfield Peverel	42	51.47 N	0.35 E
Hatfield Swamp ≋	276	40.50 N	74.20 W
Hathāla	123	32.03 N	70.34 E
Hathaway Pines	226	38.07 N	120.28 W
Hatherleigh	42	50.49 N	4.04 W
Hathersage	44	53.19 N	1.38 W
Hāthras	124	27.36 N	78.03 E
Hātia ⩊	124	22.30 N	91.15 E
Ḥāṭibah, Ra's >	144	21.55 N	38.58 E
Ha Tien	110	10.23 N	104.29 E
Hatillo	240m	18.29 N	66.49 W
Ha Tinh	110	18.20 N	105.54 E
Hatinoe → Hachinohe	92	40.30 N	141.29 E
Hatiozi → Hachiōji	94	35.39 N	139.20 E
Hatip	130	37.46 N	32.25 E
Hātisāla	272b	22.33 N	88.32 E
Hato, Bocht van ⊂	241s	12.13 N	68.58 W
Hatogaya	94	35.50 N	139.44 E
Hato Mayor [del Rey]	238	18.46 N	69.15 W
Hato Rey	240m	18.25 N	66.03 W
Hatoyama	94	35.59 N	139.20 E
Hāt Pīplia	124	22.46 N	76.18 E
Hatsukaichi	96	34.21 N	132.20 E
Hatsu-shima I	94	35.02 N	139.10 E
Hatsutomi	268	35.46 N	140.01 E
Hatta	124	24.07 N	79.36 E
Hattab, Oued el V	36	35.23 N	9.32 E
Hattah-Kulkyne National Park ♦	166	34.40 S	142.30 E
Hattem	52	52.28 N	6.04 E
Hatten, Dtsch.	52	53.02 N	8.22 E
Hatten, Fr.	56	48.54 N	7.59 E
Hattenhofen	60	48.13 N	11.07 E
Hatteras	192	35.13 N	75.41 W
Hatteras, Cape >	192	35.13 N	75.32 W
Hatteras Island I	192	35.25 N	75.30 W
Hattiesburg	194	31.19 N	89.17 W
Hatting	41	55.51 N	9.46 E
Hattingen	56	51.23 N	7.10 E
Hattingspruit	158	28.09 S	30.11 E
Hatton, Eng., U.K.	262	53.20 N	2.36 W
Hatton, Scot., U.K.	46	57.25 N	1.54 W
Hatton, Al., U.S.	194	34.33 N	87.24 W
Hatton, N.D., U.S.	198	47.38 N	97.27 W
Hatton ⊶[8]	260	51.28 N	0.25 W
Hatton Fields	226	36.33 N	121.54 W
Hattorf [am Harz]	52	51.39 N	10.14 E
Hattori, Nihon	270	34.46 N	135.27 E
Hattori, Nihon	270	34.52 N	135.36 E
Hattstatt	58	48.01 N	7.17 E
Hattstedt	41	54.31 N	9.01 E
Hatunsaray	130	37.35 N	32.21 E
Hatvan	30	47.40 N	19.41 E
Hat Yai	110	7.01 N	100.28 E
Hatzfeld ⊶[8]	263	51.17 N	7.11 E
Hatzic	224	49.09 N	122.15 W
Hatzic Lake ⊜	224	49.10 N	122.14 W
Haubourdin	50	50.36 N	2.59 E
Haubstadt	194	38.12 N	87.34 W
Hāudullāpur	272b	22.25 N	88.33 E
Hauge	26	58.18 N	6.15 E
Haugesund	26	59.25 N	5.18 E
Haugh of Urr	44	54.58 N	3.52 W
Haughton Green	262	53.27 N	2.06 W
Haugsdorf	61	48.42 N	16.05 E
Hau Hoi Wan ⊂	100	22.28 N	113.56 E
Hauhungaroa Range ⩚	172	38.50 S	175.34 E
Haukeligrend	26	59.45 N	7.31 E
Haukipudas	26	65.11 N	25.21 E
Haukivesi ⊜	26	62.06 N	28.28 E
Haukivuori	26	62.01 N	27.13 E
Hauldres, Ru des ≃	261	48.37 N	2.28 E
Haulerwijk	52	53.04 N	6.20 E
Haultain ≃	184	55.51 N	106.46 W
Haune ≃	56	50.52 N	9.43 E
Haunersdorf	60	48.36 N	12.43 E
Haunstetten	58	48.18 N	10.54 E
Haunts Creek ⩊	276	40.37 N	73.31 W
Hauppauge	210	40.49 N	73.12 W
Hauptsrus	158	26.33 S	26.18 E
Hauraki Gulf ⊂	172	36.20 S	175.05 E
Hauroko, Lake ⊜	172	46.00 S	167.20 E
Hauru, Pointe >	174s	17.29 S	149.55 W
Haus	64	47.25 N	13.49 E
Hausa	273a	6.37 N	3.21 E
Hausach	58	48.17 N	8.10 E
Hausham	64	47.45 N	11.50 E
Hausruck ⩚	60	48.07 N	13.35 E
Haussee ⊜	264a	52.38 N	13.41 E
Haussömmern	54	51.11 N	10.49 E
Haut, Isle au I	188	44.03 N	68.38 W
Haut Atlas ⩚	148	31.30 N	6.00 W
Haut-Bout	261	48.32 N	1.55 E
Haute Colme, Canal de la ≍	50	50.50 N	2.12 E
Hautecombe, Abbaye de ⚑[1]	62	45.45 N	5.50 E
Haute-Corse □[5]	36	42.30 N	9.00 E
Haute-Garonne □[5]	32	43.25 N	1.30 E
Haute-Kotto □[5]	152	7.00 N	23.00 E
Haute-Loire □[5]	32	45.05 N	3.50 E
Hauteluce	62	45.45 N	6.35 E
Haute-Marne □[5]	58	48.05 N	5.10 E
Hauterive	186	49.12 N	68.16 W
Hauterives	62	45.15 N	5.02 E
Hautes-Alpes □[5]	62	44.40 N	6.30 E
Haute-Sangha □[5]	152	4.30 N	16.00 E
Haute-Saône □[5]	58	47.40 N	6.10 E
Haute-Savoie □[5]	32	46.00 N	6.20 E
Haute Seine, Canal de la ≍	50	48.34 N	3.43 E
Hautes Fagnes ⩚	56	50.30 N	6.05 E
Hautes-Pyrénées □[5]	32	43.00 N	0.10 E
Haute Sûre, Lac de la ⊜[1]	56	49.52 N	5.52 E
Haute-Vienne □[5]	32	45.50 N	1.15 E
Hauteville-Lompnes	58	45.58 N	5.36 E
Haute Volta → Burkina Faso □[1]	150	13.00 N	1.30 W
Haut-Folin ∧	32	47.00 N	4.02 E
Haut-Kœnigsbourg, Château du ⊥	58	48.14 N	7.22 E
Haut-Mbomou □[5]	140	6.00 N	26.00 E
Hautmont	50	50.15 N	3.56 E
Haut-Ogooué □[4]	152	1.00 S	13.50 E
Haut-Rhin □[5]	58	47.53 N	7.13 E
Hauts-de-Seine □[5]	261	48.50 N	2.11 E
Hautvillers	50	49.05 N	3.57 E
Haut-Zaïre □[4]	154	2.20 N	27.00 E
Hauula	229c	21.36 N	157.54 W
Hauzenberg	60	48.39 N	13.38 E
Hauz Rāni ⊶[8]	272a	28.32 N	77.13 E
Havana, Ar., U.S.	194	35.06 N	93.31 W
Havana, Fl., U.S.	192	30.37 N	84.24 W
Havana, Il., U.S.	194	40.18 N	90.03 W
Havana, N.D., U.S.	198	45.57 N	97.37 W
Havana → La Habana	240p	23.08 N	82.22 W
Havane, La → La Habana	240p	23.08 N	82.22 W
Havannah, Canal de la ⩊	175f	22.22 S	167.01 E
Havant	42	50.51 N	0.59 W
Havasu, Lake ⊜[1]	200	34.30 N	114.20 W
Havasu Creek ≃	200	36.19 N	112.46 W
Havasupai Indian Reservation ⊶[4]	200	36.13 N	112.40 W
Havdrup	41	55.32 N	12.08 E
Havel ≃	54	52.53 N	11.58 E
Havelange	56	50.23 N	5.14 E
Havelberg	54	52.50 N	12.04 E
Havelberg ∧[2]	264a	52.28 N	13.12 E
Haveli	123	30.27 N	73.42 E
Haveliān	123	34.03 N	73.10 E
Havel-Kanal ≍	264a	52.36 N	13.12 E
Havelland ⊶[1]	54	52.25 N	12.45 E
Havelländischer Grosser Hauptkanal ≍	264a	52.37 N	13.03 E
Havelländisches Luch ≋	54	52.40 N	12.40 E
Havelock, On., Can.	212	44.26 N	77.53 W
Havelock, N.Z.	172	41.17 S	173.46 E
Havelock, N.C., U.S.	192	34.52 N	76.54 W
Havelock Island I	110	11.58 N	93.00 E
Havelock North	172	39.40 S	176.53 E
Haven	198	37.53 N	97.46 W
Haverford	285	40.00 N	75.17 W
Haverford College ⚑[2]	285	40.00 N	75.18 W
Haverfordwest	42	51.49 N	4.58 W
Haverhill, Eng., U.K.	42	52.05 N	0.26 E
Haverhill, Ma., U.S.	207	42.46 N	71.04 W
Haverhill Airport ⊗	283	42.48 N	71.04 W
Haverhill-Riverside Airport ⊗	283	42.46 N	71.02 W
Hāveri	122	14.48 N	75.24 E
Haverigg	44	54.11 N	3.17 W
Havering ⊶[8]	42	51.34 N	0.14 E
Havering-atte-Bower ⊶[8]	260	51.37 N	0.11 E
Havering's Grove	260	51.38 N	0.23 E
Havern ⊜	26	62.17 N	15.07 E
Haverö	26	62.24 N	15.05 E
Haverstraw	210	41.11 N	73.57 W
Havertown	208	39.58 N	75.18 W
Haviland, Ks., U.S.	198	37.37 N	99.06 W
Haviland, Oh., U.S.	216	41.01 N	84.35 W
Haviland Brook ≃	276	41.07 N	73.33 W
Ḥavīq	128	38.10 N	48.54 E
Havířov	30	49.47 N	18.27 E
Havixbeck	52	51.58 N	7.25 E
Hävla	40	58.55 N	15.52 E
Havlíčkův Brod	30	49.36 N	15.35 E
Havnbjerg	41	55.02 N	9.48 E
Havnsø	41	55.45 N	11.20 E
Havran	130	39.33 N	27.06 E
Havré, Bel.	50	50.28 N	4.02 E
Havre, Mt., U.S.	202	48.32 N	109.40 W
Havre-Aubert	186	47.14 N	61.51 W
Havre Aubert, Île du I	186	47.14 N	61.57 W
Havre aux Maisons, Île du I	186	47.25 N	61.47 W
Havre de Grace	208	39.32 N	76.05 W
Havre de Grace Heights	208	39.35 N	76.07 W
Havre → Le Havre	50	49.30 N	0.08 E
Havre North	202	48.36 N	109.41 W
Havre-Saint-Pierre	186	50.14 N	63.36 W
Havsa	130	41.33 N	26.49 E
Havza	130	40.58 N	35.41 E
Haw ≃	192	35.36 N	79.03 W
Hawaii □[3]	229d	20.00 N	157.45 W
Hawaii I	229d	19.30 N	155.30 W
Hawaiian Gardens	280	33.49 N	118.04 W
Hawaiian Islands II	229d	20.30 N	157.30 W
Hawaiian Ridge ⟡[3]	14	24.00 N	165.00 W
Hawaii Volcanoes National Park ♦	229d	19.23 N	155.17 W
Hawal ≃	146	10.00 N	12.05 E
Hawarden, Sk., Can.	184	51.23 N	106.36 W
Hawarden, N.Z.	172	42.56 S	172.38 E
Hawarden, Wales, U.K.	44	53.11 N	3.02 W
Hawarden, Ia., U.S.	198	42.59 N	96.29 W
Ḥawashīyah, Wādī V	140	28.31 N	32.58 E
Haw Creek ≃	218	39.11 N	85.55 W
Hawea, Lake ⊜	172	44.30 S	169.17 E
Hawera	172	39.35 S	174.17 E
Hawes	44	54.18 N	2.12 W
Hawesville	194	37.54 N	86.45 W
Haweswater Reservoir ⊜	44	54.32 N	2.48 W
Ḥawf, Jabal ⩚[2]	273c	29.55 N	31.21 E
Ḥawf, Wādī V	142	29.53 N	31.18 E
Hawi	229d	20.14 N	155.50 W
Hawick	44	55.25 N	2.47 W
Hawk Creek ≃	198	44.44 N	95.25 W

Symbols in the index entries represent the broad categories identified in the key at the right. Symbols with superior numbers (⩚[1]) identify subcategories (see complete key on page *I · 1).*

Symbole im Register stellen die rechts im Schlüssel erklärten Kategorien dar. Symbole mit hochgestellten Ziffern (⩚[1]) bezeichnen Unterabteilungen einer Kategorie (vgl. vollständiger Schlüssel auf Seite *I · 1).*

Los símbolos incluídos en el texto del índice representan las grandes categorias identificadas con la clave a la derecha. Los símbolos con numeros en su parte superior (⩚[1]) identifican las subcategorías (véase la clave completa en la página *I · 1).*

Les symboles de l'index représentent les catégories indiquées dans la légende à droite. Les symboles suivis d'un indice (⩚[1]) représentent des sous-catégories (voir légende complète à la page *I · 1).*

Os símbolos incluídos no texto do índice representam as grandes categorias identificadas com a chave à direita. Os símbolos com números em sua parte superior (⩚[1]) identificam as subcategorias (veja-se a chave completa à página *I · 1).*

∧ Mountain	Berg	Montaña	Montagne	Montanha
⩚ Mountains	Gebirge	Montañas	Montagnes	Montanhas
)(Pass	Paß	Paso	Col	Passo
V Valley, Canyon	Tal, Cañon	Valle, Cañón	Vallée, Canyon	Vale, Canhão
≚ Plain	Ebene	Llano	Plaine	Planície
> Cape	Kap	Cabo	Cap	Cabo
I Island	Insel	Isla	Île	Ilha
II Islands	Inseln	Islas	Îles	Ilhas
⊥ Other Topographic Features	Andere Topographische Objekte	Otros Elementos Topográficos	Autres données topographiques	Outros acidentes topográficos

ESPAÑOL — Nombre | Página | Lat.°′ | Long.°′ W = Oeste
FRANÇAIS — Nom | Page | Lat.°′ | Long.°′ W = Ouest
PORTUGUÊS — Nome | Página | Lat.°′ | Long.°′ W = Oeste

Hawkdun Range ⩕ 172 44.46 S 170.00 E
Hawke, Cape > 166 32.13 S 152.34 E
Hawke Bay ⊂ 172 39.20 S 177.30 E
Hawker 166 31.53 S 138.25 E
Hawkes, Mount ∧ 9 83.56 S 55.45 W
Hawkes Brook ≃ 283 42.45 N 71.08 W
Hawkesbury 206 45.36 N 74.37 W
Hawkesbury ≃ 170 33.30 S 151.10 E
Hawkesbury Island I 182 53.38 N 129.00 W
Hawkes Pond ◎ 283 42.30 N 71.02 W
Hawkeye 190 42.56 N 91.57 W
Hawkhurst 42 51.02 N 0.30 E
Hawking 42 51.06 N 1.10 E
Hawkins, Tx., U.S. 222 32.35 N 95.12 W
Hawkins, Wi., U.S. 190 45.30 N 90.43 W
Hawkins, Lake ◎[1] 222 32.38 N 95.15 W
Hawkins Island I 180 60.30 N 146.00 W
Hawkinsville 192 32.17 N 83.28 W
Hawk Junction 190 48.05 N 84.34 W
Hawk Lake 184 49.48 N 93.59 W
Haw Knob ∧ 192 35.19 N 84.02 W
Hawk Point 219 38.58 N 91.07 W
Hawk Run 214 40.55 N 78.12 W
Hawksbill ∧ 188 38.33 N 78.23 W
Hawksbill Creek ⊂ 192 26.32 N 78.43 W
Hawks Nest Point > 238 24.09 N 75.32 W
Hawkwell 260 51.36 N 0.40 E
Hawkwood 166 25.47 S 150.50 E
Hawley, Eng., U.K. 260 51.25 N 0.14 E
Hawley, Mn., U.S. 198 46.52 N 96.18 W
Hawley, Pa., U.S. 210 41.28 N 75.10 W
Hawleyton 210 42.01 N 75.55 W
Hawleyville 207 41.25 N 73.21 W
Haworth, Eng., U.K. 44 53.49 N 1.57 W
Haworth, N.J., U.S. 276 40.57 N 73.59 W
Haw Par Villa ▼ 271c 1.16 N 103.47 E
Hawr 142 27.52 N 30.44 E
Ḥawrān, Wādī V 128 33.58 N 42.34 E
Ḥawsh ʿĪsā 142 30.55 N 30.17 E
Hawthorn, Austl. 274b 37.49 S 145.02 E
Hawthorn, Pa., U.S. 214 41.01 N 79.17 W
Hawthorne, Ca., U.S. 228 33.54 N 118.21 W
Hawthorne, Fl., U.S. 192 29.35 N 82.05 W
Hawthorne, Nv., U.S. 204 38.31 N 118.37 W
Hawthorne, N.J., U.S. 210 40.56 N 74.09 W
Hawthorne, N.Y., U.S. 210 41.06 N 73.47 W
Hawthorne Lake ◎ 276 41.03 N 74.35 W
Hawthorne Municipal Airport ⊠ 280 33.55 N 118.20 W
Hawthorne Race Course ♠ 278 41.50 N 87.45 W
Hawthorn Woods 278 42.13 N 88.03 W
Ḥawwārah 132 32.32 N 35.54 E
Hawwārat ʿAdlān 142 29.12 N 30.58 E
Hawwārat al-Maqṭaʿ 142 29.15 N 30.54 E
Hawza 148 27.06 N 10.55 W
Hawzen 144 13.56 N 39.28 E
Haxby 44 54.01 N 1.04 W
Haxey 44 53.29 N 0.50 W
Haxtun 198 40.38 N 102.37 W
Hay 166 34.30 S 144.51 E
Hay ≃, Austl. 166 25.14 S 138.00 E
Hay ≃, Can. 176 60.52 N 115.44 W
Hay ≃, Wi., U.S. 190 44.59 N 91.51 W
Hay, Cape > 176 74.25 N 113.00 W
Hay, Mount ∧, Austl. 162 23.28 S 133.05 E
Hay, Mount ∧, Austl. 170 33.37 S 150.26 E
Hay, Mount ∧, N.A. 180 59.15 N 137.37 W
Hay, South Fork ≃ 190 45.03 N 91.57 W
Haya 164 3.27 S 129.33 E
Haya ≃, Nihon 94 35.14 N 139.09 E
Haya ≃, Nihon 94 35.25 N 138.27 E
Hayachine-san ∧ 92 39.34 N 141.29 E
Hayakawa 94 35.25 N 138.22 E
Hayama, Nihon 94 35.16 N 139.35 E
Hayama, Nihon 96 33.26 N 133.13 E
Hayang 98 35.55 N 128.47 E
Hayange 56 49.20 N 6.03 E
HaYarden — Jordan ≃ 132 31.46 N 35.33 E
Hayashima 96 34.36 N 133.50 E
Hayastan — Armenia □[1] 22 40.00 N 45.00 E
Hayasui-seto ≍ 96 33.18 N 131.59 E
Haybān 140 11.13 N 30.31 E
Haybān, Jabal ∧ 140 11.15 N 30.31 E
Hay Bay ⊂ 212 44.10 N 76.55 W
Haybes 56 50.00 N 4.43 E
Haydān, Wādī al- V 132 31.27 N 35.36 E
Haydarlı 130 38.16 N 30.23 E
Hayden, Az., U.S. 200 33.00 N 110.47 W
Hayden, Co., U.S. 200 40.29 N 107.15 W
Hayden, In., U.S. 218 38.58 N 85.44 W
Hayden Peak ∧ 202 42.59 N 116.39 W
Haydenville, Ma., U.S. 207 42.22 N 72.42 W
Haydenville, Oh., U.S. 188 39.28 N 82.19 W
Haydock 44 53.28 N 2.39 W
Haydock Park Race Course ♠ 262 53.29 N 2.37 W
Haydon Bridge 44 54.58 N 2.14 W
Haye, La — 's-Gravenhage 52 52.06 N 4.18 E
Hayes 194 30.06 N 92.55 W
Hayes ◆[8], Eng., U.K. 260 51.31 N 0.25 W
Hayes ◆[8], Eng., U.K. 260 51.23 N 0.01 E
Hayes ≃, Mb., Can. 184 57.03 N 92.09 W
Hayes ≃, N.T., Can. 176 67.18 N 95.02 W
Hayes, Mount ∧ 180 63.37 N 146.43 W
Hayes Center 198 40.30 N 101.01 W
Hayes State Memorial ⊥ 214 41.21 N 83.08 W
Hayesville, N.C., U.S. 192 35.02 N 83.49 W
Hayesville, Oh., U.S. 214 40.46 N 82.15 W
Hayesville, Or., U.S. 224 44.59 N 122.58 W
Hayfield, Eng., U.K. 262 53.23 N 1.57 W
Hayfield, Mn., U.S. 190 43.53 N 92.50 W
Hayford Peak ∧ 204 36.40 N 115.11 W
Hayfork 204 40.33 N 123.10 W
Hayfork Bally ∧ 204 40.39 N 123.13 W
Hayfork Creek ≃ 204 40.37 N 123.26 W
Hay Island I 212 44.53 N 80.58 W
Hayk, Lake ◎ 144 11.21 N 39.43 E
Haykota 144 15.10 N 37.03 E
Hay Lake ◎ 212 45.23 N 78.11 W
Hay Lakes 182 53.13 N 113.03 W
Hayle 42 50.11 N 5.23 W
Haymakers Run ≃ 279b 40.25 N 79.43 W
Haymana 130 39.27 N 32.30 E
Haynes 194 34.53 N 90.47 W
Haynes Creek ≃ 285 39.53 N 74.50 W
Haynesville, La., U.S. 194 32.57 N 93.08 W
Haynesville, Va., U.S. 208 37.57 N 76.40 W
Hayneville 194 32.11 N 86.34 W
Haynin 144 15.50 N 48.19 E
Hay-on-Wye 42 52.04 N 3.07 W
Hay Point > 166 21.17 S 149.18 E
Hayrabolu 130 41.12 N 27.06 E
Hay River 176 60.51 N 115.40 W
Hays, Ab., Can. 182 50.06 N 111.48 W
Hays, Ks., U.S. 198 38.52 N 99.19 W
Hays, Mt., U.S. 202 47.59 N 108.41 W
Hays □[6] 222 30.02 N 97.45 W
Hays ◆[8] 279b 40.23 N 79.56 W
Hayshah, Sabkhat al- ⊞ 146 31.45 N 15.20 E
Hays Mill Creek ≃ 285 39.44 N 74.50 W
Hay Springs 198 42.41 N 102.41 W
Haystack Mountain ∧ 204 41.39 N 115.38 W
Haysville, Ks., U.S. 198 37.33 N 97.21 W
Haysville, Pa., U.S. 279b 40.32 N 80.09 W
Hayti, Mo., U.S. 194 36.14 N 89.44 W
Hayti, Pa., U.S. 208 39.59 N 75.51 W
Hayti, S.D., U.S. 198 44.39 N 97.12 W
Hayward, Ca., U.S. 226 37.40 N 122.04 W
Hayward, Wi., U.S. 190 46.00 N 91.29 W
Hayward Brook ≃ 283 42.22 N 71.20 W
Hayward Municipal Airport ⊠ 282 37.40 N 122.08 W
Haywards Heath 42 51.00 N 0.06 W
Haywood 184 49.40 N 98.12 W
Ḥayy, Jabal al- ∧ 142 29.43 N 31.35 E
HaẒafon □[5] 132 32.50 N 35.20 E
Hazār, Kūh-e ∧ 128 29.30 N 57.18 E
Hazard 192 37.14 N 83.11 W
Hazardville 207 41.59 N 72.32 W
Hazar Gölü ◎ 130 38.30 N 39.25 E
Hazārībāg 124 23.59 N 85.21 E
Hazārībāg Plateau ⩕[1] 124 24.00 N 85.10 E
Haze, Cape > 220 26.46 N 82.10 W
Hazebrouck 50 50.43 N 2.32 E
Hazel ≃ 188 38.33 N 77.51 W
Hazelbrook 170 33.44 S 150.27 E
Hazel Crest 278 41.34 N 87.41 W
Hazel Dell 224 45.40 N 122.39 W
Hazel Green 190 42.31 N 90.26 W
Hazelgrove, Austl. 170 33.40 S 149.52 E
Hazel Grove, Eng., U.K. 44 53.23 N 2.08 W
Hazel Hurst 214 41.42 N 78.35 W
Hazel Kirk 279b 40.11 N 79.57 W
Hazel Park 216 42.27 N 83.06 W
Hazel Park Raceway ♠ 281 42.29 N 83.05 W
Hazelton, B.C., Can. 182 55.15 N 127.40 W
Hazelton, Id., U.S. 202 42.35 N 114.08 W
Hazelton, N.D., U.S. 198 46.29 N 100.16 W
Hazelton Mountains ⩕ 182 54.30 N 128.20 W
Hazelton Peak ∧ 202 44.06 N 107.03 W
Hazelwood, Mo., U.S. 219 38.46 N 90.22 W
Hazelwood, N.C., U.S. 192 35.28 N 83.00 W
Hazelwood ◆[8] 279b 40.25 N 79.56 W
Hazen, Ar., U.S. 194 34.46 N 91.34 W
Hazen, Nv., U.S. 226 39.33 N 119.02 W
Hazen, N.D., U.S. 198 47.17 N 101.37 W
Hazen, Pa., U.S. 214 41.12 N 78.58 W
Hazen Bay ⊂ 180 61.00 N 165.10 W
Ḥaẕerim 132 31.14 N 34.43 E
Hazlehurst, Ga., U.S. 192 31.52 N 82.35 W
Hazlehurst, Ms., U.S. 194 31.51 N 90.23 W
Hazlet, Sk., Can. 184 50.25 N 108.36 W
Hazlet, N.J., U.S. 208 40.26 N 74.13 W
Hazleton, Ia., U.S. 190 42.37 N 91.54 W
Hazleton, Pa., U.S. 210 40.57 N 75.58 W
Hazlett, Lake ◎ 162 21.30 S 128.48 E
Ḥaẕor HaGelilit 132 32.59 N 35.33 E
Hazro, Pāk. 123 33.54 N 72.29 E
Hazro, Tür. 130 38.15 N 40.47 E
Hazu 94 34.47 N 137.08 E
He ≃, Zhg. 100 27.05 N 114.59 E
He ≃, Zhg. 102 23.26 N 111.30 E
Heacham 42 52.55 N 0.30 E
Head ≃ 212 44.44 N 79.15 W
Head Bay d'Espoir ⊂ 186 47.56 N 55.45 W
Headcorn 42 51.11 N 0.37 E
Headford 48 53.28 N 9.05 W
Head Lake ◎ 212 44.45 N 78.55 W
Headland 194 31.21 N 85.20 W
Headlands 154 18.14 S 32.03 E
Headley, Eng., U.K. 42 51.07 N 0.50 W
Headley, Eng., U.K. 260 51.17 N 0.16 W
Headley, Mount ∧ 202 47.44 N 115.15 W
Head of the Harbor 276 40.54 N 73.10 W
Heald Green 262 53.22 N 2.14 W
Heald Moor ◆[3] 262 53.44 N 2.10 W
Healdsburg 204 38.36 N 122.52 W
Healdton 196 34.13 N 97.29 W
Healesville 169 37.40 S 145.31 E
Healing 44 53.34 N 0.10 W
Healy, Ak., U.S. 180 63.52 N 148.58 W
Healy, Ks., U.S. 198 38.36 N 100.37 W
Healy, Mount ∧ 180 63.46 N 149.01 W
Healy Lake ◎ 212 45.10 N 79.55 W
Heani, Mont ∧ 174x 9.47 S 139.04 W
Heanna 174m 26.19 N 127.54 E
Heanor 44 53.01 N 1.22 W
Heany Junction 154 20.06 S 28.54 E
Heard Island I 6 53.06 S 73.30 E
Heard Pond ◎ 283 42.21 N 71.22 W
Hearne 222 30.52 N 96.35 W
Hearst 176 49.41 N 83.40 W
Hearst Island I 9 69.25 S 62.10 W
Hearst San Simeon State Historical Park ♠ 226 35.42 N 121.10 W
Heart ≃, Ab., Can. 182 56.14 N 117.17 W
Heart ≃, N.D., U.S. 198 46.47 N 100.51 W
Heart Lake ◎, Ab., Can. 182 55.02 N 111.30 W
Heart Lake ◎, On., Can. 275b 43.44 N 79.48 W
Heart Lake Indian Reserve ◆[4] 182 55.02 N 111.30 W
Heart Pond ◎ 283 42.34 N 71.23 W
Heart's Content 186 47.53 N 53.22 W
Heath, Ma., U.S. 207 42.40 N 72.49 W
Heath, Oh., U.S. 214 40.02 N 82.28 W
Heath, Tx., U.S. 222 32.50 N 96.29 W
Heath ≃ 248 12.31 S 68.38 W
Heath, Pointe > 186 49.05 N 61.42 W
Heathcote, Austl. 169 36.55 S 144.42 E
Heathcote, Austl. 274a 34.05 S 151.01 E
Heathcote Brook ≃ 276 40.23 N 74.37 W
Heath End 42 51.22 N 1.09 W
Heatherton 274b 37.58 S 145.06 E
Heathfield 42 50.59 N 0.17 E
Heathmont 274b 37.49 S 145.15 E
Heath Springs 192 34.35 N 80.40 W
Heathsville 208 37.55 N 76.28 W
Heatley 262 53.24 N 2.27 W
Heaton Hall ⊥ 262 53.32 N 2.15 W
Heaton Moor 262 53.25 N 2.11 W
Heaven, Temple of ▼[1] 271a 39.53 N 116.25 E
Heavener 194 34.53 N 94.36 W
Heaverham 260 51.18 N 0.15 E
Heaviley 262 53.24 N 2.09 W
Hebaochang 107 29.33 N 105.32 E
Hebao Dao I 100 21.52 N 113.09 E
Hebbronville 196 27.18 N 98.40 W
Hebburn 44 54.59 N 1.30 W
Hebbville 284b 39.20 N 77.46 W
Hebden Bridge 44 53.45 N 2.00 W
Hebden Water ≃ 262 53.44 N 2.00 W
Hebei, Zhg. 104 40.43 N 122.12 E
Hebei, Zhg. 104 41.01 N 123.51 E
Hebei (Hopeh) □[4] 98 38.00 N 116.00 E
Hebeitun 105 39.35 N 117.07 E
Hebel 166 28.59 S 147.48 E
Heber, Az., U.S. 200 34.25 N 110.35 W
Heber, Ca., U.S. 204 32.44 N 115.32 W
Heber City 200 40.30 N 111.24 W
Heber Springs 194 35.29 N 92.01 W
Hebgen Lake ◎[1] 202 44.47 N 111.14 W
Hebi 98 35.59 N 114.11 E
Hebian 107 30.29 N 105.08 E
Hebo, Or., U.S. 224 45.13 N 123.51 W
Hebo, Zhg. 102 31.29 N 98.58 E
Hebo, Mount ∧ 224 45.12 N 123.45 W
Hébridas, Islas — Hebrides II 46 57.00 N 6.30 W
Hebrides II 22 57.00 N 6.30 W
Hebrides, Sea of the ⊤[2] 46 57.07 N 6.55 W
Hebron, Nf., Can. 176 58.12 N 62.38 W
Hebron, Ct., U.S. 207 41.39 N 72.21 W
Hebron, Il., U.S. 216 42.28 N 88.25 W
Hebron, In., U.S. 216 41.19 N 87.12 W
Hebron, Ky., U.S. 218 39.03 N 84.42 W
Hebron, Md., U.S. 208 38.25 N 75.41 W
Hebron, Ne., U.S. 198 40.09 N 97.35 W
Hebron, N.D., U.S. 198 46.54 N 102.02 W
Hebron, Pa., U.S. 208 40.21 N 76.24 W
Hebron, Tx., U.S. 222 33.01 N 96.52 W
Hebron, Wi., U.S. 216 42.56 N 88.42 W
Hebron — Al-Khalīl 132 31.32 N 35.06 E
Hebu 100 27.50 N 115.22 E
Hebutu 104 42.19 N 122.20 E
Heby 40 59.56 N 16.53 E
Hecao 105 40.21 N 116.47 E
Hecate Strait ≍ 182 53.00 N 131.00 W
Hecelchakán 232 20.10 N 90.08 W
Heceta Island I 180 55.45 N 133.35 W
Hechi 102 24.42 N 108.02 E
Hechiceros 196 28.33 N 103.38 W
Hechingen 58 48.21 N 8.58 E
Hechtel 56 51.08 N 5.21 E
Hechthausen 52 53.38 N 9.14 E
Hechuan 107 30.00 N 106.16 E
Heckelberg 54 52.44 N 13.50 E
Hecker 219 38.18 N 90.00 W
Heckington 42 52.59 N 0.18 W
Hecklingen 54 51.51 N 11.32 E
Heckscher State Park ♠ 210 40.43 N 73.10 W
Hecla, Mb., Can. 184 51.08 N 96.40 W
Hecla, S.D., U.S. 198 45.52 N 98.09 W
Hecla Island I 184 51.08 N 96.45 W
Hecla Provincial Park ♠ 184 51.12 N 96.35 W
Hectanooga 186 44.06 N 66.02 W
Hector, N.Z. 172 41.36 S 171.53 E
Hector, Mn., U.S. 198 44.44 N 94.42 W
Hector, Mount ∧ 172 40.57 S 175.17 E
Heda 94 34.58 N 138.46 E
Hedal 26 60.37 N 9.42 E
Hedaru 154 4.30 S 37.54 E
Heddal ▼[1] 26 59.35 N 9.11 E
Hedding 285 40.06 N 74.44 W
Hédé, Fr. 32 48.18 N 1.48 W
Hede, Sve. 26 62.25 N 13.30 E
Hedehusene 41 55.39 N 12.12 E
Hedel 52 51.45 N 5.15 E
Hedemora 40 60.17 N 15.59 E
Hedemünden 56 51.23 N 9.46 E
Hedensted 41 55.46 N 9.42 E
Hedersleben 54 51.51 N 11.15 E
Hedesunda 40 60.24 N 16.59 E
Hedesundafjärdarna ◎ 40 60.20 N 17.00 E
He Devil ∧ 202 45.21 N 116.33 W
Hedge End 42 50.54 N 1.18 W
Hedgerley 260 51.35 N 0.36 W
Hedian 100 32.45 N 114.18 E
Hedley, B.C., Can. 182 49.21 N 120.04 W
Hedley, Tx., U.S. 196 34.52 N 100.39 W
Hedmark □[6] 26 61.30 N 11.45 E
Hednesford 42 52.43 N 2.00 W
Hedo 174m 26.51 N 128.16 E
Hedo-misaki > 174m 26.52 N 128.16 E
Hedon 44 53.44 N 0.12 W
Hedrick 190 41.10 N 92.18 W
Hedströmmen ≃ 40 59.28 N 16.04 E
Hedutne 272c 19.10 N 73.06 E
Hedwig Village 222 29.47 N 95.27 W
Heek 52 52.07 N 7.06 E
Heel 52 51.11 N 5.53 E
Heel Point > 174a 19.19 N 166.37 E
Heemskerk 52 52.31 N 4.40 E
Heemstede 52 52.21 N 4.37 E
Heepen 52 52.01 N 8.35 E
Heer, Bel. 56 50.10 N 4.50 E
Heer, Ned. 56 50.50 N 5.44 E
Heerde 52 52.23 N 6.03 E
Heerdt ◆[8] 263 51.13 N 6.43 E
Heerenveen 52 52.57 N 5.55 E
Heeren-Werve 52 51.35 N 7.38 E
Heerhugowaard 52 52.40 N 4.50 E
Heerkan 107 29.32 N 103.56 E
Heerlen 56 50.54 N 5.59 E
Heesch 52 51.44 N 5.32 E
Heeslingen 52 53.19 N 9.20 E
Heessen 52 51.42 N 7.50 E
Heeze 52 51.24 N 5.35 E
Ḥefa (Haifa) 132 32.50 N 35.00 E
Ḥefa □[5] 132 32.35 N 35.00 E
Ḥefa, Mifraẕ ⊂ 132 32.52 N 35.03 E
Ḥefa, Sede-Teʿufa ⊠ 132 32.49 N 35.02 E
Hefei 100 31.51 N 117.17 E
Hefengchang 107 30.26 N 104.43 E
Heffron Park ♠ 274a 33.57 S 151.15 E
Heflin 194 33.38 N 85.35 W
Hegang 89 47.24 N 130.22 E
Hegau ◆[1] 58 47.50 N 8.45 E
Hégenheim 58 47.34 N 7.32 E
Hegewisch ◆[8] 278 41.40 N 87.33 W
Hegins 208 40.39 N 76.29 W
Hegra 26 63.28 N 11.07 E
Hegura-jima I 92 37.51 N 136.55 E
Heguri 270 34.38 N 135.42 E
Hegyeshalom 61 47.55 N 17.10 E
Hehlen 52 51.59 N 9.28 E
Heho 110 20.43 N 96.49 E
Hehou 100 28.40 N 114.28 E
Hei ≃, Zhg. 102 40.18 N 99.26 E
Hei ≃, Zhg. 105 40.44 N 116.27 E
Heicheng (Karakhoto) ⊥ 102 41.47 N 101.03 E
Heichengzhen 102 36.16 N 106.06 E
Heichonglu 104 42.10 N 121.01 E
Heidayingzi 102 40.52 N 116.12 E
Heidberg ∧[2] 263 51.15 N 7.11 E
Heide 30 54.12 N 9.06 E
Heide ◆[8], Dtsch. 263 51.26 N 7.01 E
Heide ◆[8], Dtsch. 263 51.31 N 6.52 E
Heideck 60 49.08 N 11.07 E
Heidelberg, Austl. 169 37.45 S 145.04 E
Heidelberg, On., Can. 212 43.31 N 80.37 W
Heidelberg, Dtsch. 56 49.25 N 8.43 E
Heidelberg, S. Afr. 158 34.06 S 20.59 E
Heidelberg, S. Afr. 158 26.32 S 28.18 E
Heidelberg, Ms., U.S. 194 31.53 N 88.59 W
Heidelberg, Pa., U.S. 279b 40.23 N 80.05 W
Heidelberg □[5] 273d 26.19 S 28.16 E
Heidelberg, Schloss ⊥ 56 49.24 N 8.42 E
Heidelsheim 56 49.06 N 8.38 E
Heiden, Dtsch. 52 51.59 N 8.50 E
Heiden, Schw. 58 47.27 N 9.33 E
Heiden, Port ⊂ 180 56.55 N 158.45 W
Heidenau, Dtsch. 52 53.19 N 9.39 E
Heidenau, Dtsch. 54 50.59 N 13.52 E
Heidenheim 56 49.01 N 10.44 E
Heidenheim an der Brenz 56 48.40 N 10.08 E
Heidenheimer 222 31.01 N 97.18 W
Heidenoldendorf 52 51.57 N 8.50 E
Heidenreichstein 61 48.52 N 15.07 E
Heider Ditch ≍ 279a 41.31 N 82.01 W
Heiderscheid 56 49.53 N 5.54 E
Heidhausen ◆[8] 263 51.23 N 7.01 E
Heidhof ◆[8] 263 51.11 N 7.11 E
Heidlersburg 208 39.57 N 77.09 W
Heidouwo 105 39.42 N 117.15 E
Heigenbrücken 56 50.02 N 9.23 E
Heigoutaicun 104 41.30 N 123.01 E
Heigun-tō I 96 33.47 N 132.14 E
Heihai — Har Hu ◎ 102 38.15 N 97.40 E
Heihe — Aihui 89 50.16 N 127.28 E
Heijō — P'yŏngyang 98 39.01 N 125.45 E
Heikega-dake ∧ 96 34.19 N 131.54 E
Heikendorf 54 54.22 N 10.12 E
Heil 263 51.38 N 7.35 E
Heilangkou 105 39.37 N 117.24 E
Heilbron 158 27.21 S 27.58 E
Heilbronn 56 49.08 N 9.13 E
Heilenbecke-Stausee ◎[1] 263 51.15 N 7.22 E
Heiligenberg 58 47.49 N 9.19 E
Heiligenblut 64 47.02 N 12.50 E
Heiligendamm 54 54.08 N 11.50 E
Heiligenhafen 54 54.22 N 10.58 E
Heiligenhaus 56 51.19 N 6.59 E
Heiligensee ◆[8] 264a 52.36 N 13.13 E
Heiligenstadt, Dtsch. 56 51.23 N 10.09 E
Heiligenstadt, Dtsch. 60 49.51 N 11.10 E
Heilin 98 35.01 N 118.58 E
Hei Ling Chau I 271d 22.15 N 114.02 E
Heilong (Amur) ≃ 89 52.56 N 141.10 E
Heilongguan 102 36.19 N 111.11 E
Heilongjiang □[4] 89 48.00 N 128.00 E
Heilongtan, Zhg. 105 40.44 N 116.31 E
Heilongtan, Zhg. 105 40.02 N 116.11 E
Heilongtan Shuiku ◎[1] 107 30.03 N 104.02 E
Heiloo 52 52.36 N 4.43 E
Heilsbronn 56 49.20 N 10.47 E
Heiltz-le-Maurupt 56 48.48 N 4.49 E
Heilungkiang — Heilongjiang □[4] 89 48.00 N 128.00 E
Heilwood 214 40.37 N 78.54 W
Heimaey I 24a 63.26 N 20.17 W
Heimbach 56 50.38 N 6.28 E
Heimbuchenthal 56 49.53 N 9.17 E
Heimburg 54 51.49 N 10.54 E
Heimdal 26 63.21 N 10.22 E
Heimenkirch 58 47.37 N 9.53 E
Heimsheim 56 48.48 N 8.51 E
Heinävesi 26 62.26 N 28.36 E
Heinersdorf, Dtsch. 54 52.27 N 14.13 E
Heinersdorf, Dtsch. 264a 52.23 N 13.20 E
Heinersdorf ◆[8] 264a 52.34 N 13.27 E
Heiniuyingzi 98 41.07 N 120.19 E
Heino 52 52.26 N 6.14 E
Heinola 26 61.13 N 26.02 E
Heinrichshorst 54 52.20 N 11.42 E
Heinsberg 56 51.03 N 6.05 E
Heiquan 102 39.32 N 99.42 E
Heirnkut 110 25.14 N 94.45 E
Heisfelde 52 53.15 N 7.26 E
Heishan 104 41.41 N 122.07 E
Heishanguan 98 38.33 N 113.41 E
Heishantou, Zhg. 89 50.13 N 119.28 E
Heishantou, Zhg. 98 42.28 N 125.33 E
Heishui 98 42.09 N 119.28 E
Heishuisi 102 36.08 N 108.42 E
Heisingen ◆[8] 263 51.25 N 7.04 E
Heisler 182 52.41 N 112.13 W
Heislerville 208 39.13 N 74.59 W
Heissen ◆[8] 263 51.26 N 6.56 E
Heist-aan-Zee 50 51.21 N 3.15 E
Heist-op-den-Berg 56 51.05 N 4.43 E
Heitang 102 26.29 N 105.09 E
Heitersheim 58 47.53 N 7.40 E
Heiwa 94 35.12 N 136.44 E
Heiyanghebao 105 39.07 N 118.15 E
Heiyantang 102 27.28 N 101.11 E
Heiyanzi 105 39.13 N 118.08 E
Hejaz — Al-Ḥijāz ◆[1] 118 24.30 N 38.30 E
Hejiachang 107 29.24 N 104.56 E
Hejian, Zhg. 98 38.26 N 116.05 E
Hejian, Zhg. 105 39.25 N 116.25 E
Hejiang 107 28.49 N 105.50 E
Hejiangzhen 107 29.16 N 104.16 E
Hejiaqiao 100 27.24 N 113.21 E
Hejiawopeng 104 41.32 N 122.07 E
Hejiaying 105 39.55 N 118.19 E
Hejiazhen 107 29.52 N 104.26 E
Hejin 102 35.39 N 110.40 E
Hejlsminde 41 55.22 N 9.37 E
Hejnsvig 41 55.41 N 8.59 E
Hekelgem 50 50.54 N 4.06 E
Hekili Point > 229a 20.48 N 156.37 W
Hekimhan 130 38.49 N 37.56 E
Hekinan 94 34.51 N 136.58 E
Hekla ∧[1] 24a 64.00 N 19.39 W
Hekou, Zhg. 100 31.22 N 114.26 E
Hekou, Zhg. 102 36.09 N 103.22 E
Hekou, Zhg. 102 28.22 N 108.14 E
Hekou, Zhg. 102 29.57 N 111.04 E
Hekou, Zhg. 102 22.38 N 103.56 E
Hekouchang 107 29.21 N 104.21 E
Hekouji 100 32.09 N 116.04 E
Hekoujie 102 26.31 N 100.29 E
Hekpoort 158 25.55 S 27.38 E
Hel 30 54.37 N 18.48 E
Helagsfjället ∧ 26 62.55 N 12.27 E
Helaluo 102 33.56 N 102.10 E
Helangou 104 41.00 N 123.25 E
Helan Shan ⩕ 102 38.40 N 105.57 E
Helbe ≃ 54 51.13 N 11.01 E
Helbra 54 51.33 N 11.29 E
Helchteren 56 51.03 N 5.22 E
Heldburg 54 50.17 N 10.44 E
Helden 56 51.07 N 7.56 E
Heldra 56 51.07 N 10.11 E
Heldrungen 54 51.18 N 11.13 E
Helechos, Cañada de los ≃ 286a 19.22 N 99.12 W
Helemano Stream ≃ 229c 21.35 N 158.06 W
Helen, Mount ∧ 166 21.34 S 141.13 E
Helena, Ar., U.S. 194 34.31 N 90.35 W
Helena, Mt., U.S. 202 46.35 N 112.02 W
Helena, N.Y., U.S. 206 44.55 N 74.44 W
Helena, Oh., U.S. 214 41.21 N 83.17 W
Helena, Ok., U.S. 196 36.32 N 98.16 W
Helena ≃ 168a 31.54 S 116.00 E
Helena River Reservoir ◎[1] 168a 31.59 S 116.13 E
Helendale 228 34.45 N 117.18 W
Helenenberg 56 49.51 N 6.32 E
Helenental V 264b 48.01 N 16.11 E
Helen Island I 108 2.58 N 131.49 E
Helensburgh, Austl. 170 34.11 S 150.59 E
Helensburgh, Scot., U.K. 46 56.01 N 4.44 W
Helen Springs 162 18.26 S 133.52 E
Helensville 172 36.40 S 174.28 E
Helenville 216 43.01 N 88.41 W
Helenwood 192 36.25 N 84.32 W
Ḥeleẕ 132 31.35 N 34.40 E
Helfenberg 61 48.32 N 14.08 E
Helfenstein 208 40.45 N 76.27 W
Helfta 54 51.30 N 11.34 E
Helgaå ≃ 26 55.53 N 14.08 E
Helgenæs >[1] 41 56.08 N 10.32 E
Helgoland I 30 54.12 N 7.53 E
Helgoländer Bucht ⊂ 30 54.10 N 8.04 E
Heli 89 47.05 N 130.16 E
Helicoide ◆[9] 286c 10.29 N 66.55 W
Helidon 171a 27.33 S 152.08 E
Heliodora 256 22.04 S 45.32 W
Heliópolis 287a 22.45 S 43.25 W
Heliopolis ⊥ 142 30.08 N 31.17 E
Heliopolis Aerodrome ⊠ 273c 30.04 N 31.19 E
Heliopolis — Miṣr al-Jadīdah ◆[8] 273c 30.06 N 31.20 E
Heliopolis Racing Club ♠ 273c 30.06 N 31.19 E
Heliuji 100 33.02 N 116.57 E
Helixi 106 30.40 N 118.59 E
Hell 26 63.26 N 10.54 E
Hellam 208 40.00 N 76.36 W
Hellberge ⩕[2] 54 52.34 N 11.17 E
Hellbrunn, Schloss ⊥ 64 47.46 N 13.04 E
Hellebæk 41 56.04 N 12.34 E
Ḥelleh ≃ 128 29.10 N 50.40 E
Hellen Blazes, Lake ◎ 220 28.01 N 80.47 W
Hellendoorn 52 52.24 N 6.26 E
Hellenthal 56 50.29 N 6.26 E
Hellerau ◆[8] 54 51.07 N 13.44 E
Hellern 52 52.15 N 7.58 E
Hellersen 263 51.12 N 7.39 E
Hellertown 208 40.34 N 75.20 W
Hellesylt 26 62.05 N 6.54 E
Hellevad 41 55.05 N 9.13 E
Hellevoetsluis 52 51.49 N 4.08 E
Hell Gate ≍ 276 40.47 N 73.56 W
Hell Hole Reservoir ◎[1] 226 39.04 N 120.22 W
Hellifield 44 54.01 N 2.12 W
Hellín 34 38.31 N 1.41 W
Helli Ness > 46a 60.02 N 1.10 W
Hellmonsödt 61 48.26 N 14.18 E
Hell Point > 186 44.16 N 64.15 W
Hells Canyon V 202 45.20 N 116.45 W
Hellsee ◎ 264a 52.45 N 13.35 E
Hells Gate V 182 49.47 N 121.27 W
Hell-Ville 157b 13.25 S 48.16 E
Hellweg ◆[1] 52 51.36 N 8.32 E
Helm 226 36.31 N 120.05 W
Helmand □[4] 128 31.00 N 64.00 E
Helmand ≃ 128 31.12 N 61.34 E
Helmbrechts 54 50.14 N 11.43 E
Helmcken Falls L 182 51.57 N 120.11 W
Helme ≃ 54 51.20 N 11.20 E
Helmeringhausen 156 25.54 S 16.57 E
Helmetta 276 40.22 N 74.25 W
Helmetta Pond ◎ 276 40.23 N 74.26 W
Helmond 52 51.29 N 5.40 E
Helmsburg 218 39.16 N 86.18 W
Helmsdale 46 58.07 N 3.40 W
Helmsdale ≃ 46 58.07 N 3.40 W
Helmshore 262 53.41 N 2.20 W
Helmsley 44 54.14 N 1.04 W
Helmstedt 54 52.13 N 11.00 E
Helnæs I 41 55.08 N 10.02 E
Helong 98 42.32 N 128.59 E
Helper 200 39.41 N 110.51 W
Helpmekaar 158 28.29 S 30.29 E
Helpter Berg ∧[2] 54 53.30 N 13.36 E
Helsby 44 53.16 N 2.46 W
Helsby Hill ∧[2] 262 53.16 N 2.46 W
Helsingborg 41 56.03 N 12.42 E
Helsinge 41 56.01 N 12.12 E
Helsingfors — Helsinki 26 60.10 N 24.58 E
Helsingør (Elsinore) 41 56.02 N 12.37 E
Helsinki (Helsingfors) 26 60.10 N 24.58 E
Helska, Mierzeja >[2] 30 54.45 N 18.39 E
Helston 42 50.05 N 5.16 W
Heltonville 218 38.55 N 86.22 W
Helvecia 252 31.06 S 60.05 W
Helvellyn ∧ 44 54.31 N 3.01 W
Helvick Head > 48 52.03 N 7.33 W
Helvoirt 52 51.38 N 5.13 E
Hem ≃ 50 50.51 N 2.06 E
Ḥemar, Naḥal V 132 31.08 N 35.22 E
Hemau 60 49.03 N 11.47 E
Hemāvati ≃ 122 12.31 N 76.27 E
Hembe 152 1.54 N 22.42 E
Hemel Hempstead 42 51.46 N 0.28 W
Hemelingen ◆[8] 52 53.03 N 8.53 E
Hemeln 52 51.30 N 9.36 E
Hemer 56 51.23 N 7.46 E
Hemet 228 33.44 N 116.58 W
Hemfjärden ⊂ 40 59.17 N 15.20 E
Hemford 186 44.30 N 64.47 W
Hemfurth-Edersee 56 51.10 N 9.02 E
Hemiksem 50 51.09 N 4.21 E
Héming 58 48.42 N 6.57 E
Hemingford 198 42.19 N 103.04 W
Hemingway 192 33.45 N 79.26 W
Hemlock, In., U.S. 216 40.25 N 86.03 W
Hemlock, N.Y., U.S. 210 42.47 N 77.36 W
Hemlock Lake ◎ 210 42.43 N 77.37 W
Hemmerde 52 51.33 N 7.48 E
Hemmerden 263 51.07 N 6.36 E
Hemmingen-Westerfeld 52 52.19 N 9.45 E
Hemmoor 52 53.41 N 9.08 E
Hemphill 194 31.20 N 93.50 W
Hempnall 42 52.30 N 1.19 E
Hempstead, N.Y., U.S. 210 40.42 N 73.37 W
Hempstead, Tx., U.S. 222 30.05 N 96.04 W
Hempstead Harbor ⊂ 276 40.50 N 73.39 W
Hempstead Lake ◎ 276 40.41 N 73.38 W
Hempstead Lake State Park ♠ 276 40.41 N 73.38 W
Hemsby 42 52.41 N 1.42 E
Hemse 26 57.14 N 18.22 E
Hemsedal 26 60.52 N 8.34 E
Hemsön I 26 62.43 N 18.05 E
Hemstreet Park 210 42.54 N 73.41 W
Hemsworth 44 53.38 N 1.21 W
Hemujing 98 37.54 N 115.22 E
Henan 102 34.35 N 101.34 E
Henan (Honan) □[4] 90 34.00 N 114.00 E
Hen and Chickens II 172 35.55 S 174.45 E
Henares ≃ 34 40.24 N 3.30 W
Henbury, Austl. 162 24.35 S 133.15 E
Henbury, Eng., U.K. 262 53.15 N 2.11 W
Hendek 130 40.48 N 30.45 E
Henderson, Arg. 252 36.18 S 61.43 W
Henderson, In., U.S. 218 39.40 N 85.31 W
Henderson, Ky., U.S. 194 37.50 N 87.35 W
Henderson, Mn., U.S. 190 44.31 N 93.54 W
Henderson, Ne., U.S. 198 40.46 N 97.48 W
Henderson, Nv., U.S. 204 36.02 N 114.58 W
Henderson, N.Y., U.S. 212 43.51 N 76.11 W
Henderson, N.C., U.S. 192 36.19 N 78.23 W
Henderson, Tn., U.S. 194 35.26 N 88.38 W
Henderson, Tx., U.S. 222 32.09 N 94.47 W
Henderson □[6] 222 32.13 N 95.50 W
Henderson Bay ⊂, N.Y., U.S. 212 43.54 N 76.10 W
Henderson Bay ⊂, Wa., U.S. 224 47.18 N 122.42 W
Henderson Creek ≃ 190 40.52 N 91.02 W
Henderson Island I 6 24.22 S 128.19 W
Hendersonville, N.C., U.S. 192 35.19 N 82.27 W
Hendersonville, Pa., U.S. 214 40.18 N 80.09 W
Hendersonville, Tn., U.S. 194 36.18 N 86.37 W
Hendījān 128 30.14 N 49.43 E
Hendon ◆[8] 260 51.35 N 0.14 W
Hendorābī, Jazīreh-ye I 128 26.40 N 53.37 E
Hendricks, Mn., U.S. 198 44.30 N 96.25 W
Hendricks, W.V., U.S. 188 39.04 N 79.37 W
Hendricks □[6] 218 39.46 N 86.26 W
Hendrik Verwoerddam ◎[1] 158 30.40 S 25.40 E
Hendrina 158 26.11 S 29.45 E
Hendry □[6] 220 26.36 N 81.13 W
Hendrysburg 214 40.04 N 81.10 W
Hendy 42 51.43 N 4.04 W
Henefer 200 41.01 N 111.29 W
Henfield 42 50.56 N 0.17 W
Heng ≃, Zhg. 102 28.40 N 104.25 E
Heng ≃, Zhg. 107 28.57 N 105.22 E
Hengām, Jazīreh-ye I 128 26.39 N 55.53 E
Henganofi 164 6.15 S 145.35 E
Hengchow — Hengyang 102 26.54 N 112.36 E
Hengdaochuan 98 41.15 N 125.31 E
Hengdaohe 104 42.02 N 123.51 E
Hengdaohezi 89 43.13 N 126.44 E
Hengdaozi 89 43.18 N 127.18 E
Hengdong 100 27.03 N 112.57 E
Hengelo 52 52.15 N 6.45 E
Hengersberg 60 48.47 N 13.03 E
Hengfan 106 30.20 N 119.45 E
Hengfeng 100 28.24 N 117.34 E
Henggang 100 29.32 N 115.27 E
Henggouzi 89 43.12 N 124.47 E
Henghutou 104 42.05 N 124.00 E
Hengjie 106 31.13 N 119.30 E
Hengjing 106 31.11 N 120.32 E
Hengjinghong 106 30.34 N 120.59 E
Hengli 100 23.12 N 114.37 E
Henglin 106 31.42 N 120.06 E
Henglu 98 41.26 N 126.04 E
Henglutou 106 30.19 N 119.19 E
Hengmian 106 31.09 N 121.38 E
Hengoed 42 51.39 N 3.10 W
Hengsen 263 51.29 N 7.38 E
Heng Sha I 106 31.20 N 121.50 E
Hengshan, Zhg. 100 27.15 N 112.51 E
Hengshan, Zhg. 102 37.56 N 108.53 E
Hengshan, Zhg. 106 31.01 N 120.32 E
Heng Shan ∧ 100 27.16 N 112.35 E
Heng Shan ⩕ 102 39.30 N 113.45 E
Hengshanchang 107 30.33 N 105.24 E
Hengshanqiao 106 31.46 N 120.07 E
Hengshanxia 106 30.18 N 118.44 E
Hengshi, Zhg. 100 26.05 N 114.38 E
Hengshi, Zhg. 100 23.52 N 113.15 E
Hengshi, Zhg. 100 29.32 N 114.41 E
Hengshui 98 37.43 N 115.40 E
Hengsteysee ◎[1] 263 51.25 N 7.28 E
Hengtangshi 106 31.41 N 121.02 E
Hengtianchi 107 29.07 N 105.01 E
Hengtianxi 107 29.05 N 105.03 E
Hengxi, Zhg. 100 29.42 N 121.35 E
Hengxi, Zhg. 100 28.46 N 120.29 E
Hengxi, Zhg. 106 31.43 N 118.46 E
Hengxian 102 22.42 N 109.13 E
Hengxiang 106 32.12 N 120.15 E
Hengxikou 100 29.26 N 121.26 E
Hengyang 102 26.54 N 112.36 E
Hénin-Beaumont 50 50.25 N 2.56 E
Henley Beach 168b 34.55 S 138.30 E
Henley-in-Arden 42 52.17 N 1.46 W
Henley-on-Thames 42 51.32 N 0.56 W
Henlopen, Cape > 208 38.48 N 75.05 W
Henlow 42 52.02 N 0.18 W
Hennan ◎ 26 62.06 N 15.46 E
Hennaya 34 34.58 N 1.22 W
Henneberg 54 50.29 N 10.21 E
Hennebont 32 47.48 N 3.17 W
Hennef 56 50.46 N 7.16 E
Hennen 56 51.27 N 7.39 E
Hennenman 158 27.59 S 27.01 E
Hennepin 190 41.15 N 89.21 W
Hennepin, Point > 281 42.12 N 83.09 W
Hennersdorf 264b 48.07 N 16.22 E
Hennessey 196 36.06 N 97.53 W
Hennessey, Lake ◎[1] 226 38.29 N 122.22 W
Hennickendorf 54 52.30 N 13.51 E
Henniez 58 46.44 N 6.54 E
Hennigsdorf 54 52.38 N 13.12 E
Henniker 188 43.10 N 71.49 W
Henning, Il., U.S. 216 40.18 N 87.42 W
Henning, Mn., U.S. 198 46.19 N 95.26 W
Henning, Tn., U.S. 194 35.40 N 89.34 W
Henri ≃ 206 46.30 N 71.47 W
Henri, Cap > 186 49.48 N 64.23 W
Henri-Chapelle 56 50.40 N 5.56 E
Henrichemont 50 47.18 N 2.32 E
Henrichenburg 263 51.35 N 7.19 E
Henrico □[6] 208 37.30 N 77.20 W
Henrietta, N.Y., U.S. 210 43.03 N 77.36 W
Henrietta, N.C., U.S. 192 35.15 N 81.47 W
Henrietta, Tx., U.S. 196 33.49 N 98.11 W
Henrietta Maria, Cape > 176 55.09 N 82.20 W
Henri Pittier, Parque Nacional ♠ 246 10.25 N 67.43 W
Henry, Il., U.S. 190 41.06 N 89.21 W
Henry, S.D., U.S. 198 44.52 N 97.27 W
Henry □[6], In., U.S. 218 39.55 N 85.22 W
Henry □[6], Ky., U.S. 218 38.26 N 85.09 W
Henry □[6], Oh., U.S. 216 41.20 N 84.04 W
Henry ≃ 162 22.40 S 115.40 E
Henry, Cape > 208 36.55 N 76.01 W
Henry, Mount ∧ 202 48.53 N 115.31 W
Henry, Mount ∧[2] 274a 33.50 S 150.38 E
Henry, Point > 162 34.29 S 119.23 E
Henry Cowell Redwoods State Park ♠ 226 37.02 N 122.03 W
Henryetta 196 35.26 N 95.58 W
Henry Island I 224 48.35 N 123.11 W
Henry Kater, Cape > 176 69.05 N 66.44 W
Henry Mountains ⩕ 200 38.00 N 110.50 W
Henrys Bend 214 41.28 N 79.37 W
Henrys Fork ≃, U.S. 200 41.00 N 109.39 W
Henrys Fork ≃, Id., U.S. 202 43.45 N 111.56 W
Henryville, P.Q., Can. 206 45.08 N 73.11 W
Henryville, In., U.S. 218 38.32 N 85.46 W
Henry W. Coe State Park ♠ 226 37.12 N 121.30 W
Hensall 190 43.26 N 81.30 W
Henshaw, Lake ◎[1] 204 33.15 N 116.45 W
Hensley 194 34.30 N 92.12 W
Hensley Lake ◎[1] 226 37.07 N 119.53 W
Henslow, Cape > 175e 9.56 S 160.38 E
Henson Creek ≃ 284b 38.46 N 77.00 W
Hensonville 210 42.17 N 74.13 W
Henstedt-Ulzburg 52 53.47 N 9.58 E
Henstridge 42 50.59 N 2.24 W
Hentiesbaai 156 22.08 S 14.18 E
Henty 166 35.31 S 147.02 E
Henzada 110 17.38 N 95.28 E
Hepburn 184 52.31 N 106.43 W
Hepburn Springs 169 37.19 S 144.09 E
Hephzibah 192 33.18 N 82.05 W
Heping, Zhg. 100 27.10 N 117.18 E
Heping, Zhg. 100 22.01 N 112.59 E
Heping, Zhg. 100 23.17 N 116.29 E
Heping, Zhg. 100 24.28 N 114.58 E
Heping, Zhg. 106 30.50 N 119.54 E
Heppenheim 56 49.39 N 8.38 E
Heppner 202 45.21 N 119.33 W
Heptonstall 262 53.45 N 2.01 W
Heptonstall Moor ≃ 262 53.46 N 2.05 W
Hepu (Lianzhou) 102 21.39 N 109.11 E
Hepworth 212 44.37 N 81.09 W
Heqiao, Zhg. 100 32.55 N 118.22 E
Heqiao, Zhg. 106 31.30 N 119.53 E
Heqing 102 26.34 N 100.12 E
Hequ 102 39.26 N 111.08 E
Héraðsflói ⊂ 24a 65.45 N 14.10 W
Hera Lacinia, Tempio di ⊥ 68 39.01 N 17.13 E
Herāt 128 34.20 N 62.12 E
Herāt □[4] 128 34.30 N 62.00 E
Hérault □[5] 32 43.40 N 3.30 E
Hérault ≃ 32 43.17 N 3.26 E
Herbasse ≃ 62 45.02 N 4.57 E
Herbault 50 47.36 N 1.08 E
Herbede 56 51.25 N 7.16 E
Herbern 52 51.44 N 7.39 E
Herbert, Sk., Can. 184 50.26 N 107.12 W
Herbert, N.Z. 172 45.14 S 170.47 E
Herbert ≃ 166 18.32 S 146.17 E
Herbert, Mount ∧ 172 43.41 S 172.44 E
Herbertabad 110 11.43 N 92.37 E
Herbert Hoover National Historic Site ⊥ 190 41.38 N 91.23 W
Herbertingen 58 48.04 N 9.26 E
Herbert Island I 180 52.45 N 170.10 W
Herberton 166 17.23 S 145.23 E
Herbertsdale 158 34.01 S 21.46 E
Herbeumont 56 49.47 N 5.14 E
Herbignac 32 47.27 N 2.19 W
Herb Lake 184 54.47 N 99.47 W
Herblay 50 49.00 N 2.10 E
Herblet Lake ◎ 184 54.56 N 99.54 W
Herbolzheim 58 48.13 N 7.47 E
Herborn 56 50.40 N 8.17 E
Herbrechtingen 56 48.37 N 10.10 E
Herbringhauser-Stausee ◎[1] 263 51.14 N 7.16 E
Herbsleben 54 51.07 N 10.50 E
Herbstein 56 50.34 N 9.20 E
Herceg-Novi 38 42.27 N 18.32 E
Herculaneum 219 38.16 N 90.22 W
Hércules, Méx. 232 28.02 N 103.48 W

English	Deutsch	Español	Français	Português
≃ River	Fluß	Río	Rivière	Rio
Canal	Kanal	Canal	Canal	Canal
L Waterfall, Rapids	Wasserfall, Stromschnellen	Cascada, Rápidos	Chute d'eau, Rapides	Cascata, Rápidos
≍ Strait	Meeresstraße	Estrecho	Détroit	Estreito
⊂ Bay, Gulf	Bucht, Golf	Bahía, Golfo	Baie, Golfe	Baía, Golfo
◎ Lake, Lakes	See, Seen	Lago, Lagos	Lac, Lacs	Lago, Lagos
⊞ Swamp	Sumpf	Pantano	Marais	Pântano
Ice Features, Glacier	Eis- und Gletscherformen	Accidentes Glaciales	Formes glaciaires	Acidentes glaciares
⊤ Other Hydrographic Features	Andere Hydrographische Objekte	Otros Elementos Hidrográficos	Autres données hydrographiques	Outros acidentes hidrográficos
Submarine Features	Untermeerische Objekte	Accidentes Submarinos	Formes de relief sous-marin	Acidentes submarinos
□ Political Unit	Politische Einheit	Unidad Política	Entité politique	Unidade política
▼ Cultural Institution	Kulturelle Institution	Institución Cultural	Institution culturelle	Instituição cultural
⊥ Historical Site	Historische Stätte	Sitio Histórico	Site historique	Sítio histórico
♠ Recreational Site	Erholungs- und Ferienort	Sitio de Recreo	Centre de loisirs	Área de Lazer
⊠ Airport	Flughafen	Aeropuerto	Aéroport	Aeroporto
Military Installation	Militäranlage	Instalación Militar	Installation militaire	Instalação militar
◆ Miscellaneous	Verschiedenes	Misceláneo	Divers	Diversos

ENGLISH / DEUTSCH

Name	Page / Seite	Lat. °′ / Breite °′	Long. °′ / Länge °′ E = Ost
Hercules, Ca., U.S.	282	38.01 N	122.17 W
Herdecke	56	51.24 N	7.26 E
Herdorf	56	50.46 N	7.56 E
Herđubreið ∧	24a	65.13 N	16.18 W
Heredia	236	10.00 N	84.07 W
Heredia □[4]	236	10.30 N	84.00 W
Hereford, Eng., U.K.	42	52.04 N	2.43 W
Hereford, Az., U.S.	200	31.26 N	110.05 W
Hereford, Md., U.S.	208	39.35 N	76.39 W
Hereford, Tx., U.S.	196	34.48 N	102.23 W
Hereford and Worcester □[6]	42	52.10 N	2.30 W
Hereford Cathedral ♁[1]	42	52.04 N	2.43 W
Hereford Mountain ∧	206	45.05 N	71.36 W
Hereke	130	40.48 N	29.39 E
Herekino	172	35.15 S	173.13 E
Herencia	34	39.21 N	3.22 W
Herent	56	50.54 N	4.40 E
Herentals	56	51.11 N	4.50 E
Hereroland Oos □[5]	156	21.00 S	20.00 E
Hereroland Wes □[5]	156	20.30 S	18.15 E
Herfølge	41	55.25 N	12.10 E
Herford	52	52.06 N	8.40 E
Hergatz	58	47.39 N	9.50 E
Hergisdorf	54	51.32 N	11.28 E
Hergla	36	36.02 N	10.31 E
Herhahn	56	50.33 N	6.26 E
Héricourt	58	47.35 N	6.45 E
Hérimoncourt	58	47.26 N	6.53 E
Heringen	54	51.27 N	10.52 E
Heringsdorf	54	54.18 N	11.00 E
Herington	198	38.40 N	96.56 W
Heriot	172	45.50 S	169.16 E
Herisau	58	47.23 N	9.17 E
Heritage Range ⋏	9	79.30 S	84.00 W
Herk ≃	56	50.58 N	5.07 E
Herk-de-Stad	56	50.56 N	5.10 E
Herkimer	210	43.01 N	74.59 W
Herkimer □[6]	210	43.02 N	74.59 W
Herlen → Kerulen ≃	90	48.48 N	117.00 E
Herleshausen	56	51.00 N	10.09 E
Herlev	41	55.43 N	12.27 E
Herlong	204	40.09 N	120.08 W
Herlufmagle	41	55.19 N	11.46 E
Herlufsholm	41	55.15 N	11.46 E
Hermagor	64	46.37 N	13.22 E
Herman, Mn., U.S.	198	45.48 N	96.08 W
Herman, Ne., U.S.	198	41.40 N	96.12 W
Herman, Pa., U.S.	214	40.50 N	79.49 W
Herman, Lake ⊜	282	38.05 N	122.09 W
Hermana Mayor Island I	116	15.48 N	119.48 E
Hermanas	196	27.13 N	101.14 W
Herman Eksteen Park ♠	273d	26.10 S	28.02 E
Herma Ness ›	46a	60.50 N	0.55 W
Hermann	219	38.42 N	91.26 W
Hermannsburg, Austl.	162	23.57 S	132.45 E
Hermannsburg, Dtsch.	52	52.50 N	10.05 E
Hermannsburg Aboriginal Reserve ◆[4]	162	24.00 S	132.45 E
Hermanns-Denkmal ⊥	52	51.55 N	8.50 E
Hermannskogel ∧	264b	48.16 N	16.18 E
Hermannstadt → Sibiu	38	45.48 N	24.09 E
Hermano Peak ∧	200	37.13 N	108.48 W
Hermansverk	26	61.11 N	6.51 E
Hermansville	190	45.42 N	87.36 W
Hermanus	158	34.25 S	19.16 E
Hermanville	194	31.57 N	90.50 W
Hermeray	261	48.38 N	1.41 E
Hermes	50	49.22 N	2.15 E
Hermeskeil	56	49.39 N	6.56 E
Hermidale	166	31.33 S	146.43 E
Hermies	50	50.07 N	3.02 E
Herminie	214	40.15 N	79.43 W
Hermiston	202	45.50 N	119.17 W
Hermitage, Nf., Can.	186	47.33 N	55.56 W
Hermitage, Eng., U.K.	42	51.27 N	1.16 W
Hermitage, Ar., U.S.	194	33.26 N	92.10 W
Hermitage, Mo., U.S.	194	37.56 N	93.18 W
Hermitage Bay ⊂	186	47.35 N	56.05 W
Hermitage Park	284c	39.05 N	77.04 W
Hermite, Isla I	254	55.52 S	67.20 W
Hermit Islands II	164	1.30 S	145.05 E
Hermleigh	196	32.38 N	100.46 W
Hermon, S. Afr.	158	33.27 S	18.59 E
Hermon, N.Y., U.S.	212	44.28 N	75.13 W
Hermon, Mount → Shaykh, Jabal ash- ∧	132	33.26 N	35.51 E
Hermosa Beach	280	33.51 N	118.23 W
Hermosillo, Méx.	200	32.30 N	114.59 W
Hermosillo, Méx.	232	29.04 N	110.58 W
Hermoso, Cerro ∧	246	1.10 S	78.12 W
Hermsdorf	54	50.54 N	11.52 E
Hermsdorf ◆[8]	264a	52.37 N	13.18 E
Hermyingyi	110	14.15 N	98.21 E
Hernád ≃	30	47.56 N	21.08 E
Hernals ◆[8]	264b	48.13 N	16.20 E
Hernandarias	252	25.22 S	54.45 W
Hernández	234	23.01 N	102.01 W
Hernandez Reservoir ⊜[1]	226	36.22 N	120.49 W
Hernando, Arg.	252	32.25 S	63.44 W
Hernando, Fl., U.S.	220	28.54 N	82.22 W
Hernando, Ms., U.S.	194	34.49 N	89.59 W
Hernando □[6]	220	28.34 N	82.22 W
Hernando de Magallanes, Parque Nacional ♠	254	54.15 S	72.00 W
Hernani	116	11.20 N	125.37 E
Herndon, Ca., U.S.	226	36.49 N	119.54 W
Herndon, Ks., U.S.	198	39.54 N	100.47 W
Herndon, Pa., U.S.	210	40.42 N	76.50 W
Herndon, Va., U.S.	208	38.58 N	77.23 W
Herndon Canal ≊	226	36.46 N	119.46 W
Herne	52	51.32 N	7.13 E
Herne Bay	42	51.23 N	1.08 E
Herne Hill	168a	31.50 S	116.01 E
Herning	41	56.08 N	8.59 E
Hernwood Heights	284b	39.22 N	77.50 W
Heroica Zitácuaro	234	19.24 N	100.22 W
Herongate	260	51.36 N	0.21 E
Herongen	56	51.24 N	6.15 E
Heron Island I	166	23.26 S	151.55 E
Heron Lake	198	43.47 N	95.19 W
Hérons, Île aux I	275a	45.25 N	73.35 W
Heronsgate	260	51.38 N	0.31 W
Hérouville	261	49.06 N	2.08 E
Hérouville-Saint-Clair	32	49.12 N	0.21 W
Herpf	54	50.34 N	10.20 E
Herradura	252	26.29 S	58.18 W
Herräng	40	60.08 N	18.39 E
Herreid	198	45.50 N	100.04 W
Herrenalb	56	48.48 N	8.26 E
Herrenberg	56	48.35 N	8.52 E
Herrenchiemsee, Schloss ⊥	64	47.52 N	12.23 E
Herrera	252	28.29 S	63.04 W
Herrera □[4]	236	7.54 N	80.38 W
Herrera del Duque	34	39.10 N	5.03 W
Herrera de Pisuerga	34	42.36 N	4.20 W
Herrick, Austl.	166	41.06 S	147.52 E
Herrick, Il., U.S.	219	39.13 N	88.59 W
Herrick Creek ≃	182	54.20 N	121.30 W
Herrick Grove	212	44.04 N	76.12 W
Herricks	276	40.45 N	73.40 W
Herrieden	56	49.14 N	10.30 E
Herrin	194	37.48 N	89.01 W
Herring Bay ⊂	208	38.44 N	76.33 W
Herring Brook ≃	283	42.10 N	70.44 W
Herring Cove, N.S., Can.	186	44.34 N	63.34 W
Herring Cove, Ak., U.S.	182	55.21 N	131.41 W
Herring Creek ≃	208	37.49 N	77.07 W
Herringen	52	51.40 N	7.44 E
Herring Run ≃	284b	39.18 N	76.31 W
Herring Run Park ♠	284b	39.19 N	76.33 W
Herritslev	41	54.42 N	11.41 E
Herrljunga	26	58.05 N	13.02 E
Herrnburg	54	53.47 N	10.45 E
Herrnhut	54	51.01 N	14.44 E
Herrsching am Ammersee	60	48.00 N	11.10 E
Herrs Island I	279b	40.28 N	79.58 W
Herrskogen	40	59.32 N	16.15 E
Herry	50	47.13 N	2.57 E
Hersbruck	60	49.30 N	11.26 E
Herschbach	56	50.34 N	7.44 E
Herscheid	56	51.10 N	7.44 E
Herschel, Sk., Can.	184	51.38 N	108.21 W
Herschel, Transkei	158	30.37 S	27.12 E
Herschel Island I	180	69.35 N	139.05 W
Herscher	216	41.03 N	88.06 W
Herselt	56	51.03 N	4.53 E
Herserange	56	49.31 N	5.47 E
Hersham	260	51.22 N	0.23 W
Hershey, Ne., U.S.	198	41.09 N	101.00 W
Hershey, Pa., U.S.	208	40.17 N	76.39 W
Hersman	219	39.57 N	90.44 W
Herstadberg	40	58.38 N	16.10 E
Herstal	56	50.40 N	5.38 E
Herstmonceux	42	50.53 N	0.20 E
Herten	52	51.35 N	7.07 E
Hertford, Eng., U.K.	42	51.48 N	0.05 W
Hertford, N.C., U.S.	192	36.11 N	76.27 W
Hertford □[6]	208	36.28 N	77.01 W
Hertfordshire □[6]	42	51.50 N	0.10 W
Hertingfordbury	260	51.48 N	0.06 W
Hertsmere □[8]	260	51.41 N	0.17 W
Hertzogville	158	28.08 S	25.33 E
Heruncun	104	40.58 N	123.27 E
Hervás	34	40.16 N	5.51 W
Herve	56	50.38 N	5.48 E
Hervest	263	51.40 N	7.01 E
Hervey Bay ⊂	166	25.00 S	153.00 E
Herxheim	56	49.09 N	8.13 E
Héry, Fr.	50	47.54 N	3.38 E
Héry, Fr.	62	45.46 N	6.28 E
Herzberg, Dtsch.	54	52.54 N	12.58 E
Herzberg, Dtsch.	54	51.41 N	13.14 E
Herzberg am Harz	52	51.39 N	10.20 E
Herzebrock	52	51.53 N	8.14 E
Herzfelde	54	52.29 N	13.50 E
Herzhausen	56	51.11 N	8.53 E
Herzliyya	132	32.10 N	34.51 E
Herznach	58	47.28 N	8.03 E
Herzogenaurach	56	49.34 N	10.53 E
Herzogenbuchsee	58	47.12 N	7.41 E
Herzogenburg	61	48.17 N	15.42 E
Herzogenrath	56	50.52 N	6.06 E
Herzsprung	54	53.04 N	12.28 E
Heṣār, Kūh-e ⋏	120	34.50 N	66.30 E
Hesarak	267d	35.47 N	51.19 E
Hesdin	50	50.22 N	2.02 E
Hesel	52	53.18 N	7.35 E
Hesepe	52	52.26 N	7.58 E
Heshachang	107	30.37 N	105.40 E
Heshan	110	23.52 N	108.52 E
Heshangqiao	100	34.15 N	113.47 E
Heshengqiao	100	30.00 N	114.22 E
Heshi, Zhg.	100	25.04 N	118.37 E
Heshi, Zhg.	107	29.10 N	104.22 E
Heshui, Zhg.	100	24.24 N	114.56 E
Heshui, Zhg.	102	22.48 N	112.29 E
Heshuijian	100	30.33 N	116.05 E
Heshun, Zhg.	100	27.30 N	117.24 E
Heshun, Zhg.	102	37.21 N	113.35 E
Heshuo	86	42.15 N	86.53 E
Hesketh Bank	262	53.42 N	2.51 W
Hesketh Out Marsh ≋	262	53.43 N	2.55 W
Heskin Green	262	53.38 N	2.42 W
Hesler	218	38.28 N	84.47 W
Hesperange	56	49.34 N	6.09 E
Hesperia, Ca., U.S.	228	34.25 N	117.18 W
Hesperia, Mi., U.S.	190	43.34 N	86.02 W
Hesperus Mountain ∧	200	37.27 N	108.05 W
Hess ≃	180	63.34 N	133.57 W
Hesselager	41	55.10 N	10.45 E
Hesselberg ∧	56	49.04 N	10.32 E
Hesselø I	41	56.12 N	11.43 E
Hesselte	52	52.25 N	7.22 E
Hessen	54	52.02 N	10.15 E
Hessen □[3]	30	50.30 N	9.15 E
Hessen Cassal	216	41.00 N	85.05 W
Hessenthal	56	49.55 N	9.17 E
Hessisch Lichtenau	56	51.12 N	9.43 E
Hessisch Oldendorf	52	52.10 N	9.15 E
Hessle	44	53.44 N	0.26 W
Hesso	166	32.08 S	137.27 E
Hess Tablemount ✣[3]	14	17.50 N	174.15 W
Hesston, Ks., U.S.	198	38.08 N	97.25 W
Hesston, Pa., U.S.	214	40.26 N	78.07 W
Heston ◆[8]	260	51.29 N	0.22 W
Heswall	44	53.20 N	3.06 W
Het ≃	110	20.49 N	104.01 E
Hetai	102	23.22 N	112.19 E
Hetanbu	100	28.21 N	117.11 E
Hetang, Zhg.	100	26.40 N	119.09 E
Hetang, Zhg.	106	31.43 N	120.27 E
Hetang, Zhg.	107	28.58 N	106.03 E
Hetaundā	124	85.02 N	27.26 E
Hetch Hetchy Aqueduct ≊[1]	226	37.29 N	122.19 W
Hetch Hetchy Reservoir ⊜[1]	226	37.57 N	119.43 W
Hethersett	42	52.36 N	1.11 E
Hetian, Zhg.	100	25.41 N	116.26 E
Hetian, Zhg.	100	23.19 N	115.38 E
Het Loo, Paleis ♁	52	52.14 N	5.56 E
Hetou	100	24.18 N	113.29 E
Hetoudian	98	37.02 N	120.35 E
Hettange-Grande	56	49.24 N	6.09 E
Hettenleidelheim	56	49.32 N	8.04 E
Hettick	219	39.21 N	90.02 W
Hettingen	58	48.13 N	9.14 E
Hettinger	198	46.00 N	102.38 W
Hetton-le-Hole	44	54.50 N	1.27 W
Hettstedt	54	51.38 N	11.30 E
Hetupu	100	30.50 N	116.03 E
Hetzendorf ◆[8]	264b	48.10 N	16.18 E
Hetzerath	56	49.52 N	6.49 E
Het Zoute	50	51.21 N	3.18 E
Heuchin	50	50.28 N	2.16 E
Heudeber	54	51.54 N	10.50 E
Heule	50	50.50 N	3.14 E
Heuningspruit	158	27.26 S	27.28 E
Heusden, Bel.	50	51.02 N	3.48 E
Heusden, Bel.	56	51.02 N	5.16 E
Heustreu	56	50.21 N	10.15 E
Heusweiler	56	49.20 N	6.55 E
Heuvelton	212	44.37 N	75.24 W
Hève, Cap de la ›	50	49.31 N	0.04 E
Heven	263	51.26 N	7.17 E
Heverlee	56	50.52 N	4.42 E
Heves	30	47.36 N	20.17 E
Heves □[6]	30	47.50 N	20.15 E
Hevlín	61	48.45 N	16.23 E
Ḥevron, Naḥal V	132	31.15 N	34.50 E
Hewanorra International Airport ⊠	241f	13.45 N	60.56 W
Hewitt, N.J., U.S.	210	41.08 N	74.18 W
Hewitt, Tx., U.S.	222	31.27 N	97.11 W
Hewittsville	219	39.32 N	89.19 W
Hewlett, N.Y., U.S.	276	40.38 N	73.41 W
Hewlett, Va., U.S.	208	37.55 N	77.35 W
Hewlett Bay Park	276	40.38 N	73.42 W
Hewlett Harbor	276	40.38 N	73.41 W
Hewlett Neck	276	40.37 N	73.42 W
Hewlett Point ›	276	40.50 N	73.45 W
Hewopu	104	41.14 N	122.24 E
Hewu	100	26.41 N	113.40 E
Hexen Kopf ∧	58	47.01 N	10.28 E
Hexham	44	54.58 N	2.06 W
Hexi, Zhg.	100	24.52 N	117.15 E
Hexi, Zhg.	102	24.09 N	102.39 E
Hexi, Zhg.	106	31.03 N	119.49 E
Hexian, Zhg.	100	31.43 N	118.22 E
Hexian, Zhg.	102	24.15 N	111.43 E
Hexibao	102	38.34 N	102.11 E
Hexingchang	107	30.05 N	104.35 E
Hexingjie	106	31.55 N	120.36 E
Hexiwu	105	39.38 N	116.58 E
Hex Rivierberge ⋏	158	33.25 S	19.37 E
Hextable	260	51.25 N	0.11 E
Hexton	172	38.37 S	177.58 E
Heyan	104	42.30 N	120.29 E
Heyang, Zhg.	98	35.27 N	118.33 E
Heyang, Zhg.	102	35.15 N	110.06 E
Heybeli ◆[8]	267b	40.53 N	29.05 E
Heybeli Ada I	267b	40.53 N	29.05 E
Heybridge, Eng., U.K.	260	51.44 N	0.41 E
Heybridge, Eng., U.K.	260	51.40 N	0.22 E
Heyburn	202	42.33 N	113.45 W
Heyerode	54	51.10 N	10.25 E
Heyrieux	62	45.38 N	5.03 E
Heysham	44	54.02 N	2.54 W
Heyuan	100	23.44 N	114.41 E
Heywood, Austl.	166	38.08 S	141.38 E
Heywood, Eng., U.K.	44	53.36 N	2.13 W
Heyworth	216	40.18 N	88.58 W
Heze (Caozhou)	98	35.17 N	115.27 E
Hezhang	102	27.00 N	104.37 E
Hezhao	98	37.08 N	115.17 E
Hezhen	100	29.56 N	120.10 E
Hezheng	102	35.25 N	103.10 E
Hezijian	105	40.13 N	116.03 E
Hezixu	100	24.54 N	115.14 E
Hezuo	102	34.58 N	102.57 E
Hiale	110	15.55 N	107.34 E
Hialeah	220	25.51 N	80.16 W
Hialeah Park Race Track ♠	220	25.51 N	80.17 W
Hiaohexi	100	31.21 N	114.02 E
Hiawassee	192	34.56 N	83.45 W
Hiawatha, Ks., U.S.	198	39.51 N	95.32 W
Hiawatha, Ut,. U.S.	200	39.29 N	111.00 W
Hiba-Dōgo-Taishaku-kokutei-kōen ♠	96	35.07 N	133.08 E
Hibaldstow	44	53.31 N	0.32 W
Hibbing	190	47.25 N	92.56 W
Hibbs, Point ›	166	42.38 S	145.15 E
Hibernia	276	40.57 N	74.30 W
Hibernia Reef ✣[2]	160	12.00 S	123.23 E
Hibiki-nada ⊤[2]	96	34.00 N	130.30 E
Hiburi-shima I	96	33.10 N	132.17 E
Hibuson Island I	116	10.27 N	125.29 E
Hickam Air Force Base ■	229c	21.20 N	157.57 W
Hickey, Mount ∧	169	37.22 S	145.19 E
Hickman, Ca., U.S.	226	37.37 N	120.45 W
Hickman, Ky., U.S.	194	36.34 N	89.11 W
Hickman, Ne., U.S.	198	40.37 N	96.37 W
Hickman, Pa., U.S.	279b	40.23 N	80.09 W
Hickman's Harbour	186	48.06 N	53.44 W
Hickory, Ms., U.S.	194	32.19 N	89.01 W
Hickory, N.C., U.S.	192	35.43 N	81.20 W
Hickory, Pa., U.S.	214	40.18 N	80.18 W
Hickory Corners	216	42.26 N	85.22 W
Hickory Creek ≃, Il., U.S.	278	41.30 N	88.06 W
Hickory Creek ≃, Mi., U.S.	216	42.05 N	86.29 W
Hickory Creek ≃, Tx., U.S.	222	31.29 N	95.07 W
Hickory Flat	194	34.36 N	89.11 W
Hickory Hills	216	41.43 N	87.49 W
Hickory Run State Park ♠	210	41.02 N	75.41 W
Hickory Township	214	41.15 N	80.27 W
Hicks, Point ›	166	37.48 S	149.17 E
Hicks Bay	172	37.36 S	178.18 E
Hickson Lake ⊜	184	56.17 N	104.25 W
Hicksville, N.Y., U.S.	210	40.46 N	73.31 W
Hicksville, Oh., U.S.	216	41.17 N	84.45 W
Hico	196	31.58 N	98.02 W
Hicpochee, Lake ⊜	220	26.50 N	81.10 W
Hida ≃	94	35.26 N	137.03 E
Hida → Hita	96	33.19 N	130.56 E
Hidaka, Nihon	94	35.54 N	139.21 E
Hidaka, Nihon	96	35.28 N	134.47 E
Hidaka, Nihon	96	33.55 N	135.09 E
Hidaka ≃	96	33.52 N	135.09 E
Hidaka-sammyaku ⋏	92a	42.35 N	142.45 E
Hida-Kiso-gawa-kokutei-kōen ♠	94	35.37 N	137.15 E
Hida-kōchi ⋏[1]	94	36.16 N	137.05 E
Hidalgo, Méx.	232	27.47 N	99.52 W
Hidalgo, Méx.	232	25.59 N	100.27 W
Hidalgo, Méx.	232	24.15 N	99.26 W
Hidalgo □[3]	234	20.30 N	99.00 W
Hidalgo del Parral	232	26.56 N	105.40 W
Hida-sammyaku ⋏	94	36.25 N	137.40 E
Hiddenhausen	52	52.08 N	8.38 E
Hidden Hills	228	34.09 N	118.43 W
Hiddensee I	54	54.33 N	13.07 E
Hidden Valley, Ca., U.S.	226	38.46 N	121.09 W
Hidden Valley, Tx., U.S.	222	29.54 N	95.25 W
Hiddesen	52	51.55 N	8.50 E
Hiddinghausen	263	51.22 N	7.17 E
Hıdırbaba	130	38.47 N	39.00 E
Hidrolândia	255	16.58 S	49.14 W
Hidrolina	255	14.37 S	49.25 W
Hieflau	61	47.36 N	14.44 E
Hienghène	175f	20.41 S	164.56 E
Hierapolis → Pamukkale ⊥	130	37.58 N	29.19 E
Hierges	56	50.06 N	4.44 E
Hierro (Ferro) I	148	27.45 N	18.00 W
Hiesfeld	263	51.33 N	6.46 E
Hietzing ◆[8]	264b	48.11 N	16.18 E
Higashi	174m	26.38 N	128.09 E
Higashi ◆[8]	270	34.41 N	135.31 E
Higashibetsuin	270	34.56 N	135.34 E
Higashifuji-enshūjō ■	94	35.17 N	138.51 E
Higashihiroshima	96	34.26 N	132.42 E
Higashiichiki	92	31.40 N	130.20 E
Higashiiyayama	96	33.52 N	133.54 E
Higashiizu	94	34.48 N	139.04 E
Higashi-jima I	174f	24.47 N	141.23 E
Higashikurume	268	35.45 N	139.32 E
Higashimatsuyama	94	36.02 N	139.24 E
Higashimonzen	268	35.56 N	139.40 E
Higashimurayama	94	35.46 N	139.29 E
Higashinada ◆[8]	270	34.43 N	135.16 E
Higashinakano	268	35.38 N	139.25 E
Higashinari ◆[8]	270	34.40 N	135.33 E
Higashine	92	38.26 N	140.24 E
Higashinose	270	34.55 N	135.30 E
Higashiōizumi ◆[8]	268	35.45 N	139.36 E
Higashiōsaka	96	34.39 N	135.35 E
Higashishirakawa	94	35.39 N	137.19 E
Higashisumiyoshi ◆[8]	270	34.37 N	135.32 E
Higashitokonoo-san ∧	96	35.25 N	134.55 E
Higashitsuno	96	33.23 N	133.02 E
Higashiura, Nihon	94	34.59 N	136.58 E
Higashiura, Nihon	270	34.33 N	135.00 E
Higashiyama ◆[8]	270	35.00 N	135.48 E
Higashiyamato	268	35.44 N	139.26 E
Higashiyodogawa ◆[8]	270	34.44 N	135.31 E
Higashiyoshino	94	34.24 N	135.58 E
Higbee	194	39.18 N	92.30 W
Higganum	207	41.29 N	72.33 W
Higgins	196	36.07 N	100.02 W
Higgins, Mount ∧	224	48.19 N	121.45 W
Higgins Lake ⊜	190	44.30 N	84.45 W
Higginsport	218	38.47 N	83.58 W
Higginsville, Austl.	162	31.45 S	121.43 E
Higginsville, Mo., U.S.	194	39.04 N	93.43 W
Higgs' Hope	158	29.19 S	23.16 E
Higham Ferrers	42	52.18 N	0.36 W
Higham Upshire	260	51.26 N	0.28 E
Highbank	222	31.10 N	96.50 W
High Bank Creek ≃	216	42.37 N	85.11 W
High Bar Indian Reserve ◆[4]	182	51.06 N	122.00 W
High Beach	260	51.39 N	0.02 E
High Bentham	44	54.08 N	2.30 W
High Bluff Island I	212	43.58 N	77.45 W
Highbridge, Eng., U.K.	42	51.13 N	2.49 W
High Bridge, N.J., U.S.	210	40.40 N	74.53 W
Highbury	164	16.25 S	143.09 E
Highcliff	279b	40.32 N	80.03 W
Higher Ballam	262	53.46 N	2.59 W
Higher Broughton ◆[8]	262	53.30 N	2.15 W
Higher Hogshead ∧[2]	262	53.42 N	2.09 W
Higher Penwortham	262	53.45 N	2.44 W
Higher Walton, Eng., U.K.	44	53.44 N	2.39 W
Higher Walton, Eng., U.K.	262	53.22 N	2.37 W
Higher Whitley	262	53.19 N	2.35 W
Highett	274b	37.57 S	145.03 E
High Falls	210	41.50 N	74.08 W
High Falls ∟	212	43.56 N	75.23 W
High Force ∟	44	54.38 N	2.13 W
Highgate	214	42.30 N	81.49 W
Highgate Center	206	44.56 N	73.02 W
Highgate Springs	206	44.58 N	73.06 W
Highgrove	228	34.01 N	117.20 W
High Halstow	260	51.27 N	0.34 E
High Hesket	44	54.48 N	2.48 W
High Hill	219	38.52 N	91.23 W
High Hill ∧[2]	276	40.49 N	73.25 W
High Hill ≃, Can.	184	56.45 N	110.30 W
High Hill ≃, Mb., Can.	184	55.52 N	94.42 W
High Hill Lake ⊜	184	55.34 N	95.40 W
High Island I, H.K.	271d	22.22 N	114.21 E
High Island I, Mi., U.S.	190	45.42 N	85.40 W
High Island Creek ≃	190	44.35 N	93.54 W
High Island Reservoir ⊜[1]	271d	22.23 N	114.21 W
Highland, Ca., U.S.	228	34.07 N	117.12 W
Highland, Il., U.S.	219	38.44 N	89.40 W
Highland, In., U.S.	216	41.33 N	87.27 W
Highland, Ks., U.S.	198	39.51 N	95.16 W
Highland, Md., U.S.	208	39.11 N	76.57 W
Highland, Mi., U.S.	281	42.38 N	83.37 W
Highland, N.Y., U.S.	210	41.43 N	73.57 W
Highland, Oh., U.S.	218	39.21 N	83.36 W
Highland, Pa., U.S.	279b	40.33 N	80.04 W
Highland □[4]	46	57.40 N	5.00 W
Highland □[6]	218	39.12 N	83.37 W
Highland Beach	220	26.25 N	80.04 W
Highland City	220	27.58 N	81.53 W
Highland Creek ≃, On., Can.	275b	43.46 N	79.08 W
Highland Creek ≃, Ca., U.S.	226	38.24 N	121.14 W
Highland Falls	210	41.22 N	73.58 W
Highland Heights, Ky., U.S.	218	39.04 N	84.27 W
Highland Heights, Oh., U.S.	214	41.33 N	81.28 W
Highland Hills	278	41.52 N	88.01 W
Highland Home	194	31.57 N	86.18 W
Highland Lake, Il., U.S.	278	42.21 N	88.04 W
Highland Lake, Ma., U.S.	283	42.41 N	72.37 W
Highland Lake, N.Y., U.S.	210	41.32 N	74.51 W
Highland Lake ⊜, Ct., U.S.	207	41.54 N	73.06 W
Highland Lake ⊜, Il., U.S.	278	42.22 N	88.04 W
Highland Lake ⊜, N.J., U.S.	276	41.10 N	74.28 W
Highland Lakes	210	41.10 N	74.28 W
Highland-on-the-Lake	284a	42.42 N	79.59 W
Highland Park, Il., U.S.	216	42.10 N	87.48 W
Highland Park, Md., U.S.	284c	38.54 N	76.54 W
Highland Park, Mi., U.S.	216	42.24 N	83.05 W
Highland Park, N.J., U.S.	210	40.29 N	74.25 W
Highland Park, Pa., U.S.	210	40.38 N	77.35 W
Highland Park, Tx., U.S.	222	32.50 N	96.48 W
Highland Park ◆[8]	280	34.07 N	118.13 W
Highland Park ♠, Ma., U.S.	283	42.30 N	70.55 W
Highland Park ♠, Pa., U.S.	279b	40.29 N	79.55 W
Highland Peak ∧	226	38.33 N	119.45 W
Highland Point ›	220	25.30 N	81.12 W
Highlands, N.J., U.S.	208	40.24 N	73.59 W
Highlands, N.C., U.S.	192	35.03 N	83.11 W
Highlands, Tx., U.S.	222	29.49 N	95.03 W
Highlands □[6]	220	27.20 N	81.16 W
Highlands Hammock State Park ♠	220	27.28 N	81.33 W
Highland Silver Lake ⊜[1]	219	38.47 N	89.39 W
Highlands North ◆[8]	273d	26.09 S	28.05 E
Highland Springs	208	37.32 N	77.19 W
Highlands Reservoir ⊜[1]	222	29.50 N	95.02 W
Highland State Recreation Area ♠	216	42.39 N	83.33 W
Highlandtown ◆[8]	284b	39.17 N	76.33 W
High Laver	260	51.45 N	0.13 E
High Legh	262	53.21 N	2.27 W
Highley	42	52.27 N	2.23 W
Highmore	198	44.31 N	99.26 W
High Ongar	260	51.43 N	0.16 E
High Park ♠	275b	43.39 N	79.28 W
High Peak □[8]	262	53.23 N	1.55 W
High Peak ∧, Pil.	116	15.29 N	120.07 E
High Peak ∧, N.Y., U.S.	210	42.09 N	74.05 W
High Peak ◆[1]	44	53.22 N	1.50 W
High Point, Fl., U.S.	220	27.55 N	82.42 W
High Point, N.C., U.S.	192	35.57 N	80.00 W
Highpoint, Oh., U.S.	218	39.14 N	84.24 W
High Point ∧, N.J., U.S.	210	41.19 N	74.40 W
High Point ∧, Wy., U.S.	202	41.37 N	107.47 W
High Point State Park ♠	210	41.18 N	74.41 W
High Prairie	182	55.26 N	116.29 W
High Ridge	219	38.27 N	90.32 W
High River	182	50.35 N	113.52 W
High Rock	192	26.36 N	76.18 W
High Rock ∧	188	39.33 N	79.06 W
Highrock Indian Reserve ◆[4]	184	55.54 N	100.30 W
Highrock Lake ⊜, Mb., Can.	184	55.45 N	100.30 W
Highrock Lake ⊜, Sk., Can.	184	57.04 N	105.30 W
High Rock Lake ⊜[1]	192	35.40 N	80.17 W
High Seat ∧	44	54.24 N	2.18 W
High Spire	208	40.12 N	76.47 W
High Springs	192	29.49 N	82.35 W
High Street ∧	44	54.29 N	2.52 W
Hightown	44	53.31 N	3.03 W
Hightstown	208	40.16 N	74.31 W
High View	210	41.33 N	74.27 W
Highwater	206	45.01 N	72.26 W
Highway City	226	36.49 N	119.54 W
High Willhays ∧	42	50.41 N	3.59 W
Highwood, Il., U.S.	216	42.11 N	87.48 W
Highwood, Mt., U.S.	202	47.35 N	110.47 W
Highwood ≃	182	50.49 N	113.47 W
Highwood Baldy ∧	202	47.27 N	110.37 W
Highwood Creek ≃	202	47.40 N	111.00 W
Highwood Mountains ⋏	202	47.25 N	110.30 W
Highworth	42	51.38 N	1.43 W
High Wycombe	42	51.38 N	0.46 W
Higlet	154	1.04 S	40.19 E
Higuera Blanca	234	19.42 N	105.10 W
Higuera de Abuya	232	24.16 N	107.04 W
Higuera de Zaragoza	232	25.59 N	109.16 W
Higueras	196	25.58 N	100.01 W
Higüero, Punta ›	240m	18.22 N	67.16 W
Higüey	238	18.37 N	68.42 W
Higuito ≃	236	14.43 N	88.40 W
Hihétro	150	7.32 N	1.06 E
Hihyā	142	30.40 N	31.36 E
Hii ≃	96	35.26 N	132.54 E
Hiidenportin kansallispuisto ♠	26	63.50 N	28.59 E
Hiiraan □[4]	144	4.00 N	45.30 E
Hiiumaa I	76	58.52 N	22.40 E
Hījānah, Buḥayrat al- ⊜	132	33.18 N	36.36 E
Híjar	34	41.10 N	0.27 W
Hiji	96	33.22 N	131.32 E
Hiji ≃	96	33.36 N	132.29 E
Hijikawa	96	33.27 N	132.41 E
Hijiri-dake ∧	94	35.26 N	138.10 E
Hikami	96	35.10 N	135.02 E
Hikari, Nihon	94	35.39 N	140.30 E
Hikari, Nihon	96	33.58 N	131.56 E
Hikarigaoka	268	35.50 N	139.58 E
Hikawa	96	35.25 N	132.50 E
Hikawa Shrine ♁[1]	268	35.54 N	139.38 E
Hiketa	96	34.13 N	134.24 E
Hiki ≃	96	33.33 N	135.27 E
Hikigawa	96	33.34 N	135.27 E
Hikimi	96	34.34 N	132.01 E
Hikimi ≃	96	34.37 N	131.48 E
Hikiura	270	34.33 N	134.58 E
Hikone	94	35.15 N	136.15 E
Hikone-jō ⊥	94	35.15 N	136.14 E
Hiko-san ∧	96	33.27 N	130.54 E
Hikueru I[1]	14	17.36 S	142.37 W
Hikurangi	172	35.36 S	174.18 E
Hikurangi ∧	172	37.55 S	178.04 E
Hikutaia	172	37.17 S	175.39 E
Hikutivake	174v	18.56 S	169.53 W
Hila	112	7.35 S	127.24 E
Hilaban Island I	116	12.03 N	125.34 E
Hilāl, Jabal ⋏	132	30.40 N	34.00 E
Hilāl, Ra's al- ›	146	32.57 N	22.10 E
Hilbersdorf	54	50.55 N	13.23 E
Hilbert	190	44.08 N	88.09 W
Hilbre Islands II	262	53.23 N	3.13 W
Hilbre Point ›	262	53.23 N	3.12 W
Hilchenbach	56	51.00 N	8.06 E
Hilda	184	50.28 N	110.03 W
Hildburghausen	54	50.25 N	10.44 E
Hilden	56	51.10 N	6.56 E
Hildenborough	260	51.13 N	0.15 E
Hilders	56	50.34 N	10.00 E
Hildesheim	52	52.09 N	9.57 E
Hildreth	198	40.20 N	99.02 W
Hilgen	263	51.06 N	7.09 E
Hilialawa	114	0.41 N	97.53 E
Hiligeo	114	1.22 N	97.10 E
Hiliotaluwa	114	0.44 N	97.53 E
Hill □[6]	222	32.02 N	97.10 W
Hillaby, Mount ∧	241g	13.12 N	59.35 W
Hill Air Force Base ■	202	41.05 N	111.58 W
Hillandale, S. Afr.	158	33.06 S	20.36 E
Hillandale, Md., U.S.	284c	39.01 N	76.58 W
Hillandale Heights	284c	39.01 N	76.59 W
Hill Bank	232	17.35 N	88.42 W
Hillburn	210	41.08 N	74.10 W
Hill City, Ks., U.S.	198	39.21 N	99.50 W
Hill City, Mn., U.S.	190	46.59 N	93.35 W
Hill City, S.D., U.S.	198	43.55 N	103.34 W
Hill Creek ≃	200	39.55 N	109.40 W
Hillcrest, Il., U.S.	216	41.57 N	89.04 W
Hillcrest, N.Y., U.S.	210	41.07 N	74.02 W
Hillcrest, N.Y., U.S.	210	42.09 N	75.53 W
Hillcrest Center	228	35.23 N	118.57 W
Hillcrest Heights	284c	38.49 N	76.57 W
Hillcrest Mines	182	49.34 N	114.23 W
Hillcrest Orchard	216	41.51 N	83.29 W
Hillcrest Park	226	38.07 N	122.16 W
Hill Cumorah ⊥	210	43.01 N	77.15 W
Hille, Dtsch.	52	52.20 N	8.44 E
Hille, Sve.	40	60.44 N	17.11 E
Hillegom	52	52.18 N	4.35 E
Hillegossen	52	51.59 N	8.37 E
Hillerød	41	55.56 N	12.19 E
Hillers Creek ≃	219	38.38 N	91.54 W
Hillesheim	56	50.18 N	6.38 E
Hilli	124	25.17 N	89.01 E
Hilliard, Fl., U.S.	192	30.41 N	81.55 W
Hilliard, Oh., U.S.	218	40.02 N	83.09 W
Hilliards	214	41.05 N	79.50 W
Hillingdon ◆[8]	42	51.32 N	0.27 W
Hillisburg	216	40.17 N	86.20 W
Hill Island Lake ⊜	176	60.29 N	109.50 W
Hillister	194	30.40 N	94.23 W
Hillman	190	45.03 N	83.54 W
Hillman ≃	168a	33.26 S	116.48 E
Hillmersdorf	54	51.42 N	13.29 E
Hill of Fearn	46	57.45 N	3.56 W
Hills	198	43.31 N	96.21 W
Hills and Dales	214	39.42 N	84.13 W
Hillsboro, Il., U.S.	219	39.09 N	89.29 W
Hillsboro, Ks., U.S.	198	38.21 N	97.12 W
Hillsboro, Ky., U.S.	218	38.18 N	83.40 W
Hillsboro, Md., U.S.	208	38.55 N	75.56 W
Hillsboro, Mo., U.S.	219	38.13 N	90.33 W
Hillsboro, N.H., U.S.	188	43.06 N	71.53 W
Hillsboro, N.M., U.S.	200	32.55 N	107.33 W
Hillsboro, N.D., U.S.	198	47.24 N	97.03 W
Hillsboro, Oh., U.S.	218	39.12 N	83.36 W
Hillsboro, Or., U.S.	224	45.31 N	122.59 W
Hillsboro, Tx., U.S.	222	32.00 N	97.07 W
Hillsboro, Wi., U.S.	190	43.39 N	90.20 W
Hillsboro Beach	220	26.18 N	80.05 W
Hillsboro Canal ≊	220	26.19 N	80.05 W
Hillsborough, N.B., Can.	186	45.56 N	64.39 W
Hillsborough, N. Ire., U.K.	48	54.28 N	6.05 W
Hillsborough, Ca., U.S.	226	37.34 N	122.22 W
Hillsborough, N.C., U.S.	192	36.04 N	79.06 W
Hillsborough □[6], Fl., U.S.	220	27.55 N	82.15 W
Hillsborough □[6], N.H., U.S.	207	42.49 N	71.41 W
Hillsborough ≃	220	27.56 N	82.27 W
Hillsborough, Cape ›	166	20.54 S	149.03 E
Hillsborough Bay ⊂, P.E., Can.	186	46.10 N	63.05 W
Hillsborough Bay ⊂, Fl., U.S.	220	27.52 N	82.27 W
Hillsborough River State Park ♠	220	28.09 N	82.14 W
Hillsburgh	212	43.47 N	80.09 W
Hills Creek Lake ⊜[1]	202	43.40 N	122.26 W
Hillsdale, Mi., U.S.	216	41.55 N	84.37 W
Hillsdale, N.J., U.S.	276	41.00 N	74.02 W
Hillsdale, N.Y., U.S.	210	42.10 N	73.31 W
Hillsdale, Pa., U.S.	214	40.45 N	78.53 W
Hillsdale □[6]	216	41.53 N	84.36 W
Hillsdale ◆[9]	282	37.32 N	122.18 W
Hillsdale Lake ⊜[1]	198	38.40 N	94.55 W
Hills Flat	226	39.14 N	121.03 W
Hillsgrove	210	41.27 N	76.42 W
Hillside, Austl.	162	21.44 S	119.23 E
Hillside, Scot., U.K.	46	56.44 N	2.29 W
Hillside, Il., U.S.	278	41.52 N	87.54 W
Hillside, N.J., U.S.	276	40.42 N	74.13 W
Hillside ◆[8]	276	40.42 N	73.47 W
Hillside Gardens	216	42.16 N	84.27 W
Hillside Heights	285	39.41 N	75.41 W
Hillside Lake	210	41.36 N	73.50 W
Hillston	166	33.29 S	145.32 E
Hillsville, Pa., U.S.	214	41.00 N	80.29 W
Hillsville, Va., U.S.	192	36.45 N	80.44 W
Hillswick	46a	60.28 N	1.30 W
Hilltop	208	39.49 N	75.04 W
Hilltop Center ◆[9]	282	37.59 N	122.19 W
Hilltown, N. Ire., U.K.	48	54.12 N	6.09 W
Hilltown, Pa., U.S.	208	40.20 N	75.14 W
Hillview	219	39.27 N	90.33 W
Hillview Reservoir ⊜[1]	276	40.55 N	73.52 W
Hillwood	284c	38.52 N	77.10 W
Hilmar	226	37.25 N	120.51 W
Hilo	229d	19.43 N	155.05 W
Hilo Bay ⊂	229d	19.44 N	155.05 W
Hilonghilong, Mount ∧	116	9.06 N	125.44 E
Hilongos	116	10.23 N	124.45 E
Hilpotstein	60	49.12 N	11.12 E
Hilpsford Point ›	44	54.03 N	3.12 W
Hils ∧	52	51.55 N	9.40 E
Hilshire Village	222	29.49 N	95.26 W
Hiltaba, Mount ∧	162	32.09 S	135.03 E
Hilter	52	52.08 N	8.08 E
Hilton, N.Y., U.S.	210	43.17 N	77.47 W
Hilton, Pa., U.S.	208	40.00 N	76.49 W
Hilton Head Island I	192	32.12 N	80.45 W
Hiltpoltstein	60	49.40 N	11.19 E
Hiltrop ◆[8]	263	51.30 N	7.15 E
Hiltrup	52	51.54 N	7.38 E
Hilvan	130	37.35 N	38.57 E
Hilvarenbeek	52	51.29 N	5.09 E
Hilversum	52	52.14 N	5.10 E
Hima	192	37.07 N	83.46 W
Himāchal Pradesh □[3]	120	32.00 N	77.00 E
Himalayas ⋏	120	28.00 N	84.00 E
Himāl Chulī ∧	124	28.25 N	84.39 E
Himamaylan	116	10.06 N	122.52 E
Himanka	26	64.04 N	23.39 E
Himarë	38	40.07 N	19.44 E
Himatnagar	120	23.36 N	72.57 E
Himberg	61	48.05 N	16.26 E
Hime ≃	94	37.02 N	137.49 E
Himeji	96	34.49 N	134.42 E
Hime-shima I	96	33.43 N	131.40 E
Himeville	158	29.44 S	29.31 E
Himi	94	36.51 N	136.59 E
Himmelbjerget ∧[2]	41	56.06 N	9.42 E
Himmelgeist ◆[8]	263	51.10 N	6.49 E
Himmelpforten	52	53.36 N	9.18 E
Himmelsthür	52	52.09 N	9.55 E
Himmerfjärden ⊂[2]	40	59.00 N	17.43 E
Himmerland ◆[1]	26	56.50 N	9.45 E
Himmetdede	130	38.55 N	35.07 E
Himrod	210	42.35 N	76.57 W
Ḥimṣ (Homs)	130	34.44 N	36.43 E
Ḥimṣ □[8]	130	34.15 N	38.00 E
Hinabangan	116	11.42 N	125.04 E
Ḥīnah	132	33.21 N	35.56 E
Hinako, Kepulauan II	114	0.52 N	97.21 E
Hinase	96	34.44 N	134.16 E
Hinatuan	116	8.23 N	126.20 E
Hinatuan Island I	116	9.47 N	125.43 E
Hinatuan Passage ⋓	116	9.45 N	125.47 E
Hinche	238	19.09 N	72.01 W
Hinchinbrook Entrance ⋓	180	60.25 N	146.50 W
Hinchinbrook Island I, Austl.	166	18.23 S	146.17 E
Hinchinbrook Island I, Ak., U.S.	180	60.22 N	146.30 W
Hinchinbrook Island National Park ♠	166	18.20 S	146.20 E
Hinckley, Eng., U.K.	42	52.33 N	1.21 W
Hinckley, Il., U.S.	216	41.46 N	88.38 W
Hinckley, Mn., U.S.	190	46.00 N	92.56 W
Hinckley, Oh., U.S.	214	41.14 N	81.45 W
Hinckley, Ut,. U.S.	200	39.19 N	112.40 W
Hinckley Reservoir ⊜[1]	210	43.20 N	75.05 W
Hindan ≃	272a	28.30 N	77.27 E
Hindang	116	10.26 N	124.44 E
Hindaun	124	26.43 N	77.01 E
Hindelang	58	47.30 N	10.22 E
Hindelbank	58	47.03 N	7.32 E
Hindeloopen	52	52.56 N	5.24 E
Hindenburg → Zabrze	30	50.18 N	18.46 E
Hindhead	42	51.07 N	0.44 W
Hindley	44	53.32 N	2.35 W
Hindley Green	262	53.31 N	2.32 W
Hindman	192	37.20 N	82.58 W
Hindmarsh, Lake ⊜	166	36.03 S	141.55 E
Hindmarsh Island I	168b	35.32 S	138.52 E
Hindmarsh Valley	168b	35.30 S	138.38 E
Hindon	42	51.06 N	2.08 W
Hinds	172	44.00 S	171.34 E
Hindsholm ›[1]	41	55.33 N	10.40 E
Hinds Lake ⊜	186	48.57 N	57.00 W
Hindu Kush ⋏	120	36.00 N	71.30 E
Hindūmalkot	123	30.09 N	73.55 E
Hindupur	122	13.49 N	77.29 E
Hi-Nella	285	39.50 N	75.01 W
Hines	202	43.33 N	119.04 W
Hines Creek	182	56.15 N	118.36 W
Hines Creek ≃	182	55.54 N	118.37 W
Hines Peak ∧	228	34.31 N	119.05 W
Hinesville	192	31.50 N	81.35 W
Hinganghāt	122	20.34 N	78.50 E
Hingatungan	116	10.35 N	125.11 E
Hingham, Eng., U.K.	42	52.35 N	0.59 E
Hingham, Ma., U.S.	207	42.14 N	70.53 W
Hingham Bay ⊂	207	42.17 N	70.55 W
Hingham Harbor ⊂	283	42.15 N	70.53 W
Hingol ≃	128	25.23 N	65.28 E
Hingoli	122	19.43 N	77.09 E
Hinigaran	116	10.17 N	122.51 E
Hınıs	130	39.22 N	41.44 E
Hınıs ≃	130	39.18 N	42.12 E
Hinkley	228	34.56 N	117.11 W
Hinkson Creek ≃	219	38.56 N	92.23 W
Hinkston Creek ≃	188	38.18 N	84.14 W
Hinnerjoki	26	61.00 N	22.00 E
Hinnerup	41	56.16 N	10.04 E
Hinnøya I	24	68.30 N	16.00 E
Hino, Nihon	94	35.00 N	136.15 E
Hino, Nihon	94	35.41 N	139.24 E
Hino, Nihon	96	35.14 N	133.27 E
Hino ≃, Nihon	94	35.09 N	136.02 E
Hino ≃, Nihon	94	36.04 N	136.11 E
Hino ≃, Nihon	96	35.27 N	133.23 E
Hinoba-an	116	9.35 N	122.28 E
Hinode	94	35.45 N	139.14 E
Hinoemata	94	37.01 N	139.23 E
Hinohara	94	35.43 N	139.09 E
Hinojosa del Duque	34	38.30 N	5.09 W
Hinokage	92	32.39 N	131.24 E
Hinomi-saki ›, Nihon	96	33.53 N	135.04 E
Hinomi-saki ›, Nihon	96	35.26 N	132.38 E
Hinsbeck	56	51.21 N	6.17 E
Hinsdale, Il., U.S.	216	41.48 N	87.56 W
Hinsdale, Ma., U.S.	207	42.26 N	73.07 W
Hinsdale, Mt., U.S.	202	48.23 N	107.05 W
Hinsdale, N.H., U.S.	207	42.47 N	72.29 W
Hinsdale, N.Y., U.S.	210	42.10 N	78.23 W
Hinsel ◆[8]	263	51.26 N	7.05 E
Hinsen ⊜	40	60.39 N	16.05 E
Hinte	52	53.25 N	7.11 E
Hinterbichl	64	47.01 N	12.20 E
Hinterbrühl	61	48.05 N	16.15 E
Hinterhermsdorf	54	50.55 N	14.22 E
Hinterrhein	58	46.32 N	9.12 E
Hinterrhein ≃	58	46.49 N	9.25 E
Hintersdorf	264b	48.18 N	16.13 E
Hintersee	54	53.37 N	14.16 E
Hinterstoder	61	47.41 N	14.09 E
Hintertux	64	47.07 N	11.41 E
Hinterweidenthal	56	49.12 N	7.45 E
Hinterzarten	58	47.54 N	8.06 E

Symbols in the index entries represent the broad categories identified in the key at the right. Symbols with superior numbers (⋏[1]) identify subcategories (see complete key on page *I · 1*).

Symbole im Register stellen die rechts im Schlüssel erklärten Kategorien dar. Symbole mit hochgestellten Ziffern (⋏[1]) bezeichnen Unterabteilungen einer Kategorie (vgl. vollständiger Schlüssel auf Seite *I · 1*).

Los símbolos incluídos en el texto del índice representan las grandes categorias identificadas con la clave a la derecha. Los símbolos con numeros en su parte superior (⋏[1]) identifican las subcategorías (véase la clave completa en la página *I · 1*).

Les symboles de l'index représentent les catégories indiquées dans la légende à droite. Les symboles suivis d'un indice (⋏[1]) représentent des sous-catégories (voir légende complète à la page *I · 1*).

Os símbolos incluídos no texto do índice representam as grandes categorias identificadas com a chave à direita. Os símbolos com números em sua parte superior (⋏[1]) identificam as subcategorias (veja-se a chave completa à página *I · 1*).

Symbol	English	Deutsch	Español	Français	Português
∧	Mountain	Berg	Montaña	Montagne	Montanha
⋏	Mountains	Gebirge	Montañas	Montagnes	Montanhas
)(	Pass	Paß	Paso	Col	Passo
V	Valley, Canyon	Tal, Cañon	Valle, Cañón	Vallée, Canyon	Vale, Canhão
≚	Plain	Ebene	Llano	Plaine	Planície
›	Cape	Kap	Cabo	Cap	Cabo
I	Island	Insel	Isla	Île	Ilha
II	Islands	Inseln	Islas	Îles	Ilhas
⊥	Other Topographic Features	Andere Topographische Objekte	Otros Elementos Topográficos	Autres données topographiques	Outros acidentes topográficos

ESPAÑOL

Nombre	Página	Lat.°′	Long.°′ W = Oeste
Hinton, Ab., Can.	182	53.25 N	117.34 W
Hinton, Mo., U.S.	219	39.03 N	92.21 W
Hinton, Ok., U.S.	196	35.28 N	98.21 W
Hinton, W.V., U.S.	192	37.40 N	80.53 W
Hi-numa ⊜	94	36.16 N	140.30 E
Hinuma ≃	94	36.16 N	140.28 E
Hinundayan	116	10.21 N	125.15 E
Hinwil	58	47.18 N	8.51 E
Hinzik	84	40.08 N	40.58 E
Hípico, Club ♠	286e	33.28 S	70.41 W
Hipólito	232	25.41 N	101.26 W
Hipólito Yrigoyen	252	32.55 S	66.20 W
Hippolytushoef	52	52.54 N	4.57 E
Hirado	92	33.22 N	129.33 E
Hirado-shima I	92	33.20 N	129.30 E
Hiraiwa-hana ›	174f	24.48 N	141.18 E
Hiraizumi	92	38.59 N	141.07 E
Hirakata, Nihon	96	34.48 N	135.38 E
Hirakata, Nihon	268	35.56 N	139.33 E
Hirakawa	270	34.52 N	135.47 E
Hīrākud	122	21.31 N	83.57 E
Hīrākud Reservoir ⊜[1]	120	21.35 N	83.50 E
Hiram, Me., U.S.	188	43.52 N	70.48 W
Hiram, Oh., U.S.	214	41.18 N	81.08 W
Hiraman ≃	154	1.07 S	39.55 E
Hirano	175d	24.35 N	124.19 E
Hirano ◆[8]	270	34.36 N	135.34 E
Hirao	96	33.56 N	132.04 E
Hirao-dai ♠	96	33.45 N	130.52 E
Hiraoka → Higashiōsaka	96	34.39 N	135.35 E
Hīrāpur	124	24.22 N	79.13 E
Hirara	175d	24.48 N	125.17 E
Hirata, Nihon	94	35.15 N	136.38 E
Hirata, Nihon	96	35.26 N	132.49 E
Hiratsuka	94	35.19 N	139.21 E
Hiraya	94	35.19 N	137.37 E
Hirfanlı Barajı ⊜[1]	130	39.10 N	33.35 E
Hirhafok	148	23.49 N	5.45 E
Hiriyūr	122	13.58 N	76.36 E
Ḥirjillah	132	33.22 N	36.18 E
Hîrlău	38	47.25 N	26.54 E
Hirokawa, Nihon	96	33.15 N	130.32 E
Hirokawa, Nihon	96	34.01 N	135.11 E
Hirok Sāmi	128	26.02 N	63.25 E
Hiromi	96	33.15 N	132.41 E
Hiroo	92a	42.17 N	143.19 E
Hirooka	268	35.15 N	140.04 E
Hirosaki	92	40.35 N	140.28 E
Hiroschima → Hiroshima	96	34.24 N	132.27 E
Hirose	96	35.22 N	133.10 E
Hiroshima	96	34.24 N	132.27 E
Hiroshima □[5]	96	34.30 N	133.00 E
Hiro-shima I	96	34.22 N	133.43 E
Hiroshima-wan ⊂	96	34.06 N	132.20 E
Hirosima → Hiroshima	96	34.24 N	132.27 E
Hirota	270	34.45 N	135.21 E
Hirsau	56	48.44 N	8.44 E
Hirschaid	56	49.49 N	10.59 E
Hirschau	60	49.33 N	11.57 E
Hirschbach	54	50.33 N	10.44 E
Hirschberg	54	50.24 N	11.49 E
Hirschberg → Jelenia Góra	30	50.55 N	15.46 E
Hirschfeld	54	51.23 N	13.37 E
Hirschfelde, Dtsch.	54	50.57 N	14.53 E
Hirschfelde, Dtsch.	264a	52.38 N	13.48 E
Hirschhorn	56	49.27 N	8.53 E
Hirschstetten ◆[8]	264b	48.14 N	16.29 E
Hirshfeld Brook ≃	276	40.57 N	74.02 W
Hirsingue	58	47.35 N	7.15 E
Hirson	50	49.55 N	4.05 E
Hîrşova	38	44.41 N	27.57 E
Hirsts Hill ∧	171a	27.13 S	152.06 E
Hirtshals	26	57.35 N	9.58 E
Hirtzfelden	58	47.55 N	7.27 E
Hirukawa	94	35.31 N	137.23 E
Hiru-zen ∧	96	35.19 N	133.40 E
Hirwaun	42	51.45 N	3.30 W
Hisābpur	272b	22.51 N	88.32 E
Hisai, Nihon	94	34.40 N	136.28 E
Hisai, Nihon	270	34.25 N	135.28 E
Hisār	123	29.10 N	75.43 E
Hisarönü	130	41.33 N	32.02 E
Ḥisbān	132	31.48 N	35.48 E
Hisiu	164	9.05 S	146.45 E
Hisn al-ʿAbr	144	16.05 N	47.22 E
Ḥiṣn al-Qarn	144	15.11 N	49.05 E
Hispaniola I	238	19.00 N	71.00 W
Hispar Glacier ⊼	123	36.05 N	75.20 E
Histon	42	52.15 N	0.06 E
Hisua	124	24.50 N	85.25 E
Ḥisyah	130	34.24 N	36.45 E
Hīt	128	33.38 N	42.49 E
Hita	96	33.19 N	130.56 E
Hitachi	94	36.36 N	140.39 E
Hitachi-ōta	94	36.32 N	140.31 E
Hitati → Hitachi	94	36.36 N	140.39 E
Hitchcock	222	29.20 N	95.00 W
Hitchin	42	51.57 N	0.17 W
Hitchins	218	38.16 N	82.55 W
Hither Green ◆[8]	260	51.27 N	0.01 W
Hither Hills State Park ♠	207	41.01 N	72.01 W
Hitiaa	174s	17.36 S	149.18 W
Hitokura	270	34.55 N	135.25 E
Hitotsubashi University ⊍[2]	268	35.42 N	139.27 E
Hitoyoshi	92	32.13 N	130.45 E
Hitra I	26	63.33 N	8.45 E
Hittarp	41	56.06 N	12.38 E
Hittisau	58	47.27 N	9.57 E
Hitzacker	54	53.09 N	11.02 E
Hitze-Berge ⋏[2]	264a	52.35 N	13.07 E
Hiu I	175f	13.10 S	166.35 E
Hiuchiga-take ∧	94	36.57 N	139.17 E
Hiuchi-nada ⊤[2]	96	34.05 N	133.20 E
Hiūnchuli Pātan ∧	124	28.50 N	82.37 E
Hiva Oa I	174x	9.45 S	139.00 W
Hi Vista	228	34.44 N	117.47 W
Hiwa	96	34.59 N	132.59 E
Hiwannee	194	31.48 N	88.41 W
Hiwasa	96	33.44 N	134.32 E
Hiwassee ≃	192	35.19 N	84.47 W
Hiwassee Lake ⊜[1]	192	35.10 N	84.05 W
Hixon	182	53.27 N	122.36 W
Hixson	192	35.09 N	85.14 W
Hiyoshi, Nihon	94	35.53 N	137.45 E
Hiyoshi, Nihon	96	33.20 N	132.48 E
Hiyoshi, Nihon	96	35.09 N	135.31 E
Hiyoshi ◆[8]	268	35.33 N	139.39 E
Ḥiyyon, Naḥal V	132	30.12 N	35.07 E
Hizaonna	174m	26.24 N	127.50 E
Hjälmare kanal ≋	40	59.24 N	15.56 E
Hjälmaren ⊜	40	59.15 N	15.45 E
Hjälmaresund ʊ	40	59.15 N	16.06 E
Hjarnø I	41	55.50 N	10.05 E
Hjelm I	41	56.08 N	10.48 E
Hjelmelandsvågen	26	59.14 N	6.11 E
Hjeltefjorden ⊂[2]	26	60.40 N	4.55 E
Hjembæk	41	55.42 N	11.25 E
Hjo	26	58.18 N	14.17 E
Hjøllund	41	56.05 N	9.25 E
Hjordkær	41	55.01 N	9.19 E
Hjørring	26	57.28 N	9.59 E
Hjortkvarn	40	58.53 N	15.25 E
Hjørundfjorden ⊂[2]	26	62.21 N	6.23 E
Hkakabo Razi ∧	102	28.20 N	97.32 E
Hkok (Kok) ≃	110	20.14 N	100.09 E
Hlabisa	158	28.08 S	31.52 E
Hlaingbwe	110	17.08 N	97.50 E
Hlatikulu	158	27.00 S	31.25 E
Hlegu	110	17.06 N	96.14 E
Hlinsko	30	49.45 N	15.55 E
Hlobane	158	27.42 S	31.00 E
Hlohovec	30	48.25 N	17.47 E
Hluboká ⊥	61	49.05 N	14.25 E

FRANÇAIS

Nom	Page	Lat.°′	Long.°′ W = Ouest
Hluboká nad Vltavou	61	49.03 N	14.27 E
Hluboš	60	49.45 N	14.02 E
Hlučín	30	49.54 N	18.12 E
Hluhluwe	158	28.01 S	32.15 E
Hluhluwe Game Reserve ◆[4]	158	28.05 S	32.04 E
Hluti	158	27.13 S	31.35 E
Hmawbi	110	17.06 N	96.02 E
H. Neely Henry Lake ⊜[1]	194	33.55 N	86.05 W
Ho	150	6.35 N	0.30 E
Hoa Binh	110	20.50 N	105.20 E
Hoa Da	110	11.11 N	108.33 E
Hoagland	216	40.56 N	84.59 W
Hoagland Ditch ≋	216	40.48 N	86.48 W
Hoanib ≃	156	19.27 S	12.46 E
Hoare Bay ⊂	176	65.20 N	62.30 W
Hoarusib ≃	156	19.03 S	12.36 E
Hoa Thoi	269c	10.44 N	106.35 E
Hoback ≃	202	43.19 N	110.44 W
Hobart, Austl.	166	42.53 S	147.19 E
Hobart, In., U.S.	216	41.31 N	87.15 W
Hobart, N.Y., U.S.	210	42.22 N	74.40 W
Hobart, Ok., U.S.	196	35.01 N	99.05 W
Hobart, Wa., U.S.	224	47.25 N	121.58 W
Hobbs, In., U.S.	216	40.17 N	85.57 W
Hobbs, N.M., U.S.	196	32.42 N	103.08 W
Hobbs Coast ⩡[2]	9	74.45 S	131.00 W
Hobe Sound	220	27.03 N	80.08 W
Hobgood	192	36.01 N	77.23 W
Hobhole Drain ≋	44	52.59 N	0.02 E
Hobhouse	158	29.31 S	27.08 E
Hobo	246	2.35 N	75.27 W
Hoboken, Bel.	50	51.10 N	4.21 E
Hoboken, N.J., U.S.	210	40.44 N	74.01 W
Hoboksar	86	46.47 N	85.43 E
Hobq Shamo ◆[2]	102	40.30 N	107.55 E
Hobro	26	56.38 N	9.48 E
Hobson	202	47.00 N	109.52 W
Hobson Lake ⊜	182	52.30 N	120.20 W
Hobsons Bay ⊂	274b	37.51 S	144.56 E
Hoburgen ›	26	56.55 N	18.07 E
Hobyo	144	5.21 N	48.32 E
Hocaköy	130	41.03 N	30.17 E
Hocalar	130	38.34 N	30.00 E
Hocalı	130	38.41 N	27.41 E
Hochalmspitze ∧	64	47.01 N	13.19 E
Hochandochtla Mountain ∧	180	65.32 N	154.50 W
Höchberg	56	49.49 N	9.51 E
Hochburg	60	48.07 N	12.52 E
Hochdahl	56	51.13 N	6.56 E
Hochdorf	58	47.10 N	8.17 E
Höchenschwand	58	47.44 N	8.10 E
Hochfeiler (Gran Pilastro) ∧	64	46.58 N	11.44 E
Hochfeld	156	21.28 S	17.58 E
Hochfeld ◆[8]	263	51.25 N	6.46 E
Hochfelden	56	48.45 N	7.34 E
Hochfilzen	64	47.28 N	12.37 E
Hochfinstermünz	58	46.56 N	10.29 E
Hochgern ∧	64	47.45 N	12.30 E
Hochgolling ∧	64	47.16 N	13.45 E
Hochheide ◆[8]	263	51.27 N	6.41 E
Hochheim, Dtsch.	56	50.01 N	8.20 E
Hochheim, Tx., U.S.	222	29.19 N	97.17 W
Hochiss ∧	64	47.27 N	11.46 E
Hochkirch	54	51.09 N	14.34 E
Hochkönig ∧	64	47.25 N	13.04 E
Hochkreuz ∧	64	46.49 N	13.04 E
Hochlantsch ∧	61	47.21 N	15.25 E
Hochlar	263	51.36 N	7.10 E
Hochneukirch	56	51.06 N	6.26 E
Hochobir ∧	61	46.30 N	14.29 E
Hochreichhart ∧	61	47.22 N	14.41 E
Hochries ∧	64	47.45 N	12.14 E
Hochschwab ∧	61	47.37 N	15.09 E
Hochschwab ⋏	61	47.36 N	15.05 E
Hochsimmer ∧	56	50.21 N	7.12 E
Hochspeyer	56	49.26 N	7.54 E
Höchst, Dtsch.	56	49.48 N	8.59 E
Höchst, Öst.	58	47.28 N	9.38 E
Höchst ◆[8]	56	50.07 N	8.33 E
Höchstadt an der Aisch	56	49.42 N	10.44 E
Höchstädt an der Donau	56	48.36 N	10.34 E
Höchsten ◆[8]	263	51.27 N	7.29 E
Höchstenbach	56	50.38 N	7.44 E
Hochstuhl (Veliki Stol) ∧	61	46.26 N	14.10 E
Hochtor)(	64	47.05 N	12.51 E
Hoch'uan → Hechuan	107	30.00 N	106.16 E
Ho Chung	271d	22.22 N	114.14 E
Hochvogel ∧	58	47.23 N	10.26 E
Hochwildstelle ∧	64	47.20 N	13.50 E
Hockenheim	56	49.19 N	8.33 E
Hockeroda	54	50.35 N	11.26 E
Hockessin	285	39.47 N	75.41 W
Hocking ≃	188	39.12 N	81.45 W
Hocking Hills State Park ♠	188	39.30 N	82.32 W
Hockley, Eng., U.K.	42	51.37 N	0.40 E
Hockley, Tx., U.S.	222	30.02 N	95.51 W
Hockomock Swamp ≡	283	41.59 N	71.05 W
Hôḍ ◆[1]	150	16.10 N	8.40 W
Hodal	124	27.54 N	77.22 E
Hōdatsu-zan ∧	94	36.47 N	136.49 E
Hodder ≃	44	53.50 N	2.25 W
Hoddesdon	42	51.46 N	0.01 W
Hoddlesden	262	53.42 N	2.26 W
Hodeida → Al-Ḥudaydah	144	14.48 N	42.57 E
Hodenhagen	52	52.46 N	9.35 E
Hodge	194	32.16 N	92.43 W
Hodgenville	194	37.34 N	85.44 W
Hodges, Lake ⊜[1]	228	33.03 N	117.05 W
Hodges Brook ≃	283	41.58 N	71.14 W
Hodges Hill ∧[2]	186	49.04 N	55.53 W
Hodgeville	184	50.08 N	106.58 W
Hodgkins	278	41.46 N	87.51 W
Hodgson	184	51.13 N	97.34 W
Hodgson ≃	164	14.48 S	134.35 E
Hodgson, Mount ∧[2]	162	22.26 S	121.10 E
Hod HaSharon	132	32.09 N	34.53 E
Hodh ech Chargui □[4]	150	18.10 N	7.15 W
Hodh el Gharbi □[4]	150	16.30 N	10.00 W
Hódmezővásárhely	30	46.25 N	20.20 E
Hodmo V	144	10.41 N	46.13 E
Hodna, Chott el ⊜	148	35.25 N	4.45 E
Hodna, Monts du ⋏	34	35.50 N	4.50 E
Hodna, Plaine du ⌣	34	35.38 N	4.30 E
Hodnet	42	52.51 N	2.35 W
Hodogaya ◆[8]	268	35.27 N	139.36 E
Hodogaya Baseball Ground ♠	268	35.27 N	139.35 E
Hodonín	30	48.51 N	17.08 E
Hodoš	61	46.50 N	16.20 E
Hodzana ≃	180	66.15 N	147.48 W
Hoed	41	56.19 N	10.49 E
Hoedekenskerke	52	51.25 N	3.55 E
Hoehne	198	37.16 N	104.22 W
Hoeksche Waard I	52	51.45 N	4.30 E
Hoek van Holland	52	51.59 N	4.09 E
Hoeningen	263	51.05 N	6.41 E
Hoensbroek	56	50.55 N	5.55 E
Hœrdt	58	48.42 N	7.47 E
Hoerstgen	263	51.30 N	6.27 E
Hoeryŏng	98	42.27 N	129.44 E
Hoeyang	98	38.43 N	127.36 E
Hof, Dtsch.	54	50.18 N	11.55 E
Hof, Ísland	24a	64.34 N	14.39 W
Hofburg ⊍	264b	48.12 N	16.22 E
Höfđakaupstaður	24a	65.50 N	20.19 W
Hofei → Hefei	100	31.51 N	117.17 E
Höfen	56	50.32 N	6.15 E
Hoffman, Il., U.S.	219	38.32 N	89.16 W

PORTUGUÊS

Nome	Página	Lat.°′	Long.°′ W = Oeste
Hoffman, Mn., U.S.	198	45.49 N	95.47 W
Hoffman Estates	216	42.02 N	88.04 W
Hoffman Island I	276	40.35 N	74.03 W
Hoffmans	210	42.54 N	74.05 W
Hoffman Station	284a	43.04 N	78.50 W
Hoffnung	263	51.07 N	7.13 E
Hofgeismar	52	51.30 N	9.22 E
Hofheim	56	50.07 N	8.26 E
Hofheim in Unterfranken	56	50.08 N	10.31 E
Hofkirchen an der Trattnach	60	48.13 N	13.44 E
Höflein an der Donau	264b	48.21 N	16.17 E
Hofmeyr	158	31.39 S	25.50 E
Höfn	24a	64.17 N	15.10 W
Hofors	40	60.33 N	16.17 E
Hofsjökull ⊼	24a	64.48 N	18.50 W
Hofstade	50	50.58 N	4.02 E
Hofstede ◆[8]	263	51.30 N	7.12 E
Hofstra University ⊍[2]	276	40.43 N	73.36 W
Hōfu	96	34.03 N	131.34 E
Hofuf → Al-Hufūf	128	25.22 N	49.34 E
Hofweier	58	48.25 N	7.55 E
Hog, Tanjong ›	116	5.18 N	119.16 E
Hogalbāria	126	23.53 N	88.51 E
Höganäs	41	56.12 N	12.33 E
Hogan Lake ⊜	190	45.52 N	78.30 W
Hogansburg	206	44.58 N	74.39 W
Hogansville	192	33.10 N	84.54 W
Hogatza ≃	180	66.00 N	155.29 W
Hogback Mountain ∧, U.S.	207	42.43 N	72.25 W
Hogback Mountain ∧, Mt., U.S.	202	44.54 N	112.07 W
Hogback Mountain ∧, Ne., U.S.	198	41.40 N	103.44 W
Hogback Mountain ∧, S.C., U.S.	192	35.10 N	82.17 W
Högbo	40	60.40 N	16.48 E
Hog Canyon V	226	35.42 N	120.35 W
Hog Creek ≃	222	31.32 N	97.18 W
Hoge Veluwe, Nationale Park de ♠	52	52.02 N	5.55 E
Högfors	40	59.59 N	15.01 E
Hoggar → Ahaggar ⋏	148	23.00 N	6.30 E
Hoghton	262	53.44 N	2.35 W
Hoghton Tower ⊥	262	53.44 N	2.34 W
Hog Island I, Ma., U.S.	283	42.40 N	70.46 W
Hog Island I, Mi., U.S.	190	45.48 N	85.22 W
Hog Island I, Vt., U.S.	206	44.57 N	73.13 W
Hog Island I, Va., U.S.	208	37.25 N	75.41 W
Hog Island Bay ⊂	208	37.27 N	75.46 W
Hogoro	154	5.57 S	36.27 E
Hog Point ›	208	37.12 N	76.41 W
Hogs Back ⩡[4]	42	51.13 N	0.40 W
Högsby	26	57.10 N	16.02 E
Högsjö	40	59.02 N	15.41 E
Hoh ≃	224	47.45 N	124.29 W
Hoh, South Fork ≃	224	47.46 N	124.01 W
Hohe Acht ∧	56	50.23 N	7.00 E
Hohebach	56	49.22 N	9.44 E
Hohegeiss	54	51.40 N	10.40 E
Hohenau	252	27.05 S	55.45 W
Hohenau an der March	61	48.36 N	16.55 E
Höhenberg	61	48.46 N	14.53 E
Hohenbrunn	60	48.03 N	11.42 E
Hohenbucko	54	51.46 N	13.28 E
Hohenbudberg ◆[8]	263	51.23 N	6.40 E
Hohenburg	60	49.16 N	11.30 E
Hohendorf	54	54.01 N	13.44 E
Hohenebra	54	51.18 N	10.49 E
Hohenems	58	47.22 N	9.41 E
Hohenfels	60	49.12 N	11.51 E
Hohenfurch	58	47.51 N	10.54 E
Hohengüstow	54	53.14 N	13.59 E
Hohenhameln	52	52.15 N	10.03 E
Hohenheide	263	51.29 N	7.47 E
Hohenkammer	60	48.25 N	11.32 E
Hohenkirchen, Dtsch.	52	53.39 N	7.55 E
Hohenkirchen, Dtsch.	54	50.51 N	10.41 E
Hohenkirchen, Dtsch.	54	53.51 N	11.17 E
Hohenkirchen, Dtsch.	56	51.23 N	9.29 E
Hohenleipisch	54	51.30 N	13.34 E
Hohenleuben	54	50.43 N	12.03 E
Hohenlimburg	56	51.21 N	7.35 E
Hohenlimburg, Schloss ⊥	263	51.21 N	7.34 E
Hohenlinden	60	48.09 N	12.00 E
Hohenmölsen	54	51.09 N	12.06 E
Hohen Neuendorf	54	52.40 N	13.16 E
Hohenpolding	60	48.23 N	12.08 E
Hohensalza → Inowrocław	30	52.48 N	18.15 E
Hohenschönhausen ◆[8]	264a	52.33 N	13.30 E
Hohenseeden	54	52.19 N	12.01 E
Hohenseefeld	54	51.53 N	13.18 E
Hohenstaufen	56	48.44 N	9.43 E
Hohenstein-Ernstthal	54	50.48 N	12.42 E
Hohensyburg ⊥	56	51.25 N	7.29 E
Hohentauern	61	47.26 N	14.29 E
Hohenthurm	54	51.31 N	12.05 E
Hohenthurn	64	46.33 N	13.40 E
Hohentwiel ∧	58	47.46 N	8.49 E
Hohenwald	194	35.32 N	87.33 W
Hohenwart	60	48.36 N	11.23 E
Hohenwarte-Stausee ⊜[1]	54	50.32 N	11.30 E
Hohenwarthe	54	52.13 N	11.42 E
Hohenwutzen	54	52.51 N	14.07 E
Hohenzethen	54	53.03 N	10.49 E
Hohenzollern, Burg ⊥	58	48.19 N	8.58 E
Hohenzollernkanal ≋	264a	52.32 N	13.20 E
Hoher Bogen ∧	60	49.15 N	12.55 E
Hoher Dachstein ∧	64	47.28 N	13.35 E
Hoher Freschen ∧	58	47.18 N	9.46 E
Hohe Rhön ⋏	56	50.30 N	10.00 E
Hoher Ifen ∧	58	47.21 N	10.05 E
Hoherlehme	264a	52.19 N	13.37 E
Hoher Mechtin ∧[2]	54	53.03 N	10.55 E
Hoher Riffler ∧	58	47.07 N	10.22 E
Hoher Sonnblick ∧	64	47.03 N	12.57 E
Hoher Zinken ∧	64	47.40 N	13.20 E
Hohe Tauern ⋏	64	47.10 N	12.45 E
Hohe Warte (Monte Coglians) ∧	64	46.37 N	12.53 E
Hoh Head ›	224	47.46 N	124.29 W
Hohhot	102	40.51 N	111.40 E
Höhn	56	50.37 N	8.00 E
Hohndorf	54	50.45 N	12.40 E
Hohne	52	52.35 N	10.22 E
Hohneck, Le ∧	58	48.02 N	7.01 E
Hohnstein	54	50.59 N	14.10 E
Hohoe	150	7.09 N	0.28 E
Hōhoku	96	34.17 N	130.57 E
Ho-Ho-Kus	276	40.59 N	74.06 W
Hohokus Brook ≃	276	40.57 N	74.06 W
Hoholitna ≃	180	61.31 N	157.00 W
Hoh Sai Hu ⊜	120	35.43 N	92.45 E
Höhscheid ◆[8]	263	51.09 N	7.04 E
Hohultslätt	26	56.58 N	15.39 E
Hohwacht	54	54.19 N	10.41 E
Hohwachter Bucht ⊂	41	54.20 N	10.45 E
Hoh Xil Hu ⊜	120	35.35 N	91.06 E
Hoh Xil Shan ⋏	120	35.20 N	90.00 E
Hoi An	110	15.52 N	108.19 E
Hoihow → Haikou	102	20.03 N	110.19 E
Hoima	154	1.26 N	31.21 E
Hoisdorf	52	53.39 N	10.20 E
Hoisington	198	38.31 N	98.46 W
Hoisten	263	51.08 N	6.42 E
Hoi Xuan	110	20.22 N	105.07 E
Hojāi	120	26.00 N	92.51 E
Højby, Dan.	41	55.55 N	11.37 E
Højby, Dan.	41	55.20 N	10.27 E
Höje	40	59.54 N	13.33 E
Højer	26	54.58 N	8.43 E
Højerup	41	55.17 N	12.27 E
Hōjō, Nihon	96	33.58 N	132.46 E
Hōjō, Nihon	96	34.54 N	134.56 E
Hōjō → Kasai	96	34.56 N	134.50 E
Hokah	190	43.45 N	91.20 W
Hokang → Hegang	89	47.24 N	130.17 E
Hökåsen	40	59.40 N	16.35 E
Hokendauqua	208	40.39 N	75.29 W
Hökensås ⋏[2]	26	58.11 N	14.08 E
Hokes Bluff	194	33.59 N	85.51 W
Hōki ≃	94	36.47 N	140.08 E
Hokianga Harbour ⊂	172	35.32 S	173.22 E
Hokitika	172	42.43 S	170.58 E
Hokkaidō □[5]	92a	44.00 N	143.00 E
Hokkaidō I	92a	44.00 N	143.00 E
Hokksund	26	59.47 N	9.59 E
Hoko ≃	224	48.17 N	124.22 W
Hōkōji	270	34.52 N	135.07 E
Hököpinge	41	55.30 N	13.00 E
Hokota	94	36.09 N	140.31 E
Hok So Wan	271d	22.13 N	114.14 E
Hokubo	96	34.57 N	133.38 E
Hokudan	96	34.32 N	134.56 E
Hokura ≃	94	37.10 N	138.16 E
Hokuriku-tunnel ◆[5]	94	35.42 N	136.10 E
Hokusei	94	35.09 N	136.31 E
Hola	154	1.29 S	40.02 E
Holalkere	122	14.02 N	76.11 E
Holanda → Netherlands □[1]	30	52.15 N	5.30 E
Holbæk	41	55.43 N	11.43 E
Holbeach	42	52.49 N	0.01 E
Holbeach Marsh ≡	42	52.52 N	0.05 E
Holberg	182	50.39 N	128.00 W
Holborn ◆[8]	260	51.31 N	0.07 W
Holbrook, Austl.	171b	35.44 S	147.19 E
Holbrook, Az., U.S.	200	34.54 N	110.09 W
Holbrook, Il., U.S.	278	41.32 N	87.38 W
Holbrook, Md., U.S.	284b	39.24 N	76.51 W
Holbrook, Ma., U.S.	207	42.09 N	71.00 W
Holbrook, Ne., U.S.	198	40.18 N	100.00 W
Holbrook, N.Y., U.S.	210	40.48 N	73.04 W
Holbrook, Lake ⊜[1]	222	32.42 N	95.33 W
Holbrook Mountain ∧[2]	212	44.25 N	77.51 W
Holckenhavn	41	55.17 N	10.47 E
Holcomb, Il., U.S.	216	42.04 N	89.06 W
Holcomb, N.Y., U.S.	210	42.54 N	77.25 W
Holcomb Creek ≃	228	34.17 N	117.08 W
Holden, Ab., Can.	182	53.14 N	112.14 W
Holden, Ma., U.S.	207	42.21 N	71.51 W
Holden, Mo., U.S.	194	38.42 N	93.59 W
Holden, Ut,. U.S.	200	39.05 N	112.16 W
Holden, W.V., U.S.	188	37.49 N	82.03 W
Holden, Mount ∧[2]	216	41.40 N	87.03 W
Holdenstedt	52	52.55 N	10.31 E
Holden Village	224	48.12 N	120.47 W
Holdenville	196	35.04 N	96.23 W
Holder	220	28.58 N	82.25 W
Holderness ›[1]	44	53.47 N	0.10 W
Holdfast	184	50.58 N	105.25 W
Holdich	254	45.57 S	68.13 W
Holdingford	190	45.43 N	94.28 W
Holdorf	52	52.35 N	8.07 E
Holdrege	198	40.26 N	99.22 W
Holeby	41	54.43 N	11.28 E
Hole in the Mountain Peak ∧	204	40.55 N	115.05 W
Hole Narsipur	122	12.47 N	76.15 E
Holešov	30	49.20 N	17.35 E
Holetown	241g	13.11 N	59.39 W
Holgate, S. Afr.	158	33.59 S	22.21 E
Holgate, Oh., U.S.	216	41.14 N	84.07 W
Holguín	240p	20.53 N	76.15 W
Holguín □[4]	240p	20.55 N	75.50 W
Hol-Hol	144	11.19 N	42.57 E
Holíč	30	48.49 N	17.10 E
Holiday Beach Provincial Park ♠	214	42.02 N	83.05 W
Holiday Hills	216	42.18 N	88.13 W
Holiday Lake Amusement Park ♠	285	40.02 N	74.56 W
Holiday Shores	219	38.55 N	89.56 W
Holitna ≃	180	61.40 N	157.12 W
Höljes	26	60.54 N	12.36 E
Hollabrunn	61	48.34 N	16.05 E
Holladay	200	40.40 N	111.49 W
Holland, Mb., Can.	184	49.36 N	98.53 W
Holland, Mi., U.S.	216	42.47 N	86.06 W
Holland, N.Y., U.S.	210	42.38 N	78.32 W
Holland, Oh., U.S.	216	41.37 N	83.42 W
Holland, Pa., U.S.	285	40.10 N	74.59 W
Holland, Tx., U.S.	222	30.53 N	97.24 W
Holland, Va., U.S.	208	36.41 N	76.47 W
Holland □[9]	52	52.20 N	4.45 E
Holland ≃	212	44.12 N	79.31 W
Holland, Mount ∧[2]	162	32.12 S	119.44 E
Hollandale	194	33.10 N	90.51 W
Holland Creek ≃	169	36.43 S	146.06 E
Hollande, Étangs de ⊜	261	48.44 N	1.48 E
Holland Fen ≡	44	53.00 N	0.10 W
Hollandia → Jayapura	164	2.32 S	140.42 E
Holland Landing	212	44.06 N	79.29 W
Holland → Netherlands □[1]	30	52.15 N	5.30 E
Holland Park	171a	27.31 S	153.03 E
Holland Patent	210	43.14 N	75.15 W
Holland Point ›	208	38.43 N	76.32 W
Holland Pond State Park ♠	207	42.04 N	72.09 W
Hollandsbird Island I	156	24.45 S	14.34 E
Hollandsch Diep ʊ	52	51.42 N	4.30 E
Hollandstoun	46	59.21 N	2.26 W
Holland Straits ʊ	208	38.08 N	76.02 W
Holland Tunnel ◆[5]	276	40.44 N	74.02 W
Hollansburg	218	39.59 N	84.47 W
Holleben	54	51.26 N	11.53 E
Hollenfels, Château ⊥	56	49.43 N	6.03 E
Höllengebirge ⋏	64	47.48 N	13.39 E
Hollenstedt	52	53.22 N	9.43 E
Hollenstein an der Ybbs	61	47.48 N	14.46 E
Höllensteinberg ∧	264b	48.06 N	16.11 E
Höllental V	61	47.45 N	15.47 E
Hollern	52	53.36 N	9.32 E
Holleton	162	31.57 S	119.02 E
Holley	210	43.13 N	78.01 W
Hollfeld	60	49.56 N	11.18 E
Hollick-Kenyon Plateau ⋏[1]	9	79.00 S	97.00 W
Holliday, Mo., U.S.	219	39.29 N	92.07 W
Holliday, Tx., U.S.	196	33.49 N	98.42 W
Holliday Creek ≃	196	33.55 N	98.28 W
Holliday Park ♠	281	42.21 N	83.24 W
Hollidaysburg	214	40.25 N	78.23 W
Hollingbourne	260	51.16 N	0.38 E
Hollingstedt	41	54.27 N	9.19 E
Hollingworth	262	53.28 N	1.59 W
Hollingworth Lake ⊜	262	53.38 N	2.06 W
Hollins, Eng., U.K.	262	53.34 N	2.17 W
Hollins, Va., U.S.	192	37.20 N	79.56 W
Hollins Green	262	53.25 N	2.27 W
Hollinswood	284c	38.55 N	77.13 W
Hollis, N.H., U.S.	207	42.44 N	71.35 W
Hollis, Ok., U.S.	196	34.41 N	99.54 W
Hollis ◆[8]	276	40.43 N	73.46 W
Hollister	226	36.51 N	121.24 W
Hollister, Mount ∧[2]	162	22.08 S	114.01 E
Holliston	207	42.12 N	71.25 W
Hollman, Cape ›	164	4.59 S	150.06 E
Holloman Air Force Base ■	200	32.51 N	106.05 W
Holloway	214	40.10 N	81.08 W
Holloway Terrace	285	39.42 N	75.32 W
Hollow Rock	194	36.02 N	88.16 W
Hollowville	210	42.12 N	73.42 W
Hollsopple	214	40.13 N	78.56 W
Hollum	52	53.26 N	5.37 E
Höllviken ⊂	41	55.26 N	12.54 E
Höllviksnäs	41	55.25 N	12.57 E
Holly, Co., U.S.	198	38.03 N	102.07 W
Holly, Mi., U.S.	216	42.47 N	83.37 W
Holly, Wa., U.S.	224	47.34 N	122.58 W
Holly, Mount ∧[2]	285	40.00 N	74.47 W
Holly Brook	285	39.59 N	74.48 W
Holly Grove	194	34.35 N	91.11 W
Holly Hill, Fl., U.S.	192	29.14 N	81.02 W
Holly Hill, S.C., U.S.	192	33.19 N	80.24 W
Holly Park, N.J., U.S.	208	39.53 N	74.10 W
Holly Park, Va., U.S.	284c	38.50 N	77.17 W
Holly Pond ⊜	276	41.03 N	73.30 W
Holly River State Park ♠	188	38.40 N	80.21 W
Holly Run ≃	285	39.47 N	75.03 W
Holly Springs	194	34.46 N	89.26 W
Holly State Recreation Area ♠	216	42.49 N	83.32 W
Hollywood, Ire.	48	53.06 N	6.35 W
Hollywood, Fl., U.S.	220	26.00 N	80.08 W
Hollywood, Md., U.S.	208	38.20 N	76.34 W
Hollywood, Pa., U.S.	285	40.05 N	75.06 W
Hollywood ◆[8]	228	34.06 N	118.21 W
Hollywood, Mount ∧	280	34.08 N	118.18 W
Hollywood Bowl ♠	280	34.07 N	118.20 W
Hollywood-Burbank Airport ⊠	228	34.12 N	118.21 W
Hollywood Heights	219	38.39 N	89.59 W
Hollywood Indian Reservation ◆[4]	220	26.02 N	80.13 W
Hollywood Park Race Track ♠	280	33.57 N	118.20 W
Hollywood Reservoir ⊜[1]	280	34.07 N	118.20 W
Holman	176	70.43 N	117.43 W
Hólmavík	24a	65.43 N	21.43 W
Holmdel	208	40.20 N	74.11 W
Holme, Dan.	41	56.07 N	10.11 E
Holme, Eng., U.K.	262	53.33 N	1.50 W
Holme ≃	44	53.41 N	1.43 W
Holme Chapel	262	53.45 N	2.11 W
Holmen, Nor.	26	60.40 N	10.22 E
Holmen, Wi., U.S.	190	43.57 N	91.15 W
Holme-on-Spaulding-Moor	44	53.50 N	0.46 W
Holmes, N.Y., U.S.	210	41.31 N	73.39 W
Holmes, Pa., U.S.	285	39.54 N	75.19 W
Holmes □[6]	214	40.33 N	81.55 W
Holmes, Mount ∧	202	44.49 N	110.51 W
Holmes Beach	220	27.31 N	82.43 W
Holmesburg ◆[8]	285	40.02 N	75.03 W
Holmes Chapel	44	53.12 N	2.22 W
Holmes Creek ≃	194	30.30 N	85.47 W
Holmesglen	274b	37.53 S	145.06 E
Holmes Harbor ⊂	224	48.04 N	122.32 W
Holmes Lake ⊜	184	57.05 N	96.45 W
Holmes Reef ✢[2]	164	16.27 S	148.00 E
Holmes Run ≃	284c	38.48 N	77.07 W
Holmes Run Acres	284c	38.51 N	77.13 W
Holmestrand	26	59.29 N	10.18 E
Holmesville, N.Y., U.S.	210	42.31 N	75.24 W
Holmesville, Oh., U.S.	214	40.37 N	81.55 W
Holmeswood	262	53.39 N	2.52 W
Holmfirth	44	53.35 N	1.46 W
Holmia	246	4.58 N	59.35 W
Holmön I	26	63.47 N	20.53 E
Holmsbu	26	59.33 N	10.27 E
Holmsjön ⊜, Sve.	26	62.41 N	16.33 E
Holmsjön ⊜, Sve.	26	62.25 N	15.20 E
Holmsund	26	63.42 N	20.21 E
Hölö	40	59.01 N	17.35 E
Holod	38	46.47 N	22.08 E
Holoit, Punta ›	232	21.37 N	88.08 W
Ḥolon	132	32.01 N	34.46 E
Holoog	156	27.22 S	17.55 E
Holopaw	220	28.08 N	81.04 W
Holroyd	274a	33.50 S	150.58 E
Holroyd ≃	164	14.10 S	141.36 E
Holsloot	52	52.44 N	6.48 E
Holstebro	26	56.21 N	8.38 E
Holsted	41	55.30 N	8.55 E
Holstein	198	42.29 N	95.32 W
Holsteinborg ⊥	41	55.13 N	11.28 E
Holsteinische Schweiz ◆[1]	54	54.11 N	10.36 E
Holsteinsborg (Sisimiut)	176	66.55 N	53.40 W
Holsterhausen	263	51.41 N	6.57 E
Holston ≃	192	35.57 N	83.51 W
Holston, North Fork ≃	192	36.33 N	82.36 W
Holston High Knob ∧	192	36.27 N	82.05 W
Holsworthy	42	50.49 N	4.21 W
Holt, Eng., U.K.	42	52.55 N	1.05 E
Holt, Wales, U.K.	44	53.05 N	2.53 W
Holt, Al., U.S.	194	33.14 N	87.29 W
Holt, Ca., U.S.	226	37.56 N	121.26 W
Holt, Fl., U.S.	194	30.42 N	86.44 W
Holt, Mi., U.S.	216	42.38 N	84.30 W
Holt Creek ≃	198	42.28 N	98.50 W
Holte	41	55.49 N	12.28 E
Holtemme ≃	54	51.57 N	11.10 E
Holten	52	52.17 N	6.25 E
Holten ◆[8]	263	51.31 N	6.48 E
Holtenau ◆[8]	54	54.22 N	10.08 E
Holter Lake ⊜[1]	202	46.55 N	111.57 W
Holthausen, Dtsch.	52	52.33 N	7.17 E
Holthausen, Dtsch.	263	51.23 N	7.13 E
Holthausen ◆[8]	263	51.34 N	7.26 E
Holthusen	52	53.08 N	7.18 E
Holton, In., U.S.	218	39.04 N	85.23 W
Holton, Ks., U.S.	198	39.27 N	95.44 W
Holtorf	52	52.40 N	9.13 E
Holts Summit	219	38.39 N	92.07 W
Holtsville	210	40.49 N	73.02 W
Holtug	41	55.21 N	12.25 E
Holtville	204	32.48 N	115.22 W
Holtwick	52	52.00 N	7.05 E
Holtwood	208	39.50 N	76.19 W
Holwerd	52	53.22 N	5.54 E
Holycross, Ire.	48	52.38 N	7.52 W
Holy Cross, Ak., U.S.	180	62.12 N	159.47 W
Holy Cross Mountain ∧	182	53.47 N	120.47 W
Holyhead	44	53.19 N	4.38 W
Holyhead Bay ⊂	44	53.23 N	4.37 W
Holy Island I, Eng., U.K.	44	55.41 N	1.48 W
Holy Island I, Scot., U.K.	46	55.32 N	5.04 W
Holy Island I, Wales, U.K.	44	53.18 N	4.37 W
Holy Island I, Ma., U.S.	283	42.43 N	70.50 W
Holyoke, Co., U.S.	198	40.35 N	102.18 W
Holyoke, Ma., U.S.	207	42.12 N	72.37 W
Holyrood	198	38.35 N	98.24 W
Holyrood Palace ⊍	46	55.56 N	3.12 W
Holýšov	60	49.36 N	13.05 E
Holywell	44	53.17 N	3.13 W
Holywell Green	262	53.41 N	1.52 W
Holywood	48	54.38 N	5.50 W
Holzbüttgen	263	51.12 N	6.37 E
Holzen	56	51.26 N	7.31 E
Holzgau	58	47.16 N	10.21 E
Holzgerlingen	56	48.38 N	9.00 E
Holzhausen, Dtsch.	52	52.17 N	8.32 E
Holzhausen, Dtsch.	52	52.13 N	8.01 E
Holzhausen, Dtsch.	52	52.01 N	8.44 E
Holzhausen, Dtsch.	54	51.18 N	12.28 E
Holzhausen an der Haide	56	50.13 N	7.55 E
Holzheim	56	51.09 N	6.39 E
Holzkirchen	64	47.52 N	11.42 E
Holzminden	52	51.50 N	9.27 E
Holzweissig	54	51.36 N	12.18 E
Holzwickede	52	51.30 N	7.36 E
Hom ≃	158	28.51 S	18.37 E
Homa Bay	154	0.31 S	34.27 E
Homalin	110	24.52 N	94.55 E
Homathko ≃	182	50.55 N	124.50 W
Homathko Icefield ⊼	182	51.05 N	124.30 W
Homberg, Dtsch.	56	50.43 N	8.59 E
Homberg, Dtsch.	56	51.02 N	9.24 E
Homberg, Dtsch.	56	51.28 N	6.43 E
Homberg, Dtsch.	263	51.18 N	6.56 E
Hombori	150	15.17 N	1.42 W
Hombori Tondo ∧	150	15.16 N	1.40 W
Hombourg-Haut	56	49.08 N	6.46 E
Hombre Muerto, Salar del ⌣	252	25.23 S	67.06 W
Hombruch ◆[8]	263	51.29 N	7.26 E
Homburg	56	49.19 N	7.20 E
Homburg → Bad Homburg vor der Höhe	56	50.13 N	8.37 E
Home, Pa., U.S.	214	40.44 N	79.06 W
Home, Wa., U.S.	224	47.17 N	122.46 W
Homeacre	214	40.51 N	79.55 W
Home Bay ⊂, N.T., Can.	176	68.45 N	67.10 W
Home Bay ⊂, Kiribati	174d	0.53 S	169.35 E
Homebush Bay ⊂	274a	33.50 S	151.05 E
Home Corner	216	40.31 N	85.38 W
Homécourt	56	49.14 N	5.59 E
Home Creek ≃	196	31.29 N	99.14 W
Homedale, Id., U.S.	202	43.37 N	116.55 W
Homedale, Oh., U.S.	214	40.04 N	83.02 W
Home Gardens	228	33.52 N	117.31 W
Home Hill	166	19.40 S	147.25 E
Homeland, Ca., U.S.	228	33.44 N	117.07 W
Homeland, Fl., U.S.	220	27.49 N	81.49 W
Homeland Canal ≋	226	35.57 N	119.27 W
Homeland Park	192	34.27 N	82.41 W
Home Place	218	39.56 N	86.08 W
Homer, Ak., U.S.	180	59.39 N	151.33 W
Homer, Ga., U.S.	192	34.20 N	83.29 W
Homer, La., U.S.	194	32.47 N	93.03 W
Homer, Mi., U.S.	216	42.08 N	84.48 W
Homer, Ne., U.S.	198	42.19 N	96.29 W
Homer, N.Y., U.S.	210	42.38 N	76.10 W
Homer, Oh., U.S.	214	40.15 N	82.31 W
Homer, Tx., U.S.	222	31.18 N	94.36 W
Homer City	214	40.32 N	79.09 W
Homert ∧[2]	263	51.11 N	7.39 E
Homer Tunnel ◆[5]	172	44.45 S	168.00 E
Homerville, Ga., U.S.	192	31.02 N	82.44 W
Homerville, Oh., U.S.	214	41.02 N	82.08 W
Homer Wash V	204	34.20 N	115.02 W
Homer Youngs Peak ∧	202	45.19 N	113.41 W
Home Seamount ✢[3]	14	12.55 S	175.37 W
Homestead, Austl.	166	20.22 S	145.39 E
Homestead, Fl., U.S.	220	25.28 N	80.28 W
Homestead, Pa., U.S.	279b	40.24 N	79.54 W
Homestead Air Force Base ■	220	25.29 N	80.23 W
Homestead National Monument of America ♠	198	40.14 N	96.54 W
Homestead Valley	282	37.54 N	122.32 W
Hometown, Il., U.S.	278	41.44 N	87.43 W
Hometown, Pa., U.S.	210	40.49 N	75.59 W
Homewood, Al., U.S.	194	33.28 N	86.48 W
Homewood, Ca., U.S.	226	39.05 N	120.09 W
Homewood, Il., U.S.	216	41.33 N	87.39 W
Homewood, Oh., U.S.	218	39.23 N	84.33 W
Homewood ◆[8]	279b	40.27 N	79.54 W
Homewood Acres	278	41.34 N	87.43 W
Homeworth	214	40.50 N	81.03 W
Hominy	196	36.24 N	96.23 W
Hominy Creek ≃	196	36.20 N	96.00 W
Hommersåk	26	58.58 N	5.42 E
Hommura	92	34.22 N	139.15 E
Homnābād	122	17.46 N	77.08 E
Homochitto ≃	194	31.09 N	91.31 W
Homoíne	156	23.52 S	35.09 E
Homonhon Island I	116	10.44 N	125.43 E
Homosassa	220	28.46 N	82.36 W
Homosassa Bay ⊂	220	28.45 N	82.43 W
Homosassa Springs	220	28.48 N	82.35 W
Homs → Al-Khums	146	32.39 N	14.16 E
Homs → Ḥimṣ	130	34.44 N	36.43 E
Honai	96	33.30 N	132.25 E
Honaker	192	37.00 N	81.58 W
Honami	96	33.36 N	130.42 E
Honan → Henan □[4]	90	34.00 N	114.00 E
Honan → Luoyang	102	34.41 N	112.28 E
Honāvar	122	14.17 N	74.27 E
Honaz	130	37.45 N	29.17 E
Honbetsu	92a	43.07 N	143.37 E
Hon Chong	110	10.10 N	104.37 E
Honda	246	5.12 N	74.45 W
Honda, Bahía ⊂, Col.	246	12.21 N	71.47 W
Honda, Bahía ⊂, Cuba	240p	22.57 N	83.10 W
Honda, Cañada ≃	258	33.57 S	59.21 W
Honda Bay ⊂	116	9.53 N	118.49 E
Honddu ≃, U.K.	42	51.54 N	2.58 W
Honddu ≃, Wales, U.K.	42	51.57 N	3.23 W
Hondeklipbaai	156	30.20 S	17.18 E
Honderfontein	158	32.12 S	21.22 E
Hon Dien, Nui ∧	110	11.33 N	108.38 E
Hondo, Ab., Can.	182	55.04 N	114.02 W
Hondo, Nihon	92	32.27 N	130.12 E
Hondo, N.M., U.S.	200	33.23 N	105.16 W
Hondo, Tx., U.S.	196	29.20 N	99.08 W
Hondo ≃, Méx.	286a	19.26 N	99.15 W
Hondo ≃, N.A.	232	18.29 N	88.19 W
Hondo, Arroyo ≃	226	37.28 N	121.47 W
Hondo, Rio ≃, Ca., U.S.	280	33.55 N	118.10 W
Hondo, Rio ≃, N.M., U.S.	196	33.22 N	104.24 W
Hondo Creek ≃	196	28.45 N	99.11 W
Hondoji Temple ⊍[1]	268	35.51 N	139.56 E
Hondschoote	50	50.59 N	2.35 E
Hondsrug ⋏[2]	52	52.55 N	6.50 E
Honduras □[1], N.A.	230	15.00 N	86.30 W
Honduras □[1], N.A.	236	15.00 N	86.30 W
Honduras, Cabo de ›	236	16.01 N	86.02 W
Honduras, Gulf of ⊂	230	16.10 N	87.50 W
Honduras, Port ⊂	236	16.13 N	88.41 W
Honea Path	192	34.26 N	82.23 W
Hönebach	56	50.56 N	9.56 E
Hønefoss	26	60.10 N	10.18 E
Honeoye	210	42.47 N	77.31 W
Honeoye Creek ≃	210	42.58 N	77.43 W
Honeoye Falls	210	42.57 N	77.35 W
Honeoye Lake ⊜	210	42.45 N	77.31 W
Honesdale	210	41.34 N	75.15 W
Honey Brook	208	40.05 N	75.54 W
Honey Creek	216	42.44 N	88.18 W
Honey Creek ≃, Ia., U.S.	190	42.09 N	93.03 W
Honey Creek ≃, Mo., U.S.	194	39.53 N	93.34 W
Honey Creek ≃, Oh., U.S.	214	41.05 N	83.12 W
Honey Creek ≃, Pa., U.S.	208	40.36 N	77.35 W
Honey Creek ≃, Wi., U.S.	216	42.41 N	88.17 W

≃	River	Fluß	Río	Rivière	Rio
≋	Canal	Kanal	Canal	Canal	Canal
⌞	Waterfall, Rapids	Wasserfall, Stromschnellen	Cascada, Rápidos	Chute d'eau, Rapides	Cascata, Rápidos
ʊ	Strait	Meeresstraße	Estrecho	Détroit	Estreito
⊂	Bay, Gulf	Bucht, Golf	Bahía, Golfo	Baie, Golfe	Baía, Golfo
⊜	Lake, Lakes	See, Seen	Lago, Lagos	Lac, Lacs	Lago, Lagos
≡	Swamp	Sumpf	Pantano	Marais	Pântano
⊼	Ice Features, Glacier	Eis- und Gletscherformen	Accidentes Glaciales	Formes glaciaires	Acidentes glaciares
⊤	Other Hydrographic Features	Andere Hydrographische Objekte	Otros Elementos Hidrográficos	Autres données hydrographiques	Outros acidentes hidrográficos

✢	Submarine Features	Untermeerische Objekte	Accidentes Submarinos	Formes de relief sous-marin	Acidentes submarinos
□	Political Unit	Politische Einheit	Unidad Politica	Entité politique	Unidade política
⊍	Cultural Institution	Kulturelle Institution	Institución Cultural	Institution culturelle	Instituição cultural
⊥	Historical Site	Historische Stätte	Sitio Histórico	Site historique	Sitio histórico
♠	Recreational Site	Erholungs- und Ferienort	Sitio de Recreo	Centre de loisirs	Area de Lazer
⊠	Airport	Flughafen	Aeropuerto	Aéroport	Aeroporto
■	Military Installation	Militäranlage	Instalación Militar	Installation militaire	Instalação militar
◆	Miscellaneous	Verschiedenes	Misceláneo	Divers	Diversos

ENGLISH / DEUTSCH

Name	Page	Lat.°′	Long.°′
Honeydew	273d	26.05 S	27.55 E
Honeygo Run ≃	284b	39.22 N	76.25 W
Honey Grove	196	33.35 N	95.54 W
Honey Lake ⊜	204	40.16 N	120.19 W
Honeymoon Bay	224	48.49 N	124.10 W
Honeyville	200	41.38 N	112.04 W
Honfleur	50	49.25 N	0.14 E
Høng	41	55.31 N	11.18 E
Hong ≃	100	32.25 N	115.35 E
Honga	152	15.09 S	15.12 E
Hon Gai	110	20.57 N	107.05 E
Hong'an	100	31.18 N	114.37 E
Honga River c	208	38.19 N	76.10 W
Hongawa	96	33.43 N	133.19 E
Hongchang	100	34.05 N	113.20 E
Hongch'ŏn	98	37.42 N	127.52 E
Hongchoudai	100	29.03 N	121.11 E
Hongcun, Zhg.	100	27.10 N	116.48 E
Hongcun, Zhg.	106	31.01 N	119.15 E
Höngen	56	51.02 N	5.56 E
Honggun	98	40.46 N	128.27 E
Honghai Wan c	100	22.40 N	115.10 E
Honghe	102	23.23 N	102.35 E
Honghu	100	29.48 N	113.27 E
Hong Hu ⊜	100	29.52 N	113.23 E
Honghuaerji	89	48.15 N	120.01 E
Honghuaji	100	33.52 N	114.26 E
Honghualiangzi	89	48.06 N	123.12 E
Honghuamu	89	48.33 N	125.39 E
Hongjiang, Zhg.	100	26.49 N	120.03 E
Hongjiang, Zhg.	102	27.07 N	109.56 E
Hong Kong □[2], Asia	90	22.15 N	114.10 E
Hong Kong □[2], Asia	100	22.15 N	114.10 E
Hong Kong I	271d	22.15 N	114.11 E
Hong Kong, University of ✓[2]	271d	22.17 N	114.08 E
Hong Kong → Victoria	271d	22.17 N	114.09 E
Hongkou Park ♦	269b	31.16 N	121.28 E
Honglai	100	25.08 N	118.32 E
Honglanbu	106	31.37 N	118.57 E
Honglinqiao	106	30.59 N	118.59 E
Hongliutai	85	39.48 N	77.26 E
Hongliuyuan	102	41.04 N	95.26 E
Honglongdian	106	30.30 N	119.00 E
Honglongtang	105	40.41 N	117.37 E
Honglu	100	25.44 N	119.20 E
Hongluan	100	28.31 N	117.01 E
Hongluo Shan ∧	104	40.56 N	120.42 E
Hongluoxian	104	41.01 N	120.53 E
Hongmeichang	105	39.50 N	115.51 E
Hongmendu	102	26.10 N	102.37 E
Hongmenkou	102	27.22 N	100.30 E
Hongmenpu	107	30.37 N	104.08 E
Hongmiaozi	107	28.47 N	104.02 E
Hong Ngu	110	10.48 N	105.21 E
Hongō, Nihon	96	34.24 N	132.59 E
Hongō, Nihon	96	34.17 N	132.02 E
Hongō ◆[8]	268	35.42 N	139.47 E
Hongpailou	107	30.38 N	104.01 E
Hongqi	89	44.23 N	126.32 E
Hongqiao, Zhg.	100	28.14 N	121.01 E
Hongqiao, Zhg.	105	39.50 N	117.44 E
Hongqiao, Zhg.	106	31.29 N	121.49 E
Hongqiao, Zhg.	269b	31.12 N	121.22 E
Hongqiao Ji Chang ✈	106	31.12 N	121.20 E
Hong → Red ≃	110	20.17 N	106.34 E
Hongrie → Hungary □[1]	30	47.00 N	20.00 E
Hongshan, Zhg.	89	48.02 N	129.00 E
Hongshan, Zhg.	98	36.37 N	118.00 E
Hongshanzi	98	42.34 N	117.14 E
Hongshi, Zhg.	89	43.00 N	127.04 E
Hongshi, Zhg.	98	41.21 N	119.32 E
Hongshidou	104	41.52 N	122.11 E
Hongshili	98	40.41 N	125.03 E
Hongshui	102	37.24 N	104.00 E
Hongshui ≃	102	23.45 N	109.30 E
Hongshuichuan	105	40.06 N	117.55 E
Hongshuyangzi	105	40.36 N	116.36 E
Hongsŏng	98	36.36 N	126.39 E
Hongtang	100	26.06 N	119.14 E
Hongtian	100	25.52 N	117.15 E
Hongtong	102	36.19 N	111.39 E
Hongtuwan	98	41.03 N	113.39 E
Hongtu Zhang ∧	100	23.46 N	115.56 E
Honguedo, Détroit d' ℧	186	49.15 N	64.00 W
Hongwŏn	98	40.02 N	127.57 E
Hongxin	100	32.43 N	117.47 E
Hongxing	105	39.48 N	116.27 E
Hongxingqiao	106	30.55 N	119.52 E
Hongyang, Zhg.	100	26.32 N	119.27 E
Hongyang, Zhg.	100	23.28 N	116.13 E
Hongyanzi	104	40.38 N	120.31 E
Hongyōtoku	268	35.41 N	139.55 E
Hongze	100	33.19 N	118.53 E
Hongze Hu ⊜	100	33.16 N	118.34 E
Honiara	175e	9.26 S	159.57 E
Honiton	42	50.48 N	3.13 W
Hon-jima I	96	34.23 N	133.47 E
Honjō, Nihon	92	39.23 N	140.03 E
Honjō, Nihon	94	36.24 N	138.01 E
Honjō, Nihon	94	36.14 N	139.11 E
Honkamäki ∧[2]	26	62.58 N	27.05 E
Hon-kawane	94	35.07 N	138.09 E
Honker Bay c	282	38.04 N	121.56 W
Hönne ≃	263	51.28 N	7.46 E
Honnecourt-sur-Escaut	50	50.02 N	3.12 E
Honningsvåg	24	70.59 N	25.59 E
Hönö	26	57.42 N	11.39 E
Honokaa	229d	20.04 N	155.28 W
Honokahua	229a	21.00 N	156.39 W
Honokawai	229a	20.57 N	156.41 W
Honolulu	229c	21.18 N	157.51 W
Honolulu □[6]	229c	21.19 N	157.52 W
Honolulu International Airport ✈	229c	21.20 N	157.55 W
Honomu	229d	19.52 N	155.07 W
Honouliuli	229c	21.22 N	158.02 W
Hönow	54	52.32 N	13.38 E
Hon Quan	110	11.39 N	106.36 E
Honshū I	92	36.00 N	138.00 E
Hontoon Island State Park ♦	220	28.59 N	81.22 W
Höntrop ◆[8]	263	51.27 N	7.08 E
Honuapo Bay c	229d	19.05 N	155.33 W
Hoo	260	51.25 N	0.34 E
Hood	226	38.22 N	121.31 W
Hood □[6]	222	32.25 N	97.45 W
Hood ≃, N.T., Can.	176	67.26 N	108.53 W
Hood ≃, Or., U.S.	224	45.42 N	121.30 W
Hood, East Fork ≃	224	45.36 N	121.38 W
Hood, Mount ∧	224	45.23 N	121.41 W
Hood, West Fork ≃	224	45.36 N	121.38 W
Hood Canal c	224	47.35 N	123.00 W
Hood Canal Floating Bridge ◆[5]	224	47.52 N	122.38 W
Hoodoo Peak ∧	202	48.15 N	120.19 W
Hood Point >, Austl.	162	34.23 S	119.34 E
Hood Point >, Pap. N. Gui.	164	10.05 S	147.45 E
Hood Pond ⊜	283	42.40 N	70.57 W
Hood River	224	45.42 N	121.31 W
Hoodsport	224	47.24 N	123.08 W
Hoods Range ✗	166	28.35 S	144.30 E
Hoof	56	51.17 N	9.20 E
Hoogerheide	52	51.25 N	4.20 E
Hoogeveen	52	52.43 N	6.29 E
Hoogeveense Vaart ≃	52	52.42 N	6.11 E
Hoogezand-Sappemeer	52	53.09 N	6.47 E
Hoogkerk	52	53.13 N	6.30 E
Hooglede	50	50.59 N	3.05 E
Hoogstede	52	52.34 N	6.56 E
Hoogstraten	56	51.24 N	4.46 E
Hoogte	158	27.28 S	28.03 E
Hoogvliet	52	51.52 N	4.21 E
Hook	42	51.17 N	0.58 W
Hook ◆[8]	260	51.22 N	0.18 W
Hooker	196	36.51 N	101.12 W
Hooker, Bi'r ⊤[4]	142	30.23 N	30.20 E
Hooker Creek	162	18.20 S	130.40 E
Hooker Creek Aboriginal Reserve ◆[4]	162	18.10 S	130.25 E
Hook Head >	48	52.07 N	6.55 W
Hookina	166	31.45 S	138.20 E
Hook Island I	166	20.08 S	148.55 E
Hook Mountain State Park ♦	276	41.09 N	73.55 W
Hook Norton	42	51.59 N	1.29 W
Hook Point >	166	25.48 S	153.05 E
Hooks	194	33.28 N	94.15 W
Hooksiel	52	53.38 N	8.01 E
Hoolehua	229a	21.10 N	157.04 W
Hoonah	180	58.07 N	135.26 W
Hoopa	204	41.03 N	123.40 W
Hoopa Valley Indian Reservation ◆[4]	204	41.08 N	123.40 W
Hooper	198	41.36 N	96.32 W
Hooper Bay	180	61.31 N	166.06 W
Hooper Islands II	208	38.20 N	76.13 W
Hooper Strait ℧	208	38.12 N	76.03 W
Hoopersville	208	38.15 N	76.10 W
Hoopes Reservoir ⊜[1]	285	39.47 N	75.37 W
Hoopeston	216	40.28 N	87.40 W
Hooping Harbour	186	50.37 N	56.17 W
Hoople	198	48.32 N	97.38 W
Hoopstad	158	27.54 S	25.58 E
Hoopstick Brook ≃	276	40.39 N	74.41 W
Höör	41	55.56 N	13.32 E
Hoorn	52	52.38 N	5.04 E
Hoorn, Kap → Hornos, Cabo de >	254	55.59 S	67.16 W
Hoosac Range ✗	207	42.45 N	73.02 W
Hoosac Tunnel ◆[5]	207	42.41 N	73.03 W
Hoosic ≃	210	42.54 N	73.39 W
Hoosick	210	42.52 N	73.20 W
Hoosick Falls	210	42.54 N	73.21 W
Hooton	262	53.18 N	2.57 W
Hoot Owl Estates	285	39.53 N	74.50 W
Hoover Dam ◆[6]	200	36.00 N	114.27 W
Hoover Reservoir ⊜[1]	214	40.08 N	82.53 W
Hooversville	214	40.08 N	78.54 W
Hopa	130	41.25 N	41.24 E
Hopatcong	210	40.55 N	74.39 W
Hopatcong, Lake ⊜	210	40.57 N	74.38 W
Hopatcong State Park ♦	276	40.55 N	74.40 W
Hop Bottom	210	41.42 N	75.46 W
Hop Brook ≃	276	40.19 N	74.08 W
Hope, B.C., Can.	182	49.23 N	121.26 W
Hope, Ak., U.S.	180	60.55 N	149.38 W
Hope, Ar., U.S.	194	33.40 N	93.35 W
Hope, In., U.S.	218	39.18 N	85.46 W
Hope, N.J., U.S.	210	40.54 N	74.58 W
Hope, N.D., U.S.	198	47.19 N	97.43 W
Hope, R.I., U.S.	207	41.44 N	71.33 W
Hope, Ben ∧	46	58.24 N	4.37 W
Hope, Loch ⊜	46	58.27 N	4.39 W
Hope, Point >	180	68.21 N	166.50 W
Hope Bay c	212	44.55 N	81.08 W
Hopedale, Nf., Can.	176	55.28 N	60.13 W
Hopedale, Il., U.S.	194	40.25 N	89.24 W
Hopedale, La., U.S.	194	29.49 N	89.39 W
Hopedale, Ma., U.S.	207	42.07 N	71.32 W
Hopedale, Oh., U.S.	214	40.19 N	80.54 W
Hope Farm	210	41.44 N	73.40 W
Hopefield	158	33.04 S	18.22 E
Hopeh → Hebei □[4]	98	38.00 N	116.00 E
Hope Island I, B.C., Can.	182	50.55 N	127.53 W
Hope Island I, On., Can.	212	44.55 N	80.12 W
Hopeland	208	40.14 N	76.16 W
Hopelawn	276	40.31 N	74.17 W
Hopelchén	232	19.46 N	89.51 W
Hopeman	46	57.42 N	3.25 W
Hope Mills	192	34.58 N	78.56 W
Hopes Advance, Cap >	176	61.04 N	69.34 W
Hopetoun, Austl.	162	33.57 S	120.07 E
Hopetoun, Austl.	166	35.44 S	142.22 E
Hopetown	158	29.34 S	24.03 E
Hope Vale Aboriginal Reserve ◆[4]	164	15.10 S	145.15 E
Hope Valley, Austl.	168b	34.50 S	138.44 E
Hope Valley, R.I., U.S.	207	41.30 N	71.43 W
Hopewell, N.J., U.S.	208	40.23 N	74.45 W
Hopewell, Pa., U.S.	214	40.08 N	78.16 W
Hopewell, Va., U.S.	208	37.18 N	77.17 W
Hopewell Islands II	176	58.25 N	78.00 W
Hopewell Junction	210	41.35 N	73.48 W
Hopewell Village National Historic Site ⊥	208	40.12 N	75.46 W
Hopfgarten	64	47.27 N	12.10 E
Hopfgarten in Defereggen	64	46.55 N	12.31 E
Hopi Buttes ∧	200	35.20 N	110.15 W
Hopi → Hebi	98	35.59 N	114.11 E
Hopi Indian Reservation ◆[4]	200	35.45 N	110.35 W
Hopkins, Mi., U.S.	216	42.37 N	85.45 W
Hopkins, Mo., U.S.	194	40.33 N	94.49 W
Hopkins □[6]	222	33.07 N	95.35 W
Hopkins ≃	166	38.24 S	142.31 E
Hopkins, Lake ⊜	162	24.15 S	128.50 E
Hopkins Creek ≃	284a	43.17 N	78.46 W
Hopkinsville	194	36.51 N	87.29 W
Hopkinton, Ia., U.S.	190	42.20 N	91.14 W
Hopkinton, Ma., U.S.	207	42.13 N	71.31 W
Hopkinton, R.I., U.S.	207	41.27 N	71.46 W
Hopland	204	38.58 N	123.06 W
Hopólito Bouchard	252	34.43 S	63.31 W
Hoppegarten	264a	52.31 N	13.40 E
Hoppenrade	264a	52.32 N	12.56 E
Hoppo → Hepu	102	21.39 N	109.11 E
Hopsten	52	52.23 N	7.36 E
Hoptrup	41	55.11 N	9.28 E
Ho Pui	271d	22.25 N	114.03 E
Hopwood, Mount ∧	166	21.49 S	144.26 E
Hoque	152	14.39 S	13.54 E
Hoquiam	224	46.58 N	123.53 W
Hoquiam, East Fork ≃	224	46.58 N	123.54 W
Hora Califo	144	8.49 N	43.07 E
Horace Mountain ∧	180	67.40 N	149.06 W
Horado	94	35.36 N	136.50 E
Hōrai	94	34.56 N	137.34 E
Horancia	144	6.31 N	38.44 E
Horasan	130	40.03 N	42.11 E
Horatio	194	33.56 N	94.21 W
Horatio Gardens	278	42.10 N	87.57 W
Horažďovice	60	49.20 N	13.43 E
Horb am Neckar	58	48.26 N	8.41 E
Horbelev	41	54.49 N	12.04 E
Horbourg	58	48.05 N	7.23 E
Hörby	41	55.51 N	13.39 E
Horconcitos	236	8.19 N	82.10 W
Hordaland □[6]	26	60.15 N	6.30 E
Hörde ◆[8]	263	51.29 N	7.30 E
Horden	44	54.46 N	1.18 W
Horden ≃	164	3.50 S	141.25 E
Horezu	38	45.08 N	23.59 E
Horgen	58	47.15 N	8.36 E
Hořice	30	50.22 N	15.38 E
Horicon	190	43.27 N	88.37 W
Horigane	268	35.50 N	139.27 E
Horine	219	38.16 N	90.25 W
Horinger	102	40.23 N	111.53 E
Horinouchi	94	37.14 N	138.56 E
Horinouchi ◆[8]	268	35.41 N	139.40 E
Horizon Tablemount ◆[3]	14	19.40 N	168.30 W
Horizontina	252	27.37 S	54.19 W
Horka	54	51.16 N	14.56 E
Hörken	40	60.02 N	14.56 E
Horley	42	51.11 N	0.11 W
Horlick Mountains ✗	9	85.23 S	121.00 W
Horloff ≃	56	50.20 N	8.52 E
Hormigueros	240m	18.09 N	67.08 W
Hormoz, Jazīreh-ye I	128	27.04 N	56.28 E
Hormozgān □[4]	128	27.50 N	56.00 E
Hormuz, Strait of ℧	128	26.34 N	56.15 E
Horn, Dtsch.	52	51.52 N	8.56 E
Horn, Öst.	61	48.40 N	15.40 E
Horn ◆[8]	52	53.38 N	10.05 E
Horn >	24a	66.28 N	22.28 W
Horn ≃, N.T., Can.	176	61.30 N	118.01 W
Horn ≃, Europe	56	49.15 N	7.20 E
Horn, Ben ∧[2]	46	58.01 N	4.02 W
Horn, Cape → Hornos, Cabo de >	254	55.59 S	67.16 W
Hornaday ≃	180	69.22 N	123.50 W
Hornafjörður c	24a	64.17 N	15.16 W
Hornavan ⊜	24	66.10 N	17.30 E
Hornbach	56	49.11 N	7.22 E
Hornbæk	41	56.05 N	12.28 E
Hornbeak	194	36.19 N	89.17 W
Hornbeck	194	31.19 N	93.23 W
Hornberg	58	48.13 N	8.13 E
Hornbrook	204	41.55 N	122.33 W
Hornburg	54	52.01 N	10.36 E
Hornby, On., Can.	275b	43.34 N	79.50 W
Hornby, N.Z.	172	43.33 S	172.32 E
Hornby Bay c	176	66.35 N	117.50 W
Horncastle	44	53.13 N	0.07 W
Hornchurch ◆[8]	260	51.34 N	0.12 E
Horndal	40	60.18 N	16.25 E
Horndean	42	50.55 N	1.00 W
Horndon on the Hill	260	51.31 N	0.25 E
Horne	41	55.06 N	10.11 E
Horne, Îles de II	14	14.16 S	178.05 W
Hornebach ≃	263	51.39 N	7.38 E
Horneburg, Dtsch.	52	53.30 N	9.34 E
Horneburg, Dtsch.	263	51.38 N	7.18 E
Hörnefors	26	63.38 N	19.54 E
Hornell	210	42.19 N	77.39 W
Hornepayne	176	49.13 N	84.47 W
Hornerstown	208	40.06 N	74.30 W
Hornhausen	54	52.02 N	11.10 E
Horn Head >	48	55.14 N	7.59 W
Horn Hill	260	51.37 N	0.32 W
Horní Jiřetín	54	50.35 N	13.32 E
Hornindal	26	61.58 N	6.31 E
Hornindalsvatnet ⊜	26	61.56 N	6.22 E
Hørning	41	56.05 N	10.03 E
Hörningsholm	40	59.03 N	17.40 E
Horní Počernice	54	50.06 N	14.38 E
Hornisgrinde ∧	56	48.36 N	8.12 E
Horn Island I, Austl.	164	10.37 S	142.17 E
Horn Island I, Ms., U.S.	194	30.13 N	88.38 W
Horní Slavkov	54	50.07 N	12.46 E
Horní Stropnice	61	48.46 N	14.44 E
Hornito, Cerro ∧	236	8.39 N	82.09 W
Hornitos	226	37.30 N	120.14 W
Horní Vltavice	60	48.57 N	13.46 E
Horn Lake	194	34.58 N	90.02 W
Horn Lake ⊜	212	45.24 N	79.36 W
Hornos, Cabo de (Cape Horn) >	254	55.59 S	67.16 W
Hornos, Isla I	254	55.57 S	67.17 W
Hornos, Islas de II	288	34.25 S	57.55 W
Hornow	54	51.38 N	14.31 E
Hornoy	50	49.51 N	1.54 E
Horn Plateau ✗[1]	176	62.15 N	119.15 W
Horn Pond ⊜	283	42.28 N	71.09 W
Hornsby, Austl.	170	33.42 S	151.06 E
Hornsby, Il., U.S.	219	39.10 N	89.45 W
Hornsbyville	208	37.11 N	76.28 W
Hornsea	44	53.55 N	0.10 W
Hornsey ◆[8]	260	51.35 N	0.07 W
Hornslet	41	56.19 N	10.20 E
Hornstorf	54	53.54 N	11.32 E
Hornsyld	41	55.45 N	9.51 E
Horntown	208	37.58 N	75.28 W
Hornu	50	50.26 N	3.49 E
Horoshiri-dake ∧	92a	42.43 N	142.41 E
Horotiu	172	37.43 S	175.12 E
Hořovice	60	49.50 N	13.54 E
Horqin Youyi Qianqi (Ulan Hot)	89	46.05 N	122.05 E
Horqin Youyi Zhongqi	89	45.09 N	121.24 E
Horqin Zuoyi Houqi	89	42.58 N	122.20 E
Horqin Zuoyi Zhongqi	89	44.07 N	123.18 E
Horqueta	252	23.24 S	56.53 W
Horrabridge	42	50.31 N	4.05 W
Horrelville	172	43.20 S	172.20 E
Horrem	263	51.06 N	6.48 E
Hörsching	61	48.14 N	14.11 E
Horse ≃	184	56.43 N	111.23 W
Horseback Knob ∧[2]	218	39.14 N	83.06 W
Horse Cave	194	37.10 N	85.54 W
Horse Creek	200	41.25 N	105.11 W
Horse Creek ≃, U.S.	198	41.57 N	103.58 W
Horse Creek ≃, Co., U.S.	198	38.05 N	103.19 W
Horse Creek ≃, Fl., U.S.	220	27.06 N	81.58 W
Horse Creek ≃, Il., U.S.	219	39.45 N	89.34 W
Horse Creek ≃, Mo., U.S.	194	37.46 N	93.53 W
Horsefly	182	52.20 N	121.24 W
Horsefly Lake ⊜	182	52.25 N	121.00 W
Horsehead Creek ≃	198	43.17 N	103.22 W
Horsehead Lake ⊜	198	47.02 N	99.47 W
Horseheads	210	42.10 N	76.49 W
Horse Islands II	186	50.13 N	55.45 W
Horsell	260	51.19 N	0.34 W
Horseneck Brook ≃	276	41.01 N	73.38 W
Horsens	41	55.52 N	9.52 E
Horsens Fjord c	41	55.50 N	10.05 E
Horseshoe Bend, Ar., U.S.	194	36.15 N	91.43 W
Horseshoe Bend, Id., U.S.	202	43.55 N	116.12 W
Horseshoe Bend National Military Park ♦	194	33.00 N	85.46 W
Horseshoe Cove c	276	40.27 N	74.00 W
Horseshoe Creek ≃	198	42.27 N	104.58 W
Horseshoe Falls ↓	284a	43.05 N	79.04 W
Horseshoe Lake ⊜, Mb., Can.	184	52.12 N	95.50 W
Horseshoe Lake ⊜, Mi., U.S.	281	42.24 N	83.45 W
Horseshoe Lake ⊜, N.J., U.S.	276	40.52 N	74.38 W
Horse Shoe Reef ◆[2]	240m	18.40 N	64.12 W
Horsfjärden c	40	59.04 N	18.09 E
Horsford	42	52.41 N	1.15 E
Horsforth	44	53.51 N	1.39 W
Horsham, Austl.	166	36.43 S	142.13 E
Horsham, Eng., U.K.	42	51.04 N	0.21 W
Horsham, Pa., U.S.	208	40.10 N	75.07 W
Hørsholm	41	55.53 N	12.30 E
Hörsingen	54	52.16 N	11.09 E
Horsley	274a	33.51 S	150.51 E
Horslunde	41	54.54 N	11.14 E
Horšovský Týn	60	49.32 N	12.56 E
Horst, Dtsch.	52	53.48 N	9.37 E
Horst, Dtsch.	54	53.22 N	10.37 E
Horst, Ned.	52	51.27 N	6.04 E
Horst ◆[8]	263	51.32 N	7.02 E
Horsted Keynes	42	51.02 N	0.01 W
Hörstel	52	52.18 N	7.35 E
Horstmar, Dtsch.	52	52.05 N	7.17 E
Horstmar, Dtsch.	263	51.36 N	7.33 E
Horsunlu	130	37.55 N	28.36 E
Horta	148a	38.32 N	28.38 W
Horta □[5]	148a	38.30 N	29.00 W
Horta ◆[8]	266d	41.26 N	2.00 E
Hortaleza ◆[8]	266a	40.28 N	3.39 W
Horten	26	59.25 N	10.30 E
Hortobágy ◆[1]	30	47.35 N	21.00 E
Hortobágyi Nemzeti Park ♦	30	47.30 N	21.10 E
Horton, Eng., U.K.	260	51.28 N	0.32 W
Horton, In., U.S.	218	40.05 N	86.09 W
Horton, Ks., U.S.	198	39.39 N	95.31 W
Horton, Mi., U.S.	216	42.09 N	84.31 W
Horton ≃	180	70.00 N	126.53 W
Horton in Ribblesdale	44	54.09 N	2.17 W
Horton Kirby	260	51.23 N	0.15 E
Horton Lake ⊜	180	67.29 N	122.31 W
Hortonville, N.Y., U.S.	210	41.46 N	75.02 W
Hortonville, Wi., U.S.	190	44.20 N	88.38 W
Horumersiel	52	53.41 N	8.00 E
Hørup	41	54.56 N	9.55 E
Hørve	41	55.45 N	11.28 E
Horw	58	47.01 N	8.18 E
Horwich	44	53.37 N	2.33 W
Horwood Lake ⊜	190	48.03 N	82.20 W
Hory Matky Boží	60	49.16 N	13.27 E
Hōryūji Temple ✓[1]	270	34.36 N	135.44 E
Hosaina	144	7.38 N	37.52 E
Hösbach	56	50.00 N	9.12 E
Hosei University ✓[2]	268	35.42 N	139.44 E
Hösel	56	51.19 N	6.54 E
Hosena	54	51.27 N	14.01 E
Hoséré Vokré ∧	146	8.20 N	13.15 E
Hoseynābād	128	35.33 N	47.08 E
Hoseynīyeh-ye Khodā-Dād	128	32.42 N	48.14 E
Hosford	192	30.23 N	84.47 W
Hoshāb	128	26.01 N	63.56 E
Hoshangābād	124	22.45 N	77.43 E
Hoshangābād Plain ≚	124	22.35 N	77.25 E
Hoshiārpur, India	123	31.32 N	75.54 E
Hoshiarpur, India	272a	28.35 N	77.22 E
Hoshigajō ∧	96	34.31 N	134.19 E
Hosingen	56	50.01 N	6.05 E
Hosjö	40	60.35 N	15.46 E
Hoskins	164	5.27 S	150.30 E
Hosmer, B.C., Can.	182	49.35 N	114.57 W
Hosmer, S.D., U.S.	198	45.34 N	99.28 W
Hosoe	94	34.49 N	137.39 E
Hospental	58	46.37 N	8.34 E
Hospers	198	43.04 N	95.54 W
Hospet	122	15.16 N	76.24 E
Hospital	48	52.29 N	8.25 W
Hospital de Orbigo	34	42.28 N	5.53 W
Hossegor	32	43.40 N	1.27 W
Hosston	194	32.53 N	93.52 W
Hosta Butte ∧	200	35.35 N	108.12 W
Hoste, Isla I	254	55.15 S	69.00 W
Hostěradice	61	48.57 N	16.15 E
Hostetter	214	40.16 N	79.24 W
Hostigrām	272b	22.26 N	88.31 E
Hostivař ◆[8]	54	50.01 N	14.32 E
Hostivice	54	50.04 N	14.15 E
Hošťka	54	50.30 N	14.20 E
Hostomice	54	50.35 N	13.46 E
Hostotipaquillo	234	21.04 N	104.04 W
Hostouň	60	49.34 N	12.46 E
Hosūr	122	12.43 N	77.49 E
Hot	110	18.06 N	98.36 E
Hota	268	35.08 N	139.51 E
Hotagen	26	63.59 N	14.15 E
Hotagen ⊜	26	63.53 N	14.29 E
Hotagsfjällen ∧	26	64.20 N	14.30 E
Hotaka	94	36.20 N	137.53 E
Hotaka-dake ∧	94	36.17 N	137.39 E
Hotamış	130	37.36 N	33.13 E
Hotan	120	37.08 N	79.54 E
Hotan ≃	90	40.30 N	80.45 E
Hotarele	38	44.10 N	26.22 E
Hotazel	158	27.15 S	23.00 E
Hotchkiss	200	38.47 N	107.43 W
Hotchkissville	207	41.34 N	73.13 W
Hot Creek Range ✗	204	38.30 N	116.25 W
Hötensleben	54	52.08 N	11.01 E
Hotevilla	200	35.55 N	110.40 W
Hotham ≃	168a	32.58 S	116.22 E
Hotham Inlet c	180	66.45 N	162.00 W
Hotham Peak ∧	180	66.48 N	160.42 W
Hoting	26	64.07 N	16.10 E
Hot Springs, Mt., U.S.	202	47.36 N	114.40 W
Hot Springs, N.C., U.S.	192	35.53 N	82.49 W
Hot Springs, S.D., U.S.	198	43.25 N	103.28 W
Hot Springs, Va., U.S.	192	37.59 N	79.49 W
Hot Springs National Park	194	34.30 N	93.04 W
Hot Springs Peak ∧, Ca., U.S.	204	40.22 N	120.07 W
Hot Springs Peak ∧, Nv., U.S.	204	41.22 N	117.26 W
Hot Springs State Park ♦	202	43.40 N	108.10 W
Hot Springs → Truth or Consequences	200	33.08 N	107.15 W
Hot Sulphur Springs	200	40.04 N	106.06 W
Hottah Lake ⊜	176	65.04 N	118.29 W
Hottentotbaai c	156	26.05 S	14.58 E
Hottentotskloof	158	33.15 S	19.40 E
Hotton	56	50.16 N	5.27 E
Hötzum	54	52.13 N	10.37 E
Houaïlou	175f	21.17 S	165.38 E
Houamuang	110	20.09 N	103.38 E
Houbaishu	106	31.49 N	119.10 E
Houbao	98	41.54 N	125.14 E
Houcheng	106	31.55 N	120.26 E
Houdahepao	104	41.49 N	123.01 E
Houdain	50	50.27 N	2.32 E
Houdan	50	48.47 N	1.36 E
Houdelaincourt	58	48.33 N	5.28 E
Houdeng-Aimeries	50	50.29 N	4.08 E
Houeillès	32	44.12 N	0.02 E
Houffalize	56	50.08 N	5.47 E
Hougang	271c	1.22 N	103.54 E
Hough Green	262	53.23 N	2.47 W
Houghton, Mi., U.S.	190	47.07 N	88.34 W
Houghton, N.Y., U.S.	210	42.25 N	78.09 W
Houghton, Wa., U.S.	224	47.40 N	122.12 W
Houghton Estates ◆[8]	273d	26.10 S	28.04 E
Houghton Green	262	53.25 N	2.34 W
Houghton Lake	190	44.18 N	84.45 W
Houghton Lake ⊜, Sk., Can.	184	52.23 N	105.08 W
Houghton Lake ⊜, Mi., U.S.	190	44.20 N	84.45 W
Houghton-le-Spring	44	54.51 N	1.28 W
Houghton Regis	42	51.55 N	0.31 W
Houguangzhengtai	104	41.13 N	122.07 E
Hougujiazi	104	42.21 N	123.22 E
Houhuangtukan	104	41.02 N	122.29 E
Houille ≃	56	50.08 N	4.49 E
Houillères de la Sarre, Canal des ≍	56	48.42 N	6.55 E
Houilles	261	48.56 N	2.11 E
Houjiangfushan	105	40.03 N	117.09 E
Houjiaping	107	30.02 N	104.38 E
Houjiaying	105	39.51 N	117.15 E
Houjie	100	22.58 N	113.39 E
Houjiumen	104	42.38 N	123.18 E
Houkou	98	37.34 N	115.09 E
Houliujia	104	40.47 N	122.19 E
Houlka	194	34.02 N	89.01 W
Houlton	188	46.07 N	67.50 W
Houluan	105	39.13 N	116.32 E
Houma, Tonga	174w	21.09 S	175.19 W
Houma, La., U.S.	194	29.35 N	90.43 W
Houma, Zhg.	102	35.36 N	111.21 E
Houmanzhoutun	104	42.29 N	123.14 E
Houmen	100	22.51 N	115.09 E
Houmet Essouq	148	33.59 N	10.51 E
Houmont Park	222	29.50 N	95.13 W
Hound Creek ≃	202	47.13 N	111.23 W
Houndé	150	11.30 N	3.31 W
Hounslow ◆[8]	42	51.29 N	0.22 W
Houplines	50	50.42 N	2.55 E
Houqianjiayu	104	40.50 N	120.41 E
Houqiao	105	40.04 N	116.39 E
Hourn, Loch c	46	57.08 N	5.36 W
Housatonic	207	42.15 N	73.22 W
Housatonic ≃	207	41.10 N	73.07 W
House	196	34.38 N	103.54 W
House ≃	184	56.13 N	112.31 W
House of Seven Gables ⊥	283	42.32 N	70.53 W
Houserville	214	40.50 N	77.50 W
House Springs	219	38.24 N	90.34 W
Houshan	106	31.03 N	120.21 E
Houston, B.C., Can.	182	54.24 N	126.38 W
Houston, De., U.S.	208	38.55 N	75.30 W
Houston, Mn., U.S.	190	43.45 N	91.34 W
Houston, Ms., U.S.	194	33.53 N	88.59 W
Houston, Mo., U.S.	194	37.19 N	91.57 W
Houston, Oh., U.S.	216	40.15 N	84.20 W
Houston, Pa., U.S.	214	40.14 N	80.12 W
Houston, Tx., U.S.	222	29.45 N	95.21 W
Houston □[6]	222	31.20 N	95.20 W
Houston ≃	194	30.16 N	93.13 W
Houston, Lake ⊜[1]	222	29.58 N	95.07 W
Houston County Lake ⊜[1]	222	31.25 N	95.35 W
Houston Creek ≃	218	38.13 N	84.15 W
Houston Intercontinental Airport ✈	222	29.59 N	95.27 W
Houston Ship Channel ≍	222	29.21 N	94.47 W
Hout ≃	156	23.04 S	29.36 E
Houtbaai	158	34.03 S	18.21 E
Houthalen	56	51.02 N	5.22 E
Houthulst	50	50.59 N	2.57 E
Houtkop	158	26.36 S	27.52 E
Houtkraal	158	30.23 S	24.05 E
Houtman Abrolhos II	162	28.43 S	113.48 E
Houtskär I	26	60.12 N	21.22 E
Houtzdale	214	40.49 N	78.21 W
Houwuliangdian	104	41.31 N	121.55 E
Houwutaigou	104	41.46 N	121.42 E
Houx	261	48.34 N	1.37 E
Houxijie	100	28.46 N	118.49 E
Houxinlitun	104	41.05 N	122.33 E
Houxinqiu	104	42.34 N	122.43 E
Houyatai	104	41.26 N	121.49 E
Houying	105	39.42 N	118.18 E
Houyingzi	98	40.24 N	123.50 E
Houzhangcun	105	40.08 N	116.11 E
Houzhou	106	31.35 N	119.22 E
Houzitun	104	41.04 N	121.18 E
Hov	41	55.55 N	10.16 E
Hova	40	58.52 N	14.13 E
Hovborg	41	55.36 N	8.57 E
Høve, Dan.	41	55.50 N	11.30 E
Hove, Eng., U.K.	42	50.49 N	0.10 W
Hovedgård	41	55.57 N	9.58 E
Hövelhof	52	51.49 N	8.40 E
Hoven, Dan.	41	55.51 N	8.46 E
Hoven, S.D., U.S.	198	45.14 N	99.46 W
Hovenweep National Monument ♦	200	37.25 N	109.04 W
Hovmantorp	26	56.47 N	15.08 E
Hovran ⊜	40	60.16 N	16.03 E
Hovsta	40	59.21 N	15.13 E
Howa, Ouadi (Wādī Howar) ∨	140	17.30 N	27.08 E
Howakil I	144	15.10 N	40.16 E
Howar, Wādī (Ouadi Howa) ∨	140	17.30 N	27.08 E
Howard, Austl.	166	25.19 S	152.34 E
Howard, Ks., U.S.	198	37.28 N	96.15 W
Howard, Oh., U.S.	214	40.24 N	82.19 W
Howard, Pa., U.S.	214	41.00 N	77.39 W
Howard, S.D., U.S.	198	44.00 N	97.31 W
Howard, Wi., U.S.	190	44.32 N	88.05 W
Howard □[6], In., U.S.	216	40.29 N	86.08 W
Howard □[6], Md., U.S.	208	39.16 N	76.48 W
Howard Beach ◆[8]	276	40.40 N	73.51 W
Howard City	190	43.23 N	85.28 W
Howard Draw ∨	196	30.08 N	101.35 W
Howard Hanson Reservoir ⊜[1]	224	47.15 N	121.45 W
Howard Heights	284b	39.17 N	76.50 W
Howardian Hills ✗[2]	44	54.07 N	1.00 W
Howard Island I	164	12.10 S	135.24 E
Howard Lake	190	45.03 N	94.04 W
Howard Prairie Lake ⊜[1]	202	42.15 N	122.20 W
Howard University ✓[2]	284c	38.55 N	77.01 W
Howden	44	53.45 N	0.52 W
Howe, In., U.S.	216	41.43 N	85.25 W
Howe, Tx., U.S.	196	33.30 N	96.37 W
Howe, Cape >	166	37.31 S	149.59 E
Howe Caverns ⊥[5]	210	42.42 N	74.25 W
Howe Green	260	51.42 N	0.32 E
Howe Island I	212	44.17 N	76.15 W
Howeke	150	4.50 N	7.45 W
Howell	216	42.36 N	83.55 W
Howell Airport ✈	278	41.39 N	87.45 W
Howell Island I	219	38.40 N	90.42 W
Howells	198	41.43 N	97.00 W
Howells Pond ⊜	276	41.03 N	74.42 W
Howes Cave	210	42.41 N	74.23 W
Howe Sound ℧	182	49.22 N	123.18 W
Howe's Range ✗	170	33.08 S	150.47 E
Howes Valley	170	32.50 S	150.51 E
Howey In The Hills	220	28.43 N	81.47 W
Howick, P.Q., Can.	206	45.11 N	73.51 W
Howick, S. Afr.	158	29.28 S	30.14 E
Howitt, Mount ∧	166	37.10 S	146.40 E
Howland	188	45.14 N	68.39 W
Howland Island I	14	0.48 N	176.38 W
Howley	186	49.10 N	57.07 W
Howley, Mount ∧	186	48.17 N	58.26 W
Howmore	46	57.18 N	7.23 W
Howqua ≃	169	37.14 S	146.08 E
Howrah → Hāora	126	22.35 N	88.20 E
Howse Peak ∧	182	51.49 N	116.41 W
Howser	182	50.18 N	116.57 W
Howson Peak ∧	182	54.25 N	127.44 W
Howth	48	53.23 N	6.04 W
Howth Head >	48	53.22 N	6.03 W
Ho Xa	110	17.04 N	107.02 E
Hoxie, Ar., U.S.	194	36.03 N	90.58 W
Hoxie, Ks., U.S.	198	39.21 N	100.26 W
Höxter	52	51.46 N	9.23 E
Hoxtolgay	86	46.35 N	86.01 E
Hoxton Park	274a	33.55 S	150.51 E
Hoxton Park Aerodrome ✈	274a	33.54 S	150.50 E
Hoy I	46	58.51 N	3.18 W
Hoya, Dtsch.	52	52.48 N	9.08 E
Hōya, Nihon	94	35.43 N	139.34 E
Høyanger	26	61.13 N	6.05 E
Hoyerswerda	54	51.26 N	14.14 E
Hoylake	44	53.23 N	3.11 W
Hoyleton, Austl.	168b	34.01 S	138.33 E
Hoyleton, Il., U.S.	219	38.27 N	89.16 W
Hoym	54	51.47 N	11.19 E
Hoyos	34	40.10 N	6.43 W
Hōyo-shotō II	96	33.52 N	132.18 E
Höytiäinen ⊜	26	62.48 N	29.39 E
Hoyt Lakes	190	47.31 N	92.08 W
Hoytville, Mi., U.S.	216	42.45 N	84.53 W
Hoytville, Oh., U.S.	216	41.11 N	83.47 W
Hozain ≃	50	48.16 N	4.06 E
Hozat	130	39.07 N	39.14 E
Hozumi	94	35.24 N	136.41 E
Hpru-so	110	19.25 N	97.08 E
Hracholusky, údolní nádrž ⊜[1]	60	49.47 N	13.07 E
Hradec Králové	30	50.12 N	15.50 E
Hrádek	61	48.46 N	16.16 E
Hrádek nad Nisou	54	50.48 N	14.51 E
Hradiště ∧	54	50.13 N	13.08 E
Hranice, Česko.	30	49.33 N	17.44 E
Hranice, Česko.	54	50.15 N	12.10 E
Hrdlovka	54	50.36 N	13.40 E
Hřensko	54	50.50 N	14.14 E
Hriňová	30	48.36 N	19.31 E
Hrob	54	50.39 N	13.44 E
Hron ≃	30	47.49 N	18.45 E
Hronov	30	50.29 N	16.12 E
Hrotovice	61	49.06 N	16.07 E
Hrubieszów	30	50.49 N	23.55 E
Hrubý Jeseník ✗	30	50.00 N	17.20 E
Hrušovany	61	48.50 N	16.23 E
Hrvatska → Croatia □[1]	36	45.10 N	15.30 E
Hsenwi	110	23.18 N	97.58 E
Hsiakuan → Xiaguan	102	25.34 N	100.14 E
Hsiamen → Xiamen	100	24.28 N	118.07 E
Hsiangt'an → Xiangtan	100	27.51 N	112.54 E
Hsiangyang → Xiangfan	102	32.03 N	112.01 E
Hsian → Xi'an	102	34.15 N	108.52 E
Hsiaohungt'ou Yü I	100	21.57 N	121.36 E
Hsichih	269d	25.04 N	121.39 E
Hsichi Yü I	100	23.15 N	119.37 E
Hsich'üan Tao I	100	25.59 N	119.56 E
Hsientung	269d	25.09 N	121.44 E
Hsienyang → Xianyang	102	34.22 N	108.42 E
Hsi-hseng	110	20.09 N	97.15 E
Hsihu	100	23.58 N	120.28 E
Hsilo	100	23.48 N	120.27 E
Hsilo ≃	100	23.50 N	120.15 E
Hsim ≃	110	20.48 N	98.31 E
Hsinch'eng	100	24.08 N	121.39 E
Hsinchu	100	24.48 N	120.58 E
Hsinchuang	100	25.02 N	121.27 E
Hsinghua → Xinghua	100	32.57 N	119.50 E
Hsingt'ai → Xingtai	98	37.04 N	114.29 E
Hsinhailien → Lianyungang	98	34.39 N	119.16 E
Hsinhsiang → Xinxiang	98	35.20 N	113.51 E
Hsinhua	100	23.02 N	120.18 E
Hsining → Xining	102	36.38 N	101.55 E
Hsinking → Changchun	89	43.53 N	125.19 E
Hsinpeit'ou ◆[8]	269d	25.09 N	121.30 E
Hsinp'u → Lianyungang	98	34.39 N	119.16 E
Hsinshih	100	23.05 N	120.17 E
Hsintien	100	24.57 N	121.32 E
Hsintien ≃	269d	25.02 N	121.29 E
Hsinyang → Xinyang	100	32.08 N	114.04 E
Hsipaw	110	22.37 N	97.18 E
Hsiukuluan ≃	100	23.28 N	121.30 E
Hsiyü	100	23.36 N	119.30 E
Hsüanhua → Xuanhua	105	40.37 N	115.03 E
Hsüch'ang → Xuchang	100	34.03 N	113.49 E
Hsüchou → Xuzhou	98	34.16 N	117.11 E
Hsüehchia	100	23.14 N	120.10 E
Hsüeh Shan ∧	100	24.23 N	121.13 E
Hsuphāng	110	20.18 N	98.42 E
Hua'an	100	25.02 N	117.34 E
Huab ≃	156	20.52 S	13.25 E
Huabu	100	29.00 N	118.20 E
Huacaña	248	14.02 S	74.02 W
Huacao	269b	31.14 N	121.19 E
Huacaraje	248	13.33 S	63.45 W
Huachacalla	248	18.45 S	68.17 W
Huacheng	100	24.04 N	115.38 E
Huachi	102	36.43 N	107.52 E
Huachi, Laguna ⊜	248	14.11 S	63.30 W
Huachipa	286d	12.00 S	76.56 W
Huacho	248	11.07 S	77.37 W
Huachón	248	10.40 S	75.57 W
Huachos	248	13.12 S	75.31 W
Huachuca City	200	31.37 N	110.20 W
Huaco	252	30.09 S	68.31 W
Huacrachuco	248	8.39 S	77.05 W
Huade	98	41.46 N	114.16 E
Huadian	89	42.58 N	126.43 E
Huading Shan ∧	100	29.15 N	121.05 E
Huafeng	106	32.14 N	121.16 E
Huagutang	106	30.55 N	119.18 E
Hua Hin	110	12.34 N	99.58 E
Huai ≃, Zhg.	98	37.28 N	114.55 E
Huai ≃, Zhg.	100	32.58 N	118.17 E
Huaiá-Miçu ≃	250	10.52 S	53.15 W
Huai'an (Chaigoubu), Zhg.	98	40.39 N	114.27 E
Huai'an, Zhg.	100	33.32 N	119.10 E
Huaibin	100	32.28 N	115.24 E
Huaide	89	43.32 N	124.50 E
Huaidezhen, Zhg.	89	43.54 N	124.47 E
Huaidezhen, Zhg.	107	28.59 N	105.15 E
Huaihuazhenshi	106	31.05 N	119.41 E
Huaiji	102	24.01 N	112.18 E
Huailai (Shacheng)	105	40.23 N	115.33 E
Huailin	100	31.26 N	117.36 E
Huaillati	248	14.05 S	72.31 W
Huainan	100	32.40 N	117.00 E
Huaining	100	30.25 N	116.38 E
Huairou	105	40.19 N	116.37 E
Huaite → Huaide	89	43.32 N	124.50 E
Huaitunas, Lagunas ⊜	248	13.06 S	66.00 W
Huaiyang	100	33.44 N	114.53 E
Huai Yot	110	7.45 N	99.37 E
Huaiyuan	100	32.57 N	117.12 E
Huaiyu Shan ✗	100	28.50 N	117.50 E
Huaji	100	32.46 N	115.20 E
Huajiang	102	25.50 N	110.21 E
Huajianzi	104	40.48 N	122.12 E
Huajiapuzi	104	40.52 N	123.14 E
Huajiayingzi	104	42.20 N	121.00 E
Huajimic	234	21.42 N	104.20 W
Huajintepec	234	16.36 N	98.14 W
Huajuapan de León	234	17.48 N	97.46 W
Huakou	100	25.13 N	117.35 E
Hualahuises	232	24.53 N	99.41 W
Hualalai ∧[1]	229d	19.42 N	155.52 W
Hualañé	252	34.59 S	71.49 W
Hualapai Indian Reservation ◆[4]	200	35.38 N	113.30 W
Hualapai Mountains ✗	200	34.50 N	113.55 W
Hualapai Peak ∧	200	35.04 N	113.54 W
Hualfín	252	27.14 S	66.50 W
Hualgayoc	248	6.46 S	78.37 W
Hualien	100	23.59 N	121.36 E
Hualien ≃	100	23.57 N	121.36 E
Hualingpuzi	104	41.31 N	123.54 E
Huallaga ≃	248	5.10 S	75.32 W
Huallamarca, Museo ✓	286d	12.05 S	77.02 W
Huallanca, Perú	248	8.49 S	77.52 W
Huallanca, Perú	248	9.51 S	76.56 W
Huallayabamba ≃	248	7.04 S	77.10 W
Hualmay	248	11.06 S	77.38 W
Hualong	102	36.05 N	102.36 E
Huamanquiquia	248	13.44 S	74.15 W
Huamantla	234	19.19 N	97.56 W
Huambo (Nova Lisboa)	152	12.44 S	15.47 E
Huambo □[5]	152	12.30 S	15.40 E
Huambos	248	6.28 S	78.58 W
Huameiao	100	26.32 N	115.47 E

Symbols in the index entries represent the broad categories identified in the key at the right. Symbols with superior numbers (✗[1]) identify subcategories (see complete key on page *I · 1*).

Symbole im Register stellen die rechts im Schlüssel erklärten Kategorien dar. Symbole mit hochgestellten Ziffern (✗[1]) bezeichnen Unterabteilungen einer Kategorie (vgl. vollständiger Schlüssel auf Seite *I · 1*).

Los símbolos incluídos en el texto del índice representan las grandes categorias identificadas con la clave a la derecha. Los símbolos con numeros en su parte superior (✗[1]) identifican las subcategorias (véase la clave completa en la página *I · 1*).

Les symboles de l'index représentent les catégories indiquées dans la légende à droite. Les symboles suivis d'un indice (✗[1]) représentent des sous-catégories (voir légende complète à la page *I · 1*).

Os símbolos incluídos no texto do índice representam as grandes categorias identificadas com a chave à direita. Os símbolos com números em sua parte superior (✗[1]) identificam as subcategorias (veja-se a chave completa à página *I · 1*).

∧	Mountain	Berg	Montaña	Montagne	Montanha
✗	Mountains	Gebirge	Montañas	Montagnes	Montanhas
)(	Pass	Paß	Paso	Col	Passo
∨	Valley, Canyon	Tal, Cañon	Valle, Cañón	Vallée, Canyon	Vale, Canhão
≚	Plain	Ebene	Llano	Plaine	Planície
>	Cape	Kap	Cabo	Cap	Cabo
I	Island	Insel	Isla	Île	Ilha
II	Islands	Inseln	Islas	Îles	Ilhas
⊥	Other Topographic Features	Andere Topographische Objekte	Otros Elementos Topográficos	Autres données topographiques	Outros acidentes topográficos

ESPAÑOL: Nombre · Página · Lat.°′ · Long.°′ W = Oeste
FRANÇAIS: Nom · Page · Lat.°′ · Long.°′ W = Ouest
PORTUGUÊS: Nome · Página · Lat.°′ · Long.°′ W = Oeste

Nombre / Nom / Nome	Página / Page	Lat.°′	Long.°′
Huamei Shan ∧	100	25.28 N	113.58 E
Huamuxtitlán	234	17.49 N	98.34 W
Huan ≃	100	30.40 N	114.05 E
Huanan	89	46.13 N	130.32 E
Huancabamba, Perú	248	10.21 S	75.32 W
Huancabamba, Perú	248	5.14 S	79.28 W
Huancané	248	15.12 S	69.46 W
Huancapi	248	13.41 S	74.04 W
Huancarama	248	13.39 S	73.05 W
Huancarqui	248	16.06 S	72.29 W
Huancavelica	248	12.46 S	75.02 W
Huancavelica □5	248	13.00 S	75.00 W
Huancaybamba	248	9.05 S	76.50 W
Huancayo	248	12.04 S	75.14 W
Huanchaca	248	20.20 S	66.39 W
Huanchaca, Serranía de ⋀	248	14.30 S	60.39 W
Huandacareo	234	19.59 N	101.17 W
Huando	248	12.29 S	74.58 W
Huang ≃, Asia	110	17.49 N	101.33 E
Huang ≃, T'aiwan	269d	25.14 N	121.37 E
Huang (Yellow) ≃, Zhg.	90	37.32 N	118.19 E
Huang'aicun	106	31.43 N	118.40 E
Huang'an	98	35.28 N	115.42 E
Huang'anshi	100	29.06 N	113.34 E
Huangbai	98	41.17 N	126.21 E
Huangbaozi	102	39.54 N	99.26 E
Huangbeipu	104	42.21 N	123.25 E
Huangcaoping	100	25.42 N	113.27 E
Huangchong	100	22.18 N	113.03 E
Huangchuan	100	32.09 N	115.03 E
Huangcun	105	39.56 N	116.11 E
Huangdaizhen	106	31.26 N	120.33 E
Huangdan	107	29.10 N	103.44 E
Huangda Yang Ʉ	100	30.03 N	122.26 E
Huangdi, Zhg.	98	40.14 N	120.15 E
Huangdi, Zhg.	105	40.57 N	118.24 E
Huangdu, Zhg.	106	30.47 N	118.51 E
Huangdu, Zhg.	106	31.16 N	121.13 E
Huangduqiao	100	29.18 N	120.55 E
Huanggai Hu ⊜	100	29.44 N	113.23 E
Huanggang	100	30.27 N	114.52 E
Huanggangji	98	34.39 N	116.03 E
Huanggangkou	100	28.32 N	114.33 E
Huanggang Shan ∧	100	27.50 N	117.45 E
Huanggangshi	100	33.09 N	115.55 E
Huangguayingzi	104	41.46 N	120.46 E
Huangguoshu	102	26.02 N	105.32 E
Huang Hai → Yellow Sea ╤2	90	36.00 N	123.00 E
Huanghe Kou ≃1	98	37.54 N	118.48 E
Huangho → Huang ≃	90	37.32 N	118.19 E
Huanghu	106	30.27 N	119.48 E
Huanghua	98	38.22 N	117.21 E
Huanghuadianzi	104	41.44 N	122.48 E
Huanghuashi	100	28.14 N	113.14 E
Huangjialing	104	42.12 N	122.55 E
Huangjialu	106	31.00 N	121.45 E
Huangjiatun	104	41.11 N	122.54 E
Huangjiazhai	106	32.01 N	121.36 E
Huangjinbu	100	28.27 N	116.47 E
Huangjing	106	31.39 N	121.06 E
Huangjinggou	107	29.37 N	104.35 E
Huangjinjing	107	29.44 N	104.38 E
Huangjinzi	89	50.02 N	127.20 E
Huangjuezhen	107	29.50 N	106.27 E
Huangkan	105	40.22 N	116.28 E
Huangkeng	100	27.35 N	117.39 E
Huangkou	102	42.46 N	93.58 E
Huanglaomen	100	29.30 N	115.49 E
Huangli	106	31.39 N	119.42 E
Huanglian	107	29.17 N	106.18 E
Huangling	102	35.41 N	109.09 E
Huanglingji	100	30.25 N	114.03 E
Huanglong, Zhg.	100	31.58 N	112.28 E
Huanglong, Zhg.	102	35.45 N	109.42 E
Huanglongxi	107	30.19 N	103.58 E
Huangmao	100	28.07 N	114.04 E
Huangmapi	100	23.30 N	114.33 E
Huangmei	100	30.04 N	115.56 E
Huangnihe, Zhg.	89	43.32 N	127.59 E
Huangnihe, Zhg.	100	31.06 N	117.22 E
Huangpi, Zhg.	100	30.53 N	114.22 E
Huangpi, Zhg.	100	26.39 N	115.51 E
Huangpu ≃	106	31.24 N	121.31 E
Huangqi	100	26.21 N	119.54 E
Huangqiao	106	32.15 N	120.13 E
Huangqiao ≃	106	32.00 N	120.20 E
Huangshahe	102	26.03 N	110.58 E
Huangshajie	100	29.03 N	113.08 E
Huangshan	98	36.57 N	122.18 E
Huangshanguan	98	37.32 N	120.16 E
Huangshapu, Zhg.	100	26.50 N	113.26 E
Huangshapu, Zhg.	100	25.08 N	112.44 E
Huangshaqiao	100	28.56 N	114.40 E
Huangshatuo	104	41.12 N	122.31 E
Huangshi, Zhg.	100	25.23 N	119.04 E
Huangshi, Zhg.	100	30.13 N	115.05 E
Huangshi, Zhg.	102	29.00 N	111.02 E
Huangshidu	100	27.44 N	116.44 E
Huangshiguan	100	26.15 N	115.54 E
Huangshui	107	30.32 N	103.55 E
Huangtan, Zhg.	100	27.44 N	119.58 E
Huangtan, Zhg.	100	26.41 N	117.17 E
Huangtan ≃	100	24.48 N	116.31 E
Huangtang, Zhg.	100	23.44 N	114.58 E
Huangtang, Zhg.	106	31.46 N	120.21 E
Huangtang, Zhg.	106	31.47 N	119.40 E
Huangtang Hu ⊜	100	30.00 N	114.12 E
Huangtankou	100	28.50 N	118.53 E
Huangtantuan	100	30.53 N	113.33 E
Huangtian	100	23.52 N	114.58 E
Huangtianfan	100	29.10 N	120.08 E
Huangtu, Zhg.	100	27.36 N	118.00 E
Huangtu, Zhg.	106	31.52 N	120.03 E
Huangtuchang	107	30.41 N	104.18 E
Huangtugang	100	31.25 N	115.05 E
Huangtukan	104	41.21 N	122.45 E
Huangtuliangzi	98	41.14 N	118.39 E
Huangtuling	100	27.18 N	113.30 E
Huangtupo	105	39.47 N	116.16 E
Huanguelén	252	37.02 S	61.57 W
Huangwan	106	30.22 N	120.48 E
Huangxian	98	37.38 N	120.29 E
Huangxu	106	32.06 N	119.37 E
Huangyaguan	105	40.14 N	117.26 E
Huangyan	100	28.39 N	121.15 E
Huangyang Shan ⋀	105	40.20 N	115.00 E
Huangyanzhuang	105	40.01 N	118.21 E
Huangyuan	102	36.40 N	101.12 E
Huangyuzeng	104	42.05 N	124.11 E
Huangze	100	29.35 N	120.55 E
Huangze Yang Ʉ	100	30.36 N	122.28 E
Huangzhai	100	29.27 N	120.00 E
Huangzhong	102	36.31 N	101.40 E
Huangzhu	110	19.29 N	110.24 E
Huangzhuang, Zhg.	100	34.05 N	112.15 E
Huangzhuang, Zhg.	105	39.29 N	117.31 E
Huangzhuang, Zhg.	105	39.53 N	117.05 E
Huangzhuang Wa ⊜	105	39.33 N	117.33 E
Huaning	102	24.14 N	102.56 E
Huaniugouzi	104	41.34 N	122.35 E
Huaniupuzi	104	41.23 N	123.31 E
Huanjiang	102	24.54 N	108.21 E
Huanren	98	41.14 N	125.21 E
Huanta	248	12.56 S	74.15 W
Huantai (Suozhen)	98	36.59 N	118.06 E
Huantan	100	31.49 N	113.04 E
Huántar	248	9.26 S	77.15 W
Huánuco	248	9.55 S	76.14 W
Huánuco □5	248	9.30 S	75.50 W
Huanuni	248	18.16 S	66.51 W
Huanxi	100	26.34 N	113.36 E
Huanxian	102	36.39 N	107.18 E
Huanxiang ≃	105	39.34 N	117.45 E
Huanxiling	104	41.17 N	123.54 E
Huanzo, Cordillera de ⋀	248	14.30 S	73.20 W
Huapango, Presa ⊜1	234	20.00 N	99.40 W
Huapí, Serranías ⋀	236	12.30 N	85.00 W
Huap'ing Yü I	100	25.26 N	121.56 E
Huaqiao, Zhg.	100	28.56 N	121.27 E
Huaqiao, Zhg.	100	29.32 N	117.11 E
Huaqiao, Zhg.	102	27.28 N	110.02 E
Huaqiao, Zhg.	107	30.28 N	103.52 E
Huaqiaozhen	107	30.47 N	106.41 E
Huaqiying	106	32.10 N	118.38 E
Huara	248	19.59 S	69.47 W
Huaral	248	11.30 S	77.12 W
Huaráz	248	9.32 S	77.32 W
Huari	248	9.20 S	77.14 W
Huariaca	248	10.27 S	76.07 W
Huaribamba	248	12.16 S	74.57 W
Huarina	248	16.12 S	68.38 W
Huarmey	248	10.04 S	78.10 W
Huarochirí	248	12.09 S	76.14 W
Huarocondo	248	13.25 S	72.13 W
Huarong	100	29.30 N	112.34 E
Huasaga ≃	246	3.42 S	76.26 W
Hua Sai	110	8.02 N	100.18 E
Huascarán, Nevado ∧	248	9.07 S	77.37 W
Huasco	252	28.28 S	71.14 W
Huasco ≃	252	28.27 S	71.13 W
Huashan	98	34.39 N	116.44 E
Huashaoying	98	40.12 N	114.36 E
Huashi	106	31.50 N	120.28 E
Huatabampo	232	26.50 N	109.38 W
Huatangpu	100	25.48 N	112.52 E
Huating	102	35.09 N	106.38 E
Huatong, Zhg.	98	40.03 N	121.56 E
Huatong, Zhg.	102	23.01 N	106.36 E
Huatusco	234	19.09 N	96.57 W
Huauchinango	234	20.11 N	98.03 W
Huaura	248	11.04 S	77.36 W
Huaura ≃	248	11.06 S	77.39 W
Huautla, Méx.	234	21.02 N	98.17 W
Huautla, Méx.	234	18.08 N	96.51 W
Huaxian (Daokou), Zhg.	98	35.37 N	114.32 E
Huaxian, Zhg.	100	23.22 N	113.12 E
Huaxian, Zhg.	102	34.30 N	109.40 E
Huayan	107	30.01 N	105.02 E
Huayang	107	30.32 N	104.04 E
Huayangzhen	102	33.25 N	107.44 E
Huaying Shan ∧	107	30.10 N	106.42 E
Huayingtai	104	40.43 N	122.19 E
Huayllay	248	11.01 S	76.21 W
Huayna Potosí, Nevado ∧	248	16.16 S	68.11 W
Huaytará	248	13.36 S	75.22 W
Hua Yü I	100	23.24 N	119.19 E
Huayuan, Zhg.	98	42.17 N	127.07 E
Huayuan, Zhg.	100	31.16 N	113.58 E
Huayuan, Zhg.	102	28.34 N	109.13 E
Huayuanzui	100	33.00 N	118.16 E
Huayunca, Nevado ∧	248	14.39 S	72.28 W
Huayuri, Pampa de ≚	248	14.30 S	75.30 W
Huazhou	102	21.40 N	110.33 E
Huazi	104	41.25 N	123.29 E
Huazigou	104	41.50 N	121.01 E
Huazikou	106	32.13 N	118.57 E
Hubārah, Wādī V	142	27.21 N	31.39 E
Hubaytah, Bi'r ╤4	142	30.27 N	32.27 E
Hubbard, Ia., U.S.	190	42.18 N	93.18 W
Hubbard, Oh., U.S.	214	41.09 N	80.34 W
Hubbard, Or., U.S.	224	45.10 N	122.48 W
Hubbard, Tx., U.S.	222	31.50 N	96.47 W
Hubbard Creek ≃	196	32.54 N	98.53 W
Hubbard Creek Reservoir ⊜1	196	32.45 N	99.00 W
Hubbard Lake ⊜	190	44.49 N	83.34 W
Hubbards	186	44.38 N	64.04 W
Hubbardston	207	42.28 N	72.00 W
Hubbell	190	47.10 N	88.25 W
Hubbell Trading Post National Historical Site ⊥	200	35.43 N	109.33 W
Hubbelrath ✦8	263	51.16 N	6.55 E
Hubei (Hupeh) □4	90	31.00 N	112.00 E
Huben, Öst.	64	47.03 N	10.58 E
Huben, Öst.	64	46.56 N	12.34 E
Huberdeau	206	45.58 N	74.38 W
Huber Heights	218	39.50 N	84.07 W
Hublersburg	210	40.58 N	77.37 W
Hubli-Dhārwār	122	15.21 N	75.10 E
Hubuleng	102	41.19 N	111.08 E
Hucaogang	106	32.00 N	120.29 E
Hucclecote	42	51.51 N	2.11 W
Huch'ang	98	41.25 N	127.03 E
Hucheng	100	25.26 N	118.27 E
Huchi	100	31.08 N	117.40 E
Huchow → Huzhou	106	30.52 N	120.06 E
Huckarde ✦8	263	51.32 N	7.24 E
Hückelhoven	56	51.04 N	6.10 E
Hückeswagen	56	51.08 N	7.20 E
Hucking	260	51.18 N	0.39 E
Huckingen ✦8	263	51.22 N	6.43 E
Huckitta Creek ≃	162	22.38 S	135.30 E
Huckleberry Island I	276	40.53 N	73.45 W
Huckleberry Mountain ∧	202	43.51 N	122.19 W
Huckleberry Mountain ∧2	212	44.28 N	75.28 W
Hucknall	42	53.02 N	1.11 W
Hucqueliers	50	50.34 N	1.54 E
Hucun	105	39.02 N	115.56 E
Hudangtou	106	30.48 N	121.22 E
Huddart Park ♦	282	37.26 N	122.19 W
Hudderfield Narrow Canal ≅	262	53.29 N	2.06 W
Huddersfield	44	53.39 N	1.47 W
Huddinge	40	59.14 N	17.59 E
Huddle Park Municipal Golf Course ♦	273d	26.09 S	28.07 E
Huddunge	40	60.03 N	16.59 E
Hude	52	53.07 N	8.27 E
Huder	89	50.00 N	121.37 E
Hudgin Creek ≃	194	33.40 N	91.59 W
Hūdī	140	17.42 N	34.17 E
Hudiksvall	26	61.44 N	17.07 E
Hudong	100	22.51 N	115.56 E
Hudson, P.Q., Can.	206	45.27 N	74.09 W
Hudson, Il., U.S.	216	40.36 N	88.59 W
Hudson, In., U.S.	216	41.31 N	85.04 W
Hudson, Ia., U.S.	190	42.24 N	92.27 W
Hudson, Md., U.S.	208	38.35 N	76.15 W
Hudson, Ma., U.S.	207	42.23 N	71.34 W
Hudson, Mi., U.S.	216	41.51 N	84.21 W
Hudson, N.H., U.S.	207	42.45 N	71.26 W
Hudson, N.Y., U.S.	210	42.15 N	73.47 W
Hudson, N.C., U.S.	192	35.50 N	81.29 W
Hudson, Oh., U.S.	214	41.14 N	81.26 W
Hudson, S.D., U.S.	198	43.07 N	96.27 W
Hudson, Tx., U.S.	222	31.19 N	94.50 W
Hudson, Wi., U.S.	190	44.58 N	92.45 W
Hudson, Wy., U.S.	200	42.54 N	108.34 W
Hudson □6	276	40.44 N	74.02 W
Hudson ≃, U.S.	188	40.42 N	74.02 W
Hudson ≃, Ga., U.S.	192	34.14 N	83.10 W
Hudson, Cerro ∧	254	46.04 S	73.10 W
Hudson, Lake ⊜1	194	36.20 N	95.05 W
Hudson Bay	184	52.52 N	102.25 W
Hudson Bay ⊂	176	60.00 N	86.00 W
Hudson-Bayonet Point	220	28.21 N	82.41 W
Hudson Falls	210	43.18 N	73.35 W
Hudson Highlands State Park ♦	210	41.26 N	73.58 W
Hudson Hope	182	56.02 N	121.55 W
Hudson Lake	216	41.42 N	86.32 W
Hudson Mountains ⋀	9	74.32 S	99.20 W
Hudsons Peak ∧	171b	36.26 S	149.10 E
Hudson Strait Ʉ	176	62.30 N	72.00 W
Hudsonville	216	42.52 N	85.51 W
Hudwin Lake ⊜	184	53.12 N	95.42 W
Hue	110	16.28 N	107.36 E
Huebra ≃	34	41.02 N	6.48 W
Huechucuicui, Punta ≻	254	41.47 S	74.02 W
Huechulafquen, Lago ⊜	254	39.46 S	71.28 W
Huechuraba	286e	33.21 S	70.40 W
Huedin	38	46.52 N	23.02 E
Huehuetán	236	15.01 N	92.22 W
Huehuetenango	236	15.20 N	91.28 W
Huehuetenango □5	236	15.40 N	91.35 W
Huehuetlán El Chico	234	18.21 N	98.42 W
Huejúcar	234	22.21 N	103.13 W
Huejuquilla El Alto	234	22.36 N	103.52 W
Huejutla de Reyes	234	21.08 N	98.25 W
Huelgoat	32	48.22 N	3.45 W
Huelma	34	37.39 N	3.27 W
Huelva	34	37.16 N	6.57 W
Huelva □4	34	37.30 N	6.55 W
Huelva, Río de ≃	34	37.27 N	6.00 W
Huenque ≃	248	16.12 S	69.44 W
Huentelauquén	252	31.35 S	71.32 W
Huércal-Overa	34	37.23 N	1.57 W
Huerfano ≃	198	38.14 N	104.15 W
Huerfano Mountain ∧	200	36.26 N	107.51 W
Huerhuero Creek ≃	226	35.40 N	120.42 W
Huerlumada	120	32.45 N	90.00 E
Huerva ≃	34	41.39 N	0.52 W
Huesca	34	42.08 N	0.25 W
Huesca □4	34	42.05 N	0.10 W
Huéscar	34	37.49 N	2.32 W
Hueston Woods State Park ♦	218	39.34 N	84.44 W
Huetamo de Núñez	234	18.35 N	100.53 W
Huete	34	40.08 N	2.41 W
Huey	219	38.36 N	89.17 W
Hueyapan de Ocampo	234	18.07 N	95.09 W
Hueytown	194	33.27 N	86.59 W
Hufengzhen	107	29.43 N	106.07 E
Hüffenhardt	56	49.18 N	9.04 E
Huffman	222	30.01 N	95.05 W
Huffman Dam ✦6	218	39.48 N	84.05 W
Hüfingen	58	47.55 N	8.29 E
Hufrat an-Nahās	140	9.45 N	24.19 E
Hufu	106	31.16 N	119.47 E
Hügel, Villa ⊕	263	51.25 N	7.01 E
Huggins, Mount ∧	9	78.17 S	162.28 E
Hugh ≃	162	25.01 S	134.01 E
Hugh Butler Lake ⊜1	198	40.22 N	100.42 W
Hughenden	166	20.51 S	144.12 E
Hughes, Austl.	162	30.42 S	129.31 E
Hughes, Ak., U.S.	180	66.03 N	154.16 W
Hughes, Ar., U.S.	194	34.56 N	90.28 W
Hughes ≃	184	56.46 N	100.01 W
Hughes, South Fork ≃	188	39.08 N	81.20 W
Hughes Airport ⊠	280	33.58 N	118.25 W
Hughes Creek ≃	169	36.53 S	145.08 E
Hughes Springs	222	33.05 N	94.38 W
Hughesville, Md., U.S.	208	38.31 N	76.47 W
Hughesville, Pa., U.S.	210	41.14 N	76.43 W
Hugh Keenleyside Dam ✦6	182	49.20 N	117.49 W
Hughson	226	37.36 N	120.52 W
Hughsonville	210	41.35 N	73.56 W
Hugh Town	42a	49.55 N	6.17 W
Hugli ≃	126	21.55 N	88.05 E
Hugli-Chinsurah	126	22.54 N	88.24 E
Hugo, Co., U.S.	198	39.08 N	103.28 W
Hugo, Ok., U.S.	196	34.00 N	95.30 W
Hugo Lake ⊜1	196	34.05 N	95.25 W
Hugoton	198	37.10 N	101.20 W
Hugou	100	33.23 N	117.08 E
Huguenot	210	41.25 N	74.38 W
Huguenot Lake ⊜	276	40.56 N	73.47 W
Huhehot → Hohhot	102	40.51 N	111.40 E
Huhsi	100	23.35 N	119.39 E
Hui'an, Zhg.	100	25.04 N	118.47 E
Huian, Zhg.	106	31.47 N	121.45 E
Huiarau Range ⋀	172	38.45 S	177.00 E
Huib-Hoch Plateau ⋀1	156	27.00 S	16.45 E
Huibie Yang Ʉ	100	30.08 N	121.44 E
Huibu	100	28.18 N	115.15 E
Huichang, Zhg.	100	25.34 N	115.49 E
Huichang, Zhg.	105	39.04 N	115.04 E
Huichapan	234	20.23 N	99.39 W
Hŭich'ŏn	98	40.10 N	126.17 E
Huichou → Huizhou	100	23.05 N	114.24 E
Huichuan	102	35.11 N	104.02 E
Huicungo	248	7.17 S	76.48 W
Huidong	102	26.41 N	102.36 E
Huidui	105	39.04 N	117.16 E
Huihe, Zhg.	89	48.12 N	119.17 E
Huihe, Zhg.	106	31.45 N	121.43 E
Huiji ≃	100	33.53 N	115.36 E
Huíla	152	15.04 S	13.32 E
Huíla □5, Ang.	152	15.00 S	15.00 E
Huila □5, Col.	246	2.30 N	75.45 W
Huila, Nevado del ∧	246	3.00 N	76.00 W
Huilai	100	23.04 N	116.18 E
Huili	102	26.43 N	102.10 E
Huiliuji	100	32.50 N	115.58 E
Huillapima	252	28.44 S	65.59 W
Huilong, Zhg.	100	27.30 N	118.24 E
Huilong, Zhg.	100	25.22 N	116.24 E
Huilong, Zhg.	100	24.09 N	113.58 E
Huilong, Zhg.	107	30.28 N	105.26 E
Huilong, Zhg.	107	30.35 N	105.49 E
Huilongchang, Zhg.	107	29.41 N	104.17 E
Huilongchang, Zhg.	107	30.18 N	103.39 E
Huilongchang, Zhg.	107	30.41 N	106.34 E
Huilongchang, Zhg.	107	29.17 N	105.01 E
Huimanguillo	234	17.51 N	93.23 W
Huimin	98	37.29 N	117.29 E
Huinan (Chaoyang)	98	42.40 N	126.00 E
Huínaymarca, Lago ⊜	248	16.20 S	68.50 W
Huinca Renancó	252	34.50 S	64.23 W
Hüinghausen	263	51.11 N	7.48 E
Huining	102	35.41 N	105.08 E
Huisachal	196	26.47 N	101.07 W
Huisduinen	52	52.56 N	4.44 E
Huishan	106	31.35 N	120.16 E
Huishui	102	26.07 N	106.24 E
Huismes	50	47.14 N	0.15 E
Huisne ≃	50	47.59 N	0.11 E
Huissen	52	51.57 N	5.56 E
Huistepec	234	16.39 N	98.20 W
Huiten Nur ⊜	120	35.30 N	92.00 E
Huiting	98	34.05 N	116.04 E
Huitiupan	234	17.13 N	92.39 W
Huitong	102	26.54 N	109.31 E
Huitongqiao	102	24.43 N	98.56 E
Huittinen (Lauttakylä)	26	61.11 N	22.42 E
Huitzilán	234	19.58 N	97.41 W
Huitzo	234	17.15 N	96.52 W
Huitzuco de los Figueroa	234	18.18 N	99.21 W
Huixian	102	33.47 N	106.16 E
Huixtla	232	15.09 N	92.28 W
Huiyang → Huizhou	100	23.05 N	114.24 E
Huiyao	100	27.16 N	118.05 E
Huize	102	26.27 N	103.09 E
Huizen	52	52.17 N	5.14 E
Huizhou	100	23.05 N	114.24 E
Hujia, Zhg.	104	41.20 N	121.52 E
Hujia, Zhg.	106	31.25 N	121.37 E
Hujiadian	107	29.41 N	104.07 E
Hujiajie	104	41.06 N	122.10 E
Hujiasi	107	29.16 N	105.13 E
Hujiawopu	104	42.34 N	122.11 E
Hujiayu	105	39.28 N	115.27 E
Hujiazhuang, Zhg.	105	39.51 N	117.07 E
Hujiazhuang, Zhg.	269b	31.21 N	121.25 E
Hujie	102	24.56 N	100.32 E
Hukeng	100	27.29 N	114.18 E
Hukou	100	29.45 N	116.13 E
Hŭksan-chedo II	98	34.30 N	125.20 E
Hukui → Fukui	94	36.04 N	136.13 E
Hukūmah	140	13.52 N	36.07 E
Hukuntsi	156	24.02 S	21.48 E
Hukuoka → Fukuoka	96	33.35 N	130.24 E
Hukusima → Fukushima	92	37.45 N	140.28 E
Hukuyama → Fukuyama	96	34.29 N	133.22 E
Hula, 'Émeq ≡1	132	33.08 N	35.37 E
Hulahula ≃	180	70.00 N	144.01 W
Hulan	89	46.00 N	126.38 E
Hulan ≃	89	45.55 N	126.41 E
Hulan Ergi	89	47.13 N	123.39 E
Hulbert, Mi., U.S.	190	46.21 N	85.09 W
Hulbert, Ok., U.S.	194	35.55 N	95.08 W
Hulberton	210	43.15 N	78.04 W
Hulda	132	31.50 N	34.53 E
Huldrefossen ⌞	26	61.28 N	5.58 E
Hulei	100	24.50 N	116.48 E
Huleia Stream ≃	229b	21.57 N	159.22 W
Hulett	198	44.40 N	104.36 W
Hulín, Česko.	30	49.19 N	17.28 E
Hulin, Zhg.	89	45.46 N	132.59 E
Hulin ≃, Zhg.	89	45.19 N	124.06 E
Hulin ≃, Zhg.	89	44.55 N	122.35 E
Huliu ≃	98	40.10 N	114.33 E
Hull, P.Q., Can.	212	45.26 N	75.43 W
Hull, Il., U.S.	219	39.43 N	91.13 W
Hull, Ia., U.S.	198	43.11 N	96.08 W
Hull, Ma., U.S.	207	42.18 N	70.54 W
Hull, Tx., U.S.	222	30.09 N	94.39 W
Hull □6	212	45.40 N	75.35 W
Hull ≃	44	53.44 N	0.19 W
Hullavington	42	51.33 N	2.09 W
Hull Bay ⊂	283	42.18 N	70.53 W
Hullbridge	42	51.37 N	0.38 E
Hull → Kingston upon Hull	44	53.45 N	0.20 W
Hullo	76	59.00 N	23.14 E
Hulmeville	285	40.08 N	74.55 W
Hüls, Dtsch.	56	51.22 N	6.30 E
Hüls, Dtsch.	263	51.40 N	7.08 E
Hülscheid	56	51.16 N	7.34 E
Hülser Berg ✦8	263	51.24 N	6.31 E
Hülser Berg ∧2	263	51.23 N	6.33 E
Hulst	52	51.17 N	4.03 E
Hult	40	58.40 N	16.07 E
Hultsfred	26	57.29 N	15.50 E
Huludao	104	40.43 N	121.00 E
Hulufa	105	39.42 N	116.12 E
Hulun → Hailar	89	49.12 N	119.42 E
Hulun Nur ⊜	88	49.01 N	117.32 E
Huluyu	105	40.14 N	116.53 E
Hulwān	142	29.51 N	31.20 E
Hulwān Observatory ⊕3	142	29.52 N	31.21 E
Huma, Tonga	174w	21.19 S	174.57 E
Huma, Zhg.	89	51.43 N	126.38 E
Huma ≃	89	51.40 N	126.44 E
Humacao	240m	18.09 N	65.50 W
Humahuaca	252	23.12 S	65.21 W
Humaitá, Bra.	248	7.31 S	63.02 W
Humaitá, Para.	252	27.03 S	58.33 W
Humaitá ≃	248	8.16 S	72.44 W
Humansdorp	158	34.02 S	24.46 E
Humansville	194	37.47 N	93.34 W
Humara, Jabal al- ∧	140	16.16 N	30.59 E
Humarock	283	42.08 N	70.41 W
Humaydah	140	14.22 N	22.31 E
Humayingzi	98	41.06 N	116.48 E
Humayun's Tomb ⊥	272a	28.36 N	77.15 E
Humbe	152	16.40 S	14.55 E
Humbe, Serra do ⋀	152	12.13 S	15.25 E
Humbeek	50	50.58 N	4.23 E
Humber ≃, On., Can.	212	43.38 N	79.28 W
Humber ≃, Eng., U.K.	44	53.40 N	0.10 W
Humber, Mouth of the ≃1	44	53.32 N	0.08 E
Humber Bay ⊂	275b	43.38 N	79.29 W
Humber Bridge ✦5	44	53.42 N	0.27 W
Humberside □6	44	53.55 N	0.40 W
Humberston	44	53.32 N	0.02 W
Humberto de Campos	250	2.37 S	43.27 W
Humber Valley Park ♦	275b	43.39 N	79.30 W
Humbird	190	44.31 N	90.53 W
Humble, Dan.	41	54.50 N	10.42 E
Humble, Tx., U.S.	222	29.59 N	95.15 W
Humboldt, Sk., Can.	184	52.12 N	105.07 W
Humboldt, Az., U.S.	200	34.30 N	112.14 W
Humboldt, Il., U.S.	194	39.36 N	88.19 W
Humboldt, Ia., U.S.	198	42.43 N	94.12 W
Humboldt, Ks., U.S.	198	37.48 N	95.26 W
Humboldt, Ne., U.S.	198	40.09 N	95.56 W
Humboldt, S.D., U.S.	198	43.38 N	97.04 W
Humboldt, Tn., U.S.	194	35.49 N	88.54 W
Humboldt ∧	175f	21.53 S	166.25 E
Humboldt ≃	204	40.02 N	118.31 W
Humboldt, North Fork ≃	204	40.56 N	115.32 W
Humboldt, Planetario ⊕	286c	10.30 N	66.50 W
Humboldt, South Fork ≃	204	40.47 N	115.53 W
Humboldt Bay ⊂	204	40.47 N	124.11 W
Humboldt Lake ⊜	204	39.58 N	118.38 W
Humboldt Mountains ⋀	9	71.45 S	11.30 E
Humboldt Park ♦	278	41.54 N	87.42 W
Humboldt Redwoods State Park ♦	204	40.19 N	124.00 W
Humboldt Salt Marsh ≡	204	39.50 N	117.55 W
Hume, Ca., U.S.	204	36.47 N	118.55 W
Hume, N.Y., U.S.	210	42.29 N	78.08 W
Hume, Lake ⊜1	166	36.06 S	147.05 E
Hume and Hovell Lookout ♦	169	37.15 S	144.59 E
Humeburn	166	27.24 S	145.14 E
Hūmedān	128	25.24 N	59.39 E
Hu Men ⊂1	100	22.44 N	113.40 E
Humenné	30	48.56 N	21.55 E
Húmera	266a	40.26 N	3.47 W
Humeston	190	40.51 N	93.29 W
Humlā Karnālī ≃	124	29.38 N	81.52 E
Humlebæk	41	55.58 N	12.33 E
Hummelo	52	52.00 N	6.14 E
Hummelstown	208	40.16 N	76.43 W
Hummels Wharf	210	40.49 N	76.50 W
Hümmling ⋀	52	52.52 N	7.31 E
Humos, Isla I	254	45.38 S	73.59 W
Humpata	152	15.02 S	13.24 E
Hümpfershausen	56	50.40 N	10.13 E
Humphrey, Ar., U.S.	194	34.25 N	91.42 W
Humphrey, Ne., U.S.	198	41.41 N	97.29 W
Humphreys, Mount ∧	204	37.17 N	118.40 W
Humphreys Peak ∧	200	35.20 N	111.40 W
Humpolec	30	49.32 N	15.22 E
Humppila	26	60.56 N	23.22 E
Humptulips	224	47.13 N	123.57 W
Humptulips ≃	224	47.03 N	124.03 W
Humptulips, East Fork ≃	224	47.15 N	123.54 W
Humptulips, West Fork ≃	224	47.15 N	123.54 W
Humptulips Ridge ∧	224	47.20 N	123.45 W
Humpty Doo	164	12.38 S	131.15 E
Humula	171b	35.29 S	147.45 E
Humuya ≃	236	15.01 N	87.44 W
Hūn	146	29.07 N	15.56 E
Hun ≃, Zhg.	98	41.01 N	122.27 E
Hun ≃, Zhg.	98	40.52 N	125.42 E
Hunabasi → Funabashi	94	35.42 N	139.59 E
Húnaflói ⊂	24a	65.50 N	20.50 W
Hunan □4	102	28.00 N	111.00 E
Hunayshāt, Ghurd al- ⍊8	142	30.07 N	29.47 E
Hunchun	98	42.54 N	130.22 E
Huncoat	262	53.46 N	2.20 W
Hundeluft	54	51.58 N	12.20 E
Hundested	41	55.58 N	11.52 E
Hundewāli	123	31.55 N	72.38 E
Hundorp	26	61.33 N	9.54 E
Hundred	188	39.41 N	80.27 W
Hundred End	262	53.42 N	2.53 W
Hundslund	41	55.55 N	10.04 E
Hundstein ∧	64	47.20 N	12.54 E
Hundwil	58	47.22 N	9.19 E
Hunedoara	38	45.45 N	22.54 E
Hunedoara □6	38	45.45 N	23.00 E
Hünfeld	56	50.40 N	9.46 E
Hungary (Magyarország) □1, Europe	22	47.00 N	20.00 E
Hungary (Magyarország) □1, Europe	30	47.00 N	20.00 E
Hungchiang → Hongjiang	102	27.07 N	109.56 E
Hungen	56	50.28 N	8.54 E
Hungerford, Austl.	166	29.00 S	144.25 E
Hungerford, Eng., U.K.	42	51.26 N	1.30 W
Hungerford, Tx., U.S.	222	29.24 N	96.05 W
Hŭngho-ri	98	37.14 N	127.44 E
Hŭngin-ni	98	39.03 N	126.26 E
Hung Long	269c	10.40 N	106.39 E
Hungmao	100	24.55 N	120.58 E
Hŭngnam	98	39.50 N	127.38 E
Hungría → Hungary □1	30	47.00 N	20.00 E
Hungry Hill ∧	48	51.41 N	9.48 W
Hungry Horse	202	48.23 N	114.03 W
Hungry Horse Dam ✦6	202	48.14 N	114.04 W
Hungry Horse Reservoir ⊜1	202	48.15 N	113.50 W
Hungry Lake ⊜	212	44.48 N	76.53 W
Hungry Law ∧2	44	55.21 N	2.24 W
Hung Yen	110	20.39 N	106.04 E
Hunhe	104	41.43 N	123.22 E
Huningue	58	47.36 N	7.35 E
Hunish, Rubha ≻	46	57.41 N	6.21 W
Huni Valley	150	5.28 N	1.55 W
Hunjiang (Badaojiang)	98	41.56 N	126.29 E
Hunker	279b	40.12 N	79.38 W
Hunkurāb, Ra's ≻	140	24.34 N	35.10 E
Hunlen Falls ⌞	182	52.17 N	125.47 W
Hunmanby	44	54.10 N	0.19 W
Hunn ⊜	40	58.51 N	15.57 E
Hunneberg ∧2	26	58.20 N	12.27 E
Hunnebostrand	26	58.27 N	11.18 E
Hunnewell	219	39.40 N	91.51 W
Hunnewell Lake ⊜	219	39.42 N	91.52 W
Hunsberge ⋀	156	27.45 S	17.12 E
Hunseby	41	54.48 N	11.32 E
Hunspach	56	48.57 N	7.57 E
Hunsrück ⋀	56	49.50 N	6.40 E
Hunstanton	42	52.57 N	0.30 E
Hunstein Range ⋀	164	4.30 S	142.40 E
Hunsūr	122	12.18 N	76.17 E
Hunswinkel	263	51.05 N	7.48 E
Hunt □6	222	33.03 N	96.05 W
Hunte ≃	52	52.30 N	8.19 E
Hunter, N.Y., U.S.	210	42.13 N	74.13 W
Hunter, N.D., U.S.	198	47.11 N	97.13 W
Hunter ≃, Austl.	170	32.50 S	151.42 E
Hunter ≃, N.Z.	172	44.22 S	169.25 E
Hunter, Île I	14	22.24 S	172.03 E
Hunter, Mount ∧	180	62.57 N	151.05 W
Hunter, Port ⊂	170	32.55 S	151.48 E
Hunterdon □6	208	40.31 N	74.52 W
Hunter Island I, Austl.	166	40.32 S	144.45 E
Hunter Island I, B.C., Can.	182	51.55 N	128.05 W
Hunter Island I, N.Y., U.S.	276	40.53 N	73.47 W
Hunter Mountain ∧	210	42.10 N	74.14 W
Hunter Mountains ⋀	172	45.42 S	167.25 E
Hunter Range ⋀	170	32.50 S	150.50 E
Hunter Ridge ✢3	14	21.30 S	174.30 E
Hunter River	186	46.21 N	63.21 W
Hunters	182	48.07 N	118.12 W
Hunters Bay ⊂	110	19.57 N	93.19 E
Hunters Creek Village	222	29.46 N	95.24 W
Huntersfield Mountain ∧	210	42.21 N	74.21 W
Hunters Hill	274a	33.50 S	151.09 E
Hunters Point ≻	282	37.43 N	122.22 W
Hunter's Quay	46	55.58 N	4.55 W
Hunters Road	154	19.09 S	29.48 E
Hunters Run	208	40.05 N	77.11 W
Huntersville	192	35.25 N	80.50 W
Huntertown	216	41.13 N	85.10 W
Hunterville	172	39.56 S	175.34 E
Hunter Wash V	200	36.17 N	108.34 W
Huntingburg	194	38.17 N	86.57 W
Huntingdon, B.C., Can.	224	49.00 N	122.16 W
Huntingdon, P.Q., Can.	206	45.05 N	74.10 W
Huntingdon, Eng., U.K.	42	52.20 N	0.12 W
Huntingdon, Pa., U.S.	214	40.29 N	78.00 W
Huntingdon, Tn., U.S.	194	36.00 N	88.25 W
Huntingdon □6, P.Q., Can.	206	45.05 N	74.00 W
Huntingdon □6, Pa., U.S.	214	40.29 N	78.01 W
Huntingdon Valley	285	40.07 N	75.03 W
Huntingdon Valley Creek ≃	285	40.07 N	75.04 W
Hunting Island State Park ♦	192	32.20 N	80.30 W
Hunting Ridge	284c	38.55 N	77.12 W
Huntington, Eng., U.K.	44	54.01 N	1.04 W
Huntington, In., U.S.	216	40.52 N	85.29 W
Huntington, Ma., U.S.	207	42.14 N	72.52 W
Huntington, N.Y., U.S.	210	40.51 N	73.25 W
Huntington, Or., U.S.	202	44.21 N	117.15 W
Huntington, Tx., U.S.	222	31.16 N	94.34 W
Huntington, Ut,. U.S.	200	39.19 N	110.57 W
Huntington, Va., U.S.	284c	38.48 N	77.15 W
Huntington, W.V., U.S.	188	38.25 N	82.26 W
Huntington □6	216	40.53 N	85.30 W
Huntington Bay	276	40.53 N	73.24 W
Huntington Bay ⊂	276	40.55 N	73.25 W
Huntington Beach, Ca., U.S.	228	33.39 N	117.59 W
Huntington Beach, N.Y., U.S.	276	40.54 N	73.23 W
Huntington Creek ≃, Nv., U.S.	204	40.37 N	115.43 W
Huntington Creek ≃, Pa., U.S.	210	41.06 N	76.22 W
Huntington Creek ≃, Ut,. U.S.	200	39.09 N	110.55 W
Huntington Harbor ⊂	276	40.54 N	73.26 W
Huntington Lake	226	37.15 N	119.14 W
Huntington Lake ⊜1, Ca., U.S.	226	37.14 N	119.12 W
Huntington Lake ⊜1, In., U.S.	216	40.50 N	85.25 W
Huntington Library ⊕3	280	34.08 N	118.07 W
Huntington Mills	210	41.11 N	76.14 W
Huntington Park	228	33.58 N	118.13 W
Huntington Park ♦	279a	41.29 N	81.56 W
Huntington Station	210	40.51 N	73.24 W
Huntington Woods	281	42.28 N	83.10 W
Huntingtown	208	38.36 N	76.36 W
Hunting Valley	279a	41.31 N	81.23 W
Huntingville	206	45.20 N	71.51 W
Huntland	194	35.03 N	86.16 W
Huntley, Il., U.S.	216	42.10 N	88.25 W
Huntley, Mt., U.S.	202	45.53 N	108.18 W
Huntly, N.Z.	172	37.33 S	175.10 E
Huntly, Scot., U.K.	46	57.27 N	2.47 W
Hunt Mountain ∧	202	44.44 N	107.45 W
Hunton	260	51.13 N	0.28 E
Huntsburg	214	41.32 N	81.03 W
Hunt's Cross ✦8	262	53.21 N	2.51 W
Hunts Point	224	47.39 N	122.14 W
Huntsville, On., Can.	212	45.20 N	79.13 W
Huntsville, Al., U.S.	194	34.43 N	86.35 W
Huntsville, Ar., U.S.	194	36.05 N	93.44 W
Huntsville, Il., U.S.	219	40.11 N	90.52 W
Huntsville, In., U.S.	218	40.00 N	85.43 W
Huntsville, Mo., U.S.	194	39.26 N	92.33 W
Huntsville, Oh., U.S.	216	40.26 N	83.49 W
Huntsville, Tn., U.S.	192	36.24 N	84.29 W
Huntsville, Tx., U.S.	222	30.43 N	95.33 W
Huntsville, Ut,. U.S.	200	41.15 N	111.46 W
Huntsville State Park ♦	222	30.37 N	95.32 W
Hunū, Kathīb al- ⍊8	142	30.37 N	32.49 E
Hunucmá	232	21.01 N	89.52 W
Hunut	130	40.39 N	41.09 E
Hünxe	52	51.38 N	6.46 E
Hünxerwald ♦	263	51.40 N	6.50 E
Hunyani ≃	154	15.37 S	30.39 E
Hunyuan	98	39.48 N	113.41 E
Hun-yung	98	42.53 N	130.12 E
Hunza □9	123	36.30 N	75.00 E
Hunza ≃	123	35.55 N	74.22 E
Huocheng	86	44.12 N	80.26 E
Huoergeluo	89	45.35 N	120.56 E
Huokou	100	26.28 N	119.16 E
Huolong	106	32.04 N	121.17 E
Huolongmen	89	49.48 N	125.47 E
Huolu	98	38.05 N	114.18 E
Huong Hoa	110	16.37 N	106.45 E
Huong Khe	110	18.13 N	105.41 E
Huong Thuy	110	16.25 N	107.40 E
Huon Gulf ⊂	164	7.10 S	147.25 E
Huon Peninsula ≻1	164	6.25 S	147.25 E
Huonville	166	43.01 S	147.02 E
Huoqiu	100	32.20 N	116.16 E
Huorili	89	49.00 N	124.41 E
Huoshan	100	31.25 N	116.20 E
Huo Shan ∧	100	31.06 N	116.12 E
Huoshaoliao	100	25.00 N	121.45 E
Huotong	100	26.53 N	119.25 E
Huotong ≃	100	26.50 N	119.32 E
Huotuolaihuduke	102	40.19 N	104.18 E
Huoxian, Zhg.	102	36.37 N	111.40 E
Huoxian, Zhg.	105	39.46 N	116.46 E
Huoyan	100	33.42 N	113.40 E
Hupeh → Hubei □4	90	31.00 N	112.00 E
Huqiao	106	31.25 N	119.24 E
Hura	126	23.18 N	86.39 E
Hūrand	84	38.51 N	47.22 E
Hurāsāgar ≃	126	24.04 N	89.40 E
Huraydīn, Wādī V	132	30.59 N	33.53 E
Huraymilā	128	25.08 N	46.08 E
Hūrayn	142	30.39 N	31.08 E
Hurd, Cape ≻	190	45.13 N	81.44 W
Hurdalssjøen ⊜	26	60.20 N	11.05 E
Hurdiyo	144	10.33 N	51.08 E
Hurdland	219	40.09 N	92.18 W
Hurdsfield	262	53.16 N	2.06 W
Hurepoix ✦1	261	48.40 N	2.10 E
Hure Qi	98	42.44 N	121.40 E
Hurffville	285	39.46 N	75.07 W
Huri ∧2	154	3.41 N	37.51 E
Huriel	32	46.23 N	2.29 E
Hurleg Hu ⊜	102	37.20 N	96.54 E
Hurley, Ms., U.S.	194	30.39 N	88.29 W
Hurley, N.M., U.S.	200	32.41 N	108.07 W
Hurley, N.Y., U.S.	210	41.55 N	74.03 W
Hurley, S.D., U.S.	198	43.16 N	97.05 W
Hurley, Wi., U.S.	190	46.26 N	90.11 W
Hurleyville	210	41.44 N	74.40 W
Hurlford	46	55.36 N	4.28 W
Hurliness	46	58.47 N	3.15 W
Hurlingham	258	34.36 S	58.38 W
Hurlock	208	38.37 N	75.51 W
Hurmāgai	128	28.18 N	64.26 E
Huron, Ca., U.S.	226	36.12 N	120.06 W
Huron, Oh., U.S.	214	41.22 N	82.33 W
Huron, S.D., U.S.	198	44.21 N	98.12 W
Huron □6, On., Can.	212	43.45 N	81.10 W
Huron □6, Oh., U.S.	214	41.15 N	82.37 W
Huron ≃, Mi., U.S.	216	42.03 N	83.14 W
Huron ≃, Oh., U.S.	214	41.23 N	82.33 W
Huron, East Branch ≃	214	41.17 N	82.38 W
Huron, Lake ⊜	190	44.30 N	82.15 W
Huron, Point ≻	214	42.34 N	82.47 W
Huron, West Branch ≃	214	41.17 N	82.38 W
Huron Gardens	216	42.38 N	83.20 W
Huron Mountains ⋀2	190	46.50 N	87.55 W
Hurons, Rivière des ≃	206	45.28 N	73.16 W
Hurricane, Ak., U.S.	180	62.59 N	149.38 W
Hurricane, Ut,. U.S.	200	37.10 N	113.17 W
Hurricane, W.V., U.S.	188	38.25 N	82.01 W
Hurricane Bayou ≃	222	31.21 N	95.35 W
Hurricane Cliffs ⍊4	200	37.20 N	113.10 W
Hurricane Creek ≃, Ar., U.S.	194	34.05 N	92.23 W
Hurricane Creek ≃, Ga., U.S.	192	31.23 N	82.19 W
Hurricane Creek ≃, Il., U.S.	219	38.53 N	89.13 W
Hurricane Lake ⊜	198	48.25 N	99.30 W
Hurricane Wash V	200	37.00 N	113.23 W
Hurshi	126	24.17 N	88.28 E
Hursley	42	51.02 N	1.24 W
Hurso	144	9.38 N	41.38 E
Hurst	222	32.49 N	97.10 W
Hurstbourne Tarrant	42	51.17 N	1.23 W
Hurstbridge	169	37.38 S	145.12 E
Hurst Green	260	51.15 N	0.01 E
Hurstpierpoint	42	50.56 N	0.11 W
Hurstville	170	33.58 S	151.06 E
Hurstwood Reservoir ⊜1	262	53.47 N	2.10 W
Hurt	192	37.05 N	79.17 W
Hurtado ≃	252	30.35 S	71.11 W
Hurtaut ≃	50	49.42 N	4.01 E
Hürth	56	50.52 N	6.51 E
Hurtsboro	194	32.14 N	85.24 W
Hurunui ≃	172	42.55 S	173.17 E
Hurup	26	56.45 N	8.25 E
Hurworth-on-Tees	44	54.29 N	1.31 W
Husainābād	124	24.32 N	84.01 E
Husainīwāla	123	30.59 N	74.34 E
Husainpur	124	24.25 N	90.40 E
Húsavík	24a	66.04 N	17.18 W
Husby-Långhundra	40	59.45 N	18.01 E
Huse → Higashiōsaka	96	34.39 N	135.35 E
Husen ✦8	263	51.33 N	7.36 E
Hushan, Zhg.	89	45.35 N	130.35 E
Hushan, Zhg.	100	28.36 N	118.59 E
Hushan, Zhg.	100	22.09 N	113.10 E
Husheib	140	14.54 N	35.07 E
Hushi	107	28.57 N	105.22 E
Hushiha	98	40.52 N	116.59 E
Hushitai	104	41.57 N	123.30 E
Hushu, Zhg.	106	31.52 N	118.59 E
Hushu, Zhg.	106	30.18 N	120.08 E
Huși	38	46.40 N	28.04 E
Husinec	60	49.03 N	13.58 E
Huskisson	170	35.02 S	150.40 E
Huskvarna	26	57.48 N	14.16 E

≃ River	Fluß	Río	Rivière	Rio	✢ Submarine Features	Untermeerische Objekte	Accidentes Submarinos	Formes de relief sous-marin	Acidentes submarinos
≅ Canal	Kanal	Canal	Canal	Canal	□ Political Unit	Politische Einheit	Unidad Politica	Entité politique	Unidade política
⌞ Waterfall, Rapids	Wasserfall, Stromschnellen	Cascada, Rápidos	Chute d'eau, Rapides	Cascata, Rápidos	⊕ Cultural Institution	Kulturelle Institution	Institución Cultural	Institution culturelle	Institução cultural
Ʉ Strait	Meeresstraße	Estrecho	Détroit	Estreito	⊥ Historical Site	Historische Stätte	Sitio Histórico	Site historique	Sitio histórico
⊂ Bay, Gulf	Bucht, Golf	Bahía, Golfo	Baie, Golfe	Baía, Golfo	♦ Recreational Site	Erholungs- und Ferienort	Sitio de Recreo	Centre de loisirs	Area de Lazer
⊜ Lake, Lakes	See, Seen	Lago, Lagos	Lac, Lacs	Lago, Lagos	⊠ Airport	Flughafen	Aeropuerto	Aéroport	Aeroporto
≡ Swamp	Sumpf	Pantano	Marais	Pântano	■ Military Installation	Militäranlage	Instalación Militar	Installation militaire	Instalação militar
⍓ Ice Features, Glacier	Eis- und Gletscherformen	Accidentes Glaciales	Formes glaciaires	Acidentes glaciares	✦ Miscellaneous	Verschiedenes	Misceláneo	Divers	Diversos
╤ Other Hydrographic Features	Andere Hydrographische Objekte	Otros Elementos Hidrográficos	Autres données hydrographiques	Outros acidentes hidrográficos					

Name	Page	Lat.°'	Long.°'
Huslia	180	65.42 N	156.25 W
Hussar	182	51.03 N	112.41 W
Hussigny-Godbrange	56	49.29 N	5.52 E
Hustisford	190	43.21 N	88.36 W
Huston ≃	220	25.42 N	81.17 W
Hustontown	214	40.03 N	78.02 W
Hustopeče	61	48.57 N	16.44 E
Husum, Dtsch.	41	54.28 N	9.03 E
Husum, Sve.	26	63.20 N	19.10 E
Husum, Wa., U.S.	224	45.47 N	121.29 W
Hutaimbaru	114	1.34 N	99.44 E
Hutangqiao	106	31.46 N	119.57 E
Hutan Melintang	114	3.53 N	100.56 E
Hutanopan	114	0.41 N	99.42 E
Hutaym, Ḥarrat ⩡[9]	128	26.15 N	40.20 E
Hutberg ∧[2]	54	52.09 N	14.33 E
Hutchins	222	32.39 N	96.43 W
Hutchinson, S. Afr.	158	31.30 S	23.09 E
Hutchinson, Ks., U.S.	198	38.03 N	97.55 W
Hutchinson, Mn., U.S.	190	44.53 N	94.22 W
Hutchinson, Pa., U.S.	214	40.13 N	79.44 W
Hutchinson ≃	276	40.52 N	73.50 W
Hutchinson Island I	220	27.25 N	80.17 W
Hutch Mountain ∧	200	34.47 N	111.22 W
Hutou, Zhg.	100	25.15 N	118.03 E
Hutou, Zhg.	100	26.04 N	118.46 E
Hutou, Zhg.	106	31.37 N	119.37 E
Hutou, Zhg.	106	32.14 N	120.17 E
Hutouya	98	37.13 N	119.46 E
Hutsonville	194	39.06 N	87.39 W
Hüttau	64	47.25 N	13.18 E
Hütteldorf ◆[8]	264b	48.12 N	16.16 E
Hüttener Berge ⋏[2]	41	54.26 N	9.40 E
Hüttenheim ◆[8]	263	51.22 N	6.43 E
Hüttental	56	50.54 N	8.02 E
Hutte Sauvage, Lac de la ⊜	176	56.15 N	64.45 W
Huttig	194	33.02 N	92.10 W
Hütting	60	48.48 N	11.07 E
Hutto	222	30.33 N	97.33 W
Hutton, Eng., U.K.	260	51.38 N	0.22 E
Hutton, Eng., U.K.	262	53.44 N	2.46 W
Hutton, Mount ∧	166	25.51 S	148.20 E
Hutton Rudby	44	54.27 N	1.17 W
Huttonsville	212	43.38 N	79.48 W
Huttrop ◆[8]	263	51.27 N	7.03 E
Hüttschlag	64	47.10 N	13.14 E
Huttwil	58	47.07 N	7.51 E
Hutubi	86	44.07 N	86.57 E
Hutuo ≃	98	38.14 N	116.05 E
Hutwisch ∧	61	47.28 N	16.13 E
Huu	115b	8.48 S	118.25 E
Huvalu Forest ◆[3]	174v	19.03 S	169.51 W
Huveaune ≃	62	43.15 N	5.23 E
Huvudskär I	40	58.57 N	18.34 E
Huwan	100	31.41 N	114.53 E
Huwei	100	23.43 N	120.26 E
Huwun	144	4.23 N	40.08 E
Ḥuwwārah	132	32.09 N	35.15 E
Huxford	194	31.13 N	87.28 W
Huxi	100	26.12 N	114.44 E
Huxian	102	34.09 N	108.32 E
Huxley	182	51.56 N	113.14 W
Huy	56	50.31 N	5.14 E
Huy ∧	54	51.57 N	10.57 E
Huyangzhen	100	32.25 N	112.45 E
Huyton-with-Roby	262	53.25 N	2.52 W
Huyuesi	106	30.23 N	118.45 E
Hüyük	130	37.57 N	31.37 E
Huyutou	100	26.44 N	119.49 E
Hūzgān	128	31.27 N	48.04 E
Huzhen	100	28.50 N	120.15 E
Huzhou	106	30.52 N	120.06 E
Huzhu	102	37.00 N	102.00 E
Huzhuangtun	104	40.43 N	122.33 E
Huzi	100	30.56 N	113.42 E
Huzisawa → Fujisawa	94	35.21 N	139.29 E
Hvalsø	41	55.36 N	11.50 E
Hvannadalshnúkur ∧	24a	64.01 N	16.41 W
Hvar	36	43.10 N	16.27 E
Hvar, Otok I	36	43.09 N	16.45 E
Hvarski Kanal ⊔	36	43.15 N	16.37 E
Hveragerði	24a	64.03 N	21.10 W
Hvide Sande	26	55.59 N	8.08 E
Hvidovre	41	55.39 N	12.29 E
Hvittingfoss	26	59.29 N	10.01 E
Hvolsvöllur	24a	63.45 N	20.10 W
Hwach'ŏn	98	38.06 N	127.41 E
Hwach'ŏn-chŏsuji ⊜[1]	98	38.07 N	127.52 E
Hwach'ŏn-ni	98	39.01 N	126.02 E
Hwainan → Huainan	100	32.40 N	117.00 E
Hwaining → Anqing	100	30.31 N	117.02 E
Hwange	154	18.22 S	26.29 E
Hwange National Park ♦	154	19.00 S	26.35 E
Hwanggong-ni	98	40.03 N	129.27 E
Hwanghae Namdo □[4]	98	38.15 N	125.30 E
Hwanghae Pukdo □[4]	98	38.30 N	126.25 E
Hwang Ho → Huang ≃	90	37.32 N	118.19 E
Hwangju	98	38.42 N	125.46 E
Hwangshih → Huangshi	100	30.13 N	115.05 E
Hyak	224	47.23 N	121.23 W
Hyakuna	174m	26.08 N	127.48 E
Hyakuri-ga-dake ∧	94	35.23 N	135.49 E
Hyakuri-kichi, Kōkū-jieitai- ■	94	36.11 N	140.25 E
Hyannis, Ma., U.S.	207	41.39 N	70.17 W
Hyannis, Ne., U.S.	198	42.00 N	101.45 W
Hyannis Port	207	41.38 N	70.18 W
Hyattsville	208	38.57 N	76.56 W
Hyattville	202	44.14 N	107.36 W
Hybla Valley	208	38.44 N	77.05 W
Hyco ≃	192	36.40 N	78.45 W
Hyco Lake ⊜[1]	192	36.30 N	79.05 W
Hydaburg	182	55.12 N	132.49 W
Hyde, N.Z.	172	45.18 S	170.15 E
Hyde, Eng., U.K.	44	53.27 N	2.04 W
Hyde, Pa., U.S.	214	41.00 N	78.28 W
Hyden, Austl.	162	32.27 S	118.53 E
Hyden, Ky., U.S.	192	37.10 N	83.22 W
Hyde Park, Guy.	246	6.30 N	58.16 W
Hyde Park, N.Y., U.S.	210	41.47 N	73.56 W
Hyde Park, Vt., U.S.	188	44.35 N	72.37 W
Hyde Park ◆[8], Il., U.S.	278	41.48 N	87.36 W
Hyde Park ◆[8], Ma., U.S.	283	42.15 N	71.08 W
Hyde Park ♦, Austl.	274a	33.53 S	151.13 E
Hyde Park ♦, Eng., U.K.	260	51.30 N	0.10 W
Hyde Park ♦, N.Y., U.S.	284a	43.06 N	79.01 W
Hyder	182	55.55 N	130.01 W
Hyderābād, India	122	17.23 N	78.29 E
Hyderābād, Pāk.	120	25.22 N	68.22 E
Hydetown	214	41.40 N	79.44 W
Hydra → Ídhra I	38	37.20 N	23.32 E
Hydraulic	182	52.36 N	121.42 W
Hydro	196	35.21 N	98.22 W
Hydrographers Passage ⊔	166	20.45 S	150.15 E
Hyen ⊜	40	60.36 N	16.12 E
Hyères	62	43.07 N	6.07 E
Hyères, Îles d' II	62	43.00 N	6.20 E
Hyères-Plage	62	43.06 N	6.10 E
Hyesan	98	41.23 N	128.12 E
Hyland ≃	180	59.50 N	128.10 W
Hylestad	26	59.05 N	7.32 E
Hyllekrog I	41	54.36 N	11.30 E
Hyllinge, Dan.	41	55.16 N	11.37 E
Hyllinge, Sve.	41	56.06 N	12.51 E
Hyllstofta	41	56.08 N	13.16 E
Hyltebruk	26	57.00 N	13.14 E
Hymaya ≃	232	24.31 N	107.41 W
Hymera	194	39.11 N	87.18 W
Hyndburn □[8]	262	53.45 N	2.23 W
Hyndman	188	39.49 N	78.43 W
Hyndman Peak ∧	202	43.45 N	114.08 W
Hynish Bay ⊂	46	56.28 N	6.50 W
Hyōgo □[5]	96	35.00 N	135.00 E
Hyōgo ◆[8]	270	34.39 N	135.10 E
Hyŏn-ni	98	37.57 N	128.20 E
Hyōno-sen ∧	96	35.21 N	134.31 E
Hyōnosen-Ushiroyama-Nagisan-kokutei-kōen ♦	96	35.15 N	134.30 E
Hyŏpch'ŏn	98	35.35 N	128.08 E
Hyrum	200	41.38 N	111.51 W
Hyrynsalmi	26	64.40 N	28.32 E
Hysham	202	46.17 N	107.14 W
Hythe, Ab., Can.	182	55.20 N	119.33 W
Hythe, Eng., U.K.	42	51.05 N	1.05 E
Hythe, Eng., U.K.	42	50.51 N	1.24 W
Hythe End	260	51.27 N	0.32 W
Hyūga	92	32.25 N	131.38 E
Hyūga-nada ⊤[2]	92	32.00 N	131.35 E
Hyvinge → Hyvinkää	26	60.38 N	24.52 E
Hyvinkää	26	60.38 N	24.52 E
I			
Iacanga	255	21.54 S	49.01 W
Iaciara	255	14.09 S	46.40 W
Iaco (Yaco) ≃	248	9.03 S	68.34 W
Iaçu	255	12.45 S	40.13 W
Iaeger	192	37.27 N	81.48 W
Iago	222	29.17 N	95.58 W
Iakora	157b	23.06 S	46.40 E
Ialomiţa □[6]	38	44.40 N	27.20 E
Ialomiţa ≃	38	44.42 N	27.51 E
Ialomiţei, Balta ≚	38	44.30 N	28.00 E
Iamonia, Lake ⊜	192	30.38 N	84.14 W
Ianaivo ≃	157b	22.56 S	46.54 E
Ianakafy	157b	23.21 S	45.28 E
Ianga	146	9.07 N	18.11 E
Iango	152	9.11 S	17.39 E
Iano, Monte ∧	267a	41.46 N	12.44 E
Iapó ≃	252	24.30 S	50.24 W
Iapu	255	19.26 S	42.13 W
Iaşi	38	47.10 N	27.35 E
Iaşi □[6]	38	47.15 N	27.15 E
Iato	70	37.58 N	13.07 E
Iatt, Lake ⊜[1]	194	31.35 N	92.40 W
Iauaretê	246	0.36 N	69.12 W
Iazu	38	44.44 N	27.25 E
Ib ≃	120	21.34 N	83.48 E
Iba, Pil.	116	15.20 N	119.58 E
Iba, Zaïre	152	3.05 S	17.38 E
'Ibādah, Wādī V	142	27.49 N	30.54 E
Ibadan	150	7.17 N	3.30 E
Ibagué	246	4.27 N	75.14 W
Ibaiti	255	23.50 S	50.10 W
Ibajay	116	11.49 N	122.10 E
Ibajay ≃	116	11.49 N	122.10 E
Ibaka	152	4.16 S	23.12 E
Ibambi	154	2.22 N	27.37 E
Ibanda	154	0.08 S	30.29 E
Ibăneşti	38	48.04 N	26.22 E
Ibans, Laguna de ⊂	236	15.53 N	84.52 W
Ibanshe	152	4.58 S	21.30 E
Ibapah Peak ∧	200	39.50 N	113.55 W
Ibar ≃	38	43.44 N	20.45 E
Ibara	96	34.36 N	133.28 E
Ibaraki, Nihon	94	36.17 N	140.26 E
Ibaraki, Nihon	96	34.49 N	135.34 E
Ibaraki □[5]	94	36.30 N	140.30 E
Ibarra	246	0.21 N	78.07 W
Ibarreta	252	25.13 S	59.51 W
Ibb	144	14.01 N	44.10 E
Ibba	154	4.48 N	29.06 E
Ibba ≃	140	7.09 N	28.41 E
Ibbenbüren	52	52.16 N	7.43 E
Ibeke Gembo	152	1.24 S	18.51 E
Ibembo	152	2.38 N	23.37 E
Ibenga ≃	152	2.20 N	18.08 E
Iberá, Esteros del ≚	252	28.05 S	57.05 W
Iberia, Mo., U.S.	194	38.05 N	92.17 W
Iberia, Oh., U.S.	214	40.40 N	82.51 W
Ibérica, Península ›[1]	10	40.00 N	5.00 W
Ibérico, Sistema ⋏	34	41.00 N	2.30 W
Ibertioga	256	21.25 S	43.58 W
Iberville	206	45.18 N	73.14 W
Iberville □[6]	206	45.15 N	73.10 W
Iberville, Mont d' (Mount Caubvick) ∧	176	58.53 N	63.43 W
Ibese	273a	6.33 N	3.29 E
Ibeto	150	10.29 N	5.09 E
Ibi	150	8.12 N	9.45 E
Ibi ≃	94	35.03 N	136.42 E
Ibiá	255	19.29 S	46.32 W
Ibiapina	250	3.55 S	40.54 W
Ibicaraí	255	14.51 S	39.36 W
Ibicuí	255	14.51 S	39.59 W
Ibicuí ≃	252	29.25 S	56.47 W
Ibicuicito, Arroyo ≃	258	33.49 S	58.49 W
Ibicuy	258	33.44 S	59.10 W
Ibicuy ≃[1]	258	33.48 S	59.10 W
Ibigawa	94	35.29 N	136.34 E
Ibipira	250	6.31 S	44.38 W
Ibiquera	255	12.38 S	40.57 W
Ibiraci	255	20.28 S	47.08 W
Ibiraçu	255	19.50 S	40.22 W
Ibirama	252	27.04 S	49.31 W
Ibirapuã	255	17.39 S	40.07 W
Ibirapuera ◆[8]	287b	23.37 S	46.40 W
Ibirapuera, Parque ♦	287b	23.35 S	46.39 W
Ibirapuitã ≃	252	29.22 S	55.57 W
Ibirataia	255	14.04 S	39.38 W
Ibiri	154	4.56 S	32.33 E
Ibirubá	252	28.38 S	53.06 W
Ibitiara	255	12.39 S	42.13 W
Ibitinga	255	21.45 S	48.49 W
Ibitiúra De Minas	256	22.04 S	46.26 W
Ibiúna	256	23.39 S	47.13 W
Ibiza → Eivissa I	34	39.00 N	1.25 E
Iblei, Monti ⋏	70	37.10 N	14.50 E
Ibnahs	142	30.34 N	31.07 E
Ibn Hāni', Ra's ›	130	35.35 N	35.43 E
Ibn Sarrār, Bi'r ⊤[4]	144	19.30 N	42.41 E
Ibo	154	12.20 S	40.35 E
Ibo ≃	96	34.46 N	134.35 E
Ibondo	154	2.38 S	32.40 E
Ibonma	164	3.28 S	133.28 E
Ibor ≃	34	39.49 N	5.33 W
Ibotirama	255	12.11 S	43.13 W
Iboundji, Mont ∧	152	1.08 S	11.48 E
Ibrah, Wādī V	140	10.36 N	24.58 E
Ibrāhīmīyah, Qārah al- ≊	142	29.10 N	31.10 E
Ibresi	80	55.18 N	47.03 E
'Ibrī	128	23.14 N	56.30 E
İbriktepe	130	41.00 N	26.30 E
Ibshān	142	31.10 N	31.10 E
Ibshawāy	142	29.22 N	30.41 E
Ibstock	42	52.42 N	1.23 W
Ibta'	132	32.47 N	36.09 E
Ibu	174m	26.45 N	128.19 E
Ibuki	94	35.24 N	136.23 E
Ibuki-jima I	96	34.08 N	133.32 E
Ibuki-sanchi ⋏	94	35.35 N	136.18 E
Ibuki-yama ∧	94	35.25 N	136.24 E
Iburg	52	52.09 N	8.02 E
Ibusuki	92	31.16 N	130.39 E
Ibwe Munyama	154	16.09 S	28.34 E
Ibychen, gora ∧	88	51.36 N	109.45 E
Ica	248	14.04 S	75.42 W
Ica □[5]	248	14.20 S	75.30 W
Ičа ≃, Lat.	76	56.52 N	26.59 E
Ica ≃, Perú	248	14.54 S	75.34 W
Iča ≃, Ross.	86	55.30 N	77.13 E
Içá (Putumayo) ≃, S.A.	246	3.07 S	67.58 W
Icabarú ≃	246	4.45 N	62.15 W
Icacos Point ›	241r	10.03 N	61.56 W
Icadambanauan Island I	116	10.49 N	119.38 E
Icamaquã ≃	252	28.34 S	56.00 W
Icamole	196	25.55 N	100.43 W
Içana	246	0.21 N	67.19 W
Içana (Isana) ≃	246	0.26 N	67.19 W
Icaño, Arg.	252	28.54 S	65.19 W
Icaño, Arg.	252	28.41 S	62.54 W
Icatu	250	2.46 S	44.04 W
Iceberg Pass)(	200	40.25 N	105.45 W
Ice House Reservoir ⊜[1]	226	38.49 N	120.23 W
İçel (Mersin)	130	36.48 N	34.38 E
İçel □[4]	130	36.45 N	34.00 E
Iceland (Ísland) □[1], Europe	22	65.00 N	18.00 W
Iceland (Ísland) □[1], Europe	24a	65.00 N	18.00 W
Iceland Basin ✦[1]	10	59.00 N	23.00 W
Icém	255	20.21 S	49.12 W
Ice Mountain ∧	182	54.25 N	121.08 W
Ičera	88	58.32 N	109.47 E
Ichaikaronji	122	16.42 N	74.28 E
Ichāmati ≃, Asia	126	22.35 N	88.57 E
Ichāmati ≃, Bngl.	126	24.00 N	89.15 E
Ichang → Yichang	102	30.42 N	111.17 E
Ichawaynochaway Creek ≃	192	31.10 N	84.28 W
Ich Bajan Ajrag uul ∧	88	47.55 N	95.02 E
Ichbulag	102	45.21 N	113.10 E
Ich Buural uul ∧	88	48.00 N	94.30 E
Ichchāpuram	122	19.07 N	84.42 E
Ichdžargalan	102	45.31 N	108.48 E
Ichenhausen	58	48.22 N	10.18 E
Ichenheim	58	48.26 N	7.49 E
Ichhapur	126	22.50 N	88.24 E
Ichhāwar	124	23.01 N	77.01 E
Ichi ≃	96	34.46 N	134.41 E
Ichiba	96	34.05 N	134.17 E
Ichihara	94	35.31 N	140.05 E
Ichikai	94	36.32 N	140.06 E
Ichikawa, Nihon	94	35.44 N	139.55 E
Ichikawa, Nihon	96	34.59 N	134.46 E
Ichikawa-daimon	94	35.34 N	138.30 E
Ichilo ≃	248	15.57 S	64.42 W
Ichinohe	92	40.13 N	141.17 E
Ichinomiya, Nihon	94	35.18 N	136.48 E
Ichinomiya, Nihon	94	34.41 N	137.26 E
Ichinomiya, Nihon	94	35.22 N	140.22 E
Ichinomiya, Nihon	94	35.39 N	138.41 E
Ichinomiya, Nihon	96	35.07 N	134.34 E
Ichinomiya, Nihon	96	34.28 N	134.51 E
Ichinomiya, Nihon	96	32.57 N	131.07 E
Ichinomoto	270	34.37 N	135.50 E
Ichinose	270	34.53 N	135.10 E
Ichinoseki	92	38.55 N	141.08 E
Ichino-tani ⊥	96	34.39 N	135.07 E
Ichiu	96	33.57 N	134.04 E
Ichkeul, Lac ⊜	36	37.10 N	9.40 E
Ichoa ≃	248	15.44 S	65.15 W
Ichoca	248	17.12 S	67.17 W
Ich'on, C.M.I.K.	98	38.30 N	126.50 E
Ich'ŏn, Taehan	98	37.17 N	127.27 E
Ich Ovoo uul ∧	90	44.40 N	95.08 E
Ichtamir	88	47.30 N	100.52 E
Ichtegem	50	51.06 N	3.00 E
Ichtershausen	54	50.52 N	10.58 E
Ich'un → Yichun	90	47.42 N	128.55 E
Ich Uul, Mong.	88	48.33 N	98.40 E
Ich Uul, Mong.	88	49.27 N	101.27 E
Icicle Creek ≃	224	47.34 N	120.40 W
Ičinskaja Sopka, vulkan ∧[1]	74	55.42 N	157.35 E
Ička, gora ∧[2]	80	51.13 N	50.15 E
Ickenham ◆[8]	260	51.34 N	0.27 W
Ickern	263	51.36 N	7.21 E
Ickesburg	208	40.27 N	77.21 W
Icking	64	47.57 N	11.25 E
İçme	130	38.37 N	39.34 E
Ičn'a	78	50.52 N	32.24 E
Icó	250	6.24 S	38.51 W
Icoca	152	6.11 S	16.19 E
Iconha	255	20.48 S	40.48 W
Icy Bay ⊂	180	60.00 N	141.15 W
Icy Cape ›	180	70.20 N	161.52 W
Icy Strait ⊔	180	58.18 N	135.30 W
Ida	216	41.54 N	83.34 W
Ida, Mount ∧, Austl.	162	29.14 S	120.25 E
Ida, Mount ∧, Jam.	241q	17.58 N	77.43 W
Idabel	194	33.53 N	94.49 W
Idaga Hamus	144	14.12 N	39.48 E
Ida Grove	198	42.20 N	95.28 W
Idah	150	7.07 N	6.43 E
Idaho □[3], U.S.	178	45.00 N	115.00 W
Idaho □[3], U.S.	202	45.00 N	115.00 W
Idaho City	202	43.49 N	115.50 W
Idaho Falls	202	43.28 N	112.02 W
Idaho National Engineering Laboratory ⋓[3]	202	43.40 N	112.45 W
Idaho Springs	200	39.44 N	105.00 W
Idalou	196	33.39 N	101.40 W
Idanha-a-Nova	34	39.55 N	7.14 W
Idāppādi	122	11.35 N	77.51 E
Idar	120	23.50 N	73.00 E
Idarkopf ∧	56	49.51 N	7.16 E
Idar-Oberstein	56	49.42 N	7.19 E
Idarwald ◆[3]	56	49.49 N	7.12 E
Idaville, In., U.S.	216	40.45 N	86.38 W
Idaville, Or., U.S.	224	45.30 N	123.51 W
Iddo ◆[8]	273a	6.28 N	3.23 E
Ide	96	34.47 N	135.49 E
Idel'	24	64.08 N	34.14 E
Idelès	148	23.58 N	5.53 E
Idemba	152	2.38 S	11.38 E
Iden	54	52.46 N	11.55 E
Ider	88	48.13 N	97.23 E
Iderijn ≃	88	49.16 N	100.41 E
Idermeg	88	47.40 N	111.05 E
Idfīnā	142	31.18 N	30.31 E
Idfū	140	24.58 N	32.52 E
Ídhi Óros ∧	38	35.18 N	24.43 E
Ídhra	38	37.20 N	23.29 E
Ídhra I	38	37.20 N	23.32 E
Idi	114	4.57 N	97.46 E
Idice ≃	64	44.35 N	11.49 E
Idi-cut	114	4.59 N	97.42 E
Ididole	144	5.53 N	43.36 E
Idifina Barrage ◆[6]	142	31.17 N	30.31 E
İdil	130	37.21 N	41.54 E
Idimu	273a	6.35 N	3.17 E
Idio	116	11.37 N	122.06 E
Idiofa	152	5.02 S	19.36 E
Iditarod ≃	180	63.02 N	158.58 W
Idjwi, Île I	154	2.09 S	29.04 E
Idkerberget	40	60.23 N	15.14 E
Idkū	142	31.18 N	30.18 E
Idkū, Buḥayrat ⊜	142	31.16 N	30.17 E
Idle ≃	44	53.27 N	0.49 W
Idle Hill	260	51.15 N	0.08 E
Idlib	130	35.55 N	36.38 E
Idlib □[8]	130	35.50 N	36.40 E
Idmū	142	28.09 N	30.41 E
Idnah	132	31.34 N	34.59 E
Idodi	154	7.47 S	35.11 E
Idomogu	273a	6.43 N	3.30 E
Idracowra	162	25.00 S	133.47 E
Idre	26	61.52 N	12.43 E
Idria	226	36.25 N	120.40 W
Idrica	76	56.21 N	28.53 E
Idrigill Point ›	46	57.20 N	6.35 W
Idrija	36	46.00 N	14.01 E
Idrijca ≃	64	46.09 N	13.45 E
Idrinskoje	86	54.21 N	92.07 E
Idro	64	45.44 N	10.29 E
Idro, Lago d' ⊜	64	45.47 N	10.30 E
Idroscalo ⊜	266b	45.28 N	9.18 E
Idstedt	41	54.35 N	9.31 E
Idstein	56	50.13 N	8.16 E
Idutywa	158	32.02 S	28.16 E
Idyllwild	204	33.45 N	116.43 W
Idylside	216	41.31 N	88.07 W
Idylwood	284c	38.54 N	77.12 W
Idževan	84	40.53 N	45.07 E
Ie	174m	26.42 N	127.48 E
Iecava	76	56.36 N	24.12 E
Iecava ≃	76	56.41 N	23.42 E
Ielsi	66	41.30 N	14.48 E
Ienne	66	41.53 N	13.10 E
Iepê	255	22.40 S	51.05 W
Ieper (Ypres)	50	50.51 N	2.53 E
Ierápetra	38	35.00 N	25.45 E
Ierisós	38	40.24 N	23.52 E
Ierzu	71	39.47 N	9.31 E
Ieshima	96	34.40 N	134.32 E
Ie-shima I	174m	26.43 N	127.47 E
Ieshima-shotō II	96	34.40 N	134.32 E
Iesolo	64	45.32 N	12.38 E
Ie-suidō ⊔	174m	26.42 N	127.51 E
If, Château d' ⊥	62	43.17 N	5.19 E
Ifakara	154	8.08 S	36.41 E
Ifako	273a	6.39 N	3.20 E
Ifalik I[1]	108	7.15 N	144.27 E
Ifanadiana	157b	21.19 S	47.39 E
Ife	150	7.30 N	4.30 E
Iferouâne	150	19.04 N	8.24 E
Iferten → Yverdon	58	46.47 N	6.39 E
Iffezheim	56	48.49 N	8.08 E
Ifni □[9]	148	29.15 N	10.08 W
Ifôghas, Adrar des ⋏	150	20.00 N	2.00 E
Ifon	150	6.58 N	5.45 E
Ifould Lake ⊜	162	30.53 S	132.09 E
Ifrane	148	33.32 N	5.06 W
Ifrane □[4]	148	33.15 N	5.05 W
Ifta	56	51.04 N	10.11 E
Ifugao □[4]	116	16.45 N	121.15 E
Iga	94	34.49 N	136.13 E
Iga ≃	94	34.45 N	136.01 E
Igal	30	46.31 N	17.55 E
Igalula, Tan.	154	5.14 S	33.00 E
Igalula, Tan.	154	5.38 S	32.38 E
Igan	112	2.49 N	111.43 E
Igan ≃	112	2.51 N	111.39 E
Iganga	154	0.37 N	33.29 E
Iganmu ◆[8]	273a	6.29 N	3.22 E
Iganna	150	7.59 N	3.14 E
Igaporã	255	13.46 S	42.43 W
Igara	250	10.24 S	40.07 W
Igaraí	256	21.25 S	46.49 W
Igara Paraná ≃	246	2.09 S	71.47 W
Igarapé-Açu	250	1.07 S	47.37 W
Igarapé Grande	250	4.41 S	44.58 W
Igarapé-Miri	250	1.59 S	48.58 W
Igaratá	256	23.12 S	46.07 W
Igarka	74	67.28 N	86.35 E
Igarra	150	7.18 N	6.07 E
Igarukiro	154	3.08 S	33.31 E
Igatpuri	122	19.42 N	73.33 E
Igaun	273a	6.42 N	3.23 E
Igawa	154	8.35 S	34.28 E
Igbaja	150	8.23 N	4.52 E
Igbobi	273a	6.32 N	3.22 E
Igboho	150	8.51 N	3.45 E
Igbologun	273a	6.25 N	3.20 E
Igbo-Ora	150	7.26 N	3.17 E
Igbor	150	7.27 N	8.34 E
Igdir, Īrān	84	39.20 N	47.30 E
Iğdır, Tür.	84	39.55 N	44.02 E
Iğdır, Tür.	130	40.16 N	35.38 E
Iğdır, Tür.	130	41.14 N	33.07 E
Igdy	128	39.54 N	56.54 E
Igea Marina	66	44.08 N	12.29 E
Igel	56	49.42 N	6.32 E
Igelfors	40	58.51 N	15.41 E
Igelsberg	58	48.32 N	8.26 E
Igel'vejem ≃	180	65.40 N	172.50 W
Igersheim	56	49.29 N	9.49 E
Iggensbach	60	48.44 N	13.08 E
Iggesund	26	61.38 N	17.04 E
Igharghar, Oued V, Afr.	148	20.25 N	6.10 E
Igharghar, Oued V, Alg.	148	28.03 N	6.15 E
Ightham	260	51.17 N	0.17 E
Ightham Mote ⊥	260	51.15 N	0.16 E
Igikpak, Mount ∧	180	67.25 N	154.58 W
Igirma	88	56.59 N	103.37 E
Igiugig	180	59.20 N	155.55 W
Iglau → Jihlava	30	49.24 N	15.36 E
Iglesia	252	30.24 S	69.13 W
Iglesias	71	39.19 N	8.32 E
Iglesiente ◆[1]	71	39.18 N	8.40 E
Igli	148	30.25 N	2.12 W
Iglino	86	54.50 N	56.26 E
Igloolik	176	69.24 N	81.49 W
Iglovo	82	55.47 N	36.40 E
Igls	64	47.14 N	11.25 E
Ignacej	78	47.41 N	28.40 E
Ignacio, Ca., U.S.	226	38.05 N	122.32 W
Ignacio, Co., U.S.	200	37.06 N	107.37 W
Ignacio de la Llave	234	18.43 N	95.59 W
Ignacio Zaragoza, Méx.	232	29.35 N	107.30 W
Ignacio Zaragoza, Méx.	234	23.55 N	103.42 W
Ignacio Zaragoza, Méx.	234	23.15 N	98.50 W
Ignalina	76	55.21 N	26.10 E
Ignatjevcy	80	57.32 N	51.39 E
Ignatovka	80	53.57 N	47.38 E
Ignatovo	82	56.10 N	37.32 E
İğneada	130	41.52 N	27.58 E
İğneada Burnu ›	130	41.54 N	28.03 E
Igney	58	48.17 N	6.24 E
Ignon ≃	58	47.31 N	5.10 E
Igny	261	48.45 N	2.14 E
Igodovo	80	58.01 N	42.21 E
Igombe ≃	154	4.38 S	31.40 E
Igoumenítsa	38	39.30 N	20.16 E
Igra	80	57.33 N	53.04 E
Igreja Nova	250	10.07 S	36.39 W
Iguaçu ≃, Bra.	256	22.45 S	43.14 W
Iguaçu ≃, S.A.	252	25.36 S	54.36 W
Iguaçu, Cataratas do (Iguassu Falls) ∟	252	25.41 S	54.26 W
Iguaí	255	14.45 S	40.04 W
Iguala	234	18.21 N	99.32 W
Igualada	34	41.35 N	1.38 E
Iguana ≃	246	7.54 N	65.46 W
Iguape	252	24.43 S	47.33 W
Iguará ≃	250	3.28 S	43.55 W
Iguassu Falls → Iguaçu, Cataratas 99do ∟	252	25.41 S	54.26 W
Iguatemi	255	23.40 S	54.34 W
Iguatemi ≃	255	23.55 S	54.10 W
Iguatu	250	6.22 S	39.18 W
Iguazú, Parque Nacional ♦	252	25.35 S	54.20 W
Iguéla	152	1.55 S	9.19 E
Iguéla, Lagune ⊂	152	1.55 S	9.25 E
Iguetti, Sebkhet ≚	148	25.05 N	9.50 W
Iguîdi, 'Erg ⩡[8]	148	26.35 N	5.40 W
Iguig	116	17.45 N	121.44 E
Igumale	150	6.49 N	7.59 E
Igumnovo	82	55.37 N	38.18 E
Igvak, Cape ›	180	57.26 N	156.00 W
Igžej	88	53.59 N	103.10 E
Ihavandiffulu Atoll I[1]	122	7.00 N	72.55 E
Iheya-shima I	93b	27.04 N	127.58 E
Ihiala	150	5.51 N	6.51 E
Ihirène, Oued V	148	20.25 N	4.35 E
Ihle ≃	54	52.17 N	11.52 E
Ihlienworth	52	53.44 N	8.55 E
Ihlow	52	53.25 N	7.27 E
Ihmert	56	51.20 N	7.44 E
Ihnāsiyat al-Madīnah	142	29.05 N	30.56 E
Ihorombe	157b	23.00 S	47.33 E
Ihosy	157b	22.24 S	46.08 E
Ihosy ≃	157b	21.44 S	45.53 E
Ihotry, Lac ⊜	157b	21.56 S	43.41 E
Ihringen	58	48.02 N	7.39 E
Ihrlerstein	60	48.56 N	11.52 E
İhsangazi	130	41.11 N	33.33 E
Ih Tal	89	43.13 N	122.15 E
Ihtiman	38	42.26 N	23.49 E
Ihu	164	7.55 S	145.25 E
Ihugh	150	7.02 N	9.00 E
Ihwah	142	29.03 N	31.00 E
Iida	94	35.31 N	137.50 E
Iidaan	144	6.06 N	48.59 E
Iijima	94	35.40 N	137.56 E
Iijoki ≃	24	65.20 N	25.17 E
Iiktu, gora ∧	86	49.51 N	87.40 E
Iinan	94	34.27 N	136.24 E
Iinashi ≃	96	35.27 N	133.13 E
Iioka	94	35.42 N	140.43 E
Iisaku	76	59.06 N	27.19 E
Iisalmi	26	63.34 N	27.11 E
Iisvesi	26	62.40 N	27.02 E
Iitaka	94	34.26 N	136.21 E
Iittala	26	61.04 N	24.10 E
Iiyama	94	36.51 N	138.22 E
Iizuka	96	33.38 N	130.41 E
Ij ≃	88	52.34 N	96.10 E
Ija ≃	88	55.05 N	101.05 E
Ijâfene ◆[2]	134	20.30 N	8.00 W
Ijaiye	273a	6.40 N	3.18 E
Ijaji	144	8.59 N	37.13 E
Ijara	154	1.36 S	40.31 E
Ijebu-Igbo	150	6.56 N	4.01 E
Ijebu-Ode	150	6.50 N	3.56 E
Ijesa-Tedo	273a	6.30 N	3.19 E
Ijin	98	42.05 N	130.08 E
Ijira	94	35.31 N	136.44 E
IJmuiden	52	52.27 N	4.36 E
IJssel ≃	52	52.35 N	5.50 E
IJsselmeer (Zuiderzee) ⊤[2]	52	52.45 N	5.25 E
IJsselmuiden	52	52.34 N	5.56 E
IJsselstein	52	52.02 N	5.03 E
Ijuí	252	28.23 S	53.55 W
Ijuí ≃	252	27.58 S	55.20 W
Iju Junction	273a	6.40 N	3.19 E
Ijuw	174b	0.30 S	166.57 E
Iju Water Works ⋓[3]	273a	6.40 N	3.20 E
IJzendijke	52	51.19 N	3.38 E
IJzer (Yser) ≃	50	51.09 N	2.43 E
Ik ≃	80	55.55 N	52.36 E
Ika	88	59.18 N	106.12 E
Ikaalinen	26	61.46 N	23.03 E
Ikaho	94	36.30 N	138.55 E
Ikalamavony	157b	21.09 S	46.35 E
Ikali	152	2.02 S	21.02 E
Ikalou	152	4.03 S	11.48 E
Ikamatua	172	42.16 S	171.41 E
Ikamba	273b	4.22 S	15.16 E
Ikang	150	4.50 N	8.32 E
Ikara	150	11.12 N	8.15 E
Ikare	150	7.32 N	5.45 E
Ikaría I	38	37.41 N	26.20 E
Ikari-dam ◆[6]	94	36.52 N	139.42 E
Ikari-ko ⊜	94	36.56 N	139.41 E
Ikaruga	96	34.36 N	135.44 E
Ikast	41	56.08 N	9.10 E
Ikatan	180	54.45 N	163.19 W
Ikatskij chrebet ⋏	88	54.00 N	111.00 E
Ikawa	94	35.13 N	138.15 E
Ikawa-dam ◆[6]	94	35.12 N	138.13 E
Ikawhenua Range ⋏	172	38.20 S	176.56 E
Ikazaki	96	33.32 N	132.39 E
Ikeda, Nihon	92a	42.55 N	143.27 E
Ikeda, Nihon	94	35.53 N	136.21 E
Ikeda, Nihon	94	35.26 N	136.34 E
Ikeda, Nihon	94	36.25 N	137.53 E
Ikeda, Nihon	96	34.49 N	135.25 E
Ikeda, Nihon	96	34.01 N	133.48 E
Ikegawa	96	33.36 N	133.11 E
Ikej	88	54.12 N	100.04 E
Ikeja	150	6.36 N	3.21 E
Ikeja □[8]	273a	6.30 N	3.25 E
Ikela	152	1.11 S	23.16 E
Ikélemba	152	1.14 N	16.31 E
Ikelemba ≃	152	0.07 N	18.17 E
Ikema-jima I	175d	24.56 N	125.16 E
Ikerre	150	7.31 N	5.14 E
Ike-shima I	174m	26.23 N	128.00 E
Ikeura	270	34.30 N	135.25 E
Iki I	92	33.47 N	129.43 E
Iki-Burul	80	45.49 N	44.39 E
Ikimba, Lake ⊜	154	1.28 S	31.30 E
Īkinjī Maryūt	142	31.00 N	29.45 E
Ikire	150	7.23 N	4.12 E
Ikirun	150	7.55 N	4.41 E
İkizce	130	39.36 N	32.40 E
İkizdere, Tür.	84	40.47 N	40.33 E
İkizdere, Tür.	130	40.47 N	40.33 E
Iko	152	0.35 S	16.01 E
Ikole	150	7.49 N	5.30 E
Ikolik, Cape ›	180	57.17 N	154.48 W
Ikom	150	5.58 N	8.42 E
Ikoma, Nihon	96	34.41 N	135.42 E
Ikoma, Tan.	154	2.04 S	34.37 E
Ikoma-sanchi ⋏	270	34.40 N	135.40 E
Ikoma-tunnel ◆[5]	270	34.41 N	135.41 E
Ikoma-yama ∧	270	34.40 N	135.41 E
Ikon-Chal'	84	44.18 N	41.55 E
Ikopa ≃	157b	17.01 S	46.45 E
Ikorec ≃	78	50.58 N	39.45 E
Ikorodu	150	6.37 N	3.31 E
Ikot Ekpene	150	5.12 N	7.40 E
Ikoy ≃	152	0.53 S	10.36 E
Ikoyi ◆[8]	273a	6.27 N	3.26 E
Ikoyi Island I	273a	6.27 N	3.26 E
Ikoyi Prison ⋓	273a	6.25 N	3.25 E
Ikozi	154	2.32 S	27.37 E
Ikpikpuk ≃	180	70.50 N	154.25 W
Ikra	126	23.42 N	87.07 E
Ikr'anoje	80	46.06 N	47.45 E
Ikrāsh	142	30.45 N	31.30 E
Ikša	82	56.10 N	37.31 E
Iksa ≃	86	57.48 N	82.36 E
Ikti, Cape ›	180	56.00 N	158.30 W
Ikuata	273a	6.25 N	3.22 E
Ikuchi-shima I	96	34.17 N	133.07 E
Ikuji-hana ›	94	36.54 N	137.25 E
Ikuktlitlig Mountain ∧	180	59.16 N	161.27 W
Ikungu	154	1.34 S	33.40 E
Ikuno	96	35.10 N	134.48 E
Ikuno ◆[8]	270	34.39 N	135.34 E
Ikurangi, Mount ∧[2]	174k	21.13 S	159.45 W
Ikusaka	94	36.25 N	137.56 E
Ikusu ≃	273b	4.24 S	15.14 E
Ikuta	268	35.36 N	139.32 E
Ikva ≃, Magy.	61	47.42 N	16.58 E
Ikva ≃, Ukr.	78	50.33 N	25.24 E
Ikwah	142	30.41 N	31.28 E
Ila, Nig.	150	8.01 N	4.55 E
Ila, Zaïre	152	2.53 S	21.05 E
Ilabaya	248	17.25 S	70.31 W
Ilacaon Point ›	116	11.00 N	123.12 E
Ilagala	154	5.12 S	29.50 E
Ilagan	116	17.10 N	121.54 E
Ilagan ≃	116	17.09 N	121.54 E
Ilaiyānkudi	122	9.38 N	78.38 E
Ilaka, Madag.	157b	19.33 S	48.52 E
Ilaka, Madag.	157b	20.20 S	47.09 E
Īlām, Īrān	128	33.38 N	46.26 E
Ilām, Nepāl	124	26.55 N	87.56 E
Īlām □[4]	128	33.15 N	46.45 E
Ilām Bāzār	126	23.38 N	87.32 E

DEUTSCH

Name	Seite	Breite°'	Länge°' E = Ost
Ilam → Sri Lanka □[1]	122	7.00 N	81.00 E
Ilan	100	24.46 N	121.45 E
Ilan ≃	100	24.43 N	121.49 E
Ilanskij	88	56.14 N	96.03 E
Ilanz	58	46.46 N	9.12 E
Ilara	273a	6.42 N	3.27 E
Ilaro	150	6.53 N	3.03 E
Ilasco	219	39.40 N	91.18 W
Ilave	248	16.06 S	69.41 W
Iława	30	53.37 N	19.33 E
Ilawe-Ekiti	150	7.37 N	5.06 E
Ilay	58	46.37 N	5.53 E
Ilbenge	74	62.49 N	124.24 E
Ilberstedt	54	51.48 N	11.40 E
Il Catalano	71	39.53 N	8.17 E
Ilchester, Eng., U.K.	42	51.01 N	2.41 W
Ilchester, Md., U.S.	284b	39.15 N	76.45 W
Ildefonso, Islas II	254	55.44 S	69.26 W
Île-à-la-Crosse	184	55.27 N	107.53 W
Île-à-la-Crosse, Lac ⊜	184	55.40 N	107.45 W
Ilebo (Port-Francqui)	152	4.19 S	20.35 E
Île-Cadieux	275a	45.25 N	74.01 W
Île-de-France □[9]	50	49.00 N	2.20 E
Île-de-Montréal □[6]	206	45.30 N	73.40 W
Île-Jésus □[6]	206	45.35 N	73.45 W
Ilek	80	51.30 N	53.22 E
Ilek ≃	72	51.30 N	53.20 E
Ilen ≃	48	51.33 N	9.19 W
Île-Perrot	206	45.23 N	73.57 W
Ileret	154	4.19 N	36.13 E
Îles, Grand lac des ⊜	206	46.43 N	73.30 W
Îles, Lac des ⊜, P.Q., Can.	206	46.06 N	74.02 W
Îles, Lac des ⊜, Sk., Can.	184	54.26 N	109.25 W
Ilesha	150	7.38 N	4.45 E
Ilesha Ibarida	150	8.56 N	3.25 E
Ilet' ≃	80	55.56 N	48.14 E
Ilevskij Pogost	24	60.41 N	43.46 E
Ileza	24	60.43 N	43.54 E
Ilfeld	54	51.34 N	10.47 E
Ilford, Austl.	170	32.58 S	149.51 E
Ilford, Mb., Can.	184	56.04 N	95.35 W
Ilford ◆[8]	260	51.33 N	0.05 E
Ilfov □[6]	38	44.30 N	26.15 E
Ilfracombe, Austl.	166	23.30 S	144.30 E
Ilfracombe, Eng., U.K.	42	51.13 N	4.08 W
Il Fuorn	58	46.40 N	10.12 E
Ilga ≃	88	55.00 N	105.04 E
Ilgaz	130	40.56 N	33.38 E
Ilgaz Dağları ⋏	130	41.00 N	33.35 E
Ilgın	130	38.17 N	31.55 E
Ilha ◆[8]	256	23.00 S	43.33 W
Ilhabela	256	23.47 S	45.21 W
Ilha das Flores	250	10.27 S	36.33 W
Ilha Grande, Baía da ⊂	256	23.09 S	44.30 W
Ilhas, Cachoeira das ∟	250	1.03 S	57.33 W
Ilha Solteira, Represa de ⊜[1]	255	20.20 S	51.20 W
Ílhavo	34	40.36 N	8.40 W
Ilhea Point ›	156	23.25 S	14.27 E
Ilhéos → Ilhéus	255	14.49 S	39.02 W
Ilhéus	255	14.49 S	39.02 W
Ili ≃	86	45.24 N	74.02 E
Ilia	38	45.56 N	22.39 E
Iliamna	180	59.45 N	154.54 W
Iliamna Lake ⊜	180	59.30 N	155.00 W
Ilian, Mount ∧	116	10.26 N	119.33 E
Iliatenco	234	16.58 N	98.40 W
İliç	130	39.28 N	38.34 E
Ilıca, Tür.	130	39.52 N	27.46 E
Ilıca, Tür.	130	39.57 N	41.07 E
Ilicínia	255	20.56 S	45.50 W
Iliff	198	40.45 N	103.03 W
Iliff, Lake ⊜	276	41.02 N	74.43 W
Iligan	116	8.14 N	124.14 E
Iligan Bay ⊂	116	8.25 N	124.05 E
Ilijan	116	13.38 N	121.04 E
Ilijsk	85	43.53 N	77.10 E
Ilim ≃	88	57.38 N	102.34 E
Ilimsk	88	56.46 N	103.52 E
Ilin	116	12.15 N	121.02 E
Ilinge	158	31.59 S	27.02 E
Ilin Island I	116	12.14 N	121.05 E
Ilinka	82	54.04 N	38.12 E
Ilinza ∧	246	0.40 S	78.42 W
Ilion	210	43.00 N	75.02 W
Ilio Point ›	229a	21.13 N	157.15 W
Ilioúpolis	267c	37.56 N	23.45 E
Ilir	88	55.13 N	100.40 E
Ilirska Bistrica	36	45.34 N	14.15 E
Ilisós ≃	267c	37.57 N	23.41 E
Ilizi	148	26.29 N	8.28 E
Ilja	76	54.25 N	27.18 E
Iljak	86	60.11 N	77.59 E
Iljič	85	40.50 N	68.27 E
Iljičovsk	78	46.18 N	30.39 E
Iljincy	78	49.07 N	29.12 E
Iljinka	80	48.32 N	41.05 E
Iljino	76	55.57 N	31.40 E
Iljinskij, Ross.	24	61.02 N	32.41 E
Iljinskij, Ross.	86	58.35 N	55.41 E
Iljinskij, Ross.	88	52.05 N	114.10 E
Iljinskij, Ross.	89	47.58 N	142.12 E
Iljinskij, Ross.	265b	55.37 N	38.06 E
Iljinskij Pogost	82	55.28 N	38.54 E
Iljinskoje, Ross.	76	56.58 N	37.11 E
Iljinskoje, Ross.	76	58.47 N	44.36 E
Iljinskoje, Ross.	76	53.14 N	35.26 E
Iljinskoje, Ross.	76	57.19 N	38.32 E
Iljinskoje, Ross.	80	56.29 N	52.49 E
Iljinskoje, Ross.	82	54.59 N	36.11 E
Iljinskoje, Ross.	82	56.34 N	35.57 E
Iljinskoje, Ross.	265b	55.46 N	37.15 E
Iljinskoje-Chovanskoje	80	56.58 N	39.46 E
Iljinsko-Podomskoje	24	61.08 N	47.56 E
Iljinsko-Zaborskoje	80	57.16 N	44.23 E
Iljiny gory ⋏[2]	76	56.34 N	34.12 E
Il'ka	88	51.43 N	108.32 E
Ilkal	122	15.58 N	76.08 E
Ilkeston	42	52.59 N	1.18 W
Il'kino	80	55.13 N	41.36 E
Ilkley	44	53.55 N	1.50 W
Ill ≃, Fr.	58	48.40 N	7.53 E
Ill ≃, Öst.	58	47.17 N	9.33 E
Illabot Creek ≃	224	48.29 N	121.30 W
Illampu, Nevado ∧	248	15.50 S	68.34 W
Illana Bay ⊂	116	7.25 N	123.45 E
Illapel	252	31.38 S	71.10 W
Illarionovo	78	48.25 N	35.16 E
Illasi	64	45.28 N	11.10 E
Illawarra, Lake ⊂	170	34.32 S	150.50 E
Illbillee, Mount ∧	162	27.02 S	132.30 E
Ille-et-Vilaine □[5]	32	48.10 N	1.30 W
Illéla	150	14.28 N	5.15 E
Iller ≃	58	48.23 N	9.58 E
Illertissen	58	48.13 N	10.06 E
Illescas, Esp.	34	40.07 N	3.50 W
Illescas, Méx.	234	23.13 N	102.07 W
Illfurth	58	47.40 N	7.16 E
Illhaeusern	58	48.11 N	7.26 E
Illi, Ba ≃	146	10.44 N	15.21 E
Illiers	50	48.18 N	1.15 E
Illimani, Nevado ∧	248	16.50 S	67.54 W
Illimo	248	6.28 S	79.51 W
Illingen	56	48.57 N	8.55 E
Illingworth	262	53.45 N	1.54 W
Illinois □[3], U.S.	178	40.00 N	89.00 W
Illinois □[3], U.S.	194	40.00 N	89.00 W
Illinois ≃, U.S.	194	35.30 N	95.06 W
Illinois ≃, Co., U.S.	200	40.45 N	106.18 W
Illinois ≃, Il., U.S.	194	38.58 N	90.27 W
Illinois ≃, Or., U.S.	202	42.33 N	124.03 W
Illinois and Michigan Canal ≊	278	41.32 N	88.05 W

Symbols in the index entries represent the broad categories identified in the key at the right. Symbols with superior numbers (⋏[1]) identify subcategories (see complete key on page *I · 1*).

Symbole im Register stellen die rechts im Schlüssel erklärten Kategorien dar. Symbole mit hochgestellten Ziffern (⋏[1]) bezeichnen Unterabteilungen einer Kategorie (vgl. vollständiger Schlüssel auf Seite *I · 1*).

Los símbolos incluídos en el texto del índice representan las grandes categorías identificadas con la clave a la derecha. Los símbolos con numeros en su parte superior (⋏[1]) identifican las subcategorías (véase la clave completa en la página *I · 1*).

Les symboles de l'index représentent les catégories indiquées dans la légende à droite. Les symboles suivis d'un indice (⋏[1]) représentent des sous-catégories (voir légende complète à la page *I · 1*).

Os símbolos incluídos no texto do índice representam as grandes categorias identificadas com a chave à direita. Os símbolos com números em sua parte superior (⋏[1]) identificam as subcategorias (veja-se a chave completa à página *I · 1*).

Symbol	English	Deutsch	Español	Français	Português
∧	Mountain	Berg	Montaña	Montagne	Montanha
⋏	Mountains	Gebirge	Montañas	Montagnes	Montanhas
)(	Pass	Paß	Paso	Col	Passo
V	Valley, Canyon	Tal, Cañon	Valle, Cañón	Vallée, Canyon	Vale, Canhão
≚	Plain	Ebene	Llano	Plaine	Planície
›	Cape	Kap	Cabo	Cap	Cabo
I	Island	Insel	Isla	Île	Ilha
II	Islands	Inseln	Islas	Îles	Ilhas
⩡	Other Topographic Features	Andere Topographische Objekte	Otros Elementos Topográficos	Autres données topographiques	Outros acidentes topográficos

ESPAÑOL — Nombre · Página · Lat.°′ · Long.°′ W = Oeste
FRANÇAIS — Nom · Page · Lat.°′ · Long.°′ W = Ouest
PORTUGUÊS — Nome · Página · Lat.°′ · Long.°′ W = Oeste

Illinois at Chicago, University of ⊍2 278 41.52 N 87.39 W
Illinois Beach State Park ♦ 216 42.26 N 87.48 W
Illinois Institute of Technology ⊍2 278 41.50 N 87.38 W
Illinois Peak ʌ 202 47.02 N 115.04 W
Illiopolis 219 39.51 N 89.14 W
Illkirch-Graffenstaden 58 48.32 N 7.43 E
Illminster 42 50.56 N 2.55 W
Illo 150 11.33 N 3.42 E
Illovo, S. Afr. 158 30.05 S 30.50 E
Illovo, S. Afr. 273d 26.08 S 28.03 E
Illzach 58 47.47 N 7.20 E
Ilm ≃, Dtsch. 54 51.07 N 11.40 E
Ilm ≃, Dtsch. 60 48.49 N 11.45 E
Ilmajoki 26 62.44 N 22.34 E
Il'men', ozero ⊜ 76 58.17 N 31.20 E
Ilmenau 54 50.41 N 10.55 E
Ilmenau ≃ 54 53.23 N 10.10 E
Il'menskij zapovednik ♦ 86 55.16 N 60.17 E
Il'mino 80 53.47 N 45.40 E
Ilo 248 17.38 S 71.20 W
Ilobasco 236 13.51 N 88.51 W
Ilobu 150 7.51 N 4.30 E
Iloc Island I 116 11.18 N 119.41 E
Ilocos Norte □4 116 18.10 N 120.45 E
Ilocos Sur □4 116 17.05 N 120.35 E
Iloilo 116 10.42 N 122.34 E
Iloilo □4 116 11.00 N 122.35 E
Iloilo Strait ⊔ 116 10.43 N 122.36 E
Ilomantsi 24 62.40 N 30.55 E
Ilondola Mission 154 10.42 S 31.47 E
Ilongero 154 4.40 S 34.52 E
Ilop 164 2.54 S 141.13 E
Ilopango, Lago de ⊜ 236 13.40 N 89.03 W
Ilora 150 7.45 N 3.50 E
Ilorin 150 8.30 N 4.32 E
Ilovajsk 83 47.56 N 38.13 E
Ilovatka 80 50.31 N 45.55 E
Ilovka 78 50.43 N 38.38 E
Ilovl'a 80 49.18 N 43.59 E
Ilovl'a ≃ 80 49.14 N 43.54 E
Iłowa 30 51.30 N 15.12 E
Il Palone ʌ 64 46.02 N 11.04 E
Il'pyrskij 74 59.56 N 164.10 E
Ilsan-ni 271b 37.41 N 126.46 E
Ilse ≃ 54 52.06 N 10.35 E
Ilshofen 56 49.10 N 9.55 E
Il'skij 78 44.51 N 38.35 E
Ilskov 41 56.14 N 9.06 E
Il Telegrafo ʌ 66 42.22 N 11.10 E
Ilten 52 52.21 N 9.55 E
Ilu 152 4.12 N 23.02 E
Ilubabor □4 144 7.50 N 35.00 E
Iluhăr 126 22.48 N 90.06 E
Ilūkste 76 55.58 N 26.18 E
Ilverich 263 51.17 N 6.42 E
Ilwaco 224 46.19 N 124.03 W
Ilwaki 112 7.56 S 126.26 E
Ilwŏl-san ʌ 98 36.50 N 129.06 E
Ilyasbey 130 40.13 N 29.52 E
Ilz 61 47.05 N 15.55 E
Ilz ≃ 60 48.35 N 13.29 E
Iłża 30 51.11 N 21.14 E
Ima 88 55.13 N 115.55 E
Ima ≃ 96 33.45 N 131.01 E
Imabari 96 34.03 N 133.00 E
Imabu ≃ 250 0.44 S 57.22 W
Imadomi 268 35.28 N 140.06 E
Imaichi 94 36.43 N 139.41 E
Imajō 94 35.46 N 136.12 E
Imajuku 268 35.58 N 139.21 E
Imajuku ✦8 268 35.29 N 139.32 E
Imaki 270 34.24 N 135.46 E
Imaloto ≃ 157b 23.27 S 45.13 E
Imambara ⊍1 272b 22.54 N 88.25 E
Imambaj I 86 43.13 N 60.25 E
Imandan-Makit, gora ʌ 88 54.07 N 117.43 E
Imandra, ozero ⊜ 24 67.30 N 33.00 E
Imanombo 157b 24.26 S 45.49 E
Imantau 86 52.58 N 68.22 E
Imari 92 33.16 N 129.53 E
Imaruí 252 28.21 S 48.49 W
Imaruí, Lagoa do c 252 28.21 S 48.52 W
Imasa 140 18.01 N 36.12 E
Imatra 26 61.10 N 28.46 E
Imavere 76 58.44 N 25.48 E
Imazu 94 35.24 N 136.02 E
Imbābah ✦8 142 30.04 N 31.13 E
Imbabura □4 246 0.22 N 78.25 W
Imba-numa ⊜ 94 35.45 N 140.12 E
Imbariê 256 22.39 S 43.13 W
Imbituba 252 28.14 S 48.40 W
Imbituva 252 25.12 S 50.35 W
Imboaçu, Canal ≚ 287a 22.48 S 43.04 W
Imboden 194 36.12 N 91.10 W
Imbonga 152 0.43 S 19.46 E
Imbundi 152 5.44 S 16.16 E
Ime, Beinn ʌ 46 56.14 N 4.49 W
Imeni Abaja 86 50.44 N 69.30 E
Imeni Babuškina 76 59.45 N 43.07 E
Imeni 0206 Bakinskich Komissarov 84 39.19 N 49.12 E
Imeni Čapajeva 85 43.28 N 76.50 E
Imeni C'urupy 82 55.30 N 38.39 E
Imeni Džambula, Kaz. 86 45.26 N 74.24 E
Imeni Džambula, Kaz. 86 47.43 N 74.09 E
Imeni Frunze 86 46.23 N 77.20 E
Imeni Il-Go Okt'abr'a 88 55.54 N 119.36 E
Imeni Kalinina, Kaz. 85 43.16 N 74.03 E
Imeni Kalinina, Kyrg. 85 41.28 N 76.22 E
Imeni Kalinina, Ross. 80 51.51 N 52.43 E
Imeni Kalinina, Uzb. 86 43.40 N 59.07 E
Imeni Karla Libknechta 78 51.37 N 35.27 E
Imeni Kirova, Kaz. 86 46.27 N 77.13 E
Imeni Kirova, Ross. 74 59.42 N 128.12 E
Imeni Leninskogo Komsomola 86 50.45 N 66.44 E
Imeni Marta 86 46.57 N 58.58 E
Imeni Michajla Ivanoviča Kalinina 80 57.59 N 45.07 E
Imeni Molodogvardejcev 86 54.03 N 70.44 E
Imeni Panfilova 85 43.23 N 77.07 E
Imeni Poliny Osipenko 89 52.25 N 136.28 E
Imeni Sardarova Karachana 85 38.26 N 68.46 E
Imeni Šeredy 83 46.52 N 40.03 E
Imeni Ševčenko 86 45.58 N 61.04 E
Imeni Stepana Razina 86 54.54 N 44.18 E
Imeni Tel'mana 89 48.36 N 134.59 E
Imeni Timir'azeva 86 53.39 N 65.31 E
Imeni Vladimira Il'iča Lenina 80 53.36 N 46.58 E
Imeni Vorovskogo, Ross. 80 55.43 N 41.06 E
Imeni Vorovskogo, Ross. 82 55.43 N 38.20 E
Imeni XXI Partsjezda 86 50.43 N 67.50 E
Imeni Žel'abova 76 58.57 N 36.36 E
Imera ≃ 70 37.59 N 13.49 E
Imerimandroso 157b 17.23 S 48.38 E
Imese 152 2.07 N 18.06 E
Imgenbroich 56 50.34 N 6.16 E
Imi 144 6.28 N 42.18 E
Imías 240p 20.04 N 74.38 W
Imilac 252 24.14 S 68.53 W
Imilili ⚲4 148 23.18 N 15.54 W
Imi-n'Tanout 148 31.10 N 8.50 W
Imišli 84 39.52 N 48.04 E
Imittós 267c 37.57 N 23.45 E
Imittós Óros ʌ 267c 37.55 N 23.47 E
Imja-do I 98 35.05 N 126.05 E
Imjin-gang ≃ 98 37.47 N 126.40 E
Imlay 204 40.39 N 118.08 W
Imlay City 190 43.01 N 83.04 W
Imlaystown 208 40.10 N 74.31 W
Imler 214 40.12 N 78.31 W
Immarna 162 30.30 S 132.09 E
Immendingen 58 47.56 N 8.44 E
Immenhausen 56 51.25 N 9.28 E
Immensen 52 52.23 N 10.04 E
Immenstaad 58 47.40 N 9.22 E
Immenstadt 58 47.33 N 10.13 E
Immigrath 263 51.06 N 6.57 E
Immingham 44 53.36 N 0.13 W
Immokalee 220 26.25 N 81.25 W
Imnaha ≃ 202 45.49 N 116.46 W
Imo □3 150 5.30 N 7.25 E
Imo ≃ 150 4.36 N 7.35 E
Imogiri 115a 7.55 S 110.23 E
Imokt'an 98 38.50 N 126.41 E
Imola 66 44.21 N 11.42 E
Imonda 164 3.20 S 141.10 E
Imore 273a 6.26 N 3.17 E
Imoro 273a 6.43 N 3.30 E
Im Ostholz ✦8 263 51.26 N 7.12 E
Imotski 36 43.27 N 17.13 E
Imp'a 98 35.59 N 126.49 E
Impasugong 116 8.19 N 125.00 E
Impe 152 2.44 S 15.17 E
Impendle 158 29.37 S 29.55 E
Imperatore, Campo ≚ 66 42.25 N 13.40 E
Imperatriz 250 5.32 S 47.29 W
Imperia 62 43.53 N 8.03 E
Imperia □4 62 43.58 N 7.47 E
Imperial, Sk., Can. 184 51.22 N 105.27 W
Imperial, Perú 248 13.04 S 76.21 W
Imperial, Ca., U.S. 204 32.50 N 115.34 W
Imperial, Mo., U.S. 219 38.22 N 90.22 W
Imperial, Ne., U.S. 198 40.31 N 101.38 W
Imperial, Pa., U.S. 214 40.26 N 80.14 W
Imperial, Tx., U.S. 196 31.16 N 102.41 W
Imperial ≃ 254 38.48 S 73.24 W
Imperial Beach 228 32.35 N 117.06 W
Imperial Dam ✦6 204 32.55 N 114.30 W
Imperial de Aragón, Canal ≚ 34 42.02 N 1.33 W
Imperiale 68 40.07 N 16.35 E
Imperial Mills 182 55.00 N 111.44 W
Imperial Palace ⊍ 268 35.41 N 139.45 E
Imperial Valley ∨ 204 32.50 N 115.30 W
Impfingen 56 49.10 N 8.07 E
Impfondo 152 1.37 N 18.04 E
Imphāl 120 24.49 N 93.57 E
Impilachti 24 61.40 N 31.04 E
Impruneta 66 43.41 N 11.15 E
Impulo 152 13.53 S 13.39 E
İmralı Adası I 130 40.32 N 28.32 E
İmranlı 130 39.54 N 38.07 E
Imroz 130 40.11 N 25.55 E
Imsil 98 35.37 N 127.15 E
Imst 64 47.14 N 10.44 E
Imtān 132 32.24 N 36.49 E
Imuris 232 30.47 N 110.52 W
Imuruan Bay c 116 10.40 N 119.16 E
Imuruk Basin ⊜ 180 65.06 N 165.36 W
Imuruk Lake ⊜ 180 65.36 N 163.10 W
Imute 273a 6.42 N 3.29 E
Imwŏn-ni 98 37.15 N 129.20 E
Ina, Nihon 94 35.59 N 140.03 E
Ina, Nihon 96 37.10 N 139.32 E
Ina, Nihon 94 35.50 N 137.57 E
Ina, Nihon 268 35.59 N 139.38 E
In'a, Ross. 74 59.24 N 144.48 E
In'a, Ross. 86 50.48 N 86.37 E
In'a, Ross. 86 53.31 N 82.40 E
Ina, Il., U.S. 194 38.09 N 88.54 W
Ina ≃, Nihon 94 37.16 N 139.33 E
Ina ≃, Nihon 96 34.43 N 135.28 E
Ina ≃, Pol. 54 53.32 N 14.38 E
In'a ≃, Ross. 74 59.23 N 144.54 E
In'a ≃, Ross. 86 54.59 N 82.59 E
Inaba 270 34.26 N 135.27 E
Inabe 94 35.07 N 136.33 E
Ina-bonchi ≚1 94 35.45 N 137.57 E
Inabu 94 35.13 N 137.30 E
Inaccessible Island I 10 37.17 S 12.45 W
Inada 270 34.54 N 135.08 E
Inagawa 96 34.53 N 135.22 E
Inagawan 116 9.33 N 118.39 E
Inage 268 35.38 N 140.05 E
Inagi 268 35.38 N 139.30 E
Inajá 250 8.54 S 37.49 W
Inajá ≃ 250 8.53 S 49.44 W
In'akino 80 54.26 N 41.07 E
Inakona 175e 9.45 S 160.02 E
Inala 171a 27.35 S 152.58 E
Inamangando ≃ 152 14.03 S 12.23 E
Inambari ≃ 248 12.41 S 69.44 W
In Amguel 148 23.40 N 5.10 E
Inami, Nihon 94 36.33 N 136.58 E
Inami, Nihon 96 34.45 N 134.54 E
Inami, Nihon 96 33.48 N 135.13 E
In Amnas 148 28.05 N 9.30 E
Inampulugan Island I 116 10.28 N 122.42 E
Inamuragasaki Point ⟩ 268 35.18 N 139.32 E
Inanda 273d 26.07 S 28.03 E
Inangahua Junction 172 41.51 S 171.57 E
Inanwatan 164 2.08 S 132.10 E
Iñapari 248 10.57 S 69.35 W
Inaparok 164 8.15 S 141.55 E
In'aptuk, gora ʌ 88 56.22 N 110.17 E
Inari 24 68.54 N 27.01 E
Inarigda 74 63.14 N 107.27 E
Inarijärvi ⊜ 24 69.00 N 28.00 E
Inas, Gunong ʌ 114 5.15 N 100.56 E
Inasa 94 34.50 N 137.40 E
Inatsuki 96 33.36 N 130.43 E
Inauini ≃ 248 8.33 S 67.24 W
Inawaia 164 8.40 S 146.35 E
Inawashiro-ko ⊜ 92 37.29 N 140.06 E
I-n-Azaoua ⚲4 148 20.49 N 7.30 E
Inazawa 94 35.15 N 136.47 E
Inba 94 35.46 N 140.14 E
Inba-numa ⊜ 94 35.45 N 140.12 E
In Belbel 148 27.54 N 1.10 E
Inca 34 39.43 N 2.54 E
Inca de Oro 252 26.45 S 69.54 W
Incaguasi 252 29.13 S 71.03 W
Incahuasi, Nevado de ʌ 252 27.02 S 68.18 W
Ince 262 53.17 N 2.49 W
Ince Blundell 262 53.31 N 3.02 W
İnce Burun ⟩ 130 42.06 N 34.56 E
Ince-in-Makerfield 262 53.32 N 2.37 W
İncekum Burnu ⟩ 130 36.13 N 33.58 E
İncesu 130 38.38 N 35.11 E
Inch 48 52.08 N 9.59 W
I-n-Chaouag ≃ 150 16.23 N 0.10 E
Inchard, Loch c 46 58.27 N 5.04 W
Inchas Military Base ▪ 142 30.20 N 31.27 E
Inchbare 46 56.47 N 2.38 W
Inchcape I 46 56.26 N 2.23 W
Inchelium 182 48.17 N 118.11 W
Inchiri □4 150 19.50 N 15.00 W
Inchmarnock I 46 55.47 N 5.09 W
Inchnadamph 46 58.09 N 4.59 W
Inch'ŏn 98 37.28 N 126.38 E
Inch'ŏn □4 98 37.28 N 126.38 E
Inchture 46 56.26 N 3.10 W
Inchwagh Lake ⊜ 281 42.27 N 83.41 W
İncirliova 130 37.50 N 27.43 E
Incisa in Val d'Arno 66 43.40 N 11.27 E
Incline Village 226 39.16 N 119.56 W
Incomáti (Komati) ≃ 156 25.46 S 32.43 E
Inconfidência 256 22.16 S 43.13 W
Inconfidentes 256 22.20 S 46.20 W
Inčoun 180 66.18 N 170.17 W
Incudine 64 46.14 N 10.22 E
Incudine, Monte ʌ 36 41.51 N 9.12 E
Incy 24 65.48 N 40.26 E
Indaal, Loch c 46 55.45 N 6.21 W
Indaiá ≃ 255 18.27 S 45.22 W
Indaiatuba 256 23.05 S 47.14 W
Indalsälven ≃ 26 62.31 N 17.27 E
Indanan 116 5.58 N 120.59 E
Indaparapeo 234 19.47 N 100.58 W
Inda Silase 144 14.05 N 38.20 E
Indaw 110 23.40 N 94.46 E
Indawgyi Lake ⊜ 110 25.10 N 96.19 E
Indé 232 25.54 N 105.13 W
Inde ≃ 56 50.54 N 6.21 E
Inde — India □1 118 20.00 N 77.00 E
Indemini 58 46.06 N 8.50 E
Independence, Ca., U.S. 204 36.48 N 118.11 W
Independence, In., U.S. 216 40.20 N 87.10 W
Independence, Ia., U.S. 190 42.28 N 91.53 W
Independence, Ks., U.S. 198 37.13 N 95.42 W
Independence, Ky., U.S. 218 38.56 N 84.32 W
Independence, La., U.S. 194 30.38 N 90.30 W
Independence, Mo., U.S. 194 39.05 N 94.24 W
Independence, Oh., U.S. 279a 41.23 N 81.38 W
Independence, Or., U.S. 202 44.51 N 123.11 W
Independence, Pa., U.S. 214 40.15 N 80.31 W
Independence, Tx., U.S. 222 30.19 N 96.21 W
Independence, Va., U.S. 192 36.37 N 81.09 W
Independence, Wi., U.S. 190 44.21 N 91.25 W
Independence ≃ 188 43.45 N 75.20 W
Independence Creek ≃ 196 30.27 N 101.44 W
Independence Hall ⊥ 285 39.57 N 75.09 W
Independence Lake ⊜1 226 39.26 N 120.18 W
Independence Mountains ʌ 204 41.15 N 115.55 W
Independencia, Bol. 248 17.07 S 66.53 W
Independência, Bra. 250 5.23 S 40.19 W
Independencia, Chile 286e 33.23 S 70.40 W
Independencia, Perú 286d 11.59 S 77.02 W
Independencia, Isla I 248 14.15 S 76.12 W
Independenţa 38 43.58 N 28.05 E
Inder, ozero ⊜ 80 48.27 N 51.54 E
Inderborskij 80 48.33 N 51.44 E
In der Bredde 263 51.20 N 7.23 E
İnderesi 130 37.50 N 35.40 E
Index 224 47.49 N 121.33 W
Index, Mount ʌ 224 47.46 N 121.35 W
Indi 122 17.10 N 75.58 E
India (Bhārat) □1 118 20.00 N 77.00 E
India Brook ≃ 276 40.47 N 74.37 W
India Gate ⊥ 272a 28.37 N 77.18 E
Indialantic 220 28.05 N 80.34 W
Indian ≃, On., Can. 212 45.16 N 76.14 W
Indian ≃, On., Can. 212 44.13 N 78.08 W
Indian ≃, De., U.S. 208 38.36 N 75.10 W
Indian ≃, Ma., U.S. 283 42.47 N 70.58 W
Indian ≃, Mi., U.S. 190 45.59 N 86.15 W
Indian ≃, N.Y., U.S. 212 44.24 N 75.39 W
Indiana 214 40.37 N 79.09 W
Indiana □6 214 40.37 N 79.09 W
Indiana □3, U.S. 178 40.00 N 86.15 W
Indiana □3, U.S. 194 40.00 N 86.15 W
Indiana Dunes National Lakeshore ♦ 216 41.40 N 87.00 W
Indiana Dunes State Park ♦ 216 41.40 N 87.02 W
Indian Agricultural Research Institute ⊍3 272a 28.38 N 77.10 E
Indiana Harbor c 278 41.40 N 87.27 W
Indiana Harbor Canal ≚ 278 41.40 N 87.27 W
Indianapolis 218 39.46 N 86.09 W
Indianapolis International Airport ✈ 218 39.43 N 86.16 W
Indianapolis Motor Speedway ♦ 218 39.48 N 86.14 W
Indian Bayou ≃ 194 34.14 N 91.52 W
Indian Brook 186 46.23 N 60.32 W
Indian Caverns ⌓5 214 40.38 N 78.05 W
Indian Church 232 17.45 N 88.40 W
Indian Creek 278 42.14 N 87.59 W
Indian Creek ≃, U.S. 218 39.19 N 84.38 W
Indian Creek ≃, Ca., U.S. 228 35.18 N 118.26 W
Indian Creek ≃, Il., U.S. 216 41.26 N 88.46 W
Indian Creek ≃, Il., U.S. 219 39.56 N 90.32 W
Indian Creek ≃, Il., U.S. 278 42.11 N 87.55 W
Indian Creek ≃, In., U.S. 216 40.55 N 86.42 W
Indian Creek ≃, In., U.S. 218 38.10 N 86.14 W
Indian Creek ≃, In., U.S. 218 38.43 N 85.06 W
Indian Creek ≃, In., U.S. 218 39.23 N 86.29 W
Indian Creek ≃, Md., U.S. 284c 38.59 N 76.55 W
Indian Creek ≃, Mo., U.S. 194 36.33 N 94.29 W
Indian Creek ≃, Mo., U.S. 219 39.10 N 91.11 W
Indian Creek ≃, N.M., U.S. 200 36.11 N 108.23 W
Indian Creek ≃, N.Y., U.S. 276 40.43 N 73.06 W
Indian Creek ≃, Oh., U.S. 218 39.19 N 84.38 W
Indian Creek ≃, Oh., U.S. 279a 41.17 N 81.31 W
Indian Creek ≃, S.D., U.S. 198 44.39 N 103.19 W
Indian Creek ≃, Tn., U.S. 194 35.13 N 88.08 W
Indian Creek Lake ⊜1 222 31.44 N 95.58 W
Indianford 216 42.49 N 88.55 W
Indian Grave Mountain ʌ2 192 32.59 N 84.21 W
Indian Harbor Beach 220 28.08 N 80.35 W
Indian Head, Sk., Can. 184 50.32 N 103.40 W
Indian Head, Md., U.S. 208 38.36 N 77.09 W
Indian Head ≃ 283 42.04 N 70.52 W
Indian Head Park 278 41.47 N 87.54 W
Indian Head Pond ⊜ 283 42.03 N 70.51 W
Indian Heights 216 40.25 N 86.07 W
Indian Island I 224 48.04 N 122.43 W
Indian Kentuck Creek ≃ 218 38.43 N 85.16 W
Indian Lake, Mi., U.S. 216 41.59 N 86.12 W
Indian Lake, N.Y., U.S. 188 43.46 N 74.16 W
Indian Lake ⊜, On., Can. 190 47.08 N 82.08 W
Indian Lake ⊜, Mi., U.S. 190 45.59 N 86.20 W
Indian Lake ⊜, Mi., U.S. 216 42.09 N 85.29 W
Indian Lake ⊜, Mi., U.S. 216 42.00 N 86.13 W
Indian Lake ⊜, N.J., U.S. 276 40.53 N 74.29 W
Indian Lake ⊜, Oh., U.S. 216 40.29 N 83.53 W
Indian Lake Estates 220 27.48 N 81.19 W
Indian Lakes ⊜ 216 41.33 N 85.25 W
Indian Lake State Park ♦ 216 40.29 N 83.52 W
Indian Mills Brook ≃ 285 39.47 N 74.44 W
Indian Mills Lake ⊜ 285 39.48 N 74.44 W
Indian Neck 207 41.15 N 72.48 W
Indian Ocean ⚲1 4 10.00 S 70.00 E
Indian Ocean ⚲1 6 10.00 S 70.00 E
Indianola, Ia., U.S. 190 41.21 N 93.33 W
Indianola, Ms., U.S. 194 33.27 N 90.39 W
Indianola, Ne., U.S. 198 40.14 N 100.25 W
Indianola, Pa., U.S. 279b 40.34 N 79.51 W
Indianola, Wa., U.S. 224 47.45 N 122.31 W
Indianópolis 255 19.02 S 47.55 W
Indianópolis ✦8 287b 23.36 S 46.38 W
Indian Peak ʌ, Ut., U.S. 200 38.16 N 113.53 W
Indian Peak ʌ, Wy., U.S. 202 44.47 N 109.51 W
Indian Point ⟩ 212 44.37 N 78.49 W
Indian Prairie Canal ≚ 220 27.02 N 80.57 W
Indian Queen Estates 284c 38.46 N 77.02 W
Indian River 190 45.24 N 84.36 W
Indian River □6 220 27.43 N 80.36 W
Indian River ≃ 220 28.00 N 80.30 W
Indian River Bay c 208 38.36 N 75.05 W
Indian River Inlet c 208 38.37 N 75.03 W
Indian Rock ʌ 224 45.59 N 120.49 W
Indian Rock Dam ✦6 208 39.57 N 76.45 W
Indian Rock Paintings ⊥ 224 46.38 N 120.31 W
Indian Rocks Beach 220 27.52 N 82.51 W
Indian Springs, Nv., U.S. 204 36.34 N 115.40 W
Indian Springs, Va., U.S. 284c 38.49 N 77.10 W
Indian Stream ≃ 206 45.03 N 71.26 W
Indiantown 220 27.01 N 80.29 W
Indian Town Point ⟩ 240c 17.06 N 61.40 W
Indian Valley Reservoir ⊜1 226 39.07 N 122.32 W
Indian Village, In., U.S. 218 40.10 N 85.22 W
Indian Village, N.Y., U.S. 210 42.57 N 76.10 W
Indiaporã 255 19.57 S 50.17 W
Indiaroba 250 11.32 S 37.31 W
Indibir 144 8.05 N 37.58 E
Indico, Océano — Indian Ocean ⚲1 6 10.00 S 70.00 E
Indien, Océan — Indian Ocean ⚲1 6 10.00 S 70.00 E
Indien, territoires britanniques de l'Océan — British Indian Ocean Territory □2 12 7.00 S 72.00 E
Indien — India □1 118 20.00 N 77.00 E
Indiera Alta 240m 18.09 N 66.53 W
Indiga 24 67.41 N 49.00 E
Indigirka ≃ 74 70.48 N 148.54 E
Inđija 38 45.03 N 20.05 E
Indin 120 20.16 N 92.57 E
Indio 204 33.43 N 116.12 W
Indio ≃, Nic. 236 10.57 N 83.44 W
Indio ≃, Pan. 236 9.12 N 80.11 W
Indio, Punta ⟩ 258 35.16 S 57.13 W
Indios, Canal de los ⊔ 240p 21.56 N 83.16 W
Indira Gandhi Canal ≚ 120 31.10 N 75.00 E
Indira Gandhi International Airport ✈ 272a 28.35 N 77.07 E
Indischer Ozean — Indian Ocean ⚲1 6 10.00 S 70.00 E
Indispensable Reefs ✦2 160 12.40 S 160.25 E
Indispensable Strait ⊔ 175e 9.00 S 160.30 E
Indochina ✦1 12 16.00 N 107.00 E
Indo — Indus ≃ 120 24.20 N 67.47 E
Indom 24 64.36 N 55.22 E
Indonesia □1 108 5.00 S 120.00 E
Indonesia, University of ⊍2 269e 6.12 S 106.51 E
Indonesia in Miniature ♦ 269e 6.08 S 106.49 E
Indonesian Culture, Museum of ⊍3 269e 6.09 N 106.49 E
Indonésie — Indonesia □1 108 5.00 S 120.00 E
Indonesien — Indonesia □1 108 5.00 S 120.00 E
Indooroopilly 171a 27.30 S 152.58 E
Indore 120 22.43 N 75.50 E
Indpur 126 23.10 N 86.56 E
Indragiri ≃ 112 0.22 S 103.26 E
Indramayu 115a 6.20 S 108.19 E
Indramayu, Ujung ⟩ 115a 6.14 S 108.17 E
Indrapuri 114 5.26 N 95.27 E
Indrāvati ≃ 122 18.44 N 80.16 E
Indre □5 32 46.45 N 1.30 E
Indre ≃ 32 47.16 N 0.19 E
Indre-et-Loire □5 32 47.15 N 0.45 E
Indrois ≃ 50 47.13 N 0.56 E
Indungo 152 14.48 S 16.17 E
Induno Olona 62 45.52 N 8.51 E
Indura 76 53.27 N 23.53 E
Indur — Indore 120 22.43 N 75.50 E
Indus ≃ 120 24.20 N 67.47 E
Industry, Il., U.S. 194 40.20 N 90.36 W
Industry, Pa., U.S. 214 40.39 N 80.25 W
Industry, Tx., U.S. 222 29.58 N 96.30 W
Indwe 158 31.27 S 27.23 E
Indwe ≃ 158 32.01 S 27.21 E
Ine 96 35.39 N 135.17 E
İnebolu 130 41.58 N 33.46 E
İnece 130 41.41 N 27.04 E
İnecik 130 40.56 N 27.16 E
In Ecker 148 24.09 N 5.03 E
İnegöl 130 40.05 N 29.31 E
Inerie, Gunung ʌ 115b 8.52 S 120.56 E
Inés, Monte ʌ 254 48.29 S 69.40 W
Ineu 38 46.26 N 21.49 E
Inez, Ky., U.S. 192 37.51 N 82.32 W
Inez, Tx., U.S. 222 28.54 N 96.47 W
Inez, Lake ⊜ 276 41.01 N 74.17 W
Infanta, Pil. 116 15.50 N 119.55 E
Infanta, Pil. 116 14.45 N 121.39 E
Infante, Kaap ⟩ 158 34.29 S 20.51 E
Inferior, Laguna c 234 16.20 N 94.40 W
Inferno, Cachoeira do ⊾ 250 1.00 S 56.04 W
Infiernillo, Presa del ⊜1 234 18.35 N 101.45 W
Infiesto 34 43.21 N 5.22 W
Infreschi, Punta degli ⟩ 68 39.59 N 15.25 E
Ing ≃ 110 20.13 N 100.27 E
Ingá 250 7.17 S 35.36 W
Ingabu 110 17.49 N 95.16 E
Ingaí 256 21.24 S 44.55 W
Ingaí ≃ 256 21.23 S 44.52 W
Ingal 150 16.47 N 6.56 E
Ingalls 218 39.57 N 85.48 W
Ingalls Creek ≃ 224 47.28 N 120.39 W
Ingalls Park 216 41.32 N 88.03 W
Inganda 152 0.05 S 20.57 E
Inganno ≃ 70 38.04 N 14.37 E
Ingarö I 40 59.16 N 18.28 E
Ingatestone 42 51.41 N 0.22 E
Ingatestone Hall ⊥ 260 51.39 N 0.23 E
Ingelfingen 56 49.18 N 9.39 E
Ingelheim 56 49.59 N 8.05 E
Ingelmunster 50 50.55 N 3.15 E
Ingelstad 26 56.45 N 14.55 E
Ingende 152 0.15 S 18.57 E
Ingeniería, Universidad Nacional de ⊍2 286d 12.02 S 77.02 W
Ingeniero Budge ✦8 288 34.43 S 58.28 W
Ingeniero Jacobacci 254 41.18 S 69.35 W
Ingeniero Juan Allan 258 34.53 S 58.11 W
Ingeniero Luiggi 252 35.25 S 64.29 W
Ingeniero Luis A. Huergo 252 39.05 S 67.14 W
Ingeniero Maschwitz 258 34.23 S 58.44 W
Ingeniero Romulo Otamendi 258 34.13 S 58.54 W
Ingeniero White 252 38.47 S 62.16 W
Ingeniero Williams 258 34.54 S 59.22 W
Ingenio La Esperanza 252 24.13 S 64.51 W
Ingenio Santa Ana 252 27.28 S 65.41 W
Ingeringbach ≃ 61 47.12 N 14.49 E
Ingersheim 58 48.06 N 7.18 E
Ingersoll 212 43.02 N 80.53 W
Ingham 166 18.39 S 146.10 E
Ingham □6 216 42.37 N 84.22 W
Ingička 85 39.52 N 67.20 E
Ingleborough ʌ 44 54.11 N 2.23 W
Ingleburn 170 34.00 S 150.52 E
Inglesa, Costa — English Coast ✦2 9 73.45 S 73.00 W
Ingleside, Austl. 274a 33.41 S 151.13 E
Ingleside, On., Can. 206 45.00 N 75.00 W
Ingleside, Il., U.S. 216 42.23 N 88.09 W
Ingleside, Tx., U.S. 196 27.52 N 97.12 W
Ingleside ✦8 282 37.43 N 122.28 W
Ingleton 44 54.10 N 2.27 W
Inglewood, Austl. 166 28.25 S 151.05 E
Inglewood, Austl. 166 36.34 S 143.52 E
Inglewood, On., Can. 212 43.47 N 79.56 W
Inglewood, N.Z. 172 39.09 S 174.12 E
Inglewood, Ca., U.S. 228 33.57 N 118.21 W
Inglewood, Wa., U.S. 224 47.44 N 122.15 W
Inglewood Forest ✦3 44 54.45 N 2.50 W
Inglis, Mb., Can. 184 50.57 N 101.15 W
Inglis, Fl., U.S. 220 29.02 N 82.40 W
Inglis Lock ✦5 220 29.02 N 82.37 W
Ingoda ≃ 88 51.42 N 115.48 E
Ingogo 158 27.32 S 29.56 E
Ingoldmells 44 53.11 N 0.20 E
Ingolstadt 60 48.46 N 11.27 E
Ingomar 279b 40.35 N 80.05 W
Ingonish 186 46.42 N 60.22 W
Ingornachoix Bay c 186 50.38 N 57.20 W
Ingraham, Lake ⊜ 220 25.09 N 81.08 W
Ingrāj Bāzār 124 25.00 N 88.09 E
Ingram, Pa., U.S. 279b 40.26 N 80.04 W
Ingram, Tx., U.S. 196 30.04 N 99.14 W
Ingram Bay c 208 37.48 N 76.17 W
Ingrave 260 51.36 N 0.21 E
Ingrid Christensen Coast ✦2 9 69.30 S 76.00 E
In Guezzam 150 19.32 N 5.42 E
Ingul ≃ 78 47.00 N 31.59 E
Ingulec 78 47.43 N 33.14 E
Ingulec ≃ 78 46.41 N 32.48 E
Ingulo-Kamenka 78 48.17 N 32.30 E
Inguri ≃ 84 42.24 N 41.33 E
Ingushetia — Čečnja-Ingušetija □3 84 43.15 N 45.40 E
Inguzet 86 58.50 N 83.52 E
Ingvallsbenning 40 60.15 N 15.53 E
Ingwavuma 158 27.09 S 32.00 E
Ingwe 154 13.02 S 26.25 E
Ingwiller 56 48.52 N 7.29 E
Inhaca, Ilha da I 158 26.03 S 32.57 E
Inhafenga 156 20.35 S 33.53 E
Inhambane 156 23.51 S 35.29 E
Inhambane □5 156 23.00 S 34.30 E
Inhambane, Baía de c 156 23.58 S 35.51 E
Inhambupe 255 11.47 S 38.21 W
Inhaminga 156 18.24 S 35.00 E
Inhanduí ≃ 255 21.37 S 52.59 W
Inhapim 255 19.33 S 42.07 W
Inharrime 156 24.29 S 35.01 E
Inharrime ≃ 156 24.29 S 35.01 E
Inhassoro 156 21.33 S 35.11 E
Inhaúma 255 19.29 S 44.22 W
Inhaúma ✦8 287a 22.52 S 43.17 W
İnhisar 130 40.03 N 30.23 E
Inhoaíba ✦8 256 22.54 S 43.36 W
Inhomirim 256 22.35 S 43.10 W
Inhomirim ≃ 287a 22.41 S 43.13 W
Inhuma 250 6.40 S 41.42 W
Inhumas 255 16.22 S 49.30 W
Ini ≃ 146 9.30 N 12.20 E
Iniesta 34 39.26 N 1.45 W
Inimutaba 255 18.45 S 44.22 W
Ining — Yining 86 43.54 N 81.21 E
Inírida ≃ 246 3.55 N 67.52 W
Inisa 150 7.52 N 4.20 E
Inishbofin I, Ire. 48 53.37 N 10.15 W
Inishbofin I, Ire. 48 55.09 N 8.11 W
Inishcrone 48 54.12 N 9.06 W
Inisheer I 48 53.02 N 9.32 W
Inishkea North I 48 54.08 N 10.12 W
Inishkea South I 48 54.07 N 10.13 W
Inishmaan I 48 53.05 N 9.32 W
Inishmore I 48 53.07 N 9.45 W
Inishmurray I 48 54.26 N 8.40 W
Inishowen ⟩1 48 55.12 N 7.20 W
Inishowen Head ⟩ 48 55.14 N 6.56 W
Inishshark I 48 53.37 N 10.18 W
Inishtrahull I 48 55.26 N 7.14 W
Inishturk I 48 53.43 N 10.08 W
Inistioge 48 52.29 N 7.04 W
Initao 116 8.30 N 124.18 E
Inje 98 38.05 N 128.09 E
Injibara 144 11.00 N 36.59 E
Injune 166 25.51 S 148.34 E
Inkeroinen 26 60.42 N 26.51 E
Inketete 152 2.37 S 21.53 E
Inkisi (Zadi) ≃ 152 4.46 S 14.52 E
Inkom 202 42.47 N 112.15 W
Inkster, Mi., U.S. 216 42.17 N 83.18 W
Inkster, N.D., U.S. 198 48.09 N 97.38 W
Inland Kaikoura Range ʌ 172 42.00 S 173.40 E
Inland Lake ⊜, Mb., Can. 184 52.17 N 99.42 W
Inland Lake ⊜, Ak., U.S. 180 66.27 N 159.47 W
Inland Sea — Seto-naikai ⚲2 96 34.20 N 133.30 E
Inle Lake ⊜ 110 20.32 N 96.55 E
Inman, Ks., U.S. 198 38.13 N 97.46 W
Inman, S.C., U.S. 192 35.02 N 82.05 W
Inman Mills 192 35.02 N 82.06 W
Inman Valley 168b 35.30 S 138.28 E
Inn (En) ≃ 32 48.35 N 13.28 E
Innamincka 166 27.45 S 140.44 E
Innbach ≃ 61 48.18 N 14.07 E
Innellan 44 55.54 N 4.57 W
Innerbraz 58 47.09 N 9.55 E
Inner Bay c 214 42.37 N 80.24 W
Inner Channel ⊔ 232 16.35 N 88.17 W
Innerferrera 58 46.31 N 9.28 E
Innerfragant 64 46.58 N 13.04 E
Inner Harbor c 276 40.52 N 73.28 W
Inner Hebrides II 46 56.30 N 6.00 W
Innerkip 212 43.13 N 80.42 W
Innerleithen 46 55.38 N 3.05 W
Inner Mongolia — Nei Monggol Zizhiqu □4 90 43.00 N 115.00 E
Inner Sister Island I 166 39.42 S 147.55 E
Inner Sound ⊔ 46 57.25 N 5.56 W
Innerste ≃ 52 52.15 N 9.50 E
Innerstetalsperre ✦6 52 51.55 N 10.17 E
Innerthal 58 47.06 N 8.56 E
Innertkirchen 58 46.42 N 8.14 E
Innervillgraten 64 46.48 N 12.23 E
Innichen — San Candido 64 46.44 N 12.17 E
Inning 60 48.05 N 11.09 E
Innisfail, Austl. 166 17.32 S 146.02 E
Innisfail, Ab., Can. 182 52.02 N 113.57 W
Innisfil Creek ≃ 212 44.08 N 79.49 W
Innisfree 182 53.22 N 111.32 W
Innisplain 171a 28.10 S 152.55 E
Innokent'jevka 89 49.42 N 136.57 E
Innokent'jevskij 89 48.37 N 140.10 E
Innoko ≃ 180 62.14 N 159.45 W
Innolovo 265a 59.47 N 29.59 E
Innoshima 96 34.17 N 133.11 E
Inno-shima I 96 34.19 N 133.10 E
Innsbruck 64 47.16 N 11.24 E
Innviertel ✦1 60 48.10 N 13.15 E
Inny ≃, Ire. 48 53.33 N 7.48 W
Inny ≃, Eng., U.K. 42 50.35 N 4.17 W
Ino, Nihon 96 33.33 N 133.26 E
Ino, Va., U.S. 208 37.46 N 76.48 W
Inoã 256 22.55 S 42.57 W
Inobonto 112 0.52 N 123.57 E
Inocência 255 19.47 S 51.48 W
Inokashira Park ✦8 268 35.42 N 139.34 E
Inokovka 80 52.33 N 42.34 E
Inola 196 36.09 N 95.30 W
Ino-misaki ⟩ 96 33.01 N 133.06 E
Inongo 152 1.57 S 18.16 E
Inoni 152 3.04 S 15.39 E
İnönü 130 39.48 N 30.09 E
Inoue 270 34.48 N 135.03 E
Inowrocław 30 52.48 N 18.15 E
Inozemcevo 84 44.06 N 43.06 E
Inp'ung-dong 98 41.25 N 126.34 E
Inrath ✦8 263 51.21 N 6.32 E
In Rhar 148 27.10 N 1.59 E
Ins 58 47.00 N 7.06 E
In Salah 148 27.12 N 2.28 E
Insan-ni 98 41.01 N 127.21 E
Insar 80 53.52 N 44.21 E
Insar ≃ 80 54.43 N 45.18 E
Insch 46 57.21 N 2.37 W
Inscription, Cape ⟩ 162 25.29 S 112.59 E
Inscription Point ⟩ 274a 34.00 S 151.13 E
Insel Man — Isle of Man □2 44 54.15 N 4.30 W
Inshar 150 8.49 N 9.40 E
Inshās ar-Raml 142 30.23 N 31.27 E
Insjön 26 60.41 N 15.05 E
Ińsko 30 53.27 N 15.33 E
In Sokki, Oued ∨ 148 29.37 N 4.13 E
Inspiration 200 33.24 N 110.52 W
Insterburg — Černʼachovsk 76 54.38 N 21.49 E
Instow 184 49.44 N 108.16 W
Insurgente José María Morelos, Parque Nacional ♦ 234 19.35 N 100.55 W
Inta 24 66.02 N 60.08 E
Intendente Alvear 252 35.14 S 63.35 W
İntepe 130 40.00 N 26.20 E
Intercession City 220 28.15 N 81.30 W
Intercourse 208 40.02 N 76.06 W
Interlagos ✦8 287b 23.42 S 46.42 W
Interlaken, Schw. 58 46.41 N 7.51 E
Interlaken, Ma., U.S. 210 42.18 N 73.19 W
Interlaken, N.J., U.S. 208 40.14 N 74.01 W
Interlaken, N.Y., U.S. 210 42.37 N 76.43 W
Interlândia 255 16.12 S 49.02 W
Internacional (Guarulhos), Aeroporto ✈ 287b 23.29 S 46.28 W
International Amphitheatre ⊍ 278 41.49 N 87.39 W
International Falls 190 48.36 N 93.24 W
International Peace Garden ♦ 198 49.00 N 100.04 W
International Trade Fair ♦ 267d 35.47 N 51.24 E
Interstate State Park ♦ 190 45.23 N 92.40 W
Inthanon, Doi ʌ 110 18.35 N 98.29 E
Intibucá 236 14.16 N 88.10 W
Intibucá □5 236 14.20 N 88.15 W
Intipucá 236 13.12 N 88.04 W
Intiyaco 252 28.39 S 60.05 W
Intracoastal Waterway ≚, U.S. 192 24.33 N 81.46 W
Intracoastal Waterway ≚, U.S. 196 26.04 N 97.12 W
Intragna 58 46.10 N 8.42 E
Intrånget 40 60.20 N 16.09 E
Introbio 62 45.57 N 9.27 E
Introdacqua 66 42.00 N 13.54 E
Intschön — Inch'ŏn 98 37.28 N 126.38 E
Intu 112 0.15 S 115.21 E
Intuto 246 3.39 S 74.44 W
Inubō-saki ⟩ 94 35.42 N 140.52 E
Inukai 96 33.04 N 131.38 E
Inukjuak 176 58.27 N 78.06 W
Inútil, Bahía c 254 53.30 S 69.50 W
Inuvik 180 68.25 N 133.30 W
Inuya ≃ 248 10.41 S 73.30 W
Inuyama 94 35.23 N 136.56 E
In'va ≃ 86 58.59 N 55.40 E
Inver 46 57.49 N 3.55 W
Inverallochy 46 57.40 N 1.55 W
Inveralochy 170 34.57 S 149.39 E
Inveraray 46 56.13 N 5.05 W
Inverarish 46 57.21 N 6.04 W
Inverarity 46 56.35 N 2.53 W
Inverbervie 46 56.51 N 2.17 W
Invercargill 172 46.24 S 168.21 E
Inverdruie 46 57.10 N 3.48 W
Inverell 166 29.47 S 151.07 E
Invergarry 46 57.02 N 4.47 W
Invergordon 46 57.42 N 4.10 W
Inverkeilor 46 56.38 N 2.32 W
Inverkeithing 46 56.02 N 3.25 W
Inverkeithny 46 57.30 N 2.38 W
Inverleigh 169 38.06 S 144.03 E
Inverloch 169 38.38 S 145.43 E
Invermay 184 51.48 N 103.09 W
Invermere 182 50.30 N 116.02 W
Invermoriston 46 57.13 N 4.38 W
Inverness, N.S., Can. 186 46.14 N 61.18 W
Inverness, P.Q., Can. 206 46.15 N 71.31 W
Inverness, Scot., U.K. 46 57.27 N 4.15 W
Inverness, Ca., U.S. 204 38.06 N 122.51 W
Inverness, Fl., U.S. 220 28.50 N 82.19 W
Inverness, Il., U.S. 216 42.07 N 88.05 W
Inverness, Ms., U.S. 194 33.21 N 90.35 W
Inveruglas 46 56.15 N 4.43 W
Inveruno 62 45.31 N 8.51 E
Inverurie 46 57.17 N 2.23 W
Inverway 162 17.50 S 129.38 E
Investigator Group II 162 33.45 S 134.30 E
Investigator Shoal ✦2 108 8.09 N 114.44 E
Investigator Strait ⊔ 166 35.25 S 137.10 E
Inwood, Mb., Can. 184 50.30 N 97.30 W
Inwood, On., Can. 214 42.49 N 81.59 W
Inwood, Fl., U.S. 220 28.02 N 81.45 W
Inwood, Ia., U.S. 198 43.18 N 96.25 W
Inwood, N.Y., U.S. 276 40.37 N 73.44 W
Inwood Hill Park ♦ 276 40.52 N 73.56 W
Inyanga 154 18.13 S 32.46 E
Inyanga Mountains ʌ 154 18.00 S 33.00 E

Symbol	English	Deutsch	Español	Français	Português
≃	River	Fluß	Río	Rivière	Rio
≚	Canal	Kanal	Canal	Canal	Canal
⊾	Waterfall, Rapids	Wasserfall, Stromschnellen	Cascada, Rápidos	Chute d'eau, Rapides	Cascata, Rápidos
⊔	Strait	Meeresstraße	Estrecho	Détroit	Estreito
c	Bay, Gulf	Bucht, Golf	Bahía, Golfo	Baie, Golfe	Baía, Golfo
⊜	Lake, Lakes	See, Seen	Lago, Lagos	Lac, Lacs	Lago, Lagos
≋	Swamp	Sumpf	Pantano	Marais	Pântano
⊼	Ice Features, Glacier	Eis- und Gletscherformen	Accidentes Glaciales	Formes glaciaires	Acidentes glaciares
⚲	Other Hydrographic Features	Andere Hydrographische Objekte	Otros Elementos Hidrográficos	Autres données hydrographiques	Outros acidentes hidrográficos
✦	Submarine Features	Untermeerische Objekte	Accidentes Submarinos	Formes de relief sous-marin	Acidentes submarinos
□	Political Unit	Politische Einheit	Unidad Política	Entité politique	Unidade política
⊍	Cultural Institution	Kulturelle Institution	Institución Cultural	Institution culturelle	Instituição cultural
⊥	Historical Site	Historische Stätte	Sitio Histórico	Site historique	Sítio histórico
♦	Recreational Site	Erholungs- und Ferienort	Sitio de Recreo	Centre de loisirs	Área de Lazer
✈	Airport	Flughafen	Aeropuerto	Aéroport	Aeroporto
▪	Military Installation	Militäranlage	Instalación Militar	Installation militaire	Instalação militar
✦	Miscellaneous	Verschiedenes	Misceláneo	Divers	Diversos

Name	Page	Lat.°′	Long.°′
Inyangani ∧	154	18.20 S	32.50 E
Inyan Kara Mountain ∧	198	44.13 N	104.21 W
Inyantue	154	18.32 S	26.41 E
Inyati	154	19.39 S	28.54 E
Inyo, Mount ∧	204	36.44 N	117.59 W
Inyokern	204	35.38 N	117.48 W
Inyo Mountains ⋀	204	36.40 N	118.10 W
Inyonga	154	6.43 S	32.04 E
Inywa	110	23.56 N	96.17 E
Inza	80	53.51 N	46.21 E
Inza ≃	80	53.54 N	45.44 E
Inzago	62	45.32 N	9.29 E
Inzai	94	35.50 N	140.09 E
Inzana Lake ⊜	182	54.58 N	124.40 W
Inžavino	80	52.19 N	42.30 E
Inzell	64	47.46 N	12.44 E
Inzer	86	54.14 N	57.34 E
Inzer ≃	86	54.30 N	56.28 E
Inzersdorf ◆[8]	264b	48.09 N	16.21 E
Inzia ≃	152	3.45 S	17.57 E
Ioanna, gora ∧	180	64.50 N	178.08 E
Ioánnina	38	39.40 N	20.50 E
Ioco	224	49.18 N	122.52 W
Iō-jima (Iwo Jima) I	174f	24.47 N	141.20 E
Iokanga ≃	24	68.00 N	39.43 E
Iola, Ks., U.S.	198	37.55 N	95.23 W
Iola, Pa., U.S.	210	45.08 N	76.32 W
Iola, Tx., U.S.	222	30.46 N	96.05 W
Iola, Wi., U.S.	190	44.30 N	89.07 W
Iolgo, chrebet ⋀	86	51.30 N	86.25 E
Iolotan'	72	37.18 N	62.21 E
Ioma	164	8.20 S	147.50 E
Iôna, Ang.	152	16.50 S	12.20 E
Iona, N.S., Can.	186	45.58 N	60.48 W
Iona, Id., U.S.	202	43.31 N	111.55 W
Iona I	46	56.19 N	6.25 W
Iôna, Parque Nacional do ♦	152	16.30 S	12.00 E
Iona, Sound of ʮ	46	56.19 N	6.24 W
Iona College ✝[2]	276	40.56 N	73.47 W
Ione, Ca., U.S.	226	38.21 N	120.55 W
Ione, Or., U.S.	202	45.30 N	119.50 W
Ione, Wa., U.S.	202	48.44 N	117.24 W
Ionia, Mi., U.S.	216	42.59 N	85.04 W
Ionia, N.Y., U.S.	210	42.56 N	77.30 W
Ionia □[6]	216	42.56 N	85.04 W
Ionian Islands → Iónioi Nísoi II	38	38.30 N	20.30 E
Ionian Sea ▾[2]	22	39.00 N	19.00 E
Ionia State Recreation Area ♦	216	42.58 N	85.36 W
Ionico, Mare → Ionian Sea ▾[2]	22	39.00 N	19.00 E
Ionienne, Mer → Ionian Sea ▾[2]	22	39.00 N	19.00 E
Iónioi Nísoi II	38	38.30 N	20.30 E
Ionisches Meer → Ionian Sea ▾[2]	22	39.00 N	19.00 E
Ionivejem ≃	180	66.12 N	174.00 W
Iony, ostrov I	74	56.26 N	143.25 E
Ioppolo	68	38.35 N	15.53 E
Ioppolo Giancaxio	70	37.23 N	13.33 E
Iordan	85	39.58 N	71.46 E
Iori ≃	84	41.03 N	46.17 E
Iorskoje ploskogorje ⋀[1]	84	41.20 N	46.00 E
Iory	85	39.30 N	67.53 E
Íos	38	36.44 N	25.17 E
Íos I	38	36.42 N	25.24 E
Ioscoe, Lake ⊜	276	41.02 N	74.19 W
Iosegun ≃	182	54.44 N	117.11 W
Iosegun Lake	182	54.29 N	116.50 W
Iō-shima I	93b	30.48 N	130.18 E
Iota	194	30.19 N	92.29 W
Iovlevo	82	56.10 N	38.20 E
Iowa	194	30.14 N	93.00 W
Iowa □[3]	178	42.15 N	93.15 W
Iowa ≃	190	41.10 N	91.02 W
Iowa, South Fork ≃	190	42.18 N	93.04 W
Iowa City	190	41.39 N	91.31 W
Iowa Falls	190	42.31 N	93.15 W
Iowa Park	196	33.57 N	98.40 W
Iō-zen ∧	94	36.31 N	136.48 E
Ipa ≃	76	52.13 N	29.08 E
Ipala	154	4.30 S	32.53 E
Ipameri	255	17.43 S	48.09 W
Ipanema ◆[8]	256	22.59 S	43.12 W
Ipanema ≃	250	9.53 S	37.15 W
Ipanguaçu	250	5.30 S	36.52 W
Ipat	24	66.13 N	56.33 E
Ipatinga	255	19.30 S	42.32 W
Ipatovo	80	45.43 N	42.53 E
Ipaumirim	250	6.47 S	38.43 W
Ipava	194	40.21 N	90.19 W
Ípeiros □[9]	38	39.40 N	20.50 E
Ipel' (Ipoly) ≃	30	47.49 N	18.52 E
Iperu	150	6.52 N	3.38 E
Iphigenia Bay ⊂	180	55.40 N	133.55 W
Iphofen	56	49.42 N	10.15 E
Ipiabas	256	22.23 S	43.53 W
Ipiales	246	0.50 N	77.37 W
Ipiaú	255	14.08 S	39.44 W
Ipiíba	256	22.52 S	42.57 W
Ipil	116	7.47 N	122.35 E
Ipin → Yibin	107	28.47 N	104.38 E
Ipirá	255	12.10 S	39.44 W
Ipiranga, Bra.	252	25.01 S	50.35 W
Ipiranga, Bra.	287a	22.43 S	43.12 W
Ipiranga ◆[8]	287b	23.36 S	46.35 W
Ipiranga ≃, Bra.	256	23.21 S	45.10 W
Ipiranga ≃, Bra.	287a	22.48 S	43.37 W
Ipiranga, Canal ≍	287a	22.46 S	43.37 W
Ipiranga, Museu do ✝	287b	23.35 S	46.36 W
Ipita	248	19.20 S	63.32 W
Ipitinga ≃	250	0.02 N	53.01 W
Ipixuna	250	4.22 S	44.34 W
Ipixuna ≃, Bra.	248	7.11 S	71.51 W
Ipixuna ≃, Bra.	248	5.45 S	63.02 W
Ipixuna ≃, Bra.	248	6.16 S	61.52 W
Ipixuna, Igarapé ≃	250	4.32 S	52.40 W
Ipoh	114	4.35 N	101.05 E
Ipojuca ≃	250	8.25 S	34.58 W
Ipokera	154	8.03 S	35.41 E
Ipole	154	5.47 S	32.44 E
Ipoly (Ipel') ≃	30	47.49 N	18.52 E
Iporá, Bra.	255	16.28 S	51.07 W
Iporã, Bra.	255	23.59 S	53.37 W
Ipota	175f	18.48 S	169.16 E
Ippari ≃	70	36.52 N	14.26 E
Ippinghausen	56	51.17 N	9.08 E
Ipplepen	42	50.29 N	3.38 W
Ippy	152	6.15 N	21.12 E
İpsala	130	40.55 N	26.23 E
Ipswich, Austl.	171a	27.36 S	152.46 E
Ipswich, Eng., U.K.	42	52.04 N	1.10 E
Ipswich, Ma., U.S.	207	42.40 N	70.50 W
Ipswich, S.D., U.S.	198	45.26 N	99.01 W
Ipswich ≃	207	42.42 N	70.48 W
Ipswich Bay ⊂	207	42.41 N	70.42 W
Ipu	250	4.20 S	40.42 W
Ipubi	250	7.39 S	40.07 W
Ipueiras	250	4.33 S	40.43 W
Ipuh	112	3.00 S	101.30 E
Ipuiúna	256	22.06 S	46.11 W
Ipun, Isla I	254	44.37 S	74.46 W
Ipupiara	255	11.49 S	42.37 W
Iput' ≃	76	52.26 N	31.02 E
Iqaluit	176	63.44 N	68.28 W
Iqe ≃	102	38.14 N	94.18 E
Iqfahṣ	142	28.47 N	30.49 E
Iquaçu, Parque Nacional do ♦	252	25.30 S	53.50 W
Iquique	248	20.13 S	70.10 W
Iquitos	246	3.46 S	73.15 W
Ira	196	32.35 N	101.00 W
Iraan, Pil.	116	9.04 N	117.42 E
Iraan, Tx., U.S.	196	30.54 N	101.53 W
Ira Banda	152	5.57 N	22.04 E
Irabu	175d	24.50 N	125.09 E
Irabu-jima I	175d	24.50 N	125.10 E
Iracajá, Cachoeira do ⌊	248	10.29 S	64.05 W
Iracema	250	5.48 S	38.18 W
Iracoubo	250	5.29 N	53.13 W
Irago-misaki ›	94	34.35 N	137.01 E
Irago-suidō ʮ	94	34.35 N	137.00 E
Iraí	252	27.11 S	53.15 W
Irajá ◆[8]	287a	22.51 S	43.19 W
Irajá ≃	287a	22.49 S	43.17 W
Irajol'	24	64.27 N	55.08 E
Irak → Iraq □[1]	128	33.00 N	44.00 E
Iráklion, Ellás	38	35.20 N	25.09 E
Iráklion, Ellás	267c	38.04 N	23.46 E
Iran (Īrān) □[1], Asia	118	32.00 N	53.00 E
Iran (Īrān) □[1], Asia	128	32.00 N	53.00 E
Iran, Pegunungan ⋀	112	2.05 N	114.55 E
Iran National Arts Museum ✝	267d	35.41 N	51.27 E
Īrānshahr	128	27.13 N	60.41 E
Irapa	246	10.34 N	62.35 W
Irapuato	234	20.41 N	101.21 W
Iraq (Al-'Irāq) □[1], Asia	118	33.00 N	44.00 E
Iraq (Al-'Irāq) □[1], Asia	128	33.00 N	44.00 E
Irará	255	12.02 S	38.46 W
Iratapuru ≃	250	0.36 S	52.35 W
Irati	252	25.27 S	50.39 W
Irati ≃	34	42.35 N	1.16 W
Irauçuba	250	3.45 S	39.47 W
Irazú, Volcán ∧[1]	236	9.58 N	83.53 W
Irba	88	58.07 N	99.00 E
Irbejskoje	88	55.39 N	95.28 E
Irbeni väin (Irbes jūras šaurums) ʮ	76	57.48 N	22.05 E
Irbes jūras šaurums (Irbeni väin) ʮ	76	57.48 N	22.05 E
Irbid	132	32.33 N	35.51 E
Irbid □[8]	132	32.30 N	35.45 E
Irbīl	128	36.11 N	44.01 E
Irbīl □[4]	128	36.10 N	44.00 E
Irbit	86	57.41 N	63.03 E
Irby	262	53.21 N	3.07 W
Irchester	42	52.16 N	0.38 W
Irdning	61	47.33 N	14.01 E
Irdyn'	78	49.23 N	31.44 E
Ire, Mount ∧	175e	9.10 S	161.05 E
Irebu	152	0.37 S	17.45 E
Irecê	250	11.18 S	41.52 W
Iregua ≃	34	42.27 N	2.24 W
Ireland (Éire) □[1], Europe	22	53.00 N	8.00 W
Ireland (Éire) □[1], Europe	48	53.00 N	8.00 W
Ireland Brook ≃	276	40.25 N	74.29 W
Iren' ≃	86	57.27 N	56.56 E
Irene, S. Afr.	158	25.53 S	28.13 E
Irene, S.D., U.S.	198	43.05 N	97.10 W
Irene, Tx., U.S.	222	31.59 N	96.52 W
Irene, Mount ∧	172	45.10 S	167.22 E
Ireng (Maú) ≃	246	3.33 N	59.51 W
Iresick Brook ≃	276	40.24 N	74.22 W
Ireton	198	42.58 N	96.19 W
Irfon ≃	42	52.09 N	3.24 W
Irgakly	84	44.22 N	44.45 E
Irgiz	86	48.37 N	61.16 E
Irgiz ≃	86	48.13 N	62.08 E
Iri	98	35.56 N	126.57 E
Irian Jaya □[4]	164	5.00 S	138.00 E
Iriba	146	15.07 N	22.15 E
Irié	150	8.17 N	9.11 W
Iriga	116	13.25 N	123.25 E
Irigny	62	45.40 N	4.49 E
Irîgui ◆[1]	150	16.43 N	5.30 W
Iriklinskij	86	51.39 N	58.38 E
Iringa	154	7.46 S	35.42 E
Iringa □[4]	154	9.00 S	35.00 E
Irinjālakuda	122	10.20 N	76.14 E
Iriomote-jima I	175d	24.20 N	123.50 E
Iriona	236	15.57 N	85.11 W
Iriri ≃, Bra.	250	3.52 S	52.37 W
Iriri ≃, Bra.	287a	22.41 S	43.05 W
Iriri Novo ≃	250	8.46 S	53.22 W
Irische See → Irish Sea ▾[2]	28	53.30 N	5.20 W
Irish, Mount ∧	204	37.38 N	115.24 W
Irish Sea ▾[2]	28	53.30 N	5.20 W
Irishtown	166	40.55 S	145.08 E
Irituia	250	1.46 S	47.26 W
Iriyamazu	268	35.16 N	139.39 E
Irkās, Wādī V	142	28.57 N	32.00 E
Irkeštam	85	39.41 N	73.55 E
Irkinejeva ≃	88	58.30 N	96.48 E
Irkinejevo	88	58.30 N	96.49 E
Irklijev	78	49.32 N	32.18 E
Irklijevskaja	78	45.51 N	39.39 E
Irkoutsk → Irkutsk	88	52.16 N	104.20 E
Irkut ≃	88	52.18 N	104.15 E
Irkutsk	88	52.16 N	104.20 E
Irkutsk Oblast' □[4]	88	56.00 N	106.00 E
Irlam	44	53.28 N	2.25 W
Irlanda, Mar de → Irish Sea ▾[2]	28	53.30 N	5.20 W
Irlande, Mer d' → Irish Sea ▾[2]	28	53.30 N	5.20 W
Irlande → Ireland □[1]	48	53.00 N	8.00 W
Irland → Ireland □[1]	48	53.00 N	8.00 W
Irma	182	52.55 N	111.14 W
Irmauw	164	7.25 S	131.42 E
Irminger Basin ✦[1]	10	61.00 N	35.00 W
Irminio ≃	70	36.46 N	14.36 E
Irmino ◆[8]	83	48.36 N	38.36 E
Irnijärvi ⊜	26	65.36 N	29.05 E
Irnsum	52	53.05 N	5.47 E
Iro, Lac ⊜	146	10.06 N	19.25 E
Iroise ⊂	32	48.15 N	4.55 W
Iron Baron	166	32.59 S	137.09 E
Iron Belt	190	46.24 N	90.19 W
Iron Bottom Sound ʮ	175e	9.15 S	160.00 E
Iron Bridge, On., Can.	190	46.17 N	83.14 W
Iron Bridge, Eng., U.K.	42	52.38 N	2.29 W
Iron Bridge Dam ◆[6]	222	32.50 N	95.54 W
Iron City	194	35.01 N	87.34 W
Iron Cove ⊂	274a	33.52 S	151.10 E
Iron Creek ≃	182	52.43 N	111.14 W
Irondale, Al., U.S.	194	33.32 N	86.42 W
Irondale, Mo., U.S.	194	37.49 N	90.40 W
Irondale, Oh., U.S.	214	40.34 N	80.43 W
Irondale ≃	212	44.49 N	78.37 W
Irondequoit	210	43.12 N	77.36 W
Irondequoit Bay ⊂	210	43.12 N	77.32 W
Iron Gate V	38	44.41 N	22.31 E
Iron Gate Reservoir ⊜[1]	38	44.30 N	22.00 E
Ironia	276	40.49 N	74.37 W
Iron Knob	166	32.44 S	137.08 E
Iron Mountain	190	45.49 N	88.03 W
Iron Mountain ∧, Az., U.S.	200	33.27 N	111.10 W
Iron Mountain ∧, Ca., U.S.	280	34.17 N	117.43 W
Iron Mountains ⋀	192	36.30 N	81.50 W
Iron Range	164	12.42 S	143.18 E
Iron Range National Park ♦	164	12.44 S	143.16 E
Iron River, Mi., U.S.	190	46.05 N	88.38 W
Iron River, Wi., U.S.	190	46.33 N	91.24 W
Iron Springs	208	39.46 N	77.25 W
Ironton, Mn., U.S.	190	46.28 N	93.58 W
Ironton, Mo., U.S.	194	37.35 N	90.37 W
Ironton, Oh., U.S.	188	38.32 N	82.40 W
Ironwood	190	46.27 N	90.10 W
Ironworks Creek ≃	285	40.10 N	74.59 W
Iroquois, On., Can.	212	44.51 N	75.19 W
Iroquois, Il., U.S.	216	40.50 N	87.35 W
Iroquois, S.D., U.S.	198	44.22 N	97.51 W
Iroquois □[6]	216	40.47 N	87.44 W
Iroquois ≃	216	41.05 N	87.49 W
Iroquois Falls	190	48.46 N	80.41 W
Iroquois Lock and Dam ◆[5]	212	44.45 N	75.23 W
Irosin	116	12.42 N	124.02 E
Írottkő (Geschriebenstein) ∧	61	47.21 N	16.26 E
Irō-zaki ›	94	34.36 N	138.51 E
Irpen'	78	50.31 N	30.15 E
Irpen' ≃	78	50.34 N	30.16 E
Irrawaddy, Mouths of the ≃[1]	110	15.45 N	94.50 E
Irrawaddy → Ayeyarwady ≃	110	20.32 N	96.55 E
Irregully Creek ≃	162	23.06 S	116.21 E
Irrel	56	49.51 N	6.28 E
Irricana	182	51.19 N	113.37 W
Irrigon	202	45.53 N	119.29 W
Irša ≃	78	50.45 N	29.30 E
Iršava	78	48.20 N	23.03 E
Irschenberg	64	47.50 N	11.55 E
Irsee	58	47.54 N	10.34 E
Irsina	68	40.45 N	16.15 E
Irt ≃	44	54.22 N	3.26 W
Irtek ≃	80	51.28 N	52.39 E
Irthing ≃	44	54.55 N	2.50 W
Irthlingborough	42	52.20 N	0.37 W
Irtyš	86	54.29 N	74.22 E
Irtyš (Ertix) ≃	74	61.04 N	68.52 E
Irtysch → Irtyš ≃	72	61.04 N	68.52 E
Irtysh → Irtyš ≃	72	61.04 N	68.52 E
Irtyšsk	86	53.21 N	75.27 E
Irubaj	80	50.11 N	51.21 E
Iruma	94	35.50 N	139.24 E
Iruma ≃	94	35.57 N	139.30 E
Iruma Air Base ■	268	35.50 N	139.24 E
Iruma-kichi, Kaijō-jieitai- ■	94	35.50 N	139.24 E
Irumu	154	1.27 N	29.52 E
Irún	34	43.21 N	1.47 W
Irupana	248	16.28 S	67.28 W
Irurzun	34	42.55 N	1.50 W
Irú Tepuy ∧	246	5.25 N	61.02 W
Irvine, Ab., Can.	184	49.57 N	110.16 W
Irvine, Scot., U.K.	46	55.37 N	4.40 W
Irvine, Ca., U.S.	228	33.40 N	117.49 W
Irvine, Ky., U.S.	192	37.42 N	83.58 W
Irvine, Pa., U.S.	214	41.50 N	79.17 W
Irvine ≃	46	55.37 N	4.41 W
Irvine, Mount ∧	210	42.03 N	78.40 W
Irvine Creek ≃	212	43.41 N	80.25 W
Irvine Park ♦	280	33.48 N	117.45 W
Irvines Landing	182	49.38 N	124.03 W
Irvinestown	48	54.28 N	7.38 W
Irving, Il., U.S.	219	39.12 N	89.24 W
Irving, N.Y., U.S.	214	42.34 N	79.07 W
Irving, Tx., U.S.	222	32.48 N	96.56 W
Irving Park ◆[8]	278	41.57 N	87.43 W
Irvington, Il., U.S.	219	38.26 N	89.10 W
Irvington, Ky., U.S.	194	37.52 N	86.17 W
Irvington, N.J., U.S.	210	40.43 N	74.13 W
Irvington, N.Y., U.S.	210	41.02 N	73.51 W
Irvington, Oh., U.S.	218	39.51 N	84.15 W
Irvington, Va., U.S.	208	37.39 N	76.25 W
Irvington ◆[8]	284b	39.17 N	76.41 W
Irvona	214	40.46 N	78.33 W
Irwell ≃	44	53.27 N	2.17 W
Irwin, Austl.	162	29.12 S	115.04 E
Irwin, Oh., U.S.	218	40.07 N	83.29 W
Irwin, Pa., U.S.	279b	40.19 N	79.42 W
Irwin ≃	162	29.15 S	114.56 E
Irwin, Point ›	162	35.04 S	116.56 E
Irwindale	280	34.06 N	117.56 W
Irwinton	192	32.48 N	83.10 W
Is	86	58.48 N	59.43 E
Is, Jabal ∧	140	21.49 N	35.39 E
Isa	150	13.14 N	6.24 E
'Īsā, Ra's ›	144	15.11 N	42.39 E
Isaac ≃	166	22.52 S	149.20 E
Isaac Lake ⊜, B.C., Can.	182	53.10 N	120.50 W
Isaac Lake ⊜, On., Can.	212	44.47 N	81.14 W
Isaba	34	42.52 N	0.55 W
Isabel, Pil.	116	10.56 N	124.26 E
Isabel, S.D., U.S.	198	45.23 N	101.25 W
Isabel □[4]	175e	7.55 S	159.10 E
Isabela, Pil.	116	10.12 N	122.59 E
Isabela (Basilan), Pil.	116	6.42 N	121.58 E
Isabela, P.R.	240m	18.30 N	67.01 W
Isabela □[4]	116	17.00 N	122.00 E
Isabela, Cabo ›	238	19.56 N	71.01 W
Isabela, Canal ʮ	246a	0.20 S	90.55 W
Isabela, Isla I, Ec.	246a	0.30 S	91.06 W
Isabela, Isla I, Méx.	234	21.51 N	105.55 W
Isabela de Sagua	240p	22.57 N	80.01 W
Isabelia, Cordillera ⋀	236	13.45 N	85.15 W
Isabella Indian Reservation ◆[4]	190	43.41 N	84.48 W
Isabella Lake ⊜	212	45.24 N	79.49 W
Isabella Lake ⊜[1]	204	35.40 N	118.26 W
Isabelle ≃	190	47.50 N	91.41 W
Isábena ≃	34	42.11 N	0.21 E
Isaccea	38	45.16 N	28.28 E
Ísafjarðardjúp ⊂[2]	24a	66.10 N	23.00 W
Ísafjörður	24a	66.08 N	23.13 W
Isāgarh	124	24.50 N	77.53 E
Isagatedo	273a	6.32 N	3.20 E
Isahaya	92	32.50 N	130.03 E
Isak	114	4.28 N	96.55 E
Isaka, Tan.	154	3.54 S	32.56 E
Isaka, Zaïre	152	2.35 S	18.48 E
Isaka-Buku	152	3.55 S	22.03 E
Īsa Khel	123	32.41 N	71.17 E
Isakly	80	54.08 N	51.32 E
Isakovka	86	55.45 N	74.24 E
Isakovo, Ross.	76	55.11 N	34.40 E
Isakovo, Ross.	76	60.30 N	41.13 E
Isakovo, Ross.	82	54.36 N	37.02 E
Isakovo, Ross.	265b	55.59 N	37.23 E
Işalniţa	38	44.24 N	23.44 E
Isalo, Massif de l' ⋀	157b	22.45 S	45.15 E
Isalo, Parc National de l' ♦	157b	22.45 S	45.15 E
Isana (Içana) ≃	246	0.26 N	67.19 W
Īsānagar	124	27.54 N	81.13 E
Isandhlwana ⊥	158	28.21 S	30.39 E
Isandja Etat	152	2.59 S	22.00 E
Isando	273d	26.09 S	28.12 E
Isanga	152	1.26 S	22.18 E
Isangano National Park ♦	154	11.10 S	30.40 E
Isangel	175f	19.32 S	169.16 E
Isangi	152	0.46 N	24.15 E
Is'angulovo	86	52.12 N	56.36 E
Isanlu Makutu	150	8.17 N	5.46 E
Isan-ni	98	40.46 N	128.55 E
Isanti	190	45.29 N	93.14 W
Isar ≃	60	48.49 N	12.58 E
Isara	150	6.59 N	3.41 E
Isarco (Eisack) ≃	64	46.27 N	11.18 E
Isarco, Valle V	64	46.45 N	11.37 E
Isarog, Mount ∧	116	13.39 N	123.23 E
Isasi	273a	6.40 N	3.23 E
Isawa	94	35.39 N	138.38 E
Isbergues	50	50.37 N	2.27 E
Isbister	46a	60.36 N	1.19 W
İscehisar	130	38.51 N	30.45 E
Iščeino	76	52.57 N	38.50 E
Iščerskaja	84	43.43 N	45.08 E
Ischgl	58	47.01 N	10.17 E
Ischia	68	40.44 N	13.57 E
Ischia, Isola d' I	68	40.43 N	13.54 E
Ischia di Castro	66	42.33 N	11.45 E
Ischim → Išim ≃	86	57.45 N	71.12 E
Ischitella	68	41.54 N	15.54 E
Ischma → Ižma ≃	24	65.19 N	52.54 E
Ischodnaja, gora ∧	180	64.50 N	173.26 W
Ischua	210	42.15 N	78.24 W
Ischua Creek ≃	210	42.10 N	78.23 W
Iscuandé ≃	246	2.38 N	78.04 W
Isdell ≃	162	16.27 S	124.51 E
Isdes	50	47.40 N	2.15 E
Ise (Uji-yamada)	94	34.29 N	136.42 E
Ise ≃	54	52.30 N	10.33 E
Isefjord ⊂	41	55.52 N	11.49 E
Isehara	94	35.24 N	139.18 E
Išejevka	80	54.25 N	48.16 E
Iseke	154	6.25 S	35.01 E
Isel ≃	64	46.50 N	12.47 E
Iselin, N.J., U.S.	210	40.34 N	74.19 W
Iselin, Pa., U.S.	214	40.33 N	79.23 W
Iselle	58	46.12 N	8.12 E
Iseltwald	58	46.43 N	7.58 E
Isen	60	48.13 N	12.04 E
Isen ≃	60	48.15 N	12.40 E
Isenbajevo	80	56.03 N	53.25 E
Isenbüttel	52	52.26 N	10.34 E
Isenyela	154	8.36 S	33.30 E
Iseo	64	45.39 N	10.03 E
Iseo, Lago d' ⊜	64	45.43 N	10.04 E
Iseramagazi	154	4.40 S	32.09 E
Iseran, Col de l')(	62	45.25 N	7.02 E
Isère □[5]	62	45.10 N	5.50 E
Isère ≃	62	44.59 N	4.51 E
Iseri	273a	6.39 N	3.23 E
Iseri-Oke	273a	6.38 N	3.23 E
Iseri-Osun	273a	6.31 N	3.17 E
Iserlohn	56	51.22 N	7.41 E
Isernhagen	52	52.26 N	9.51 E
Isernia	66	41.36 N	14.14 E
Isernia □[4]	66	41.40 N	14.15 E
Isesaki	94	36.19 N	139.12 E
Ise-Shima-kokuritsu-kōen ♦	92	34.23 N	136.48 E
Iset' ≃	86	56.36 N	66.24 E
Isetskoje	86	56.29 N	65.21 E
Ise-wan ⊂	94	34.43 N	136.43 E
Iseyin	150	7.58 N	3.36 E
Isezaki → Isesaki	92	36.19 N	139.12 E
Isfahan → Eşfahān	128	32.40 N	51.38 E
Isfana	85	39.50 N	69.31 E
Isfana ≃	85	40.13 N	69.26 E
Isfara	85	40.07 N	70.38 E
'Isfiyā	132	32.43 N	35.04 E
Ishenga Oswe	152	3.46 S	22.34 E
Isheri-Olofin	273a	6.35 N	3.17 E
Isherton	246	2.19 N	59.22 W
Ishi ≃	270	34.35 N	135.38 E
Ishibashi	94	36.26 N	139.52 E
Ishibe	94	35.00 N	136.04 E
Ishigaki	175d	24.20 N	124.09 E
Ishigaki-shima I	175d	24.24 N	124.12 E
Ishige	94	36.07 N	139.58 E
Ishii	96	34.04 N	134.26 E
Ishikari ≃	92a	43.15 N	141.23 E
Ishikari-dake ∧	92a	43.33 N	143.02 E
Ishikari-heiya ≚	92a	43.15 N	141.23 E
Ishikari-sanchi ⋀	92a	43.35 N	143.00 E
Ishikari-wan ⊂	92a	43.25 N	141.01 E
Ishikawa, Nihon	94	37.09 N	140.27 E
Ishikawa, Nihon	174m	26.25 N	127.50 E
Ishikawa □[5]	94	36.45 N	136.45 E
Ishiki	94	34.48 N	137.01 E
Ishikiri	270	34.41 N	135.39 E
I-shima I	96	33.51 N	134.49 E
Ishinomaki	92	38.25 N	141.18 E
Ishinomaki-wan ⊂	92	38.18 N	141.18 E
Ishioka	94	36.11 N	140.16 E
Ishiyama	270	34.58 N	135.55 E
Ishizuchi-san ∧	96	33.46 N	133.07 E
Ishkumān	123	36.32 N	73.49 E
Ishmant	142	29.12 N	31.11 E
Ishpeming	190	46.29 N	87.40 W
Ishuizu ≃	270	34.33 N	135.27 E
Ishurdi	124	24.08 N	89.05 E
Isidro Casanova	288	34.42 S	58.35 W
Isigny	32	49.19 N	1.06 W
Işık Dağı ∧	130	38.21 N	36.32 E
Işıklı	130	38.19 N	29.51 E
Işıklı Burnu ›	267b	41.14 N	29.15 E
Isili	71	39.44 N	9.06 E
Isil'kul'	86	54.55 N	71.16 E
Išim	86	56.09 N	69.27 E
Išim ≃	86	57.45 N	71.12 E
Išimbaj	86	53.28 N	56.02 E
Išimka	86	51.24 N	67.08 E
Išimskaja step' ≚	86	55.00 N	70.00 E
Isimu	112	0.40 N	122.51 E
Isinga	88	52.55 N	112.00 E
Isiolo	154	0.21 N	37.35 E
Isiolo Game Reserve ◆[4]	154	0.32 N	37.34 E
Isipingo	158	29.59 S	30.56 E
Isipingo Beach	158	29.59 S	30.57 E
Isiro (Paulis)	154	2.47 N	27.37 E
Isis	166	25.12 S	152.13 E
Isisford	166	24.16 S	144.26 E
Iskandar	85	41.36 N	69.43 E
Iskâr ≃	38	43.44 N	24.27 E
Iskâr, jazovir ⊜[1]	38	42.28 N	23.35 E
Iškašim	123	36.44 N	71.37 E
Iskaten', chrebet ⋀	180	66.30 N	179.00 W
Iškejevo	80	55.51 N	50.56 E
İskele	130	35.17 N	33.52 E
İskenderun	130	36.37 N	36.07 E
İskenderun Körfezi (Gulf of Alexandretta) ⊂	130	36.30 N	35.40 E
Iske-R'az'ap	80	54.36 N	49.42 E
İskilip	130	40.45 N	34.29 E
Iski-Naukat	85	40.16 N	72.36 E
Iskininskij	80	47.13 N	52.41 E
Iskitim	86	54.38 N	83.18 E
Iskona ≃	82	55.34 N	36.05 E
Iskushuban	144	10.17 N	50.14 E
Iskut ≃	180	56.42 N	131.45 W
Isla	234	18.01 N	95.30 W
Isla ≃	46	57.30 N	2.47 W
Isla, Salar de la ≚	252	25.49 S	68.53 W
Isla Cristina	34	37.12 N	7.19 W
Isla de Maipo	252	33.45 S	70.54 W
İslâhiye	130	37.03 N	36.36 E
Islāmābād	123	33.42 N	73.10 E
Islāmābād → Anantnāg	123	33.44 N	75.09 E
Isla Mala	258	34.12 S	56.21 W
Islāmkot	120	24.42 N	70.11 E
Islamorada	220	24.55 N	80.37 W
Islāmpur, India	122	17.03 N	74.16 E
Islāmpur, India	124	25.09 N	85.12 E
Islāmpur, India	124	26.16 N	88.12 E
Islāmpur, India	126	21.43 N	87.39 E
Islāmpur, India	126	24.09 N	88.28 E
Isla Mujeres	232	21.12 N	86.43 W
Island	194	37.26 N	87.08 W
Island □[6]	224	48.07 N	122.36 W
Island ≃	262	53.44 N	2.51 W
Island Bay ⊂	116	9.06 N	118.10 E
Island Beach State Park ♦	208	39.50 N	74.06 W
Island Bend	171b	36.19 S	148.29 E
Island Creek	283	42.00 N	70.43 W
Island Falls, Sk., Can.	184	55.32 N	102.21 W
Island Falls, Me., U.S.	188	46.00 N	68.16 W
Island Heights	208	39.56 N	74.09 W
Islandia → Iceland □[1]	24a	65.00 N	18.00 W
Island → Iceland □[1]	24a	65.00 N	18.00 W

ENGLISH Name	Page	Lat.°′	Long.°′
Island Lagoon ⊜	166	31.30 S	136.40 E
Island Lake, Mb., Can.	184	53.58 N	94.47 W
Island Lake, Il., U.S.	216	42.17 N	88.12 W
Island Lake, Mi., U.S.	281	42.31 N	83.44 W
Island Lake ⊜	184	53.47 N	94.25 W
Island Lake State Recreation Area ♦	216	42.30 N	83.43 W
Island Park, Id., U.S.	202	44.24 N	111.19 W
Island Park, N.Y., U.S.	276	40.36 N	73.39 W
Island Park, R.I., U.S.	207	41.37 N	71.13 W
Island Park Reservoir ⊜[1]	202	44.25 N	111.29 W
Island Point ›	162	30.20 S	115.02 E
Island Pond	188	44.48 N	71.52 W
Island Pond ⊜	186	48.25 N	56.23 W
Islands, Bay of ⊂, Nf., Can.	186	49.10 N	58.15 W
Islands, Bay of ⊂, N.Z.	172	35.12 S	174.10 E
Island View	216	40.31 N	83.53 W
Isla Patrulla	252	32.59 S	54.35 W
Islas de la Bahía □[5]	236	16.20 N	86.30 W
Islas Malvinas → Falkland Islands □[2]	254	51.45 S	59.00 W
Isla Verde	252	33.14 S	62.24 W
Isla Vista	204	34.25 N	119.50 W
Islay I	46	55.46 N	6.10 W
Islay, Punta ›	248	17.01 S	72.07 W
Islay, Rhinns of ›[1]	46	55.45 N	6.25 W
Islay, Sound of ʮ	46	55.50 N	6.06 W
Isle	190	46.08 N	93.28 W
Isle ≃, Fr.	32	44.55 N	0.15 W
Isle ≃, Eng., U.K.	42	50.59 N	2.53 W
Isle-Adam, Forêt de l' ♦	261	49.05 N	2.15 E
Isle-aux-Morts	186	47.35 N	58.59 W
Isle of Hope	192	31.58 N	81.05 W
Isle of Man □[2], Europe	22	54.15 N	4.30 W
Isle of Man □[2], Europe	44	54.15 N	4.30 W
Isle of Man (Ronaldsway) Airport ⊠	44	54.06 N	4.36 W
Isle of Palms	192	32.47 N	79.48 W
Isle of Wight	208	36.54 N	76.42 W
Isle of Wight □[6], Eng., U.K.	42	50.40 N	1.20 W
Isle of Wight □[6], Va., U.S.	208	36.50 N	76.42 W
Isle of Wight Bay ⊂	208	38.22 N	75.06 W
Isle Royale National Park ♦	190	48.00 N	89.00 W
Isles, Lake of the ⊜	212	44.19 N	75.59 W
Isle Saint George	214	41.43 N	82.49 W
Islesboro Island I	188	44.20 N	68.53 W
Isleta	200	34.54 N	106.41 W
Isleta Indian Reservation ◆[4]	200	34.55 N	106.45 W
Isleton	226	38.09 N	121.36 W
Islets-Caribou	186	49.30 N	67.14 W
Isleworth ◆[8]	260	51.28 N	0.20 W
Islington	207	42.13 N	71.11 W
Islington ◆[8], On., Can.	275b	43.39 N	79.32 W
Islington ◆[8], Eng., U.K.	42	51.34 N	0.06 W
Islip, Eng., U.K.	42	51.50 N	1.14 W
Islip, N.Y., U.S.	276	40.43 N	73.12 W
Islip Terrace	276	40.44 N	73.11 W
Islivig	46	58.05 N	7.11 W
Isloč' ≃	76	53.55 N	26.13 E
Islón	252	29.54 S	71.12 W
Isluga, Volcán ∧[1]	248	19.10 S	68.51 W
Ismael Cortinas (Arroyo Grande)	258	33.58 S	57.06 W
Ismailia → Al-Ismā'īlīyah	142	30.35 N	32.16 E
Ismā'īlīyah ◆[8]	273c	30.03 N	31.14 E
Ismā'īlīyah, Tur'at al- ≍	142	30.04 N	31.16 E
İsmailli	130	38.56 N	27.13 E
Ismailly	84	40.47 N	48.09 E
Ismailovo	80	55.34 N	54.39 E
Ismaning	60	48.14 N	11.41 E
Isnā	140	25.18 N	32.33 E
Isny	58	47.41 N	10.02 E
Isoanala	157b	23.50 S	45.44 E
Isobe	94	34.22 N	136.49 E
Isogo ◆[8]	268	35.23 N	139.37 E
Isojoki	26	62.07 N	21.58 E
Isoka	154	10.10 S	32.35 E
Isokyrö	26	63.00 N	22.19 E
Isola, Fr.	62	44.11 N	7.03 E
Isola, Ms., U.S.	194	33.15 N	90.35 W
Isola, Monte ∧	64	45.42 N	10.05 E
Isola d'Asti	62	44.50 N	8.11 E
Isola del Cantone	62	44.39 N	8.57 E
Isola del Gran Sasso d'Italia	66	42.30 N	13.40 E
Isola della Scala	64	45.16 N	11.00 E
Isola del Liri	66	41.41 N	13.34 E
Isola di Capo Rizzuto	68	38.58 N	17.06 E
Isola Dovarese	64	45.10 N	10.18 E
Isola Farnese ◆[8]	66	42.01 N	12.23 E
Isola Vicentina	64	45.38 N	11.25 E
Isoletta	66	41.30 N	13.34 E
Isolillock Peak ∧	224	49.18 N	121.27 W
Isolo	273a	6.32 N	3.19 E
Isone	58	46.08 N	8.59 E
Isonzo (Soča) ≃	64	45.47 N	13.32 E
Isorella	64	45.18 N	10.19 E
Iso-Syöte ∧[2]	26	65.37 N	27.35 E
Iso-zaki ›	94	36.23 N	140.38 E
Ispani	68	40.08 N	15.34 E
Isparta	130	37.46 N	30.33 E
Isparta □[4]	130	38.00 N	31.00 E
Isperih	38	43.43 N	26.50 E
Ispica	70	36.47 N	14.55 E
Ispica, Cava d' ⊥[5]	70	36.51 N	14.51 E
Ispikān	128	26.14 N	62.12 E
İspir	130	40.29 N	41.00 E
Ispra	62	45.49 N	8.37 E
Ispringen	56	48.55 N	8.40 E
Israel (Yisra'el) □[1], Asia	118	31.30 N	35.00 E
Israel (Yisra'el) □[1], Asia	132	31.30 N	35.00 E
Israel ≃	188	44.29 N	71.35 W
Issa	80	53.52 N	44.51 E
Issa ≃	76	56.58 N	28.47 E
Issano	246	5.49 N	59.25 W
Issaquah	224	47.31 N	122.01 W
Issaran, Ra's ›	142	28.48 N	32.47 E
Issel (Oude IJssel) ≃	52	52.00 N	6.10 E
Isselburg	52	51.51 N	6.28 E
Isselhorst	52	51.57 N	8.24 E
Isser, Oued ≃, Alg.	34	36.52 N	3.48 E
Isser, Oued ≃, Alg.	34	35.08 N	1.28 W
Issia	150	6.29 N	6.35 W
Issigeac	32	44.44 N	0.36 E
Issime	62	45.41 N	7.51 E
Issogne	62	45.39 N	7.41 E
Issoire	32	45.33 N	3.15 E
Issole ≃	62	43.27 N	6.12 E
Issou	261	48.59 N	1.48 E
Issoudun	32	46.57 N	2.00 E
Issum	52	51.32 N	6.25 E
Issuna	154	5.23 S	34.46 E
Is-sur-Tille	58	47.31 N	5.06 E
Issy	50	48.49 N	2.17 E
Issyk	85	43.22 N	77.28 E
Issyk-Kul' (Rybačje)	85	42.26 N	76.12 E
Issyk-Kul' □[4]	85	42.15 N	77.15 E
Issyk-Kul', ozero ⊜	85	42.25 N	77.15 E
Issy-les-Moulineaux	261	48.49 N	2.17 E
Īstādeh-ye Moqor, Āb-e ⊜	120	32.32 N	67.57 E

DEUTSCH Name	Seite	Breite°′	Länge°′ E = Ost
Istana Presidential Palace ✝	269e	6.10 S	106.49 E
İstanbul, Tür.	130	41.01 N	28.58 E
İstanbul, Tür.	267b	41.01 N	28.58 E
İstanbul □[4]	130	41.10 N	28.45 E
Istanbul (Yeşilköy) International Airport ⊠	267b	40.58 N	28.49 E
İstanbul Boğazı (Bosporus) ʮ	130	41.06 N	29.04 E
Istanbul University ✝[2]	267b	41.00 N	28.58 E
Iṣṭanhā	142	30.28 N	31.07 E
Istead Rise	260	51.24 N	0.22 E
Isteren ⊜	26	61.58 N	11.48 E
Isthmus Bay ⊂	212	45.00 N	81.15 W
Istiaía	38	38.57 N	23.09 E
İstinye ◆[8]	267b	41.06 N	29.03 E
Istisu	84	39.57 N	45.59 E
Istmina	246	5.10 N	76.39 W
Isto, Mount ∧	180	69.12 N	143.48 W
Istobensk	80	58.25 N	48.48 E
Istobnoje, Ross.	78	51.08 N	37.21 E
Istobnoje, Ross.	78	51.16 N	38.39 E
Istok	38	42.47 N	20.29 E
Istokpoga, Lake ⊜	220	27.22 N	81.17 W
Istra	82	55.55 N	36.52 E
Istra ›[1]	36	45.15 N	14.00 E
Istra ≃	82	55.44 N	37.08 E
Istrana	64	45.41 N	12.07 E
Istres	62	43.31 N	4.59 E
Istria → Istra ›[1]	36	45.15 N	14.00 E
Istrinskoje vodochranilišče ⊜[1]	82	56.04 N	36.49 E
Isulan	116	6.34 N	124.37 E
Isumi	94	35.17 N	140.19 E
Isumi ≃	94	35.18 N	140.25 E
Isumrud Strait ʮ	164	4.45 S	145.50 E
Isunba	273a	6.27 N	3.17 E
Iswarīpur	126	22.19 N	89.07 E
Iswepe	158	26.50 S	30.31 E
Itá	252	25.29 S	57.21 W
Itabaiana, Bra.	250	7.20 S	35.20 W
Itabaiana, Bra.	250	10.41 S	37.26 W
Itabaiana, Bra.	250	11.16 S	37.47 W
Itabapoana	255	21.18 S	40.58 W
Itabashi ◆[8]	268	35.45 N	139.43 E
Itaberá	255	23.51 S	49.09 W
Itaberaba	255	12.32 S	40.18 W
Itaberaí	255	16.02 S	49.48 W
Itabi	250	10.08 S	37.06 W
Itabira	255	19.37 S	43.13 W
Itaboca	256	22.03 S	44.05 W
Itaboraí	256	22.45 S	42.52 W
Itaboraí □[7]	287a	22.43 S	43.00 W
Itabuna	255	14.48 S	39.16 W
Itacaiuna ≃	250	5.21 S	49.08 W
Itacajá	250	8.19 S	47.46 W
Itacambiruçu ≃	255	16.44 S	42.45 W
Itacaré	255	14.18 S	39.00 W
Itacoatiara	250	3.08 S	58.25 W
Itacoatiara, Ponta de ›	287a	22.59 S	43.02 W
Itacurubí del Rosario	252	24.29 S	56.41 W
Itacurussá	256	22.55 S	43.55 W
Itacurussá, Ilha de I	256	22.56 S	43.53 W
Itaeté	255	12.59 S	40.58 W
Itagacaba ≃	256	22.34 S	44.56 W
Itagi	255	14.10 S	40.01 W
Itaguaçu	255	19.48 S	40.51 W
Itaguaí	256	22.52 S	43.47 W
Itaguajé	255	22.37 S	51.59 W
Itaguara	255	20.23 S	44.29 W
Itaguaré, Pico do ∧	256	22.30 S	45.10 W
Itaguari ≃	255	14.11 S	44.40 W
Itaguaru	255	15.44 S	49.37 W
Itaguatins	250	5.47 S	47.29 W
Itagüí	246	6.10 N	75.36 W
Itaí	255	23.24 S	49.06 W
Itá-Ibaté	252	27.26 S	57.20 W
Itaiçaba	250	4.40 S	37.51 W
Itaim	256	22.24 S	45.53 W
Itaim ≃, Bra.	250	7.02 S	42.02 W
Itaim ≃, Bra.	256	23.07 S	45.08 W
Itaim ≃, Bra.	256	22.19 S	45.51 W
Itainópolis	250	7.24 S	41.31 W
Itaiópolis	252	26.20 S	49.56 W
Itaipava	256	22.23 S	43.08 W
Itaipu, Bra.	256	22.58 S	43.02 W
Itaipu, Bra.	287a	22.44 S	43.26 W
Itaipu, Lagoa de ⊂	287a	22.58 S	43.02 W
Itaipu, Ponta de ›	287a	22.59 S	43.03 W
Itaipu, Represa de ⊜[1]	252	25.00 S	54.30 W
Itäisen Suomenlahden kansallispuisto ♦	26	60.15 N	27.00 E
Itaituba	250	4.17 S	55.59 W
Itajá	255	19.07 S	51.37 W
Itajaí	252	26.53 S	48.39 W
Itajaí do Sul ≃	252	27.12 S	49.39 W
Itajipora	256	22.19 S	46.28 W
Itajubá	256	22.26 S	45.27 W
Itaju do Colônia	255	15.09 S	39.44 W
Itajuípe	255	14.41 S	39.22 W
Itaka, Ross.	88	53.53 N	118.42 E
Itaka, Tan.	154	8.52 S	32.47 E
Itaki	273a	6.43 N	3.17 E
Itako	94	35.56 N	140.33 E
Itakura, Nihon	94	36.13 N	139.36 E
Itakura, Nihon	94	37.03 N	138.18 E
Itala Game Reserve ◆[4]	158	27.31 S	31.19 E
Italia → Italy □[1]	36	42.50 N	12.50 E
Itálica ⊥	34	37.30 N	6.05 W
Italie → Italy □[1]	36	42.50 N	12.50 E
Italien → Italy □[1]	36	42.50 N	12.50 E
Italy	222	32.11 N	96.53 W
Italy (Italia) □[1], Europe	22	42.50 N	12.50 E
Italy (Italia) □[1], Europe	36	42.50 N	12.50 E
Itamaraju	255	17.05 S	39.31 W
Itamarandiba	255	17.51 S	42.51 W
Itamarandiba ≃	255	17.18 S	42.48 W
Itamarati de Minas	256	21.25 S	42.49 W
Itamari	255	13.47 S	39.37 W
Itamataré	250	2.16 S	46.24 W
Itambacuri	255	18.01 S	41.42 W
Itambé	255	15.15 S	40.37 W
Itambi	256	22.44 S	42.58 W
Itami	96	34.46 N	135.25 E
Itami, Camp ■	270	34.47 N	135.24 E
Itamonte	256	22.17 S	44.53 W
Itampolo	157b	24.41 S	43.57 E
Itānagar	120	27.09 N	93.33 E
Itandéua, Lago ⊜	250	2.01 S	55.10 W
Itandrano	157b	21.47 S	45.17 E
Itanhaém	255	24.11 S	46.47 W
Itanhandu	256	22.18 S	44.57 W
Itanhauã ≃	248	4.45 S	63.48 W
Itanhém	255	17.09 S	40.20 W
Itanhomi	255	19.10 S	41.52 W
Itano	96	34.07 N	134.28 E
Itaobim	255	16.34 S	41.30 W
Itaocaia	287a	22.58 S	43.01 W
Itapaci	255	14.57 S	49.34 W
Itapagipe	255	19.54 S	49.22 W
Itapajé	250	3.41 S	39.34 W
Itapanhaú ≃	256	23.51 S	46.10 W
Itaparaná ≃	248	5.47 S	63.03 W
Itaparica, Ilha de I	255	13.00 S	38.42 W
Itaparica, Represa de ⊜[1]	250	8.50 S	38.40 W
Itapaya	248	17.34 S	66.21 W
Itapé	255	14.54 S	39.26 W
Itapebi	255	15.56 S	39.32 W
Itapecerica	255	20.28 S	45.07 W

Symbols in the index entries represent the broad categories identified in the key at the right. Symbols with superior numbers (⋀[1]) identify subcategories (see complete key on page *I · 1)*.

Symbole im Register stellen die rechts im Schlüssel erklärten Kategorien dar. Symbole mit hochgestellten Ziffern (⋀[1]) bezeichnen Unterabteilungen einer Kategorie (vgl. vollständiger Schlüssel auf Seite *I · 1)*.

Los símbolos incluídos en el texto del índice representan las grandes categorias identificadas con la clave a la derecha. Los símbolos con numeros en su parte superior (⋀[1]) identifican las subcategorías (véase la clave completa en la página *I · 1)*.

Les symboles de l'index représentent les catégories indiquées dans la légende à droite. Les symboles suivis d'un indice (⋀[1]) représentent des sous-catégories (voir légende complète à la page *I · 1)*.

Os símbolos incluídos no texto do índice representam as grandes categorias identificadas com a chave à direita. Os símbolos com números em sua parte superior (⋀[1]) identificam as subcategorias (veja-se a chave completa à página *I · 1)*.

∧ Mountain	Berg	Montaña	Montagne	Montanha
⋀ Mountains	Gebirge	Montañas	Montagnes	Montanhas
)(Pass	Paß	Paso	Col	Passo
V Valley, Canyon	Tal, Cañon	Valle, Cañón	Vallée, Canyon	Vale, Canhão
≚ Plain	Ebene	Llano	Plaine	Planície
› Cape	Kap	Cabo	Cap	Cabo
I Island	Insel	Isla	Île	Ilha
II Islands	Inseln	Islas	Îles	Ilhas
⊥ Other Topographic Features	Andere Topographische Objekte	Otros Elementos Topográficos	Autres données topographiques	Outros acidentes topográficos

ESPAÑOL | FRANÇAIS | PORTUGUÊS

Nombre / Nom / Nome	Página / Page / Página	Lat.°′	Long.°′ W = Oeste / W = Ouest / W = Oeste
Itapecerica da Serra	256	23.43 S	46.50 W
Itapecerica da Serra □7	287b	23.44 S	46.52 W
Itapecuru-Mirim	250	3.24 S	44.20 W
Itapemirim	255	21.01 S	40.50 W
Itapera	250	2.32 S	43.47 W
Itaperina, Pointe ≻	157b	24.59 S	47.06 E
Itaperuna	255	21.12 S	41.54 W
Itapetim	250	7.22 S	37.11 W
Itapetinga	255	15.15 S	40.15 W
Itapetininga	255	23.36 S	48.03 W
Itapetininga ≃	255	23.35 S	48.27 W
Itapeva, Bra.	255	23.58 S	48.52 W
Itapeva, Bra.	256	22.46 S	46.13 W
Itapevi	256	23.33 S	46.56 W
Itapevi □7	287b	23.31 S	46.55 W
Itapicuru	250	11.19 S	38.15 W
Itapicuru ≃, Bra.	250	2.52 S	44.12 W
Itapicuru ≃, Bra.	250	11.47 S	37.32 W
Itapipoca	250	3.30 S	39.35 W
Itapira	256	22.26 S	46.50 W
Itapiranga, Bra.	250	2.45 S	58.01 W
Itapiranga, Bra.	252	27.08 S	53.43 W
Itapirapuã	255	15.52 S	50.36 W
Itapitanga	255	14.26 S	39.34 W
Itapiúna	250	4.33 S	38.57 W
Itápolis	255	21.35 S	48.46 W
Itaporã	255	22.01 S	54.54 W
Itaporã de Goiás	250	8.02 S	48.39 W
Itaporanga, Bra.	250	7.18 S	38.10 W
Itaporanga, Bra.	255	23.42 S	49.29 W
Itaporanga d'Ajuda	250	10.59 S	37.18 W
Itapúa □5	252	26.50 S	55.50 W
Itapuranga	255	15.35 S	49.59 W
Itaquaí ≃	246	4.20 S	70.12 W
Itaquaquecetuba	256	23.29 S	46.21 W
Itaquaquecetuba □7	287b	23.28 S	46.20 W
Itaquara	255	13.27 S	39.57 W
Itaquari	255	20.20 S	40.22 W
Itaquaxiara	287b	23.47 S	46.51 W
Itaquaxiara, Ribeirão ≃	287b	23.44 S	46.47 W
Itaquera ◆8	256	23.32 S	46.27 W
Itaquera, Ribeirão ≃	287b	23.28 S	46.26 W
Itaqui	252	29.08 S	56.33 W
Itaquyry	252	24.56 S	55.13 W
Itarantim	255	15.39 S	40.03 W
Itararé	255	24.07 S	49.20 W
Itārsi	124	22.37 N	77.45 E
Itarumã	255	18.42 S	51.25 W
Itasca, Il., U.S.	278	41.58 N	88.00 W
Itasca, Tx., U.S.	222	32.09 N	97.08 W
Itasca, Lake ⊜	198	47.11 N	95.12 W
Itasca State Park ♠	198	47.18 N	95.18 W
Itata ≃	252	36.23 S	72.52 W
Itatí	252	27.16 S	58.15 W
Itatiaia	256	22.30 S	44.34 W
Itatiaia, Parque Nacional do ♠	256	22.28 S	44.37 W
Itatiba	256	23.00 S	46.51 W
Itatinga	255	23.07 S	48.36 W
Itatira	250	4.30 S	39.37 W
Itatka	86	56.49 N	85.37 E
Itatolo	273b	4.09 S	15.15 E
Itatskij	86	56.04 N	89.05 E
Itatupã	250	0.37 S	51.12 W
Itaú	250	5.50 S	37.59 W
Itaueira	250	7.36 S	43.02 W
Itaueira ≃	250	6.41 S	42.55 W
Itaúna	255	20.04 S	44.34 W
Itaúna, Morro do ʌ2	287a	22.46 S	43.02 W
Itāwa	124	25.32 N	76.22 E
Itazuke-kūkō ⊠	96	33.35 N	130.28 E
Itbayat Island I	108	20.46 N	121.50 E
Itéa	38	38.26 N	22.24 E
Itenes (Guaporé) ≃	248	11.54 S	65.01 W
Ith ʌ	52	52.05 N	9.35 E
Ithaca, Mi., U.S.	190	43.17 N	84.36 W
Ithaca, N.Y., U.S.	210	42.26 N	76.29 W
Itháki	38	38.23 N	20.42 E
Itháki I	38	38.24 N	20.42 E
Ithan Creek ≃	285	40.00 N	75.21 W
Ithnayn	142	30.41 N	32.21 E
Ithon ≃	42	52.12 N	3.27 W
Itigi	154	5.42 S	34.29 E
Itikawa → Ichikawa	94	35.44 N	139.55 E
Itimādpur	124	27.15 N	78.12 E
Itimbiri ≃	152	2.02 N	22.44 E
Itinga	255	16.36 S	41.47 W
Itinga ≃	255	16.35 S	41.45 W
Itinomiya → Ichinomiya	94	35.18 N	136.48 E
Itipo	152	0.50 S	18.35 E
Itiquira	255	17.12 S	54.07 W
Itiquira ≃	248	17.21 S	55.37 W
Itirapina	255	22.15 S	47.49 W
Itire	273a	6.31 N	3.21 E
Itiruçu	255	13.31 S	40.09 W
Itiúba	250	10.43 S	39.51 W
Itkillik ≃	180	70.08 N	150.57 W
Itlar'	82	56.51 N	39.17 E
Itlīdim	142	27.52 N	30.48 E
Itmīdah	142	30.46 N	31.20 E
Itmuryn, ozero ⊜	80	49.30 N	52.22 E
Itō	94	34.58 N	139.05 E
Itobi	256	21.44 S	46.58 W
Itobo	154	4.10 S	33.01 E
Itoculo	154	14.42 S	40.18 E
Itoigawa	94	37.02 N	137.51 E
Itoko	152	1.00 S	21.45 E
Itomamo, Lac ⊜	186	49.11 N	70.28 W
Itoman	174m	26.08 N	127.40 E
Iton ≃	50	49.09 N	1.12 E
Itonamas ≃	248	12.28 S	64.24 W
Itororó	255	15.07 S	40.06 W
Itri	66	41.17 N	13.32 E
Iṭsā	142	29.15 N	30.48 E
Itsukaichi, Nihon	94	35.44 N	139.13 E
Itsukaichi, Nihon	96	34.24 N	132.22 E
Itsuki	92	32.24 N	130.50 E
Itsuku-shima I	96	34.16 N	132.19 E
Itsuwa	92	32.30 N	130.10 E
Itta Bena	194	33.29 N	90.19 W
Ittel, Oued V	148	34.19 N	6.01 E
Itter ≃	263	51.09 N	6.52 E
Ittersum	52	52.28 N	6.07 E
Itteville	261	48.31 N	2.21 E
Ittiri	71	40.36 N	8.34 E
Itú	255	23.16 S	47.19 W
Itu ≃	252	29.25 S	55.51 W
Ituaçu	255	13.49 S	41.18 W
Ituango	246	7.04 N	75.45 W
Ituberá	255	13.44 S	39.09 W
Itucumã ≃	248	6.59 S	69.48 W
Itueta	255	19.23 S	41.11 W
Ituí	256	21.32 S	42.55 W
Ituí ≃	246	4.38 S	70.19 W
Ituim ≃	252	28.35 S	51.20 W
Ituiutaba	255	18.58 S	49.28 W
Itula	154	3.29 S	27.52 E
Itumbiara	255	18.25 S	49.13 W
Itumirim	256	21.19 S	44.53 W
Itum-Kale	84	42.43 N	45.35 E
Ituna	184	51.10 N	103.30 W
Itungi Port	154	9.35 S	33.56 E
Ituni	246	5.30 N	58.14 W
Itupararanga, Reprêsa de ⊜1	256	23.37 S	47.16 W
Itupeva	256	23.09 S	47.04 W
Itupeva, Rio da ≃	256	22.03 S	47.15 W
Itupiranga	250	5.09 S	49.20 W
Ituporanga	252	27.25 S	49.36 W
Iturama	255	19.44 S	50.11 W
Iturbe	252	26.01 S	56.30 W
Iturbide	232	19.40 N	89.37 W
Ituri ≃	154	1.40 N	27.01 E
Iturup, ostrov (Etorofu-tō) I	92a	44.35 N	147.10 E
Itutinga	256	21.18 S	44.40 W
Ituverava	255	20.20 S	47.47 W
Ituxi ≃	248	7.18 S	64.51 W
Ituzaingó, Arg.	252	27.36 S	56.41 W
Ituzaingó, Arg.	258	34.40 S	58.40 W
Ituzaingó, Ur.	258	34.25 S	56.26 W
Itwa	124	27.20 N	82.42 E
Ityāy al-Bārūd	142	30.53 N	30.40 E
Ityopiya → Ethiopia □1	144	9.00 N	39.00 E
Itz ≃	56	49.58 N	10.52 E
Itzehoe	52	53.55 N	9.31 E
Iubundha ≃	126	24.06 N	90.20 E
Iuka, Il., U.S.	219	38.37 N	88.47 W
Iuka, Ms., U.S.	194	34.48 N	88.11 W
Iul'tin	180	67.50 N	178.48 W
Iul'tin, gora ʌ	180	67.50 N	178.25 W
Iúna	255	20.21 S	41.32 W
Iupeba	256	23.41 S	46.22 W
Iva	192	34.18 N	82.39 W
Ivaceviči	76	52.43 N	25.21 E
Ivačovo	76	60.32 N	36.22 E
Ivahona	157b	23.27 S	46.10 E
Ivaí ≃	255	23.18 S	53.42 W
Ivaiporã	252	24.15 S	51.45 W
Ivajlovgrad	38	41.32 N	26.08 E
Ivakoany, Massif de l' ⋏	157b	23.50 S	46.25 E
Ivalo	24	68.42 N	27.30 E
Ivalojoki ≃	24	68.43 N	27.36 E
Ivancevo	82	55.58 N	36.07 E
Ivančice	61	49.06 N	16.23 E
Ivancovo	82	56.39 N	35.50 E
Ivanec	36	46.13 N	16.08 E
Ivane-Puste	78	48.39 N	26.11 E
Ivangorod	76	59.24 N	28.10 E
Ivangrad	38	42.50 N	19.52 E
Ivanhoe, Austl.	166	32.54 S	144.18 E
Ivanhoe, Austl.	274b	37.46 S	145.03 E
Ivanhoe, Ca., U.S.	226	36.23 N	119.13 W
Ivanhoe, Il., U.S.	278	42.17 N	88.02 W
Ivanhoe, Mn., U.S.	198	44.27 N	96.14 W
Ivanhoe, Va., U.S.	192	36.50 N	80.58 W
Ivanhoe ≃	190	48.40 N	82.11 W
Ivanhoe Lake ⊜	190	48.05 N	82.38 W
Ivanica	78	50.47 N	32.36 E
Ivanić Grad	36	45.42 N	16.24 E
Ivaniči	78	50.39 N	24.20 E
Ivanišči, Ross.	76	56.36 N	35.13 E
Ivanišči, Ross.	80	55.46 N	40.26 E
Ivanjci	61	46.38 N	15.54 E
Ivanjica	38	43.35 N	20.14 E
Ivankov	78	50.56 N	29.54 E
Ivankovcy	89	49.06 N	134.28 E
Ivan'kovo	82	54.44 N	37.57 E
Ivan'kovskij	80	56.39 N	40.05 E
Ivan'kovskoje vodochranilišče ⊜1	82	56.37 N	36.32 E
Ivanof Bay	180	55.54 N	159.29 W
Ivano-Frankovo	78	49.55 N	23.43 E
Ivano-Frankovsk	78	48.55 N	24.43 E
Ivano-Frankovsk □4	78	48.45 N	24.30 E
Ivanopol'	78	49.52 N	28.12 E
Ivanopolje	83	48.28 N	37.46 E
Ivano-Šamševo	83	46.52 N	39.54 E
Ivanov	78	49.28 N	28.21 E
Ivanovka, Kyrg.	85	42.54 N	75.05 E
Ivanovka, Ross.	80	52.51 N	53.48 E
Ivanovka, Ross.	80	51.54 N	43.46 E
Ivanovka, Ross.	80	52.15 N	41.35 E
Ivanovka, Ross.	88	50.22 N	128.02 E
Ivanovka, Ross.	89	43.58 N	132.30 E
Ivanovka, Ukr.	78	46.43 N	34.33 E
Ivanovka, Ukr.	78	46.58 N	30.28 E
Ivanovka, Ukr.	83	48.14 N	38.58 E
Ivanovka, Ukr.	83	47.35 N	37.19 E
Ivanovo, Bela.	76	52.09 N	25.32 E
Ivanovo, Ross.	80	57.00 N	40.59 E
Ivanovo Oblast' □4	76	57.00 N	41.00 E
Ivanovo-Voznesensk → Ivanovo	80	57.00 N	40.59 E
Ivanovskaja, Ross.	24	60.48 N	55.52 E
Ivanovskaja, Ross.	78	45.17 N	38.29 E
Ivanovskoje, Ross.	76	59.17 N	28.49 E
Ivanovskoje, Ross.	78	51.37 N	34.57 E
Ivanovskoje, Ross.	82	55.05 N	37.50 E
Ivanovskoje, Ross.	82	54.55 N	36.50 E
Ivanovskoje, Ross.	82	55.52 N	36.55 E
Ivanovskoje, Ross.	82	56.23 N	37.07 E
Ivanovskoje, Ross.	265a	59.46 N	30.47 E
Ivan-Ozero	82	54.04 N	38.20 E
Ivan-Ozero, ozero ⊜	82	54.07 N	38.17 E
Ivanpah Lake ⊜	204	35.35 N	115.25 W
Ivantejevka, Ross.	80	52.16 N	49.07 E
Ivantejevka, Ross.	82	55.58 N	37.55 E
Ivantejevo	76	57.48 N	33.09 E
Ivato	157b	20.37 S	47.12 E
Ivatuba	255	23.37 S	52.13 W
Ivdel'	72	60.42 N	60.24 E
Ivel ≃	42	52.10 N	0.18 W
Ivenec	76	53.53 N	26.45 E
Iver	260	51.31 N	0.30 W
Iver Heath	260	51.32 N	0.31 W
Iverny	261	49.00 N	2.47 E
Ivigtut	176	61.12 N	48.10 W
Ivindo ≃	152	0.09 S	12.09 E
Ivinghoe	42	51.50 N	0.37 W
Ivinheima ≃	255	23.14 S	53.42 W
Ivje	76	53.56 N	25.46 E
Ivn'a	78	51.04 N	36.08 E
Ivnica	78	50.09 N	29.03 E
Ivohibe	157b	22.29 S	46.52 E
Ivolginsk	88	51.45 N	107.14 E
Ivón ≃	248	11.06 S	66.08 W
Ivondro	157b	24.47 S	46.52 E
Ivor	208	36.54 N	76.54 W
Ivorogbo	150	5.30 N	6.21 E
Ivory Coast (Côte d'Ivoire) □1, Afr.	134	8.00 N	5.00 W
Ivory Coast (Côte d'Ivoire) □1, Afr.	150	8.00 N	5.00 W
Ivory Coast ⊥2	150	5.10 N	5.00 W
Ivoryton	207	41.20 N	72.26 W
Ivösjön ⊜	26	56.06 N	14.27 E
Ivot, Ross.	76	53.42 N	34.12 E
Ivot, Ukr.	78	51.58 N	33.28 E
Ivotka ≃	78	51.57 N	33.22 E
Ivrea	62	45.28 N	7.52 E
İvrindi	130	39.34 N	27.29 E
Ivry-la-Bataille	50	48.53 N	1.28 E
Ivry [-sur-Seine]	50	48.49 N	2.23 E
Ivujivik	176	62.24 N	77.55 W
Ivybridge	42	50.23 N	3.56 W
Ivy Hatch	260	51.16 N	0.16 E
Ivyland	285	40.12 N	75.04 W
Iwade	96	34.15 N	135.19 E
Iwafune, Nihon	94	36.19 N	139.40 E
Iwafune, Nihon	270	34.44 N	135.54 E
Iwagi	96	34.15 N	133.09 E
Iwai	94	36.03 N	139.54 E
Iwai-shima I	96	33.47 N	131.58 E
Iwaizumi	92	39.50 N	141.48 E
Iwaki (Taira)	94	37.03 N	140.55 E
Iwaki ≃	92	41.01 N	140.22 E
Iwaki-san ʌ	92	40.39 N	140.18 E
Iwakuni	96	34.09 N	132.11 E
Iwakuni Marine Corps Air Station ■	96	34.08 N	132.14 E
Iwakura	94	35.17 N	136.52 E
Iwama	94	36.18 N	140.16 E
Iwami, Nihon	96	34.53 N	132.26 E
Iwami, Nihon	96	35.35 N	134.20 E
Iwami-kōgen ʌ1	96	35.00 N	132.30 E
Iwami-kokubun-ji ⊕1	96	34.56 N	132.08 E
Iwamizawa	92a	43.12 N	141.46 E
Iwamura	94	35.22 N	137.26 E
Iwanai	92a	42.58 N	140.30 E
Iwanowo → Ivanovo	80	57.00 N	40.59 E
Iwanuma	92	38.06 N	140.52 E
Iwaoka ◆8	270	34.44 N	134.58 E
Iwase, Nihon	94	36.21 N	140.06 E
Iwase, Nihon	268	35.17 N	139.52 E
Iwata	94	34.42 N	137.48 E
Iwataki	96	35.34 N	135.09 E
Iwate □5	92	39.37 N	141.22 E
Iwate-san ʌ	92	39.51 N	141.00 E
Iwatsuki	94	35.57 N	139.42 E
Iwaya	270	34.35 N	135.02 E
Iwaya → Awaji	96	34.35 N	135.01 E
Iwayama	270	34.52 N	135.52 E
Iwazono	270	34.45 N	135.19 E
Iwo	150	7.38 N	4.11 E
Iwo Jima → Iō-jima I	174f	24.47 N	141.20 E
Iwŏn	98	40.19 N	128.39 E
Iwuy	50	50.14 N	3.19 E
Ixcán ≃	236	16.07 N	91.05 W
Ixchiguán	236	15.12 N	91.53 W
Ixelles	56	50.50 N	4.22 E
Ixhuatlán	234	19.04 N	96.59 W
Ixiamas	248	13.45 S	68.09 W
Iximché ⊥	236	14.44 N	90.59 W
Ixmiquilpan	234	20.29 N	99.14 W
Ixonia	216	43.09 N	88.36 W
Ixopo	158	30.08 S	30.00 E
Ixtahuacán	236	15.25 N	91.46 W
Ixtapa	234	17.39 N	101.36 W
Ixtapa, Punta ≻	234	17.39 N	101.40 W
Ixtapan de la Sal	234	18.50 N	99.41 W
Ixtepec	234	16.34 N	95.06 W
Ixtlahuacán del Río	234	20.52 N	103.15 W
Ixtlán	234	20.11 N	102.24 W
Ixtlán de Juárez	234	17.20 N	96.29 W
Ixtlán del Río	234	21.02 N	104.22 W
Ixworth	42	52.18 N	0.50 E
Iya ≃	96	33.58 N	133.47 E
'Iyādh	144	14.59 N	46.51 E
'Iyāl Bakhīt	140	13.25 N	28.41 E
Iyang	98	34.53 N	127.01 E
Iyang, Gili I	115a	6.59 S	114.10 E
Iyang → Yiyang	102	28.36 N	112.20 E
Iyo	96	33.46 N	132.42 E
Iyo-mishima	96	33.58 N	133.33 E
Iyo-nada ⊤2	96	33.40 N	132.20 E
Iž ≃	80	55.58 N	52.38 E
Izabal	236	15.24 N	89.08 W
Izabal □5	236	15.30 N	89.00 W
Izabal, Lago de ⊜	236	15.30 N	89.10 W
'Izab al-Başārīṭah	142	31.23 N	31.47 E
Īzad Khvāst	128	31.31 N	52.07 E
Izalco	236	13.45 N	89.40 W
'Izam, Jabal al- ʌ	132	30.51 N	35.46 E
Izamal	232	20.56 N	89.01 W
Izapa ⊥	232	14.55 N	92.10 W
Iz'aslav	78	50.07 N	26.51 E
'Izbat Abū Şuql	132	31.09 N	33.49 E
Izberbaš	84	42.33 N	47.52 E
Izbica, Pol.	30	50.54 N	23.09 E
Izbica, Pol.	30	54.42 N	17.26 E
Izd'oškovo	76	55.08 N	33.37 E
Izegem	50	50.55 N	3.12 E
Īzeh	128	31.50 N	49.50 E
Izena-shima I	174m	26.56 N	127.56 E
Izendy	86	45.48 N	59.28 E
Izernore	58	46.13 N	5.33 E
Iževsk	80	56.51 N	53.14 E
Iževskoje	80	54.34 N	40.53 E
Izkī	128	22.56 N	57.46 E
Ižma	24	65.02 N	53.55 E
Ižma ≃	24	65.19 N	52.54 E
Izmail	78	45.21 N	28.50 E
Izmajlovo	80	53.43 N	47.14 E
Izmajlovo ◆8	265b	55.48 N	37.46 E
Izmajlovo Park ♠	265b	55.46 N	37.47 E
Izmalkovo	76	52.41 N	37.58 E
İzmir	130	38.25 N	27.09 E
İzmir □4	130	38.30 N	27.15 E
İzmir Körfezi c	130	38.30 N	26.50 E
İzmit (Kocaeli)	130	40.46 N	29.55 E
İzmit Körfezi c	130	40.45 N	29.35 E
Ižmorskij	86	56.11 N	86.38 E
Iznajar, Embalse de ⊜1	34	37.15 N	4.30 W
Iznalloz	34	37.23 N	3.31 W
İznik	130	40.26 N	29.43 E
İznik Gölü ⊜	130	40.26 N	29.30 E
Iznoski	76	54.59 N	35.19 E
Izola	64	45.32 N	13.40 E
Izoplit	82	56.38 N	36.12 E
Izopo, Punta ≻	236	15.48 N	87.23 W
Ižora ≃	265a	59.48 N	30.36 E
Izozog, Bañados del ☷	248	18.48 S	62.10 W
Izra'	132	32.51 N	36.15 E
Izsák	30	46.48 N	19.22 E
Iztacalco ◆8	286a	19.23 N	99.07 W
Iztaccíhuatl, Volcán ʌ1	234	19.11 N	98.39 W
Iztaccíhuatl y Popocatéptl, Parques Nacionales ♠	234	19.10 N	98.38 W
Iztapa	236	13.56 N	90.43 W
Iztapalapa ◆8	286a	19.21 N	99.06 W
Izucar de Matamoros	234	18.36 N	98.28 W
Izu-hantō ≻1	94	34.45 N	139.00 E
Izuhara	92	34.12 N	129.17 E
Iz'um	83	49.12 N	37.19 E
Izumi, Nihon	92	32.05 N	130.22 E
Izumi, Nihon	92	38.20 N	140.53 E
Izumi, Nihon	94	35.54 N	136.40 E
Izumi, Nihon	96	34.55 N	134.55 E
Izumi, Nihon	96	34.29 N	135.26 E
Izumi ◆8	268	35.25 N	139.30 E
Izumi-ōtsu	96	34.30 N	135.24 E
Izumi-sano	96	34.25 N	135.19 E
Izumizaki	94	37.09 N	140.17 E
Izumo	96	35.22 N	132.46 E
Izumo ≃	94	34.38 N	136.33 E
Izumo-kokubun-ji ⊕1	96	35.26 N	133.06 E
Izumrud	86	57.05 N	61.23 E
Izu-nagaoka	94	35.02 N	138.56 E
Izushi	96	35.28 N	134.52 E
Izu-shotō II	6	32.00 N	140.00 E
Izu Trench ✢1	6	31.00 N	142.00 E
Izuwara	270	34.53 N	135.32 E
Izvarino	83	48.17 N	39.52 E
Izvestij CIK, ostrova II	74	75.55 N	82.30 E
Izvestkovyj	89	48.59 N	131.33 E
Izvorul Muntelui, Lacul ⊜1	38	47.00 N	26.00 E
Izynžul'	86	52.24 N	90.13 E
J			
Ja'ār, Birkat al- ⊜	142	30.28 N	30.10 E
Jääsjärvi ⊜	26	61.36 N	26.07 E
Jaba, Ityo.	144	6.17 N	35.12 E
Jaba, Pap. N. Gui.	175e	6.32 S	155.12 E
Jabā, Sūrīy.	132	33.10 N	35.56 E
Jabal, Bahr al- → Mountain Nile ≃	136	9.30 N	30.30 E
Jabal Abyad Plateau ⋏1	140	19.00 N	29.00 E
Jabal al-Awliyā'	140	15.14 N	32.30 E
Jabal al-Awliyā', Khazzān (White Nile Dam) ◆6	140	15.14 N	32.29 E
Jabalambre ʌ	34	40.06 N	1.03 W
Jabal an-Nūr	142	28.57 N	31.02 E
Jabal Aṭ-Ṭayr	142	28.14 N	30.45 E
Jabal Dūd	140	13.25 N	33.09 E
Jabal Lubnān □4	132	33.50 N	35.40 E
Jabalón ≃	34	38.53 N	4.05 W
Jabal os Sarāj	120	35.07 N	69.14 E
Jabalpur	124	23.10 N	79.57 E
Jabal Qerri	140	16.15 N	32.48 E
Jabal 'Uwaybid	142	30.09 N	32.12 E
Jabālyah	132	31.32 N	34.29 E
Jabal Zuqar, Jazīrat I	144	14.00 N	42.45 E
Jabbān, Arḍ al- ◆1	132	32.08 N	36.35 E
Jabbeke	50	51.11 N	3.05 E
Jabbi	123	32.24 N	72.06 E
Jabbū, Qā' ☷	132	29.35 N	36.13 E
Jabbūl, Sabkhat al- ⊜	130	36.03 N	37.39 E
Jabel	54	53.32 N	12.32 E
Jabi	114	2.32 N	102.48 E
Jabiru	164	12.40 S	132.53 E
Jabjabah, Wādī V	140	22.37 N	33.17 E
Jablah	130	35.21 N	35.55 E
Jablanac	36	44.42 N	14.54 E
Jablanica	36	43.39 N	17.45 E
Jablanica ≃	38	43.07 N	21.57 E
Jablaničko Jezero ⊜1	36	43.40 N	17.50 E
Jablines	261	48.55 N	2.46 E
Jabločnoje	78	50.18 N	35.14 E
Jabločnyj	89	47.10 N	142.04 E
Jablonec nad Nisou	30	50.44 N	15.10 E
Jablonica	30	48.37 N	17.25 E
Jabłonka	30	49.29 N	19.41 E
Jablonné v Podještědí	54	50.48 N	14.47 E
Jablonoj → Jablonovyj chrebet ⋏	88	53.30 N	115.00 E
Jablonov	78	48.24 N	24.57 E
Jablonovo	88	51.51 N	112.49 E
Jablonovyj chrebet ⋏	88	53.30 N	115.00 E
Jabłonowo	30	53.24 N	19.09 E
Jablonowy-Gebirge → Jablonovyj chrebet ⋏	88	53.30 N	115.00 E
Jablunkov	30	49.35 N	18.47 E
Jaboatão	250	8.07 S	35.01 W
Jaboncillos Creek ≃	196	27.23 N	97.45 W
Jabonga	116	9.20 N	125.32 E
Jaborandi	255	20.40 S	48.25 W
Jaboticabal	255	21.16 S	48.19 W
Jabrat Sa'īd ⊤4	140	16.06 N	31.50 E
Jabron ≃	62	44.33 N	4.45 E
Jabron, Torrent le ≃	62	44.09 N	5.57 E
Jabung	115a	5.29 S	105.40 E
Jabung, Tanjung ≻	112	1.01 S	104.22 E
Jaca	34	42.34 N	0.33 W
Jacala	234	21.01 N	99.11 W
Jacaleapa	236	14.00 N	86.40 W
Jacaltenango	236	15.40 N	91.44 W
Jacana	274b	37.42 S	144.55 E
Jacaraci	255	14.51 S	42.26 W
Jacaré ≃, Bra.	248	5.49 S	63.35 W
Jacaré ≃, Bra.	250	10.10 S	41.58 W
Jacaré ≃, Bra.	255	13.50 S	40.42 W
Jacareí	256	23.19 S	45.58 W
Jacareí ≃	256	22.54 S	46.28 W
Jacarepaguá ◆8	256	22.56 S	43.20 W
Jacarepaguá, Lagoa de c	256	22.59 S	43.24 W
Jacarezinho	255	23.09 S	49.59 W
Jaceel V	144	10.25 N	51.01 E
Jaceruba	256	22.35 S	43.34 W
Jáchal ≃	252	30.44 S	68.08 W
Jachenau	64	47.36 N	11.25 E
Jachniki	78	50.26 N	33.10 E
Jachroma	82	56.17 N	37.30 E
Jachroma ≃	82	56.31 N	37.07 E
Jáchymov	54	50.20 N	12.55 E
Jaciara	255	15.59 S	54.57 W
Jacinto	255	16.10 S	40.17 W
Jacinto Aráuz	252	38.04 S	63.26 W
Jacinto City	222	29.46 N	95.14 W
Jacinto Machado	252	29.00 S	49.46 W
Jaciparaná	248	9.15 S	64.23 W
Jaciparaná ≃	248	9.22 S	64.22 W
Jackass Creek ≃	226	37.22 N	119.23 W
Jack Creek ≃	202	42.59 N	121.32 W
Jackfish Lake ⊜	184	53.05 N	108.25 W
Jackhead Harbour	184	51.52 N	97.16 W
Jack Lake ⊜	212	44.42 N	78.03 W
Jack London State Historical Park ♠	226	38.21 N	122.32 W
Jackman	188	45.38 N	70.15 W
Jackman Creek ≃	224	48.30 N	121.43 W
Jack Mountain ʌ, Mt., U.S.	202	46.21 N	112.18 W
Jack Mountain ʌ, Wa., U.S.	224	48.47 N	120.57 W
Jackpot	204	41.59 N	114.40 W
Jacksboro, Tn., U.S.	192	36.19 N	84.11 W
Jacksboro, Tx., U.S.	196	33.13 N	98.09 W
Jacks Creek ≃	208	40.35 N	77.33 W
Jacks Fork ≃	194	37.12 N	91.17 W
Jacks Island I	279b	40.37 N	79.43 W
Jacks Mountain ʌ	210	40.45 N	77.30 W
Jackson, Al., U.S.	194	31.30 N	87.53 W
Jackson, Ca., U.S.	226	38.20 N	120.46 W
Jackson, Ga., U.S.	192	33.17 N	83.57 W
Jackson, Ky., U.S.	192	37.33 N	83.23 W
Jackson, La., U.S.	194	30.50 N	91.13 W
Jackson, Mi., U.S.	216	42.14 N	84.24 W
Jackson, Mn., U.S.	198	43.37 N	94.59 W
Jackson, Ms., U.S.	194	32.17 N	90.11 W
Jackson, Mo., U.S.	194	37.22 N	89.39 W
Jackson, N.J., U.S.	208	40.08 N	74.19 W
Jackson, N.C., U.S.	192	36.23 N	77.25 W
Jackson, Oh., U.S.	188	39.03 N	82.38 W
Jackson, Pa., U.S.	210	41.50 N	75.36 W
Jackson, S.C., U.S.	192	33.19 N	81.47 W
Jackson, Tn., U.S.	194	35.36 N	88.48 W
Jackson, Wy., U.S.	200	43.28 N	110.45 W
Jackson □6, In., U.S.	218	38.53 N	86.03 W
Jackson □6, Mi., U.S.	216	42.15 N	84.24 W
Jackson □6, Tx., U.S.	222	29.00 N	96.35 W
Jackson ≃	188	37.47 N	79.46 W
Jackson, Cape ≻	172	41.00 S	174.18 E
Jackson, Lake ⊜, Fl., U.S.	192	30.30 N	84.17 W
Jackson, Lake ⊜, Fl., U.S.	220	27.29 N	81.28 W
Jackson, Lake ⊜, Fl., U.S.	220	27.55 N	81.10 W
Jackson, Mount ʌ, Ant.	9	71.23 S	63.22 W
Jackson, Mount ʌ, Austl.	162	30.15 S	119.16 E
Jackson, Port c	170	33.50 S	151.16 E
Jackson Bay c	172	43.58 S	168.42 E
Jackson Brook ≃	276	40.53 N	74.34 W
Jackson Butte ʌ	226	38.20 N	120.43 W
Jackson Center, Oh., U.S.	216	40.27 N	84.02 W
Jackson Center, Pa., U.S.	214	41.16 N	80.09 W
Jackson Creek ≃, Can.	184	49.18 N	100.50 W
Jackson Creek ≃, Ca., U.S.	226	38.18 N	121.01 W
Jackson Creek ≃, Il., U.S.	216	41.26 N	88.10 W
Jackson Head ≻	172	43.58 S	168.37 E
Jackson Heights ◆8	276	40.45 N	73.53 W
Jackson Lake ⊜	202	43.55 N	110.40 W
Jackson Lake ⊜1	192	33.22 N	83.52 W
Jackson Meadows Reservoir ⊜1	226	39.29 N	120.32 W
Jackson Mountain ʌ	188	44.46 N	70.32 W
Jackson Park ♠, On., Can.	281	42.17 N	83.01 W
Jackson Park ♠, Il., U.S.	278	41.47 N	87.35 W
Jackson's Arm	186	49.52 N	56.47 W
Jacksons Creek ≃	169	37.40 S	144.48 E
Jacksonville, Al., U.S.	194	33.48 N	85.45 W
Jacksonville, Ar., U.S.	194	34.51 N	92.06 W
Jacksonville, Fl., U.S.	192	30.19 N	81.39 W
Jacksonville, Il., U.S.	219	39.44 N	90.13 W
Jacksonville, N.J., U.S.	285	40.03 N	74.46 W
Jacksonville, N.Y., U.S.	210	42.31 N	76.37 W
Jacksonville, N.C., U.S.	192	34.45 N	77.25 W
Jacksonville, Or., U.S.	202	42.18 N	122.57 W
Jacksonville, Tx., U.S.	222	31.57 N	95.16 W
Jacksonville, Vt., U.S.	207	42.47 N	72.49 W
Jacksonville, Lake ⊜1	222	31.55 N	95.17 W
Jacksonville Beach	192	30.17 N	81.23 W
Jacksonville Naval Air Station ■	192	30.14 N	81.41 W
Jacks Reef	210	43.06 N	76.25 W
Jacks Run ≃	279b	40.13 N	79.35 W
Jacktown Acres	279b	40.19 N	79.45 W
Jacmel	238	18.14 N	72.32 W
Jaco	232	27.50 N	104.00 W
Jacob, Morne ʌ	240e	14.46 N	61.06 W
Jacobābād	120	28.17 N	68.26 E
Jacobina	250	11.11 S	40.31 W
Jacob Island I	212	44.28 N	78.28 W
Jacob Riis Park ♠	276	40.34 N	73.52 W
Jacobs Creek ≃	214	40.07 N	79.44 W
Jacobsdal	158	29.13 S	24.41 E
Jacobus	208	39.53 N	76.43 W
Jacona de Plancarte	234	19.57 N	102.16 W
Jacques, Lac à ⊜	180	66.10 N	127.25 W
Jacques-Cartier	275a	45.31 N	73.29 W
Jacques-Cartier ≃	206	46.40 N	71.45 W
Jacques-Cartier, Détroit de Ʉ	186	50.00 N	63.30 W
Jacques-Cartier, Mont ʌ	186	48.59 N	65.57 W
Jacques-Cartier, Pont ◆5	275a	45.31 N	73.32 W
Jacquet River	186	47.55 N	66.00 W
Jacqueville	150	5.12 N	4.25 W
Jacquinot Bay c	164	5.35 S	151.30 E
Jacu ≃, Bra.	250	6.13 S	35.09 W
Jacú ≃, Bra.	256	23.05 S	45.08 W
Jacu, Rio do ≃	287b	23.29 S	46.27 W
Jacuba ≃	255	18.25 S	52.28 W
Jacuecanga	256	23.01 S	44.13 W
Jacuí ≃	252	30.02 S	51.15 W
Jacuípe ≃	255	12.30 S	39.05 W
Jacumba	204	32.37 N	116.11 W
Jacundá	250	4.33 S	49.28 W
Jacundá ≃	250	1.57 S	50.26 W
Jacupiranga	252	24.42 S	48.00 W
Jacuriaí ≃	250	10.57 S	39.35 W
Jacutinga	256	22.17 S	46.37 W
Jada	146	8.46 N	12.09 E
Jada'ah, Jabal ʌ2	142	29.58 N	30.40 E
Jādabpur	126	22.29 N	88.23 E
Jaddi, Rās ≻	128	25.14 N	63.31 E
Jade	52	53.20 N	8.14 E
Jade Buddha, Temple of the ⊕1	269b	31.14 N	121.26 E
Jadebusen c	52	53.30 N	8.10 E
Jäder	40	59.25 N	16.41 E
Jäderfors	40	60.41 N	16.40 E
Jade Run ≃	285	39.56 N	74.45 W
Jadīdah	128	34.01 N	42.28 E
Jadito Wash V	200	35.22 N	110.50 W
J.A.D. Jensens Nunatakker ʌ	176	62.45 N	48.00 W
Jadotville → Likasi	154	10.59 S	26.44 E
Jadraque	34	40.55 N	2.55 W
Jadrin	80	55.56 N	46.12 E
Jadromino	82	55.57 N	36.36 E
Jādū	146	31.57 N	12.01 E
Jaduty	78	51.22 N	32.19 E
Jægerspris	41	55.51 N	11.59 E
Jaeger Summit ʌ	154	2.52 S	35.47 E
Jaén, Esp.	34	37.46 N	3.47 W
Jaén, Perú	248	5.42 S	78.47 W
Jaén □4	34	38.00 N	3.30 E
Jæren ◆1	26	58.45 N	5.45 E
Jāfarābād, India	120	20.52 N	71.22 E
Ja'farābād, Īrān	128	35.43 N	50.43 E
Jāfarpur	126	22.29 N	89.06 E
Jāfarpur ◆8	272a	28.40 N	77.01 E
Jaffa, Cape ≻	166	36.58 S	139.40 E
Jaffa, Tel Aviv- → Tel Aviv-Yafo	132	32.04 N	34.46 E
Jaffna	122	9.40 N	80.00 E
Jaffna Lagoon c	122	9.35 N	80.15 E
Jaffrey	207	42.48 N	72.01 W
Jafr, Qā' al- ⊥7	132	30.17 N	36.20 E
Jagādhri	124	30.10 N	77.18 E
Jägala ≃	76	59.29 N	25.09 E
Jagalūr	122	14.32 N	76.21 E
Jāgan	120	28.05 N	68.30 E
Jagannāthganj Ghāt	124	24.45 N	89.49 E
Jagannāthpūr	272b	22.43 N	88.19 E
Jagati	126	23.54 N	89.06 E
Jagatnagar	272b	22.47 N	88.13 E
Jagatpur ◆8	272a	28.44 N	77.14 E
Jagatsingpur	120	20.16 N	86.10 E
Jagdalpur	122	19.04 N	82.02 E
Jagdīspur	124	25.29 N	84.25 E
Jagel	41	54.27 N	9.32 E
Jagel'urta, gora ʌ2	24	67.33 N	38.02 E
Jagenbach	61	48.38 N	15.02 E
Jägerndorf → Krnov	30	50.05 N	17.41 E
Jagersfontein	158	29.44 S	25.29 E
Jaggayyapeta	122	16.54 N	80.06 E
Jagged Mountain ʌ	180	58.38 N	162.02 W
Jagīn ≃	128	25.35 N	58.18 E
Jagnob ≃	85	39.15 N	68.35 E
Jagny-sous-Bois	261	49.05 N	2.27 E
Jagodnoje, Ross.	74	62.33 N	149.40 E
Jagodnoje, Ross.	80	53.36 N	49.04 E
Jagodnyj	86	59.44 N	65.04 E
Jagorlyckij zaliv c	78	46.24 N	31.50 E
Jagotin	78	50.17 N	31.46 E
Jagraon	123	30.47 N	75.29 E
Jagst ≃	56	49.14 N	9.11 E
Jagsthausen	56	49.19 N	9.28 E
Jagstzell	56	49.02 N	10.05 E
Jagtiāl	122	18.48 N	78.56 E
Jaguaquara	255	13.32 S	39.58 W
Jaguarão	252	32.34 S	53.23 W
Jaguarão (Yaguarón) ≃	252	32.39 S	53.12 W
Jaguarari	250	10.16 S	40.12 W
Jaguaretama	250	5.37 S	38.46 W
Jaguari	252	29.30 S	54.41 W
Jaguari ≃, Bra.	256	22.41 S	47.17 W
Jaguari ≃, Bra.	256	23.10 S	45.55 W
Jaguariaíva	252	24.15 S	49.42 W
Jaguaribara	250	5.40 S	38.37 W
Jaguaribe	250	5.53 S	38.37 W
Jaguaribe ≃	250	4.25 S	37.45 W
Jaguari-Mirim ≃	256	21.59 S	47.17 W
Jaguaripe	255	13.06 S	38.53 W
Jaguariúna	256	22.41 S	46.59 W
Jaguaruna	252	28.36 S	49.02 W
Jagüé	252	28.38 S	68.24 W
Jagüey Grande	240p	22.32 N	81.08 W
Jāguli	126	22.56 N	88.32 E
Jāgulia	272b	22.44 N	88.32 E
Jagungal, Mount ʌ	171b	36.09 S	148.23 E
Jagunovskij	86	55.17 N	85.59 E
Jahānābād, India	124	25.13 N	84.59 E
Jahānābād, Pāk.	123	32.11 N	72.29 E
Jahāngīra	123	33.58 N	72.13 E
Jahāngīrābād	124	28.25 N	78.06 E
Jahangirpur ◆8	272a	28.44 N	77.13 E
Jahānia	123	30.02 N	71.49 E
Jahannam, Qārat ʌ2	142	29.19 N	30.09 E
Jahdānīyah, Wādī al- V	132	30.12 N	36.22 E
Jahnsdorf	54	50.44 N	12.51 E
Jahrom	128	28.31 N	53.33 E
Jahú → Jaú	255	22.18 S	48.33 W
Jaicós	250	7.21 S	41.08 W
Jaidak	120	31.58 N	66.43 E
Jaihti ≃	126	24.08 N	86.48 E
Jaijon	123	31.21 N	76.09 E
Jailolo	108	1.05 N	127.30 E
Jaimanitas ≃	286b	23.05 N	82.29 W
Jainca	102	35.59 N	102.02 E
Jainti	124	26.42 N	89.36 E
Jaintiāpur	120	25.08 N	92.07 E
Jaipur	120	26.55 N	75.49 E
Jaipur Hāt	124	25.06 N	89.01 E
Jais	124	26.15 N	81.32 E
Jaisalmer	120	26.55 N	70.54 E
Jaito	123	30.28 N	74.53 E
Jaja	86	56.12 N	86.26 E
Jaja ≃	86	56.58 N	86.23 E
Jājapur	120	20.51 N	86.20 E
Jājarkoṭ	124	28.42 N	82.12 E
Jājarm	128	36.58 N	56.27 E
Jajce	36	44.21 N	17.16 E
Jajichi	174m	26.47 N	128.13 E
Jajjha	123	28.45 N	70.34 E
Jajl'u	86	51.48 N	87.36 E
Jajpan	85	40.23 N	70.48 E
Jajsan	86	50.51 N	56.14 E
Jajva	86	59.20 N	57.15 E
Jajva ≃	86	59.13 N	56.40 E
Ják	61	47.08 N	16.35 E
Jakarta, Indon.	115a	6.10 S	106.48 E
Jakarta, Indon.	269e	6.10 S	106.48 E
Jakarta, Teluk c	115a	6.05 S	106.48 E
Jakarta Kota Station ◆5	269e	6.08 S	106.49 E
Jakarta Raya □4	115a	6.10 S	106.45 E
Jakdūl ⊜	140	17.39 N	32.59 E
Jake Creek Mountain ʌ	204	41.13 N	116.54 W
Jakenan	115a	6.45 S	111.11 E
Jākhal	123	29.48 N	75.50 E
Jakhāu	120	23.13 N	68.43 E
Jakkonen	24	66.33 N	29.52 E
Jakobsberg	40	59.26 N	17.50 E
Jakobsdalsberget ʌ2	40	58.41 N	16.07 E
Jakobshavn (Ilulissat)	176	69.13 N	51.06 W
Jakobstad (Pietarsaari)	26	63.40 N	22.42 E
Jakovleviči	76	54.20 N	30.31 E
Jakovlevka	89	44.26 N	133.28 E
Jakovlevo, Ross.	78	50.51 N	36.27 E
Jakovlevo, Ross.	82	54.48 N	37.26 E
Jakša	24	61.48 N	56.49 E
Jakšanga	80	58.23 N	45.56 E
Jakšur-Bodja	80	57.11 N	53.09 E
Jakupica ⋏	38	41.43 N	21.26 E
Jakutija □3	74	67.00 N	125.00 E
Jakutsk	74	62.00 N	129.40 E
Jal	196	32.06 N	103.11 W
Jalacingo	234	19.48 N	97.18 W
Jalaid Qi	89	46.40 N	122.55 E
Jalājil	128	25.41 N	45.28 E
Jalālābād, Afg.	120	34.26 N	70.28 E
Jalālābād, India	123	30.37 N	74.15 E
Jalālābād, India	124	27.43 N	79.40 E
Jalālah al-Baḥrīyah, Jabal ⋏1	142	29.20 N	32.00 E
Jalālat al-Qiblīyah, Jabal al- ⋏	142	28.42 N	32.22 E
Jalālpur, India	124	26.19 N	82.44 E
Jalālpur, Pāk.	123	32.38 N	74.12 E
Jalālpur Pīrwāla	123	29.30 N	71.13 E
Jalama	84	41.44 N	48.34 E
Jalan'	86	58.21 N	91.53 E
Jalán ≃	236	14.39 N	86.12 W
Jalan Besar Stadium ♠	271c	1.18 N	103.52 E
Jalandhar	123	31.19 N	75.34 E
Jalangi	126	24.08 N	88.42 E
Jalangi ≃	126	23.25 N	88.22 E
Jalan Kayu	271c	1.24 N	103.52 E
Jalapa, Guat.	236	14.38 N	89.59 W
Jalapa, Méx.	234	17.43 N	92.49 W
Jalapa, Nic.	236	13.55 N	86.08 W
Jalapa □5	236	14.35 N	89.55 W
Jalasjärvi	26	62.30 N	22.45 E
Jalaud ≃	116	10.45 N	122.40 E
Jālaun	124	26.09 N	79.21 E
Jal'čiki	80	55.09 N	48.01 E
Jalcocotán	234	21.28 N	105.07 W
Jalda	126	21.56 N	87.30 E
Jaleaca de Catalán	234	17.26 N	99.51 W
Jalesar	124	27.29 N	78.19 E
Jaleshwar	126	21.49 N	87.13 E
Jaleśwar	124	26.38 N	85.48 E
Jālgaon, India	122	21.01 N	75.34 E
Jālgaon, India	122	21.03 N	76.32 E
Jal'gelevo	265a	59.44 N	29.57 E
Jalhay	56	50.34 N	5.58 E
Jalingo	146	8.53 N	11.22 E
Jalirpār	126	23.13 N	89.58 E
Jalisco □3	234	20.20 N	103.40 W
Jallas ≃	34	42.54 N	9.08 W
Jallieu	62	45.35 N	5.16 E
Jālna	122	19.50 N	75.53 E
Jalón ≃	34	41.47 N	1.04 W
Jālor	120	25.21 N	72.37 E
Jalostotitlán	234	21.12 N	102.28 W
Jalpa	234	21.38 N	102.58 W
Jalpa de Méndez	234	18.08 N	93.05 W
Jalpāiguri	124	26.31 N	88.44 E
Jalpan de Serra	234	21.14 N	99.29 W
Jalpug ≃	78	45.41 N	28.35 E
Jalpug, ozero ⊜	78	45.25 N	28.37 E
Jalta (Yalta), Ukr.	78	44.30 N	34.10 E
Jalta, Ukr.	83	46.58 N	37.16 E
Jaltepec ≃	234	17.26 N	94.59 W
Jáltipan de Morelos	234	17.58 N	94.42 W
Jaltuškov	78	48.58 N	27.30 E
Jaluit I1	14	6.00 N	169.35 E
Jalūlā'	128	34.16 N	45.10 E
Jalutorovsk	86	56.40 N	66.18 E
Jam, Ross.	82	55.29 N	37.45 E
Jam, Uzb.	85	40.07 N	68.11 E
Jām ≃	128	35.10 N	61.06 E
Jama	83	48.52 N	38.06 E
Jamaame (Margherita)	144	0.04 N	42.45 E
Jamaare ≃	146	12.06 N	10.14 E
Jāmāibāti	272b	22.51 N	88.08 E
Jamaica	240p	20.12 N	75.09 W
Jamaica ◆8	276	40.42 N	73.47 W
Jamaica □1, N.A.	230	18.15 N	77.30 W
Jamaica □1, N.A.	241q	18.15 N	77.30 W
Jamaica Bay c	210	40.36 N	73.51 W
Jamaica Channel Ʉ	238	18.00 N	75.30 W
Jamaica Plain ◆8	283	42.19 N	71.06 W
Jamaika → Jamaica □1	241q	18.15 N	77.30 W
Jamaïque → Jamaica □1	241q	18.15 N	77.30 W
Jamal, poluostrov ≻1	74	70.00 N	70.00 E
Jam-Alin', chrebet ⋏	89	53.00 N	134.36 E
Jamālīyah ◆8	273c	30.03 N	31.16 E
Jamalo-Neneckij □3	72	67.00 N	75.00 E
Jamālpur, Bngl.	124	24.55 N	89.56 E
Jamālpur, India	124	25.18 N	86.30 E
Jamālpurganj	126	23.04 N	87.59 E
Jamanchalinka	80	47.40 N	51.35 E
Jamanota ʌ2	241s	12.29 N	69.57 W
Jamantau, gora ʌ	86	54.15 N	58.06 E
Jamanxim ≃	250	4.43 S	56.18 W
Jamapará	256	21.55 S	42.43 W
Jamari ≃	248	8.27 S	63.30 W
Jamarovka	88	50.38 N	110.16 E
Jamašurma	80	55.58 N	49.36 E
Jamay	234	20.18 N	102.43 W
Jamba	152	13.50 S	15.30 E

	English	Deutsch	Español	Français	Português
≃	River	Fluß	Río	Rivière	Rio
≊	Canal	Kanal	Canal	Canal	Canal
∟	Waterfall, Rapids	Wasserfall, Stromschnellen	Cascada, Rápidos	Chute d'eau, Rapides	Cascata, Rápidos
Ʉ	Strait	Meeresstraße	Estrecho	Détroit	Estreito
c	Bay, Gulf	Bucht, Golf	Bahía, Golfo	Baie, Golfe	Baía, Golfo
⊜	Lake, Lakes	See, Seen	Lago, Lagos	Lac, Lacs	Lago, Lagos
☷	Swamp	Sumpf	Pantano	Marais	Pântano
⍓	Ice Features, Glacier	Eis- und Gletscherformen	Accidentes Glaciales	Formes glaciaires	Acidentes glaciares
⊤	Other Hydrographic Features	Andere Hydrographische Objekte	Otros Elementos Hidrográficos	Autres données hydrographiques	Outros acidentes hidrográficos
✢	Submarine Features	Untermeerische Objekte	Accidentes Submarinos	Formes de relief sous-marin	Acidentes submarinos
□	Political Unit	Politische Einheit	Unidad Politica	Entité politique	Unidade política
⊕	Cultural Institution	Kulturelle Institution	Institución Cultural	Institution culturelle	Institução cultural
⊥	Historical Site	Historische Stätte	Sitio Histórico	Site historique	Sitio histórico
♠	Recreational Site	Erholungs- und Ferienort	Sitio de Recreo	Centre de loisirs	Area de Lazer
⊠	Airport	Flughafen	Aeropuerto	Aéroport	Aeroporto
■	Military Installation	Militäranlage	Instalación Militar	Installation militaire	Instalação militar
◆	Miscellaneous	Verschiedenes	Misceláneo	Divers	Diversos

Jāmbād 126 22.42 N 86.35 E
Jambeiro 256 23.16 S 45.41 W
Jambeiro, Serra do ⩘[2] 256 23.13 S 45.38 W
Jambelí, Canal de ⋈ 246 3.00 S 80.00 W
Jamberoo 170 34.39 S 150.47 E
Jambes 56 50.28 N 4.52 E
Jambi 112 1.36 S 103.37 E
Jambi □[4] 112 1.30 S 103.00 E
Jambin 166 24.12 S 150.22 E
Jamboaye ≐ 114 5.16 N 97.29 E
Jambol 38 42.29 N 26.30 E
Jambongan, Pulau I 116 6.40 N 117.27 E
Jambuair, Tanjung › 114 5.16 N 97.30 E
Jambusar 120 22.03 N 72.48 E
James ≐, Austl. 166 20.36 S 137.41 E
James ≐, Ab., Can. 182 51.55 N 114.34 W
James ≐, U.S. 198 42.52 N 97.18 W
James ≐, Mo., U.S. 194 36.45 N 93.30 W
James ≐, Va., U.S. 192 36.57 N 76.26 W
James, Isla I 254 44.57 S 74.07 W
James, Lake ⊜ 216 41.42 N 85.02 W
James, Lake ⊜[1] 192 35.45 N 81.55 W
James Bay ⊂ 176 53.30 N 80.30 W
Jamesburg 208 40.21 N 74.26 W
James Bypass ≊ 226 36.41 N 120.16 W
James City, N.C., U.S. 192 35.05 N 77.02 W
James City, Pa., U.S. 214 41.37 N 78.50 W
James City □[6] 208 37.17 N 76.48 W
James Craik 252 32.09 S 63.28 W
James Creek 214 40.23 N 78.10 W
James Gardens ♦ 275b 43.40 N 79.31 W
James Island, B.C., Can. 224 48.37 N 123.22 W
James Island, S.C., U.S. 192 32.44 N 79.57 W
James Island I 208 38.31 N 76.20 W
Jameson Raid Memorial ⊥ 273d 26.11 S 27.49 E
James Point › 192 25.21 N 76.24 W
Jamesport 194 39.58 N 93.48 W
James Price Point › 162 17.30 S 122.08 E
James Ranges ⩘ 162 24.06 S 132.30 E
James River Bridge ✦[5] 208 37.00 N 76.30 W
James Ross, Cape › 176 74.40 N 114.25 W
James Ross Island I 9 64.15 S 57.45 W
James Ross Strait ⋈ 176 69.40 N 95.30 W
James Smith Indian Reserve ✦[4] 184 53.08 N 104.52 W
Jamestown, Austl. 166 33.12 S 138.36 E
Jamestown, Ire. 48 53.55 N 8.02 W
Jamestown, S. Afr. 158 31.06 S 26.45 E
Jamestown, Ca., U.S. 226 37.57 N 120.25 W
Jamestown, Ks., U.S. 198 39.35 N 97.51 W
Jamestown, Ky., U.S. 194 36.59 N 85.03 W
Jamestown, Mi., U.S. 216 42.50 N 85.51 W
Jamestown, N.Y., U.S. 214 42.05 N 79.14 W
Jamestown, N.C., U.S. 192 35.59 N 79.56 W
Jamestown, N.D., U.S. 198 46.54 N 98.42 W
Jamestown, Oh., U.S. 218 39.39 N 83.44 W
Jamestown, Pa., U.S. 214 41.29 N 80.26 W
Jamestown, R.I., U.S. 207 41.29 N 71.22 W
Jamestown, Tn., U.S. 194 36.25 N 84.55 W
Jamestown ⊥ 208 37.12 N 76.46 W
Jamestown Festival Park ♦ 208 37.14 N 76.48 W
Jamestown Island I 208 37.12 N 76.46 W
Jamestown Reservoir ⊜[1] 198 47.15 N 98.40 W
Jamesville, N.Y., U.S. 210 42.59 N 76.04 W
Jamesville, Va., U.S. 208 37.30 N 75.55 W
Jamet, Lac ⊜ 206 46.34 N 74.30 W
Jametz 56 49.26 N 5.23 E
Jamieson ≐ 169 37.18 S 146.08 E
Jaminauá ≐ 248 9.20 S 70.59 W
Jaminsk 76 52.46 N 28.16 E
Jaminskij 80 50.21 N 42.14 E
Jāmira ≐ 126 21.45 N 87.02 E
Jamira ≐[1] 126 21.35 N 88.28 E
Jamison 208 40.16 N 75.05 W
Jamison City 210 41.18 N 76.22 W
Jamison Town 274a 33.46 S 150.41 E
Jam-Ižora 265a 59.42 N 30.36 E
Jām Jodhpur 120 21.54 N 70.01 E
Jamkhandi 122 16.31 N 75.18 E
Jamki 86 59.33 N 66.47 E
Jamkino 82 55.55 N 38.24 E
Jamm 76 58.26 N 28.03 E
Jammalamadugu 122 14.50 N 78.24 E
Jammerbugten ⊂ 26 57.20 N 9.30 E
Jammerland Bugt ⊂ 41 55.35 N 11.05 E
Jammu 123 32.42 N 74.52 E
Jammu Airport ⊠ 123 32.42 N 74.51 E
Jammu and Kashmīr □[2] 120 34.00 N 76.00 E
Jamnagar 120 22.28 N 70.04 E
Jamoigne 56 49.42 N 5.25 E
Jamor ≐ 266c 38.42 N 9.15 W
Jampang-kulon 115a 7.16 S 106.37 E
Jampol', Ukr. 78 49.58 N 26.14 E
Jampol', Ukr. 78 51.57 N 33.46 E
Jampol', Ukr. 78 48.16 N 28.17 E
Jampol', Ukr. 83 48.56 N 37.58 E
Jāmpur, India 272b 22.56 N 88.12 E
Jāmpur, Pāk. 123 29.39 N 70.36 E
Jämsä 26 61.52 N 25.12 E
Jamsah 140 27.38 N 33.35 E
Jämsänkoski 26 61.55 N 25.11 E
Jamshedpur 126 22.48 N 86.11 E
Jamsk 74 59.35 N 154.10 E
Jamskaja Sloboda 82 55.29 N 36.01 E
Jāmtāra 126 23.57 N 86.48 E
Jämtland □[9] 26 63.30 N 14.00 E
Jämtlands Län □[6] 24 63.00 N 14.40 E
Jamuāni 126 21.57 N 86.14 E
Jamuga 82 56.24 N 36.40 E
Jamūi 124 24.55 N 86.13 E
Jamuna ≐, Bngl. 124 23.51 N 89.45 E
Jamuna ≐, India 272b 22.57 N 88.35 E
Jamundí 246 3.15 N 76.32 W
Jāmuria 126 23.44 N 87.02 E
Jāmurki 126 24.09 N 90.02 E
Jana ≐ 74 71.31 N 136.32 E
Janāi 272b 22.43 N 88.16 E
Janāj 142 31.00 N 30.46 E
Janajkino 80 50.43 N 51.06 E
Janakpur 124 26.39 N 85.55 E
Janakpur □[8] 124 27.15 N 86.00 E
Janas 266c 38.49 N 9.26 W
Janauacá, Lago ⊜ 246 3.28 S 60.17 W
Janaúba 255 15.48 S 43.19 W
Janaucu, Ilha I 250 0.30 N 50.10 W
Janaul 86 56.16 N 54.56 E
Jand 123 33.26 N 72.01 E
Janda, Laguna de la ⊜ 34 36.15 N 5.51 W
Jandaia 255 17.06 S 50.07 W
Jandaia do Sul 255 23.36 S 51.39 W
Jandaíra 250 11.34 S 37.47 W
Jandalī, Wādī al- V 142 30.05 N 31.52 E
Jandaq 128 34.02 N 54.26 E
Jandelsbrunn 60 48.44 N 13.42 E
Jandiāla 123 31.36 N 75.03 E
Jandiatuba ≐ 246 3.28 S 68.42 W
Jandira 256 23.31 S 46.54 W
Jandira □[7] 287b 23.32 S 46.54 W
Jandowae 166 26.47 S 151.06 E
Jandrakinot 180 64.54 N 172.32 W
Jándula ≐ 34 38.03 N 4.06 W
Jándula, Embalse de ⊜[1] 34 38.30 N 4.00 W
Janeiro, Rio de ≐ 250 11.51 S 45.09 W
Jane Peak ∧ 172 45.20 S 168.19 E
Janes Island I 208 38.00 N 75.52 W
Janes Island State Park ♦ 208 38.00 N 75.52 W
Janesville, Ca., U.S. 204 40.17 N 120.31 W
Janesville, Mn., U.S. 190 44.06 N 93.42 W
Janesville, Wi., U.S. 216 42.40 N 89.01 W
Jangal Bādhāl 126 23.07 N 89.21 E
Jangamo 156 24.06 S 35.21 E
Jangany 157b 23.14 S 45.27 E
Jangarej 24 68.46 N 61.25 E
Jangel'skij 86 53.08 N 58.59 E
Jangeru 112 2.20 S 116.29 E
Jangiabad 85 41.08 N 70.05 E
Jangi-Bazar 85 41.40 N 70.53 E
Jangijer 85 40.17 N 68.50 E
Jangijul' 85 41.07 N 69.03 E
Jangikišlak 85 40.25 N 67.10 E
Jangikurgan, Uzb. 85 40.34 N 71.09 E
Jangikurgan, Uzb. 85 41.12 N 71.44 E
Jangipāra 126 22.45 N 88.04 E
Jangīpur 124 24.28 N 88.04 E
Jangong 114 4.23 N 96.48 E
Jangoon 122 17.43 N 79.11 E
Jangulovo 80 56.26 N 50.25 E
Janikowo 30 52.45 N 18.07 E
Janīn 132 32.28 N 35.18 E
Janina → Ioánnina 38 39.40 N 20.50 E
Janino 265a 59.56 N 30.36 E
Janisjarvi, ozero ⊜ 24 61.59 N 30.57 E
Janiuay 116 10.58 N 122.30 E
Janja 38 44.40 N 19.15 E
Janjina, Hrv. 36 42.56 N 17.26 E
Janjina, Madag. 157b 20.30 S 45.50 E
Janka 126 21.52 N 87.56 E
Jankan, chrebet ⩘ 88 55.45 N 118.00 E
Jankāpur 126 21.54 N 87.23 E
Jan Kempdorp (Andalusia) 158 27.55 S 24.51 E
Jan Lake ⊜ 184 54.55 N 102.55 W
Janlohong 112 2.15 N 117.03 E
Jan Mayen I 12 71.00 N 8.20 W
Jan Mayen Ridge ✦[3] 10 69.00 N 8.00 W
Jannaale 144 1.48 N 44.42 E
Jannali 274a 34.01 S 151.04 E
Jannali Park ♦ 274a 34.01 S 151.03 E
Janos 232 30.54 N 108.10 W
Jánoshalma 30 46.18 N 19.20 E
Jánosháza 30 47.08 N 17.10 E
János-hegy ∧ 264c 47.31 N 18.58 E
Jánossomorja 61 47.47 N 17.08 E
Janoviči 76 55.17 N 30.42 E
Janowiec Wielkopolski 30 52.46 N 17.31 E
Janów Lubelski 30 50.43 N 22.24 E
Jānsath 124 29.20 N 77.51 E
Jansen 184 51.47 N 104.43 W
Jansenville 158 32.56 S 24.40 E
Janskij 74 68.28 N 134.48 E
Janskij zaliv ⊂ 74 71.50 N 136.00 E
Jantarnyj 76 54.52 N 19.57 E
Jantetelco 234 18.42 N 98.46 W
Jantikovo 80 55.32 N 47.48 E
Jantra ≐ 38 43.38 N 25.34 E
Januária 255 15.29 S 44.22 W
Januário Cicco 250 6.09 S 35.35 W
Jan Van Riebeeck Park ♦ 273d 26.10 S 27.59 E
Janvarcevo 80 51.26 N 52.15 E
Janville 50 48.12 N 1.53 E
Janville-sur-Juine 261 48.31 N 2.16 E
Janvry 261 48.39 N 2.09 E
Jany-Kurgan 85 43.55 N 67.15 E
Janzé 32 47.58 N 1.30 W
Janzūr 142 30.41 N 31.02 E
Jaora 120 23.38 N 75.08 E
Japan (Nihon) □[1], Asia 90 36.00 N 138.00 E
Japan (Nihon) □[1], Asia 92 36.00 N 138.00 E
Japan, Sea of ⊤[2] 90 40.00 N 135.00 E
Japan Basin ✦[1] 12 40.00 N 135.00 E
Japanisches Meer → Japan, Sea of ⊤[2] 90 40.00 N 135.00 E
Japan Trench ✦[1] 6 37.00 N 143.00 E
Japaratinga 250 9.05 S 35.15 W
Japaratuba 250 10.35 S 36.57 W
Japeri 256 22.39 S 43.40 W
Japi 250 6.27 S 35.56 W
Japim 248 7.37 S 72.54 W
Japla 124 24.33 N 84.01 E
Japoatã 250 10.20 S 36.48 W
Japón, Mar del → Japan, Sea of ⊤[2] 90 40.00 N 135.00 E
Japon → Japan □[1] 92 36.00 N 138.00 E
Japtiksal'a 74 69.21 N 72.32 E
Japuíba 256 22.35 S 42.42 W
Japurá 246 1.48 S 66.30 W
Japurá (Caquetá) ≐ 246 3.08 S 64.46 W
Jaqué 246 7.31 N 78.10 W
Jaqueri-mirim ≐ 287b 23.31 S 46.51 W
Jaquí 248 15.30 S 74.26 W
Jar 80 58.15 N 52.06 E
Jār, Jabal ∧ 128 24.34 N 38.18 E
Jarābulus 130 36.49 N 38.01 E
Jarad 144 18.59 N 41.24 E
Jaradū 142 29.18 N 30.42 E
Jaraguá 255 15.45 S 49.20 W
Jaraguá ✦[8] 287b 23.27 S 46.44 W
Jaraguá, Pico do ∧ 287b 23.26 S 46.46 W
Jaraguá do Sul 252 26.29 S 49.04 W
Jaraicejo 34 39.40 N 5.49 W
Jaraiz de la Vera 34 40.04 N 5.45 W
Jaral del Progreso 234 20.22 N 101.04 W
Jarales 200 34.36 N 106.45 W
Jarama ≐ 34 40.02 N 3.39 W
Jarama, Canal del ≊ 266a 40.18 N 3.32 W
Jaramānah 132 33.29 N 36.21 E
Jaramillo 254 47.11 S 67.09 W
Jaramor 80 56.07 N 48.44 E
Jaran' ≐ 80 57.35 N 48.14 E
Jarandilla 34 40.08 N 5.39 W
Jaraniyo 144 10.42 N 39.55 E
Jaransk 80 57.19 N 47.54 E
Jarānwāla 123 31.20 N 73.26 E
Jarash 132 32.17 N 35.54 E
Jaraucu ≐ 250 1.48 S 52.22 W
Jarawī, Wādī V 142 29.47 N 31.19 E
Jarbah, Jabal al- ∧ 142 30.16 N 32.03 E
Jarbah, Wāḥat ⊤[4] 140 29.21 N 25.20 E
Jarbidge ≐ 202 42.19 N 115.39 W
Järbo 40 60.43 N 16.36 E
Jarcevo 76 55.04 N 32.41 E
Jardas al-ʿAbīd 146 32.19 N 20.56 E
Jardim, Bra. 248 21.28 S 56.09 W
Jardim, Bra. 250 7.35 S 39.16 W
Jardim América ✦[8] 287b 23.34 S 46.41 W
Jardim de Piranhas 250 6.22 S 37.20 W
Jardim do Seridó 250 6.35 S 36.46 W
Jardim Paraiso 256 22.48 S 43.35 W
Jardim Paulista ✦[8] 287b 23.35 S 46.40 W
Jardín América 252 27.03 S 55.14 W
Jardine ≐ 164 10.55 S 142.13 E
Jardine River National Park ♦ 164 11.20 S 142.40 E
Jardines de la Reina, Archipiélago de los II 240p 20.50 N 78.55 W
Jardinópolis 255 21.02 S 47.46 W
Jardymly 84 38.55 N 48.15 E
Jaredi 150 12.46 N 5.05 E
Jaremča 78 48.27 N 24.33 E
Jaren'ga, Ross. 24 63.27 N 53.26 E
Jarenga, Ross. 24 62.43 N 49.30 E
Jarensk 24 62.11 N 49.02 E
Järfälla 40 59.24 N 17.50 E
Jargalang 89 43.06 N 122.54 E
Jargara 78 46.27 N 28.27 E
Jargeau 50 47.52 N 2.07 E
Jari ≐, Bra. 248 5.07 S 62.21 W
Jari ≐, Bra. 250 1.09 S 51.54 W
Jari, Lago ⊜ 246 5.00 S 62.19 W
Jāria Jhānjail 124 25.02 N 90.39 E
Jaridih 124 23.38 N 86.04 E
Jarinu 256 23.06 S 46.44 W
Jarīr, Wādī al- V 128 25.38 N 42.30 E
Jarkino 88 59.08 N 99.23 E
Jarkovo 86 57.24 N 67.05 E
Jarkul'-Mat'uškino 86 55.51 N 76.06 E
Järlåsa 40 59.53 N 17.12 E
Jarmen 54 53.55 N 13.20 E
Jarmolincy 78 49.12 N 26.50 E
Järna 40 59.06 N 17.34 E
Jarnac 32 45.41 N 0.10 W
Jarny 56 49.09 N 5.53 E
Jaro 116 11.11 N 124.47 E
Jarochta 88 58.58 N 98.58 E
Jarocin 30 51.59 N 17.31 E
Jaroměř 30 50.21 N 15.55 E
Jaroměřice 61 49.05 N 15.53 E
Jaropolec 82 56.08 N 35.49 E
Jaroslavec 78 51.33 N 33.40 E
Jaroslavl' 80 57.37 N 39.52 E
Jaroslavl' Oblast' □[4] 76 57.45 N 39.00 E
Jaroslavl' Station ✦[5] 265b 55.47 N 37.39 E
Jaroslavskaja 84 44.36 N 40.27 E
Jaroslavskij 89 44.10 N 132.13 E
Jarosław 30 50.02 N 22.42 E
Jarovaja 83 49.03 N 37.37 E
Järpen 26 63.21 N 13.29 E
Jarrahdale 168a 32.21 S 116.04 E
Jarratt 208 36.48 N 77.28 W
Jarreau 194 30.39 N 91.29 W
Jarrell 222 30.49 N 97.36 W
Jarrettsville 208 39.36 N 76.28 W
Jarrīs 142 27.55 N 30.46 E
Jarrow 44 54.59 N 1.29 W
Jarry, Parc ♦ 275a 45.32 N 73.38 W
Jar-Sale 74 66.50 N 70.50 E
Jarsomovy 86 60.15 N 73.38 E
Jartai Yanchi ⊜ 102 39.43 N 105.41 E
Jaru 248 10.26 S 62.27 W
Jaru ≐ 248 10.05 S 61.59 W
Jarud Qi 89 44.37 N 120.58 E
Jaruu 88 48.08 N 96.45 E
Järva-Jaani 76 59.02 N 25.53 E
Järvakandi 76 58.47 N 24.49 E
Järvelä 26 60.52 N 25.17 E
Järvenpää 26 60.28 N 25.06 E
Jarvie 182 54.27 N 113.59 W
Jarville-la-Malgrange 58 48.40 N 6.13 E
Jarvis 212 42.53 N 80.06 W
Jarvisburg 192 36.12 N 75.52 W
Jarvis Island I 14 0.23 S 160.02 W
Järvsö 26 61.43 N 16.10 E
Jarwa 124 27.39 N 82.31 E
Jasaan 116 8.39 N 124.45 E
Jasai 272c 18.56 N 73.01 E
Jašalta 80 46.20 N 42.17 E
Jasašnaja Tašla 80 53.55 N 48.16 E
Jaša Tomić 38 45.27 N 20.51 E
Jasdan 120 22.02 N 71.12 E
Jasel'da ≐ 76 52.07 N 26.28 E
Jasenevo ✦[8] 265b 55.36 N 37.33 E
Jasenki 78 51.32 N 38.12 E
Jasenovoje 82 54.10 N 36.47 E
Jasenovskij 83 48.10 N 39.10 E
Jasenskaja 78 46.22 N 38.16 E
Jashpurnagar 124 22.54 N 84.09 E
Jāshpur Pāts ✦[1] 124 22.55 N 84.00 E
Jasidih 124 24.31 N 86.39 E
Jasień 30 51.46 N 15.01 E
Jasienica 54 53.37 N 14.32 E
Jasikan 150 7.24 N 0.28 E
Jašil'kul', ozero ⊜ 120 37.45 N 72.55 E
Jasin 114 2.19 N 102.26 E
Jasin'a 78 48.16 N 24.20 E
Jasinga 115a 6.29 S 106.27 E
Jasinovataja 83 48.08 N 37.51 E
Jasinovka 83 48.08 N 37.57 E
Jāsk 128 25.38 N 57.46 E
Jaskhar 272c 18.54 N 72.59 E
Jaškino, Ross. 80 52.41 N 53.26 E
Jaškino, Ross. 86 55.54 N 85.26 E
Jaskino, Ross. 265b 55.40 N 37.16 E
Jaškul' 80 46.11 N 45.21 E
Jaškul' ≐ 80 46.15 N 45.05 E
Jasło 30 49.45 N 21.29 E
Jasmine Estates 220 28.17 N 82.42 W
Jasmund ›[1] 54 54.32 N 13.35 E
Jasnaja Pol'ana ⊥ 82 54.05 N 37.32 E
Jasnogorka 83 48.47 N 37.33 E
Jasnogorsk 82 54.29 N 37.42 E
Jasnomorskij 89 46.45 N 141.54 E
Jasnyj, Ross. 86 51.04 N 59.58 E
Jasnyj, Ross. 89 53.17 N 127.59 E
Jason Islands II 254 51.05 S 61.00 W
Jason Peninsula ›[1] 9 66.10 S 61.00 W
Jasonville 194 39.09 N 87.11 W
Jasper, Ab., Can. 182 52.53 N 118.05 W
Jasper, Al., U.S. 194 33.49 N 87.16 W
Jasper, Ar., U.S. 194 36.00 N 93.11 W
Jasper, Fl., U.S. 192 30.31 N 82.56 W
Jasper, Ga., U.S. 192 34.28 N 84.25 W
Jasper, In., U.S. 194 38.23 N 86.55 W
Jasper, Mi., U.S. 216 41.48 N 84.02 W
Jasper, Mn., U.S. 198 43.51 N 96.23 W
Jasper, Mo., U.S. 194 37.20 N 94.18 W
Jasper, N.Y., U.S. 210 42.07 N 77.30 W
Jasper, Tn., U.S. 194 35.04 N 85.37 W
Jasper, Tx., U.S. 194 30.55 N 93.59 W
Jasper □[6] 216 40.57 N 87.09 W
Jasper Lake ⊜ 182 53.07 N 118.00 W
Jasper National Park ♦ 182 52.53 N 118.03 W
Jaspur 124 29.17 N 78.49 E
Jasra 124 25.17 N 81.48 E
Jassans-Riottier 58 45.59 N 4.45 E
Jassar 123 32.06 N 74.57 E
Jassy ≐ 85 40.46 N 73.05 E
Jassy → Iași 38 47.10 N 27.35 E
Jastarnia 30 54.43 N 18.40 E
Jastrebarsko 36 45.40 N 15.39 E
Jastrebovka, Ross. 78 51.27 N 37.32 E
Jastrebovka, Ross. 82 54.36 N 36.24 E
Jastrowie 30 53.26 N 16.49 E
Jaswantnagar 124 26.53 N 78.55 E
Jászapáti 30 47.31 N 20.09 E
Jászberény 30 47.30 N 19.55 E
Jász-Nagykun-Szolnok □[6] 30 47.12 N 20.11 E
Jataí 255 17.53 S 51.43 W
Jatapu ≐ 246 2.13 S 58.17 W
Jatate ≐ 232 16.15 N 91.17 W
Jati, Bra. 250 7.41 S 39.01 W
Jāti, Pāk. 120 24.21 N 68.16 E
Jatibarang 115a 6.28 S 108.17 E
Jatibonico 240p 21.56 N 79.10 W
Jatibonico del Sur ≐ 240p 21.33 N 79.09 W
Jatilawang 115a 7.32 S 109.06 E
Jatiluhur, Waduk ⊜[1] 115a 6.35 S 107.20 E
Jatinegara ✦[8] 269e 6.13 S 106.52 E
Jatiroto 115a 8.07 S 113.21 E
Jatisrono 115a 7.49 S 111.07 E
Jatiwangi 115a 6.44 S 108.15 E
Jatni 120 20.10 N 85.42 E
Jatniel 273d 26.07 S 28.19 E
Jatobá ≐ 255 12.23 S 54.07 W
Jatobá, Ribeirão ≐ 256 21.28 S 42.49 W
Jatoi Janūbi 123 29.31 N 70.51 E
Jātrāpur 126 22.44 N 89.45 E
Jatt (Tel Gat) 132 32.24 N 35.02 E
Jatznick 54 53.35 N 13.56 E
Jáu, Ang. 152 15.12 S 13.31 E
Jaú, Bra. 255 22.18 S 48.33 W
Jaú ≐ 246 1.54 S 61.26 W
Jaú, Parque Nacional do ♦ 246 2.30 S 63.00 W
Jauaperi ≐ 246 1.26 S 61.35 W
Jauerling ∧ 61 48.20 N 15.20 E
Jaugrām 126 23.06 N 88.05 E
Jauja 248 11.48 S 75.30 W
Jauli 272a 28.44 N 77.21 E
Jaumave 234 23.25 N 99.23 W
Jaunde → Yaoundé 152 3.52 N 11.31 E
Jaune, Mer → Yellow Sea ⊤[2] 90 36.00 N 123.00 E
Jaungulbene 76 57.04 N 26.36 E
Jaunjelgava 76 56.37 N 25.05 E
Jaunpass)(58 46.36 N 7.20 E
Jaunpiebalga 76 57.11 N 26.03 E
Jaunpils 76 56.44 N 23.01 E
Jaunpur 124 25.44 N 82.41 E
Jaupaci 255 16.18 S 50.54 W
Jauquara ≐ 248 15.06 S 57.06 W
Jáuregui 258 34.36 S 59.10 W
Jauru 250 11.06 S 57.30 W
Jauru ≐, Bra. 248 16.22 S 57.46 W
Jauru ≐, Bra. 255 18.40 S 54.36 W
Jausiers 62 44.25 N 6.44 E
Jauza ≐, Ross. 82 56.25 N 36.05 E
Jauza ≐, Ross. 265b 55.45 N 37.38 E
Java 198 45.30 N 99.53 W
Java Center 210 42.39 N 78.23 W
Javādi Hills ⩘[2] 122 12.35 N 78.50 E
Java → Jawa I 115a 7.30 S 110.00 E
Javan 85 38.19 N 69.02 E
Javari (Yavarí) ≐ 242 4.21 S 70.02 W
Javas 80 54.26 N 42.51 E
Java Sea → Jawa, Laut ⊤[2] 112 5.00 S 110.00 E
Java Trench ✦[1] 12 10.30 S 110.00 E
Java Village 210 42.40 N 78.26 W
Jävenitz 54 52.31 N 11.30 E
Javier, Isla I 254 47.06 S 74.24 W
Javkino 78 47.16 N 32.37 E
Javlenka 86 54.21 N 68.27 E
Javor ⩘ 38 44.05 N 18.55 E
Javořice ∧ 61 49.14 N 15.20 E
Javorie ∧ 30 48.27 N 19.18 E
Javorná 60 49.13 N 13.18 E
Javorník 30 50.23 N 17.00 E
Javorov 78 49.56 N 23.23 E
Javorová skála ∧ 30 49.31 N 14.30 E
Javr ≐ 24 68.09 N 30.06 E
Jävre 26 65.09 N 21.59 E
Jawa (Java) I 115a 7.30 S 110.00 E
Jawa, Laut (Java Sea) ⊤[2] 112 5.00 S 110.00 E
Jawa Barat □[4] 115a 7.00 S 107.00 E
Jawʿāiyāt, Jabal al- ∧ 132 31.26 N 36.26 E
Jawāla Mukhi 123 31.53 N 76.19 E
Jawa Tengah □[4] 115a 7.30 S 110.00 E
Jawa Timur □[4] 115a 8.00 S 113.00 E
Jawbar 132 33.31 N 36.19 E
Jawf, Wādī V 144 15.50 N 45.30 E
Jawi 112 0.48 S 109.16 E
Jawor 30 51.03 N 16.11 E
Jaworzno 30 50.13 N 19.15 E
Jay, Fl., U.S. 194 30.57 N 87.09 W
Jay, Ok., U.S. 196 36.25 N 94.47 W
Jay □[6] 216 40.26 N 84.59 W
Jaya, Puncak ∧ 164 4.05 S 137.11 E
Jayanca 248 6.24 S 79.50 W
Jayapura (Sukarnapura) 164 2.32 S 140.42 E
Jayb, Wādī al- (Haʿ Arava) V 132 30.58 N 35.24 E
Jay Cooke State Park ♦ 190 46.41 N 92.23 W
Jay Creek Aboriginal Reserve ✦[4] 162 23.45 S 133.35 E
Jaydebpur 124 24.00 N 90.26 E
Jaynagar 126 22.36 N 90.42 E
Jaynagar Majilpur 126 22.11 N 88.25 E
Jaynes 200 32.16 N 111.01 W
Jay Peak ∧ 188 44.55 N 72.32 W
Jaypur, India 122 18.51 N 82.35 E
Jaypur, India 126 23.03 N 87.27 E
Jayrūd 130 33.49 N 36.44 E
Jayton 196 33.15 N 100.34 W
Jayuya 240m 18.13 N 66.36 W
Jaywick 42 51.47 N 1.08 E
Jaz 80 54.54 N 45.13 E
Jaželbicy 76 58.02 N 32.58 E
Jazevec 24 65.43 N 46.30 E
Jazgulem ≐ 85 38.12 N 71.21 E
Jazīrat Muḥammad 273c 30.07 N 31.12 E
Jazjavan 85 40.39 N 71.44 E
Jažma 24 66.56 N 44.29 E
Jaz Mūrīān, Hāmūn-e ⊜ 128 27.20 N 58.55 E
Jazovaja 86 49.27 N 85.20 E
Jazykovo 80 54.18 N 47.24 E
Jazzīn 132 33.32 N 35.34 E
Jbāʿ 132 33.29 N 35.31 E
J.B. Thomas, Lake ⊜[1] 196 32.35 N 101.10 W
J. C. Murphey Lake ⊜ 216 40.58 N 87.30 W
Jdiouia 34 35.57 N 0.50 E
Jeanerette 194 29.54 N 91.39 W
Jeanesville 210 40.56 N 75.58 W
Jeannette 214 40.19 N 79.36 W
Jebba 150 9.08 N 4.50 E
Jebel 38 45.33 N 21.14 E
Jebeniana 148 35.02 N 10.55 E
Jeber-Bergfrieden 54 51.59 N 12.20 E
Jeberos 248 5.17 S 76.13 W
Jebri 120 27.18 N 65.44 E
Jebus 112 1.44 S 105.29 E
Jechegnadzor 84 39.46 N 45.21 E
Jéci, Serra ∧ 154 12.48 S 35.12 E
Jedane, Oued ti-n- V 148 24.55 N 6.30 E
Jedarma 88 58.44 N 102.36 E
Jedburgh 44 55.29 N 2.34 W
Jedburgh Abbey ⊌[1] 44 55.27 N 2.34 W
Jeddah → Jiddah 144 21.30 N 39.12 E
Jeddore Lake ⊜[1] 186 48.03 N 55.55 W
Jedelevo 80 53.24 N 47.45 E
Jedepo 150 5.16 N 8.20 W
Jedincy 78 48.10 N 27.19 E
Jedisa 84 42.31 N 44.16 E
Jedlesee ✦[8] 264b 48.16 N 16.23 E
Jednevo 82 56.06 N 36.14 E
Jedogon 88 54.15 N 100.15 E
Jedrovo 76 57.55 N 33.38 E
Jędrzejów 30 50.39 N 20.18 E
Jedwabne 30 53.17 N 22.19 E
Jed Water ≐ 46 55.32 N 2.33 W
Jeetzel (Jeetze) ≐ 54 53.09 N 11.04 E
Jefawa 140 10.57 N 23.48 E
Jeffara (Al-Jifārah) ≚ 146 32.30 N 11.45 E
Jeffers 198 44.03 N 95.11 W
Jefferson, Ga., U.S. 192 34.07 N 83.34 W
Jefferson, In., U.S. 216 40.17 N 86.36 W
Jefferson, Ia., U.S. 198 42.00 N 94.22 W
Jefferson, Md., U.S. 208 39.21 N 77.31 W
Jefferson, Ma., U.S. 207 42.21 N 71.52 W
Jefferson, N.J., U.S. 285 39.45 N 75.13 W
Jefferson, N.Y., U.S. 210 42.14 N 73.54 W
Jefferson, N.Y., U.S. 210 42.29 N 74.37 W
Jefferson, N.C., U.S. 192 36.25 N 81.28 W
Jefferson, Oh., U.S. 214 41.44 N 80.46 W
Jefferson, Or., U.S. 202 44.43 N 123.00 W
Jefferson, Pa., U.S. 279b 40.18 N 80.03 W
Jefferson, S.C., U.S. 192 34.39 N 80.23 W
Jefferson, S.D., U.S. 198 42.36 N 96.33 W
Jefferson, Tx., U.S. 194 32.45 N 94.20 W
Jefferson, Wi., U.S. 216 43.00 N 88.48 W
Jefferson □[6], Il., U.S. 219 38.19 N 88.55 W
Jefferson □[6], In., U.S. 218 38.44 N 85.23 W
Jefferson □[6], Ky., U.S. 218 38.14 N 85.10 W
Jefferson □[6], Mo., U.S. 219 38.20 N 90.34 W
Jefferson □[6], N.Y., U.S. 212 43.59 N 75.55 W
Jefferson □[6], Oh., U.S. 214 40.22 N 80.37 W
Jefferson □[6], Pa., U.S. 214 41.09 N 79.05 W
Jefferson □[6], Wa., U.S. 224 47.50 N 122.36 W
Jefferson □[6], Wi., U.S. 216 43.02 N 88.46 W
Jefferson ≐ 202 45.56 N 111.30 W
Jefferson, Mount ∧, U.S. 202 44.34 N 111.30 W
Jefferson, Mount ∧, Nv., U.S. 204 38.46 N 116.55 W
Jefferson, Mount ∧, Or., U.S. 202 44.40 N 121.47 W
Jefferson City, Mo., U.S. 219 38.34 N 92.10 W
Jefferson City, Tn., U.S. 192 36.07 N 83.29 W
Jefferson Farms 285 39.40 N 75.34 W
Jefferson Manor 284c 38.47 N 77.04 W
Jefferson Park ✦[8] 278 41.59 N 87.46 W
Jefferson Proving Ground ■ 218 38.50 N 85.25 W
Jeffersonton 188 38.38 N 77.55 W
Jeffersontown 218 38.11 N 85.33 W
Jefferson Village 284c 38.52 N 77.10 W
Jeffersonville, Ga., U.S. 192 32.41 N 83.20 W
Jeffersonville, In., U.S. 218 38.16 N 85.44 W
Jeffersonville, N.Y., U.S. 210 41.46 N 74.56 W
Jeffersonville, Oh., U.S. 218 39.39 N 83.33 W
Jeffrey City 200 42.29 N 107.49 W
Jeffreys Bay 158 34.02 S 24.54 E
Jeffries Creek ≐ 192 34.05 N 79.32 W
Jefimovka 80 52.13 N 52.03 E
Jefimovskij 76 59.30 N 35.02 E
Jefremov 76 53.09 N 38.07 E
Jefremova 82 56.13 N 38.59 E
Jefremovka 83 47.19 N 38.29 E
Jefremovo-Stepanovka 78 48.43 N 40.50 E
Jefremovskaja 82 55.25 N 38.59 E
Jega 150 12.15 N 4.23 E
Jegenstorf 58 47.03 N 7.30 E
Jegindybulak, Kaz. 86 49.45 N 76.23 E
Jegindybulak, Kaz. 86 48.42 N 81.48 E
Jegizkara, gora ∧ 86 46.24 N 64.09 E
Jegorjevka 89 50.42 N 127.42 E
Jegorjevsk 82 55.23 N 39.02 E
Jegorlyk ≐ 80 46.33 N 41.52 E
Jehol → Chengde 105 40.58 N 117.53 E
Jeja ≐ 78 46.41 N 38.36 E
Jejsk 78 46.42 N 38.16 E
Jejskij liman ⊂ 78 46.42 N 38.25 E
Jeju → Cheju 90 33.31 N 126.32 E
Jejur 272b 22.53 N 88.08 E
Jēkabpils 76 56.29 N 25.51 E
Jekaterinburg (Sverdlovsk) 86 56.51 N 60.36 E
Jekaterinburg Oblast' □[4] 86 58.00 N 62.00 E
Jekaterinino 76 55.49 N 33.58 E
Jekaterininskoje 86 56.53 N 74.34 E
Jekaterinoslav → Dnepropetrovsk 78 48.27 N 34.59 E
Jekaterinoslavka 89 50.23 N 129.08 E
Jekaterinovka, Kaz. 86 54.36 N 70.58 E
Jekaterinovka, Ross. 78 46.42 N 38.46 E
Jekaterinovka, Ross. 80 53.04 N 49.28 E
Jekaterinovka, Ross. 80 46.32 N 41.42 E
Jekaterinovka, Ross. 80 52.03 N 44.21 E
Jekaterinovka, Ross. 83 47.33 N 38.23 E
Jekaterinovka ✦[8] 265b 55.46 N 37.23 E
Jekaterinovskaja 78 46.20 N 39.58 E
Jekateriny, proliv ⋈, Ross. 74 44.30 N 146.45 E
Jekateriny, proliv ⋈, Ross. 92a 44.25 N 146.40 E
Jekimoviči 76 54.07 N 33.18 E
Jekpindykurylys 80 47.49 N 47.17 E
Jekyll Island I 192 31.04 N 81.25 W
Jekyll Island State Park ♦ 192 31.02 N 81.25 W
Jelabuga 80 55.47 N 52.04 E
Jelai ≐, Indon. 112 2.59 S 110.45 E
Jelai ≐, Malay. 114 4.04 N 102.20 E
Jelan', Ross. 80 52.13 N 44.11 E
Jelan', Ross. 80 50.57 N 43.44 E
Jelan', Ross. 83 48.41 N 39.47 E
Jelan', Ross. 86 57.39 N 63.42 E
Jelan' ≐, Ross. 78 51.07 N 41.25 E
Jelan' ≐, Ross. 80 50.57 N 43.44 E
Jelan' ≐, Ross. 80 51.07 N 41.26 E
Jelancy 88 52.49 N 106.25 E
Jelanec 78 47.42 N 31.51 E
Jelanka 86 55.37 N 75.18 E
Jelan'-Koleno 78 51.09 N 41.14 E
Jelan'-Kolenovskij 78 51.10 N 41.10 E
Jelat'ma 80 54.58 N 41.45 E
Jelaur, Ross. 80 54.34 N 50.21 E
Jelaur, Ross. 80 53.50 N 48.48 E
Jelchovka 80 53.51 N 50.18 E
Jel'covka 86 53.15 N 86.15 E
Jel'cy, Ross. 76 56.40 N 33.51 E
Jel'cy, Ross. 82 56.11 N 38.46 E
Jelec 76 52.37 N 38.30 E
Jeleckij 24 67.03 N 64.10 E
Jelenia Góra (Hirschberg) 30 50.55 N 15.46 E
Jelenia Góra □[4] 30 51.10 N 15.30 E
Jelenskij 76 53.29 N 35.23 E
Jelep La Pass)(124 27.23 N 88.51 E
Jelgava 76 56.39 N 23.42 E
Jelgavkrasti 76 57.28 N 24.26 E
Jelisejevka 78 47.02 N 36.24 E
Jelizarovo, Ross. 80 58.33 N 44.50 E
Jelizarovo, Ukr. 78 48.12 N 34.33 E
Jelizavetgradka 78 48.48 N 32.24 E
Jelizavetinka 86 51.28 N 71.12 E
Jelizavetopol'skoje 86 52.51 N 60.36 E
Jelizavetovka 78 46.39 N 38.53 E
Jelizavety, mys › 89a 54.26 N 142.42 E
Jelizovo 76 53.24 N 29.01 E
Jelli 154 5.22 N 31.48 E
Jellico 192 36.35 N 84.07 W
Jelling 41 55.45 N 9.26 E
Jelloway 214 40.33 N 82.18 W
Jelm Mountain ∧ 200 41.06 N 105.58 W
Jel'n'a 76 54.35 N 33.11 E
Jelnat' 80 57.20 N 42.49 E
Jel'niki 80 54.37 N 43.53 E
Jeloguj ≐ 74 63.13 N 87.45 E
Jel'onovka, Ukr. 83 47.50 N 37.40 E
Jel'onovka, Ukr. 83 48.39 N 38.01 E
Jelošnoje 86 55.27 N 66.44 E
Jelovo 80 57.03 N 54.54 E
Jels 41 55.21 N 9.12 E
Jelšanka, Ross. 80 51.49 N 46.23 E
Jelšanka, Ross. 80 52.35 N 47.59 E
Jelšanka Pervaja 80 52.53 N 52.02 E
Jelšava 30 48.39 N 20.14 E
Jel'sk 78 51.48 N 29.09 E
Jema ≐ 144 10.09 N 38.20 E
Jemaa 150 9.27 N 8.23 E
Jemaja, Pulau I 112 2.55 N 105.45 E
Jemaluang 114 2.17 N 103.52 E
Jemantajevo 80 53.34 N 53.50 E
Jemanželinsk 86 54.45 N 61.20 E
Jember 115a 8.10 S 113.42 E
Jemca 24 63.04 N 40.20 E
Jemca ≐ 24 63.15 N 41.20 E
Jemeljanovka 78 45.32 N 34.53 E
Jemeljanovo 86 56.11 N 92.40 E
Jemel'stan 24 61.13 N 52.29 E
Jemen, Volksrepublik → Yemen □[1] 144 15.00 N 47.00 E
Jemen → Yemen □[1] 144 15.00 N 47.00 E
Jemez ≐ 200 35.22 N 106.31 W
Jemez Canyon Reservoir ⊜[1] 200 35.28 N 106.39 W
Jemez Indian Reservation ✦[4] 200 35.35 N 106.45 W
Jemez Springs 200 35.46 N 106.41 W
Jemgum 52 53.16 N 7.23 E
Jemil'čino 78 50.52 N 27.48 E
Jeminary 86 47.32 N 85.38 E
Jemmal 148 35.38 N 10.46 E
Jemnice 61 49.01 N 15.35 E
Jempang, Kenohan ⊜ 112 0.26 S 116.12 E
Jena, Dtsch. 54 50.56 N 11.35 E
Jena, La., U.S. 194 31.40 N 92.08 W
Jenakijevo 83 48.14 N 38.13 E
Jenašimskij Polkan, gora ∧ 74 59.50 N 92.52 E
Jenaz 58 46.55 N 9.45 E
Jenbach 64 47.24 N 11.47 E
Jenbek 86 48.53 N 77.12 E
Jendarata 114 3.55 N 100.57 E
Jendongin 88 53.27 N 113.01 E
Jendouba (Souk el Arba) 148 36.30 N 8.47 E
Jendouba □[8] 148 36.30 N 8.45 E
Jeneponto 112 5.41 S 119.42 E
Jenera 216 40.54 N 83.44 W
Jeniang 114 5.49 N 100.38 E
Jenisej (Yenisey) ≐ 72 71.50 N 82.40 E
Jenisejsk 86 58.27 N 92.10 E
Jenisejskij kr'až ⩘ 74 59.00 N 93.00 E
Jenisejskij zaliv ⊂ 74 72.30 N 80.00 E
Jenison 216 42.54 N 85.47 W
Jenkins, Ky., U.S. 192 37.10 N 82.37 W
Jenkins, Tx., U.S. 222 32.59 N 94.44 W
Jenkins, Mount ∧ 162 25.36 S 129.41 E
Jenkinson Lake ⊜[1] 226 38.44 N 120.33 W
Jenkinsville 192 34.16 N 81.17 W
Jenkintown 208 40.05 N 75.07 W
Jenks 196 36.01 N 95.58 W
Jenli 100 23.15 N 120.08 E
Jenners 214 40.08 N 79.02 W
Jennersdorf 61 46.57 N 16.08 E
Jennerstown 214 40.10 N 79.04 W
Jennifer Branch ≐ 284b 39.25 N 76.30 W
Jennings, Fl., U.S. 192 30.36 N 83.05 W
Jennings, La., U.S. 194 30.13 N 92.39 W
Jennings, Mo., U.S. 219 38.43 N 90.15 W
Jennings □[6] 218 38.59 N 85.36 W
Jennings Creek ≐ 216 40.53 N 84.17 W
Jennings Lodge 224 45.23 N 122.36 W
Jenotajevka 80 47.15 N 47.03 E
Jenpeg Dam ✦[6] 184 54.33 N 98.02 W
Jensen 200 40.22 N 109.20 W
Jensen Beach 220 27.15 N 80.13 W
Jens Munk Island I 176 69.42 N 79.30 W
Jens Munks Ø I 176 64.40 N 40.30 W
Jenu 112 0.36 S 109.52 E
Jen'uka 88 57.58 N 121.42 E
Jeonju → Chŏnju 98 35.49 N 127.08 E
Jepač 24 66.58 N 61.22 E
Jepara 115a 6.35 S 110.39 E
Jeparit 166 36.09 S 141.59 E
Jepelacio 248 6.07 S 76.57 W
Jepichin 80 48.16 N 45.14 E
Jepifan' 76 53.49 N 38.33 E
Jeppener 258 35.17 S 58.12 W
Jeptha Knob ∧[2] 218 38.11 N 85.07 W
Jepua (Jeppo) 26 63.24 N 22.37 E
Jequeri 255 20.27 S 42.40 W
Jequetepeque ≐ 248 7.21 S 79.36 W
Jequié 255 13.51 S 40.05 W
Jequitaí 255 17.15 S 44.28 W
Jequitinhonha 255 16.26 S 41.00 W
Jequitinhonha ≐ 255 15.51 S 38.53 W
Jerachtur 80 54.43 N 41.09 E
Jerada 148 34.17 N 2.13 W
Jeradou 36 36.15 N 10.23 E
Jerangle 171b 35.52 S 149.22 E
Jeransang 114 3.52 N 102.22 E
Jerantut 114 3.56 N 102.22 E
Jerba, Île de I 148 33.48 N 10.54 E
Jerbar 140 5.39 N 31.05 E
Jerbent 128 39.19 N 58.36 E
Jerbogačon 74 61.16 N 108.00 E
Jercevo 24 60.48 N 40.05 E
Jerdenevo 82 54.55 N 36.27 E
Jerécuaro 234 20.09 N 100.31 W
Jeremejevka 83 46.58 N 39.33 E
Jeremejevo 82 55.57 N 37.01 E
Jérémie 238 18.39 N 74.07 W
Jeremino 82 56.27 N 37.58 E
Jeremoabo 250 10.04 S 38.21 W
Jeremy Hill ∧[2] 207 42.45 N 71.21 W
Jeremy Point › 207 41.53 N 70.04 W
Jerevan 84 40.11 N 44.30 E
Jerez ≐ 234 22.15 N 103.11 W
Jerez de García Salinas 234 22.39 N 103.00 W
Jerez de la Frontera 34 36.41 N 6.08 W
Jerez de los Caballeros 34 38.19 N 6.46 W
Jergač 86 57.28 N 56.39 E
Jergeni ⩘[2] 80 47.00 N 44.00 E
Jergeninskij 80 47.07 N 44.28 E
Jericho, Austl. 166 23.36 S 146.08 E
Jericho, N.J., U.S. 285 39.48 N 75.09 W
Jericho, N.Y., U.S. 210 40.47 N 73.32 W
Jericho → Arīḥā 132 31.52 N 35.27 E
Jericho Dam ⊜[1] 158 26.39 S 30.28 E
Jerichow 54 52.30 N 12.01 E
Jericó, Bra. 250 6.33 S 37.48 W
Jericó, Col. 246 5.47 N 75.47 W
Jericoacoara, Ponta de › 250 2.48 S 40.29 W
Jerid, Chott ≡ 148 33.42 N 8.26 E
Jerik ≐ 83 48.59 N 38.30 E
Jerilderie 166 35.22 S 145.44 E
Jerimoth Hill ∧[2] 207 41.52 N 71.47 W
Jerki 78 48.59 N 31.00 E
Jermak 86 52.02 N 76.55 E
Jermakovo 80 53.11 N 49.38 E
Jermakovskaja 80 48.03 N 41.17 E
Jermakovskoje 86 53.16 N 92.24 E
Jermekejevo 80 54.05 N 53.40 E
Jermentau 86 51.38 N 73.10 E
Jermentau ⩘ 86 51.10 N 73.10 E
Jermica 24 66.56 N 52.15 E
Jermilovka 86 57.40 N 72.55 E
Jermiš' 80 54.46 N 42.16 E
Jermolajevo, Ross. 86 55.13 N 92.10 E
Jermolajevo, Ross. 86 52.46 N 55.47 E
Jermolino, Ross. 82 56.48 N 37.49 E
Jermolino, Ross. 82 55.12 N 36.36 E
Jermolino, Ross. 82 55.57 N 36.54 E
Jermolino, Ross. 86 57.20 N 64.43 E
Jermyn 210 41.31 N 75.32 W
Jernhatten ∧[2] 41 56.15 N 10.48 E
Jernih 114 4.25 N 97.43 E
Jeroaquara 255 15.23 S 50.25 W
Jerofej Pavlovič 89 53.58 N 122.01 E
Jerome, Az., U.S. 200 34.44 N 112.06 W
Jerome, Id., U.S. 202 42.43 N 114.31 W
Jerome, Il., U.S. 219 39.46 N 89.41 W
Jerome, Mi., U.S. 216 42.01 N 84.28 W
Jerome, Pa., U.S. 214 40.12 N 78.59 W
Jeromesville 214 40.48 N 82.11 W
Jer'omino 86 58.35 N 79.25 E
Jerónimos, Mosteiro dos ⊌[1] 266c 38.42 N 9.12 W
Jeröö 88 49.45 N 106.40 E
Jeröö ≐ 88 49.54 N 106.08 E

Symbols in the index entries represent the broad categories identified in the key at the right. Symbols with superior numbers (⩘[1]) identify subcategories (see complete key on page *I · 1)*.

Symbole im Register stellen die rechts im Schlüssel erklärten Kategorien dar. Symbole mit hochgestellten Ziffern (⩘[1]) bezeichnen Unterabteilungen einer Kategorie (vgl. vollständiger Schlüssel auf Seite *I · 1)*.

Los símbolos incluídos en el texto del índice representan las grandes categorias identificadas con la clave a la derecha. Los símbolos con numeros en su parte superior (⩘[1]) identifican las subcategorías (véase la clave completa en la página *I · 1)*.

Les symboles de l'index représentent les catégories indiquées dans la légende à droite. Les symboles suivis d'un indice (⩘[1]) représentent des sous-catégories (voir légende complète à la page *I · 1)*.

Os símbolos incluídos no texto do índice representam as grandes categorias identificadas com a chave à direita. Os símbolos com números em sua parte superior (⩘[1]) identificam as subcategorias (veja-se a chave completa à página *I · 1)*.

	English	Deutsch	Español	Français	Português
∧	Mountain	Berg	Montaña	Montagne	Montanha
⩘	Mountains	Gebirge	Montañas	Montagnes	Montanhas
)(	Pass	Paß	Paso	Col	Passo
V	Valley, Canyon	Tal, Cañon	Valle, Cañón	Vallée, Canyon	Vale, Canhão
≚	Plain	Ebene	Llano	Plaine	Planície
›	Cape	Kap	Cabo	Cap	Cabo
I	Island	Insel	Isla	Île	Ilha
II	Islands	Inseln	Islas	Îles	Ilhas
⏏	Other Topographic Features	Andere Topographische Objekte	Otros Elementos Topográficos	Autres données topographiques	Outros acidentes topográficos

ESPAÑOL: Nombre | Página | Lat.°′ | Long.°′ W = Oeste
FRANÇAIS: Nom | Page | Lat.°′ | Long.°′ W = Ouest
PORTUGUÊS: Nome | Página | Lat.°′ | Long.°′ W = Oeste

Jeropol 74 65.15 N 168.40 E
Jerpoint Abbey ⊥ 48 52.29 N 7.08 W
Jerry City 216 41.15 N 83.36 W
Jerry Slough ≐ 226 35.33 N 119.31 W
Jersey 214 40.03 N 82.46 W
Jersey □6 219 39.07 N 90.20 W
Jersey □2, Europe 22 49.15 N 2.10 W
Jersey □2, Europe 43b 49.15 N 2.10 W
Jersey City 210 40.43 N 74.04 W
Jersey City State College ⊍2 276 40.43 N 74.05 W
Jersey Mountain ∧ 202 45.29 N 115.34 W
Jersey Shore 210 41.12 N 77.16 W
Jersey Village 222 29.52 N 95.35 W
Jerseyville 219 39.07 N 90.19 W
Jerši 76 54.24 N 34.12 E
Jeršiči 76 53.40 N 32.44 E
Jeršov 80 51.20 N 48.17 E
Jeršovka 86 54.07 N 64.59 E
Jeršovo 82 55.46 N 36.52 E
Jeršovskij 86 52.29 N 59.08 E
Jertarskij 86 56.47 N 64.18 E
Jerte ≐ 34 39.58 N 6.17 W
Jerteh 114 5.45 N 102.30 E
Jertoma 24 63.32 N 47.48 E
Jerumenha 250 7.05 S 43.30 W
Jerusalem Airport ⊠ 132 31.52 N 35.12 E
Jerusalem → Yerushalayim 132 31.46 N 35.14 E
Jerusalim (Talusan) 116 7.26 N 122.49 E
Jeruslan ≐ 80 50.15 N 45.42 E
Jervaulx Abbey ⊍1 44 54.16 N 1.43 W
Jervis, Cape ≻ 168b 35.38 S 138.06 E
Jervis Bay 170 35.08 S 150.42 E
Jervis Bay c 170 35.05 S 150.44 E
Jervis Inlet c 182 49.46 N 124.10 W
Jervois Range ⩗ 162 22.38 S 136.05 E
Jerxheim 54 52.05 N 10.54 E
Jerykly 80 55.11 N 51.26 E
Jerzens 58 47.10 N 10.45 E
Jesaulovka 83 48.03 N 39.02 E
Jesenankaty ≐ 80 50.32 N 51.47 E
Jesenice, Česko. 54 50.04 N 13.29 E
Jesenice, Slo. 61 46.27 N 14.04 E
Jesenice, údolní nádrž ⊜1 60 50.04 N 12.27 E
Jeseník 30 50.14 N 17.13 E
Jesenoviči 76 57.17 N 34.14 E
Jesensaj 80 49.54 N 51.28 E
Ješera 84 43.04 N 40.55 E
Jeserig bei Wiesenburg 54 52.05 N 12.27 E
Jesi 66 43.31 N 13.14 E
Jesil' 86 51.58 N 66.24 E
Jes'ki 76 57.56 N 36.23 E
Jesönbulag → Altaj 90 46.20 N 96.18 E
Jessej 74 68.29 N 102.10 E
Jesselton → Kota Kinabalu 112 5.59 N 116.04 E
Jessen 54 51.47 N 12.58 E
Jessentuki 84 44.03 N 42.51 E
Jesser Point ≻ 158 27.32 S 32.40 E
Jessheim 26 60.09 N 11.11 E
Jessnitz 54 51.41 N 12.17 E
Jessore 124 23.10 N 89.13 E
Jessup, Md., U.S. 208 39.08 N 76.46 W
Jessup, Pa., U.S. 210 41.28 N 75.33 W
Jessup Park ♦ 280 34.15 N 118.24 W
Jestetten 58 47.39 N 8.34 E
Jestřebí 54 50.38 N 14.36 E
Jésuite, Lac du ⊜ 206 46.53 N 72.36 W
Jesup, Ga., U.S. 192 31.36 N 81.53 W
Jesup, Ia., U.S. 190 42.28 N 92.03 W
Jesup, Lake ⊜ 220 28.43 N 81.14 W
Jesús 252 27.03 S 55.47 W
Jésus, Île I 206 45.35 N 73.45 W
Jesús Carranza 234 17.26 N 95.02 W
Jesús de Otoro 236 14.26 N 87.59 W
Jesús María, Arg. 252 30.59 S 64.06 W
Jesús María, Méx. 232 25.06 N 107.28 W
Jesús María, Méx. 234 21.58 N 102.21 W
Jesús María, Perú 286d 12.04 S 77.04 W
Jesús María ≐ 234 21.51 N 104.42 W
Jesús María, Punta ≻ 258 34.39 S 56.55 W
Jesús Menéndez 240p 21.10 N 76.29 W
Jet 196 36.39 N 98.10 W
Jeta, Ilha de I 150 11.53 N 16.15 W
Jetafe 116 10.09 N 124.09 E
Jetmore 198 38.05 N 99.53 W
Jet Propulsion Laboratory ⊍3 280 34.12 N 118.11 W
Jetpur 120 21.44 N 70.37 E
Jetřichovice 54 50.49 N 14.25 E
Jett 218 38.11 N 84.49 W
Jette 50 50.52 N 4.20 E
Jettingen 58 48.23 N 10.26 E
Jeumont 50 50.18 N 4.06 E
Jeune Landing 182 50.27 N 127.30 W
Jeunieb 114 5.10 N 96.29 E
Jeuram 114 4.14 N 96.18 E
Jever 52 53.34 N 7.54 E
Jeverland ◆1 52 53.35 N 8.00 E
Jevgaščino 86 56.26 N 74.41 E
Jevgenjevka 85 43.31 N 77.40 E
Jevíčko 30 49.38 N 16.43 E
Jevišovice 61 48.59 N 16.00 E
Jevišovka ≐ 61 48.49 N 16.28 E
Jevlach 84 40.36 N 47.09 E
Jevlaš'ovo 80 53.07 N 46.51 E
Jevnaker 26 60.15 N 10.28 E
Jevpatorija 78 45.12 N 33.22 E
Jevra 86 59.56 N 64.27 E
Jevrej □3 89 48.30 N 132.00 E
Jevsug 83 49.13 N 39.18 E
Jevsug ≐ 83 48.47 N 39.19 E
Jewel Cave National Monument ♦ 198 43.42 N 103.50 W
Jewell, Ia., U.S. 190 42.18 N 93.38 W
Jewell, Ks., U.S. 198 39.40 N 98.09 W
Jewell, N.Y., U.S. 210 43.13 N 75.48 W
Jewell, Oh., U.S. 216 41.20 N 84.17 W
Jewell, Or., U.S. 224 45.56 N 123.30 W
Jewell Ridge 192 37.11 N 81.47 W
Jewell Village 218 39.10 N 85.51 W
Jewett, Il., U.S. 194 39.13 N 88.15 W
Jewett, Oh., U.S. 214 40.22 N 81.00 W
Jewett, Tx., U.S. 222 31.22 N 96.09 W
Jewett City 207 41.36 N 71.58 W
Jewett Creek ≐ 212 44.22 N 75.45 W
Jewett Lake ⊜ 184 56.09 N 104.40 W
Jewettville 284a 42.43 N 78.52 W
Jey ◆8 267d 35.41 N 51.21 E
Jeyretān 120 37.10 N 67.20 E
Jezerce ∧ 38 42.26 N 19.49 E
Jezerišče 76 55.50 N 29.59 E
Jezerní hora ∧ 60 49.10 N 13.11 E
Ježicha 80 58.06 N 47.40 E
Jeziorany 30 53.58 N 20.46 E
Ježovo 80 58.02 N 52.14 E
Jezreel, Valley of → Yizre'el, 'Émeq ⊻ 132 32.36 N 35.14 E
J. G. Strijdomdam ⊜1 158 27.25 S 32.05 E
Jhābua 120 22.46 N 74.36 E
Jhāhtipahāri 126 23.22 N 86.54 E
Jha Jha 124 24.46 N 86.22 E
Jhajjar 124 28.37 N 76.39 E
Jhal 120 28.17 N 67.27 E
Jhālakāti 124 22.39 N 90.12 E
Jhālārāpātan 124 24.33 N 76.10 E
Jhālāwār 124 24.36 N 76.09 E
Jhalida 124 23.22 N 85.58 E
Jhal Jhao 120 26.18 N 65.35 E
Jhālod 120 23.06 N 74.09 E
Jhang Sadar 123 31.16 N 72.19 E
Jhānsi 124 25.26 N 78.35 E
Jhānsi Post 123 33.52 N 71.24 E
Jhāpā 124 26.29 N 87.51 E
Jhārgrām 126 22.27 N 86.59 E
Jharia 126 23.45 N 86.24 E
Jhārpokhariā 126 22.10 N 86.38 E
Jhārsuguda 120 21.51 N 84.02 E
Jhawāriān 123 32.22 N 72.38 E
Jhelum 123 32.56 N 73.44 E
Jhelum ≐ 123 31.12 N 72.08 E
Jhenida 124 23.33 N 89.10 E
Jhenkāri 272b 22.46 N 88.18 E
Jhikergacha 126 23.07 N 89.07 E
Jhikra 126 22.37 N 87.55 E
Jhilimili 126 22.49 N 86.37 E
Jhil Kuranga ◆8 272a 28.40 N 77.17 E
Jhilla ≐1 126 21.58 N 88.56 E
Jhinkpāni 124 22.25 N 85.47 E
Jhok Rind 120 31.27 N 70.26 E
Jhumra 123 31.34 N 73.11 E
Jhunjhunūn 120 28.08 N 75.24 E
Jiaban, Zhg. 102 25.10 N 107.03 E
Jiaban, Zhg. 102 25.38 N 107.07 E
Jiabong 116 11.46 N 124.57 E
Jiacha 120 29.11 N 92.44 E
Jiading 106 31.23 N 121.15 E
Jiāganj 126 24.14 N 88.16 E
Jiagedan 89 51.35 N 120.55 E
Jiahashitai 89 46.25 N 122.17 E
Jiahe 102 25.43 N 112.05 E
Jiajiachang, Zhg. 107 29.44 N 105.06 E
Jiajiachang, Zhg. 107 30.26 N 104.21 E
Jiajiagou, Zhg. 104 41.44 N 120.58 E
Jiajiagou, Zhg. 104 42.20 N 121.46 E
Jiajiang 107 29.45 N 103.34 E
Jiajiayuan 106 32.18 N 120.55 E
Jiakou 100 30.10 N 119.03 E
Jiakou Wa ≡ 105 38.58 N 116.50 E
Jiali 120 30.47 N 93.24 E
Jialing ≐ 102 29.34 N 106.35 E
Jialou 100 32.54 N 113.26 E
Jialu 106 30.26 N 118.50 E
Jialu ≐ 100 33.38 N 114.36 E
Jiamingzhen 107 29.16 N 105.20 E
Jiamusi (Kiamusze) 89 46.50 N 130.21 E
Jiamuyingzi 104 41.56 N 121.43 E
Ji'an, Zhg. 98 41.06 N 126.08 E
Ji'an, Zhg. 100 27.07 N 114.58 E
Jian ≐, Zhg. 100 26.38 N 118.12 E
Jian ≐, Zhg. 104 40.59 N 121.51 E
Jian'an 89 43.04 N 125.03 E
Jianba 106 31.59 N 120.35 E
Jianbi 106 32.11 N 119.35 E
Jianchang, Zhg. 98 40.51 N 119.46 E
Jianchang, Zhg. 98 39.58 N 122.35 E
Jianchang, Zhg. 98 41.16 N 124.29 E
Ji'anchang, Zhg. 107 30.31 N 106.02 E
Jianchangying 98 40.06 N 118.49 E
Jianchapu 105 39.06 N 116.31 E
Jianchaxi, Zhg. 102 28.08 N 108.04 E
Jianchaxi, Zhg. 107 30.22 N 104.03 E
Jianchuan 102 26.34 N 99.53 E
Jiande 100 29.29 N 119.16 E
Jiang'an 107 28.44 N 105.05 E
Jiangba 100 33.08 N 118.45 E
Jiangbei (Lianglukou) 107 29.44 N 106.38 E
Jiangbeixu 100 26.20 N 115.26 E
Jiangbian 102 24.03 N 103.37 E
Jiangbianzhai 102 23.49 N 100.11 E
Jiangcheng, Zhg. 102 22.40 N 101.48 E
Jiangcheng, Zhg. 105 38.52 N 115.22 E
Jiangcun 100 28.17 N 117.49 E
Jiangdi 102 25.08 N 104.45 E
Jiangdihe 102 25.55 N 101.31 E
Jiangdu 100 32.26 N 119.34 E
Jiangduo 100 32.22 N 120.15 E
Jiange 102 32.06 N 105.29 E
Jianggezhuang 98 39.27 N 119.09 E
Jianghua (Shuikou) 102 24.58 N 111.38 E
Jianghuaqiao 106 32.05 N 120.00 E
Jiangji 100 32.19 N 115.44 E
Jiangjia, Zhg. 106 31.40 N 121.09 E
Jiangjia, Zhg. 106 31.58 N 121.28 E
Jiangjiadian 104 41.41 N 121.03 E
Jiangjiagou 104 41.44 N 121.44 E
Jiangjiaji 100 31.59 N 115.16 E
Jiangjiatun, Zhg. 104 41.42 N 122.02 E
Jiangjiatun, Zhg. 104 41.42 N 122.25 E
Jiangjin 107 29.17 N 106.15 E
Jiangjing 100 25.34 N 119.25 E
Jiangjunmiao 86 44.43 N 90.05 E
Jiangjunqiao 102 31.18 N 100.55 E
Jiangkou, Zhg. 100 29.43 N 121.25 E
Jiangkou, Zhg. 100 27.44 N 114.49 E
Jiangkou, Zhg. 100 27.27 N 118.03 E
Jiangkou, Zhg. 100 25.29 N 119.12 E
Jiangkou, Zhg. 100 27.21 N 115.31 E
Jiangkou, Zhg. 102 23.31 N 110.17 E
Jiangkou, Zhg. 102 29.38 N 110.20 E
Jiangkou, Zhg. 102 27.37 N 108.48 E
Jiangkou, Zhg. 102 30.26 N 111.42 E
Jiangkou, Zhg. 102 33.39 N 107.12 E
Jiangkou, Zhg. 107 30.14 N 103.55 E
Jiangkouji 100 32.50 N 116.16 E
Jiangkoutang 100 27.30 N 112.44 E
Jiangle 100 26.42 N 117.25 E
Jiangliadian 98 42.33 N 117.27 E
Jiangling 102 30.20 N 112.06 E
Jianglingxi 102 31.28 N 107.13 E
Jiangmen 100 22.35 N 113.05 E
Jiangmifeng 89 43.58 N 126.45 E
Jiangning 106 31.58 N 118.50 E
Jiangpu 100 32.04 N 118.37 E
Jiangqiao 89 46.48 N 123.45 E
Jiangqiaotou 106 30.37 N 120.38 E
Jiangshan 100 28.45 N 118.37 E
Jiangshan ≐ 100 28.57 N 118.50 E
Jiangshe 106 31.34 N 120.08 E
Jiangshui 98 37.13 N 113.59 E
Jiangsu (Kiangsu) □4 90 33.00 N 120.00 E
Jiangtian 100 25.52 N 119.34 E
Jiangtun, Zhg. 102 23.41 N 112.37 E
Jiangtun, Zhg. 104 41.37 N 122.22 E
Jiangwakou 105 39.31 N 117.42 E
Jiangwan, Zhg. 100 29.25 N 118.02 E
Jiangwan, Zhg. 106 31.18 N 121.29 E
Jiangwan Airport ⊠ 269b 31.20 N 121.30 E
Jiangxi 102 22.51 N 101.50 E
Jiangxi (Kiangsi) □4 100 28.00 N 116.00 E
Jiangxiacun 106 31.44 N 121.50 E
Jiangxiang 100 32.16 N 117.37 E
Jiangxikou 100 27.36 N 118.23 E
Jiangya 102 29.17 N 110.39 E
Jiangyi 100 29.12 N 115.46 E
Jiangyin 106 31.55 N 120.16 E
Jiangyou 102 31.47 N 104.45 E
Jiangyu, Zhg. 98 36.16 N 118.40 E
Jiangyu, Zhg. 100 27.50 N 112.46 E
Jiangyuanzhen 107 30.35 N 103.48 E
Jiangzaogang 106 32.01 N 121.03 E
Jiangzhasiji 120 30.28 N 88.55 E
Jiangzhong 120 29.10 N 93.32 E
Jianhe, Zhg. 102 26.27 N 108.33 E
Jianhe, Zhg. 105 39.14 N 118.03 E
Jianhu 100 33.28 N 119.50 E
Jianli 100 29.49 N 112.53 E
Jianling 100 32.45 N 113.12 E
Jianning 100 26.50 N 116.49 E
Jian'ou 100 27.03 N 118.19 E
Jianping (Yebaishou) 98 41.24 N 119.37 E
Jianqiao 106 30.20 N 120.12 E
Jianqigou 104 40.54 N 123.17 E
Jianshan, Zhg. 100 29.14 N 120.44 E
Jianshan, Zhg. 100 29.58 N 120.16 E
Jian Shan ∧ 104 41.49 N 121.44 E
Jianshi 102 30.36 N 109.38 E
Jianshui 102 23.38 N 102.49 E
Jiantiao 100 29.04 N 121.36 E
Jiantou 105 39.26 N 115.41 E
Jiantouji 98 34.35 N 117.34 E
Jianyang, Zhg. 100 27.22 N 118.04 E
Jianyang, Zhg. 100 33.27 N 119.40 E
Jianyang, Zhg. 107 30.24 N 104.32 E
Jiao ≐ 100 26.48 N 119.42 E
Jiaocheng 102 37.33 N 112.02 E
Jiaodao 105 39.39 N 116.06 E
Jiaodianzi 104 41.32 N 121.49 E
Jiaodonggou 104 40.50 N 123.58 E
Jiaohe, Zhg. 89 43.42 N 127.19 E
Jiaohe, Zhg. 98 38.01 N 116.17 E
Jiaojiapuzi 104 40.47 N 123.48 E
Jiaolai ≐, Zhg. 89 43.43 N 123.05 E
Jiaolai ≐, Zhg. 98 37.07 N 119.35 E
Jiaolai ≐, Zhg. 98 42.47 N 120.44 E
Jiaoling 100 24.41 N 116.10 E
Jiaomei 100 24.32 N 117.54 E
Jiaonan (Wanggezhuang) 98 35.51 N 119.59 E
Jiao Shan I 106 31.21 N 120.06 E
Jiaoshanhe 100 29.38 N 112.33 E
Jiaoxi 106 31.49 N 120.10 E
Jiaoxian 98 36.18 N 119.58 E
Jiaoyang 100 27.56 N 119.16 E
Jiaozhou Wan c 98 36.10 N 120.15 E
Jiaozhuang 100 33.14 N 114.02 E
Jiaozuo 102 35.15 N 113.13 E
Jiapu 106 31.06 N 119.56 E
Jiashan, Zhg. 100 32.47 N 118.00 E
Jiashan, Zhg. 106 30.51 N 120.54 E
Jiashi 85 39.28 N 76.45 E
Jiashun Hu ⊜ 120 34.35 N 86.05 E
Jiasi 107 29.06 N 106.24 E
Jiatan 107 30.12 N 106.29 E
Jiatianchang 107 29.09 N 106.16 E
Jiawang 98 34.27 N 117.27 E
Jiaxian, Zhg. 100 33.58 N 113.13 E
Jiaxian, Zhg. 102 38.01 N 110.31 E
Jiaxiang 98 35.25 N 116.21 E
Jiaxing 106 30.46 N 120.45 E
Jiayin 89 48.53 N 130.24 E
Jiayu 100 29.58 N 113.55 E
Jiayun Hu ⊜ 120 35.02 N 85.40 E
Jiaze 106 31.42 N 119.47 E
Jiazhai 98 34.33 N 115.48 E
Jiazhuang 105 39.19 N 117.22 E
Jiazi 100 22.55 N 116.04 E
Jiazier 85 38.40 N 76.33 E
Jibacoa ≐ 240p 20.15 N 77.12 W
Jibagalle 144 8.04 N 48.39 E
Jibalei 144 10.09 N 50.53 E
Jibannagar 126 23.25 N 88.50 E
Jíbaro ≐ 286b 23.03 N 82.23 W
Jibat ∧ 144 8.45 N 37.29 E
Jibiya 150 13.05 N 7.12 E
Jiboa ≐ 236 13.22 N 89.04 W
Jibóia, Ilha da I 256 23.03 S 44.22 W
Jibuti → Djibouti 144 11.36 N 43.09 E
Jicamarca, Quebrada ⊻ 286d 12.02 S 76.57 W
Jicarilla Apache Indian Reservation ◆4 200 36.40 N 107.00 W
Jicarón, Isla I 246 7.16 N 81.47 W
Jicatuyo ≐ 236 14.59 N 88.16 W
Jicheng 105 39.23 N 116.17 E
Jičín 30 50.26 N 15.21 E
Jicotea ≐ 286b 23.01 N 82.14 W
Jidād 140 11.05 N 24.44 E
Jiddah (Jeddah) 144 21.30 N 39.12 E
Jidingxilin 120 32.52 N 92.21 E
Jidy, Wādī al- ⊻ 142 30.13 N 32.46 E
Jiebu 100 28.15 N 115.02 E
Jiedong 100 26.02 N 113.00 E
Jiegou 100 33.21 N 117.55 E
Jiehe 98 35.16 N 117.04 E
Jieji 100 33.33 N 118.24 E
Jiejiang 106 31.58 N 120.43 E
Jiejinkou 89 47.57 N 132.50 E
Jielingkou 98 40.09 N 119.15 E
Jielongchang 107 29.13 N 106.32 E
Jiemian 100 25.56 N 118.02 E
Jiepai, Zhg. 100 26.41 N 112.46 E
Jiepai, Zhg. 100 29.34 N 115.06 E
Jiepai, Zhg. 106 30.55 N 119.32 E
Jiepai, Zhg. 107 29.28 N 104.43 E
Jiepaiji 100 32.15 N 117.50 E
Jiesheng 100 22.45 N 115.25 E
Jieshi, Zhg. 100 22.51 N 115.49 E
Jieshi, Zhg. 107 29.27 N 105.17 E
Jieshi Wan c 100 22.46 N 115.40 E
Jieshou, Zhg. 100 33.18 N 115.20 E
Jieshou, Zhg. 100 27.22 N 117.40 E
Jieshou, Zhg. 100 33.00 N 119.27 E
Jiexi 100 23.28 N 115.56 E
Jiexiu 102 37.05 N 111.51 E
Jieyang 100 23.35 N 116.21 E
Jiezhongdian 100 32.41 N 112.29 E
Jieznas 76 54.36 N 24.10 E
Jifjāfah, Bi'r ⊤4 140 30.27 N 33.11 E
Jiftūn, Jazā'ir II 140 27.13 N 33.56 E
Jiggalong 162 23.25 S 120.47 E
Jiggalong Creek ≐ 162 22.53 S 120.14 E
Jigongying 102 26.18 N 104.48 E
Jigongzhen 98 34.02 N 115.32 E
Jiguaní 240p 20.22 N 76.26 W
Jiguanshan, Zhg. 98 40.32 N 123.55 E
Jiguanshan, Zhg. 104 42.08 N 124.15 E
Jiguanshan, Zhg. 104 41.18 N 123.36 E
Jigüey, Bahía de c 240p 22.08 N 78.05 W
Jigzhi 102 33.28 N 101.29 E
Jihe 100 32.15 N 112.48 E
Jiheier 85 38.11 N 75.46 E
Jihlava 30 49.24 N 15.36 E
Jihlava ≐ 61 48.55 N 16.37 E
Jihočeský Kraj □4 30 49.05 N 14.30 E
Jihomoravský Kraj □4 30 49.10 N 16.40 E
Jiiqley 144 4.25 N 45.22 E
Jijel 148 36.48 N 5.46 E
Jijel □5 148 36.45 N 6.00 E
Jijia ≐ 38 46.54 N 28.05 E
Jijiadianzi 98 35.31 N 118.59 E
Jijiamiao 107 29.18 N 104.06 E
Jijiapuzi 104 41.16 N 124.12 E
Jijiashi 106 32.08 N 120.18 E
Jijiaying 105 40.20 N 115.24 E
Jijiga 144 9.22 N 42.47 E
Jikawo 144 8.22 N 33.46 E
Jikawo ≐ 144 8.22 N 33.47 E
Jike 102 31.00 N 99.41 E
Jilalin 89 51.19 N 119.55 E
Jilantai 102 39.47 N 105.45 E
Jilbānah, Bi'r al- ⊤4 142 30.55 N 32.29 E
Jilemutu 89 52.14 N 120.47 E
Jilib 144 0.29 N 42.46 E
Jilibulake 120 33.05 N 93.10 E
Jili Hu ⊜ 86 46.57 N 87.27 E
Jilin (Kirin) 89 43.51 N 126.33 E
Jilin (Kirin) □4 90 44.00 N 126.00 E
Jiliu ≐ 89 52.04 N 120.48 E
Jill, Kediet ej ∧ 148 22.38 N 12.33 W
Jill, Sebkhet ej ⊜ 148 22.47 N 12.53 W
Jiloca ≐ 34 41.21 N 1.39 W
Jilotepec de Abasolo 234 19.58 N 99.32 W
Jilotlán de los Dolores 234 19.14 N 102.59 W
Jílové 54 50.46 N 14.07 E
Jima 144 7.36 N 36.50 E
Jimbaran 115b 8.46 S 115.11 E
Jimbolia 38 45.47 N 20.43 E
Jimboomba 171a 27.50 S 153.02 E
Jimei 100 24.37 N 118.07 E
Jimena de la Frontera 34 36.26 N 5.27 W
Jiménez, Méx. 232 29.02 N 100.41 W
Jiménez, Méx. 232 27.08 N 104.55 W
Jimenez, Pil. 116 8.20 N 123.50 E
Jiménez, Arroyo ≐ 288 34.44 S 58.13 W
Jiménez, Laguna de ⊜ 258 35.26 S 59.01 W
Jiménez del Téul 234 23.10 N 104.05 W
Jimeta 146 9.16 N 12.27 E
Jimi ≐ 164 5.20 S 144.20 E
Jimingcun 105 39.19 N 116.09 E
Jiminghe 100 30.36 N 115.32 E
Jim Ned Creek ≐ 196 31.50 N 99.07 W
Jimo 98 36.23 N 120.27 E
Jimsar 86 44.00 N 89.04 E
Jim Thorpe 210 40.52 N 75.43 W
Jimuganayaji 85 38.36 N 75.39 E
Jin (Gam) ≐, Asia 110 21.55 N 105.12 E
Jin ≐, Zhg. 100 28.24 N 115.49 E
Jin ≐, Zhg. 100 26.51 N 117.46 E
Jin ≐, Zhg. 100 24.54 N 118.35 E
Jināh 140 25.20 N 30.31 E
Jinan (Tsinan), Zhg. 98 36.40 N 116.57 E
Jin'an, Zhg. 100 28.38 N 119.18 E
Jinbang 100 25.01 N 118.01 E
Jinbo ≐ 107 28.54 N 103.40 E
Jincang 89 43.20 N 130.30 E
Jince 60 49.47 N 13.59 E
Jinchanggouliang 98 41.56 N 120.19 E
Jincheng, Zhg. 102 35.30 N 112.50 E
Jincheng, Zhg. 104 41.12 N 121.25 E
Jinchengshai 102 26.43 N 111.00 E
Jincheng Shan ∧ 107 30.47 N 106.32 E
Jinchuan 102 31.25 N 102.08 E
Jinchuanqiao 102 27.18 N 101.48 E
Jincun 106 31.08 N 119.49 E
Jīnd 123 29.19 N 76.19 E
Jindabyne 171b 36.25 S 148.38 E
Jindabyne, Lake ⊜1 171b 36.22 S 148.37 E
Jindaichang 107 29.43 N 104.49 E
Jindālī, Bi'r ⊤4 142 29.55 N 31.40 E
Jindřichovice 54 50.15 N 12.37 E
Jindřichův Hradec 30 49.09 N 15.00 E
Jinfeng 100 26.01 N 119.36 E
Jinfosi 102 39.29 N 99.00 E
Jing ≐, Zhg. 86 44.52 N 82.50 E
Jing ≐, Zhg. 102 34.28 N 109.00 E
Jing'an 100 28.52 N 115.20 E
Jin'gangpo 107 29.38 N 106.25 E
Jingangtou 100 27.54 N 113.40 E
Jingangtuo 107 29.10 N 106.07 E
Jing'anji 98 34.30 N 116.55 E
Jingbian 102 37.25 N 108.21 E
Jingbohu ⊜ 89 43.54 N 128.54 E
Jingcheng 100 24.36 N 117.30 E
Jingde 100 30.19 N 118.31 E
Jingdezhen (Kingtechen) 100 29.16 N 117.11 E
Jingdong 102 24.28 N 100.52 E
Jingellic 171b 35.56 S 147.42 E
Jingeryu 105 39.43 N 115.36 E
Jinggang 100 28.28 N 112.46 E
Jinggangshan (Ciping) 100 26.36 N 114.05 E
Jinggongqiao 100 29.45 N 117.11 E
Jinggu 102 23.32 N 100.41 E
Jingguanzhen 107 29.55 N 106.33 E
Jinghai, Zhg. 100 23.03 N 116.31 E
Jinghai, Zhg. 105 38.56 N 116.55 E
Jinghaiwei 98 36.52 N 122.13 E
Jinghe 86 44.39 N 82.50 E
Jinghong 102 22.01 N 100.49 E
Jinghuiling 105 40.22 N 117.27 E
Jingjiang, Zhg. 102 26.19 N 100.33 E
Jingjiang, Zhg. 106 32.01 N 120.15 E
Jingjiayu 104 41.40 N 123.51 E
Jingle 102 38.24 N 111.54 E
Jinglou 100 32.39 N 112.56 E
Jingmen 102 31.00 N 112.09 E
Jingning, Zhg. 100 27.59 N 119.38 E
Jingning, Zhg. 102 35.25 N 105.56 E
Jingou 104 41.38 N 120.35 E
Jingoutun 98 41.03 N 117.27 E
Jingshan 100 31.02 N 113.05 E
Jingtai 102 37.17 N 104.09 E
Jingu 100 25.13 N 118.07 E
Jingxi 102 23.08 N 106.29 E
Jingxian, Zhg. 98 37.42 N 116.16 E
Jingxian, Zhg. 100 30.42 N 118.24 E
Jingxian, Zhg. 102 26.40 N 109.25 E
Jingxin 100 24.14 N 115.56 E
Jingxing, Zhg. 89 47.04 N 123.01 E
Jingxing, Zhg. 98 38.02 N 114.08 E
Jingyan 107 29.40 N 104.04 E
Jingyu 98 42.22 N 126.50 E
Jingyuan, Zhg. 102 36.38 N 104.37 E
Jingyuan, Zhg. 102 35.30 N 106.48 E
Jingzhi 98 36.19 N 119.23 E
Jingzichang 107 29.00 N 104.41 E
Jinhae → Chinhae 98 35.09 N 128.40 E
Jinhu 100 33.00 N 119.02 E
Jinhua 100 29.07 N 119.39 E
Jinhua ≐ 100 29.06 N 119.39 E
Jinhui 106 30.59 N 121.29 E
Jining, Zhg. 98 35.25 N 116.36 E
Jining, Zhg. 102 40.57 N 113.02 E
Jinja 154 0.26 N 33.12 E
Jinjiadian 98 41.39 N 118.18 E
Jinjiang, Zhg. 100 24.50 N 118.35 E
Jinjiang, Zhg. 110 26.19 N 100.33 E
Jinjiawopeng 104 41.38 N 122.16 E
Jinjiawopu 104 42.32 N 122.10 E
Jinjiazhen 89 42.49 N 123.40 E
Jinjing, Zhg. 100 28.31 N 113.25 E
Jinjing, Zhg. 100 24.37 N 118.36 E
Jinjini 150 7.26 N 2.39 W
Jinju → Chinju 98 35.11 N 128.05 E
Jinkeng 100 27.15 N 117.14 E
Jinkichi-mori ∧ 96 33.41 N 134.07 E
Jinkou, Zhg. 98 36.35 N 120.46 E
Jinkou, Zhg. 100 30.22 N 114.10 E
Jinkou, Zhg. 100 29.18 N 115.15 E
Jinkuang 102 28.20 N 101.54 E
Jinlijing 107 29.48 N 104.45 E
Jinlingsi 104 41.42 N 120.49 E
Jinlingyu 105 40.06 N 117.32 E
Jinlingzhen 98 36.49 N 118.11 E
Jinlonggou 89 51.45 N 125.51 E
Jinmachi-chūtonchi, Rikujō-jieitai- ■ 92 38.25 N 140.27 E
Jinmu Jiao ≻ 110 18.09 N 109.34 E
Jinnah Barrage ◆6 123 32.57 N 71.30 E
Jinning 102 24.41 N 102.35 E
Jinniu, Zhg. 100 31.24 N 117.12 E
Jinniu, Zhg. 100 29.59 N 114.38 E
Jinotega 236 13.06 N 86.00 W
Jinotega □5 236 14.00 N 85.25 W
Jinotepe 236 11.51 N 86.12 W
Jinping, Zhg. 102 26.38 N 109.03 E
Jinping, Zhg. 102 22.50 N 103.10 E
Jinpingchang 107 28.54 N 104.43 E
Jinpo 105 39.18 N 115.15 E
Jinqian ≐ 102 32.52 N 110.01 E
Jinqiao 100 31.46 N 116.50 E
Jinrui 100 27.57 N 114.12 E
Jinseki 96 34.48 N 133.11 E
Jinsen → Inch'ŏn 98 37.28 N 126.38 E
Jinsha, Zhg. 100 26.12 N 118.39 E
Jinsha, Zhg. 102 27.18 N 106.10 E
Jinsha, Zhg. 106 32.06 N 121.05 E
Jinsha (Yangtze) ≐ 102 28.50 N 104.36 E
Jinshan, Zhg. 89 51.51 N 126.30 E
Jinshan, Zhg. 106 30.54 N 121.09 E
Jinshanwei 106 30.44 N 121.19 E
Jinshanxiang 107 30.35 N 104.52 E
Jinshanzui 106 30.44 N 121.22 E
Jinshi 102 29.39 N 111.52 E
Jinshijing 107 29.23 N 104.08 E
Jinshuzhen 106 31.23 N 120.24 E
Jinsiniangqiao 106 30.43 N 121.15 E
Jinta 102 40.03 N 98.53 E
Jintan 106 31.45 N 119.34 E
Jintang, Zhg. 102 30.54 N 104.19 E
Jintang, Zhg. 102 30.19 N 102.19 E
Jintian 100 27.10 N 114.27 E
Jintotolo Channel ⊌ 116 11.48 N 123.05 E
Jintotolo Island I 116 11.51 N 123.08 E
Jinxi, Zhg. 100 27.54 N 116.43 E
Jinxi, Zhg. 104 40.45 N 120.50 E
Jinxian, Zhg. 98 38.02 N 115.02 E
Jinxian, Zhg. 98 39.04 N 121.40 E
Jinxian, Zhg. 100 28.22 N 116.14 E
Jinxian (Dalinghe), Zhg. 104 41.11 N 121.22 E
Jinxiang, Zhg. 98 35.05 N 116.18 E
Jinxiang, Zhg. 100 27.26 N 120.35 E
Jin-ya ⊥ 94 36.06 N 137.15 E
Jinyun 100 28.40 N 120.03 E
Jinz, Qā' al- ≚ 132 30.45 N 36.04 E
Jinze 106 31.02 N 120.56 E
Jinzhai 100 31.44 N 115.54 E
Jinzhaizhen 100 31.32 N 115.46 E
Jinzhen 100 33.39 N 118.17 E
Jinzhong ≐ 105 39.08 N 117.42 E
Jinzhou (Chinchou) 104 41.07 N 121.08 E
Jinzisi 107 29.09 N 106.22 E
Jinzū ≐ 94 36.46 N 137.13 E
Jiō 270 34.58 N 135.28 E
Ji-Paraná 248 10.52 S 61.57 W
Jipijapa 246 1.20 S 80.35 W
Jipioca, Ilha I 250 1.53 N 50.12 W
Jiquí ≐ 240p 21.22 N 78.32 W
Jiquilisco 236 13.19 N 88.35 W
Jiquilisco, Bahía de c 236 13.10 N 88.28 W
Jiquilpan de Juárez 234 19.59 N 102.43 W
Jiquipilas 234 16.40 N 93.39 W
Jiquipilco 234 19.32 N 99.36 W
Jiquiriçá ≐ 255 13.12 S 38.57 W
Jirāfī, Wādī al- (Nahal Paran) ⊻ 132 30.24 N 35.10 E
Jirbān 140 11.03 N 30.36 E
Jiřetín 54 50.50 N 14.35 E
Jiri ≐ 120 24.42 N 93.06 E
Jiřikov 54 50.59 N 14.35 E
Jirjā 140 26.20 N 31.53 E
Jirkov 54 50.30 N 13.27 E
Jīroft 128 28.40 N 57.46 E
Jīsh (Gush Halav) 132 33.02 N 35.27 E
Jishou 102 28.17 N 109.29 E
Jishui, Zhg. 100 27.14 N 115.06 E
Jishui, Zhg. 100 33.46 N 115.24 E
Jisr ash-Shughūr 130 35.48 N 36.19 E
Jitan 100 24.56 N 115.43 E
Jitarning 162 32.48 S 117.59 E
Jitaúna 255 14.01 S 39.57 W
Jitianzhen 107 30.19 N 104.01 E
Jitotol 234 17.02 N 92.52 W
Jitra 114 6.16 N 100.25 E
Jituo 120 34.15 N 82.05 E
Jiu ≐ 38 43.47 N 23.48 E
Jiubao 100 25.57 N 115.48 E
Jiubingtai 104 41.39 N 124.07 E
Jiucheng, Zhg. 98 38.12 N 117.18 E
Jiucheng, Zhg. 105 39.23 N 116.44 E
Jiuchuchang 107 29.55 N 104.38 E
Jiudaoliang 102 31.35 N 110.12 E
Jiudhara 126 22.24 N 89.44 E
Jiudian 106 32.10 N 120.57 E
Jiudongle 102 38.49 N 101.05 E
Jiudu 106 30.31 N 119.53 E
Jiufanxian 98 35.51 N 115.41 E
Jiufeng, Zhg. 100 24.20 N 117.02 E
Jiufeng, Zhg. 100 25.33 N 119.08 E
Jiugang 105 39.03 N 116.12 E
Jiugongan 102 29.52 N 112.00 E
Jiugongkou 105 39.50 N 114.43 E
Jiugong Shan ∧ 100 29.26 N 114.42 E
Jiuguan, Zhg. 98 37.26 N 121.53 E
Jiuguan, Zhg. 106 30.51 N 120.16 E
Jiuguantao 98 36.40 N 115.25 E
Jiuhe 100 23.32 N 115.04 E
Jiuhongshui 102 37.14 N 103.57 E
Jiuhu 98 37.03 N 117.36 E
Jiuhuai'an 98 40.24 N 114.31 E
Jiuhuajie 100 30.25 N 117.51 E
Jiuhuaxian 100 23.30 N 113.16 E
Jiuhuinan 98 42.37 N 126.14 E
Jiujiang, Zhg. 100 29.44 N 115.59 E
Jiujiang, Zhg. 100 29.36 N 115.52 E
Jiujiang, Zhg. 100 22.51 N 113.02 E
Jiujiawopeng 104 40.59 N 121.22 E
Jiujiji 98 35.09 N 114.48 E
Jiujing 107 29.05 N 103.54 E
Jiukou 100 30.52 N 112.38 E
Jiuli 107 29.32 N 103.32 E
Jiulian Shan ⩗ 100 24.40 N 114.46 E
Jiuliguan 100 31.50 N 114.14 E
Jiuling Shan ⩗ 100 28.46 N 114.45 E
Jiulong, Zhg. 100 24.08 N 112.55 E
Jiulong, Zhg. 102 29.00 N 101.50 E
Jiulong ≐, Zhg. 100 25.59 N 117.18 E
Jiulong ≐, Zhg. 100 24.28 N 117.48 E
Jiulongchang 107 29.32 N 106.05 E
Jiulonggang 100 32.38 N 117.03 E
Jiulong → Kowloon 271d 22.18 N 114.10 E
Jiulongpo 107 29.29 N 106.32 E
Jiulongzhen 106 31.54 N 121.34 E
Jiumen 98 40.42 N 120.27 E
Jiumianyang 100 30.16 N 113.13 E
Jiumiao 104 42.24 N 121.36 E
Jiumu 100 28.11 N 118.27 E
Jiuninghe 105 39.28 N 117.46 E
Jiuningyang 100 25.38 N 117.21 E
Jiupu, Zhg. 100 32.50 N 118.45 E
Jiupu, Zhg. 105 40.21 N 115.18 E
Jiuquan (Suzhou) 102 39.45 N 98.34 E
Jiurongcheng 98 37.21 N 122.32 E
Jiushangshui 100 33.32 N 114.32 E
Jiushan Liedao II 100 29.26 N 122.12 E
Jiushenqiu 100 33.11 N 115.08 E
Jiusiyang 100 33.41 N 118.39 E
Jiusongyu 105 40.27 N 116.58 E
Jiutai 89 44.08 N 125.50 E
Jiuwuqing 105 39.31 N 116.52 E
Jiuxian, Zhg. 98 37.53 N 117.06 E
Jiuxian, Zhg. 100 31.11 N 118.04 E
Jiuxian, Zhg. 100 33.15 N 115.35 E
Jiuxian, Zhg. 100 25.14 N 116.31 E
Jiuxian, Zhg. 100 33.32 N 113.17 E
Jiuxian, Zhg. 100 25.54 N 113.22 E
Jiuxian, Zhg. 107 30.27 N 103.51 E
Jiuxian, Zhg. 107 29.51 N 106.13 E
Jiuxian ≐ 100 25.07 N 116.24 E
Jiuxiangcheng 100 33.13 N 114.49 E
Jiuyingkou 105 39.42 N 114.44 E
Jiuyingzi 104 42.03 N 121.38 E
Jiuyuanqu 102 35.09 N 111.51 E
Jiuyuhang 106 30.17 N 119.56 E
Jiuyunjie 86 44.12 N 88.05 E
Jiuzhan 89 43.57 N 126.29 E
Jiuzhen 100 24.05 N 117.42 E
Jiuzhou 105 39.30 N 116.33 E
Jiuzhuangwo 105 40.11 N 115.36 E
Jiwangmiao 269b 31.14 N 121.17 E
Jiwangtun 104 41.02 N 122.58 E
Jīwani 128 25.03 N 61.45 E
Jiwen 89 50.32 N 123.15 E
Jixi, Zhg. 89 45.17 N 130.59 E
Jixi, Zhg. 100 30.06 N 118.35 E
Jixian, Zhg. 98 35.26 N 114.05 E
Jixian, Zhg. 98 37.36 N 115.31 E
Jixian, Zhg. 105 40.03 N 117.24 E
Jixiangsi 107 30.39 N 105.32 E
Jixiashi 100 28.22 N 118.44 E
Jixingji 100 32.55 N 116.46 E
Jiyang, Zhg. 98 36.59 N 117.11 E
Jiyang, Zhg. 100 27.10 N 118.07 E
Jiyang, Zhg. 105 39.38 N 115.59 E
Jiyi 102 35.50 N 110.23 E
Jiyuan 102 35.08 N 112.35 E
Jiyun ≐ 105 39.07 N 117.43 E
Jiz', Wādī al- ⊻ 144 16.19 N 52.00 E
Jīzah, Ahrāmāt al- (Pyramids of Giza) ⊥ 142 29.59 N 31.08 E
Jīzah, Tur'at al- ≍ 273c 29.50 N 31.16 E
Jīzān 144 16.54 N 42.29 E
Jizayy 142 30.28 N 30.51 E
Jize 98 36.54 N 114.52 E
Jizera ≐ 54 50.10 N 14.43 E
Jizl, Wādī al- ⊻ 128 25.38 N 38.21 E
Jizō-dake ∧ 94 36.36 N 139.28 E
Jizō-zaki ≻ 96 35.34 N 133.20 E
Joaçaba 252 27.10 S 51.30 W
Joachimsthal 54 52.58 N 13.44 E
Joachimsthal → Jáchymov 54 50.20 N 12.55 E
Joaíma 255 16.39 S 41.02 W
Joal Fadiout 150 14.10 N 16.51 W
Joana Coeli 250 1.58 S 49.23 W
Joana Peres 250 3.18 S 49.42 W
Joanes 250 0.51 S 48.31 W
Joanicó 258 34.36 S 56.15 W
Joanna 192 34.24 N 81.48 W
Joanópolis 256 22.56 S 46.17 W
João Câmara 250 5.32 S 35.48 W
João Mendes ≐ 287a 22.57 S 43.03 W
João Neiva 255 19.45 S 40.24 W
João Pessoa 250 7.07 S 34.52 W
João Pinheiro 255 17.45 S 46.10 W
Joaquim Egídio 256 22.53 S 46.59 W
Joaquim Távora 255 23.30 S 49.58 W
Joaquin 194 31.58 N 94.03 W
Joaquin Miller Park ♦ 282 37.49 N 122.11 W
Joaquín Suárez 258 34.44 S 56.02 W
Joaquín V. González 252 25.05 S 64.11 W
Job 62 45.37 N 3.45 E
Jobabo 240p 20.54 N 77.17 W
Jobat 120 22.25 N 74.34 E
Jobo Point ≻ 116 8.42 N 126.15 E
Jobos 240m 17.58 N 66.10 W
Jobos, Bahía de c 240m 17.56 N 66.13 W
Job Peak ∧ 204 39.35 N 118.14 W
Jobstown 285 40.02 N 74.41 W
Jochberg 64 47.23 N 12.24 E
Jock ≐ 212 45.16 N 75.43 W
Jocketa 54 50.33 N 12.10 E
Jockgrim 56 49.06 N 8.17 E
Jocko ≐ 202 47.20 N 114.17 W
Jocolí 252 32.35 S 68.41 W
Jo Co Marsh ≡ 276 40.37 N 73.47 W
Jocón 236 15.17 N 86.58 W
Jocoro 236 13.37 N 88.01 W
Jocotán 236 14.49 N 89.23 W
Jocotepec 234 20.18 N 103.26 W
Jocotitlán 234 19.42 N 99.48 W
Jódar 34 37.50 N 3.21 W
Jodhpur 120 26.17 N 73.02 E
Jodiya 120 22.42 N 70.18 E
Jodoigne 56 50.43 N 4.52 E
Jodrell Bank Radio Telescope ⊍3 262 53.14 N 2.18 W
Joe ≐ 220 25.17 N 81.05 W
Joe Batt's Arm 186 49.44 N 54.10 W
Joel 158 28.42 S 28.21 E
Joensuu 26 62.36 N 29.46 E
Joetsu 94 37.06 N 138.15 E
Jœuf 56 49.14 N 6.01 E
Jofane 156 21.17 S 34.16 E
Joffre, Mount ∧ 182 50.32 N 115.13 W
Jōganzi ≐ 94 36.46 N 137.18 E
Jōga-shima I 94 35.08 N 139.37 E
Jōgawara 268 35.42 N 139.22 E
Jōge 96 34.42 N 133.07 E
Jogeshvari ◆8 272c 19.08 N 72.51 E
Jogeshvari Cave •5 272c 19.08 N 72.51 E
Jõgeva 76 58.45 N 26.24 E
Jog Falls ∟ 122 14.13 N 74.45 E
Joggins 186 45.42 N 64.27 W
Joghatāy 128 36.36 N 57.01 E
Jogindarnagar 123 31.59 N 76.46 E
Jogjakarta → Yogyakarta 115a 7.48 S 110.22 E
Jogui ≐ 255 23.45 S 54.40 W
Jōhana 94 36.31 N 136.54 E
Johannesburg, S. Afr. 158 26.12 S 28.05 E
Johannesburg, S. Afr. 273d 26.12 S 28.05 E
Johannesburg, Ca., U.S. 228 35.22 N 117.38 W
Johannesburg □5 273d 26.13 S 28.02 E
Johannesburg (Jan Smuts) Airport ⊠ 273d 26.08 S 28.14 E
Johanngeorgenstadt 54 50.26 N 12.43 E
Johanniskreuz 56 49.20 N 7.49 E
Johannisthal ◆8 264a 52.26 N 13.30 E
Jōhen 92 32.57 N 132.35 E
Johi 120 26.41 N 67.37 E
Johilla ≐ 124 23.37 N 81.14 E
John ≐ 180 66.55 N 151.35 W
John Boyd Thacher State Park ♦ 210 42.38 N 74.01 W
John Carroll University ⊍2 279a 41.29 N 81.32 W
John Day 202 44.24 N 118.57 W
John Day ≐ 202 45.44 N 120.39 W
John Day, Middle Fork ≐ 202 44.55 N 119.18 W
John Day, North Fork ≐ 202 44.45 N 119.38 W
John Day, South Fork ≐ 202 44.28 N 119.31 W
John Day Dam ◆6 224 45.43 N 120.41 W
John Day Fossil Beds National Monument ♦ 202 44.34 N 119.39 W
John F. Kennedy International Airport ⊠ 210 40.38 N 73.47 W
John F. Kennedy National Historical Site ⊥ 283 42.21 N 71.08 W
John F. Kennedy Space Center ⊍3 220 28.40 N 80.40 W
John Forrest National Park ♦ 168a 31.53 S 116.06 E
John Hancock Center ⊍ 278 41.55 N 87.37 W
John H. Kerr Reservoir ⊜1 192 36.35 N 78.35 W
John J. Duffy Preserve ♦ 278 41.39 N 87.55 W
John Martin Reservoir ⊜1 198 38.05 N 103.02 W
John McLaren Park ♦ 282 37.43 N 122.25 W
John Muir National Historical Site ⊥ 282 37.59 N 122.08 W
Johnny Run ≐ 216 41.17 N 88.21 W
John o' Groats 46 58.38 N 3.05 W
John Pennekamp Coral Reef State Park ♦ 220 25.11 N 80.15 W
John Redmond Reservoir ⊜1 198 38.18 N 95.55 W
Johns ≐ 224 46.54 N 124.01 W
Johns Creek ≐ 192 37.30 N 80.06 W
Johnshaven 46 56.47 N 2.20 W
Johns Hopkins University ⊍2 284b 39.20 N 76.37 W
Johns Island I 192 32.40 N 80.05 W
Johnson, Ar., U.S. 194 36.07 N 94.09 W
Johnson, Ks., U.S. 198 37.34 N 101.45 W
Johnson, Ne., U.S. 198 40.24 N 95.59 W
Johnson, N.Y., U.S. 210 41.22 N 74.30 W
Johnson, Vt., U.S. 188 44.38 N 72.40 W
Johnson □6, In., U.S. 218 39.29 N 86.03 W
Johnson □6, Tx., U.S. 222 32.20 N 97.20 W
Johnson, Mount ∧ 226 36.37 N 121.19 W
Johnson Bay c 208 38.03 N 75.20 W
Johnsonburg, N.J., U.S. 210 40.58 N 74.53 W
Johnsonburg, N.Y., U.S. 210 42.44 N 78.18 W
Johnsonburg, Pa., U.S. 214 41.29 N 78.40 W

Symbol	English	Deutsch	Español	Français	Português
≐	River	Fluß	Río	Rivière	Rio
☰	Canal	Kanal	Canal	Canal	Canal
∟	Waterfall, Rapids	Wasserfall, Stromschnellen	Cascada, Rápidos	Chute d'eau, Rapides	Cascata, Rápidos
⊌	Strait	Meeresstraße	Estrecho	Détroit	Estreito
c	Bay, Gulf	Bucht, Golf	Bahía, Golfo	Baie, Golfe	Baía, Golfo
⊜	Lake, Lakes	See, Seen	Lago, Lagos	Lac, Lacs	Lago, Lagos
≡	Swamp	Sumpf	Pantano	Marais	Pântano
⊓	Ice Features, Glacier	Eis- und Gletscherformen	Accidentes Glaciales	Formes glaciaires	Acidentes glaciares
⊤	Other Hydrographic Features	Andere Hydrographische Objekte	Otros Elementos Hidrográficos	Autres données hydrographiques	Outros acidentes hidrográficos

Symbol	English	Deutsch	Español	Français	Português
✣	Submarine Features	Untermeerische Objekte	Accidentes Submarinos	Formes de relief sous-marin	Acidentes submarinos
□	Political Unit	Politische Einheit	Unidad Política	Entité politique	Unidade política
⊍	Cultural Institution	Kulturelle Institution	Institución Cultural	Institution culturelle	Instituição cultural
⊥	Historical Site	Historische Stätte	Sitio Histórico	Site historique	Sítio histórico
♦	Recreational Site	Erholungs- und Ferienort	Sitio de Recreo	Centre de loisirs	Área de Lazer
⊠	Airport	Flughafen	Aeropuerto	Aéroport	Aeroporto
■	Military Installation	Militäranlage	Instalación Militar	Installation militaire	Instalação militar
◆	Miscellaneous	Verschiedenes	Misceláneo	Divers	Diversos

Johnson City, N.Y., U.S. 210 42.06 N 75.57 W
Johnson City, Tn., U.S. 192 36.18 N 82.21 W
Johnson City, Tx., U.S. 196 30.16 N 98.24 W
Johnson Creek, N.Y., U.S. 210 43.15 N 78.31 W
Johnson Creek, Wi., U.S. 216 43.04 N 88.46 W
Johnson Creek ≃, Id., U.S. 202 44.58 N 115.30 W
Johnson Creek ≃, Ky., U.S. 218 38.27 N 84.04 W
Johnson Creek ≃, N.Y., U.S. 210 43.22 N 78.16 W
Johnson Creek ≃, Tx., U.S. 222 32.02 N 94.59 W
Johnson Creek ≃, Wa., U.S. 224 46.35 N 121.42 W
Johnsondale 204 35.58 N 118.32 W
Johnson Drain ≋ 281 42.26 N 83.28 W
Johnson Draw V, Tx., U.S. 196 31.58 N 101.41 W
Johnson Draw V, Tx., U.S. 196 30.08 N 101.07 W
Johnson Hall State Historic Site ⊥ 210 43.01 N 74.23 W
Johnson Park ♠ 276 40.30 N 74.27 W
Johnson Point › 241h 13.07 N 61.12 W
Johnsons Crossing 180 60.29 N 133.16 W
Johnsons Point › 240c 17.02 N 61.53 W
Johnsons Pond ⊜ 283 42.44 N 71.03 W
Johnsons Station 222 32.42 N 97.08 W
Johnsonville, N.Z. 172 41.14 S 174.47 E
Johnsonville, N.Y., U.S. 210 42.55 N 73.31 W
Johnsonville, S.C., U.S. 192 33.49 N 79.26 W
Johnston, Wales, U.K. 42 51.46 N 5.00 W
Johnston, Ia., U.S. 190 41.40 N 93.41 W
Johnston, R.I., U.S. 207 41.46 N 71.21 W
Johnston, S.C., U.S. 192 33.49 N 81.48 W
Johnston, Lake ⊜ 162 32.25 S 120.30 E
Johnston Atoll I[1] 14 16.45 N 169.32 W
Johnston City 194 37.49 N 88.55 W
Johnstone 46 55.50 N 4.31 W
Johnstone Peak ∧ 280 34.10 N 117.48 W
Johnstone Strait ⊔ 182 50.25 N 126.00 W
Johnston Falls ∟ 154 10.35 S 28.40 E
Johnstown, Co., U.S. 200 40.20 N 104.54 W
Johnstown, N.Y., U.S. 210 43.00 N 74.22 W
Johnstown, Oh., U.S. 214 40.09 N 82.41 W
Johnstown, Pa., U.S. 214 40.19 N 78.55 W
Johnstown Center 216 42.42 N 88.50 W
Johnstown Flood National Memorial ⊥ 214 40.21 N 78.47 W
John Tyler Arboretum ♠ 285 39.56 N 75.26 W
Jōhoku 94 36.28 N 140.22 E
Johol 114 2.36 N 102.16 E
Johor □[3] 114 2.00 N 103.30 E
Johor ≃ 114 1.27 N 104.02 E
Johor, Selat ⊔ 271c 1.28 N 103.48 E
Johor Baharu 114 1.28 N 103.45 E
Jöhstadt 54 50.30 N 13.05 E
Joice Island I 282 38.08 N 122.02 W
Joigny 50 47.59 N 3.24 E
Joiner 194 35.30 N 90.08 W
Joinerville 222 32.11 N 94.55 W
Joinvile 252 26.18 S 48.50 W
Joinville 58 48.27 N 5.08 E
Joinville, Lac ⊜ 206 46.18 N 75.12 W
Joinville Island I 9 63.15 S 55.45 W
Joinville-le-Pont 261 48.49 N 2.28 E
Jōjima 96 33.15 N 130.26 E
Jojogan 115a 6.58 S 111.46 E
Jojutla 234 18.37 N 99.11 W
Joka 272b 22.27 N 88.18 E
Jokau 140 8.24 N 33.49 E
Jokioinen 26 60.49 N 23.28 E
Jokkmokk 24 66.37 N 19.50 E
Jökulsá á Brú ≃ 24a 65.41 N 14.13 W
Jökulsårgljúfur National Park ♠ 24a 66.00 N 16.20 W
Jolārpettai 122 12.34 N 78.35 E
Jolfā 128 38.57 N 45.38 E
Joliet, Il., U.S. 216 41.31 N 88.04 W
Joliet, Mt., U.S. 202 45.29 N 108.58 W
Joliet Correctional Center ⊍ 278 41.33 N 88.04 W
Joliett 208 40.37 N 76.27 W
Joliette 206 46.01 N 73.27 W
Joliette □[6] 206 46.25 N 74.00 W
Jolietville 218 40.03 N 86.15 W
Jöllenbeck 52 52.11 N 8.45 E
Jollyville 222 30.27 N 97.47 W
Jolo 116 6.03 N 121.00 E
Jolo Group II 116 6.00 N 121.09 E
Jolo Island I 116 5.58 N 121.06 E
Jølstravatnet ⊜ 26 61.32 N 6.13 E
Jomalig Island I 116 14.42 N 122.22 E
Jomba 102 31.27 N 98.15 E
Jombang 115a 7.33 S 112.14 E
Jombo ≃ 152 10.36 S 17.32 E
Jona 58 47.14 N 8.52 E
Jonacatepec 234 18.41 N 98.48 W
Jonah 222 30.38 N 97.32 W
Jönåker 40 58.44 N 16.40 E
Jonathan Dickinson State Park ♠ 220 27.01 N 80.08 W
Jonava 76 55.05 N 24.17 E
Jones, Pil. 116 16.33 N 121.42 E
Jones, Mi., U.S. 216 41.54 N 85.48 W
Jones, Ok., U.S. 196 35.33 N 97.17 W
Jones ≃ 283 42.00 N 70.42 W
Jones and Laughlin Steel Corporation ⊍[3], Pa., U.S. 279b 40.26 N 79.58 W
Jones and Laughlin Steel Corporation ⊍[3], Pa., U.S. 279b 40.37 N 80.14 W
Jones Beach State Park ♠ 210 40.35 N 73.31 W
Jonesboro, Ar., U.S. 194 35.50 N 90.42 W
Jonesboro, Ga., U.S. 192 33.31 N 84.21 W
Jonesboro, Il., U.S. 194 37.27 N 89.16 W
Jonesboro, In., U.S. 216 40.28 N 85.37 W
Jonesboro, La., U.S. 194 32.14 N 92.42 W
Jonesboro, Tn., U.S. 192 36.17 N 82.28 W
Jonesburg 219 38.51 N 91.18 W
Jones Creek 222 28.58 N 95.27 W
Jones Creek ≃, On., Can. 212 44.30 N 75.49 W
Jones Creek ≃, Tx., U.S. 222 29.08 N 96.03 W
Jones Falls ≃ 284b 39.18 N 76.37 W
Jones Falls, North Branch ≃ 284b 39.25 N 76.42 W
Jones Inlet ⊂ 210 40.35 N 73.34 W
Jones Mill 194 34.27 N 92.50 W
Jones Mountains ⋏ 9 73.32 S 94.00 W
Jonesport 188 44.31 N 67.35 W
Jones Sound ⊔ 176 76.00 N 85.00 W
Jonestown 194 34.19 N 90.27 W
Jonesville, In., U.S. 218 39.04 N 85.53 W
Jonesville, La., U.S. 194 31.37 N 91.49 W
Jonesville, Mi., U.S. 216 41.59 N 84.40 W
Jonesville, N.Y., U.S. 210 42.55 N 73.49 W
Jonesville, N.C., U.S. 192 36.14 N 80.50 W
Jonesville, S.C., U.S. 192 34.50 N 81.40 W
Jonesville, Va., U.S. 192 36.41 N 83.06 W
Jong ≃ 150 7.32 N 12.23 W
Jonglei Canal ≋ 136 9.21 N 31.32 E
Jongunjärvi ⊜ 26 65.17 N 27.15 E
Jónico, Mar → Ionian Sea ⊤[2] 22 39.00 N 19.00 E
Joniškėlis 76 56.02 N 24.10 E
Joniškis 76 56.14 N 23.37 E
Jonkersberg 158 33.55 S 22.15 E
Jönköping 26 57.47 N 14.11 E
Jönköpings Län □[6] 26 57.30 N 14.30 E
Jonquière 186 48.24 N 71.15 W
Jonquières 62 44.07 N 4.54 E
Jonsdorf 54 50.51 N 14.43 E
Jonstorp 41 56.14 N 12.40 E
Jonuta 232 18.05 N 92.08 W
Jonvilliers 261 48.34 N 1.42 E
Jonzac 32 45.27 N 0.26 W
Joondalup, Lake ⊜ 168a 31.45 S 115.47 E
Joplin, Mo., U.S. 194 37.05 N 94.30 W
Joplin, Mt., U.S. 202 48.33 N 110.46 W
Joppa, Il., U.S. 194 37.12 N 88.50 W
Joppa, Md., U.S. 208 39.26 N 76.21 W
Jóquei Clube ♠ 287b 23.35 S 46.41 W
Joquicingo 234 19.03 N 99.33 W
Jora 124 26.20 N 77.49 E
Jordan, Pil. 116 10.40 N 122.35 E
Jordan, Mn., U.S. 190 44.40 N 93.37 W
Jordan, Mt., U.S. 202 47.19 N 106.54 W
Jordan, N.Y., U.S. 210 43.03 N 76.28 W
Jordan (Al-Urdun) □[1], Asia 118 31.00 N 36.00 E
Jordan (Al-Urdun) □[1], Asia 128 31.00 N 36.00 E
Jordan (Nahr al-Urdunn) (HaYarden) ≃, Asia 132 31.46 N 35.33 E
Jordan ≃, B.C., Can. 224 48.26 N 124.08 W
Jordan ≃, Ut,. U.S. 200 40.49 N 112.08 W
Jordan Creek ≃ 202 42.52 N 117.38 W
Jordânia 255 15.54 S 40.11 W
Jordania → Jordan □[1] 128 31.00 N 36.00 E
Jordanie → Jordan □[1] 128 31.00 N 36.00 E
Jordanien → Jordan □[1] 128 31.00 N 36.00 E
Jordan Lake ⊜ 216 42.46 N 85.09 W
Jordanów 30 49.40 N 19.50 E
Jordans 260 51.37 N 0.36 W
Jordan Valley 202 42.58 N 117.03 W
Jordanville 210 42.55 N 74.57 W
Jordão ≃ 252 25.46 S 52.07 W
Jordbro 40 59.09 N 18.07 E
Jördenstorf 54 53.52 N 12.37 E
Jordet 26 61.25 N 12.09 E
Jorge Chávez, Aeropuerto Internacional ⊠ 286d 12.02 S 77.07 W
Jorge Grego, Ilha I 256 23.13 S 44.09 W
Jorge Montt, Isla I 254 51.20 S 74.45 W
Jorge V, Costa de → George V Coast ⊥[2] 9 68.30 S 147.30 E
Jorge VI, Estrecho de → George VI Sound ⊔ 9 71.00 S 68.00 W
Jorhāt 120 26.46 N 94.13 E
Jork 52 53.32 N 9.41 E
Jörlfeld 41 54.38 N 9.15 E
Jorm 120 36.52 N 70.51 E
Jörn 26 65.04 N 20.02 E
Jornado del Muerto ◆[2] 200 33.20 N 106.50 W
Joroinen 26 62.11 N 27.50 E
Jorong 112 3.58 S 114.56 E
Jørpeland 26 59.01 N 6.03 E
J'orzovka 80 48.56 N 44.38 E
Jos 150 9.55 N 8.53 E
Jose Abad Santos 116 5.38 N 125.27 E
José Batlle y Ordóñez 252 33.28 S 55.07 W
José Bonifácio 255 21.03 S 49.41 W
José Cardel 234 19.22 N 96.22 W
José C. Paz 258 34.30 S 58.45 W
José de Freitas 250 4.45 S 42.35 W
José de San Martín 254 44.02 S 70.29 W
José Enrique Rodó (Drabble) 258 33.41 S 57.34 W
José Francisco Vergara 252 22.28 S 69.38 W
Joselândia 248 16.32 S 56.12 W
José Martí, Aeropuerto Internacional ⊠ 286b 23.00 N 82.24 W
Jose Panganiban 116 14.17 N 122.41 E
José Pedro Varela 252 33.27 S 54.32 W
Joseph 202 45.21 N 117.13 W
Joseph, Lac ⊜ 176 52.45 N 65.15 W
Joseph, Lake ⊜ 212 45.10 N 79.44 W
Joseph Bonaparte Gulf ⊂ 164 14.15 S 128.30 E
Joseph City 200 34.57 N 110.20 W
Joseph Creek ≃ 202 46.03 N 117.01 W
Joseph Davis State Park ♠ 284a 43.13 N 79.03 W
Josephine, Pa., U.S. 214 40.29 N 79.11 W
Josephine, Tx., U.S. 222 33.04 N 96.19 W
Josephine, Lake ⊜ 220 27.24 N 81.26 W
Josephine Peak ∧ 280 34.17 N 118.09 W
Josephstaal 164 4.44 S 145.01 E
José Santos Arévalo 258 35.10 S 59.14 W
Joshīmath 120 30.34 N 79.34 E
Jōshin-Etsu-kōgen-kokuritsu-kōen ♠ 94 36.46 N 138.40 E
Joshua 222 32.28 N 97.23 W
Joshuas Creek ≃ 275b 43.29 N 79.37 W
Joshua Tree 204 34.08 N 116.18 W
Joshua Tree National Monument ♠ 204 33.55 N 116.00 W
Joshua Trees State Park ♠ 228 34.41 N 117.47 W
Joškar-Ola 80 56.38 N 47.52 E
Jos Plateau ⋏[1] 150 9.30 N 9.00 E
Jossa 56 50.14 N 9.35 E
Josselin 32 47.57 N 2.33 W
Jossigny 50 48.50 N 2.45 E
Jostedalsbreen ⊓ 26 61.40 N 7.00 E
Jost Van Dyke I 240m 18.28 N 64.45 W
Jōtō ◆[8] 270 34.42 N 135.34 E
Jotunheimen ⋏ 26 61.38 N 8.18 E
Jotunheimen Nasjonalpark ♠ 26 61.35 N 8.30 E
Jouarre 50 48.56 N 3.08 E
Jouars-Pontchartrain 261 48.47 N 1.54 E
Joubertina 158 33.50 S 23.51 E
Joué-lès-Tours 50 47.21 N 0.40 E
Jougne 58 46.46 N 6.24 E
Jouques 62 43.38 N 5.38 E
Jourdanton 196 28.55 N 98.32 W
Joure 52 52.57 N 5.47 E
Joutsa 26 61.44 N 26.07 E
Joutseno 26 61.06 N 28.30 E
Joutsijärvi 24 66.40 N 28.00 E
Joux, Lac de ⊜ 58 46.38 N 6.18 E
Joux, Vallée de V 58 46.35 N 6.15 E
Jouy 50 48.31 N 1.33 E
Jouy-en-Josas 261 48.46 N 2.10 E
Jouy-le-Moutier 261 49.01 N 2.03 E
Jouy-le-Potier 50 47.45 N 1.49 E
Jovellanos 240p 22.48 N 81.12 W
Jovellar 116 13.04 N 123.36 E
Jovet, Mont ∧ 62 45.30 N 6.39 E
Joveyn ≃ 128 36.48 N 56.28 E
Joviânia 255 17.49 S 49.30 W
Jowai 120 25.27 N 92.12 E
Jowhar 144 2.46 N 45.31 E
Jowlaenga, Mount ∧ 162 17.21 S 122.56 E
Jowzjān □[4] 120 36.30 N 66.00 E
Joy 190 41.12 N 90.55 W
Joy, Mount ∧ 180 63.46 N 132.55 W
Joyce 194 31.56 N 92.35 W
Joyeuse 62 44.29 N 4.14 E
Jōyō 96 34.51 N 135.47 E
Joyous Pavilion Park ♠ 271a 39.52 N 116.22 E
Joyuda 240m 18.07 N 67.11 W
Józefów 30 52.09 N 21.12 E
J. Percy Priest Lake ⊜[1] 194 36.05 N 86.30 W
Ju ≃, Zhg. 100 30.38 N 114.51 E
Ju ≃, Zhg. 105 39.45 N 117.35 E
Juaba 250 2.23 S 49.33 W
Juagdan 116 10.00 N 124.35 E
Juami ≃ 246 1.45 S 67.30 W
Juanacatlán 234 20.31 N 103.10 W
Juana Díaz 240m 18.03 N 66.31 W
Juan Aldama 232 24.19 N 103.21 W
Juan Anchorena ◆[8] 288 34.29 S 58.30 W
Juan Atucha 258 35.32 S 59.21 W
Juan B. Arruabarrena 252 30.20 S 58.19 W
Juan Bautista Alberdi 252 27.35 S 65.37 W
Juan Blanco, Arroyo ≃ 258 35.05 S 57.26 W
Juancheng 98 35.35 N 115.29 E
Juan de Fuca, Strait of ⊔ 224 48.18 N 124.00 W
Juan de Garay 254 38.52 S 64.34 W
Juan de Mena 252 24.55 S 56.44 W
Juan de Nova, Île I 138 17.03 S 42.45 E
Juan Díaz Covarrubias 234 18.07 N 95.09 W
Juan E. Barra 252 37.48 S 60.29 W
Juan Eugenio 232 25.10 N 103.20 W
Juan Fernández, Archipiélago II 244 33.00 S 80.00 W
Juan González Grande, Arroyo ≃ 258 34.00 S 58.14 W
Juan González Romero ◆[8] 286a 19.30 N 99.04 W
Juangriego 246 11.05 N 63.57 W
Juan Gualberto Gómez 240p 22.52 N 81.33 W
Juan Guerra 248 6.35 S 76.21 W
Juanita 224 47.42 N 122.13 W
Juan Jorba 252 33.37 S 65.16 W
Juan José Castelli 252 25.57 S 60.37 W
Juán José Perez 248 15.14 S 68.58 W
Juanjuí 248 7.11 S 76.45 W
Juankoski 26 63.04 N 28.21 E
Juan-les-Pins 62 43.34 N 7.06 E
Juan L. Lacaze 258 34.26 S 57.27 W
Juan N. Fernández 252 38.00 S 59.16 W
Juan Perez Sound ⊔ 182 52.30 N 131.18 W
Juan Ramírez, Isla I 234 21.50 N 97.40 W
Juan Rodríguez Clara 234 18.00 N 95.25 W
Juan Tronconi 258 35.30 S 59.15 W
Juan Viñas 236 9.54 N 83.45 W
Juárez, Méx. 232 27.37 N 100.44 W
Juárez, Méx. 232 30.19 N 108.05 W
Juárez, Méx. 234 17.39 N 93.10 W
Juárez, Cerro ∧ 234 20.37 N 99.17 W
Juárez, Sierra ⋏ 234 17.30 N 96.30 W
Juárez, Sierra de ⋏ 232 32.00 N 115.50 W
Juárez → Ciudad Juárez 232 31.44 N 106.29 W
Juarzon 150 5.20 N 8.52 W
Juatinga, Ponta de › 256 23.17 S 44.30 W
Juazeirinho 250 7.04 S 36.35 W
Juàzeiro 250 9.25 S 40.30 W
Juazeiro do Norte 250 7.12 S 39.20 W
Jūbā 154 4.51 N 31.37 E
Juba ≃ 248 14.59 S 57.44 W
Jubachstausee ⊜[1] 263 51.10 N 7.37 E
Jūbāl, Maḍīq ⊔ 140 27.40 N 33.55 E
Jubal, Strait of → Jūbāl, Maḍīq ⊔ 140 27.40 N 33.55 E
Jubayl (Byblos) 130 34.07 N 35.39 E
Jubaysho 144 5.48 N 37.22 E
Jubayt 140 18.57 N 36.50 E
Jubba (Genale) ≃ 144 0.15 S 42.38 E
Jubbada Dhexe □[4] 144 1.00 N 43.00 E
Jubbada Hoose □[4] 144 0.00 42.00 E
Jubbah 128 28.02 N 40.56 E
Jubb al-Jarrāḥ 130 34.49 N 37.19 E
Jubbātā al-Khashab 132 33.13 N 35.49 E
Jubb Jannīn 132 33.37 N 35.47 E
Jubbulpore → Jabalpur 124 23.10 N 79.57 E
Jubilee Downs 162 18.22 S 125.17 E
Jubilee Lake ⊜, Austl. 162 29.12 S 126.38 E
Jubilee Lake ⊜, Nf., Can. 186 48.04 N 55.11 W
Jubones ≃ 246 3.13 S 79.57 W
Jūbu-san ∧ 270 34.50 N 135.55 E
Juby, Cap › 148 27.58 N 12.55 W
Júcar (Xúquer) ≃ 34 39.09 N 0.14 W
Juçara 255 15.53 S 50.51 W
Júcaro 240p 21.37 N 78.51 W
Jucás 250 6.32 S 39.32 W
Jüchen 56 51.06 N 6.30 E
Juchhöh 54 50.24 N 11.52 E
Juchipila 234 21.25 N 103.07 W
Juchipila ≃ 234 21.03 N 103.25 W
Juchitán de Zaragoza 234 16.26 N 95.01 W
Juchitepec 234 19.06 N 98.53 W
Juchitlán 234 20.05 N 104.07 W
Juchnov 76 54.45 N 35.14 E
Juchoviči 76 56.02 N 28.39 E
Jucuapa 236 13.31 N 88.24 W
Jucurucu ≃ 255 17.21 S 39.13 W
Jucurutu 250 6.02 S 37.01 W
Judaea □[9] 132 31.35 N 35.00 E
Judas, Punta › 236 9.31 N 84.32 W
Judaydat al-Khās 132 33.24 N 36.33 E
Judaydat ʿArṭūz 132 33.26 N 36.10 E
Juddah → Jiddah 144 21.30 N 39.12 E
Jude Island I 186 47.15 N 54.49 W
Judenau 61 48.17 N 16.00 E
Judenburg 61 47.10 N 14.40 E
Judges Hill ∧[2] 283 42.12 N 70.49 W
Judian 102 27.20 N 99.36 E
Judinki, Ross. 82 54.37 N 37.17 E
Judinki, Ross. 82 55.27 N 35.48 E
Judino, Ross. 76 58.43 N 39.17 E
Judino, Ross. 80 55.51 N 48.55 E
Judino, Ross. 82 54.09 N 38.19 E
Judino, Ross. 265b 55.40 N 37.12 E
Judío, Rambla del ≃ 34 38.15 N 1.27 W
Judique 186 45.52 N 61.30 W
Judith ≃ 202 47.44 N 109.38 W
Judith, Point › 207 41.22 N 71.29 W
Judith Gap 202 46.40 N 109.45 W
Judith Mountains ⋏ 202 47.12 N 109.15 W
Judith Peak ∧ 202 47.13 N 109.13 W
Judoma ≃ 74 59.08 N 135.06 E
Judson, S.C., U.S. 192 34.50 N 82.27 W
Judson, Tx., U.S. 222 32.35 N 94.45 W
Judsonia 194 35.16 N 91.38 W
Jue ≃ 100 31.42 N 113.20 E
Juehedian 105 39.26 N 117.06 E
Juelsminde 41 55.43 N 10.01 E
Juexi 100 29.27 N 121.57 E
Juexizhen 107 28.55 N 104.16 E
Jufari ≃ 246 1.13 S 62.00 W
Jufayr, Bi'r al- ⊤[4] 142 30.49 N 32.40 E
Jufrah, Wādī al- V 142 30.24 N 31.35 E
Jug 86 57.43 N 56.10 E
Jug ≃ 24 60.45 N 46.20 E
Jughna 140 12.24 N 25.06 E
Jugo-Kamskij 86 57.42 N 55.35 E
Jugon 32 48.25 N 2.20 W
Jugo-Osetija (South Ossetia) □[9] 84 42.20 N 44.00 E
Jugoslavija → Yugoslavia □[1] 22 44.00 N 21.00 E
Jugoslawien → Yugoslavia □[1] 22 44.00 N 21.00 E
Jugo-Zapad ◆[8] 265b 55.40 N 37.32 E
Juḥā 144 16.41 N 42.54 E
Jühnsdorf 264a 52.18 N 13.23 E
Jühnsdorfer Heide ◆[3] 264a 52.19 N 13.24 E
Juhu ◆[8] 272c 19.07 N 72.49 E
Juhua Dao I 98 40.29 N 120.47 E
Juhu Airport ⊠ 272c 19.06 N 72.50 E
Jui 272c 19.01 N 73.05 E
Juidongshan 100 23.46 N 117.31 E
Juigalpa 236 12.05 N 85.24 W
Juillac 32 45.19 N 1.19 E
Juilly 261 49.01 N 2.42 E
Juína ≃ 248 12.36 S 58.57 W
Juine ≃ 50 48.32 N 2.23 E
Juist 52 53.40 N 6.59 E
Juist I 52 53.40 N 7.00 E
Juisui 100 23.30 N 121.21 E
Juiz de Fora 256 21.45 S 43.20 W
Jūjō Base ■ 268 35.45 N 139.43 E
Jujurieux 58 46.02 N 5.25 E
Jujuy □[4] 252 23.00 S 66.00 W
Jujuy → San Salvador de Jujuy 252 24.11 S 65.18 W
Jukagirskoje ploskogorje ⋏[1] 74 66.00 N 155.00 E
Jukamenskoje 80 57.53 N 52.15 E
Jukonda ≃ 86 59.38 N 67.26 E
Juksa 86 56.55 N 85.10 E
Juksejevo 24 59.52 N 54.19 E
Jukskei ≃ 273d 26.06 S 28.06 E
Jukta 74 63.23 N 105.41 E
Jula ≃ 24 63.49 N 44.44 E
Julāna 124 29.08 N 76.25 E
Julayfah, Bi'r al- ⊤[4] 142 30.43 N 29.35 E
Julbach 60 48.40 N 13.52 E
Juldybajevo 86 52.20 N 57.52 E
Julebu 98 40.09 N 113.36 E
Julesburg 198 40.59 N 102.15 W
Juli 248 16.13 S 69.27 W
Juliaca 248 15.30 S 70.08 W
Julia Creek 166 20.39 S 141.45 E
Julia Creek ≃ 166 20.00 S 141.11 E
Julian 214 40.52 N 77.56 W
Juliana, Lake ⊜ 220 28.07 N 81.48 W
Julianakanaal ≋ 56 51.05 N 5.50 E
Julian Alps ⋏ 36 46.00 N 14.00 E
Juliana Top ∧ 250 3.41 N 56.32 W
Julianehåb (Qaqortoq) 176 60.43 N 46.01 W
Julia Pfeiffer Burns State Park ♠ 226 36.10 N 120.40 W
Jülich 56 50.55 N 6.21 E
Juliénas 58 46.14 N 4.43 E
Juliette, Lake ⊜[1] 192 33.05 N 83.50 W
Julijske Alpe → Julian Alps ⋏ 36 46.00 N 14.00 E
Julimes 232 28.25 N 105.27 W
Júlio de Castilhos 252 29.14 S 53.41 W
Julio Prestes, Estação ◆[5] 287b 23.32 S 46.38 W
Julita ⊍ 40 59.09 N 16.02 E
Juliuhe 104 42.03 N 122.55 E
Juliustown 285 40.00 N 74.40 W
Julu 98 37.13 N 115.01 E
Juma 24 65.07 N 33.16 E
Juma ≃ 98 39.34 N 115.42 E
Jumaguzino 86 52.54 N 56.23 E
Jumapolo 115a 7.42 S 111.00 E
Jumaševo 80 54.59 N 54.25 E
Jumay, Volcán ∧[1] 236 14.41 N 89.59 W
Jumbilla 248 5.54 S 77.45 W
Jumbo 154 17.28 S 30.55 E
Jumbo, Raas › 144 1.39 S 41.36 E
Jumboo 144 0.15 S 42.38 E
Jumbo Peak ∧ 204 36.12 N 114.11 W
Jumeauville 261 48.55 N 1.47 E
Jumentos Cays II 238 22.42 N 75.55 W
Jumet 50 50.26 N 4.25 E
Jumièges 50 49.26 N 0.49 E
Jumilla 34 38.29 N 1.17 W
Jumlā 124 29.17 N 82.10 E
Jummayzat Banī ʿAmr 142 30.48 N 31.32 E
Jump ≃ 190 45.17 N 91.05 W
Jump, North Fork ≃ 190 45.25 N 90.40 W
Jump, South Fork ≃ 190 45.25 N 90.40 W
Jumt uul ∧ 102 44.29 N 97.10 E
Jūn 132 33.35 N 35.27 E
Jun ≃ 100 25.57 N 118.03 E
Jūnāgadh 120 21.31 N 70.28 E
Junan (Shizilu) 98 35.11 N 118.51 E
Junayfah 142 30.12 N 32.25 E
Junaynah, Ra's al- ∧ 140 29.01 N 33.58 E
Juncal, Isla I 258 33.58 S 58.24 W
Juncal do Norte ≡ 266c 38.52 N 8.59 W
Juncal do Sul ≡ 266c 38.51 N 8.58 W
Juncheng 98 38.57 N 114.41 E
Juncos 240m 18.14 N 65.55 W
Junction, Tx., U.S. 196 30.29 N 99.46 W
Junction, Ut,. U.S. 200 38.14 N 112.13 W
Junction City, Ar., U.S. 194 33.00 N 92.43 W
Junction City, Il., U.S. 219 38.34 N 89.07 W
Junction City, Ks., U.S. 198 39.01 N 96.49 W
Junction City, Ky., U.S. 194 37.35 N 84.47 W
Junction City, Or., U.S. 202 44.13 N 123.12 W
Junction City, Wa., U.S. 224 46.58 N 123.46 W
Jundah 166 24.50 S 143.04 E
Jundiaí 256 23.11 S 46.52 W
Jundiaí ≃, Bra. 256 23.32 S 46.15 W
Jundiaí ≃, Bra. 256 23.11 S 47.16 W
Jundiaí do Sul 255 23.27 S 50.17 W
Jundiaí-mirim ≃ 256 23.10 S 46.56 W
Jundiapeba 256 23.33 S 46.15 W
Jundu Shan ⋏ 105 40.30 N 116.05 E
Juneau, Ak., U.S. 180 58.20 N 134.27 W
Juneau, Wi., U.S. 190 43.24 N 88.42 W
Junee 166 34.52 S 147.35 E
June in Winter, Lake ⊜ 220 27.18 N 81.24 W
June Lake 226 37.46 N 119.04 W
June Park 220 28.04 N 80.41 W
Jungapeo de Juárez 234 19.27 N 100.29 W
Jungar Qi 102 39.49 N 111.10 E
Jungbluth Ditch ≋ 279a 41.27 N 82.07 W
Jungfernheide ◆[3] 264a 52.34 N 13.17 E
Jungfern-Inseln → Virgin Islands □[2] 240m 18.20 N 64.50 W
Jungfern-See ⊜ 264a 52.25 N 13.05 E
Jungfrau ∧ 58 46.32 N 7.58 E
Jungfraujoch ◆[5] 58 46.33 N 7.58 E
Junggar Pendi (Dzungarian Basin) ≚[1] 86 45.00 N 88.00 E
Jungle Habitat ♠ 276 41.08 N 74.21 W
Junglinster 56 49.43 N 6.15 E
Jungshāhi 120 24.51 N 67.46 E
Juniata 198 40.35 N 98.30 W
Juniata □[6] 208 40.34 N 77.24 W
Juniata ◆[8] 285 40.01 N 75.07 W
Juniata ≃ 188 40.24 N 77.01 W
Juniata, Frankstown Branch ≃ 214 40.34 N 78.03 W
Juniata, Raystown Branch ≃ 214 40.25 N 77.58 W
Juniata Gap 214 40.33 N 78.26 W
Juniata Terrace 208 40.35 N 77.34 W
Junín, Arg. 252 34.35 S 60.57 W
Junín, Ec. 246 0.56 S 80.13 W
Junín, Perú 248 11.10 S 76.00 W
Junín □[5] 248 11.30 S 75.00 W
Junín, Lago de ⊜ 248 11.02 S 76.06 W
Junín de los Andes 254 39.56 S 71.05 W
Junior 188 38.59 N 79.57 W
Juniper 186 46.33 N 67.13 W
Junipero Serra Peak ∧ 226 36.08 N 121.25 W
Juniville 50 49.24 N 4.23 E
Jūniyah 130 33.59 N 35.38 E
Junk Bay ⊂ 271d 22.17 N 114.15 E
Jun Kharchanai 123 36.52 N 75.01 E
Junk Island I 271d 22.17 N 114.16 E
Junkou 100 26.42 N 116.49 E
Junlian 102 28.08 N 104.35 E
Junliangcheng 105 39.04 N 117.27 E
Junling 100 28.17 N 116.28 E
Junnar 122 19.12 N 73.53 E
Juno Beach 220 26.52 N 80.04 W
Junokommunarskoje ◆[8] 83 48.13 N 38.18 E
Junqalī □[4] 140 7.30 N 32.20 E
Junqueiro 250 9.56 S 36.29 W
Junqueirópolis 255 21.32 S 51.26 W
Junsele 26 63.41 N 16.54 E
Juntas 236 10.16 N 85.00 W
Jun Ul Shan ⋏ 102 37.30 N 97.00 E
Junxian 102 32.31 N 111.30 E
Jūō 94 36.40 N 140.41 E
Juodkrantė 76 55.33 N 21.08 E
Juodupė 76 56.05 N 25.37 E
Juojärvi ⊜ 26 62.43 N 28.33 E
Juozapinės kalnas ∧[2] 76 54.32 N 25.37 E
Juparanã, Lagoa ⊜ 255 19.35 S 40.18 W
Jupilingo ≃ 236 14.48 N 89.14 W
Jupille 56 50.39 N 5.38 E
Jupiter 220 26.56 N 80.05 W
Jupiter ≃ 186 49.29 N 63.37 W
Jupiter Inlet ⊂ 220 26.57 N 80.04 W
Jupiter Island I 220 27.04 N 80.07 W
Juqueri ≃ 256 23.24 S 46.52 W
Juqueri, Reservatório do ⊜[1] 256 23.20 S 46.38 W
Juqueriquerê, Serra do ⋏ 256 23.43 S 45.37 W
Juquiá 252 24.19 S 47.38 W
Juquiá ≃ 256 23.56 S 47.09 W
Juquiá, Ponta do › 252 24.25 S 47.00 W
Juquiá-guaçu ≃ 256 24.00 S 47.16 W
Juquitiba 256 23.57 S 47.03 W
Jur 74 59.52 N 137.39 E
Jur ≃ 140 8.39 N 29.18 E
Jura □[3] 58 47.20 N 7.15 E
Jura □[5] 58 46.50 N 5.50 E
Jura ⋏ 58 46.45 N 6.30 E
Jura I 46 56.00 N 5.50 W
Jūra ≃ 76 55.03 N 22.09 E
Jura, Sound of ⊔ 46 55.57 N 5.48 W
Juramento 255 16.50 S 43.35 W
Juratiški 76 54.02 N 25.54 E
Jurayrah, Jabal al- ∧ 128 24.06 N 39.16 E
Jurays wa ʿIzbatuhā 142 30.19 N 30.55 E
Jurbarkas 76 55.05 N 22.48 E
Jurcevo 76 60.02 N 32.36 E
Juréia 256 21.17 S 46.22 W
Jurenino 76 59.24 N 42.47 E
Jurevići 78 51.57 N 29.32 E
Jurf ad-Darāwīsh 132 30.42 N 35.52 E
Jurga 86 55.42 N 84.51 E
Jurgamyš 86 55.21 N 64.28 E
Jurgenson Woods ♠ 278 41.34 N 87.36 W
Jurien 162 30.19 S 115.02 E
Juriesfontein 158 31.40 S 22.08 E
Juring 164 6.26 S 134.20 E
Jurino 80 56.18 N 46.18 E
Jurja 24 59.03 N 49.14 E
Jurjevec 80 57.18 N 43.06 E
Jurjevka, Ukr. 78 48.44 N 36.02 E
Jurjevka, Ukr. 83 48.30 N 39.00 E
Jurjev-Pol'skij 80 56.30 N 39.41 E
Jurjevskoje 82 55.05 N 36.13 E
Jurjev → Tartu 76 58.23 N 26.43 E
Jurla 86 59.17 N 54.19 E
Jurlovo, Ross. 82 55.54 N 37.16 E
Jurlovo, Ross. 82 55.19 N 35.52 E
Jūrmala 76 56.58 N 23.42 E
Jurong, Sing. 271c 1.19 N 103.43 E
Jurong, Zhg. 106 31.57 N 119.10 E
Jurong ≃ 271c 1.18 N 103.44 E
Jurong, Selat ⊔ 271c 1.18 N 103.42 E
Jurovo, Ross. 80 57.30 N 43.50 E
Jurovo, Ross. 82 55.30 N 38.22 E
Jurovo, Ukr. 78 51.22 N 27.50 E
Jurovskoje 86 59.29 N 69.02 E
Jursla 40 58.40 N 16.11 E
Jurty 88 56.03 N 97.37 E
Juruá 246 3.27 S 66.03 W
Juruá ≃ 242 2.37 S 65.44 W
Juruaia 256 21.15 S 46.35 W
Juruá-mirim ≃ 248 8.08 S 72.48 W
Juruena ≃ 248 7.20 S 58.03 W
Jurujuba, Enseada de ⊂ 287a 22.56 S 43.07 W
Jurumirim, Represa ⊜[1] 255 23.20 S 49.15 W
Jurumkuvejem ≃ 180 66.14 N 173.35 E
Jurupari ≃ 248 7.45 S 70.10 W
Jurupari, Arquipélago II 250 0.07 N 50.30 W
Jurupari, Ilha de I 250 0.20 N 50.07 W
Juruti 250 2.09 S 56.04 W
Jur'uzan' 86 54.52 N 58.26 E
Jur'uzan' ≃ 86 55.42 N 57.00 E
Jurva 26 62.41 N 21.59 E
Jušala 86 57.04 N 64.17 E
Juscelândia 255 15.20 S 51.19 W
Jusepín 246 9.45 N 63.31 W
Jushiguan 102 24.47 N 97.38 E
Jūshiyama 94 35.06 N 136.46 E
Juskatla 182 53.37 N 132.18 W
Jus'ki 80 56.39 N 53.05 E
Juškovo 76 59.46 N 45.11 E
Juškozero 24 64.44 N 32.06 E
Jūsō ◆[8] 270 34.43 N 135.28 E
Jussey 58 47.49 N 5.54 E
Justa 80 47.07 N 46.18 E
Justice 278 41.44 N 87.50 W
Justin 222 33.05 N 97.18 W
Justineberg ∧[2] 40 58.43 N 15.04 E
Justiniano Posse 252 32.53 S 62.40 W
Justo Daract 252 33.52 S 65.11 W
Justus 214 40.42 N 81.35 W
Jušut ≃ 80 56.12 N 48.23 E
Jus'va 24 58.56 N 54.57 E
Jutaí 248 5.11 S 68.54 W
Jutaí ≃ 242 2.43 S 66.57 W
Jutaza 80 54.35 N 53.16 E
Jütchendorf 264a 52.16 N 13.10 E
Jüterbog 54 51.59 N 13.04 E
Juththah, Jabal al- ∧ 132 30.12 N 35.36 E
Juti 255 22.52 S 54.37 W
Jutiapa 236 14.17 N 89.54 W
Jutiapa □[5] 236 14.10 N 89.50 W
Juticalpa 236 14.42 N 86.15 W
Jutiquile 236 14.45 N 86.08 W
Jutland → Jylland ◆[1] 26 56.00 N 9.15 E
Jutogh 123 31.06 N 77.07 E
Jutrosin 30 51.40 N 17.10 E
Juupajoki 26 61.47 N 24.27 E
Juuru 76 59.04 N 24.59 E
Juva 26 61.54 N 27.51 E
Juventud, Isla de la (Isla de Pinos) I 240p 21.40 N 82.50 W
Juvisy-sur-Orge 50 48.41 N 2.23 E
Juvuln ⊜ 26 63.43 N 13.09 E
Juwana 115a 6.42 S 111.09 E
Juwangi 115a 7.10 S 110.45 E
Juxi 100 27.30 N 119.08 E
Juxian 98 35.37 N 118.54 E
Juxing 106 31.56 N 121.33 E
Juyanhai → Gaxun Nur ⊜ 102 42.22 N 100.34 E
Juye 98 35.23 N 116.06 E
Jūyom 128 28.34 N 53.56 E
Juyongguan 105 40.18 N 116.04 E
Juža 80 56.35 N 42.01 E
Juzennecourt 58 48.11 N 4.59 E
Juzi ≃ 98 40.18 N 123.35 E
Juziers 261 49.00 N 1.51 E
Južna Morava ≃ 38 43.41 N 21.24 E
Južno-Aleksandrovka 88 55.51 N 96.10 E
Južno-Aličurskij chrebet ⋏ 120 37.30 N 73.20 E
Južno-Golodnostepskij kanal ≋ 85 40.15 N 69.08 E
Južno-Jenisejskij 86 58.48 N 94.39 E
Južno-Mujskij chrebet ⋏ 88 55.40 N 114.00 E
Južno-Sachalinsk 89 46.58 N 142.42 E
Južno-Suchokumsk 84 44.37 N 45.34 E
Južno-Ural'sk 86 54.26 N 61.15 E
Južnyj, Kaz. 86 49.21 N 73.01 E
Južnyj, Ross. 80 56.08 N 44.09 E
Južnyj, Ross. 80 47.20 N 41.51 E
Južnyj, Ross. 86 53.14 N 83.42 E
Južnyj, Ross. 86 53.33 N 60.02 E
Južnyj, mys › 74 57.45 N 156.45 E
Južnyj-Alamyšik 85 40.46 N 72.38 E
Južnyj Bug ≃ 78 46.59 N 31.58 E
Južnyj Prijut 84 43.12 N 41.55 E
Južnyj Ural ⋏ 86 54.00 N 58.30 E
Juzovka → Doneck 83 48.00 N 37.48 E
Jwālahari ◆[8] 272a 28.40 N 77.06 E
Jwayyā 132 33.14 N 35.19 E
Jyderup 41 55.40 N 11.26 E
Jylland (Jutland) ◆[1] 26 56.00 N 9.15 E
Jyllinge 41 55.45 N 12.07 E
Jyväskylä 26 62.14 N 25.44 E

K

K2 (Qogir Feng) ∧ 123 35.53 N 76.30 E
Ka ≃ 150 11.40 N 4.10 E
Kaaawa 229c 21.33 N 157.51 W
Kaabong 154 3.31 N 34.08 E
Kaachka 128 37.21 N 59.36 E
Kaala ∧ 229c 21.31 N 158.09 W
Kaalaea 229c 21.28 N 157.51 W
Kaala-Gomén 175f 20.40 S 164.25 E
Kaalspruit 158 29.15 S 26.10 E
Kaapahu Bay ⊂ 229a 20.39 N 156.05 W
Kaapmuiden 156 25.33 S 31.20 E
Kaappunt › 158 34.21 S 18.30 E
Kaapstad → Cape Town 158 33.55 S 18.22 E
Kaarli 76 59.24 N 26.27 E
Kaarssen 54 53.12 N 11.02 E
Kaarst 56 51.14 N 6.37 E
Kaaterskill Creek ≃ 210 42.13 N 73.53 W
Kaatoan, Mount ∧ 116 8.07 N 124.55 E
Kaatsheuvel 52 51.40 N 5.02 E
Kaavi 26 62.59 N 28.30 E
Kaba 150 10.09 N 11.40 W
Kaba ≃ 86 47.53 N 86.12 E
Kaba, Goulbin V 150 13.42 N 6.19 E
Kabacan 116 7.08 N 124.49 E
Kabacan ≃ 116 7.08 N 124.50 E
Kabadak 126 22.13 N 89.19 E
Kabadak ≃[1] 126 22.13 N 89.18 E
Kabadüz 130 40.53 N 37.56 E
Kabaena, Pulau I 112 5.15 S 121.55 E
Kabaena, Selat ⊔ 112 5.00 S 122.00 E
Kabah ⊥ 232 20.07 N 89.29 W
Kabala 150 9.35 N 11.33 W
Kabale 154 1.15 S 29.59 E
Kabalebo ≃ 250 5.02 N 57.21 W
Kabalega Falls ∟ 154 2.17 N 31.41 E
Kabalega Falls National Park ♠ 154 2.15 N 31.50 E
Kabali, Indon. 112 1.42 S 121.54 E
Kabalı, Tür. 130 41.52 N 35.05 E
Kabalo 154 6.03 S 26.55 E
Kabambare 154 4.42 S 27.43 E
Kaban' 86 54.39 N 66.28 E
Kabangu Kuta 154 14.00 S 24.03 E
Kabanjahe 114 3.06 N 98.30 E
Kabanje 83 49.13 N 38.12 E
Kabankalan 116 9.59 N 122.49 E
Kabanovka 80 53.39 N 51.18 E
Kabanovo 86 55.20 N 70.52 E
Kabansk 88 52.03 N 106.39 E
Kabardinka 78 44.39 N 37.57 E
Kabardino-Balkarija □[3] 84 43.30 N 43.30 E
Kabasalan 116 7.48 N 122.45 E
Kabayan 116 16.37 N 120.51 E
Kabba 150 7.50 N 6.03 E
Kabbani ≃ 122 12.13 N 76.54 E
Kåbdalis 24 66.10 N 20.00 E
Kabd aṣ-Ṣārim ◆[1] 130 34.34 N 39.33 E
Kabd Warqah ◆[1] 130 34.20 N 39.37 E
Kabel ◆[8] 263 51.24 N 7.29 E
Kabenung Lake ⊜ 190 48.16 N 85.00 W
Kabetogama Lake ⊜ 190 48.28 N 92.59 W
Kabeya 154 5.40 S 27.58 E
Kab-hegy ∧ 30 47.03 N 17.39 E
Kabia ≃ 146 9.54 N 15.10 E
Kabid, Wādī V 132 30.08 N 36.31 E
Kabinakagami Lake ⊜ 190 48.54 N 84.25 W
Kabin Buri 110 13.59 N 101.43 E
Kabinda 152 6.08 S 24.29 E
Kabinu 112 4.00 N 116.05 E
Kabir 112 8.17 S 124.13 E
Kabira 175d 24.27 N 124.08 E
Kabīr Kili 123 33.11 N 71.19 E
Kabīr Kūh ⋏ 128 33.25 N 46.45 E
Kabīrwāla 123 30.24 N 71.52 E
Kabkābīyah 140 13.39 N 24.05 E
Kablow 264a 52.18 N 13.44 E
Kablower Ziegelei 264a 52.19 N 13.43 E
Kablukovo, Ross. 82 56.50 N 36.12 E
Kablukovo, Ross. 82 56.02 N 38.10 E
Kablumgu, Cape › 164 6.20 S 150.00 E
Kabna 140 19.10 N 32.41 E
Kabo 152 7.39 N 18.37 E
Kabobo 154 5.07 S 29.03 E
Kaboe ≃ 158 28.55 S 19.17 E
Kābol 120 34.31 N 69.12 E
Kābol □[4] 120 34.30 N 69.15 E
Kābol ≃ 120 33.55 N 72.14 E
Kabompo 154 13.36 S 24.12 E
Kabompo ≃ 138 14.10 S 23.11 E
Kabondo-Dianda 154 8.53 S 25.40 E
Kabongo, Zaïre 154 7.19 S 25.35 E
Kabongo, Zaïre 154 8.43 S 28.11 E
Kabongo-Lunda, Chutes ∟ 152 7.34 S 17.17 E
Kaboro 152 6.59 N 17.33 E
Kabot 150 10.48 N 14.57 W
Kabotshome 154 3.46 S 26.54 E
Kabou, Centraf. 152 5.20 N 21.43 E
Kabou, Togo 150 9.27 N 0.49 E
Kaboudia, Rass › 148 35.14 N 11.10 E
Kaboul → Kābol 120 34.31 N 69.12 E
Kabr 140 10.54 N 26.50 E
Kabri 132 33.01 N 35.09 E
Kabūdarāhang 128 35.12 N 48.44 E
Kabūd Gonbad 128 37.00 N 59.45 E
Kābul → Kābol 120 34.30 N 69.11 E
Kabunda 154 12.25 S 29.22 E
Kabunga 154 1.42 S 28.08 E
Kabura ≃ 94 36.17 N 139.04 E
Kaburuang, Pulau I 108 3.48 N 126.48 E
Kabūshīyah 140 16.53 N 33.42 E
Kabwanga 152 7.01 S 22.37 E
Kabwe (Broken Hill) 154 14.27 S 28.27 E
Kabwe-Katanda 152 7.59 S 24.29 E
Kabyčovka 83 49.28 N 39.45 E
Kabylie ◆[1] 34 36.30 N 4.30 E
Kača 78 44.47 N 33.32 E
Kačalinskaja 80 49.07 N 44.03 E
Kačanik 38 42.13 N 21.14 E
Kačanovo 76 57.28 N 27.46 E
Kacbachskij 86 52.58 N 59.40 E
Kačerginė 76 54.56 N 23.44 E
Kacha ≃[1] 126 22.23 N 89.54 E
Kachagalau ∧ 154 2.19 N 35.03 E

Symbols in the index entries represent the broad categories identified in the key at the right. Symbols with superior numbers (⋏[1]) identify subcategories (see complete key on page *I · 1).*

Symbole im Register stellen die rechts im Schlüssel erklärten Kategorien dar. Symbole mit hochgestellten Ziffern (⋏[1]) bezeichnen Unterabteilungen einer Kategorie (vgl. vollständiger Schlüssel auf Seite *I · 1).*

Los símbolos incluídos en el texto del índice representan las grandes categorias identificadas con la clave a la derecha. Los símbolos con numeros en su parte superior (⋏[1]) identifican las subcategorías (véase la clave completa en la página *I · 1).*

Les symboles de l'index représentent les catégories indiquées dans la légende à droite. Les symboles suivis d'un indice (⋏[1]) représentent des sous-catégories (voir légende complète à la page *I · 1).*

Os símbolos incluídos no texto do índice representam as grandes categorias identificadas com a chave à direita. Os símbolos com números em sua parte superior (⋏[1]) identificam as subcategorias (veja-se a chave completa à página *I · 1).*

∧ Mountain	Berg	Montaña	Montagne	Montanha
⋏ Mountains	Gebirge	Montañas	Montagnes	Montanhas
)(Pass	Paß	Paso	Col	Passo
V Valley, Canyon	Tal, Cañon	Valle, Cañón	Vallée, Canyon	Vale, Canhão
≚ Plain	Ebene	Llano	Plaine	Planície
› Cape	Kap	Cabo	Cap	Cabo
I Island	Insel	Isla	Île	Ilha
II Islands	Inseln	Islas	Îles	Ilhas
⊥ Other Topographic Features	Andere Topographische Objekte	Otros Elementos Topográficos	Autres données topographiques	Outros acidentes topográficos

ESPAÑOL / FRANÇAIS / PORTUGUÊS

Nombre / Nom / Nome	Página / Page	Lat.°′	Long.°′ W = Oeste / W = Ouest
Kach'ang-ni	98	38.24 N	126.11 E
Kachati	84	42.30 N	41.46 E
Kachchh, Gulf of ⊂	120	22.36 N	69.30 E
Kachemak Bay ⊂	180	59.35 N	151.30 W
Kachess Lake ⊜[1]	224	47.20 N	121.14 W
Kachhwa	124	25.13 N	82.43 E
Kachi	84	41.26 N	46.56 E
Kachia	150	9.53 N	7.58 E
Kachib	84	42.25 N	46.36 E
Kachin □[3]	102	26.00 N	97.30 E
Kach'i-ri	98	34.27 N	126.08 E
Kachisi	144	9.39 N	37.50 E
Kachovka	78	46.47 N	33.30 E
Kachovskoje vodochranilišče ⊜[1]	78	47.25 N	34.10 E
Kachowka-Stausee → Kachovskoje vodochranilišče ⊜[1]	78	47.25 N	34.10 E
K'achta	88	50.26 N	106.25 E
Kachua, Bngl.	126	22.39 N	89.53 E
Kachua, Bngl.	126	23.21 N	90.54 E
Kachul	78	45.54 N	28.11 E
Kačiry	86	53.05 N	76.07 E
Kačkanar	86	58.42 N	59.38 E
Kačkanar, gora ∧	86	58.47 N	59.23 E
Kaçkar Daği ∧	130	40.50 N	41.10 E
Kačkarovka	78	47.06 N	33.44 E
Kačug	88	53.58 N	105.52 E
Kada ≃	88	55.03 N	102.04 E
Kadada ≃	80	53.09 N	46.01 E
Kadaingti	110	17.37 N	97.32 E
Kadaiyanallūr	122	9.05 N	77.21 E
Kadamatt Island I	122	11.14 N	72.47 E
Kadaň	54	50.20 N	13.15 E
Kadanai (Kadaney) ≃	120	31.02 N	66.09 E
Kadaney (Kadanai) ≃	120	31.02 N	66.09 E
Kadan Kyun I	110	12.30 N	98.22 E
Kadapongan, Pulau I	112	4.43 S	115.44 E
Kadassa ≃	115b	9.24 S	120.02 E
Kaddam ⊜[1]	122	19.07 N	78.46 E
Kade	150	6.05 N	0.50 W
Kadéï ≃	152	3.31 N	16.05 E
Kadena	174m	26.22 N	127.45 E
Kadena Airfield ✈	174m	26.22 N	127.45 E
Kadeshiki	80	58.08 N	49.11 E
Kadetrenden (Kadet Rinne) ⊔	41	54.30 N	12.15 E
Kadet Rinne (Kadetrenden) ⊔	41	54.30 N	12.15 E
Kadgo, Lake ⊜	162	26.42 S	127.18 E
Kadi	120	23.18 N	72.20 E
Kadiana	150	10.45 N	6.30 W
Kadıköy	130	40.46 N	26.46 E
Kadina	168b	33.58 S	137.43 E
Kading ≃	110	18.19 N	104.00 E
Kadınhanı	130	38.15 N	32.14 E
Kadiolo	150	10.33 N	5.46 W
Kadipaten	115a	6.46 S	108.10 E
Kādīpur	124	26.10 N	82.23 E
Kadiri	122	14.07 N	78.10 E
Kadirli	130	37.23 N	36.05 E
Kadışehri	130	40.00 N	35.49 E
Kadiyevka → Stachanov	83	48.34 N	38.40 E
Kadja, Ouadi (Wādī Kaja) V	146	12.02 N	22.28 E
Kadkan	128	35.35 N	58.50 E
Kadnikov	76	59.30 N	40.20 E
Kadnikovskij	76	60.19 N	40.15 E
Kado	150	7.39 N	9.44 E
Ka-do I	98	39.33 N	124.40 E
Kadodo	140	11.04 N	29.31 E
Kadogawa	92	32.28 N	131.39 E
Kadoka	198	43.50 N	101.30 W
Kadom	80	54.34 N	42.30 E
Kadoma, Nihon	270	34.44 N	135.35 E
Kadoma, Zimb.	154	18.21 S	29.55 E
Kadoškino	80	54.01 N	44.25 E
Kadov	60	49.24 N	13.47 E
Kaduj	76	59.12 N	37.09 E
Kadumbul ≃	115b	9.42 S	120.32 E
Kaduna	150	10.33 N	7.27 E
Kaduna □[3]	150	10.30 N	7.45 E
Kaduna ≃	150	8.45 N	5.45 E
Kāduqlī	140	11.01 N	29.43 E
Kadūr	122	13.34 N	76.01 E
Kadyj	80	57.47 N	43.11 E
Kadykčan	74	63.02 N	146.50 E
Kadyšovo	80	54.20 N	46.45 E
Kadžerom	24	64.41 N	55.54 E
Kadži-Saj	85	42.08 N	77.10 E
Kaech'ŏn	98	39.42 N	125.53 E
Kaédi	150	16.09 N	13.30 W
Kaedo-ri	98	34.35 N	127.39 E
Kaegudeck Lake ⊜	186	48.07 N	55.11 W
Kaélé	146	10.07 N	14.27 E
Kaena Point ≻	229c	21.35 N	158.17 W
Kaeo	172	35.06 S	173.47 E
Kaesŏng	98	37.59 N	126.33 E
Kāf	128	31.24 N	37.24 E
Kafakumba	152	9.41 S	23.44 E
Kafan	84	39.13 N	46.24 E
Kafanchan	150	9.36 N	8.17 E
Kaffraria □[9]	158	31.30 S	28.30 E
Kaffrine	150	14.06 N	15.33 W
Kafia Kingi	140	9.16 N	24.25 E
Kafin	150	9.30 N	7.04 E
Kafinda	154	12.39 S	30.20 E
Kafin Madaki	150	10.41 N	9.46 E
Kafirévs, Ákra ≻	38	38.09 N	24.36 E
Kafirnigan ≃	120	36.58 N	68.02 E
Kafo ≃	154	1.08 N	31.05 E
Kafr ad-Dawwār	142	31.08 N	30.07 E
Kafr ad-Difrāwī	142	31.03 N	30.40 E
Kafr al-'Ā'id	142	30.27 N	31.35 E
Kafr al-Baṭṭīkh	142	31.24 N	31.44 E
Kafr al-Jarā'idah	142	31.13 N	31.16 E
Kafr ash-Shaykh	142	31.07 N	30.56 E
Kafr ash-Shaykh □[4]	142	31.15 N	30.50 E
Kafrat Ṭā'il Mūsā	142	30.53 N	29.44 E
Kafr at-Tamīmī	142	30.37 N	31.21 E
Kafr az-Zayyāt	142	30.49 N	30.49 E
Kafr Diyamā	142	30.48 N	30.52 E
Kafr el-Zaiyat → Kafr az-Zayyāt	142	30.49 N	30.49 E
Kafr Ḥakīm	273c	30.05 N	31.07 E
Kafr Ḥūnah	132	33.29 N	35.35 E
Kafr Kanna	132	32.45 N	35.20 E
Kafr Kilā al-Bāb	142	30.41 N	31.09 E
Kafr Nabrakh	132	33.42 N	35.38 E
Kafr Naffākh	132	33.04 N	35.44 E
Kafr Nāsij	132	33.09 N	36.03 E
Kafr Rabī'	142	30.42 N	30.50 E
Kafr Sa'd	142	31.19 N	31.39 E
Kafr Salīm	142	31.09 N	30.06 E
Kafr Ṣaqr	142	30.48 N	31.37 E
Kafr Shanawān	142	30.30 N	31.01 E
Kafr Shibīn	142	30.18 N	31.18 E
Kafr Shīmā	132	33.49 N	35.32 E
Kafr Shukr	142	30.33 N	31.16 E
Kafr Sūsah	132	33.29 N	36.16 E
Kafr Takhārīm	130	36.07 N	36.31 E
Kafr Ṭarkhān al-Gharbī	142	29.29 N	31.13 E
Kafr Yasif	132	32.57 N	35.10 E
Kafue	154	15.47 S	28.11 E
Kafue ≃	154	15.56 S	28.55 E
Kafue Flats ⁂	154	15.40 S	27.25 E
Kafue Gorge V	154	15.54 S	28.34 E
Kafue National Park ♠	154	15.00 S	25.45 E
Kafulwe Mission	154	9.00 S	29.02 E
Kafumba	152	5.23 S	18.55 E
Kafwira	154	12.10 S	27.33 E
Kaga	94	36.18 N	136.18 E
Kaga Bandoro	152	6.59 N	19.11 E
Kagalaska Island I	180	51.47 N	176.23 W
Kagal'nickaja	83	46.53 N	40.09 E
Kagal'nik	83	47.05 N	39.19 E
Kagal'nik ≃	83	47.04 N	39.18 E
Kagami	96	33.37 N	133.26 E
Kagamigahara	94	35.24 N	136.54 E
Kagamil Island I	180	53.00 N	169.43 W
Kagamino	96	35.05 N	133.56 E
Kāgān, Pāk.	123	34.47 N	73.32 E
Kagan, Uzb.	128	39.43 N	64.33 E
Kagan Valley V	123	34.25 N	73.17 E
Kagarko	150	9.29 N	7.41 E
Kagarlyk	78	49.51 N	30.50 E
Kagawa	96	34.15 N	134.02 E
Kagawa □[5]	96	34.15 N	134.00 E
Kagawong, Lake ⊜	190	45.49 N	82.18 W
Kagaznagar	122	19.18 N	79.50 E
Kåge	26	64.50 N	20.59 E
Kagelike	120	37.20 N	87.02 E
Kagera (Akagera) ≃	154	0.57 S	31.47 E
Kågeröd	41	56.01 N	13.06 E
Kâgheṭ ⬥[1]	148	24.00 N	7.30 W
Kâğıthane ⬥[8]	267b	41.04 N	28.58 E
Kagitumba	154	1.04 S	30.27 E
Kağızman	84	40.09 N	43.08 E
Käglan ⋏[2]	40	59.23 N	15.31 E
Kagmar	140	14.24 N	30.25 E
Kagopal	146	8.17 N	16.27 E
Kagoshima	92	31.36 N	130.33 E
Kagoshima □[5]	93b	29.00 N	129.30 E
Kagoshima-wan ⊂	92	31.25 N	130.38 E
Kagran ⬥[8]	264b	48.15 N	16.27 E
Kagulu	154	1.15 N	33.18 E
Kagyo-ri	98	34.25 N	126.48 E
Kahalīya, Jabal ∧	142	29.55 N	32.09 E
Kahaluu	229c	21.27 N	157.50 W
Kahama	154	3.50 S	32.36 E
Kahana Bay ⊂	229c	21.34 N	157.52 W
Kahayan ≃	112	3.20 S	114.04 E
Kahe	154	3.30 S	37.26 E
Kahemba	152	7.17 S	19.00 E
Kahia	154	6.21 S	28.24 E
Kahiu Point ≻	229a	21.13 N	156.58 W
Kaḥk	142	29.25 N	30.38 E
Kahl ≃	56	50.04 N	9.00 E
Kahla	54	50.48 N	11.35 E
Kahl am Main	56	50.04 N	9.00 E
Kahlenberg ∧[2]	264b	48.16 N	16.21 E
Kahler Asten ∧	56	51.11 N	8.29 E
Kahlersberg ∧	64	47.32 N	13.02 E
Kāhna	123	31.22 N	74.22 E
Kahnūj	128	27.58 N	57.45 E
Kahoka	194	40.25 N	91.43 W
Kahoku, Nihon	96	33.39 N	133.47 E
Kahoku, Nihon	96	33.06 N	130.41 E
Kahoku-gata ⊜	94	36.40 N	136.41 E
Kahoolawe I	229a	20.33 N	156.37 W
Kahouanne, Îlet à I	241o	16.22 N	61.47 W
Kahoué, Mont ∧	150	7.06 N	7.15 W
Kahramanmaraş	130	37.36 N	36.55 E
Kahraman Maraş □[4]	130	38.00 N	37.05 E
Kahror Pakka	123	29.37 N	71.55 E
Kahshe Lake ⊜	212	44.52 N	79.16 W
Kâhta	130	37.46 N	38.36 E
Kahuku	229c	21.40 N	157.57 W
Kahuku Point ≻	229c	21.43 N	157.59 W
Kahului	229a	20.54 N	156.28 W
Kahului Airport ✈	229a	20.54 N	156.26 W
Kahului Bay ⊂	229a	20.54 N	156.28 W
Kahurangi Point ≻	172	40.47 S	172.13 E
Kahūta	123	33.35 N	73.23 E
Kahuzi-Biega, Parc National de ♠	154	1.50 N	28.40 E
Kahyŏn-bong ∧	271b	37.38 N	126.39 E
Kahyŏn-ni	271b	37.32 N	126.44 E
Kai	164	2.15 S	136.32 E
Kai, Kepulauan II	164	5.35 S	132.45 E
Kai, Tanjung ≻	112	2.52 S	118.45 E
Kaia, Wādī V	140	11.31 N	24.15 E
Kaiai, Jabal ∧	140	19.54 N	36.48 E
Kaiama	150	9.37 N	3.58 E
Kaiapit	164	6.15 S	146.15 E
Kaiapoi	172	43.23 S	172.40 E
Kaibab Indian Reservation ⬥[4]	200	36.55 N	112.40 W
Kaibab Plateau ⋏[1]	200	36.30 N	112.15 W
Kaibara	96	35.08 N	135.05 E
Kai Beab	164	7.29 S	139.40 E
Kaibing	61	47.12 N	15.50 E
Kaibito Plateau ⋏[1]	200	36.40 N	111.20 W
Kaichengqiao	100	31.18 N	117.44 E
Kaida	94	35.56 N	137.36 E
Kaidori	268	35.37 N	139.27 E
Kaidu ≃	90	41.55 N	86.38 E
Kaiedin	140	9.45 N	32.11 E
Kaieteur Fall ⌞	246	5.10 N	59.28 W
Kaieteur National Park ♠	246	5.10 N	59.45 W
Kaifeng	98	34.51 N	114.21 E
Kaifu	96	33.35 N	134.21 E
Kaifu ≃	96	33.35 N	134.22 E
Kaihe	98	35.42 N	116.20 E
Kaihu	172	35.46 S	173.42 E
Kaihua	100	29.09 N	118.23 E
Kai Iwi	172	39.51 S	174.56 E
Kaijian	102	23.42 N	111.48 E
Kaijiang	102	31.05 N	107.55 E
Kaijo → Kaesŏng	98	37.59 N	126.33 E
Kai Kecil I	164	5.45 S	132.40 E
Kaikohe	172	35.25 S	173.48 E
Kaikoura	172	42.25 S	173.41 E
Kaikoura Peninsula ≻[1]	172	42.26 S	173.42 E
Kaikukang	89	53.07 N	124.46 E
Kailahun	150	8.17 N	10.34 W
Kailāshahar	120	24.20 N	92.01 E
Kailas → Kangrinboqê Feng ∧	120	31.04 N	81.18 E
Kaili	102	26.35 N	107.55 E
Kailu	89	43.36 N	121.14 E
Kailua	229c	21.24 N	157.44 W
Kailua Bay ⊂	229c	21.25 N	157.44 W
Kailua Kona	229d	19.22 N	155.59 W
Kaim ≃	164	6.40 S	141.45 E
Kaimai Range ⋏	172	37.45 S	175.55 E
Kaïmaktsalán ∧	38	40.58 N	21.48 E
Kaimana	164	3.39 S	133.45 E
Kaimanawa Mountains ⋏	172	39.15 S	175.54 E
Kaiman-Inseln → Cayman Islands □[2]	238	19.30 N	80.40 W
Kaimenshan	104	41.03 N	123.08 E
Kaimganj	124	27.34 N	79.21 E
Kaimon-dake ∧	92	31.11 N	130.32 E
Kain	50	50.38 N	3.22 E
Käina	76	58.50 N	22.45 E
Kainab ≃	158	28.31 S	19.35 E
Kainach ≃	61	46.54 N	15.31 E
Kainan, Nihon	96	33.36 N	134.22 E
Kainan, Nihon	96	34.09 N	135.12 E
Kainantu	164	6.15 S	145.55 E
Kainda	85	42.50 N	73.41 E
Kai-Ndunda	152	5.42 S	12.42 E
Kaingan ≃	115a	7.44 S	107.54 E
Kainji Lake ⊜[1]	150	10.30 N	4.35 E
Kaioba	112	5.20 S	122.37 E
Kaipara Harbour ⊂	172	36.25 S	174.13 E
Kaiparowits Plateau ⋏[1]	200	37.20 N	111.15 W
Kaiping, Zhg.	102	22.23 N	112.35 E
Kaiping, Zhg.	105	39.41 N	118.16 E
Kaipuri, Pulau I	164	1.51 S	137.01 E
Kairābani	126	24.08 N	87.02 E
Kairaku-en ♠	94	36.22 N	140.27 E
Kairāna	124	29.24 N	77.12 E
Kairatu	164	3.21 S	128.22 E
Kairiru Island I	164	3.20 S	143.35 E
Kairo → Al-Qāhirah	142	30.03 N	31.15 E
Kairouan	148	35.41 N	10.07 E
Kairouan □[8]	148	35.30 N	9.55 E
Kairuku	164	8.50 S	146.35 E
Kairy	78	46.57 N	33.43 E
Kaisarganj	124	27.15 N	81.33 E
Kaisariani	267c	37.58 N	23.47 E
Kaisariani Monastery ʊ[1]	267c	37.58 N	23.47 E
Kaisergebirge ⋏	64	47.36 N	12.20 E
Kaisermühlen ⬥[8]	264b	48.14 N	16.26 E
Kaiser Pass)(	226	37.17 N	119.06 W
Kaisersesch	56	50.14 N	7.08 E
Kaiserslautern	56	49.26 N	7.46 E
Kaiserstuhl ⋏[2]	58	48.06 N	7.40 E
Kaiserswerth ⬥[8]	263	51.18 N	6.44 E
Kaiser-Wilhelm-Museum ʊ	263	51.20 N	6.34 E
Kaishantun	98	42.43 N	129.43 E
Kaisheim	56	48.46 N	10.48 E
Kaišiadorys	76	54.52 N	24.27 E
Kait, Tanjung ≻	112	3.14 S	106.05 E
Kaita	96	34.20 N	132.32 E
Kaitaia	172	35.07 S	173.16 E
Kaitaichi-chūtonchi, Rikujō-jieitai- ■	96	34.21 N	132.32 E
Kai Tak Airport ✈	271d	22.20 N	114.12 E
Kaitangata	172	46.18 S	169.51 E
Kaitersberg ⋏	60	49.11 N	12.57 E
Kaithal	124	29.48 N	76.23 E
Kaituma ≃	246	8.11 N	59.41 W
Kaiwaka	172	36.10 S	174.27 E
Kaiwatu	164	8.07 S	127.49 E
Kaiwi Channel ⊔	229b	21.15 N	157.30 W
Kaixian	102	31.13 N	108.25 E
Kaiyang	102	26.58 N	106.40 E
Kaiyuan, Zhg.	102	23.44 N	103.11 E
Kaiyuan, Zhg.	104	42.32 N	124.01 E
Kaiyuancheng	98	42.37 N	124.04 E
Kaiyuh Mountains ⋏	180	64.00 N	158.00 W
Kaizhou	104	41.22 N	121.19 E
Kaizu	94	35.13 N	136.38 E
Kaizuka	96	34.27 N	135.21 E
Kaja, Wādī (Ouadi Kadja) V	146	12.02 N	22.28 E
Kajaani	26	64.14 N	27.41 E
Kajabbi	166	20.02 S	140.02 E
Kajakī, Band-e ⊜[1]	128	32.22 N	65.16 E
Kajang, Indon.	112	5.20 S	120.21 E
Kajang, Malay.	114	2.59 N	101.47 E
Kajang, Gunong ∧	114	2.46 N	104.09 E
Kajasan	86	55.12 N	62.16 E
Kajasula	84	44.19 N	44.59 E
Kajen	115a	7.02 S	109.34 E
Kajgy	86	50.55 N	64.43 E
Kajiado	154	1.51 S	36.47 E
Kajikazawa	94	35.33 N	138.27 E
Kajiki	92	31.44 N	130.40 E
Kājlāgarh	126	22.02 N	87.47 E
Kajmanačicha	86	53.32 N	75.11 E
Kajmonovo	88	56.50 N	104.54 E
Kajmysovy	86	59.48 N	76.31 E
Kajnar	86	49.12 N	77.25 E
Kajo Kaji	154	3.53 N	31.40 E
Kajrakkum	85	40.16 N	69.49 E
Kajrakkumskoje vodochranilišce ⊜[1]	85	40.20 N	70.10 E
Kajrakty	86	48.31 N	73.14 E
Kajsackoje	80	49.44 N	46.51 E
Kājū ≃	128	25.34 N	61.13 E
Kājulia	126	23.01 N	89.57 E
Kajuru	150	10.21 N	7.40 E
Kaka, Centraf.	140	6.01 N	26.30 E
Kākā, Sūd.	140	10.36 N	32.11 E
Kaka, Lae o ≻	229a	20.31 N	156.33 W
Kakabeka Falls ⌞	190	48.24 N	89.37 W
Kakabia, Pulau I	112	6.54 S	122.13 E
Kakadu National Park ♠	164	13.00 S	132.45 E
Kakagi Lake ⊜	184	49.13 N	93.52 W
Kakamas	158	28.45 S	20.33 E
Kakamega	154	0.17 N	34.45 E
Kakamigahara	94	35.24 N	136.54 E
Kakana	110	9.07 N	92.49 E
Kakanui Mountains ⋏	172	45.09 S	170.26 E
Kaka Point	172	46.23 S	169.47 E
Kakaramea	172	39.43 S	174.27 E
Kakasa	164	9.20 S	148.45 E
Kakata	150	6.35 N	10.19 W
Kakatahi	172	39.41 S	175.20 E
Kākdwīp	126	21.53 N	88.11 E
Kake, Nihon	96	34.36 N	132.19 E
Kake, Ak., U.S.	180	56.58 N	133.56 W
Kakegawa	94	34.46 N	138.01 E
Kakehashi ≃	94	36.25 N	136.25 E
Kakelwe	154	4.49 S	29.00 E
Kakenge	152	4.51 S	21.55 E
Kakeya	96	35.11 N	132.49 E
Kakhonak	180	59.26 N	154.51 W
Kakhra	126	21.38 N	87.27 E
Kākī	128	28.19 N	51.34 E
Kākināda	122	16.56 N	82.13 E
Kakino	80	55.12 N	44.53 E
Kakinoki	96	34.26 N	131.52 E
Kakisa Lake ⊜	176	60.55 N	117.40 W
Kakizaki	92	37.15 N	138.25 E
Kako ≃, Guy.	246	5.46 N	60.35 W
Kako ≃, Nihon	96	34.44 N	134.49 E
Kakoaka	156	18.40 S	24.22 E
Kakogawa	96	34.46 N	134.51 E
Kakrāla	272a	28.33 N	77.25 E
Kāksa	126	23.28 N	87.28 E
Kaktovik	180	70.08 N	143.37 W
Kakuda	92	37.58 N	140.47 E
Kakui-shima I	96	34.43 N	134.19 E
Kakuma	154	3.43 N	34.52 E
Kakunodate	92	39.35 N	140.34 E
Kakus ≃	112	2.46 N	113.01 E
Kakwa ≃	182	54.36 N	118.28 W
Kala	146	12.05 N	14.27 E
Kala ≃	122	8.18 N	79.50 E
Kalaa Kebira	148	35.52 N	10.32 E
Kalaallit Nunaat → Greenland □[2]	16	70.00 N	40.00 W
Kalaa Sghira	36	35.49 N	10.33 E
Kālābāgh	123	32.58 N	71.34 E
Kalabahi	112	8.13 S	124.31 E
Kalabáka	38	39.42 N	21.43 E
Kalabakan	112	4.25 N	117.29 E
Kalabo	152	14.57 S	22.40 E
Kalabula	86	43.24 N	83.06 E
Kalač	78	50.25 N	41.01 E
Kalačinsk	86	55.03 N	74.34 E
Kalač-Kurtlak	80	49.00 N	42.26 E
Kalač-na-Donu	80	48.43 N	43.31 E
Kalačskaja vozvyšennost' ⋏[1]	80	50.30 N	41.30 E
Kaladan ≃	110	20.09 N	92.57 E
Kaladar	212	44.39 N	77.07 W
Kalae	229a	21.10 N	157.00 W
Ka Lae ≻	229d	18.55 N	155.41 W
Kalaena ≃	112	2.40 S	120.53 E
Kalagan	89	50.30 N	119.55 E
Kalagwe	110	22.31 N	96.31 E
Kalahari Desert ⬥[2]	156	24.00 S	21.30 E
Kalahari Gemsbok National Park ♠	156	25.30 S	20.30 E
Kalaheo	229b	21.55 N	159.31 W
Kālaia	126	22.23 N	90.36 E
Kalai-Chumb	85	38.28 N	70.46 E
Kalai-Mor	128	35.39 N	62.33 E
Kalais	80	52.38 N	42.38 E
Kalaiyā	124	27.02 N	85.00 E
Kalajka	88	58.28 N	111.46 E
Kalajoki	26	64.15 N	23.57 E
Kalajoki ≃	26	64.17 N	23.55 E
Kalakamate	156	20.39 S	27.21 E
Kalakan	88	55.08 N	116.45 E
Kalakan ≃	88	55.07 N	116.46 E
Kalakepen	114	2.45 N	97.50 E
Kalām	123	35.32 N	72.35 E
Kalama, Wa., U.S.	224	46.00 N	122.50 W
Kalama, Zaïre	154	2.55 S	28.33 E
Kalama ≃	224	46.02 N	122.52 W
Kalama, Pulau I	112	3.15 N	125.28 E
Kalámai	38	37.04 N	22.07 E
Kalamákion	267c	37.55 N	23.43 E
Kalamalka Lake ⊜	182	50.09 N	119.22 W
Kalamariá	38	40.35 N	22.58 E
Kalamazoo	216	42.17 N	85.35 W
Kalamazoo □[6]	216	42.14 N	85.32 W
Kalamazoo ≃	216	42.40 N	86.10 W
Kalamazoo, North Branch ≃	216	42.14 N	84.44 W
Kalamazoo, South Branch ≃	216	42.14 N	84.44 W
Kalamazoo Lake ⊂	216	42.39 N	86.13 W
Kalamb	122	19.03 N	73.57 E
Kalamba	152	0.26 S	18.17 E
Kalambau, Pulau I	112	4.55 S	115.39 E
Kalambo Falls ⌞	154	8.36 S	31.14 E
Kalamboli	272c	19.01 N	73.06 E
Kalamitskij zaliv ⊂	78	45.05 N	33.23 E
Kalamo	216	42.32 N	85.01 W
Kalampáka	38	39.42 N	21.39 E
Kalampising	112	3.44 N	116.42 E
Kalamunda	168a	31.57 S	116.03 E
Kalamunda National Park ♠	168a	31.59 S	116.04 E
Kalana	150	10.47 N	8.12 W
Kalančak	78	46.16 N	33.17 E
Kalandula	152	9.06 S	15.57 E
Kalange-Bushimaie ≃	152	7.55 S	23.11 E
Kalanguj	88	51.01 N	116.31 E
Kalankalan	150	10.07 N	8.54 W
Kalannie	162	30.21 S	117.04 E
Kalanshiyū ar-Ramlī al-Kabīr, Sarīr ⋄[8]	146	28.00 N	23.00 E
Kālānwāli	123	29.51 N	74.57 E
Kalao, Pulau I	112	7.18 S	120.58 E
Kalaong	116	6.04 N	124.28 E
Kalaotoa, Pulau I	112	7.22 S	121.47 E
Kalapana	229d	19.21 N	154.58 W
Kalāpāra	126	21.59 N	90.14 E
Kalar ≃	88	55.23 N	116.18 E
Kalar, Kūh-e ∧	128	31.50 N	50.53 E
Kalaraš	78	47.16 N	28.19 E
Kälarne	26	62.59 N	16.05 E
Kālāroa	126	22.52 N	89.02 E
Kalasarv	84	39.11 N	48.03 E
Kalasi	86	48.43 N	86.59 E
Kalasin, Indon.	112	0.12 N	114.16 E
Kalasin, Thai	110	16.29 N	103.30 E
Kalašnikovo	76	57.17 N	35.13 E
Kalāt	120	29.02 N	66.35 E
Kalatungan Mountain ∧	116	7.58 N	124.47 E
Kalaupapa	229a	21.11 N	156.59 W
Kalaupapa National Historical Park ♠	229a	21.12 N	156.58 W
Kalaupapa Peninsula ≻[1]	229a	21.13 N	156.58 W
Kalauri	84	41.49 N	45.42 E
Kalaus ≃	80	45.43 N	44.07 E
Kalaus-Kr'akovka	83	48.46 N	38.52 E
Kalavárdha	38	36.20 N	27.57 E
Kalávrita	38	38.01 N	22.06 E
Kalaw	110	20.38 N	96.34 E
Kalawao □[6]	229a	21.12 N	156.58 W
Kal'azin	76	57.15 N	37.52 E
Kalb, Nahr al- ≃	132	33.57 N	35.35 E
Kalb, Ra's al- ≻	144	14.02 N	48.41 E
Kalbā'	128	25.03 N	56.21 E
Kalbar	171a	27.56 S	152.37 E
Kalbarri	162	27.42 S	114.09 E
Kalbarri National Park ♠	162	27.45 S	114.25 E
Kalbe	54	52.40 N	11.25 E
Kalbinskij chrebet ⋏	86	49.10 N	83.00 E
Kalchās	120	29.21 N	69.42 E
Kal'čik ≃	83	47.07 N	37.36 E
Kaldırım ≃	267b	41.10 N	29.12 E
Kaldygajty ≃	80	49.20 N	52.38 E
Kale, Tür.	130	36.14 N	29.59 E
Kale, Tür.	130	40.23 N	39.39 E
Kale, Tür.	130	37.26 N	28.51 E
Kalecik, Tür.	130	40.06 N	33.25 E
Kalecik, Tür.	130	37.17 N	39.02 E
Kaleden	182	49.23 N	119.35 W
Kaledupa, Pulau I	112	5.32 S	123.47 E
Kalegauk Island I	110	15.32 N	97.40 E
Kalehe	154	2.06 S	28.55 E
Kaleindaung ≃	110	18.50 N	94.00 E
Kalema, Tan.	154	1.12 S	31.50 E
Kalema, Zaïre	152	4.08 S	24.15 E
Kalemie (Albertville)	154	5.56 S	29.12 E
Kalemyo	120	23.12 N	94.10 E
Kalene Hill	152	11.11 S	24.10 E
Kaleščatovka	83	49.35 N	39.55 E
Kaletwa	110	21.45 N	92.48 E
Kalety	30	50.34 N	18.54 E
Kalevala	24	65.13 N	31.08 E
Kalewa	110	23.12 N	94.17 E
Kale Water ≃	46	55.32 N	2.28 W
Kaleybar	128	38.47 N	47.02 E
Kálfafell	24a	63.58 N	17.40 W
Kalga	88	50.57 N	118.48 E
Kalgačicha	24	63.20 N	36.44 E
Kalgan	162	34.53 S	118.01 E
Kalgan → Zhangjiakou	105	40.50 N	114.53 E
Kalgin Island I	180	60.28 N	151.55 W
Kalgoorlie	162	30.45 S	121.28 E
Kalhe	272c	18.52 N	73.06 E
Kali	150	12.10 N	11.29 W
Kāli ≃[1]	126	23.40 N	89.12 E
Kālia	126	23.03 N	89.38 E
Kāliāganj	124	25.38 N	88.19 E
Kāliāghaj ≃	126	22.10 N	87.50 E
Kāliākair	126	24.05 N	90.14 E
Kaliakra, nos ≻	38	43.21 N	28.27 E
Kalianda	115a	5.45 S	105.38 E
Kalianget	115a	7.03 S	113.56 E
Kalibek, ozero ⊜	86	53.52 N	70.40 E
Kālībhīt Hills ⋏[2]	124	22.10 N	77.30 E
Kalibo	116	11.43 N	122.22 E
Kalida	216	40.59 N	84.12 W
Kalifornien, Golf von → California, Golfo de ⊂	232	28.00 N	112.00 W
Kālī Gaṇḍakī ≃	124	27.42 N	84.25 E
Kāliganga ≃	126	23.43 N	90.15 E
Kālīganj, Bngl.	126	23.25 N	89.08 E
Kālīganj, Bngl.	126	23.55 N	90.34 E
Kālīganj, Bngl.	126	22.28 N	89.02 E
Kāliganj, India	126	23.44 N	88.14 E
Kalihiwai ≃	229b	22.13 N	159.26 W
Kalijati	115a	6.32 S	107.40 E
Kālikāpur, Bngl.	126	22.43 N	89.26 E
Kālikāpur, Bngl.	126	23.46 N	89.55 E
Kālikāpur, India	126	22.37 N	86.17 E
Kālikāpur, India	272b	22.29 N	88.32 E
Kalikino, Ross.	76	52.57 N	39.50 E
Kalikino, Ross.	80	52.55 N	54.05 E
Kalima, Zaïre	154	2.34 S	26.37 E
Kalima, Zhg.	104	41.32 N	122.40 E
Kalimantan Barat □[4]	112	0.30 N	110.00 E
Kalimantan → Borneo I	112	0.30 N	114.00 E
Kalimantan Selatan □[4]	112	2.30 S	115.30 E
Kalimantan Tengah □[4]	112	2.00 S	113.30 E
Kalimantan Timur □[4]	112	1.30 N	116.30 E
Kálimnos	38	36.57 N	26.59 E
Kálimnos I	38	37.00 N	27.00 E
Kālimpang	124	27.04 N	88.29 E
Kalina, Pointe de ≻	273b	4.18 S	15.16 E
Kālīnadi ≃	122	14.50 N	74.08 E
Kālinagar	126	22.26 N	88.51 E
Kalinga-Apayao □[4]	116	17.50 N	121.10 E
Kalinga Bil ⊜	272b	22.33 N	88.33 E
Kalinin	80	47.11 N	42.10 E
Kalininabad	85	39.45 N	69.08 E
Kaliningrad (Königsberg), Ross.	76	54.43 N	20.30 E
Kaliningrad, Ross.	82	55.55 N	37.49 E
Kaliningrad Oblast' □[4]	76	54.45 N	21.15 E
Kalinino, Ross.	78	45.07 N	39.00 E
Kalinino, Ross.	80	46.21 N	48.53 E
Kalinino, Ross.	86	57.20 N	56.20 E
Kalinino, Ross.	89	49.24 N	129.20 E
Kalinino, Ukr.	83	47.27 N	37.28 E
Kalininsk, Kyrg.	85	42.29 N	72.06 E
Kalininsk, Ross.	80	51.30 N	44.28 E
Kalininskaja, Ross.	78	45.29 N	38.40 E
Kalininskaja, Ross.	80	47.52 N	42.15 E
Kalininskij	83	48.01 N	39.36 E
Kalininskoje, Kyrg.	85	42.50 N	73.49 E
Kalininskoje, Ukr.	78	47.07 N	32.59 E
Kalinin → Tver'	82	56.52 N	35.55 E
Kalinkoviči	76	52.08 N	29.21 E
Kalinku	154	11.12 S	33.12 E
Kalinovik	38	43.31 N	18.26 E
Kalinovka, Kaz.	86	49.58 N	55.22 E
Kalinovka, Ross.	78	51.54 N	34.28 E
Kalinovka, Ukr.	78	50.14 N	30.14 E
Kalinovka, Ukr.	78	49.27 N	28.32 E
Kalinovo, Ross.	82	54.54 N	37.17 E
Kalinovo, Ukr.	83	48.34 N	38.31 E
Kālipur	272b	22.41 N	88.17 E
Kaliro	154	0.54 N	33.30 E
Kalis	144	8.23 N	49.05 E
Kalisat	115a	8.08 S	113.48 E
Kalisch → Kalisz	30	51.46 N	18.06 E
Kāli Sindh ≃	124	25.32 N	76.17 E
Kalispell	202	48.11 N	114.18 W
Kalistraticha	86	52.59 N	83.35 E
Kalisz	30	51.46 N	18.06 E
Kalisz □[4]	30	51.40 N	17.45 E
Kalisz Pomorski	30	53.19 N	15.54 E
Kalitva ≃	78	48.10 N	40.46 E
Kaliua	154	5.04 S	31.48 E
Kaliveli Tank ⊜[1]	122	12.05 N	79.50 E
Kaliwiro	115a	7.27 S	109.51 E
Kaliwungu	115a	6.57 S	110.14 E
Kalix	26	65.51 N	23.08 E
Kalixälven ≃	24	65.50 N	23.11 E
Kālka	123	30.50 N	76.56 E
Kālkāji ⬥[8]	272a	28.33 N	77.16 E
Kalkaman	86	51.58 N	76.02 E
Kalkan	130	36.15 N	29.24 E
Kalkar	52	51.44 N	6.18 E
Kalkaska	190	44.44 N	85.10 W
Kalkfeld	156	20.53 S	16.11 E
Kalkfontein	156	22.08 S	20.53 E
Kalkfonteindam ⊜[1]	158	29.30 S	25.15 E
Kalkhorst	54	53.58 N	11.02 E
Kalkım	130	39.48 N	27.13 E
Kālkini	126	23.06 N	90.16 E
Kalkmond	158	28.40 S	20.26 E
Kalkrand	156	24.03 S	17.33 E
Kalksburg ⬥[8]	264b	48.08 N	16.15 E
Kalk-See ⊜	264a	52.26 N	13.46 E
Kalkstasie	158	30.00 S	18.55 E
Kalkum ⬥[8]	263	51.18 N	6.46 E
Kalkutta → Calcutta	126	22.32 N	88.22 E
Kalkwerf	158	28.39 S	21.43 E
Kall	56	50.32 N	6.32 E
Kallakkurichchi	122	11.44 N	78.58 E
Kallakoopah Creek ≃	166	27.29 S	138.15 E
Kållandsö I	26	58.40 N	13.09 E
Kallang ≃	271c	1.19 N	103.52 E
Kallar Kahār	123	32.47 N	72.42 E
Kallaste	76	58.39 N	27.09 E
Kallavesi ⊜	26	62.50 N	27.45 E
Kalletal	52	52.06 N	8.56 E
Källfallet	40	59.50 N	15.31 E
Kallhäll	40	59.27 N	17.48 E
Kalliecahoolie Lake ⊜	184	54.14 N	95.29 W
Kallinge	26	56.14 N	15.17 E
Kallista	274b	37.53 S	145.22 E
Kallithéa	267c	37.57 N	23.42 E
Kallmünz	60	49.09 N	11.58 E
Kallnach	58	47.01 N	7.14 E
Kallsjön ⊜	26	63.37 N	13.00 E
Kalmakkora	86	44.03 N	78.44 E
Kalmakkyrgan ≃	86	46.58 N	64.30 E
Kalmar	26	56.40 N	16.22 E
Kalmar Län □[6]	26	57.20 N	16.00 E
Kalmarsund ⊔	26	56.40 N	16.25 E
Kalmit ∧	56	49.19 N	8.05 E
Kal'mius ≃	83	47.05 N	37.34 E
Kalmthout	50	51.23 N	4.28 E
Kalmyckije Mysy	86	51.53 N	82.16 E
Kalmykia → Kalmykija □[3]	72	46.30 N	45.30 E
Kalmykija □[3]	72	46.30 N	45.30 E
Kalmykov	80	49.01 N	42.49 E
Kalmykovka, Ukr.	83	49.17 N	38.39 E
Kalmykovka, Ukr.	83	49.17 N	39.52 E
Kalmykovo	80	49.03 N	51.47 E
Kālna	126	23.13 N	88.22 E
Kalnciems	76	56.50 N	23.37 E
Kal'niboloto	78	48.44 N	31.00 E
Kalnibolotskaja	78	46.01 N	40.28 E
Kalničko Gorje ⋏	36	46.10 N	16.30 E
Kalo	164	10.00 S	147.45 E
Kálócfa	61	46.45 N	16.34 E
Kalocsa	30	46.32 N	18.59 E
Kalofer	38	42.37 N	24.59 E
Kalohi Channel ⊔	229a	21.00 N	156.56 W
Kaloko	154	6.47 S	25.48 E
Kalol, India	120	22.36 N	73.27 E
Kālol, India	120	23.15 N	72.29 E
Kalole	154	3.42 S	27.22 E
Kalolio	112	0.11 S	121.38 E
Kaloli Point ≻	229d	19.38 N	154.57 W
Kalomo	154	17.02 S	26.30 E
Kalomo ≃	154	17.57 S	26.24 E
Kalona	190	41.28 N	91.42 W
Kalonda	152	4.48 S	17.33 E
Kalone Peak ∧	182	52.38 N	126.37 W
Kalonga	154	9.10 S	27.25 E
Kalorama	274b	37.49 S	145.22 E
Kaloran	115a	7.15 S	110.15 E
Kalø Vig ⊂	41	56.15 N	10.25 E
Kalpáki	38	39.55 N	20.20 E
Kalpeni Island I	122	10.05 N	73.38 E
Kālpi	124	26.07 N	79.44 E
Kāl Qal'eh	128	32.38 N	62.32 E
Kalri	123	31.39 N	72.33 E
Kalsdorf bei Graz	61	46.57 N	15.28 E
Kalskag	180	61.30 N	160.23 W
Kalsūbai ∧	122	19.36 N	73.43 E
Kaltag	180	64.20 N	158.44 W
Kaltan	86	53.30 N	87.17 E
Kaltbrunn	58	47.12 N	9.02 E
Kalte Herberge ∧	56	50.03 N	7.59 E
Kalteneber	56	51.19 N	10.08 E
Kaltenhouse	56	48.48 N	7.50 E
Kaltenkirchen	52	53.50 N	9.58 E
Kaltenleutgeben	264b	48.07 N	16.12 E
Kaltennordheim	56	50.38 N	10.10 E
Kaltensundheim	56	50.36 N	10.10 E
Kalter Gang ≃	264b	48.02 N	16.25 E
Kalthof	263	51.26 N	7.40 E
Kal'tino	265a	59.58 N	30.40 E
Kaltungo	146	9.50 N	11.19 E
Kaluga	82	54.31 N	36.16 E
Kaluga Oblast' □[4]	76	54.30 N	35.30 E
Kalugino, Kaz.	80	48.22 N	51.33 E
Kalugino, Ross.	82	54.59 N	37.11 E
Kalukalukuang, Pulau I	112	5.14 S	117.38 E
Kālu Khuhar	120	25.08 N	67.46 E
Kalulushi	154	12.50 S	28.03 E
Kalumba, Mount ∧	166	31.49 S	146.22 E
Kalumburu	164	14.18 S	126.39 E
Kalumburu Aboriginal Reserve ⬥[4]	164	14.15 S	126.50 E
Kalundborg	41	55.41 N	11.06 E
Kalundborg Fjord ⊂	41	55.41 N	11.00 E
Kālundri	272c	18.59 N	73.08 E
Kalundu, Zaïre	154	3.26 S	29.08 E
Kalundu, Zam.	154	10.16 S	29.24 E
Kalungwishi ≃	154	9.01 S	28.57 E
Kalūr Kot	123	32.09 N	71.16 E
Kaluš	78	49.03 N	24.23 E
Kałuszyn	30	52.13 N	21.49 E
Kalutara	122	6.35 N	79.58 E
Kalvåg	26	61.46 N	4.53 E
Kalvarija	76	54.21 N	23.14 E
K'alvaz	84	38.39 N	48.18 E
Kalvehave	41	55.00 N	12.10 E
Kälviä	26	63.52 N	23.26 E
Kalwa	272c	19.12 N	72.59 E
Kalwang	61	47.26 N	14.46 E
Kalwaria Zebrzydowska	30	49.52 N	19.41 E
Kalyān	122	19.15 N	73.09 E
Kalyāndurg	122	14.33 N	77.06 E
Kam ≃	146	8.15 N	11.00 E
Kama, Mya.	110	19.02 N	95.06 E
Kama, Ross.	80	56.19 N	54.06 E
Kama, Ross.	86	60.08 N	62.10 E
Kama, Zaïre	154	3.32 S	27.07 E
Kama ≃, Ross.	72	55.45 N	52.00 E
Kama ≃, Ross.	86	55.35 N	76.54 E
Kamachumu	154	1.35 S	31.37 E
Kamado-zaki ≻	96	33.04 N	132.02 E
Kamae	92	32.48 N	131.56 E
Kamagaya	94	35.45 N	140.01 E
Kamaiki Point ≻	229a	20.46 N	156.50 W
Kamaishi	92	39.16 N	141.53 E
Kama-iwa I	174f	24.47 N	141.17 E
Kamajai	76	55.49 N	25.30 E
Kamakou ∧	229a	21.07 N	156.52 W
Kamakura	94	35.19 N	139.33 E
Kamakwie	150	9.30 N	12.14 W
Kamal	115a	7.10 S	112.42 E
Kamālia	123	30.44 N	72.39 E
Kamamaung	110	17.21 N	97.40 E
Kāman, India	124	27.39 N	77.16 E
Kaman, Tür.	130	39.22 N	33.44 E
Kaman ≃	110	14.48 N	106.51 E
Kamana	154	5.59 S	24.56 E
Kamanashi ≃	94	35.33 N	138.28 E
Kamango	154	0.39 N	29.53 E
Kamaniskeg Lake ⊜	212	45.25 N	77.42 W
Kamanjab	156	19.35 S	14.51 E
Kamapanda	152	12.00 S	24.10 E
Kamara Forest ♠	264c	47.26 N	19.00 E
Kamarān I	144	15.21 N	42.35 E
Kamaran, Hadjer ∧	146	12.41 N	21.46 E
Kamarang ≃	246	5.53 N	60.35 W
Kāmāreddi	122	18.19 N	78.21 E
Kāmārhāti	272b	22.40 N	88.22 E
Kamarik	130	39.37 N	39.18 E
Kāmārkhāli Ghāt	126	23.32 N	89.33 E
Kāmārkunda	272b	22.49 N	88.13 E
Kamas	200	40.38 N	111.16 W
Kamata ⬥[8]	268	35.33 N	139.43 E
Kamatsi Lake ⊜	184	56.10 N	102.15 W
Kamay	196	33.51 N	98.48 W
Kamba	150	11.53 N	3.36 E
Kamba Kota	152	7.10 N	17.54 E
Kambalda	162	31.12 S	121.40 E
Kambam	122	9.44 N	77.18 E
Kambang	112	1.42 S	100.42 E
Kambanga	152	13.23 S	23.03 E
Kambar	120	27.36 N	68.00 E
Kambara	94	35.07 N	138.36 E
Kambara Island I	175g	18.57 S	178.57 W
Kambara-tunnel ⬥[5]	94	35.02 N	138.31 E
Kambarka	80	56.17 N	54.12 E
Kambia	150	9.07 N	12.55 W
Kambja	76	58.14 N	26.42 E
Kambolé	150	8.45 N	1.36 E
Kambole Mission	154	8.46 S	30.46 E
Kambove	154	10.52 S	26.38 E
Kambu	115b	8.23 S	118.20 E
Kambuye	152	7.18 S	22.50 E
Kamčatka ≃	74	56.15 N	162.30 E
Kamčatka, poluostrov (Kamchatka) ≻[1]	74	56.00 N	160.00 E
Kamčatskij poluostrov ≻[1]	74	56.15 N	163.00 E
Kamčatskij zaliv ⊂	74	55.35 N	162.21 E
Kamchatka → Kamčatka, poluostrov ≻[1]	74	56.00 N	160.00 E
Kâmchay Méa	110	11.35 N	105.40 E
Kamčija ≃	38	43.02 N	27.53 E
Kāmdebpur, India	272b	22.47 N	88.30 E
Kāmdebpur, India	272b	22.54 N	88.20 E
Kāmdeysh	123	35.24 N	71.20 E
Kameari ⬥[8]	268	35.46 N	139.51 E
Kameda	92	37.52 N	139.07 E
Kameel	158	26.38 S	24.58 E
Kamegamori ∧	96	33.47 N	133.12 E
Kameido ⬥[8]	268	35.42 N	139.50 E
Kamelik ≃	80	52.06 N	49.30 E
Kamen', Bela.	76	55.01 N	28.53 E
Kamen, Dtsch.	52	51.35 N	7.40 E
Kamen', gora ∧	74	69.06 N	94.48 E
Kamenda	154	6.28 S	24.33 E
Kamenec	76	52.24 N	23.49 E
Kamenec-Podol'skij	78	48.41 N	26.36 E
Kameng ≃	120	26.38 N	92.54 E
Kamenický Šenov	54	50.45 N	14.29 E
Kamenjak, Rt ≻	36	44.46 N	13.55 E
Kamenka, Kaz.	80	51.07 N	50.19 E
Kamenka, Kaz.	85	42.55 N	72.50 E
Kamenka, Kaz.	86	52.22 N	69.04 E
Kamenka, Mol.	78	48.03 N	28.42 E
Kamenka, Ross.	24	65.54 N	44.05 E
Kamenka, Ross.	78	50.43 N	39.25 E
Kamenka, Ross.	80	56.11 N	45.35 E
Kamenka, Ross.	80	57.23 N	41.49 E
Kamenka, Ross.	80	53.13 N	44.03 E
Kamenka, Ross.	80	52.04 N	41.49 E
Kamenka, Ross.	82	54.43 N	38.19 E
Kamenka, Ross.	82	56.11 N	37.18 E
Kamenka, Ross.	82	55.13 N	36.59 E
Kamenka, Ross.	86	58.33 N	95.51 E
Kamenka, Ross.	89	44.28 N	136.01 E
Kamenka, Ross.	265a	59.59 N	30.53 E
Kamenka, Ukr.	78	49.02 N	32.06 E
Kamenka, Ukr.	83	49.38 N	39.22 E
Kamenka, Ukr.	83	49.07 N	37.18 E
Kamenka, Ukr.	83	47.25 N	37.42 E
Kamenka ⬥[8]	265a	60.03 N	30.11 E
Kamenka ≃, Ross.	83	47.30 N	38.54 E
Kamenka ≃, Ross.	88	58.33 N	95.51 E
Kamenka ≃, Ross.	265a	60.01 N	30.12 E
Kamenka ≃, Ukr.	78	49.47 N	30.01 E
Kamenka ≃, Ukr.	78	47.39 N	34.02 E
Kamenka ≃, Ukr.	83	49.35 N	39.05 E
Kamenka-Bugskaja	78	50.07 N	24.20 E
Kamenka-Dneprovskaja	78	47.29 N	34.25 E
Kamen'-Kaširskij	78	51.38 N	24.58 E
Kamen'-na-Obi	86	53.47 N	81.20 E
Kamennogorsk	24	60.58 N	29.07 E
Kamennoje, Ukr.	78	51.31 N	27.38 E
Kamennoje, Ukr.	78	47.53 N	35.25 E
Kamennomostskij	84	44.18 N	40.12 E
Kamennye Mogily, zapovednik ♠	78	47.18 N	37.04 E
Kamennyj Brod, Ross.	83	47.26 N	39.51 E
Kamennyj Brod, Ukr.	78	50.25 N	27.49 E
Kamennyj Jar	80	48.27 N	45.34 E
Kamenolomni	83	47.40 N	40.13 E
Kamen'-Rybolov	89	44.46 N	132.02 E
Kamensk	88	51.58 N	106.36 E
Kamenskij	80	50.53 N	45.29 E
Kamenskoje, Ross.	74	62.30 N	166.12 E

Symbol	English	Deutsch	Español	Français	Português
≃	River	Fluß	Río	Rivière	Rio
≍	Canal	Kanal	Canal	Canal	Canal
⌞	Waterfall, Rapids	Wasserfall, Stromschnellen	Cascada, Rápidos	Chute d'eau, Rapides	Cascata, Rápidos
⊔	Strait	Meeresstraße	Estrecho	Détroit	Estreito
⊂	Bay, Gulf	Bucht, Golf	Bahía, Golfo	Baie, Golfe	Baía, Golfo
⊜	Lake, Lakes	See, Seen	Lago, Lagos	Lac, Lacs	Lago, Lagos
⁂	Swamp	Sumpf	Pantano	Marais	Pântano
⌂	Ice Features, Glacier	Eis- und Gletscherformen	Accidentes Glaciales	Formes glaciaires	Acidentes glaciares
⊤	Other Hydrographic Features	Andere Hydrographische Objekte	Otros Elementos Hidrográficos	Autres données hydrographiques	Outros acidentes hidrográficos

Symbol	English	Deutsch	Español	Français	Português
✤	Submarine Features	Untermeerische Objekte	Accidentes Submarinos	Formes de relief sous-marin	Acidentes submarinos
□	Political Unit	Politische Einheit	Unidad Politica	Entité politique	Unidade política
ʊ	Cultural Institution	Kulturelle Institution	Institución Cultural	Institution culturelle	Instituição cultural
⊥	Historical Site	Historische Stätte	Sitio Histórico	Site historique	Sitio histórico
♠	Recreational Site	Erholungs- und Ferienort	Sitio de Recreo	Centre de loisirs	Área de Lazer
✈	Airport	Flughafen	Aeropuerto	Aéroport	Aeroporto
■	Military Installation	Militäranlage	Instalación Militar	Installation militaire	Instalação militar
⬥	Miscellaneous	Verschiedenes	Misceláneo	Divers	Diversos

ENGLISH: Name | Page | Lat.°′ | Long.°′ — DEUTSCH: Name | Seite | Breite°′ | Länge°′ E = Ost

Kamenskoje, Ross. 82 55.16 N 36.50 E
Kamenskoje, Ukr. 78 45.49 N 29.16 E
Kamensk-Šachtinskij 83 48.21 N 40.19 E
Kamensk-Ural'skij 86 56.28 N 61.54 E
Kamenz 54 51.16 N 14.06 E
Kameoka 96 35.00 N 135.35 E
Kamerik 52 52.06 N 4.54 E
Kamerunberg → Cameroon Mountain ∧ 152 4.12 N 9.11 E
Kamerun → Cameroon □1 134 6.00 N 12.00 E
Kames 46 55.54 N 5.15 W
Kameškovo 80 56.21 N 41.00 E
Kāmet ∧ 120 30.54 N 79.37 E
Kameur, Bahr ≃ 146 9.26 N 20.50 E
Kameyama 94 34.51 N 136.27 E
Kami, Nihon 94 34.41 N 137.42 E
Kami, Nihon 96 35.05 N 134.53 E
Kamiah 202 46.13 N 116.01 W
Kamiak Butte ∧ 202 46.52 N 117.10 W
Kamiakotani 270 34.56 N 135.23 E
Kamiasō 268 35.35 N 139.30 E
Kamień Krajeński 30 53.33 N 17.32 E
Kamienna ≃ 30 51.06 N 21.47 E
Kamienna Góra 30 50.47 N 16.01 E
Kamień Pomorski 30 53.58 N 14.46 E
Kamieńsk 30 51.12 N 19.30 E
Kamieskroon 156 30.09 S 17.56 E
Kamifukuoka 94 35.52 N 139.32 E
Kamigōri 96 34.52 N 134.22 E
Kamigyō ◆8 270 35.02 N 135.45 E
Kamiichi 94 36.42 N 137.22 E
Kamiishihara 268 35.39 N 139.32 E
Kamiiso 92a 41.49 N 140.39 E
Kamiita 96 34.07 N 134.24 E
Kami-jima I 94 34.33 N 136.59 E
Kamikamagari-jima I 96 34.11 N 132.44 E
Kamikatsu 96 33.53 N 134.24 E
Kamikawa, Nihon 92a 43.51 N 142.46 E
Kamikawa, Nihon 94 36.13 N 139.07 E
Kamikitazawa ◆8 268 35.40 N 139.38 E
Kamikume 270 34.55 N 135.03 E
Kâmil 130 41.07 N 34.47 E
Kamilukuak Lake ⊜ 176 62.22 N 101.40 W
Kamimaki 270 34.34 N 135.43 E
Kamimizo 268 35.33 N 139.22 E
Kamina 154 8.44 S 25.00 E
Kaminaka, Nihon 94 35.28 N 135.51 E
Kaminaka, Nihon 96 33.48 N 134.22 E
Kaminak Lake ⊜ 176 62.10 N 95.00 W
Kaminaljuyú ⊥ 236 14.38 N 90.33 W
Kaminoho 94 35.37 N 137.03 E
Kaminokawa 94 36.26 N 139.55 E
Kaminokuni 92a 41.48 N 140.06 E
Kaminoseki 96 33.49 N 132.07 E
Kaminoyama 92 38.09 N 140.17 E
Kaminskij 80 57.10 N 41.28 E
Kaminuriak Lake ⊜ 176 63.00 N 95.40 W
Kamioka 94 36.16 N 137.18 E
Kamiotawa 270 34.54 N 135.31 E
Kamioyamada 268 35.35 N 139.24 E
Kámiros ⊥ 38 36.19 N 27.57 E
Kamisato 94 36.15 N 139.09 E
Kamishak Bay ⊂ 180 59.15 N 153.45 W
Kamishii 94 36.04 N 136.24 E
Kamishinden 270 34.49 N 135.30 E
Kamisunagawa 92a 43.30 N 142.00 E
Kamitaira 94 36.24 N 136.54 E
Kamitakara 94 36.17 N 137.22 E
Kamitakino 270 34.57 N 134.59 E
Kamitomi 268 35.49 N 139.31 E
Kamitonda 96 33.43 N 135.27 E
Kamitsuruma 268 35.31 N 139.25 E
Kamitsushima 92 34.50 N 129.28 E
Kamituga 154 3.04 S 28.11 E
Kamiura 96 33.03 N 131.55 E
Kamiyahagi 94 35.18 N 137.29 E
Kamiyama 96 33.58 N 134.23 E
Kamiyamada 94 36.28 N 138.09 E
Kamiyama-jima I 174m 26.15 N 127.35 E
Kamiyugi 268 35.37 N 139.23 E
Kamīzgān 84 38.58 N 47.44 E
Kamkhat Muḩaywir ∧2 132 31.08 N 36.30 E
Kamku 120 27.30 N 96.30 E
Kamla (Kamlā) ≃ 124 25.37 N 86.40 E
Kamlach ≃ 58 48.30 N 10.22 E
Kamloops 182 50.40 N 120.20 W
Kamloops Indian Reserve ◆4 182 50.42 N 120.20 W
Kamloops Lake ⊜ 182 50.43 N 120.33 W
Kammon-kaikyō ꓤ 96 33.56 N 130.56 E
Kammon-kyō ◆5 96 33.56 N 130.55 E
Kammuri-yama ∧ 96 34.28 N 132.05 E
Kamnik 36 46.13 N 14.37 E
Kamniokan 88 56.17 N 111.57 E
Kamo, Haya. 84 40.22 N 45.08 E
Kamo, N.Z. 172 35.41 S 174.19 E
Kamo, Nihon 92 37.39 N 139.03 E
Kamo, Nihon 94 34.50 N 138.46 E
Kamo, Nihon 96 34.45 N 135.52 E
Kamo, Nihon 96 35.10 N 134.04 E
Kamo, Nihon 96 35.20 N 132.55 E
Kamo, Nihon 270 34.55 N 135.13 E
Kamo ≃, Nihon 94 35.06 N 140.06 E
Kamo ≃, Nihon 96 33.56 N 133.09 E
Kamo ≃, Nihon 270 34.56 N 135.44 E
Kamoa Mountains ⋏ 246 1.37 N 59.00 W
Kamoda-misaki › 96 33.50 N 134.45 E
Kamogata 96 34.32 N 133.35 E
Kamogawa, Nihon 94 35.06 N 140.06 E
Kamogawa, Nihon 96 34.51 N 133.49 E
Kamohio Bay ⊂ 229a 20.31 N 156.36 W
Kamojima 96 34.04 N 134.21 E
Kāmoke 123 31.58 N 74.13 E
Kamoshida ◆8 268 35.34 N 139.30 E
Kamoto 96 33.00 N 130.45 E
Kamp 56 50.14 N 7.37 E
Kamp ≃ 61 48.23 N 15.48 E
Kāmpa 272b 22.56 N 88.28 E
Kampala 154 0.19 N 32.25 E
Kampar 114 4.18 N 101.09 E
Kampar ≃ 112 0.32 N 103.08 E
Kamparkalns ∧2 76 57.18 N 22.47 E
Kampar Kanan ≃ 112 0.16 N 101.41 E
Kampen 52 52.33 N 5.54 E
Kampene 154 3.36 S 26.40 E
Kampfe, Lake ⊜ 276 41.02 N 74.21 W
Kamphaeng, Khao ∧ 110 14.37 N 99.18 E
Kamphaeng Phet 110 16.28 N 99.30 E
Kampil 124 27.37 N 79.17 E
Kampinoski Park Narodowy ♦ 30 52.20 N 20.35 E
Kampire Dior ∧ 123 36.38 N 74.23 E
Kamp-Lintfort 52 51.30 N 6.31 E
Kamp'o 98 35.48 N 129.29 E
Kampolombo, Lake ⊜ 154 11.37 S 29.42 E
Kampong Ayer Puteh 114 4.16 N 103.12 E
Kampong Baharu 114 3.43 N 103.17 E
Kampong Benta 114 3.32 N 103.22 E
Kampong Buloh 114 5.32 N 102.45 E
Kâmpóng Cham 110 12.00 N 105.27 E
Kampong Chenor 114 3.29 N 102.36 E
Kâmpóng Chhnăng 110 12.15 N 104.40 E
Kampong Dong 114 3.54 N 101.54 E
Kampong Guchil 114 5.33 N 102.14 E
Kampong Jabor 114 3.57 N 103.20 E
Kampong Jerangau 114 4.51 N 103.12 E
Kampong Kandang 114 2.11 N 102.18 E
Kâmpóng Kântuŏt 110 11.26 N 104.49 E
Kampong Kenyam 114 4.31 N 102.28 E
Kampong Kuala Kemaman 114 4.14 N 103.27 E
Kampong Lamir 114 3.36 N 103.21 E
Kampong Lawa 114 5.40 N 101.42 E
Kampong Mengkarak 114 3.19 N 102.27 E
Kampong Merang 114 5.32 N 102.57 E
Kampong Nuri 114 5.02 N 102.23 E
Kampong Penarek 114 5.37 N 102.48 E
Kampong Raja 114 5.48 N 102.35 E
Kampong Renggong 114 4.33 N 102.35 E
Kâmpóng Saôm 110 10.38 N 103.30 E
Kâmpóng Saôm, Chhâk ⊂ 110 10.50 N 103.32 E
Kampong Sebuyau 112 1.31 N 110.56 E
Kampong Sekendi 114 3.43 N 100.56 E
Kampong Surau 114 5.49 N 100.54 E
Kampong Tanjong Batu 114 3.12 N 103.27 E
Kampong Tebing Runtoh 271c 1.26 N 103.40 E
Kâmpóng Thum 110 12.42 N 104.54 E
Kâmpóng Trâlach 110 11.54 N 104.47 E
Kampong Ulu 110 10.03 N 98.33 E
Kampong Ulu Chalok 114 5.26 N 102.50 E
Kâmpôt 110 10.37 N 104.11 E
Kampsville 194 39.18 N 90.37 W
Kampti 150 10.08 N 3.27 W
Kâmpŭchéa → Cambodia □1 110 13.00 N 105.00 E
Kampung ≃ 164 5.44 S 138.24 E
Kampungbaru 112 1.12 S 102.57 E
Kampville 219 38.51 N 90.33 W
Kāmrānga 126 23.14 N 90.47 E
Kamrau, Teluk ⊂ 164 3.32 S 133.37 E
Kamsack 184 51.34 N 101.54 W
Kamsdorf 54 50.38 N 11.28 E
Kamskij 24 60.04 N 53.13 E
Kamskoje Ustje 80 55.13 N 49.16 E
Kamskoje vodochranilišče ⊜1 86 58.52 N 56.15 E
Kamslybas, ozero ⊜ 86 46.12 N 61.48 E
Kamsu-ri 98 38.03 N 125.54 E
Kamsuuma 144 0.15 N 42.47 E
Kāmthi 120 21.14 N 79.12 E
Kam Tin 271d 22.27 N 114.03 E
Kamuchawie Lake ⊜ 184 56.18 N 101.59 W
Kamudilo 154 7.42 S 27.18 E
Kamuela (Waimea) 229d 20.01 N 155.48 W
Kamui-misaki › 92a 43.20 N 140.21 E
Kámuk, Cerro ∧ 236 9.17 N 83.04 W
Kamuli 154 0.57 N 33.07 E
Kamundan ≃ 164 2.17 S 132.39 E
Kamutambaie ≃ 152 7.17 S 23.41 E
Kamwandu 152 6.04 S 22.42 E
Kamyšet 88 55.12 N 98.42 E
Kamyšev, Ross. 80 46.39 N 42.38 E
Kamyšev, Ross. 80 46.53 N 42.31 E
Kamyševacha, Ukr. 78 47.43 N 35.32 E
Kamyševacha, Ukr. 83 48.42 N 38.23 E
Kamyševatskaja 78 46.25 N 37.57 E
Kamyševskaja 80 47.37 N 41.49 E
Kamyšin 80 50.06 N 45.24 E
Kamyškurgon 85 40.34 N 70.24 E
Kamyšla 80 54.07 N 52.10 E
Kamyšlov 86 56.52 N 62.43 E
Kamyslybas 86 46.11 N 61.57 E
Kamyšnaja ≃ 83 48.55 N 39.55 E
Kamyšnoje 86 51.58 N 61.47 E
Kamyšovyj 80 46.26 N 45.12 E
Kamyš-Samarskich Ozer, razlivy ≋ 80 48.50 N 50.50 E
Kamyz'ak 80 46.07 N 48.05 E
Kamyz'ak ≃ 80 46.00 N 48.06 E
Kan, Īrān 128 35.45 N 51.16 E
Kan, Sūd. 140 9.01 N 31.47 E
Kan ≃ 86 56.31 N 93.47 E
Kana ≃ 154 18.30 S 27.22 E
Kanaaupscow ≃ 176 53.39 N 77.09 W
Kanab 200 37.02 N 112.31 W
Kanab Creek ≃ 200 36.24 N 112.38 W
Kanab Plateau ⋏1 200 36.40 N 112.45 W
Kanada 96 33.41 N 130.47 E
Kanada → Canada □1 176 60.00 N 95.00 W
Kanadej 80 53.10 N 47.30 E
Kanae 94 35.30 N 137.49 E
Kanafis 140 9.48 N 25.40 E
Kanaga Island I 180 51.45 N 177.10 W
Kanaga Volcano ∧1 180 51.50 N 177.09 W
Kanagawa □5 94 35.30 N 139.30 E
Kanagawa ◆8 268 35.28 N 139.38 E
Kanagi 96 34.53 N 132.11 E
Kanai 268 35.35 N 139.28 E
Kānāipur 126 23.33 N 89.47 E
Kanairiktok ≃ 176 55.05 N 60.20 W
Kanā'is, Ra's al- › 140 31.15 N 27.51 E
Kanajevka, Ross. 80 53.07 N 45.35 E
Kanajevka, Ross. 80 52.12 N 49.40 E
Kanaka Creek ≃ 226 39.25 N 120.57 W
Kanakapura 122 12.33 N 77.25 E
Kanakeswar 126 23.09 N 90.25 E
Kanákia I 267c 37.55 N 23.24 E
Kanākir 132 33.15 N 36.05 E
Kanal 64 46.05 N 13.38 E
Kanal-Inseln → Channel Islands II 28 49.20 N 2.20 W
Kanam 164 3.25 S 152.10 E
Kanamachi ◆8 268 35.46 N 139.53 E
Kanamori 268 35.32 N 139.28 E
Kanan 270 34.29 N 135.38 E
Kananaskis ≃ 182 51.05 N 115.03 W
Kananga (Luluabourg) 152 5.54 S 22.25 E
Kananggar 115b 10.03 S 120.22 E
Kanangra-Boyd National Park ♦ 170 34.00 S 150.06 E
Kananikol'skoje 86 52.47 N 57.29 E
Kanaoka 270 34.33 N 135.32 E
Kanapou Bay ⊂ 229a 20.33 N 156.33 W
Kanarase-yama ∧ 96 33.26 N 131.15 E
Kanarraville 200 37.32 N 113.10 W
Kanaš 80 55.31 N 47.30 E
Kanasagō 94 36.33 N 140.28 E
Kanata 212 45.19 N 75.54 W
Kanaudi 124 23.36 N 81.23 E
Kanava, Ross. 24 61.07 N 54.58 E
Kanava, Ross. 80 47.13 N 45.24 E
Kanavka 80 50.19 N 48.33 E
Kanawha 190 42.56 N 93.47 W
Kanawha ≃ 188 38.50 N 82.08 W
Kanaya, Nihon 94 34.49 N 138.08 E
Kanaya, Nihon 96 34.04 N 135.15 E
Kanaya, Nihon 268 35.10 N 139.50 E
Kanayama 94 35.39 N 137.09 E
Kanazawa 94 36.34 N 136.39 E
Kanazawa ◆8 268 35.20 N 139.38 E
Kanazu 94 36.13 N 136.14 E
Kanbalu 110 23.12 N 95.31 E
Kanbauk 110 14.36 N 98.02 E
Kančalan ≃ 180 65.08 N 176.25 E
Kanchanaburi 110 14.01 N 99.32 E
Kanchanadit 110 9.10 N 99.28 E
Kānchenjunga (Kañchanjanggā) ∧ 124 27.42 N 88.08 E
Kānchipuram 122 12.50 N 79.43 E
Kanchow → Ganzhou 100 25.54 N 114.55 E
Kānchrāpāra 126 22.57 N 88.28 E
Kańczuga 30 49.59 N 22.24 E
Kanda 96 33.47 N 130.59 E
Kanda ◆8 268 35.42 N 139.46 E
Kandabulak 80 53.58 N 50.44 E
Kandāghāt 123 30.59 N 77.07 E
Kandahar 184 51.46 N 104.21 W
Kandāhu 120 27.33 N 69.24 E
Kanda-Kanda 152 6.56 S 23.36 E
Kandala 152 6.02 S 19.24 E
Kandalakša 24 67.09 N 32.21 E
Kandalakšskaja guba ⊂ 24 66.55 N 32.45 E
Kandalakšskij zapovednik ♦ 24 68.50 N 37.30 E
Kandang 114 3.03 N 97.20 E
Kandangan 112 2.47 S 115.16 E
Kandanghaur 115a 6.21 S 108.06 E
Kandat 86 57.08 N 89.02 E
Kandava 76 57.05 N 22.49 E
Kandavu Island I 175g 19.03 S 178.13 E
Kandavu Passage ꓤ 175g 18.45 S 178.00 E
Kandé 150 9.57 N 1.03 E
Kandel 56 49.05 N 8.11 E
Kandel ∧ 58 48.04 N 8.01 E
Kander ≃ 58 46.43 N 7.38 E
Kandern 58 47.43 N 7.40 E
Kandersteg 58 46.30 N 7.40 E
Kandhkot 120 28.14 N 69.11 E
Kāndhla 124 29.19 N 77.16 E
Kandi, Bénin 150 11.08 N 2.56 E
Kandi, India 126 23.57 N 88.02 E
Kandi, Tanjung › 112 1.19 N 121.28 E
Kandia ≃ 123 35.28 N 73.18 E
Kandiāro 120 27.04 N 68.13 E
Kandik ≃ 180 65.24 N 142.34 W
Kandilli ◆8 267b 41.04 N 29.03 E
Kandıra 130 41.04 N 30.09 E
Kandivli ◆8 272c 19.12 N 72.51 E
Kandla 120 23.02 N 70.14 E
Kando ≃ 96 35.22 N 132.40 E
Kandor, Ouadi V 146 17.13 N 20.52 E
Kandos 170 32.52 S 149.58 E
Kāndra 126 23.44 N 87.58 E
Kandrāch 120 25.29 N 65.29 E
Kandreho 157b 17.29 S 46.06 E
Kandrian 164 6.15 S 149.35 E
Kandry 80 54.34 N 54.07 E
Kandufuri I 122 7.05 N 72.48 E
Kandute I 122 6.20 N 72.57 E
Kandy 122 7.18 N 80.38 E
Kane, Il., U.S. 219 39.11 N 90.21 W
Kane, Pa., U.S. 214 41.39 N 78.48 W
Kane □6 216 41.53 N 88.18 W
Kaneda 268 35.28 N 139.22 E
Kaneilio Point › 229c 21.27 N 158.12 W
Kanektok ≃ 180 59.45 N 161.55 W
Kanem □5 146 15.00 N 16.00 E
Kanemi 116 6.55 N 123.58 E
Kaneohe 229c 21.25 N 157.48 W
Kaneohe Bay ⊂ 229c 21.28 N 157.49 W
Kaneohe Bay Marine Corps Air Station ■ 229c 21.27 N 157.46 W
Kaneville 216 41.50 N 88.31 W
Kanevskaja 78 46.05 N 38.57 E
Kaneyama 94 35.28 N 137.06 E
Kanfanar 64 45.07 N 13.51 E
Kang 156 23.41 S 22.50 E
Kangaba 150 11.56 N 8.25 W
Kangal 130 39.15 N 37.24 E
Kangalassy 74 62.23 N 129.59 E
Kangān 128 27.50 N 52.03 E
Kānganheri ◆8 272a 28.33 N 76.59 E
Kanganpur 123 30.46 N 74.08 E
Kangar 114 6.26 N 100.12 E
Kangaré 150 11.35 N 8.10 W
Kangarilla 168b 35.09 S 138.40 E
Kangaroo ≃ 170 34.46 S 150.18 E
Kangaroo Creek Reservoir ⊜1 168b 34.52 S 138.46 E
Kangaroo Flat 168b 34.33 S 138.40 E
Kangaroo Ground 274b 37.41 S 145.13 E
Kangaroo Island I 166 35.50 S 137.06 E
Kangaroo Valley 170 34.44 S 150.32 E
Kangasala 26 61.28 N 24.05 E
Kangasniemi 26 61.59 N 26.38 E
Kangāvar 128 34.30 N 47.58 E
Kangaz 78 46.07 N 28.33 E
Kangbao 98 41.53 N 114.40 E
Kangding 102 30.03 N 102.02 E
Kangdong 98 39.09 N 126.05 E
Kangdu 100 27.00 N 116.36 E
Kangean, Kepulauan II 112 6.55 S 115.30 E
Kangean, Pulau I 112 6.54 S 115.20 E
Kangen ≃ 140 6.47 N 33.09 E
Kanggezhuang 105 40.26 N 116.44 E
Kanggup'o 98 41.07 N 127.31 E
Kanggye 98 40.58 N 126.34 E
Kanggyŏng 98 36.10 N 127.00 E
Kanghwa 98 37.45 N 126.30 E
Kanghwa-do I 98 37.40 N 126.27 E
Kanghwa-man ⊂ 98 37.20 N 126.35 E
Kangil 88 52.15 N 116.20 E
Kangiqsualujjuaq 176 58.41 N 65.57 W
Kangiqsujuaq 176 61.36 N 71.58 W
Kangirsuk 176 60.01 N 70.01 W
Kangjin 98 34.39 N 126.45 E
Kangjinjing 89 46.12 N 126.48 E
Kangkar Lenggor 114 2.16 N 103.44 E
Kangkar Teberau 114 1.32 N 103.45 E
Kangley 216 41.09 N 88.53 W
Kangly 85 40.07 N 67.54 E
Kangmaer 124 30.45 N 85.34 E
Kangmar 120 28.34 N 89.51 E
Kangnam ◆8 271b 37.30 N 127.01 E
Kangnam-sanmaek ⋏ 98 40.30 N 125.30 E
Kangnichumike 120 33.10 N 80.59 E
Kangnŭng 98 37.45 N 128.54 E
Kango 152 0.09 N 10.08 E
Kangoku-iwa I 174f 24.48 N 141.17 E
Kangombe 152 14.03 S 23.40 E
Kangongo 152 17.57 S 21.02 E
Kangowa 152 9.55 S 22.48 E
Kangping 98 42.44 N 123.21 E
Kāngpokpi 120 25.08 N 93.58 E
Kangpu 102 27.43 N 99.00 E
Kāngra 123 32.06 N 76.16 E
Kangrinboqê Feng ∧ 120 31.29 N 80.45 E
Kangshan 100 22.48 N 120.17 E
Kangsŏ 98 38.58 N 125.26 E
Kangsŏ-ri 98 38.06 N 126.58 E
Kangto ∧ 120 27.52 N 92.30 E
Kangtuyingzi 104 41.47 N 121.31 E
Känguruh-Insel → Kangaroo Island I 166 35.50 S 137.06 E
Kangwŏn Do □4, C.M.I.K. 98 38.45 N 127.35 E
Kangwŏn Do □4, Taehan 98 37.45 N 128.15 E
Kangxianzhuang 105 39.06 N 116.27 E
Kangyidaung 110 16.56 N 94.54 E
Kangzhuang 105 40.23 N 115.53 E
Kanhar ≃ 124 24.28 N 83.08 E
Kanheri Caves ⊥5 272c 19.13 N 72.52 E
Kanholmsfjärden ꓤ 40 59.20 N 18.47 E
Kanhsien → Ganzhou 100 25.54 N 114.55 E
Kani, C. Iv. 150 8.29 N 6.36 W
Kani, Mya. 110 22.26 N 94.50 E
Kani, Nihon 94 35.22 N 137.04 E
Kaniama 152 7.31 S 24.11 E
Kaniamba 154 7.27 S 26.57 E
Kanibadam 85 40.17 N 70.25 E
Kanie 94 35.08 N 136.48 E
Kaniepa 154 9.00 S 27.21 E
Kaniere 172 42.45 S 171.00 E
Kaniere, Lake ⊜ 172 42.50 S 171.09 E
Kaniet Islands II 164 0.53 S 145.30 E
Kanifay 174q 9.32 N 138.06 E
Kanigiri 122 15.24 N 79.31 E
Kanihāula ◆8 272a 28.44 N 77.01 E
Kanin 54 52.17 N 12.50 E
Kanin, poluostrov ›1 24 68.00 N 45.00 E
Kanina 124 28.20 N 76.19 E
Kaningo 154 0.49 S 38.32 E
Kanin-Kamen' ∧ 24 68.18 N 45.00 E
Kanin Nos 24 68.39 N 43.14 E
Kanin Nos, mys › 24 68.39 N 43.16 E
Kaniva 166 36.23 S 141.15 E
Kanjiža 38 46.04 N 20.04 E
Kānjur ◆8 272c 19.08 N 72.56 E
Kanjut Sār ∧ 123 36.14 N 75.22 E
Kankaanpää 26 61.48 N 22.25 E
Kankakee 216 41.07 N 87.51 W
Kankakee □6 216 41.07 N 87.52 W
Kankakee ≃ 216 41.23 N 88.16 W
Kankakee River State Park ♦ 216 41.12 N 87.59 W
Kankan 150 10.23 N 9.18 W
Kankar ◆8 272a 28.46 N 77.06 E
Kankéla 150 10.50 N 6.40 W
Kānker 122 20.17 N 81.29 E
Kankō → Hamhŭng 98 39.54 N 127.32 E
Kankossa 150 15.56 N 11.31 W
Kankunskij 74 57.37 N 126.08 E
Kanlıavşar 130 37.13 N 38.16 E
Kanlıca ◆8 267b 41.06 N 29.04 E
Kanmaw Kyun I 110 11.40 N 98.28 E
Kanmen 100 28.06 N 121.16 E
Kanmuri-jima I 96 35.41 N 135.25 E
Kanmuri-yama ∧ 92 34.28 N 132.05 E
Kanna ≃ 94 36.17 N 139.09 E
Kannabe 96 34.32 N 133.23 E
Kannabi-san ∧2 270 34.48 N 135.44 E
Kannack 110 14.07 N 108.37 E
Kannad 122 20.16 N 75.08 E
Kanna-kō ⊂ 174m 26.28 N 127.58 E
Kannami 94 35.05 N 138.57 E
Kannapolis 192 35.29 N 80.37 W
Kannauj 124 27.04 N 79.55 E
Kanniyākumari 122 8.05 N 77.34 E
Kannod 124 22.40 N 76.44 E
Kannonkoski 26 62.58 N 25.15 E
Kannon-zaki › 268 35.15 N 139.45 E
Kannose ≃ 96 34.54 N 132.49 E
Kannus 26 63.54 N 23.54 E
Kano, Nig. 150 12.00 N 8.30 E
Kano, Nihon 96 34.14 N 131.49 E
Kano □3 150 11.45 N 9.00 E
Kano ≃, Nig. 150 11.50 N 8.31 E
Kano ≃, Nihon 94 35.05 N 138.52 E
Kanona 210 42.22 N 77.22 W
Kanoneiland 158 28.39 S 21.05 E
Kanonerskij, ostrov I 265a 59.54 N 30.13 E
Kanonji 96 34.07 N 133.39 E
Kanopolis 198 38.42 N 98.09 W
Kanopolis Lake ⊜1 198 38.38 N 98.00 W
Kanorado 198 39.19 N 102.02 W
Kanosh 200 38.48 N 112.26 W
Kanouse Brook ≃ 276 41.02 N 74.26 W
Kanouse Mountain ∧ 276 41.04 N 74.25 W
Kan'ov 78 49.44 N 31.28 E
Kan'ovka 24 67.08 N 39.40 E
Kanovlei 156 19.10 S 19.23 E
Kan'ovskoje vodochranilišče ⊜1 78 50.00 N 31.20 E
Kanowit 112 2.06 N 112.09 E
Kanoya 92 31.23 N 130.51 E
Kanō-zan ∧2 268 35.15 N 139.57 E
Kanpetlet 110 21.12 N 94.02 E
Kanpoli 272c 19.04 N 73.09 E
Kānpur 124 26.28 N 80.21 E
Kanra 94 36.13 N 138.55 E
Kansa ≃ 94 34.55 N 137.34 E
Kansaj 85 40.30 N 69.41 E
Kansanshi 154 12.05 S 26.26 E
Kānsāripāra 272b 22.56 N 88.14 E
Kansas, Il., U.S. 194 39.33 N 87.56 W
Kansas, Oh., U.S. 214 41.14 N 83.17 W
Kansas □3, U.S. 178 38.45 N 98.15 W
Kansas □3, U.S. 198 38.45 N 98.15 W
Kansas ≃ 198 39.07 N 94.36 W
Kansas City, Ks., U.S. 198 39.06 N 94.37 W
Kansas City, Mo., U.S. 194 39.05 N 94.34 W
Kansau 110 23.50 N 93.35 E
Kansei Gakuin University ⊍2 270 34.46 N 135.21 E
Kansei University ⊍2 270 34.46 N 135.31 E
Kansenia 154 10.19 S 26.02 E
Kanshan 106 30.12 N 120.25 E
Kanshi 100 24.56 N 116.54 E
Kansk 86 56.13 N 95.41 E
Kansŏng 98 38.22 N 128.29 E
Kansu 85 39.45 N 75.02 E
Kansu → Gansu □4 102 37.00 N 103.00 E
Kansyat 164 2.15 S 138.51 E
Kant 85 42.55 N 74.55 E
Kantabrisches Gebirge → Cantábrica, Cordillera ⋏ 34 43.00 N 5.00 W
Kantalvi 272c 18.54 N 73.03 E
Kantang 110 7.25 N 99.31 E
Kāntāphor 124 22.35 N 76.34 E
Kantchari 150 12.29 N 1.31 E
Kantché 150 13.33 N 8.28 E
Kantemirovka, Kaz. 85 42.51 N 70.20 E
Kantemirovka, Ross. 83 49.41 N 39.51 E
Kānth 124 29.04 N 78.38 E
Kantharalak 110 14.39 N 104.39 E
Kānthi Coastal Plain ≚ 126 21.45 N 87.45 E
Kantishna ≃ 180 64.45 N 149.58 W
Kantner 214 40.06 N 78.56 W
Kantō-heiya ≚ 94 36.00 N 139.30 E
Kanton (Canton) I 174h 2.50 S 171.40 W
Kanton → Guangzhou 100 23.06 N 113.16 E
Kantorp 40 59.01 N 16.28 E
Kantō-sanchi ⋏, Nihon 92 35.50 N 138.50 E
Kantō-sanchi ⋏, Nihon 94 35.59 N 138.43 E
Kantuanji 100 32.59 N 116.19 E
Kantubek 86 45.07 N 59.16 E
Kantu-long 110 19.57 N 97.36 E
Kantunilkín 232 21.06 N 87.29 W
Kanturk 48 52.10 N 8.55 W
Kanuku Mountains ⋏ 246 3.12 N 59.30 W
Kanuma 94 36.33 N 139.44 E
Kanus 156 27.54 S 18.40 E
Kanuti ≃ 180 66.26 N 153.02 W
Kan'utino 76 55.33 N 33.14 E
Kanye 156 24.59 S 25.19 E
Kanygtokynmangkyn, laguna ⊂ 180 69.20 N 178.45 E
Kanyu 156 20.05 S 24.39 E
Kanyutkwin 110 18.21 N 96.30 E
Kanzaki ≃ 270 34.42 N 135.25 E
Kanzanavolok 24 62.23 N 36.58 E
Kanzenze 154 10.31 S 25.12 E
Kanzi 98 39.34 N 122.39 E
Kaohiung → Kaohsiung 100 22.38 N 120.17 E
Kaohsiung 100 22.38 N 120.17 E
Kaohsiunghsien 100 22.38 N 120.21 E
Kaoje 150 11.14 N 4.07 E
Kaoka Bay ⊂ 175e 9.42 S 160.40 E
Kaokoland □5 156 18.15 S 13.00 E
Kaoko Otavi 156 18.14 S 13.40 E
Kaoko Veld ⋏1 156 20.00 S 14.00 E
Kaolack 150 14.09 N 16.04 W
Kaolack □4 150 14.00 N 15.30 W
Kaolin 285 39.48 N 75.43 W
Kaolun → Kowloon 271d 22.18 N 114.10 E
Kaoma 154 14.47 S 24.48 E
Kaongweshi ≃ 152 7.53 S 22.20 E
Kaoping → Changzhi 102 36.11 N 113.08 E
Kaoshanji 105 40.11 N 117.17 E
Kaoshanpu 100 30.54 N 114.32 E
Kaouadja ≃ 140 6.45 N 24.15 E
Kaouar ◆1 146 19.00 N 12.40 E
Kao Valley V 158 28.54 S 18.06 E
Kapaa 229b 22.04 N 159.19 W
Kapadvanj 120 23.01 N 73.04 E
Kapahiang 112 3.39 S 102.34 E
Kapal 86 45.08 N 79.03 E
Kapalong 116 7.35 N 125.42 E
Kapan 112 9.44 S 124.17 E
Kapanga, Zaïre 152 8.21 S 22.35 E
Kapanga, Zaïre 152 5.04 S 16.58 E
Kapangan 116 16.35 N 120.35 E
Kapaonik ⋏ 38 43.20 N 20.50 E
Kāpāsia 126 24.07 N 90.32 E
Kapatagan 116 7.52 N 123.44 E
Kapatu 154 9.43 S 30.42 E
Kapčagaj 85 43.53 N 77.12 E
Kapčagajskoje vodochranilišče ⊜1 86 43.50 N 78.00 E
Kapchorwa 154 1.24 N 34.27 E
Kapedo 154 1.10 N 36.06 E
Kapelle 52 51.28 N 3.58 E
Kapellen, Bel. 50 51.19 N 4.26 E
Kapellen, Dtsch. 56 51.25 N 6.35 E
Kapellen, Dtsch. 263 51.08 N 6.38 E
Kapellen, Öst. 61 47.38 N 15.37 E
Kapelle-op-den-Bos 50 51.01 N 4.22 E
Kapellerfeld 264b 48.19 N 16.30 E
Kapelln 61 48.15 N 15.45 E
Kapellskär 40 59.43 N 19.04 E
Kapema 154 10.42 S 28.24 E
Kapenguria 154 1.04 N 35.07 E
Kapfenberg 61 47.26 N 15.18 E
Kapia 152 4.17 S 19.46 E
Kapıdağ Yarımadası ›1 130 40.28 N 27.50 E
Kapikik Lake ⊜ 184 51.32 N 91.57 W
Kapikog Lake ⊜ 212 45.09 N 79.53 W
Kapilmuni 126 22.42 N 89.20 E
Kapingamarangi I1 14 1.04 N 154.46 E
Kapiri Mposhi 154 13.58 S 28.41 E
Kāpīsā □4 120 34.45 N 69.30 E
Kapiskau ≃ 176 52.47 N 81.55 W
Kapit 112 2.01 N 112.56 E
Kapitanovka 78 48.54 N 31.42 E
Kapiti Island I 172 40.52 S 174.54 E
Kapiura ≃ 164 5.45 S 150.35 E
Kapka, Massif du ⋏ 146 15.07 N 21.45 E
Kapkataš 85 40.23 N 74.20 E
Kapkatas, chrebet ⋏ 85 41.50 N 76.10 E
Kapkinka 80 48.08 N 43.51 E
Kaplan 194 29.59 N 92.17 W
Kaplice 61 48.45 N 14.30 E
Kapoe 110 9.35 N 98.40 E
Kapoeta 154 4.47 N 33.35 E
Kapona 154 7.11 S 29.09 E
Kaponga 172 39.26 S 174.09 E
Kaporskoje 265a 59.45 N 29.58 E
Kapos ≃ 30 46.44 N 18.30 E
Kaposvár 30 46.22 N 17.47 E
Kaposvar Creek ≃ 184 50.31 N 101.55 W
Kapotn'a ◆8 265b 55.38 N 37.48 E
Kapowsin 224 46.59 N 122.13 W
Kapowsin, Lake ⊜ 224 46.58 N 122.13 W
Kapp 26 60.42 N 10.52 E
Kappar 128 25.19 N 62.42 E
Kappel 56 50.00 N 7.21 E
Kappeln 41 54.40 N 9.56 E
Kappelshamn 26 57.51 N 18.47 E
Kapps 156 22.22 S 17.52 E
Kapralicha 86 56.11 N 67.15 E
Kaprijke 50 51.13 N 3.36 E
Kaprun 64 47.16 N 12.46 E
Kapsabet 154 0.12 N 35.06 E
Kapsan 98 41.04 N 128.19 E
Kapstadt → Cape Town 158 33.55 S 18.22 E
Kaptai 120 22.21 N 92.17 E
Kaptipada 126 21.31 N 86.32 E
Kaptol 36 45.26 N 17.44 E
Kapuas ≃, Indon. 112 0.25 S 109.40 E
Kapuas ≃, Indon. 112 3.01 S 114.20 E
Kapuas Hulu, Pegunungan ⋏ 112 1.15 N 113.30 E
Kapulo 154 8.18 S 29.15 E
Kapunda 168b 34.21 S 138.54 E
Kapūrthala 123 31.23 N 75.23 E
Kapur Utara, Pegunungan ⋏ 115a 6.52 S 111.30 E
Kapuskasing 176 49.25 N 82.26 W
Kapuskasing ≃ 176 49.49 N 82.00 W
Kapuskasing Lake ⊜ 190 48.30 N 82.55 W
Kapustin Jar 80 48.36 N 45.45 E
Kapustino 78 48.57 N 31.14 E
Kapuvár 30 47.36 N 17.02 E
Kap Verde → Cape Verde □1 150a 16.00 N 24.00 W
Kapyrevščina 76 55.15 N 32.53 E
Kapytdžuch, gora ∧ 84 39.13 N 46.00 E
Kara 74 69.14 N 65.00 E
Kara ≃ 150 10.01 N 0.25 E
Karaali 130 39.40 N 32.57 E
Karaaul 86 48.57 N 79.15 E
Karababa Dağı ∧ 130 39.31 N 36.10 E
Karabachskij chrebet ⋏ 84 39.42 N 46.36 E
Karabagl'ar 84 39.26 N 45.12 E
Kara-Balta 85 42.50 N 73.52 E
Karabanovo 82 56.19 N 38.42 E
Karabaš, Ross. 80 54.42 N 52.36 E
Karabaš, Ross. 86 55.29 N 60.14 E
Karabau 80 48.26 N 52.54 E
Karabekaul 128 38.30 N 64.08 E
Karabiğa 130 40.24 N 27.18 E
Karabil', vozvyšennost' ⋏1 128 36.25 N 64.00 E
Kara-Bogaz-Gol, zaliv ⊂ 72 41.00 N 53.15 E
Karabudachkent 84 42.41 N 47.34 E
Karabük 130 41.12 N 32.37 E
Karabula 88 58.08 N 97.23 E
Karabula ≃ 88 58.22 N 97.02 E
Karabulak, Kaz. 85 42.32 N 69.46 E
Karabulak, Kaz. 86 44.54 N 78.30 E
Karabulak, Kaz. 86 47.34 N 84.41 E
Karabulak, Kyrg. 85 39.51 N 69.38 E
Karabulduk 130 40.50 N 38.34 E
Karaburun 130 38.37 N 26.31 E
Karabutak 86 49.59 N 60.10 E
Karacabey 130 40.13 N 28.21 E
Karacadağ, Tür. 130 37.43 N 39.37 E
Karacadağ, Tür. 130 41.57 N 27.40 E
Karaca Dağ ∧ 130 37.40 N 39.50 E
Karačaj ≃ 84 41.28 N 49.00 E
Karačajevo-Čerkesija □3 84 44.00 N 42.00 E
Karačajevsk 84 43.45 N 41.54 E
Karacaköy 130 41.24 N 28.22 E
Karačala 84 39.48 N 48.57 E
Karacaoğlan 130 41.31 N 27.07 E
Karacasu 130 37.43 N 28.37 E
Karacaviran 130 39.44 N 38.08 E
Karaçay 130 36.10 N 36.02 E
Karaçayır 130 39.55 N 37.01 E
Karačev 76 53.07 N 35.00 E
Karachay → Karačajevo-Čerkesija □3 84 44.00 N 42.00 E
Karāchi 120 24.52 N 67.03 E
Karachtaj 85 40.55 N 69.46 E
Karači 80 57.59 N 50.28 E
Karād 122 17.17 N 74.12 E
Kara Dağ ∧ 130 40.22 N 39.05 E
Karadarja ≃ 85 40.54 N 71.45 E
Karadeniz → Black Sea ⊤2 22 43.00 N 35.00 E
Karadere 130 40.40 N 30.50 E
Karadirek 130 38.34 N 30.11 E
Karaftit 88 54.12 N 111.54 E
Karagaj, Kaz. 80 48.39 N 47.38 E
Karagaj, Ross. 80 58.16 N 54.56 E
Karagajly 86 49.20 N 75.48 E
Karaganda 86 49.50 N 73.10 E
Karaganda □8 86 50.00 N 74.00 E
Karagel 128 39.23 N 53.11 E
Karagičevskij 80 50.11 N 42.55 E
Karaginskij, ostrov I 74 58.50 N 164.00 E
Karaginskij zaliv ⊂ 74 58.50 N 164.00 E
Karagola Road 124 25.29 N 87.23 E
Karagöl Dağı ∧ 130 40.32 N 38.10 E
Kara Gölü ⊜ 130 36.42 N 29.50 E
Karagoš, gora ∧ 86 51.44 N 89.24 E
Karagužicha 86 50.47 N 83.00 E
Karahallı 130 38.20 N 29.32 E
Karaia 124 25.54 N 78.01 E
Karaičev 80 48.37 N 42.13 E
Karaidel' 86 55.50 N 56.53 E
Karaidel'skij 86 55.49 N 57.05 E
Kāraikāl 122 10.55 N 79.50 E
Kāraikkudi 122 10.04 N 78.47 E
Karaisalı 130 37.16 N 35.03 E
Karaitivu I 122 8.23 N 79.47 E
Karaj 128 35.48 N 50.59 E
Karaj ≃ 267d 35.35 N 51.11 E
Karajantak 85 40.03 N 67.54 E
Karak 114 3.24 N 102.02 E
Karakabak 86 50.33 N 75.09 E
Karakain 85 41.26 N 74.19 E
Kara-Kala 128 38.26 N 56.18 E
Karakalpak Respublika □3 86 43.00 N 59.00 E
Karakaralong, Pulau II 112 4.30 N 125.30 E
Karakastek 85 43.08 N 76.06 E
Karakavak 85 39.41 N 72.43 E
Karakax ≃ 120 37.00 N 79.45 E
Karakaya Barajı ⊜1 130 38.25 N 38.45 E
Karakeçi 130 37.26 N 39.26 E
Karakeçili 130 39.36 N 33.23 E
Karakelong, Pulau I 108 4.15 N 126.48 E
Karakemer 85 42.55 N 75.20 E
Karakendža 85 39.14 N 71.31 E
Karakitang, Pulau I 112 3.11 N 125.32 E
Karakoin, ozero ⊜ 86 46.10 N 68.45 E
Karakojsu ≃ 84 42.33 N 46.58 E
Karakojun ≃ 85 41.10 N 75.45 E
Karakol (Prževal'sk) 85 42.29 N 78.24 E
Karakolka 85 41.32 N 77.23 E
Karakoram Pass)(120 35.30 N 77.50 E
Karakoram Range ⋏ 120 35.30 N 77.00 E
Karakoro ≃ 150 14.43 N 12.03 W
Karaksar 88 51.16 N 115.58 E
Karakudžur ≃ 85 41.59 N 75.42 E
Karakul', Ross. 86 57.26 N 70.51 E
Karakul', Taj. 85 39.02 N 73.33 E
Karakul', Uzb. 128 39.32 N 63.50 E
Karakul', ozero ⊜ 85 39.05 N 73.25 E
Karakulak 130 39.59 N 40.01 E
Kara-Kul'dža 85 40.37 N 73.35 E
Karakul'dža ≃ 85 40.39 N 73.26 E
Karakulino 80 56.01 N 53.43 E
Karakul'skoje 86 54.04 N 62.26 E
Karakum 86 46.49 N 79.33 E
Karakumskij kanal ≚ 128 37.35 N 61.50 E
Karakumy ◆2 72 39.00 N 60.00 E
Karakuni 270 34.28 N 135.28 E
Karakurt 130 40.10 N 42.36 E
Karala ◆8 272a 28.44 N 77.02 E
Karalat 80 45.55 N 48.18 E
Karalon 88 57.02 N 115.52 E
Karalundi 162 26.07 S 118.41 E
Karam 88 55.09 N 107.37 E
Karama ≃ 112 2.18 S 119.06 E
Karamağara 130 39.42 N 35.31 E
Karamai → Karamay 86 45.30 N 84.55 E
Karaman 130 37.11 N 33.14 E
Karaman □4 130 37.00 N 33.00 E
Karamanlı 130 37.22 N 29.49 E
Karamay 86 45.30 N 84.55 E
Karambu 112 3.51 S 116.04 E
Karamea 172 41.15 S 172.07 E
Karamea ≃ 172 41.16 S 172.06 E
Karamea Bight ⊂3 172 41.30 S 171.40 E
Karamıkbataklığı ≋ 130 38.25 N 30.50 E
Karamnisa Nāla ⊜1 124 25.42 N 83.25 E
Karamoja □5 154 2.50 N 34.15 E
Karamola, gora ∧ 86 47.58 N 66.35 E
Karamürsel 130 40.42 N 29.36 E
Karamurt 85 42.19 N 69.58 E
Karamyš ≃ 80 51.20 N 45.00 E
Karamyševo, Ross. 76 57.45 N 28.45 E
Karamyševo, Ross. 82 54.46 N 36.07 E
Karamyševo, Ross. 88 57.34 N 100.55 E
Karamzino 76 56.00 N 34.33 E
Karang, Gunung ∧ 115a 6.16 S 106.03 E
Karang, Tanjung › 112 0.38 S 119.44 E
Karangagung 112 2.22 S 104.27 E
Karangampel 115a 6.28 S 108.27 E
Karangana 150 12.13 N 5.02 W
Karangasem 115b 8.27 S 115.37 E
Karangbinangun 115a 7.01 S 112.30 E
Karangbolang, Ujung › 115a 7.46 S 109.02 E
Karangbolong 115a 7.45 S 109.28 E
Karanggede 115a 7.22 S 110.37 E
Karangkates, Waduk ⊜1 115a 8.11 S 112.34 E
Karangkobar 115a 7.16 S 109.44 E
Karangnunggal 115a 7.38 S 108.06 E
Karangpandan 115a 7.37 S 111.04 E
Karangsembung 115a 6.51 S 108.39 E
Kāranja 122 20.29 N 77.29 E
Karanjia 120 21.47 N 85.58 E
Karanpura 123 29.50 N 73.27 E
Karaoba, Kaz. 86 53.17 N 65.06 E
Karaoba, Kaz. 86 47.03 N 56.20 E
Karaoğlan 130 39.14 N 39.13 E
Karaoj 86 45.54 N 74.45 E
Karaozek, Kaz. 85 43.43 N 77.23 E
Karaozek, Kaz. 86 45.03 N 65.18 E
Karaozek, Uzb. 86 43.16 N 58.40 E
Karapınar, Tür. 130 37.43 N 33.33 E
Karapınar, Tür. 130 41.30 N 32.12 E
Karapyši 78 49.38 N 30.47 E
Karaš 80 56.54 N 39.24 E
Karas, Pulau I 164 3.27 S 132.40 E
Karasaj 85 41.34 N 77.49 E
Kara-Sal ≃ 80 47.22 N 43.38 E
Karaşar 130 40.20 N 32.00 E
Karasay 120 36.47 N 83.48 E
Karasburg 156 28.00 S 18.43 E
Karasburg □5 156 28.00 S 18.45 E
Kara Sea → Karskoje more ⊤2 72 76.00 N 80.00 E
Karašengel' 86 47.29 N 75.35 E
Karašjåkka ≃ 24 69.26 N 25.49 E
Karasjok 24 69.27 N 25.30 E
Karaskan 85 41.03 N 71.49 E
Karasor, ozero ⊜, Kaz. 86 51.57 N 75.45 E
Karasor, ozero ⊜, Kaz. 86 49.54 N 75.32 E
Karasu, Azer. 84 40.11 N 48.41 E
Karasu, Kaz. 86 52.40 N 65.28 E
Karasu, Kaz. 86 51.20 N 62.21 E
Kara-Su, Kyrg. 85 40.44 N 72.53 E
Karasu, Kyrg. 85 43.03 N 73.57 E
Karasu, Nihon 94 34.39 N 136.32 E
Karasu, Tür. 130 41.06 N 30.41 E
Karasu ≃, Nihon 94 36.15 N 139.17 E
Karasu ≃, Tür. 130 39.07 N 38.44 E
Karasuk 86 53.44 N 78.02 E
Karasuk ≃ 86 53.35 N 77.30 E
Karasuyama 94 36.39 N 140.09 E
Karata 84 42.35 N 46.21 E
Karatal, Kaz. 86 45.07 N 77.54 E
Karatal, Kaz. 86 47.36 N 85.12 E
Karatal ≃ 86 46.26 N 77.10 E
Karataş, Tür. 130 36.36 N 35.21 E
Karataş, Tür. 130 38.34 N 28.17 E
Karataş Burun › 130 36.35 N 35.22 E
Karatau 85 43.10 N 70.28 E
Karatau, chrebet ⋏, Kaz. 72 43.50 N 68.30 E
Karatau, chrebet ⋏, Taj. 85 38.10 N 69.00 E
Karateginskij chrebet ⋏ 85 38.50 N 69.40 E
Karatepe Milli Parkı ♦ 130 37.17 N 36.13 E
Karatia 126 24.14 N 89.58 E
Karatobe 80 49.41 N 53.31 E
Karatogaj 86 48.42 N 59.40 E
Karaton 86 46.25 N 53.30 E
Karatoya ≃ 124 24.13 N 89.36 E
Karatschi → Karāchi 120 24.52 N 67.03 E

Symbols in the index entries represent the broad categories identified in the key at the right. Symbols with superior numbers (⋏1) identify subcategories (see complete key on page *I · 1).*

Symbole im Register stellen die rechts im Schlüssel erklärten Kategorien dar. Symbole mit hochgestellten Ziffern (⋏1) bezeichnen Unterabteilungen einer Kategorie (vgl. vollständiger Schlüssel auf Seite *I · 1).*

Los símbolos incluídos en el texto del índice representan las grandes categorias identificadas con la clave a la derecha. Los símbolos con numeros en su parte superior (⋏1) identifican las subcategorías (véase la clave completa en la página *I · 1).*

Les symboles de l'index représentent les catégories indiquées dans la légende à droite. Les symboles suivis d'un indice (⋏1) représentent des sous-catégories (voir légende complète à la page *I · 1).*

Os símbolos incluídos no texto do índice representam as grandes categorias identificadas com a chave à direita. Os símbolos com números em sua parte superior (⋏1) identificam as subcategorias (veja-se a chave completa à página *I · 1).*

	English	Deutsch	Español	Français	Português
∧	Mountain	Berg	Montaña	Montagne	Montanha
⋏	Mountains	Gebirge	Montañas	Montagnes	Montanhas
)(	Pass	Paß	Paso	Col	Passo
V	Valley, Canyon	Tal, Cañon	Valle, Cañón	Vallée, Canyon	Vale, Canhão
≚	Plain	Ebene	Llano	Plaine	Planície
›	Cape	Kap	Cabo	Cap	Cabo
I	Island	Insel	Isla	Île	Ilha
II	Islands	Inseln	Islas	Îles	Ilhas
⊥	Other Topographic Features	Andere Topographische Objekte	Otros Elementos Topográficos	Autres données topographiques	Outros acidentes topográficos

ESPAÑOL · FRANÇAIS · PORTUGUÊS

Nombre / Nom / Nome	Página / Page / Página	Lat.°′	Long.°′ W = Oeste / W = Ouest / W = Oeste
Karatsu	92	33.26 N	129.58 E
Karaturuk	85	43.33 N	77.59 E
Karatuzskoje	86	53.36 N	92.53 E
Karau	164	3.45 S	144.20 E
Karaul	74	70.06 N	83.08 E
Karauli	124	26.30 N	77.01 E
Karault'ob'o	85	40.33 N	75.57 E
Karaunk'ur ≃	85	40.54 N	72.20 E
Karaurğan	130	40.15 N	42.17 E
Karauzak	86	42.59 N	60.02 E
Karauzek	80	47.15 N	48.25 E
Karavan	85	41.30 N	71.45 E
Karavannoje, Ross.	80	45.59 N	47.08 E
Karavannoje, Ross.	80	57.47 N	47.41 E
Karavás	38	36.21 N	22.57 E
Karave	272c	19.01 N	73.01 E
Karawa	152	3.20 N	20.18 E
Karawang	115a	6.19 S	107.17 E
Karawang, Tanjung ›	115a	5.56 S	107.00 E
Karawanken ⋏	36	46.30 N	14.25 E
Karayaka	130	40.45 N	36.37 E
Karayazı	130	39.41 N	42.08 E
Karaye	150	11.48 N	8.02 E
Karayün	130	39.41 N	37.19 E
Karažal	86	48.02 N	70.49 E
Karbalā'	128	32.36 N	44.02 E
Karbalā' □[4]	128	32.00 N	42.15 E
Karbenning	40	60.02 N	16.04 E
Kårberg	40	58.58 N	14.57 E
Karbeyaz	130	36.02 N	36.12 E
Kårböle	26	61.59 N	15.19 E
Karby	40	59.34 N	18.13 E
Karcag	30	47.19 N	20.56 E
Karczew	30	52.06 N	21.15 E
Kardail ≃	80	50.43 N	42.54 E
Kardašova Řečice	61	49.11 N	14.53 E
Kardeljevo	36	43.04 N	17.26 E
Karden	56	50.11 N	7.17 E
Kardhámaina	38	36.47 N	27.09 E
Kardhámila	38	38.32 N	26.05 E
Kardhítsa	38	39.21 N	21.55 E
Kärdla	76	59.00 N	22.45 E
Kardymovo	76	54.54 N	32.26 E
Kârdžali	38	41.39 N	25.22 E
Kardžin	84	43.16 N	44.16 E
Karea	272b	22.42 N	88.33 E
Kareeberge ⋏	158	30.53 S	21.57 E
Kareedouw	158	33.57 S	24.18 E
Kareli	84	42.01 N	43.54 E
Karelia □[9]	24	63.00 N	32.00 E
Karelia → Karelija □[3]	24	64.00 N	32.30 E
Karelija □[3]	24	64.00 N	32.30 E
Karel'skij Gorodok	76	58.04 N	36.30 E
Karema, Pap. N. Gui.	164	9.12 S	147.14 E
Karema, Tan.	154	6.49 S	30.26 E
Karen	110	12.51 N	92.53 E
Karenga ≃	88	54.28 N	116.32 E
Karepino	24	61.02 N	57.02 E
Karera	272a	28.41 N	77.23 E
Karesuando	24	68.25 N	22.30 E
Kärevere	76	58.26 N	26.29 E
Kāreyz-e Elyās	128	35.25 N	61.20 E
Kargali	80	55.12 N	50.54 E
Kargalinskaja	84	43.44 N	46.30 E
Karganaj	180	65.21 N	175.25 E
Kargapazarı Dağları ⋏	130	40.07 N	41.35 E
Kargapolje	86	55.57 N	64.27 E
Kargasok	86	59.07 N	80.53 E
Kargat	86	55.10 N	80.17 E
Kargat ≃	86	54.37 N	78.12 E
Kargı	130	41.08 N	34.30 E
Kargil	123	34.34 N	76.06 E
Karginskaja	80	49.21 N	41.38 E
Karginskij ≃	265a	59.50 N	30.01 E
Kargopol'	24	61.30 N	38.58 E
Karguéri	146	13.27 N	10.25 E
Karhal	124	27.01 N	78.57 E
Karhijärvi ⊜	26	61.35 N	22.30 E
Karhula	26	60.31 N	26.57 E
Kari	146	11.14 N	10.34 E
Karia-Ba-Mohammed	148	34.19 N	5.10 W
Kariaí	38	40.16 N	24.15 E
Karianga	157b	22.22 S	47.26 E
Kariba	154	16.30 S	28.45 E
Kariba, Lake ⊜[1]	154	17.00 S	28.00 E
Karibib	156	21.58 S	15.51 E
Karibib □[5]	156	22.20 S	16.00 E
Karibisches Meer → Caribbean Sea Ŧ[2]	230	15.00 N	73.00 W
Karibumba	154	0.22 N	29.22 E
Kariega ≃	158	33.03 S	23.28 E
Karigasniemi	24	69.24 N	25.50 E
Karikari, Cape ›	172	34.47 S	173.24 E
Karimata	175d	24.54 N	125.17 E
Karimata, Kepulauan II	112	1.25 S	109.05 E
Karimata, Pulau I	112	1.36 S	108.55 E
Karimata, Selat (Karimata Strait) Ų	112	2.05 S	108.40 E
Karīmganj	120	24.52 N	92.21 E
Karīmnagar	122	18.26 N	79.09 E
Karīmpur	126	23.58 N	88.37 E
Karimun, Pulau I	114	1.03 N	103.22 E
Karimunjawa, Kepulauan II	115a	5.50 S	110.25 E
Karimunjawa, Pulau I	115a	5.51 S	110.27 E
Karin, Som.	144	10.59 N	49.13 E
Karin, Som.	144	10.51 N	45.47 E
Karino	82	54.42 N	38.56 E
Karin Seamount ⊹[3]	14	17.55 N	168.58 W
Karinskoje	82	55.42 N	36:41 E
Karintorf	80	58.33 N	50.11 E
Karis (Karjaa)	26	60.05 N	23.40 E
Karise	41	55.18 N	12.13 E
Karisimbi, Volcan ∧[1]	154	1.30 S	29.27 E
Káristos	38	38.00 N	24.24 E
Kariya	94	34.59 N	136.59 E
Kariye Museum ʊ[1]	267b	41.01 N	28.55 E
Kārīz	128	34.49 N	60.47 E
Karjaa → Karis	26	60.05 N	23.40 E
Karjepolje	24	65.34 N	43.40 E
Kārkal	122	13.12 N	74.59 E
Karkalaj	80	57.00 N	52.24 E
Karkaralinsk	86	49.23 N	75.21 E
Karkar Dūmān ◆[8]	272a	28.39 N	77.18 E
Karkar Island I	164	4.40 S	146.00 E
Karkas, Kūh-e ∧	128	33.29 N	51.50 E
Karkheh ≃	128	31.46 N	47.55 E
Karkīndar	128	25.47 N	59.15 E
Karkinitskij zaliv c	78	45.55 N	33.00 E
Karkkila	26	60.32 N	24.11 E
Karkku	26	61.25 N	23.01 E
Karkom, Har ∧	132	30.17 N	34.44 E
Karkonoski Park Narodowy ♦	30	50.45 N	15.35 E
Kärla	76	58.20 N	22.15 E
Karlholmsbruk	40	60.31 N	17.35 E
Karlik Shan ∧	102	43.08 N	94.20 E
Karlino	30	54.03 N	15.51 E
Karlıova	130	39.18 N	41.01 E
Karlobag	36	44.32 N	15.05 E
Karlo-Libknechtovsk	83	48.42 N	38.04 E
Karlo-Marksovo	83	48.16 N	38.09 E
Karloske ≃	184	55.41 N	93.56 W
Karlovac	36	45.29 N	15.34 E
Karlovka	78	49.27 N	35.08 E
Karlovo	38	42.38 N	24.48 E
Karlovy Vary (Carlsbad)	54	50.11 N	12.52 E
Karlsbad → Karlovy Vary	54	50.11 N	12.52 E
Karlsborg, Sve.	26	58.32 N	14.31 E
Karlsborg, Sve.	26	65.48 N	23.17 E
Karlsburg → Alba Iulia	38	46.04 N	23.35 E
Karlsby	40	58.38 N	15.08 E
Karlsfeld	60	48.13 N	11.28 E
Karlshafen	52	51.38 N	9.27 E
Karlshamn	26	56.10 N	14.51 E
Karlshorst ◆[8]	264a	52.29 N	13.32 E
Karlshorst, Trabrennbahn ♦	264a	52.29 N	13.31 E
Karlshuld	60	48.41 N	11.18 E
Karlskoga	40	59.20 N	14.31 E
Karlskrona	26	56.10 N	15.35 E
Karlslunde Strand	41	55.34 N	12.14 E
Karlsöarna II	26	57.17 N	17.58 E
Karlsruhe	56	49.03 N	8.24 E
Karlsruhe □[5], Dtsch.	56	49.20 N	8.45 E
Karlsruhe □[5], Dtsch.	58	48.30 N	8.30 E
Karlstad, Sve.	40	59.22 N	13.30 E
Karlstad, Mn., U.S.	198	48.34 N	96.31 W
Karlstadt	56	49.57 N	9.45 E
Karlstift	61	48.35 N	14.45 E
Karluk, Ross.	88	53.27 N	105.58 E
Karluk, Ak., U.S.	180	57.34 N	154.28 W
Karl'uk, Uzb.	85	38.12 N	67.42 E
Karma	150	13.40 N	1.49 E
Karma, Ouadi ∨	146	15.38 N	20.01 E
Karmah	140	19.38 N	30.25 E
Karmāla	122	18.25 N	75.12 E
Karmanovka	80	49.24 N	50.22 E
Karmanovo	76	55.52 N	34.52 E
Karmansbo	40	59.42 N	15.44 E
Karmatānr	126	24.05 N	86.42 E
Karmel, Har (Mount Carmel) ∧	132	32.44 N	35.02 E
Karmi'el	132	32.55 N	35.18 E
Karmiyya	132	31.36 N	34.33 E
Karmøy I	26	59.15 N	5.15 E
Karnack	194	32.40 N	94.10 W
Karnak	194	37.17 N	88.58 W
Karnak → Al-Karnak	140	25.43 N	32.39 E
Karnāl	124	29.41 N	76.59 E
Karnāla Fort ⊥	272c	18.53 N	73.07 E
Karṇālī □[8]	124	29.30 N	82.30 E
Karṇālī ≃	124	28.15 N	81.05 E
Karnap ◆[8]	263	51.31 N	7.01 E
Karnaphuli Reservoir ⊜[1]	120	22.42 N	92.12 E
Karnātaka □[3]	122	14.00 N	76.00 E
Karnauchovka	78	48.28 N	34.44 E
Karnes □[6]	222	29.00 N	97.47 W
Karnes City	196	28.53 N	97.54 W
Karni	150	10.40 N	2.37 W
Karniki	82	54.12 N	38.05 E
Karnische Alpen (Alpi Carniche) ⋏	64	46.40 N	13.00 E
Karnobat	38	42.39 N	26.59 E
Karns City	214	41.00 N	79.44 W
Kärnten □[3]	30	46.50 N	13.50 E
Karnzow	54	52.59 N	12.26 E
Karoi	154	16.50 S	29.40 E
Karokh	128	34.28 N	62.35 E
Karoli	124	22.55 N	79.04 E
Karolinenhof ◆[8]	264a	52.23 N	13.38 E
Karomatan	116	7.46 N	123.44 E
Karompa Lompo, Pulau I	112	7.15 S	121.45 E
Karon	126	24.07 N	86.44 E
Karonga	154	9.56 S	33.56 E
Karonie	162	30.58 S	122.32 E
Karoonda	166	35.06 S	139.54 E
Karor	123	31.13 N	70.57 E
Karora	140	17.42 N	38.22 E
Karos	158	28.24 S	21.35 E
Karosa	112	1.48 S	119.20 E
Karoso, Tanjung ›	115b	9.33 S	118.50 E
Karotho Post	154	5.11 N	35.50 E
Karou	150	15.07 N	0.39 E
Karow, Dtsch.	54	52.20 N	12.15 E
Karow, Dtsch.	54	53.32 N	12.15 E
Karow ◆[8]	264a	52.37 N	13.29 E
Karpathen → Carpathian Mountains ⋏	22	48.00 N	24.00 E
Kárpathos, Ellás	38	35.30 N	27.14 E
Kárpathos, Ellás	130	35.31 N	27.12 E
Kárpathos I	38	35.40 N	27.10 E
Karpenísion	38	38.55 N	21.40 E
Karpinsk	86	59.45 N	60.01 E
Karpogory	24	64.00 N	44.24 E
Karpovka, Ukr.	83	49.10 N	37.43 E
Karpovka, Ukr.	83	47.57 N	39.36 E
Karpovo, Ross.	76	60.02 N	36.43 E
Karpovo, Ross.	82	55.35 N	38.34 E
Karpunicha	80	57.42 N	45.20 E
Karpuninskij	86	58.43 N	61.50 E
Karpuzlu	130	37.33 N	27.50 E
Karratha	162	20.44 S	116.51 E
Karrats Fjord c[2]	176	71.20 N	54.00 W
Karrebæksminde	41	55.11 N	11.40 E
Karres	58	47.13 N	10.47 E
Kärrgruvan	40	60.05 N	15.56 E
Karridale	162	34.13 S	115.05 E
Kars	84	40.36 N	43.05 E
Kars □[4]	84	40.35 N	43.00 E
Kars ≃	84	40.37 N	43.41 E
Karša	80	49.48 N	51.27 E
Karsakpaj	86	47.49 N	66.41 E
Karsakuwigamak Lake ⊜	184	56.22 N	99.30 W
Kärsämäki	26	63.58 N	25.46 E
Karsantı	130	37.33 N	35.24 E
Kārsava	76	56.47 N	27.40 E
Karsdorf	54	51.17 N	11.39 E
Karši	128	38.53 N	65.48 E
Karsin	30	53.54 N	17.56 E
Karšinskaja step' ≚	128	39.10 N	65.00 E
Karskije Vorota, proliv Ų	72	70.30 N	58.00 E
Karskoje more (Kara Sea) Ŧ[2]	72	76.00 N	80.00 E
Karsovaj	80	58.14 N	53.11 E
Kårsta, Sve.	40	59.39 N	18.14 E
Kärsta, Sve.	40	59.40 N	16.49 E
Karstädt	54	53.09 N	11.44 E
Karst → Kras ⋏[1]	64	45.48 N	14.00 E
Karstula	26	62.52 N	24.47 E
Karsun	80	54.11 N	46.59 E
Kartajol'	24	64.32 N	53.14 E
Kartala ∧	157a	11.45 S	43.22 E
Kartaly	86	53.03 N	60.40 E
Kartārpur	123	31.27 N	75.30 E
Karthaus	214	41.07 N	78.07 W
Kartlijskij chrebet ⋏	84	42.10 N	44.55 E
Kartosuro	115a	7.33 S	110.44 E
Karttula	26	62.53 N	26.58 E
Kartuzy	30	54.20 N	18.12 E
Kartzow	54	52.29 N	12.58 E
Käru	76	58.50 N	25.11 E
Karuah ≃	170	32.39 S	151.58 E
Karufa	164	3.50 S	133.27 E
Karuizawa	94	36.21 N	138.38 E
Karukuwisa	156	18.56 S	19.40 E
Karumai	92	40.19 N	141.28 E
Karumba	166	17.29 S	140.50 E
Kārūn ≃	128	30.26 N	48.10 E
Karungi	26	66.03 N	23.57 E
Karungu	154	0.51 S	34.09 E
Karuni	115b	9.26 S	119.19 E
Karunjie	164	16.18 S	127.12 E
Karunki	26	66.02 N	24.01 E
Karup	41	56.18 N	9.10 E
Karup ≃	41	56.18 N	9.10 E
Karūr	122	10.57 N	78.05 E
Karuscia, Punta ›	70	36.49 N	11.59 E
Karvala	265a	59.41 N	30.09 E
Karviná	30	49.50 N	18.30 E
Kārwār	122	14.48 N	74.08 E
Karwendel ⋏	64	47.27 N	11.20 E
Karwi	124	25.12 N	80.54 E
Karym	86	60.07 N	66.41 E
Karymskoje, Ross.	88	51.37 N	114.21 E
Karymskoje, Ross.	88	54.07 N	101.49 E
Karza	86	58.35 N	80.50 E
Karzachi	84	41.15 N	43.16 E
Kas, Sūd.	140	12.30 N	24.17 E
Kaş, Tür.	130	36.12 N	29.38 E
Kas ≃	86	59.40 N	90.00 E
Kasaan	182	55.32 N	132.24 W
Kasabi	152	14.48 S	23.42 E
Kasach ≃	84	40.03 N	43.52 E
Kasadi ≃	272c	19.01 N	73.03 E
Kasa-do I	98	34.28 N	126.03 E
Kasado-shima I	96	33.57 N	131.51 E
Kasagi	94	34.45 N	135.56 E
Kasagi-sanchi ⋏	270	34.37 N	135.56 E
Kasagi-yama ∧	94	35.31 N	137.21 E
Kasahara	94	35.17 N	137.09 E
Kasahata	268	35.54 N	139.25 E
Kasai	96	34.56 N	134.50 E
Kasai ◆[8]	268	35.39 N	139.53 E
Kasai (Cassai) ≃, Afr.	152	3.02 S	16.57 E
Kāsai ≃, India	124	22.09 N	87.50 E
Kasai-Occidental □[4]	152	5.30 S	21.40 E
Kasai-Oriental □[4]	152	4.00 S	23.30 E
Kasaji	152	10.22 S	23.27 E
Kasakake	94	36.23 N	139.17 E
Kasama, Nihon	94	36.23 N	140.16 E
Kasama, Zam.	154	10.13 S	31.12 E
Kasamatsu	94	35.22 N	136.46 E
Kasan	128	39.02 N	65.35 E
Kasan-dong	98	41.18 N	126.55 E
Kasane	156	17.50 S	25.05 E
Kasanga	154	8.28 S	31.09 E
Kasangale	152	6.20 S	22.42 E
Kasangeshi ≃	152	8.24 S	21.56 E
Kasangulu	152	4.36 S	15.10 E
Kasanka National Park ♦	154	12.35 S	30.12 E
Kasan → Kazan'	80	55.49 N	49.08 E
Kasano-misaki ›	94	36.21 N	136.18 E
Kasansaj	85	41.15 N	71.32 E
Kasansaj ≃	85	40.57 N	71.30 E
Kasaoka	96	34.30 N	133.30 E
Kāsaragod	122	12.30 N	75.00 E
Kasari ≃	76	58.45 N	23.49 E
Kašary	78	49.03 N	41.00 E
Kasatori-yama ∧, Nihon	94	34.44 N	136.18 E
Kasatori-yama ∧, Nihon	96	33.33 N	132.55 E
Kasauli	123	30.55 N	76.57 E
Kasba	124	25.51 N	87.33 E
Kasbagoas	126	24.11 N	88.30 E
Kasba Kamarda	126	21.46 N	87.21 E
Kasba Lake ⊜	176	60.18 N	102.07 W
Kasba Mirgoda	126	21.42 N	87.28 E
Kasba Nārāyangarh	126	22.10 N	87.23 E
Kasba Patāspur	126	22.02 N	87.32 E
Kasba-Tadla	148	32.34 N	6.18 W
Kaschau → Košice	30	48.43 N	21.15 E
Kåseberga	26	55.23 N	14.04 E
Kaseda	92	31.25 N	130.19 E
Kasempa	154	13.27 S	25.50 E
Kasenga	154	10.22 S	28.38 E
Kasenyi	154	1.24 N	30.26 E
Kasese, Ug.	154	0.10 N	30.05 E
Kasese, Zaïre	154	1.38 S	27.07 E
Kaset Sombun	110	16.17 N	101.57 E
Kasfareet Military Base ■	142	30.15 N	32.24 E
Kāsganj	124	27.49 N	78.39 E
Kashabowie Lake ⊜	190	48.42 N	90.25 W
Kashaf ≃	128	35.58 N	61.07 E
Kashagawigamog Lake ⊜	212	44.59 N	78.37 W
Kāshān	128	33.59 N	51.29 E
Kashasha	154	1.44 S	31.37 E
Kashegelok	180	60.50 N	157.50 W
Kashgar → Kashi	85	39.29 N	75.59 E
Kashi	85	39.29 N	75.59 E
Kashiba	96	34.33 N	135.42 E
Kashihara	96	34.30 N	135.46 E
Kashiji Plain ≚	152	13.20 S	22.30 E
Kashileshi ≃	152	9.46 S	23.05 E
Kashima, Nihon	92	33.07 N	130.06 E
Kashima, Nihon	94	35.58 N	140.38 E
Kashima, Nihon	94	36.58 N	136.55 E
Kashima, Nihon	96	35.30 N	133.01 E
Kashima-jingū ʊ[1]	94	35.59 N	140.40 E
Kashima-nada Ŧ[2]	94	36.15 N	140.45 E
Kashima-Yariga-take ∧	94	36.37 N	137.45 E
Kashimo	94	35.43 N	137.23 E
Kāshināthpur	126	23.58 N	89.37 E
Kashing → Jiaxing	106	30.46 N	120.45 E
Kashio ◆[8]	268	35.25 N	139.33 E
Kāshīpur, India	124	29.13 N	78.57 E
Kāshipur, India	126	23.26 N	86.40 E
Kashitu	154	13.42 S	28.40 E
Kashiwa	94	35.52 N	139.59 E
Kashiwara	96	34.35 N	135.37 E
Kashiwazaki, Nihon	92	37.22 N	138.33 E
Kashiwazaki, Nihon	268	35.56 N	139.42 E
Kāshmar	128	35.12 N	58.27 E
Kashmir, Vale of ∨	123	34.00 N	75.00 E
Kashmir → Jammu and Kashmīr □[2]	120	34.00 N	76.00 E
Kashmor	120	28.26 N	69.35 E
Kashmūnd Ghar ⋏	123	34.42 N	70.31 E
Kashunuk ≃	180	61.18 N	165.36 W
Kashwakamak Lake ⊜	212	44.50 N	77.04 W
Kasia	124	26.45 N	83.55 E
Kāsiāni	126	23.14 N	89.45 E
Kasiāri	126	22.08 N	87.14 E
Kasidiji ≃	152	7.57 S	23.12 E
Kasigau ∧	154	3.50 S	38.40 E
Kasigluk	180	60.52 N	162.32 W
Kasilof	180	60.24 N	151.18 W
Kasilovo	78	50.38 N	35.37 E
Kasimbar	112	0.09 S	120.00 E
Kasimov	80	54.56 N	41.24 E
Kāsimpur, Bngl.	126	23.59 N	90.19 E
Kāsimpur, India	272b	22.46 N	88.31 E
Kašin	76	57.21 N	37.37 E
Kāsināthpur	272b	22.35 N	88.31 E
Kasinge	154	6.20 S	26.59 E
Kasinka	156	18.13 S	24.22 E
Kāsipur	272b	22.25 N	88.10 E
Kašira	82	54.51 N	38.10 E
Kaširka ≃	82	54.52 N	38.13 E
Kasiruta, Pulau I	108	0.25 S	127.12 E
Kasiui, Pulau I	164	4.30 S	131.40 E
Kasiwa → Kashiwa	94	35.52 N	139.59 E
Kaskabulak	86	49.34 N	79.52 E
Kaškadarja □[8]	128	39.00 N	66.00 E
Kaskaden-Kette → Cascade Range ⋏	202	45.00 N	121.30 W
Kaskana	85	40.45 N	69.36 E
Kaskaskia ≃	194	37.59 N	89.56 W
Kaskaskia, East Fork ≃	219	38.43 N	89.09 W
Kaskaskia, North Fork ≃	219	38.46 N	89.09 W
Kaskattama ≃	176	57.03 N	90.07 W
Kaskelen	85	43.12 N	76.37 E
Kaskelen ≃	85	43.53 N	77.08 E
Kaskinen → Kaskö	26	62.23 N	21.13 E
Kaskö (Kaskinen)	26	62.23 N	21.13 E
Kašlagač ≃	83	47.45 N	37.16 E
Kaslātu ∧	124	23.58 N	84.54 E
Kasli	86	55.53 N	60.46 E
Kaslo	182	49.55 N	116.55 W
Kasn'a	76	55.24 N	34.20 E
Kasn'a ≃	76	55.51 N	34.25 E
Kaso ≃	115a	7.25 S	106.40 E
Kasongo	154	4.27 S	26.40 E
Kasongo-Lunda	152	6.28 S	16.49 E
Kásos I	38	35.22 N	26.56 E
Kasota	190	44.18 N	93.57 W
Kašperovka	78	49.26 N	29.41 E
Kaspi	84	41.57 N	44.25 E
Kaspijsk	84	42.52 N	47.38 E
Kaspijskij	22	45.22 N	47.24 E
Kaspijskoje more → Caspian Sea Ŧ[2]	72	42.00 N	50.30 E
Kaspische Senke → Prikaspijskaja nizmennost' ≚	80	48.00 N	52.00 E
Kaspisches Meer → Caspian Sea Ŧ[2]	72	42.00 N	50.30 E
Kaspl'a	76	55.00 N	31.38 E
Kaspl'a ≃	76	55.24 N	30.43 E
Kasr, Ra's ›	140	18.02 N	38.35 E
Kasrik	130	38.13 N	41.54 E
Kassab	130	35.56 N	35.59 E
Kassai → Cassai (Kasai) ≃	152	3.02 S	16.57 E
Kassa → Košice	30	48.43 N	21.15 E
Kassalā	140	15.28 N	36.24 E
Kassalā □[4]	140	15.00 N	35.00 E
Kassándra ›[1]	38	40.06 N	23.22 E
Kassándras, Kólpos c	38	40.06 N	23.30 E
Kassel	56	51.19 N	9.29 E
Kassel □[5]	56	51.10 N	9.20 E
Kasserine	148	35.11 N	8.48 E
Kasserine □[8]	148	35.00 N	8.45 E
Kasshabog Lake ⊜	212	44.38 N	77.58 W
Kassikaityu ≃	246	1.49 N	58.32 W
Kassinger	140	18.45 N	31.54 E
Kassîr, Sabkhat al- ⊜	130	35.03 N	41.07 E
Kasslerfeld ◆[8]	263	51.26 N	6.45 E
Kasson	190	44.01 N	92.45 W
Kassou	150	11.35 N	2.03 W
Kassoum	150	13.05 N	3.18 W
Kastamonu	130	41.22 N	33.47 E
Kastamonu □[4]	130	41.40 N	33.45 E
Kastanéai	38	41.38 N	26.28 E
Kastelholm	26	60.14 N	20.04 E
Kastellaun	56	50.04 N	7.26 E
Kastellórizon I	130	36.08 N	29.34 E
Kasterlee	56	51.15 N	4.57 E
Kastiyu, Puntan ›	174n	14.57 N	145.40 E
Kastl, Dtsch.	60	49.22 N	11.42 E
Kastl, Dtsch.	60	49.50 N	11.54 E
Kastorf	52	53.44 N	10.34 E
Kastoría	38	40.31 N	21.15 E
Kastorías, Límni ⊜	38	40.30 N	21.17 E
Kastornoje	78	51.50 N	38.06 E
Kastrávion, Tekhnití Límni ⊜[1]	38	38.50 N	21.20 E
Kastrup Lufthavn ⊠	41	55.38 N	12.39 E
Kasuga, Nihon	94	35.28 N	136.29 E
Kasuga, Nihon	96	33.32 N	130.27 E
Kasuga, Nihon	96	35.10 N	135.06 E
Kasugai, Nihon	94	35.14 N	136.58 E
Kasugai, Nihon	94	35.39 N	138.39 E
Kasuga-kōkūkichi, Kaijō-jieitai- ■	96	33.31 N	130.28 E
Kasuga Shrine ʊ[1]	270	34.41 N	135.51 E
Kasuka	158	33.40 S	26.41 E
Kasukabe	94	35.58 N	139.45 E
Kasukawa	94	36.24 N	139.13 E
Kasulu	154	4.34 S	30.06 E
Kasumi	96	35.38 N	134.38 E
Kasumiga-ura ⊜	94	36.00 N	140.25 E
Kasum-Ismailov	84	40.36 N	46.47 E
Kasumkent	84	41.41 N	48.07 E
Kasungan	112	1.58 S	113.24 E
Kasungu	154	13.01 S	33.30 E
Kasungu National Park ♦	154	12.55 S	33.15 E
Kasupe	154	15.10 S	35.15 E
Kasūr	123	31.07 N	74.27 E
Kaszuby ◆[1]	30	54.10 N	18.15 E
Kata	88	58.46 N	102.40 E
Kataba	154	16.05 S	25.10 E
Kataeregi	150	9.22 N	6.17 E
Katagum	146	12.17 N	10.21 E
Katahdin, Mount ∧	188	45.55 N	68.55 W
Katai	272c	19.10 N	73.05 E
Katajevo	88	50.57 N	108.41 E
Katajsk	86	56.18 N	62.35 E
Katako-Kombe	152	3.24 S	24.25 E
Katakura	270	34.29 N	135.31 E
Katakwi	154	1.55 N	33.57 E
Katale	154	4.59 S	31.03 E
Katalla	180	60.12 N	144.31 W
Katanda	154	0.50 S	29.22 E
Katanga □[9]	138	10.00 S	26.00 E
Katanga ≃	74	60.08 N	102.13 E
Katangi	124	23.27 N	79.47 E
Katanglad Mountains ⋏	116	8.06 N	124.54 E
Katangli	89	51.42 N	143.14 E
Katanimara	126	22.17 N	87.11 E
Katanning	162	33.42 S	117.33 E
Katano	270	34.47 N	135.40 E
Katano-hana ›	174f	24.49 N	141.20 E
Katanti	154	2.18 S	27.08 E
Kataoka	270	35.03 N	135.58 E
Katapakishi	152	8.15 S	22.49 E
Katara, Depresión de → Qaṭṭārah, Munkhafaḍ al- ≚[7]	140	30.00 N	27.30 E
Katârniān Ghāt	124	28.20 N	81.09 E
Katar → Qatar □[1]	128	25.00 N	51.10 E
Katase	268	35.19 N	139.29 E
Katashina	94	36.46 N	139.14 E
Katašin	76	52.36 N	32.10 E
Katav-Ivanovsk	86	54.45 N	58.12 E
Katayama	268	35.46 N	139.34 E
Katchall Island I	110	7.57 N	93.22 E
Katchewanooka Lake ⊜	212	44.27 N	78.16 W
Katchin-wan c	174m	26.18 N	127.53 E
Katchirga	150	14.03 N	0.06 E
Katchiungo	152	12.35 S	16.13 E
Katech	84	41.39 N	46.34 E
Kateel ≃	180	65.28 N	157.35 W
Katélé	150	10.38 N	5.37 W
Katena-wan c	174m	26.50 N	128.05 E
Katepwa Beach	184	50.42 N	103.38 W
Katerbow	54	52.59 N	12.39 E
Kateríni	38	40.16 N	22.30 E
Katerinopol'	78	48.56 N	30.59 E
Katerloch ⊥[5]	61	47.16 N	15.32 E
Katernberg ◆[8], Dtsch.	263	51.16 N	7.06 E
Katernberg ◆[8], Dtsch.	263	51.29 N	7.04 E
Katesbridge	48	54.18 N	6.08 W
Kates Needle ∧	180	57.03 N	132.03 W
Katešovo	82	54.08 N	37.00 E
Katete, Malaŵi	154	12.17 S	33.39 E
Katete, Zam.	154	14.05 S	32.07 E
Katghora	124	22.30 N	82.33 E
Katha	110	24.11 N	96.21 E
Kathangor, Jabal ∧	140	5.45 N	33.59 E
Katherine	164	14.28 S	132.16 E
Katherine ≃	164	14.39 S	131.42 E
Katherine Creek ≃	166	23.48 S	143.42 E
Katherine Gorge National Park ♦	164	14.10 S	132.30 E
Kāthgodām	124	29.16 N	79.32 E
Kathiār	120	25.32 N	87.35 E
Kāthiāwār Peninsula ›[1]	120	22.00 N	71.00 E
Kathīb, Ra's ›	144	14.55 N	42.53 E
Kathla	123	31.59 N	76.47 E
Kathleen	220	28.07 N	82.01 W
Kathleen Valley	162	27.23 S	120.38 E
Kathlow	54	51.43 N	14.29 E
Kāṭhmāṇḍau	124	27.43 N	85.19 E
Kathmandu → Kāṭhmāṇḍau	124	27.43 N	85.19 E
Kathor	120	21.18 N	72.56 E
Kathrabbā	132	31.08 N	35.37 E
Kathua	123	32.22 N	75.31 E
Kāthuli	126	23.52 N	88.40 E
Kati	150	12.44 N	8.04 W
Kātiādi	126	24.15 N	90.48 E
Katibas ≃	112	2.01 N	112.33 E
Katihār	124	25.32 N	87.35 E
Katikati	172	37.33 S	175.55 E
Katima Mulilo	152	17.27 S	24.14 E
Katimik Lake ⊜	184	52.54 N	99.22 W
Katiola	150	8.08 N	5.06 W
Katipunan	116	8.31 N	123.17 E
Katiti Aboriginal Land Reserve ◆[4]	162	25.10 S	131.15 E
Kātlang	123	34.22 N	72.05 E
Katlehong	273d	26.19 S	28.09 E
Katlenburg-Duhm	52	51.41 N	10.06 E
Katmai, Mount ∧	180	58.17 N	154.56 W
Katmai National Park ♦	180	58.30 N	155.00 W
Kātmāndu → Kāṭhmāṇḍau	124	27.43 N	85.19 E
Katni	80	57.59 N	47.46 E
Katni → Murwāra	124	23.51 N	80.24 E
Káto Akhaïa	38	38.09 N	21.32 E
Kātol	120	21.16 N	78.35 E
Katompi	154	6.11 S	26.20 E
Katonah	210	41.16 N	73.41 W
Katonga ≃	154	0.34 N	31.50 E
Katon-Karagaj	86	49.11 N	85.37 E
Katoomba	170	33.42 S	150.18 E
Katopa	154	2.45 S	25.06 E
Katori-jingū ʊ[1]	94	35.52 N	140.30 E
Katoúna	38	38.47 N	21.07 E
Katovice	60	49.16 N	13.49 E
Katowice	30	50.16 N	19.00 E
Katowice □[4]	30	50.15 N	19.00 E
Katra	123	32.59 N	74.57 E
Kātrās	126	23.48 N	86.17 E
Katričev	80	49.23 N	45.33 E
Kātrīnā, Jabal ∧	140	28.31 N	33.57 E
Katrine, Loch ⊜	46	56.15 N	4.31 W
Katrineholm	40	59.00 N	16.12 E
Katsch, Golf von → Kachchh, Gulf of c	120	22.36 N	69.30 E
Katschbach ≃	61	47.08 N	14.17 E
Katschberg)(	64	47.03 N	13.37 E
Katsepe	157b	15.45 S	46.15 E
Katshungu	154	2.27 S	27.23 E
Katsina	150	13.00 N	7.32 E
Katsina □[3]	150	12.20 N	7.45 E
Katsina Ala	150	7.10 N	9.17 E
Katsina Ala ≃	152	7.48 N	8.52 E
Katsunuma	94	35.39 N	138.44 E
Katsura ◆[8]	270	34.59 N	135.42 E
Katsura ≃, Nihon	94	35.36 N	139.15 E
Katsura ≃, Nihon	94	34.53 N	135.42 E
Katsura ≃, Nihon	96	34.02 N	134.35 E
Katsura ≃, Nihon	270	34.53 N	135.42 E
Katsuragi	96	34.15 N	135.30 E
Katsuragi-san ∧	96	34.20 N	135.27 E
Katsushika ◆[8]	268	35.43 N	139.51 E
Katsuta, Nihon	94	36.24 N	140.30 E
Katsuta, Nihon	96	35.04 N	134.11 E
Katsuura, Nihon	94	35.08 N	140.18 E
Katsuura, Nihon	96	33.56 N	134.30 E
Katsuyama, Nihon	94	36.03 N	136.30 E
Katsuyama, Nihon	96	35.05 N	133.41 E
Kattakurgan	72	39.55 N	66.15 E
Kattara-Senke → Qaṭṭārah, Munkhafaḍ al- ≚[7]	140	30.00 N	27.30 E
Kattarp	41	56.09 N	12.46 E
Katta-Taldyk	85	40.19 N	73.12 E
Kattaviá	38	35.57 N	27.46 E
Kattegat Ų	26	57.00 N	11.00 E
Katternberg ◆[8]	263	51.09 N	7.02 E
Katthammarsvik	26	57.26 N	18.50 E
Kattowitz → Katowice	30	50.16 N	19.00 E
Kattrup	41	55.57 N	9.56 E
Kāttuputtūr	122	10.59 N	78.14 E
Katul, Jabal ∧	140	14.16 N	29.23 E
Katuma	154	6.10 S	30.34 E
Katumba	154	7.45 S	25.18 E
Katun' ≃	86	52.25 N	85.05 E
Katunino	80	58.01 N	45.39 E
Katunki	80	56.50 N	43.14 E
Kātūria	124	24.44 N	86.43 E
Katu Shan ∧	86	45.40 N	82.55 E
Katusice	54	50.26 N	14.50 E
Kātwa	126	23.39 N	88.08 E
Katwijk aan de Rijn	52	52.11 N	4.26 E
Katwijk aan Zee	52	52.13 N	4.24 E
Katy	222	29.47 N	95.49 W
Katyn	76	54.47 N	31.44 E
Kąty Wrocławskie	30	51.02 N	16.46 E
Katzenbuckel ∧	56	49.28 N	9.02 E
Katzenelnbogen	56	50.17 N	7.59 E
Katzenfurt	56	50.37 N	8.21 E
Katzhütte	54	50.33 N	11.03 E
Kaua ≃	156	19.24 S	22.03 E
Kauai □[6]	229b	21.59 N	159.22 W
Kauai I	229b	22.00 N	159.30 W
Kauai Channel Ų	229b	21.45 N	158.50 W
Kaub	56	50.05 N	7.46 E
Kau Desert ◆[2]	229d	19.21 N	155.19 W
Kaufbeuren	58	47.53 N	10.37 E
Kaufering	58	48.05 N	10.52 E
Kaufman	222	32.35 N	96.18 W
Kaufman □[6]	222	32.38 N	96.18 W
Kaufungen	56	51.17 N	9.38 E
Kaugama	150	12.28 N	9.44 E
Kauhajoki	26	62.26 N	22.11 E
Kauhanevan-Pohjankankaan kansallispuisto ♦	26	62.08 N	22.25 E
Kauhava	26	63.06 N	23.05 E
Kauiki Head ›	229a	20.45 N	155.59 W
Kaukapakapa	172	36.37 S	174.30 E
Kaukasus → Bol'šoj Kavkaz ⋏	84	42.30 N	45.00 E
Kaukauna	190	44.16 N	88.16 W
Kaukau Veld ⋏[1]	156	19.30 S	20.30 E
Kaukhāli	126	22.38 N	90.04 E
Kaukura I[1]	14	15.45 S	146.42 W
Kaula I	229d	21.45 N	160.30 W
Kaulakahi Channel Ų	229b	22.00 N	159.53 W
Kaulille	56	51.11 N	5.31 E
Kauliranta	24	66.27 N	23.41 E
Kaŭl-li	98	37.58 N	124.37 E
Kaulsdorf	54	50.37 N	11.26 E
Kaulsdorf ◆[8]	264a	52.31 N	13.33 E
Kaulsdorf-Süd ◆[8]	264a	52.29 N	13.34 E
Kaumakani	229b	21.55 N	159.37 W
Kaumalapau	229a	20.47 N	156.59 W
Kaunakakai	229a	21.05 N	157.01 W
Kaunas	76	54.54 N	23.54 E
Kauneonga Lake	210	41.41 N	74.50 W
Kauner Tal ∨	64	47.01 N	10.44 E
Kaunghein	110	25.40 N	95.26 E
Kauniainen → Grankulla	26	60.13 N	24.45 E
Kaununui ›	229b	21.56 N	160.10 W
Kaup	164	3.50 S	144.00 E
Kaupanger	26	61.11 N	7.14 E
Kaura Namoda	150	12.35 N	6.35 E
Kauriyāla Ghāt	124	28.23 N	81.02 E
Kauru	150	10.33 N	8.12 E
Kausa	272c	19.10 N	73.02 E
Kau Sai Chau I	271d	22.22 N	114.18 E
Kausala	26	60.54 N	26.22 E
Kaušany	78	46.38 N	29.25 E
Kaustinen	26	63.32 N	23.42 E
Kauswagan	116	8.11 N	124.05 E
Kautokeino	24	69.00 N	23.02 E
Kauttua	26	61.06 N	22.10 E
Kau-ye Kyun I	110	11.01 N	98.32 E
Kavača	74	60.16 N	169.51 E
Kavacık	130	39.40 N	28.30 E
Kavadarci	38	41.26 N	22.00 E
Kavajë	38	41.11 N	19.33 E
Kavak, Tür.	130	38.24 N	39.26 E
Kavak, Tür.	130	41.05 N	36.03 E
Kavak, Tür.	130	39.18 N	37.30 E
Kavakbaşı	130	38.29 N	41.49 E
Kavaklıdere	130	37.26 N	28.22 E
Kavála	38	40.56 N	24.25 E
Kavalerovo	89	44.15 N	135.04 E
Kāvali	122	14.55 N	79.59 E
Kavango □[5]	156	18.30 S	20.15 E
Kavaratti	122	10.34 N	72.39 E
Kavaratti Island I	122	10.33 N	72.38 E
Kavarna	38	43.25 N	28.20 E
Kavendou, Mont ∧	150	10.41 N	12.12 W
Kāveri ≃	122	11.09 N	79.52 E
Kāveri Falls ʟ	122	12.18 N	77.17 E
Kaverino, Ross.	80	54.10 N	41.47 E
Kaverino, Ross.	82	56.11 N	36.15 E
Kavieng	164	2.35 S	150.50 E
Kavimba	156	18.02 S	24.38 E
Kavīr, Dasht-e ◆[2]	128	34.40 N	54.30 E
Kavkazskij zapovednik ♦	84	43.55 N	40.30 E
Kävlinge	41	55.48 N	13.06 E
Kävlingeån ≃	41	55.47 N	13.06 E
Kavungo	152	11.31 S	23.03 E
Kavuu ≃	154	7.40 S	31.46 E
Kavykuči-Gazimurskije	88	51.22 N	118.10 E
Kaw, Guy. fr.	250	4.29 N	52.02 W
Kaw, Ok., U.S.	196	36.46 N	96.50 W
Kawa	110	17.05 N	96.28 E
Kawaba	94	36.41 N	139.07 E
Kawabe, Nihon	94	35.29 N	137.04 E
Kawabe, Nihon	96	33.55 N	135.11 E
Kawachi, Nihon	94	36.24 N	136.38 E
Kawachi, Nihon	94	36.37 N	139.56 E
Kawachi, Nihon	94	35.53 N	140.15 E
Kawachi-nagano	96	34.27 N	135.34 E
Kawagama Lake ⊜	212	45.18 N	78.45 W
Kawage	94	34.47 N	136.33 E
Kawagoe	94	35.55 N	139.29 E
Kawaguchi	94	35.48 N	139.43 E
Kawaguchiko	94	35.30 N	138.46 E
Kawaguchi-ko ⊜	94	35.31 N	138.45 E
Kawahara	96	35.24 N	134.12 E
Kawai, Nihon	94	36.18 N	137.07 E
Kawai, Nihon	270	34.35 N	135.45 E
Kawaihae Bay c	229d	20.02 N	155.50 W
Kawaihoa ›	229b	21.47 N	160.12 W
Kawaikini ∧	229b	22.05 N	159.29 W
Kawailoa	229c	21.36 N	158.05 W
Kawailoa Beach	229c	21.37 N	158.04 W
Kawajiri	96	34.14 N	132.42 E
Kawakami, Nihon	94	35.58 N	138.35 E
Kawakami, Nihon	96	34.44 N	133.29 E
Kawakami, Nihon	96	35.17 N	133.39 E
Kawakawa	172	35.23 S	174.04 E
Kawakubo	270	34.54 N	135.38 E
Kawali	115a	7.11 S	108.22 E
Kawama Mission	154	10.04 S	28.37 E
Kawamata	92	37.39 N	140.36 E
Kawambwa	154	9.47 S	29.05 E
Kawamoto, Nihon	94	36.09 N	139.17 E
Kawamoto, Nihon	96	34.59 N	132.30 E
Kawane	94	34.57 N	138.05 E
Kawanishi, Nihon	94	37.09 N	138.45 E
Kawanishi, Nihon	96	34.49 N	135.24 E
Kawanishi, Nihon	270	34.35 N	135.47 E
Kawanoe	96	34.01 N	133.34 E
Kawara, Nihon	96	33.40 N	130.51 E
Kawara, Nihon	270	34.59 N	135.18 E
Kawara Débé	150	12.20 N	3.26 E
Kawarai	268	35.25 N	140.05 E
Kawardha	124	22.01 N	81.15 E
Kawartha Park	212	44.32 N	78.12 W
Kawasaki, Nihon	94	35.32 N	139.43 E
Kawasaki, Nihon	96	33.35 N	130.49 E
Kawasaki-kō c	268	35.30 N	139.47 E
Kawasaki Stadium ♦	268	35.32 N	139.43 E
Kawashima, Nihon	94	35.21 N	136.50 E
Kawashima, Nihon	94	35.59 N	139.30 E
Kawashima, Nihon	96	34.04 N	134.19 E
Kawashima ◆[8]	268	35.28 N	139.35 E
Kawashiri-misaki ›	96	34.26 N	130.58 E
Kawatana	92	33.04 N	129.52 E
Kawauchi	96	33.48 N	132.55 E
Kawau Island I	172	36.25 S	174.51 E
Kawawa ◆[8]	268	35.31 N	139.33 E
Kawayan	116	11.41 N	124.21 E
Kawazu	94	34.44 N	138.59 E
Kawbein	110	16.33 N	97.52 E
Kawdut	110	15.31 N	97.47 E
Kawe	164	7.50 S	138.14 E
Kawe, Pulau I	164	0.03 S	130.07 E
Kaweenakumik Lake ⊜	184	52.52 N	99.30 W
Kaweka ∧	172	39.17 S	176.23 E
Kaweka Range ⋏	172	39.15 S	176.20 E
Kawerau	172	38.03 S	176.43 E
Kawhia	172	38.04 S	174.49 E
Kawhia Harbour c	172	38.05 S	174.50 E
Kawich Peak ∧	204	37.58 N	116.27 W
Kawich Range ⋏	204	37.40 N	116.30 W
Kawin	164	2.45 S	150.45 E
Kawinda	115b	8.07 S	118.04 E
Kawit	269f	14.27 N	120.54 E
Kawkabān	144	15.40 N	43.52 E
Kawkareik	110	16.33 N	98.14 E
Kaw Lake ⊜[1]	196	36.55 N	96.57 W
Kawludo	110	18.29 N	97.19 E
Kawm	140	13.31 N	22.50 E
Kawm al-Farā'in (Buto) ⊥	142	31.11 N	30.45 E
Kawm ar-Rāhib	142	28.20 N	30.37 E
Kawm Birah	273c	30.05 N	31.08 E
Kawm Dafanah (Daphnæ) ⊥	142	30.52 N	32.11 E
Kawm Ḥamādah	142	30.46 N	30.42 E
Kawm Ishfīn	273c	30.11 N	31.15 E
Kawm Ishū	142	31.07 N	30.00 E
Kawm Ju'ayf (Naucratis) ⊥	142	30.54 N	30.36 E
Kawm Umbū	140	24.28 N	32.57 E
Kawnglanghpu	102	27.04 N	98.21 E
Kawnipi Lake ⊜	190	48.24 N	91.14 W
Kawthaung	110	9.59 N	98.33 E
Kax ≃	86	43.40 N	81.45 E
Kaxgar ≃	85	39.40 N	78.00 E
Kaya, Burkina	150	13.05 N	1.05 W
Kaya, Nihon	96	35.30 N	135.06 E
Kayaapu	112	5.26 S	102.24 E
Kayadibi, Tür.	130	39.29 N	36.43 E
Kayadibi, Tür.	130	39.55 N	34.15 E
Kayah □[3]	110	19.15 N	97.30 E
Kayak Island I	180	59.52 N	144.30 W
Kāyalpattinam	122	8.34 N	78.07 E
Kāyamba	272b	22.41 N	88.32 E
Kayambi	154	9.27 S	31.58 E
Kayan	110	16.54 N	96.34 E
Kayan ≃	112	2.55 N	117.35 E
Kayangel Islands II	108	8.04 N	134.43 E
Kayang-san ∧[2]	271b	37.33 N	126.43 E
Kāyankulam	122	9.11 N	76.30 E
Kayapa	116	16.22 N	120.53 E
Kayapınar	130	37.34 N	41.10 E
Kayaş	130	39.56 N	32.58 E
Kaya-san ∧	98	35.49 N	128.07 E

≃ River	Fluß	Río	Rivière	Rio
≊ Canal	Kanal	Canal	Canal	Canal
ʟ Waterfall, Rapids	Wasserfall, Stromschnellen	Cascada, Rápidos	Chute d'eau, Rapides	Cascata, Rápidos
Ų Strait	Meeresstraße	Estrecho	Détroit	Estreito
c Bay, Gulf	Bucht, Golf	Bahía, Golfo	Baie, Golfe	Baía, Golfo
⊜ Lake, Lakes	See, Seen	Lago, Lagos	Lac, Lacs	Lago, Lagos
≚ Swamp	Sumpf	Pantano	Marais	Pântano
⍓ Ice Features, Glacier	Eis- und Gletscherformen	Accidentes Glaciales	Formes glaciaires	Acidentes glaciares
Ŧ Other Hydrographic Features	Andere Hydrographische Objekte	Otros Elementos Hidrográficos	Autres données hydrographiques	Outros acidentes hidrográficos

⊹ Submarine Features	Untermeerische Objekte	Accidentes Submarinos	Formes de relief sous-marin	Acidentes submarinos
□ Political Unit	Politische Einheit	Unidad Politica	Entité politique	Unidade política
ʊ Cultural Institution	Kulturelle Institution	Institución Cultural	Institution culturelle	Institução cultural
⊥ Historical Site	Historische Stätte	Sitio Histórico	Site historique	Sitio histórico
♦ Recreational Site	Erholungs- und Ferienort	Sitio de Recreo	Centre de loisirs	Area de Lazer
⊠ Airport	Flughafen	Aeropuerto	Aéroport	Aeroporto
■ Military Installation	Militäranlage	Instalación Militar	Installation militaire	Instalação militar
◆ Miscellaneous	Verschiedenes	Misceláneo	Divers	Diversos

ENGLISH — Name | Page | Lat.°′ | Long.°′
DEUTSCH — Name | Seite | Breite°′ | Länge°′ E = Ost

Kaya-san Kukrip Kongwŏn ♦ 98 35.47 N 128.06 E
Kaycee 200 43.42 N 106.38 W
Kayeli 164 3.23 S 127.06 E
Kayembe-Mukulu 152 9.03 S 23.57 E
Kayen 115a 6.54 S 110.59 E
Kayenta 200 36.43 N 110.15 W
Kayes, Congo 152 4.25 S 11.41 E
Kayes, Mali 150 14.27 N 11.26 W
Kayes □[4] 150 14.00 N 11.00 W
Kay Gardens 285 39.45 N 75.25 W
Kayima 150 8.53 N 11.10 W
Kayin □[3] 110 17.30 N 97.45 E
Kayış Dağı ∧ 267b 40.59 N 29.10 E
Kaymakçı 130 38.10 N 28.08 E
Kaymaz, Tür. 130 39.31 N 31.11 E
Kaymaz, Tür. 130 40.55 N 30.18 E
Kayna 54 50.59 N 12.14 E
Kaynar 130 38.55 N 36.28 E
Kayō, Nihon 96 34.51 N 133.42 E
Kayō, Nihon 174m 26.33 N 128.07 E
Kayoa, Pulau I 164 0.05 S 127.25 E
Kayombo 154 9.36 S 25.37 E
Kaypak 130 37.08 N 36.27 E
Kay Point › 180 69.18 N 138.22 W
Kayser Gebergte ⋀ 250 3.03 N 56.35 W
Kayseri 130 38.43 N 35.30 E
Kayseri □[4] 130 38.30 N 35.55 E
Kaysersberg 58 48.08 N 7.15 E
Kaysville 200 41.02 N 111.56 W
Kayuadi, Pulau I 112 6.49 S 120.47 E
Kayuagung 112 3.24 S 104.50 E
Kayumas 115a 7.50 S 114.08 E
Kayuta Lake ⊜ 210 43.25 N 75.12 W
Kayuyu 154 3.39 S 26.21 E
Kazach 84 41.06 N 45.22 E
Kazachskij melkosopočnik ⋀[2] 86 49.00 N 72.00 E
Kazachstan → Kazakhstan □[1] 72 48.00 N 68.00 E
Kazačij 83 46.58 N 40.03 E
Kazačinskoje, Ross. 86 57.49 N 93.17 E
Kazačinskoje, Ross. 88 56.16 N 107.36 E
Kazačja Lopan' 78 50.21 N 36.11 E
Kazačje 74 70.44 N 136.13 E
Kazačji Lageri 78 46.42 N 32.59 E
Kazačka 80 51.28 N 43.56 E
Kazackij 86 49.20 N 58.31 E
Kazackoje 78 51.18 N 33.29 E
Kazakdarja 86 43.27 N 59.46 E
Kazakevičevo 89 48.17 N 134.46 E
Kazakhstan □[1], Asia 72 48.00 N 68.00 E
Kazakhstan □[1], Asia 86 47.00 N 76.00 E
Kazaki 76 52.38 N 38.16 E
Kazaklija 78 46.00 N 28.37 E
Kazakstan → Kazakhstan □[1] 72 48.00 N 68.00 E
Kazal'cevo 86 59.18 N 80.30 E
Kazalinsk 86 45.46 N 62.07 E
Kazan' 80 55.49 N 49.08 E
Kazan ≃ 176 64.02 N 95.30 W
Kazanbulak 84 40.38 N 46.41 E
Kazancı 130 36.30 N 32.53 E
Kazandžik 128 39.16 N 55.32 E
Kazanka, Kaz. 86 53.20 N 67.27 E
Kazanka, Ukr. 78 47.50 N 32.49 E
Kazanka ≃ 80 55.48 N 49.01 E
Kazanlâk 38 42.38 N 25.21 E
Kazan Lake ⊜ 184 55.33 N 108.21 W
Kazanlı 130 36.50 N 34.45 E
Kazanovka 76 53.46 N 38.34 E
Kazan-rettō (Volcano Islands) II 14 25.00 N 141.00 E
Kazanskaja 78 49.48 N 41.09 E
Kazanskoje, Ross. 82 54.59 N 37.39 E
Kazanskoje, Ross. 86 55.38 N 69.14 E
Kazan' Station ✦[5] 265b 55.46 N 37.40 E
Kazantip, mys › 78 45.28 N 35.51 E
Kazarman 85 41.24 N 74.03 E
Kazatin 78 49.43 N 28.50 E
Kazatkul' 86 55.02 N 76.03 E
Kazbegi 84 42.39 N 44.39 E
Kazbek, gora ∧ 84 42.42 N 44.31 E
Kaz Dağı ∧ 130 39.42 N 26.50 E
Kazembe 154 12.11 S 32.37 E
Kāzerūn 128 29.37 N 51.38 E
Kazgorodok, Kaz. 86 49.56 N 71.36 E
Kazgorodok, Kaz. 86 52.53 N 70.42 E
Kažim 24 60.20 N 51.30 E
Kazi-Magomed 84 40.03 N 48.56 E
Kazimierza Wielka 30 50.16 N 20.30 E
Kazimierz Dolny 30 51.20 N 21.58 E
Kazincbarcika 30 48.16 N 20.37 E
Kazinka, Ross. 76 52.32 N 39.42 E
Kazinka, Ross. 78 50.14 N 37.50 E
Kāzipāra 272b 22.43 N 88.31 E
Kāzīr Char 126 22.46 N 90.33 E
Kaziza 152 10.42 S 23.52 E
Kazlų Rūda 76 54.46 N 23.30 E
Kaz'minskoje 84 44.35 N 41.41 E
Kaznačejevo 82 54.31 N 37.16 E
Kazo 94 36.07 N 139.36 E
Kaz'onnyj Torec ≃ 83 48.54 N 37.46 E
Kaztalovka 80 49.46 N 48.42 E
Kazuma Pan National Park ♦ 154 18.15 S 25.33 E
Kazumba 152 6.25 S 22.02 E
Kazungula 154 17.45 S 25.20 E
Kazuno 92 40.11 N 140.47 E
Kazvin → Qazvīn 128 36.16 N 50.00 E
Kazy 128 39.13 N 57.30 E
Kazym 74 63.40 N 67.14 E
Kazym ≃ 74 63.54 N 65.50 E
Kazyr ≃ 86 53.47 N 92.53 E
Kbal Dâmrei 110 14.07 N 105.21 E
Kbelnice 60 49.18 N 13.59 E
Kbely ✦[8] 54 50.07 N 14.32 E
Kcynia 30 53.00 N 17.30 E
Kdyně 60 49.23 N 13.02 E
Kéa 38 37.38 N 24.21 E
Kéa I 38 37.34 N 24.22 E
Keaau 229d 19.37 N 155.02 W
Keady 48 54.15 N 6.42 W
Keahole Point › 229d 19.44 N 156.03 W
Keal, Loch na ⊂ 46 56.28 N 6.04 W
Kealaikahiki, Lae o › 229a 20.32 N 156.42 W
Kealaikahiki Channel ʯ 229a 20.37 N 156.50 W
Kealakekua Bay ⊂ 229d 19.28 N 155.56 W
Kealia 229b 22.06 N 159.18 W
Keams Canyon 200 35.48 N 110.11 W
Keanae 229a 20.51 N 156.09 W
Keanapapa Point › 229a 20.54 N 157.04 W
Kean College of New Jersey ⊕[2] 276 40.41 N 74.14 W
Keansburg 208 40.25 N 74.12 W
Kearney, Mo., U.S. 194 39.22 N 94.21 W
Kearney, Ne., U.S. 198 40.41 N 99.04 W
Kearney, Pa., U.S. 214 40.08 N 78.12 W
Kearns 200 40.39 N 111.59 W
Kearny, Az., U.S. 200 33.03 N 110.54 W
Kearny, N.J., U.S. 210 40.46 N 74.08 W
Kearsley 262 53.32 N 2.23 W
Kearsley Creek ≃ 216 43.04 N 83.40 W
Keasbey 276 40.31 N 74.19 W
Keb' ≃ 76 57.44 N 28.28 E
Kebajoran ✦[8] 269e 6.13 S 106.46 E
Keban 130 38.48 N 38.45 E
Keban Barajı ⊜[1] 130 38.50 N 39.20 E
Kebanyartimur 115a 7.09 S 112.52 E
Kébara 152 2.27 S 14.25 E
Kebbi 150 12.08 N 4.44 E
Kebeiti 120 36.47 N 79.29 E
Kébémer 150 15.22 N 16.27 W
Kébi, Mayo ≃ 146 9.18 N 13.33 E
Kebili 148 33.42 N 8.58 E
Kebîr, Oued el ≃ 34 36.50 N 6.07 E
Kebnekaise ∧ 24 67.53 N 18.33 E
Kebock Head › 46 58.01 N 6.20 W
Kebri Dehar 144 6.47 N 44.17 E
Kebumen 115a 7.40 S 109.39 E
Keb'uty 80 45.50 N 44.14 E
Keče 85 43.14 N 71.22 E
Kecel 30 46.32 N 19.16 E
Kech ≃ 128 26.00 N 62.44 E
Kechika ≃ 176 59.36 N 127.05 W
Keçiborlu 130 37.57 N 30.18 E
Kecksburg 214 40.11 N 79.28 W
Kecskemét 30 46.54 N 19.42 E
Kedabek 84 40.34 N 45.49 E
Kedah □[3] 114 6.00 N 100.40 E
Kėdainiai 76 55.17 N 24.00 E
Kédange-sur-Canner 56 49.19 N 6.20 E
Kedārnāth 124 30.44 N 79.04 E
Kedārpur 126 23.18 N 90.27 E
Kedges Straits ʯ 208 38.03 N 76.02 W
Kedgwick 186 47.39 N 67.21 W
Kedgwick ≃ 186 47.40 N 67.29 W
Kédhron 38 39.13 N 22.03 E
Kedian 100 31.23 N 112.51 E
Kediri 115a 7.49 S 112.01 E
Kedjebi 150 8.12 N 0.25 E
Kedon 74 64.08 N 159.14 E
Kedong 89 48.02 N 126.15 E
Kédougou 150 12.33 N 12.11 W
Kedrasju 24 64.36 N 60.24 E
Kedrovka 86 55.32 N 86.03 E
Kedu 102 26.33 N 104.21 E
Kedungdung 115a 7.06 S 113.15 E
Kedungjati 115a 7.10 S 110.37 E
Kedungwuni 115a 6.58 S 109.39 E
Kedvavom 24 64.15 N 53.27 E
Kędzierzyn Kozle 30 50.20 N 18.12 E
Keecheus Lake ⊜ 224 47.22 N 121.22 W
Keefer 218 38.32 N 84.38 W
Keefers 182 50.02 N 121.33 W
Keego Harbor 216 42.36 N 83.20 W
Keelby 44 53.34 N 0.15 W
Keele 42 53.00 N 2.17 W
Keele ≃ 180 64.24 N 124.50 W
Keele Peak ∧ 180 63.26 N 130.19 W
Keeley Lake ⊜ 184 54.54 N 108.08 W
Keeling Islands → Cocos Islands □[2] 12 12.10 S 96.55 E
Keels 186 48.36 N 53.24 W
Keelung → Chilung 100 25.08 N 121.44 E
Keen, Mount ∧ 46 56.58 N 2.54 W
Keene, On., Can. 212 44.15 N 78.10 W
Keene, Ca., U.S. 228 35.13 N 118.33 W
Keene, Ky., U.S. 192 37.56 N 84.38 W
Keene, N.H., U.S. 188 42.56 N 72.16 W
Keene, Oh., U.S. 214 40.21 N 81.52 W
Keene, Tx., U.S. 222 32.23 N 97.19 W
Keenesburg 200 40.06 N 104.31 W
Keeney Knob ∧ 192 37.47 N 80.42 W
Keeneyville 278 41.59 N 88.07 W
Keep River National Park ♦ 164 15.48 S 129.03 E
Keerbergen 56 51.00 N 4.37 E
Keer-Weer, Cape › 164 13.58 S 141.30 E
Keeseg ∧ 64 46.58 N 12.14 E
Keeseville 188 44.30 N 73.28 W
Keesler Air Force Base ■ 194 30.26 N 88.55 W
Keetmanshoop 156 26.36 S 18.08 E
Keetmanshoop □[5] 156 26.30 S 19.00 E
Keewatin, On., Can. 184 49.46 N 94.34 W
Keewatin, Mn., U.S. 190 47.23 N 93.04 W
Kefa □[4] 144 6.50 N 36.00 E
Kefallinía I 38 38.15 N 20.35 E
Kéfalos 38 36.45 N 27.00 E
Kefamenanu 112 9.27 S 124.29 E
Kefar ʿAzza 132 31.29 N 34.32 E
Kefar Blum 132 33.10 N 35.36 E
Kefar ʿEẕyon 132 31.39 N 35.08 E
Kefar Naḥum (Capernaum) ⊥ 132 32.53 N 35.34 E
Kefar Sava 132 32.10 N 34.54 E
Kefar Shammay 132 32.57 N 35.27 E
Kefar Szold 132 33.11 N 35.39 E
Kefar Vitkin 132 32.23 N 34.53 E
Kefar Warburg 132 31.43 N 34.44 E
Kefar Yona 132 32.19 N 34.55 E
Kefermarkt 61 48.26 N 14.32 E
Keffi 150 8.51 N 7.52 E
Keffin Hausa 150 12.15 N 9.58 E
Keflavík 24a 64.02 N 22.36 W
Keftya 144 13.54 N 37.07 E
Kega 24 65.10 N 36.54 E
Ke Ga, Mui ›, Viet 110 12.53 N 109.28 E
Ke Ga, Mui ›, Viet 110 10.42 N 107.58 E
Kegalla 122 7.15 N 80.21 E
Kégashka 186 50.12 N 61.17 W
Kégashka, Lac ⊜ 186 50.20 N 61.25 W
Kegejli 86 42.45 N 59.35 E
Kegičovka 78 49.17 N 35.46 E
Kegnæs ›[1] 41 54.52 N 9.59 E
Kegon-no-taki ⌊ 94 36.44 N 139.31 E
Kegonsa, Lake ⊜ 216 42.58 N 89.15 W
Kegonzhake 120 33.00 N 87.53 E
Keg River 176 57.48 N 117.52 W
Kegums 76 56.46 N 24.45 E
Kegworth 42 52.50 N 1.16 W
Kehdingen, Land ✦[1] 52 53.45 N 9.15 E
Kehiwin Indian Reserve ✦[4] 182 54.07 N 110.48 W
Kehl 56 48.35 N 7.50 E
Kehlen 58 47.41 N 9.33 E
Kehoe 218 38.28 N 83.03 W
Kehra 76 59.20 N 25.20 E
Kehrigk 54 52.09 N 13.55 E
Ke-hsi Mānsām 110 21.56 N 97.50 E
Keig 46 57.15 N 2.39 W
Keighley 44 53.52 N 1.54 W
Keihoku 96 35.09 N 135.38 E
Keijō → Sŏul 98 37.33 N 126.58 E
Keila 76 59.18 N 24.25 E
Keilor 169 37.43 S 144.50 E
Keimoes 158 28.41 S 21.00 E
Kei Mouth 158 32.41 S 28.22 E
Keio University ⊕[2] 268 35.38 N 139.45 E
Kei Road 158 32.42 S 27.32 E
Keiser 194 35.40 N 90.05 W
Keiskammahoek 158 32.41 S 27.09 E
Keiskammapunt › 158 32.40 S 27.10 E
Keïta 150 14.46 N 5.46 E
Kéita, Bahr ≃ 146 9.14 N 18.21 E
Keitele 26 63.11 N 26.22 E
Keitele ⊜ 26 62.55 N 26.00 E
Keith, Austl. 166 36.06 S 140.21 E
Keith, Scot., U.K. 46 57.32 N 2.57 W
Keith Arm ⊂ 176 65.20 N 122.15 W
Keithley Creek 182 52.45 N 121.24 W
Keithsburg 190 41.05 N 90.56 W
Keiyasi 175g 17.54 S 177.45 E
Keizer 224 44.59 N 123.01 W
Kejaman 112 2.39 N 113.45 E
Kejimkujik National Park ♦ 186 44.21 N 65.18 W
Kejngypil'gyn, laguna ⊂ 180 63.30 N 178.50 E
Kejni, gora ∧ 180 64.30 N 174.54 W
Kejvy ⋀ 24 67.35 N 38.00 E
Kekaha 229b 21.58 N 159.42 W
Kekek ≃ 190 48.24 N 75.48 W
Kekerengu 172 42.00 S 174.01 E
Kékes ∧ 30 47.55 N 20.02 E
Kekeyaer 85 38.02 N 75.05 E
Kek Lok Si ⊕[1] 114 5.23 N 100.14 E
Kekpāra 126 22.27 N 86.35 E
Kekri 120 25.58 N 75.09 E
Kekurnoi, Cape › 180 57.44 N 155.15 W
Kelafo 144 5.40 N 44.20 E
Kelai ≃ 112 2.10 N 117.29 E
Kelan 102 38.43 N 111.32 E
Kelanang 114 2.48 N 101.26 E
Kelang 114 3.02 N 101.27 E
Kelang, Pulau I, Indon. 164 3.12 S 127.44 E
Kelang, Pulau I, Malay. 114 3.00 N 101.18 E
Kelani ≃ 122 6.58 N 79.52 E
Kelantan 114 0.51 N 101.40 E
Kelantan □[3] 114 5.20 N 102.00 E
Kelantan ≃ 114 6.11 N 102.15 E
Kelapa 112 1.52 S 105.42 E
Kelasuri 84 43.08 N 41.13 E
Kelat 218 38.32 N 84.19 W
Kelayres 210 40.54 N 76.00 W
Kelb, Ouadi V 146 15.19 N 18.51 E
Kel'badžar 84 40.07 N 46.02 E
Kelberg 56 50.17 N 6.55 E
Kelbia, Sebkhet ⊜ 36 35.51 N 10.16 E
Kelbra 54 51.26 N 11.02 E
Keld Ula ∧ 86 43.20 N 85.25 E
Kel'd'ušovo 80 55.01 N 44.59 E
Keleft 128 37.21 N 66.15 E
Kelegou 98 41.57 N 118.11 E
Kélékélé 273b 4.20 S 15.08 E
Kelem 144 4.48 N 35.58 E
Kelenföld ✦[8] 264c 47.28 N 19.03 E
Kelenken, gora ∧ 180 66.07 N 170.52 W
Keles, Tür. 130 39.55 N 29.14 E
Keles, Uzb. 85 41.24 N 69.12 E
Keles ≃ 85 41.02 N 68.37 E
Keleti-főcsatorna ≍ 30 48.01 N 21.20 E
Keleti Pályaudvar ✦[5] 264c 47.30 N 19.06 E
Kelheim 60 48.55 N 11.52 E
Kelibia 148 36.51 N 11.06 E
Kelkheim 56 50.08 N 8.26 E
Kelkit 130 40.08 N 39.27 E
Kelkit ≃ 130 40.46 N 36.32 E
Kell 219 38.30 N 88.54 W
Kellé 152 0.06 S 14.33 E
Kellen 52 51.48 N 6.10 E
Kellenhusen 54 54.11 N 11.03 E
Keller, Tx., U.S. 222 32.56 N 97.15 W
Keller, Va., U.S. 208 37.37 N 75.45 W
Keller, Wa., U.S. 182 48.04 N 118.41 W
Kellerberg 64 46.40 N 13.42 E
Kellerberrin 162 31.38 S 117.43 E
Kellerjoch ∧ 64 47.19 N 11.46 E
Keller Lake ⊜, N.T., Can. 176 64.00 N 121.30 W
Keller Lake ⊜, Sk., Can. 184 56.04 N 106.46 W
Kellerovka 86 53.50 N 69.17 E
Keller Peak ∧ 228 34.12 N 117.03 W
Kellett, Cape › 176 71.59 N 125.34 W
Kellettville 214 41.33 N 79.16 W
Kelleys Island 214 41.36 N 82.42 W
Kelleys Island I 214 41.36 N 82.42 W
Kelliher 184 51.15 N 103.44 W
Kellinghusen 52 53.57 N 9.43 E
Kellmünz 58 48.07 N 10.08 E
Kelloe 44 54.43 N 1.28 W
Kellogg, Id., U.S. 202 47.32 N 116.07 W
Kellogg, Ia., U.S. 190 41.43 N 92.54 W
Kellogg, Mn., U.S. 190 44.18 N 91.59 W
Kellogg Marsh 224 48.05 N 122.07 W
Kelloggsville 214 41.52 N 80.36 W
Kellojärvi ⊜ 26 64.16 N 29.03 E
Kelloselkä 24 66.56 N 28.50 E
Kells, N. Ire., U.K. 44 54.48 N 6.13 E
Kells, N. Ire., U.K. 48 54.48 N 6.13 E
Kells → Ceanannus Mór 48 53.44 N 6.53 W
Kelly Air Force Base ■ 196 29.24 N 98.35 W
Kelly Lake ⊜ 180 65.30 N 126.10 W
Kelly Run ≃, Pa., U.S. 279b 40.15 N 79.55 W
Kelly Run ≃, Pa., U.S. 279b 40.13 N 79.45 W
Kellyville, Austl. 274a 33.43 S 150.57 E
Kellyville, Ok., U.S. 196 35.56 N 96.12 W
Kelmė 76 55.38 N 22.56 E
Kel'mency 78 48.27 N 26.50 E
Kelmet 144 16.04 N 38.55 E
Kelmscott 168a 32.07 S 116.01 E
Kelo 146 9.19 N 15.48 E
Kelolokan 112 1.08 N 117.54 E
Kelottijärvi 24 68.31 N 22.04 E
Kelowna 182 49.53 N 119.29 W
Kelsall 44 53.13 N 2.43 W
Kelsey Bay 182 50.24 N 125.57 W
Kelsey Head › 42 50.24 N 5.08 W
Kelsey Lake ⊜ 184 53.37 N 101.02 W
Kelseyville 204 38.58 N 122.50 W
Kelso, Scot., U.K. 46 55.36 N 2.25 W
Kelso, Wa., U.S. 224 46.08 N 122.54 W
Kelsterbach 56 50.04 N 8.32 E
Kel'temašat 85 42.30 N 70.17 E
Kelty 46 56.08 N 3.23 W
Keluang 114 2.02 N 103.19 E
Keluang, Tanjung › 112 3.02 S 110.39 E
Kelud, Gunung ∧ 115a 7.56 S 112.18 E
Keluo ≃ 89 49.22 N 125.15 E
Keluotun 89 49.16 N 125.44 E
Kelvedon 42 51.51 N 0.42 E
Kelvedon Hatch 260 51.40 N 0.16 E
Kelvington 184 52.10 N 103.30 W
Kelvin Seamount ✢[3] 16 38.50 N 64.00 W
Kelyexeed 144 8.46 N 49.12 E
Kelzenberg 263 51.07 N 6.30 E
Kem' 24 64.57 N 34.36 E
Kem' ≃, Ross. 24 64.57 N 34.41 E
Kem' ≃, Ross. 86 58.31 N 92.04 E
Kema 112 1.23 N 125.04 E
Kema ≃, Ross. 76 60.16 N 37.20 E
Kema ≃, Ross. 76 59.21 N 44.29 E
Ké Macina 150 13.58 N 5.22 W
Kémah, Congo 273b 4.11 S 15.13 E
Kemah, Tür. 130 39.36 N 39.02 E
Kemah, Tx., U.S. 222 29.32 N 95.01 W
Kemaliye 130 39.16 N 38.29 E
Kemalpaşa, Tür. 130 41.30 N 41.30 E
Kemalpaşa, Tür. 130 38.25 N 27.26 E
Kemano 182 53.34 N 127.56 W
Kemasik 114 4.25 N 103.27 E
Kemayan 114 3.08 N 102.22 E
Kemayoran Airport ⊠ 269e 6.09 S 106.51 E
Kembani 112 1.34 S 122.54 E
Kembé 152 4.36 N 21.54 E
Kemberg 54 51.46 N 12.38 E
Kemblesville 208 39.45 N 75.50 W
Kembolcha 144 11.02 N 39.43 E
Kembs 58 47.41 N 7.30 E
Kembul 164 5.55 S 150.40 E
Kemčug ≃ 86 57.14 N 90.31 E
Kemena ≃ 112 3.10 N 113.03 E
Kemeneshát ⋀[2] 61 46.58 N 16.40 E
Kemer, Tür. 130 36.38 N 29.21 E
Kemer, Tür. 130 36.36 N 30.34 E
Kemer, Tür. 130 37.21 N 30.04 E
Kemer ≃ 267b 41.04 N 29.07 E
Kemer Barajı ⊜[1] 130 37.34 N 28.31 E
Kemerburgaz ✦[8] 267b 41.09 N 28.54 E
Kemerhisar 130 37.49 N 34.36 E
Kemerovo 86 55.20 N 86.05 E
Kemerovo Oblast' □[4] 86 55.00 N 87.00 E
Kemi 26 65.49 N 24.32 E
Kemie 26 62.14 N 30.20 E
Kemijärvi 24 66.40 N 27.25 E
Kemijärvi ⊜ 24 66.36 N 27.24 E
Kemijoki ≃ 24 65.47 N 24.30 E
Kemiö → Kimito 26 60.10 N 22.45 E
Keml'a 80 54.42 N 45.15 E
Kemmel 50 50.47 N 2.49 E
Kemmelberg ∧[2] 50 50.47 N 2.50 E
Kemmerer 200 41.47 N 110.32 W
Kemminghausen ✦[8] 263 51.34 N 7.29 E
Kemmuna (Comino) I 36 36.00 N 14.20 E
Kemnader See ⊜ 263 51.25 N 7.15 E
Kemnath 60 49.52 N 11.54 E
Kemnay 46 57.14 N 2.27 W
Kemnitz 54 54.04 N 13.31 E
Kémo-Gribingui □[5] 152 6.00 N 19.00 E
Kemp 222 32.26 N 96.13 W
Kemp, Lake ⊜[1] 196 33.45 N 99.13 W
Kemparana 150 12.50 N 4.56 W
Kemp Coast ⊥[2] 9 67.10 S 58.00 E
Kempele 26 64.55 N 25.30 E
Kempen 56 51.22 N 6.25 E
Kempen ✦[1] 56 51.10 N 5.20 E
Kempener Land ✦[1] 263 51.19 N 6.29 E
Kempenfelt Bay ⊂ 212 44.23 N 79.36 W
Kempenich 56 50.25 N 7.07 E
Kemper → Quimper 32 48.00 N 4.06 W
Kempisch Kanaal ≍ 56 51.10 N 4.49 E
Kemp Mill 284c 39.02 N 77.01 W
Kempner 196 31.05 N 98.00 W
Kemp Peninsula ›[1] 9 73.08 S 60.15 W
Kemps Bay 238 24.02 N 77.33 W
Kemps Creek ≃ 274a 33.51 S 150.46 E
Kempsey, Austl. 166 31.05 S 152.50 E
Kempsey, Eng., U.K. 42 52.08 N 2.12 W
Kempston 42 52.07 N 0.30 W
Kempt, Lac ⊜ 176 47.25 N 74.22 W
Kempten (Allgäu) 58 47.43 N 10.19 E
Kempton, Il., U.S. 216 40.56 N 88.14 W
Kempton, In., U.S. 216 40.17 N 86.13 W
Kempton Park 158 26.06 S 28.14 E
Kempton Park □[5] 273d 26.06 S 28.14 E
Kempton Park Race Course ♦ 260 51.25 N 0.23 W
Kemptville 212 45.01 N 75.38 W
Kemptville Creek ≃ 212 45.03 N 75.39 W
Kemsing 260 51.18 N 0.14 E
Kemubu 114 5.18 N 102.01 E
Kemujan, Pulau I 115a 5.48 S 110.28 E
Kemul, Kong ∧ 112 1.52 N 116.11 E
Ken ≃ 124 25.46 N 80.31 E
Ken, Loch ⊜ 44 55.02 N 4.02 W
Ken, Water of ≃ 44 55.04 N 4.08 W
Kena ≃ 24 62.05 N 39.06 E
Kenai 180 60.33 N 151.15 W
Kenai Fjords National Park ♦ 180 59.45 N 150.00 W
Kenai Mountains ⋀ 180 60.00 N 150.00 W
Kenai Peninsula ›[1] 180 60.10 N 150.00 W
Kenamuke Swamp ≡ 140 6.15 N 33.48 E
Kenansville, Fl., U.S. 220 27.52 N 80.59 W
Kenansville, N.C., U.S. 192 34.57 N 77.57 W
Kenaral 85 42.32 N 72.08 E
Kenašči 80 50.32 N 53.20 E
Kenashiga-sen ∧ 96 35.14 N 133.31 E
Kenaston 184 51.30 N 106.18 W
Kenberma 283 42.17 N 70.52 W
Kenbridge 192 36.57 N 78.07 W
Kenda 126 23.12 N 86.32 E
Kendai 124 22.45 N 82.37 E
Kendal, Sk., Can. 184 50.15 N 103.37 W
Kendal, Indon. 115a 6.55 S 110.12 E
Kendal, S. Afr. 158 26.04 S 28.58 E
Kendal, Eng., U.K. 44 54.20 N 2.45 W
Kendall, Austl. 166 31.38 S 152.43 E
Kendall, Fl., U.S. 220 25.40 N 80.19 W
Kendall, Mi., U.S. 216 42.22 N 85.49 W
Kendall, N.Y., U.S. 210 43.20 N 78.02 W
Kendall, Wi., U.S. 190 43.47 N 90.22 W
Kendall □[6] 216 41.38 N 88.27 W
Kendall, Cape › 176 63.36 N 87.09 W
Kendall, Mount ∧ 172 41.22 S 172.24 E
Kendall Park 208 40.31 N 74.24 W
Kendallville 216 41.26 N 85.15 W
Kendari 112 3.57 S 122.35 E
Kendari, Teluk ⊂ 112 3.57 S 122.38 E
Kendawangan 112 2.32 S 110.12 E
Kende 150 11.30 N 4.12 E
Kendenup 162 34.29 S 117.39 E
Kendghāta 126 24.05 N 87.10 E
Kendikolu I 122 5.57 N 73.24 E
Kendiktas ⋀ 85 43.35 N 74.45 E
Kendleton 222 29.27 N 96.00 W
Kendrāparha 120 20.30 N 86.25 E
Kendrew 158 32.31 S 24.30 E
Kendrick, Fl., U.S. 192 29.22 N 82.12 W
Kendrick, Id., U.S. 202 46.36 N 116.38 W
Kendrick Creek ≃ 226 38.00 N 119.50 W
Kendua 272b 22.34 N 88.10 E
Kendu Bay 154 0.22 S 34.39 E
Kendujhargarh 120 21.38 N 85.35 E
Kendyrlik 86 47.30 N 85.12 E
Kenedy 196 28.49 N 97.50 W
Kenefick 222 30.07 N 94.51 W
Kenema 150 7.52 N 11.12 W
Kenes, Kaz. 85 43.41 N 67.49 E
Kenes, Kaz. 85 43.59 N 73.35 E
Kenesaw 198 40.37 N 98.39 W
Kenga 86 57.27 N 80.57 E
Kenga ≃ 86 58.05 N 80.37 E
Kenge 152 4.52 S 16.59 E
Kengeja 154 5.25 S 39.44 E
Kēng Hkam, Mya. 110 21.01 N 98.29 E
Keng Hkam, Mya. 110 21.27 N 97.03 E
Kengkou, Zhg. 100 29.48 N 117.22 E
Kengkou, Zhg. 100 28.27 N 120.26 E
Kengtian 100 25.54 N 119.26 E
Kēng Tung 110 21.17 N 99.36 E
Kengun-chūtonchi, Rikujō-jieitai- ■ 92 32.46 N 130.45 E
Kenhardt 158 29.19 S 21.12 E
Kenhorst 208 40.18 N 75.57 W
Kenia 152 2.43 S 17.04 E
Kenia → Kenya □[1] 154 1.00 N 38.00 E
Kenia → Kirinyaga ∧ 154 0.10 S 37.20 E
Kéniéba 150 12.50 N 11.14 W
Kenilworth, Eng., U.K. 42 52.21 N 1.34 W
Kenilworth, Il., U.S. 278 42.05 N 87.43 W
Kenilworth, N.J., U.S. 276 40.40 N 74.17 W
Kenilworth, Pa., U.S. 208 40.14 N 75.38 W
Kenilworth, Ut., U.S. 200 39.41 N 110.48 W
Kenilworth Castle ⊥ 42 52.21 N 1.34 W
Keningau 112 5.20 N 116.10 E
Kenitra 148 34.16 N 6.40 W
Kenitra □[4] 148 34.30 N 6.00 W
Kenley ✦[8] 260 51.19 N 0.06 W
Kenli (Xishuanghe) 98 37.40 N 118.35 E
Kenly 192 35.35 N 78.07 W
Kenmare, Ire. 48 51.53 N 9.35 W
Kenmare, N.D., U.S. 198 48.40 N 102.04 W
Kenmare River ≃ 48 51.45 N 10.00 W
Kenmawr 279b 40.28 N 80.06 W
Kenmore, Scot., U.K. 46 56.34 N 3.59 W
Kenmore, N.Y., U.S. 210 42.57 N 78.52 W
Kenmore, Wa., U.S. 224 47.45 N 122.14 W
Kennard, In., U.S. 218 39.54 N 85.31 W
Kennard, Pa., U.S. 214 41.28 N 80.20 W
Kennard, Tx., U.S. 222 31.22 N 95.11 W
Kennebec 198 43.54 N 99.51 W
Kennebec ≃ 188 44.00 N 69.50 W
Kennebecasis Bay ⊂ 186 45.25 N 66.00 W
Kennebec Lake ⊜ 212 44.43 N 77.00 W
Kennebunk 188 43.23 N 70.32 W
Kennedale 222 32.38 N 97.13 W
Kennedy, Al., U.S. 194 33.35 N 87.59 W
Kennedy, N.Y., U.S. 214 42.09 N 79.06 W
Kennedy, Zimb. 154 18.52 S 27.10 E
Kennedy, Cape → Canaveral, Cape › 220 28.27 N 80.32 W
Kennedy, Mount ∧, B.C., Can. 182 50.49 N 125.33 W
Kennedy, Mount ∧, Yk., Can. 180 60.30 N 139.00 W
Kennedy Entrance ʯ 180 59.00 N 152.00 W
Kennedy Lake ⊜ 182 49.05 N 125.40 W
Kennedy Peak ∧ 110 23.19 N 93.45 E
Kennedy Range ⋀ 162 24.30 S 115.00 E
Kennedyville 208 39.18 N 75.59 W
Kennemerduinen, Nationale Park de ♦ 52 52.25 N 4.35 E
Kenner 194 29.59 N 90.14 W
Kennerdell 214 41.16 N 79.51 W
Kennet ≃ 42 51.28 N 0.57 W
Kennetcook 186 45.11 N 63.44 W
Kenneth City 220 27.49 N 82.44 W
Kennett 194 36.14 N 90.03 W
Kennett ≃ 42 52.26 N 0.28 E
Kennett Square 208 39.50 N 75.42 W
Kennewick 202 46.12 N 119.08 W
Kenney 219 40.06 N 89.05 W
Kenney Dam ✦[6] 182 53.37 N 124.58 W
Kennington, Eng., U.K. 42 51.10 N 0.54 E
Kennington, Eng., U.K. 42 51.43 N 1.15 W
Kennisis Lake ⊜ 212 45.13 N 78.39 W
Kenn Reef ✢[2] 160 21.12 S 155.46 E
Kenny 222 30.03 N 96.20 W
Kennydale 224 47.31 N 122.12 W
Kennywood Park ♦ 279b 40.23 N 79.52 W
Kénogami 186 48.26 N 71.14 W
Kenogami ≃ 176 51.06 N 84.28 W
Kénogami, Lac ⊜ 186 48.20 N 71.23 W
Kenogamissi Lake ⊜ 190 48.15 N 81.31 W
Keno Hill 180 63.55 N 135.18 W
Kenora 184 49.47 N 94.29 W
Kenosha 216 42.35 N 87.49 W
Kenosha □[6] 216 42.35 N 88.03 W
Kenova 188 38.23 N 82.34 W
Kenoza Lake 210 41.44 N 74.57 W
Kenoza Lake ⊜ 283 42.47 N 71.03 W
Kenozero, ozero ⊜ 24 62.03 N 38.14 E
Ken Rock 216 42.15 N 89.03 W
Kensal 198 47.18 N 98.43 W
Kense 86 46.49 N 68.20 E
Kensett 194 35.13 N 91.40 W
Kensico Lake ⊜ 276 41.07 N 73.45 W
Kensico Reservoir ⊜[1] 210 41.05 N 73.46 W
Kensington, Austl. 274a 33.55 S 151.14 E
Kensington, P.E., Can. 186 46.26 N 63.38 W
Kensington, Ca., U.S. 226 37.54 N 122.16 W
Kensington, Ct., U.S. 207 41.38 N 72.46 W
Kensington, Ks., U.S. 198 39.46 N 99.01 W
Kensington, Md., U.S. 284c 39.01 N 77.04 W
Kensington, Oh., U.S. 214 40.44 N 80.57 W
Kensington ✦[8], S. Afr. 273d 26.12 S 28.06 E
Kensington ✦[8], N.Y., U.S. 276 40.39 N 73.58 W
Kensington ✦[8], Pa., U.S. 285 39.58 N 75.08 W
Kensington and Chelsea ✦[8] 260 51.29 N 0.11 W
Kensington Estates 284c 39.02 N 77.05 W
Kensington Metropolitan Park ♦ 281 42.32 N 83.39 W
Kensington Park 220 27.22 N 82.31 W
Kent, S.L. 150 8.10 N 13.10 W
Kent, Ct., U.S. 207 41.43 N 73.28 W
Kent, N.Y., U.S. 210 43.20 N 78.08 W
Kent, Oh., U.S. 214 41.09 N 81.21 W
Kent, Or., U.S. 224 45.11 N 120.41 W
Kent, Wa., U.S. 224 47.22 N 122.14 W
Kent □[6], On., Can. 214 42.25 N 82.10 W
Kent □[6], Eng., U.K. 42 51.15 N 0.40 E
Kent □[6], De., U.S. 208 39.10 N 75.32 W
Kent □[6], Md., U.S. 208 39.13 N 76.04 W
Kent □[6], Mi., U.S. 216 42.56 N 85.33 W
Kent □[6], R.I., U.S. 207 41.40 N 71.38 W
Kent ≃ 44 54.15 N 2.48 W
Kent, Vale of V 42 51.10 N 0.30 E
Kent Acres 208 39.07 N 75.31 W
Kentallen 46 56.39 N 5.15 W
Kentani 158 32.31 S 28.19 E
Kentau 85 43.36 N 68.36 E
Kent Bridge 214 42.31 N 82.04 W
Kent County Airport ⊠ 216 42.54 N 85.39 W
Kentfield 282 37.57 N 122.33 W
Kent Group II 166 39.27 S 147.20 E
Kenthurst 274a 33.40 S 151.00 E
Kent Island I 208 38.55 N 76.20 W
Kent Lake ⊜ 216 42.32 N 83.40 W
Kentland, In., U.S. 216 40.46 N 87.26 W
Kentland, Md., U.S. 284c 38.55 N 76.53 W
Kenton, Eng., U.K. 42 50.38 N 3.28 W
Kenton, De., U.S. 208 39.13 N 75.39 W
Kenton, Mi., U.S. 190 46.29 N 88.53 W
Kenton, Oh., U.S. 216 40.38 N 83.36 W
Kenton, Tn., U.S. 194 36.12 N 89.00 W
Kenton □[6] 218 38.56 N 84.33 W
Kent Park 283 42.06 N 70.41 W
Kent Park ♦ 273d 26.08 S 28.04 E
Kent Peninsula ›[1] 176 68.30 N 107.00 W
Kent Point › 208 38.50 N 76.22 W
Kentucky □[3] 178 37.30 N 85.15 W
Kentucky ≃ 218 38.41 N 85.11 W
Kentucky, Middle Fork ≃ 192 37.35 N 83.40 W
Kentucky, North Fork ≃ 192 37.34 N 83.42 W
Kentucky, South Fork ≃ 192 37.34 N 83.42 W
Kentucky Horse Park ♦ 218 38.08 N 84.31 W
Kentucky Lake ⊜[1] 194 36.25 N 88.05 W
Kent Village 284c 38.55 N 76.53 W
Kentville 186 45.05 N 64.30 W
Kentwood, La., U.S. 194 30.56 N 90.30 W
Kentwood, Mi., U.S. 216 42.52 N 85.38 W
Kent Woodlands 282 37.57 N 122.34 W
Kenvil 276 40.52 N 74.37 W
Kenwick 168a 32.02 S 115.58 E
Kenwood, Ca., U.S. 226 38.25 N 122.33 W
Kenwood, Md., U.S. 284b 39.21 N 76.31 W
Kenwood, Oh., U.S. 218 39.12 N 84.22 W
Kenwood ✦[8] 278 41.49 N 87.36 W
Kenwood ⊥ 260 51.34 N 0.10 W
Kenya □[1] 154 1.00 N 38.00 E
Kenya, Mount → Kirinyaga ∧ 154 0.10 S 37.20 E
Kenyon, Eng., U.K. 262 53.27 N 2.34 W
Kenyon, Mn., U.S. 190 44.16 N 92.59 W
Kenyon, R.I., U.S. 207 41.26 N 71.37 W
Ken-zaki › 268 35.08 N 139.41 E
Kenzingen 58 48.11 N 7.46 E
Kenzou 152 4.10 N 15.02 E
Keokea 229a 20.42 N 156.21 W
Keokuk 190 40.23 N 91.23 W
Keoladeo National Park ♦ 124 27.10 N 77.20 E
Keonchi 124 22.38 N 81.47 E
Keo Neua, Col de)(110 18.23 N 105.09 E
Keon Park 274b 37.42 S 145.01 E
Keosauqua 190 40.43 N 91.57 W
Keota, Ia., U.S. 190 41.21 N 91.57 W
Keota, Ok., U.S. 196 35.15 N 94.55 W
Keowee, Lake ⊜[1] 192 34.45 N 82.55 W
Kepa (Mittagskogel) ∧ 61 46.31 N 13.57 E
Kepala Batas 114 5.31 N 100.26 E
Kepanjen 115a 8.07 S 112.34 E
Kepi 164 6.32 S 139.19 E
Kępice 30 54.15 N 16.52 E
Kepina 24 65.24 N 41.50 E
Keping Shan ⋀ 85 40.00 N 77.10 E
Kępno 30 51.17 N 17.59 E
Kepo 112 2.56 S 106.33 E
Keppel Bay ⊂ 166 23.21 S 150.55 E
Keppel Harbour ⊂ 271c 1.16 N 103.50 E
Kepsut 130 39.41 N 28.09 E
Keptown 219 39.05 N 88.40 W
Kequan 98 36.04 N 114.00 E
Kerala □[3] 122 10.00 N 76.30 E
Keram ≃ 164 4.07 S 144.07 E
Keramian, Pulau I 112 5.04 S 114.36 E
Kerandin 112 0.12 S 104.46 E
Kerang 166 35.44 S 143.55 E
Keranyo 144 5.04 N 38.18 E
Keratéa 38 37.48 N 23.59 E
Keratsínion 267c 37.58 N 23.37 E
Keraudren, Cape › 162 19.57 S 119.45 E
Kerava 26 60.24 N 25.07 E
Keravat 164 4.19 S 152.01 E
Kerbat ≃ 114 5.01 N 102.51 E
Kerbela → Karbalā' 128 32.36 N 44.02 E
Kerbi ≃ 89 52.28 N 136.25 E
Kerby 202 42.11 N 123.39 W
Kerč' 78 45.22 N 36.27 E
Kerčel' 86 59.18 N 64.46 E
Kerčemja 24 61.28 N 53.50 E
Kerčenskij poluostrov ›[1] 78 45.15 N 36.00 E
Kerčenskij proliv ʯ 78 45.22 N 36.38 E
Kerčevskij 24 59.55 N 56.17 E
Kerch → Kerč' 78 45.22 N 36.27 E
Kerckhoff Lake ⊜[1] 226 37.09 N 119.31 W
Kéré 154 5.16 N 26.11 E
Kéré ≃ 140 5.19 N 25.40 E
Kerec, mys › 24 65.20 N 39.40 E
Kerej, ozero ⊜ 86 50.08 N 68.45 E
Kerema 164 8.00 S 145.45 E
Keremeos 182 49.12 N 119.50 W
Kerem Maharal 132 32.39 N 34.59 E
Kerempe Burnu › 130 42.01 N 33.21 E
Keren 144 15.46 N 38.28 E
Kerend 128 34.16 N 46.15 E
Kerens 222 32.07 N 96.13 W
Kerepes 264c 47.34 N 19.18 E
Keret' 24 66.16 N 33.34 E
Keret', ozero ⊜ 24 65.55 N 32.56 E
Kerewan 150 13.29 N 16.10 W
Kerga 24 62.39 N 46.00 E
Kergez 84 40.18 N 49.38 E
Kerguélen, Îles II 6 49.15 S 69.10 E
Kerguelen Plateau ✢[3] 6 55.00 S 75.00 E
Kerhonkson 210 41.46 N 74.17 W
Kerian ≃ 114 5.10 N 100.26 E
Kericho 154 0.22 S 35.17 E
Keri Kera 140 12.21 N 32.46 E
Kerikeri 172 35.13 S 173.58 E
Kerimäki 26 61.55 N 29.17 E
Kerinci, Gunung ∧ 112 1.42 S 101.16 E
Kerio ≃ 154 2.59 N 36.07 E
Keríon 38 37.40 N 20.48 E
Keritang 112 0.51 S 102.39 E
Keriya ≃ 120 38.30 N 82.10 E
Kerka ≃ 61 46.28 N 16.36 E
Kerkafalva 61 46.46 N 16.30 E
Kerkdriel 52 51.46 N 5.20 E
Kerkebet 144 16.18 N 37.24 E
Kerken 56 51.27 N 6.22 E
Kerkenna, Îles II 148 34.44 N 11.12 E
Kerkhove 50 50.48 N 3.30 E
Kerkhoven 198 45.11 N 95.19 W
Kerki, Ross. 24 63.43 N 54.05 E
Kerki, Turk. 128 37.50 N 65.12 E
Kérkira (Corfu) 38 39.36 N 19.56 E
Kérkira I 38 39.40 N 19.42 E
Kerkrade [-Holz] 56 50.52 N 6.04 E
Kerling 114 3.35 N 101.36 E
Kermadec Islands II 14 29.16 S 177.55 W
Kermadec Ridge ✢[3] 14 30.30 S 178.30 W
Kermadec Trench ✢[1] 14 30.00 S 177.00 W
Kermajärvi ⊜ 26 62.28 N 28.40 E
Kermān, Īrān 128 30.17 N 57.05 E
Kerman, Ca., U.S. 226 36.43 N 120.04 W
Kermān □[4] 128 29.00 N 57.30 E
Kermit 196 31.51 N 103.05 W
Kermit Roosevelt Seamount ✢[3] 16 39.35 N 146.00 W
Kermode, Mount ∧ 182 52.57 N 131.51 W
Kern □[6] 228 35.20 N 118.55 W
Kern ≃ 204 35.13 N 119.17 W
Kern, South Fork ≃ 204 35.40 N 118.27 W
Kern City 228 35.18 N 119.05 W
Kernersville 192 36.07 N 80.04 W
Kernforschungszentrum ⊕[3] 56 49.07 N 8.26 E
Kernhof 61 47.49 N 15.32 E
Kern Island Canal ≍ 228 35.22 N 119.01 W
Kern Lake Bed ⊜ 228 35.10 N 119.05 W
Kern River Channel ≃[1] 226 35.49 N 119.40 W
Kernville 204 35.45 N 118.25 W
Keroh 114 5.43 N 101.00 E
Keros 24 60.44 N 52.50 E
Kérou 150 10.50 N 2.06 E
Kérouané 150 9.16 N 9.01 W
Kerowagi 164 5.50 S 144.50 E
Kerpen 56 50.52 N 6.41 E
Kerpinen' 78 46.47 N 28.22 E
Kerr 214 41.03 N 78.25 W
Kerrera I 46 56.23 N 5.34 W
Kerridge 262 53.17 N 2.06 W
Kerridge Hill ∧[2] 262 53.17 N 2.06 W
Kerrobert 184 51.55 N 109.08 W
Kerrtown 214 41.38 N 80.10 W
Kerruish Park ♦ 279a 41.26 N 81.34 W
Kerrville 196 30.02 N 99.08 W
Kerry 42 52.30 N 3.16 W
Kerry □[6] 48 52.10 N 9.30 W
Kerry Head › 48 52.25 N 9.57 W
Kersa 144 9.28 N 41.53 E
Kersbrook 168b 34.47 S 138.51 E
Kersey 214 41.21 N 78.35 W
Kershaw 192 34.33 N 80.35 W
Kersinyane 150 15.24 N 10.10 W
Kersley 182 52.49 N 122.25 W
Kerspestausee ⊜[1] 263 51.08 N 7.30 E
Kerstenhausen 56 51.04 N 9.13 E
Kert, Oued ≃ 34 35.15 N 3.15 W
Kertamulia 112 0.23 S 109.09 E
Kerteh 114 4.31 N 103.27 E
Kerteminde 41 55.27 N 10.40 E
Kertosono 115a 7.35 S 112.06 E
Kerulen (Cherlen) (Herlen) ≃ 90 48.48 N 117.00 E
Kerva 80 55.37 N 39.35 E
Kerzaz 148 29.30 N 1.37 W
Kerzendorf 264a 52.16 N 13.17 E
Keržencc 80 56.28 N 44.26 E
Keržencc ≃ 80 56.05 N 45.03 E
Kerzers 58 46.58 N 7.12 E
Kesabpur 126 22.55 N 89.13 E
Ke Sach 110 9.46 N 105.59 E
Kesagami Lake ⊜ 176 50.23 N 80.15 W
Kesälahti 26 61.54 N 29.50 E
Keşan 130 40.51 N 26.37 E
Keşap 130 40.55 N 38.31 E
Kesbern 263 51.20 N 7.42 E
Kesch, Piz ∧ 58 46.38 N 9.52 E
Kesem ≃ 144 9.14 N 40.06 E
Kesennuma 92 38.54 N 141.35 E
Kesh 48 54.32 N 7.43 W
Keshan 89 48.02 N 125.51 E
Keshena 190 44.53 N 88.38 W
Keshendeh 120 36.05 N 66.51 E
Keshequa Creek ≃ 210 42.43 N 77.50 W
Keshod 120 21.18 N 70.15 E
Keşiş Dağları ⋀ 130 39.50 N 39.45 E
Keskastel 56 48.58 N 7.02 E
Keskin 130 39.41 N 33.37 E
Keski-Suomen lääni □[4] 26 62.30 N 25.30 E
Keskozero 24 61.24 N 33.12 E
Keskuvejem, gora ∧ 180 66.12 N 177.40 W
Kes'ma 76 58.27 N 37.04 E
Kesova Gora 76 57.35 N 37.17 E
Kespur 126 22.35 N 87.29 E
Kesra 36 35.49 N 9.22 E
Kessebüren 263 51.31 N 7.43 E
Kessel 56 51.08 N 4.37 E

Symbols in the index entries represent the broad categories identified in the key at the right. Symbols with superior numbers (⋀[1]) identify subcategories (see complete key on page *I · 1*).

Symbole im Register stellen die rechts im Schlüssel erklärten Kategorien dar. Symbole mit hochgestellten Ziffern (⋀[1]) bezeichnen Unterabteilungen einer Kategorie (vgl. vollständiger Schlüssel auf Seite *I · 1*).

Los símbolos incluidos en el texto del índice representan las grandes categorias identificadas con la clave a la derecha. Los símbolos con numeros en su parte superior (⋀[1]) identifican las subcategorías (véase la clave completa en la página *I · 1*).

Les symboles de l'index représentent les catégories indiquées dans la légende à droite. Les symboles suivis d'un indice (⋀[1]) représentent des sous-catégories (voir légende complète à la page *I · 1*).

Os símbolos incluídos no texto do índice representam as grandes categorias identificadas com a chave à direita. Os símbolos com números em sua parte superior (⋀[1]) identificam as subcategorias (veja-se a chave completa à página *I · 1*).

	English	Deutsch	Español	Français	Português
∧	Mountain	Berg	Montaña	Montagne	Montanha
⋀	Mountains	Gebirge	Montañas	Montagnes	Montanhas
)(	Pass	Paß	Paso	Col	Passo
V	Valley, Canyon	Tal, Cañon	Valle, Cañón	Vallée, Canyon	Vale, Canhão
≃	Plain	Ebene	Llano	Plaine	Planície
›	Cape	Kap	Cabo	Cap	Cabo
I	Island	Insel	Isla	Île	Ilha
II	Islands	Inseln	Islas	Îles	Ilhas
⊥	Other Topographic Features	Andere Topographische Objekte	Otros Elementos Topográficos	Autres données topographiques	Outros acidentes topográficos

ESPAÑOL — Nombre | Página | Lat.°′ | Long.°′ W = Oeste
FRANÇAIS — Nom | Page | Lat.°′ | Long.°′ W = Ouest
PORTUGUÊS — Nome | Página | Lat.°′ | Long.°′ W = Oeste

Nombre / Nom / Nome	Página / Page	Lat.°′	Long.°′
Kesselsdorf	54	51.02 N	13.35 E
Kessingland	42	52.25 N	1.42 E
Kesswil	58	47.36 N	9.20 E
Kestel Gölü ⊜	130	37.24 N	30.28 E
Kestell	158	28.19 S	28.38 E
Kesten'ga	24	65.55 N	31.47 E
Kestilä	26	64.21 N	26.17 E
Keston ◆ 8	260	51.22 N	0.02 E
Keswick, On., Can.	212	44.15 N	79.28 W
Keswick, Eng., U.K.	44	54.37 N	3.08 W
Keszthely	30	46.46 N	17.15 E
Ket' ≃	86	58.55 N	81.32 E
Keta	150	5.55 N	1.00 E
Keta ≃	94	34.56 N	137.50 E
Keta, ozero ⊜	74	68.44 N	90.00 E
Ketaka	96	35.30 N	134.03 E
Keta Lagoon c	150	5.54 N	0.56 E
Ketam, Pulau I	271c	1.24 N	103.57 E
Ketama	34	34.50 N	4.37 W
Ketang	100	22.58 N	115.28 E
Ketapang, Indon.	112	1.52 S	109.59 E
Ketapang, Indon.	115a	6.54 S	113.17 E
Ketapang, Indon.	115a	5.44 S	105.48 E
Ketaun	112	3.23 S	101.49 E
Ketčenery	80	47.18 N	44.31 E
Ketchikan	182	55.21 N	131.35 W
Ketchum	202	43.40 N	114.21 W
Kete Krachi	150	7.46 N	0.03 W
Ketelmeer ⊜	52	52.35 N	5.45 E
Keti Bandar	120	24.08 N	67.27 E
Ketingwan ∧	154	0.40 N	35.50 E
Ketoj, ostrov I	74	47.20 N	152.28 E
Kétou	150	7.22 N	2.36 E
Ketovo	86	55.21 N	65.18 E
Kętrzyn (Rastenburg)	30	54.06 N	21.23 E
Ketsch	56	49.22 N	8.31 E
Ketta	152	1.28 N	15.56 E
Kettering, Eng., U.K.	42	52.24 N	0.44 W
Kettering, Md., U.S.	284c	38.53 N	76.49 W
Kettering, Oh., U.S.	218	39.41 N	84.10 W
Kettinge	41	54.42 N	11.45 E
Kettle ≃, Mb., Can.	184	56.23 N	94.34 W
Kettle ≃, N.A.	182	48.42 N	118.07 W
Kettle ≃, Mn., U.S.	190	45.52 N	92.45 W
Kettle Creek ≃, On., Can.	212	42.40 N	81.13 W
Kettle Creek ≃, Pa., U.S.	210	41.18 N	77.51 W
Kettle Creek State Park ♠	214	41.23 N	77.56 W
Kettle Falls	202	48.36 N	118.03 W
Kettleman City	226	36.00 N	119.57 W
Kettleman Hills ∧∧ 2	226	36.00 N	120.00 W
Kettle Rapids Dam ◆ 6	184	56.23 N	94.38 W
Kettlersville	216	40.22 N	84.16 W
Kettleshulme	262	53.19 N	2.01 W
Kettlewell	44	54.09 N	2.02 W
Kettwig	56	51.22 N	6.56 E
Kęty	30	49.53 N	19.13 E
Ketzin	54	52.28 N	12.50 E
Keudemane	114	5.15 N	96.55 E
Keudepasi	114	4.18 N	95.56 E
Keudeteunom	114	4.27 N	95.48 E
Keudeunga	114	5.01 N	95.22 E
Keuka Lake ⊜	210	42.27 N	77.10 W
Keuka Lake, West Branch c	210	42.33 N	77.09 W
Keuka Park	210	42.37 N	77.06 W
Keukenhof ♠	52	52.16 N	4.33 E
Keul'	88	58.25 N	102.49 E
Keula	54	51.20 N	10.31 E
Keum ≃	86	59.32 N	70.35 E
Keurboomsrivier	158	34.00 S	23.24 E
Keurusselkä ⊜	26	62.10 N	24.40 E
Keuruu	26	62.16 N	24.42 E
Kevdo-Mel'sitovo	80	53.09 N	43.54 E
Kevelaer	52	51.35 N	6.15 E
Kevin	202	48.44 N	111.57 W
Kevsala	80	45.48 N	42.41 E
Kew, Austl.	169	37.49 S	145.02 E
Kew, T./C. Is.	238	21.54 N	72.02 W
Kewanee	190	41.14 N	89.55 W
Kewanna	216	41.01 N	86.25 W
Kewaunee	190	44.27 N	87.30 W
Keweenaw Bay c	190	46.56 N	88.23 W
Keweenaw Peninsula › 1	190	47.12 N	88.25 W
Keweenaw Point ›	190	47.30 N	87.50 W
Kew Gardens ♠, On., Can.	275b	43.40 N	79.18 W
Kew Gardens ♠, Eng., U.K.	260	51.28 N	0.18 W
Key, Lough ⊜	48	54.00 N	8.15 W
Keyala	154	4.27 N	32.52 E
Keyangkeer Shan ∧	120	31.20 N	87.13 E
Keya Paha ≃	198	42.54 N	99.00 W
Key Biscayne	220	25.42 N	80.10 W
Keyes, Ca., U.S.	226	37.33 N	120.54 W
Keyes, Ok., U.S.	196	36.48 N	102.15 W
Keyesport	219	38.44 N	89.17 W
Keyhole Reservoir ⊜ 1	198	44.21 N	104.51 W
Keyhole State Park ♠	198	44.19 N	104.48 W
Keyihe	89	50.40 N	122.27 E
Keyingham	44	53.42 N	0.07 W
Key Largo	220	25.04 N	80.28 W
Key Largo I	220	25.16 N	80.19 W
Keymer	42	50.55 N	0.08 W
Keynes Hill ∧ 2	168b	34.37 S	139.06 E
Keyneton	168b	34.34 S	139.08 E
Keynsham	42	51.26 N	2.30 W
Keynshamburg	154	19.15 S	29.39 E
Keyport, N.J., U.S.	276	40.25 N	74.12 W
Keyport, Wa., U.S.	224	47.42 N	122.38 W
Keyport Harbor c	276	40.26 N	74.12 W
Keysborough	274b	38.00 S	145.10 E
Keysbrook	168a	32.26 S	115.59 E
Keyser	188	39.26 N	78.58 W
Keystone, In., U.S.	216	40.36 N	85.16 W
Keystone, Ia., U.S.	190	41.59 N	92.11 W
Keystone, S.D., U.S.	198	43.53 N	103.25 W
Keystone, W.V., U.S.	192	37.24 N	81.27 W
Keystone Lake ⊜ 1, Ok., U.S.	196	36.15 N	96.25 W
Keystone Lake ⊜ 1, Pa., U.S.	214	40.45 N	79.15 W
Keystone Peak ∧	200	31.53 N	111.13 W
Keystone State Park ♠	214	40.23 N	79.24 W
Keysville, Fl., U.S.	220	27.52 N	82.06 W
Keysville, Va., U.S.	192	37.02 N	78.29 W
Keytesville	194	39.26 N	92.56 W
Key West	220	24.33 N	81.46 W
Key West Island I	220	24.33 N	81.47 W
Key West Naval Air Station ■	220	24.34 N	81.41 W
Keyworth	42	52.52 N	1.05 W
Kez	80	57.53 N	53.43 E
Kezar Stadium ♠	282	37.46 N	122.27 W
Kezi	154	20.58 S	28.32 E
Kezilesu Zizhizhou □ 8	85	40.00 N	75.30 E
Kežma	88	58.59 N	101.09 E
Kežmarok	30	49.08 N	20.25 E
Kgalagadi □ 5	156	25.00 S	22.00 E
Kgatleng □ 5	156	24.28 S	26.05 E
Kgokgole ≃	158	26.44 S	22.28 E
Kgun Lake ⊜	180	61.32 N	163.45 W
Khaanziir, Ras ›	144	10.55 N	45.47 E
Khabab	132	33.00 N	36.16 E
Khabīr, Kūh-e ∧	128	28.48 N	56.26 E
Khābūr, Nahr al- (Habur) ≃	130	35.08 N	40.26 E
Khādar	272a	28.33 N	77.22 E
Khadari, Wādī al- V	140	10.29 N	26.15 E
Khadaungnge Taung ∧	110	18.57 N	94.37 E
Khadki (Kirkee)	122	18.34 N	73.52 E
Khadra	34	36.15 N	0.35 E
Khafūrī, Wādī V	142	29.37 N	32.04 E
Khagaria	124	25.30 N	86.29 E
Khagdon ≃ 1	126	22.09 N	90.05 E
Khāgrāmuri	272b	22.26 N	88.14 E
Khaïdhárion	267c	37.33 N	22.53 E
Khair	124	27.57 N	77.50 E
Khairābād	124	27.32 N	80.45 E
Khairāgarh	120	21.25 N	80.58 E
Khairbani	126	24.14 N	87.05 E
Khairna	272c	19.06 N	73.01 E
Khairpur, Pāk.	120	27.32 N	68.46 E
Khairpur, Pāk.	123	29.35 N	72.14 E
Khairwāra	120	23.59 N	73.35 E
Khajrāho	120	24.50 N	79.58 E
Khajuri	126	21.52 N	87.58 E
Khajuri ◆ 8	272a	28.43 N	77.16 E
Khakassia → Chakasija □ 3	86	53.00 N	90.00 E
Kha Khaeng ≃	110	14.55 N	99.07 E
Khakhea	156	24.51 S	23.20 E
Khalándrion	267c	38.01 N	23.48 E
Khalatse	123	34.20 N	76.49 E
Khālidī, Khirbat al- ⊥	132	29.39 N	35.14 E
Khalkhāl	128	37.37 N	48.32 E
Khalkhalah	132	33.04 N	36.32 E
Khálki I	130	36.17 N	27.35 E
Khalkidhikí □ 9	38	40.25 N	23.27 E
Khalkís	38	38.28 N	23.36 E
Khālsar	120	34.31 N	77.41 E
Khambhāliya	120	22.12 N	69.39 E
Khambhāt	120	22.18 N	72.37 E
Khambhāt, Gulf of c	122	21.00 N	72.30 E
Khāmgaon	122	20.41 N	76.34 E
Khamir	144	16.05 N	43.55 E
Khāmis, Ash-Shallāl al- (Fifth Cataract) ⌊	140	18.23 N	33.47 E
Khamīs Mushayṭ	144	18.18 N	42.44 E
Khamkeut	110	18.15 N	104.43 E
Khamma	70	36.47 N	12.02 E
Khammam	122	17.15 N	80.09 E
Khamsah	142	30.25 N	32.23 E
Khan ≃, Lao	110	19.54 N	102.09 E
Khan ≃, Namibia	156	22.37 S	14.56 E
Khāna	126	23.20 N	87.44 E
Khānābād	120	36.41 N	69.07 E
Khān Abū Shāmāt	132	33.40 N	36.54 E
Khānākul	126	22.43 N	87.51 E
Khān al-Baghdādī	128	33.51 N	42.33 E
Khānaqīn	128	34.21 N	45.22 E
Khān Arnabah	132	33.11 N	35.53 E
Khancoban	171b	36.12 S	148.05 E
Khandaghosh	126	23.13 N	87.41 E
Khandela	120	27.36 N	75.30 E
Khandwa	124	21.50 N	76.20 E
Khān-e Chahār Bāgh, Afg.	120	35.58 N	69.38 E
Khān-e Chahār Bāgh, Afg.	128	37.00 N	65.14 E
Khāneh Khvodī	128	36.02 N	55.59 E
Khānewāl	123	30.18 N	71.56 E
Khāngāh Dogrān	123	31.50 N	73.37 E
Khāngarh, Pāk.	120	28.22 N	71.43 E
Khāngarh, Pāk.	123	29.55 N	71.10 E
Khangkhai	110	19.28 N	103.15 E
Khaniá	38	35.31 N	24.02 E
Khaníon, Kólpos c	38	35.34 N	23.48 E
Khānkurda	126	22.00 N	87.25 E
Khanna	123	30.42 N	76.13 E
Khannā, Qāʿ ≡	132	32.04 N	36.26 E
Khānozai	120	30.37 N	67.19 E
Khānpur, India	272b	22.40 N	88.16 E
Khānpur, Pāk.	123	28.39 N	70.39 E
Khānpur ◆ 8, India	272a	28.34 N	77.01 E
Khānpur ◆ 8, India	272a	28.31 N	77.14 E
Khān Shaykhūn	130	35.26 N	36.38 E
Khanty-Mansiysk → Chanty-Mansijsk	74	61.00 N	69.06 E
Khān Yūnus	132	31.21 N	34.19 E
Khao Laem Reservoir ⊜ 1	110	14.50 N	98.30 E
Khao Saming	110	12.21 N	102.27 E
Khao Sok National Park ♠	110	8.55 N	98.35 E
Khao Yoi	110	13.14 N	99.50 E
Khapalu	123	35.10 N	76.20 E
Khaptad National Park ♠	124	29.28 N	81.10 E
Kharab, Ghoubet al c	144	11.30 N	42.35 E
Kharabā	132	32.34 N	36.27 E
Kharagdiha	124	24.25 N	86.10 E
Kharagpur, India	124	25.07 N	86.33 E
Kharagpur, India	126	22.20 N	87.20 E
Kharak	123	33.07 N	71.06 E
Khārān	120	28.35 N	65.25 E
Kharānoq	128	32.20 N	54.39 E
Kharar, India	123	30.45 N	76.39 E
Kharar, India	126	22.42 N	87.41 E
Khāravli ∧ 2	272c	18.54 N	72.55 E
Kharāyij, Sabkhat al- ⊜	130	35.40 N	37.20 E
Kharaz, Jabal ∧	144	12.44 N	44.09 E
Kharbatā	132	31.57 N	35.04 E
Kharbine → Harbin	89	45.45 N	126.41 E
Khardaha	126	22.44 N	88.22 E
Khārghar	272c	19.03 N	73.04 E
Kharg Island → Khārk, Jazīreh-ye I	128	29.15 N	50.20 E
Khargon	120	21.49 N	75.36 E
Khāriān Cantonment	123	32.49 N	73.52 E
Khariār Road	122	20.54 N	82.31 E
Khārijah, Al-Wāḥāt al- ⊤ 4	140	25.20 N	30.35 E
Kharīm, Jabal ∧	132	30.17 N	33.58 E
Kharīṭ, Wādī al- V	140	24.26 N	33.03 E
Khārk, Jazīreh-ye (Kharg Island) I	128	29.15 N	50.20 E
Kharkov → Char'kov	78	50.00 N	36.15 E
Kharmān, Kūh-e ∧	128	29.13 N	53.35 E
Kharri	272b	22.55 N	88.14 E
Kharsāwān	124	22.48 N	85.50 E
Kharsia	124	21.58 N	83.07 E
Khartoum → Al-Kharṭūm	140	15.36 N	32.32 E
Khartoum North → Al-Kharṭūm Baḥrī	140	15.38 N	32.33 E
Khartum → Al-Kharṭūm	140	15.36 N	32.32 E
Kharumwa	154	3.12 S	32.39 E
Khāsbāti	272b	22.55 N	88.25 E
Khasebake	156	20.41 S	24.29 E
Khāsh, Afg.	128	31.31 N	62.52 E
Khāsh, Īrān	128	28.14 N	61.14 E
Khāsh ≃	128	31.11 N	62.05 E
Khāsh, Dasht-e ◆ 2	128	31.50 N	62.30 E
Khashab, Jabal al- ∧ 2	142	29.56 N	31.01 E
Khashm al-Qirbah	140	14.58 N	35.55 E
Khashm al-Qirbah, Khazzān ⊜ 1	140	14.40 N	35.55 E
Khashshab, Tur'at al- ≅	273c	29.53 N	31.17 E
Khashum	140	12.27 N	28.02 E
Khāş Konar	120	34.39 N	70.54 E
Khaskovo → Haskovo	38	41.56 N	25.33 E
Khatauli	124	29.17 N	77.43 E
Khātegaon	124	22.36 N	76.55 E
Khātra	126	22.59 N	86.51 E
Khatt, Oued al V	148	26.45 N	13.03 W
Khaur	123	33.16 N	72.28 E
Khāvda	120	23.51 N	69.43 E
Khawrah	144	14.26 N	46.09 E
Khawsa	110	15.03 N	97.50 E
Khayāla ◆ 8	272a	28.40 N	77.06 E
Khaybar, Ḩarrat ▴ 9	128	25.30 N	39.45 E
Khayerpur	272b	22.35 N	88.33 E
Khayl, Kathīb al- ▴ 8	142	30.33 N	32.28 E
Khayra Bil ⊜	272b	22.52 N	88.29 E
Khayrasole	126	23.48 N	87.16 E
Khayung ≃	110	15.07 N	104.42 E
Kheardaha	272b	22.29 N	88.28 E
Khe Bo	110	19.08 N	104.41 E
Khed	122	17.43 N	73.23 E
Khefapur	272a	28.30 N	77.05 E
Khejurdaha	272b	22.59 N	88.10 E
Khemis	148	36.16 N	2.13 E
Khemis el Khechna	34	36.39 N	3.20 E
Khemisset	148	33.50 N	6.03 W
Khemisset □ 4	148	33.50 N	6.05 W
Khem Karan	123	31.09 N	74.34 E
Khemmarat	110	16.03 N	105.13 E
Khenchla	148	35.28 N	7.11 E
Khenifra	148	33.00 N	5.40 W
Khenifra □ 4	148	32.35 N	5.10 W
Khenjān	120	35.36 N	70.59 E
Khenyen	272b	22.59 N	88.19 E
Khera ◆ 8	272a	28.46 N	77.08 E
Kheri	124	27.54 N	80.48 E
Kheri Branch ≅	124	28.11 N	80.25 E
Kherli	124	27.12 N	77.02 E
Kherrata	148	36.31 N	5.26 E
Khersān ≃	128	31.33 N	50.22 E
Kherson → Cherson	78	46.38 N	32.35 E
Khetia	120	21.40 N	74.35 E
Khevāj	120	38.13 N	71.02 E
Khewāri	120	26.36 N	68.52 E
Khewra	123	32.39 N	73.01 E
Kheyr Khāneh	128	34.57 N	63.37 E
Khichīwāra Plateau ∧∧ 1	124	24.25 N	77.30 E
Khichripur ◆ 8	272a	28.37 N	77.19 E
Khilchipur	124	24.02 N	76.34 E
Khilkāpur	272b	22.46 N	88.29 E
Khimki → Chimki	82	55.54 N	37.26 E
Khíos	38	38.22 N	26.08 E
Khíos I	38	38.22 N	26.00 E
Khipro	120	25.50 N	69.22 E
Khirbat al-Ghazālah	132	32.44 N	36.12 E
Khirbat ʿAwwād	132	32.19 N	36.43 E
Khirbat Qanāfār	132	33.38 N	35.43 E
Khirbat Umm as-Surab	132	32.26 N	36.19 E
Khirbitā	142	30.45 N	30.40 E
Khiri Mat	110	16.50 N	99.48 E
Khirpai	126	22.42 N	87.37 E
Khirr, Wādī al- V	128	31.51 N	44.29 E
Khisfīn	132	32.51 N	35.49 E
Khiuri Khala ∧	124	29.58 N	81.18 E
Khiva → Chiva	72	41.24 N	60.22 E
Khlong Khlung	110	16.12 N	99.43 E
Khlong Thom	110	7.56 N	99.09 E
Khlong Yai	110	11.46 N	102.54 E
Khlung	110	12.27 N	102.14 E
Khmel'nitskiy → Chmel'nickij	78	49.25 N	27.00 E
Khoai, Hon I	110	8.26 N	104.50 E
Khogali	140	6.08 N	27.47 E
Khojāng ∧	124	28.41 N	85.09 E
Khok Kloi	110	8.17 N	98.19 E
Khok Pho	110	6.43 N	101.06 E
Khoksa	126	23.48 N	89.17 E
Khok Samrong	110	15.04 N	100.44 E
Kholargós	267c	38.00 N	23.48 E
Kholm	120	36.42 N	67.41 E
Kholombidzo Falls ⌊	154	15.54 S	34.44 E
Khomām	128	37.22 N	49.40 E
Khomas Hochland ∧∧ 1	156	22.30 S	16.30 E
Khomeyn	128	33.38 N	50.04 E
Khomeynīshahr	128	32.41 N	51.31 E
Khomodimo	156	22.46 S	23.52 E
Khondmāl Hills ∧∧ 2	122	20.20 N	84.00 E
Khong → Mekong ≃	12	10.33 N	105.24 E
Khoni	272c	19.10 N	73.07 E
Khon Kaen	110	16.26 N	102.50 E
Khóra	38	37.04 N	21.43 E
Khorāsān □ 4	128	35.00 N	58.00 E
Khóra Sfakíon	38	35.12 N	24.09 E
Khordha	120	20.11 N	85.37 E
Khorel	272b	22.42 N	88.19 E
Khorramābād	128	33.30 N	48.20 E
Khorram Daraq	128	36.26 N	48.36 E
Khorramshahr	128	30.25 N	48.11 E
Khoru	272b	22.51 N	88.31 E
Khossanto	150	13.08 N	11.58 W
Khouribga	148	32.54 N	6.57 W
Khouribga □ 4	148	32.50 N	6.30 W
Khowai	120	24.06 N	91.38 E
Khowāng	120	27.16 N	94.53 E
Khowst	120	33.22 N	69.57 E
Khrisokhoús, Kólpos c	130	35.06 N	32.25 E
Khrisoúpolis	38	40.58 N	24.42 E
Khudiān	123	30.59 N	74.17 E
Khuff	128	24.57 N	44.42 E
Khugaung	110	26.07 N	98.18 E
Khūgīānī Šānī	120	31.31 N	66.12 E
Khuis	156	26.37 S	21.45 E
Khuīyāla	120	27.14 N	70.30 E
Khu Khan	110	14.42 N	104.12 E
Khulna	124	22.48 N	89.33 E
Khulna □ 5	126	22.45 N	89.30 E
Khŭm Bathéay	110	11.59 N	104.57 E
Khumbur Khūlē Ghar ∧	120	32.49 N	68.47 E
Khungdugang ∧	124	27.31 N	89.02 E
Khūnjerāb Pass)(	123	36.52 N	75.27 E
Khun Tan, Doi ∧	110	18.30 N	99.20 E
Khunti	124	23.05 N	85.17 E
Khūr	128	32.57 N	58.26 E
Khurai	124	24.03 N	78.19 E
Khuralji Khās ◆ 8	272a	28.39 N	77.17 E
Khuria Tank ⊜ 1	124	22.25 N	81.36 E
Khurigāchi	272b	22.49 N	88.20 E
Khurīyā Murīyā, Jazāʾir II	118	17.30 N	56.00 E
Khurja	124	28.15 N	77.51 E
Khurli	120	28.59 N	65.52 E
Khurramshahr → Khorramshahr	128	30.25 N	48.11 E
Khūsf	128	32.46 N	58.53 E
Khushāb	123	32.18 N	72.21 E
Khushālgarh	123	33.30 N	71.54 E
Khushk Khurd ◆ 8	272a	28.46 N	77.10 E
Khutubi ≃	86	44.45 N	86.25 E
Khuwayy	140	13.05 N	29.14 E
Khuzdār	120	27.48 N	66.37 E
Khūzestān □ 4	128	31.00 N	49.00 E
Khvāf	128	34.33 N	60.08 E
Khvājeh Moḥammad, Kūh-e ∧∧	120	36.22 N	70.17 E
Khvājeh Ra'ūf	120	33.19 N	64.43 E
Khvor	128	33.47 N	55.03 E
Khvormūj	128	28.39 N	51.23 E
Khvoy	128	38.33 N	44.58 E
Khwae Noi ≃	110	14.01 N	99.32 E
Khyber Pass)(	123	34.05 N	71.10 E
Kia	175e	7.33 S	158.26 E
Kialwe	154	9.22 S	27.08 E
Kiama, Austl.	170	34.41 S	150.51 E
Kiama, Zaïre	152	7.15 S	17.44 E
Kiamba	116	5.59 N	124.37 E
Kiambi	154	7.20 S	28.01 E
Kiamboni, Kap → Jumbo, Raas ›	144	1.39 S	41.36 E
Kiambu	154	1.10 S	36.50 E
Kiamesha Lake	210	41.41 N	74.40 W
Kiamichi ≃	194	33.57 N	95.14 W
Kiamika ≃	206	46.38 N	75.15 W
Kiamika, Barrage ◆ 6	206	46.37 N	75.08 W
Kiamika, Réservoir ⊜ 1	206	46.40 N	75.05 W
Kiamusze → Jiamusi	89	46.50 N	130.21 E
Kiana	180	66.59 N	160.25 W
Kiandra	171b	35.53 S	148.30 E
Kiangara	157b	17.58 S	47.02 E
Kiangarow, Mount ∧	166	26.49 S	151.33 E
Kiangsi → Jiangxi □ 4	100	28.00 N	116.00 E
Kiangsu → Jiangsu □ 4	90	33.00 N	120.00 E
Kian → Ji'an	100	27.07 N	114.58 E
Kiantajärvi ⊜	26	65.03 N	29.07 E
Kiaohsien → Jiaoxian	98	36.18 N	119.58 E
Kibæk	41	56.02 N	8.51 E
Kibaha	154	6.46 S	38.55 E
Kibali ≃	154	3.37 N	28.34 E
Kibali-Sturi Game Reserve ◆ 4	154	2.45 N	29.33 E
Kibamba	154	4.53 S	26.33 E
Kibanga Port	154	0.11 N	32.52 E
Kibangou	152	3.27 S	12.21 E
Kibanseke	273b	4.26 S	15.23 E
Kibar	120	32.20 N	78.01 E
Kibara	154	2.09 S	33.27 E
Kibāsī	128	30.34 N	47.50 E
Kibau Iyayi	154	8.52 S	34.32 E
Kibawe	116	7.34 N	125.00 E
Kibaya	154	5.18 S	36.34 E
Kibenga	152	7.55 S	17.35 E
Kibeni	164	7.25 S	143.48 E
Kiberashi	154	5.23 S	37.26 E
Kiberege	154	7.57 S	36.52 E
Kibi	150	6.10 N	0.33 W
Kibi-kōgen ∧∧ 1	96	34.45 N	133.15 E
Kibila	154	8.14 S	26.23 E
Kibiti	154	7.44 S	38.57 E
Kibler Park	273d	26.18 S	28.00 E
Kiboga	154	1.02 N	30.58 E
Kiboko	154	2.15 S	37.42 E
Kibombo	154	3.54 S	25.55 E
Kibondo	154	3.35 S	30.42 E
Kibouendé, Congo	273b	4.19 S	15.11 E
Kibouendé, Congo	273b	4.17 S	15.09 E
Kibouendé I	273b	4.11 S	15.09 E
Kibouendé II	273b	4.12 S	15.09 E
Kibre Mengist	144	5.52 N	39.00 E
Kıbrısçık	130	40.25 N	31.51 E
Kıbrıs → Cyprus □ 1	130	35.00 N	33.00 E
Kibumbu	154	3.32 S	29.45 E
Kibungo	154	2.10 S	30.32 E
Kibuye, Bdi.	154	3.40 S	29.59 E
Kibuye, Rw.	154	2.03 S	29.21 E
Kibwesa	154	6.28 S	29.57 E
Kibwezi	154	2.25 S	37.58 E
Kibworth Harcourt	42	52.32 N	0.59 W
Kičevo	38	41.31 N	20.57 E
Kichčik	74	53.24 N	156.03 E
Kichijōji	268	35.42 N	139.35 E
Kickany	78	46.47 N	29.36 E
Kickapoo ≃	190	43.05 N	90.53 W
Kickapoo Creek ≃, Il., U.S.	194	40.08 N	89.27 W
Kickapoo Creek ≃, Il., U.S.	219	40.08 N	89.27 W
Kickapoo Creek ≃, Tx., U.S.	196	31.31 N	99.58 W
Kickapoo Creek ≃, Tx., U.S.	222	30.47 N	95.08 W
Kickapoo Creek ≃, Tx., U.S.	222	32.16 N	95.28 W
Kicking Horse Pass)(	182	51.27 N	116.18 W
Kičkino	80	47.05 N	44.02 E
Kičma	80	57.12 N	48.55 E
Kicman'	78	48.27 N	25.44 E
Kičmengskij Gorodok	24	59.59 N	45.48 E
Kičuj ≃	80	55.13 N	51.16 E
Kidal	150	18.26 N	1.24 E
Kidapawan	116	7.01 N	125.03 E
Kidatu	154	7.42 S	36.57 E
Kidbrooke ◆ 8	260	51.28 N	0.02 E
Kidderminster	42	52.23 N	2.14 W
Kidderpore ◆ 8	272b	22.31 N	88.19 E
Kidderpore Docks ◆ 5	272b	22.33 N	88.19 E
Kidd's Beach	158	33.09 S	27.42 E
Kidepo National Park ♠	154	3.50 N	33.40 E
Kidete, Tan.	154	6.25 S	37.16 E
Kidete, Tan.	154	6.39 S	36.42 E
Kidira	150	14.28 N	12.13 W
Kidlington	42	51.50 N	1.17 W
Kidnappers, Cape ›	172	39.39 S	177.07 E
Kido	164	9.15 S	146.55 E
Kidričevo	61	46.24 N	15.47 E
Kidron	214	40.44 N	81.45 W
Kidsgrove	44	53.06 N	2.15 W
Kidston	166	18.53 S	144.10 E
Kidugallo	154	6.47 S	38.12 E
Kidul, Pegunungan ∧∧	115a	8.13 S	111.30 E
Kidwelly	42	51.45 N	4.18 W
Kiefersfelden	64	47.37 N	12.11 E
Kiekebusch	264a	52.21 N	13.33 E
Kiel, Dtsch.	41	54.20 N	10.08 E
Kiel, Wi., U.S.	190	43.54 N	88.02 W
Kiel Canal → Nord-Ostsee-Kanal ≅	30	53.53 N	9.08 E
Kielce	30	50.52 N	20.37 E
Kielce □ 4	30	50.30 N	20.30 E
Kielder	44	55.14 N	2.35 W
Kielder Reservoir ⊜ 1	44	55.11 N	2.30 W
Kieler Bucht (Kiel Bay) c	41	54.35 N	10.35 E
Kieler Förde c	41	54.24 N	10.12 E
Kiembara	150	13.15 N	2.44 W
Kienberg	264a	52.40 N	12.54 E
Kienge	154	10.34 S	27.33 E
Kienitz	54	52.40 N	14.26 E
Kiens → Chienes	64	46.48 N	11.50 E
Kiental	58	46.35 N	7.43 E
Kierling	264b	48.19 N	16.17 E
Kierspe	56	51.08 N	7.35 E
Kierspe-Bahnhof	263	51.08 N	7.37 E
Kiester	190	43.32 N	93.42 W
Kieta	175e	6.13 S	155.38 E
Kietrz	30	50.05 N	18.01 E
Kietz	54	52.34 N	14.36 E
Kiev → Kijev	78	50.26 N	30.31 E
Kiev Station ◆ 5	265b	55.45 N	37.34 E
Kiew → Kijev	78	50.26 N	30.31 E
Kifaya	150	12.10 N	13.04 W
Kiffa	150	16.37 N	11.24 W
Kifisiá	38	38.04 N	23.48 E
Kifisós ≃, Ellás	38	38.26 N	23.15 E
Kifisós ≃, Ellás	267c	38.06 N	23.45 E
Kifrī	128	34.42 N	44.58 E
Kifrī, Jabal ∧	142	27.48 N	32.50 E
Kigač ≃	80	46.28 N	49.12 E
Kigali	154	1.57 S	30.04 E
Kiği	130	39.19 N	40.21 E
Kigille	140	8.40 N	34.02 E
Kigoma	154	4.52 S	29.38 E
Kigoma □ 4	154	4.30 S	30.30 E
Kigun, Cape ›	180	52.00 N	175.21 W
Kigwa	154	5.10 S	33.08 E
Kihei	229a	20.47 N	156.27 W
Kihikihi	172	38.02 S	175.21 E
Kihniö	26	62.12 N	23.11 E
Kihnu I	76	58.08 N	24.00 E
Kiholo Bay c	229d	19.52 N	155.56 W
Kihundo	154	9.25 S	38.59 E
Kihurio	154	4.28 S	38.04 E
Kii-hantō › 1	92	34.00 N	135.45 E
Kiik	86	47.31 N	72.55 E
Kiikkaškan	86	49.28 N	77.04 E
Kiiminginjoki ≃	26	65.12 N	25.18 E
Kii-nagashima	92	34.12 N	136.20 E
Kiirun → Chilung	100	25.08 N	121.44 E
Kii-sanchi ∧∧	92	34.00 N	135.50 E
Kii-suidō ⊔	96	33.55 N	134.55 E
Kija ≃	86	56.52 N	86.39 E
Kijabe	154	0.56 S	36.34 E
Kijakty, ozero ⊜	86	50.00 N	69.15 E
Kijal	114	4.21 N	103.29 E
Kijaly	86	54.17 N	69.41 E
Kijasovo	80	56.21 N	53.07 E
Kijev (Kiev)	78	50.26 N	30.31 E
Kijev □ 4	78	50.15 N	30.30 E
Kijevka, Kaz.	86	50.16 N	71.34 E
Kijevka, Ross.	80	46.05 N	42.57 E
Kijevka, Ross.	80	50.46 N	48.28 E
Kijevskoje	78	45.03 N	37.52 E
Kijevskoje vodochranilišče ⊜ 1	78	51.00 N	30.25 E
Kijima-chosuichi ⊜	96	35.04 N	132.44 E
Kijimadaira	94	36.51 N	138.24 E
Kijima-dam ◆ 6	96	35.05 N	132.44 E
Kijma	86	51.35 N	67.34 E
Kijoka	174m	26.42 N	128.09 E
Kikagati	154	1.02 S	30.40 E
Kikai-shima I	93b	28.19 N	129.59 E
Kikale	154	7.50 S	39.12 E
Kikati ≃	152	14.48 S	12.28 E
Kikenka ≃	265a	59.52 N	30.04 E
Kikerino	76	59.28 N	29.35 E
Kikerk Lake ⊜	176	67.20 N	113.20 W
Kikimi	273b	4.26 S	15.25 E
Kikimorka	80	58.10 N	49.27 E
Kikinda	38	45.50 N	20.28 E
Kikládhes (Cyclades) II	38	37.30 N	25.00 E
Kiklah	146	32.05 N	12.41 E
Kiknur	80	57.19 N	47.14 E
Kikombo, Zaïre	152	5.59 S	18.09 E
Kikombo, Zaïre	152	5.40 S	18.48 E
Kikongo	152	4.16 S	17.11 E
Kikori	164	7.25 S	144.15 E
Kikori ≃	164	7.10 S	144.05 E
Kikorze	54	53.39 N	15.01 E
Kiku ≃	94	34.39 N	138.04 E
Kikuchi	96	32.59 N	130.49 E
Kikuchi ≃	96	32.56 N	130.35 E
Kikugawa, Nihon	94	34.45 N	138.05 E
Kikugawa, Nihon	96	34.07 N	131.02 E
Kikuka	96	33.02 N	130.46 E
Kikuma	96	34.03 N	132.53 E
Kikuna	268	35.10 N	139.40 E
Kikusui	96	32.58 N	130.36 E
Kikvidze, Ross.	80	50.53 N	42.46 E
Kikvidze, Ross.	80	50.44 N	43.03 E
Kikvorsberg ∧∧	158	31.17 S	25.20 E
Kikwit	152	5.02 S	18.49 E
Kil	26	59.30 N	13.19 E
Kilaån ≃	40	58.44 N	17.01 E
Kilafors	26	61.14 N	16.34 E
Kila Kila	164	9.30 S	147.10 E
Kīlakkarai	122	9.14 N	78.47 E
Kilambé, Cerro ∧	236	13.34 N	85.42 W
Kilauea	229b	22.12 N	159.24 W
Kilauea Crater ▴ 6	229d	19.25 N	155.17 W
Kilauea Point ›	229b	22.14 N	159.24 W
Kilb	61	48.06 N	15.24 E
Kilbaha	48	52.33 N	9.52 W
Kilbarchan	46	55.50 N	4.33 W
Kılbasan	130	37.20 N	33.12 E
Kilbeggan	48	53.22 N	7.29 W
Kilbirnie	46	55.46 N	4.41 W
Kilbourne, Il., U.S.	219	40.09 N	90.01 W
Kilbourne, Oh., U.S.	214	40.20 N	82.58 W
Kilbrannan Sound ⊔	46	55.40 N	5.25 W
Kilbride	46	57.05 N	7.27 W
Kilbuck Mountains ∧∧	180	60.50 N	159.45 W
Kilbuck Run ≃	279b	40.31 N	80.08 W
Kilcar	48	54.38 N	8.35 W
Kilchberg	58	47.19 N	8.33 E
Kilchis ≃	224	45.30 N	123.52 W
Kilchoan	46	56.42 N	6.06 W
Kilchreest	48	53.10 N	8.38 W
Kilchrenan	46	56.21 N	5.11 W
Kilchu	98	40.58 N	129.20 E
Kilcock	48	53.24 N	6.40 W
Kilcolgan	48	53.13 N	8.52 W
Kilconnell	48	53.20 N	8.25 W
Kilcoole	48	53.06 N	6.04 W
Kilcormac	48	53.10 N	7.43 W
Kilcoy	171a	26.57 S	152.33 E
Kilcreggan	46	55.59 N	4.50 W
Kilcullen	48	53.08 N	6.45 W
Kildare (Saint-Ambroise-de-Kildare), P.Q., Can.	206	46.05 N	73.32 W
Kildare, Ire.	48	53.10 N	6.55 W
Kildare □ 6	48	53.15 N	6.45 W
Kildare, Cape ›	186	46.52 N	63.58 W
Kildeer	278	42.10 N	88.03 W
Kil'din, ostrov I	24	69.22 N	34.12 E
Kil'dinstroj	24	68.48 N	33.06 E
Kildonan, B.C., Can.	182	49.00 N	125.00 W
Kildonan, Scot., U.K.	46	58.10 N	3.51 W
Kildonan, Zimb.	154	17.21 S	30.37 E
Kildonan, Strath of V	46	58.09 N	3.51 W
Kildorrery	48	52.14 N	8.26 W
Kildrummy Castle ⊥	46	57.14 N	2.52 W
Kildurk	164	16.26 S	129.37 E
Kilemary	80	56.47 N	46.52 E
Kilembe, Ug.	154	0.12 N	30.00 E
Kilembe, Zaïre	152	5.42 S	19.55 E
Kilfenora	48	52.59 N	9.13 W
Kilfinnane	48	52.21 N	8.28 W
Kilgard	224	49.03 N	122.12 W
Kilgarvan	48	51.54 N	9.27 W
Kilgore, Oh., U.S.	214	40.28 N	81.00 W
Kilgore, Tx., U.S.	222	32.23 N	94.52 W
Kilham	44	54.04 N	0.23 W
Kili I	14	5.39 N	169.04 E
Kilian Island I	176	73.35 N	107.53 W
Kilibo	150	8.34 N	2.36 E
Kılıç	130	40.38 N	29.23 E
Kilifi	154	3.38 S	39.51 E
Kilija	78	45.27 N	29.16 E
Kilikollūr	122	8.54 N	76.39 E
Kilima	154	0.59 S	29.12 E
Kilimanjaro □ 4	154	3.45 S	37.45 E
Kilimanjaro ∧	154	3.04 S	37.22 E
Kilimanjaro Game Reserve ◆ 4	154	3.05 S	37.20 E
Kilimatinde	154	5.51 S	34.57 E
Kilimavony	157b	23.48 S	43.41 E
Kilimli	130	41.28 N	31.50 E
Kilindoni	154	7.55 S	39.39 E
Kilingi-Nõmme	76	58.09 N	24.58 E
Kilis	130	36.44 N	37.05 E
Kilkare Woods	282	37.38 N	121.55 W
Kilkee	48	52.41 N	9.38 W
Kilkeel	48	54.04 N	6.00 W
Kilkelly	48	53.53 N	8.51 W
Kilkenny (Cill Chainnigh)	48	52.39 N	7.15 W
Kilkenny □ 6	48	52.40 N	7.20 W
Kilkerrin	48	53.33 N	8.34 W
Kilkhampton	42	50.53 N	4.29 W
Kilkieran	48	53.19 N	9.43 W
Kilkieran Bay c	48	53.15 N	9.45 W
Kilkís	38	41.00 N	22.53 E
Killadoon	48	53.42 N	9.56 W
Killadysert	48	52.41 N	9.06 W
Killala	48	54.13 N	9.13 W
Killala Bay c	48	54.15 N	9.10 W
Killaloe	48	52.48 N	8.27 W
Killaloe Station	190	45.33 N	77.25 W
Killam	182	52.47 N	111.51 W
Killara	274a	33.46 S	151.09 E
Killarney, Austl.	166	28.20 S	152.18 E
Killarney, Mb., Can.	184	49.12 N	99.42 W
Killarney, On., Can.	190	45.58 N	81.31 W
Killarney, Ire.	48	52.03 N	9.30 W
Killarney, Lake ⊜	240b	25.03 N	77.27 W
Killarney, Lakes of ⊜	48	52.01 N	9.30 W
Killarney Heights	274a	33.46 S	151.13 E
Killarney Provincial Park ♠	190	46.05 N	81.30 W
Killashandra	48	54.00 N	7.32 W
Killavally	48	53.45 N	9.23 W
Killawog	210	42.24 N	76.01 W
Killbear Provincial Park ♠	212	45.21 N	80.12 W
Kill Buck, N.Y., U.S.	210	42.10 N	78.41 W
Killbuck, Oh., U.S.	214	40.29 N	81.59 W
Killbuck Creek ≃, Il., U.S.	216	42.10 N	89.06 W
Killbuck Creek ≃, In., U.S.	218	40.07 N	85.41 W
Killbuck Creek ≃, Oh., U.S.	214	40.20 N	81.57 W
Killdeer	198	47.22 N	102.45 W
Killean	46	55.39 N	5.40 W
Killearn	46	56.03 N	4.22 W
Killeen	222	31.07 N	97.43 W
Killen	194	34.51 N	87.32 W
Killenaule	48	52.34 N	7.40 W
Killeter	48	54.40 N	7.41 W
Kıllıdağ ∧	130	40.21 N	42.10 E
Killik ≃	180	69.00 N	153.58 W
Killilan	46	57.19 N	5.25 W
Killimor	48	53.10 N	8.17 W
Killin	46	56.28 N	4.19 W
Killington Peak ∧	188	43.36 N	72.49 W
Killingworth	207	41.21 N	72.33 W
Killíni	38	37.55 N	21.09 E
Killíni ∧	38	37.57 N	22.23 E
Killiniq Island I	176	60.24 N	64.40 W
Killinkoski	26	62.24 N	23.52 E
Killorglin	48	52.06 N	9.47 W
Killough	48	54.16 N	5.39 W
Killpecker Creek ≃	202	41.35 N	109.14 W
Killucan	48	53.31 N	7.07 W
Kill Van Kull ⊔	276	40.39 N	74.05 W
Killybegs	48	54.38 N	8.27 W
Killyleagh	48	54.24 N	5.39 W
Kilmacolm	46	55.54 N	4.38 W
Kilmacthomas	48	52.12 N	7.25 W
Kilmaine	48	53.34 N	9.09 W
Kilmallock	48	52.23 N	8.34 W
Kilmaluag	46	57.41 N	6.17 W
Kilmarnock, Scot., U.K.	46	55.36 N	4.30 W
Kilmarnock, Va., U.S.	208	37.42 N	76.22 W
Kilmartin	46	56.07 N	5.29 W
Kilmar Tor ∧ 2	42	50.33 N	4.28 W
Kilmaurs	46	55.39 N	4.32 W
Kilmelford	46	56.16 N	5.29 W
Kil'mez', Ross.	80	56.57 N	51.04 E
Kil'mez', Ross.	80	57.04 N	51.21 E
Kil'mez' ≃	80	56.58 N	50.28 E
Kilmichael	194	33.26 N	89.34 W
Kilmichael Point ›	48	52.44 N	6.10 W
Kilmore	169	37.18 S	144.57 E
Kilmore Creek ≃	216	40.20 N	86.38 W
Kilmory	46	57.03 N	6.22 W
Kilnaleck	48	53.52 N	7.19 W
Kilninver	46	56.20 N	5.31 W
Kilo	115b	8.21 S	118.24 E
Kilokri ◆ 8	272a	28.35 N	77.16 E
Kiloli	154	6.50 S	33.23 E
Kilombero ≃	154	8.31 S	37.22 E
Kilomines	154	1.48 N	30.14 E
Kilondo	154	9.46 S	34.21 E
Kilosa	154	6.50 S	36.59 E
Kilpisjärvi	24	69.03 N	20.48 E
Kilrea	48	54.58 N	6.35 W
Kilrenny	46	56.14 N	2.41 W
Kilrush	48	52.39 N	9.30 W
Kilsbergen ∧∧ 2	40	59.20 N	14.47 E
Kilsmo	40	59.04 N	15.31 E
Kilsyth, Austl.	274b	37.48 S	145.19 E
Kilsyth, Scot., U.K.	46	55.59 N	4.04 W
Kiltealy	48	52.34 N	6.45 W
Kiltimagh	48	53.51 N	9.01 W
Kiltoom	48	53.28 N	8.01 W
Kilttān Island I	122	11.29 N	73.00 E
Kiltu-ri	98	34.35 N	127.20 E
Kilwa	154	9.18 S	28.25 E
Kilwa Island I	154	9.20 S	28.33 E
Kilwa Kivinje	154	8.45 S	39.24 E
Kilwa Masoko	154	8.56 S	39.31 E
Kilwinning	46	55.40 N	4.42 W
Kim	198	37.14 N	103.21 W
Kim ≃	152	5.28 N	11.07 E
Kima	154	1.26 S	26.43 E
Kimaam	164	7.58 S	138.53 E
Kimamba	154	6.47 S	37.08 E
Kimande	154	7.22 S	35.30 E
Kīmān Fāris (Crocodilopolis) (Arsinoe) ⊥	142	29.19 N	30.50 E
Kimba	166	33.09 S	136.25 E
Kimball, Mn., U.S.	190	45.19 N	94.18 W
Kimball, Ne., U.S.	198	41.14 N	103.39 W
Kimball, S.D., U.S.	198	43.44 N	98.57 W
Kimball, Mount ∧	180	63.14 N	144.39 W
Kimbanda	152	4.07 S	17.59 E
Kimbe	164	5.31 S	150.10 E
Kimbe Bay c	164	5.30 S	150.30 E
Kimberley, B.C., Can.	182	49.41 N	115.59 W
Kimberley, S. Afr.	158	28.43 S	24.46 E
Kimberley, Eng., U.K.	44	52.59 N	1.16 W
Kimberley Downs	162	17.24 S	124.22 E
Kimberley Plateau ∧∧ 1	160	17.00 S	127.00 E
Kimberling City	194	36.38 N	93.28 W
Kimberly, Id., U.S.	202	42.32 N	114.21 W
Kimberly, Wi., U.S.	190	44.16 N	88.20 W
Kimberton	208	40.08 N	75.34 W
Kimbolton, N.Z.	172	40.03 S	175.47 E
Kimbolton, Eng., U.K.	42	52.18 N	0.24 W
Kimbolton, Oh., U.S.	214	40.09 N	81.34 W
Kimbongo	152	6.08 S	18.01 E
Kimbwala	273b	4.22 S	15.12 E
Kimch'aek (Sŏngjin)	98	40.41 N	129.12 E
Kimch'ŏn	98	36.07 N	128.05 E
Kimerka ≃	82	56.52 N	37.22 E
Kimhae	98	35.14 N	128.52 E
Kimhwa	98	38.26 N	127.36 E
Kími	38	38.37 N	24.06 E
Kimil'tej	88	54.08 N	101.59 E
Kimito (Kemiö)	26	60.10 N	22.45 E
Kimito I	26	60.07 N	22.40 E
Kimi-tōge ∧ 2	270	34.43 N	135.06 E
Kimi-tōge)(	96	34.23 N	135.37 E
Kimitsu	94	35.20 N	139.54 E
Kimiwan Lake ⊜	182	55.45 N	116.54 W
Kimje	98	35.48 N	126.52 E
Kim Kim ≃	271c	1.26 N	103.58 E
Kimmell	216	41.23 N	85.32 W
Kim-me-ni-oli Wash V	200	36.07 N	108.11 W
Kímolos I	38	36.48 N	24.34 E
Kimongo	152	4.29 S	12.58 E
Kimovsk	76	53.58 N	38.32 E
Kimpangu	152	5.51 S	15.01 E
Kim Plan	279b	40.20 N	79.44 W
Kimp'o	271b	37.37 N	126.43 E
Kimp'o Airport ⊠	271b	37.33 N	126.48 E
Kimpombo	273b	4.17 S	15.10 E
Kimpō-zan ∧	94	35.53 N	138.38 E
Kimry	82	56.52 N	37.21 E
Kimsquit	182	52.49 N	126.58 W
Kimstad	40	58.32 N	15.58 E
Kimu ≃	268	35.56 N	139.57 E
Kimuenza	273b	4.27 S	15.17 E
Kimvula	152	5.44 S	15.58 E
Kimwanga	154	7.08 S	28.42 E
Kin	174m	26.26 N	127.55 E
Kinabalian, Mount ∧	116	8.14 N	125.25 E
Kinabalu, Gunong ∧	112	6.05 N	116.33 E

Symbol	English	Deutsch	Español	Français	Português
≃	River	Fluß	Río	Rivière	Rio
≅	Canal	Kanal	Canal	Canal	Canal
⌊	Waterfall, Rapids	Wasserfall, Stromschnellen	Cascada, Rápidos	Chute d'eau, Rapides	Cascata, Rápidos
⊔	Strait	Meeresstraße	Estrecho	Détroit	Estreito
c	Bay, Gulf	Bucht, Golf	Bahía, Golfo	Baie, Golfe	Baía, Golfo
⊜	Lake, Lakes	See, Seen	Lago, Lagos	Lac, Lacs	Lago, Lagos
≡	Swamp	Sumpf	Pantano	Marais	Pântano
⌂	Ice Features, Glacier	Eis- und Gletscherformen	Accidentes Glaciales	Formes glaciaires	Acidentes glaciares
⊤	Other Hydrographic Features	Andere Hydrographische Objekte	Otros Elementos Hidrográficos	Autres données hydrographiques	Outros acidentes hidrográficos

Symbol	English	Deutsch	Español	Français	Português
✦	Submarine Features	Untermeerische Objekte	Accidentes Submarinos	Formes de relief sous-marin	Acidentes submarinos
□	Political Unit	Politische Einheit	Unidad Politica	Entité politique	Unidade política
∪	Cultural Institution	Kulturelle Institution	Institución Cultural	Institution culturelle	Instituição cultural
⊥	Historical Site	Historische Stätte	Sitio Histórico	Site historique	Sitio histórico
♠	Recreational Site	Erholungs- und Ferienort	Sitio de Recreo	Centre de loisirs	Area de Lazer
⊠	Airport	Flughafen	Aeropuerto	Aéroport	Aeroporto
■	Military Installation	Militäranlage	Instalación Militar	Installation militaire	Instalação militar
◆	Miscellaneous	Verschiedenes	Misceláneo	Divers	Diversos

Name	Page	Lat.°′	Long.°′
Kinabalu National Park ♦	112	6.05 N	116.33 E
Kinabatangan ≃	112	5.42 N	118.23 E
Kınalı ◆[8]	267b	40.55 N	29.03 E
Kınalı Ada I	267b	40.55 N	29.03 E
Kinangaly ∧	157b	19.12 S	45.40 E
Kinango	154	4.08 S	39.19 E
Kinapusan Island I	116	5.13 N	120.40 E
Kinara	164	2.16 S	132.44 E
Kinasa	94	36.42 N	138.01 E
Kinaūni	272a	28.39 N	77.23 E
Kinbasket Lake ⊜[1]	182	51.58 N	118.03 W
Kinbrace	46	58.15 N	3.56 W
Kinbuck	46	56.13 N	3.57 W
Kincaid, Sk., Can.	184	49.39 N	107.00 W
Kincaid, Il., U.S.	219	39.35 N	89.24 W
Kincardine, On., Can.	190	44.11 N	81.38 W
Kincardine, Scot., U.K.	46	56.04 N	3.44 W
Kinchafoonee Creek ≃	192	31.38 N	84.10 W
Kinchang	110	26.32 N	98.02 E
Kinchara	272b	22.53 N	88.32 E
Kinchega National Park ♦	166	32.30 S	142.20 E
Kincheloe Air Force Base ■	190	46.15 N	84.28 W
Kincolith	182	55.00 N	129.57 W
Kincraig	46	57.08 N	3.55 W
Kinda, Zaïre	152	4.47 S	21.48 E
Kinda, Zaïre	154	9.18 S	25.04 E
Kindadal	112	1.35 S	123.11 E
Kindanba	152	3.44 S	14.31 E
Kindarun Mountain ∧	170	32.49 S	150.41 E
Kindberg	61	47.31 N	15.27 E
Kinde	190	43.56 N	82.59 W
Kindeje	152	7.07 S	13.44 E
Kindel'a	80	51.36 N	52.58 E
Kindel'a ≃	80	51.30 N	52.45 E
Kindelbrück	54	51.16 N	11.05 E
Kindele	152	8.39 S	24.11 E
Kinder	194	30.29 N	92.51 W
Kinderhook, Il., U.S.	219	39.42 N	91.09 W
Kinderhook, Mi., U.S.	216	41.48 N	85.00 W
Kinderhook, N.Y., U.S.	210	42.23 N	73.41 W
Kinderhook Creek ≃	210	42.19 N	73.45 W
Kinder Reservoir ⊜[1]	262	53.23 N	1.55 W
Kinder Scout ∧	44	53.23 N	1.52 W
Kindersley	184	51.27 N	109.10 W
Kindia	150	10.04 N	12.51 W
Kindikan	88	56.02 N	115.15 E
Kinding	60	49.00 N	11.23 E
Kindley Field ⊠	240a	32.22 N	64.40 W
Kindred	198	46.38 N	97.01 W
Kindu	154	2.57 S	25.56 E
Kindykty, ozero ⊜	86	51.15 N	62.14 E
Kinel'	80	53.14 N	50.39 E
Kinel'-Čerkasy	80	53.29 N	51.29 E
Kinel'skije jary ⋏[1]	80	53.42 N	52.00 E
Kineo, Mount ∧	188	45.42 N	69.44 W
Kinesi	154	1.28 S	33.52 E
Kinešma	80	57.26 N	42.09 E
Kineton	42	52.10 N	1.30 W
Kinfauns	46	56.22 N	3.21 W
King	192	36.16 N	80.21 W
King □[6]	224	47.26 N	121.48 W
King ≃, Austl.	164	14.41 S	131.59 E
King ≃, Austl.	169	36.41 S	146.25 E
King, Lake ⊜	162	25.38 S	120.06 E
King, Mont ∧	212	45.29 N	75.52 W
King, Mount ∧	166	25.10 S	147.31 E
Kingabwa ◆[8]	273b	4.19 S	15.20 E
King and Queen □[6]	208	37.42 N	76.50 W
King and Queen Court House	208	37.40 N	76.52 W
Kingaroy	166	26.33 S	151.50 E
Kingarth	46	55.46 N	5.03 W
King City, On., Can.	212	43.56 N	79.32 W
King City, Ca., U.S.	226	36.12 N	121.07 W
King City, Mo., U.S.	194	40.03 N	94.31 W
King Cove	180	55.04 N	162.19 W
Kingdom City	219	38.58 N	91.56 W
King Edward ≃	164	14.14 S	126.35 E
Kingersheim	58	47.48 N	7.20 E
King Ferry	210	42.39 N	76.37 W
Kingfield	188	44.57 N	70.09 W
Kingfisher	196	35.51 N	97.55 W
King George	208	38.16 N	77.11 W
King George □[6]	208	38.15 N	77.10 W
King George, Mount ∧	182	50.35 N	115.24 W
King George Bay C	254	51.33 S	60.37 W
King George Island I	9	62.00 S	58.15 W
King George Islands II	176	57.20 N	78.25 W
King George's Dock ◆[5]	272b	22.32 N	88.18 E
King George Sound ⊔	162	35.03 S	117.57 E
King George's Reservoir ⊜[1]	260	51.39 N	0.01 W
King George VI Reservoir ⊜[1]	260	51.27 N	0.32 W
King Hill	202	43.00 N	115.12 W
Kinghorn	46	56.04 N	3.10 W
Kingie ≃	46	57.04 N	5.08 W
Kingisepp	76	59.22 N	28.36 E
King Island I, Austl.	166	39.50 S	144.00 E
King Island I, B.C., Can.	182	52.12 N	127.42 W
King Island I, Ak., U.S.	180	64.58 N	168.05 W
Kinglake National Park ♦	169	37.35 S	145.25 E
King Lear Peak ∧	204	41.12 N	118.34 W
King Leopold Ranges ⋏	160	17.30 S	125.45 E
Kingman, Az., U.S.	200	35.11 N	114.03 W
Kingman, Ks., U.S.	198	37.38 N	98.06 W
Kingman Reef ✦[2]	14	6.24 N	162.22 W
King Mountain ∧, B.C., Can.	180	58.17 N	128.54 W
King Mountain ∧, Ok., U.S.	196	34.52 N	99.17 W
King Mountain ∧, Or., U.S.	202	42.42 N	123.14 W
King Mountain ∧, Or., U.S.	202	43.49 N	118.52 W
King of Prussia	208	40.05 N	75.23 W
King of Prussia Plaza ◆[9]	285	40.05 N	75.25 W
Kingoma	152	5.11 S	13.34 E
Kingoma-Ngoma	152	5.50 S	16.49 E
Kingombe, Zaïre	154	3.56 S	26.35 E
Kingombe, Zaïre	154	7.24 S	26.11 E
Kingoonya	162	30.54 S	135.18 E
Kingoué	152	3.43 S	14.09 E
King Peak ∧	204	40.10 N	124.08 W
Kingri	120	30.27 N	69.49 E
Kings, Il., U.S.	216	42.00 N	89.06 W
Kings, Ms., U.S.	194	32.23 N	90.51 W
Kings □[6], Ca., U.S.	226	36.20 N	119.39 W
Kings □[6], N.Y., U.S.	210	40.42 N	74.00 W
Kings ≃, Ar., U.S.	194	36.29 N	93.35 W
Kings ≃, Ca., U.S.	226	36.03 N	119.49 W
Kings ≃, Nv., U.S.	204	41.31 N	118.08 W
Kings, Middle Fork ≃	204	36.50 N	118.52 W
Kings, North Fork ≃, Ca., U.S.	204	36.52 N	119.08 W
Kings, North Fork ≃, Ca., U.S.	226	36.18 N	119.52 W
Kings, South Fork ≃	226	36.18 N	119.52 W
King Salmon	180	58.41 N	156.39 W
King Salmon ≃	180	58.15 N	157.30 W
Kingsbarns	46	56.18 N	2.39 W
Kings Beach	226	39.14 N	120.01 W
Kingsbridge	42	50.17 N	3.46 W
Kingsburg	226	36.30 N	119.33 W
Kingsbury, Eng., U.K.	42	52.35 N	1.40 W
Kingsbury, In., U.S.	216	41.31 N	86.42 W
Kingsbury ◆[8]	260	51.35 N	0.17 W
Kings Canyon National Park ♦	204	36.48 N	118.30 W
Kingsclere	42	51.20 N	1.14 W
Kingscote	168b	35.40 S	137.38 E
Kingscourt	48	53.53 N	6.48 W
Kings Creek	218	40.10 N	83.44 W
Kings Creek ≃, Austl.	171a	27.57 S	151.42 E
Kings Creek ≃, Tx., U.S.	222	32.25 N	96.15 W
King's Cross Station ◆[5]	260	51.32 N	0.07 W
Kings Dominion ♦	208	37.51 N	77.27 W
Kingsdown, Eng., U.K.	42	51.11 N	1.25 E
Kingsdown, Eng., U.K.	260	51.21 N	0.17 E
Kings Falls ⌊	212	43.55 N	75.38 W
Kingsford, Austl.	274a	33.56 S	151.14 E
Kingsford, Mi., U.S.	190	45.47 N	88.04 W
Kingsford Heights	216	41.29 N	86.42 W
Kingsford Smith Airport ⊠	170	33.57 S	151.11 E
Kingsgate	182	49.00 N	116.11 W
Kingsgrove	274a	33.57 S	151.06 E
Kingshill	241n	17.44 N	64.48 W
Kingshouse	46	56.21 N	4.19 W
Kings Island ♦	218	39.21 N	84.16 W
Kingskerswell	42	50.30 N	3.33 W
Kingsland, Eng., U.K.	42	52.15 N	2.47 W
Kingsland, Ar., U.S.	194	33.51 N	92.17 W
Kingsland, Ga., U.S.	192	30.47 N	81.41 W
Kingsland, Tx., U.S.	196	30.40 N	98.26 W
Kingsland, Va., U.S.	208	37.24 N	77.26 W
Kings Langley	42	51.43 N	0.28 W
Kingsley, S. Afr.	158	27.55 S	30.33 E
Kingsley, Eng., U.K.	42	53.01 N	1.59 W
Kingsley, Eng., U.K.	262	53.16 N	2.40 W
Kingsley, Ia., U.S.	198	42.35 N	95.58 W
Kingsley, Mi., U.S.	190	44.35 N	85.32 W
Kingsley, Pa., U.S.	210	41.46 N	75.45 W
Kingsley Dam ◆[6]	198	41.11 N	101.39 W
King's Lynn	42	52.45 N	0.24 E
Kings Manor	285	40.05 N	75.21 W
Kingsmere Lake ⊜	184	54.06 N	106.27 W
Kings Mills	218	39.21 N	84.14 W
Kings Mountain	192	35.14 N	81.20 W
Kings Mountain National Military Park ♦	192	35.07 N	81.33 W
King Solomon's Mines → Mikhrot Shelomo Hamelekh ⊥	132	29.45 N	34.56 E
King Sound ⊔	162	17.00 S	123.30 E
Kings Park, N.Y., U.S.	210	40.53 N	73.16 W
Kings Park, Va., U.S.	284c	38.48 N	77.14 W
Kings Park ♦	168a	31.57 S	115.49 E
Kings Peak ∧	200	40.46 N	110.22 W
Kings Plaza ◆[9]	276	40.37 N	73.55 W
King's Point, Nf., Can.	186	49.35 N	56.11 W
Kings Point, N.Y., U.S.	210	40.49 N	73.44 W
Kingsport	192	36.32 N	82.33 W
King's Sutton	42	52.01 N	1.16 W
Kingsteignton	42	50.33 N	3.35 W
King Sterndale	262	53.15 N	1.52 W
Kingsthorpe	171a	27.29 S	151.49 E
Kingston, Austl.	171a	27.40 S	153.07 E
Kingston, N.S., Can.	186	44.59 N	64.57 W
Kingston, On., Can.	212	44.14 N	76.30 W
Kingston, Jam.	241q	18.00 N	76.48 W
Kingston, N.Z.	172	45.20 S	168.42 E
Kingston, Norf. I.	174c	29.03 S	167.58 E
Kingston, Ga., U.S.	192	34.14 N	84.56 W
Kingston, Il., U.S.	216	42.06 N	88.46 W
Kingston, Ma., U.S.	207	41.59 N	70.43 W
Kingston, Mo., U.S.	194	39.38 N	94.02 W
Kingston, N.J., U.S.	276	40.22 N	74.36 W
Kingston, N.Y., U.S.	210	41.55 N	73.59 W
Kingston, Oh., U.S.	218	39.28 N	82.54 W
Kingston, Ok., U.S.	196	33.59 N	96.43 W
Kingston, Pa., U.S.	210	41.15 N	75.53 W
Kingston, R.I., U.S.	207	41.29 N	71.31 W
Kingston, Tn., U.S.	192	35.52 N	84.30 W
Kingston, Wa., U.S.	224	47.48 N	122.30 W
Kingston Bay C	283	42.00 N	70.42 W
Kingston Mills	212	44.17 N	76.27 W
Kingston Southeast	166	36.50 S	139.51 E
Kingston upon Hull	44	53.45 N	0.20 W
Kingston [upon Thames]	28	51.25 N	0.19 W
Kingston [upon Thames] ◆[8]	42	51.25 N	0.19 W
Kingstown	241h	13.09 N	61.14 W
Kingstown → Dún Laoghaire	48	53.17 N	6.08 W
Kingstree	192	33.40 N	79.49 W
Kingsville, Austl.	274b	37.49 S	144.52 E
Kingsville, On., Can.	214	42.02 N	82.45 W
Kingsville, Md., U.S.	284b	39.26 N	76.25 W
Kingsville, Oh., U.S.	214	41.53 N	80.41 W
Kingsville, Tx., U.S.	196	27.30 N	97.51 W
Kingsville Naval Air Station ■	196	27.31 N	97.47 W
Kingswear	42	50.21 N	3.34 W
Kingswinford	42	52.29 N	2.10 W
Kingswood, Austl.	274a	33.46 S	150.43 E
Kingswood, S. Afr.	158	27.29 S	25.46 E
Kingswood, Eng., U.K.	42	51.27 N	2.22 W
Kingswood, Eng., U.K.	260	51.17 N	0.13 W
Kingswood Park	285	40.07 N	74.51 W
King's Worthy	42	51.06 N	1.18 W
Kingtechen → Jingdezhen	100	29.16 N	117.11 E
Kington	42	52.12 N	3.01 W
Kingunda	152	6.34 S	16.58 E
Kingungi	152	5.24 S	17.56 E
Kingussie	46	57.05 N	4.03 W
King William	208	37.41 N	77.00 W
King William □[6]	208	37.42 N	77.05 W
King William Island I	176	69.00 N	97.30 W
King William's Town	158	32.51 S	27.22 E
Kingwood, Tx., U.S.	222	29.54 N	95.18 W
Kingwood, W.V., U.S.	188	39.28 N	79.41 W
Kinh Duc	110	11.49 N	107.58 E
Kinhwa → Jinhua	100	29.07 N	119.39 E
Kınık	130	39.05 N	27.23 E
Kinira ≃	158	31.12 S	29.17 E
Kinistino	184	52.57 N	105.00 W
Kinjar Khās	123	29.55 N	70.58 E
Kinkala	152	4.22 S	14.46 E
Kinker Creek ≃	282	38.02 N	121.52 W
Kinkony, Lac ⊜	157b	16.08 S	45.50 E
Kinkora	285	40.07 N	74.45 W
Kinleith	172	38.16 S	175.54 E
Kinloch	46	57.01 N	6.17 W
Kinlochbervie	46	58.28 N	5.03 W
Kinlocheil	46	56.51 N	5.20 W
Kinlochewe	46	57.36 N	5.20 W
Kinloch Hourn	46	57.06 N	5.22 W
Kinlochleven	46	56.42 N	4.58 W
Kinloch Rannoch	46	56.42 N	4.11 W
Kinloss	46	57.37 N	3.34 W
Kinmount	212	44.47 N	78.39 W
Kinmundy	219	38.46 N	88.50 W
Kinn	26	61.36 N	4.45 E
Kinna	26	57.30 N	12.41 E
Kinnaird	182	49.17 N	117.39 W
Kinnaird Head ›	46	57.42 N	2.00 W
Kinnegad	48	53.26 N	7.05 W
Kinnekulle ∧[2]	26	58.35 N	13.23 E
Kinnelon	210	40.59 N	74.23 W
Kinnel Water ≃	44	55.08 N	3.25 W
Kinneret	132	32.43 N	35.33 E
Kinneret, Yam (Sea of Galilee) ⊜	132	32.48 N	35.35 E
Kinneret-Negev Conduit ≍[1]	132	32.52 N	35.32 E
Kinnerley	42	52.47 N	2.59 W
Kinniconick Creek ≃	218	38.37 N	83.09 W
Kinnula	26	63.22 N	24.58 E
Kino ≃	96	34.13 N	135.09 E
Kinoe	96	34.14 N	132.55 E
Kinogitan	116	9.00 N	124.48 E
Kinojévis ≃	190	48.23 N	78.21 W
Kinomoto	94	35.30 N	136.13 E
Kinonge ≃	206	45.39 N	74.55 W
Kinoni	154	0.39 S	30.27 E
Kinosaki	96	35.37 N	134.49 E
Kinpoku-san ∧	92	38.05 N	138.22 E
Kinrola	166	23.46 S	148.45 E
Kinross, S. Afr.	158	26.22 S	29.03 E
Kinross, Scot., U.K.	46	56.13 N	3.27 W
Kin-saki ›	174m	26.26 N	127.57 E
Kinsale, Ire.	48	51.42 N	8.32 W
Kinsale, Va., U.S.	208	38.01 N	76.34 W
Kinsale, Old Head of ›	48	51.36 N	8.32 W
Kinsale Harbour C	48	51.41 N	8.30 W
Kinsarvik	26	60.23 N	6.43 E
Kinschasa → Kinshasa	152	4.18 S	15.18 E
Kinshasa (Léopoldville), Zaïre	152	4.18 S	15.18 E
Kinshasa (Léopoldville), Zaïre	273b	4.18 S	15.18 E
Kinshasa □[4]	152	4.18 S	15.18 E
Kinshasa (Ndjili) Airport ⊠, Zaïre	273b	4.23 S	15.27 E
Kinshasa (Ndolo) Airport ⊠, Zaïre	273b	4.20 S	15.19 E
Kinshasa-Est ◆[8]	273b	4.18 S	15.18 E
Kinshasa-Ouest ◆[8]	273b	4.20 S	15.15 E
Kinsley	198	37.55 N	99.24 W
Kinsman, Il., U.S.	216	41.11 N	88.34 W
Kinsman, Oh., U.S.	214	41.27 N	80.36 W
Kinston, Al., U.S.	194	31.12 N	86.10 W
Kinston, N.C., U.S.	192	35.15 N	77.34 W
Kintamani	115b	8.14 S	115.19 E
Kintamo, Rapides de ⌊	273b	4.19 S	15.15 E
Kintampo	150	8.03 N	1.43 W
Kintap	112	3.51 S	115.13 E
Kintari, Mont ∧[2]	273b	4.08 S	15.23 E
Kintélé	273b	4.09 S	15.21 E
Kintinian	150	11.36 N	9.23 W
Kintinku	154	5.53 S	35.14 E
Kintobongo-Bunge	154	8.54 S	26.23 E
Kintore	46	57.13 N	2.21 W
Kintore, Mount ∧	162	26.34 S	130.30 E
Kintore Range ⋏	162	23.25 S	129.20 E
Kintsana	273b	4.19 S	15.10 E
Kintus	86	60.09 N	71.25 E
Kintyre ›[1]	46	55.32 N	5.35 W
Kintyre, Mull of ›	46	55.17 N	5.55 W
Kinu ≃	94	35.56 N	139.57 E
Kinuseo Falls ⌊	182	54.47 N	121.12 W
Kinuso	182	55.20 N	115.25 W
Kinvarra	48	53.08 N	8.55 W
Kinver	42	52.27 N	2.14 W
Kin-wan C	174m	26.25 N	127.54 E
Kinwood	222	29.56 N	95.23 W
Kinyangiri	154	4.27 S	34.37 E
Kinyeti ∧	154	3.57 N	32.54 E
Kinzia	152	3.36 S	18.26 E
Kinzig ≃, Dtsch.	56	50.08 N	8.54 E
Kinzig ≃, Dtsch.	58	48.37 N	7.49 E
Kinzua	202	44.59 N	120.03 W
Kinzua Creek ≃	214	41.47 N	78.50 W
Kinzua Dam ◆[6]	214	41.50 N	79.01 W
Kioga-See → Kyoga, Lake ⊜	154	1.30 N	33.00 E
Kioshkokwi Lake ⊜	190	46.05 N	78.52 W
Kioto → Kyōto	94	35.00 N	135.45 E
Kiowa, Co., U.S.	198	39.20 N	104.27 W
Kiowa, Ks., U.S.	198	37.01 N	98.29 W
Kiowa, Ok., U.S.	196	34.43 N	95.53 W
Kiowa Creek ≃, U.S.	196	36.46 N	99.55 W
Kiowa Creek ≃, Co., U.S.	198	40.20 N	104.05 W
Kipahigan Lake ⊜	184	55.20 N	101.55 W
Kipandi	152	5.19 S	16.46 E
Kipanga	154	6.14 S	35.21 E
Kiparissía	38	37.14 N	21.40 E
Kiparissiakós Kólpos C	38	37.37 N	21.24 E
Kipatimu	154	8.29 S	38.56 E
Kipawa ≃	190	47.03 N	79.23 W
Kipawa, Lac ⊜	190	46.55 N	79.00 W
Kipawa, Réserve ♦	190	47.15 N	78.15 W
Kipembawe	154	7.39 S	33.24 E
Kipengere Range ⋏	154	9.10 S	34.15 E
Kiperčeny	78	47.32 N	28.50 E
Kipijevo	24	65.40 N	54.30 E
Kipili	154	7.26 S	30.36 E
Kipini	154	2.32 S	40.31 E
Kipling	184	50.10 N	102.38 W
Kipnuk	180	59.56 N	164.03 W
Kippax	44	53.46 N	1.22 W
Kippen	46	56.08 N	4.11 W
Kippenheim	58	48.17 N	7.49 E
Kippure ∧	48	53.10 N	6.20 W
Kípros → Cyprus □[1]	130	35.00 N	33.00 E
Kipsdorf	54	50.47 N	13.32 E
Kipton	214	41.16 N	82.18 W
Kipushi	154	11.46 S	27.14 E
Kipushia, Zaïre	154	6.10 S	25.12 E
Kipushia, Zaïre	154	12.58 S	29.30 E
Kira, Nihon	94	34.49 N	137.05 E
Kir'a, Ross.	80	55.04 N	46.53 E
Kirakira	175e	10.27 S	161.55 E
Kirandul	122	18.40 N	81.16 E
Kirane	150	15.25 N	10.14 W
Kiranlık	130	39.07 N	41.41 E
Kiranomena	157b	18.17 S	46.03 E
Kīratpur	124	29.31 N	78.12 E
Kiraz	130	38.13 N	28.13 E
Kirazlı	130	40.02 N	26.41 E
Kırbaçbayırı ∧	267b	40.56 N	29.10 E
Kırbaşı	130	40.01 N	31.50 E
Kirbla	76	58.44 N	23.57 E
Kirby Muxloe	42	52.38 N	1.13 W
Kirbys Creek ≃	208	36.28 N	77.06 W
Kirbyville	194	30.39 N	93.53 W
Kırçal	130	41.39 N	35.16 E
Kırcasalih	130	41.23 N	26.48 E
Kirchardt	56	49.12 N	8.59 E
Kirchbach in Steiermark	61	46.54 N	15.44 E
Kirchberg, Dtsch.	54	50.37 N	12.32 E
Kirchberg, Dtsch.	56	49.12 N	9.58 E
Kirchberg, Dtsch.	56	49.56 N	7.24 E
Kirchberg, Dtsch.	60	48.54 N	13.11 E
Kirchberg, Schw.	58	47.05 N	7.35 E
Kirchberg, Schw.	58	47.25 N	9.03 E
Kirch-Berg ∧[2]	264a	52.27 N	13.02 E
Kirchberg am Wagram	61	48.26 N	15.53 E
Kirchberg an der Pielach	61	48.02 N	15.26 E
Kirchberg in Tirol	64	47.27 N	12.19 E
Kirchbichl	64	47.31 N	12.05 E
Kirchderne ◆[8]	263	51.33 N	7.30 E
Kirchdorf, Dtsch.	52	52.36 N	8.49 E
Kirchdorf, Dtsch.	54	54.00 N	11.26 E
Kirchdorf an der Krems	61	47.56 N	14.07 E
Kirchdorf im Wald	60	48.55 N	13.16 E
Kirchen	56	50.48 N	7.53 E
Kirchende	263	51.25 N	7.26 E
Kirchenlaibach	60	49.53 N	11.46 E
Kirchenlamitz	54	50.09 N	11.56 E
Kirchenthumbach	60	49.45 N	11.43 E
Kirchhain	56	50.49 N	8.55 E
Kirchham	60	48.21 N	13.16 E
Kirchheiligen	54	51.11 N	10.42 E
Kirchheimbolanden	56	49.40 N	8.00 E
Kirchheim in Schwaben	58	48.10 N	10.30 E
Kirchheim unter Teck	56	48.39 N	9.27 E
Kirchhellen	52	51.36 N	6.55 E
Kirchhellen Heide ◆[3]	263	51.36 N	6.53 E
Kirchhofen	264a	52.22 N	13.53 E
Kirchhörde ◆[8]	263	51.27 N	7.27 E
Kirchhundem	56	51.05 N	8.05 E
Kirchlengern	52	52.12 N	8.35 E
Kirchlinde ◆[8]	263	51.32 N	7.22 E
Kirchlinteln	52	52.56 N	9.19 E
Kirchmöser	54	52.22 N	12.25 E
Kirchroth	60	48.57 N	12.33 E
Kirchschlag in der Buckligen Welt	61	47.31 N	16.18 E
Kirchveischede	56	51.05 N	7.59 E
Kirchwalsede	52	53.01 N	9.23 E
Kirchwerder ◆[8]	52	53.25 N	10.11 E
Kirchzarten	58	47.58 N	7.56 E
Kircubbin	48	54.29 N	5.32 W
Kirda	85	41.06 N	69.00 E
Kirdāsah	142	30.02 N	31.07 E
Kireç	130	39.33 N	28.22 E
Kirej ≃	88	54.12 N	100.40 E
Kirejevo	80	50.01 N	44.29 E
Kirejevsk	76	53.56 N	37.56 E
Kirejkovo	76	53.38 N	35.49 E
Kirenga ≃	88	57.47 N	108.07 E
Kirensk	88	57.46 N	108.08 E
Kirghizia → Kyrgyzstan □[1]	72	41.30 N	75.00 E
Kirgili	85	40.24 N	71.43 E
Kirgizija → Kyrgyzstan □[1]	72	41.30 N	75.00 E
Kirgiziya → Kyrgyzstan □[1]	72	41.30 N	75.00 E
Kirgiz-Mijaki	86	53.38 N	54.47 E
Kirgizskij chrebet ⋏	85	42.30 N	74.00 E
Kiri	152	1.27 S	19.00 E
Kiribati □[1]	14	5.00 S	170.00 W
Kiribati II	14	0.30 S	174.00 E
Kiries West	158	26.34 S	19.00 E
Kiriga-mine ∧	94	36.06 N	138.12 E
Kırıkhan, Tür.	130	39.32 N	41.20 E
Kırıkhan, Tür.	130	36.32 N	36.19 E
Kirikiri Prisons ʊ	273a	6.27 N	3.19 E
Kırıkkale	130	39.50 N	33.31 E
Kırıkkale □[4]	130	40.00 N	33.45 E
Kirikovka	78	50.22 N	35.07 E
Kirillov	76	59.52 N	38.23 E
Kirillovka	265b	55.57 N	37.20 E
Kirillovo, Ross.	80	57.07 N	45.27 E
Kirillovo, Ross.	80	53.47 N	42.40 E
Kirillovskoje	76	60.28 N	29.17 E
Kirin → Jilin	89	43.51 N	126.33 E
Kirin → Jilin □[4]	90	44.00 N	126.00 E
Kirinyaga (Mount Kenya) ∧	154	0.10 S	37.20 E
Kirishima-Yaku-kokuritsu-kōen ♦	92	31.55 N	130.51 E
Kirishima-yama ∧	92	31.56 N	130.52 E
Kiriši	76	59.27 N	32.02 E
Kiritimati (Christmas Island) I[1]	174o	1.52 N	157.20 W
Kiriwina Island I	164	8.35 S	151.05 E
Kiriwina Islands II	164	8.35 S	151.05 E
Kirizume-tōge ∧[2]	270	34.56 N	135.16 E
Kirjanovskaja Kontora	88	58.18 N	104.13 E
Kirka	130	39.17 N	30.33 E
Kirkabister	46a	60.07 N	1.08 W
Kırkağaç	130	39.06 N	27.40 E
Kirkbride	44	54.54 N	3.12 W
Kirkburton	44	53.37 N	1.42 W
Kirkby	44	53.29 N	2.54 W
Kirkby in Ashfield	44	53.06 N	1.15 W
Kirkby Lonsdale	44	54.13 N	2.36 W
Kirkby Malzeard	44	54.11 N	1.38 W
Kirkbymoorside	44	54.16 N	0.55 W
Kirkby Stephen	44	54.28 N	2.20 W
Kirkcaldy	46	56.07 N	3.10 W
Kirkcolm	44	54.58 N	5.05 W
Kirkconnel	44	55.23 N	4.00 W
Kirkcudbright	44	54.50 N	4.03 W
Kirkcudbright Bay C	44	54.48 N	4.04 W
Kirkdale ◆[8]	262	53.26 N	2.59 W
Kirkeby	41	56.09 N	9.27 E
Kirkee → Khadki	122	18.34 N	73.52 E
Kirkenær	26	60.28 N	12.03 E
Kirkenes	24	69.40 N	30.03 E
Kirke Stillinge	41	55.26 N	11.15 E
Kirkham	44	53.47 N	2.53 W
Kirkhill	46	57.28 N	4.26 W
Kirkintilloch	46	55.57 N	4.10 W
Kirkjubæjarklaustur	24a	63.47 N	18.04 W
Kirkkonummi → Kyrkslätt	26	60.07 N	24.26 E
Kirkland, P.Q., Can.	275a	45.27 N	73.52 W
Kirkland, Il., U.S.	216	42.05 N	88.51 W
Kirkland, Tx., U.S.	196	34.23 N	100.04 W
Kirkland, Wa., U.S.	224	47.40 N	122.12 W
Kirkland Creek ≃	200	34.32 N	113.00 W
Kirkland Lake	190	48.09 N	80.02 W
Kırklar Dağı ∧	130	40.32 N	40.35 E
Kırklareli	130	41.44 N	27.12 E
Kırklareli □[4]	130	41.40 N	27.30 E
Kirklees □[8]	262	53.36 N	1.52 W
Kirkleyditch	262	53.18 N	2.12 W
Kirklin	194	40.11 N	86.21 W
Kirkliston	46	55.58 N	3.25 W
Kirk Michael, I. of Man	44	54.17 N	4.35 W
Kirkmichael, Scot., U.K.	46	56.43 N	3.29 W
Kirkmuirhill	46	55.40 N	3.55 W
Kirkness Lake ⊜	184	51.32 N	93.56 W
Kirkpatrick, Mount ∧	9	84.20 S	166.19 E
Kirkpatrick Lake ⊜	182	51.52 N	111.18 W
Kirk Sandall	44	53.33 N	1.04 W
Kirksville, Il., U.S.	219	39.34 N	88.40 W
Kirksville, Mo., U.S.	194	40.11 N	92.34 W
Kirkton	46	56.13 N	2.55 W
Kirkton of Culsalmond	46	57.23 N	2.34 W
Kirkton of Glenisla	46	56.44 N	3.17 W
Kirktown of Auchterless	46	57.27 N	2.28 W
Kirkūk	128	35.28 N	44.28 E
Kirkville	210	43.05 N	75.57 W
Kirkwall	46	58.59 N	2.58 W
Kirkwood, S. Afr.	158	33.24 S	25.26 E
Kirkwood, De., U.S.	208	39.34 N	75.41 W
Kirkwood, Il., U.S.	190	40.51 N	90.44 W
Kirkwood, Mo., U.S.	219	38.35 N	90.24 W
Kirkwood, N.J., U.S.	285	39.50 N	75.01 W
Kirkwood, N.Y., U.S.	210	42.02 N	75.48 W
Kirmir ≃	130	40.07 N	31.43 E
Kirn	56	49.47 N	7.28 E
Kirnāhar	126	23.45 N	87.52 E
Kirotshe	154	1.37 S	29.02 E
Kirov, Ross.	76	54.05 N	34.20 E
Kirov, Ross.	80	58.38 N	49.42 E
Kirova, zaliv C	84	39.09 N	49.03 E
Kirovabad → Gjandža	84	40.40 N	46.22 E
Kirovakan	84	40.48 N	44.30 E
Kirovgrad	86	57.26 N	60.04 E
Kirovka	86	47.07 N	82.00 E
Kirovo, Bela.	78	51.29 N	29.24 E
Kirovo, Ross.	86	55.33 N	63.46 E
Kirovo, Ukr.	78	47.41 N	35.46 E
Kirovo, Ukr.	83	48.23 N	37.55 E
Kirovo, Ukr.	83	48.50 N	38.03 E
Kirovo, Uzb.	85	40.26 N	70.34 E
Kirov Oblast' □[4]	24	59.00 N	50.00 E
Kirovo-Čepeck	80	58.33 N	50.01 E
Kirovograd	78	48.30 N	32.18 E
Kirovograd □[4]	78	48.30 N	32.00 E
Kirovsk, Azer.	84	38.48 N	48.43 E
Kirovsk, Bela.	76	53.16 N	29.29 E
Kirovsk, Ross.	24	67.37 N	33.35 E
Kirovsk, Ross.	265a	59.52 N	31.00 E
Kirovsk, Turk.	128	37.42 N	60.23 E
Kirovsk, Ukr.	83	49.01 N	37.56 E
Kirovsk, Ukr.	83	48.38 N	38.39 E
Kirovskij, Azer.	84	40.26 N	49.51 E
Kirovskij, Kaz.	86	44.52 N	78.12 E
Kirovskij, Ross.	74	54.18 N	155.47 E
Kirovskij, Ross.	80	45.51 N	48.07 E
Kirovskij, Ross.	89	54.26 N	126.55 E
Kirovskij, Ross.	89	45.07 N	133.30 E
Kirovskije ostrova II	265a	59.58 N	30.15 E
Kirovskoje, Kyrg.	85	42.39 N	71.35 E
Kirovskoje, Ukr.	78	48.33 N	34.53 E
Kirovskoje, Ukr.	78	45.14 N	35.13 E
Kirovskoje, Ukr.	83	48.09 N	38.21 E
Kirov Stadium ♦	265a	59.58 N	30.14 E
Kirov Theatre ʊ	265a	59.55 N	30.18 E
Kirpičnyj Zavod	265a	60.01 N	30.48 E
Kirpil'skaja	78	45.23 N	39.43 E
Kirriemuir	46	56.41 N	3.01 W
Kirs	86	59.21 N	52.14 E
Kirsanov	80	52.38 N	42.43 E
Kirsanovka	80	52.30 N	52.53 E
Kirschau	54	51.04 N	14.27 E
Kırşehir	130	39.09 N	34.10 E
Kırşehir □[4]	130	39.20 N	34.10 E
Kīrthar National Park ♦	120	25.50 N	67.40 E
Kīrthar Range ⋏	120	27.00 N	67.10 E
Kirtland, N.M., U.S.	200	36.44 N	108.21 W
Kirtland, Oh., U.S.	214	41.37 N	81.21 W
Kirtland Air Force Base ■	200	35.02 N	106.37 W
Kirtland Hills	214	41.37 N	81.24 W
Kirtle Water ≃	44	54.58 N	3.05 W
Kirton	42	52.56 N	0.04 W
Kirton in Lindsey	44	53.28 N	0.36 W
Kirtorf	56	50.46 N	9.06 E
Kiruna	24	67.51 N	20.16 E
Kirundu	154	0.44 S	25.32 E
Kirurumo	154	5.53 S	34.11 E
Kirvin	222	31.46 N	96.20 W
Kirwan Heights	279b	40.22 N	80.06 W
Kirwee	172	43.30 S	172.13 E
Kirwin	198	39.40 N	99.07 W
Kirwin Reservoir ⊜[1]	198	39.39 N	99.10 W
Kiryandongo	154	1.53 N	32.03 E
Kiryū	94	36.24 N	139.20 E
Kirza	86	54.14 N	81.40 E
Kiržač	82	56.09 N	38.52 E
Kiržač ≃	82	55.52 N	39.04 E
Kisa, Nihon	96	34.43 N	132.59 E
Kisa, Sve.	26	57.59 N	15.37 E
Kisai	94	36.06 N	139.35 E
Kisaichi	270	34.46 N	135.42 E
Kisakata	92	39.13 N	139.54 E
Kisaki	154	7.28 S	37.36 E
Kis Alföld =	61	47.35 N	17.00 E
Kišaly	76	54.23 N	43.12 E
Kisambo	152	6.25 S	18.14 E
Kisanga	154	2.29 N	26.35 E
Kisangani (Stanleyville)	154	0.30 S	25.12 E
Kisantu	152	5.07 S	15.05 E
Kisar, Pulau I	112	8.05 S	127.10 E
Kisaralik ≃	180	60.51 N	161.16 W
Kisaran	114	2.59 N	99.37 E
Kisarawe	154	6.54 S	39.04 E
Kisarazu	94	35.23 N	139.55 E
Kisarazu-Kichi, Kōkū-jieitai ■	94	35.24 N	139.55 E
Kisawa	96	33.49 N	134.18 E
K.I. Sawyer Air Force Base ■	190	46.21 N	87.25 W
Kisbér	30	47.30 N	18.02 E
Kisbey	184	49.38 N	102.41 W
Kise ≃	94	35.06 N	138.53 E
Kiselevsk → Kisel'ovsk	86	54.00 N	86.39 E
Kisel'ovka	80	47.18 N	44.07 E
Kisel'ovsk	86	54.00 N	86.39 E
Kisengwa	154	6.00 S	25.50 E
Kisen-yama ∧[2]	270	34.54 N	135.51 E
Kiser Lake ⊜	218	40.11 N	83.58 W
Kīsh, Jazīreh-ye I	128	26.32 N	53.56 E
Kishanda	154	1.42 S	31.34 E
Kishanganga ≃	123	34.22 N	73.30 E
Kishanganj	124	26.07 N	87.56 E
Kishangarh	120	27.52 N	70.34 E
Kishangarh ◆[8]	272a	28.31 N	77.08 E
Kishangarh Bās	120	26.34 N	74.52 E
Kishb, Harrat al- ⊥[9]	144	23.00 N	41.25 E
Kishi, Nig.	150	9.05 N	3.52 E
Kishi, Zaïre	154	10.04 S	26.26 E
Kishida ≃	96	35.38 N	134.27 E
Kishigawa	96	34.13 N	135.20 E
Kishikas ≃	184	52.45 N	91.43 W
Kishimoto	96	35.23 N	133.25 E
Kishinev → Kišin'ov	38	47.00 N	28.50 E
Kishiwada	96	34.28 N	135.22 E
Kishorganj	124	24.26 N	90.46 E
Kishorn, Loch C	46	57.21 N	5.41 W
Kishtwār	123	33.19 N	75.46 E
Kishwaukee ≃	216	42.11 N	89.08 W
Kishwaukee, South Branch ≃	216	42.12 N	88.59 W
Kisia	152	4.35 S	18.22 E
Kisigo ≃	154	7.03 S	35.50 E
Kisii	154	0.41 S	34.46 E
Kisiju	154	7.24 S	39.20 E
Kiši-Karoj, ozero ⊜	86	54.03 N	71.20 E
Kisika-zaki ›	93b	30.50 N	131.04 E
Kısıklı ◆[8]	267b	41.01 N	29.03 E
Kišin	78	51.08 N	27.41 E
Kišin'ov (Kishinev)	38	47.00 N	28.50 E
Kısır Dağı ∧	84	40.58 N	43.04 E
Kısırkaya ◆[8]	267b	41.14 N	28.58 E
Kısırmandıra ◆[8]	267b	41.14 N	28.49 E
Kisiwada → Kishiwada	96	34.28 N	135.22 E
Kisiwani	154	4.08 S	37.57 E
Kisizi	154	1.00 S	29.56 E
Kiska Island I	181a	52.00 N	177.30 E
Kiskatinaw ≃	182	56.06 N	120.08 W
Kiska Volcano ∧[1]	181a	52.07 N	177.36 E
Kis-Kevély ∧[2]	264c	47.38 N	18.59 E
Kiski Lake ⊜	184	54.46 N	98.55 W
Kiskimere	279b	40.37 N	79.35 W
Kiskiminetas ≃	214	40.41 N	79.40 W
Kiskittogisu Lake ⊜	184	54.13 N	98.20 W
Kiskitto Lake ⊜	184	54.16 N	98.34 W
Kiskörei-víztároló ⊜[1]	30	47.35 N	20.40 E
Kiskőrös	30	46.38 N	19.17 E
Kiskunfélegyháza	30	46.43 N	19.52 E
Kiskunhalas	30	46.26 N	19.30 E
Kiskunmajsa	30	46.30 N	19.45 E
Kiskunsági Nemzeti Park ♦	30	46.40 N	19.25 E
Kisl'akovka	78	46.44 N	31.59 E
Kisl'akovskaja	78	46.27 N	39.40 E
Kislovka	83	49.38 N	37.53 E
Kislovo	80	49.54 N	45.25 E
Kislovodsk	84	43.55 N	42.44 E
Kismaayo	144	0.22 S	42.32 E
Kismet	276	40.38 N	73.12 W
Kisnema	76	60.20 N	37.39 E
Kiso, Nihon	94	35.56 N	137.47 E
Kiso, Nihon	268	35.34 N	139.26 E
Kiso ≃	94	35.02 N	136.45 E
Kisofukushima	94	35.51 N	137.42 E
Kisogawa	94	35.20 N	136.47 E
Kisoripur	126	22.05 N	88.34 E
Kisoro	154	1.17 S	29.41 E
Kiso-sammyaku ⋏	94	35.43 N	137.50 E
Kisozaki	94	35.04 N	136.44 E
Kispest ◆[8]	264c	47.27 N	19.08 E
Kispiox	182	55.21 N	127.41 W
Kispiox ≃	182	55.16 N	127.41 W
Kispiox Mountain ∧	182	55.25 N	127.57 W
Kissamos	38	35.30 N	23.38 E
Kissena Park ♦	276	40.45 N	73.49 W
Kisseynew Lake ⊜	184	54.58 N	101.35 W
Kissidougou	150	9.11 N	10.06 W
Kissimmee	220	28.17 N	81.24 W
Kissimmee ≃	220	27.10 N	80.53 W
Kissimmee, Lake ⊜	220	27.55 N	81.16 W
Kissing	60	48.18 N	10.59 E
Kississing	184	55.07 N	101.07 W
Kississing Lake ⊜	184	55.10 N	101.20 W
Kisslegg	58	47.47 N	9.53 E
Kissū, Jabal ∧	140	21.35 N	25.09 E
Kista	80	46.05 N	43.06 E
Kistanje	36	43.59 N	15.58 E
Kistarcsa	264c	47.33 N	19.16 E
Kistendej	80	52.08 N	43.39 E
Kistigan Lake ⊜	184	54.38 N	92.37 W
Kistler	214	40.22 N	77.51 W
Kisújszállás	30	47.13 N	20.46 E
Kisuki	96	35.17 N	132.54 E
Kisumu	154	0.06 S	34.45 E
Kisvárda	30	48.13 N	22.05 E
Kiswere	154	9.26 S	39.33 E
Kita	150	13.03 N	9.29 W
Kita ◆[8], Nihon	268	35.45 N	139.44 E
Kita ◆[8], Nihon	270	34.42 N	135.30 E
Kita ◆[8], Nihon	270	35.03 N	135.45 E
Kita ◆[8], Nihon	270	34.45 N	135.08 E
Kitaaiki	94	36.04 N	138.34 E
Kita-Daitō-jima I	90	25.57 N	131.18 E
Kitafuji-enshūjō ■	94	35.25 N	138.48 E
Kitagata	94	35.26 N	136.41 E
Kitagawa	96	33.27 N	134.03 E
Kitagi-shima I	96	34.23 N	133.32 E
Kitaibaraki	94	36.48 N	140.45 E
Kitain Temple ʊ[1]	268	35.54 N	139.30 E
Kita-Iō-jima I	14	25.26 N	141.17 E
Kitairiso	268	35.50 N	139.26 E
Kitajima	96	34.05 N	134.35 E
Kitakami	92	39.18 N	141.07 E
Kitakami ≃	92	38.25 N	141.19 E
Kitakami-kōchi ⋏	92	39.30 N	141.30 E
Kitakata	92	37.39 N	139.52 E
Kitakyuschu → Kitakyūshū	96	33.53 N	130.50 E
Kitakyūshū	96	33.53 N	130.50 E
Kitakyushu-kokutei-kōen ♦	96	33.45 N	130.50 E
Kitale	154	1.01 N	35.00 E
Kitamachi ◆[8]	268	35.46 N	139.39 E
Kitamba ◆[8]	273b	4.19 S	15.14 E
Kitami	92a	43.48 N	143.54 E
Kitami-sanchi ⋏	92a	44.22 N	142.43 E
Kitamoto	94	36.02 N	139.32 E
Kita-Nagato-kaigan-kokutei-kōen ♦	96	34.24 N	131.16 E
Kitanakagusuku	174m	26.21 N	127.51 E
Kitanda, Zaïre	154	6.36 S	26.27 E
Kitanda, Zaïre	154	9.59 S	27.28 E
Kitangari	154	10.39 S	39.20 E
Kitangiri, Lake ⊜	154	4.05 S	34.19 E
Kitangua	152	6.17 S	20.22 E
Kitano, Nihon	96	33.20 N	130.35 E
Kitano, Nihon	268	35.47 N	139.26 E
Kitanoshinden	268	35.48 N	139.26 E
Kitatachibana	94	36.29 N	139.03 E
Kitatajima	268	35.56 N	139.30 E
Kitatawara	270	34.44 N	135.42 E
Kitaura	94	36.04 N	140.32 E
Kita-ura ⊜	94	36.00 N	140.34 E
Kitava Island I	164	8.40 S	151.20 E
Kitaya	154	10.39 S	40.10 E
Kit Carson, Ca., U.S.	226	38.41 N	120.07 W
Kit Carson, Co., U.S.	198	38.45 N	102.47 W
Kitchener, Austl.	162	31.02 S	124.11 E
Kitchener, On., Can.	212	43.27 N	80.29 W
Kitee	26	62.06 N	30.09 E
Kitega → Gitega	154	3.26 S	29.56 E
Kiteiyab	140	17.12 N	33.43 E
Kitenda	152	6.53 S	17.21 E
Kitenevo	82	56.21 N	36.13 E
Kitengo	152	7.26 S	24.08 E
Kitéssa	154	5.20 N	25.20 E
Kitgum	154	3.18 N	32.53 E
Kíthira	38	36.09 N	23.00 E
Kíthira I	38	36.20 N	22.58 E
Kíthnos	38	37.26 N	24.26 E
Kíthnos I	38	37.25 N	24.28 E
Kitimat	182	54.03 N	128.33 W
Kitimat ≃	182	54.06 N	128.38 W
Kitimat Ranges ⋏	182	53.30 N	128.50 W
Kitinen ≃	24	67.08 N	27.29 E
Kitíou, Akrotírion ›	130	34.48 N	33.36 E
Kitlope ≃	182	53.10 N	127.45 W
Kitlope Lake ⊜	182	53.07 N	127.47 W
Kitō, Nihon	94	34.42 N	138.03 E
Kitō, Nihon	96	33.46 N	134.12 E
Kitoj ≃	88	52.39 N	103.56 E
Kitridge Point ›	241g	13.09 N	59.25 W
Kitsap □[6]	224	47.41 N	122.44 W
Kitscoty	184	53.20 N	110.20 W
Kit's Coty House ʊ	260	51.19 N	0.30 E
Kitshua-Nseke	152	4.26 S	19.36 E
Kitsuki	92	33.25 N	131.37 E
Kitsuregawa	94	36.43 N	140.01 E
Kittanning	214	40.48 N	79.31 W
Kittatinny Mountain ∧	210	41.10 N	74.55 W
Kittatinny Tunnel ◆[5]	214	40.09 N	77.41 W
Kittendorf	54	53.37 N	12.54 E
Kittery	188	43.05 N	70.44 W
Kitt Green	262	53.33 N	2.41 W
Kittilä	24	67.40 N	24.54 E
Kittitas	202	46.59 N	120.24 W
Kittitas □[6]	224	47.13 N	121.01 W
Kitt Peak National Observatory ʊ[3]	200	31.58 N	111.36 W
Kittsee	61	48.05 N	17.04 E
Kitu	154	7.38 S	27.42 E
Kitui	154	1.22 S	38.01 E
Kitumbeine ∧[1]	154	2.44 S	36.16 E
Kitunda	154	6.48 S	33.13 E
Kitutu	154	3.17 S	28.05 E
Kitwanga	182	55.06 N	128.03 W
Kitwangar Indian Reserve ◆[4]	182	55.06 N	128.04 W
Kitwe	154	12.49 S	28.13 E
Kitwitwi	156	17.25 S	18.25 E
Kityang → Jieyang	100	23.35 N	116.21 E
Kitzbühel	64	47.27 N	12.23 E
Kitzbüheler Alpen ⋏	64	47.20 N	12.20 E
Kitzingen	56	49.44 N	10.09 E
Kitzscher	54	51.09 N	12.33 E
Kiukiang → Jiujiang	100	29.44 N	115.59 E
Kiukiu, Pointe ›	174x	9.47 S	139.09 W
Kiul	124	25.09 N	86.06 E
Kiunga, Kenya	154	1.45 S	41.29 E
Kiunga, Pap. N. Gui.	164	6.10 S	141.15 E
Kiuruvesi	26	63.39 N	26.37 E
Kiuschu → Kyūshū I	92	33.00 N	131.00 E
Kivak	180	64.16 N	172.57 W
Kivalina	180	67.44 N	164.33 W
Kivercy	78	50.50 N	25.27 E
Kiveriči	76	57.22 N	36.36 E
Kivijärvi	26	63.04 N	25.03 E
Kivijärvi ⊜	26	63.10 N	25.09 E
Kivik	26	55.41 N	14.15 E
Kiviõli	76	59.21 N	26.57 E
Kivu □[4]	154	2.30 S	27.00 E
Kivu, Lac ⊜	154	2.00 S	29.10 E
Kiwaba N'zogi	152	8.57 S	16.32 E
Kiwai Island I	164	8.30 S	143.25 E

Symbols in the index entries represent the broad categories identified in the key at the right. Symbols with superior numbers (⋏[1]) identify subcategories (see complete key on page *I · 1).*

Symbole im Register stellen die rechts im Schlüssel erklärten Kategorien dar. Symbole mit hochgestellten Ziffern (⋏[1]) bezeichnen Unterabteilungen einer Kategorie (vgl. vollständiger Schlüssel auf Seite *I · 1).*

Los símbolos incluídos en el texto del índice representan las grandes categorias identificadas con la clave a la derecha. Los símbolos con numeros en su parte superior (⋏[1]) identifican las subcategorías (véase la clave completa en la página *I · 1).*

Les symboles de l'index représentent les catégories indiquées dans la légende à droite. Les symboles suivis d'un indice (⋏[1]) représentent des sous-catégories (voir légende complète à la page *I · 1).*

Os símbolos incluídos no texto do índice representam as grandes categorias identificadas com a chave à direita. Os símbolos com números em sua parte superior (⋏[1]) identificam as subcategorias (veja-se a chave completa à página *I · 1).*

English	Deutsch	Español	Français	Português
∧ Mountain	Berg	Montaña	Montagne	Montanha
⋏ Mountains	Gebirge	Montañas	Montagnes	Montanhas
)(Pass	Paß	Paso	Col	Passo
V Valley, Canyon	Tal, Cañon	Valle, Cañón	Vallée, Canyon	Vale, Canhão
= Plain	Ebene	Llano	Plaine	Planície
› Cape	Kap	Cabo	Cap	Cabo
I Island	Insel	Isla	Île	Ilha
II Islands	Inseln	Islas	Îles	Ilhas
⊥ Other Topographic Features	Andere Topographische Objekte	Otros Elementos Topográficos	Autres données topographiques	Outros acidentes topográficos

ESPAÑOL

Nombre	Página	Lat.°'	Long.°' W = Oeste
Kiwalik	180	66.02 N	161.50 W
Kiwanis Lake	214	41.28 N	81.09 W
Kiyama	96	33.25 N	130.32 E
Kīyāmakī Dāgh ∧	84	38.47 N	45.51 E
Kiyan	174m	26.05 N	127.40 E
Kiyan-zaki >	174m	26.05 N	127.39 E
Kıyıköy	130	41.38 N	28.05 E
Kiyiu Lake ⊜	184	51.38 N	108.55 W
Kiyl ≃	86	49.25 N	54.50 E
Kiyokawa	94	35.29 N	139.17 E
Kiyomi	94	36.07 N	137.11 E
Kiyosawa	94	35.03 N	138.15 E
Kiyose	94	35.47 N	139.32 E
Kiyosu	94	35.13 N	136.50 E
Kiyosumi-yama ∧	94	35.09 N	140.09 E
Kiyotani	270	34.52 N	134.59 E
Kiyotsu ≃	94	37.03 N	138.41 E
Kizel	86	59.03 N	57.40 E
Kizevatovo	80	53.13 N	45.18 E
Kızıl ≃	130	41.44 N	35.58 E
Kızıl Adalar II	130	40.52 N	29.05 E
Kızılcabölük	130	37.37 N	29.01 E
Kızılcadağ	130	37.01 N	29.58 E
Kızılcahamam	130	40.28 N	32.39 E
Kızılçakçak	84	40.46 N	43.37 E
Kızıldağ Milli Parkı ♠	130	37.58 N	31.28 E
Kızıldikme	130	39.05 N	37.01 E
Kızılhisar	130	37.33 N	29.18 E
Kızılırmak	130	40.21 N	33.59 E
Kızılören	130	37.52 N	32.07 E
Kizil'skoje	86	52.44 N	58.54 E
Kızılsu	130	37.28 N	42.13 E
Kiziltašskij liman ⊂	78	45.07 N	37.05 E
Kızıltepe	130	37.12 N	40.36 E
Kızıltoprak ◆[8]	267b	40.58 N	29.03 E
Kizil'unt	84	43.12 N	46.53 E
Kızılyaka	130	37.09 N	32.54 E
Kižimiz, gora ∧	24	63.12 N	58.48 E
Kizimkazi	154	6.27 S	39.28 E
Kižinga	88	51.51 N	109.55 E
Kizir ≃	86	53.51 N	93.06 E
Kızkalesi ⊥	130	36.28 N	34.04 E
Kızkulesi ◆[5]	267b	41.01 N	29.00 E
Kizl'ar	84	43.50 N	46.40 E
Kizl'arskij zaliv ⊂	84	44.33 N	46.55 E
Kizner	80	56.17 N	51.31 E
Kiz'oma	24	61.08 N	44.50 E
Kizu	96	34.44 N	135.49 E
Kizu ≃	94	34.53 N	135.42 E
Kizuki	268	35.34 N	139.40 E
Kizuri	270	34.39 N	135.34 E
Kizyl-Ajak	128	37.40 N	65.23 E
Kizyl-Arvat	128	38.58 N	56.15 E
Kizyl-Atrek	128	37.36 N	54.46 E
Kizyl-Su	128	39.48 N	53.01 E
Kjellerup	41	56.17 N	9.26 E
Kjøbenhavn → København	41	55.40 N	12.35 E
Kjustendil	38	42.17 N	22.41 E
Klaarstroom	158	33.20 S	22.32 E
Klaaswaal	52	51.46 N	4.26 E
Klabat, Gunung ∧	112	1.28 N	125.02 E
Kladanj	38	44.13 N	18.41 E
Kladbišči	80	55.32 N	45.33 E
Kläden	54	52.38 N	11.39 E
Kladkovo	82	55.24 N	38.51 E
Kladno	54	50.08 N	14.05 E
Kladovo	38	44.37 N	22.37 E
Kladow ◆[8]	264a	52.27 N	13.09 E
Kladruby	60	49.43 N	12.59 E
Klaeng	110	12.47 N	101.39 E
Klagan	112	5.58 N	117.27 E
Klagenfurt	61	46.37 N	14.18 E
Klågerup	41	55.36 N	13.15 E
Klagshamn	41	55.32 N	12.55 E
Klagstorp	41	55.24 N	13.22 E
Klahoose Indian Reserve ◆[4]	182	50.31 N	124.19 W
Klaipėda (Memel)	76	55.43 N	21.07 E
Klakah	115a	7.59 S	113.15 E
Klamath	204	41.31 N	124.02 W
Klamath ≃	204	41.33 N	124.04 W
Klamath Falls	202	42.13 N	121.46 W
Klamath Marsh ≡	202	42.54 N	121.44 W
Klamath Mountains ⋀	204	41.40 N	123.20 W
K. Lamido	146	9.21 N	11.12 E
Klämmingen ⊜	40	59.07 N	17.15 E
Klammpass)(	64	47.17 N	13.05 E
Klamono	164	1.08 S	131.30 E
Klangenan	115a	6.42 S	108.26 E
Klang → Kelang	114	3.02 N	101.27 E
Klangpi	110	22.59 N	93.20 E
Klarälven (Trysilelva) ≃	26	59.23 N	13.32 E
Kl'as'ma	265b	55.59 N	37.50 E
Klášterec	54	50.24 N	13.10 E
Kl'asticy	76	55.53 N	28.36 E
Klaten	115a	7.42 S	110.35 E
Klatovy	60	49.24 N	13.18 E
Klausdorf, Dtsch.	54	54.20 N	13.01 E
Klausdorf, Dtsch.	54	54.18 N	10.15 E
Klausenburg → Cluj-Napoca	38	46.47 N	23.36 E
Klausenpass)(	58	46.52 N	8.51 E
Kl'avlino	80	54.17 N	52.01 E
Klawer	158	31.44 S	18.36 E
Klawock	182	55.33 N	133.06 W
Klazienaveen	52	52.44 N	7.00 E
Kl'az'ma	82	55.58 N	37.27 E
Kl'az'ma ≃	80	56.10 N	42.58 E
Kl'az'minskoje vodochranilišče ⊜[1]	265b	55.59 N	37.35 E
Kleberg	222	32.40 N	96.37 W
Kleck	76	53.04 N	26.38 E
Kłecko	30	52.38 N	17.26 E
Kleczew	30	52.23 N	18.10 E
Kledering ◆[8]	264b	48.08 N	16.26 E
Kleef	263	51.11 N	6.56 E
Kleena Kleene	182	51.57 N	124.50 W
Kleinasien → Asia Minor □[9]	22	39.00 N	32.00 E
Kleinbeeren	264a	52.22 N	13.20 E
Kleinbegin	158	28.50 S	21.36 E
Klein-Blesbokspruit ≃	273d	26.16 S	28.29 E
Kleinbodungen	54	51.28 N	10.32 E
Klein Bonaire I	241s	12.10 N	68.18 W
Klein Bünzow	54	53.53 N	13.48 E
Kleinburg	275b	43.50 N	79.38 W
Klein Curaçao I	241s	12.00 N	68.40 W
Kleine Elster ≃	54	51.32 N	13.23 E
Kleine Emme ≃	58	47.04 N	8.17 E
Kleine Emscher ≃	263	51.31 N	6.43 E
Kleine Erlauf ≃	61	48.07 N	15.08 E
Kleineichen	263	51.08 N	7.21 E
Kleine Laber ≃	60	48.55 N	12.31 E
Kleinenberg	52	51.35 N	8.58 E
Kleinenbroich	263	51.12 N	6.35 E
Kleinengstingen	58	48.23 N	9.18 E
Kleiner Jasmunder Bodden ⊂	54	54.28 N	13.32 E
Kleiner Ravens-Berg ∧[2]	264a	52.22 N	13.04 E
Kleiner Wannsee ⊜	264a	52.25 N	13.10 E
Kleiner Zern-See ⊜	264a	52.26 N	12.55 E
Kleine Spree ≃	54	51.31 N	14.24 E
Kleines Walsertal V	64	47.23 N	10.12 E
Kleinfeltersville	208	40.18 N	76.15 W
Kleinglödnitz	61	46.51 N	14.08 E
Kleinhammer	263	51.14 N	7.46 E
Klein-Jukskei ≃	273d	26.08 S	27.56 E
Klein-Karas	156	27.32 S	18.06 E
Klein Karroo → Little Karroo ⋀[1]	158	33.45 S	21.30 E
Klein Kienitz	264a	52.18 N	13.29 E
Kleinlützel	58	47.26 N	7.25 E
Kleinmachnow	54	52.24 N	13.15 E
Klein Marzehns	54	52.01 N	12.37 E
Kleinmond	158	34.21 S	19.03 E
Klein-Olifants ≃	158	25.41 S	29.19 E

FRANÇAIS

Nom	Page	Lat.°'	Long.°' W = Ouest
Kleinschönebeck	264a	52.29 N	13.43 E
Klein-Soutpan	158	30.26 S	22.26 E
Klein-Vis ≃	158	33.05 S	26.00 E
Klein Wanzleben	54	52.04 N	11.21 E
Klein Ziethen	264a	52.23 N	13.27 E
Klein Ziethener-Berge ∧[2]	264a	52.22 N	13.26 E
Klekovača ∧	36	44.26 N	16.31 E
Klementjevka	86	50.16 N	80.56 E
Klementjevo	82	55.38 N	36.01 E
Klemme	190	43.00 N	93.36 W
Klemtu	182	52.36 N	128.31 W
Klenovka	80	57.45 N	54.19 E
Klenovo	82	55.19 N	37.21 E
Klerksdorp	158	26.58 S	26.39 E
Klerkskraal	158	26.15 S	27.10 E
Klesov	78	51.19 N	26.54 E
Klésso	150	10.57 N	3.59 W
Klet' ∧	61	48.52 N	14.17 E
Kletn'a	76	53.23 N	33.12 E
Kletskij	80	49.19 N	43.04 E
Kletsko-Počtovskij	80	49.36 N	43.03 E
Klettgau ◆[1]	58	47.40 N	8.25 E
Klettwitz	54	51.32 N	13.53 E
Klevan'	78	50.44 N	26.02 E
Kleve	52	51.48 N	6.09 E
Klevenka	80	52.07 N	49.33 E
Kley ◆[8]	263	51.30 N	7.22 E
Klibreck, Ben ∧	46	58.14 N	4.22 W
Kličev	76	53.29 N	29.21 E
Klička	88	50.26 N	118.00 E
Klickitat	224	45.49 N	121.09 W
Klickitat □[6]	224	45.50 N	121.07 W
Klickitat ≃	224	45.42 N	121.17 W
Kliedbruch ◆[1]	263	51.22 N	6.33 E
Klietz	54	52.40 N	12.04 E
Klimino	88	58.39 N	98.42 E
Klimoviči	76	53.37 N	31.58 E
Klimovo, Ross.	76	52.23 N	32.11 E
Klimovo, Ross.	82	55.22 N	38.52 E
Klimovsk	82	55.22 N	37.32 E
Klimovskoje	82	54.42 N	37.48 E
Klimov Zavod	76	54.50 N	34.55 E
Klimpfjäll	24	65.04 N	14.52 E
Klin, Ross.	82	56.20 N	36.44 E
Klin, Ross.	82	55.19 N	36.20 E
Klinaklini ≃	182	51.05 N	125.36 W
Klin-Bel'din	82	54.45 N	39.13 E
Klincovka	80	51.41 N	49.11 E
Klincy	76	52.47 N	32.14 E
Kline Ditch ≊	279a	41.28 N	82.04 W
Kling	116	5.58 N	124.42 E
Klingbach ≃	56	49.10 N	8.20 E
Klingenberg	54	50.55 N	13.31 E
Klingenberg am Main	56	49.47 N	9.11 E
Klingenmünster	56	49.08 N	8.01 E
Klingenthal	54	50.21 N	12.28 E
Klinger Lake ⊜	216	41.47 N	85.33 W
Klingerstown	208	40.40 N	76.41 W
Klinghardtberge ∧	156	27.18 S	15.48 E
Klingnau	58	47.35 N	8.15 E
Klink	54	53.29 N	12.37 E
Klinkino	83	47.17 N	38.15 E
Klínovec ∧	54	50.24 N	12.58 E
Klinsko-Dmitrovskaja gr'ada ∧	82	56.15 N	37.30 E
Klintehamn	26	57.24 N	18.12 E
Klintsy → Klincy	76	52.47 N	32.14 E
Klip ≃, S. Afr.	158	27.03 S	29.03 E
Klip ≃, S. Afr.	273d	26.19 S	27.53 E
Klipbakken	158	28.50 S	21.21 E
Klipdale	158	34.19 S	19.57 E
Klipdam	158	27.35 S	19.56 E
Kliplev	41	54.56 N	9.25 E
Klippan	41	56.08 N	13.06 E
Klipplaat	158	33.02 S	24.21 E
Klippoortjie	273d	26.13 S	28.10 E
Klipriviersberg ⋀	273d	26.17 S	28.02 E
Kliptown	273d	26.17 S	27.53 E
Klipwerf	158	31.09 S	19.52 E
Kliškovcy	78	48.26 N	26.15 E
Klisura	38	42.42 N	24.27 E
Klitmøller	26	57.02 N	8.31 E
Klitten	54	51.20 N	14.36 E
Klixbüll	41	54.48 N	8.53 E
Ključ	36	44.32 N	16.47 E
Klobbicke	264a	52.46 N	13.48 E
Klobouky	61	49.00 N	16.52 E
Kłobuck	30	50.55 N	18.57 E
Klobuticy	76	58.35 N	29.35 E
Kłodawa	30	52.16 N	18.55 E
Kłodzko	30	50.27 N	16.39 E
Kløfta	26	60.04 N	11.09 E
Kłomnice	30	50.56 N	19.21 E
Klondike	216	40.28 N	86.57 W
Klondike □[9]	180	63.30 N	139.00 W
Klondike ≃	180	64.05 N	139.26 W
Klöntaler See ⊜	58	47.02 N	8.58 E
Klooga	76	59.19 N	24.16 E
Kloosterveen	52	52.59 N	6.33 E
Kloosterzande	52	51.22 N	4.02 E
Kloster	54	54.35 N	13.06 E
Klosterfelde	54	52.48 N	13.28 E
Klosterhardt ◆[8]	263	51.31 N	6.53 E
Klösterle	58	47.08 N	10.05 E
Klostermansfeld	54	51.35 N	11.29 E
Klosterneuburg	61	48.18 N	16.20 E
Kloster Oesede	52	52.12 N	8.07 E
Klosters	58	46.54 N	9.53 E
Klostertal V	58	47.08 N	9.59 E
Kloster Zinna	54	52.01 N	13.07 E
Kloten, Schw.	58	47.27 N	8.35 E
Kloten, Sve.	40	59.54 N	15.17 E
Klotz, Lac ⊜	176	60.32 N	73.40 W
Klötze	54	52.38 N	11.10 E
Kloulklubed	175b	7.02 N	134.15 E
Klouto	150	6.57 N	0.34 E
Kluane ≃	180	61.53 N	139.43 W
Kluane Lake ⊜	180	61.15 N	138.40 W
Kluane National Park ♠	180	60.45 N	139.30 W
Kluang	112	2.41 S	103.54 E
Kl'učevaja	24	65.16 N	41.32 E
Kl'učevskaja Sopka, vulkan ∧[1]	74	56.04 N	160.38 E
Kl'učevskij	88	53.33 N	119.26 E
Kluchorskij, pereval)(	84	43.15 N	41.54 E
Kl'uči, Ross.	74	56.18 N	160.51 E
Kl'uči, Ross.	80	51.59 N	46.31 E
Kl'uči, Ross.	80	51.26 N	45.11 E
Kl'uči, Ross.	86	52.16 N	79.10 E
Kl'učovka, Kyrg.	85	42.34 N	71.48 E
Kl'učovka, Ross.	86	51.22 N	55.48 E
Kluczbork	30	50.59 N	18.13 E
Kluess	54	53.46 N	12.14 E
Kluet ≃	114	3.04 N	97.20 E
Kl'ukvenka	86	58.34 N	85.55 E
Klukwan	180	59.24 N	135.54 W
Klundert	52	51.40 N	4.32 E
Klungkung	115b	8.32 S	115.24 E
Klüppelberg	56	51.06 N	7.28 E
Klüterthöhle ⊥[5]	52	51.18 N	7.21 E
Klutina Lake ⊜	180	61.37 N	146.55 W
Klütz	54	53.58 N	11.10 E
Knaben gruver	26	58.39 N	7.04 E
Knaddah	130	35.45 N	36.12 E
Kn'aginino	80	55.49 N	45.03 E
Knaik ≃	46	56.14 N	3.52 W
Knapdaar	158	30.43 S	26.09 E
Knapdale ◆[1]	46	55.55 N	5.30 W
Knaphill	260	51.19 N	0.37 W
Knapp	190	44.57 N	92.04 W
Knapp Creek	210	42.00 N	78.30 W
Knappenberg	61	46.56 N	14.35 E
Knäred	26	56.32 N	13.19 E
Knaresborough	44	54.00 N	1.27 W
Knargram	126	24.01 N	87.59 E
Knauertown	285	40.10 N	75.44 W
Knauthain ◆[8]	54	51.16 N	12.18 E

PORTUGUÊS

Nome	Página	Lat.°'	Long.°' W = Oeste
Kn'ažaja Bajgora	76	52.23 N	40.02 E
Kn'azevka	86	57.35 N	74.10 E
Kn'ažji Gory	76	56.05 N	35.14 E
Kn'ažovo	76	59.40 N	43.54 E
Knebel	41	56.13 N	10.30 E
Knebworth	42	51.52 N	0.12 W
Kneehills Creek ≃	182	51.30 N	112.50 W
Knee Lake ⊜, Mb., Can.	184	55.03 N	94.40 W
Knee Lake ⊜, Sk., Can.	184	55.51 N	107.00 W
Knesebeck	54	52.41 N	10.42 E
Knesselare	50	51.08 N	3.25 E
Knetzgau	56	50.00 N	10.33 E
Knevicy	76	57.56 N	32.14 E
Kneža	38	43.30 N	24.05 E
Knić	38	43.55 N	20.43 E
Knickerbocker	196	31.16 N	100.38 W
Kniebis	58	48.28 N	8.17 E
Knife ≃	198	47.20 N	101.23 W
Knife Lake ⊜	184	53.47 N	91.20 W
Knife River Indian Villages National Historical Site ⊥	198	47.21 N	101.23 W
Knight Inlet ⊂	182	50.41 N	125.40 W
Knight Island I	180	60.20 N	147.45 W
Knighton	42	52.21 N	3.03 W
Knightsen	226	37.58 N	121.40 W
Knights Landing	226	38.47 N	121.43 W
Knightstown	218	39.47 N	85.31 W
Knightville Dam ◆[6]	207	42.17 N	72.52 W
Knik Arm ⊂	180	61.25 N	149.45 W
Knin	36	44.02 N	16.12 E
Knippa	196	29.18 N	99.38 W
Knislinge	26	56.11 N	14.05 E
Knittelfeld	61	47.14 N	14.50 E
Knittlingen	56	49.01 N	8.45 E
Knivsbjerg ∧[2]	41	55.08 N	9.27 E
Knivsta	40	59.43 N	17.48 E
Knjaževac	38	43.34 N	22.16 E
Knob, Cape >	162	34.32 S	119.16 E
Knobby Head >	162	29.40 S	114.58 E
Knob Noster	194	38.45 N	93.33 W
Knob Peak ∧	116	12.28 N	121.21 E
Knoc	48	52.38 N	9.20 W
Knock	46	57.33 N	2.45 W
Knockholt	260	51.18 N	0.06 E
Knockholt Pound	260	51.19 N	0.08 E
Knocklayd ∧	48	55.09 N	6.15 W
Knocklong	48	52.26 N	8.24 W
Knockmealdown Mountains ⋀	48	52.10 N	8.00 W
Knokke	50	51.21 N	3.17 E
Knole ⊥	260	51.16 N	0.12 E
Knolls Green	262	53.19 N	2.18 W
Knollwood, Ct., U.S.	207	41.16 N	72.23 W
Knollwood, Il., U.S.	278	42.17 N	87.53 W
Knollwood, Md., U.S.	284c	39.02 N	76.58 W
Knollwood Park	216	42.14 N	84.22 W
Knon ⊜	40	60.12 N	13.40 E
Knossós ⊥	38	35.20 N	25.10 E
Knottingley	44	53.43 N	1.14 W
Knott's Berry Farm ♠	280	33.50 N	118.00 W
Knotts Island	208	36.31 N	75.56 W
Knotty Ash ◆[8]	262	53.25 N	2.54 W
Knotty Green	260	51.37 N	0.39 W
Knowland State Arboretum and Park ♠	282	37.45 N	122.09 W
Knowle	42	52.23 N	1.43 W
Knowlesville	210	43.14 N	78.19 W
Knowlton Lake ⊜	212	44.28 N	76.41 W
Knowltonwood	285	39.53 N	75.24 W
Knowsley	262	53.27 N	2.51 W
Knowsley □[8]	262	53.27 N	2.50 W
Knowsley Hall ʋ	262	53.26 N	2.50 W
Knowsley Park ♠	262	53.27 N	2.49 W
Knox, In., U.S.	216	41.17 N	86.37 W
Knox, N.Y., U.S.	210	42.40 N	74.07 W
Knox, Pa., U.S.	214	41.14 N	79.32 W
Knox □[6], Mo., U.S.	219	40.08 N	92.09 W
Knox □[6], Oh., U.S.	214	40.23 N	82.29 W
Knox, Cape >	182	54.11 N	133.04 W
Knoxboro	210	42.58 N	75.36 W
Knox City, Mo., U.S.	219	40.08 N	92.00 W
Knox City, Tx., U.S.	196	33.25 N	99.49 W
Knox Coast ⊥[2]	9	66.30 S	105.00 E
Knox Dale	214	41.05 N	79.02 W
Knoxfield	274b	37.53 S	145.15 E
Knox Lake ⊜[1]	214	40.31 N	82.30 W
Knoxville, Ga., U.S.	192	32.43 N	83.59 W
Knoxville, Il., U.S.	190	40.54 N	90.17 W
Knoxville, Ia., U.S.	190	41.19 N	93.06 W
Knoxville, Pa., U.S.	210	41.57 N	77.26 W
Knoxville, Tn., U.S.	192	35.57 N	83.55 W
Knuckles ∧	122	7.24 N	80.48 E
Knudshoved Odde >[1]	41	55.03 N	11.45 E
Knüll ∧	56	50.53 N	9.24 E
Knutby	40	59.55 N	18.15 E
Knuthenborg	41	54.50 N	11.30 E
Knutsford	44	53.19 N	2.22 W
Knysna	158	34.02 S	23.02 E
Knyszyn	30	53.19 N	22.55 E
Koala Sanctuary ◆[4]	274a	33.40 S	151.10 E
Koani	154	6.08 S	39.17 E
Kob'	88	55.25 N	101.24 E
Koba	112	2.29 S	106.24 E
Kob'aj	74	63.34 N	126.30 E
Kőbánya ◆[8]	264c	47.29 N	19.10 E
Kobarid	36	46.15 N	13.35 E
Kobar Sink ⊥[7]	144	13.35 N	40.50 E
Kobayashi	92	31.59 N	130.59 E
Kōbe, Nihon	96	34.41 N	135.10 E
Kōbe, Nihon	270	34.41 N	135.10 E
Kōbe-kō ⊂	270	34.40 N	135.12 E
Kobel'aki	78	49.09 N	34.12 E
København (Copenhagen)	41	55.40 N	12.35 E
København □[6]	41	55.45 N	12.25 E
Kōbe University ʋ[2]	270	34.43 N	135.14 E
Kobi	84	42.33 N	44.32 E
Koblenz, Dtsch.	56	50.21 N	7.35 E
Koblenz, Schw.	58	47.37 N	8.14 E
Koblenz □[5]	56	50.10 N	7.30 E
Kobo, Ityo.	144	12.11 N	39.33 E
Kobo, Zaïre	152	4.54 S	17.09 E
Ko-boke ♠	96	33.50 N	133.46 E
Koboko	154	3.25 N	30.58 E
Koboldo	89	52.58 N	132.42 E
Kobona	76	60.01 N	31.36 E
Kobou ≃	152	6.13 N	23.19 E
Kobowen Swamp ≡	144	5.38 N	33.54 E
Koboža	76	58.49 N	35.01 E
Koboža ≃	76	58.52 N	36.17 E
Kobra	24	60.03 N	50.44 E
Kobrin	76	52.13 N	24.21 E
Kobrinskoje	76	59.25 N	30.07 E
Kobroor, Pulau I	164	6.12 S	134.32 E
Kobuchizawa	94	35.52 N	138.19 E
Kobuga-hara ♠	94	36.40 N	139.35 E
Kobuk	180	66.54 N	156.52 W
Kobuk ≃	180	66.45 N	161.00 W
Kobuk Valley National Park ♠	180	67.20 N	159.00 W
Kobuleti	84	41.50 N	41.47 E
Kobushiga-take ∧	94	35.54 N	138.44 E
Kobylanka	54	53.19 N	14.50 E
Kobylin	30	51.43 N	17.13 E
Kobyl'nik	76	54.56 N	26.41 E
Kobyžča	78	50.49 N	31.30 E
Kocaali	130	41.03 N	30.52 E
Kocaaliler	130	37.19 N	30.44 E
Kocaavşar ≃	130	40.08 N	27.57 E
Kocaeli □[4]	130	40.55 N	29.55 E
Kocaeli → İzmit	130	40.46 N	29.55 E
Koçali	130	37.55 N	38.15 E
Kočani	38	41.55 N	22.25 E
Koçarlı	130	37.45 N	27.42 E
Kocasinan ◆[8]	267b	41.01 N	28.50 E
Koçbaşı Tepe ∧	84	39.25 N	43.21 E
Kočečum ≃	74	64.17 N	101.10 E
Kočelajevo	80	54.01 N	44.02 E
Kočemary	80	54.50 N	40.58 E
Kočen'ajevka	80	53.52 N	46.59 E
Kočen'ga, Ross.	76	60.09 N	43.33 E
Kočenga, Ross.	88	55.55 N	104.06 E
Kočenga ≃	88	55.55 N	104.06 E
Kočerdyk	86	54.35 N	62.58 E
Kočerga	88	55.15 N	103.46 E
Kočerov	78	50.21 N	29.21 E
Kočetovka, Ross.	80	55.16 N	46.07 E
Kočetovka, Ross.	80	52.58 N	40.29 E
Kočevar	76	60.26 N	42.11 E
Kočevje	36	45.38 N	14.52 E
Kočevo	86	59.36 N	54.18 E
Koch'am-ni	98	41.06 N	129.23 E
Kŏch'ang, Taehan	98	35.26 N	126.42 E
Kŏch'ang, Taehan	98	35.41 N	127.55 E
Kochanoviči	76	55.52 N	28.08 E
Kochanovo	76	54.28 N	30.01 E
Koch Bihār	124	26.19 N	89.26 E
Kochel	64	47.39 N	11.22 E
Kochelsee ⊜	64	47.38 N	11.20 E
Kochena	158	27.00 S	18.50 E
Kocher ≃	56	49.14 N	9.12 E
Kōchi, Nihon	96	33.33 N	133.33 E
Kōchi, Nihon	96	34.28 N	132.53 E
Kōchi □[5]	96	33.40 N	133.30 E
Kōchi-dani ♠	94	34.34 N	136.10 E
Kochinda	174m	26.08 N	127.43 E
Koch Island I	176	69.38 N	78.15 W
Kochiu → Gejiu	90	23.22 N	103.06 E
Kochma	80	56.56 N	41.06 E
Koch Peak ∧	202	45.02 N	111.28 W
Kochugaon	124	26.34 N	90.04 E
Kock	30	51.39 N	22.27 E
Kočki, Ross.	86	52.24 N	80.40 E
Kočki, Ross.	86	54.20 N	80.29 E
Kočkor-Ata	85	41.04 N	72.29 E
Kočkorka	85	42.14 N	75.45 E
Kocksoord	273d	26.13 S	27.39 E
Kočkurovo	80	54.02 N	45.26 E
Kočmes	24	66.12 N	60.44 E
Kočon'ovo	86	55.02 N	82.12 E
Kočov	60	49.49 N	12.44 E
Kočubej	84	44.24 N	46.33 E
Kočubejevskoje	84	44.41 N	41.41 E
Kōda, Nihon	94	34.52 N	137.10 E
Kōda, Nihon	96	34.42 N	132.45 E
Kodačdikost	24	63.11 N	55.49 E
Kodaikānal	122	10.14 N	77.29 E
Kodaira	94	35.44 N	139.29 E
Kodama	94	36.11 N	139.08 E
Kodar, chrebet ⋀	88	57.15 N	118.10 E
Kodāri	124	27.56 N	85.56 E
Kodarma	124	24.28 N	85.36 E
Kodera ◆[8]	270	34.41 N	135.04 E
Kodersdorf	54	51.15 N	14.53 E
Kodi	152	3.34 S	22.12 E
Kodiak	180	57.48 N	152.23 W
Kodiak Island I	180	57.30 N	153.30 W
Kodiang	114	6.24 N	100.18 E
Kodinār	120	20.47 N	70.42 E
Kodino	24	63.43 N	39.41 E
Kodo ≃	152	7.05 N	19.10 E
Kodo, Jabal ∧	140	12.26 N	23.38 E
Kodok	140	9.53 N	32.07 E
Kodori ≃	84	42.47 N	41.10 E
Kodorskij chrebet ⋀	84	43.00 N	42.00 E
Kodra	78	50.36 N	29.34 E
Kodry ⋀[2]	78	47.10 N	28.25 E
Kodyma	78	48.07 N	29.07 E
Kodyma ≃	78	48.01 N	30.48 E
Kodžori	84	41.40 N	44.41 E
Koegas	158	29.16 S	22.20 E
Koehn Lake ⊜	228	35.20 N	117.53 W
Koekelare	50	51.05 N	2.58 E
Koekenaap	158	31.30 S	18.18 E
Koeltztown	219	38.19 N	92.03 W
Koenigsmacker	56	49.24 N	6.17 E
Koersel	56	51.04 N	5.16 E
Koes	156	25.59 S	19.08 E
Kofa Mountains ⋀	200	33.20 N	114.00 W
Kofçaz	130	41.58 N	27.12 E
Kofeld	58	47.44 N	9.41 E
Köfering	60	48.56 N	12.12 E
Koffiefontein	158	29.30 S	25.00 E
Kofiau, Pulau I	164	1.11 S	129.50 E
Köflach	61	47.04 N	15.05 E
Koforidua	150	6.03 N	0.17 W
Kōfu, Nihon	94	35.39 N	138.35 E
Kōfu, Nihon	96	35.17 N	133.30 E
Koga, Nihon	94	36.11 N	139.43 E
Koga, Nihon	96	33.40 N	130.30 E
Koga, Tan.	154	6.14 S	32.25 E
Kogaluc ≃	176	59.40 N	77.35 W
Kogaluc, Baie ⊂	176	59.20 N	77.50 W
Kogaluk ≃	176	56.12 N	61.44 W
Kogan	166	27.03 S	150.46 E
Kogane	268	35.50 N	139.56 E
Koganei	94	35.42 N	139.32 E
Kogarah	274a	33.58 S	151.08 E
Kogarah Bay ⊂	274a	33.59 S	151.07 E
Køge, Dan.	41	55.27 N	12.11 E
Kōge, Nihon	96	35.24 N	134.15 E
Køge Bugt ⊂, Dan.	41	55.30 N	12.20 E
Køge Bugt ⊂, Kal. Nun.	176	65.00 N	40.30 W
Kogil'nik ≃	78	45.51 N	29.38 E
Kogin Baba	146	7.55 N	11.30 E
Koglhof	61	47.19 N	15.40 E
Kogon ≃	150	11.09 N	14.42 W
Kogoni	150	14.44 N	6.02 W
Kŏgŭm-do I	98	34.27 N	127.11 E
Kohak	128	25.44 N	62.33 E
Kohala Mountains ⋀	229d	20.05 N	155.45 W
Kohama-shima I	175d	24.19 N	123.59 E
Kohāt	123	33.35 N	71.26 E
Kohāt ≃	123	33.24 N	71.48 E
Kohatk Wash V	200	32.38 N	111.55 W
Kohila	76	59.10 N	24.45 E
Kohīma	120	25.40 N	94.07 E
Kohistān □[9]	123	35.03 N	72.52 W
Kohlberg ∧[2]	263	51.18 N	7.46 E
Kohler	190	43.44 N	87.46 W
Kohlstädt	52	51.50 N	8.52 E
Kohoku	94	35.26 N	136.15 E
Kōhoku ◆[8]	268	35.31 N	139.38 E
Kohren-Sahlis	54	51.01 N	12.36 E
Kohsān	128	34.39 N	61.12 E
Kohtla-Järve	76	59.24 N	27.15 E
Kohu → Kōfu	94	35.39 N	138.35 E
Kohukohu	172	35.21 S	173.32 E
Kohŭng	98	34.37 N	127.16 E
Kohunlich ⊥	232	18.27 N	89.01 W
Kohuratahi	172	39.06 S	174.46 E
Koide	94	37.13 N	138.57 E
Koidern	180	61.58 N	140.25 W
Koidu	150	8.38 N	10.59 W
Koigi	76	58.50 N	25.45 E
Koihoa	110	8.12 N	93.29 E
Koil-Aligarh → Alīgarh	124	27.53 N	78.05 E
Koimbani	157a	11.37 S	43.23 E
Koindu	150	8.26 N	10.19 W
Koin-ni	98	40.28 N	126.22 E
Koito ≃	94	35.21 N	139.52 E
Kojandy	86	49.51 N	75.40 E
Kojda	24	66.23 N	42.31 E
Kŏje-do I	98	34.52 N	128.37 E
Kojetin	30	49.21 N	17.18 E
Kojgorodok	24	60.26 N	50.58 E
Ko-jima I	92a	41.22 N	139.48 E
Kojima-ko ⊜[1]	96	34.37 N	134.00 E
Kojŏ	98	38.57 N	127.51 E
Kojonup	162	33.50 S	117.09 E
Kojsary	85	42.33 N	78.10 E
Kojsug	83	47.07 N	39.41 E
Kojtas, Kaz.	86	51.32 N	76.15 E
Kojtaš, Uzb.	85	40.11 N	67.19 E
Kok (Hkok) ≃	110	20.14 N	100.09 E
Kōka	94	34.54 N	136.13 E
Koka, Lake ⊜[1]	144	8.23 N	39.05 E
Kokai ≃	94	35.52 N	140.08 E
K'okajgyr	85	40.43 N	75.37 E
Kokalaat	86	49.47 N	64.15 E
Kokand	85	40.33 N	70.57 E
Kokanee Glacier Provincial Park ♠	182	49.47 N	117.10 W
Kokankišlak	85	40.56 N	72.30 E
Kökar I	26	59.56 N	20.55 E
Kokas	164	2.42 S	132.26 E
Kokašice	60	49.53 N	12.57 E
Kokava nad Rimavicou	30	48.34 N	19.50 E
Kokawa	96	34.16 N	135.24 E
K'okbel'	85	40.17 N	72.55 E
Kokčetav	86	53.17 N	69.25 E
Kokčetav □[8]	86	53.30 N	70.00 E
Kokčetavskaja vozvyšennost' ⋀[1]	86	52.50 N	69.00 E
Kokee State Park ♠	229b	22.08 N	159.40 W
Kokemäenjoki ≃	26	61.33 N	21.42 E
Kokemäki	26	61.15 N	22.21 E
Kokenau	164	4.43 S	136.26 E
Ko Kha	110	18.11 N	99.24 E
Kokhav HaYarden (Belvoir) ⊥	132	32.36 N	35.31 E
Kókhi, Ákra >	267c	37.53 N	23.27 E
Koki	150	15.30 N	15.59 W
Kokinu	268	35.59 N	139.59 E
Kokiu → Gejiu	102	23.22 N	103.06 E
Kok-Jangak	85	41.02 N	73.12 E
Kokka	140	20.00 N	30.35 E
Kokkilai Lagoon ⊂	122	9.00 N	80.56 E
Kokkola (Karleby)	26	63.50 N	23.07 E
Kokku	98	40.22 N	128.44 E
Koknese	76	56.39 N	25.29 E
Koko	150	11.26 N	4.32 E
Kokoda	164	8.52 S	147.45 E
Koko Head >	229c	21.16 N	157.42 W
Kokola	154	0.47 N	29.36 E
Kokole Point >	229b	21.59 N	159.46 W
Kokolik ≃	180	69.46 N	163.00 W
Kokolopozo	150	5.08 N	6.05 W
K'ok'omeren ≃	85	41.43 N	73.54 E
Kokomo, Hi., U.S.	229a	20.52 N	156.18 W
Kokomo, In., U.S.	216	40.29 N	86.08 W
Kokomo, Ms., U.S.	194	31.11 N	90.00 W
Kokong	156	24.27 S	23.03 E
Kokonoe	96	33.10 N	131.10 E
Koko Nor → Qinghai Hu ⊜	102	36.50 N	100.20 E
Kokopo	164	4.20 S	152.15 E
Kokorevka	76	52.35 N	34.16 E
Kokosing ≃	214	40.22 N	82.12 W
Kokos-Inseln → Cocos (Keeling) Islands □[2]	14	12.10 S	96.55 E
Kokoškino	265b	55.38 N	37.11 E
Kokpāra Narsinghgarh	126	22.31 N	86.33 E
Kokpaš	86	51.12 N	87.45 E
Kokpekty	86	48.45 N	82.24 E
Kokrājhār	124	26.24 N	90.16 E
Kokrines	180	64.56 N	154.42 W
Kokrines Hills ⋀[2]	180	65.15 N	154.00 W
Koksa ≃	86	50.16 N	85.36 E
Kokšaalatau, chrebet ⋀	72	41.00 N	78.00 E
Koksan	98	38.46 N	126.40 E
Koksaraj	85	42.40 N	68.08 E
Kokšekol', ozero ⊜	86	46.05 N	62.00 E
Koksijde	50	51.07 N	2.38 E
Koksilah	224	48.40 N	123.38 W
Koksilah ≃	224	48.45 N	123.39 W
Koksoak ≃	176	58.32 N	68.10 W
Koksŏng	98	35.17 N	127.17 E
Koksovyj	78	48.12 N	40.39 E
Kokstad	158	30.32 S	29.29 E
Koksu, Kaz.	85	41.27 N	68.01 E
Koksu, Kaz.	86	44.59 N	77.56 E
Koktal	86	44.09 N	79.48 E
Koktas, Kaz.	86	47.33 N	70.55 E
Koktas, Kaz.	86	45.59 N	73.32 E
Kok-Taš, Kyrg.	85	41.12 N	72.25 E
Kokterek	80	49.25 N	49.15 E
Koktubek	86	48.07 N	56.51 E
Kokubu, Nihon	92	31.44 N	130.46 E
Kokubu, Nihon	96	34.56 N	132.07 E
Kokubunji, Nihon	94	36.22 N	139.51 E
Kokubunji, Nihon	96	34.18 N	133.58 E
Kokubunji, Nihon	268	35.42 N	139.29 E
Kokubunji Temple ʋ[1]	268	35.44 N	139.55 E
Kokufu	96	35.28 N	134.16 E
Kokuj	88	52.13 N	117.33 E
Kokujbel' ≃	85	38.21 N	72.46 E
Kokžar	86	49.01 N	60.10 E
Kol ≃	128	26.59 N	55.47 E
Kola, Indon.	164	5.26 S	134.29 E
Kola, Ross.	24	68.53 N	33.01 E
Kola ≃	24	68.53 N	33.02 E
Kolachel	122	8.10 N	77.15 E
Kolāchi ≃	120	27.08 N	67.02 E
Kol'adovka	83	49.05 N	39.12 E
Kolageran	84	40.58 N	44.37 E
Kolahun	150	8.24 N	10.02 W
Kolaka	112	4.03 S	121.36 E
Kolambo	152	7.34 S	21.58 E
Kolambugan	116	8.07 N	123.55 E
Kolangār	120	34.02 N	69.01 E
Kola Peninsula → Kol'skij poluostrov >[1]	24	67.30 N	37.00 E
Kolār	122	13.08 N	78.08 E
Kolāras	124	25.14 N	77.36 E
Kolār Gold Fields	122	12.55 N	78.17 E
Kolari	24	67.20 N	23.48 E
Kolarovgrad → Šumen	38	43.16 N	26.55 E
Kolárovo	30	47.52 N	18.02 E
Kolašin	38	42.49 N	19.31 E
Kolāyat	120	27.50 N	72.57 E
Kolbači	89	54.22 N	123.02 E
Kolbäck	40	59.34 N	16.15 E
Kolbäcksån ≃	40	59.32 N	16.16 E
Kol'baj, gora ∧[2]	86	43.43 N	53.57 E
Kolbano	112	10.02 S	124.31 E
Kolbasna	78	47.47 N	29.13 E
Kolbča	76	53.39 N	29.14 E
Kolberg → Kołobrzeg	30	54.12 N	15.33 E
Kolbermoor	64	47.51 N	12.04 E
Kolbio	144	1.10 S	41.15 E
Kolbnitz	64	46.52 N	13.19 E
Kolbotn	26	59.49 N	10.48 E
Kolbuszowa	30	50.15 N	21.47 E
Kolby Kås	41	55.48 N	10.33 E
Kolchida ≡	84	42.15 N	42.00 E
Kolchozabad	120	37.27 N	68.31 E
Kol'covo	82	54.27 N	36.40 E
Kol'čuga	82	55.43 N	37.12 E
Kol'čugino	80	56.18 N	39.23 E
Kołczewo	54	53.58 N	14.38 E
Kolda	150	12.53 N	14.57 W
Kolda □[4]	150	12.50 N	14.50 W
Kolding	41	55.31 N	9.29 E
Kolding Fjord ⊂	41	55.30 N	9.35 E
Kole, Zaïre	152	3.27 S	22.29 E
Kole, Zaïre	154	2.07 N	25.26 E
Kolea	34	36.38 N	2.46 E
Kolebīra	124	22.43 N	84.42 E
Kole Kalyan ◆[8]	272c	19.06 N	72.51 E
Kolenfeld	52	52.24 N	9.27 E
Koleno	80	51.52 N	44.07 E
Kolenté	150	10.06 N	12.37 W
Kolenté (Great Scarcies) ≃	150	8.55 N	13.08 W
Kolga	76	59.32 N	25.42 E
Kolgujev, ostrov I	24	69.05 N	49.15 E
Kolhāpur, India	122	16.06 N	78.16 E
Kolhāpur, India	122	16.42 N	74.13 E
Kolho	26	62.08 N	24.31 E
Koli	76	59.30 N	34.30 E
Koli ∧[2]	26	63.06 N	29.48 E
Koli, Jabal ∧	140	14.05 N	25.31 E
Kolia	150	9.46 N	6.28 W
Koliba (Corubal) ≃	150	11.57 N	15.06 W
Koliganek	180	59.48 N	157.25 W
Kolima ⊜	26	63.16 N	25.50 E
Kolimbine ≃	150	14.26 N	11.23 W
Kolín	30	50.01 N	15.13 E
Kolka	76	57.45 N	22.35 E
Kølkær	41	56.04 N	9.06 E
Kolkasrags >	76	57.47 N	22.36 E
Kolki, Ukr.	78	51.37 N	26.37 E
Kolki, Ukr.	78	51.07 N	25.41 E
Kolkwitz	54	51.45 N	14.15 E
Kollbach ≃	60	48.36 N	12.58 E
Kölleda	54	51.11 N	11.15 E
Kollegāl	122	12.09 N	77.07 E
Kolleru Lake ⊜	122	16.39 N	81.13 E
Kollum	52	53.16 N	6.09 E
Kollund	41	54.51 N	9.27 E
Kolmanskop	156	26.40 S	15.12 E
Kolmården	40	58.40 N	16.23 E
Kolmården ⋀[2]	40	58.41 N	16.35 E
Kolmårdens Djurpark ♠	40	58.40 N	16.29 E
Kolmogorovo	86	59.15 N	91.20 E
Köln (Cologne)	56	50.56 N	6.59 E
Köln □[5]	56	50.55 N	6.40 E
Köln-Bonn, Flughafen ⊠	56	50.50 N	7.10 E
Kolno	30	53.25 N	21.56 E
Kolo, Niger	150	13.14 N	2.20 E
Koło, Pol.	30	52.12 N	18.38 E
Kolo, Tan.	154	4.44 S	35.50 E
Koloa	229b	21.54 N	159.28 W
Kolobovo	80	56.42 N	41.21 E
Kołobrzeg	30	54.12 N	15.33 E
Koloč' ≃	82	55.34 N	35.52 E
Kolochau	54	51.44 N	13.16 E
Kolodn'a	76	54.48 N	32.09 E
Kologriv	76	58.51 N	44.17 E
Kologrivovka	80	51.44 N	45.20 E
Kolojar	80	52.34 N	46.58 E
Kolok (Golok) ≃	114	6.15 N	102.05 E
Kolokani	150	13.35 N	8.02 W
Koloko	150	11.05 N	5.19 W
Kolokol'covka, Ross.	80	52.36 N	49.48 E
Kolokol'covka, Ross.	80	51.12 N	44.36 E
Kololo	144	7.29 N	41.58 E
Kolom'agi ◆[8]	265a	60.00 N	30.17 E
Kolom'agi Airport ⊠	265a	60.01 N	30.17 E
Kolomak	78	49.50 N	35.18 E
Kolombangara Island I	175e	8.00 S	157.05 E
Kolomea → Kolomyja	78	48.32 N	25.04 E
Kolomenka ≃	82	55.06 N	38.46 E
Kolomenskaja Sloboda	82	54.22 N	38.15 E
Kolomenskoje ◆[8]	265b	55.40 N	37.41 E
Kolomna	82	55.05 N	38.49 E
Kolomyja	78	48.32 N	25.04 E
Kolondiéba	150	11.05 N	6.54 W
Kolonga	174w	21.08 S	175.04 W
Kolonia	174r	6.58 N	158.13 E
Kolonie Stolp	264a	52.28 N	13.46 E
Kolono	112	4.18 S	122.41 E
Kolonodale	112	2.00 S	121.19 E
Kolora	272b	22.55 N	88.22 E
Kolosib	120	24.14 N	92.42 E
Kol'osnoje	78	46.02 N	29.56 E
Kolosovka	86	56.28 N	73.36 E
Kolovai	174w	21.06 S	175.20 W
Kolovertnoje	80	50.36 N	51.06 E
Kolowana Watobo, Teluk ⊂	112	5.00 S	123.06 E
Kolozsvár → Cluj-Napoca	38	46.47 N	23.36 E
Kolp' ≃	76	59.20 N	36.49 E
Kolpaševo	86	58.20 N	82.50 E
Kolpino	76	59.45 N	30.36 E
Kölpinsee ⊜	54	53.30 N	12.34 E
Kolpny	76	52.15 N	37.02 E
Kölsa	54	51.28 N	12.13 E
Kol'skij poluostrov (Kola Peninsula) >[1]	24	67.30 N	37.00 E
Kolsnaren ⊜	40	59.02 N	16.01 E
Kolsva	40	59.36 N	15.50 E
Kol'togan	85	43.51 N	67.25 E
Koltovskaja	80	52.47 N	44.16 E
Koltubanovskij	80	52.57 N	52.02 E
Koltuši	265a	59.56 N	30.40 E
Kol'ubakino	82	55.40 N	36.32 E
Kolubara ≃	38	44.40 N	20.15 E
Kol'učinskaja guba ⊂	180	66.40 N	174.30 W
Koluel Kayke	254	46.43 S	68.14 W
Kolumbien → Colombia □[1]	246	4.00 N	72.00 W
Kol'upanovo	82	54.26 N	36.14 E
Koluškino	78	48.39 N	40.56 E
Koluszki	30	51.44 N	19.49 E
Koluton	86	51.43 N	69.25 E
Koluton ≃	86	51.42 N	69.10 E
Kolva ≃	24	65.55 N	57.15 E
Kolvereid	24	64.51 N	11.32 E
Kølvrå	41	56.18 N	9.08 E
Kolwezi	154	10.43 S	25.28 E
Kolyberovo	82	55.16 N	38.44 E
Kolyčevo	82	55.30 N	37.52 E
Kolyma ≃	74	69.30 N	161.00 E
Kolymskaja	74	68.44 N	158.44 E
Kolymskaja nizmennost' ≡	74	68.30 N	154.00 E
Kolyšlej	80	52.42 N	44.32 E
Kolyšovo	82	54.54 N	36.57 E
Kolyvan', Ross.	86	51.18 N	82.34 E
Kolyvan', Ross.	86	55.18 N	82.45 E
Kom ∧	38	43.10 N	23.03 E
Kom ≃	152	2.18 N	11.40 E
Koma, Ityo.	144	8.27 N	36.52 E
Koma, Mya.	110	15.39 N	98.12 E
Koma, Ross.	86	55.02 N	91.19 E
Koma ≃	94	35.59 N	139.26 E
Komadougou Yobé (Komadugu Yobe) ≃	146	13.43 N	13.20 E
Komadugu Gana ≃	146	13.05 N	12.24 E
Komadugu Yobe (Komadougou Yobé) ≃	146	13.43 N	13.20 E
Komae	94	35.38 N	139.35 E
Komagane	94	35.43 N	137.55 E
Komaga-take ∧, Nihon	92a	42.04 N	140.41 E
Komaga-take ∧, Nihon	94	35.45 N	138.14 E
Komaga-take ∧, Nihon	94	35.47 N	137.48 E
Komagome ◆[8]	268	35.44 N	139.45 E
Komaki	94	35.17 N	136.55 E
Komandorskije ostrova II	74	55.00 N	167.00 E
Komandorski Village	226	37.43 N	121.54 W
Komariči	76	52.27 N	34.47 E
Komarin	78	51.26 N	30.31 E
Komarniki	78	49.00 N	23.04 E
Komárno, Slov.	30	47.45 N	18.09 E
Komarno, Ukr.	78	49.38 N	23.42 E
Komárom	30	47.44 N	18.08 E
Komárom-Esztergom □[6]	30	47.40 N	18.15 E
Komarovka	78	51.14 N	32.07 E

Symbol	English	Deutsch	Español	Français	Português
≃	River	Fluß	Río	Rivière	Rio
≊	Canal	Kanal	Canal	Canal	Canal
∟	Waterfall, Rapids	Wasserfall, Stromschnellen	Cascada, Rápidos	Chute d'eau, Rapides	Cascata, Rápidos
)(	Strait	Meeresstraße	Estrecho	Détroit	Estreito
⊂	Bay, Gulf	Bucht, Golf	Bahía, Golfo	Baie, Golfe	Baía, Golfo
⊜	Lake, Lakes	See, Seen	Lago, Lagos	Lac, Lacs	Lago, Lagos
≡	Swamp	Sumpf	Pantano	Marais	Pântano
⊓	Ice Features, Glacier	Eis- und Gletscherformen	Accidentes Glaciales	Formes glaciaires	Acidentes glaciares
⊤	Other Hydrographic Features	Andere Hydrographische Objekte	Otros Elementos Hidrográficos	Autres données hydrographiques	Outros acidentes hidrográficos
⊹	Submarine Features	Untermeerische Objekte	Accidentes Submarinos	Formes de relief sous-marin	Acidentes submarinos
□	Political Unit	Politische Einheit	Unidad Politica	Entité politique	Unidade política
ʋ	Cultural Institution	Kulturelle Institution	Institución Cultural	Institution culturelle	Instituição cultural
⊥	Historical Site	Historische Stätte	Sitio Histórico	Site historique	Sitio histórico
♠	Recreational Site	Erholungs- und Ferienort	Sitio de Recreo	Centre de loisirs	Area de Lazer
⊠	Airport	Flughafen	Aeropuerto	Aéroport	Aeroporto
▪	Military Installation	Militäranlage	Instalación Militar	Installation militaire	Instalação militar
◆	Miscellaneous	Verschiedenes	Misceláneo	Divers	Diversos

ENGLISH Name	Page	Lat.°′	Long.°′
DEUTSCH Name	Seite	Breite°′	Länge°′ E = Ost

Name	Page	Lat.°′	Long.°′
Komarovo	76	58.39 N	33.26 E
Komarovy	86	60.26 N	75.50 E
Komati (Incomáti) ≃	156	25.46 S	32.43 E
Komatipoort	156	25.25 S	31.55 E
Komatsu, Nihon	94	36.24 N	136.27 E
Komatsu, Nihon	96	33.53 N	133.07 E
Komatsu-kūkō ⊠	94	36.24 N	136.26 E
Komatsushima	96	34.00 N	134.35 E
Kombissiri	150	12.04 N	1.20 W
Kombone	152	4.37 N	9.19 E
Komdhārā	272b	22.53 N	88.14 E
Kome Island I	154	0.06 S	32.45 E
Komen	64	45.49 N	13.44 E
Komenda	150	5.03 N	1.29 W
Komenoi	268	35.55 N	140.01 E
Komering ≃	112	2.59 S	104.50 E
Komeshia	154	8.01 S	27.07 E
Komfane	164	5.39 S	134.44 E
Komga	158	32.35 S	27.55 E
Komi □3	72	64.00 N	54.00 E
Kominato → Amatsu-kominato	94	35.07 N	140.10 E
Kominternovskoje	78	46.49 N	30.56 E
Komin Yanga	150	11.42 N	0.08 E
Komi-Perm'ackij Avtonomnyj Okrug □8	24	60.00 N	54.30 E
Komissarovka, Ross.	83	48.07 N	40.09 E
Komissarovka, Ukr.	83	48.23 N	38.32 E
Komissarovo	89	44.59 N	131.46 E
Komissarovskij	80	47.29 N	42.59 E
Komkans	158	31.16 S	18.09 E
Komló	30	46.12 N	18.16 E
Kommadagga	158	33.09 S	25.55 E
Kommandodrif	158	27.30 S	26.14 E
Kommandokraal	158	33.06 S	22.51 E
Kommetjie	158	34.08 S	18.21 E
Kommunal'naja	88	52.03 N	115.06 E
Kommunar, Ross.	80	58.10 N	43.33 E
Kommunar, Ross.	86	54.20 N	89.18 E
Kommunarka	265b	55.34 N	37.29 E
Kommunary	26	60.54 N	29.47 E
Kommunizma, pik ∧	85	38.57 N	72.01 E
Komo ≃	152	0.09 N	9.50 E
Komodo	115b	8.35 S	119.30 E
Komodo, Pulau I	115b	8.36 S	119.30 E
Komoé ≃	150	5.12 N	3.44 W
Komoé, Parc National de la ♠	150	9.00 N	3.30 W
Komoka	214	42.57 N	81.26 W
Komono, Congo	152	3.15 S	13.14 E
Komono, Nihon	94	35.00 N	136.31 E
Komoran, Pulau I	164	8.18 S	138.45 E
Komoren → Comoros □1	157a	12.10 S	44.10 E
Komorin, Kap → Comorin, Cape >	122	8.04 N	77.34 E
Komorn → Komárno	30	47.45 N	18.09 E
Komoro	94	36.19 N	138.26 E
Komotau → Chomutov	54	50.28 N	13.26 E
Komotiní	38	41.08 N	25.25 E
Kompanejevka	78	48.15 N	32.12 E
Kompasberg ∧	158	31.45 S	24.32 E
Kompiam	164	5.20 S	143.55 E
Kompot	112	0.24 N	124.10 E
Kom → Qom	128	34.39 N	50.54 E
Komrat	78	46.18 N	28.38 E
Komsomolabad	85	38.52 N	69.57 E
Komsomolec	86	53.45 N	62.02 E
Komsomolec, ostrov I	74	80.30 N	95.00 E
Komsomolec, zaliv c	72	45.30 N	52.45 E
Komsomol'sk, Ross.	80	57.02 N	40.21 E
Komsomol'sk, Ross.	86	55.38 N	88.11 E
Komsomol'sk, Ross.	86	57.27 N	86.02 E
Komsomol'sk, Turk.	128	39.02 N	63.36 E
Komsomol'skij, Kaz.	86	47.20 N	53.42 E
Komsomol'skij, Kaz.	86	51.40 N	66.39 E
Komsomol'skij, Ross.	80	54.27 N	45.49 E
Komsomol'skij, Ross.	89	50.22 N	142.10 E
Komsomol'skij, Ukr.	83	47.40 N	37.26 E
Komsomol'sk-na-Amure	89	50.35 N	137.02 E
Komsomol'sk-na-Ust'urte	86	44.03 N	58.20 E
Komsomol'skoje, Ross.	80	55.16 N	47.33 E
Komsomol'skoje, Ross.	80	50.46 N	47.03 E
Komsomol'skoje, Ross.	88	52.29 N	111.06 E
Komsomol'skoje, Ukr.	78	49.35 N	36.30 E
Komsomol'skoje, Ukr.	78	49.43 N	28.40 E
Komsomol'skoje, Ukr.	83	47.40 N	38.05 E
Komsomol'skoj Pravdy, ostrova II	74	77.20 N	107.40 E
Kŏmun-do I	98	34.02 N	127.19 E
Kömürcüpinar ◆8	267b	41.15 N	28.51 E
Komusan	98	42.08 N	129.41 E
Komyšn'a	78	50.12 N	33.41 E
Kona, India	272b	22.37 N	88.18 E
Kona, Mali	150	14.57 N	3.53 W
Kona Coast ⊥2	229d	19.25 N	155.55 W
Konagkend	84	41.04 N	48.37 E
Konakovo	82	56.42 N	36.46 E
Konakpınar, Tür.	130	39.26 N	27.53 E
Konakpınar, Tür.	130	38.53 N	37.22 E
Konan, C. Iv.	150	8.21 N	8.00 W
Kōnan, Nihon	94	35.20 N	136.53 E
Kōnan, Nihon	94	34.56 N	136.11 E
Kōnan ◆8	268	35.22 N	139.35 E
Konan → Hŭngnam	98	39.50 N	127.38 E
Konar (Kunar) ≃	123	34.25 N	70.32 E
Konārak	120	19.54 N	86.07 E
Konār Dam ◆6	124	23.58 N	85.45 E
Konarhā □4	120	35.15 N	71.00 E
Konawa	196	34.57 N	96.45 W
Končanskoje-Suvorovskoje	76	58.39 N	34.04 E
Konceba	78	48.07 N	29.56 E
Konch	124	25.59 N	79.09 E
Konda	74	61.20 N	63.58 E
Konda ≃, Ross.	86	60.40 N	69.46 E
Konda ≃, Ross.	88	53.30 N	113.32 E
Kondagaon	122	19.36 N	81.40 E
Konde	154	4.57 S	39.45 E
Kondega	76	60.14 N	33.30 E
Kondiaronk, Lac ⊜	190	46.56 N	76.45 W
Kondinin	162	32.30 S	118.16 E
Kondinskoje	86	59.40 N	67.22 E
Kondli ◆8	272a	28.37 N	77.19 E
Kondoa	154	4.54 S	35.47 E
Kondol'	80	52.49 N	45.03 E
Kondolole	154	1.20 N	25.58 E
Kondopoga	24	62.12 N	34.17 E
Kondorfa	61	46.54 N	16.24 E
Kondratjevo, Ross.	76	60.38 N	28.08 E
Kondratjevo, Ross.	88	57.21 N	98.11 E
Kondrovka	80	54.36 N	43.17 E
Kondrovo	82	54.48 N	35.56 E
Konduga	146	11.39 N	13.24 E
Kondukūr	122	15.13 N	79.55 E
Kondurča ≃	80	53.31 N	50.24 E
Kondūz	120	37.45 N	68.51 E
Kondūz □4	120	36.45 N	68.30 E
Koné	175f	21.04 S	164.52 E
Koné, Passe de ⊔	175f	21.08 S	164.41 E
Konecbor	24	64.52 N	57.44 E
Konergino	180	65.54 N	178.50 W
Konfara	150	11.55 N	8.50 W
Kong, C. Iv.	150	9.09 N	4.37 W
Køng, Dan.	41	55.07 N	11.50 E
Kông ≃	110	13.32 N	105.58 E
Kŏng, Kaôh I	110	11.20 N	103.00 E
Kongakut ≃	180	69.48 N	141.50 W
Kongbo	152	4.44 N	21.23 E
Kongcheng	100	31.02 N	117.05 E
Kongeå ≃	41	55.23 N	8.40 E
Kongens Lyngby	41	55.46 N	12.31 E
Kongfang	100	27.58 N	116.53 E
Kongiganak	180	59.58 N	162.45 W
Konginkangas	26	62.46 N	25.48 E
Kongjiamatou	105	39.07 N	116.10 E
Kongjiatun	104	40.42 N	124.04 E
Kongjiawopeng	89	43.58 N	122.41 E
Kongjiazhuang	105	40.47 N	114.48 E
Kongju	98	36.27 N	127.07 E
Konglong	100	29.56 N	115.54 E
Konglongshan	105	40.33 N	117.17 E
Konglu	102	27.16 N	97.56 E
Kongmoon → Jiangmen	100	22.35 N	113.05 E
Kongo, Republik → Zaire □1	138	4.00 S	25.00 E
Kongo → Congo ≃	138	6.04 S	12.24 E
Kongō-Ikoma-kokutei-kōen ♠	96	34.28 N	135.40 E
Kongolo, Zaïre	154	5.26 S	24.49 E
Kongolo, Zaïre	154	5.23 S	27.00 E
Kongor	140	7.10 N	31.21 E
Kongō-sanchi ⋏	270	34.27 N	135.41 E
Kongoussi	150	13.19 N	1.32 W
Kongō-zan ∧	96	34.25 N	135.41 E
Kongsberg	26	59.39 N	9.39 E
Kongsvinger	26	60.12 N	12.00 E
Kongsvoll	26	62.18 N	9.37 E
Kongtan	107	29.10 N	104.42 E
Kongur Shan ∧, Zhg.	85	38.37 N	75.20 E
Kongwa	154	6.12 S	36.25 E
Kongyangcun	106	31.23 N	118.54 E
Kongzhen	106	31.29 N	119.00 E
Koni	154	10.42 S	27.15 E
Koni ≃	150	13.05 N	5.37 W
Koniakari	150	14.34 N	10.54 W
Konice	30	49.35 N	16.53 E
Koniecpol	30	50.48 N	19.41 E
Königgrätz → Hradec Králové	30	50.12 N	15.50 E
Königheim	56	49.37 N	9.35 E
Königin Alexandra-Kette → Queen Alexandra Range ⋏	9	84.00 S	168.00 E
Königin Fabiola-Gebirge → Queen Fabiola Mountains ⋏	9	71.30 S	35.40 E
Königin Mary-Küste → Queen Mary Coast ⊥2	9	67.00 S	96.00 E
Königin Maud-Land → Queen Maud Land ◆1	9	72.30 S	12.00 E
König-Otto-Höhle ⊥5	60	49.15 N	11.42 E
Königsbach	56	48.58 N	8.36 E
Königsberg	56	50.05 N	10.34 E
Königsberg → Kaliningrad	76	54.43 N	20.30 E
Königsborn	263	51.33 N	7.41 E
Königsbrück	54	51.16 N	13.54 E
Königsbrunn, Dtsch.	58	48.16 N	10.53 E
Königsbrunn, Öst.	264b	48.21 N	16.25 E
Königsdorf	64	47.49 N	11.28 E
Königsee	54	50.39 N	11.05 E
Königsfelden v1	58	47.29 N	8.14 E
Königsfeld im Schwarzwald	58	48.08 N	8.25 E
Königshain	54	51.11 N	14.52 E
Königshardt ◆8	263	51.33 N	6.51 E
Königsheim	58	48.06 N	8.51 E
Königslutter	54	52.15 N	10.49 E
Königsmoor ◆3	52	53.15 N	9.40 E
Königssee	64	47.33 N	12.58 E
Königssee ⊜	64	47.36 N	12.59 E
Königsstuhl ⊥4	54	54.34 N	13.40 E
Königstein, Dtsch.	54	50.55 N	14.04 E
Königstein, Dtsch.	56	50.11 N	8.29 E
Königstein, Dtsch.	60	49.37 N	11.38 E
Königstetten	264b	48.18 N	16.09 E
Königswalde	54	50.33 N	13.02 E
Königswartha	54	51.18 N	14.20 E
Königswiesen	61	48.24 N	14.50 E
Königswinter	56	50.40 N	7.11 E
Königs Wusterhausen	54	52.18 N	13.37 E
Konin	30	52.13 N	18.16 E
Konin □4	30	52.20 N	18.20 E
Konispol	38	39.39 N	20.10 E
Kónitsa	38	40.02 N	20.45 E
Köniz	58	46.56 N	7.25 E
Konjic	38	43.39 N	17.57 E
Konka ≃	78	47.40 N	35.22 E
Könkämäälven ≃	24	68.29 N	22.17 E
Konkapot ≃	210	42.03 N	73.20 W
Konkiep ≃	156	28.03 S	17.21 E
Konkō	96	34.32 N	133.37 E
Kon'-Kolodez'	76	52.08 N	39.11 E
Konkouré ≃	150	9.58 N	13.42 W
Kon'kovo	83	47.20 N	38.10 E
Konkudera	88	57.33 N	112.30 E
Konkug University v2	271b	37.32 N	127.05 E
Konnagar	126	22.42 N	88.22 E
Könnern	54	51.40 N	11.46 E
Konnevesi ⊜	26	62.40 N	26.35 E
Konnur	122	16.12 N	74.45 E
Kōno	94	35.49 N	136.04 E
Konobejevo	82	55.24 N	38.40 E
Konohana ◆8	270	34.41 N	135.26 E
Kōnoike	270	34.42 N	135.37 E
Konolfingen	58	46.53 N	7.38 E
Konongo	150	6.37 N	1.11 W
Konoša	24	60.58 N	40.15 E
Kōno-shima I	96	34.28 N	133.31 E
Kōnosu	94	36.03 N	139.31 E
Konotop	78	51.14 N	33.12 E
Konovalovka	80	53.06 N	51.34 E
Kon'ovo, Ross.	24	62.08 N	39.16 E
Kon'ovo, Ross.	86	56.18 N	70.43 E
Konqi ≃	90	40.40 N	90.10 E
Konradshöhe ◆8	264a	52.35 N	13.14 E
Konradsreuth	54	50.16 N	11.50 E
Konsankoro	150	9.02 N	9.00 W
Konsen-daichi ⋏1	92a	43.25 N	144.52 E
Końskie	30	51.12 N	20.26 E
Konstabel	158	33.16 S	20.17 E
Konstantinopel → İstanbul	130	41.01 N	28.58 E
Konstantinovka, Ross.	80	56.41 N	50.53 E
Konstantinovka, Ross.	265a	59.47 N	30.08 E
Konstantinovka, Ukr.	78	49.57 N	35.07 E
Konstantinovka, Ukr.	78	47.51 N	31.09 E
Konstantinovka, Ukr.	83	48.32 N	37.43 E
Konstantinovka, Ukr.	83	47.52 N	37.24 E
Konstantinovo	82	56.33 N	38.02 E
Konstantinovsk	80	47.35 N	41.06 E
Konstantinovskij	76	57.50 N	39.36 E
Konstantinovskije Porogi	76	60.34 N	37.04 E
Konstantynów Łódzki	30	51.45 N	19.20 E
Konstanz	58	47.40 N	9.10 E
Kontagora	150	10.24 N	5.28 E
Kontcha	152	7.58 N	12.14 E
Kontejevo	80	58.26 N	41.21 E
Kontha	110	19.30 N	96.03 E
Kontich	50	51.08 N	4.27 E
Kontiolahti	26	62.46 N	29.51 E
Kontiomäki	26	64.21 N	28.09 E
Kon Tum	110	14.21 N	108.00 E
Kontum, Plateau du ⋏1	110	13.55 N	108.05 E
Kōnu	96	34.42 N	133.05 E
Kon'uchovo	86	55.08 N	70.38 E
Konus, gora ∧	180	67.34 N	178.10 E
Konya	130	37.52 N	32.31 E
Konya □4	130	38.00 N	33.00 E
Konyr	80	50.25 N	53.25 E
Konyrat	80	49.36 N	47.01 E
Konyrolen	86	44.16 N	79.19 E
Konyševka	78	51.51 N	35.18 E
Konystanu	80	48.51 N	53.20 E
Konz	56	49.42 N	6.34 E
Konza	154	1.45 S	37.07 E
Konžakovskij Kamen', gora ∧	86	59.38 N	59.08 E
Konzell	60	49.04 N	12.43 E
Koocanusa, Lake ⊜1	202	49.00 N	115.10 W
Koog [aan de Zaan]	52	52.27 N	4.49 E
Kookynie	162	29.20 S	121.29 E
Koolamarra	166	20.12 S	140.14 E
Koolatah	164	15.53 S	142.27 E
Koolau Range ⋏	229c	21.35 N	158.00 W
Kooloonong	166	34.53 S	143.09 E
Koolskamp	50	51.00 N	3.12 E
Koolyanobbing	162	30.50 S	119.35 E
Koolywurtie	168b	34.38 S	137.37 E
Koombana Bay c	168a	33.18 S	115.36 E
Koonap ≃	158	33.03 S	26.39 E
Koondrook	166	35.39 S	144.08 E
Koonga	76	58.35 N	24.12 E
Koonibba	162	31.58 S	133.27 E
Koontz Lake	216	41.25 N	86.29 W
Koontz Lake ⊜	216	41.25 N	86.28 W
Koopan-Noord	158	26.53 S	20.41 E
Koopan-Suid	158	27.15 S	20.22 E
Koopmansfontein	158	28.14 S	24.01 E
Koorawatha	166	34.02 S	148.33 E
Koorda	162	30.50 S	117.29 E
Koosa	76	58.33 N	27.07 E
Koosfontein	158	27.22 S	25.27 E
Koosharem	200	38.30 N	111.52 W
Kooskia	202	46.08 N	115.58 W
Koossa	150	9.32 N	8.32 W
Kootenai (Kootenay) ≃	182	49.15 N	117.39 W
Kootenay (Kootenai) ≃	182	49.15 N	117.39 W
Kootenay Indian Reserve ◆4	182	49.37 N	115.45 W
Kootenay Lake ⊜	182	49.35 N	116.50 W
Kootenay National Park ♠	182	51.00 N	116.00 W
Kootjieskolk	158	31.15 S	20.21 E
Kootwijk	52	52.12 N	5.45 E
Koo-wee-rup	169	38.12 S	145.30 E
Kopa	85	43.32 N	75.50 E
Kopa ≃	85	43.40 N	76.15 E
Kopāganj	124	26.01 N	83.34 E
Kopāi ≃	126	23.48 N	87.47 E
Kopajgorod	78	48.51 N	27.48 E
Kopanbulak	86	48.56 N	80.52 E
Kopang	115b	8.39 S	116.21 E
Kopanovka	80	47.27 N	46.48 E
Kopanskaja	78	46.17 N	38.29 E
Kopapan	80	50.20 N	50.26 E
Kopargaon	122	19.53 N	74.29 E
Koparkhairna	272c	19.06 N	72.59 E
Koparpāda	272c	19.02 N	73.04 E
Kópasker	24a	66.20 N	16.24 W
Kopatkeviči	76	52.19 N	28.49 E
Kópavogur	24a	64.06 N	21.50 W
Kopceviči	76	52.14 N	28.19 E
Kopé, Mont ∧2	150	4.59 N	7.27 W
Kopejsk	86	55.07 N	61.37 E
Kopenhagen → København	41	55.40 N	12.35 E
Köpenick ◆8	54	52.27 N	13.34 E
Köpenick, Schloss v	264a	52.27 N	13.34 E
Koper	36	45.33 N	13.44 E
Köpernitz	54	53.04 N	12.56 E
Kopervik	26	59.17 N	5.18 E
Kopetdag, chrebet ⋏	128	37.50 N	58.00 E
Kopeysk → Kopejsk	86	55.07 N	61.37 E
Kop Geçidi)(	130	40.03 N	40.33 E
Kopice	54	53.44 N	14.32 E
Köping	40	59.31 N	16.00 E
Kopisty	54	50.34 N	13.35 E
Kopjevo	86	55.03 N	89.50 E
Koplik	38	42.13 N	19.26 E
Köpmanholmen	26	63.10 N	18.34 E
Kopnino	82	56.53 N	38.29 E
Kopondei, Tanjung >	115b	8.04 S	122.52 E
Koporje	76	59.44 N	29.01 E
Koporskaja guba c	76	59.52 N	28.55 E
Koppal	122	15.21 N	76.09 E
Koppang	26	61.34 N	11.04 E
Koppány ≃	30	46.35 N	18.26 E
Kopparberg	40	59.52 N	14.59 E
Kopparbergs Län □6	26	61.00 N	14.30 E
Koppel	214	40.50 N	80.19 W
Kopperå	26	63.24 N	11.51 E
Kopperby	41	54.38 N	9.56 E
Kopperl	222	32.04 N	97.30 W
Koppi	89	48.32 N	140.07 E
Koppi ≃	89	48.33 N	140.08 E
Koppies	158	27.20 S	27.30 E
Koppom	26	59.43 N	12.09 E
Kopri	272c	19.11 N	72.58 E
Koprivnica	36	46.10 N	16.50 E
Köprü ≃	130	36.50 N	31.10 E
Köprülü Kanyon Milli Parkı ♠	130	37.20 N	31.18 E
Köprüören	130	39.30 N	29.47 E
Kopt'ovo	80	56.43 N	40.31 E
Kopyčincy	78	49.06 N	25.55 E
Kopyl'	76	53.09 N	27.05 E
Kopylovka	86	58.40 N	82.22 E
Kopylovo, Ross.	24	60.35 N	45.02 E
Kopylovo, Ross.	82	56.26 N	36.25 E
Kopys'	76	54.19 N	30.18 E
Kor ≃	128	29.36 N	53.18 E
Kōra	94	35.12 N	136.15 E
Koraa Shiir	144	3.18 N	46.16 E
Korab ⋏	38	41.47 N	20.34 E
Kor Aban	144	3.58 N	42.44 E
Korablino	80	53.55 N	40.01 E
Korahe	144	6.35 N	44.23 E
Kor'akovka	86	52.24 N	77.08 E
Kor'akskaja Sopka, vulkan ∧1	74	53.20 N	158.43 E
Kor'akskoje nagorje ⋏	74	62.30 N	172.00 E
Kōrakuen ♠	96	34.38 N	133.53 E
Korakuen Stadium ♠	268	35.43 N	139.45 E
Korallenmeer → Coral Sea ⊽2	14	20.00 S	158.00 E
Koralpe ⋏	61	46.50 N	14.58 E
Korannaberg ⋏	158	27.25 S	22.32 E
Korapun	164	5.25 S	152.00 E
Korāput	122	18.49 N	82.43 E
Korarou, Lac ⊜	150	15.15 N	3.16 W
Koratla	122	18.49 N	78.43 E
Korat → Nakhon Ratchasima	110	14.58 N	102.07 E
Kor'ažma	24	61.18 N	47.06 E
Korba, India	124	22.21 N	82.41 E
Korba, Tun.	36	36.35 N	10.52 E
Korbach	56	51.16 N	8.52 E
Korbeta	144	13.03 N	39.43 E
Korbol	146	10.01 N	17.43 E
Korbous	36	36.49 N	10.35 E
Korbu, Gunong ∧	114	4.43 N	101.17 E
Korçë	38	40.37 N	20.46 E
Korcovo	76	58.52 N	42.13 E
Korčula	36	42.58 N	17.08 E
Korčula, Otok I	36	42.57 N	16.50 E
Korčulanski Kanal ⊔	36	43.03 N	16.40 E
Kordestān □4	128	35.30 N	47.00 E
Kord Kūy	128	36.48 N	54.07 E
Kordovo	86	54.06 N	93.17 E
Korea, North □1, Asia	90	40.00 N	127.00 E
Korea, North □1, Asia	98	40.00 N	127.00 E
Korea, South □1, Asia	90	36.30 N	128.00 E
Korea, South □1, Asia	98	36.30 N	128.00 E
Korea Bay c	98	39.00 N	124.00 E
Korea Strait ⊔	90	34.00 N	129.00 E
Korea University v2	271b	37.36 N	127.02 E
Korec	78	50.37 N	27.09 E
Korekozevo	82	54.20 N	36.11 E
Korelakša	24	65.33 N	32.22 E
Koreliči	76	53.34 N	26.08 E
Korem	144	12.30 N	39.30 E
Koré Mayroua	150	13.18 N	3.55 E
Koren (Die Wurzen))(	64	46.31 N	13.45 E
Korenkovo	78	45.07 N	36.24 E
Koren'ovo, Ross.	78	51.25 N	34.55 E
Koren'ovo, Ross.	265b	55.40 N	38.00 E
Korenovsk	78	45.29 N	39.28 E
Korf	74	60.19 N	165.50 E
Korfovskij	89	48.13 N	135.03 E
Korga	158	30.12 S	20.28 E
Korgan	130	40.44 N	37.13 E
Korgašino	82	54.45 N	37.41 E
Kõrgessaare	76	58.59 N	22.28 E
Korgonskij chrebet ⋏	86	50.45 N	84.30 E
Korgus	140	19.13 N	33.29 E
Korhogo	150	9.27 N	5.38 W
Kōri	270	34.47 N	135.39 E
Koridhallós	267c	37.59 N	23.39 E
Korido	164	0.50 S	135.35 E
Koriella	169	37.10 S	145.39 E
Korienzé	150	15.24 N	3.47 W
Korim	164	0.54 S	136.02 E
Korima, Oued el V	148	33.51 N	0.23 W
Koringberg	158	33.01 S	18.40 E
Koringplaas	158	32.48 S	20.58 E
Korinth	41	55.08 N	10.21 E
Korinthiakós Kólpos c	38	38.19 N	22.04 E
Kórinthos (Corinth)	38	37.56 N	22.56 E
Korínthou, Dhiórix ≌	38	37.57 N	22.56 E
Kőris-hegy ∧	30	47.18 N	17.45 E
Koritsa → Korçë	38	40.37 N	20.46 E
Köritz	54	52.51 N	12.27 E
Kōriyama	92	37.24 N	140.23 E
Kōriyama → Yamato-kōriyama	96	34.38 N	135.47 E
Korizo, Passe de)(	146	22.28 N	15.27 E
Korkino, Ross.	86	54.54 N	61.23 E
Korkino, Ross.	88	54.23 N	105.14 E
Korkinskoje, ozero ⊜	265a	59.55 N	30.44 E
Korkuteli	130	37.04 N	30.13 E
Korla	90	41.44 N	86.09 E
Korl'aki	80	57.06 N	46.57 E
Korliki	74	61.31 N	82.22 E
Korma, Bela.	76	53.08 N	30.48 E
Korma, Bela.	76	52.21 N	31.31 E
Körmend	61	47.01 N	16.37 E
Kormilovka	86	55.00 N	74.06 E
Kormovoje	80	46.17 N	43.30 E
Kornat, Otok I	36	43.50 N	15.16 E
Körnebach ≃	263	51.35 N	7.38 E
Kornejevka, Kaz.	86	54.01 N	68.27 E
Kornejevka, Kaz.	86	50.12 N	74.19 E
Kornejevka, Ross.	80	51.45 N	48.46 E
Kornelimünster	56	50.43 N	6.11 E
Körner, Dtsch.	54	51.13 N	10.35 E
Korner, Mt., U.S.	182	48.59 N	112.15 W
Kornešty	78	47.22 N	27.59 E
Korneuburg	61	48.21 N	16.20 E
Kórnik	30	52.17 N	17.04 E
Kornilovo	86	53.32 N	81.05 E
Kornin	78	50.06 N	29.32 E
Kornouchovo	80	55.33 N	49.53 E
Korn'ovo	265a	60.03 N	30.45 E
Kornsjø	26	58.57 N	11.39 E
Kornwestheim	56	48.52 N	9.11 E
Koro, C. Iv.	150	8.34 N	7.28 W
Koro, Mali	150	14.04 N	3.05 W
Koro I	175g	17.19 S	179.23 E
Koroba	164	5.40 S	142.45 E
Koroča	78	50.48 N	37.11 E
Korodougou Markala	150	12.26 N	6.17 W
Köroğlu Tepesi ∧	130	40.31 N	31.53 E
Korogwe	154	5.09 S	38.29 E
Koroit	166	38.17 S	142.22 E
Korolenko, gora ∧	88	58.15 N	115.01 E
Korolevskij Belok, gora ∧	86	51.00 N	83.43 E
Korol'ovo	78	48.09 N	23.08 E
Korol'ovščina	76	55.49 N	31.45 E
Korom, Bahr ≃	146	10.35 N	19.45 E
Koromba ∧	175g	17.53 S	177.34 E
Koromiri I	174k	21.15 S	159.43 W
Koromo → Toyota	94	35.05 N	137.09 E
Koronadal	116	6.30 N	124.51 E
Koróni	38	36.48 N	21.56 E
Korónia, Límni ⊜	38	40.41 N	23.05 E
Koronowo	30	53.19 N	17.57 E
Korop	78	51.34 N	32.56 E
Koropélé	152	4.44 N	17.11 E
Koropíon	38	37.54 N	23.53 E
Koror	175b	7.20 N	134.29 E
Koror I	175b	7.20 N	134.30 E
Kororoit Creek ≃	274b	37.52 S	144.52 E
Körös ≃	30	46.43 N	20.12 E
Koro Sea ⊽2	175g	18.00 S	179.50 E
Korosten'	78	50.57 N	28.39 E
Korostyšev	78	50.19 N	29.03 E
Korotkova	88	56.43 N	107.55 E
Korotojak	78	50.59 N	39.10 E
Koro Toro	146	16.05 N	18.30 E
Korotovo	76	58.57 N	37.28 E
Korotyš	76	52.22 N	37.27 E
Korovincy	78	50.48 N	33.45 E
Korovin Island I	180	55.25 N	160.15 W
Korovino, Ross.	78	51.25 N	36.45 E
Korovino, Ross.	80	53.49 N	53.03 E
Korovin Volcano ∧1	180	52.22 N	174.10 W
Korovou	175g	17.57 S	178.21 E
Koroyanitu ∧	175g	17.40 S	177.35 E
Korožečna ≃	76	57.32 N	38.18 E
Korpilahti	26	62.01 N	25.33 E
Korpo (Korppoo)	26	60.10 N	21.34 E
Korså	40	60.38 N	16.08 E
Korsakov	89	46.38 N	142.46 E
Korsakovo	76	53.16 N	37.21 E
Korschenbroich	56	51.11 N	6.31 E
Korselbränna	26	64.27 N	15.35 E
Korševo	78	51.11 N	40.07 E
Korsika → Corse I	36	42.00 N	9.00 E
Korsnäs, Suomi	26	62.47 N	21.12 E
Korsnäs, Sve.	40	60.35 N	15.43 E
Korsør	41	55.20 N	11.09 E
Korsør Nor c	41	55.20 N	11.11 E
Korsun'	83	48.12 N	38.05 E
Koršunovo	88	58.37 N	110.10 E
Korsun'-Ševčenkovskij	78	49.26 N	31.16 E
Korsze	30	54.10 N	21.09 E
Kortgene	52	51.34 N	3.48 E
Kortilisy	78	51.51 N	24.25 E
Kortkeros	24	61.49 N	51.28 E
Kortrijk (Courtrai)	50	50.50 N	3.16 E
Kortuz, gora ∧	86	54.33 N	91.56 E
Koruçam Burnu >	130	35.24 N	32.56 E
Korucu	130	39.28 N	27.22 E
Kor'ukovka	78	51.46 N	32.14 E
Korumburra	169	38.26 S	145.49 E
Korwai	124	24.08 N	78.03 E
Kōryō	96	34.33 N	135.45 E
Koryŏng	98	35.44 N	128.15 E
Koryst'	78	50.35 N	27.01 E
Koryta	60	49.24 N	13.13 E
Korženevskoj, pik ∧	85	39.04 N	72.00 E
Korženeuc'	78	48.13 N	27.02 E
Korževka	80	54.12 N	46.22 E
Kos	38	36.53 N	27.18 E
Kos I	38	36.50 N	27.10 E
Kosa, Ityo.	144	7.51 N	36.51 E
Kosa, Ross.	24	59.56 N	54.55 E
Kosa, Ross.	88	54.47 N	108.52 E
Kosa ≃, Ross.	24	60.11 N	55.10 E
Kosa ≃, Ross.	80	58.26 N	51.15 E
Kosa ⊥	150	15.50 N	7.00 W
Koš-Agač	86	50.00 N	88.40 E
Kosai	94	34.43 N	137.33 E
Kosaja, šivera ∟	88	58.24 N	97.48 E
Kosaja Gora	82	54.07 N	37.33 E
Kosaka	92	40.19 N	140.44 E
Kosan	98	38.52 N	127.24 E
Košankol'	80	49.56 N	48.11 E
Koščagyl	86	46.51 N	53.48 E
Kösching	60	48.49 N	11.30 E
Kościan	30	52.06 N	16.38 E
Kościerzyna	30	54.08 N	18.00 E
Kosciusko	194	33.03 N	89.35 W
Kosciusko □6	216	41.14 N	85.51 W
Kosciusko, Mount ∧	171b	36.27 S	148.16 E
Kosciusko National Park ♠	166	36.10 S	148.15 E
Kös Dağı ∧	130	40.59 N	34.25 E
Kosdaulet, peski ◆2	80	47.45 N	49.30 E
Kose, Eesti	76	59.11 N	25.10 E
Kose, Nihon	270	34.25 N	135.46 E
Köse, Tür.	130	40.13 N	39.39 E
Kösedağı ∧	130	39.54 N	42.39 E
Kösefakılı	130	39.36 N	34.09 E
Košelevka	82	55.09 N	38.05 E
Košelicha	80	55.02 N	43.33 E
Košerovo	82	55.38 N	38.22 E
Koserow	54	54.03 N	13.59 E
Kosha	140	20.49 N	30.32 E
Koshien Stadium ♠	270	34.42 N	135.22 E
Koshigaya	94	35.54 N	139.48 E
Koshigoe	268	35.18 N	139.30 E
Koshikijima-rettō II	92	31.45 N	129.49 E
Koshino	94	36.02 N	136.01 E
Koshk-e Kohneh	128	34.52 N	62.31 E
Koshkonong	194	36.35 N	91.38 W
Koshkonong, Lake ⊜	216	42.52 N	88.58 W
Koshkonong Creek ≃	216	42.53 N	88.59 W
Koshlong Lake ⊜	212	44.58 N	78.29 W
Kōshoku	94	36.32 N	138.06 E
Koshu → Kwangju	98	35.09 N	126.54 E
Kosī □8	124	27.15 N	87.15 E
Kosi ≃	124	25.26 N	87.22 E
Košice	30	48.43 N	21.15 E
Kosigi	122	15.51 N	77.16 E
Kosi Kalan	124	27.48 N	77.26 E
Kosikovo	76	59.52 N	43.23 E
Kosimeer ⊜	158	26.55 S	32.52 E
Kosino, Ross.	80	58.23 N	51.17 E
Kosino, Ross.	82	55.43 N	37.52 E
Kosju	24	65.38 N	59.03 E
Kosju ≃	24	66.18 N	59.53 E
Kosjuvom	24	66.17 N	59.50 E
Köşk	130	37.51 N	28.03 E
Koskaecodde Lake ⊜	186	48.00 N	55.20 W
Koškar	80	47.27 N	53.29 E
Koški, Ross.	80	54.12 N	50.28 E
Koski, Suomi	26	60.39 N	23.09 E
Koškino	80	56.20 N	50.49 E
Koskol'	86	49.31 N	67.05 E
Koskuduk	86	44.06 N	77.22 E
Koskullskulle	24	67.12 N	20.50 E
Koslan	24	63.28 N	48.52 E
Köslin → Koszalin	30	54.12 N	16.09 E
Kosmonosy	54	50.26 N	15.00 E
Kosmynino	80	57.35 N	40.46 E
Kosoba, gora ∧	86	48.15 N	79.40 E
Kosogor	80	57.07 N	47.34 E
Kosoj, porog ∟, Ross.	86	57.30 N	95.30 E
Kosoj, porog ∟, Ross.	88	57.44 N	96.20 E
Kosolapovo	80	56.57 N	49.37 E
Kosŏng, C.M.I.K.	98	38.40 N	128.19 E
Kosŏng, Taehan	98	34.58 N	128.18 E
Kosov	78	48.19 N	25.05 E
Kosovo-Metohija □4	38	42.35 N	21.00 E
Kosovska Mitrovica	38	42.53 N	20.52 E
Kosový potok ≃	60	49.46 N	12.48 E
Kosrae I	14	5.19 N	162.59 E
Kösreli	130	37.11 N	35.59 E
Kossdorf	54	51.29 N	13.14 E
Kosse	222	31.18 N	96.38 W
Kössen	64	47.40 N	12.24 E
Kossindi	152	3.51 N	16.19 E
Kösslarn	60	48.22 N	13.07 E
Kossol Passage ⊔	175b	7.52 N	134.36 E
Kossol Reef ✣2	175b	7.57 N	134.41 E
Kossou, Lac de ⊜1	150	7.25 N	5.45 W
Kossovo	76	52.45 N	25.09 E
Kossuth	214	41.17 N	79.35 W
Kosta	26	56.51 N	15.23 E
Kostajnica	36	45.14 N	16.33 E
Košt'any	54	50.39 N	13.45 E
Koš-Tegirmen	85	42.47 N	73.53 E
Kostelec nad Labem	54	50.11 N	14.35 E
Kostenec	38	42.16 N	23.49 E
Koster	158	25.57 S	26.42 E
Kosterevo	80	55.56 N	39.37 E
Kosteröarna I	26	58.54 N	11.02 E
Kostešty	78	46.52 N	28.44 E
Kostešty-Stynka, vodochranilišče (Lacul Stînca-Costești) ⊜1	38	47.55 N	27.10 E
Koštice	54	50.24 N	13.55 E
Kostino, Ross.	80	52.11 N	51.20 E
Kostino, Ross.	80	52.24 N	51.39 E
Kostino, Ross.	82	56.18 N	37.43 E
Kostino, Ross.	265b	55.55 N	37.51 E
Kostino-Otdelec	78	51.33 N	41.26 E
Kost'kovo	76	60.02 N	33.14 E
Košt'ob'o	85	41.06 N	74.15 E
Kostomukša	24	64.41 N	30.49 E
Kostonjärvi ⊜	26	65.47 N	28.27 E
Kostopol'	78	50.53 N	26.26 E
Kostriževka	78	48.38 N	25.41 E
Kostroma	76	57.46 N	40.55 E
Kostroma ≃	24	57.47 N	40.55 E
Kostroma Oblast' □4	24	58.30 N	44.00 E
Kostrovo	82	55.53 N	36.42 E
Kostrzyn	30	52.37 N	14.39 E
Kost'ukoviči	76	53.20 N	32.03 E
Kost'ukovka	76	52.32 N	30.56 E
Kosugaya ◆8	268	35.22 N	139.33 E
Kosuge	94	35.45 N	138.57 E
Kosugi	94	36.43 N	137.06 E
Kosum Phisai	110	16.13 N	103.01 E
Koszalin (Köslin)	30	54.12 N	16.09 E
Koszalin □4	30	54.00 N	16.00 E
Kőszeg	61	47.23 N	16.33 E
Koszyce	30	50.11 N	20.35 E
Kota, India	120	25.11 N	75.50 E
Kota, India	124	22.18 N	82.02 E
Kota, Malay.	114	5.35 N	100.23 E
Kota, Malay.	114	2.31 N	102.10 E
Kotaagung	112	5.30 S	104.38 E
Kotabaharu, Indon.	112	0.48 S	111.33 E
Kota Baharu, Malay.	114	6.08 N	102.15 E
Kotabangun	112	0.16 S	116.35 E
Kotabaru, Indon.	112	3.14 S	116.13 E
Kotabaru, Indon.	112	1.08 S	101.43 E
Kotabaru → Jayapura	164	2.32 S	140.42 E
Kota Belud	112	6.25 N	116.31 E
Kotabumi	112	4.50 S	104.54 E
Kotabunan	112	0.49 N	124.38 E
Kotadabok	112	0.30 S	104.33 E
Kot Addu	123	30.28 N	70.58 E
Kotagiri	122	11.26 N	76.53 E
Kot'ajevka	80	46.33 N	48.46 E
Kotake	96	33.41 N	130.43 E
Kota Kinabalu (Jesselton)	112	5.59 N	116.04 E
Kota Kota → Nkhotakota	154	12.57 S	34.17 E
Kotālpur	126	23.02 N	87.36 E
Kotamobagu	112	0.46 N	124.19 E
Kotanemel', gora ∧	86	47.43 N	77.18 E
Kotapinang	114	1.53 N	100.05 E
Kotari ⋏	36	44.05 N	15.30 E
Kotaringin	114	0.53 N	102.03 E
Kota Sarang Semut	114	5.59 N	100.24 E
Kotatengah	114	1.05 N	100.33 E
Kota Tinggi	114	1.44 N	103.54 E
Kotawaringin	112	2.29 S	111.25 E
Kotchāndpur	124	23.24 N	89.01 E
Kotcho Lake ⊜	176	59.05 N	121.10 W
Kot Chutta	123	29.53 N	70.39 E
Kotdwāra	124	29.45 N	78.32 E
Kotel	38	42.53 N	26.27 E
Kotel'nič	80	58.18 N	48.20 E
Kotel'niki	82	55.39 N	37.52 E
Kotel'nikovo	80	47.38 N	43.09 E
Kotel'nyj, ostrov I	74	75.45 N	138.44 E
Kotel'va	78	50.05 N	34.45 E
Kot Fateh	123	30.07 N	75.05 E
Köthen	54	51.45 N	11.58 E
Kotido	154	3.00 N	34.06 E
Koti → Kōchi	96	33.33 N	133.33 E
Kotikovo	89	49.08 N	144.13 E
Kotka	26	60.28 N	26.55 E
Kot Kapūra	123	30.35 N	74.54 E
Kotkino	24	67.02 N	51.03 E
Kotla	123	32.15 N	76.02 E
Kotl'akovo	82	56.17 N	35.49 E
Kotlas	24	61.16 N	46.35 E
Kotli	123	33.31 N	73.55 E
Kotlik	180	63.02 N	163.33 W
Kotlin, ostrov I	76	60.00 N	29.46 E
Kotly	76	59.36 N	28.45 E
Kot Mūmin	123	32.11 N	73.02 E
Kotō	94	35.08 N	136.14 E
Kōtō ◆8	268	35.41 N	139.48 E
Koto ≃, Nihon	96	33.58 N	131.13 E
Kotō ≃, Nihon	96	34.21 N	134.02 E
Kotobiki-san ∧	96	35.03 N	132.47 E
Kotohira	96	34.11 N	133.49 E
Kotohira-gu v1	96	34.11 N	133.49 E
Kotohira-yama ∧	96	34.11 N	133.48 E
Kotonami	96	34.10 N	133.56 E
Koton-Karifi	150	8.08 N	6.48 E
Kotonkoro	150	11.02 N	5.58 E
Kotor	38	42.25 N	18.46 E
Kotoriba	36	46.21 N	16.49 E
Kotorovo	80	54.54 N	41.35 E
Kotor Varoš	36	44.37 N	17.23 E
Kotouba	150	8.41 N	3.12 W
Kotovka	78	49.08 N	34.57 E
Kotovo	80	50.18 N	44.50 E
Kotovsk, Ross.	80	52.36 N	41.32 E
Kotovsk, Ukr.	78	47.45 N	29.33 E
Kot Pūtli	124	27.43 N	76.12 E
Kotra, India	120	24.22 N	73.10 E
Kotra, India	272b	22.46 N	88.34 E
Kot Rādha Kishan	123	31.10 N	74.06 E
Kotri	120	25.22 N	68.18 E
Kotri Allāhrakhio	120	24.24 N	67.50 E
Kotrung → Uttarpara-Kotrung	272b	22.40 N	88.21 E
Kötschach [-Mauthen]	64	46.40 N	13.00 E
Kot Sultān	123	30.46 N	70.56 E
Kōtsu-zan ∧	96	34.01 N	134.12 E
Kottagūdem	122	17.33 N	80.38 E
Kottas Mountains ⋏	9	74.20 S	12.00 W
Kottayam	122	9.35 N	76.31 E
Kotte → Sri Jayawardenepura	122	6.54 N	79.54 E
Kottingbrunn	61	47.57 N	16.14 E
Kotto ≃	136	4.14 N	22.02 E
Kotton	144	9.35 N	50.28 E
Kottūru	122	14.49 N	76.13 E
Kotuj ≃	74	71.55 N	102.05 E
Kot'užen'	78	47.51 N	28.36 E
Kotwālīpāra	126	22.59 N	89.59 E
Kotzebue	180	66.53 N	162.39 W
Kotzebue Sound ⊔	180	66.20 N	163.00 W
Kötzting	60	49.11 N	12.52 E
Koualé	150	11.24 N	7.01 W
Kou'an	106	32.19 N	119.52 E
Kouandé	150	10.20 N	1.42 E
Kouango	152	4.58 N	19.59 E
Kouassi-Datékro	150	7.49 N	3.31 W
Koubansaki	273b	4.22 S	15.09 E
Koubia	150	11.35 N	11.54 W
Kouchibouguac National Park ♠	186	46.50 N	65.00 W
Koudougou	150	12.15 N	2.22 W
Kouéré	150	10.27 N	3.59 W
Kouffo ≃	150	6.35 N	1.59 E
Kouga	146	9.56 N	21.03 E
Kouga ≃	158	33.37 S	22.14 E
Kougaberge ⋏	158	33.40 S	23.50 E
Kougarok Mountain ∧	180	65.41 N	165.13 W
K'ouhu	100	23.35 N	120.11 E
Kouilou □5	152	4.30 S	12.00 E
Kouilou ≃	152	4.28 S	11.41 E
Koukdjuak ≃	176	66.45 N	73.09 W
Kouki	152	7.10 N	17.18 E
Koúklia	130	34.42 N	32.34 E
Koukourou ≃	152	7.32 N	19.42 E
Koukourou-Bamingui, Réserve de Faune du ◆4	152	7.20 N	20.00 E
Koula ≃	229b	21.54 N	159.36 W
Koulamoutou	152	1.08 S	12.29 E
Koulikoro	150	12.53 N	7.33 W
Koulikoro □4	150	13.00 N	8.00 W
Koulouguidi	150	13.27 N	11.03 W
Koulountou ≃	150	13.15 N	13.37 W
Koumac	175f	20.33 S	164.17 E
Koumac, Grand Récif de ✣2	175f	20.32 S	164.04 E
Koumala	166	21.37 S	149.15 E
Koumaméyong	152	0.11 N	11.51 E
Koumankou	150	12.06 N	6.08 W
Koumbakara	150	12.42 N	14.29 W
Koumbal	146	9.26 N	22.39 E
Koumbala ≃	146	9.14 N	20.42 E
Koumbia, Burkina	150	11.14 N	3.42 W
Koumbia, Guinée	150	11.48 N	13.30 W
Koumbisaleh ⊥	150	15.46 N	7.59 W
Koumbouma	150	10.24 N	12.56 W
Koumi	94	36.05 N	138.29 E
Koumpentoum	150	13.59 N	14.34 W
Koumra	146	8.55 N	17.33 E
Koundara	150	12.29 N	13.18 W
Koundé	152	6.07 N	14.38 E
Koundian ⊥	150	13.10 N	10.41 W
Koundougou	150	11.44 N	4.31 W
Koun-Fao	150	7.29 N	3.15 W
Koungheul	150	13.59 N	14.48 W
Koungoulou	152	3.32 S	13.20 E
Kouniohou	150	7.40 N	0.48 E
Kounradskij	86	46.59 N	75.00 E
Kountze	194	30.22 N	94.18 W
Koupé, Mont ∧	152	4.47 N	9.43 E
Koupéla	150	12.11 N	0.21 W
Kouragué	150	12.18 N	10.02 W
Kourak	86	54.50 N	84.40 E
Kouriles, Détroit des → Pervyj Kuril'skij proliv ⊔	74	50.50 N	156.36 E
Kouri-shima I	174m	26.42 N	128.01 E
Kourou	250	5.09 N	52.39 W
Kouroukoto	150	12.35 N	10.05 W
Kourouma	150	11.37 N	4.48 W
Kourouninkoto	150	13.52 N	9.35 W

Symbols in the index entries represent the broad categories identified in the key at the right. Symbols with superior numbers (⋏1) identify subcategories (see complete key on page *I · 1).*

Symbole im Register stellen die rechts im Schlüssel erklärten Kategorien dar. Symbole mit hochgestellten Ziffern (⋏1) bezeichnen Unterabteilungen einer Kategorie (vgl. vollständiger Schlüssel auf Seite *I · 1).*

Los símbolos incluídos en el texto del índice representan las grandes categorias identificadas con la clave a la derecha. Los símbolos con numeros en su parte superior (⋏1) identifican las subcategorías (véase la clave completa en la página *I · 1).*

Les symboles de l'index représentent les catégories indiquées dans la légende à droite. Les symboles suivis d'un indice (⋏1) représentent des sous-catégories (voir légende complète à la page *I · 1).*

Os símbolos incluídos no texto do índice representam as grandes categorias identificadas com a chave à direita. Os símbolos com números em sua parte superior (⋏1) identificam as subcategorias (veja-se a chave completa à página *I · 1).*

∧ Mountain	Berg	Montaña	Montagne	Montanha
⋏ Mountains	Gebirge	Montañas	Montagnes	Montanhas
)(Pass	Paß	Paso	Col	Passo
V Valley, Canyon	Tal, Cañon	Valle, Cañón	Vallée, Canyon	Vale, Canhão
≚ Plain	Ebene	Llano	Plaine	Planície
> Cape	Kap	Cabo	Cap	Cabo
I Island	Insel	Isla	Île	Ilha
II Islands	Inseln	Islas	Îles	Ilhas
⊥ Other Topographic Features	Andere Topographische Objekte	Otros Elementos Topográficos	Autres données topographiques	Outros acidentes topográficos

ESPAÑOL · FRANÇAIS · PORTUGUÊS

Nombre / Nom / Nome	Página / Page	Lat.°′	Long.°′ W = Oeste / Ouest
Kouroussa	150	10.39 N	9.53 W
Koury	150	12.11 N	4.48 W
Koussanar	150	13.52 N	14.05 W
Koussané, Mali	150	14.53 N	11.14 W
Koussane, Sén.	150	14.08 N	12.26 W
Kousser, Massif de ʌ	148	32.02 N	5.59 W
Koussi, Emi ʌ	146	19.50 N	18.30 E
Koussili	150	13.30 N	11.38 W
Koutia Ba	150	14.11 N	14.28 W
Koutiala	150	12.23 N	5.28 W
Kouto	150	9.53 N	6.25 W
Koutou	98	38.35 N	114.24 E
Koutoumo, Île I	175f	22.40 S	167.33 E
Kouts	216	41.19 N	87.01 W
Kouvola	26	60.52 N	26.42 E
Kouya ≏	150	10.09 N	9.45 W
Kouyou ≏	152	0.45 S	16.38 E
Kova	88	58.18 N	100.21 E
Kova ≏	88	58.18 N	100.18 E
Kovada Milli Parkı ♠	130	37.32 N	30.53 E
Kovaksa	80	55.31 N	43.30 E
Koval'ovka	78	47.16 N	31.43 E
Kovarskas	76	55.26 N	24.55 E
Kovarzino	76	60.09 N	38.33 E
Kovdor	24	67.34 N	30.22 E
Kovdozero, ozero ⊜	24	66.47 N	32.00 E
Kovel'	78	51.14 N	24.41 E
Kovernino	80	57.07 N	43.49 E
Kovilpatti	122	9.10 N	77.52 E
Kovin	38	44.45 N	20.59 E
Kovno → Kaunas	76	54.54 N	23.54 E
Kovpyta	78	51.23 N	30.50 E
Kovrina Vtoraja	80	47.01 N	41.44 E
Kovrov	80	56.22 N	41.18 E
Kovševata	78	49.29 N	30.38 E
Kovsug ≏	83	48.48 N	39.17 E
Kovūr	122	14.29 N	79.59 E
Kovvur	122	17.01 N	81.44 E
Kovylkin	80	48.16 N	41.28 E
Kovylkino	80	54.02 N	43.56 E
Kovža	24	61.09 N	38.58 E
Kovžinskij Zavod	76	60.24 N	37.04 E
Kowal	30	52.32 N	19.09 E
Kowalewo Pomorskie	30	53.10 N	18.53 E
Kowangge	115b	8.16 S	118.32 E
Kowanyama	164	15.28 S	141.44 E
Kowanyama Aboriginal Reserve ◆ [4]	164	15.15 S	141.45 E
Kowār	126	24.13 N	86.11 E
Koweït → Kuwait □ [1]	128	29.30 N	47.45 E
Kowel → Kovel'	78	51.14 N	24.41 E
Kowghān ≏	128	34.15 N	62.57 E
Kowhitirangi	172	42.52 S	171.01 E
Kowie → Port Alfred	158	33.36 S	26.55 E
Kowkcheh ≏	120	37.10 N	69.23 E
Kowloon City	271d	22.19 N	114.11 E
Kowloon Peak ʌ	271d	22.21 N	114.13 E
Kowmung ≏	170	33.52 S	150.16 E
Kowŏn	98	39.26 N	127.14 E
Kowt-e 'Ashrow	120	34.27 N	68.48 E
Koxtag	120	37.23 N	78.05 E
Kōya	96	34.12 N	135.35 E
Koyadaira	96	33.56 N	134.13 E
Kōyaguchi	96	34.18 N	135.33 E
Koyama ◆ [8]	268	35.37 N	139.43 E
Koyama-ike ⊜	96	35.30 N	134.09 E
Kōyama-misaki ›	96	34.40 N	131.36 E
Koyambattur → Coimbatore	122	11.00 N	76.58 E
Koyang-ni	98	37.42 N	126.56 E
Kōya-Ryūjin-kokutei-kōen ♠	96	34.10 N	135.35 E
Köyceğiz	130	36.57 N	28.41 E
Köyceğiz Gölü ⊜	130	36.55 N	28.40 E
Koyna Reservoir ⊜ [1]	122	17.25 N	73.45 E
Koyra ≏ [1]	126	22.27 N	89.16 E
Koyuk	180	64.56 N	161.08 W
Koyuk ≏	180	64.55 N	161.12 W
Koyukuk	180	64.53 N	157.43 W
Koyukuk ≏	180	64.56 N	157.30 W
Koyukuk, Middle Fork ≏	180	67.03 N	151.04 W
Koyukuk, North Fork ≏	180	67.03 N	151.04 W
Koyukuk, South Fork ≏	180	66.35 N	151.57 W
Koyulhisar	130	40.18 N	37.51 E
Koža	80	57.47 N	48.57 E
Kozakai	94	34.48 N	137.22 E
Kōzaki	94	35.54 N	140.24 E
Kō-zaki ›	92	34.05 N	129.13 E
Kozaklı	130	39.14 N	34.49 E
Kōzan, Nihon	96	34.35 N	133.03 E
Kozan, Tür.	130	37.27 N	35.49 E
Kozáni	38	40.18 N	21.47 E
Kožanka	78	49.58 N	29.46 E
Koz'any, Bela.	76	55.18 N	26.52 E
Kožany, Ross.	76	52.48 N	31.44 E
Kozara ⋏	36	45.00 N	16.50 E
Kozarac	36	44.58 N	16.51 E
Kozdinga	24	63.43 N	47.32 E
Kozelec	78	50.55 N	31.08 E
Kozel'ščina	78	49.13 N	33.51 E
Kozel'sk	82	54.02 N	35.48 E
Koževnikovo	86	56.16 N	84.00 E
Kozhikode → Calicut	122	11.15 N	75.46 E
Koziegłowy	30	50.36 N	19.09 E
Kozienice	30	51.35 N	21.33 E
Kožim	24	65.48 N	59.28 E
Kozin	78	50.14 N	30.39 E
Kozino	265b	55.54 N	37.11 E
Kozjak (Possruck) ⋏	61	46.37 N	15.28 E
Kozlov	78	49.33 N	25.20 E
Kozlov Bereg	76	58.57 N	27.44 E
Kozlovka, Ross.	78	51.39 N	41.16 E
Kozlovka, Ross.	78	50.52 N	40.27 E
Kozlovka, Ross.	80	55.52 N	48.14 E
Kozlovka, Ross.	80	52.33 N	45.41 E
Kozlovo, Ross.	76	57.34 N	35.29 E
Kozlovo, Ross.	82	56.31 N	36.16 E
Kozlovščina	76	53.19 N	25.18 E
Kozlu, Tür.	130	41.26 N	31.46 E
Kozlu, Tür.	130	40.37 N	36.30 E
Kozluk	130	38.11 N	41.29 E
Koźmin	30	51.50 N	17.28 E
Koz'mino	24	61.56 N	48.19 E
Koz'modemjansk	80	56.20 N	46.36 E
Koz'mogorodskoje	24	65.32 N	44.55 E
Kozova	78	49.26 N	25.09 E
Kožpos'olok	24	63.10 N	38.06 E
Kožuchovo	265b	55.43 N	37.54 E
Kożuchów	30	51.45 N	15.35 E
Kozuka	268	35.09 N	139.57 E
Kōzuki	96	34.59 N	134.20 E
Kozukue ◆ [8]	268	35.30 N	139.36 E
Kozul'ka	86	56.10 N	91.24 E
Kožurla	86	55.21 N	79.02 E
Kōzu-shima I	92	34.13 N	139.10 E
Kozuya	270	34.52 N	135.45 E
Kpandae	150	8.28 N	0.01 W
Kpandu	150	7.00 N	0.18 E
Kpong	150	6.09 N	0.04 E
Kpo Range ⋏	150	7.15 N	10.15 W
Kra, Isthmus of ⊥ [3]	110	10.20 N	99.00 E
Kraai ≏	158	30.40 S	26.45 E
Kraaifontein	158	33.50 S	18.43 E
Kraal	158	26.34 S	28.26 E
Kraankuil	158	29.52 S	24.10 E
Krabbendijke	52	51.26 N	4.07 E
Krabi	110	8.04 N	98.55 E
Krâchéh	110	12.29 N	106.01 E
Krackow	54	53.20 N	14.16 E
Kraftsdorf	54	50.52 N	11.55 E
Kragan	115a	6.42 S	111.37 E
Kragenæs	41	54.55 N	11.22 E
Kragerø	26	58.52 N	9.25 E
Kraghave	41	54.48 N	11.53 E
Kragujevac	38	44.01 N	20.55 E
Krahenhöhe ◆ [8]	263	51.10 N	7.06 E
Kraiburg	60	48.10 N	12.26 E
Kraichgau □ [9]	56	49.10 N	8.50 E
Krainburg → Kranj	36	46.15 N	14.21 E
Krainka	82	54.07 N	36.21 E
Krai-Russkije	80	57.23 N	46.50 E
Krajčikovo	86	56.16 N	73.20 E
Krajenka	30	53.19 N	17.00 E
Krajeva	89	44.54 N	131.08 E
Krajneje	80	47.29 N	46.01 E
Krajnik Dolny	54	53.05 N	14.25 E
Krajnovka	84	43.57 N	47.24 E
Krakatau ʌ [1]	115a	6.07 S	105.24 E
Krakatoa → Krakatau ʌ [1]	115a	6.07 S	105.24 E
Krakau → Kraków	30	50.03 N	19.58 E
Krâkôr	110	12.32 N	104.12 E
Krakovec	78	49.57 N	23.07 E
Krakovo	80	53.36 N	50.51 E
Krakow, Dtsch.	54	53.39 N	12.16 E
Kraków, Pol.	30	50.03 N	19.58 E
Kraków □ [4]	30	49.50 N	20.00 E
Krakower See ⊜	54	53.37 N	12.17 E
Kraksaan	115a	7.46 S	113.25 E
Kraksdorf	54	54.18 N	11.04 E
Kralendijk	241s	12.10 N	68.17 W
Kralice	61	49.11 N	16.12 E
Kraljevica	36	45.16 N	14.34 E
Kraljevo	38	43.43 N	20.41 E
Kralovice	60	49.59 N	13.29 E
Královské Vinohrady ◆ [8]	54	50.01 N	14.29 E
Kralupy nad Vltavou	54	50.11 N	14.18 E
Kralupy u Chomutova	54	50.25 N	13.20 E
Králův Dvůr	60	49.56 N	14.02 E
Kramatorsk	83	48.43 N	37.32 E
Kramer	216	40.20 N	87.17 W
Kramfors	26	62.56 N	17.47 E
Krammer ɰ [1]	52	51.38 N	4.15 E
Krampen	61	47.40 N	15.32 E
Krampnitz	264a	52.28 N	13.04 E
Krampnitzsee ⊜	264a	52.27 N	13.03 E
Kramsach	64	47.27 N	11.52 E
Kranebitten, Flughafen ⊠	64	47.16 N	11.20 E
Kranenburg	52	51.47 N	6.03 E
Krångede	26	63.09 N	16.05 E
Kranichfeld	54	50.51 N	11.12 E
Kranídhion	38	37.22 N	23.10 E
Kranj	36	46.15 N	14.21 E
Kranji, Sing.	271c	1.26 N	103.46 E
Kranji, Sing.	271c	1.26 N	103.45 E
Kranji ≏	271c	1.26 N	103.45 E
Kranji Reservoir ⊜ [1]	271c	1.26 N	103.45 E
Kranji War Memorial ⊥	271c	1.26 N	103.45 E
Kranjska Gora	64	46.29 N	13.47 E
Kransaja Pol'ana	84	43.41 N	40.13 E
Kranskop	158	29.00 S	30.47 E
Kranskop ʌ	158	27.43 S	29.41 E
Kranzberg	156	21.55 S	15.43 E
Krapina	36	46.10 N	15.52 E
Krapivinskij	86	55.00 N	86.49 E
Krapivna	76	53.38 N	35.31 E
Krapkowice	30	50.29 N	17.56 E
Krapperup	41	56.16 N	12.31 E
Krapuh	114	3.39 N	98.10 E
Kras ⋏ [1]	64	45.48 N	14.00 E
Krasavino	24	60.58 N	46.26 E
Krasavka	80	51.11 N	43.24 E
Krasieo ≏	110	14.49 N	100.05 E
Krasilov	78	49.39 N	26.59 E
Krasino	72	70.45 N	54.27 E
Krasivaja Meča ≏	76	52.55 N	39.03 E
Krasivka	80	52.16 N	42.31 E
Krasivoje	86	51.54 N	66.46 E
Kraskino	89	42.44 N	130.48 E
Kraskovo	265b	55.39 N	37.59 E
Krāslava	76	55.54 N	27.10 E
Kraslice	54	50.18 N	12.31 E
Krasnaja ≏	83	49.01 N	38.15 E
Krasnaja Gora, Ross.	76	53.01 N	31.37 E
Krasnaja Gora, Ross.	76	60.16 N	35.42 E
Krasnaja Gorbatka	80	55.52 N	41.46 E
Krasnaja Gorka	80	56.12 N	43.04 E
Krasnaja Jaranga	180	65.40 N	172.50 W
Krasnaja Jaruga	78	50.48 N	35.39 E
Krasnaja Pachra	82	55.27 N	37.17 E
Krasnaja Pol'ana, Ross.	80	56.15 N	51.09 E
Krasnaja Pol'ana, Ross.	80	46.06 N	41.30 E
Krasnaja Pol'ana, Ross.	80	52.13 N	53.38 E
Krasnaja Pol'ana, Ukr.	78	47.33 N	37.05 E
Krasnaja Popovka	83	49.08 N	38.09 E
Krasnaja Sloboda, Azer.	84	41.24 N	48.31 E
Krasnaja Sloboda, Bela.	76	52.51 N	27.10 E
Krasnaja Talovka	83	48.51 N	39.51 E
Krasnaja Vol'a	76	52.23 N	27.04 E
Krasnaja Zar'a	76	52.47 N	37.41 E
Krásná Lípa	54	50.54 N	14.31 E
Krasn'anka	80	51.04 N	47.56 E
Krasneno	180	64.38 N	174.48 E
Kraśnik	30	50.56 N	22.13 E
Krasnoarmejsk, Kaz.	86	53.50 N	69.42 E
Krasnoarmejsk, Ross.	80	51.02 N	45.42 E
Krasnoarmejsk, Ross.	82	56.08 N	38.08 E
Krasnoarmejsk, Ukr.	83	48.17 N	37.11 E
Krasnoarmejskaja	78	45.23 N	38.12 E
Krasnoarmejskij, Ross.	74	69.35 N	172.00 E
Krasnoarmejskij, Ross.	80	47.01 N	42.12 E
Krasnoarmejskoje, Ross.	80	55.46 N	47.11 E
Krasnoarmejskoje, Ross.	80	52.44 N	50.02 E
Krasnoarmejskoje, Ukr.	83	47.14 N	37.56 E
Krasnoborsk, Ross.	24	61.34 N	45.53 E
Krasnoborsk, Ross.	80	53.46 N	48.04 E
Krasnobród	30	50.33 N	23.13 E
Krasnobrodskij	86	54.10 N	86.28 E
Krasnodar	78	45.02 N	39.00 E
Krasnodar Kraj □ [8]	78	45.30 N	39.00 E
Krasnodarskij	83	48.15 N	39.51 E
Krasnodarskoje vodochranilišče ⊜ [1]	78	45.06 N	39.31 E
Krasnodon	83	48.17 N	39.48 E
Krasnofarfornyj	76	59.08 N	31.51 E
Krasnoflotskoje	80	50.04 N	41.14 E
Krasnogorka	85	43.15 N	75.10 E
Krasnogorodskoje	76	56.50 N	28.17 E
Krasnogorovka	83	48.00 N	37.31 E
Krasnogorsk, Ross.	82	55.50 N	37.20 E
Krasnogorsk, Ross.	89	48.24 N	142.06 E
Krasnogorskij, Ross.	80	56.09 N	48.20 E
Krasnogorskij, Ross.	86	54.36 N	61.15 E
Krasnogorskij, Uzb.	85	41.09 N	69.39 E
Krasnogorskoje, Ross.	80	57.42 N	52.30 E
Krasnogorskoje, Ross.	86	52.18 N	86.12 E
Krasnogovardejskij	86	57.22 N	62.20 E
Krasnograd	78	49.22 N	35.27 E
Krasnogvardejsk	85	39.46 N	67.16 E
Krasnogvardejskij	82	54.04 N	37.46 E
Krasnogvardejskoje, Kaz.	86	51.24 N	69.18 E
Krasnogvardejskoje, Ross.	78	50.39 N	38.24 E
Krasnogvardejskoje, Ross.	80	45.51 N	41.31 E
Krasnogvardejskoje, Ukr.	78	45.29 N	34.17 E
Krasnoil'sk	78	48.01 N	25.34 E
Krasnojar	80	48.54 N	51.46 E
Krasnojarka, Ross.	86	55.20 N	73.04 E
Krasnojarka, Ross.	86	59.26 N	60.30 E
Krasnoj Armii, proliv ɰ	74	80.00 N	94.35 E
Krasnojarovo	89	51.27 N	128.28 E
Krasnojarsk	86	56.01 N	92.50 E
Krasnojarskij	86	51.58 N	59.55 E
Krasnojarsk Kraj □ [8]	86	56.00 N	92.22 E
Krasnojarskoje vodochranilišče ⊜ [1]	86	55.00 N	92.00 E
Krasnoje, Bela.	76	54.14 N	27.05 E
Krasnoje, Mol.	78	46.38 N	29.50 E
Krasnoje, Ross.	24	59.12 N	47.49 E
Krasnoje, Ross.	76	53.06 N	33.55 E
Krasnoje, Ross.	76	52.51 N	38.47 E
Krasnoje, Ross.	78	50.21 N	38.50 E
Krasnoje, Ross.	78	46.44 N	39.34 E
Krasnoje, Ross.	78	50.56 N	38.41 E
Krasnoje, Ross.	82	54.26 N	38.38 E
Krasnoje, Ross.	86	54.37 N	85.23 E
Krasnoje, Ukr.	83	48.23 N	39.31 E
Krasnoje, Ukr.	83	48.25 N	37.19 E
Krasnoje, ozero ⊜	74	64.30 N	174.24 E
Krasnoje Echo	80	55.48 N	40.42 E
Krasnoje Gorodišče	82	54.04 N	38.44 E
Krasnoje-na-Volge	80	57.31 N	41.14 E
Krasnoje Selo, Ross.	80	48.02 N	45.13 E
Krasnoje Selo, Ross.	80	48.46 N	42.20 E
Krasnoje Selo, Ross.	265a	59.44 N	30.05 E
Krasnoje Znam'a, Ross.	76	57.26 N	35.13 E
Krasnoje Znam'a, Turk.	128	36.58 N	62.30 E
Krasnokamsk	86	58.04 N	55.48 E
Krasnokutsk, Kaz.	86	53.01 N	75.59 E
Krasnokutsk, Ukr.	78	50.06 N	35.09 E
Krasnolesje	76	54.24 N	22.23 E
Krasnolesnyj	78	51.53 N	39.35 E
Krasnoluki	76	54.37 N	28.50 E
Krasnomajskij	76	57.37 N	34.22 E
Krasnookt'abr'skij, Kyrg.	85	42.50 N	74.18 E
Krasnookt'abr'skij, Ross.	80	56.40 N	47.45 E
Krasnookt'abr'skij, Ross.	80	48.53 N	44.45 E
Krasnooskol'skoje vodochranilišče ⊜ [1]	83	49.17 N	37.37 E
Krasnoostrovskij	76	60.18 N	28.40 E
Krasnopavlovka	78	49.08 N	36.19 E
Krasnoperekopsk	78	45.57 N	33.47 E
Krasnopolje, Bela.	76	53.20 N	31.24 E
Krasnopolje, Ukr.	78	50.46 N	35.16 E
Krasnorečenskij	89	44.41 N	135.14 E
Krasnoščelje	24	67.21 N	37.02 E
Krasnoščokovo	86	51.40 N	82.45 E
Krasnosel'kup	74	65.41 N	82.28 E
Krasnosel'skoje	78	45.25 N	32.42 E
Krasnosielc	30	53.03 N	21.10 E
Krasnoslobodsk, Ross.	80	54.26 N	43.48 E
Krasnoslobodsk, Ross.	80	48.42 N	44.34 E
Krasnotorka	83	48.41 N	37.31 E
Krasnoturansk	86	54.16 N	91.29 E
Krasnoturjinsk	86	59.46 N	60.12 E
Krasnoufimsk	86	56.37 N	57.46 E
Krasnoural'sk	86	58.21 N	60.03 E
Krasnousol'skij	86	53.54 N	56.27 E
Krasnovidovo	80	55.21 N	49.04 E
Krasnovišersk	24	60.23 N	56.59 E
Krasnovka, Ross.	83	48.47 N	40.07 E
Krasnovka, Ukr.	83	47.24 N	37.26 E
Krasnovodsk	128	40.00 N	53.00 E
Krasnovodskij poluostrov › [1]	128	40.30 N	53.15 E
Krasnovodskij zaliv ⊂	128	39.55 N	53.15 E
Krasnoyarsk → Krasnojarsk	86	56.01 N	92.50 E
Krasnozatonskij	24	61.41 N	50.58 E
Krasnozavodsk	82	56.27 N	38.13 E
Krasnoznamensk	76	54.57 N	22.30 E
Krasnoznamenskij	86	51.03 N	69.30 E
Krasnoz'orskoje	86	53.59 N	79.14 E
Krásný Dvůr	54	50.10 N	13.24 E
Krasnyj, Ross.	76	54.34 N	31.26 E
Krasnyj, Ross.	92a	46.15 N	141.15 E
Krasnyj Aul	86	51.03 N	81.02 E
Krasnyj Bazar	84	39.41 N	46.58 E
Krasnyj Bogatyr'	80	56.02 N	41.08 E
Krasnyj Bor, Ross.	80	55.17 N	43.59 E
Krasnyj Bor, Ross.	80	55.53 N	53.06 E
Krasnyj Bor, Ross.	265a	59.41 N	30.41 E
Krasnyj Cholm, Ross.	76	58.03 N	37.07 E
Krasnyj Cholm, Ross.	80	54.11 N	40.42 E
Krasnyj Cholm, Ross.	86	51.35 N	54.09 E
Krasnyj Čuduk	80	46.18 N	46.56 E
Krasnyj Čikoj	88	50.22 N	108.15 E
Krasnyje Baki	80	57.08 N	45.10 E
Krasnyje Barrikady	80	46.14 N	47.53 E
Krasnyje Četai	80	55.42 N	46.09 E
Krasnyje Gory	76	58.57 N	29.29 E
Krasnyje Okny	78	47.32 N	29.27 E
Krasnyje Partizany	78	50.57 N	31.47 E
Krasnyje Tkači	80	57.30 N	39.45 E
Krasnyj Gorodok	76	57.11 N	33.44 E
Krasnyj Gul'aj	80	54.01 N	48.22 E
Krasnyj Jar, Kaz.	86	53.20 N	69.14 E
Krasnyj Jar, Ross.	80	46.33 N	48.21 E
Krasnyj Jar, Ross.	80	53.30 N	50.22 E
Krasnyj Jar, Ross.	80	51.38 N	46.25 E
Krasnyj Jar, Ross.	80	50.37 N	45.47 E
Krasnyj Jar, Ross.	80	50.42 N	44.46 E
Krasnyj Jar, Ross.	86	55.54 N	86.57 E
Krasnyj Jar, Ross.	86	55.14 N	72.56 E
Krasnyj Jar, Ross.	86	57.07 N	84.33 E
Krasnyj Kl'ič	86	55.26 N	56.12 E
Krasnyj Kut, Ross.	80	50.57 N	46.58 E
Krasnyj Kut, Ukr.	83	48.12 N	38.48 E
Krasnyj Liman, Ross.	78	51.32 N	39.50 E
Krasnyj Liman, Ukr.	83	48.59 N	37.49 E
Krasnyj Log	78	51.23 N	39.46 E
Krasnyj Luč, Ross.	76	57.04 N	30.05 E
Krasnyj Luč, Ukr.	83	48.08 N	38.56 E
Krasnyj Majak	80	56.03 N	41.23 E
Krasnyj Manyč, Ross.	80	46.33 N	42.10 E
Krasnyj Manyč, Ross.	80	45.31 N	44.42 E
Krasnyj Manyč, Ross.	80	46.59 N	41.07 E
Krasnyj Meliorator	80	50.02 N	46.06 E
Krasnyj Okt'abr', Kaz.	86	46.50 N	75.59 E
Krasnyj Okt'abr', Ross.	80	51.33 N	45.42 E
Krasnyj Okt'abr', Ross.	80	56.06 N	41.23 E
Krasnyj Okt'abr', Ross.	82	55.37 N	36.30 E
Krasnyj Okt'abr', Ross.	82	56.07 N	38.53 E
Krasnyj Okt'abr', Ross.	86	55.37 N	64.48 E
Krasnyj Okt'abr', Ukr.	83	48.15 N	38.12 E
Krasnyj Okt'abr', Ukr.	83	48.56 N	39.23 E
Krasnyj Oskol	83	49.11 N	37.26 E
Krasnyj Partizan	80	46.20 N	43.10 E
Krasnyj Perekop	78	46.41 N	33.46 E
Krasnyj Profintern	80	57.45 N	40.27 E
Krasnyj Rog	76	52.57 N	33.45 E
Krasnyj Steklovar	80	56.13 N	48.47 E
Krasnyj Stroitel' ◆ [8]	265b	55.35 N	37.37 E
Krasnyj Sulin	83	47.54 N	40.03 E
Krasnyj Tekstil'ščik	80	51.23 N	45.50 E
Krasnyj Tkač	82	55.28 N	39.05 E
Krasnystaw	30	50.59 N	23.10 E
Krasnyy Luch → Krasnyj Luč	83	48.08 N	38.56 E
Krasucha	76	57.23 N	33.12 E
Kras'ukovskaja	83	47.31 N	40.06 E
Kraszna (Crasna) ≏	38	48.09 N	22.20 E
Kratovo	38	42.05 N	22.11 E
Krauchenwies	58	48.01 N	9.14 E
Kraul Mountains ⋏	9	73.10 S	14.10 W
Krauschwitz	54	51.31 N	14.41 E
Kräuterin ⋏	61	47.41 N	15.05 E
Krautheim	56	49.23 N	9.38 E
Kravaře, Česko.	30	49.56 N	18.01 E
Kravaře, Česko.	54	50.38 N	14.23 E
Kray ◆ [8]	263	51.28 N	7.05 E
Kražiai	76	55.36 N	22.40 E
Krbava ◆ [1]	36	44.40 N	15.35 E
Kreamer Island I	220	26.46 N	80.44 W
Kreba	54	51.20 N	14.40 E
Krebs	196	34.55 N	95.42 W
Krečetovo	24	60.56 N	38.30 E
Krečevicy	76	58.37 N	31.21 E
Krefeld	56	51.20 N	6.34 E
Kregme	41	55.57 N	12.04 E
Kreiensen	52	51.51 N	9.58 E
Kreischa	54	50.56 N	13.45 E
Kremastón, Tekhnití Límni ⊜ [1]	38	38.55 N	21.30 E
Kremenčug	78	49.04 N	33.25 E
Kremenčugskoje vodochranilišče ⊜ [1]	78	49.20 N	32.30 E
Kremenec	78	50.07 N	25.45 E
Kremennaja	83	49.03 N	38.14 E
Kremen'ovka	83	47.20 N	37.29 E
Kremenskoj	80	47.49 N	41.08 E
Kremenskoje	82	55.06 N	35.57 E
Kremlin ⊍	265b	55.45 N	37.37 E
Kremmen	54	52.45 N	13.01 E
Kremmling	200	40.03 N	106.23 W
Kremnica	30	48.43 N	18.54 E
Krempe	52	53.50 N	9.29 E
Krems ≏, Öst.	61	48.14 N	14.19 E
Krems ≏, Öst.	61	48.25 N	15.36 E
Krems an der Donau	61	48.25 N	15.36 E
Kremsbrücke	64	46.57 N	13.37 E
Kremsmünster	61	48.03 N	14.08 E
Krenitzin Islands II	180	54.08 N	166.00 W
Krensitz	54	51.29 N	12.27 E
Krepenskij	83	48.06 N	39.03 E
Krepkaja ≏	83	47.35 N	39.23 E
Krepoljin	38	44.16 N	21.37 E
Kreščonka	86	55.52 N	80.06 E
Kresgeville	210	40.54 N	75.30 W
Kress	196	34.22 N	101.45 W
Kressbronn	58	47.35 N	9.36 E
Kressey Lake ⊜	285	39.44 N	75.07 W
Kresta, zaliv ⊂	180	66.00 N	179.15 W
Krestcy, Ross.	76	58.15 N	32.31 E
Krestcy, Ross.	76	58.23 N	39.00 E
Krestjanskij	85	40.32 N	69.02 E
Krestjanskoje	80	45.34 N	42.56 E
Krest-Major	74	67.37 N	144.45 E
Krestovaja Guba	72	74.07 N	55.33 E
Krestovo-Gorodišče	80	54.10 N	48.36 E
Krestovyj, pereval)(	84	42.32 N	44.28 E
Kresty	82	55.16 N	37.06 E
Kreta → Kríti I	38	35.29 N	24.42 E
Kretek	115a	7.59 S	110.19 E
Kretinga	76	55.53 N	21.13 E
Kreuth	64	47.38 N	11.44 E
Kreuzau	56	50.45 N	6.29 E
Kreuzberg	263	51.09 N	7.27 E
Kreuzberg ◆ [8]	264a	52.30 N	13.23 E
Kreuzberg ʌ	56	50.22 N	9.58 E
Kreuzeck-Gruppe ⋏	64	46.51 N	13.06 E
Kreuzen	64	46.40 N	13.35 E
Kreuzlingen	58	47.39 N	9.11 E
Kreuznach → Bad Kreuznach	56	49.52 N	7.51 E
Kreuztal	56	50.58 N	7.59 E
Krevo	76	54.19 N	26.17 E
Kreyenhagen	54	52.55 N	10.52 E
Krian	115a	7.24 S	112.35 E
Kría Vrísi	38	40.41 N	22.18 E
Kribi	152	2.57 N	9.55 E
Kričov	76	53.42 N	31.43 E
Kriebstein, Burg ⊥	54	51.02 N	13.00 E
Krieglach	61	47.33 N	15.34 E
Kriel	158	26.16 S	29.14 E
Kriens	58	47.02 N	8.17 E
Krigujgun, mys ›	180	65.30 N	171.05 W
Kriljon, mys ›	89	45.53 N	142.05 E
Křimice	60	49.46 N	13.15 E
Krim-Krim	146	8.58 N	15.48 E
Krim → Krymskij poluostrov › [1]	78	45.00 N	34.00 E
Krimmler Wasserfälle ⌞	64	47.12 N	12.10 E
Krimnicksee ⊜	264a	52.18 N	13.39 E
Krimpen aan de IJssel	52	51.54 N	4.35 E
Krimskij	80	47.39 N	40.44 E
Krinicčno-Lugskoje	83	47.45 N	39.12 E
Kriničk i	78	48.22 N	34.27 E
Kriničnaja	83	48.08 N	38.02 E
Kriničnoje	78	45.32 N	28.40 E
Krishna ≏	122	15.57 N	80.59 E
Krishna, Mouths of the ≏ [1]	122	15.43 N	80.55 E
Krishnachaadrapur	126	21.50 N	86.49 E
Krishnagiri	122	12.32 N	78.14 E
Krishnamāti	272b	22.40 N	88.32 E
Krishnanagar, India	126	23.24 N	88.30 E
Krishnanagar, India	126	23.13 N	87.33 E
Krishnapur, Bngl.	126	23.30 N	89.56 E
Krishnapur, India	272b	22.36 N	88.26 E
Krishnarāja Sāgara ⊜ [1]	122	12.30 N	76.26 E
Krishnarājpet	122	12.40 N	76.30 E
Krishnarāmpur	126	22.43 N	88.14 E
Kristdala	26	57.24 N	16.11 E
Kristiania → Oslo	26	59.55 N	10.45 E
Kristianopel	26	56.15 N	16.02 E
Kristiansand	26	58.10 N	8.00 E
Kristianstad	26	56.02 N	14.08 E
Kristianstads Län □ [6]	26	56.15 N	14.00 E
Kristiansund	26	63.07 N	7.45 E
Kristiinankaupunki → Kristinestad	26	62.17 N	21.23 E
Kristineberg	26	65.04 N	18.35 E
Kristinehamn	40	59.20 N	14.07 E
Kristinestad (Kristiinankaupunki)	26	62.17 N	21.23 E
Kríti (Crete) I	38	35.29 N	24.42 E
Kritikón Pélagos (Sea of Crete) ᴛ [2]	38	35.46 N	23.54 E
Kritzendorf	264b	48.20 N	16.18 E
Kriul'any	78	47.13 N	29.09 E
Kriuša	82	54.28 N	36.24 E
Kriv'ačka	80	58.40 N	45.27 E
Krivaja ≏	38	44.27 N	18.09 E
Krivaja, kosa › [2]	83	47.02 N	38.06 E
Krivaja Ruda	78	49.31 N	32.59 E
Kriv'anskaja	83	47.24 N	40.10 E
Kriva Palanka	38	42.12 N	22.20 E
Krivcy	82	55.28 N	38.12 E
Kriviči	76	54.43 N	27.17 E
Krivinka	86	51.08 N	78.10 E
Krivodol	38	43.23 N	23.29 E
Krivoj Buzan	80	46.31 N	48.33 E
Krivoje Ozero	78	47.56 N	30.21 E
Krivoj Rog	78	47.55 N	33.21 E
Krivoj Torec ≏	83	48.39 N	37.32 E
Křivoklát	60	50.02 N	13.54 E
Krivonosovo	78	49.55 N	39.16 E
Krivorožje, Ross.	78	48.51 N	40.45 E
Krivorožje, Ukr.	78	48.31 N	38.40 E
Krivorožje, Ukr.	83	48.31 N	38.40 E
Krivošeino	86	57.20 N	83.57 E
Krivošin	76	52.52 N	26.08 E
Krivoy Rog → Krivoj Rog	78	47.55 N	33.21 E
Kriwoi-Rog → Krivoj Rog	78	47.55 N	33.21 E
Križevci	36	46.02 N	16.33 E
Krizskoje	83	49.28 N	39.38 E
Krk, Otok I	36	45.05 N	14.35 E
Krkonošský národní park ♠	30	50.45 N	15.35 E
Krn ʌ	64	46.16 N	13.40 E
Krnov	30	50.05 N	17.41 E
Krobia	30	51.47 N	16.58 E
Krøderen ⊜	26	60.15 N	9.38 E
Krogager	41	55.42 N	8.51 E
Krögis	54	51.07 N	13.22 E
Krokek	40	58.40 N	16.24 E
Kroken	24	65.22 N	14.20 E
Krokodil ≏, S. Afr.	156	24.12 S	26.52 E
Krokodil ≏, S. Afr.	156	25.26 S	31.58 E
Krokom	26	63.19 N	14.30 E
Krokowa	30	54.48 N	18.11 E
Krolevec	78	51.33 N	33.23 E
Kröller-Müller, Rijksmuseum ⊍	52	52.05 N	5.50 E
Krölpa	54	50.41 N	11.32 E
Krom ≏	158	30.53 S	19.01 E
Krombi Pits	156	19.30 S	25.02 E
Kroměříž	30	49.18 N	17.24 E
Krommenie	52	52.29 N	4.45 E
Krompachy	30	48.56 N	20.52 E
Kromy	76	52.43 N	35.46 E
Kronach	54	50.14 N	11.20 E
Kronberg	56	50.10 N	8.30 E
Kronborg ⊥	41	56.02 N	12.38 E
Krone	263	51.27 N	7.20 E
Krong Ana ⊜ [1]	110	12.30 N	108.00 E
Krŏng Kaôh Kŏng	110	11.37 N	102.59 E
Krŏng Kêb	110	10.29 N	104.19 E
Kronobergs Län □ [6]	26	56.40 N	14.40 E
Kronoby (Kruunupyy)	26	63.43 N	23.02 E
Kronockaja Sopka, vulkan ʌ [1]	74	54.44 N	160.31 E
Kronockij zaliv ⊂	74	54.12 N	160.36 E
Kronoki	74	54.36 N	161.10 E
Kronshagen	41	54.20 N	10.05 E
Kronštadt	76	59.59 N	29.45 E
Kronstadt → Brașov	38	45.39 N	25.37 E
Kronwa	110	15.25 N	98.26 E
Kroondal	158	25.45 S	27.19 E
Kroonstad	158	27.46 S	27.12 E
Kröpelin	54	54.04 N	11.48 E
Kropotkin, Ross.	72	45.26 N	40.34 E
Kropotkin, Ross.	88	58.30 N	115.17 E
Kropotkina, gora ʌ	88	53.43 N	117.32 E
Kropp	41	54.24 N	9.31 E
Kroppefjäll ʌ [2]	26	58.40 N	12.13 E
Kroppenstedt	54	51.56 N	11.18 E
Kropstädt	54	51.58 N	12.44 E
Kropufino	76	60.23 N	39.10 E
Krościenko	30	49.27 N	20.26 E
Kröslin	54	54.07 N	13.45 E
Krošn'a	78	50.18 N	28.39 E
Krośniewice	30	52.16 N	19.10 E
Krosno	30	49.42 N	21.46 E
Krosno □ [4]	30	49.30 N	22.00 E
Krosno Odrzańskie	30	52.04 N	15.05 E
Krossen	54	50.58 N	11.59 E
Krostitz	54	51.28 N	12.27 E
Krotoszyn	30	51.42 N	17.26 E
Krotovka	80	53.18 N	51.12 E
Krotovo	86	56.57 N	69.20 E
Krotz Springs	194	30.32 N	91.45 W
Kröv	56	49.59 N	7.05 E
Kroya	115a	7.38 S	109.14 E
Krško	36	45.58 N	15.29 E
Krsy	60	49.54 N	13.03 E
Kr'učkov	80	48.01 N	45.40 E
Kr'učkovo	76	57.03 N	35.34 E
Kruckow	54	53.54 N	13.14 E
Krudenburg	263	51.39 N	6.45 E
Kruenggeukueh	114	5.15 N	97.02 E
Kruengluak	114	2.50 N	97.45 E
Kruft	56	50.23 N	7.20 E
Kruger National Park ♠	156	24.00 S	31.40 E
Krugersdorp	158	26.05 S	27.35 E
Krugersdorp □ [5]	273d	26.05 S	27.35 E
Krugersdorp Race Course ♠	273d	26.08 S	27.45 E
Krugersdorp West	273d	26.06 S	27.45 E
Krugloje, Bela.	76	54.15 N	29.48 E
Krugloje, Ross.	83	47.01 N	39.15 E
Kruglooz'ornoje	86	55.13 N	79.01 E
Kruglooz'ornyj	80	51.06 N	51.17 E
Kruglyži	80	58.31 N	47.42 E
Krugzell	58	47.47 N	10.16 E
Krui	112	5.11 S	103.56 E
Kruidfontein	158	32.51 S	21.57 E
Kruiningen	52	51.27 N	4.02 E
Kruis, Kaap ›	156	21.49 S	13.57 E
Kruisfontein	158	34.00 S	24.43 E
Kruishoutem	50	50.54 N	3.31 E
Kruisland	52	51.34 N	4.24 E
Kruisrivier	158	33.26 S	21.55 E
Kruisvallei	158	33.53 S	23.10 E
Krujë	38	41.30 N	19.48 E
Krukira, Laguna de ⊂	236	13.56 N	83.30 W
Kr'ukov	80	47.24 N	42.28 E
Kr'ukovo, Ross.	74	66.30 N	159.31 E
Kr'ukovo, Ross.	82	55.59 N	37.10 E
Kr'ukovo, Ross.	82	55.28 N	36.32 E
Kr'ukovo, Ross.	83	47.40 N	39.13 E
Krukut, Kali ≏	269e	6.12 S	106.48 E
Krulevščina	76	55.02 N	27.45 E
Krumasye	164	1.40 S	133.09 E
Krumbach, Dtsch.	58	47.58 N	9.02 E
Krumbach, Dtsch.	58	48.14 N	10.22 E
Krumme Lanke ⊜	264a	52.27 N	13.14 E
Krummendammer Heide ◆ [3]	264a	52.28 N	13.39 E
Krummenerl	263	51.05 N	7.45 E
Krummensee	264a	52.36 N	13.42 E
Krumme Steyrling ≏	61	47.54 N	14.14 E
Krummhörn	52	53.26 N	7.06 E
Krummhörn ◆ [1]	52	53.25 N	7.10 E
Krumovgrad	38	41.28 N	25.39 E
Krumroy	214	39.58 N	81.24 W
Krün	64	47.30 N	11.16 E
Krung Thep (Bangkok), Thai	110	13.45 N	100.31 E
Krung Thep (Bangkok), Thai	269a	13.45 N	100.31 E
Krung Thep Mahanakhon □ [4]	269a	13.47 N	100.43 E
Krung Thon Bridge ◆ [5]	269a	13.47 N	100.30 E
Krupá	54	50.08 N	13.41 E
Krupec	78	51.38 N	34.21 E
Krüpel-See ⊜	264a	52.18 N	13.42 E
Krupka	54	50.43 N	13.46 E
Krupki	76	54.19 N	29.08 E
Kruså	41	54.50 N	9.25 E
Kruščica jezero ⊜ [1]	36	44.39 N	15.19 E
Krusenstern, Cape ›	180	67.07 N	163.43 W
Kruševac	38	43.35 N	21.20 E
Kruševo	38	41.22 N	21.14 E
Krušinovka	76	53.14 N	29.50 E
Krušné hory (Erzgebirge) ⋏	54	50.30 N	13.15 E
Kruszwica	30	52.41 N	18.19 E
Krutaja, Ross.	24	63.02 N	54.38 E
Krutaja, Ross.	86	57.24 N	76.27 E
Krutaja Gorka	86	55.25 N	73.15 E
Krutcy	76	57.10 N	29.23 E
Krutec, Ross.	76	60.17 N	39.25 E
Krutec, Ross.	82	56.10 N	38.33 E
Kruticha, Ross.	86	53.58 N	81.14 E
Kruticha, Ross.	86	56.49 N	77.10 E
Krutinka	86	56.01 N	71.31 E
Krutoje	76	52.26 N	37.28 E
Krutoj Log	86	57.53 N	58.14 E
Krutoj Majdan	80	55.35 N	44.04 E
Krutyje Verchi	82	54.19 N	36.26 E
Kruunupyy → Kronoby	26	63.43 N	23.02 E
Kruzenšterna, proliv ɰ	74	48.30 N	153.50 E
Kruzof Island I	180	57.10 N	135.40 W
Krydor	184	52.47 N	107.03 W
Krylatskoje ◆ [8]	265b	55.45 N	37.26 E
Krylbo	40	60.08 N	16.13 E
Krylovskaja	78	46.07 N	39.19 E
Krym	83	47.19 N	39.31 E
Krym, Respublika □ [3]	78	45.00 N	34.00 E
Krymsk	78	44.56 N	37.59 E
Krymskij	78	47.40 N	40.46 E
Krymskije gory ⋏	78	44.45 N	34.25 E
Krymskij poluostrov (Crimea) › [1]	78	45.00 N	34.00 E
Krymskij Zapovednik ◆ [4]	78	44.42 N	34.12 E
Krymskoje	83	48.45 N	38.48 E
Krynica	30	49.25 N	20.56 E
Krynka ≏	83	47.36 N	38.47 E
Kryžina, chrebet ⋏	88	54.00 N	95.00 E
Kryžopol'	78	48.23 N	28.52 E
Krzepice	30	50.58 N	18.44 E
Krzeszowice	30	50.09 N	19.39 E
Krzeszyce	54	52.36 N	15.01 E
Krzna ≏	30	52.08 N	23.31 E
Krzywiń	30	51.58 N	16.49 E
Krzyż	30	52.54 N	16.01 E
Ksar Chellala	148	35.13 N	2.18 E
Ksar el Barka	150	18.24 N	12.13 W
Ksar-el-Kebir	148	35.01 N	5.54 W
Ksar-el-Seghir	34	35.50 N	5.32 W
Ksar Hellal	36	35.39 N	10.54 E
Ksaverovka	78	50.03 N	30.12 E
Ksel, Djebel ʌ	148	33.44 N	1.10 E
Kšen' ≏	76	52.23 N	37.44 E
Ksenjevka	88	53.34 N	118.44 E
Ksenofontova	24	60.58 N	56.12 E
Kšenskij	78	51.52 N	37.43 E
Książ Wielkopolski	30	52.05 N	17.14 E
Ksob, Oued ≏	36	35.49 N	7.53 E
Ksour, Monts des ⋏	148	32.45 N	0.30 W
Ksour Essaf	148	35.25 N	11.00 E
Kstovo	80	56.11 N	44.11 E
Kū', Wādī al- V	140	13.37 N	25.15 E
Kuah	114	6.19 N	99.51 E
Kuai ≏	100	33.09 N	117.32 E
Kuala, Indon.	112	2.55 N	105.48 E
Kuala, Indon.	114	3.32 N	98.24 E
Kualabee	114	4.24 N	96.03 E
Kuala Berang	114	5.04 N	103.01 E
Kualacenako	112	0.28 S	102.40 E
Kuala Kangsar	114	4.46 N	100.56 E
Kualakapuas	112	3.01 S	114.21 E
Kuala Kedah	114	6.06 N	100.18 E
Kuala Kelawang	114	2.56 N	102.05 E
Kuala Kerai	114	5.32 N	102.12 E
Kuala Kerau	114	3.43 N	102.22 E
Kualakeriau	112	0.50 N	113.20 E
Kuala Ketil	114	5.36 N	100.39 E
Kuala Kubu Baharu	114	3.34 N	101.39 E
Kuala Kurau	114	5.01 N	100.26 E
Kualakurun	112	1.07 S	113.53 E
Kualalangsa	114	4.32 N	98.01 E
Kuala Lipis	114	4.11 N	102.03 E
Kuala Lumpur	114	3.10 N	101.42 E
Kuala Lumpur □ [3]	114	3.10 N	101.42 E
Kualamanjual	112	1.25 S	112.00 E
Kuala Nerang	114	6.15 N	100.36 E
Kualapesaguan	112	2.01 S	110.08 E
Kuala Pilah	114	2.44 N	102.15 E
Kualapuu	229a	21.09 N	157.02 W
Kuala Selangor	114	3.21 N	101.15 E
Kualasimpang	114	4.17 N	98.03 E
Kuala Terengganu	114	5.20 N	103.08 E
Kualu ≏	114	2.45 N	100.00 E
Kuamut	112	5.13 N	117.30 E
Kuamut ≏	112	5.13 N	117.32 E
Kuanbang	98	40.29 N	120.04 E
Kuancheng, Zhg.	98	40.37 N	118.31 E
Kuancheng, Zhg.	105	40.38 N	118.27 E
Kuandang	112	0.52 N	122.55 E
Kuandian	98	40.43 N	124.44 E
Kuando → Cuando ≏	152	18.27 S	23.32 E
Kuanhsi	100	24.48 N	121.10 E
Kuanmiao	100	22.58 N	120.19 E
Kuanshan	100	23.03 N	121.09 E
Kuan Shan ʌ	100	23.14 N	120.54 E
Kuantan	114	3.48 N	103.20 E
Kuantan ≏	114	3.50 N	103.17 E
Kuanyin	100	25.02 N	121.04 E
Kuanyün → Guanyun	98	34.20 N	119.17 E
Kuanza → Cuanza ≏	152	9.19 S	13.08 E
Kuba	84	41.22 N	48.31 E
Kuba → Cuba □ [1]	240p	21.30 N	80.00 W
Kuban' ≏	72	45.20 N	37.30 E
Kubatly	84	39.22 N	46.34 E
Kubbī	140	11.08 N	25.14 E
Kubbum	140	11.47 N	23.47 E
Kubena ≏	76	59.36 N	39.39 E
Kubenskoje	76	59.26 N	39.40 E
Kubenskoje, ozero ⊜	76	59.40 N	39.25 E
Kubiki	94	37.11 N	138.20 E
Kubinka	82	55.35 N	36.43 E
Kubitzer Bodden ⊂	54	54.24 N	13.12 E
Küblis	58	46.55 N	9.47 E
Kubn'a ≏	80	55.31 N	48.27 E
Kubokawa	96	33.12 N	133.08 E
Kubor, Mount ʌ	164	6.05 S	144.45 E
Kubr' ≏	82	56.52 N	38.17 E
Kubrat	38	43.48 N	26.30 E
Kubu	115b	8.16 S	115.35 E
Kubuchaj	88	50.30 N	114.48 E
Kubu Gajah	114	5.10 N	100.41 E
Kubumesaai	112	1.31 N	115.06 E
Kubutambahan	115b	8.05 S	115.10 E
Kučema	24	65.37 N	42.28 E
Kučen'ajevo	80	54.44 N	46.24 E
Kučevo	38	44.27 N	21.44 E
Kuchaiburi	126	22.16 N	86.10 E
Kuchāman	120	27.09 N	74.52 E
Kuch'ang-ni	98	40.09 N	124.46 E
Kuchelebai	154	1.29 N	35.01 E
Kuchen Spitze ʌ	58	47.03 N	10.14 E
Kuchinarai	110	16.32 N	104.04 E
Kuching	112	1.33 N	110.20 E
Kuchinoerabu-jima I	93b	30.28 N	130.12 E
Kuchino-shima I	93b	29.57 N	129.57 E
Kuchiwa	96	34.53 N	132.55 E
Kuchl	64	47.37 N	13.09 E
Kūchnay Darweyshān	128	30.59 N	64.11 E
Kuchterin Lug	89	52.25 N	128.05 E
Kuchtinka	82	54.29 N	38.10 E
Kučino	265b	55.45 N	37.58 E
Kučkak	85	40.15 N	70.20 E
Kučki	80	53.01 N	44.29 E
Kuçovë	38	40.48 N	19.54 E
Küçük Ağrı Dağı ʌ	84	39.40 N	44.25 E
Küçükbahçe	130	38.33 N	26.24 E
Küçükbakkal ◆ [8]	267b	40.58 N	29.06 E
Küçükçekmece ◆ [8]	267b	40.59 N	28.46 E

Symbol	English	Deutsch	Español	Français	Português
≏	River	Fluß	Río	Rivière	Rio
≊	Canal	Kanal	Canal	Canal	Canal
⌞	Waterfall, Rapids	Wasserfall, Stromschnellen	Cascada, Rápidos	Chute d'eau, Rapides	Cascata, Rápidos
ɰ	Strait	Meeresstraße	Estrecho	Détroit	Estreito
⊂	Bay, Gulf	Bucht, Golf	Bahía, Golfo	Baie, Golfe	Baía, Golfo
⊜	Lake, Lakes	See, Seen	Lago, Lagos	Lac, Lacs	Lago, Lagos
≡	Swamp	Sumpf	Pantano	Marais	Pântano
⊓	Ice Features, Glacier	Eis- und Gletscherformen	Accidentes Glaciales	Formes glaciaires	Acidentes glaciares
ᴛ	Other Hydrographic Features	Andere Hydrographische Objekte	Otros Elementos Hidrográficos	Autres données hydrographiques	Outros acidentes hidrográficos
✢	Submarine Features	Untermeerische Objekte	Accidentes Submarinos	Formes de relief sous-marin	Acidentes submarinos
□	Political Unit	Politische Einheit	Unidad Politica	Entité politique	Unidade política
⊍	Cultural Institution	Kulturelle Institution	Institución Cultural	Institution culturelle	Institução cultural
⊥	Historical Site	Historische Stätte	Sitio Histórico	Site historique	Sitio histórico
♠	Recreational Site	Erholungs- und Ferienort	Sitio de Recreo	Centre de loisirs	Area de Lazer
⊠	Airport	Flughafen	Aeropuerto	Aéroport	Aeroporto
■	Military Installation	Militäranlage	Instalación Militar	Installation militaire	Instalação militar
◆	Miscellaneous	Verschiedenes	Misceláneo	Divers	Diversos

Name	Page	Lat.°′	Long.°′
Küçükçekmece Gölü ⊜	267b	41.00 N	28.46 E
Küçükköy •[8]	267b	41.04 N	28.54 E
Küçükkuyu	130	39.32 N	26.36 E
Kučukskoje, ozero ⊜	86	52.42 N	79.46 E
Kucur, Tanjung >	115a	8.39 S	114.34 E
Kučurgan ≃	78	46.43 N	29.53 E
Kūd	123	33.05 N	75.17 E
Kuda ≃	88	52.25 N	104.08 E
Kudaka-jima I	174m	26.09 N	127.54 E
Kudamatsu	96	34.00 N	131.52 E
Kudanggou	104	41.06 N	124.00 E
Kudap	114	1.17 N	102.26 E
Kudara, Ross.	88	52.13 N	106.39 E
Kudara, Taj.	85	38.25 N	72.41 E
Kudara ≃	85	38.19 N	72.28 E
Kudara-Somon	88	50.10 N	107.25 E
Kudat	112	6.53 N	116.50 E
Kudejevskij	86	54.52 N	56.46 E
Kudene	164	6.14 S	134.39 E
Kudever'	76	56.47 N	29.23 E
Kudinovo	82	55.45 N	38.12 E
Kudirkos Naumiestis	76	54.46 N	22.53 E
Kudongho	98	35.31 N	126.29 E
Kudoyama	96	34.17 N	135.34 E
Kudremukh ∧	122	13.08 N	75.16 E
Kudrovo	265a	59.54 N	30.31 E
Kudus	115a	6.48 S	110.50 E
Kudyat al-Islām	142	27.32 N	30.45 E
Kudymkar	86	59.01 N	54.37 E
Kuee Ruins ⊥	229d	19.21 N	155.23 W
Kueishan Tao I	100	24.51 N	121.57 E
Kueisui → Hohhot	102	40.51 N	111.40 E
Kueiyang → Guiyang	102	26.35 N	106.43 E
Kuekvun' ≃	180	69.14 N	179.25 E
Kuënlun → Kunlun Shan ⋏	120	36.30 N	88.00 E
Kuerbin	89	49.25 N	128.59 E
K'uerhlo → Korla	90	41.44 N	86.09 E
Kufayr az-Zayt	132	33.26 N	35.44 E
Kufayr Yābūs	132	33.42 N	36.01 E
Kufrinjah	132	32.18 N	35.42 E
Kufstein	64	47.35 N	12.10 E
Kufūr Bilshāy	142	30.51 N	30.48 E
Kufūr Najm	142	30.44 N	31.35 E
Kuga, Nihon	96	34.05 N	132.05 E
Kuga, Nihon	96	33.56 N	132.16 E
Kuga, Zhg.	90	41.43 N	82.54 E
Kugaluk ≃	180	69.10 N	131.00 W
Kugaly	86	44.29 N	78.40 E
Kugarčino	80	55.33 N	50.29 E
Kugart ≃	85	40.52 N	72.53 E
Kugas	85	38.21 N	70.48 E
Kugej	83	46.53 N	39.19 E
Kugesi	80	56.02 N	47.18 E
Kugmallit Bay ⊂	180	69.33 N	133.25 W
Kugojeja ≃	78	46.34 N	39.38 E
Kuguno	94	36.03 N	137.16 E
Kuḥaylī	140	19.25 N	32.50 E
Kühbach	60	48.29 N	11.11 E
Kūhdasht	128	33.32 N	47.36 E
Kūh Lab, Ra's-e >	128	25.17 N	60.28 E
Kuḥlīyah, Wādī V	142	30.05 N	31.58 E
Kühlungsborn	54	54.09 N	11.43 E
Kuhmo	26	64.08 N	29.31 E
Kuhmoinen	26	61.34 N	25.11 E
Kühnhausen	54	51.02 N	10.58 E
Kühnsdorf	61	46.37 N	14.37 E
Kūhpāyeh	128	32.43 N	52.26 E
Kühren	54	51.20 N	12.50 E
Kuhstedt	52	53.23 N	8.58 E
Kui	164	7.30 S	147.15 E
Kuibyschew → Samara	80	53.12 N	50.09 E
Kuidesu	98	41.46 N	119.29 E
Kuidou	100	25.10 N	118.11 E
Kuikkol', ozero ⊜	86	50.57 N	64.30 E
Kuikui, Lae o >	229a	20.36 N	156.35 W
Kuilāpāl	126	22.50 N	86.38 E
Kuinre	52	52.47 N	5.50 E
Kuiseb ≃	156	22.59 S	14.31 E
Kuishi-yama ∧, Nihon	96	33.51 N	133.35 E
Kuishi-yama ∧, Nihon	96	33.40 N	133.31 E
Kuitan	100	23.05 N	115.58 E
Kuiten Uul ∧	86	49.08 N	87.49 E
Kuito	152	12.22 S	16.56 E
Kuiu Island I	180	56.45 N	134.10 W
Kuivaniemi	26	65.35 N	25.11 E
Kuivastu	76	58.35 N	23.22 E
Kuja, Ross.	24	67.46 N	53.10 E
Kuja, Ross.	24	65.05 N	40.06 E
Kujal'nickij liman ⊜	78	46.40 N	30.42 E
Kujang	98	39.52 N	126.01 E
Kujani Game Reserve •[4]	150	7.10 N	0.50 W
Kujawy •[1]	30	52.45 N	18.30 E
Kujbyšev	86	55.27 N	78.19 E
Kujbyševka	78	47.37 N	31.42 E
Kujbyševo, Ross.	83	47.49 N	38.55 E
Kujbyševo, Ukr.	78	44.38 N	33.52 E
Kujbyševo, Ukr.	78	47.22 N	36.39 E
Kujbyševo, Uzb.	85	40.22 N	71.17 E
Kujbyšev → Samara	80	53.12 N	50.09 E
Kujbyševskij, Kaz.	86	53.15 N	66.51 E
Kujbyševskij, Uzb.	72	37.52 N	68.44 E
Kujbyševskij Zaton	80	55.09 N	49.12 E
Kujbyševskoje vodochranilišče ⊜[1]	80	54.30 N	48.30 E
Kujeda	86	56.26 N	55.35 E
Kujgan	86	45.25 N	74.10 E
Kujgenkol'	80	49.17 N	47.59 E
Kuji	92	40.11 N	141.46 E
Kuji ≃	94	36.29 N	140.37 E
Kujirai	268	35.56 N	139.27 E
Kujl'uk	85	41.15 N	69.20 E
Kujman'	76	52.52 N	39.16 E
Kujŏng-ni	98	37.53 N	125.54 E
Kujtun	88	54.21 N	101.29 E
Kujū	96	33.01 N	131.18 E
Kujūkuri	94	35.32 N	140.25 E
Kujūkuri-hama ⊥[2]	94	35.35 N	140.30 E
Kujū-san ∧	96	33.05 N	131.15 E
Kuk ∧	64	46.16 N	13.45 E
Kuk ≃	180	70.36 N	160.00 W
Kukaklek Lake ⊜	180	59.09 N	155.20 W
Kukalaya ≃	236	13.39 N	83.37 W
Kukan	89	49.12 N	133.28 E
Kukarino	82	55.31 N	35.59 E
Kukawa	146	12.56 N	13.35 E
Kukerin	162	33.11 S	118.05 E
Kukës	38	42.05 N	20.24 E
Kuke Shan ⋏	85	40.00 N	75.00 E
Kuki	94	36.04 N	139.40 E
Kukipi	164	8.10 S	146.05 E
Kukkola	26	65.59 N	24.04 E
Kukmirn	61	47.04 N	16.13 E
Kukmor	80	56.13 N	50.54 E
Kukoboj	76	58.42 N	39.54 E
Kukol'	76	59.52 N	32.35 E
Kükong → Shaoguan	100	24.50 N	113.37 E
Kukpowruk ≃	180	69.35 N	163.00 W
Kukpuk ≃	180	68.23 N	166.20 W
Kukshi	120	22.12 N	74.45 E
Kukuj	76	59.21 N	32.33 E
Kuku-Nor → Qinghai Hu ⊜	102	36.50 N	100.20 E
Kukup	114	1.19 N	103.27 E
Kuku Point >	174a	19.18 N	166.34 E
Kukuri Mukuri Char I	126	21.56 N	90.39 E
Kukuštan	86	57.38 N	56.30 E
Kula, Blg.	38	43.53 N	22.31 E
Kula, Jugo.	38	45.36 N	19.32 E
Kula, Tür.	130	38.32 N	28.40 E
Kula, Hi., U.S.	229a	20.52 N	156.40 W
Kul'ab	120	37.55 N	69.46 E
Kul'ab □[4]	85	38.15 N	69.45 E
Kulāchi	123	31.56 N	70.27 E
Kulagi	76	52.56 N	32.24 E
Kula Gulf ʯ	175e	8.05 S	157.18 E
Kulai	114	1.40 N	103.36 E
Kulaj	86	57.42 N	75.15 E
Kula Kangri ∧	124	28.03 N	90.27 E
Kulākh	144	21.18 N	40.41 E
Kulakovo, Ross.	82	55.06 N	37.28 E
Kulakovo, Ross.	86	58.06 N	93.57 E
Kulakši	86	47.12 N	55.24 E
Kulal, Mount ∧	154	2.43 N	36.56 E
Kulanak	85	41.22 N	75.31 E
Kulandy	86	46.08 N	59.31 E
Kulanutpes ≃	86	50.21 N	69.08 E
Kular	74	70.41 N	134.22 E
Kulassein Island I	116	6.25 N	120.41 E
Kulaura	120	24.32 N	92.03 E
Kulautuva	76	54.58 N	23.38 E
Kulaykilī	140	11.21 N	25.36 E
Kul'či	89	53.33 N	139.36 E
Kuldīga	76	56.58 N	21.59 E
Kuldja → Yining	86	43.54 N	81.21 E
Kul'dur	89	49.13 N	131.38 E
Kule	156	23.05 S	20.05 E
Kulebaki	80	55.24 N	42.32 E
Kulejevo	86	59.40 N	80.59 E
Kulen Vakuf	36	44.34 N	16.06 E
Kulešovka	83	47.05 N	39.33 E
Kulevčinskij	86	53.12 N	61.26 E
Kulgām	123	33.39 N	75.01 E
Kulgera	162	25.50 S	133.18 E
Kulgunino	86	53.35 N	56.56 E
Kuligi	80	58.11 N	53.46 E
Kulikov	78	49.58 N	24.04 E
Kulikovka, Ross.	80	52.14 N	47.36 E
Kulikovka, Ukr.	78	51.23 N	31.37 E
Kulikovo	76	52.14 N	39.35 E
Kulikovskij	80	50.51 N	42.34 E
Kulim	114	5.22 N	100.34 E
Kulin	162	32.40 S	118.10 E
Kuliushucun	105	40.07 N	116.34 E
Kulju	26	61.23 N	23.46 E
Kulkyne Creek ≃	166	30.16 S	144.12 E
Kullaberg ⋏[2]	41	56.18 N	12.30 E
Kullamaa	76	58.53 N	24.05 E
Küllenhahn •[8]	263	51.14 N	7.08 E
Küllstedt	56	51.16 N	10.17 E
Kullu	123	31.58 N	77.06 E
Kulm	198	46.18 N	98.57 W
Kulmbach	54	50.06 N	11.27 E
Kulnura	170	33.14 S	151.13 E
Kuloj, Ross.	24	64.58 N	43.28 E
Kuloj, Ross.	24	61.02 N	42.29 E
Kuloj ≃, Ross.	24	66.03 N	43.22 E
Kuloj ≃, Ross.	76	60.25 N	42.30 E
Kuloli	85	39.22 N	68.03 E
Kulongshan	98	41.43 N	116.54 E
Kulongshanpuzi	104	41.16 N	123.59 E
Kulotino	76	58.27 N	33.21 E
Kulp	130	38.30 N	41.02 E
Kulpahar	124	25.19 N	79.39 E
Kulpara	168b	34.04 S	138.02 E
Kulpawn ≃	150	10.21 N	1.05 W
Kulpi	126	22.06 N	88.15 E
Kul'pino	82	56.18 N	37.09 E
Kulpmont	208	40.47 N	76.28 W
Kulpsville	285	40.15 N	75.20 W
Kul'sary	86	46.59 N	54.01 E
Kulsbjerge ⋏[2]	41	55.01 N	12.01 E
Külsheim	56	49.40 N	9.31 E
Kültepe ⊥	130	38.44 N	35.34 E
Kulti	126	23.44 N	86.51 E
Kultikri	126	22.10 N	87.09 E
Kultuk	88	51.44 N	103.42 E
Kulu	130	39.06 N	33.05 E
Kuluha, Jabal ∧	140	15.31 N	23.25 E
Kulumadau	164	9.03 S	152.43 E
Kulunda	86	52.35 N	78.57 E
Kulunda ≃	86	52.59 N	79.48 E
Kulundinskaja step' ⌣	86	53.00 N	79.00 E
Kulundinskoje, ozero ⊜	86	53.00 N	79.36 E
Kuluqi	89	50.23 N	124.13 E
Kulwin	166	35.02 S	142.33 E
Kum ≃	130	38.38 N	27.32 E
Kuma	96	33.39 N	132.54 E
Kuma ≃, Nihon	92	32.30 N	130.34 E
Kuma ≃, Ross.	72	44.56 N	47.00 E
Kuma ≃, Ross.	86	59.32 N	66.45 E
Kumagaya	94	36.08 N	139.23 E
Kumai, Indon.	112	3.23 S	112.33 E
Kumai, Indon.	112	2.44 S	111.43 E
Kumai, Teluk ⊂	112	3.00 S	111.43 E
Kumaishi	92a	42.08 N	139.59 E
Kumajri	84	40.48 N	43.50 E
Kumakanda	88	52.44 N	116.55 E
Kumalarang	116	7.44 N	123.08 E
Kumamba, Kepulauan II	164	1.36 S	138.45 E
Kumamoto	92	32.48 N	130.43 E
Kumamoto □[5]	96	32.58 N	130.55 E
Kumano, Nihon	92	33.54 N	136.05 E
Kumano, Nihon	96	34.20 N	132.34 E
Kumano ≃	92	33.44 N	136.01 E
Kumano-nada ⫪[2]	92	33.47 N	136.20 E
Kumanovo	38	42.08 N	21.43 E
Kumār ≃[1], Bngl.	126	23.11 N	90.10 E
Kumār ≃[1], Bngl.	126	23.31 N	89.28 E
Kumara, N.Z.	172	42.38 S	171.11 E
Kumara, Ross.	89	51.37 N	126.47 E
Kumārapālaiyam	122	11.28 N	77.43 E
Kumardhubi	126	23.48 N	86.43 E
Kumarganj	126	22.59 N	87.44 E
Kumārghāt	120	24.04 N	92.04 E
Kumārgrām	124	26.37 N	89.50 E
Kumāri ≃	126	22.57 N	86.48 E
Kumārkhāli	124	23.51 N	89.15 E
Kumarl	162	32.47 S	121.33 E
Kumasi	150	6.41 N	1.35 W
Kumatori	270	34.24 N	135.22 E
Kumawa, Pegunungan ⋏	164	3.50 S	132.50 E
Kumba	152	4.38 N	9.25 E
Kumbakonam	122	10.58 N	79.23 E
Kumba Pits	156	18.45 S	24.45 E
Kumbar	140	12.03 N	30.16 E
Kumbarilla	166	27.19 S	150.53 E
Kumbe	164	8.21 S	140.13 E
Kumbel'	85	42.30 N	73.11 E
Kümch'ŏn	98	38.10 N	126.29 E
Kum-Dag	128	39.16 N	54.35 E
Kumdah ⫪[4]	144	20.23 N	45.05 E
Kumdan ∧	123	35.09 N	77.35 E
Kumdanlı	130	38.19 N	30.59 E
Kume	96	35.03 N	133.54 E
Kume-jima I	93b	26.20 N	126.47 E
Kumenan	96	34.56 N	133.58 E
Kumeny	80	58.07 N	49.56 E
Kŭm-gang ≃	98	36.00 N	126.40 E
Kŭmgang-san ∧	98	38.35 N	128.10 E
Kŭmhwa	98	38.17 N	127.28 E
Kumi	154	1.29 N	33.56 E
Kumihama	96	35.36 N	134.55 E
Kuminovskoje	86	57.48 N	64.07 E
Kuminskij	86	58.40 N	66.04 E
Kumiyama	270	34.53 N	135.45 E
Kumizawa •[8]	268	35.23 N	139.31 E
Kumköy •[8]	267b	41.15 N	29.02 E
Kumla	40	59.08 N	15.08 E
Kumli	84	43.58 N	46.04 E
Kumlinge I	26	60.16 N	20.47 E
Kumluca, Tür.	130	36.22 N	30.18 E
Kumluca, Tür.	130	41.27 N	32.28 E
Kummelnäs	40	59.21 N	18.17 E
Kummerow	54	54.17 N	12.53 E
Kummerower See ⊜	54	53.49 N	12.52 E
Kümmersbruck	60	49.25 N	11.53 E
Kumo	146	10.03 N	11.13 E
Kŭmŏ-do I	98	34.31 N	127.45 E
Kumon Range ⋏	102	26.30 N	97.15 E
Kumora	88	55.53 N	111.13 E
Kumosō-yama ∧	96	33.54 N	134.18 E
Kumotori-yama ∧	94	35.51 N	138.57 E
Kumphawapi	110	17.07 N	103.01 E
Kumrābād	126	24.10 N	87.16 E
Kumru	130	40.53 N	37.17 E
Kŭmsan	98	36.07 N	127.30 E
Kŭmsan-ni	98	37.55 N	125.41 E
Kumsenga	154	3.47 S	30.25 E
Kumta	122	14.25 N	74.24 E
Kumu	154	3.04 N	25.09 E
Kumu ≃	114	1.24 N	100.43 E
Kumuch	84	42.11 N	47.07 E
Kumukahi, Cape >	229d	19.31 N	154.49 W
Kumukuli	120	37.33 N	88.50 E
Kumusi ≃	164	8.35 S	148.00 E
Kümüx	86	42.14 N	88.11 E
Kumzār	128	26.20 N	56.25 E
Kuna	202	43.29 N	116.25 W
Kunar (Konar) ≃	123	34.25 N	70.32 E
Kunašak	86	55.43 N	61.36 E
Kunashiri-tō → Kunašir, ostrov I	92a	44.10 N	146.00 E
Kunašir, ostrov (Kunashiri-tō) I	92a	44.10 N	146.00 E
Kun'batar	84	44.17 N	45.34 E
Kuncheng Hu ⊜	106	31.35 N	120.45 E
Kunchhā	124	28.08 N	84.20 E
Kunc'ovo •[8]	265b	55.44 N	37.26 E
Kunda, Eesti	76	59.29 N	26.32 E
Kunda, Zaïre	154	3.57 S	26.35 E
Kunda Hills ⋏[2]	122	11.10 N	76.30 E
Kundahit	126	23.58 N	87.10 E
Kundam	124	23.13 N	80.21 E
Kundāpura	122	13.38 N	74.42 E
Kundar ≃	120	31.56 N	69.19 E
Kundat	86	55.14 N	87.51 E
Kundelungu, Parc National de ♠	154	10.30 S	27.45 E
Kunderu ≃	122	14.38 N	78.42 E
Kundi	154	1.08 S	40.41 E
Kundiān	123	32.27 N	71.28 E
Kundiawa	164	6.00 S	145.00 E
Kundima	164	4.14 S	143.52 E
Kundl	64	47.28 N	11.59 E
Kundla	120	21.20 N	71.18 E
Kundr'učje ≃	83	47.52 N	40.15 E
Kundur, Pulau I	112	0.45 N	103.26 E
Kunene (Cunene) ≃	152	17.20 S	11.50 E
Kunersdorf, Forst •[3]	264a	52.17 N	12.59 E
Kunes	24	70.21 N	26.31 E
Künes ≃	86	43.55 N	80.55 E
Kunga ≃[1]	126	21.45 N	89.30 E
Kungälv	26	57.52 N	11.58 E
Kungana	146	7.50 N	10.42 E
Kungchuling → Huaide	89	43.32 N	124.50 E
Kungej-Alatau, chrebet ⋏	85	42.50 N	77.00 E
Kunggyü Yumco ⊜	124	30.35 N	82.09 E
Kunghit Island I	182	52.06 N	131.04 W
Kunghsi	100	24.37 N	121.16 E
Kung-pei-tien	269d	25.06 N	121.38 E
Kungrad	86	43.06 N	58.54 E
Kungsängen	40	59.29 N	17.45 E
Kungsängen flygplats ⊠	40	58.36 N	16.15 E
Kungsbacka	26	57.29 N	12.04 E
Kungsgården	40	60.36 N	16.37 E
Kungshamn	26	58.22 N	11.15 E
Kungsör	40	59.25 N	16.05 E
Kungu	152	2.47 N	19.12 E
Kungur	86	57.25 N	56.57 E
Kunhār ≃	123	34.17 N	73.29 E
Kunhegyes	30	47.22 N	20.38 E
Kunhing	110	21.18 N	98.26 E
Kuni	94	36.35 N	138.38 E
Kunia	229c	21.29 N	158.07 W
Kunigami	174m	26.45 N	128.10 E
Kunimi	96	33.41 N	131.36 E
Kuningan	115a	6.59 S	108.29 E
Kunisaki	96	33.33 N	131.45 E
Kunisaki-hantō >[1]	96	33.30 N	131.40 E
Kunitachi	268	35.41 N	139.26 E
Kuni Vyselki	82	54.18 N	38.41 E
Kunja	76	56.18 N	30.59 E
Kunja ≃, Ross.	76	57.09 N	31.10 E
Kunja ≃, Ross.	82	56.31 N	38.12 E
Kunjāh	123	32.32 N	73.59 E
Kunje	83	49.23 N	37.15 E
Kunkle	216	41.38 N	84.30 W
Kunkletown	210	40.51 N	75.27 W
Kunkuri	124	22.45 N	83.57 E
Kunlong	110	23.25 N	98.39 E
Kunlun Shan ⋏	120	36.30 N	88.00 E
Kunming	102	25.05 N	102.40 E
Kunming Hu ⊜	271a	39.59 N	116.15 E
Kunmunya Aboriginal Reserve •[4]	164	15.45 S	124.45 E
Kunnamkulam	122	10.39 N	76.05 E
Kunost'	76	60.01 N	37.38 E
Kunovice	30	49.03 N	17.29 E
Kunow	54	53.00 N	12.07 E
Kunowice	54	52.20 N	14.50 E
Kunrau	54	52.35 N	11.01 E
Kunsan	98	35.58 N	126.41 E
Kunshan	106	31.23 N	120.57 E
Kunszentmárton	30	46.51 N	20.18 E
Kuntair	150	13.32 N	16.13 W
Kuntaur	150	13.40 N	14.48 W
Kuntiki	86	58.29 N	76.24 E
Kunting	100	29.48 N	121.56 E
Kuntshankoie	152	3.20 S	23.34 E
Kuntuolun	102	45.13 N	115.21 E
Kununurra	164	15.47 S	128.44 E
Kunwi	98	36.15 N	128.34 E
Kunya	150	12.14 N	8.34 E
Kunyo	144	6.17 N	42.33 E
Kunžak	61	49.07 N	15.11 E
Künzell	56	50.33 N	9.42 E
Künzelsau	56	49.16 N	9.41 E
Künzing	60	48.40 N	13.05 E
Kunzulu	152	3.29 S	16.09 E
Kuocang Shan ⋏	100	28.36 N	120.30 E
Kuohsing	100	24.02 N	120.51 E
Kuokegan	120	37.30 N	89.55 E
Kuolajarvi	24	66.58 N	29.12 E
Kuop I[1]	175c	7.03 N	151.56 E
Kuopio	26	62.54 N	27.41 E
Kuopion lääni □[4]	26	63.00 N	27.30 E
Kuortane	26	62.48 N	23.30 E
Kupa ≃	36	45.28 N	16.24 E
Kup'abal	271b	37.37 N	126.54 E
Kupang	112	10.10 S	123.35 E
Kupang, Teluk ⊂	112	10.04 S	123.40 E
Kup'ansk	83	49.42 N	37.38 E
Kupanskoje	82	56.51 N	38.43 E
Kup'ansk-Uzlovoj	83	49.39 N	37.39 E
Kuparuk ≃	180	70.25 N	148.55 W
Kupava	80	51.07 N	42.57 E
Kupavna	265b	55.45 N	38.08 E
Kuper Island I	224	48.58 N	123.39 W
Kupferberg	263	51.09 N	7.27 E
Kupferdreh •[8]	263	51.23 N	7.05 E
Kupfermühle	41	54.50 N	9.24 E
Kupferzell	56	49.14 N	9.41 E
Kupiano	164	10.05 S	148.11 E
Kupičev	78	51.00 N	24.44 E
Kupino	86	54.22 N	77.18 E
Kupiškis	76	55.50 N	24.58 E
Küplü, Tür.	130	40.06 N	30.00 E
Küplü, Tür.	130	41.07 N	26.21 E
Kupol, gora ∧	180	68.38 N	174.45 E
Kuppenheim	56	48.49 N	8.15 E
Kupper Airport ⊠	276	40.31 N	74.36 W
Kupreanof	180	56.49 N	132.57 W
Kupreanof Island I	180	56.50 N	133.30 W
Kupreanof Point >	180	55.34 N	159.35 W
Kupres	36	44.00 N	17.17 E
Küps	54	50.11 N	11.16 E
Kupuri	89	54.44 N	130.30 E
Kur ≃	89	48.44 N	134.14 E
Kur, Pulau I	164	5.20 S	132.00 E
Kura (Kuruçay) ≃, Asia	84	39.24 N	49.19 E
Kura ≃, Ross.	84	44.06 N	44.57 E
Kurabuchi	94	36.25 N	138.48 E
Kur'ačeje	83	48.10 N	39.37 E
Kur'ačevka, Ukr.	83	49.39 N	38.42 E
Kur'ačevka, Ukr.	83	49.22 N	39.36 E
Kurach	84	41.36 N	47.46 E
Kurach ≃	84	41.40 N	48.11 E
Kurachovka	83	48.02 N	37.23 E
Kurachovo	83	47.59 N	37.16 E
Kuragaty	85	43.06 N	72.59 E
Kuragaty ≃	85	43.57 N	73.34 E
Kuragino	86	53.53 N	92.40 E
Kurahashi	96	34.06 N	132.30 E
Kurahashi-jima I	96	34.08 N	132.31 E
Kuraj	86	56.42 N	95.29 E
Kurajlysaj	80	50.07 N	51.51 E
Kurakaki	270	34.59 N	135.28 E
Kurakino, Ross.	80	52.33 N	44.03 E
Kurakino, Ross.	82	54.30 N	35.48 E
Kurakovo	82	54.05 N	37.14 E
Kūrāli	123	30.50 N	76.35 E
Kuram	85	43.33 N	78.08 E
Kuramā', Ḥarrat ⊥[9]	128	24.30 N	40.15 E
Kurama-yama ∧	96	35.07 N	135.46 E
Kuraminskij chrebet ⋏	85	40.45 N	70.10 E
Kuramo Waters ⊂	273a	6.26 N	3.26 E
Kuranami	268	35.27 N	140.00 E
Kuraon	124	24.59 N	82.05 E
Kurar •[8]	272c	19.11 N	72.52 E
Kurašasaj	86	50.18 N	56.55 E
Kurashiki	96	34.35 N	133.46 E
Kurasiki → Kurashiki	96	34.35 N	133.46 E
Kurate	96	33.47 N	130.41 E
Kurauli	124	27.24 N	78.59 E
Kuraymah	140	18.33 N	31.51 E
Kurayoshi	96	35.26 N	133.49 E
Kurayyimah	132	32.16 N	35.36 E
Kurba	80	57.34 N	39.32 E
Kurba ≃	88	52.02 N	108.30 E
Kurbağa Gölü ⊜	130	38.21 N	35.17 E
Kurbağalı ≃	267b	40.59 N	29.02 E
Kurbatovo	86	55.34 N	91.10 E
Kurbulik	88	53.45 N	108.57 E
Kurčaloj	84	43.12 N	46.05 E
Kurchatov	78	51.39 N	35.36 E
Kur-Čilik ≃	85	43.50 N	78.06 E
Kurčum	86	48.37 N	83.40 E
Kurdaj	85	43.21 N	74.59 E
K'urdamir	84	40.21 N	48.08 E
Kurdgelauri	84	41.58 N	45.32 E
Kurdistan □[9]	128	37.00 N	45.00 E
Kurdufān al-Janūbīyah □[4]	140	11.00 N	30.00 E
Kurdufān ash-Shamālīyah □[4]	140	14.00 N	29.45 E
Kurd'umovka	83	48.28 N	37.59 E
Kurduvādi	122	18.05 N	75.26 E
Kure, Austl.	164	15.27 S	124.33 E
Kure, Nihon	96	34.14 N	132.34 E
Küre, Tür.	130	41.48 N	33.43 E
Kure Atoll I[1]	14	28.25 N	178.25 W
Küre Dağları ⋏	130	41.45 N	34.00 E
Kurejka ≃	74	66.30 N	87.12 E
Kurejskaja	88	58.56 N	111.20 E
Kuren'	78	51.09 N	32.44 E
Kurenalus	26	65.21 N	26.59 E
Kurenec	76	54.33 N	26.57 E
Kuresaare	76	58.15 N	22.28 E
Kurgal'džinskij	86	50.36 N	70.01 E
Kurgan	86	55.26 N	65.18 E
Kurgan Mečetnyj, gora ∧[2]	83	48.06 N	39.21 E
Kurgan Oblast' □[4]	86	55.30 N	64.30 E
Kurgan-T'ube	120	37.50 N	68.48 E
Kurgan T'ube □[4]	85	38.15 N	68.50 E
Kurgasyn	86	49.15 N	66.43 E
Kurgatej	88	54.23 N	99.27 E
Kurgolovo	76	59.46 N	28.06 E
Kuria I	14	0.14 N	173.25 E
Kuria Muria Islands → Khurīyā Murīyā, Jazā'ir II	118	17.30 N	56.00 E
Kuriasol	126	22.06 N	86.39 E
Kuridala	166	21.17 S	140.30 E
Kurīgrām	124	25.49 N	89.39 E
Kurihama	268	35.13 N	139.43 E
Kurihashi	94	36.08 N	139.42 E
Kurikka	26	62.37 N	22.25 E
Kurilen → Kuril'skije ostrova II	74	46.10 N	152.00 E
Kurilen-Strasse → Pervyj Kuril'skij proliv ʯ	74	50.50 N	156.36 E
Kuriles, Islas → Kuril'skije ostrova II	74	46.10 N	152.00 E
Kuril Islands → Kuril'skije ostrova II	74	46.10 N	152.00 E
Kurilovka	80	50.44 N	48.02 E
Kuril'sk	74	45.14 N	147.53 E
Kuril'skije ostrova (Kuril Islands) II	74	46.10 N	152.00 E
Kuril Strait → Pervyj Kuril'skij proliv ʯ	74	50.50 N	156.36 E
Kuril Trench ✦[1]	6	47.00 N	155.00 E
Kuřim	30	49.18 N	16.32 E
Kurimoto	94	35.49 N	140.30 E
Ku-Ring-Gai Chase National Park ♠	170	33.38 S	151.15 E
Kurinjippadi	122	11.34 N	79.36 E
Kurinskaja kosa >[2]	84	39.03 N	49.13 E
Kurinwás ≃	236	12.49 N	83.41 W
Kuripapango	172	39.23 S	176.21 E
Kuriyama, Nihon	92a	43.03 N	141.47 E
Kuriyama, Nihon	94	36.52 N	139.37 E
Kurja, Ross.	24	61.42 N	57.09 E
Kurja, Ross.	86	51.36 N	82.19 E
Kurjanovskaja	76	60.19 N	41.33 E
Kurkijoki	26	61.18 N	29.54 E
Kurkino, Ross.	76	53.26 N	38.40 E
Kurkino, Ross.	265b	55.53 N	37.23 E
Kurkliai	76	55.25 N	25.03 E
Kurl •[8]	263	51.35 N	7.35 E
Kurla •[8]	272c	19.05 N	72.53 E
Kurlackoje	83	47.21 N	39.03 E
Kurleja	88	52.11 N	119.11 E
Kurlin	80	51.48 N	51.00 E
Kurlovskij	80	55.27 N	40.36 E
Kurmanajevka	80	52.31 N	52.06 E
Kurmani	126	22.47 N	89.53 E
Kurmankol'	80	49.09 N	48.27 E
Kurmenty	85	42.48 N	78.15 E
Kurmuk	140	10.33 N	34.17 E
Kurnell	274a	34.01 S	151.13 E
Kurnell Peninsula >[1]	274a	34.02 S	15.11 E
Kurnool	122	15.50 N	78.03 E
Kurobane	94	36.51 N	140.07 E
Kurobe	94	36.51 N	137.26 E
Kurobe ≃	94	36.55 N	137.25 E
Kurobe-dam •[6]	94	36.36 N	137.38 E
Kurodashō	96	35.01 N	135.00 E
Kurogi	96	33.12 N	130.40 E
Kurohone	94	36.30 N	139.17 E
Kuroishi	92	40.38 N	140.36 E
Kuroiso	94	36.58 N	140.03 E
Kuroo-tōge)(	96	35.11 N	134.12 E
Kuropatkino, Ross.	80	46.32 N	45.20 E
Kuropatkino, Uzb.	85	39.57 N	67.27 E
Kurort-Darasun	88	51.12 N	113.44 E
Kurose	96	34.19 N	132.40 E
Kurose ≃	96	34.13 N	132.36 E
Kuro-shima I, Nihon	93b	30.50 N	129.57 E
Kuro-shima I, Nihon	175d	24.19 N	124.05 E
Kurosu	268	35.51 N	139.23 E
Kurovo	82	55.49 N	36.00 E
Kurovskoje	82	55.34 N	38.55 E
Kurow	172	44.44 S	170.28 E
Kuroya	268	35.55 N	139.44 E
Kurrajong	170	33.33 S	150.40 E
Kurram	120	30.06 N	66.31 E
Kurram ≃	123	32.36 N	71.20 E
Kurri Kurri	170	32.49 S	151.29 E
Kuršab ≃	85	40.46 N	73.06 E
Kursavka	84	44.28 N	42.31 E
Kursela	124	25.27 N	87.15 E
Kuršėnai	76	56.00 N	22.56 E
Kurseong	120	26.53 N	88.17 E
Kursk	78	51.42 N	36.12 E
Kurskaja	84	44.03 N	44.27 E
Kurskaja kosa >[2]	76	55.18 N	21.00 E
Kurskij zaliv ⊂	76	55.00 N	21.00 E
Kursk Oblast' □[4]	78	51.40 N	36.00 E
Kursk Station •[5]	265b	55.46 N	37.40 E
Kuršumlija	38	43.08 N	21.17 E
Kurşunlu, Tür.	130	40.51 N	33.16 E
Kurşunlu, Tür.	130	38.40 N	37.51 E
Kurtalan	130	37.57 N	41.42 E
Kurtamyš	86	54.55 N	64.27 E
Kurtatsch → Cortaccia	64	46.19 N	11.13 E
Kürten, Dtsch.	56	51.03 N	7.16 E
Kurten, Tx., U.S.	222	30.47 N	96.16 W
Kurthasanlı	130	38.20 N	32.11 E
Kurth Lake ⊜	222	31.26 N	94.42 W
Kūrtī	140	18.07 N	31.33 E
Kurtino	82	54.59 N	38.17 E
Kurtinskoje vodochranilišče ⊜[1]	85	43.50 N	76.20 E
Kurtistown	229d	19.36 N	155.03 W
Kurtoğlu Burnu >	130	36.35 N	28.50 E
Kurtušibinskij chrebet ⋏	88	52.10 N	93.30 E
Kurty ≃	85	44.05 N	76.20 E
Kurtz	218	38.58 N	86.12 W
Kuru, Sūd.	140	7.43 N	26.31 E
Kuru, Suomi	26	61.52 N	23.44 E
Kuru ≃	140	9.08 N	26.57 E
Kurucaşile	130	41.50 N	32.43 E
Kuruçay	130	39.39 N	38.29 E
Kuruçay (Kura) ≃	84	39.24 N	49.19 E
Kuruçeşme •[8]	267b	41.03 N	29.02 E
Kuruktag ⋏	90	41.30 N	90.00 E
Kurum	164	4.45 S	145.55 E
Kuruman	158	27.28 S	23.28 E
Kuruman ≃	158	26.56 S	20.39 E
Kurumanheuwels ⋏[2]	158	27.40 S	23.25 E
Kurumdy, gora ∧	85	39.28 N	73.32 E
Kurume	96	33.19 N	130.31 E
Kurumkan	88	54.18 N	110.18 E
Kurun ≃	144	5.30 N	34.17 E
Kurunegala	122	7.29 N	80.22 E
Kurungbaja, Tanjung >	115b	8.15 S	120.35 E
Kurung Tank ⊜[1]	124	22.19 N	82.14 E
Kurunzulaj	88	51.00 N	117.10 E
Kuruqi	89	48.58 N	123.50 E
Kurur, Jabal ∧	140	20.31 N	31.32 E
Kurusaj	85	40.35 N	69.24 E
Kurushima-kaikyo ʯ	96	34.07 N	133.00 E
Kuruson-zan ∧	96	34.12 N	130.58 E
Kurylys	86	48.38 N	60.47 E
Kuryongp'o	98	35.59 N	129.32 E
Kurzeme □[9]	76	56.50 N	22.30 E
Kusa	86	55.20 N	59.29 E
Kusabe	270	34.31 N	135.29 E
Kuşadası	130	37.51 N	27.15 E
Kuşadası Körfezi ⊂	130	37.50 N	27.08 E
Kusak ≃	86	47.50 N	75.45 E
Kušalino	76	57.07 N	36.05 E
Kusan-ni, Taehan	98	37.43 N	128.49 E
Kusan-ni, Taehan	271b	37.29 N	126.45 E
Kusatsu, Nihon	94	36.37 N	138.36 E
Kusatsu, Nihon	94	35.00 N	135.57 E
Kusawa Lake ⊜	180	60.20 N	136.15 W
Kusaybah, Bi'r ⫪[4]	140	22.41 N	29.55 E
Kuščovskaja	78	46.33 N	39.37 E
Kuse	96	35.04 N	133.45 E
Kusel	56	49.32 N	7.24 E
Kušen'ki	78	48.53 N	34.07 E
Kusey	54	52.36 N	11.05 E
Kuş Gölü ⊜	130	40.10 N	27.57 E
Kuş Gölü Milli Parkı ♠	130	40.15 N	27.55 E
Kushaka	150	10.32 N	6.48 E
Kushālgarh	120	23.10 N	74.27 E
Kusheriki	150	10.33 N	6.28 E
Kushi	174m	26.33 N	128.06 E
Kushida ≃	94	34.36 N	136.34 E
Kushigata	94	35.36 N	138.28 E
Kushihiki	268	35.55 N	139.36 E
Kushikino	92	31.44 N	130.16 E
Kushima	92	31.29 N	131.14 E
Kushimoto	92	33.28 N	135.47 E
Kushira	270	34.28 N	135.43 E
Kushiro	92a	42.58 N	144.23 E
Kushog Lake ⊜	212	45.05 N	78.48 W
Kushtia	124	23.55 N	89.07 E
Kushui	102	42.11 N	94.25 E
Kusiro → Kushiro	92a	42.58 N	144.23 E
Kusiyāra ≃	120	24.36 N	91.44 E
Kuška	128	35.16 N	62.20 E
Kuška ≃	128	36.00 N	62.40 E
Kuskokwim ≃	180	60.17 N	162.27 W
Kuskokwim, North Fork ≃	180	63.06 N	154.37 W
Kuskokwim, South Fork ≃	180	63.06 N	154.37 W
Kuskokwim Bay ⊂	180	59.45 N	162.25 W
Kuskokwim Mountains ⋏	180	62.30 N	156.00 W
Kuskovo •[8]	265b	55.44 N	37.49 E
Kuškušara	24	64.58 N	40.21 E
Kuśmā	124	28.14 N	83.41 E
Kušmurun	86	52.27 N	64.36 E
Kušmurun, ozero ⊜	86	52.40 N	64.48 E
Küsnacht	58	47.19 N	8.35 E
Kušnarenkovo	86	55.06 N	55.22 E
Kušnica	78	48.27 N	23.14 E
Kusŏng	98	39.59 N	125.15 E
Kusria	272b	22.58 N	88.14 E
Kussharo-ko ⊜	92a	43.38 N	144.21 E
Küssnacht am Rigi	58	47.05 N	8.27 E
Kustanaj	86	53.10 N	63.35 E
Kustanaj □[8]	86	53.00 N	63.00 E
Kustar'ovka	80	54.16 N	42.16 E
Küsten-Gebirge → Coast Mountains ⋏	176	55.00 N	129.00 W
Küstenkanal ≊	52	52.57 N	7.18 E
Küsten-Ketten → Coast Ranges ⋏	178	41.00 N	123.30 W
Kusthalia	126	23.29 N	87.03 E
Kūstī	140	13.10 N	32.40 E
Kusu, Nihon	94	34.55 N	136.38 E
Kusu, Nihon	96	33.16 N	131.09 E
Kušugum	78	47.42 N	35.14 E
Kušum ≃	80	48.54 N	50.32 E
Kusumba	272b	22.27 N	88.24 E
Kusumbāni ∧	126	21.57 N	86.26 E
Kušumskij	80	51.38 N	48.21 E
Kusung	98	36.18 N	128.55 E
Kusunoki	96	34.03 N	131.15 E
K'us'ur	74	70.39 N	127.15 E
Kušva	86	58.18 N	59.45 E
Kut, Ko I	110	11.40 N	102.35 E
Kuta	150	9.52 N	6.43 E
Kuta ≃	88	56.46 N	105.40 E
Kutabaru	112	0.44 S	102.56 E
Kutabuloh	114	3.28 N	97.04 E
Kutacane	114	3.30 N	97.48 E
Kütahya	130	39.25 N	29.59 E
Kütahya □[4]	130	39.20 N	29.30 E
Kutais	78	44.32 N	39.18 E

Name	Seite	Breite°′	Länge°′ E = Ost
Kutaisi	84	42.15 N	42.40 E
Kutāmat al-Ghābah	142	30.55 N	30.54 E
Kutanibong	114	3.53 N	96.22 E
Kutaradja → Banda Aceh	114	5.34 N	95.20 E
Kutarere	172	38.03 S	177.09 E
Kutasawang	114	5.08 N	96.54 E
Kutch, Rann of (Rann of Kachchh) •[1]	120	24.05 N	70.10 E
Kutchan	92a	42.54 N	140.45 E
Kutcharo-ko ⊜	92a	45.09 N	142.19 E
Kutejnikovo, Ross.	83	47.34 N	39.46 E
Kutejnikovo, Ukr.	83	47.49 N	38.18 E
Kutenholz	52	53.29 N	9.19 E
Kutima	88	57.10 N	108.16 E
Kutima ≃	88	57.08 N	108.14 E
Kutina	36	45.29 N	16.46 E
Kutiyāna	120	21.38 N	69.59 E
Kutkai	110	23.27 N	97.56 E
Kutluškino	80	55.14 N	50.24 E
Kutná Hora	30	49.57 N	15.16 E
Kutno	30	52.15 N	19.23 E
Kutoarjo	115a	7.43 S	109.54 E
Kutomara	88	51.06 N	118.49 E
Kutse Game Reserve •[4]	156	23.30 S	24.05 E
Kutsuki	94	35.21 N	135.55 E
Küttigen	58	47.25 N	8.03 E
Kuttura	24	68.24 N	26.28 E
Kuttusoja	24	67.46 N	28.50 E
Kuttuzi	265a	59.45 N	30.04 E
Kutu	152	2.44 S	18.09 E
Kutubdia Island I	120	21.50 N	91.52 E
Kutubu, Lake ⊜	164	6.23 S	143.18 E
Kutukovo	80	54.26 N	40.31 E
Kutulik	88	53.21 N	102.48 E
Kutulo, Lagh ≃	154	2.08 N	40.56 E
Kutuluk ≃	80	53.19 N	51.09 E
Kutum	140	14.12 N	24.40 E
Kutu-Moke	152	3.12 S	17.21 E
Kúty, Slov.	30	48.40 N	17.03 E
Kuty, Ukr.	78	48.16 N	25.10 E
Kutztown	210	40.31 N	75.46 W
Kuujjuaq	176	58.06 N	68.25 W
Kuuli-Majak	128	40.14 N	52.42 E
Kuurne	50	50.51 N	3.17 E
Kuusamo	26	65.58 N	29.11 E
Kuusankoski	26	60.54 N	26.38 E
Kuva	85	40.32 N	72.05 E
Kuvak-Nikol'skoje	80	53.37 N	43.30 E
Kuvandyk	86	51.28 N	57.21 E
Kuvango	152	14.28 S	16.20 E
Kuvasaj	85	40.18 N	71.58 E
Kuvet ≃	180	69.14 N	175.00 E
Kuvšinovo	76	57.02 N	34.10 E
Kuwabara	270	34.53 N	135.15 E
Kuwait (Al-Kuwayt) □[1], Asia	118	29.30 N	47.45 E
Kuwait (Al-Kuwayt) □[1], Asia	128	29.30 N	47.45 E
Kuwait → Al-Kuwayt	128	29.20 N	47.59 E
Kuwait Bay → Kuwayt, Jūn al- ⊂	128	29.30 N	48.00 E
Kuwana	94	35.04 N	136.42 E
Kuwayt, Jūn al- (Kuwait Bay) ⊂	128	29.30 N	48.00 E
Kuyāli	126	22.31 N	86.11 E
Kuybyshev → Samara	80	53.12 N	50.09 E
Kuye ≃	102	38.30 N	110.44 E
Kūysanjaq	128	36.05 N	44.38 E
Kuyucak, Tür.	130	37.51 N	38.21 E
Kuyucak, Tür.	130	37.55 N	28.28 E
Kuyuwini ≃	246	2.16 N	58.16 W
Kuyuyukak, Cape >	180	56.54 N	156.50 W
Kuzaranda	24	62.22 N	35.37 E
Kuze	94	35.33 N	136.30 E
Kuze •[8]	270	34.57 N	135.43 E
Kuzedejevo	86	53.20 N	87.10 E
Kuzemin	78	50.09 N	34.39 E
Kuzemovka	83	49.31 N	37.59 E
Kužener	80	56.48 N	48.56 E
Kuženkino	76	57.44 N	33.59 E
Kuzitrin ≃	180	65.10 N	165.28 W
Kuzkejevo	80	55.46 N	52.48 E
Kuz'miniči	76	54.16 N	33.42 E
Kuz'minka ≃	265a	59.48 N	30.31 E
Kuz'minki •[8]	265b	55.42 N	37.48 E
Kuz'mino, Ross.	82	55.09 N	37.53 E
Kuz'mino, Ross.	82	56.36 N	37.55 E
Kuzmiščevo	82	54.46 N	37.12 E
Kuz'movka	74	62.19 N	92.02 E
Kuznečicha	80	54.43 N	49.38 E
Kuznečikovo	82	56.13 N	36.35 E
Kuzneck	80	53.07 N	46.36 E
Kuzneckij Alatau ⋏	86	54.45 N	88.00 E
Kuzneck → Novokuzneck	86	53.45 N	87.06 E
Kuznečnoje	26	61.09 N	29.52 E
Kuznecova	89	46.16 N	138.03 E
Kuznecovka	76	56.18 N	28.33 E
Kuznecovo, Ross.	82	55.30 N	38.21 E
Kuznecovo, Ross.	82	55.27 N	36.57 E
Kuznecovo, Ross.	86	59.15 N	63.28 E
Kuznecovo-Michajlovka	83	47.27 N	38.13 E
Kuznecovskij	80	47.25 N	40.57 E
Kuznecy	82	55.51 N	38.40 E
Kuznetsk → Kuzneck	80	53.07 N	46.36 E
Kuznetsovsk	78	51.22 N	25.53 E
Kuzomen', Ross.	24	64.17 N	42.53 E
Kuzomen', Ross.	24	66.17 N	36.54 E
Kuzovatovo	80	53.33 N	47.41 E
Kuzucubelen	130	36.51 N	34.27 E
Kuzuha	270	34.52 N	135.41 E
Kuzuryū ≃	94	36.13 N	136.08 E
Kuzuu	94	36.24 N	139.37 E
Kuzyaka	130	41.14 N	33.44 E
Kvænangen ⊂[2]	24	70.05 N	21.13 E
Kværndrup	41	55.10 N	10.32 E
Kvaisi	84	42.31 N	43.40 E
Kvaløy I	24	69.40 N	18.30 E
Kvaløya I	24	70.37 N	23.52 E
Kvam	26	61.40 N	9.42 E
Kvanløse	41	55.39 N	11.41 E
Kvanndal	26	60.29 N	6.36 E
Kvareli	84	41.56 N	45.54 E
Kvarner ⊂	36	44.45 N	14.15 E
Kvarnerić ʯ	36	44.45 N	14.35 E
Kvarnsveden	40	60.31 N	15.24 E
Kvarntorp	40	59.08 N	15.15 E
Kvarsa	80	56.58 N	53.57 E
Kvarsebo	40	58.39 N	16.39 E
Kvašenki	82	56.48 N	37.33 E
Kvenna ≃	26	60.01 N	7.56 E
Kverkfjöll ∧	24a	64.43 N	16.38 W
Kvichak Bay ⊂	180	58.48 N	157.30 W
Kvicksund	40	59.27 N	16.19 E
Kvidinge	41	56.08 N	13.04 E
Kvien ⊜	40	60.24 N	13.48 E
Kvikkjokk	24	66.55 N	17.50 E
Kvilda	60	49.01 N	13.35 E
Kvina ≃	26	58.17 N	6.56 E
Kvismare kanal ≊	40	59.12 N	15.11 E
Kvissleby	26	62.17 N	17.21 E
Kvistbro	40	59.09 N	14.49 E
Kvistgård	41	55.59 N	12.30 E
Kvitok	88	56.03 N	98.30 E
Kwa ≃	152	3.10 S	16.11 E
Kwachaga	154	5.38 S	38.08 E
Kwada	164	6.09 S	141.53 E
Kwahae-ri •[8]	271b	37.33 N	126.50 E
Kwahu Plateau ⋏[1]	150	6.30 N	0.30 W
Kwai → Khwae Noi ≃	110	14.00 N	99.33 E
Kwajalein I[1]	14	9.05 N	167.20 E
Kwajok	140	8.19 N	28.00 E
Kwakoegron	250	5.15 N	55.20 W

Symbols in the index entries represent the broad categories identified in the key at the right. Symbols with superior numbers (⋏[1]) identify subcategories (see complete key on page *I · 1).*

Symbole im Register stellen die rechts im Schlüssel erklärten Kategorien dar. Symbole mit hochgestellten Ziffern (⋏[1]) bezeichnen Unterabteilungen einer Kategorie (vgl. vollständiger Schlüssel auf Seite *I · 1).*

Los símbolos incluídos en el texto del índice representan las grandes categorias identificadas con la clave a la derecha. Los símbolos con numeros en su parte superior (⋏[1]) identifican las subcategorías (véase la clave completa en la página *I · 1).*

Les symboles de l'index représentent les catégories indiquées dans la légende à droite. Les symboles suivis d'un indice (⋏[1]) représentent des sous-catégories (voir légende complète à la page *I · 1).*

Os símbolos incluídos no texto do índice representam as grandes categorias identificadas com a chave à direita. Os símbolos com números em sua parte superior (⋏[1]) identificam as subcategorias (veja-se a chave completa à página *I · 1).*

English	Deutsch	Español	Français	Português
∧ Mountain	Berg	Montaña	Montagne	Montanha
⋏ Mountains	Gebirge	Montañas	Montagnes	Montanhas
)(Pass	Paß	Paso	Col	Passo
V Valley, Canyon	Tal, Cañon	Valle, Cañón	Vallée, Canyon	Vale, Canhão
⌣ Plain	Ebene	Llano	Plaine	Planície
> Cape	Kap	Cabo	Cap	Cabo
I Island	Insel	Isla	Île	Ilha
II Islands	Inseln	Islas	Îles	Ilhas
⊥ Other Topographic Features	Andere Topographische Objekte	Otros Elementos Topográficos	Autres données topographiques	Outros acidentes topográficos

ESPAÑOL — Nombre | Página | Lat.°′ | Long.°′ W = Oeste
FRANÇAIS — Nom | Page | Lat.°′ | Long.°′ W = Ouest
PORTUGUÊS — Nome | Página | Lat.°′ | Long.°′ W = Oeste

Kwale, Kenya 154 4.11 S 39.27 E
Kwale, Nig. 150 5.46 N 6.26 E
Kwambilo ≃ 273b 4.25 S 15.20 E
Kwa-Mbonambi 158 28.36 S 32.05 E
Kwamisa ∧ 150 7.08 N 1.53 W
Kwamouth 152 3.10 S 16.12 E
Kwa Mtoro 154 5.14 S 35.26 E
Kwanak-san ∧ 271b 37.27 N 126.58 E
Kwando (Cuando) ≃ 152 18.27 S 23.32 E
Kwangchow — Guangzhou 100 23.06 N 113.16 E
Kwangju 98 35.09 N 126.54 E
Kwangju □⁴ 98 35.09 N 126.55 E
Kwango (Cuango) ≃ 152 3.14 S 17.23 E
Kwangsi Chuang Autonomous Region — Guangxi Zhuangzu Zizhiqu □⁴ 102 24.00 N 109.00 E
Kwangtung — Guangdong □⁴ 90 23.00 N 113.00 E
Kwangwazi 154 7.47 S 38.15 E
Kwangyang 98 34.59 N 127.34 E
Kwania, Lake ◎ 154 1.45 N 32.45 E
Kwanmo-bong ∧ 98 41.42 N 129.13 E
Kwansan-ni 271b 37.43 N 126.51 E
Kwanto Plain — Kantō-heiya ≐ 94 36.00 N 139.30 E
Kwara □³ 150 8.45 N 5.00 E
Kware 150 13.12 N 5.14 E
Kwa-Thema 273d 26.18 S 28.23 E
Kwatisore 164 3.15 S 134.57 E
Kweichow — Guizhou □⁴ 102 27.00 N 107.00 E
Kweihwa — Hohhot 102 40.51 N 111.40 E
Kweijang — Guiyang 102 26.35 N 106.43 E
Kweilin — Guilin 102 25.17 N 110.17 E
Kweisui — Hohhot 102 40.51 N 111.40 E
Kweiyang — Guiyang 102 26.35 N 106.43 E
Kwekwe 154 18.55 S 29.49 E
Kweneng □⁵ 156 24.00 S 24.00 E
Kwenge (Caengo) ≃ 152 4.50 S 18.42 E
Kwesimintim 150 4.54 N 1.47 W
Kwethluk 180 60.49 N 161.27 W
Kwethluk ≃ 180 60.46 N 161.26 W
Kwidzyn 30 53.45 N 18.56 E
Kwigillingok 180 59.51 N 163.08 W
Kwiguk 180 62.45 N 164.28 W
Kwiha 144 13.31 N 39.32 E
Kwikila 164 9.48 S 147.41 E
Kwilu (Cuilo) ≃ 152 3.22 S 17.22 E
Kwinana 168a 32.15 S 115.48 E
Kwitaro ≃ 246 3.19 N 58.47 W
Kwobrup 162 33.37 S 117.46 E
Kwoka, Gunung ∧ 164 0.31 S 132.27 E
Kwolla 150 9.00 N 9.15 E
Kwun Tong 271d 22.19 N 114.12 E
Kyabé 146 9.27 N 18.57 E
Kyabra 166 26.18 S 143.10 E
Kyabra Creek ≃ 166 25.36 S 142.55 E
Kyabram 166 36.19 S 145.03 E
Kyaikkami 110 16.04 N 97.34 E
Kyaiklat 110 16.26 N 95.44 E
Kyaikto 110 17.18 N 97.01 E
Kya-in 110 16.02 N 98.08 E
Kyaka 154 1.16 S 31.25 E
Kyalite 166 34.57 S 143.29 E
Kyancutta 166 33.08 S 135.34 E
Ky Anh 110 18.05 N 106.18 E
Kyat-aw 110 12.29 N 98.19 E
Kyaukhnyat 110 18.15 N 97.31 E
Kyaukkyi 110 18.19 N 96.46 E
Kyaukme 110 22.32 N 97.02 E
Kyaukpa 110 13.05 N 98.59 E
Kyaukpyu, Mya. 110 19.05 N 93.52 E
Kyaukpyu, Mya. 110 19.26 N 93.33 E
Kyaukse 110 21.36 N 96.08 E
Kyauktaw 110 20.51 N 92.59 E
Kyaunggon 110 17.06 N 95.11 E
Kybartai 76 54.39 N 22.45 E
Kybean 171b 36.22 S 149.25 E
Kybeyan Range ∧ 171b 36.10 S 149.30 E
Kyburz 226 38.47 N 120.18 W
Kydra 171b 36.27 S 149.23 E
Kyeamba 171b 35.26 S 147.37 E
Kyeamba Creek ≃ 171b 35.06 S 147.29 E
Kyebang-san ∧ 98 37.43 N 128.29 E
Kyegegwa 154 0.29 N 31.03 E
Kyeikdon 110 16.00 N 98.24 E
Kyeintali 110 18.00 N 94.29 E
Kyenjojo 154 0.37 N 30.38 E
Kyeryong-san Kukrip Kongwŏn ♦ 98 36.21 N 127.13 E
Kyes Peak ∧ 224 47.57 N 121.19 W
Kyffhäuser-Denkmal ɪ 54 51.23 N 11.06 E
Kyffhäuser Gebirge ∧ 54 51.23 N 11.05 E
Kyidaunggan 110 19.53 N 96.12 E
Kyindwe 110 20.58 N 93.51 E
Kyje ✦⁸ 54 50.04 N 14.32 E
Kyjov 30 49.01 N 17.08 E
Kykladen — Kikládhes ɪɪ 38 37.30 N 25.00 E
Kykotsmovi Village 200 35.52 N 110.37 W
Kykva 80 57.22 N 53.50 E
Kylās ∧ 124 25.18 N 90.45 E
Kyle, Sk., Can. 184 50.50 N 108.02 W
Kyle, S.D., U.S. 198 43.25 N 102.10 W
Kyle, Tx., U.S. 196 29.59 N 97.52 W
Kyle □⁹ 46 55.29 N 4.24 W
Kyle, Lake ◎¹ 154 20.14 S 31.00 E
Kyleakin 46 57.16 N 5.44 W
Kyle of Lochalsh 46 57.17 N 5.43 W
Kylerhea 46 57.14 N 5.41 W
Kylertown 214 41.00 N 78.10 W
Kylestrome 46 58.16 N 5.02 W
Kyll ≃ 56 49.48 N 6.42 E
Kyllburg 56 50.02 N 6.35 E
Kym ≃ 42 52.14 N 0.17 W
Kymen lääni □⁴ 26 61.00 N 28.00 E
Kymijoki ≃ 26 60.30 N 26.52 E
Kyn 86 57.52 N 58.38 E
Kyndby 41 55.48 N 11.56 E
Kyneton 169 37.15 S 144.27 E
Kynnefjäll ∧² 26 58.42 N 11.41 E
Kynšperk nad Ohří 54 50.04 N 12.32 E
Kynuna 166 21.35 S 141.55 E
Kyodong-do ɪ 98 37.45 N 126.16 E
Kyoga, Lake ◎ 154 1.30 N 33.00 E
Kyōga-misaki › 96 35.46 N 135.13 E
Kyogle 166 28.37 S 153.00 E
Kyoha-ri 271b 37.46 N 126.46 E
Kyohyŏn-ni 271b 37.43 N 126.58 E
Kyom ≃ 140 8.58 N 28.13 E
Kyŏmip'o — Songnim 98 38.44 N 125.38 E
Kyonan 94 35.07 N 139.50 E
Kyondo 110 16.35 N 98.03 E
Kyŏnggi Do □⁴ 98 37.30 N 127.15 E
Kyŏnggi-man ⊂ 98 37.25 N 126.00 E
Kyŏngju 98 35.51 N 129.14 E
Kyŏngju Kukrip Kongwŏn ♦ 98 35.47 N 129.15 E
Kyŏngsan 98 35.48 N 128.43 E
Kyŏngsang Namdo □⁴ 98 35.15 N 128.30 E
Kyŏngsang Pukdo □⁴ 98 36.15 N 128.45 E
Kyŏngsŏng 98 41.35 N 129.36 E
Kyŏngsŏng — Sŏul 98 37.33 N 126.58 E
Kyŏngwŏn 98 42.48 N 130.09 E
Kyŏnkhadun 110 16.04 N 95.38 E
Kyonmange 110 16.30 N 95.50 E
Kyonpyaw 110 17.18 N 95.12 E
Kyotera 154 0.33 S 31.19 E
Kyōto, Nihon 94 35.00 N 135.45 E
Kyōto, Nihon 270 35.00 N 135.45 E
Kyōto □⁵ 94 35.05 N 135.45 E
Kyōto-bonchi ∧ 270 35.03 N 135.45 E
Kyōto Race Track ♦ 270 34.54 N 135.44 E
Kyōto University ʊ² 270 35.02 N 135.46 E
Kyōwa 94 36.19 N 140.03 E
Kyŏyomi-dake ∧ 96 33.31 N 131.02 E
Kypšak, ozero ◎ 86 50.09 N 68.28 E
Kyra 88 49.36 N 111.58 E
Kyra ≃ 88 49.24 N 112.19 E
Kyrčany 80 57.37 N 50.10 E
Kyren 88 51.41 N 102.08 E
Kyrenia — Girne 130 35.20 N 33.19 E
Kyrgyzstan □¹, Asia 72 41.30 N 75.00 E
Kyrgyzstan □¹, Asia 85 41.30 N 75.00 E
Kyritz 54 52.56 N 12.23 E
Kyrkheden 40 60.10 N 13.29 E
Kyrkkazyk 85 42.30 N 72.20 E
Kyrksæterøra 26 63.17 N 9.06 E
Kyrkslätt (Kirkkonummi) 26 60.07 N 24.26 E
Kyrö 26 60.42 N 22.45 E
Kyrönjoki ≃ 26 63.14 N 21.45 E
Kyrösjärvi ◎ 26 61.45 N 23.10 E
Kyröskoski 26 61.40 N 23.11 E
Kyrta 24 64.04 N 57.42 E
Kyrykkuduk 80 49.51 N 51.54 E
Ky Son 110 19.24 N 104.08 E
Kyštovka 86 56.33 N 76.38 E
Kyštym 86 55.42 N 60.34 E
Kysykkamys 80 49.14 N 50.19 E
Kyte ≃ 190 42.00 N 89.19 W
Kytlym 86 59.30 N 59.12 E
Kytmanovo 86 53.28 N 85.28 E
Kyūhōji 270 34.38 N 135.35 E
Kyunchaung 110 15.33 N 98.15 E
Kyundon 110 20.31 N 95.44 E
Kyungyi ɪ 110 15.04 N 97.44 E
Kyunhla 110 23.21 N 95.18 E
Kyuquot 182 50.02 N 127.23 W
Kyuquot Sound ⊂ 182 50.05 N 127.15 W
Kyūroku-jima ɪ 92 40.32 N 139.29 E
Kyū-shizudani-gakkō ɪ 96 34.45 N 134.13 E
Kyūshū ɪ 92 33.00 N 131.00 E
Kyushu-Palau Ridge ✦³ 14 20.00 N 136.00 E
Kyūshū-sanchi ∧ 92 32.35 N 131.17 E
Kywebwe 110 18.42 N 96.25 E
Kywong 166 34.59 S 146.44 E
Kyyjärvi 26 63.02 N 24.34 E
Kyyvesi ◎ 26 61.58 N 27.07 E
Kyzas 86 52.20 N 89.20 E
Kyzyl 88 51.42 N 94.27 E
Kyzylagadžskij zapovednik ✦⁴ 84 39.10 N 49.00 E
Kyzylagaš 86 45.54 N 81.37 E
Kyzylaryk 85 43.26 N 72.04 E
Kyzylbejit 85 41.30 N 72.24 E
Kyzyl-Chaja 86 50.03 N 89.54 E
Kyzyl-Chem (Šišchid) ≃ 88 51.21 N 96.58 E
Kyzyl-Džar 85 41.17 N 72.02 E
Kyzyljengek 85 41.57 N 74.56 E
Kyzylespe 86 47.27 N 73.53 E
Kyzylkak, ozero ◎ 86 53.25 N 73.48 E
Kyzyl-Kija 85 40.16 N 72.08 E
Kyzyl-Kommuna 86 48.44 N 67.32 E
Kyzylkum ✦² 72 42.00 N 64.00 E
Kyzylkup 128 40.38 N 53.58 E
Kyzyl-Mažalyk 86 51.10 N 90.32 E
Kyzylmazar 85 39.39 N 68.25 E
Kyzyloba 80 49.37 N 50.38 E
Kyzylsu ≃ 85 39.17 N 71.23 E
Kyzyltas, gory ∧ 86 48.30 N 74.50 E
Kyzyltau 86 47.53 N 72.05 E
Kyzylt'ob'o 85 42.13 N 75.16 E
Kyzyltu, Kaz. 86 47.46 N 59.08 E
Kyzyltu, Kaz. 86 47.43 N 76.12 E
Kyzyltu, Kyrg. 85 42.11 N 76.40 E
Kyzyluj 86 48.07 N 65.28 E
Kyzylžar 86 48.17 N 69.39 E
Kzyl-Kuga 80 48.28 N 53.01 E
Kzyl-Orda 86 44.48 N 65.28 E
Kzyl-Orda □⁸ 86 45.00 N 64.00 E
Kzyltu 86 53.38 N 72.20 E

L

La'a 102 29.44 N 101.26 E
Laa an der Thaya 61 48.43 N 16.23 E
Laaben 61 48.06 N 15.52 E
Laaber 60 49.04 N 11.53 E
Laaberberg 60 48.46 N 12.01 E
Laab im Walde 264b 48.09 N 16.11 E
Laacher See ◎ 56 50.25 N 7.16 E
Laaerberg ∧² 264b 48.09 N 16.24 E
Laage 54 53.56 N 12.20 E
La Aguja, Cabo de › 246 11.18 N 74.12 W
Laakajärvi ◎ 26 63.50 N 27.55 E
Laaken ✦⁸ 263 51.15 N 7.15 E
Laakirchen 64 47.58 N 13.49 E
La Albuera 34 38.43 N 6.49 W
La Alcarria ✦¹ 34 40.45 N 2.45 W
La Aldea 230 20.54 N 101.29 W
La Aldehuela 266a 40.18 N 3.36 W
La Algaba 34 37.28 N 6.01 W
La Almarcha 34 39.41 N 2.22 W
La Almunia de Doña Godina 34 41.29 N 1.22 W
Laanecoorie Reservoir ◎¹ 169 36.52 S 143.53 E
La Antigua, Salina ≐ 252 30.00 S 66.06 W
La Antorcha, Cerro ∧ 234 21.43 N 102.45 W
Laar ✦⁸ 263 51.28 N 6.43 E
La Araucanía □⁴ 252 38.45 S 72.30 W
La Arena, Pan. 236 7.58 N 80.28 W
La Arena, Perú 248 5.20 S 80.44 W
Laas Caanood 144 8.28 N 47.21 E
La Ascensión 232 24.20 N 99.55 W
Laas Dawaco 144 10.28 N 49.05 E
Laas Dhaareed 144 10.13 N 46.08 E
Laase 54 53.04 N 11.18 E
Laas — Lasa 64 46.37 N 10.42 E
Laas Qoray 144 11.10 N 48.13 E
La Asunción 246 11.02 N 63.53 W
La Atravesada, Loma ∧² 232 29.57 N 112.12 W
Laatzen 52 52.19 N 9.47 E
Laau Point › 229a 21.06 N 157.19 W
La Aurora 286e 33.36 S 70.38 W
La Azufrosa 196 28.14 N 100.50 W
Laba ≃ 78 45.11 N 39.42 E
La Babia 232 28.34 N 102.04 W
Labadie 219 38.31 N 90.51 W
Labadieville 194 29.50 N 90.57 W
La Baie 186 48.19 N 70.53 W
La Balme-de-Sillingy 58 45.58 N 6.02 E
La Balme-les-Grottes 62 45.51 N 5.20 E
Laban 208 37.23 N 76.17 W
La Banda 252 27.44 S 64.15 W
La Bandera, Cerro ∧ 232 24.35 N 105.07 W
La Bañeza 34 42.18 N 5.54 W
La Barca 234 20.17 N 102.34 W
La Barceloneta ✦⁸ 266d 41.22 N 2.11 E
La Barge 200 42.16 N 110.11 W
La Barge Creek ≃ 200 42.14 N 110.10 W
La Barra 236 12.54 N 83.32 W
La Barre-en-Ouche 50 48.57 N 0.40 E
La Barrita 236 14.05 N 91.03 W
La Barr Meadows 226 39.11 N 121.02 W
Labason 116 8.04 N 122.31 E
La Bassée 50 50.32 N 2.48 E
Labastide-Murat 32 44.39 N 1.34 E
La Bastide-Puylaurent 62 44.36 N 3.54 E
La Bâte 261 48.35 N 2.01 E
La Baule-Escoublac 32 47.17 N 2.24 W
La Bazoche-Gouet 50 48.08 N 0.59 E
L'Abbé 261 48.34 N 1.50 E
Labdah (Leptis Magna) ɪ 146 32.38 N 14.18 E
Labé 150 11.19 N 12.17 W
Labe (Elbe) ≃ 30 53.50 N 9.00 E
Labégude 62 44.39 N 4.22 E
La Bégude-Blanche 62 43.55 N 6.08 E
La Bégude-de-Mazenc 62 44.32 N 4.56 E
Labelle, P.Q., Can. 206 46.16 N 74.44 W
La Belle, Fl., U.S. 220 26.45 N 81.26 W
La Belle, Mo., U.S. 219 40.07 N 91.54 W
Labelle □⁶ 206 46.20 N 75.00 W
Labelle, Lac ◎, P.Q., Can. 206 46.13 N 74.52 W
La Belle, Lac ◎, Wi., U.S. 216 43.08 N 88.31 W
Labengke, Pulau ɪ 112 3.27 S 122.25 E
La Bérarde 62 44.56 N 6.18 E
Laberge, Lake ◎ 180 61.11 N 135.12 W
La Berra ∧ 58 46.41 N 7.11 E
Laberweinting 60 48.48 N 12.19 E
La Besace 56 49.34 N 4.58 E
Labette Creek ≃ 198 37.03 N 95.05 W
Labi 112 4.25 N 114.22 E
La Biche ≃ 182 55.01 N 112.44 W
Labico 66 41.47 N 12.53 E
Labin 36 45.05 N 14.07 E
Labinsk 84 44.38 N 40.44 E
Labis 114 2.23 N 103.02 E
La Bisbal 34 41.57 N 3.03 E
Łabiszyn 30 52.57 N 17.55 E
Lablābah, Wādī al- V 273c 30.02 N 31.19 E
La Blanca 286e 33.31 S 70.41 W
La Blanca Grande, Laguna ◎ 252 38.26 S 63.55 W
Labnā ɪ 232 20.11 N 89.34 W
Labo 116 14.09 N 122.51 E
Labo ≃ 116 14.11 N 122.56 E
Labo, Mount ∧ 116 14.01 N 122.48 E
Laboe 54 54.24 N 10.15 E
La Boissière 261 48.46 N 1.59 E
La Boissière-Ecole 261 48.41 N 1.39 E
La Bollène-Vésubie 62 43.59 N 7.20 E
La Bonneville-sur-Iton 50 49.00 N 1.02 E
Laboratory 214 40.09 N 80.13 W
Laborde, Arg. 252 33.09 S 62.51 W
La Borde, Fr. 261 48.32 N 2.50 E
Laborec ≃ 30 48.36 N 22.00 E
Laborie 241f 13.45 N 61.00 W
Labouchere, Mount ∧ 162 25.12 S 118.18 E
Labouheyre 32 44.13 N 0.55 W
Laboulaye 252 34.07 S 63.24 W
La Bouverie 50 50.24 N 3.52 E
La Boyera, Ven. 286c 10.23 N 66.57 W
La Boyera, Ven. 286c 10.25 N 66.50 W
Lābpur 126 23.50 N 87.49 E
Labrador ✦¹ 176 54.00 N 62.00 W
Labrador Basin ✦¹ 176 61.00 N 55.00 W
Labrador City 176 52.57 N 66.55 W
Labrador Sea ⊤² 176 57.00 N 53.00 W
Lábrea, Bra. 248 7.16 S 64.47 W
La Brea, Trin. 241r 10.15 N 61.37 W
Labrède 32 44.41 N 0.31 W
La Bresse 58 48.00 N 6.53 E
La Brévine 58 46.59 N 6.36 E
Labrieville, Réserve ♦ 186 49.20 N 69.40 W
La Brigue 62 44.04 N 7.37 E
La Brillanne 62 43.55 N 5.53 E
Labrit 32 44.07 N 0.33 W
La Broquerie 184 49.28 N 96.27 W
Labroye 50 50.17 N 1.59 E
Labry 56 49.10 N 5.52 E
Labuan, Pulau ɪ 112 5.21 N 115.13 E
Labuha 164 0.37 S 127.29 E
Labuhan 115a 6.22 S 105.50 E
Labuhanbajo 115b 8.29 S 119.54 E
Labuhanbatu 114 2.12 N 100.12 E
Labuhanbilik 114 2.31 N 100.10 E
Labuhandeli 114 3.45 N 98.41 E
Labuhanhaji, Indon. 114 3.33 N 97.00 E
Labuhanhaji, Indon. 115b 8.42 S 116.34 E
Labuhanmarege 112 7.06 S 120.40 E
Labuhanmaringgai 115a 5.21 S 105.48 E
Labuhanruku 114 3.13 N 99.35 E
Labuk ≃ 112 5.54 N 117.30 E
Labuk, Telukan ⊂ 116 6.07 N 117.46 E
Labu Kananga 115b 8.08 S 117.47 E
Labutta 110 16.09 N 94.46 E
Labytnangi 72 66.39 N 66.21 E
Lač, Ross. 24 63.18 N 54.28 E
Laç, Shq. 38 41.38 N 19.43 E
Lac □⁵ 146 13.30 N 14.15 E
Lača, ozero ◎ 24 61.20 N 38.48 E
La Cadena 196 25.53 N 104.12 W
L'Acadie 275a 45.19 N 73.21 W
L'Acadie ≃ 206 45.29 N 73.16 W
La Cadière-d'Azur 62 43.12 N 5.46 E
Lacadivas, Islas — Lakshadweep ɪɪ 122 10.00 N 73.00 E
Laca Jahuira ≃ 248 19.21 S 67.54 W
La Cal ≃ 248 17.27 S 58.15 W
Lac-à-la-Tortue 206 46.37 N 72.38 W
La Calera, Chile 252 32.47 S 71.12 W
La Calera, Perú 286d 12.12 S 76.54 W
Lac-Allard 186 50.33 N 63.25 W
Lacamas Creek ≃ 224 45.37 N 122.26 W
Lacamas Lake ◎ 224 45.37 N 122.26 W
La Campana, Esp. 34 37.34 N 5.26 W
La Campana, Méx. 234 22.45 N 105.35 W
La Cañada 234 20.37 N 100.19 W
La Cañada, Cerro ∧ 234 21.24 N 99.13 W
La Cañada Flintridge 228 34.12 N 118.12 W
La Canada Verde Creek ≃ 280 33.52 N 118.02 W
Lacanau 32 44.59 N 1.05 W
Lacanau, Lac de ⊂ 32 44.58 N 1.07 W
La Candelaria, Arg. 252 26.06 S 65.06 W
La Candelaria, Méx. 200 31.07 N 106.29 W
La Cañiza 34 42.13 N 8.16 W
La Canourgue 62 44.26 N 3.13 E
Lacantún ≃ 232 16.36 N 90.39 W
La Capelle-en-Thiérache 50 49.58 N 3.55 E
La Capelle-lès-Boulogne 50 50.44 N 1.42 E
La Capelle-Marival 32 44.44 N 1.54 E
La Carlota, Arg. 252 33.25 S 63.18 W
La Carlota, Pil. 116 10.25 N 122.55 E
Lacarne 214 41.31 N 83.03 W
La Carolina 34 38.15 N 3.37 W
La Casita 234 23.43 N 104.46 W
La Castellana 116 10.20 N 123.03 E
Lacaune 32 43.43 N 2.42 E
Lac-Bellemare 206 46.44 N 73.08 W
Lac-Brome 206 45.13 N 72.31 W
Laccadive, Minicoy, and Amīndīvi Islands — Lakshadweep □³ 122 10.00 N 73.00 E
Laccadive Islands — Lakshadweep ɪɪ 122 10.00 N 73.00 E
Lacchiarella 64 45.19 N 9.08 E
Lacco Ameno 68 40.45 N 13.54 E
Lac Courte Oreilles Indian Reservation ✦⁴ 190 45.55 N 91.19 W
Lac du Flambeau 190 45.59 N 89.51 W
Lac du Flambeau Indian Reservation ✦⁴ 190 45.59 N 89.53 W
Laceby 44 53.32 N 0.10 W
Lacedonia 68 41.03 N 15.25 E
La Ceiba, Hond. 236 15.47 N 86.50 W
La Ceiba, Ven. 246 9.28 N 71.04 W
La Celle-les-Bordes 261 48.38 N 1.57 E
La Celle-Saint-Cloud 261 48.51 N 2.08 E
La Celle-Saint-Cyr 50 47.58 N 3.18 E
La Center, Ky., U.S. 194 37.04 N 88.58 W
La Center, Wa., U.S. 224 45.52 N 122.40 W
Lacepede Bay ⊂ 166 36.47 S 139.45 E
Lacerdónia 156 18.01 S 35.30 E
Laces (Latsch) 64 46.37 N 10.52 E
Lac-Etchemin 186 46.24 N 70.30 W
Lacey 224 47.02 N 122.49 W
Lacey Creek ≃ 278 41.50 N 88.03 W
Laceyville 210 41.39 N 76.10 W
Lac-Frontière 186 46.42 N 70.00 W
La Chaise-Dieu 62 45.19 N 3.42 E
La Chambre 62 45.22 N 6.18 E
La Chapelle-d'Angillon 50 47.22 N 2.26 E
La Chapelle-en-Vercors 62 44.58 N 5.25 E
La Chapelle-Gauthier 261 48.33 N 2.54 E
La Chapelle-la-Reine 50 48.19 N 2.35 E
La Chapelle-Saint-Luc 50 48.20 N 4.03 E
La Chapelle-Vendômoise 50 47.40 N 1.15 E
La Charité-sur-Loire 50 47.11 N 3.01 E
La Chartre-sur-le-Loir 50 47.44 N 0.35 E
La Châtaigneraie 32 46.39 N 0.44 W
La Châtre 32 46.35 N 1.59 E
Lachaussée, Étang de ◎ 56 49.02 N 5.48 E
La Chaux-de-Fonds 58 47.06 N 6.50 E
Lachay, Punta › 248 11.18 S 77.39 W
Lach Dennis 262 53.15 N 2.26 W
Lachdenpochja 24 61.31 N 30.08 E
Lachen 58 47.12 N 8.51 E
Lachenaie 275a 45.42 N 73.34 W
Lachendorf 52 52.37 N 10.14 E
Lachhmangarh Sīkar 120 27.49 N 75.02 E
L'achi 80 55.20 N 41.56 E
Lachine 206 45.26 N 73.40 W
Lachine, Canal de ⊔ 275a 45.26 N 73.40 W
Lachine, Rapides de ⌐ 275a 45.25 N 73.36 W
La Chira, Punta › 286d 12.13 S 77.03 W
La Chivera 286c 10.37 N 66.54 W
Lachkaltsap Indian Reserve ✦⁴ 182 55.03 N 129.34 W
Lachlan ≃ 166 34.21 S 143.57 E
La Chorrera, Col. 246 0.44 S 73.01 W
La Chorrera, Pan. 236 8.53 N 79.47 W
L'achoviči, Bela. 76 52.23 N 27.55 E
L'achoviči, Bela. 76 53.02 N 26.16 E
L'achovskije ostrova ɪɪ 74 73.30 N 141.00 E
La Choza 258 34.47 S 59.07 W
La Choza, Arroyo ≃ 258 34.40 S 58.58 W
Lachta ✦⁸ 265a 60.00 N 30.09 E
Lachtinskij Razliv, ozero ◎ 265a 60.00 N 30.11 E
Lachute 206 45.38 N 74.20 W
Lachva 76 52.13 N 27.04 E
La Ciénaga 252 27.30 S 66.57 W
La Ciénega 234 16.54 N 96.46 W
Lâçin 130 40.47 N 34.54 E
La Cinta Creek ≃ 196 35.24 N 104.06 W
La Ciotat 62 43.10 N 5.36 E
La Cisterna 286e 33.33 S 70.41 W
La Citadelle ɪ 238 19.35 N 72.14 W
La Ciudad 234 23.44 N 105.42 W
Lack 48 54.33 N 7.35 W
Lackawanna 210 42.49 N 78.49 W
Lackawanna □⁶ 210 41.24 N 75.40 W
Lackawanna ≃ 210 41.21 N 75.47 W
Lackawanna, Lake ◎ 276 40.57 N 74.42 W
Lackawanna State Park ♦ 210 41.33 N 75.44 W
Lackawaxen 210 41.29 N 74.59 W
Lackawaxen ≃ 210 41.29 N 74.59 W
Lackey 208 37.14 N 76.33 W
Lackland Air Force Base ■ 196 29.27 N 98.37 W
Läckö 26 58.41 N 13.13 E
Lackoje 76 58.05 N 38.08 E
Lac La Belle 216 43.09 N 88.32 W
Lac la Biche 182 54.46 N 111.58 W
Lac la Hache 182 51.49 N 121.28 W
Lac la Ronge Provincial Park ♦ 184 55.15 N 104.55 W
La Clayette 32 46.18 N 4.19 E
Laclede, Id., U.S. 182 48.10 N 116.45 W
La Clede, Il., U.S. 219 38.53 N 88.43 W
Laclede, Mo., U.S. 194 39.47 N 93.10 W
La Clotilde 252 27.08 S 60.40 W
La Clusaz 58 45.54 N 6.25 E
La Cluse 58 46.10 N 5.34 E
La Cluse-et-Mijoux 58 46.53 N 6.23 E
Lacmalac 171b 35.19 S 148.19 E
Lac-Masson 206 46.02 N 74.04 W
Lac-Mégantic 188 45.36 N 70.53 W
Lacob ti-duyong, Mount ∧ 116 17.35 N 121.09 E
La Cocha 252 27.47 S 65.34 W
Lacolle 206 45.05 N 73.22 W
La Colle 206 45.04 N 73.20 W
La Colle-sur-Loup 62 43.41 N 7.06 E
La Colmena 286a 19.36 N 99.18 W
La Colorada 232 28.41 N 110.25 W
La Columna — Bolívar, Pico ∧ 246 8.30 N 71.02 W
La Coma 232 24.28 N 98.19 W
Lacombe, Ab., Can. 182 52.28 N 113.44 W
Lacombe, La., U.S. 194 30.18 N 89.56 W
Lacon 190 41.01 N 89.24 W
Lacona, Ia., U.S. 190 41.11 N 93.22 W
Lacona, N.Y., U.S. 212 43.38 N 76.04 W
La Concepción, Pan. 236 8.31 N 82.37 W
La Concepción, Ven. 246 10.38 N 71.50 W
La Condamine-Châtelard 62 44.27 N 6.45 E
Laconi 71 39.51 N 9.03 E
Laconia 188 43.31 N 71.28 W
La Conner 224 48.23 N 122.29 W
La Consulta 252 33.44 S 69.07 W
Lacoochee 220 28.27 N 82.10 W
La Coruña 34 43.22 N 8.23 W
La Coruña □⁴ 34 43.10 N 8.25 W
Lacoste, Fr. 62 43.50 N 5.16 E
La Coste, Tx., U.S. 196 29.19 N 98.49 W
La Côte-Saint-André 62 45.23 N 5.15 E
La Courneuve 261 48.56 N 2.23 E
La Couronne 32 45.37 N 0.06 E
La Courtine 32 45.42 N 2.16 E
Lac qui Parle ≃ 198 45.01 N 95.53 W
Lac qui Parle, West Branch ≃ 198 44.55 N 96.02 W
La Crau 62 43.09 N 6.04 E
Lacre Punt › 241s 12.02 N 68.15 W
La Crescent 190 43.49 N 91.18 W
La Crescenta 280 34.13 N 118.14 W
La Croft 214 40.39 N 80.35 W
Lacroix-Saint-Ouen 50 49.21 N 2.47 E
La Crosse, In., U.S. 216 41.19 N 86.53 W
La Crosse, Ks., U.S. 198 38.31 N 99.18 W
La Crosse, Va., U.S. 192 36.41 N 78.05 W
Lacrosse, Wa., U.S. 202 46.49 N 117.53 W
La Crosse, Wi., U.S. 190 43.48 N 91.14 W
La Crosse ≃ 190 43.48 N 91.14 W
La Cruz, Arg. 252 29.10 S 56.38 W
La Cruz, Col. 246 1.35 N 76.58 W
La Cruz, C.R. 236 11.04 N 85.39 W
La Cruz, Méx. 196 28.33 N 100.48 W
La Cruz, Ur. 258 33.56 S 56.15 W
La Cruz, Cerro ∧ 234 17.55 N 101.31 W
La Cruz de Río Grande 236 13.06 N 84.10 W
Lac-Saguay 206 46.30 N 75.09 W
Lac Seul 184 50.20 N 92.16 W
Lac Seul Indian Reserve ✦⁴ 184 50.15 N 92.10 W
La Cuchilla 234 18.54 N 103.19 W
La Cuesta, C.R. 236 8.30 N 82.50 W
La Cuesta, Méx. 234 20.10 N 104.51 W
La Cuesta, P.R. 240m 18.25 N 66.49 W
La Cumbre, Arg. 252 30.58 S 64.30 W
La Cumbre, Ven. 286c 10.32 N 66.57 W
La Cumbre, Volcán ∧¹ 246a 0.20 S 91.30 W
La Cure 58 46.28 N 6.05 E
Lacy Fork ≃ 222 32.24 N 96.08 W
La Cygne 198 38.21 N 94.45 W
Lacy-Lakeview 222 31.37 N 97.06 W
Lada, Teluk ⊂ 115a 6.29 S 105.44 E
Ladainha 255 17.39 S 41.44 W
Ladākh □⁹ 120 35.10 N 76.10 E
Ladākh Range ∧ 120 34.00 N 78.00 E
Ladan 78 50.31 N 32.35 E
La Dang, Ko ɪ 114 6.33 N 99.18 E
Ladang Jagor 114 4.42 N 101.35 E
Ladara 114 1.28 N 97.28 E
Ladário 248 19.01 S 57.35 W
Ladbergen 52 52.08 N 7.44 E
Ladby 41 55.26 N 10.38 E
Ladd 190 41.22 N 89.13 W
Låddenhøj ∧² 41 56.13 N 9.48 E
Ladder Creek ≃ 198 38.48 N 100.52 W
Laddingford 260 51.12 N 0.25 E
Laddonia 219 39.14 N 91.38 W
Ladeburg 264a 52.42 N 13.35 E
La Défense ʊ 261 48.53 N 2.15 E
La Dehesa 286e 33.22 S 70.33 W
La Dent d'Oche ∧ 58 46.21 N 6.44 E
Ladera Heights 280 33.59 N 118.22 W
La Désirade ɪ 241o 16.19 N 61.03 W
Lādhi 38 41.27 N 26.17 E
Ladhurka 126 23.22 N 86.32 E
La Digue ɪ 138 4.21 S 55.50 E
Lâdik 130 40.55 N 35.55 E
Ladinger Spitze ∧ 61 46.51 N 14.39 E
L'adiny 24 61.33 N 38.20 E
Ladismith 158 33.30 S 21.16 E
Ladispoli 66 41.56 N 12.05 E
Lādīz 128 28.56 N 61.19 E
Ladner 224 49.05 N 123.05 W
Lādnūn 120 27.39 N 74.23 E
Ladoga 194 39.54 N 86.48 W
Ladoga, Lake — Ladožskoje ozero ◎ 24 61.00 N 31.30 E
La Dolorita 286c 10.29 N 66.47 W
Ladon 50 48.00 N 2.32 E
Ladonia 196 33.25 N 95.56 W
La Dorada 246 5.27 N 74.40 W
La Dormida 252 33.21 S 67.55 W
Lado Sarāi ✦⁸ 272a 28.32 N 77.12 E
L'adova 78 48.28 N 27.37 E
Ladovskaja Balka 80 45.38 N 41.25 E
Ladožskaja 78 45.19 N 39.54 E
Ladožskoje Ozero 76 60.08 N 31.04 E
Ladožskoje ozero (Lake Ladoga) ◎ 24 61.00 N 31.30 E
Lādpur ✦⁸ 272a 28.44 N 76.59 E
Ladrillero, Golfo ⊂ 254 49.20 S 75.37 W
Ladson 192 32.59 N 80.06 W
Ladue 219 38.38 N 90.23 W
Ladue ≃ 180 63.09 N 140.25 W
Laduozong 102 31.27 N 97.19 E
Laduškin 76 54.36 N 20.11 E
Ladva 24 61.21 N 34.34 E
Ladva-Vetka 24 61.33 N 34.27 E
Ladwa 124 29.59 N 77.03 E
L'ady, Bela. 76 54.36 N 31.10 E
Lady, Fr. 261 48.35 N 2.54 E
L'ady, Ross. 76 58.38 N 28.47 E
Lady Ann Strait ⌐ 176 75.40 N 79.50 W
Ladybank 46 56.16 N 3.08 W
Lady Barron 166 40.12 S 148.14 E
Ladybower Reservoir ◎¹ 44 53.20 N 1.45 W
Ladybrand 158 29.19 S 27.25 E
Lady Elliot Island ɪ 166 24.07 S 152.42 E
Lady Evelyn Lake ◎ 190 47.20 N 80.10 W
Lady Frere 158 31.44 S 27.16 E
Lady Grey 158 30.45 S 27.13 E
Lady Lake 220 28.55 N 81.55 W
Ladysmith, Austl. 171b 35.12 S 147.31 E
Ladysmith, B.C., Can. 182 48.58 N 123.49 W
Ladysmith, S. Afr. 158 28.34 S 29.45 E
Ladysmith, Wi., U.S. 190 45.27 N 91.06 W
Ladyžinka 86 51.00 N 68.42 E
Ladyžin 78 48.41 N 29.15 E
Ladžanurges 84 42.37 N 42.50 E
Lae 164 6.45 S 147.00 E
Lae ɪ¹ 14 8.56 N 166.14 E
Laem, Khao ∧ 110 14.27 N 101.30 E
Laem Ngop 110 12.10 N 102.26 E
La Encantada 232 25.17 N 101.04 W
La Encarnacion 234 23.23 N 98.01 W
Laer 52 52.03 N 7.21 E
Laer ✦⁸ 263 51.28 N 7.16 E
Lærdalsøyri 26 61.06 N 7.29 E
La Escondida 196 26.17 N 99.46 W
La Esmeralda, Méx. 232 27.17 N 103.39 W
La Esmeralda, Para. 252 22.13 S 62.38 W
La Esmeralda, Ven. 246 3.10 N 65.33 W
Læsø ɪ 26 57.16 N 11.01 E
La Esperanza, Cuba 240p 22.46 N 83.44 W
La Esperanza, Hond. 236 14.20 N 88.10 W
La Esperanza, Méx. 196 26.46 N 104.00 W
La Esperanza, Méx. 200 32.06 N 114.47 W
La Esperanza, Perú 248 8.05 S 79.04 W
La Esperanza, P.R. 240m 18.22 N 66.07 W
La Estación ✦⁸ 266a 40.27 N 3.48 W
La Estrada 34 42.41 N 8.29 W
La Estrella, Bol. 248 16.30 S 63.45 W
La Estrella, Ven. 286c 10.25 N 66.48 W
La Estrella, Cerro ∧ 286a 19.20 N 99.05 W
Lafa 89 43.50 N 127.19 E
La Falda 252 31.05 S 64.30 W
La Farge 190 43.34 N 90.38 W
LaFargeville 212 44.11 N 75.57 W
Lafayette, Fr. 62 45.35 N 5.04 E
Lafayette, Al., U.S. 194 32.53 N 85.24 W
Lafayette, Ca., U.S. 226 37.53 N 122.07 W
Lafayette, Co., U.S. 198 39.59 N 105.05 W
Lafayette, Ga., U.S. 192 34.42 N 85.16 W
Lafayette, In., U.S. 216 40.25 N 86.52 W
Lafayette, La., U.S. 194 30.13 N 92.01 W
Lafayette, Mn., U.S. 190 44.26 N 94.23 W
Lafayette, N.J., U.S. 210 41.05 N 74.41 W
La Fayette, N.Y., U.S. 210 42.54 N 76.06 W
Lafayette, Oh., U.S. 216 40.46 N 83.49 W
Lafayette, Or., U.S. 224 45.14 N 123.06 W
Lafayette, R.I., U.S. 207 41.34 N 71.28 W
Lafayette, Tn., U.S. 194 36.31 N 86.01 W
La Fayette, Tx., U.S. 222 32.54 N 94.51 W
Lafayette, Mount ∧ 188 44.10 N 71.38 W
Lafayette Hill 285 40.05 N 75.15 W
Lafayette Reservoir ◎¹ 282 37.53 N 122.08 W
Lafayette Water Tunnel ✦⁵ 282 37.54 N 122.12 W
La Fé 240p 21.45 N 82.45 W
La Fère 50 49.40 N 3.22 E
La Feria 196 26.09 N 97.49 W
Laferrere 288 34.45 S 58.35 W
La Ferrière-sur-Risle 50 48.59 N 0.48 E
La Ferté-Alais 50 48.29 N 2.21 E
La Ferté-Bernard 50 48.11 N 0.40 E
La Ferté-Frênel 50 48.50 N 0.30 E
La Ferté-Gaucher 50 48.47 N 3.18 E
La Ferté-Imbault 50 47.23 N 1.58 E
La Ferté-Macé 32 48.36 N 0.22 W
La Ferté-Milon 50 49.10 N 3.07 E
La Ferté-Saint-Aubin 50 47.43 N 1.56 E
La Ferté-sous-Jouarre 50 48.57 N 3.08 E
Laferté-sur-Amance 58 47.50 N 5.42 E
La Ferté-Vidame 50 48.37 N 0.55 E
La Ferté-Villeneuil 50 47.59 N 1.21 E
Lafferty 214 40.06 N 81.01 W
Laffrey 62 45.02 N 5.46 E
Lafia 150 8.30 N 8.30 E
Lafiagi 150 8.52 N 5.25 E
Laflamme ≃ 190 48.56 N 77.18 W
Laflèche, P.Q., Can. 275a 45.30 N 73.28 W
Lafleche, Sk., Can. 184 49.43 N 106.35 W
La Flèche, Fr. 32 47.42 N 0.05 W
La Floresta 266d 41.27 N 2.04 E
La Florida, Chile 286e 33.33 S 70.34 W
La Florida, Esp. 266d 41.31 N 2.12 E
La Florida, Guat. 232 16.33 N 90.27 W
Lafnitz ≃ 61 46.57 N 16.16 E
La Foa 175f 21.43 S 165.50 E
La Foce 62 44.08 N 9.47 E
La Follette 192 36.22 N 84.07 W
Lafon 154 5.02 N 32.27 E
Lafontaine, P.Q., Can. 206 45.48 N 74.01 W
La Fontaine, In., U.S. 216 40.40 N 85.43 W
Lafontaine, Parc ♦ 275a 45.32 N 73.34 W
Lafourche, Bayou ≃ 194 29.05 N 90.14 W
La Foux, Fr. 62 43.16 N 6.35 E
La Foux, Fr. 62 44.17 N 6.34 E
La Fragua 252 26.05 S 64.20 W
La Francia 252 31.24 S 62.38 W
La Fregeneda 34 40.59 N 6.52 W
La Frette-sur-Seine 261 48.58 N 2.11 E
La Fría 246 8.13 N 72.15 W
Lafrimbolle 58 48.36 N 7.01 E
La Fuente de San Esteban 34 40.48 N 6.15 W
Laga, Monti della ∧ 66 42.37 N 13.24 E
La Gacilly 28 47.46 N 2.09 W
Lagaip ≃ 164 5.05 S 142.40 E
La Galite ɪ 36 37.32 N 8.56 E
La Gallareta 252 29.34 S 60.23 W
La Gallega 34 41.54 N 3.16 W
Lagan 26 56.55 N 13.59 E
Lagan ≃, Sve. 26 56.33 N 12.56 E
Lagan ≃, N. Ire., U.K. 48 54.37 N 5.53 W
Lagangzong 120 28.05 N 91.04 E
Lagantu 102 42.20 N 108.22 E
La Garde 62 43.07 N 6.01 E
La Garde-Freinet 62 43.19 N 6.28 E
La Garenne-Colombes 261 48.55 N 2.15 E
Lagarina, Val V 64 45.50 N 11.10 E
Lagarto, Bra. 250 10.54 S 37.41 W
Lagarto, C.R. 236 10.07 N 84.56 W
Lagarto Creek ≃ 196 28.08 N 97.56 W
Lagawe 116 16.49 N 121.06 E
Lagay 116 14.06 N 122.12 E
Lagayan 116 17.43 N 120.42 E
Lage, Dtsch. 52 51.59 N 8.48 E
Lage, Esp. 34 43.13 N 9.00 W
Lage, Zhg. 120 29.26 N 85.51 E
Lagedu 102 26.24 N 101.11 E
Lågen ≃, Nor. 26 59.03 N 10.05 E
Lågen ≃, Nor. 26 61.08 N 10.25 E
Lägerdorf 52 53.53 N 9.34 E
Lages 252 27.48 S 50.19 W
Lageuen 114 4.44 N 95.31 E
Lage Zwaluwe 52 51.43 N 4.41 E
Laggan 46 57.02 N 4.16 W
Laggan, Loch ◎¹ 46 56.57 N 4.28 W
Laggan Bay ⊂ 46 55.41 N 6.19 W
Lagginhorn ∧ 58 46.11 N 8.01 E
Laghmān □⁴ 120 35.00 N 70.15 E
Laghouat 148 33.50 N 2.59 E
Laghouat □⁵ 148 32.00 N 3.30 E
Laghy 48 54.37 N 8.05 W
Lagič 84 40.51 N 48.24 E
La Giettaz 62 45.52 N 6.30 E
La Giganta, Cerro ∧ 234 21.08 N 101.19 W
La Giustiniana ✦⁸ 267a 41.59 N 12.24 E
La Gleize 56 50.25 N 5.51 E
La Gloria 246 8.37 N 73.48 W
Lagnieu 62 45.54 N 5.21 E
Lagny 50 48.52 N 2.43 E
Lagny-le-Sec 261 49.05 N 2.45 E
Lago 68 39.10 N 16.09 E
Lago, Mount ∧ 224 48.51 N 120.32 W
Lagoa Branca 256 21.54 S 47.02 W
Lagoa da Prata 255 20.01 S 45.33 W
Lagoa Formosa 255 18.47 S 46.24 W
Lago Argentino — Calafate 254 50.20 S 72.18 W
Lagoa Santa 255 19.38 S 43.53 W
Lagoa Vermelha 252 28.13 S 51.32 W
Lago Blanco 254 45.55 S 71.15 W
Lago da Pedra 250 4.45 S 45.10 W
Lagodechi 84 41.49 N 46.18 E
Lagodechskij zapovednik ♦ 84 41.53 N 46.22 E
Lagoinha 256 23.06 S 45.11 W
Lagolândia 255 15.37 S 49.02 W
Lagolovo 265a 59.42 N 30.00 E
Lagonegro 68 40.07 N 15.46 E
Lagonglong 116 8.48 N 124.47 E
Lagonoy 116 13.44 N 123.31 E
Lagonoy Gulf ⊂ 116 13.35 N 123.45 E
Lagopesole, Castel di ɪ 68 40.48 N 15.45 E
Lago Posadas 254 47.32 S 71.45 W
Lagorai, Catena del ∧ 64 46.18 N 11.25 E
Lago Ranco 254 40.20 S 72.38 W
La Gorgue 50 50.38 N 2.42 E
Lagos, Ang. 152 16.04 S 17.03 E
Lagos, Nig. 150 6.27 N 3.24 E
Lagos, Nig. 273a 6.27 N 3.24 E
Lagos, Port. 34 37.06 N 8.40 W
Lagos □³ 150 6.30 N 3.30 E
Lagos (Ikeja) Airport ⊠ 273a 6.35 N 3.20 E
Lagos, University of ʊ² 273a 6.32 N 3.24 E
Lagosanto 66 44.46 N 12.08 E
Lagos de Moreno 234 21.21 N 101.55 W
Lagos Harbour ⊂ 273a 6.26 N 3.24 E
Lagos Island ɪ 273a 6.27 N 3.24 E
Lagos Lagoon ⊂ 273a 6.30 N 3.26 E
Lagos Terminus ✦⁵ 273a 6.28 N 3.23 E
La Gouèra 148 20.48 N 17.08 W
La Goulette 148 36.49 N 10.18 E
Lago Viedma 254 49.48 S 72.07 W
La Granadella 34 41.21 N 0.40 E
La Grand'Combe 62 44.13 N 4.02 E
La Grande 202 45.19 N 118.05 W
La Grande Deux, Réservoir ◎¹ 176 53.40 N 76.55 W
La Grande Moucherolle ∧ 62 45.00 N 5.34 E
La Grande Quatre, Réservoir ◎¹ 176 54.00 N 73.15 W
La Grange, Austl. 162 18.41 S 121.45 E
LaGrange, Ca., U.S. 226 37.40 N 120.28 W
La Grange, Ga., U.S. 192 33.02 N 85.01 W
La Grange, Il., U.S. 216 41.48 N 87.52 W
Lagrange, In., U.S. 216 41.38 N 85.25 W
La Grange, Ky., U.S. 218 38.24 N 85.22 W
La Grange, Mo., U.S. 219 40.02 N 91.29 W
La Grange, N.C., U.S. 192 35.18 N 77.47 W
Lagrange, Oh., U.S. 214 41.14 N 82.07 W
La Grange, Tx., U.S. 222 29.54 N 96.52 W
Lagrange, Wy., U.S. 198 41.38 N 104.10 W
Lagrange □⁶ 216 41.39 N 85.25 W
Lagrange Bay ⊂ 162 18.38 S 121.42 E
La Grange Highlands 278 41.48 N 87.51 W
La Grange Lock and Dam ✦⁵ 219 39.57 N 90.32 W
La Grange Park 278 41.50 N 87.52 W
Lagrangeville 210 41.39 N 73.46 W

≃ River / Fluß / Río / Rivière / Rio
⊔ Canal / Kanal / Canal / Canal / Canal
⌐ Waterfall, Rapids / Wasserfall, Stromschnellen / Cascada, Rápidos / Chute d'eau, Rapides / Cascata, Rápidos
⌐ Strait / Meeresstraße / Estrecho / Détroit / Estreito
⊂ Bay, Gulf / Bucht, Golf / Bahía, Golfo / Baie, Golfe / Baía, Golfo
◎ Lake, Lakes / See, Seen / Lago, Lagos / Lac, Lacs / Lago, Lagos
≐ Swamp / Sumpf / Pantano / Marais / Pântano
⌧ Ice Features, Glacier / Eis- und Gletscherformen / Accidentes Glaciales / Formes glaciaires / Acidentes glaciares
⊤ Other Hydrographic Features / Andere Hydrographische Objekte / Otros Elementos Hidrográficos / Autres données hydrographiques / Outros acidentes hidrográficos

✦ Submarine Features / Untermeerische Objekte / Accidentes Submarinos / Formes de relief sous-marin / Acidentes submarinos
□ Political Unit / Politische Einheit / Unidad Política / Entité politique / Unidade política
ʊ Cultural Institution / Kulturelle Institution / Institución Cultural / Institution culturelle / Instituição cultural
ɪ Historical Site / Historische Stätte / Sitio Histórico / Site historique / Sítio histórico
♦ Recreational Site / Erholungs- und Ferienort / Sitio de Recreo / Centre de loisirs / Area de Lazer
⊠ Airport / Flughafen / Aeropuerto / Aéroport / Aeroporto
■ Military Installation / Militäranlage / Instalación Militar / Installation militaire / Instalação militar
✦ Miscellaneous / Verschiedenes / Misceláneo / Divers / Diversos

Name	Page	Lat. °′	Long. °′
La Granja	286e	33.32 S	70.39 W
La Gran Piedra ∧	240p	20.01 N	75.38 W
La Gran Sabana ≚	246	5.30 N	61.30 W
La Grave	62	45.03 N	6.18 E
La Grita	246	8.08 N	71.59 W
Lagro	216	40.50 N	85.43 W
La Groise	50	50.05 N	3.41 E
La Grue Bayou ≃	194	34.05 N	91.10 W
Lagu	102	26.26 N	101.30 E
La Guadeloupe (Saint-Évariste)	188	45.57 N	70.56 W
La Guajira □[5]	246	11.30 N	72.30 W
La Guajira, Península de ≻[1]	246	12.00 N	71.40 W
La Guardia, Arg.	252	29.33 S	65.27 W
La Guardia, Bol.	248	17.54 S	63.20 W
Laguardia, Esp.	34	42.33 N	2.35 W
La Guardia, Esp.	34	41.54 N	8.53 W
La Guardia Airport ⊠	210	40.46 N	73.53 W
La Gudiña	34	42.04 N	7.08 W
La Guêpière	261	48.35 N	1.50 E
La Guerche-de-Bretagne	32	47.56 N	1.14 W
La Guerche-sur-l'Aubois	32	46.57 N	2.57 E
Laguiole	32	44.41 N	2.51 E
Laguna, Bra.	252	28.29 S	48.47 W
Laguna, N.M., U.S.	200	35.02 N	107.22 W
Laguna □[4]	116	14.10 N	121.20 E
Laguna ≃	226	38.16 N	121.23 W
Laguna, Arroyo de la ≃	282	37.35 N	121.53 W
Laguna, Ilha da I	250	1.40 S	51.00 W
Laguna Beach	228	33.32 N	117.46 W
Laguna Blanca	240p	20.27 N	76.07 W
Laguna Blanca, Parque Nacional ♦	254	39.00 S	70.18 W
Laguna Creek ≃	200	36.54 N	109.45 W
Laguna Dam ◆[6]	200	32.50 N	114.31 W
Laguna de Pozuelos, Monumento Natural ♦, Arg.	248	22.20 S	66.00 W
Laguna de Pozuelos, Monumento Natural ♦, Arg.	252	22.20 S	66.00 W
Laguna Hills	228	33.36 N	117.42 W
Laguna Indian Reservation ◆[4]	200	35.00 N	107.20 W
Laguna Lake ⊜	226	35.16 S	120.42 W
Laguna Larga	252	31.46 S	63.48 W
Laguna Limpia	252	26.29 S	59.41 W
Laguna Niguel	228	33.31 N	117.43 W
Laguna Paiva	252	31.19 S	60.39 W
Laguna Park	222	31.52 N	97.23 W
Lagunas	248	5.14 S	75.38 W
Laguna San Rafael, Parque Nacional ♦	254	47.00 S	73.30 W
Lagunas de Chacagua, Parque Nacional ♦	234	16.00 N	97.00 W
Lagunas de Montebello, Parque Nacional ♦	236	16.05 N	91.45 W
Lagunas de Zempoala, Parque Nacional ♦	234	19.08 N	99.20 W
Lagundo	64	46.41 N	11.08 E
Lagunillas, Bol.	248	19.38 S	63.43 W
Lagunillas, Méx.	234	21.34 N	99.35 W
Lagunillas, Ven.	246	8.31 N	71.24 W
Lagunillás, Laguna ⊜	248	15.44 S	70.43 W
Lagunillas → Ciudad Ojeda	246	10.12 N	71.19 W
Laguntara ⊂	236	15.35 N	84.05 W
L'agušje	86	54.24 N	77.59 E
Laguyu	104	41.43 N	123.49 E
Laha	89	48.10 N	124.39 E
La Habana (Havana), Cuba	240p	23.08 N	82.22 W
La Habana (Havana), Cuba	286b	23.08 N	82.22 W
La Habana □[4]	240p	22.45 N	82.10 W
La Habana, Universidad de ⚑[2]	286b	23.08 N	82.22 W
La Habra	228	33.55 N	117.56 W
La Habra Heights	280	33.57 N	117.57 W
Lahad Datu	112	5.02 N	118.19 E
Lahad Datu, Telukan ⊂	112	4.50 N	118.30 E
Lahaina	229a	20.52 N	156.40 W
Laham	112	0.22 N	115.24 E
Lahār	124	26.12 N	78.57 E
La Harpe, Il., U.S.	190	40.35 N	90.58 W
La Harpe, Ks., U.S.	198	37.55 N	95.17 W
Lāharpur	124	27.43 N	80.54 E
Lahaska	208	40.21 N	75.02 W
Lahat, Indon.	112	3.48 S	103.32 E
Lahat, Malay.	114	4.33 N	101.02 E
La Hauteville	261	48.42 N	1.37 E
La Havane → La Habana	240p	23.08 N	82.22 W
LaHave ≃	186	44.14 N	64.20 W
La Haye-du-Puits	32	49.18 N	1.33 W
La Haye → 's-Gravenhage	52	52.06 N	4.18 E
La Häy-les-Rosas	261	48.47 N	2.21 E
Lähden	52	52.45 N	7.34 E
Lāhe	110	26.20 N	95.26 E
Laheria Sarai	124	26.07 N	85.54 E
Lahewa	114	1.24 N	97.11 E
Lahfān, Bi'r ⫪[4]	132	31.01 N	33.52 E
Lahi, Ava ж	174w	21.02 S	175.11 W
La Higuera	252	29.30 S	71.17 W
Laḥij	144	13.02 N	44.54 E
Lāhījān	128	37.12 N	50.01 E
Lāhithah	132	32.59 N	36.35 E
Lahn ≃	56	50.18 N	7.37 E
Lahnstein	56	50.19 N	7.36 E
Laholm	26	56.31 N	13.02 E
Laholmsbukten ⊂	26	56.35 N	12.50 E
La Honda	226	37.19 N	122.16 W
La Honda Creek ≃	282	37.18 N	122.16 W
Lahontan Reservoir ⊜[1]	226	39.23 N	119.09 W
Lahontan State Recreation Area ♦	226	39.28 N	119.03 W
Lāhor	123	34.03 N	72.22 E
Lahore	123	31.35 N	74.18 E
Lahor → Lahore	123	31.35 N	74.18 E
La Horqueta	246	3.06 N	72.50 W
La Horqueta, Arroyo ≃	288	34.41 S	58.51 W
La Houssaye-en-Brie	261	48.45 N	2.53 E
Lahr	58	48.20 N	7.52 E
Lahri	120	29.11 N	68.13 E
Lāhrūd	128	38.30 N	47.49 E
Laḥṭah, Wādī V	142	29.44 N	32.45 E
Lahti	26	60.58 N	25.40 E
La Huaca	248	4.54 S	80.57 W
La Huacana	234	18.58 N	101.49 W
La Huerta, Méx.	234	19.28 N	104.39 W
La Huerta, N.M., U.S.	196	32.27 N	104.13 W
La Hunière	261	48.36 N	1.52 E
Lahuy Island I	116	13.56 N	123.50 E
Laï	146	9.24 N	16.18 E
Laiagam	164	5.30 S	143.20 E
Lai'an	100	32.27 N	118.25 E
Laibach → Ljubljana	36	46.03 N	14.31 E
Laibin	102	23.42 N	109.22 E
Lai Chau	110	22.02 N	103.10 E
Laichingen	58	48.29 N	9.41 E
Laichow Bay → Laizhou Wan ⊂	98	37.36 N	119.30 E
Laide	46	57.52 N	5.32 W
Laidley	171a	27.38 S	152.24 E
Laidley Creek ≃	171a	27.31 S	152.24 E
Laidon, Loch ⊜	46	56.39 N	4.40 W
Laie	229c	21.39 N	157.55 W
Laifang	100	25.56 N	116.54 E
Laifeng, Zhg.	102	29.31 N	109.15 E
Laifeng, Zhg.	107	30.14 N	105.17 E
Laifengzhen	107	29.26 N	106.13 E
L'Aigle	50	48.45 N	0.38 E
L'Aigle Creek ≃	194	33.12 N	92.08 W
Laignes	50	47.50 N	4.22 E
Laigou	100	33.56 N	117.06 E
Laigueglia	62	43.58 N	8.09 E
Laihia	26	62.58 N	22.01 E
Lai-hka	110	21.16 N	97.40 E
Lailly-en-Val	50	47.46 N	1.41 E
Laïmbélé, Mont ∧	175f	16.20 S	167.31 E
Lainate	266b	45.34 N	9.02 E
Lainbach	61	47.38 N	14.46 E
La Independencia, Bahía de ⊂	248	14.15 S	76.10 W
Laingsburg, S. Afr.	158	33.11 S	20.51 E
Laingsburg, Mi., U.S.	216	42.53 N	84.21 W
Lainioälven ≃	24	67.22 N	23.39 E
La Inmaculada	232	29.55 N	111.48 W
Laino Borgo	68	39.57 N	15.59 E
Lainsitz (Lužnice) ≃	61	49.13 N	14.42 E
Lainville	261	49.04 N	1.49 E
Lainz ◆[8]	264b	48.11 N	16.17 E
Lainzer Tiergarten ♦	264b	48.10 N	16.14 E
Lair, Scot., U.K.	46	57.29 N	5.20 W
Lair, Ky., U.S.	218	38.20 N	84.18 W
Laird Hill	222	32.21 N	94.54 W
Lairdsville	210	41.14 N	76.37 W
Lairg	46	58.01 N	4.25 W
Laïri	146	10.49 N	17.06 E
Laïri, Batha de ≃	146	12.28 N	16.45 E
Laïriri, Pic ∧	175f	15.27 S	166.48 E
Lais, Indon.	112	0.47 N	120.27 E
Lais, Indon.	112	3.32 S	102.03 E
Lais, Pil.	116	6.20 N	125.39 E
Laisamis	154	1.36 N	37.48 E
Laiševo	80	55.24 N	49.32 E
Laishan	98	37.24 N	121.23 E
Laishui	105	39.23 N	115.42 E
Laissac	32	44.23 N	2.49 E
Laissey	58	47.18 N	6.14 E
Laisu	107	29.16 N	105.47 E
Laisvall	24	66.05 N	17.10 E
Laitan	107	29.06 N	106.10 E
Laitila	26	60.53 N	21.41 E
Laives (Leifers)	64	46.26 N	11.20 E
Laiwu	98	36.12 N	117.38 E
Laiwui	164	1.22 S	127.40 E
Laixi (Shuiji)	98	36.51 N	120.29 E
Laiya	116	13.40 N	121.24 E
Laiyang	98	36.58 N	120.44 E
Laiyuan, Zhg.	98	39.18 N	114.44 E
Laiyuan, Zhg.	100	25.36 N	117.01 E
Laizhou Wan (Laichow Bay) ⊂	98	37.36 N	119.30 E
Laja ≃, Chile	252	37.16 S	72.43 W
Laja ≃, Méx.	234	20.30 N	100.46 W
Laja ≃, Ross.	24	66.20 N	56.16 E
Laja, Laguna de la ⊜	252	37.21 S	71.19 W
Laja, Salto del ↳	252	37.22 S	71.25 W
Lajajalpan ≃	234	20.17 N	97.32 W
La Jalca	248	6.29 S	77.43 W
La Jara	200	37.16 N	105.57 W
La Jara ◆[1]	34	39.42 N	4.54 W
La Jara Canyon V	200	36.50 N	107.30 W
La Jara Creek ≃	200	37.22 N	105.46 W
La Jarrie	32	46.08 N	1.00 W
Lajas, Cuba	240p	22.25 N	80.18 W
Lajas, P.R.	240m	18.03 N	67.04 W
La Javie	62	44.10 N	6.21 E
Laje	255	13.10 S	39.25 W
Laje, Ilha da I	287a	22.57 S	43.09 W
Laje, Ponta da ≻	266c	38.40 N	9.19 W
Laje, Ribeira de ≃	266c	38.41 N	9.19 W
Lajeado	252	29.27 S	51.58 W
Lajeado Velho ◆[8]	287b	23.32 S	46.23 W
Lajedo	250	8.40 S	36.19 W
Lajes	250	5.41 S	36.14 W
Lajes, Ribeirão das ≃	256	22.38 S	43.42 W
Lajinha	255	20.09 S	41.37 W
Laji Shan ⋀	102	36.13 N	102.15 E
Lajkovo	265b	55.42 N	37.13 E
La Jolla, Ca., U.S.	204	32.51 N	117.16 W
La Jolla, Ca., U.S.	228	32.51 N	117.16 W
La Jolla, Point ≻	228	32.51 N	117.17 W
Lajord	184	50.14 N	104.09 W
La Jose	214	40.50 N	78.41 W
Lajosmizse	30	47.02 N	19.34 E
La Joya, Méx.	196	26.26 N	101.08 W
La Joya, Perú	248	16.44 S	71.51 W
La Joya, Cerro ∧	234	20.06 N	101.38 W
La Joya, Laguna ⊂	234	15.55 N	93.40 W
La Joya de Atotonilco	234	23.35 N	104.20 W
Lajta (Leitha) ≃	61	47.54 N	17.17 E
Lajtamak	86	58.25 N	67.25 E
Lajturi	84	41.55 N	41.55 E
La Junta	198	37.59 N	103.32 W
Lakaband	120	31.00 N	69.30 E
Lakahia, Teluk ⊂	164	4.00 S	134.38 E
Lakamané	150	14.31 N	9.55 W
Lakar Kūh ∧	128	31.02 N	57.06 E
Lakatoro	175f	16.07 S	167.25 E
Lake	194	32.20 N	89.19 W
Lake □[6], Ca., U.S.	226	39.01 N	122.33 W
Lake □[6], Fl., U.S.	220	28.42 N	81.39 W
Lake □[6], Il., U.S.	216	42.22 N	87.50 W
Lake □[6], In., U.S.	216	41.25 N	87.22 W
Lake □[6], Oh., U.S.	214	41.43 N	81.15 W
Lake Accotink Park ♦	284c	38.48 N	77.14 W
Lake Albert	171b	35.10 S	147.23 E
Lake Alfred	220	28.05 N	81.43 W
Lake Alpine	226	38.28 N	120.00 W
Lake Andes	198	43.09 N	98.32 W
Lake Angelus	281	42.42 N	83.19 W
Lake Ariel	210	41.27 N	75.23 W
Lake Arrowhead	228	34.14 N	117.11 W
Lake Arthur, La., U.S.	194	30.04 N	92.40 W
Lake Arthur, N.M., U.S.	196	32.59 N	104.21 W
Lake Barcroft	284c	38.51 N	77.09 W
Lake Bathurst	170	35.01 S	149.36 E
Lake Benton	198	44.15 N	96.17 W
Lake Beseck	207	41.31 N	72.44 W
Lake Bluff	216	42.16 N	87.50 W
Lake Brownwood	196	31.49 N	99.02 W
Lake Buena Vista	220	28.23 N	81.31 W
Lake Butler	192	30.01 N	82.20 W
Lake Cable	214	40.52 N	81.27 W
Lake Camm	162	32.59 S	119.35 E
Lake Cargelligo	166	33.18 S	146.23 E
Lake Carmel	210	41.27 N	73.40 W
Lake Charles	194	30.13 N	93.13 W
Lake Chelan National Recreation Area ♦	224	48.20 N	120.40 W
Lake City, Ar., U.S.	194	35.48 N	90.26 W
Lake City, Co., U.S.	200	38.01 N	107.18 W
Lake City, Fl., U.S.	192	30.11 N	82.38 W
Lake City, Il., U.S.	219	39.45 N	88.43 W
Lake City, Ia., U.S.	198	42.16 N	94.44 W
Lake City, Mi., U.S.	190	44.20 N	85.12 W
Lake City, Mn., U.S.	190	44.26 N	92.16 W
Lake City, Pa., U.S.	214	42.00 N	80.20 W
Lake City, S.C., U.S.	192	33.52 N	79.45 W
Lake City, Tn., U.S.	192	36.13 N	84.09 W
Lake Clarke Shores	220	26.39 N	80.04 W
Lake Clark National Park ♦	180	60.30 N	153.15 W
Lake Coleridge	172	43.22 S	171.32 E
Lake Como, N.Y., U.S.	210	42.41 N	76.18 W
Lake Como, Pa., U.S.	210	41.51 N	75.20 W
Lake Corpus Christi State Park ♦	196	28.05 N	97.52 W
Lake Cowichan	224	48.50 N	124.03 W
Lake Creek ≃	222	30.16 N	95.29 W
Lake Crescent	224	48.06 N	123.50 W
Lake Crystal	190	44.06 N	94.13 W
Lake Dalecarlia	216	41.20 N	87.24 W
Lake Dallas	222	33.07 N	97.02 W
Lake Delta	210	43.17 N	75.28 W
Lake Delton	190	43.36 N	89.47 W
Lakedemonovka	83	47.12 N	38.33 E
Lake Dennison State Park ♦	207	42.38 N	72.05 W
Lake District ◆[1]	44	54.30 N	3.10 W
Lake District National Park ♦	44	54.30 N	3.05 W
Lake Eliza	216	41.26 N	87.10 W
Lake Elsinore	228	33.38 N	117.20 W
Lake Elsinore State Recreation Area ♦	228	33.41 N	117.22 W
Lake Entrance ж	170	33.05 S	151.39 E
Lake Errock	224	49.13 N	122.02 W
Lake Eyre National Park ♦	166	28.30 S	137.30 E
Lake Fairfax County Park ♦	284c	38.58 N	77.19 W
Lake Fenton	216	42.52 N	83.43 W
Lakefield, On., Can.	212	44.26 N	78.16 W
Lakefield, S. Afr.	273d	26.11 S	28.18 E
Lakefield, Mn., U.S.	198	43.40 N	95.10 W
Lakefield National Park ♦	164	15.00 S	144.05 E
Lake Forest, Fl., U.S.	192	25.58 N	80.11 W
Lake Forest, Il., U.S.	216	42.12 N	87.53 W
Lake Forest, N.J., U.S.	276	40.58 N	74.36 W
Lake Forest Park	224	47.45 N	122.17 W
Lake Fork	219	39.58 N	89.21 W
Lake Fork ≃, Il., U.S.	219	40.05 N	89.25 W
Lake Fork ≃, Ut., U.S.	200	40.13 N	110.07 W
Lake Fork, North Fork ≃	219	39.56 N	89.14 W
Lake Fork Creek ≃	222	32.36 N	95.21 W
Lake Fork Reservoir ⊜[1]	222	32.50 N	95.35 W
Lake Geneva	216	42.36 N	88.26 W
Lake George	188	43.25 N	73.42 W
Lake Grace	162	33.06 S	118.28 E
Lake Grinnell	276	41.06 N	74.38 W
Lake Grove	276	40.51 N	73.06 W
Lake Hamilton	220	28.07 N	81.42 W
Lake Harbor	220	26.42 N	80.48 W
Lake Harbour	176	62.51 N	69.53 W
Lake Harmony	210	41.04 N	75.36 W
Lake Havasu City	200	34.29 N	114.19 W
Lake Havasu State Park ♦	200	34.29 N	114.21 W
Lake Helen	220	28.58 N	81.14 W
Lake Hiawatha	210	40.52 N	74.22 W
Lake Hill	210	42.04 N	74.11 W
Lake Hills, In., U.S.	216	41.28 N	87.27 W
Lake Hills, Wa., U.S.	224	47.36 N	122.08 W
Lake Hopatcong	210	40.55 N	74.39 W
Lake Hughes	228	34.40 N	118.26 W
Lake Huntington	210	41.41 N	75.00 W
Lakehurst	208	40.00 N	74.18 W
Lakehurst Naval Air Station ■	208	40.01 N	74.18 W
Lake Illawarra	170	34.33 S	150.52 E
Lake Intervale	276	40.53 N	74.25 W
Lake in the Hills	216	42.10 N	88.19 W
Lake Isabella	204	35.39 N	118.28 W
Lake Jackson	222	29.02 N	95.26 W
Lake Jem	220	28.45 N	81.40 W
Lakekamu ≃	164	8.10 S	146.15 E
Lake Katrine	210	41.59 N	73.59 W
Lake King	162	33.05 S	119.40 E
Lake Lackawanna	210	40.57 N	74.42 W
Lakeland, Fl., U.S.	220	28.03 N	81.57 W
Lakeland, Ga., U.S.	192	31.02 N	83.04 W
Lakeland, Mi., U.S.	216	42.28 N	83.51 W
Lakeland, N.Y., U.S.	210	43.06 N	76.15 W
Lakeland Park	216	42.21 N	88.17 W
Lakeland Village	228	33.39 N	117.22 W
Lake Lenape	210	41.01 N	74.44 W
Lake Linden	190	47.11 N	88.26 W
Lake Lookover	276	41.09 N	74.24 W
Lake Loramie State Park ♦	216	40.23 N	84.20 W
Lake Louise, Ab., Can.	182	51.26 N	116.11 W
Lake Louise, Wa., U.S.	224	47.05 N	122.36 W
Lake Lucerne	214	41.24 N	81.21 W
Lake Luzerne	210	43.18 N	73.50 W
Lake Mackay Reserve ◆[4]	162	22.00 S	129.45 E
Lake Magdalene	220	28.05 N	82.28 W
Lake Malawi National Park ♦	154	14.00 S	34.55 E
Lake Manyara National Park ♦	154	3.30 S	36.25 E
Lake Mary	220	28.45 N	81.19 W
Lakemba	274a	33.55 S	151.05 E
Lakemba Island I	175g	18.13 S	178.47 W
Lakemba Passage ж	175g	17.53 S	178.32 W
Lake Mead National Recreation Area ♦	200	36.00 N	114.30 W
Lake Meredith National Recreation Area ♦	196	35.40 N	101.40 W
Lake Mills, Ia., U.S.	190	43.25 N	93.31 W
Lake Mills, Wi., U.S.	216	43.04 N	88.54 W
Lake Milton	214	41.06 N	80.58 W
Lake Minchumina	180	63.53 N	152.19 W
Lake Monroe	220	28.50 N	81.19 W
Lakemont, N.Y., U.S.	210	42.31 N	76.56 W
Lakemont, Pa., U.S.	214	40.28 N	78.23 W
Lakemoor	216	42.20 N	88.12 W
Lakemore	214	41.01 N	81.25 W
Lake Mountain ∧	169	37.31 S	145.54 E
Lake Murray	164	7.00 S	141.29 E
Lake Murray State Park ♦	196	34.01 N	97.00 W
Laken ◆[8]	50	50.52 N	4.25 E
Lake Nakuru National Park ♦	154	0.20 S	36.05 E
Lake Nash	166	21.00 S	137.55 E
Lake Nepessing	216	43.02 N	83.22 W
Lakenheath	42	52.25 N	0.31 E
Lake Norden	198	44.34 N	97.12 W
Lake Normandy Estates	284c	39.03 N	77.11 W
Lake Odessa	216	42.47 N	85.08 W
Lake of the Ozarks State Park ♦	194	38.08 N	92.40 W
Lake of the Woods	216	41.26 N	86.14 W
Lake on the Mountain Provincial Park ♦	212	44.02 N	77.05 W
Lake Orion	216	42.47 N	83.14 W
Lake Orion Heights	216	42.46 N	83.18 W
Lake Oroville State Recreational Area ♦	226	39.32 N	121.27 W
Lake Oswego	224	45.25 N	122.39 W
Lake Ozark	194	38.11 N	92.38 W
Lakepa	174v	18.59 S	169.48 W
Lake Panasoffkee	220	28.46 N	82.07 W
Lake Paringa	172	43.43 S	169.29 E
Lake Park, Fl., U.S.	220	26.48 N	80.04 W
Lake Park, Ia., U.S.	198	43.27 N	95.19 W
Lake Park, Mn., U.S.	198	46.53 N	96.05 W
Lake Pine	208	39.52 N	74.51 W
Lake Placid, Fl., U.S.	220	27.17 N	81.21 W
Lake Placid, N.Y., U.S.	188	44.16 N	73.58 W
Lake Pleasant	188	43.28 N	74.25 W
Lakeport, Ca., U.S.	204	39.02 N	122.54 W
Lakeport, Mi., U.S.	190	43.07 N	82.30 W
Lakeport, N.Y., U.S.	210	43.09 N	75.52 W
Lake Preston	198	44.21 N	97.22 W
Lake Providence	194	32.48 N	91.10 W
Lake Pukaki	172	44.11 S	170.09 E
Lakeridge, Nv., U.S.	226	39.02 N	119.56 W
Lake Ridge, N.J., U.S.	276	40.24 N	74.15 W
Lake Riviera	208	40.03 N	74.10 W
Lake Ronkonkoma	276	40.50 N	73.07 W
Lake Saint Louis	219	38.48 N	90.45 W
Lake Sammamish State Park ♦	224	47.33 N	122.03 W
Lake San Marcos	228	33.09 N	117.12 W
Lake Sawyer	224	47.20 N	122.03 W
Lakes Bay ⊂	208	39.22 N	74.30 W
Lakes District	224	47.10 N	122.31 W
Lakes Entrance	166	37.53 S	147.59 E
Lake Shawnee	276	40.59 N	74.36 W
Lakeshore, Ca., U.S.	226	37.15 N	119.12 W
Lake Shore, Md., U.S.	208	39.06 N	76.29 W
Lake Shore, Mi., U.S.	216	42.38 N	86.14 W
Lakeshore, Ms., U.S.	194	30.14 N	89.26 W
Lake Shore, Wa., U.S.	224	45.42 N	122.42 W
Lakeside, N.S., Can.	186	44.38 N	63.41 W
Lakeside, S. Afr.	273d	26.06 S	28.09 E
Lakeside, Az., U.S.	200	34.09 N	109.58 W
Lakeside, Ca., U.S.	228	32.51 N	116.55 W
Lakeside, Ct., U.S.	207	41.25 N	73.13 W
Lakeside, Ct., U.S.	207	41.40 N	73.14 W
Lakeside, Mi., U.S.	216	41.51 N	86.40 W
Lakeside, Mt., U.S.	202	48.01 N	114.13 W
Lakeside, Oh., U.S.	214	41.32 N	82.44 W
Lakeside, Or., U.S.	202	43.34 N	124.10 W
Lakeside, Va., U.S.	208	37.36 N	77.28 W
Lakeside ◆[9]	281	42.37 N	83.00 W
Lakeside Village	222	32.02 N	97.30 W
Lake Station	216	41.34 N	87.14 W
Lake Stevens	224	48.01 N	122.04 W
Lake Stockholm	276	41.04 N	74.31 W
Lake Success	276	40.46 N	73.43 W
Lake Superior Provincial Park ♦	190	47.32 N	84.50 W
Lake Swannanoa	276	41.01 N	74.31 W
Lake Taghkanic State Park ♦	210	42.06 N	73.43 W
Lake Tahoe Airport ⊠	226	38.54 N	120.00 W
Lake Tahoe-Nevada State Park ♦	226	39.13 N	119.55 W
Lake Tamarack	210	41.06 N	74.32 W
Lake Tekapo	172	44.01 S	170.30 E
Lake Telemark	276	40.57 N	74.30 W
Lake Temescal Regional Park ♦	282	37.51 N	122.14 W
Laketon	216	40.58 N	85.50 W
Laketown	200	41.49 N	111.19 W
Lake Varley	162	32.46 S	119.27 E
Lake View, Ar., U.S.	194	34.24 N	90.50 W
Lakeview, Ca., U.S.	228	33.50 N	117.07 W
Lakeview, Ga., U.S.	192	34.58 N	85.15 W
Lake View, Ia., U.S.	198	42.18 N	95.03 W
Lakeview, Mi., U.S.	190	43.26 N	85.16 W
Lake View, N.Y., U.S.	210	42.42 N	78.56 W
Lakeview, Oh., U.S.	216	40.29 N	83.56 W
Lakeview, Or., U.S.	202	42.11 N	120.20 W
Lake View, S.C., U.S.	192	34.20 N	79.09 W
Lakeview, Tx., U.S.	194	29.55 N	93.54 W
Lakeview, Tx., U.S.	196	34.40 N	100.42 W
Lakeview, Wa., U.S.	224	47.10 N	122.30 W
Lakeview ◆[8]	278	41.57 N	87.39 W
Lakeview Mountain ∧, B.C., Can.	182	49.03 N	120.09 W
Lakeview Mountain ∧, Wa., U.S.	224	46.22 N	121.24 W
Lakeview Park ♦	285	40.12 N	75.32 W
Lake Village, Ar., U.S.	194	33.19 N	91.16 W
Lake Village, In., U.S.	216	41.08 N	87.27 W
Lakeville, Ct., U.S.	207	41.57 N	73.26 W
Lakeville, In., U.S.	216	41.31 N	86.16 W
Lakeville, Mi., U.S.	214	42.49 N	83.09 W
Lakeville, Mn., U.S.	190	44.38 N	93.14 W
Lakeville, N.Y., U.S.	210	42.50 N	77.42 W
Lakeville, Oh., U.S.	214	40.40 N	82.07 W
Lakeville Lake ⊜	214	42.50 N	83.09 W
Lake Wales	220	27.54 N	81.35 W
Lake Whitney State Park ♦	222	31.55 N	97.22 W
Lake Wilson	198	43.59 N	95.57 W
Lake Winola	210	41.30 N	75.50 W
Lakewood, Ca., U.S.	228	33.51 N	118.07 W
Lakewood, Co., U.S.	200	39.42 N	105.04 W
Lakewood, Il., U.S.	216	39.19 N	88.54 W
Lakewood, Mi., U.S.	216	42.18 N	85.31 W
Lakewood, N.J., U.S.	208	40.05 N	74.13 W
Lakewood, N.Y., U.S.	214	42.06 N	79.20 W
Lakewood, Oh., U.S.	214	41.28 N	81.47 W
Lakewood, Pa., U.S.	210	41.51 N	75.22 W
Lakewood, Wa., U.S.	224	48.09 N	122.12 W
Lakewood, Wi., U.S.	190	45.18 N	88.31 W
Lakewood Center ◆[9]	280	33.51 N	118.09 W
Lakewood Park	198	48.04 N	98.56 W
Lakewood Park ♦	279a	41.29 N	81.47 W
Lakewood Shores	216	41.17 N	88.10 W
Lake Worth, Fl., U.S.	220	26.36 N	80.03 W
Lake Worth, Tx., U.S.	222	32.49 N	97.27 W
Lake Zurich	216	42.11 N	88.05 W
Lakhdaria	34	36.34 N	3.35 E
Lākheri	124	25.40 N	76.10 E
Lakhīmpur	124	27.57 N	80.46 E
Lakhipur, India	120	24.48 N	93.01 E
Lakhipur, India	124	26.02 N	90.18 E
Lakhish	132	31.34 N	34.51 E
Lakhish V	132	31.49 N	34.38 E
Lakhnādon	124	22.36 N	79.36 E
Lakhya ≃	126	23.35 N	90.31 E
L'aki	84	40.34 N	47.26 E
Laki ≃	115a	7.30 S	107.25 E
Lakin	198	37.56 N	101.15 W
Lakinsk	80	56.01 N	39.57 E
Lakkadiven → Lakshadweep II	122	10.00 N	73.00 E
Lakki	123	32.36 N	70.55 E
Laknau → Lucknow	124	26.51 N	80.55 E
Lakonikós Kólpos ⊂	38	36.25 N	22.37 E
Lakor, Pulau I	164	8.14 S	128.10 E
Lakota, C. Iv.	150	5.51 N	5.41 W
Lakota, Ia., U.S.	190	43.22 N	94.05 W
Lakota, N.D., U.S.	198	48.02 N	98.20 W
Laksefjorden ⊂[2]	24	70.58 N	27.00 E
Lakselv	24	70.04 N	24.56 E
Lakshadweep □[8]	122	10.00 N	73.00 E
Lakshadweep II	122	10.00 N	73.00 E
Lakshadweep Sea ⫪[2]	12	7.00 N	76.00 E
Lākshām	124	23.14 N	91.08 E
Lakshamannāth	126	21.51 N	87.13 E
Lakshmanpur	272b	22.38 N	88.16 E
Lakshmeshwar	122	15.08 N	75.28 E
Lakshmi, Char I	126	21.57 N	90.33 E
Lakshmikantapur	126	22.07 N	88.20 E
Lakshmi Narayan Temple ⚑[1]	272a	28.38 N	77.12 E
Lakshmīpur	126	22.57 N	90.50 E
Lakshmisāgar	126	22.55 N	87.01 E
Lala	116	7.59 N	123.46 E
Lalafuta ≃	154	13.57 S	24.41 E
La Laguna → San Cristóbal de la Laguna	148	28.29 N	16.19 W
La Lagunita	234	23.41 N	105.44 W
La Laja	252	37.16 S	72.42 W
La Lajilla	232	26.47 N	99.37 W
Lāla Mūsa	123	32.42 N	73.58 E
Lalana ≃	234	17.49 N	95.09 W
Lalapansi	154	19.16 S	30.15 E
Lâlapaşa	130	41.50 N	26.44 E
Lalatuncun	104	41.44 N	122.00 E
La Lava	248	19.55 S	65.38 W
Lalbenque	32	44.20 N	1.33 E

ENGLISH / **DEUTSCH**

Name	Page	Lat. °′	Long. °′
L'Albufera ⊜	34	39.20 N	0.22 W
Laleham, Austl.	166	23.58 S	148.46 E
Laleham, Eng., U.K.	260	51.25 N	0.30 W
Lāleh Zār, Kūh-e ∧	128	29.24 N	56.45 E
La Leona	196	25.52 N	101.05 W
La Leonesa	252	27.03 S	58.43 W
Lalera	152	0.22 N	11.28 E
Lalevade-d'Ardèche	62	44.39 N	4.19 E
Lālganj	124	25.52 N	85.11 E
Lālgarh	126	22.35 N	87.03 E
Lāliān	123	31.49 N	72.48 E
Lalibela	144	12.02 N	39.02 E
La Libertad, El Sal.	236	13.29 N	89.19 W
La Libertad, Guat.	232	16.47 N	90.07 W
La Libertad, Hond.	236	14.43 N	87.36 W
La Libertad, Nic.	236	12.13 N	85.10 W
La Libertad □[5]	248	8.00 S	78.30 W
La Ligua	252	32.27 S	71.14 W
La Lima, Hond.	236	15.24 N	87.56 W
La Lima, It.	66	44.04 N	10.46 E
La Limpia, Laguna ⊜	258	35.37 S	57.49 W
Lalín	34	42.39 N	8.07 W
Lalin ≃	89	45.29 N	125.26 E
Lalinde	32	44.51 N	0.44 E
Lalindi	115b	10.12 S	120.10 E
Lalindu ≃	112	3.28 S	122.05 E
La Línea	34	36.10 N	5.19 W
L'alino	82	54.29 N	39.06 E
Lalitpur	124	24.41 N	78.25 E
La Llagosta	266d	41.31 N	2.12 E
Lalla Khedidja, Tamgout de ∧	34	36.27 N	4.15 E
Lal Lal Reservoir ⊜[1]	169	37.40 S	144.04 E
Lālmanir Hāt	124	25.54 N	89.27 E
Lālmohan	126	22.13 N	90.42 E
Laloa	112	4.50 S	121.54 E
La Loche	184	56.29 N	109.27 W
La Loche ≃	184	56.09 N	109.08 W
La Loche, Lac ⊜	184	56.25 N	109.30 W
Laloki	164	9.25 S	147.15 E
La Londe	62	43.08 N	6.14 E
La Lora ⋀[1]	34	42.45 N	4.00 W
Lalor Park	274a	33.45 S	150.56 E
La Loupe	50	48.28 N	1.01 E
Lalouvesc	62	45.07 N	4.32 E
La Louvière	50	50.28 N	4.11 E
L'Alpe-d'Huez	62	45.06 N	6.04 E
Lālpur, Bngl.	126	24.11 N	88.58 E
Lālpur, India	120	22.12 N	69.58 E
Lal'sk	24	60.44 N	47.34 E
Lālsot	124	26.34 N	76.20 E
Lālua	126	21.57 N	90.18 E
La Luz, Méx.	196	25.52 N	97.37 W
La Luz, Méx.	232	24.12 N	97.52 W
La Luz, Nic.	236	13.44 N	84.47 W
La Luz, N.M., U.S.	200	32.58 N	105.56 W
Lam	60	49.12 N	13.03 E
Lama ≃, Ross.	82	56.29 N	36.10 E
Lama ≃, Zhg.	104	42.11 N	123.29 E
Lama, ozero ⊜	74	69.30 N	90.30 E
L'Amable Lake ⊜	212	45.01 N	77.49 W
La Macarena, Parque Nacional ♦	246	2.40 N	73.45 W
La Macarena, Serranía de ⋀	246	2.45 N	73.55 W
La Maddalena	71	41.13 N	9.24 E
Lama dei Peligni	66	42.02 N	14.11 E
La Madeleine	50	50.39 N	3.04 E
Lamadong	98	40.39 N	119.39 E
La Madrague	62	43.14 N	5.22 E
La Madrid, Arg.	252	27.38 S	65.15 W
Lamadrid, Méx.	196	27.05 N	101.50 W
Lamag	112	5.29 N	117.49 E
La Magdalena, Río de ≃	286a	19.21 N	99.11 W
Lamagoumen	105	40.52 N	116.39 E
Lamahuang	104	42.27 N	121.33 E
La Mailleraye-sur-Seine	50	49.29 N	0.46 E
Lamainong	114	3.49 N	96.46 E
La Majada	286c	10.27 N	67.01 W
Lama-Kara	150	9.33 N	1.12 E
La Malbaie	186	47.39 N	70.10 W
La Malinche, Parque Nacional ♦	234	19.15 N	98.05 W
Lamaline	186	46.52 N	55.49 W
La Malmaison ⊥	261	48.52 N	2.10 E
Lamaload Reservoir ⊜[1]	262	53.16 N	2.02 W
Lama Mocogno	64	44.18 N	10.45 E
La Mancha ◆[1]	34	38.50 N	3.00 W
La Mancha, Canal de → English Channel ж	28	50.20 N	1.00 W
Lamandau ≃	112	2.42 S	111.34 E
Lamap	175f	16.26 S	167.43 E
Lamar, Co., U.S.	198	38.05 N	102.37 W
Lamar, Mo., U.S.	194	37.29 N	94.16 W
Lamar, Pa., U.S.	210	41.01 N	77.32 W
Lamar, S.C., U.S.	192	34.10 N	80.03 W
Lamar ≃	202	44.56 N	110.24 W
La Marañosa	266a	40.17 N	3.35 W
Lamarche	58	48.04 N	5.47 E
Lamarche-sur-Saône	58	47.16 N	5.23 E
Lamari ≃	164	6.54 S	145.25 E
La Mariposa, Embalse ⊜[1]	286c	10.24 N	66.56 W
La Mariscala	252	34.03 S	54.47 W
La Marmora, Punta ∧	71	39.59 N	9.20 E
La Marolle-en-Sologne	50	47.35 N	1.47 E
La Maroma	196	28.34 N	100.45 W
Lamarque, Arg.	252	39.24 S	65.42 W
La Marque, Tx., U.S.	222	29.22 N	94.58 W
La Marsa	36	36.53 N	10.20 E
La Martre	62	43.46 N	6.36 E
Lamas	248	6.25 S	76.35 W
La Masica	236	15.37 N	87.07 W
Lamastre	62	44.59 N	4.35 E
La Matanza □[5]	288	34.46 S	58.37 W
La Matanza → San Justo	258	34.40 S	58.33 W
Lama Temple ⚑[1]	271a	39.56 N	116.25 E
La Mauricie, Parc National de (La Mauricie National Park) ♦	206	46.50 N	73.00 W
La Maya, Cuba	240p	20.10 N	75.39 W
Lamaya, Zhg.	102	29.50 N	99.53 E
Lamayingzi	104	42.09 N	121.50 E
Lambach	60	48.05 N	13.53 E
Lamballe	32	48.28 N	2.31 W
Lambaréné	152	0.42 S	10.13 E
Lambari	256	21.58 S	45.21 W
Lambari ≃, Bra.	255	19.30 S	45.00 W
Lambari ≃, Bra.	256	21.47 S	45.13 W
Lambasa	175g	16.26 S	179.24 E
Lambayeque	248	6.42 S	79.55 W
Lambayeque □[5]	248	6.20 S	80.00 W
Lambayeque ≃	248	6.43 S	79.54 W
Lambay Island I	48	53.29 N	6.01 W
Lambe	273a	6.42 N	3.21 E
Lambersart	50	50.39 N	3.02 E
Lambert, Ms., U.S.	194	34.12 N	90.17 W
Lambert, Mt., U.S.	198	47.41 N	104.37 W
Lambert, Cape ≻, Austl.	162	20.35 S	117.10 E
Lambert, Cape ≻, Pap. N. Gui.	164	4.12 S	151.32 E
Lambert Glacier ⊓	9	71.00 S	70.00 E
Lamberton	198	44.13 N	95.15 W
Lambert-Saint Louis International Airport ⊠	219	38.45 N	90.22 W
Lambertsbaai → Lambert's Bay	158	32.05 S	18.17 E
Lambert's Bay	158	32.05 S	18.17 E
Lambertville, Mi., U.S.	216	41.45 N	83.37 W
Lambertville, N.J., U.S.	208	40.21 N	74.56 W
Lambesc	62	43.39 N	5.16 E
Lambeth	214	42.54 N	81.18 W
Lambeth ◆[8]	42	51.30 N	0.07 W
L'ambir'	80	54.17 N	45.07 E
Lambo Katenga	154	5.02 S	28.48 E
Lambomakondro	157b	22.41 S	44.44 E
Lambourn	42	51.31 N	1.31 W
Lambourne ≃	42	51.24 N	1.18 W
Lambourne End	260	51.38 N	0.08 E
Lambrama	248	13.52 S	72.46 W
Lambrate ◆[8]	266b	45.29 N	9.15 E
Lambrecht	56	50.08 N	8.56 E
Lambrechten	60	48.19 N	13.31 E
Lambrechts Drift	158	28.31 S	21.43 E
Lambro ≃	62	45.08 N	9.32 E
Lambro, Parco ♦	266b	45.30 N	9.15 E
Lambs Creek	210	41.51 N	77.06 W
Lambs Terrace	285	39.46 N	75.02 W
Lambton	273d	26.15 S	28.10 E
Lambton □[6]	214	42.45 N	82.15 W
Lambton, Cape ≻	176	71.05 N	123.10 W
Lambu	164	3.09 S	151.41 E
Lambunao	116	11.03 N	122.29 E
L'amca	24	64.27 N	37.04 E
Lamdessar	164	7.12 S	131.58 E
Lame, Nig.	150	10.23 N	9.13 E
Lamé, Tchad	146	9.15 N	14.32 E
La Meca → Makkah	144	21.27 N	39.49 E
La Mecque → Makkah	144	21.27 N	39.49 E
Lame Deer	202	45.37 N	106.39 W
La Media Luna, Arrecifes de ✧[2]	236	15.13 N	82.36 W
La Méditerranée → Mediterranean Sea ⫪[2]	10	35.00 N	20.00 E
Lamego	34	41.06 N	7.49 W
La Meije ∧	62	45.00 N	6.18 E
Lameirão, Morro do ∧[2]	287a	22.54 S	43.31 W
La Membrolle-sur-Choisille	50	47.26 N	0.38 E
La Mendieta	252	24.19 S	64.58 W
L'amen'ga	76	59.51 N	44.31 E
Lamentin	241o	16.16 N	61.38 W
Lamèque	186	47.47 N	64.38 W
Lamèque, Île I	186	47.48 N	64.36 W
La Merced, Arg.	252	28.10 S	65.41 W
La Merced, Arg.	252	24.58 S	65.29 W
La Merced, Perú	248	11.03 S	75.19 W
Lameroo	166	35.20 S	140.31 E
La Mesa, Pan.	236	8.09 N	81.11 W
La Mesa, Ca., U.S.	228	32.46 N	117.01 W
La Mesa, N.M., U.S.	200	32.07 N	106.42 W
Lamesa, Tx., U.S.	196	32.44 N	101.57 W
La Mesa Dam ◆[6]	269f	14.43 N	121.04 E
La Meta ∧	66	41.41 N	13.56 E
Lamía	38	38.54 N	22.26 E
L'amin ≃	74	61.18 N	71.48 E
Lamine ≃	194	38.59 N	92.51 W
La Minerve	206	46.15 N	74.56 W
Laming ≃	61	47.25 N	15.16 E
Lamington ≃	210	40.38 N	74.41 W
Lamington, Mount ∧[1]	164	8.56 S	148.10 E
Lamington National Park ♦	166	28.15 S	153.12 E
La Mira	234	18.02 N	102.19 W
La Mirada	228	33.55 N	118.00 W
La Mirada Creek ≃	280	33.53 N	118.01 W
La Misión	204	32.05 N	116.50 W
Lamitan	116	6.39 N	122.08 E
Lamlam, Mount ∧[2]	174p	13.20 N	144.40 E
Lamlash	46	55.32 N	5.08 W
Lamma Island I	271d	22.12 N	114.07 E
Lammefjord ⊂	41	55.48 N	11.43 E
Lammerlaw Top ∧	172	45.40 S	169.38 E
Lammermuir ◆[1]	46	55.50 N	2.25 W
Lammermuir Hills ⋀[2]	46	55.50 N	2.44 W
Lammeulo	114	5.15 N	95.56 E
Lammhulf	26	57.10 N	14.35 E
Lammi	26	61.05 N	25.01 E
Lamming Mills	182	53.22 N	120.18 W
Lamogai	164	5.50 S	149.20 E
La Moille, Il., U.S.	190	41.31 N	89.16 W
Lamoille, Nv., U.S.	204	40.43 N	115.28 W
Lamoille ≃	188	44.35 N	73.10 W
La Moine ≃	194	39.59 N	90.31 W
La Moine, East Fork ≃	194	40.24 N	90.56 W
Lamoka Lake ⊜	210	42.24 N	77.05 W
La Molina	286d	12.05 S	76.57 W
Lamon Bay ⊂	116	14.25 N	122.00 E
Lamone ≃	66	44.31 N	12.15 E
Lamongan	115a	7.07 S	112.25 E
Lamongan, Gunung ∧	115a	7.58 S	113.20 E
Lamoni	190	40.37 N	93.56 W
Lamont, Ab., Can.	182	53.46 N	112.48 W
Lamont, Ca., U.S.	228	35.15 N	118.54 W
Lamont, Ia., U.S.	190	42.35 N	91.38 W
Lamont, Mi., U.S.	216	43.01 N	86.09 W
Lamont, Ok., U.S.	196	36.41 N	97.33 W
La Monte	194	38.46 N	93.25 W
La Mosquitia □[9]	236	15.00 N	83.45 W
La Mothe, Lac ⊜[1]	186	48.46 N	71.09 W
La Mothe-Achard	32	46.37 N	1.40 W
Lamotrek I[1]	14	7.30 N	146.20 E
La Mott	285	40.04 N	75.08 W
La Motte, Lac ⊜	190	48.24 N	78.03 W
Lamotte-Beuvron	50	47.36 N	2.01 E
La Motte-Chalançon	62	44.29 N	5.23 E
La Motte-du-Caire	62	44.21 N	6.02 E
Lamoura	58	46.24 N	5.58 E
La Moure	198	46.21 N	98.17 W
La Moustique ≃	241o	16.11 N	61.35 W
Lampa	248	15.21 S	70.22 W
Lampang	110	18.18 N	99.31 E
Lampasas	196	31.03 N	98.10 W
Lampasas ≃	196	30.59 N	97.24 W
Lampazos de Naranjo	232	27.01 N	100.31 W
Lampedusa	70a	35.30 N	12.56 E
Lampedusa, Isola di I	70a	35.31 N	12.35 E
Lampertheim	56	49.35 N	8.28 E
Lampeter, Wales, U.K.	42	52.07 N	4.05 W
Lampeter, Pa., U.S.	208	39.58 N	76.14 W
Lamphun	110	18.35 N	99.01 E
Lampinsaari	26	64.25 N	25.09 E
Lampione, Isolotto di I	70a	35.34 N	12.19 E
Lampman	184	49.23 N	102.45 W
Lamprechtshausen	64	47.59 N	12.57 E
Lampung □[4]	112	5.00 S	105.00 E
Lampung, Teluk ⊂	115a	5.40 S	105.20 E
Lamskoje	76	52.57 N	38.02 E
Lamspringe	52	51.58 N	10.00 E
Lamstedt	52	53.38 N	9.05 E
Lāmta	124	22.08 N	80.07 E
Lam Tong Hoi Hap ж	271d	22.15 N	114.15 E
Lamu, Kenya	154	2.16 S	40.54 E
Lāmu, Mya.	110	19.14 N	94.10 E
Lamud	248	6.09 S	77.55 W
La Muerte, Cerro ∧	236	9.33 N	83.44 W
Lam Uk Wei	271d	22.26 N	114.22 E
La Mure	62	44.54 N	5.47 E
Lamure-sur-Azergues	58	46.04 N	4.30 E
La Mutua	234	22.23 N	99.18 W
Lan' ≃, Bela.	76	52.09 N	27.18 E
Lan ≃, Zhg.	104	41.14 N	123.32 E
Lan, Loi ∧	110	19.40 N	97.55 E
Lana	64	46.37 N	11.09 E
Lanai I	229a	20.50 N	156.55 W
Lanai City	229a	20.49 N	156.55 W
Lanaihale ∧	229a	20.49 N	156.52 W
Lanaken	56	50.53 N	5.39 E
Lanalhue, Lago ⊜	252	37.55 S	73.18 W
La Nana, Bayou ≃	222	31.27 N	94.43 W
Lanao del Norte □[4]	116	8.10 N	124.00 E
Lanao del Sur □[4]	116	7.50 N	124.25 E

Symbols in the index entries represent the broad categories identified in the key at the right. Symbols with superior numbers (⋀[1]) identify subcategories (see complete key on page *I · 1).*

Symbole im Register stellen die rechts im Schlüssel erklärten Kategorien dar. Symbole mit hochgestellten Ziffern (⋀[1]) bezeichnen Unterabteilungen einer Kategorie (vgl. vollständiger Schlüssel auf Seite *I · 1).*

Los símbolos incluídos en el texto del índice representan las grandes categorias identificadas con la clave a la derecha. Los símbolos con numeros en su parte superior (⋀[1]) identifican las subcategorías (véase la clave completa en la página *I · 1).*

Les symboles de l'index représentent les catégories indiquées dans la légende à droite. Les symboles suivis d'un indice (⋀[1]) représentent des sous-catégories (voir légende complète à la page *I · 1).*

Os símbolos incluídos no texto do índice representam as grandes categorias identificadas com a chave à direita. Os símbolos com números em sua parte superior (⋀[1]) identificam as subcategorias (veja-se a chave completa à página *I · 1).*

∧ Mountain	Berg	Montaña	Montagne	Montanha
⋀ Mountains	Gebirge	Montañas	Montagnes	Montanhas
)(Pass	Paß	Paso	Col	Passo
V Valley, Canyon	Tal, Cañon	Valle, Cañón	Vallée, Canyon	Vale, Canhão
≚ Plain	Ebene	Llano	Plaine	Planície
≻ Cape	Kap	Cabo	Cap	Cabo
I Island	Insel	Isla	Île	Ilha
II Islands	Inseln	Islas	Îles	Ilhas
⊥ Other Topographic Features	Andere Topographische Objekte	Otros Elementos Topográficos	Autres données topographiques	Outros acidentes topográficos

ESPAÑOL — Nombre / Página / Lat.°′ / Long.°′ W = Oeste
FRANÇAIS — Nom / Page / Lat.°′ / Long.°′ W = Ouest
PORTUGUÊS — Nome / Página / Lat.°′ / Long.°′ W = Oeste

La Napoule 62 43.31 N 6.56 E
Lanarce 62 44.44 N 4.00 E
Lanark, On., Can. 212 45.01 N 76.22 W
Lanark, Scot., U.K. 46 55.41 N 3.46 W
Lanark, Il., U.S. 190 42.06 N 89.50 W
Lanark, Pa., U.S. 208 40.33 N 75.26 W
Lanark □6 212 45.05 N 76.20 W
La Nartelle 62 43.19 N 6.39 E
Lanas 112 5.20 N 116.30 E
La Nava de Ricomalillo 34 39.39 N 4.59 W
Lanbi Kyun I 110 10.50 N 98.15 E
Lanboyan Point ≻ 116 8.18 N 122.56 E
Lancang 102 23.00 N 100.02 E
Lancang → Mekong ≃ 12 10.33 N 105.24 E
Lancashire 285 39.49 N 75.29 W
Lancashire □6 44 53.45 N 2.40 W
Lancashire Plain ≛ 44 53.40 N 2.45 W
Lancaster, On., Can. 206 45.08 N 74.30 W
Lancaster, Eng., U.K. 44 54.03 N 2.48 W
Lancaster, Ca., U.S. 228 34.41 N 118.08 W
Lancaster, Ky., U.S. 192 37.37 N 84.34 W
Lancaster, Ma., U.S. 207 42.27 N 71.40 W
Lancaster, Mn., U.S. 198 48.51 N 96.48 W
Lancaster, Mo., U.S. 194 40.31 N 92.31 W
Lancaster, N.H., U.S. 188 44.29 N 71.34 W
Lancaster, N.Y., U.S. 210 42.54 N 78.40 W
Lancaster, Oh., U.S. 188 39.43 N 82.36 W
Lancaster, Pa., U.S. 208 40.02 N 76.18 W
Lancaster, S.C., U.S. 192 34.43 N 80.46 W
Lancaster, Tx., U.S. 222 32.38 N 96.47 W
Lancaster, Va., U.S. 208 37.46 N 76.28 W
Lancaster, Wi., U.S. 190 42.50 N 90.42 W
Lancaster □6, Pa., U.S. 208 40.02 N 76.19 W
Lancaster □6, Va., U.S. 208 37.45 N 76.30 W
Lancaster Canal ≍ 262 53.46 N 2.43 W
Lancaster Sound Ʋ 176 74.13 N 84.00 W
Lancaster Village 285 39.45 N 75.35 W
Lančchuti 84 42.06 N 42.01 E
Lance Creek 200 43.01 N 104.38 W
Lance Creek ≃ 198 43.22 N 104.16 W
Lancefield 169 37.17 S 144.44 E
Lancelin 162 31.02 S 115.20 E
Lancelot, Mount ∧ 162 26.13 S 123.12 E
Lancey 62 45.14 N 5.53 E
Lanchang 114 3.30 N 102.11 E
Lanchester 44 54.49 N 1.44 W
Lanchow → Lanzhou 102 36.03 N 103.41 E
Lanciano 66 42.14 N 14.23 E
Lancin, Fr. 62 45.43 N 5.24 E
Lančin, Ukr. 78 48.34 N 24.45 E
Lancing 42 50.50 N 0.19 W
Lanco 254 39.24 S 72.46 W
Lancones 246 4.35 S 80.30 W
Lancun 98 36.24 N 120.10 E
Łańcut 30 50.05 N 22.13 E
Lancy 58 46.11 N 6.07 E
Lândana 152 5.13 S 12.08 E
Landang Gua 116 6.58 N 122.15 E
Landau 56 49.12 N 8.07 E
Landau an der Isar 60 48.40 N 12.43 E
Landay 128 30.31 N 63.47 E
Land Between the Lakes ♠ 194 36.55 N 88.05 W
Landeck 58 47.08 N 10.34 E
Landen 56 50.45 N 5.05 E
Landenberg 208 39.47 N 75.46 W
Landenhausen 56 50.36 N 9.28 E
Lander 200 42.49 N 108.43 W
Lander ≃ 162 20.25 S 132.00 E
Landerneau 32 48.27 N 4.15 W
Landes □5 32 44.20 N 1.00 W
Landes ◆1 32 44.15 N 1.00 W
Landesbergen 52 52.33 N 9.07 E
Landeskrone ∧2 54 51.08 N 14.56 E
Landess 216 40.37 N 85.34 W
Landete 34 39.54 N 1.22 W
Landham Brook ≃ 283 42.22 N 71.25 W
Landhausen 263 51.24 N 7.45 E
Landi 98 36.35 N 119.59 E
Landi Kotal 123 34.06 N 71.09 E
Landina 86 59.12 N 67.02 E
Landing 210 40.54 N 74.40 W
Landing Lake ⊜ 184 55.17 N 97.26 W
Landis, Sk., Can. 184 52.12 N 108.28 W
Landis, N.C., U.S. 192 35.32 N 80.36 W
Landisburg 208 40.20 N 77.18 W
Landisville 208 40.06 N 76.25 W
Landivisiau 32 48.31 N 4.04 W
Landkey 42 51.04 N 4.00 W
Landkirchen 54 54.27 N 11.08 E
Lando 192 34.46 N 81.00 W
Land O'Lakes, Fl., U.S. 220 28.11 N 82.34 W
Land O'Lakes, Wi., U.S. 190 46.10 N 89.13 W
Landor 162 25.09 S 116.54 E
Landos 62 44.51 N 3.50 E
Landösjön ⊜ 26 63.35 N 14.04 E
Landover Estates 284c 38.56 N 76.54 W
Landover Hills 284c 38.57 N 76.53 W
Landover Mall ◆9 284c 38.55 N 76.51 W
Landquart 58 46.58 N 9.33 E
Landquart ≃ 58 46.58 N 9.32 E
Landrecies 50 50.08 N 3.42 E
Landres 56 49.19 N 5.48 E
Landreth Draw V 196 31.14 N 102.29 W
Landriano 62 45.19 N 9.15 E
Landri Sales 250 7.16 S 43.55 W
Landro (Höhlenstein) 64 46.39 N 12.14 E
Landrum 192 35.10 N 82.11 W
Landry 62 45.34 N 6.45 E
Landsberg 54 51.31 N 12.10 E
Landsberg am Lech 58 48.05 N 10.55 E
Landsberg an der Warthe → Gorzów Wielkopolski 30 52.44 N 15.15 E
Landsborough 166 26.49 S 152.58 E
Landsborough Creek ≃ 166 22.30 S 144.33 E
Landsbro 26 57.22 N 14.54 E
Land's End ≻, Eng., U.K. 42 50.03 N 5.44 W
Lands End ≻, Ca., U.S. 228 33.28 N 118.36 W
Lands End ≻, R.I., U.S. 207 41.27 N 71.19 W
Landshut 60 48.33 N 12.09 E
Landskrona 41 55.52 N 12.50 E
Landsman Creek ≃ 198 39.35 N 102.19 W
Landsmeer 52 52.26 N 4.52 E
Landštejn 61 49.00 N 15.13 E
Landstuhl 56 49.25 N 7.34 E
Landweg 263 51.29 N 7.37 E
Landwehrbach ≃ 263 51.26 N 6.26 E
Lane 219 40.07 N 88.51 W
Lane ≃ 50 47.17 N 0.05 E
Lane City 222 29.13 N 96.02 W
Lane Cove 274a 33.49 S 151.10 E
Lane Cove ≃ 274a 33.48 S 151.09 E
Lane Cove River Park ♠ 274a 33.47 S 151.09 E
La Negra 252 23.45 S 70.19 W
Lane Mountain ∧ 228 35.05 N 116.56 W
Lanersbach 64 47.09 N 11.44 E
Lanesboro, Ma., U.S. 207 42.31 N 73.14 W
Lanesboro, Mn., U.S. 190 43.43 N 91.58 W
Lanesboro, Pa., U.S. 210 41.57 N 75.35 W
Lanester 32 47.46 N 3.21 W
Lanesville, In., U.S. 218 38.14 N 85.59 W
Lanesville, N.Y., U.S. 210 42.08 N 74.16 W
Lanesville, Va., U.S. 208 37.37 N 76.59 W
Lanett 194 32.52 N 85.11 W
La Neuveville 58 47.04 N 7.06 E
Laneville 222 31.58 N 94.49 W
Lanexa 208 37.24 N 76.55 W
Lanezi Lake ⊜ 182 53.03 N 120.56 W
Lang 184 49.56 N 104.23 W
La'nga Co ⊜ 124 30.42 N 81.16 E
Langadhás 38 40.45 N 23.04 E
Langádhia 38 37.41 N 22.02 E
Langa-Langa 152 3.54 S 15.56 E
Langan Creek ≃ 216 40.57 N 87.49 W
Langano, Lake ⊜ 144 7.35 N 38.48 E
Langao 102 32.13 N 109.02 E
Langar, Afg. 120 37.02 N 73.47 E
L'angar, Kyrg. 85 40.25 N 73.07 E
L'angar, Taj. 123 37.02 N 72.42 E
Langara 112 4.02 S 123.00 E
Langara Island I 182 54.14 N 133.00 W
Langarūd 128 37.11 N 50.10 E
L'angasovo 80 58.32 N 49.30 E
Langat ≃ 114 2.54 N 101.22 E
Langau 61 48.49 N 15.42 E
Langavat, Loch ⊜ 46 58.04 N 6.48 W
Långban 40 59.51 N 14.15 E
Langbank 184 50.05 N 102.20 W
Lang Bay 182 49.47 N 124.21 W
Langberg ∧∧ 158 28.20 S 22.35 E
Langburkersdorf 54 51.02 N 14.14 E
Langda 102 31.12 N 96.59 E
Langdai 102 26.06 N 105.20 E
Langdon 198 48.45 N 98.22 W
Langdondale 214 40.08 N 78.15 W
Langdon Hills 260 51.34 N 0.25 E
Langeac 32 45.06 N 3.30 E
Langeais 50 47.20 N 0.24 E
Langebaan 158 33.06 S 18.02 E
Langeberg ∧∧ 158 33.55 S 20.30 E
Lange Berge ∧∧2 56 50.20 N 10.55 E
Langebrück 54 51.07 N 13.50 E
Langeland I 41 55.00 N 10.50 E
Langelandsbælt Ʋ 41 54.50 N 10.55 E
Längelmävesi ⊜ 26 61.32 N 24.22 E
Langeloth 214 40.21 N 80.24 W
Langelsheim 52 51.56 N 10.19 E
Langemark 50 50.55 N 2.55 E
Langen, Dtsch. 52 53.36 N 8.35 E
Langen, Dtsch. 56 49.59 N 8.41 E
Langenargen 58 47.35 N 9.32 E
Langenau, Dtsch. 54 50.50 N 13.18 E
Langenau, Dtsch. 58 48.30 N 10.07 E
Langenberg, Dtsch. 52 51.46 N 8.19 E
Langenberg, Dtsch. 56 51.21 N 7.09 E
Langenbernsdorf 54 50.45 N 12.19 E
Langenbielau → Bielawa 30 50.41 N 16.38 E
Langenbochum 263 51.37 N 7.07 E
Langenbruck 58 47.21 N 7.46 E
Langenburg, Sk., Can. 184 50.50 N 101.43 W
Langenburg, Dtsch. 56 49.15 N 9.50 E
Langendorf 54 51.11 N 11.58 E
Langendreer ◆8 263 51.28 N 7.19 E
Langeneichstädt 54 51.20 N 11.41 E
Langenfeld, Dtsch. 56 51.07 N 6.56 E
Längenfeld, Öst. 64 47.04 N 10.58 E
Langenhagen 52 52.27 N 9.44 E
Langenhessen 54 50.45 N 12.22 E
Langenhorn 41 54.41 N 8.53 E
Langenhorst 263 51.22 N 7.02 E
Langenlois 61 48.28 N 15.40 E
Langennaundorf 54 51.36 N 13.20 E
Langenneufnach 58 48.16 N 10.36 E
Langenselbold 56 50.10 N 9.02 E
Langensteinach 56 49.30 N 10.10 E
Langenthal 58 47.13 N 7.47 E
Langenwang 61 47.34 N 15.37 E
Langenweddingen 54 52.02 N 11.31 E
Langenwetzendorf 54 50.41 N 12.05 E
Langenzenn 56 49.30 N 10.48 E
Langenzersdorf 61 48.18 N 16.22 E
Langeoog 52 53.45 N 7.29 E
Langeoog I 52 53.46 N 7.32 E
Langerfeld ◆8 263 51.16 N 7.15 E
Langer See ⊜ 264a 52.25 N 13.38 E
Langerwehe 56 50.49 N 6.22 E
Langeskov 41 55.22 N 10.36 E
Langesund 26 59.00 N 9.45 E
Langevåg 26 62.27 N 6.12 E
Langewiesen 54 50.40 N 10.58 E
Langfang → Anci 105 39.31 N 116.41 E
Langfjorden ⊂2 26 62.43 N 7.30 E
Langford, B.C., Can. 224 48.27 N 123.30 W
Langford, Eng., U.K. 260 51.45 N 0.40 E
Langford, N.Y., U.S. 210 42.35 N 78.51 W
Langford, S.D., U.S. 198 45.36 N 97.49 W
Langförden 52 52.47 N 8.14 E
Langgam 112 0.15 N 101.43 E
Langgapayung 114 1.43 N 99.59 E
Langgöns 56 50.30 N 8.40 E
Långhalsen ⊜ 40 58.56 N 16.41 E
Langham 184 52.22 N 106.57 W
Langhe □9 62 44.30 N 8.00 E
Langhirano 64 44.37 N 10.16 E
Langho 262 53.48 N 2.27 W
Langholm 44 55.09 N 3.00 W
Langhorne 208 40.10 N 74.55 W
Langhorne Acres 284c 38.51 N 77.16 W
Langhorne Creek 168b 35.18 S 139.02 E
Langhorne Gardens 285 40.11 N 74.53 W
Langhorne Manor 285 40.10 N 74.55 W
Langhorne Terrace 285 40.10 N 74.57 W
Langji Shan I 100 28.32 N 121.36 E
Langjökull ⊓ 24a 64.42 N 20.12 W
Langju 100 27.52 N 116.36 E
Lang Ka, Doi ∧ 110 19.00 N 99.24 E
Langkawi, Pulau I 114 6.22 N 99.50 E
Langkesi, Kepulauan II 112 5.18 S 124.20 E
Langklip 158 28.12 S 20.20 E
Langkrans 158 27.47 S 31.03 E
Langlade I 186 46.50 N 56.20 W
Lang Lang ≃ 169 38.17 S 145.31 E
Langley, B.C., Can. 224 49.06 N 122.39 W
Langley, Eng., U.K. 260 51.30 N 0.33 W
Langley, Eng., U.K. 260 51.14 N 0.35 E
Langley, Eng., U.K. 262 53.15 N 2.05 W
Langley, Ok., U.S. 196 36.27 N 95.02 W
Langley, S.C., U.S. 192 33.31 N 81.50 W
Langley, Wa., U.S. 224 48.02 N 122.24 W
Langley Air Force Base ■ 208 37.05 N 76.21 W
Langley Forest 284c 38.57 N 77.10 W
Langley Hill ∧2 282 37.20 N 122.14 W
Langley Park 284c 38.59 N 76.58 W
Langleyville 219 39.34 N 89.21 W
Langlo ≃ 166 26.26 S 146.05 E
Langlois 202 42.55 N 124.26 W
Langmazong 120 30.52 N 89.58 E
Lang Mo 110 17.14 N 106.27 E
Långnäs 26 60.06 N 20.17 E
Langnau 58 46.57 N 7.47 E
Langogne 62 44.43 N 3.51 E
Langon 32 44.33 N 0.15 W
Langøya I 24 68.44 N 14.50 E
Langping 102 30.38 N 110.21 E
Langport 42 51.02 N 2.50 W
Langqiao 100 30.30 N 118.24 E
Langquaid 60 48.49 N 12.03 E
Langreo → Sama [de Langreo] 34 43.18 N 5.41 W
Langres 58 47.52 N 5.20 E
Langres, Plateau de ∧∧1 58 47.41 N 5.03 E
Langruth 184 50.24 N 98.38 W
Langruzong 120 31.50 N 91.25 E
Langsa 114 4.28 N 97.58 E
Langsa, Teluk ⊂ 114 4.35 N 98.00 E
Langschede 263 51.29 N 7.43 E
Långsele 26 63.11 N 17.04 E
Langshan, Zhg. 102 41.12 N 107.22 E
Langshan, Zhg. 105 40.22 N 115.41 E
Långshyttan 40 60.27 N 16.01 E
Långsjön ⊜ 40 59.00 N 17.27 E
Langsnek ⊥ 158 27.28 S 29.55 E
Lang Son 110 21.50 N 106.44 E
Langstaff 275b 43.50 N 79.25 W
Langst-Kierst 263 51.18 N 6.43 E
Lang Suan 110 9.57 N 99.04 E
Långsvan ⊜ 40 59.43 N 15.49 E
Langtang National Park ♠ 124 28.10 N 85.30 E
Langtian 100 25.11 N 113.28 E
Langting 120 25.30 N 93.07 E
Langton 212 42.45 N 80.35 W
Langtoutun 89 46.51 N 121.54 E
Langtuozi 104 41.01 N 121.43 E
Langu 100 27.56 N 118.11 E
Langue 236 13.37 N 87.39 W
Languedoc □9 32 44.00 N 4.00 E
Langui Layo, Laguna de ⊜ 248 14.29 S 71.13 W
L'Anguille ≃ 194 34.44 N 90.40 W
Langula 54 51.09 N 10.25 E
Langundu, Tanjung ≻ 115b 8.49 S 118.58 E
Langwarden 52 53.36 N 8.19 E
Langwedel 52 52.59 N 9.12 E
Langweer 52 52.57 N 5.43 E
Langweid 58 48.29 N 10.51 E
Langweiler 56 49.40 N 7.31 E
Langwies 58 46.49 N 9.43 E
Langwo 104 41.13 N 121.44 E
Langwozhuang 105 39.05 N 115.37 E
Langxi 106 31.08 N 119.10 E
Langxi ≃ 106 31.10 N 118.59 E
Langzhong 102 31.35 N 105.59 E
Langzishan 104 41.02 N 123.23 E
Lanham 284c 38.58 N 76.51 W
Lanhil Island I 116 6.46 N 122.22 E
Lanibga, Mount ∧ 116 10.27 N 123.56 E
Lanigan 184 51.52 N 105.02 W
Lanigan Creek ≃ 184 51.23 N 105.13 W
Lanín, Parque Nacional ♠ 254 39.36 S 71.24 W
Lanín, Volcán ∧1 254 39.38 S 71.30 W
Lanjiang 107 30.24 N 105.11 E
Lankao (Lanfeng) 98 34.50 N 114.49 E
Lanker See ⊜ 54 54.12 N 10.17 E
Lankeys Creek 171b 35.49 S 147.39 E
Länkipohja 26 61.44 N 24.48 E
Lanklaar 56 51.01 N 5.44 E
Lank-Latum 263 51.18 N 6.41 E
Lankou 100 23.59 N 115.05 E
Lankoviri 146 9.00 N 11.25 E
Lankwitz ◆8 264a 52.26 N 13.21 E
Lanling 89 45.15 N 126.12 E
Lannabruk 40 59.14 N 14.56 E
Lannach 61 46.56 N 15.19 E
Lännaholm 40 59.53 N 17.57 E
Lannaja 78 49.21 N 35.16 E
Lannemezan 32 43.08 N 0.23 E
Lannilis 32 48.34 N 4.31 W
Lannion 32 48.44 N 3.28 W
Lannon 216 43.08 N 88.09 W
L'Annonciation 206 46.25 N 74.52 W
Lanoka Harbor 208 39.52 N 74.10 W
Lanoraie 206 45.58 N 73.13 W
La Noria 258 35.10 S 58.48 W
Lanovcy 78 49.52 N 26.05 E
Lanping 102 26.29 N 99.23 E
Lanqibao 104 40.56 N 122.25 E
Lanqikoucun 104 40.52 N 122.26 E
Lanqipuzi 104 42.12 N 123.15 E
Lanquín 236 15.34 N 89.58 W
Lans, Montagnes de ∧∧ 62 44.52 N 5.29 E
Lansdale 208 40.14 N 75.17 W
Lansdowne, Austl. 162 17.53 S 126.39 E
Lansdowne, Austl. 274a 33.54 S 150.59 E
Lansdowne, On., Can. 212 44.24 N 76.01 W
Lansdowne, India 124 29.50 N 78.41 E
Lansdowne, Md., U.S. 284b 39.14 N 76.39 W
Lansdowne, Pa., U.S. 285 39.56 N 75.16 W
L'Anse, Mi., U.S. 190 46.45 N 88.27 W
Lanse, Pa., U.S. 214 40.59 N 78.08 W
L'Anse-aux-Meadows National Historic Park ♠ 186 51.36 N 55.32 W
L'anse Creuse Bay ⊂ 214 42.34 N 82.49 W
L'Anse Indian Reservation ◆4 190 46.48 N 88.22 W
Lans-en-Vercors 62 45.07 N 5.35 E
Lansford, N.D., U.S. 198 48.37 N 101.22 W
Lansford, Pa., U.S. 210 40.49 N 75.52 W
Lanshan 102 25.18 N 111.52 E
Lanshantou 98 35.07 N 119.21 E
Lansing, Il., U.S. 216 41.33 N 87.32 W
Lansing, Ia., U.S. 190 43.21 N 91.12 W
Lansing, Ks., U.S. 198 39.14 N 94.54 W
Lansing, Mi., U.S. 216 42.43 N 84.33 W
Lansing, N.Y., U.S. 210 42.32 N 76.30 W
Lansing, Oh., U.S. 214 40.04 N 80.47 W
Lansing ◆8 275b 43.45 N 79.25 W
Lansing, Lake ⊜ 216 42.46 N 84.25 W
Lansing Municipal Airport ⊠ 278 41.32 N 87.32 W
Lanškroun 30 49.55 N 16.37 E
Lanslebourg 62 45.17 N 6.52 E
Lanslevillard 62 45.17 N 6.55 E
Lanstrop ◆8 263 51.34 N 7.34 E
Lantana 220 26.35 N 80.03 W
Lantang 100 23.25 N 114.56 E
Lantau Island I 100 22.17 N 113.59 E
Lanta Yai, Ko I 110 7.35 N 99.05 E
Lanterne ≃ 58 47.44 N 6.03 E
Lantewa 146 12.16 N 11.44 E
Lantian 102 34.03 N 109.12 E
Lantianba 107 28.52 N 105.26 E
Lantianchang 271a 39.58 N 116.17 E
Lantsch 58 46.41 N 9.34 E
Lantsch → Laces 64 46.37 N 10.52 E
Lantschou → Lanzhou 102 36.03 N 103.41 E
Lantzville 224 49.15 N 124.05 W
La Nurra ◆1 71 40.45 N 8.15 E
Lanús 258 34.43 S 58.24 W
Lanús □5 288 34.42 S 58.28 W
Lanusei 71 39.53 N 9.32 E
Lanuvio 66 41.40 N 12.42 E
Lanuza 116 9.14 N 126.04 E
Lanuza Bay ⊂ 116 9.17 N 126.04 E
Lanxi, Zhg. 89 46.15 N 126.14 E
Lanxi, Zhg. 100 29.12 N 119.28 E
Lanxian 102 38.22 N 111.46 E
Lány 54 50.06 N 13.58 E
Lan Yü I 100 22.03 N 121.32 E
Lanzada 64 46.15 N 9.51 E
Lanzarote I 148 29.00 N 13.40 W
Lanzendorf 264b 48.06 N 16.26 E
Lanzhou (Lanchow) 102 36.03 N 103.41 E
Lanzo Torinese 62 45.16 N 7.28 E
Lao ≃, It. 68 39.47 N 15.48 E
Lao ≃, Thai 110 19.55 N 99.54 E
Lao ≃, Zhg. 100 29.11 N 116.00 E
Laoag 116 18.12 N 120.36 E
Laoag ≃ 116 18.12 N 120.31 E
Laoang 116 12.34 N 125.00 E
Laoang Island I 116 12.35 N 125.01 E
Lao Bao 110 16.37 N 106.36 E
Laobian, Zhg. 104 41.58 N 123.10 E
Laobian, Zhg. 104 40.42 N 122.21 E
Lao Cai 110 22.30 N 103.57 E
Laochang, Zhg. 102 24.34 N 104.11 E
Laochang, Zhg. 107 29.30 N 106.36 E
Laocheng 104 42.37 N 124.04 E
Laodafang 104 41.40 N 122.40 E
Laodao ≃ 100 28.16 N 112.58 E
Laodaodian 89 51.16 N 126.40 E
Laofengkou 86 46.11 N 83.38 E
Laofu 98 42.13 N 118.17 E
Laogang 106 31.01 N 121.49 E
Laoge 100 32.49 N 119.52 E
Laoguan 100 27.38 N 113.36 E
Laoguanpu 104 40.53 N 120.51 E
Laoha ≃ 90 43.24 N 120.39 E
Laohaotuo 104 41.25 N 122.46 E
Laoheba 107 28.51 N 103.49 E
Laoheishan 89 43.45 N 130.52 E
Laoheshangtai 104 40.43 N 120.49 E
Laohokow → Guanghua 102 32.25 N 111.36 E
Laohuk'ou 100 24.53 N 121.03 E
Laohumiao 271a 39.58 N 116.20 E
Laohutuozi 104 42.25 N 122.34 E
Laois □6 48 53.00 N 7.24 W
Laojunguan 105 40.22 N 114.47 E
Laojunmiao → Yumen 102 39.56 N 97.51 E
Laoka 89 52.47 N 125.52 E
Laolao, Bahia ⊂ 174n 15.08 N 145.46 E
Lao → Laos □1 110 18.00 N 105.00 E
Lao Ling ∧ 89 43.27 N 130.11 E
Laolong ≃ 106 32.11 N 120.00 E
Laolongtan 107 30.01 N 104.48 E
Laomocun 106 30.51 N 119.11 E
Laon 50 49.34 N 3.40 E
Laona, N.Y., U.S. 214 42.25 N 79.19 W
Laona, Wi., U.S. 190 45.33 N 88.40 W
La Orchila, Isla I 246 11.48 N 66.09 W
La Orotava 148 28.23 N 16.31 W
La Oroya 248 11.32 S 75.54 W
Laos (Lao) □1, Asia 108 18.00 N 105.00 E
Laos (Lao) □1, Asia 110 18.00 N 105.00 E
Laoshan (Licun) 98 36.10 N 120.25 E
Laoshan Wan ⊂ 98 36.24 N 120.45 E
Laosolu 114 3.11 N 98.02 E
Laotto 216 41.17 N 85.12 W
Laou, Oued ≃ 34 35.29 N 5.04 W
Laowushi 106 31.43 N 121.00 E
Laoxinkou 100 30.12 N 112.50 E
Laoyemiao 98 41.03 N 119.53 E
Laoyezhuang 106 32.16 N 120.04 E
Laoyingpan 100 26.34 N 115.10 E
Laozha 106 31.35 N 121.07 E
Laozhen 100 31.34 N 118.19 E
Laozhong 98 33.56 N 114.51 E
Laozhuangzi 105 39.44 N 118.05 E
Laozishan 100 33.11 N 118.36 E
Lapa 252 25.45 S 49.42 W
Lapa ◆8, Bra. 287a 22.55 S 43.11 W
Lapa ◆8, Bra. 287b 23.32 S 46.42 W
Lapac Island I 116 5.32 N 120.47 E
Lapai 150 9.06 N 6.45 E
Lapaich, Sgurr na ∧ 46 57.21 N 5.04 W
Lapalisse 32 46.15 N 3.38 E
La Palma, Col. 246 5.22 N 74.24 W
La Palma, Cuba 240p 22.45 N 83.33 W
La Palma, El Sal. 236 14.19 N 89.11 W
La Palma, Méx. 234 17.05 N 99.29 W
La Palma, Méx. 234 20.09 N 102.46 W
La Palma, Pan. 246 8.25 N 78.09 W
La Palma, Pan. 246 7.42 N 80.12 W
La Palma, Ca., U.S. 280 33.50 N 118.02 W
La Palma I 148 28.40 N 17.52 W
La Palma ≃ 240p 23.03 N 80.54 W
La Palma de Cervelló 266d 41.25 N 1.58 E
La Palma del Condado 34 37.23 N 6.33 W
La Palmita 196 25.57 N 99.18 W
La Paloma 252 34.40 S 54.10 W
La Palud 62 43.47 N 6.20 E
La Pampa □4 252 37.00 S 66.00 W
La Panza Range ∧∧ 226 35.18 N 120.18 W
Lapão 250 11.24 S 41.50 W
La Paragua 246 6.50 N 63.20 W
Laparan Island I 116 5.54 N 119.59 E
La Parota 234 18.20 N 101.08 W
La Pasión, Laguna ⊂ 234 15.59 N 97.40 W
La Pasión, Río de ≃ 232 16.28 N 90.33 W
La Patrie 206 45.24 N 71.15 W
La Paz, Arg. 252 30.45 S 59.39 W
La Paz, Arg. 252 33.28 S 67.33 W
La Paz, Bol. 248 16.30 S 68.09 W
La Paz, Col. 246 10.23 N 73.10 W
La Paz, Hond. 236 14.16 N 87.40 W
La Paz, Méx. 232 24.10 N 110.18 W
La Paz, Méx. 234 23.41 N 100.43 W
La Paz, Pil. 116 8.19 N 125.43 E
Lapaz, In., U.S. 216 41.28 N 86.18 W
La Paz, Ur. 258 34.46 S 56.15 W
La Paz, Ur. 258 34.21 S 57.18 W
La Paz □5, Bol. 248 15.30 S 68.00 W
La Paz □5, Hond. 236 14.15 N 87.50 W
La Paz, Bahía ⊂ 232 24.09 N 110.25 W
La Paz, Río de ≃ 248 16.27 S 67.19 W
La Paz Centro 236 12.20 N 86.41 W
Lape 115b 8.39 S 117.37 E
La Pedrera 246 1.18 S 69.43 W
Lapeer 216 43.03 N 83.19 W
Lapeer □6 216 43.00 N 83.20 W
Lapel 218 40.04 N 85.50 W
La Penne-sur-Huveaune 62 43.17 N 5.31 E
La Perla, Méx. 196 28.18 N 104.33 W
La Perla, Méx. 232 28.18 N 104.38 W
La Perla, Perú 286d 12.05 S 77.08 W
La Perouse 170 33.59 S 151.14 E
La Perouse, Bahía ⊂ 174z 27.04 S 109.18 W
La Perouse Bay ⊂ 229a 20.35 N 156.25 W
La Perouse Strait Ʋ 89 45.45 N 142.00 E
La Pesca 234 23.46 N 97.47 W
La Pesse 58 46.18 N 5.51 E
La Petite-Pierre 56 48.52 N 7.19 E
Lapford 42 50.55 N 3.47 W
Lapham Hill ∧2 216 43.02 N 88.24 W
L'apičev 80 48.30 N 43.32 E
La Piedad de Cabadas 234 20.21 N 102.00 W
La Pimienta 234 21.28 N 99.01 W
La Pine 202 43.40 N 121.30 W
Lapinin Island I 116 10.06 N 124.34 E
Lapinjärvi (Lappträsk) 26 60.38 N 26.13 E
Lapin lääni □4 24 68.00 N 27.00 E
Lapinlahti 26 63.22 N 27.24 E
Lapino 82 54.57 N 37.49 E
La Pintada 236 8.36 N 80.27 W
La Pintana 286e 33.37 S 70.38 W
La Pizzuta ∧ 70 38.00 N 13.16 E
La Place, Il., U.S. 219 39.48 N 88.43 W
La Place, La., U.S. 194 30.03 N 90.28 W
Lap Lae 110 17.39 N 100.02 E
La Plaine 240d 15.20 N 61.15 W
Lapland □9 24 68.00 N 25.00 E
Laplandija 24 68.16 N 33.19 E
Laplandskij Zapovednik ◆4 24 67.50 N 32.10 E
La Plata, Arg. 258 34.55 S 57.57 W
La Plata, Col. 246 2.23 N 75.53 W
La Plata, Md., U.S. 208 38.31 N 76.58 W
La Plata, Mo., U.S. 194 40.01 N 92.29 W
La Plata □5 288 34.55 S 58.04 W
La Plata ≃ 200 36.54 N 108.15 W
La Plata, Lago ⊜ 254 44.53 S 71.50 W
La Plata, Lago ⊜1 240m 18.20 N 66.14 W
La Plata, Universidad Nacional de ʊ2 288 35.55 S 57.57 W
La Plata Peak ∧ 200 39.02 N 106.28 W
La Playa ◆8 286b 23.06 N 82.27 W
La Playa Corrida de San Juan, Punta ≻ 234 18.36 N 103.42 W
La Plonge Indian Reserve ◆4 184 55.15 N 107.36 W
La Plume 210 41.34 N 75.45 W
La Pobla de Segur 34 42.14 N 0.59 E
La Pocatière 186 47.22 N 70.02 W
La Poile 186 47.41 N 58.24 W
La Poile Bay ⊂ 186 47.38 N 58.20 W
Lapominka 24 64.48 N 40.28 E
La Pomme 62 43.25 N 5.35 E
Laponie → Lapland □9 24 68.00 N 25.00 E
Laporte, Co., U.S. 200 40.38 N 105.08 W
La Porte, In., U.S. 216 41.36 N 86.43 W
La Porte, Oh., U.S. 279a 41.19 N 82.05 W
Laporte, Pa., U.S. 210 41.25 N 76.30 W
La Porte, Tx., U.S. 222 29.39 N 95.01 W
La Porte □6 216 41.36 N 86.43 W
La Porte City 190 42.18 N 92.11 W
Laposo, Bulu ∧ 112 4.29 S 119.47 E
La Potherie, Lac ⊜ 176 58.50 N 72.24 W
Lapoutroie 58 48.09 N 7.10 E
La Poveda 266a 40.19 N 3.29 W
La Poza Grande 232 25.50 N 112.05 W
Lappago (Lappach) 64 46.55 N 11.48 E
Lappajärvi 26 63.12 N 23.38 E
Lappajärvi ⊜ 26 63.08 N 23.40 E
Lappeenranta 26 61.04 N 28.11 E
Lappfjärd (Lapväärtti) 26 62.15 N 21.32 E
Lappi 26 61.06 N 21.50 E
Lappland → Lapland □9 24 68.00 N 25.00 E
Lappträsk → Lapinjärvi 26 60.38 N 26.13 E
La Prairie 206 45.25 N 73.30 W
Laprairie □6 206 45.20 N 73.35 W
La Prele Creek ≃ 198 42.50 N 105.30 W
La Presa ≃ 232 24.25 N 111.34 W
Laprida, Arg. 252 37.33 S 60.49 W
Laprida, Arg. 252 28.23 S 64.33 W
La Pryor 196 28.57 N 99.51 W
Lapšanga 80 57.27 N 45.03 E
Lâpseki 130 40.20 N 26.41 E
Lapta 130 35.20 N 33.10 E
Laptev Sea → Laptevych, more ⊤2 74 76.00 N 126.00 E
Laptevych, more (Laptev Sea) ⊤2 74 76.00 N 126.00 E
Lapua 26 62.57 N 23.00 E
Lapuanjoki ≃ 26 63.34 N 22.30 E
La Puebla de Cazalla 34 37.14 N 5.19 W
La Puebla de Montalbán 34 39.52 N 4.21 W
La Puente 228 34.01 N 117.56 W
La Puerta 252 28.10 S 65.48 W
Lapu-Lapu (Opon) 116 10.19 N 123.57 E
La Punt 58 46.35 N 9.55 E
La Punta 286d 12.05 S 77.11 W
La Purísima, Chile 286e 33.34 S 70.39 W
La Purísima, Méx. 232 26.10 N 112.04 W
Lăpuș 38 47.30 N 24.01 E
La Push 224 47.54 N 124.38 W
Lapuyan 116 7.36 N 123.12 E
Lapväärtti → Lappfjärd 26 62.15 N 21.32 E
Lapwai 202 46.24 N 116.48 W
Łapy 30 53.00 N 22.53 E
La Queue-en-Brie 261 48.47 N 2.35 E
La Queue-lès-Yvelines 261 48.48 N 1.46 E
La Quiaca 252 22.06 S 65.37 W
L'Aquila 66 42.22 N 13.22 E
L'Aquila □4 66 42.05 N 13.40 E
Lār 128 27.41 N 54.17 E
Lara 169 38.01 S 144.24 E
Lara □3 246 10.10 N 69.50 W
Larabanga 150 9.13 N 1.51 W
Laracha 34 43.15 N 8.35 W
Larache 148 35.12 N 6.10 W
Laragne-Montéglin 62 44.19 N 5.49 E
Lārak, Jazīreh-ye I 128 26.52 N 56.22 E
Laramate 248 14.15 S 74.52 W
La Rambla 34 37.36 N 4.44 W
Laramie 200 41.18 N 105.35 W
Laramie ≃ 200 42.12 N 104.32 W
Laramie Mountains ∧∧ 200 42.00 N 105.40 W
Laramie Peak ∧ 200 42.17 N 105.27 W
Laranjaí ≃ 255 23.12 S 53.45 W
Laranjal 255 21.22 S 42.28 W
Laranjeiras 250 10.48 S 37.10 W
Laranjeiras ◆8 287a 22.56 S 43.11 W
Laranjeiras do Sul 252 25.25 S 52.25 W
Larantuka 115b 8.21 S 122.59 E
Laraos 248 12.17 S 75.50 W
Larap 116 14.18 N 122.39 E
Larat 164 7.09 S 131.45 E
Larat, Pulau I 164 7.10 S 131.50 E
Laravale 171a 28.05 S 152.56 E
La Raya, Abra)(248 14.35 S 70.59 W
L'Arbaa Naït Irathen 34 36.38 N 4.12 E
Larb Creek ≃ 202 48.25 N 107.16 W
L'Arbresle 62 45.50 N 4.37 E
Lärbro 26 57.47 N 18.47 E
Larbut, Jazīrat I 140 18.47 N 37.33 E
Larche, Col de (Colle della Maddalena))(62 44.25 N 6.53 E
Larchmont 210 40.55 N 73.45 W
Larchmont Harbor ⊂ 276 40.55 N 73.45 W
Larchwood 198 43.27 N 96.26 W
Lardaro 64 45.58 N 10.39 E
Larde 154 16.28 S 39.43 E
Lardeau 182 50.09 N 116.57 W
Larderello 66 43.14 N 10.53 E
Larder Lake ⊜ 190 48.05 N 79.36 W
Lardier, Cap ≻ 62 43.09 N 6.37 E
L'Ardoise 186 45.37 N 60.45 W
Lardy 261 48.31 N 2.16 E
Lare 154 0.20 N 37.56 E
Laredo, Esp. 34 43.24 N 3.25 W
Laredo, Tx., U.S. 196 27.30 N 99.30 W
Laredo Sound Ʋ 182 52.32 N 128.53 W
La Reforma, Méx. 232 25.06 N 108.05 W
La Reforma, Méx. 234 16.34 N 97.51 W
La Reina 286e 33.27 S 70.33 W
Laren 52 52.15 N 5.14 E
Larena 116 9.15 N 123.35 E
La Réole 32 44.35 N 0.02 W
Lares, Perú 248 13.04 S 72.05 W
Lares, P.R. 240m 18.18 N 66.53 W
Larga 78 48.23 N 26.50 E
Larga, Laguna ⊜ 196 27.30 N 97.25 W
Large, Île du I 275a 45.19 N 73.52 W
Largentière 62 44.32 N 4.18 E
L'Argentière-la-Bessée 62 44.47 N 6.33 E
Lar Gerd 120 35.29 N 66.40 E
Largo 220 27.54 N 82.47 W
Largo, Cañon V 200 36.40 N 107.43 W
Largo, Cayo I 240p 21.38 N 81.28 W
Largo Creek ≃ 200 34.29 N 108.51 W
Largoward 46 56.15 N 2.51 W
Largs 46 55.48 N 4.52 W
Largue ≃ 62 43.51 N 5.52 E
Lari, It. 66 43.34 N 10.35 E
Lari, Perú 248 15.37 S 71.46 W
Lariang 112 1.26 S 119.17 E
Lariang ≃ 112 1.25 S 119.17 E
La Ricamarie 62 45.24 N 4.22 E
Larimer 214 40.21 N 79.44 W
Larimore 198 47.54 N 97.37 W
Larino, It. 66 41.48 N 14.54 E
Larino, Ukr. 83 47.53 N 37.56 E
La Rioja 252 29.26 S 66.51 W
La Rioja □4, Arg. 252 30.00 S 67.30 W
La Rioja □4, Esp. 34 42.15 N 2.30 W
Lárisa 38 39.38 N 22.25 E
Larisa Station ◆5 267c 37.58 N 23.42 E
Larjak 74 61.16 N 80.15 E
Larjan 76 59.30 N 33.47 E
Larjegan ≃ 86 60.30 N 77.44 E
Lārkāna 120 27.33 N 68.13 E
Larkhall 46 55.45 N 3.59 W
Lark Harbour 186 49.06 N 58.23 W
Larkhill 42 51.12 N 1.50 W
Larkspur 226 37.56 N 122.30 W
Larksville 210 41.14 N 75.55 W
Larnaca → Lárnax 130 34.55 N 33.38 E
Lárnakos, Kólpos ⊂ 130 34.55 N 33.45 E
Lárnax (Larnaca) 130 34.55 N 33.38 E
Larne 48 54.51 N 5.49 W
Larned 198 38.10 N 99.05 W
Larne Lough ⊜ 48 54.47 N 5.45 W
Laro 146 8.17 N 12.18 E
La Robla 34 42.48 N 5.37 W
La Roca de la Sierra 34 39.07 N 6.41 W
La Roche 58 46.42 N 7.08 E
La Roche-Bernard 32 47.31 N 2.18 W
La Roche-de-Rame 62 44.45 N 6.35 E
La Roche-Derrien 28 48.45 N 3.16 W
La Roche-des-Arnauds 62 44.34 N 5.57 E
La Roche-en-Ardenne 56 50.11 N 5.35 E
La Roche-en-Brenil 50 47.22 N 4.10 E
La Rochefoucauld 32 45.45 N 0.23 E
La Roche-Guyon 50 49.05 N 1.38 E
La Rochelle 32 46.10 N 1.10 W
Laroche-Saint-Cydroine 50 47.58 N 3.31 E
La Roche-sur-Foron 58 46.04 N 6.19 E
La Roche-sur-Yon 32 46.40 N 1.26 W
La Rochette, Fr. 62 45.28 N 6.07 E
La Rochette, Fr. 261 48.30 N 2.40 E
Larochette, Lux. 56 49.47 N 6.15 E
La Roda 34 39.13 N 2.09 W
La Romaine 186 50.13 N 60.40 W
La Romana 238 18.25 N 68.58 W
Larona 112 2.45 S 121.20 E
La Ronge 184 55.06 N 105.17 W
Laroquebrou 32 44.58 N 2.11 E
La Roquebrussanne 62 43.20 N 5.59 E
Larose 194 29.34 N 90.22 W
La Rosita 236 13.53 N 84.24 W
La Route 261 48.48 N 2.47 E
Larrabee State Park ♠ 224 48.41 N 122.29 W
Larreynaga 236 12.40 N 86.34 W
Larrey Point ≻ 162 19.58 S 119.07 E
Larrimah 164 15.35 S 133.12 E
Larringes 58 46.22 N 6.35 E
Larrison Creek ≃ 222 31.27 N 95.03 W
Larroque 252 33.02 S 59.01 W
Larrys Creek ≃ 210 41.13 N 77.13 W
Larrys River 186 45.13 N 61.23 W
Larsen Air Park ⊠ 281 42.11 N 83.33 W
Larsen Bay 180 57.33 N 154.00 W
Larsen Ice Shelf ⊓ 9 68.30 S 62.30 W
Larteh Aheneasi 150 5.56 N 0.04 E
La Rubia 252 30.06 S 61.48 W
La Rue, Oh., U.S. 214 40.35 N 83.23 W
Larue, Tx., U.S. 222 32.07 N 95.41 W
La Rumorosa 204 32.34 N 116.06 W
Laruns 32 42.59 N 0.25 W
Larus Lake ⊜ 184 51.17 N 94.40 W
Larvik 26 59.04 N 10.00 E
Larwill 216 41.10 N 85.37 W
Larzac, Causse du ∧∧1 32 44.00 N 3.15 E
Lasa (Laas) 64 46.37 N 10.42 E
La Sabana 252 27.52 S 59.57 W
Las Adjuntas 286c 10.26 N 67.01 W
La Sagne 58 47.03 N 6.48 E
La Sal 200 38.18 N 109.14 W
La Salada, Laguna ⊜ 234 22.28 N 98.20 W
La Salette-Fallavaux 62 44.51 N 5.59 E
La Salle, On., Can. 214 42.14 N 83.06 W
La Salle, P.Q., Can. 206 45.26 N 73.38 W
Lasalle, Fr. 62 44.03 N 3.51 E
La Salle, It. 62 45.45 N 7.04 E
La Salle, Co., U.S. 200 40.20 N 104.42 W
La Salle, Il., U.S. 216 41.20 N 89.06 W
La Salle □6 216 41.21 N 88.51 W
La Salle ≃ 184 49.45 N 97.08 W
Lasalle, Parc ♠ 275a 45.26 N 73.40 W
La Salle College ʊ2 285 40.02 N 75.09 W
La Salle Gardens 216 42.39 N 83.21 W
Las Almejas, Bahía ⊂ 232 24.29 N 111.44 W
La Sal Mountains ∧∧ 200 38.30 N 109.10 W
Lasan 112 1.14 N 115.13 E
Lasanga Island I 164 7.25 S 147.16 E
Las Animas 198 38.04 N 103.13 W
La Santa, Cerro ∧ 240m 18.07 N 66.03 W
Las Arenas 240m 18.02 N 67.09 W
La Sarraz 58 46.40 N 6.31 E
La Sarre 190 48.48 N 79.12 W
La Sarre ≃ 190 48.43 N 79.16 W
Las Arrias 252 30.21 S 63.35 W
La Sauceda 196 28.26 N 100.38 W
La Saulce 62 44.25 N 6.01 E
Las Auras 196 26.25 N 99.20 W
Las Aves, Isla I 238 15.42 N 63.38 W
Las Aves, Islas II 246 12.00 N 67.30 W
Las Ballenas, Canal de Ʋ 232 29.10 N 113.29 W
Lasberg 61 48.28 N 14.32 E
Las Blancas 196 25.42 N 97.35 W
Las Bonitas 246 7.52 N 65.40 W
Las Breñas 252 27.05 S 61.05 W
Låsby 41 56.09 N 9.49 E
Las Cabezas de San Juan 34 36.59 N 5.56 W
Las Cabras 252 34.18 S 71.19 W
Las Cañas ≃ 234 22.29 N 105.36 W
Lascano 252 33.40 S 54.12 W
Lascar, Volcán ∧1 252 23.23 S 67.45 W
Lascari 70 38.00 N 13.56 E
Las Casas → San Cristóbal de las Casas 234 16.45 N 92.38 W
Las Catitas 252 33.18 S 68.02 W
Las Catonas, Arroyo ≃ 288 34.37 S 58.43 W
Lascaux, Grotte de ⊥5 32 45.01 N 1.08 E
Las Cejas 252 26.53 S 64.44 W
L'Ascension 206 46.33 N 74.50 W
L'aščevka 78 49.33 N 32.41 E
Las Chacras 258 35.05 S 59.10 W
Las Choapas 234 17.55 N 94.05 W
La Scie 186 49.57 N 55.36 W
Las Coloradas 254 39.33 S 70.35 W
Las Condes 286e 33.22 S 70.31 W
Lascone, Monte ∧2 267a 41.59 N 12.23 E
Las Cruces 200 32.18 N 106.46 W
Las Cuevas 232 29.38 N 101.19 W
Las Delicias 232 15.58 N 91.50 W
La Selle, Morne ∧ 238 18.22 N 71.59 W
La Selva Beach 226 36.55 N 121.51 W
Lasem 115a 6.42 S 111.26 E
La Serena 252 29.54 S 71.16 W
La Serena ◆1 34 38.45 N 5.30 W
La Seyne 32 43.06 N 5.53 E
La Seyne-sur-Mer 62 43.06 N 5.53 E
Las Flores, Arg. 252 36.03 S 59.07 W
Las Flores, Arg. 252 30.19 S 69.12 W
Las Flores, Méx. 234 18.22 N 93.10 W
Las Flores, P.R. 240m 18.03 N 66.22 W
Las Flores, Ven. 286c 10.34 N 66.56 W
Las Flores, Arroyo ≃ 252 35.36 S 59.01 W
Las Flores, Cerro ∧ 234 16.43 N 95.30 W
Las Flores Canyon V 280 34.03 N 118.38 W
Las Flores Chica, Laguna ⊜ 258 35.30 S 59.01 W
Las Flores Grande, Laguna ⊜ 258 35.34 S 59.02 W
Las Garcitas 252 26.35 S 59.48 W
Las Guacamayas 234 18.02 N 102.12 W
Las Guayabas 232 24.00 N 97.45 W
Lasham 42 51.11 N 1.03 W
Las Harquetas, Arroyo ≃ 288 34.29 S 58.38 W
Lashburn 184 53.08 N 109.36 W
Lāsh-e Joveyn 128 31.43 N 61.37 E
Las Heras, Arg. 252 32.51 S 68.49 W
Las Heras, Arg. 254 46.33 S 68.57 W
Lashio 110 22.56 N 97.45 E
Lashkar Gāh 128 31.35 N 64.21 E

≃ River	Fluß	Río	Rivière	Rio	
≍ Canal	Kanal	Canal	Canal	Canal	
⌊ Waterfall, Rapids	Wasserfall, Stromschnellen	Cascada, Rápidos	Chute d'eau, Rapides	Cascata, Rápidos	
Ʋ Strait	Meeresstraße	Estrecho	Détroit	Estreito	
⊂ Bay, Gulf	Bucht, Golf	Bahía, Golfo	Baie, Golfe	Baía, Golfo	
⊜ Lake, Lakes	See, Seen	Lago, Lagos	Lac, Lacs	Lago, Lagos	
≛ Swamp	Sumpf	Pantano	Marais	Pântano	
⊓ Ice Features, Glacier	Eis- und Gletscherformen	Accidentes Glaciales	Formes glaciaires	Acidentes glaciares	
⊤ Other Hydrographic Features	Andere Hydrographische Objekte	Otros Elementos Hidrográficos	Autres données hydrographiques	Outros acidentes hidrográficos	

✦ Submarine Features	Untermeerische Objekte	Accidentes Submarinos	Formes de relief sous-marin	Acidentes submarinos
□ Political Unit	Politische Einheit	Unidad Politica	Entité politique	Unidade política
ʊ Cultural Institution	Kulturelle Institution	Institución Cultural	Institution culturelle	Institução cultural
⊥ Historical Site	Historische Stätte	Sitio Histórico	Site historique	Sitio histórico
♠ Recreational Site	Erholungs- und Ferienort	Sitio de Recreo	Centre de loisirs	Area de Lazer
⊠ Airport	Flughafen	Aeropuerto	Aéroport	Aeroporto
■ Military Installation	Militäranlage	Instalación Militar	Installation militaire	Instalação militar
◆ Miscellaneous	Verschiedenes	Misceláneo	Divers	Diversos

Lashkar → Gwalior 124 26.13 N 78.10 E
Las Hormigas 232 25.30 N 98.44 W
Lasht 123 36.48 N 73.01 E
Lasia, Pulau I 114 2.10 N 96.39 E
La Sierra, Montaña ⋏ 236 14.04 N 87.54 W
Las Iglesias 196 27.35 N 101.21 W
Las Iglesias, Cerro ∧ 232 26.16 N 106.38 W
La Sila ⋏ 68 39.15 N 16.30 E
La Siligata 66 43.56 N 12.45 E
La Silla de Caracas ∧ 286c 10.33 N 66.51 W
Łasin 30 53.32 N 19.05 E
Lašino 80 58.16 N 49.59 E
Lāsjerd 128 35.24 N 53.04 E
Łask 30 51.36 N 19.07 E
Łaskarzew 30 51.48 N 21.35 E
L'askel'a 24 61.45 N 30.59 E
Laško 36 46.09 N 15.14 E
L'askoviči 78 52.07 N 28.09 E
Las Lajas, Arg. 252 38.31 S 70.22 W
Las Lajas, Pan. 236 8.15 N 81.52 W
Las Lajitas 252 24.41 S 64.15 W
Las Lomas 246 4.40 S 80.15 W
Las Lomitas 252 24.42 S 60.36 W
Lašma 80 54.56 N 41.09 E
Las Malvinas 252 34.50 S 68.15 W
Lašmanka 80 54.44 N 51.28 E
Las Mareas 240m 17.56 N 66.09 W
Las Margaritas 232 16.19 N 91.59 W
Las Margaritas, Laguna ⊜ 258 35.28 S 57.56 W
Las Marianas 258 35.04 S 59.31 W
Las Marías 240m 18.15 N 67.00 W
Las Marismas ≡ 34 37.00 N 6.15 W
Las Mayas 286c 10.26 N 66.56 W
Las Mercedes 246 9.07 N 66.24 W
Las Mesas de San Isidro 234 21.55 N 100.15 W
Las Minas 286c 10.27 N 66.52 W
Las Minas, Cerro ∧ 236 14.33 N 88.39 W
Las Minillas, Cerro ∧ 286e 33.31 S 70.29 W
Las Moras Creek ≃ 196 29.00 N 100.39 W
Las Mulas, Laguna ⊜ 258 35.32 S 57.54 W
Las Navas 116 12.21 N 125.02 E
Las Nieves 232 26.24 N 105.22 W
Las Nopaleras, Cerro ∧ 232 25.08 N 103.14 W
La Solana 34 38.56 N 3.14 W
La Soledad, Cerro ∧ 232 26.32 N 107.17 W
Lasolo 112 3.29 S 122.04 E
Lasolo ≃ 112 3.28 S 122.06 E
Las Ortegas, Arroyo ≃ 288 34.45 S 58.32 W
Las Ovejas 252 37.01 S 70.45 W
Las Palmas, Arg. 252 27.04 S 58.42 W
Las Palmas, Arg. 258 34.05 S 59.10 W
Las Palmas, Pan. 236 8.08 N 81.27 W
Las Palmas, P.R. 240m 17.59 N 66.02 W
Las Palmas □4 148 28.25 N 14.15 W
Las Palmas de Gran Canaria 148 28.06 N 15.24 W
Las Palomas 200 31.44 N 107.37 W
Las Perdices, Canal ≊ 286e 33.31 S 70.33 W
La Spezia 62 44.07 N 9.50 E
La Spezia □4 62 44.15 N 9.42 E
Las Piedras, P.R. 240m 18.11 N 65.52 W
Las Piedras, Ur. 258 34.44 S 56.13 W
Las Piedras, Río de ≃ 248 12.30 S 69.14 W
Las Piñas, Pil. 269f 14.29 N 120.59 E
Las Piñas, P.R. 240m 18.15 N 65.55 W
Las Plumas 254 43.43 S 67.15 W
Lasqueti Island I 182 49.29 N 124.17 W
Las Raices Creek ≃ 196 28.09 N 99.02 W
Las Ratas, Cerro ∧ 234 18.37 N 103.37 W
Las Rejas 286e 33.28 S 70.44 W
Las Rosas, Arg. 252 32.28 S 61.34 W
Las Rosas, Chile 286e 33.35 S 70.37 W
Las Rosas, Méx. 232 16.24 N 92.23 W
Las Rozas de Madrid 266a 40.29 N 3.52 W
Las Sales, Canal ≊ 286a 19.26 N 99.03 W
Lassan 54 53.57 N 13.50 E
Lassance 255 17.54 S 44.34 W
Lassater 222 32.49 N 94.30 W
Lassay 32 48.26 N 0.30 W
Lassee 61 48.13 N 16.49 E
Lassellsville 210 43.03 N 74.36 W
Lassen Peak ∧1 204 40.29 N 121.31 W
Lassen Volcanic National Park ♦ 204 40.30 N 121.19 W
Lassigny 50 49.35 N 2.51 E
Lassnitz ≃ 61 46.46 N 15.32 E
Lassnitzhöhe 61 47.05 N 15.35 E
Lasso ∧2 174n 15.02 N 145.38 E
L'Assomption 206 45.50 N 73.25 W
L'Assomption □6 206 45.48 N 73.35 W
L'Assomption ≃ 206 45.43 N 73.29 W
Lasswade 46 55.53 N 3.08 W
Lassy 261 49.06 N 2.27 E
Las Tablas 246 7.46 N 80.17 W
Lastarrio, Parque Nacional ♦ 254 44.50 S 72.05 W
Las Tinajas 252 27.27 S 62.55 W
Last Mountain ∧ 184 51.07 N 104.54 W
Last Mountain Lake ⊜ 184 51.05 N 105.10 W
Las Toscas 252 28.21 S 59.17 W
Lastoursville 152 0.49 S 12.42 E
Lastovo, Otok I 36 42.45 N 16.53 E
Lastovski Kanal ⊔ 36 42.50 N 16.59 E
Lastra a Signa 66 43.46 N 11.06 E
Las Trampas Creek ≃ 282 37.53 N 122.03 W
Las Trampas Peak ∧ 282 37.50 N 122.03 W
Las Trampas Regional Park ♦ 282 37.50 N 122.03 W
Las Trampas Ridge ∧ 282 37.49 N 122.02 W
Lästringe 40 58.54 N 17.18 E
Las Truchas 234 17.55 N 102.12 W
Lastrup 52 52.48 N 7.52 E
Las Tunas 240p 20.58 N 76.57 W
Las Tunas □4 240p 21.00 N 77.00 W
Las Tunas, Arroyo ≃ 288 34.27 S 58.41 W
Las Tunas, Punta > 240m 18.30 N 66.38 W
Las Tunas Beach ♦ 280 34.02 N 118.36 W
Las Tunas Grandes, Laguna ⊜ 252 35.58 S 62.25 W
La Suze 32 47.54 N 0.02 E
Las Varas, Méx. 232 29.29 N 108.01 W
Las Varas, Méx. 234 21.10 N 105.10 W
Las Varillas 252 31.52 S 62.43 W
Las Vegas, P.R. 240m 18.11 N 67.02 W
Las Vegas, Nv., U.S. 204 36.10 N 115.08 W
Las Vegas, N.M., U.S. 200 35.36 N 105.13 W
Las Vegas, Ven. 246 9.35 N 68.37 W
Las Vigas de Ramirez 234 19.38 N 97.05 W
La Tabatière 186 50.50 N 58.58 W
Latacunga 246 0.56 S 78.37 W
Latady Island I 9 70.45 S 74.35 W
La Tagua 246 0.03 S 74.40 W
Latakia □9 130 35.20 N 36.00 E
Latakia → Al-Lādhiqīyah 130 35.31 N 35.47 E
Latambar 123 33.07 N 70.52 E
Lata Mountain ∧ 174y 14.14 S 169.29 W
La Tapona 234 22.48 N 100.38 W
Låtefossen ∟ 26 59.57 N 6.37 E
Latehar 124 23.45 N 84.30 E
Lately Common 262 53.29 N 2.30 W
Latera 66 42.38 N 11.50 E
Laterina 66 43.31 N 11.43 E
Laterns 58 47.16 N 9.43 E
Laterrière 186 48.18 N 71.06 W
Laterza 68 40.37 N 16.48 E
La Teste-de-Buch 32 44.38 N 1.09 W
La Tetilla, Cerro ∧ 234 20.21 N 104.59 W
Latexo 222 31.24 N 95.29 W
Latgale □9 76 56.20 N 27.10 E
Latham, Austl. 162 29.45 S 116.26 E
Latham, Il., U.S. 219 39.58 N 89.10 W
Latham, N.Y., U.S. 210 42.44 N 73.45 W
Latham, Oh., U.S. 218 39.06 N 83.15 W
Lathan ≃ 50 47.27 N 0.08 E
Lathen 52 52.52 N 7.19 E
Latheron 46 58.17 N 3.23 W
Lāthi 120 21.43 N 71.23 E
Lathrop, Ca., U.S. 226 37.49 N 121.16 W
Lathrop, Mo., U.S. 194 39.32 N 94.19 W
Lathrup Village 281 42.29 N 83.14 W
La Thuile 62 45.43 N 6.57 E
La Tiama 286c 10.26 N 66.46 W
Latian, Mount ∧ 116 6.13 N 125.30 E
Latiano 68 40.33 N 17.43 E
Latimer, Eng., U.K. 260 51.41 N 0.33 W
Latimer, Ia., U.S. 190 42.45 N 93.22 W
Latina 66 41.28 N 12.52 E
Latina □4 66 41.27 N 13.06 E
Latiri 140 9.10 N 25.43 E
Latisana 64 45.47 N 13.00 E
Latjuga 24 64.16 N 48.46 E
Latnaja 78 51.43 N 38.55 E
La Toma 252 33.03 S 65.37 W
Laton 226 36.26 N 119.41 W
Latonovo 83 47.29 N 38.38 E
Latorica ≃ 30 48.28 N 21.50 E
Latornell ≃ 182 54.58 N 118.00 W
La Torrecilla ∧ 240m 18.12 N 66.20 W
La Tortuga, Isla I 246 10.56 N 65.20 W
Latouche Island I 180 60.00 N 147.55 W
Latouche Treville, Cape > 162 18.27 S 121.49 E
La Tour 62 43.57 N 7.11 E
La Tour-d'Aigues 62 43.44 N 5.33 E
La Tour-d'Auvergne 32 45.32 N 2.41 E
La Tour-de-Peilz 58 46.27 N 6.49 E
La Tour-du-Pin 62 45.34 N 5.27 E
La Tourette Park ♦ 276 40.35 N 74.08 W
Latowicz 30 52.02 N 21.48 E
Lat Phrao, Khlong ≊ 269a 13.48 N 100.35 E
La Tremblade 32 45.46 N 1.08 W
La Trimouille 32 46.28 N 1.02 E
La Trinidad, Arg. 252 27.24 S 65.31 W
La Trinidad, Nic. 236 12.58 N 86.14 W
La Trinidad, Pil. 116 16.28 N 120.35 E
La Trinidad, Ven. 286c 10.27 N 66.52 W
La Trinidad de Orichuna 246 7.07 N 69.45 W
La Trinitaria 232 16.07 N 92.03 W
La Trinité 240e 14.44 N 60.58 W
Latrobe, Austl. 166 41.14 S 146.24 E
Latrobe, Pa., U.S. 214 40.19 N 79.22 W
La Trobe ≃ 169 38.10 S 146.32 E
Latrobe University ⊕2 274b 37.43 S 145.03 E
La Tronche 62 45.12 N 5.44 E
Latronico 68 40.05 N 16.01 E
Latta 192 34.20 N 79.25 W
Lattarico 68 39.28 N 16.08 E
Lattasburg 214 40.53 N 82.06 W
Latterbach 58 46.40 N 7.35 E
Lattingtown 276 40.54 N 73.36 W
Latty 216 41.05 N 84.35 W
La Tuilerie 261 48.34 N 2.08 E
La Tuilière 62 44.11 N 5.32 E
Latuna 112 8.23 S 124.06 E
La Tuque 176 47.26 N 72.47 W
Lātūr 122 18.24 N 76.35 E
La Turbie 62 43.45 N 7.24 E
Latvia (Latvija) □1, Europe 22 57.00 N 25.00 E
Latvia (Latvija) □1, Europe 76 57.00 N 25.00 E
Lau, Nig. 146 9.13 N 11.17 E
Lau, Pap. N. Gui. 164 5.50 S 151.20 E
Laubach 56 50.33 N 8.59 E
Lau Basin ⊹1 14 20.00 S 177.00 W
Laubusch 54 51.28 N 14.10 E
Laubuseschbach 56 50.24 N 8.20 E
Lauca ≃ 248 19.10 S 68.10 W
Lauca, Parque Nacional ♦ 248 18.20 S 69.15 W
Laucha 54 51.13 N 11.41 E
Lauchhammer 54 51.30 N 13.47 E
Lauchheim 56 48.52 N 10.14 E
Lauda-Königshofen 56 49.34 N 9.41 E
Lauder 46 55.43 N 2.45 W
Lauderdale 194 32.31 N 88.30 W
Lauderdale V 46 55.43 N 2.42 W
Lauderdale-by-the-Sea 220 26.12 N 80.07 W
Lauderdale Lakes 220 26.09 N 80.12 W
Lauderhill 220 26.08 N 80.12 W
Laudun 62 44.06 N 4.40 E
Lauenbrück 52 53.12 N 9.33 E
Lauenburg 52 53.22 N 10.33 E
Lauenburg → Lebork 30 54.33 N 17.44 E
Lauenförde 52 51.39 N 9.23 E
Lauenstein, Dtsch. 52 52.04 N 9.33 E
Lauenstein, Dtsch. 54 50.47 N 13.49 E
Lauenstein, Dtsch. 54 50.31 N 11.20 E
Lauer ≃ 56 50.18 N 10.10 E
Lauerzer See ⊜ 58 47.02 N 8.36 E
Lauf an der Pegnitz 60 49.30 N 11.17 E
Läufelfingen 58 47.24 N 7.51 E
Laufen, Dtsch. 64 47.57 N 12.56 E
Laufen, Schw. 58 47.25 N 7.30 E
Laufenburg (Baden), Dtsch. 58 47.35 N 8.04 E
Laufenburg (Baden), Schw. 58 47.33 N 8.04 E
Laufersfort, Schloss ⊥ 263 51.25 N 6.37 E
Lauffen am Neckar 56 49.05 N 9.10 E
Laugharne 42 51.47 N 4.28 W
Laughery Creek ≃ 218 39.02 N 84.53 W
Laughlen, Mount ∧ 162 23.23 S 134.23 E
Laughlin Air Force Base ■ 196 29.22 N 100.47 W
Laughlin Peak ∧ 196 36.38 N 104.12 W
Laughlintown 214 40.13 N 79.12 W
Lau Group II 175g 18.20 S 178.30 W
Lauingen 56 48.34 N 10.25 E
Lauis → Lugano 58 46.01 N 8.58 E
Laukaa 26 62.25 N 25.57 E
Laukuva 76 55.37 N 22.14 E
Laul'u 89 45.46 N 135.16 E
Laun 110 10.07 N 98.46 E
Launceston, Austl. 166 41.26 S 147.08 E
Launceston, Eng., U.K. 42 50.38 N 4.21 W
Laundi, Tanjung > 115b 9.28 S 120.12 E
Laune ≃ 48 52.07 N 9.48 W
Launglon 110 13.58 N 98.07 E
Laungowāl 123 30.13 N 75.41 E
La Unión, Chile 254 40.17 S 73.05 W
La Unión, Col. 246 1.36 N 77.09 W
La Unión, El Sal. 236 13.20 N 87.51 W
La Unión, Esp. 34 37.37 N 0.52 W
La Unión, Méx. 234 17.58 N 101.49 W
La Unión, Perú 248 9.46 S 76.48 W
La Unión, Perú 248 5.24 S 80.45 W
La Union, Pil. 116 6.42 N 126.05 E
La Union, N.M., U.S. 200 31.57 N 106.39 W
La Unión, Ven. 246 8.13 N 67.46 W
La Unión, Ven. 286c 10.25 N 66.48 W
La Union □4 116 16.35 N 120.25 E
Launois-sur-Vence 56 49.39 N 4.32 E
Launsdorf 61 46.46 N 14.27 E
Laupen 58 46.54 N 7.14 E
Laupendahl •−8 263 51.21 N 6.56 E
Laupheim 58 48.14 N 9.52 E
Laur 116 15.35 N 121.11 E
Laura, Austl. 164 15.34 S 144.28 E
Laura, Oh., U.S. 218 39.59 N 84.24 W
La Urbana 246 7.08 N 66.56 W
Laureana di Borrello 68 38.30 N 16.05 E
Laurel, De., U.S. 208 38.33 N 75.34 W
Laurel, Fl., U.S. 220 27.07 N 82.27 W
Laurel, In., U.S. 218 39.30 N 85.11 W
Laurel, Md., U.S. 208 39.05 N 76.50 W
Laurel, Ms., U.S. 194 31.41 N 89.07 W
Laurel, Mt., U.S. 202 45.40 N 108.46 W
Laurel, Ne., U.S. 198 42.25 N 97.05 W
Laurel, Va., U.S. 208 37.38 N 77.30 W
Laurel, Wa., U.S. 224 45.57 N 121.23 W
Laurel ≃ 192 36.57 N 84.18 W
Laurel, Mount ∧2 285 39.56 N 74.53 W
Laurel Bay 192 32.33 N 80.44 W
Laureldale, N.J., U.S. 208 39.29 N 74.41 W
Laureldale, Pa., U.S. 208 40.23 N 75.55 W
Laureles 252 31.22 S 55.51 W
Laureles, Isla de los I 258 33.45 S 59.23 W
Laurel Gardens 279b 40.31 N 80.01 W
Laurel Hill, Austl. 171b 35.37 S 148.05 E
Laurel Hill, N.C., U.S. 192 34.48 N 79.32 W
Laurel Hill ∧ 214 40.15 N 79.05 W
Laurel Hollow 276 40.52 N 73.28 W
Laurel Reservoir ⊜1 276 41.10 N 73.33 W
Laurel Ridge State Park ♦ 188 39.58 N 79.23 W
Laurel River Lake ⊜1 192 36.55 N 84.15 W
Laurel Run 210 41.13 N 75.51 W
Laurel Run ≃ 208 40.20 N 77.20 W
Laurel Springs 285 39.49 N 75.00 W
Laurelton 210 40.52 N 77.11 W
Laurelville, Oh., U.S. 188 39.28 N 82.44 W
Laurelville, Pa., U.S. 214 40.09 N 79.29 W
Laurenburg 56 50.20 N 7.54 E
Laurence Harbor 276 40.27 N 74.14 W
Laurencekirk 46 56.50 N 2.29 W
Laurens, Ia., U.S. 198 42.50 N 94.51 W
Laurens, N.Y., U.S. 210 42.32 N 75.06 W
Laurens, S.C., U.S. 192 34.29 N 82.00 W
Laurentides 206 45.51 N 73.46 W
Laurentides, Les ⋏1 176 48.00 N 71.00 W
Laurentides, Parc Provincial des ♦ 186 47.40 N 71.30 W
Laurenzana 68 40.28 N 15.58 E
Lauria 68 40.02 N 15.50 E
Lau Ridge ⊹3 14 21.00 S 178.30 W
Laurie Island I 9 60.45 S 44.35 W
Laurie Lake ⊜ 184 56.34 N 101.54 W
Laurier, Mb., Can. 184 50.54 N 99.33 W
Laurier, P.Q., Can. 206 46.32 N 71.38 W
Laurière 32 46.05 N 1.28 E
Laurierville 206 46.18 N 71.39 W
Laurinburg 192 34.46 N 79.27 W
Laurino 68 40.20 N 15.20 E
Laurito 68 40.10 N 15.24 E
Lauritsala 26 61.04 N 28.16 E
Lauritzen Bay ⊂ 9 69.05 S 156.50 E
Laurium 190 47.14 N 88.26 W
Lauriya Nandangarh 124 26.59 N 84.24 E
Lauro, Monte ∧ 70 37.07 N 14.49 E
Laurys Station 208 40.43 N 75.32 W
Lausanne 58 46.31 N 6.38 E
Lauscha 54 50.28 N 11.10 E
Laut 86 59.18 N 66.02 E
Laut, Pulau I, Indon. 112 3.40 S 116.10 E
Laut, Pulau I, Indon. 112 4.43 N 107.59 E
Laut, Selat ⊔ 112 3.25 S 116.03 E
Lauta 54 51.27 N 14.04 E
Lautaro 252 38.31 S 72.27 W
Lautaro, Volcán ∧1 254 49.00 S 73.32 W
Lautem 112 8.22 S 126.54 E
Lautenbach 58 47.57 N 7.09 E
Lautenthal 52 51.52 N 10.17 E
Lauter ≃, Dtsch. 56 49.39 N 7.35 E
Lauter ≃, Europe 56 48.58 N 8.11 E
Lauterach 58 47.29 N 9.44 E
Lauterbach, Dtsch. 56 50.38 N 9.24 E
Lauterbach, Dtsch. 58 48.14 N 8.20 E
Lauterbourg 56 48.59 N 8.11 E
Lauterbrunnen 58 46.36 N 7.55 E
Lauterecken 56 49.39 N 7.35 E
Lauterhofen 60 49.22 N 11.37 E
Lauter [Sachsen] 54 50.33 N 12.44 E
Laut Kecil, Kepulauan II 112 4.50 S 115.45 E
Lautoka 175g 17.37 S 177.27 E
Lauttakylä → Huittinen 26 61.11 N 22.42 E
Laut Tawar, Danau ⊜ 114 4.38 N 96.54 E
Lauwe 50 50.48 N 3.11 E
Lauwerszee ⊂ 52 53.20 N 6.12 E
Lauzerte 32 44.15 N 1.08 E
Lauzon 206 46.50 N 71.10 W
Lauzun 32 44.38 N 0.28 E
Lava (Łyna) ≃ 76 54.37 N 21.14 E
Lava, Nosy I 157b 14.33 S 47.36 E
Lava Beds National Monument ♦ 204 41.42 N 121.30 W
Lavaca □6 222 29.22 N 96.55 W
Lavaca ≃ 196 28.50 N 96.36 W
Lavaca Bay ⊂ 196 28.35 N 96.35 W
La Vacherie 62 44.53 N 5.11 E
Lavagh More ∧ 48 54.45 N 8.05 W
Lavagna 62 44.18 N 9.20 E
Lavagna ≃ 62 44.21 N 9.20 E
Lava Hot Springs 202 42.37 N 112.00 W
Lavaisse 252 33.49 S 65.25 W
Laval, P.Q., Can. 206 45.35 N 73.45 W
Laval, Fr. 32 48.04 N 0.46 W
Laval-des-Rapides •−8 275a 45.33 N 73.42 W
La Valette-du-Var 62 43.08 N 5.59 E
La Valette → Valletta 36 35.54 N 14.31 E
La Vall d'Uixo 34 39.49 N 0.14 W
Lavalle, Arg. 252 29.01 S 59.11 W
Lavalle, Arg. 252 28.12 S 65.08 W
Lavalleja → Minas 252 34.23 S 55.14 W
Lavallette 208 39.58 N 74.04 W
La Valley 200 37.06 N 105.20 W
Laval-Ouest •−8 275a 45.33 N 73.52 W
Lavaltrie 206 45.53 N 73.17 W
Lavamünd 61 46.39 N 14.56 E
Lāvān, Jazīreh-ye I 128 26.48 N 53.15 E
Lavan, Naḥal V 132 30.57 N 34.21 E
Lavanono 157b 25.24 S 44.55 E
Lavant ≃ 61 46.38 N 14.57 E
Lavapié, Punta > 252 37.09 S 73.35 W
Lávara 38 41.16 N 26.22 E
Lavaraty 157b 23.16 S 46.59 E
Lavardac 32 44.11 N 0.18 E
Lavarone 64 45.56 N 11.15 E
Lavassaare 76 58.31 N 24.22 E
Lava-Tudo ≃ 252 28.26 S 50.25 W
Laveaga Peak ∧ 226 36.53 N 121.11 W
La Vecilla de Curueño 34 42.51 N 5.24 W
La Vega 238 19.13 N 70.31 W
La Vega •−8 286c 10.28 N 66.57 W
Lavela 24 63.38 N 45.31 E
La Vela, Cabo de > 246 12.15 N 72.11 W
La Vela de Coro 246 11.27 N 69.34 W
Lavelanet 32 42.56 N 1.51 E
Lavelle 208 40.46 N 76.22 W
Lavello 68 41.03 N 15.48 E
Laven 41 56.07 N 9.43 E
La Venada 196 25.50 N 97.30 W
Lavendon 42 52.11 N 0.40 W
Lavenham 42 52.06 N 0.47 E
Laveno 58 45.55 N 8.37 E
Lavenone 64 45.44 N 10.26 E
La Venta ≃ 234 16.59 N 93.46 W
La Venta ⊥ 234 18.08 N 94.03 W
Laventie 50 50.38 N 2.46 E
La Ventura 232 24.38 N 100.54 W
Laver ≃ 44 54.08 N 1.30 W
Lavéra 62 43.23 N 5.02 E
La Vera •−1 34 40.20 N 5.30 W
La Verde, Arg. 252 27.08 S 59.23 W
La Verde, Arg. 258 34.44 S 59.16 W
Laverdière, Lac ⊜ 206 46.50 N 74.28 W
L'Averdy, Cape > 175e 5.33 S 155.04 E
La Vérendrye, Réserve ♦ 190 47.30 N 77.30 W
La Vergne 194 36.00 N 86.34 W
La Verna ⊕1 66 43.42 N 11.54 E
La Verne, Ca., U.S. 280 34.06 N 117.46 W
Laverne, Ok., U.S. 196 36.42 N 99.53 W
La Vernia 196 29.21 N 98.07 W
Laverock 285 40.05 N 75.11 W
La Verpillière 62 45.38 N 5.09 E
La Verrière 261 48.45 N 1.57 E
Lavers Hill 169 38.40 S 143.24 E
Laverton, Austl. 162 28.38 S 122.25 E
Laverton, Austl. 169 37.52 S 144.45 E
Laverton Royal Australian Air Force Base ■ 169 37.52 S 144.43 E
La Veta 200 37.30 N 105.00 W
Lavezares 116 12.32 N 124.20 E
Lavezzi, Îles II 71 41.20 N 9.15 E
Lavezzola 66 44.34 N 11.52 E
Lavia 26 61.36 N 22.36 E
Laviano 68 40.47 N 15.18 E
Lavic Lake ⊜ 204 34.40 N 116.21 W
La Victoria, Perú 286d 12.04 S 77.02 W
La Victoria, Ven. 246 10.14 N 67.20 W
Lavieille, Lake ⊜ 190 45.51 N 78.14 W
Lavik 26 61.06 N 5.30 E
La Vila Joiosa 34 38.30 N 0.14 W
La Villa 64 46.36 N 11.54 E
La Villa ≃ 236 7.59 N 80.23 W
La Ville-du-Bois 261 48.40 N 2.16 E
La Villeneuve-Saint-Martin 261 49.04 N 1.58 E
Lavillette 186 47.16 N 65.18 W
Lavin 58 46.46 N 10.06 E
La Viña, Arg. 252 25.27 S 65.35 W
Lavina, Mt., U.S. 202 46.17 N 108.56 W
Lavinio Lido di Enea 66 41.30 N 12.05 E
Laviolette, Lac ⊜ 206 46.51 N 73.58 W
La Virginia 246 4.54 N 75.53 W
Lavis 64 46.08 N 11.07 E
La Vista 198 41.11 N 96.01 W
Lavon 222 33.02 N 96.26 W
Lavonia 192 34.26 N 83.06 W
Lavon Lake ⊜1 222 33.05 N 96.28 W
Lavougba 152 5.46 N 23.21 E
La Voulte-sur-Rhône 62 44.48 N 4.47 E
Lavoûte-sur-Loire 62 45.07 N 3.54 E
Lavoutte, Anse ⊂ 241f 14.06 N 60.56 W
Lavradia 266c 38.40 N 9.03 W
Lavras 256 21.14 S 45.00 W
Lavras ≃ 287a 23.00 S 43.33 W
Lavras da Mangabeira 250 6.45 S 38.57 W
Lavras do Sul 252 30.49 S 53.55 W
Lavrentija 180 65.35 N 171.00 W
Lavrentija, zaliv ⊂ 180 65.40 N 171.15 W
Lavrinhas 256 22.35 S 44.54 W
Lávrion 38 37.44 N 24.04 E
Lavumisa 158 27.19 S 31.54 E
Lavushi Manda National Park ♦ 154 12.20 S 30.50 E
Lawa 116 6.12 N 125.41 E
Lawai 229b 21.55 N 159.30 W
Lawang 115a 7.49 S 112.42 E
La Wantzenau 58 48.40 N 7.50 E
La Ward 222 28.51 N 96.28 W
Lawas 112 4.51 N 115.24 E
Lawatu 112 2.53 S 120.18 E
Lawdar 144 13.53 N 45.52 E
Lawele 112 5.13 S 122.57 E
Lawers, Ben ∧ 46 56.34 N 4.13 W
Laweueng 114 5.31 N 95.52 E
Lawford Lake ⊜ 184 54.30 N 96.43 W
Lawgi 166 24.34 S 150.39 E
Lawin 114 5.18 N 101.04 E
Lawin, Pulau I 164 1.31 S 128.44 E
Lawit, Gunong ∧ 114 5.25 N 102.35 E
Lawksawk 110 21.15 N 96.52 E
Lawler 190 43.04 N 92.09 W
Lawlor, Mount ∧ 280 34.16 N 118.06 W
Lawn, Nf., Can. 186 46.57 N 55.32 W
Lawn, Pa., U.S. 208 40.13 N 76.32 W
Lawn, Tx., U.S. 196 32.08 N 99.49 W
Lawn Bay ⊂ 186 46.53 N 55.35 W
Lawndale, Ca., U.S. 228 33.53 N 118.21 W
Lawndale, Il., U.S. 219 40.13 N 89.17 W
Lawndale, N.C., U.S. 192 35.24 N 81.33 W
Lawndale •−8, Il., U.S. 278 41.51 N 87.43 W
Lawndale •−8, Pa., U.S. 285 40.03 N 75.05 W
Lawnes Creek ≃ 208 37.08 N 76.40 W
Lawn Hill 166 18.35 S 138.35 E
Lawn Hill Creek ≃ 166 18.03 S 139.09 E
Lawn Hill National Park ♦ 166 18.45 S 138.27 E
Lawnside 285 39.51 N 75.01 W
Lawowa 112 4.26 S 122.56 E
Lawqah 128 29.49 N 42.45 E
Lawra 150 10.39 N 2.52 W
Lawrence, N.Z. 172 45.55 S 169.41 E
Lawrence, In., U.S. 218 39.50 N 86.01 W
Lawrence, Ks., U.S. 198 38.58 N 95.14 W
Lawrence, Ma., U.S. 207 42.42 N 71.09 W
Lawrence, Mi., U.S. 216 42.13 N 86.03 W
Lawrence, Ne., U.S. 198 40.17 N 98.15 W
Lawrence, N.Y., U.S. 276 40.36 N 73.43 W
Lawrence, Pa., U.S. 279b 40.18 N 80.09 W
Lawrence, Tx., U.S. 222 32.45 N 96.21 W
Lawrence □6, In., U.S. 218 38.52 N 86.29 W
Lawrence □6, Pa., U.S. 214 41.00 N 80.20 W
Lawrence, Lake ⊜ 224 46.51 N 122.34 W
Lawrence Brook ≃ 276 40.29 N 74.24 W
Lawrenceburg, In., U.S. 218 39.05 N 84.51 W
Lawrenceburg, Ky., U.S. 218 38.02 N 84.54 W
Lawrenceburg, Tn., U.S. 194 35.14 N 87.20 W
Lawrence Fork ≃ 198 41.36 N 103.14 W
Lawrence Institute of Technology ⊕2 281 42.28 N 83.15 W
Lawrence Marsh ≡ 276 40.36 N 73.42 W
Lawrence Municipal Airport ⊠ 283 42.43 N 71.07 W
Lawrence Park 214 42.09 N 80.01 W
Lawrencepur 123 33.50 N 72.30 E
Lawrenceville, Il., U.S. 194 38.43 N 87.40 W
Lawrenceville, N.J., U.S. 208 40.17 N 74.43 W
Lawrenceville, Pa., U.S. 210 42.00 N 77.08 W
Lawrenceville, Va., U.S. 192 36.45 N 77.50 W
Lawrenceville •−8 279b 40.28 N 79.57 W
Lawson, Austl. 170 33.43 S 150.26 E
Lawson, Mo., U.S. 194 39.26 N 94.12 W
Lawson Heights 214 40.18 N 79.23 W
Lawsonia 208 37.58 N 75.50 W
Lawsons Creek ≃ 170 32.35 S 149.43 E
Lawtey 192 30.02 N 82.04 W
Lawton, Ky., U.S. 218 38.16 N 83.13 W
Lawton, Mi., U.S. 216 42.10 N 85.50 W
Lawton, N.D., U.S. 198 48.18 N 98.22 W
Lawton, Ok., U.S. 196 34.36 N 98.23 W
Lawton •−8 286b 23.06 N 82.21 W
Lawu, Gunung ∧ 115a 7.38 S 111.11 E
Lawyer Creek ≃ 202 46.14 N 116.01 W
Lawyersville 210 42.42 N 74.30 W
Lawz, Jabal al- ∧ 128 28.40 N 35.18 E
Laxå 40 58.59 N 14.37 E
Laxay 46 58.09 N 6.35 W
Laxenburg 264b 48.04 N 16.21 E
Laxenburger Park ♦ 264b 48.04 N 16.22 E
Laxey 44 54.14 N 4.23 W
Laxford, Loch ⊂ 46 58.23 N 5.06 W
Lax Kw'alaams 182 54.33 N 130.25 W
Laxou 58 48.41 N 6.09 E
Layang Layang 114 1.49 N 103.29 E
Laye ≃ 62 43.54 N 5.48 E
La Yesca 234 21.19 N 104.02 W
Layhill 208 39.05 N 77.03 W
Laylā 144 22.17 N 46.45 E
Lay Lake ⊜1 194 33.10 N 86.35 W
Layou 241h 13.12 N 61.17 W
Layou ≃ 240d 15.23 N 61.26 W
La'youn □4 148 27.55 N 12.15 W
Lay-Saint-Christophe 56 48.45 N 6.12 E
Laysan Island I 14 25.50 N 171.50 W
Layton, N.J., U.S. 210 41.13 N 74.50 W
Layton, Ut,. U.S. 200 41.03 N 111.58 W
Laytons Lake ⊜ 285 39.42 N 75.26 W
Laytonville 204 39.41 N 123.28 W
Laytown 48 53.40 N 6.14 W
Laž 80 57.11 N 49.14 E
La Zarca 232 25.50 N 104.44 W
Lazarev 89 52.13 N 141.32 E
Lazarevo 80 56.49 N 50.15 E
Lazarevskoje 84 43.55 N 39.20 E
Lazarivo 157b 23.54 S 44.59 E
Lazaro Cárdenas, Méx. 196 25.23 N 103.10 W
Lázaro Cárdenas, Méx. 232 30.33 N 115.56 W
Lázaro Cárdenas, Méx. 234 17.57 N 102.12 W
Lázaro Cárdenas, Presa ⊜1 232 25.35 N 105.02 W
Lazdijai 76 54.14 N 23.31 E
Lazha 102 26.26 N 101.50 E
Lazhulong 120 35.08 N 81.33 E
Lazi 116 9.08 N 123.38 E
Lazio □4 66 42.00 N 12.30 E
Lazise 64 45.30 N 10.44 E
Lazo 89 43.25 N 133.55 E
Lazorki 78 50.06 N 32.39 E
La Zorra, Quebrada ≃ 286c 10.36 N 67.03 W
Lazovskij zapovednik ♦ 89 43.00 N 133.55 E
Lazzaro 68 37.58 N 15.40 E
Lazzate 266b 45.40 N 9.05 E
Lea ≃ 42 51.30 N 0.01 E
Léach 110 12.21 N 103.46 E
Leach ≃ 42 51.41 N 1.39 W
Leach Pond ⊜ 283 42.04 N 71.09 W
Leachville 194 35.56 N 90.15 W
Leacock 208 40.05 N 76.12 W
Lead 198 44.21 N 103.45 W
Leadbetter Point > 224 46.38 N 124.03 W
Leadburn 46 55.47 N 3.14 W
Leadenham 44 53.05 N 0.34 W
Leaden Roding 260 51.48 N 0.19 E
Leader 184 50.53 N 109.31 W
Leader Water ≃ 46 55.36 N 2.41 W
Leadgate 44 54.52 N 1.48 W
Lead Hill ∧2 194 37.06 N 92.38 W
Leadhills 44 55.25 N 3.47 W
Leadon ≃ 42 51.53 N 2.16 W
Leadore 202 44.40 N 113.21 W
Leadville 200 39.15 N 106.17 W
Leaf ≃, Mn., U.S. 198 46.29 N 94.53 W
Leaf ≃, Ms., U.S. 194 31.00 N 88.45 W
Leaf Lake ⊜ 184 53.02 N 102.07 W
Leaghur, Lake ⊜ 166 33.35 S 143.04 E
League, Slieve ∧ 48 54.39 N 8.44 W
League City 222 29.30 N 95.05 W
Leakesville 194 31.09 N 88.33 W
Leakey 196 29.43 N 99.45 W
Leakin Park ♦ 284b 39.18 N 76.42 W
Leak Run ≃ 279b 40.27 N 79.47 W
Leaksville 192 36.29 N 79.53 W
Lealman 220 27.49 N 82.40 W
Lealui 152 15.10 S 23.02 E
Leam ≃ 42 52.17 N 1.14 W
Leamington 214 42.03 N 82.36 W
Leamington Spa → Royal Leamington Spa 42 52.18 N 1.31 W
Le'an 100 27.24 N 115.48 E
Leán ≃ 236 15.47 N 87.20 W
Leander Point > 162 29.16 S 114.56 E
Leandro 250 5.59 S 44.55 W
Leandro N. Alem 252 27.36 S 55.19 W
Leane, Lough ⊜ 48 52.05 N 9.35 W
Leannan ≃ 48 55.02 N 7.38 W
Leano, Monte ∧ 66 41.20 N 13.13 E
Learmonth 162 22.15 S 114.05 E
Leary 192 31.29 N 84.30 W
Leaside □8 275b 43.42 N 79.22 W
Leask 184 53.00 N 106.45 W
Leatherhead 42 51.18 N 0.20 W
Leatherman Peak ∧ 202 44.05 N 113.44 W
Leatherwood Creek ≃ 218 38.49 N 86.30 W
Lea Town 262 53.46 N 2.48 W
Leavenworth, Ks., U.S. 198 39.18 N 94.55 W
Leavenworth, Wa., U.S. 224 47.35 N 120.39 W
Leavesden Aerodrome ⊠ 260 51.42 N 0.27 W
Leavittsburg 214 41.14 N 80.52 W
Leawood 194 37.03 N 94.31 W
Łeba 30 54.47 N 17.33 E
Łeba ≃ 30 54.47 N 17.33 E
Lebach 56 49.24 N 6.54 E
Lebak 116 6.32 N 124.03 E
Lebam 224 46.33 N 123.32 W
Lébamba 152 2.12 S 11.30 E
Lebango 152 0.22 N 14.49 E
Lebanon, Ct., U.S. 207 41.38 N 72.13 W
Lebanon, Il., U.S. 219 38.36 N 89.48 W
Lebanon, In., U.S. 218 40.02 N 86.28 W
Lebanon, Ks., U.S. 198 39.48 N 98.33 W
Lebanon, Ky., U.S. 194 37.34 N 85.15 W
Lebanon, Mo., U.S. 194 37.40 N 92.39 W
Lebanon, N.H., U.S. 188 43.38 N 72.15 W
Lebanon, N.J., U.S. 210 40.38 N 74.50 W
Lebanon, N.Y., U.S. 210 42.47 N 75.39 W
Lebanon, Oh., U.S. 218 39.26 N 84.12 W
Lebanon, Or., U.S. 202 44.32 N 122.54 W
Lebanon, Pa., U.S. 208 40.20 N 76.24 W
Lebanon, S.D., U.S. 198 45.04 N 99.46 W
Lebanon, Tn., U.S. 194 36.12 N 86.17 W
Lebanon, Va., U.S. 192 36.54 N 82.04 W
Lebanon □6 208 40.20 N 76.25 W
Lebanon (Lubnān) □1, Asia 118 34.00 N 36.00 E
Lebanon (Lubnān) □1, Asia 128 34.00 N 36.00 E
Lebanon Junction 194 37.50 N 85.43 W
Lebanon Mountains → Lubnān, Jabal ⋏ 132 34.00 N 36.00 E
Lebanon Springs 210 42.29 N 73.23 W
Le Ban-Saint-Martin 56 49.07 N 6.09 E
Le Bar-sur-le-Loup 62 43.42 N 6.59 E
Leb'ažje, Kaz. 86 51.28 N 77.46 E
Leb'ažje, Ross. 80 57.25 N 49.32 E
Leb'ažje, Ross. 86 55.16 N 66.29 E
Lebbeke 50 51.00 N 4.08 E
Le Béage 62 44.51 N 4.07 E
Le Beausset 62 43.12 N 5.48 E
Lebec 228 34.50 N 118.51 W
Lebed'an' 76 53.01 N 39.09 E
Lebedevka, Kaz. 86 50.09 N 54.07 E
Lebedevka, Ross. 80 51.06 N 47.09 E
Lebedevka, Ross. 86 56.48 N 66.57 E
Lebedi 78 51.17 N 37.38 E
Lebedin, Ukr. 78 48.59 N 31.31 E
Lebedin, Ukr. 78 50.36 N 34.30 E
Lebedino 80 55.14 N 49.50 E
Leben, Oued el V 148 34.37 N 10.01 E
Lebesby 24 70.34 N 26.59 E
Le Bessat 62 45.22 N 4.31 E
Le Bihan Falls ∟ 158 29.51 S 28.03 E
Le Biot 58 46.16 N 6.38 E
Lebir ≃ 114 5.33 N 102.12 E
Le Blanc 32 46.38 N 1.04 E
Le Blanc-Mesnil 261 48.56 N 2.28 E
Le Bleymard 62 44.29 N 3.44 E
Leblon •−8 287a 22.59 S 43.13 W
Lebo, Ks., U.S. 198 38.25 N 95.51 W
Lebo, Zaïre 152 4.29 N 23.57 E
Le Bois-de-Cise 50 50.05 N 1.26 E
Le Bois-Dieu 261 48.39 N 1.43 E
Le Bois-d'Oingt 58 45.55 N 4.35 E
Lebombo Mountains ⋏2 156 25.15 S 32.00 E
Lebongtandai 112 3.01 S 101.54 E
Le Boréon 62 44.07 N 7.17 E
Lębork 30 54.33 N 17.44 E
Le Boulay 261 48.47 N 1.40 E
Le Bourg-d'Oisans 62 45.03 N 6.02 E
Le Bourget 261 48.56 N 2.26 E
Le Bourget-du-Lac 62 45.39 N 5.52 E
Le Brassus 58 46.35 N 6.13 E
Lebrija 34 36.55 N 6.04 W
Lebrija ≃ 246 8.08 N 73.47 W
Le Broc 62 43.49 N 7.10 E
Le Brugeron 62 45.43 N 3.43 E
Łebsko, Jezioro ⊂ 30 54.44 N 17.24 E
Lebu 252 37.37 S 73.39 W
Le Bugue 32 44.55 N 0.56 E
Le Buisson de Massoury ≡ 261 48.30 N 2.43 E
Lebus 54 52.25 N 14.32 E
Le Caire → Al-Qāhirah 142 30.03 N 31.15 E
Le Camp-du-Castellet 62 43.15 N 5.45 E
Le Cannet 62 43.34 N 7.01 E
Lecanto 220 28.51 N 82.29 W
Le Cap → Cape Town 158 33.55 S 18.22 E
Le Cap → Cap-Haïtien 238 19.45 N 72.12 W
Le Carbet 240e 14.43 N 61.11 W
Le Cateau 50 50.06 N 3.33 E
Le Catelet 50 50.00 N 3.15 E
Lecce 68 40.23 N 18.11 E
Lecce □4 68 40.13 N 18.10 E
Lecce, Tavoliere di ≚ 68 40.30 N 17.35 E
Lecce nei Marsi 66 41.56 N 13.41 E
Lečchumskij chrebet ⋏ 84 42.45 N 43.05 E
Lecco 62 45.51 N 9.23 E
Lecco, Lago di ⊜ 58 45.55 N 9.19 E
Le Center 190 44.23 N 93.43 W
Lech 58 47.12 N 10.09 E
Lech ≃ 30 48.44 N 10.56 E
Le Châble, Fr. 58 46.06 N 6.06 E
Le Châble, Schw. 58 46.05 N 7.12 E
L'Échalp 62 44.45 N 7.00 E
Le Chambon-Feugerolles 62 45.24 N 4.19 E
Le Chambon-sur-Lignon 62 45.03 N 4.18 E
Le Champ-Renault 261 49.06 N 2.31 E
Lechang 100 25.09 N 113.21 E
Le Chasseral ∧ 58 47.08 N 7.03 E
Le-Château-d'Oléron 32 45.53 N 1.11 W
Le Châtelard, Fr. 62 45.41 N 6.08 E
Le Châtelard, Schw. 58 46.04 N 6.58 E
Le Châtelet 32 46.39 N 2.17 E
Le Châtelet-en-Brie 50 48.30 N 2.48 E
Lechbruck 58 47.42 N 10.47 E
Leche, Laguna de la ⊂ 240p 22.13 N 78.38 W
Le Chêne-Rogneux 261 48.46 N 1.46 E
Le Chesnay 261 48.50 N 2.07 E
Le Chesne 56 49.31 N 4.46 E
Le Cheylard 62 44.54 N 4.25 E
Lechfeld ≚ 58 48.10 N 10.50 E
Lechiguanas, Islas de las II 252 33.26 S 59.42 W
Lechlade 42 51.43 N 1.41 W
Lechleiten 58 47.16 N 10.12 E
Lechta 24 60.49 N 48.28 E
Lechtaler Alpen ⋏ 64 47.15 N 10.30 E
Lechuga, Arroyo ≃ 286b 23.01 N 82.16 W
Lechuguilla, Cerro ∧ 234 22.19 N 104.15 W
Lecinone, Monte ∧ 267a 41.59 N 12.48 E
Leck 41 54.46 N 8.58 E
Le Claire 190 41.36 N 90.21 W
Lecompte 194 31.05 N 92.24 W
Leconfield 44 53.52 N 0.27 W
Léconi 152 1.35 S 14.14 E
Lecontes Mills 214 41.05 N 78.17 W
Le Cornate ∧ 66 43.10 N 10.57 E
Le Coudray-Montceaux 261 48.34 N 2.31 E
Le Coudray-Saint-Germer 50 49.25 N 1.50 E
Le Creusot 58 46.48 N 4.26 E
Le Croci di Acerno)(68 40.47 N 15.02 E
Le Croisic 32 47.18 N 2.31 W
Le Crotoy 50 50.13 N 1.37 E
Łęczna 30 51.19 N 22.52 E
Łęczyca 30 52.04 N 19.13 E
Leda ≃ 52 53.12 N 7.26 E
Ledaig 46 56.30 N 5.23 W
Led'anaja, gora ∧ 74 61.53 N 171.09 E
Ledang, Gunong ∧ 114 2.22 N 102.37 E
Ledava ≃ 61 46.29 N 16.35 E
Ledbetter 222 30.09 N 96.48 W
Ledbury 42 52.02 N 2.25 W
Lede 50 50.58 N 3.58 E
Ledenice 61 48.57 N 14.37 E
Lederach 285 40.16 N 75.24 W
Le Deschaux 58 46.57 N 5.30 E
Ledesma 34 41.05 N 6.00 W
Ledgewood 276 40.52 N 74.39 W
Ledi, Ben ∧ 46 56.15 N 4.19 W
Le Diamant 240e 14.29 N 61.02 W
Lediba 152 3.03 S 16.32 E
Lédignan 62 43.59 N 4.06 E
Ledkovo 24 67.14 N 50.30 E
Lednice 61 48.48 N 16.48 E
Ledo, India 120 27.18 N 95.44 E
Ledo, Indon. 112 1.02 N 109.36 E
Lêdo, Cabo > 152 9.41 S 13.12 E
Ledong 110 18.45 N 109.12 E
Le Donjon 32 46.21 N 3.48 E
Le Dorat 32 46.13 N 1.05 E
Le Doré, Lac ⊜ 186 51.17 N 61.23 W
Ledra ≃ 64 46.13 N 13.02 E
Ledsham 262 53.16 N 2.58 W
Ledu 102 36.32 N 102.25 E
Leduc 182 53.16 N 113.33 W
Ledung 114 2.45 N 99.59 E
Ledyard Bay ⊂ 180 69.30 N 164.30 W
Lędyczek 30 53.33 N 16.58 E
Lee, Il., U.S. 216 41.48 N 88.56 W
Lee, Ma., U.S. 207 42.18 N 73.14 W
Lee □6, Fl., U.S. 220 26.34 N 81.55 W
Lee □6, Il., U.S. 216 41.50 N 89.29 W
Lee □6, Tx., U.S. 222 30.20 N 96.55 W
Lee ≃ 48 51.54 N 8.22 W
Lee Boulevard Heights 284c 38.52 N 77.09 W
Lee Center 210 43.18 N 75.31 W
Leechburg 214 40.37 N 79.36 W
Leechburg Airport ⊠ 279b 40.37 N 79.34 W
Leech Lake ⊜, Sk., Can. 184 51.04 N 102.30 W
Leech Lake ⊜, Mn., U.S. 190 47.09 N 94.23 W
Leech Lake Indian Reservation •−4 190 47.30 N 94.27 W
Leechtown 224 48.30 N 123.42 W
Leedey 196 35.52 N 99.20 W
Leedom Estates 285 39.41 N 75.35 W
Leeds, Eng., U.K. 44 53.50 N 1.35 W
Leeds, Al., U.S. 194 33.32 N 86.32 W
Leeds, N.Y., U.S. 210 42.15 N 73.54 W
Leeds, N.D., U.S. 198 48.17 N 99.26 W
Leeds and Bradford (Yeadon) Airport ⊠ 44 53.52 N 1.38 W
Leeds and Grenville □6 212 44.45 N 75.50 W

Symbols in the index entries represent the broad categories identified in the key at the right. Symbols with superior numbers (⋏1) identify subcategories (see complete key on page *I* · *1*).

Symbole im Register stellen die rechts im Schlüssel erklärten Kategorien dar. Symbole mit hochgestellten Ziffern (⋏1) bezeichnen Unterabteilungen einer Kategorie (vgl. vollständiger Schlüssel auf Seite *I* · *1*).

Los símbolos incluídos en el texto del índice representan las grandes categorias identificadas con la clave a la derecha. Los símbolos con numeros en su parte superior (⋏1) identifican las subcategorías (véase la clave completa en la página *I* · *1*).

Les symboles de l'index représentent les catégories indiquées dans la légende à droite. Les symboles suivis d'un indice (⋏1) représentent des sous-catégories (voir légende complète à la page *I* · *1*).

Os símbolos incluídos no texto do índice representam as grandes categorias identificadas com a chave à direita. Os símbolos com números em sua parte superior (⋏1) identificam as subcategorias (veja-se a chave completa à página *I* · *1*).

∧ Mountain	Berg	Montaña	Montagne	Montanha
⋏ Mountains	Gebirge	Montañas	Montagnes	Montanhas
)(Pass	Paß	Paso	Col	Passo
V Valley, Canyon	Tal, Cañon	Valle, Cañón	Vallée, Canyon	Vale, Canhão
≚ Plain	Ebene	Llano	Plaine	Planície
> Cape	Kap	Cabo	Cap	Cabo
I Island	Insel	Isla	Île	Ilha
II Islands	Inseln	Islas	Îles	Ilhas
♦ Other Topographic Features	Andere Topographische Objekte	Otros Elementos Topográficos	Autres données topographiques	Outros acidentes topográficos

ESPAÑOL

Nombre	Página	Lat. °′	Long. °′ W = Oeste
Leeds and Liverpool Canal ≊	262	53.25 N	2.59 W
Leeds Point	208	39.29 N	74.25 W
Leedstown	42	50.10 N	5.22 W
Leegebruch	54	52.43 N	13.11 E
Leek, Ned.	52	53.09 N	6.24 E
Leek, Eng., U.K.	44	53.06 N	2.01 W
Leelanau, Lake ⊜	190	44.55 N	85.43 W
Leelanau Peninsula ›[1]	190	45.10 N	85.35 W
Leeming	44	54.17 N	1.32 W
Leenaun	48	53.36 N	9.45 W
Leende	52	51.21 N	5.33 E
Lee-on-the-Solent	42	50.47 N	1.12 W
Lee Park	210	41.14 N	75.55 W
Leeper	214	41.22 N	79.18 W
Leer	52	53.14 N	7.26 E
Leerdam	52	51.54 N	5.05 E
Leerhafe	52	53.32 N	7.47 E
Leersum	52	52.01 N	5.26 E
Lees	262	53.32 N	2.04 W
Leesburg, Fl., U.S.	220	28.48 N	81.52 W
Leesburg, Ga., U.S.	192	31.43 N	84.10 W
Leesburg, In., U.S.	216	41.19 N	85.51 W
Leesburg, N.J., U.S.	208	39.15 N	74.59 W
Leesburg, Oh., U.S.	218	39.20 N	83.33 W
Leesburg, Tx., U.S.	222	32.59 N	95.05 W
Leesburg, Va., U.S.	208	39.06 N	77.33 W
Lees Creek ≃	218	39.21 N	83.29 W
Leese	52	52.30 N	9.06 E
Leesport	208	40.27 N	75.58 W
Lees Summit	194	38.55 N	94.23 W
Leeste	52	52.59 N	8.49 E
Leeston	172	43.46 S	172.18 E
Leesville, Il., U.S.	216	41.01 N	87.33 W
Leesville, In., U.S.	218	38.51 N	86.18 W
Leesville, La., U.S.	194	31.08 N	93.15 W
Leesville, Oh., U.S.	214	40.27 N	81.13 W
Leesville, S.C., U.S.	192	33.54 N	81.30 W
Leesville, Tx., U.S.	222	29.24 N	97.45 W
Leesville Lake ⊜[1], Oh., U.S.	214	40.30 N	81.10 W
Leesville Lake ⊜[1], Va., U.S.	192	37.05 N	79.25 W
Leeton	166	34.33 S	146.24 E
Leetonia	214	40.52 N	80.45 W
Leetsdale	214	40.33 N	80.12 W
Leeudoringstad	158	27.15 S	26.10 E
Leeu-Gamka	158	32.47 S	21.59 E
Leeupan ⩦	273d	26.14 S	28.19 E
Leeuwarden	52	53.12 N	5.46 E
Leeuwin, Cape ›	162	34.22 S	115.08 E
Lee Vining	226	37.57 N	119.07 W
Leeward Islands II	238	17.00 N	63.00 W
Le Faouët	28	48.02 N	3.29 W
Le Fayet	58	45.55 N	6.42 E
Lefèvre, Pointe ›	175f	20.54 S	167.01 E
Leffe	62	45.48 N	9.53 E
Lefferts, Lake ⊜	276	40.25 N	74.14 W
Léfini ≃	152	2.57 S	16.10 E
Léfini, Réserve de Chasse de la ◆[4]	152	2.58 S	15.25 E
Lefke	130	35.07 N	32.51 E
Le Focette	64	43.55 N	10.13 E
Leforest	50	50.26 N	3.04 E
Lefors	196	35.26 N	100.48 W
Le François	240e	14.37 N	60.54 W
Le Freney-d'Oisans	62	45.02 N	6.07 E
Lefroy	212	44.16 N	79.34 W
Lefroy, Lake ⊜	162	31.15 S	121.40 E
Leftrook Lake ⊜	184	56.05 N	98.36 W
Lega Hida	144	7.56 N	41.04 E
Legal	182	53.57 N	113.35 W
Leganés	34	40.19 N	3.45 W
Le Gardeur	206	45.45 N	73.28 W
Legaspi	116	13.08 N	123.44 E
Legau	58	47.51 N	10.07 E
Legden	52	52.02 N	7.07 E
Legendre ≃	206	45.44 N	71.08 W
Legendre Island I	162	20.23 S	116.54 E
Leggett, Ca., U.S.	204	39.51 N	123.42 W
Leggett, Tx., U.S.	222	30.49 N	94.52 W
Leghorn → Livorno	66	43.33 N	10.19 E
Legion Mine	154	21.23 S	28.33 E
Legion of Honor, Palace of the ʋ	282	37.47 N	122.30 W
Legionowo	30	52.25 N	20.56 E
Legnago	64	45.11 N	11.18 E
Legnano	62	45.36 N	8.54 E
Legnica (Liegnitz)	30	51.13 N	16.09 E
Legnica □[4]	30	51.25 N	16.10 E
Le Gosier	241o	16.12 N	61.30 W
Le Grand	226	37.13 N	120.14 W
LeGrand, Cape ›	162	34.01 S	122.06 E
Le Grand-Lucé	50	47.52 N	0.28 E
Le Grand-Quevilly	50	49.25 N	1.02 E
Le Grand-Serre	62	45.16 N	5.06 E
Le Grand Wintersberg ∧[2]	56	48.59 N	7.37 E
Le Grau-du-Roi	62	43.32 N	4.08 E
Le Gua	62	45.01 N	5.37 E
Le Guelta	34	36.22 N	0.50 E
Leguga	154	3.23 N	25.02 E
Legume	166	28.25 S	152.19 E
Legundi, Pulau I	115a	5.50 S	105.16 E
Leh	123	34.10 N	77.35 E
Le Havre	50	49.30 N	0.08 E
Lehčevo	38	43.32 N	23.32 E
Le Hérie-la-Viéville	50	49.49 N	3.38 E
Lehesten	54	50.29 N	11.28 E
Lehi	200	40.23 N	111.50 W
Lehigh, Ia., U.S.	190	42.21 N	94.03 W
Lehigh, Ok., U.S.	196	34.28 N	96.12 W
Lehigh □[6]	208	40.36 N	75.29 W
Lehigh ≃	210	40.41 N	75.12 W
Lehigh Acres	220	26.37 N	81.37 W
Lehighton	210	40.50 N	75.42 W
Lehinch	48	52.56 N	9.21 W
Lehnin	54	52.19 N	12.44 E
Lehnitz	54	52.44 N	13.15 E
Lehnitz See ⊜	264a	52.45 N	13.16 E
Leho	140	7.07 N	33.52 E
Le Hohwald	58	48.24 N	7.20 E
Le Houlme	50	49.31 N	1.02 E
Lehr	198	45.59 N	99.32 W
Lehra Gāga	123	29.55 N	75.49 E
Lehrbach	56	50.47 N	9.04 E
Lehrberg	56	49.21 N	10.30 E
Lehre	54	52.19 N	10.40 E
Lehrte	52	52.22 N	9.59 E
Lehstedt	52	52.14 N	10.12 E
Lehtimäki	26	62.47 N	23.55 E
Lehtrār Bāla	123	33.42 N	73.26 E
Lehtse	76	59.15 N	25.50 E
Lehua I	229b	22.01 N	160.06 W
Lehututu	156	23.58 S	21.51 E
Lei ≃	100	26.54 N	112.39 E
Leiah	123	30.58 N	70.56 E
Leião	266c	38.44 N	9.18 W
Leibnitz	61	46.47 N	15.32 E
Leibo	102	28.19 N	103.21 E
Leicester, Eng., U.K.	42	52.38 N	1.05 W
Leicester, Ma., U.S.	207	42.14 N	71.54 W
Leicester, N.Y., U.S.	210	42.46 N	77.53 W
Leicestershire □[6]	42	52.40 N	1.10 W
Leichardt	274a	33.53 S	151.07 E
Leichhardt ≃	166	17.35 S	139.48 E
Leichhardt Falls ʟ	166	18.14 S	139.53 E
Leichhardt Range ʎ	166	20.40 S	147.25 E
Leichlingen	56	51.06 N	7.01 E
Leiden	52	52.09 N	4.30 E
Leiderdorp	52	52.09 N	4.32 E
Leidschendam	52	52.05 N	4.24 E
Leie (Lys) ≃	50	51.03 N	3.43 E
Leiferde	52	52.26 N	10.26 E
Leigh, N.Z.	172	36.17 S	174.49 E
Leigh, Eng., U.K.	44	53.30 N	2.33 W
Leigh, Eng., U.K.	260	51.12 N	0.13 E
Leigh ≃	169	38.06 S	144.03 E

FRANÇAIS

Nom	Page	Lat. °′	Long. °′ W = Ouest
Leigh Canal ≊	262	53.28 N	2.21 W
Leigh Creek	166	30.28 S	138.25 E
Leighlinbridge	48	52.44 N	6.59 W
Leigh-on-Sea	42	51.33 N	0.38 E
Leighton	194	34.42 N	87.31 W
Leighton Buzzard	42	51.55 N	0.40 W
Leikanger	26	61.10 N	6.52 E
Leiktho	110	19.13 N	96.35 E
Leimbach	54	51.36 N	11.28 E
Leimstruth	56	50.59 N	8.19 E
Lein ≃	56	48.54 N	10.01 E
Leinan	184	50.30 N	107.46 W
Leinburg	60	49.27 N	11.19 E
Leine ≃	52	52.43 N	9.36 E
Leinefelde	54	51.23 N	10.20 E
Leinfelden-Echterdingen	56	48.41 N	9.08 E
Leinster	162	27.51 S	120.36 E
Leinster □[9]	48	53.05 N	7.00 W
Leinster, Mount ∧	48	52.37 N	6.44 W
Leintwardine	42	52.23 N	2.51 W
Leipalingis	76	54.05 N	23.51 E
Leipheim	58	48.27 N	10.13 E
Leipoldtville	158	32.14 S	18.30 E
Leipsic, De., U.S.	208	39.14 N	75.31 W
Leipsic, In., U.S.	218	38.40 N	86.22 W
Leipsic, Oh., U.S.	216	41.05 N	83.59 W
Leipsic ≃	208	39.15 N	75.24 W
Leipzig	54	51.19 N	12.20 E
Leiria	34	39.45 N	8.48 W
Leirvik	26	59.45 N	5.30 E
Leisach	64	46.48 N	12.45 E
Leishendian	107	28.58 N	106.40 E
Leisi	76	58.34 N	22.39 E
Leisler, Mount ∧	162	23.28 S	129.17 E
Leisnig	54	51.09 N	12.56 E
Leiston	42	52.12 N	1.34 E
Leisure City	220	25.29 N	80.25 W
Leitariegos, Puerto de)(	34	43.00 N	6.25 W
Leitchfield	194	37.28 N	86.17 W
Leiters Ford	216	41.07 N	86.23 W
Leith	46	55.59 N	3.10 W
Leith, Water of ≃	46	55.59 N	3.11 W
Leitha (Lajta) ≃	61	47.54 N	17.17 E
Leithagebirge ʎ	61	47.52 N	16.35 E
Leithe ◆[8]	263	51.29 N	7.06 E
Leith Hill ∧[2]	42	51.11 N	0.23 W
Leitre	164	2.50 S	141.40 E
Leitrim	48	54.00 N	8.04 W
Leitrim □[6]	48	54.20 N	8.20 W
Leitzkau	54	52.03 N	11.57 E
Leixi	100	27.10 N	112.52 E
Leixlip	48	53.22 N	6.29 W
Leiyang	100	26.24 N	112.51 E
Lei Yue Mun ʯ	271d	22.16 N	114.14 E
Leizhou Bandao ›[1]	102	21.15 N	110.09 E
Leizhuang	98	39.47 N	118.34 E
Lejasciems	76	57.17 N	26.35 E
Lek ≃	52	51.55 N	4.34 E
Lékana	152	2.19 S	14.36 E
Le Kef → El Kef	148	36.11 N	8.43 E
Lékéti ≃	152	1.36 S	14.57 E
Lekhainá	38	37.56 N	21.17 E
Lekir	114	4.07 N	100.44 E
Lekitobi	112	1.58 S	124.33 E
Lekkeroog	158	30.43 S	20.00 E
Lekkerwater	156	23.38 S	17.14 E
Lekma ≃	80	58.18 N	52.04 E
Łęknice	54	51.35 N	14.45 E
Lékoni ≃	152	1.11 S	13.16 E
Lekotero	152	0.46 S	23.51 E
Lékoumou □[5]	152	3.00 S	13.30 E
Le Kreïder	148	34.06 N	0.02 E
Le Kremlin-Bicêtre	261	48.49 N	2.21 E
Leksand	26	60.44 N	14.59 E
Leksberg	40	59.41 N	13.49 E
Leksozero, ozero ⊜	24	63.46 N	30.58 E
Leksvik	26	63.40 N	10.37 E
Lela	152	5.03 S	12.29 E
Le Lac-d'Issarlès	62	44.49 N	4.04 E
Le Lamentin	240e	14.37 N	61.01 W
Leland, Il., U.S.	216	41.37 N	88.48 W
Leland, Mi., U.S.	190	45.01 N	85.45 W
Leland, Ms., U.S.	194	33.24 N	90.53 W
Leland Grove	219	39.47 N	89.41 W
Leland Lake ⊜	224	47.53 N	122.53 W
Lelång ⊜	26	59.08 N	12.10 E
Lelant	42	50.11 N	5.26 W
Le Laus	62	44.31 N	6.09 E
Le Lauzet-Ubaye	62	44.26 N	6.26 E
Le Lavandou	62	43.08 N	6.22 E
Lel'čicy	78	51.47 N	28.19 E
Leleiwi Point ›	229d	19.44 N	155.00 W
Leleque	254	42.23 S	71.03 W
Leles	115a	7.07 S	107.53 E
Lelewau	112	3.02 S	121.05 E
Lélex	58	46.18 N	5.57 E
Le Liège	50	47.13 N	1.06 E
Le Limbé	238	19.42 N	72.24 W
Leling	98	37.45 N	117.12 E
Lelingluang	164	7.09 S	131.43 E
Lelintah	164	2.03 S	130.16 E
Le Lion-d'Angers	32	47.38 N	0.43 W
Leli Shan ∧	120	33.26 N	81.42 E
Le Locle	58	47.03 N	6.45 E
Lelogama	112	9.44 S	123.57 E
Le Lorrain	240e	14.50 N	61.04 W
Le Luc	62	43.23 N	6.19 E
Le Lude	50	47.39 N	0.09 E
Lelydrop	250	5.42 N	55.16 W
Lelystad	52	52.31 N	5.27 E
Lema	150	12.57 N	4.14 E
Le Madonie ʎ	70	37.52 N	13.58 E
Lemahabang	115a	6.17 S	107.27 E
Le Maire, Estrecho de ʯ	254	54.50 S	65.00 W
Léman, Lac → Geneva, Lake ⊜	58	46.25 N	6.30 E
Lemankoa	175e	5.02 S	154.35 E
Le Mans	50	48.00 N	0.12 E
Le Marin	240e	14.28 N	60.53 W
Le Markstein	58	47.56 N	7.02 E
Le Mars	198	42.47 N	96.09 W
Lema Shilindi	144	4.55 N	42.02 E
Lemay	219	38.32 N	90.17 W
Lemay, Lac ⊜	186	50.35 N	68.25 W
Lembach	56	49.00 N	7.48 E
Lembach im Mühlkreis	60	48.29 N	13.53 E
Lemba-Gaba	273b	4.27 S	15.18 E
Lembak	112	0.52 N	117.32 E
Lembang	115a	6.49 S	107.36 E
Lembeck	52	51.45 N	7.00 E
Lembeek	50	50.43 N	4.13 E
Lembeh, Pulau I	112	1.26 N	125.13 E
Lembeni	154	3.47 S	37.37 E
Lemberg, Sk., Can.	184	50.44 N	103.13 W
Lemberg, Fr.	56	49.00 N	7.23 E
Lemberg ∧	58	48.09 N	8.45 E
Lemberg → L'vov	78	49.50 N	24.00 E
Lembruch	52	52.31 N	8.22 E
Lembu, Gunung ∧	114	4.12 N	97.24 E
Lemdiyya	148	36.12 N	2.50 E
Lemdiyya □[5]	148	35.50 N	3.00 E
Leme	255	22.12 S	47.24 W
Leme, Morro do ∧[2]	287a	22.58 S	43.10 W
Le Mée-sur-Seine	261	48.32 N	2.38 E
Lemei Rock ∧	224	46.01 N	121.46 W
Lemele	52	52.27 N	6.25 E
Le Mêle-sur-Sarthe	50	48.31 N	0.21 E
Lemene ≃	64	45.37 N	12.53 E
Lemeris, Cape ›	164	3.15 S	152.03 E
Le Merlerault	50	48.42 N	0.18 E
Lemery	116	13.53 N	120.55 E
Lemeškino	80	51.01 N	44.27 E
Le Mesle	261	48.43 N	1.41 E
Le Mesnil-Amelot	261	49.01 N	2.36 E

PORTUGUÊS

Nome	Página	Lat. °′	Long. °′ W = Oeste
Le Mesnil-Aubry	261	49.03 N	2.24 E
Le Mesnil-le-Roi	261	48.56 N	2.08 E
Le Mesnil-Saint-Denis	261	48.45 N	1.58 E
Le Mesnil-sur-Oger	50	48.57 N	4.01 E
Lemesós (Limassol)	130	34.40 N	33.02 E
Lemešovka	78	52.04 N	31.38 E
Lemeta	180	64.52 N	147.44 W
Lemförde	52	52.28 N	8.22 E
Lemfu	152	5.18 S	15.13 E
Lemgo	52	52.02 N	8.54 E
Lemhi ≃	202	45.12 N	113.53 W
Lemhi Pass)(	202	44.58 N	113.27 W
Lemhi Range ʎ	202	44.30 N	113.25 W
Lemie	62	45.14 N	7.17 E
Lemierzyce	54	52.35 N	14.56 E
Lemieux Islands II	176	64.30 N	64.40 W
Lemin	102	21.11 N	109.42 E
Leming	196	29.04 N	98.29 W
Lemitar	200	34.09 N	106.54 W
Lemke	52	52.39 N	9.09 E
Lemland I	26	60.03 N	20.09 E
Lemmatsi	76	58.20 N	26.37 E
Lemmenjoen kansallispuisto ♠	24	68.40 N	26.00 E
Lemmer	52	52.50 N	5.42 E
Lemmon	198	45.56 N	102.09 W
Lemmon, Mount ∧	200	32.26 N	110.47 W
Lemnos → Límnos I	38	39.54 N	25.21 E
Lemoenshoek	158	33.51 S	20.51 E
Lemoine, Lac ⊜	190	48.00 N	78.00 W
Lemon, Lake ⊜	218	39.16 N	86.25 W
Le Monastier	62	44.56 N	4.00 E
Lemoncove	204	36.23 N	119.01 W
Lemon Creek ≃	276	40.31 N	74.12 W
Le Monêtier-les-Bains	62	44.59 N	6.31 E
Lemon Grove	228	32.44 N	117.01 W
Lemon Heights	280	33.46 N	117.48 W
Lemont, Il., U.S.	216	41.40 N	88.00 W
Lemont, Pa., U.S.	214	40.49 N	77.49 W
Le Montet	32	46.25 N	3.03 E
Le Mont-Saint-Michel ʋ[1]	32	48.38 N	1.32 W
Lemoore	226	36.18 N	119.46 W
Lemoore Naval Air Station ■	226	36.15 N	119.57 W
Lemoro	112	1.25 S	121.05 E
Le Moule	241o	16.20 N	61.21 W
Le Moutier	261	48.50 N	1.42 E
LeMoyne, P.Q., Can.	275a	45.31 N	73.29 W
Lemoyne, Oh., U.S.	214	41.30 N	83.28 W
Lemoyne, Pa., U.S.	208	40.15 N	76.54 W
Lempa ≃	236	13.14 N	88.49 W
Lempäälä	26	61.19 N	23.45 E
Lempe	112	1.40 S	120.14 E
Lempira □[5]	236	14.20 N	88.40 W
Lemro ≃	110	20.25 N	93.20 E
Lemsid	148	26.32 N	13.49 W
Lemukutan, Pulau I	112	0.45 N	108.43 E
Le Murge ʎ[1]	68	40.52 N	16.42 E
Lemutan	112	3.03 N	115.49 E
Le Muy	62	43.28 N	6.33 E
Lemva ≃	24	66.30 N	61.48 E
Lemvig	26	56.32 N	8.18 E
Lemyethna	110	17.36 N	95.09 E
Len ≃	260	51.16 N	0.31 E
Lena, Il., U.S.	190	42.22 N	89.49 W
Lena, Wi., U.S.	190	44.57 N	88.02 W
Lena ≃	74	72.25 N	126.40 E
Lenangguar	115b	8.44 S	117.24 E
Lenape	285	39.55 N	75.38 W
Lenart	61	46.35 N	15.50 E
Lenasia	273d	26.17 S	27.50 E
Lenawee □[6]	216	41.53 N	84.04 W
Lencloître	32	46.49 N	0.20 E
Lençóis	255	12.34 S	41.23 W
Lençois Maranhenses, Parque Nacional dos ♠	250	2.25 S	43.15 W
Lend	64	47.18 N	13.04 E
Lenda ≃	154	1.20 N	28.01 E
Lendava	61	46.34 N	16.27 E
Lendelede	50	50.53 N	3.14 E
Lendery	24	63.26 N	31.03 E
Lendinara	64	45.05 N	11.36 E
Lendorf	64	46.50 N	13.26 E
Lendringsen	56	51.24 N	7.49 E
Le Neubourg	50	49.09 N	0.55 E
Lenga	114	2.17 N	102.49 E
Lengduqiao	106	30.27 N	119.15 E
Lengede	52	52.12 N	10.18 E
Lengefeld	54	50.43 N	13.11 E
Lengelscheid	263	51.08 N	7.40 E
Lengenfeld, Dtsch.	54	50.34 N	12.22 E
Lengenfeld, Dtsch.	56	51.13 N	10.13 E
Lenger	85	42.12 N	69.54 E
Lengerich, Dtsch.	52	52.11 N	7.50 E
Lengerich, Dtsch.	52	52.33 N	7.32 E
Lenggor ≃	114	2.25 N	103.37 E
Lenggries	64	47.41 N	11.34 E
Lenghu	90	38.30 N	93.15 E
Lengjiagou	104	41.40 N	121.37 E
Lengkong	115a	7.32 S	112.04 E
Lenglingen ⊜	26	64.14 N	13.45 E
Lengnau	58	47.11 N	7.22 E
Lengoué	152	1.13 N	15.43 E
Lengoué ≃	152	0.49 N	15.47 E
Lengshuichang	107	29.27 N	106.26 E
Lengshuikeng	100	27.55 N	117.08 E
Lengshuitan	102	26.27 N	111.35 E
Lengua de Vaca, Punta ›	252	30.14 S	71.38 W
Lengulu	154	3.15 N	26.30 E
Lengwe National Park ♠	154	16.15 S	34.45 E
Lengzipu	104	41.42 N	122.47 E
Lenham	42	51.14 N	0.43 E
Lenhartsville	208	40.34 N	75.53 W
Lenhovda	26	57.00 N	15.17 E
Lenina, gora ∧[2]	265b	55.42 N	37.31 E
Lenina, ozero ⊜	78	48.33 N	35.12 E
Lenina, pik ∧	85	39.20 N	72.55 E
Leninabad → Chudžand	85	40.17 N	69.37 E
Leninakan → Kumajri	84	40.48 N	43.50 E
Lenin Central Stadium ♠	265b	55.43 N	37.33 E
Lenin-Džol	85	41.03 N	72.38 E
Leningori	84	42.07 N	44.29 E
Leningrad Oblast' □[4]	24	60.00 N	32.00 E
Leningrado → Sankt-Peterburg	76	59.55 N	30.15 E
Leningrad → Sankt-Peterburg	76	59.55 N	30.15 E
Leningradskaja	78	46.19 N	39.24 E
Leningradskaja ʋ[3]	9	69.30 S	159.23 E
Leningradskij	85	38.06 N	70.01 E
Leningradskoje	86	53.33 N	71.35 E
Lenino	78	45.18 N	35.47 E
Lenino ◆[8]	265b	55.37 N	37.41 E
Leninogorsk, Kaz.	86	50.27 N	83.32 E
Leninogorsk, Ross.	80	54.36 N	52.30 E
Leninpol'	85	42.29 N	71.55 E
Leninsk, Kaz.	86	45.40 N	63.20 E
Leninsk, Ross.	80	46.08 N	43.46 E
Leninsk, Ross.	80	48.42 N	45.11 E
Leninsk, Ross.	86	54.55 N	59.54 E
Leninsk, Uzb.	85	40.38 N	72.15 E
Leninskaja Sloboda	80	56.05 N	44.28 E
Leninskij, Kaz.	86	52.13 N	76.47 E
Leninskij, Mol.	78	47.53 N	28.23 E
Leninskij, Ross.	80	46.31 N	44.28 E
Leninskij, Ross.	80	56.34 N	45.56 E
Leninskij, Ross.	82	54.18 N	37.28 E
Leninskij, Ukr.	83	48.05 N	39.31 E
Leninsk-Kuzneckij	86	54.38 N	86.10 E
Leninskoje, Kaz.	80	49.03 N	49.56 E
Leninskoje, Kaz.	85	41.45 N	69.23 E
Leninskoje, Kaz.	86	50.44 N	57.53 E
Leninskoje, Kaz.	86	54.04 N	65.22 E
Leninskoje, Kyrg.	85	40.42 N	73.11 E
Leninskoje, Ross.	80	58.19 N	47.06 E
Leninskoje, Ross.	89	47.56 N	132.38 E
Leninskoje, Ukr.	78	45.16 N	35.54 E
Leninskoje, Ukr.	78	51.27 N	33.18 E
Lenin-Stausee → Kujbyševskoje vodochranilišče ⊜[1]	80	54.30 N	48.30 E
Leninžol	80	49.20 N	47.05 E
Lenk	58	46.28 N	7.27 E
Lenkerville	208	40.32 N	76.58 W
Len'ki	86	52.57 N	80.26 E
Lenkoran'	84	38.45 N	48.50 E
Lenmalu	164	1.44 S	130.13 E
Lennard, Mount ∧[2]	168a	33.21 S	115.53 E
Lenne ≃	56	51.25 N	7.30 E
Lennegebirge ʎ	52	51.15 N	8.00 E
Lennep	56	51.11 N	7.15 E
Lennep ◆[8]	52	51.12 N	7.15 E
Lennestadt	56	51.08 N	8.01 E
Lenni	285	39.54 N	75.27 W
Lennon	216	42.59 N	83.56 W
Lennonville	162	27.58 S	117.50 E
Lennox, Ca., U.S.	228	33.56 N	118.21 W
Lennox, S.D., U.S.	198	43.21 N	96.53 W
Lennox □[9]	46	56.02 N	4.15 W
Lennox, Isla I	254	55.18 S	66.50 W
Lennox and Addington □[6]	212	44.30 N	77.00 W
Lennoxtown	46	55.59 N	4.12 W
Lennoxville	206	45.22 N	71.51 W
Leno	64	45.22 N	10.13 E
Lenoir	192	35.54 N	81.32 W
Lenoir City	192	35.47 N	84.15 W
Le Noirmont	58	47.13 N	6.58 E
Lenola	66	41.24 N	13.28 E
Lenora	60	48.56 N	13.48 E
Lenore Lake ⊜	184	52.30 N	105.00 W
Le Nouvion-en-Thiérache	50	50.01 N	3.47 E
Lenox, Ga., U.S.	192	31.16 N	83.27 W
Lenox, Ia., U.S.	198	40.52 N	94.33 W
Lenox, Ma., U.S.	207	42.22 N	73.17 W
Lenox, Tn., U.S.	194	36.05 N	89.29 W
Lenox Dale	207	42.20 N	73.14 W
Lens	50	50.26 N	2.50 E
Lensahn	54	54.13 N	10.52 E
Lensk	74	61.00 N	114.50 E
Lenskoje	86	58.09 N	63.11 E
Lenswood	168b	34.55 S	138.49 E
Lentate sul Seveso	266b	45.41 N	9.07 E
Lentechi	84	42.48 N	42.44 E
Lenti	61	46.37 N	16.33 E
Lenting	60	48.48 N	11.28 E
Lentini	70	37.17 N	15.00 E
Lentner	219	39.43 N	92.09 W
Lentua ⊜	26	64.14 N	29.36 E
Lentvaris	76	54.39 N	25.03 E
Lenwood	228	34.53 N	117.07 W
Lenya	110	11.28 N	99.00 E
Lenya ≃	110	11.40 N	98.43 E
Lenz	273d	26.19 S	27.49 E
Lenzburg	58	47.23 N	8.11 E
Lenzen	54	53.05 N	11.28 E
Lenzerheide (Lai)	58	46.44 N	9.33 E
Lenzinghausen	52	52.07 N	8.28 E
Lenzkirch	58	47.52 N	8.12 E
Léo, Burkina	150	11.06 N	2.06 W
Leo, In., U.S.	216	41.13 N	85.00 W
Leoben	61	47.23 N	15.06 E
Leo Carrillo State Beach ♠	228	34.03 N	118.56 W
Léogâne	238	18.31 N	72.38 W
Leogang	64	47.26 N	12.45 E
Leola, Ar., U.S.	194	34.10 N	92.35 W
Leola, Pa., U.S.	208	40.05 N	76.11 W
Leola, S.D., U.S.	198	45.43 N	98.56 W
Leominster, Eng., U.K.	42	52.14 N	2.45 W
Leominster, Ma., U.S.	207	42.31 N	71.45 W
León, Esp.	34	42.36 N	5.34 W
Léon, Fr.	32	43.53 N	1.18 W
León, Nic.	236	12.26 N	86.53 W
Leon, Pil.	116	10.47 N	122.23 E
Leon, Ia., U.S.	190	40.44 N	93.44 W
Leon, Ks., U.S.	198	37.41 N	96.46 W
Leon, N.Y., U.S.	210	42.18 N	79.01 W
León □[4]	34	42.35 N	6.00 W
León □[5]	236	12.35 N	86.35 W
Leon □[6]	222	31.18 N	95.55 W
León □[9]	34	42.00 N	6.00 W
Leon ≃	196	30.59 N	97.24 W
Leon, Arroyo ≃	282	37.28 N	122.25 W
León, Montes de ʎ	34	42.30 N	6.18 W
Leona	222	31.09 N	95.58 W
Leona ≃	196	28.45 N	99.11 W
Leona, Punta ›	236	9.41 N	84.41 W
Leonard, Mi., U.S.	214	42.51 N	83.08 W
Leonard, Mo., U.S.	219	39.53 N	92.10 W
Leonard, N.D., U.S.	198	46.39 N	97.14 W
Leonard, Tx., U.S.	196	33.22 N	96.14 W
Leonardo	276	40.25 N	74.03 W
Leonardo da Vinci, Aeroporto Intercontinentale ⊠	66	41.48 N	12.13 E
Leonardsburg	214	40.21 N	82.59 W
Leonardsville	210	42.48 N	75.15 W
Leonardtown	208	38.17 N	76.38 W
Leonardville, Namibia	156	23.29 S	18.49 E
Leonardville, Ks., U.S.	198	39.21 N	96.51 W
Leona Vicario	200	32.10 N	115.10 W
Leonberg	56	48.48 N	9.01 E
Leonbronn	56	49.03 N	8.53 E
Leondale	273d	26.18 S	28.12 E
Leondárion	267c	37.59 N	23.51 E
León [de los Aldamas]	234	21.07 N	101.40 W
Leonding	61	48.16 N	14.15 E
Leone	174u	14.20 S	170.47 W
Leone, Golfo del → Lion, Golfe du ⊂	32	43.00 N	4.00 E
Leone, Monte ∧	58	46.15 N	8.06 E
Leones	252	32.39 S	62.18 W
Leonessa	66	42.34 N	12.58 E
Leonforte	70	37.38 N	14.23 E
Leongatha	169	38.29 S	145.57 E
León Guzmán	196	25.31 N	103.34 W
Leonia	276	40.51 N	73.59 W
Leonicha	76	59.37 N	38.51 E
Leonidas	216	42.01 N	85.21 W
Leonídhion	38	37.10 N	22.52 E
Leonidovo	89	49.17 N	142.50 E
Leon Junction	222	31.20 N	97.36 W
Leonora	162	28.53 S	121.20 E
Leonovo	82	55.26 N	38.42 E
Leontjevka	85	43.03 N	69.50 E
Leontjevo	76	58.58 N	36.37 E
Leonville	194	30.28 N	91.58 W
Leopard	285	40.01 N	75.27 W
Leopold	169	38.11 S	144.28 E
Leopold and Astrid Coast ±[2]	9	67.10 S	84.10 E
Leopoldau ◆[8]	264b	48.16 N	16.27 E
Leopold Downs	162	17.52 S	125.25 E
Léopold II, Lac → Mai-Ndombe, Lac ⊜	152	2.00 S	18.20 E
Leopoldina	256	21.32 S	42.38 W
Leopoldkanaal ≊	50	51.14 N	3.46 E
Leopoldo de Bulhões	255	16.37 S	48.46 W
Leopoldo y Astrid, Costa → Leopold and Astrid Coast ±[2]	9	67.10 S	84.10 E
Leopoldsburg	56	51.07 N	5.15 E
Leopoldsdorf	264b	48.06 N	16.24 E
Leopoldshagen	54	53.46 N	13.53 E
Leopoldstadt ◆[8]	264b	48.13 N	16.23 E
Léopoldville → Kinshasa	152	4.18 S	15.18 E
Leoti	198	38.28 N	101.21 W
Leoville	184	53.37 N	107.35 W
Leovo	78	46.29 N	28.15 E
Le Pailly	58	47.48 N	5.25 E
Le Palais	32	47.21 N	3.09 W
Lepanto, C.R.	236	9.57 N	85.02 W
Lepanto, Ar., U.S.	194	35.36 N	90.19 W
Lepanto → Návpaktos	38	38.23 N	21.50 E
Lepar, Pulau I	112	2.57 S	106.50 E
Le Parcq	50	50.23 N	2.06 E
Le Pâté	261	48.32 N	2.18 E
Lepe	34	37.15 N	7.12 W
Le Péage-de-Roussillon	62	45.22 N	4.48 E
Le Pecq	261	48.54 N	2.07 E
Lepel'	76	54.53 N	28.42 E
Le Pellerin	32	47.12 N	1.45 W
Lepembusu, Keli ∧	115b	8.40 S	121.49 E
Le Perray-en-Yuelines	261	48.42 N	1.51 E
Le Perreux-sur-Marne	261	48.51 N	2.30 E
Lepeški	82	56.05 N	38.07 E
Le Petit-Clamart ʋ	261	48.47 N	2.14 E
Le Petit-Couronne	50	49.23 N	1.01 E
Le Petit-Quevilly	50	49.26 N	1.02 E
Lephepe	156	23.20 S	25.50 E
Lépi	152	12.52 S	15.26 E
Le Piastre	66	44.00 N	10.50 E
Lepihué	254	41.37 S	73.36 W
Le Pin	261	48.55 N	2.38 E
Le Pin-au-Haras	50	48.44 N	0.09 E
L'Épine, Fr.	56	48.58 N	4.28 E
L'Épine, Fr.	261	48.32 N	2.21 E
Leping	100	28.57 N	117.05 E
Lepini, Monti ʎ	66	41.35 N	13.00 E
Lépin-le-Lac	62	45.32 N	5.47 E
L'Épiphanie	206	45.51 N	73.30 W
Lepl'avo	78	49.48 N	31.32 E
Le Plessis-aux-Bois	261	49.00 N	2.46 E
Le Plessis-Belleville	50	49.06 N	2.46 E
Le Plessis-Bouchard	261	49.00 N	2.14 E
Le Plessis-Pâté	261	48.37 N	2.20 E
Le Plessis-Trévise	261	48.49 N	2.34 E
Lépo, Lagoa de ⊜	152	17.08 S	19.00 E
Le Poët	62	44.17 N	5.53 E
Le Pont	58	46.40 N	6.20 E
Le Pont-de-Beauvoisin	62	45.32 N	5.40 E
Le Pont-de-Montvert	62	44.22 N	3.45 E
Le Pontel	261	48.49 N	1.53 E
Lepontine, Alpi ʎ	58	46.25 N	8.40 E
Leporano	68	40.23 N	17.20 E
Le Port	157c	20.55 S	55.18 E
Le Portel	50	50.42 N	1.34 E
Le Port-Marly	261	48.53 N	2.06 E
Le Pouzin	62	44.45 N	4.45 E
Leppävirta	26	62.29 N	27.47 E
Lepperton	172	39.04 S	174.13 E
Leppin	54	52.53 N	11.34 E
Leppington	274a	33.58 S	150.49 E
Le Pradet	62	43.06 N	6.01 E
Lepreau, Point ›	186	45.04 N	66.27 W
Le Prêcheur	240e	14.48 N	61.14 W
Le Pré-Saint-Gervais	261	48.53 N	2.25 E
Le Prese	58	46.18 N	10.04 E
Lepsinsk	86	45.32 N	80.37 E
Lepsy, Kaz.	86	46.18 N	78.20 E
Lepsy, Kaz.	86	46.15 N	78.55 E
Le Puy	62	45.02 N	3.53 E
Le Quesnoy	50	50.15 N	3.38 E
Léraba ≃	150	9.42 N	4.35 W
Le Raincy	261	48.54 N	2.31 E
Le Rayol-Canadel-sur-Mer	62	43.10 N	6.28 E
Le Raysville	210	41.51 N	76.11 W
Lerberget	41	56.11 N	12.33 E
Lercara Friddi	70	37.45 N	13.36 E
Lerche ◆[8]	263	51.37 N	7.43 E
Lerderderg ≃	169	37.42 S	144.30 E
Lerdo → Ciudad Lerdo	196	25.32 N	103.32 W
Léré, Fr.	50	47.28 N	2.52 E
Léré, Mali	150	15.43 N	4.55 W
Lere, Nig.	150	9.43 N	9.21 E
Léré, Tchad	146	9.39 N	14.13 E
Lereh	164	3.08 S	139.54 E
Lerek ∧	114	3.47 N	102.47 E
Le Reposoir	58	46.00 N	6.33 E
Leri ≃	42	52.32 N	4.02 W
Leribe	158	28.58 S	28.00 E
Lerici	64	44.04 N	9.55 E
Lérida	246	0.10 N	70.42 W
Lérida → Lleida	34	41.37 N	0.37 E
Lerik	84	38.46 N	48.25 E
Lérins, Îles de II	62	43.31 N	7.03 E
Lerma	34	42.02 N	3.45 W
Lerma ≃	234	20.13 N	102.46 W
Lermontovka	89	47.10 N	134.20 E
Lermoos	64	47.24 N	10.53 E
Lerno, Monte ∧	71	40.37 N	9.10 E
Le Robert	240e	14.41 N	60.57 W
Léros I, Ellás	38	37.08 N	26.52 E
Léros I, Ellás	267c	37.59 N	23.34 E
Lérouville	56	48.47 N	5.33 E
Leroux Wash V	200	34.54 N	110.12 W
Le Roy, Il., U.S.	216	40.21 N	88.45 W
Leroy, In., U.S.	216	41.22 N	87.16 W
Le Roy, Ks., U.S.	198	38.05 N	95.38 W
Le Roy, Mn., U.S.	190	43.30 N	92.30 W
Le Roy, N.Y., U.S.	210	42.58 N	77.59 W
Le Roy, Pa., U.S.	210	41.41 N	76.43 W
Leroy, Tx., U.S.	222	31.44 N	97.01 W
Lerum	26	57.46 N	12.16 E
Le Russey	58	47.10 N	6.44 E
Lerwick	46a	60.09 N	1.09 W
Léry	206	45.21 N	73.48 W
Lesa	62	45.50 N	8.34 E
Les Abrets	62	45.32 N	5.35 E
Les Abymes	241o	16.16 N	61.31 W
Lesage, Lac ⊜	206	46.19 N	75.03 W
Le Saint-Esprit	240e	14.34 N	60.57 W
Les Aix-d'Angillon	50	47.12 N	2.34 E
Les Allues	62	45.26 N	6.33 E
Les Alluets-le-Roi	261	48.55 N	1.55 E
Les Andelys	50	49.15 N	1.25 E
Les Anses-d'Arlets	240e	14.29 N	61.05 W
Le Sappy-en-Chartreuse	62	45.16 N	5.47 E
Les Arcs	62	43.27 N	6.29 E
Lesatima, Oldoinyo ∧	154	0.19 S	36.37 E
Le Sauze	62	44.22 N	6.41 E
Les Baux-en-Provence	62	43.45 N	4.48 E
Les Bézards	50	47.48 N	2.44 E
Les Bordes	261	48.39 N	1.58 E
Les Borges Blanques	34	41.31 N	0.52 E
Lesbos → Lésvos I	38	39.10 N	26.20 E
Les Bouchoux	58	46.18 N	5.49 E
Les Bréviaires	261	48.42 N	1.49 E
Lesbury	44	55.24 N	1.36 W
L'Escarène	62	43.50 N	7.21 E
Les Cayes	238	18.12 N	73.45 W
Les Chaises	261	48.39 N	1.42 E
Les Chapieux	62	45.42 N	6.44 E
Leschenault, Cape ›	162	31.18 S	115.27 E
Leschenault Estuary ⊂[1]	168a	33.15 S	115.42 E
Lesches	261	48.54 N	2.47 E
Leščinovka	78	49.16 N	34.14 E
Les Clayes-sous-Bois	261	48.49 N	1.59 E
Les Contamines-Montjoie	62	45.50 N	6.44 E
Les Diablerets	58	46.21 N	7.10 E
Les Diablerets ∧	58	46.19 N	7.12 E
Lesdiboderi	146	8.28 N	12.35 E
Les Echarmeaux	58	46.10 N	4.27 E
Les Échelles	62	45.26 N	5.45 E
Les Écureuils	206	46.39 N	71.43 W
Le Semnoz ∧	62	45.48 N	6.07 E
Leseru	154	0.35 N	35.10 E
Les Essarts	32	46.46 N	1.14 W
Les Essarts-le-Roi	261	48.43 N	1.54 E
Les Estables	62	44.54 N	4.10 E
Les Étangs	56	49.09 N	6.23 E
Les Fonts	266d	41.32 N	2.02 E
Les Fourgs	58	46.50 N	6.25 E
Les Galleries d'Anjou ◆[9]	275a	45.35 N	73.34 W
Les Gâtines	261	48.48 N	1.58 E
Les Gets	58	46.09 N	6.40 E
Les Granges-le-Roi	261	48.30 N	2.01 E
Les Grésillons	261	48.56 N	2.01 E
Les Halles	62	45.43 N	4.26 E
Leshan	107	29.34 N	103.45 E
Les Haudères	58	46.05 N	7.31 E
Les Hautes-Rivières	56	49.53 N	4.50 E
Les Herbiers	32	46.52 N	1.01 W
Les Houches	62	45.53 N	6.48 E
Lesignano de'Bagni	64	44.39 N	10.18 E
Lésigny	261	48.45 N	2.37 E
Lesima, Monte ∧	62	44.41 N	9.15 E
Lesina	68	41.52 N	15.21 E
Lesina, Lago di ⊂	68	41.53 N	15.26 E
Les Islettes	56	49.06 N	5.00 E
Lesjaskog	26	62.15 N	8.22 E
Lesjöfors	40	59.59 N	14.11 E
Lesken	84	43.16 N	43.48 E
Les'ki	78	49.19 N	32.13 E
Lesko	30	49.29 N	22.21 E
Leskovac	38	42.59 N	21.57 E
Leskov Island I	18	56.40 S	28.10 W
Les Laumes	58	47.32 N	4.27 E
Les Lecques	62	43.11 N	5.40 E
Leslie, S. Afr.	158	26.27 S	28.55 E
Leslie, Scot., U.K.	46	56.12 N	3.13 W
Leslie, Ar., U.S.	194	35.49 N	92.33 W
Leslie, Ga., U.S.	192	31.57 N	84.05 W
Leslie, Mi., U.S.	216	42.27 N	84.25 W
Leslie, W.V., U.S.	188	38.02 N	80.43 W
Les Lilas	261	48.53 N	2.25 E
Les Loges	261	48.34 N	2.03 E
Les Loges-en-Josas	261	48.46 N	2.09 E
Lesmahagow	46	55.39 N	3.55 W
Les Marécottes	58	46.07 N	7.00 E
Les Mées	62	44.02 N	5.59 E
Les Mesnuls	50	48.45 N	1.50 E
Lesmo	266b	45.39 N	9.18 E
Les Molières	261	48.40 N	2.04 E
Les Monges ∧	62	44.16 N	6.12 E
Lesmont	50	48.26 N	4.25 E
Les Mosses	58	46.24 N	7.07 E
Lesmurdie Falls National Park ♠	168a	32.01 S	116.04 E
Les Mureaux	261	49.00 N	1.55 E
Leśna	30	51.02 N	15.16 E
Lesna ≃	76	52.10 N	23.33 E
Lesnaja	76	52.59 N	25.46 E
Lesneven	32	48.34 N	4.19 W
Les Neyrolles	58	46.08 N	5.38 E
Lešnica	38	44.39 N	19.19 E
Lesnoj, Ross.	24	59.48 N	52.08 E
Lesnoj, Ross.	80	54.11 N	40.27 E
Lesnoj, Ross.	86	56.57 N	67.15 E
Lesnoj ◆[8]	265a	60.00 N	30.19 E
Lesnoje	76	58.17 N	35.32 E
Lesnoje Konobejevo	80	54.02 N	41.55 E
Lesnoje Mat'unino	80	53.27 N	47.26 E
Lesnoj Gorodok	265b	55.39 N	37.13 E
Lesnoj park ♠	265a	59.59 N	30.21 E
Lesný ∧	60	50.02 N	12.37 E
Lesnyje Pol'any, Ross.	24	58.58 N	52.26 E
Lesnyje Pol'any, Ross.	265b	55.57 N	37.53 E
Lesogorsk, Ross.	80	55.06 N	43.56 E
Lesogorsk, Ross.	88	56.03 N	99.33 E
Lesogorsk, Ross.	89	49.27 N	142.08 E
Lesogorskij	24	61.02 N	28.53 E
Lesong, Gunong ∧	114	2.44 N	103.17 E
Lesopil'noje	89	46.44 N	134.20 E
Lesosibirsk	86	58.16 N	92.29 E
Lesotho □[1], Afr.	138	29.30 S	28.30 E
Lesotho □[1], Afr.	158	29.30 S	28.30 E
Lesovščina	78	50.47 N	28.35 E
Lesozavodsk	89	45.28 N	133.27 E
Lesozavodskij	24	66.44 N	32.49 E
Lesparre-Médoc	32	45.18 N	0.56 W
Les Pavillons-sous-Bois	261	48.55 N	2.30 E
Les Pieux	32	49.31 N	1.48 W
Les Planches-en-Montagne	58	46.40 N	6.01 E
Les Ponts-de-Martel	58	46.54 N	6.41 E
Les Posets ∧	34	42.39 N	0.25 E
Les Praz-de-Chamonix	58	45.56 N	6.52 E
Lesquin	50	50.35 N	3.07 E
Les Riceys	50	47.59 N	4.22 E
Les Roches-l'Evêque	50	47.47 N	0.53 E
Les Rousses	58	46.29 N	6.04 E
Les Ruelles	261	48.40 N	1.37 E
Les Sables-d'Olonne	32	46.30 N	1.47 W
Lessach	64	47.11 N	13.49 E
Les Saintes II	241o	15.52 N	61.37 W
Les Salles-sur-Verdon	62	43.46 N	6.12 E
Lessay	32	49.13 N	1.32 W
Les Scaffarels	62	43.57 N	6.41 E
Lesse ≃	56	50.14 N	4.54 E
Lessebo	26	56.45 N	15.16 E
Lessen → Lessines	50	50.43 N	3.50 E
Lesser Antilles II	238	15.00 N	61.00 W
Lesser Khingan Range → Xiao Hinggan Ling ʎ	89	48.45 N	127.00 E
Lesser Slave ≃	182	55.10 N	114.03 W
Lesser Slave Lake ⊜	182	55.25 N	115.30 W
Lesser Sunda Islands → Tenggara, Nusa II	108	9.00 S	120.00 E
Lessines (Lessen)	50	50.43 N	3.50 E
Lessini, Monti ʎ	64	45.41 N	11.13 E
L'Estaque	62	43.22 N	5.20 E
Leste ≃	250	6.20 S	57.46 W
Lester, Pa., U.S.	285	39.52 N	75.17 W
Lester, Wa., U.S.	224	47.12 N	121.29 W
Lester B. Pearson International Airport ⊠	212	43.41 N	79.38 W
Les Tessiers	62	44.24 N	4.16 E
Les Thilliers-en-Vexin	50	49.14 N	1.36 E
Lestijärvi	26	63.32 N	24.39 E
Lestijoki ≃	26	64.04 N	23.38 E
Lestkov	60	49.54 N	12.52 E
Lestock	184	51.18 N	104.00 W
L'Estréchure	62	44.06 N	3.47 E
Les Trois-Îlets	240e	14.32 N	61.02 W
Les Trois Lacs ⊜	206	45.48 N	71.54 W
Le Sueur	190	44.30 N	93.52 W
Le Sueur ≃	190	44.07 N	94.03 W
Lesueur, Mount ∧[2]	162	30.10 S	115.11 E
Lešukonskoje	24	64.54 N	45.40 E
Les Ulis	261	48.41 N	2.11 E
Lesung, Tanjung ›	115a	6.28 S	105.40 E
Lesunovo	80	55.40 N	43.07 E
Les Vans	62	44.24 N	4.08 E
Les Verrières	58	46.54 N	6.30 E
Lésvos I	38	39.10 N	26.20 E
Leszno	30	51.51 N	16.35 E
Leszno □[4]	30	51.45 N	16.45 E
Letälven ≃	40	59.05 N	14.20 E
L'Étang-la-Ville	261	48.52 N	2.05 E

Symbol	English	Deutsch	Español	Français	Português
≃	River	Fluß	Río	Rivière	Rio
≊	Canal	Kanal	Canal	Canal	Canal
ʟ	Waterfall, Rapids	Wasserfall, Stromschnellen	Cascada, Rápidos	Chute d'eau, Rapides	Cascata, Rápidos
ʯ	Strait	Meeresstraße	Estrecho	Détroit	Estreito
⊂	Bay, Gulf	Bucht, Golf	Bahía, Golfo	Baie, Golfe	Baía, Golfo
⊜	Lake, Lakes	See, Seen	Lago, Lagos	Lac, Lacs	Lago, Lagos
⩦	Swamp	Sumpf	Pantano	Marais	Pântano
⊼	Ice Features, Glacier	Eis- und Gletscherformen	Accidentes Glaciales	Formes glaciaires	Acidentes glaciares
⫪	Other Hydrographic Features	Andere Hydrographische Objekte	Otros Elementos Hidrográficos	Autres données hydrographiques	Outros acidentes hidrográficos
✣	Submarine Features	Untermeerische Objekte	Accidentes Submarinos	Formes de relief sous-marin	Acidentes submarinos
□	Political Unit	Politische Einheit	Unidad Politica	Entité politique	Unidade política
ʋ	Cultural Institution	Kulturelle Institution	Institución Cultural	Institution culturelle	Instituição cultural
⊥	Historical Site	Historische Stätte	Sitio Histórico	Site historique	Sitio histórico
♠	Recreational Site	Erholungs- und Ferienort	Sitio de Recreo	Centre de loisirs	Area de Lazer
⊠	Airport	Flughafen	Aeropuerto	Aéroport	Aeroporto
■	Military Installation	Militäranlage	Instalación Militar	Installation militaire	Instalação militar
◆	Miscellaneous	Verschiedenes	Misceláneo	Divers	Diversos

Letcher 198 43.53 N 98.08 W
Letchmore Heath 260 51.40 N 0.20 W
Letchworth 42 51.58 N 0.14 W
Letchworth State Park ♠ 210 42.42 N 77.56 W
Letea, Ostrovul I 38 45.20 N 29.20 E
Le Teil 62 44.33 N 4.41 E
Le Temple 261 49.00 N 1.58 E
Letenye 30 46.26 N 16.43 E
Le Tertre-Saint-Denis 261 48.56 N 1.36 E
Lethbridge, Austl. 274a 33.44 S 150.48 E
Lethbridge, Ab., Can. 182 49.42 N 112.50 W
Lethbridge, Nf., Can. 186 48.21 N 53.52 W
Le Theil-sur-Huisne 50 48.16 N 0.42 E
Lethem 246 3.23 N 59.48 W
Le Thillay 261 49.00 N 2.28 E
Le Thillot 58 47.53 N 6.46 E
Le Tholy 58 48.05 N 6.45 E
Le Thor 62 43.56 N 5.00 E
Le Thoronet 62 43.27 N 6.18 E
Leti, Kepulauan II 164 8.13 S 127.50 E
Leti, Pulau I 112 8.12 S 127.41 E
Letičev 78 49.23 N 27.37 E
Leticia 246 4.09 S 69.57 W
Leting 98 39.27 N 118.53 E
Letino 68 41.26 N 14.17 E
Letjiesbos 158 32.34 S 22.16 E
Letka 24 59.36 N 49.22 E
Letlhakane 156 21.27 S 25.30 E
Letlhakeng 156 24.08 S 25.02 E
Letmathe 56 51.22 N 7.37 E
Letn'aja Zolotica 24 64.57 N 36.50 E
Letnerečenskij 24 64.17 N 34.23 E
Le Touquet-Paris-Plage 50 50.31 N 1.35 E
Le Touvet 62 45.21 N 5.57 E
Letovo 265b 55.34 N 37.24 E
Letpadan 110 17.47 N 95.45 E
Le Trait 50 49.28 N 0.49 E
Le Trayas 62 43.28 N 6.55 E
Le Tremblay-sur-Mauldre 261 48.47 N 1.53 E
Le Tréport 50 50.04 N 1.22 E
Letschin 54 52.39 N 14.21 E
Letsôk-aw Kyun I 110 11.37 N 98.15 E
Letter 52 52.24 N 9.38 E
Letterfrack 48 53.33 N 10.00 W
Letterkenny 48 54.57 N 7.44 W
Lettermullan 48 53.13 N 9.42 W
Letterston 42 51.56 N 5.00 W
Lettonie
— Latvia □[1] 72 57.00 N 25.00 E
Letts 218 39.14 N 85.35 W
Letung 112 2.58 N 105.42 E
Letzlingen 54 52.26 N 11.29 E
Leu 38 44.11 N 24.00 E
Léua 152 11.34 S 20.32 E
Leubnitz 54 50.43 N 12.21 E
Leubsdorf 54 50.48 N 13.08 E
Leuca 68 39.48 N 18.21 E
Leucadia 228 33.04 N 117.18 W
Leucate, Étang de c 32 42.51 N 3.00 E
Leuchars 46 56.23 N 2.53 W
Leuchtenberg 60 49.36 N 12.15 E
Leudeville 261 48.34 N 2.20 E
Leuenberger Forst ◆[3] 264a 52.40 N 13.53 E
Leuglay 58 47.49 N 4.48 E
Leuk 58 46.19 N 7.38 E
Leukerbad 58 46.23 N 7.38 E
Leulumoega 175a 13.49 S 171.55 W
Leumeah 274a 34.03 S 150.50 E
Leuna 54 51.19 N 12.01 E
Leupoldsgrün 54 50.17 N 11.47 E
Leura 170 33.43 S 150.20 E
Leura, Mount ʌ[2] 169 38.15 S 143.09 E
Leuser, Gunung ʌ 114 3.45 N 97.11 E
Leušinskij Tuman, ozero ⊜ 86 59.42 N 65.35 E
Leutenberg 54 50.34 N 11.28 E
Leutersdorf 54 50.57 N 14.40 E
Leutershausen 56 49.18 N 10.24 E
Leutesdorf 56 50.27 N 7.23 E
Leutkirch 58 47.49 N 10.01 E
Leuven (Louvain) 56 50.53 N 4.42 E
Leuville-sur-Orge 261 48.37 N 2.16 E
Leuwiliang 115a 6.34 S 106.37 E
Leuze, Bel. 50 50.36 N 3.36 E
Leuze, Bel. 56 50.34 N 4.54 E
Levack 190 46.38 N 81.23 W
Levádhia 38 38.25 N 22.54 E
Levaja Mama ≃ 88 57.10 N 111.54 E
Le Val-d'Ajol 58 47.55 N 6.29 E
Le Val-d'Albian 261 48.45 N 2.11 E
Levallois-Perret 261 48.54 N 2.18 E
Le Val-Saint-Germain 261 48.34 N 2.04 E
Levan 200 39.33 N 111.51 W
Levanger 26 63.45 N 11.18 E
Levanna, Monte ʌ 62 45.24 N 7.12 E
Levant, Île du I 62 43.03 N 6.28 E
Levante, Riviera di ±[2] 62 44.15 N 9.30 E
Levanto 62 44.10 N 9.38 E
Levanzo 70 37.59 N 12.20 E
Levanzo, Isola di I 70 38.00 N 12.20 E
Levaši 84 42.27 N 47.20 E
Le Vauclin 240e 14.33 N 60.51 W
Levdym 86 60.29 N 66.19 E
Leveaux Mountain ʌ[2] 190 47.37 N 90.47 W
Levél 61 47.54 N 17.12 E
Level, Isla I 254 44.29 S 74.23 W
Level Green 279b 40.24 N 79.43 W
Levelland 196 33.35 N 102.22 W
Levelock 180 59.07 N 156.52 W
Level Park 216 42.22 N 85.18 W
Leven, Eng., U.K. 44 53.53 N 0.19 W
Leven, Scot., U.K. 46 56.12 N 3.00 W
Leven ≃, Eng., U.K. 44 54.14 N 3.01 W
Leven ≃, Eng., U.K. 44 54.31 N 1.21 W
Leven, Loch ⊜, Scot., U.K. 46 56.41 N 5.07 W
Leven, Loch ⊜, Scot., U.K. 46 56.12 N 3.22 W
Leven Point › 158 27.55 S 32.35 E
Levens 62 43.52 N 7.13 E
Levenshulme ◆[8] 262 53.27 N 2.10 W
Levent 130 38.27 N 37.52 E
Leventina, Valle V 58 46.25 N 8.52 E
Leveque, Cape › 162 16.24 S 122.56 E
Leverano 68 40.17 N 18.00 E
Leverburgh 46 57.45 N 7.00 W
Leveretts Chapel 222 32.19 N 94.55 W
Levering 190 45.38 N 84.47 W
Leverkusen 56 51.03 N 6.59 E
Levern 52 52.22 N 8.26 E
Lever Park ♠ 262 53.37 N 2.34 W
Le Vésinet 261 48.54 N 2.08 E
Le Vésuve
— Vesuvio ʌ[1] 68 40.49 N 14.26 E
Leviathan Peak ʌ 226 38.41 N 119.37 W
Levice 30 48.13 N 18.37 E
Levicha 86 57.36 N 59.55 E
Levick, Mount ʌ 9 74.08 S 163.12 E
Levico 64 46.01 N 11.18 E
Levie 36 41.42 N 9.07 E
Levier 58 46.57 N 6.08 E
Le Vigan 32 43.59 N 3.35 E
Levin 172 40.37 S 175.17 E
Levino 76 60.29 N 37.30 E
Lévis 206 46.48 N 71.11 W
Lévis □[6] 206 46.40 N 71.15 W
Levisa Fork ≃ 192 38.06 N 82.36 W
Lévis-Saint Nom 261 48.43 N 1.58 E
Levítha I 38 37.00 N 26.28 E
Levittown, P.R. 240m 18.27 N 66.14 W
Levittown, N.Y., U.S. 210 40.43 N 73.30 W
Levittown, Pa., U.S. 208 40.09 N 74.49 W
Levittown Discount World ◆[9] 285 40.09 N 74.49 W
Levittown
— Willingboro 208 40.03 N 74.53 W
Lévka Óri ʌ 38 35.18 N 24.01 E
Levkás 38 38.50 N 20.41 E
Levkás I 38 38.39 N 20.27 E
Levkímmi 38 39.25 N 20.04 E
Levoča 30 49.02 N 20.36 E
Levokumskoje 84 44.48 N 44.39 E
Levroux 32 46.59 N 1.37 E
Levski 38 43.22 N 25.08 E
Lev Tolstoj 76 53.13 N 39.27 E
Levuka 175g 17.41 S 178.50 E
Lėvuo ≃ 76 56.04 N 24.23 E
Levyj Tuzlov ≃ 83 47.35 N 39.23 E
Lewapaku 115b 9.43 S 119.55 E
Lewbeach 210 42.00 N 74.47 W
Lewe 110 19.38 N 96.07 E
Lewedorp 52 51.30 N 3.45 E
Lewellen 198 41.19 N 102.08 W
Lewer ≃ 156 25.30 S 17.45 E
Lewes, Eng., U.K. 42 50.52 N 0.01 E
Lewes, De., U.S. 208 38.46 N 75.08 W
Lewin Brzeski 30 50.46 N 17.37 E
Lewis, Ia., U.S. 198 41.18 N 95.04 W
Lewis, Ks., U.S. 198 37.56 N 99.15 W
Lewis □[6], Ky., U.S. 218 38.32 N 83.21 W
Lewis □[6], Mo., U.S. 219 40.08 N 91.45 W
Lewis □[6], N.Y., U.S. 212 43.47 N 75.29 W
Lewis □[6], Wa., U.S. 224 46.35 N 122.22 W
Lewis ≃ 224 45.51 N 122.48 W
Lewis, Butt of › 46 58.31 N 6.16 W
Lewis, East Fork ≃ 224 45.52 N 122.43 W
Lewis, Isle of I 46 58.10 N 6.40 W
Lewis, Mount ʌ 204 40.24 N 116.51 W
Lewis and Clark ≃ 224 46.10 N 123.52 W
Lewis and Clark Cavern State Park ♠ 202 45.49 N 111.13 W
Lewis and Clark Lake ⊜[1] 198 42.50 N 97.45 W
Lewis and Clark Range ⋏ 202 47.30 N 113.00 W
Lewisberry 208 40.08 N 76.52 W
Lewisburg, Ky., U.S. 194 36.59 N 86.56 W
Lewisburg, Oh., U.S. 218 39.50 N 84.32 W
Lewisburg, Pa., U.S. 210 40.57 N 76.53 W
Lewisburg, Tn., U.S. 194 35.26 N 86.47 W
Lewisburg, W.V., U.S. 188 37.48 N 80.26 W
Lewis Center 214 40.12 N 83.01 W
Lewis Creek ≃, Ca., U.S. 226 35.17 N 120.58 W
Lewis Creek ≃, In., U.S. 218 39.22 N 85.51 W
Lewis Creek Reservoir ⊜[1] 222 30.26 N 95.32 W
Lewisdale 284c 38.58 N 76.58 W
Lewisetta 208 38.01 N 76.28 W
Lewis Gut c 276 41.09 N 73.09 W
Lewisham 273d 26.07 S 27.49 E
Lewisham ◆[8] 42 51.27 N 0.01 E
Lewisham Location 273d 26.10 S 27.47 E
Lewis-Lockport Airport ⊠ 278 41.36 N 88.05 W
Lewis Pass)(172 42.23 S 172.24 E
Lewisport 194 37.56 N 86.54 W
Lewisporte 186 49.15 N 55.03 W
Lewis Range ⋏, Austl. 162 20.20 S 128.40 E
Lewis Range ⋏, Mt., U.S. 202 48.35 N 113.40 W
Lewis Run 214 41.52 N 78.39 W
Lewis Run ≃ 279b 40.17 N 79.55 W
Lewis Smith Lake ⊜[1] 194 34.05 N 87.07 W
Lewiston, Ca., U.S. 204 40.43 N 122.48 W
Lewiston, Id., U.S. 202 46.25 N 117.01 W
Lewiston, Me., U.S. 188 44.06 N 70.12 W
Lewiston, Mi., U.S. 190 44.53 N 84.18 W
Lewiston, Mn., U.S. 190 43.59 N 91.52 W
Lewiston, N.Y., U.S. 210 43.10 N 79.02 W
Lewiston, Ut,. U.S. 200 41.58 N 111.51 W
Lewiston Orchards 202 46.23 N 116.59 W
Lewistown, Il., U.S. 194 40.23 N 90.09 W
Lewistown, Md., U.S. 208 39.32 N 77.24 W
Lewistown, Mo., U.S. 219 40.05 N 91.48 W
Lewistown, Mt., U.S. 202 47.03 N 109.25 W
Lewistown, Oh., U.S. 216 40.25 N 83.53 W
Lewistown, Pa., U.S. 208 40.35 N 77.34 W
Lewisville, N.B., Can. 186 46.06 N 64.46 W
Lewisville, Ar., U.S. 194 33.21 N 93.34 W
Lewisville, In., U.S. 218 39.48 N 85.21 W
Lewisville, Pa., U.S. 208 39.43 N 75.53 W
Lewisville, Tx., U.S. 222 33.02 N 96.59 W
Lewisville Dam ◆[6] 222 33.05 N 96.55 W
Lewisville Lake ⊜[1] 196 33.08 N 97.00 W
Lewoleba 112 8.23 S 123.24 E
Lewotobi-lakilaki, Ili ʌ 115b 8.32 S 122.46 E
Lewvan 184 50.00 N 104.06 W
Lexa 194 34.35 N 90.44 W
Lexington, Ga., U.S. 192 33.52 N 83.06 W
Lexington, Il., U.S. 216 40.38 N 88.47 W
Lexington, In., U.S. 218 38.39 N 85.37 W
Lexington, Ky., U.S. 218 38.02 N 84.30 W
Lexington, Ma., U.S. 207 42.26 N 71.13 W
Lexington, Mi., U.S. 190 43.16 N 82.31 W
Lexington, Ms., U.S. 194 33.06 N 90.03 W
Lexington, Mo., U.S. 194 39.11 N 93.52 W
Lexington, Ne., U.S. 198 40.46 N 99.44 W
Lexington, N.Y., U.S. 210 42.15 N 74.22 W
Lexington, N.C., U.S. 192 35.49 N 80.15 W
Lexington, Oh., U.S. 214 40.40 N 82.34 W
Lexington, Ok., U.S. 196 35.00 N 97.20 W
Lexington, Or., U.S. 202 45.26 N 119.41 W
Lexington, S.C., U.S. 192 33.58 N 81.14 W
Lexington, Tn., U.S. 194 35.39 N 88.23 W
Lexington, Tx., U.S. 222 30.25 N 97.01 W
Lexington, Va., U.S. 192 37.47 N 79.26 W
Lexington Park 208 38.16 N 76.27 W
Lexington Reservoir ⊜[1] 226 37.12 N 121.59 W
Lexton 169 37.17 S 143.31 E
Leybourne 260 51.18 N 0.25 E
Leyburn 44 54.19 N 1.49 W
Leyden
— Leiden 52 52.09 N 4.30 E
Leye 102 24.48 N 106.34 E
Leyland 44 53.42 N 2.42 W
Leyond ≃ 184 51.40 N 96.32 W
Léyou ≃ 152 1.07 S 13.08 E
Leyre ≃ 32 44.39 N 1.01 W
Leysdown-on-Sea 42 51.24 N 0.55 E
Leysin 58 46.21 N 7.01 E
Leyte 116 11.23 N 124.29 E
Leyte □[4] 116 10.50 N 124.55 E
Leyte I 116 10.50 N 124.50 E
Leyte Gulf c 116 10.50 N 125.25 E
Leyton ◆[8] 260 51.33 N 0.01 W
Leyu 106 31.55 N 120.43 E
Lèz ≃ 62 44.13 N 4.43 E
Lèz ≊ 62 43.31 N 3.55 E
Leža 76 58.56 N 40.45 E
Leža ≃ 76 59.15 N 40.10 E
Leżajsk 30 50.16 N 22.24 E
Lezama 246 9.43 N 66.24 W
Lézarde ≃ 240e 14.36 N 61.01 W
Lézat 58 46.30 N 5.56 E
Lèze ≃ 62 43.40 N 5.28 E
Lezhë 38 41.47 N 19.39 E
Lezhi 107 30.17 N 105.02 E
Ležn'ovo 80 56.46 N 40.53 E
Lezzeno 58 45.56 N 9.11 E
L'gov 78 51.43 N 35.17 E
Lhasa 120 29.40 N 91.09 E
Lhasa ≃ 120 29.21 N 90.45 E
L'Hautil 261 49.00 N 2.01 E
Lhazê 120 29.10 N 87.42 E
L'Hillil 34 35.41 N 0.19 E
Lhokkruet 114 4.52 N 95.24 E
Lhoknga 114 5.29 N 95.15 E
Lhokseumawe 114 5.10 N 97.08 E
Lhoksukon 114 5.03 N 97.19 E
L'Hôpital-sous-Rochefort 62 45.46 N 3.56 E
Lhorong 102 30.45 N 96.09 E
L'Hospitalet de Llobregat 34 41.22 N 2.08 E
Lhotse ʌ 124 27.57 N 86.56 E
Lhozhag 120 28.24 N 90.49 E
Lhuis 62 45.45 N 5.32 E
Lhuntsi Dzong 120 27.39 N 91.09 E
Lhünzê 120 28.25 N 92.31 E
Li 110 17.48 N 98.57 E
Li ≃, Thai 110 18.26 N 98.42 E
Li ≃, Zhg. 100 33.11 N 115.07 E
Li ≃, Zhg. 102 29.24 N 112.01 E
Lian ≃, Zhg. 100 24.02 N 113.18 E
Lian ≃, Zhg. 100 25.46 N 115.38 E
Lian ≃, Zhg. 102 24.02 N 113.18 E
Lian ≃, Zhg. 102 27.48 N 112.52 E
Liancheng 100 25.44 N 116.46 E
Liancourt 50 49.20 N 2.28 E
Liane ≃ 50 50.43 N 1.36 E
Liang 164 3.30 S 128.19 E
Lianga 116 8.38 N 126.06 E
Lianga Bay c 116 8.37 N 126.12 E
Liang'anchang 107 30.30 N 104.56 E
Liangbao 102 34.37 N 110.45 E
Liangbingbao 89 45.48 N 128.19 E
Liangbingtai 89 43.12 N 128.47 E
Liangbuaya 112 0.05 N 116.46 E
Liangchahe 107 29.03 N 106.18 E
Liangcheng 98 35.35 N 119.35 E
Liangcun 100 26.36 N 115.34 E
Liangdang 102 33.56 N 106.12 E
Liangdawa 105 40.39 N 117.37 E
Liangfengwu 107 30.11 N 105.22 E
Lianggezhuang 105 39.21 N 115.22 E
Lianghe, Zhg. 89 45.09 N 128.45 E
Lianghe, Zhg. 102 24.51 N 98.25 E
Liangheguan 102 32.52 N 109.19 E
Lianghekou, Zhg. 102 33.42 N 104.25 E
Lianghekou, Zhg. 102 29.14 N 108.40 E
Lianghekou, Zhg. 102 31.27 N 102.13 E
Lianghekou, Zhg. 107 28.55 N 106.03 E
Liangiu 98 35.12 N 117.47 E
Liangjia 107 29.29 N 105.33 E
Liangjiadian 98 39.10 N 121.54 E
Liangjiafang 98 41.04 N 117.18 E
Liangjianfang 105 40.45 N 117.20 E
Liangjiang 102 23.23 N 108.22 E
Liangjiangkou 98 42.38 N 128.05 E
Liangjiawazi 104 40.40 N 120.42 E
Liangjiazi 104 42.13 N 122.31 E
Liangkou 100 23.43 N 113.43 E
Lianglukou 107 29.18 N 106.15 E
Liangmen 98 35.34 N 114.54 E
Liangmentou 100 28.58 N 121.12 E
Liangmushi 106 30.46 N 119.35 E
Liangpa 102 24.10 N 106.13 E
Liangpeng 106 30.47 N 119.38 E
Liangping 102 30.41 N 107.49 E
Liang Shan ʌ 102 23.45 N 99.45 E
Liangshui ≃ 271a 39.49 N 116.40 E
Liangtian 100 25.37 N 113.00 E
Liangtinghe 100 30.20 N 116.12 E
Liangtoumen 100 29.31 N 120.45 E
Liangtun 98 40.14 N 122.34 E
Liangwangzhuang 105 39.01 N 116.58 E
Liangxiangzhen 105 39.44 N 116.08 E
Liangying 100 23.14 N 116.21 E
Liangyuan 100 32.00 N 117.34 E
Liangzhu 106 30.23 N 120.03 E
Liangzi Hu ⊜ 100 30.16 N 114.34 E
Lianhe 98 42.36 N 125.37 E
Lian Hu ⊜ 106 32.02 N 119.32 E
Lianhua 100 27.07 N 113.57 E
Lianhuachi 105 40.28 N 116.33 E
Lianhuapao 89 45.32 N 129.50 E
Lianhua Shan ⋏ 100 23.40 N 116.00 E
Lianjiang, Zhg. 100 26.12 N 119.31 E
Lianjiang, Zhg. 102 21.38 N 110.15 E
Lianjiechang 107 29.41 N 104.30 E
Liannan (Sanjiang) 102 24.38 N 112.10 E
Lianozovo ◆[8] 265b 55.54 N 37.35 E
Lianping 100 24.22 N 114.31 E
Lianpu 100 26.02 N 118.38 E
Lianshanguan 104 40.58 N 123.46 E
Lianshi 106 30.42 N 120.26 E
Lianshui 100 33.47 N 119.16 E
Liansiji 98 33.58 N 114.24 E
Liantang 106 31.37 N 120.38 E
Lianxian 102 24.48 N 112.25 E
Lianyin 89 53.28 N 123.51 E
Lianyuan (Lantian) 102 27.42 N 111.19 E
Lianyungang, Zhg. 98 34.44 N 119.30 E
Lianyungang (Xinpu), Zhg. 98 34.39 N 119.16 E
Lianyun Shan ʌ 100 28.32 N 113.50 E
Lianzhou
— Hepu 102 21.39 N 109.11 E
Liao ≃ 90 40.50 N 121.48 E
Liaobinta 104 42.08 N 123.04 E
Liaocheng 98 36.30 N 115.59 E
Liaodong Bandao (Liaotung Peninsula) ›[1] 98 40.00 N 122.20 E
Liaodong Wan (Gulf of Liaotung) c 98 40.30 N 121.30 E
Liaohe Kou c[1] 104 40.42 N 122.05 E
Liaojiangshi 100 26.05 N 113.17 E
Liaoning □[4] 90 41.00 N 123.00 E
Liaotung, Gulf of
— Liaodong Wan c 98 40.30 N 121.30 E
Liaotung Peninsula
— Liaodong Bandao ›[1] 98 40.00 N 122.20 E
Liaoyang 104 41.17 N 123.11 E
Liaoyangwopu 89 43.00 N 123.28 E
Liaoyuan 89 42.54 N 125.07 E
Liaozhong 104 41.31 N 122.44 E
Liapádhes 38 39.40 N 19.44 E
Liāquatpur 123 28.56 N 70.57 E
Liard ≃ 176 61.52 N 121.18 W
Liāri 120 25.41 N 66.29 E
Liart 50 49.46 N 4.20 E
Liat, Pulau I 112 2.53 S 107.05 E
Liathach ʌ 46 57.35 N 5.29 W
Lib I 14 8.19 N 167.25 E
Libagon 116 10.18 N 125.03 E
Libanga 152 0.19 N 18.41 E
Liban
— Lebanon □[1] 128 34.00 N 36.00 E
Líbano 246 4.55 N 75.04 W
Libano
— Lebanon □[1] 128 34.00 N 36.00 E
Libanon
— Lebanon □[1] 128 34.00 N 36.00 E
Libau
— Liepāja 76 56.31 N 21.01 E
Libby 202 48.23 N 115.33 W
Libby Dam ◆[6] 202 48.24 N 115.20 W
Libčeves 54 50.26 N 13.50 E
Libčice nad Vltavou 54 50.10 N 14.20 E
Liběchov 54 50.20 N 14.28 E
Libenge 152 3.39 N 18.38 E
Liberal, Ks., U.S. 198 37.02 N 100.55 W
Liberal, Mo., U.S. 194 37.33 N 94.31 W
Liberdade 256 22.01 S 44.19 W
Liberdade ◆[8] 287b 23.35 S 46.37 W
Liberdade ≃, Bra. 248 7.10 S 71.51 W
Liberdade ≃, Bra. 250 9.40 S 52.17 W
Liberec 30 50.46 N 15.03 E
Liberia 236 10.38 N 85.27 W
Liberia □[1], Afr. 134 6.30 N 9.30 W
Liberia □[1], Afr. 150 6.30 N 9.30 W
Liberta 240c 17.02 N 61.47 W
Libertad, Arg. 258 34.42 S 58.41 W
Libertad, Ur. 258 34.38 S 56.39 W
Libertad, Ven. 246 8.20 N 69.37 W
Libertad, Ven. 246 9.23 N 68.44 W
Libertador □[5] 286c 10.27 N 66.57 W
Libertador General Bernardo O'Higgins □[4] 252 34.30 S 71.00 W
Libertador General San Martín 252 23.48 S 64.48 W
Liberty, Il., U.S. 219 39.53 N 91.06 W
Liberty, In., U.S. 218 39.38 N 84.55 W
Liberty, Ky., U.S. 194 37.19 N 84.56 W
Liberty, Ms., U.S. 194 31.09 N 90.48 W
Liberty, Mo., U.S. 194 39.14 N 94.25 W
Liberty, Ne., U.S. 198 40.05 N 96.28 W
Liberty, N.Y., U.S. 210 41.48 N 74.44 W
Liberty, N.C., U.S. 192 35.51 N 79.34 W
Liberty, Pa., U.S. 210 41.34 N 77.06 W
Liberty, Pa., U.S. 279b 40.20 N 79.51 W
Liberty, S.C., U.S. 192 34.47 N 82.41 W
Liberty, Tx., U.S. 222 30.03 N 94.47 W
Liberty □[6] 222 30.12 N 94.50 W
Liberty Acres 280 34.04 N 118.12 W
Liberty Center, In., U.S. 216 40.41 N 85.16 W
Liberty Center, Oh., U.S. 216 41.26 N 84.00 W
Liberty City 222 32.27 N 94.57 W
Liberty Corner 276 40.39 N 74.34 W
Liberty Ditch ≊ 226 36.31 N 120.02 W
Liberty Farms 226 38.19 N 121.42 W
Liberty Hill 196 30.40 N 97.55 W
Liberty Island I 276 40.41 N 74.03 W
Liberty Lake ⊜[1] 208 39.25 N 76.53 W
Liberty Manor 284b 39.21 N 76.47 W
Liberty Mills 216 41.02 N 85.44 W
Liberty Park 216 41.26 N 87.22 W
Libertytown 208 39.29 N 77.14 W
Liberty Tree Mall ◆[9] 283 42.33 N 70.57 W
Liberty Tunnel ◆[5] 279b 40.26 N 80.01 W
Libertyville 216 42.16 N 87.57 W
Líbeznice 54 50.10 N 14.30 E
Libia
— Libya □[1] 146 27.00 N 17.00 E
Libibi 152 14.42 S 17.44 E
Libishan 106 30.45 N 119.20 E
Lībīyah, Aṣ-Ṣaḥrā' al- (Libyan Desert) ◆[2] 136 24.00 N 25.00 E
Lībiyā
— Libya □[1] 146 27.00 N 17.00 E
Liblín 60 49.55 N 13.32 E
Libni, Jabal ʌ[2] 132 30.44 N 33.50 E
Libo 102 25.28 N 107.53 E
Libobo, Tanjung › 164 0.54 S 128.28 E
Liboc ≃ 54 50.10 N 13.31 E
Libochovice 54 50.22 N 14.03 E
Libode 158 31.33 S 29.02 E
Liboi 154 0.24 N 40.57 E
Liboko 152 2.43 N 21.28 E
Libomyšl 60 49.52 N 14.00 E
Libona 116 8.20 N 124.44 E
Liboumba ≃ 152 0.38 N 12.54 E
Libourne 32 44.55 N 0.14 W
Libramont 56 49.55 N 5.23 E
Library 214 40.18 N 80.02 W
Librazhd 38 41.11 N 20.19 E
Libres 234 19.28 N 97.41 W
Libreville 152 0.23 N 9.27 E
Librizzi 70 38.06 N 14.57 E
Libro Point › 116 11.26 N 119.29 E
Libu 102 23.41 N 111.30 E
Libucan Island I 116 11.54 N 124.39 E
Libuganon ≃ 116 7.27 N 125.47 E
Libunga 154 1.49 N 26.35 E
Liburung 112 3.55 S 120.09 E
Libušín 54 50.09 N 14.04 E
Libya (Lībiyā) □[1], Afr. 136 27.00 N 17.00 E
Libya (Lībiyā) □[1], Afr. 146 27.00 N 17.00 E
Libyan Desert
— Lībīyah, Aṣ-Ṣaḥrā' al- ◆[2] 136 24.00 N 25.00 E
Libyan Plateau
— Aḍ-Ḍiffah ⋏[1] 140 30.30 N 25.30 E
Libye
— Libya □[1] 146 27.00 N 17.00 E
Libyen
— Libya □[1] 146 27.00 N 17.00 E
Libysche Wüste
— Lībīyah, Aṣ-Ṣaḥrā' al- ◆[2] 136 24.00 N 25.00 E
Licancábur, Volcán ʌ[1] 248 22.50 S 67.50 W
Licantén 252 34.59 S 72.00 W
Licata 70 37.06 N 13.56 E
Licciana Nardi 64 44.16 N 10.02 E
Lice 130 38.28 N 40.39 E
Lich 56 50.33 N 8.50 E
Lichačova, mys › 89 42.44 N 132.51 E
Lichaja ≃ 83 48.08 N 40.15 E
Lichang 107 28.53 N 104.26 E
Licheng 102 36.30 N 113.21 E
Lichères-Près-Aigremont 50 47.43 N 3.51 E
Lichfield 42 52.42 N 1.48 W
Lichinga 154 13.18 S 35.14 E
Lichitiseni 38 46.23 N 27.17 E
Lichoborka ≃ 265b 55.50 N 37.38 E
Lichoslavl' 76 57.07 N 35.28 E
Lichovka 78 48.41 N 33.55 E
Lichovskoj 83 48.07 N 40.12 E
Lichtaart 56 51.14 N 4.54 E
Lichte 54 50.31 N 11.10 E
Lichtenau 56 48.43 N 8.01 E
Lichtenberg, Dtsch. 54 50.23 N 11.40 E
Lichtenberg, Fr. 56 48.55 N 7.29 E
Lichtenberg ◆[8] 264a 52.31 N 13.29 E
Lichtenburg 158 26.08 S 26.08 E
Lichtendorf 263 51.28 N 7.37 E
Lichtenfels 56 50.09 N 11.04 E
Lichtenplatz ◆[8] 263 51.15 N 7.12 E
Lichtenrade ◆[8] 264a 52.23 N 13.25 E
Lichtensee 54 51.23 N 13.22 E
Lichtensteig 58 47.19 N 9.05 E
Lichtenstein 54 50.45 N 12.37 E
Lichtenstein, Schloss ʊ 58 48.24 N 9.15 E
Lichtentanne 54 50.42 N 12.25 E
Lichtenvoorde 52 51.59 N 6.34 E
Lichterfelde ◆[8] 264a 52.26 N 13.19 E
Lichtervelde 50 51.02 N 3.09 E
Lichuan, Zhg. 100 27.18 N 116.53 E
Lichuan, Zhg. 102 30.18 N 108.51 E
Lick Creek ≃, Il., U.S. 219 39.42 N 89.41 W
Lick Creek ≃, In., U.S. 218 38.33 N 86.31 W
Lick Creek ≃, Mo., U.S. 219 39.31 N 91.39 W
Lick Creek ≃, Oh., U.S. 216 41.21 N 84.25 W
Lick Creek ≃, Tn., U.S. 192 36.11 N 83.10 W
Lickershamn 26 57.50 N 18.31 E
Licking 194 37.29 N 91.51 W
Licking □[6] 214 40.10 N 82.30 W
Licking ≃, Ky., U.S. 188 39.06 N 84.30 W
Licking ≃, Oh., U.S. 214 40.03 N 82.20 W
Licking, North Fork ≃, Ky., U.S. 218 38.35 N 84.13 W
Licking, North Fork ≃, Oh., U.S. 214 40.03 N 82.23 W
Licking, South Fork ≃ 218 38.41 N 84.20 W
Lickingville 214 41.23 N 79.22 W
Lick Observatory ʊ[3] 226 37.22 N 121.37 W
Ličko Polje ≚ 36 44.35 N 15.25 E
Lick Run ≃, Pa., U.S. 210 41.12 N 77.32 W
Lick Run ≃, Pa., U.S. 279b 40.17 N 79.57 W
Licodia Eubea 70 37.09 N 14.42 E
Licosa, Punta › 68 40.15 N 14.54 E
Licun 98 38.32 N 117.08 E
Licungo ≃ 154 17.40 S 37.15 E
Lid' 76 59.39 N 35.05 E
Lida 76 53.53 N 25.18 E
Lidan ≃ 26 58.31 N 13.09 E

ENGLISH				DEUTSCH			
Name	Page	Lat.°′	Long.°′	Name	Seite	Breite°′	Länge°′ E = Ost

Lidao 98 37.15 N 122.32 E
Lidarentuncun 104 41.32 N 123.12 E
Lidcombe 274a 33.52 S 151.03 E
Liddel Water ≃ 44 55.04 N 2.57 W
Liddesdale V 44 55.12 N 2.46 W
Liddon Gulf c 176 75.03 N 113.00 W
Liden 26 62.42 N 16.48 E
Lidesi 100 33.33 N 115.53 E
Lidgerwood 198 46.04 N 97.09 W
Lidgetton 158 29.25 S 30.05 E
Lidian 107 28.57 N 103.44 E
Lídice, Bra. 256 22.51 S 44.12 W
Lídice, Pan. 236 8.45 N 79.54 W
Lidice ⊥ 54 50.03 N 14.08 E
Lidingö 40 59.22 N 18.08 E
Lidköping 26 58.30 N 13.10 E
Lido 64 45.25 N 12.22 E
Lido, Litorale di ±[2] 64 45.23 N 12.21 E
Lido, Porto di c 64 45.26 N 12.25 E
Lido Beach 276 40.35 N 73.38 W
Lido di Camaiore 64 43.54 N 10.13 E
Lido di Castel Fusano ◆[8] 66 41.43 N 12.20 E
Lido di Iesolo 64 45.30 N 12.39 E
Lido di Metaponto 68 40.22 N 16.50 E
Lido di Ostia ◆[8] 66 41.44 N 12.14 E
Lido di Pomposa 66 44.45 N 12.14 E
Lido di Siponto 68 41.37 N 15.55 E
Lido Key I 220 27.19 N 82.35 W
Lidsjön ⊜ 40 58.55 N 16.51 E
Lidu 107 30.35 N 106.04 E
Lidzbark 30 53.17 N 19.49 E
Lidzbark Warmiński 30 54.09 N 20.35 E
Liebenau, Dtsch. 52 52.36 N 9.05 E
Liebenau, Öst. 61 48.32 N 14.49 E
Liebenbergsvlei ≃ 158 27.20 S 28.31 E
Liebenburg 52 52.01 N 10.26 E
Liebenwalde 54 52.52 N 13.23 E
Lieberhausen 56 51.03 N 7.40 E
Lieberose 54 51.59 N 14.17 E
Liebertwolkwitz 54 51.17 N 12.28 E
Liebig, Mount ʌ 162 23.18 S 131.22 E
Liebstadt 54 50.52 N 13.51 E
Liechtenstein □[1], Europe 22 47.09 N 9.35 E
Liechtenstein □[1], Europe 58 47.09 N 9.35 E
Liechtensteinklamm V 64 47.18 N 13.12 E
Liedberg 263 51.10 N 6.32 E
Liedekerke 50 50.52 N 4.05 E
Liège (Luik) 56 50.38 N 5.34 E
Liège □[4] 56 50.30 N 5.30 E
Liège, Aéroport ⊠ 56 50.39 N 5.30 E
Liegnitz
— Legnica 30 51.13 N 16.09 E
Lieja
— Liège 56 50.38 N 5.34 E
Lieksa 26 63.19 N 30.01 E
Lielais Liepu kalns ʌ[2] 76 56.25 N 27.50 E
Lielupe ≃ 76 57.01 N 23.56 E
Lielvārde 76 56.43 N 24.51 E
Liemienzhen 107 30.29 N 106.05 E
Lienart 154 3.04 N 25.31 E
Lienchou
— Hepu 102 21.39 N 109.11 E
Lienen 52 52.09 N 7.58 E
Lienz 64 46.50 N 12.47 E
Liepāja 76 56.31 N 21.01 E
Liepājas ezers ⊜ 76 56.27 N 21.03 E
Liepe 54 53.58 N 13.56 E
Liepna 76 57.25 N 27.25 E
Liepnitzsee ⊜ 264a 52.45 N 13.30 E
Lièpvre 58 48.16 N 7.17 E
Lier (Lierre) 50 51.08 N 4.34 E
Lierenfeld ◆[8] 263 51.13 N 6.51 E
Lierna 58 45.57 N 9.18 E
Liernais 50 47.12 N 4.17 E
Lierneux 56 50.18 N 5.48 E
Liershizhai 104 41.49 N 123.43 E
Liesborn 52 51.43 N 8.15 E
Lieser ≃, Dtsch. 56 49.55 N 7.01 E
Lieser ≃, Öst. 64 46.47 N 13.39 E
Lieshout 52 51.32 N 5.35 E
Liesing ◆[8] 264b 48.08 N 16.17 E
Liesing ≃ 264b 48.08 N 16.28 E
Liesingbach ≃ 61 47.20 N 15.02 E
Liesjärven kansallispuisto ♠ 26 60.40 N 23.54 E
Lieskau 54 51.37 N 13.48 E
Liesse 50 49.37 N 3.48 E
Liessies 50 50.07 N 4.05 E
Liestal 58 47.29 N 7.44 E
Liești 38 45.38 N 27.32 E
Lietuva
— Lithuania □[1] 72 56.00 N 24.00 E
Lietzow 54 54.29 N 13.30 E
Lieurey 50 49.14 N 0.29 E
Lieusaint 261 48.38 N 2.33 E
Lieutel ≃ 261 48.49 N 1.52 E
Lieutenant Robert J. Palenscar Memorial Airport ⊠ 285 39.51 N 75.03 W
Liévin 50 50.25 N 2.46 E
Lièvre, Rivière du ≃ 176 45.31 N 75.26 W
Lièvres, Île aux I 186 47.51 N 69.44 W
Liezen 61 47.35 N 14.15 E
Lifanga 152 0.19 N 21.57 E
Liffey ≃ 48 53.21 N 6.16 W
Liffol-le-Grand 58 48.19 N 5.35 E
Lifford 48 54.50 N 7.29 W
Liffré 32 48.13 N 1.30 W
Lifjell ʌ 26 59.30 N 8.52 E
Lifoku 152 0.04 S 21.18 E
Lifou I 175f 20.53 S 167.13 E
Lifoula 273b 4.06 S 15.25 E
Lifton 42 50.39 N 4.17 W
Liftwood 285 39.47 N 75.31 W
Lifune ≃ 152 8.21 S 13.22 E
Ligačovo 265b 55.56 N 37.15 E
Ligang 100 30.04 N 121.52 E
Ligao, Pil. 116 13.14 N 123.32 E
Ligao, Pil. 116 6.17 N 124.09 E
Ligasa 152 0.42 N 23.45 E
Ligezhuang, Zhg. 105 39.49 N 115.56 E
Ligezhuang, Zhg. 105 39.42 N 118.12 E
Light ≃ 168b 34.35 S 138.22 E
Lightfoot 208 37.20 N 76.45 W
Lighthouse Beach ±[2] 273a 6.24 N 3.22 E
Lighthouse Point 220 26.16 N 80.05 W
Lighthouse Point ›, On., Can. 214 41.50 N 82.38 W
Lighthouse Point ›, Fl., U.S. 192 29.54 N 84.21 W
Lighthouse Point ›, Mi., U.S. 190 45.13 N 85.32 W
Lighthouse Reef ✣[2] 232 17.20 N 87.32 W
Lightning Creek ≃, Sk., Can. 184 49.12 N 101.43 W
Lightning Creek ≃, N.A. 224 48.50 N 121.03 W
Lightning Creek ≃, Wy., U.S. 198 43.11 N 104.44 W
Lightning Ridge 166 29.26 S 147.59 E
Lightstreet 210 41.02 N 76.25 W
Lightsville 216 40.18 N 84.42 W
Ligist 61 46.59 N 15.12 E
Lignano Pineta 64 45.40 N 13.07 E
Lignano Sabbiadoro 64 45.42 N 13.09 E
Lignières 32 46.45 N 2.11 E
Lignite 198 48.52 N 102.33 W
Lignon ≃ 62 45.44 N 4.08 E
Lignumvitae Key I 220 24.55 N 80.42 W
Ligny-en-Barrois 58 48.41 N 5.20 E
Ligny-en-Cambrésis 50 50.06 N 3.22 E
Ligny-le-Châtel 50 47.54 N 3.45 E
Ligny-le-Ribault 50 47.41 N 1.47 E
Ligonha ≃ 154 16.54 S 39.09 E
Ligonier, In., U.S. 216 41.27 N 85.35 W
Ligonier, Pa., U.S. 214 40.14 N 79.14 W
Ligovka 78 49.08 N 36.03 E
Ligovo 76 60.13 N 31.48 E
Ligovo ◆[8] 265a 59.50 N 30.12 E
Ligovskij kanal ≊ 265a 59.47 N 30.10 E
Liguantu 105 40.24 N 115.45 E
Ligueil 32 47.03 N 0.49 E
Ligui 232 25.43 N 111.16 W
Ligure, Mar
— Ligurian Sea ⊤[2] 36 43.30 N 9.00 E
Liguria □[4] 62 44.30 N 8.50 E
Liguria, Mar de
— Ligurian Sea ⊤[2] 36 43.30 N 9.00 E
Ligurian Sea ⊤[2] 36 43.30 N 9.00 E
Ligurisches Meer
— Ligurian Sea ⊤[2] 36 43.30 N 9.00 E
Lihir Group II 164 3.05 S 152.40 E
Lihir Island I 164 3.05 S 152.35 E
Lihou Reef and Cays ✣[2] 166 17.25 S 151.40 E
Lihu 100 23.23 N 116.03 E
Lihue 229b 21.58 N 159.22 W
Lihue Airport ⊠ 229b 21.59 N 159.21 W
Lihuel Calel, Parque Nacional ♠, Arg. 252 37.58 S 65.32 W
Lihuel Calel, Parque Nacional ♠, Arg. 254 37.58 S 65.32 W
Lihula 76 58.41 N 23.50 E
Liji, Zhg. 100 31.59 N 115.51 E
Liji, Zhg. 100 33.48 N 117.48 E
Lijia, Zhg. 98 37.49 N 118.01 E
Lijia, Zhg. 104 41.43 N 122.20 E
Lijiaba 107 29.37 N 105.33 E
Lijiadian 104 42.07 N 121.14 E
Lijiajie 107 29.49 N 105.30 E
Lijiakou 105 39.12 N 116.29 E
Lijiang 102 26.57 N 100.15 E
Lijiapuzi 104 40.59 N 123.38 E
Lijiaqiao, Zhg. 105 40.03 N 116.40 E
Lijiaqiao, Zhg. 105 39.47 N 117.47 E
Lijiaqiao, Zhg. 106 31.38 N 120.00 E
Lijiatun 104 41.19 N 121.23 E
Lijiatuo 107 29.28 N 106.33 E
Lijiawobao 104 41.00 N 122.26 E
Lijiaxiang 106 30.57 N 119.59 E
Lijiazao 105 39.17 N 118.19 E
Lijin, Zhg. 98 37.29 N 118.16 E
Lijin, Zhg. 104 41.40 N 121.20 E
Lik ≃ 110 18.31 N 102.31 E
Likako 152 0.15 N 21.00 E
Likang 100 22.47 N 120.29 E
Likasi (Jadotville) 154 10.59 S 26.44 E
Likati 152 3.21 N 23.53 E
Likati ≃ 152 2.53 N 24.03 E
Likely 182 52.37 N 121.34 W
Likėnai 76 56.12 N 24.37 E
Likete 152 0.43 S 21.25 E
Likhu ≃ 124 27.15 N 86.12 E
Liki 112 1.36 S 101.11 E
Likimi 152 2.50 N 20.45 E
Likino 82 55.38 N 37.08 E
Likino-Dulevo 82 55.43 N 38.58 E
Liknes 26 58.19 N 6.59 E
Likoma Island I 154 12.05 S 34.45 E
Likou, Zhg. 100 29.53 N 117.28 E
Likou, Zhg. 100 33.51 N 113.20 E
Likou, Zhg. 106 31.24 N 120.37 E
Likouala □[5] 152 2.00 N 17.30 E
Likouala ≃ 152 1.13 S 16.48 E
Likouala aux Herbes ≃ 152 0.50 S 17.11 E
Likova ≃ 265b 55.34 N 37.21 E
Likstammen ⊜ 40 58.58 N 17.12 E
Liku 174v 19.02 S 169.47 W
Likupang 112 1.41 N 125.04 E
Likus ≃ 236 14.14 N 83.35 W
Likuyu 154 10.20 S 36.14 E
Lilanchengzhen 105 39.12 N 116.43 E
Lilanga 152 0.34 S 23.55 E
Lilasi 124 29.22 N 84.30 E
Lilbert 222 31.44 N 94.54 W
Lilbourn 194 36.35 N 89.36 W
L'Île-Bouchard 32 47.07 N 0.25 E
Lilenga 152 0.54 N 22.06 E
L'Île-Rousse 32 42.38 N 8.56 E
Lili 106 31.00 N 120.42 E
Lilian Point › 174d 0.53 S 169.35 E
Lilienfeld 61 48.03 N 15.36 E
Lilienthal 52 53.08 N 8.55 E
Liling 100 27.40 N 113.30 E
Lilio 116 14.08 N 121.26 E
Liljendal 40 60.08 N 14.04 E
Lilla Bharwana 123 32.34 N 72.45 E
Lilla Edet 26 58.08 N 12.08 E
Lillån 40 59.19 N 15.13 E
Lillby 26 63.28 N 23.00 E
Lille 50 50.38 N 3.04 E
Lillebælt ʮ 41 55.20 N 9.45 E
Lillebonne 50 49.31 N 0.33 E
Lillehammer 26 61.08 N 10.30 E
Lille-Lesquin, Aéroport ⊠ 50 50.35 N 3.07 E
Lillerød 41 55.52 N 12.22 E
Lillers 50 50.34 N 2.29 E
Lillesand 26 58.15 N 8.24 E
Lilleshall 42 52.44 N 2.21 W
Lillestrøm 26 59.57 N 11.05 E
Lille Værløse 41 55.47 N 12.23 E
Lillhärdal 26 61.51 N 14.04 E
Lillian 222 32.30 N 97.11 W
Lillington 192 35.23 N 78.48 W
Lillinonah Lake ⊜[1] 207 41.28 N 73.21 W
Lilli Pilli 274a 34.04 S 151.07 E
Lillo 34 39.43 N 3.18 W
Lillooet 182 50.42 N 121.56 W
Lillooet ≃ 182 49.45 N 122.08 W
Lillooet Lake ⊜ 182 50.13 N 122.29 W
Lilly 214 40.25 N 78.37 W
Lilly Creek ≃ 222 32.47 N 94.56 W
Liloan 116 10.09 N 125.07 E
Lilongwe 154 13.59 S 33.44 E
Lilo Viejo 252 26.56 S 62.58 W
Liloy 116 8.08 N 122.40 E
Liluāh 272b 22.35 N 88.23 E
Lily 192 37.01 N 84.04 W
Lily Cache Creek ≃ 278 41.41 N 88.07 W
Lilydale, Austl. 166 41.15 S 147.13 E
Lilydale, Austl. 169 37.45 S 145.21 E
Lily Dale, N.Y., U.S. 214 42.21 N 79.19 W
Lilyfield 274a 33.52 S 151.10 E
Lilyvale 273d 26.06 S 28.25 E
Lim ≃, Afr. 152 7.54 N 15.46 E
Lim ≃, Europe 38 43.45 N 19.13 E
Lima, Arg. 258 34.03 S 59.12 W
Lima, Para. 252 23.54 S 56.20 W
Lima, Perú 248 12.03 S 77.03 W
Lima, Perú 286d 12.03 S 77.03 W
Lima, Sve. 26 60.56 N 13.26 E
Lima, Il., U.S. 219 40.11 N 91.23 W
Lima, Mt., U.S. 202 44.38 N 112.35 W
Lima, N.Y., U.S. 210 42.54 N 77.36 W
Lima, Oh., U.S. 216 40.44 N 84.06 W
Lima, Pa., U.S. 285 39.55 N 75.26 W
Lima □[5] 248 12.00 S 76.35 W
Lima (Limia) ≃, Europe 34 41.41 N 8.50 W
Lima ≃, It. 64 44.00 N 10.35 E
Lima, Punta › 240m 18.11 N 65.41 W
Lima Center 216 42.47 N 88.49 W
Limache 252 33.01 S 71.16 W
Lima Duarte 256 21.51 S 43.48 W
Liman, Ross. 80 45.47 N 47.14 E
Liman, Ukr. 78 49.36 N 36.27 E
Liman, Ukr. 78 45.41 N 29.45 E
Liman, Ukr. 83 49.21 N 38.57 E
Liman, Yis. 132 33.03 N 35.06 E
Liman ≃ 115a 6.29 S 105.48 E
Limanowa 30 49.43 N 20.26 E
Limanskoje 78 46.38 N 30.00 E
Limão ◆[8] 287b 23.30 S 46.40 W
Limapuluh 114 3.10 N 99.26 E
Lima Reservoir ⊜[1] 202 44.38 N 112.17 W
Limarí ≃ 252 30.44 S 71.43 W

Symbols in the index entries represent the broad categories identified in the key at the right. Symbols with superior numbers (⋏[1]) identify subcategories (see complete key on page *I · 1*).

Symbole im Register stellen die rechts im Schlüssel erklärten Kategorien dar. Symbole mit hochgestellten Ziffern (⋏[1]) bezeichnen Unterabteilungen einer Kategorie (vgl. vollständiger Schlüssel auf Seite *I · 1*).

Los símbolos incluídos en el texto del índice representan las grandes categorias identificadas con la clave a la derecha. Los símbolos con numeros en su parte superior (⋏[1]) identifican las subcategorías (véase la clave completa en la página *I · 1*).

Les symboles de l'index représentent les catégories indiquées dans la légende à droite. Les symboles suivis d'un indice (⋏[1]) représentent des sous-catégories (voir légende complète à la page *I · 1*).

Os símbolos incluídos no texto do índice representam as grandes categorias identificadas com a chave à direita. Os símbolos com números em sua parte superior (⋏[1]) identificam as subcategorias (veja-se a chave completa à página *I · 1*).

ʌ Mountain	Berg	Montaña	Montagne	Montanha
⋏ Mountains	Gebirge	Montañas	Montagnes	Montanhas
)(Pass	Paß	Paso	Col	Passo
V Valley, Canyon	Tal, Cañon	Valle, Cañón	Vallée, Canyon	Vale, Canhão
≚ Plain	Ebene	Llano	Plaine	Planície
› Cape	Kap	Cabo	Cap	Cabo
I Island	Insel	Isla	Île	Ilha
II Islands	Inseln	Islas	Îles	Ilhas
± Other Topographic Features	Andere Topographische Objekte	Otros Elementos Topográficos	Autres données topographiques	Outros acidentes topográficos

ESPAÑOL — Nombre | Página | Lat.°′ | Long.°′ W = Oeste

FRANÇAIS — Nom | Page | Lat.°′ | Long.°′ W = Ouest

PORTUGUÊS — Nome | Página | Lat.°′ | Long.°′ W = Oeste

Limas	112	0.14 N	104.31 E
Limasawa Island I	116	9.56 N	125.05 E
Limassa	152	4.14 N	22.02 E
Limassol → Lemesós	130	34.40 N	33.02 E
Limavady	48	55.03 N	6.57 W
Limaville	214	40.59 N	81.09 W
Limay, Fr.	50	49.00 N	1.44 E
Limay, Pil.	116	14.34 N	120.36 E
Limay ≃	254	38.59 S	68.00 W
Limay Mahuida	252	37.12 S	66.42 W
Limbach-Oberfrohna	54	50.51 N	12.45 E
Limbadi	68	38.33 N	15.58 E
Limbang	112	4.45 N	115.00 E
Limbang ≃	112	4.50 N	115.01 E
Limbani	248	14.08 S	69.42 W
Limbara, Monte Λ	71	40.51 N	9.10 E
Limbaži	76	57.31 N	24.42 E
Līmbdi	120	22.34 N	71.48 E
Limbe	154	15.49 S	35.03 E
Limbiate	62	45.36 N	9.07 E
Limboto	112	0.37 N	122.57 E
Limbourg	56	50.37 N	5.56 E
Limbrick	262	53.38 N	2.36 W
Limbueta	152	12.30 S	18.42 E
Limbunya	164	17.14 S	129.50 E
Limburg □[4], Bel.	56	51.00 N	5.30 E
Limburg □[4], Ned.	52	51.14 N	5.50 E
Limburg an der Lahn	56	50.23 N	8.04 E
Limburgerhof	56	49.25 N	8.24 E
Lim Chu Kang	271c	1.26 N	103.43 E
Limecrest	218	39.54 N	83.48 W
Limefield	262	53.37 N	2.18 W
Limeira	255	22.34 S	47.24 W
Limekiln Canyon V	280	34.18 N	118.33 W
Lime Lake	210	42.26 N	78.29 W
Limen	100	27.07 N	119.19 E
Limena	64	45.29 N	11.50 E
Limentra ≃	64	44.14 N	11.03 E
Limerick, Sk., Can.	184	49.40 N	106.15 W
Limerick (Luimneach), Ire.	48	52.40 N	8.38 W
Limerick, Pa., U.S.	285	40.14 N	75.32 W
Limerick □[6]	48	52.30 N	8.45 W
Limerick Lake ⊜	212	44.54 N	77.37 W
Limerock	207	41.55 N	71.28 W
Lime Springs	190	43.27 N	92.17 W
Limestone, Austl.	162	21.11 S	119.50 E
Limestone, Fl., U.S.	220	27.21 N	81.53 W
Limestone, Me., U.S.	186	46.54 N	67.49 W
Limestone, N.Y., U.S.	210	42.01 N	78.37 W
Limestone, Pa., U.S.	214	41.08 N	79.20 W
Limestone □[6]	222	31.35 N	96.35 W
Limestone ≃	184	56.31 N	94.07 W
Limestone, Lake ⊜[1]	222	31.25 N	96.20 W
Limestone Bay c	184	53.50 N	98.50 W
Limestone Canyon V	280	33.45 N	117.41 W
Limestone Creek ≃	210	43.06 N	75.58 W
Limestone Lake ⊜, Mb., Can.	184	56.35 N	96.00 W
Limestone Lake ⊜, Sk., Can.	184	54.36 N	103.18 W
Limestone Point >[1]	184	53.50 N	98.50 W
Limestone Point Lake ⊜	184	55.07 N	100.32 W
Lime Street Station ◆[5]	262	53.25 N	2.59 W
Lime Village	180	61.21 N	155.28 W
Limfjorden Ʉ	26	56.55 N	9.10 E
Limhamn ◆[8]	41	55.35 N	12.54 E
Limia (Lima) ≃	34	41.41 N	8.50 W
Limina	70	37.56 N	15.17 E
Liminka	26	64.49 N	25.24 E
Liminzhen	98	34.31 N	115.56 E
Limit Brook ≃	283	42.42 N	71.25 W
Limmared	26	57.32 N	13.21 E
Limmaren ⊜	40	59.44 N	18.43 E
Limmen	52	52.34 N	4.41 E
Limmen Bight c[3]	164	14.45 S	135.40 E
Limmen Bight ≃	164	15.07 S	135.44 E
Límnos I	38	39.54 N	25.21 E
Limoeiro	250	7.52 S	35.27 W
Limoeiro do Norte	250	5.08 S	38.05 W
Limoges, On., Can.	212	45.20 N	75.15 W
Limoges, Fr.	32	45.50 N	1.16 E
Limoges-Fourches	261	48.38 N	2.40 E
Limogne	32	44.24 N	1.46 E
Limón, Hond.	236	15.52 N	85.33 W
Limon, Co., U.S.	198	39.15 N	103.41 W
Limón □[4]	236	10.00 N	83.15 W
Limonar	240p	22.57 N	81.24 W
Limone Piemonte	62	44.12 N	7.34 E
Limone sul Garda	64	45.49 N	10.47 E
Limours	50	48.39 N	2.05 E
Limousin, Plateaux du ⩘[1]	32	45.30 N	1.15 E
Limoux	32	43.04 N	2.14 E
Limpopo ≃	156	25.15 S	33.30 E
Limpsfield	42	51.16 N	0.01 E
Limski kanal c	64	45.07 N	13.38 E
Limu	102	25.02 N	110.51 E
Limuru	154	1.06 S	36.39 E
Linachamari	24	69.40 N	31.20 E
Līnah	128	28.42 N	43.48 E
Lin'an	106	30.14 N	119.43 E
Linanäs	40	59.28 N	18.31 E
Linao Bay c	116	6.45 N	124.00 E
Linapacan Island I	116	11.27 N	119.49 E
Linapacan Strait Ʉ	116	11.37 N	119.56 E
Linares, Chile	252	35.51 S	71.36 W
Linares, Col.	246	1.23 N	77.31 W
Linares, Esp.	34	38.05 N	3.38 W
Linares, Méx.	232	24.52 N	99.34 W
Linariá	38	37.24 N	24.57 E
Linaro, Capo >	66	42.02 N	11.50 E
Linas	261	48.38 N	2.16 E
Linas, Monte Λ	71	39.27 N	8.37 E
Linas-Montlhéry, Domaine Militaire de ■	261	48.37 N	2.13 E
Linate, Aeroporto di ⊠	62	45.27 N	9.16 E
Lincai	100	33.50 N	114.56 E
Lincang	102	23.45 N	102.20 E
Lince	286d	12.06 S	77.03 W
Linch	200	43.36 N	106.11 W
Lincheng, Zhg.	98	37.27 N	114.29 E
Lincheng, Zhg.	106	30.55 N	119.47 E
Linch'ing → Linqing	98	36.53 N	115.41 E
Lincoln, Arg.	252	34.52 S	61.32 W
Lincoln, On., Can.	212	43.10 N	79.29 W
Lincoln, N.Z.	172	43.39 S	172.29 E
Lincoln, Eng., U.K.	44	53.14 N	0.33 W
Lincoln, Ar., U.S.	194	35.56 N	94.25 W
Lincoln, Ca., U.S.	226	38.53 N	121.17 W
Lincoln, De., U.S.	208	38.52 N	75.25 W
Lincoln, Il., U.S.	219	40.08 N	89.21 W
Lincoln, In., U.S.	216	40.37 N	86.12 W
Lincoln, Ks., U.S.	198	39.02 N	98.08 W
Lincoln, Me., U.S.	188	45.21 N	68.30 W
Lincoln, Ma., U.S.	207	42.25 N	71.18 W
Lincoln, Mi., U.S.	190	44.41 N	83.24 W
Lincoln, Mo., U.S.	194	38.23 N	93.20 W
Lincoln, Mt., U.S.	202	46.57 N	112.40 W
Lincoln, Ne., U.S.	198	40.48 N	96.40 W
Lincoln, N.H., U.S.	188	44.02 N	71.40 W
Lincoln, Pa., U.S.	208	40.12 N	76.12 W
Lincoln, Pa., U.S.	279b	40.18 N	79.51 W
Lincoln, R.I., U.S.	207	41.54 N	71.25 W
Lincoln, Tx., U.S.	222	30.17 N	96.52 W
Lincoln □[6], Mo., U.S.	219	39.05 N	90.57 W
Lincoln □[6], Or., U.S.	224	44.59 N	123.52 W
Lincoln, Mount Λ	200	39.21 N	106.07 W
Lincoln Acres	228	32.40 N	117.04 W
Lincoln Boyhood National Memorial ⊥	194	38.10 N	86.58 W
Lincoln Cathedral ʊ[1]	44	53.14 N	0.33 W
Lincoln Center ʊ	276	40.46 N	73.59 W
Lincoln City	224	44.57 N	124.00 W
Lincoln Creek ≃, Ne., U.S.	198	40.54 N	97.06 W
Lincoln Creek ≃, Wa., U.S.	224	46.45 N	123.02 W
Lincolndale	210	41.19 N	73.43 W
Lincoln Estates	278	41.31 N	87.49 W
Lincoln Heights, Oh., U.S.	214	40.47 N	82.30 W
Lincoln Heights, Oh., U.S.	218	39.15 N	84.28 W
Lincoln Heights, Pa., U.S.	279b	40.19 N	79.37 W
Lincoln Home National Historical Site ⊥	219	39.47 N	89.38 W
Lincolnia Heights	284c	38.50 N	77.09 W
Lincoln Memorial ⊥	284c	38.53 N	77.03 W
Lincoln Park, Co., U.S.	200	38.25 N	105.13 W
Lincoln Park, Ga., U.S.	192	32.52 N	84.19 W
Lincoln Park, Mi., U.S.	216	42.15 N	83.10 W
Lincoln Park, N.J., U.S.	276	40.55 N	74.18 W
Lincoln Park, N.Y., U.S.	210	41.57 N	74.00 W
Lincoln Park ♠, Ca., U.S.	282	37.46 N	122.30 W
Lincoln Park ♠, Il., U.S.	278	41.56 N	87.38 W
Lincoln Park Airport ⊠	276	40.57 N	74.19 W
Lincoln Place ◆[8]	279b	40.22 N	79.55 W
Lincoln Sea ⊤[2]	16	83.00 N	56.00 W
Lincolnshire	216	42.11 N	87.54 W
Lincolnshire □[6]	28	52.55 N	0.22 W
Lincoln's New Salem State Park ♠	219	39.58 N	89.52 W
Lincoln Tomb State Memorial ⊥	219	39.50 N	89.39 W
Lincolnton, Ga., U.S.	192	33.47 N	82.28 W
Lincolnton, N.C., U.S.	192	35.28 N	81.15 W
Lincoln Tunnel ◆[5]	276	40.46 N	74.01 W
Lincoln University	208	39.48 N	75.55 W
Lincoln Village, Ca., U.S.	226	38.00 N	121.19 W
Lincoln Village, Oh., U.S.	218	39.57 N	83.08 W
Lincolnville	214	41.47 N	79.51 W
Lincolnwood	278	42.00 N	87.43 W
Lincolnwood Hills	278	41.31 N	87.54 W
Linconia	285	40.08 N	74.59 W
Lincroft	208	40.19 N	74.07 W
Lind	202	46.58 N	118.36 W
Linda, Ross.	80	56.37 N	44.07 E
Linda, Ca., U.S.	226	39.07 N	121.32 W
Linda-a-Velha	266c	38.43 N	9.14 W
Lindale, Ga., U.S.	192	34.11 N	85.10 W
Lindale, Tx., U.S.	222	32.30 N	95.24 W
Lindau, Dtsch.	41	54.36 N	9.47 E
Lindau, Dtsch.	52	51.39 N	10.07 E
Lindau, Dtsch.	54	52.02 N	12.06 E
Lindau, Dtsch.	58	47.33 N	9.41 E
Lindbergh	219	39.02 N	92.08 W
Lindbergh Field ⊠	228	32.44 N	117.11 W
Lind Coulee V	202	47.00 N	119.10 W
Linde ≃	74	64.57 N	124.36 E
Lindelse	41	54.52 N	10.44 E
Linden, Guy.	246	6.00 N	58.18 W
Linden, Al., U.S.	194	32.18 N	87.47 W
Linden, Ca., U.S.	226	38.01 N	121.05 W
Linden, In., U.S.	194	40.11 N	86.54 W
Linden, Mi., U.S.	216	42.48 N	83.46 W
Linden, N.J., U.S.	210	40.37 N	74.14 W
Linden, Pa., U.S.	210	41.14 N	77.08 W
Linden, Pa., U.S.	279b	40.14 N	80.08 W
Linden, Tn., U.S.	194	35.37 N	87.50 W
Linden, Tx., U.S.	194	33.00 N	94.21 W
Linden ◆[8]	273d	26.08 S	28.00 E
Linden Airport ⊠	276	40.37 N	74.15 W
Lindenberg, Dtsch.	54	53.02 N	12.07 E
Lindenberg, Dtsch.	54	52.36 N	13.31 E
Lindenberg, Dtsch.	54	52.12 N	14.07 E
Lindenberg im Allgäu	58	47.36 N	9.53 E
Linden-Dahlhausen ◆[8]	263	51.26 N	7.09 E
Lindenfels	56	49.41 N	8.47 E
Lindenhorst ◆[8]	263	51.33 N	7.27 E
Lindenhurst, Il., U.S.	216	42.24 N	88.01 W
Lindenhurst, N.Y., U.S.	210	40.41 N	73.22 W
Lindenhurst, Pa., U.S.	285	40.14 N	74.54 W
Linden Park	216	40.13 N	85.23 W
Lindenthal	54	51.24 N	12.20 E
Lindenwold	208	39.49 N	74.59 W
Lindenwood, Il., U.S.	216	42.03 N	89.02 W
Lindenwood, In., U.S.	218	39.41 N	86.09 W
Linderhausen	263	51.18 N	7.17 E
Linderhof, Schloss ⊥	64	47.34 N	10.57 E
Lindern	52	52.50 N	7.46 E
Linderöd	41	55.56 N	13.49 E
Linderödsåsen ⩘[2]	26	55.53 N	13.56 E
Lindesay, Mount Λ[2]	162	34.49 S	117.18 E
Lindesberg	40	59.35 N	15.15 E
Lindesnäs	40	60.20 N	14.32 E
Lindesnes >	26	58.00 N	7.02 E
Lindfield, Austl.	274a	33.47 S	151.10 E
Lindfield, Eng., U.K.	42	51.01 N	0.05 W
Lindfors	40	59.36 N	13.49 E
Lindholmen	40	59.35 N	18.06 E
Lindhorst	52	52.21 N	9.17 E
Líndhos	38	36.06 N	28.04 E
Líndhos ⊥	38	36.06 N	28.05 E
Lindi	154	10.00 S	39.43 E
Lindi □[4]	154	9.15 S	38.45 E
Lindi ≃	154	0.33 N	25.05 E
Lindian	89	47.11 N	124.52 E
Lindis Pass)(	172	44.36 S	169.40 E
Lindkirchen	60	48.40 N	11.47 E
Lindlar	56	51.01 N	7.23 E
Lindley, S. Afr.	158	28.00 S	27.57 E
Lindley, N.Y., U.S.	210	42.02 N	77.08 W
Lind National Park ♠	166	37.35 S	149.05 E
Lindö	40	58.37 N	16.15 E
Lindóia	256	22.31 S	46.39 W
Lindome	26	57.34 N	12.05 E
Lindon	198	39.44 N	103.24 W
Lindong, Zhg.	100	26.03 N	118.49 E
Lindong, Zhg.	105	39.51 N	117.41 E
Lindow	54	52.58 N	13.00 E
Lind Point >	240m	18.20 N	64.48 W
Lindre, Étang de ⊜[1]	56	48.47 N	6.45 E
Lindsay, On., Can.	212	44.21 N	78.44 W
Lindsay, Ca., U.S.	204	36.12 N	119.05 W
Lindsay, Ne., U.S.	198	41.42 N	97.41 W
Lindsay, Ok., U.S.	196	34.50 N	97.36 W
Lindsborg	198	38.34 N	97.40 W
Lindsey	214	41.25 N	83.13 W
Lindved	41	55.47 N	9.35 E
Lindy Lake	276	41.05 N	74.22 W
Lineboro	208	39.43 N	76.50 W
Line Creek ≃	194	33.34 N	88.42 W
Line Islands II	14	0.05 N	157.00 W
Line Lexington	208	40.17 N	75.16 W
Line Mountain Λ	210	40.45 N	76.37 W
Linesville	214	41.39 N	80.25 W
Lineville, Al., U.S.	194	33.18 N	85.45 W
Lineville, Ia., U.S.	190	40.34 N	93.31 W
Línevo	86	54.05 N	83.24 E
Linfen	102	36.05 N	111.32 E
Linfield	208	40.13 N	75.34 W
Linford	260	51.29 N	0.25 E
Ling ≃	46	57.19 N	5.27 W
Ling'an	106	30.36 N	120.30 E
Linganamakki Reservoir ⊜[1]	122	14.04 N	74.54 E
Lingao	102	19.54 N	109.40 E
Lingayen	116	16.01 N	120.14 E
Lingayen Gulf c	116	16.15 N	120.14 E
Lingbi	100	33.33 N	117.33 E
Lingbo	26	61.03 N	16.41 E
Lingchuan, Zhg.	102	25.26 N	110.15 E
Lingchuan, Zhg.	102	35.46 N	113.26 E
Lingda	106	31.12 N	119.18 E
Lingdale	44	54.32 N	0.57 W
Lingdianzhen	106	31.51 N	121.25 E
Lingdou	100	26.22 N	118.56 E
Lingen	52	52.31 N	7.19 E
Lingesestausee ⊜[1]	263	51.06 N	7.32 E
Lingfengwei	100	24.44 N	115.35 E
Lingfield	42	51.11 N	0.01 W
Lingga, Kepulauan II	112	0.05 S	104.35 E
Lingga, Pulau I	112	0.12 S	104.35 E
Lingham Lake ⊜	212	44.46 N	77.25 W
Linghe	98	36.23 N	119.03 E
Linghu	106	30.44 N	120.10 E
Lingig	116	8.02 N	126.24 E
Lingjiachang	107	29.28 N	104.54 E
Lingjiaqiao	106	30.09 N	120.04 E
Lingkar Dzong	124	28.45 N	90.36 E
Lingkou, Zhg.	100	29.16 N	120.38 E
Lingkou, Zhg.	106	31.57 N	119.38 E
Lingle	200	42.08 N	104.20 W
Linglestown	208	40.21 N	76.48 W
Lingling	102	26.13 N	111.37 E
Linglongta	98	40.54 N	119.59 E
Lingma	102	23.22 N	107.53 E
Lingolsheim	58	48.34 N	7.41 E
Lingomo	152	0.38 N	21.59 E
Lingqiu	98	39.24 N	114.13 E
Lingshan, Zhg.	98	36.33 N	120.27 E
Lingshan, Zhg.	102	22.28 N	109.17 E
Lingshanwei	98	35.58 N	120.13 E
Lingshi	102	36.54 N	111.43 E
Lingshou	98	38.18 N	114.24 E
Lingshui	110	18.31 N	110.01 E
Lingtangqiao	100	32.43 N	119.14 E
Linguaglossa	70	37.50 N	15.08 E
Linguère	150	15.24 N	15.07 W
Lingwala	273b	4.22 S	15.17 E
Lingwood	42	52.37 N	1.29 E
Lingwu	102	38.06 N	106.21 E
Lingxian, Zhg.	98	37.21 N	116.34 E
Lingxian, Zhg.	100	26.30 N	113.46 E
Lingxiazhu	100	29.03 N	119.46 E
Lingyuan	98	41.15 N	119.16 E
Lingzhuangzi	105	39.04 N	117.09 E
Lingzinan	105	39.29 N	115.15 E
Linh, Ngoc Λ	110	15.04 N	107.59 E
Linhai	100	28.51 N	121.07 E
Linhares	255	19.25 S	40.04 W
Linh Cam	110	18.31 N	105.34 E
Linhe	102	40.51 N	107.30 E
Linhezhuang	105	40.04 N	117.39 E
Linhigh	284b	39.21 N	76.31 W
Linhó	266c	38.46 N	9.23 W
Linhsia → Linxia	102	35.35 N	103.13 E
Linhuaiguan	100	32.55 N	117.40 E
Linhuanji	100	33.42 N	116.33 E
Lini → Linyi	98	35.04 N	118.22 E
Linjiang, Zhg.	98	41.44 N	126.55 E
Linjiang, Zhg.	100	27.50 N	118.26 E
Linjiang, Zhg.	100	28.04 N	115.21 E
Linjiang, Zhg.	102	33.01 N	105.01 E
Linjiangchang	107	29.14 N	105.58 E
Linjianghu	100	28.41 N	117.54 E
Linjiangsi	107	30.15 N	104.37 E
Linjiatai	104	40.43 N	123.57 E
Linkenheim	56	49.07 N	8.24 E
Linköping	26	58.25 N	15.37 E
Linkou	89	45.15 N	130.16 E
Linksfield ◆[8]	273d	26.10 S	28.06 E
Linksmakalnis	76	54.45 N	23.55 E
Linksness	46	58.56 N	3.19 W
Linkuva	76	56.05 N	23.59 E
Linkwood	208	38.32 N	75.57 W
Linli	102	29.18 N	111.30 E
Linlithgow	46	55.59 N	3.37 W
Linmeyer	273d	26.16 S	28.04 E
Linn, Ks., U.S.	198	39.40 N	97.05 W
Linn, Mo., U.S.	219	38.29 N	91.51 W
Linn ◆[8]	263	51.20 N	6.38 E
Linnancang	105	39.50 N	117.37 E
Linnansaaren kansallispuisto ♠	26	62.07 N	28.31 E
Linndale	279a	41.27 N	81.46 W
Linne	52	51.10 N	5.57 E
Linnell	226	36.21 N	119.11 W
Linnés Hammarby ⊥	40	59.49 N	17.46 E
Linn Grove	216	40.38 N	85.01 W
Linnhe, Loch c	46	56.39 N	5.21 W
Linnich	56	50.59 N	6.16 E
Linntown	210	40.58 N	76.54 W
Linnville Bayou ≃	222	28.57 N	95.42 W
Linosa	70a	35.51 N	12.52 E
Linosa, Isola di I	70a	35.51 N	12.52 E
Linovica	78	50.28 N	32.22 E
Lin'ovo	80	50.53 N	44.51 E
Linow	54	53.06 N	12.49 E
Linping → Yuhang	106	30.25 N	120.18 E
Linpu	100	30.03 N	120.15 E
Linqi, Zhg.	98	35.48 N	113.53 E
Linqi, Zhg.	100	29.51 N	119.06 E
Linqing	98	36.53 N	115.41 E
Linqu	98	36.32 N	118.31 E
Linquan	100	33.06 N	115.13 E
Linru	100	34.11 N	112.49 E
Linruzhen	100	34.17 N	112.35 E
Lins	255	21.40 S	49.45 W
Linshan	100	30.09 N	120.59 E
Linshanhe	100	30.44 N	114.52 E
Linshengpu	104	41.34 N	123.20 E
Linshui	102	30.21 N	106.59 E
Linslade	42	51.55 N	0.41 W
Linstead	241q	18.08 N	77.02 W
Linta ≃	157b	25.02 S	44.05 E
Lintan	102	34.37 N	103.40 E
Lintao	102	35.27 N	103.46 E
Linté	152	5.24 N	11.42 E
Linth ≃	58	47.07 N	9.07 E
Linthal, Fr.	58	47.56 N	7.08 E
Linthal, Schw.	58	46.55 N	9.00 E
Linthicum Heights	284b	39.12 N	76.39 W
Linthkanal ≊	58	47.13 N	8.57 E
Linthwaite	262	53.37 N	1.51 W
Lintingkou	105	39.39 N	117.30 E
Linton, Austl.	169	37.41 S	143.34 E
Linton, N.Z.	172	40.26 S	175.33 E
Linton, Eng., U.K.	42	52.06 N	0.17 E
Linton, Eng., U.K.	260	51.13 N	0.31 E
Linton, In., U.S.	194	39.02 N	87.09 W
Linton, N.D., U.S.	198	46.16 N	100.13 W
Lintong	102	34.21 N	109.11 E
Linton Park ♠	260	51.13 N	0.31 E
Linum	264a	52.46 N	12.53 E
Linville, Austl.	171a	26.51 S	152.16 E
Linville, N.C., U.S.	192	36.03 N	81.52 W
Linwood, Austl.	168b	34.21 S	138.46 E
Linwood, In., U.S.	218	40.12 N	85.41 W
Linwood, Ma., U.S.	207	42.05 N	71.38 W
Linwood, N.J., U.S.	208	39.20 N	74.34 W
Linwood, Pa., U.S.	285	39.49 N	75.24 W
Linworth	214	40.06 N	83.04 W
Linwu, Zhg.	98	36.14 N	119.17 E
Linwu, Zhg.	102	25.16 N	112.20 E
Linxi, Zhg.	90	43.30 N	118.00 E
Linxi, Zhg.	98	36.52 N	115.32 E
Linxia	102	35.35 N	103.13 E
Linxian, Zhg.	98	36.04 N	113.50 E
Linxian, Zhg.	102	37.58 N	110.59 E
Linxiang	100	29.28 N	113.30 E
Linyanti	156	18.04 S	24.01 E
Linyanti ≃	156	17.58 S	24.16 E
Linyi, Zhg.	98	35.04 N	118.22 E
Linyi, Zhg.	98	37.13 N	116.51 E
Linyi, Zhg.	102	35.15 N	110.59 E
Linying	100	33.50 N	113.57 E
Linyüan	100	22.30 N	120.23 E
Linyü → Shanhaiguan	98	40.01 N	119.44 E
Linz, Dtsch.	56	50.34 N	7.17 E
Linz, Öst.	61	48.18 N	14.18 E
Linze, Zhg.	100	33.03 N	119.38 E
Linze, Zhg.	102	39.19 N	100.17 E
Linzgau ◆[1]	58	47.45 N	9.16 E
Linzhai	100	24.18 N	115.03 E
Linzhang	98	36.21 N	114.36 E
Linzhi	120	29.25 N	94.22 E
Linzikou	100	28.42 N	112.46 E
Linzolo	152	4.25 S	15.07 E
Lioko, Zaïre	152	0.02 N	22.04 E
Lioko, Zaïre	152	1.25 N	23.07 E
Lio Matoh	112	3.10 N	115.14 E
Liomer	50	49.51 N	1.49 E
Lion, Golfe du c	32	43.00 N	4.00 E
Lionel Town	241q	17.48 N	77.14 W
Lioni	68	40.52 N	15.11 E
Lion Rock Λ[2]	271d	22.22 N	114.11 E
Lion Rock Tunnel ◆[5]	271d	22.21 N	114.09 E
Lions Den	154	17.16 S	30.02 E
Lion's Head	212	44.59 N	81.15 W
Lionville	208	40.03 N	75.39 W
Lioppa	112	7.40 S	126.00 E
Liouesso	152	1.02 N	15.43 E
Liozno	76	55.02 N	30.48 E
Lipa	116	13.57 N	121.10 E
Lipan	196	32.31 N	98.03 W
Lipany	30	49.10 N	20.58 E
Lipari	70	38.28 N	14.57 E
Lipari, Isola I	70	38.29 N	14.56 E
Lipatkain	112	0.01 S	101.13 E
Lipayan	104	42.13 N	123.23 E
Lipcy	78	50.13 N	36.25 E
Lipeck	76	52.37 N	39.35 E
Lipeck Oblast' □[4]	76	52.30 N	39.00 E
Lipeckoje Vtoroje	78	47.46 N	29.41 E
Liperi	26	62.32 N	29.22 E
Lipetsk → Lipeck	76	52.37 N	39.35 E
Lipez, Cerro Λ	248	21.53 S	66.52 W
Liphook	42	51.05 N	0.49 W
Lipiany	30	53.00 N	14.59 E
Lipicy	76	53.22 N	37.17 E
Lipin Bor	76	60.16 N	37.57 E
Liping	102	26.17 N	109.00 E
Lipis ≃	114	4.10 N	102.04 E
Lipiyu	104	41.09 N	123.36 E
Lipka ≃	265b	55.45 N	37.11 E
Lipkany	78	48.16 N	26.48 E
Lipki	76	53.58 N	37.42 E
Lipník nad Bečvou	30	49.31 N	17.35 E
Lipniški	76	54.00 N	25.37 E
Lipno	30	52.51 N	19.10 E
Lipno, údolní Nádrž ⊜[1]	61	48.43 N	14.04 E
Lipno nad Vltavou	61	48.38 N	14.14 E
Lipoa Point >	229a	21.02 N	156.38 W
Lipova	38	46.05 N	21.40 E
Lipovaja Dolina	78	50.35 N	33.48 E
Lipovcy	89	44.11 N	131.44 E
Lipovec	78	49.14 N	29.03 E
Lipovka, Ross.	78	50.52 N	40.02 E
Lipovka, Ross.	80	52.26 N	46.11 E
Lipovka, Ross.	80	49.46 N	44.56 E
Lippborg	52	51.40 N	8.02 E
Lippe ≃	52	51.39 N	6.38 E
Lipperode	52	51.41 N	8.22 E
Lippetal	52	51.40 N	8.06 E
Lippoldsberg	52	51.37 N	9.33 E
Lippstadt	52	51.40 N	8.19 E
Lipscomb	196	36.14 N	100.16 W
Lipsko	30	51.09 N	21.39 E
Lipsoí I, Ellás	38	37.20 N	26.45 E
Lipsoí I, Ellás	130	37.20 N	26.45 E
Lipton	184	50.54 N	103.50 W
Liptovská Teplička	30	48.59 N	20.06 E
Liptovský Mikuláš	30	49.06 N	19.37 E
Liptrap, Cape >	166	38.54 S	145.55 E
Lipu	102	24.25 N	110.29 E
Lipu La)(	124	30.21 N	81.05 E
Liqiao	107	29.03 N	104.48 E
Lira, Ug.	154	2.15 N	32.54 E
Lira, Ven.	286c	10.26 N	66.46 W
Liranga	152	0.40 S	17.36 E
Lirangdian	105	39.14 N	116.14 E
Lircay	248	12.56 S	74.43 W
Liren	100	33.55 N	118.47 E
Lirentuncun	104	41.24 N	122.59 E
Liri ≃	66	41.25 N	13.52 E
Liro	175f	16.27 S	168.13 E
Liro ≃	58	46.18 N	9.23 E
Lisakovsk	86	52.36 N	62.37 E
Lisala	152	2.09 N	21.31 E
Lisavy	82	56.33 N	38.32 E
Lisboa (Lisbon), Port.	34	38.43 N	9.08 W
Lisboa (Lisbon), Port.	266c	38.43 N	9.08 W
Lisboa □[5]	266c	38.48 N	9.16 W
Lisbon, Il., U.S.	216	41.29 N	88.29 W
Lisbon, Md., U.S.	208	39.20 N	77.04 W
Lisbon, N.H., U.S.	188	44.12 N	71.54 W
Lisbon, N.D., U.S.	198	46.26 N	97.40 W
Lisbon, Oh., U.S.	214	40.46 N	80.46 W
Lisbon Falls	188	43.59 N	70.03 W
Lisbon → Lisboa	34	38.43 N	9.08 W
Lisbonne → Lisboa	34	38.43 N	9.08 W
Lisburn	48	54.31 N	6.03 W
Lisburne, Cape >	180	68.52 N	166.14 W
Lisburne Peninsula >[1]	180	68.30 N	165.15 W
Liscannor Bay c	48	52.55 N	9.25 W
Liscarney	48	53.43 N	9.35 W
Liscia ≃	71	41.11 N	9.19 E
Liscia, Lago di ⊜	71	41.00 N	9.16 E
Lisdoonvarna	48	53.01 N	9.15 W
Lisec	78	48.52 N	24.36 E
Liseleje	41	56.01 N	11.59 E
Lishan, Zhg.	100	31.50 N	113.16 E
Lishan, Zhg.	104	41.10 N	123.00 E
Lishangzhuang	105	39.35 N	118.11 E
Lishanke	98	40.41 N	119.53 E
Lishe	100	29.48 N	121.28 E
Lishe ≃	102	24.18 N	101.32 E
Lishi, Zhg.	102	37.32 N	111.09 E
Lishi, Zhg.	106	31.14 N	120.37 E
Lishi, Zhg.	107	29.10 N	105.42 E
Lishizhen, Zhg.	107	29.04 N	106.15 E
Lishizhen, Zhg.	107	29.20 N	105.24 E
Lishu	89	43.21 N	124.37 E
Lishui, Zhg.	100	28.27 N	119.54 E
Lishui, Zhg.	106	31.39 N	119.01 E
Lishuzhen	89	45.05 N	130.41 E
Lisianski Island I	14	26.02 N	174.00 W
Lisica ≃	86	58.34 N	85.11 E
Lisičansk	83	48.55 N	38.26 E
Lisichansk → Lisičansk	83	48.55 N	38.26 E
Lisicy	82	56.47 N	36.21 E
Lisieux, Sk., Can.	184	49.17 N	105.59 W
Lisieux, Fr.	50	49.09 N	0.14 E
Lisij Nos	265a	60.01 N	30.00 E
Líšina	60	49.37 N	13.10 E
Lisitu	154	9.39 S	34.39 E
Lisizhuang	105	38.55 N	115.07 E
Lisja	80	57.15 N	54.22 E
Liska ≃	80	48.32 N	43.08 E
Liskeard	42	50.28 N	4.28 W
Liski, Ross.	78	50.56 N	39.29 E
Liski, Ross.	78	50.59 N	39.30 E
Lískova	60	49.25 N	12.43 E
L'Isle, Schw.	58	46.37 N	6.25 E
Lisle, Il., U.S.	216	41.48 N	88.04 W
Lisle, N.Y., U.S.	210	42.21 N	76.00 W
L'Isle-Adam	50	49.07 N	2.14 E
L'Isle Jourdain	32	46.14 N	0.41 E
L'Isle-sur-la-Sorgue	62	43.55 N	5.03 E
L'Isle-sur-le-Doubs	58	47.27 N	6.35 E
L'Isle-sur-Serein	50	47.35 N	4.00 E
Lisman	194	32.10 N	88.16 W
Lismore, Austl.	166	28.48 S	153.17 E
Lismore, Austl.	169	37.58 S	143.20 E
Lismore, N.S., Can.	186	45.42 N	62.16 W
Lismore, Ire.	48	52.08 N	7.55 W
Lismore Castle ⊥	48	52.08 N	7.52 W
Lismore Island I	46	56.29 N	5.33 W
Lisnaskea	48	54.15 N	7.27 W
Lišn'ovka	78	51.28 N	25.25 E
Lisö >[1]	40	58.55 N	17.45 E
Lišov	61	49.01 N	14.37 E
Liss	42	51.03 N	0.55 W
Lissabon → Lisboa	34	38.43 N	9.08 W
Lissberg	56	50.22 N	9.05 E
Lisse	52	52.15 N	4.33 E
Lisses	261	48.36 N	2.26 E
Lissewege	50	51.18 N	3.11 E
Lissie	222	29.33 N	96.13 W
Lissingen	56	50.14 N	6.38 E
Lissone	62	45.37 N	9.14 E
Lissy	261	48.38 N	2.42 E
Lista	80	47.44 N	45.54 E
Lista >[1]	26	58.07 N	6.40 E
Lister ≃	263	51.05 N	7.45 E
Lištica	36	43.23 N	17.36 E
Listowel, On., Can.	212	43.44 N	80.57 W
Listowel, Ire.	48	52.27 N	9.29 W
Listv'anka	88	51.52 N	104.51 E
Listv'anskij	86	54.27 N	83.29 E
Lisui	105	40.05 N	116.44 E
Lit	26	63.19 N	14.49 E
Lita	100	27.22 N	116.34 E
Litang, Malay.	112	5.20 N	118.31 E
Litang, Zhg.	102	23.11 N	109.05 E
Litang, Zhg.	102	30.00 N	100.16 E
Litang ≃	102	28.04 N	101.30 E
Litani ≃	250	3.40 N	54.00 W
Līṭānī, Nahr al- ≃	132	33.20 N	35.14 E
Litava ≃	61	49.02 N	16.36 E
Litcham	42	52.44 N	0.47 E
Litchfield, Ct., U.S.	207	41.44 N	73.11 W
Litchfield, Il., U.S.	219	39.10 N	89.39 W
Litchfield, Mi., U.S.	216	42.02 N	84.45 W
Litchfield, Mn., U.S.	190	45.07 N	94.31 W
Litchfield, Ne., U.S.	198	41.09 N	99.09 W
Litchfield, Oh., U.S.	214	41.10 N	82.02 W
Litchfield □[6]	207	41.45 N	73.11 W
Litchfield Park	200	33.29 N	112.21 W
Litchville	198	46.39 N	98.11 W
Literberry	219	39.51 N	90.12 W
Līth, Wādī al- V	144	20.40 N	40.35 E
Litherland	44	53.28 N	2.59 W
Lithgow	170	33.29 S	150.09 E
Lithia	220	27.51 N	82.10 W
Líthinon, Ákra >	38	34.55 N	24.44 E
Lithonia	192	33.42 N	84.06 W
Lithuania (Lietuva) □[1], Europe	22	56.00 N	24.00 E
Lithuania (Lietuva) □[1], Europe	76	56.00 N	24.00 E
Litian	100	26.58 N	114.10 E
Litija	36	46.03 N	14.50 E
Litin	78	49.20 N	28.05 E
Litipāra	124	24.42 N	87.37 E
Lititz	208	40.09 N	76.18 W
Litke	89	53.57 N	140.15 E
Litókhoron	38	40.06 N	22.30 E
Litoko	154	1.13 S	24.47 E
Litoměřice	54	50.35 N	14.09 E
Litomyšl	30	49.52 N	16.19 E
Litoo	154	9.54 S	38.24 E
Litouqiao	106	31.15 N	118.54 E
Litovel	30	49.42 N	17.05 E
Litovko	89	49.15 N	135.11 E
Litschau	61	48.57 N	15.03 E
Littau	58	47.03 N	8.16 E
Little ≃, Austl.	169	38.01 S	144.35 E
Little ≃, On., Can.	281	42.20 N	82.56 W
Little ≃, U.S.	194	33.37 N	93.52 W
Little ≃, U.S.	194	35.32 N	90.25 W
Little ≃, Al., U.S.	194	31.18 N	87.46 W
Little ≃, Al., U.S.	194	34.16 N	85.40 W
Little ≃, Ct., U.S.	207	41.36 N	72.03 W
Little ≃, Ga., U.S.	192	33.14 N	83.24 W
Little ≃, Ga., U.S.	192	30.51 N	83.21 W
Little ≃, Ga., U.S.	192	33.39 N	82.32 W
Little ≃, In., U.S.	216	40.53 N	85.32 W
Little ≃, Ky., U.S.	194	36.51 N	87.58 W
Little ≃, La., U.S.	194	31.38 N	91.49 W
Little ≃, Ma., U.S.	283	42.37 N	70.42 W
Little ≃, Ma., U.S.	283	42.46 N	70.51 W
Little ≃, N.Y., U.S.	210	43.18 N	75.43 W
Little ≃, N.C., U.S.	192	35.15 N	78.42 W
Little ≃, N.C., U.S.	192	35.21 N	78.02 W
Little ≃, Ok., U.S.	196	35.00 N	96.25 W
Little ≃, S.C., U.S.	192	34.10 N	81.11 W
Little ≃, S.C., U.S.	192	33.56 N	82.25 W
Little ≃, S.C., U.S.	192	34.11 N	81.45 W
Little ≃, Tn., U.S.	192	35.51 N	83.57 W
Little ≃, Tx., U.S.	222	30.51 N	96.41 W
Little ≃, Va., U.S.	192	37.05 N	80.32 W
Little ≃, Va., U.S.	208	37.49 N	77.26 W
Little, Mountain Fork ≃	194	33.57 N	94.34 W
Little Abaco I	238	26.53 N	77.43 W
Little Alfold ≃	61	47.30 N	17.00 E
Little Amwell	260	51.47 N	0.02 W
Little Andaman I	110	10.45 N	92.30 E
Little Arkansas ≃	198	37.43 N	97.22 W
Little Auglaize ≃	216	41.07 N	84.25 W
Little Averill Lake ⊜	206	44.57 N	71.44 W
Little Baddow	260	51.44 N	0.35 E
Little Barrier Island I	172	36.12 S	175.05 E
Little Bay	186	47.41 N	58.24 W
Little Bay c	276	40.48 N	73.47 W
Little Bay Islands	186	49.39 N	55.47 W
Little Bear ≃	200	41.42 N	111.57 W
Little Bear Creek ≃	196	37.43 N	101.43 W
Little Bear Creek Reservoir ⊜[1]	194	34.25 N	87.57 W
Little Beaver Creek ≃, U.S.	198	46.17 N	103.56 W
Little Beaver Creek ≃, U.S.	198	39.49 N	101.03 W
Little Beaver Creek ≃, U.S.	214	40.38 N	80.31 W
Little Beaver Creek ≃, Wa., U.S.	224	48.54 N	121.06 W
Little Beaver Creek, Middle Fork ≃	214	40.43 N	80.37 W
Little Beaver Creek, North Fork ≃	214	40.43 N	80.33 W
Little Beaver Creek, West Fork ≃	214	40.43 N	80.37 W
Little Belt → Lillebælt Ʉ	41	55.20 N	9.45 E
Little Belt Mountains ⩘	202	46.45 N	110.35 W
Little Berkhamsted	260	51.45 N	0.08 W
Little Bighorn ≃	202	45.44 N	107.34 W
Little Billabong	171b	35.35 S	147.32 E
Little Bitter Lake → Murrah aṣ-Ṣughrā, Al-Buḥayrah al- ⊜	142	30.13 N	32.33 E
Little Bitterroot ≃	202	47.30 N	114.19 W
Little Black ≃, U.S.	194	36.25 N	90.45 W
Little Black ≃, Ak., U.S.	180	66.26 N	143.49 W
Little Black Bear Indian Reserve ◆[4]	184	51.00 N	103.23 W
Little Blackfoot ≃	202	46.31 N	112.48 W
Little Blue ≃, U.S.	198	39.41 N	96.40 W
Little Blue ≃, In., U.S.	218	39.32 N	85.46 W
Littleborough	44	53.39 N	2.05 W
Little Bow ≃	182	49.53 N	112.29 W
Little Brazos ≃	222	30.38 N	96.31 W
Little Brokenstraw Creek ≃	214	41.50 N	79.23 W
Little Brosna ≃	48	53.10 N	8.05 W
Little Buffalo ≃	176	61.00 N	113.46 W
Little Bullhead	184	51.40 N	96.51 W
Little Burstead	260	51.36 N	0.24 E
Little Calumet ≃	278	41.39 N	87.34 W
Little Catalina	186	48.33 N	53.02 W
Little Cayman I	238	19.41 N	80.03 W
Little Cedar ≃	190	42.57 N	92.31 W
Little Chalfont	260	51.40 N	0.34 W
Little Chartiers Creek ≃	279b	40.17 N	80.08 W
Little Choptank River c	208	38.32 N	76.13 W
Little Churchill ≃	184	57.15 N	95.21 W
Little Chute	190	44.16 N	88.19 W
Little Coco Island I	110	14.00 N	93.13 E
Little Colorado ≃	200	36.11 N	111.48 W
Little Compton	207	41.30 N	71.10 W
Little Cooley	214	41.44 N	79.53 W
Little Cottonwood ≃	198	44.15 N	94.20 W
Little Creek	208	39.10 N	75.26 W
Little Creek ≃	285	39.56 N	74.48 W
Little Creek Naval Amphibious Base ■	208	36.55 N	76.10 W
Little Creek Reservoir ⊜[1]	208	37.20 N	76.50 W
Little Cumbrae Island I	46	55.43 N	4.57 W
Little Current	190	45.58 N	81.56 W
Little Current ≃	176	50.57 N	84.36 W
Little Cypress Bayou ≃	194	32.41 N	94.15 W
Little Cypress Creek ≃	222	32.39 N	94.42 W
Little Darby Creek ≃	218	39.53 N	83.13 W
Little Dart ≃	42	50.54 N	3.51 W
Little Deep Creek ≃	198	48.35 N	100.52 W
Little Deer Creek ≃, In., U.S.	216	40.36 N	86.28 W
Little Deer Creek ≃, Pa., U.S.	279b	40.33 N	79.50 W
Little Deschutes ≃	202	43.51 N	121.27 W
Little Desert ◆[2]	166	36.35 S	141.20 E
Little Desert National Park ♠	166	36.25 S	141.25 E
Little Diomede Island I	180	65.45 N	168.57 W
Little Don ≃	275b	43.42 N	79.20 W
Little Dry Creek ≃, Ca., U.S.	226	39.22 N	121.52 W
Little Dry Creek ≃, Mt., U.S.	202	47.21 N	106.22 W
Little Ease Run ≃	285	39.39 N	75.04 W
Little Eau Pleine ≃	190	44.40 N	89.41 W
Little Egg Harbor c	208	39.35 N	74.18 W
Little Elkhart ≃	216	41.43 N	85.49 W
Little End	260	51.41 N	0.14 E
Little Etobicoke Creek ≃	275b	43.37 N	79.34 W
Little Exuma I	238	23.27 N	75.37 W
Little Fabius ≃	219	39.59 N	91.59 W
Little Falls, Mn., U.S.	190	45.58 N	94.21 W
Little Falls, N.J., U.S.	276	40.52 N	74.12 W
Little Falls, N.Y., U.S.	210	43.02 N	74.51 W
Little Falls ≃	208	39.36 N	76.38 W
Little Falls Dam ◆[6]	284c	38.57 N	77.08 W
Little Farms	218	39.57 N	83.10 W
Little Ferry	276	40.51 N	74.02 W
Littlefield	196	33.55 N	102.19 W
Little Flatrock ≃	218	39.26 N	85.33 W
Littlefork	190	48.23 N	93.33 W
Little Fork ≃	190	48.31 N	93.35 W
Little Fort	182	51.25 N	120.12 W
Little Genesee	210	42.02 N	78.13 W
Little Gold ≃	162	18.01 S	126.29 E
Little Gunpowder Falls ≃	208	39.23 N	76.22 W
Littlehampton	42	50.48 N	0.33 W
Little Harbour Deep	186	50.15 N	56.33 W
Little Haw Creek ≃	192	29.23 N	81.24 W
Little Hawk Lake ⊜	212	45.10 N	78.42 W
Little Hoosic ≃	210	42.49 N	73.20 W
Little Hope	214	42.06 N	79.49 W
Little Hulton	262	53.32 N	2.25 W
Little Humboldt ≃	204	41.00 N	117.43 W
Little Humboldt, North Fork ≃	204	41.24 N	117.10 W
Little Humboldt, South Fork ≃	204	41.24 N	117.10 W
Little Hurricane Creek ≃	192	31.23 N	82.19 W
Little Inagua I	238	21.30 N	73.00 W
Little Indian Creek ≃, Il., U.S.	216	41.31 N	88.46 W
Little Indian Creek ≃, In., U.S.	218	38.12 N	86.08 W
Little Island Pond ⊜	283	42.43 N	71.17 W
Littlejohns Creek ≃	226	37.52 N	121.14 W
Little Juniata ≃	214	40.34 N	78.03 W
Little Juniata Creek ≃	208	40.23 N	77.02 W
Little Kanawha ≃	188	39.16 N	81.34 W
Little Kanawha, West Fork ≃	188	38.57 N	81.16 W
Little Karroo (Klein Karroo) ⩘[1]	158	33.45 S	21.30 E
Little Kentucky ≃	218	38.41 N	85.12 W
Little Klickitat ≃	224	45.51 N	121.04 W
Little Koniuji Island I	180	55.01 N	159.26 W
Little Lake ⊜, On., Can.	212	44.26 N	79.40 W
Little Lake ⊜, La., U.S.	194	29.30 N	90.10 W
Little Laramie ≃	200	41.28 N	105.44 W
Little Laver	260	51.46 N	0.14 E
Little Leigh	262	53.17 N	2.35 W
Little Lever	262	53.34 N	2.22 W
Little Limestone Lake ⊜	184	53.46 N	99.18 W
Little London	241q	18.15 N	78.13 W
Little Lost ≃	202	43.46 N	112.58 W
Little Lun ≃	116	6.02 N	125.17 E
Little Mahoning Creek ≃	214	40.49 N	79.00 W
Little Maitland ≃	212	43.52 N	81.18 W
Little Manatee ≃	220	27.42 N	82.28 W
Little Manatee, South Fork ≃	220	27.39 N	82.18 W
Little Manistee ≃	190	44.15 N	86.19 W
Little Manitou Lake ⊜	184	51.45 N	105.30 W
Little Marco Pass c	220	26.01 N	81.46 W
Little Marsh	210	41.53 N	77.24 W
Little Meadows	210	41.59 N	76.08 W
Little Mecatina ≃	176	50.28 N	59.35 W
Little Medicine Bow ≃	200	41.58 N	106.18 W
Little Mexico	196	30.57 N	102.52 W
Little Miami ≃	218	39.05 N	84.26 W
Little Miami, East Fork ≃	218	39.09 N	84.18 W
Little Miami, North Fork ≃	218	39.48 N	83.47 W
Littlemill	46	57.32 N	3.49 W
Little Mississippi ≃	212	45.17 N	77.35 W
Little Missouri ≃, U.S.	198	47.30 N	102.25 W
Little Missouri ≃, Ar., U.S.	194	33.49 N	92.54 W
Little Mountain Λ	208	40.47 N	76.40 W
Little Muddy ≃, Il., U.S.	194	37.50 N	89.11 W
Little Muddy ≃, N.D., U.S.	198	48.12 N	103.36 W
Little Mulberry Creek ≃	194	32.26 N	86.51 W
Little Naches ≃	224	46.58 N	121.08 W

≃ River	Fluß	Río	Rivière	Rio
≊ Canal	Kanal	Canal	Canal	Canal
∟ Waterfall, Rapids	Wasserfall, Stromschnellen	Cascada, Rápidos	Chute d'eau, Rapides	Cascata, Rápidos
Ʉ Strait	Meeresstraße	Estrecho	Détroit	Estreito
c Bay, Gulf	Bucht, Golf	Bahía, Golfo	Baie, Golfe	Baía, Golfo
⊜ Lake, Lakes	See, Seen	Lago, Lagos	Lac, Lacs	Lago, Lagos
≡ Swamp	Sumpf	Pantano	Marais	Pântano
⊓ Ice Features, Glacier	Eis- und Gletscherformen	Accidentes Glaciales	Formes glaciaires	Acidentes glaciares
⊤ Other Hydrographic Features	Andere Hydrographische Objekte	Otros Elementos Hidrográficos	Autres données hydrographiques	Outros acidentes hidrográficos

✣ Submarine Features	Untermeerische Objekte	Accidentes Submarinos	Formes de relief sous-marin	Acidentes submarinos
□ Political Unit	Politische Einheit	Unidad Politica	Entité politique	Unidade política
ʊ Cultural Institution	Kulturelle Institution	Institución Cultural	Institution culturelle	Instituição cultural
⊥ Historical Site	Historische Stätte	Sitio Histórico	Site historique	Sitio histórico
♠ Recreational Site	Erholungs- und Ferienort	Sitio de Recreo	Centre de loisirs	Area de Lazer
⊠ Airport	Flughafen	Aeropuerto	Aéroport	Aeroporto
■ Military Installation	Militäranlage	Instalación Militar	Installation militaire	Instalação militar
◆ Miscellaneous	Verschiedenes	Misceláneo	Divers	Diversos

ENGLISH

DEUTSCH

Name	Page	Lat.°′	Long.°′
Little Nahant	283	42.25 N	70.56 W
Little Namaqualand □[9]	156	29.00 S	17.00 E
Little Neck	283	42.42 N	70.48 W
Little Neck ◆[8]	276	40.46 N	73.44 W
Little Neck Bay c	276	40.47 N	73.46 W
Little Nemaha ≃	198	40.19 N	95.40 W
Little Neshaminy Creek ≃	285	40.15 N	75.02 W
Little Niangua ≃	194	38.04 N	92.54 W
Little Nicobar I	110	7.20 N	93.40 E
Little Ohoopee ≃	192	32.27 N	82.24 W
Little Osage ≃	194	38.02 N	94.14 W
Little Otter Creek ≃	212	42.44 N	80.51 W
Little Ouse ≃	42	52.30 N	0.22 E
Little Panoche Creek ≃	226	36.50 N	120.42 W
Little Patuxent ≃	284b	39.11 N	76.52 W
Little Paxton	42	52.15 N	0.15 W
Little Peconic Bay c	207	40.59 N	72.24 W
Little Pee Dee ≃	192	33.42 N	79.11 W
Little Pic ≃	190	48.48 N	86.37 W
Little Pine and Lucky Man Indian Reserve ◆[4]	184	52.56 N	109.05 W
Little Pine Creek ≃, Pa., U.S.	210	41.18 N	77.22 W
Little Pine Creek ≃, Pa., U.S.	279b	40.31 N	79.57 W
Little Pine Island I	220	26.36 N	82.05 W
Little Pine Key I	220	24.44 N	81.19 W
Little Pine State Park ♠	210	41.22 N	77.20 W
Little Pipe Creek ≃	208	39.36 N	77.16 W
Little Platte ≃	194	39.24 N	94.41 W
Little Plum Creek ≃	279b	40.30 N	79.51 W
Little Popo Aggie ≃	202	42.54 N	108.35 W
Little Porcupine Creek ≃, Mt., U.S.	202	46.18 N	106.34 W
Little Porcupine Creek ≃, Mt., U.S.	202	48.02 N	106.04 W
Littleport	42	52.28 N	0.19 E
Little Portage Creek ≃	216	42.00 N	85.27 W
Little Powder ≃	198	45.28 N	105.20 W
Little Pucketa Creek ≃	279b	40.33 N	79.45 W
Little Quill Lake ⊜	184	51.55 N	104.05 W
Little Rann of Kachchh ≚	120	23.25 N	71.15 E
Little Red ≃	194	35.11 N	91.27 W
Little Red, Middle Fork ≃	194	35.37 N	92.11 W
Little Red Deer ≃	182	52.04 N	114.09 W
Little Red River Indian Reserve ◆[4]	184	53.30 N	105.58 W
Little Redstone Lake ⊜	212	45.13 N	78.34 W
Little River, Austl.	169	37.58 S	144.30 E
Little River, N.Z.	172	43.46 S	172.47 E
Little River, Ks., U.S.	198	38.23 N	98.00 W
Little River, Tx., U.S.	222	30.59 N	97.22 W
Little Rock, Ar., U.S.	194	34.44 N	92.17 W
Littlerock, Ca., U.S.	228	34.31 N	117.59 W
Little Rock, Il., U.S.	216	41.43 N	88.34 W
Little Rock, Ia., U.S.	198	43.26 N	95.52 W
Littlerock, Wa., U.S.	224	46.54 N	123.01 W
Little Rock ≃	198	43.16 N	96.15 W
Little Rock Air Force Base ■	194	34.55 N	92.10 W
Little Rock Creek ≃	228	34.28 N	118.01 W
Little Rock Wash V	228	34.42 N	118.02 W
Little Rocky Mountains ⋀	202	47.50 N	108.10 W
Little Rouge Creek ≃	212	43.48 N	79.08 W
Little Ruaha ≃	154	7.17 S	35.28 E
Little Sable Point ›	190	43.38 N	86.32 W
Little Sac ≃	194	37.39 N	93.46 W
Little Sachigo Lake ⊜	184	54.09 N	92.11 W
Little Saint Bernard Pass → Petit-Saint-Bernard, Col du)(	62	45.41 N	6.53 E
Little Salkehatchie ≃	192	32.37 N	80.53 W
Little Salmon ≃, Id., U.S.	202	45.25 N	116.19 W
Little Salmon ≃, N.Y., U.S.	212	43.32 N	76.16 W
Little Salmon, North Branch ≃	212	43.24 N	76.09 W
Little Salmon, South Branch ≃	212	43.24 N	76.09 W
Little Salmon Lake ⊜	180	62.12 N	134.45 W
Little Salt Lake ⊜	200	37.55 N	112.53 W
Little Sandy ≃	188	38.35 N	82.51 W
Little Sandy, East Fork ≃	188	38.30 N	82.50 W
Little Sandy Creek ≃	200	42.06 N	109.27 W
Little Sandy Desert ◆[2]	162	24.20 S	120.50 E
Little Saskatchewan ≃	184	49.52 N	100.07 W
Little Scarcies ≃	150	8.51 N	13.09 W
Little Scioto ≃, Oh., U.S.	214	40.31 N	83.12 W
Little Scioto ≃, Oh., U.S.	218	38.46 N	82.53 W
Little Sewickley Creek ≃, Pa., U.S.	279b	40.15 N	79.45 W
Little Sewickley Creek ≃, Pa., U.S.	279b	40.33 N	80.12 W
Little Silver	276	40.20 N	74.02 W
Little Sioux ≃	198	41.49 N	96.04 W
Little Sioux, West Fork ≃	198	42.04 N	96.00 W
Little Sitkin Island I	181a	51.55 N	178.30 E
Little Smoky ≃	182	55.42 N	117.38 W
Little Snake ≃	200	40.27 N	108.26 W
Little Sodus Bay c	210	43.20 N	76.43 W
Little Southwest Miramichi ≃	186	46.57 N	65.50 W
Little Stanney	262	53.15 N	2.53 W
Little Stony Creek ≃	226	39.20 N	122.31 W
Little Stour ≃	42	51.19 N	1.15 E
Littlestown	208	39.44 N	77.05 W
Little Stukeley	42	52.21 N	0.13 W
Little Sugarloaf ∧[2]	274b	37.41 S	145.19 E
Little Sur ≃	226	36.20 N	121.54 W
Little Sutton	262	53.17 N	2.57 W
Little Swatara Creek ≃	208	40.24 N	76.29 W
Little Tallapoosa ≃	192	33.18 N	85.34 W
Little Tanaga Island I	180	51.48 N	176.10 W
Little Tennessee ≃	192	35.47 N	84.15 W
Little Thurrock	260	51.28 N	0.21 E
Little Timber Creek ≃	285	39.53 N	75.08 W
Little Tinicum Island I	285	39.51 N	75.17 W
Little Tobago I, Br. Vir. Is.	240m	18.26 N	64.51 W
Little Tobago I, Trin.	241r	11.18 N	60.30 W
Little Toby Creek ≃	214	41.22 N	78.49 W
Littleton, Eng., U.K.	260	51.24 N	0.28 W
Littleton, Co., U.S.	200	39.36 N	105.00 W
Littleton, Ma., U.S.	207	42.32 N	71.30 W
Littleton, N.H., U.S.	188	44.18 N	71.46 W
Littleton, N.C., U.S.	192	36.26 N	77.54 W
Littleton, W.V., U.S.	188	39.41 N	80.31 W
Little Traverse Bay c	190	45.24 N	85.03 W
Little Truckee ≃	226	39.25 N	120.05 W
Little Turtle ≃	184	48.46 N	92.36 W
Little Turtle State Recreation Area ♠	216	40.50 N	85.26 W
Little Valley	210	42.15 N	78.48 W
Little Vermilion ≃	216	41.20 N	89.05 W
Little Vermilion Lake ⊜	184	51.16 N	93.50 W
Little Vienna Estates	284c	38.54 N	77.18 W
Little Wabash ≃	194	37.54 N	88.05 W
Little Walsingham	42	52.54 N	0.51 E
Little Waltham	260	51.47 N	0.29 E
Little Warley	260	51.35 N	0.19 E
Little Washita ≃	196	34.58 N	97.51 W
Little Wellington, Isla I	254	48.30 S	74.45 W
Little White ≃	198	43.44 N	100.40 W
Little White Mountain ∧	182	49.42 N	119.20 W
Little White Salmon ≃	224	45.43 N	121.38 W
Little Wichita ≃	196	33.54 N	97.59 W
Little Wichita, East Fork ≃	196	33.52 N	98.07 W
Little Wind ≃	202	42.57 N	108.29 W
Little Wind, North Fork ≃	202	43.01 N	108.53 W
Little Wind, South Fork ≃	202	43.01 N	108.53 W
Little Wolf ≃	190	44.23 N	88.48 W
Little Wood ≃	202	42.57 N	114.21 W
Little York, In., U.S.	218	38.42 N	85.54 W
Little York, N.Y., U.S.	210	42.42 N	76.10 W
Little Zab (Zāb-e Kūchek) (Az-Zāb aṣ-Ṣaghīr) ≃	128	35.12 N	43.25 E
Littoral □[4]	152	4.13 N	10.25 E
Litunga	152	13.17 S	16.43 E
Litvínov	54	50.37 N	13.36 E
Litvinovka	83	49.18 N	39.27 E
Litvinovo	76	59.34 N	38.01 E
Litvinskoje	86	50.42 N	72.42 E
Litzmannstadt → Łódź	30	51.46 N	19.30 E
Liu ≃, Zhg.	98	41.48 N	122.43 E
Liu ≃, Zhg.	98	42.45 N	126.04 E
Liu ≃, Zhg.	98	40.38 N	118.09 E
Liu ≃, Zhg.	102	23.52 N	109.45 E
Liu ≃, Zhg.	105	40.38 N	118.09 E
Liu ≃, Zhg.	106	31.31 N	121.18 E
Liuanzhuang	105	39.14 N	117.11 E
Liuba	102	33.32 N	107.07 E
Liubotong	100	31.26 N	116.00 E
Liucao	106	31.07 N	121.41 E
Liuchen	102	23.09 N	110.29 E
Liucheng, Zhg.	100	24.03 N	115.08 E
Liucheng, Zhg.	100	28.36 N	119.34 E
Liucheng, Zhg.	102	24.32 N	109.21 E
Liuchengba	102	27.27 N	102.53 E
Liuch'iu Hsü I	100	22.21 N	120.22 E
Liuchow → Liuzhou	102	24.19 N	109.24 E
Liucun	106	30.44 N	119.23 E
Liucura	252	38.39 S	71.05 W
Liudaogou	98	41.34 N	127.12 E
Liudaohe	105	40.39 N	116.12 E
Liudongqiao	106	31.03 N	119.32 E
Liudu	100	26.44 N	119.33 E
Liuduo	100	34.01 N	120.17 E
Liuduzhuang	105	39.27 N	117.50 E
Liuerbao	104	41.13 N	122.55 E
Liufang	100	27.56 N	116.22 E
Liufangling	100	30.27 N	114.27 E
Liufentzu	269d	24.57 N	121.35 E
Liugezhuang, Zhg.	98	38.33 N	116.30 E
Liugezhuang, Zhg.	105	40.03 N	118.16 E
Liugou	105	40.57 N	118.18 E
Liugu ≃	98	40.22 N	120.26 E
Liuguan	100	29.56 N	113.08 E
Liuguantun	104	41.20 N	121.21 E
Liuhang	106	31.21 N	121.22 E
Liuhe, Zhg.	98	42.15 N	125.43 E
Liuhe, Zhg.	100	33.20 N	112.48 E
Liuhe, Zhg.	100	30.46 N	113.12 E
Liuhe, Zhg.	100	30.20 N	115.36 E
Liuhe, Zhg.	100	32.22 N	118.49 E
Liuhe, Zhg.	105	39.31 N	118.17 E
Liuhe, Zhg.	106	31.30 N	121.15 E
Liuhegou	104	41.56 N	122.44 E
Liuheita	104	42.09 N	123.56 E
Liuhejie	102	24.26 N	101.35 E
Liuhekou	105	40.39 N	118.09 E
Liuheng Dao I	100	29.43 N	122.08 E
Liuhuang	100	23.58 N	116.28 E
Liuhudang	104	42.31 N	122.22 E
Liujia	102	24.54 N	107.49 E
Liujiachang	107	29.46 N	103.49 E
Liujiachuan	105	40.07 N	114.47 E
Liujiadai	106	31.57 N	120.23 E
Liujiadian	89	50.07 N	124.17 E
Liujiadu	106	32.15 N	120.33 E
Liujiafen	105	39.58 N	115.47 E
Liujiagangzi	104	41.28 N	122.33 E
Liujiagou	98	37.47 N	120.53 E
Liujiahe, Zhg.	100	32.06 N	113.21 E
Liujiahe, Zhg.	104	40.40 N	123.58 E
Liujiang	98	40.04 N	119.34 E
Liujiashan	105	40.14 N	114.49 E
Liujiatun, Zhg.	104	41.52 N	122.44 E
Liujiatun, Zhg.	104	41.51 N	122.05 E
Liujiatun, Zhg.	104	42.08 N	122.44 E
Liujiawopeng	104	42.16 N	123.01 E
Liujiazhai	269b	31.21 N	121.27 E
Liujiazhen	106	32.04 N	121.30 E
Liujiazi, Zhg.	98	41.00 N	120.13 E
Liujiazi, Zhg.	104	42.36 N	122.15 E
Liujiazi, Zhg.	104	41.48 N	123.47 E
Liujingcun	105	39.27 N	115.26 E
Liujisu	105	40.01 N	117.13 E
Liukeshu	86	44.59 N	90.12 E
Liuku	102	25.48 N	98.52 E
Liuli	154	11.05 S	34.38 E
Liulicun	271a	39.56 N	116.28 E
Liulidian	106	31.31 N	119.17 E
Liuligou	104	41.24 N	121.29 E
Liulihezhen	105	39.36 N	116.01 E
Liulin	100	31.34 N	113.14 E
Liuliwei	100	24.20 N	114.03 E
Liulongtai	104	41.32 N	120.56 E
Liumachang	107	29.51 N	104.54 E
Liumaogou	89	48.12 N	127.13 E
Liupangtun	104	41.36 N	123.28 E
Liupan Shan ⋀	102	35.40 N	106.40 E
Liuqianhutun	104	42.01 N	123.41 E
Liuqiao	106	32.11 N	120.51 E
Liuquan, Zhg.	98	34.27 N	117.20 E
Liuquan, Zhg.	105	39.22 N	116.18 E
Liurenba	100	29.57 N	114.49 E
Liushi, Zhg.	98	38.33 N	115.44 E
Liushi, Zhg.	100	28.03 N	120.51 E
Liushilipu	100	32.45 N	115.58 E
Liushi Shan ∧	120	36.15 N	82.05 E
Liushouying	98	39.48 N	119.19 E
Liushudian	98	35.54 N	119.30 E
Liushudixia	104	42.26 N	121.14 E
Liushui	89	44.17 N	124.15 E
Liushuigou	100	31.34 N	112.27 E
Liushuquan	105	39.21 N	118.06 E
Liusiqiao	100	29.47 N	116.21 E
Liusong	105	39.40 N	117.08 E
Liuta	98	35.52 N	115.18 E
Liutai	98	41.20 N	113.43 E
Liutaizi	104	41.46 N	122.39 E
Liutang	102	24.58 N	110.21 E
Liutiaozhaicun	104	41.29 N	123.12 E
Liutuan	98	36.56 N	119.22 E
Liutuhutun	104	40.44 N	120.32 E
Liuwanglou	98	34.48 N	116.28 E
Liuwa Plain ≚	152	14.30 S	22.40 E
Liuwa Plain National Park ♠	152	14.30 S	22.40 E
Liuwei	106	32.16 N	119.28 E
Liuwudian	100	24.36 N	118.13 E
Liuxi ≃	100	23.22 N	112.54 E
Liuxia	106	30.15 N	120.03 E
Liuyang	100	28.09 N	113.38 E
Liuyang ≃	100	28.13 N	112.58 E
Liuyuan	98	36.10 N	114.34 E
Liuyuankou	98	34.54 N	114.20 E
Liuzhai	102	25.15 N	107.20 E
Liuzhou	102	24.19 N	109.24 E
Liuzhuang	100	33.10 N	120.19 E
Livada	38	47.52 N	23.07 E
Livadija	89	42.50 N	132.39 E
Livanátai	38	38.42 N	23.03 E
Līvāni	76	56.22 N	26.11 E
Livanjsko Polje ≚	36	43.55 N	16.45 E
Livanovka	86	52.06 N	61.59 E
Livarot	50	49.01 N	0.09 E
Lively, On., Can.	190	46.26 N	81.09 W
Lively, Va., U.S.	208	37.47 N	76.31 W
Lively Island I	254	52.02 S	58.30 W
Livengood	180	65.32 N	148.33 W
Livenka, Ross.	78	50.26 N	38.18 E
Livenka, Ross.	78	50.44 N	40.14 E
Livenza ≃	64	45.35 N	12.51 E
Live Oak, Ca., U.S.	226	39.16 N	121.39 W
Live Oak, Fl., U.S.	192	30.17 N	82.59 W
Live Oak Creek ≃	196	30.39 N	101.42 W
Liverdun	56	48.45 N	6.03 E
Liverdy-en-Brie	261	48.42 N	2.47 E
Livergnano	66	44.19 N	11.21 E
Liveringa	162	18.03 S	124.10 E
Livermore, Ca., U.S.	226	37.40 N	121.46 W
Livermore, Ia., U.S.	190	42.52 N	94.11 W
Livermore, Ky., U.S.	194	37.29 N	87.07 W
Livermore, Mount ∧	196	30.38 N	104.10 W
Livermore Falls	188	44.28 N	70.11 W
Liverpool, Austl.	170	33.54 S	150.56 E
Liverpool, N.S., Can.	186	44.02 N	64.43 W
Liverpool, Eng., U.K.	44	53.25 N	2.55 W
Liverpool, Eng., U.K.	262	53.25 N	2.55 W
Liverpool, In., U.S.	216	41.34 N	87.18 W
Liverpool, N.Y., U.S.	210	43.06 N	76.13 W
Liverpool, Pa., U.S.	208	40.34 N	76.59 W
Liverpool, Tx., U.S.	222	29.18 N	95.17 W
Liverpool □[8]	262	53.25 N	2.55 W
Liverpool ≃	164	12.02 S	134.13 E
Liverpool (Speke) Airport ⊠	44	53.21 N	2.52 W
Liverpool, Cape ›	176	73.38 N	78.06 W
Liverpool, University of ⊛[2]	262	53.24 N	2.58 W
Liverpool Bay c, N.T., Can.	180	69.45 N	130.00 W
Liverpool Bay c, N.S., Can.	186	44.02 N	64.41 W
Liverpool Bay c, Eng., U.K.	44	53.30 N	3.16 W
Liverpool Football Ground ♠	262	53.26 N	2.57 W
Liverpool Heights	210	43.07 N	76.13 W
Liverpool Range ⋀	166	31.40 S	150.30 E
Livet-et-Gavet	62	45.06 N	5.56 E
Livigno	64	46.32 N	10.04 E
Livilliers	261	49.06 N	2.06 E
Lívingston, Guat.	236	15.50 N	88.45 W
Livingston, Scot., U.K.	46	55.53 N	3.32 W
Livingston, Al., U.S.	194	32.35 N	88.11 W
Livingston, Ca., U.S.	226	37.23 N	120.43 W
Livingston, Il., U.S.	194	38.58 N	89.45 W
Livingston, Ky., U.S.	192	37.17 N	84.12 W
Livingston, La., U.S.	194	30.30 N	90.44 W
Livingston, Mt., U.S.	202	45.39 N	110.33 W
Livingston, N.J., U.S.	210	40.47 N	74.18 W
Livingston, N.Y., U.S.	210	42.09 N	73.47 W
Livingston, Tn., U.S.	194	36.23 N	85.19 W
Livingston, Tx., U.S.	222	30.42 N	94.55 W
Livingston, Wi., U.S.	190	42.54 N	90.25 W
Livingston □[6], Il., U.S.	216	40.53 N	88.38 W
Livingston □[6], Mi., U.S.	216	42.38 N	83.50 W
Livingston □[6], N.Y., U.S.	210	42.48 N	77.49 W
Livingstone	154	17.50 S	25.53 E
Livingstone, Chutes de (Livingstone Falls) ⊥	152	4.50 S	14.30 E
Livingstone, Lake ⊜[1]	222	30.50 N	95.30 W
Livingstone Falls → Livingstone, Chutes de ⊥	152	4.50 S	14.30 E
Livingstone Lake ⊜	212	45.22 N	78.43 W
Livingstonia	154	10.36 S	34.07 E
Livingston Island I	9	62.35 S	60.30 W
Livingston Mall ◆[9]	276	40.47 N	74.21 W
Livingston Manor	210	41.54 N	74.49 W
Livno	36	43.50 N	17.01 E
Livny	76	52.25 N	37.37 E
Livojoki ≃	26	65.24 N	26.48 E
Livonia, In., U.S.	218	38.34 N	86.17 W
Livonia, La., U.S.	194	30.33 N	91.33 W
Livonia, Mi., U.S.	216	42.22 N	83.21 W
Livonia, N.Y., U.S.	210	42.49 N	77.40 W
Livonia Center	210	42.49 N	77.38 W
Livonia Mall ◆[9]	281	42.26 N	83.20 W
Livorno (Leghorn)	66	43.33 N	10.19 E
Livorno □[4]	66	43.14 N	10.35 E
Livorno Ferraris	62	45.17 N	8.05 E
Livourne → Livorno	66	43.33 N	10.19 E
Livramento do Brumado	255	13.39 S	41.50 W
Livramento → Santana do Livramento	252	30.53 S	55.31 W
Livron-sur-Drôme	62	44.46 N	4.51 E
Livry-Gargan	261	48.56 N	2.33 E
Livry-sur-Seine	261	48.31 N	2.41 E
Liwa	112	5.04 S	104.06 E
Liwale	154	9.46 S	37.56 E
Liwale Chini	154	9.41 S	38.01 E
Liwan	154	4.54 N	35.40 E
Liwonde	154	14.52 S	35.28 E
Liwonde National Park ♠	154	14.50 S	35.20 E
Liwung ≃	115a	6.08 S	106.49 E
Lixi, Zhg.	100	29.15 N	114.46 E
Lixi, Zhg.	100	27.39 N	116.19 E
Lixian, Zhg.	98	38.29 N	115.34 E
Lixian, Zhg.	102	34.11 N	105.02 E
Lixian, Zhg.	102	29.30 N	111.37 E
Lixian, Zhg.	105	39.33 N	116.26 E
Lixian → Black ≃	110	21.15 N	105.20 E
Lixin, Zhg.	100	33.06 N	116.08 E
Lixin, Zhg.	100	26.52 N	116.42 E
Lixing	100	33.28 N	115.28 E
Lixingzhuang	105	39.25 N	117.56 E
Lixoúrion	38	38.12 N	20.26 E
Lixus ⊥	34	35.16 N	6.13 W
Liyang, Zhg.	98	37.28 N	113.37 E
Liyang, Zhg.	106	31.26 N	119.29 E
Liyuanbao	100	25.16 N	112.55 E
Liyujiang	100	25.57 N	113.15 E
Lizard	42	49.58 N	5.12 W
Lizarda	250	9.36 S	46.41 W
Lizard Head Peak ∧	200	42.47 N	109.11 W
Lizard Island I	164	14.40 S	145.28 E
Lizard Point ›	42	49.56 N	5.13 W
Lizard Point Indian Reserve ◆[4]	184	50.40 N	100.57 W
Lize	107	30.08 N	106.11 E
Lizhai	106	31.34 N	121.45 E
Lizhou	102	28.08 N	102.10 E
Lizhu	100	29.56 N	120.30 E
Lizhuang, Zhg.	100	34.24 N	116.30 E
Lizhuang, Zhg.	107	28.47 N	104.46 E
Lizhuangqiao	106	31.48 N	119.37 E
Lizino	83	49.33 N	38.51 E
Lizinovka	78	50.08 N	39.28 E
Liziwei	107	30.19 N	106.39 E
Lizy-sur-Ourcq	50	49.01 N	3.02 E
Lizzana	64	45.51 N	11.03 E
Lizzanello	68	40.18 N	18.13 E
Lizzano	68	40.23 N	17.27 E
Lizzano in Belvedere	64	44.10 N	10.53 E
Ljalovo	82	56.03 N	37.14 E
Ljan	26	59.51 N	10.48 E
Ljubelj (Loiblpass))(	61	46.26 N	14.16 E
Ljubija	36	44.56 N	16.37 E
Ljubimec	38	41.50 N	26.05 E
Ljubinje	38	42.57 N	18.05 E
Ljubljana	36	46.03 N	14.31 E
Ljubovija	38	44.11 N	19.22 E
Ljubuški	36	43.12 N	17.33 E
Ljugarn	26	57.19 N	18.42 E
Ljunga	40	58.31 N	16.21 E
Ljungan ≃	26	62.19 N	17.23 E
Ljungaverk	26	62.29 N	16.03 E
Ljungby	26	56.50 N	13.56 E
Ljungbyhed	41	56.04 N	13.12 E
Ljungbyholm	26	56.38 N	16.10 E
Ljungdalen	26	62.51 N	12.47 E
Ljungsbro	26	58.31 N	15.30 E
Ljungskile	26	58.14 N	11.55 E
Ljusdal	26	61.50 N	16.05 E
Ljusfallshammar	40	58.47 N	15.29 E
Ljusnan ≃	26	61.12 N	17.08 E
Ljusnaren ⊜	40	59.51 N	14.56 E
Ljusne	26	61.13 N	17.08 E
Ljusterö I	40	59.31 N	18.37 E
Ljutomer	61	46.31 N	16.12 E
Llagas Creek ≃	226	36.58 N	121.31 W
Llaima, Volcán ∧[1]	252	38.43 S	71.43 W
Llamara, Salar de ≚	248	21.13 S	69.40 W
Llanaber	42	52.45 N	4.05 W
Llanaelhaearn	42	52.59 N	4.24 W
Llanarth	42	52.12 N	4.18 W
Llanarthney	42	51.52 N	4.09 W
Llanbedrog	42	52.52 N	4.29 W
Llanberis, Pass of V	44	53.06 N	4.04 W
Llanbister	42	52.21 N	3.18 W
Llanboidy	42	51.54 N	4.36 W
Llanbryde	46	57.37 N	3.13 W
Llanbrynmair	42	52.37 N	3.57 W
Llançà	34	42.22 N	3.09 E
Llancanelo, Laguna ⊜	252	35.35 S	69.09 W
Llandaff	42	51.30 N	3.14 W
Llandaff Cathedral ⊛[1]	42	51.29 N	3.15 W
Llanddewi Brefi	42	52.10 N	3.57 W
Llandeilo	42	51.52 N	3.59 W
Llandilo	274a	33.43 S	150.45 E
Llandinam	42	52.29 N	3.26 W
Llandissilio	42	51.53 N	4.44 W
Llandovery	42	51.59 N	3.48 W
Llandrindod Wells	42	52.15 N	3.23 W
Llandudno	44	53.19 N	3.49 W
Llandybie	42	51.50 N	4.00 W
Llandysul	42	52.02 N	4.19 W
Llanelli	42	51.42 N	4.10 W
Llanelltyd	42	52.45 N	3.54 W
Llanelly	169	36.44 S	143.51 E
Llanenddwyn	42	52.49 N	4.06 W
Llanerchymedd	44	53.20 N	4.22 W
Llanes	34	43.25 N	4.45 W
Llanfaethlu	44	53.21 N	4.32 W
Llanfair-Caereinion	42	52.39 N	3.20 W
Llanfairfechan	44	53.15 N	3.58 W
Llanfairpwllgwyngyll	44	53.13 N	4.12 W
Llanfrynach	42	51.56 N	3.21 W
Llanfyllin	42	52.46 N	3.17 W
Llanfynydd	42	51.56 N	4.06 W
Llanfyrnach	42	51.57 N	4.35 W
Llangadog	42	51.56 N	3.53 W
Llangefni	44	53.16 N	4.18 W
Llangennech	42	51.41 N	4.04 W
Llangollen	42	52.58 N	3.10 W
Llangollen Estates	208	39.39 N	75.37 W
Llangranog	42	52.09 N	4.29 W
Llangurig	42	52.25 N	3.36 W
Llangwyryfon	42	52.19 N	4.03 W
Llangynog	42	52.50 N	3.25 W
Llanharan	42	51.33 N	3.25 W
Llanidloes	42	52.27 N	3.32 W
Llanilar	42	52.21 N	4.01 W
Llanllyfni	44	53.03 N	4.17 W
Llano	196	30.45 N	98.40 W
Llano ≃	196	30.35 N	98.25 W
Llano Colorado	204	31.38 N	115.55 W
Llanon	42	52.17 N	4.10 W
Llanos ≚	246	5.00 N	70.00 W
Llanpumsaint	42	51.56 N	4.18 W
Llanquihue	254	41.15 S	73.01 W
Llanquihue, Lago ⊜	254	41.08 S	72.48 W
Llanrhaeadr-ym-Mochnant	42	52.51 N	3.17 W
Llanrhidian	42	51.37 N	4.11 W
Llanrhystud	42	52.18 N	4.09 W
Llanrwst	44	53.08 N	3.48 W
Llansantffraid-ym-Mechain	42	52.47 N	3.08 W
Llansawel	42	52.01 N	4.00 W
Llantrisant	42	51.33 N	3.23 W
Llantwit Major	42	51.25 N	3.30 W
Llanuwchllyn	42	52.52 N	3.41 W
Llanwenog	42	52.06 N	4.12 W
Llanwrda	42	51.58 N	3.53 W
Llanwrtyd Wells	42	52.07 N	3.38 W
Llanybydder	42	52.04 N	4.09 W
Llata	248	9.25 S	76.47 W
Llavallol ◆[8]	288	34.48 S	58.28 W
Llay	44	53.06 N	2.59 W
Lleida	34	41.37 N	0.37 E
Lleida □[4]	34	42.00 N	1.10 E
Llentrisca, Cap ›	34	38.51 N	1.14 E
Llera de Canales	234	23.19 N	99.01 W
Llerena	34	38.14 N	6.01 W
Lleulleu, Lago ⊜	252	38.09 S	73.20 W
Lleyn Peninsula ›[1]	42	52.54 N	4.30 W
Llica	248	19.52 S	68.16 W
Llico	252	34.46 S	72.05 W
Lliria	34	39.38 N	0.36 W
Llivia	32	42.28 N	1.59 E
Llobregat ≃	34	41.19 N	2.09 E
Llobregat, Delta del ≚[2]	266d	41.17 N	2.08 E
Llorente	116	11.25 N	125.33 E
Llorente ≃	116	11.25 N	125.33 E
Llorona, Punta ›	236	8.39 N	83.45 W
Lloyd	218	38.37 N	82.51 W
Lloyd Harbor	210	40.54 N	73.27 W
Lloyd Harbor c	276	40.55 N	73.27 W
Lloydminster	184	53.17 N	110.00 W
Lloyd Neck ›[1]	276	40.56 N	73.28 W
Lloyd Point ›	210	40.57 N	73.29 W
Lloyds ≃	186	48.33 N	57.13 W
Llucena	34	40.08 N	0.17 W
Llucmajor	34	39.29 N	2.54 E
Llullaillaco, Volcán ∧[1]	252	24.43 S	68.33 W
Llusco	248	14.21 S	72.07 W
Lluta ≃	248	18.24 S	70.19 W
Llyn Brianne Reservoir ⊜[1]	42	52.08 N	3.45 W
Llyswen	42	52.02 N	3.17 W
Llys-y-frân Reservoir ⊜[1]	42	51.53 N	4.51 W
Lnáře	60	49.28 N	13.47 E
Lo (Panlong) ≃	110	21.18 N	105.25 E
Loa	200	38.24 N	111.38 W
Loa ≃, Chile	244	21.26 S	70.04 W
Loa ≃, Congo	273b	4.20 S	15.11 E
Loami	194	39.40 N	89.51 W
Loanda, Bra.	255	22.54 S	53.10 W
Loanda, Gabon	152	0.55 S	9.00 E
Loanda → Luanda	152	8.48 S	13.14 E
Loande ≃	152	8.41 S	17.56 E
Loange (Luangue) ≃	152	4.17 S	20.02 E
Loango Buele	152	5.10 S	12.59 E
Loanhead	46	55.53 N	3.09 W
Loanja ≃	154	17.22 S	24.48 E
Loano	62	44.08 N	8.15 E
Loantaka Brook ≃	276	40.43 N	74.28 W
Lo Aranguiz	286e	33.23 S	70.40 W
Loay	116	9.36 N	124.01 E
Lob' ≃	82	56.29 N	35.51 E
Lobamba	158	26.27 S	31.12 E
Loban	24	65.44 N	45.25 E
Loban' ≃	80	56.58 N	51.12 E
Lobanovo	76	53.04 N	38.14 E
Lobanovskije Vyselki	82	54.18 N	38.58 E
Lo Barnechea	286e	33.21 S	70.31 W
Lobaski	80	54.38 N	45.09 E
Lobatos	234	22.49 N	103.24 W
Lobatse	156	25.11 S	25.40 E
Löbau	54	51.05 N	14.40 E
Lobau ≚	264b	48.10 N	16.32 E
Lobaye □[5]	152	4.00 N	18.30 E
Lobaye ≃	152	3.41 N	18.35 E
Lobbes	50	50.21 N	4.15 E
Lobbs Run ≃	279b	40.15 N	79.55 W
Lobdell Lake ⊜	216	42.48 N	83.48 W
Löbejün	54	51.38 N	11.53 E
Lobelville	194	35.46 N	87.47 W
Lo Benitez	286e	33.34 S	70.42 W
Lobenstein	54	50.26 N	11.38 E
Lobería	252	38.09 S	58.47 W
Lo Bernales	286e	33.34 S	70.34 W
Löberöd	41	55.47 N	13.30 E
Lobethal	168b	34.54 S	138.52 E
Łobez	30	53.39 N	15.36 E
Lobito	152	12.20 S	13.34 E
Lobitos	246	4.26 S	81.17 W
Lobitos Creek ≃	282	37.22 N	122.24 W
Lobkoviči	76	53.50 N	31.45 E
Lobn'a	82	56.01 N	37.30 E
Löbnitz, Dtsch.	54	51.35 N	12.28 E
Löbnitz, Dtsch.	54	54.17 N	12.43 E
Lobo, Indon.	164	3.45 S	134.05 E
Lobo, Pil.	116	13.39 N	121.13 E
Lobo ≃	150	6.02 N	6.47 W
Loboko	152	0.45 S	16.38 E
Lobos	258	35.11 S	59.06 W
Lobos, Cay I	238	22.24 N	77.32 W
Lobos, Isla I	232	27.20 N	110.36 W
Lobos, Isla de I, Esp.	148	28.45 N	13.49 W
Lobos, Isla de I, Méx.	234	21.27 N	97.13 W
Lobos, Laguna de ⊜	258	35.17 S	59.07 W
Lobos, Point ›	226	37.47 N	122.31 W
Lobos, Punta ›	248	21.01 S	70.11 W
Lobos de Afuera, Islas II	248	6.57 S	80.42 W
Lobos de Tierra, Isla I	248	6.27 S	80.52 W
Lo Boza	286e	33.23 S	70.46 W
Lobskoje	24	62.45 N	35.16 E
Lobstädt	54	51.08 N	12.29 E
Löbtau ◆[8]	54	51.03 N	13.42 E
Loburg	54	52.07 N	12.05 E
Lobva	86	59.12 N	60.30 E
Łobżenica	30	53.16 N	17.15 E
Locana	62	45.25 N	7.27 E
Locana, Val di V	62	45.25 N	7.27 E
Locarno	58	46.10 N	8.48 E
Lo Castillo, Aeropuerto ⊠	286e	33.23 S	70.36 W
Locate Triulzi	62	45.21 N	9.13 E
Loccum	52	52.27 N	9.08 E
Loceri	71	39.51 N	9.35 E
Loch	169	38.22 S	145.43 E
Lochaber ◆[1]	46	56.57 N	5.06 W
Lochailort	46	56.53 N	5.40 W
Lochaline	46	56.32 N	5.47 W
Locharbriggs	44	55.06 N	3.35 W
Lochar Water ≃	44	54.59 N	3.27 W
Lochboisdale	46	57.09 N	7.19 W
Lochcarron	46	57.24 N	5.30 W
Lochdon	46	56.26 N	5.41 W
Lochearn	284b	39.21 N	76.43 W
Lochearnhead	46	56.23 N	4.17 W
Lochem	52	52.09 N	6.25 E
Loches	50	47.08 N	1.00 E
Lochgair	46	56.03 N	5.20 W
Loch Garman → Wexford	48	52.20 N	6.27 W
Lochgelly	46	56.08 N	3.19 W
Lochgilphead	46	56.03 N	5.26 W
Lochgoilhead	46	56.10 N	4.54 W
Lochiel	168b	33.56 S	138.10 E
Lochindorb ⊜	46	57.24 N	3.43 W
Lochino	265b	55.42 N	37.19 E
Lochinvar National Park ♠	154	15.55 S	27.15 E
Lochinver	46	58.09 N	5.15 W
Lochmaben	44	55.08 N	3.27 W
Lochmaddy	46	57.36 N	7.11 W
Lochnagar ∧	46	56.57 N	3.16 W
Lochovice	60	49.51 N	13.59 E
Lochranza	46	55.42 N	5.18 W
Loch Raven Dam ◆[6]	284b	39.26 N	76.33 W
Loch Raven Reservoir ⊜[1]	208	39.27 N	76.34 W
Lochristi	50	51.06 N	3.50 E
Lochsa ≃	202	46.08 N	115.36 W
Loch Sheldrake	210	41.46 N	74.39 W
Loch Sport	166	38.03 S	147.36 E
Lochvica	78	50.22 N	33.16 E
Lochwinnoch	46	55.48 N	4.39 W
Lochy, Loch ⊜	46	56.57 N	4.53 W
Lock	166	33.34 S	135.46 E
Lock and Dam No. 20 ◆[6], U.S.	219	40.09 N	91.30 W
Lock and Dam No. 21 ◆[6], U.S.	219	39.54 N	91.26 W
Lock and Dam No. 22 ◆[6], U.S.	219	39.39 N	91.16 W
Lock and Dam No. 24 ◆[6], U.S.	219	39.22 N	90.55 W
Lock and Dam No. 25 ◆[6], U.S.	219	39.01 N	90.41 W
Locke, Ca., U.S.	226	38.15 N	121.31 W
Locke, In., U.S.	216	41.28 N	86.00 W
Locke, N.Y., U.S.	210	42.39 N	76.25 W
Lockeford	226	38.10 N	121.09 W
Lockenhaus	61	47.24 N	16.25 E
Lockeport	186	43.42 N	65.07 W
Lockerbie	44	55.07 N	3.22 W
Lockesburg	194	33.58 N	94.10 W
Lockhart, Austl.	166	35.14 S	146.43 E
Lockhart, Fl., U.S.	220	28.37 N	81.26 W
Lockhart, Tx., U.S.	222	29.53 N	97.40 W
Lockhart River Aboriginal Reserve ◆[4]	164	13.00 S	143.15 E
Lock Haven	210	41.08 N	77.26 W
Lockheed Aircraft Corporation ⊛[3], Ca., U.S.	280	34.12 N	118.22 W
Lockheed Aircraft Corporation ⊛[3], Ca., U.S.	282	37.25 N	122.02 W
Lockington	216	40.12 N	84.13 W
Lock Mountain ∧	214	40.25 N	78.18 W
Lockney	196	34.07 N	101.26 W
Löcknitz	54	53.27 N	14.12 E
Löcknitz ≃, Dtsch.	54	53.07 N	11.16 E
Löcknitz ≃, Dtsch.	264a	52.25 N	13.49 E
Lockport, Mb., Can.	184	50.05 N	96.56 W
Lockport, Il., U.S.	216	41.35 N	88.03 W
Lockport, La., U.S.	194	29.39 N	90.32 W
Lockport, N.Y., U.S.	210	43.10 N	78.41 W
Lockport Lock ◆[5]	278	41.35 N	88.04 W
Locks Heath	42	50.52 N	1.15 W
Locksley Park	210	42.45 N	78.52 W
Lockvattnet ⊜	40	59.03 N	17.05 E
Lockview	279b	40.10 N	79.55 W
Lockwood, Ca., U.S.	226	35.56 N	121.05 W
Lockwood, Mo., U.S.	194	37.23 N	93.57 W
Lockwood Corners	214	41.00 N	81.34 W
Lockyer Creek ≃	171a	27.25 S	152.36 E
Locminé	28	47.53 N	2.50 W
Loc Ninh	110	11.51 N	106.36 E
Loco, Bayou ≃	222	31.28 N	94.44 W
Locon	50	50.34 N	2.40 E
Locorotondo	68	40.45 N	17.20 E
Locri	68	38.14 N	16.16 E
Locri Epizefiri ⊥	68	38.12 N	16.13 E
Locroja	248	12.41 S	74.26 W
Locsin	116	13.09 N	123.43 E
Locumba	248	17.36 S	70.46 W
Locumba ≃	248	17.54 S	70.57 W
Locust	208	40.18 N	73.59 W
Locust Creek ≃	194	39.40 N	93.17 W
Locust Fork ≃	194	33.33 N	87.11 W
Locust Grove, N.Y., U.S.	276	40.48 N	73.30 W
Locust Grove, Ok., U.S.	196	36.12 N	95.10 W
Locust Lake State Park ♠	208	40.46 N	76.08 W
Locust Point ›	276	40.49 N	73.48 W
Locust Valley	210	40.53 N	73.36 W
Lod (Lydda)	132	31.58 N	34.54 E
Lod, Nemel-Te'ufa (Ben Gurion Airport) ⊠	132	31.59 N	34.53 E
Loda	216	40.31 N	88.04 W
Lodal Creek ≃	285	40.14 N	75.27 W
Löddeköpinge	41	55.46 N	13.01 E
Loddon	42	52.32 N	1.29 E
Loddon ≃, Austl.	166	35.32 S	143.52 E
Loddon ≃, Eng., U.K.	42	51.30 N	0.53 W
Lodè	71	40.35 N	9.32 E
Lodejnoje Pole	76	60.44 N	33.30 E
Lodenau	54	51.24 N	14.57 E
Löderburg	54	51.52 N	11.32 E
Lodève	32	43.43 N	3.19 E
Lodge Creek ≃	202	48.35 N	109.10 W
Lodge Grass	202	45.18 N	107.21 W
Lodgepole, Ab., Can.	182	53.06 N	115.19 W
Lodgepole, Ne., U.S.	198	41.08 N	102.38 W
Lodgepole Creek ≃	198	40.57 N	102.22 W
Lodhāsuli	126	22.19 N	87.03 E
Lodhrān	123	29.32 N	71.38 E
Lodi, It.	62	45.19 N	9.30 E
Lodi, Ca., U.S.	226	38.07 N	121.16 W
Lodi, N.J., U.S.	210	40.52 N	74.05 W
Lodi, N.Y., U.S.	210	42.36 N	76.49 W
Lodi, Oh., U.S.	214	41.02 N	82.00 W
Lodi, Wi., U.S.	190	43.18 N	89.31 W
Lodi Park ♠	272a	28.36 N	77.13 E
Lodi Vecchio	62	45.18 N	9.24 E
Lodja	152	3.29 S	23.26 E
Lodosa	34	42.25 N	2.05 W
Lodoyo	115a	8.10 S	112.13 E
Lodrone	64	45.50 N	10.32 E
Lods	58	47.03 N	6.15 E
Lodsch → Łódź	30	51.46 N	19.30 E
Lodwar	154	3.07 N	35.36 E
Łódź	30	51.46 N	19.30 E
Łódź □[4]	30	51.50 N	19.25 E
Loe Āgra	123	34.35 N	71.43 E
Loei	110	17.29 N	101.35 E
Loei ≃	110	17.51 N	101.37 E
Loen	26	61.52 N	6.52 E
Loenen	52	52.07 N	6.01 E
Loengo	154	4.45 S	26.27 E
Loeriesfontein	158	30.56 S	19.26 E
Lo Espejo	286e	33.32 S	70.43 W
Lo Espejo, Canal ≚	286e	33.32 S	70.43 W
Lofa ≃	150	6.36 N	11.08 W
Lofer	64	47.35 N	12.41 E
Löffingen	58	47.53 N	8.20 E
Lofoten II	24	68.30 N	15.00 E
Lofoten Basin ◆[1]	10	70.00 N	4.00 E
Lofthouse	44	53.44 N	1.29 W
Lofthus	26	60.20 N	6.40 E
Loftus, Austl.	274a	34.03 S	151.03 E
Loftus, Eng., U.K.	44	54.33 N	0.53 W
Lofty, Mount ∧, Austl.	168b	34.59 S	138.42 E
Lofty, Mount ∧, Austl.	274b	37.43 S	145.17 E
Log	80	49.29 N	43.52 E
Loga, Dtsch.	52	53.14 N	7.29 E
Loga, Niger	150	13.37 N	3.14 E
Logačovka	80	52.23 N	52.21 E
Logan, Ia., U.S.	198	41.38 N	95.47 W
Logan, Ks., U.S.	198	39.39 N	99.34 W
Logan, N.M., U.S.	196	35.22 N	103.25 W
Logan, Oh., U.S.	188	39.32 N	82.24 W
Logan, Ut,. U.S.	200	41.44 N	111.50 W
Logan, W.V., U.S.	188	37.50 N	81.59 W
Logan □[6], Il., U.S.	219	40.09 N	89.22 W
Logan □[6], Oh., U.S.	216	40.22 N	83.46 W
Logan ◆[8]	285	40.02 N	75.09 W
Logan ≃, Austl.	171a	27.43 S	153.18 E
Logan ≃, Ab., Can.	182	55.09 N	111.42 W
Logan ≃, Ut,. U.S.	200	41.44 N	111.57 W
Logan, Mount ∧, Yk., Can.	180	60.34 N	140.24 W
Logan, Mount ∧, Wa., U.S.	224	48.32 N	120.57 W
Logan Creek ≃, Ca., U.S.	226	39.22 N	122.06 W
Logan Creek ≃, Mo., U.S.	194	37.11 N	90.49 W
Logan Creek ≃, Ne., U.S.	198	41.37 N	96.29 W
Logandale	204	36.35 N	114.29 W
Logan International Airport ⊠	283	42.22 N	71.00 W
Logan Lake ⊜	212	44.52 N	78.59 W
Logan Martin Lake ⊜[1]	194	33.40 N	86.15 W
Logan Mountains ⋀	180	61.45 N	128.38 W
Logan Pass)(	202	48.42 N	113.43 W
Logansport, In., U.S.	216	40.45 N	86.21 W
Logansport, La., U.S.	194	31.58 N	93.59 W
Logan Square ◆[8]	278	41.56 N	87.42 W
Loganton	210	41.02 N	77.18 W
Loganville, Ga., U.S.	192	33.50 N	83.54 W
Loganville, Pa., U.S.	208	39.52 N	76.42 W
Logärden ⊜	40	60.37 N	16.00 E
Lögdeälven ≃	26	63.33 N	19.25 E
Logduz	76	60.00 N	44.41 E
Loge ≃, Ang.	152	10.12 S	17.00 E
Loge ≃, Ang.	152	7.49 S	13.06 E
Logia	164	2.55 S	151.27 E
Loginovo	82	55.42 N	38.44 E
Logirim	154	4.43 N	33.14 E
Logišin	76	52.20 N	25.59 E
Lognes	261	48.50 N	2.38 E
Lognes-Émerainville, Aérodrome de ⊠	261	48.49 N	2.37 E
Logo	154	5.20 N	30.18 E
Logojsk	76	54.12 N	27.49 E
Logone ≃	146	12.06 N	15.02 E
Logone Birni	146	11.47 N	15.06 E
Logone Gana	146	11.33 N	15.09 E
Logone-Occidental □[5]	146	8.50 N	16.00 E
Logone Occidental ≃	146	9.07 N	16.26 E
Logone-Oriental □[5]	146	8.15 N	16.20 E
Logone Oriental ≃	146	9.07 N	16.26 E
Logoualé	150	7.07 N	7.33 W
Logovskij	80	48.26 N	43.23 E
Log pod Mangartom	64	46.24 N	13.36 E
Logroño	34	42.28 N	2.27 W
Logrosán	34	39.20 N	5.29 W
Løgstør	26	56.58 N	9.15 E
Logtāk Lake ⊜	120	24.33 N	93.50 E
Løgten	41	56.17 N	10.19 E
Logudoro ◆[1]	71	40.35 N	8.40 E
Logue Brook Dam ◆[6]	168a	33.00 S	115.57 E
Løgumgårde	41	55.05 N	8.57 E
Løgumkloster	41	55.03 N	8.57 E
Logumukum	154	0.27 N	36.05 E
Logy Creek ≃	224	46.11 N	120.35 W
Loh I	175f	13.21 S	166.38 E
Lohāgara	126	23.11 N	89.39 E
Lohals	41	55.08 N	10.55 E
Lohārdaga	124	23.26 N	84.41 E
Lohāru	120	28.27 N	75.49 E
Lohatlha	158	28.02 S	23.04 E
Lohausen ◆[8]	263	51.16 N	6.44 E
Lohauserholz ◆[8]	263	51.39 N	7.48 E
Lohberg	263	51.35 N	6.46 E
Löhdorf ◆[8]	263	51.09 N	7.01 E
Lo Hermida	286e	33.29 S	70.33 W
Lohfelden	56	51.16 N	9.32 E
Lohheide ◆[8]	263	51.30 N	6.40 E
Lohiān	123	31.10 N	75.11 E
Lohiniva	24	67.10 N	24.58 E

Symbols in the index entries represent the broad categories identified in the key at the right. Symbols with superior numbers (⋀[1]) identify subcategories (see complete key on page *I · 1*).

Symbole im Register stellen die rechts im Schlüssel erklärten Kategorien dar. Symbole mit hochgestellten Ziffern (⋀[1]) bezeichnen Unterabteilungen einer Kategorie (vgl. vollständiger Schlüssel auf Seite *I · 1*).

Los símbolos incluídos en el texto del índice representan las grandes categorias identificadas con la clave a la derecha. Los símbolos con numeros en su parte superior (⋀[1]) identifican las subcategorías (véase la clave completa en la página *I · 1*).

Les symboles de l'index représentent les catégories indiquées dans la légende à droite. Les symboles suivis d'un indice (⋀[1]) représentent des sous-catégories (voir légende complète à la page *I · 1*).

Os símbolos incluídos no texto do índice representam as grandes categorias identificadas com a chave à direita. Os símbolos com números em sua parte superior (⋀[1]) identificam as subcategorias (veja-se a chave completa à página *I · 1*).

∧	Mountain	Berg	Montaña	Montagne	Montanha
⋀	Mountains	Gebirge	Montañas	Montagnes	Montanhas
)(	Pass	Paß	Paso	Col	Passo
V	Valley, Canyon	Tal, Cañon	Valle, Cañón	Vallée, Canyon	Vale, Canhão
≚	Plain	Ebene	Llano	Plaine	Planície
›	Cape	Kap	Cabo	Cap	Cabo
I	Island	Insel	Isla	Île	Ilha
II	Islands	Inseln	Islas	Îles	Ilhas
⊥	Other Topographic Features	Andere Topographische Objekte	Otros Elementos Topográficos	Autres données topographiques	Outros acidentes topográficos

ESPAÑOL — Nombre | Página | Lat.°′ | Long.°′ W = Oeste
FRANÇAIS — Nom | Page | Lat.°′ | Long.°′ W = Ouest
PORTUGUÊS — Nome | Página | Lat.°′ | Long.°′ W = Oeste

Lohit ≏ 120 27.48 N 95.28 E
Lohja 26 60.15 N 24.05 E
Lohjanharju ʌ 26 60.15 N 24.30 E
Lohjanjärvi ⊜ 26 60.15 N 23.55 E
Löhlbach 56 51.04 N 8.58 E
Lohmar 56 50.50 N 7.13 E
Lohme, Dtsch. 54 54.35 N 13.37 E
Löhme, Dtsch. 264a 52.37 N 13.40 E
Lohmen, Dtsch. 54 50.59 N 13.59 E
Lohmen, Dtsch. 54 53.41 N 12.05 E
Lohmühle 263 51.31 N 6.40 E
Lohne, Dtsch. 52 52.42 N 8.12 E
Löhne, Dtsch. 52 52.11 N 8.41 E
Löhnen 263 51.36 N 6.39 E
Lohnsburg 60 48.09 N 13.24 E
Loho → Luohe 100 33.35 N 114.01 E
Lohr am Main 56 50.00 N 9.34 E
Lohrville 198 42.16 N 94.32 W
Lohsa 54 51.23 N 14.24 E
Loi ≏ 110 21.19 N 100.44 E
Loi, Phou ʌ 110 20.16 N 103.12 E
Loiano 66 44.16 N 11.19 E
Loiblpass (Ljubelj))(61 46.26 N 14.16 E
Loiborsoit 154 3.52 S 36.26 E
Loi-kaw 110 19.41 N 97.13 E
Loile ≏ 152 0.52 S 20.12 E
Loimaa 26 60.51 N 23.03 E
Loimijoki ≏ 26 61.13 N 22.38 E
Loi Mwe 110 21.11 N 99.46 E
Loing ≏ 50 48.23 N 2.48 E
Loing, Canal du ≊ 50 48.22 N 2.50 E
Loir ≏ 32 47.33 N 0.32 W
Loira → Loire ≏ 32 47.16 N 2.11 W
Loire 62 45.33 N 4.48 E
Loire □[5] 32 45.30 N 4.00 E
Loire ≏ 32 47.16 N 2.11 W
Loire, Canal latéral à la ≊ 50 47.37 N 2.44 E
Loire-Atlantique □[5] 32 47.20 N 1.35 W
Loiret □[5] 50 47.55 N 2.20 E
Loiret ≏ 50 47.52 N 1.48 E
Loir-et-Cher □[5] 50 47.30 N 1.30 E
Loïs, Lac ⊜ 190 48.34 N 78.44 W
Loisach ≏ 64 47.56 N 11.27 E
Loisdale 284c 38.46 N 77.11 W
Loisia 58 46.29 N 5.27 E
Loison ≏ 56 49.30 N 5.17 E
Loitz 54 53.58 N 13.07 E
Loíza, Lago ⊜[1] 240m 18.17 N 66.00 W
Loíza Aldea 240m 18.26 N 65.53 W
Loja, Ec. 246 4.00 S 79.13 W
Loja, Esp. 34 37.10 N 4.09 W
Loja □[4] 246 4.10 S 79.30 W
Lojang → Luoyang 102 34.41 N 112.28 E
Lojev 78 51.56 N 30.46 E
Lojga 24 61.05 N 44.37 E
Lojno 24 59.44 N 52.39 E
Løjt Kirkeby 41 55.05 N 9.28 E
Loka, Sūd. 154 4.16 N 31.01 E
Loka, Zaïre 152 0.20 N 17.57 E
Loka brunn 40 59.36 N 14.28 E
Lokači 78 50.44 N 24.39 E
Lokako 152 2.14 S 21.45 E
Lokalema 152 1.59 N 22.17 E
Lokan ≏ 116 5.25 N 117.44 E
Lokandu 154 2.31 S 25.47 E
Lokan tekojärvi ⊜[1] 24 67.55 N 27.40 E
Lokbatan 84 40.20 N 49.43 E
Løken 26 59.48 N 11.29 E
Lokeren 50 51.06 N 4.00 E
Loket 54 50.09 N 12.43 E
Lokichar 154 2.23 N 35.39 E
Lokichokio 154 4.12 N 34.21 E
Lokitaung 154 4.16 N 35.45 E
Lokka 24 67.49 N 27.44 E
Løkken 26 57.22 N 9.43 E
Løkken verk 26 63.08 N 9.42 E
Lokn'a 76 56.50 N 30.09 E
Loknaš ≏ 82 56.11 N 36.04 E
Loko 150 8.02 N 7.49 E
Lokofa-Bokolongo 152 0.12 N 19.22 E
Lokoja 150 7.47 N 6.45 E
Lokolama 152 2.34 S 19.53 E
Lokolenge 152 1.11 N 22.40 E
Lokolo ≏ 152 0.43 S 19.40 E
Lokomo 152 2.41 N 15.19 E
Lokoro ≏ 152 1.43 S 18.23 E
Lokossa 150 6.38 N 1.43 E
Lokosso 150 10.19 N 3.40 W
Lokot', Ross. 76 52.34 N 34.34 E
Lokot', Ross. 86 51.11 N 81.11 E
Lokoua ≏ 273b 4.06 S 15.16 E
Loksa 76 59.35 N 25.45 E
Loks Land I 176 62.26 N 64.38 W
Loktyši 76 52.50 N 26.43 E
Lokve 64 46.01 N 13.49 E
Loky 157b 12.47 S 49.39 E
Lol 140 6.26 N 29.37 E
Lol ≏ 140 9.13 N 28.59 E
Lóla, Ang. 152 14.22 S 13.42 E
Lola, Guinée 150 7.48 N 8.32 W
Lola, Mount ʌ 226 39.26 N 120.22 W
Lolengi 152 0.07 N 20.59 E
Loleta 204 40.38 N 124.13 W
Lolingo 152 0.55 N 22.38 E
Loliondo 154 2.03 S 35.37 E
Lolita 222 28.50 N 96.32 W
Lolland I 41 54.46 N 11.30 E
Lollar 56 50.39 N 8.42 E
Lolo, Mt., U.S. 202 46.45 N 114.04 W
Lolo, Zaïre 152 2.13 N 23.00 E
Lolo ≏ 152 1.07 S 12.28 E
Lolobau Island I 164 4.55 S 151.10 E
Lolo Creek ≏, Id., U.S. 202 46.26 N 116.10 W
Lolo Creek ≏, Mt., U.S. 202 46.45 N 114.03 W
Lolodorf 152 3.14 N 10.44 E
Lolo Pass)(202 46.38 N 114.35 W
Lolotique 236 13.33 N 88.21 W
Lolowai 175f 15.18 S 168.00 E
Loltong 175f 15.33 S 168.08 E
Lolvavana, Passage ʯ 175f 15.26 S 168.12 E
Lolwa 154 1.22 N 29.31 E
Lolworth Range ⩚ 166 20.20 S 145.15 E
Lom, Blg. 38 43.49 N 23.14 E
Lom, Česko. 54 50.37 N 13.40 E
Lom, Nor. 26 61.50 N 8.33 E
Lom, Ross. 80 57.54 N 39.12 E
Lom ʌ 60 49.54 N 13.12 E
Lom ≏, Afr. 152 5.20 N 13.24 E
Lom ≏, Blg. 38 43.50 N 23.15 E
Loma 144 6.55 N 37.34 E
Loma, Point ≻ 228 32.41 N 117.14 W
Loma Blanca, Chile 286e 33.30 S 70.47 W
Loma Blanca, Méx. 200 31.35 N 106.17 W
Loma Bonita 234 18.07 N 95.53 W
Loma Echegareña 234 22.53 N 105.51 W
Lomakino 85 40.05 N 68.10 E
Lomako ≏ 152 0.50 N 20.50 E
Loma Linda 228 34.02 N 117.15 W
Lomaloma 175g 17.17 S 178.59 W
Lomami ≏ 138 0.46 N 24.16 E
Loma Mountains ⩚ 150 9.10 N 11.07 W
Loma Ridge ʌ 280 33.45 N 117.43 W
Lomas, Bahía ⊂ 254 52.35 S 69.05 W
Lomas Alegres 234 17.38 N 92.36 W
Lomas Chapultepec ◆[8] 286a 19.26 N 99.13 W
Lomas del Real 234 22.30 N 97.54 W
Lomas de Monreal 200 31.17 N 110.56 W
Lomas de Zamora 258 34.46 S 58.24 W
Lomas de Zamora □[5] 288 34.45 S 58.24 W
Loma Verde 258 35.16 S 58.24 W
Lomax, Il., U.S. 190 40.41 N 91.04 W
Lomax, Tx., U.S. 222 29.41 N 95.04 W

Łomazy 30 51.55 N 23.10 E
Lomazzo 62 45.42 N 9.02 E
Lomba ≏ 152 15.36 S 21.32 E
Lombagin 112 0.55 N 124.04 E
Lombard 216 41.52 N 88.00 W
Lombardia □[4] 36 45.40 N 9.30 E
Lombardy East 273d 26.07 S 28.08 E
Lombe 152 9.27 S 16.13 E
Lomblen, Pulau I 112 8.25 S 123.30 E
Lombo do Tejo, Mouchão do I 266c 38.52 N 9.00 W
Lombok 115b 8.30 S 116.40 E
Lombok I 115b 8.45 S 116.30 E
Lombok, Selat ʯ 115b 8.30 S 115.50 E
Lombong 114 1.48 N 103.51 E
Lomé 150 6.08 N 1.13 E
Lomela 152 2.18 S 23.17 E
Lomela ≏ 152 0.14 S 20.42 E
Lomellina □[9] 62 45.15 N 8.45 E
Lomello 62 45.07 N 8.47 E
Lometa 196 31.13 N 98.23 W
Lomi 24 67.05 N 16.09 E
Lomié 152 3.10 N 13.37 E
Lomira 190 43.35 N 88.26 W
Lo Miranda 252 34.11 S 70.54 W
Lomita 228 33.47 N 118.18 W
Lom Kao 110 16.53 N 101.14 E
Lomma 41 55.41 N 13.05 E
Lommabukten ⊂ 41 55.40 N 12.58 E
Lommatzsch 54 51.12 N 13.18 E
Lomme 50 50.39 N 2.59 E
Lomme ≏ 56 50.08 N 5.10 E
Lommel 56 51.14 N 5.18 E
Lomnice ≏ 60 49.26 N 14.04 E
Lomnice nad Popelkou 30 50.32 N 15.22 E
Lomond 182 50.21 N 112.39 W
Lomond, Loch ⊜, N.S., Can. 186 45.46 N 60.35 W
Lomond, Loch ⊜, On., Can. 190 48.15 N 89.20 W
Lomond, Loch ⊜, Scot., U.K. 46 56.08 N 4.38 W
Lomond, Loch ⊜, Il., U.S. 278 42.17 N 88.01 W
Lomonosov 265a 59.55 N 29.46 E
Lomonosov Moscow State University ʊ[2] 265b 55.43 N 37.32 E
Lomonosovskij 86 52.50 N 66.28 E
Lomovatka 83 48.27 N 38.34 E
Lomovoje 24 64.01 N 40.40 E
Lompobatang, Gunung ʌ 112 5.20 S 119.55 E
Lompoc 204 34.38 N 120.27 W
Lom Sak 110 16.47 N 101.15 E
Lomy 88 52.17 N 117.59 E
Łomża 30 53.11 N 22.05 E
łomża □[4] 30 53.00 N 22.15 E
Lonaconing 188 39.33 N 78.58 W
Lonate Pozzolo 62 45.36 N 8.45 E
Lonato 64 45.27 N 10.29 E
Lonāvale 122 18.45 N 73.25 E
Lončakovo 89 47.05 N 134.10 E
Loncoche 254 39.22 S 72.38 W
Loncon ≏ 64 45.42 N 12.47 E
Loncopué 252 38.04 S 70.37 W
Londela-Kaye 152 4.51 S 13.24 E
Londerzeel 50 51.00 N 4.18 E
Londinières 50 49.50 N 1.24 E
Londo 154 2.03 N 25.43 E
Londoko 89 49.02 N 131.59 E
London, On., Can. 212 42.59 N 81.14 W
London, Kiribati 174o 1.58 N 157.28 W
London, Eng., U.K. 42 51.30 N 0.10 W
London, Eng., U.K. 260 51.30 N 0.10 W
London, Ar., U.S. 194 35.19 N 93.15 W
London, Ca., U.S. 226 36.30 N 119.25 W
London, Ky., U.S. 192 37.07 N 84.05 W
London, Oh., U.S. 218 39.53 N 83.26 W
London, Tx., U.S. 196 30.41 N 99.35 W
London, Wi., U.S. 216 43.03 N 89.01 W
London (Gatwick) Airport ⊠, Eng., U.K. 42 51.09 N 0.21 W
London (Heathrow) Airport ⊠, Eng., U.K. 42 51.27 N 0.28 W
London Colney 260 51.43 N 0.18 W
Londonderry, N.S., Can. 186 45.29 N 63.36 W
Londonderry (Derry), N. Ire., U.K. 48 54.59 N 7.20 W
Londonderry, N.H., U.S. 207 42.51 N 71.22 W
Londonderry, Oh., U.S. 214 39.16 N 82.47 W
Londonderry, Cape ≻ 164 13.45 S 126.55 E
Londonderry, Isla I 254 55.03 S 70.35 W
Londontowne 208 38.59 N 76.32 W
London Zoo ♦ 260 51.32 N 0.09 W
Londres 252 27.43 S 67.07 W
Londres → London 42 51.30 N 0.10 W
Londrina 255 23.18 S 51.09 W
Lonedell 219 38.18 N 90.50 W
Lone Grove 196 34.10 N 97.15 W
Lonely Lake ⊜ 184 51.09 N 99.05 W
Lonelyville 276 40.39 N 73.11 W
Lone Mountain ʌ 204 38.02 N 117.29 W
Lone Oak, Ky., U.S. 194 37.02 N 88.39 W
Lone Oak, Tx., U.S. 222 33.01 N 95.57 W
Lone Pine 204 36.36 N 118.03 W
Lone Pine Koala Sanctuary ♦ 171a 27.32 S 152.57 E
Lone Rock 190 43.11 N 90.11 W
Lone Star 222 32.56 N 94.43 W
Lone Tree 190 41.29 N 91.25 W
Lone Tree Creek ≏, U.S. 200 40.25 N 104.35 W
Lone Tree Creek ≏, Ca., U.S. 226 37.53 N 121.14 W
Lone Wolf 196 34.59 N 99.14 W
Long 110 18.05 N 99.50 E
Long ≏, Fr. 50 47.41 N 0.28 E
Long ≏, Zhg. 100 23.26 N 114.38 E
Long ≏, Zhg. 102 24.32 N 109.15 E
Long ≏, Zhg. 105 39.23 N 116.49 E
Longa 152 14.42 S 18.32 E
Longa ≏, Ang. 152 16.25 N 19.04 E
Longa ≏, Ang. 152 10.15 S 13.30 E
Longá ≏, Bra. 250 3.09 S 41.56 W
Longa, proliv ʯ 74 70.20 N 178.00 E
Longairo 154 4.30 N 32.17 E
Long Akah 112 3.19 N 114.47 E
Long'an 102 25.03 N 109.00 E
Longana 175f 15.20 S 167.55 E
Long'anqiao 89 47.31 N 124.27 E
Longare 64 45.29 N 11.36 E
Longarone 64 46.16 N 12.18 E
Long Arroyo V 196 33.04 N 104.17 W
Longasy 24 61.58 N 35.09 E
Longaví 252 35.58 S 71.41 W
Longbangun 112 0.36 N 115.11 E
Long Bar Harbor 208 39.27 N 76.15 W
Long Barn 226 38.05 N 120.08 W
Long Bay ⊂, Austl. 274a 33.58 S 151.16 E
Long Bay ⊂, U.S. 192 33.35 N 78.45 W
Long Beach, Ca., U.S. 228 33.46 N 118.11 W
Long Beach, In., U.S. 216 41.44 N 86.51 W
Long Beach, Ms., U.S. 194 30.21 N 89.09 W
Long Beach, N.Y., U.S. 210 40.35 N 73.39 W
Long Beach, Wa., U.S. 224 46.21 N 124.03 W
Long Beach ⊥[2] 208 39.39 N 74.11 W
Long Beach Breakwater ◆[5] 280 33.43 N 118.09 W

Long Beach Middle Harbor ⊂ 280 33.45 N 118.13 W
Long Beach Municipal Airport ⊠ 280 33.49 N 118.09 W
Long Beach Naval Station ■ 280 33.45 N 118.14 W
Longbeleh 112 0.16 N 116.11 E
Long Belepai 112 2.45 N 114.04 E
Longbenton 44 55.02 N 1.35 W
Longboat Key 220 27.24 N 82.39 W
Longboat Key I 220 27.23 N 82.39 W
Long Branch, N.J., U.S. 208 40.18 N 73.59 W
Longbranch, Wa., U.S. 224 47.12 N 122.45 W
Long Branch □[8] 275b 43.35 N 79.32 W
Long Branch ≏ 219 39.23 N 91.49 W
Long Branch Lake ⊜[1] 194 39.49 N 92.31 W
Longbu 100 25.32 N 115.24 E
Long Buckby 42 52.19 N 1.04 W
Long Cane Creek ≏ 192 33.57 N 82.24 W
Long Canyon V 226 38.59 N 120.41 W
Long Cay I 238 22.37 N 74.20 W
Longchamp, Hippodrome de ♦ 261 48.51 N 2.14 E
Longchamps, Arg. 258 34.52 S 58.23 W
Longchamps, Bel. 56 50.03 N 5.42 E
Longchang, Zhg. 104 40.53 N 123.08 E
Longchang, Zhg. 107 29.21 N 105.17 E
Longchaumois 58 46.27 N 5.56 E
Longchêne 261 48.38 N 2.00 E
Longchuan, Zhg. 100 24.07 N 115.17 E
Longchuan, Zhg. 102 24.14 N 97.45 E
Longchuan (Shweli) ≏ 102 23.56 N 96.17 E
Long Creek, Il., U.S. 219 39.48 N 88.50 W
Long Creek, Or., U.S. 202 44.42 N 119.06 W
Long Creek ≏ 184 49.07 N 103.00 W
Long Crendon 42 51.47 N 1.01 W
Longcun 100 23.34 N 115.33 E
Longde 102 35.28 N 106.22 E
Longdendale V 262 53.29 N 1.56 W
Long Ditton 260 51.23 N 0.20 W
Longdongtuo 107 29.59 N 106.21 E
Longdor, gora ʌ 88 58.24 N 116.47 E
Longdou 100 27.25 N 117.24 E
Longdu 106 31.51 N 118.56 E
Long Eaton 42 52.54 N 1.15 W
Longeau 58 47.46 N 5.18 E
Long Eddy 210 41.51 N 75.08 W
Longfellow National Historical Site ⊥ 283 42.23 N 71.08 W
Longfengchang 107 30.26 N 105.38 E
Longfengkan 104 41.51 N 124.01 E
Longfengyutun 104 40.39 N 122.57 E
Longfield 260 51.24 N 0.18 E
Longford, Austl. 166 38.10 S 147.05 E
Longford, Ire. 48 53.44 N 7.47 W
Longford, Md., U.S. 284b 39.25 N 76.39 W
Longford □[6] 48 53.40 N 7.40 W
Longford Park ♦ 262 53.27 N 2.17 W
Longframlington 44 55.18 N 1.47 W
Longgang, Zhg. 100 29.38 N 114.57 E
Longgang, Zhg. 100 33.22 N 120.04 E
Longgang, Zhg. 102 24.41 N 101.09 E
Longgangzi 104 42.09 N 123.26 E
Long Green 208 39.28 N 76.31 W
Long Grove 216 42.11 N 88.00 W
Longguan 105 40.47 N 115.34 E
Longgudu 100 27.45 N 116.14 E
Longguntur 112 0.13 N 112.12 E
Long Harbour 186 47.26 N 53.48 W
Long Harbour ⊂, Nf., Can. 186 47.44 N 55.01 W
Long Harbour ⊂, H.K. 271d 22.27 N 114.20 E
Longhorn Cavern State Park ♦ 196 30.20 N 98.30 W
Longhorsley 44 55.15 N 1.46 W
Longhoughton 44 55.26 N 1.36 W
Long Hu ⊜ 100 29.58 N 116.10 E
Longhua, Zhg. 98 41.17 N 117.37 E
Longhua, Zhg. 100 22.42 N 113.59 E
Longhua, Zhg. 100 23.37 N 114.14 E
Longhua, Zhg. 106 31.09 N 121.26 E
Longhua Airport ⊠ 269b 31.10 N 121.26 E
Longhua Pagoda ʊ[1] 269b 31.11 N 121.26 E
Longhui, Zhg. 100 25.32 N 114.47 E
Longhui (Taohuaping), Zhg. 102 27.00 N 110.59 E
Longhui, Zhg. 107 29.32 N 104.48 E
Longhutang 106 31.52 N 119.59 E
Longi 70 38.01 N 14.45 E
Longido 154 2.44 S 36.41 E
Longiram 112 0.02 S 115.38 E
Long Island I, Antig. 240c 17.08 N 61.45 W
Long Island I, Austl. 166 22.09 S 149.54 E
Long Island I, Ba. 238 23.15 N 75.07 W
Long Island I, Nf., Can. 186 47.35 N 54.05 W
Long Island I, N.T., Can. 176 54.50 N 79.20 W
Long Island I, N.S., Can. 186 44.20 N 66.15 W
Long Island I, Ak., U.S. 182 54.54 N 132.45 W
Long Island I, Ma., U.S. 283 42.19 N 70.58 W
Long Island I, N.Y., U.S. 188 40.50 N 73.00 W
Long Island I, Wa., U.S. 224 46.27 N 123.58 W
Long Island City ◆[8] 276 40.45 N 73.56 W
Long Island MacArthur Airport ⊠ 210 40.48 N 73.06 W
Long Island Sound ʯ 188 41.05 N 72.58 W
Long Island University (C.W. Post Center) ʊ[2], N.Y., U.S. 276 40.49 N 73.36 W
Long Island University ʊ[2], N.Y., U.S. 276 40.41 N 73.59 W
Longitudinal, Valle V 252 36.00 S 72.00 W
Long Jetty 170 33.22 S 151.29 E
Longji 107 29.23 N 106.04 E
Longjiadian 104 42.10 N 120.47 E
Longjiang, Zhg. 89 47.19 N 123.12 E
Longjiang, Zhg. 100 22.59 N 116.13 E
Longjiang, Zhg. 100 22.53 N 113.04 E
Longjiang, Zhg. 107 29.48 N 105.03 E
Longjie 107 29.53 N 104.32 E
Longjin 100 28.37 N 116.37 E
Longjing 100 23.53 N 112.52 E
Longjohn Slough ≏ 278 41.43 N 87.53 W
Longjumeau 50 48.42 N 2.18 E
Longka 120 33.12 N 79.47 E
Longkamp 56 49.53 N 7.07 E
Longkangji 100 33.09 N 116.54 E
Long Ke 271d 22.23 N 114.22 E
Long Key I, Fl., U.S. 220 27.44 N 82.45 W
Long Key I, Fl., U.S. 220 24.49 N 80.49 W
Long King Creek ≏ 222 30.34 N 94.58 W
Longkou, Zhg. 98 37.38 N 120.18 E
Longkou, Zhg. 100 32.56 N 114.57 E
Longkou, Zhg. 100 29.57 N 113.47 E
Longkou, Zhg. 100 26.11 N 115.15 E
Longkouqiao 85 39.40 N 77.09 E
Long Lake, Il., U.S. 216 42.22 N 88.08 W
Long Lake, N.Y., U.S. 188 43.58 N 74.25 W
Long Lake, Tx., U.S. 222 31.39 N 95.47 W
Long Lake ⊜, On., Can. 212 44.41 N 76.45 W
Long Lake ⊜, Mi., U.S. 190 45.12 N 83.30 W
Long Lake ⊜, Mi., U.S. 281 42.37 N 83.44 W

Long Lake ⊜, Mi., U.S. 281 42.36 N 83.28 W
Long Lake ⊜, N.Y., U.S. 188 44.04 N 74.20 W
Long Lake ⊜, N.D., U.S. 198 46.43 N 100.07 W
Long Lake ⊜, Wa., U.S. 224 47.03 N 122.47 W
Long Lake ⊜[1] 202 47.50 N 117.40 W
Long Lake Creek ≏ 198 46.40 N 100.13 W
Long Lake Shores 281 42.35 N 83.19 W
Long Lama 112 3.46 N 114.24 E
Longlaville 56 49.32 N 5.47 E
Longleaf 194 31.00 N 92.34 W
Long Leaf Park 192 34.12 N 77.56 W
Longleat ʊ 42 51.12 N 2.17 W
Longlegged Lake ⊜ 184 50.46 N 94.08 W
Longli 102 26.26 N 106.58 E
Longlin 102 24.49 N 105.31 E
Longling 102 24.39 N 98.40 E
Longmeadow 207 42.03 N 72.35 W
Long Melford 42 52.05 N 0.43 E
Longmen, Zhg. 89 48.55 N 126.54 E
Longmen, Zhg. 100 29.53 N 119.57 E
Longmen, Zhg. 100 24.56 N 118.04 E
Longmen, Zhg. 100 25.06 N 116.58 E
Longmen, Zhg. 100 23.44 N 114.15 E
Longmen, Zhg. 107 29.12 N 106.13 E
Longmen, Zhg. 107 29.27 N 104.59 E
Longmenchang 107 30.53 N 106.10 E
Longmensuo 98 40.56 N 115.54 E
Longmenzhang 107 28.59 N 106.13 E
Longming 102 22.59 N 107.11 E
Longmire 224 46.45 N 121.49 W
Long Moc 110 18.51 N 105.01 E
Longmont 200 40.10 N 105.06 W
Longmorn 46 57.36 N 3.17 W
Long Mountain ʌ 194 36.41 N 92.26 W
Long Mountain ʌ[2] 42 52.39 N 3.09 W
Longmu 100 24.16 N 115.28 E
Longnan 100 24.54 N 114.48 E
Longnawan 112 1.54 N 114.53 E
Long Neck ≻[1] 276 41.03 N 73.29 W
Long Neck Point ≻ 276 41.02 N 73.29 W
Longniddry 46 55.58 N 2.53 W
Longnüsi 107 30.23 N 106.11 E
Longny-au-Perche 50 48.32 N 0.45 E
Longobucco 68 39.27 N 16.37 E
Longperrier 261 49.03 N 2.40 E
Long Pine 198 42.32 N 99.42 W
Longping 100 29.53 N 115.41 E
Long Plains 168b 34.21 S 138.22 E
Long Point, Austl. 274a 34.01 S 150.54 E
Long Point, Il., U.S. 216 41.00 N 88.54 W
Long Point ≻, Ba. 240b 25.01 N 77.20 W
Long Point ≻, Nf., Can. 186 48.48 N 58.46 W
Long Point ≻, N.S., Can. 186 46.51 N 60.18 W
Long Point ≻, On., Can. 212 44.06 N 76.29 W
Long Point ≻, On., Can. 212 44.32 N 80.18 W
Long Point ≻, Pil. 116 9.39 N 118.20 E
Long Point ≻, Ca., U.S. 280 33.44 N 118.23 W
Long Point ≻, Vir. Is., U.S. 240m 18.18 N 64.53 W
Long Point ≻[1], Mb., Can. 184 53.02 N 98.40 W
Long Point ≻[1], On., Can. 214 42.34 N 80.15 W
Long Point Bay ⊂ 212 42.40 N 80.14 W
Long Point Creek ≏ 216 41.02 N 88.48 W
Long Point Provincial Park ♦ 214 42.35 N 80.35 W
Long Pond ⊜, U.S. 283 42.41 N 71.21 W
Long Pond ⊜, Ma., U.S. 207 41.43 N 70.04 W
Long Pond ⊜, Ma., U.S. 207 41.48 N 70.57 W
Longpont, Fr. 50 49.16 N 3.13 E
Longpont, Fr. 261 48.38 N 2.17 E
Longport 208 39.18 N 74.31 W
Long Prairie 198 45.58 N 94.51 W
Long Prairie ≏ 198 46.20 N 94.36 W
Longpré-les-Corps-Sants 50 50.01 N 1.59 E
Long Preston 44 54.02 N 2.15 W
Longqiantai 104 41.23 N 120.52 E
Longqu, Zhg. 98 34.16 N 114.49 E
Longqu, Zhg. 98 34.54 N 116.47 E
Longquan 100 28.04 N 119.07 E
Longquan ≏ 100 28.17 N 119.44 E
Longquanguan 98 38.55 N 113.51 E
Longquan Shan ⩚ 107 30.25 N 104.15 E
Longquanyi 107 30.34 N 104.16 E
Longquanzhen 107 30.21 N 104.39 E
Long Range Mountains ⩚ 186 49.20 N 57.30 W
Longreach 166 23.26 S 144.15 E
Long Reach ⊂ 186 45.26 N 66.09 W
Long Reach ʯ 212 44.07 N 77.04 W
Long Reef ✢[2] 164 11.11 S 151.40 E
Long Reef Point ≻ 274a 33.45 S 151.19 E
Longridge 44 53.51 N 2.36 W
Long Run ≏, Il., U.S. 278 41.37 N 88.03 W
Long Run ≏, Pa., U.S. 279b 40.20 N 79.48 W
Long-Sault 206 45.02 N 74.53 W
Long Sault Dam ◆[6] 206 45.00 N 74.45 W
Long Sault Islands II 206 45.00 N 74.55 W
Longsegah 112 2.15 N 116.42 E
Longshan, Zhg. 100 33.36 N 116.18 E
Longshan, Zhg. 102 29.28 N 109.20 E
Longshansuo 100 30.05 N 121.33 E
Longsheng, Zhg. 102 25.48 N 110.00 E
Longsheng, Zhg. 107 30.36 N 105.21 E
Longshizhen, Zhg. 107 30.12 N 106.26 E
Longshizhen, Zhg. 107 29.23 N 105.10 E
Longshu 107 29.33 N 105.45 E
Longs Peak ʌ 200 40.15 N 105.37 W
Long Stratton 42 52.29 N 1.14 E
Long Sutton 42 52.47 N 0.08 E
Longtaichang 107 30.04 N 105.34 E
Longtan, Zhg. 100 23.40 N 113.24 E
Longtan, Zhg. 102 28.20 N 108.52 E
Longtan, Zhg. 106 32.11 N 119.04 E
Longtan, Zhg. 106 31.20 N 118.45 E
Longtansi 107 30.42 N 104.10 E
Longtanzhen 107 29.19 N 104.35 E
Long Teru 112 3.52 N 114.15 E
Long Thanh 110 10.47 N 106.57 E
Longtian 100 25.38 N 119.28 E
Longtian'an 106 31.10 N 120.49 E
Long Tom ≏ 202 44.23 N 123.15 W
Longton, Eng., U.K. 44 53.43 N 2.48 W
Longton, Eng., U.K. 262 53.43 N 2.48 W
Longton, Ks., U.S. 198 37.22 N 96.04 W
Longtou 98 38.51 N 121.18 E
Longtoupu 100 27.54 N 113.12 E
Longtouwei 100 25.14 N 115.24 E
Longtown 44 55.01 N 2.58 W
Long Truong 269c 10.49 N 106.49 E
Longué 32 47.23 N 0.06 W
Longueau 50 49.52 N 2.21 E
Longuenesse 50 50.44 N 2.14 E
Longuesse 261 49.04 N 1.56 E
Longueuil 206 45.32 N 73.30 W
Longueville, Austl. 274a 33.50 S 151.10 E
Longueville, Fr. 50 48.31 N 3.15 E
Longueville-sur-Scie 50 49.48 N 1.06 E
Longuyon 56 49.26 N 5.36 E
Long Valley 210 40.47 N 74.46 W
Long Valley Creek ≏, Ca., U.S. 226 39.03 N 122.34 W
Long Valley Creek ≏, Nv., U.S. 226 39.31 N 119.39 W
Longvic 58 47.17 N 5.04 E
Longview, Ab., Can. 182 50.32 N 114.14 W

Longview, N.C., U.S. 192 35.43 N 81.23 W
Longview, Tx., U.S. 222 32.30 N 94.44 W
Longview, Wa., U.S. 224 46.08 N 122.56 W
Longview Heights 222 32.30 N 94.41 W
Longvilliers 261 48.35 N 2.00 E
Longvilly 56 50.01 N 5.50 E
Longwai 112 0.42 N 116.39 E
Longwan 105 38.57 N 116.10 E
Longwangmiao, Zhg. 98 36.12 N 115.13 E
Longwangmiao, Zhg. 102 40.36 N 95.52 E
Longwangmiao, Zhg. 104 41.38 N 121.04 E
Longwangmiao, Zhg. 104 42.35 N 123.42 E
Longwarry 169 38.07 S 145.46 E
Longwen 100 24.36 N 116.21 E
Longwo 100 23.28 N 115.17 E
Longwokou 106 32.18 N 119.52 E
Longwood 220 28.42 N 81.20 W
Longwood Gardens ♦ 285 39.52 N 75.40 W
Longwood Lake 276 40.59 N 74.52 W
Longwood Park 192 34.55 N 79.42 W
Longworth 182 53.55 N 121.28 W
Longwy 56 49.31 N 5.46 E
Longxi, Zhg. 102 34.56 N 104.47 E
Longxi, Zhg. 107 29.59 N 106.09 E
Longxian, Zhg. 102 34.51 N 106.59 E
Longxian, Zhg. 107 29.09 N 105.50 E
Longxi → Zhangzhou 100 24.33 N 117.39 E
Long Xuyen 110 10.23 N 105.25 E
Longyan 100 25.08 N 117.02 E
Longyao 98 37.23 N 114.41 E
Longyou 100 29.02 N 119.10 E
Longyou ≏ 106 32.08 N 120.38 E
Longyuanba 100 24.56 N 114.27 E
Longzhaogou 98 40.49 N 124.36 E
Longzhen 89 48.41 N 126.42 E
Longzhou 102 22.22 N 106.52 E
Loni 272a 28.45 N 77.17 E
Lonigo 64 45.23 N 11.23 E
Löningen 52 52.44 N 7.46 E
Lonja ≏ 36 45.27 N 16.41 E
Lonkala 152 4.37 S 23.14 E
Lönnewitz 54 51.34 N 13.11 E
Lonny 56 49.49 N 4.35 E
Lonoke 194 34.47 N 91.53 W
Lonquimay, Volcán ʌ[1] 252 38.22 S 71.34 W
Lönsboda 26 56.24 N 14.19 E
Lønsdal 24 66.44 N 15.28 E
Lonsdale 190 44.28 N 93.25 W
Lonsdale, Point ≻ 169 38.17 S 144.37 E
Lons-le-Saunier 58 46.40 N 5.33 E
Lonton 110 25.06 N 96.17 E
Lontra ≏ 250 6.37 S 48.39 W
Lontra, Ribeirão da ≏ 255 21.28 S 53.37 W
Lonua ≏ 152 1.16 N 22.38 E
Lonzhen 107 30.00 N 103.59 E
Loo 84 43.43 N 39.36 E
Looc 116 12.16 N 121.59 E
Looe 42 50.21 N 4.28 W
Loogootee 194 38.40 N 86.54 W
Looking Glass ≏ 216 42.52 N 84.54 W
Lookout 210 41.47 N 75.11 W
Lookout, Cape ≻, N.C., U.S. 192 34.35 N 76.32 W
Lookout, Cape ≻, Or., U.S. 224 45.20 N 124.00 W
Lookout, Point ≻, Austl. 171a 27.26 S 153.33 E
Lookout, Point ≻, Md., U.S. 208 38.02 N 76.19 W
Lookout Mountain ʌ, U.S. 194 34.25 N 85.40 W
Lookout Mountain ʌ, Or., U.S. 202 44.20 N 120.22 W
Lookout Mountain ʌ, Or., U.S. 224 45.21 N 121.31 W
Lookout Mountain ʌ, Wa., U.S. 224 48.40 N 122.22 W
Lookout Pass)(202 47.27 N 115.42 W
Lookout Point Lake ⊜[1] 202 43.52 N 122.40 W
Lookout Ridge ⩚ 180 69.07 N 158.36 W
Loolmalassin ʌ[1] 154 3.03 S 35.49 E
Loomis, Ca., U.S. 226 38.49 N 121.12 W
Loomis, Ne., U.S. 198 40.28 N 99.30 W
Loomis, Wa., U.S. 182 48.49 N 119.37 W
Loon 116 9.48 N 123.47 E
Loon ≏ 184 55.50 N 101.59 W
Loon Creek ≏ 202 44.49 N 114.49 W
Loongana 162 30.57 S 127.02 E
Loon Lake ⊜, Can. 184 55.51 N 102.00 W
Loon Lake ⊜, Mi., U.S. 281 42.41 N 83.22 W
Loon Lake ⊜[1] 226 39.00 N 120.18 W
Loon op Zand 52 51.38 N 5.04 E
Loop 196 32.55 N 102.25 W
Loop ◆[8] 278 41.53 N 87.38 W
Loop Head ≻ 48 52.34 N 9.56 W
Loos 50 50.37 N 3.01 E
Loosdorf 61 48.12 N 15.24 E
Loosduinen ◆[8] 52 52.04 N 4.13 E
Loose, Dtsch. 41 54.31 N 9.53 E
Loose, Eng., U.K. 260 51.14 N 0.31 E
Loose Creek 219 38.30 N 91.57 W
Lop 120 37.02 N 80.15 E
Lop ≏ 110 13.18 N 107.37 E
Lopandino 76 52.28 N 34.49 E
Lopanka 80 46.24 N 40.59 E
Lopar'ovo 80 58.20 N 42.41 E
Lopasn'a ≏ 82 54.51 N 37.52 E
Lopatiči 76 53.34 N 30.53 E
Lopatin, Ross. 84 43.53 N 47.41 E
Lopatin, Ukr. 78 50.13 N 24.50 E
Lopatina, gora ʌ 89 50.52 N 143.10 E
Lopatino, Ross. 80 52.37 N 45.47 E
Lopatino, Ross. 82 54.45 N 37.00 E
Lopatino, Ross. 89 48.24 N 142.15 E
Lopatinskij 82 55.21 N 38.34 E
Lopatka, mys ≻ 74 50.52 N 156.40 E
Lopatovo 76 56.08 N 29.12 E
Lop Buri 110 14.48 N 100.37 E
Lopé-Okanda, Réserve de Chasse de ◆[4] 152 0.30 S 11.40 E
Lopévi I 175f 16.30 S 168.21 E
López, Méx. 232 27.00 N 105.02 W
Lopez, Pa., U.S. 210 41.27 N 76.20 W
Lopez, Wa., U.S. 224 48.31 N 122.54 W
López, Arroyo de ≏ 258 35.26 S 57.35 W
Lopez, Cap ≻ 152 0.37 S 8.43 E
Lopez Bay ⊂ 116 13.56 N 122.12 E
Lopez Island I 224 48.30 N 122.54 W
Lopez Lake ⊜[1] 226 35.12 N 120.28 W
Lopik 52 51.58 N 4.56 E
Lop Nor → Lop Nur ⊜ 90 40.20 N 90.15 E
Lop Nur (Lop Nor) ⊜ 90 40.20 N 90.15 E
Lopori ≏ 152 1.14 N 19.49 E
Lopotovo 82 56.04 N 36.49 E
Loppersum 52 53.19 N 6.45 E
Loppi 26 60.43 N 24.27 E
Lo Prado 286e 33.26 S 70.45 W
Lopšen'ga 24 64.58 N 37.41 E
L'Opton Ruisseau ≏ 261 48.52 N 1.29 E
Lopt'uga 24 63.16 N 47.56 E
Lopuchovka, Ross. 80 51.59 N 44.42 E
Lopuchovka, Ross. 80 50.37 N 44.29 E
Łopuszno 30 50.57 N 20.15 E
Lora 123 33.53 N 73.17 E
Lora ≏ 246 9.25 N 72.25 W
Lora, Hāmūn-i- ⊜ 128 29.20 N 64.50 E
Lora Creek ≏ 162 28.10 S 135.22 E
Lora del Río 34 37.39 N 5.32 W
Lorain 214 41.27 N 82.10 W
Lorain □[6] 214 41.22 N 82.06 W
Lorain County Regional Airport ⊠ 279a 41.20 N 82.11 W
Loraine, Ca., U.S. 228 35.19 N 118.25 W

Loraine, Il., U.S. 219 40.09 N 91.13 W
Loraine, Tx., U.S. 196 32.24 N 100.42 W
Loralai 120 30.22 N 68.36 E
Loramie, Lake ⊜[1] 216 40.23 N 84.18 W
Loramie Creek ≏ 216 40.11 N 84.14 W
Lorca 34 37.40 N 1.42 W
Lorch, Dtsch. 56 48.49 N 9.40 E
Lorch, Dtsch. 56 50.02 N 7.48 E
Lorchhausen 56 50.03 N 7.47 E
Lord Howe Island I 160 31.33 S 159.05 E
Lord Howe Rise ✢[3] 14 32.00 S 162.00 E
Lord Howe Seamounts ✢[3] 14 28.00 S 159.00 E
Lord Mayor Bay ⊂ 176 69.44 N 92.00 W
Lordsburg 200 32.21 N 108.42 W
Lord's Cricket Ground ♦ 260 51.32 N 0.10 W
Lordstown 214 41.09 N 80.53 W
Lords Valley 210 41.23 N 75.04 W
Loreauville 194 30.03 N 91.44 W
Loreley ♦ 56 50.08 N 7.44 E
Lorena, Bra. 256 22.44 S 45.08 W
Lorena, Tx., U.S. 222 31.23 N 97.13 W
Lorengau 164 2.00 S 147.15 E
Lorentz ≏ 164 5.23 S 138.04 E
Lorentzen 56 48.57 N 7.10 E
Lorenzago di Cadore 64 46.29 N 12.28 E
Lorenzo 196 33.40 N 101.32 W
Lorenzo Geyres (Queguay) 252 32.05 S 57.55 W
Loreo 64 45.04 N 12.11 E
Lorestān □[4] 128 33.30 N 48.30 E
Loreto, Arg. 252 27.46 S 57.17 W
Loreto, Bol. 248 15.13 S 64.40 W
Loreto, Bra. 250 7.05 S 45.09 W
Loreto, It. 66 43.26 N 13.36 E
Loreto, Méx. 232 26.01 N 111.21 W
Loreto, Méx. 234 22.16 N 101.58 W
Loreto, Para. 252 23.16 S 57.11 W
Loreto, Pil. 116 8.12 N 125.45 E
Loreto, Pil. 116 10.21 N 125.34 E
Loreto □[5] 246 3.00 S 75.00 W
Loreto Aprutino 66 42.26 N 13.59 E
Loreto Mocagua 246 3.48 S 70.15 W
Lorette, Mb., Can. 184 49.44 N 96.52 W
Lorette, Fr. 62 45.31 N 4.35 E
Loretteville 206 46.51 N 71.21 W
Loretto, Ky., U.S. 194 37.38 N 85.24 W
Loretto, Pa., U.S. 214 40.30 N 78.37 W
Loretto, Tn., U.S. 194 35.04 N 87.26 W
Loretto → Loreto 66 43.26 N 13.36 E
Lorgues 62 43.29 N 6.22 E
Lorian Swamp ≡ 154 0.40 N 39.35 E
Lorica 246 9.14 N 75.49 W
Lorida 220 27.26 N 81.15 W
Lorient 32 47.45 N 3.22 W
L'Orignal 206 45.37 N 74.42 W
Lorimer Park ♦ 285 40.06 N 75.05 W
Lorimor 194 41.07 N 94.03 W
Loring, Aeródromo de ⊠ 266a 40.22 N 3.47 W
Loring Air Force Base ■ 186 46.57 N 67.54 W
Lorino 180 65.30 N 171.43 W
Loriol-sur-Drôme 62 44.45 N 4.49 E
Loris 192 34.03 N 78.53 W
Lorman 194 31.49 N 91.03 W
L'Orme 261 48.39 N 1.41 E
Lormes 50 47.17 N 3.49 E
Lorn, Firth of ⊂[1] 46 56.20 N 5.45 W
Lorna Glen 162 26.14 S 121.33 E
Lorne, Austl. 169 38.33 S 143.59 E
Lorne, N.B., Can. 186 47.53 N 66.08 W
Loro Ciuffenna 66 43.35 N 11.38 E
Loronyo 154 4.39 N 32.38 E
Lorquin 58 48.40 N 7.00 E
Lörrach 58 47.37 N 7.40 E
Lorraine □[9] 32 49.00 N 6.00 E
Lorrez-le-Bocage 50 48.14 N 2.54 E
Lorris 50 47.53 N 2.31 E
Lorsch 56 49.39 N 8.34 E
Lorsica 62 44.26 N 9.16 E
Lorup 52 52.55 N 7.38 E
Lorze ≏ 58 47.15 N 8.25 E
Los 26 61.44 N 15.10 E
Los, Îles de II 150 9.30 N 13.48 W
Losa, Nuraghe ⊥ 71 40.07 N 8.46 E
Losada ≏ 246 2.12 N 73.55 W
Los Aguacates 286c 10.35 N 66.48 W
Los Alamitos 280 33.48 N 118.04 W
Los Alamitos Armed Forces Reserve Center ■ 280 33.47 N 118.03 W
Los Alamitos Race Course ♦ 280 33.48 N 118.03 W
Los Alamos, Ca., U.S. 204 34.44 N 120.16 W
Los Alamos, N.M., U.S. 200 35.53 N 106.19 W
Los Aldamas 232 26.03 N 99.11 W
Los Alerces, Parque Nacional ♦ 254 42.50 S 71.52 W
Los Altos, Méx. 196 26.14 N 98.28 W
Los Altos, Ca., U.S. 226 37.23 N 122.06 W
Los Altos Hills 226 37.22 N 122.08 W
Los Amates, Guat. 236 15.16 N 89.06 W
Los Amates, Méx. 234 18.08 N 102.15 W
Los Americanos, Barra I 232 24.50 N 97.35 W
Los Andes 252 32.50 S 70.37 W
Los Ángeles, Chile 252 37.28 S 72.21 W
Los Angeles, Ca., U.S. 228 34.03 N 118.14 W
Los Angeles, Ca., U.S. 280 34.03 N 118.14 W
Los Angeles □[6] 228 34.20 N 118.10 W
Los Angeles ≏ 228 33.46 N 118.12 W
Los Angeles Aqueduct ≊[1] 204 35.22 N 118.05 W
Los Angeles Coliseum and Sports Arena ♦ 280 34.01 N 118.17 W
Los Angeles Convention Center ʊ 280 34.03 N 118.17 W
Los Angeles County Fairgrounds ♦ 280 34.05 N 117.46 W
Los Angeles County Museum of Art ʊ 280 34.05 N 118.22 W
Los Angeles Harbor ⊂ 280 33.42 N 118.16 W
Los Angeles International Airport ⊠ 228 33.56 N 118.24 W
Los Antiguos 254 46.33 S 71.37 W
Losantville 218 40.01 N 85.10 W
Losap I[1] 14 6.54 N 152.44 E
Los Arabos 240p 22.44 N 80.43 W
Losarang 115a 6.24 S 108.10 E
Los Aros 234 22.46 N 102.57 W
Los Banos 226 37.03 N 120.50 W
Los Banos Creek ≏ 226 37.20 N 120.57 W
Los Banos Creek, North Fork ≏ 226 36.57 N 121.07 W
Los Banos Creek, South Fork ≏ 226 36.57 N 121.07 W
Los Banos Reservoir ⊜[1] 226 36.59 N 120.57 W
Los Berros 252 31.57 S 68.39 W
Los Blancos 252 23.36 S 62.36 W
Los Bolones, Cerro ʌ, Méx. 232 16.50 N 92.38 W
Los Bolones, Cerro ʌ, Méx. 234 16.39 N 92.34 W
Los Cardales 258 34.20 S 58.59 W
Los Cerrillos, Arg. 252 31.57 S 65.28 W
Los Cerrillos, Ur. 258 34.37 S 56.22 W
Los Cerrillos, Aeropuerto ⊠ 286e 33.30 S 70.43 W

Symbol	English	Deutsch	Español	Français	Português
≏	River	Fluß	Río	Rivière	Rio
≊	Canal	Kanal	Canal	Canal	Canal
⌊	Waterfall, Rapids	Wasserfall, Stromschnellen	Cascada, Rápidos	Chute d'eau, Rapides	Cascata, Rápidos
ʯ	Strait	Meeresstraße	Estrecho	Détroit	Estreito
⊂	Bay, Gulf	Bucht, Golf	Bahía, Golfo	Baie, Golfe	Baía, Golfo
⊜	Lake, Lakes	See, Seen	Lago, Lagos	Lac, Lacs	Lago, Lagos
≡	Swamp	Sumpf	Pantano	Marais	Pântano
⊓	Ice Features, Glacier	Eis- und Gletscherformen	Accidentes Glaciales	Formes glaciaires	Acidentes glaciares
⊤	Other Hydrographic Features	Andere Hydrographische Objekte	Otros Elementos Hidrográficos	Autres données hydrographiques	Outros acidentes hidrográficos
✢	Submarine Features	Untermeerische Objekte	Accidentes Submarinos	Formes de relief sous-marin	Acidentes submarinos
□	Political Unit	Politische Einheit	Unidad Politica	Entité politique	Unidade política
ʊ	Cultural Institution	Kulturelle Institution	Institución Cultural	Institution culturelle	Instituição cultural
⊥	Historical Site	Historische Stätte	Sitio Histórico	Site historique	Sitio histórico
♦	Recreational Site	Erholungs- und Ferienort	Sitio de Recreo	Centre de loisirs	Area de Lazer
⊠	Airport	Flughafen	Aeropuerto	Aéroport	Aeroporto
■	Military Installation	Militäranlage	Instalación Militar	Installation militaire	Instalação militar
◆	Miscellaneous	Verschiedenes	Misceláneo	Divers	Diversos

Los Cerritos Center ◆[9] 280 33.52 N 118.05 W
Los Chacos 248 14.33 S 62.11 W
Löschenrod 56 50.30 N 9.41 E
Los Chiles 236 11.02 N 84.43 W
Los Conquistadores 252 30.36 S 58.28 W
Los Coronados, Islas II 204 32.25 N 117.15 W
Los Coyotes Indian Reservation ◆[4] 204 33.20 N 116.35 W
Los Cuatro Álamos 286e 33.32 S 70.44 W
Los Dos Caminos 286c 10.31 N 66.50 W
Los Ebanos 196 26.14 N 98.34 W
Loseley House ⊥ 260 51.13 N 0.36 W
Los Esclavos ≃ 236 13.50 N 90.20 W
Losevo 78 50.40 N 40.02 E
Los Flamencos, Laguna ⊜ 258 35.36 S 58.42 W
Los Frailes, Picacho ∧ 234 23.53 N 106.03 W
Los Frentones 252 26.25 S 61.25 W
Los Fresnos 196 26.04 N 97.29 W
Los Garzas 196 26.23 N 99.46 W
Los Gatos 226 37.13 N 121.58 W
Los Gatos Creek ≃, Ca., U.S. 226 36.13 N 120.08 W
Los Gatos Creek ≃, Ca., U.S. 226 37.20 N 121.54 W
Los Glaciares, Parque Nacional ♦ 254 49.52 S 73.05 W
Los Guerras 196 26.25 N 99.05 W
Loshan → Leshan 107 29.34 N 103.45 E
Losheim 56 49.30 N 6.44 E
Los Hermanos, Islas II 246 11.45 N 64.25 W
Los Herreras 196 25.55 N 99.24 W
Los Huacales, Cerro ∧ 234 22.19 N 101.34 W
Losi 273a 6.40 N 3.31 E
Łosice 30 52.14 N 22.43 E
Los Idolos, Parque Arqueológico de ⊥ 246 1.55 N 76.10 W
Lošinj, Otok I 36 44.36 N 14.24 E
Losinoborskaja 86 58.27 N 89.28 E
Losino-Petrovskij 82 55.52 N 38.12 E
Losinovka 78 50.51 N 31.54 E
Los Jazmines, Presa ⊜[1] 286a 19.25 N 99.16 W
Los Juríes 252 28.28 S 62.06 W
Loškar'ovka 78 47.57 N 34.12 E
Loskopdam ⊜[1] 156 25.23 S 29.20 E
Loskop Dam Game Reserve ◆[4] 156 25.23 S 29.20 E
Los Lagos 254 39.51 S 72.50 W
Los Lagos □[4] 254 41.45 S 73.00 W
Los Llanos 240m 18.03 N 66.24 W
Los Llanos [de Aridane] 148 28.39 N 17.54 W
Los López 196 26.15 N 99.05 W
Los Lunas 200 34.48 N 106.43 W
Los Manglares de Tumbes, Santuario Nacional ♦ 246 2.25 S 80.20 W
Los Maribios, Cordillera ⋌ 236 12.35 N 86.50 W
Los Médanos, Istmo de ⊥[3] 241s 11.35 N 69.45 W
Los Menucos 254 40.50 S 68.08 W
Los Micos, Laguna de ϲ 236 15.45 N 87.36 W
Los'mino 76 55.04 N 34.24 E
Los Mochis 232 25.45 N 108.57 W
Los Molinos 204 40.01 N 122.05 W
Los Muermos 254 41.24 S 73.29 W
Los Naranjos 286c 10.27 N 66.48 W
Los Navalmorales 34 39.43 N 4.38 W
Lošnica 76 54.17 N 28.46 E
Los Nietos 280 33.58 N 118.04 W
Løsning 41 55.48 N 9.42 E
Los Nogales 196 26.16 N 99.43 W
Losolava 175f 14.11 S 167.34 E
Los Olmos Creek ≃, Tx., U.S. 196 27.20 N 97.40 W
Los Olmos Creek ≃, Tx., U.S. 196 26.21 N 98.48 W
Los Osos 226 35.19 N 120.50 W
Los Oyameles 234 19.43 N 97.32 W
Los Padillas 200 34.58 N 106.41 W
Los Palacios, Arg. 252 29.22 S 68.11 W
Los Palacios, Cuba 240p 22.35 N 83.15 W
Los Palacios y Villafranca 34 37.10 N 5.56 W
Los Perros, Arroyo ≃ 288 34.37 S 58.46 W
Los Pinos ◆[8] 286b 23.04 N 82.23 W
Los Pinos ≃ 200 36.56 N 107.36 W
Los Placeres del Oro 234 18.13 N 100.54 W
Los Polvorines 288 34.30 S 58.41 W
Los Quillayes 286e 33.34 S 70.37 W
Los Quirquinchos 252 33.22 S 61.43 W
Los Rábanos 240m 18.11 N 66.50 W
Los Ramones 196 25.42 N 99.37 W
Los Remedios ≃ 286a 19.31 N 99.05 W
Los Reyes de Salgado 234 19.35 N 102.29 W
Los Reyes la Paz 286a 19.21 N 98.58 W
Los Ríos □[4] 246 1.30 S 79.25 W
Los Rodríguez 232 27.11 N 101.21 W
Los Roques, Islas II 246 11.50 N 66.45 W
Lossa 54 51.13 N 11.25 E
Lossa ≃ 54 51.18 N 11.10 E
Los Santos □[4] 236 7.55 N 80.25 W
Los Santos de Maimona 34 38.27 N 6.23 W
Los Sauces 252 37.58 S 72.50 W
Lossburg 58 48.25 N 8.27 E
Lössel 263 51.21 N 7.39 E
Losser 52 52.15 N 7.00 E
Los Serranos 228 33.59 N 117.42 W
Lossie ≃ 46 57.43 N 3.16 W
Lossiemouth 46 57.43 N 3.18 W
Lössnitz 54 50.37 N 12.43 E
Lost ≃, U.S. 202 41.56 N 121.30 W
Lost ≃, In., U.S. 194 38.33 N 86.49 W
Lost ≃, Mn., U.S. 198 47.51 N 96.02 W
Lost ≃, W.V., U.S. 188 39.05 N 78.36 W
Lostant 216 41.09 N 89.04 W
Los Taques 246 11.50 N 70.16 W
Lost Bridge State Recreation Area ♦ 216 40.45 N 85.37 W
Lost Creek ≃, Al., U.S. 194 33.38 N 87.14 W
Lost Creek ≃, Ar., U.S. 194 34.10 N 92.31 W
Lost Creek ≃, Oh., U.S. 218 39.58 N 84.09 W
Lost Creek ≃, Ut,. U.S. 200 41.04 N 111.32 W
Lost Creek ≃, Wy., U.S. 200 42.01 N 108.11 W
Lost Draw V 196 32.58 N 102.02 W
Los Telares 252 28.59 S 63.26 W
Los Teques 246 10.21 N 67.02 W
Los Testigos, Islas II 246 11.22 N 63.06 W
Lost Hills 226 35.36 N 119.41 W
Lostine ≃ 202 45.33 N 117.29 W
Lost Lake ⊜, Or., U.S. 224 45.29 N 121.49 W
Lost Lake ⊜, Wa., U.S. 224 47.20 N 121.24 W
Lost Nation 190 41.57 N 90.49 W
Lostock ≃ 262 53.40 N 2.48 W
Lostock Gralam 262 53.16 N 2.28 W
Los Trancos Creek ≃ 282 37.25 N 122.12 W
Los Trancos Woods 282 37.21 N 122.12 W
Lost River Range ⋌ 202 44.10 N 113.35 W
Lost Trail Pass)(202 45.41 N 113.57 W
Lostwithiel 42 50.25 N 4.40 W
Losuia 164 8.32 S 151.04 E
Los Vidrios 232 31.59 N 113.28 W
Los Vilos 252 31.55 S 71.31 W
Los Yébenes 34 39.34 N 3.53 W
Lot □[5] 32 44.35 N 1.40 E
Lot ≃ 32 44.18 N 0.20 E
Lota 252 37.05 S 73.10 W
Lotagipi Swamp (Lotikipi Plain) ≚ 144 4.36 N 34.55 E
Lotak 112 0.11 S 115.54 E
Lotbinière □[6] 206 46.30 N 71.40 W
Lotela, Lake ⊜ 220 27.34 N 81.29 W
Løten 26 60.49 N 11.19 E
Lot-et-Garonne □[5] 32 44.20 N 0.20 E
Lotfābād 128 37.32 N 59.20 E
Lothair, S. Afr. 158 26.26 S 30.27 E
Lothair, Ky., U.S. 192 37.14 N 83.10 W
Lothian □[4] 46 55.55 N 3.05 W
Lothringen → Lorraine □[9] 32 49.00 N 6.00 E
Lotikipi Plain (Lotagipi Swamp) ≚ 144 4.36 N 34.55 E
Loto 152 2.49 S 22.29 E
Loto ≃ 152 1.55 S 22.09 E
Lotofaga 175a 13.59 S 171.50 W
Lotoi ≃ 152 1.35 S 18.30 E
Lotorp 40 58.44 N 15.50 E
Lotošino 76 56.14 N 35.38 E
Lotrului, Munții ⋌ 38 45.30 N 23.52 E
Lotsane ≃ 156 22.41 S 28.11 E
Lötschberg Tunnel ◆[5] 58 46.25 N 7.45 E
Lötschental V 58 46.25 N 7.50 E
Lotseninsel I 41 54.40 N 10.01 E
Lott 222 31.12 N 97.02 W
Lotta ≃ 24 68.36 N 31.06 E
Lotte 52 52.17 N 7.55 E
Lottivue 214 42.40 N 82.46 W
Löttringhausen ◆[8] 263 51.27 N 7.27 E
Lottsburg 208 37.57 N 76.31 W
Lotts Creek ≃ 192 32.09 N 81.47 W
Lottsford Branch ≃ 284c 38.55 N 76.49 W
Lottstetten 58 47.38 N 8.34 E
Lotuke, Jabal ∧ 154 4.07 N 33.48 E
Lotung 100 24.41 N 121.46 E
Lotzorai 71 39.58 N 9.39 E
Louang Namtha 110 20.57 N 101.25 E
Louangphrabang 110 19.52 N 102.08 E
L'Ouarsenis, Massif de ⋌ 34 35.40 N 1.50 E
Loubaresse 62 44.36 N 4.03 E
Loube, Montagne de la ∧ 62 43.22 N 5.59 E
Loubetsi 152 3.12 S 12.10 E
Louchi 24 66.04 N 33.00 E
Loučim 60 49.22 N 13.07 E
Loučná ∧ 54 50.39 N 13.37 E
Loude 98 35.54 N 117.18 E
Loudéac 32 48.10 N 2.45 W
Louden Cove ϲ 276 41.05 N 73.43 W
Loudes 62 45.05 N 3.45 E
Loudima Poste 152 4.07 S 13.04 E
Loudon 192 35.43 N 84.20 W
Loudonville, N.Y., U.S. 210 42.42 N 73.45 W
Loudonville, Oh., U.S. 214 40.38 N 82.14 W
Loudoun □[6] 208 39.05 N 77.30 W
Loudun 32 47.01 N 0.05 E
Loué 32 48.00 N 0.09 W
Loue ≃ 58 47.01 N 5.27 E
Louga 150 15.37 N 16.13 W
Louga □[4] 150 15.25 N 15.30 W
Louge 252 36.57 S 61.40 W
Louge ≃ 32 43.27 N 1.20 E
Lougguéré ≃ 150 15.35 N 14.47 W
Loughborough 42 52.47 N 1.11 W
Loughborough Lake ⊜ 212 44.23 N 76.30 W
Loughermore ∧[2] 48 54.59 N 7.05 W
Loughman 220 28.14 N 81.34 W
Loughor 42 51.40 N 4.04 W
Loughor ≃ 42 51.40 N 4.04 W
Loughrea 48 53.12 N 8.34 W
Loughros More Bay ϲ 48 54.47 N 8.35 W
Loughton 260 51.39 N 0.03 E
Louhans 58 46.38 N 5.13 E
Louin 194 32.04 N 89.15 W
Louisa, Ky., U.S. 192 38.06 N 82.36 W
Louisa, Va., U.S. 192 38.01 N 78.00 W
Louisa, Lake ⊜, On., Can. 212 45.28 N 78.30 W
Louisa, Lake ⊜, Fl., U.S. 220 28.29 N 81.44 W
Louisbourg 186 45.55 N 59.58 W
Louis Bull Indian Reserve ◆[4] 182 52.53 N 113.31 W
Louisburg, Ks., U.S. 198 38.37 N 94.40 W
Louisburg, N.C., U.S. 192 36.05 N 78.18 W
Louisburgh 48 53.46 N 9.51 W
Louisdale 186 45.36 N 61.04 W
Louise, Ms., U.S. 194 32.58 N 90.35 W
Louise, Tx., U.S. 222 29.06 N 96.25 W
Louise, Lac ⊜, P.Q., Can. 206 45.46 N 74.25 W
Louise, Lac ⊜, P.Q., Can. 206 45.43 N 71.25 W
Louise, Lake ⊜ 180 62.20 N 146.30 W
Louise Island I 182 52.58 N 131.50 W
Louiseville 206 46.15 N 72.57 W
Louis Gentil → Youssoufia 148 32.16 N 8.33 W
Louisiade Archipelago II 160 11.00 S 153.00 E
Louisiana 219 39.26 N 91.03 W
Louisiana □[3], U.S. 178 31.15 N 92.15 W
Louisiana □[3], U.S. 194 31.15 N 92.15 W
Louisiana ʊ 41 55.58 N 12.33 E
Lou Island I 164 2.25 S 147.20 E
Louis Trichardt 156 23.01 S 29.43 E
Louisvale 158 28.33 S 21.12 E
Louisville, On., Can. 214 42.28 N 82.07 W
Louisville, Al., U.S. 194 31.47 N 85.33 W
Louisville, Ga., U.S. 192 33.00 N 82.24 W
Louisville, Il., U.S. 194 38.46 N 88.30 W
Louisville, Ky., U.S. 218 38.15 N 85.45 W
Louisville, Ms., U.S. 194 33.07 N 89.03 W
Louisville, Ne., U.S. 198 40.59 N 96.09 W
Louisville, Oh., U.S. 214 40.50 N 81.15 W
Louisville Ridge ◆[3] 14 31.00 S 172.30 W
Louisville Seamount ◆[3] 14 31.15 S 172.15 W
Louis-XIV, Pointe ≻ 176 54.37 N 79.45 W
Loujiaying 98 42.04 N 116.04 E
Loukanga 273b 4.20 S 15.09 E
Loukkos, Oued ≃ 34 35.12 N 6.09 W
Loukoua ≃ 273b 4.09 S 15.08 E
Loulé 34 37.08 N 8.02 W
Loum 152 4.43 N 9.44 E
Loumou 273b 4.08 S 15.09 E
Lount Lake ⊜ 184 50.10 N 94.20 W
Louny 54 50.19 N 13.46 E
Loup ≃, Fr. 62 43.38 N 7.09 E
Loup ≃, Ne., U.S. 198 41.24 N 97.19 W
Loup, Gorge du V 56 49.47 N 6.23 E
Loup, Rivière du ≃ 206 46.13 N 72.55 W
Loup City 198 41.16 N 98.57 W
Loups Marins, Lacs des ⊜ 176 56.30 N 73.45 W
Lourches 50 50.19 N 3.21 E
Lourdes, Nf., Can. 186 48.39 N 59.00 W
Lourdes, Fr. 32 43.06 N 0.03 W
Lourel de Baixo 266c 38.49 N 9.22 W
Lourenço 250 2.30 N 51.40 W
Lourenço Marques → Maputo 156 25.58 S 32.35 E
Lourenço Velho 256 22.22 S 45.19 W
Lourenço Velho ≃, Bra. 256 23.26 S 45.35 W
Lourenço Velho ≃, Bra. 256 22.22 S 45.31 W
Loures 34 38.50 N 9.10 W
Loures ≃ 266c 38.50 N 9.08 W
Lourinhã 34 39.14 N 9.19 W
Lourmarin 62 43.46 N 5.22 E
Lourosa 34 40.19 N 7.56 W
Loury 50 48.00 N 2.05 E
Lousã, Port. 34 40.07 N 8.15 W
Lousa, Port. 266c 38.53 N 9.12 W
Louse Creek ≃ 198 46.22 N 100.57 W
Lou Shan ∧ 89 45.15 N 128.58 E
Louta 150 13.30 N 3.10 W
Loutang 106 31.26 N 121.12 E
Loutézou, Île de I 273b 4.22 S 15.10 E
Louth, Austl. 166 30.32 S 145.07 E
Louth, Ire. 44 53.57 N 6.33 W
Louth, Ire. 48 53.57 N 6.33 W
Louth, Eng., U.K. 44 53.22 N 0.01 W
Louth □[6] 48 53.55 N 6.30 W
Louth Bay ϲ 166 34.34 S 136.02 E
Louti, Mayo ≃ 146 9.38 N 13.56 E
Loutit Bay ϲ 169 38.33 S 144.00 E
Loutrá Aidhipsoú 38 38.51 N 23.02 E
Loutre ≃ 219 38.42 N 91.25 W
Loutre, Bayou de ≃ 194 32.41 N 92.08 W
Loutrópirgos 267c 38.02 N 23.28 E
Louvain → Leuven 56 50.53 N 4.42 E
Louveciennes 261 48.52 N 2.07 E
Louveigné 56 50.32 N 5.42 E
Louveira 256 23.04 S 46.58 W
Louviers, Fr. 50 49.13 N 1.10 E
Louviers, Co., U.S. 200 39.28 N 105.00 W
Louvre ʊ 261 48.52 N 2.20 E
Louvres 50 49.02 N 2.30 E
Louvroil 50 50.16 N 3.58 E
Louwsburg 158 27.37 S 31.07 E
Lou Yaeger, Lake ⊜[1] 219 39.10 N 89.37 W
Lövånger 26 64.22 N 21.18 E
Lovászi 61 46.33 N 16.34 E
Lovat' ≃ 76 58.14 N 31.28 E
Lovcy 82 55.00 N 39.15 E
Love 184 53.29 N 104.09 W
Loveč 38 43.08 N 24.43 E
Love Clough 262 53.44 N 2.17 W
Lovedale 279b 40.17 N 79.52 W
Lovejoy 219 38.39 N 90.10 W
Lovelady 222 31.08 N 95.27 W
Loveland, Co., U.S. 200 40.23 N 105.04 W
Loveland, Oh., U.S. 218 39.16 N 84.16 W
Lovell 202 44.50 N 108.23 W
Lovell Island I 283 42.20 N 70.56 W
Lovelock 204 40.10 N 118.28 W
Lovely 192 37.49 N 82.24 W
Love Point ≻ 208 39.02 N 76.18 W
Lovere 64 45.49 N 10.04 E
Lovering, Lac ⊜ 206 45.10 N 72.09 W
Lovero 64 46.14 N 10.14 E
Loves Green 260 51.43 N 0.24 E
Loves Park 216 42.19 N 89.03 W
Loviisa → Lovisa 26 60.27 N 26.14 E
Lovilia 190 41.08 N 92.54 W
Loving, N.M., U.S. 196 32.17 N 104.05 W
Loving, Tx., U.S. 196 33.16 N 98.31 W
Lovingston 192 37.45 N 78.52 W
Lovington, Il., U.S. 219 39.42 N 88.37 W
Lovington, N.M., U.S. 196 32.56 N 103.20 W
Lovisa (Loviisa) 26 60.27 N 26.14 E
Lövő 61 47.30 N 16.47 E
Lovö I 40 59.20 N 17.50 E
Lovoi ≃ 154 8.14 S 26.39 E
Lovosice 54 50.31 N 14.03 E
Lovozero, Ross. 24 68.00 N 35.00 E
Lovozero, Ross. 24 65.00 N 29.50 E
Lovozero, ozero ⊜ 24 67.54 N 35.12 E
Lovrenc 61 46.32 N 15.23 E
Lövstabruk 40 60.24 N 17.53 E
Lövstabukten ϲ 40 60.35 N 17.45 E
Lövstad slott ⊥ 40 58.33 N 16.02 E
Lóvua, Ang. 152 11.36 S 23.53 E
Lóvua, Ang. 152 7.20 S 20.16 E
Lovua (Lóvua) ≃ 152 6.07 S 20.35 E
Low 188 45.48 N 75.57 W
Low, Cape ≻ 176 63.07 N 85.18 W
Lowa 154 1.24 S 25.51 E
Lowa ≃ 154 1.24 S 25.51 E
Lowāda 126 22.27 N 87.37 E
Lowat → Lovat' ≃ 76 58.14 N 31.28 E
Lowber 279b 40.15 N 79.46 W
Lowden 190 41.51 N 90.55 W
Lowder Brook ≃ 283 43.14 N 71.11 W
Lowell, Ar., U.S. 194 36.15 N 94.07 W
Lowell, In., U.S. 216 41.17 N 87.25 W
Lowell, Ma., U.S. 207 42.38 N 71.19 W
Lowell, Mi., U.S. 216 42.56 N 85.20 W
Lowell, Or., U.S. 202 43.55 N 122.46 W
Lowell, Lake ⊜[1] 202 43.33 N 116.40 W
Lowell, University of ʊ[2] 283 42.39 N 71.20 W
Lowell-Dracut State Forest ♦ 283 42.40 N 71.22 W
Lowelli 140 5.59 N 33.45 E
Lowellville 214 41.02 N 80.32 W
Löwen ≃ 158 26.51 S 18.17 E
Löwenberg 54 52.54 N 13.08 E
Löwenbruch 264a 52.18 N 13.19 E
Löwen → Leuven 56 50.53 N 4.42 E
Löwenstein 56 49.06 N 9.22 E
Lowe Pond ⊜ 283 42.41 N 70.59 W
Lower Aetna Lake ⊜ 285 39.51 N 74.48 W
Lower Arrow Lake ⊜ 182 49.40 N 118.08 W
Lower Bay ϲ 208 40.33 N 74.02 W
Lower Bear River Reservoir ⊜[1] 226 38.33 N 120.14 W
Lower Bershire Valley 276 40.54 N 74.37 W
Lower Beverley Lake ⊜ 212 44.36 N 76.09 W
Lower Broughton ◆[8] 262 53.29 N 2.15 W
Lower Brule Indian Reservation ◆[4] 198 44.05 N 99.44 W
Lower Buckhorn Lake ⊜ 212 44.33 N 78.17 W
Lower Burrell 214 40.33 N 79.45 W
Lower California → Baja California ≻[1] 232 28.00 N 113.30 W
Lower Chittering 168a 31.34 S 116.06 E
Lower Crystal Springs Reservoir ⊜[1] 226 37.32 N 122.22 W
Lower Darwen 262 53.43 N 2.28 W
Lower Egypt → Misr Bahrī □[9] 140 31.00 N 31.00 E
Lower Eltham Park ♦ 274b 37.45 S 145.09 E
Lower Elwha Indian Reservation ◆[4] 224 48.09 N 123.33 W
Lower Fort Garry National Historic Park ♦ 184 50.07 N 96.55 W
Lower Ganga Canal ≊ 124 26.27 N 80.17 E
Lower Gap ϲ 212 44.10 N 76.35 W
Lower Halstow 260 51.22 N 0.40 E
Lower Hay Lake ⊜ 212 45.25 N 78.13 W
Lower Higham 260 51.26 N 0.28 E
Lower Huron Metropolitan Park ♦ 281 42.12 N 83.25 W
Lower Hutt 172 41.13 S 174.55 E
Lower Kalskag 180 61.31 N 160.22 W
Lower Keechi Creek ≃ 222 31.08 N 95.46 W
Lower Klamath Lake ⊜ 204 41.55 N 121.42 W
Lower Lake 226 38.55 N 122.36 W
Lower Lake ⊜ 204 41.15 N 120.02 W
Lower Loteni 158 29.32 S 29.36 E
Lower Manitou Lake ⊜ 184 49.15 N 93.00 W
Lower Matecumbe Key I 220 24.51 N 80.43 W
Lower Montville 276 40.54 N 74.22 W
Lower Mystic Lake ⊜ 283 42.26 N 71.09 W
Lower Nazeing 260 51.44 N 0.01 E
Lower Otay Lake ⊜[1] 228 32.37 N 116.55 W
Lower Paia 229a 20.55 N 156.23 W
Lower Paudash Lake ⊜ 212 44.58 N 78.01 W
Lower Peirce Reservoir ⊜[1] 271c 1.22 N 103.49 E
Lower Peover 262 53.16 N 2.23 W
Lower Place 262 53.36 N 2.09 W
Lower Plenty 274b 37.44 S 145.06 E
Lower Portland 170 33.27 S 150.53 E
Lower Post 176 59.55 N 128.30 W
Lower Red Lake ⊜ 198 48.00 N 94.50 W
Lower River Rouge ≃ 281 42.18 N 83.14 W
Lower Rouge Parkway ♦ 281 42.18 N 83.20 W
Lower Saxony → Niedersachsen □[3] 30 52.40 N 9.00 E
Lower Stoke 260 51.27 N 0.38 E
Lower Trajan's Wall ⊥ 38 45.40 N 28.30 E
Lower Ugashik Lake ⊜ 180 57.30 N 156.56 W
Lower Van Norman Lake ⊜[1] 280 34.17 N 118.29 W
Lower West Pubnico 186 43.38 N 65.48 W
Lower Whitley 262 53.18 N 2.35 W
Lower Wood's Harbour 186 43.31 N 65.44 W
Lowery, Lake ⊜ 220 28.07 N 81.41 W
Lower Zambezi International Game Park ◆[4] 154 15.30 S 29.35 E
Lowestoft 42 52.29 N 1.45 E
Lowgar □[4] 120 33.50 N 69.00 E
Lowick 44 55.38 N 2.00 W
Łowicz 30 52.07 N 19.56 E
Lowman 210 42.02 N 76.44 W
Lowmoor 192 37.47 N 79.53 W
Lowood 171a 27.28 S 152.35 E
Lowrah (Pishīn Lora) ≃ 120 29.09 N 64.55 E
Lowries Run ≃ 279b 40.30 N 80.05 W
Low Rocky Point ≻ 166 43.00 S 145.30 E
Lowry Air Force Base ■ 198 39.43 N 104.53 W
Lowry City 194 38.08 N 93.43 W
Lowther ≃ 44 54.39 N 2.44 W
Lowther Hills ⋌[2] 44 55.19 N 3.38 W
Lowton 262 53.28 N 2.35 W
Lowton Common 262 53.29 N 2.33 W
Lowville, N.Y., U.S. 212 43.47 N 75.29 W
Lowville, Pa., U.S. 214 42.01 N 79.49 W
Loxahatchee 220 26.49 N 80.13 W
Loxley 194 30.37 N 87.45 W
Loxstedt 52 53.28 N 8.38 E
Loxten 52 52.03 N 8.08 E
Loxton, Austl. 166 34.27 S 140.35 E
Loxton, S. Afr. 158 31.30 S 22.22 E
Loyal 190 44.44 N 90.29 W
Loyal, Loch ⊜ 46 58.23 N 4.22 W
Loyalhanna 214 40.19 N 79.21 W
Loyalhanna Creek ≃ 214 40.28 N 79.27 W
Loyalhanna Lake ⊜[1] 214 40.25 N 79.28 W
Loyalsock Creek ≃ 210 41.14 N 76.56 W
Loyalton 204 39.40 N 120.14 W
Loyalty Islands → Loyauté, Îles II 175f 21.00 S 167.00 E
Loyang 271c 1.22 N 103.58 E
Loyang → Luoyang 102 34.41 N 112.28 E
Loyauté, Îles (Loyalty Islands) II 175f 21.00 S 167.00 E
Loyne, Loch ⊜ 46 57.06 N 5.00 W
Loyola College ʊ[2] 284b 39.21 N 76.37 W
Loyola Marymount University ʊ[2] 280 33.58 N 118.25 W
Loyola University ʊ[2] 278 42.00 N 87.39 W
Loyoro 154 3.21 N 34.16 E
Loysburg 214 40.10 N 78.23 W
Loysville 208 40.22 N 77.21 W
Lozano 258 34.51 S 59.03 W
Lozère □[5] 32 44.30 N 3.30 E
Lozère, Mont ∧ 62 44.25 N 3.46 E
Loznica 38 44.32 N 19.13 E
Ložnikovo, Ross. 86 56.54 N 73.56 E
Ložnikovo, Ross. 88 51.22 N 117.03 E
Lozno-Aleksandrovka 78 49.50 N 38.44 E
Loznoje 80 49.17 N 44.26 E
L'Ozone ◆[8] 273b 4.21 S 15.14 E
Lozovaja, Kaz. 86 53.17 N 77.45 E
Lozovaja, Ukr. 78 48.54 N 36.20 E
Lozovaja, Ukr. 83 49.28 N 37.54 E
Lozovoje, Ukr. 78 49.18 N 27.18 E
Lozovoje, Ukr. 83 49.13 N 37.36 E
Lozovskij 83 48.33 N 38.54 E
Lozoyuela 34 40.55 N 3.37 W
Loz'va ≃ 86 59.36 N 62.20 E
Lozzo di Cadore 64 46.29 N 12.27 E
Lu 62 45.00 N 8.29 E
Lu ≃ 100 27.04 N 115.00 E
Lua ≃ 152 2.46 N 18.26 E
Luabo 156 18.30 S 36.10 E
Luabu ≃ 152 2.46 S 18.19 E
Luachimo ≃ 152 6.33 S 20.59 E
Luaha-sibuha 110 0.31 S 98.28 E
Luala ≃ 154 17.57 S 36.30 E
Lualaba ≃ 154 0.26 N 25.20 E
Luali 152 5.06 S 12.29 E
Lualoje ≃ 152 12.18 S 21.38 E
Luama ≃ 154 4.46 S 26.53 E
Luambe National Park ♦ 154 12.25 S 32.15 E
Luambimba ≃ 152 15.00 S 22.48 E
Luampa 154 15.03 S 24.28 E
Luampa ≃ 154 14.33 S 24.10 E
Lu'an 100 31.44 N 116.31 E
Luan ≃ 98 39.20 N 119.10 E
Luana ≃ 152 7.56 S 21.06 E
Luan Balu 114 2.38 N 96.13 E
Luancheng, Zhg. 98 37.53 N 114.39 E
Luancheng, Zhg. 102 22.45 N 108.51 E
Luanchuan 102 33.51 N 111.36 E
Luancundo ≃ 152 16.25 S 21.27 E
Luanda 152 8.48 S 13.14 E
Luanda □[5] 152 9.00 S 13.15 E
Luando ≃ 152 10.19 S 16.40 E
Luando, Réserva do ◆[4] 152 11.10 S 17.30 E
Luang, Khao ∧ 110 8.31 N 99.47 E
Luang, Thale ϲ 110 7.30 N 100.15 E
Luang Chiang Dao, Doi ∧ 110 19.23 N 98.54 E
Luanginga (Luanguinga) ≃ 152 15.11 S 22.56 E
Luang Prabang → Louangphrabang 110 19.52 N 102.08 E
Luang Prabang Range ⋌ 110 18.30 N 101.15 E
Luangue 152 7.19 S 19.38 E
Luangue (Loange) ≃ 152 4.17 S 20.02 E
Luanguinga (Luanginga) ≃ 152 15.11 S 22.56 E
Luangwa (Aruângua) ≃ 154 15.36 S 30.25 E
Luanhaizi 120 34.27 N 93.12 E
Luanhe 105 40.57 N 117.44 E
Luannan (Bencheng) 98 39.32 N 118.39 E
Luanping (Anjiangying) 98 40.57 N 117.20 E
Luanshishan 104 42.10 N 123.41 E
Luanshya 154 13.08 S 28.24 E
Luán Toro 252 36.12 S 65.06 W
Luanxian 98 39.45 N 118.44 E
Luanza 154 8.42 S 28.42 E
Luapula □[4] 154 10.55 S 29.00 E
Luapula ≃ 154 9.26 S 28.33 E
Luar, Danau ⊜ 112 0.55 N 112.15 E
Luarca 34 43.32 N 6.32 W
Luashi 152 10.56 S 23.37 E
Luashi ≃ 152 10.41 S 22.55 E
Luassinga ≃ 152 15.47 S 18.50 E
Luati 152 14.35 S 21.13 E
Luatira 152 12.52 S 17.14 E
Luau 152 10.42 S 22.12 E
Lua-Vindu ≃ 152 3.38 N 19.16 E
Luba 152 3.27 N 8.33 E
Lubaantun ⊥ 232 16.17 N 88.58 W
Lubaczów 30 50.10 N 23.07 E
Lubalo 152 9.12 S 19.16 E
Lubalo ≃ 152 7.22 S 19.20 E
Lubamiti 152 2.29 S 17.47 E
L'uban', Bela. 76 52.37 N 29.08 E
L'uban', Bela. 76 52.48 N 27.59 E
Lubań, Pol. 30 51.08 N 15.18 E
L'uban', Ross. 76 59.21 N 31.13 E
Lubāna 76 56.54 N 26.43 E
Lubang 116 13.52 N 120.07 E
Lubang Island I 116 13.46 N 120.11 E
Lubang Islands II 116 13.46 N 120.15 E
Lubango 152 14.55 S 13.30 E
Lubanowo 54 53.09 N 14.36 E
Lubāns ⊜ 76 56.46 N 26.53 E
Lubansenshi ≃ 154 11.21 S 30.35 E
Lub'any 80 56.02 N 51.24 E
Lubao 100 23.22 N 112.55 E
L'ubar 78 49.55 N 27.44 E
Lübars, Dtsch. 54 52.39 N 12.02 E
Lübars, Dtsch. 54 52.10 N 12.09 E
Lübars ◆[8] 264a 52.37 N 13.22 E
Lubartów 30 51.28 N 22.38 E
L'ubašovka 78 47.51 N 30.15 E
Lubawa 30 53.30 N 19.45 E
Lubaynī, Bahr al- ≊ 273c 29.56 N 31.11 E
Lübbecke 52 52.18 N 8.36 E
Lübben 54 51.56 N 13.53 E
Lübbenau 54 51.52 N 13.57 E
Lubber Brook ≃ 283 42.33 N 71.09 W
Lubbers Run ≃ 276 40.56 N 74.43 W
Lübbesee ⊜ 54 53.05 N 13.34 E
Lubbock 196 33.34 N 101.51 W
Lübbow 54 52.54 N 11.10 E
Lubbub Creek ≃ 194 33.04 N 88.10 W
L'ubča 76 53.45 N 26.03 E
L'ubeč, Ukr. 78 51.42 N 30.39 E
Lubec, Me., U.S. 188 44.51 N 66.59 W
Lübeck 52 53.52 N 10.40 E
Lübecker Bucht ϲ 54 54.00 N 10.55 E
Lubefu 152 4.43 S 24.25 E
Lubefu ≃ 152 4.10 S 23.00 E
Lubelska, Wyżyna ⋌[2] 30 51.00 N 23.00 E
Lubembe (Luembe) ≃ 152 6.37 S 21.05 E
Lubenec 54 50.06 N 13.20 E
Lüben → Lubin 30 51.24 N 16.13 E
L'ubercy 82 55.41 N 37.53 E
Lubéron, Montagne du ⋌ 62 43.48 N 5.22 E
Lubersac 32 45.27 N 1.24 E
L'ubešov 78 51.46 N 25.31 E
Lübesse 54 53.29 N 11.28 E
Lubi ≃ 152 4.58 S 23.26 E
Lubiana → Ljubljana 36 46.03 N 14.31 E
Lubic Island I 116 10.58 N 120.44 E
L'ubickoje 80 51.46 N 49.19 E
Lubień Kujawski 30 52.25 N 19.10 E
Lubilash ≃ 152 6.02 S 23.45 E
Lubile 154 2.55 S 26.45 E
L'ubim 80 58.22 N 40.41 E
L'ubimovka, Kaz. 86 52.15 N 66.45 E
L'ubimovka, Ross. 78 51.31 N 35.37 E
L'ubimovka, Ukr. 78 46.47 N 33.34 E
L'ubimyj 83 47.53 N 39.28 E
Lubin, Pol. 30 51.24 N 16.13 E
Lubin, Pol. 54 53.50 N 14.25 E
L'ubino 86 57.30 N 88.47 E
L'ubinskij 86 55.09 N 72.42 E
Lubishi ≃ 152 6.54 S 24.09 E
Lubja ≃ 265a 59.58 N 30.30 E
Lublin 30 51.15 N 22.35 E
Lublin □[4] 30 51.30 N 22.30 E
Lubliniec 30 50.40 N 18.41 E
L'ublino ◆[8] 265b 55.41 N 37.44 E
Lubmin 54 54.08 N 13.37 E
Lubnān, Jabal (Lebanon Mountains) ⋌ 132 34.00 N 36.00 E
Lubnān → Lebanon □[1] 128 34.00 N 36.00 E
L'ubnica 76 57.58 N 32.42 E
Lubny 78 50.01 N 33.00 E
L'ubochna 76 53.31 N 34.23 E
Lubok China 114 2.27 N 102.04 E
Lubomierz 30 51.01 N 15.30 E
L'uboml' 78 51.14 N 24.01 E
Luboń 30 52.23 N 16.54 E
Lubondai 152 6.34 S 22.39 E
Lubondoi 154 8.02 S 26.31 E
L'ubostan' 78 51.19 N 35.44 E
L'ubotin 78 49.57 N 35.57 E
Lubraniec 30 52.33 N 18.50 E
Lubsko 30 51.46 N 14.59 E
Lubsza ≃ 54 51.56 N 14.43 E
Lübtheen 54 53.18 N 11.04 E
Lubu, Indon. 112 0.46 S 122.30 E
Lubu, Zhg. 102 23.09 N 112.13 E
Lubuagan 116 17.21 N 121.10 E
L'ubučany 82 55.15 N 37.33 E
Lubudi, Zaïre 152 6.51 S 21.18 E
Lubudi, Zaïre 154 9.57 S 25.58 E
Lubudi ≃, Zaïre 152 4.03 S 21.23 E
Lubudi ≃, Zaïre 154 9.13 S 25.38 E
Lubue 152 4.09 S 19.52 E
Lubue ≃ 152 4.10 S 19.53 E
Lubukambacang 112 0.37 S 101.25 E
Lubukbatang 112 4.03 S 104.12 E
Lubukbertubung 112 0.02 N 102.08 E
Lubuklinggau 112 3.18 S 102.52 E
Lubukpakam 114 3.33 N 98.52 E
Lubukraya, Dolok ∧ 114 1.29 N 99.13 E
Lubuksikaping 112 0.08 N 100.10 E
Lubumbaschi → Lubumbashi 154 11.40 S 27.28 E
Lubumbashi (Élisabethville) 154 11.40 S 27.28 E
Lubunda 154 5.10 S 26.40 E
Lubutu 154 0.44 S 26.35 E
Luby 54 50.12 N 12.25 E
L'ubytino 76 58.49 N 33.23 E
Lübz 54 53.27 N 12.01 E
Lučak 85 38.23 N 67.25 E
Lucala 152 9.16 S 15.15 E
Lucala ≃, Ang. 152 9.37 S 14.14 E
Lucala ≃, Ang. 152 6.38 S 12.34 E
Lucan, On., Can. 190 43.11 N 81.24 W
Lucan, Ire. 48 53.22 N 6.27 W
Lucanas 248 14.36 S 74.15 W
Lucania □[9] 68 40.30 N 16.00 E
Lucania, Mount ∧ 180 61.01 N 140.28 W
Lucano 152 11.16 S 21.38 E
Lucaogou 102 42.26 N 96.55 E
Lucapa 152 8.36 S 20.54 E
Lucas, Ia., U.S. 190 41.01 N 93.27 W
Lucas, Ks., U.S. 198 39.03 N 98.32 W
Lucas, Oh., U.S. 214 40.45 N 82.30 W
Lucas, Tx., U.S. 222 33.05 N 96.35 W
Lucas □[6] 214 41.39 N 83.32 W
Lucas González 252 32.24 S 59.33 W
Lucas Heights 274a 34.02 S 150.58 E
Lucas Valley 282 38.03 N 122.35 W
Lucasville 218 38.52 N 82.59 W
Lucban 116 14.06 N 121.33 E
Lucca 66 43.50 N 10.29 E
Lucca □[4] 64 44.02 N 10.27 E
Lucca Sicula 70 37.35 N 13.18 E
Lucé 50 48.26 N 1.28 E
Luce, Water of ≃ 44 54.52 N 4.48 W
Lucea 241q 18.27 N 78.10 W
Luce Bay ϲ 44 54.47 N 4.50 W
Luce Bayou ≃ 222 30.03 N 95.07 W
Lucedale 194 30.55 N 88.35 W
Lucena, Esp. 34 37.24 N 4.29 W
Lucena, Pil. 116 13.56 N 121.37 E
Lucenay-L'Évêque 32 47.05 N 4.15 E
Luc-en-Diois 62 44.37 N 5.27 E
Lučenec 30 48.20 N 19.40 E
Lucens 58 46.42 N 6.50 E
Luceque 152 14.41 S 15.04 E
Lucera 68 41.30 N 15.20 E
Lucéram 62 43.53 N 7.22 E
Lucerne, Ca., U.S. 204 39.05 N 122.47 W
Lucerne, In., U.S. 216 40.52 N 86.24 W
Lucerne, Lake → Vierwaldstätter See ⊜ 58 47.00 N 8.28 E
Lucerne Lake ⊜ 228 34.31 N 116.57 W
Lucerne → Luzern 58 47.03 N 8.18 E
Lucernemines 214 40.33 N 79.09 W
Lucerne Valley 228 34.26 N 116.58 W
Lucero 200 30.49 N 106.30 W
Lucero, Lake ⊜ 200 32.42 N 106.25 W
Lučesa ≃ 76 55.10 N 30.11 E
Luch 80 57.01 N 42.15 E
Luch ≃ 80 56.14 N 42.25 E
Luchang 102 26.23 N 102.18 E
Luchena ≃ 34 37.44 N 1.50 W
Lucheng, Zhg. 102 24.21 N 106.00 E
Lücheng, Zhg. 106 31.55 N 119.44 E
Lucheng, Zhg. 106 31.47 N 120.02 E
Luché-Pringé 50 47.42 N 0.05 E
Lucheringo ≃ 154 11.43 S 36.17 E
Luchibe ≃ 152 12.07 S 21.13 E
Luchico (Lushiko) ≃ 152 6.13 S 19.40 E
Luchou 269d 25.05 N 121.28 E
Luchovicy 82 54.59 N 39.03 E
Lüchow 54 52.58 N 11.10 E
Luchow → Luzhou 107 28.54 N 105.27 E
Lüchtringen 52 51.47 N 9.25 E
Luchuan 102 22.19 N 110.11 E
Luci 100 29.52 N 119.47 E
Luciara 250 10.27 S 50.32 W
Lucie ≃ 250 3.35 N 57.38 W
Lucikou 100 28.56 N 116.04 E
Lučin 76 53.01 N 30.01 E
Lucinda, Austl. 166 18.32 S 146.20 E
Lucinda, Pa., U.S. 214 41.19 N 79.22 W
Lucindale 166 36.59 S 140.22 E
Lucio Vázquez 234 22.47 N 99.46 W
Lucipara, Kepulauan II 164 5.30 S 127.33 E
Lucira 152 13.51 S 12.31 E
Lucito 66 41.44 N 14.41 E
Luci Yu I 100 25.07 N 119.22 E
Luck, Ukr. 78 50.44 N 25.20 E
Luck, Wi., U.S. 190 45.34 N 92.28 W
Luck, Mount ∧[2] 162 28.47 S 123.33 E
Lucka 54 51.06 N 12.20 E
Luckau 54 51.51 N 13.43 E
Luckeesarai 124 25.11 N 86.05 E
Luckenwalde 54 52.05 N 13.10 E
Luckey 214 41.27 N 83.29 W
Luckhoff 158 29.44 S 24.43 E
Luckiamute ≃ 202 44.45 N 123.09 W
Luck Lake ⊜ 184 51.05 N 107.07 W
Lucknow, On., Can. 190 43.57 N 81.31 W
Lucknow, India 124 26.51 N 80.55 E
Lucknow, Pa., U.S. 208 40.20 N 76.54 W
Lucknow Branch ≊ 124 27.57 N 80.03 E
Lucky Lake 184 51.00 N 107.10 W
Lucky Peak Lake ⊜[1] 202 43.33 N 116.00 W
Luco dei Marsi 66 41.58 N 13.28 E
Lucomagno, Passo del)(58 46.33 N 8.49 E
Luçon, Fr. 32 46.27 N 1.10 W
Lucon, Pa., U.S. 285 40.14 N 75.25 W
Luconha ≃ 152 12.54 S 21.15 E
Lucun, Zhg. 98 36.12 N 118.01 E
Lucun, Zhg. 106 30.49 N 119.26 E
Lucunga ≃ 152 6.57 S 12.48 E
Lucungu ≃ 152 6.41 S 14.26 E
Lucusse 152 12.32 S 20.48 E
Lucy Creek 166 22.25 S 136.20 E
Lüda → Dalian 98 38.53 N 121.35 E
Luda Kamčija ≃ 38 43.03 N 27.29 E
Ludao 89 43.51 N 129.19 E
Ludbreg 36 46.15 N 16.37 E
Luddan 123 29.54 N 72.34 E
Luddenden 262 53.44 N 1.56 W
Luddenham 274a 33.53 S 150.41 E
Luddesdown 260 51.22 N 0.24 E
Lüdenscheid 56 51.13 N 7.38 E
Lüder ≃ 56 50.31 N 9.27 E
Lüderitz, Dtsch. 54 52.30 N 11.44 E
Lüderitz, Namibia 156 26.38 S 15.10 E
Lüderitz □[5] 156 26.30 S 15.45 E
Lüdersdorf 54 53.47 N 10.46 E
Ludgershall 42 51.16 N 1.37 W
Ludgo 40 58.55 N 17.08 E
Ludhiāna 123 30.54 N 75.51 E
Ludian 102 27.11 N 103.33 E
Luding 102 29.55 N 102.15 E
Lüdinghausen 52 51.46 N 7.26 E
Ludington 190 43.57 N 86.27 W
Ludingtonville 210 41.29 N 73.39 W
L'udinovo 76 53.52 N 34.27 E
L'udkovo 76 54.36 N 34.43 E
Ludlam Bay ϲ 208 39.10 N 74.42 W
Ludlow, Eng., U.K. 42 52.22 N 2.43 W
Ludlow, Il., U.S. 216 40.23 N 88.08 W
Ludlow, Ky., U.S. 218 39.05 N 84.32 W
Ludlow, Ma., U.S. 207 42.09 N 72.28 W
Ludlow, Pa., U.S. 214 41.43 N 78.56 W
Ludlow, Vt., U.S. 188 43.23 N 72.42 W
Ludlow Falls 218 40.00 N 84.20 W
Ludlowville 210 42.33 N 76.32 W
Ludogorie ◆[1] 38 43.46 N 26.56 E
Ludonghe 102 25.53 N 103.33 E
Ludoni 76 58.12 N 29.21 E
Ludowici 192 31.42 N 81.44 W
Luduș 38 46.29 N 24.05 E
Ludvika 40 60.09 N 15.11 E
Ludwigkanal ≊ 60 49.05 N 11.27 E
Ludwigsburg 56 48.53 N 9.11 E
Ludwigsfelde 54 52.17 N 13.16 E
Ludwigsfelder-Heide ◆[3] 264a 52.18 N 13.14 E
Ludwigshafen 56 49.29 N 8.26 E
Ludwigshafen am Bodensee 58 47.49 N 9.03 E
Ludwigslust 54 53.19 N 11.30 E
Ludwigsort → Laduškin 76 54.36 N 20.11 E
Ludwigsstadt 54 50.30 N 11.23 E
Ludwigstein, Burg ⊥ 56 51.20 N 9.55 E
Ludza 76 56.33 N 27.43 E
Lue 170 32.39 S 149.51 E
Luebo 152 5.21 S 21.25 E
Lueders 196 32.48 N 99.37 W
Lueg, Pass)(64 47.34 N 13.12 E
Lueki 154 3.22 S 25.51 E
Luele ≃ 152 7.55 S 20.09 E
Luemba 154 3.42 S 28.40 E
Luembe (Lubembe) ≃, Afr. 152 6.37 S 21.05 E
Luembé ≃, Zaïre 154 6.43 S 24.11 E
Luena, Ang. 152 11.47 S 19.52 E
Luena, Zaïre 154 9.27 S 25.47 E
Luena ≃, Ang. 152 12.31 S 22.34 E
Luena ≃, Zam. 152 14.45 S 23.25 E
Luena Flats ≡ 152 14.50 S 23.20 E
Luengué ≃ 152 16.54 S 21.52 E
Luenha (Ruenya) ≃ 154 16.24 S 33.48 E
Lueo ≃ 152 9.06 S 23.51 E

Symbols in the index entries represent the broad categories identified in the key at the right. Symbols with superior numbers (⋌[1]) identify subcategories (see complete key on page *I · 1).*

Symbole im Register stellen die rechts im Schlüssel erklärten Kategorien dar. Symbole mit hochgestellten Ziffern (⋌[1]) bezeichnen Unterabteilungen einer Kategorie (vgl. vollständiger Schlüssel auf Seite *I · 1).*

Los símbolos incluídos en el texto del índice representan las grandes categorias identificadas con la clave a la derecha. Los símbolos con numeros en su parte superior (⋌[1]) identifican las subcategorías (véase la clave completa en la página *I · 1).*

Les symboles de l'index représentent les catégories indiquées dans la légende à droite. Les symboles suivis d'un indice (⋌[1]) représentent des sous-catégories (voir légende complète à la page *I · 1).*

Os símbolos incluídos no texto do índice representam as grandes categorias identificadas com a chave à direita. Os símbolos com números em sua parte superior (⋌[1]) identificam as subcategorias (veja-se a chave completa à página *I · 1).*

	English	Deutsch	Español	Français	Português
∧	Mountain	Berg	Montaña	Montagne	Montanha
⋌	Mountains	Gebirge	Montañas	Montagnes	Montanhas
)(	Pass	Paß	Paso	Col	Passo
V	Valley, Canyon	Tal, Cañon	Valle, Cañón	Vallée, Canyon	Vale, Canhão
≚	Plain	Ebene	Llano	Plaine	Planície
≻	Cape	Kap	Cabo	Cap	Cabo
I	Island	Insel	Isla	Île	Ilha
II	Islands	Inseln	Islas	Îles	Ilhas
⊥	Other Topographic Features	Andere Topographische Objekte	Otros Elementos Topográficos	Autres données topographiques	Outros acidentes topográficos

ESPAÑOL — Nombre, Página, Lat. °′, Long. °′ W = Oeste
FRANÇAIS — Nom, Page, Lat. °′, Long. °′ W = Ouest
PORTUGUÊS — Nome, Página, Lat. °′, Long. °′ W = Oeste

Luepa 246 5.43 N 61.31 W
Lueta 152 7.19 S 22.06 E
Lueta ≃ 152 7.04 S 21.40 E
Lueyang 102 33.20 N 106.10 E
Lüfangsicun 104 41.25 N 123.22 E
Lufeng, Zhg. 100 22.57 N 115.38 E
Lufeng, Zhg. 102 25.07 N 102.07 E
Lufico 152 6.24 S 13.23 E
Lufira ≃ 154 8.16 S 26.27 E
Lufkin 222 31.20 N 94.43 W
Luftekopf ʌ [2] 56 50.05 N 7.37 E
Lufubu ≃ 154 8.36 S 30.47 E
Lufuidje ≃ 152 12.52 S 22.47 E
Lufupa 154 10.37 S 24.56 E
Lufupa ≃ 154 14.37 S 26.12 E
Luga 76 58.44 N 29.52 E
Luga ≃ 76 59.40 N 28.18 E
Lugagnano Val d'Arda 62 44.49 N 9.50 E
Lugan' ≃ 83 48.37 N 39.27 E
Lugančik ≃ 83 48.35 N 39.32 E
Lugang, Zhg. 100 31.17 N 118.22 E
Lugang, Zhg. 100 27.23 N 115.36 E
Luganga 154 7.31 S 35.32 E
Lugano 58 46.01 N 8.58 E
Lugano, Lago di ⊛ 58 46.00 N 9.00 E
Lugansk (Vorošilovgrad) 83 48.34 N 39.20 E
Lugansk □ [4] 78 49.00 N 39.00 E
Luganskoje 83 48.26 N 38.15 E
Luganville 175f 15.32 S 167.10 E
Lugards Falls ⌊ 154 3.03 S 38.42 E
Lugareño 240p 21.33 N 77.28 W
Lugarno 274a 33.59 S 151.03 E
Lugau 54 50.44 N 12.44 E
Lügde 52 51.57 N 9.15 E
Lugela 154 16.25 S 36.43 E
Lugenda 154 12.30 S 37.43 E
Lugenda ≃ 154 11.25 S 38.33 E
Lugg ≃ 42 52.02 N 2.38 W
Luggarus → Locarno 58 46.10 N 8.48 E
Luginino 76 57.43 N 35.17 E
Luginy 78 51.04 N 28.24 E
Lugnano in Teverina 66 42.34 N 12.20 E
Lugnaquillia Mountain ʌ 48 52.58 N 6.27 W
Lugnås 40 58.39 N 13.42 E
Lugny 58 46.28 N 4.49 E
Lugo, Esp. 34 43.00 N 7.34 W
Lugo, It. 66 44.25 N 11.54 E
Lugo □ [4] 34 43.00 N 7.25 W
Lugoj 38 45.41 N 21.54 E
Lugongshi 106 31.38 N 121.12 E
Lugos → Lugoj 38 45.41 N 21.54 E
Lugouqiao 105 39.51 N 116.13 E
Lugovaja Subbota 86 59.52 N 69.45 E
Lugovoj, Kaz. 85 42.56 N 72.45 E
Lugovoj, Ross. 86 59.44 N 65.55 E
Lugovoje 85 42.55 N 72.43 E
Lugovskij 88 58.02 N 112.54 E
Lugovskoje 80 50.38 N 46.28 E
Lugu 102 28.21 N 102.09 E
Lugulu ≃ 154 2.17 S 26.32 E
Lugunga ʌ 154 6.47 S 36.19 E
Luguru 154 2.55 S 33.58 E
Lugus Island I 116 5.41 N 120.50 E
Luhanka 26 61.47 N 25.42 E
Luhe 60 49.35 N 12.09 E
Luhe ≃ 52 53.18 N 10.11 E
Lühedian 100 32.33 N 114.28 E
Lühmannsdorf 54 54.00 N 13.38 E
Luhombero ≃ 154 8.24 S 37.12 E
Luhsien → Luzhou 107 28.54 N 105.27 E
Luhuo 102 31.26 N 100.48 E
Lui ≃, Ang. 152 8.41 S 17.56 E
Lui ≃, Zam. 152 16.21 S 23.18 E
Lui, Beinn ʌ 46 56.24 N 4.49 W
Luia 152 8.26 S 21.45 E
Luia (Ruya) ≃, Afr. 154 16.34 S 33.12 E
Luia ≃, Ang. 152 8.24 S 21.42 E
Lúia ≃, Moç. 154 15.34 S 32.58 E
Luiana 152 17.23 S 23.03 E
Luiana ≃ 152 17.27 S 23.14 E
Luichart, Loch ⊛ 46 57.37 N 4.46 W
Luido 156 21.31 S 34.41 E
Luie ≃ 152 4.33 S 17.41 E
Luik → Liège 56 50.38 N 5.34 E
Luilaka ≃ 152 0.52 S 20.12 E
Luilu ≃ 152 6.22 S 23.50 E
Luimbale 152 12.15 S 15.19 E
Luimneach → Limerick 48 52.40 N 8.38 W
Luing I 46 56.13 N 5.40 W
Luino 58 46.00 N 8.44 E
Luio ≃ 152 13.15 S 21.39 E
Luipaardsvlei 273d 26.16 S 27.42 E
Luiro ≃ 24 67.08 N 27.29 E
Luisant 50 48.25 N 1.29 E
Luís Correia 250 2.53 S 41.40 W
Luisen-Berg ʌ [2] 264a 52.27 N 13.07 E
Luisenthal 54 50.47 N 10.43 E
Luís Gomes 250 6.25 S 38.23 W
Luis Guillón 288 34.48 S 58.27 W
Luishia 154 11.10 S 27.02 E
Luis Moya, Méx. 234 22.25 N 102.15 W
Luis Moya, Méx. 234 23.05 N 103.56 W
Luis Muñoz Marin, Aeropuerto Internacional ⊠ 240m 18.27 N 66.00 W
Luis Peña, Cayo de I 240m 18.18 N 65.20 W
Luis Pereira, Arroyo ≃ 258 34.33 S 57.02 W
Luita 152 8.04 S 19.25 E
Luitpold Coast ⚓ [2] 9 78.30 S 32.00 W
Luiza 152 7.12 S 22.25 E
Luiza ≃ 152 7.35 S 22.40 E
Luizavo ≃ 152 11.42 S 23.12 E
Luizi 154 6.03 S 27.28 E
Luiziânia 255 21.41 S 50.17 W
Luján, Arg. 252 33.03 S 68.52 W
Luján, Arg. 252 32.22 S 65.57 W
Luján, Arg. 258 34.34 S 59.07 W
Luján ≃ 288 34.26 S 58.32 W
Lujia, Zhg. 106 31.15 N 121.37 E
Lujia, Zhg. 106 31.19 N 121.03 E
Lujia, Zhg. 269b 31.22 N 121.18 E
Lujiabang 106 31.20 N 121.01 E
Lujiachang 107 30.14 N 105.34 E
Lujiagangzi 104 42.05 N 122.59 E
Lujiang 100 31.14 N 117.17 E
Lujiao 100 29.10 N 112.52 E
Lujiaoxi 107 28.55 N 105.48 E
Lujiaqiao, Zhg. 106 31.47 N 120.27 E
Lujiaqiao, Zhg. 107 28.50 N 106.21 E
Lujiatun, Zhg. 98 40.14 N 122.11 E
Lujiatun, Zhg. 104 41.58 N 122.38 E
Lujiatun, Zhg. 104 41.10 N 121.56 E
Lujiatun, Zhg. 104 42.18 N 124.15 E
Lujiazhou 100 28.16 N 114.35 E
L'uk 80 56.55 N 52.48 E
Lukachukai Wash V 200 36.39 N 109.36 W
Lukačok 89 53.03 N 132.16 E
Lukala 152 5.31 S 14.32 E
Lukang 100 24.03 N 120.25 E
Lukanga, Zaïre 152 1.00 S 18.08 E
Lukanga, Zaïre 152 1.41 S 18.09 E
Lukanga Swamp ⩩ 154 14.25 S 27.45 E
Luk'anovo 82 54.52 N 37.25 E
Lukašin 84 40.12 N 44.01 E
Lukaškin Jar 86 60.20 N 78.24 E
Luke, Mount ʌ 162 27.13 S 116.48 E
Luke Air Force Base ■ 200 33.32 N 112.22 W
Lukenie ≃ 152 2.44 S 18.09 E
Lukens, Mount ʌ 280 34.16 N 118.14 W
Lukeville 200 31.52 N 112.48 W
Luki 76 53.29 N 26.15 E
Lukino, Ross. 82 55.26 N 37.04 E
Lukino, Ross. 82 55.50 N 36.49 E
Lukka 140 14.33 N 23.42 E
Luknovo 80 56.12 N 42.03 E
Lukojanov 80 55.02 N 44.30 E
Lukolela, Zaïre 152 5.23 S 24.32 E
Lukolela, Zaïre 152 1.03 S 17.12 E
Lukong 107 29.31 N 105.39 E
Lukoshi ≃ 152 10.05 S 22.59 E
Lukosi 154 18.30 S 26.30 E
Lukoškino 82 55.19 N 37.16 E
Lukou, Zhg. 100 27.14 N 114.04 E
Lukou, Zhg. 106 31.48 N 118.52 E
Lukoupu 100 29.30 N 113.26 E
Lukouyu 100 28.24 N 113.18 E
Lukov 78 51.13 N 24.19 E
Lukovit 38 43.12 N 24.10 E
Lukovskaja 80 50.35 N 41.52 E
Łuków 30 51.56 N 22.23 E
Lükqün 86 42.44 N 89.42 E
Lukuga ≃ 154 5.40 S 26.55 E
Lukula 152 5.23 S 12.57 E
Lukula ≃, Afr. 152 5.08 S 12.28 E
Lukula ≃, Zaïre 152 4.13 S 17.58 E
Lukuledi ≃ 154 10.05 S 39.42 E
Lukulu 152 14.25 S 23.12 E
Lukulu ≃ 154 10.56 S 31.05 E
Lukumburu 154 9.45 S 35.09 E
Lukunga ≃ 273b 4.25 S 15.14 E
Lukuni 152 5.52 S 17.11 E
Lukusashi ≃ 154 14.38 S 30.00 E
Lukusuzi National Park ♠ 154 12.50 S 32.35 E
Lula, It. 71 40.28 N 9.29 E
Lula, Ms., U.S. 194 34.27 N 90.28 W
Lula, Zaïre 152 5.22 S 16.02 E
Luleå 26 65.34 N 22.10 E
Luleälven ≃ 24 65.35 N 22.03 E
Lüleburgaz 130 41.24 N 27.21 E
Lules 252 26.56 S 65.21 W
Luliang 102 25.05 N 103.36 E
Lüliang Shan ∧ 102 37.25 N 111.20 E
Luliāni 123 31.15 N 74.25 E
Luliao 269d 25.07 N 121.39 E
Luling 222 29.40 N 97.38 W
Lullingstone Castle ⊥ 260 51.21 N 0.12 E
Lulo ≃ 152 9.25 S 18.14 E
Lulong 98 39.54 N 118.50 E
Lulonga 152 0.37 N 18.23 E
Lulonga ≃ 152 0.43 N 18.23 E
Lulu ≃ 152 1.18 N 23.42 E
Lulua ≃ 152 5.02 S 21.07 E
Luluabourg → Kananga 152 5.54 S 22.25 E
Lulu Island I, B.C., Can. 224 49.09 N 123.05 W
Lulu Island I, Ak., U.S. 182 55.28 N 133.30 W
Luluo 98 37.06 N 113.58 E
Lulworth, Mount ʌ 162 26.53 S 117.42 E
Lumai 152 13.31 S 21.21 E
Lumajang 115a 8.08 S 113.13 E
Lumajangdong Co ⊛ 120 34.00 N 81.45 E
Lumaku, Gunong ʌ 112 4.52 N 115.38 E
Lumaling 120 29.53 N 92.37 E
Lumb 262 53.42 N 1.58 W
Lumbala ≃ 152 12.38 S 22.34 E
Lumbala Kaquengue 152 12.39 S 22.34 E
Lumbala N'guimbo 152 14.08 S 21.25 E
Lumbangaraga 114 1.53 N 99.04 E
Lumbanlobu 114 2.31 N 99.08 E
Lumbe ≃ 152 16.42 S 23.42 E
Lumber ≃ 192 34.12 N 79.10 W
Lumber City 192 31.55 N 82.40 W
Lumberport 188 39.22 N 80.20 W
Lumberton, Ms., U.S. 194 31.00 N 89.27 W
Lumberton, N.J., U.S. 285 39.57 N 74.48 W
Lumberton, N.C., U.S. 192 34.37 N 79.00 W
Lumberton, Tx., U.S. 194 30.16 N 94.10 W
Lumbinī □ [8] 124 27.45 N 83.30 E
Lumbis 112 4.18 N 116.15 E
Lumbo 154 15.00 S 40.44 E
Lumbovka 24 67.44 N 40.30 E
Lumbrales 34 40.56 N 6.43 W
Lumbrein 58 46.41 N 9.08 E
Lumbres 50 50.42 N 2.08 E
Lumbwa 154 0.12 S 35.28 E
Lumby 182 50.15 N 118.58 W
Lumding 120 25.45 N 93.10 E
Lumege ≃ 152 11.55 S 20.58 E
Lumerau ≃ 116 5.21 N 118.53 E
Lumi 164 3.29 S 142.02 E
Lumiei ≃ 64 46.24 N 12.51 E
Luminárias 256 21.30 S 44.54 W
Luminosa 256 22.35 S 45.38 W
Lumintao ≃ 116 12.43 N 120.55 E
Lummen 56 50.59 N 5.12 E
Lummi Bay ⊂ 224 48.46 N 122.41 W
Lummi Indian Reservation ◆ [4] 224 48.48 N 122.38 W
Lummi Island 224 48.42 N 122.40 W
Lummi Island I 224 48.42 N 122.40 W
Lumphanan 46 57.07 N 2.41 W
Lumphăt 110 13.30 N 106.59 E
Lumphini Park ♠ 269a 13.44 N 100.33 E
Lumpkin 192 32.03 N 84.47 W
Lumpun ≃ 80 57.01 N 51.22 E
Lumsån ≃ 40 59.59 N 15.26 E
Lumsås 41 55.57 N 11.31 E
Lumsden, Nf., Can. 186 49.19 N 53.37 W
Lumsden, Sk., Can. 184 50.34 N 104.53 W
Lumsden, N.Z. 172 45.44 S 168.27 E
Lumsden, Scot., U.K. 46 57.15 N 2.52 W
Lumsheden 40 60.43 N 16.15 E
Lums Pond State Park ♠ 208 39.34 N 75.43 W
Lumu, Indon. 112 2.11 S 119.09 E
Lumu, Zhg. 106 31.22 N 120.37 E
Lumuna 154 3.46 S 26.24 E
Lumuna ≃ 152 16.59 S 21.25 E
Lumut, Indon. 114 1.33 N 98.56 E
Lumut, Malay. 114 4.14 N 100.38 E
Lumut, Tanjung › 112 3.50 S 105.57 E
Lumwana 154 11.50 S 25.10 E
Lün, Mong. 88 47.24 N 102.52 E
Lün, Mong. 88 47.52 N 105.15 E
Luna, Pil. 116 16.51 N 120.23 E
Luna, Pil. 116 18.18 N 121.21 E
Luna ≃ 246 4.32 S 60.41 W
Lunada Bay ⊂ 280 33.46 N 118.25 W
Lunain ≃ 50 48.20 N 2.47 E
Lunamatrona 71 39.39 N 8.54 E
Lunan 102 24.49 N 103.16 E
Lunan Bay ⊂ 46 56.39 N 2.28 W
Lunano 66 43.44 N 12.26 E
Luna Pier 216 41.48 N 83.26 W
Lūnāvāda 120 23.08 N 73.37 E
Luncarty 46 56.27 N 3.28 W
Lund, B.C., Can. 182 49.58 N 124.44 W
Lund, Sve. 41 55.42 N 13.11 E
Lund, Nv., U.S. 204 38.51 N 115.00 W
Lunda ≃, Ang. 152 6.07 S 13.52 E
L'unda ≃, Ross. 80 56.32 N 46.03 E
Lundåkrabukten ⊂ 41 55.48 N 12.53 E
Lundale 188 37.48 N 81.44 W
Lunda Norte □ [5] 152 8.45 S 19.45 E
Lundar 184 50.42 N 98.02 W
Lunda Sul □ [5] 152 10.00 S 20.30 E
Lundazi 154 12.19 S 33.13 E
Lundby 41 55.07 N 11.53 E
Lunde 41 55.29 N 10.21 E
Lundeborg 41 55.08 N 10.47 E
Lunden 41 54.20 N 9.01 E
Lunderskov 41 55.29 N 9.18 E
Lundevatn ⊛ 26 58.22 N 6.36 E
Lundi ≃ 154 21.43 S 32.34 E
Lundsberg 40 59.30 N 14.10 E
Lundsfjärden ⊛ 40 59.38 N 14.41 E
Lundy I 42 51.10 N 4.40 W
Lundys Lane 214 41.53 N 80.21 W
Lune ≃ 44 54.02 N 2.50 W
Lüneburg 52 53.15 N 10.23 E
Lüneburg □ [5] 52 53.15 N 10.00 E
Lüneburger Heide ◆ [1] 52 53.10 N 10.20 E
Lunel 62 43.41 N 4.08 E
Lünen 52 51.36 N 7.32 E
Lunenburg, N.S., Can. 186 44.23 N 64.19 W
Lunenburg, Ma., U.S. 207 42.35 N 71.43 W
Lunenburg, Va., U.S. 192 36.57 N 78.15 W
Luneray 50 49.50 N 0.55 E
Lünern 263 51.33 N 7.46 E
Lunéville 56 48.36 N 6.30 E
Lunga I 46 56.13 N 5.42 W
Lunga ≃, Ang. 152 5.59 S 16.20 E
Lunga ≃, Zam. 154 14.34 S 26.25 E
Lungälven ≃ 40 59.34 N 14.10 E
Lunga Reservoir ⊛ [1] 208 38.32 N 77.28 W
Lungau ◆ [1] 64 47.07 N 13.39 E
Lungavilla 62 45.02 N 9.04 E
Lungch'i → Zhangzhou 100 24.33 N 117.39 E
Lunge 152 12.12 S 16.05 E
Lunge'nake 120 31.45 N 85.55 E
Lungern 58 46.47 N 8.10 E
Lunggar 120 31.10 N 84.00 E
Lunghezza ◆ [8] 267a 41.55 N 12.35 E
Lungi 150 8.38 N 13.13 W
Lunglei 120 22.53 N 92.44 E
Lungro 68 39.44 N 16.07 E
Lungsang 124 29.51 N 88.41 E
Lungt'an 100 24.52 N 121.12 E
Lungué-Bungo (Lungwebungu) ≃ 152 14.19 S 23.14 E
Lunguya 154 3.23 S 32.24 E
Lungwebungu (Lungué-Bungo) ≃ 152 14.19 S 23.14 E
Lūni 120 26.00 N 73.00 E
Lūni ≃ 120 24.41 N 71.15 E
Luni ⊥ 64 44.04 N 10.01 E
Lunia-Bubi 154 7.30 S 24.49 E
Lunigiana ◆ [1] 64 44.15 N 9.50 E
Lunin 76 52.18 N 26.38 E
Luninec 76 52.15 N 26.48 E
Lunino, Ross. 80 53.35 N 45.14 E
Lunino, Ross. 82 54.09 N 38.29 E
Lunjiao 100 22.53 N 113.13 E
Lūnkaransar 120 28.29 N 73.44 E
Lunnaja, gora ʌ 180 68.14 N 174.20 E
Lunndörrsfjällen ʌ 26 63.00 N 13.00 E
Lunno 76 53.27 N 24.16 E
Lunongzha 106 31.59 N 120.55 E
Lunsar 150 8.41 N 12.32 W
Lunsemfwa ≃ 154 14.54 S 30.12 E
Lunt 262 53.31 N 2.59 W
Lunteren 52 52.05 N 5.37 E
Lunyuk 115b 8.57 S 117.14 E
Lunz am See 61 47.51 N 15.03 E
Lunzenau 54 50.58 N 12.45 E
Lunzhen 98 36.47 N 116.34 E
Luo ≃, Zhg. 102 34.48 N 113.04 E
Luo ≃, Zhg. 102 34.42 N 110.15 E
Luoba, Zhg. 100 24.51 N 114.13 E
Luoba, Zhg. 107 29.08 N 106.11 E
Luobei (Fengxiang) 89 47.34 N 130.50 E
Luobo 102 28.22 N 101.38 E
Luobu 102 24.30 N 109.40 E
Luobumiao 102 40.19 N 107.30 E
Luochanghe 100 31.01 N 117.18 E
Luocheng, Zhg. 102 24.51 N 108.59 E
Luocheng, Zhg. 107 29.23 N 104.01 E
Luochuan 102 35.55 N 109.26 E
Luoci 102 25.19 N 102.18 E
Luodian 106 31.25 N 121.20 E
Luoding 102 22.47 N 111.31 E
Luoduzhen 107 30.22 N 106.35 E
Luofa 105 39.25 N 116.50 E
Luofang, Zhg. 100 28.40 N 115.04 E
Luofang, Zhg. 100 27.52 N 115.06 E
Luofu, Zaïre 154 0.10 S 29.14 E
Luofu, Zhg. 100 24.32 N 115.35 E
Luogang, Zhg. 100 23.11 N 113.30 E
Luogang, Zhg. 100 24.25 N 115.38 E
Luogosanto 71 41.03 N 9.13 E
Luoguhe 89 53.18 N 121.30 E
Luohan Shan ʌ 100 25.51 N 119.13 E
Luohe 100 33.35 N 114.01 E
Luoheya 98 35.46 N 118.54 E
Luohua 100 26.35 N 118.43 E
Luoji 100 32.06 N 117.16 E
Luojiachang 107 30.49 N 106.32 E
Luojiang 102 31.21 N 104.28 E
Luojiatang 106 30.18 N 120.13 E
Luojiatun, Zhg. 98 40.11 N 118.34 E
Luojiatun, Zhg. 104 42.06 N 122.44 E
Luojiatun, Zhg. 104 40.55 N 122.04 E
Luojiawei 100 26.55 N 115.02 E
Luoke 100 24.07 N 114.28 E
Luokeng 100 24.32 N 113.23 E
Luokou, Zhg. 100 28.54 N 117.24 E
Luokou, Zhg. 100 25.46 N 115.39 E
Luolong 107 28.49 N 104.46 E
L'Uomo di Cagna ʌ 71 41.33 N 9.04 E
Luonan 102 34.05 N 110.04 E
Luoning 102 34.25 N 111.42 E
Luoping 102 24.59 N 104.21 E
Luoqi 102 29.48 N 106.56 E
Luoqiao 100 26.28 N 119.01 E
Luoquanzhen 107 29.50 N 104.31 E
Luoshan, Zhg. 100 32.13 N 114.32 E
Luoshan, Zhg. 100 29.41 N 113.18 E
Luoshan, Zhg. 105 39.55 N 117.33 E
Luoshe, Zhg. 106 31.39 N 120.11 E
Luoshe, Zhg. 106 30.41 N 120.04 E
Luoshuihe 98 39.27 N 114.19 E
Luossa ≃ 152 8.24 S 17.03 E
Luotian 100 30.48 N 115.22 E
Luotuodian 100 32.13 N 113.49 E
Luotuoqiao 100 29.56 N 121.32 E
Luotuo Shan ʌ 104 42.14 N 121.42 E
Luowenba 102 31.48 N 107.48 E
Luowenyu 105 40.16 N 117.57 E
Luoxi 100 29.05 N 114.58 E
Luoxiao Shan ∧ 100 26.00 N 114.00 E
Luoyang (Loyang), Zhg. 102 34.41 N 112.28 E
Luoyang, Zhg. 106 31.39 N 120.05 E
Luoyuan 100 26.31 N 119.32 E
Luoyuan Wan ⊂ 100 26.25 N 119.43 E
Luoyukou 102 38.23 N 110.43 E
Luozhexi 107 29.02 N 103.54 E
Luozi 152 4.57 S 14.08 E
Lupala 156 17.50 S 19.06 E
Lupani 154 18.54 S 27.44 E
Lupao 116 15.53 N 120.54 E
Lupar ≃ 112 1.30 N 111.00 E
Łupawa 30 54.26 N 17.24 E
Lupberg 60 49.09 N 11.45 E
Lupembe 154 9.15 S 35.15 E
Lupeni 38 45.22 N 23.13 E
Lupire 152 14.36 S 19.29 E
Lupiro 154 8.23 S 36.40 E
Lupon 116 6.54 N 126.00 E
Luppa 54 51.20 N 12.57 E
Luputa 152 7.10 S 23.42 E
Luqiao, Zhg. 100 32.34 N 117.14 E
Luqiao, Zhg. 100 28.35 N 121.22 E
Luqu 102 34.41 N 102.22 E
Luque 34 37.33 N 4.16 W
Luquillo 240m 18.22 N 65.43 W
Luquillo, Sierra de ∧ 240m 18.17 N 65.47 W
Lūrah ≃ 120 31.33 N 66.33 E
Luray 188 38.39 N 78.27 W
Lure 58 47.41 N 6.30 E
Lure, Montagne de ∧ 62 44.07 N 5.47 E
Lureco ≃ 154 12.28 S 37.40 E
Luremo 152 8.31 S 17.50 E
Lurgan 48 54.28 N 6.20 W
Luribay 248 17.06 S 67.39 W
Lurigancho 286d 12.02 S 77.01 W
Lurín 248 12.17 S 76.52 W
Lúrio 154 13.35 S 40.30 E
Lúrio ≃ 154 13.35 S 40.32 E
Lurisia 62 44.18 N 7.42 E
Lurnea 274a 33.56 S 150.54 E
Lurö I 26 58.48 N 13.14 E
Lürrip ◆ [8] 263 51.12 N 6.28 E
Lusahunga 154 2.52 S 31.15 E
Lusaka, Zaïre 154 7.10 S 29.27 E
Lusaka, Zam. 154 15.25 S 28.17 E
Lusaka □ [4] 154 15.25 S 29.00 E
Lusakert 84 40.23 N 44.36 E
Lusambo 152 4.58 S 23.27 E
Lusancay Islands and Reefs II 164 8.25 S 150.20 E
Lusanga 152 4.50 S 18.44 E
Lusangaye 154 4.54 S 26.00 E
Lusangi 154 4.37 S 27.08 E
Luscar 182 53.04 N 117.24 W
Luseke 152 2.51 S 23.08 E
Luseland 184 52.05 N 109.24 W
Lusen ʌ 60 48.56 N 13.31 E
Lusenga Plain National Park ♠ 154 9.30 S 29.10 E
Lusengo 152 1.46 N 19.29 E
Luserna San Giovanni 62 44.48 N 7.15 E
Lush, Mount ʌ 164 17.02 S 127.30 E
Lushan, Zhg. 100 33.45 N 112.53 E
Lushan, Zhg. 102 30.15 N 102.58 E
Lu Shan ʌ 100 29.31 N 115.58 E
Lu Shan ∧ 98 36.05 N 118.05 E
Lushanguanliju 100 29.33 N 115.58 E
Lushi 102 34.05 N 111.01 E
Lushiko (Luchico) ≃ 152 6.13 S 19.40 E
Lüshikou 100 29.16 N 120.17 E
Lushnje 38 40.56 N 19.42 E
Lushoto 154 4.47 S 38.17 E
Lushui 102 26.00 N 98.51 E
Lüshun (Port Arthur) 98 38.48 N 121.16 E
Lüsi 106 32.03 N 121.36 E
Lusi ≃ 115a 7.05 S 110.55 E
Lusiana 64 45.47 N 11.34 E
Lusignan 32 46.26 N 0.07 E
Lusignan, Lac ⊛ 206 46.40 N 74.09 W
Lusigny-sur-Barse 50 48.15 N 4.16 E
Lusikisiki 158 31.25 S 29.30 E
L'uşino 76 52.38 N 26.31 E
Lusk, Ire. 48 53.32 N 6.10 W
Lusk, Wy., U.S. 200 42.45 N 104.27 W
Lus-la-Croix-Haute 62 44.40 N 5.42 E
Lusongwa 152 12.58 S 24.16 E
Luspebryggan 24 67.01 N 19.51 E
Lussac-les-Châteaux 32 46.24 N 0.44 E
Lussan 62 44.09 N 4.22 E
Luṣṣān, Wādī V 132 30.30 N 34.18 E
Lustenau 58 47.26 N 9.39 E
Luster 26 61.26 N 7.24 E
Lustin 56 50.23 N 4.53 E
Lustrafjorden ⊂ [2] 26 61.20 N 7.22 E
Lüstringen 52 52.16 N 8.08 E
Lusutfu (Maputo) (Great Usutu) ≃ 158 26.11 S 32.42 E
Luswishi ≃ 154 13.55 S 27.24 E
Lūt, Dasht-e ◆ [2] 128 32.00 N 58.00 E
L'uta ≃ 76 58.37 N 28.40 E
Lü-ta → Dalian 98 38.53 N 121.35 E
Lutago (Luttach) 64 46.57 N 11.55 E
Lutai 100 33.32 N 115.03 E
Lütan, Zhg. 98 34.07 N 114.27 E
Lütan, Zhg. 100 28.57 N 119.46 E
Lutang 100 25.39 N 112.46 E
Lutao 116 10.00 N 124.04 E
Lü Tao I 100 22.40 N 121.29 E
Lutcher 194 30.02 N 90.41 W
Lute 284c 39.04 N 77.03 W
Lutembo 152 13.26 S 21.16 E
Lutembo ≃ 152 12.03 S 22.15 E
L'uten'ka 78 50.13 N 34.02 E
Lutesville 194 37.18 N 89.58 W
Lutéte ≃ 152 9.21 S 15.14 E
Lutexu ≃ 273b 4.24 S 15.12 E
Lütgendortmund ◆ [8] 263 51.30 N 7.21 E
Luthe 52 52.26 N 9.28 E
Luther, Mi., U.S. 190 44.02 N 85.40 W
Luther, Ok., U.S. 196 35.39 N 97.11 W
Luther Lake ⊛ 212 43.55 N 80.26 W
Luthersburg 214 41.03 N 78.43 W
Lutherville-Timonium 284b 39.25 N 76.37 W
Luthrie 46 56.21 N 3.05 W
Luti 175e 7.14 S 156.59 E
Lutian, Zhg. 100 26.33 N 114.38 E
Lütian, Zhg. 100 23.48 N 113.56 E
Lütjenburg 54 54.17 N 10.35 E
Lütjensee 52 53.39 N 10.22 E
Luton, Eng., U.K. 42 51.53 N 0.25 W
Luton, Eng., U.K. 260 51.22 N 0.32 E
Lutong 112 4.28 N 114.00 E
Lutosn'a ≃ 82 56.26 N 36.52 E
Lutou 100 32.16 N 112.53 E
Lutry 58 46.30 N 6.41 E
Lutshi 154 4.09 S 26.30 E
Lutshima ≃ 152 5.22 S 18.59 E
Lutsk → Luck 78 50.44 N 25.20 E
Luttach → Lutago 64 46.57 N 11.55 E
Lutter am Barenberge 52 51.59 N 10.16 E
Lutterbach 58 47.46 N 7.17 E
Lutterworth 42 52.28 N 1.10 W
Lüttich → Liège 56 50.38 N 5.34 E
Luttrell 192 36.11 N 83.44 W
Lüttringhausen ◆ [8] 263 51.13 N 7.14 E
Lutuai ≃ 152 12.33 S 20.16 E
Lutugino 83 48.24 N 39.13 E
Lutz 220 28.09 N 82.27 W
Lützel 56 50.58 N 8.10 E
Lutzelbourg 56 48.44 N 7.15 E
Lützelflüh 58 47.00 N 7.41 E
Lützen 54 51.15 N 12.08 E
Lutzerath 56 50.07 N 7.00 E
Lutz Hill 284b 39.20 N 76.32 W
Lützow 54 53.40 N 11.11 E
Lützow-Holm Bay ⊂ 9 69.10 S 37.30 E
Lutzputs 158 28.03 S 20.40 E
Lützschena 54 51.23 N 12.16 E
Lutzville 158 31.33 S 18.22 E
Luud, Waadi V 144 10.17 N 50.14 E
Luuq 144 3.48 N 42.33 E
Luus 102 45.30 N 105.45 E
Luverne, Al., U.S. 194 31.42 N 86.15 W
Lu Verne, Ia., U.S. 190 42.54 N 94.04 W
Luverne, Mn., U.S. 198 43.39 N 96.12 W
Luvo 152 5.51 S 14.05 E
Luvo ≃ 152 10.18 S 17.08 E
Luvua 154 8.48 S 25.19 E
Lúvua ≃, Ang. 152 11.57 S 22.30 E
Luvua ≃, Zaïre 154 6.46 S 26.58 E
Luvuvhu ≃ 156 22.40 S 30.55 E
Luwegu ≃ 154 8.31 S 37.23 E
Luwingu 154 10.15 S 29.55 E
Luwuk 112 0.56 S 122.47 E
Luwuk → Banggai 112 1.34 S 123.30 E
Luxana Bay ⊂ 182 52.03 N 131.00 W
Luxapallila Creek ≃ 194 33.28 N 88.26 W
Luxembourg 56 49.36 N 6.09 E
Luxembourg □ [4] 56 50.00 N 5.30 E
Luxembourg □ [1], Europe 22 49.45 N 6.05 E
Luxembourg □ [1], Europe 56 49.45 N 6.05 E
Luxembourg, Aéroport de ⊠ 56 49.37 N 6.10 E
Luxembourg, Jardin du ♠ 261 48.51 N 2.19 E
Luxemburg 190 44.32 N 87.42 W
Luxemburg → Luxembourg □ [1] 56 49.45 N 6.05 E
Luxemburgo → Luxembourg □ [1] 56 49.45 N 6.05 E
Luxeuil-les-Bains 58 47.49 N 6.23 E
Luxi, Zhg. 102 24.32 N 103.41 E
Luxi (Mangshi), Zhg. 102 24.20 N 98.25 E
Lüxia 100 26.41 N 120.06 E
Luxian 107 28.55 N 105.29 E
Luxiang, Zhg. 106 31.32 N 120.45 E
Lüxiang, Zhg. 106 30.50 N 121.10 E
Luxi Dao I 100 27.59 N 121.11 E
Luxikou 100 29.54 N 113.42 E
Luxmanor 284c 39.02 N 77.07 W
Luxor 214 40.20 N 79.28 W
Luxora 194 35.45 N 89.55 W
Luxor → Al-Uqṣur 140 25.41 N 32.39 E
Luxu 106 31.01 N 120.50 E
Lu Xun Museum ⊍ 269b 31.16 N 121.28 E
Lüxuqiao 106 31.50 N 119.31 E
Luy ≃ 32 43.39 N 1.08 W
Luyan 106 30.25 N 120.53 E
Lüyang 104 41.23 N 121.40 E
Luyanó ≃ 286b 23.07 N 82.21 W
Luyeh 100 22.55 N 121.08 E
Luyi 100 33.53 N 115.28 E
Luynes 50 47.23 N 0.33 E
Luyu 106 31.34 N 121.41 E
Luyuan, Zhg. 106 31.51 N 120.38 E
Luyuan, Zhg. 271a 39.54 N 116.27 E
Luz, Bra. 255 19.48 S 45.40 W
Luz, Bra. 287a 22.48 S 43.05 W
Luz ◆ [8] 266c 38.46 N 9.10 W
Luz, Estação da ◆ [5] 287b 23.32 S 46.38 W
Luz, Isla I 254 45.30 S 73.59 W
Luz, Ponta da › 287a 22.47 S 43.05 W
Luza, Ross. 24 62.42 N 37.06 E
Luza, Ross. 24 60.39 N 47.10 E
Luža, Ross. 76 59.58 N 31.56 E
Luža ≃ 82 55.03 N 36.35 E
Luzarches 50 49.07 N 2.25 E
Luzern 58 47.03 N 8.18 E
Luzern □ [3] 58 47.05 N 8.05 E
Luzerne 210 41.17 N 75.54 W
Luzerne □ [6] 210 41.14 N 75.53 W
Luzhai, Zhg. 102 24.31 N 109.50 E
Luzhai, Zhg. 269b 31.20 N 121.22 E
Luzhi 106 31.16 N 120.52 E
Luzhou 107 28.54 N 105.27 E
Luziânia 255 16.15 S 47.56 W
Lužické hory ∧ 54 50.48 N 14.40 E
Luzilândia 250 3.28 S 42.22 W
Lužki, Bela. 76 55.21 N 27.52 E
Lužki, Ross. 82 54.51 N 37.36 E
Lužná 54 50.06 N 13.45 E
Lužnice ≃, Europe 30 49.14 N 14.23 E
Lužnice (Lainsitz) ≃, Europe 61 49.13 N 14.42 E
Lužniki ◆ [8] 265b 55.43 N 37.33 E
Luzon I 116 16.00 N 121.00 E
Luzon Strait ɥ 108 20.30 N 121.00 E
Lužskaja guba ⊂ 76 59.45 N 28.20 E
Luzy 32 46.48 N 3.58 E
Luzzara 64 44.58 N 10.41 E
Luzzi 68 39.27 N 16.17 E
L'va ≃ 78 52.00 N 27.36 E
L'va Tolstogo 82 54.37 N 36.03 E
L'vov 78 49.50 N 24.00 E
L'vov □ [4] 78 49.30 N 24.00 E
L'vovskij 82 55.19 N 37.31 E
Lwówek 30 52.28 N 16.10 E
Lwówek Śląski 30 51.07 N 15.35 E
Lwów → L'vov 78 49.50 N 24.00 E
Lyall, Mount ʌ 172 45.17 S 167.34 E
Lyallpur → Faisalabad 123 31.25 N 73.05 E
Lyantonde 154 0.24 S 31.09 E
Lybster 46 58.18 N 3.18 W
Lycaonia □ [9] 130 37.50 N 33.15 E
Lychen 54 53.12 N 13.19 E
Lycia □ [9] 130 36.20 N 30.00 E
Lyckeby 26 56.12 N 15.39 E
Lyck → Ełk 30 53.50 N 22.22 E
Lyčkovo, Ross. 76 57.55 N 32.24 E
Lyčkovo, Ukr. 78 49.06 N 35.12 E
Lycksele 26 64.36 N 18.40 E
Lycoming □ [6] 210 41.14 N 77.00 W
Lycoming Creek ≃ 210 41.13 N 77.02 W
Lydd 42 50.57 N 0.55 E
Lydda → Lod 132 31.58 N 34.54 E
Lydden ≃ 42 50.56 N 2.22 W
Lydenburg 156 25.10 S 30.29 E
Lydenburgh County Park ♠ 276 40.50 N 73.14 W
Lydford 42 50.39 N 4.06 W
Lydgate 262 53.44 N 2.07 W
Lydham 42 52.31 N 2.58 W
Lydia □ [9] 130 38.40 N 27.30 E
Lydia Mills 192 34.28 N 81.55 W
Lydiate 262 53.32 N 2.57 W
Lydick 216 41.42 N 86.22 W
Lydney 42 51.44 N 2.32 W
Lye Green 260 51.43 N 0.35 W
Lyell, Mount ʌ, Can. 182 51.57 N 117.06 W
Lyell, Mount ʌ, Ca., U.S. 226 37.44 N 119.16 W
Lyell Brown, Mount ʌ 162 23.21 S 130.24 E
Lyell Island I 182 52.40 N 131.30 W
Lyerly 192 34.24 N 85.24 W
Lyford 196 26.24 N 97.47 W
Lygnern ⊛ 26 57.29 N 12.20 E
Lykens 208 40.34 N 76.42 W
Lykošino 76 58.07 N 33.43 E
Lyle, Mn., U.S. 190 43.30 N 92.56 W
Lyle, Wa., U.S. 224 45.41 N 121.17 W
Lyles 194 35.55 N 87.20 W
Lyman, Ne., U.S. 198 41.55 N 104.02 W
Lyman, S.C., U.S. 192 34.56 N 82.07 W
Lyman, Wa., U.S. 224 48.31 N 122.03 W
Lyman, Wy., U.S. 200 41.19 N 110.17 W
Lymbel'karamo 86 60.15 N 83.32 E
Lyme 207 41.18 N 72.19 W
Lyme Bay ⊂ 42 50.38 N 3.00 W
Lyme Hall ⊥ 262 53.20 N 2.03 W
Lyme Park ♠ 262 53.21 N 2.04 W
Lyme Regis 42 50.44 N 2.57 W
Lyminge 42 51.08 N 1.05 E
Lymington 42 50.46 N 1.33 W
Lymkoj 86 59.31 N 70.22 E
Lymm 262 53.23 N 2.29 W
Lympne 42 51.05 N 1.02 E
Lympstone 42 50.39 N 3.25 W
Lyn 212 44.35 N 75.47 W
Łyna (Lava) ≃ 76 54.37 N 21.14 E
Lynæs 41 55.57 N 11.52 E
Lynbrook 276 40.39 N 73.41 W
Lynch, Ky., U.S. 192 36.57 N 82.55 W
Lynch, Ne., U.S. 198 42.49 N 98.27 W
Lynch, Lac ⊛ 190 46.25 N 77.05 W
Lynchburg, Oh., U.S. 218 39.14 N 83.47 W
Lynchburg, S.C., U.S. 192 34.03 N 80.04 W
Lynchburg, Tn., U.S. 194 35.16 N 86.22 W
Lynchburg, Va., U.S. 192 37.24 N 79.08 W
Lynches ≃ 192 33.50 N 79.22 W
Lynchville 214 41.26 N 78.34 W
Lynd ≃ 164 16.28 S 143.18 E
Lynde Creek ≃ 212 43.51 N 78.57 W
Lynden, On., Can. 212 43.14 N 80.09 W
Lynden, Wa., U.S. 224 48.56 N 122.27 W
Lyndhurst, Austl. 166 19.12 S 144.23 E
Lyndhurst, Austl. 166 30.17 S 138.21 E
Lyndhurst, Austl. 274b 38.03 S 145.15 E
Lyndhurst, Eng., U.K. 42 50.52 N 1.34 W
Lyndhurst, N.J., U.S. 276 40.48 N 74.07 W
Lyndhurst, Oh., U.S. 214 41.31 N 81.29 W
Lyndoch 168b 34.37 S 138.53 E
Lyndon, Austl. 162 23.37 S 115.15 E
Lyndon, Ks., U.S. 198 38.38 N 95.41 W
Lyndon, Ky., U.S. 218 38.15 N 85.36 W
Lyndon ≃ 162 23.29 S 114.06 E
Lyndon B. Johnson, Lake ⊛ [1] 196 30.35 N 98.25 W
Lyndon B. Johnson Historical Park ⊥ 196 30.15 N 98.38 W
Lyndon B. Johnson Space Center ⊍ [3] 222 29.34 N 95.05 W
Lyndonville, N.Y., U.S. 210 43.19 N 78.23 W
Lyndonville, Vt., U.S. 188 44.32 N 72.00 W
Lyndora 214 40.51 N 79.55 W
Lyne 260 51.23 N 0.33 W
Lyne ≃, Eng., U.K. 44 55.12 N 1.31 W
Lyne ≃, Eng., U.K. 44 54.58 N 3.01 W
Lyneham 42 51.31 N 1.58 W
Lynemouth 44 55.12 N 1.31 W
Lyne Water ≃ 46 55.39 N 3.16 W
Lynga 80 57.17 N 53.04 E
Lyngdal 26 58.08 N 7.05 E
Lynge 41 55.51 N 12.17 E
Lyngen 24 69.34 N 20.10 E
Lyngen ⊂ [2] 24 69.58 N 20.30 E
Lyngør 26 58.38 N 9.10 E
Lynher ≃ 42 50.28 N 4.12 W
Lynmouth 42 51.15 N 3.50 W
Lynn, Al., U.S. 194 34.02 N 87.32 W
Lynn, In., U.S. 218 40.02 N 84.56 W
Lynn, Ma., U.S. 207 42.28 N 70.57 W
Lynn ≃ 212 42.47 N 80.12 W
Lynn Canal ⊂ 180 58.50 N 135.15 W
Lynndyl 200 39.31 N 112.22 W
Lynne Acres 284b 39.21 N 76.45 W
Lynnfield 207 42.32 N 71.02 W
Lynn Garden 192 36.34 N 82.34 W
Lynn Harbor ⊂ 283 42.27 N 70.57 W
Lynn Haven 194 30.14 N 85.38 W
Lynn Lake 184 56.51 N 101.03 W
Lynnville 190 41.34 N 92.47 W
Lynnwood, Pa., U.S. 210 41.14 N 75.56 W
Lynnwood, Pa., U.S. 214 40.07 N 79.51 W
Lynnwood, Wa., U.S. 224 47.49 N 122.18 W
Lynn Woods ♠ 283 42.29 N 70.59 W
Lynton 42 51.15 N 3.50 W
Lyntupy 76 55.03 N 26.19 E
Lynwood, Ca., U.S. 228 33.55 N 118.12 W
Lynwood, Il., U.S. 278 41.32 N 87.32 W
Lynx Lake ⊛ 176 62.25 N 106.15 W
Lyø I 41 55.02 N 10.10 E
Lyon 62 45.45 N 4.51 E
Lyon □ [6] 226 39.00 N 119.15 W
Lyon ≃ 46 56.37 N 4.01 W
Lyon, Gare ◆ [5] 261 48.51 N 2.23 E
Lyon, Glen V 46 56.35 N 4.20 W
Lyon, Loch ⊛ 46 56.32 N 4.36 W
Lyon Inlet ⊂ 176 66.32 N 83.53 W
Lyon Mountain 188 44.43 N 73.54 W
Lyon Mountain ʌ 188 44.41 N 73.53 W
Lyonnais □ [9] 62 45.45 N 4.30 E
Lyonnais, Monts du ∧ 62 45.40 N 4.30 E
Lyons, Co., U.S. 200 40.13 N 105.16 W
Lyons, Ga., U.S. 192 32.12 N 82.19 W
Lyons, Il., U.S. 216 41.48 N 87.49 W
Lyons, In., U.S. 194 38.59 N 87.04 W
Lyons, Ks., U.S. 198 38.20 N 98.12 W
Lyons, Mi., U.S. 216 42.58 N 84.56 W
Lyons, Ne., U.S. 198 41.56 N 96.28 W
Lyons, N.Y., U.S. 210 43.03 N 76.59 W
Lyons, Oh., U.S. 216 41.41 N 84.04 W
Lyons, Tx., U.S. 222 30.23 N 96.34 W
Lyons, Wi., U.S. 216 42.39 N 88.21 W
Lyons ≃ 162 25.02 S 115.09 E
Lyon-Satolas, Aéroport de ⊠ 62 45.43 N 5.04 E
Lyons Creek ≃ 284a 43.03 N 79.04 W
Lyons Falls 212 43.37 N 75.22 W
Lyons-la-Forêt 50 49.24 N 1.28 E
Lyons Plains 207 41.13 N 73.21 W
Lyons Run ≃ 279b 40.25 N 79.43 W
Lyon Station 208 40.28 N 75.45 W
Lyonsville 276 40.57 N 74.25 W
Lyracrumpane 48 52.20 N 9.30 W
Lyrestad 40 58.48 N 14.04 E
Lys (Leie) ≃, Europe 50 51.03 N 3.43 E
Lys ≃, It. 62 45.36 N 7.47 E
Lysá ʌ 60 49.29 N 12.42 E
Lysaja Gora 78 48.11 N 31.06 E
Lysaker 26 59.54 N 10.36 E
Lys'anka 78 49.16 N 30.50 E
Lysá pod Makytou 30 49.12 N 18.13 E
Lysefjorden ⊂ [2] 26 59.00 N 6.14 E
Lysekil 26 58.16 N 11.26 E
Łysica ʌ 30 50.54 N 20.55 E
Lysjön ⊛ 40 60.07 N 14.18 E
Lyskovo 80 56.04 N 45.02 E
Lysogorka 83 47.42 N 39.12 E
Lyss 58 47.04 N 7.18 E
Lysterfield 274b 37.56 S 145.18 E
Lysterfield ʌ [2] 274b 37.56 S 145.16 E
Lysterfield Reservoir ⊛ [1] 274b 37.58 S 145.18 E
Lyster Station 206 46.22 N 71.37 W
Lys'va 86 58.07 N 57.47 E
Lys'va ≃ 80 58.15 N 54.47 E
Lysyje Gory 80 51.32 N 44.46 E
Lytham Saint Anne's 44 53.45 N 2.57 W
Lytkarino 82 55.35 N 37.54 E
Lytle 196 29.13 N 98.47 W
Lytle Creek ≃ 228 34.09 N 117.23 W
Lyttelton, N.Z. 172 43.35 S 172.42 E
Lyttelton, S. Afr. 158 25.50 S 28.11 E
Lytton 182 50.14 N 121.34 W
Lytton Springs 222 30.00 N 97.37 W
Lyubertsy → L'ubercy 82 55.41 N 37.53 E

M

Ma ≃ 110 19.47 N 105.56 E
Ma, Oued el V, Alg. 148 27.45 N 7.45 W
Ma, Oued el V, Maur. 148 24.03 N 9.10 W
Maadid, Djebel ʌ 34 35.52 N 4.46 E
Maalaea Bay ⊂ 229a 20.47 N 156.29 W
Ma'alot-Tarshiḥa 132 33.01 N 35.17 E
Maam Cross 48 53.27 N 9.31 W
Ma'ān 132 30.12 N 35.44 E
Ma'ān □ [8] 132 30.20 N 36.30 E
Maaninka 26 63.09 N 27.18 E
Ma'anshan, Zhg. 100 31.42 N 118.30 E
Maanshan, Zhg. 107 29.52 N 104.59 E
Ma-ao 116 10.29 N 122.59 E
Maap I 174q 9.35 N 138.11 E
Maar 140 6.54 N 31.33 E
Maardu 76 59.28 N 25.02 E
Maarianhamina → Mariehamn 26 60.06 N 19.57 E
Ma'ārik, Qārat al- ʌ [2] 142 29.59 N 30.52 E
Ma'arrat an-Nu'mān 130 35.38 N 36.40 E
Ma'arrat Miṣrīn 130 36.01 N 36.40 E
Ma'arrat Ṣaydnāyā 132 33.41 N 36.23 E
Maarssen 52 52.08 N 5.08 E
Maas 48 54.50 N 8.22 W
Maas (Meuse) ≃ 30 51.49 N 5.01 E
Maasbracht 52 51.08 N 5.53 E
Maasdam 52 51.47 N 4.32 E
Maaseik 56 51.06 N 5.48 E
Maasholm 41 54.41 N 9.59 E
Maasin 116 10.08 N 124.50 E
Maasmechelen 56 50.58 N 5.42 E
Maasniel 52 51.13 N 6.01 E

≃ River	Fluß	Río	Rivière	Rio	✦ Submarine Features	Untermeerische Objekte	Accidentes Submarinos / Formes de relief sous-marin / Acidentes submarinos
≊ Canal	Kanal	Canal	Canal	Canal	□ Political Unit	Politische Einheit	Unidad Politica / Entité politique / Unidade política
⌊ Waterfall, Rapids	Wasserfall, Stromschnellen	Cascada, Rápidos	Chute d'eau, Rapides	Cascata, Rápidos	⊍ Cultural Institution	Kulturelle Institution	Institución Cultural / Institution culturelle / Instituição cultural
ɥ Strait	Meeresstraße	Estrecho	Détroit	Estreito	⊥ Historical Site	Historische Stätte	Sitio Histórico / Site historique / Sitio histórico
⊂ Bay, Gulf	Bucht, Golf	Bahía, Golfo	Baie, Golfe	Baía, Golfo	♠ Recreational Site	Erholungs- und Ferienort	Sitio de Recreo / Centre de loisirs / Area de Lazer
⊛ Lake, Lakes	See, Seen	Lago, Lagos	Lac, Lacs	Lago, Lagos	⊠ Airport	Flughafen	Aeropuerto / Aéroport / Aeroporto
⩩ Swamp	Sumpf	Pantano	Marais	Pântano	■ Military Installation	Militäranlage	Instalación Militar / Installation militaire / Instalação militar
⊞ Ice Features, Glacier	Eis- und Gletscherformen	Accidentes Glaciales	Formes glaciaires	Acidentes glaciares	◆ Miscellaneous	Verschiedenes	Misceláneo / Divers / Diversos
⚓ Other Hydrographic Features	Andere Hydrographische Objekte	Otros Elementos Hidrográficos	Autres données hydrographiques	Outros acidentes hidrográficos			

ENGLISH — Name · Page · Lat.°′ · Long.°′
DEUTSCH — Name · Seite · Breite°′ · Länge°′ E = Ost

Maassluis 52 51.55 N 4.15 E
Maastricht 56 50.52 N 5.43 E
Maave 156 21.03 S 34.47 E
Ma-ayon ≃ 116 11.25 N 122.46 E
Maba 100 32.59 N 118.48 E
Maba, Ouadi V 146 15.10 N 21.00 E
Mababe Depression ⊥[7] 156 18.50 S 24.15 E
Mabaduan 164 9.16 S 142.44 E
Mabaho, Mount ∧ 116 9.15 N 125.42 E
Mabaia 152 7.13 S 14.03 E
Mabalacat 116 15.14 N 120.34 E
Mabalane 156 23.37 S 32.31 E
Mabana 224 48.05 N 122.24 W
Mabanga 152 1.30 N 19.06 E
Mabank 222 32.21 N 96.06 W
Mabaoquan 105 40.09 N 115.53 E
Ma'barot 132 32.22 N 34.54 E
Mabaruma 246 8.12 N 59.47 W
Mabashi 268 35.49 N 139.55 E
Mabau 112 2.14 S 111.54 E
Mabay 240p 20.16 N 76.40 W
Mabber, Ras › 144 9.28 N 50.50 E
Mabel Creek 162 29.01 S 134.17 E
Mabeleapodi 156 20.58 S 22.36 E
Mabel Lake ⊜ 182 50.35 N 118.44 W
Maben 194 33.33 N 89.05 W
Mabenga-Cité 152 3.39 S 18.40 E
Mabenge 152 4.14 N 24.09 E
Maberry, Loch ⊜ 44 55.02 N 4.41 W
Mabeti ≃ 92 40.31 N 141.31 E
Mabeul 36 36.27 N 10.46 E
Mabi, Nihon 96 34.38 N 133.41 E
Mabi, Zhg. 100 26.21 N 119.36 E
Mabi, Zhg. 102 35.59 N 112.15 E
Mabian 107 28.48 N 103.41 E
Mabian ≃ 107 29.08 N 103.58 E
Mablethorpe 44 53.21 N 0.15 E
Mableton 192 33.49 N 84.34 W
Mabole ≃ 150 9.01 N 12.44 W
Maboma 154 2.32 N 28.13 E
Mabonto 150 8.52 N 11.49 W
Mabote 156 22.03 S 34.09 E
Mabou 186 46.05 N 61.22 W
Mabrak, Jabal ∧ 132 30.13 N 35.29 E
Mabrous ⊤[4] 146 21.13 N 13.38 E
Mabrūk, Lībiyā 146 29.50 N 17.10 E
Mabrūk, Sūd. 140 8.07 N 29.25 E
Mabton 202 46.12 N 119.59 W
Mabuasehube Game Reserve ◆[4] 156 25.10 S 22.10 E
Mabuguai 100 29.49 N 112.42 E
Mabuki 154 2.59 S 33.11 E
Mabuni 174m 26.05 N 127.43 E
Mabwe 154 8.39 S 26.31 E
Mača, Ross. 74 59.54 N 117.35 E
Maca, Ven. 286c 10.28 N 66.48 W
Maca, Cerro ∧ 254 45.06 S 73.12 W
Macachín 252 37.09 S 63.39 W
Macaco, Morro do ∧[2] 287a 22.56 S 43.07 W
Macacos, Ilha dos I 250 1.20 S 50.35 W
Macacu ≃ 256 22.42 S 43.02 W
Macaé 255 22.23 S 41.47 W
Macaíba 250 5.51 S 35.21 W
Macajalar Bay c 116 8.37 N 124.38 E
Macajuba 255 12.09 S 40.22 W
Macalaya 116 12.53 N 123.46 E
Macalelon 116 13.45 N 122.08 E
Macalister 182 52.27 N 122.24 W
Macalister ≃ 166 38.02 S 146.59 E
Macalister, Mount ∧ 170 34.27 S 149.45 E
Macallum Lake ⊜ 184 55.02 N 108.25 W
Macaloge 154 12.25 S 35.25 E
MacAlpine Lake ⊜ 176 66.40 N 103.15 W
Macamic, Lac ⊜ 190 48.48 N 78.59 W
Macan, Kepulauan II 112 7.00 S 121.00 E
Macão 34 39.33 N 8.00 W
Macao → Macau □[2] 100 22.10 N 113.33 E
Macapá 250 0.02 N 51.03 W
Macará 246 4.23 S 79.57 W
Macarani 255 15.33 S 40.24 W
Macarao 286c 10.26 N 67.02 W
Macarao ≃ 286c 10.26 N 67.01 W
Macareo, Caño ≃[1] 246 9.47 N 61.37 W
Macari ≃ 250 1.52 N 50.31 W
MacArthur, Pil. 116 10.50 N 125.00 E
MacArthur, Il., U.S. 278 41.39 N 87.44 W
Macas 246 2.19 S 78.07 W
Macatawa ≃ 216 42.48 N 86.05 W
Macatawa, Lake c 216 42.47 N 86.10 W
Macaterick, Loch ⊜ 44 55.12 N 4.26 W
Macau, Bra. 250 5.07 S 36.38 W
Macau (Aomen), Macau 100 22.14 N 113.35 E
Macau □[2], Asia 90 22.10 N 113.33 E
Macau □[2], Asia 100 22.10 N 113.33 E
Macau, Ilha I 156 20.55 S 35.05 E
Macauã ≃ 248 9.13 S 68.44 W
Macaúbas 255 13.02 S 42.42 W
Macaya, Pic ∧ 238 18.25 N 74.00 W
Macaza ≃ 206 46.21 N 74.47 W
Maccarese ◆[8] 267a 41.53 N 12.13 E
Maccarese, Bonifica di ◆[1] 267a 41.51 N 12.13 E
Macchiagodena 66 41.33 N 14.24 E
MacClenny 192 30.16 N 82.07 W
Macclesfield, Austl. 168b 35.10 S 138.50 E
Macclesfield, Eng., U.K. 44 53.16 N 2.07 W
Macclesfield □[8] 262 53.17 N 2.15 W
Macclesfield Canal ≋ 262 53.24 N 2.03 W
Macclesfield Forest ◆[3] 262 53.15 N 2.03 W
Macdhui, Ben ∧ 158 30.39 S 27.58 E
MacDill Air Force Base ▪ 220 27.51 N 82.29 W
Macdonald ≃ 170 33.23 S 150.59 E
MacDonald, Lake ⊜ 162 23.30 S 129.00 E
MacDonald Downs 162 22.27 S 135.13 E
Macdonald Lake ⊜ 212 45.14 N 78.34 W
MacDonald Pass)(202 46.34 N 112.18 W
Macdonald Range ⋏ 182 49.12 N 114.46 W
MacDonnell Ranges ⋏ 162 23.45 S 133.20 E
Macdonnel Peninsula ›[1] 168b 35.47 S 138.00 E
MacDowell Lake ⊜ 184 52.15 N 92.45 W
Macduff 46 57.40 N 2.29 W
Macdui, Ben ∧ 46 57.05 N 3.38 W
Mačecha 80 50.48 N 43.17 E
Mačechi 78 49.31 N 34.26 E
Maceday Lake ⊜ 281 42.42 N 83.26 W
Macedo de Cavaleiros 34 41.32 N 6.58 W
Macedon, Austl. 169 37.25 S 144.34 E
Macedon, N.Y., U.S. 210 43.04 N 77.17 W
Macedonia, Ct., U.S. 207 41.47 N 73.30 W
Macedonia, Oh., U.S. 214 41.18 N 81.30 W
Macedonia □[9] 38 41.00 N 23.00 E
Macedonia □[1], Europe 22 41.50 N 22.00 E
Macedonia (Makedonija) □[1], Europe 38 41.50 N 22.00 E
Macedonia Brook State Park ♦ 207 41.47 N 73.29 W
Maceió 250 9.40 S 35.43 W
Maceira 266c 38.52 N 9.19 W
Macenta 150 8.33 N 9.28 W
Maceo 246 6.33 N 74.47 W
Macerata 66 43.18 N 13.27 E
Macerata □[4] 66 43.12 N 13.10 E
Macerata Feltria 66 43.48 N 12.26 E
MacFarlane ≃ 176 59.12 N 107.58 W
Macfarlane, Lake ⊜ 166 31.55 S 136.42 E
Macfarlane, Mount ∧ 172 43.56 S 169.23 E
Macgillycuddy's Reeks ⋏ 48 51.55 N 9.45 W
MacGregor 184 49.57 N 98.49 W
Machacamarca 248 18.10 S 67.02 W
Machache ∧ 158 29.21 S 27.55 E
Machachi 246 0.30 S 78.34 W
Machačkala 84 42.58 N 47.30 E
Machada, Mata Nacional da ♦ 266c 38.36 N 9.02 W
Machadinho ≃ 248 9.00 S 61.52 W
Machado 256 21.41 S 45.56 W
Machado ≃, Bra. 248 8.03 S 62.52 W
Machado ≃, Bra. 256 21.38 S 45.52 W
Machadodorp 156 25.40 S 30.14 E
Machagai 252 26.56 S 60.03 W
Machaila 156 22.15 S 32.55 E
Machakos 154 1.31 S 37.16 E
Machala 246 3.16 S 79.58 W
Machalí 252 34.11 S 70.40 W
Machalilla, Parque Nacional ♦ 246 1.30 S 80.45 W
Machalino 80 53.05 N 46.14 E
Māchalpur 124 24.08 N 76.18 E
Machaneng 156 23.10 S 27.26 E
Machang, Malay. 114 5.46 N 102.13 E
Machang, Zhg. 98 34.06 N 119.02 E
Machang, Zhg. 98 42.05 N 119.42 E
Machanga 156 20.58 S 34.59 E
Machangcun 105 38.54 N 115.26 E
Machangfu 102 25.14 N 103.45 E
Machang Jianhe ≃ 105 39.00 N 117.40 E
Machaquilá ≃ 236 16.13 N 90.01 W
Machattie, Lake ⊜ 166 24.50 S 139.48 E
Machault 50 49.21 N 4.30 E
Machava 156 25.54 S 32.29 E
Machaze 156 20.51 S 33.26 E
Machecoul 32 47.00 N 1.50 W
Macheke 154 18.05 S 31.51 E
Machelen 50 50.55 N 4.26 E
Macheng 100 31.13 N 115.00 E
Macherio 266b 45.38 N 9.16 E
Mācherla 122 16.29 N 79.26 E
Machern 54 51.21 N 12.37 E
Machery 261 48.36 N 2.05 E
Machesna Mountain ∧ 226 35.17 N 120.14 W
Machesney Park 216 42.20 N 89.03 W
Māchhīwāra 123 30.55 N 76.12 E
Machhlīshahr 124 25.41 N 82.25 E
Machias, Me., U.S. 188 44.42 N 67.27 W
Machias, N.Y., U.S. 210 42.25 N 78.30 W
Machias ≃ 188 44.43 N 67.22 W
Machias Bay c 188 44.40 N 67.20 W
Machichaco, Cabo › 34 43.27 N 2.45 W
Machichi ≃ 184 57.03 N 92.06 W
Machico 148 32.42 N 16.46 W
Machida 94 35.32 N 139.27 E
Machile ≃ 154 17.26 S 25.02 E
Machilīpatnam (Bandar) 122 16.10 N 81.08 E
Machindžauri 84 41.40 N 41.43 E
Machiques 246 10.04 N 72.34 W
Machiya ≃ 94 35.01 N 136.42 E
Machkund ⊜[1] 122 18.26 N 82.35 E
Machmud-Mekteb 84 44.26 N 45.13 E
Machn'ovo 86 58.27 N 61.42 E
Macho, Arroyo del V 196 33.36 N 104.28 W
Machočen, porog ᒪ 88 57.23 N 121.29 E
Machona, Laguna c 234 18.20 N 93.40 W
Machrihanish 46 55.26 N 5.45 W
Machtaly 85 41.22 N 68.02 E
Machupicchu 248 13.07 S 72.34 W
Machupicchu ⊥ 248 13.07 S 72.34 W
Machupo ≃ 248 12.34 S 64.25 W
Machynlleth 42 52.35 N 3.51 W
Maciá, Arg. 252 32.10 S 59.23 W
Macia, Moç. 156 25.03 S 33.10 E
Maciel, Arroyo ≃, Ur. 258 33.42 S 57.59 W
Maciel, Arroyo ≃, Ur. 258 33.36 S 56.31 W
Măcin 38 45.15 N 28.08 E
Macina → Massina ◆[1] 150 14.30 N 5.00 W
Macintyre ≃ 166 28.38 N 149.41 E
Maçka 130 40.48 N 39.38 E
Mačkassy 80 52.46 N 45.34 E
Mackay, Austl. 166 21.09 S 149.11 E
Mackay, Id., U.S. 202 43.54 N 113.36 W
MacKay ≃ 184 57.03 N 111.55 W
Mackay, Lake ⊜ 162 22.30 S 129.00 E
MacKay Lake ⊜ 176 63.55 N 110.25 W
Mackenrode 54 51.33 N 10.33 E
Mackenzie 246 6.00 N 58.17 W
Mackenzie ≃, Austl. 166 23.38 S 149.46 E
Mackenzie ≃, N.T., Can. 176 69.15 N 134.08 W
MacKenzie Bay c, Ant. 9 68.20 S 71.15 E
Mackenzie Bay c, Can. 180 69.00 N 136.30 W
Mackenzie Delta ≚[2] 180 68.50 N 135.25 W
Mackenzie Mountains ⋏ 180 64.00 N 130.00 W
Mackeyville 210 41.03 N 77.28 W
Mackinac, Straits of ᑌ 190 45.49 N 84.42 W
Mackinac Bridge ◆[5] 190 45.50 N 84.45 W
Mackinac Island 190 45.50 N 84.37 W
Mackinac Island I 190 45.51 N 84.38 W
Mackinac Island State Park ♦ 190 45.52 N 84.40 W
Mackinaw 190 40.32 N 89.21 W
Mackinaw ≃ 194 40.33 N 89.44 W
Mackinaw City 190 45.47 N 84.43 W
Mackinnon Road 154 3.44 S 39.03 E
Macklin 184 52.20 N 109.56 W
Mačkovci 61 46.47 N 16.09 E
M'ačkovo, Ross. 82 55.13 N 38.40 E
M'ačkovo, Ross. 82 56.21 N 39.03 E
Macksville, Austl. 166 30.43 S 152.55 E
Macksville, Ks., U.S. 198 38.57 N 98.58 W
Maclean 166 29.28 S 153.13 E
Macleantown 158 32.47 S 27.45 E
Maclear 158 31.02 S 28.23 E
Macleay ≃ 166 30.52 S 153.01 E
Macleod 274b 37.43 S 145.04 E
Macleod, Lake ⊜ 162 24.00 S 113.35 E
Maclovia Herrera 232 29.05 N 105.08 W
Macmillan ≃ 180 62.52 N 135.55 W
Macocolo 152 6.47 S 16.08 E
Macolin 58 47.09 N 7.14 E
Macolla, Punta › 241s 12.06 N 70.13 W
Macolo 152 7.05 S 16.48 E
Macomb 190 40.27 N 90.40 W
Macomb □[6] 214 42.40 N 82.54 W
Macomb Mall ◆[9] 281 42.32 N 82.55 W
Macomer 71 40.16 N 8.47 E
Macomia 154 12.15 S 40.08 E
Macon, Bel. 50 50.03 N 4.13 E
Mâcon, Fr. 58 46.18 N 4.50 E
Macon, Ga., U.S. 192 32.50 N 83.37 W
Macon, Il., U.S. 219 39.42 N 88.59 W
Macon, Ms., U.S. 194 33.06 N 88.33 W
Macon, Mo., U.S. 194 39.44 N 92.28 W
Macon □[6], Il., U.S. 219 39.51 N 89.32 W
Macon □[6], Mo., U.S. 219 39.50 N 92.20 W
Macon, Bayou ≃ 194 31.55 N 91.33 W
Macon Creek ≃ 216 41.58 N 83.38 W
Macondo 152 12.35 S 23.44 E
Macondo ≃ 152 13.23 S 23.03 E
Mâconnais, Monts du ⋏ 58 46.18 N 4.45 E
Macorís, Cabo › 238 19.47 N 70.28 W
Macosquin 48 55.06 N 6.43 W
Macossa 156 17.52 S 33.56 E
Macouba, Pointe de › 240e 14.53 N 61.09 W
Macoun Lake ⊜ 184 56.32 N 103.50 W
Macoupin □[6] 219 39.17 N 89.53 W
Macoupin Creek ≃ 219 39.11 N 90.36 W
Macovane 156 21.28 S 35.04 E
Macpherson, Mount ∧[2] 162 21.49 S 121.35 E
Macquarie ≃, Austl. 166 41.44 S 147.08 E
Macquarie ≃, Austl. 166 30.07 S 147.24 E
Macquarie, Lake ⊜ 170 33.05 S 151.35 E
Macquarie Fields 274a 33.59 S 150.53 E
Macquarie Harbour c 166 42.19 S 145.23 E
Macquarie Island I 9 54.30 S 158.56 E
Macquarie Marshes ≡ 166 30.50 S 147.32 E
Macquarie Pass National Park ♦ 170 34.34 S 150.39 E
Macquarie Ridge ✦[3] 9 57.00 S 159.00 E
Macquarie University ⊕[2] 274a 33.46 S 151.06 E
MacRitchie Reservoir ⊜[1] 271c 1.21 N 103.50 E
Mac. Robertson Land ◆[1] 9 68.10 S 65.00 E
Macrohon 116 10.05 N 124.56 E
Macroom 48 51.54 N 8.57 W
Mactan Island I 116 10.18 N 123.58 E
MacTier 212 45.08 N 79.47 W
Macuco de Minas 256 21.46 S 44.47 W
Macucuau ≃ 246 0.37 S 61.24 W
Macuelizo 236 15.18 N 88.31 W
Macugnaga 58 45.58 N 7.58 E
Macujer 246 0.23 N 72.55 W
Macul 286e 33.30 S 70.34 W
Maculabo Island I 116 14.24 N 122.49 E
Macumba ≃ 162 27.52 S 137.12 E
Macungie 208 40.30 N 75.33 W
Macunqiao 100 33.50 N 116.13 E
Macuro 246 10.39 N 61.56 W
Macusani 248 14.05 S 70.26 W
Macuspana 234 17.46 N 92.36 W
Macusse 152 17.51 S 20.21 E
Macuto 286c 10.37 N 66.53 W
Macuze 156 17.42 S 37.11 E
Macy 216 40.57 N 86.07 W
Mad ≃, On., Can. 212 44.25 N 79.54 W
Mad ≃, Ca., U.S. 204 40.57 N 124.07 W
Mad ≃, N.Y., U.S. 212 43.20 N 75.44 W
Mad ≃, Oh., U.S. 188 39.46 N 84.11 W
Mad ≃, Vt., U.S. 188 44.18 N 72.41 W
Mada ≃ 150 7.59 N 7.55 E
Ma'dabā 132 31.43 N 35.48 E
Madagascar (Madagasikara) □[1], Afr. 138 19.00 S 46.00 E
Madagascar (Madagasikara) □[1], Afr. 157b 19.00 S 46.00 E
Madagascar Basin ✦[1] 12 27.00 S 53.00 E
Madagascar Plateau ✦[3] 10 30.00 S 45.00 E
Madagasikara → Madagascar □[1] 157b 19.00 S 46.00 E
Madagaskar → Madagascar □[1] 157b 19.00 S 46.00 E
Madagiz 84 40.19 N 46.44 E
Madagoi, Bohol V 144 0.44 N 42.56 E
Madā'in Ṣāliḥ 128 26.48 N 37.53 E
Madajevo 80 54.48 N 44.31 E
Madama 146 21.58 N 13.39 E
Madame, Isle I 186 45.33 N 61.02 W
Madan 38 41.30 N 24.57 E
Madanapalle 122 13.33 N 78.30 E
Madang, Pap. N. Gui. 164 5.15 S 145.50 E
Madang, Zhg. 100 29.58 N 116.40 E
Madang □[5] 164 5.00 S 145.30 E
Madanpur 272b 22.40 N 88.32 E
Madanpur Dabās ◆[8] 272a 28.43 N 77.02 E
Madaoua 150 14.05 N 5.58 E
Mādār Gāng ≃[1] 126 22.12 N 89.04 E
Mādāri Hāt 124 26.42 N 89.17 E
Mādārīpur 124 23.10 N 90.12 E
Madarounfa 150 13.18 N 7.09 E
Mādārpur 272b 22.54 N 88.27 E
Madau Island I 164 8.58 S 152.28 E
Madawaska, On., Can. 212 45.30 N 77.59 W
Madawaska, Me., U.S. 186 47.21 N 68.19 W
Madawaska ≃ 212 45.27 N 76.21 W
Madawaska Highlands ⋏[1] 212 45.15 N 77.35 W
Madawaska Lake ⊜ 212 45.20 N 78.23 W
Madaxmaroodi 144 2.39 N 44.36 E
Madaya, Mya. 110 22.13 N 96.07 E
Maḍāyā, Sūrīy. 132 33.41 N 36.06 E
Madbar 140 6.19 N 30.40 E
Mad Creek ≃ 210 42.55 N 77.59 W
Maddalena, Colle della (Col de Larche))(62 44.25 N 6.53 E
Maddalena, Isola I 71 41.14 N 9.25 E
Maddaloni 68 41.02 N 14.23 E
Maddela 116 16.21 N 121.41 E
Madden, Mount ∧ 162 33.12 S 119.51 E
Maddington 168a 32.03 S 115.59 E
Maddock 198 47.57 N 99.31 W
Maddy, Loch c 46 57.36 N 7.08 W
Made 52 51.41 N 4.46 E
Madeir 140 7.50 N 29.12 E
Madeira 218 39.11 N 84.21 W
Madeira I 148 32.44 N 17.00 W
Madeira ≃ 242 3.22 S 58.45 W
Madeira, Arquipélago da II 148 32.40 N 16.45 W
Madeira Beach 220 27.48 N 82.48 W
Madeirinha ≃ 248 8.31 S 60.46 W
Madeirinha, Paraná ≃[1] 246 3.25 S 58.51 W
M'adel' 76 54.53 N 26.57 E
Mädelegabel ∧ 58 47.18 N 10.18 E
Madeleine, Îles de la II 186 47.30 N 61.45 W
Madeleine, Pointe › 275a 45.27 N 73.57 W
Madeleine-Centre 186 49.15 N 65.21 W
Madeley, Eng., U.K. 42 52.59 N 2.20 W
Madeley, Eng., U.K. 42 52.39 N 2.28 W
Madelia 190 44.03 N 94.25 W
Madeline Island I 190 46.50 N 90.40 W
Maden, Tür. 130 38.23 N 39.40 E
Maden, Tür. 130 40.11 N 40.25 E
Madenijet 86 47.53 N 78.37 E
Madera, Méx. 232 29.12 N 108.07 W
Madera, Ca., U.S. 226 36.57 N 120.03 W
Madera, Pa., U.S. 214 40.49 N 78.26 W
Madera □[6] 226 37.15 N 119.45 W
Madera Canal ≋ 226 37.05 N 119.59 W
Madera Lake ⊜[1] 226 37.02 N 119.59 W
Madera Peak ∧ 226 37.32 N 119.23 W
Maderas, Islas → Madeira, Arquipélago da II 148 32.40 N 16.45 W
Maderas, Volcán ∧[1] 236 11.27 N 85.31 W
Maderno 64 45.38 N 10.35 E
Madgaon (Margao) 122 15.18 N 73.57 E
Madh ◆[8] 272c 19.08 N 72.47 E
Madhepura 124 25.55 N 86.47 E
Madhkūr, Bi'r ⊤[4] 142 30.42 N 32.32 E
Mādhopur 123 32.22 N 75.36 E
Madhubani 124 26.22 N 86.05 E
Madhudaha 272b 22.31 N 88.25 E
Madhugiri 122 13.40 N 77.12 E
Madhumati ≃[1] 126 22.53 N 89.52 E
Madhupar 126 22.54 N 86.28 E
Madhupur 126 24.16 N 86.39 E
Madhya Bhārat Pathār ◆[1] 124 25.00 N 77.00 E
Madhyamgrām 272b 22.42 N 88.27 E
Madhya Pradesh □[3] 118 23.00 N 79.00 E
Madia 154 7.08 S 26.00 E
Madian 106 32.15 N 119.58 E
Madibi 152 4.18 S 18.24 E
Madibira 154 8.12 S 34.49 E
Madibogo 158 26.25 S 25.10 E
Madida 98 42.57 N 130.48 E
Madidi ≃ 248 12.32 S 66.52 W
Madill 196 34.05 N 96.46 W
Madimba, Ang. 152 6.31 S 14.21 E
Madimba, Zaïre 152 4.58 S 15.08 E
Madina 150 13.24 N 8.51 W
Madina do Boé 150 11.45 N 14.13 W
Madinani 150 9.37 N 6.57 W
Madīnat al-Abyār 146 32.11 N 20.36 E
Madīnat ash-Sha'b (Al-Ittiḥad) 144 12.50 N 44.56 E
Madīnat ath Thawrah 130 35.52 N 38.34 E
Madine, Lac de ⊜ 56 48.54 N 5.42 E
Madingo 152 4.07 S 11.22 E
Madingou 152 4.09 S 13.34 E
Madingzi 104 42.08 N 120.52 E
Madi Opei 154 3.37 N 33.05 E
Madirobe 157b 16.04 S 46.15 E
Madirovalo 157b 16.26 S 46.30 E
Madison, Al., U.S. 194 34.41 N 86.44 W
Madison, Ca., U.S. 226 38.41 N 121.58 W
Madison, Ct., U.S. 207 41.16 N 72.35 W
Madison, Fl., U.S. 192 30.28 N 83.24 W
Madison, Ga., U.S. 192 33.35 N 83.28 W
Madison, Il., U.S. 219 38.40 N 90.09 W
Madison, In., U.S. 218 38.44 N 85.22 W
Madison, Ks., U.S. 198 38.08 N 96.08 W
Madison, Me., U.S. 188 44.47 N 69.52 W
Madison, Md., U.S. 208 38.30 N 76.13 W
Madison, Mn., U.S. 198 45.00 N 96.11 W
Madison, Mo., U.S. 219 39.28 N 92.12 W
Madison, Ne., U.S. 198 41.49 N 97.27 W
Madison, N.J., U.S. 210 40.45 N 74.25 W
Madison, N.Y., U.S. 210 42.53 N 75.30 W
Madison, N.C., U.S. 192 36.23 N 79.57 W
Madison, Oh., U.S. 214 41.46 N 81.03 W
Madison, Pa., U.S. 279b 40.15 N 79.41 W
Madison, S.D., U.S. 198 44.00 N 97.06 W
Madison, Va., U.S. 188 38.22 N 78.15 W
Madison, W.V., U.S. 188 38.04 N 81.49 W
Madison, Wi., U.S. 216 43.04 N 89.24 W
Madison □[6], Il., U.S. 219 38.49 N 89.58 W
Madison □[6], In., U.S. 218 40.10 N 85.41 W
Madison □[6], N.Y., U.S. 210 43.05 N 75.42 W
Madison □[6], Oh., U.S. 218 39.53 N 83.27 W
Madison □[6], Tx., U.S. 222 30.58 N 95.55 W
Madison ≃ 202 45.56 N 111.30 W
Madison, West Fork ≃ 202 44.55 N 111.35 W
Madisonburg, Oh., U.S. 214 40.51 N 81.55 W
Madisonburg, Pa., U.S. 210 40.55 N 77.31 W
Madison Heights, Mi., U.S. 216 42.29 N 83.06 W
Madison Heights, Va., U.S. 192 37.25 N 79.07 W
Madison Mills 218 39.40 N 83.20 W
Madison-on-the-Lake 214 41.42 N 81.24 W
Madison Park 276 40.26 N 74.19 W
Madison Range ⋏ 202 45.15 N 111.20 W
Madison Square Garden ♦ 276 40.45 N 74.00 W
Madisonville, Ky., U.S. 194 37.19 N 87.29 W
Madisonville, La., U.S. 194 30.24 N 90.09 W
Madisonville, Tn., U.S. 192 35.31 N 84.21 W
Madisonville, Tx., U.S. 222 30.56 N 95.54 W
Madiun 115a 7.37 S 111.31 E
Madiun ≃ 115a 7.23 S 111.27 E
Madiyi 102 28.14 N 110.30 E
Madjingo 152 1.23 N 14.06 E
Madjoari 150 11.26 N 1.15 E
Madley, Mount ∧ 162 24.31 S 123.58 E
Madoc 212 44.30 N 77.28 W
Mado Gashi 154 0.44 N 39.10 E
Madoi 102 34.53 N 98.24 E
Madol 140 9.02 N 27.46 E
Madon ≃ 58 48.36 N 6.06 E
Madona 76 56.51 N 26.13 E
Madonna (Unserfrau) 64 46.43 N 10.52 E
Madonna della Guardia ⊕[1] 62 44.29 N 8.51 E
Madonna della Quercia ⊕[1] 66 42.25 N 12.06 E
Madonna dell'Olmo 62 44.25 N 7.32 E
Madonna del Sasso ⊕[1] 58 46.11 N 8.33 E
Madonna di Campiglio 64 46.14 N 10.49 E
Madonna di Tirano 64 46.13 N 10.09 E
Madora 76 53.09 N 30.11 E
Madougou 150 14.24 N 3.05 W
Madrakah 144 21.59 N 39.59 E
Madrakah, Ra's al- › 118 19.00 N 57.50 E
Madras, India 122 13.05 N 80.17 E
Madras, Or., U.S. 202 44.38 N 121.07 W
Madras → Tamil Nādu □[3] 122 11.00 N 78.15 E
Madre, Laguna c, Méx. 232 25.00 N 97.40 W
Madre, Laguna c, Tx., U.S. 196 27.00 N 97.35 W
Madre, Sierra ⋏ 116 16.20 N 122.00 E
Madre de Chiapas, Sierra ⋏ 232 15.30 N 92.35 W
Madre de Deus de Minas 256 21.29 S 44.20 W
Madre de Dios □[5] 248 12.00 S 70.15 W
Madre de Dios ≃ 248 10.23 S 65.24 W
Madre de Dios, Isla I 254 50.15 S 75.05 W
Madre del Sur, Sierra ⋏ 234 17.00 N 100.00 W
Madre Occidental, Sierra ⋏ 232 25.00 N 105.00 W
Madre Oriental, Sierra ⋏ 232 22.00 N 99.30 W
Madre Vieja ≃ 236 14.01 N 91.26 W
Madrid, Col. 246 4.44 N 74.16 W
Madrid, Esp. 34 40.24 N 3.41 W
Madrid, Esp. 266a 40.24 N 3.41 W
Madrid, Pil. 116 9.15 N 126.00 E
Madrid, Al., U.S. 194 31.02 N 85.23 W
Madrid, Ia., U.S. 190 41.52 N 93.49 W
Madrid, Ne., U.S. 198 40.51 N 101.32 W
Madrid □[4], Esp. 34 40.30 N 3.40 W
Madrid □[4], Esp. 34 40.30 N 3.40 W
Madridejos, Esp. 34 39.28 N 3.32 W
Madridejos, Pil. 116 11.18 N 123.44 E
Madrigalejo 34 39.09 N 5.37 W
Madrillon 284c 38.55 N 77.14 W
Madriz □[5] 236 13.30 N 86.30 W
Madroñera 34 39.26 N 5.46 W
Madruga 240p 22.55 N 81.51 W
Madrūsah 146 24.48 N 14.32 E
Madsen 184 50.58 N 93.55 W
Madsūs, Bi'r ⊤[4] 142 29.15 N 32.19 E
Maducang Island I 116 10.42 N 120.15 E
Maduda 152 4.55 S 13.06 E
Maduo 152 1.24 S 20.44 E
Madura 162 31.55 S 127.00 E
Madura I 115a 7.00 S 113.20 E
Madura, Selat ᑌ 115a 7.25 S 113.25 E
Madurai 122 9.56 N 78.07 E
Madura → Madurai 122 9.56 N 78.07 E
Madurāntakam 122 12.31 N 79.54 E
Madureira, Serra de ⋏ 287a 22.49 S 43.31 W
Maduru ≃ 122 7.52 N 81.31 E
Madwar al-Bighāl ∧[2] 142 29.09 N 29.54 E
Madžalis 84 42.08 N 47.50 E
Mãe, Ilha da I 287a 22.59 S 43.04 W
Maeander Reef ✦[2] 116 8.05 N 119.18 E
Maebaru 92 33.33 N 130.12 E
Maebashi 94 36.23 N 139.04 E
Maeda 270 34.55 N 135.08 E
Mãe dos Homens 256 22.52 S 46.37 W
Maegye-ri 98 34.45 N 126.18 E
Mae Hong Son 110 19.16 N 97.56 E
Mae Klong ≃ 110 13.21 N 100.00 E
Maenclochog 42 51.54 N 4.48 W
Maengsan 98 39.40 N 126.30 E
Maeno ◆[8] 268 35.46 N 139.42 E
Maenza 66 41.31 N 13.11 E
Mae Ramat 110 16.58 N 98.31 E
Mae Rim 110 18.54 N 98.57 E
Maerkansu 85 39.19 N 73.53 E
Ma'erna 102 31.13 N 102.02 E
Maershan ∧ 102 26.18 N 100.20 E
Mae Sariang 110 18.10 N 97.56 E
Maeser 200 40.28 N 109.35 W
Mae Sot 110 16.43 N 98.34 E
Maesteg 42 51.37 N 3.40 W
Maestra, Sierra ⋏ 240p 20.00 N 76.45 W
Maestre de Campo Island I 116 12.56 N 121.42 E
Maestu 34 42.44 N 2.27 W
Mae Tha 110 18.28 N 99.08 E
Maevarano ≃ 157b 14.35 S 47.58 E
Maevatanana 157b 16.56 S 46.49 E
Maéwo I 175f 15.10 S 168.10 E
Ma'fan 146 25.55 N 14.29 E
Mafang 105 40.02 N 117.01 E
Mafangchang 107 29.24 N 106.06 E
Mafangcun 105 40.09 N 116.24 E
Ma Faro ✦[2] 122 5.50 N 73.26 E
Mafeking 184 52.41 N 101.06 W
Mafembage 152 14.32 S 21.42 E
Mafengtun 104 40.49 N 122.54 E
Mafeteng 158 29.51 S 27.15 E
Maffliers 261 49.05 N 2.19 E
Maffra 166 37.58 S 146.59 E
Mafia Channel ᑌ 154 8.10 S 39.40 E
Mafia Island I 154 7.50 S 39.50 E
Mafikeng 156 25.53 S 25.39 E
Mafou ≃ 150 10.32 N 10.08 W
Mafra, Bra. 252 26.07 S 49.49 W
Mafra, Port. 34 38.56 N 9.20 W
Magadan 74 59.34 N 150.48 E
Magadi 154 1.54 S 36.17 E
Magadi, Lake ⊜ 154 1.52 S 36.17 E
Magaguadavic Lake ⊜ 186 45.43 N 67.12 W
Magai-butsu ⊕[1] 96 33.05 N 131.45 E
Magalhães Bastos ◆[8] 287a 22.53 S 43.23 W
Magalhães de Almeida 250 3.24 S 42.12 W
Magaliesberg ⋏ 158 25.50 S 27.30 E
Magallanes 116 12.50 N 123.50 E
Magallanes, Estrecho de (Strait of Magellan) ᑌ 254 54.00 S 71.00 W
Magallanes → Punta Arenas 254 53.09 S 70.55 W
Magallanes y de la Antártica Chilena □[4] 254 53.00 S 72.00 W
Maganga 154 0.51 N 26.22 E
Magangué 246 9.14 N 74.45 W
Magansk 88 55.52 N 93.15 E
Maganuy ≃ 116 6.55 N 124.30 E
Magara, India 126 22.34 N 87.34 E
Mağara, Tür. 130 36.43 N 33.52 E
Magaramkent 84 41.37 N 48.21 E
Magaria 150 13.00 N 8.54 E
Magat ≃ 116 17.02 N 121.49 E
Magazine Mountain ∧ 194 35.10 N 93.38 W
Magazzolo ≃ 70 37.25 N 13.15 E
Magboro 273a 6.43 N 3.24 E
Magburaka 150 8.43 N 11.57 W
Magdagači 89 53.27 N 125.48 E
Magdalena, Arg. 258 35.04 S 57.32 W
Magdalena, Bol. 248 13.20 S 64.08 W
Magdalena, Méx. 234 20.55 N 103.57 W
Magdalena, Perú 248 6.21 S 77.49 W
Magdalena, Perú 286d 12.06 S 77.05 W
Magdalena, N.M., U.S. 200 34.07 N 107.14 W
Magdalena □[5] 246 10.00 N 74.00 W
Magdalena ≃, Col. 246 11.06 N 74.51 W
Magdalena ≃, Méx. 232 30.48 N 112.32 W
Magdalena, Bahía c 232 24.35 N 112.00 W
Magdalena, Isla I, Chile 254 44.40 S 73.10 W
Magdalena, Isla I, Méx. 232 24.55 N 112.15 W
Magdalena, Punta › 246 3.56 N 77.21 W
Magdalena Contreras ◆[8] 286a 19.18 N 99.17 W
Magdalena de Kino 232 30.38 N 110.57 W
Magdalena Peñasco 234 17.14 N 97.34 W
Magdalena Teitipac 234 16.54 N 96.34 W
Magdalena Tequisistlán 234 16.22 N 95.15 W
Magdalen Laver 260 51.45 N 0.11 E
Magdalinovka 78 48.55 N 34.54 E
Magdeborn 54 51.14 N 12.26 E
Magdeburg 54 52.07 N 11.38 E
Magdeburger Börde ≚ 54 52.00 N 11.30 E
Magdeburgo → Magdeburg 54 52.07 N 11.38 E
Magdiwang 116 12.30 N 122.31 E
Magdonskij, porog ᒪ 88 57.45 N 100.55 E
Māge 110 26.33 N 98.33 E
Magé □[7] 287a 22.41 S 43.07 W
Magee 194 31.52 N 89.44 W
Magee, Island ›[1] 48 54.49 N 5.42 W
Magelang 115a 7.28 S 110.13 E
Magellan, Strait of → Magallanes, Estrecho de ᑌ 254 54.00 S 71.00 W
Magellan-Strasse → Magallanes, Estrecho de ᑌ 254 54.00 S 71.00 W
Magén 132 31.18 N 34.26 E
Magenta 62 45.28 N 8.53 E
Magenta, Lake ⊜ 162 33.26 S 119.10 E
Magerov 78 50.08 N 23.43 E
Magerøy I 24 71.03 N 25.45 E
Magetan 115a 7.39 S 111.20 E
Magezhuang 105 40.08 N 117.59 E
Maggia 58 46.15 N 8.42 E
Maggia ≃ 58 46.09 N 8.48 E
Maggia, Valle V 58 46.17 N 8.40 E
Maggie Creek ≃ 204 40.43 N 116.05 W
Maggiorasca, Monte ∧ 62 44.33 N 9.29 E
Maggiore ≃, It. 267a 43.43 N 13.06 E
Maggiore ≃, It. 267a 41.54 N 12.16 E
Maggiore, Lago ⊜ 36 46.00 N 8.40 E
Maggiore, Monte ∧ 68 41.14 N 14.12 E
Maghāghah 142 28.39 N 30.50 E
Maghama 150 15.31 N 12.51 W
Maghar 132 32.53 N 35.24 E
Maghdūshah 132 33.31 N 35.23 E
Maghera 48 54.51 N 6.40 W
Magherafelt 48 54.45 N 6.36 W
Maghniyya 148 34.50 N 1.50 W
Magholpur ◆[8] 272a 28.42 N 77.06 E
Maghull 44 53.32 N 2.57 W
Magician Lake ⊜ 216 42.04 N 86.10 W
Magic Mountain ♦ 228 34.26 N 118.36 W
Magic Reservoir ⊜[1] 202 43.17 N 114.23 W
Magill, Lac ⊜ 206 45.35 N 71.17 W
Magill Heights 279b 40.37 N 79.52 W
Magill Lake ⊜ 184 54.45 N 94.58 W
Mágina ∧ 34 37.43 N 3.28 W
Maginu 268 35.35 N 139.36 E
Magione 66 43.08 N 12.12 E
Magisano 68 39.01 N 16.27 E
Magiscatzín 234 22.48 N 98.42 W
Magiss Lake ⊜ 184 52.59 N 91.40 W
Maglaj 38 44.33 N 18.06 E
Magliana ◆[8] 267a 41.50 N 12.25 E
Magliana, Fosso ≃ 267a 41.49 N 12.25 E
Magliano dei Marsi 66 42.05 N 13.22 E
Magliano in Toscana 66 42.36 N 11.17 E
Magliano Sabina 66 42.22 N 12.29 E
Maglie 68 40.07 N 18.19 E
Maglód 264c 47.27 N 19.21 E
M'aglovo 265a 59.53 N 30.41 E
Magnago 266b 45.35 N 8.48 E
Magnanville 261 48.58 N 1.41 E
Magnet 184 51.19 N 99.30 W
Magnetawan ≃ 190 45.46 N 80.37 W
Magnetic Island I 166 19.08 S 146.50 E
Magnetic Springs 214 40.21 N 83.16 W
Magnetischer Nordpol → North Magnetic Pole ◆ 16 77.19 N 101.49 W
Magnetischer Südpol → South Magnetic Pole ◆ 9 65.18 S 139.30 E
Magnières 58 48.27 N 6.34 E
Magnitka 86 55.21 N 59.43 E
Magnitogorsk 86 53.27 N 59.04 E
Magnitostroj 80 51.43 N 53.05 E
Magnolia, Ar., U.S. 194 33.16 N 93.14 W
Magnolia, De., U.S. 208 39.04 N 75.28 W
Magnolia, Ma., U.S. 283 42.35 N 70.43 W
Magnolia, Mn., U.S. 198 43.38 N 96.04 W
Magnolia, Ms., U.S. 194 31.08 N 90.27 W
Magnolia, N.J., U.S. 285 39.51 N 75.02 W
Magnolia, Oh., U.S. 214 40.39 N 81.17 W
Magnolia, Tx., U.S. 222 30.13 N 95.45 W
Magnor 26 59.57 N 12.12 E
Magny-en-Vexin 50 49.09 N 1.47 E
Magny-le-Hongre 261 48.52 N 2.49 E
Magny-les-Hameaux 261 48.44 N 2.04 E
Mago 89 53.15 N 140.13 E
Magog 206 45.16 N 72.09 W
Magog ≃ 206 45.24 N 71.54 W
Magog, Lake ⊜ 206 45.18 N 72.03 W
Magoito 266c 38.52 N 9.26 W
Magome ◆[8] 268 35.35 N 139.43 E
Mago National Park ♦ 144 5.30 N 36.15 E
Magonoy 116 6.54 N 124.33 E
Magoro 154 1.44 N 34.06 E
Magothy Bay c 208 37.10 N 75.55 W
Magothy River c 208 39.04 N 76.28 W
Magoúla 267c 38.04 N 23.32 E
Magoye 154 16.00 S 27.37 E
Magozal, Méx. 232 21.34 N 97.59 W
Magozal, Méx. 234 21.34 N 97.59 W
M'agozero 76 60.21 N 34.50 E
Magpie 186 50.19 N 64.30 W
Magpie ≃, On., Can. 190 47.56 N 84.50 W
Magpie ≃, P.Q., Can. 186 50.19 N 64.27 W
Magpie, Lac ⊜ 186 51.00 N 64.41 W
Magpie Ouest ≃ 186 51.02 N 64.42 W
Magra 126 22.59 N 88.22 E
Magra ≃ 64 44.03 N 9.58 E
Magra Hāt 126 22.14 N 88.23 E
Magrath 182 49.25 N 112.52 W
Magrè (Margreid) 64 46.17 N 11.12 E
Magro ≃ 34 39.11 N 0.25 W
Magruder Mountain ∧ 204 37.25 N 117.33 W
Magsaysay (Linugos) 116 9.01 N 125.11 E
Magsingal 116 17.41 N 120.25 E
Magu ≃ 250 2.56 S 41.55 W
Maguan 102 22.59 N 104.19 E
Maguanying 271a 39.52 N 116.17 E
Maguari, Cabo › 250 0.18 S 48.22 W
Magude 156 25.02 S 32.40 E
Magudu 158 27.31 S 31.40 E
Magueyes 196 25.44 N 97.47 W
Maguindanao □[4] 116 6.55 N 124.20 E
Magumeri 146 12.08 N 12.50 E
Māgura 124 23.29 N 89.25 E
Maguru 150 12.28 N 6.35 E
Maguse Lake ⊜ 176 61.40 N 95.10 W
Maguzhan 120 31.15 N 88.00 E
Magway, Mya. 110 20.09 N 94.55 E
Magway, Mya. 110 20.30 N 94.30 E
Magwe 154 4.08 N 32.17 E
Magwood Park ♦ 275b 43.39 N 79.30 W
Magyarország → Hungary □[1] 30 47.00 N 20.00 E
Mahābād 128 36.45 N 45.43 E
Mahābaleshwar 122 17.55 N 73.40 E
Mahabe 157b 17.05 S 45.20 E
Mahābhārat Lek ⋏ 124 27.40 N 84.30 E
Mahabo, Madag. 157b 23.40 S 46.08 E
Mahabo, Madag. 157b 20.23 S 44.40 E
Mahād 122 18.05 N 73.25 E
Mahadday Weyn 144 2.58 N 45.32 E
Mahādebpur 126 23.51 N 89.53 E
Mahādeo Hills ⋏[2] 122 22.22 N 78.34 E
Mahādeo Range ⋏ 122 17.50 N 74.15 E
Mahaffey 214 40.52 N 78.43 W
Mahagi 154 2.18 N 30.59 E
Mahagi Port 154 2.09 N 31.14 E
Mahai 102 38.17 N 94.13 E
Mahaica-Berbice □[4] 246 6.20 N 57.50 W
Mahaicony Village 246 6.36 N 57.48 W
Mahajamba ≃ 157b 15.33 S 47.08 E
Mahajamba, Helodranon' i c 157b 15.24 S 47.05 E
Mahājan 123 28.47 N 73.50 E
Mahajanga 157b 15.43 S 46.19 E
Mahajanga □[4] 157b 17.00 S 46.00 E
Mahajilo ≃ 157b 19.42 S 45.22 E
Mahajjah 132 32.57 N 36.14 E
Mahākālī □[8] 124 29.30 N 80.30 E
Mahākālī (Sārda) ≃ 124 27.21 N 81.23 E
Mahakam ≃ 112 0.35 S 117.17 E
Mahālandi 126 24.04 N 88.07 E
Mahalatswe 156 23.05 S 26.51 E
Mahalla el-Kubra → Al-Maḥallah al-Kubrā 142 30.58 N 31.10 E
Maḥallāt 128 33.55 N 50.27 E
Maḥallat Kayl 142 31.01 N 30.17 E
Maḥallat Marḥūm 142 30.48 N 30.57 E
Maḥallat Minūf 142 30.53 N 30.58 E
Maḥallat Zayyād 142 31.02 N 31.14 E
Maham 124 28.59 N 76.18 E
Mahamba 158 27.07 S 31.10 E
Mahānadi ≃ 118 20.19 N 86.45 E
Mahānadpati 126 23.00 N 88.16 E
Mahānanda ≃ 124 24.29 N 88.18 E
Mahanay Island I 116 10.12 N 124.14 E
Mahanoro 157b 19.54 S 48.48 E
Mahanoy City 208 40.48 N 76.08 W
Mahanoy Creek ≃ 208 40.42 N 76.51 W
Mahantango Creek ≃ 208 40.47 N 76.56 W
Mahantango Mountain ∧ 208 40.40 N 76.45 W
Mahao 89 43.10 N 127.59 E
Mahape 272c 19.07 N 73.01 E
Mahārājganj, India 124 27.09 N 83.34 E
Mahārājganj, India 124 26.07 N 84.29 E
Mahārājpur, India 124 25.01 N 79.44 E
Mahārājpur, India 272a 28.39 N 77.20 E
Mahārāshtra □[3] 122 19.00 N 76.00 E
Maḥārīq, Wādī V 142 27.48 N 31.47 E
Mahārlū, Daryācheh-ye ⊜ 128 29.25 N 52.50 E
Mahāsamund 120 21.06 N 82.06 E
Maha Sarakham 110 16.11 N 103.18 E
Maha Sawat, Khlong ≋ 269a 13.47 N 100.28 E
Mahasoa 157b 22.12 S 46.06 E
Mahasolo 157b 19.07 S 46.22 E
Mahates 246 10.14 N 75.12 W
Mahatsinjo 157b 21.26 S 45.51 E
Maḥaṭṭat al-Ḥafīf 132 32.12 N 37.08 E
Mahaut 240d 15.21 N 61.25 W
Mahavavy ≃, Madag. 157b 15.57 S 45.54 E
Mahavavy ≃, Madag. 157b 13.00 S 48.55 E
Mahaweli ≃ 122 8.27 N 81.13 E
Mahaxai 110 17.25 N 105.12 E
Maḥbas, Wādī al- V 140 15.50 N 29.45 E
Mahbūbābād 122 17.37 N 80.01 E
Mahbūbnagar 122 16.44 N 77.59 E
Mahd adh-Dhahab 128 23.30 N 40.52 E
Mahdāt, Bi'r al- ⊤[4] 142 30.44 N 32.32 E
Mahdia, Guy. 246 5.16 N 59.09 W
Mahdia, Tun. 148 35.30 N 11.04 E

Symbols in the index entries represent the broad categories identified in the key at the right. Symbols with superior numbers (⋏[1]) identify subcategories (see complete key on page *I · 1).*

Symbole im Register stellen die rechts im Schlüssel erklärten Kategorien dar. Symbole mit hochgestellten Ziffern (⋏[1]) bezeichnen Unterabteilungen einer Kategorie (vgl. vollständiger Schlüssel auf Seite *I · 1).*

Los símbolos incluídos en el texto del índice representan las grandes categorias identificadas con la clave a la derecha. Los símbolos con numeros en su parte superior (⋏[1]) identifican las subcategorías (véase la clave completa en la página *I · 1).*

Les symboles de l'index représentent les catégories indiquées dans la légende à droite. Les symboles suivis d'un indice (⋏[1]) représentent des sous-catégories (voir légende complète à la page *I · 1).*

Os símbolos incluídos no texto do índice representam as grandes categorias identificadas com a chave à direita. Os símbolos com números em sua parte superior (⋏[1]) identificam as subcategorias (veja-se a chave completa à página *I · 1).*

Symbol	English	Deutsch	Español	Français	Português
∧	Mountain	Berg	Montaña	Montagne	Montanha
⋏	Mountains	Gebirge	Montañas	Montagnes	Montanhas
)(	Pass	Paß	Paso	Col	Passo
V	Valley, Canyon	Tal, Cañon	Valle, Cañón	Vallée, Canyon	Vale, Canhão
≚	Plain	Ebene	Llano	Plaine	Planície
›	Cape	Kap	Cabo	Cap	Cabo
I	Island	Insel	Isla	Île	Ilha
II	Islands	Inseln	Islas	Îles	Ilhas
⊥	Other Topographic Features	Andere Topographische Objekte	Otros Elementos Topográficos	Autres données topographiques	Outros acidentes topográficos

ESPAÑOL — Nombre / Página / Lat.°′ / Long.°′ W = Oeste
FRANÇAIS — Nom / Page / Lat.°′ / Long.°′ W = Ouest
PORTUGUÊS — Nome / Página / Lat.°′ / Long.°′ W = Oeste

Mahdia □8 148 35.18 N 10.45 E
Mahe 122 11.42 N 75.32 E
Mahébourg 157c 20.24 S 57.42 E
Mahé Island I 138 4.40 S 55.28 E
Mahendraganj 124 25.20 N 89.45 E
Mahendragarh 124 28.17 N 76.09 E
Mahendra Giri ʌ 122 18.58 N 84.21 E
Mahendranagar 124 28.52 N 80.17 E
Mahenge, Tan. 154 8.41 S 36.43 E
Mahenge, Tan. 154 7.38 S 36.16 E
Maheno 172 45.10 S 170.50 E
Mahesāna 120 23.36 N 72.24 E
Mahesgādi 272b 22.39 N 88.33 E
Maheshmunda 126 24.13 N 86.24 E
Maheshtala 272b 22.30 N 88.15 E
Maheshwar 120 22.11 N 75.35 E
Mahespur 124 23.21 N 88.55 E
Mahgawān 124 26.29 N 78.37 E
Mahi ≃ 120 22.16 N 72.58 E
Mahia Peninsula ≻1 172 39.10 S 177.53 E
Mahiāri 272b 22.35 N 88.14 E
Māhikpur 272b 22.32 N 88.14 E
Mahilāra 126 22.56 N 90.16 E
Māhīm ◆8 272c 19.03 N 72.49 E
Māhīm ≃ 272c 19.03 N 72.51 E
Māhīm Bay c 272c 19.02 N 72.50 E
Mahina, Mali 150 13.46 N 10.51 W
Mahina, Poly. fr. 174s 17.31 S 149.30 W
Mahinerangi, Lake ⊜ 172 45.51 S 169.57 E
Mahinog 116 9.09 N 124.47 E
Mahīshādal 126 22.11 N 87.59 E
Mahishdānga 272b 22.54 N 88.11 E
Mahlabatini 158 28.14 S 31.30 E
Mahlangasi 158 27.37 S 31.42 E
Mahlberg 58 48.17 N 7.48 E
Mahlow 54 52.22 N 13.24 E
Mahlsdorf 54 52.47 N 11.13 E
Mahlsdorf-Süd ◆8 264a 52.29 N 13.36 E
Mahmūdābād, India 124 27.18 N 81.07 E
Maḥmūdābād, Īrān 128 36.38 N 52.15 E
Maḥmūd-e Rāqī 120 35.01 N 69.20 E
Maḥmūdīyah, Tur'at al- ≅ 142 31.11 N 29.53 E
Mahmudiye 130 39.30 N 31.00 E
Mahmūdpur, India 272a 28.46 N 77.22 E
Mahmudpur, India 272b 22.41 N 88.09 E
Mahmutbey ◆8 267b 41.03 N 28.49 E
Mahmutşevketpaşa 130 41.05 N 29.19 E
Mahmutşevketpaşa ◆8 267b 41.09 N 29.11 E
Mahnomen 198 47.18 N 95.58 W
Mahoba 124 25.17 N 79.52 E
Mahogany Mountain ʌ 202 43.14 N 117.16 W
Mahomet 216 40.11 N 88.24 W
Mahone Bay 186 44.27 N 64.23 W
Mahone Bay c 186 44.30 N 64.15 W
Mahoning □6 214 41.06 N 80.39 W
Mahoning ≃ 214 40.58 N 80.23 W
Mahoning, West Branch ≃ 214 41.12 N 80.57 W
Mahoning Creek ≃ 214 40.55 N 79.27 W
Mahoning Creek Lake ⊜1 214 40.50 N 79.10 W
Mahony Lake ⊜ 180 65.30 N 125.20 W
Mahood Falls 182 51.50 N 120.39 W
Mahood Lake ⊜ 182 51.55 N 120.24 W
Mahopac 210 41.22 N 73.44 W
Mahopac Falls 210 41.22 N 73.46 W
Mahora 34 39.13 N 1.44 W
Mahoras Brook ≃ 276 40.25 N 74.08 W
Mahrāt, Jabal ʌʌ1 144 17.05 N 51.30 E
Mahrauli ◆8 272a 28.31 N 77.11 E
Mahrauni 124 24.35 N 78.43 E
Mähren → Morava □9 30 49.20 N 17.00 E
Mahres 148 34.32 N 10.30 E
Mähring 60 49.55 N 12.32 E
Mahuiling 100 29.24 N 115.48 E
Māhul ◆8 272c 19.01 N 72.53 E
Mahulia 126 22.39 N 86.24 E
Mahur Island I 164 2.50 S 152.40 E
Mahuta 154 10.52 S 39.27 E
Mahuva 120 21.05 N 71.48 E
Mahwa 124 27.03 N 76.56 E
Mahwah 276 41.06 N 74.09 W
Mahwah ≃ 276 41.06 N 74.10 W
Mai, Île de I 275a 45.36 N 73.50 W
Maia, Am. Sam. 174y 14.13 S 169.28 W
Maia, Port. 34 41.14 N 8.37 W
Mai Aini 144 14.47 N 39.06 E
Maiala National Park ♠ 171a 27.19 S 152.46 E
Maianga 152 14.12 S 21.45 E
Maiano 64 46.11 N 13.04 E
Maiauatá 250 1.51 S 49.02 W
Maicao 246 11.23 N 72.13 W
Maîche 58 47.15 N 6.48 E
Maichen 102 20.29 N 109.59 E
Maici ≃ 248 6.30 S 61.43 W
Maicuru ≃ 250 2.14 S 54.17 W
Maida 68 38.51 N 16.22 E
Maidan ♠ 272b 22.33 N 88.21 E
Maiden 192 35.34 N 81.12 W
Maidenhead 42 51.32 N 0.44 W
Maiden Newton 42 50.46 N 2.35 W
Maidstone, Austl. 274b 37.47 S 144.52 E
Maidstone, On., Can. 214 42.13 N 82.53 W
Maidstone, Sk., Can. 184 53.06 N 109.18 W
Maidstone, Eng., U.K. 42 51.17 N 0.32 E
Maidstone □8 260 51.17 N 0.35 E
Maiduguri 146 11.51 N 13.10 E
Maie 154 2.46 N 30.34 E
Maiella, Montagna della ʌʌ 66 42.05 N 14.07 E
Maienfeld 58 47.00 N 9.32 E
Maierato 68 38.42 N 16.11 E
Maifeld □9 56 50.20 N 7.20 E
Maigatari 150 12.46 N 9.27 E
Maignelay 50 49.33 N 2.31 E
Maigo 116 8.10 N 123.57 E
Mai Gudo ʌ 144 7.29 N 37.12 E
Maigue ≃ 48 52.39 N 8.48 W
Maihar 124 24.16 N 80.45 E
Maihara 94 35.19 N 136.17 E
Maijoma 196 28.55 N 104.21 W
Maikala Plateau ʌʌ1 124 22.30 N 81.00 E
Maikala Range ʌʌ 122 22.30 N 81.30 E
Maikammer 56 49.18 N 9.07 E
Maiko ≃ 154 0.14 N 25.33 E
Maiko, Parc National de la ♠ 154 3.30 N 27.45 E
Maikoor, Pulau I 164 6.15 S 134.15 E
Mailand → Milano 62 45.28 N 9.12 E
Mailāni 124 28.17 N 80.21 E
Mailasqui 256 23.33 S 47.04 W
Maili 229c 21.25 N 158.10 W
Maillane 62 43.50 N 4.47 E
Mailley-et-Chazelot 58 47.32 N 6.03 E
Maillezais 32 46.22 N 0.44 W
Mailly-le-Camp 50 48.40 N 4.13 E
Mailly-le-Château 50 47.36 N 3.38 E
Mailly-Maillet 50 50.04 N 2.36 E
Mailsi 123 29.48 N 72.11 E
Maimbung 116 5.56 N 121.02 E
Mai Mefales 144 14.59 N 38.16 E
Mā'īn 132 31.41 N 35.44 E
Main ≃, Dtsch. 30 50.00 N 8.18 E
Main ≃, N. Ire., U.K. 48 54.43 N 6.18 W
Maināguri 124 26.34 N 88.49 E
Mainau I 58 47.42 N 9.11 E
Mainburg 60 48.38 N 11.47 E
Main Camp 174o 2.01 N 157.25 W
Main Canal ≅, Ca., U.S. 226 37.25 N 121.05 W
Main Canal ≅, Ca., U.S. 226 37.23 N 120.26 W
Main Canal ≅, Wa., U.S. 224 47.07 N 120.44 W
Main Channel ꓴ 190 45.22 N 81.50 W
Maincourt-sur-Yvette 261 48.43 N 1.58 E
Main Creek ≃ 276 40.34 N 74.11 W
Maincy 261 48.33 N 2.42 E
Mai-Ndombe, Lac ⊜ 152 2.00 S 18.20 E
Main-Donau-Kanal ≅ 60 49.02 N 11.36 E
Main Duck Island I 212 43.56 N 76.37 W
Maine 210 42.11 N 76.03 W
Maine □9 32 48.15 N 0.05 W
Maine □3, U.S. 178 45.15 N 69.15 W
Maine □3, U.S. 188 45.15 N 69.15 W
Maine ≃ 48 52.09 N 9.45 W
Maine, Gulf of c 178 43.00 N 68.00 W
Maine-et-Loire □5 32 47.25 N 0.30 W
Mainesburg 210 41.47 N 77.07 W
Mainé-Soroa 146 13.12 N 12.02 E
Maineville 218 39.18 N 84.13 W
Mainguerin 261 48.32 N 1.51 E
Mainhardt 56 49.04 N 9.33 E
Mainit 116 9.32 N 125.32 E
Mainit, Lake ⊜ 116 9.26 N 125.32 E
Mainland 285 40.15 N 75.22 W
Mainland I, Scot., U.K. 46 59.00 N 3.15 W
Mainland I, Scot., U.K. 46a 60.16 N 1.16 W
Mainleus 54 50.06 N 11.22 E
Mainoru 164 14.02 S 134.05 E
Mainpuri 124 27.14 N 79.01 E
Main Range National Park ♠ 171a 28.01 S 152.22 E
Maintal 56 50.09 N 8.54 E
Maintenon 50 48.35 N 1.35 E
Maintirano 157b 18.03 S 44.01 E
Main Topsail ʌ 186 49.08 N 56.33 W
Mainvilliers 50 48.27 N 1.28 E
Mainz 56 50.01 N 8.16 E
Maio I 150a 15.15 N 23.10 W
Maiolati Spontini 66 43.28 N 13.06 E
Maiori 68 40.39 N 14.38 E
Maiori, Nuraghe ⊥ 71 40.56 N 9.06 E
Maipa 164 8.21 S 146.33 E
Maipo ≃ 252 33.37 S 71.39 W
Maipo, Volcán ʌ1 252 34.10 S 69.50 W
Maipú, Arg. 252 36.52 S 57.52 W
Maipú, Arg. 252 32.58 S 68.47 W
Maipú, Chile 252 33.31 S 70.46 W
Maiqihamiao 89 43.22 N 120.46 E
Maiquetía 246 10.36 N 66.57 W
Maira ≃ 62 44.49 N 7.38 E
Maira, Valle ∨ 62 44.30 N 7.08 E
Mairābāri 120 26.28 N 92.26 E
Mairi 250 11.43 S 40.08 W
Mairinque 256 23.33 S 47.10 W
Mairiporã 256 23.19 S 46.35 W
Mairiporã □7 287b 23.24 S 46.37 W
Mairipotaba 255 17.18 S 49.28 W
Maisach 60 48.13 N 11.16 E
Maisaka 94 34.41 N 137.37 E
Maishi 100 29.11 N 113.58 E
Maišiagala 76 54.52 N 25.04 E
Maiskhāl Island I 120 21.36 N 91.56 E
Maison de Pierre, Lac de la ⊜ 206 46.53 N 74.42 W
Maisonneuve, Parc ♠ 275a 45.33 N 73.34 W
Maisons-Alfort 261 48.48 N 2.26 E
Maisons-Laffitte 50 48.57 N 2.09 E
Maisons-Laffitte, Château de ⊥ 261 48.57 N 2.09 E
Maisse 50 48.24 N 2.23 E
Maissin 56 49.58 N 5.11 E
Maitani 270 34.49 N 135.22 E
Maitengwe 156 20.06 S 27.13 E
Maitengwe ≃ 156 19.59 S 26.26 E
Maithon Reservoir ⊜1 126 23.50 N 86.43 E
Maitland, Austl. 168b 34.22 S 137.40 E
Maitland, Austl. 170 32.44 S 151.33 E
Maitland, N.S., Can. 186 45.19 N 63.30 W
Maitland, On., Can. 212 44.38 N 75.37 W
Maitland, Fl., U.S. 220 28.37 N 81.21 W
Maitland ≃ 190 43.45 N 81.43 W
Maitland, Lake ⊜ 162 27.11 S 121.03 E
Maixie 100 27.38 N 115.29 E
Maíz ≃ 236 11.17 N 83.52 W
Maíz, Islas del II 236 12.15 N 83.00 W
Maizefield 158 26.28 S 29.31 E
Maizhokunggar 120 29.50 N 91.45 E
Maizières-lès-Metz 56 49.13 N 6.09 E
Maizières-lès-Vic 58 48.43 N 6.46 E
Maizuru 96 35.28 N 135.24 E
Maja ≃, Ross. 74 60.24 N 134.30 E
Maja ≃, Ross. 89 54.31 N 134.41 E
Majābirah, Minqār al- ⩡4 142 30.16 N 29.49 E
Majačka ≃ 83 48.44 N 37.33 E
Majačnyj 86 52.41 N 55.44 E
Majadahonda 266a 40.29 N 3.52 W
Majagua 240p 21.55 N 79.00 W
Majagual 246 8.33 N 74.38 W
Majaki, Ukr. 78 46.25 N 30.16 E
Majaki, Ukr. 83 48.57 N 37.37 E
Majalaya 115a 7.03 S 107.45 E
Majalengka 115a 6.50 S 108.13 E
Majana, Ensenada de c 240p 22.41 N 82.45 W
Majanji 154 0.15 N 33.59 E
Majari ≃ 246 3.29 N 60.58 W
Majayjay 116 14.09 N 121.28 E
Majchura 85 39.02 N 68.35 E
Majdantal 85 43.41 N 68.02 E
Majd el Kurūm 132 32.55 N 35.15 E
Majé 256 22.39 S 43.02 W
Majeigha 140 11.33 N 24.40 E
Majenang 115a 7.18 S 108.45 E
Majene 112 3.33 S 118.57 E
Majenica 216 40.46 N 85.27 W
Majevica ʌʌ 38 44.30 N 18.55 E
Maji 144 6.11 N 35.38 E
Majia 100 32.32 N 118.50 E
Majia ≃ 98 38.09 N 117.53 E
Majiacun 106 30.08 N 119.58 E
Majiahe 102 35.20 N 104.46 E
Majian, Zhg. 100 29.19 N 119.36 E
Majian, Zhg. 100 29.43 N 120.00 E
Majiang, Zhg. 102 23.48 N 111.09 E
Majiang, Zhg. 110 26.28 N 107.28 E
Majiangzong 120 30.27 N 90.03 E
Majiaoba 102 32.14 N 104.35 E
Majiaping 102 36.31 N 103.20 E
Majiasi 105 39.03 N 117.05 E
Majiawopu 104 41.46 N 121.06 E
Majiayan 100 27.26 N 112.56 E
Majiazhai 104 42.22 N 124.04 E
Majiazhou 100 26.46 N 114.47 E
Majidun Creek ≃ 273a 6.38 N 3.28 E
Majie, Zhg. 102 23.50 N 105.07 E
Majie, Zhg. 102 25.03 N 103.45 E
Majin 100 29.18 N 118.24 E
Majin ≃ 100 29.00 N 118.21 E
Majinzhuangzi 104 41.55 N 123.53 E
Maji Shan I 106 31.26 N 120.06 E
Majītha 123 31.46 N 74.57 E
Majja 74 61.44 N 130.18 E
Majkain 86 51.27 N 75.52 E
Majkop 84 44.35 N 40.07 E
Majkor 86 59.01 N 55.54 E
Majlibaš 86 45.49 N 62.39 E
Majli-Saj 85 41.17 N 72.29 E
Majlispur 126 24.13 N 90.53 E
Majmak 85 42.40 N 71.15 E
Majna, Ross. 80 54.07 N 47.37 E
Majna, Ross. 86 53.00 N 91.28 E
Majnan 272b 22.59 N 88.09 E
Majnic, ozero ⊜ 180 63.15 N 176.40 E
Majno-Gytkino 180 63.36 N 176.30 E
Majŏn-ni, C.M.I.K. 98 39.06 N 127.07 E
Majŏn-ni, Taehan 271b 37.36 N 126.41 E
Major, Puig ʌ 34 39.48 N 2.48 E
Majorca → Mallorca I 34 39.30 N 3.00 E
Major Creek ≃ 169 36.51 S 145.05 E
Major Isidoro 250 9.32 S 37.00 W
Majorque, Île → Mallorca I 34 39.30 N 3.00 E
Majrūr 140 14.01 N 30.27 E
Majrūr, Wādī ∨ 140 15.44 N 26.26 E
Majsk 86 57.49 N 77.16 E
Majskij, Ross. 83 47.43 N 40.03 E
Majskij, Ross. 84 43.38 N 44.04 E
Majskij, Ross. 89 52.18 N 129.38 E
Majskij, Ross. 89 49.00 N 140.10 E
Majskoje, Kaz. 86 50.55 N 78.15 E
Majskoje, Ross. 82 56.08 N 37.55 E
Majtan 86 45.46 N 74.20 E
Majtobe 85 43.01 N 70.35 E
Māju 126 22.37 N 88.05 E
Majuba Hill ⊥ 158 27.28 S 29.51 E
Majuqiao 105 39.46 N 116.32 E
Majuro I1 14 7.09 N 171.12 E
Majuzigou 104 41.49 N 121.38 E
Maka 150 13.40 N 14.17 W
Makabana 152 2.48 S 12.29 E
Makabe 94 36.16 N 140.06 E
Makadasa ≃ 116 7.22 N 124.36 E
Makaha, Hi., U.S. 229c 21.28 N 158.13 W
Makaha, Zimb. 154 17.17 S 32.37 E
Makaha Point ≻ 229b 22.08 N 159.44 W
Makah Indian Reservation ◆4 224 48.20 N 124.41 W
Makahuena Point ≻ 229b 21.52 N 159.27 W
Makak 152 3.33 N 11.02 E
Makala 273b 4.25 S 15.17 E
Makalamabedi 156 20.19 S 23.51 E
Makale 112 3.06 S 119.51 E
Makallé 252 27.13 S 59.17 W
Makālu ʌ 124 27.54 N 87.06 E
Makamba 154 4.08 S 29.49 E
Makanapur 272a 28.38 N 77.21 E
Makanči 86 46.48 N 82.00 E
Makanya 154 4.20 S 37.51 E
Makanza 152 1.36 N 19.07 E
Makaoo Indian Reserve ◆4 184 53.40 N 110.02 W
Makapu Point ≻ 174v 18.59 S 169.56 W
Makapuu Head ≻ 229c 21.19 N 157.39 W
Makarakomburu, Mount ʌ 175e 9.43 S 160.02 E
Makarakskij 86 55.36 N 88.03 E
Makarapan Mountain ʌ 246 4.00 N 58.51 W
Makarewa 172 46.20 S 168.21 E
Makari 146 12.35 N 14.28 E
Makar-Ib 24 63.39 N 49.24 E
Makaricha 24 66.15 N 58.20 E
Makarje 80 58.35 N 48.11 E
Makarjev 80 57.52 N 43.48 E
Makarjevo 80 56.06 N 45.06 E
Makarov, Ross. 89 48.38 N 142.48 E
Makarov, Ukr. 78 50.28 N 29.49 E
Makarovo, Ross. 80 52.18 N 43.20 E
Makarovo, Ross. 82 54.22 N 36.40 E
Makarovo, Ross. 88 57.29 N 107.52 E
Makarska 36 43.18 N 17.02 E
Makasar, Selat (Makassar Strait) ꓴ 112 2.00 S 117.30 E
Makasar → Ujungpandang 112 5.07 S 119.24 E
Makaševka 80 51.30 N 42.36 E
Makassar Strait → Makasar, Selat ꓴ 112 2.00 S 117.30 E
Makasuko 154 6.00 S 34.56 E
Makat 80 47.39 N 53.19 E
Makatea I 14 15.50 S 148.15 W
Makati 269f 14.34 N 121.02 E
Makaw, Mya. 110 26.27 N 96.42 E
Makaw, Zaïre 152 3.29 S 18.19 E
Makawao 229a 20.51 N 156.18 W
Makaweli 229b 21.55 N 159.38 W
Makay, Massif du ʌʌ 157b 21.15 S 45.15 E
Makaya 152 3.22 S 18.02 E
Makedonija → Macedonia □1 38 41.50 N 22.00 E
Makefu 174v 18.59 S 169.55 W
Makejevka, Ukr. 78 50.40 N 31.50 E
Makejevka, Ukr. 83 48.02 N 37.58 E
Makejevka, Ukr. 83 49.14 N 37.59 E
Makemie Park 208 37.55 N 75.34 W
Makemo I1 14 16.35 S 143.40 W
Makena 229a 20.39 N 156.27 W
Makeni 150 8.53 N 12.03 W
Makere 154 4.17 S 30.25 E
Maketu 172 37.46 S 176.27 E
Makeyevka → Makejevka 83 48.02 N 37.58 E
Makgadikgadi ≚ 156 20.45 S 25.30 E
Makgadikgadi Pans Game Reserve ◆4 156 20.30 S 24.45 E
Makhachkala → Machačkala 84 42.58 N 47.30 E
Makhad 123 33.08 N 71.44 E
Makhaleng ≃ 158 30.20 S 27.23 E
Mākhālpur 272b 22.56 N 88.10 E
Makham 110 12.40 N 102.12 E
Makhdūmnagar 124 26.28 N 82.46 E
Makhfar al-Quwayrah 132 29.48 N 35.19 E
Makhfar Ramn 132 29.42 N 35.25 E
Makhrūq, Wādī al- ∨ 132 31.30 N 37.10 E
Makhyah, Wādī ∨ 144 17.40 N 49.01 E
Maki, Indon. 164 3.11 S 134.14 E
Maki, Nihon 92 37.45 N 138.53 E
Maki, Nihon 94 37.05 N 138.23 E
Maki, Nihon 270 34.52 N 135.04 E
Makika, Lua ⩡6 229a 20.34 N 156.34 W
Makikihi 172 44.38 S 171.09 E
Makilala 116 6.55 N 125.05 E
Makindu 154 2.17 S 37.49 E
Makino, Nihon 94 35.28 N 136.05 E
M'akino, Ross. 265b 55.48 N 37.22 E
Makinsk 86 52.37 N 70.26 E
Makio-dam ◆6 94 35.50 N 137.36 E
Makioka 94 35.45 N 138.43 E
Makira □4 175e 11.00 S 162.30 E
Makira Harbour c 175e 10.25 S 161.29 E
M'akiševo 76 56.34 N 28.53 E
M'akit 74 61.24 N 152.09 E
Makkah (Mecca) 144 21.27 N 39.49 E
Makkavejevo 88 51.44 N 113.58 E
Makkum 52 53.04 N 5.24 E
Makó, Magy. 30 46.13 N 20.29 E
Mako, Sén. 150 12.52 N 12.21 W
Makoaneng ʌ 158 29.47 S 28.57 E
Makobe Lake ⊜ 190 47.27 N 80.25 W
Makoka 154 2.34 S 25.29 E
Makok-ni 271b 37.43 N 126.38 E
Makokou 152 0.34 N 12.52 E
Makoli 154 17.27 S 26.05 E
Makongai Island I 175g 17.27 S 178.58 E
Makongo 154 3.25 N 26.22 E
Makongolosi 154 8.24 S 33.09 E
Makopse 84 43.59 N 39.13 E
Makorako ʌ 172 39.09 S 176.02 E
Makoro 154 3.08 N 29.44 E
Makoshika State Park ♠ 198 47.03 N 104.41 W
Makošino 78 51.27 N 32.18 E
Makotuku 172 40.07 S 176.14 E
Makoua 152 0.01 N 15.39 E
Makov 30 49.23 N 18.30 E
Makovskoje 86 58.12 N 90.52 E
Maków Mazowiecki 30 52.52 N 21.06 E
Maków Podhalański 30 49.44 N 19.41 E
Makrai 124 22.04 N 77.06 E
Makrampur 126 22.44 N 90.14 E
Makrāna 120 27.03 N 74.43 E
Makran Coast ⩡2 128 25.15 N 61.00 E
M'aksa 76 58.54 N 38.12 E
Maksaticha 76 57.48 N 35.53 E
Maksimicha 88 53.15 N 108.43 E
Maksimkin Jar 86 58.42 N 86.48 E
Maksimoviči 78 51.13 N 29.37 E
Maksimovka, Ross. 80 52.59 N 51.10 E
Maksimovka, Ross. 89 46.04 N 137.51 E
Maksimovka, Ukr. 83 47.38 N 37.34 E
Maksimovo 82 56.20 N 35.58 E
Maksudangarh 124 24.03 N 77.15 E
Maktar 148 35.51 N 9.12 E
Maktau 154 3.24 S 38.08 E
Mākū, Īrān 128 39.17 N 44.31 E
Maku, Zhg. 105 39.33 N 114.46 E
Makuhari 268 35.39 N 140.03 E
Makuliro 154 9.35 S 37.26 E
Makumbako 154 8.51 S 34.50 E
Makumbi 152 5.51 S 20.41 E
Makung (P'enghu) 100 23.34 N 119.34 E
Makunudu I 122 6.25 N 72.41 E
Makunudu Atoll I1 122 6.20 N 72.36 E
Makuragi-san ʌ 96 35.32 N 133.08 E
Makurazaki 92 31.16 N 130.19 E
Makurdi 150 7.45 N 8.32 E
Makushin Volcano ʌ1 180 53.53 N 166.50 W
Makušino 86 55.13 N 67.13 E
Makuyuni 154 3.33 S 36.06 E
Makwa Lake ⊜ 184 54.04 N 109.15 W
Makwassie 158 27.26 S 26.00 E
Makwende-Bayo 154 7.08 S 28.06 E
Makwiro 154 17.58 S 30.28 E
Māl, India 124 26.52 N 88.44 E
Mal, Maur. 150 16.58 N 13.23 W
Mala, Perú 248 12.39 S 76.38 W
Malå, Sve. 26 65.11 N 18.44 E
Mala ≃ 248 12.40 S 76.41 W
Mala, Punta ≻ 246 7.28 N 80.00 W
Malabang 116 7.38 N 124.03 E
Malabar, Austl. 274a 33.58 S 151.15 E
Malabar, Fl., U.S. 220 28.00 N 80.33 W
Malabar Coast ⩡2 122 11.00 N 75.00 E
Malabar Farm State Park ♠ 214 40.38 N 82.25 W
Malabar Hill ʌ2 272c 18.57 N 72.48 E
Malabar Point ≻ 272c 18.57 N 72.47 E
Malabo 152 3.45 N 8.47 E
Mal Abrigo 258 34.09 S 56.57 W
Malabrigo Point ≻ 116 13.36 N 121.15 E
Malabuyoc 116 9.39 N 123.19 E
Malaca, Estrecho de → Malacca, Strait of ꓴ 110 2.30 N 101.20 E
Malacacheta 255 17.50 S 42.05 W
Malacañang Palace υ 269f 14.36 N 120.59 E
Malacatepec, Volcán ʌ1 286a 19.10 N 99.16 W
Malacca, Strait of ꓴ 110 2.30 N 101.20 E
Malachovka 82 55.39 N 38.00 E
Malachovo, Ross. 82 54.45 N 37.27 E
Malachovo, Ross. 82 54.22 N 37.31 E
Malachovskij 80 49.08 N 41.43 E
Malacky 30 48.27 N 17.00 E
Mālād ◆8 272c 19.11 N 72.51 E
Malad ≃ 200 41.35 N 112.07 W
Malad City 202 42.11 N 112.15 W
Malad Creek ≃ 272c 19.08 N 72.48 E
Malafede ≃ 267a 41.47 N 12.24 E
Málaga, Col. 246 6.42 N 72.44 W
Málaga, Esp. 34 36.43 N 4.25 W
Malaga, Ca., U.S. 226 36.42 N 119.46 W
Malaga, N.J., U.S. 208 39.34 N 75.02 W
Malaga, N.M., U.S. 196 32.13 N 104.04 W
Málaga □4 34 36.50 N 4.40 W
Malagarasi 154 5.06 S 30.50 E
Malagarasi ≃ 154 5.12 S 29.47 E
Malagash 186 45.46 N 63.23 W
Malagasy Republic → Madagascar □1 157b 19.00 S 46.00 E
Malago ≃ 116 10.55 N 123.02 E
Malagón 34 39.10 N 3.51 W
Malagón ≃ 34 37.35 N 7.29 W
Malagrotta ◆8 66 41.53 N 12.20 E
Mal'agurt 80 57.39 N 52.32 E
Malahat 224 48.32 N 123.34 W
Malahide 48 53.27 N 6.09 W
Malaimbandy 157b 20.20 S 45.36 E
Malaisie → Malaysia □1 112 2.30 N 112.30 E
Malaita □4 175e 9.00 S 161.00 E
Malaita I 175e 9.00 S 161.00 E
Malaja Beloz'orka 78 47.14 N 34.56 E
Malaja Bessergenovka 83 47.09 N 38.36 E
Malaja Borščovka 82 56.33 N 36.53 E
Malaja Bykovka 80 51.54 N 47.45 E
Malaja Čuja ≃ 88 58.56 N 112.13 E
Malaja Devica 78 50.41 N 32.10 E
Malaja Doroginka 82 54.06 N 38.56 E
Malaja Dubna 82 55.52 N 38.58 E
Malaja Istra ≃ 82 55.54 N 36.50 E
Malaja Ižmora 80 53.32 N 42.48 E
Malaja Janisol' 83 47.22 N 37.20 E
Malaja Jekaterinovka 80 51.26 N 44.17 E
Malaja Kinel' ≃ 80 53.29 N 51.30 E
Malaja Kokšaga ≃ 80 56.09 N 47.53 E
Malaja Konkudera ≃ 88 57.26 N 112.37 E
Malaja Kuril'skaja Gr'ada (Habomai-Shotō) II 92a 43.30 N 146.10 E
Malaja Laba ≃ 84 44.16 N 40.53 E
Malaja Neva ≃1 265a 59.57 N 30.15 E
Malaja Ochta ◆8 265a 59.56 N 30.24 E
Malaja Orlovka 80 47.18 N 41.24 E
Malaja Pera 24 64.11 N 54.47 E
Malaja Serdoba 80 52.28 N 44.56 E
Malaja Sestra ≃ 82 56.17 N 35.57 E
Malaja Tokmačevka 78 47.32 N 35.54 E
Malaja Višera 76 58.51 N 32.14 E
Malaja Viska 78 48.39 N 31.38 E
Malaka, Sempitan ꓴ 114 5.44 N 95.30 E
Malakāl 140 9.31 N 31.39 E
Malaka → Melaka 114 2.12 N 102.15 E
Malākand 123 34.34 N 71.56 E
Mala Kapela ʌʌ 36 44.50 N 15.30 E
Malakka, Strasse von → Malacca, Strait of ꓴ 110 2.30 N 101.20 E
Malakoff, Fr. 261 48.49 N 2.19 E
Malakoff, Tx., U.S. 222 32.10 N 96.00 W
Malakpur ◆8 272a 28.42 N 77.12 E
Malakula □8 175f 16.20 S 167.20 E
Malakula I 175f 16.15 S 167.30 E
Malakwāl 123 32.34 N 73.13 E
Malala 164 5.15 S 147.10 E
Malalag 116 6.36 N 125.24 E
Malalbergo 64 44.43 N 11.32 E
Malamala 112 3.21 S 120.55 E
Mala Mala Game Reserve ◆4 156 24.52 S 31.30 E
Malamaui Island I 116 6.44 N 121.58 E
Malambo 246 10.52 N 74.47 W
Malambo, Arroyo ≃ 258 33.43 S 58.46 W
Malambunga 116 9.02 N 117.38 E
Malamocco 64 45.22 N 12.20 E
Malampaya Sound ꓴ 116 10.51 N 119.20 E
Malān 110 25.37 N 96.21 E
Malān, Rās ≻ 128 25.18 N 65.11 E
Malanao Island I 116 9.27 N 118.37 E
Malanas ≃ 116 17.41 N 120.43 E
Mālancha 272b 22.55 N 88.26 E
Mālancha ≃1 126 21.40 N 89.20 E
Mālandighi 126 23.33 N 87.24 E
Malandji 152 5.56 S 22.18 E
Malang 115a 7.59 S 112.37 E
Malang, Gunung ʌ 115a 7.02 S 107.01 E
Malangali 154 8.34 S 34.51 E
Malangas 116 7.37 N 123.01 E
Malanggwā 124 26.52 N 85.34 E
Malangka, Tanjung ≻ 112 1.20 N 120.48 E
Malan Guan)(105 40.16 N 117.39 E
Malanipa Island I 116 6.53 N 122.16 E
Malanje 152 9.32 S 16.20 E
Malanje □5 152 9.30 S 16.30 E
Malanut Bay c 116 9.16 N 117.59 E
Malanville 150 11.52 N 3.23 E
Malanyu 105 40.11 N 117.42 E
Malanzán 252 30.48 S 66.37 W
Mała Panew ≃ 30 50.44 N 17.52 E
Malapantao, Mount ʌ 116 9.54 N 122.37 E
Malapardis Brook ≃ 276 40.49 N 74.25 W
Mälaren ⊜ 40 59.30 N 17.12 E
Malargüe 252 35.28 S 69.35 W
Mälar-See → Mälaren ⊜ 40 59.30 N 17.12 E
Malartic 190 48.08 N 78.08 W
Malartic, Lac ⊜ 190 48.15 N 78.07 W
Malasia → Malaysia □1 112 2.30 N 112.30 E
Malasiqui 116 15.55 N 120.25 E
Malaspina 254 44.56 S 66.54 W
Malaspina Glacier ⊓ 180 59.50 N 140.30 W
Malaspina Strait ꓴ 182 49.44 N 124.20 W
Malassis 261 48.38 N 2.03 E
Malāṭīyah 142 28.42 N 30.51 E
Malatya 130 38.21 N 38.19 E
Malatya □4 130 38.30 N 38.10 E
Malau 175f 15.10 S 166.48 E
Malaucène 62 44.10 N 5.08 E
Malaunay 50 49.32 N 1.02 E
Malaut 123 30.13 N 74.29 E
Malavalli 122 12.23 N 77.05 E
Malawali, Pulau I 116 7.03 N 117.18 E
Malawi □1, Afr. 138 13.30 S 34.00 E
Malawi □1, Afr. 154 13.30 S 34.00 E
Malawi, Lake → Nyasa, Lake ⊜ 154 12.00 S 34.30 E
Malawiya 140 15.16 N 36.12 E
Malayagiri ʌ 120 21.23 N 85.16 E
Malayal 116 7.12 N 121.57 E
Malaya → Semenanjung Malaysia □9 114 4.00 N 102.00 E
Malaybalay 116 8.09 N 125.05 E
Malāyer 128 34.17 N 48.50 E
Malay Peninsula ≻1 110 6.00 N 101.00 E
Malay Reef ✦2 166 17.59 S 149.18 E
Malaysia □1, Asia 108 2.30 N 112.30 E
Malaysia □1, Asia 112 2.30 N 112.30 E
Malazgirt 130 39.09 N 42.31 E
Malbaie ≃ 186 47.39 N 70.09 W
Malbaie, La c 186 48.35 N 64.14 W
Malbon 166 21.04 S 140.18 E
Malbooma 162 30.41 S 134.11 E
Malborghetto Valbruna 64 46.30 N 13.26 E
Malbork 30 54.02 N 19.01 E
Malbrán 252 29.21 S 62.27 W
Malbuisson 58 46.48 N 6.18 E
Malbun 58 47.35 N 9.33 E
Malcesine 64 45.46 N 10.48 E
Mal'cevo 265b 55.56 N 37.57 E
Mal'čevskaja 78 49.04 N 40.21 E
Mal'čevsko-Polnenskaja 83 48.58 N 40.12 E
Malchanskij chrebet ʌʌ 88 50.45 N 109.30 E
Malchin 54 53.44 N 12.46 E
Malchiner See ⊜ 54 53.43 N 12.38 E
Malching 60 48.19 N 13.12 E
Malchow 54 53.28 N 12.25 E
Malchow ◆8 264a 52.35 N 13.29 E
Malčin 88 49.44 N 93.18 E
Malcolm 162 28.56 S 121.30 E
Malcolm, Point ≻ 162 33.48 S 123.45 E
Malcolm Island I 182 50.40 N 127.00 W
Malcom 190 41.42 N 92.33 W
Malcompeth → Mahābaleshwar 122 17.55 N 73.40 E
Malcontenta 64 45.25 N 12.13 E
Malczyce 30 51.14 N 16.29 E
Māldah 124 25.02 N 88.09 E
Maldegem 50 51.13 N 3.27 E
Malden, Ma., U.S. 207 42.25 N 71.04 W
Malden, Mo., U.S. 194 36.33 N 89.57 W
Malden I 14 4.03 S 154.59 W
Malden ≃ 283 42.24 N 71.05 W
Malden Bridge 210 42.28 N 73.35 W
Malden on Hudson 210 42.06 N 73.56 W
Maldivas → Maldives □1 12 3.15 N 73.00 E
Maldive Islands → Maldives □1 12 3.15 N 73.00 E
Mal di Ventre, Isola di I 71 39.59 N 8.18 E
Maldives □1 12 3.15 N 73.00 E
Maldon, Austl. 169 37.00 S 144.04 E
Maldon, Eng., U.K. 42 51.45 N 0.40 E
Maldon □8 260 51.43 N 0.40 E
Maldonado 252 34.54 S 54.57 W
Maldonado, Punta ≻ 234 16.20 N 98.35 W
Male, It. 64 46.21 N 10.55 E
Male', Mald. 12 4.10 N 73.30 E
Male, Mya. 110 23.02 N 95.58 E
Maléa, Ákra ≻ 38 36.26 N 23.12 E
Malea, Dolok ʌ 114 0.56 N 99.38 E
Malebo, Pool ⊜ 152 4.17 S 15.20 E
Malediven → Maldives □1 12 3.15 N 73.00 E
Mālegaon 122 20.33 N 74.32 E
Malegno, It. 64 45.56 N 10.14 E
Malegno, It. 64 46.40 N 11.08 E
Malehra 124 24.34 N 79.19 E
Maleit, Lake ⊜ 140 7.55 N 28.35 E
Malejevka 78 47.29 N 32.43 E
Malek, Kaz. 85 40.47 N 68.37 E
Malek, Sūd. 140 6.04 N 31.36 E
Malé Karpaty ʌʌ 30 48.30 N 17.20 E
Malek Dīn 120 32.25 N 68.04 E
Malek Kandī 128 37.09 N 46.06 E
Malek Sīāh, Kūh-e ʌ 128 29.51 N 60.52 E
Malela, Zaïre 154 2.28 S 26.09 E
Malela, Zaïre 154 4.22 S 26.08 E
Malema 154 14.57 S 37.20 E
Malen'ga 24 63.50 N 36.25 E
Malengoya 154 3.32 N 25.25 E
Malente 54 54.10 N 10.33 E
Maleo 62 45.10 N 9.46 E
Māler Kotla 124 30.31 N 75.53 E
Malesco 58 46.08 N 8.30 E
Malesherbes 50 48.18 N 2.25 E
Malestroit 32 47.49 N 2.23 W
Maleta 88 50.50 N 108.25 E
Maletto 70 37.49 N 14.52 E
Malfa 70 38.35 N 14.50 E
Malgas 158 34.18 S 20.35 E
Malgersdorf 60 48.32 N 12.45 E
Malgobek 84 43.32 N 44.34 E
Malgomaj ⊜ 26 64.47 N 16.12 E
Malha Wells 140 15.08 N 26.12 E
Malheur ≃ 202 44.03 N 116.59 W
Malheur, North Fork ≃ 202 43.45 N 118.04 W
Malheur, South Fork ≃ 202 43.33 N 118.10 W
Malheureux, Cap ≻ 157c 19.59 S 57.36 E
Malheur Lake ⊜ 202 43.20 N 118.45 W
Mali, Guinée 150 12.05 N 12.18 W
Mali, Zaïre 154 2.48 S 26.08 E
Mali □1, Afr. 134 17.00 N 4.00 W
Mali □1, Afr. 150 17.00 N 4.00 W
Mali ≃ 102 25.43 N 97.29 E
Maliangping 102 31.29 N 111.20 E
Malianjingzi 102 41.32 N 95.23 E
Malibamatšo ≃ 158 29.20 S 29.28 E
Malibu 228 34.02 N 118.42 W
Malibu Lake ⊜1 228 34.07 N 118.45 W
Malien ≃ 269d 25.11 N 121.41 E
Malienkang 269d 25.10 N 121.39 E
Maligay Bay c 116 7.30 N 123.14 E
Malighati 126 22.33 N 87.40 E
Maligne ≃ 182 52.56 N 118.02 W
Maligne Lake ⊜ 182 52.40 N 117.31 W
Malīhābād 124 26.55 N 80.43 E
Māliḥah, Wādī ∨ 142 29.21 N 32.35 E
Malik 112 0.34 S 123.14 E
Malik, Wādī al- ∨ 140 18.02 N 30.58 E
Mali Kyun I 110 13.06 N 98.16 E
Malili 112 2.38 S 121.06 E
Målilla 26 57.23 N 15.48 E
Malimba, Monts ʌʌ 154 7.32 S 29.30 E
Malim Nawar 114 4.21 N 101.07 E
Malimono 116 9.34 N 125.25 E
Malin, Ire. 48 55.18 N 7.15 W
Malin, Ukr. 78 50.46 N 29.15 E
Malin, Or., U.S. 202 42.00 N 121.24 W
Malinalco ⊥ 234 18.57 N 99.30 W
Malinaltepec 234 17.03 N 98.40 W
Malinau 112 3.35 N 116.38 E
Malin Beg 48 54.40 N 8.48 W
Malindang, Mount ʌ 116 8.13 N 123.38 E
Malindi 154 3.13 S 40.07 E
Malindi Marine National Park ♠ 154 3.15 S 40.10 E
Malines → Mechelen 50 51.02 N 4.28 E
Malinga 152 2.25 S 12.14 E
Malingping 115a 6.46 S 106.01 E
Malingsbosjön ⊜ 40 59.55 N 15.27 E
Malin Head ≻ 48 55.23 N 7.24 W
Malinki 82 54.05 N 38.59 E
Malinniki 82 56.17 N 38.24 E
Malino, Indon. 112 5.15 S 119.51 E
Malino, Ross. 82 55.06 N 38.11 E
Malino, Ross. 265b 55.58 N 37.13 E
Malino, Bukit ʌ 112 0.45 N 120.47 E
Malinoa I 174w 21.02 S 175.08 W
Malinovka, Ross. 80 51.47 N 43.26 E
Malinovka, Ross. 86 53.24 N 87.17 E
Malinovka, Ukr. 78 49.47 N 36.43 E
Malinta 216 41.19 N 84.02 W
Malinyi 154 8.56 S 36.08 E
Malipāra 272b 22.57 N 88.14 E
Mali Rajinac ʌ 36 44.48 N 15.02 E
Malita 116 6.25 N 125.36 E
Malitbog 116 10.10 N 125.00 E
Maliuchang 107 29.05 N 104.07 E
Maliuping 107 29.55 N 106.23 E
Ma Liu Shui 271d 22.25 N 114.12 E
Malivo 82 55.07 N 39.02 E
Maliwun 110 10.14 N 98.37 E
Malizhen 102 23.10 N 104.35 E
Maljamar 196 32.51 N 103.46 W
Malka, Ross. 74 53.20 N 157.30 E
Malka, Ross. 84 43.47 N 43.21 E
Malka ≃ 84 43.44 N 44.15 E
Malkāpur 120 20.53 N 76.12 E
Malkara 130 40.53 N 26.54 E
Malkerns 158 26.32 S 31.11 E
Malko Târnovo 38 41.59 N 27.32 E
Mallāḥ 132 32.30 N 36.51 E
Mallaig, Ab., Can. 182 54.13 N 111.22 W
Mallaig, Scot., U.K. 46 57.00 N 5.50 W
Mallala 168b 34.26 S 138.30 E
Mallaoua 150 13.02 N 9.36 E
Mallapunyah 164 16.59 S 135.49 E
Mallaranny 48 53.54 N 9.49 W
Mallard Reservoir ⊜1 282 38.01 N 122.03 W
Mallawī 142 27.44 N 30.50 E
Mallee Cliffs National Park ♠ 166 34.15 S 142.40 E
Mallemort 62 43.44 N 5.11 E
Mallersdorf 60 48.47 N 12.16 E
Mallery Lake ⊜ 176 63.55 N 98.25 W
Malles Venosta (Mals) 64 46.41 N 10.32 E
Mallet 252 25.55 S 50.50 W
Mallig 116 17.08 N 121.41 E
Malligasta 252 29.11 S 67.26 W
Mallina 162 20.53 S 118.02 E
Malling 41 56.02 N 10.10 E
Mallnitz 64 46.59 N 13.10 E
Mallorca I 34 39.30 N 3.00 E
Mallorytown 212 44.29 N 75.53 W
Mallow 48 52.08 N 8.39 W
Mallwood 216 42.51 N 89.02 W
Malm 26 64.04 N 11.13 E
Malmbäck 26 57.35 N 14.28 E
Malmberget 24 67.10 N 20.40 E
Malmédy 56 50.25 N 6.02 E
Malmesbury, S. Afr. 158 33.28 S 18.44 E
Malmesbury, Eng., U.K. 42 51.36 N 2.06 W
Malmesbury, Vale of ∨ 42 51.22 N 2.10 W
Malmköping 40 59.08 N 16.44 E
Malmlången ⊜ 40 59.27 N 14.42 E
Malmö 41 55.36 N 13.00 E
Malmöhus Län □6 26 55.45 N 13.30 E
Malmsbury 169 37.12 S 144.23 E
Malmsbury Reservoir ⊜1 169 37.13 S 144.22 E
Malmslätt 26 58.25 N 15.30 E
Malmstrom Air Force Base ■ 202 47.30 N 111.10 W
Malmyž 80 56.31 N 50.41 E
Malna 116 8.08 N 124.27 E
Malnate 62 45.48 N 8.53 E
Malnoue 261 48.50 N 2.36 E
Malo 64 45.39 N 11.24 E
Malo I 175f 15.40 S 167.11 E
Malo, Arroyo ≃ 258 33.43 S 58.52 W
Maloarchangel'sk 76 52.24 N 36.30 E
Maloarchangel'skoje 88 50.24 N 108.50 E
Maloba 154 6.18 S 27.39 E
Malodel'skaja 80 50.11 N 43.53 E
Maloduša 76 52.09 N 30.14 E
Maloelap I1 14 8.45 N 171.03 E
Malo-Iljinovka ◆8 83 48.38 N 37.59 E
Maloja 58 46.24 N 9.41 E
Malojapass)(58 46.24 N 9.41 E
Malojaroslavec 82 55.01 N 36.28 E
Malojaz 86 55.13 N 58.09 E
Maloje Goloustnoje 88 52.18 N 105.18 E
Malojekaterinovka 78 47.39 N 35.16 E
Maloje Kozino 80 56.26 N 43.41 E
Maloje Polesje ◆1 78 50.10 N 25.00 E
Maloje-Ščerbedino 80 51.59 N 42.50 E
Maloje Skuratovo 76 53.33 N 37.00 E
Malokirsanovka 83 47.28 N 38.31 E
Malokrasnojarka 86 56.28 N 76.01 E
Malo-les-Bains 50 51.03 N 2.24 E
Malolo 154 7.18 S 36.35 E
Malolos, Guam 174p 13.18 N 144.46 E
Malolos, Pil. 116 14.51 N 120.49 E
Malom 164 3.10 S 151.50 E
Maloma 158 27.00 S 31.40 E
Malombe, Lake ⊜ 154 14.38 S 35.12 E
Malomichajlovka 78 48.06 N 36.23 E
Malonabatovskij 80 48.57 N 43.40 E
Malone, Fl., U.S. 192 30.57 N 85.09 W
Malone, N.Y., U.S. 188 44.50 N 74.17 W
Malone, Tx., U.S. 222 31.55 N 96.54 W
Malone, Wa., U.S. 224 46.58 N 123.20 W
Malonga 152 10.24 S 23.10 E
Malonno 64 46.07 N 10.18 E
Malonty 61 48.41 N 14.35 E
Małopolska ◆1 30 50.10 N 21.30 E
Malor'azancevo 83 48.53 N 38.23 E
Malorita 78 51.47 N 24.05 E
Malorossijskij 86 53.12 N 62.30 E
Malošujka 24 63.45 N 37.22 E
Malott 182 48.16 N 119.42 W
Måløv 41 55.45 N 12.20 E
Małowice 30 51.34 N 15.27 E
Måløy 26 61.56 N 5.07 E
Malozemel'skaja Tundra ◆1 24 67.50 N 51.00 E
Malpaisillo 236 12.35 N 86.41 W
Malpartida de Plasencia 34 39.59 N 6.02 W
Malpas, Austl. 166 34.43 S 140.37 E
Malpas, Eng., U.K. 44 53.01 N 2.46 W

≃	River	Fluß	Río	Rivière	Rio
≅	Canal	Kanal	Canal	Canal	Canal
⌐	Waterfall, Rapids	Wasserfall, Stromschnellen	Cascada, Rápidos	Chute d'eau, Rapides	Cascata, Rápidos
ꓴ	Strait	Meeresstraße	Estrecho	Détroit	Estreito
c	Bay, Gulf	Bucht, Golf	Bahía, Golfo	Baie, Golfe	Baía, Golfo
⊜	Lake, Lakes	See, Seen	Lago, Lagos	Lac, Lacs	Lago, Lagos
≚	Swamp	Sumpf	Pantano	Marais	Pântano
⊓	Ice Features, Glacier	Eis- und Gletscherformen	Accidentes Glaciales	Formes glaciaires	Acidentes glaciares
⌐	Other Hydrographic Features	Andere Hydrographische Objekte	Otros Elementos Hidrográficos	Autres données hydrographiques	Outros acidentes hidrográficos

✦	Submarine Features	Untermeerische Objekte	Accidentes Submarinos	Formes de relief sous-marin	Acidentes submarinos
□	Political Unit	Politische Einheit	Unidad Politica	Entité politique	Unidade politica
υ	Cultural Institution	Kulturelle Institution	Institución Cultural	Institution culturelle	Instituição cultural
⊥	Historical Site	Historische Stätte	Sitio Histórico	Site historique	Sitio histórico
♠	Recreational Site	Erholungs- und Ferienort	Sitio de Recreo	Centre de loisirs	Area de Lazer
✈	Airport	Flughafen	Aeropuerto	Aéroport	Aeroporto
■	Military Installation	Militäranlage	Instalación Militar	Installation militaire	Instalação militar
◆	Miscellaneous	Verschiedenes	Misceláneo	Divers	Diversos

Malpaso 234 22.37 N 102.46 W
Malpe 122 13.21 N 74.43 E
Malpelo, Isla de I 242 3.59 N 81.35 W
Malpensa, Aeroporto della ⊗ 62 45.38 N 8.44 E
Malpeque Bay c 186 46.30 N 63.47 W
Malprabha ≃ 122 16.12 N 76.03 E
Mālpura 120 26.17 N 75.23 E
Målsåker slott ⊥ 40 59.23 N 17.18 E
Malsch 56 48.53 N 8.19 E
Malše (Maltsch) ≃ 61 48.58 N 14.28 E
Målselva ≃ 24 69.14 N 18.30 E
Mals
— Malles Venosta 64 46.41 N 10.32 E
Malta, Bra. 250 6.54 S 37.31 W
Malta, Öst. 64 46.57 N 13.30 E
Malta, Il., U.S. 216 41.56 N 88.52 W
Malta, Mt., U.S. 202 48.21 N 107.52 W
Malta, Oh., U.S. 188 39.38 N 81.51 W
Malta □¹, Europe 22 35.50 N 14.35 E
Malta □¹, Europe 36 35.50 N 14.35 E
Malta I 36 35.53 N 14.27 E
Malta ≃ 76 56.44 N 26.53 E
Malta Channel ⊔ 36 36.20 N 15.00 E
Maltahöhe 156 24.50 S 17.00 E
Maltahöhe □⁵ 156 25.00 S 16.30 E
Maltatal V 64 47.03 N 13.24 E
Maltby 44 53.26 N 1.11 W
Malte Brun ʌ 172 43.34 S 170.18 E
Malte
— Malta □¹ 36 35.50 N 14.35 E
Maltepe ✦⁸ 267b 40.55 N 29.08 E
Malton 44 54.08 N 0.48 W
Malton ✦⁸ 275b 43.42 N 79.38 W
Maltrata 234 18.48 N 97.16 W
Maltsch (Malše) ≃ 61 48.58 N 14.28 E
Malugou 89 43.39 N 128.27 E
Maluku □⁴ 164 5.00 S 130.00 E
Maluku (Moluccas) II 108 2.00 S 128.00 E
Maluku, Laut (Molucca Sea) ⌒² 108 0.00 125.00 E
Maluku-Maes 152 4.06 S 15.31 E
Ma'lūlā 130 33.50 N 36.33 E
Ma'lūlā, Jabal ʌ 132 33.54 N 36.36 E
Malu Mare 38 44.15 N 23.51 E
Malumfashi 150 11.47 N 7.37 E
Malunda 112 3.00 S 118.50 E
Malung 26 60.40 N 13.44 E
Maluso 116 6.33 N 121.53 E
Malūt 140 10.26 N 32.12 E
Maluti 126 24.09 N 87.41 E
Maluwe 150 8.40 N 2.17 W
Maluzhen 106 31.20 N 121.16 E
Malvaglia 58 46.25 N 8.59 E
Malvaglio 266b 45.31 N 8.47 E
Malvagna 70 37.55 N 15.04 E
Mālvan 122 16.04 N 73.28 E
Malveira 266c 38.45 N 9.27 W
Malvern, Austl. 274b 37.52 S 145.02 E
Malvern, Ar., U.S. 194 34.21 N 92.48 W
Malvern, Ia., U.S. 198 41.00 N 95.35 W
Malvern, Oh., U.S. 214 40.41 N 81.10 W
Malvern, Pa., U.S. 285 40.02 N 75.31 W
Malvern ✦⁸ 273d 26.12 S 28.06 E
Malverne 276 40.40 N 73.40 W
Malvern Hills ʌ² 42 52.05 N 2.21 W
Malvérnia 156 22.06 S 31.42 E
Malvern Link 42 52.08 N 2.18 W
Malvinas 252 29.37 S 58.59 W
Malvinas, Islas
— Falkland Islands □² 254 51.45 S 59.00 W
Malvito 68 39.36 N 16.03 E
Malwal 140 9.19 N 31.35 E
Mālwa Plateau ʌ¹ 124 23.50 N 77.30 E
Malybaj 85 43.30 N 78.25 E
Malý Dunaj ≃ 30 47.45 N 18.09 E
Malyj Alabuchi 80 51.33 N 42.10 E
Malyj Čany, ozero ⊜ 86 54.33 N 78.02 E
Malyje Gorod'atiči 76 52.33 N 28.20 E
Malyje Jagury 80 45.26 N 43.01 E
Malyje Kamkaly 86 44.44 N 71.31 E
Malyje Karmakuly 72 72.23 N 52.44 E
Malyje Porogi 265a 59.47 N 30.42 E
Malyj Civil' ≃ 80 55.54 N 47.28 E
Malyj Nesvetaj ≃ 83 47.32 N 39.49 E
Malyj, ostrov I 76 60.02 N 28.02 E
Malyj An'uj ≃ 74 68.30 N 160.49 E
Malyj Čeremšan ≃ 80 54.18 N 50.01 E
Malyj Chamar-Daban, chrebet ʌ 88 51.00 N 105.00 E
Malyj Irgiz ≃ 80 52.12 N 47.58 E
Malyj Jenisej (Ka-Chem) ≃ 88 51.43 N 94.26 E
Malyj Jugan ≃ 86 60.40 N 73.54 E
Malyj Kavkaz ʌ 84 41.00 N 44.35 E
Malyj Kundyš ≃ 80 56.22 N 47.53 E
Malyj Šantar, ostrov I 89 54.30 N 137.36 E
Malyj Sarybulak 86 52.10 N 72.35 E
Malyj Tajmyr, ostrov I 74 78.08 N 107.12 E
Malyj T'uters, ostrov I 76 59.49 N 26.56 E
Malyj Uran ≃ 80 52.30 N 53.01 E
Malyj Uzen' ≃ 80 48.50 N 49.39 E
Malyj Zelenčuk ≃ 84 44.24 N 41.56 E
Malyn' 82 54.36 N 38.40 E
Malyševo 76 57.50 N 35.36 E
Malzéville 58 48.43 N 6.12 E
Mama 88 58.18 N 112.54 E
Mama ≃ 88 58.18 N 112.55 E
Ma Ma Creek ≃ 171a 27.35 S 152.13 E
Mamadyš 80 55.44 N 51.25 E
Mamagota 175e 6.46 S 155.24 E
Mamahuolang 104 42.24 N 124.12 E
Mamajiecun 104 41.26 N 122.51 E
Mamakan 88 57.48 N 114.01 E
Mamaku 172 38.06 S 176.05 E
Mamakwash Lake ⊜ 184 51.38 N 92.56 W
Mamala Bay c 229a 21.18 N 157.57 W
Mamalu Bay c 229a 20.37 N 156.09 W
Mamanguape 250 6.50 S 35.07 W
Mama'o, Hakau ⌒² 174w 21.00 S 175.12 W
Mamara 248 14.14 S 72.35 W
Mamaroneck 210 40.56 N 73.43 W
Mamaroneck ≃ 276 40.57 N 73.44 W
Mamaroneck Harbor c 276 40.56 N 73.43 W
Mamasa 112 2.56 S 119.22 E
Mamasa ≃ 112 3.30 S 119.42 E
Mamba 94 36.07 N 138.55 E
Mambai 255 14.28 S 46.07 W
Mambajao 116 9.15 N 124.43 E
Mambajao, Mount ʌ 116 9.10 N 124.44 E
Mambali 154 4.33 S 32.41 E
Mambalot 116 8.51 N 117.55 E
Mambare ≃ 164 8.20 S 147.55 E
Mambasa 154 1.21 N 29.03 E
Mamberamo ≃ 164 1.26 S 137.53 E
Mambéré ≃ 152 3.31 N 16.03 E
Mambili ≃ 152 0.07 N 16.08 E
Mambrui 154 3.07 S 40.09 E
Mambucaba 256 23.01 S 44.31 W
Mambucaba ≃ 256 23.02 S 44.32 W
Mamburao 116 13.14 N 120.35 E
Mambusao ≃ 116 11.24 N 122.41 E
Mamdūh, Rujm ʌ 132 32.14 N 36.15 E
Mamedkala 84 42.10 N 48.10 E
Mamehaktebo 112 0.08 N 115.32 E
Mamelodi 158 25.43 S 28.18 E
Ma-Me-O Beach 182 52.58 N 113.59 W
Mamera 286c 10.27 N 66.59 W
Mamera, Quebrada ≃ 286c 10.27 N 66.59 W
Mamers 50 48.21 N 0.23 E
Mamfe 152 5.46 N 9.17 E
Mamiá ≃ 250 1.55 S 55.07 W
Mamiá, Lago ⊜ 246 4.15 S 63.03 W
Mamiao 98 35.04 N 116.10 E
Mamie 192 36.07 N 75.50 W
Mamiña 248 20.05 S 69.14 W
Maminigui 150 7.24 N 5.50 W
Mamirolle 58 47.12 N 6.10 E
Mamisonskij, pereval ✕ 84 42.43 N 43.48 E
Maml'utka 86 54.57 N 68.35 E
Mammendorf 60 48.12 N 11.09 E
Mammola 68 38.22 N 16.15 E
Mammoth, Az., U.S. 200 32.43 N 110.38 W
Mammoth, W.V., U.S. 188 38.15 N 81.22 W
Mammoth Cave National Park ♦ 194 37.08 N 86.13 W
Mammoth Lakes 204 37.38 N 118.58 W
Mammoth Pool Reservoir ⊜¹ 226 37.20 N 119.20 W
Mammoth Spring 194 36.29 N 91.32 W
Mamoiada 71 40.13 N 9.17 E
Mamonovo, Ross. 265b 55.36 N 37.49 E
Mamonovo, Ross. 265b 55.41 N 37.19 E
Mamont 279b 40.29 N 79.36 W
Mamontovo, Ross. 86 52.43 N 81.37 E
Mamontovo, Ross. 86 51.45 N 81.25 E
Mamoré ≃ 248 10.23 S 65.23 W
Mamori, Lago ⊜ 246 3.38 S 60.07 W
Mamoriá ≃ 248 7.30 S 66.21 W
Mamou, Guinée 150 10.23 N 12.05 W
Mamou, La., U.S. 194 30.38 N 92.25 W
Mamoutzou 157a 12.47 S 45.14 E
Mampikony 157b 16.06 S 47.38 E
Mampong 150 7.04 N 1.24 W
Mamrāš 84 41.44 N 48.19 E
Mamre 158 33.30 S 18.29 E
Mamry, Jezioro ⊜ 30 54.08 N 21.42 E
Mamuchi 98 35.41 N 118.17 E
Mamué 152 13.35 S 13.13 E
Mamuil, Paso de ✕ 254 39.35 S 71.28 W
Mamuju 112 2.41 S 118.54 E
Mamulique 196 26.08 N 100.20 W
Ma'mūn 140 12.15 N 22.41 E
Mamuno 156 22.16 S 20.01 E
Mamuripi (Manuripe) ≃ 248 11.06 S 67.36 W
Mamuru ≃ 250 2.42 S 56.44 W
Mamykovo 80 54.38 N 50.37 E
Mamyl' 24 61.57 N 56.41 E
Man, C. Iv. 150 7.24 N 7.33 W
Man, India 120 33.51 N 78.32 E
Man, W.V., U.S. 192 37.44 N 81.52 W
Man (Île de)
— Isle of Man □² 44 54.15 N 4.30 W
Man, Isle of
— Isle of Man □² 44 54.15 N 4.30 W
Mana, Guy. fr. 250 5.40 N 53.47 W
Mana, Hi., U.S. 229b 22.02 N 159.46 W
Mana ≃, Guy. fr. 250 5.44 N 53.54 W
Mana ≃, Ross. 86 55.57 N 92.28 E
Manabí □⁴ 246 0.40 S 80.05 W
Manacacías ≃ 246 4.23 N 72.04 W
Manacapuru 246 3.18 S 60.37 W
Manacapuru ≃ 246 3.18 S 60.38 W
Manacle Point ⌃ 42 50.03 N 5.03 W
Manacor 34 39.34 N 3.12 E
Manado 112 1.29 N 124.51 E
Managua 236 12.09 N 86.17 W
Managua □⁵ 236 12.00 N 86.25 W
Managua, Aeropuerto ⊗ 286b 23.00 N 82.17 W
Managua, Lago de ⊜ 236 12.20 N 86.20 W
Manahawkin 208 39.41 N 74.15 W
Manahawkin Bay c 208 39.40 N 74.12 W
Manaia 172 39.33 S 174.08 E
Manā'if, Bi'r al- ⌒⁴ 142 30.31 N 32.12 E
Manajenki 76 53.42 N 36.27 E
Manakalampona ʌ 157b 15.23 S 48.50 E
Manakara 157b 22.08 S 48.01 E
Manakau 172 40.43 S 175.13 E
Manakau ʌ 172 42.14 S 173.37 E
Manākhah 144 15.07 N 43.44 E
Manalapan Brook ≃ 276 40.24 N 74.23 W
Manāli 123 32.15 N 77.10 E
Manama
— Al-Manāmah 128 26.13 N 50.35 E
Manamansalo I 26 64.21 N 27.04 E
Manambaho ≃ 157b 17.41 S 44.04 E
Manambato, Madag. 157b 13.14 S 49.43 E
Manambato, Madag. 157b 13.43 S 49.07 E
Manambolo ≃ 157b 19.18 S 44.24 E
Manambolosy 157b 16.02 S 49.40 E
Manam Island I 164 4.05 S 145.05 E
Manámo, Caño ≃¹ 246 9.55 N 62.16 W
Manamoc Island I 116 11.19 N 120.41 E
Manana Island I 229c 21.20 N 157.40 W
Manantantana ≃ 157b 21.25 S 45.33 E
Manaoag 116 13.30 N 120.34 E
Mananara 157b 16.10 S 49.46 E
Mananara ≃ 157b 23.21 S 47.42 E
Mananjary 157b 19.19 S 45.23 E
Manankoro 157b 21.13 S 48.20 E
Manantenina 150 10.28 N 7.28 W
Manantiales Behr 157b 24.17 S 47.19 E
Manaoag 254 45.41 S 67.31 W
Manaos 116 16.03 N 120.29 E
— Manaus 246 3.08 S 60.01 W
Manapatrana 157b 21.40 S 47.35 E
Manapiare ≃ 246 5.04 N 66.30 W
Manapire ≃ 246 7.42 N 66.07 W
Manapla 116 10.58 N 123.07 E
Mana Point ⌃ 229b 22.03 N 159.47 W
Mana Pools National Park ♦ 154 16.00 S 28.35 E
Manapouri 172 45.34 S 167.36 E
Manapouri, Lake ⊜ 172 45.30 S 167.30 E
Manappārai 122 10.36 N 78.25 E
Manaquiri, Lago ⊜ 246 3.29 S 60.31 W
Manār ≃ 122 18.39 N 77.44 E
Manaravolo 157b 23.59 S 45.39 E
Manas, Som. 144 2.57 N 43.28 E
Manas, Zhg. 86 44.18 N 86.13 E
Manās ≃, Asia 120 26.13 N 90.38 E
Manas ≃, Zhg. 86 45.38 N 85.12 E
Manas, gora ʌ 85 42.18 N 71.01 E
Manasarowar Lake
— Mapam Yumco ⊜ 120 30.42 N 81.27 E
Manas Hu ⊜ 86 45.45 N 85.55 E
Manāslu ʌ 124 28.33 N 84.33 E
Manasota Key I 220 26.58 N 82.23 W
Manasquan 208 40.07 N 74.02 W
Manasquan ≃ 208 40.06 N 74.02 W
Manassa 200 37.10 N 105.56 W
Manassas 208 38.45 N 77.28 W
Manassas National Battlefield Park ♦ 208 38.50 N 77.32 W
Manassas Park 208 38.46 N 77.27 W
Manastash Creek ≃ 224 46.59 N 120.35 W
Manastash Creek, North Fork ≃ 224 46.57 N 120.44 W
Manastash Creek, South Fork ≃ 224 46.57 N 120.44 W
Manastash Ridge ʌ 224 46.55 N 120.30 W
Manatang 112 8.26 S 124.28 E
Manatawny 208 40.17 N 75.41 W
Manatawny Creek ≃ 208 40.14 N 75.39 W
Manatee ≃⁶ 220 27.26 N 82.25 W
Manatee ≃ 220 27.32 N 82.38 W
Manatee, Lake ⊜¹ 220 27.29 N 82.20 W
Manatí, Col. 246 10.27 N 74.58 W
Manatí, Cuba 240p 21.19 N 76.56 W
Manatí, P.R. 240m 18.26 N 66.29 W
Manatí ≃ 240m 18.29 N 66.29 W
Manatí, Bahía de c 240p 21.24 N 76.48 W
Manatuto 112 8.30 S 126.01 E
Manaul 116 12.27 N 121.25 E
Manaure 110 18.51 N 93.44 E
Manaus 246 3.08 S 60.01 W
Manavgat 130 36.47 N 31.26 E
Manawa 190 44.27 N 88.55 W
Mānāwāla 123 31.35 N 73.41 E
Manawan Lake ⊜ 184 55.24 N 103.14 W
Manāwar 120 22.14 N 75.05 E
Manawatu ≃ 172 40.28 S 175.13 E
Manawoka, Pulau I 164 4.05 S 131.20 E
Manay 116 7.13 N 126.32 E
Manayunk ✦⁸ 285 40.01 N 75.13 W
Manazuru 94 35.09 N 139.08 E
Manazuru-misaki ⌃ 94 35.08 N 139.10 E
Manban 102 23.04 N 103.11 E
Mānbāzār 126 23.04 N 86.39 E
Manbian 102 24.19 N 100.32 E
Manbij 130 36.31 N 37.57 E
Manby 44 53.22 N 0.06 E
Mancelona 190 44.54 N 85.03 W
Mancha Blanca 254 40.47 S 65.27 W
Mancha Real 34 37.47 N 3.37 W
Manchaug 207 42.05 N 71.44 W
Mancha □⁵ 32 49.00 N 1.10 W
Mancheng 105 38.56 N 115.20 E
Mancherāl 122 18.52 N 79.26 E
Manchester, Eng., U.K. 44 53.28 N 2.15 W
Manchester, Eng., U.K. 262 53.28 N 2.15 W
Manchester, Ct., U.S. 207 41.46 N 72.31 W
Manchester, Ga., U.S. 192 32.51 N 84.37 W
Manchester, Il., U.S. 219 39.33 N 90.20 W
Manchester, Ia., U.S. 190 42.29 N 91.27 W
Manchester, Ky., U.S. 192 37.09 N 83.45 W
Manchester, Md., U.S. 208 39.39 N 76.53 W
Manchester, Ma., U.S. 207 42.34 N 70.46 W
Manchester, Mi., U.S. 216 42.09 N 84.02 W
Manchester, N.H., U.S. 188 42.59 N 71.27 W
Manchester, N.Y., U.S. 210 42.58 N 77.13 W
Manchester, Oh., U.S. 218 38.41 N 83.36 W
Manchester, Pa., U.S. 208 40.03 N 76.43 W
Manchester, Tn., U.S. 194 35.28 N 86.05 W
Manchester, Vt., U.S. 210 43.09 N 73.04 W
Manchester, Wa., U.S. 224 47.33 N 122.33 W
Manchester □⁸ 262 53.27 N 2.13 W
Manchester Airport ⊗ 44 53.21 N 2.15 W
Manchester Bridge 210 41.41 N 73.52 W
Manchester City Football Ground ♦ 262 53.27 N 2.14 W
Manchester Docks ✦⁵ 262 53.28 N 2.17 W
Manchester Race Course ♦ 262 53.30 N 2.16 W
Manchester Ship Canal ☲ 262 53.19 N 2.57 W
Manchester United Football Ground ♦ 262 53.28 N 2.18 W
Manching 60 48.43 N 11.30 E
Manchioneal 241q 18.02 N 76.17 W
Manchón 236 14.23 N 92.02 W
Manchouli
— Manzhouli 88 49.35 N 117.22 E
Manchuria □⁹ 90 47.00 N 125.00 E
Manciano 66 42.35 N 11.31 E
Mancieulles 56 49.17 N 5.53 E
Máncora 246 4.06 S 81.05 W
Mancos 200 37.20 N 108.17 W
Mancos ≃ 200 36.59 N 108.59 W
Mand 128 26.07 N 62.03 E
Mand ≃, India 120 21.42 N 83.15 E
Mand ≃, Īrān 128 28.11 N 51.17 E
Manda, India 126 22.06 N 86.14 E
Manda, Tan. 154 7.58 S 32.26 E
Manda, Tan. 154 8.30 S 32.44 E
Manda, Tan. 154 10.28 S 34.35 E
Manda, Tchad 146 9.12 N 18.10 E
Manda, Jabal ʌ 140 8.39 N 24.27 E
Mandabe, Madag. 157b 21.03 S 44.55 E
Mandabe, Madag. 157b 20.55 S 45.49 E
Mandach 102 44.28 N 108.11 E
Mandaguari 255 23.32 S 51.42 W
Mandai Orchard Gardens ♦ 271c 1.24 N 103.47 E
Manda Island I 154 2.15 S 40.57 E
Mandal 26 58.02 N 7.27 E
Mandal, Jibāl ʌ² 140 12.09 N 29.31 E
Mandala, Puncak ʌ 164 4.44 S 140.20 E
Mandalay 110 22.00 N 96.05 E
Mandalay □⁸ 110 21.00 N 96.00 E
Mandalay 116 41.01 N 84.20 W
Mandale Station ✦⁵ 272c 19.03 N 72.56 E
Mandalgov' 102 45.45 N 106.12 E
Mandalī 128 33.45 N 45.32 E
Mandalkia 272b 22.43 N 88.08 E
Mandal-Ovoo 102 44.35 N 104.05 E
Mandalselva ≃ 26 58.02 N 7.28 E
Mandaluyong 269f 14.35 N 121.02 E
Mandan 198 46.49 N 100.53 W
Mandanici 70 38.00 N 15.19 E
Mandāoli ✦⁸ 272a 28.38 N 77.18 E
Mandaon 116 12.14 N 123.17 E
Mandapur 126 23.00 N 88.29 E
Mandar, Teluk c 112 3.40 S 119.15 E
Mandara Mountains (Monts Mandara) ʌ 146 10.45 N 13.40 E
Mandas 71 39.38 N 9.07 E
Mandatoriccio 68 39.28 N 16.50 E
Mandau ≃ 114 0.48 N 101.47 E
Mandaue 116 10.20 N 123.56 E
Mandāwar 124 29.30 N 78.08 E
Mandeb, Bab el ⊔ 144 12.40 N 43.20 E
Mandehu 102 42.07 N 121.33 E
Mandel 128 33.17 N 61.52 E
Mandélia 146 11.43 N 15.15 E
Mandelieu 62 43.33 N 6.56 E
Mandello del Lario 58 45.55 N 9.19 E
Mandera 154 3.56 N 41.52 E
Manderfeld 56 50.20 N 6.20 E
Manderscheid 56 50.05 N 6.49 E
Manderson 202 44.16 N 107.57 W
Mandeure 58 47.27 N 6.48 E
Mandeville, P.Q., Can. 206 46.22 N 73.22 W
Mandeville, Jam. 241q 18.02 N 77.30 W
Mandeville, N.Z. 172 46.00 S 168.49 E
Mandeville, La., U.S. 194 30.21 N 90.03 W
Mandi 123 31.43 N 76.55 E
Mandiana 150 10.38 N 8.41 W
Mandiangin 112 2.01 S 102.58 E
Mandi Angin, Gunong ʌ 114 4.42 N 102.52 E
Mandi Bahāuddīn 123 32.35 N 73.30 E
Mandi Būrewāla 123 30.09 N 72.41 E
Mandi Dabwāli 123 29.58 N 74.42 E
Mandié 154 16.30 S 33.30 E
Mandimba 154 14.21 S 35.39 E
Mandini 158 29.09 S 31.23 E
Mandioli, Pulau I 108 0.44 S 127.14 E
Mandioré, Lagoa ⊜ 248 18.08 S 57.33 W
Mandira ⊜¹ 124 22.20 N 84.35 E
Mandiri ≃ 115a 7.02 S 106.32 E
Mandi Sādiqganj 123 30.10 N 73.44 E
Mandjafa 146 11.11 N 15.25 E
Mandjé, Lac ⊜ 152 2.50 S 10.22 E
Mandji 152 1.36 S 10.26 E
Mandla 120 22.36 N 80.23 E
Mandora 162 19.44 S 120.51 E
Mandoto 157b 19.34 S 46.17 E
Mandoul ≃ 146 8.56 N 17.58 E
Mandouri 150 10.51 N 0.49 E
Mandra, Ellás 267c 38.04 N 23.30 E
Māndrā, India 272b 22.55 N 88.07 E
Mandra, Pāk. 123 33.22 N 73.14 E
Mandrare ≃ 157b 25.10 S 46.27 E
Mandres-les-Roses 261 48.42 N 2.33 E
Mandriola ✦⁸ 267a 41.45 N 12.30 E
Mandriole 62 44.36 N 12.15 E
Mandrioli, Passo dei ✕ 64 43.48 N 11.55 E
Mandritsara 157b 15.50 S 48.49 E
Mandronarivo 157b 21.07 S 45.38 E
Māndu 120 22.22 N 75.23 E
Mandu, Ribeirão do ≃ 256 22.14 S 45.55 W
Manduba, Ponta ⌃ 256 24.05 S 46.18 W
Manduhu 104 41.36 N 122.38 E
Mandun 102 22.17 N 100.05 E
Mandurah 168a 32.32 S 115.43 E
Manduria 68 40.24 N 17.38 E
Māndvi, India 120 21.15 N 73.18 E
Māndvi, India 120 22.50 N 69.22 E
Mandvi ✦⁸ 272c 18.57 N 72.50 E
Mandya 122 12.33 N 76.54 E
Mané 150 12.59 N 1.21 W
Måne ≃ 26 59.00 N 9.40 E
Manea 42 52.30 N 0.11 E
Manebach 54 50.41 N 10.51 E
Manek Urai 114 5.23 N 102.14 E
Manendragarh 124 23.13 N 82.13 E
Manera 157b 22.55 S 44.20 E
Manerbio 64 45.21 N 10.08 E
Manětin 60 49.59 N 13.14 E
Manevič 78 51.17 N 25.33 E
Manfalūṭ 142 27.19 N 30.58 E
Manfredonia 68 41.38 N 15.55 E
Manfredonia, Golfo di c 68 41.35 N 16.05 E
Manga, Bra. 255 14.46 S 43.56 W
Manga, Burkina 150 11.40 N 1.04 W
Manga, Ur. 258 34.49 S 56.06 W
Manga ✦¹ 146 15.00 N 14.00 E
Mangabeiras, Chapada das ʌ² 250 10.00 S 46.30 W
Mangagoy 116 8.11 N 126.21 E
Mangahao ≃ 172 40.23 S 175.50 E
Mangai 164 2.45 S 151.05 E
Mangaia I 14 21.55 S 157.55 W
Mangakino 172 38.22 S 175.47 E
Mangala 152 1.02 N 23.50 E
Mangalagiri 122 16.26 N 80.33 E
Mangaldai 120 26.26 N 92.02 E
Mangaldan 116 16.04 N 120.24 E
Mangalia 38 43.50 N 28.35 E
Mangalkot 126 23.33 N 87.54 E
Mangalmé 146 12.21 N 19.37 E
Mangalore 122 12.52 N 74.53 E
Mangalpaita 126 23.19 N 89.11 E
Mangalvedha 122 17.31 N 75.28 E
Mangamahu 172 39.49 S 175.22 E
Manganês ≃ 250 10.21 S 48.27 W
Manganji 268 35.40 N 139.26 E
Mangaoka 157b 12.19 S 49.07 E
Mangapehi 172 38.31 S 175.18 E
Mangaratiba 256 22.57 S 44.02 W
Mangarin, Monte (Mangrt) ʌ 64 46.25 N 13.40 E
Mangatarem 116 15.47 N 120.17 E
Mangawān 124 24.41 N 81.33 E
Mangaweka 172 39.48 S 175.47 E
Mangaweka ʌ 172 39.49 S 176.05 E
Mangcao Point ⌃ 116 11.02 N 123.54 E
Mangchang 102 25.08 N 107.21 E
Mangde ≃ 124 27.35 N 90.28 E
Mange, S.L. 150 8.55 N 12.51 W
Mange, Zaïre 152 0.54 N 20.30 E
Mange, Zhg. 102 32.25 N 83.35 E
Mangeigne 146 10.31 N 21.19 E
Mangerton Mountain ʌ 48 51.57 N 9.29 W
Mangfall ≃ 64 47.51 N 12.08 E
Manggar 112 2.53 S 108.16 E
Manggeng 114 3.36 N 96.55 E
Manggonggri 164 3.30 S 133.19 E
Mangguar, Tanjung ⌃ 164 2.53 S 134.51 E
Mangham 194 32.18 N 91.46 W
Mangichu ≃ 126 23.24 N 90.48 E
Mangindrano 157b 14.17 S 48.58 E
Mangin Range ʌ 110 24.20 N 95.42 E
Mangistau □⁸ 86 44.00 N 54.30 E
Mangkalihat, Tanjung ⌃ 112 1.02 N 118.59 E
Mangkutana 112 2.24 S 120.48 E
Manglares, Cabo ⌃ 246 1.36 N 79.02 W
Mangla Reservoir ⊜¹ 123 33.10 N 73.40 E
Manglaur 124 29.48 N 77.52 E
Manglisi 84 41.43 N 44.24 E
Mangnai 120 37.40 N 91.50 E
Mangniu ≃, Zhg. 104 41.45 N 120.53 E
Mangniu ≃, Zhg. 105 39.04 N 115.26 E
Mangnuiyingzi 104 41.01 N 121.54 E
Mango 220 28.00 N 82.19 W
Mangochi 154 14.28 S 35.16 E
Mango Island I 175g 17.27 S 179.09 W
Mangoky ≃, Madag. 157b 21.29 S 43.41 E
Mangoky ≃, Madag. 157b 23.27 S 45.13 E
Mangole, Pulau I 112 1.53 S 125.50 E
Mangombe 154 1.25 S 26.54 E
Mangone 68 39.12 N 16.20 E
Mangonia Park 220 26.46 N 80.05 W
Mangonui 172 34.59 S 173.32 E
Mangoplah 171b 35.23 S 147.15 E
Mangoro ≃ 157b 20.00 S 48.45 E
Mangotsfield 42 51.28 N 2.28 W
Mangoupa 140 5.53 N 24.40 E
Māngrol 120 21.07 N 70.07 E
Mangrove Cay I 238 24.10 N 77.45 W
Mangrove Creek ≃ 170 33.28 S 151.10 E
Mangrove Creek Dam ✦⁶ 170 33.13 S 151.07 E
Mangrove Mountain 170 33.19 S 151.14 E
Mangrove Point ⌃ 220 26.56 N 82.08 W
Mangrt (Monte Mangart) ʌ 64 46.25 N 13.40 E
Mangrullo, Cuchilla ʌ² 258 34.34 S 56.42 W
Mangrūl Pīr 122 20.19 N 77.21 E
Mångsälven ≃ 40 59.59 N 14.36 E
Mangshi 112 2.10 S 104.00 E
Mangu ≃ 273b 4.24 S 15.24 E
Mangualde 34 40.36 N 7.46 W
Mangueira, Lagoa c 252 33.06 S 52.48 W
Mangueirinha 255 25.57 S 52.09 W
Manguéni, Plateau du ʌ¹ 146 22.35 N 12.40 E
Mangui 89 52.03 N 122.13 E
Manguito 240p 22.35 N 80.55 W
Mangulile 236 15.03 N 86.49 W
Mangum 196 34.52 N 99.30 W
Mangupung I 152 5.13 S 19.35 E
Mangup, Ross. 76 51.36 N 38.28 E
Mangut, Ross. 88 49.46 N 112.38 E
Mangya 98 37.40 N 90.50 E
Man'gyŏng 98 35.52 N 126.48 E
Manhan ≃ 207 42.17 N 72.38 W
Manhartsberg ʌ 61 48.32 N 15.44 E
Manhasset 276 40.47 N 73.42 W
Manhasset Bay c 276 40.50 N 73.43 W
Manhasset Hills 276 40.46 N 73.41 W
Manhasset Neck ⌃¹ 276 40.50 N 73.42 W
Manhattan, Il., U.S. 216 41.25 N 87.59 W
Manhattan, Ks., U.S. 198 39.11 N 96.34 W
Manhattan, Mt., U.S. 202 45.51 N 111.19 W
Manhattan □⁸ 276 40.47 N 73.58 W
Manhattan Beach 228 33.53 N 118.24 W
Manhattan Beach State Park ♦ 280 33.54 N 118.25 W
Manhattan Bridge ✦⁵ 276 40.42 N 73.59 W
Manhattan College ✦² 276 40.53 N 73.54 W
Manheim 208 40.09 N 76.23 W
Manhiça 156 25.24 S 32.48 E
Mān Hpāng 110 22.41 N 98.36 E
Manhuaçu 255 20.15 S 42.02 W
Manhumirim 255 20.22 S 41.57 W
Maní, P.R. 240m 18.15 N 67.10 W
Māni, Zaïre 154 6.27 S 25.20 E
Māni', Jabal al- ʌ 132 33.19 N 36.17 E
Mania ≃ 157b 19.42 S 45.22 E
Maniago 64 46.10 N 12.43 E
Maniamba 154 12.43 S 35.00 E
Manianga 273b 4.10 S 15.19 E
Manica □⁵ 156 19.00 S 33.15 E
Manicahan 116 7.01 N 122.12 E
Manicaland □⁴ 154 19.30 S 32.15 E
Manicani Island I 116 10.59 N 125.38 E
Manicaragua 240p 22.09 N 79.58 W
Manic Deux, Réservoir ⊜¹ 186 49.25 N 68.25 W
Manicoré 248 5.49 S 61.17 W
Manicoré ≃ 248 5.51 S 61.19 W
Manicouagan ≃ 186 49.11 N 68.13 W
Manicouagan, Réservoir ⊜¹ 186 51.30 N 68.19 W
Manic Trois, Réservoir ⊜¹ 186 50.00 N 68.40 W
Manifold ⌃ 44 53.03 N 1.47 W
Maniganggo 102 32.01 N 99.11 E
Manignan 150 10.00 N 7.50 W
Manigotagan 184 51.06 N 96.18 W
Manigotagan ≃ 184 51.07 N 96.20 W
Manihāri 124 25.21 N 87.38 E
Manihiki I¹ 14 10.24 S 161.01 W
Manika, Plateau de la ʌ¹ 154 10.00 S 26.00 E
Manikanäli 126 23.19 N 87.03 E
Mānikganj 124 23.52 N 90.00 E
Mānikpur 124 25.04 N 81.07 E
Manila, Pil. 116 14.35 N 121.00 E
Manila, Pil. 269f 14.35 N 121.00 E
Manila, Ar., U.S. 194 35.52 N 90.10 W
Manila, Ut., U.S. 200 40.59 N 109.43 W
Manila Bay c 116 14.30 N 120.45 E
Manila Cathedral ✝¹ 269f 14.35 N 120.59 E
Manila International Airport ⊗ 269f 14.31 N 121.01 E
Manilla, Austl. 166 30.45 S 150.43 E
Manilla, In., U.S. 218 39.34 N 85.37 W
Manilla, Ia., U.S. 198 41.53 N 95.13 W
Manille
— Manila 116 14.35 N 121.00 E
Manily 74 62.29 N 165.36 E
Mani Majra 123 30.43 N 76.50 E
Manimbaya, Tanjung ⌃ 112 0.01 N 119.36 E
Manimpé 150 14.09 N 5.31 W
Maningory ≃ 157b 17.13 S 49.28 E
Maningrida 164 12.03 S 134.13 E
Maninjau, Danau ⊜ 112 0.20 S 100.11 E
Manino 76 53.58 N 34.20 E
Manipa, Pulau I 164 3.17 S 127.35 E
Manipa, Selat ⊔ 164 3.20 S 127.23 E
Manipur □³ 120 25.00 N 94.00 E
Manipur ≃ 110 22.52 N 94.05 E
Manique de Baixo 266c 38.44 N 9.22 W
Maniquin Island I 116 11.36 N 121.45 E
Manirāmpur 126 23.01 N 89.14 E
Manisa 130 38.36 N 27.26 E
Manisa □⁴ 130 38.50 N 28.10 E
Manissauá-Miçu ≃ 250 10.58 S 53.20 W
Manistee 190 44.14 N 86.19 W
Manistee ≃ 190 44.15 N 86.21 W
Manistique 190 45.57 N 86.14 W
Manistique ≃ 190 45.57 N 86.15 W
Manistique, West Branch ≃ 190 46.02 N 86.09 W
Manistique Lake ⊜ 190 46.15 N 85.45 W
Manito 190 40.25 N 89.46 W
Manitoba □⁴, Can. 176 54.00 N 97.00 W
Manitoba □⁴, Can. 184 54.00 N 97.00 W
Manitoba, Lake ⊜ 184 51.00 N 98.45 W
Manitou 184 49.15 N 98.31 W
Manitou ≃, On., Can. 184 48.58 N 93.20 W
Manitou ≃, P.Q., Can. 186 50.18 N 65.15 W
Manitou, Lac ⊜, P.Q., Can. 186 50.29 N 63.54 W
Manitou, Lac ⊜, P.Q., Can. 186 50.54 N 65.18 W
Manitou, Lac ⊜, P.Q., Can. 206 46.03 N 74.23 W
Manitou, Lake ⊜, On., Can. 190 45.48 N 82.00 W
Manitou, Lake ⊜, In., U.S. 216 41.03 N 86.11 W
Manitou Beach, Sk., Can. 184 51.43 N 105.26 W
Manitou Beach, Mi., U.S. 216 41.58 N 84.19 W
Manitou Lake ⊜, On., Can. 190 46.01 N 79.00 W
Manitou Lake ⊜, Sk., Can. 184 52.45 N 109.45 W
Manitoulin Island I 190 45.50 N 82.20 W
Manitou Springs 200 38.51 N 104.55 W
Manitouwabing Lake ⊜ 212 45.29 N 79.54 W
Manitowaning 190 45.45 N 81.49 W
Manitowik Lake ⊜ 190 48.10 N 84.24 W
Manitowish Waters 190 46.09 N 89.53 W
Manitowoc 190 44.05 N 87.39 W
Manitowoc ≃ 190 44.05 N 87.39 W
Maniwaki 188 46.23 N 75.58 W
Manīyā 142 30.50 N 30.59 E
Manizales 246 5.05 N 75.32 W
Manja, Madag. 157b 21.26 S 44.20 E
Manjā, Urd. 132 31.45 N 35.51 E
Manjacaze 156 24.44 S 33.53 E
Manjakandriana 157b 18.55 S 47.47 E
Manjeri 122 11.07 N 76.07 E
Manjiang 98 41.57 N 127.36 E
Manjimup 162 34.14 S 116.09 E
Manjing 107 29.55 N 104.07 E
Mānjra ≃ 122 18.49 N 77.52 E
Manjuyod 116 9.41 N 123.09 E
Mank 61 48.06 N 15.20 E
Mankanaj 86 48.58 N 60.58 E
Mankarbo 80 60.14 N 17.28 E
Man Kāt 110 22.05 N 98.01 E
Mankato, Ks., U.S. 198 39.47 N 98.12 W
Mankato, Mn., U.S. 190 44.09 N 93.59 W
Mankayane 158 26.42 S 31.00 E
Mankeri 85 42.55 N 69.50 E
Mankera 123 31.23 N 71.26 E
Mankim 152 5.01 N 12.00 E
Mankinholes 262 53.42 N 2.03 W
Mankono 150 8.04 N 6.12 W
Mankota 184 49.25 N 107.04 W
Man'kovka, Ukr. 78 48.58 N 30.20 E
Man'kovka, Ukr. 83 49.34 N 38.27 E
Man'kovo 83 49.24 N 40.17 E
Man'kovo-Ber'ozovskaja 80 48.47 N 41.33 E
Mankoya 154 14.47 S 24.48 E
Mānkundu 272b 22.50 N 88.22 E
Mānkur, India 126 22.30 N 87.54 E
Mānkur, India 126 23.20 N 87.33 E
Manlaj 102 44.07 N 106.50 E
Manley 262 53.14 N 2.45 W
Manley Hot Springs 180 65.00 N 150.37 W
Manleys Corner 283 42.03 N 71.04 W
Manlius 210 43.00 N 75.58 W
Manlleu 34 42.00 N 2.17 E
Manly, Austl. 170 33.48 S 151.17 E
Manly, Austl. 171a 27.28 S 153.11 E
Manly, Ia., U.S. 190 43.17 N 93.12 W
Manly Warringah War Memorial Park ♦ 274a 33.46 S 151.15 E
Manmād 122 20.15 N 74.27 E
Mann ≃ 164 12.20 S 134.07 E
Mann, Mount ʌ 162 25.59 S 129.42 E
Manna, Indon. 112 4.27 S 102.55 E
Mān Nā, Mya. 110 23.27 N 97.14 E
Mannahill 166 32.26 S 139.59 E
Mannar 122 8.59 N 79.54 E
Mannar, Gulf of c 122 8.30 N 79.00 E
Mannārgudi 122 10.40 N 79.26 E
Mannar Island I 122 9.03 N 79.50 E
Mann Creek ≃ 281 42.32 N 83.44 W
Männedorf 58 47.15 N 8.42 E
Mannersdorf am Leithagebirge 61 47.58 N 16.36 E
Mannersdorf an der Rabnitz 61 47.25 N 16.31 E
Mannford 196 36.09 N 96.23 W
Mannheim 56 49.29 N 8.29 E
Manni 120 34.48 N 87.15 E
Manning, Ia., U.S. 198 41.54 N 95.03 W
Manning, N.D., U.S. 198 47.13 N 102.46 W
Manning, S.C., U.S. 192 33.41 N 80.12 W
Manning, Cape ⌃ 174o 2.02 N 157.26 W
Manning Provincial Park ♦ 224 49.07 N 120.54 W
Manning Strait ⊔ 175e 7.24 S 158.00 E
Mannington 188 39.31 N 80.20 W
Manningtree 42 51.57 N 1.04 E
Mannō 96 34.11 N 133.51 E
Mann Ranges ʌ 162 26.00 S 129.30 E
Mannsville 212 43.42 N 76.03 W
Mannswörth ✦⁸ 264b 48.09 N 16.31 E
Mannu 71 39.18 N 8.58 E
Mannu ≃ 71 40.50 N 8.23 E
Mannu, Capo ⌃ 71 40.47 N 8.09 E
Mannu, Monte ʌ 71 40.23 N 8.25 E
Mannum 166 34.55 S 139.18 E
Mannus 171b 35.48 S 147.57 E
Mannus Creek ≃ 171b 35.58 S 148.03 E
Mannville 182 53.20 N 111.10 W
Mano 150 8.02 N 12.06 W
Mano ≃ 150 6.56 N 11.31 W
Manoa 248 9.40 S 65.27 W
Manoel Ribas 252 24.31 S 51.39 W
Manohardi 126 24.08 N 90.43 E
Manoharpur, India 124 22.23 N 85.12 E
Manoharpur, India 126 21.59 N 87.18 E
Manokin ≃ 208 38.05 N 75.55 W
Manokotak 180 58.40 N 159.09 W
Manokwari 164 0.52 S 134.05 E
Manolo Fortich (Maluko) 116 8.25 N 124.58 E
Manoma ≃ 89 49.18 N 136.37 E
Manombo 157b 22.57 S 43.28 E
Manomet 207 41.55 N 70.34 W
Manomet Hill ʌ² 207 41.55 N 70.36 W
Manong 114 4.36 N 100.53 E
Manonga ≃ 154 4.08 S 34.12 E
Manono 154 7.18 S 27.25 E
Manono I 175a 13.50 S 172.05 W
Manora 168b 34.00 S 138.49 E
Manoppello 66 42.15 N 14.03 E
Manor, Sk., Can. 184 49.36 N 102.05 W
Manor, Pa., U.S. 214 40.20 N 79.40 W
Manor, Tx., U.S. 222 30.20 N 97.33 W
Manorbier 42 51.39 N 4.48 W
Manorhamilton 48 54.18 N 8.10 W
Manorhaven 276 40.50 N 73.42 W
Manor Hill 214 40.38 N 77.55 W
Manori ✦⁸ 272c 19.12 N 72.47 E
Manori Creek c 272c 19.12 N 72.48 E
Manorina National Park ♦ 171a 27.23 S 152.47 E
Manori Point ⌃ 272c 19.11 N 72.47 E
Manorom 110 11.38 N 99.04 E
Manorville 214 40.47 N 79.31 W
Manosque 62 43.50 N 5.47 E
Manotick 212 45.13 N 75.41 W
Manouane ≃ 186 49.30 N 71.11 W
Manouane, Lac ⊜ 186 50.41 N 70.45 W
Manouanis ≃ 186 50.28 N 70.08 W
Manouanis, Lac ⊜ 186 50.51 N 70.43 W
Manown 279b 40.13 N 79.54 W
Manpaka 273b 4.18 S 15.12 E
Manpitou 100 22.17 N 112.52 E
Manp'o 98 41.10 N 126.17 E
Mānpur, India 122 20.22 N 80.43 E
Mānpur, India 124 23.46 N 81.08 E
Manqabād 142 27.12 N 31.07 E
Manqatīn 142 28.20 N 30.40 E
Manquehue, Cerro ʌ 286e 33.21 S 70.36 W
Manra I¹ 14 4.27 S 171.15 W
Manresa 34 41.44 N 1.50 E
Manresa Island I 276 41.04 N 73.25 W
Mānsa, India 120 23.26 N 72.40 E
Mānsa, India 123 29.59 N 75.23 E
Mansa (Fort Rosebery), Zam. 154 11.12 S 28.53 E
Mansabá 150 12.18 N 15.15 W
Mansafis 142 28.00 N 30.49 E
Mansalay 116 12.31 N 121.26 E
Mansara 150 13.20 N 4.39 W
Manse ≃ 50 47.08 N 0.25 E
Manseau 206 46.22 N 72.00 W
Mānsehra 123 34.20 N 73.12 E
Mansein 110 25.12 N 95.58 E
Mansel Island I 176 62.00 N 79.50 W
Mansfeld 54 51.35 N 11.27 E
Mansfield, Austl. 169 37.03 S 146.05 E
Mansfield, Eng., U.K. 44 53.09 N 1.11 W
Mansfield, Ar., U.S. 194 35.04 N 94.13 W
Mansfield, Ga., U.S. 192 33.31 N 83.44 W
Mansfield, Il., U.S. 216 40.12 N 88.30 W
Mansfield, La., U.S. 194 32.02 N 93.42 W
Mansfield, Ma., U.S. 207 42.02 N 71.13 W
Mansfield, Mo., U.S. 194 37.06 N 92.34 W
Mansfield, N.J., U.S. 285 40.05 N 74.43 W
Mansfield, Oh., U.S. 214 40.45 N 82.30 W
Mansfield, Pa., U.S. 210 41.48 N 77.04 W
Mansfield, Tx., U.S. 222 32.33 N 97.08 W
Mansfield, Mount ʌ 188 44.33 N 72.49 W
Mansfield Center 207 41.45 N 72.11 W
Mansfield Hollow Lake ⊜¹ 207 41.45 N 72.11 W
Mansfield Hollow State Park ♦ 207 41.46 N 72.10 W
Mansfield Municipal Airport ⊗ 283 42.00 N 71.12 W
Mansfield Woodhouse 44 53.11 N 1.12 W
Man Shan I 106 31.14 N 120.17 E
Mansieville Location 273d 26.05 S 27.45 E
Mansinhapur 272b 22.39 N 88.09 E
Mansión 236 10.06 N 85.22 W
Manskoje belogorje ʌ 88 54.35 N 94.00 E
Mansle 32 45.53 N 0.11 E
Manso ≃ 248 14.42 S 56.16 W
Mansôa 150 12.10 N 14.36 W
Manson, Ia., U.S. 198 42.32 N 94.32 W
Manson, Wa., U.S. 182 47.53 N 120.09 W
Manson ≃ 182 55.42 N 123.47 W
Manson Creek 182 55.41 N 124.29 W
Mansonville 206 45.03 N 72.23 W
Mansourah 36 36.04 N 4.28 E
Mansucum 246 9.02 N 77.49 W
Mansura 194 31.03 N 92.02 W
Mansura
— Al-Manṣūrah 142 31.03 N 31.23 E
Manṣūrīyah, Tur'at al- ☲ 142 31.03 N 31.24 E
Mansurovo 82 55.52 N 36.36 E
Mansus, Ec. 246 0.57 S 80.44 W
Manta, It. 62 44.37 N 7.29 E
Manta, Bahía de c 246 0.54 S 80.42 W
Mantabuan Island I 116 5.02 N 120.13 E
Mantagao ≃ 184 51.50 N 97.48 W
Mantalingajan, Mount ʌ 116 8.48 N 117.40 E
Mantalingajan Range ʌ 116 8.46 N 117.40 E
Mantanani Besar, Pulau I 112 6.45 N 116.17 E
Mantangule Island I 116 8.10 N 117.10 E
Mantantale 152 2.10 S 20.06 E
Mantanzas 123 4.27 S 123.45 E
Mantaro ≃ 248 12.15 S 73.58 W
Manteca 226 37.47 N 121.12 W
Mantecal 246 7.33 N 69.09 W
Mantel 60 49.39 N 12.03 E
Mantena 255 18.47 S 40.59 W

Symbols in the index entries represent the broad categories identified in the key at the right. Symbols with superior numbers (ʌ¹) identify subcategories (see complete key on page *I · 1*).

Symbole im Register stellen die rechts im Schlüssel erklärten Kategorien dar. Symbole mit hochgestellten Ziffern (ʌ¹) bezeichnen Unterabteilungen einer Kategorie (vgl. vollständiger Schlüssel auf Seite *I · 1*).

Los símbolos incluidos en el texto del índice representan las grandes categorías identificadas con la clave a la derecha. Los símbolos con numeros en su parte superior (ʌ¹) identifican las subcategorías (véase la clave completa en la página *I · 1*).

Les symboles de l'index représentent les catégories indiquées dans la légende à droite. Les symboles suivis d'un indice (ʌ¹) représentent des sous-catégories (voir légende complète à la page *I · 1*).

Os símbolos incluídos no texto do índice representam as grandes categorias identificadas com a chave à direita. Os símbolos com números em sua parte superior (ʌ¹) identificam as subcategorias (veja-se a chave completa à página *I · 1*).

	English	Deutsch	Español	Français	Português
ʌ	Mountain	Berg	Montaña	Montagne	Montanha
ʌ	Mountains	Gebirge	Montañas	Montagnes	Montanhas
✕	Pass	Paß	Paso	Col	Passo
V	Valley, Canyon	Tal, Cañon	Valle, Cañón	Vallée, Canyon	Vale, Canhão
≃	Plain	Ebene	Llano	Plaine	Planície
⌃	Cape	Kap	Cabo	Cap	Cabo
I	Island	Insel	Isla	Île	Ilha
II	Islands	Inseln	Islas	Îles	Ilhas
✦	Other Topographic Features	Andere Topographische Objekte	Otros Elementos Topográficos	Autres données topographiques	Outros acidentes topográficos

ESPAÑOL — Nombre, Página, Lat. °′, Long. °′ W = Oeste
FRANÇAIS — Nom, Page, Lat. °′, Long. °′ W = Ouest
PORTUGUÊS — Nome, Página, Lat. °′, Long. °′ W = Oeste

Nombre / Nom / Nome	Página / Page	Lat. °′	Long. °′ W = Oeste
Manteno	216	41.15 N	87.49 W
Manteo	192	35.54 N	75.40 W
Mantes-Chérence, Aérodrome de ⊠	261	49.05 N	1.41 E
Mantes-la-Jolie	50	48.59 N	1.43 E
Mantes-la-Ville	261	48.58 N	1.42 E
Manteswar	126	23.26 N	88.06 E
Manteuil-le-Haudouin	50	49.08 N	2.48 E
Manthelan	50	47.08 N	0.47 E
Manti	200	39.16 N	111.38 W
Manticao	116	8.24 N	124.17 E
Mantilla ⬥[8]	286b	23.04 N	82.20 W
Mantin	114	2.49 N	101.54 E
Mantiqueira, Serra da ⩘	256	22.00 S	44.45 W
Mantok	112	1.09 S	123.14 E
Manton	190	44.24 N	85.23 W
Mantorville	190	44.04 N	92.45 W
Mantos Blancos	252	23.25 S	70.05 W
Mantou	104	42.27 N	122.26 E
Mantova	64	45.09 N	10.48 E
Mantova □[4]	64	45.10 N	10.47 E
Māntri	126	21.39 N	86.49 E
Mänttä	26	62.02 N	24.38 E
Mantua, Cuba	240p	22.17 N	84.17 W
Mantua, N.J., U.S.	208	39.47 N	75.10 W
Mantua, Oh., U.S.	214	41.17 N	81.13 W
Mantua, Va., U.S.	284c	38.51 N	77.15 W
Mantua ≃	240p	22.12 N	84.25 W
Mantua Creek ≃	285	39.51 N	75.14 W
Mantua Creek, Chestnut Branch ≃	285	39.47 N	75.10 W
Mantua Creek, Porch Branch ≃	285	39.46 N	75.07 W
Mantua Hills	284c	38.51 N	77.16 W
Mantua → Mantova	64	45.09 N	10.48 E
Mantua Terrace	285	39.48 N	75.10 W
Manturovo, Ross.	78	51.28 N	37.07 E
Manturovo, Ross.	80	58.20 N	44.46 E
Mäntyharju	26	61.25 N	26.53 E
Mäntyluoto	26	61.35 N	21.29 E
Manu	248	12.15 S	70.50 W
Manú ≃	248	12.16 S	70.51 W
Manu, Parque Nacional del ♠	248	12.15 S	71.40 W
Manuae I[1], Cook Is.	14	19.21 S	158.56 W
Manuae I[1], Poly. fr.	14	16.30 S	154.40 W
Manua Islands II	174y	14.13 S	169.35 W
Manuel	234	22.44 N	98.19 W
Manuel Alves ≃	250	11.19 S	48.28 W
Manuel Alves Grande ≃	250	7.27 S	47.35 W
Manuel Antonio, Parque Nacional ♠	236	9.25 N	84.10 W
Manuel Avila Camacho, Presa ⊜[1]	234	18.55 N	98.10 W
Manuel Benavides	232	29.05 N	103.55 W
Manuel Derqui	252	27.50 S	58.48 W
Manuel Duarte	256	22.06 S	43.34 W
Manuel Ribeiro	256	22.54 S	42.47 W
Manuel Rodríguez, Isla I	254	52.35 S	73.50 W
Manuel Urbano	248	8.53 S	69.18 W
Manués-Açu ≃	250	3.22 S	57.44 W
Manuguru	122	17.59 N	80.43 E
Manuhangi I[1]	14	19.12 S	141.16 W
Manuherikia ≃	172	45.16 S	169.24 E
Manui, Pulau I	112	3.35 S	123.08 E
Manuilovskaja	76	60.29 N	40.40 E
Manu Island I	164	1.17 S	143.35 E
Manūjān	128	27.24 N	57.32 E
Manuk ≃	115a	6.14 S	108.13 E
Manuk, Pulau I	164	5.33 S	130.18 E
Manukan	116	8.31 N	123.06 E
Manukau	172	37.02 S	174.54 E
Manukau Harbour ⊂	172	37.01 S	174.44 E
Manulla ≃	48	53.57 N	9.12 W
Manulu Lagoon ⊂	174o	1.56 N	157.20 W
Manumuskin ≃	208	39.18 N	75.00 W
Manundi, Tanjung ›	164	0.38 S	135.22 E
Manunui	172	38.53 S	175.20 E
Manuoha ∧	172	38.39 S	177.07 E
Manuripe (Mamuripi) ≃	248	11.06 S	67.36 W
Manuripi ≃	248	11.42 S	67.16 W
Manursing Island I	276	40.58 N	73.40 W
Manursing Island Park ♠	276	40.58 N	73.40 W
Manus □[5]	164	2.00 S	147.00 E
Mānushmuria	126	22.22 N	86.47 E
Manus Island I	164	2.05 S	147.00 E
Manutahi	172	39.40 S	174.24 E
Manutuke	172	38.41 S	177.55 E
Manvel, N.D., U.S.	198	48.04 N	97.10 W
Manvel, Tx., U.S.	222	29.28 N	95.22 W
Manville, N.J., U.S.	210	40.32 N	74.35 W
Manville, R.I., U.S.	207	41.58 N	71.28 W
Mānwat	122	19.18 N	76.30 E
Many	194	31.34 N	93.29 W
Manyal Shīḥah	273c	29.57 N	31.14 E
Manyana	156	23.23 S	21.44 E
Manyani	154	3.05 S	38.30 E
Manyara, Lake ⊜	154	3.35 S	35.50 E
Manyas	130	40.02 N	27.58 E
Manyberries	184	49.24 N	110.42 W
Manyč ≃	72	47.15 N	40.00 E
Manyč-Gudilo, ozero ⊜	80	46.24 N	42.38 E
Manyeleti Game Reserve ⬥[4]	156	25.42 S	31.30 E
Many Island Lake ⊜	184	50.08 N	110.03 W
Manyoni	154	5.45 S	34.50 E
Many Peaks	166	24.33 S	151.23 E
Manytsch → Manyč ≃	72	47.15 N	40.00 E
Manz'a	86	58.29 N	96.15 E
Mānzai	120	30.07 N	68.52 E
Manzanares	34	39.00 N	3.22 W
Manzanares ≃	34	40.19 N	3.32 W
Manzanares, Canal del ≅	266a	40.23 N	3.41 W
Manzanillo, Cuba	240p	20.21 N	77.07 W
Manzanillo, Méx.	234	19.03 N	104.20 W
Manzanillo, Bahía ⊂	234	19.04 N	104.22 W
Manzanillo, Bahía de ⊂	234	19.12 N	104.43 W
Manzanillo, Punta ›, Pan.	236	9.38 N	79.32 W
Manzanillo, Punta ›, Ven.	241s	11.32 N	69.17 W
Manzanillo Bay ⊂	238	19.45 N	71.46 W
Manzanita, Or., U.S.	224	45.43 N	123.56 W
Manzanita, Wa., U.S.	224	47.42 N	122.33 W
Manzano, It.	64	45.59 N	13.23 E
Manzano, N.M., U.S.	200	34.38 N	106.20 W
Manzanola	198	38.06 N	103.51 W
Manzano Peak ∧	200	34.35 N	106.26 W
Manželija	78	49.19 N	33.38 E
Manzhouli	88	49.35 N	117.22 E
Manziana	66	42.08 N	12.08 E
Manzil	128	29.15 N	63.05 E
Manzilah, Birkat al- ⊜	142	31.08 N	31.56 E
Manzilah, Buḥayrat al- ⊜	142	31.15 N	32.00 E
Manzini	158	26.30 S	31.25 E
Manzone	258	34.29 S	58.52 W
Manzurka	88	53.30 N	106.04 E
Maó, Esp.	34	39.53 N	4.15 E
Mao, Rep. Dom.	238	19.34 N	71.05 W
Mao, Tchad	136	14.07 N	15.19 E
Maoba	102	30.02 N	108.59 E
Maocifan	100	31.40 N	112.53 E
Maocun	98	34.25 N	117.16 E
Maodianzi, Zhg.	107	30.42 N	104.25 E
Maodianzi, Zhg.	107	29.45 N	104.55 E
Mao'ertuo	107	29.19 N	106.24 E
Maojiagou	104	40.58 N	120.51 E
Maojiaji	100	31.32 N	114.16 E
Maojiakou	100	29.53 N	112.58 E
Maojiaping	105	40.34 N	114.43 E
Maojiapuzi	104	41.10 N	123.32 E
Maojiatun	104	41.05 N	121.58 E
Maojiazao	98	39.53 N	113.26 E
Maoke, Pegunungan ⩘	164	4.00 S	138.00 E
Maolin, Zhg.	89	43.58 N	123.24 E
Maolin, Zhg.	100	30.32 N	118.14 E
Maomao Shan ∧	102	37.12 N	103.10 E
Maoming	102	21.39 N	110.54 E
Maomu	102	40.18 N	99.28 E
Ma On Shan ∧	271d	22.25 N	114.15 E
Ma On Shan Tsuen	271d	22.24 N	114.14 E
Maoping	102	30.23 N	110.33 E
Maopora, Pulau I	112	7.35 S	127.35 E
Maoshan	105	40.17 N	117.26 E
Mao Shan ⩘	106	31.43 N	119.17 E
Maoshi	100	26.57 N	113.05 E
Maospati	115a	7.36 S	111.26 E
Maouri, Dallol V	150	12.05 N	3.32 E
Maowen	102	31.30 N	103.39 E
Maoxing	89	45.32 N	124.33 E
Mao Yü I	100	23.19 N	119.19 E
Maozhou	105	38.51 N	116.06 E
Mapaga	112	0.06 S	119.48 E
Mapam Yumco ⊜	120	30.42 N	81.27 E
Mapan	112	2.21 S	111.10 E
Mapanda	152	9.32 S	24.16 E
Mapane	112	1.24 S	120.40 E
Mapanza	154	16.15 S	26.55 E
Mapaoni ≃	250	1.55 N	54.13 W
Mapari ≃, Bra.	246	1.49 S	66.48 W
Mapari ≃, Bra.	250	0.45 N	53.07 W
Mapastepec	234	15.26 N	92.54 W
Mapaville	219	38.14 N	90.29 W
Mapi	164	7.07 S	139.23 E
Mapi ≃	164	7.00 S	139.16 E
Mapia, Kepulauan II	108	0.50 N	134.20 E
Mapida	112	0.33 S	119.46 E
Mapimí	232	25.49 N	103.51 W
Mapimí, Bolsón de ⬥[2]	232	26.30 N	104.00 W
Mapimí, Bufa de ∧	196	25.47 N	103.48 W
Maping, Zhg.	100	24.16 N	117.54 E
Maping, Zhg.	100	31.36 N	113.32 E
Mapinga	154	6.36 S	39.04 E
Mapinhane	156	22.19 S	35.03 E
Mapire	246	7.45 N	64.42 W
Mapiri	248	15.15 S	68.10 W
Mapiri ≃	248	9.52 S	66.21 W
Mapixari, Ilha I	246	2.10 S	65.08 W
Maple ⬥[8]	275b	43.51 N	79.31 W
Maple ≃, U.S.	198	45.47 N	98.33 W
Maple ≃, Ia., U.S.	198	42.00 N	95.59 W
Maple ≃, Mi., U.S.	190	42.59 N	84.57 W
Maple ≃, Mn., U.S.	190	44.05 N	94.00 W
Maple ≃, N.D., U.S.	198	46.56 N	96.55 W
Maple Airfield ⊠	275b	43.51 N	79.32 W
Maple Bay	224	48.49 N	123.36 W
Maple Bluff	216	43.07 N	89.22 W
Maple Creek	184	49.55 N	109.27 W
Maple Creek ≃	198	41.33 N	96.27 W
Maplecrest	210	42.17 N	74.11 W
Maple Cross	260	51.37 N	0.30 W
Mapledale	214	41.23 N	79.51 W
Maple Falls	224	48.55 N	122.04 W
Maple Glen	285	40.11 N	75.11 W
Maple Grove, On., Can.	212	43.55 N	78.44 W
Maple Grove, P.Q., Can.	206	45.19 N	73.50 W
Maple Heights	214	41.24 N	81.33 W
Maple Lake	190	45.13 N	94.00 W
Maple Lake ⊜	212	45.06 N	78.40 W
Maple Lane	216	41.45 N	86.14 W
Maple Leaf Gardens ♠	275b	43.40 N	79.23 W
Maple Meadow Brook ≃	283	42.33 N	71.09 W
Maple Mount	194	37.42 N	87.26 W
Maple Park	216	41.55 N	88.36 W
Maples	216	41.01 N	84.58 W
Maple Shade	285	39.57 N	74.59 W
Maple Springs	214	42.12 N	79.25 W
Maplesville	194	32.47 N	86.52 W
Mapleton, S. Afr.	158	26.20 S	28.14 E
Mapleton, Ia., U.S.	198	42.09 N	95.47 W
Mapleton, Mn., U.S.	190	43.55 N	93.57 W
Mapleton, Or., U.S.	202	44.01 N	123.51 W
Mapleton, Ut,. U.S.	200	40.07 N	111.34 W
Mapleton Depot	214	40.24 N	77.57 W
Maple Valley	224	47.25 N	122.03 W
Mapleville	207	41.56 N	71.38 W
Maplewood, Mo., U.S.	219	38.36 N	90.19 W
Maplewood, N.J., U.S.	276	40.43 N	74.14 W
Maplewood, Oh., U.S.	216	40.23 N	84.02 W
Maplewood, Wa., U.S.	224	47.30 N	122.07 W
Maplewood Terrace	279b	40.17 N	79.32 W
Mapocho ≃	286e	33.25 S	70.47 W
Mapocho, Estación ⬥[5]	286e	33.26 S	70.40 W
Mapoi	154	5.28 N	27.40 E
Mapoon Aboriginal Reserve ⬥[4]	164	11.40 S	142.25 E
Mappsville	208	37.51 N	75.34 W
Maprik	164	3.40 S	143.05 E
Mapuera ≃	250	1.05 S	57.02 W
Mapujiang	105	40.24 N	114.56 E
Mapulanguene	156	24.29 S	32.06 E
Mapumulo	158	29.11 S	31.02 E
Maputa	158	26.59 S	32.46 E
Maputo	156	25.58 S	32.35 E
Maputo □[5]	156	26.00 S	32.25 E
Maputo (Great Usutu) (Lusutfu) ≃	158	26.11 S	32.42 E
Maputo, Baia de ⊂	158	25.48 S	32.51 E
Maqên Gangri ∧	102	34.55 N	99.18 E
Maqiangou	105	39.30 N	115.02 E
Maqiao, Zhg.	100	29.48 N	114.22 E
Maqiao, Zhg.	106	30.28 N	120.42 E
Maqna	128	28.24 N	34.45 E
Maqṭeïr ⍑[4]	148	22.10 N	10.50 W
Maquan ≃	124	29.35 N	84.10 E
Maqueda	34	40.04 N	4.22 W
Maqueda Bay ⊂	116	11.44 N	124.58 E
Maqueda Channel ψ	116	13.42 N	124.01 E
Maquela do Zombo	152	6.03 S	15.07 E
Maquereau, Pointe au ›	186	48.12 N	64.47 W
Maquilaú ≃	246	1.23 N	63.24 W
Maquiling, Mount ∧	116	14.08 N	121.12 E
Maquinchao	254	41.15 S	68.44 W
Maquinchao ≃	254	41.13 S	69.25 W
Maquoketa	190	42.04 N	90.39 W
Maquoketa ≃	190	42.11 N	90.19 W
Maquoketa, North Fork ≃	190	42.05 N	90.40 W
Mar, Laguna ⊂	286b	23.05 N	82.30 W
Mar, Serra do ±[4]	252	26.00 S	48.00 W
Mara, India	120	28.11 N	94.06 E
Mara, Perú	248	14.06 S	72.07 W
Mara, Zhg.	120	28.11 N	94.08 E
Mara □[4]	154	1.45 S	34.30 E
Mara ≃, Afr.	154	1.31 S	33.56 E
Mara ≃, Ross.	88	58.06 N	104.06 E
Maraã, Bra.	246	1.50 S	65.22 W
Maraa, Poly. fr.	174s	17.46 S	149.34 W
Marabá	250	5.21 S	49.07 W
Marabahan	112	3.00 S	114.45 E
Marabut	116	11.07 N	125.13 E
Maracá, Ilha de I, Bra.	246	3.25 N	61.40 W
Maracá, Ilha de I, Bra.	250	2.05 N	50.25 W
Maracaçumé ≃	250	1.23 S	45.42 W
Maracaí	255	22.36 S	50.39 W
Maracaibo	246	10.40 N	71.37 W
Maracaibo, Lago de ⊜	246	9.50 N	71.30 W
Maracaju	255	21.38 S	55.09 W
Maracaju, Serra de ⩘[2]	255	20.45 S	55.00 W
Maracalagonis	71	39.17 N	9.13 E
Maracanã	250	0.46 S	47.27 W
Maracanã ⬥[8]	287a	22.54 S	43.14 W
Maracanã ≃	248	8.22 S	59.41 W
Maracanã, Estádio do ♠	287a	22.55 S	43.14 W
Maracanaú	250	3.52 S	38.38 W
Maracás	255	13.26 S	40.27 W
Maracay	246	10.15 N	67.36 W
Maracossic Creek ≃	208	37.53 N	77.11 W
Marādah	146	29.14 N	19.13 E
Maradi	150	13.29 N	7.06 E
Maradi □[5]	150	14.00 N	7.00 E
Maradi, Goulbin ≃	150	13.38 N	6.20 E
Marāghah, Sabkhat al- ⊜	130	35.39 N	37.39 E
Marāgheh	128	37.23 N	46.13 E
Maragiu, Capo ›	71	40.20 N	8.23 E
Maragogi	250	9.01 S	35.13 W
Maragogipe	255	12.46 S	38.55 W
Marahoué, Parc National de la ♠	150	7.00 N	6.00 W
Mārahra	124	27.44 N	78.35 E
Marahuaca, Cerro ∧	246	3.34 N	65.27 W
Maraial	250	8.47 S	35.50 W
Maraiche Lake ⊜	184	54.28 N	102.01 W
Marainviller	58	48.35 N	6.36 E
Maraisburg → Roodepoort-Maraisburg	273d	26.11 S	27.56 E
Marais des Cygnes ≃	194	38.02 N	94.14 W
Marais Temps Clair ⊜	219	38.54 N	90.24 W
Marajó, Baía de ⊂	250	1.00 S	48.30 W
Marajó, Ilha de I	250	1.00 S	49.30 W
Marakabei	158	29.32 S	28.09 E
Ma'rakah	132	33.16 N	35.18 E
Mārākand	84	38.52 N	45.14 E
Marakwini	164	3.42 S	141.31 E
Maralal	154	1.06 N	36.42 E
Maralaleng	156	25.47 S	22.45 E
Maralal Game Sanctuary ⬥[4]	154	1.09 N	36.38 E
Maraldy	86	52.26 N	77.45 E
Marali	152	6.01 N	18.24 E
Maralik	84	40.35 N	43.52 E
Maralinga	162	30.10 S	131.35 E
Maralinga Lands ⬥[4]	162	29.15 S	130.50 E
Maram	120	25.25 N	94.06 E
Maramag	116	7.46 N	125.00 E
Maramasike I	175e	9.32 S	161.27 E
Marambaia ≃	256	21.44 S	46.25 W
Marambaia, Ilha da I	256	23.04 S	43.58 W
Marambaia, Pico da ∧	256	23.04 S	43.59 W
Marambaia, Restinga de ±[2]	256	23.04 S	43.45 W
Marambio ʊ[3]	9	64.14 S	56.43 W
Marampa	150	8.41 N	12.28 W
Maramsilli Reservoir ⊜[1]	122	20.32 N	81.41 E
Maramureş □[6]	38	47.40 N	24.00 E
Maran	114	3.35 N	102.46 E
Mārān, Koh-i- ∧	120	29.26 N	66.48 E
Marana, Mali	150	14.38 N	11.55 W
Marana, Az., U.S.	200	32.26 N	111.13 W
Maranalgo	162	29.23 S	117.48 E
Maranboy	164	14.30 S	132.45 E
Maranchón	34	41.03 N	2.12 W
Marand	128	38.26 N	45.46 E
Maranello	64	44.32 N	10.52 E
Marang, Malay.	114	5.12 N	103.13 E
Marang, Mya.	110	10.27 N	98.47 E
Marangá ≃	287a	22.51 S	43.23 W
Marangani	248	14.22 S	71.10 W
Marangas	116	8.40 N	117.38 E
Marange-Zondrange	56	49.07 N	6.32 E
Maranguape	250	3.53 S	38.40 W
Maranhão □[3]	250	5.00 S	45.00 W
Maranhão ≃	255	13.51 S	48.20 W
Marano	266b	45.38 N	8.38 E
Marano, Laguna di ⊂	64	45.44 N	13.10 E
Maranoa ≃	166	27.50 S	148.37 E
Marano di Napoli	68	40.54 N	14.11 E
Marano Lagunare	64	45.46 N	13.10 E
Marañón ≃	242	4.30 S	73.27 W
Marano sul Panaro	64	44.27 N	10.58 E
Marano Vicentino	64	45.41 N	11.25 E
Marans	32	46.19 N	1.00 W
Maraoli ⬥[8]	272c	19.03 N	72.54 E
Marapanim	250	0.42 S	47.42 W
Marapendi, Lagoa de ⊂	287a	23.01 S	43.24 W
Marapi ≃	250	0.37 N	55.58 W
Marapicu, Morro do ∧	287a	22.50 S	43.36 W
Mararoa ≃	172	45.34 S	167.36 E
Mararui	154	1.56 S	41.18 E
Maras	248	13.20 S	72.09 W
Marasany	80	57.27 N	54.25 E
Marasende, Pulau I	112	5.08 S	118.09 E
Mărăşeşti	38	45.52 N	27.14 E
Maraş → Kahramanmaraş	130	37.36 N	36.55 E
Maratasã ≃	250	4.14 S	42.15 W
Maratea	68	39.59 N	15.45 E
Marathon, Austl.	166	20.49 S	143.34 E
Marathon, On., Can.	190	48.43 N	86.23 W
Marathón, Ellás	38	38.10 N	23.58 E
Marathon, Fl., U.S.	220	24.42 N	81.05 W
Marathon, N.Y., U.S.	210	42.26 N	76.01 W
Marathon, Tx., U.S.	196	30.12 N	103.15 W
Marathon, Wi., U.S.	190	44.55 N	89.50 W
Maratua, Pulau I	112	2.15 N	118.36 E
Marau, Bra.	252	28.27 S	52.12 W
Maraú, Bra.	255	14.06 S	39.00 W
Marauiá ≃	246	0.23 S	65.13 W
Marausa	70	37.56 N	12.30 E
Maravari	175e	7.51 S	156.42 E
Maravatío de Ocampo	234	19.54 N	100.27 W
Maravilha	252	26.47 S	53.09 W
Maravillas	232	27.22 N	104.29 W
Maravillas Creek ≃	196	29.34 N	102.47 W
Mara Vista	207	41.33 N	70.34 W
Marav Lake ⊜	120	29.04 N	69.18 E
Maravovo	175e	9.17 S	159.38 E
Marāwah	146	32.29 N	21.25 E
Marawi, Pil.	116	8.01 N	124.18 E
Marawī, Sūd.	140	18.29 N	31.49 E
Marawwah I	128	24.18 N	53.18 E
Maraye-en-Othe	50	48.10 N	3.51 E
Marayes	252	31.29 S	67.20 W
Marayong	274a	33.45 S	150.54 E
Maraza	84	40.33 N	48.56 E
Marazion	42	50.08 N	5.28 W
Marbach, Dtsch.	54	51.02 N	13.13 E
Marbach, Dtsch.	56	50.37 N	9.43 E
Marbach, Schw.	58	46.52 N	7.55 E
Marbach am Neckar	56	48.56 N	9.14 E
Marbache	56	48.48 N	6.05 E
Marbais	50	50.33 N	4.31 E
Marbeck	52	51.49 N	6.52 E
Marbella	34	36.31 N	4.53 W
Marble, Mn., U.S.	190	47.19 N	93.17 W
Marble, N.C., U.S.	192	35.10 N	83.55 W
Marble, Pa., U.S.	214	41.20 N	79.26 W
Marble Arch ⊥	146	30.29 N	18.35 E
Marble Bar	162	21.11 S	119.44 E
Marble Canyon V	200	36.30 N	111.50 W
Marble Falls	196	30.34 N	98.16 W
Marble Hall	156	24.57 S	29.13 E
Marblehead, Il., U.S.	219	39.50 N	91.22 W
Marblehead, Ma., U.S.	207	42.30 N	70.51 W
Marblehead, Oh., U.S.	214	41.32 N	82.44 W
Marblehead Neck ›[1]	283	42.29 N	70.51 W
Marble Hill	194	37.18 N	89.58 W
Marble Lake ⊜	216	41.54 N	84.54 W
Marblemount	224	48.31 N	121.26 W
Marble Rock	190	42.57 N	92.52 W
Marbleton	206	45.37 N	71.35 W
Marburg, Austl.	171a	27.34 S	152.35 E
Marburg, Dtsch.	56	50.49 N	8.46 E
Marburg, S. Afr.	158	30.44 S	30.26 E
Marburg, Lake ⊜[1]	208	39.48 N	76.53 W
Marburg an der Drau → Maribor	36	46.33 N	15.39 E
Marbury	208	38.34 N	77.09 W
Marc ≃	50	50.43 N	3.50 E
Marca, Ponta da ›	152	16.31 S	11.42 E
Marcal ≃	30	47.41 N	17.32 E
Marcala	236	14.07 N	88.00 W
Marcali	30	46.35 N	17.25 E
Marcallo con Casone	266b	45.29 N	8.52 E
Marcaria	64	45.07 N	10.32 E
Marceau, Lac ⊜	186	51.25 N	66.41 W
Marcedusa	68	39.02 N	16.50 E
Marcelin	184	52.55 N	106.47 W
Marceline	194	39.42 N	92.56 W
Marcelino Ramos	252	27.28 S	51.54 W
Marcella	276	40.59 N	74.28 W
Marcellina	66	42.01 N	12.48 E
Marcellus, Mi., U.S.	216	42.01 N	85.48 W
Marcellus, N.Y., U.S.	210	42.59 N	76.20 W
Marcellus Falls	210	43.00 N	76.20 W
Marcevo	83	47.15 N	38.53 E
March	42	52.33 N	0.06 E
March (Morava) ≃	30	48.10 N	16.59 E
Marcha	74	60.37 N	123.18 E
Marcha ≃	74	63.28 N	118.50 E
March Air Force Base ■	228	33.54 N	117.15 W
Marchais	261	48.31 N	2.03 E
Marchal	152	5.16 S	14.58 E
Marchamat	85	40.30 N	72.19 E
Marchand	214	40.51 N	79.02 W
Marchaux	58	47.19 N	6.08 E
Marche □[4]	66	43.30 N	13.15 E
Marche □[9]	32	46.05 N	2.10 E
Marche-en-Famenne	56	50.12 N	5.20 E
Marchegg	61	48.17 N	16.55 E
Marche-les-Dames	56	50.29 N	4.58 E
Marchémoret	261	49.03 N	2.46 E
Marchena	34	37.20 N	5.24 W
Marchena, Isla I	246a	0.21 N	90.29 W
Marchenoir	50	47.49 N	1.24 E
Marchesato	68	39.07 N	16.58 E
Marchfeld ⬥[1]	264b	48.17 N	16.31 E
Marchienne-au-Pont	50	50.24 N	4.23 E
Marchinbar Island I	164	11.15 S	136.45 E
Marching	60	48.49 N	11.43 E
Mar Chiquita, Laguna ⊂	252	37.37 S	57.24 W
Mar Chiquita, Laguna ⊜	252	30.42 S	62.36 W
Marchtrenk	61	48.11 N	14.07 E
Marciana	66	42.47 N	10.10 E
Marciana Marina	66	42.48 N	10.12 E
Marcianise	68	41.02 N	14.17 E
Marciano della Chiana	66	43.18 N	11.47 E
Marčichina Buda	78	51.58 N	34.03 E
Marcigny	32	46.17 N	4.02 E
Marcillac-Vallon	32	44.29 N	2.28 E
Marcilloles	62	45.20 N	5.11 E
Marcilly	261	49.02 N	2.53 E
Marcilly-la-Campagne	50	48.50 N	1.13 E
Marcilly-le-Hayer	50	48.21 N	3.38 E
Marcilly-sur-Eure	50	48.49 N	1.21 E
Marck	50	50.57 N	1.57 E
Marckolsheim	58	48.10 N	7.33 E
Marco, Bra.	250	3.08 S	40.09 W
Marco, It.	64	45.51 N	11.01 E
Marco, Fl., U.S.	220	25.58 N	81.43 W
Marcoing	50	50.07 N	3.11 E
Marco Island I	220	25.55 N	81.45 W
Marcola	202	44.10 N	122.51 W
Marcolino, Igarapé ≃	250	11.03 S	58.35 W
Marcona	248	15.03 S	75.01 W
Marco Polo, Aeroporto ⊠	64	45.30 N	12.21 E
Marco Polo Bridge ⬥[5]	271a	39.52 N	116.12 E
Marcos Juárez	252	32.42 S	62.06 W
Marcos Paz	258	34.46 S	58.50 W
Marcos Paz □[5]	288	34.49 S	58.49 W
Marcotte, Lac ⊜	206	46.47 N	73.12 W
Marcoussis	261	48.39 N	2.14 E
Marcq	261	48.52 N	1.49 E
Marcq-en-Barœul	50	50.40 N	3.05 E
Marčugi	82	55.21 N	38.33 E
Marcus	198	42.49 N	95.48 W
Marcus Baker, Mount ∧	180	61.26 N	147.45 W
Marcus Hook	208	39.49 N	75.25 W
Marcus Hook Creek ≃	285	39.49 N	75.25 W
Marcus Island → Minami-Tori-shima I	14	24.18 N	153.58 E
Marcy, Mount ∧	188	44.07 N	73.56 W
Marda	162	30.13 S	119.17 E
Mardakert	84	40.12 N	46.48 E
Mardalsfossen ∟	26	62.30 N	8.07 E
Mardān	123	34.12 N	72.02 E
Mardarovka	78	47.32 N	29.44 E
Mar de Cães, Vala de ≅	266c	38.51 N	8.59 W
Mar de Espanha	256	21.52 S	43.00 W
Mardela Springs	208	38.27 N	75.45 W
Mar del Plata	252	38.00 S	57.33 W
Marden	42	51.10 N	0.29 E
Mardie	162	21.11 S	115.57 E
Mardin	130	37.18 N	40.44 E
Mardin □[4]	128	37.25 N	41.00 E
Mar Dyke ≃	260	51.29 N	0.14 E
Maré I	175f	21.30 S	168.00 E
Mare a Brăilei, Insula I	38	45.00 N	28.00 E
Marea de Portillo	240p	19.55 N	77.11 W
Marecchia ≃	66	44.04 N	12.34 E
Marechal Cândido Rondon	252	24.34 S	54.04 W
Marechal Deodoro	250	9.43 S	35.54 W
Marechal Taumaturgo	248	8.57 S	72.48 W
Maree, Loch ⊜	46	57.42 N	5.30 W
Mareeba	166	17.00 S	145.26 E
Mareetsane	158	26.09 S	25.25 E
Mareil-en-France	261	49.04 N	2.26 E
Mareil-le-Guyon	261	48.47 N	1.51 E
Mareil-Marly	261	48.53 N	2.05 E
Mare Island I	226	38.06 N	122.16 W
Mare Island Naval Shipyard ■	226	38.06 N	122.17 W
Mare Island Strait ψ	282	38.06 N	122.17 W
Mareje, Gunung ∧	115b	8.46 S	116.08 E
Marek	112	4.48 S	120.21 E
Maremma ⬥[1]	66	42.30 N	11.30 E
Marene	62	44.39 N	7.44 E
Marengo, Il., U.S.	216	42.14 N	88.36 W
Marengo, In., U.S.	218	38.22 N	86.20 W
Marengo, Ia., U.S.	190	41.47 N	92.04 W
Marengo, Mi., U.S.	216	42.17 N	84.51 W
Marengo, Oh., U.S.	214	40.24 N	82.49 W
Marengo ⬥[1]	62	44.55 N	8.40 E
Marengo ⊥	62	44.49 N	8.40 E
Marengo Cave ±[5]	218	38.23 N	86.21 W
Marenisco	190	46.22 N	89.41 W
Marennes	32	45.50 N	1.06 W
Marerano	157b	21.23 S	44.52 E
Maresias	256	23.48 S	45.33 W
Marettimo	70	37.58 N	12.04 E
Marettimo, Isola I	70	37.58 N	12.03 E
Mareuil-en-Brie	50	48.57 N	3.45 E
Mareuil-lès-Meaux	261	48.56 N	2.52 E
Mareuil-sur-Aÿ	50	49.03 N	4.02 E
Mareuil-sur-Belle	32	45.28 N	0.28 E
Marevo	76	57.19 N	32.05 E
Marey-sur-Tille	58	47.35 N	5.03 E
Marfa	196	30.18 N	104.01 W
Marfinka	83	47.36 N	38.32 E
Marfino	80	46.25 N	48.44 E
Mar Forest ⬥[3]	46	57.00 N	3.35 W
Margai Caka ⊜	120	35.00 N	87.00 E
Margam, Īrān	84	39.09 N	44.57 E
Margam, Wales, U.K.	42	51.34 N	3.44 W
Marganec	78	47.38 N	34.40 E
Margao → Madgaon	122	15.18 N	73.57 E
Margaree	186	46.24 N	61.05 W
Margaree Harbour	186	46.26 N	61.07 W
Margaret ≃	162	18.10 S	125.37 E
Margaret, Mount ∧	224	46.18 N	122.08 W
Margaret Bay	182	51.20 N	127.29 W
Margaret Creek ≃	166	29.26 S	137.07 E
Margarethenhöhe ⬥[8]	263	51.26 N	6.58 E
Margaret River, Austl.	162	33.57 S	115.04 E
Margaret River, Austl.	162	18.38 S	126.52 E
Margaret Roding	260	51.47 N	0.19 E
Margaretting	260	51.41 N	0.25 E
Margarettsville	208	36.32 N	77.21 W
Margaretville	210	42.08 N	74.38 W
Margarita, Bahía → Marguerite Bay ⊂	9	68.30 S	68.30 W
Margarita, Isla I	246	9.05 N	74.30 W
Margarita, Isla de I	246	11.00 N	64.00 W
Margarita Belén	252	27.16 S	58.58 W
Margarita Peak ∧	228	33.26 N	117.23 W
Margaritovka	83	46.55 N	38.52 E
Margate, S. Afr.	158	30.55 S	30.15 E
Margate, Eng., U.K.	42	51.24 N	1.24 E
Margate, Fl., U.S.	220	26.14 N	80.12 W
Margate City	208	39.19 N	74.30 W
Margecany	30	48.54 N	21.01 E
Margelan → Margilan	85	40.28 N	71.44 E
Margeride, Monts de la ⩘	32	44.50 N	3.30 E
Margès	62	45.09 N	5.03 E
Mārgherita	120	27.17 N	95.41 E
Margherita di Savoia	68	41.23 N	16.09 E
Margherita → Jamaame	144	0.04 N	42.45 E
Margherita Peak ∧	154	0.22 N	29.51 E
Marghī	120	34.58 N	66.31 E
Marghita	38	47.21 N	22.21 E
Margi ≃	70	37.16 N	14.58 E
Margilan	85	40.28 N	71.44 E
Margit Híd ⬥[5]	264c	47.31 N	19.02 E
Margit-sziget I	264c	47.32 N	19.03 E
Margny-lès-Compiègne	50	49.26 N	2.49 E
Margone	62	45.13 N	7.11 E
Margonin	30	52.59 N	17.05 E
Margos	248	10.04 S	76.26 W
Margosatubig	116	7.34 N	123.10 E
Margot Lake ⊜	184	52.28 N	93.10 W
Mārgow, Dasht-e ⬥[2]	128	30.45 N	63.10 E
Margreid → Magrè	64	46.17 N	11.12 E
Marguerite, Pic → Margherita Peak ∧	154	0.22 N	29.51 E
Marguerite Bay ⊂	9	68.30 S	68.30 W
Marguerittes	62	43.51 N	4.27 E
Margut	56	49.35 N	5.16 E
Margyang	124	29.57 N	90.09 E
Mari	164	9.10 S	141.40 E
Maria	116	9.12 N	123.39 E
Maria, Îles II	14	21.48 S	154.41 W
Mariabrunn ⬥[8]	264b	48.12 N	16.14 E
María Cleofas, Isla I	234	21.16 N	106.14 W
Maria da Fé	256	22.18 S	45.23 W
María Elena	252	22.21 S	69.40 W
Maria Enzersdorf	61	48.06 N	16.17 E
Maria Gail	64	46.36 N	13.52 E
Mariager	26	56.39 N	10.00 E
Mariāhu	124	25.37 N	82.37 E
María Ignacia (Vela)	252	37.24 S	59.30 W
Maria Island I, Austl.	164	14.52 S	135.40 E
Maria Island I, Austl.	166	42.39 S	148.04 E
Maria Island National Park ♠	166	42.39 S	148.06 E
Mariakani	154	3.52 S	39.28 E
Maria Laach ʊ[1]	56	50.24 N	7.14 E
María la Baja	246	9.59 N	75.17 W
Maria Lanzendorf	264b	48.06 N	16.25 E
Maria Luggau	64	46.42 N	12.45 E
María Madre, Isla I	234	21.35 N	106.33 W
María Magdalena, Isla I	234	21.25 N	106.24 W
Marian, Lake ⊜	220	27.52 N	81.06 W
Mariana	255	20.23 S	43.25 W
Mariana Basin ✣[1]	14	17.30 N	145.00 E
Mariana Islands II	108	16.00 N	145.30 E
Mariana Ridge ✣[3]	14	17.00 N	146.00 E
Mariana Trench ✣[1]	14	15.00 N	147.30 E
Mariāni	120	26.40 N	94.20 E
Marian Lake ⊜	176	63.00 N	116.10 W
Marianna, Ar., U.S.	194	34.46 N	90.45 W
Marianna, Fl., U.S.	192	30.46 N	85.13 W
Mariannelund	26	57.37 N	15.34 E
Mariannhill	158	29.52 S	30.50 E
Mariano Acosta	258	34.43 S	58.48 W
Mariano Comense	62	45.42 N	9.11 E
Mariano del Friuli	64	45.55 N	13.27 E
Mariano I. Loza	252	29.22 S	58.12 W
Mariano J. Haedo	288	34.38 S	58.36 W
Mariano Moreno	252	38.44 S	70.01 W
Mariano Moreno → Moreno	258	34.39 S	58.48 W
Marianopoli	70	37.36 N	13.55 E
Mariánské Lázně	60	49.59 N	12.43 E
Mariar	164	2.48 S	132.50 E
Mariarano	157b	15.29 S	46.42 E
Marias ≃	202	47.56 N	110.30 W
Marias, Dry Fork ≃	202	48.22 N	111.45 W
Marías, Islas II	234	21.25 N	106.28 W
Maria Saal	61	46.41 N	14.21 E
Marias Pass)(	202	48.19 N	113.21 W
Maria Stein	216	40.24 N	84.28 W
María Teresa	252	34.01 S	61.54 W
Maria-Theresiopel → Subotica	38	46.06 N	19.39 E
Mariato, Punta ›	246	7.13 N	80.53 W
Maria van Diemen, Cape ›	172	34.28 S	172.39 E
Mariaville	210	42.49 N	74.08 W
Mariazell	61	47.47 N	15.19 E
Ma'rib	144	15.30 N	45.20 E
Maribo	41	54.46 N	11.31 E
Maribojoc Bay ⊂	116	9.42 N	123.50 E
Maribor	61	46.33 N	15.39 E
Maribyrnong	274b	37.46 S	144.54 E
Marica, Blg.	38	42.02 N	25.50 E
Maricá, Bra.	256	22.55 S	42.49 W
Marica, Ross.	78	51.45 N	35.16 E
Maricá □[7]	287a	22.57 S	42.59 W
Marica (Évros) (Meriç) ≃	38	40.52 N	26.12 E
Maricá, Lagoa de ⊂	256	22.56 S	42.50 W
Maricaban Island I	116	13.39 N	120.53 E
Maricao	240m	18.11 N	66.59 W
Maricás, Ilhas II	256	23.01 S	42.55 W
Maricha Bil ⊜	272b	22.55 N	88.31 E
Marico ≃	156	24.12 S	26.52 E
Maricopa, Az., U.S.	200	33.03 N	112.02 W
Maricopa, Ca., U.S.	204	35.03 N	119.24 W
Maricopa Indian Reservation ⬥[4]	200	33.02 N	112.05 W
Maricunga, Salar de ≚	252	26.55 S	69.05 W
Maridagao ≃	116	7.13 N	124.41 E
Marīdī	154	4.55 N	29.28 E
Maridi ≃	140	6.05 N	29.24 E
Marié ≃	246	0.27 S	66.26 W
Marie Byrd Land ⬥[1]	9	80.00 S	120.00 W
Marie Curtis Park ♠	275b	43.35 N	79.33 W
Mariedamm	40	58.51 N	15.09 E
Mariefred	40	59.16 N	17.13 E
Marie-Galante I	241o	15.56 N	61.16 W
Mariehamn	26	60.06 N	19.57 E
Marieholm	41	55.52 N	13.09 E
Mariel	240p	22.59 N	82.45 W
Marie Lake ⊜	184	54.37 N	110.18 W
Marie-Lefranc, Lac ⊜	206	46.08 N	75.00 W
Mari El → Marij El □[3]	80	56.30 N	48.00 E
Mariembourg	50	50.06 N	4.31 E
Marienbad → Mariánské Lázně	60	49.59 N	12.43 E
Marienbaum	52	51.41 N	6.22 E
Marienberg, Dtsch.	54	50.39 N	13.10 E
Marienberg, Dtsch.	56	50.39 N	7.57 E
Marienberg, Pap. N. Gui.	164	3.55 S	144.15 E
Marien-Berg ∧[2]	264a	52.22 N	13.32 E
Marienborn	54	52.12 N	11.08 E
Marienburg → Malbork	30	54.02 N	19.01 E
Mariendorf ⬥[8]	264a	52.26 N	13.23 E
Marienfelde ⬥[8]	264a	52.25 N	13.22 E
Marienhafe	52	53.31 N	7.16 E
Marienheide	56	51.05 N	7.32 E
Mariental, Dtsch.	54	52.16 N	10.59 E
Mariental, Namibia	156	24.36 S	17.59 E
Mariental □[5]	156	25.00 S	19.00 E
Marienville	214	41.28 N	79.07 W
Maries □[6]	219	38.15 N	91.56 W
Maries ≃	194	38.30 N	92.01 W
Mariestad	40	58.43 N	13.51 E
Marieta ≃	246	5.02 N	66.38 W
Marietta, Ga., U.S.	192	33.57 N	84.33 W
Marietta, In., U.S.	218	39.26 N	85.53 W
Marietta, Mn., U.S.	198	45.00 N	96.25 W
Marietta, Oh., U.S.	188	39.24 N	81.27 W
Marietta, Ok., U.S.	196	33.56 N	97.06 W
Marietta, Pa., U.S.	208	40.03 N	76.33 W
Marietta, Tx., U.S.	222	33.10 N	94.33 W
Marietta, Wa., U.S.	224	48.47 N	122.34 W
Marieville	206	45.26 N	73.10 W
Mariga ≃	150	9.40 N	5.55 E
Marigliano	66	40.56 N	14.27 E
Marignane	62	43.25 N	5.13 E
Marignier	58	46.06 N	6.31 E
Marigny-le-Châtel	50	48.24 N	3.44 E
Marigny-L'Église	50	47.22 N	3.56 E
Marigot, Dom.	240d	15.32 N	61.18 W
Marigot, Guad.	238	18.04 N	63.06 W
Marihatag	116	8.48 N	126.18 E
Mariinsk	86	56.13 N	87.45 E
Mariinskoje	89	51.43 N	140.13 E
Marijampole	76	54.33 N	23.21 E
Marijec	80	56.32 N	49.50 E
Marij El □[3]	80	56.30 N	48.00 E
Marikana	158	25.42 S	27.30 E
Marikina	269f	14.38 N	121.06 E
Marikina ≃	269f	14.33 N	121.04 E
Marília	255	22.13 S	49.56 W
Marilla	210	42.50 N	78.33 W
Mari-Malmyž	80	56.30 N	50.52 E
Marimari ≃	246	3.58 S	58.49 W
Marimba	152	8.28 S	17.08 E
Marín	34	42.23 N	8.42 W
Marin □[6]	226	38.03 N	122.33 W
Marina	226	36.41 N	121.48 W
Marina ⬥[8]	282	37.47 N	122.27 W
Marina del Rey	280	33.50 N	118.25 W
Marina del Rey ⊂	280	33.58 N	118.27 W
Marina di Andora	62	43.57 N	8.08 E
Marina di Campo	66	42.44 N	10.14 E
Marina di Caronia	70	38.02 N	14.28 E
Marina di Carrara	64	44.02 N	10.02 E
Marina di Cecina	66	43.18 N	10.29 E
Marina di Gioiosa Ionica	68	38.18 N	16.20 E
Marina di Grosseto	66	42.43 N	10.59 E
Marina di Massa	64	44.00 N	10.06 E
Marina di Minturno	66	41.16 N	13.45 E
Marina di Orosei	71	40.22 N	9.43 E
Marina di Palma ⬥[8]	70	37.10 N	13.43 E
Marina di Pietrasanta	64	43.56 N	10.12 E
Marina di Pisa	66	43.40 N	10.16 E
Marina di Ragusa	70	36.47 N	14.33 E
Marina di Ravenna	66	44.29 N	12.17 E
Marina Fall ∟	246	5.22 N	59.29 W
Marin City	282	37.52 N	122.21 W
Marinduque □[4]	116	13.25 N	121.55 E
Marinduque Island I	116	13.24 N	121.58 E
Marine	219	38.47 N	89.46 W
Marine City	214	42.43 N	82.29 W
Marine-Ehrenmal ⊥	54	54.23 N	10.15 E
Marineland of the Pacific ʊ[3]	228	33.44 N	118.24 W
Marinella	70	37.35 N	12.50 E
Marine Museum ʊ	280	33.43 N	118.17 W
Marineo	70	37.57 N	13.25 E
Marine Park ♠	283	42.20 N	71.01 W
Marine Parkway Bridge ⬥[5]	276	40.34 N	73.53 W
Mariners Museum ʊ	208	37.03 N	76.30 W
Marines	50	49.09 N	1.59 E
Marinette	190	45.06 N	87.37 W
Maringá	255	23.25 S	51.55 W
Maringa ≃	152	1.14 N	19.48 E
Maringouin	194	30.29 N	91.31 W
Marínguè	154	17.55 S	34.24 E
Marinha Grande	34	39.45 N	8.56 W
Marinho ≃	287a	23.00 S	43.27 W
Marin Mall ⬥[9]	282	37.56 N	122.31 W
Marino, It.	66	41.46 N	12.39 E
Marino, Vanuatu	175f	15.00 S	168.09 E
Marinovka, Ross.	80	48.41 N	43.49 E
Marinovka, Ukr.	78	47.46 N	30.53 E
Marinovka, Ukr.	83	47.54 N	38.51 E
Marin Peninsula ›[1]	282	37.51 N	122.31 W
Marinskij Posad	80	56.07 N	47.43 E
Marintu	112	0.34 N	110.00 E
Marinwood	226	38.02 N	122.32 W
Mario, Monte ∧[2]	267a	41.55 N	12.27 E
Marion, Austl.	168b	35.01 S	138.34 E
Marion, Al., U.S.	194	32.37 N	87.19 W
Marion, Ar., U.S.	194	35.12 N	90.11 W
Marion, Ct., U.S.	207	41.33 N	72.55 W
Marion, Il., U.S.	194	37.43 N	88.55 W
Marion, In., U.S.	216	40.33 N	85.39 W
Marion, Ia., U.S.	190	42.02 N	91.35 W
Marion, Ks., U.S.	198	38.20 N	97.01 W
Marion, Ky., U.S.	194	37.19 N	88.04 W
Marion, La., U.S.	194	32.54 N	92.14 W
Marion, Ma., U.S.	207	41.42 N	70.45 W
Marion, Mi., U.S.	190	44.06 N	85.08 W
Marion, Ms., U.S.	194	32.25 N	88.38 W
Marion, N.Y., U.S.	210	43.08 N	77.11 W
Marion, N.C., U.S.	192	35.41 N	82.00 W
Marion, N.D., U.S.	198	46.36 N	98.19 W
Marion, Oh., U.S.	214	40.35 N	83.07 W
Marion, S.C., U.S.	192	34.10 N	79.24 W
Marion, S.D., U.S.	198	43.25 N	97.15 W
Marion, Va., U.S.	192	36.50 N	81.30 W
Marion, Wi., U.S.	190	44.40 N	88.53 W
Marion □[6], Fl., U.S.	220	29.00 N	82.03 W
Marion □[6], Il., U.S.	219	38.38 N	88.57 W
Marion □[6], In., U.S.	218	39.46 N	86.09 W
Marion □[6], Mo., U.S.	219	39.50 N	91.37 W
Marion □[6], Oh., U.S.	214	40.35 N	83.08 W

≃	River	Fluß	Río	Rivière	Rio
≅	Canal	Kanal	Canal	Canal	Canal
∟	Waterfall, Rapids	Wasserfall, Stromschnellen	Cascada, Rápidos	Chute d'eau, Rapides	Cascata, Rápidos
ψ	Strait	Meeresstraße	Estrecho	Détroit	Estreito
⊂	Bay, Gulf	Bucht, Golf	Bahía, Golfo	Baie, Golfe	Baía, Golfo
⊜	Lake, Lakes	See, Seen	Lago, Lagos	Lac, Lacs	Lago, Lagos
☰	Swamp	Sumpf	Pantano	Marais	Pântano
⍌	Ice Features, Glacier	Eis- und Gletscherformen	Accidentes Glaciales	Formes glaciaires	Acidentes glaciares
⍑	Other Hydrographic Features	Andere Hydrographische Objekte	Otros Elementos Hidrográficos	Autres données hydrographiques	Outros acidentes hidrográficos

✣	Submarine Features	Untermeerische Objekte	Accidentes Submarinos	Formes de relief sous-marin	Acidentes submarinos
□	Political Unit	Politische Einheit	Unidad Politica	Entité politique	Unidade política
ʊ	Cultural Institution	Kulturelle Institution	Institución Cultural	Institution culturelle	Instituição cultural
⊥	Historical Site	Historische Stätte	Sitio Histórico	Site historique	Sitio histórico
♠	Recreational Site	Erholungs- und Ferienort	Sitio de Recreo	Centre de loisirs	Area de Lazer
⊠	Airport	Flughafen	Aeropuerto	Aéroport	Aeroporto
■	Military Installation	Militäranlage	Instalación Militar	Installation militaire	Instalação militar
⬥	Miscellaneous	Verschiedenes	Misceláneo	Divers	Diversos

ENGLISH / DEUTSCH

Name	Page / Seite	Lat.°′ / Breite°′	Long.°′ / Länge°′ E = Ost
Marion □[6], Or., U.S.	224	45.06 N	122.47 W
Marion □[6], Tx., U.S.	222	32.48 N	94.33 W
Marion, Lake ⊜	220	28.05 N	81.32 W
Marion, Lake ⊜[1]	192	33.30 N	80.25 W
Marion Bay c	166	42.48 S	147.55 E
Marion Center	214	40.46 N	79.03 W
Marion Downs	166	23.22 S	139.39 E
Marion Heights	210	40.48 N	76.28 W
Marion Hill	214	40.44 N	80.18 W
Marion Junction	194	32.26 N	87.14 W
Marion Lake ⊜[1]	198	38.24 N	97.08 W
Marion Reef ✧[2]	166	19.10 S	152.17 E
Marion Station	208	38.02 N	75.46 W
Marionville	194	37.00 N	93.38 W
Mariópolis	252	26.20 S	52.33 W
Maripa	246	7.26 N	65.09 W
Maripá de Minas	256	21.48 S	42.58 W
Maripasoula	250	3.38 N	54.02 W
Maripipi Island I	116	11.47 N	124.19 E
Mariposa	226	37.29 N	119.57 W
Mariposa □[6]	226	37.29 N	119.58 W
Mariposa Creek ≃	226	37.14 N	120.26 W
Mariposa Slough ≃	226	37.12 N	120.46 W
Mariquita	246	5.12 N	74.54 W
Marisa	112	0.28 N	121.56 E
Marisa ≃	112	0.28 N	121.56 E
Mariscal Estigarribia	252	22.02 S	60.38 W
Marisco, Ponta do ›	287a	23.01 S	43.17 W
Mariškino	82	55.21 N	38.37 E
Marissa	219	38.15 N	89.45 W
Maritime Alps (Alpes Maritimes) (Alpi Marittime) ⋏	62	44.15 N	7.10 E
Maritimes, Alpes → Maritime Alps ⋏	62	44.15 N	7.10 E
Marittime, Alpi → Maritime Alps ⋏	62	44.15 N	7.10 E
Mari-Turek	80	56.47 N	49.36 E
Maritzburg → Pietermaritzburg	158	29.37 S	30.16 E
Mariupol' (Ždanov)	83	47.06 N	37.33 E
Mariusa, Caño ≃[1]	246	9.43 N	61.26 W
Mariusa, Isla I	241r	9.39 N	61.19 W
Marīvān	128	35.31 N	46.10 E
Mariveles	116	14.26 N	120.29 E
Märjamaa	76	58.54 N	24.26 E
Marjanovka, Ross.	86	54.58 N	72.38 E
Marjanovka, Ukr.	78	50.28 N	24.48 E
Marjanskaja	78	45.06 N	38.38 E
Marjevka	86	53.46 N	67.24 E
Marjina Gorka	76	53.31 N	28.09 E
Marjinka	83	47.56 N	37.31 E
Marjino, Ross.	82	54.28 N	37.12 E
Marjino, Ross.	89	48.31 N	130.38 E
Marjino, Ross.	265a	59.50 N	29.56 E
Marjino, Ross.	265a	59.54 N	31.00 E
Marjino, Ross.	265b	55.52 N	37.18 E
Marjinskaja	84	43.53 N	43.29 E
Marjinsko	76	58.49 N	28.32 E
Mār Jirjis, Jūn c	132	33.54 N	35.33 E
Marj 'Uyūn	132	33.22 N	35.35 E
Marka, Som.	144	1.43 N	44.53 E
Mārkā, Urd.	132	31.59 N	35.59 E
Markā I	144	18.13 N	41.19 E
Mark Acres	279b	40.21 N	79.42 W
Markakol', ozero ⊜	86	48.45 N	85.48 E
Markala	150	13.41 N	6.05 W
Markam	102	29.40 N	98.30 E
Markansu	85	39.18 N	73.20 E
Mārkāpur	122	15.44 N	79.17 E
Markaryd	26	56.26 N	13.36 E
Markazī □[4]	128	34.30 N	50.30 E
Markdale	212	44.19 N	80.39 W
Markdorf	58	47.43 N	9.23 E
Marked Tree	194	35.31 N	90.25 W
Markelo	52	52.14 N	6.30 E
Markelovo	86	56.42 N	83.33 E
Marken I	52	52.28 N	5.03 E
Markendorf	54	51.59 N	13.10 E
Markermeer ⊜	52	52.33 N	5.15 E
Markesan	190	43.42 N	88.59 W
Märket I	40	60.18 N	19.08 E
Market Bosworth	42	52.37 N	1.24 W
Market Deeping	42	52.41 N	0.19 W
Market Drayton	42	52.54 N	2.29 W
Market Harborough	42	52.29 N	0.55 W
Markethill	48	54.18 N	6.31 W
Market Lavington	42	51.18 N	1.59 W
Market Rasen	44	53.24 N	0.21 W
Market Weighton	44	53.52 N	0.40 W
Markfield	42	52.40 N	1.17 W
Markgröningen	56	48.54 N	9.05 E
Markham, On., Can.	212	43.52 N	79.16 W
Markham, Il., U.S.	278	41.35 N	87.41 W
Markham, Tx., U.S.	222	28.57 N	96.04 W
Markham ≃	164	6.35 S	146.25 E
Markham, Mount ʌ	9	82.51 S	161.21 E
Markham Bay c	176	63.30 N	71.48 W
Markinch	46	56.12 N	3.08 W
Märkisch Buchholz	54	52.07 N	13.46 E
Markit	85	38.55 N	77.38 E
Markkleeberg	54	51.17 N	12.23 E
Markland Dam ◆[6]	218	38.47 N	84.58 W
Markle, In., U.S.	216	40.50 N	85.20 W
Markle, Pa., U.S.	279b	40.34 N	79.39 W
Markleeville	226	38.41 N	119.46 W
Markleville	218	39.58 N	85.36 W
Markley Canyon V	282	38.00 N	121.50 W
Marknesse	52	52.43 N	5.52 E
Markneukirchen	54	50.18 N	12.19 E
Markoldendorf	52	51.48 N	9.46 E
Markópoulon	267c	37.54 N	23.54 E
Markounda	152	7.37 N	16.59 E
Markovka	83	49.31 N	39.34 E
Markovo, Ross.	74	64.40 N	170.25 E
Markovo, Ross.	80	57.01 N	40.30 E
Markovo, Ross.	82	55.52 N	39.17 E
Markovo, Ross.	88	57.20 N	107.04 E
Markoy	150	14.39 N	0.02 E
Markranstädt	54	51.18 N	12.13 E
Marks, Ross.	80	51.42 N	46.46 E
Marks, Ms., U.S.	194	34.15 N	90.16 W
Marks Tey	42	51.52 N	0.47 E
Marksuhl	56	50.55 N	10.11 E
Marksville	194	31.07 N	92.03 W
Markt Bibart	56	49.39 N	10.26 E
Marktbreit	56	49.40 N	10.08 E
Markt Erlbach	56	49.29 N	10.38 E
Marktheidenfeld	56	49.50 N	9.36 E
Markt Indersdorf	60	48.22 N	11.23 E
Marktl	60	48.15 N	12.51 E
Marktleugast	54	50.10 N	11.38 E
Marktleuthen	54	50.08 N	12.00 E
Marktoberdorf	58	47.47 N	10.37 E
Marktredwitz	30	50.00 N	12.06 E
Markt Rettenbach	58	47.57 N	10.23 E
Marktschellenberg	64	47.42 N	13.02 E
Markt Schwaben	60	48.11 N	11.51 E
Mark Twain Cave ⊥[5]	219	39.42 N	91.21 W
Mark Twain Lake ⊜[1]	219	39.30 N	91.45 W
Mark Twain State Park ♠	219	39.29 N	91.48 W
Markulešty	78	47.52 N	28.14 E
Markundi	140	11.33 N	23.49 E
Markvue Manor	279b	40.20 N	79.46 W
Mark West Creek ≃	226	38.30 N	122.42 W
Marl	52	51.38 N	7.05 E
Marlasi	164	5.30 S	134.38 E
Marlboro, Ab., Can.	182	53.33 N	116.45 W
Marlboro, N.J., U.S.	208	40.18 N	74.14 W
Marlboro, N.Y., U.S.	210	41.36 N	73.58 W
Marlboro, Oh., U.S.	214	40.53 N	81.12 W
Marlboro, Pa., U.S.	285	39.54 N	75.42 W
Marlborough, Austl.	166	22.49 S	149.53 E
Marlborough, Guy.	246	7.29 N	58.38 W
Marlborough, Eng., U.K.	42	51.26 N	1.43 W
Marlborough, Ct., U.S.	207	41.37 N	72.27 W
Marlborough, Ma., U.S.	207	42.20 N	71.33 W
Marlborough Downs ⋏[1]	42	51.30 N	1.45 W
Marldon	42	50.28 N	3.36 W
Marle	50	49.44 N	3.46 E
Marlenheim	58	48.37 N	7.30 E
Marles-en-Brie	261	48.44 N	2.53 E
Marles-les-Mines	50	50.30 N	2.31 E
Marlette	190	43.19 N	83.04 W
Marlette Lake ⊜	226	39.10 N	119.54 W
Marley, Il., U.S.	278	41.33 N	87.55 W
Marley, Md., U.S.	208	39.09 N	76.35 W
Marley Creek ≃	278	41.31 N	87.57 W
Marley Neck ›[1]	284b	39.12 N	76.33 W
Marlieux	58	46.04 N	5.04 E
Marlin	222	31.18 N	96.53 W
Marlinton	188	38.13 N	80.05 W
Marl-Loemühle, Flughafen ⊠	263	51.39 N	7.10 E
Marlow, Dtsch.	54	54.09 N	12.34 E
Marlow, Eng., U.K.	42	51.35 N	0.48 W
Marlow, Ok., U.S.	196	34.38 N	97.57 W
Marlpit Hill	260	51.13 N	0.04 E
Marlton	208	39.53 N	74.55 W
Marlton Heights	285	39.40 N	75.21 W
Marly	50	50.20 N	3.32 E
Marly, Forêt de ♠	261	48.50 N	2.00 E
Marly-la-Ville	261	49.05 N	2.30 E
Marly-le-Roi	50	48.52 N	2.05 E
Marma, Sve.	26	61.16 N	16.52 E
Marma, Sve.	40	60.30 N	17.25 E
Marmaduke	194	36.11 N	90.22 W
Marmagne	58	46.50 N	4.21 E
Marmande	32	44.30 N	0.10 E
Marmara, Sea of → Marmara Denizi ≂[2]	130	40.40 N	28.15 E
Marmara Adası I	130	40.38 N	27.37 E
Marmara Denizi (Sea of Marmara) ≂[2]	130	40.40 N	28.15 E
Marmara Ereğlisi	130	40.58 N	27.57 E
Marmara Gölü ⊜	130	38.37 N	28.02 E
Marmaris	130	36.51 N	28.16 E
Marmarītā	130	34.47 N	36.15 E
Marmarth	198	46.17 N	103.55 W
Marmaton ≃	194	38.00 N	94.19 W
Marmelopolis	256	22.27 S	45.10 W
Marmelos	248	6.08 S	61.50 W
Marmelos, Rio dos ≃	248	6.06 S	61.46 W
Marmet	188	38.14 N	81.34 W
Marmion Lake ⊜[1]	190	48.54 N	91.30 W
Marmirolo	64	45.13 N	10.45 E
Marmolada ʌ	64	46.26 N	11.51 E
Marmora, On., Can.	212	44.29 N	77.41 W
Marmora, N.J., U.S.	208	39.16 N	74.38 W
Marmore	66	42.33 N	12.43 E
Marmore ≃	62	45.44 N	7.37 E
Marmore, Cascàta delle ∟	66	42.33 N	12.43 E
Marmot Bay c	180	58.00 N	152.20 W
Marmot Island I	180	58.13 N	151.51 W
Marmoutier	58	48.41 N	7.23 E
Mar Muerto, Laguna c	234	16.10 N	94.10 W
Marnate	266b	45.38 N	8.54 E
Marnay	58	47.17 N	5.46 E
Marnaz	58	46.04 N	6.32 E
Marne, Dtsch.	52	53.57 N	9.00 E
Marne, Mi., U.S.	216	43.02 N	85.49 W
Marne □[5]	32	48.55 N	4.10 E
Marne ≃, Austl.	168b	34.40 S	139.18 E
Marne ≃, Fr.	32	48.49 N	2.24 E
Marne à la Saône, Canal de la ≍	58	48.44 N	4.36 E
Marne au Rhin, Canal de la ≍	56	48.35 N	7.47 E
Marneuli	84	41.28 N	44.50 E
Marnhull	42	50.58 N	2.18 W
Marnitz	54	53.19 N	11.56 E
Maroa, Il., U.S.	219	40.02 N	88.57 W
Maroa, Ven.	246	2.43 N	67.33 W
Maroala	157b	15.23 S	47.59 E
Maroantsetra	157b	15.26 S	49.44 E
Marobi Raghza	120	32.36 N	69.52 E
Maroc → Morocco □[1]	148	32.00 N	5.00 W
Maroelaboom	156	19.15 S	18.53 E
Marofandilia	157b	20.07 S	44.34 E
Maroglio ≃	70	37.03 N	14.15 E
Marokko → Morocco □[1]	148	32.00 N	5.00 W
Marol ◆[8]	272c	19.07 N	72.53 E
Marolambo	157b	20.02 S	48.07 E
Maroldsweisach	56	50.12 N	10.39 E
Marolles-en-Brie	261	48.44 N	2.33 E
Marolles-en-Hurepoix	261	48.34 N	2.18 E
Marolles-les-Braults	50	48.15 N	0.19 E
Maromandia	157b	14.13 S	48.08 E
Maromme	50	49.28 N	1.02 E
Maromokotro ʌ	157b	14.01 S	48.59 E
Marondera	154	18.10 S	31.36 E
Marone	64	45.44 N	10.05 E
Marong	102	31.07 N	99.20 E
Maronghi Creek ≃	171a	26.58 S	152.22 E
Maroni (Marowijne) ≃	250	5.45 N	53.58 W
Maroon	171a	28.10 S	152.44 E
Maroon, Mount ʌ	171a	28.13 S	152.44 E
Maroondah Aqueduct ≍[1]	274b	37.42 S	145.01 E
Maros	112	5.00 S	119.34 E
Maros (Mureș) ≃	38	46.15 N	20.13 E
Maroseranana	157b	18.32 S	48.51 E
Marostica	64	45.45 N	11.39 E
Marosvásárhely → Tîrgu Mureș	38	46.33 N	24.33 E
Marotandrano	157b	16.10 S	48.50 E
Marotiri, Îles II	14	27.55 S	143.26 W
Marotta	66	43.46 N	13.08 E
Maroua	146	10.36 N	14.20 E
Maroubra	274a	33.57 S	151.16 E
Marouini ≃	250	3.18 N	54.04 W
Marovato, Madag.	157b	13.59 S	48.36 E
Marovato, Madag.	157b	15.48 S	48.05 E
Marovato, Madag.	157b	16.28 S	48.25 E
Marovoay	157b	16.06 S	46.39 E
Marovoay Nord	157b	16.57 S	44.34 E
Marowijne □[5]	250	5.40 N	54.20 W
Marowijne (Maroni) ≃	250	5.45 N	53.58 W
Marpent	50	50.18 N	4.05 E
Marple	44	53.24 N	2.03 W
Marquam	224	45.04 N	122.41 W
Marquand	194	37.25 N	90.10 W
Marquard	158	28.54 S	27.28 E
Marquardt	54	52.27 N	12.57 E
Marquartstein	64	47.45 N	12.28 E
Marquesas Islands → Marquises, Îles II	6	9.00 S	139.30 W
Marquesas Keys II	220	24.34 N	82.08 W
Marquette, Ks., U.S.	198	38.33 N	97.50 W
Marquette, Mi., U.S.	190	46.32 N	87.23 W
Marquette Park ♠	278	41.46 N	87.42 W
Márquez, Perú	286d	11.57 S	77.08 W
Marquez, Tx., U.S.	222	31.14 N	96.15 W
Marquion	50	50.13 N	3.05 E
Marquis	241k	12.06 N	61.37 W
Marquis, Cape ›	241f	14.03 N	60.54 W
Marquise	50	50.49 N	1.42 E
Marquises, Îles (Marquesas Islands) II	6	9.00 S	139.30 W
Marrabel	168b	34.08 S	138.53 E
Marra Creek ≃	166	30.05 S	147.05 E
Marradi	66	44.04 N	11.37 E
Marradong	168a	32.52 S	116.27 E
Marrah, Jabal ʌ	140	13.04 N	24.21 E
Marra Hills ⋏[2]	140	6.05 N	27.33 E
Marrakech	148	31.38 N	8.00 W
Marrakech □[4]	148	31.30 N	8.05 W
Marramarra National Park ♠	170	33.32 S	151.04 E
Marrawah	166	40.56 S	144.41 E
Marree	166	29.39 S	138.04 E
Marrero	194	29.53 N	90.06 W
Marrickville	274a	33.55 S	151.09 E
Marromeu	156	18.20 S	35.56 E
Marrowstone Island I	224	48.04 N	122.41 W
Marrubiu	71	39.45 N	8.38 E
Marruecos → Morocco □[1]	148	32.00 N	5.00 W
Marrupa	154	13.08 S	37.30 E
Mars	214	40.41 N	80.00 W
Marsā al-Burayqah	146	30.25 N	19.34 E
Marsabit	154	2.20 N	37.59 E
Marsabit National Park ♠	154	2.20 N	38.00 E
Marsac-en-Livradois	62	45.29 N	3.44 E
Marṣafā wa Kafr Aḥmad Ḥashīsh	142	30.25 N	31.15 E
Marsal	56	48.48 N	6.36 E
Marsala	70	37.48 N	12.26 E
Marsā Maṭrūḥ	140	31.21 N	27.14 E
Marsā Maṭrūḥ □[4]	142	29.00 N	30.00 E
Marsange ≃	261	48.43 N	2.45 E
Marsangue ≃	261	48.40 N	2.47 E
Marsannay-la-Côte	58	47.16 N	4.59 E
Marsanne	62	44.39 N	4.52 E
Marsassoum	150	12.50 N	16.00 W
Mars'aty	86	60.05 N	60.29 E
Marscheid ◆[8]	263	51.14 N	7.14 E
Marsciano	66	42.54 N	12.20 E
Marsden, Austl.	166	33.45 S	147.32 E
Marsden, Eng., U.K.	262	53.36 N	1.56 W
Marsden, Point ›	168b	35.35 S	137.38 E
Marsden Park	274a	33.42 S	150.50 E
Marsdiep ⊔	52	52.59 N	4.45 E
Marseille	62	43.18 N	5.24 E
Marseille-en-Beauvaisis	50	49.35 N	1.57 E
Marseille-Marignane, Aéroport de ⊠	62	43.27 N	5.13 E
Marseilles, Il., U.S.	216	41.19 N	88.42 W
Marseilles, Oh., U.S.	214	40.42 N	83.23 W
Marsella → Marseille	62	43.18 N	5.24 E
Marsfield	274a	33.47 S	151.07 E
Marsfjället ʌ	24	65.05 N	15.28 E
Marshall, Liber.	150	6.10 N	10.23 W
Marshall, Ar., U.S.	194	35.54 N	92.37 W
Marshall, Il., U.S.	194	39.23 N	87.41 W
Marshall, Mi., U.S.	216	42.16 N	84.57 W
Marshall, Mn., U.S.	198	44.26 N	95.47 W
Marshall, Mo., U.S.	194	39.07 N	93.11 W
Marshall, N.C., U.S.	192	35.47 N	82.41 W
Marshall, Tx., U.S.	194	32.32 N	94.22 W
Marshall, Va., U.S.	188	38.51 N	77.51 W
Marshall, Wi., U.S.	216	43.10 N	89.04 W
Marshall □[6], Il., U.S.	216	41.02 N	89.24 W
Marshall □[6], In., U.S.	216	41.21 N	86.19 W
Marshall ≃	162	22.59 S	136.59 E
Marshall Bennett Islands II	164	8.50 S	151.50 E
Marshallberg	192	34.43 N	76.30 W
Marshall Canyon Regional Park ♠	280	34.09 N	117.43 W
Marshall Gold Discovery State Historical Park ♠	226	38.48 N	120.53 W
Marshall Hall	208	38.41 N	77.06 W
Marshall Islands □[1]	14	11.00 N	168.00 E
Marshall Islands II	14	9.00 N	168.00 E
Marshalls Creek	210	41.03 N	75.08 W
Marshallton, De., U.S.	208	39.43 N	75.39 W
Marshallton, Pa., U.S.	210	40.47 N	76.33 W
Marshallton, Pa., U.S.	285	39.57 N	75.41 W
Marshalltown	190	42.02 N	92.54 W
Marshallville, Ga., U.S.	192	32.27 N	83.56 W
Marshallville, Oh., U.S.	214	40.54 N	81.44 W
Marshbank Metropolitan Park ♠	281	42.36 N	83.23 W
Marsh Creek ≃, Ca., U.S.	282	37.53 N	121.49 W
Marsh Creek ≃, Mi., U.S.	281	42.06 N	83.13 W
Marsh Creek ≃, Pa., U.S.	214	41.03 N	77.36 W
Marsh Creek ≃, Pa., U.S.	285	40.03 N	75.43 W
Marsh Creek ≃, Wi., U.S.	216	42.13 N	89.04 W
Marsh Creek Lake ⊜[1]	208	40.04 N	75.44 W
Marshes Creek ≃	276	40.36 N	74.13 W
Marshfield, Eng., U.K.	42	51.28 N	2.19 W
Marshfield, Ma., U.S.	207	42.05 N	70.42 W
Marshfield, Mo., U.S.	194	37.20 N	92.54 W
Marshfield, Wi., U.S.	190	44.40 N	90.10 W
Marshfield Airport ⊠	283	42.06 N	70.40 W
Marshfield Center	283	42.07 N	70.43 W
Marshfield Hills	207	42.08 N	70.44 W
Marsh Harbour	238	26.33 N	77.03 W
Marsh Hill	210	41.29 N	76.58 W
Mars Hill, In., U.S.	218	39.43 N	86.09 W
Mars Hill, Me., U.S.	186	46.30 N	67.52 W
Mars Hill, N.C., U.S.	192	35.49 N	82.32 W
Marsh Island I	194	29.35 N	91.53 W
Marsh Lake ⊜	180	60.25 N	134.18 W
Marsh Peak ʌ	200	40.43 N	109.50 W
Marshside	262	53.40 N	2.58 W
Marshville	192	34.59 N	80.22 W
Marshyhope Creek ≃	208	38.32 N	75.45 W
Marsica ◆[1]	66	41.50 N	13.45 E
Marsico Nuovo	68	40.25 N	15.44 E
Marsico Vetere	68	40.23 N	15.49 E
Marsillargues	62	43.40 N	4.11 E
Marsimang, Tanjung ›	164	3.27 S	130.49 E
Marsing	202	43.32 N	116.48 W
Marske-by-the-Sea	44	54.36 N	1.01 W
Mars-la-Tour	56	49.06 N	5.54 E
Marson	56	48.55 N	4.32 E
Marssum	52	53.12 N	5.42 E
Märsta	40	59.37 N	17.51 E
Marstal	41	54.51 N	10.31 E
Marsteller	214	40.39 N	78.48 W
Märstetten	58	47.36 N	9.04 E
Marston	262	53.16 N	2.30 W
Marston Moor ≚	44	53.57 N	1.17 W
Marston Moor Battlesite ⊥	44	53.57 N	1.17 W
Marstons Mills	207	41.39 N	70.25 W
Marstrand	26	57.53 N	11.35 E
Marsyāngdī ≃	124	28.05 N	84.28 E
Mart	222	31.32 N	96.50 W
Marta	66	42.32 N	11.55 E
Marta ≃	66	42.14 N	11.42 E
Martaban	110	16.32 N	97.37 E
Martaban, Gulf of c	110	16.30 N	97.00 E
Martano	68	40.12 N	18.18 E
Martap	152	6.54 N	13.03 E
Martapura, Indon.	112	3.25 S	114.51 E
Martapura, Indon.	112	4.19 S	104.22 E
Marte	146	12.22 N	13.51 E
Marteg ≃	42	52.20 N	3.33 W
Martel, Fr.	32	44.56 N	1.37 E
Martel, Oh., U.S.	214	40.40 N	82.55 W
Martelange	56	49.50 N	5.44 E
Martell	226	38.22 N	120.48 W
Martello	64	46.34 N	10.47 E
Martello, Val V	64	46.31 N	10.45 E
Martemjanovskij	86	55.54 N	80.22 E
Marten ◆[8]	263	51.31 N	7.23 E
Marten Lake ⊜	190	46.42 N	79.41 W
Marten Mountain ʌ	182	55.28 N	114.43 W
Marte R. Gomez, Presa ⊜[1]	196	26.10 N	99.00 W
Martfeld	52	52.52 N	9.04 E
Marthaguy Creek ≃	166	30.16 S	147.35 E
Martha Lake	224	47.51 N	122.20 W
Marthall	262	53.17 N	2.18 W
Martham	42	52.42 N	1.38 E
Marthasville	219	38.37 N	91.03 W
Martha's Vineyard I	207	41.25 N	70.40 W
Martí, Cuba	240p	21.09 N	77.27 W
Martí, Cuba	240p	22.57 N	80.55 W
Martí, Pico ʌ	240p	20.01 N	76.35 W
Martignacco	64	46.05 N	13.08 E
Martignat	58	46.13 N	5.36 E
Martigny	58	46.06 N	7.04 E
Martigny-les-Bains	58	48.06 N	5.49 E
Martigues	62	43.24 N	5.03 E
Martil	34	35.37 N	5.17 W
Martim Francisco	256	22.31 S	46.57 W
Martin, Slov.	30	49.05 N	18.55 E
Martin, Ky., U.S.	192	37.34 N	82.45 W
Martin, Mi., U.S.	216	42.32 N	85.38 W
Martin, N.D., U.S.	198	47.49 N	100.06 W
Martin, Oh., U.S.	214	41.33 N	83.20 W
Martin, S.D., U.S.	198	43.10 N	101.43 W
Martin, Tn., U.S.	194	36.20 N	88.51 W
Martin □[6]	220	27.07 N	80.31 W
Martín ≃	34	41.18 N	0.19 W
Martín, Arroyo ≃	288	34.51 S	58.04 W
Martin, Isle I	46	57.55 N	5.14 W
Martina	58	46.53 N	10.30 E
Martina Franca	68	40.42 N	17.21 E
Martinborough	172	41.13 S	175.28 E
Martín Chico, Punta ›	258	34.10 S	58.13 W
Martindale	196	29.50 N	97.51 W
Martindale Creek ≃, Austl.	170	32.32 S	150.42 E
Martindale Creek ≃, In., U.S.	218	39.48 N	85.09 W
Martindale Pond ⊜	284a	43.11 N	79.16 W
Martin-Église	50	49.54 N	1.09 E
Martinengo	62	45.34 N	9.46 E
Mărtinești	38	45.30 N	27.18 E
Martinez, Ca., U.S.	226	38.01 N	122.07 W
Martinez, Ga., U.S.	192	33.31 N	82.04 W
Martínez ◆[8]	258	34.29 S	58.30 W
Martínez de la Torre	234	20.04 N	97.03 W
Martín García, Isla I	258	34.13 S	58.15 W
Martinho Campos	255	19.20 S	45.13 W
Martinica → Martinique □[2]	240e	14.40 N	61.00 W
Martini Creek ≃	282	37.33 N	122.31 W
Martinique □[2], N.A.	230	14.40 N	61.00 W
Martinique □[2], N.A.	240e	14.40 N	61.00 W
Martinique Passage ⊔	238	15.10 N	61.15 W
Martin Lake ⊜[1], Al., U.S.	194	32.50 N	85.55 W
Martin Lake ⊜[1], Tx., U.S.	222	32.15 N	94.35 W
Martin Marietta Corporation ⊛[3]	284b	39.20 N	76.26 W
Martinniemi	26	65.13 N	25.18 E
Martinópole	250	3.15 S	40.41 W
Martin Peninsula ›[1]	9	74.25 S	114.10 W
Martín Pérez ≃	286b	23.07 N	82.20 W
Martin Point ›	180	70.08 N	143.16 W
Martin Run ≃	279a	41.27 N	82.12 W
Martins	250	6.05 S	37.55 W
Martinsberg	61	48.22 N	15.09 E
Martins Brook ≃	283	42.34 N	71.06 W
Martinsburg, Mo., U.S.	219	39.06 N	91.38 W
Martinsburg, N.Y., U.S.	212	43.44 N	75.28 W
Martinsburg, Oh., U.S.	214	40.16 N	82.21 W
Martinsburg, Pa., U.S.	214	40.18 N	78.19 W
Martinsburg, W.V., U.S.	188	39.27 N	77.57 W
Martins Creek	208	40.47 N	75.11 W
Martins Creek ≃	210	41.37 N	75.46 W
Martinscroft	262	53.24 N	2.31 W
Martins Ferry	214	40.05 N	80.43 W
Martins Mills	222	32.25 N	95.47 W
Martins Pond ⊜	283	42.36 N	71.08 W
Martinstein	56	49.48 N	7.32 E
Martinsthal	56	50.03 N	8.07 E
Martinsville, Austl.	170	33.03 S	151.25 E
Martinsville, Il., U.S.	194	39.20 N	87.52 W
Martinsville, In., U.S.	218	39.25 N	86.25 W
Martinsville, N.J., U.S.	276	40.36 N	74.34 W
Martinsville, Oh., U.S.	218	39.19 N	83.48 W
Martinsville, Va., U.S.	192	36.41 N	79.52 W
Martinton	216	40.55 N	87.44 W
Martintown	206	45.09 N	74.42 W
Martin Van Buren National Historic Site ⊥	210	42.22 N	73.43 W
Martin Vaz, Ilhas II	244	20.30 S	28.51 W
Martis	71	40.47 N	8.49 E
Martisovo	76	56.34 N	31.55 E
Martock	42	50.59 N	2.46 W
Martofte	41	55.33 N	10.40 E
Marton, N.Z.	172	40.05 S	175.23 E
Marton, Eng., U.K.	262	53.12 N	2.13 W
Martorell	266d	41.28 N	1.56 E
Martorelles de Baix	266d	41.32 N	2.14 E
Martos	34	37.43 N	3.58 W
Martovaja	78	49.57 N	36.57 E
Martre, Lac la ⊜	176	63.15 N	117.55 W
Martti	24	67.28 N	28.28 E
Martūbah	146	32.35 N	22.46 E
Martuk	86	50.46 N	56.31 E
Martuni, Azer.	84	39.48 N	47.06 E
Martuni, Haya.	84	40.08 N	45.19 E
Martvili	84	42.25 N	42.22 E
Martville	210	43.17 N	76.38 W
Martynoviči	78	51.17 N	29.37 E
Martynovka	78	49.38 N	31.18 E
Martynovo	80	50.43 N	50.23 E
Martynovskij	80	50.29 N	42.18 E
Maru	150	12.22 N	6.22 E
Marua	164	9.30 S	149.20 E
Marudi	112	4.11 N	114.19 E
Marudu, Telukan c	112	6.45 N	116.55 E
Marugame	96	34.17 N	133.47 E
Maruggio	68	40.19 N	17.34 E
Maruia	172	42.11 S	172.13 E
Maruia ≃	172	41.47 S	172.12 E
Maruim	250	10.45 S	37.05 W
Maruko	94	36.19 N	138.16 E
Marula	154	20.26 S	28.06 E
Marulan	170	34.43 S	150.00 E
Marulan South	170	34.46 S	150.02 E
Marum	52	53.08 N	6.16 E
Marum, Mont ʌ	175f	16.15 S	168.07 E
Marunga	152	17.27 S	20.02 E
Marungu	154	3.44 S	30.48 E
Marungu ⋏	154	7.42 S	30.00 E
Maruoka	94	36.09 N	136.16 E
Mårup	41	55.57 N	10.35 E
Marusino	265b	55.42 N	37.59 E
Maruškino	82	55.36 N	37.12 E
Ma'rūt	120	31.34 N	67.03 E
Marutea I[1]	14	17.00 S	143.10 W
Maruyama	94	35.01 N	139.58 E
Maruyama ≃	96	35.39 N	134.50 E
Marv Dasht	128	29.50 N	52.40 E
Marve ◆[8]	272c	19.12 N	72.49 E
Marvejols	32	44.33 N	3.18 E
Marvell	194	34.33 N	90.54 W
Marvel Loch	162	31.28 S	119.28 E
Marviken	40	58.34 N	16.51 E
Marvila ◆[8]	266c	38.44 N	9.06 W
Marville	56	49.27 N	5.27 E
Marvin Creek ≃	214	41.48 N	78.26 W
Marvine, Mount ʌ	200	38.40 N	111.39 W
Mar Vista ◆[8]	280	34.00 N	118.27 W
Mārwār	120	25.44 N	73.36 E
Marwayne	184	53.32 N	110.20 W
Marwitz	264a	52.41 N	13.09 E
Marwitzer Heide ◆[3]	264a	52.40 N	13.06 E
Marwood	214	40.48 N	79.47 W
Marxhagen	54	53.37 N	12.36 E
Marxloh ◆[8]	263	51.31 N	6.46 E
Mary	128	37.36 N	61.50 E
Mary □[8]	128	37.30 N	62.30 E
Mary ≃, Austl.	164	12.53 S	131.38 E
Mary ≃, Austl.	166	25.26 S	152.55 E
Mary Anne Group II	162	21.13 S	115.32 E
Maryborough, Austl.	166	25.32 S	152.42 E
Maryborough, Austl.	169	37.03 S	143.45 E
Maryborough → Port Laoise	48	53.02 N	7.17 W
Mary D	208	40.45 N	76.04 W
Marydale	158	29.23 S	22.05 E
Marydel	208	39.06 N	75.44 W
Maryfield	184	49.48 N	101.32 W
Maryhill	224	45.41 N	120.49 W
Mary Jane, Lake ⊜	220	28.22 N	81.11 W
Mary Kathleen	166	20.49 S	139.58 E
Maryknoll	210	41.11 N	73.50 W
Mary Lake ⊜	212	45.15 N	79.15 W
Maryland	210	42.32 N	74.53 W
Maryland □[3], U.S.	178	39.00 N	76.45 W
Maryland □[3], U.S.	188	39.00 N	76.45 W
Maryland, University of (Baltimore County Campus) ⊛[2], Md., U.S.	284b	39.15 N	76.43 W
Maryland, University of ⊛[2], Md., U.S.	284c	38.59 N	76.57 W
Maryland City	208	39.05 N	76.49 W
Maryland Gardens Park ♠	275b	43.47 N	79.32 W
Maryland Heights	219	38.42 N	90.25 W
Maryland Historical Society ⊛	284b	39.18 N	76.37 W
Maryland Line	208	39.42 N	76.39 W
Maryland Park	284c	38.53 N	76.54 W
Marylebone	262	53.34 N	2.38 W
Maryneal	196	32.14 N	100.27 W
Marypark	46	57.26 N	3.21 W
Maryport	44	54.43 N	3.30 W
Marys ≃, Il., U.S.	194	37.53 N	89.47 W
Marys ≃, Nv., U.S.	204	41.04 N	115.16 W
Marys Creek ≃	202	42.18 N	115.48 W
Mary's Igloo	180	65.09 N	165.04 W
Marys Peak ʌ	202	44.30 N	123.33 W
Marystown	186	47.10 N	55.09 W
Marysvale	200	38.26 N	112.13 W
Marysville, Austl.	169	37.31 S	145.45 E
Marysville, B.C., Can.	182	49.38 N	115.57 W
Marysville, N.B., Can.	186	45.59 N	66.35 W
Marysville, Ca., U.S.	226	39.08 N	121.35 W
Marysville, Ks., U.S.	198	39.50 N	96.38 W
Marysville, Mi., U.S.	214	42.54 N	82.29 W
Marysville, Oh., U.S.	214	40.14 N	83.22 W
Marysville, Pa., U.S.	208	40.20 N	76.55 W
Marysville, Wa., U.S.	224	48.03 N	122.10 W
Maryūṭ, Buḥayrat ⊜	142	31.08 N	29.56 E
Maryvale	171a	28.05 S	152.15 E
Maryvale ◆[8]	275b	43.46 N	79.18 W
Maryville, Mo., U.S.	194	40.20 N	94.52 W
Maryville, Tn., U.S.	192	35.45 N	83.58 W
Marywell	46	57.02 N	2.42 W
Marywood	216	41.48 N	88.18 W
Marzabotto	64	44.20 N	11.12 E
Marzagão	255	17.59 S	48.39 W
Marzahn ◆[8]	264a	52.33 N	13.33 E
Marzahna	54	52.00 N	12.46 E
Marzahne	54	52.31 N	12.31 E
Marzal, Aven de ⊥[5]	62	44.22 N	4.31 E
Marzo, Punta ›	246	6.50 N	77.42 W
Marzolara	64	44.38 N	10.10 E
Marzūq	146	25.55 N	13.55 E
Marzūq, Ḥamādat ◆[2]	146	26.10 N	12.45 E
Marzūq, Ṣaḥrā' ◆[2]	146	24.30 N	13.00 E
Masa	152	3.45 S	15.29 E
Masachapa	236	11.47 N	86.31 W
Mas'adah (Cæsarea Philippi)	132	33.14 N	35.45 E
Masada → Meẕada, Ḥorvot ⊥	132	31.19 N	35.21 E
Más Afuera, Isla → Alejandro Selkirk, Isla I	244	33.45 S	80.46 W
Masagua	236	14.12 N	90.51 W
Masaguisi	116	12.41 N	121.32 E
Masai	114	1.29 N	103.53 E
Masai Mara Game Reserve ◆[4]	154	1.15 S	35.15 E
Masai Steppe ⋏[1]	154	4.45 S	37.00 E
Masak	85	43.37 N	78.18 E
Masaka	154	0.20 S	31.44 E
Masaki, Nihon	96	33.47 N	132.42 E
Masaki, Nihon	268	35.13 N	140.02 E
Masalembu Besar, Pulau I	112	5.34 S	114.26 E
Masally	84	39.03 N	48.40 E
Masalok, Puntan ›	174n	15.01 N	145.41 E
Masamba	112	2.32 S	120.20 E
Masan	98	35.11 N	128.32 E
Masangwe ʌ	154	5.28 S	30.05 E
Masānjor	126	24.07 N	87.19 E
Masapelid Island I	116	9.42 N	125.39 E
Masapun	112	7.47 S	126.38 E
Masaṟah	142	27.29 N	30.50 E
Masaran	115a	7.28 S	110.55 E
Ma'ṣarat Samālūṭ	142	28.19 N	30.43 E
Masaryktown	220	28.26 N	82.27 W
Masasi	154	10.43 S	38.48 E
Masatepe	236	11.55 N	86.09 W
Más a Tierra, Isla → Róbinson Crusoe, Isla I	244	33.38 S	78.52 W
Masaya	236	11.58 N	86.06 W
Masaya □[5]	236	12.00 N	86.10 W
Masba	146	11.30 N	13.00 E
Masbate	116	12.22 N	123.36 E
Masbate □[4]	116	12.20 N	123.30 E
Masbate Island I	116	12.15 N	123.30 E
Masbate Pass ⊔	116	12.30 N	123.35 E
Mascali	70	37.45 N	15.12 E
Mascarene Basin ✧[1]	12	15.00 S	56.00 E
Mascarene Islands II	157c	21.00 S	57.00 E
Mascarene Plateau ✧[3]	12	10.00 S	60.00 E
Mascasín	252	31.22 S	66.59 W
Maschen	52	53.24 N	10.02 E
Maschito	68	40.54 N	15.50 E
Mascot, Austl.	274a	33.56 S	151.12 E
Mascot, Tn., U.S.	192	36.03 N	83.44 W
Mascota	234	20.32 N	104.49 W
Mascota ≃	234	20.38 N	104.59 W
Mascotte	220	28.35 N	81.53 W
Mascouche	206	45.45 N	73.36 W
Mascouche ≃	206	45.41 N	73.40 W
Mascoutah	219	38.29 N	89.47 W
Mascuppic Lake ⊜	283	42.41 N	71.23 W
Mase	102	27.16 N	104.08 E
Masefield	184	49.09 N	107.48 W
Masela, Pulau I	164	8.09 S	129.50 E
Masenberg ʌ	61	47.21 N	15.53 E
Maser	64	45.48 N	11.59 E
Maserada sul Piave	64	45.45 N	12.17 E
Maseru	158	29.28 S	27.30 E
Masevaux	58	47.47 N	7.00 E
Maševka	78	49.26 N	34.52 E
Maševo	78	52.06 N	32.48 E
Masha	100	27.26 N	117.50 E
Mashaba	154	20.02 S	30.29 E
Mashaba Mountains ⋏	154	18.45 S	30.32 E
Mash'abbe' Sade	132	31.00 N	34.47 E
Mashābih I	128	25.37 N	36.29 E
Mashalah	142	30.44 N	31.08 E
Masham	44	54.13 N	1.40 W
Mashan, Zhg.	89	45.13 N	130.35 E
Mashan, Zhg.	100	27.33 N	113.46 E
Mashan, Zhg.	102	23.50 N	108.16 E
Mashar	140	9.14 N	26.52 E
Mashbury	260	51.47 N	0.24 E
Mashel ≃	224	46.51 N	122.20 W
Mashenqiao	105	40.04 N	117.36 E
Masherbrum ʌ	123	35.43 N	76.18 E
Mashgharah	132	33.32 N	35.39 E
Mashhad, Īrān	128	36.18 N	59.36 E
Mash-had, Yis.	132	32.44 N	35.19 E
Mashi, Nig.	150	13.00 N	7.54 E
Mashi, Zhg.	100	29.05 N	114.22 E
Mashi, Zhg.	100	25.01 N	114.09 E
Mashike	92a	43.51 N	141.31 E
Mashiko	94	36.28 N	140.06 E
Mashita ≃	94	35.40 N	137.10 E
Mashīz	128	29.56 N	56.37 E
Mashkai ≃	128	26.02 N	65.19 E
Māshkel, Hāmūn-i- ⊜	128	28.15 N	63.00 E
Māshkel, Rūd-i- (Māshkīd) ≃	128	28.02 N	63.25 E
Mashki Chāh	128	29.01 N	62.27 E
Māshkīd (Rūd-i-Māshkel) ≃	128	28.02 N	63.25 E
Mashonaland North □[4]	154	16.30 S	30.00 E
Mashonaland South □[4]	154	18.15 S	30.45 E
Mashpee	207	41.38 N	70.28 W
Mashra'ur-Raqq	140	8.25 N	29.16 E
Mashtūl as-Sūq	142	30.22 N	31.22 E
Mashū-ko ⊜	92a	43.35 N	144.32 E
Masibi	152	11.08 S	22.42 E
Masihi	114	2.47 N	99.40 E
Masīlah, Wādī al- V	144	15.10 N	51.08 E
Masi-Manimba	152	4.46 S	17.55 E
Masin	164	6.15 S	139.19 E
Masina	272b	22.55 N	88.32 E
Masindi	154	1.41 N	31.43 E
Masini Port	154	1.42 N	32.05 E
Masinloc	116	15.32 N	119.57 E
Masīr	142	31.03 N	31.00 E
Maṣīrah I	118	20.25 N	58.50 E
Maṣīrah, Khalīj c	118	20.10 N	58.15 E
Masis	84	40.00 N	44.29 E
Masisea	248	8.36 S	74.19 W
Masisi	154	1.24 S	28.49 E
Masjed-e Soleymān	128	31.58 N	49.18 E
Masjid Tanah	114	2.21 N	102.07 E
Mask, Lough ⊜	48	53.35 N	9.20 W
Maska	150	11.20 N	7.20 E
Maskan, Ras ›	144	11.10 N	43.33 E
Maskanah	130	36.01 N	38.05 E
Maskin	128	23.35 N	56.39 E
Maškino	82	54.53 N	36.08 E
Maskinongé □[6]	206	46.35 N	73.30 W
Maskinongé ≃, P.Q., Can.	206	46.10 N	73.01 W
Maskinongé ≃, P.Q., Can.	206	45.49 N	74.40 W
Maskinongé, Lac ⊜	206	46.19 N	73.23 W
Maškoviči	82	54.11 N	36.17 E
Masku	26	60.34 N	22.06 E
Maskūtān	128	26.51 N	59.49 E
Maskwa ≃	184	50.33 N	96.08 W
Masl'anino	86	54.20 N	84.13 E
Masl'anskaja	86	55.56 N	70.08 E
Maslova	265a	59.47 N	30.48 E
Maslovka	78	51.33 N	39.14 E
Maslovo	86	60.07 N	60.30 E
Masnières	50	50.07 N	3.13 E
Maso	150	7.14 N	2.53 W
Masoala	157b	15.59 S	50.10 E
Masoala, Cap ›	157b	15.59 S	50.13 E
Masoala, Presqu'île de ›[1]	157b	15.40 S	50.12 E
Masoarivo	157b	19.03 S	44.19 E
Masomeloka	157b	20.17 S	48.37 E
Mason, Mi., U.S.	216	42.34 N	84.26 W
Mason, Oh., U.S.	218	39.21 N	84.18 W
Mason, Tn., U.S.	194	35.24 N	89.31 W
Mason, Tx., U.S.	196	30.44 N	99.13 W
Mason, W.V., U.S.	188	39.01 N	82.01 W
Mason □[6], Il., U.S.	219	40.18 N	90.04 W
Mason □[6], Ky., U.S.	218	38.35 N	83.48 W
Mason □[6], Wa., U.S.	224	47.20 N	123.09 W
Mason, Lake ⊜	162	27.39 S	119.34 E
Mason Bay c	172	46.56 S	167.44 E
Mason City, Il., U.S.	219	40.12 N	89.41 W
Mason City, Ia., U.S.	190	43.09 N	93.12 W
Mason City, Ne., U.S.	198	41.13 N	99.18 W
Masone	62	44.30 N	8.42 E
Masonicus Brook ≃	276	41.06 N	74.09 W
Mason Lake ⊜	224	47.20 N	122.57 W
Masons Creek ≃	285	39.59 N	74.51 W
Mason Valley V	226	39.07 N	119.10 W
Masonville, N.J., U.S.	285	39.59 N	74.52 W
Masonville, N.Y., U.S.	210	42.15 N	75.23 W
Maspeth ◆[8]	276	40.43 N	73.55 W
Masqat (Muscat)	128	23.37 N	58.35 E
Maṣra'	142	27.14 N	31.02 E
Massa	64	44.01 N	10.09 E
Massa-Carrara □[4]	64	44.15 N	10.03 E
Massachusetts □[3], U.S.	178	42.15 N	71.50 W
Massachusetts □[3], U.S.	207	42.15 N	71.50 W
Massachusetts (Boston), University of ⊛[2]	283	42.19 N	71.03 W
Massachusetts Bay c	207	42.20 N	70.50 W
Massachusetts Correctional Institution ⊛	283	42.07 N	71.18 W
Massachusetts Institute of Technology ⊛[2]	283	42.21 N	71.06 W
Massaciuccoli, Lago di ⊜	66	43.50 N	10.20 E
Massacre Lake ⊜	204	41.39 N	119.35 W
Massa Fermana	66	43.09 N	13.28 E
Massa Fiscaglia	66	44.48 N	12.01 E
Massafra	68	40.35 N	17.07 E
Massaguet	146	12.28 N	15.26 E
Massakory	146	13.00 N	15.44 E
Massalassef	146	11.43 N	17.08 E
Massa Lombarda	66	44.27 N	11.49 E
Massa Lubrense	68	40.36 N	14.20 E
Massa Marittima	66	43.03 N	10.53 E
Massa Martana	66	42.46 N	12.31 E
Massandra	78	44.32 N	34.12 E
Massangano	152	9.37 S	14.15 E
Massangena	156	21.32 S	32.57 E
Massapê	250	3.31 S	40.19 W
Massapequa	210	40.40 N	73.28 W
Massapequa Park	276	40.40 N	73.27 W
Massapequa Reserve County Park ♠	276	40.42 N	73.27 W
Massapoag Brook ≃	283	42.09 N	71.09 W
Massapoag Lake ⊜	283	42.06 N	71.11 W
Massara	156	18.20 S	34.09 E
Massarosa	66	43.52 N	10.20 E
Massasoit State Park ♠	207	41.53 N	71.01 W
Massaua → Mitsiwa	144	15.38 N	39.28 E
Massawa → Mitsiwa	144	15.38 N	39.28 E
Massawippi ≃	206	45.22 N	71.51 W
Massawippi, Lake ⊜	206	45.14 N	72.00 W
Massay	50	47.09 N	2.00 E
Massé, Ruisseau ≃	275a	45.28 N	73.17 W
Massello	62	44.57 N	7.04 E
Massen	52	51.32 N	7.38 E
Massena, Ia., U.S.	198	41.15 N	94.46 W
Massena, N.Y., U.S.	206	44.55 N	74.53 W
Massenya	146	11.24 N	16.10 E
Masset	182	54.02 N	132.09 W
Masset Inlet c	182	53.42 N	132.20 W
Masseube	32	43.26 N	0.35 E
Massey	190	46.12 N	82.05 W
Massiac	32	45.15 N	3.12 E
Massiaru	76	58.00 N	24.35 E
Massico, Monte ʌ	68	41.10 N	13.55 E

Symbols in the index entries represent the broad categories identified in the key at the right. Symbols with superior numbers (⋏[1]) identify subcategories (see complete key on page *I · 1*).

Symbole im Register stellen die rechts im Schlüssel erklärten Kategorien dar. Symbole mit hochgestellten Ziffern (⋏[1]) bezeichnen Unterabteilungen einer Kategorie (vgl. vollständiger Schlüssel auf Seite *I · 1*).

Los símbolos incluídos en el texto del índice representan las grandes categorias identificadas con la clave a la derecha. Los símbolos con numeros en su parte superior (⋏[1]) identifican las subcategorías (véase la clave completa en la página *I · 1*).

Les symboles de l'index représentent les catégories indiquées dans la légende à droite. Les symboles suivis d'un indice (⋏[1]) représentent des sous-catégories (voir légende complète à la page *I · 1*).

Os símbolos incluídos no texto do índice representam as grandes categorias identificadas com a chave à direita. Os símbolos com números em sua parte superior (⋏[1]) identificam as subcategorias (veja-se a chave completa à página *I · 1*).

ʌ Mountain	Berg	Montaña	Montagne	Montanha
⋏ Mountains	Gebirge	Montañas	Montagnes	Montanhas
)(Pass	Paß	Paso	Col	Passo
V Valley, Canyon	Tal, Cañon	Valle, Cañón	Vallée, Canyon	Vale, Canhão
≚ Plain	Ebene	Llano	Plaine	Planície
› Cape	Kap	Cabo	Cap	Cabo
I Island	Insel	Isla	Île	Ilha
II Islands	Inseln	Islas	Îles	Ilhas
⊥ Other Topographic Features	Andere Topographische Objekte	Otros Elementos Topográficos	Autres données topographiques	Outros acidentes topográficos

ESPAÑOL Nombre	Página	Lat.°′	Long.°′ W = Oeste

FRANÇAIS Nom	Page	Lat.°′	Long.°′ W = Ouest

PORTUGUÊS Nome	Página	Lat.°′	Long.°′ W = Oeste

Massieville 218 39.16 N 82.58 W
Massif Central → Central, Massif ⋏ 32 45.00 N 3.10 E
Massillon 214 40.48 N 81.32 W
Massima Camp 152 1.27 S 11.42 E
Massina 273b 4.22 S 15.22 E
Massina ✦1 150 14.30 N 5.00 W
Massinga 156 23.20 S 35.25 E
Massingir 156 23.51 S 32.04 E
Massive, Mount ∧ 200 39.12 N 106.28 W
Masson, Lac ⊜ 206 46.03 N 74.02 W
Masson Island I 9 66.08 S 96.34 E
Massy 261 48.44 N 2.17 E
Mastābah 144 20.49 N 39.20 E
Maštaga 84 40.32 N 50.00 E
Masterson 196 35.38 N 101.58 W
Masterton 172 40.57 S 175.40 E
Mas-Thibert 62 43.34 N 4.44 E
Mastic Point 192 25.03 N 77.57 W
Mastigouche ≃ 206 46.20 N 73.24 W
Mastigouche Nord ≃ 206 46.24 N 73.25 W
Mastūj 123 36.17 N 72.31 E
Mastūj ≃ 123 35.54 N 71.49 E
Mastung 120 29.48 N 66.51 E
Mastūrah 128 23.06 N 38.50 E
Masu 146 12.10 N 13.19 E
Masua 126 24.16 N 90.46 E
Masuda 96 34.40 N 131.51 E
Masuho 94 35.34 N 138.28 E
Masuika 152 7.37 S 22.32 E
Masuku 154 17.12 S 27.07 E
Māsūleh 128 37.10 N 48.59 E
Masulipatam → Machilīpatnam 122 16.10 N 81.08 E
Masura 126 23.16 N 90.24 E
Masurai, Gunung ∧ 112 2.30 S 101.51 E
Masury 214 41.12 N 80.32 W
Masvingo 154 20.05 S 30.50 E
Maşyāf 130 35.03 N 36.21 E
Maszewo, Pol. 30 53.29 N 15.02 E
Maszewo, Pol. 54 52.06 N 14.55 E
Mat ≃ 38 41.39 N 19.34 E
Mata, Indon. 115b 8.12 S 122.56 E
Mata, Zaïre 152 7.53 S 21.58 E
Mata Amarilla 254 49.36 S 71.13 W
Mataba, Mount ∧ 269f 14.42 N 121.10 E
Matabeleland North □4 154 19.00 S 27.15 E
Matabeleland South □4 154 21.00 S 29.15 E
Mātābhānga 124 26.20 N 89.13 E
Matabuena 34 41.10 N 3.40 W
Matachel ≃ 34 38.50 N 6.17 W
Matachewan 190 47.56 N 80.39 W
Matacuni ≃ 246 3.02 N 65.16 W
Matad 88 46.58 N 115.18 E
Mata de Plátano, Quebrada ≃ 286c 10.35 N 66.46 W
Matadero Creek ≃ 282 37.26 N 122.08 W
Mata de São João 255 12.31 S 38.17 W
Matadi 152 5.49 S 13.27 E
Matador 196 34.00 N 100.49 W
Matagalpa 236 12.55 N 85.55 W
Matagalpa □5 236 13.00 N 85.30 W
Matagami 176 49.45 N 77.38 W
Matag-ob 116 11.07 N 124.29 E
Matagorda 196 28.41 N 95.58 W
Matagorda □6 222 28.57 N 96.00 W
Matagorda Bay c 196 28.35 N 96.20 W
Matagorda Island I 196 28.15 N 96.30 W
Matagorda Peninsula >1 196 28.32 N 96.07 W
Mata Grande 250 9.07 S 37.44 W
Matahiae, Pointe > 174s 17.49 S 149.17 W
Mataiea 174s 17.45 S 149.23 W
Mataiva I1 14 14.53 S 148.40 W
Mataj 86 45.53 N 78.43 E
Matajing 107 29.32 N 104.00 E
Matak, Pulau I 112 3.18 N 106.16 E
Matakana, Austl. 166 33.00 S 145.54 E
Matakana, N.Z. 172 36.21 S 174.43 E
Matakana Island I 172 37.35 S 176.05 E
Matakitaki ≃ 172 41.48 S 172.19 E
Matala 152 14.46 S 15.04 E
Matale 122 7.28 N 80.37 E
Matam 150 15.40 N 13.15 W
Matama 96 33.36 N 131.28 E
Matama, Cerro ∧ 236 9.47 N 83.15 W
Matamata 172 37.49 S 175.47 E
Matameye 150 13.26 N 8.28 E
Matamoras 210 41.22 N 74.42 W
Matamoros, Méx. 232 25.53 N 97.30 W
Matamoros, Méx. 232 25.32 N 103.15 W
Matan 112 1.52 S 110.00 E
Matana 154 3.46 S 29.41 E
Matana, Danau ⊜ 112 2.28 S 121.20 E
Matanalem, Cape > 164 2.28 S 149.57 E
Matandu ≃ 154 8.45 S 39.19 E
Matane 186 48.51 N 67.32 W
Matang, Malay. 114 4.49 N 100.41 E
Matang, Zhg. 100 29.17 N 113.05 E
Matang, Zhg. 100 32.20 N 121.04 E
Matangi 172 37.49 S 175.25 E
Matani 84 42.06 N 45.13 E
Matanni 123 33.48 N 71.34 E
Matanuska ≃ 180 61.30 N 149.15 W
Matanza, Aeródromo ⊠ 288 34.44 S 58.30 W
Matanza, Río de la ≃ 258 34.42 S 58.28 W
Matanzas, Cuba 240p 23.03 N 81.35 W
Matanzas, Méx. 234 21.37 N 101.38 W
Matanzas □4 240p 22.40 N 81.20 W
Matanzas, Bahía de c 240p 23.04 N 81.30 W
Matanza → San Justo 258 34.40 S 58.33 W
Matapa 156 23.11 S 24.39 E
Matapalo, Cabo > 236 8.23 N 83.19 W
Matape ≃ 232 28.25 N 110.26 W
Matapédia 186 47.58 N 66.57 W
Matapédia, Lac ⊜ 186 48.33 N 67.33 W
Matapi ≃ 250 0.03 S 51.12 W
Mata Point > 174v 19.07 S 169.51 W
Matapu 172 39.29 S 174.14 E
Mataquito ≃ 252 34.59 S 72.12 W
Matará, Perú 248 7.16 S 78.16 W
Matara, S. Lan. 122 5.56 N 80.33 E
Mataram 115b 8.35 S 116.07 E
Matarani 248 17.00 S 72.06 W
Mataranka 164 14.56 S 133.07 E
Matārimah, Ra's > 142 29.27 N 32.42 E
Matarinao Bay c 116 11.14 N 125.34 E
Mataró 34 41.32 N 2.27 E
Matarraña ≃ 34 41.14 N 0.22 E
Matas ∧ 266d 41.30 N 2.16 E
Matasiri, Pulau I 112 4.48 S 115.48 E
Mätäsvaara 26 63.26 N 29.36 E
Matata 172 37.53 S 176.45 E
Matatepai, Pointe > 174x 9.43 S 139.02 W
Matatiele 158 30.24 S 28.43 E
Mātātīla Dam ✦6 124 25.06 N 78.22 E
Matatindoc Point > 116 9.43 N 122.23 E
Matatula, Cape > 174u 14.15 S 170.34 W
Mataura 172 46.11 S 168.52 E
Mataurá ≃, Bra. 248 5.30 S 60.45 W
Mataura ≃, N.Z. 172 46.34 S 168.43 E
Matāutu 175a 13.57 S 171.56 W
Mataval, Baie de c 174s 17.30 S 149.30 W
Matavera 174k 21.13 S 159.44 W
Mataveri 174z 27.10 S 109.27 E
Mataveri Airstrip ⊠ 174z 27.10 S 109.25 W
Matawai 172 38.21 S 177.32 E
Matawan 208 40.24 N 74.13 W
Matawin ≃ 206 46.54 N 72.56 W
Matāy 142 28.25 N 30.46 E
Matbūl 142 31.05 N 31.02 E
Matča 85 39.27 N 69.39 E
Matchaponix Brook ≃ 276 40.23 N 74.23 W
Matchi-Manitou, Lac ⊜ 190 48.00 N 77.04 W
Matching 260 51.47 N 0.13 E
Matching Green 260 51.47 N 0.14 E
Matching Tye 260 51.47 N 0.12 E
Mateare 236 12.14 N 86.26 W
Mateba, Île de I 152 5.54 S 12.50 E
Matehuala 234 23.39 N 100.39 W
Mateke Hills ⋏2 154 21.48 S 31.00 E
Mateko 152 4.03 S 18.55 E
Matelica 66 43.15 N 13.00 E
Matemo, Ilha I 154 12.13 S 40.36 E
Matera 68 40.40 N 16.37 E
Matera □4 68 40.30 N 16.25 E
Materborn 52 51.46 N 6.06 E
Matese, Lago del ⊜ 68 41.25 N 14.25 E
Matese, Monti del ⋏ 66 41.27 N 14.22 E
Mátészalka 30 47.57 N 22.19 E
Matete ≃ 273b 4.24 S 15.20 E
Matetsi 154 18.16 S 25.56 E
Mateur 148 37.03 N 9.40 E
Matewan 192 37.37 N 82.09 W
Matfield 207 42.02 N 70.59 W
Matfors 26 62.21 N 17.02 E
Matha 32 45.52 N 0.19 W
Mathbaria 126 22.18 N 89.57 E
Mathematicians Seamounts ✤3 16 15.00 N 111.00 W
Mather, Mb., Can. 184 49.06 N 99.07 W
Mather, Ca., U.S. 226 37.53 N 119.52 W
Mather, Pa., U.S. 188 39.56 N 80.04 W
Mather Air Force Base ■ 226 38.34 N 121.18 W
Mather Gorge V 284c 38.59 N 77.15 W
Matheson 190 48.32 N 80.28 W
Matheson Island 184 51.44 N 96.56 W
Matheu 258 34.22 S 58.50 W
Mathews 208 37.26 N 76.19 W
Mathews □6 208 37.25 N 76.20 W
Mathews, Lake ⊜ 228 33.51 N 117.26 W
Mathi 62 45.15 N 7.32 E
Mathis 196 28.05 N 97.49 W
Māthle 272b 22.35 N 88.14 E
Mathry 42 51.57 N 5.05 W
Mathura, India 122 10.57 N 78.27 E
Mathura, India 124 27.30 N 77.41 E
Mathura Bil ⊜ 272b 22.56 N 88.29 E
Mathurai → Madurai 122 9.56 N 78.07 E
Mathurāpur, Bngl. 126 24.02 N 88.47 E
Mathurāpur, Bngl. 126 23.17 N 89.15 E
Mati 116 6.57 N 126.13 E
Matiacoali 150 12.22 N 1.02 E
Matiakhola 126 23.16 N 86.56 E
Mātiāli 124 26.56 N 88.49 E
Matiāri 120 25.36 N 68.27 E
Matias Barbosa 256 21.53 S 43.20 W
Matías Romero 234 16.53 N 95.02 W
Mātibhānga 126 22.49 N 89.56 E
Matícora ≃ 246 11.03 N 71.09 W
Matiere 172 38.45 S 175.06 E
Matignon 32 48.36 N 2.18 W
Matiguás 236 12.50 N 85.28 W
Matinecock 276 40.53 N 73.38 W
Matinenda Lake ⊜ 190 46.22 N 82.57 W
Matinha 250 3.06 S 45.02 W
Matinicock Point > 276 40.54 N 73.38 W
Matinicus Island I 188 43.54 N 68.55 W
Matino 68 40.02 N 18.08 E
Matipó 255 20.17 S 42.21 W
Maţir Ţāris 142 29.22 N 30.54 E
Matiyure ≃ 246 7.36 N 67.39 W
Matjiesfontein 158 33.14 S 20.35 E
Matkasel'kja 26 61.58 N 30.33 E
Mātla ≃1 126 22.04 N 88.38 E
Matlab Bāzār 126 23.20 N 90.43 E
Matlacha 220 26.37 N 82.05 W
Matlacha Pass ⊔ 220 26.37 N 82.04 W
Matlamanyane 156 19.33 S 25.57 E
Matlapa 234 21.15 N 98.50 W
M'atlevo 76 54.54 N 35.39 E
Mātli 120 25.02 N 68.39 E
Matlock, Eng., U.K. 44 53.08 N 1.32 W
Matlock, Wa., U.S. 224 47.14 N 123.25 W
Matlock, Mount ∧ 169 37.35 S 146.11 E
Matmata 148 33.33 N 9.58 E
Matnog 116 12.35 N 124.05 E
Mato 154 8.01 S 24.55 E
Mato ≃ 246 7.09 N 65.07 W
Mato, Cerro ∧ 246 7.15 N 65.14 W
Matoaca 208 37.13 N 77.28 W
Matobe 112 2.42 S 100.11 E
Matočkin Šar 72 73.16 N 56.27 E
Matočkin Šar, proliv ⊔ 72 73.20 N 55.21 E
Mato Grosso □3 242 12.00 S 57.00 W
Mato Grosso, Planalto do ⋏1 242 15.30 S 56.00 W
Mato Grosso do Sul □3 242 20.00 S 55.00 W
Matola-Rio 156 25.58 S 32.26 E
Matombo 154 7.03 S 37.46 E
Mato Mole, Serra do ⋏2 256 23.00 S 46.12 W
Matong 164 5.35 S 151.45 E
Matonipi ≃ 186 51.21 N 69.45 W
Matope 154 15.20 S 34.59 E
Matopo Hills ⋏2 154 20.36 S 28.28 E
Matopos 154 20.24 S 28.28 E
Matos ≃ 248 14.07 S 65.25 W
Matosinhos 34 41.11 N 8.42 W
Matoso, Ponta do > 287a 22.50 S 43.11 W
Matou, T'aiwan 100 23.11 N 120.14 E
Matou, Zhg. 98 36.29 N 114.26 E
Matou, Zhg. 100 25.14 N 118.22 E
Matou, Zhg. 100 29.49 N 115.35 E
Matou, Zhg. 100 30.48 N 118.29 E
Matou, Zhg. 105 39.46 N 116.49 E
Matou, Zhg. 105 39.18 N 116.45 E
Matou, Zhg. 105 39.33 N 116.07 E
Matouji 98 35.02 N 115.07 E
Matour 58 46.18 N 4.29 E
Matoury 250 4.51 N 52.20 W
Matouxi 107 30.15 N 106.31 E
Matouying 98 39.18 N 118.47 E
Matouzhen, Zhg. 98 34.39 N 118.18 E
Matouzhen, Zhg. 100 33.32 N 118.56 E
Mato Verde 255 15.23 S 42.52 W
Matozinhos 255 19.35 S 44.07 W
Mátra ⋏ 30 47.55 N 20.00 E
Maţraḩ 128 23.38 N 58.34 E
Matraville 274a 33.54 S 151.18 E
Matrei am Brenner 64 47.08 N 11.27 E
Matrei in Osttirol 64 47.00 N 12.32 E
Matru 150 7.36 N 12.11 W
Matsap 158 28.38 S 22.47 E
Matsapha 158 26.29 S 31.23 E
Matsari 152 5.21 N 12.14 E
Matsena 150 13.05 N 10.05 E
Matsiatra ≃ 157b 21.25 S 45.33 E
Matsieng 158 29.36 S 27.32 E
Matsknutsgårdarna 40 60.28 N 15.22 E
Matsqui 224 49.12 N 122.25 W
Matsubara 96 34.34 N 135.33 E
Matsubushi 268 35.55 N 139.49 E
Matsuda 94 35.21 N 139.09 E
Matsudai 94 37.08 N 138.37 E
Matsudo 94 35.47 N 139.54 E
Matsudo Race Track ♠ 268 35.48 N 139.55 E
Matsue 96 35.28 N 133.04 E
Matsugasaki 268 35.53 N 139.58 E
Matsuida 94 36.19 N 138.48 E
Matsukawa, Nihon 94 36.25 N 137.51 E
Matsukawa, Nihon 94 35.36 N 137.55 E
Matsumae 92 41.26 N 140.07 E
Matsu → Matsu Tao I 100 26.09 N 119.56 E
Matsumoto 94 36.14 N 137.58 E
Matsuno 96 33.13 N 132.42 E
Matsunoyama 94 37.05 N 138.37 E
Matsuo 94 35.38 N 140.28 E
Matsuōji 268 35.08 N 140.01 E
Matsuoka 94 36.05 N 136.18 E
Matsuo-san ∧ 270 34.38 N 135.44 E
Matsusaka 94 34.34 N 136.32 E
Matsushima 92 38.22 N 141.04 E
Matsu Tao I 100 26.09 N 119.56 E
Matsutō 94 36.31 N 136.34 E
Matsuura 92 33.22 N 129.42 E
Matsuyama 96 33.50 N 132.45 E
Matsuzaki 94 34.45 N 138.47 E
Matta ≃ 208 38.07 N 77.26 W
Mattagami ≃ 176 50.43 N 81.29 W
Mattagami Heights 190 48.29 N 81.22 W
Mattagami Lake ⊜ 190 47.54 N 81.35 W
Mattamuskeet, Lake ⊜ 192 35.30 N 76.11 W
Mattapan ✦8 283 42.16 N 71.06 W
Mattapoisett 207 41.39 N 70.49 W
Mattaponi 208 37.32 N 76.46 W
Mattaponi ≃ 208 37.31 N 76.47 W
Mattarana 62 44.15 N 9.37 E
Mattarello 64 46.00 N 11.07 E
Mattawa, On., Can. 190 46.19 N 78.42 W
Mattawa, Wa., U.S. 202 46.44 N 119.54 W
Mattawa ≃ 190 46.19 N 78.43 W
Mattawamkeag 188 45.30 N 68.21 W
Mattawamkeag ≃ 188 45.30 N 68.24 W
Mattawan 216 42.12 N 85.47 W
Mattawana 214 40.30 N 77.44 W
Mattawoman Creek ≃ 208 38.34 N 77.12 W
Matterhorn (Cervino) ∧, Europe 58 45.59 N 7.43 E
Matterhorn ∧, Nv., U.S. 204 41.49 N 115.23 W
Mattersburg 61 47.44 N 16.25 E
Mattertal V 58 46.10 N 7.49 E
Matteson 216 41.30 N 87.42 W
Matteson Lake ⊜ 216 41.56 N 85.12 W
Matthew Flinders Memorial ⊥ 169 38.19 S 145.04 E
Matthews 216 40.23 N 85.29 W
Matthews Mountain ∧2 194 37.29 N 90.21 W
Matthews Ridge 246 7.30 N 60.10 W
Matthew Town 238 20.57 N 73.40 W
Matthias Church ♉1 264c 47.30 N 19.02 E
Matthiessen State Park ♠ 216 41.17 N 89.01 W
Maţţī, Sabkhat ⊜ 128 23.30 N 52.00 E
Mattie, Lake ⊜ 220 28.08 N 81.46 W
Mattig ≃ 60 48.16 N 13.04 E
Mattighofen 60 48.06 N 13.09 E
Mattinata 68 41.42 N 16.03 E
Mattishall 42 52.39 N 1.02 E
Mattituck 207 40.59 N 72.32 W
Mattole ≃ 204 40.18 N 124.21 W
Mattoon, Il., U.S. 194 39.28 N 88.22 W
Mattoon, Wi., U.S. 190 45.00 N 89.02 W
Mattox Creek ≃ 208 38.12 N 76.58 W
Mattox Draw V 198 38.03 N 101.11 W
Mattsee 64 47.58 N 13.06 E
Mattsee ⊜ 60 47.59 N 13.07 E
Mattydale 210 43.05 N 76.08 W
Matu 112 2.41 N 111.32 E
Matua 112 2.59 S 110.45 E
Matuba 156 24.27 S 32.55 E
Matucana 248 11.51 S 76.24 W
Matudo → Matsudo 94 35.47 N 139.54 E
Matue → Matsue 96 35.28 N 133.04 E
Matuku Island I 175g 19.10 S 179.46 E
Matumoto → Matsumoto 94 36.14 N 137.58 E
Matungo ≃ 152 16.25 S 21.27 E
Matunuck 207 41.23 N 71.32 W
Matuog 116 9.55 N 123.09 E
Matura Bay c 241r 10.38 N 61.01 W
Maturín 246 9.45 N 63.11 W
Maturino 76 59.06 N 37.55 E
Matusadona National Park ♠ 154 16.25 S 28.35 E
Matusov 78 49.03 N 31.34 E
Matutina 255 19.13 S 45.58 W
Matuto 154 14.46 S 35.59 E
Matutum, Mount ∧ 116 6.22 N 125.05 E
Matuzaka → Matsusaka 94 34.34 N 136.32 E
Matvejevka 80 53.32 N 53.29 E
Matvejev Kurgan 83 47.35 N 38.52 E
Matvejevo, Ross. 76 58.38 N 43.30 E
Matvejevo, Ross. 86 57.47 N 57.51 E
Mátyásföld ✦8 264c 47.31 N 19.13 E
Matyra ≃ 76 52.38 N 39.38 E
Matyševo 80 50.49 N 44.12 E
Mau 124 25.17 N 81.23 E
Maú (Ireng) ≃ 246 3.33 N 59.51 W
Mauá, Bra. 256 23.40 S 46.27 W
Maúa, Moç. 154 13.51 S 37.10 E
Mauá □7 287b 23.40 S 46.27 W
Mau Aimma 124 25.42 N 81.55 E
Mauban 116 14.12 N 121.44 E
Maubara 112 8.37 S 125.12 E
Maubeuge 50 50.17 N 3.58 E
Mauchamps 261 48.32 N 2.12 E
Mauchline 46 55.31 N 4.24 W
Maud, Scot., U.K. 46 57.31 N 2.06 W
Maud, Mo., U.S. 219 39.37 N 92.15 W
Maud, Oh., U.S. 218 39.21 N 84.23 W
Maud, Ok., U.S. 196 35.08 N 96.46 W
Maud, Tx., U.S. 194 33.20 N 94.21 W
Maud, Point > 162 23.06 S 113.45 E
Maudaha 124 25.41 N 80.07 E
Maude 166 34.28 S 144.18 E
Maudétour-en-Vexin 261 49.06 N 1.47 E
Mau-é-ele 156 24.21 S 34.07 E
Mauensee 58 47.10 N 8.04 E
Mauer ✦8 264b 48.09 N 16.16 E
Mauerbach 264b 48.15 N 16.10 E
Mauerbach ≃ 264b 48.12 N 16.14 E
Mauerkirchen 60 48.11 N 13.08 E
Maués 250 3.24 S 57.42 W
Maués ≃ 246 3.22 S 57.44 W
Maug ≃ 116 8.20 N 125.53 E
Mauganj 124 24.41 N 81.53 E
Mauga Silisili ∧ 175a 13.35 S 172.27 W
Maughold 44 54.18 N 4.17 W
Maug Islands II 108 20.01 N 145.13 E
Mauguio 62 43.37 N 4.01 E
Mauguio, Étang de c 62 43.35 N 4.02 E
Maui □6 229a 20.53 N 156.30 W
Maui I 229a 20.45 N 156.15 W
Mauk 115a 6.04 S 106.30 E
Mauke I 14 20.09 S 157.23 W
Maulbach 56 50.43 N 9.04 E
Maulbronn 56 49.00 N 8.49 E
Maulde 50 50.30 N 3.26 E
Mauldin 192 34.46 N 82.18 W
Mauldre ≃ 261 48.58 N 1.49 E
Maule 50 48.55 N 1.51 E
Maule □4 252 35.30 S 71.30 W
Maule ≃ 252 35.19 S 72.25 W
Maule, Laguna del ⊜ 252 36.04 S 70.30 W
Mauléon 32 46.56 N 0.45 W
Mauléon-Licharre 32 43.14 N 0.53 W
Maulette 261 48.48 N 1.37 E
Maullín 254 41.38 S 73.37 W
Maulvi Bāzār 120 24.29 N 91.47 E
Maumaupaki ∧ 172 36.58 S 175.35 E
Maumee 214 41.33 N 83.39 W
Maumee ≃ 216 41.42 N 83.28 W
Maumee Bay c 214 41.43 N 83.26 W
Maumelle, Lake ⊜1 194 34.55 N 92.40 W
Maumere 115b 8.37 S 122.14 E
Maun 156 20.00 S 23.25 E
Maunabo 240m 18.01 N 65.54 W
Mauna Kea ∧1 229d 19.50 N 155.28 W
Maunaloa 229a 21.08 N 157.13 W
Mauna Loa ∧1 229d 19.29 N 155.36 W
Maunalua Bay c 229c 21.17 N 157.44 W
Maunath Bhanjan 124 25.57 N 83.33 E
Maunatlala 156 22.32 S 27.28 E
Maunesha ≃ 216 43.13 N 88.57 W
Maungahaumi ∧ 172 38.18 S 177.40 E
Maunga Roa ∧ 174k 21.13 S 159.48 W
Maungatapere 172 35.45 S 174.12 E
Maungaturoto 172 36.06 S 174.22 E
Maungdaw 110 20.50 N 92.21 E
Maungmagan 110 14.09 N 98.06 E
Maungu 154 3.33 S 38.45 E
Maunoir, Lac ⊜ 180 67.30 N 125.00 W
Maupihaa I1 14 16.50 S 153.55 W
Maupin 224 45.10 N 121.04 W
Maur 123 30.05 N 75.15 E
Mau Rānīpur 124 25.15 N 79.08 E
Maurecourt 261 49.00 N 2.04 E
Maure-de-Bretagne 32 47.54 N 1.59 W
Mauregard 261 49.02 N 2.35 E
Maurepas 261 48.45 N 1.55 E
Maurepas, Lake ⊜ 194 30.15 N 90.30 W
Maures ⋏ 62 43.16 N 6.23 E
Mauretanien → Mauritania □1 134 20.00 N 12.00 W
Mauri ≃ 248 17.18 S 68.41 W
Mauria, Passo della)(64 46.27 N 12.31 E
Mauriac 32 45.13 N 2.20 E
Maurice (Île) → Mauritius □1 157c 20.17 S 57.33 E
Maurice ≃ 208 39.13 N 75.02 W
Maurice, Lake ⊜ 162 29.28 S 130.58 E
Maurice K. Goddard State Park ♠ 214 41.23 N 81.10 W
Mauricetown 208 39.17 N 74.58 W
Mauriceville 172 40.47 S 175.42 E
Mauricio → Mauritius □1 157c 20.17 S 57.33 E
Maurienne V 62 45.13 N 6.30 E
Maurino, Canal ≍ 286e 33.34 S 70.32 W
Mauritania (Mauritanie) □1 134 20.00 N 12.00 W
Mauritanie → Mauritania □1 134 20.00 N 12.00 W
Mauriti 250 7.23 S 38.46 W
Mauritius □1, Afr. 138 20.17 S 57.33 E
Mauritius □1, Afr. 157c 20.17 S 57.33 E
Mauritius I 157c 20.17 S 57.33 E
Mauron 32 48.05 N 2.18 W
Maurs 32 44.43 N 2.11 E
Maurui 154 5.07 S 38.23 E
Maury ≃ 192 37.37 N 79.27 W
Maury Channel ⊔ 176 75.44 N 94.40 W
Maury Island >1 224 47.20 N 122.24 W
Maussane 62 43.43 N 4.48 E
Mauston 190 43.47 N 90.04 W
Mautala 126 22.25 N 89.05 E
Mautau, Pointe > 174x 9.42 S 138.58 W
Mautern an der Donau 61 48.24 N 15.35 E
Mauterndorf 64 47.08 N 13.40 E
Mautern in Steiermark 61 47.24 N 14.50 E
Mauth 60 48.53 N 13.35 E
Mauthausen 61 48.14 N 14.32 E
Mauthen 64 46.40 N 13.00 E
Mauvais Coulee V 198 48.21 N 99.06 W
Mauvaise Terre Creek ≃ 219 39.43 N 90.38 W
Mauvaise Terre Lake ⊜1 219 39.42 N 90.12 W
Mauvezin 32 43.44 N 0.55 E
Mava 164 6.50 S 141.25 E
Mavaca ≃ 246 2.31 N 65.11 W
Mavanza 156 22.43 S 35.08 E
Māvelikara 122 9.16 N 76.33 E
Maverick 200 33.43 N 109.32 W
Mavinga 152 15.50 S 20.21 E
Mavita 156 19.33 S 33.10 E
Mavonde 156 18.32 S 33.02 E
Mavuradona Mountains ⋏ 154 16.30 S 31.20 E
Mawa 154 2.43 N 26.42 E
Mawai 114 1.52 N 103.57 E
Ma Wan I 271d 22.21 N 114.03 E
Mawāna 124 29.06 N 77.55 E
Mawangkanli Shan ∧ 120 34.19 N 80.03 E
Mawangtang 106 30.42 N 120.42 E
Mawasangka 112 5.17 S 122.18 E
Mawchi 110 18.49 N 97.09 E
Maw-daung Pass)(110 11.47 N 99.39 E
Mawdesley 262 53.38 N 2.46 W
Mawdesley Lake ⊜ 184 54.01 N 100.39 W
Mawgan 42 50.06 N 5.12 W
Mawi 272a 28.39 N 77.25 E
Mawiwi 154 3.06 N 27.40 E
Māwiyah 144 13.35 N 44.21 E
Mawjib, Wādī al- V 132 31.28 N 35.34 E
Mawkhi 110 16.17 N 98.53 E
Mawlaik 110 23.38 N 94.24 E
Mawlamyaing → Mawlamyine 110 16.30 N 97.38 E
Mawlamyine (Moulmein) 110 16.30 N 97.38 E
Mawr, Wādī V 144 15.41 N 42.42 E
Mawshij 144 13.43 N 43.17 E
Mawson ♉3 9 67.40 S 63.43 E
Mawson Escarpment ⫯4 9 73.05 S 68.10 E
Mawson Peninsula >1 9 68.35 S 154.11 E
Maw Taung ∧ 110 11.39 N 99.35 E
Mawuba 102 29.50 N 108.11 E
Max 198 47.49 N 101.17 W
Maxaranguape 250 5.31 S 35.16 W
Maxatawny 208 40.33 N 75.41 W
Maxcanú 232 20.35 N 89.59 W
Maxéville 58 48.43 N 6.10 E
Maxglan, Flughafen ⊠ 64 47.48 N 13.02 E
Maxhütte Haidhof 60 49.12 N 12.05 E
Maxiang 100 24.41 N 118.15 E
Maximo 214 40.53 N 81.11 W
Maximo Paz 258 34.56 S 58.37 W
Maxinkuckee, Lake ⊜ 216 41.12 N 86.24 W
Maxixe 156 23.51 S 35.21 E
Maxon Creek ≃ 196 29.53 N 102.24 W
Maxton 192 34.44 N 79.20 W
Maxville 206 45.17 N 74.51 W
Maxwell, Ca., U.S. 226 39.16 N 122.11 W
Maxwell, In., U.S. 218 39.51 N 85.46 W
Maxwell, Ia., U.S. 190 41.53 N 93.23 W
Maxwell, Ne., U.S. 198 41.04 N 100.31 W
Maxwell, N.M., U.S. 196 36.32 N 104.32 W
Maxwell, Tx., U.S. 222 29.53 N 97.48 W
Maxwell Air Force Base ■ 194 32.23 N 86.21 W
Maxwell Bay c 176 74.35 N 89.00 W
May 196 31.59 N 98.55 W
May ≃, Austl. 162 17.07 S 123.50 E
May ≃, Ab., Can. 182 55.43 N 111.22 W
May ≃, Pap. N. Gui. 164 4.35 S 141.35 E
May, Cape >1 208 38.58 N 74.55 W
May, Isle of I 46 56.11 N 2.34 W
May, Mount ∧ 182 54.02 N 119.58 W
Maya, Pulau I 112 1.10 S 109.35 E
May Aché 146 12.00 N 15.44 E
Mayaguana I 238 22.23 N 72.57 W
Mayaguana Passage ⊔ 238 22.32 N 73.15 W
Mayagüez 240m 18.12 N 67.09 W
Mayagüez, Aeropuerto ⊠ 240m 18.15 N 67.09 W
Mayagüez, Bahía de c 240m 18.12 N 67.10 W
Mayahi 150 13.58 N 7.40 E
Mayajigua 240p 22.14 N 79.04 W
Mayaka 152 5.17 N 16.52 E
Mayala 273b 4.21 S 15.09 E
Mayales, Punta > 236 11.52 N 85.26 W
Mayama 152 3.51 S 14.54 E
Mayamba 152 4.46 S 16.52 E
Mayāmey 128 36.24 N 55.42 E
Maya Mountains ⋏ 232 16.40 N 88.50 W
Mayang 102 27.41 N 109.35 E
Mayang-do I 98 40.00 N 128.12 E
Mayantoc 116 15.37 N 120.23 E
Mayao 106 30.50 N 120.23 E
Mayapan ⊥ 232 20.38 N 89.27 W
Māyāpur 272b 22.27 N 88.08 E
Mayarí 240p 20.40 N 75.41 W
Mayarí Arriba 240p 20.25 N 75.32 W
Mayaro Bay c 241r 10.15 N 60.58 W
Maya-san ∧ 96 34.44 N 135.12 E
Maybee 216 42.00 N 83.30 W
Maybeury 192 37.22 N 81.22 W
Maybole 44 55.21 N 4.41 W
Maybrook 210 41.29 N 74.13 W
Maychew 144 13.02 N 39.34 E
Maydelle 222 31.48 N 95.18 W
Maydena 166 42.55 S 146.30 E
Maydh 144 11.00 N 47.07 E
Maydī 144 16.20 N 42.46 E
Maydolong 116 11.30 N 125.30 E
Maydūm 142 29.22 N 31.10 E
Mayen 56 50.19 N 7.13 E
Mayence → Mainz 56 50.01 N 8.16 E
Mayenne 32 48.18 N 0.37 W
Mayenne □5 32 48.05 N 0.40 W
Mayenne ≃ 32 47.30 N 0.33 W
Mayer 200 34.23 N 112.14 W
Mayerling 61 48.03 N 16.06 E
Mayersville 194 32.54 N 91.03 W
Mayerthorpe 182 53.57 N 115.08 W
Mayet 50 47.46 N 0.17 E
Mayfair ✦8, S. Afr. 273d 26.12 S 28.01 E
Mayfair ✦8, Pa., U.S. 285 40.02 N 75.03 W
Mayfield, N.Z. 172 43.49 S 171.25 E
Mayfield, Eng., U.K. 42 51.01 N 0.15 E
Mayfield, Eng., U.K. 44 53.01 N 1.45 W
Mayfield, Scot., U.K. 46 55.52 N 3.02 W
Mayfield, In., U.S. 218 40.11 N 85.21 W
Mayfield, Ky., U.S. 194 36.44 N 88.38 W
Mayfield, N.Y., U.S. 210 43.06 N 74.15 W
Mayfield, Oh., U.S. 279a 41.33 N 81.26 W
Mayfield, Pa., U.S. 210 41.32 N 75.32 W
Mayfield, Ut,. U.S. 200 39.06 N 111.42 W
Mayfield Creek ≃ 194 36.57 N 89.05 W
Mayfield Dam ✦6 224 46.30 N 122.35 W
Mayfield Heights 214 41.31 N 81.27 W
Mayfield Lake ⊜1 224 46.31 N 122.32 W
Mayflower 194 34.57 N 92.25 W
Mayford 260 51.18 N 0.34 W
May Inlet c 176 76.15 N 100.45 W
Māyir, Sūrīy. 130 36.23 N 37.02 E
Māyir, Sūrīy. 130 36.28 N 37.11 E
May Jirgui 150 13.44 N 8.08 E
Maykop → Majkop 84 44.35 N 40.07 E
Mayland 42 51.39 N 0.47 E
Maymont 184 52.33 N 107.40 W
Maymūn, Wādī V 146 30.10 N 10.27 E
Maymyo 110 22.02 N 96.28 E
Mayna 126 22.14 N 87.47 E
Maynāmati 124 23.29 N 91.07 E
Maynard, Ia., U.S. 190 42.46 N 91.52 W
Maynard, Ma., U.S. 207 42.26 N 71.27 W
Maynard, Oh., U.S. 214 40.07 N 80.53 W
Maynardville 192 36.15 N 83.47 W
Mayne 224 48.51 N 123.18 W
Mayne ≃ 166 23.34 S 141.18 E
Mayne Island I 224 48.51 N 123.17 W
Maynooth 48 53.23 N 6.35 W
Mayo, Yk., Can. 180 63.35 N 135.54 W
Mayo, Fl., U.S. 192 30.03 N 83.10 W
Mayo, Md., U.S. 208 38.53 N 76.30 W
Mayo □6 48 53.54 N 9.15 W
Mayo ≃, Arg. 254 45.46 S 69.43 W
Mayo ≃, Col. 246 1.40 N 77.21 W
Mayo ≃, Méx. 232 26.45 N 109.47 W
Mayo ≃, Perú 248 6.37 S 76.16 W
Mayoba 154 17.13 S 26.16 E
Mayo Bay c 116 6.56 N 126.22 E
Mayodan 192 36.24 N 79.58 W
Mayo Faran 146 8.57 N 12.04 E
Mayo-Kébbi □5 146 10.00 N 15.30 E
Mayoko, Congo 152 2.18 S 12.49 E
Mayoko, Zaïre 152 1.05 S 23.49 E
Mayo Lake ⊜ 180 63.46 N 135.10 W
Mayo Ndaga 146 6.54 N 11.25 E
Mayon Volcano ∧1 116 13.15 N 123.41 E
Mayor Buratovich 252 39.15 S 62.37 W
Mayo Reservoir ⊜1 192 36.00 N 78.53 W
Mayor Island I 172 37.18 S 176.16 E
Mayor Pablo Lagerenza 248 19.58 S 60.45 W
Mayotte □2, Afr. 138 12.50 S 45.10 E
Mayotte □2, Afr. 157a 12.50 S 45.10 E
Mayoyao 116 16.59 N 121.14 E
Mayoyoque 246 0.41 N 75.18 W
Maypearl 222 32.19 N 97.01 W
May Pen 241q 17.58 N 77.14 W
Mayport Naval Station ■ 192 30.22 N 81.24 W
Mayraira Point > 116 18.39 N 120.51 E
Mayrán, Desierto de ✦2 196 25.45 N 102.45 W
Mayres 62 44.40 N 4.07 E
Mayrhofen 64 47.10 N 11.52 E
Mays 218 39.45 N 85.26 W
Maysah, Tall al- ∧ 132 31.08 N 35.40 E
Maysān □4 128 32.00 N 47.00 E
Maysfield 222 30.54 N 96.51 W
Mays Landing 208 39.27 N 74.43 W
Mays Lick 218 38.31 N 83.50 W
Maysville, Ky., U.S. 218 38.38 N 83.44 W
Maysville, Mo., U.S. 194 39.53 N 94.21 W
Maysville, N.C., U.S. 192 34.54 N 77.13 W
Maysville, Ok., U.S. 196 34.49 N 97.24 W
Maythalūn 132 32.21 N 35.16 E
Maytiguid Island I 116 11.03 N 119.36 E
Maytown 208 40.04 N 76.35 W
Mayu 100 27.48 N 120.26 E
Mayumba 152 3.25 S 10.39 E
Mayung 114 0.49 N 103.03 E
Māyūram 122 11.06 N 79.40 E
Mayville, Mi., U.S. 190 43.20 N 83.21 W
Mayville, N.Y., U.S. 214 42.15 N 79.30 W
Mayville, N.D., U.S. 198 47.29 N 97.19 W
Mayville, Wi., U.S. 190 43.29 N 88.32 W
Maywood, Ca., U.S. 280 33.59 N 118.11 W
Maywood, Il., U.S. 216 41.52 N 87.50 W
Maywood, Mo., U.S. 219 39.57 N 91.36 W
Maywood, Ne., U.S. 198 40.39 N 100.37 W
Maywood, N.J., U.S. 276 40.54 N 74.03 W
Maywood, N.Y., U.S. 210 42.42 N 73.52 W
Maywood Race Track ♠ 278 41.44 N 87.50 W
Mayyit, Al-Bahr al- → Dead Sea ⊜ 132 31.30 N 35.30 E
Maza, Arg. 252 36.50 S 63.19 W
Maza, Ross. 80 57.14 N 44.13 E
Mazabuka 154 15.51 S 27.46 E
Mazagan → El-Jadida 148 33.16 N 8.30 W
Mazagão 250 0.07 S 51.17 W
Mazagaon ✦8 272c 18.57 N 72.50 E
Mazagão Velho 250 0.13 S 51.25 W
Ma'zah, Jabal ∧ 130 35.51 N 40.38 E
Mazamet 32 43.30 N 2.24 E
Mazamitla 234 19.55 N 103.02 W
Mazán ≃ 246 3.28 S 73.11 W
Māzandarān □4 128 36.30 N 53.30 E
Mazanovo 89 51.40 N 128.52 E
Mazār, Jabal ∧ 132 33.34 N 36.03 E
Mazar, Oued V 148 31.50 N 1.36 E
Mazara, Val di ✦1 70 37.50 N 13.00 E
Mazara del Vallo 70 37.39 N 12.35 E
Mazār-e Sharīf 120 36.42 N 67.06 E
Mazargues 62 43.15 N 5.24 E
Mazaro ≃ 70 37.39 N 12.35 E
Mazarredo 254 47.05 S 66.42 W
Mazarrón 34 37.36 N 1.19 W
Mazarrón, Golfo de c 34 37.30 N 1.18 W
Mazarsu 85 41.56 N 72.40 E
Mazaruni ≃ 246 6.25 N 58.38 W
Mazatenango 236 14.32 N 91.30 W
Mazatlán 234 23.13 N 106.25 W
Mazatlán Villa de Flores 234 18.02 N 96.54 W
Mazatzal Mountains ⋏ 200 34.00 N 111.55 W
Mazatzal Peak ∧ 200 34.03 N 111.28 W
Maze 94 35.52 N 137.10 E
Maze ≃ 94 35.40 N 137.10 E
Mažeikiai 76 56.19 N 22.20 E
Mazenod 184 49.53 N 106.14 W
Mazeppa, Mn., U.S. 190 44.16 N 92.32 W
Mazeppa, Pa., U.S. 210 40.59 N 76.59 W
Mazha 100 23.27 N 114.00 E
Māzhān, Īrān 128 32.35 N 59.01 E
Mazhan, Zhg. 98 36.04 N 118.45 E
Mazhangfang, Zhg. 104 40.44 N 120.53 E
Mazhangfang, Zhg. 104 42.23 N 122.26 E
Mazhuang, Zhg. 98 37.47 N 115.17 E
Mazhuang, Zhg. 100 32.54 N 114.03 E
Mazhuang, Zhg. 105 39.11 N 116.15 E
Mazhūr, Khubb al- ⫯8 128 27.45 N 43.55 E
Mazıdağı 130 37.30 N 40.30 E
Mazigou 105 40.28 N 114.48 E
Mazilovo ✦8 265b 55.44 N 37.26 E
Mazīnān 128 36.18 N 56.46 E
Mazinaw Lake ⊜ 212 44.55 N 77.12 W
Mazirbe 76 57.41 N 22.21 E
Mazoco 154 11.40 S 35.48 E
Mazoe ≃ 154 16.32 S 33.25 E
Mazomanie 190 43.10 N 89.47 W
Mazomba ≃ 256 22.53 S 43.45 W
Mazon 216 41.14 N 88.25 W
Mazon ≃ 216 41.21 N 88.25 W
Mazon, East Fork ≃ 216 41.11 N 88.18 W
Mazon, West Fork ≃ 216 41.15 N 88.21 W
Mazong Shan ∧ 102 41.28 N 97.10 E
Mazong Shan ⋏ 102 41.30 N 97.30 E
Mazou ≃ 50 47.15 N 2.59 E
Mazra'at-Bayt Jinn 132 33.19 N 35.55 E
Mazsalaca 76 57.52 N 25.03 E
Mazul'skij 86 56.16 N 90.28 E
Mazunga 154 21.45 S 29.52 E
Mazury ✦1 30 53.45 N 21.00 E
Mazzarino 70 37.18 N 14.13 E
Mazzarrà Sant'andrea 70 38.05 N 15.08 E
Mazzin 64 46.27 N 11.42 E
Mba 175g 17.33 S 177.41 E
Mbabala Island I 154 11.18 S 29.44 E
Mbabane 158 26.18 S 31.06 E
Mbabo, Tchabal ∧ 152 7.16 N 12.09 E
Mbacké 150 14.48 N 15.55 W
Mbaéré ≃ 152 3.47 N 17.31 E
Mbage 140 5.30 N 25.13 E
M'bahiakro 150 7.27 N 4.20 W
Mbaïki 152 3.53 N 18.00 E
Mbakaou, Barrage de ✦5 152 6.15 N 12.46 E
Mbala, Centraf. 152 7.48 N 20.51 E
Mbala (Abercorn), Zam. 154 8.50 S 31.22 E
Mbalam 152 2.13 N 13.49 E
Mbale 154 1.05 N 34.10 E
Mbali 152 2.50 S 16.12 E
Mbali ≃ 152 4.26 N 18.20 E
Mbalizi 154 8.56 S 33.22 E
Mbalmayo 152 3.31 N 11.30 E
Mbalouro ≃ 273b 4.09 S 15.21 E
Mbalourou 273b 4.09 S 15.21 E
Mbam ≃ 152 4.24 N 11.17 E
Mbamba Bay 154 11.17 S 34.46 E
Mbamou, Île I 152 4.13 S 15.25 E
Mbamou, Pointe > 273b 4.16 S 15.19 E
Mbandaka (Coquilhatville) 152 0.04 N 18.16 E
Mbanga 152 4.30 N 9.34 E
Mbanika Island I 175e 9.05 S 159.12 E
M'banza Congo 152 6.16 S 14.15 E
Mbanza-Ngungu 152 5.15 S 14.52 E
Mbarangandu ≃ 154 8.57 S 37.24 E
Mbarara 154 0.37 S 30.39 E
Mbari ≃ 152 4.34 N 22.43 E
Mbarizunga Game Reserve ✦4 154 4.45 N 28.06 E
Mbashe ≃ 158 32.15 S 28.53 E
Mbassay 146 7.39 N 15.40 E
Mbate 154 8.52 S 39.10 E
M'batto 150 6.28 N 4.22 W
Mbava Island I 175e 7.49 S 156.33 E
Mbé, Cam. 152 7.43 N 13.30 E
Mbé, Congo 152 3.18 S 15.54 E
Mbé ≃ 152 0.27 N 9.41 E
Mbemba 154 10.03 S 38.36 E
Mbengga I 175g 18.23 S 178.08 E
M'bengué 150 10.00 N 5.54 W
Mbéré 146 10.49 N 15.44 E
Mbéré ≃ 152 7.45 N 15.36 E
Mberengwa 154 20.30 S 29.53 E
Mbereshi Mission 154 9.45 S 28.46 E
Mberubu 150 6.10 N 7.38 E
Mbeya 154 8.54 S 33.27 E
Mbeya □4 154 8.00 S 33.30 E
Mbi ≃ 152 4.26 N 18.16 E
Mbia 140 6.15 N 29.19 E
M'bigou 152 1.53 S 11.56 E
Mbinda 152 2.00 S 12.55 E
Mbindawina 152 15.57 S 23.18 E
Mbinga 154 10.56 S 35.01 E
Mbini 152 1.35 N 9.37 E
Mbini ≃ 152 1.35 N 9.37 E
Mbirira 154 4.21 S 30.10 E
Mbirizi 154 0.23 S 31.27 E
Mbogo 154 7.26 S 33.26 E
Mboie 152 6.56 S 21.54 E
Mbola 175e 9.37 S 160.39 E
Mboli 152 4.08 N 23.09 E
Mbomou □5 152 5.00 N 23.30 E
Mbomou (Bomu) ≃ 136 4.08 N 22.26 E
Mbonge 152 4.33 N 9.05 E
Mboro, Sén. 150 15.09 N 16.54 W
Mboro, Sūd. 140 6.18 N 28.45 E
Mborokua I 175e 9.00 S 158.40 E
Mborong 115b 8.49 S 120.37 E
Mboté 152 3.56 S 12.43 E
Mbotou ≃ 152 6.49 N 24.14 E
Mbouda 152 5.38 N 10.15 E
Mboula 152 4.27 N 16.29 E
Mbour 150 14.24 N 16.58 W
Mbout 150 16.02 N 12.35 W
Mbrès 152 6.40 N 19.48 E
M'Bridge ≃ 152 7.14 S 12.52 E
Mbua 175g 16.48 S 178.37 E
Mbua Bay c 175g 16.49 S 178.35 E
Mbuji-Mayi (Bakwanga) 152 6.09 S 23.38 E
Mbulu 154 3.51 S 35.32 E
Mbulula 154 5.26 S 27.26 E
Mbuluzane ≃ 158 26.08 S 31.52 E
Mbuluzi ≃ 158 26.08 S 31.52 E
Mbuma 154 3.32 N 24.50 E
Mburucuyá 252 28.03 S 58.14 W
Mbutha 175g 16.39 S 179.50 E
Mbwemkuru ≃ 154 9.29 S 39.39 E
McAdam 186 45.36 N 67.20 W
McAdam National Park ♠ 164 7.15 S 145.40 E
McAdams Peak ∧2 219 38.58 N 90.32 W
McAdoo 210 40.54 N 75.59 W
McAdoo Heights 210 40.54 N 76.01 W
McAfee 210 41.10 N 74.32 W
McAlester 196 34.56 N 95.46 W

	English	Deutsch	Español	Français	Português
≃	River	Fluß	Río	Rivière	Rio
≍	Canal	Kanal	Canal	Canal	Canal
↘	Waterfall, Rapids	Wasserfall, Stromschnellen	Cascada, Rápidos	Chute d'eau, Rapides	Cascata, Rápidos
⊔	Strait	Meeresstraße	Estrecho	Détroit	Estreito
c	Bay, Gulf	Bucht, Golf	Bahía, Golfo	Baie, Golfe	Baía, Golfo
⊜	Lake, Lakes	See, Seen	Lago, Lagos	Lac, Lacs	Lago, Lagos
≡	Swamp	Sumpf	Pantano	Marais	Pântano
⊟	Ice Features, Glacier	Eis- und Gletscherformen	Accidentes Glaciales	Formes glaciaires	Acidentes glaciares
⊤	Other Hydrographic Features	Andere Hydrographische Objekte	Otros Elementos Hidrográficos	Autres données hydrographiques	Outros acidentes hidrográficos

	English	Deutsch	Español	Français	Português
✤	Submarine Features	Untermeerische Objekte	Accidentes Submarinos	Formes de relief sous-marin	Acidentes submarinos
□	Political Unit	Politische Einheit	Unidad Politica	Entité politique	Unidade política
♉	Cultural Institution	Kulturelle Institution	Institución Cultural	Institution culturelle	Instituição cultural
⊥	Historical Site	Historische Stätte	Sitio Histórico	Site historique	Sitio histórico
♠	Recreational Site	Erholungs- und Ferienort	Sitio de Recreo	Centre de loisirs	Area de Lazer
⊠	Airport	Flughafen	Aeropuerto	Aéroport	Aeroporto
■	Military Installation	Militäranlage	Instalación Militar	Installation militaire	Instalação militar
✦	Miscellaneous	Verschiedenes	Misceláneo	Divers	Diversos

Name	Page	Lat.°′	Long.°′
McAlisterville	208	40.38 N	77.16 W
McAllen	196	26.12 N	98.13 W
McAlpine	208	39.16 N	76.50 W
McAlpine Dam ◆[6]	218	38.16 N	85.47 W
McAlveys Fort	214	40.39 N	77.50 W
McArthur	188	39.14 N	82.28 W
McArthur ≃	164	15.54 S	136.40 E
McArthur River	164	16.27 S	136.07 E
McAuley	184	50.16 N	101.23 W
McBain	190	44.11 N	85.12 W
McBee	192	34.28 N	80.15 W
McBeth	222	29.11 N	95.30 W
McBeth Fjord ⊂[2]	176	69.38 N	68.30 W
McBride	182	53.18 N	120.10 W
McCall	202	44.54 N	116.05 W
McCall Creek	194	31.30 N	90.41 W
McCallum	186	47.38 N	56.15 W
McCallum Creek ≃	169	37.03 S	143.49 E
McCamey	196	31.08 N	102.13 W
McCammon	202	42.39 N	112.11 W
McCandless, Pa., U.S.	214	40.35 N	80.01 W
McCandless, Pa., U.S.	279b	40.34 N	80.02 W
McCarteney Creek ≃	202	47.13 N	120.05 W
McCarthy	180	61.26 N	142.55 W
McCauley Island I	182	53.40 N	130.15 W
McCaysville	192	34.59 N	84.22 W
McChord Air Force Base ■	224	47.08 N	122.29 W
McClarens Run ≃	279b	40.27 N	80.12 W
McClarty Lake ⊜	184	54.28 N	100.20 W
McCleary	224	47.03 N	123.15 W
McClees Creek ≃	276	40.22 N	74.03 W
McClellan Air Force Base ■	226	38.39 N	121.23 W
McClellan Creek ≃	196	35.22 N	100.34 W
McClellanville	192	33.05 N	79.27 W
McClintock, Mount ʌ	9	80.13 S	157.26 E
McCloud	204	41.15 N	122.08 W
McCloud ≃	204	40.46 N	122.18 W
McClure, Il., U.S.	194	37.19 N	89.26 W
McClure, Oh., U.S.	216	41.22 N	83.56 W
McClure, Pa., U.S.	210	40.42 N	77.18 W
McClure, Lake ⊜[1]	226	37.37 N	120.16 W
McClusky	198	47.29 N	100.26 W
McColl	192	34.40 N	79.32 W
McComas	192	37.23 N	81.17 W
McComb, Ms., U.S.	194	31.14 N	90.27 W
McComb, Oh., U.S.	216	41.06 N	83.47 W
McConaughy, Lake ⊜[1]	198	41.15 N	101.50 W
McConnell Air Force Base ■	198	37.38 N	97.15 W
McConnell Range ʌʌ	180	64.00 N	123.50 W
McConnellsburg	188	39.55 N	77.59 W
McConnells Mill	279b	40.15 N	80.15 W
McConnells Mill State Park ♦	214	40.57 N	80.11 W
McConnellstown	214	40.27 N	78.05 W
McConnellsville	210	43.16 N	75.42 W
McConnelsville	188	39.38 N	81.51 W
McCook, Il., U.S.	278	41.48 N	87.50 W
McCook, Ne., U.S.	198	40.12 N	100.37 W
McCordsville	218	39.53 N	85.55 W
McCormick	192	33.54 N	82.17 W
McCormick Place ✤	278	41.51 N	87.37 W
McCoy	224	45.03 N	123.13 W
McCoy Creek ≃	202	43.02 N	118.50 W
McCoy Lake ⊜	184	52.35 N	92.19 W
McCraney Creek ≃	219	39.39 N	91.12 W
McCreary	184	50.46 N	99.30 W
McCrory	194	35.15 N	91.12 W
McCulloch, Mount ʌ	162	25.10 S	129.52 E
McCullom Lake	216	42.22 N	88.18 W
McCullough	279b	40.22 N	79.38 W
McCullough Mountain ʌ	204	35.36 N	115.11 W
McCune	198	37.21 N	95.00 W
McCurtain	196	35.08 N	94.58 W
McCusker ≃	184	55.32 N	108.40 W
McCutchenville	214	40.59 N	83.15 W
McDade	222	30.17 N	97.15 W
McDavid	194	30.51 N	87.19 W
McDermitt	204	41.59 N	117.43 W
McDermott	218	38.50 N	83.03 W
McDonald, Ks., U.S.	198	39.47 N	101.22 W
McDonald, Pa., U.S.	214	40.22 N	80.14 W
McDonald, Lac ⊜	206	45.52 N	74.35 W
McDonald, Lake ⊜	202	48.35 N	113.55 W
McDonald Park ♦	282	37.18 N	122.17 W
McDonogh	284b	39.24 N	76.46 W
McDonough, Ga., U.S.	192	33.26 N	84.08 W
McDonough, N.Y., U.S.	210	42.30 N	75.46 W
McDouall Peak	162	29.51 S	134.55 E
McDougal, Mount ʌ	200	42.54 N	110.36 W
McDowell Peak ʌ	200	33.40 N	111.50 W
McElhattan	210	41.09 N	77.22 W
McElmo Creek ≃	200	37.13 N	109.12 W
Mc Ennen Airport ⊠	281	42.12 N	83.37 W
Mcensk	76	53.17 N	36.35 E
McEwen	194	36.06 N	87.37 W
McEwensville	210	41.05 N	76.49 W
McFadden	200	41.39 N	106.07 W
McFarland, Ca., U.S.	226	35.40 N	119.13 W
McFarland, Wi., U.S.	216	43.00 N	89.17 W
McGavock Lake ⊜	184	56.32 N	101.25 W
McGehee	194	33.37 N	91.23 W
McGill	204	39.24 N	114.46 W
McGill, Université ✤[2]	275a	45.30 N	73.35 W
McGillivray, Lac ⊜	190	46.04 N	77.06 W
McGinnis Slough Wildlife Refuge ◆[4]	278	41.39 N	87.52 W
McGovern	214	40.14 N	80.13 W
McGrann	214	40.47 N	79.31 W
McGrath	180	62.58 N	155.38 W
McGraw	210	42.35 N	76.05 W
McGregor, On., Can.	214	42.09 N	82.58 W
McGregor, S. Afr.	158	33.57 S	19.50 E
McGregor, Ia., U.S.	190	43.01 N	91.10 W
McGregor, Tx., U.S.	222	31.26 N	97.24 W
McGregor ≃	182	54.11 N	122.00 W
McGregor Creek ≃	214	42.24 N	82.11 W
McGregor Lake ⊜	182	50.31 N	112.53 W
McGregor Range ʌʌ	166	26.40 S	142.45 E
McGuffey	216	40.41 N	83.47 W
McGuire, Mount ʌ	202	45.10 N	114.36 W
McGuire Air Force Base ■	208	40.02 N	74.35 W
McGuire Reservoir ⊜	224	45.19 N	123.26 W
M'Chedallah	34	36.21 N	4.16 E
McHenry, Il., U.S.	216	42.20 N	88.16 W
McHenry, Ms., U.S.	194	30.42 N	89.08 W
McHenry □[6]	216	42.19 N	88.27 W
Mcherrah ◆[1]	148	27.00 N	4.40 W
Mchinga	154	9.44 S	39.42 E
Mchinji	154	13.41 S	32.55 E
Mchungo	154	7.42 S	39.17 E
McInnes Lake ⊜	184	52.12 N	93.45 W
McIntosh, Al., U.S.	194	31.15 N	88.01 W
McIntosh, Il., U.S.	216	42.03 N	88.23 W
McIntosh, Mn., U.S.	198	47.38 N	95.53 W
McIntosh, S.D., U.S.	198	45.55 N	101.20 W
McIntosh Lake ⊜	184	55.45 N	105.08 W
McIntyre	214	40.34 N	79.17 W
McIntyre Bay ⊂	182	54.05 N	131.55 W
McKay, Mount ʌ	162	22.26 S	120.01 E
McKay Creek ≃	202	45.40 N	118.50 W
McKean	214	41.59 N	80.09 W
McKean □[6]	214	41.49 N	78.27 W
McKeand ≃	176	65.26 N	68.10 W
McKee	192	37.25 N	83.59 W
McKee City	208	39.27 N	74.38 W
McKee Creek ≃	219	39.46 N	90.36 W
McKeesport	214	40.20 N	79.51 W
McKees Rocks	214	40.27 N	80.03 W
McKenna	224	46.56 N	122.33 W
McKenzie, Al., U.S.	194	31.32 N	86.42 W
McKenzie, Tn., U.S.	194	36.07 N	88.31 W
McKenzie ≃	202	44.07 N	123.06 W
McKenzie Bridge	202	44.10 N	122.09 W
McKenzie Creek ≃	212	43.02 N	79.53 W
McKenzie Island	184	51.05 N	93.48 W
McKenzie Lake ⊜, On., Can.	212	45.22 N	78.02 W
McKenzie Lake ⊜, Sk., Can.	184	54.12 N	102.30 W
McKerrow, Lake ⊜	172	44.26 S	168.03 E
McKillip Ditch ≊	216	40.50 N	86.51 W
McKinlay	166	21.16 S	141.17 E
McKinlay ≃	166	20.50 S	141.28 E
McKinley, Mount ʌ	180	63.04 N	151.00 W
McKinley Airport ⊠	281	42.33 N	82.58 W
McKinley Park ♦	279b	40.25 N	80.00 W
McKinleyville, Ca., U.S.	204	40.56 N	124.05 W
McKinleyville, W.V., U.S.	214	40.15 N	80.36 W
McKinney	222	33.11 N	96.36 W
McKittrick, Ca., U.S.	226	35.18 N	119.37 W
McKittrick, Mo., U.S.	219	38.44 N	91.27 W
McKittrick Summit ʌ	226	35.18 N	119.46 W
McKnight Lake ⊜	184	56.03 N	101.08 W
McKnightstown	208	39.52 N	77.20 W
McKnight Village	279b	40.31 N	80.00 W
McKownville	210	42.41 N	73.50 W
McLain	194	31.06 N	88.49 W
McLaren Vale	168b	35.14 S	138.32 E
McLarty Hills ʌʌ[2]	162	19.29 S	123.33 E
McLaughlin	198	45.48 N	100.48 W
McLaughlin ≃	184	53.46 N	97.38 W
McLaughlin Run ≃	279b	40.22 N	80.07 W
McLaurin	194	31.10 N	89.13 W
McLean, Sk., Can.	184	50.30 N	104.04 W
McLean, Il., U.S.	194	40.18 N	89.10 W
McLean, N.Y., U.S.	210	42.33 N	76.17 W
McLean, Tx., U.S.	196	35.13 N	100.35 W
McLean, Va., U.S.	208	38.56 N	77.10 W
McLean □[6]	216	40.29 N	88.45 W
McLean Hamlet	284c	38.56 N	77.13 W
McLean Lake ⊜	184	56.27 N	109.15 W
McLean Mountain ʌ	186	47.07 N	68.50 W
McLeansboro	194	38.05 N	88.32 W
McLennan	182	55.42 N	116.54 W
McLennan □[6]	222	31.35 N	97.13 W
McLeod ≃	182	54.08 N	115.42 W
McLeod Bay ⊂	176	62.53 N	110.00 W
McLeodganj	123	30.15 N	73.42 E
McLeod Lake	182	54.59 N	123.02 W
M'Clintock Channel ⊔	176	72.00 N	102.00 W
McLoughlin, Mount ʌ	202	42.27 N	122.19 W
McLoughlin Bay ⊂	176	67.50 N	99.00 W
McLoughlin House National Historic Site ⊥	224	45.20 N	122.33 W
McLouth	198	39.11 N	95.12 W
McLure	182	51.03 N	120.14 W
M'Clure Strait ⊔	176	74.30 N	116.00 W
McMahan	222	29.51 N	97.31 W
McMahon	184	50.05 N	107.32 W
McMasterville	206	45.33 N	73.15 W
McMichael Art Collection ✤	275b	43.50 N	79.37 W
McMillan, Lake ⊜[1]	196	32.40 N	104.20 W
McMinnville, Or., U.S.	224	45.12 N	123.11 W
McMinnville, Tn., U.S.	194	35.41 N	85.46 W
McMurdo ✤[3]	9	77.50 S	166.25 E
McMurdo Sound ⊔	9	77.30 S	165.00 E
McMurray	214	40.17 N	80.05 W
McNair	222	29.48 N	95.02 W
McNary	200	34.04 N	109.51 W
McNeil, Ar., U.S.	194	33.20 N	93.12 W
McNeil, Tx., U.S.	222	30.27 N	97.43 W
McNeil, Mount ʌ	182	54.35 N	130.14 W
McNeil Island I	224	47.13 N	122.41 W
McNeill	194	30.40 N	89.38 W
McNulty	224	45.50 N	122.50 W
McPhail ≃	184	52.44 N	96.31 W
McPhee Bay ⊂	212	44.35 N	79.19 W
McPhee Reservoir ⊜[1]	200	37.32 N	108.35 W
McPherson	198	38.22 N	97.39 W
McPherson Range ʌʌ	166	28.20 S	153.00 E
McQueeney	196	29.35 N	98.02 W
McRae, Ar., U.S.	194	35.06 N	91.49 W
McRae, Ga., U.S.	192	32.04 N	82.54 W
McRae, Mount ʌ	162	22.17 S	117.35 E
McRae Point Provincial Park ♦	212	44.34 N	79.19 W
McRoberts	192	37.12 N	82.40 W
McSherrystown	208	39.48 N	77.00 W
McVeigh	192	37.32 N	82.15 W
McVeytown	214	40.30 N	77.44 W
McVickers Brook ≃	276	40.45 N	74.38 W
McVille	198	47.45 N	98.10 W
McWilliams	194	31.49 N	87.05 W
Mdandu	154	9.09 S	34.42 E
Mdantsana	158	32.56 S	27.42 E
M'Daourouch	36	36.05 N	7.49 E
Meacham	184	52.08 N	105.45 W
Mead	198	41.14 N	96.30 W
Mead, Lake ⊜[1]	200	36.05 N	114.25 W
Meade, Ks., U.S.	198	37.17 N	100.20 W
Meade, Mi., U.S.	214	42.43 N	82.52 W
Meade ≃	180	70.50 N	156.25 W
Meaden Peak ʌ	200	40.46 N	107.03 W
Meade Peak ʌ	202	42.30 N	111.15 W
Meadie, Loch ⊜	46	58.20 N	4.33 W
Meadow, Tx., U.S.	196	33.20 N	102.12 W
Meadow, Ut,. U.S.	200	38.53 N	112.24 W
Meadowbank Park ♦	274a	33.49 S	151.06 E
Meadowbrook, Il., U.S.	219	38.54 N	90.01 W
Meadowbrook, In., U.S.	216	41.03 N	85.03 W
Meadow Brook ≃, Ma., U.S.	283	42.03 N	70.58 W
Meadow Brook ≃, Pa., U.S.	285	40.07 N	75.04 W
Meadow Creek ≃	202	46.03 N	115.18 W
Meadow Flat	170	33.26 S	149.56 E
Meadow Island I	276	40.36 N	73.33 W
Meadow Lake	184	54.08 N	108.26 W
Meadow Lake ⊜, Sk., Can.	184	54.07 N	108.20 W
Meadow Lake ⊜, N.Y., U.S.	276	40.44 N	73.50 W
Meadow Lake Provincial Park ♦	184	54.28 N	109.10 W
Meadow Lands	214	40.13 N	80.13 W
Meadowlands Sports Complex ♦	276	40.49 N	74.05 W
Meadowlark Airport ⊠	280	33.43 N	118.02 W
Meadowood, De., U.S.	285	39.43 N	75.47 W
Meadowood, Md., U.S.	284c	39.04 N	77.00 W
Meadows	168b	35.11 S	138.46 E
Meadows, Island of I	276	40.34 N	74.12 W
Meadows Field ⊠	226	35.26 N	119.03 W
Meadowvale ◆[8]	275b	43.37 N	79.43 W
Meadow Valley Wash V	204	36.39 N	114.35 W
Meadowview	192	36.46 N	81.52 W
Meadow Vista	226	39.06 N	121.01 W
Meads Creek ≃	210	42.10 N	77.07 W
Meadville, Ms., U.S.	194	31.28 N	90.53 W
Meadville, Mo., U.S.	194	39.47 N	93.18 W
Meadville, Pa., U.S.	214	41.38 N	80.09 W
Meaford	212	44.36 N	80.35 W
Meaghers Grant	186	44.55 N	63.15 W
Me-akan-dake ʌ	92a	43.23 N	144.01 E
Mealasta Isle I	46	58.05 N	7.08 W
Mealhada	34	40.22 N	8.27 W
Méan	56	50.22 N	5.20 E
Meana	128	36.55 N	60.30 E
Meana Sardo	71	39.57 N	9.04 E
Meandarra	166	27.20 S	149.53 E
Meander Creek Reservoir ⊜[1]	214	41.09 N	80.47 W
Meander River	176	59.02 N	117.42 W
Mearim ≃	250	3.04 S	44.35 W
Measham	42	52.43 N	1.29 W
Meath □[6]	48	53.35 N	6.40 W
Meath □[9]	48	53.40 N	7.00 W
Meaux	50	48.57 N	2.52 E
Meaux-Esbly, Aérodrome de ⊠	261	48.55 N	2.50 E
Mebane	192	36.05 N	79.16 W
Mebisere	273a	6.42 N	3.31 E
Mebtoûh, Oued el ≃	34	35.16 N	0.32 W
Meča ≃	82	54.50 N	39.10 E
Meca, La → Makkah	144	21.27 N	39.49 E
Mecanhelas	154	15.12 S	35.54 E
Mecatán	234	21.32 N	105.08 W
Mecatlán	234	20.13 N	97.41 W
Mecaya ≃	246	0.29 N	75.11 W
Mecca → Makkah	144	21.27 N	39.49 E
Mečebilovo	78	49.04 N	36.41 E
Mečetinskaja	78	46.46 N	40.27 E
Mečetka	78	50.54 N	40.05 E
Mechanic Falls	188	44.06 N	70.23 W
Mechanicsburg, Il., U.S.	219	39.48 N	89.24 W
Mechanicsburg, In., U.S.	218	40.09 N	86.28 W
Mechanicsburg, Oh., U.S.	218	40.04 N	83.33 W
Mechanicsburg, Pa., U.S.	208	40.12 N	77.00 W
Mechanicstown, N.Y., U.S.	210	41.27 N	74.24 W
Mechanicstown, Oh., U.S.	214	40.37 N	80.57 W
Mechanicsville, Ia., U.S.	190	41.54 N	91.15 W
Mechanicsville, Md., U.S.	208	38.26 N	76.44 W
Mechanicsville, Va., U.S.	192	37.36 N	77.22 W
Mechanicville	210	42.54 N	73.41 W
Mechara	144	8.32 N	40.22 E
Mechelen (Malines)	50	51.02 N	4.28 E
Mechel'ta	84	42.48 N	46.30 E
Mechernich	56	50.35 N	6.38 E
Mechī □[8]	124	27.15 N	87.45 E
Mechī ≃	124	26.14 N	87.58 E
Mechita	252	35.04 S	60.24 W
Mechlin → Mechelen	50	51.02 N	4.28 E
Mechonskoje	86	56.09 N	64.34 E
Mechra Safsaf	34	34.52 N	2.36 W
Mechren'ga	24	61.46 N	40.57 E
Mechrenga ≃	24	63.15 N	41.20 E
Mechriyya	148	33.35 N	0.18 W
Mechroha	36	36.21 N	7.51 E
Mecidiye, Tür.	130	40.38 N	26.32 E
Mecidiye, Tür.	130	38.53 N	27.42 E
Mečigmen	180	65.28 N	172.05 W
Mečigmeskij zaliv ⊂	180	65.25 N	172.00 W
Meçitözü	130	40.31 N	35.19 E
Meckelfeld	52	53.25 N	10.01 E
Meckenbeuren	58	47.42 N	9.34 E
Meckenheim	56	50.37 N	7.07 E
Meckering	162	31.38 S	117.01 E
Meckesheim	56	49.19 N	8.49 E
Meckinghoven	263	51.37 N	7.19 E
Mecklenburg, Dtsch.	54	53.47 N	11.28 E
Mecklenburg, N.Y., U.S.	210	42.27 N	76.43 W
Mecklenburg □[9]	54	53.30 N	13.00 E
Mecklenburger Bucht ⊂	54	54.20 N	11.40 E
Mecklenburgische Seenplatte ◆[1]	54	53.30 N	12.00 E
Mecklenburg-Vorpommern □[3]	30	53.45 N	12.30 E
Meclov	60	49.31 N	12.52 E
Meco	210	43.03 N	74.23 W
Mecoacán	234	18.23 N	93.07 W
Mecoacán, Laguna ⊂	234	18.22 N	93.09 W
Meconta	154	14.49 S	39.50 E
Mecox Bay ⊂	207	40.54 N	72.20 W
Mecque, La → Makkah	144	21.27 N	39.49 E
Mecsek ʌʌ	30	46.15 N	18.05 E
Mecubúri	154	14.39 S	38.54 E
Mecubúri ≃	154	14.10 S	40.31 E
Mecúfi	154	13.17 S	40.30 E
Mecula	154	12.04 S	37.40 E
Meda, It.	62	45.40 N	9.09 E
Meda, Port.	34	40.58 N	7.16 W
Medak	122	18.02 N	78.16 E
Medākul	126	23.03 N	90.11 E
Médan, Fr.	261	48.57 N	2.00 E
Medan, Indon.	114	3.35 N	98.40 E
Medang	114	2.06 N	101.38 E
Medang, Pulau I	115b	8.09 S	117.23 E
Medang, Tanjung ›	114	2.08 N	101.39 E
Médanos	252	38.50 S	62.41 W
Medanosa, Punta ›	254	48.06 S	65.55 W
Medaryville	216	41.04 N	86.53 W
Mede	62	45.06 N	8.44 E
Medebach	56	51.12 N	8.42 E
Medeiros Neto	255	17.20 S	40.14 W
Medel, Val V	58	46.37 N	8.50 E
Medellín, Col.	246	6.15 N	75.35 W
Medellin, Pil.	116	11.08 N	123.58 E
Medelpad □[9]	26	62.40 N	16.15 E
Medemblik	52	52.46 N	5.06 E
Měděnec	54	50.25 N	13.05 E
Medenica	78	49.26 N	23.45 E
Médenine	148	33.21 N	10.30 E
Médenine □[8]	148	32.00 N	10.00 E
Mederdra	150	16.55 N	15.39 W
Medesano	64	44.45 N	10.08 E
Medevi	40	58.40 N	14.57 E
Medfield	207	42.11 N	71.18 W
Medford, Ma., U.S.	207	42.25 N	71.06 W
Medford, N.J., U.S.	208	39.54 N	74.49 W
Medford, N.Y., U.S.	210	40.49 N	73.00 W
Medford, Ok., U.S.	196	36.48 N	97.44 W
Medford, Or., U.S.	202	42.19 N	122.52 W
Medford, Wi., U.S.	190	45.08 N	90.20 W
Medford Farms	285	39.52 N	74.45 W
Medford Lakes	285	39.51 N	74.48 W
Medfra	180	63.06 N	154.44 W
Medgidia	38	44.15 N	28.16 E
Medgyes → Mediaș	38	46.10 N	24.21 E
Medi	154	5.04 N	30.44 E
Media	208	39.55 N	75.23 W
Mediapolis	190	41.00 N	91.09 W
Mediaș	38	46.10 N	24.21 E
Medical Lake	202	47.34 N	117.40 W
Medicina	66	44.28 N	11.38 E
Medicine Bow	200	41.53 N	106.12 W
Medicine Bow ≃	200	42.00 N	106.40 W
Medicine Bow Mountains ʌʌ	200	41.10 N	106.10 W
Medicine Bow Peak ʌ	200	41.21 N	106.19 W
Medicine Creek ≃, Mo., U.S.	194	39.43 N	93.24 W
Medicine Creek ≃, Ne., U.S.	198	40.17 N	100.10 W
Medicine Creek ≃, S.D., U.S.	198	44.06 N	99.42 W
Medicine Hat	184	50.03 N	110.40 W
Medicine Knoll Creek ≃	198	44.19 N	100.05 W
Medicine Lake	198	48.30 N	104.30 W
Medicine Lake ⊜	198	48.28 N	104.24 W
Medicine Lodge	198	37.16 N	98.34 W
Medicine Lodge ≃	196	36.49 N	98.20 W
Medicine Rocks State Park ♦	198	46.01 N	104.35 W
Medina, Bra.	255	16.15 S	41.29 W
Medina, Pil.	116	8.55 N	125.01 E
Medina, N.Y., U.S.	210	43.13 N	78.23 W
Medina, N.D., U.S.	198	46.53 N	99.17 W
Medina, Oh., U.S.	214	41.08 N	81.51 W
Medina, Tx., U.S.	196	29.48 N	99.15 W
Medina, Wa., U.S.	224	47.37 N	122.13 W
Medina □[6]	214	41.08 N	81.52 W
Medina ≃	196	29.12 N	98.20 W
Medina → Al-Madīnah	128	24.28 N	39.36 E
Medinaceli	34	41.10 N	2.26 W
Medina del Campo	34	41.18 N	4.55 W
Medina de Ríoseco	34	41.53 N	5.02 W
Médina Gonasse	150	13.08 N	13.45 W
Medinah	278	41.59 N	88.01 W
Medina Lake ⊜[1]	196	29.35 N	98.58 W
Médina Sabak	150	13.36 N	15.35 W
Medina-Sidonia	34	36.27 N	5.55 W
Medinat al-Faiyum → Al-Fayyūm	142	29.19 N	30.50 E
Medininkai	76	54.32 N	25.40 E
Medinīpur	126	22.26 N	87.20 E
Medino	164	9.40 S	149.40 E
Medio, Arroyo del ≃	258	33.49 S	57.43 W
Medio, Punta ›	252	27.07 S	70.57 W
Medio Creek ≃	196	28.19 N	97.19 W
Mediterranean Sea ▼[2]	10	35.00 N	20.00 E
Mediterraneo, Mare → Mediterranean Sea ▼[2]	10	35.00 N	20.00 E
Medjana	34	36.08 N	4.41 E
Medje	154	2.25 N	27.18 E
Medjerda, Monts de la ʌʌ	36	36.35 N	8.15 E
Medkovec	38	43.37 N	23.10 E
Mednogorsk	86	51.24 N	57.37 E
Mednoje	76	56.56 N	35.29 E
Mednyj, ostrov I	74	54.45 N	167.35 E
Médoc ◆[1]	32	45.20 N	1.00 W
Mêdog	120	29.20 N	95.15 E
Medolla	64	44.51 N	11.04 E
Medora, Il., U.S.	219	39.11 N	90.09 W
Medora, In., U.S.	218	38.49 N	86.10 W
Medora, N.D., U.S.	198	46.54 N	103.31 W
Médouneu	152	0.57 N	10.47 E
Medow	54	53.50 N	13.32 E
Medstead, Sk., Can.	184	53.19 N	108.02 W
Medstead, Eng., U.K.	42	51.08 N	1.04 W
Medua	126	22.38 N	90.44 E
Meductic	186	46.00 N	67.29 W
Medulla	220	27.58 N	81.58 W
Međumurje ◆[1]	61	46.25 N	16.30 E
Meduna ≃	64	45.49 N	12.34 E
Medveđa	38	42.50 N	21.35 E
Medvedevo, Ross.	76	60.02 N	43.01 E
Medvedevo, Ross.	80	56.37 N	47.47 E
Medvedevo, Ross.	86	60.37 N	77.21 E
Medvedevskoje	76	58.58 N	35.58 E
Medvedica ≃, Ross.	76	57.05 N	37.32 E
Medvedica ≃, Ross.	80	49.35 N	42.41 E
Medvedickij	80	50.47 N	44.43 E
Medvědí hora ʌ	60	48.59 N	13.25 E
Medvedkovo ◆[8]	265b	55.53 N	37.38 E
Medvedok	80	57.23 N	50.05 E
Medvedovskaja	78	45.27 N	39.01 E
Medvenka, Ross.	78	51.26 N	36.07 E
Medvenka, Ross.	82	54.15 N	37.42 E
Medvežij, ostrov I	89	54.41 N	136.18 E
Medvežinka	83	48.10 N	39.31 E
Medvežje, ozero ⊜	86	55.07 N	68.00 E
Medvežjegorsk	24	62.55 N	34.23 E
Medvežji ostrova II	74	70.52 N	161.26 E
Medvežji ozera ⊜	265b	55.52 N	38.00 E
Medvežji Oz'ora	265b	55.52 N	37.59 E
Medvežskaja	24	64.57 N	57.34 E
Medviagalis ʌ[2]	76	55.38 N	22.45 E
Medvin	78	49.23 N	30.47 E
Medv'onka ≃	265b	55.44 N	37.12 E
Medway, Ma., U.S.	207	42.08 N	71.23 W
Medway, Oh., U.S.	218	39.53 N	83.59 W
Medway □[8]	260	51.24 N	0.31 E
Medway ≃, N.S., Can.	186	44.08 N	64.36 W
Medway ≃, Eng., U.K.	42	51.27 N	0.44 E
Medyn'	82	54.58 N	35.52 E
Medynka ≃	82	54.44 N	36.02 E
Medynskij Zavorot, mys ›	24	68.58 N	59.17 E
Medžibož	78	49.26 N	27.25 E
Medzilaborce	30	49.16 N	21.55 E
Meeberrie	162	26.58 S	115.58 E
Meekatharra	162	26.36 S	118.29 E
Meeker, Co., U.S.	200	40.02 N	107.54 W
Meeker, Oh., U.S.	214	40.39 N	83.18 W
Meeks Bay	226	39.02 N	120.08 W
Meelpaeg Lake ⊜[1]	186	48.16 N	56.35 W
Meenaar	168a	31.38 S	116.53 E
Meentheena	162	21.17 S	120.28 E
Meer	56	51.27 N	4.44 E
Meeralpen → Maritime Alps ʌʌ	62	44.15 N	7.10 E
Meerane	54	50.51 N	12.28 E
Meerbeck	263	51.28 N	6.39 E
Meerbeke	50	50.50 N	4.02 E
Meerbusch	56	51.15 N	6.41 E
Meerhout	56	51.08 N	5.05 E
Meerhusener Moor ◆[3]	52	53.35 N	7.30 E
Meerkerk	52	51.45 N	5.00 E
Meerle	52	51.28 N	4.48 E
Meersburg	58	47.41 N	9.16 E
Meerssen	56	50.53 N	5.45 E
Meerut	124	28.59 N	77.42 E
Meese ≃	42	52.40 N	2.39 W
Meeteetse	202	44.09 N	108.52 W
Mega, Indon.	164	0.41 S	131.53 E
Mega, Ityo.	144	4.07 N	38.16 E
Mega, Pulau I	112	4.00 S	101.02 E
Megalo	144	6.55 N	41.48 E
Megálon Khoríon	38	36.27 N	27.21 E
Megalópolis	38	37.24 N	22.08 E
Meganom, mys ›	78	44.48 N	35.05 E
Mégantic □[6]	206	46.10 N	71.30 W
Mégantic, Lac ⊜	188	45.32 N	70.53 W
Mégantic, Mont ʌ	206	45.28 N	71.09 W
Mégara	38	38.01 N	23.21 E
Megargel	196	33.27 N	98.56 W
Mégaron, Kólpos ⊂	267c	37.56 N	23.20 E
Megaruma ≃	154	13.28 S	40.32 E
Megasini ʌ	126	21.38 N	86.21 E
Meget	88	52.24 N	104.03 E
Megève	62	45.52 N	6.37 E
Mégevette	58	46.12 N	6.30 E
Megezez ʌ	144	9.17 N	39.32 E
Megget Reservoir ⊜[1]	46	55.29 N	3.17 W
Meghālaya □[3]	120	25.30 N	91.15 E
Meghna ≃	120	22.50 N	90.50 E
Megi-jima I	96	34.24 N	134.03 E
Mégiscane ≃	190	48.29 N	77.08 W
Mégiscane, Lac ⊜	190	48.35 N	75.55 W
Meglino, ozero ⊜	76	58.25 N	35.07 E
Megra, Ross.	24	66.09 N	41.37 E
Megra, Ross.	76	60.10 N	37.13 E
Megri	84	38.56 N	46.16 E
Meguro ◆[8]	268	35.38 N	139.42 E
Meguro ≃	268	35.37 N	139.45 E
Mehadia	38	44.55 N	22.22 E
Méhaigne ≃	56	50.32 N	5.13 E
Mehaïguene, Oued V	148	32.15 N	2.59 E
Mehakit	112	2.51 S	115.57 E
Mehar	120	27.11 N	67.49 E
Meharry, Mount ʌ	162	22.59 S	118.35 E
Mehdia	148	35.26 N	1.40 E
Mehede	40	60.27 N	17.24 E
Mehedinți □[6]	38	44.30 N	22.50 E
Meheisa	140	19.37 N	32.57 E
Mehekar	122	20.09 N	76.34 E
Mehendiganj	126	22.49 N	90.32 E
Meherpur	124	23.46 N	88.38 E
Meherrin ≃	192	36.26 N	76.57 W
Mehetia I	14	17.52 S	148.03 W
Mehidpur	120	23.49 N	75.40 E
Mehikoorma	76	58.14 N	27.28 E
Mehlteuer	54	50.32 N	12.02 E
Mehlville	219	38.30 N	90.19 W
Mehnagar	124	25.53 N	83.07 E
Mehndāwal	124	26.59 N	83.07 E
Mehoopany	210	41.34 N	76.04 W
Mehoopany Creek ≃	210	41.34 N	76.03 W
Mehpālpur ◆[8]	272a	28.33 N	77.08 E
Mehr	52	51.43 N	6.29 E
Mehrābād	128	36.53 N	47.55 E
Mehrābād ◆[8]	267d	35.40 N	51.20 E
Mehram Nagar ◆[8]	272a	28.34 N	77.07 E
Mehrān	128	33.07 N	46.10 E
Mehrān ≃	128	26.52 N	55.24 E
Mehring	56	49.48 N	6.49 E
Mehrīz	128	31.35 N	54.28 E
Mehrow	264a	52.34 N	13.37 E
Mehrum	263	51.35 N	6.37 E
Mè-hsa-tè	110	19.33 N	97.38 E
Mehtarlām	120	34.39 N	70.10 E
Mehun-sur-Yèvre	50	47.09 N	2.13 E
Mei ≃, Zhg.	100	24.24 N	116.34 E
Mei ≃, Zhg.	100	26.00 N	115.23 E
Mei ≃, Zhg.	105	39.21 N	117.50 E
Meia Meia	154	5.49 S	35.48 E
Meia Ponte, Rio da ≃	255	18.32 S	49.36 W
Meichang	105	39.22 N	117.10 E
Meichuan	100	30.10 N	115.36 E
Meicun, Zhg.	100	25.30 N	116.56 E
Meicun, Zhg.	106	30.22 N	119.01 E
Meicun, Zhg.	106	30.40 N	119.04 E
Meicun, Zhg.	106	31.33 N	120.24 E
Meide	263	51.11 N	6.55 E
Meiderich ◆[8]	263	51.28 N	6.46 E
Meidling ◆[8]	264b	48.11 N	16.20 E
Meierij ◆[1]	52	51.35 N	5.40 E
Meierkaisong	120	30.54 N	84.31 E
Meiersberg	263	51.17 N	6.57 E
Meig ≃	46	57.34 N	4.41 W
Meiganga	152	6.31 N	14.11 E
Meigle	46	56.35 N	3.09 W
Meigs	192	31.04 N	84.05 W
Meigs Field ⊠	278	41.51 N	87.36 W
Meihsien → Meixian	100	24.21 N	116.08 E
Meihua	100	26.02 N	119.40 E
Meihuajie	100	25.14 N	113.05 E
Meijel	52	51.21 N	5.53 E
Meijino-Mori-Minō-kokutei-kōen ♦	94	34.51 N	135.29 E
Meiji Shrine ✤[1]	268	35.41 N	139.42 E
Meikeng	100	23.59 N	114.05 E
Meikle Millyea ʌ	44	55.07 N	4.19 W
Meikle Says Law ʌ	46	55.55 N	2.40 W
Meiktila	110	20.52 N	95.52 E
Meila	54	51.09 N	13.13 E
Meilen	58	47.16 N	8.38 E
Meili	106	31.42 N	120.53 E
Meilie	100	26.18 N	117.38 E
Meilin, Zhg.	100	23.18 N	115.58 E
Meilin, Zhg.	106	30.35 N	119.04 E
Meillerie	58	46.24 N	6.43 E
Meilong	100	22.56 N	115.17 E
Meilunyingzi	104	42.18 N	122.10 E
Meina	62	45.47 N	8.32 E
Meine	52	52.23 N	10.32 E
Meiners Oaks	228	34.26 N	119.17 W
Meinerzhagen	56	51.06 N	7.38 E
Meiningen	54	50.34 N	10.25 E
Meinung	100	22.54 N	120.32 E
Meio, Ilha do I	287a	23.02 S	43.17 W
Meiringen	58	46.43 N	8.12 E
Meisburg	56	50.06 N	6.41 E
Meisenheim	56	49.42 N	7.40 E
Meishan, Zhg.	106	31.06 N	119.43 E
Meishan, Zhg.	107	30.02 N	103.49 E
Meissen	54	51.10 N	13.28 E
Meissendorf	52	52.43 N	9.50 E
Meiss Lake ⊜	204	41.52 N	122.04 W
Meissner ʌ	56	51.12 N	9.50 E
Meitan	102	27.46 N	107.35 E
Meitian	100	25.21 N	112.47 E
Meitingen	56	48.32 N	10.50 E
Meiwa	94	34.33 N	136.39 E
Meixi	106	30.48 N	119.45 E
Meixian, Zhg.	100	24.21 N	116.08 E
Meixian, Zhg.	100	28.52 N	113.38 E
Meiyao	89	49.37 N	124.30 E
Meiyino	140	6.12 N	34.40 E
Meizhai	102	25.30 N	108.50 E
Meizhou	100	23.50 N	117.20 E
Meizhou Dao I	100	25.06 N	119.07 E
Meizhou Wan ⊂	100	25.06 N	119.00 E
Meizhu	106	31.16 N	119.13 E
Meječkyn, ostrov I	180	65.26 N	178.00 W
Mejerda, Oued (Oued Medjerda) ≃	36	37.07 N	10.13 E
Mejez el Bab	148	36.39 N	9.37 E
Mejia	126	23.34 N	87.06 E
Mejicanos	236	13.43 N	89.12 W
Mejillones	252	23.06 S	70.27 W
Mejillones, Península ›[1]	252	23.17 S	70.34 W
Mejillones del Sur, Bahía de ⊂	252	23.03 S	70.27 W
Mejnypil'gyno	74	62.32 N	177.02 E
Mejorada del Campo	266a	40.24 N	3.29 W
Meka	162	27.26 S	116.48 E
Mekada, Garaet el ⊞	36	36.48 N	8.00 E
Mékambo	152	1.01 N	13.56 E
Mekele	144	13.33 N	39.30 E
Mekerra, Oued ≃	34	35.00 N	0.45 W
Mekhé	150	15.07 N	16.38 W
Mekhliganj	124	26.21 N	88.55 E
Mekhtar	120	30.28 N	69.22 E
Mékinac ≃	206	46.51 N	72.46 W
Mekka → Makkah	144	21.27 N	39.49 E
Meknès	148	33.53 N	5.37 W
Meknès □[4]	148	33.50 N	5.30 W
Mekong ≃	12	10.33 N	105.24 E
Mekongga, Gunung ʌ	112	3.38 S	121.15 E
Mekongga, Pegunungan ʌʌ	112	3.35 S	121.15 E
Mékôngk → Mekong ≃	12	10.33 N	105.24 E
Mekoryuk	180	60.23 N	166.12 W
Mékrou ≃	150	12.24 N	2.49 E
Mel	64	46.04 N	12.05 E
Melado ≃	252	35.43 S	71.05 W
Melah, Oued el V, Alg.	148	28.21 N	6.00 E
Melah, Oued el V, Tun.	148	34.03 N	8.06 E
Melah, Sebkhet el ⊜	148	29.05 N	1.10 W
Melaka	114	2.12 N	102.15 E
Melaka □[3]	114	2.15 N	102.15 E
Melalap	112	5.14 N	116.00 E
Melandro ≃	68	40.37 N	15.27 E
Melanesia II	14	13.00 S	164.00 E
Melanesian Basin ✦[1]	14	0.05 N	160.35 E
Melappālaiyam	122	8.42 N	77.43 E
Melara	64	45.03 N	11.11 E
Melaune	54	51.11 N	14.44 E
Melawi ≃	112	0.05 N	111.29 E
Melayu ≃	271c	1.27 N	103.42 E
Melbern	216	41.28 N	84.39 W
Melbost	46	58.15 N	6.22 W
Melbourn	42	52.05 N	0.01 E
Melbourne, Austl.	169	37.49 S	144.58 E
Melbourne, Austl.	274b	37.49 S	144.58 E
Melbourne, On., Can.	214	42.49 N	81.33 W
Melbourne, Eng., U.K.	42	52.49 N	1.25 W
Melbourne, Ar., U.S.	194	36.03 N	91.54 W
Melbourne, Fl., U.S.	220	28.04 N	80.36 W
Melbourne, Ia., U.S.	190	41.56 N	93.06 W

Name	Seite	Breite°′	Länge°′ E = Ost
Melbourne, University of ✤[2]	274b	37.48 S	144.58 E
Melbourne Beach	220	28.04 N	80.33 W
Melbourne Island I	176	68.30 N	104.45 W
Melbourne Regional Airport ⊠	220	28.06 N	80.38 W
Mel'cany	80	54.28 N	44.43 E
Melcher	190	41.13 N	93.14 W
Melchor, Isla I	254	45.08 S	73.57 W
Melchor Múzquiz	232	27.53 N	101.31 W
Melchor Ocampo	196	26.03 N	99.33 W
Melchor Romero ◆[8]	258	34.56 S	58.03 W
Melchtal	58	46.50 N	8.17 E
Melcroft	214	40.03 N	79.24 W
Melderskin ʌ	26	60.01 N	6.05 E
Meldola	66	44.07 N	12.05 E
Meldorf	30	54.05 N	9.05 E
Meldrum Bay	190	45.56 N	83.07 W
Meldrum Creek	182	52.07 N	122.20 W
Mélé, Centraf.	146	9.46 N	21.33 E
Mele, India	272b	22.49 N	88.09 E
Mele, It.	62	44.27 N	8.45 E
Mélé, Baie ⊂	175f	17.43 S	168.15 E
Mele, Capo ›	62	43.57 N	8.10 E
Melechovo	80	56.17 N	41.17 E
Meleck	86	57.25 N	90.12 E
Meleden	144	10.25 N	49.51 E
Melegnano	62	45.21 N	9.19 E
Meleješt'	78	46.59 N	29.33 E
Melekeok	175b	7.29 N	134.38 E
Melekess → Dimitrovgrad	80	54.14 N	49.39 E
Melela ≃	154	17.04 S	38.36 E
Melena del Sur	240p	22.47 N	82.09 W
Melendiz Dağı ʌ	130	38.07 N	34.25 E
Melendugno	68	40.16 N	18.20 E
Melenki	80	55.20 N	41.38 E
Meleškoviči	78	51.56 N	28.59 E
Meleuz	86	52.58 N	55.55 E
Mélèzes, Rivière aux ≃	176	57.40 N	69.29 W
Melfa	208	37.39 N	75.45 W
Melfa ≃	66	41.30 N	13.35 E
Melfi, It.	68	41.00 N	15.39 E
Melfi, Tchad	146	11.04 N	17.56 E
Melfort, Sk., Can.	184	52.52 N	104.36 W
Melfort, Zimb.	154	17.59 S	31.19 E
Melfort, Loch ⊂	46	56.15 N	5.31 W
Melgaço, Bra.	250	1.47 S	50.44 W
Melgaço, Port.	34	42.07 N	8.16 W
Melgar	246	4.12 N	74.39 W
Melghir, Chott ⊜	148	34.20 N	6.20 E
Mel'guny	80	52.09 N	40.52 E
Melhus	26	63.17 N	10.16 E
Meli ≃	150	8.16 N	10.42 W
Meliane, Oued ≃	36	36.46 N	10.18 E
Meliau	112	0.08 S	110.18 E
Meliau, Gunong ʌ	116	5.50 N	117.14 E
Melibocus ʌ	56	49.42 N	8.40 E
Melichovo, Ross.	78	50.42 N	36.48 E
Melichovo, Ross.	82	55.07 N	37.39 E
Melicuccà	68	38.18 N	15.53 E
Melide, Esp.	34	42.55 N	8.00 W
Melide, Schw.	58	45.57 N	8.57 E
Meligalás	38	37.13 N	21.59 E
Melilla	34	35.19 N	2.58 W
Melilli	70	37.11 N	15.07 E
Melimoyu, Cerro ʌ	254	44.05 S	72.52 W
Melincué	252	33.39 S	61.27 W
Melipilla	252	33.42 S	71.13 W
Mélisey	58	47.45 N	6.35 E
Melissa	68	39.18 N	17.01 E
Melissano	68	39.58 N	18.07 E
Melíssia	267c	38.03 N	23.50 E
Melita	184	49.16 N	101.00 W
Melito di Porto Salvo	68	37.55 N	15.47 E
Melitopol'	78	46.50 N	35.22 E
Melívoia	38	39.45 N	22.48 E
Melk	61	48.14 N	15.20 E
Melk ≃	61	48.14 N	15.19 E
Melk ✤[1]	61	48.14 N	15.20 E
Melka Teka	144	6.05 N	43.08 E
Melkbosstrand	158	33.43 S	18.27 E
Melksham	42	51.23 N	2.09 W
Mella ≃	64	45.13 N	10.13 E
Mellansel	26	63.26 N	18.19 E
Mellau	58	47.21 N	9.53 E
Melle, Dtsch.	52	52.12 N	8.20 E
Melle, Fr.	32	46.13 N	0.09 W
Melleck	64	47.40 N	12.45 E
Mellègue, Oued ≃	36	36.32 N	8.51 E
Mellen	190	46.19 N	90.39 W
Mellendorf	52	52.33 N	9.43 E
Mellenville	210	42.15 N	73.40 W
Mellerud	26	58.42 N	12.28 E
Mellette	198	45.09 N	98.29 W
Mellier ≃	56	49.43 N	5.32 E
Melling	262	53.30 N	2.56 W
Mellingen	54	50.56 N	11.23 E
Mellish Reef I[1]	160	17.25 S	155.50 E
Mellish Rise ✦[3]	14	17.00 S	156.00 E
Mellit	140	14.08 N	25.33 E
Mellone, Monte ʌ	267a	41.50 N	12.43 E
Mellong Range ʌʌ	170	33.06 S	150.43 E
Mellon Udrigle	46	57.55 N	5.39 W
Mellor	262	53.46 N	2.32 W
Mellor Brook	262	53.47 N	2.33 W
Mellösa	40	59.06 N	16.33 E
Mellrichstadt	56	50.26 N	10.18 E
Mellum I	52	53.40 N	8.10 E
Melmerby	44	54.44 N	2.35 W
Melmore	214	41.02 N	83.07 W
Melmoth	158	28.38 S	31.24 E
Mel'nica-Podol'skaja	78	48.37 N	26.10 E
Mělník	54	50.20 N	14.29 E
Mel'nikovo, Ross.	26	61.05 N	29.22 E
Mel'nikovo, Ross.	86	56.34 N	84.05 E
Mel'nikovo, Taj.	85	40.19 N	70.19 E
Melo	252	32.22 S	54.11 W
Melo ≃	248	21.27 S	57.52 W
Melo, Ilha de I	150	11.02 N	15.13 W
Melocheville	206	45.19 N	73.56 W
Meloco	154	13.25 S	39.08 E
Melolo	115b	9.53 S	120.40 E
Melolo ≃	115b	9.52 S	120.41 E
Melong	152	5.07 N	9.57 E
Melos → Mílos I	38	36.41 N	24.15 E
Melovaja ≃	83	49.23 N	40.16 E
Melovatka	83	49.21 N	38.11 E
Melovoje	83	49.22 N	40.06 E
Melovoj Syrt ʌ	80	52.15 N	52.35 E
Melozitna ≃	180	64.46 N	155.29 W
Melrose, Austl.	162	27.56 S	121.19 E
Melrose, Austl.	166	32.42 S	146.58 E
Melrose, Scot., U.K.	46	55.36 N	2.44 W
Melrose, Ma., U.S.	207	42.27 N	71.04 W
Melrose, Mn., U.S.	198	45.40 N	94.48 W
Melrose, N.M., U.S.	196	34.25 N	103.37 W
Melrose, N.Y., U.S.	210	42.50 N	73.37 W
Melrose, Oh., U.S.	216	41.05 N	84.25 W
Melrose, Wi., U.S.	190	44.07 N	90.59 W
Melrose ◆[8]	276	40.49 N	73.55 W
Melrose Abbey ✤[1]	46	55.37 N	2.45 W
Melrose Park, Fl., U.S.	220	26.06 N	80.12 W
Melrose Park, Il., U.S.	216	41.54 N	87.51 W
Melrose Park, N.Y., U.S.	212	42.54 N	76.32 W
Melrose Park, Pa., U.S.	285	40.04 N	75.08 W
Mels	58	47.03 N	9.25 E
Melstone	202	46.35 N	107.52 W
Melsungen	56	51.08 N	9.32 E
Meltaus	24	66.54 N	25.22 E
Meltham, Eng., U.K.	44	53.35 N	1.51 W
Meltham, Eng., U.K.	262	53.36 N	1.51 W
Melton, Austl.	168b	34.05 S	137.59 E
Melton, Austl.	169	37.41 S	144.35 E
Melton Constable	42	52.53 N	1.01 E

Symbols in the index entries represent the broad categories identified in the key at the right. Symbols with superior numbers (ʌʌ[1]) identify subcategories (see complete key on page *I · 1*).

Symbole im Register stellen die rechts im Schlüssel erklärten Kategorien dar. Symbole mit hochgestellten Ziffern (ʌʌ[1]) bezeichnen Unterabteilungen einer Kategorie (vgl. vollständiger Schlüssel auf Seite *I · 1*).

Los símbolos incluídos en el texto del índice representan las grandes categorias identificadas con la clave a la derecha. Los símbolos con numeros en su parte superior (ʌʌ[1]) identifican las subcategorías (véase la clave completa en la página *I · 1*).

Les symboles de l'index représentent les catégories indiquées dans la légende à droite. Les symboles suivis d'un indice (ʌʌ[1]) représentent des sous-catégories (voir légende complète à la page *I · 1*).

Os símbolos incluídos no texto do índice representam as grandes categorias identificadas com a chave à direita. Os símbolos com números em sua parte superior (ʌʌ[1]) identificam as subcategorias (veja-se a chave completa à página *I · 1*).

ʌ Mountain	Berg	Montaña	Montagne	Montanha
ʌʌ Mountains	Gebirge	Montañas	Montagnes	Montanhas
)(Pass	Paß	Paso	Col	Passo
V Valley, Canyon	Tal, Cañon	Valle, Cañón	Vallée, Canyon	Vale, Canhão
≚ Plain	Ebene	Llano	Plaine	Planície
› Cape	Kap	Cabo	Cap	Cabo
I Island	Insel	Isla	Île	Ilha
II Islands	Inseln	Islas	Îles	Ilhas
⊥ Other Topographic Features	Andere Topographische Objekte	Otros Elementos Topográficos	Autres données topographiques	Outros acidentes topográficos

ESPAÑOL

Nombre	Página	Lat.°′	Long.°′ W = Oeste
Melton Hill Lake ⊜[1]	192	36.00 N	84.15 W
Melton Mowbray	42	52.46 N	0.53 W
Melton Reservoir ⊜[1]	169	37.43 S	144.32 E
Melúa	246	3.55 N	72.50 W
Meluan	112	1.52 N	111.56 E
Meluco	154	12.36 S	39.38 E
Melúli ≃	154	16.28 S	39.44 E
Melun, Fr.	50	48.32 N	2.40 E
Melun, Mya.	110	20.14 N	93.24 E
Melunga	152	17.16 S	16.24 E
Melūr	122	10.03 N	78.20 E
Melvaig	46	57.48 N	5.49 W
Melvern	198	38.30 N	95.38 W
Melvern Lake ⊜[1]	198	38.30 N	95.50 W
Melvich	46	58.33 N	3.55 W
Melville, Austl.	168a	32.03 S	115.49 E
Melville, Sk., Can.	184	50.55 N	102.48 W
Melville, La., U.S.	194	30.41 N	91.44 W
Melville, N.Y., U.S.	276	40.47 N	73.24 W
Melville ◆[8]	273d	26.11 S	28.00 E
Melville, Cape ≻, Austl.	164	14.11 S	144.30 E
Melville, Cape ≻, Pil.	116	7.49 N	117.01 E
Melville, Détroit de → Viscount Melville Sound Ɥ	176	74.10 N	108.00 W
Melville, Lake ⊜	176	53.45 N	59.30 W
Melville Bugt ⊂	16	75.30 N	63.00 W
Melville Hall Airport ⊠	240d	15.33 N	61.18 W
Melville Hills ⋏[2]	180	69.15 N	124.00 W
Melville Island I, Austl.	164	11.40 S	131.00 E
Melville Island I, N.T., Can.	16	75.15 N	110.00 W
Melville Island Aboriginal Reserve ◆[4]	164	11.40 S	131.00 E
Melville Peninsula ≻[1]	176	68.00 N	84.00 W
Melville Sound Ɥ, N.T., Can.	176	68.05 N	107.30 W
Melville Sound Ɥ, On., Can.	212	44.57 N	81.05 W
Melvin, Il., U.S.	216	40.34 N	88.15 W
Melvin, Ky., U.S.	192	37.21 N	82.41 W
Melvin, Tx., U.S.	196	31.13 N	99.35 W
Melvin, Lough ⊜	48	54.26 N	8.10 W
Melvindale	214	42.16 N	83.10 W
Melvin Lake ⊜	184	57.08 N	100.15 W
Melyana	148	36.15 N	2.15 E
Mélykút	30	46.13 N	19.24 E
Melzo	62	45.30 N	9.25 E
Memala	112	1.44 S	112.36 E
Mêmar Co ⊜	120	34.15 N	82.20 E
Memāri	126	23.12 N	88.07 E
Memba	154	14.11 S	40.30 E
Membalong	112	3.09 S	107.38 E
Memboro	115b	9.22 S	119.32 E
Membre	56	49.52 N	4.54 E
Même ≃	50	48.11 N	0.39 E
Memel	158	27.43 S	29.30 E
Mēmele ≃	76	56.24 N	24.10 E
Memel → Klaipėda	76	55.43 N	21.07 E
Memel → Nemunas ≃	76	55.18 N	21.23 E
Memewin, Lac ⊜	190	46.29 N	78.42 W
Memmert I	52	53.39 N	6.53 E
Memmingen	58	47.59 N	10.11 E
Memo ≃	246	9.16 N	66.40 W
Memori, Tanjung ≻	164	0.52 S	134.08 E
Memorial Bridge ◆[5]	269a	13.44 N	100.30 E
Memorial Stadium ♠	284b	39.20 N	76.36 W
Mémót	110	11.49 N	106.11 E
Mempawah	112	0.22 N	108.58 E
Memphis, Fl., U.S.	220	27.32 N	82.33 W
Memphis, In., U.S.	218	38.29 N	85.45 W
Memphis, Mi., U.S.	214	42.54 N	82.46 W
Memphis, Mo., U.S.	194	40.27 N	92.10 W
Memphis, Tn., U.S.	194	35.08 N	90.02 W
Memphis, Tx., U.S.	196	34.43 N	100.32 W
Memphis → Mīt Ruhaynah ⊥	142	29.51 N	31.15 E
Memphis Naval Air Station ■	194	35.21 N	89.52 W
Memphremagog, Lake ⊜	206	45.05 N	72.15 W
Memsie	46	57.39 N	2.02 W
Mena, Ityo.	144	6.25 N	39.51 E
Mena, Ukr.	78	51.31 N	32.13 E
Mena, Ar., U.S.	194	34.35 N	94.14 W
Menado → Manado	112	1.29 N	124.51 E
Menaggio	58	46.01 N	9.14 E
Menahga	198	46.45 N	95.06 W
Menai	274a	34.01 S	151.01 E
Menai Bridge	44	53.14 N	4.10 W
Menai Strait Ɥ	44	53.12 N	4.12 W
Ménaka	150	15.55 N	2.24 E
Menaldum	52	53.12 N	5.39 E
Menan	202	43.43 N	111.59 W
Menands	210	42.41 N	73.43 W
Menangina	162	29.50 S	121.54 E
Menantico Creek ≃	208	39.20 N	75.00 W
Menarandra ≃	157b	25.17 S	44.30 E
Menard	196	30.55 N	99.47 W
Menard □[6]	219	40.01 N	89.51 W
Menard Creek ≃	222	30.29 N	94.50 W
Menars	50	47.38 N	1.24 E
Menasha	190	44.12 N	88.26 W
Menate	112	0.14 S	113.02 E
Menawashei	140	12.40 N	24.59 E
Menchang	105	38.54 N	117.01 E
Menčikury	78	47.04 N	34.48 E
Mencué	254	40.25 S	69.38 W
Mend	89	43.40 N	123.08 E
Mendanau, Pulau I	112	2.51 S	107.26 E
Mendarik, Pulau I	112	1.18 N	107.02 E
Mendatai	102	38.51 N	94.39 E
Mendatica	62	44.05 N	7.49 E
Mendawai	112	2.59 S	113.16 E
Mendawai ≃	112	3.17 S	113.21 E
Mendaya	115a	8.23 S	114.42 E
Mende	32	44.30 N	3.30 E
Mendebo ⋏	144	6.50 N	39.40 E
Mendel' ≃	86	58.13 N	90.08 E
Mendelejevsk	80	55.54 N	52.20 E
Menden	56	51.26 N	7.47 E
Menden ◆[8]	263	51.24 N	6.54 E
Mendenhall, Ms., U.S.	194	31.57 N	89.52 W
Mendenhall, Pa., U.S.	285	39.51 N	75.38 W
Mendenhall, Cape ≻	180	59.51 N	166.15 W
Mendes	256	22.32 S	43.44 W
Méndez	232	25.07 N	98.34 W
Mendez-Nuñez	116	14.08 N	120.54 E
Mendham	210	40.46 N	74.36 W
Mendi, Ityo.	144	9.50 N	35.06 E
Mendi, Pap. N. Gui.	164	6.10 S	143.40 E
Mendig	56	50.21 N	7.15 E
Mendip Hills ⋏[2]	42	51.15 N	2.40 W
Mendlesham	42	52.16 N	1.05 E
Mendocino	204	39.18 N	123.47 W
Mendocino, Cape ≻	204	40.25 N	124.25 W
Mendocino Fracture Zone ✣	16	40.00 N	145.00 W
Mendola ≃	70	37.44 N	13.32 E
Mendon, Il., U.S.	219	40.05 N	91.17 W
Mendon, Ma., U.S.	207	42.06 N	71.33 W
Mendon, Mi., U.S.	216	42.00 N	85.27 W
Mendon, N.Y., U.S.	210	43.00 N	77.34 W
Mendon, Oh., U.S.	216	40.40 N	84.31 W
Mendon, Pa., U.S.	279b	40.11 N	79.41 W
Mendota, Ca., U.S.	226	36.45 N	120.22 W
Mendota, Il., U.S.	216	41.32 N	89.07 W
Mendota, Lake ⊜	216	43.05 N	89.25 W
Mendoza, Arg.	252	32.53 S	68.49 W
Mendoza, Perú	248	6.20 S	77.24 W
Mendoza, Ur.	258	34.17 S	56.13 W
Mendoza □[4]	252	34.30 S	68.30 W
Mendoza ≃	252	32.21 S	68.18 W

FRANÇAIS

Nom	Page	Lat.°′	Long.°′ W = Ouest
Mendoza, Arroyo de ≃	258	34.21 S	56.18 W
Mendrisio	58	45.52 N	8.59 E
Mend'ukino	82	54.47 N	38.51 E
Mendung	112	0.31 N	103.13 E
Ménéac	32	48.09 N	2.28 W
Mene de Mauroa	246	10.43 N	71.01 W
Mene Grande	246	9.49 N	70.56 W
Menemen	130	38.36 N	27.04 E
Menen	50	50.48 N	3.07 E
Meneng Point ≻	174b	0.32 S	166.57 E
Menes	115a	6.23 S	105.55 E
Menfi	70	37.36 N	12.58 E
Mengalum, Pulau I	112	6.16 N	115.12 E
Mengban	102	23.08 N	100.19 E
Mengbang	102	21.28 N	101.19 E
Mengcheng	100	33.17 N	116.33 E
Mengchi ≃	107	29.47 N	104.56 E
Mengcun	98	38.06 N	117.05 E
Mengdapu	104	41.35 N	123.12 E
Mengede ◆[8]	263	51.34 N	7.23 E
Mengeh Jek	120	37.02 N	66.07 E
Mengen, Dtsch.	58	48.03 N	9.20 E
Mengen, Tür.	130	40.56 N	32.04 E
Mengeringhausen	56	51.22 N	8.59 E
Mengersgereuth-Hämmern	54	50.24 N	11.07 E
Menges Mills	208	39.52 N	76.54 W
Menggala	112	4.28 S	105.17 E
Menggu	102	26.34 N	102.57 E
Menggubao	104	42.27 N	122.23 E
Menggudai	102	38.10 N	108.15 E
Menghai	102	22.00 N	100.26 E
Menghe	106	32.03 N	119.47 E
Menghun	102	21.44 N	100.23 E
Mengjiacun	106	31.33 N	118.46 E
Mengjiagang	89	46.22 N	130.40 E
Mengjiatai	104	42.06 N	123.21 E
Mengjiawan	102	38.35 N	109.25 E
Mengjiawopeng	104	41.22 N	121.51 E
Mengjiayuanjia	105	40.52 N	118.08 E
Mengjiazhai	269b	31.18 N	121.19 E
Mengka	102	25.10 N	98.01 E
Mengkibol	114	1.58 N	103.20 E
Mengkuang	114	3.11 N	102.24 E
Menglian	102	22.20 N	99.38 E
Menglinghausen ◆[8]	263	51.28 N	7.25 E
Mengluchang	107	29.19 N	103.35 E
Mengmucun	106	31.59 N	119.01 E
Mengong	152	2.56 N	11.25 E
Mengqigou	104	42.00 N	121.08 E
Mengshan	102	24.07 N	110.33 E
Meng Shan ⋏, Zhg.	98	35.44 N	117.45 E
Meng Shan ⋏, Zhg.	104	41.50 N	121.10 E
Mengtong	107	30.44 N	105.53 E
Mengulek, gora ∧	86	50.58 N	89.30 E
Mengwang	102	22.26 N	100.34 E
Mengyin	98	35.45 N	117.57 E
Mengzhe	102	22.02 N	100.16 E
Mengzhi	102	24.10 N	99.46 E
Mengzi	102	23.22 N	103.20 E
Menihek Lakes ⊜	176	54.00 N	66.35 W
Ménil-la-Tour	56	48.46 N	5.52 E
Menindee	166	32.24 S	142.26 E
Menindee Lake ⊜	166	32.21 S	142.20 E
Meningie	166	35.42 S	139.20 E
Menjiaqiangzi	104	42.29 N	121.19 E
Menkoutang	106	31.01 N	119.27 E
Menlo	224	46.37 N	123.38 W
Menlo Park	226	37.27 N	122.10 W
Menlo Park Mall ◆[9]	276	40.32 N	74.20 W
Menlo Park Terrace	276	40.32 N	74.20 W
Mennecy	261	48.34 N	2.26 E
Mennetou-sur-Cher	50	47.16 N	1.53 E
Mennighüffen	52	52.13 N	8.43 E
Menno	198	43.14 N	97.34 W
Meno, Indon.	164	3.52 S	135.31 E
Meno, Ok., U.S.	196	36.23 N	98.10 W
Menominee	190	45.06 N	87.36 W
Menominee ≃	190	45.05 N	87.36 W
Menominee Indian Reservation ◆[4]	190	45.00 N	88.45 W
Menomonee ≃	216	43.02 N	87.54 W
Menomonee Falls	216	43.10 N	88.07 W
Menomonie	190	44.52 N	91.55 W
Menongue	152	14.36 S	17.48 E
Menor, Mar ⊂	34	37.43 N	0.48 W
Menorca I	34	40.00 N	4.00 E
Mens	62	44.49 N	5.45 E
Menslage	52	52.41 N	7.49 E
Menston	44	53.53 N	1.44 W
Menstrup	41	55.13 N	11.36 E
Mentana	66	42.02 N	12.38 E
Mentasta Lake	180	62.55 N	143.45 W
Mentasta Mountains ⋏	180	62.40 N	143.07 W
Mentawai, Kepulauan II	108	2.00 S	99.30 E
Mentawai, Selat Ɥ	108	1.45 S	100.00 E
Mentekab	114	3.29 N	102.21 E
Menteke, peski ◆[2]	80	47.20 N	50.40 E
Menteng ◆[8]	269e	6.12 S	106.50 E
Menteroda	54	51.18 N	10.33 E
Menthon-Saint-Bernard	62	45.51 N	6.12 E
Menton	62	43.47 N	7.30 E
Mentone, Austl.	274b	37.59 S	145.05 E
Mentone, Ca., U.S.	228	34.05 N	117.08 W
Mentone, In., U.S.	216	41.10 N	86.02 W
Mentone, Tx., U.S.	196	31.42 N	103.36 W
Mentone → Menton	62	43.47 N	7.30 E
Mentor, Ky., U.S.	218	38.53 N	84.14 W
Mentor, Oh., U.S.	214	41.39 N	81.20 W
Mentor-on-the-Lake	214	41.42 N	81.21 W
Mentougou	105	39.56 N	116.03 E
Mentzdam ⊜[1]	158	33.10 S	25.09 E
Menucourt	261	49.02 N	1.59 E
Menuma	94	36.13 N	139.23 E
Men'uša	76	58.23 N	30.42 E
Menyamya	164	7.10 S	146.00 E
Menyapa, Gunung ∧	112	1.05 N	116.05 E
Menyuan	102	37.27 N	101.48 E
Menza ≃	88	50.14 N	108.38 E
Menzel Bourguiba	148	37.10 N	9.48 E
Menzel Bou Zelfa	36	36.41 N	10.36 E
Menzel Djemil	36	37.14 N	9.55 E
Menzelen	52	51.37 N	6.32 E
Menzelerheide	263	51.37 N	6.31 E
Menzelinsk	80	55.43 N	53.08 E
Menzel Temime	148	36.47 N	10.59 E
Menzenschwand	58	47.49 N	8.04 E
Menzies	162	29.41 S	121.02 E
Menzies, Mount ∧	9	73.30 S	61.50 E
Menziken	58	47.14 N	8.12 E
Meobbaai ⊂	156	24.25 S	14.34 E
Meola Āgri	272a	28.42 N	77.23 E
Meolo	64	45.37 N	12.27 E
Meon ≃	42	50.48 N	1.15 W
Meopham	260	51.22 N	0.22 E
Meopham Station	260	51.23 N	0.21 E
Meoqui	232	28.17 N	105.29 W
Meota	184	53.02 N	108.27 W
Méouge ≃	62	44.16 N	5.50 E
Méounes-lès-Montrieux	62	43.17 N	5.58 E
Mepal	42	52.24 N	0.07 E
Mepisckaro, gora ∧	84	41.50 N	42.40 E
Meppel	52	52.42 N	6.11 E
Meppen	52	52.41 N	7.17 E
Meqerghane, Sebkha ≡	148	26.19 N	1.20 E
Meqruur	174q	9.31 N	138.09 E
Mequinenza, Embalse de ⊜[1]	34	41.20 N	0.05 E
Mequon	216	43.13 N	87.59 W
Mer	50	47.42 N	1.30 E
Mera ≃	58	46.11 N	9.25 E
Merah	112	0.50 N	116.48 E
Merai	164	4.50 S	152.20 E

PORTUGUÊS

Nome	Página	Lat.°′	Long.°′ W = Oeste
Meråker	26	63.26 N	11.45 E
Merakurak	115a	6.53 S	111.59 E
Meramangye, Lake ⊜	162	28.25 S	132.13 E
Merambéllou, Kólpos ⊂	38	35.14 N	25.47 E
Meramec ≃	194	38.23 N	90.21 W
Meramec Caverns ⊥[5]	219	38.15 N	91.06 W
Meramec State Park ♠	219	38.14 N	91.05 W
Meran	273a	6.38 N	3.16 E
Meranggau	112	0.12 S	110.17 E
Merangin ≃	112	2.09 S	102.47 E
Meran → Merano	64	46.40 N	11.09 E
Merano (Meran)	64	46.40 N	11.09 E
Merapi, Gunung ∧	115a	8.03 S	114.15 E
Merapoh	114	4.41 N	101.59 E
Merasheen	186	47.25 N	54.21 W
Merasheen Island I	186	47.30 N	54.15 W
Merate	62	45.42 N	9.25 E
Meratus, Pegunungan ⋏	112	2.45 S	115.40 E
Merauke	164	8.28 S	140.20 E
Merauke ≃	164	8.30 S	140.24 E
Merbabu, Gunung ∧	115a	7.27 S	110.26 E
Merbau, Indon.	114	2.16 N	99.50 E
Merbau, Indon.	114	1.07 N	102.33 E
Merbein	166	34.11 S	142.04 E
Mercaderes	246	1.47 N	77.10 W
Merca → Marka	144	1.43 N	44.53 E
Mercantour, Parc National du ♠	62	44.10 N	7.00 E
Mercāra	122	12.25 N	75.44 E
Mercatale	66	43.15 N	12.08 E
Mercato San Severino	68	40.47 N	14.46 E
Mercato Saraceno	66	43.57 N	12.12 E
Merced	226	37.18 N	120.28 W
Merced □[6]	226	37.15 N	120.40 W
Merced ≃	226	37.21 N	120.58 W
Merced, Lake ⊜	282	37.43 N	122.29 W
Merced, North Fork ≃	226	37.37 N	120.03 W
Merced, South Fork ≃	226	37.39 N	119.53 W
Merced Airport ⊠	226	37.17 N	120.31 W
Mercedario, Cerro ∧	252	31.59 S	70.07 W
Mercedes, Arg.	252	29.12 S	58.05 W
Mercedes, Arg.	252	33.40 S	65.28 W
Mercedes, Arg.	258	34.39 S	59.27 W
Mercedes, Pil.	116	14.07 N	123.01 E
Mercedes, Tx., U.S.	196	26.08 N	97.54 W
Mercedes, Ur.	252	33.16 S	58.01 W
Mercer, N.Z.	172	37.16 S	175.03 E
Mercer, Mo., U.S.	194	40.30 N	93.31 W
Mercer, Oh., U.S.	216	40.40 N	84.35 W
Mercer, Pa., U.S.	214	41.13 N	80.14 W
Mercer, Wi., U.S.	190	46.09 N	90.03 W
Mercer □[6], N.J., U.S.	208	40.13 N	74.45 W
Mercer □[6], Oh., U.S.	216	40.33 N	84.34 W
Mercer □[6], Pa., U.S.	214	41.14 N	80.15 W
Mercer Island	224	47.35 N	122.15 W
Mercersburg	188	39.49 N	77.54 W
Mercerville	208	40.14 N	74.41 W
Mercês, Bra.	256	21.12 S	43.21 W
Mercês, Port.	266c	38.47 N	9.19 W
Merchants Bay ⊂	176	67.10 N	62.50 W
Merchants Millpond ⊜	208	36.26 N	76.41 W
Merchantville	285	39.56 N	75.04 W
Merchong ≃	114	3.03 N	103.27 E
Merchtem	50	50.58 N	4.14 E
Mercier (Saint-Philomène)	275a	45.19 N	73.45 W
Mercier, Pont ◆[5]	275a	45.25 N	73.39 W
Mercoal	182	53.10 N	117.05 W
Mercogliano	68	40.55 N	14.44 E
Mercury	204	36.40 N	115.59 W
Mercury Islands II	172	36.35 S	175.55 E
Mercy, Cape ≻	176	64.53 N	63.32 W
Mercy Bay ⊂	176	74.05 N	119.00 W
Mercy-le-Bas	56	49.23 N	5.45 E
Merdeka Bridge ◆[5]	271c	1.18 N	103.53 E
Méré, Fr.	261	48.47 N	1.49 E
Mere, Eng., U.K.	42	51.06 N	2.16 W
Mere, Eng., U.K.	262	53.20 N	2.25 W
Mere Brow	262	53.40 N	2.53 W
Mereckij	85	43.48 N	74.42 E
Mereclough	262	53.46 N	2.11 W
Meredale	273d	26.17 S	27.59 E
Meredith, Austl.	169	37.51 S	144.04 E
Meredith, N.H., U.S.	188	43.39 N	71.30 W
Meredith, Cape ≻	254	52.15 S	60.39 W
Meredith, Lake ⊜[1]	196	35.36 N	101.42 W
Meredosia	219	39.50 N	90.34 W
Meredosia Lake ⊜	219	39.52 N	90.33 W
Mereeg	144	3.46 N	47.18 E
Merefa	78	49.49 N	36.03 E
Méré Lava I	175f	14.25 S	168.03 E
Merelbeke	50	51.00 N	3.45 E
Merenkurkku (Norra Kvarken) Ɥ	26	63.36 N	20.43 E
Mereny	78	46.58 N	29.04 E
Merevari ≃	246	4.28 N	63.57 W
Méréville	50	48.19 N	2.05 E
Merewa	144	7.40 N	37.00 E
Merewether	170	32.57 S	151.46 E
Mereworth	260	51.15 N	0.23 E
Mergenevo	80	49.56 N	51.17 E
Mergozzo	58	45.58 N	8.26 E
Mergui (Myeik)	110	12.26 N	98.36 E
Mergui Archipelago II	110	12.00 N	98.00 E
Merḥavya	132	32.36 N	35.19 E
Meria	272b	22.59 N	88.20 E
Meribah	166	34.42 S	140.51 E
Méribel	62	45.25 N	6.34 E
Meriç	130	41.11 N	26.25 E
Meriç (Marica) (Évros) ≃	38	40.52 N	26.12 E
Méricourt	50	50.24 N	2.52 E
Mérida, Esp.	34	38.55 N	6.20 W
Mérida, Méx.	200	32.39 N	114.58 W
Mérida, Méx.	232	20.58 N	89.37 W
Merida, Pil.	116	10.55 N	124.32 E
Mérida, Ven.	246	8.36 N	71.08 W
Mérida □[3]	246	8.30 N	71.10 W
Mérida, Cordillera de ⋏	246	8.40 N	71.00 W
Meridale	210	42.22 N	74.57 W
Meriden, Eng., U.K.	42	52.26 N	1.37 W
Meriden, Ct., U.S.	207	41.32 N	72.48 W
Meriden, N.J., U.S.	276	40.57 N	74.28 W
Meridian, Ca., U.S.	226	39.09 N	121.55 W
Meridian, Ga., U.S.	192	31.27 N	81.22 W
Meridian, Id., U.S.	202	43.36 N	116.23 W
Meridian, Ms., U.S.	194	32.21 N	88.42 W
Meridian, N.Y., U.S.	210	43.09 N	76.32 W
Meridian, Pa., U.S.	214	40.51 N	79.58 W
Meridian, Tx., U.S.	222	31.55 N	97.39 W
Meridian Hills	218	39.53 N	86.09 W
Meridian Naval Air Station ■	194	32.33 N	88.34 W
Meridianville	194	34.51 N	86.34 W
Mériel	261	49.05 N	2.12 E
Mérignac	32	44.50 N	0.42 W
Merigold	194	33.50 N	90.43 W
Merikarvia	26	61.51 N	21.30 E
Merille, Laga ≃	154	1.25 N	38.26 E
Merimbula	166	36.53 S	149.54 E
Merín, Laguna (Lagoa Mirim) ⊂	252	32.45 S	52.50 W
Merinda	166	20.01 S	148.10 E
Mering	60	48.16 N	10.59 E
Meringa	146	10.44 N	12.09 E
Merin Gubai	144	1.26 N	44.20 E
Meringur	166	34.24 S	141.16 E
Merino	198	40.28 N	103.21 W
Merinos	252	32.24 S	56.54 W
Merion Station	285	39.59 N	75.15 W
Merir I	108	4.19 N	132.19 E
Merishausen	58	47.45 N	8.37 E
Merit	222	33.13 N	96.17 W
Merivale Gardens	212	45.19 N	75.44 W
Meriwether Farms	285	39.58 N	75.34 W
Merizo	174p	13.16 N	144.40 E
Merke	85	42.52 N	73.11 E
Merkel	196	32.28 N	100.00 W
Merkem	50	50.57 N	2.51 E
Merkendorf	56	49.12 N	10.42 E
Merkinė	76	54.10 N	24.10 E
Merklin	60	49.34 N	13.07 E
Merklingen	58	48.30 N	9.44 E
Merkourovoúni ∧	267c	37.54 N	23.48 E
Merksem	50	51.15 N	4.27 E
Merksplas	56	51.22 N	4.52 E
Merkulovići	76	52.58 N	30.36 E
Merkys ≃	76	54.10 N	24.11 E
Merlara	64	45.10 N	11.26 E
Merlejevo	82	55.05 N	37.13 E
Merlimau, Pulau I	271c	1.17 N	103.42 E
Merlimont-Plage	50	50.28 N	1.35 E
Merlin, On., Can.	214	42.14 N	82.14 W
Merlin, Or., U.S.	202	42.31 N	123.25 W
Merlin Seamount ✣[3]	14	9.05 S	150.44 W
Merlo, Arg.	252	32.21 S	65.02 W
Merlo, Arg.	258	34.40 S	58.45 W
Merlo □[5]	288	34.40 S	58.45 W
Merlo, Aeródromo ⊠	288	34.41 S	58.45 W
Merlynston	274b	37.43 S	144.58 E
Mermaid Beach	171a	28.03 S	153.27 E
Mern	41	55.03 N	12.04 E
Merna	198	41.29 N	99.45 W
Mernye	30	46.30 N	17.50 E
Meroe ⊥	140	16.56 N	33.43 E
Meron	132	32.59 N	35.26 E
Meron, Hare ∧	132	32.58 N	35.25 E
Meros, Ponta dos ≻	256	23.13 S	44.21 W
Merotai Besar	112	4.26 N	117.46 E
Merouana	34	35.38 N	5.55 E
Merouane, Chott ⊜	148	34.00 N	6.02 E
Mer'oža	76	59.02 N	36.23 E
Merredin	162	31.29 S	118.16 E
Merrick	276	40.39 N	73.33 W
Merrick ∧	44	55.08 N	4.29 W
Merrick Bay ⊂	276	40.38 N	73.33 W
Merrickville	212	44.55 N	75.50 W
Merri Creek ≃	169	37.48 S	145.01 E
Merriewold Lake	210	41.22 N	74.12 W
Merrifield	284c	38.52 N	77.13 W
Merrill, Ia., U.S.	198	42.43 N	96.14 W
Merrill, Mi., U.S.	190	43.24 N	84.19 W
Merrill, Or., U.S.	202	42.01 N	121.35 W
Merrill, Wi., U.S.	190	45.10 N	89.41 W
Merrillan	190	44.27 N	90.50 W
Merrill C. Meigs Field ⊠	278	41.52 N	87.37 W
Merrill Lake ⊜	212	44.55 N	77.24 W
Merrillville	216	41.28 N	87.19 W
Merrimac	207	42.49 N	71.00 W
Merrimack ≃	188	42.49 N	70.49 W
Merrimack College ◗[2]	283	42.40 N	71.08 W
Merrimac Terrace	283	42.49 N	71.00 W
Merriman, S. Afr.	158	31.13 S	23.38 E
Merriman, Ne., U.S.	198	42.55 N	101.42 W
Merrionette Park	278	41.41 N	87.42 W
Merriott	42	50.54 N	2.48 W
Merritt, B.C., Can.	182	50.07 N	120.47 W
Merritt, Wa., U.S.	224	47.47 N	120.51 W
Merritt, Lake ⊜[1]	282	37.48 N	122.16 W
Merritt Island	220	28.21 N	80.42 W
Merritt Island I	220	28.33 N	80.40 W
Merritt Reservoir ⊜[1]	198	42.35 N	100.55 W
Merriwa	166	32.08 S	150.21 E
Mer Rouge	194	32.46 N	91.47 W
Merrow	207	41.49 N	72.18 W
Merrygoen	166	31.50 S	149.14 E
Merrylands	274a	33.50 S	150.59 E
Merrymount Park ♠	283	42.16 N	71.01 W
Merryville	194	30.45 N	93.32 W
Mersa Fatma	144	14.55 N	40.20 E
Mersa Matruh → Marsā Maṭrūḥ	140	31.21 N	27.14 E
Mersch	56	49.46 N	6.06 E
Merscheid ◆[8]	263	51.10 N	7.01 E
Merse V	46	55.39 N	2.15 W
Merse ≃	66	43.05 N	11.22 E
Mersea Island I	42	51.47 N	0.55 E
Merseburg	54	51.21 N	11.59 E
Mersey ≃, Austl.	166	41.10 S	146.22 E
Mersey ≃, N.S., Can.	186	44.02 N	64.43 W
Mersey ≃, Eng., U.K.	44	53.25 N	3.00 W
Merseyside □[6]	44	53.25 N	2.50 W
Mersey Tunnel ◆[5]	262	53.24 N	3.00 W
Mersing	114	2.26 N	103.50 E
Mersin → İçel	130	36.48 N	34.38 E
Mers-les-Bains	50	50.04 N	1.23 E
Mērsrags	76	57.21 N	23.07 E
Merstham	260	51.16 N	0.09 W
Merta	120	26.39 N	74.02 E
Merta Road	120	26.43 N	73.55 E
Merthyr Tydfil	42	51.46 N	3.23 W
Merti	154	1.04 N	38.40 E
Mertingen	56	48.39 N	10.47 E
Mértola	34	37.38 N	7.40 W
Merton, Austl.	169	36.59 S	145.42 E
Merton, Wi., U.S.	216	43.08 N	88.18 W
Merton ◆[8]	42	51.25 N	0.12 W
Mertz Glacier Tongue ʭ	9	67.40 S	144.45 E
Mertzon	196	31.16 N	100.49 W
Mertztown	208	40.30 N	75.40 W
Méru, Fr.	50	49.14 N	2.08 E
Meru, Kenya	154	0.03 N	37.39 E
Meru, Mount ∧	154	3.14 S	36.45 E
Meru National Park ♠	154	0.10 N	38.15 E
Meruoca	250	3.28 S	40.28 W
Mervans	58	46.48 N	5.11 E
Merville	50	50.38 N	2.38 E
Mervin	184	53.20 N	108.53 W
Merv → Mary	128	37.36 N	61.50 E
Merwede	158	31.38 S	23.48 E
Merweville	158	32.40 S	21.31 E
Merwin, Lake ⊜[1]	224	45.59 N	122.26 W
Merxleben	54	51.07 N	10.40 E
Mery	82	55.49 N	36.36 E
Méry-la-Bataille	50	49.33 N	2.38 E
Méry-sur-Oise	261	49.04 N	2.11 E
Méry-sur-Seine	50	48.30 N	3.53 E
Merzdorf	54	51.23 N	14.32 E
Merzhausen	58	47.58 N	7.49 E
Merzifon	130	40.53 N	35.29 E
Merzig	56	49.27 N	6.36 E
Mesa, Micron.	175c	7.21 N	151.51 E
Mesa, Moç.	154	13.00 S	39.33 E
Mesa, S. Afr.	158	26.29 S	26.59 E
Mesa, Az., U.S.	200	33.25 N	111.49 W
Mesa ≃	34	41.15 N	1.48 W
Mesa, Cerro ∧	254	48.46 S	71.29 W
Mesabi Range ⋏[2]	190	47.30 N	92.50 W
Mesachie Lake	224	48.49 N	124.07 W
Mesa del Nayar	234	22.16 N	104.35 W
Mesa de Santa Rita	234	23.04 N	105.31 W
Mesagne	68	40.33 N	17.49 E
Mes'agutovo	86	55.35 N	58.20 E
Mesaména	152	3.44 N	12.50 E
Mesa Mountain ∧	200	37.55 N	106.38 W
Mesarás, Kólpos ⊂	38	34.58 N	24.36 E
Mesa Verde National Park ♠	200	37.13 N	108.30 W
Mescalero	200	33.09 N	105.46 W
Mescalero Apache Indian Reservation ◆[4]	200	33.12 N	105.40 W
Meščerino, Ross.	76	53.37 N	37.23 E
Meščerino, Ross.	82	55.11 N	38.21 E
Meščerskij	265b	55.40 N	37.25 E
Meščerskoje	82	55.17 N	37.38 E
Meschede	56	51.20 N	8.17 E
Meschetskij chrebet ⋏	84	41.48 N	42.30 E
Mescit Tepe ∧	130	40.22 N	41.11 E
Meščovsk	76	54.19 N	35.17 E
Meščura	24	63.20 N	50.52 E
Mese	58	46.17 N	9.21 E
Mèsè Atet	110	18.38 N	97.39 E
Mesen-Bucht → Mezenskaja guba ⊂	24	66.40 N	43.45 E
Mesero	266b	45.30 N	8.51 E
Mesewa → Mitsiwa	144	15.38 N	39.28 E
Mesfinto	144	13.20 N	37.19 E
Mesgarābād	267d	35.37 N	51.31 E
Mesgouez, Lac ⊜	176	51.24 N	75.05 W
Meshed → Mashhad	128	36.18 N	59.36 E
Meshgīn Shahr	128	38.24 N	47.40 E
Meshomasic Mountain ∧	207	41.38 N	72.32 W
Meshoppen	210	41.34 N	76.03 W
Meshoppen Creek ≃	210	41.37 N	76.03 W
Mesick	190	44.24 N	85.42 W
Mesier, Canal Ɥ	254	48.20 S	74.33 W
Mesilinka ≃	182	56.09 N	124.28 W
Mesilla	200	32.16 N	106.48 W
Mesillas, Méx.	234	23.14 N	106.03 W
Mesillas, Méx.	234	23.33 N	103.35 W
Mesima ≃	68	38.30 N	16.15 E
Meskiana	148	35.39 N	7.41 E
Meskiana, Oued ≃	36	35.49 N	7.53 E
Meskine	146	11.25 N	15.21 E
Meškuičiai	76	56.05 N	23.28 E
Meskum	114	1.34 N	102.01 E
Meslay-du-Maine	32	47.57 N	0.33 W
Meslay-le-Grenet	50	48.22 N	1.23 E
Mesnil-Val-Plage	50	50.03 N	1.20 E
Mesocco	58	46.23 N	9.14 E
Mesola	66	44.55 N	12.14 E
Mesolcina, Valle V	58	46.20 N	9.10 E
Mesolóngion	38	38.21 N	21.17 E
Mesomikenda Lake ⊜	190	47.40 N	81.53 W
Mesopotamia	214	41.27 N	80.57 W
Mesopotamia □[9]	128	34.00 N	44.00 E
Mesoraca	68	39.05 N	16.48 E
Mesóyia □[9]	267c	37.56 N	23.53 E
Mespelbrunn ⊥	56	49.54 N	9.19 E
Mesquita, Bra.	255	19.13 S	42.35 W
Mesquita, Bra.	256	22.48 S	43.26 W
Mesquite, Nv., U.S.	204	36.48 N	114.03 W
Mesquite, Tx., U.S.	222	32.46 N	96.35 W
Messach Mellet ⋏[2]	146	24.30 N	11.35 E
Messalo ≃	154	11.40 S	40.26 E
Messaoud, Oued V	148	27.28 N	0.21 W
Messdorf	54	52.43 N	11.33 E
Messina, It.	70	38.11 N	15.33 E
Messina, S. Afr.	156	22.23 S	30.00 E
Messina □[4]	70	38.03 N	14.52 E
Messina, Stretto di Ɥ	70	38.15 N	15.35 E
Messinge ≃	154	11.34 S	35.25 E
Messingham	44	53.32 N	0.39 W
Messíni	38	37.04 N	22.00 E
Messíni ⊥	38	37.11 N	21.57 E
Messiniakós Kólpos ⊂	38	36.58 N	22.00 E
Messix Peak ∧	202	41.29 N	112.31 W
Messkirch	58	47.59 N	9.07 E
Messojacha ≃	74	67.52 N	77.27 E
Messondo	152	3.43 N	10.28 E
Messtetten	58	48.11 N	8.58 E
Messy	261	48.58 N	2.42 E
Mestá	38	38.15 N	25.55 E
Mesta (Néstos) ≃	38	40.41 N	24.44 E
Mestasa	148	35.07 N	4.25 W
Městečko	60	50.03 N	13.52 E
Mestghanem	148	35.51 N	0.07 E
Mestghanem □[5]	148	36.00 N	0.30 E
Mestia	84	43.03 N	42.43 E
Mestlin	54	53.35 N	11.56 E
Město Touškov	60	49.46 N	13.15 E
Mestre	64	45.29 N	12.15 E
Mestrino	64	45.26 N	11.45 E
Mesudiye	130	40.28 N	37.46 E
Mesuji ≃	112	4.08 S	105.52 E
Mesum	52	52.13 N	7.29 E
Meszah Peak ∧	180	58.28 N	131.26 W
Meta, It.	68	40.39 N	14.24 E
Meta, Mo., U.S.	219	38.18 N	92.09 W
Meta □[5]	246	3.30 N	73.00 W
Meta ≃	246	6.12 N	67.28 W
Métabief	58	46.47 N	6.21 E
Metagācha	272b	22.38 N	88.31 E
Metahara	144	8.54 N	39.55 E
Meta Incognita Peninsula ≻[1]	176	62.45 N	68.30 W
Metairie	194	29.59 N	90.09 W
Metaline Falls	202	48.51 N	117.22 W
Metallifere, Colline ⋏	66	43.15 N	11.00 E
Metallostroj	265a	59.47 N	30.33 E
Metamora, Il., U.S.	190	40.47 N	89.21 W
Metamora, In., U.S.	218	39.26 N	85.08 W
Metamora, Mi., U.S.	216	42.56 N	83.17 W
Metamora, Oh., U.S.	216	41.42 N	83.54 W
Metán	252	25.29 S	64.57 W
Metangula	154	12.43 S	34.49 E
Metapán	236	14.20 N	89.27 W
Metapontum ⊥	68	40.23 N	16.50 E
Metarica	154	14.20 S	36.48 E
Metates	234	23.46 N	106.02 W
Metaurilia	66	43.49 N	13.03 E
Metauro ≃	66	43.50 N	13.03 E
Metcalfe	212	45.14 N	75.28 W
Metchosin	224	48.22 N	123.33 W
Metechi	84	41.55 N	44.21 E
Metedeconk, South Branch ≃	208	40.04 N	74.09 W
Meteghan	186	44.11 N	66.10 W
Metelen	52	52.08 N	7.12 E
Metema	144	12.57 N	36.12 E
Metéora ◗[1]	38	39.46 N	21.36 E
Meteor Crater ⊥[6]	200	35.02 N	111.02 W
Meteor Seamount ✣[3]	8	48.00 S	8.30 E
Metepec, Méx.	234	19.15 N	99.36 W
Metepec, Méx.	234	18.56 N	98.28 W
Metharaw	110	16.12 N	98.08 E
Metheringham	44	53.08 N	0.24 W
Methil	46	56.10 N	3.01 W
Methler	263	51.35 N	7.37 E
Methlick	46	57.25 N	2.14 W
Methóni	38	36.50 N	21.43 E
Methow	182	48.07 N	120.00 W
Methow ≃	202	48.03 N	119.53 W
Methuen	207	42.43 N	71.11 W
Methven, N.Z.	172	43.38 S	171.39 E
Methven, Scot., U.K.	46	56.25 N	3.34 W
Methwold	42	52.31 N	0.33 E
Metica ≃	246	4.09 N	72.55 W
Metiskow	184	52.24 N	110.38 W
Metković	36	43.03 N	17.39 E
Metlakatla, B.C., Can.	182	54.20 N	130.27 W
Metlakatla, Ak., U.S.	182	55.08 N	131.35 W
Metlaoui	148	34.20 N	8.24 E
Metlatonoc	234	17.11 N	98.20 W
Metlika	36	45.39 N	15.19 E
Metlili, Oued V	148	31.54 N	4.53 E
Metlili ech Chaâmba	148	32.18 N	3.40 E
Metnitz	61	46.59 N	14.13 E
Meto, Bayou ≃	194	34.05 N	91.26 W
Metolius ≃	202	44.36 N	121.17 W
Metompkin Bay ⊂	208	37.43 N	75.35 W
Metompkin Inlet ⊂	208	37.41 N	75.35 W
Metro	115a	5.05 S	105.20 E
Metropolis	194	37.09 N	88.43 W
Metropolitan	190	46.00 N	87.53 W
Metropolitan Beach ♠	281	42.35 N	82.48 W
Metropolitan Museum of Art ◗	276	40.47 N	73.58 W
Metropolitan Oakland International Airport ⊠	226	37.43 N	122.13 W
Metschow	54	53.49 N	12.58 E
Metsematluku	156	24.01 S	24.40 E
Metsera	154	2.35 S	26.07 E
Métsovon	38	39.46 N	21.11 E
Mettawa	278	42.14 N	87.56 W
Metten	60	48.52 N	12.55 E
Mettendorf	56	49.57 N	6.19 E
Metter	192	32.23 N	82.03 W
Mettet	56	50.19 N	4.40 E
Mettetal Airport ⊠	281	42.21 N	83.27 W
Mettingen	52	52.18 N	7.46 E
Mettlach	56	49.30 N	6.36 E
Mettmach	60	48.10 N	13.21 E
Mettmann	56	51.15 N	6.58 E
Mettray	50	47.27 N	0.39 E
Mettuppālaiyam	122	11.18 N	76.57 E
Mettūr	122	11.48 N	77.48 E
Metu	144	8.20 N	35.36 E
Metuchen	210	40.32 N	74.21 W
Metuge	154	12.58 S	40.20 E
Metulla	132	33.16 N	35.35 E
Metundo, Ilha I	154	11.10 S	40.41 E
Metz	56	49.08 N	6.10 E
Metzervisse	56	49.19 N	6.17 E
Metzger	224	45.26 N	122.45 W
Metzingen	56	48.32 N	9.17 E
Metzkausen	263	51.16 N	6.57 E
Metztitlán	234	20.36 N	98.45 W
Metztitlán, Laguna ⊜	234	20.40 N	98.50 W
Meu ≃	32	48.02 N	1.47 W
Meudon	261	48.48 N	2.14 E
Meudon, Bois de ♠	261	48.47 N	2.12 E
Meul ≃	158	27.56 S	28.50 E
Meulaboh	114	4.09 N	96.08 E
Meulan	50	49.01 N	1.54 E
Meulebeke	50	50.57 N	3.17 E
Meung-sur-Loire	50	47.50 N	1.42 E
Meureubo ≃	114	4.09 N	96.09 E
Meureudu	114	5.16 N	96.16 E
Meursault	58	46.59 N	4.46 E
Meurthe ≃	32	48.47 N	6.09 E
Meurthe-et-Moselle □[5]	32	48.35 N	6.10 E
Meuse	58	47.59 N	5.33 E
Meuse □[5]	56	49.00 N	5.30 E
Meuse (Maas) ≃	30	51.49 N	5.01 E
Meuselwitz	54	51.02 N	12.17 E
Meuvette ≃	50	48.45 N	1.08 E
Meux Creek ≃	212	44.07 N	81.02 W
Mevagissey	42	50.16 N	4.48 W
Mevang	152	0.07 N	11.05 E
Mewāt Plain ≡	124	27.40 N	77.15 E
Mexborough	44	53.30 N	1.17 W
Mexia	222	31.40 N	96.28 W
Mexia Lake ⊜[1]	222	31.39 N	96.36 W
Mexiana, Ilha I	250	0.02 S	49.35 W
Mexicali	232	32.40 N	115.29 W
Mexican Hat	200	37.09 N	109.52 W
Mexico, In., U.S.	216	40.49 N	86.06 W
Mexico, Me., U.S.	188	44.33 N	70.32 W
Mexico, Mo., U.S.	219	39.10 N	91.52 W
Mexico, N.Y., U.S.	212	43.27 N	76.13 W
Mexico, Pa., U.S.	208	40.32 N	77.21 W
México □[3]	234	19.20 N	99.45 W
Mexico (México) □[1], N.A.	230	23.00 N	102.00 W
Mexico (México) □[1], N.A.	232	23.00 N	102.00 W
México, Golfo de → Mexico, Gulf of ⊂	230	25.00 N	90.00 W
Mexico, Gulf of ⊂	230	25.00 N	90.00 W
Mexico Basin ✣[1]	16	25.00 N	92.00 W
Mexico Bay ⊂	212	43.31 N	76.17 W
Mexico Beach	192	29.58 N	85.24 W
Mexico City → Ciudad de México	234	19.24 N	99.09 W
Mexiko, Golf von → Mexico, Gulf of ⊂	230	25.00 N	90.00 W
Mexiko → Ciudad de México	234	19.24 N	99.09 W
Mexiko → Mexico □[1]	232	23.00 N	102.00 W
Meximieux	58	45.54 N	5.12 E
Mexique, Golfe du → Mexico, Gulf of ⊂	230	25.00 N	90.00 W
Mexique → Mexico □[1]	230	23.00 N	102.00 W
Mexticacán	234	21.13 N	102.43 W
Mey, Castle of ⊥	46	58.38 N	3.14 W
Meyanodas	164	7.38 S	131.38 E
Meycauayan	116	14.44 N	120.58 E
Meydan	130	38.21 N	41.47 E
Meydancık	130	41.25 N	42.14 E
Meydān-e Gel ≡	128	29.04 N	54.50 E
Meydān Khvolah	120	33.36 N	69.51 E
Meyenburg	54	53.18 N	12.14 E
Meyers Chuck	182	55.44 N	132.15 W
Meyersdale	188	39.48 N	79.01 W
Meyers Lake	214	40.52 N	81.24 W
Meyersville	222	28.55 N	97.21 W
Meyerton	158	26.33 S	28.01 E
Meyísti I	130	36.08 N	29.34 E
Meymac	32	45.32 N	2.09 E
Meymaneh	120	35.55 N	64.47 E
Meymeh	128	33.27 N	51.10 E
Meymeh ≃	128	32.05 N	47.16 E
Meynypilgino	180	62.32 N	177.02 E
Meyo Centre	152	2.33 N	11.02 E
Meyrargues	62	43.38 N	5.32 E
Meyrin	58	46.14 N	6.05 E
Meyronne	184	49.39 N	106.50 W
Meyrueis	32	44.10 N	3.26 E
Meyungs	175b	7.20 N	134.27 E
Meža ≃	61	46.35 N	15.02 E
Meẓada, Ḥorvot (Masada) ⊥	132	31.19 N	35.21 E
Mezapa	236	15.33 N	87.23 W
Mezcala	234	17.56 N	99.37 W
Mezcala ≃	234	18.00 N	99.47 W
Mezcalapa	234	17.37 N	93.22 W
Mezcalapa ≃	234	18.00 N	92.54 W
Mezdra	38	43.09 N	23.42 E
Meždurečensk	86	53.42 N	88.03 E
Meždurečenskij	86	59.36 N	65.53 E
Mèze	32	43.25 N	3.36 E
Mézel	62	43.59 N	6.12 E
Mezen'	24	65.50 N	44.13 E
Mezen' ≃	24	66.11 N	43.59 E
Mézenc, Mont ∧	62	44.55 N	4.11 E
Mezenskaja guba ⊂	24	66.40 N	43.45 E
Meževaja	78	48.16 N	36.44 E
Mežgorje	78	48.32 N	23.30 E
Meziadin Lake ⊜	182	56.04 N	129.18 W
Mežica	61	46.31 N	14.52 E
Mézières-en-Brenne	32	46.49 N	1.13 E
Mézières-sur-Seine	261	48.58 N	1.48 E
Mézilhac	62	44.48 N	4.21 E
Mézin	32	44.03 N	0.16 E
Mezinovskij	76	55.30 N	40.21 E
Mežirič	78	50.43 N	34.29 E
Mezőberény	30	46.50 N	21.02 E
Mezőcsát	30	47.49 N	20.55 E
Mezőkovácsháza	30	46.25 N	20.55 E
Mezőkövesd	30	47.50 N	20.34 E
Mezőtúr	30	47.00 N	20.38 E
Mežoz'ornyj	86	54.09 N	59.23 E
Mezquital	234	23.29 N	104.23 W
Mezquital ≃	232	22.35 N	104.54 W
Mezquital del Oro	234	21.10 N	103.23 W
Mezquitic	234	22.23 N	103.41 W

Symbol	English	Deutsch	Español	Français	Português
≃	River	Fluß	Río	Rivière	Rio
≍	Canal	Kanal	Canal	Canal	Canal
∟	Waterfall, Rapids	Wasserfall, Stromschnellen	Cascada, Rápidos	Chute d'eau, Rapides	Cascata, Rápidos
Ɥ	Strait	Meeresstraße	Estrecho	Détroit	Estreito
⊂	Bay, Gulf	Bucht, Golf	Bahía, Golfo	Baie, Golfe	Baía, Golfo
⊜	Lake, Lakes	See, Seen	Lago, Lagos	Lac, Lacs	Lago, Lagos
≡	Swamp	Sumpf	Pantano	Marais	Pântano
ʭ	Ice Features, Glacier	Eis- und Gletscherformen	Accidentes Glaciales	Formes glaciaires	Acidentes glaciares
⊤	Other Hydrographic Features	Andere Hydrographische Objekte	Otros Elementos Hidrográficos	Autres données hydrographiques	Outros acidentes hidrográficos
✣	Submarine Features	Untermeerische Objekte	Accidentes Submarinos	Formes de relief sous-marin	Acidentes submarinos
□	Political Unit	Politische Einheit	Unidad Política	Entité politique	Unidade política
◗	Cultural Institution	Kulturelle Institution	Institución Cultural	Institution culturelle	Instituição cultural
⊥	Historical Site	Historische Stätte	Sitio Histórico	Site historique	Sitio histórico
♠	Recreational Site	Erholungs- und Ferienort	Sitio de Recreo	Centre de loisirs	Area de Lazer
⊠	Airport	Flughafen	Aeropuerto	Aéroport	Aeroporto
■	Military Installation	Militäranlage	Instalación Militar	Installation militaire	Instalação militar
◆	Miscellaneous	Verschiedenes	Misceláneo	Divers	Diversos

ENGLISH — Name · Page · Lat.°′ · Long.°′
DEUTSCH — Name · Seite · Breite°′ · Länge°′ E = Ost

Name	Page	Lat.°′	Long.°′
Mezraa	130	41.12 N	35.08 E
Mézy	261	49.00 N	1.53 E
Mezzana	64	46.19 N	10.48 E
Mezzano	64	46.09 N	11.48 E
Mezzenile	62	45.17 N	7.23 E
Mezzocorona	64	46.13 N	11.07 E
Mezzoiuso	70	37.52 N	13.28 E
Mezzola, Lago di ⊜	58	46.12 N	9.26 E
Mezzoldo	58	46.01 N	9.40 E
Mezzolombardo	64	46.13 N	11.05 E
Mezzomerico	266b	45.37 N	8.36 E
Mfangano Island I	154	0.28 S	34.01 E
Mfolozi ≃	158	28.25 S	32.26 E
Mfou	152	3.43 N	11.38 E
Mfuwe	154	13.04 S	31.46 E
Mgači	89	51.05 N	142.17 E
Mgeni ≃	158	29.48 S	31.02 E
Mgeta	154	8.19 S	36.08 E
Mglin	76	53.04 N	32.51 E
M'goun, Irhil ∧	148	31.31 N	6.25 W
M'hai, B'nom ∧	110	11.21 N	107.50 E
Mhasvād	122	17.38 N	74.47 E
Mhlatuze ≃	158	28.47 S	32.06 E
Mhlume	158	26.02 S	31.50 E
Mholach, Beinn ∧[2]	46	58.14 N	6.31 W
Mhòr, Beinn ∧	46	57.17 N	7.19 W
Mhòr, Loch ⊜	46	57.14 N	4.26 W
Mhow	120	22.33 N	75.46 E
Mi ≃, Zhg.	98	37.12 N	119.10 E
Mi ≃, Zhg.	100	27.09 N	112.51 E
Mia, Oued V	148	30.47 N	4.54 E
Miacatlán	234	18.46 N	99.22 W
Mia-dong ◆[8]	271b	37.37 N	127.01 E
Miagao	116	10.39 N	122.14 E
Miahuatlán de Porfirio Díaz	234	16.20 N	96.36 W
Miajadas	34	39.09 N	5.54 W
Miaméré	146	8.52 N	19.50 E
Miami, Mb., Can.	184	49.21 N	98.11 W
Miami, Az., U.S.	200	33.23 N	110.52 W
Miami, Fl., U.S.	220	25.46 N	80.11 W
Miami, In., U.S.	216	40.36 N	86.06 W
Miami, Ok., U.S.	196	36.52 N	94.52 W
Miami, Tx., U.S.	196	35.42 N	100.38 W
Miami □[6], In., U.S.	216	40.45 N	86.04 W
Miami □[6], Oh., U.S.	218	40.02 N	84.13 W
Miami ≃	224	45.33 N	123.53 W
Miami Beach, On., Can.	212	44.13 N	79.29 W
Miami Beach, Fl., U.S.	220	25.47 N	80.07 W
Miami Canal ≊	220	25.47 N	80.15 W
Miami Creek ≃	226	37.21 N	119.44 W
Miami International Airport ⊠	220	25.48 N	80.17 W
Miami Lakes	220	25.53 N	80.18 W
Miamisburg	218	39.38 N	84.17 W
Miamisburg Mound State Memorial ⊥	218	39.38 N	84.17 W
Miami Shores	220	25.51 N	80.11 W
Miami Springs	220	25.49 N	80.17 W
Miami State Recreation Area ♦	216	40.40 N	85.55 W
Miamiville	218	39.13 N	84.18 W
Miān Channūn	123	30.27 N	72.22 E
Mianchi	102	34.48 N	111.49 E
Mīāndoāb	128	36.58 N	46.06 E
Miandrivazo	157b	19.31 S	45.28 E
Mianduhe	89	49.05 N	121.06 E
Miane	64	45.57 N	12.06 E
Mīāneh	128	37.26 N	47.42 E
Miang, Phu ∧	110	17.42 N	101.01 E
Miangas, Pulau I	108	5.35 N	126.35 E
Mianhu	100	23.28 N	116.09 E
Mianhuadi	104	41.15 N	120.49 E
Miāni	123	32.32 N	73.04 E
Miāni Hōr C	120	25.34 N	66.19 E
Mianning	102	28.39 N	102.09 E
Mianus ≃	207	41.03 N	73.35 W
Mianus, East Branch ≃	276	41.06 N	73.35 W
Mianus Reservoir ⊜[1]	276	41.08 N	73.37 W
Miānwāli	123	32.35 N	71.33 E
Mianxian	102	33.09 N	106.48 E
Mianyang, Zhg.	100	30.23 N	113.25 E
Mianyang, Zhg.	102	31.30 N	104.49 E
Mianzhu	102	31.20 N	104.09 E
Miao Dao I	98	37.56 N	120.45 E
Miaodao Qundao II	98	38.10 N	120.40 E
Miao'ergou	86	45.32 N	83.52 E
Miaofengshan	105	40.04 N	116.13 E
Miaogou	104	41.12 N	120.40 E
Miaojiagou	104	42.16 N	123.22 E
Miaojiatun	104	40.54 N	120.55 E
Miaokou	98	35.48 N	114.09 E
Miaoli	100	24.34 N	120.49 E
Miao Ling ⋏	102	26.15 N	107.26 E
Miaopu	106	31.00 N	118.44 E
Miaoqian	100	30.33 N	117.44 E
Miaotou	106	30.58 N	120.33 E
Miaowan	100	33.07 N	114.41 E
Miaoyang	98	40.49 N	124.24 E
Miaozhen	106	31.43 N	121.21 E
Miaozigou	107	30.17 N	104.35 E
Miarayon	116	8.04 N	124.50 E
Miarinarivo, Madag.	157b	16.38 S	48.15 E
Miarinarivo, Madag.	157b	18.57 S	46.55 E
Miarinavaratra	157b	20.13 S	47.31 E
Miasa	94	36.34 N	137.53 E
Miass	86	54.59 N	60.06 E
Miass ≃	86	56.06 N	64.30 E
Miasteczko Krajeńskie	30	53.06 N	17.01 E
Miastko	30	54.01 N	17.00 E
Miboro-dam ◆[6]	94	36.08 N	136.55 E
Mibu	94	36.25 N	139.48 E
Mibu ≃	94	35.49 N	137.57 E
Mica	156	24.10 S	30.48 E
Mica Mountain ∧	200	32.13 N	110.33 W
Micang Shan ⋏	102	32.45 N	107.20 E
Micanopy	192	29.30 N	82.16 W
Micaúne	156	18.18 S	36.35 E
Mičavičevnik	24	64.14 N	57.58 E
Miccosukee, Lake ⊜[1]	192	30.34 N	83.58 W
Miccosukee Indian Reservation ◆[4]	220	26.10 N	80.50 W
Michael, Mount ∧	164	6.25 S	145.20 E
Michael J. Kirwan Reservoir ⊜[1]	214	41.10 N	81.10 W
Michajlo-Koc'ubinskoje	78	51.27 N	31.04 E
Michajlov	82	54.14 N	39.02 E
Michajlovka, Kaz.	85	43.06 N	71.36 E
Michajlovka, Kaz.	85	42.50 N	75.42 E
Michajlovka, Kaz.	86	53.51 N	76.32 E
Michajlovka, Kyrg.	85	42.37 N	78.20 E
Michajlovka, Ross.	78	49.53 N	39.38 E
Michajlovka, Ross.	80	47.38 N	46.54 E
Michajlovka, Ross.	80	50.05 N	43.15 E
Michajlovka, Ross.	86	51.49 N	79.45 E
Michajlovka, Ross.	86	56.26 N	78.53 E
Michajlovka, Ross.	88	50.26 N	104.10 E
Michajlovka, Ross.	88	55.30 N	114.09 E
Michajlovka, Ross.	88	51.07 N	119.20 E
Michajlovka, Ross.	88	52.57 N	103.18 E
Michajlovka, Ross.	89	49.13 N	129.56 E
Michajlovka, Ross.	89	43.56 N	132.00 E
Michajlovka, Ross.	265a	60.04 N	30.14 E
Michajlovka, Ross.	265a	59.43 N	30.01 E
Michajlovka, Ukr.	78	49.19 N	36.28 E
Michajlovka, Ukr.	78	47.16 N	35.14 E
Michajlovka, Ukr.	83	48.30 N	38.54 E
Michajlovka, Ukr.	83	48.09 N	37.22 E
Michajlovka, Ukr.	83	48.44 N	37.16 E
Michajlovo	80	56.56 N	45.04 E
Michajlovo-Aleksandrovskij	83	49.13 N	40.15 E
Michajlovskaja	80	50.58 N	41.52 E
Michajlovskaja Celina, zapovednik ♦	78	50.45 N	34.10 E
Michajlovskij, Kaz.	86	50.17 N	55.23 E
Michajlovskij, Ross.	76	60.05 N	43.29 E
Michajlovskij, Ross.	86	51.41 N	79.47 E
Michajlovskoje, Ross.	76	58.23 N	37.40 E
Michajlovskoje, Ross.	80	56.11 N	45.47 E
Michajlovskoje, Ross.	82	55.50 N	36.20 E
Michajlovskoje, Ross.	265b	55.35 N	37.35 E
Michalevo	82	55.27 N	38.26 E
Michali	82	55.17 N	39.05 E
Michalkovo	82	54.11 N	37.33 E
Michalovce	30	48.45 N	21.55 E
Michalovy Hory	60	49.55 N	12.47 E
Michanoviči	76	53.45 N	27.40 E
Michaud, Point ›	186	45.34 N	60.40 W
Micheal Peak ∧	182	53.35 N	126.26 W
Michejevo	88	57.10 N	104.53 E
Michel	182	49.43 N	114.49 W
Michelago	171b	35.43 S	149.10 E
Michelau	56	50.10 N	11.06 E
Micheldever	42	51.09 N	1.15 W
Micheldorf in Oberösterreich	61	47.52 N	14.08 E
Michelsneukirchen	60	49.08 N	12.33 E
Michelson, Mount ∧	180	69.19 N	144.17 W
Michel'sonovskij	265b	55.42 N	37.54 E
Michelstadt	56	49.41 N	9.00 E
Michendorf	54	52.18 N	13.01 E
Miches	238	18.59 N	69.03 W
Micheta	84	41.52 N	44.44 E
Michiana	216	41.46 N	86.48 W
Michiana Regional Airport ⊠	216	41.42 N	86.19 W
Michigamme ≃	190	46.04 N	88.13 W
Michigan	198	48.01 N	98.07 W
Michigan □[3], U.S.	178	44.00 N	85.00 W
Michigan □[3], U.S.	190	44.00 N	85.00 W
Michigan ≃	200	40.52 N	106.20 W
Michigan, Lake ⊜	190	44.00 N	87.00 W
Michigan, University of ⊛[2]	281	42.17 N	83.44 W
Michigan Center	216	42.13 N	84.19 W
Michigan City	216	41.42 N	86.53 W
Michigan International Speedway ♦	216	42.03 N	84.15 W
Michigan Stadium ♦	281	42.16 N	83.45 W
Michigan State Fair Grounds ♦	281	42.27 N	83.07 W
Michigantown	216	40.19 N	86.23 W
Michika	146	10.38 N	13.24 E
Michillinda	280	34.07 N	118.05 W
Michinmahuida, Volcán ∧[1]	254	42.49 S	72.28 W
Michipicoten Bay C	190	47.55 N	84.56 W
Michipicoten Island I	190	47.45 N	85.45 W
Michnevo	82	55.07 N	37.58 E
Michninskaja	24	60.26 N	46.14 E
Michoacán	204	32.28 N	115.20 W
Michoacán □[3]	234	19.10 N	101.50 W
Michoacanejo	234	21.33 N	102.36 W
Michów	30	51.32 N	22.19 E
Michurinsk → Mičurinsk	80	52.54 N	40.30 E
Mickle Fell ∧	44	54.37 N	2.18 W
Mickleham	260	51.16 N	0.19 W
Mickleover	42	52.54 N	1.32 W
Mickleton, Eng., U.K.	42	52.05 N	1.46 W
Mickleton, N.J., U.S.	285	39.47 N	75.14 W
Mickle Trafford	262	53.13 N	2.50 W
Mickleyville	218	39.45 N	86.16 W
Mico ≃	236	12.11 N	84.16 W
Mico, Montañas del ⋏	236	15.30 N	88.55 W
Miconge	152	4.26 S	12.51 E
Micoud	241f	13.50 N	60.54 W
Micronesia II	14	11.00 N	159.00 E
Micronesia, Federated States of □[1]	14	5.00 N	152.00 E
Mičurin	38	42.10 N	27.51 E
Mičurinsk	80	52.54 N	40.30 E
Midai, Pulau I	112	3.00 N	107.47 E
Midale	184	49.22 N	103.27 W
Midar	148	34.58 N	3.30 W
Mid-Atlantic Ridge ✢[3]	8	0.00	20.00 W
Midbar Yehuda → Wilderness of Judæa ◆[2]	132	31.30 N	35.18 E
Middalya	162	23.55 S	114.45 E
Middelburg, Ned.	52	51.30 N	3.37 E
Middelburg, S. Afr.	158	25.47 S	29.28 E
Middelburg, S. Afr.	158	31.30 S	25.00 E
Middelfart	41	55.30 N	9.45 E
Middelharnis	52	51.45 N	4.11 E
Middelkerke	50	51.11 N	2.49 E
Middelkerke, Vliegveld ⊠	50	51.12 N	2.52 E
Middelpos	158	31.55 S	20.13 E
Middelstum	52	53.20 N	6.38 E
Middelwater	156	23.17 S	30.16 E
Middelwit	156	24.58 S	27.00 E
Middenbeemster	52	52.33 N	4.55 E
Middenin	158	27.43 S	28.02 E
Middenmeer	52	52.47 N	5.00 E
Middle ≃, B.C., Can.	182	54.50 N	125.08 W
Middle ≃, Ca., U.S.	226	38.03 N	121.31 W
Middle ≃, Ia., U.S.	194	41.29 N	93.24 W
Middle ≃, Mn., U.S.	198	48.22 N	97.04 W
Middle ≃, Mo., U.S.	219	38.39 N	91.53 W
Middle Alkali Lake ⊜	204	41.28 N	120.04 W
Middle America Trench ✢[1]	16	15.00 N	95.00 W
Middle Andaman I	110	12.30 N	92.50 E
Middle Barton	42	51.56 N	1.22 W
Middle Bass	214	41.41 N	82.50 W
Middle Bass Island I	214	41.41 N	82.49 W
Middle-Bay	186	51.28 N	57.30 W
Middle Bay C	276	40.37 N	73.36 W
Middleboro	207	41.53 N	70.54 W
Middle Bosque ≃	222	31.31 N	97.16 W
Middlebourne	188	39.29 N	80.54 W
Middlebranch	214	40.54 N	81.20 W
Middle Breakwater ◆[5]	280	33.43 N	118.13 W
Middlebro	184	49.01 N	95.21 W
Middle Brook	186	48.45 N	54.13 W
Middle Brook ≃, N.J., U.S.	276	40.39 N	74.41 W
Middle Brook ≃, N.J., U.S.	276	40.33 N	74.33 W
Middle Brook, East Branch ≃	276	40.35 N	74.33 W
Middle Brook, West Branch ≃	276	40.35 N	74.33 W
Middleburg, Md., U.S.	208	39.35 N	77.12 W
Middleburg, N.Y., U.S.	210	42.36 N	74.20 W
Middleburg, Oh., U.S.	216	40.17 N	83.34 W
Middleburg, Pa., U.S.	208	40.47 N	77.02 W
Middleburg Heights	214	41.22 N	81.48 W
Middlebury, Ct., U.S.	207	41.31 N	73.07 W
Middlebury, In., U.S.	216	41.40 N	85.42 W
Middlebury, Vt., U.S.	188	44.00 N	73.10 W
Middlebush	276	40.29 N	74.32 W
Middle Caicos I	238	21.47 N	71.43 W
Middle Cape ›	220	25.09 N	81.09 W
Middle Castor ≃	212	45.16 N	75.24 W
Middle Channel ≃[1], N.T., Can.	180	69.21 N	135.33 W
Middle Channel ≃[1], Mi., U.S.	281	42.33 N	82.42 W
Middle Concho ≃	196	31.27 N	100.25 W
Middle Creek ≃, U.S.	208	39.41 N	76.18 W
Middle Creek ≃, Pa., U.S.	210	40.46 N	76.52 W
Middle Creek ≃, Pa., U.S.	210	41.28 N	75.11 W
Middle Fabius ≃	194	39.58 N	91.35 W
Middle Falls	210	43.07 N	73.32 W
Middlefield, Ct., U.S.	207	41.31 N	72.42 W
Middlefield, N.Y., U.S.	210	42.41 N	74.50 W
Middlefield, Oh., U.S.	214	41.27 N	81.04 W
Middle Fork Reservoir ⊜[1]	218	39.51 N	84.51 W
Middle Ground I	272c	18.55 N	72.51 E
Middle Ground ✢[2]	174g	28.15 N	177.25 W
Middle Grove, Mo., U.S.	219	39.24 N	92.16 W
Middle Grove, N.Y., U.S.	210	43.05 N	73.55 W
Middle Haddam	207	41.33 N	72.33 W
Middleham	44	54.17 N	1.49 W
Middle Harbour C	274a	33.48 S	151.14 E
Middle Head ›	274a	33.50 S	151.16 E
Middle Hope	210	41.34 N	74.01 W
Middle Island	210	40.53 N	72.56 W
Middle Island I	162	34.07 S	123.12 E
Middle Level Main Drain ≊	42	52.43 N	0.22 E
Middle Loup ≃	198	41.17 N	98.23 W
Middle Maitland ≃	212	43.53 N	81.19 W
Middlemarch	172	45.31 S	170.07 E
Middlemount	166	22.49 S	148.40 E
Middle Musquodoboit	186	45.03 N	63.09 W
Middle Nodaway ≃	194	40.54 N	95.00 W
Middle Pease ≃	196	34.15 N	100.07 W
Middle Point	216	40.51 N	84.27 W
Middleport, N.Y., U.S.	210	43.12 N	78.28 W
Middleport, Oh., U.S.	188	39.00 N	82.02 W
Middleport, Pa., U.S.	208	40.44 N	76.05 W
Middle Raccoon ≃	198	41.34 N	94.12 W
Middle Reservoir ⊜[1]	283	42.27 N	71.07 W
Middle River	208	39.20 N	76.26 W
Middle River C	208	39.19 N	76.25 W
Middle River Neck ›[1]	284b	39.22 N	76.23 W
Middle River Rouge ≃	281	42.20 N	83.15 W
Middle Rouge Parkway ♦	281	42.21 N	83.21 W
Middle Run ≃	285	39.41 N	75.43 W
Middlesboro	192	36.36 N	83.43 W
Middlesbrough	44	54.35 N	1.14 W
Middlesex, Belize	232	17.02 N	88.31 W
Middlesex, N.J., U.S.	276	40.34 N	74.29 W
Middlesex, N.Y., U.S.	210	42.42 N	77.16 W
Middlesex, N.C., U.S.	192	35.47 N	78.12 W
Middlesex □[6], On., Can.	212	43.00 N	81.08 W
Middlesex □[6], Ct., U.S.	207	41.33 N	72.39 W
Middlesex □[6], Ma., U.S.	207	42.30 N	71.25 W
Middlesex □[6], N.J., U.S.	208	40.29 N	74.27 W
Middlesex □[6], Va., U.S.	208	37.40 N	76.35 W
Middlesex Fells Reservation ♦	283	42.27 N	71.07 W
Middlesex Reservoir ⊜[1]	276	40.37 N	74.19 W
Middle Stewiacke	186	45.13 N	63.08 W
Middle Swan	168a	31.52 S	116.00 E
Middle Thames ≃	212	42.59 N	80.58 W
Middleton, Austl.	166	22.22 S	141.32 E
Middleton, N.S., Can.	186	44.57 N	65.04 W
Middleton, Eng., U.K.	42	52.43 N	0.28 E
Middleton, Eng., U.K.	44	53.33 N	2.13 W
Middleton, Ma., U.S.	207	42.35 N	71.01 W
Middleton, Mi., U.S.	190	43.11 N	84.42 W
Middleton, Tn., U.S.	194	35.03 N	88.53 W
Middleton, Wi., U.S.	216	43.05 N	89.30 W
Middleton-in-Teesdale	44	54.38 N	2.04 W
Middleton Island I	180	59.25 N	146.25 W
Middleton-on-the-Wolds	44	53.56 N	0.33 W
Middleton Pond ⊜	283	42.36 N	71.02 W
Middleton Reef I[1]	160	29.28 S	159.06 E
Middleton Saint George	44	54.30 N	1.28 W
Middletown, N. Ire., U.K.	48	54.18 N	6.50 W
Middletown, Ca., U.S.	226	38.45 N	122.36 W
Middletown, Ct., U.S.	207	41.33 N	72.39 W
Middletown, De., U.S.	208	39.26 N	75.43 W
Middletown, Il., U.S.	219	40.11 N	89.35 W
Middletown, In., U.S.	218	40.03 N	85.32 W
Middletown, Ky., U.S.	218	38.14 N	85.32 W
Middletown, Md., U.S.	208	39.26 N	77.32 W
Middletown, Mo., U.S.	219	39.07 N	91.24 W
Middletown, N.J., U.S.	208	40.23 N	74.07 W
Middletown, N.Y., U.S.	210	41.26 N	74.25 W
Middletown, Oh., U.S.	218	39.30 N	84.23 W
Middletown, Pa., U.S.	208	40.11 N	76.43 W
Middletown, R.I., U.S.	207	41.32 N	71.17 W
Middletown, Va., U.S.	188	39.01 N	78.16 W
Middletown Park	218	40.09 N	85.26 W
Middle Tuolumne ≃	226	37.50 N	120.01 W
Middleville, Mi., U.S.	216	42.42 N	85.27 W
Middleville, N.Y., U.S.	210	43.08 N	74.58 W
Middleville, N.Y., U.S.	276	43.08 N	74.58 W
Middlewich	44	53.11 N	2.27 W
Middle Yegua Creek ≃	222	30.19 N	96.47 W
Middle Yuba ≃	226	39.22 N	121.12 W
Midelt	148	32.41 N	4.43 W
Midfield	222	28.56 N	96.13 W
Midge Hall	262	53.42 N	2.45 W
Midgic	186	45.59 N	64.18 W
Mid Glamorgan □[6]	42	51.40 N	3.30 W
Midgley	262	53.44 N	1.58 W
Midhurst, On., Can.	212	44.27 N	79.44 W
Midhurst, Eng., U.K.	42	50.59 N	0.45 W
Midi, Aiguille du ∧	62	45.52 N	6.53 E
Midi, Canal du ≊	32	43.26 N	1.58 E
Midi de Bigorre, Pic du ∧	32	42.56 N	0.08 E
Mid Illovo	158	29.59 S	30.25 E
Mid-Indian Basin ✢[1]	12	10.00 S	80.00 E
Mid-Indian Ridge ✢[3]	6	30.00 S	75.00 E
Midland, Austl.	168a	31.53 S	116.00 E
Midland, On., Can.	212	44.45 N	79.53 W
Midland, Ca., U.S.	204	33.52 N	114.48 W
Midland, Mi., U.S.	190	43.36 N	84.14 W
Midland, N.C., U.S.	192	35.13 N	80.30 W
Midland, Oh., U.S.	218	39.18 N	83.54 W
Midland, Pa., U.S.	214	40.37 N	80.26 W
Midland, Pa., U.S.	214	40.37 N	80.26 W
Midland, S.D., U.S.	198	44.04 N	101.09 W
Midland, Tx., U.S.	196	31.59 N	102.04 W
Midland, Wa., U.S.	224	47.10 N	122.24 W
Midland Bay C	212	44.47 N	79.52 W
Midland Beach ◆[8]	276	40.34 N	74.05 W
Midland City	219	40.09 N	89.08 W
Midland Park, Mi., U.S.	216	42.23 N	85.22 W
Midland Park, N.J., U.S.	276	40.59 N	74.08 W
Midland Park Lake ⊜	212	44.44 N	79.53 W
Midlands □[4]	154	19.00 S	29.45 E
Midleton	48	51.55 N	8.10 W
Midlothian, Il., U.S.	216	41.37 N	87.43 W
Midlothian, Tx., U.S.	222	32.28 N	96.59 W
Midlothian Creek ≃	278	41.39 N	87.40 W
Midlum	52	53.43 N	8.37 E
Midnapore	182	50.55 N	114.05 W
Midnapore Canal ≊	126	22.25 N	87.53 E
Midnapore Plain ≚	126	22.00 N	87.45 E
Mid-Ohio Sports Car Course ♦	214	40.40 N	82.38 W
Midongy Nord	157b	20.45 S	46.13 E
Midongy Sud	157b	23.35 S	47.01 E
Midori	96	34.43 N	132.37 E
Midori ◆[8]	268	35.32 N	139.34 E
Midori ≃	92	32.42 N	130.37 E
Midou ≃	32	43.54 N	0.30 W
Mid-Pacific Mountains ✢[3]	14	20.00 N	170.00 E
Midpines	226	37.32 N	119.55 W
Midreshet Ben Gurion	132	30.21 N	34.46 E
Midsayap	116	7.12 N	124.32 E
Midshipman Point ›	282	38.07 N	122.27 W
Midsland	52	53.22 N	5.16 E
Midsomer Norton	42	51.18 N	2.28 W
Midu	102	25.22 N	100.31 E
Midvale, De., U.S.	285	39.39 N	75.37 W
Midvale, Id., U.S.	202	44.28 N	116.44 W
Midvale, Oh., U.S.	214	40.26 N	81.22 W
Midville	192	32.49 N	82.14 W
Midway, B.C., Can.	182	49.01 N	118.47 W
Midway, B.C., Can.	202	49.01 N	118.46 W
Midway, Al., U.S.	194	32.04 N	85.31 W
Midway, In., U.S.	216	41.37 N	85.55 W
Midway, Ky., U.S.	218	38.09 N	84.41 W
Midway, Pa., U.S.	279b	40.22 N	80.17 W
Midway, Tx., U.S.	222	31.02 N	95.45 W
Midway, Ut,. U.S.	200	40.30 N	111.28 W
Midway City	280	33.45 N	118.00 W
Midway Islands □[2], Oc.	6	28.13 N	177.22 W
Midway Islands □[2], Oc.	174g	28.13 N	177.22 W
Midway Mall ◆[9]	279a	41.24 N	82.07 W
Midway Naval Station ■	174g	28.13 N	177.26 W
Midway Park	192	34.43 N	77.21 W
Midwest	200	43.24 N	106.16 W
Midwest City	196	35.26 N	97.23 W
Midwolda	52	53.12 N	7.00 E
Midyan ◆[1]	128	27.40 N	35.35 E
Midyat	130	37.25 N	41.23 E
Midyobe	152	1.21 N	10.18 E
Midžor (Midžur) ∧	38	43.23 N	22.42 E
Mie	96	32.58 N	131.35 E
Mie □[5]	92	34.30 N	136.30 E
Miechów	30	50.23 N	20.01 E
Miedwie, Jezioro ⊜	54	53.17 N	14.52 E
Międzybórz	30	51.24 N	17.40 E
Międzychód	30	52.36 N	15.55 E
Międzylesie	30	50.10 N	16.40 E
Międzyrzec Podlaski	30	52.00 N	22.47 E
Międzyrzecz	30	52.28 N	15.35 E
Międzyzdroje	30	53.55 N	14.28 E
Miehuapu	105	39.11 N	117.44 E
Miejska Górka	30	51.40 N	16.58 E
Miélan	32	43.26 N	0.19 E
Mielec	30	50.18 N	21.25 E
Mielno	30	54.16 N	16.01 E
Mien ⊜	26	56.25 N	14.51 E
Mienga	152	17.17 S	19.48 E
Mienhua Yü I	100	25.29 N	122.06 E
Mient'ienhuo Shan ∧	269d	25.11 N	121.30 E
Mier	232	26.26 N	99.09 W
Miercurea-Ciuc	38	46.22 N	25.48 E
Mieres	34	43.15 N	5.46 W
Mierlo	52	51.27 N	5.37 E
Mieroszów	30	50.41 N	16.10 E
Miersdorf	264a	52.20 N	13.37 E
Miersig	38	46.53 N	21.51 E
Mier y Noriega	234	23.25 N	100.07 W
Miesaituo	120	35.52 N	93.40 E
Miesbach	64	47.47 N	11.50 E
Miesenbach	61	47.22 N	15.46 E
Mieso	144	9.15 N	40.48 E
Mieste	54	52.28 N	11.11 E
Miesterhorst	54	52.27 N	11.09 E
Mieszkowice	30	52.46 N	14.30 E
Mifflin, Oh., U.S.	214	40.47 N	82.22 W
Mifflin, Pa., U.S.	208	40.34 N	77.24 W
Mifflin □[6]	210	40.40 N	77.33 W
Mifflinburg	210	40.55 N	77.02 W
Mifflintown	208	40.34 N	77.23 W
Mifflinville	210	41.01 N	76.18 W
Miftāḥ, Wādī V	142	30.15 N	31.46 E
Migdal	132	32.50 N	35.30 E
Migdal Ha'Emeq	132	32.41 N	35.15 E
Migdol	158	26.54 S	25.27 E
Migennes	50	47.58 N	3.31 E
Migliarino	66	44.46 N	11.56 E
Migliaro	64	44.48 N	11.58 E
Miglionico	68	40.34 N	16.30 E
Mignano Monte Lungo	68	41.23 N	13.58 E
Mignone ≃	66	42.11 N	11.44 E
Mignovillard	58	46.48 N	6.08 E
Migori ≃	154	0.59 S	34.15 E
Miguel Alemán, Presa ⊜[1]	234	18.13 N	96.32 W
Miguel Alves	250	4.10 S	42.54 W
Miguel Auza	232	24.18 N	103.25 W
Miguel Calmon	250	11.26 S	40.36 W
Miguel Couto	287a	22.43 S	43.27 W
Miguel de la Borda	236	9.09 N	80.19 W
Migueles, Arroyo de los ≃	266a	40.20 N	3.32 W
Miguelete	258	34.01 S	57.39 W
Miguelete, Arroyo ≃	258	34.14 S	57.54 W
Miguel Hidalgo, Presa ⊜[1]	232	26.30 N	108.35 W
Miguelópolis	255	20.12 S	48.03 W
Miguel Pereira	256	22.27 S	43.22 W
Miguel Riglos	252	36.51 S	63.42 W
Migulinskaja	80	49.42 N	41.16 E
Migvie	46	57.08 N	2.56 W
Migyaunglaung	110	14.40 N	98.09 E
Mihăești	38	45.07 N	25.00 E
Mihai Viteazu	38	44.39 N	28.41 E
Mihajlovgrad	38	43.25 N	23.13 E
Mihalgazi	130	40.02 N	30.34 E
Mihalıççık	130	39.52 N	31.30 E
Mihama, Nihon	94	34.46 N	136.54 E
Mihama, Nihon	94	35.36 N	135.56 E
Mihama, Nihon	96	33.54 N	135.08 E
Mihara, Nihon	96	34.24 N	133.05 E
Mihara, Nihon	96	34.17 N	134.46 E
Mihara, Nihon	96	34.32 N	135.34 E
Mihara-yama ∧	94	34.43 N	139.23 E
Mihla	54	51.04 N	10.20 E
Miho	94	36.00 N	140.18 E
Mihonoseki	96	35.34 N	133.19 E
Miho-wan C	96	35.30 N	133.23 E
Mihuangzhuang	105	39.07 N	116.12 E
Mijaly	86	48.57 N	53.42 E
Mijares ≃	34	39.55 N	0.01 W
Mijdaḥah	144	14.00 N	48.26 E
Mijdrecht	52	52.13 N	4.52 E
Mijiang	98	43.01 N	130.08 E
Mijoux	58	46.22 N	6.00 E
Mikabo-yama ∧	94	36.09 N	138.55 E
Mikame	96	33.25 N	132.27 E
Mikamo, Nihon	96	35.09 N	133.37 E
Mikamo, Nihon	96	34.05 N	133.57 E
Mikasa	92a	43.14 N	141.53 E
Mikaševiči	76	52.13 N	27.28 E
Mikata	94	35.33 N	135.55 E
Mikata-ko ⊜	94	35.34 N	135.53 E
Mikatou	273b	4.16 S	15.08 E
Mikawa, Nihon	94	36.29 N	136.29 E
Mikawa, Nihon	96	33.37 N	132.58 E
Mikawa-wan C	94	34.43 N	137.10 E
Mikawa-wan-kokutei-kōen ♦	94	34.42 N	137.10 E
Mikazuki	96	34.58 N	134.27 E
Mikese	154	6.46 S	37.54 E
Mikhaylov, Cape ›	9	66.51 S	118.33 E
Mikhrot Shelomo Hamelekh (Timna') (King Solomon's Mines) ⊥	132	29.45 N	34.56 E
Miki, Nihon	96	34.48 N	134.59 E
Miki, Nihon	96	34.17 N	134.05 E
Mikínai ⊥	38	37.44 N	22.45 E
Mikindani	154	10.17 S	40.07 E
Mikinduri	154	0.07 N	37.50 E
Mikkabi	94	34.48 N	137.33 E
Mikkaichi	270	34.26 N	135.35 E
Mikkeli	26	61.41 N	27.15 E
Mikkelin lääni □[4]	26	62.00 N	27.30 E
Mikkwa ≃	176	58.25 N	114.45 W
Mikołajki	30	53.49 N	21.36 E
Mikołów	30	50.11 N	18.55 E
Mikomeseng	152	2.08 N	10.37 E
Mikomoto-jima I	94	34.34 N	138.56 E
Míkonos	38	37.26 N	25.20 E
Míkonos I	38	37.29 N	25.25 E
Mikope	152	5.03 S	20.48 E
Mikre	38	43.02 N	24.31 E
Mikrí Préspa, Límni ⊜	38	40.46 N	21.04 E
Miksimil	126	22.52 N	89.23 E
Mikšino	76	57.15 N	35.43 E
Mikstat	30	51.32 N	17.59 E
Mikulášovice	54	50.58 N	14.20 E
Mikulincy	78	49.24 N	25.38 E
Mikulino	76	55.02 N	31.07 E
Mikulkin, mys ›	24	67.48 N	46.40 E
Mikulov	61	48.49 N	16.39 E
Mikumi	154	7.24 S	36.59 E
Mikumi National Park ♦	154	7.12 S	37.05 E
Mikun'	24	62.21 N	50.06 E
Mikuni	94	36.13 N	136.09 E
Mikuni-sammyaku ⋏	94	36.50 N	138.40 E
Mikuni-tōge)(	94	36.46 N	138.50 E
Mikuni-yama ∧	94	35.59 N	138.43 E
Mikura-jima I	92	33.52 N	139.36 E
Mila	34	36.27 N	6.16 E
Milaca	190	45.45 N	93.39 W
Miladummadulu Atoll I[1]	122	6.15 N	73.15 E
Milagre	256	21.18 S	47.00 W
Milagres	250	7.17 S	38.57 W
Milagro	246	2.07 S	79.36 W
Milagros	116	12.13 N	123.30 E
Milam □[6]	222	30.47 N	96.57 W
Milan, Ga., U.S.	192	32.01 N	83.03 W
Milan, In., U.S.	218	39.07 N	85.07 W
Milan, Mi., U.S.	216	42.05 N	83.40 W
Milan, Mn., U.S.	198	45.06 N	95.54 W
Milan, Mo., U.S.	194	40.12 N	93.07 W
Milan, N.M., U.S.	200	35.10 N	107.53 W
Milan, Oh., U.S.	214	41.17 N	82.36 W
Milan, Pa., U.S.	210	41.54 N	76.32 W
Milan, Tn., U.S.	194	35.55 N	88.45 W
Milando	152	8.45 S	17.36 E
Milan Federal Correctional Institution ⊛	281	42.06 N	83.40 W
Milang	168b	35.25 S	138.58 E
Milan → Milano	62	45.28 N	9.12 E
Milano (Milan), It.	62	45.28 N	9.12 E
Milano (Milan), It.	266b	45.28 N	9.12 E
Milano, Tx., U.S.	222	30.43 N	96.52 W
Milano □[4]	62	45.30 N	9.30 E
Milanoa	157b	13.35 S	49.47 E
Milano Marittima	66	44.16 N	12.21 E
Milanville	210	41.40 N	75.04 W
Milâs	130	37.19 N	27.47 E
Milaševiči	78	51.39 N	27.56 E
Mil'atino, Ross.	76	54.29 N	34.18 E
Mil'atino, Ross.	82	55.41 N	35.48 E
Milazzo	70	38.13 N	15.14 E
Milazzo, Capo di ›	70	38.16 N	15.14 E
Milazzo, Golfo di C	70	38.15 N	15.20 E
Milbank	198	45.13 N	96.38 W
Milbanke Sound ⊔	182	52.18 N	128.33 W
Milborne Port	42	50.58 N	2.27 W
Milbuk	116	6.10 N	124.16 E
Milburn	196	34.14 N	96.32 W
Milburn Creek ≃	276	40.38 N	73.36 W
Milden	184	51.30 N	107.31 W
Mildenau	54	50.35 N	13.04 E
Mildenhall	42	52.21 N	0.30 E
Milders	64	47.06 N	11.16 E
Mildmay	212	44.03 N	81.07 W
Mildred, Il., U.S.	219	39.46 N	89.38 W
Mildred, Pa., U.S.	210	41.28 N	76.22 W
Mildura	166	34.12 S	142.09 E
Mile	102	24.26 N	103.26 E
Miléai	38	39.20 N	23.09 E
Milena	70	37.28 N	13.44 E
Milendella	168b	34.49 S	139.12 E
Milepa	154	11.43 S	36.20 E
Miles, Austl.	166	26.40 S	150.11 E
Miles, Tx., U.S.	196	31.35 N	100.10 W
Miles ≃	283	42.40 N	70.51 W
Milesburg	214	40.56 N	77.47 W
Miles City	202	46.24 N	105.50 W
Miles Creek C	208	38.46 N	76.12 W
Miles Creek ≃	226	37.12 N	120.21 W
Mile Seven Hundred Thirty Three	180	60.03 N	131.07 W
Milešovka ∧	54	50.33 N	13.56 E
Milestone	184	50.00 N	104.30 W
Milesville	279b	40.12 N	79.52 W
Milet (Miletus) ⊥	130	37.28 N	27.15 E
Mileto	68	38.36 N	16.04 E
Miletto, Monte ∧	68	41.27 N	14.22 E
Miletus → Milet ⊥	130	37.28 N	27.15 E
Mileura	162	26.23 S	117.20 E
Milevsko	30	49.27 N	14.22 E
Milford, Eng., U.K.	42	51.11 N	0.38 W
Milford, Ct., U.S.	207	41.13 N	73.04 W
Milford, De., U.S.	208	38.54 N	75.25 W
Milford, Il., U.S.	216	40.37 N	87.41 W
Milford, In., U.S.	216	41.24 N	85.50 W
Milford, Ia., U.S.	198	43.19 N	95.08 W
Milford, Ky., U.S.	218	38.34 N	84.09 W
Milford, Me., U.S.	188	44.56 N	68.38 W
Milford, Md., U.S.	284b	39.21 N	76.44 W
Milford, Ma., U.S.	207	42.08 N	71.31 W
Milford, Mi., U.S.	216	42.35 N	83.35 W
Milford, N.H., U.S.	207	42.50 N	71.38 W
Milford, N.J., U.S.	210	40.34 N	75.05 W
Milford, N.Y., U.S.	210	42.35 N	74.56 W
Milford, Oh., U.S.	218	39.10 N	84.17 W
Milford, Pa., U.S.	210	41.19 N	74.48 W
Milford, Tx., U.S.	222	32.07 N	96.57 W
Milford, Ut,. U.S.	200	38.23 N	113.00 W
Milford, Va., U.S.	208	38.01 N	77.22 W
Milford Brook ≃	276	40.19 N	74.17 W
Milford Center	218	40.10 N	83.26 W
Milford Cross Roads	285	39.43 N	75.44 W
Milford Haven	42	51.40 N	5.02 W
Milford Haven C	42	51.42 N	5.03 W
Milford Lake ⊜[1]	198	39.15 N	97.00 W
Milford on Sea	42	50.44 N	1.36 W
Milford Ridge	284b	39.21 N	76.45 W
Milford Sound	172	44.40 S	167.54 E
Milford Sound ⊔	172	44.35 S	167.47 E
Milford Station	186	45.03 N	63.26 W
Milgis ≃	154	1.48 N	38.06 E
Milgoo ∧	162	28.51 S	118.07 E
Mil'guvejem ≃	180	68.22 N	171.30 E
Milḥ, Baḥr al- ⊜	128	32.40 N	43.35 E
Milḥat Ashqar ⊜	128	35.18 N	41.55 E
Milḥat Ashqar ≕	130	35.18 N	41.55 E
Milhaud	62	43.47 N	4.18 E
Mili I[1]	14	6.08 N	171.55 E
Milian ≃	112	5.13 N	117.25 E
Milibangalala, Ponta ›	158	26.26 S	32.56 E
Milicia ≃	70	38.04 N	13.33 E
Milicz	30	51.32 N	17.17 E
Milieu, Rivière du ≃	206	46.47 N	73.56 W
Milīj	142	30.36 N	31.03 E
Milim	164	5.10 S	152.00 E
Milín	60	49.39 N	14.02 E
Miling	162	30.30 S	116.21 E
Milis	71	40.03 N	8.38 E
Militello in Val di Catania	70	37.16 N	14.48 E
Militello Rosmarino	70	38.03 N	14.41 E
Milk ≃	202	48.05 N	106.15 W
Milk Creek ≃, Co., U.S.	200	40.24 N	107.45 W
Milk Creek ≃, Or., U.S.	224	45.15 N	122.41 W
Milk Hill ∧[2]	42	51.23 N	1.51 W
Mil'kovo	74	54.43 N	158.37 E
Milk River	182	49.09 N	112.05 W
Milk River Ridge Reservoir ⊜[1]	182	49.22 N	112.35 W
Mill	52	51.41 N	5.47 E
Mill ≃, Ct., U.S.	276	41.08 N	73.16 W
Mill ≃, Ma., U.S.	207	42.18 N	72.37 W
Mill ≃, Ma., U.S.	283	42.38 N	70.41 W
Mill ≃, Ma., U.S.	283	42.12 N	70.57 W
Mill ≃, Ma., U.S.	283	42.08 N	71.21 W
Mill ≃, Ma., U.S.	283	42.44 N	70.52 W
Mill ≃, N.Y., U.S.	276	40.38 N	73.39 W
Millard	198	41.13 N	96.07 W
Millau	32	44.06 N	3.05 E
Mill Bay	224	48.39 N	123.34 W
Millboro	192	37.59 N	79.36 W
Millbourne	285	39.58 N	75.15 W
Millbrae	226	37.35 N	122.23 W
Millbrook, On., Can.	212	44.09 N	78.27 W
Millbrook, Eng., U.K.	42	50.20 N	4.13 W
Millbrook, Ma., U.S.	283	42.03 N	70.41 W
Millbrook, N.J., U.S.	276	40.52 N	74.33 W
Millbrook, N.Y., U.S.	210	41.47 N	73.41 W
Mill Brook ≃, Ma., U.S.	283	42.31 N	71.18 W
Mill Brook ≃, N.J., U.S.	276	40.53 N	74.32 W
Mill Brook ≃, N.J., U.S.	276	40.25 N	74.06 W
Mill Brook ≃, N.J., U.S.	276	40.29 N	74.23 W
Millburn	276	40.44 N	74.18 W
Millbury, Ma., U.S.	207	42.11 N	71.45 W
Millbury, Oh., U.S.	214	41.33 N	83.25 W
Mill City	202	44.45 N	122.29 W
Mill Creek, Pa., U.S.	214	40.26 N	77.56 W
Millcreek, Ut,. U.S.	200	40.27 N	111.54 W
Mill Creek, W.V., U.S.	188	38.43 N	79.58 W
Mill Creek ≃, Austl.	274a	33.59 S	151.01 E
Mill Creek ≃, Ca., U.S.	226	36.49 N	119.21 W
Mill Creek ≃, Ca., U.S.	228	34.05 N	117.06 W
Mill Creek ≃, De., U.S.	285	39.42 N	75.39 W
Mill Creek ≃, Il., U.S.	219	39.50 N	91.24 W
Mill Creek ≃, In., U.S.	194	39.30 N	86.57 W
Mill Creek ≃, In., U.S.	216	41.01 N	86.36 W
Mill Creek ≃, Ia., U.S.	198	42.47 N	95.31 W
Mill Creek ≃, Ks., U.S.	198	39.55 N	96.56 W
Mill Creek ≃, Ky., U.S.	218	38.28 N	84.20 W
Mill Creek ≃, N.J., U.S.	276	40.48 N	74.03 W
Mill Creek ≃, N.J., U.S.	285	40.02 N	74.55 W
Mill Creek ≃, N.Y., U.S.	212	43.57 N	76.08 W
Mill Creek ≃, Oh., U.S.	214	41.06 N	80.40 W
Mill Creek ≃, Oh., U.S.	214	40.14 N	83.09 W
Mill Creek ≃, Oh., U.S.	218	39.06 N	84.32 W
Mill Creek ≃, Oh., U.S.	279a	41.25 N	81.38 W
Mill Creek ≃, Or., U.S.	224	45.36 N	121.11 W
Mill Creek ≃, Pa., U.S.	208	40.00 N	76.18 W
Mill Creek ≃, Pa., U.S.	210	41.53 N	77.08 W
Mill Creek ≃, Pa., U.S.	214	41.09 N	79.03 W
Mill Creek ≃, Pa., U.S.	285	40.03 N	75.16 W
Mill Creek ≃, Pa., U.S.	285	40.08 N	74.52 W
Mill Creek ≃, Tx., U.S.	222	32.46 N	95.46 W
Mill Creek ≃, Tx., U.S.	222	29.50 N	96.07 W
Mill Creek ≃, Tx., U.S.	222	30.08 N	95.37 W
Mill Creek ≃, Va., U.S.	208	38.09 N	77.10 W
Mill Creek, North Fork ≃	224	45.33 N	121.18 W
Mill Creek, South Fork ≃	224	45.36 N	121.12 W
Millcreek Township	214	42.05 N	80.10 W
Milldale	207	41.33 N	72.53 W
Milledgeville, Ga., U.S.	192	33.04 N	83.13 W
Milledgeville, Il., U.S.	190	41.57 N	89.46 W
Milledgeville, Oh., U.S.	218	39.36 N	83.35 W
Mille Îles, Rivière des ≃	206	45.42 N	73.32 W
Mille Lacs, Lac des ⊜	190	48.50 N	90.30 W
Mille Lacs Kathio State Park ♦	190	46.08 N	93.43 W
Mille Lacs Lake ⊜	190	46.15 N	93.40 W
Millemont	261	48.49 N	1.45 E
Millen	192	32.48 N	81.56 W
Millendon	168a	31.48 S	116.02 E
Miller, Mo., U.S.	194	37.13 N	93.50 W
Miller, S.D., U.S.	198	44.31 N	98.59 W
Miller □[6]	219	38.15 N	92.15 W
Miller, Mount ∧	180	60.25 N	142.23 W
Miller City	216	41.06 N	84.08 W
Miller Creek ≃	282	38.02 N	122.30 W
Miller House	180	65.32 N	145.11 W
Miller Mountain ∧	204	38.03 N	118.12 W
Millerovo, Ross.	78	48.55 N	40.25 E
Millerovo, Ross.	83	47.49 N	39.15 E
Miller Peak ∧	200	31.23 N	110.17 W
Miller Place	210	40.58 N	73.00 W
Millers ≃	207	42.35 N	72.30 W
Millersburg, In., U.S.	216	41.31 N	85.41 W
Millersburg, In., U.S.	218	41.31 N	85.41 W
Millersburg, Ky., U.S.	218	38.18 N	84.08 W
Millersburg, Mi., U.S.	190	45.20 N	84.03 W
Millersburg, Oh., U.S.	214	40.33 N	81.55 W
Millersburg, Pa., U.S.	208	40.32 N	76.57 W
Millers Creek ≃	196	33.27 N	99.14 W
Miller Seamount ✢[3]	16	53.30 N	144.20 W
Millers Falls	207	42.34 N	72.29 W
Millers Ferry	194	32.05 N	87.22 W
Millers Flat	172	45.40 S	169.25 E
Millers Island	284b	39.14 N	76.24 W
Millers Pond ⊜	276	40.51 N	73.12 W
Millersport	188	39.54 N	82.32 W
Millers Run ≃	279b	40.22 N	80.07 W
Millerstown	210	40.32 N	77.09 W
Millersville, Il., U.S.	219	39.25 N	89.07 W
Millersville, Oh., U.S.	214	41.18 N	83.16 W
Millersville, Pa., U.S.	208	39.59 N	76.21 W
Millerton, N.Y., U.S.	210	41.57 N	73.30 W
Millerton, Pa., U.S.	210	41.59 N	76.56 W
Millerton Lake ⊜[1]	226	37.01 N	119.41 W
Millerton Lake State Recreation Area ♦	226	37.02 N	119.37 W
Millertown	186	48.49 N	56.33 W
Millertown Junction	186	49.01 N	56.21 W
Millesimo	62	44.22 N	8.12 E
Millet	182	53.06 N	113.28 W
Millett, Mi., U.S.	216	42.42 N	84.38 W
Millett, Tx., U.S.	196	28.35 N	99.12 W
Milleur Point ›	44	55.01 N	5.06 W

Symbols in the index entries represent the broad categories identified in the key at the right. Symbols with superior numbers (⋏[1]) identify subcategories (see complete key on page *I · 1).*

Symbole im Register stellen die rechts im Schlüssel erklärten Kategorien dar. Symbole mit hochgestellten Ziffern (⋏[1]) bezeichnen Unterabteilungen einer Kategorie (vgl. vollständiger Schlüssel auf Seite *I · 1).*

Los símbolos incluídos en el texto del índice representan las grandes categorias identificadas con la clave a la derecha. Los símbolos con numeros en su parte superior (⋏[1]) identifican las subcategorías (véase la clave completa en la página *I · 1).*

Les symboles de l'index représentent les catégories indiquées dans la légende à droite. Les symboles suivis d'un indice (⋏[1]) représentent des sous-catégories (voir légende complète à la page *I · 1).*

Os símbolos incluídos no texto do índice representam as grandes categorias identificadas com a chave à direita. Os símbolos com números em sua parte superior (⋏[1]) identificam as subcategorias (veja-se a chave completa à página *I · 1).*

∧	Mountain	Berg	Montaña	Montagne	Montanha
⋏	Mountains	Gebirge	Montañas	Montagnes	Montanhas
)(	Pass	Paß	Paso	Col	Passo
V	Valley, Canyon	Tal, Cañon	Valle, Cañón	Vallée, Canyon	Vale, Canhão
≚	Plain	Ebene	Llano	Plaine	Planície
›	Cape	Kap	Cabo	Cap	Cabo
I	Island	Insel	Isla	Île	Ilha
II	Islands	Inseln	Islas	Îles	Ilhas
⊥	Other Topographic Features	Andere Topographische Objekte	Otros Elementos Topográficos	Autres données topographiques	Outros acidentes topográficos

ESPAÑOL · FRANÇAIS · PORTUGUÊS

Nombre / Nom / Nome	Página / Page / Página	Lat.°′	Long.°′ W = Oeste / W = Ouest / W = Oeste
Millevaches, Plateau de ⩕[1]	32	45.30 N	2.10 E
Millford	48	55.07 N	7.43 W
Mill Green	260	51.41 N	0.22 E
Mill Grove	216	40.25 N	85.17 W
Mill Hall	210	41.06 N	77.29 W
Millheim	210	40.53 N	77.28 W
Mill Hill ◆[8]	260	51.37 N	0.13 W
Mill Hill ∧[2]	262	53.25 N	1.54 W
Millhousen	218	39.13 N	85.26 W
Millican	222	30.28 N	96.12 W
Millicent	166	37.36 S	140.22 E
Milligan, Fl., U.S.	194	30.45 N	86.38 W
Milligan, Ne., U.S.	198	40.30 N	97.23 W
Milligan Gulch ∨	200	33.37 N	107.02 W
Milligantown	279b	40.33 N	79.41 W
Milliken	275b	43.49 N	79.18 W
Millingen aan de Rijn	52	51.52 N	6.02 E
Millington, Il., U.S.	216	41.34 N	88.36 W
Millington, Md., U.S.	208	39.15 N	75.50 W
Millington, Mi., U.S.	190	43.16 N	83.31 W
Millington, N.J., U.S.	210	40.40 N	74.31 W
Millington, Tn., U.S.	194	35.20 N	89.53 W
Millinocket	188	45.39 N	68.42 W
Millionnyj	89	54.30 N	126.19 E
Millis	207	42.10 N	71.21 W
Mill Island I, Ant.	9	65.30 S	100.40 E
Mill Island I, N.T., Can.	176	64.00 N	78.00 W
Millisle	48	54.36 N	5.32 W
Mill Lake ⊜	212	45.22 N	80.00 W
Millmerran	166	27.52 S	151.16 E
Millmont	210	40.53 N	77.08 W
Mill Neck	276	40.52 N	73.34 W
Mill Neck ≻[1]	276	40.53 N	73.33 W
Mill Neck Creek ⊂	276	40.54 N	73.33 W
Millom	44	54.13 N	3.18 W
Mill Pond ⊜	276	40.53 N	73.22 W
Millport, Scot., U.K.	46	55.46 N	4.55 W
Millport, Al., U.S.	194	33.33 N	88.04 W
Millport, N.Y., U.S.	210	42.16 N	76.50 W
Millport, Pa., U.S.	214	41.55 N	78.07 W
Millrift	210	41.25 N	74.45 W
Mill River	207	42.06 N	73.16 W
Mill Run Acres	284c	38.58 N	77.17 W
Millry	194	31.38 N	88.18 W
Mills, Pa., U.S.	214	41.57 N	77.41 W
Mills, Wy., U.S.	202	42.50 N	106.21 W
Mills, Lake ⊜[1]	224	47.59 N	123.36 W
Millsboro	208	38.35 N	75.17 W
Mills Creek ≃, Austl.	166	22.23 S	143.05 E
Mills Creek ≃, Ca., U.S.	282	37.27 N	122.25 W
Mills Lake ⊜	176	61.30 N	118.10 W
Mills Mansion State Historic Site ⊥	210	41.52 N	73.57 W
Millstadt	219	38.27 N	90.05 W
Millstatt	64	46.48 N	13.35 E
Millstätter See ⊜	64	46.47 N	13.35 E
Millstone	276	40.29 N	74.35 W
Millstone ≃	276	40.33 N	74.34 W
Millstream, Austl.	162	21.35 S	117.04 E
Millstream, B.C., Can.	224	48.30 N	123.31 W
Millstream Chichester National Park ♠	162	21.25 S	117.20 E
Millstreet	48	52.03 N	9.04 W
Milltown, Scot., U.K.	46	57.14 N	2.52 W
Milltown, In., U.S.	218	38.20 N	86.16 W
Milltown, Mt., U.S.	202	46.52 N	113.52 W
Milltown, N.J., U.S.	208	40.27 N	74.26 W
Milltown, Wi., U.S.	190	45.31 N	92.30 W
Milltown Malbay	48	52.50 N	9.23 W
Millvale	279b	40.28 N	79.58 W
Mill Valley	226	37.54 N	122.32 W
Mill Village	214	41.53 N	79.58 W
Millville, Ma., U.S.	207	42.01 N	71.34 W
Millville, N.J., U.S.	208	39.24 N	75.02 W
Millville, Oh., U.S.	218	39.24 N	84.40 W
Millville, Pa., U.S.	210	41.07 N	76.31 W
Millville Lake	283	42.48 N	71.13 W
Millville Lake ⊜	283	42.48 N	71.13 W
Millwood, Md., U.S.	284c	38.53 N	76.53 W
Millwood, N.Y., U.S.	210	41.11 N	73.48 W
Millwood, Va., U.S.	188	39.04 N	78.02 W
Millwood Lake ⊜[1]	194	33.45 N	94.00 W
Milly-la-Forêt	50	48.24 N	2.28 E
Milly-Lamartine	58	46.21 N	4.42 E
Milmay	208	39.26 N	74.51 W
Milmersdorf	54	53.06 N	13.38 E
Milmine	219	39.54 N	88.39 W
Milmont Park	285	39.53 N	75.20 W
Milne Bay □[5]	164	10.00 S	152.30 E
Milne Bay ⊂	164	10.22 S	150.30 E
Milner	224	49.20 N	122.42 W
Milnesville	210	40.59 N	75.59 W
Milngavie	46	55.57 N	4.20 W
Milnor	198	46.15 N	97.27 W
Milnrow	44	53.37 N	2.06 W
Milnthorpe	44	54.14 N	2.46 W
Milo, Ab., Can.	182	50.34 N	112.53 W
Milo, Ia., U.S.	190	41.17 N	93.26 W
Milo, Me., U.S.	188	45.15 N	68.59 W
Milo ≃	150	11.04 N	9.14 W
Milon-la-Chapelle	261	48.44 N	2.03 E
Mílos	38	36.45 N	24.27 E
Mílos I	38	36.41 N	24.15 E
Miloslaviči	76	53.41 N	32.15 E
Miloslavskoje	76	53.34 N	39.24 E
Miłosław	30	52.13 N	17.29 E
Milow, Dtsch.	54	53.11 N	11.32 E
Milow, Dtsch.	54	52.31 N	12.18 E
Milpa Alta ◆[8]	286a	19.11 N	99.01 W
Milparinka	166	29.44 S	141.53 E
Milpitas	226	37.25 N	121.54 W
Milpitas Wash ∨	204	33.18 N	114.44 W
Milroy, In., U.S.	218	39.29 N	85.28 W
Milroy, Pa., U.S.	208	40.42 N	77.35 W
Milseburg ∧	56	50.32 N	9.53 E
Mil'skaja ravnina ≚	84	40.00 N	48.00 E
Milspe	263	51.18 N	7.21 E
Miltach	60	49.09 N	12.46 E
Miltenberg	56	49.42 N	9.15 E
Miltitz	54	51.19 N	12.16 E
Milton, Austl.	170	35.19 S	150.26 E
Milton, On., Can.	212	43.31 N	79.53 W
Milton, N.Z.	172	46.07 S	169.58 E
Milton, Eng., U.K.	42	52.14 N	0.09 E
Milton, De., U.S.	208	38.46 N	75.18 W
Milton, Fl., U.S.	194	30.37 N	87.02 W
Milton, Il., U.S.	219	39.34 N	90.39 W
Milton, In., U.S.	218	39.47 N	85.09 W
Milton, In., U.S.	218	38.58 N	85.01 W
Milton, Ia., U.S.	190	40.40 N	92.09 W
Milton, Ky., U.S.	218	38.43 N	85.22 W
Milton, Ma., U.S.	207	42.15 N	71.05 W
Milton, N.J., U.S.	276	41.02 N	74.32 W
Milton, N.Y., U.S.	210	41.39 N	73.57 W
Milton, N.D., U.S.	198	48.37 N	98.02 W
Milton, Pa., U.S.	210	41.00 N	76.50 W
Milton, Vt., U.S.	188	44.38 N	73.06 W
Milton, Wa., U.S.	224	47.14 N	122.18 W
Milton, W.V., U.S.	188	38.26 N	82.07 W
Milton, Wi., U.S.	216	42.46 N	88.56 W
Milton, Lake ⊜	214	41.06 N	80.58 W
Milton Abbot	42	50.35 N	4.15 W
Milton-Freewater	202	45.55 N	118.23 W
Milton Harbor ⊂	276	40.57 N	73.42 W
Milton Keynes	42	52.02 N	0.42 W
Milton Point ≻	276	40.57 N	73.42 W
Miltonvale	198	39.20 N	97.26 W
Miltou	146	10.14 N	17.26 E
Miltzow	54	54.12 N	13.13 E
Milumba	154	7.06 S	31.04 E
Miluo	100	28.50 N	113.04 E
Miluo ≃	100	28.50 N	113.06 E
Mil'utinskaja	80	48.38 N	41.40 E
Mil'utkej, gora ∧	180	65.42 N	178.03 W
Milverton, On., Can.	212	43.34 N	80.55 W
Milverton, Eng., U.K.	42	51.02 N	3.16 W
Milwaukee	216	43.02 N	87.54 W
Milwaukee □[6]	216	43.02 N	87.58 W
Milwaukee ≃	190	43.02 N	87.54 W
Milwaukee Bay ⊂	216	43.02 N	87.53 W
Milwaukie	224	45.26 N	122.38 W
Mim	150	6.54 N	2.34 W
Mima	96	33.17 N	132.36 E
Mimasaka	96	35.00 N	134.10 E
Mimbres ≃	200	32.13 N	107.28 W
Mimbres Mountains ⩕	200	32.45 N	107.45 W
Mimi ≃	92	32.20 N	131.37 E
Mimico ◆[8]	275b	43.37 N	79.30 W
Mimico Creek ≃	275b	43.37 N	79.29 W
Mimizan	32	44.12 N	1.14 W
Mimmaya	92	41.12 N	140.26 E
Mimoň	54	50.40 N	14.44 E
Mimongo	152	1.11 S	11.36 E
Mimoso, Bra.	248	16.17 S	55.48 W
Mimoso, Bra.	255	15.10 S	48.05 W
Mimoso do Sul	255	21.04 S	41.22 W
Mims	220	28.39 N	80.50 W
Mimuro-yama ∧	96	35.14 N	134.28 E
Min ≃, Zhg.	100	26.05 N	119.32 E
Min ≃, Zhg.	102	28.46 N	104.38 E
Mina, Méx.	196	26.01 N	100.32 W
Mina, Nv., U.S.	204	38.23 N	118.06 W
Mina ≃	112	10.09 S	124.12 E
Mîna, Oued ≃	34	35.47 N	0.30 E
Mīnā' al-Aḥmadī	128	29.04 N	48.08 E
Mīnāb	128	27.09 N	57.05 E
Mīnāb ≃	128	27.01 N	56.53 E
Minabe	96	33.46 N	135.19 E
Minabegawa	96	33.47 N	135.20 E
Mina El Limón	236	12.45 N	86.44 W
Minago ≃	184	54.34 N	98.08 W
Minahasa ≻[1]	112	1.00 N	124.35 E
Minãj ≃[1]	126	22.31 N	89.22 E
Minakami	94	36.46 N	138.58 E
Minakuchi	94	34.58 N	136.10 E
Minam ≃	202	45.37 N	117.43 W
Minamata	92	32.13 N	130.24 E
Minami	94	35.39 N	136.57 E
Minami ◆[8], Nihon	268	35.24 N	139.36 E
Minami ◆[8], Nihon	270	34.40 N	135.31 E
Minami ◆[8], Nihon	270	34.58 N	135.45 E
Minami ≃	94	35.30 N	135.49 E
Minamiaiki	94	36.02 N	138.33 E
Minami-Alps-kokuritsu-kōen ♠	94	35.40 N	138.13 E
Minamiashigara	94	35.19 N	139.07 E
Minami-Bōsō-kokutei-kōen ♠	94	35.10 N	140.05 E
Minamichita	94	34.44 N	136.52 E
Minami-Daitō-jima I	90	25.50 N	131.15 E
Minami-Iō-jima I	14	24.14 N	141.28 E
Minamiizu	94	34.39 N	138.50 E
Minamimaki	94	36.00 N	138.30 E
Minaminasu	94	36.39 N	140.06 E
Minamisenju ◆[8]	268	35.44 N	139.48 E
Minamishinano	94	35.19 N	137.56 E
Minami-Tori-shima (Marcus Island) I	14	24.18 N	153.58 E
Minano	94	36.04 N	139.06 E
Mina Pirquitas	252	22.41 S	66.31 W
Minard, S. Afr.	158	31.17 S	27.35 E
Minard, Scot., U.K.	46	56.07 N	5.15 W
Minas, Cuba	240p	21.29 N	77.37 W
Minas, Indon.	114	0.50 N	101.29 E
Minas, Ur.	252	34.23 S	55.14 W
Minas, Sierra de las ⩕	236	15.10 N	89.40 W
Minas Basin ⊂	186	45.20 N	64.00 W
Minas Channel ʮ	186	45.15 N	64.45 W
Minas de Barroterán	232	27.40 N	101.20 W
Minas de Corrales	252	31.35 S	55.28 W
Minas de Matahambre	240p	22.35 N	83.57 W
Minas de Oro	236	14.46 N	87.20 W
Minas de Ríotinto	34	37.42 N	6.35 W
Minas Gerais □[3]	255	18.00 S	44.00 W
Minas Novas	255	17.15 S	42.36 W
Mînăstirea	38	44.13 N	26.54 E
Minatare	198	41.48 N	103.30 W
Minatitlán	234	17.59 N	94.31 W
Minato	268	35.13 N	139.52 E
Minato ◆[8], Nihon	268	35.39 N	139.45 E
Minato ◆[8], Nihon	270	34.39 N	135.26 E
Minato ≃	268	35.13 N	139.52 E
Minbāl	142	28.24 N	30.41 E
Minbu	110	20.11 N	94.52 E
Minbulak	85	41.30 N	75.53 E
Minbya	110	20.22 N	93.15 E
Minbyin	110	19.17 N	93.32 E
Minchināābād	123	30.10 N	73.34 E
Minchinhampton	42	51.42 N	2.10 W
Minchumina, Lake ⊜	180	63.52 N	152.15 W
Mincio ≃	64	45.04 N	10.59 E
Minco	196	35.18 N	97.56 W
Minčol ∧	30	49.15 N	20.59 E
Mind'ak	86	54.02 N	58.48 E
Mindanao I	116	8.00 N	125.00 E
Mindanao ≃	116	7.07 N	124.24 E
Mindego Creek ≃	282	37.18 N	122.15 W
Mindego Hill ∧[2]	282	37.18 N	122.13 W
Mindel ≃	58	48.31 N	10.23 E
Mindelheim	58	48.03 N	10.29 E
Mindelo	150a	16.53 N	25.00 W
Mindemoya	190	45.44 N	82.10 W
Minden, On., Can.	212	44.55 N	78.43 W
Minden, Dtsch.	52	52.17 N	8.55 E
Minden, La., U.S.	194	32.36 N	93.17 W
Minden, Ne., U.S.	198	40.29 N	98.56 W
Minden, Nv., U.S.	226	38.57 N	119.45 W
Minden, W.V., U.S.	188	37.58 N	81.07 W
Minden City	190	43.40 N	82.46 W
Mindenmines	194	37.28 N	94.35 W
Minderoo	162	22.00 S	115.02 E
Mindif	146	10.24 N	14.26 E
Mindiptana	164	5.45 S	140.42 E
Mindon	110	19.21 N	94.44 E
Mindoro I	116	12.50 N	121.05 E
Mindoro Occidental □[4]	116	13.00 N	121.00 E
Mindoro Oriental □[4]	116	13.00 N	121.20 E
Mindoro Strait ʮ	116	12.20 N	120.40 E
Mindouli	152	4.17 S	14.21 E
Mindourou, Cam.	152	4.06 N	14.34 E
Mindourou, Cam.	152	3.25 N	13.32 E
Minduri	256	21.41 S	44.37 W
Mindživan	84	39.03 N	46.42 E
Mine, Ityo.	144	8.20 N	40.09 E
Mine, Nihon	96	33.17 N	130.26 E
Mine, Nihon	96	34.10 N	131.13 E
Minear Lake ⊜	278	42.17 N	87.57 W
Minebank Run ≃	284b	39.25 N	76.32 W
Mine Brook ≃, Ma., U.S.	283	42.08 N	71.26 W
Mine Brook ≃, Ma., U.S.	283	42.09 N	71.15 W
Mine Brook ≃, N.J., U.S.	276	40.41 N	74.38 W
Mine Centre	190	48.45 N	92.37 W
Minehead	42	51.13 N	3.29 W
Mine Hill	210	40.52 N	74.35 W
Mineiros	255	17.34 S	52.34 W
Mineo	70	37.16 N	14.42 E
Mineola, N.Y., U.S.	210	40.44 N	73.38 W
Mineola, Tx., U.S.	222	32.39 N	95.29 W
Miner ≃	180	66.30 N	138.25 W
Mineral	224	46.43 N	122.10 W
Mineral City	214	40.36 N	81.21 W
Mineral Creek ≃	224	46.45 N	122.08 W
Mineral de Cucharas	234	22.52 N	105.19 W
Mineral del Monte	234	20.08 N	98.40 W
Mineral de Pozos	234	21.14 N	100.29 W
Mineral'nyje Vody	84	44.12 N	43.08 E
Mineral Point, Pa., U.S.	214	40.23 N	78.50 W
Mineral Point, Wi., U.S.	190	42.51 N	90.10 W
Mineral Ridge	214	41.08 N	80.46 W
Mineral Springs, Ar., U.S.	194	33.52 N	93.54 W
Mineral Springs, Pa., U.S.	214	41.00 N	78.22 W
Mineral Wells	196	32.48 N	98.06 W
Minerbe	64	45.14 N	11.20 E
Minerbio	64	44.37 N	11.29 E
Minersville, Pa., U.S.	208	40.41 N	76.16 W
Minersville, Ut,. U.S.	200	38.12 N	112.55 W
Mine Run ≃	285	40.15 N	75.28 W
Minerva, Ky., U.S.	218	38.42 N	83.55 W
Minerva, Oh., U.S.	214	40.43 N	81.06 W
Minerva, Tx., U.S.	222	30.46 N	96.59 W
Minerva, Embalse ⊜[1]	240p	22.25 N	79.48 W
Minerva Park	214	40.04 N	83.00 W
Minervino Murge	68	41.05 N	16.05 E
Minesing Swamp ⋕	212	44.23 N	79.51 W
Minetto	210	43.23 N	76.28 W
Mineville	188	44.05 N	73.31 W
Mineyama	96	35.37 N	135.04 E
Minfeng	120	37.05 N	82.40 E
Minga	154	11.08 S	27.57 E
Mingala	152	5.06 N	21.49 E
Mingan	186	50.18 N	64.02 W
Mingan ≃	186	50.18 N	63.59 W
Mingan, Îles de II	186	50.12 N	63.35 W
Mingan Archipelago National Park ♠	186	50.12 N	63.35 W
Mingan Mountains ⩕	116	15.29 N	121.24 E
Mingāora	123	34.47 N	72.22 E
Mingardo ≃	68	40.02 N	15.18 E
Mingary	166	32.08 S	140.44 E
Mingcheng	89	43.11 N	125.59 E
Mingečaur	84	40.45 N	47.03 E
Mingečaurskoje vodochranilišče ⊜[1]	84	40.50 N	46.50 E
Mingela	166	19.53 S	146.38 E
Mingenew	162	29.11 S	115.26 E
Mingera Creek ≃	166	20.38 S	138.10 E
Minggang	100	32.29 N	114.03 E
Minggao	100	34.20 N	112.15 E
Minghuang	106	31.41 N	119.56 E
Mingin	110	22.52 N	94.39 E
Mingjuesi	106	31.34 N	118.53 E
Minglanilla	34	39.32 N	1.36 W
Ming Ming	164	5.30 S	146.10 E
Mingo, Congo	152	1.55 S	14.59 E
Mingo, Oh., U.S.	216	40.13 N	83.38 W
Mingo Creek ≃, Pa., U.S.	279b	40.13 N	79.57 W
Mingo Creek ≃, Pa., U.S.	285	40.10 N	75.32 W
Mingo Junction	214	40.19 N	80.36 W
Mingorría	34	40.45 N	4.40 W
Mingoville	214	40.56 N	77.39 W
Mingoyo	154	10.06 S	39.38 E
Mingrel'skaja	78	45.01 N	38.20 E
Mingshantou	100	29.18 N	112.33 E
Mingshui, Zhg.	89	47.10 N	125.55 E
Mingshui, Zhg.	102	42.06 N	96.04 E
Mingulay I	46	56.49 N	7.38 W
Mingwan	106	31.04 N	120.17 E
Mingxi	100	26.24 N	117.13 E
Mingyuegou	89	43.07 N	128.54 E
Mingyuelu	85	39.34 N	75.26 E
Minhang	106	31.01 N	121.24 E
Minhla, Mya.	110	19.58 N	95.03 E
Minhla, Mya.	110	17.59 N	95.43 E
Minho □[9]	34	41.40 N	8.30 W
Minho (Miño) ≃	34	41.52 N	8.51 W
Minhou	100	26.12 N	119.06 E
Minianko	150	9.58 N	8.22 W
Minićevo	38	43.41 N	22.18 E
Minicoy Island I	122	8.17 N	73.02 E
Minier	194	40.26 N	89.18 W
Minigwal, Lake ⊜	162	29.35 S	123.12 E
Minija ≃	76	55.21 N	21.17 E
Minilya	162	23.51 S	113.58 E
Minilya ≃	162	23.56 S	113.51 E
Minimarg	123	34.47 N	75.05 E
Minīn	132	33.39 N	36.18 E
Miniota	184	50.08 N	101.00 W
Minisinakwa Lake ⊜	190	47.40 N	81.43 W
Ministikwan Lake ⊜	184	54.01 N	109.39 W
Ministro Ramos Mexía	254	40.30 S	67.17 W
Ministro Rivadavia	288	34.51 S	58.22 W
Minitonas	184	52.07 N	101.00 W
Minj	164	5.54 S	144.39 E
Minjar	86	55.04 N	57.33 E
Minjary, Mount ∧	171b	35.14 S	148.08 E
Minjiadianzi	104	41.35 N	121.41 E
Minjiaji	100	31.08 N	115.01 E
Minkamman	140	6.03 N	31.32 E
Min'kovo	76	59.42 N	43.28 E
Min-Kuš	85	41.41 N	74.28 E
Minlaton	168b	34.46 S	137.36 E
Minle, Zhg.	100	22.59 N	112.58 E
Minle, Zhg.	102	38.27 N	100.56 E
Minna	150	9.37 N	6.33 E
Minna Bluff ≻[1]	9	78.32 S	166.30 E
Minna-shima I, Nihon	174m	26.39 N	127.49 E
Minna-shima I, Nihon	175d	24.45 N	124.42 E
Minneapolis, Ks., U.S.	198	39.07 N	97.42 W
Minneapolis, Mn., U.S.	190	44.58 N	93.15 W
Minnechaduza Creek ≃	198	42.54 N	100.29 W
Minnedosa	184	50.14 N	99.51 W
Minnehaha	224	45.39 N	122.37 W
Minnehaha, Lake ⊜	220	28.31 N	81.46 W
Minneola, Fl., U.S.	220	28.35 N	81.45 W
Minneola, Ks., U.S.	198	37.26 N	100.00 W
Minneola, Lake ⊜	220	28.34 N	81.46 W
Minneosa Creek ≃	196	35.31 N	102.48 W
Minneota	198	44.34 N	95.59 W
Minnertsga	52	53.15 N	5.35 E
Minnesota □[3]	178	46.00 N	94.15 W
Minnesota ≃	178	44.54 N	93.10 W
Minnesota Lake	190	43.50 N	93.49 W
Minnewanka, Lake ⊜	182	51.15 N	115.20 W
Minnewaukan	198	48.04 N	99.15 W
Minnie Creek	162	24.02 S	115.42 E
Minnigaff	44	54.58 N	4.30 W
Minnipa	162	32.51 S	135.09 E
Minnitaki Lake ⊜	184	49.58 N	92.00 W
Minnoch, Water of ≃	44	55.02 N	4.33 W
Mino, Nihon	94	35.32 N	136.55 E
Minō, Nihon	96	34.50 N	135.28 E
Miño (Minho) ≃, Europe	34	41.52 N	8.51 W
Minō ≃, Nihon	270	34.47 N	134.57 E
Minoa	210	43.04 N	76.00 W
Minobu	94	35.22 N	138.26 E
Minobu-san ∧	94	35.24 N	138.25 E
Minobu-sanchi ⩕	94	35.14 N	138.20 E
Minocqua	190	45.52 N	89.42 W
Minokamo	94	35.26 N	137.01 E
Mino-Mikawa-kōgen ⩕[1]	94	35.11 N	137.23 E
Minong	190	46.05 N	91.49 W
Minonk	216	40.54 N	89.02 W
Minooka	216	41.27 N	88.16 W
Minorca → Menorca I	34	40.00 N	4.00 E
Minori	94	36.14 N	140.21 E
Minorsville	218	38.20 N	84.42 W
Minoshō	270	34.39 N	135.49 E
Minot, Ma., U.S.	283	42.14 N	70.45 W
Minot, N.D., U.S.	198	48.13 N	101.17 W
Minot Air Force Base ■	198	48.26 N	101.21 W
Minowa	94	35.55 N	137.59 E
Minqiao	100	32.53 N	119.13 E
Minqin	102	38.42 N	103.11 E
Minqing	100	26.12 N	118.51 E
Minquadale	285	39.42 N	75.34 W
Minquan	98	34.41 N	115.11 E
Minquiers, Plateau des II	32	48.57 N	2.09 W
Minsen	52	53.42 N	7.58 E
Min Shan ⩕	102	33.35 N	103.00 E
Minshāt adh-Dhahab	142	28.00 N	30.42 E
Minshat al-Amir Muhammad 'Ali	142	29.10 N	30.38 E
Minshāt al-Bakkārī	273c	30.01 N	31.08 E
Minshāt al-Ikhwah	142	30.56 N	31.21 E
Minshāt al-Mughālaqah	142	27.44 N	30.47 E
Minshāt Būlīn	142	31.11 N	30.10 E
Minshāt Sulṭān	142	30.32 N	30.55 E
Minsk	76	53.54 N	27.34 E
Minsk □[8]	76	53.45 N	27.45 E
Minskaja vozvyšennost' ⩕[1]	76	54.00 N	27.10 E
Mińsk Mazowiecki	30	52.11 N	21.34 E
Minster, Eng., U.K.	42	51.20 N	1.19 E
Minster, Eng., U.K.	42	51.26 N	0.49 E
Minster, Oh., U.S.	216	40.24 N	84.23 W
Minsterley	42	52.39 N	2.55 W
Minta	152	4.35 N	12.48 E
Mintaka Pass)(	123	37.00 N	74.50 E
Mintard	263	51.22 N	6.54 E
Mintaro	168b	33.55 S	138.43 E
Mint Canyon	228	34.26 N	118.25 W
Mintlaw	46	57.31 N	2.00 W
Minto, Austl.	274a	34.01 S	150.51 E
Minto, Mb., Can.	184	49.25 N	100.01 W
Minto, N.B., Can.	186	46.05 N	66.05 W
Minto, Yk., Can.	180	62.34 N	136.51 W
Minto, Ak., U.S.	180	65.09 N	149.21 W
Minto, N.D., U.S.	198	48.17 N	97.22 W
Minto, Lac ⊜	176	57.13 N	75.00 W
Minto, Mount ∧	9	71.55 S	169.33 E
Minto Inlet ⊂	176	71.20 N	117.00 W
Mintom II	152	2.42 N	13.17 E
Minton	184	49.10 N	104.35 W
Mintoum	152	0.27 N	12.16 E
Minturn	200	39.35 N	106.25 W
Minturnae ⊥	68	41.14 N	13.45 E
Minturno	66	41.15 N	13.45 E
Minūf	142	30.28 N	30.56 E
Minulovo	265a	60.03 N	30.45 E
Minumadai-yōsui ≅	268	35.50 N	139.42 E
Minur'uk	85	40.56 N	73.22 E
Minusinsk	86	53.43 N	91.42 E
Minutang	120	28.13 N	96.32 E
Minute Man National Historical Park ♠	207	42.27 N	71.17 W
Minvoul	152	2.09 N	12.08 E
Minwakh	144	16.50 N	48.05 E
Minxian	102	34.26 N	104.02 E
Minya → Al-Minyā	142	28.06 N	30.45 E
Minyā al-Qamḥ	142	30.31 N	31.21 E
Minya Konka → Gongga Shan ∧	102	29.35 N	101.51 E
Minyat an-Naṣr	142	31.07 N	31.39 E
Minyat as-Sīrij ◆[8]	273c	30.05 N	31.15 E
Minyat Sandūb	142	31.00 N	31.23 E
Minžir	78	46.40 N	28.19 E
Minzow	54	53.23 N	12.30 E
Mio	190	44.39 N	84.07 W
Mioglia	62	44.29 N	8.25 E
Mionica	38	44.15 N	20.05 E
Miory	76	55.37 N	27.38 E
Mipi	120	28.57 N	95.48 E
Miquan	86	44.06 N	87.35 E
Miquelon I	186	47.03 N	56.20 W
Miquihuana	234	23.34 N	99.47 W
Miquon	285	40.04 N	75.16 W
Mir, Bela.	76	53.27 N	26.28 E
Mir, Cuba	240p	20.46 N	76.36 W
Mīr, Miṣr	142	27.27 N	30.44 E
Mir, Niger	146	14.05 N	11.59 E
Mira	34	40.26 N	8.44 W
Mira ≃, N.S., Can.	186	46.03 N	60.00 W
Mira ≃, Col.	246	1.36 N	79.01 W
Mira ≃, Port.	34	37.43 N	8.47 W
Mīrābād	128	30.25 N	61.50 E
Mira Bay ⊂	186	46.02 N	59.56 W
Mirabeau	62	43.42 N	5.39 E
Mirabel	206	45.39 N	74.05 W
Mirabel, Aéroport International de ⊠	206	45.41 N	74.02 W
Mirabella Eclano	68	41.02 N	14.59 E
Mirabella Imbaccari	70	37.19 N	14.27 E
Mirabello, Ippodromo ♠	266b	45.36 N	9.17 E
Mirabello Monferrato	62	45.02 N	8.31 E
Miracema do Tocantins	250	9.33 S	48.24 W
Mirada Hills → La Mirada	228	33.54 N	118.01 W
Mirador	250	6.22 S	44.22 W
Mirador, Cerro ∧	286d	11.57 S	77.02 W
Mirador, Paso de)(	254	40.42 S	71.56 W
Miradouro	255	20.53 S	42.21 W
Miraflores, Arg.	252	28.36 S	65.55 W
Miraflores, Col.	246	5.12 N	73.12 W
Miraflores, Col.	246	1.25 N	72.13 W
Miraflores, Perú	286d	12.07 S	77.02 W
Miraflores, Esclusas de ◆[5]	236	9.00 N	79.36 W
Miraflores, Palacio ʋ	286c	10.31 N	66.55 W
Mīrah, Wādī al- ∨	128	32.26 N	41.42 E
Miraí	256	21.12 S	42.37 W
Miraj	122	16.50 N	74.38 E
Miraki	85	39.02 N	67.10 E
Miraleste	228	33.46 N	118.19 W
Mira Loma	228	34.01 N	117.31 W
Miramar, Arg.	252	38.16 S	57.51 W
Miramar, Arg.	252	30.54 S	62.40 W
Miramar, C.R.	236	10.06 N	84.44 W
Miramar, Fr.	62	43.30 N	6.57 E
Miramar, Moç.	156	23.50 S	35.34 E
Miramar, Fl., U.S.	220	25.59 N	80.13 W
Miramar ◆[8]	286b	23.07 N	82.25 W
Miramar, Laguna ⊜	236	16.23 N	91.16 W
Miramare	66	44.02 N	12.38 E
Miramare, Aeroporto di ⊠	66	44.02 N	12.35 E
Miramare, Castello di ⊥	64	45.42 N	13.43 E
Miramar Naval Air Station ■	228	32.52 N	117.07 W
Miramas	62	43.35 N	5.00 E
Mirambeau	32	45.23 N	0.34 W
Miramichi Bay ⊂	186	47.08 N	65.08 W
Mira Monte	228	36.42 N	119.03 W
Mīram Shāh	120	33.01 N	70.04 E
Mīrān	123	31.24 N	70.43 E
Miranda, Austl.	274a	34.02 S	151.06 E
Miranda, Bra.	248	20.14 S	56.22 W
Miranda, Col.	246	3.15 N	76.14 W
Miranda, Ca., U.S.	204	40.14 N	123.49 W
Miranda □[3]	246	10.15 N	66.25 W
Miranda ≃	248	19.25 S	57.20 W
Miranda, Aerodromo ⊠	286c	10.29 N	66.50 W
Miranda de Ebro	34	42.41 N	2.57 W
Miranda do Douro	34	41.30 N	6.16 W
Mirande	32	43.31 N	0.25 E
Mirandela	34	41.29 N	7.11 W
Mirando City	196	27.26 N	99.00 W
Mirandola	64	44.53 N	11.04 E
Mirano	64	45.30 N	12.07 E
Mirantão	256	22.15 S	44.30 W
Mirante do Paranapanema	255	22.17 S	51.54 W
Mirapuxi ≃	255	13.06 S	51.10 W
Mirasaka	96	34.46 N	132.58 E
Mira Taglio	64	45.26 N	12.08 E
Miravalles, Volcán ∧[1]	236	10.45 N	85.10 W
Miravete, Puerto de)(	34	39.43 N	5.43 W
Mīr Bacheh Kowt	120	34.45 N	69.08 E
Mirbāṭ	118	17.00 N	54.45 E
Mirboo North	169	38.24 S	146.10 E
Mirebeau-sur-Bèze	58	47.24 N	5.19 E
Mirecourt	58	48.18 N	6.08 E
Miren	64	45.54 N	13.37 E
Mirfield	44	53.40 N	1.41 W
Mirgorod	78	49.58 N	33.36 E
Mirgorodka	80	50.58 N	53.33 E
Miri	112	4.23 N	113.59 E
Miriam Vale	166	24.20 S	151.34 E
Mirim, Lagoa (Laguna Merín) ⊂	252	32.45 S	52.50 W
Mirimichi, Lake ⊜	283	42.02 N	71.18 W
Mírina	38	39.52 N	25.04 E
Miriñay ≃	252	30.10 S	57.39 W
Mirinzal	250	2.01 S	44.43 W
Miritiparaná ≃	246	1.11 S	70.02 W
Miriyama	164	3.57 S	141.45 E
Mīrjāveh	128	29.01 N	61.28 E
Mirke ◆[8]	263	51.16 N	7.09 E
Mirna ≃	64	45.19 N	13.36 E
Mirnock ∧	64	46.46 N	13.43 E
Mirnoje Ozero	86	57.44 N	78.45 E
Mirnyj, Ross.	74	62.33 N	113.53 E
Mirnyj, Ross.	80	53.30 N	50.18 E
Mirnyj, Ukr.	78	50.57 N	28.34 E
Mirnyy ʋ[3]	9	66.33 S	93.00 E
Mirond Lake ⊜	184	55.06 N	102.47 W
Mironeasa	38	46.58 N	27.25 E
Mironovka	78	49.39 N	30.59 E
Mironovo	88	58.19 N	109.38 E
Mironovskij	83	48.29 N	38.17 E
Miropol'	78	50.07 N	27.41 E
Miropolje	78	51.02 N	35.16 E
Miroslav	61	48.57 N	16.18 E
Mirosławiec	30	53.21 N	16.05 E
Mirošov	60	49.41 N	13.40 E
Mirotice	60	49.26 N	14.02 E
Mirovice	60	49.31 N	14.02 E
Mirovoje	78	47.45 N	34.45 E
Mirovskoje	78	48.05 N	33.23 E
Mirow	54	53.16 N	12.49 E
Mīrpur, Bngl.	126	23.47 N	90.21 E
Mīrpur, Bngl.	126	23.56 N	88.59 E
Mīrpur, Pāk.	123	33.11 N	73.47 E
Mīrpur Batoro	120	24.44 N	68.16 E
Mīrpur Bībīwāri	120	28.32 N	67.44 E
Mīrpur Khās	120	25.32 N	69.00 E
Mīrpur Sakro	120	24.33 N	67.37 E
Mirria	150	13.43 N	9.07 E
Mirror	182	52.28 N	113.07 W
Mirror Lake ⊜, Ma., U.S.	283	42.05 N	71.20 W
Mirror Lake ⊜, N.J., U.S.	276	40.29 N	74.22 W
Mirtağ	130	38.23 N	41.56 E
Mirto	70	38.05 N	14.45 E
Mirtóön Pélagos ⍑[2]	38	36.51 N	23.18 E
Miryang	98	35.31 N	128.44 E
Miry Run ≃	285	40.15 N	74.49 W
Mirza-Aki	85	40.45 N	73.25 E
Mirzaani	84	41.23 N	46.09 E
Mirzāganj	126	22.21 N	90.14 E
Mīrzākalu	126	22.29 N	90.48 E
Mirzāpur, Bngl.	126	24.06 N	90.06 E
Mirzāpur, India	124	25.09 N	82.35 E
Mirzāpur, India	272b	22.50 N	88.24 E
Mis	64	46.12 N	11.57 E
Misa ≃	66	43.43 N	13.14 E
Misāḥah, Bi'r ⍑[4]	140	22.12 N	27.57 E
Misailovo	265b	55.34 N	37.49 E
Misaka	94	35.38 N	138.40 E
Misaka-tōge)(	96	33.42 N	132.52 E
Misaki, Nihon	94	35.18 N	140.22 E
Misaki, Nihon	96	33.23 N	132.07 E
Misaki, Nihon	96	34.19 N	135.09 E
Misaki → Miura	94	35.08 N	139.37 E
Misakubo	94	35.09 N	137.52 E
Misallah, Ra's ≻	142	29.50 N	32.36 E
Misamis Occidental □[4]	116	8.20 N	123.42 E
Misamis Oriental □[4]	116	8.45 N	125.00 E
Misano Adriatico	66	43.57 N	12.39 E
Misantla	234	19.56 N	96.50 W
Misasa	96	35.24 N	133.54 E
Misasagi → Fujiidera	96	34.34 N	135.36 E
Misato, Nihon	94	36.23 N	138.57 E
Misato, Nihon	94	34.43 N	136.24 E
Misato, Nihon	94	36.15 N	137.54 E
Misato, Nihon	96	34.09 N	135.22 E
Misato, Nihon	268	35.50 N	139.53 E
Misawa	92	40.41 N	141.24 E
Misbourne ≃	260	51.34 N	0.29 W
Misburg	52	52.23 N	9.51 E
Miscou Centre	186	47.57 N	64.34 W
Miscou Island I	186	47.57 N	64.33 W
Miscou Point ≻	186	48.03 N	64.32 W
Mišelevka	88	52.51 N	103.09 E
Misema ≃	190	47.54 N	79.53 W
Mi-sen ∧	96	34.16 N	132.19 E
Misenheimer	192	35.29 N	80.17 W
Miseno	68	40.47 N	14.05 E
Misericórdia, Serra da ∧	287a	22.51 S	43.17 W
Misery, Mount ∧	169	37.24 S	143.36 E
Misgār	123	36.47 N	74.47 E
Mish'āb, Ra's al- ≻	128	28.12 N	48.39 E
Mishagua ≃	248	11.13 S	72.59 W
Mishan	89	45.33 N	131.52 E
Mishawaka	216	41.39 N	86.09 W
Mishawum Lake ⊜	283	42.30 N	71.08 W
Mishbiḥ, Jabal ∧	140	22.38 N	34.44 E
Misheguk Mountain ∧	180	68.15 N	161.03 W
Mishe-Mokwa, Lake ⊜	285	39.52 N	74.48 W
Mishibishu Lake ⊜	190	48.05 N	85.25 W
Mishicot	190	44.14 N	87.38 W
Mishima	94	35.07 N	138.55 E
Mi-shima I	96	34.46 N	131.09 E
Mishima → Settsu	96	34.46 N	135.33 E
Mishmar HaNegev	132	31.21 N	34.43 E
Mishmi Hills ⩕[2]	120	29.00 N	96.00 E
Mishō	96	32.57 N	132.34 E
Mishqal, Jabal al- ∧	132	31.53 N	36.08 E
Mišicha	88	51.38 N	105.35 E
Misikan	120	35.45 N	89.25 E
Misilmeri	70	38.02 N	13.27 E
Misima Island I	164	10.40 S	152.45 E
Misinto	266b	45.40 N	9.05 E
Misiones □[4]	252	27.00 S	55.00 W
Misiones □[5]	252	27.00 S	57.00 W
Misión San Francisco de Laishí	252	26.14 S	58.38 W
Misión San Vicente	232	31.20 N	116.15 W
Misirevo	82	56.16 N	36.45 E
Miskī	140	14.51 N	24.13 E
Miski, Enneri ∨	146	20.00 N	17.55 E
Miškino, Ross.	86	55.20 N	63.55 E
Miškino, Ross.	265a	59.42 N	30.45 E
Miskito Channel ʮ	236	14.20 N	83.08 W
Miskitos, Cayos II	236	14.23 N	82.46 W
Miskitos Reef ✦[2]	236	14.28 N	82.42 W
Miskolc	30	48.06 N	20.47 E
Misli	130	38.10 N	34.52 E
Mislinja	61	46.28 N	15.14 E
Mislinja ≃	61	46.35 N	15.02 E
Mislippi	146	10.00 N	15.37 E
Mislivna ∧	61	48.40 N	14.44 E
Mismār	140	18.13 N	35.38 E
Mismār, Jabal ∧	140	18.06 N	35.42 E
Mismi, Nevado ∧	248	15.30 S	71.42 W
Mišn'ovo	76	53.58 N	36.21 E
Misoke	154	1.06 S	28.38 E
Misool, Pulau I	164	1.52 S	130.10 E
Mispillion ≃	208	38.57 N	75.20 W
Misquamaebin Lake ⊜	184	53.30 N	91.05 W
Misquamicut	207	41.20 N	71.49 W
Miṣr al-Jadīdah (Heliopolis) ◆[8]	273c	30.06 N	31.20 E
Miṣr al-Qadīmah (Old Cairo) ◆[8]	273c	30.00 N	31.14 E
Misrātah	146	32.23 N	15.06 E
Miṣr Baḥrī □[9]	140	31.00 N	31.00 E
Miṣr → Egypt □[1]	140	27.00 N	30.00 E
Misrikh	124	27.27 N	80.31 E
Missanello	68	40.17 N	16.10 E
Missão Santa Cruz	152	16.14 S	21.57 E
Missão Velha	250	7.15 S	39.08 W
Misserghin	34	35.37 N	0.45 W
Missinaibi ≃	176	50.44 N	81.29 W
Missinaibi Lake ⊜	190	48.23 N	83.40 W
Missinaibi Lake Provincial Park ♠	190	48.25 N	83.35 W
Mission, S.D., U.S.	198	43.18 N	100.39 W
Mission, Tx., U.S.	196	26.12 N	98.19 W
Mission ◆[8]	282	37.45 N	122.25 W
Mission Bay ⊂	228	32.47 N	117.15 W
Mission Beach	166	17.52 S	146.06 E
Mission City	224	49.08 N	122.18 W
Mission Creek ≃	282	37.32 N	121.55 W
Mission Hills ◆[8]	280	34.16 N	118.27 W
Mission Mountain ∧[2]	194	36.02 N	94.35 W
Mission Peak ∧	282	37.31 N	121.53 W
Mission Range ⩕	202	47.30 N	113.55 W
Mission Texas State Historic Park ♠	222	31.33 N	95.15 W
Mission Valley	222	28.54 N	97.12 W
Mission Viejo	228	33.36 N	117.40 W
Missisquoi □[6]	206	45.10 N	72.55 W
Missisquoi ≃	206	45.00 N	73.08 W
Missisquoi Bay ⊂	206	45.05 N	73.10 W
Missisquoi-Nord ≃	206	45.02 N	72.26 W
Mississagagon Lake ⊜	212	44.52 N	77.05 W
Mississagi ≃	190	46.10 N	83.01 W
Mississagi Provincial Park ♠	190	46.35 N	82.45 W
Mississagua ≃	212	44.34 N	78.20 W
Mississagua Lake ⊜	212	44.42 N	78.19 W
Mississauga	212	43.35 N	79.39 W
Mississinewa ≃	216	40.46 N	86.02 W
Mississinewa Lake ⊜[1]	216	40.42 N	85.52 W
Mississippi □[3], U.S.	178	32.50 N	89.30 W
Mississippi □[3], U.S.	194	32.50 N	89.30 W
Mississippi ≃, On., Can.	212	45.26 N	76.16 W
Mississippi ≃, U.S.	178	29.00 N	89.15 W
Mississippi Bay ⊂	162	34.00 S	122.17 E
Mississippi Delta ≚[2]	194	29.10 N	89.15 W
Mississippi Lake ⊜	212	45.05 N	76.12 W
Mississippi Sound ʮ	194	30.15 N	88.40 W
Mississippi State	194	33.26 N	88.47 W
Missolonghi → Mesolóngion	38	38.21 N	21.17 E
Missoula	202	46.52 N	113.59 W
Missouri □[3], U.S.	178	38.30 N	93.30 W
Missouri □[3], U.S.	194	38.30 N	93.30 W
Missouri ≃	178	38.50 N	90.08 W
Missouri, Coteau du ⩕[2]	198	46.00 N	99.30 W
Missouri Buttes ∧	198	44.37 N	104.47 W
Missouri City	222	29.37 N	95.32 W
Missouri Creek ≃	219	40.07 N	90.43 W
Missouri Valley	198	41.33 N	95.53 W
Mistake, Mount ∧	171a	27.52 S	152.20 E
Mistake Creek	164	17.06 S	129.04 E
Mistake Creek ≃	166	21.38 S	146.50 E
Mistake Mountains ⩕	171a	27.52 S	152.22 E
Mistaken Point ≻	186	46.38 N	53.10 W
Mistanipisipou ≃	186	51.32 N	61.50 W
Mistassibi ≃	176	48.53 N	72.13 W
Mistassibi Nord-Est ≃	186	49.50 N	71.56 W
Mistassini	176	50.25 N	73.52 W
Mistassini, Lac ⊜	176	51.00 N	73.37 W
Mistatim	184	52.52 N	103.22 W
Mistawasis Indian Reserve ◆[4]	184	53.06 N	106.48 W
Mistelbach, Dtsch.	60	49.55 N	11.31 E
Mistelbach, Öst.	61	48.34 N	16.35 E
Mistelgau	60	49.55 N	11.28 E
Misteln ⊜	40	59.07 N	16.57 E
Misterbianco	70	37.31 N	15.00 E
Misterei	140	13.07 N	22.09 E
Misteriosa Bank ✦[2]	238	18.50 N	83.50 W
Misterton, Eng., U.K.	42	50.52 N	2.47 W
Misterton, Eng., U.K.	44	53.27 N	0.51 W
Misti, Volcán ∧[1]	248	16.18 S	71.24 W
Mistikokan ≃	184	57.01 N	91.27 W
Mistley	42	51.56 N	1.05 E
Mistrás ⊥	38	37.04 N	22.21 E
Mistretta	70	37.56 N	14.22 E
Misugi	94	34.33 N	136.16 E
Misumi, Nihon	92	32.37 N	130.27 E
Misumi, Nihon	96	34.46 N	131.58 E
Misumi, Nihon	96	34.22 N	131.15 E
Misumi ≃	96	34.47 N	131.56 E
Misurina	64	46.35 N	12.15 E
Mišurin Rog	78	48.50 N	33.58 E
Mišutino, Ross.	76	59.31 N	36.01 E
Mišutino, Ross.	82	56.23 N	38.06 E
Mita, Punta ≻	234	20.47 N	105.33 W
Mīt Abū Ghālib	142	31.17 N	31.40 E
Mita Hills Dam ◆[6]	154	14.15 S	29.06 E
Mit'ajevo, Ross.	82	55.16 N	36.32 E
Mit'ajevo, Ross.	86	60.17 N	61.06 E
Mitaka	94	35.40 N	139.33 E
Mitake, Nihon	94	35.25 N	137.08 E
Mitake, Nihon	94	35.51 N	137.37 E
Mit'akinka ≃	83	48.35 N	39.50 E
Mit'akino	82	54.24 N	38.50 E
Mit'akinskaja	83	48.36 N	39.47 E
Mīt al-'Āmil	142	30.54 N	31.21 E
Mitatib	140	16.03 N	36.11 E
Mitau → Jelgava	76	56.39 N	23.42 E
Mīt Badr Ḥalāwah	142	30.51 N	31.14 E
Mīt Bashshār	142	30.31 N	31.24 E
Mitcham, Austl.	168b	34.59 S	138.36 E
Mitcham, Austl.	274b	37.49 S	145.12 E
Mitcham ◆[8]	260	51.24 N	0.10 W
Mitcheldean	42	51.53 N	2.30 W
Mitchell, Austl.	166	26.29 S	147.58 E
Mitchell, On., Can.	212	43.28 N	81.12 W
Mitchell, Il., U.S.	219	38.46 N	90.06 W
Mitchell, In., U.S.	218	38.43 N	86.28 W
Mitchell, Ne., U.S.	198	41.56 N	103.48 W
Mitchell, Or., U.S.	202	44.34 N	120.09 W
Mitchell, S.D., U.S.	198	43.42 N	98.01 W
Mitchell ≃, Austl.	164	15.12 S	141.35 E
Mitchell ≃, Austl.	164	14.28 S	125.43 E
Mitchell ≃, Austl.	166	37.53 S	147.41 E
Mitchell, Lake ⊜[1]	194	32.50 N	86.30 W
Mitchell, Mount ∧	192	35.46 N	82.16 W
Mitchell and Alice Rivers National Park ♠	164	15.30 S	142.05 E
Mitchell Bay ⊂	214	42.28 N	82.26 W
Mitchell Corners	212	43.57 N	78.48 W
Mitchell Field ⊠	278	41.55 N	88.15 W
Mitchell Lake ⊜, B.C., Can.	182	52.53 N	120.36 W
Mitchell Lake ⊜, On., Can.	212	44.34 N	78.58 W
Mitchell Point ≻	214	42.26 N	82.26 W
Mitchellville	190	41.40 N	93.21 W
Mitchelstown	48	52.16 N	8.16 W
Mīt Fāris	142	31.02 N	31.36 E
Mīt Ghamr	142	30.43 N	31.16 E
Mīt Ḥalfah	273c	30.10 N	31.14 E
Mīt Ḥamal	142	30.26 N	31.32 E
Mithapur	120	22.25 N	69.00 E
Mitha Tiwāna	123	32.15 N	72.07 E
Mithi	120	24.44 N	69.48 E
Míthimna	38	39.22 N	26.10 E

	English	Deutsch	Español	Français	Português
≃	River	Fluß	Río	Rivière	Rio
≅	Canal	Kanal	Canal	Canal	Canal
⌞	Waterfall, Rapids	Wasserfall, Stromschnellen	Cascada, Rápidos	Chute d'eau, Rapides	Cascata, Rápidos
ʮ	Strait	Meeresstraße	Estrecho	Détroit	Estreito
⊂	Bay, Gulf	Bucht, Golf	Bahía, Golfo	Baie, Golfe	Baía, Golfo
⊜	Lake, Lakes	See, Seen	Lago, Lagos	Lac, Lacs	Lago, Lagos
⋕	Swamp	Sumpf	Pantano	Marais	Pântano
⍓	Ice Features, Glacier	Eis- und Gletscherformen	Accidentes Glaciales	Formes glaciaires	Acidentes glaciares
⍑	Other Hydrographic Features	Andere Hydrographische Objekte	Otros Elementos Hidrográficos	Autres données hydrographiques	Outros acidentes hidrográficos
✦	Submarine Features	Untermeerische Objekte	Accidentes Submarinos	Formes de relief sous-marin	Acidentes submarinos
□	Political Unit	Politische Einheit	Unidad Politica	Entité politique	Unidade política
ʋ	Cultural Institution	Kulturelle Institution	Institución Cultural	Institution culturelle	Instituição cultural
⊥	Historical Site	Historische Stätte	Sitio Histórico	Site historique	Sitio histórico
♠	Recreational Site	Erholungs- und Ferienort	Sitio de Recreo	Centre de loisirs	Area de Lazer
⊠	Airport	Flughafen	Aeropuerto	Aéroport	Aeroporto
■	Military Installation	Militäranlage	Instalación Militar	Installation militaire	Instalação militar
◆	Miscellaneous	Verschiedenes	Misceláneo	Divers	Diversos

Name / Name	Page / Seite	Lat.°′ / Breite°′	Long.°′ / Länge°′ E = Ost
Mitiaro I	14	19.49 S	157.43 W
Mitidja, Plaine de la ≚	34	36.45 N	3.00 E
Mitilíni	38	39.06 N	26.32 E
Mitino	265b	55.51 N	37.21 E
Mitis, Lac ⊜	186	48.17 N	67.45 W
Mitishto ≃	184	54.50 N	98.58 W
Mitiškovo	76	54.40 N	33.31 E
Mitiwanga	214	41.22 N	82.27 W
Mitkof Island I	180	56.45 N	132.50 W
Mitla ⊥	234	16.55 N	96.17 W
Mitla, Laguna ⊂	234	17.03 N	100.25 W
Mitla, Mamarr (Mitla Pass))(	142	30.00 N	32.53 E
Mitla Pass → Mitla, Mamarr)(	142	30.00 N	32.53 E
Mito, Nihon	94	34.49 N	137.19 E
Mito, Nihon	94	36.22 N	140.28 E
Mito, Nihon	96	34.40 N	131.59 E
Mitō, Nihon	96	34.13 N	131.21 E
Mito, Nihon	268	35.10 N	139.37 E
Mitomi	94	35.47 N	138.44 E
Mitoya	96	35.17 N	132.52 E
Mitra, Monte ∧	152	1.23 N	9.57 E
Mitra do Bispo ∧	256	22.10 S	44.34 W
Mitre ∧	172	40.48 S	175.27 E
Mitre, Península ≻[1]	254	54.48 S	65.40 W
Mitre Peak ∧	172	44.38 S	167.50 E
Mitrofania Island I	180	55.51 N	158.49 W
Mitrofanovka	78	49.58 N	39.42 E
Mitrofanovo	24	63.13 N	56.00 E
Mīt Ruhaynah	273c	29.51 N	31.15 E
Mīt Ruhaynah (Memphis) ⊥	142	29.51 N	31.15 E
Mitry-le-Neuf	261	48.57 N	2.36 E
Mitry-Mory	261	48.59 N	2.37 E
Mitsamiouli	157a	11.23 S	43.18 E
Mitsinjo	157b	16.01 S	45.52 E
Mitsio, Nosy I	157b	12.54 S	48.36 E
Mitsiwa (Massawa)	144	15.38 N	39.28 E
Mitsiwa Channel ⋓	144	15.30 N	40.00 E
Mitsu, Nihon	96	34.47 N	134.33 E
Mitsu, Nihon	96	34.48 N	133.56 E
Mitsubori	268	35.56 N	139.56 E
Mitsue	94	34.29 N	136.10 E
Mitsugi	96	34.30 N	133.09 E
Mitsuike Park ♦	268	35.31 N	139.39 E
Mitsukaidō	94	36.01 N	139.59 E
Mitsuke	92	37.32 N	138.56 E
Mitsumarenge-dake ∧	94	36.23 N	137.35 E
Mitsushima	92	34.16 N	129.19 E
Mitsuzaku	268	35.25 N	140.00 E
Mitsuzawa Park Race Track ♦	268	35.27 N	139.36 E
Mitta, Oued el V	148	34.20 N	6.44 E
Mittagong	170	34.27 S	150.27 E
Mittagskogel (Kepa) ∧	61	46.31 N	13.57 E
Mittainville	261	48.40 N	1.39 E
Mitta Mitta ≃	171b	36.12 S	147.11 E
Mitte ◂[8]	264a	52.31 N	13.24 E
Mittelberg, Dtsch.	58	47.38 N	10.25 E
Mittelberg, Öst.	58	47.20 N	10.10 E
Mittelfischach	56	49.02 N	9.52 E
Mittelfranken □[5]	56	49.20 N	10.40 E
Mittellandkanal ≍	30	52.16 N	11.41 E
Mittelmeer → Mediterranean Sea ▼[2]	10	35.00 N	20.00 E
Mittelsaida	54	50.46 N	13.18 E
Mittelstetten	60	48.15 N	11.06 E
Mittenwald	64	47.27 N	11.15 E
Mittenwalde, Dtsch.	54	53.11 N	13.39 E
Mittenwalde, Dtsch.	54	52.16 N	13.32 E
Mitterndorf	64	47.33 N	13.55 E
Mittersill	64	47.16 N	12.29 E
Mitterskirchen	60	48.21 N	12.44 E
Mitterteich	60	49.57 N	12.15 E
Mittewald an der Drau	64	46.46 N	12.36 E
Mittweida	54	50.59 N	12.59 E
Mitú	246	1.08 N	70.03 W
Mitumba, Monts ⋏	154	6.00 S	29.00 E
Mituo	107	28.53 N	105.37 E
Mitwaba	154	8.38 S	27.20 E
Mitwitz	56	50.15 N	11.12 E
Mityana	154	0.24 N	32.03 E
Mīt Yazīd	142	30.30 N	31.20 E
Mitzic	152	0.47 N	11.34 E
Miura	94	35.08 N	139.37 E
Miura-chosuichi ⊜[1]	94	35.49 N	137.23 E
Miura-dam ◂[6]	94	35.49 N	137.24 E
Miura-hantō ≻[1]	94	35.15 N	139.39 E
Mius	80	51.26 N	47.56 E
Mius ≃	83	47.18 N	38.49 E
Miusinsk	83	48.05 N	38.53 E
Miusskij liman ⊂[1]	83	47.15 N	38.40 E
Miwa, Nihon	94	35.11 N	136.47 E
Miwa, Nihon	94	36.39 N	140.18 E
Miwa, Nihon	96	35.12 N	135.14 E
Miwa, Nihon	96	34.39 N	132.51 E
Miwa, Nihon	96	34.13 N	132.06 E
Miwa, Nihon	270	34.31 N	135.51 E
Mi-Wuk Village	226	38.05 N	120.13 W
Mixcoac ◂[8]	286a	19.23 N	99.12 W
Mixcoac, Presa de ⊜[1]	286a	19.22 N	99.14 W
Mixco Viejo ⊥	236	14.52 N	90.40 W
Mixian	100	34.31 N	113.22 E
Mixin	107	30.23 N	105.46 E
Mixquiahuala	234	20.14 N	99.13 W
Mixtán	234	17.55 N	95.51 W
Mixteco ≃	234	18.11 N	98.30 W
Mixtlán	234	20.26 N	104.25 W
Miya	94	36.05 N	137.15 E
Miya ≃, Nihon	94	34.32 N	136.44 E
Miya ≃, Nihon	94	36.28 N	137.15 E
Miyagawa, Nihon	94	36.19 N	137.09 E
Miyagawa, Nihon	94	34.22 N	136.21 E
Miyagi □[5]	92	38.22 N	140.52 E
Miyagi-jima I	174m	26.21 N	127.57 E
Miyāh, Wādī al- V	140	25.00 N	33.23 E
Miyahara	268	35.56 N	139.37 E
Miyajima	96	34.18 N	132.19 E
Miyake	270	34.35 N	135.47 E
Miyake-jima I	92	34.05 N	139.32 E
Miyako	92	39.38 N	141.57 E
Miyakojima ◂[8]	270	34.43 N	135.33 E
Miyako-jima I	175d	24.47 N	125.20 E
Miyakonojō	92	31.44 N	131.04 E
Miyako-rettō II	175d	24.24 N	125.00 E
Miyama, Nihon	92	34.06 N	136.14 E
Miyama, Nihon	94	36.00 N	136.22 E
Miyama, Nihon	94	35.33 N	136.45 E
Miyama, Nihon	96	35.16 N	135.33 E
Miyama, Nihon	96	33.59 N	135.22 E
Miyāni	120	21.51 N	69.23 E
Miyanojō	92	31.54 N	130.27 E
Miyanoura-dake ∧	93b	30.20 N	130.31 E
Miyara	175d	24.20 N	124.14 E
Miyata	96	33.44 N	130.40 E
Miyazaki, Nihon	92	31.54 N	131.26 E
Miyazaki, Nihon	94	35.56 N	136.05 E
Miyazakino-hana ≻	96	34.04 N	135.05 E
Miyazu	96	35.32 N	135.11 E
Miyi	102	27.00 N	102.08 E
Miyoshi, Nihon	96	33.57 N	133.03 E
Miyoshi, Nihon	96	34.48 N	132.51 E
Miyoshi, Nihon	96	34.02 N	133.52 E
Miyoshi, Nihon	268	35.50 N	139.31 E
Miyota	94	36.18 N	138.30 E
Miyun	105	40.22 N	116.50 E
Miyun Shuiku ⊜[1]	105	40.30 N	116.58 E
Mizan Teferi	144	6.53 N	35.28 E
Mizdah	146	31.26 N	12.59 E
Mize	194	31.52 N	89.33 W
Mizen Head ≻, Ire.	48	52.51 N	6.01 W
Mizen Head ≻, Ire.	48	51.27 N	9.49 W
Miževiči	76	52.59 N	25.05 E
Mizhi	102	37.49 N	110.02 E
Mizil	38	45.00 N	26.26 E
Mizoč	78	50.24 N	26.09 E
Mizoguchi	96	35.21 N	133.26 E
Mizonokuchi	268	35.36 N	139.37 E
Mizonuma	268	35.48 N	139.36 E
Mizoram □[3]	120	23.30 N	93.00 E
Mizpah	208	39.29 N	74.50 W
Mizpah Creek ≃	198	46.16 N	105.17 W
Mizpé Ramon	132	30.36 N	34.48 E
Mizque	248	17.56 S	65.19 W
Mizque ≃	248	18.39 S	64.20 W
Mizue ◂[8]	268	35.41 N	139.54 E
Mizuho, Nihon	94	35.46 N	139.21 E
Mizuho, Nihon	96	35.10 N	135.22 E
Mizuho, Nihon	96	34.51 N	132.31 E
Mizukaidō → Mitsukaidō	94	36.01 N	139.59 E
Mizuko	268	35.50 N	139.34 E
Mizumaki	96	33.51 N	130.42 E
Mizunami	94	35.22 N	137.15 E
Mizunoko-jima I	96	33.02 N	132.11 E
Mizusawa	92	39.08 N	141.08 E
Mizushima-nada ⊂	96	34.25 N	133.40 E
Mizutori	270	34.47 N	135.45 E
Mizuwake-tōge)(	96	33.15 N	131.17 E
Mjälgen	40	60.33 N	15.07 E
Mjällom	26	62.59 N	18.26 E
Mjangad	86	48.15 N	91.57 E
Mjanyana	158	31.50 S	28.10 E
Mjölby	26	58.19 N	15.08 E
Mjøndalen	26	59.45 N	10.01 E
Mjörn ⊜	26	57.54 N	12.25 E
Mjøsa ⊜	26	60.40 N	11.00 E
Mkalama	154	4.07 S	34.38 E
Mkata	154	5.47 S	38.17 E
Mkhondvo ≃	158	26.39 S	31.25 E
Mkokotoni	154	5.52 S	39.15 E
Mkomazi ≃	158	30.12 S	30.50 E
Mkomazi Game Reserve ◂[4]	154	4.10 S	38.10 E
Mkulwe	154	8.35 S	32.19 E
Mkumvura ≃	154	15.55 S	31.07 E
Mkunumbi	154	2.18 S	40.42 E
Mkushi	154	13.40 S	29.20 E
Mkushi ≃	154	14.40 S	29.07 E
Mkushi River	154	13.32 S	29.45 E
Mkuze	158	27.37 S	32.02 E
Mkuze ≃	158	27.53 S	32.29 E
Mkuzi Game Reserve ◂[4]	158	27.40 S	32.15 E
Mkwaja	154	5.47 S	38.51 E
Mkwaya	154	10.06 S	39.40 E
Mladá Boleslav	54	50.23 N	14.59 E
Mladenovac	38	44.26 N	20.42 E
Mladotice	60	49.58 N	13.18 E
Mlala Hills ⋏[2]	154	6.47 S	31.45 E
M'Lang	116	6.55 N	124.53 E
M'Lang ≃	116	6.52 N	124.45 E
Mlanje Peak → Sapitwa ∧	154	15.57 S	35.36 E
Mlava ≃	38	44.45 N	21.13 E
Mława	30	53.06 N	20.23 E
Mlawula	158	26.11 S	32.01 E
Mliba	158	26.14 S	31.36 E
Mlinov	78	50.31 N	25.37 E
Mljet, Otok I	36	42.45 N	17.30 E
Mljet Nacionalni Park ♦	36	42.47 N	17.25 E
Mljetski Kanal ⋓	36	42.48 N	17.35 E
Mmabatho	138	25.51 S	25.38 E
Mmadinare	156	21.57 S	27.52 E
Mnazi	154	8.54 S	39.06 E
Mnevniki ◂[8]	265b	55.45 N	37.28 E
Mnichov	60	50.03 N	12.49 E
Mníšek pod Brdy	30	49.52 N	14.16 E
Mo	24	66.15 N	14.08 E
Mo ≃	150	8.45 N	0.11 E
Moa	240p	20.40 N	74.56 W
Moa ≃, Afr.	150	6.59 N	11.36 W
Moa ≃, Bra.	248	7.39 S	72.41 W
Moa, Pulau I	164	8.10 S	127.56 E
Moab	200	38.34 N	109.32 W
Moabi	152	2.15 S	11.00 E
Moaco ≃	248	7.41 S	68.18 W
Moa Island I	164	10.12 S	142.16 E
Moala Island I	175g	18.36 S	179.53 E
Moalboal	116	9.56 N	123.23 E
Moama	166	36.07 S	144.47 E
Moamba	156	25.35 S	32.13 E
Moana	168b	35.13 S	138.29 E
Moanda	152	1.34 S	13.11 E
Moanza	152	5.25 S	17.30 E
Moar Lake ⊜	184	52.00 N	95.09 W
Moate	48	53.23 N	7.43 W
Moatize	154	16.08 S	33.45 E
Moawhango	172	39.35 S	175.52 E
Moba, Nig.	273a	6.27 N	3.28 E
Moba, Zaïre	154	7.03 S	29.47 E
Mobara	94	35.25 N	140.18 E
Mobārakpur	126	22.58 N	89.10 E
Mobaye	152	4.19 N	21.11 E
Mobayi-Mbongo	152	4.18 N	21.11 E
Mobberley	262	53.19 N	2.20 W
Mobeetie	196	35.31 N	100.26 W
Mobeka	152	1.53 N	19.46 E
Mobenzélé	152	0.54 N	17.51 E
Moberly	194	39.25 N	92.26 W
Moberly ≃	182	56.12 N	120.55 W
Moberly Lake	182	55.48 N	121.45 W
Moberly Lake ⊜	182	55.49 N	121.45 W
Mobile, Al., U.S.	194	30.41 N	88.02 W
Mobile, Az., U.S.	200	33.03 N	112.16 W
Mobile ≃	194	30.29 N	88.01 W
Mobile Bay ⊂	194	30.25 N	88.00 W
Mobjack	208	37.23 N	76.21 W
Mobjack Bay ⊂	208	37.19 N	76.21 W
Mobridge	198	45.32 N	100.25 W
Moca, P.R.	240m	18.24 N	67.07 W
Moca, Rep. Dom.	238	19.24 N	70.31 W
Moča ≃	82	55.25 N	37.28 E
Mocajuba	250	2.35 S	49.30 W
Mocal ≃	236	14.00 N	88.33 W
Močalejevka	80	53.38 N	51.46 E
Močališče	80	56.21 N	48.23 E
Moçambique	154	15.03 S	40.45 E
Moçambique → Mozambique □[1]	138	18.15 S	35.00 E
Mocanaqua	210	41.08 N	76.08 W
Mocanguê Grande, Ilha I	287a	22.52 S	43.08 W
Mocassins, Lac des ⊜	206	46.35 N	74.25 W
Mo Cay	110	10.08 N	106.20 E
Moccasin, Ca., U.S.	226	37.49 N	120.18 W
Moccasin, Il., U.S.	219	39.09 N	88.45 W
Moc Chau	110	20.51 N	104.37 E
Moccoidumis	144	1.36 N	44.26 E
Mocha, Isla I	252	38.22 S	73.56 W
Mocha → Al-Makhā'	144	13.19 N	43.15 E
Moche ≃	248	8.10 S	79.03 W
Moche ⊥	248	8.06 S	79.05 W
Mocheng	106	31.35 N	120.43 E
Mochh	123	32.45 N	71.31 E
Mochigase	96	35.20 N	134.12 E
Mochitlan	234	17.30 N	99.18 W
Mochizuki	94	36.16 N	138.22 E
Mocho, Arroyo ≃	226	37.41 N	121.55 W
Mochov	54	50.08 N	14.50 E
Mochtín	60	49.22 N	13.21 E
Mochudi	156	24.28 S	26.05 E
Močily	82	54.20 N	38.41 E
Mocímboa da Praia	154	11.20 S	40.21 E
Mocímboa do Rovuma	154	11.20 S	39.18 E
Möckeln ⊜, Sve.	26	56.40 N	14.10 E
Möckeln ⊜, Sve.	40	59.18 N	14.30 E
Möckern	54	52.08 N	11.57 E
Mockfjärd	40	60.30 N	14.58 E
Mockhorn Island I	208	37.13 N	75.53 W
Möckmühl	56	49.19 N	9.22 E
Mockrehna	54	51.30 N	12.49 E
Mocksville	192	35.53 N	80.33 W
Moclips	224	47.14 N	124.12 W
Môco, Serra do ∧	152	12.28 S	15.10 E
Mocoa	246	1.09 N	76.37 W
Mococa	256	21.28 S	47.01 W
Mocoduene	156	23.40 S	35.10 E
Mocoretá	252	30.38 S	57.58 W
Mocorito	232	25.29 N	107.55 W
Moctezuma, Méx.	232	29.48 N	109.42 W
Moctezuma, Méx.	234	22.45 N	101.05 W
Moctezuma ≃, Méx.	232	29.09 N	109.40 W
Moctezuma ≃, Méx.	234	21.59 N	98.34 W
Mocuba	154	16.50 S	36.59 E
Močurica ≃	38	42.31 N	26.32 E
Modane	62	45.12 N	6.40 E
Modāsa	120	23.28 N	73.18 E
Modau ≃	56	49.49 N	8.28 E
Modbury	42	50.21 N	3.53 W
Modder ≃	158	29.02 S	24.37 E
Modderbee	273d	26.10 S	28.24 E
Modder East	273d	26.11 S	28.26 E
Modderfontein	273d	26.06 S	28.09 E
Modderfontein ≃	273d	26.13 S	28.10 E
Modderrivier	158	29.02 S	24.38 E
Model City	284a	43.11 N	78.59 W
Modena, It.	64	44.40 N	10.55 E
Modena, N.Y., U.S.	210	41.40 N	74.07 W
Modena □[4]	64	44.30 N	10.54 E
Moder ≃	56	48.49 N	8.06 E
Möderbrugg	61	47.17 N	14.29 E
Modern Art, Museum of ☗	276	40.46 N	73.58 W
Modeste, Mount ∧	224	48.37 N	124.06 W
Modesto, Ca., U.S.	226	37.38 N	120.59 W
Modesto, Il., U.S.	219	39.29 N	89.59 W
Modesto City-County Airport ⊠	226	37.39 N	120.57 W
Modesto Main Canal ≍	226	37.39 N	120.27 W
Modesto Reservoir ⊜[1]	226	37.26 N	121.58 W
Modica	70	36.52 N	14.46 E
Modigliana	66	44.09 N	11.47 E
Modinagar	124	28.51 N	77.37 E
Modione ≃	70	37.34 N	12.49 E
Modjamboli	152	2.28 N	22.06 E
Modjeska	280	33.43 N	117.37 W
Mödling	61	48.05 N	16.17 E
Mödling ≃	264b	48.04 N	16.22 E
Modoc	218	40.02 N	85.07 W
Modon ≃	50	47.16 N	1.27 E
Modowi	164	4.05 S	134.39 E
Modra, Slov.	30	48.21 N	17.17 E
Modra, Tchad	146	20.43 N	17.42 E
Modra špilja ±[5]	36	43.00 N	16.02 E
Mödrath	56	50.53 N	6.43 E
Modriča	38	44.57 N	18.18 E
Modřice	61	49.07 N	16.37 E
Mo Duc	110	14.57 N	108.53 E
Modugno	68	41.05 N	16.47 E
Moe	169	38.10 S	146.15 E
Moe ≃, Austl.	169	38.08 S	146.17 E
Moe ≃, P.Q., Can.	206	45.19 N	71.49 W
Moecherville	216	41.44 N	88.17 W
Moeda	255	20.20 S	44.03 W
Moehau ∧	172	36.35 S	175.24 E
Moel Fferna ∧	42	52.57 N	3.18 W
Moelv	26	60.56 N	10.42 E
Moema	255	19.50 S	45.24 W
Moen	50	50.46 N	3.24 E
Moen I	175c	7.26 N	151.52 E
Moena	64	46.22 N	11.39 E
Moengo	250	5.37 N	54.24 W
Moen-jo-Daro ⊥	120	27.18 N	68.15 E
Moenkopi	200	36.06 N	111.13 W
Moenkopi Wash V	200	35.54 N	111.26 W
Moeraki Point ≻	172	45.22 S	170.52 E
Moerbeke, Bel.	50	50.45 N	3.55 E
Moerbeke, Bel.	50	51.10 N	3.56 E
Moerdijk	52	51.43 N	4.38 E
Moerewa	172	35.23 S	174.02 E
Moergestel	52	51.33 N	5.11 E
Moero, Lago → Mweru, Lake ⊜	154	9.00 S	28.45 E
Moers	56	51.27 N	6.37 E
Moersbach ≃	263	51.33 N	6.36 E
Moesa ≃	58	46.13 N	9.03 E
Moffat	44	55.20 N	3.27 W
Moffat Peak ∧	172	45.02 S	168.07 E
Moffatt	222	31.12 N	97.28 W
Moffatt, Lac ⊜	206	45.34 N	71.19 W
Moffat Water ≃	44	55.18 N	3.25 W
Moffet Point ≻	180	55.26 N	162.32 W
Moffett Field Naval Air Station ■	226	37.24 N	122.03 W
Moffit	198	46.40 N	100.17 W
Mofoluku	273a	6.33 N	3.20 E
Moga	123	30.48 N	75.10 E
Mogadiscio → Muqdisho	144	2.04 N	45.22 E
Mogadishu → Muqdisho	144	2.04 N	45.22 E
Mogadore	214	41.02 N	81.23 W
Mogadore Reservoir ⊜[1]	214	41.04 N	81.21 W
Mogador → Essaouira	148	31.30 N	9.47 W
Mogadouro	34	41.20 N	6.39 W
Mogalakwena ≃	156	23.00 S	28.40 E
Mogalo	152	3.10 N	19.04 E
Mogami ≃	92	38.55 N	139.48 E
Mogan Shan ∧	106	30.36 N	119.52 E
Mogapinyana	156	22.19 S	27.27 E
Mogaung	110	25.18 N	96.56 E
Mogdy	89	50.35 N	133.51 E
Mogees	285	40.06 N	75.19 W
Møgeltønder	41	54.56 N	8.49 E
Mogenstrup	41	55.11 N	11.53 E
Mogent ≃	266d	41.33 N	2.15 E
Moggio Udinese	64	46.25 N	13.12 E
Mogi, Serra do ⋏	287b	23.47 S	46.20 W
Mogielnica	30	51.42 N	20.43 E
Mogila-Bel'mak, gora ∧[2]	78	47.20 N	36.35 E
Mogila-Mečetnaja, gora ∧[2]	83	48.16 N	38.53 E
Mogilev → Mogil'ov	76	53.54 N	30.21 E
Mogilno	30	52.40 N	17.58 E
Mogil'ov, Bela.	76	53.54 N	30.21 E
Mogil'ov, Ukr.	78	48.52 N	34.29 E
Mogil'ov □[8]	76	53.45 N	30.30 E
Mogil'ov-Podol'skij	78	48.27 N	27.48 E
Mogincual	154	15.35 S	40.25 E
Moglal, Wādī V	140	19.18 N	34.29 E
Moglia	64	44.56 N	10.55 E
Mogliano Veneto	64	45.33 N	12.14 E
Mogoča	88	53.44 N	119.44 E
Mogoča ≃	76	58.00 N	36.26 E
Mogočin	86	57.43 N	83.34 E
Mogod	88	48.24 N	103.00 E
Mogogh	140	8.26 N	31.19 E
Mogojto	88	54.25 N	110.27 E
Mogojtuj	88	51.17 N	114.55 E
Mogok	110	22.55 N	96.30 E
Mogollon Mountains ⋏	200	33.25 N	108.40 W
Mogollon Rim ±[4]	200	34.25 N	110.50 W
Mogor	120	32.52 N	67.47 E
Mogorella	71	39.52 N	8.51 E
Mogoro	71	39.41 N	8.47 E
Mogotes	246	6.30 N	72.58 W
Mogotón ∧	236	13.45 N	86.23 W
Mograt Island I	140	19.30 N	33.15 E
Mogroum	146	11.06 N	15.25 E
Moguer	34	37.16 N	6.50 W
Mogyoród	264c	47.36 N	19.15 E
Mogyoródi-patak ≃	264c	47.36 N	19.05 E
Mogzon	88	51.45 N	111.58 E
Mohács	30	45.59 N	18.42 E
Mohaka	172	39.07 S	177.11 E
Mohaka ≃	172	39.07 S	177.12 E
Mohall	198	48.45 N	101.30 W
Moḥammadābād	128	30.53 N	61.28 E
Mohammedia (Fedala)	148	33.44 N	7.24 W
Mohana	124	25.54 N	77.45 E
Mohangi	154	0.03 N	29.05 E
Mohania	124	25.11 N	83.37 E
Mohanpur, Bngl.	126	23.24 N	90.36 E
Mohanpur, India	126	21.51 N	87.26 E
Mohanpur, India	272a	28.44 N	77.10 E
Mohave, Lake ⊜[1]	204	35.25 N	114.38 W
Mohawk, Mi., U.S.	190	47.18 N	88.21 W
Mohawk, N.Y., U.S.	210	43.00 N	75.00 W
Mohawk ≃	210	42.47 N	73.42 W
Mohawk, East Branch ≃	212	43.22 N	75.28 W
Mohawk, Lake ⊜	276	41.02 N	74.41 W
Mohawk Dam ◂[6]	214	40.20 N	82.05 W
Mohawk Mountain ∧	207	41.49 N	73.17 W
Mohawk Point ≻	212	42.51 N	79.29 W
Mohe	89	53.29 N	122.19 E
Moheda	26	57.00 N	14.34 E
Mohegan	207	41.28 N	72.06 W
Mohegan Lake	210	41.19 N	73.51 W
Mohelnice	30	49.46 N	16.55 E
Moher, Cliffs of ±[4]	48	52.57 N	9.26 W
Mohican ≃	214	40.22 N	82.09 W
Mohican, Black Fork ≃	214	40.35 N	82.17 W
Mohican, Cape ≻	180	60.12 N	167.28 W
Mohican, Clear Fork ≃	214	40.35 N	82.12 W
Mohican, Jerome Fork ≃	214	40.45 N	82.23 W
Mohican, Lake Fork ≃	214	40.27 N	82.12 W
Mohican, Muddy Fork ≃	214	40.45 N	82.08 W
Mohican State Park ♦	214	40.37 N	82.16 W
Mohicanville Dam ◂[6]	214	40.44 N	82.09 W
Mohili ◂[8]	272c	19.06 N	72.53 E
Mohill	48	53.54 N	7.52 W
Mohlakeng	273d	26.13 S	27.42 E
Möhlau	54	51.44 N	12.21 E
Möhlin	58	47.34 N	7.51 E
Möhne ≃	52	51.27 N	7.57 E
Möhnestausee ⊜[1]	52	51.29 N	8.08 E
Mohns Ridge ✦[3]	16	72.30 N	5.00 E
Mohnton	208	40.17 N	75.59 W
Mohnyin	110	24.47 N	96.22 E
Moho ≃	236	16.04 N	88.52 W
Mohokare (Caledon) ≃	158	30.31 S	26.05 E
Moholm	40	58.37 N	14.02 E
Mohon	56	49.45 N	4.44 E
Mohorn	54	51.00 N	13.28 E
Mohoro	154	8.08 S	39.10 E
Möhringen	58	47.57 N	8.46 E
Mohrsville	208	40.28 N	75.59 W
Moi	26	58.28 N	6.32 E
Moiano, It.	68	40.39 N	14.28 E
Moiano, It.	68	41.05 N	14.32 E
Moindou	175f	21.42 S	165.41 E
Moinești	38	46.28 N	26.29 E
Moingbi	140	5.46 N	28.49 E
Moinkum	85	43.48 N	73.41 E
Mointy	86	47.13 N	73.21 E
Moio Alcantara	70	37.54 N	15.03 E
Moiporá	255	16.34 S	50.42 W
Moira	48	54.30 N	6.17 W
Moira ≃	212	44.09 N	77.23 W
Moiraba	250	2.27 S	49.25 W
Moira Lake ⊜	212	44.29 N	77.27 W
Moirans	62	45.20 N	5.34 E
Moirans-en-Montagne	58	46.26 N	5.44 E
Mõisaküla	76	58.06 N	25.11 E
Moisdon	32	47.37 N	1.22 W
Moisejeviči	76	53.13 N	28.17 E
Moisejevka, Ross.	86	58.05 N	76.16 E
Moisejevka, Ukr.	83	49.14 N	39.51 E
Moisejevo Alabuška	76	51.54 N	42.06 E
Moisenay	261	48.34 N	2.44 E
Moisés Ville	252	30.43 S	61.29 W
Moisie	186	50.11 N	66.05 W
Moisie ≃	176	50.11 N	66.05 W
Moisie, Baie de ⊂	186	50.16 N	65.56 W
Moisling ◂[8]	52	53.50 N	10.38 E
Moison Creek ≃	281	42.18 N	82.40 W
Moissac	32	44.06 N	1.05 E
Moïssala	146	8.21 N	17.46 E
Moisselles	261	49.03 N	2.20 E
Moisson	261	49.05 N	1.40 E
Moisson, Forêt de ♦	261	49.03 N	1.39 E
Moissy-Cramayel	261	48.38 N	2.36 E
Moita	34	38.39 N	8.59 W
Moitaco	246	8.01 N	64.21 W
Moivre ≃	56	48.52 N	4.28 E
Mojácar	34	37.08 N	1.51 W
Mojana, Brazo ≃[1]	246	9.02 N	74.46 W
Mojave	228	35.03 N	118.10 W
Mojave ≃	204	35.06 N	116.04 W
Mojave Desert ◂[2]	204	35.00 N	117.00 W
Mojave River Forks Reservoir ⊜[1]	228	34.20 N	117.15 W
Moji	85	38.59 N	74.24 E
Mojiang	102	23.28 N	101.39 E
Mojicuaçu ≃	255	20.53 S	48.10 W
Moji das Cruzes	256	23.31 S	46.11 W
Mojiguaçu	256	22.22 S	46.57 W
Mojimirim	256	22.26 S	46.57 W
Mojjero ≃	74	68.44 N	103.42 E
Mojnalyk	88	51.18 N	95.33 E
Mojo	144	8.36 N	39.07 E
Mojoagung	115a	7.34 S	112.21 E
Mojokerto	115a	7.28 S	112.26 E
Mojosari	115a	7.31 S	112.33 E
Mojstrana	64	46.27 N	13.56 E
Moju	250	1.53 S	48.46 W
Moju ≃	250	1.40 S	48.25 W
Mōka	94	36.26 N	140.01 E
Mokai	172	38.32 S	175.54 E
Mokāma	124	25.24 N	85.55 E
Mokambo	154	12.25 S	28.21 E
Mokane	219	38.40 N	91.52 W
Mokapu Peninsula ≻[1]	229c	21.27 N	157.45 W
Mokaria	152	2.00 N	23.20 E
Mokarta, Castello di ⊥	70	37.48 N	12.45 E
Mokau	172	38.41 S	174.37 E
Mokau ≃	172	38.42 S	174.37 E
Moke	102	30.14 N	100.01 E
Mokelumne ≃	226	38.13 N	121.28 W
Mokelumne, Middle Fork ≃	226	38.22 N	120.37 W
Mokelumne, North Fork ≃	226	38.22 N	120.37 W
Mokelumne, South Fork ≃	226	38.23 N	120.35 W
Mokelumne Aqueduct ≍[1]	226	37.54 N	122.07 W
Mokelumne Hill	226	38.18 N	120.42 W
Mokena	216	41.31 N	87.53 W
Mokhotlong	158	29.22 S	29.02 E
Mokil I[1]	14	6.40 N	159.47 E
Mokimbo	154	6.20 S	28.42 E
Mokino	80	57.27 N	49.11 E
Moklakan	88	54.56 N	118.56 E
Möklinta	40	60.05 N	16.32 E
Moknine	148	35.38 N	10.54 E
Mokochu, Khao ∧	110	15.56 N	99.06 E
Mokohinau Islands II	172	35.55 S	175.07 E
Mokokchūng	120	26.20 N	94.32 E
Mokolo, Cam.	146	10.45 N	13.48 E
Mokolo, Zaïre	152	1.57 N	18.05 E
Mokolo ≃	156	23.14 S	27.43 E
Mokombe	152	0.14 S	23.48 E
Mokoreta ≃	172	46.21 S	168.51 E
Mokou	273b	4.13 S	15.13 E
Mokpalin	110	17.26 N	96.53 E
Mokp'o	98	34.48 N	126.22 E
Mokraja Jel'muta	80	46.51 N	41.41 E
Mokraja Ol'chovka	80	50.28 N	44.59 E
Mokraja Sura ≃	78	48.19 N	35.09 E
Mokraja Volnovacha ≃	83	47.30 N	37.15 E
Mokrany	78	51.50 N	24.14 E
Mokrisset	34	34.59 N	5.20 W
Mokro-Jelančik	83	47.42 N	38.31 E
Mokrous	80	51.14 N	47.37 E
Mokrousovo	86	55.48 N	66.45 E
Mokrušinskoje	86	57.31 N	93.11 E
Mokryje Jaly ≃	78	48.05 N	36.44 E
Mokryj Gašun	80	46.53 N	42.45 E
Mokryj Jelančik ≃	83	47.08 N	38.20 E
Mokryj Kor	82	54.34 N	37.58 E
Mokša ≃	80	54.44 N	41.53 E
Mokšan	80	53.26 N	44.37 E
Moku	154	2.57 N	29.22 E
Mokuleia	229c	21.35 N	158.09 W
Mokumbusu	152	1.44 N	21.04 E
Mokvin	78	50.57 N	26.48 E
Mokwa	150	9.20 N	5.02 E
Mol	56	51.11 N	5.06 E
Mola di Bari	68	41.04 N	17.05 E
Molale	144	10.08 N	39.42 E
Molalla	224	45.08 N	122.34 W
Molalla ≃	224	45.18 N	122.43 W
Molalla, North Fork ≃	224	45.05 N	122.29 W
Molanda	152	2.28 N	20.48 E
Molango	234	20.53 N	98.46 W
Molanosa	184	54.30 N	105.33 W
Moláoi	38	36.48 N	22.52 E
Molara, Isola I	71	40.52 N	9.43 E
Molaretto	62	45.10 N	7.00 E
Molat, Otok I	36	44.15 N	14.49 E
Molbergen	52	52.51 N	7.55 E
Molčanovka	83	46.52 N	38.37 E
Molčanovo	86	57.35 N	83.48 E
Mold	44	53.10 N	3.08 W
Moldary	86	50.47 N	78.29 E
Moldau → Vltava ≃	30	50.21 N	14.30 E
Moldavia □[9]	38	47.00 N	27.15 E
Moldavia → Moldova □[1]	38	47.00 N	29.00 E
Moldavija → Moldova □[1]	38	47.00 N	29.00 E
Molde	26	62.44 N	7.11 E
Moldotau, chrebet ⋏	85	41.35 N	74.40 E
Moldova □[1], Europe	22	47.00 N	29.00 E
Moldova □[1], Europe	38	47.00 N	29.00 E
Moldova ≃	38	46.54 N	26.58 E
Moldova Nouă	38	44.44 N	21.40 E
Moldoveanu, Vîrful ∧	38	45.36 N	24.44 E
Môle ≃, Fr.	62	43.15 N	6.32 E
Mole ≃, Eng., U.K.	42	50.57 N	3.54 W
Mole ≃, Eng., U.K.	42	51.24 N	0.21 W
Môle, Cap du ≻	238	19.50 N	73.25 W
Mole Creek	166	41.33 S	146.24 E
Moledet	132	32.35 N	35.26 E
Molega Lake ⊜	186	44.22 N	64.53 W
Mole Game Reserve ◂[4]	150	9.30 N	2.00 W
Molegbe	152	4.14 N	20.53 E
Molenbeek-St.-Jean	50	50.51 N	4.19 E
Molepolole	156	24.25 S	25.30 E
Moléson ∧	58	46.33 N	7.01 E
Molėtai	76	55.14 N	25.25 E
Mole Valley □[8]	260	51.16 N	0.18 W
Molfetta	68	41.12 N	16.36 E
Molibagu	112	0.23 N	123.59 E
Molières-sur-Cèze	62	44.15 N	4.09 E
Molimiao	89	43.34 N	121.54 E
Molina	252	35.07 S	71.17 W
Molina de Aragón	34	40.51 N	1.53 W
Molina de Segura	34	38.03 N	1.12 W
Molina di Ledro	64	45.56 N	10.46 E
Molinara	68	41.18 N	14.54 E
Moline, Il., U.S.	190	41.30 N	90.30 W
Moline, Ks., U.S.	198	37.21 N	96.18 W
Moline, Mi., U.S.	216	42.44 N	85.39 W
Molinella	64	44.37 N	11.40 E
Molinges	58	46.21 N	5.46 E
Molingguan	106	31.50 N	118.50 E
Molini di Tures (Mühlen)	64	46.54 N	11.56 E
Molinière Point ≻	241k	12.05 N	61.45 W
Molino	194	30.43 N	87.18 W
Molino de Rosas ◂[8]	286a	19.22 N	99.13 W
Molinos	252	25.25 S	66.19 W
Molins de Rei	34	41.25 N	2.01 E
Moliro	154	8.13 S	30.34 E
Molise □[4]	66	41.35 N	14.30 E
Moliterno	68	40.14 N	50.52 E
Mölkau	54	51.20 N	12.26 E
Molkom	40	59.36 N	13.43 E
Möll ≃	64	46.50 N	13.26 E
Mollahasan	130	39.22 N	42.37 E
Mollāhāt	126	22.56 N	89.48 E
Mollakendi	130	38.36 N	39.20 E
Mollaro	64	46.16 N	11.05 E
Möllbrücke	64	46.50 N	13.22 E
Mölle	41	56.17 N	12.29 E
Möllen	263	51.35 N	6.42 E
Möllenbeck, Dtsch.	54	53.17 N	11.44 E
Möllenbeck, Dtsch.	54	53.23 N	13.20 E
Mollendo	248	17.02 S	72.01 W
Möllensee ⊜	264a	52.26 N	13.51 E
Mollepata	248	13.31 S	72.32 W
Moller, Port ⊂	180	55.51 N	160.25 W
Möllersdorf	264b	48.02 N	16.18 E
Mollet del Vallès	266d	41.33 N	2.13 E
Mollia	62	45.49 N	8.02 E
Molliens-Vidame	50	49.53 N	2.01 E
Mollington	262	53.13 N	2.55 W
Mollis	58	47.05 N	9.04 E
Mölln, Dtsch.	54	53.37 N	10.41 E
Molln, Öst.	61	47.53 N	14.15 E
Mollösund	26	58.04 N	11.28 E
Mollusk	208	37.43 N	76.32 W
Molly Ann Brook ≃	276	40.55 N	74.11 W
Mölnbo	40	59.03 N	17.25 E
Mölndal	26	57.39 N	12.01 E
Mölnlycke	26	57.39 N	12.09 E
Mölntorp	40	59.33 N	16.15 E
Molocaboc Island I	116	10.58 N	123.34 E
Moločansk	78	47.12 N	35.36 E
Molochio	68	38.18 N	16.02 E
Moločnaja ≃	78	46.42 N	35.20 E
Moločnoje	76	59.17 N	39.41 E
Moločnoje, ozero ⊜	78	46.30 N	35.20 E
Molócuè ≃	154	17.03 S	38.52 E
Molodečno	76	54.19 N	26.49 E
Molodežnaja ☗[3]	9	67.35 S	46.35 E
Molodi	82	55.17 N	37.31 E
Molodo	150	14.14 N	6.02 W
Molodogvardejsk	83	48.20 N	39.40 E
Molodoj Tud	76	56.26 N	33.36 E
Molod'ožnyj	89	50.23 N	136.48 E
Mologa ≃	76	58.50 N	37.11 E
Molokai I	229a	21.07 N	157.00 W
Molokai Fracture Zone ✦	16	23.00 N	130.00 W
Molokča ≃	82	56.15 N	38.45 E
Molokini I	229a	20.38 N	156.30 W
Molokovo, Ross.	76	58.10 N	36.45 E
Molokovo, Ross.	82	55.34 N	37.52 E
Moloma ≃	24	58.20 N	48.28 E
Molong	166	33.06 S	148.52 E
Molonglo ≃	171b	35.15 S	148.58 E
Molopo ≃	156	28.30 S	20.13 E
Molotkoviči	76	52.07 N	25.56 E
Molotov → Perm'	86	58.00 N	56.15 E
Molotovsk → Severodvinsk	24	64.34 N	39.50 E
Molou	146	13.42 N	21.44 E
Moloundou	152	2.03 N	15.10 E
Molowaie	152	5.47 S	23.20 E
Moloy	58	47.32 N	4.55 E
Molsheim	58	48.32 N	7.29 E
Molson Lake ⊜	184	54.12 N	96.45 W
Molteno	158	31.22 S	26.22 E
Moltrasio	58	45.52 N	9.05 E
Molu, Pulau I	164	6.45 S	131.33 E
Moluca, Mar de la → Maluku, Laut ▼[2]	108	0.00	125.00 E
Molucas, Islas → Maluku II	108	2.00 S	128.00 E
Molucca Sea → Maluku, Laut ▼[2]	108	0.00	125.00 E
Moluccas → Maluku II	108	2.00 S	128.00 E
Molukken → Maluku II	108	2.00 S	128.00 E
Molumbo	154	15.27 S	30.15 E
Molundo	116	7.56 N	124.23 E
Moluques → Maluku II	108	2.00 S	128.00 E
Molveno, Lago di ⊜	64	46.08 N	10.57 E
Molvoticy	76	57.25 N	32.20 E
Molžaninovo	82	55.56 N	37.22 E
Moma, Moç.	154	16.44 S	39.14 E
Moma, Zaïre	152	1.36 S	23.57 E
Moma ≃	74	66.26 N	143.06 E
Momanga	156	18.12 S	21.42 E
Momats ≃	164	5.20 S	137.47 E
Momax	234	21.56 N	103.19 W
Momba ≃	154	8.28 S	32.40 E
Mombaça	250	5.45 S	39.38 W
Mombaça, Corrego ≃	287b	23.46 S	46.47 W
Mombachito, Cerro ∧	236	12.24 N	85.34 W
Mombacho, Volcán ∧[1]	236	11.50 N	85.58 W
Mombango	152	1.45 N	24.26 E
Mombaruzzo	62	44.46 N	8.27 E
Mombasa	154	4.03 S	39.40 E
Mombetsu	92a	44.21 N	143.22 E
Mombo	154	4.53 S	38.17 E
Mombongo	152	1.39 N	23.09 E
Momboyo ≃	152	0.16 S	19.00 E
Mombuey	34	42.02 N	6.20 W
Mombum	164	8.23 S	138.51 E
Momčilgrad	38	41.32 N	25.25 E
Momence	216	41.10 N	87.39 W
Momfafa, Tanjung ≻	164	0.18 S	131.20 E
Momi	175g	17.55 S	177.17 E
Momignies	50	50.02 N	4.10 E
Mommark	41	54.55 N	10.03 E
Mommenheim	56	48.45 N	7.39 E
Momo	152	1.52 N	11.48 E
Momotombo, Volcán ∧[1]	236	12.26 N	86.33 W
Momozaka	270	34.51 N	135.02 E
Mompog Island I	116	13.31 N	122.11 E
Mompog Pass ⋓	116	13.34 N	122.13 E
Mompono	152	0.04 N	21.48 E
Mompós	246	9.14 N	74.26 W
Momskij chrebet ⋏	74	66.00 N	146.00 E
Mon	110	18.31 N	96.38 E
Mon □[8]	110	17.30 N	97.00 E
Møn I	41	55.00 N	12.20 E
Mon ≃	110	20.20 N	94.54 E
Mona	200	39.48 N	111.51 W
Mona, Canal de la ⋓	238	18.30 N	67.45 W
Mona, Isla de I	238	18.05 N	67.54 W
Mona, Punta ≻	236	9.38 N	82.37 W
Monaca	214	40.41 N	80.16 W
Monach, Sound of ⋓	46	57.34 N	7.35 W
Monach Islands II	46	57.31 N	7.40 W
Monachovo	83	48.09 N	38.07 E
Monaci, Fiume dei ≃	70	37.24 N	14.48 E
Monaco	62	43.42 N	7.23 E
Monaco □[1], Europe	22	43.45 N	7.25 E
Monaco □[1], Europe	62	43.45 N	7.25 E
Monadhliath Mountains ⋏	46	57.10 N	4.00 W
Monadnock Mountain ∧	207	42.52 N	72.07 W
Monagas □[3]	246	9.20 N	63.00 W
Monaghan	48	54.15 N	6.58 W
Monaghan □[6]	48	54.10 N	7.00 W
Monagrillo	236	7.59 N	80.26 W
Monahans	196	31.35 N	102.53 W
Monahans Draw V	196	31.55 N	101.46 W
Monahans Sandhills State Park ♦	196	31.38 N	102.50 W
Monakino	89	43.24 N	133.29 E
Mona Lake ⊜	216	43.11 N	86.17 W
Monamolin	48	52.33 N	6.20 W
Monango	198	46.10 N	98.35 W
Monapo	154	14.57 S	40.17 E
Monapo ≃	154	15.07 S	40.33 E
Mona Quimbundo	152	9.55 S	19.58 E
Monar, Loch ⊜	46	57.25 N	5.06 W
Monarch	192	34.43 N	81.35 W
Monarch Mountain ∧	182	51.54 N	125.53 W
Monarch Pass)(	200	38.30 N	106.19 W
Monaro Range ⋏	171b	36.22 S	149.03 E
Monarto South	168b	35.08 S	139.08 E
Monaš	80	46.58 N	50.36 E
Monashee Mountains ⋏	182	50.30 N	118.30 W
Monashee Provincial Park ♦	182	50.28 N	118.11 W
Monash University ☗[2]	274b	37.55 S	145.08 E
Monasterace	68	38.27 N	16.33 E
Monasterevin	48	53.07 N	7.02 W
Monasterolo di Savigliano	62	44.40 N	7.37 E
Monastir, It.	71	39.23 N	9.02 E
Monastir, Tun.	148	35.47 N	10.50 E
Monastir □[8]	148	35.15 N	10.45 E
Monastir → Bitola	38	41.01 N	21.20 E
Monastyrišče	78	49.00 N	29.49 E
Monastyriska	78	49.06 N	25.11 E
Monastyrščina	76	54.21 N	31.50 E
Monatélé	152	4.16 N	11.12 E
Mona Vale	170	33.41 S	151.18 E
Monbulk	274b	37.52 S	145.25 E
Monbulk Creek ≃	274b	37.54 S	145.15 E
Moncada	116	15.44 N	120.34 E
Moncalieri	62	45.00 N	7.41 E
Moncalvo	62	45.03 N	8.16 E
Monção, Bra.	250	3.30 S	45.15 W
Monção, Port.	34	42.05 N	8.29 W
Monceau-sur-Sambre	50	50.25 N	4.22 E
Mončegorsk	24	67.54 N	32.58 E
Mönchdorf	61	48.21 N	14.48 E
Mönchengladbach	56	51.12 N	6.28 E
Mönchengladbach, Flughafen ⊠	263	51.14 N	6.29 E
Mönchhof	61	47.52 N	16.56 E
Monchique	34	37.19 N	8.33 W
Mönchweiler	58	48.06 N	8.25 E
Moncks Corner	192	33.11 N	80.00 W
Monclova	232	26.54 N	101.25 W
Moncontour	32	48.21 N	2.39 W
Moncoutant	32	46.43 N	0.35 W
Moncton	186	46.06 N	64.47 W
Mondaí	252	27.05 S	53.25 W
Mondaino	66	43.51 N	12.41 E
Mondavio	66	43.40 N	12.58 E
Monday ≃	252	25.33 S	54.41 W
Mondego ≃	34	40.09 N	8.52 W
Mondego, Cabo ≻	34	40.11 N	8.55 W
Mondello	70	38.13 N	13.20 E
Mondeodo	112	3.33 S	122.12 E
Mondeor	273d	26.17 S	28.00 E
Mondimbi	152	1.43 N	22.58 E
Mondo, Tan.	154	4.59 S	35.54 E
Mondo, Tchad	146	13.47 N	15.32 E
Mondolè, Monte ∧	62	44.13 N	7.46 E
Mondolfo	66	43.45 N	13.06 E
Mondombe	152	0.53 S	22.45 E
Mondoñedo	34	43.26 N	7.22 W
Mondorf-les-Bains	56	49.31 N	6.16 E
Mondoro	150	14.40 N	1.57 W

Symbols in the index entries represent the broad categories identified in the key at the right. Symbols with superior numbers (⋏[1]) identify subcategories (see complete key on page *I · 1).*

Symbole im Register stellen die rechts im Schlüssel erklärten Kategorien dar. Symbole mit hochgestellten Ziffern (⋏[1]) bezeichnen Unterabteilungen einer Kategorie (vgl. vollständiger Schlüssel auf Seite *I · 1).*

Los símbolos incluídos en el texto del índice representan las grandes categorias identificadas con la clave a la derecha. Los símbolos con numeros en su parte superior (⋏[1]) identifican las subcategorías (véase la clave completa en la página *I · 1).*

Les symboles de l'index représentent les catégories indiquées dans la légende à droite. Les symboles suivis d'un indice (⋏[1]) représentent des sous-catégories (voir légende complète à la page *I · 1).*

Os símbolos incluídos no texto do índice representam as grandes categorias identificadas com a chave à direita. Os símbolos com números em sua parte superior (⋏[1]) identificam as subcategorias (veja-se a chave completa à página *I · 1).*

∧ Mountain	Berg	Montaña	Montagne	Montanha
⋏ Mountains	Gebirge	Montañas	Montagnes	Montanhas
)(Pass	Paß	Paso	Col	Passo
V Valley, Canyon	Tal, Cañon	Valle, Cañón	Vallée, Canyon	Vale, Canhão
≚ Plain	Ebene	Llano	Plaine	Planície
≻ Cape	Kap	Cabo	Cap	Cabo
I Island	Insel	Isla	Île	Ilha
II Islands	Inseln	Islas	Îles	Ilhas
± Other Topographic Features	Andere Topographische Objekte	Otros Elementos Topográficos	Autres données topographiques	Outros acidentes topográficos

ESPAÑOL — Nombre | Página | Lat.°′ | Long.°′ W = Oeste
FRANÇAIS — Nom | Page | Lat.°′ | Long.°′ W = Ouest
PORTUGUÊS — Nome | Página | Lat.°′ | Long.°′ W = Oeste

Mondoubleau 50 47.59 N 0.54 E
Mondovi 190 44.34 N 91.40 W
Mondragon, Fr. 62 44.14 N 4.43 E
Mondragon, Pil. 116 12.31 N 124.45 E
Mondragone 68 41.07 N 13.53 E
Mondrain Island I 162 34.08 S 122.15 E
Mondsee 64 47.52 N 13.21 E
Mondsee @ 64 47.49 N 13.23 E
Monds Island I 285 39.50 N 75.19 W
Mondy 88 51.40 N 100.59 E
Monee 216 41.25 N 87.45 W
Moneglia 62 44.14 N 9.30 E
Monemvasia 38 36.41 N 23.03 E
Monero 200 36.54 N 106.52 W
Moneron, ostrov I 89 46.17 N 141.15 E
Monesiglio 62 44.28 N 8.07 E
Monessen 214 40.08 N 79.53 W
Monesterio 34 38.05 N 6.16 W
Monestier-de-Clermont 62 44.54 N 5.38 E
Monetnyj 86 57.03 N 60.53 E
Monett 194 36.55 N 93.55 W
Monette 194 35.53 N 90.20 W
Money Creek ≃ 216 40.40 N 88.58 W
Moneygall 48 52.53 N 7.57 W
Moneymore 48 54.42 N 6.40 W
Monfalcone 64 45.49 N 13.32 E
Monferrato □[9] 62 44.55 N 8.05 E
Monflanquin 32 44.32 N 0.46 E
Monforte 34 39.03 N 7.26 W
Monforte de Lemos 34 42.31 N 7.30 W
Monforte San Giorgio 70 38.09 N 15.23 E
Monfort Heights 218 39.12 N 84.37 W
Monga 152 4.12 N 22.49 E
Mongaguá 256 24.06 S 46.37 W
Mongai-Musenge 152 4.04 S 19.34 E
Mongala ≃ 152 1.53 N 19.46 E
Mongalla 154 5.12 N 31.46 E
Mongalla Game Reserve ✦[4] 154 5.12 N 31.33 E
Mongandjo 152 1.21 N 24.20 E
Mongarlowe ≃ 170 35.15 S 149.52 E
Mongat 266d 41.28 N 2.17 E
Mongaup ≃ 210 41.25 N 74.45 W
Mongaup Valley 210 41.40 N 74.47 W
Mongbwalu 154 1.57 N 30.02 E
Mongbyŏn-ni 271b 37.40 N 126.44 E
Mong Cai 110 21.32 N 107.58 E
Monge ∧ 266c 38.46 N 9.26 W
Monger, Îles II 186 51.05 N 58.45 W
Mongeri 150 8.19 N 11.44 W
Mongers Lake @ 162 29.15 S 117.05 E
Monggon Qulu 89 48.35 N 119.49 E
Monggŭmp'o 98 38.09 N 124.47 E
Mŏng Hai 110 20.46 N 99.49 E
Mŏng Hawm 110 23.51 N 98.20 E
Monghidoro 66 44.13 N 11.19 E
Mŏng Hpāyak 110 20.53 N 99.54 E
Mŏng Hsat 110 20.32 N 99.15 E
Monghyr → Munger 124 25.23 N 86.28 E
Mongi ≃ 164 6.35 S 147.35 E
Mongiana 68 38.31 N 16.19 E
Mongibello → Etna, Monte ∧[1] 70 37.46 N 15.00 E
Mongiuffi 70 37.55 N 15.17 E
Mŏng Küng 110 21.36 N 97.32 E
Mŏng Ma 110 21.37 N 99.54 E
Mŏng Mit 110 23.07 N 96.41 E
Mŏng Nai 110 20.31 N 97.52 E
Mŏng Nawng 110 21.39 N 98.08 E
Mongo, Tchad 146 12.11 N 18.42 E
Mongo, In., U.S. 216 41.41 N 85.17 W
Mongo ≃ 150 9.34 N 12.11 W
Mongoj 88 53.57 N 113.50 E
Mongol Altajn nuruu ∧∧ 90 46.30 N 93.00 E
Mongol Ard Uls → Mongolia □[1] 90 46.00 N 105.00 E
Mongolei → Mongolia □[1] 90 46.00 N 105.00 E
Mongol els ✦[2] 88 47.45 N 94.30 E
Mongolia (Mongol Ard Uls) □[1] 90 46.00 N 105.00 E
Mongolie → Mongolia □[1] 90 46.00 N 105.00 E
Mongomo 152 1.38 N 11.19 E
Mŏngŏn Mor't 88 48.11 N 108.29 E
Mongororo 146 12.01 N 22.28 E
Mongoumba 152 3.38 N 18.36 E
Mŏng Pai 110 19.44 N 97.05 E
Mŏng Pan 110 20.19 N 98.22 E
Mŏng Pawn 110 20.49 N 97.28 E
Mŏng Ping 110 21.22 N 99.02 E
Mongpong ≃ 116 12.44 N 120.48 E
Mongrando 62 45.31 N 8.00 E
Mŏng Si 110 23.40 N 98.23 E
Mong Tung Hang 271d 22.20 N 114.02 E
Mongu 152 15.15 S 23.09 E
Mongua 152 16.43 S 15.23 E
Monguelfo (Welsberg) 64 46.45 N 12.06 E
Monguno 146 12.40 N 13.38 E
Mŏng Yai 110 22.25 N 98.02 E
Mŏng Yawng 110 21.11 N 100.22 E
Monheim, Dtsch. 56 48.50 N 10.51 E
Monheim, Dtsch. 56 51.05 N 6.53 E
Moniaive 44 55.12 N 3.55 W
Mönichkirchen 61 47.31 N 16.02 E
Monico 190 45.34 N 89.09 W
Monida Pass)(202 44.33 N 112.18 W
Mon Idée 50 49.53 N 4.23 E
Monie 152 4.00 S 17.22 E
Monie Bay c 208 38.13 N 75.51 W
Monie Creek ≃ 208 38.14 N 75.50 W
Monifieth 46 56.29 N 2.49 W
Monimail 46 56.18 N 3.08 W
Moninger 214 40.14 N 80.13 W
Monino 82 55.50 N 38.11 E
Moniquirá 246 5.52 N 73.36 W
Mõniste 76 57.35 N 26.33 E
Monistrol-d'Allier 62 44.57 N 3.38 E
Monistrol-sur-Loire 62 45.17 N 4.10 E
Monitor Range ∧∧ 204 38.45 N 116.30 W
Monitor Valley V 204 39.00 N 116.40 W
Monívea 48 53.23 N 8.43 W
Monjolo 256 22.49 S 42.57 W
Monk, Pointe ≻ 275a 45.29 N 73.57 W
Monkayo 116 7.50 N 126.03 E
Mönkebude 54 53.46 N 13.57 E
Monken Hadley ✦[8] 260 51.40 N 0.11 W
Monkey Bay 154 14.05 S 34.55 E
Monkey River 236 16.22 N 88.29 W
Mońki 30 53.24 N 22.49 E
Monkira 166 24.49 S 140.34 E
Monkoto 152 1.38 S 20.39 E
Monks Heath 262 53.16 N 2.14 W
Monkton 212 43.35 N 81.05 W
Monmouth, Wales, U.K. 42 51.50 N 2.43 W
Monmouth, Il., U.S. 190 40.54 N 90.38 W
Monmouth, In., U.S. 216 40.52 N 84.57 W
Monmouth, Or., U.S. 202 44.50 N 123.13 W
Monmouth □[6] 208 40.16 N 74.17 W
Monmouth Beach 276 40.19 N 73.58 W
Monmouth Hills 276 40.24 N 74.00 W
Monmouth Junction 208 40.22 N 74.32 W
Monmouth Mountain ∧ 182 51.00 N 123.47 W
Monnickendam 52 52.27 N 5.02 E
Monnow ≃ 42 51.48 N 2.42 W
Mono □[5] 150 6.45 N 1.50 E
Mono □[6] 226 38.18 N 119.22 W
Mono ≃ 150 6.17 N 1.51 E
Mono, Caño ≃ 246 4.25 N 67.47 W
Mono, Punta ≻ 236 11.36 N 83.39 W
Monobe 96 33.42 N 133.53 E
Monobe ≃ 96 33.32 N 133.41 E
Monocacy ≃ 208 39.13 N 77.27 W
Monocacy Station 208 40.16 N 75.46 W
Monogarovo 82 54.42 N 38.45 E
Mono Island I 175e 7.21 S 155.34 E
Mono Lake @ 204 38.00 N 119.00 W
Monolith 228 35.07 N 118.22 W
Monomoy Island I 207 41.35 N 69.59 W
Monomoy Point ≻ 207 41.33 N 70.02 W
Monon 216 40.52 N 86.52 W
Monona, Ia., U.S. 190 43.03 N 91.23 W
Monona, Wi., U.S. 216 43.03 N 89.20 W
Monona, Lake @ 216 43.03 N 89.22 W
Monongah 214 40.12 N 79.55 W
Monongahela ≃ 188 40.27 N 80.00 W
Monongahela Brook ≃ 285 39.47 N 75.09 W
Monopoli 68 40.57 N 17.19 E
Monor 30 47.21 N 19.27 E
Mono Road Station 275b 43.51 N 79.51 W
Monóver 34 38.26 N 0.50 W
Monowai, Lake @ 172 45.52 S 167.27 E
Monponsett 207 42.01 N 70.50 W
Monponsett Pond @ 283 42.01 N 70.51 W
Monreal 34 42.42 N 1.30 W
Monreal del Campo 34 40.47 N 1.21 W
Monreale 70 38.05 N 13.17 E
Monreale, Castello di ⊥ 71 39.38 N 8.49 E
Monroe, Ct., U.S. 207 41.19 N 73.12 W
Monroe, Fl., U.S. 220 25.52 N 81.06 W
Monroe, Ga., U.S. 192 33.47 N 83.42 W
Monroe, In., U.S. 216 40.44 N 84.56 W
Monroe, Ia., U.S. 190 41.31 N 93.06 W
Monroe, La., U.S. 194 32.30 N 92.07 W
Monroe, Mi., U.S. 216 41.54 N 83.23 W
Monroe, Ne., U.S. 198 41.28 N 97.35 W
Monroe, N.J., U.S. 276 41.06 N 74.38 W
Monroe, N.Y., U.S. 210 41.19 N 74.11 W
Monroe, N.C., U.S. 192 34.59 N 80.32 W
Monroe, Oh., U.S. 218 39.26 N 84.21 W
Monroe, Or., U.S. 202 44.18 N 123.17 W
Monroe, Ut., U.S. 200 38.37 N 112.07 W
Monroe, Va., U.S. 192 37.30 N 79.07 W
Monroe, Wa., U.S. 224 47.51 N 121.58 W
Monroe, Wi., U.S. 190 42.36 N 89.38 W
Monroe □[6], Fl., U.S. 220 25.10 N 81.10 W
Monroe □[6], Il., U.S. 219 38.20 N 90.09 W
Monroe □[6], In., U.S. 218 39.10 N 86.26 W
Monroe □[6], Mi., U.S. 216 41.55 N 83.26 W
Monroe □[6], Mo., U.S. 219 39.30 N 92.00 W
Monroe □[6], N.Y., U.S. 210 43.10 N 77.36 W
Monroe □[6], Pa., U.S. 210 40.59 N 75.12 W
Monroe, Lake @ 220 28.52 N 81.16 W
Monroe Bridge 207 42.43 N 72.56 W
Monroe Center, Ct., U.S. 207 41.20 N 73.12 W
Monroe Center, Il., U.S. 216 42.06 N 89.00 W
Monroe City, In., U.S. 194 38.36 N 87.21 W
Monroe City, Mo., U.S. 219 39.39 N 91.44 W
Monroe City, Tx., U.S. 222 29.47 N 94.35 W
Monroe Lake @[1] 218 39.05 N 86.25 W
Monroe Manor 216 41.36 N 86.40 W
Monroeton 210 41.43 N 76.30 W
Monroeville, Al., U.S. 194 31.31 N 87.19 W
Monroeville, In., U.S. 216 40.58 N 84.52 W
Monroeville, N.J., U.S. 208 39.37 N 75.09 W
Monroeville, Oh., U.S. 214 41.14 N 82.41 W
Monroeville, Pa., U.S. 214 40.26 N 79.47 W
Monroeville Mall ✦[9] 279b 40.26 N 79.48 W
Monrovia, Liber. 150 6.18 N 10.47 W
Monrovia, Ca., U.S. 228 34.08 N 117.59 W
Monrovia, In., U.S. 218 39.34 N 86.28 W
Monrovia Mountain Park ♦ 280 34.10 N 118.10 W
Monrovia Peak ∧ 280 34.13 N 117.58 W
Mons (Bergen), Bel. 50 50.27 N 3.56 E
Mons, Fr. 62 43.41 N 6.43 E
Monschau 56 50.33 N 6.14 E
Monse 112 4.07 S 123.15 E
Monsefú 248 6.52 S 79.52 W
Monselice 64 45.14 N 11.45 E
Monsenhor Hipólito 250 6.59 S 41.07 W
Monsenhor Paulo 256 21.46 S 45.33 W
Monsenhor Tabosa 250 4.47 S 40.04 W
Monserrato 71 39.15 N 9.08 E
Monsey 210 41.06 N 74.04 W
Monsheim, Dtsch. 56 49.38 N 8.12 E
Mönsheim, Dtsch. 56 48.52 N 8.52 E
Møns Klint ≛[4] 41 54.58 N 12.33 E
Monsols 58 46.13 N 4.31 E
Monson, Me., U.S. 188 45.17 N 69.30 W
Monson, Ma., U.S. 207 42.06 N 72.19 W
Monster 52 52.02 N 4.10 E
Mönsterås 26 57.02 N 16.26 E
Monsummano Terme 66 43.52 N 10.49 E
Montà 62 44.48 N 7.57 E
Montabaur 56 50.26 N 7.50 E
Montafon V 58 47.02 N 9.57 E
Montagano 66 41.39 N 14.40 E
Montagnana 64 45.14 N 11.28 E
Montagnareale 70 38.07 N 14.57 E
Montagne d'Ambre, Parque National de la ♦ 157b 12.40 S 49.05 E
Montagnola 66 43.17 N 11.11 E
Montagrier 32 45.16 N 0.29 E
Montagu 158 33.45 S 20.08 E
Montague, P.E., Can. 186 46.10 N 62.39 W
Montague, Ca., U.S. 204 41.43 N 122.31 W
Montague, Ma., U.S. 207 42.32 N 72.32 W
Montague, Mi., U.S. 190 43.25 N 86.21 W
Montague, Tx., U.S. 196 33.40 N 97.43 W
Montague, Isla I 232 31.45 N 114.48 W
Montague City 207 42.35 N 72.35 W
Montague Island I 180 60.00 N 147.30 W
Montague Peak ∧ 180 60.15 N 147.01 W
Montagu Island I 18 58.25 S 26.20 W
Montaigle, Château de ⊥ 50 50.18 N 4.49 E
Montaigu 32 46.59 N 1.19 W
Montaigut-en-Combraille 32 46.11 N 2.48 E
Montainville 261 48.53 N 1.52 E
Montaione 66 43.33 N 10.55 E
Montaj-Taš 86 43.23 N 71.34 E
Montalba 222 31.53 N 95.38 W
Montalbán 34 40.50 N 0.48 W
Montalbancito 286c 10.28 N 66.59 W
Montalbano Elicona 70 38.02 N 15.01 E
Montalbano Ionico 68 40.17 N 16.34 E
Montalcino 66 43.03 N 11.29 E
Montaldo di Cosola 62 44.42 N 9.11 E
Montale 66 43.56 N 11.01 E
Montalegre 34 41.49 N 7.48 W
Montalet-le-Bois 261 49.03 N 1.50 E
Montalieu-Vercieu 62 45.49 N 5.24 E
Montallegro 70 37.23 N 13.21 E
Mont Alto 208 39.50 N 77.33 W
Montalto ∧ 68 38.10 N 15.55 E
Montalto delle Marche 66 42.59 N 13.36 E
Montalto di Castro 66 42.21 N 11.37 E
Montalto Ligure 62 43.56 N 7.51 E
Montalto Uffugo 68 39.25 N 16.10 E
Montalvin Manor 226 37.59 N 122.21 W
Montalvo 228 34.15 N 119.12 W
Montana, Schw. 58 46.18 N 7.29 E
Montana, Ak., U.S. 180 62.05 N 150.04 W
Montana □[3], U.S. 178 47.00 N 110.00 W
Montana □[3], U.S. 202 47.00 N 110.00 W
Montana de Oro State Park ♦ 226 35.15 N 120.50 W
Montana Indian Reserve ✦[4] 182 52.43 N 113.25 W
Montanaro 62 45.14 N 7.51 E
Montánchez 34 39.13 N 6.09 W
Montandon 210 40.58 N 76.51 W
Montanha 255 18.08 S 40.21 W
Montano Antilia 68 40.10 N 15.22 E
Montara 226 37.33 N 122.31 W
Montara Beach ♦ 282 37.33 N 122.31 W
Montara Mountain ∧∧ 282 37.32 N 122.27 W
Montargil 34 39.05 N 8.10 W
Montargis 50 48.00 N 2.45 E
Montataire 50 49.16 N 2.26 E
Montauban 32 44.01 N 1.21 E
Montauban, Lac @ 206 46.52 N 72.10 W
Montauban-les-Mines 206 46.50 N 72.20 W
Montauk 207 41.02 N 71.57 W
Montauk, Lake @ 207 41.04 N 71.55 W
Montauk Point ≻ 207 41.04 N 71.52 W
Montauroux 62 43.37 N 6.46 E
Monta Vista 226 37.19 N 122.03 W
Montazzoli 66 41.57 N 14.26 E
Montbard 50 47.37 N 4.20 E
Montbarrey 58 47.01 N 5.39 E
Montbazon 50 47.17 N 0.43 E
Montbéliard 58 47.31 N 6.48 E
Mont Belvieu 222 29.50 N 94.53 W
Montbenoît 58 46.59 N 6.28 E
Montblanc 34 41.22 N 1.10 E
Mont Blanc, Tunnel du ✦[5] 58 45.50 N 6.53 E
Mont-Bonvillers 56 49.20 N 5.51 E
Montbovon 58 46.29 N 7.03 E
Montbozon 58 47.28 N 6.16 E
Montbrison 62 45.36 N 4.03 E
Montbron 32 45.40 N 0.30 E
Montbronn 56 48.59 N 7.19 E
Montcada i Reixas 266d 41.29 N 2.11 E
Montcalm □[6] 206 46.20 N 74.20 W
Montceau-les-Mines 58 46.40 N 4.22 E
Montcenis 58 46.47 N 4.23 E
Mont Cenis, Col du)(62 45.15 N 6.54 E
Mont Cenis, Lac du @ 62 45.14 N 6.55 E
Montcevelles, Lac @ 186 51.07 N 60.38 W
Montchanin, Fr. 58 46.45 N 4.27 E
Montchanin, De., U.S. 285 39.47 N 75.35 W
Montchauvet 261 48.54 N 1.38 E
Montclair, Ca., U.S. 228 34.06 N 117.41 W
Montclair, N.J., U.S. 210 40.49 N 74.12 W
Montclair State College ✪[2] 276 40.51 N 74.12 W
Mont Clare 285 40.08 N 75.30 W
Montcornet 50 49.41 N 4.01 E
Montdale 210 41.32 N 75.37 W
Mont-de-Marsan 32 43.53 N 0.30 W
Montdidier 50 49.39 N 2.34 E
Mont-Dore 175f 22.16 S 166.34 E
Monte, Castel del ⊥ 68 41.05 N 16.16 E
Monte, Laguna del @, Arg. 252 37.00 S 62.28 W
Monte, Laguna del @, Arg. 258 35.28 S 58.49 W
Montea ∧ 68 39.40 N 15.57 E
Monte Adone, Galleria di ✦[5] 64 44.21 N 11.25 E
Monteagle 194 35.15 N 85.50 W
Monteagudo 248 19.49 S 63.59 W
Monte Albán ⊥ 234 17.02 N 96.45 W
Monte Alegre, Bra. 250 2.01 S 54.04 W
Monte Alegre, Bra. 250 6.04 S 35.20 W
Monte Alegre de Goiás 255 13.14 S 47.10 W
Monte Alegre de Minas 255 18.52 S 48.52 W
Monte Alegre de Sergipe 250 10.02 S 37.33 W
Monte Alegre do Piauí 250 9.46 S 45.18 W
Monte Alegre do Sul 256 22.40 S 46.41 W
Monte Azul 255 15.09 S 42.53 W
Monte Azul Paulista 255 20.55 S 48.38 W
Montebello, P.Q., Can. 206 45.39 N 74.56 W
Montebello, It. 62 45.00 N 9.06 E
Montebello, P.R. 240m 18.22 N 66.31 W
Montebello, Ca., U.S. 228 34.00 N 118.06 W
Montebello Iónico 68 37.59 N 15.45 E
Monte Bello Islands II 162 20.25 S 115.32 E
Montebello Vicentino 64 45.27 N 11.23 E
Montebelluna 64 45.47 N 12.03 E
Monte Belo 256 21.20 S 46.23 W
Montebruno 62 44.31 N 9.15 E
Monte Buey 252 32.55 S 62.27 W
Montecalvo Irpino 68 41.11 N 15.02 E
Monte Campatri 267a 41.48 N 12.44 E
Montecarlo 252 26.34 S 54.47 W
Monte Carlo ✦[8] 62 43.44 N 7.25 E
Monte Carmelo 255 18.43 S 47.29 W
Montecarotto 66 43.31 N 13.04 E
Monte Caseros 252 30.15 S 57.39 W
Montecassiano 66 43.21 N 13.26 E
Montecassino, Abbazia di ✪[1] 66 41.29 N 13.48 E
Montecastrilli 66 42.39 N 12.29 E
Montecatini-Terme 66 43.53 N 10.46 E
Monte Cavallo 66 42.59 N 13.00 E
Montecchio 66 43.51 N 12.46 E
Montecchio Emilia 64 44.42 N 10.27 E
Montecchio Maggiore 64 45.30 N 11.24 E
Montecelio 66 42.01 N 12.44 E
Montechiaro d'Asti 62 45.01 N 8.07 E
Montechiarugolo 64 44.42 N 10.25 E
Monte Chingolo ✦[8] 288 34.45 S 58.20 W
Monteciccardo 66 43.49 N 12.48 E
Montecilfone 66 41.54 N 14.50 E
Montecillos, Cordillera de ∧∧ 236 14.25 N 87.51 W
Montecito 204 34.26 N 119.37 W
Monte Comán 252 34.36 S 67.54 W
Montecorice 68 40.14 N 14.59 E
Montecorvino Pugliano 68 40.41 N 14.57 E
Montecorvino Rovella 68 40.42 N 14.59 E
Montecosaro 66 43.19 N 13.37 E
Monte Creek 182 50.39 N 119.57 W
Montecreto 64 44.14 N 10.41 E
Montecristi, Ec. 246 1.03 S 80.40 W
Monte Cristi, Rep. Dom. 238 19.52 N 71.39 W
Monte Cristo 248 14.43 S 61.14 W
Montecristo, Isola di I 36 42.20 N 10.19 E
Montecuccolo ✪[1] 64 44.19 N 10.50 E
Montedinove 66 42.58 N 13.35 E
Monte di Procida 68 40.48 N 14.03 E
Monte do Carmo 250 10.45 S 48.07 W
Montedoro 70 37.27 N 13.49 E
Monte Escobedo 234 22.18 N 103.35 W
Monte Estoril 266c 38.42 N 9.24 W
Montefalcione 68 40.58 N 14.53 E
Montefalco 66 42.54 N 12.39 E
Montefalcone di Val Fortore 68 41.20 N 15.00 E
Montefano 66 43.25 N 13.26 E
Montefeltro ✦[1] 66 43.50 N 12.15 E
Montefiascone 66 42.32 N 12.02 E
Montefiorino 64 44.22 N 10.37 E
Monteforte d'Alpone 64 45.25 N 11.17 E
Monteforte Irpino 68 40.54 N 14.42 E
Montefrío 34 37.19 N 4.01 W
Montegallo 66 42.50 N 13.19 E
Montegiordano 68 40.02 N 16.32 E
Montegiorgio 66 43.08 N 13.32 E
Monte Giovi, Passo di (Jaufen Pass))(64 46.50 N 11.19 E
Montego Bay 241q 18.28 N 77.55 W
Montegranaro 66 43.14 N 13.38 E
Monte Grande 252 30.06 S 70.31 W
Monte Grimano 66 43.52 N 12.29 E
Montegrotto Terme 64 45.19 N 11.46 E
Montegut 194 29.28 N 90.33 W
Monteiasi 68 40.30 N 17.23 E
Monteiro 250 7.53 S 37.07 W
Monteiro Lobato 256 22.58 S 45.50 W
Monteith, Mount ∧ 182 55.45 N 122.30 W
Montejicar 34 37.34 N 3.30 W
Montejinni 164 16.40 S 131.45 E
Montelavar 266c 38.51 N 9.20 W
Monteleone di Puglia 68 41.10 N 15.15 E
Monteleone di Spoleto 66 42.39 N 12.58 E
Monteleone Rocco Doria 71 40.29 N 8.34 E
Monteleone Sabino 66 42.14 N 12.51 E
Montelepre 70 38.05 N 13.10 E
Montelíbano 246 8.05 N 75.29 W
Montélimar 62 44.34 N 4.45 E
Montelindo ≃ 252 23.56 S 57.12 W
Montella 68 40.51 N 15.01 E
Montellano 34 37.00 N 5.34 W
Montello, Nv., U.S. 204 41.15 N 114.11 W
Montello, Wi., U.S. 190 43.47 N 89.19 W
Monteluco ✪[1] 66 42.43 N 12.45 E
Montelungo 64 44.24 N 9.54 E
Montelupo Fiorentino 66 43.44 N 11.01 E
Montemaggiore Belsito 70 37.51 N 13.46 E
Montemagno 62 44.59 N 8.20 E
Monte Maíz 252 33.12 S 62.36 W
Montemarano 68 40.55 N 15.00 E
Montemarciano 66 43.38 N 13.19 E
Montemayor, Meseta de ∧∧[1] 254 44.20 S 66.10 W
Montemesola 68 40.34 N 17.20 E
Montemiletto 68 41.01 N 14.54 E
Montemilone 68 41.02 N 15.38 E
Montemor 266c 38.49 N 9.12 W
Montemor ∧ 266c 38.49 N 9.12 W
Montemorelos 232 25.12 N 99.49 W
Montemor-o-Novo 34 38.39 N 8.13 W
Montemor-o-Velho 34 40.10 N 8.41 W
Montemuro ∧ 34 40.58 N 7.56 W
Montemurro 68 40.18 N 15.59 E
Montendre 32 45.17 N 0.24 W
Montenegro 252 29.42 S 51.28 W
Montenegro → Crna Gora □[3] 38 42.30 N 19.18 E
Montenero 66 43.30 N 10.21 E
Montenero ∧ 68 39.13 N 16.35 E
Montenero di Bisaccia 66 41.57 N 14.47 E
Monteodorisio 66 42.05 N 14.39 E
Monte Oliveto Maggiore, Abbazia del ✪[1] 66 43.12 N 11.32 E
Monte Pascoal, Parque Nacional de ♦ 255 16.54 S 39.24 W
Monte Patria 252 30.42 S 70.58 W
Montepescali 66 42.53 N 11.05 E
Monte Porzio Catone 267a 41.49 N 12.43 E
Monteprandone 66 42.55 N 13.50 E
Montepuez 154 13.07 S 39.00 E
Montepuez ≃ 154 12.32 S 40.27 E
Montepulciano 66 43.05 N 11.47 E
Monte Quemado 252 25.48 S 62.52 W
Monterado 112 0.45 N 109.08 E
Monterchi 66 43.29 N 12.07 E
Montereale 66 42.31 N 13.15 E
Montereale Valcellina 64 46.10 N 12.39 E
Montereau 50 47.51 N 2.34 E
Montereau-Faut-Yonne 50 48.23 N 2.57 E
Montereau-sur-le-Jard 261 48.35 N 2.40 E
Monterey, Ca., U.S. 226 36.36 N 121.53 W
Monterey, In., U.S. 216 41.09 N 86.28 W
Monterey, Ky., U.S. 218 38.25 N 84.52 W
Monterey, Ma., U.S. 207 42.10 N 73.12 W
Monterey, N.Y., U.S. 210 42.18 N 77.03 W
Monterey, Tn., U.S. 194 36.08 N 85.16 W
Monterey, Va., U.S. 188 38.24 N 79.34 W
Monterey □[6] 226 36.40 N 121.38 W
Monterey Bay c 226 36.45 N 121.55 W
Monterey Park 228 34.03 N 118.07 W
Monterey Peninsula Airport ⊠ 226 36.35 N 121.51 W
Montería 246 8.46 N 75.53 W
Monteriggioni 66 43.23 N 11.13 E
Montero 248 17.20 S 63.15 W
Monte Romano 66 42.16 N 11.54 E
Monteroni d'Arbia 66 43.14 N 11.25 E
Monteroni di Lecce 68 40.19 N 18.06 E
Monteros 252 27.10 S 65.30 W
Monterosso al Mare 62 44.09 N 9.39 E
Monterosso Almo 70 37.05 N 14.46 E
Monterosso Calabro 68 38.43 N 16.17 E
Monterotondo 66 42.03 N 12.37 E
Monterotondo Marittimo 66 43.09 N 10.51 E
Monterrey, Méx. 232 25.40 N 100.19 W
Monterrey, Méx. 234 16.05 N 93.23 W
Monterrico, Hipódromo de ♦ 286d 12.06 S 76.59 W
Monterubbiano 66 43.05 N 13.43 E
Montes Altos 250 5.50 S 47.04 W
Monte San Biagio 66 41.21 N 13.21 E
Monte San Giovanni Campano 66 41.38 N 13.31 E
Montesano, It. 36 40.16 N 15.43 E
Montesano, Wa., U.S. 224 46.58 N 123.36 W
Montesano sulla Marcellana 68 40.16 N 15.42 E
Monte San Savino 66 43.20 N 11.43 E
Monte Santa Maria Tiberina 66 43.26 N 12.09 E
Monte Sant'Angelo 68 41.42 N 15.57 E
Monte Santo 250 10.26 S 39.20 W
Monte Santo de Minas 256 21.12 S 46.59 W
Monte Santu, Capo di ≻ 71 40.05 N 9.44 E
Montesarchio 68 41.04 N 14.38 E
Montescaglioso 68 40.33 N 16.40 E
Montes Claros 255 16.43 S 43.52 W
Montescudaio 66 43.18 N 10.40 E
Montese 64 44.16 N 10.56 E
Monte Sereno 226 37.15 N 122.01 W
Monte Sião 256 22.26 S 46.34 W
Montesilvano Marina 66 42.31 N 14.09 E
Montespaccato ✦[8] 267a 41.54 N 12.23 E
Montespertoli 66 43.38 N 11.04 E
Montespluga 58 46.30 N 9.21 E
Montets, Col des)(58 46.00 N 6.55 E
Monteux 62 44.02 N 5.00 E
Montevago 70 37.42 N 12.58 E
Montevallo 194 33.06 N 86.51 W
Montevarchi 66 43.31 N 11.34 E
Monteverde 68 41.00 N 15.32 E
Monte Verde ≃ 256 21.55 S 43.33 W
Monteverde Nuovo ✦[8] 267a 41.51 N 12.27 E
Montevergine, Santuario di ✪[1] 68 40.55 N 14.45 E
Montevideo, Mn., U.S. 198 44.56 N 95.43 W
Montevideo, Ur. 258 34.53 S 56.11 W
Montevideo □[5] 258 34.50 S 56.12 W
Montevideo, Cerro de ∧[2] 258 33.54 S 56.15 W
Monte Vista 200 37.34 N 106.08 W
Montévrain 261 48.53 N 2.45 E
Montezemolo 62 44.22 N 8.08 E
Montezuma, Ga., U.S. 192 32.18 N 84.01 W
Montezuma, In., U.S. 194 39.47 N 87.22 W
Montezuma, Ia., U.S. 190 41.35 N 92.31 W
Montezuma, Ks., U.S. 198 37.35 N 100.26 W
Montezuma, N.Y., U.S. 210 43.00 N 76.42 W
Montezuma, Oh., U.S. 216 40.29 N 84.33 W
Montezuma Castle National Monument ♦ 200 34.38 N 110.49 W
Montezuma Creek ≃ 200 37.17 N 109.20 W
Montezuma Hills ∧∧[2] 282 38.07 N 121.51 W
Montezuma Slough ≃ 226 38.04 N 121.52 W
Montfaucon, Fr. 56 49.17 N 5.08 E
Montfaucon, Fr. 62 45.10 N 4.18 E
Montfaucon, Schw. 58 47.17 N 7.03 E
Montfermeil 261 48.54 N 2.34 E
Montfleur 58 46.19 N 5.26 E
Montfort, Fr. 32 48.08 N 1.58 W
Montfort, Wi., U.S. 190 42.58 N 90.25 W
Montfort-l'Amaury 50 48.47 N 1.49 E
Montfort-le-Rotrou 50 48.03 N 0.25 E
Montfort-sur-Risle 50 49.18 N 0.40 E
Montfrin 62 43.53 N 4.36 E
Montgé 261 49.02 N 2.45 E
Montgenèvre 62 44.56 N 6.43 E
Montgenèvre, Col de)(62 44.56 N 6.44 E
Montgeron 261 48.42 N 2.27 E
Montgeroult 261 49.05 N 2.00 E
Montgesoye 58 47.05 N 6.12 E
Montgomery, Wales, U.K. 42 52.33 N 3.03 W
Montgomery, Al., U.S. 194 32.23 N 86.18 W
Montgomery, Il., U.S. 216 41.43 N 88.20 W
Montgomery, La., U.S. 194 31.40 N 92.53 W
Montgomery, Mi., U.S. 216 41.46 N 84.48 W
Montgomery, Mn., U.S. 190 44.26 N 93.34 W
Montgomery, N.Y., U.S. 210 41.31 N 74.14 W
Montgomery, Oh., U.S. 218 39.13 N 84.21 W
Montgomery, Pa., U.S. 210 41.10 N 76.52 W
Montgomery, Tx., U.S. 222 30.23 N 95.42 W
Montgomery, W.V., U.S. 188 38.11 N 81.19 W
Montgomery □[6], Il., U.S. 219 39.09 N 89.29 W
Montgomery □[6], Md., U.S. 208 39.05 N 77.09 W
Montgomery □[6], Mo., U.S. 219 38.57 N 91.27 W
Montgomery □[6], N.Y., U.S. 210 42.57 N 74.22 W
Montgomery □[6], Oh., U.S. 218 39.45 N 84.15 W
Montgomery □[6], Pa., U.S. 208 40.07 N 75.21 W
Montgomery □[6], Tx., U.S. 222 30.18 N 95.30 W
Montgomery City 219 38.58 N 91.30 W
Montgomery Dam ✦[6] 214 40.39 N 80.24 W
Montgomery Knolls 284b 39.14 N 76.48 W
Montgomery Mall ✦[9] 284c 39.01 N 77.09 W
Montgomery → Sāhīwāl 123 30.40 N 73.06 E
Montgomery Square 284c 39.04 N 77.09 W
Montgomeryville 285 40.15 N 75.15 W
Montgomeryville Airport ⊠ 285 40.15 N 75.14 W
Montguyon 32 45.13 N 0.11 W
Monthermé 56 49.53 N 4.44 E
Monthey 58 46.15 N 6.57 E
Monthois 56 49.19 N 4.43 E
Monthureux-sur-Saône 58 48.02 N 5.58 E
Monthyon 261 49.00 N 2.50 E
Monti 71 40.49 N 9.19 E
Monticelli d'Ongina 64 45.05 N 9.56 E
Monticello, Ar., U.S. 194 33.37 N 91.47 W
Monticello, Fl., U.S. 192 30.32 N 83.52 W
Monticello, Ga., U.S. 192 33.18 N 83.41 W
Monticello, Il., U.S. 194 40.01 N 88.34 W
Monticello, In., U.S. 216 40.44 N 86.45 W
Monticello, Ia., U.S. 190 42.14 N 91.11 W
Monticello, Ky., U.S. 194 36.49 N 84.50 W
Monticello, Mn., U.S. 190 45.18 N 93.47 W
Monticello, Ms., U.S. 194 31.33 N 90.06 W
Monticello, Mo., U.S. 219 40.07 N 91.42 W
Monticello, N.Y., U.S. 210 41.39 N 74.41 W
Monticello, Ut,. U.S. 200 37.52 N 109.20 W
Monticello, Wi., U.S. 190 42.44 N 89.35 W
Monticello ⊥ 188 38.00 N 78.30 W
Monticello Conte Otto 64 45.35 N 11.35 E
Monticello Dam ✦[6] 226 38.30 N 122.07 W
Monticello Woods 284c 38.47 N 77.10 W
Montichiari 64 45.25 N 10.23 E
Monticiano 66 43.08 N 11.11 E
Montiel, Campo de ≚ 34 38.46 N 2.44 W
Montier-en-Der 58 48.29 N 4.46 E
Montieri 66 43.08 N 11.01 E
Montieri, Poggio di ∧ 66 43.08 N 11.00 E
Montiers-sur-Saulx 58 48.32 N 5.16 E
Montignac 32 45.04 N 1.10 E
Montigny 58 48.31 N 6.48 E
Montigny-Devant-Sassey 56 49.26 N 5.09 E
Montigny-le-Bretonneux 261 48.46 N 2.02 E
Montigny-le-Roi 58 48.00 N 5.30 E
Montigny-lès-Cormeilles 261 48.59 N 2.12 E
Montigny-lès-Metz 56 49.06 N 6.09 E
Montigny-sur-Aube 58 47.57 N 4.46 E
Montijo, Esp. 34 38.55 N 6.37 W
Montijo, Pan. 236 7.59 N 81.03 W
Montijo, Port. 34 38.42 N 8.58 W
Montijo, Aeroporto ⊠ 266c 38.42 N 9.02 W
Montijo, Golfo de c 246 7.40 N 81.07 W
Montilla 34 37.35 N 4.38 W
Montividiu 255 17.24 S 51.14 W
Montivilliers 50 49.33 N 0.12 E
Montjay-la-Tour 261 48.55 N 2.40 E
Montjoie, Lac @, P.Q., Can. 206 46.17 N 75.08 W
Montjoie, Lac @, P.Q., Can. 206 45.25 N 72.06 W
Mont-Joli 186 48.35 N 68.11 W
Montjovet 62 45.43 N 7.40 E
Montjuich, Estadio de ♦ 266d 41.22 N 2.09 E
Montjuich, Faro de ✦[5] 266d 41.21 N 2.11 E
Montjuich, Parque de ♦ 266d 41.21 N 2.09 E
Mont-Laurier 176 46.33 N 75.30 W
Montlebon 58 47.02 N 6.37 E
Montlhéry 50 48.38 N 2.16 E
Montlhéry, Tour de ✪ 261 48.38 N 2.16 E
Montlhéry, Tour de ♦ 261 48.38 N 2.16 E
Montlignon 261 49.01 N 2.17 E
Montlouet 261 48.31 N 1.43 E
Mont-Louis 32 42.31 N 2.07 E
Montlouis-sur-Loire 50 47.23 N 0.50 E
Montluçon 32 46.21 N 2.36 E
Montluel 62 45.51 N 5.03 E
Montmagny, P.Q., Can. 186 46.59 N 70.33 W
Montmagny, Fr. 261 48.58 N 2.21 E
Montmajour, Abbaye de ✪[1] 62 43.43 N 4.40 E
Montmartre ✦[8] 261 48.53 N 2.21 E
Montmédy 56 49.31 N 5.22 E
Montmélian 62 45.30 N 6.04 E
Montmeló 266d 41.33 N 2.15 E
Montmerle-sur-Saône 58 46.05 N 4.46 E
Montmin 62 45.48 N 6.16 E
Montmirail, Fr. 50 48.52 N 3.32 E
Montmirail, Fr. 50 48.06 N 0.48 E
Montmirey-le-Château 58 47.13 N 5.32 E
Montmoreau-Saint-Cybard 32 45.24 N 0.08 E
Montmorenci 216 40.28 N 87.02 W
Montmorency, Austl. 274b 37.43 S 145.07 E
Montmorency, Fr. 261 49.00 N 2.20 E
Montmorency ≃ 186 46.53 N 71.07 W
Montmorency, Forêt de ♦ 261 49.02 N 2.16 E
Montmorency → Beauport 186 46.52 N 71.11 W
Montmorillon 32 46.26 N 0.52 E
Montmort 50 48.55 N 3.49 E
Monto 166 24.52 S 151.07 E
Montodine 62 45.17 N 9.42 E
Montoggio 62 44.31 N 9.03 E
Montoire-sur-le-Loir 50 47.45 N 0.52 E
Montone 66 43.22 N 12.20 E
Montone ≃, It. 64 44.24 N 12.14 E
Montone ≃, It. 66 43.22 N 12.20 E
Montopoli in Val d'Arno 66 43.40 N 10.45 E
Mont Orford, Parc du ♦ 206 45.22 N 72.05 W
Montorio al Vomano 66 42.35 N 13.38 E
Montorio nei Frentani 66 41.46 N 14.55 E
Montoro 34 38.01 N 4.23 W
Mont'Orso, Galleria di ✦[5] 66 41.20 N 13.15 E
Montour □[6] 210 40.58 N 76.37 W
Montour Falls 210 42.20 N 76.50 W
Montour Run ≃, Pa., U.S. 279b 40.36 N 79.57 W
Montour Run ≃, Pa., U.S. 279b 40.31 N 80.08 W
Montoursville 210 41.15 N 76.55 W
Mont Park 274b 37.43 S 145.04 E
Montparnasse, Gare ✦[5] 261 48.51 N 2.19 E
Mont Peko, Parc National du ♦ 150 7.00 N 7.15 W
Montpelier, Jam. 241q 18.22 N 77.56 W
Montpelier, Id., U.S. 202 42.19 N 111.17 W
Montpelier, In., U.S. 216 40.33 N 85.16 W
Montpelier, Md., U.S. 284c 39.04 N 76.51 W
Montpelier, Ms., U.S. 194 33.43 N 88.56 W
Montpelier, Oh., U.S. 216 41.35 N 84.36 W
Montpelier, Vt., U.S. 188 44.15 N 72.34 W
Montpellier 62 43.36 N 3.53 E
Montpellier-Fréjorgues, Aéroport de ⊠ 62 43.33 N 4.00 E
Montpezat-sous-Bauzon 62 44.43 N 4.12 E
Mont-Pichet 261 48.53 N 2.54 E
Montpon-Ménesterol 32 45.00 N 0.10 E
Montpont-en-Bresse 58 46.33 N 5.09 E
Montréal, P.Q., Can. 206 45.31 N 73.34 W
Montréal, P.Q., Can. 275a 45.31 N 73.34 W
Montréal, Fr. 50 47.32 N 4.02 E
Montreal, Wi., U.S. 190 46.25 N 90.14 W
Montreal ≃, On., Can. 190 47.14 N 84.39 W
Montreal ≃, On., Can. 190 47.08 N 79.27 W
Montreal ≃, Sk., Can. 184 55.06 N 105.19 W
Montreal ≃, U.S. 190 46.44 N 90.25 W
Montréal, Base des Forces Canadiennes ■ 275a 45.31 N 73.25 W
Montréal, Île de I 206 45.30 N 73.40 W
Montréal, Université de ✪[2] 275a 45.30 N 73.37 W
Montréal-Est 206 45.38 N 73.31 W
Montreal International Airport ⊠ 206 45.28 N 73.45 W
Montreal Lake 184 54.03 N 105.46 W
Montreal Lake @ 184 54.20 N 105.40 W
Montreal Lake Indian Reserve ✦[4] 184 54.00 N 105.45 W
Montréal-Nord 206 45.36 N 73.38 W
Montréal-Quest 275a 45.27 N 73.39 W
Montreal Water Works Aqueduct ≊[1] 275a 45.26 N 73.36 W
Montrésor 50 47.09 N 1.12 E
Montresta 71 40.22 N 8.30 E
Montret 58 46.41 N 5.07 E
Montreuil 261 48.52 N 2.26 E
Montreuil-Bellay 32 47.08 N 0.09 W
Montreuil-sous-Bois 50 48.52 N 2.26 E
Montreuil-sur-Mer 50 50.28 N 1.46 E
Montreux 58 46.26 N 6.55 E
Montrevel-en-Bresse 58 46.20 N 5.08 E
Montrichard 50 47.21 N 1.11 E
Montriond 58 46.12 N 6.41 E
Mont-Rolland 206 45.57 N 74.07 W
Montrond-les-Bains 62 45.38 N 4.14 E
Montrose, Austl. 274b 37.49 S 145.21 E
Montrose, Scot., U.K. 46 56.43 N 2.29 W
Montrose, Ca., U.S. 228 34.12 N 118.13 W
Montrose, Co., U.S. 200 38.28 N 107.52 W
Montrose, Ia., U.S. 190 40.31 N 91.24 W
Montrose, Mi., U.S. 190 43.10 N 83.53 W
Montrose, N.Y., U.S. 210 41.15 N 73.56 W
Montrose, Oh., U.S. 214 41.08 N 81.37 W
Montrose, Pa., U.S. 210 41.50 N 75.52 W
Montrose, S.D., U.S. 198 43.41 N 97.11 W
Montrose Harbor c 278 41.58 N 87.38 W
Montrose Hill 279b 40.30 N 79.51 W
Montross 208 38.05 N 76.49 W
Montrouge 261 48.49 N 2.19 E
Mont-Royal 206 45.31 N 73.39 W
Mont Royal, Parc ♦ 275a 45.31 N 73.35 W
Mont Royal Tunnel ✦[5] 275a 45.31 N 73.38 W
Montry 261 48.53 N 2.50 E
Monts 50 47.17 N 0.37 E
Monts, Pointe des ≻ 186 49.20 N 67.23 W
Mont-Saint-Aignan 50 49.28 N 1.05 E
Mont-Sainte-Anne, Parc du ♦ 186 47.08 N 70.55 W
Mont-Saint-Hilaire 206 45.34 N 73.11 W
Mont-Saint-Martin 56 49.32 N 5.47 E
Mont-Saint-Michel → Le Mont-Saint-Michel ✪[1] 32 48.38 N 1.32 W
Mont-Saint-Vincent 58 46.38 N 4.29 E
Montsauche 50 47.13 N 4.01 E
Montsec 56 48.53 N 5.43 E
Montserrat □[2], N.A. 230 16.45 N 62.12 W
Montserrat □[2], N.A. 238 16.45 N 62.12 W
Montserrat, Monasterio de ✪[1] 34 41.36 N 1.49 E
Montsoult 261 49.04 N 2.19 E
Montsûrs 28 48.08 N 0.33 W
Mont-sur-Vaudrey 58 46.58 N 5.36 E
Mont-Tremblant, Parc provincial du ♦ 206 46.42 N 74.20 W
Montuenga 34 41.03 N 4.37 W
Montvale, N.J., U.S. 276 41.02 N 74.01 W
Montvale, Va., U.S. 192 37.23 N 79.43 W
Montverde 220 28.36 N 81.41 W
Montville, Ct., U.S. 207 41.27 N 72.08 W
Montville, N.J., U.S. 276 40.54 N 74.23 W
Montville, Oh., U.S. 214 41.36 N 81.03 W
Montville Airpark ⊠ 276 40.56 N 74.20 W
Monument, S. Afr. 273d 26.06 S 27.43 E
Monument, Or., U.S. 202 44.49 N 119.25 W
Monument, Pa., U.S. 214 41.07 N 77.42 W
Monument Beach 207 41.43 N 70.36 W
Monument Draw V, U.S. 196 32.27 N 102.20 W
Monument Draw V, Tx., U.S. 196 30.51 N 102.33 W
Monument Hill State Historic Site ⊥ 222 29.53 N 96.54 W

≃ River	Fluß	Río	Rivière	Rio
≊ Canal	Kanal	Canal	Canal	Canal
ʟ Waterfall, Rapids	Wasserfall, Stromschnellen	Cascada, Rápidos	Chute d'eau, Rapides	Cascata, Rápidos
)(Strait	Meeresstraße	Estrecho	Détroit	Estreito
c Bay, Gulf	Bucht, Golf	Bahía, Golfo	Baie, Golfe	Baía, Golfo
@ Lake, Lakes	See, Seen	Lago, Lagos	Lac, Lacs	Lago, Lagos
≡ Swamp	Sumpf	Pantano	Marais	Pântano
☐ Ice Features, Glacier	Eis- und Gletscherformen	Accidentes Glaciales	Formes glaciaires	Acidentes glaciares
≊ Other Hydrographic Features	Andere Hydrographische Objekte	Otros Elementos Hidrográficos	Autres données hydrographiques	Outros acidentes hidrográficos

✧ Submarine Features	Untermeerische Objekte	Accidentes Submarinos	Formes de relief sous-marin	Acidentes submarinos
□ Political Unit	Politische Einheit	Unidad Politica	Entité politique	Unidade política
✪ Cultural Institution	Kulturelle Institution	Institución Cultural	Institution culturelle	Institução cultural
⊥ Historical Site	Historische Stätte	Sitio Histórico	Site historique	Sitio histórico
♦ Recreational Site	Erholungs- und Ferienort	Sitio de Recreo	Centre de loisirs	Area de Lazer
⊠ Airport	Flughafen	Aeropuerto	Aéroport	Aeroporto
■ Military Installation	Militäranlage	Instalación Militar	Installation militaire	Instalação militar
✦ Miscellaneous	Verschiedenes	Misceláneo	Divers	Diversos

Name	Page	Lat.°′	Long.°′
Monumento	256	22.44 S	43.51 W
Monument Peak ∧, Co., U.S.	200	39.43 N	107.55 W
Monument Peak ∧, Id., U.S.	202	42.07 N	114.14 W
Monument Valley V	200	37.05 N	110.20 W
Monundilla, Mount ∧	170	32.45 S	150.29 E
Monveda	152	2.57 N	21.27 E
Monymusk	46	57.13 N	2.31 W
Monyo	110	17.59 N	95.30 E
Monywa	110	22.05 N	95.08 E
Monza	62	45.35 N	9.16 E
Monze	154	16.16 S	27.28 E
Monzen	92	37.17 N	136.46 E
Monzie	46	56.24 N	3.48 W
Monzón, Esp.	34	41.55 N	0.12 E
Monzón, Perú	248	9.10 S	76.23 W
Moóca ⊸[8]	287b	23.33 S	46.35 W
Moóca, Ribeirão da ≃	287b	23.36 S	46.35 W
Moodie Island I	176	64.37 N	65.30 W
Moodus	207	41.30 N	72.27 W
Moodus Reservoir ⊜[1]	207	41.30 N	72.24 W
Moody	222	31.18 N	97.21 W
Moody Air Force Base ■	192	30.59 N	83.11 W
Moody Wood Dale Airport ⊠	278	41.59 N	87.58 W
Mooers	206	44.58 N	73.35 W
Mooi ≃, S. Afr.	158	28.45 S	30.34 E
Mooi ≃, S. Afr.	158	26.53 S	26.56 E
Mooirivier	158	29.13 S	29.50 E
Mook	52	51.45 N	5.54 E
Mookane	156	24.59 S	24.33 E
Mooketsi	156	23.35 S	30.05 E
Moolawatana	166	29.55 S	139.43 E
Moolman	158	27.10 S	30.53 E
Mooloogool	162	26.06 S	119.05 E
Moon	214	40.31 N	80.14 W
Moon ≃	212	45.08 N	79.59 W
Moon, Mountains of the → Ruwenzori Range ⋀	154	0.23 N	29.54 E
Moonachie	276	40.50 N	74.02 W
Moonachie Creek ≃	276	40.48 N	74.03 W
Moonah Creek ≃	166	22.03 S	138.33 E
Moon Crest	279b	40.32 N	80.11 W
Moondarra Reservoir ⊜[1]	169	38.04 S	146.22 E
Moonee Valley Racecourse ♦	274b	37.46 S	144.56 E
Moonie	166	27.43 S	150.22 E
Moonie ≃	166	29.19 S	148.43 E
Moon Island I, On., Can.	212	45.09 N	80.01 W
Moon Island I, Ma., U.S.	283	42.18 N	71.00 W
Moon Run	214	40.27 N	80.06 W
Moonta	168b	34.04 S	137.35 E
Moor, Kepulauan II	164	2.57 S	135.45 E
Moora	162	30.39 S	116.00 E
Moorabbin	169	37.56 S	145.02 E
Moorabbin Airport ⊠	274b	37.59 S	145.09 E
Mooraberree	166	25.14 S	140.59 E
Moorabool ≃	169	38.09 S	144.19 E
Moorarie	162	25.56 S	117.35 E
Moorburg	52	53.17 N	7.53 E
Moorcroft	198	44.15 N	104.56 W
Moordorf	52	53.28 N	7.23 E
Moordrecht	52	51.59 N	4.40 E
Moore, Austl.	171a	26.53 S	152.18 E
Moore, Eng., U.K.	262	53.21 N	2.38 W
Moore, Id., U.S.	202	43.44 N	113.21 W
Moore, Mt., U.S.	202	46.58 N	109.41 W
Moore, Ok., U.S.	196	35.20 N	97.29 W
Moore, Tx., U.S.	196	29.03 N	99.01 W
Moore ≃	162	31.22 S	115.29 E
Moore, Lake ⊜	162	29.50 S	117.35 E
Moorea I	174s	17.32 S	149.50 W
Moorebank	274a	33.56 S	150.56 E
Moore Creek ≃	212	45.29 N	77.58 W
Moorefield, Ky., U.S.	218	38.16 N	83.55 W
Moorefield, Oh., U.S.	214	40.12 N	81.10 W
Moorefield, W.V., U.S.	188	39.03 N	78.58 W
Moore Haven	220	26.49 N	81.05 W
Moore Haven Lock ⊸[5]	220	26.51 N	81.05 W
Moore Lake ⊜, On., Can.	212	45.26 N	78.01 W
Moore Lake ⊜, On., Can.	212	44.48 N	78.48 W
Moore Lake ⊜, Mi., U.S.	281	42.37 N	83.36 W
Mooreland, In., U.S.	218	39.59 N	85.15 W
Mooreland, Ok., U.S.	196	36.26 N	99.12 W
Moore Point ≻	275b	43.48 N	79.03 W
Moore Reservoir ⊜[1]	188	44.25 N	71.50 W
Mooresburg	210	40.59 N	76.43 W
Moores Creek National Battlefield ♦	192	34.24 N	78.08 W
Moores Hill	218	39.06 N	85.05 W
Moore Station	222	32.11 N	95.35 W
Moorestown	208	39.58 N	74.56 W
Moorestown Mall ⊸[9]	285	39.56 N	74.58 W
Mooresville, In., U.S.	218	39.36 N	86.22 W
Mooresville, N.C., U.S.	192	35.35 N	80.48 W
Mooreville	281	42.06 N	83.44 W
Moorfoot Hills ⋀[2]	46	55.45 N	3.02 W
Moorhead, Mn., U.S.	198	46.52 N	96.46 W
Moorhead, Ms., U.S.	194	33.27 N	90.30 W
Mooring	222	30.41 N	96.33 W
Mooringsport	194	32.41 N	93.57 W
Moormerland	52	53.20 N	7.27 E
Moornanyah Lake ⊜	166	33.02 S	143.58 E
Moorooka	171a	27.32 S	153.02 E
Mooroolbark	274b	37.47 S	145.19 E
Moorpark	228	34.17 N	118.53 W
Moorreesburg	158	33.08 S	18.40 E
Moorrege	52	53.40 N	9.39 E
Moorriem	52	53.15 N	8.19 E
Moorsel	50	50.57 N	4.06 E
Moorside	262	53.34 N	2.04 W
Moorslede	50	50.53 N	3.04 E
Moosach ⊸[8]	60	48.11 N	11.31 E
Moosbrunn	264b	48.01 N	16.28 E
Moosburg, Dtsch.	30	48.29 N	11.57 E
Moosburg, Öst.	61	46.39 N	14.10 E
Moosburg an der Isar	60	48.29 N	11.57 E
Moose ≃, Me., U.S.	188	45.40 N	69.42 W
Moose ≃, N.Y., U.S.	212	43.37 N	75.22 W
Moose Creek	206	45.15 N	74.58 W
Moose Creek ≃	206	45.23 N	75.04 W
Moosehead Lake ⊜	188	45.40 N	69.40 W
Mooseheart	216	41.49 N	88.20 W
Moose Heights	182	53.05 N	122.30 W
Moose Hill ∧[2]	283	42.07 N	71.13 W
Moose Island I	184	51.42 N	97.10 W
Moose Jaw	184	50.23 N	105.32 W
Moose Jaw ≃	184	50.34 N	105.17 W
Moose Lake, Mb., Can.	184	53.43 N	100.20 W
Moose Lake, Mn., U.S.	190	46.27 N	92.45 W
Moose Lake ⊜, Ab., Can.	182	54.15 N	110.55 W
Moose Lake ⊜, Mb., Can.	184	53.55 N	99.45 W
Moose Lake ⊜, On., Can.	212	45.09 N	78.28 W
Mooselookmeguntic Lake ⊜	188	44.53 N	70.48 W
Moose Mountain ∧	184	49.45 N	102.37 W
Moose Mountain Creek ≃	184	49.12 N	102.10 W
Moose Mountain Provincial Park ♦	184	49.48 N	102.25 W
Moose Pass	180	60.29 N	149.22 W
Moos → Moso	64	46.41 N	12.23 E
Moos → Moso in Passiria	64	46.50 N	11.10 E
Moosomin	184	50.07 N	101.40 W
Moosomin Indian Reserve ⊸[4]	184	53.06 N	108.14 W
Moosonee	176	51.17 N	80.39 W
Moosup	207	41.42 N	71.52 W
Mooti	144	0.35 N	41.56 E
Moots Creek ≃	216	40.32 N	86.47 W
Mootwingee National Park ♦	166	31.07 S	142.23 E
Mopane	156	22.37 S	29.52 E
Mopeia Velha	156	17.59 S	35.44 E
Mopipi	156	21.07 S	24.55 E
Mopo	100	33.07 N	113.02 E
Moppo → Mokp'o	98	34.48 N	126.22 E
Mopti	150	14.30 N	4.12 W
Mopti □[4]	150	14.40 N	4.15 W
Moqokorei	144	4.04 N	46.08 E
Moquegua	248	17.12 S	70.56 W
Moquegua □[5]	248	16.50 S	70.55 W
Mór	30	47.23 N	18.12 E
Mor ≃	126	24.01 N	88.03 E
Mòr, Glen V	46	57.10 N	4.40 W
Mor, Sgurr ∧	46	57.42 N	5.03 W
Mora, Cam.	146	11.03 N	14.09 E
Mora, Esp.	34	39.41 N	3.46 W
Mora, India	272c	18.54 N	72.56 E
Mora, Port.	34	38.56 N	8.10 W
Mora, Sve.	26	61.00 N	14.33 E
Mora, Mn., U.S.	190	45.52 N	93.17 W
Mora, N.M., U.S.	200	35.58 N	105.19 W
Mora ≃	196	35.44 N	104.23 W
Mora, Arroyo de la ≃	196	34.05 N	104.18 W
Moraby	40	60.23 N	15.35 E
Morača, Manastir ⊍[1]	38	42.44 N	19.20 E
Morada	226	38.01 N	121.15 W
Morādābād	124	28.50 N	78.47 E
Morada Nova	250	5.07 S	38.23 W
Morada Nova de Minas	255	18.37 S	45.22 W
Moradel, Montaña de ∧	236	15.06 N	86.16 W
Mora de Rubielos	34	40.15 N	0.45 W
Moraduccio	66	44.10 N	11.29 E
Morafenobe	157b	17.49 S	44.55 E
Morąg	30	53.56 N	19.56 E
Moraga	226	37.50 N	122.08 W
Mórahalom	30	46.13 N	19.54 E
Moraine	218	39.42 N	84.13 W
Moraine Hills State Park ♦	216	42.18 N	88.15 W
Moraine State Park ♦	214	40.56 N	80.07 W
Morainvilliers	261	48.56 N	1.56 E
Morākhi ≃	126	24.01 N	88.10 E
Morākhi Reservoir ⊜[1]	126	24.10 N	87.15 E
Mor'akovskij Zaton	86	56.45 N	84.41 E
Moral de Calatrava	34	38.50 N	3.35 W
Moraleda, Canal ⊔	254	44.30 S	73.30 W
Morales, Guat.	236	15.29 N	88.49 W
Morales, Perú	248	6.28 S	76.28 W
Morales, Arroyo ≃	258	34.48 S	58.36 W
Morales, Laguna ⊂	234	23.35 N	97.47 W
Moramanga	157b	18.56 S	48.12 E
Moran, Ks., U.S.	198	37.54 N	95.10 W
Moran, Mi., U.S.	190	45.59 N	84.49 W
Moran, Tx., U.S.	196	32.33 N	99.10 W
Moran ≃	164	15.16 S	125.33 E
Moranbah	166	22.00 S	148.02 E
Morangis	261	48.42 N	2.20 E
Morangup Hill ∧[2]	168a	31.41 S	116.19 E
Morann	214	40.48 N	78.21 W
Morano Calabro	68	39.50 N	16.08 E
Morano sul Po	62	45.10 N	8.22 E
Moran State Park ♦	224	48.41 N	122.52 W
Morant Bay	241q	17.53 N	76.25 W
Morant Cays II	238	17.24 N	75.59 W
Morant Point ≻	241q	17.55 N	76.10 W
Morar, Loch ⊜	46	56.57 N	5.43 W
Mörarp	41	56.04 N	12.52 E
Morasverdes	34	40.36 N	6.16 W
Morat, Lac de (Murtensee) ⊜	58	46.55 N	7.05 E
Moratalla	34	38.12 N	1.53 W
Morattico	208	37.47 N	76.37 W
Moratuwa	122	6.46 N	79.53 E
Morava □[9]	30	49.30 N	17.00 E
Morava (March) ≃	30	48.10 N	16.59 E
Morāveh Tappeh	128	37.55 N	55.57 E
Moravia, C.R.	236	9.51 N	83.26 W
Moravia, Ia., U.S.	190	40.53 N	92.48 W
Moravia, N.Y., U.S.	210	42.42 N	76.25 W
Moravia → Morava □[9]	30	49.20 N	17.00 E
Moravian Indian Reserve ⊸[4]	214	42.34 N	81.53 W
Moravská Dyje ≃	61	48.51 N	15.30 E
Moravská Ostrava → Ostrava	30	49.50 N	18.17 E
Moravská Třebová	30	49.45 N	16.40 E
Moravské Budějovice	61	49.03 N	15.49 E
Moravský Krumlov	61	49.03 N	16.19 E
Morawa	162	29.13 S	116.00 E
Morawhanna	246	8.16 N	59.45 W
Moraya	248	21.45 S	65.32 W
Morayfield	171a	27.07 S	152.57 E
Moray Firth ⊂[1]	46	57.50 N	3.30 W
Morazán, Guat.	236	14.56 N	90.09 W
Morazán, Hond.	236	15.17 N	87.34 W
Morbach	56	49.48 N	7.07 E
Morbegno	36	46.08 N	9.34 E
Morbi	120	22.49 N	70.50 E
Morbihan □[5]	32	47.55 N	2.50 W
Mörbisch am See	61	47.45 N	16.40 E
Morbras ≃	261	48.47 N	2.29 E
Mörbylånga	26	56.31 N	16.23 E
Morcenx	32	44.02 N	0.55 W
Morciano di Romagna	66	43.55 N	12.38 E
Morcone	68	41.20 N	14.40 E
Morcote	58	45.56 N	8.55 E
Morcy	80	51.18 N	47.51 E
Morden	184	49.11 N	98.05 W
Morden ⊸[8]	260	51.24 N	0.12 W
Mordialloc	169	38.00 S	145.05 E
Mordino	24	61.21 N	51.52 E
Mordoğan	130	38.30 N	26.37 E
Mordovija □[3]	80	54.30 N	44.00 E
Mordovo, Ross.	80	51.07 N	45.48 E
Mordovo, Ross.	80	52.05 N	40.46 E
Mordovo-Adel'akovo	80	53.47 N	51.36 E
Mordovskij Buguruslan	80	53.48 N	52.31 E
Mordovskij Zapovednik ⊸[4]	80	54.48 N	43.20 E
Mordves	82	54.34 N	38.13 E
Mordvinia → Mordovija □[3]	80	54.30 N	44.00 E
Mordy	30	52.13 N	22.31 E
More, Ben ∧, Scot., U.K.	46	56.21 N	4.35 W
More, Ben ∧, Scot., U.K.	46	56.25 N	6.01 W
More, Loch ⊜	46	58.17 N	4.52 W
More Assynt, Ben ∧	46	58.08 N	4.53 W
Moreau ≃, Mo., U.S.	219	38.33 N	92.06 W
Moreau ≃, S.D., U.S.	198	45.18 N	100.43 W
Moreau, North Fork ≃	198	45.09 N	102.50 W
Moreau, South Fork ≃	198	45.09 N	102.50 W
Moreau Peak ∧	198	45.21 N	103.43 W
Moreauville	194	31.02 N	91.58 W
Morec	80	51.03 N	44.03 E
Morecambe	44	54.04 N	2.53 W
Morecambe Bay ⊂	44	54.07 N	3.00 W
Moree, Austl.	166	29.28 S	149.51 E
Morée, Fr.	50	47.54 N	1.14 E
Morehead, Pap. N. Gui.	164	8.40 S	141.35 E
Morehead, Ky., U.S.	218	38.11 N	83.25 W
Morehead ≃	164	9.00 S	141.25 E
Morehead City	192	34.43 N	76.43 W
Morehouse	194	36.50 N	89.41 W
Moreira César	256	22.55 S	45.22 W
Moreland, Austl.	274b	37.45 S	144.58 E
Moreland, Ga., U.S.	192	33.17 N	84.46 W
Moreland, Ky., U.S.	194	37.30 N	84.48 W
Moreland Hills	279a	41.27 N	81.29 W
Morelia	234	19.42 N	101.07 W
Morell	186	46.25 N	62.42 W
Morella, Austl.	166	22.59 S	143.52 E
Morella, Esp.	34	40.37 N	0.06 W
Morello ≃	70	37.29 N	14.08 E
Morelos, Méx.	196	28.25 N	100.53 W
Morelos, Méx.	232	26.42 N	107.40 W
Morelos, Méx.	234	22.53 N	102.37 W
Morelos □[3]	234	18.45 N	99.00 W
Moremi Wildlife Reserve ⊸[4]	156	19.10 S	23.15 E
Morena	124	26.30 N	78.09 E
Morena, Sierra ∧	282	37.25 N	122.18 W
Morena, Sierra ⋀	34	38.00 N	5.00 W
Morenci, Az., U.S.	200	33.04 N	109.21 W
Morenci, Mi., U.S.	216	41.43 N	84.13 W
Moreni	38	45.00 N	25.39 E
Moreno, Arg.	258	34.39 S	58.48 W
Moreno, Ca., U.S.	228	33.55 N	117.09 W
Moreno □[5]	288	34.36 S	58.48 W
Moreno, Bahía ⊂	252	23.35 S	70.30 W
Møre og Romsdal □[6]	26	62.40 N	7.50 E
Mores	71	40.33 N	8.50 E
Moresby Island I, B.C., Can.	182	52.50 N	131.55 W
Moresby Island I, B.C., Can.	224	48.40 N	123.20 W
Mores Island I	238	26.18 N	77.33 W
Moresnet	56	50.43 N	5.59 E
Morestel	62	45.40 N	5.28 E
Moreton, Austl.	164	12.28 S	142.38 E
Moreton, Eng., U.K.	44	53.24 N	3.07 W
Moreton, Eng., U.K.	260	51.44 N	0.14 E
Moreton, Cape ≻	171a	27.02 S	153.28 E
Moreton Bay ⊂	171a	27.20 S	153.15 E
Moretonhampstead	42	50.40 N	3.45 W
Moreton-in-Marsh	42	51.59 N	1.42 W
Moreton Island I	171a	27.10 S	153.25 E
Moreton Island National Park ♦	171a	27.09 S	153.25 E
Moret-sur-Loing	50	48.22 N	2.49 E
Moretta	62	44.46 N	7.32 E
Moreuil	50	49.46 N	2.29 E
Morey Park	210	42.33 N	73.43 W
Morey Peak ∧	204	38.37 N	116.17 W
Morez	58	46.31 N	6.02 E
Morfa Nefyn	42	52.56 N	4.33 W
Mörfelden-Walldorf	56	49.58 N	8.34 E
Morga	80	54.26 N	46.29 E
Morgan, Austl.	166	34.02 S	139.40 E
Morgan, Ga., U.S.	192	31.32 N	84.35 W
Morgan, Ky., U.S.	218	38.36 N	84.23 W
Morgan, Mn., U.S.	198	44.25 N	94.55 W
Morgan, Pa., U.S.	279b	40.22 N	80.08 W
Morgan, Tx., U.S.	222	32.01 N	97.37 W
Morgan, Ut,. U.S.	200	41.02 N	111.40 W
Morgan □[6], Il., U.S.	219	39.44 N	90.14 W
Morgan □[6], In., U.S.	218	39.30 N	86.25 W
Morgan, Mount ∧	171b	35.44 S	148.47 E
Morgan City, Al., U.S.	194	34.28 N	86.34 W
Morgan City, La., U.S.	194	29.41 N	91.12 W
Morgan Creek ≃	196	32.19 N	100.55 W
Morganfield	194	37.41 N	87.55 W
Morgan Hill	226	37.07 N	121.39 W
Morganito	246	5.04 N	67.44 W
Morgan Park ⊸[8]	278	41.42 N	87.40 W
Morgan's Bay	158	32.43 S	28.20 E
Morgan's Point	222	29.41 N	94.59 W
Morgans Point ≻	212	42.52 N	79.21 W
Morgan State College ⊍[2]	284b	39.21 N	76.35 W
Morgantina ⊥	70	37.25 N	14.29 E
Morganton	192	35.44 N	81.41 W
Morgantown, In., U.S.	218	39.22 N	86.15 W
Morgantown, Ky., U.S.	194	37.13 N	86.41 W
Morgantown, Md., U.S.	208	38.21 N	76.58 W
Morgantown, Ms., U.S.	194	31.34 N	91.20 W
Morgantown, Ms., U.S.	194	31.18 N	89.54 W
Morgantown, Oh., U.S.	218	39.08 N	83.13 W
Morgantown, Pa., U.S.	208	40.09 N	75.54 W
Morgantown, W.V., U.S.	188	39.37 N	79.57 W
Morganville	208	40.23 N	74.15 W
Morgan Whyalla Pipeline ≖[1]	168b	33.48 S	138.56 E
Morganza	194	30.44 N	91.35 W
Morgårdshammar	40	60.09 N	15.23 E
Morgauši	80	55.58 N	46.47 E
Morgenzon	158	26.45 S	29.36 E
Morges	58	46.31 N	6.30 E
Morgex	62	45.45 N	7.02 E
Morghāb (Murgab) ≃	128	38.18 N	61.12 E
Morghar	126	23.40 N	89.37 E
Morghūm, Kūh-e ∧	128	33.06 N	57.30 E
Morgongåva	40	59.56 N	16.57 E
Morgongiori	71	39.45 N	8.46 E
Morguilla, Punta ≻	252	37.46 S	73.40 W
Morhange	56	48.55 N	6.38 E
Mori, It.	64	45.51 N	10.59 E
Mori, Nihon	92a	42.06 N	140.35 E
Mori, Nihon	94	34.50 N	137.56 E
Mori, Nihon	270	34.32 N	135.00 E
Mori ≃	164	10.00 S	148.30 E
Moriah	241r	11.15 N	60.43 W
Moriah, Mount ∧	204	39.17 N	114.12 W
Morialta Conservation Park ♦	168b	34.55 S	138.40 E
Moriarty	200	34.59 N	106.02 W
Moriarty, Mount ∧	224	49.08 N	124.26 W
Morib	114	2.45 N	101.26 E
Moribaya	150	9.53 N	9.33 W
Morice ≃	182	54.24 N	126.45 W
Morice Lake ⊜	182	54.00 N	127.37 W
Morichal Largo ≃	246	9.27 N	62.25 W
Moricsala rezervāts ♦	76	57.17 N	22.11 E
Morie, Loch ⊜	46	57.44 N	4.28 W
Morienval	50	49.18 N	2.56 E
Morigerati	68	40.08 N	15.33 E
Moriguchi	96	34.44 N	135.34 E
Morija	158	29.34 S	27.31 E
Moriki	150	12.52 N	6.30 E
Morin Dawa	89	48.28 N	124.27 E
Moringen	52	51.42 N	9.52 E
Morino, It.	66	41.53 N	13.25 E
Morino, Ross.	76	57.54 N	30.22 E
Morinville	182	53.48 N	113.39 W
Morioka	92	39.42 N	141.09 E
Morīri, Tso ⊜	120	32.54 N	78.20 E
Morisset	170	33.06 S	151.29 E
Moriston ≃	46	57.12 N	4.36 W
Moritzburg ⊥	54	51.09 N	13.40 E
Morivione ⊸[8]	266b	45.26 N	9.12 E
Moriya	94	35.56 N	140.00 E
Moriyama	94	35.04 N	135.59 E
Moriyama-chūtonchi, Rikujō-jieitai- ■	94	35.12 N	136.57 E
Moriyoshi-zan ∧	92	39.58 N	140.33 E
Morki	80	56.25 N	49.01 E
Morkill ≃	182	53.42 N	120.30 W
Morkiny Gory	76	57.33 N	36.18 E
Mörkö I	40	58.59 N	17.40 E
Morkoka ≃	74	65.10 N	115.52 E
Mørkøv	41	55.40 N	11.32 E
Morlaix	32	48.35 N	3.50 W
Morlanwelz	50	50.27 N	4.14 E
Morles	56	50.38 N	9.51 E
Morley, Eng., U.K.	44	53.46 N	1.36 W
Morley, Mi., U.S.	190	43.29 N	85.26 W
Morley, N.Y., U.S.	212	44.40 N	75.12 W
Morley Green	262	53.20 N	2.16 W
Mörlunda	26	57.19 N	15.51 E
Mormal'	76	52.45 N	29.53 E
Mormanno	68	39.53 N	16.00 E
Mormant	50	48.36 N	2.53 E
Mormoiron	62	44.04 N	5.11 E
Mormon Bar	226	37.28 N	119.57 W
Mormon Lake ⊜	200	34.57 N	111.27 W
Mormon Peak ∧	204	36.57 N	114.30 W
Mormon Reservoir ⊜[1]	202	43.16 N	114.49 W
Mormon Slough ≃	226	37.57 N	121.18 W
Mormon Station Historical State Monument ♦	226	39.00 N	119.50 W
Mormugao	122	15.24 N	73.48 E
Morna	272a	28.35 N	77.22 E
Mornant	62	45.37 N	4.40 E
Mornas	62	44.12 N	4.44 E
Morne-à-l'Eau	241o	16.21 N	61.31 W
Morne Trois Pitons National Park ♦	240d	15.19 N	61.19 W
Morney	166	25.22 S	141.28 E
Morningdale	207	42.18 N	71.45 W
Morningside	284c	38.50 N	76.53 W
Morningside Park ♦	275b	43.47 N	79.12 W
Morningstar ≃	48	52.27 N	8.41 W
Morning Sun	190	41.05 N	91.15 W
Mornington	169	38.13 S	145.03 E
Mornington, Isla I	254	49.45 S	75.23 W
Mornington Island I	164	16.33 S	139.24 E
Mornington Island Aboriginal Land Trust ⊸[4]	164	16.20 S	139.20 E
Mornington Peninsula ≻[1]	169	38.20 S	145.05 E
Morno	150	8.41 N	1.31 W
Mornou, Hadjer ∧	146	17.12 N	23.08 E
Moro, Indon.	114	0.46 N	103.43 E
Moro, Or., U.S.	224	45.29 N	120.43 W
Moro ≃	150	7.25 N	11.03 W
Morobe	164	7.45 S	147.35 E
Morobe □[5]	164	7.00 S	146.30 E
Moroč'	76	52.34 N	27.36 E
Moroč' ≃	76	52.35 N	27.35 E
Morocco	216	40.56 N	87.27 W
Morocco (Al-Magreb) □[1], Afr.	134	32.00 N	5.00 W
Morocco (Al-Magreb) □[1], Afr.	148	32.00 N	5.00 W
Morococala	248	18.10 S	66.44 W
Morococha	248	11.37 S	76.09 W
Moro Creek ≃	194	33.18 N	92.22 W
Morogoro	154	6.49 S	37.40 E
Morogoro □[4]	154	8.00 S	37.15 E
Moro Gulf ⊂	116	6.51 N	123.00 E
Moroka	273d	26.16 S	27.52 E
Morokweng	158	26.12 S	23.45 E
Moroleón	234	20.08 N	101.12 W
Morombe	157b	21.45 S	43.22 E
Morón, Arg.	258	34.39 S	58.37 W
Morón, Cuba	240p	22.06 N	78.38 W
Mörön, Mong.	88	48.15 N	100.23 E
Mörön, Mong.	88	47.24 N	110.16 E
Mörön, Mong.	88	49.38 N	100.10 E
Morón, Ven.	246	10.29 N	68.11 W
Morón □[5]	288	34.37 S	58.37 W
Mörön ≃	88	47.14 N	110.37 E
Morón, Aeródromo ⊠	288	34.41 S	58.38 W
Morón, Arroyo ≃	288	34.33 S	58.37 W
Morona ≃	246	4.45 S	77.04 W
Morona-Santiago □[4]	246	2.30 S	78.00 W
Morondava	157b	20.17 S	44.17 E
Morón de Almazán	34	41.25 N	2.25 W
Morón de la Frontera	34	37.08 N	5.27 W
Morones, Sierra ⋀	234	21.45 N	103.10 W
Morong	116	14.41 N	120.16 E
Morongo Indian Reservation ⊸[4]	204	33.59 N	116.50 W
Moroni, Comores	157a	11.41 S	43.16 E
Moroni, Ut,. U.S.	200	39.31 N	111.35 W
Moron Us ≃, Zhg.	90	34.42 N	94.50 E
Moron Us ≃, Zhg.	120	34.42 N	94.50 E
Moros ≃	34	41.03 N	4.15 W
Morošečnoje	74	56.24 N	156.12 E
Morotai I	108	2.20 N	128.25 E
Moroto	154	2.32 N	34.39 E
Moroto ∧	154	2.32 N	34.46 E
Morouba	152	6.11 N	20.13 E
Morovis	240m	18.20 N	66.24 W
Morovsk	78	51.06 N	30.50 E
Morowali	112	1.52 S	121.30 E
Moroyama	94	35.56 N	139.19 E
Morozkovo	86	59.29 N	61.01 E
Morozovka, Ross.	78	50.09 N	39.38 E
Morozovka, Ukr.	83	49.28 N	39.54 E
Morozovsk	80	48.22 N	41.50 E
Morozovskaja	24	61.10 N	50.18 E
Morpeth, On., Can.	214	42.23 N	81.51 W
Morpeth, Eng., U.K.	44	55.10 N	1.41 W
Morphett Vale	168b	35.07 S	138.31 E
Morra, Monte ∧	267a	42.02 N	12.50 E
Morral	214	40.41 N	83.12 W
Morral, Arroyo del ≃	266d	41.29 N	2.03 E
Morrelganj	126	22.28 N	89.51 E
Morrice	216	42.50 N	84.11 W
Morrill	198	41.57 N	103.55 W
Morrilton	194	35.09 N	92.44 W
Morrin	182	51.40 N	112.47 W
Morrinhos, Bra.	250	3.14 S	40.07 W
Morrinhos, Bra.	255	17.44 S	49.07 W
Morrinsville	172	37.39 S	175.32 E
Morris, Mb., Can.	184	49.21 N	97.22 W
Morris, Ct., U.S.	207	41.41 N	73.11 W
Morris, Il., U.S.	216	41.21 N	88.25 W
Morris, In., U.S.	218	39.16 N	85.10 W
Morris, Mn., U.S.	198	45.35 N	95.54 W
Morris, N.Y., U.S.	210	42.32 N	75.14 W
Morris, Ok., U.S.	196	35.36 N	95.51 W
Morris, Pa., U.S.	210	41.36 N	77.18 W
Morris □[6], N.J., U.S.	210	40.48 N	74.29 W
Morris □[6], Tx., U.S.	222	33.05 N	94.45 W
Morris ≃	184	49.21 N	97.22 W
Morris, Mount ∧	162	26.09 S	131.04 E
Morrisburg	212	44.54 N	75.11 W
Morrisdale	214	40.56 N	78.13 W
Morris Dam ⊸[6]	280	34.11 N	117.53 W
Morris Jesup, Kap ≻	16	83.38 N	33.52 W
Morris Lake ⊜	276	41.03 N	74.37 W
Morrison, Arg.	252	32.36 S	62.50 W
Morrison, Il., U.S.	190	41.48 N	89.57 W
Morrison, Mo., U.S.	219	38.40 N	91.38 W
Morrison, Point ≻	168b	35.44 S	137.47 E
Morrison Creek ≃	275b	43.28 N	79.39 W
Morrison Lake ⊜, On., Can.	212	44.52 N	79.28 W
Morrison Lake ⊜, Mi., U.S.	216	42.53 N	85.13 W
Morrisonville	219	39.25 N	89.27 W
Morris Park ♦	285	39.59 N	75.15 W
Morris Plains	210	40.49 N	74.28 W
Morris Reservoir ⊜[1]	228	34.12 N	117.52 W
Morris Run	210	41.40 N	77.01 W
Morristown, Az., U.S.	200	33.51 N	112.37 W
Morristown, Il., U.S.	216	42.10 N	89.03 W
Morristown, In., U.S.	218	39.40 N	85.41 W
Morristown, Mn., U.S.	190	44.14 N	93.26 W
Morristown, N.J., U.S.	210	40.47 N	74.28 W
Morristown, N.Y., U.S.	212	44.35 N	75.38 W
Morristown, Oh., U.S.	214	40.04 N	81.05 W
Morristown, S.D., U.S.	198	45.56 N	101.43 W
Morristown, Tn., U.S.	192	36.12 N	83.17 W
Morristown Airport ⊠	276	40.48 N	74.25 W
Morristown National Historical Park ♦	210	40.46 N	74.32 W
Morrisville, N.Y., U.S.	210	42.53 N	75.38 W
Morrisville, Pa., U.S.	208	40.12 N	74.47 W
Morrisville, Vt., U.S.	188	44.33 N	72.35 W
Morrito	236	11.37 N	85.05 W
Morro	246	2.39 S	80.19 W
Morro, Castillo del (Morro Castle) ⊥	286b	23.09 N	82.21 W
Morro, Punta ≻	232	19.39 N	90.42 W
Morro Agudo	287a	22.45 S	43.29 W
Morro Bay	226	35.21 N	120.50 W
Morro Bay ⊂	226	35.20 N	120.51 W
Morro Bay State Park ♦	226	35.20 N	120.52 W
Morro Creek ≃	226	35.23 N	120.52 W
Morro do Chapéu	250	11.33 S	41.09 W
Morro d'Oro	66	42.39 N	13.54 E
Morro Mazatán	234	16.07 N	95.27 W
Morrone del Sannio	66	41.43 N	14.47 E
Morropón	248	5.15 S	80.00 W
Morros	250	2.52 S	44.03 W
Morrosquillo, Golfo de ⊂	246	9.35 N	75.40 W
Morrow, La., U.S.	194	30.49 N	92.04 W
Morrow, Oh., U.S.	218	39.21 N	84.07 W
Morrow □[6]	214	40.33 N	82.50 W
Morrow Island I	282	38.07 N	122.05 W
Morrow Mountain State Park ♦	192	35.23 N	80.05 W
Morrow Point Reservoir ⊜[1]	200	38.25 N	107.30 W
Mörrum	26	56.11 N	14.45 E
Morrumbala	154	17.22 S	35.36 E
Morrumbene	156	23.39 S	35.20 E
Mörrumsån ≃	26	56.09 N	14.44 E
Mors I	26	56.50 N	8.45 E
Morsains	50	48.48 N	3.32 E
Morsang-sur-Orge	261	48.40 N	2.21 E
Moršansk	80	53.26 N	41.49 E
Morsbach	56	50.52 N	7.43 E
Mörsch	56	48.58 N	8.17 E
Morschwiller-le-Bas	58	47.45 N	7.16 E
Morščichino	265b	55.56 N	37.20 E
Morse, Sk., Can.	184	50.25 N	107.03 W
Morse, La., U.S.	194	30.07 N	92.29 W
Morse, Tx., U.S.	196	36.04 N	101.29 W
Morse Mill	219	38.17 N	90.40 W
Mörsenbroich ⊸[8]	263	51.15 N	6.48 E
Morse Reservoir ⊜[1]	218	40.06 N	86.02 W
Morses Pond ⊜	283	42.18 N	71.19 W
Morsi	120	21.21 N	78.00 E
Morskaja Masel'ga	24	63.06 N	34.54 E
Morskoj Bir'učok, ostrov I	84	44.42 N	47.02 E
Morson	184	49.03 N	94.18 W
Morsott	36	35.40 N	8.01 E
Morstein	285	40.01 N	75.35 W
Mort	272a	28.43 N	77.25 E
Morta	272a	28.44 N	77.27 E
Mortagne	32	48.31 N	0.33 E
Mortagne ≃	58	48.33 N	6.27 E
Mortagne-au-Perche	50	48.31 N	0.33 E
Mortagne-sur-Sèvre	32	47.00 N	0.57 W
Mortain	32	48.39 N	0.56 W
Mortana	162	33.02 S	134.07 E
Mortara	62	45.15 N	8.44 E
Morteau	58	47.04 N	6.37 E
Mortefontaine	50	49.07 N	2.36 E
Mortegliano	64	45.57 N	13.10 E
Morte Point ≻	42	51.11 N	4.13 W
Morteratsch, Piz ∧	58	46.22 N	9.51 E
Morteros	252	30.42 S	62.00 W
Mortes, Rio das ≃, Bra.	255	11.45 S	50.44 W
Mortes, Rio das ≃, Bra.	256	21.18 S	43.58 W
Mortesoro	140	10.12 N	34.09 E
Mort-Homme, Forêt du ⊸[3]	56	49.15 N	5.15 E
Mortimer	42	51.22 N	1.04 W
Mortlach	184	50.28 N	106.03 W
Mortlake, Austl.	166	38.05 S	142.48 E
Mortlake, Austl.	274a	33.51 S	151.07 E
Mortlake ⊸[8]	260	51.28 N	0.16 W
Mortlock ≃	168a	31.42 S	116.55 E
Mortlock North ≃	168a	31.38 S	116.42 E
Mortola Inferiore	62	43.47 N	7.33 E
Morton, Il., U.S.	190	40.36 N	89.27 W
Morton, Mn., U.S.	198	44.33 N	94.59 W
Morton, Ms., U.S.	194	32.21 N	89.39 W
Morton, N.Y., U.S.	210	43.20 N	78.00 W
Morton, Pa., U.S.	285	39.55 N	75.20 W
Morton, Tx., U.S.	196	33.43 N	102.45 W
Morton, Wa., U.S.	224	46.33 N	122.16 W
Morton, Mount ∧[2]	274b	37.56 S	145.20 E
Morton Arboretum ⊸[4]	278	41.49 N	88.04 W
Morton Craig Range ⋀	162	28.12 S	124.41 E
Morton Grove	216	42.02 N	87.46 W
Morton National Park ♦	170	35.00 S	150.10 E
Mortons Gap	194	37.14 N	87.28 W
Mortorio, Isola I	71	41.05 N	9.36 E
Mortornès del Vallès	266d	41.33 N	2.16 E
Mortrée	50	48.38 N	0.05 E
Mörtschach	64	46.55 N	12.55 E
Mortsel	50	51.10 N	4.28 E
M'ortvyj Donec ≃	83	47.15 N	39.14 E
Morty	80	55.49 N	51.44 E
Morua	175f	16.54 S	168.32 E
Morumbi ⊸[8]	287b	23.36 S	46.42 E
Morumbi, Estádio do ♦	287b	23.37 S	46.43 W
Morungaba	256	22.52 S	46.48 W
Morungole ∧	154	3.49 N	34.02 E
Moruya	166	35.55 S	150.05 E
Morvan ⋀	32	47.05 N	4.00 E
Morvant	241r	10.39 N	61.28 W
Morven, Austl.	166	26.25 S	147.07 E
Morven, N.Z.	172	44.50 S	171.07 E
Morven, Ga., U.S.	192	30.56 N	83.29 W
Morven, N.C., U.S.	192	34.51 N	80.00 W
Morven ∧, Scot., U.K.	46	57.07 N	3.02 W
Morven ∧, Scot., U.K.	46	58.14 N	3.42 W
Morwell	169	38.14 S	146.24 E
Morwell ≃	169	38.10 S	146.23 E
Morwenstow	42	50.54 N	4.33 W
Moryń	30	52.49 N	14.13 E
Morženga	76	59.37 N	40.12 E
Morzhovoi	180	54.55 N	163.18 W
Morzine	58	46.11 N	6.43 E
Moržovec, ostrov I	24	66.44 N	42.35 E
Moša ≃, Ross.	24	62.25 N	39.46 E
M'oša ≃, Ross.	80	55.25 N	49.22 E
Mosal'sk	76	54.29 N	34.59 E
Mosambik → Mozambique □[1]	138	18.15 S	35.00 E
Mošanicy	82	54.56 N	38.23 E
Mosås	40	59.12 N	15.08 E
Mosbach	56	49.21 N	9.08 E
Mosborough	44	53.19 N	1.22 W
Mosby	26	58.14 N	7.54 E
Mosby Woods	284c	38.52 N	77.18 W
Moscavide	266c	38.47 N	9.06 W
Mosciano Sant'Angelo	66	42.45 N	13.53 E
Moščnyj, ostrov I	76	60.01 N	27.50 E
Moscos Islands II	110	14.00 N	97.45 E
Moscou → Moskva	82	55.45 N	37.35 E
Moscow, Id., U.S.	202	46.43 N	116.59 W
Moscow, In., U.S.	218	39.29 N	85.34 W
Moscow, Oh., U.S.	218	38.51 N	84.13 W
Moscow, Pa., U.S.	210	41.20 N	75.31 W
Moscow, Tx., U.S.	222	30.55 N	94.50 W
Moscow Air Terminal ⊠	265b	55.48 N	37.32 E
Moscow Circus ♦	265b	55.43 N	37.33 E
Moscow Mills	219	38.56 N	90.55 W
Moscow → Moskva	82	55.45 N	37.35 E
Moscow Station ⊸[5]	265a	59.56 N	30.22 E
Moscow Victory Park ♦	265a	59.52 N	30.20 E
Moscow Zoo ♦	265b	55.46 N	37.34 E
Moscufo	66	42.25 N	14.03 E
Moscú → Moskva	82	55.45 N	37.35 E
Mosel	54	50.47 N	12.28 E
Mosel (Moselle) ≃	32	50.22 N	7.36 E
Moselebe ≃	156	25.03 S	23.13 E
Moselle, Ms., U.S.	194	31.30 N	89.16 W
Moselle, Mo., U.S.	219	38.23 N	90.54 W
Moselle □[5]	56	49.00 N	6.30 E
Moselle (Mosel) ≃	32	50.22 N	7.36 E
Moselotte ≃	58	48.01 N	6.38 E
Mošenskoje	76	58.31 N	34.35 E
Mosermandl ∧	64	47.12 N	13.24 E
Mosers River	186	44.59 N	62.15 W
Moses Lake	202	47.07 N	119.16 W
Moses Lake ⊜[1]	202	47.10 N	119.20 W
Moses Point	180	64.42 N	162.03 W
Moses Power Plant ⊸[6]	284a	43.09 N	79.02 W
Mosetse	156	20.37 S	26.32 E
Mosgiel	172	45.53 S	170.21 E
Moshannon	214	41.02 N	78.00 W
Moshannon Creek ≃	214	41.04 N	78.06 W
Moshanpu	100	29.34 N	112.41 E
Moshaweng ≃	158	26.35 S	22.50 E
Mosheim, Tn., U.S.	192	36.11 N	82.57 W
Mosheim, Tx., U.S.	222	31.38 N	97.36 W
Moshi	154	3.21 S	37.20 E
Moshi ≃	150	9.18 N	4.38 E
Moshiyu	104	41.15 N	124.05 E
Mosier	224	45.41 N	121.23 W
Mosier Hill ∧[2]	214	40.06 N	80.24 W
Mosina	30	52.16 N	16.51 E
Mosinee	190	44.47 N	89.42 W
Mosjøen	24	65.50 N	13.10 E
Moskal'onki	86	54.59 N	71.54 E
Moskal'vo	89	53.35 N	142.30 E
Moskau → Moskva	82	55.45 N	37.35 E
Moskenesøya I	24	67.59 N	13.00 E
Moskháton	267c	37.57 N	23.41 E
Moškino	80	57.45 N	45.20 E
Moskito-Golf → Mosquitos, Golfo de los ⊂	236	9.00 N	81.15 W
Moškovo	86	55.18 N	83.37 E
Moskovskaja Slav'anka	265a	59.45 N	30.30 E
Moskovskaja vozvyšennost' ⋀[1]	76	56.15 N	37.30 E
Moskva (Moscow), Ross.	82	55.45 N	37.35 E
Moskva (Moscow), Ross.	265b	55.45 N	37.35 E
Moskva ≃	76	55.05 N	38.50 E
Moskva, Gorod □[7]	265b	55.45 N	37.35 E
Moskva, pik ∧	85	38.57 N	71.49 E
Moskva Oblast' □[4]	76	55.30 N	37.30 E
Moskvy, kanal imeni ≖	82	56.43 N	37.08 E
Mosman	170	33.49 S	151.14 E
Mosman Park	168a	32.01 S	115.46 E
Mošny	78	49.32 N	31.44 E
Moso (Moos)	64	46.41 N	12.23 E
Moso in Passiria (Moos)	64	46.50 N	11.10 E
Mošok	80	55.48 N	41.17 E
Mosolovo	80	54.17 N	40.32 E
Mosomane	156	24.04 S	26.15 E
Mosoni-Duna ≃	61	47.54 N	17.17 E
Mosonmagyaróvár	30	47.51 N	17.17 E
Mosonszolnok	61	47.51 N	17.11 E
Mosopa	156	24.50 S	25.31 E
Mospino	83	47.53 N	38.03 E
Mosqueiro	250	1.10 S	48.28 W
Mosquera	246	2.30 N	78.29 W
Mosquero	196	35.46 N	103.57 W
Mosquic, Lac ⊜	206	46.39 N	74.28 W
Mosquito, Punta ≻	246	9.07 N	77.53 W
Mosquito, Riacho ≃	252	22.02 S	57.57 W
Mosquito Brook ≃	283	42.40 N	71.02 W
Mosquito Creek ≃, Ia., U.S.	198	41.11 N	95.50 W
Mosquito Creek ≃, Oh., U.S.	214	41.10 N	80.45 W
Mosquito Creek ≃, Pa., U.S.	214	41.07 N	78.07 W
Mosquito Creek Lake ⊜[1]	214	41.22 N	80.45 W
Mosquito Creek State Park ♦	214	41.22 N	80.45 W
Mosquito Indian Reserve ⊸[4]	184	52.30 N	108.15 W
Mosquito Lagoon ⊂	220	28.45 N	80.45 W
Mosquitos, Costa de □[9]	236	13.00 N	83.45 W
Mosquitos, Golfo de los ⊂	236	9.00 N	81.15 W
Moss	26	59.26 N	10.42 E
Mossaka	152	1.13 S	16.48 E
Mossâmedes	255	16.07 S	50.11 W
Mossbank, Sk., Can.	184	49.55 N	105.59 W
Moss Bank, Eng., U.K.	262	53.29 N	2.44 W
Mossbank, Scot., U.K.	46a	60.27 N	1.12 W
Moss Bank Park ♦	262	53.36 N	2.28 W
Moss Beach	282	37.32 N	122.31 W
Mossburn	172	45.40 S	168.15 E
Mosselbaai (Mossel Bay)	158	34.11 S	22.08 E
Mosselbaai ⊂	158	34.06 S	22.20 E
Mossendjo	152	2.57 S	12.44 E
Mosses, Col des)(	58	46.24 N	7.06 E
Mossgiel	166	33.15 S	144.34 E
Moss Hill	222	30.15 N	94.45 W
Mossig ≃	58	48.33 N	7.30 E
Mössingen	58	48.24 N	9.03 E
Moss Landing	226	36.48 N	121.47 W
Mossleigh	182	50.43 N	113.20 W
Mossley	262	53.32 N	2.02 W
Mossley Hill ⊸[8]	262	53.23 N	2.55 W
Mossman	164	16.28 S	145.22 E
Mossmans Brook ≃	276	41.03 N	74.27 W
Moss Moor ⊸[3]	262	53.37 N	2.00 W
Moss Mountain ∧	194	34.50 N	92.40 W
Mossø ⊜	41	56.02 N	9.48 E
Mosson ≃	62	43.33 N	3.54 E
Mossoró	250	5.11 S	37.20 W
Mosso Santa Maria	62	45.38 N	8.08 E
Moss Point	194	30.24 N	88.32 W
Moss Point ≻	279a	41.37 N	81.32 W
Moss Side	262	53.46 N	2.57 W
Mossuril	154	14.58 S	40.42 E
Moss Vale	170	34.33 S	150.22 E
Mossy ≃, Mb., Can.	184	51.39 N	99.55 W
Mossy ≃, Sk., Can.	184	54.05 N	103.00 W
Mossyrock	224	46.31 N	122.29 W
Mossyrock Dam ⊸[6]	224	46.32 N	122.25 W
Most	54	50.32 N	13.39 E
Mosta	80	56.32 N	42.10 E
Mostar	36	43.20 N	17.49 E
Mostardas, Bra.	252	31.06 S	50.57 W
Mostardas, Bra.	256	23.44 S	46.38 W
Møsting, Kap ≻	176	64.00 N	41.00 W
Mostiska	78	49.48 N	23.09 E
Mostiștea ≃	38	44.15 N	27.10 E
Mostizzolo	64	46.24 N	11.01 E

Symbols in the index entries represent the broad categories identified in the key at the right. Symbols with superior numbers (⋀[1]) identify subcategories (see complete key on page *I · 1).*

Symbole im Register stellen die rechts im Schlüssel erklärten Kategorien dar. Symbole mit hochgestellten Ziffern (⋀[1]) bezeichnen Unterabteilungen einer Kategorie (vgl. vollständiger Schlüssel auf Seite *I · 1).*

Los símbolos incluídos en el texto del índice representan las grandes categorias identificadas con la clave a la derecha. Los símbolos con numeros en su parte superior (⋀[1]) identifican las subcategorías (véase la clave completa en la página *I · 1).*

Les symboles de l'index représentent les catégories indiquées dans la légende à droite. Les symboles suivis d'un indice (⋀[1]) représentent des sous-catégories (voir légende complète à la page *I · 1).*

Os símbolos incluídos no texto do índice representam as grandes categorias identificadas com a chave à direita. Os símbolos com números em sua parte superior (⋀[1]) identificam as subcategorias (veja-se a chave completa à página *I · 1).*

∧	Mountain	Berg	Montaña	Montagne	Montanha
⋀	Mountains	Gebirge	Montañas	Montagnes	Montanhas
)(	Pass	Paß	Paso	Col	Passo
V	Valley, Canyon	Tal, Cañon	Valle, Cañón	Vallée, Canyon	Vale, Canhão
≚	Plain	Ebene	Llano	Plaine	Planície
≻	Cape	Kap	Cabo	Cap	Cabo
I	Island	Insel	Isla	Île	Ilha
II	Islands	Inseln	Islas	Îles	Ilhas
⊥	Other Topographic Features	Andere Topographische Objekte	Otros Elementos Topográficos	Autres données topographiques	Outros acidentes topográficos

ESPAÑOL — Nombre | Página | Lat.°′ | Long.°′ W = Oeste

FRANÇAIS — Nom | Page | Lat.°′ | Long.°′ W = Ouest

PORTUGUÊS — Nome | Página | Lat.°′ | Long.°′ W = Oeste

Mostki	**83**	49.19 N	38.30 E
Most na Soči	**64**	46.09 N	13.44 E
Mostok	**76**	53.59 N	30.28 E
Móstoles	**266a**	40.19 N	3.51 W
Mostoos Hills ⩘ 2	**184**	55.00 N	109.15 W
Mostovaja	**76**	56.13 N	33.08 E
Mostovka	**86**	58.10 N	65.31 E
Mostovoje	**78**	47.24 N	30.59 E
Mostovskoj	**84**	44.25 N	40.48 E
Mostovskoje	**86**	55.46 N	66.22 E
Mostrim (Edgeworthstown)	**48**	53.42 N	7.36 W
Mostva ≃	**78**	52.00 N	27.33 E
Mosty	**76**	53.25 N	24.32 E
Mostyn, Malay.	**112**	4.40 N	118.11 E
Mostyn, Wales, U.K.	**44**	53.19 N	3.16 W
Mosul → Al-Mawṣil	**128**	36.20 N	43.08 E
Møsvatnet ⊜	**26**	59.52 N	8.05 E
Mota	**144**	11.02 N	37.52 E
Mota I	**175f**	13.49 S	167.42 E
Motaba ≃	**152**	2.03 N	18.03 E
Mota del Cuervo	**34**	39.30 N	2.52 W
Mota del Marqués	**34**	41.38 N	5.10 W
Motagua ≃	**236**	15.44 N	88.14 W
Motala	**26**	58.33 N	15.03 E
Motala ström ≃	**40**	58.38 N	16.10 E
Mota Lava I	**175f**	13.40 S	167.40 E
Motane I	**174x**	9.59 S	138.49 W
Motatán	**246**	9.24 N	70.36 W
Motaze	**156**	24.48 S	32.52 E
Motegi	**94**	36.32 N	140.11 E
Mote Park ♦	**260**	51.17 N	0.34 E
Moteve, Cap >	**174x**	9.58 S	139.02 W
Moth	**124**	25.43 N	78.57 E
Mother Brook ≊	**283**	42.15 N	71.10 W
Motherwell	**46**	55.48 N	4.00 W
Motihāri	**124**	26.39 N	84.55 E
Motilla del Palancar	**34**	39.34 N	1.53 W
Motiong	**116**	11.47 N	125.00 E
Motiti Island I	**172**	37.38 S	176.26 E
Motjärnshyttan	**40**	59.56 N	13.58 E
Motloutse	**156**	21.28 S	27.24 E
Motloutse ≃	**156**	22.15 S	29.00 E
Moto-ara ≃	**94**	35.53 N	139.50 E
Motobu	**174m**	26.39 N	127.54 E
Motol'	**76**	52.19 N	25.36 E
Motola, Monte ∧	**68**	40.22 N	15.26 E
Motopu	**174x**	9.55 S	139.03 W
Motor Island I	**284a**	42.58 N	78.56 W
Motorki	**80**	56.53 N	51.29 E
Motorovo	**86**	56.31 N	71.10 E
Motosu	**94**	35.29 N	136.40 E
Motosu-ko ⊜	**94**	35.28 N	138.35 E
Motou	**106**	32.18 N	120.34 E
Motovilovo	**80**	55.36 N	43.51 E
Motovun	**64**	45.20 N	13.50 E
Motoyama	**96**	33.45 N	133.35 E
Moto-yama ∧ 2	**174f**	24.48 N	141.20 E
Motozintla de Mendoza	**232**	15.22 N	92.14 W
Motril	**34**	36.45 N	3.31 W
Motrone	**64**	43.54 N	10.12 E
Motru	**38**	44.50 N	23.00 E
Mott	**198**	46.22 N	102.19 W
Motta	**64**	45.36 N	11.29 E
Motta Camastra	**70**	37.54 N	15.10 E
Motta d'Affermo	**70**	37.59 N	14.18 E
Motta di Livenza	**64**	45.47 N	12.36 E
Mottafollone	**68**	39.39 N	16.04 E
Motta Montecorvino	**68**	41.30 N	15.07 E
Motta San Giovanni	**70**	38.00 N	15.41 E
Motta Sant'Anastasia	**70**	37.31 N	14.58 E
Motta Visconti	**62**	45.17 N	8.59 E
Möttingen	**56**	48.48 N	10.35 E
Mottingham ◆ 8	**260**	51.26 N	0.03 E
Mottisfont	**42**	51.02 N	1.32 W
Mottola	**68**	40.38 N	17.03 E
Mottram in Longdendale	**262**	53.27 N	2.01 W
Motts Creek ≃	**276**	40.38 N	73.45 W
Mottville, Mi., U.S.	**216**	41.48 N	85.45 W
Mottville, N.Y., U.S.	**210**	42.59 N	76.27 W
Motu ≃	**172**	37.51 S	177.35 E
Motueka	**172**	41.07 S	173.00 E
Motueka ≃	**172**	41.05 S	173.01 E
Motul [de Felipe Carrillo Puerto]	**232**	21.06 N	89.17 W
Motu One I 1	**14**	15.48 S	154.33 W
Motupe	**248**	6.09 S	79.44 W
Motupena Point >	**175e**	6.32 S	155.09 E
Motutapu I	**174k**	21.14 S	159.43 W
Motygino	**86**	58.11 N	94.40 E
Motyklejka	**74**	59.26 N	148.38 E
Motyžin	**78**	50.23 N	29.55 E
Motyzlej	**80**	54.54 N	42.54 E
Mou	**175f**	21.05 S	165.26 E
Mouanko	**152**	3.39 N	9.49 E
Mouans-Sartoux	**62**	43.37 N	6.58 E
Mouaskar	**148**	35.45 N	0.01 E
Mouaskar □ 5	**148**	35.10 N	0.00
Mouchard	**58**	46.58 N	5.48 E
Mouchoir Bank ✦ 2	**238**	20.57 N	70.42 W
Mouchoir Passage ʯ	**238**	21.10 N	71.00 W
Moúdhros	**38**	39.52 N	25.16 E
Mouding	**102**	25.24 N	101.35 E
Moudjéria	**150**	17.53 N	12.20 W
Moudon	**58**	46.40 N	6.48 E
Moudongouma ≃	**152**	1.36 N	17.24 E
Mouila	**152**	1.52 S	11.01 E
Mouit	**150**	16.35 N	13.05 W
Mouka	**152**	7.16 N	21.52 E
Moukden → Shenyang	**104**	41.48 N	123.27 E
Moulamein	**166**	35.05 S	144.02 E
Moulay-bou-Selham	**34**	34.53 N	6.15 W
Moulay-Idriss	**148**	34.02 N	5.27 W
Mouldsworth	**262**	53.14 N	2.44 W
Moule à Chique, Cap >	**241f**	13.43 N	60.57 W
Moulhoulé	**144**	12.36 N	43.12 E
Moulin, Île du I	**275a**	45.41 N	73.32 W
Moulin-des-Ponts	**58**	46.21 N	5.19 E
Moulineaux	**50**	49.21 N	0.58 E
Moulinet	**62**	43.57 N	7.25 E
Moulins	**32**	46.34 N	3.20 E
Moulins-la-Marche	**50**	48.39 N	0.29 E
Moulmeingyun	**110**	16.23 N	95.16 E
Moulmein → Mawlamyine	**110**	16.30 N	97.38 E
Moulouya, Oued ≃	**148**	35.05 N	2.25 W
Moulton, Eng., U.K.	**44**	53.13 N	2.31 W
Moulton, Al., U.S.	**194**	34.28 N	87.17 W
Moulton, Ia., U.S.	**190**	40.41 N	92.40 W
Moulton, Tx., U.S.	**222**	29.34 N	97.09 W
Moultrie	**192**	31.10 N	83.47 W
Moultrie □ 6	**219**	39.36 N	88.37 W
Moultrie, Lake ⊜ 1	**192**	33.20 N	80.05 W
Mouly	**175f**	20.42 S	166.25 E
Mound	**222**	31.21 N	97.38 W
Mound Bayou	**194**	33.52 N	90.43 W
Mound City, Il., U.S.	**194**	37.05 N	89.09 W
Mound City, Ks., U.S.	**198**	38.08 N	94.48 W
Mound City, Mo., U.S.	**194**	40.07 N	95.13 W
Mound City, S.D., U.S.	**198**	45.43 N	100.04 W
Mound City Group National Monument ♦	**218**	39.23 N	83.00 W
Mound Lake ⊜	**219**	40.05 N	90.17 W
Moundou	**146**	8.34 N	16.05 E
Moundridge	**198**	38.12 N	97.31 W
Mounds, Il., U.S.	**194**	37.06 N	89.11 W
Mounds, Ok., U.S.	**196**	35.52 N	96.03 W
Mounds State Park ♦	**218**	40.07 N	85.37 W
Mounds State Recreation Area ♦	**218**	39.30 N	84.59 W
Moundsville	**188**	39.55 N	80.44 W
Moundville	**194**	32.59 N	87.37 W
Moungali ◆ 8	**273b**	4.15 S	15.17 E
Moung Roessei	**110**	12.46 N	103.27 E
Mounianzé ≃	**152**	0.32 N	12.52 E
Mounier, Mont ∧	**62**	44.09 N	6.58 E
Mounlapamôk	**110**	14.20 N	105.52 E
Mount Aetna	**208**	40.25 N	76.18 W
Mountain	**190**	45.11 N	88.28 W
Mountain □ 4	**116**	17.20 N	121.10 E
Mountain ≃	**180**	65.41 N	128.50 W
Mountainair	**200**	34.31 N	106.14 W
Mountainaire	**200**	35.05 N	111.39 W
Mountain Ash	**42**	51.42 N	3.24 W
Mountain Brook	**194**	33.30 N	86.45 W
Mountain Chute Dam ◆ 6	**212**	45.11 N	76.54 W
Mountain City, Ga., U.S.	**192**	34.55 N	83.23 W
Mountain City, Nv., U.S.	**204**	41.50 N	115.57 W
Mountain City, Tn., U.S.	**192**	36.28 N	81.48 W
Mountain Creek	**194**	32.43 N	86.29 W
Mountain Creek ≃, Pa., U.S.	**208**	40.09 N	77.11 W
Mountain Creek ≃, Tx., U.S.	**222**	32.42 N	96.58 W
Mountain Creek Lake ⊜ 1	**222**	32.43 N	96.58 W
Mountain Dale	**210**	41.41 N	74.31 W
Mountain Grove	**194**	37.07 N	92.15 W
Mountain Home, Ar., U.S.	**194**	36.20 N	92.23 W
Mountain Home, Id., U.S.	**202**	43.07 N	115.41 W
Mountainhome, Pa., U.S.	**210**	41.11 N	75.17 W
Mountain Home Air Force Base ■	**202**	43.03 N	115.52 W
Mountain Iron	**190**	47.31 N	92.37 W
Mountain Lake, Fl., U.S.	**220**	27.57 N	81.36 W
Mountain Lake, Mn., U.S.	**198**	43.56 N	94.55 W
Mountain Lake ⊜, On., Can.	**212**	44.42 N	81.03 W
Mountain Lake ⊜, On., Can.	**212**	44.59 N	78.43 W
Mountain Lake ⊜, N.J., U.S.	**276**	40.53 N	74.27 W
Mountain Lakes	**210**	40.53 N	74.26 W
Mountain Lodge	**210**	41.23 N	74.09 W
Mountain Nile (Baḥr al-Jabal) ≃	**136**	9.30 N	30.30 E
Mountain Park	**182**	52.55 N	117.14 W
Mountain Pine	**194**	34.34 N	93.10 W
Mountain Point	**182**	55.18 N	131.32 W
Mountain Ranch	**226**	38.14 N	120.33 W
Mountainside	**208**	40.40 N	74.21 W
Mountain Spring Lakes	**276**	41.02 N	74.23 W
Mountain Valley Lake ⊜	**279b**	40.18 N	79.35 W
Mountain View, Ar., U.S.	**194**	35.52 N	92.07 W
Mountain View, Ca., U.S.	**226**	37.23 N	122.04 W
Mountain View, Mo., U.S.	**194**	36.59 N	91.42 W
Mountain View, Ok., U.S.	**196**	35.05 N	98.44 W
Mountain View, Wy., U.S.	**200**	41.16 N	110.20 W
Mountain View, Wy., U.S.	**200**	42.51 N	106.23 W
Mountain View Acres	**228**	34.31 N	117.24 W
Mountain Village	**180**	62.05 N	163.44 W
Mountain Zebra National Park ♦	**158**	32.16 S	25.29 E
Mount Airy, Md., U.S.	**208**	39.22 N	77.09 W
Mount Airy, N.C., U.S.	**192**	36.29 N	80.36 W
Mount Airy ◆ 8	**285**	40.04 N	75.12 W
Mount Albert	**212**	44.08 N	79.19 W
Mount Alford	**171a**	28.04 S	152.36 E
Mount Alida	**158**	29.09 S	30.18 E
Mount Angel	**224**	45.04 N	122.47 W
Mount Ann Park ♦	**283**	42.37 N	70.44 W
Mount Arlington	**210**	40.55 N	74.38 W
Mount Assiniboine Provincial Park ♦	**182**	50.54 N	115.40 W
Mount Auburn	**219**	39.46 N	89.16 W
Mount Augustus	**162**	24.19 S	116.54 E
Mount Ayliff	**158**	30.54 S	29.20 E
Mount Ayr, In., U.S.	**216**	40.57 N	87.18 W
Mount Ayr, Ia., U.S.	**198**	40.42 N	94.14 W
Mount Baldy	**280**	34.14 N	117.40 W
Mount Barker, Austl.	**162**	34.38 S	117.40 E
Mount Barker, Austl.	**168b**	35.04 S	138.52 E
Mount Bellew Bridge	**48**	53.28 N	8.29 W
Mount Berry	**194**	34.17 N	85.11 W
Mount Bethel	**210**	40.54 N	75.07 W
Mount Blanchard	**216**	40.53 N	83.33 W
Mount Bold Reservoir ⊜ 1	**168b**	35.07 S	138.42 E
Mount Brydges	**214**	42.54 N	81.29 W
Mount Buffalo National Park ♦	**166**	36.45 S	146.45 E
Mount Buller	**169**	37.10 S	146.27 E
Mount Calm	**222**	31.45 N	96.53 W
Mount Carleton Provincial Park ♦	**186**	47.23 N	66.50 W
Mount Carmel, Nf., Can.	**186**	47.09 N	53.29 W
Mount Carmel, Il., U.S.	**194**	38.24 N	87.45 W
Mount Carmel, Ky., U.S.	**218**	38.29 N	83.38 W
Mount Carmel, Oh., U.S.	**218**	39.06 N	84.18 W
Mount Carmel, Pa., U.S.	**208**	40.47 N	76.24 W
Mount Carmel Heights	**218**	39.07 N	84.18 W
Mount Carroll	**190**	42.05 N	89.58 W
Mount Cavenagh	**162**	25.58 S	133.15 E
Mount Charles	**275b**	43.41 N	79.40 W
Mount Clare	**188**	39.13 N	80.21 W
Mount Clemens	**214**	42.35 N	82.52 W
Mount Colah	**274a**	33.41 S	151.07 E
Mount Compass	**168b**	35.22 S	138.37 E
Mount Cook	**172**	43.44 S	170.06 E
Mount Cook National Park ♦	**172**	43.35 S	170.15 E
Mount Coot-tha Park ♦	**171a**	27.28 S	152.56 E
Mount Cory	**216**	40.56 N	83.50 W
Mount Crawford	**168b**	34.40 S	138.57 E
Mount Crosby	**171a**	27.32 S	152.48 E
Mount Currie Indian Reserve ◆ 4	**182**	50.19 N	122.42 W
Mount Dandenong	**274b**	37.50 S	145.22 E
Mount Dennis ◆ 8	**275b**	43.42 N	79.30 W
Mount Desert Island I	**188**	44.20 N	68.20 W
Mount Diablo Creek ≃	**282**	38.02 N	122.02 W
Mount Diablo State Park ♦	**226**	37.51 N	121.55 W
Mount Dora	**220**	28.48 N	81.38 W
Mount Doreen	**162**	22.03 S	131.18 E
Mount Druitt	**274a**	33.46 S	150.49 E
Mount Eaton	**214**	40.42 N	81.42 W
Mount Eba	**166**	30.12 S	135.40 E
Mount Eden	**226**	37.38 N	122.06 W
Mount Edgecumbe	**180**	57.03 N	135.21 W
Mount Edwards	**171a**	28.01 S	152.31 E
Mount Elgon National Park ♦	**154**	1.07 N	34.44 E
Mount Elizabeth	**164**	16.15 S	126.12 E
Mount Emu Creek ≃	**169**	38.18 S	142.55 E
Mount Enterprise	**222**	31.55 N	94.41 W
Mount Ephraim	**285**	39.52 N	75.05 W
Mount Evelyn	**274b**	37.47 S	145.23 E
Mount Fern	**276**	40.52 N	74.34 W
Mount Field National Park ♦	**166**	42.40 S	146.35 E
Mount Fletcher	**158**	30.40 S	28.30 E
Mount Forest	**212**	43.59 N	80.44 W
Mount Freedom	**210**	40.49 N	74.34 W
Mount Frere	**158**	31.00 S	28.58 E
Mount Gambier	**166**	37.50 S	140.46 E
Mount Garnet	**166**	17.41 S	145.07 E
Mount Gay	**188**	37.51 N	82.00 W
Mount Gilead, N.C., U.S.	**192**	35.12 N	80.00 W
Mount Gilead, Oh., U.S.	**214**	40.32 N	82.49 W
Mount Gravatt	**171a**	27.33 S	153.06 E
Mount Greenwood ◆ 8	**278**	41.42 N	87.43 W
Mount Gunson	**162**	31.27 S	137.11 E
Mount Hagen	**164**	5.50 S	144.15 E
Mount Hawke	**42**	50.17 N	5.12 W
Mount Hawthorn	**168a**	31.55 S	115.50 E
Mount Healthy	**218**	39.14 N	84.32 W
Mount Hebron	**284b**	39.18 N	76.50 W
Mount Helena	**168a**	31.53 S	116.13 E
Mount Hermon, Ca., U.S.	**226**	37.03 N	122.04 W
Mount Hermon, Ma., U.S.	**207**	42.40 N	72.29 W
Mount Holly, N.J., U.S.	**208**	39.59 N	74.47 W
Mount Holly, N.C., U.S.	**192**	35.17 N	81.00 W
Mount Holly Springs	**208**	40.07 N	77.11 W
Mount Hope, Austl.	**166**	34.07 S	135.23 E
Mount Hope, On., Can.	**212**	43.09 N	79.55 W
Mount Hope, Ks., U.S.	**198**	37.52 N	97.39 W
Mount Hope, N.J., U.S.	**276**	40.56 N	74.33 W
Mount Hope, Oh., U.S.	**214**	40.38 N	81.47 W
Mount Hope, W.V., U.S.	**188**	37.53 N	81.09 W
Mount Hope Lake ⊜	**276**	40.56 N	74.32 W
Mount Horeb	**190**	43.00 N	89.44 W
Mount Houston	**222**	29.54 N	95.18 W
Mount Howitt	**166**	26.31 S	142.16 E
Mount Hunter Rivulet ≃	**274a**	34.02 S	150.40 E
Mount Ida	**194**	34.33 N	93.38 W
Mount Isa	**166**	20.44 S	139.30 E
Mount Jackson, Pa., U.S.	**214**	40.58 N	80.26 W
Mount Jackson, Va., U.S.	**188**	38.44 N	78.38 W
Mount Jewett	**214**	41.43 N	78.38 W
Mount Juliet	**194**	36.12 N	86.31 W
Mount Kaputar National Park ♦	**166**	30.16 S	150.10 E
Mount Kenya National Park ♦	**154**	0.09 S	37.19 E
Mount Kisco	**210**	41.12 N	73.43 W
Mount Kokeby	**168a**	32.13 S	116.58 E
Mountlake Terrace	**224**	47.47 N	122.18 W
Mount Laurel	**285**	39.56 N	74.54 W
Mount Lebanon	**214**	40.21 N	80.02 W
Mount Liberty	**214**	40.21 N	82.38 W
Mount Lofty Ranges ⩘	**168b**	34.45 S	139.00 E
Mount Magnet	**162**	28.04 S	117.49 E
Mount Manara	**166**	32.29 S	143.56 E
Mount Margaret, Austl.	**162**	28.47 S	122.11 E
Mount Margaret, Austl.	**166**	26.54 S	143.21 E
Mount Marion	**210**	42.02 N	73.59 W
Mount Martha	**169**	38.17 S	145.01 E
Mount Maunganui	**172**	37.37 S	176.11 E
Mount McKinley National Park → Denali National Park ♦	**180**	63.15 N	150.30 W
Mount Mee	**171a**	27.04 S	152.46 E
Mountmellick	**48**	53.07 N	7.20 W
Mount Misery Point >	**276**	40.58 N	73.05 W
Mount Mistake National Park ♦	**171a**	27.53 S	152.20 E
Mount Molloy	**164**	16.41 S	145.20 E
Mount Monger	**162**	30.59 S	121.53 E
Mount Moorosi	**158**	30.16 S	27.53 E
Mount Morgan	**166**	23.39 S	150.23 E
Mount Morris, Il., U.S.	**190**	42.03 N	89.25 W
Mount Morris, Mi., U.S.	**190**	43.07 N	83.41 W
Mount Morris, N.Y., U.S.	**210**	42.43 N	77.52 W
Mount Morris Dam ◆ 6	**210**	42.44 N	77.53 W
Mount Mulligan	**166**	16.51 S	144.52 E
Mount Nebo	**279b**	40.33 N	80.06 W
Mountnessing	**260**	51.39 N	0.21 E
Mount Olive, Il., U.S.	**219**	39.04 N	89.43 W
Mount Olive, Ms., U.S.	**194**	31.45 N	89.39 W
Mount Olive, N.C., U.S.	**192**	35.11 N	78.04 W
Mount Oliver	**279b**	40.28 N	79.59 W
Mount Olivet	**218**	38.31 N	84.02 W
Mount Orab	**218**	39.01 N	83.55 W
Mount Penn	**208**	40.20 N	75.54 W
Mount Perry	**166**	25.11 S	151.39 E
Mount Pleasant, Austl.	**168b**	34.47 S	139.02 E
Mount Pleasant, On., Can.	**212**	43.05 N	80.19 W
Mount Pleasant, In., U.S.	**218**	38.07 N	86.31 W
Mount Pleasant, Ia., U.S.	**190**	40.57 N	91.33 W
Mount Pleasant, Mi., U.S.	**190**	43.35 N	84.46 W
Mount Pleasant, N.C., U.S.	**192**	35.23 N	80.26 W
Mount Pleasant, Oh., U.S.	**214**	40.11 N	80.48 W
Mount Pleasant, Pa., U.S.	**214**	40.08 N	79.32 W
Mount Pleasant, S.C., U.S.	**192**	32.47 N	79.51 W
Mount Pleasant, Tn., U.S.	**194**	35.32 N	87.12 W
Mount Pleasant, Tx., U.S.	**222**	33.09 N	94.58 W
Mount Pleasant, Ut,. U.S.	**200**	39.32 N	111.27 W
Mount Pleasant Mills	**208**	40.43 N	77.01 W
Mount Pleasant Park ♦	**284b**	39.22 N	76.35 W
Mount Pocono	**210**	41.07 N	75.21 W
Mount Pritchard	**274a**	33.54 S	150.54 E
Mount Prospect, S. Afr.	**158**	27.29 S	29.53 E
Mount Prospect, Il., U.S.	**216**	42.03 N	87.56 W
Mount Pulaski	**219**	40.00 N	89.16 W
Mount Rainier	**284c**	38.56 N	76.57 W
Mount Rainier National Park ♦	**224**	46.52 N	121.43 W
Mountrath	**48**	53.00 N	7.27 W
Mount Repose	**218**	39.10 N	84.14 W
Mount Revelstoke National Park ♦	**182**	51.06 N	118.00 W
Mount Riddock	**162**	23.03 S	134.40 E
Mount Robson Provincial Park ♦	**182**	52.58 N	118.50 W
Mount Rogers National Recreation Area ♦	**192**	36.42 N	81.30 W
Mount Roskill	**172**	36.55 S	174.45 E
Mount Royal	**285**	39.49 N	75.13 W
Mount Rushmore National Memorial ⊥	**198**	43.50 N	103.24 W
Mount Saint Helens National Volcanic Monument ♦	**224**	46.12 N	122.11 W
Mount Sandiman	**162**	24.24 S	115.23 E
Mount Sarah	**162**	26.57 S	135.22 E
Mount Savage	**188**	39.41 N	78.52 W
Mount's Bay ⊂	**42**	50.03 N	5.25 W
Mount Selinda	**154**	20.25 S	32.43 E
Mount Selman	**222**	32.04 N	95.17 W
Mount Seymour Provincial Park ♦	**182**	49.23 N	122.57 W
Mount Shasta	**204**	41.18 N	122.18 W
Mount Sinai	**276**	40.57 N	73.02 W
Mount Sinai Harbor ⊂	**276**	40.57 N	73.02 W
Mount Sinai Ridge ∧	**218**	39.04 N	84.58 W
Mount Somers	**172**	43.43 S	171.24 E
Mountsorrel	**42**	52.44 N	1.07 W
Mount Spokane State Park ♦	**202**	47.58 N	117.13 W
Mount Sterling, Il., U.S.	**219**	39.59 N	90.45 W
Mount Sterling, Ky., U.S.	**192**	38.03 N	83.56 W
Mount Sterling, Mo., U.S.	**219**	38.28 N	91.38 W
Mount Sterling, Oh., U.S.	**218**	39.43 N	83.15 W
Mount Stewart, P.E., Can.	**186**	46.22 N	62.52 W
Mount Stewart, S. Afr.	**158**	33.10 S	24.26 E
Mount Stromlo Observatory ʊ 3	**171b**	35.20 S	149.00 E
Mount Summit	**218**	40.00 N	85.23 W
Mount Surprise	**166**	18.09 S	144.19 E
Mount Sylvia	**171a**	27.44 S	152.14 E
Mount Tamalpais State Park ♦	**226**	37.54 N	122.34 W
Mount Torrens	**168b**	34.52 S	138.57 E
Mount Tremper	**210**	42.03 N	74.17 W
Mount Uniacke	**186**	44.54 N	63.50 W
Mount Union	**214**	40.23 N	77.52 W
Mount Upton	**210**	42.25 N	75.23 W
Mount Vernon, Austl.	**162**	24.13 S	118.14 E
Mount Vernon, Al., U.S.	**194**	31.05 N	88.00 W
Mount Vernon, Ga., U.S.	**192**	32.10 N	82.35 W
Mount Vernon, Il., U.S.	**219**	38.19 N	88.54 W
Mount Vernon, In., U.S.	**194**	37.55 N	87.53 W
Mount Vernon, Ia., U.S.	**190**	41.55 N	91.25 W
Mount Vernon, Ky., U.S.	**192**	37.21 N	84.20 W
Mount Vernon, Md., U.S.	**208**	38.14 N	75.49 W
Mount Vernon, Mo., U.S.	**194**	37.06 N	93.49 W
Mount Vernon, N.Y., U.S.	**210**	42.45 N	78.53 W
Mount Vernon, N.Y., U.S.	**210**	40.54 N	73.50 W
Mount Vernon, Oh., U.S.	**214**	40.23 N	82.29 W
Mount Vernon, Or., U.S.	**202**	44.25 N	119.06 W
Mount Vernon, Pa., U.S.	**279b**	40.17 N	79.48 W
Mount Vernon, S.D., U.S.	**198**	43.42 N	98.15 W
Mount Vernon, Tx., U.S.	**222**	33.11 N	95.13 W
Mount Vernon, Wa., U.S.	**224**	48.25 N	122.19 W
Mount Vernon ⊥	**208**	38.47 N	77.06 W
Mount Victoria	**170**	33.35 S	150.15 E
Mount Victory	**216**	40.32 N	83.31 W
Mount View	**207**	41.38 N	71.24 W
Mountville	**208**	40.02 N	76.26 W
Mount Vision	**210**	42.35 N	75.04 W
Mount Washington	**284b**	39.23 N	76.41 W
Mount Washington ◆ 8	**284b**	39.22 N	76.40 W
Mount Waverley	**274b**	37.53 S	145.08 E
Mount Wedge, Austl.	**162**	22.45 S	132.09 E
Mount Wedge, Austl.	**162**	33.29 S	135.10 E
Mount Wellington	**172**	36.54 S	174.51 E
Mount Wilhelm National Park ♦	**164**	5.45 S	145.05 E
Mount William National Park ♦	**166**	40.56 S	148.15 E
Mount Willoughby	**162**	27.58 S	134.08 E
Mount Wilson Observatory ʊ 3	**228**	34.14 N	118.03 W
Mount Wolf	**208**	40.03 N	76.42 W
Mount Zion	**219**	39.46 N	88.53 W
Mounyaz	**146**	10.41 N	21.18 E
Moura, Austl.	**166**	24.35 S	149.58 E
Moura, Bra.	**246**	1.27 S	61.38 W
Moura, Port.	**34**	38.08 N	7.27 W
Moura, Tchad	**146**	13.47 N	21.13 E
Moura Brasil	**256**	22.07 S	43.09 W
Mouraya	**146**	11.27 N	20.59 E
Mourdi, Dépression du ⠂7	**146**	18.10 N	23.00 E
Mourdiah	**150**	14.28 N	7.28 W
Mouriès	**62**	43.41 N	4.52 E
Mourindi	**152**	2.32 S	10.48 E
Mourmelon-le-Grand	**50**	49.08 N	4.22 E
Mourne ≃	**48**	54.49 N	7.28 W
Mourne Beg ≃	**48**	54.41 N	7.39 W
Mourne Mountains ⩘	**48**	54.10 N	6.04 W
Mousa I	**46a**	60.00 N	1.11 W
Mouscron	**50**	50.44 N	3.13 E
Mousgougou	**146**	10.47 N	16.09 E
Moussa Ali ∧	**144**	12.28 N	42.24 E
Mousseaux-sur-Seine	**261**	49.03 N	1.39 E
Moussey	**58**	48.40 N	6.47 E
Moussoro	**146**	13.39 N	16.29 E
Moussy-le-Neuf	**261**	49.04 N	2.36 E
Moussy-le-Vieux	**261**	49.03 N	2.38 E
Moustiers-Sainte-Marie	**62**	43.51 N	6.13 E
Moustique, Morne ∧	**241o**	16.06 N	61.44 W
Mouthe	**58**	46.43 N	6.12 E
Mouthier-Haute-Pierre	**58**	47.02 N	6.16 E
Moutier	**58**	47.17 N	7.23 E
Moûtiers	**62**	45.29 N	6.32 E
Moutiers-au-Perche	**50**	48.29 N	0.51 E
Moutnice	**61**	49.02 N	16.46 E
Moutohora	**172**	38.17 S	177.32 E
Moutomoukadi	**152**	4.41 S	13.15 E
Moutong	**112**	0.28 N	121.13 E
Mouy	**50**	49.19 N	2.19 E
Mouydir ⩘	**148**	24.45 N	4.05 E
Mouyondzi	**152**	3.58 S	13.57 E
Mouzákion	**38**	39.26 N	21.40 E
Mouzarak	**146**	13.11 N	15.58 E
Mouzon	**56**	49.36 N	5.05 E
Mouzon ≃	**58**	48.21 N	5.41 E
Moville, Ire.	**48**	55.11 N	7.03 W
Moville, Ia., U.S.	**198**	42.29 N	96.04 W
Mowang	**100**	30.31 N	113.34 E
Moweaqua	**219**	39.37 N	89.01 W
Mowein	**140**	7.36 N	28.11 E
Mowry Slough ≃	**282**	37.29 N	122.03 W
Mowrystown	**218**	39.02 N	83.44 W
Mowu	**100**	26.50 N	117.42 E
Moxhe	**56**	50.38 N	5.05 E
Moxi	**107**	30.18 N	105.41 E
Moxico □ 5	**152**	13.00 S	20.30 E
Moxotó ≃	**250**	9.19 S	38.14 W
Moy	**48**	54.27 N	6.42 W
Moy ≃	**48**	54.12 N	9.08 W
Moy, Cnoc ∧ 2	**46**	55.22 N	5.46 W
Moya, Comores	**157a**	12.18 S	44.27 E
Moya, Perú	**248**	12.24 S	75.10 W
Moyagee	**162**	27.45 S	117.54 E
Moyahua	**234**	21.16 N	103.10 W
Moyale, Ityo.	**144**	3.30 N	39.07 E
Moyale, Kenya	**154**	3.32 N	39.03 E
Moyamba	**150**	8.10 N	12.26 W
Moycullen	**48**	53.21 N	9.09 W
Moydans	**62**	44.24 N	5.30 E
Moÿ-de-l'Aisne	**50**	49.45 N	3.22 E
Moye Dao I	**98**	36.55 N	122.32 E
Moyen Atlas ⩘	**148**	33.30 N	5.00 W
Moyen-Chari □ 5	**146**	9.00 N	18.00 E
Moyenmoutier	**58**	48.23 N	6.55 E
Moyenne-Sido	**146**	8.13 N	18.43 E
Moyenneville	**50**	50.04 N	1.45 E
Moyen-Ogooué □ 4	**152**	0.30 S	10.30 E
Moyenvic	**56**	48.47 N	6.33 E
Moyeuvre-Grande	**56**	49.15 N	6.02 E
Moyie	**182**	49.17 N	115.50 W
Moyie ≃	**202**	48.42 N	116.11 W
Moyie Springs	**202**	48.43 N	116.11 W
Moylan	**285**	39.54 N	75.23 W
Moyle ≃	**48**	52.24 N	7.39 W
Moyo	**154**	3.39 N	31.43 E
Moyo ≃	**115b**	8.26 S	117.28 E
Moyo, Pulau I	**115b**	8.15 S	117.34 E
Moyobamba	**248**	6.03 S	76.58 W
Moyock	**208**	36.31 N	76.10 W
Moyogalpa	**236**	11.32 N	85.42 W
Moyowosi ≃	**154**	4.50 S	31.24 E
Moyu	**120**	37.17 N	79.44 E
Moyuta, Volcán ∧ 1	**236**	14.02 N	90.06 W
M'oža ≃, Europe	**76**	55.27 N	30.43 E
M'oža ≃, Ross.	**80**	58.23 N	44.54 E
Možajevka	**83**	48.44 N	39.45 E
Možajsk	**82**	55.30 N	36.01 E
Možajskij	**265a**	59.43 N	30.07 E
Možajskoje vodochranilišče ⊜ 1	**82**	55.35 N	35.50 E
Mozambique (Moçambique) □ 1	**138**	18.15 S	35.00 E
Mozambique Channel ʯ	**138**	19.00 S	41.00 E
Mozambique → Moçambique	**154**	15.03 S	40.42 E
Mozambique Plateau ✦ 3	**10**	32.00 S	35.00 E
Mozarlândia	**255**	14.47 S	50.35 W
Možarovka	**86**	51.09 N	59.05 E
Možarov Majdan	**80**	55.37 N	45.53 E
Možary	**80**	53.53 N	41.02 E
Mozdok	**84**	43.44 N	44.38 E
Možga	**80**	56.23 N	52.17 E
Mozhabong Lake ⊜	**190**	46.57 N	82.05 W
Mozia ⊥	**70**	37.52 N	12.28 E
Mozichang	**107**	29.20 N	103.53 E
Mozolevo	**76**	59.19 N	33.51 E
Mozu	**270**	34.34 N	135.29 E
Mozuli	**76**	56.36 N	28.11 E
Mozyr'	**78**	52.03 N	29.14 E
Mozzanica	**62**	45.29 N	9.41 E
Mozzano	**66**	42.50 N	13.31 E
Mozzate	**266b**	45.41 N	8.57 E
Mpaka	**158**	26.26 S	31.47 E
Mpala	**154**	6.45 S	29.31 E
Mpama ≃	**152**	0.57 S	15.39 E
Mpanda	**154**	6.22 S	31.02 E
Mpé	**152**	2.54 S	14.43 E
Mpese	**152**	5.14 S	15.33 E
Mpessoba	**150**	12.40 N	5.43 W
Mphoengs	**154**	21.10 S	27.51 E
Mpigi	**154**	0.13 N	32.42 E
Mpika	**154**	11.54 S	31.26 E
Mpila ◆ 8	**273b**	4.14 S	15.18 E
Mpoka	**152**	1.26 S	17.02 E
Mpoko ≃	**152**	4.19 N	18.33 E
Mporokoso	**154**	9.23 S	30.05 E
Mpouya	**152**	2.37 S	16.13 E
Mpraeso	**150**	6.35 N	0.44 W
Mpui	**154**	8.21 S	31.50 E
Mpulungu	**154**	8.46 S	31.07 E
Mpwapwa	**154**	6.21 S	36.29 E
Mqanduli	**158**	31.48 S	28.46 E
Mrągowo	**30**	53.52 N	21.19 E
Mrakovo	**86**	52.43 N	56.38 E
M'Ramani	**157a**	12.21 S	44.32 E
Mranggen	**115a**	7.01 S	110.31 E
Mras-Su ≃	**86**	53.45 N	87.49 E
Mrhila, Jebel ∧	**36**	35.25 N	9.14 E
Mrijo	**154**	5.10 S	36.15 E
Mrkonjić Grad	**36**	44.25 N	17.05 E
Mrkopalj	**36**	45.19 N	14.51 E
Mrocza	**30**	53.14 N	17.36 E
Msagali	**154**	6.21 S	36.18 E
M'Saken	**148**	35.44 N	10.35 E
Msata	**154**	6.20 S	38.23 E
Mšec	**54**	50.10 N	13.54 E
Mšeno	**54**	50.27 N	14.38 E
M'Sila	**148**	35.46 N	4.31 E
M'Sila □ 5	**148**	35.00 N	4.20 E
M'Sila, Oued ≃	**34**	35.46 N	4.34 E
Mšinskaja	**76**	59.01 N	29.57 E
Msoro	**154**	13.36 S	31.55 E
Msta	**76**	57.55 N	34.29 E
Msta ≃	**76**	58.25 N	31.20 E
Mstera	**80**	56.23 N	41.56 E
Mstislavl'	**76**	54.02 N	31.42 E
Mstiž	**76**	54.34 N	28.10 E
Mszana Dolna	**30**	49.42 N	20.05 E
Mszczonów	**30**	51.58 N	20.31 E
Mtakataka	**154**	14.12 S	34.32 E
Mtakuja	**154**	7.22 S	30.37 E
Mtama	**154**	10.18 S	39.22 E
Mtamvuna ≃	**158**	31.06 S	30.12 E
Mtarazi National Park ♦	**154**	18.36 S	32.50 E
Mtata ≃	**158**	31.58 S	29.10 E
Mtelo ∧	**154**	1.39 N	35.23 E
Mtilikwe ≃	**154**	21.09 S	31.30 E
Mtito Andei	**154**	2.41 S	38.10 E
Mtowabaga	**154**	2.30 S	35.53 E
Mtsensk → Mcensk	**76**	53.17 N	36.35 E
Mtubatuba	**158**	28.30 S	32.08 E
Mtunzini	**158**	28.57 S	31.46 E
Mtwara	**154**	10.16 S	40.11 E
Mtwara □ 4	**154**	11.00 S	39.00 E
Mtyangimbori	**154**	10.16 S	35.31 E
Mu ≃, Mya.	**110**	21.56 N	95.38 E
Mu ≃, Nihon	**92a**	42.33 N	141.56 E
Mu, Cerro ∧	**246**	9.29 N	73.07 W
Muʿa	**174w**	21.11 S	175.07 W
Muacandala	**152**	10.02 S	19.40 E
Mualama	**154**	16.53 S	38.17 E
Mualang	**112**	0.42 N	111.18 E
Muʿallaqah, Lubnān	**132**	33.50 N	35.54 E
Mu ʿAllaqah, Sūd.	**140**	13.28 N	23.57 E
Muan	**98**	34.58 N	126.26 E
Muaná	**250**	1.32 S	49.13 W
Muanda	**152**	5.56 S	12.21 E
Muangai	**152**	12.32 S	19.51 E
Muang Bèng	**110**	20.22 N	101.44 E
Muang Hay	**110**	21.03 N	101.49 E
Muang Hinboun	**110**	17.35 N	104.36 E
Muang Hôngsa	**110**	19.43 N	101.20 E
Muang Houn	**110**	20.09 N	101.27 E
Muang Hounxianghoung	**110**	21.37 N	102.18 E
Muang Huang	**110**	18.45 N	103.42 E
Muang Khammouan	**110**	17.24 N	104.48 E
Muang Khao	**110**	19.47 N	103.29 E
Muang Khi	**110**	18.27 N	101.46 E
Muang Không	**110**	14.07 N	105.51 E
Muang Khôngxédôn	**110**	15.34 N	105.49 E
Muang La	**110**	20.52 N	102.07 E
Muang Liap	**110**	18.29 N	101.40 E
Muang Long	**110**	20.57 N	100.48 E
Muang Meung	**110**	20.43 N	100.28 E
Muang Ngoy, Lao	**102**	20.43 N	102.41 E
Muang Ngoy, Lao	**110**	20.43 N	102.41 E
Muang Nong	**110**	16.22 N	106.30 E
Muang Ou Nua	**110**	22.18 N	101.48 E
Muang Ou Tai	**110**	22.07 N	101.48 E
Muang Pakbèng	**110**	19.54 N	101.08 E
Muang Pak-Lay	**110**	18.12 N	101.25 E
Muang Paktha	**110**	20.06 N	100.36 E
Muang Pakxan	**110**	18.22 N	103.39 E
Muang Peun	**110**	20.13 N	103.52 E
Muang Phalan	**110**	16.39 N	105.34 E
Muang Phiang	**110**	19.06 N	101.32 E
Muang Phônthong	**110**	15.05 N	105.39 E
Muang Phoun	**110**	19.07 N	102.43 E
Muang Sam Sip	**110**	15.31 N	104.44 E
Muang Sing	**110**	21.11 N	101.09 E
Muang Soum	**110**	18.45 N	102.36 E
Muang Souvannakhili	**110**	15.23 N	105.49 E
Muang Souy	**110**	19.33 N	102.52 E
Muang Sung	**110**	20.19 N	102.27 E
Muang Thadua	**110**	19.26 N	101.50 E
Muang Thatèng	**110**	15.26 N	106.23 E
Muang Thathôm	**110**	19.00 N	103.36 E
Muang Va	**110**	21.53 N	102.19 E
Muang Vangviang	**110**	18.56 N	102.27 E
Muang Vapi	**110**	15.40 N	105.55 E
Muang Xaignabouri	**110**	19.15 N	101.45 E
Muang Xamtong	**110**	19.51 N	103.51 E
Muang Xay	**110**	20.42 N	101.59 E
Muang Xépôn	**110**	16.41 N	106.14 E
Muang Xon	**110**	20.27 N	103.19 E
Muang Yo	**110**	21.31 N	101.51 E
Muang You	**110**	19.49 N	102.50 E
Muanza	**156**	18.59 S	34.48 E
Muar (Bandar Maharani)	**114**	2.02 N	102.34 E
Muar ≃	**114**	2.03 N	102.35 E
Muara	**112**	5.02 N	115.02 E
Muaraaman	**112**	3.07 S	102.12 E
Muaraancalung	**112**	0.27 N	116.41 E
Muarabeliti	**112**	3.15 S	103.02 E
Muarabenangin	**112**	0.58 S	115.19 E
Muarabinuangeun	**115a**	6.50 S	105.53 E
Muarabulian	**112**	1.43 S	103.15 E
Muarabungo	**112**	1.28 S	102.07 E
Muaradua	**112**	4.32 S	104.05 E
Muaraenim	**112**	3.39 S	103.48 E
Muaragusung	**112**	1.35 N	117.17 E
Muarajuloi	**112**	0.12 S	114.03 E
Muarakaman	**112**	0.09 S	116.43 E
Muarakelingi	**112**	3.05 S	103.14 E
Muarakumpe	**112**	1.24 S	104.00 E
Muaralabuh	**112**	1.29 S	101.03 E
Muaralakitan	**112**	2.51 S	103.19 E
Muaralasan	**112**	1.48 N	117.12 E
Muaralembu	**112**	0.24 S	101.21 E
Muaramawai	**112**	0.37 N	116.49 E
Muarapangean	**112**	2.38 N	116.41 E
Muarapantai	**112**	0.45 S	101.43 E
Muarapayang	**112**	1.32 S	115.48 E
Muararupit	**112**	2.44 S	102.54 E
Muarasabak	**112**	1.08 S	103.51 E
Muarasiberut	**108**	1.36 S	99.11 E
Muarasipongi	**112**	0.37 N	99.51 E
Muaratais	**114**	1.17 N	99.21 E
Muaratebo	**112**	1.30 S	102.26 E
Muarateladang	**112**	2.50 S	103.58 E
Muaratembesi	**112**	1.42 S	103.07 E
Muaratewe	**112**	0.57 S	114.53 E
Muaratuhup	**112**	0.37 S	114.50 E
Muaratunan	**112**	1.24 S	116.39 E
Muarawahau	**112**	1.02 N	116.52 E
Muāri, Rās >	**120**	24.49 N	66.40 E
Muasdale	**46**	55.36 N	5.41 W
Muá Ximica	**152**	9.50 S	18.41 E
Mubārakpur	**124**	26.05 N	83.18 E
Mubārakpur Dabās ◆ 8	**272a**	28.43 N	77.03 E
Mubayyad ⊤ 4	**142**	30.55 N	32.48 E
Mubende	**154**	0.35 N	31.23 E
Mubi	**146**	10.18 N	13.20 E
Mubur, Pulau I	**112**	3.20 N	106.12 E
Mucaitá ≃	**250**	6.59 S	42.40 W
Mucajaí ≃	**246**	2.25 N	60.52 W
Mucambo	**250**	3.54 S	40.44 W
Mucári	**152**	9.30 S	16.54 E
Muccan	**162**	20.38 S	120.04 E
Muccia	**66**	43.05 N	13.02 E
Much	**56**	50.54 N	7.25 E
Mucha	**269d**	24.59 N	121.34 E
Muchangpu	**100**	31.55 N	116.35 E
Muchanovo	**82**	56.31 N	38.20 E
Muchavec ≃	**76**	52.05 N	23.39 E
Much Dewchurch	**42**	51.59 N	2.46 W
Muchea	**168a**	31.35 S	115.59 E
Mücheln	**54**	51.18 N	11.48 E
Muchen	**89**	48.10 N	136.13 E
Muchengzhen	**107**	29.47 N	103.29 E
Much Hoole	**262**	53.42 N	2.48 W
Muchinga Escarpment ⠂4	**154**	14.45 S	29.30 E
Muchinga Mountains ⩘	**154**	12.20 S	31.00 E
Muchino, Ross.	**80**	58.11 N	51.02 E
Muchino, Ross.	**89**	52.16 N	127.14 E
Muchor-Konduj	**88**	52.25 N	113.16 E
Muchrani	**84**	41.56 N	44.35 E
Muchtadir	**84**	41.41 N	48.46 E
Muchtolovo	**80**	55.27 N	43.13 E
Muchuan	**107**	28.55 N	103.58 E
Much Wenlock	**42**	52.36 N	2.34 W
Mucifal	**266c**	38.48 N	9.26 W
Mučikan	**88**	53.02 N	120.27 E
Muck I	**46**	56.50 N	6.15 W
Mücka	**54**	51.18 N	14.40 E
Muckadilla	**166**	26.35 S	148.23 E
Muckalee Creek ≃	**192**	31.38 N	84.09 W
Muckamore	**48**	54.41 N	6.10 W
Mučkapskij	**80**	51.52 N	42.28 E
Mučkas	**24**	64.02 N	48.27 E
Mücke	**56**	50.38 N	9.03 E
Muckendorf an der Donau	**264b**	48.20 N	16.09 E
Mucking	**260**	51.30 N	0.26 E
Muckle Roe I	**46a**	60.22 N	1.27 W
Muckleshoot Indian Reservation ◆ 4	**224**	47.16 N	122.09 W
Muckno Lough ⊜	**48**	54.07 N	6.42 W
Mucojo	**154**	12.04 S	40.28 E
Mucoma	**152**	15.18 S	13.39 E
Muconda	**152**	10.34 S	21.17 E
Mucope, Ang.	**152**	16.24 S	14.53 E
Mucope, Ang.	**152**	8.42 S	21.43 E
Mucrone, Monte ∧	**62**	45.36 N	7.56 E
Mucubela	**154**	16.55 S	37.52 E
Mucuchíes	**246**	8.45 N	70.55 W
M'uc'ucl'u	**84**	40.28 N	47.55 E
Mucugê	**255**	13.00 S	41.23 W
Mucuim ≃	**248**	6.33 S	64.18 W
Muculo	**152**	16.47 S	14.51 E
Muçum	**252**	29.10 S	51.53 W
Mucumbura	**154**	16.09 S	31.31 E
Mucun	**100**	26.44 N	114.00 E
Mucupia	**156**	18.01 S	36.48 E
Mucupina, Monte ∧	**236**	15.08 N	86.38 W
Mucur	**130**	39.04 N	34.23 E
Mucuri	**255**	18.05 S	39.34 W
Mucuri ≃	**255**	18.05 S	39.34 W
Mucusso	**152**	18.01 S	21.25 E
Mud ≃, Ky., U.S.	**194**	37.13 N	86.54 W
Mud ≃, W.V., U.S.	**188**	38.25 N	82.17 W
Muda ≃	**114**	5.33 N	100.22 E
Mudan ≃	**89**	46.22 N	129.33 E
Mudanjiang	**89**	44.35 N	129.36 E
Mudanya	**130**	40.22 N	28.52 E
Mudau	**56**	49.32 N	9.11 E

Symbol	English	Deutsch	Español	Français	Português
≃	River	Fluß	Río	Rivière	Rio
≊	Canal	Kanal	Canal	Canal	Canal
⌊	Waterfall, Rapids	Wasserfall, Stromschnellen	Cascada, Rápidos	Chute d'eau, Rapides	Cascata, Rápidos
ʯ	Strait	Meeresstraße	Estrecho	Détroit	Estreito
⊂	Bay, Gulf	Bucht, Golf	Bahía, Golfo	Baie, Golfe	Baía, Golfo
⊜	Lake, Lakes	See, Seen	Lago, Lagos	Lac, Lacs	Lago, Lagos
≡	Swamp	Sumpf	Pantano	Marais	Pântano
⊼	Ice Features, Glacier	Eis- und Gletscherformen	Accidentes Glaciales	Formes glaciaires	Acidentes glaciares
⊤	Other Hydrographic Features	Andere Hydrographische Objekte	Otros Elementos Hidrográficos	Autres données hydrographiques	Outros acidentes hidrográficos
✦	Submarine Features	Untermeerische Objekte	Accidentes Submarinos	Formes de relief sous-marin	Acidentes submarinos
□	Political Unit	Politische Einheit	Unidad Politica	Entité politique	Unidade política
ʊ	Cultural Institution	Kulturelle Institution	Institución Cultural	Institution culturelle	Instituição cultural
⊥	Historical Site	Historische Stätte	Sitio Histórico	Site historique	Sitio histórico
♦	Recreational Site	Erholungs- und Ferienort	Sitio de Recreo	Centre de loisirs	Area de Lazer
⊠	Airport	Flughafen	Aeropuerto	Aéroport	Aeroporto
■	Military Installation	Militäranlage	Instalación Militar	Installation militaire	Instalação militar
◆	Miscellaneous	Verschiedenes	Misceláneo	Divers	Diversos

ENGLISH: Name, Page, Lat.°′, Long.°′ — DEUTSCH: Name, Seite, Breite°′, Länge°′ E = Ost

Name	Page	Lat.°′	Long.°′
Mudaysīsāt, Jabal ∧	132	31.39 N	36.14 E
Mud Creek ≃, N.A.	206	45.01 N	72.24 W
Mud Creek ≃, U.S.	198	43.17 N	96.15 W
Mud Creek ≃, Il., U.S.	219	38.21 N	89.48 W
Mud Creek ≃, In., U.S.	216	41.06 N	86.21 W
Mud Creek ≃, In., U.S.	216	40.26 N	85.55 W
Mud Creek ≃, Ne., U.S.	198	41.01 N	98.54 W
Mud Creek ≃, N.Y., U.S.	210	42.17 N	77.13 W
Mud Creek ≃, N.Y., U.S.	210	42.59 N	77.23 W
Mud Creek ≃, N.Y., U.S.	210	43.05 N	78.43 W
Mud Creek ≃, Ok., U.S.	196	33.55 N	97.28 W
Mud Creek ≃, S.D., U.S.	198	45.11 N	98.24 W
Mud Creek ≃, Tx., U.S.	222	31.48 N	94.58 W
Muddus Nationalpark ♣	24	67.00 N	20.16 E
Muddy ≃, Nv., U.S.	204	36.27 N	114.22 W
Muddy ≃, Wa., U.S.	224	46.04 N	122.01 W
Muddy Boggy Creek ≃	196	34.03 N	95.47 W
Muddy Branch ≃	284c	39.03 N	77.18 W
Muddy Brook ≃	276	41.07 N	73.20 W
Muddy Creek ≃, U.S.	276	41.03 N	74.02 W
Muddy Creek ≃, Mo., U.S.	194	38.51 N	93.03 W
Muddy Creek ≃, Mt., U.S.	202	47.56 N	111.46 W
Muddy Creek ≃, Oh., U.S.	214	41.27 N	83.03 W
Muddy Creek ≃, Pa., U.S.	208	39.47 N	76.18 W
Muddy Creek ≃, Ut,. U.S.	200	38.24 N	110.42 W
Muddy Creek ≃, Wy., U.S.	198	42.35 N	104.57 W
Muddy Creek ≃, Wy., U.S.	200	41.59 N	106.08 W
Muddy Creek ≃, Wy., U.S.	200	41.32 N	110.13 W
Muddy Creek ≃, Wy., U.S.	200	41.01 N	107.42 W
Muddy Creek ≃, Wy., U.S.	202	43.17 N	108.14 W
Muddy Fork ≃	224	46.22 N	121.34 W
Muddy Gut ⊂	284b	39.17 N	76.26 W
Muddy Peak ∧	204	36.18 N	114.42 W
Müden, Dtsch.	52	52.52 N	10.07 E
Müden, Dtsch.	54	52.31 N	10.22 E
Mudgee	166	32.36 S	149.35 E
Mudgeeraba	171a	28.04 S	153.22 E
Mudhol	122	16.21 N	75.17 E
Mud Island I	171a	27.20 S	153.15 E
Mud Islands II	169	38.17 S	144.45 E
Mudjatik ≃	184	56.02 N	107.36 W
Mudjuga	24	63.46 N	39.15 E
Mud Lake ⊜, Id., U.S.	202	43.53 N	112.24 W
Mud Lake ⊜, Nv., U.S.	204	37.52 N	117.04 W
Mud Lake ⊜, N.Y., U.S.	212	44.30 N	75.28 W
Mud Lake Reservoir ⊜[1]	198	45.50 N	98.10 W
Mudon	110	16.15 N	97.44 E
Mudongzhen	102	29.35 N	106.51 E
Mudu	106	31.15 N	120.30 E
Mudug □[4]	144	6.15 N	48.00 E
Mudurnu	130	40.28 N	31.13 E
Mudurnu ≃	130	40.49 N	30.33 E
M'ud'ur'um ≃	85	40.53 N	76.36 E
Mueda	154	11.39 S	39.33 E
Muelle de los Bueyes	236	12.04 N	84.32 W
Mueller, Mount ∧[2]	162	19.54 S	127.51 E
Muenster	196	33.39 N	97.23 W
Mu'er	107	29.48 N	106.37 E
Muerte, Valle de la → Death Valley V	204	36.30 N	117.00 W
Muerto ≃	252	23.02 S	62.29 W
Muerto, Mar → Dead Sea ⊜	132	31.30 N	35.30 E
Mufulira	154	12.33 S	28.14 E
Mufuma	152	9.04 S	17.06 E
Mufu Shan ∧	100	29.02 N	113.54 E
Mufu Shan ⋏	100	29.00 N	114.00 E
Mugang	100	29.44 N	115.14 E
Muganskaja ravnina ≚	84	39.40 N	48.15 E
Mugazine	158	26.07 S	32.30 E
Mugegawa	94	35.31 N	136.51 E
Mugello V	66	43.55 N	11.30 E
Mügeln	54	51.14 N	13.02 E
Muger ≃	144	9.54 N	37.57 E
Müggelberge ⋏[2]	264a	52.25 N	13.39 E
Müggelheim ◆[8]	264a	52.25 N	13.40 E
Muggia	64	45.36 N	13.46 E
Muggio	266b	45.36 N	9.14 E
Mughal Sarāi	124	25.18 N	83.07 E
Mugi, Nihon	94	35.34 N	137.01 E
Mugi, Nihon	96	33.40 N	134.25 E
Mu Gia, Deo)(	110	17.40 N	105.47 E
Muginga	152	8.20 S	17.37 E
Muğla	130	37.12 N	28.22 E
Muğla □[4]	130	37.10 N	28.30 E
Mugodžarskaja	86	48.36 N	58.27 E
Mugodžary, gory ⋏[2]	86	49.00 N	58.40 E
Mugombazi	154	5.50 S	30.14 E
Mugo-ri	98	38.58 N	126.31 E
Mugrejevskij	80	56.36 N	42.21 E
Mugron	32	43.45 N	0.45 W
Mugu Karṇālī ≃	124	29.38 N	81.52 E
Mugur-Aksy	86	50.21 N	90.30 E
Mūḥ, Sabkhat al- ⊜	130	34.30 N	38.20 E
Muhala	154	5.40 S	28.43 E
Muhamdi	124	27.57 N	80.13 E
Muḥammad, Ra's ›	140	27.44 N	34.15 E
Muhammadābād	124	26.02 N	83.23 E
Muhammadpur	126	23.24 N	89.36 E
Muḥammad Qawl	140	20.54 N	37.05 E
Muḥayshir, Birkat ⊜	142	30.43 N	31.56 E
Muheza	154	5.10 S	38.47 E
Muḥīṭ, Maṣrif al- ≊	273c	30.07 N	31.06 E
Mühlacker	56	48.57 N	8.50 E
Mühlau	54	50.54 N	12.45 E
Mühlbach am Hochkönig	64	47.22 N	13.08 E
Muhlbach-sur-Munster	58	48.02 N	7.05 E
Mühlberg	54	51.26 N	13.13 E
Mühldorf	61	48.22 N	15.21 E
Mühldorf am Inn	60	48.15 N	12.32 E
Mühlenbeck	54	52.40 N	13.22 E
Mühlenbecker See ⊜	264a	52.41 N	13.24 E
Muhlenberg	210	41.14 N	76.09 W
Mühlen-Berg ∧[2]	264a	52.23 N	13.15 E
Mühlen Eichsen	54	53.45 N	11.15 E
Mühlenfliess ≃	264a	52.26 N	13.41 E
Mühlen → Molini di Tures	64	46.54 N	11.56 E
Mühlenrahmede	263	51.16 N	7.40 E
Mühlhausen, Dtsch.	54	51.12 N	10.27 E
Mühlhausen, Dtsch.	263	51.33 N	7.44 E
Mühlhausen im Täle	56	48.34 N	9.39 E
Mühlheim	56	50.07 N	8.50 E
Mühlheim an der Donau	58	48.01 N	8.53 E
Mühlig-Hofmann Mountains ⋏	9	72.00 S	5.20 E
Mühlleiten	264b	48.10 N	16.34 E
Mühltroff	54	50.32 N	11.55 E
Mühlviertel ◆[1]	30	48.25 N	14.10 E
Muhola	26	63.20 N	25.05 E
Muhoro	154	1.01 S	34.07 E
Muhos	26	64.48 N	25.59 E
Muḥradah	130	35.15 N	36.35 E
Mühringen	58	48.25 N	8.46 E
Muhu I	76	58.38 N	23.15 E
Muhula	154	13.53 S	39.30 E
Muhulu	154	1.03 S	27.17 E
Muhutwe	154	1.33 S	31.42 E
Muhu väin ⊔	76	58.45 N	23.20 E
Muhuwesi ≃	154	11.16 S	37.58 E
Muick, Loch ⊜	46	56.55 N	3.10 W
Muiden	52	52.19 N	5.04 E
Muiderslot ⊥	52	52.20 N	5.10 E
Muides-sur-Loire	50	47.40 N	1.31 E
Muié	152	14.25 S	20.36 E
Mui Hopohoponga Point ›	174w	21.09 S	175.02 W
Muikaichi	96	34.21 N	131.56 E
Muikamachi	94	37.04 N	138.53 E
Muine Bheag (Bagenalstown)	48	52.41 N	6.58 W
Muir, Mi., U.S.	216	42.59 N	84.56 W
Muir, Pa., U.S.	208	40.36 N	76.31 W
Muir, Mount ∧	180	61.06 N	148.24 W
Muir Beach	282	37.52 N	122.35 W
Muirdrum	46	56.31 N	2.42 W
Muirkirk, Scot., U.K.	46	55.31 N	4.04 W
Muirkirk, Md., U.S.	284c	39.03 N	76.53 W
Muir of Ord	46	57.31 N	4.27 W
Muiron Islands II	162	21.35 S	114.20 E
Muir Seamount ✦[3]	16	33.41 N	62.30 W
Muirtown	46	56.16 N	3.45 W
Muir Woods	282	37.53 N	122.34 W
Muir Woods National Monument ♣	226	37.54 N	122.33 W
Muiskraal	158	33.56 S	21.13 E
Muisne	246	0.36 N	80.02 W
Muite	154	14.02 S	39.00 E
Mui Wo	271d	22.16 N	113.59 E
Muizen, Bel.	50	51.01 N	4.31 E
Muizen, Bel.	56	50.46 N	5.10 E
Muja, Ityo.	144	12.02 N	39.29 E
Muja, Ross.	88	56.24 N	115.39 E
Muja ≃	88	56.24 N	115.39 E
Mujāhidpur ◆[8]	272a	28.34 N	77.13 E
Mujang-ni	98	35.26 N	126.32 E
Mujezerskij	24	63.57 N	31.55 E
Mujiapucun	104	41.06 N	122.48 E
Mujiayu	105	40.24 N	116.55 E
Mujimbeji Mission	154	12.11 S	24.57 E
Mujnak	86	43.48 N	59.02 E
Muju	98	36.02 N	127.40 E
Mujunkum, peski ◆[2]	86	44.20 N	71.00 E
Mukačevo	78	48.27 N	22.45 E
Mukah	112	2.54 N	112.06 E
Mukaishima	96	34.20 N	133.10 E
Mukalla → Al-Mukallā	144	14.32 N	49.08 E
Mukandpur ◆[8]	272a	28.44 N	77.11 E
Mukandwara	120	24.49 N	75.59 E
Mukawa	94	35.47 N	138.23 E
Mukāwir	132	31.34 N	35.38 E
Mukāwir ⊥	132	31.34 N	35.38 E
Mukawwar I	140	20.48 N	37.13 E
Mukdahan	110	16.32 N	104.43 E
Mukden → Shenyang	104	41.48 N	123.27 E
Muke Arba	144	8.57 N	42.09 E
Mukebo	154	6.49 S	28.03 E
Mukeriān	123	31.57 N	75.37 E
Mukharram al-Fawqānī	130	34.49 N	37.04 E
Mukhmās	132	31.52 N	35.17 E
Mukho	98	37.33 N	129.06 E
Mukilteo	224	47.56 N	122.18 W
Mukinbudin	162	30.54 S	118.13 E
Mukinge Hill	154	13.29 S	25.52 E
Mukō	96	34.56 N	135.42 E
Muko ≃	96	34.41 N	135.23 E
Mukomuko	112	2.35 S	101.07 E
Mukomwenze	154	6.52 S	27.16 E
Mukoshima-rettō II	14	27.37 N	142.10 E
Mukry	128	37.36 N	65.44 E
Muksi-ri	98	39.52 N	125.54 E
Muksu ≃	85	39.15 N	71.23 E
Muksūdpur	126	23.18 N	89.51 E
Muktāgācha	124	24.46 N	90.14 E
Muktsar	123	30.29 N	74.31 E
Mukuku	154	12.09 S	29.49 E
Mukuleshi ≃	154	10.21 S	24.30 E
Mukur	86	48.03 N	54.30 E
Mukusaki	115b	8.33 S	121.37 E
Mukutan	154	0.38 N	36.16 E
Mukutawa ≃	184	53.10 N	97.28 W
Mukwela	154	17.02 S	26.39 E
Mukwonago	216	42.51 N	88.19 W
Mūl	122	20.04 N	79.40 E
Mula, Esp.	34	38.03 N	1.30 W
Mula, Zhg.	102	29.40 N	100.39 E
Mula ≃, India	122	19.32 N	74.50 E
Mula ≃, India	122	18.34 N	74.20 E
Mūla ≃, Pāk.	120	27.57 N	67.36 E
Mulādi	126	22.54 N	90.25 E
Muladu I	122	7.01 N	72.59 E
Mulaly	86	45.27 N	78.19 E
Mulan	89	45.57 N	128.03 E
Muland ◆[8]	272c	19.10 N	72.57 E
Mulanda	152	14.41 S	21.48 E
Mulanje, Malaŵi	154	16.03 S	35.31 E
Mulanje, Moç.	154	16.03 S	35.45 E
Mulargia, Lago ⊜	71	39.37 N	9.14 E
Mulas, Punta ›	240m	18.09 N	65.27 W
Mulas, Punta de ›	240p	21.01 N	75.35 W
Mulatos	232	28.39 N	108.51 W
Mulayit Taung ∧	110	16.11 N	98.32 E
Mulazzo	64	44.19 N	9.53 E
Mulbāgal	122	13.10 N	78.24 E
Mulben	46	57.31 N	3.06 W
Mulberry, Ar., U.S.	194	35.30 N	94.03 W
Mulberry, Fl., U.S.	220	27.53 N	81.58 W
Mulberry, In., U.S.	216	40.20 N	86.39 W
Mulberry, Oh., U.S.	218	39.11 N	84.14 W
Mulberry ≃	194	35.28 N	94.03 W
Mulberry Creek ≃, Al., U.S.	194	32.27 N	86.52 W
Mulberry Creek ≃, Tx., U.S.	196	34.37 N	100.55 W
Mulberry Fork ≃	194	33.33 N	87.11 W
Mulberry Grove	219	38.55 N	89.16 W
Mulberry Mountain ∧	194	35.42 N	92.56 W
Mulchatna ≃	180	59.39 N	157.08 W
Mulchén	252	37.43 S	72.14 W
Mulda, Dtsch.	54	50.48 N	13.25 E
Mul'da, Ross.	24	67.28 N	63.34 E
Mulde ≃	54	51.52 N	12.15 E
Muldenstein	54	51.40 N	12.19 E
Muldersdrif se Loop ≃	273d	26.06 S	27.51 E
Muldersvlei	158	30.41 S	22.13 E
Muldoon	222	29.49 N	97.04 W
Muldraugh	194	37.56 N	85.59 W
Muldrow	194	35.24 N	94.35 W
Mule, Lac la ⊜	186	51.33 N	65.35 W
Muleba	154	1.49 S	31.40 E
Mule Creek ≃	198	37.05 N	99.00 W
Mulegé	232	26.53 N	112.01 W
Mulegns	58	46.33 N	9.37 E
Mulei	86	43.49 N	90.11 E
Mules (Mauls)	64	46.51 N	11.31 E
Mules, Pulau I	115b	8.54 S	120.17 E
Muleshoe	196	34.13 N	102.43 W
Mulevala	154	16.30 S	37.30 E
Mulga Downs	162	22.08 S	118.26 E
Mulgathing	162	30.15 S	134.00 E
Mulgathing Rocks ∧	162	30.14 S	133.58 E
Mulghar	126	22.46 N	89.45 E
Mulgoa	170	33.50 S	150.40 E
Mulgoa Creek ≃	274a	33.46 S	150.39 E
Mulgowie	171a	27.43 S	152.22 E
Mulgrave, Austl.	274b	37.56 S	145.12 E
Mulgrave, N.S., Can.	186	45.37 N	61.23 W
Mulgrave Hills ⋏[2]	180	67.42 N	163.24 W
Mulgul	162	24.49 S	118.26 E
Mulhacén ∧	34	37.03 N	3.19 W
Mulhall	196	36.03 N	97.24 W
Mülhausen → Mulhouse	58	47.45 N	7.20 E
Mülheim	56	49.54 N	7.01 E
Mülheim an der Ruhr	56	51.24 N	6.54 E
Mülheimer Ruhrtalbrüke ◆[5]	263	51.23 N	6.54 E
Mülheim-Karlich	56	50.21 N	7.28 E
Mulhouse (Mülhausen)	58	47.45 N	7.20 E
Muli	102	27.50 N	101.15 E
Muling, Zhg.	89	44.56 N	130.31 E
Muling, Zhg.	89	44.31 N	130.13 E
Muling ≃	89	45.53 N	133.30 E
Mulini, Capo ›	70	37.34 N	15.10 E
Mulino	224	45.13 N	122.34 W
Mulinu'u, Cape ›	175a	13.26 S	172.43 W
Mulita ≃	116	7.18 N	124.52 E
Mulkear ≃	48	52.40 N	8.33 W
Mūlki	122	13.06 N	74.48 E
Mull, Island of I	46	56.27 N	6.00 W
Mull, Sound of ⊔	46	56.32 N	5.50 W
Mullagh	48	53.49 N	6.57 W
Mullaghareirk Mountains ⋏	48	52.20 N	9.10 W
Mullaghcleevaun ∧	48	53.06 N	6.24 W
Mullaghmore ∧	48	54.52 N	6.51 W
Mullaloo Point ›	168a	31.48 S	115.44 E
Mullan	202	47.28 N	115.48 W
Mullen	198	42.02 N	101.02 W
Müllenbach	56	50.19 N	6.55 E
Mullengudgery	166	31.41 S	147.26 E
Mullens	192	37.34 N	81.22 W
Muller, Pegunungan ⋏	112	0.40 N	113.50 E
Muller Creek ≃	162	22.29 S	134.30 E
Muller Range ⋏	164	5.35 S	142.15 E
Mullerup	41	55.30 N	11.13 E
Mullet Key I	220	27.37 N	82.44 W
Mullet Peninsula ›[1]	48	54.12 N	10.00 W
Mullett Lake ⊜	190	45.30 N	84.30 W
Mullewa	162	28.33 S	115.31 E
Mull Head ›, Scot., U.K.	46	58.58 N	2.43 W
Mull Head ›, Scot., U.K.	46	59.23 N	2.54 W
Müllheim	58	47.48 N	7.38 E
Mullhyttan	40	59.09 N	14.41 E
Mullica ≃	208	39.33 N	74.25 W
Mullica, Alquatka Branch ≃	285	39.47 N	74.48 W
Mullica, Sleeper Branch ≃	285	39.39 N	74.40 W
Mullica Hill	208	39.44 N	75.13 W
Mulligan ≃	166	25.00 S	138.30 E
Mulliken	216	42.45 N	84.53 W
Mullin	196	31.33 N	98.40 W
Mullinahone	48	52.30 N	7.30 W
Mullinavat	48	52.21 N	7.10 W
Mullingar	48	53.32 N	7.20 W
Mullins	192	34.12 N	79.15 W
Mullinville	198	37.35 N	99.28 W
Mullion	42	50.01 N	5.15 W
Mulloon Creek ≃	171b	35.12 S	149.38 E
Mullovka	80	54.13 N	49.25 E
Müllrose	54	52.14 N	14.25 E
Mullsjö	26	57.55 N	13.53 E
Mullumbimby	166	28.33 S	153.30 E
Mullum Mullum Creek ≃	274b	37.44 S	145.10 E
Mulobezi	154	16.48 S	25.09 E
Mulonda Funda	154	11.06 S	25.28 E
Mulondo	152	15.39 S	15.14 E
Mulongo	154	7.50 S	27.00 E
Mulshi Lake ⊜	122	18.30 N	73.30 E
Multai	120	21.46 N	78.15 E
Multān	123	30.11 N	71.29 E
Multen ⊜	40	59.10 N	14.37 E
Multia	26	62.25 N	24.47 E
Multnomah □[6]	224	45.30 N	122.22 W
Multnomah Channel ≃[1]	224	45.51 N	122.52 W
Multnomah Falls ∟	224	45.35 N	122.07 W
Mulu, Gunong ∧	112	4.04 N	114.56 E
Mulumbe, Monts ⋏	154	8.16 S	28.16 E
Mulungushi	154	14.40 S	28.50 E
Mulungushi Dam ◆[6]	154	14.40 S	28.50 E
Mulvane	198	37.28 N	97.14 W
Mulwad	140	18.39 N	30.35 E
Mulyah Mountain ∧	166	30.37 S	144.31 E
Muma	152	3.24 N	23.15 E
Mumbles Head ›	42	51.35 N	3.59 W
Mumbondo	152	10.09 S	14.15 E
Mumbra	272c	19.11 N	73.01 E
Mumbwa	154	14.59 S	27.04 E
Mumcular	130	37.05 N	27.40 E
Mume	154	9.40 S	27.26 E
Mumen	102	32.09 N	106.28 E
Mumeng	164	7.00 S	146.35 E
Mumford, N.Y., U.S.	210	42.59 N	77.52 W
Mumford, Tx., U.S.	222	30.44 N	96.34 W
Mumias	154	0.20 N	34.29 E
Mümling ≃	56	49.50 N	9.09 E
Mumoni ∧	154	0.31 S	38.01 E
Mumra	80	45.47 N	47.41 E
Mumu	140	12.06 N	23.42 E
Mumungwe	156	21.59 S	26.24 E
Mun ≃	110	15.19 N	105.30 E
Mun, Jabal ∧	140	14.08 N	22.42 E
Munā, Ar. Su.	144	21.25 N	39.52 E
Muna, Méx.	232	20.29 N	89.43 W
Muna ≃	74	67.52 N	123.06 E
Muna, Pulau I	112	5.00 S	122.30 E
Muna, Selat ⊔	112	5.15 S	122.10 E
Munā al-Amīr	142	29.54 N	31.15 E
Munābāo	120	25.45 N	70.17 E
Munajly	86	46.47 N	54.31 E
Munakata	96	33.50 N	130.35 E
Munam-ni	98	38.41 N	126.54 E
Munam-san ∧	98	40.26 N	127.22 E
Munbong-ni	271b	37.43 N	126.49 E
Muncar	115a	8.26 S	114.20 E
Münchberg	54	50.11 N	11.47 E
Müncheberg	54	52.30 N	14.08 E
Münchehofe	264a	52.30 N	13.40 E
München	60	48.08 N	11.34 E
Münchenbernsdorf	54	50.49 N	11.56 E
Münchenbuchsee	58	47.01 N	7.27 E
Münchendorf	264b	48.02 N	16.23 E
München-Erding, Flughafen ⊠	60	48.22 N	11.48 E
München-Gladbach → Mönchengladbach	56	51.12 N	6.28 E
München-Riem, Flughafen ⊠	60	48.08 N	11.41 E
Münchenstein	58	47.31 N	7.37 E
Münchhausen	56	50.57 N	8.43 E
Munchique, Cerro ∧	246	2.32 N	76.57 W
Munchique, Parque Nacional ♣	246	2.30 N	77.10 W
Munch'ŏn	98	39.16 N	127.15 E
Muncie	216	40.11 N	85.23 W
Muncusun	130	38.54 N	35.38 E
Muncy	210	41.12 N	76.47 W
Muncy Creek ≃	210	41.13 N	76.48 W
Muncy Valley	210	41.21 N	76.35 W
Mundare	182	53.36 N	112.20 W
Mundaring	168a	31.54 S	116.10 E
Munday	196	33.26 N	99.37 W
Mundelein	216	42.15 N	88.00 W
Mündelheim ◆[8]	263	51.21 N	6.41 E
Münden	56	51.25 N	9.39 E
Munderfing	60	48.05 N	13.11 E
Munderkingen	58	48.14 N	9.38 E
Munderoo ∧	171b	35.48 S	147.47 E
Mundesley	42	52.53 N	1.26 E
Mundijong	168a	32.18 S	115.59 E
Mundiwindi	162	23.52 S	120.09 E
Mūndka ◆[8]	272a	28.41 N	77.02 E
Mundo ≃	34	38.19 N	1.40 W
Mundolsheim	58	48.39 N	7.42 E
Mundon Hill	260	51.41 N	0.42 E
Mundo Novo	255	11.52 S	40.28 W
Mundra	120	22.51 N	69.44 E
Mundrabilla	162	31.52 S	127.51 E
Mundubbera	166	25.36 S	151.18 E
Mundybaš	86	53.14 N	87.19 E
Mundytau, gora ∧	85	38.00 N	68.27 E
Munene	154	20.38 S	30.03 E
Munenga	152	10.02 S	14.41 E
Munera	34	39.02 N	2.28 W
Munford	194	35.26 N	89.48 W
Munfordville	194	37.16 N	85.53 W
Mungallala	166	26.27 S	147.33 E
Mungallala Creek ≃	166	28.05 S	147.15 E
Mungana	166	17.07 S	144.24 E
Mungaoli	124	24.25 N	78.06 E
Mungári	154	17.12 S	33.31 E
Mungar Junction	166	25.36 S	152.36 E
Mungau	152	13.56 S	21.55 E
Mungbere	154	2.38 N	28.30 E
Mungeli	124	22.04 N	81.41 E
Munger	124	25.23 N	86.28 E
Mungeranie	162	28.00 S	138.36 E
Mungindi	166	28.58 S	148.59 E
Munglinup	162	33.43 S	120.51 E
Mungo	152	11.49 S	16.16 E
Mungo National Park ♣	166	33.44 S	143.02 E
Mungra Badshāhpur	124	25.40 N	82.11 E
Mungun-Tajga, gora ∧	86	50.16 N	90.05 E
Mun'gyŏng	98	36.44 N	128.07 E
Munhall	214	40.23 N	79.54 W
Munhamade	154	16.37 S	36.58 E
Munhango	152	12.12 S	18.42 E
Munhango ≃	152	11.20 S	19.50 E
Munhoz	256	22.37 S	46.22 W
Munhye-ri	98	38.10 N	127.19 E
Munich → München	60	48.08 N	11.34 E
Muniesa	34	41.02 N	0.48 W
Munim ≃	250	2.45 S	44.04 W
Munirka ◆[8]	272a	28.34 N	77.10 E
Munising	190	46.24 N	86.38 W
Munith	216	42.23 N	84.15 W
Muñiz	258	34.33 S	58.42 W
Muniz Freire	255	20.28 S	41.25 W
Munkács → Mukačevo	78	48.27 N	22.45 E
Munka-Ljungby	41	56.15 N	12.58 E
Munkebjerg ∧[2]	41	55.41 N	9.37 E
Munkebo	41	55.27 N	10.34 E
Munkedal	26	58.29 N	11.41 E
Munkerud	40	59.50 N	13.31 E
Munkfors	40	59.50 N	13.32 E
Munksund	26	65.17 N	21.29 E
Munktorp	40	59.32 N	16.08 E
Munku-Sardyk, gora ∧	88	51.45 N	100.32 E
Munlochy	46	57.32 N	4.15 W
Münnerstadt	56	50.15 N	10.11 E
Munnsville	210	42.58 N	75.35 W
Muñoz	116	15.43 N	120.54 E
Munozero	24	67.05 N	34.12 E
Muñoz Gamero, Península ›[1]	254	52.30 S	73.10 W
Munpal-li	271b	37.45 N	126.43 E
Munro ◆[8]	288	34.32 S	58.31 W
Munroe Falls	214	41.08 N	81.26 W
Munro Lake ⊜	184	54.38 N	95.16 W
Munsan	98	37.51 N	126.48 E
Munsarpur	126	24.18 N	88.26 E
Munsey Park	276	40.48 N	73.41 W
Munshiganj	124	23.33 N	90.32 E
Münsing	64	47.54 N	11.22 E
Münsingen, Dtsch.	58	48.25 N	9.29 E
Münsingen, Schw.	58	46.53 N	7.34 E
Munsö I	40	59.23 N	17.35 E
Munson, Ab., Can.	182	51.34 N	112.45 W
Munson, Pa., U.S.	214	40.57 N	78.10 W
Munson Knob ∧[2]	214	40.40 N	81.54 W
Munsons Corners	210	42.35 N	76.13 W
Münster, Dtsch.	52	51.57 N	7.37 E
Munster, Dtsch.	52	52.59 N	10.05 E
Münster, Dtsch.	56	49.55 N	8.52 E
Munster, Fr.	56	48.55 N	6.54 E
Munster, Fr.	58	48.03 N	7.08 E
Münster, Schw.	58	46.29 N	8.16 E
Munster, In., U.S.	216	41.33 N	87.30 W
Münster □[5]	52	51.50 N	7.25 E
Munster □[9]	48	52.25 N	8.20 W
Munster ≃	48	52.33 N	7.12 W
Münsterkirche ☨[1]	263	51.27 N	7.01 E
Münsterland ◆[1]	52	52.00 N	7.30 E
Münsterlingen	58	47.38 N	9.14 E
Münstermaifeld	56	50.15 N	7.22 E
Muntadgin	162	31.45 S	118.34 E
Muntahak ∧	114	1.52 N	103.47 E
Munte	112	0.30 N	119.55 E
Muntele Mare, Vîrful ∧	38	46.29 N	23.14 E
Muntendam	52	53.07 N	6.53 E
Muntok	112	2.04 S	105.11 E
Mununzi	154	0.36 N	29.15 E
Munuscong Lake ⊜	190	46.10 N	84.08 W
Münzenberg	56	50.27 N	8.46 E
Münzkirchen	60	48.29 N	13.34 E
Munzur Dağları ⋏	130	39.30 N	39.10 E
Munzur Vadisi Milli Parkı ♣	130	39.25 N	39.30 E
Muolea Point ›	229a	20.41 N	156.01 W
Muong Het	110	20.49 N	104.01 E
Muong Hinh	110	19.49 N	105.03 E
Muong Khoua	110	21.05 N	102.31 E
Muong Saiapoun	110	18.24 N	101.31 E
Muong Te	110	22.28 N	102.37 E
Muonio	24	67.57 N	23.42 E
Muoro	36	40.20 N	9.20 E
Muotathal	58	46.59 N	8.46 E
Mupa	152	16.10 S	15.44 E
Mupa, Parque Nacional da ◆[4]	152	16.00 S	15.35 E
Muping	98	37.24 N	121.35 E
Mupini	156	17.50 S	19.40 E
Mup'ungjang	98	35.58 N	127.49 E
Muqaddam, Wādī V	140	18.04 N	31.30 E
Muqaṭṭaʿ	140	14.40 N	35.51 E
Muqaybirah, Bi'r al- ⊤[4]	142	30.53 N	32.50 E
Muqayshiṭ I	128	24.10 N	53.45 E
Muqdisho (Mogadishu)	144	2.04 N	45.22 E
Muqi	98	41.46 N	124.39 E
Muqsam, Jabal ∧	140	13.38 N	27.42 E
Muquequete	152	14.50 S	14.16 E
Muqui	255	20.57 S	41.20 W
Mur (Mura) ≃	30	46.18 N	16.53 E
Mura (Mur) ≃, Europe	30	46.18 N	16.53 E
Mura ≃, Ross.	88	58.27 N	98.34 E
Muradiye, Tür.	84	38.59 N	43.46 E
Muradiye, Tür.	130	38.39 N	27.21 E
Murādnagar	124	28.47 N	77.30 E
Murafa ≃	78	48.13 N	28.14 E
Murāgācha	126	23.32 N	88.24 E
Muraglione, Passo del)(	66	43.56 N	11.39 E
Murai Reservoir ⊜[1]	271c	1.24 N	103.41 E
Murajá	250	0.47 S	47.57 W
Murakami	92	38.14 N	139.29 E
Murallón, Cerro ∧	254	49.48 S	73.25 W
Murambi	154	1.46 S	30.23 E
Muramvya	154	3.16 S	29.37 E
Murana	164	3.33 S	133.49 E
Murang'a	154	0.43 S	37.09 E
Murano, Isola di I	64	45.28 N	12.21 E
Muranskij porog ∟	88	58.02 N	112.16 E
Muraoka	96	35.28 N	134.35 E
Muraši	24	59.24 N	48.55 E
Muraški	265b	55.59 N	37.45 E
Murat	32	45.07 N	2.52 E
Murat ≃	84	38.39 N	39.50 E
Murat Dağı ∧	130	38.55 N	29.43 E
Muratkovo	86	58.26 N	62.23 E
Muratlı	130	41.10 N	27.30 E
Muratovo	83	48.48 N	38.45 E
Muratpur	272b	22.59 N	88.27 E
Murau	61	47.07 N	14.10 E
Muravera	71	39.25 N	9.34 E
Muravjovka	89	49.50 N	127.44 E
Muravjovo	76	56.14 N	34.14 E
Murayama	92	38.28 N	140.22 E
Murayama-chosuichi ⊜[1]	268	35.45 N	139.25 E
Muraysah, Ra's al- ›	146	31.55 N	25.02 E
Murča	34	41.24 N	7.27 W
Murcanyo	144	11.41 N	50.27 E
Mūrcheh Khvort	128	33.06 N	51.30 E
Murchin	54	53.54 N	13.44 E
Murchison, Austl.	166	36.37 S	145.14 E
Murchison, N.Z.	172	41.48 S	172.20 E
Murchison, Tx., U.S.	222	32.17 N	95.45 W
Murchison ≃	162	27.42 S	114.09 E
Murchison, Mount ∧, Austl.	162	26.46 S	116.25 E
Murchison, Mount ∧, N.Z.	172	43.01 S	171.22 E
Murchison Falls → Kabalega Falls ∟	154	2.17 N	31.41 E
Murchison Range ⋏	162	20.11 S	134.26 E
Murcia, Esp.	34	37.59 N	1.07 W
Murcia, Pil.	116	10.36 N	123.02 E
Murcia □[4], Esp.	34	38.00 N	1.30 W
Murcia □[4], Esp.	34	38.00 N	1.30 W
Murcia □[4], Esp.	148	37.55 N	1.30 W
Murciélago, Islas II	236	10.51 N	85.57 W
Murcielagos Bay ⊂	116	8.39 N	123.33 E
Mur-de-Barrez	32	44.51 N	2.39 E
Murdeduke, Lake ⊜	169	38.11 S	143.53 E
Murder Creek ≃, Al., U.S.	194	31.04 N	87.06 W
Murder Creek ≃, N.Y., U.S.	210	43.05 N	78.31 W
Murderkill ≃	208	39.03 N	75.24 W
Murdo	198	43.53 N	100.42 W
Murdock	220	27.00 N	82.08 W
Mure	94	36.45 N	138.14 E
Mureaux, Aérodrome des ⊠	261	49.00 N	1.57 E
Mureck	61	46.42 N	15.46 E
Mürefte	130	40.40 N	27.14 E
Mureș □[6]	38	46.35 N	24.40 E
Mureș (Maros) ≃	38	46.15 N	20.13 E
Muret	32	43.28 N	1.21 E
Murewa	154	17.39 S	31.47 E
Murfreesboro, Ar., U.S.	194	34.03 N	93.41 W
Murfreesboro, N.C., U.S.	192	36.26 N	77.05 W
Murfreesboro, Tn., U.S.	194	35.50 N	86.23 W
Murg	58	47.33 N	8.01 E
Murg ≃	56	48.55 N	8.10 E
Murgab	85	38.10 N	73.59 E
Murgab (Morghāb) ≃, Asia	128	38.18 N	61.12 E
Murgab ≃, Taj.	120	38.20 N	72.30 E
Murgenella	164	11.33 S	132.55 E
Murgeni	38	46.12 N	28.01 E
Murgenthal	58	47.16 N	7.50 E
Murgha Faqīrzai	120	31.03 N	67.48 E
Murgha Kibzai	120	30.44 N	69.25 E
Murgon	166	26.15 S	151.57 E
Muri, Cook Is.	174k	21.14 S	159.43 W
Muri, Nig.	146	9.11 N	10.53 E
Muri, Schw.	58	46.56 N	7.29 E
Muri, Schw.	58	47.16 N	8.21 E
Muria, Gunung ∧	115a	6.36 S	110.53 E
Muriaé	255	21.08 S	42.22 W
Muriaé ≃	255	21.43 S	41.22 W
Murias de Paredes	34	42.51 N	6.11 W
Muribeca	250	10.26 S	36.59 W
Muribeca dos Guararapes	250	8.10 S	35.01 W
Murici	250	9.19 S	35.56 W
Muricizal ≃	250	6.40 S	48.40 W
Murīdke	123	31.48 N	74.16 E
Muriége	152	9.58 S	21.11 E
Muriel Lake ⊜	182	54.10 N	110.40 W
Murih, Pulau I	112	1.54 N	108.38 E
Murila	152	10.44 S	20.20 E
Murilo I[1]	14	8.40 N	152.11 E
Mūrinda	123	30.47 N	76.29 E
Murinja	88	54.47 N	107.21 E
Murino, Ross.	88	51.30 N	104.23 E
Murino, Ross.	265a	60.03 N	30.27 E
Murinskij ≃	265a	60.01 N	30.28 E
Muriqui	256	22.56 S	43.57 W
Muriqui ≃	287a	22.52 S	43.02 W
Murisengo	62	45.05 N	8.08 E
Mūrītāniyā → Mauritania □[1]	134	20.00 N	12.00 W
Müritz ⊜	54	53.25 N	12.43 E
Muriwai	172	38.46 S	177.55 E
Murkong Selek	120	27.49 N	95.16 E
Murlīganj	124	25.54 N	86.59 E
Murlo	66	43.09 N	11.23 E
Murmansk	24	68.58 N	33.05 E
Murmansk Oblast' □[4]	24	68.00 N	35.00 E
Murmansk Rise ✦[3]	12	75.00 N	37.00 E
Murmerwoude	52	53.16 N	6.00 E
Murmino	80	54.36 N	40.03 E
Murnau	64	47.40 N	11.12 E
Murnei	140	12.57 N	22.52 E
Murō	94	34.34 N	136.02 E
Murō-Akame-Aoyama-kokutei-kōen ♣	94	34.30 N	136.10 E
Muro Lucano	68	40.45 N	15.29 E
Murom	80	55.34 N	42.02 E
Muromcevo	86	56.23 N	75.14 E
Muroran	92a	42.18 N	140.59 E
Muros	34	42.47 N	9.02 W
Muros y Noya, Ría de ⊂[1]	34	42.45 N	9.00 W
Muroto	96	33.18 N	134.09 E
Muroto-Anan-kaigan-kokutei-kōen ♣	96	33.41 N	134.32 E
Muroto-zaki ›	96	33.15 N	134.11 E
Murovanyje Kurilovcy	78	48.43 N	27.31 E
Murowana Goślina	30	52.35 N	17.01 E
Murphy, Id., U.S.	202	43.13 N	116.33 W
Murphy, Mo., U.S.	219	38.29 N	90.29 W
Murphy, N.C., U.S.	192	35.05 N	84.02 W
Murphy Lake ⊜	182	52.03 N	121.14 W
Murphys	226	38.08 N	120.27 W
Murphysboro	194	37.45 N	89.20 W
Murphy Slough ≃	226	36.28 N	120.00 W
Murr ≃	56	48.57 N	9.16 E
Murr, Wādī V	142	28.27 N	32.18 E
Murrah, Qārat al- ∧[2]	142	30.00 N	32.41 E
Murrah al-Kubrā, Al-Buḥayrah al- (Great Bitter Lake) ⊜	142	30.20 N	32.23 E
Murrah aṣ-Ṣughrā, Al-Buḥayrah al- (Little Bitter Lake) ⊜	142	30.13 N	32.33 E
Murra Murra	166	28.16 S	146.48 E
Murrāt, Ābār ⊤[4]	140	21.03 N	32.55 E
Murray, Ia., U.S.	190	41.02 N	93.56 W
Murray, Ky., U.S.	194	36.36 N	88.18 W
Murray, Ut,. U.S.	200	40.40 N	111.53 W
Murray ≃, Austl.	166	35.22 S	139.22 E
Murray ≃, Austl.	168a	32.35 S	115.46 E
Murray ≃, B.C., Can.	182	55.40 N	121.10 W
Murray, Lake ⊜	164	7.00 S	141.30 E
Murray, Lake ⊜[1]	192	34.04 N	81.23 W
Murray, Mount ∧, Yk., Can.	180	60.54 N	128.49 W
Murray, Mount ∧, Pap. N. Gui.	164	6.46 S	144.01 E
Murray Bay → La Malbaie	186	47.39 N	70.10 W
Murray Bridge	168b	35.07 S	139.17 E
Murray Canal ≊	212	44.04 N	77.35 W
Murray City	188	39.30 N	82.09 W
Murray Downs	162	21.04 S	134.40 E
Murray Fracture Zone ✦	16	34.00 N	135.00 W
Murray Harbour	186	46.00 N	62.31 W
Murray Head ›	186	46.00 N	62.28 W
Murray Maxwell Bay ⊂	176	70.00 N	80.00 W
Murray Mouth ≃[1]	168b	35.34 S	138.54 E
Murray River	186	46.01 N	62.37 W
Murraysburg	158	31.58 S	23.47 E
Murrayville, B.C., Can.	224	49.10 N	122.36 W
Murrayville, Il., U.S.	194	39.35 N	90.15 W
Murrébuè	154	13.02 S	40.30 E
Murree	123	33.54 N	73.24 E
Mürren	58	46.34 N	7.54 E
Murrhardt	56	48.59 N	9.34 E
Murrí ≃	246	6.33 N	76.52 W
Murrieta	228	33.33 N	117.12 W
Murro di Porca, Capo ›	70	37.00 N	15.20 E
Murrumbidgee ≃	166	34.43 S	143.12 E
Murrumburrah	166	34.33 S	148.21 E
Murrupula	154	15.27 S	38.47 E
Murrurundi	166	31.46 S	150.50 E
Murry Hill	279b	40.17 N	80.09 W
Murrysville	279b	40.25 N	79.41 W
Mursal	130	39.11 N	37.59 E
Mursala, Pulau I	114	1.38 N	98.32 E
Murshidābād	126	24.11 N	88.16 E
Mürşitpınar	130	36.54 N	38.19 E
Murska Sobota	61	46.40 N	16.10 E
Murskij, porog ∟	88	58.27 N	98.30 E
Mursko Središće	61	46.31 N	16.27 E
Murtajāpur	122	20.44 N	77.23 E
Murtal	266c	38.42 N	9.22 W
Murtee	166	31.35 S	143.30 E
Murten	58	46.56 N	7.07 E
Murtensee → Morat, Lac de ⊜	58	46.55 N	7.05 E
Murter, Otok I	36	43.48 N	15.37 E
Murtle Lake ⊜	182	52.08 N	119.38 W
Murtoa	166	36.37 S	142.28 E
Murton	44	54.49 N	1.24 W
Murtosa	34	40.44 N	8.38 W
Muru	140	6.36 N	29.15 E
Muru ≃	248	8.09 S	70.45 W
Muru, Capu di ›	36	41.44 N	8.40 E
Murud	122	18.19 N	72.58 E
Murud, Gunong ∧	112	3.52 N	115.30 E
Murukta	74	67.46 N	102.01 E
Murung ≃	112	0.12 S	114.03 E
Murupara	172	38.28 S	176.42 E
Mururoa I[1]	6	21.52 S	138.55 W
Murutinga	246	3.26 S	59.12 W
Murvaul, Lake ⊜[1]	222	32.03 N	94.28 W
Murvaul Creek ≃	194	32.05 N	94.12 W
Murwāra	124	23.51 N	80.24 E
Murwillumbah	166	28.19 S	153.24 E
Mürz ≃	61	47.24 N	15.17 E
Mürzsteg	61	47.40 N	15.29 E
Mürzzuschlag	61	47.36 N	15.41 E
Muş	130	38.44 N	41.30 E
Muş □[4]	128	39.00 N	42.00 E
Musa	152	2.40 N	19.18 E
Mūša ≃, Europe	76	56.24 N	24.10 E
Musa ≃, Pap. N. Gui.	164	9.25 S	148.50 E
Mūsā, Jabal (Mount Sinai) ∧	140	28.32 N	33.59 E
Mūsā, ʿUyūn (Springs of Moses) ⊤[4]	142	29.52 N	32.39 E
Musabeyli	130	39.51 N	34.37 E
Musadi	152	2.34 S	22.47 E
Musaid	146	31.35 N	25.03 E
Mūsa Khel	123	32.38 N	71.44 E
Mūsa Khel Bāzār	120	30.52 N	69.49 E
Musala ∧	38	42.11 N	23.34 E
Musan	98	42.14 N	129.13 E
Musandam Peninsula ›[1]	128	26.18 N	56.24 E
Musao	154	7.43 S	26.17 E
Mūsā Qalʿeh	120	32.22 N	64.46 E
Mūsā Qalʿeh ≃	128	32.05 N	64.51 E
Musar	272b	22.54 N	88.14 E
Musasa	154	3.21 S	31.33 E
Musashi	96	33.30 N	131.43 E
Musashi → Iruma	94	35.50 N	139.24 E
Musashimurayama	268	35.45 N	139.23 E
Musashino	94	35.42 N	139.34 E
Musashino-daichi ⋏[1]	268	35.45 N	139.35 E
Musau	58	47.32 N	10.40 E
Musayʿīd	128	24.59 N	51.32 E
Musaymīr	144	13.27 N	44.37 E
Mūsāzai	120	30.23 N	66.32 E
Muscat and Oman → Oman □[1]	118	22.00 N	58.00 E
Muscatatuck ≃	218	38.46 N	86.10 W
Muscatatuck, Grassy Fork ≃	218	38.45 N	85.07 W
Muscatatuck, Vernon Fork ≃	218	38.46 N	85.54 W
Muscatine	190	41.25 N	91.03 W
Muscat → Masqaṭ	128	23.37 N	58.35 E
Müsch	56	50.23 N	6.49 E
Mus-Chaja, gora ∧	74	62.35 N	140.50 E
Muschu Island I	164	3.25 S	143.35 E
Muschwitz	54	51.11 N	12.07 E
Muscle Shoals	194	34.44 N	87.40 W
Musclow, Mount ∧	182	53.17 N	127.09 W
Musclow Lake ⊜	184	51.25 N	94.56 W
Muscoda	190	43.11 N	90.26 W
Musconetcong ≃	210	40.36 N	75.11 W
Musconetcong, Lake ⊜	276	40.54 N	74.42 W
Muscongus Bay ⊂	188	43.55 N	69.20 W
Muscote Bay ⊂	212	44.06 N	77.18 W
Muscowpetung Indian Reserve ◆[4]	184	50.45 N	104.15 W
Muscoy	228	34.09 N	117.20 W
Muse	214	40.17 N	80.12 W
Musengezi ≃	154	15.43 S	31.14 E
Museum, Bergbau ☨	263	51.29 N	7.13 E
Musgrave, Austl.	164	14.47 S	143.30 E
Musgrave, B.C., Can.	224	48.45 N	123.32 W
Musgrave, Mount ∧	172	43.48 S	170.43 E
Musgrave Ranges ⋏	162	26.10 S	131.50 E
Musgravetown	186	48.24 N	53.53 W
Mūshā	142	27.08 N	31.18 E
Mushābani	126	22.31 N	86.27 E
Mushāsh, Jabal al- ∧[2]	142	28.54 N	31.11 E
Mushenge	152	4.32 S	21.21 E
Mushie	152	3.01 S	16.54 E
Mushima	154	14.13 S	25.05 E
Mushin	150	6.32 N	3.22 E
Mūsi ≃, India	122	16.41 N	79.40 E
Musi ≃, Indon.	112	2.20 S	104.56 E
Musicians Seamounts ✦[3]	6	31.00 N	162.00 W
Muskauer Heide ◆[3]	54	51.25 N	14.40 E
Muskeg ≃	182	54.01 N	119.03 W
Muskeget Channel ⊔	207	41.25 N	70.20 W
Muskeget Island I	207	41.20 N	70.18 W
Muskeg Lake Indian Reserve ◆[4]	184	52.58 N	106.57 W
Muskego	216	42.54 N	88.08 W
Muskego Lake ⊜	216	42.53 N	88.07 W
Muskegon	216	43.14 N	86.14 W
Muskegon □[6]	216	43.12 N	86.08 W
Muskegon ≃	190	43.14 N	86.20 W

Symbols in the index entries represent the broad categories identified in the key at the right. Symbols with superior numbers (⋏[1]) identify subcategories (see complete key on page *I · 1*).

Symbole im Register stellen die rechts im Schlüssel erklärten Kategorien dar. Symbole mit hochgestellten Ziffern (⋏[1]) bezeichnen Unterabteilungen einer Kategorie (vgl. vollständiger Schlüssel auf Seite *I · 1*).

Los símbolos incluídos en el texto del índice representan las grandes categorias identificadas con la clave a la derecha. Los símbolos con numeros en su parte superior (⋏[1]) identifican las subcategorías (véase la clave completa en la página *I · 1*).

Les symboles de l'index représentent les catégories indiquées dans la légende à droite. Les symboles suivis d'un indice (⋏[1]) représentent des sous-catégories (voir légende complète à la page *I · 1*).

Os símbolos incluídos no texto do índice representam as grandes categorias identificadas com a chave à direita. Os símbolos com números em sua parte superior (⋏[1]) identificam as subcategorias (veja-se a chave completa à página *I · 1*).

Symbol	English	Deutsch	Español	Français	Português
∧	Mountain	Berg	Montaña	Montagne	Montanha
⋏	Mountains	Gebirge	Montañas	Montagnes	Montanhas
)(	Pass	Paß	Paso	Col	Passo
V	Valley, Canyon	Tal, Cañon	Valle, Cañón	Vallée, Canyon	Vale, Canhão
≚	Plain	Ebene	Llano	Plaine	Planície
›	Cape	Kap	Cabo	Cap	Cabo
I	Island	Insel	Isla	Île	Ilha
II	Islands	Inseln	Islas	Îles	Ilhas
⊥	Other Topographic Features	Andere Topographische Objekte	Otros Elementos Topográficos	Autres données topographiques	Outros acidentes topográficos

ESPAÑOL — Nombre | Página | Lat.°′ | Long.°′ W = Oeste
FRANÇAIS — Nom | Page | Lat.°′ | Long.°′ W = Ouest
PORTUGUÊS — Nome | Página | Lat.°′ | Long.°′ W = Oeste

Muskegon County Airport ⊠ 216 43.10 N 86.14 W
Muskegon Heights 216 43.12 N 86.14 W
Muskegon Lake ⊜ 216 43.14 N 86.17 W
Muskegon State Park ♠ 216 43.14 N 86.20 W
Mušketova, gora ∧ 88 53.35 N 113.32 E
Muskingum □[6] 214 40.06 N 81.51 W
Muskingum ≃ 188 39.27 N 81.30 W
Muskingum Brook ≃ 285 39.48 N 74.44 W
Muskira 124 25.40 N 79.48 E
Muskö I 40 59.00 N 18.06 E
Muskoday Indian Reserve ⧫[4] 184 53.06 N 105.30 W
Muskogee 196 35.44 N 95.22 W
Muskoka □[6] 212 45.05 N 79.03 W
Muskoka, Lake ⊜ 212 45.00 N 79.25 W
Muskoka, North Branch ≃ 212 45.02 N 79.19 W
Muskoka, South Branch ≃ 212 45.02 N 79.19 W
Muskosh Channel ⊔ 212 44.55 N 79.53 W
Muskowekwan Indian Reserve ⧫[4] 184 51.19 N 104.06 W
Muskrat Creek ≃ 202 43.09 N 108.11 W
Muskrat Dam Lake ⊜ 184 53.25 N 91.40 W
Muskrat Lake ⊜ 190 45.40 N 76.55 W
Muskwa ≃ 176 58.45 N 122.35 W
Muskwa Lake ⊜ 182 56.09 N 114.38 W
Muslimbāgh 120 30.49 N 67.45 E
Musl'umovo 80 55.18 N 53.12 E
Muşmuş 132 32.32 N 35.09 E
Musocco ⧫[8] 266b 45.30 N 9.08 E
Musofu Mission 154 13.31 S 29.02 E
Musoma 154 1.30 S 33.48 E
Musone ≃, It. 64 45.50 N 11.55 E
Musone ≃, It. 66 43.28 N 13.38 E
Musoshi 154 11.54 S 27.46 E
Musquanousse, Lac ⊜ 186 50.22 N 61.05 W
Musquapsink Brook ≃ 276 40.59 N 74.01 W
Musquaro, Lac ⊜ 186 50.38 N 61.05 W
Musquash ≃ 212 44.57 N 79.52 W
Musquash Brook ≃ 283 42.42 N 71.26 W
Musquashcut Pond ⊜ 283 42.13 N 70.46 W
Musquodoboit Harbour 186 44.47 N 63.09 W
Mussau Island I 164 1.30 S 149.40 E
Musselburgh 46 55.57 N 3.04 W
Musselkanaal 52 52.56 N 7.00 E
Musselshell ≃ 202 47.21 N 107.58 W
Mussende 152 10.32 S 16.05 E
Mussidan 32 45.02 N 0.22 E
Mussolo 152 9.59 S 17.19 E
Mussomeli 70 37.35 N 13.45 E
Mussoorie 124 30.27 N 78.05 E
Mussuco 152 17.08 S 19.05 E
Mussum 52 51.48 N 6.34 E
Mussuma 152 14.14 S 21.59 E
Mussy-sur-Seine 58 47.58 N 4.30 E
Mustafakemalpaşa 130 40.02 N 28.24 E
Mustafa Kemal Paşa ≃ 130 40.07 N 28.33 E
Mustafino 80 55.01 N 53.38 E
Mustahil 144 5.12 N 44.17 E
Müstair 58 46.37 N 10.27 E
Mustajevo 80 51.48 N 53.25 E
Mustajõe 76 57.59 N 26.58 E
Mustāng 124 29.11 N 83.58 E
Mustang Draw V 196 32.12 N 101.36 W
Mustang Island I 196 28.00 N 96.55 W
Mustāy 142 30.37 N 31.09 E
Musters, Lago ⊜ 254 45.27 S 69.13 W
Mustinka ≃ 198 45.45 N 96.38 W
Mustjala 76 58.28 N 22.14 E
Mustla 76 58.14 N 25.52 E
Musturud 273c 30.08 N 31.17 E
Mustvee 76 58.51 N 26.56 E
Musu-dan > 98 40.50 N 129.43 E
Musun 84 39.42 N 43.49 E
Muswellbrook 166 32.16 S 150.53 E
Muszyna 30 49.21 N 20.54 E
Mūt, Mişr 140 25.29 N 28.59 E
Mut, Tür. 130 36.39 N 33.27 E
Muta 61 46.37 N 15.10 E
Mutá, Ponta do > 255 13.52 S 38.56 W
Mu'tah 132 31.06 N 35.42 E
Mutalau 174v 18.56 S 169.50 W
Mutambara 154 19.36 S 32.33 E
Mutanchiang → Mudanjiang 89 44.35 N 129.36 E
Mutanda, Moç. 156 21.02 S 33.31 E
Mutanda, Zaïre 152 5.17 S 16.34 E
Mutanda Mission 154 12.24 S 26.16 E
Mutankiang → Mudanjiang 89 44.35 N 129.36 E
Mutarammil, Jabal al- ∧ 132 31.04 N 36.06 E
Mutare 154 18.58 S 32.40 E
Mutbīn 132 33.09 N 36.15 E
Mutějovice 54 50.09 N 13.41 E
Mutha 154 1.48 S 38.26 E
Muthill 46 56.19 N 3.50 W
Mutiko 154 1.39 S 28.12 E
Muting 164 7.23 S 140.20 E
Mutis, Gunung ∧ 112 9.34 S 124.14 E
Mutlu (Rezovska) ≃ 38 41.59 N 28.01 E
Mutoko 154 17.24 S 32.13 E
Mutombo-Mukulu 152 7.58 S 24.00 E
Mutoraj 74 61.20 N 100.30 E
Mutoto 152 5.42 S 22.42 E
Mutouchengzi 98 41.20 N 119.59 E
Mutouhao 107 28.49 N 105.04 E
Mutsamudu 157a 12.09 S 44.25 E
Mutshatsha 152 10.39 S 24.27 E
Mutsu 92 41.17 N 141.10 E
Mutsuai 268 35.08 N 139.38 E
Mutsumi 96 34.26 N 131.34 E
Mutsuura ⧫[8] 268 35.19 N 139.37 E
Mutsu-wan ⊂ 92 41.05 N 140.55 E
Muttaburra 166 22.36 S 144.33 E
Mutte Kopf ∧ 58 47.16 N 10.39 E
Muttenz 58 47.32 N 7.39 E
Mutters 64 47.14 N 11.23 E
Mutterstadt 56 49.26 N 8.21 E
Muttonbird Islands II 172 47.15 S 167.24 E
Muttontown 276 40.49 N 73.33 W
Muttra → Mathura 124 27.30 N 77.41 E
Mutual, Oh., U.S. 218 40.05 N 83.38 W
Mutual, Pa., U.S. 279b 40.14 N 79.30 W
Mutūbis 142 31.18 N 30.31 E
Mutuca, Ribeirão da ≃ 256 21.36 S 45.39 W
Mutuco, Lago ⊜ 250 1.21 N 50.24 W
Mutuípe 255 13.15 S 39.31 W
Mutum 255 19.49 S 41.26 W
Mutum ≃ 246 4.25 S 68.03 W
Mutum Biyu 146 8.38 N 10.46 E
Mutumbo 152 13.14 S 17.17 E
Mutunópolis 255 13.40 S 49.15 W
Muturi 164 2.06 S 133.43 E
Muturi ≃ 164 2.13 S 133.40 E
Mututi, Ilha do I 250 0.45 S 51.00 W
Mutzig 58 48.32 N 7.28 E
Mutzschen 54 51.16 N 12.53 E
Mu Us Shamo ⧫[2] 102 38.45 N 109.10 E
Mūvattupula 122 9.58 N 76.35 E
Muvukoni 154 0.24 S 38.14 E
Muwopu 104 41.03 N 121.12 E
Muxaluando 152 8.07 S 14.17 E
Muxihe 100 31.03 N 115.21 E
Muxima 152 9.31 S 13.56 E
Muyaga 154 3.14 S 30.33 E
Muyang 100 27.06 N 119.34 E
Muyang ≃ 100 27.00 N 119.41 E
Muyinga 154 2.51 S 30.20 E
Muymano ≃ 248 11.27 S 69.03 W
Muy Muy 236 12.46 N 85.38 W
Muyua Island I 164 9.05 S 152.50 E
Muyuka 152 4.17 N 9.25 E
Muyumba 154 7.15 S 26.59 E
Mužač' 82 54.22 N 36.21 E
Muzaffarābād 123 34.22 N 73.28 E
Muzaffargarh 123 30.04 N 71.12 E
Muzaffarnagar 124 29.28 N 77.41 E
Muzaffarpur 124 26.07 N 85.24 E
Muzambinho 256 21.22 S 46.32 W
Muzambinho ≃ 256 21.15 S 46.26 W
Muzambo ≃ 256 21.17 S 46.16 W
Muzat ≃ 90 41.15 N 83.27 E
Muzayrīb 132 32.42 N 36.01 E
Muzbek, gora ∧ 85 40.23 N 69.39 E
Muzbel' ⧫[1] 86 50.15 N 70.50 E
Muzeze 152 15.03 S 17.43 E
Muzhen 100 30.43 N 117.56 E
Muži 74 65.22 N 64.40 E
Mužiči 84 43.03 N 44.59 E
Mužiksu 86 47.42 N 84.58 E
Muzillac 32 47.33 N 2.29 W
Muzkol, chrebet ⩘ 85 38.25 N 73.30 E
Muzoka 154 16.41 S 27.19 E
Muzon, Cape > 182 54.41 N 132.44 W
Muztag ∧, Zhg. 120 36.03 N 80.07 E
Muztag ∧, Zhg. 120 36.25 N 87.25 E
Muztagata ∧ 85 38.17 N 75.11 E
Muz Tau ∧ 86 43.50 N 85.40 E
Muzūrah 142 28.53 N 30.48 E
Muzzana del Turgnano 64 45.49 N 13.08 E
Mvam 152 0.13 S 9.39 E
Mvangan 152 2.38 N 11.44 E
Mvela 154 14.46 S 35.16 E
Mvengué 152 3.17 N 11.01 E
Mvolo 140 6.03 N 29.56 E
Mvomero 154 6.20 S 37.25 E
Mvoti ≃ 158 29.24 S 31.22 E
Mvoung ≃ 152 0.04 N 12.18 E
Mvouti 152 4.15 S 12.29 E
Mvuha 154 7.12 S 37.51 E
Mvuma 154 19.19 S 30.35 E
Mwadi-Kalumba 152 7.53 S 18.46 E
Mwadui 154 3.33 S 33.36 E
Mwali (Mohéli) I 157a 12.15 S 43.45 E
Mwami 154 16.40 S 29.46 E
Mwanangumune 152 15.31 S 23.30 E
Mwango 152 6.51 S 24.13 E
Mwanza, Malaŵi 154 15.37 S 34.31 E
Mwanza, Tan. 154 2.31 S 32.54 E
Mwanza, Zaïre 154 7.54 S 26.45 E
Mwanza, Zam. 152 17.02 S 24.27 E
Mwanza □[4] 154 2.45 S 32.45 E
Mwanza Gulf ⊂ 154 2.35 S 32.51 E
Mwaya, Tan. 154 9.33 S 33.57 E
Mwaya, Tan. 154 8.55 S 36.50 E
Mweelrea ∧ 48 53.38 N 9.50 W
Mwehu 154 5.44 S 26.40 E
Mweka 152 4.51 S 21.34 E
Mwemena 154 10.19 S 27.28 E
Mwenda 154 12.01 S 28.44 E
Mwendjila 152 7.12 S 18.51 E
Mwene-Ditu 152 7.03 S 23.27 E
Mwenezi 154 21.22 S 30.45 E
Mwenga 154 3.02 S 28.26 E
Mwepo 154 11.56 S 26.11 E
Mwerasandu 154 0.59 S 30.23 E
Mwereni 154 4.20 S 39.08 E
Mweru, Lake ⊜ 154 9.00 S 28.45 E
Mweru Mantipa National Park ♠ 154 8.45 S 29.30 E
Mweru Wantipa, Lake ⊜ 154 8.45 S 29.40 E
Mwetshi 152 4.42 S 22.39 E
Mwilambwe 154 8.07 S 25.00 E
Mwilitau Islands II 164 2.50 S 146.20 E
Mwimbi 154 8.39 S 31.40 E
Mwingi 154 0.56 S 38.04 E
Mwinilunga 152 11.44 S 24.26 E
Mwitikira 154 6.31 S 35.39 E
Mwombezhi ≃ 154 12.52 S 25.00 E
Myaing 110 21.37 N 94.51 E
Myājlār 120 26.15 N 70.23 E
Myakka ≃ 220 26.56 N 82.11 W
Myakka, Lake ⊜ 220 27.16 N 82.17 W
Myakka City 220 27.20 N 82.09 W
Myakka River State Park ♠ 220 27.15 N 82.17 W
Myall Lakes National Park ♠ 166 32.28 S 152.22 E
Myall Range ⩘ 170 32.58 S 151.22 E
Myanaung 110 18.17 N 95.19 E
Myanmar → Burma □[1] 110 22.00 N 98.00 E
Myaungmya 110 16.36 N 94.56 E
Myawadi 110 16.41 N 98.31 E
Mybster 46 58.27 N 3.25 W
Myckelgensjö 26 63.34 N 17.37 E
Myebon 110 20.03 N 93.22 E
Myeik → Mergui 110 12.26 N 98.36 E
Myers, Ky., U.S. 218 38.21 N 83.57 W
Myers, N.Y., U.S. 210 42.32 N 76.32 W
Myerstown 208 40.22 N 76.19 W
Myingyan 110 21.28 N 95.23 E
Myinmoletkat Taung ∧ 110 13.28 N 98.48 E
Myitkyinā 110 25.23 N 97.24 E
Myitnge ≃ 110 21.52 N 95.59 E
Myitta 110 14.10 N 98.31 E
Myittha 110 21.25 N 96.08 E
Myittha ≃ 110 23.12 N 94.17 E
Myjava 30 48.45 N 17.34 E
Myjeldino 24 61.46 N 54.48 E
Myjlybulak 86 48.57 N 75.13 E
Myla 24 65.25 N 50.48 E
Mylau 54 50.37 N 12.16 E
Myl'džino 86 59.03 N 78.29 E
Myllendonk, Schloss ⊥ 263 51.13 N 6.29 E
Myllykoski 26 60.47 N 26.48 E
Myllymäki 26 62.32 N 24.17 E
Mylor 168b 35.03 S 138.45 E
Mymensingh 124 24.45 N 90.24 E
Mynämäki 26 60.40 N 22.00 E
Mynaral 86 45.25 N 73.41 E
Mynbulak, gora ∧ 85 41.43 N 69.49 E
Mynfontein 158 30.55 S 23.57 E
Mynydd Bach ∧[2] 42 52.15 N 4.05 W
Mynydd Eppynt ∧ 42 52.05 N 3.30 W
Mynydd Hiraethog ∧ 44 53.05 N 3.33 W
Mynydd Pencarreg ∧[2] 42 52.04 N 4.04 W
Mynydd Preseli ∧ 42 51.58 N 4.42 W
Myōgata 94 35.51 N 137.02 E
Myōgi 94 36.17 N 138.49 E
Myōgi-Arafune-Saku-kōgen-kokutei-kōen ♠ 94 36.12 N 138.10 E
Myōgi-san ∧ 94 36.17 N 138.44 E
Myo-gyi 110 21.27 N 96.22 E
Myohaung 110 20.36 N 93.10 E
Myohyang-san ∧ 98 40.02 N 126.17 E
Myohyang-sanmaek ⩘ 98 40.30 N 127.00 E
Myojin-dake ∧ 270 34.57 N 135.36 E
Myōjin-san ∧ 96 33.34 N 133.04 E
Myōken-san ∧ 96 35.24 N 134.39 E
Myōken-zan ∧ 270 34.56 N 135.28 E
Myōken-zan ∧[2] 270 34.30 N 134.57 E
Myōkō 94 36.56 N 138.13 E
Myōkō-kōgen 94 36.52 N 138.12 E
Myōkō-san ∧ 94 36.52 N 138.07 E
Myŏnmong-ni ⧫[8] 271b 37.35 N 127.05 E
Myponga 168b 35.24 S 138.28 E
Myponga Reservoir ⊜[1] 168b 35.24 S 138.26 E
Myra ⊥ 130 36.15 N 29.54 E
Mýrdalsjökull ⊓ 24a 63.40 N 19.05 W
Myrnam 182 53.40 N 111.14 W
Myroodah 162 18.08 S 124.16 E
Myrskylä (Mörskom) 26 60.40 N 25.51 E
Myrtle Beach 192 33.41 N 78.53 W
Myrtle Beach Air Force Base ■ 192 33.41 N 78.56 W
Myrtle Beach State Park ♠ 192 33.37 N 78.58 W
Myrtle Creek 202 43.01 N 123.17 W
Myrtle Grove 194 30.25 N 87.18 W
Myrtle Point 202 43.03 N 124.08 W
Myrtle Springs 222 32.37 N 95.56 W
Myrtletowne 204 40.47 N 124.04 W
Myrtleville 170 34.29 S 149.49 E
Myšega 82 54.31 N 37.02 E
Mysen 26 59.33 N 11.20 E
Mysia □[9] 130 39.15 N 28.00 E
Mysingen ⊔ 40 59.00 N 18.15 E
Myski 86 53.42 N 87.48 E
Myškino 76 57.47 N 38.27 E
Myśla ≃ 54 52.40 N 14.29 E
Myślenice 30 49.51 N 19.56 E
Myślibórz 30 52.55 N 14.52 E
Mysłowice 30 50.15 N 19.07 E
Mysore 122 12.18 N 76.39 E
Mys Šmidta 180 68.56 N 179.26 W
Mystic, Ct., U.S. 207 41.21 N 71.58 W
Mystic, Ia., U.S. 190 40.46 N 92.56 W
Mystic ≃ 283 42.23 N 71.03 W
Mystic Seaport ⊍ 207 41.22 N 71.58 W
Mys Vchodnoj 74 73.53 N 86.43 E
Mysy 24 60.34 N 53.57 E
Mys Želanija 72 76.56 N 68.35 E
Myszków 30 50.36 N 19.20 E
Myszyniec 30 53.24 N 21.21 E
Myt 80 56.48 N 42.21 E
My Tho 110 10.21 N 106.21 E
Mytholm 262 53.44 N 2.01 W
Mytholmroyd 262 53.44 N 1.59 W
Mytilene → Mitilíni 38 39.06 N 26.32 E
Mytišči 82 55.55 N 37.46 E
Mytishchi → Mytišči 82 55.55 N 37.46 E
Mytišino 76 54.48 N 34.01 E
Mýto 60 49.47 N 13.44 E
Myton 200 40.11 N 110.03 W
Mývatn ⊜ 24a 65.37 N 16.58 W
Myzovo 78 51.22 N 24.31 E
M'zab, Oued V 148 32.19 N 5.24 E
Mže ≃ 60 49.46 N 13.24 E
Mzenga 154 6.56 S 38.43 E
Mziha 154 5.54 S 37.47 E
Mzimba 154 11.52 S 33.34 E
Mzimkulu ≃ 158 30.44 S 30.28 E
Mzimvubu ≃ 158 31.38 S 29.32 E
Mzintlava ≃ 158 31.12 S 29.18 E
Mzuzu 154 11.27 S 33.55 E
Mzymta ≃ 84 43.27 N 39.56 E

N

Na I 174r 6.52 N 158.22 E
Na (Tengtiao) ≃ 110 22.05 N 103.09 E
Naab ≃ 60 49.01 N 12.02 E
Naach, Jbel ∧ 34 34.53 N 3.22 W
Naachtpunkt Brook ≃ 276 40.54 N 74.15 W
Naaldwijk 52 52.00 N 4.12 E
Naalehu 229d 19.03 N 155.35 W
Na'ām 140 9.42 N 28.27 E
Na'âma, Sebkhet en ≣ 148 33.20 N 0.16 W
Naaman Creek ≃ 285 39.48 N 75.27 W
Naaman Creek, South Branch ≃ 285 39.49 N 75.27 W
Naamans Garden 285 39.49 N 75.31 W
Naantali 26 60.27 N 22.02 E
Naarden 52 52.17 N 5.09 E
Naarn ≃ 61 48.11 N 14.49 E
Naas 48 53.13 N 6.39 W
Naas ≃ 171b 35.36 S 149.04 E
Naast, Bel. 50 50.33 N 4.05 E
Naast, Scot., U.K. 46 57.47 N 5.39 W
Na'azuz, Har ∧ 132 30.01 N 35.00 E
Nabā, Jabal an- (Mount Nebo) ∧ 132 31.46 N 35.45 E
Nababiep 156 29.36 S 17.46 E
Nabābpur 272b 22.42 N 88.12 E
Nabaganga ≃[1] 126 22.59 N 89.34 E
Nabagram 126 24.12 N 88.06 E
Nabalat Al-Hajanah 140 13.13 N 29.02 E
Nabari 94 34.37 N 136.05 E
Nabari ≃ 94 34.45 N 136.01 E
Nabarūh 142 31.06 N 31.18 E
Nabas 116 11.50 N 122.05 E
Nabasta 126 23.15 N 88.01 E
Nabawa 162 28.31 S 114.47 E
Nabb 218 38.36 N 85.38 W
Nabberu, Lake ⊜ 162 25.36 S 120.30 E
Nabburg 60 49.28 N 12.11 E
Nabeina 174t 1.26 N 173.05 E
Naberera 154 4.12 S 36.56 E
Naberežnoje 265b 55.57 N 37.58 E
Naberežnyje Čelny 80 55.42 N 52.19 E
Nabesna 180 62.22 N 143.00 W
Nabesna ≃ 180 63.03 N 141.52 W
Nabeul 148 36.27 N 10.44 E
Nabeul □[8] 148 36.35 N 10.45 E
Nābha 123 30.22 N 76.09 E
Nab Hill ∧[2] 262 53.47 N 1.57 W
Nabigou 152 1.12 S 9.31 E
Nabī Hārūn, Jabal an- ∧ 132 30.19 N 35.24 E
Nabileque ≃ 248 20.55 S 57.49 W
Nabire 164 3.22 S 135.29 E
Nabī Shu'ayb, Jabal an- ∧ 144 15.17 N 43.59 E
Nabisipi ≃ 186 50.14 N 62.13 W
Nabiswera 154 1.28 N 32.16 E
Nabī Yūnus, Ra's an- > 132 33.39 N 35.24 E
Nabnasset 207 42.36 N 71.25 W
Nabnasset Pond ⊜ 283 42.37 N 71.26 W
Nabogame 232 26.14 N 106.57 W
Naboomspruit 156 24.32 S 28.36 E
Nabordo 150 10.10 N 9.20 E
Nabou 150 11.27 N 2.43 W
Nabq 140 28.04 N 34.25 E
Nabua 116 13.24 N 123.22 E
Nabula 120 31.55 N 80.10 E
Nābulus 132 32.13 N 35.16 E
Nabunturan 116 7.35 N 125.58 E
Nacajuca 234 18.08 N 93.01 W
Nacala 154 14.34 S 40.41 E
Nacala-Velha 154 14.32 S 40.37 E
Načalovo 80 46.20 N 48.11 E
Nacaome 236 13.31 N 87.30 W
Nacastillo 234 19.35 N 104.55 W
Nacchie 144 7.23 N 40.10 E
Nacereddine 34 36.08 N 3.26 E
Nachabinka ≃ 265b 55.51 N 37.12 E
Nachabino 82 55.51 N 37.11 E
Naches 224 46.43 N 120.41 W
Naches ≃ 202 46.38 N 120.31 W
Nachičevan' 84 39.13 N 45.24 E
Nachičevanskaja Respublika □[3] 84 39.20 N 45.30 E
Nachi-katsuura 92 33.30 N 135.55 E
Nāchinda 126 21.53 N 87.46 E
Nachingwea 154 10.23 S 38.46 E
Nāchna 120 27.30 N 71.43 E
Náchod 30 50.25 N 16.10 E
Nachodka 89 42.48 N 132.52 E
Nächstebreck ⧫[8] 263 51.18 N 7.14 E
Nachterstedt 54 51.49 N 11.20 E
Nachuge 110 10.45 N 92.22 E
Nachvak Fiord ⊂[2] 176 59.03 N 63.45 W
Naci, Pil. 116 6.19 N 124.46 E
Naci, Pil. 116 14.19 N 120.46 E
Nacimiento 252 37.30 S 72.40 W
Nacimiento ≃ 226 35.49 N 120.45 W
Nacimiento, Lake ⊜[1] 226 35.45 N 121.00 W
Načinskij Golec, gora ∧ 89 52.24 N 118.53 E
Nacka 40 59.18 N 18.10 E
Naco, Méx. 232 31.20 N 109.56 W
Naco, Az., U.S. 200 31.20 N 109.56 W
Nacogdoches 222 31.36 N 94.39 W
Nacogdoches □[6] 222 31.40 N 94.45 W
Nacogdoches, Lake ⊜[1] 222 31.37 N 94.50 W
Nácori Chico 232 29.39 N 109.01 W
Nacozari de García 232 30.24 N 109.39 W
Ñacunday 252 26.01 S 54.46 W
Nada 222 29.24 N 96.23 W
Nada ⧫[8] 270 34.44 N 135.14 E
Nadābhānga 272b 22.24 N 88.14 E
Nadachi 94 37.09 N 138.06 E
Nadaleen Mountain ∧ 180 64.15 N 133.04 W
Nadasaki 96 34.32 N 133.52 E
Nádasd 61 46.58 N 16.37 E
Nadbai 124 27.14 N 77.12 E
Nadder ≃ 42 51.03 N 1.48 W
Nadela 34 42.58 N 7.30 W
Nadelkap → Agulhas, Cape > 158 34.52 S 20.00 E
Naden Harbour ⊂ 182 54.00 N 132.35 W
Nadeždinskoje 89 48.18 N 133.11 E
Nadi 140 18.40 N 33.42 E
Nadiād 120 22.42 N 72.52 E
Nādir, Mişr 142 30.33 N 30.51 E
Nadir, Vir. Is., U.S. 240m 18.19 N 64.53 W
Nădlac 38 46.10 N 20.45 E
Nador 148 35.12 N 2.55 W
Nador □[4] 148 35.09 N 3.04 W
Nadporožje 76 60.28 N 34.17 E
Nadrin 56 50.10 N 5.41 E
Nadterečnaja 84 43.37 N 45.22 E
Nadvoicy 24 63.52 N 34.15 E
Nadvornaja 78 48.38 N 24.34 E
Nadym 72 65.35 N 72.42 E
Nadym ≃ 74 66.12 N 72.00 E
Nadyrovo 80 54.53 N 52.28 E
Naeba-san ∧ 94 36.51 N 138.41 E
Nae-dong 98 37.16 N 126.27 E
Naejang-san Kukrip Kongwŏn ♠ 98 35.28 N 126.52 E
Naenwa 120 25.46 N 75.51 E
Nærbø 26 58.40 N 5.39 E
Næsby 41 55.25 N 10.22 E
Næstved 41 55.14 N 11.46 E
Nafada 146 11.08 N 11.20 E
Nafadji 150 12.37 N 11.37 W
Nafarros 266c 38.49 N 9.25 W
Nafāzah, 'Alam ∧[2] 142 30.30 N 29.42 E
Näfels 58 47.06 N 9.04 E
Nafī 128 24.57 N 43.42 E
Nafīshah 142 30.34 N 32.15 E
Naftalan 84 40.31 N 46.50 E
Naftan, Puntan I > 174n 15.05 N 145.45 E
Nāfūrah 146 29.20 N 21.20 E
Nafūsah, Jabal ⩘[2] 146 31.50 N 12.00 E
Nāg 120 27.24 N 65.08 E
Naga, Nihon 96 34.16 N 135.26 E
Naga, Pil. 116 13.37 N 123.11 E
Naga, Pil. 116 10.13 N 123.45 E
Nâga, Kreb en ⏏[4] 148 24.00 N 6.00 W
Naga, Oued en V 148 27.53 N 7.10 W
Nagaga 154 10.54 S 39.07 E
Nagahama, Nihon 94 35.23 N 136.16 E
Nagahama, Nihon 96 33.36 N 132.29 E
Nagahama, Nihon 174m 26.25 N 127.44 E
Naga Hills ⩘ 110 26.00 N 95.00 E
Nagai, Nihon 92 38.06 N 140.02 E
Nagai, Nihon 268 35.12 N 139.37 E
Nagai Island I 180 55.11 N 159.55 W
Nagai Park ♠ 270 34.36 N 135.31 E
Nagaizumi 94 35.08 N 138.54 E
Nāgāland □[3] 120 26.00 N 95.00 E
Nagambie 169 36.47 S 145.10 E
Nagannu-shima I 174m 26.16 N 127.33 E
Nagano 94 36.39 N 138.11 E
Nagano □[5] 94 36.00 N 138.00 E
Nagano-dam ⧫[6] 94 35.50 N 136.33 E
Naganohara 94 36.33 N 138.38 E
Nagao, Nihon 96 34.16 N 134.10 E
Nagao, Nihon 270 34.50 N 135.43 E
Nagao-hana > 96 35.32 N 134.01 E
Nagaoka 92 37.27 N 138.51 E
Nagaokakyō 94 34.55 N 135.42 E
Nagaon 120 26.20 N 92.40 E
Nāgappattinam 122 10.46 N 79.50 E
Nagar, India 123 32.07 N 77.10 E
Nagar, India 124 27.26 N 77.06 E
Nagara 270 34.26 N 135.44 E
Nagara ≃ 94 35.01 N 136.43 E
Nagareyama 94 35.51 N 139.54 E
Nāgārjuna Sāgar ⊜[1] 122 16.35 N 79.21 E
Nagarote 236 12.16 N 86.34 W
Nagar Pārkar 120 24.22 N 70.45 E
Nāgarpur 124 24.03 N 89.53 E
Nagar Untāri 124 24.17 N 83.30 E
Nagarzê 124 28.59 N 90.25 E
Nagas 116 13.06 N 123.18 E
Nagasaka 94 35.49 N 138.22 E
Nagasaki 92 32.48 N 129.55 E
Nagasawa 268 35.12 N 139.41 E
Nagashima 94 35.05 N 136.42 E
Naga-shima I, Nihon 96 33.49 N 132.05 E
Naga-shima I, Nihon 96 34.41 N 134.15 E
Nagashino ⊥ 94 34.56 N 137.32 E
Nagasin Lake ⊜ 190 47.44 N 83.37 W
Nagasu 96 32.56 N 130.27 E
Nagasu → Usa 96 33.31 N 131.22 E
Nagata ⧫[8] 270 34.40 N 135.09 E
Nagataki 270 34.23 N 135.20 E
Nagatino ⧫[8] 265b 55.41 N 37.41 E
Nagato, Nihon 94 36.15 N 138.16 E
Nagato, Nihon 96 34.21 N 131.10 E
Nagatsuda ⧫[8] 268 35.32 N 139.30 E
Nāgaur 120 27.12 N 73.44 E
Nāgāvali ≃ 122 18.13 N 83.56 E
Nagavskaja 80 47.47 N 42.50 E
Nagawa 94 36.05 N 137.41 E
Nagawicka Lake ⊜ 216 43.05 N 88.23 W
Nagcarlan 116 14.08 N 121.25 E
Nagda 120 23.27 N 75.25 E
Nagele 52 52.37 N 5.44 E
Nāgercoil 122 8.10 N 77.26 E
Nagi 96 35.07 N 134.11 E
Nagiba 116 13.41 N 120.53 E
Nagibino 86 55.46 N 72.43 E
Nagichot 154 4.16 N 33.34 E
Nagīna 124 29.27 N 78.27 E
Nāgirāt 126 23.38 N 89.18 E
Nagi-san ∧ 96 35.10 N 134.11 E
Nagiso 94 35.36 N 137.37 E
Nagla 272a 28.31 N 77.22 E
Naglarby 40 60.25 N 15.34 E
Nagles Mountains ⩘ 48 52.05 N 8.30 W
Nagłowice 30 50.41 N 20.06 E
Nago 174m 26.35 N 127.59 E
Nāgod 124 24.34 N 80.36 E
Nagog Pond ⊜ 283 42.31 N 71.26 W
Nagoja → Nagoya 94 35.10 N 136.55 E
Nagold 56 48.33 N 8.43 E
Nagold ≃ 56 48.52 N 8.42 E
Nagol'naja ≃ 83 47.57 N 38.58 E
Nagol'no-Tarasovka 83 48.00 N 39.29 E
Nagorje 76 56.55 N 38.16 E
Nagornoje 78 45.26 N 28.27 E
Nagorno-Karabakh □[9] 84 40.00 N 46.40 E
Nagornyj, Ross. 74 55.58 N 124.57 E
Nagornyj, Ross. 265a 59.43 N 30.16 E
Nagorsk 24 59.18 N 50.48 E
Nagorskoje 82 56.54 N 38.06 E
Nago-wan ⊂ 174m 26.34 N 127.57 E
Nagoya 94 35.10 N 136.55 E
Nagoya-kūkō ⊠ 94 35.15 N 136.55 E
Nāgpur 120 21.09 N 79.06 E
Nagqu 120 31.34 N 92.00 E
Nagrai 123 34.23 N 72.41 E
Nāgrākāta 124 26.54 N 88.55 E
Nagrota 123 32.03 N 76.05 E
Nagu I 26 60.10 N 21.48 E
Nagua 238 19.23 N 69.50 W
Naguabo 240m 18.13 N 65.44 W
Naguilian 116 17.01 N 121.50 E
Nagumbuaya Point > 116 13.34 N 124.21 E
Naguri 94 35.53 N 139.11 E
Naguri I 122 6.39 N 72.55 E
Nagyatád 30 46.14 N 17.22 E
Nagybajom 30 46.23 N 17.31 E
Nagybánya → Baia Mare 38 47.40 N 23.35 E
Nagycenk 61 47.36 N 16.42 E
Nagyecsed 30 47.52 N 22.24 E
Nagykálló 78 47.53 N 21.51 E
Nagykanizsa 30 46.27 N 17.00 E
Nagykáta 30 47.25 N 19.45 E
Nagy-Kevély ∧[2] 264c 47.37 N 18.59 E
Nagykőrös 30 47.02 N 19.43 E
Nagy-Milic ∧ 30 48.35 N 21.28 E
Nagytarcsa 264c 47.32 N 19.17 E
Nagytétény ⧫[8] 264c 47.24 N 18.58 E
Nagyvarad → Oradea 38 47.03 N 21.57 E
Naha 174m 26.13 N 127.40 E
Naha Airfield ⊠ 174m 26.13 N 127.40 E
Nahabuan 112 0.49 N 114.05 E
Nahakki 123 34.25 N 71.20 E
Nahalal 132 32.41 N 35.12 E
Nahal 'Oz 132 31.28 N 34.30 E
Naham 132 31.46 N 35.00 E
Nāhan 124 30.33 N 77.18 E
Nahang (Nihing) ≃ 128 26.00 N 62.44 E
Nahanni National Park ♠ 180 61.40 N 126.00 W
Nahant 207 42.25 N 70.55 W
Nahant Bay ⊂ 207 42.27 N 70.55 W
Nahant Beach ⏏[2] 283 42.27 N 70.56 W
Nahari 96 33.25 N 134.01 E
Nahari ≃ 96 33.25 N 134.01 E
Nahariyya 132 33.00 N 35.05 E
Naharpur ⧫[8] 272a 28.42 N 77.07 E
Nahāta 126 23.20 N 89.31 E
Nahāvand 128 34.12 N 48.22 E
Nahcotta 224 46.30 N 124.02 W
Nahe 89 48.28 N 124.52 E
Nahe ≃ 56 49.58 N 7.57 E
Nahf 132 32.56 N 35.19 E
Nahma 190 45.50 N 86.39 W
Nahmer ⧫[8] 263 51.20 N 7.35 E
Nahmer ≃ 263 51.21 N 7.35 E
Nahoe 174x 9.45 S 138.55 W
Nahoï, Cap > 175f 14.39 S 166.37 E
Nahon ≃ 50 47.14 N 1.39 E
Nahrīn 120 36.01 N 69.06 E
Nahr Ouassel, Oued ≃ 148 35.42 N 2.33 E
Nahualate ≃ 236 14.03 N 91.32 W
Nahuatzén 234 19.42 N 101.50 W
Nahuel Huapi 254 41.03 S 71.09 W
Nahuel Huapi, Lago ⊜ 254 40.58 S 71.30 W
Nahuel Huapi, Parque Nacional ♠ 254 41.00 S 71.48 W
Nahuel Niyeu 254 40.30 S 66.33 W
Nahunta 192 31.12 N 81.58 W
Nāhyā 142 30.03 N 31.07 E
Naia ≃ 66 42.46 N 12.22 E
Naica 232 27.53 N 105.31 W
Naicam 184 52.25 N 104.30 W
Nai Ga 102 27.48 N 97.30 E
Naiguatá, Pico ∧ 286c 10.33 N 66.46 W
Naihāti, Bngl. 126 22.49 N 89.37 E
Naihāti, India 126 22.54 N 88.25 E
Naij Gol ≃, Zhg. 102 36.20 N 94.49 E
Naij Gol ≃, Zhg. 120 36.20 N 94.49 E
Naikliu 112 9.30 S 123.50 E
Naikoon Provincial Park ♠ 182 53.50 N 131.50 W
Naila 54 50.19 N 11.42 E
Nailin 98 41.53 N 119.15 E
Nails Creek ≃ 222 30.16 N 96.44 W
Nailsea 42 51.26 N 2.43 W
Nailsworth 42 51.42 N 2.14 W
Nā'im, Jabal an- ∧ 132 31.04 N 35.55 E
Naiman Qi 89 42.55 N 120.43 E
Nain, Nf., Can. 176 56.32 N 61.41 W
Nā'īn, Īrān 128 32.52 N 53.05 E
Nain ⊜ 40 60.14 N 13.50 E
Naini Tāl 124 29.23 N 79.27 E
Nainpur 124 22.26 N 80.07 E
Nairai I 175g 17.49 S 179.24 E
Nairn, Scot., U.K. 46 57.35 N 3.53 W
Nairn, La., U.S. 194 29.27 N 89.38 W
Nairn ≃ 46 57.35 N 3.52 W
Nairne 168b 35.02 S 138.54 E
Nairobi 154 1.17 S 36.49 E
Nairobi Airport ⊠ 276 41.08 N 74.21 W
Nairobi National Park ♠ 154 1.24 S 36.50 E
Naissaar I 76 59.33 N 24.32 E
Naita ∧ 144 5.30 N 35.18 E
Naitamba Island I 175g 17.31 S 179.17 W
Naivasha 154 0.43 S 36.26 E
Naivasha, Lake ⊜ 154 0.46 S 36.21 E
Naivos 114 2.30 N 96.10 E
Naizifang 105 39.36 N 116.47 E
N'aizishen 89 43.41 N 127.29 E
Najac 32 44.13 N 1.59 E
Najafābād 128 32.37 N 51.21 E
Najafgarh ⧫[8] 272a 28.37 N 76.59 E
Najafgarh Drain ≊ 272a 28.43 N 77.14 E
Najasa ≃ 240p 20.42 N 77.55 W
Najd □[8] 144 21.00 N 46.00 E
Najd □[9] 118 25.00 N 44.30 E
Nájera 34 42.25 N 2.44 W
Najhā 132 33.23 N 36.22 E
Naj' Hammādī 140 26.03 N 32.15 E
Najībābād 124 29.38 N 78.20 E
Najin 98 42.15 N 130.18 E
Najinkouzi 89 50.23 N 126.57 E
Najio 270 34.50 N 135.18 E
Najstenjarvi 24 62.16 N 32.38 E
Naju 98 35.03 N 126.43 E
Najza, gora ∧ 86 49.24 N 70.42 E
Naka, Nihon 94 36.27 N 140.30 E
Naka, Nihon 96 35.02 N 134.55 E
Naka, Nihon 268 35.49 N 140.03 E
Naka, Nihon 270 34.50 N 135.48 E
Naka, Nihon 270 34.50 N 135.56 E
Naka, Nihon 270 34.42 N 135.45 E
Naka ⧫[8] 268 35.27 N 139.39 E
Naka ≃, Nihon 94 36.20 N 140.36 E
Naka ≃, Nihon 96 33.56 N 134.42 E
Naka ≃, Nihon 268 35.39 N 139.51 E
Nakadōri-shima I 92 32.57 N 129.04 E
Nakagami 268 35.49 N 139.21 E
Nakagawa 94 35.38 N 137.56 E
Nakagawa ⧫[8] 268 35.33 N 139.35 E
Nakagō 94 36.58 N 138.14 E
Nakagusuku 174m 26.15 N 127.49 E
Nakagusuku-wan ⊂ 174m 26.14 N 127.53 E
Nakagyō ⧫[8] 270 35.01 N 135.45 E
Nakaheji 96 33.47 N 135.31 E
Nakai 94 35.20 N 139.14 E
Nakaizu 94 34.57 N 139.00 E
Nakajima, Nihon 94 37.07 N 136.51 E
Nakajima, Nihon 96 33.58 N 132.07 E
Nakajima, Nihon 268 35.26 N 139.56 E
Nakajima, Nihon 268 35.18 N 139.58 E
Naka-jima I 96 33.58 N 132.37 E
Nakajō, Nihon 92 38.03 N 139.24 E
Nakajō, Nihon 94 36.36 N 138.02 E
Nakakawane 94 35.03 N 138.05 E
Nāka Khārari 120 25.15 N 66.44 E
Nakalele Point > 229a 21.02 N 156.35 W
Nākālia 126 24.02 N 89.40 E
Nakama, Nihon 96 33.50 N 130.43 E
Nakama, Nihon 174m 26.16 N 127.44 E
Nakaminato 94 36.21 N 140.36 E
Nakamura 96 32.59 N 132.56 E
Nakanai Mountains ⩘ 164 5.35 S 151.10 E
Nakano, Nihon 94 36.45 N 138.22 E
Nakano, Nihon 268 35.20 N 139.54 E
Nakano, Nihon 270 34.58 N 135.58 E
Nakano ⧫[8] 268 35.42 N 139.42 E
Nakanobu ⧫[8] 268 35.36 N 139.43 E
Nakanojō 94 36.35 N 138.51 E
Nakano-shima I 93b 29.49 N 129.52 E
Nakanoshima-suidō ⊔ 93b 29.44 N 129.49 E
Nakanougan-jima I 175d 24.11 N 123.33 E
Nakaosu 174m 26.37 N 128.02 E
Nakaōzō ⧫[8] 270 34.51 N 135.11 E
Nakape 140 5.47 N 28.37 E
Nakashibetsu 92a 43.33 N 144.59 E
Nākāsipāra 126 23.35 N 88.21 E
Nakasongola 154 1.19 N 32.28 E
Nakatō 268 35.45 N 139.24 E
Nakatomi, Nihon 94 35.28 N 138.26 E
Nakatomi, Nihon 268 35.49 N 139.30 E
Nakatosa 96 33.20 N 133.14 E
Nakatsu, Nihon 96 33.34 N 131.13 E
Nakatsu, Nihon 96 33.57 N 135.18 E
Nakatsu, Nihon 268 35.30 N 139.20 E
Nakatsu ≃ 94 37.00 N 138.39 E
Nakatsue 96 33.08 N 130.56 E
Nakatsugawa 94 35.29 N 137.30 E
Nakatsumine-yama ∧ 96 33.58 N 134.31 E
Nakauchigami 270 34.56 N 135.10 E
Naka-umi ⊂ 96 35.28 N 133.12 E
Nakayama, Nihon 96 33.38 N 132.42 E
Nakayama, Nihon 96 35.31 N 133.35 E
Nakayama ⧫[8] 268 35.31 N 139.33 E
Nakayama ≃ 96 33.55 N 133.08 E
Nakazato, Nihon 94 36.05 N 138.50 E
Nakazato, Nihon 94 37.03 N 138.42 E
Nakazuma 268 35.58 N 139.35 E
Nakéty 175f 21.33 S 166.03 E
Nakfa 144 16.43 N 38.32 E
Nakhola 120 26.07 N 92.11 E
Nakhon Nayok 110 14.12 N 101.13 E
Nakhon Pathom 110 13.49 N 100.03 E
Nakhon Phanom 110 17.24 N 104.47 E
Nakhon Ratchasima 110 14.58 N 102.07 E
Nakhon Sawan 110 15.41 N 100.07 E
Nakhon Si Thammarat 110 8.26 N 99.58 E
Nakhon Thai 110 17.07 N 100.50 E
Nakhtarana 120 23.20 N 69.15 E
Nakina 176 50.10 N 86.42 W
Nakkaş ≃ 267b 41.00 N 28.45 E
Nakło nad Notecią 30 53.08 N 17.35 E
Naknek 180 58.44 N 157.02 W
Naknek Lake ⊜ 180 58.40 N 156.15 W
Nako 150 10.38 N 3.04 W
Nakodar 123 31.07 N 75.29 E
Nakonde 154 9.20 S 32.42 E
Nakoso-no-seki-ato ⊥ 94 36.53 N 140.46 E
Nakou 100 27.09 N 117.38 E
Nakskov 41 54.50 N 11.09 E
Nakskov Fjord ⊂ 41 54.50 N 11.02 E
Näkten ⊜ 26 62.52 N 14.38 E
Naktong-gang ≃ 98 35.07 N 128.57 E
Nakūr 124 29.55 N 77.18 E
Nakuru 154 0.17 S 36.04 E
Nakuru, Lake ⊜ 154 0.22 S 36.05 E
Nakusp 182 50.15 N 117.48 W
Nāl ≃ 120 26.02 N 65.19 E
Nālāgarh 123 31.03 N 76.43 E
Nalajch 88 47.45 N 107.16 E
Nālanda 124 25.07 N 85.25 E
Nalao 102 24.22 N 105.23 E
Nalázi 156 24.03 S 33.20 E
Nalbāri 120 26.25 N 91.26 E
Nalcayec, Isla I 254 46.06 S 73.49 W
Nalchik → Nal'čik 84 43.29 N 43.37 E
Nālchiti 124 22.38 N 90.17 E
Nal'čik 84 43.29 N 43.37 E
Naldānga 126 23.26 N 89.11 E
Nāldera 123 31.11 N 77.11 E
Näldsjön ⊜ 26 63.23 N 14.17 E
Nałęczów 30 51.18 N 22.11 E
Nalgonda 122 17.03 N 79.16 E
Nalgora 126 22.52 N 90.39 E
Nalhāti 126 24.18 N 87.49 E
Naliagrām 126 23.36 N 89.37 E
Naliang 102 21.43 N 107.51 E
Nālikul 272b 22.49 N 88.11 E
Nalinnes 50 50.19 N 4.26 E
Nalisan 104 42.06 N 122.12 E
Nallamalla Hills ⩘ 122 15.30 N 78.45 E
Nalles (Nals) 64 46.32 N 11.12 E
Nallıhan 130 40.11 N 31.21 E
Na Logu 64 46.23 N 13.45 E
Nalolo 152 15.35 S 23.07 E
Nalón ≃ 34 43.32 N 6.04 W
Nalong 102 23.35 N 106.05 E
Nalusa 152 14.55 S 22.13 E
Nālūt 146 31.52 N 10.59 E
Nalžovské Hory 60 49.20 N 13.33 E
Nam ≃ 110 21.33 N 98.38 E
Namaacha 156 25.58 S 32.01 E
Namachire 152 11.26 S 22.43 E
Namacunde 152 17.18 S 15.50 E
Namacurra 154 17.29 S 37.01 E
Namadgi National Park ♠ 171b 35.45 S 148.57 E
Namak, Daryācheh-ye ⊜ 128 34.30 N 51.50 E
Namak, Kavīr-e ⧫[2] 128 34.45 N 57.45 E
Namakan Lake ⊜ 190 48.27 N 92.35 W
Nāmakkal 122 11.14 N 78.10 E
Namaksār, Kowl-e ⊜ 128 34.00 N 64.30 E
Namakula 174v 18.57 S 169.54 W
Namaland □[5] 156 25.50 S 18.00 E
Namamugi ⧫[8] 268 35.29 N 139.41 E
Namanga 154 2.33 S 36.46 E
Namangan 85 41.00 N 71.40 E
Namangan □[4] 85 41.00 N 71.15 E
Namanyere 154 7.31 S 31.03 E
Namapa 154 13.43 S 39.50 E
Namarodu, Cape > 164 3.38 S 152.30 E
Namarrói 154 15.58 S 36.55 E
Namasagali 154 1.01 N 32.57 E
Namatanai 164 3.40 S 152.25 E
Nambe Indian Reservation ⧫[4] 200 35.52 N 105.57 W
Namber 164 1.04 S 134.49 E
Nambi 162 28.54 S 121.41 E
Nambour 166 26.38 S 152.58 E
Nambouwalu 175g 16.59 S 178.42 E
Nambuangongo 152 8.01 S 14.12 E
Nambucca Heads 166 30.39 S 153.00 E
Nam Can 110 8.46 N 104.59 E
Namcha Barwa → Namjagbarwa Feng ∧ 102 29.38 N 95.04 E
Namch'ang 98 35.26 N 129.16 E
Nam Co ⊜ 120 30.42 N 90.30 E
Namdae-ch'ŏn ≃ 98 40.26 N 128.57 E
Namdanak 85 41.11 N 69.42 E
Nam Dinh 110 20.25 N 106.10 E
Nämdö I 40 59.12 N 18.41 E
Nämdöfjärden ⊔ 40 59.12 N 18.34 E
Nam Du, Quan Dao II 110 9.42 N 104.22 E
Namegawa 94 36.04 N 139.22 E
Nameh 112 2.34 N 116.21 E
Nameigos Lake ⊜ 190 48.46 N 84.43 W
Namekagon ≃ 190 46.05 N 92.06 W

	English	Deutsch	Español	Français	Português
≃	River	Fluß	Río	Rivière	Rio
≊	Canal	Kanal	Canal	Canal	Canal
⌞	Waterfall, Rapids	Wasserfall, Stromschnellen	Cascada, Rápidos	Chute d'eau, Rapides	Cascata, Rápidos
⊔	Strait	Meeresstraße	Estrecho	Détroit	Estreito
⊂	Bay, Gulf	Bucht, Golf	Bahía, Golfo	Baie, Golfe	Baía, Golfo
⊜	Lake, Lakes	See, Seen	Lago, Lagos	Lac, Lacs	Lago, Lagos
≣	Swamp	Sumpf	Pantano	Marais	Pântano
⊓	Ice Features, Glacier	Eis- und Gletscherformen	Accidentes Glaciales	Formes glaciaires	Acidentes glaciares
⊤	Other Hydrographic Features	Andere Hydrographische Objekte	Otros Elementos Hidrográficos	Autres données hydrographiques	Outros acidentes hidrográficos

	English	Deutsch	Español	Français	Português
✣	Submarine Features	Untermeerische Objekte	Accidentes Submarinos	Formes de relief sous-marin	Acidentes submarinos
□	Political Unit	Politische Einheit	Unidad Politica	Entité politique	Unidade política
⊍	Cultural Institution	Kulturelle Institution	Institución Cultural	Institution culturelle	Institução cultural
⊥	Historical Site	Historische Stätte	Sitio Histórico	Site historique	Sitio histórico
♠	Recreational Site	Erholungs- und Ferienort	Sitio de Recreo	Centre de loisirs	Area de Lazer
⊠	Airport	Flughafen	Aeropuerto	Aéroport	Aeroporto
■	Military Installation	Militäranlage	Instalación Militar	Installation militaire	Instalação militar
⧫	Miscellaneous	Verschiedenes	Misceláneo	Divers	Diversos

ENGLISH / DEUTSCH

Name | Page | Lat.°′ | Long.°′ — Name | Seite | Breite°′ | Länge°′ E = Ost

Namen → Namur 56 50.28 N 4.52 E
Namerikawa 94 36.46 N 137.20 E
Náměšť 61 49.12 N 16.10 E
Nametil 154 15.43 S 39.21 E
Namew Lake ⊜ 184 54.13 N 101.56 W
Nam-gang ≃ 98 39.03 N 125.52 E
Namhae 98 34.50 N 127.54 E
Namhae-do I 98 34.48 N 127.57 E
Namhan-gang ≃ 98 37.31 N 127.18 E
Namhkam 110 23.50 N 97.41 E
Namho-ri 98 38.07 N 125.10 E
Namhsan 110 22.58 N 97.10 E
Namiai 94 35.22 N 137.41 E
Namib Desert ⬌[2] 156 23.00 S 15.00 E
Namibe 152 15.10 S 12.09 E
Namibe □[5] 152 15.20 S 12.30 E
Namibia □[1], Afr. 138 22.00 S 17.00 E
Namibia □[1], Afr. 156 22.00 S 17.00 E
Namibie → Namibia □[1] 156 22.00 S 17.00 E
Namib-Naukluft Park ◆ 156 23.30 S 15.30 E
Namie 92 37.29 N 141.00 E
Namies 158 29.18 S 19.13 E
Namīn 128 38.25 N 48.30 E
Naminga 88 56.33 N 118.41 E
Namjagbarwa Feng ∧ 102 29.38 N 95.04 E
Nāmja La)(124 29.27 N 82.34 E
Namji-ri 98 35.23 N 128.29 E
Nāmkhāna 126 21.46 N 88.14 E
Nam Kwo Chau I 271d 22.15 N 114.21 E
Namlan 110 22.15 N 97.24 E
Nāmlāng ≃ 124 29.28 N 82.50 E
Namlea 164 3.18 S 127.06 E
Namling 120 29.41 N 89.04 E
Namlos 58 47.21 N 10.40 E
Nam Ngum Reservoir ⊜[1] 110 18.30 N 102.40 E
Namnoi, Khao ∧ 110 10.36 N 98.38 E
Namo 112 1.24 S 119.57 E
Namoi ≃ 166 30.00 S 148.07 E
Namoluk I[1] 14 5.55 N 153.08 E
Namonuito I[1] 14 8.46 N 150.02 E
Namorik I[1] 14 5.36 N 168.07 E
Namoruputh 154 4.34 N 35.57 E
Namounou 150 11.52 N 1.42 E
Namous, Oued en V 148 31.00 N 0.15 W
Namoya 154 4.01 S 27.34 E
Nampa, Ab., Can. 182 56.02 N 117.08 W
Nampa, Id., U.S. 202 43.32 N 116.33 W
Nampala 150 15.17 N 5.33 W
Nam Pat 110 17.43 N 100.41 E
Nampawng 110 22.45 N 97.52 E
Nam Phan □[9] 110 11.00 N 107.00 E
Nam Phong 110 16.42 N 102.52 E
Nampicuan 116 15.44 N 120.38 E
Namp'o 98 38.45 N 125.23 E
Nampont-Saint-Martin 50 50.21 N 1.45 E
Namp'ot'ae-san ∧ 98 41.44 N 128.24 E
Nampuecha 154 13.59 S 40.18 E
Nampula 154 15.07 S 39.15 E
Nampula □[5] 154 15.00 S 39.00 E
Namsang 110 20.53 N 97.43 E
Namsan Park ◆ 271b 37.34 N 126.59 E
Namsanyŏng-ni 98 38.59 N 127.26 E
Namsen ≃ 24 64.27 N 11.28 E
Namsi 98 39.54 N 124.36 E
Namsos 24 64.29 N 11.30 E
Nam Tok 110 14.14 N 99.04 E
Namtu 110 23.05 N 97.24 E
Namu 182 51.49 N 127.52 W
Namu I[1] 14 8.00 N 168.10 E
Namuka-I-Lau I 175g 18.51 S 178.38 W
Namúli, Serra ∧∧ 154 15.15 S 37.08 E
Namur, Bel. 56 50.28 N 4.52 E
Namur, P.Q., Can. 206 45.54 N 74.56 W
Namur □[4] 56 50.20 N 4.50 E
Namuruputh 154 4.34 N 35.57 E
Namutoni 156 18.49 S 16.55 E
Namwala 154 15.45 S 26.26 E
Namwera 154 14.22 S 35.30 E
Namwŏn 98 35.25 N 127.21 E
Namyang, C.M.I.K. 98 42.57 N 129.53 E
Namyang, Taehan 98 37.14 N 126.44 E
Namyit Island I 108 10.11 N 114.22 E
Namysłów 30 51.05 N 17.42 E
Nan 110 18.47 N 100.47 E
Nan ≃, Thai 110 15.42 N 100.09 E
Nan ≃, Zhg. 100 28.15 N 120.43 E
Nana ≃ 152 5.00 N 15.50 E
Nana Barya ≃ 146 7.59 N 17.43 E
Nana Barya, Réserve de Faune de la ⬌[4] 146 7.30 N 17.30 E
Nanacamilpa 234 19.29 N 98.33 W
Nanaimo 224 49.10 N 123.56 W
Nanaimo ≃ 224 49.08 N 123.54 W
Nanaimo Lakes ⊜ 224 49.07 N 124.11 W
Nānakheri ⬌[8] 272a 28.31 N 76.59 E
Nana Kru 150 4.50 N 8.44 W
Nanakuli 229c 21.23 N 158.09 W
Nanam 98 41.43 N 129.41 E
Nana-Mambéré □[5] 152 5.30 N 15.30 E
Nan'an 100 24.58 N 118.23 E
Nan'anba 107 28.46 N 104.38 E
Nanango 166 26.40 S 152.00 E
Nanantun 110 24.45 N 95.41 E
Nanao, Nihon 94 37.03 N 136.58 E
Nanao, T'aiwan 100 24.28 N 121.48 E
Nan'ao, Zhg. 100 23.27 N 117.02 E
Nan'ao Dao I 100 23.26 N 117.03 E
Nanao-wan C 94 37.06 N 137.00 E
Nanas Channel ≍ 271c 1.25 N 103.58 E
Nanatsu-jima II 92 37.36 N 136.53 E
Nanatsuka 94 36.44 N 136.41 E
Nanay ≃ 246 3.42 S 73.16 W
Nanba 102 32.20 N 104.58 E
Nanbaita 105 38.58 N 115.39 E
Nanbaixia 98 35.45 N 117.23 E
Nanbaozhen 106 31.32 N 121.37 E
Nanbu, Nihon 94 35.17 N 138.27 E
Nanbu, Zhg. 102 31.23 N 106.02 E
Nancaicun 105 39.28 N 117.01 E
Nancefield 273d 26.17 S 27.53 E
Nancha 89 47.08 N 129.19 E
Nanchang, Zhg. 100 28.41 N 115.53 E
Nanchang (Liantang), Zhg. 100 28.34 N 115.56 E
Nancheng, Zhg. 100 25.39 N 118.26 E
Nancheng, Zhg. 100 27.35 N 116.40 E
Nancheng → Hanzhong 102 33.08 N 107.02 E
Nanching → Nanjing 106 32.03 N 118.47 E
Nanchital 234 18.04 N 94.24 W
Nanchong 107 30.48 N 106.04 E
Nanchuan 102 29.08 N 107.07 E
Nanchuang 100 24.36 N 120.59 E
Nanch'ung → Nanchong 107 30.48 N 106.04 E
Nancowry Island I 110 7.59 N 93.32 E
Nancroix 62 45.32 N 6.46 E
Nancun, Zhg. 98 36.32 N 120.06 E
Nancun, Zhg. 98 39.46 N 114.07 E
Nancy 58 48.41 N 6.12 E
Nanda Devi ∧ 124 30.23 N 79.59 E
Nāndāha 272b 22.50 N 88.17 E
Nandaime 236 11.46 N 86.03 W
Nanda Kot ∧ 124 30.17 N 80.05 E
Nandan 96 34.15 N 134.43 E
Nandarivatu 175g 17.34 S 177.58 E
Nandashan 100 29.01 N 112.43 E
Nānded 122 19.09 N 77.20 E
Nāndgaon, India 122 20.19 N 74.39 E
Nāndgaon, India 272c 18.58 N 73.08 E
Nandi 175g 17.48 S 177.25 E
Nandi Bay C 175g 17.44 S 177.25 E
Nandi Drug ∧ 122 13.25 N 77.42 E
Nandigrām 126 22.01 N 87.58 E
Nandikotkūr 122 15.52 N 78.16 E
Nanding ≃, Asia 102 23.25 N 98.41 E
Nanding ≃, Asia 110 23.25 N 98.41 E
Nandlstadt 60 48.32 N 11.48 E
Nandom 150 10.51 N 2.45 W
N'andoma 24 61.40 N 40.12 E
Nandu 106 31.27 N 119.19 E
Nandu ≃ 110 20.04 N 110.22 E
Nanduluohe 105 40.11 N 117.13 E
Nāndūra 122 20.50 N 76.27 E
Nandurbār 122 21.22 N 74.15 E
Nanduri 175g 16.27 S 179.09 E
Nandy 261 48.35 N 2.34 E
Nandyāl 122 15.29 N 78.29 E
Nanfangquan 106 31.26 N 120.16 E
Nanfen 104 41.06 N 123.44 E
Nanfeng, Zhg. 100 27.15 N 116.32 E
Nanfeng, Zhg. 100 29.16 N 116.32 E
Nangabadau 112 1.02 N 111.54 E
Nangade 154 11.05 S 39.36 E
Nanga Eboko 152 4.41 N 12.22 E
Nangahale 115b 8.34 S 122.32 E
Nangakelawit 112 0.23 N 112.26 E
Nāngal 123 31.24 N 76.14 E
Nangalangki 112 1.15 S 111.40 E
Nangalao Island I 116 11.27 N 120.11 E
Nangal Dewat ⬌[8] 272a 28.33 N 77.06 E
Nangamau 112 0.06 S 111.55 E
Nangamesi, Teluk C 115b 9.37 S 120.20 E
Nangamuntatai 112 0.22 S 112.23 E
Nangang 100 31.22 N 116.59 E
Nan Gang C 100 23.30 N 117.00 E
Nan'gangwa 105 39.46 N 116.09 E
Nangaobat 112 0.57 N 113.13 E
Nangaocun 105 39.25 N 115.58 E
Nanga Parbat ∧ 123 35.15 N 74.36 E
Nangapinoh 112 0.20 S 111.44 E
Nangaraun 112 0.38 N 113.11 E
Nangarhār □[4] 120 34.15 N 70.30 E
Nangatayap 112 1.32 S 110.34 E
Nangezhuang 105 39.31 N 116.23 E
Nanggala Hill ∧ 175e 8.16 S 157.43 E
Nanggulan 115a 7.46 S 110.12 E
Nangi 272b 22.31 N 88.13 E
Nangin 110 10.31 N 98.31 E
Nangis 50 48.33 N 3.00 E
Nangka ≃ 269f 14.41 N 121.06 E
Nanglal ≃ 126 24.20 N 90.04 E
Nangloi ⬌[8], India 272a 28.41 N 77.05 E
Nāngloi ⬌[8], India 272a 28.40 N 77.02 E
Nangloi Jat ⬌[8] 272a 28.41 N 77.04 E
Nangnim 98 40.58 N 127.08 E
Nangnim-sanmaek ∧∧ 98 40.00 N 127.00 E
Nangō, Nihon 92 31.32 N 131.23 E
Nangō, Nihon 94 37.13 N 139.33 E
Nangola 150 12.40 N 6.36 W
Nangoma 152 15.30 S 23.08 E
Nangong 98 37.24 N 115.22 E
Nangou 89 43.17 N 128.37 E
Nangō-yama-tunnel ⬌[6] 94 35.12 N 139.10 E
Nangqên 102 32.22 N 96.21 E
Nang Rong 110 14.38 N 102.48 E
Nanguan 102 37.00 N 112.31 E
Nangweshi 152 16.26 S 23.17 E
Nanhai → Foshan 100 23.03 N 113.09 E
Nanhai → South China Sea ⊽[2] 108 10.00 N 113.00 E
Nanhe 98 37.01 N 114.41 E
Nanhedian 100 33.23 N 112.25 E
Nanhekan 107 30.24 N 103.27 E
Nanhezhao 105 39.05 N 115.56 E
Nanhsi 100 23.11 N 120.29 E
Nanhu 102 39.57 N 94.13 E
Nanhua 102 25.14 N 101.13 E
Nanhualou 104 42.30 N 123.53 E
Nanhuang 98 36.58 N 121.47 E
Nanhui 106 31.03 N 121.45 E
Nan Hulsan Hu ⊜ 102 36.39 N 96.20 E
Nanhuta Shan ∧ 100 24.22 N 121.26 E
Nanhutou 89 43.44 N 128.55 E
Nanika Lake ⊜ 182 53.45 N 127.40 W
Naniwa ⬌[8] 270 34.39 N 135.30 E
Nanjangūd 122 12.06 N 76.42 E
Nanjemoy 208 38.27 N 77.13 W
Nanjemoy Creek C 208 38.25 N 77.07 W
Nanji I 100 27.28 N 121.04 E
Nanjiang, Zhg. 100 32.44 N 120.52 E
Nanjiang, Zhg. 102 32.33 N 107.30 E
Nanjiangqiao 100 28.58 N 113.44 E
Nanjie 107 29.11 N 105.00 E
Nanjing, Zhg. 100 24.41 N 114.25 E
Nanjing, Zhg. 100 24.32 N 117.22 E
Nanjing (Nanking), Zhg. 106 32.03 N 118.47 E
Nanjing, Zhg. 107 28.49 N 105.12 E
Nanjinyi 107 30.02 N 104.42 E
Nanjirinji 154 9.39 S 39.04 E
Nanjō 94 35.50 N 136.13 E
Nanjuma ≃ 105 39.24 N 115.43 E
Nankan 96 33.03 N 130.32 E
Nankāna Sāhib 123 31.27 N 73.42 E
Nankang 100 25.42 N 114.44 E
Nankang ⬌[8] 269d 25.03 N 121.36 E
Nankin 214 40.55 N 82.17 W
Nanking → Nanjing 106 32.03 N 118.47 E
Nanko-kōen ◆ 94 37.05 N 140.14 E
Nankoku 96 33.39 N 133.44 E
Nankou 100 26.38 N 117.24 E
Nankouzhen 105 40.14 N 116.07 E
Nanku 106 31.06 N 120.37 E
Nankye 110 14.20 N 98.11 E
Nanle 98 36.04 N 115.10 E
Nanling, Zhg. 100 30.56 N 118.20 E
Nanling, Zhg. 100 23.21 N 115.25 E
Nanling, Zhg. 104 41.37 N 120.56 E
Nan Ling ∧∧ 90 25.00 N 112.00 E
Nanlinqiao 100 29.35 N 114.19 E
Nanliu ≃ 102 21.38 N 109.00 E
Nanliucun 105 40.10 N 116.04 E
Nanlongba 102 28.02 N 107.31 E
Nanlou Shan ∧ 89 43.27 N 126.42 E
Nanma 102 24.17 N 101.03 E
Nanmatang 106 32.18 N 120.38 E
Nanmeng 105 39.11 N 116.22 E
Nanmoku 94 36.10 N 138.44 E
Nannerch 262 53.13 N 3.15 W
Nannine 162 26.53 S 118.20 E
Nanning 102 22.48 N 108.20 E
Nanniwan 102 36.29 N 109.40 E
Nannō 94 35.13 N 136.36 E
Nannup 162 33.59 S 115.45 E
Nanny ≃ 48 53.40 N 6.14 W
Na Noi 110 18.19 N 100.43 E
Nānole ⬌[8] 272c 19.01 N 72.55 E
Nanoose Bay 224 49.16 N 124.12 W
Nanoose Harbour C 224 49.20 N 124.10 W
Nanoshi 272c 18.56 N 73.05 E
Nanowin ≃ 184 53.13 N 97.13 W
Nanpan ≃, Zhg. 102 25.07 N 106.00 E
Nanpan ≃, Zhg. 102 24.34 N 103.04 E
Nānpāra 124 27.52 N 81.30 E
Nanpengchang 107 29.21 N 106.38 E
Nanpi 98 38.02 N 116.42 E
Nanpiao 104 41.12 N 120.39 E
Nanping, Zhg. 89 43.24 N 129.05 E
Nanping, Zhg. 98 42.16 N 129.09 E
Nanping, Zhg. 100 26.38 N 118.10 E
Nanping, Zhg. 102 21.50 N 107.28 E
Nanping, Zhg. 102 33.07 N 104.20 E
Nanpingji 100 33.30 N 116.51 E
Nanpu 105 39.16 N 118.12 E
Nanpu ≃ 100 27.02 N 118.18 E
Nanqingtuo 105 39.37 N 117.53 E
Nanqu 104 40.44 N 122.08 E
Nanquan 98 36.24 N 120.17 E
Nanri Dao I 100 25.13 N 119.30 E
Nansa ≃ 34 43.22 N 4.29 W
Nansei 92 34.22 N 136.41 E
Nansei-shotō (Ryukyu Islands) II 90 26.30 N 128.00 E
Nansemond □[6] 208 36.43 N 76.40 W
Nansen, Lago ⊜ 254 47.57 S 72.21 W
Nan Sha I 106 31.36 N 121.22 E
Nanshahe 98 35.03 N 117.12 E
Nanshan, Zhg. 100 26.38 N 118.20 E
Nanshan, Zhg. 105 39.21 N 115.34 E
Nanshanba 100 25.34 N 116.32 E
Nanshanchengzi 98 42.09 N 125.19 E
Nanshan Island I 108 10.45 N 115.49 E
Nanshankou 102 43.09 N 93.41 E
Nanshanlingcun 105 39.09 N 117.26 E
Nanshan → Qilian Shan ∧∧ 102 39.06 N 98.40 E
Nanshuang Dao I 100 26.35 N 120.08 E
Nanshui 100 22.02 N 113.16 E
Nansifa 105 39.27 N 116.27 E
Nansio 154 2.08 S 33.03 E
Nans-les-Pins 62 43.22 N 5.47 E
Nansunzhai 269b 31.21 N 121.27 E
Nant 32 44.01 N 3.18 E
Nant ≃ 50 47.30 N 1.14 E
Nantai 104 40.55 N 122.47 E
Nantais, Lac ⊜ 176 60.59 N 74.00 W
Nantai-san ∧ 94 36.43 N 140.26 E
Nantai-zan ∧ 94 36.46 N 139.29 E
Nantang 100 26.08 N 115.12 E
Nantangdun 106 31.15 N 120.56 E
Nantangmei 105 38.51 N 114.56 E
Nantasket Beach 283 42.16 N 70.52 W
Nantawarra 168b 34.00 S 138.14 E
Nant Bran ≃ 42 51.57 N 3.28 W
Nanterre 50 48.53 N 2.12 E
Nantes 32 47.13 N 1.33 W
Nanteuil-le-Haudouin 50 49.08 N 2.48 E
Nanteuil-lès-Meaux 261 48.56 N 2.54 E
Nantian, Zhg. 100 27.57 N 119.56 E
Nantian, Zhg. 100 29.08 N 121.56 E
Nantianmen 104 40.56 N 123.04 E
Nanticoke, On., Can. 212 42.54 N 80.11 E
Nanticoke, Md., U.S. 208 38.16 N 75.54 W
Nanticoke, Pa., U.S. 210 41.12 N 76.00 W
Nanticoke ≃ 208 38.16 N 75.56 W
Nanticoke Creek ≃, On., Can. 212 42.48 N 80.04 W
Nanticoke Creek ≃, N.Y., U.S. 210 42.05 N 76.05 W
Nantmeal Village 285 40.08 N 75.42 W
Nanto 92 34.20 N 136.31 E
Nanton 182 50.21 N 113.46 W
Nantong 106 32.02 N 120.53 E
Nant'ou, T'aiwan 100 23.55 N 120.41 E
Nantou, Zhg. 100 22.33 N 113.55 E
Nantouillet 261 49.00 N 2.42 E
Nantschang → Nanchang 100 28.41 N 115.53 E
Nantua 58 46.09 N 5.37 E
Nantuantingzhuang 105 40.17 N 118.17 E
Nantucket 207 41.17 N 70.06 W
Nantucket □[6] 207 41.17 N 70.06 W
Nantucket Island I 207 41.16 N 70.03 W
Nantucket Sound ≍ 207 41.30 N 70.15 W
Nantuego 154 11.21 S 38.24 E
Nantulo 154 12.17 S 39.03 E
Nantung → Nantong 106 32.02 N 120.53 E
Nantwich 44 53.04 N 2.32 W
Nanty Glo 214 40.28 N 78.50 W
Nant-y-moch Reservoir ⊜[1] 42 52.27 N 3.50 W
Nanu 164 8.50 S 142.40 E
Nanuet 210 41.05 N 74.00 W
Nanuet Mall ⬌[9] 276 41.06 N 74.01 W
Nanuku Passage ≍ 175g 16.45 S 179.15 W
Nanumanga I 14 6.18 S 176.20 E
Nanumea I[1] 14 5.39 S 176.08 E
Nanuque 255 17.50 S 40.21 W
Nānūr 126 23.42 N 87.52 E
Nanusa, Kepulauan II 108 4.42 N 127.06 E
Nanushuk ≃ 180 69.18 N 151.00 W
Nanwan 100 32.09 N 113.57 E
Nan Wan C 100 21.55 N 120.47 E
Nanwengkouzi 89 51.10 N 125.25 E
Nanwenquan 107 29.26 N 106.35 E
Nanxi, Zhg. 100 31.31 N 115.38 E
Nanxi, Zhg. 100 26.24 N 118.24 E
Nanxi, Zhg. 107 28.51 N 104.58 E
Nanxian 102 29.20 N 112.19 E
Nanxiang 106 31.17 N 121.18 E
Nanxikou 107 30.43 N 106.07 E
Nanxin, Zhg. 98 35.33 N 117.12 E
Nanxin, Zhg. 105 39.11 N 115.38 E
Nanxing Hu ⊜ 106 31.08 N 120.48 E
Nanxinzhuang 98 36.39 N 115.15 E
Nanxiong 100 25.10 N 114.20 E
Nanxun 106 30.53 N 120.26 E
Nanya 100 26.52 N 118.19 E
Nanyandang Shan ∧ 100 27.36 N 120.04 E
Nanyang, Zhg. 100 27.24 N 119.39 E
Nanyang, Zhg. 100 33.00 N 112.32 E
Nanyang, Zhg. 100 33.25 N 120.13 E
Nanyangcun 106 31.53 N 121.43 E
Nanyanggangzi 89 48.43 N 125.27 E
Nanyang Hu ⊜ 98 35.12 N 116.41 E
Nanyang Shan ∧ 106 31.20 N 120.28 E
Nanyang Technological Institute ⊛[2] 271c 1.21 N 103.41 E
Nanyi Hu ⊜ 106 31.07 N 118.57 E
Nan-yō 92 38.03 N 140.10 E
Nanyu 100 25.59 N 119.14 E
Nanyuan 105 39.48 N 116.23 E
Nanyuan Airport ⊠ 271a 39.47 N 116.23 E
Nanyue 100 27.13 N 112.43 E
Nanyuki 154 0.01 N 37.04 E
Nanyulin 105 40.09 N 115.23 E
Nanzamu 98 41.56 N 124.23 E
Nanzha 106 31.51 N 120.15 E
Nanzhai 106 31.34 N 120.02 E
Nanzhang, Zhg. 102 31.50 N 111.41 E
Nanzhang, Zhg. 105 39.03 N 115.46 E
Nanzhao 100 33.30 N 112.27 E
Nanzhaoji 100 32.38 N 115.58 E
Nanzhen 100 26.59 N 119.57 E
Nanzhenjie 106 31.48 N 119.17 E
Nanzhila 154 16.05 S 26.07 E
Nanzhuang, Zhg. 105 40.22 N 116.21 E
Nanzhuang, Zhg. 105 40.43 N 114.58 E
Nao 152 4.35 N 15.09 E
Naoābād 272b 22.28 N 88.27 E
Naoāpāra 126 22.45 N 89.39 E
Naococane, Lac ⊜ 176 52.52 N 70.40 W
Naoetsu 94 37.11 N 138.15 E
Naogaon 124 24.47 N 88.56 E
Naoiri 96 33.04 N 131.23 E
Naokot 120 24.51 N 69.27 E
Naoli ≃ 89 47.20 N 134.10 E
Naolinco 234 19.39 N 96.51 W
Não-me-Toque 252 28.28 S 52.49 W
Naong, Bukit ∧ 112 2.40 N 112.45 E
Nāopāra 126 24.09 N 88.54 E
Naopukuria 272b 22.55 N 88.16 E
Naosap Lake ⊜ 184 54.51 N 101.24 W
Naoshima 96 34.27 N 133.59 E
Naours 50 50.02 N 2.17 E
Náousa 38 40.37 N 22.05 E
Naozhou Dao I 102 20.57 N 110.34 E
Napa 226 38.17 N 122.17 W
Napa □[6] 226 38.18 N 122.17 W
Napa ≃ 226 38.07 N 122.18 W
Napacao Point > 116 9.43 N 124.31 E
Napajedla 30 49.10 N 17.31 E
Napakiak 180 60.42 N 161.57 W
Napaku 112 2.32 N 115.58 E
Na Pali Coast State Park ◆ 229b 22.09 N 159.41 W
Napalkovo 74 70.03 N 73.47 E
Napamute 180 61.33 N 158.42 W
Napanee 212 44.15 N 76.57 W
Napanee ≃ 212 44.12 N 77.02 W
Napanoch 210 41.44 N 74.22 W
Napareuli 84 42.03 N 45.31 E
Napas 86 59.53 N 81.58 E
Napaskiak 180 60.42 N 161.45 W
Napa Valley V 226 38.18 N 122.18 W
Napavine 224 46.34 N 122.54 W
Napayauan Island I 116 12.22 N 123.14 E
Napè 110 18.18 N 105.06 E
Napenay 252 26.44 S 60.37 W
Naperville 216 41.47 N 88.08 W
Napetipi ≃ 186 51.21 N 58.08 W
Napf ∧ 58 47.00 N 7.56 E
Napido 164 0.41 S 135.23 E
Napiéolédougou 150 9.18 N 5.35 W
Napier, N.Z. 172 39.29 S 176.55 E
Napier, S. Afr. 158 34.29 S 19.53 E
Napier, Mount ∧[2] 162 17.32 S 129.10 E
Napier Mountains ∧∧ 9 66.30 S 53.40 E
Napierville 206 45.11 N 73.25 W
Napierville □[6] 206 45.10 N 73.35 W
Napinka 184 49.17 N 100.50 W
Naplate 216 41.20 N 88.54 W
Naples, Fl., U.S. 220 26.08 N 81.47 W
Naples, Id., U.S. 202 48.34 N 116.23 W
Naples, Il., U.S. 219 39.45 N 90.36 W
Naples, N.Y., U.S. 210 42.36 N 77.24 W
Naples, Tx., U.S. 222 33.12 N 94.40 W
Naples → Napoli 68 40.51 N 14.17 E
Naples Park 220 26.16 N 81.48 W
Napo 102 23.16 N 105.54 E
Napo □[4] 246 0.30 S 77.00 W
Napo ≃ 246 3.20 S 72.40 W
Napola 70 37.59 N 12.38 E
Napoleon, In., U.S. 218 39.12 N 85.19 W
Napoleon, Ky., U.S. 218 38.46 N 84.47 W
Napoleon, Mi., U.S. 216 42.10 N 84.15 W
Napoleon, N.D., U.S. 198 46.30 N 99.46 W
Napoleon, Oh., U.S. 216 41.23 N 84.07 W
Napoleonville 194 29.56 N 91.01 W
Nápoles → Napoli 68 40.51 N 14.17 E
Napoli (Naples) 68 40.51 N 14.17 E
Napoli □[4] 68 40.53 N 14.25 E
Napoli, Golfo di C 68 40.43 N 14.10 E
Napopo 154 4.12 N 28.02 E
Nappamerry 166 27.36 S 141.07 E
Nappanee 216 41.26 N 86.00 W
Nappan Island I 212 44.23 N 77.49 W
Napton on the Hill 42 52.15 N 1.24 W
Napu 115b 9.24 S 119.56 E
Napudalutai Shan ∧ 89 51.06 N 122.13 E
Naqādah 140 25.54 N 32.43 E
Naqadeh 128 36.57 N 45.23 E
Naqb, Ra's an- ∧ 132 29.50 N 35.40 E
Nar ≃ 42 52.45 N 0.24 E
Nara, Mali 150 15.10 N 7.17 W
Nara, Nihon 96 34.41 N 135.50 E
Nara □[5] 96 34.30 N 135.50 E
Nāra ≃, Pāk. 120 24.07 N 69.07 E
Nara ≃, Ross. 82 54.53 N 37.26 E
Nara-bonchi ≚[1] 270 34.38 N 135.50 E
Naracoorte 166 36.58 S 140.44 E
Naradhan 166 33.37 S 146.19 E
Narai ≃ 94 36.20 N 137.55 E
Narāil 126 23.10 N 89.30 E
Naraina ⬌[8] 272a 28.37 N 77.08 E
Naraini 124 25.11 N 80.29 E
Narainpur 126 24.03 N 86.36 E
Narakawa 94 35.59 N 137.50 E
Naramata 182 49.36 N 119.35 W
Naran 88 48.34 N 98.17 E
Naran Bulag 86 49.22 N 92.33 E
Nārang 123 31.54 N 74.31 E
Narangba 171a 27.12 S 152.58 E
Naranja 220 25.31 N 80.25 W
Naranjal, Ec. 246 2.42 S 79.37 W
Naranjal, Ven. 286c 10.28 N 67.02 W
Naranjito, Hond. 236 14.57 N 88.41 W
Naranjito, P.R. 240m 18.18 N 66.15 W
Naranjo 236 10.06 N 84.22 W
Naranjo ≃ 236 14.30 N 92.11 W
Naranjo Islands II 116 12.23 N 124.03 E
Naranjos 234 21.21 N 97.41 W
Narao 92 32.50 N 129.04 E
Nara Park ◆ 270 34.41 N 135.52 E
Narasannapeta 122 18.25 N 84.03 E
Narasapur 122 16.27 N 81.40 E
Narasaraopet 122 16.15 N 80.04 E
Narashino 94 35.41 N 140.02 E
Narasun 88 50.06 N 112.58 E
Narat 86 43.28 N 83.44 E
Narathiwat 110 6.26 N 101.50 E
Nara Visa 196 35.36 N 103.05 W
Nara Women's University ⊛[2] 270 34.42 N 135.49 E
Nārāyanganj 124 23.37 N 90.30 E
Nārāyanī □[8] 124 27.15 N 85.00 E
Nārāyaṇi ≃ 124 25.39 N 85.13 E
Nārāyanpāra 272b 22.54 N 88.19 E
Nārāyanpet 122 16.44 N 77.30 E
Nārāyanpur 272b 22.29 N 88.34 E
Narazeni 84 42.27 N 41.57 E
Narberth, Wales, U.K. 42 51.48 N 4.45 W
Narberth, Pa., U.S. 285 40.00 N 75.15 W
Narbonne 32 43.11 N 3.00 E
Narcao 71 39.10 N 8.40 E
Narcea ≃ 34 43.28 N 6.06 W
Narcondam Island I 110 13.20 N 94.16 E
Narcosli Creek ≃ 182 52.49 N 122.28 W
Nardò 68 40.11 N 18.02 E
Nare ≃ 246 6.12 N 74.35 W
Narellan 170 34.02 S 150.44 E
Narembeen 162 32.04 S 118.24 E
Narenbulake 89 49.52 N 120.23 E
Narendranagar 124 30.10 N 78.18 E
Nares Strait ≍ 16 80.30 N 68.00 W
Naretha 162 31.00 S 124.50 E
Narew ≃ 30 52.26 N 20.42 E
Nargund 122 15.43 N 75.23 E
Narhan 272c 19.08 N 73.07 E
Nāri ≃ 120 28.35 N 67.50 E
Naria 124 23.18 N 90.25 E
Nariai 270 34.53 N 135.38 E
Nariel 171b 36.26 S 147.50 E
Narijn ≃ 88 50.20 N 93.24 E
Narijnteel 102 45.57 N 101.29 E
Nārikelbāria 126 23.17 N 89.21 E
Nariman 85 40.34 N 72.48 E
Narimanabad 84 38.53 N 48.52 E
Narimba, Her Majesty's Air Station (Royal Australian Navy Airfield) ■ 274a 33.43 S 150.53 E
Narin ≃ 120 36.54 N 92.51 E
Narince 130 37.52 N 38.46 E
Narinda, Baie de C 157b 14.55 S 47.30 E
Nariño □[5] 246 1.30 N 78.00 W
Narita 94 35.47 N 140.19 E
Nariwa 96 34.47 N 133.33 E
Nariwa ≃ 96 34.46 N 133.36 E
Nar'jan-Mar 24 67.39 N 53.00 E
Nārkanda 123 31.16 N 77.27 E
Narkatiāganj 124 27.06 N 84.28 E
Närke □[9] 40 59.06 N 15.03 E
Närkes Marieberg 40 59.12 N 15.10 E
Narlı 130 37.27 N 37.09 E
Narma 80 54.46 N 42.01 E
Narmada ≃ 120 21.38 N 72.36 E
Narmada Valley V 124 22.30 N 77.00 E
Narmak ⬌[8] 267d 35.43 N 51.29 E
Narman 130 40.21 N 41.52 E
Narmušad' 80 54.40 N 41.07 E
Nar-Nar-Goon 169 38.05 S 145.34 E
Nārnaul 124 28.03 N 76.07 E
Narni 66 42.31 N 12.31 E
Naro 70 37.18 N 13.47 E
Naro ≃ 70 37.14 N 13.37 E
Naroč' ≃ 76 54.26 N 26.39 E
Naroč', ozero ⊜ 76 54.52 N 26.45 E
Narodiči 78 51.13 N 29.03 E
Narodnaja, gora ∧ 24 65.04 N 60.09 E
Naro-Fominsk 82 55.23 N 36.43 E
Naro Island I 116 11.53 N 123.40 E
Narok 154 1.05 S 35.52 E
Narol 30 50.22 N 23.21 E
Narón 34 43.32 N 8.10 W
Narooma 166 36.14 S 150.03 E
Naro-Osakovo 82 55.33 N 36.33 E
Narovčat 80 53.52 N 43.41 E
Narovl'a 78 51.48 N 29.29 E
Nārowāl 123 32.06 N 74.53 E
Närpes (Närpiö) 26 62.28 N 21.20 E
Närpiö → Närpes 26 62.28 N 21.20 E
Narrabeen 170 33.43 S 151.18 E
Narrabeen Lagoon C 274a 33.43 S 151.17 E
Narrabri 166 30.19 S 149.47 E
Narragansett 207 41.25 N 71.27 W
Narragansett Bay C 207 41.40 N 71.20 W
Narran ≃ 166 29.45 S 147.20 E
Narra Narra ∧ 171b 35.50 S 147.27 E
Narrandera 166 34.45 S 146.33 E
Narraway ≃ 182 54.48 N 119.56 W
Narraweena 274a 33.45 S 151.16 E
Narre Warren 274b 38.02 S 145.19 E
Narre Warren North 274b 37.59 S 145.19 E
Narrogin 162 32.56 S 117.10 E
Narromine 166 32.14 S 148.15 E
Narrows, Md., U.S. 208 38.58 N 76.15 W
Narrows, Va., U.S. 192 37.19 N 80.48 W
Narrowsburg 210 41.36 N 75.03 W
Närsen ⊜ 40 60.17 N 14.23 E
Narsimhapur 124 22.57 N 79.12 E
Narsinghdi 124 23.55 N 90.43 E
Narsinghgarh 124 23.42 N 77.06 E
Narsīpatnam 122 17.40 N 82.37 E
Narskije Prudy, ozero ⊜[1] 82 55.32 N 36.36 E
Narssaq 176 60.54 N 46.00 W
Nartkala 84 43.33 N 43.50 E
Nartuby ≃ 62 43.28 N 6.34 E
Naru 92 32.49 N 128.56 E
Narubis, Namibia 158 27.10 S 19.05 E
Narubis, Namibia 158 26.55 S 18.35 E
Naruko 92 38.44 N 140.43 E
Naruksovo 80 54.37 N 44.33 E
Naruo 270 34.43 N 135.23 E
Narusawa 94 35.29 N 138.41 E
Narutō, Nihon 94 35.36 N 140.25 E
Naruto, Nihon 96 34.11 N 134.37 E
Naruto-kaikyō ≍ 96 34.14 N 134.39 E
Narva, Eesti 76 59.23 N 28.12 E
Narva, Ross. 86 55.25 N 93.39 E
Narva ≃ 76 59.27 N 28.02 E
Narvacan 116 17.25 N 120.28 E
Narva-Jõesuu 76 59.27 N 28.03 E
Narva laht (Narvskij zaliv) C 76 59.30 N 27.40 E
Narvan 85 40.15 N 67.12 E
Narvik 24 68.26 N 17.25 E
Narvskij zaliv (Narva laht) C 76 59.30 N 27.40 E
Narvskoje vodochranilišče ⊜[1] 76 59.18 N 28.14 E
Narwāna 124 29.37 N 76.07 E
Narwietooma 162 23.15 S 132.35 E
Narym 86 58.58 N 81.30 E
Naryn, Kyrg. 85 41.26 N 75.59 E
Naryn, Ross. 88 50.13 N 96.27 E
Naryn □[4] 85 41.30 N 76.00 E
Naryn ≃ 85 40.54 N 71.45 E
Narynkol 72 42.43 N 80.12 E
Naryntau, gory ∧∧ 85 41.25 N 76.50 E
Naryškino 76 52.58 N 35.44 E
Naryū-zaki > 96 35.36 N 135.28 E
Narzole 62 44.35 N 7.52 E
Nås, Sve. 40 60.27 N 14.29 E
Näs, Sve. 40 58.41 N 15.50 E
Nasadkino 82 56.29 N 37.21 E
Näsåker 26 63.26 N 16.54 E
Na San, Thai 110 8.48 N 99.22 E
Na San, Viet 110 21.12 N 104.02 E
Nasarawa 150 8.30 N 7.40 E
Năsăud 38 47.17 N 24.24 E
Nasawa 175f 15.13 S 168.09 E
NASA Wallops Station ⊛[3] 208 37.52 N 75.28 W
Nasbinals 32 44.40 N 3.03 E
Naschel 252 32.55 S 65.23 W
Naseby, N.Z. 172 45.02 S 170.09 E
Naseby, Eng., U.K. 42 52.25 N 0.58 W
Naselle 224 46.21 N 123.48 W
Naselle ≃ 224 46.25 N 123.55 W
Nase → Naze 93b 28.23 N 129.30 E
Nash 194 33.27 N 94.08 W
Nashawena Island I 207 41.26 N 70.53 W
Nāshik 122 19.59 N 73.48 E
Nashoba Brook ≃ 283 42.28 N 71.24 W
Nashport 214 40.04 N 82.09 W
Nashū', Wādī an- V 146 26.25 N 14.15 E
Nashua, Ia., U.S. 190 42.57 N 92.32 W
Nashua, Mt., U.S. 202 48.07 N 106.21 W
Nashua, N.H., U.S. 207 42.45 N 71.28 W
Nashua ≃ 207 42.46 N 71.27 W
Nashuixi 102 30.09 N 108.40 E
Näshultasjön ⊜ 40 59.14 N 16.21 E
Nashville, On., Can. 275b 43.50 N 79.40 W
Nashville, Ar., U.S. 194 33.56 N 93.50 W
Nashville, Ga., U.S. 192 31.12 N 83.15 W
Nashville, Il., U.S. 219 38.20 N 89.22 W
Nashville, In., U.S. 218 39.12 N 86.15 W
Nashville, Mi., U.S. 216 42.36 N 85.05 W
Nashville, N.C., U.S. 192 35.58 N 77.57 W
Nashville, Oh., U.S. 214 40.36 N 82.07 W
Nashville, Tn., U.S. 194 36.09 N 86.47 W
Nashwaak ≃ 186 45.57 N 66.37 W
Nashwaaksis 186 45.59 N 66.39 W
Nashwah 142 30.30 N 31.29 E
Nashwauk 190 47.22 N 93.10 W
Nasia 150 10.09 N 0.48 W
Naṣīb 132 32.33 N 36.11 E
Našice 38 45.29 N 18.06 E
Nasielsk 30 52.36 N 20.48 E
Näsijärvi ⊜ 26 61.37 N 23.42 E
Nāṣir 140 8.36 N 33.04 E
Nāṣir, Buḥayrat (Lake Nasser) ⊜[1] 140 22.40 N 32.00 E
Nasīrābād, India 120 26.18 N 74.44 E
Nasīrābād, Pāk. 120 28.23 N 68.24 E
Naskaftym 80 52.57 N 45.38 E
Naskaupi ≃ 176 53.45 N 60.50 W
Näsnaren ⊜ 40 58.51 N 16.18 E
Naso 70 38.07 N 14.47 E
Nasondoye 154 10.22 S 25.06 E
Naso Point > 116 10.25 N 121.57 E
Nasorolevu ∧ 175g 16.38 S 178.42 E
Nasosnyj 84 40.37 N 49.34 E
Naṣr 142 30.36 N 30.23 E
Naṣrābād 128 34.08 N 51.26 E
Naṣrānī, Jabal an- ∧ 130 34.06 N 37.24 E
Nasriddinbek 85 40.41 N 71.55 E
Nāsriganj 124 25.03 N 84.20 E
Nass ≃ 182 55.00 N 129.50 W
Nassau, Ba. 240b 25.05 N 77.21 W
Nassau, Dtsch. 54 50.46 N 13.32 E
Nassau, Dtsch. 56 50.19 N 7.47 E
Nassau, N.Y., U.S. 210 42.30 N 73.36 W
Nassau □[6] 210 40.45 N 73.38 W
Nassau, Bahía C 254 55.25 S 67.40 W
Nassau Bay 222 29.32 N 95.05 W
Nassau Coliseum ◆ 276 40.43 N 73.36 W
Nassau International Airport ⊠ 240b 25.02 N 77.28 W
Nassau Island I 14 11.33 S 165.25 W
Nassau Shores 276 40.39 N 73.26 W
Nassawadox 208 37.28 N 75.51 W
Nassawango Creek ≃ 208 38.10 N 75.25 W
Nassenfels 60 48.48 N 11.16 E
Nassenheide 54 52.49 N 13.12 E
Nasser, Lake → Nāṣir, Buḥayrat ⊜[1] 140 22.40 N 32.00 E
Nassereith 58 47.19 N 10.50 E
Nassian 150 8.27 N 3.29 W
Nässjö 26 57.39 N 14.41 E
Nastapoca ≃ 176 56.55 N 76.33 W
Nastapoka Islands II 176 57.00 N 76.50 W
Nastasjino 82 54.28 N 38.16 E
Nastaška 78 49.39 N 30.19 E
Nastätten 56 50.12 N 7.51 E
Nastauli 272a 28.43 N 77.22 E
Nastf, Bi'r ⊽[4] 142 30.18 N 30.28 E
Nasu 94 37.01 N 140.07 E
Nasu-dake ∧, Nihon 92 37.07 N 139.58 E
Nasu-dake ∧, Nihon 94 37.09 N 139.58 E
Nasugbu 116 14.05 N 120.38 E
Nasukoin Mountain ∧ 202 48.48 N 114.35 W
Nasva 76 56.35 N 30.10 E
Nat ≃ 190 48.48 N 82.07 W
Nata, Bots. 156 20.12 S 26.12 E
Natá, Pan. 236 8.20 N 80.31 W
Nata ≃ 156 20.14 S 26.10 E
Natagaima 246 3.37 N 75.06 W
Nātāgarh 272b 22.42 N 88.25 E
Natal, Bra. 250 5.47 S 35.13 W
Natal, B.C., Can. 182 49.44 N 114.50 W
Natal, Indon. 110 0.33 N 99.07 E
Natal □[4] 158 28.40 S 30.40 E
Natal Basin ⊽[1] 10 30.00 S 40.00 E
Natalia 196 29.11 N 98.51 W
Nataljevka 83 47.10 N 38.29 E
Nataljin Jar 80 51.46 N 50.35 E
Nataljino 80 52.56 N 49.02 E
Natalkuz Lake ⊜ 182 53.26 N 125.20 W
Natalspruit ≃ 273d 26.19 S 28.10 E
Natanes Plateau ∧∧[1] 200 33.35 N 110.15 W
Natash, Wādī V 140 24.25 N 33.26 E
Natashō 96 35.24 N 135.38 E
Natashquan 186 50.12 N 61.49 W
Natashquan ≃ 176 50.06 N 61.49 W
Natashquan, Pointe de > 186 50.06 N 61.44 W
Natashquan Est ≃ 186 51.20 N 61.40 W
Natchez 194 31.33 N 91.24 W
Natchez Trace Parkway ◆ 194 32.00 N 91.00 W
Natchitoches 194 31.45 N 93.05 W
Natco Lake ⊜ 276 40.26 N 74.09 W
Natércia 256 22.07 S 45.30 W
Naters 58 46.20 N 7.59 E
Natewa Bay C 175g 16.35 S 179.40 E
Na Thawi 110 6.45 N 100.42 E
Nāthdwāra 120 24.56 N 73.49 E
Nathia Gali 123 34.04 N 73.24 E
Nathkaw 102 26.53 N 96.13 E
Nathula I 175g 16.53 S 177.25 E
Natick 207 42.17 N 71.21 W
Natick Laboratories ■ 283 42.17 N 71.22 W
Natimuk 166 36.45 S 141.57 E
Nation ≃ 182 55.28 N 123.35 W
National Agricultural Research Center ⊛[3] 284c 39.02 N 76.52 W
National Airport ⊠ 281 42.19 N 83.25 W
National Arboretum ◆ 284c 38.54 N 76.58 W
National Assembly ⊛ 269a 13.46 N 100.31 E
National Baseball Hall of Fame and Museum ⊛ 210 42.42 N 74.57 W
National City 228 32.40 N 117.05 W
National Gallery ⊛ 260 51.31 N 0.08 W
National Institute of Health ⊛ 284c 39.00 N 77.06 W
National Maritime Museum ⊛ 260 51.29 N 0.00
National Park 285 39.51 N 75.10 W
National Taiwan Normal University ⊛[2] 269d 25.02 N 121.31 E
National Taiwan University ⊛[2] 269d 25.01 N 121.32 E
National Zoological Park ◆ 284c 38.56 N 77.03 W
Natipi, Lac ⊜ 186 51.27 N 71.23 W
Natisone ≃ 64 45.57 N 13.22 E
Natitingou 150 10.19 N 1.22 E
Native Bay C 176 63.52 N 82.30 W
Natividade 250 11.43 S 47.47 W
Natividade da Serra 256 23.24 S 45.26 W
Natívitas ⬌[8] 286a 19.14 N 99.05 W
Nativity, Church of the ⊛[1] 132 31.43 N 35.12 E
Natkyizin 110 14.55 N 97.57 E
Natl 132 31.39 N 35.52 E
Natoma 198 39.11 N 99.01 W
Natong 102 23.01 N 107.50 E
Nator 124 24.25 N 88.59 E
Natori 92 38.08 N 140.55 E
Natorp 263 51.30 N 7.38 E
Natron, Lake ⊜ 154 2.25 S 36.00 E
Natrona Heights 214 40.37 N 79.43 W
Naṭrūn, Wādī an- ±[7] 142 30.25 N 30.13 E
Natsui ≃ 94 37.03 N 140.59 E
Nattai ≃ 170 34.05 S 150.25 E
Nattai River 170 34.04 S 150.27 E
Nattam 122 10.14 N 78.14 E
Nåttarö I 40 58.52 N 18.07 E
Nattaset ∧ 24 68.12 N 27.20 E
Nattaung ∧ 110 18.48 N 97.02 E
Natters 64 47.14 N 11.22 E
Nattwerder 264a 52.26 N 12.56 E
Natuchajevskaja 78 44.54 N 37.34 E
Nātudaha 126 23.39 N 88.41 E
Natukanaoka Pan ≚ 156 18.40 S 15.45 E
Natuna Besar I 112 4.00 N 108.15 E
Natuna Besar, Kepulauan II 112 4.40 N 108.00 E
Natuna Selatan, Kepulauan II 112 2.45 N 109.00 E
Natural Bridge 212 44.04 N 75.29 W
Natural Bridge ◆ 192 37.38 N 79.33 W
Natural Bridges National Monument ◆ 200 37.30 N 110.08 W
Natural Bridge State Resort Park ◆ 192 37.47 N 83.42 W
Naturaliste, Cape > 162 33.32 S 115.01 E
Naturaliste Channel ≍ 162 25.25 S 113.00 E
Naturita 200 38.13 N 108.34 W
Naturita Creek ≃ 200 38.13 N 108.32 W
Naturno (Naturns) 64 46.39 N 11.00 E
Natzungen 52 51.36 N 9.14 E
Nau 85 40.09 N 69.22 E
Nau, Cap de la > 34 38.44 N 0.14 E
Naucalpan de Juárez 286a 19.28 N 99.14 W
Naucelle 32 44.12 N 2.20 E
Naučnyj 78 44.44 N 34.01 E
Naude 272c 19.03 N 73.06 E
Nauders 58 46.53 N 10.30 E
Nauen 54 52.36 N 12.52 E
Nauener Luch ≚ 264a 52.37 N 12.55 E
Nauener Stadtforst ◆ 264a 52.38 N 12.58 E
Naugachhia 124 25.24 N 87.06 E
Naugatuck 207 41.30 N 73.05 W
Naugatuck ≃ 207 41.19 N 73.05 W
Naughton 190 46.24 N 81.12 W
Naugol'noje 82 56.22 N 38.11 E
Naui 140 18.28 N 30.43 E
Naujamiestis 76 55.41 N 24.04 E
Naujan 116 13.20 N 121.18 E
Naujan, Lake ⊜ 116 13.10 N 121.21 E
Naujoji Akmenė 76 56.19 N 22.55 E
Naukan 180 66.01 N 169.43 W
Naulavaara ∧[2] 26 63.53 N 28.13 E
Naulila 152 17.12 S 14.42 E
Naumburg, Dtsch. 54 51.09 N 11.48 E
Naumburg, Dtsch. 56 51.15 N 9.10 E
Naumovščina 76 58.23 N 28.20 E
Naunak 86 59.00 N 80.13 E

Symbols in the index entries represent the broad categories identified in the key at the right. Symbols with superior numbers (∧∧[1]) identify subcategories (see complete key on page *I · 1).*

Symbole im Register stellen die rechts im Schlüssel erklärten Kategorien dar. Symbole mit hochgestellten Ziffern (∧∧[1]) bezeichnen Unterabteilungen einer Kategorie (vgl. vollständiger Schlüssel auf Seite *I · 1).*

Los símbolos incluídos en el texto del índice representan las grandes categorias identificadas con la clave a la derecha. Los símbolos con numeros en su parte superior (∧∧[1]) identifican las subcategorías (véase la clave completa en la página *I · 1).*

Les symboles de l'index représentent les catégories indiquées dans la légende à droite. Les symboles suivis d'un indice (∧∧[1]) représentent des sous-catégories (voir légende complète à la page *I · 1).*

Os símbolos incluídos no texto do índice representam as grandes categorias identificadas com a chave à direita. Os símbolos com números em sua parte superior (∧∧[1]) identificam as subcategorias (veja-se a chave completa à página *I · 1).*

	English	Deutsch	Español	Français	Português
∧	Mountain	Berg	Montaña	Montagne	Montanha
∧∧	Mountains	Gebirge	Montañas	Montagnes	Montanhas
)(	Pass	Paß	Paso	Col	Passo
V	Valley, Canyon	Tal, Cañon	Valle, Cañón	Vallée, Canyon	Vale, Canhão
≚	Plain	Ebene	Llano	Plaine	Planície
>	Cape	Kap	Cabo	Cap	Cabo
I	Island	Insel	Isla	Île	Ilha
II	Islands	Inseln	Islas	Îles	Ilhas
±	Other Topographic Features	Andere Topographische Objekte	Otros Elementos Topográficos	Autres données topographiques	Outros acidentes topográficos

ESPAÑOL

Nombre	Página	Lat.°′	Long.°′ W = Oeste
Naundorf	54	50.56 N	13.25 E
Naunglon	110	16.48 N	97.45 E
Naungpale	110	19.33 N	97.08 E
Naunhof	54	51.16 N	12.35 E
Naupada ◆[8]	272c	19.04 N	72.50 E
Nā'ūr	132	31.53 N	35.50 E
Nauraushaun Brook ≃	276	41.03 N	73.59 W
Nauroth	56	50.42 N	7.52 E
Nauroz Kalāt	128	28.47 N	65.38 E
Naurskaja	84	43.38 N	45.19 E
Nauru □[1], Oc.	14	0.32 S	166.55 E
Nauru □[1], Oc.	174b	0.32 S	166.55 E
Naurzumskij zapovednik ♠	86	51.30 N	64.20 E
Naushahro Fīroz	120	26.50 N	68.07 E
Naushon Island I	207	41.29 N	70.45 W
Nauški	88	50.28 N	106.07 E
Nausori	175g	18.02 S	178.32 E
Naussac, Barrage de ◆[6]	62	44.46 N	3.49 E
Naustdal	26	61.31 N	5.43 E
Nauta	246	4.32 S	73.33 W
Nautanwa	124	27.26 N	83.25 E
Nautilus Park	207	41.22 N	72.05 W
Nautla	234	20.13 N	96.47 W
Nauvoo	190	40.33 N	91.23 W
Nava	232	28.25 N	100.46 W
Nava, Arroyo de la ≃	266a	40.31 N	3.46 W
Nava, Colle di)(	62	44.05 N	7.53 E
Nava del Rey	34	41.20 N	5.05 W
Navadwip	126	23.25 N	88.22 E
Navahermosa	34	39.38 N	4.28 W
Navajo	200	35.55 N	109.01 W
Navajo ≃	200	37.01 N	107.10 W
Navajo Creek ≃	200	36.59 N	111.24 W
Navajo Hopi Joint Use Area ◆[4]	200	36.15 N	110.30 W
Navajo Indian Reservation ◆[4]	200	36.25 N	110.00 W
Navajo Mountain ∧	200	37.02 N	110.52 W
Navajo National Monument ♠	200	36.40 N	110.33 W
Navajo Reservoir ⊜[1]	200	36.55 N	107.30 W
Naval	116	11.34 N	124.23 E
Navalmoral de la Mata	34	39.54 N	5.32 W
Naval Ordnance Test Station ■	228	35.32 N	117.05 W
Navalvillar de Pela	34	39.06 N	5.28 W
Navan	48	53.39 N	6.41 W
Navāpur	122	21.09 N	73.48 E
Navarin, mys ≻	180	62.16 N	179.10 E
Navarino, Isla I	254	55.05 S	67.40 W
Navarino → Pílos	38	36.55 N	21.43 E
Navarra □[4], Esp.	34	42.40 N	1.30 W
Navarra □[4], Esp.	34	42.45 N	1.30 W
Navarre, Austl.	169	36.54 S	143.07 E
Navarre, Oh., U.S.	214	40.43 N	81.31 W
Navarro	258	35.01 S	59.16 W
Navarro □[6]	222	32.05 N	96.30 W
Navarro ≃	204	39.11 N	123.45 W
Navarro, Cañada ≃	258	35.00 S	59.18 W
Navarro, Laguna ⊜	258	35.01 S	59.18 W
Navarro Mills Lake ⊜[1]	222	31.56 N	96.45 W
Navašino	80	55.32 N	42.12 E
Navasota	222	30.23 N	96.05 W
Navasota ≃	222	30.20 N	96.09 W
Navassa	192	34.15 N	78.00 W
Navassa Island I	238	18.24 N	75.01 W
Nave	64	45.35 N	10.17 E
Nävekvarn	40	58.38 N	16.49 E
Navenne	58	47.36 N	6.10 E
Naver ≃	46	58.32 N	4.15 W
Naver, Loch ⊜	46	58.17 N	4.23 W
Navesink	276	40.23 N	74.02 W
Navesink River ⊂	276	40.23 N	73.58 W
Navesnoje	76	52.17 N	37.57 E
Nâves-Parmelan	58	45.56 N	6.11 E
Navesti ≃	76	58.30 N	24.54 E
Navestock	260	51.39 N	0.13 E
Navestock Side	260	51.39 N	0.16 E
Navia, Arg.	252	34.47 S	66.35 W
Navia, Esp.	34	43.32 N	6.43 W
Navia ≃	34	43.33 N	6.44 W
Navidad	252	33.57 S	71.50 W
Navidad ≃	196	28.41 N	96.35 W
Navidad, Bahía de ⊂	234	19.17 N	104.50 W
Navidad Bank ✦[3]	238	20.00 N	68.50 W
Navio, Riacho do ≃	250	8.39 S	38.36 W
Naviraí	255	23.08 S	54.13 W
Navis	64	47.07 N	11.32 E
Naviti I	175g	17.07 S	177.15 E
Navl'a	76	52.51 N	34.30 E
Navl'a ≃	76	52.42 N	34.01 E
Năvodari	38	44.19 N	28.36 E
Navoi	72	40.15 N	65.15 E
Navojoa	232	27.06 N	109.26 W
Navolato	232	24.47 N	107.42 W
Navoloki	80	57.28 N	41.59 E
Navotas	269f	14.39 N	120.57 E
Návpaktos	38	38.23 N	21.50 E
Návplion	38	37.34 N	22.48 E
Navrongo	150	10.54 N	1.06 W
Navsāri	120	20.51 N	72.55 E
Navua	175g	18.14 S	178.10 E
Navy Island I	284a	43.04 N	79.01 W
Navy Pier ◆[5]	278	41.53 N	87.36 W
Navy Yard City	224	47.32 N	122.41 W
Nawa, Nihon	96	35.30 N	133.30 E
Nawá, Sūrīy.	132	32.53 N	36.03 E
Nawābganj, Bngl.	124	24.36 N	88.17 E
Nawābganj, Bngl.	126	23.40 N	90.10 E
Nawābganj, India	124	28.33 N	79.38 E
Nawābganj, India	124	26.52 N	82.08 E
Nawābganj, India	124	26.56 N	81.13 E
Nawābshāh	120	26.15 N	68.25 E
Nawāda	124	24.53 N	85.32 E
Nāwah	120	32.19 N	67.53 E
Nawa Kot	120	28.20 N	71.22 E
Nawalapitiya	122	7.03 N	80.32 E
Nawalgarh	120	27.51 N	75.16 E
Nawa → Naha	174m	26.13 N	127.40 E
Nawān Kot	123	31.06 N	71.32 E
Nawanshahr	123	31.07 N	76.08 E
Nawāpāra, Bngl.	126	23.02 N	89.23 E
Nawāpāra, India	122	20.58 N	81.51 E
Nawapārā, India	126	23.29 N	88.15 E
Nawasā al-Ghayṭ	142	30.58 N	31.19 E
Nawāshahr	123	34.10 N	73.16 E
Nawāṣīf, Ḥarrat ⏚[9]	144	21.20 N	42.10 E
Nawāy	142	27.47 N	30.46 E
Nawiliwili Bay ⊂	229b	21.57 N	159.21 W
Nawinda Kuta	152	16.25 S	24.28 E
Nawŏn-ni	98	36.25 N	126.40 E
Naxera	208	37.20 N	76.27 W
Naxi	107	28.47 N	105.22 E
Náxos	38	37.06 N	25.23 E
Náxos I	38	37.02 N	25.35 E
Naxos ⊥	70	37.49 N	15.17 E
Nayābās	272a	28.35 N	77.19 E
Nayāgaon	126	23.32 N	90.46 E
Nayāgarh	120	20.08 N	85.06 E
Nayāgrām	126	22.02 N	87.11 E
Nayak	120	34.44 N	66.57 E
Nayāpāra	126	21.35 N	87.01 E
Nayarit	204	32.20 N	115.19 W
Nayarit □[3]	234	22.00 N	105.00 W
Nayau Island I	175g	17.58 S	179.03 W
Nāy Band, Īrān	128	27.23 N	52.38 E
Nāy Band, Īrān	128	32.20 N	57.34 E
Nāy Band, Kūh-e ∧	128	32.26 N	57.22 E
Nayland	42	51.59 N	0.52 E
Naylor	194	36.34 N	90.36 W
Nayong	102	26.50 N	105.13 E
Nayoro	92a	44.21 N	142.28 E
Nazālī Ṭāhā'	142	28.11 N	30.42 E

FRANÇAIS

Nom	Page	Lat.°′	Long.°′ W = Ouest
Nazaré, Bra.	250	6.23 S	47.40 W
Nazaré, Bra.	255	13.02 S	39.00 W
Nazaré, Port.	34	39.36 N	9.04 W
Nazaré da Mata	250	7.44 S	35.14 W
Nazaré do Piauí	250	6.59 S	42.40 W
Nazareno	256	21.13 S	44.37 W
Nazaré Paulista	256	23.11 S	46.24 W
Nazareth, Bel.	50	50.58 N	3.36 E
Nazareth, Pa., U.S.	208	40.44 N	75.18 W
Nazareth, Vanuatu	175f	15.29 S	168.10 E
Nazareth Bank ✦[4]	12	14.30 S	60.45 E
Nazareth → Naẕerat	132	32.42 N	35.18 E
Nazário	255	16.36 S	49.54 W
Nazarjevo, Ross.	82	55.22 N	36.24 E
Nazarjevo, Ross.	265b	55.59 N	37.16 E
Nazarovo	86	56.01 N	90.26 E
Nazarovskij	78	49.33 N	40.56 E
Nazas	232	25.14 N	104.08 W
Nazas ≃	232	25.35 N	105.00 W
Nazca	248	14.50 S	74.57 W
Nazca Ridge ✦[3]	18	22.00 S	82.00 W
Naze	93b	28.23 N	129.30 E
Nazeing	260	51.44 N	0.03 E
N'azepetrovsk	86	56.03 N	59.36 E
Naẕerat (Nazareth)	132	32.42 N	35.18 E
Naẕerat 'Illit	132	32.42 N	35.19 E
Nazija	76	59.50 N	31.35 E
Nazik Gölü ⊜	130	38.50 N	42.16 E
Nazilli	130	37.55 N	28.21 E
Nazimicha	265b	55.59 N	38.08 E
Nazımiye	130	39.11 N	39.50 E
Nazimovo	86	59.30 N	90.58 E
Nazina	86	60.07 N	78.52 E
Nāzira	120	26.55 N	94.44 E
Nāzir Hāt	120	22.38 N	91.47 E
Nāzirpur	126	22.43 N	89.58 E
Nazko ≃	182	53.07 N	123.34 W
Nazlat al-'Amūdayn	142	28.14 N	30.42 E
Nazlat al-Badramān	142	27.40 N	30.44 E
Nazlat as-Sammān	273c	29.59 N	31.08 E
Nazlat Khalīfah	273c	30.01 N	31.10 E
Nazlat Qufṭan Bāshā	142	28.57 N	30.49 E
Nazlat Thābit	142	28.25 N	30.47 E
Nazran'	84	43.13 N	44.46 E
Nazret	144	8.33 N	39.16 E
Nazyvajevsk	86	55.34 N	71.21 E
N. B. C. Studios ✪[3]	280	34.09 N	118.20 W
Nchanga	154	12.30 S	27.53 E
Nchelenge	154	9.20 S	28.50 E
Ncue	152	2.01 N	10.28 E
Ndabala	154	13.28 S	29.50 E
Ndala	154	4.46 S	33.16 E
N'dalatando	152	9.18 S	14.54 E
Ndali	150	9.51 N	2.43 E
Ndanda	152	5.12 N	22.21 E
Ndande	150	15.16 N	16.30 W
Ndarassa	152	6.49 N	22.15 E
Ndélé	146	8.24 N	20.39 E
Ndélélé	152	4.02 N	14.56 E
Ndemba	152	0.11 N	14.19 E
Ndendé	152	2.23 S	11.23 E
Ndikiniméki	152	4.46 N	10.50 E
Ndindi	152	3.46 S	11.09 E
N'Djamena	146	12.07 N	15.03 E
Ndji ≃	152	6.47 N	22.14 E
Ndjili ◆[8]	273b	4.20 S	15.22 E
Ndjili ≃	273b	4.19 S	15.24 E
Ndjili, Grande Île de la I	273b	4.19 S	15.24 E
Ndjim ≃	152	4.38 N	11.24 E
Ndjo	152	1.15 S	14.30 E
Ndjolé	152	0.11 S	10.45 E
Ndogo, Lagune ⊂	152	2.35 S	10.00 E
Ndola	154	12.58 S	28.38 E
Ndolo ◆[8]	273b	4.19 S	15.19 E
Ndona	115b	8.46 S	121.45 E
Ndongo	152	2.19 S	13.38 E
Ndouba	152	0.11 S	14.09 E
Ndougou	152	1.39 S	9.40 E
Ndu	152	4.41 N	22.49 E
Nduguti	154	4.18 S	34.42 E
Nduindui	175f	15.24 S	167.46 E
Ndumbwe	154	10.14 S	39.58 E
Ndumu Game Reserve ◆[4]	158	26.53 S	32.15 E
Nduye	154	1.50 N	29.01 E
Ne	268	35.47 N	140.03 E
Nea ≃	26	63.13 N	11.02 E
Neabul Creek ≃	166	27.45 S	147.32 E
Néa Erithraía	267c	38.05 N	23.49 E
Néa Filadhélfia	267c	38.02 N	23.44 E
Neagari	94	36.27 N	136.27 E
Neagh, Lough ⊜	48	54.38 N	6.24 W
Neah Bay	224	48.22 N	124.37 W
Néa Ionía	267c	38.02 N	23.45 E
Neajlov ≃	38	44.11 N	26.12 E
Néa Khalkidhón	267c	38.02 N	23.43 E
Neale, Lake ⊜	162	24.22 S	130.00 E
Neales ≃	162	28.08 S	136.47 E
Neales Flat	168b	34.15 S	139.10 E
Néa Liósia	267c	38.02 N	23.42 E
Neamt □[6]	38	47.00 N	26.30 E
Neandertal, Naturschutzgebiet ♠	263	51.15 N	7.00 E
Néa Páfos (Paphos)	130	34.45 N	32.25 E
Neapel → Napoli	68	40.51 N	14.17 E
Néa Pendéli	267c	38.04 N	23.52 E
Néa Péramos	267c	38.00 N	23.26 E
Neápolis, Ellás	38	36.30 N	23.04 E
Neápolis, Ellás	38	35.15 N	25.37 E
Neapolis, Oh., U.S.	216	41.29 N	83.52 W
Néa Psará	38	38.23 N	23.48 E
Near Islands II	181a	52.40 N	173.30 E
Near North Side ◆[8]	278	41.54 N	87.38 W
Néa Smírni	267c	37.57 N	23.43 E
Neasons Hill	214	41.37 N	80.08 W
Neatahwanta, Lake ⊜	210	43.18 N	76.27 W
Neath	42	51.40 N	3.48 W
Neath ≃	42	51.37 N	3.50 W
Neauphle-le-Château	50	48.49 N	1.54 E
Neauphle-le-Vieux	261	48.49 N	1.52 E
Neavitt	208	38.43 N	76.16 W
Neba	94	35.15 N	137.35 E
Nebaj	236	15.24 N	91.08 W
Nebbou	150	11.18 N	1.53 W
Nebelhorn ∧	58	47.25 N	10.20 E
Nebesnaja, gora ∧	86	43.19 N	80.44 E
Nebeur	36	36.17 N	8.47 E
Nebine Creek ≃	166	29.07 S	146.56 E
Nebit-Dag	128	39.30 N	54.22 E
Neblina, Pico da ∧	246	0.48 N	66.02 W
Nebo	194	39.27 N	90.47 W
Nebo, Mount ∧	200	39.49 N	111.46 W
Nebo, Mount → Nabā, Jabal an- ∧	132	31.46 N	35.45 E
Nebolči	76	59.08 N	33.18 E
Nebra	54	51.17 N	11.34 E
Nebraska	218	39.04 N	85.28 W
Nebraska □[3], U.S.	178	41.30 N	100.00 W
Nebraska □[3], U.S.	198	41.30 N	100.00 W
Nebraska City	198	40.40 N	95.51 W
Nebrodi ⋏	70	37.54 N	14.35 E
Nebyloje	80	56.22 N	39.59 E
Nečajannoje	78	46.57 N	31.33 E
Nečajevka	80	53.17 N	44.27 E
Nečajevo	82	54.42 N	37.23 E
Necaxa ≃	234	20.16 N	97.27 W
Necedah	190	44.01 N	90.04 W
Nechajevskij	80	50.25 N	41.44 E
Nechako ≃	182	53.56 N	122.42 W
Nechako Plateau ⋏[1]	182	54.00 N	124.30 W
Nechako Range ⋏	182	53.20 N	124.30 W
Nechako Reservoir ⊜[1]	182	53.25 N	125.10 W
Neche	198	48.59 N	97.33 W
Neches	222	31.52 N	95.30 W

PORTUGUÊS

Nome	Página	Lat.°′	Long.°′ W = Oeste
Neches ≃	194	29.55 N	93.52 W
Nechí	246	8.07 N	74.46 W
Nechí ≃	246	8.08 N	74.46 W
Nechisar National Park ♠	144	6.00 N	37.50 E
Nechmeya	36	36.36 N	7.31 E
Nechranická Přehradová Nádrž ⊜[1]	54	50.20 N	13.20 E
Nechvorošča	78	49.09 N	34.44 E
Neckar ≃	30	49.31 N	8.26 E
Neckarbischofsheim	56	49.17 N	8.57 E
Neckarelz	56	49.20 N	9.06 E
Neckargemünd	56	49.23 N	8.47 E
Neckarsteinach	56	49.25 N	8.53 E
Neckarsulm	56	49.12 N	9.13 E
Neckartailfingen	56	48.36 N	9.16 E
Neckartenzlingen	56	48.35 N	9.14 E
Neck Creek ≃	276	40.36 N	74.12 W
Necker	284b	39.23 N	76.29 W
Necker Island I, Br. Vir. Is.	240m	18.33 N	64.21 W
Necker Island I, Hi., U.S.	14	23.35 N	164.42 W
Necker Ridge ✦[3]	14	22.00 N	167.15 W
Necochea	252	38.33 S	58.45 W
Necrópolis ◆	266a	40.25 N	3.38 W
Nedalssjön ⊜	26	62.56 N	12.11 E
Nedančiči	78	51.30 N	30.37 E
Ned Brown Preserve ♠	278	42.02 N	88.01 W
Nedel'noje	82	54.50 N	36.39 E
Nederland	194	29.58 N	93.59 W
Nederland → Netherlands □[1]	30	52.15 N	5.30 E
Nederlandse Antillen → Netherlands Antilles □[2]	241s	12.15 N	69.00 W
Neder-Rijn ≃[1]	52	51.58 N	5.20 E
Nederweert	52	51.17 N	5.45 E
Nederzwalm-Hermelgem	50	50.53 N	3.41 E
Nedlands	168a	31.59 S	115.49 E
Nedlitz	54	52.04 N	12.14 E
Nedlitz ◆[8]	264a	52.26 N	13.03 E
Nêdong	120	29.14 N	91.46 E
Nedre Soppero	24	68.01 N	21.44 E
Nedre Vättern ⊜	40	59.49 N	15.40 E
Nedrigajlov	78	50.50 N	33.53 E
Nédroma	148	35.01 N	1.45 W
Nedrow	210	42.58 N	76.08 W
Nedstrand	26	59.21 N	5.51 E
Neebish Island I	190	46.16 N	84.09 W
Neede	52	52.08 N	6.36 E
Needham, In., U.S.	218	39.32 N	85.58 W
Needham, Ma., U.S.	207	42.17 N	71.14 W
Needham Market	42	52.09 N	1.03 E
Needhams Point ≻	241g	13.05 N	59.36 W
Needle Mountain ∧	202	44.05 N	109.37 W
Needles	204	34.50 N	114.36 W
Needling Hill ∧[2]	168a	31.53 S	116.56 E
Needville	222	29.23 N	95.50 W
Neelyton	214	40.10 N	77.50 W
Ñeembucú □[5]	252	27.00 S	58.00 W
Neenah	190	44.11 N	88.27 W
Neepawa	184	50.13 N	99.29 W
Neerabup National Park ♠	168a	31.41 S	115.43 E
Neerim South	169	38.01 S	145.58 E
Neermoor	52	53.18 N	7.26 E
Neeroeteren	56	51.05 N	5.42 E
Neerpelt	56	51.13 N	5.25 E
Neersen	263	51.15 N	6.29 E
Nee Soon	271c	1.24 N	103.49 E
Neetze	52	53.15 N	10.39 E
Neetze ≃	54	53.20 N	10.28 E
Nefedjevo, Ross.	82	54.39 N	37.56 E
Nefedjevo, Ross.	265b	55.54 N	37.10 E
Neffs	208	40.42 N	75.37 W
Neffsville	208	40.06 N	76.18 W
Nef'odovo	86	58.48 N	72.34 E
Nefta	148	33.52 N	7.33 E
Nefteabad	85	40.12 N	70.34 E
Neftečala	84	39.23 N	49.16 E
Neftegorsk	84	44.22 N	39.42 E
Neftekumsk	84	44.45 N	44.48 E
Nefyn	42	52.57 N	4.31 W
Nefza	36	36.58 N	9.05 E
Negage	152	7.45 S	15.16 E
Négala	150	12.52 N	8.27 W
Negapatam → Nāgappattinam	122	10.46 N	79.50 E
Negara, Indon.	112	2.37 S	115.06 E
Negara, Indon.	115a	8.22 S	114.37 E
Negara ≃	112	3.00 S	114.45 E
Negast	54	54.15 N	13.01 E
Negaunee	190	46.29 N	87.36 W
Negba	132	31.40 N	34.41 E
Negele	144	5.20 N	39.36 E
Negenborn	52	51.53 N	9.34 E
Negeribatin	112	4.35 S	104.32 E
Negeri Sembilan □[3]	114	2.45 N	102.10 E
Negev Desert → HaNegev ◆[1]	132	30.30 N	34.55 E
Negishi	268	35.51 N	139.23 E
Negley	214	40.47 N	80.32 W
Negola	152	14.10 S	14.30 E
Negomano	154	11.27 S	38.31 E
Negombo	122	7.13 N	79.50 E
Negonego I[1]	14	18.47 S	141.48 W
Negoreloje	76	53.36 N	27.04 E
Negotin	38	44.14 N	22.32 E
Negra, Laguna ⊜	252	34.03 S	53.40 W
Negra, Ponta ≻	256	22.58 S	42.42 W
Negra, Punta ≻, Belize	232	16.17 N	88.34 W
Negra, Punta ≻, Perú	248	6.06 S	81.09 W
Negrais	266c	38.53 N	9.17 W
Negras, Lomas ∧[2]	286d	11.55 S	77.06 W
Negreira	34	42.54 N	8.44 W
Nègres, Pointe des ≻	240e	14.36 N	61.06 W
Negrești	38	46.50 N	27.27 E
Negrești-Oaș	38	47.52 N	23.25 E
Negrine	148	34.30 N	7.30 E
Negritos	246	4.38 S	81.19 W
Negro ≃, Arg.	254	41.02 S	62.47 W
Negro ≃, Bol.	248	9.49 S	65.42 W
Negro ≃, Bol.	248	14.11 S	63.07 W
Negro ≃, Bra.	248	5.15 S	70.53 W
Negro ≃, Bra.	248	19.13 S	57.17 W
Negro ≃, Bra.	250	9.15 S	47.34 W
Negro ≃, Bra.	252	26.01 S	50.30 W
Negro ≃, Col.	246	5.44 N	74.39 W
Negro ≃, N.A.	236	13.02 N	87.17 W
Negro ≃, Para.	252	24.23 S	57.11 W
Negro ≃, S.A.	246	3.08 S	59.55 W
Negro ≃, S.A.	252	33.24 S	58.22 W
Negro, Baia del ⊂	144	7.55 N	49.55 E
Negro, Cerro ∧, Arg.	254	46.55 S	70.12 W
Negro, Cerro ∧, Arg.	254	44.09 S	69.30 W
Negro, Cerro ∧, Méx.	234	17.19 N	97.25 W
Negro, Mar → Black Sea Ŧ[2]	22	43.00 N	35.00 E
Negros I	116	10.00 N	123.00 E
Negros Occidental □[4]	116	10.20 N	123.00 E
Negros Oriental □[4]	116	9.40 N	123.00 E
Negru-Vodă	38	43.50 N	28.12 E
Neguac	186	47.15 N	65.05 W
Nehalem	224	45.43 N	123.53 W
Nehalem ≃	224	45.40 N	123.56 W
Nehawka	198	40.49 N	95.59 W
Nehbandān	128	31.32 N	60.02 E
Neheim-Hüsten	56	51.27 N	7.57 E
Nehonsey Brook ≃	285	39.49 N	75.18 W
Néhoué, Baie de ⊂	175f	20.21 S	164.09 E
Nehru Planetarium ✪	272c	18.59 N	72.49 E
Neiba	238	18.28 N	71.25 W
Neichiang → Neijiang	107	29.35 N	105.03 E
Neidpath	184	50.13 N	107.15 W
Neige, Crêt de la ∧	58	46.16 N	5.56 E
Neiges, Piton des ∧	157c	21.05 S	55.29 E
Neihart	202	46.56 N	110.44 W
Neihe ≃	100	22.54 N	115.38 E
Neihu	269d	25.05 N	121.34 E
Neihuang	98	35.59 N	114.55 E
Neijiang	107	29.35 N	105.03 E
Neikiang → Neijiang	107	29.35 N	105.03 E
Neilburg	184	52.50 N	109.38 W
Neillsville	190	44.33 N	90.35 W
Neilston	46	55.47 N	4.27 W
Neimen	263	51.29 N	7.48 E
Nei Monggol Zizhiqu (Inner Mongolia) □[4]	90	43.00 N	115.00 E
Nein	132	32.38 N	35.21 E
Neindorf	54	52.20 N	10.50 E
Neinstedt	54	51.45 N	11.05 E
Neiqiu	98	37.17 N	114.31 E
Neira	246	5.10 N	75.32 W
Neirone	62	44.27 N	9.11 E
Neishuishan	269d	25.09 N	121.43 E
Neisse (Nysa Łużycka) (Nisa) ≃	30	52.04 N	14.46 E
Neiva	246	2.56 N	75.18 W
Neiwufuquan	105	40.11 N	117.39 E
Neixiang	102	33.12 N	111.57 E
Neixpa ≃	234	18.05 N	102.46 W
Neizeng Shan ∧	100	24.02 N	117.32 E
Neja, Ross.	80	58.24 N	46.31 E
Neja, Ross.	80	58.18 N	43.54 E
Neja ≃	80	57.48 N	43.42 E
Nejapa de Madero	234	16.37 N	95.59 W
Nejdek	54	50.17 N	12.42 E
Nejd → Najd □[9]	118	25.00 N	44.30 E
Nejo	144	9.30 N	35.30 E
Nejva ≃	86	57.54 N	62.18 E
Nejvo-Šajtanskij	86	57.44 N	61.15 E
Nekalagba	154	2.50 N	28.01 E
Nekemte	144	9.02 N	36.31 E
Nekhab ⊥	140	25.10 N	32.48 E
Nekoosa	190	44.18 N	89.54 W
Nekor, Oued ≃	34	35.14 N	3.45 W
Neko-zaki ≻	96	35.40 N	134.46 E
Nekrasino	82	56.18 N	36.33 E
Nekrasovka	265b	55.41 N	37.56 E
Nekrasovo, Ross.	80	51.10 N	45.18 E
Nekrasovo, Ross.	82	54.30 N	38.57 E
Nekrasovskoje	80	57.41 N	40.22 E
Nekselø I	41	55.47 N	11.18 E
Neksø	26	55.04 N	15.09 E
Nela Park ♠	279a	41.33 N	81.33 W
Nel'aty	88	56.29 N	115.41 E
Nelichu ∧	140	6.08 N	34.25 E
Nelidovo	76	56.13 N	32.46 E
Neligh	198	42.07 N	98.01 W
Nel'kan	74	57.40 N	136.13 E
Nellie	214	40.20 N	82.04 W
Nellikuppam	122	11.46 N	79.41 E
Nellingen	56	48.33 N	9.47 E
Nellis Air Force Base ■	204	36.14 N	115.02 W
Nelliston	210	42.56 N	74.37 W
Nellis Weapons Range ■	204	37.15 N	116.20 W
Nellore	122	14.26 N	79.58 E
Nel'ma	89	47.39 N	139.09 E
Nelson, B.C., Can.	182	49.29 N	117.17 W
Nelson, N.Z.	172	41.17 S	173.17 E
Nelson, Eng., U.K.	44	53.51 N	2.13 W
Nelson, Ne., U.S.	198	40.12 N	98.04 W
Nelson, Pa., U.S.	210	41.59 N	77.14 W
Nelson ≃	184	57.04 N	92.30 W
Nelson, Cape ≻, Austl.	166	38.26 S	141.33 E
Nelson, Cape ≻, Pap. N. Gui.	164	9.00 S	149.15 E
Nelson, Estrecho Ʉ	254	51.37 S	75.00 W
Nelson Creek ≃	222	30.56 N	95.31 W
Nelson House	184	55.47 N	98.51 W
Nelson Island I	180	60.35 N	164.45 W
Nelson-Kennedy Ledges State Park ♠	214	41.18 N	81.04 W
Nelson Lake ⊜	184	55.44 N	100.00 W
Nelson Lakes National Park ♠	172	41.50 S	172.40 E
Nelson Reservoir ⊜[1]	202	48.30 N	107.34 W
Nelson's Dockyard ⊥	240c	17.00 N	61.46 W
Nelsonville, N.Y., U.S.	210	41.25 N	73.57 W
Nelsonville, Oh., U.S.	188	39.27 N	82.14 W
Nelspoort	158	32.07 S	23.00 E
Nelspoortjie	158	29.58 S	22.25 E
Nelspruit	156	25.30 S	30.58 E
Néma, Maur.	150	16.37 N	7.15 W
Nema, Ross.	80	57.31 N	50.31 E
Néma, Dahr ⏚[4]	150	16.40 N	7.13 W
Nemadji ≃	190	46.41 N	92.02 W
Nemah	224	46.31 N	123.51 W
Nemaha	198	40.20 N	95.40 W
Neman	76	55.02 N	22.02 E
Neman (Nemunas) ≃	76	55.18 N	21.23 E
Nematābād ◆[8]	267d	35.38 N	51.21 E
Nembe	150	4.35 N	6.26 E
Nembrala	112	10.53 S	122.50 E
Nembro	62	45.45 N	9.45 E
Nemčinovka	265b	55.43 N	37.23 E
Nemda ≃, Ross.	80	57.35 N	48.56 E
Nemda ≃, Ross.	80	57.21 N	43.08 E
Nemegosenda ≃	190	48.31 N	82.53 W
Nemegt uul ⋏	102	43.40 N	101.10 E
Nemeiben Lake ⊜	184	55.20 N	105.20 W
Nemenčinė	76	54.51 N	25.29 E
Nementcha, Monts de ⋏	148	34.52 N	7.05 E
Nemeriči	76	53.51 N	33.59 E
Nemi	66	41.43 N	12.43 E
Nemi, Lago di ⊜	267a	41.43 N	12.42 E
Nemira Mare, Vîrful ∧	38	46.15 N	26.19 E
Nemirov, Ukr.	78	50.07 N	23.25 E
Nemirov, Ukr.	78	48.58 N	28.50 E
Nemirovo	82	55.54 N	36.12 E
Nemo	222	32.16 N	97.39 W
Nemoli	68	40.04 N	15.48 E
Nemor ≃	89	48.23 N	124.32 E
Nemours	50	48.16 N	2.42 E
Nemoviči	78	51.16 N	26.38 E
Nemrut Gölü ⊜	130	38.37 N	42.12 E
Nemuna, Bjeshkët e ⋏	38	42.27 N	19.47 E
Nemunas (Neman) ≃	76	55.18 N	21.23 E
Nemuro	92a	43.20 N	145.35 E
Nemuro-hantō ≻[1]	92a	43.21 N	145.42 E
Nemuro Strait Ʉ	92a	44.00 N	145.20 E
Nemzeti Museum ✪	264c	47.29 N	19.05 E
Nen ≃	89	45.25 N	124.40 E
Nena Creek ≃	224	45.07 N	121.07 W
Nenagh	48	52.52 N	8.12 W
Nenagh ≃	48	52.56 N	8.17 W
Nenana	180	64.34 N	149.07 W
Nenana ≃	180	64.30 N	149.00 W
Nenaševo	82	54.34 N	37.28 E
Nenasi	114	3.08 N	103.27 E
Nendaz	58	46.11 N	7.18 E
Nendeln	58	47.12 N	9.32 E
Nendo I	14	10.45 S	165.54 E
Nene ≃	42	52.48 N	0.13 E
Neneckij □[3]	72	67.30 N	54.00 E
Nenetsia → Neneckij □[3]	72	67.30 N	54.00 E
Nenggiri ≃	114	4.53 N	101.48 E
Nengjia	104	41.38 N	120.46 E
Nengo ≃	152	14.27 S	22.09 E
Nenneper ≃	263	51.32 N	6.26 E
Neno	154	15.24 S	34.39 E
Nentón ≃	236	15.48 N	91.52 W
Nenzing	58	47.11 N	9.42 E
Neo	94	35.38 N	136.37 E
Neo ≃	94	35.24 N	136.34 E
Neodesha	198	37.25 N	95.40 W
Neoga	194	39.19 N	88.27 W
Neola, Ia., U.S.	198	41.26 N	95.36 W
Neola, Ut,. U.S.	200	40.26 N	110.01 W
Neoneli	71	40.04 N	8.57 E
Néon Fáliron	267c	37.57 N	23.40 E
Néon Karlovásion	38	37.48 N	26.44 E
Néon Psikhikón	267c	38.00 N	23.47 E
Neopit	190	44.58 N	88.49 W
Neópolis	250	10.18 S	36.35 W
Neoshera	123	33.09 N	74.14 E
Neosho	194	36.52 N	94.22 W
Neosho ≃	194	35.48 N	95.18 W
Neotsu	224	45.00 N	123.58 W
Nepa ≃	88	59.16 N	108.16 E
Nepal (Nepāl) □[1], Asia	118	28.00 N	84.00 E
Nepal (Nepāl) □[1], Asia	124	28.00 N	84.00 E
Nepālgañj	124	28.03 N	81.37 E
Nepa Nagar	120	21.28 N	76.23 E
Nepaug Reservoir ⊜[1]	207	41.48 N	72.57 W
Nepean	212	45.18 N	75.47 W
Nepean ≃	170	33.27 S	150.53 E
Nepean, Point ≻	169	38.18 S	144.39 E
Nepean Bay ⊂	168b	35.42 S	137.44 E
Nepean Island I	174c	29.04 S	167.58 E
Nepean Reservoir ⊜[1]	170	34.22 S	150.35 E
Nepecino	82	55.12 N	38.37 E
Nepeña	248	9.10 S	78.23 W
Nepewassi Lake ⊜	190	46.20 N	80.40 W
Nephi	200	39.42 N	111.50 W
Nephin ∧	48	54.01 N	9.22 W
Nephin Beg Range ⋏	48	54.00 N	9.35 W
Nepi	66	42.14 N	12.21 E
Nepisiguit ≃	186	47.37 N	65.38 W
Nepisiguit Bay ⊂	186	47.46 N	65.32 W
Népliget ♠	264c	47.29 N	19.07 E
Nepoko ≃	154	1.40 N	27.01 E
Nepomuceno	256	21.14 S	45.15 W
Nepomuk	60	49.29 N	13.36 E
Neponset ≃	283	42.17 N	71.02 W
Neponset Reservoir ⊜[1]	283	42.05 N	71.15 W
Neponset River Reservation ♠	283	42.13 N	71.08 W
Neppermin	54	53.56 N	14.02 E
Nepr'adva ≃	76	53.40 N	38.39 E
Nép-sziget I	264c	47.34 N	19.05 E
Neptune, N.J., U.S.	208	40.12 N	74.02 W
Neptune, Oh., U.S.	216	40.36 N	84.30 W
Neptune Beach	192	30.18 N	81.23 W
Neptune City	208	40.12 N	74.02 W
Neqarot, Naḥal V	132	30.40 N	35.15 E
Nera ≃, Europe	38	44.49 N	21.22 E
Nera ≃, It.	66	42.26 N	12.24 E
Nérac	32	44.08 N	0.20 E
Nerákion	267c	38.01 N	23.27 E
Nerang	171a	28.00 S	153.20 E
Nerang ≃	171a	28.03 S	153.17 E
Neratovice	54	50.14 N	14.31 E
Nerča ≃	88	51.56 N	116.40 E
Nerchau	54	51.16 N	12.47 E
Nerčinsk	88	51.58 N	116.35 E
Nerčinskij Zavod	88	51.19 N	119.36 E
Nère ≃	50	47.34 N	2.18 E
Nerechta	80	57.28 N	40.34 E
Nerenstetten	56	48.31 N	10.06 E
Neresheim	56	48.45 N	10.15 E
Nereta	76	56.13 N	25.18 E
Nereto	66	42.49 N	13.49 E
Neretva ≃	36	43.01 N	17.27 E
Nerevoznoje	80	56.53 N	53.54 E
Nerima ◆[8]	268	35.44 N	139.39 E
Neris (Vilija) ≃	76	54.54 N	23.53 E
Nerito	66	42.32 N	13.28 E
Nerja	34	36.44 N	3.52 W
Nerka, Lake ⊜	180	59.30 N	158.45 W
Nerl', Ross.	76	57.03 N	37.59 E
Nerl', Ross.	80	56.40 N	40.24 E
Nerl' ≃, Ross.	76	57.07 N	37.39 E
Nerl' ≃, Ross.	80	56.11 N	40.34 E
Nero, ozero ⊜	80	57.07 N	39.27 E
Neroj	88	54.28 N	97.49 E
Néronde	62	45.50 N	4.14 E
Nérondes	32	47.00 N	2.49 E
Nerópolis	255	16.25 S	49.14 W
Nerriga	170	35.07 S	150.05 E
Nerrima	162	18.24 S	124.29 E
Nerrimunga Creek ≃	170	34.57 S	150.04 E
Nersingen	58	48.25 N	10.07 E
Nerskaja ≃	82	55.23 N	38.35 E
Nerul	272c	19.02 N	73.01 E
Nerus ≃	114	5.20 N	103.05 E
Nerussa ≃	76	52.33 N	33.47 E
Nerva	34	37.42 N	6.32 W
Nervi	62	44.23 N	9.02 E
Nervia ≃	62	43.47 N	7.38 E
Nerviano	266b	45.33 N	8.58 E
Nerville-la-Forêt	261	49.05 N	2.17 E
Nes, Ned.	52	53.04 N	5.51 E
Nes, Ned.	52	53.26 N	5.45 E
Nes, Nor.	26	60.34 N	9.59 E
Nes', Ross.	24	66.37 N	44.36 E
Nes, Har ∧	132	30.22 N	34.37 E
Nesbyen	26	60.34 N	9.09 E
Neščerdo, ozero ⊜	76	55.54 N	29.04 E
Neščeretovo	83	49.24 N	38.48 E
Nesco	208	39.38 N	74.41 W
Nescochague Creek ≃	285	39.39 N	74.41 W
Nescochague Creek, Great Swamp Branch ≃	285	39.41 N	74.43 W
Nesconset	276	40.51 N	73.09 W
Nescopeck	210	41.03 N	76.13 W
Nescopeck Creek ≃	210	41.03 N	76.14 W
Nescopeck Mountain ∧	210	41.03 N	76.05 W
Nesebâr	38	42.39 N	27.44 E
Neshaminy Creek ≃	208	40.04 N	74.55 W
Neshaminy Hills	285	40.10 N	74.57 W
Neshaminy Mall ◆[9]	285	40.08 N	74.57 W
Neshaminy State Park ♠	285	40.05 N	74.55 W
Neshaminy Woods	285	40.10 N	74.57 W
Neshannock Creek ≃	214	40.59 N	80.21 W
Nesher	132	32.46 N	35.03 E
Nesjøen ⊜[1]	26	63.02 N	12.01 E
Neškan	180	67.03 N	173.01 W
Neskaupstaður	24a	65.10 N	13.43 W
Neskowin	224	45.06 N	123.58 W
Neskynpil'gyn, laguna ⊂	180	66.57 N	172.45 W
Nesle	50	49.46 N	2.55 E
Nesna	24	66.12 N	13.02 E
Nespelem	182	48.10 N	118.58 W
Nesque ≃	62	43.59 N	4.59 E
Nesquehoning	210	40.51 N	75.48 W
Ness	262	53.17 N	3.03 W
Ness, Loch ⊜	46	57.15 N	4.30 W
Ness City	198	38.27 N	99.54 W
Nesse ≃	54	50.59 N	10.32 E
Nesselrode, Mount ∧	180	58.58 N	134.18 W
Nesselwang	58	47.37 N	10.30 E
Nesselwängle	58	47.29 N	10.37 E
Nesslau	58	47.13 N	9.13 E
Nessmersiel	52	53.40 N	7.21 E
Nesso	58	45.55 N	9.08 E
Neštěmice	54	50.40 N	14.07 E
Nesterkovo	76	59.10 N	30.33 E
Nesterov, Ross.	76	54.38 N	22.34 E
Nesterov, Ukr.	78	50.04 N	23.58 E
Nesterovka	80	52.26 N	53.42 E
Nesterovo, Ross.	80	54.31 N	41.49 E
Nesterovo, Ross.	82	56.45 N	36.30 E
Nesterovo, Ross.	88	52.22 N	107.53 E
Nestiary	80	56.34 N	45.21 E
Nestoita	78	47.47 N	29.21 E
Neston	44	53.18 N	3.04 W
Nestore ≃	66	43.21 N	12.15 E
Néstos (Mesta) ≃	38	40.41 N	24.44 E
Nesttun	26	60.19 N	5.20 E
Nestucca ≃	224	45.12 N	123.57 W
Nesvetaj	83	47.27 N	39.40 E
Nesviž	76	53.13 N	26.40 E
Nes Ẕiyyona	132	31.55 N	34.48 E
Netanya	132	32.20 N	34.51 E
Netarhāt	124	23.29 N	84.16 E
Netarts	224	45.26 N	123.56 W
Netarts Bay ⊂	224	45.24 N	123.56 W
Netcong	210	40.53 N	74.42 W
Nethan ≃	46	55.42 N	3.52 W
Nether Alderley	262	53.17 N	2.14 W
Netherdale	166	21.08 S	148.32 E
Netherlands (Nederland) □[1], Europe	22	52.15 N	5.30 E
Netherlands (Nederland) □[1], Europe	30	52.15 N	5.30 E
Netherlands Antilles (Nederlandse Antillen) □[2], N.A.	230	12.15 N	68.45 W
Netherlands Antilles (Nederlandse Antillen) □[2], N.A.	241s	12.15 N	68.45 W
Netherton	262	53.30 N	2.58 W
Nethy Bridge	46	57.16 N	3.38 W
Netia	154	14.48 S	39.59 E
Netley Marsh	42	50.53 N	1.32 W
Neto ≃	68	39.13 N	17.08 E
Netolice	61	49.03 N	14.12 E
Netphen	56	50.55 N	8.06 E
Netra	56	51.06 N	10.05 E
Netrakona	124	24.53 N	90.43 E
Netstal	58	47.03 N	9.03 E
Nettancourt	56	48.52 N	4.57 E
Nette	52	52.02 N	10.05 E
Nette ◆[8]	263	51.33 N	7.25 E
Nettelstedt	52	52.18 N	8.41 E
Nettetal	56	51.18 N	6.16 E
Nettilling Fiord ⊂[2]	176	66.02 N	68.12 W
Nettilling Lake ⊜	176	66.30 N	70.40 W
Nett Lake ⊜	190	48.10 N	93.10 W
Nett Lake Indian Reservation ◆[4]	190	48.06 N	93.10 W
Nettlebed	42	51.35 N	1.00 W
Nettle Creek ≃	218	40.03 N	83.48 W
Nettleden	260	51.47 N	0.32 W
Nettleham	44	53.16 N	0.29 W
Nettlestead	260	51.15 N	0.25 E
Nettlestead Green	260	51.14 N	0.25 E
Nettleton	194	34.05 N	88.37 W
Nettuno	66	41.27 N	12.39 E
Nettuno, Grotta di ⏚[5]	71	40.34 N	8.09 E
Netzschkau	54	50.36 N	12.14 E
Neualbenreuth	60	49.59 N	12.27 E
Neu-Anspach	56	50.17 N	8.29 E
Neuastenberg	56	51.10 N	8.29 E
Neubeckum	52	51.48 N	8.01 E
Neubrandenburg	54	53.33 N	13.15 E
Neubraunschweig → New Brunswick □[4]	186	46.30 N	66.15 W
Neubritannien → New Britain I	164	6.00 S	150.00 E
Neu Büddenstedt	54	52.10 N	10.31 E
Neubukow	54	54.02 N	11.40 E
Neuburg am Inn	60	48.30 N	13.27 E
Neuburg an der Donau	60	48.44 N	11.11 E
Neuchâtel	58	46.59 N	6.56 E
Neuchâtel □[3]	58	47.00 N	6.55 E
Neuchâtel, Lac de ⊜	58	46.52 N	6.50 E
Neu-Delhi → New Delhi	124	28.36 N	77.12 E
Neudenau	56	49.17 N	9.16 E
Neudietendorf	54	50.55 N	10.55 E
Neudorf, Sk., Can.	184	50.44 N	102.59 W
Neudorf, Dtsch.	54	50.29 N	12.58 E
Neudorf ◆[8]	263	51.25 N	6.47 E
Neudörfl	61	47.48 N	16.17 E
Neue Hebriden → Vanuatu □[1]	175f	16.00 S	167.00 E
Neuemühle	264a	52.18 N	13.39 E
Neuenburg, Dtsch.	52	53.23 N	7.57 E
Neuenbürg, Dtsch.	56	48.50 N	8.35 E
Neuenburg, Dtsch.	58	47.49 N	7.35 E
Neuenburg → Neuchâtel	58	46.59 N	6.56 E
Neuendettelsau	56	49.17 N	10.47 E
Neuendorf	54	54.31 N	13.05 E
Neuendorfer See ⊜	54	52.07 N	13.55 E
Neuenegg	58	46.54 N	7.18 E
Neuenhagen bei Berlin	54	52.32 N	13.41 E
Neuenhaus	52	52.30 N	6.59 E
Neuenhof ◆[8]	263	51.10 N	7.13 E
Neuenhoven	263	51.08 N	6.31 E
Neue Niers ≃	263	51.16 N	6.26 E
Neuenkamp ◆[8]	263	51.26 N	6.44 E
Neuenkirchen, Dtsch.	52	51.50 N	8.26 E
Neuenkirchen, Dtsch.	52	53.14 N	8.31 E
Neuenkirchen, Dtsch.	52	52.30 N	8.04 E
Neuenkirchen, Dtsch.	52	53.02 N	9.42 E
Neuenkirchen, Dtsch.	52	52.14 N	7.22 E
Neuenkirchen, Dtsch.	52	53.46 N	8.53 E
Neuenkirchen, Dtsch.	54	54.32 N	13.20 E
Neuenrade	56	51.17 N	7.47 E
Neuensalz	54	50.30 N	12.13 E
Neuenstadt am Kocher	56	49.14 N	9.20 E
Neuenwalde	52	53.40 N	8.40 E
Neuerburg	56	50.00 N	6.17 E
Neu-Erlaa ◆[8]	264b	48.08 N	16.19 E
Neues Palais ⊥	264a	52.24 N	13.01 E
Neu Fahrland	264a	52.26 N	13.03 E
Neufahrn bei Freising	60	48.19 N	11.40 E
Neufahrn in Niederbayern	60	48.44 N	12.11 E
Neuf-Brisach	58	48.01 N	7.32 E
Neufchâteau, Bel.	56	49.50 N	5.26 E
Neufchâteau, Fr.	58	48.21 N	5.42 E
Neufchâtel-en-Bray	50	49.44 N	1.27 E
Neufchâtel-sur-Aisne	50	49.26 N	4.02 E
Neufelden	61	48.29 N	14.00 E
Neuffen	56	48.33 N	9.22 E
Neuffossé, Canal de Ξ	50	50.45 N	2.15 E
Neufmanil	56	49.49 N	4.48 E
Neuf-Marché	50	49.25 N	1.43 E
Neufmontiers-lès-Meaux	261	48.58 N	2.50 E
Neufundland → Newfoundland □[4]	176	52.00 N	56.00 W
Neufvilles	50	50.34 N	4.00 E
Neugersdorf	54	50.59 N	14.36 E
Neuglobsow	54	53.09 N	13.02 E
Neugraben-Fischbek ◆[8]	52	53.28 N	9.52 E
Neuguinea → New Guinea I	164	5.00 S	140.00 E
Neuharlingersiel	52	53.42 N	7.42 E
Neu-Hartmannsdorf	264a	52.22 N	13.51 E
Neuhaus, Dtsch.	54	50.30 N	11.08 E
Neuhaus, Dtsch.	54	53.17 N	10.55 E
Neuhaus, Dtsch.	58	47.48 N	8.34 E
Neuhaus, Öst.	61	47.47 N	15.11 E
Neuhaus an der Oste	52	53.48 N	9.02 E
Neuhausen, Dtsch.	54	50.41 N	13.28 E
Neuhausen, Dtsch.	58	47.58 N	8.55 E
Neuhausen, Schw.	58	47.41 N	8.37 E
Neuhaus im Solling	52	51.45 N	9.31 E
Neuhaus-Schierschnitz	54	50.19 N	11.14 E
Neuheum	114	5.34 N	95.32 E
Neuhof	56	50.27 N	9.40 E

Symbol	English	Deutsch	Español	Français	Português
≃	River	Fluß	Río	Rivière	Rio
Ξ	Canal	Kanal	Canal	Canal	Canal
↳	Waterfall, Rapids	Wasserfall, Stromschnellen	Cascada, Rápidos	Chute d'eau, Rapides	Cascata, Rápidos
Ʉ	Strait	Meeresstraße	Estrecho	Détroit	Estreito
⊂	Bay, Gulf	Bucht, Golf	Bahía, Golfo	Baie, Golfe	Baía, Golfo
⊜	Lake, Lakes	See, Seen	Lago, Lagos	Lac, Lacs	Lago, Lagos
☷	Swamp	Sumpf	Pantano	Marais	Pântano
⌂	Ice Features, Glacier	Eis- und Gletscherformen	Accidentes Glaciales	Formes glaciaires	Acidentes glaciares
Ŧ	Other Hydrographic Features	Andere Hydrographische Objekte	Otros Elementos Hidrográficos	Autres données hydrographiques	Outros acidentes hidrográficos

Symbol	English	Deutsch	Español	Français	Português
✦	Submarine Features	Untermeerische Objekte	Accidentes Submarinos	Formes de relief sous-marin	Acidentes submarinos
□	Political Unit	Politische Einheit	Unidad Politica	Entité politique	Unidade política
✪	Cultural Institution	Kulturelle Institution	Institución Cultural	Institution culturelle	Institução cultural
⊥	Historical Site	Historische Stätte	Sitio Histórico	Site historique	Sitio histórico
♠	Recreational Site	Erholungs- und Ferienort	Sitio de Recreo	Centre de loisirs	Area de Lazer
⊠	Airport	Flughafen	Aeropuerto	Aéroport	Aeroporto
■	Military Installation	Militäranlage	Instalación Militar	Installation militaire	Instalação militar
◆	Miscellaneous	Verschiedenes	Misceláneo	Divers	Diversos

ENGLISH / DEUTSCH

Name / Name	Page / Seite	Lat. °′ / Breite °′	Long. °′ / Länge °′ E = Ost
Neuhof an der Zenn	56	49.27 N	10.38 E
Neuhofen	56	49.25 N	8.26 E
Neuhofen an der Krems	61	48.08 N	14.14 E
Neuillé-Pont-Pierre	50	47.33 N	0.33 E
Neuilly-en-Thelle	50	49.13 N	2.17 E
Neuilly-L'Évêque	58	47.55 N	5.26 E
Neuilly-Saint-Front	50	49.10 N	3.16 E
Neuilly-sur-Marne	261	48.51 N	2.32 E
Neuilly-sur-Seine	50	48.53 N	2.16 E
Neuirland → New Ireland I	164	3.20 S	152.00 E
Neu-Isenburg	56	50.03 N	8.41 E
Neukagran ◆[8]	264b	48.14 N	16.27 E
Neu-Kaledonien → New Caledonia □[2]	175f	21.30 S	165.30 E
Neukalen	54	53.49 N	12.47 E
Neu Kaliss	54	53.10 N	11.17 E
Neukieritzsch	54	51.10 N	12.25 E
Neukirch, Dtsch.	54	51.17 N	13.58 E
Neukirch, Dtsch.	54	51.05 N	14.20 E
Neukirch, Dtsch.	58	47.39 N	9.41 E
Neukirchen, Dtsch.	41	54.52 N	8.44 E
Neukirchen, Dtsch.	54	50.46 N	12.52 E
Neukirchen, Dtsch.	54	51.05 N	12.32 E
Neukirchen, Dtsch.	54	50.47 N	12.22 E
Neukirchen, Dtsch.	54	54.19 N	11.01 E
Neukirchen, Dtsch.	56	50.46 N	9.41 E
Neukirchen, Dtsch.	56	49.29 N	6.50 E
Neukirchen, Dtsch.	60	49.05 N	11.45 E
Neukirchen, Dtsch.	263	51.07 N	6.41 E
Neukirchen, Öst.	64	47.15 N	12.17 E
Neukirchen am Walde	60	48.24 N	13.46 E
Neukirchen bei Sulzbach-Rosenberg	60	49.32 N	11.38 E
Neukirchen-Vluyn	56	51.27 N	6.33 E
Neukloster	54	53.52 N	11.41 E
Neukölln ◆[8]	264a	52.29 N	13.27 E
Neu Kosenow	54	53.47 N	13.46 E
Neulangerwisch	264a	52.19 N	13.04 E
Neulengbach	61	48.12 N	15.55 E
Neulienken	54	53.27 N	14.22 E
Neu Lübbenau	54	52.04 N	13.53 E
Neulussheim	56	49.17 N	8.31 E
Neumagen	56	49.51 N	6.53 E
Neuman Creek ≃	284a	42.42 N	78.48 W
Neumark	54	50.39 N	12.21 E
Neumarkt am Wallersee	64	47.57 N	13.14 E
Neumarkt im Hausruckkreis	60	48.16 N	13.45 E
Neumarkt in der Oberpfalz	60	49.16 N	11.28 E
Neumarkt in Steiermark	61	47.04 N	14.25 E
Neumarkt-Sankt Veit	60	48.22 N	12.30 E
Neumarkt → Tîrgu Mureș	38	46.33 N	24.33 E
Neumarkt → Tîrgu-Secuiesc	38	46.00 N	26.08 E
Neumünster	30	54.04 N	9.59 E
Neun ≃	110	19.42 N	104.03 E
Neunburg vorm Wald	60	49.21 N	12.24 E
Neundorf	54	51.49 N	11.34 E
Neung-sur-Beuvron	50	47.32 N	1.48 E
Neunkirchen, Dtsch.	56	50.32 N	8.06 E
Neunkirchen, Dtsch.	56	49.20 N	7.10 E
Neunkirchen, Dtsch.	56	50.48 N	8.00 E
Neunkirchen, Öst.	61	47.43 N	16.05 E
Neunkirchen am Brand	60	49.37 N	11.08 E
Neunkirchen am Potzberg	56	49.30 N	7.29 E
Neunkirchen-Seelscheid	56	50.51 N	7.20 E
Neuötting	60	48.14 N	12.42 E
Neupetershain	54	51.36 N	14.09 E
Neuquén	252	38.57 S	68.04 W
Neuquén □[4]	254	39.00 S	70.00 W
Neuquén ≃	252	38.59 S	68.00 W
Neurara	252	24.10 S	68.29 W
Neuravensburg	58	47.38 N	9.46 E
Neureisenberg	264b	48.01 N	16.30 E
Neurode → Nowa Ruda	30	50.35 N	16.31 E
Neuruppin	54	52.55 N	12.48 E
Neusalza-Spremberg	54	51.02 N	14.32 E
Neusalz → Nowa Sól	30	51.48 N	15.44 E
Neu Sankt Johann	58	47.14 N	9.12 E
Neusatz → Novi Sad	38	45.15 N	19.50 E
Neuschottland → Nova Scotia □[4]	186	45.00 N	63.00 W
Neuschwanstein, Schloss ʊ	64	47.35 N	10.44 E
Neuse ≃	192	35.06 N	76.30 W
Neuseddin	264a	52.18 N	12.59 E
Neuseeland → New Zealand □[1]	172	41.00 S	174.00 E
Neusibirische Inseln → Novosibirskije ostrova II	74	75.00 N	142.00 E
Neusiedl am See	61	47.57 N	16.51 E
Neusiedler See (Fertő) ⊜	61	47.50 N	16.45 E
Neusohl → Banská Bystrica	30	48.44 N	19.07 E
Neusorg	60	49.56 N	11.58 E
Neuss	56	51.12 N	6.41 E
Neusserweyhe	263	51.13 N	6.39 E
Neustadt, On., Can.	212	44.05 N	81.00 W
Neustadt, Dtsch.	54	52.52 N	12.25 E
Neustadt, Dtsch.	54	51.01 N	14.13 E
Neustadt, Dtsch.	54	50.44 N	11.44 E
Neustadt, Dtsch.	56	50.51 N	9.07 E
Neustadt, Dtsch.	56	50.37 N	7.26 E
Neustadt ◆[8]	52	53.04 N	8.47 E
Neustadt am Rübenberge	52	52.30 N	9.28 E
Neustadt an der Aisch	56	49.34 N	10.37 E
Neustadt an der Donau	60	48.48 N	11.46 E
Neustadt an der Waldnaab	60	49.44 N	12.11 E
Neustadt an der Weinstrasse	56	49.21 N	8.08 E
Neustadt bei Coburg	56	50.19 N	11.07 E
Neustädter Bucht c	54	54.02 N	10.50 E
Neustadt-Glewe	54	53.25 N	11.36 E
Neustadt in Holstein	54	54.06 N	10.48 E
Neustettin → Szczecinek	30	53.43 N	16.42 E
Neustift am Walde ◆[8]	264b	48.15 N	16.18 E
Neustift im Stubaital	64	47.07 N	11.19 E
Neustrelitz	54	53.21 N	13.04 E
Neu Töplitz	264a	52.27 N	12.54 E
Neutral Hills ⋀[2]	184	52.10 N	110.50 W
Neutraubling	60	48.59 N	12.12 E
Neutrebbin	54	52.40 N	14.13 E
Neu-Ulm	58	48.23 N	10.01 E
Neuve-Chapelle	50	50.35 N	2.47 E
Neuves-Maisons	58	48.37 N	6.06 E
Neuvic	32	45.23 N	2.16 E
Neuville-aux-Bois	50	48.04 N	2.03 E
Neuville-de-Poitou	32	46.41 N	0.15 E
Neuville-en-Condroz	56	50.32 N	5.27 E
Neuville-lès-Dieppe	50	49.55 N	1.06 E
Neuville-sur-Oise	261	49.01 N	2.04 E
Neuville-sur-Saône	62	45.52 N	4.51 E
Neuvy-le-Roi	50	47.36 N	0.36 E
Neuvy-sur-Barangeon	50	47.19 N	2.15 E
Neuvy-sur-Loire	50	47.31 N	2.53 E
Neuwaldegg ◆[8]	264b	48.14 N	16.17 E
Neuwerk ◆[8]	263	51.13 N	6.28 E
Neuwerk I	52	53.55 N	8.30 E
Neuwied	56	50.25 N	7.27 E
Neuwiller-lès-Saverne	56	48.49 N	7.24 E
Neu Wulmstorf	52	53.28 N	9.48 E
Neuzelle	54	52.05 N	14.38 E
Neu Zittau	54	52.23 N	13.44 E
Neva ≃	265a	59.57 N	30.20 E
Névache	62	45.01 N	6.37 E
Nevada, Ia., U.S.	190	42.01 N	93.27 W
Nevada, Mo., U.S.	194	37.50 N	94.21 W
Nevada, Oh., U.S.	214	40.49 N	83.07 W
Nevada, Tx., U.S.	222	33.02 N	96.22 W
Nevada □[6]	226	39.16 N	121.01 W
Nevada □[3], U.S.	178	39.00 N	117.00 W
Nevada □[3], U.S.	204	39.00 N	117.00 W
Nevada, Sierra ⋀, Esp.	34	37.05 N	3.10 W
Nevada, Sierra ⋀, Ca., U.S.	204	38.00 N	119.15 W
Nevada City	226	39.15 N	121.00 W
Nevada Creek ≃	202	46.54 N	113.02 W
Nevado, Cerro ∧, Arg.	252	35.35 S	68.30 W
Nevado, Cerro ∧, Col.	246	3.59 N	74.04 W
Nevado de Colima, Parque Nacional del ♦	234	19.30 N	103.35 W
Nevado de Toluca, Parque Nacional ♦	234	19.10 N	99.44 W
Neval'cevo	86	58.38 N	81.53 E
Nevali	272c	19.01 N	73.07 E
Nevanka	88	56.30 N	98.54 E
Neve, Serra da ⋀	152	13.52 S	13.26 E
Nevel'	76	56.02 N	29.55 E
Nevel'sk	89	46.40 N	141.53 E
Nevel'skogo, proliv ꓴ	89	52.05 N	141.35 E
Nevendon	260	51.36 N	0.30 E
Never	89	53.58 N	124.05 E
Neverkino	80	52.47 N	46.44 E
Neverovo	80	55.07 N	44.24 E
Nevers	32	47.00 N	3.09 E
Neversink ≃	210	41.21 N	74.42 W
Neversink Reservoir ⊜[1]	210	41.48 N	74.42 W
Nevertire	166	31.52 S	147.39 E
Neves	256	22.51 S	43.06 W
Nevesinje	38	43.15 N	18.07 E
Nevėžis ≃	76	54.56 N	23.46 E
Nevežkino	80	53.07 N	43.19 E
Neviano	68	40.06 N	18.06 E
Neviano degli Arduini	64	44.35 N	10.19 E
Neviges	56	51.19 N	7.05 E
Neville Island	279b	40.31 N	80.08 W
Neville Island I	279b	40.31 N	80.08 W
Nevinnomyssk	84	44.38 N	41.56 E
Nevis I	238	17.10 N	62.34 W
Nevis ≃	46	56.50 N	5.00 W
Nevis, Ben ∧	46	56.48 N	5.01 W
Nevis, Loch c	46	57.01 N	5.43 W
Nevjansk	86	57.32 N	60.13 E
Nevlunghamn	26	58.58 N	9.52 E
Nevon	88	58.07 N	102.49 E
Nevşehir	130	38.38 N	34.43 E
Nevşehir □[4]	130	38.50 N	34.40 E
Nevskoje	76	58.08 N	30.26 E
New ≃, Belize	232	18.22 N	88.24 W
New ≃, Guy.	246	3.23 N	57.36 W
New ≃, N.A.	204	33.08 N	115.44 W
New ≃, Eng., U.K.	260	51.40 N	0.01 W
New ≃, U.S.	192	38.10 N	81.12 W
New ≃, Az., U.S.	200	33.31 N	112.18 W
New ≃, Fl., U.S.	192	29.50 N	84.40 W
New ≃, Fl., U.S.	192	29.55 N	82.25 W
New ≃, N.C., U.S.	192	34.32 N	77.20 W
New ≃, S.C., U.S.	192	32.09 N	80.50 W
New ≃, Tn., U.S.	192	36.25 N	84.38 W
New, North Fork ≃	192	36.33 N	81.21 W
Newabāgam	272b	22.48 N	88.24 E
New Abbey	44	54.59 N	3.38 W
New Addington ◆[8]	260	51.21 N	0.01 W
Newala	154	10.56 S	39.18 E
New Albany, In., U.S.	218	38.17 N	85.49 W
New Albany, Ms., U.S.	194	34.29 N	89.00 W
New Albany, Oh., U.S.	214	40.05 N	82.49 W
New Albany, Pa., U.S.	210	41.36 N	76.27 W
New Albin	190	43.29 N	91.17 W
New Alexandria, Oh., U.S.	214	40.17 N	80.40 W
New Alexandria, Pa., U.S.	214	40.24 N	79.25 W
New Alexandria, Va., U.S.	284c	38.47 N	77.03 W
New Alfa	140	15.10 N	35.40 E
New Almaden	226	37.11 N	121.49 W
New Alresford	42	51.06 N	1.10 W
New Amsterdam	246	6.15 N	57.31 W
New Angledool	166	29.07 S	147.57 E
Newark, Ar., U.S.	194	35.42 N	91.26 W
Newark, Ca., U.S.	226	37.31 N	122.02 W
Newark, De., U.S.	208	39.41 N	75.45 W
Newark, Il., U.S.	216	41.32 N	88.35 W
Newark, Md., U.S.	208	38.15 N	75.17 W
Newark, Mo., U.S.	219	39.59 N	91.59 W
Newark, N.J., U.S.	210	40.44 N	74.10 W
Newark, N.Y., U.S.	210	43.02 N	77.05 W
Newark, Oh., U.S.	214	40.04 N	82.24 W
Newark, Tx., U.S.	222	33.00 N	97.29 W
Newark Bay c, U.S.	276	40.39 N	74.09 W
Newark Bay c, N.J., U.S.	276	40.40 N	74.08 W
Newark Bay Bridge ◆[5]	276	40.42 N	74.07 W
Newark International Airport ⊠	210	40.42 N	74.10 W
Newark Lake ⊜	204	39.41 N	115.44 W
Newark-on-Trent	44	53.05 N	0.49 W
Newark Slough ≃	282	37.31 N	122.05 W
Newark Valley	210	42.13 N	76.11 W
New Athens, Il., U.S.	219	38.19 N	89.52 W
New Athens, Oh., U.S.	214	40.11 N	80.59 W
New Augusta	194	31.12 N	89.02 W
Newaukum, North Fork ≃	224	46.36 N	122.51 W
Newaukum, South Fork ≃	224	46.36 N	122.51 W
Newaygo	190	43.25 N	85.48 W
New Baden, Il., U.S.	219	38.32 N	89.42 W
New Baden, Tx., U.S.	222	31.03 N	96.26 W
New Baltimore, Mi., U.S.	214	42.40 N	82.44 W
New Baltimore, N.Y., U.S.	210	42.26 N	73.47 W
New Bavaria	216	41.12 N	84.10 W
New Bedford, Ma., U.S.	207	41.38 N	70.56 W
New Bedford, Pa., U.S.	214	41.06 N	80.30 W
New Bedford ≃	42	52.35 N	0.20 E
Newberg	224	45.18 N	122.58 W
New Berlin, Il., U.S.	219	39.43 N	89.54 W
New Berlin, N.Y., U.S.	210	42.37 N	75.19 W
New Berlin, Pa., U.S.	210	40.53 N	76.59 W
New Berlin, Wi., U.S.	216	42.58 N	88.06 W
New Berlinville	208	40.20 N	75.38 W
Newbern, Al., U.S.	194	32.35 N	87.31 W
Newbern, Il., U.S.	219	39.01 N	90.20 W
New Bern, N.C., U.S.	192	35.06 N	77.02 W
Newbern, Tn., U.S.	194	36.06 N	89.15 W
Newberry, Fl., U.S.	192	29.38 N	82.36 W
Newberry, Mi., U.S.	190	46.21 N	85.30 W
Newberry, S.C., U.S.	192	34.16 N	81.37 W
Newbery, Aeroparque ⊠, Arg.	258	34.35 S	58.24 W
Newbery, Aeroparque ⊠, Arg.	288	34.35 S	58.24 W
New Bethlehem	214	41.00 N	79.19 W
Newbiggin-by-the-Sea	44	55.11 N	1.30 W
New Bight	238	24.19 N	75.24 W
New Bloomfield, Mo., U.S.	219	38.43 N	92.05 W
New Bloomfield, Pa., U.S.	208	40.25 N	77.11 W
New Bloomington	214	40.35 N	83.19 W
Newbold Island I	285	40.08 N	74.45 W
Newboro	212	44.39 N	76.19 W
Newboro Lake ⊜	212	44.38 N	76.20 W
Newborough, Austl.	169	38.11 S	146.17 E
Newborough, Wales, U.K.	44	53.09 N	4.22 W
New Boston, Il., U.S.	190	41.10 N	90.59 W
New Boston, Mi., U.S.	216	42.09 N	83.24 W
New Boston, Oh., U.S.	218	38.45 N	82.56 W
New Boston, Tx., U.S.	194	33.27 N	94.24 W
New Braintree	207	42.19 N	72.07 W
New Braunfels	196	29.42 N	98.07 W
New Bremen	216	40.26 N	84.22 W
Newbridge → Droichead Nua	48	53.11 N	6.48 W
Newbridge on Wye	42	52.13 N	3.27 W
New Brighton, N.Z.	172	43.31 S	172.44 E
New Brighton, Eng., U.K.	262	53.26 N	3.03 W
New Brighton, Pa., U.S.	214	40.43 N	80.18 W
New Brighton ◆[8]	276	40.38 N	74.06 W
New Britain, Ct., U.S.	207	41.39 N	72.46 W
New Britain, Pa., U.S.	208	40.18 N	75.11 W
New Britain I	164	6.00 S	150.00 E
New Britain Trench ✦[1]	14	6.00 S	153.00 E
New Brockton	194	31.23 N	85.55 W
Newbrook	182	54.19 N	112.57 W
New Brooklyn County Park ♦	285	39.43 N	74.57 W
New Brunswick, In., U.S.	218	39.57 N	86.31 W
New Brunswick, N.J., U.S.	208	40.29 N	74.27 W
New Brunswick □[4], Can.	176	46.30 N	66.15 W
New Brunswick □[4], Can.	186	46.30 N	66.15 W
New Buffalo, Mi., U.S.	216	41.47 N	86.44 W
New Buffalo, Pa., U.S.	208	40.27 N	76.58 W
New Buildings	48	54.57 N	7.21 W
New Bullards Bar Lake ⊜[1]	226	39.25 N	121.08 W
Newburg, Mo., U.S.	194	37.54 N	91.54 W
Newburg, Pa., U.S.	208	40.08 N	77.32 W
Newburg, Pa., U.S.	214	40.31 N	78.25 W
Newburgh, On., Can.	212	44.19 N	76.52 W
Newburgh, Eng., U.K.	262	53.35 N	2.47 W
Newburgh, Scot., U.K.	46	56.20 N	3.15 W
Newburgh, Scot., U.K.	46	57.18 N	2.00 W
Newburgh, In., U.S.	194	37.56 N	87.24 W
Newburgh, N.Y., U.S.	210	41.30 N	74.00 W
Newburgh Heights	279a	41.27 N	81.39 W
Newburn	44	54.59 N	1.43 W
Newbury, On., Can.	214	42.41 N	81.48 W
Newbury, Eng., U.K.	42	51.25 N	1.20 W
Newbury, Ma., U.S.	207	42.49 N	70.53 W
Newbury Old Town	207	42.46 N	70.51 W
Newbury Park	228	34.11 N	118.53 W
Newburyport	207	42.48 N	70.52 W
Newby	44	54.20 N	0.28 W
Newby Bridge	44	54.16 N	2.58 W
New Caledonia (Nouvelle-Calédonie) □[2], Oc.	14	21.30 S	165.30 E
New Caledonia (Nouvelle-Calédonie) □[2], Oc.	175f	21.30 S	165.30 E
New Caledonia Basin ✦[1]	14	30.00 S	165.00 E
New Canaan	207	41.08 N	73.29 W
New Canada ◆[8]	273d	26.13 S	27.57 E
New Caney	222	30.09 N	95.13 W
New Canton	219	39.38 N	91.06 W
New-Carlisle, P.Q., Can.	186	48.01 N	65.20 W
New Carlisle, In., U.S.	216	41.42 N	86.30 W
New Carlisle, Oh., U.S.	218	39.56 N	84.01 W
New Carrollton	284c	38.58 N	76.52 W
New Cassel	276	40.45 N	73.34 W
Newcastle, Austl.	170	32.56 S	151.46 E
Newcastle, N.B., Can.	186	47.00 N	65.34 W
Newcastle, On., Can.	212	43.55 N	78.35 W
Newcastle, Ire.	48	52.16 N	7.48 W
Newcastle, S. Afr.	158	27.49 S	29.55 E
Newcastle, Eng., U.K.	42	52.26 N	3.06 W
Newcastle, N. Ire., U.K.	48	54.12 N	5.54 W
Newcastle, Ca., U.S.	226	38.53 N	121.08 W
New Castle, Co., U.S.	200	39.34 N	107.32 W
New Castle, De., U.S.	208	39.39 N	75.34 W
New Castle, In., U.S.	218	39.55 N	85.22 W
New Castle, Ky., U.S.	218	38.26 N	85.10 W
Newcastle, Ne., U.S.	198	42.33 N	96.42 W
Newcastle, Oh., U.S.	214	40.20 N	82.10 W
Newcastle, Ok., U.S.	196	35.15 N	97.36 W
New Castle, Pa., U.S.	214	41.00 N	80.20 W
Newcastle, Tx., U.S.	196	33.11 N	98.44 W
New Castle, Va., U.S.	192	37.30 N	80.06 W
Newcastle, Wy., U.S.	198	43.51 N	104.12 W
New Castle □[6]	208	39.44 N	75.33 W
Newcastle Airport ⊠	44	55.03 N	1.43 W
Newcastle Bay c	164	10.50 S	142.37 E
Newcastle Bight c[3]	170	32.51 S	151.54 E
Newcastle Creek ≃	164	17.20 S	133.23 E
Newcastle Emlyn	42	52.02 N	4.28 W
Newcastle Mine	182	51.28 N	112.46 W
Newcastleton	44	55.11 N	2.49 W
Newcastle-under-Lyme	44	53.00 N	2.14 W
Newcastle upon Tyne	44	54.59 N	1.35 W
Newcastle Waters	162	17.24 S	133.24 E
Newcastle West	48	52.27 N	9.03 W
Newcestown	48	51.47 N	8.51 W
New Chicago	216	41.34 N	87.16 W
Newchurch, Wales, U.K.	42	52.09 N	3.08 W
New Church, Va., U.S.	208	37.59 N	75.32 W
New City	210	41.08 N	73.59 W
Newclare ◆[8]	273d	26.11 S	27.58 E
New Columbia	210	41.02 N	76.52 W
New Columbus	210	41.10 N	76.18 W
Newcomerstown	214	40.16 N	81.36 W
New Concord	188	39.59 N	81.44 W
New Corydon	216	40.34 N	84.51 W
New Croton Aqueduct ≋[1]	276	41.11 N	73.49 W
New Croton Reservoir ⊜[1]	210	41.14 N	73.46 W
New Cumberland, Pa., U.S.	208	40.13 N	76.53 W
New Cumberland, W.V., U.S.	214	40.29 N	80.36 W
New Cumberland Dam ◆[6]	214	40.32 N	80.37 W
New Cumnock	44	55.24 N	4.12 W
New Dayton	182	49.25 N	112.23 W
New Deer	46	57.30 N	2.12 W
Newdegate	162	33.06 S	119.01 E
New Delhi, India	124	28.36 N	77.12 E
New Delhi, India	272a	28.36 N	77.12 E
New Delhi Railroad Station ◆[5]	272a	28.39 N	77.13 E
New Denver	182	49.59 N	117.22 W
New Derry	214	40.21 N	79.19 W
New Dundee	212	43.21 N	80.31 W
New Eagle	214	40.12 N	79.56 W
New Edinburg	194	33.45 N	92.14 W
New Effington	198	45.51 N	96.55 W
New Egypt	208	40.04 N	74.31 W
Newell, Ia., U.S.	198	42.36 N	95.00 W
Newell, S.D., U.S.	198	44.42 N	103.25 W
Newell, W.V., U.S.	214	40.37 N	80.36 W
Newell, Lake ⊜, Austl.	162	24.50 S	126.10 E
Newell, Lake ⊜, Ab., Can.	182	50.25 N	111.56 W
New Ellenton	192	33.25 N	81.41 W
Newellton	194	32.04 N	91.14 W
New Eltham ◆[8]	260	51.26 N	0.04 E
New England	198	46.32 N	102.52 W
New England National Park ♦	166	30.30 S	152.15 E
New England Range ⋀	166	30.00 S	151.50 E
Newenham, Cape ›	180	58.37 N	162.12 W
Newent	42	51.56 N	2.24 W
New Enterprise	214	40.10 N	78.25 W
New Ermelo	158	26.32 S	30.02 E
New Falconwood	284a	42.59 N	78.58 W
Newfane, N.Y., U.S.	210	43.17 N	78.42 W
Newfane, Vt., U.S.	188	42.59 N	72.39 W
New Ferry	262	53.22 N	2.59 W
Newfield, N.J., U.S.	208	39.32 N	75.01 W
Newfield, N.Y., U.S.	210	42.22 N	76.35 W
Newfield Pond ⊜	283	42.38 N	71.22 W
New Florence, Mo., U.S.	219	38.54 N	91.26 W
New Florence, Pa., U.S.	214	40.22 N	79.04 W
New Forest ◆[3]	42	50.53 N	1.35 W
New Fork ≃	200	42.33 N	109.58 W
Newfound Gap)(	192	35.37 N	83.25 W
Newfoundland, N.J., U.S.	276	40.44 N	74.29 W
Newfoundland, Pa., U.S.	210	41.19 N	75.19 W
Newfoundland □[4]	176	52.00 N	56.00 W
Newfoundland I	186	48.30 N	56.00 W
Newfoundland Basin ✦[1]	8	45.00 N	40.00 W
Newfoundland Ridge ✦[3]	8	40.30 N	48.00 W
New Franklin	194	39.01 N	92.44 W
New Freedom	208	39.44 N	76.42 W
New Galilee	214	40.50 N	80.24 W
New Galloway	44	55.05 N	4.10 W
New Garden	285	39.49 N	75.45 W
Newgate	182	49.00 N	115.10 W
Newgate Street	260	51.44 N	0.07 W
New Georgia I	175e	8.15 S	157.30 E
New Georgia Group II	175e	8.30 S	157.20 E
New Georgia Sound ꓴ	175e	8.00 S	158.10 E
New Germantown	208	40.18 N	77.34 W
New Germany	186	44.33 N	64.43 W
New Glarus	190	42.48 N	89.38 W
New Glasgow	186	45.35 N	62.39 W
New Gretna	208	39.35 N	74.27 W
New Guinea I	164	5.00 S	140.00 E
Newgulf	222	29.16 N	95.54 W
Newhalem	224	48.40 N	121.14 W
Newhalen	180	59.43 N	154.54 W
Newhall, Eng., U.K.	42	52.48 N	1.34 W
Newhall, Ca., U.S.	228	34.23 N	118.31 W
Newham ◆[8]	42	51.32 N	0.03 E
New Hamburg, On., Can.	212	43.23 N	80.42 W
New Hamburg, N.Y., U.S.	210	41.35 N	73.57 W
New Hampshire	216	40.33 N	83.57 W
New Hampshire □[3], U.S.	178	43.35 N	71.40 W
New Hampshire □[3], U.S.	188	43.35 N	71.40 W
New Hampton, Ia., U.S.	190	43.03 N	92.19 W
New Hampton, N.Y., U.S.	210	41.25 N	74.24 W
New Hanover, S. Afr.	158	29.28 S	30.28 E
New Hanover, Il., U.S.	219	38.23 N	90.13 W
New Hanover I	164	2.30 S	150.15 E
New Harmony	194	38.07 N	87.56 W
New Hartford, Ct., U.S.	207	41.52 N	72.58 W
New Hartford, Ia., U.S.	190	42.34 N	92.37 W
New Hartford, Mo., U.S.	219	39.12 N	91.16 W
New Hartford, N.Y., U.S.	210	43.04 N	75.18 W
Newhaven, Eng., U.K.	42	50.47 N	0.03 E
New Haven, Ct., U.S.	207	41.18 N	72.56 W
New Haven, Il., U.S.	194	37.54 N	88.07 W
New Haven, In., U.S.	216	41.04 N	85.00 W
New Haven, Ky., U.S.	194	37.39 N	85.35 W
New Haven, Mi., U.S.	214	42.43 N	82.48 W
New Haven, Mo., U.S.	219	38.36 N	91.13 W
New Haven, N.Y., U.S.	212	43.29 N	76.19 W
New Haven, Oh., U.S.	214	41.02 N	82.41 W
New Haven, W.V., U.S.	188	38.59 N	81.58 W
New Haven □[6]	207	41.18 N	72.56 W
New Hazelton	182	55.15 N	127.35 W
New Hebrides II	175f	16.00 S	167.00 E
New Hebrides Trench ✦[1]	14	22.30 S	170.00 E
New Hebrides → Vanuatu □[1]	175f	16.00 S	167.00 E
Newhebron	194	31.44 N	89.58 W
New Hempstead	276	41.08 N	74.03 W
New Hey	262	53.36 N	2.06 W
New Hogan Lake ⊜[1]	226	38.09 N	120.48 W
New Holland, Eng., U.K.	44	53.42 N	0.22 W
New Holland, Il., U.S.	219	40.11 N	89.36 W
New Holland, Oh., U.S.	218	39.33 N	83.15 W
New Holland, Pa., U.S.	208	40.06 N	76.05 W
New Holstein	190	43.57 N	88.05 W
New Hope, Al., U.S.	194	34.32 N	86.23 W
New Hope, Pa., U.S.	208	40.21 N	74.57 W
New Hudson	281	42.30 N	83.36 W
New Hyde Park	276	40.44 N	73.41 W
New Hythe	260	51.19 N	0.27 E
New Iberia	194	30.00 N	91.49 W
Newick	42	50.58 N	0.01 E
Newington, On., Can.	206	45.07 N	75.01 W
Newington, Eng., U.K.	42	51.05 N	1.08 E
Newington, Eng., U.K.	260	51.21 N	0.40 E
Newington, Ct., U.S.	207	41.42 N	72.43 W
Newinn	48	52.26 N	7.53 W
New Ipswich	207	42.44 N	71.51 W
New Ireland □[5]	164	3.00 S	151.30 E
New Ireland I	164	3.20 S	152.00 E
New Island I	126	21.31 N	88.12 E
New Jersey □[3], U.S.	178	40.15 N	74.30 W
New Jersey □[3], U.S.	188	40.15 N	74.30 W
New Jersey Institute of Technology ʊ[2]	276	40.45 N	74.11 W
New Johnsonville	194	36.01 N	87.58 W
New Kensington	214	40.34 N	79.45 W
New Kent	208	37.31 N	76.58 W
New Kent □[6]	208	37.30 N	77.00 W
New Kingstown	208	40.13 N	77.07 W
Newkirk	196	36.52 N	97.03 W
Newkirk Estates	285	39.42 N	75.36 W
New Knoxville	216	40.29 N	84.18 W
New Kowloon (Xinjiulong)	271d	22.20 N	114.10 E
New Lagos ◆[8]	273a	6.30 N	3.22 E
New Lake ⊜	192	35.38 N	76.20 W
Newland	192	36.05 N	81.55 W
Newland Head ›	168b	35.39 S	138.31 E
Newland Range ⋀	162	27.53 S	123.58 E
Newlands	166	21.11 S	147.54 E
Newlands ◆[8]	273d	26.11 S	27.58 E
New Lane	262	53.37 N	2.52 W
New Lebanon, N.Y., U.S.	210	42.27 N	73.23 W
New Lebanon, Oh., U.S.	218	39.45 N	84.23 W
New Lebanon, Pa., U.S.	214	41.25 N	80.04 W
New Lebanon Center	210	42.28 N	73.25 W
New Leipzig	198	46.22 N	101.56 W
New Lenox	216	41.30 N	87.57 W
New Lexington	188	39.42 N	82.12 W
New Liberty	218	38.36 N	84.54 W
New Lisbon	190	43.52 N	90.09 W
New Liskeard	190	47.30 N	79.40 W
Newllano	194	31.06 N	93.16 W
New London, Ct., U.S.	207	41.21 N	72.07 W
New London, Ia., U.S.	190	40.55 N	91.23 W
New London, Mn., U.S.	198	45.18 N	94.56 W
New London, Mo., U.S.	219	39.35 N	91.24 W
New London, N.H., U.S.	188	43.24 N	71.59 W
New London, Oh., U.S.	214	41.05 N	82.24 W
New London, Pa., U.S.	208	39.47 N	75.52 W
New London, Tx., U.S.	222	32.15 N	94.56 W
New London, Wi., U.S.	190	44.23 N	88.44 W
New London □[6]	207	41.21 N	72.07 W
New London Submarine Base ■	207	41.24 N	72.05 W
New Longton	262	53.44 N	2.45 W
Newlonsburg	279b	40.25 N	79.40 W
New Lyme	214	41.36 N	80.47 W
Newlyn, Austl.	169	37.25 S	143.59 E
Newlyn, Eng., U.K.	42	50.06 N	5.33 W
Newlyn East	42	50.22 N	5.03 W
Newmachar	46	57.16 N	2.11 W
New Machavie	158	26.48 S	26.57 E
New Madison	218	39.58 N	84.42 W
New Madrid	194	36.35 N	89.31 W
Newmains	44	55.47 N	3.53 W
Newman, Austl.	162	23.20 S	119.46 E
Newman, Ca., U.S.	226	37.18 N	121.01 W
Newman, Il., U.S.	194	39.47 N	87.59 W
Newman, Mount ∧	162	23.16 S	119.33 E
New Manchester	214	40.31 N	80.34 W
Newman Grove	198	41.45 N	97.46 W
Newmanstown	208	40.20 N	76.12 W
Newmansville	219	40.00 N	90.01 W
New Marion	218	39.00 N	85.22 W
Newmarket, Austl.	171a	27.25 S	153.01 E
Newmarket, On., Can.	212	44.03 N	79.28 W
Newmarket, Ire.	48	52.13 N	9.00 W
Newmarket, S. Afr.	273d	26.17 S	28.08 E
Newmarket, Eng., U.K.	42	52.15 N	0.25 E
New Market, Al., U.S.	194	34.54 N	86.25 W
New Market, Ia., U.S.	198	40.43 N	94.53 W
New Market, Md., U.S.	208	39.22 N	77.16 W
Newmarket, N.H., U.S.	188	43.04 N	70.56 W
New Market, N.J., U.S.	276	40.34 N	74.27 W
New Market, Va., U.S.	188	38.39 N	78.40 W
Newmarket on Fergus	48	52.45 N	8.53 W
Newmarket Race Course ♦	273d	26.17 S	28.08 E
New Marske	44	54.34 N	1.02 W
New Martinsville	188	39.38 N	80.51 W
New Meadows	202	44.58 N	116.16 W
New Melle	219	38.42 N	90.52 W
New Melones Lake ⊜[1]	226	38.00 N	120.32 W
New Memphis	219	38.29 N	89.41 W
New Mexico □[3]	178	34.30 N	106.00 W
New Miami	218	39.26 N	84.32 W
New Middletown	214	40.58 N	80.34 W
New Milford, Ct., U.S.	207	41.34 N	73.24 W
New Milford, Il., U.S.	216	42.11 N	89.04 W
New Milford, N.J., U.S.	276	40.56 N	74.01 W
New Milford, Pa., U.S.	210	41.52 N	75.43 W
New Millpond ⊜	276	40.50 N	73.13 W
New Millport	214	40.54 N	78.32 W
New Mills	44	53.23 N	2.00 W
Newmilns	46	55.37 N	4.20 W
New Milton	42	50.44 N	1.40 W
New Minden	219	38.26 N	89.22 W
New Munster	216	42.34 N	88.13 W
Newnan	192	33.22 N	84.47 W
Newnans Lake ⊜	192	29.39 N	82.13 W
Newnham	42	51.49 N	2.27 W
New Norcia	162	30.58 S	116.13 E
New Norfolk	166	42.47 S	147.03 E
New Norway	182	52.53 N	112.58 W
New Orleans	194	29.57 N	90.04 W
New Orleans Naval Air Station ■	194	29.51 N	90.01 W
New Oxford	208	39.51 N	77.03 W
New Palestine	218	39.43 N	85.53 W
New Paltz	210	41.44 N	74.05 W
New Paris, In., U.S.	216	41.30 N	85.49 W
New Paris, Oh., U.S.	218	39.51 N	84.47 W
New Paris, Pa., U.S.	214	40.06 N	78.39 W
New Philadelphia, Oh., U.S.	214	40.30 N	81.27 W
New Philadelphia, Pa., U.S.	208	40.43 N	76.06 W
New Pine Creek	202	41.59 N	120.17 W
New Pitsligo	46	57.35 N	2.11 W
New Pittsburg	214	40.50 N	82.06 W
New Plymouth, N.Z.	172	39.04 S	174.05 E
New Plymouth, Id., U.S.	202	43.58 N	116.49 W
New Point	218	39.18 N	85.19 W
New Point Comfort ›	208	37.18 N	76.17 W
Newport, Austl.	274a	33.40 S	151.19 E
Newport, Austl.	274b	37.51 S	144.53 E
Newport, P.Q., Can.	186	48.16 N	64.45 W
Newport, Ire.	48	52.42 N	8.24 W
Newport, Ire.	48	53.53 N	9.34 W
Newport, Eng., U.K.	42	50.42 N	1.18 W
Newport, Eng., U.K.	42	51.59 N	0.15 E
Newport, Eng., U.K.	42	52.47 N	2.22 W
Newport, Wales, U.K.	42	52.01 N	4.51 W
Newport, Wales, U.K.	42	51.35 N	3.00 W
Newport, Ar., U.S.	194	35.36 N	91.16 W
Newport, De., U.S.	208	39.42 N	75.36 W
Newport, In., U.S.	194	39.53 N	87.24 W
Newport, Ky., U.S.	218	39.05 N	84.29 W
Newport, Me., U.S.	188	44.50 N	69.16 W
Newport, Md., U.S.	208	38.25 N	76.54 W
Newport, Mi., U.S.	216	42.00 N	83.18 W
Newport, N.H., U.S.	188	43.21 N	72.10 W
Newport, N.J., U.S.	208	39.17 N	75.10 W
Newport, N.Y., U.S.	210	43.11 N	75.00 W
Newport, N.C., U.S.	192	34.47 N	76.51 W
Newport, Oh., U.S.	216	39.23 N	81.13 W
Newport, Or., U.S.	202	44.38 N	124.03 W
Newport, Pa., U.S.	208	40.28 N	77.07 W
Newport, R.I., U.S.	207	41.29 N	71.18 W
Newport, Tn., U.S.	192	35.58 N	83.11 W
Newport, Vt., U.S.	206	44.56 N	72.12 W
Newport, Wa., U.S.	202	48.11 N	117.02 W
Newport □[6]	207	41.35 N	71.15 W
Newport Bay c	208	38.14 N	75.13 W
Newport Beach	228	33.37 N	117.55 W
Newport Center	206	44.57 N	72.18 W
Newport Hills	224	47.32 N	122.10 W
Newport News	208	36.58 N	76.25 W
Newport-on-Tay	46	56.26 N	2.55 W
Newport Pagnell	42	52.05 N	0.44 W
New Port Richey	220	28.14 N	82.43 W
Newportville	285	40.09 N	74.53 W
Newportville Terrace	285	40.07 N	74.54 W
New Prague	190	44.32 N	93.34 W
New Preston	207	41.40 N	73.21 W
New Providence, N.J., U.S.	210	40.41 N	74.24 W
New Providence, Pa., U.S.	208	39.56 N	76.12 W
New Providence, Tn., U.S.	194	36.32 N	87.23 W
New Providence I	240b	25.02 N	77.24 W
Newquay, Eng., U.K.	42	50.25 N	5.05 W
New Quay, Wales, U.K.	42	52.13 N	4.22 W
New Redruth	273d	26.16 S	28.07 E
New Richland	190	43.53 N	93.29 W
New-Richmond, P.Q., Can.	186	48.10 N	65.52 W
New Richmond, Oh., U.S.	218	38.56 N	84.16 W
New Richmond, Wi., U.S.	190	45.07 N	92.32 W
New Riegel	214	41.03 N	83.19 W
New Rim Ditch ≋	228	35.08 N	118.58 W
New Ringgold	208	40.41 N	76.00 W
New Road	186	44.45 N	63.28 W
New Roads	194	30.42 N	91.26 W
New Rochelle	210	40.54 N	73.46 W
New Rockford	198	47.40 N	99.08 W
New Romney	42	50.59 N	0.57 E
New Ross, N.S., Can.	186	44.44 N	64.27 W
New Ross, Ire.	48	52.24 N	6.56 W
New Rossington	44	53.29 N	1.04 W
Newry, N. Ire., U.K.	48	54.11 N	6.20 W
Newry, Pa., U.S.	214	40.24 N	78.26 W
Newry, S.C., U.S.	192	34.43 N	82.54 W
New Salem, In., U.S.	218	39.32 N	85.22 W
New Salem, N.D., U.S.	198	46.50 N	101.24 W
New Salisbury	218	38.19 N	86.06 W
New Sarum → Salisbury	42	51.05 N	1.48 W
New Schwabenland ◆[1]	9	72.30 S	1.00 E
New Scone	46	56.25 N	3.24 W
Newsham Park ♦	262	53.25 N	2.56 W
New Sharon	190	41.28 N	92.39 W
New Sheffield	214	40.36 N	80.17 W
New Shrewsbury	276	40.19 N	74.04 W
New Siberian Islands → Novosibirskoje ostrova II	74	75.00 N	142.00 E
New Smyrna Beach	220	29.01 N	80.55 W
Newsome	222	32.59 N	95.08 W
Newsoms	208	36.37 N	77.07 W
New South Wales □[3]	166	33.00 S	146.00 E
New South Wales, University of ʊ[2]	274a	33.55 S	151.14 E
New South Wales Lawn Tennis Association Courts ♦	274a	33.53 S	151.14 E
New Springfield	214	40.55 N	80.36 W
New Square	276	41.08 N	74.02 W
New Stanton	214	40.13 N	79.37 W
Newstead	169	37.07 S	144.04 E
New Stuyahok	180	59.29 N	157.20 W
New Suffolk	207	41.00 N	72.28 W
New Summerfield	222	31.59 N	95.06 W
New Tazewell	192	36.27 N	83.33 W
New Terrell City Lake ⊜[1]	222	32.44 N	96.14 W
New Territories □[8]	271d	22.24 N	114.10 E
New Thunderchild Indian Reserve ◆[4]	184	53.30 N	108.50 W
Newtok	180	60.56 N	164.38 W
Newton, Eng., U.K.	44	53.57 N	2.27 W
Newton, Eng., U.K.	262	53.16 N	2.43 W
Newton, Ga., U.S.	192	31.18 N	84.20 W
Newton, Il., U.S.	194	38.59 N	88.09 W
Newton, Ia., U.S.	190	41.41 N	93.02 W
Newton, Ks., U.S.	198	38.02 N	97.20 W
Newton, Ma., U.S.	207	42.20 N	71.12 W
Newton, Ms., U.S.	194	32.19 N	89.09 W
Newton, N.J., U.S.	210	41.03 N	74.45 W
Newton, N.C., U.S.	192	35.40 N	81.13 W
Newton, Tx., U.S.	194	30.50 N	93.45 W
Newton □[6]	216	40.46 N	87.27 W
Newton Abbot	42	50.32 N	3.36 W
Newton Arlosh	44	54.53 N	3.15 W
Newton Aycliffe	44	54.36 N	1.32 W
Newton Brook ◆[8]	275b	43.48 N	79.24 W
Newton Center	283	42.20 N	71.12 W
Newton Falls, N.Y., U.S.	188	44.12 N	74.59 W
Newton Falls, Oh., U.S.	214	41.11 N	80.58 W
Newton Ferrers	42	50.18 N	4.02 W
Newton Flotman	42	52.32 N	1.16 E
Newton Hamilton	214	40.24 N	77.51 W
Newton Highlands	283	42.19 N	71.13 W
Newton-le-Willows	44	53.28 N	2.37 W
Newton Longville	42	51.58 N	0.46 W
Newton Lower Falls	283	42.19 N	71.23 W
Newtonmore	46	57.04 N	4.08 W
Newton Stewart	44	54.57 N	4.29 W
Newtonsville	218	39.11 N	84.05 W
Newton Upper Falls	283	42.19 N	71.13 W
Newtonville, On., Can.	212	43.56 N	78.30 W
Newtonville, Ma., U.S.	283	42.21 N	71.13 W
Newtonville, N.J., U.S.	208	39.33 N	74.51 W
New Toronto ◆[8]	275b	43.36 N	79.30 W
Newtown, Austl.	169	38.09 S	144.20 E
Newtown, Nf., Can.	186	49.12 N	53.31 W
Newtown, Eng., U.K.	262	53.21 N	2.00 W
Newtown, Wales, U.K.	42	52.32 N	3.19 W
Newtown, Ct., U.S.	207	41.24 N	73.18 W
Newtown, In., U.S.	216	40.12 N	87.08 W
Newtown, Ky., U.S.	218	38.13 N	84.57 W
New Town, N.D., U.S.	198	47.58 N	102.29 W
Newtown, Pa., U.S.	208	40.14 N	74.56 W
Newtown ◆[8]	274a	33.54 S	151.11 E
Newtownabbey	48	54.42 N	5.54 W
Newtownards	48	54.36 N	5.41 W
Newtownbutler	48	54.12 N	7.23 W
Newtown Creek ≃, N.Y., U.S.	276	40.44 N	73.58 W

Symbols in the index entries represent the broad categories identified in the key at the right. Symbols with superior numbers (⋀[1]) identify subcategories (see complete key on page *I · 1)*.

Symbole im Register stellen die rechts im Schlüssel erklärten Kategorien dar. Symbole mit hochgestellten Ziffern (⋀[1]) bezeichnen Unterabteilungen einer Kategorie (vgl. vollständiger Schlüssel auf Seite *I · 1)*.

Los símbolos incluídos en el texto del índice representan las grandes categorias identificadas con la clave a la derecha. Los símbolos con numeros en su parte superior (⋀[1]) identifican las subcategorías (véase la clave completa en la página *I · 1)*.

Les symboles de l'index représentent les catégories indiquées dans la légende à droite. Les symboles suivis d'un indice (⋀[1]) représentent des sous-catégories (voir légende complète à la page *I · 1)*.

Os símbolos incluídos no texto do índice representam as grandes categorias identificadas com a chave à direita. Os símbolos com números em sua parte superior (⋀[1]) identificam as subcategorias (veja-se a chave completa à página *I · 1)*.

	English	Deutsch	Español	Français	Português
∧	Mountain	Berg	Montaña	Montagne	Montanha
⋀	Mountains	Gebirge	Montañas	Montagnes	Montanhas
)(	Pass	Paß	Paso	Col	Passo
V	Valley, Canyon	Tal, Cañon	Valle, Cañón	Vallée, Canyon	Vale, Canhão
≚	Plain	Ebene	Llano	Plaine	Planície
›	Cape	Kap	Cabo	Cap	Cabo
I	Island	Insel	Isla	Île	Ilha
II	Islands	Inseln	Islas	Îles	Ilhas
⏏	Other Topographic Features	Andere Topographische Objekte	Otros Elementos Topográficos	Autres données topographiques	Outros acidentes topográficos

ESPAÑOL Nombre / FRANÇAIS Nom / PORTUGUÊS Nome	Página / Page	Lat.°′	Long.°′ W = Oeste / W = Ouest
Newtown Creek ≃, Pa., U.S.	285	40.13 N	74.56 W
Newtown Crommelin	48	54.59 N	6.13 W
Newtown Forbes	48	53.46 N	7.50 W
Newtownhamilton	48	54.12 N	6.35 W
Newtown Mount Kennedy	48	53.05 N	6.07 W
Newtown Saint Boswells	46	55.34 N	2.40 W
Newtown Square	208	39.59 N	75.24 W
Newtownstewart	48	54.43 N	7.24 W
New Tredegar	42	51.43 N	3.14 W
New Tripoli	208	40.41 N	75.45 W
New Troy	216	41.53 N	86.33 W
New Truxton	219	38.58 N	91.15 W
New Ulm, Mn., U.S.	190	44.18 N	94.27 W
New Ulm, Tx., U.S.	222	29.53 N	96.29 W
New Utrecht ◆[8]	276	40.36 N	73.59 W
New Vernon	276	40.45 N	74.30 W
New Vienna	218	39.19 N	83.41 W
Newville, In., U.S.	216	41.21 N	84.51 W
Newville, Pa., U.S.	208	40.10 N	77.23 W
New Vineyard	188	44.48 N	70.07 W
New Waltham	44	53.32 N	0.04 W
New Washington, Pil.	116	11.39 N	122.26 E
New Washington, In., U.S.	218	38.33 N	85.32 W
New Washington, Oh., U.S.	214	40.57 N	82.51 W
New Waterford, N.S., Can.	186	46.15 N	60.05 W
New Waterford, Oh., U.S.	214	40.50 N	80.36 W
New Waverly, In., U.S.	216	40.46 N	86.12 W
New Waverly, Tx., U.S.	222	30.32 N	95.29 W
New Westminster	224	49.12 N	122.55 W
New Whiteland	218	39.33 N	86.05 W
New Wilmington	214	41.07 N	80.19 W
New Windsor, Md., U.S.	208	39.32 N	77.06 W
New Windsor, N.Y., U.S.	210	41.30 N	74.01 W
New Windsor → Windsor	42	51.29 N	0.38 W
New Woodbine Racetrack ♠	275b	43.43 N	79.36 W
New Woodstock	210	42.50 N	75.51 W
New World Island I	186	49.35 N	54.40 W
New Year Creek ≃	222	30.08 N	96.12 W
New York, N.Y., U.S.	210	40.43 N	74.01 W
New York, N.Y., U.S.	276	40.43 N	74.01 W
New York □[6]	276	40.47 N	73.58 W
New York □[3], U.S.	178	43.00 N	75.00 W
New York □[3], U.S.	188	43.00 N	75.00 W
New York, City College of ⚲[2]	276	40.49 N	73.57 W
New York, Polytechnic Institute of ⚲[2]	276	40.42 N	73.59 W
New York, State University of (Stony Brook) ⚲[2], N.Y., U.S.	276	40.55 N	73.08 W
New York, State University of (Buffalo) ⚲[2], N.Y., U.S.	284a	42.57 N	78.49 W
New York, State University of, College at Buffalo ⚲[2]	284a	42.56 N	78.53 W
New York at Buffalo, State University of ⚲[2]	284a	42.56 N	78.49 W
New York Mills, Mn., U.S.	198	46.31 N	95.22 W
New York Mills, N.Y., U.S.	210	43.06 N	75.18 W
New York State Barge Canal ≊	210	43.05 N	78.43 W
New York Stock Exchange ⚲	276	40.42 N	74.01 W
New Zealand □[1]	172	41.00 S	174.00 E
Nexapa ≃	234	18.07 N	98.46 W
Nexon	32	45.41 N	1.11 E
Ney	216	41.23 N	84.32 W
Neyagawa	96	34.46 N	135.38 E
Neye	263	51.07 N	7.22 E
Neyestausee ⊜[1]	263	51.08 N	7.24 E
Ney Lake ⊜	184	54.38 N	92.25 W
Neyland	42	51.43 N	4.57 W
Neylandville	222	33.12 N	96.00 W
Neyrīz	128	29.12 N	54.19 E
Neyshābūr	128	36.12 N	58.50 E
Neyyāttinkara	122	8.24 N	77.05 E
Nezahualcóyotl	234	19.27 N	99.03 W
Nezahualcóyotl, Presa ⊜[1]	234	17.10 N	93.40 W
Nezamajevskaja	78	46.09 N	40.16 E
Nezameno-toko ♠	94	35.46 N	137.42 E
Nežárka ≃	61	49.11 N	14.41 E
Nezavertajlovka	78	46.37 N	29.56 E
Nežin	78	51.03 N	31.54 E
Nezlobnaja	84	44.08 N	43.23 E
Neznanka ≃	265b	55.34 N	37.21 E
Neznanovo	80	54.02 N	40.06 E
Nezperce	202	46.14 N	116.14 W
Nez Perce Indian Reservation ◆[4]	202	46.20 N	116.30 W
Nez Perce National Historical Park ♠	202	45.50 N	116.15 W
Nezpique, Bayou ≃	194	30.12 N	92.35 W
Nezvěstice	60	49.39 N	13.32 E
Ngabang	112	0.23 N	109.57 E
Ngabé	152	3.12 S	16.11 E
Ngabordamlu, Tanjung ›	164	6.56 S	134.11 E
Ngadda ≃	146	12.40 N	13.50 E
Ngadirojo	115a	8.13 S	111.19 E
Ngadza	152	5.10 N	20.12 E
Ngahere	172	42.24 S	171.27 E
Ngala	146	12.20 N	14.10 E
Ngale	152	2.56 N	21.20 E
Ngali	152	2.27 S	19.20 E
Ngaliema, Baie de ⊂	273b	4.19 S	15.16 E
Ngalipaeng	112	3.24 N	125.37 E
Ngaloa Harbour ⊂	175g	19.06 S	178.11 E
Ngamaba	273b	4.14 S	15.16 E
Ngamba ◆[8]	273b	4.15 S	15.18 E
Ngambé	152	4.14 N	10.37 E
Ngamdu	146	11.48 N	12.18 E
Ngami, Lake ⊜	156	20.37 S	22.40 E
Ngamiland □[5]	156	19.09 S	22.47 E
Ngamo	154	19.08 S	27.32 E
Ngamouéri	273b	4.14 S	15.14 E
Ngamring	124	29.14 N	87.10 E
Nganda ∧	154	10.25 S	33.50 E
Ngangala	154	4.42 N	31.55 E
Ngangla Ringco ⊜	120	31.40 N	83.00 E
Nganglong Kangri ∧	120	32.45 N	81.12 E
Nganglong Kangri ⩘	120	32.00 N	83.00 E
Ngangzê Co ⊜	120	31.05 N	86.55 E
Nganjuk	115a	7.36 S	111.55 E
Ngao	110	18.46 N	99.59 E
Ngaoui, Mont ∧	152	6.40 N	14.57 E
Ngaoundéré	152	7.19 N	13.35 E
Ngapali	110	18.26 N	94.19 E
Ngapara	172	44.57 S	170.45 E
Ngape	110	20.04 N	94.38 E
Ngaputaw	110	16.32 N	94.42 E
Ngara	154	2.28 S	30.39 E
Ngaramasch	175b	6.54 N	134.08 E
Ngarimbi	154	8.28 S	38.36 E
Ngaruawahia	172	37.40 S	175.09 E
Ngaruroro ≃	172	39.34 S	176.56 E
Ngasamo	154	2.33 S	33.53 E
Ngat ≃	110	19.09 N	99.01 E
Ngatangiia	174k	21.14 S	159.43 W
Ngatangiia Harbour ⊂	174k	21.14 S	159.45 W
Ngatea	172	37.17 S	175.30 E
Ngathainggyaung	110	17.24 N	95.05 E
Ngatik I[1]	14	5.51 N	157.16 E
Ngau I	175g	18.02 S	179.18 E
Ngauruhoe, Mount ∧	172	39.09 S	175.38 E
Ngau Tau Kok → Kwun Tong	271d	22.19 N	114.12 E
Ngawen	115a	7.00 S	111.18 E
Ngawi	115a	7.24 S	111.26 E
Ngay Nua	110	21.50 N	101.54 E
Ngebel	115a	7.46 S	111.37 E
Ngele	152	0.29 S	20.25 E
Ngemelis Islands II	175b	7.07 N	134.15 E
Ngerengere	154	6.45 S	38.07 E
Ngerkeel	175b	7.25 N	134.30 E
Ngermechau	175b	7.35 N	134.39 E
Ngeruktabel I	175b	7.15 N	134.24 E
Ngetbong	175b	7.37 N	134.35 E
Ngetera	146	12.31 N	12.38 E
Nggamea Island I	175g	16.46 S	179.46 W
Nggatokae Island I	175e	8.46 S	158.11 E
Nggela Pile I	175e	9.05 S	160.15 E
Nggela Sule I	175e	9.05 S	160.15 E
Nggelelevu I	175g	16.05 S	179.09 W
Nggwavuma ≃	158	26.58 S	32.17 E
Nghia Dan	110	19.18 N	105.26 E
Nghia Hanh	110	15.03 N	108.47 E
Nghia Lo	110	21.36 N	104.31 E
Ngiap ≃	110	18.24 N	103.36 E
Ngidinga	152	5.37 S	15.17 E
Ngimbang	115a	7.17 S	112.12 E
Ng'iro ∧	154	2.08 N	36.51 E
Ng'iro, Ewaso ≃, Kenya	154	0.28 N	39.55 E
Ngiro, Ewaso ≃, Kenya	154	2.04 S	36.07 E
Ngo	152	2.29 S	15.45 E
Ngoangoa ≃	140	5.48 N	25.09 E
Ngoboli	154	4.57 N	32.37 E
Ngoko ≃, Afr.	152	1.40 N	16.03 E
Ngoko ≃, Congo	152	0.25 S	15.29 E
Ngol-Kedju Hill ∧[2]	152	6.20 N	9.45 E
Ngolo	146	9.56 N	22.16 E
Ngom ≃	102	31.11 N	97.15 E
Ngomahuru	154	20.26 S	30.43 E
Ngomba	154	8.23 S	32.53 E
Ngomba ∧	154	5.43 S	35.52 E
Ngombe, Zaïre	152	6.35 S	20.42 E
Ngombe, Zaïre	273b	4.24 S	15.11 E
Ngome	158	27.46 S	31.28 E
Ngomedzap	152	3.15 N	11.12 E
Ngomeni, Ras ›	154	2.59 S	40.14 E
Ngong	154	1.22 S	36.39 E
Ngongotaha	172	38.05 S	176.12 E
Ngono ≃	154	1.08 S	31.35 E
Ngonye Falls ∟	152	16.40 S	23.35 E
Ngop	140	6.16 N	30.12 E
Ngora	154	1.27 N	33.46 E
Ngorengore	154	1.02 S	35.30 E
Ngoring Hu ⊜	102	34.50 N	97.35 E
Ngoro	115a	7.41 S	112.16 E
Ngorongoro Crater ⏚[6]	154	3.10 S	35.35 E
Ngote	154	2.14 N	30.48 E
Ngoto	152	4.00 N	17.21 E
Ngotwane ≃	156	23.35 S	26.58 E
Ngoulémakong	152	3.07 N	11.25 E
Ngouma	150	15.38 N	3.22 W
Ngounié □[4]	152	1.30 S	11.00 E
Ngounié ≃	152	0.37 S	10.18 E
Ngouri	146	13.38 N	15.22 E
Ngouroundou	152	6.27 N	22.37 E
Ngourti	146	15.19 N	13.12 E
Ngoywa	154	5.56 S	32.48 E
Ngozi	154	2.54 S	29.50 E
Ngqeleni	158	31.40 S	29.02 E
Ngudiabaka ≃	273b	4.25 S	15.11 E
Nguélémendouka	152	4.23 N	12.55 E
Ngugha ≃	156	19.21 S	23.15 E
Nguigmi	146	14.15 N	13.07 E
Nguila	152	4.43 N	11.41 E
Nguiu	164	11.45 S	130.38 E
Ngulu I[1]	108	8.27 N	137.29 E
Ngum ≃	110	18.09 N	103.06 E
Nguna, Île I	175f	17.26 S	168.21 E
Ngunga	154	3.41 S	33.34 E
Ngunju, Tanjung ›	115b	10.19 S	120.28 E
Ngunut	115a	8.06 S	112.01 E
Ngurore	146	9.18 N	12.14 E
Nguru	146	12.52 N	10.27 E
Ngwempisi ≃	158	26.42 S	31.26 E
Ngweni	158	27.56 S	32.15 E
Ngwenya ∧	158	26.11 S	31.02 E
Ngwerere	154	15.18 S	28.20 E
Ngweze ≃	154	17.40 S	25.07 E
Nha Be	269c	10.42 N	106.44 E
Nhabe ≃, Bots.	156	20.22 S	22.58 E
Nha Be ≃, Viet	269c	10.39 N	106.44 E
Nhacoongo	156	24.18 S	35.14 E
Nhamacolomo	156	18.05 S	34.26 E
Nhamundá	250	2.14 S	56.43 W
Nhamundá ≃	246	2.12 S	56.41 W
Nha Nam	110	21.27 N	106.06 E
Nhandeara	255	20.40 S	50.02 W
Nhareia	152	11.25 S	17.03 E
Nha Trang	110	12.15 N	109.11 E
Nhia ≃	152	10.15 S	14.12 E
Nhill	166	36.20 S	141.39 E
Nhlangano	158	27.06 S	31.12 E
Nhlazatshe	158	28.10 S	31.14 E
Nhoma ≃	156	18.52 S	20.53 E
Nhon Trach	269c	10.43 N	106.51 E
Nhulunbuy	164	12.11 S	136.47 E
Nhundo	152	14.25 S	21.23 E
Nhunguaçu	256	22.21 S	42.53 W
Niabembe	154	2.14 S	27.44 E
Niafounké	150	15.56 N	4.00 W
Niagara	190	45.46 N	87.59 W
Niagara □[6], On., Can.	212	43.05 N	79.20 W
Niagara □[6], N.Y., U.S.	210	43.10 N	78.42 W
Niagara ≃	212	43.15 N	79.04 W
Niagara County Historical Center ⚲	284a	43.10 N	78.43 W
Niagara Falls, On., Can.	212	43.06 N	79.04 W
Niagara Falls, On., Can.	284a	43.06 N	79.04 W
Niagara Falls, N.Y., U.S.	210	43.05 N	79.03 W
Niagara Falls, N.Y., U.S.	284a	43.05 N	79.03 W
Niagara Falls ∟	212	43.05 N	79.04 W
Niagara Falls Airport ⊠	284a	43.02 N	79.08 W
Niagara Falls International Airport ⊠	284a	43.06 N	78.56 W
Niagara-on-the-Lake	212	43.15 N	79.04 W
Niagara University ⚲[2]	284a	43.08 N	79.02 W
Niagassola	150	12.19 N	9.07 W
Niah	112	3.52 N	113.44 E
Niakaramandougou	150	8.40 N	5.17 W
Niamey	150	13.31 N	2.07 E
Niamey □[5]	150	14.00 N	2.00 E
Niamtougou	150	9.46 N	1.06 E
Nianbadu	100	28.17 N	118.28 E
Niandan ≃	150	10.30 N	10.26 W
Niandan Koro	150	11.05 N	9.15 W
Nianforando	150	9.32 N	10.31 W
Niangara	154	3.42 N	27.52 E
Niangay, Lac ⊜	150	15.50 N	3.00 W
Niangmake	102	30.14 N	99.40 E
Niangnianggong	104	41.00 N	121.13 E
Niangniangmiao	98	42.34 N	118.05 E
Niangniangwa	105	40.33 N	117.30 E
Niangoloko	150	10.17 N	4.55 W
Niangua ≃	194	37.58 N	92.48 W
Niangzizhuang	105	40.02 N	118.05 E
Nia-Nia	154	1.24 N	27.36 E
Nianpan	104	41.48 N	124.02 E
Niantic, Ct., U.S.	207	41.19 N	72.11 W
Niantic, Il., U.S.	219	39.51 N	89.10 W
Nianyugou	104	42.00 N	123.59 E
Nianyushan	100	29.11 N	117.04 E
Nianzhuang	98	34.19 N	117.47 E
Nianzigang	100	31.03 N	114.18 E
Nianzishan	89	47.32 N	122.52 E
Niapu	154	2.25 N	26.28 E
Niari □[5]	152	3.15 S	12.30 E
Niari ≃	152	3.56 S	12.12 E
Niaro	140	10.38 N	31.31 E
Nias, Pulau I	114	1.05 N	97.35 E
Niassa □[5]	154	13.30 S	36.00 E
Niatupo	246	9.33 N	78.54 W
Nibbiano	62	44.54 N	9.19 E
Nibe	26	56.59 N	9.38 E
Nibong Tebal	114	5.10 N	100.29 E
Nibra	272b	22.36 N	88.16 E
Nīca	76	56.19 N	21.04 E
Nica ≃	86	57.29 N	64.33 E
Nicaea → İznik	130	40.26 N	29.43 E
Nicaragua □[1], N.A.	230	13.00 N	85.00 W
Nicaragua □[1], N.A.	236	13.00 N	85.00 W
Nicaragua, Lago de ⊜	236	11.30 N	85.30 W
Nicaro	240p	20.42 N	75.33 W
Nicastro	68	38.59 N	16.20 E
Ničatka, ozero ⊜	88	57.45 N	117.30 E
Nice	62	43.42 N	7.15 E
Nice-Côte d'Azur, Aéroport de ⊠	62	43.40 N	7.14 E
Niceville	194	30.31 N	86.28 W
Nichelino	62	44.59 N	7.38 E
Nicheng	106	30.55 N	121.49 E
Nichihara	96	34.33 N	131.50 E
Nichinan, Nihon	92	31.36 N	131.23 E
Nichinan, Nihon	96	35.09 N	133.16 E
Nicholas □[6]	218	38.20 N	84.02 W
Nicholas Channel ʉ	238	23.25 N	80.05 W
Nicholasville	192	37.52 N	84.34 W
Nicholls	192	31.31 N	82.38 W
Nicholl's Town	238	25.08 N	78.00 W
Nichols, Ca., U.S.	282	38.02 N	121.59 W
Nichols, Fl., U.S.	220	27.54 N	82.02 W
Nichols, N.Y., U.S.	210	42.01 N	76.22 W
Nichols Brook ≃	283	42.37 N	70.59 W
Nicholson, Austl.	162	18.02 S	128.54 E
Nicholson, Ky., U.S.	218	38.54 N	84.33 W
Nicholson, Ms., U.S.	194	30.28 N	89.41 W
Nicholson, Pa., U.S.	210	41.37 N	75.46 W
Nicholson ≃, Austl.	162	17.34 S	128.38 E
Nicholson ≃, Austl.	166	17.31 S	139.36 E
Nicholson Island I	212	43.56 N	77.31 W
Nicholson Range ⩘	162	27.15 S	116.45 E
Nicholson River Aboriginal Reserve ◆[4]	162	18.00 S	137.30 E
Nichols Run ≃	284b	39.03 N	77.18 W
Nickerie □[5]	250	5.40 N	56.50 W
Nickerie ≃	250	5.59 N	57.00 W
Nickerson	198	38.08 N	98.05 W
Nickol Bay ⊂	162	20.39 S	116.52 E
Nicktown	214	40.37 N	78.48 W
Nicobar Islands II	110	8.00 N	93.30 E
Nicola	182	50.10 N	120.40 W
Nicola ≃	182	50.25 N	121.18 W
Nicolae Bălcescu	38	47.34 N	26.52 E
Nicolai Mountain ∧	224	46.05 N	123.28 W
Nicola Lake ⊜	182	50.10 N	120.25 W
Nicola Mameet Indian Reserve ◆[4]	182	50.11 N	120.49 W
Nicolaus	226	38.54 N	121.35 W
Nicolet	206	46.13 N	72.37 W
Nicolet □[6]	206	46.15 N	72.20 W
Nicolet ≃	206	46.14 N	72.39 W
Nicolet, Lac ⊜	206	45.50 N	71.33 W
Nicolet, Lake ⊜	190	46.20 N	84.15 W
Nicolet Centre ≃	206	45.46 N	71.50 W
Nicolet Sud-Ouest ≃	206	46.13 N	72.36 W
Nicoll Bay ⊂	276	40.43 N	73.07 W
Nicollet	190	44.16 N	94.11 W
Nicoll Point ›	276	40.42 N	73.09 W
Nicolosi	70	37.37 N	15.01 E
Nicosia, It.	70	37.45 N	14.24 E
Nicosia (Levkosía), Kípros	130	35.10 N	33.22 E
Nicosia (Lefkoşa), Kıbrıs	130	35.10 N	33.22 E
Nicotera	68	38.34 N	15.57 E
Nicoya	236	10.09 N	85.27 W
Nicoya, Golfo de ⊂	236	9.47 N	84.48 W
Nicoya, Península de ›[1]	236	10.00 N	85.25 W
Nictheroy → Niterói	256	22.53 S	43.07 W
Nida	76	55.18 N	21.01 E
Nida ≃	30	50.18 N	20.52 E
Nidadavole	122	16.55 N	81.40 E
Nidau	58	47.07 N	7.14 E
Nidd ≃	44	54.01 N	1.12 W
Nidda	56	50.24 N	9.00 E
Nidda ≃	56	50.06 N	8.34 E
Nidder ≃	56	50.12 N	8.47 E
Nidderau	56	50.14 N	8.52 E
Nide	102	31.51 N	96.19 E
Nideggen	56	50.47 N	6.29 E
Nidelva ≃	26	58.24 N	8.48 E
Nidwalden □[3]	58	46.55 N	8.28 E
Nidž	84	40.56 N	47.41 E
Nidzica	30	53.22 N	20.26 E
Niebüll	41	54.48 N	8.50 E
Nied ≃	56	49.23 N	6.40 E
Nied Allemande ≃	56	49.10 N	6.26 E
Nieddu, Monte ∧	71	40.45 N	9.34 E
Niederanven	56	49.39 N	6.16 E
Niederau	54	51.10 N	13.32 E
Niederaula	56	50.48 N	9.36 E
Niederbayern □[5]	60	48.45 N	12.45 E
Niederbipp	58	47.16 N	7.39 E
Niederbobritzsch	54	50.54 N	13.26 E
Niederbonsfeld	263	51.23 N	7.08 E
Niederbronn-Les-Bains	56	48.57 N	7.38 E
Niederdonk	263	51.14 N	6.41 E
Niederelfringhausen	263	51.21 N	7.10 E
Niedere Tauern ⩘	30	47.18 N	14.00 E
Niederfinow	54	52.50 N	13.55 E
Niederfrohna	54	50.53 N	12.43 E
Niederhaverbeck	52	53.09 N	9.54 E
Niederheimbach	56	50.02 N	7.48 E
Niederhone	56	51.13 N	10.06 E
Niederkassel	56	50.49 N	7.02 E
Nieder-Kassel ◆[8]	263	51.14 N	6.45 E
Niederkrüchten	56	51.12 N	6.13 E
Niederlande → Netherlands □[1]	30	52.15 N	5.30 E
Niederländische Antillen → Netherlands Antilles □[2]	241s	12.15 N	69.00 W
Niederlausitz □[9]	54	51.40 N	14.15 E
Niederlehme	54	52.19 N	13.39 E
Niedermarsberg	56	51.28 N	8.50 E
Niedermarschacht	52	53.25 N	10.21 E
Nieder-Mörlen	56	50.23 N	8.43 E
Niederndodeleben	54	52.08 N	11.30 E
Nieder-Neuendorf	264a	52.37 N	13.12 E
Niedernhall	56	49.17 N	9.36 E
Niedernwöhren	52	52.21 N	9.08 E
Niederoderwitz	54	50.57 N	14.44 E
Nieder-Ohmen	56	50.38 N	9.02 E
Nieder-Olm	56	49.55 N	8.11 E
Niederorschel	54	51.22 N	10.25 E
Niederösterreich □[3]	61	48.20 N	15.50 E
Niedersachsen □[3]	30	52.40 N	9.00 E
Niedersachswerfen	54	51.33 N	10.46 E
Niederschöneweide ◆[8]	264a	52.27 N	13.31 E
Niederschönhausen ◆[8]	54	52.35 N	13.23 E
Niedersonthofen	58	47.38 N	10.13 E
Niederstetten	56	49.24 N	9.55 E
Niederstotzingen	56	48.32 N	10.14 E
Niedersulz	61	48.29 N	16.40 E
Niederurnen	58	47.07 N	9.03 E
Niederwald	58	46.26 N	8.12 E
Niederwalgern	56	50.44 N	8.41 E
Niederweningen	58	47.30 N	8.23 E
Niederwiesa	54	50.51 N	13.01 E
Niederwürschnitz	54	50.43 N	12.45 E
Nied Française ≃	56	49.10 N	6.26 E
Niedu	100	25.28 N	114.08 E
Niefang	152	1.50 N	10.14 E
Nieheim	52	51.48 N	9.06 E
Niekerkshoop	158	29.19 S	22.51 E
Niel	50	51.07 N	4.20 E
Niellé	150	10.12 N	5.38 W
Niellim	146	9.42 N	17.49 E
Niem	152	6.12 N	15.14 E
Niemba	154	5.57 S	28.26 E
Niemegk	54	52.04 N	12.41 E
Niemeyer ◆[8]	287a	23.00 S	43.15 W
Niemodlin	30	50.39 N	17.37 E
Niéna	150	11.26 N	6.21 W
Nienberge	52	52.00 N	7.34 E
Nienborg-Wigbold	52	52.08 N	7.06 E
Nienburg, Dtsch.	52	52.38 N	9.13 E
Nienburg, Dtsch.	54	51.50 N	11.46 E
Niendorf	54	53.59 N	10.50 E
Nienhagen, Dtsch.	52	52.33 N	10.05 E
Nienhagen, Dtsch.	54	51.57 N	11.09 E
Niénokoué, Mont ∧[2]	150	5.26 N	7.10 W
Niepkuhlen ≃	263	51.29 N	6.31 E
Niepołomice	30	50.03 N	20.13 E
Nieppe	50	50.42 N	2.50 E
Nier ≃	48	52.17 N	7.48 W
Niéré	146	14.30 N	21.09 E
Niéré, Hadjer ∧	146	14.21 N	21.40 E
Niéri Ko ≃	150	13.21 N	13.23 W
Niers ≃	52	51.43 N	5.57 E
Nierst	263	51.19 N	6.43 E
Nierstein	56	49.52 N	8.20 E
Niesen ∧	58	46.39 N	7.39 E
Niesky	54	51.17 N	14.49 E
Nieszawa	30	52.50 N	18.55 E
Nieto, Cañada de ≃	258	34.00 S	58.15 W
Nieu Bethesda	158	31.51 S	24.34 E
Nieuw-Amsterdam, Ned.	52	52.44 N	6.51 E
Nieuw Amsterdam, Sur.	250	5.53 N	55.05 W
Nieuw-Buinen	52	52.57 N	6.55 E
Nieuwefontein	158	28.01 S	19.06 E
Nieuwegein	52	52.03 N	5.05 E
Nieuwe-Niedorp	52	52.45 N	4.54 E
Nieuwe-Pekela	52	53.04 N	6.58 E
Nieuweschans	52	53.11 N	7.12 E
Nieuwkoop	52	52.08 N	4.47 E
Nieuw Nickerie	250	5.57 N	56.59 W
Nieuwolda	52	53.14 N	6.59 E
Nieuwoudtville	158	31.23 S	19.07 E
Nieuwpoort, Bel.	50	51.08 N	2.45 E
Nieuwpoort, Ned. Ant.	241s	12.03 N	68.49 W
Nieuwpoort-Bad	50	51.09 N	2.42 E
Nieuw-Schoonebeek	52	52.38 N	6.59 E
Nieuw-Vennep	52	52.16 N	4.38 E
Nieuw-Weerdinge	52	52.52 N	6.59 E
Nieva ≃	246	4.35 S	77.53 W
Nievenheim	56	51.07 N	6.46 E
Nievería	286d	11.59 S	76.55 W
Nièvre □[5]	32	47.05 N	3.30 E
Nièvre ≃	50	47.10 N	3.13 E
Niga	150	13.38 N	5.27 W
Nigan	126	23.30 N	87.59 E
Niğde	130	37.59 N	34.42 E
Niğde □[4]	130	38.15 N	34.15 E
Nigei Island I	182	50.55 N	127.50 W
Nigel	158	26.30 S	28.28 E
Niger □[3]	150	10.00 N	6.00 E
Niger □[1]	134	16.00 N	8.00 E
Niger ≃	150	5.33 N	6.33 E
Niger Delta ≡[2]	150	4.50 N	6.00 E
Nigeria □[1]	134	10.00 N	8.00 E
Nigerian Museum ⚲	273a	6.20 N	3.24 E
Nigg	46	57.43 N	4.00 W
Nighāsan	124	28.14 N	80.52 E
Nightcaps	172	45.58 S	168.02 E
Nighthawk	182	48.58 N	119.38 W
Night Hawk Lake ⊜	190	48.28 N	81.00 W
Nightingale Island I	10	37.24 S	12.28 W
Nightmute	180	60.29 N	164.43 W
Nigrita	38	40.55 N	23.30 E
Nihe	104	41.27 N	121.13 E
Nihing (Nahang) ≃	128	26.00 N	62.44 E
Nihoa I	14	23.06 N	161.58 W
Nihommatsu	92	37.35 N	140.26 E
Nihonbashi ◆[8]	268	35.41 N	139.47 E
Nihon → Japan □[1]	92	36.00 N	138.00 E
Nihon-kai → Japan, Sea of ⊤[2]	90	40.00 N	135.00 E
Nihon University ⚲[2]	268	35.42 N	139.45 E
Nihtaur	124	29.20 N	78.23 E
Nihuil, Embalse del ⊜[1]	252	35.05 S	68.45 W
Niida ≃	96	33.11 N	132.58 E
Niigata	92	37.55 N	139.03 E
Niigata □[5]	94	37.08 N	138.30 E
Niihama	96	33.58 N	133.16 E
Niihari	94	36.07 N	140.09 E
Niiharu	94	36.41 N	138.55 E
Niihau I	229b	21.55 N	160.10 W
Nii-jima I	92	34.22 N	139.16 E
Niimi	96	34.59 N	133.28 E
Niinisalo	26	61.50 N	22.29 E
Niitsu	92	37.48 N	139.07 E
Niiza	94	35.48 N	139.34 E
Níjar	34	36.58 N	2.12 W
Nijiaqiao	269b	31.14 N	121.21 E
Nijil	132	30.31 N	35.33 E
Nijkerk	52	52.13 N	5.30 E
Nijlen	56	51.10 N	4.39 E
Nijmegen	52	51.50 N	5.50 E
Nijo Castle ⊥	270	35.01 N	135.45 E
Nijvel → Nivelles	50	50.36 N	4.20 E
Nijverdal	52	52.22 N	6.27 E
Níkaia	267c	37.58 N	23.39 E
Nikel'	24	69.24 N	30.12 E
Nikel'tau	86	50.23 N	58.13 E
Nikiforovo	265b	55.50 N	38.05 E
Nikiniki	112	9.49 S	124.28 E
Nikip Lake ⊜	184	52.53 N	91.53 W
Nikitovka, Ross.	78	50.23 N	38.25 E
Nikitovka, Ukr.	83	48.21 N	38.02 E
Nikitsch	61	47.32 N	16.40 E
Nikitskoje, Ross.	82	55.18 N	38.28 E
Nikitskoje, Ross.	82	55.13 N	35.46 E
Nikki	150	9.56 N	3.12 E
Nikkō	94	36.45 N	139.37 E
Nikkō-kokuritsu-kōen ♠	94	36.49 N	139.33 E
Niklā al-ʿInab	142	30.55 N	30.46 E
Niklasdorf	61	47.24 N	15.10 E
Nikobaren → Nicobar Islands II	110	8.00 N	93.30 E
Nikolai	180	62.58 N	154.09 W
Nikolajev, Ukr.	78	49.32 N	23.58 E
Nikolajev, Ukr.	78	46.58 N	32.00 E
Nikolajev □[4]	78	47.15 N	31.45 E
Nikolajevka, Kaz.	86	49.10 N	81.59 E
Nikolajevka, Ross.	80	46.21 N	47.44 E
Nikolajevka, Ross.	80	52.28 N	49.14 E
Nikolajevka, Ross.	80	52.11 N	48.04 E
Nikolajevka, Ross.	80	53.08 N	47.12 E
Nikolajevka, Ross.	83	47.18 N	38.50 E
Nikolajevka, Ross.	86	56.29 N	95.06 E
Nikolajevka, Ross.	86	54.57 N	75.44 E
Nikolajevka, Ross.	88	55.46 N	98.10 E
Nikolajevka, Ross.	89	48.34 N	134.47 E
Nikolajevka, Ukr.	78	47.38 N	33.12 E
Nikolajevka, Ukr.	78	47.06 N	34.14 E
Nikolajevka, Ukr.	78	44.58 N	33.37 E
Nikolajevka, Ukr.	78	46.23 N	29.24 E
Nikolajevka, Ukr.	78	47.33 N	30.25 E
Nikolajevka, Ukr.	78	51.04 N	34.02 E
Nikolajevka, Ukr.	83	47.39 N	37.41 E
Nikolajevka, Ukr.	83	48.51 N	37.46 E
Nikolajevka, Ukr.	83	48.46 N	38.20 E
Nikolajevo	76	58.16 N	29.29 E
Nikolajevo-Kozlovskij	83	47.13 N	38.21 E
Nikolajevsk	80	50.01 N	45.28 E
Nikolajevskaja	80	47.37 N	41.29 E
Nikolajevsk-Na-Amure	89	53.08 N	140.44 E
Nikolajevskoje, Ross.	78	45.08 N	39.36 E
Nikolajevskoje, Ross.	88	51.04 N	111.48 E
Nikolajevskoje, Ross.	88	52.21 N	117.00 E
Nikolassee ◆[8]	264a	52.26 N	13.12 E
Nikolayev → Nikolajev	78	46.58 N	32.00 E
Nikolo-Berezovec	76	58.38 N	42.17 E
Nikolo-Berjozovka	80	56.06 N	54.17 E
Nikolo-Chovanskoje	265b	55.36 N	37.27 E
Nikologory	80	56.09 N	41.59 E
Nikolo-Kropotki	82	56.44 N	37.55 E
Nikolo-L'vovsk	89	43.54 N	131.23 E
Nikolo-Makarovo	80	57.38 N	43.34 E
Nikolsdorf	64	46.47 N	12.55 E
Nikol'sk, Ross.	24	59.30 N	45.27 E
Nikol'sk, Ross.	80	53.45 N	46.05 E
Nikolski	180	52.56 N	168.52 W
Nikol'skij, Ross.	24	60.55 N	34.00 E
Nikol'skij, Ross.	86	56.18 N	68.58 E
Nikol'skij Toržok	76	59.53 N	38.46 E
Nikol'skoje, Ross.	74	55.12 N	166.00 E
Nikol'skoje, Ross.	76	52.39 N	36.04 E
Nikol'skoje, Ross.	76	55.26 N	35.04 E
Nikol'skoje, Ross.	76	59.30 N	42.32 E
Nikol'skoje, Ross.	76	59.23 N	44.36 E
Nikol'skoje, Ross.	78	50.35 N	41.10 E
Nikol'skoje, Ross.	80	47.46 N	46.24 E
Nikol'skoje, Ross.	80	52.37 N	43.49 E
Nikol'skoje, Ross.	82	54.51 N	35.53 E
Nikol'skoje, Ross.	82	54.27 N	36.24 E
Nikol'skoje, Ross.	82	54.30 N	36.50 E
Nikol'skoje, Ross.	82	54.03 N	37.10 E
Nikol'skoje, Ross.	82	54.18 N	35.53 E
Nikol'skoje, Ross.	82	55.37 N	36.41 E
Nikol'skoje, Ross.	82	55.15 N	36.04 E
Nikol'skoje, Ross.	82	56.09 N	36.43 E
Nikol'skoje, Ross.	82	55.53 N	36.26 E
Nikol'skoje, Ross.	86	57.12 N	84.21 E
Nikol'skoje, Ross.	86	52.02 N	55.43 E
Nikol'skoje, Ross.	265a	59.41 N	30.47 E
Nikol'skoje, Ross.	265b	55.46 N	37.54 E
Nikol'skoje, Ukr.	83	47.46 N	37.18 E
Nikol'skoje-na-Čeremšane	80	54.03 N	49.14 E
Nikol'skoje-na-Dnepre	78	48.12 N	35.12 E
Nikol'skoje-Ur'upino	265b	55.48 N	37.13 E
Nikonga ≃	154	4.40 S	31.28 E
Nikonorovka	83	49.07 N	39.59 E
Nikonova Gora	76	60.22 N	36.07 E
Nikonovskoje	82	55.17 N	38.10 E
Nikopol, Blg.	38	43.42 N	24.54 E
Nikopol', Ukr.	78	47.35 N	34.25 E
Niksar	130	40.36 N	36.58 E
Nīkshahr	128	26.13 N	60.12 E
Nikšić	38	42.46 N	18.56 E
Nikulino, Ross.	76	55.16 N	33.46 E
Nikulino, Ross.	80	58.05 N	44.14 E
Nikulino, Ross.	82	56.48 N	35.50 E
Nikulino ◆[8]	265b	55.40 N	37.28 E
Nikulkino	82	56.07 N	38.38 E
Nikul'skoje	82	55.10 N	38.41 E
Nikumaroro I[1]	14	4.40 S	174.32 W
Nikunau I	14	1.23 S	176.26 E
Nīl, Nahr an- → Nile ≃	140	30.10 N	31.06 E
Nila, Pulau I	164	6.44 S	129.31 E
Nilakka ⊜	26	63.07 N	26.33 E
Niland	204	33.14 N	115.31 W
Nil Blanc → White Nile ≃	140	15.38 N	32.31 E
Nile □[5]	154	3.00 N	31.30 E
Nile (Nahr an-Nīl) ≃	140	30.10 N	31.06 E
Niles, Il., U.S.	216	42.01 N	87.48 W
Niles, Mi., U.S.	216	41.49 N	86.15 W
Niles, Oh., U.S.	214	41.10 N	80.45 W
Niles Canyon V	282	37.36 N	121.56 W
Niles Pond ⊜	283	42.35 N	70.40 W
Nilgani	272b	22.46 N	88.26 E
Nilgaut, Lac ⊜	190	46.36 N	77.15 W
Nīlgiri	126	21.28 N	86.46 E
Nilka	86	43.47 N	82.20 E
Nilkitkwa ≃	182	55.27 N	126.43 W
Nillahcootie, Lake ⊜[1]	169	36.54 S	146.00 E
Nil → Nile ≃	140	30.10 N	31.06 E
Nilo Azul → Blue Nile ≃	140	15.38 N	32.31 E
Nilo Blanco → White Nile ≃	140	15.38 N	32.31 E
Nilo → Nile ≃	140	30.10 N	31.06 E
Nilópolis	256	22.49 S	43.25 W
Nilópolis □[7]	287a	22.49 S	43.26 W
Nilphāmāri	124	25.56 N	88.51 E
Nilsiä	26	63.12 N	28.05 E
Niltepec	234	16.34 N	94.37 W
Nilüfer ≃	130	40.18 N	28.27 E
Nīlwāl ◆[8]	272a	28.40 N	76.59 E
Nilwood	219	39.24 N	89.49 W
Nima	96	35.09 N	132.24 E
Nīmach	120	24.28 N	74.52 E
Niman ≃	89	51.24 N	132.45 E
Nimančik	89	52.09 N	133.47 E
Nimba, Mount ∧	150	7.37 N	8.25 W
Nimbāhera	120	24.37 N	74.41 E
Nimba Range ⩘	150	7.30 N	8.30 W
Nimboran, Pegunungan ⩘	164	2.45 S	140.20 E
Nimelen ≃	89	52.27 N	136.32 E
Nîmes	62	43.50 N	4.21 E
Nimis	64	46.12 N	13.16 E
Nimishillen Creek ≃	214	40.38 N	81.22 W
Nimisila	214	40.56 N	81.34 W
Nimisila Reservoir ⊜[1]	214	40.57 N	81.31 W
Nīm Ka Thāna	120	27.44 N	75.48 E
Nimmitabel	166	36.31 S	149.16 E
Nimmonsburg	210	42.09 N	75.55 W
Nimpkish Lake ⊜	182	50.25 N	126.59 W
Nimrod Lake ⊜[1]	194	34.55 N	93.20 W
Nīmrūz □[4]	128	30.30 N	62.00 E
Nims ≃	56	49.51 N	6.28 E
Nimta	272b	22.40 N	88.25 E
Nimule	154	3.36 N	32.03 E
Nimule National Park ♠	154	3.50 N	31.35 E
Nimy	50	50.28 N	3.57 E
Niña Bonita, Presa ⊜[1]	286b	23.02 N	82.29 W
Nīnah, Wādī V	146	30.02 N	15.22 E
Nīnawā □[4]	128	36.10 N	42.35 E
Nīnawá (Nineveh) ⊥	128	36.25 N	43.10 E
Nin Bay ⊂	116	12.13 N	123.15 E
Ninda	152	14.47 S	21.24 E
Nindigully	166	28.21 S	148.49 E
Nindirí	236	12.00 N	86.08 W
Nine Ashes	260	51.42 N	0.18 E
Nine Degree Channel ʉ	122	9.00 N	73.00 E
Ninemile Creek ≃, N.Y., U.S.	210	43.24 N	76.38 W
Ninemile Creek ≃, N.Y., U.S.	210	43.11 N	75.20 W
Ninemile Creek ≃, N.Y., U.S.	210	43.06 N	76.14 W
Nine Mile Creek ≃, Ut,. U.S.	200	39.50 N	109.53 W
Ninemile Island I	279b	40.29 N	79.52 W
Nine Mile Lake ⊜	212	44.57 N	79.34 W
Nine Mile Point ›	212	44.09 N	76.34 W
Ninepin Group II	271d	22.16 N	114.21 E
Nineteen Hundred Five Memorial Cemetery ◆	265a	59.51 N	30.27 E
Ninette	184	49.24 N	99.38 W
Ninetyeast Ridge ✣[3]	6	4.00 S	90.00 E
Ninety Mile Beach ⏚[2], Austl.	166	38.13 S	147.23 E
Ninety Mile Beach ⏚[2], N.Z.	172	34.48 S	173.00 E
Ninety Six	192	34.10 N	82.01 W
Nineveh, In., U.S.	218	39.22 N	86.05 W
Nineveh, N.Y., U.S.	210	42.12 N	75.36 W
Nineveh → Nīnawá ⊥	128	36.25 N	43.10 E
Ninfa ⊥	66	41.36 N	12.58 E
Ninfas, Punta ›	254	42.56 S	64.20 W
Ninfield	42	50.53 N	0.25 E
Ninga	184	49.13 N	99.51 W
Ningaloo	162	22.42 S	113.40 E
Ning'an	89	44.22 N	129.25 E
Ningari	150	14.40 N	3.16 W
Ningbo	100	29.52 N	121.31 E
Ningcheng (Tianyi)	98	41.33 N	119.20 E
Ningde	100	26.43 N	119.33 E
Ningdu	100	26.31 N	115.58 E
Ningerum	164	5.41 S	141.08 E
Ninggang	100	26.50 N	114.02 E
Ningguo	106	30.38 N	118.58 E
Ninghai	100	29.17 N	121.25 E
Ninghe (Lutai)	105	39.20 N	117.48 E
Ninghepu	105	40.43 N	116.07 E
Ninghua	100	26.15 N	116.38 E
Ningi	150	11.04 N	9.32 E
Ningjin, Zhg.	98	37.37 N	114.55 E
Ningjin, Zhg.	98	37.39 N	116.48 E
Ningjing Shan ⩘	102	29.45 N	98.45 E
Ningling	98	34.27 N	115.21 E
Ningming	102	22.07 N	107.05 E
Ningnan	102	27.11 N	102.36 E
Ningpo → Ningbo	100	29.52 N	121.31 E
Ningqiang	102	32.44 N	106.19 E
Ningshan	102	33.04 N	108.39 E
Ningsia Hui Autonomous Region → Ningxia Huizu Zizhiqu □[4]	102	37.00 N	106.00 E
Ningsia → Yinchuan	102	38.30 N	106.18 E
Ningwu	102	39.01 N	112.21 E
Ningxi	100	28.35 N	121.00 E
Ningxia Huizu Zizhiqu (Ningsia Hui) □[4]	102	37.00 N	106.00 E
Ningxian	102	35.31 N	108.01 E
Ningxiang	100	28.15 N	112.33 E
Ningyang	98	35.47 N	116.47 E
Ningyō-tōge)(	96	35.19 N	133.56 E
Ningyuan	102	25.37 N	111.46 E
Ningyuanbao	102	38.38 N	102.30 E
Ningyuanpu	105	40.44 N	114.54 E
Ninh Binh	110	20.15 N	105.59 E
Ninh Hoa	110	12.29 N	109.08 E
Ninhue	252	36.24 S	72.24 W
Ninigo Group II	164	1.15 S	144.15 E
Ninilchik	180	60.03 N	151.41 W
Ninnescah ≃	198	37.20 N	97.10 W
Ninnescah, North Fork ≃	198	37.34 N	97.42 W
Ninnescah, South Fork ≃	198	37.34 N	97.42 W
Ninnis Glacier Tongue ⍓	9	68.12 S	147.12 E
Ninocminda	84	41.18 N	43.35 E
Ninohe	92	40.16 N	141.18 E
Ninomiya, Nihon	94	35.18 N	139.16 E
Ninomiya, Nihon	94	36.22 N	139.58 E
Ninove	50	50.50 N	4.01 E
Niny	84	44.29 N	43.57 E
Nio	96	34.12 N	133.39 E
Nioaque	248	21.08 S	55.48 W
Nioaque ≃	248	20.46 S	56.04 W
Niobe	214	42.01 N	79.27 W
Niobrara	198	42.45 N	98.01 W
Niobrara ≃	198	42.45 N	98.00 W
Nioka	154	2.10 N	30.39 E
Nioki	152	2.43 S	17.41 E
Niokolo Koba	150	13.04 N	12.43 W
Niokolo Koba, Parc National du ♠	150	13.00 N	13.00 W
Niono	150	14.15 N	6.00 W
Nionsamoridougou	150	8.43 N	8.50 W
Nioro du Rip	150	13.45 N	15.48 W
Nioro du Sahel	150	15.15 N	9.35 W
Niort	32	46.19 N	0.27 W
Niota	192	35.30 N	84.32 W
Nioût ⊤[4]	150	16.03 N	6.52 W
Nipan	166	24.47 S	150.01 E
Nipāni	122	16.24 N	74.23 E
Nipawin	184	53.22 N	104.00 W
Nipawin Provincial Park ♠	184	54.00 N	104.40 W
Nipe, Bahía de ⊂	240p	20.47 N	75.42 W
Nipekamew ≃	184	54.59 N	104.52 W
Nipekamew Lake ⊜	184	54.24 N	104.58 W
Nipepe	154	14.01 S	37.55 E
Nipigon	190	49.01 N	88.16 W
Nipigon, Lake ⊜	176	49.50 N	88.30 W
Nipigon Bay ⊂	190	48.53 N	87.50 W
Nipin ≃	184	55.45 N	109.02 W
Nipisi Lake ⊜	182	55.47 N	114.57 W
Nipissing □[6]	212	45.30 N	78.50 W
Nipissing, Lake ⊜	190	46.17 N	80.00 W
Nipissis, Lac ⊜	186	51.02 N	66.10 W
Nipisso, Lac ⊜	186	50.52 N	65.50 W
Nipomo	204	35.02 N	120.28 W
Nippenicket, Lake ⊜	283	41.58 N	71.03 W
Nippers Harbour	186	49.48 N	55.52 W
Nippersink Creek ≃	216	42.23 N	88.22 W
Niqiu	100	33.25 N	115.38 E
Niquelândia	255	14.27 S	48.27 W
Niquero	240p	20.03 N	77.35 W
Niquivil	252	30.25 S	68.42 W
Nīr	128	38.02 N	47.59 E
Nīr, Jabal an- ⩘[2]	128	24.10 N	43.20 E
Nīra ≃	122	17.59 N	75.07 E
Nirʿam	132	31.31 N	34.35 E
Nirasaki	94	35.42 N	138.27 E
Nirayama	94	35.03 N	138.57 E
Nirgua	246	10.09 N	68.34 W
Nirim	132	31.20 N	34.24 E
Nirmal	122	19.06 N	78.21 E
Nirmāli	124	26.19 N	86.35 E
Nirsa	126	23.47 N	86.43 E
Niš	38	43.19 N	21.54 E
Nisa	34	39.31 N	7.39 W
Nisa (Neisse) (Nysa Łużycka) ≃	30	52.04 N	14.46 E
Nişāb, Ar. Su.	128	29.11 N	44.43 E
Nişāb, Yaman	144	14.31 N	46.30 E
Nišava ≃	38	43.22 N	21.46 E
Nisbet	210	41.13 N	77.07 W
Niscemi	70	37.09 N	14.23 E
Nischintāpur	272b	22.26 N	88.22 E
Nişf Thānī Bashbīsh	142	31.07 N	31.11 E
Nishan	120	33.35 N	85.30 E
Nishi ◆[8], Nihon	268	35.27 N	139.38 E
Nishi ◆[8], Nihon	270	34.41 N	135.30 E

Symbol	English	Deutsch	Español	Français	Português
≃	River	Fluß	Río	Rivière	Rio
≊	Canal	Kanal	Canal	Canal	Canal
∟	Waterfall, Rapids	Wasserfall, Stromschnellen	Cascada, Rápidos	Chute d'eau, Rapides	Cascata, Rápidos
ʉ	Strait	Meeresstraße	Estrecho	Détroit	Estreito
⊂	Bay, Gulf	Bucht, Golf	Bahía, Golfo	Baie, Golfe	Baía, Golfo
⊜	Lake, Lakes	See, Seen	Lago, Lagos	Lac, Lacs	Lago, Lagos
≡	Swamp	Sumpf	Pantano	Marais	Pântano
⍓	Ice Features, Glacier	Eis- und Gletscherformen	Accidentes Glaciales	Formes glaciaires	Acidentes glaciares
⊤	Other Hydrographic Features	Andere Hydrographische Objekte	Otros Elementos Hidrográficos	Autres données hydrographiques	Outros acidentes hidrográficos
✣	Submarine Features	Untermeerische Objekte	Accidentes Submarinos	Formes de relief sous-marin	Acidentes submarinos
□	Political Unit	Politische Einheit	Unidad Politica	Entité politique	Unidade política
⚲	Cultural Institution	Kulturelle Institution	Institución Cultural	Institution culturelle	Instituição cultural
⊥	Historical Site	Historische Stätte	Sitio Histórico	Site historique	Sitio histórico
♠	Recreational Site	Erholungs- und Ferienort	Sitio de Recreo	Centre de loisirs	Area de Lazer
⊠	Airport	Flughafen	Aeropuerto	Aéroport	Aeroporto
■	Military Installation	Militäranlage	Instalación Militar	Installation militaire	Instalação militar
◆	Miscellaneous	Verschiedenes	Misceláneo	Divers	Diversos

Nishiarai ◆[8] 268 35.47 N 139.47 E
Nishiazai 94 35.31 N 136.10 E
Nishibetsuin 270 34.58 N 135.31 E
Nishi-Chūgoku-sanchi-kokutei-kōen ♠ 96 34.40 N 132.10 E
Nishigō 96 37.09 N 140.10 E
Nishiiyayama 96 33.53 N 133.49 E
Nishiizu 94 34.46 N 138.47 E
Nishi-jima I 96 34.39 N 134.29 E
Nishikata 94 36.28 N 139.45 E
Nishikatsura 94 35.31 N 138.51 E
Nishiki 96 34.16 N 131.57 E
Nishiki ≈ 96 34.09 N 132.15 E
Nishikiori 270 34.29 N 135.34 E
Nishikyō ◆[8] 270 34.59 N 135.40 E
Nishimori ◆[8] 270 34.45 N 135.01 E
Nishinari ◆[8] 270 34.38 N 135.28 E
Nishinasuno 94 36.53 N 139.59 E
Nishinomiya 96 34.43 N 135.20 E
Nishinoomote 93b 30.44 N 131.00 E
Nishio 94 34.52 N 137.03 E
Nishitoda ◆[8] 270 34.43 N 135.00 E
Nishitosa 96 33.09 N 132.47 E
Nishiwaki 96 34.59 N 134.58 E
Nishiyodogawa ◆[8] 270 34.42 N 135.27 E
Nish — Niš 38 43.19 N 21.54 E
Nisinomiya — Nishinomiya 96 34.43 N 135.20 E
Nísiros I 38 36.35 N 27.10 E
Niska Lake ⊜ 184 55.35 N 108.38 W
Niskayuna 210 42.46 N 73.50 W
Nisling ≈ 180 62.27 N 139.30 W
Nismes 56 50.05 N 4.33 E
Nispen 52 51.29 N 4.28 E
Nisporeny 78 47.06 N 28.11 E
Nisqually ≈ 224 47.06 N 122.42 W
Nisqually Indian Reservation ◆[4] 224 47.02 N 122.42 W
Nisqually Reach c 224 47.07 N 122.45 W
Nissan ≈ 26 56.40 N 12.51 E
Nissequogue 276 40.54 N 73.12 W
Nissequogue ≈ 276 40.54 N 73.13 W
Nissequogue, Northeast Branch ≈ 276 40.50 N 73.13 W
Nissequogue River State Park ♠ 276 40.51 N 73.13 W
Nisser ⊜ 26 59.10 N 8.30 E
Nisshin 94 35.08 N 137.02 E
Nissoria 70 37.39 N 14.27 E
Nissum Bredning c 26 56.38 N 8.22 E
Nissum Fjord c[2] 26 56.21 N 8.14 E
Nisswa 190 46.31 N 94.17 W
Nistelrode 52 51.43 N 5.33 E
Nister ≈ 56 50.47 N 7.43 E
Nisutlin ≈ 180 60.10 N 132.30 W
Nita, Indon. 115b 8.40 S 122.11 E
Nita, Nihon 96 35.12 N 133.01 E
Nitalas 272c 19.06 N 73.08 E
Nitaure 76 57.10 N 25.10 E
Niterói 256 22.53 S 43.07 W
Niterói ◆[7] 287a 22.56 S 43.04 W
Nith ≈, On., Can. 212 43.12 N 80.22 W
Nith ≈, Scot., U.K. 44 55.00 N 3.35 W
Nithāri 272a 28.35 N 77.21 E
Nithāri ◆[8] 272a 28.42 N 77.03 E
Nithi River 182 54.01 N 125.01 W
Nithsdale V 44 55.14 N 3.46 W
Nitibe 112 9.19 S 124.12 E
Nitinat 224 48.55 N 124.29 W
Nitinat ≈ 224 48.49 N 124.37 W
Nitinat Lake ⊜ 182 48.45 N 124.45 W
Niton 42 50.35 N 1.16 W
Nitra 30 48.20 N 18.05 E
Nitra ≈ 30 47.46 N 18.10 E
Nitro 188 38.24 N 81.50 W
Nitry 50 47.40 N 3.53 E
Nitta 94 36.17 N 139.18 E
Nittälven ≈ 40 59.51 N 14.50 E
Nittany Mountain ∧ 210 41.00 N 77.25 W
Nittedal 26 60.04 N 10.53 E
Nittenau 60 49.12 N 12.16 E
Nittendorf 60 49.02 N 11.58 E
Niu Aunfo Point > 174w 21.04 S 175.20 W
Niubaotun 105 39.46 N 116.41 E
Niubu 100 31.02 N 117.39 E
Niuchutuncun 104 41.28 N 122.58 E
Niudouguang 100 24.51 N 115.44 E
Niue □[2], Oc. 14 19.02 S 169.52 W
Niue I[2], Oc. 174v 19.02 S 169.52 W
Niu'erhe 89 51.30 N 121.49 E
Niufentai 89 47.05 N 120.02 E
Niufozhen 107 29.23 N 105.02 E
Niuhang 100 28.44 N 115.51 E
Niuhuaxi 107 29.29 N 103.48 E
Niujie 102 27.47 N 104.16 E
Niujingjie 110 25.46 N 100.33 E
Niuke 120 30.41 N 82.01 E
Niulakita I 14 10.45 S 179.30 E
Niulan ≈ 102 27.28 N 103.10 E
Niulanshan 105 40.13 N 116.39 E
Niumaowu 98 40.58 N 124.59 E
Niupeng 106 31.32 N 121.50 E
Niupichang 107 30.35 N 103.40 E
Niushitun 98 35.18 N 114.24 E
Niut, Gunung ∧ 112 1.00 N 109.55 E
Niutan 107 29.05 N 105.21 E
Niutao I 14 6.06 S 177.17 E
Niuti 100 32.58 N 113.35 E
Niutian 100 27.17 N 115.44 E
Niutoushan 89 45.09 N 126.45 E
Niutou Shan I 100 29.07 N 121.56 E
Niutuo 106 39.15 N 116.20 E
Niutuoshan 106 31.04 N 119.37 E
Niuxichang 107 28.47 N 104.31 E
Niuxintai 104 41.21 N 123.53 E
Niuxintun 104 41.56 N 121.21 E
Niuyuanzi 105 40.20 N 117.47 E
Niuzhuang, Zhg. 98 37.21 N 118.29 E
Niuzhuang, Zhg. 104 40.58 N 122.32 E
Nivå 41 55.56 N 12.31 E
Nivala 26 63.55 N 24.58 E
Nive ≈, Austl. 166 26.02 S 146.25 E
Nive ≈, Fr. 32 43.30 N 1.29 W
Nivelles (Nijvel) 50 50.36 N 4.20 E
Nivernais □[9] 32 47.00 N 3.30 E
Nivernais, Canal du ≅ 50 47.40 N 3.40 E
Niverville, Mb., Can. 184 49.37 N 97.01 W
Niverville, N.Y., U.S. 210 42.26 N 73.40 W
Nivillers 50 49.28 N 2.10 E
Nivnoje 76 53.11 N 32.35 E
Nivskij 24 67.16 N 32.23 E
Niwāno 128 26.22 N 83.43 E
Nixa 194 37.02 N 93.17 W
Nixi 102 27.58 N 99.27 E
Nixis 107 30.08 N 106.19 E
Nixizhen 107 29.02 N 104.16 E
Nixon, Nv., U.S. 204 39.49 N 119.21 W
Nixon, Pa., U.S. 214 40.45 N 79.56 W
Nixon, Tx., U.S. 222 29.16 N 97.45 W
Niyodo 96 33.32 N 133.08 E
Niyodo ≈ 96 33.27 N 133.29 E
Niyor 114 2.05 N 103.17 E
Niyu Shan I 100 27.51 N 121.03 E
Niža 24 66.20 N 43.16 E
Nizāmābād 122 18.40 N 78.07 E
Nizamghāt 120 28.16 N 95.42 E
Nizām Sāgar ⊜[1] 122 18.10 N 77.55 E
Nižankoviči 78 49.40 N 22.47 E
Nīzgān ≈ 128 33.13 N 63.40 E
Nizhniy Tagil — Nižnij Tagil 86 57.55 N 59.57 E
Nižin 76 52.38 N 28.10 E
Nizino 265a 59.50 N 29.53 E
Nizip 130 37.01 N 37.46 E
Nízke Tatry ⋏ 30 48.54 N 19.40 E
Nízke Tatry, národní park ♠ 30 47.48 N 19.35 E
Nižn'aja 80 56.34 N 49.07 E
Nižn'aja Čvorovaja 86 59.11 N 77.31 E
Nižnaja Dobrinka 80 50.18 N 45.42 E
Nižn'aja Duvanka 83 49.35 N 38.10 E
Nižn'aja-Gerasimovka 83 48.46 N 39.44 E
Nižn'aja Grajvoronka 78 51.47 N 37.45 E
Nižn'aja Irga 86 56.51 N 57.26 E
Nižn'aja Ivanovka ◆[8] 83 48.09 N 38.46 E
Nižn'aja Karelina 88 57.55 N 107.44 E
Nižn'aja Keul'skaja, šivera ∟ 88 58.25 N 102.46 E
Nižn'aja Krynka 83 48.07 N 38.11 E
Nižn'aja Matrenka 80 52.16 N 40.06 E
Nižn'aja-Ol'chovaja 83 48.44 N 39.35 E
Nižn'aja Omka 86 55.26 N 74.55 E
Nižn'aja Omra 24 62.46 N 55.46 E
Nižn'aja Ošma 80 55.44 N 51.18 E
Nižn'aja Peša 24 66.43 N 47.36 E
Nižn'aja Pojma 88 56.11 N 97.13 E
Nižn'aja Pokrovka 80 51.40 N 50.07 E
Nižn'aja Šachtama 88 51.24 N 117.40 E
Nižn'aja Salda 86 58.05 N 60.43 E
Nižn'aja Syzran' 80 53.04 N 48.34 E
Nižn'aja Tavda 86 57.40 N 66.12 E
Nižn'aja Tunguska ≈ 74 65.48 N 88.04 E
Nižn'aja Tura 86 58.37 N 59.49 E
Nižn'aja Vol'dža 86 58.19 N 79.20 E
Nižn'aja Zaimka 88 56.09 N 98.14 E
Nižneangarsk 88 55.47 N 109.33 E
Nižnebakanskij 78 44.52 N 37.46 E
Nižne-Baranikovka 83 49.05 N 39.51 E
Nižnečujskij 85 43.12 N 74.21 E
Nižnedevick 78 51.33 N 38.20 E
Nižne-Gnilovskoj ◆[8] 83 47.11 N 39.36 E
Nižnegnutov 80 48.02 N 42.22 E
Nižnegorskij 78 45.27 N 34.44 E
Nižneilimsk 88 57.11 N 103.16 E
Nižneje 83 48.36 N 38.37 E
Nižneje Al'kejevo 80 54.46 N 50.03 E
Nižn'eje Gir'unino 88 51.12 N 116.58 E
Nižneje Kučukovo 80 56.13 N 52.57 E
Nižneje Kujto, ozero ⊜ 24 64.58 N 31.38 E
Nižneje M'ačkovo 82 55.33 N 37.59 E
Nižneje Platino 83 48.48 N 39.30 E
Nižnejepravalje ≈ 83 48.17 N 39.57 E
Nižneje Romanovo 86 59.47 N 69.35 E
Nižneje Sančelejevo 80 53.40 N 49.27 E
Nižnekamsk 80 55.32 N 51.58 E
Nižnekamskoje vodochranilišče ⊜[1] 80 55.50 N 53.00 E
Nižnekundr'učenskaja 80 47.45 N 40.57 E
Nižnelemskij 24 64.01 N 56.16 E
Nižne-Mit'akin Pervyj 83 48.41 N 40.02 E
Nižne-Nagol'naja 83 49.00 N 39.59 E
Nižneoz'ornoje 80 51.37 N 53.56 E
Nižne-Podpol'nyj 83 47.12 N 40.01 E
Nižne-Pokrovka 83 49.13 N 38.38 E
Nižnetambovskoje 89 50.54 N 138.13 E
Nižne-T'oploje 83 48.48 N 39.23 E
Nižnetroickij 80 54.20 N 53.41 E
Nižneudinsk 88 54.54 N 99.03 E
Nižnevartovsk 74 60.56 N 76.31 E
Nižnij Baskunčak 80 48.13 N 46.50 E
Nižnij Časučej 88 50.31 N 115.08 E
Nižnij Čir 80 48.22 N 43.03 E
Nižnij Čulym 86 54.37 N 78.56 E
Nižnije Černi 80 47.41 N 43.26 E
Nižnije Čeršely 80 54.40 N 52.08 E
Nižnije Ostrovcy 82 55.35 N 38.01 E
Nižnije Sergi 86 56.40 N 59.18 E
Nižnije Serogozy 78 46.50 N 34.23 E
Nižnije Timers'any 80 54.34 N 47.45 E
Nižnije V'azovyje 80 55.49 N 48.32 E
Nižnij Ingaš 88 56.12 N 96.31 E
Nižnij Kisl'aj 78 50.50 N 40.11 E
Nižnij Kuranach 74 58.49 N 125.32 E
Nižnij Lomov 80 53.32 N 43.41 E
Nižnij Mamon 78 50.11 N 40.30 E
Nižnij Novgorod (Gorky) 80 56.20 N 44.00 E
Nižnij Novgorod Oblast' □[4] 80 56.30 N 45.00 E
Nižnij Odes 24 63.40 N 54.52 E
Nižnij Ol'šan 78 50.45 N 38.55 E
Nižnij P'andž 120 37.08 N 68.32 E
Nižnij Paramonov 78 47.57 N 41.55 E
Nižnij Rogačik 78 47.21 N 34.02 E
Nižnij Serebr'akov 78 47.58 N 41.02 E
Nižnij Škaft 80 53.36 N 45.40 E
Nižnij Stan 88 52.18 N 115.44 E
Nižnij Tagil 86 57.55 N 59.57 E
Nižnij Takanyš 80 55.57 N 51.04 E
Nižnij Ufalej 86 55.55 N 59.59 E
Nižnij V'aloz'orskij 24 66.44 N 35.10 E
Nižnyj Nagol'čik 83 48.01 N 39.04 E
Nizwā 128 22.56 N 57.32 E
Nizy 78 50.47 N 34.46 E
Nizy-le-Comte 50 49.34 N 4.03 E
Nizza Monferrato 62 44.46 N 8.21 E
Nizzana 132 30.53 N 34.27 E
Nizzana, Nahal V 132 30.57 N 34.23 E
Nizzanim 132 31.43 N 34.38 E
Njassa-See — Nyasa, Lake ⊜ 154 12.00 S 34.30 E
Njazidja (Grande Comore) I 157a 11.35 S 43.20 E
Njinjo 154 8.48 S 38.54 E
Njoko ≈ 152 17.10 S 24.05 E
Njombe 154 9.20 S 34.46 E
Njombe ≈ 154 6.56 S 35.06 E
Njupeskär ∟ 26 61.38 N 12.41 E
Njurunda 26 62.16 N 17.22 E
Nkambe 152 6.38 N 10.40 E
Nkandla 158 28.37 S 31.05 E
Nkawkaw 150 6.33 N 0.47 W
Nkayi 154 19.00 S 28.54 E
Nkhata Bay 154 11.33 S 34.18 E
Nkhotakota 154 12.57 S 34.17 E
Nkolabona 152 1.14 N 11.43 E
Nkomi, Lagune c 152 1.35 S 9.17 E
Nkongsamba 152 4.57 N 9.56 E
Nkonko 154 6.20 S 34.58 E
Nkoso 152 2.45 S 22.39 E
Nkoto 152 1.56 S 19.41 E
Nkunga 152 4.41 S 18.34 E
Nkurenkuru 152 17.38 S 18.35 E
Nkwalini 158 28.45 S 31.33 E
Nmai ≈ 102 25.42 N 97.30 E
Nnewi 152 6.00 N 6.59 E
Nō 94 37.06 N 137.59 E
Noābād 272b 22.34 N 88.31 E
Noailles 50 49.20 N 2.12 E
Noākhāli 124 22.49 N 91.06 E
Noak Hill ◆[8] 260 51.37 N 0.14 E
Noale 64 45.32 N 12.04 E
Noāmundi 124 22.09 N 85.32 E
Noank 207 41.19 N 71.59 W
Noarlunga 168b 35.11 S 138.30 E
Noasca 62 45.27 N 7.19 E
Noatak 180 67.34 N 162.59 W
Noatak ≈ 180 67.00 N 162.30 W
Nobby 171a 27.51 S 151.54 E
Nobel 212 45.25 N 80.06 W
Nobeoka 92 32.35 N 131.40 E
Nobidome 268 35.48 N 139.35 E
Nobidome-yōsui ≅[1] 268 35.44 N 139.27 E
Nōbi-heiya ≚ 94 35.15 N 136.45 E
Nobili 150 11.33 N 1.12 W
Nobitz 54 50.58 N 12.29 E
Noble, Il., U.S. 194 38.41 N 88.13 W
Noble, Ok., U.S. 196 35.08 N 97.23 W
Noble □[6] 216 41.24 N 85.25 W
Noble Park 274b 37.58 S 145.10 E
Noblestown 279b 40.24 N 80.12 W
Noblesville 218 40.02 N 86.00 W
Nobleton, On., Can. 212 43.54 N 79.40 W
Nobleton, Fl., U.S. 220 28.38 N 82.15 W
Noboribetsu 92a 42.27 N 141.11 E
Noborito 268 35.37 N 139.34 E
Nobres 248 14.44 S 56.20 W
Nobsa 246 5.46 N 72.57 W
Nocatee 220 27.09 N 81.52 W
Noccundra 166 27.50 S 142.36 E
Nocé 50 48.22 N 0.42 E
Noce ≈ 64 46.09 N 11.04 E
Nocera Inferiore 68 40.44 N 14.38 E
Nocera Superiore 68 40.44 N 14.40 E
Nocera Tirinese 68 39.02 N 16.09 E
Nocera Umbra 66 43.05 N 12.47 E
Noceto 64 44.48 N 10.11 E
Nochistlán 234 21.22 N 102.51 W
Nochten 54 51.26 N 14.36 E
Noci 68 40.48 N 17.08 E
Nociglia 68 40.02 N 18.20 E
Nockamixon Lake ⊜[1] 208 40.28 N 75.14 W
Nockamixon State Park ♠ 208 40.27 N 75.16 W
Nockatunga 166 27.43 S 142.43 E
Nocona 196 33.47 N 97.43 W
Nocupétaro 234 18.48 N 101.04 W
Noda 94 35.56 N 139.52 E
Nodagawa 96 35.31 N 135.06 E
Nodaway ≈ 194 39.54 N 94.58 W
Nodera 270 34.45 N 134.56 E
Nods 58 47.06 N 6.20 E
Noé, Ouadi V 146 15.39 N 21.19 E
Noel 194 36.32 N 94.29 W
Noenieput 158 27.29 S 20.06 E
Noepoli 68 40.05 N 16.20 E
Noer 41 54.27 N 10.00 E
Noetinger 252 32.22 S 62.19 W
Nœux-les-Mines 50 50.29 N 2.40 E
Nofels 58 47.15 N 9.34 E
Nogah 132 31.37 N 34.42 E
Nogajskaja step' ≚ 84 44.17 N 45.05 E
Nogales, Chile 252 32.44 S 71.15 W
Nogales, Méx. 232 31.20 N 110.56 W
Nogales, Méx. 234 18.49 N 97.10 W
Nogales, Az., U.S. 200 31.20 N 110.56 W
Nogami 94 36.07 N 139.07 E
Nogangjin 98 39.30 N 125.23 E
Nogara, It. 64 45.11 N 11.04 E
Nogara, Ityo. 144 13.53 N 36.32 E
Nogaro 32 43.46 N 0.02 W
Nōgata 96 33.44 N 130.44 E
Nogent-en-Bassigny 58 48.02 N 5.21 E
Nogent-le-Roi 50 48.39 N 1.32 E
Nogent-le-Rotrou 50 48.19 N 0.50 E
Nogent-sur-Marne 261 48.50 N 2.29 E
Nogent-sur-Oise 50 49.16 N 2.28 E
Nogent-sur-Seine 50 48.29 N 3.30 E
Nogent-sur-Vernisson 50 47.51 N 2.45 E
Nogi 94 36.14 N 139.44 E
Nogies Creek ≈ 212 44.35 N 78.31 W
Noginsk 82 55.51 N 38.27 E
Nogisaki 268 35.57 N 139.58 E
Nogliki 89 51.48 N 143.10 E
Nogmung 102 27.30 N 97.49 E
Nogoa ≈ 166 23.33 S 148.32 E
Nōgohaku-san ∧ 94 35.46 N 136.31 E
Nogoon Nuur 86 49.33 N 90.17 E
Nogoyá 252 32.24 S 59.48 W
Nógrád □[6] 30 48.00 N 19.35 E
Noguera Pallaresa ≈ 34 42.15 N 0.54 E
Noguera Ribagorzana ≈ 34 41.40 N 0.43 E
Nohain ≈ 50 47.24 N 2.55 E
Nohar 123 29.11 N 74.46 E
Noheji 92 40.52 N 141.08 E
Nohili Point > 229b 22.04 N 159.47 W
Nohjhīl 124 27.51 N 77.39 E
Nohta 124 23.40 N 79.34 E
Nohwa-do I 98 34.12 N 126.35 E
Noicattaro 68 41.02 N 16.59 E
Noichi 96 33.33 N 133.42 E
Noir, Causse ⋏[1] 32 44.10 N 3.15 E
Noir, Isla I 254 54.29 S 73.02 W
Noire ≈, P.Q., Can. 190 45.54 N 76.57 W
Noire ≈, P.Q., Can. 206 45.33 N 72.58 W
Noire ≈, P.Q., Can. 206 46.39 N 72.08 W
Noire, Mer du — Black Sea ▼[2] 22 43.00 N 35.00 E
Noire, Montagne ∧ 206 46.14 N 74.18 W
Noire, Montagne ⋏ 32 43.28 N 2.18 E
Noirétable 62 45.49 N 3.46 E
Noirmoutier 32 47.00 N 2.15 W
Noirmoutier, Île de I 32 47.00 N 2.15 W
Noiseau 261 48.47 N 2.33 E
Noisiel 261 48.51 N 2.37 E
Noisy ≈ 212 44.19 N 80.08 W
Noisy-le-Grand 261 48.51 N 2.33 E
Noisy-le-Roi 261 48.51 N 2.04 E
Noisy-le-Sec 261 48.53 N 2.28 E
Nojember'an 84 41.12 N 45.01 E
Nojima-zaki > 94 34.56 N 139.53 E
Nojiri-ko ⊜ 94 36.49 N 138.13 E
Nojon 102 43.10 N 102.07 E
Nojon uul ⋏ 102 43.10 N 101.30 E
Nokami 96 34.15 N 135.20 E
Nokaneng 156 19.40 S 22.16 E
Nōke 270 34.26 N 135.29 E
Nokha Mandi 120 27.35 N 73.29 E
Nokia 26 61.28 N 23.30 E
Nokilalaki, Bulu ∧ 112 1.13 S 120.08 E
Nok Kundi 128 28.46 N 62.46 E
Nokogiri-yama ∧[2] 268 35.09 N 139.51 E
Nokomis, Sk., Can. 184 51.30 N 105.00 W
Nokomis, Fl., U.S. 220 27.07 N 82.26 W
Nokomis, Il., U.S. 219 39.18 N 89.17 W
Nokomis Lake ⊜ 184 56.58 N 103.02 W
Nokou 146 14.35 N 14.47 E
Nokpan-ni ◆[8] 271b 37.36 N 126.56 E
Nokrek ∧ 124 25.27 N 90.20 E
Nokuku 175f 14.53 S 166.35 E
Nola, Centraf. 152 3.32 N 16.04 E
Nola, It. 68 40.55 N 14.33 E
Nolan ≈ 222 32.07 N 97.26 W
Nolan Creek ≈ 222 31.02 N 97.26 W
Nolands Fork ≈ 218 39.41 N 85.07 W
Nolanville 222 31.05 N 97.36 W
Nolay 58 46.57 N 4.38 E
Nole 62 45.15 N 7.35 E
Noli 62 44.12 N 8.26 E
Noli, Capo di > 62 44.12 N 8.25 E
Nolichucky ≈ 192 36.07 N 83.14 W
Nolin ≈ 194 37.13 N 86.15 W
Nolin Lake ⊜[1] 194 37.20 N 86.10 W
Nolinsk 80 57.33 N 49.57 E
Nomad 164 6.18 S 142.14 E
Nomahegan Brook ≈ 276 40.41 N 74.18 W
Nomans Land I 207 41.15 N 70.49 W
Nombre de Dios, Méx. 234 23.51 N 104.14 W
Nombre de Dios, Pan. 236 9.35 N 79.28 W
Nombre de Dios, Cordillera ⋏ 236 15.35 N 86.55 W
Nome 180 64.30 N 165.24 W
Nomény 56 48.54 N 6.14 E
Nomexy 58 48.18 N 6.23 E
Nomgon, Mong. 102 45.26 N 105.08 E
Nomgon, Mong. 102 42.50 N 105.07 E
Nomgon uul ⋏ 102 42.50 N 104.20 E
Nomingue, Petit lac ⊜ 206 46.21 N 75.00 W
Nomini Bay c 208 38.09 N 76.43 W
Nominingue 206 46.24 N 75.02 W
Nominingue, Lac ⊜ 206 46.26 N 74.59 W
Nomoi Islands II 14 5.27 N 153.40 E
Nomoneas II 175c 7.24 N 151.53 E
Nomozaki 92 32.35 N 129.45 E
Nomtsas 156 24.22 S 16.47 E
Nomura 96 33.22 N 132.38 E
Nona, Lake ⊜ 220 28.24 N 81.15 W
Nonacho Lake ⊜ 176 61.42 N 109.40 W
Nonancourt 50 48.46 N 1.12 E
Nonant-le-Pin 50 48.42 N 0.13 E
Nonantola 64 44.41 N 11.02 E
Nonburg 24 65.34 N 50.32 E
Nonceveux 56 50.28 N 5.44 E
Nondalton 180 60.00 N 154.49 W
Nondwa 154 6.26 S 35.20 E
Nondweni 158 28.11 S 30.49 E
None 62 44.56 N 7.32 E
Nonette ≈ 50 49.12 N 2.24 E
None-yama ∧ 96 33.29 N 134.10 E
Nong'an 89 44.25 N 125.10 E
Nong Bua Lamphu 110 17.11 N 102.25 E
Nong Han 110 17.21 N 103.07 E
Nong Hèt 110 19.29 N 103.59 E
Nong Khai 110 17.52 N 102.44 E
Nongoma 158 27.58 S 31.35 E
Nongpoh 120 25.54 N 91.53 E
Nongstoin 120 25.31 N 91.16 E
Nonnenhorn 58 47.34 N 9.36 E
Nonnevitz 54 54.39 N 13.17 E
Nonning 166 32.30 S 136.30 E
Nonnweiler 56 49.36 N 6.58 E
Nono 144 8.32 N 37.26 E
Nonoai 252 27.21 S 52.47 W
Nonoava 232 27.28 N 106.44 W
Nonoc Island I 116 9.51 N 125.37 E
Nono de Julho, Túnel ◆[5] 287b 23.34 S 46.39 W
Nonogasta 252 29.18 S 67.30 W
Nonoichi 94 36.32 N 136.37 E
Nonouti I[1] 14 0.40 S 174.21 E
Nonsan 98 36.12 N 127.05 E
Nonsuch Bay c 240c 17.03 N 61.42 W
Non Sung 110 15.11 N 102.16 E
Nonthaburi 110 13.50 N 100.29 E
Nonthaburi □[4] 269a 13.52 N 100.27 E
Nontron 32 45.32 N 0.40 E
Nonvianuk Lake ⊜ 180 59.00 N 155.15 W
Noojee 169 37.55 S 146.00 E
Nookawarra 162 26.19 S 116.52 E
Nooksack 224 48.55 N 122.19 W
Nooksack ≈ 224 48.46 N 122.35 W
Nooksack, Middle Fork ≈ 224 48.50 N 122.08 W
Nooksack, North Fork ≈ 224 48.50 N 122.11 W
Nooksack, South Fork ≈ 224 48.50 N 122.11 W
Noonamah 164 12.38 S 131.04 E
Noonan 198 48.53 N 103.00 W
Noon Hill ∧[2] 283 42.09 N 71.19 W
Noonkanbah 162 18.30 S 124.50 E
Noorat 169 38.12 S 142.56 E
Noord-Beveland I 52 51.35 N 3.45 E
Noord-Brabant □[4] 52 51.30 N 5.00 E
Noord-Holland □[4] 52 52.40 N 4.50 E
Noordhorn 52 53.16 N 6.24 E
Noordoewer 156 28.45 S 17.37 E
Noordoost Polder ◆[1] 52 52.42 N 5.45 E
Noordpunt > 241s 12.23 N 69.10 W
Noord-Scharwoude 52 52.43 N 4.47 E
Noordwijk aan Zee 52 52.14 N 4.26 E
Noordwijk-Binnen 52 52.13 N 4.27 E
Noordwijkerhout 52 52.15 N 4.30 E
Noordwolde 52 52.54 N 6.09 E
Noormarkku 26 61.35 N 21.52 E
Noorvik 180 66.50 N 161.12 W
Noosaville 166 26.24 S 153.04 E
Nootka Island I 182 49.32 N 126.42 W
Nootka Sound ʊ 182 49.33 N 126.38 W
Nopaltepec 234 18.17 N 95.59 W
No Point, Point > 276 41.09 N 73.08 W
Nóqui 152 5.51 S 13.25 E
Nora, Sve. 40 59.31 N 15.02 E
Nora, In., U.S. 218 39.55 N 86.08 W
Nora ≈ 89 52.26 N 129.58 E
Nora ⊥ 71 39.00 N 9.01 E
Nor Ačin 84 40.19 N 44.35 E
Norah Head > 170 33.17 S 151.35 E
Nora Islands II 144 16.02 N 40.03 E
Norala 116 6.28 N 124.38 E
Noralee 182 53.59 N 126.26 W
Noranda 190 48.15 N 79.02 W
Noraskög ⋏ 40 59.39 N 14.50 E
Nora Springs 190 43.08 N 93.00 W
Norberg 40 60.04 N 15.56 E
Norberto de la Riestra 252 35.16 S 59.46 W
Norborne 194 39.18 N 93.40 W
Norcan Lake ⊜ 212 45.10 N 76.53 W
Norcatur 198 39.50 N 100.11 W
Norchia ⊥ 66 42.20 N 11.57 E
Norcia 66 42.48 N 13.05 E
Norco 228 33.56 N 117.33 W
Norcott, Mount ∧ 162 32.07 S 121.59 E
Norcross 192 33.56 N 84.12 W
Nord □[4] 146 9.00 N 13.30 E
Nord □[5] 50 50.20 N 3.40 E
Nord, Canal du ≅ 50 50.16 N 3.05 E
Nord, Cap — Nordkapp > 24 71.11 N 25.48 E
Nord, Gare ◆[5] 261 48.53 N 2.21 E
Nord, Grand lac du ⊜ 186 50.54 N 67.06 W
Nord, Petit lac du ⊜ 186 50.50 N 67.10 W
Nord, Rivière du ≈ 206 45.31 N 74.20 W
Nordamerika — North America ⊥[1] 16 45.00 N 100.00 W
Nordanholen 40 60.30 N 14.57 E
Nordausques 50 50.49 N 2.05 E
Nordaustlandet I 12 79.48 N 22.24 E
Nordbögge 263 51.37 N 7.44 E
Nordborg 41 55.03 N 9.45 E
Nordby 41 55.58 N 10.34 E
Nord Dakota — North Dakota □[3] 198 47.30 N 100.15 W
Norddeich 52 53.37 N 7.09 E
Nordegg 182 52.28 N 116.04 W
Nordegg ≈ 182 52.53 N 115.18 W
Norden, Dtsch. 52 53.36 N 7.12 E
Norden, Eng., U.K. 262 53.38 N 2.13 W
Norden, Ca., U.S. 226 39.20 N 120.22 W
Nordendorf 58 48.36 N 10.50 E
Nordenham 52 53.29 N 8.28 E
Nordenšel'da, archipelag II 74 76.45 N 96.00 E
Nordenskiold ≈ 180 62.05 N 136.18 W
Norderney 52 53.42 N 7.08 E
Norderney I 52 53.42 N 7.10 E
Norderstapel 41 54.21 N 9.14 E
Norderstedt 52 53.43 N 10.00 E
Nordfjord c[2] 26 61.54 N 5.12 E
Nordfjordeid 26 61.54 N 6.00 E
Nordfold 24 67.46 N 15.12 E
Nordfriesische Inseln — North Frisian Islands II 52 54.50 N 8.12 E
Nordfriesland ◆[1] 41 54.40 N 9.10 E
Nordgermersleben 54 52.13 N 11.20 E
Nordhalben 54 50.22 N 11.30 E
Nordhausen 54 51.30 N 10.47 E
Nordheim 222 28.55 N 97.36 W
Nordheim vor der Rhön 56 50.28 N 10.11 E
Nordhelle ∧[2] 263 51.09 N 7.46 E
Nordhorn 52 52.27 N 7.05 E
Nordic Park 278 41.57 N 88.02 W
Nordingrå 26 62.56 N 18.16 E
Nordirland — Northern Ireland □[8] 48 54.40 N 6.45 W
Nordiyya 132 32.19 N 34.54 E
Nordkanal ≅ 263 51.10 N 6.42 E
Nordkapp > 24 71.11 N 25.48 E
Nordkinnhalvøya >[1] 24 70.55 N 27.45 E
Nordkirchen 52 51.44 N 7.31 E
Nordkjosbotn 24 69.13 N 19.30 E
Nord-Korea — Korea, North □[1] 98 40.00 N 127.00 E
Nordland 224 48.03 N 122.41 W
Nordland □[6] 24 67.00 N 14.40 E
Nördliche Dwina — Severnaja Dvina ≈ 24 64.32 N 40.30 E

ENGLISH: Name | Page | Lat.°' | Long.°'

Nördliches Eismeer — Arctic Ocean ▼[1] 16 85.00 N 170.00 E
Nördlingen 56 48.51 N 10.30 E
Nordmaling 26 63.34 N 19.30 E
Nordmark 40 59.50 N 14.06 E
Nordmarka ◆[1] 26 60.00 N 10.25 E
Nordostrundingen > 16 81.36 N 12.09 W
Nord-Ostsee-Kanal ≅ 30 53.53 N 9.08 E
Nord-Ouest □[4] 152 6.30 N 10.30 E
Nordpfälzer Bergland ⋏ 56 49.40 N 7.40 E
Nordradde ≈ 52 52.43 N 7.17 E
Nordreisa 24 69.46 N 21.03 E
Nordre Strømfjord c[2] 176 67.50 N 52.00 W
Nordrhein-Westfalen □[3] 30 51.30 N 7.30 E
Nordsee — North Sea ▼[2] 22 55.20 N 3.00 E
Nordstemmen 52 52.09 N 9.46 E
Nordstrand I 41 54.30 N 8.53 E
Nordstrandischmoor I 41 54.33 N 8.48 E
Nord-Trøndelag □[6] 24 64.25 N 12.00 E
Nordvik 74 74.02 N 111.32 E
Nordwalde 52 52.05 N 7.28 E
Nordwest-Kap — North West Cape > 162 21.45 S 114.10 E
Nore 26 60.10 N 9.01 E
Nore ≈ 48 52.25 N 6.58 W
Noremberg — Nürnberg 60 49.27 N 11.04 E
Norf 263 51.09 N 6.43 E
Norf ≈ 263 51.11 N 6.44 E
Norfolk, Ct., U.S. 207 41.59 N 73.12 W
Norfolk, Ma., U.S. 283 42.07 N 71.19 W
Norfolk, Ne., U.S. 198 42.02 N 97.25 W
Norfolk, Va., U.S. 208 36.50 N 76.17 W
Norfolk □[6], On., Can. 214 42.48 N 80.25 W
Norfolk □[6], Eng., U.K. 42 52.35 N 1.00 E
Norfolk □[6], Ma., U.S. 207 42.10 N 71.15 W
Norfolk Broads ◆[1] 42 52.40 N 1.30 E
Norfolk-Insel — Norfolk Island □[2] 174c 29.02 S 167.57 E
Norfolk International Airport ⊠ 208 36.54 N 76.12 W
Norfolk Island □[2], Oc. 14 29.02 S 167.57 E
Norfolk Island □[2], Oc. 174c 29.02 S 167.57 E
Norfolk Island Aerodome ⊠ 174c 29.03 S 167.56 E
Norfolk Naval Shipyard ■ 208 36.49 N 76.18 W
Norfolk Naval Station ■ 208 36.57 N 76.18 W
Norfolk Ridge ▼[3] 14 29.00 S 168.00 E
Norfork Lake ⊜[1] 194 36.25 N 92.10 W
Norg 52 53.04 N 6.27 E
Norge 208 37.22 N 76.46 W
Norge — Norway □[1] 24 62.00 N 10.00 E
Norham 44 55.43 N 2.10 W
Norheimsund 26 60.22 N 6.08 E
Noria de Ángeles 234 22.27 N 101.56 W
Norikura-dake ∧ 94 36.06 N 137.33 E
Noril'sk 74 69.20 N 88.06 E
Noring, Gunong ∧ 114 5.24 N 101.44 E
Norland, On., Can. 212 44.43 N 78.49 W
Norland, Fl., U.S. 220 25.57 N 80.12 W
Norlane 169 38.06 S 144.21 E
Norley 262 53.15 N 2.39 W
Norlina 192 36.26 N 78.11 W
Norma, It. 66 41.35 N 12.58 E
Norma, N.J., U.S. 208 39.29 N 75.05 W
Normal, Al., U.S. 194 34.47 N 86.34 W
Normal, Il., U.S. 216 40.30 N 88.59 W
Norman, Ar., U.S. 194 34.27 N 93.40 W
Norman, In., U.S. 218 38.57 N 86.16 W
Norman, Ok., U.S. 196 35.13 N 97.26 W
Norman ≈ 166 17.28 S 140.49 E
Norman, Lake ⊜[1] 192 35.35 N 80.55 W
Normanby, Austl. 171a 27.28 S 153.01 E
Normanby, N.Z. 172 39.32 S 174.17 E
Normanby ≈ 164 14.25 S 144.08 E
Normanby Island I 164 10.05 S 151.05 E
Norman Creek c 284b 39.18 N 76.25 W
Normandie □[9] 32 49.00 N 0.05 W
Normandie, Collines de ⋏[2] 32 48.40 N 0.30 W
Normandien 158 27.57 S 29.47 E
Normandy Heights 284b 39.17 N 76.48 W
Normandy — Normandie □[9] 32 49.00 N 0.05 W
Normandy Park 224 47.27 N 122.21 W
Normangee 222 31.02 N 96.07 W
Normanhurst 274a 33.43 S 151.06 E
Normanhurst, Mount ∧ 162 25.04 S 122.32 E
Norman Island I 240m 18.20 N 64.37 W
Normannische Inseln — Channel Islands II 28 49.20 N 2.20 W
Norman Park 192 31.16 N 83.41 W
Normans Kill ≈ 210 42.36 N 73.44 W
Normanton, Austl. 166 17.40 S 141.05 E
Normanton, Eng., U.K. 44 53.41 N 1.27 W
Normanville 168b 35.27 S 138.19 E
Norman Wells 180 65.17 N 126.51 W
Nor Marsh ≋ 260 51.24 N 0.38 E
Normétal 190 48.59 N 79.23 W
Nornalup 162 35.00 S 116.49 E
Norogachi 232 27.15 N 107.07 W
Noroton ≈ 276 41.03 N 73.31 W
Noroton Point > 276 41.03 N 73.26 W
Norovlin 88 48.40 N 112.00 E
Noroy-le-Bourg 58 47.37 N 6.18 E
Norphlet 194 33.18 N 92.39 W
Norquay 184 51.53 N 102.05 W
Ñorquinco 254 41.51 S 70.54 W
Norra Barken ⊜ 40 60.07 N 15.31 E
Norra Björkfjärden c 40 59.27 N 17.28 E
Norrahammar 26 57.42 N 14.06 E
Norra Hörken ⊜ 40 60.04 N 14.53 E
Norra Kvarken (Merenkurkku) ʊ 26 63.36 N 20.43 E
Norra Kvills Nationalpark ♠ 26 57.44 N 15.37 E
Norrälgen ⊜ 40 59.50 N 14.34 E
Norra Rörum 41 56.01 N 13.30 E
Norra Storfjället ∧ 24 65.52 N 15.18 E
Norra Yngern ⊜ 40 59.09 N 17.22 E
Norrboda 40 60.28 N 18.25 E
Norrbotten □[9] 26 66.45 N 23.00 E
Norrbottens Län □[6] 24 66.00 N 20.00 E
Nørre Åby 41 55.27 N 9.54 E
Nørre Alslev 41 54.54 N 11.54 E
Nørre Broby 41 55.15 N 10.14 E
Nørre Nærå 41 55.34 N 10.17 E
Norrent-Fontes 50 50.35 N 2.24 E
Nørre Snede 41 55.58 N 9.25 E
Nørresundby 26 57.04 N 9.55 E
Nørre Vejrup 41 55.31 N 8.47 E
Norrfjärden 26 65.25 N 21.27 E
Norridge 216 41.57 N 87.49 W
Norridgewock 188 44.42 N 69.47 W
Norris 192 36.11 N 84.04 W
Norris, Lake ⊜ 220 28.57 N 81.32 W
Norris Arm 186 49.05 N 55.15 W
Norris Bridge ◆[5] 208 37.37 N 76.26 W
Norris City 194 37.58 N 88.19 W
Norris Dam State Park ♠ 192 36.14 N 84.07 W
Norrish Creek ≈ 224 49.10 N 122.08 W
Norris Lake ⊜[1] 192 36.20 N 83.55 W
Norris Point 186 49.31 N 57.53 W
Norristown 208 40.07 N 75.20 W
Norrköping 40 58.36 N 16.11 E
Norroway Brook ≈ 283 42.11 N 71.03 W
Norrskedika 40 60.17 N 18.17 E
Norrsundet 26 60.56 N 17.08 E

DEUTSCH: Name | Seite | Breite°' | Länge°' E = Ost

Norrtälje 40 59.46 N 18.42 E
Norrtäljeviken c 40 59.47 N 18.53 E
Norseman 162 32.12 S 121.46 E
Norsewood 172 40.04 S 176.13 E
Norsjå ⊜ 26 59.18 N 9.20 E
Norsjö 26 64.55 N 19.29 E
Norsk 89 52.20 N 129.55 E
Norsminde 41 56.01 N 10.16 E
Norsup 175f 16.05 S 167.23 E
Norte, Cabo >, Bra. 250 1.40 N 49.55 W
Norte, Cabo >, Chile 174z 27.03 S 109.24 W
Norte, Cabo — Nordkapp > 24 71.11 N 25.48 E
Norte, Canal ʊ 288 34.37 S 58.15 W
Norte, Canal do ʊ 250 0.30 N 50.30 W
Norte, Cayo I 240m 18.20 N 65.15 W
Norte, Estación del ◆[5], Esp. 266a 40.25 N 3.43 W
Norte, Estación del ◆[5], Esp. 266d 41.24 N 2.02 E
Norte, Mar del — North Sea ▼[2] 22 55.20 N 3.00 E
Norte, Punta > 254 42.04 S 63.45 W
Norte, Serra do ⋏[1] 248 11.20 S 59.00 W
Norte de Santander □[3] 238 9.15 N 73.00 W
Norte de Santander □[5] 246 8.00 N 73.00 W
Nortelândia 248 14.25 S 56.48 W
Nörten-Hardenberg 52 51.38 N 9.56 E
North, S.C., U.S. 192 33.36 N 81.06 W
North, Va., U.S. 208 37.26 N 76.24 W
North ≈, Nf., Can. 176 57.30 N 62.05 W
North ≈, On., Can. 212 44.44 N 79.39 W
North ≈, Al., U.S. 194 33.15 N 87.30 W
North ≈, Ia., U.S. 194 41.31 N 93.27 W
North ≈, Ma., U.S. 283 42.10 N 70.43 W
North ≈, Mo., U.S. 219 39.52 N 91.27 W
North ≈, Wa., U.S. 224 46.45 N 123.53 W
North, Cape > 186 47.02 N 60.25 W
North Abington 207 42.07 N 70.57 W
North Adams, Ma., U.S. 207 42.42 N 73.06 W
North Adams, Mi., U.S. 216 41.58 N 84.32 W
North Albany 202 44.39 N 123.06 W
Northallerton 44 54.20 N 1.26 W
Northam, Austl. 168a 31.39 S 116.40 E
Northam, S. Afr. 156 25.03 S 27.11 E
Northam, Eng., U.K. 42 51.02 N 4.12 W
North America ⊥[1] 4 45.00 N 100.00 W
North America ⊥[1] 16 45.00 N 100.00 W
North American Basin ▼[1] 8 30.00 N 60.00 W
North Amherst 207 42.24 N 72.31 W
North Amityville 276 40.41 N 73.25 W
Northampton, Austl. 162 28.21 S 114.37 E
Northampton, Eng., U.K. 42 52.14 N 0.54 W
Northampton, Md., U.S. 284c 38.52 N 76.49 W
Northampton, Ma., U.S. 207 42.19 N 72.38 W
Northampton, N.Y., U.S. 207 40.54 N 72.40 W
Northampton, Pa., U.S. 208 40.41 N 75.29 W
Northampton □[6], N.C., U.S. 208 36.28 N 77.21 W
Northampton □[6], Pa., U.S. 210 40.45 N 75.18 W
Northampton □[6], Va., U.S. 208 37.20 N 75.50 W
Northamptonshire □[6] 42 52.20 N 0.50 W
North Andaman I 110 13.15 N 92.55 E
North Andover 207 42.41 N 71.08 W
North Andrews Gardens 220 26.12 N 80.07 W
North Anna ≈ 192 37.48 N 77.25 W
North Anson 188 44.51 N 69.54 W
North Apollo 214 40.35 N 79.33 W
North Arlington 276 40.47 N 74.08 W
North Arm ≈[1] 224 49.12 N 123.10 W
North Asheboro 192 35.44 N 79.49 W
North Atlanta 192 33.51 N 84.20 W
North Attleboro 207 41.59 N 71.20 W
North Attleboro National Fish Hatchery ♠ 283 42.00 N 71.17 W
North Auburn 274a 33.50 S 151.02 E
North Augusta 192 33.30 N 81.57 W
North Aulatsivik Island I 176 59.50 N 64.00 W
North Aurora 216 41.48 N 88.19 W
North Australian Basin ▼[1] 14 14.30 S 116.30 E
Northaw 260 51.42 N 0.09 W
North Babylon 276 40.42 N 73.19 W
North Balabac Strait ʊ 116 8.10 N 117.04 E
North Baltimore 216 41.10 N 83.40 W
North Balwyn 274b 37.48 S 145.05 E
North Bannister 168a 32.35 S 116.26 E
North Bārākpur 126 22.46 N 88.22 E
North Bass Island I 214 41.43 N 82.49 W
North Battleford 184 52.47 N 108.17 W
North Bay, On., Can. 190 46.19 N 79.28 W
North Bay, N.Y., U.S. 210 43.14 N 75.45 W
North Bay, Wi., U.S. 216 42.46 N 87.47 W
North Bay c, On., Can. 212 44.53 N 79.48 W
North Bay c, Wa., U.S. 224 46.59 N 124.04 W
North Bay Village 220 25.51 N 80.08 W
North Beach 168a 31.52 S 115.45 E
North Beach ◆[8] 282 37.48 N 122.25 W
North Beach Peninsula >[1] 224 46.30 N 124.02 W
North Belle Vernon 214 40.08 N 79.52 W
North Bellmore 276 40.41 N 73.32 W
North Bend, B.C., Can. 182 49.53 N 121.27 W
North Bend, Ne., U.S. 198 41.27 N 96.46 W
North Bend, Oh., U.S. 218 39.09 N 84.44 W
North Bend, Or., U.S. 202 43.24 N 124.13 W
North Bend, Pa., U.S. 214 41.21 N 77.42 W
North Bend, Wa., U.S. 224 47.29 N 121.47 W
North Benfleet 260 51.35 N 0.32 E
North Bengal Plains ≚, Asia 124 26.15 N 88.35 E
North Bengal Plains ≚, Asia 124 26.20 N 88.30 E
North Bennington 210 42.55 N 73.14 W
North Bergen 276 40.47 N 74.02 W
North Berwick, Scot., U.K. 46 56.04 N 2.44 W
North Berwick, Me., U.S. 188 43.18 N 70.44 W
North Bethlehem 210 42.40 N 73.50 W
North Bihar Plains ≚ 124 26.20 N 86.00 E
North Billerica 207 42.35 N 71.17 W
North Bloomfield 214 41.27 N 80.52 W
North Boggy Creek ≈ 196 34.23 N 96.04 W
North Bonneville 224 45.38 N 121.58 W
Northborough 207 42.19 N 71.38 W
North Bosque ≈ 196 31.40 N 97.24 W
North Boston 210 42.41 N 78.47 W
North Bourke 166 30.03 S 145.57 E
North Box Hill 274b 37.48 S 145.07 E
North Braddock 279b 40.23 N 79.50 W
North Branch, Mi., U.S. 190 43.13 N 83.11 W
North Branch, Mn., U.S. 190 45.30 N 92.58 W
North Branch, N.J., U.S. 210 40.36 N 74.41 W

Symbols in the index entries represent the broad categories identified in the key at the right. Symbols with superior numbers (⋏[1]) identify subcategories (see complete key on page *I · 1*).

Symbole im Register stellen die rechts im Schlüssel erklärten Kategorien dar. Symbole mit hochgestellten Ziffern (⋏[1]) bezeichnen Unterabteilungen einer Kategorie (vgl. vollständiger Schlüssel auf Seite *I · 1*).

Los símbolos incluídos en el texto del índice representan las grandes categorias identificadas con la clave a la derecha. Los símbolos con numeros en su parte superior (⋏[1]) identifican las subcategorías (véase la clave completa en la página *I · 1*).

Les symboles de l'index représentent les catégories indiquées dans la légende à droite. Les symboles suivis d'un indice (⋏[1]) représentent des sous-catégories (voir légende complète à la page *I · 1*).

Os símbolos incluídos no texto do índice representam as grandes categorias identificadas com a chave à direita. Os símbolos com números em sua parte superior (⋏[1]) identificam as subcategorias (veja-se a chave completa à página *I · 1*).

	English	Deutsch	Español	Français	Português
∧	Mountain	Berg	Montaña	Montagne	Montanha
⋏	Mountains	Gebirge	Montañas	Montagnes	Montanhas
✕	Pass	Paß	Paso	Col	Passo
V	Valley, Canyon	Tal, Cañon	Valle, Cañón	Vallée, Canyon	Vale, Canhão
≚	Plain	Ebene	Llano	Plaine	Planície
>	Cape	Kap	Cabo	Cap	Cabo
I	Island	Insel	Isla	Île	Ilha
II	Islands	Inseln	Islas	Îles	Ilhas
⊥	Other Topographic Features	Andere Topographische Objekte	Otros Elementos Topográficos	Autres données topographiques	Outros acidentes topográficos

ESPAÑOL: Nombre · Página · Lat.°′ · Long.°′ W = Oeste
FRANÇAIS: Nom · Page · Lat.°′ · Long.°′ W = Ouest
PORTUGUÊS: Nome · Página · Lat.°′ · Long.°′ W = Oeste

North Branch Canal ≅ 224 47.12 N 120.40 W
North Branford 207 41.19 N 72.46 W
North Breakers ✦² 174g 28.14 N 177.25 W
Northbridge, Austl. 274a 33.49 S 151.13 E
Northbridge, Ma., U.S. 207 42.09 N 71.39 W
North Bristol 214 41.24 N 80.52 W
Northbrook, On., Can. 212 44.44 N 77.10 W
Northbrook, Il., U.S. 216 42.07 N 87.49 W
Northbrook, Pa., U.S. 285 39.55 N 75.41 W
North Brookfield, Ma., U.S. 207 42.16 N 72.05 W
North Brookfield, N.Y., U.S. 210 42.51 N 75.24 W
North Brunswick 208 40.28 N 74.28 W
North Buganda □⁵ 154 1.00 N 32.15 E
North Caicos I 238 21.56 N 71.59 W
North Caldwell 276 40.51 N 74.16 W
North Canadian ≃ 196 35.17 N 95.31 W
North Canton, Ct., U.S. 207 41.53 N 72.53 W
North Canton, Ga., U.S. 192 34.14 N 84.29 W
North Canton, Oh., U.S. 214 40.52 N 81.24 W
North Cape 216 42.47 N 88.05 W
North Cape ▸, P.E., Can. 186 47.05 N 64.00 W
North Cape ▸, N.Z. 172 34.25 S 173.02 E
North Cape ▸, Pap. N. Gui. 164 2.32 S 150.49 E
North Cape ▸, Mi., U.S. 216 41.44 N 83.25 W
North Cape May 208 38.58 N 74.57 W
North Cape → Nordkapp ▸ 24 71.11 N 25.48 E
North Captiva Island I 220 26.35 N 82.13 W
North Caribou Lake @ 176 52.50 N 90.40 W
North Carolina □³, U.S. 178 35.30 N 80.00 W
North Carolina □³, U.S. 192 35.30 N 80.00 W
North Carver 207 41.55 N 70.48 W
North Cascades National Park ◆ 224 48.30 N 121.00 W
North Castor ≃ 212 45.16 N 75.24 W
North Catasauqua 208 40.40 N 75.29 W
North Chagrin Reservation ◆ 279a 41.34 N 81.26 W
North Channel 𝔲, On., Can. 190 46.02 N 82.50 W
North Channel 𝔲, On., Can. 212 44.10 N 76.45 W
North Channel 𝔲, U.K. 44 55.10 N 5.40 W
North Channel 𝔲, N.Y., U.S. 276 40.36 N 73.53 W
North Channel ≃¹ 281 42.38 N 82.40 W
North Charleroi 214 40.09 N 79.54 W
North Charleston 192 32.51 N 79.58 W
North Chatham 210 42.29 N 73.38 W
North Chelmsford 207 42.38 N 71.23 W
North Chicago 216 42.19 N 87.50 W
North Chili 210 43.06 N 77.45 W
Northchurch 260 51.46 N 0.36 W
North City 224 47.45 N 122.18 W
North Cleveland 222 30.21 N 95.06 W
Northcliff ✦⁸ 273d 26.09 S 27.58 E
Northcliffe 162 34.36 S 116.07 E
North Clymer 214 42.04 N 79.34 W
North Cohasset 283 42.15 N 70.50 W
North Cohocton 210 42.34 N 77.28 W
North College Hill 218 39.13 N 84.33 W
North Collins 210 42.35 N 78.56 W
North Commerce Lake @ 281 42.35 N 83.30 W
North Concho ≃ 196 31.27 N 100.25 W
North Conway 188 44.03 N 71.07 W
North Cotabato □⁴ 116 7.15 N 124.50 E
Northcote 274b 37.46 S 145.00 E
North Cray ✦⁸ 260 51.26 N 0.08 E
North Creek 188 43.41 N 73.59 W
North Creek ≃ 278 41.33 N 87.37 W
Northcrest 222 31.38 N 97.06 W
North Crossett 194 33.09 N 91.56 W
North Crosswicks 285 40.10 N 74.39 W
North Croton Creek ≃ 196 33.24 N 100.00 W
North Dakota □³, U.S. 178 47.30 N 100.15 W
North Dakota □³, U.S. 198 47.30 N 100.15 W
North Dandalup 168a 32.31 S 115.58 E
North Dandalup ≃ 168a 32.36 S 115.53 E
North Dartmouth 207 41.38 N 70.58 W
North Dighton 207 41.51 N 71.07 W
North Dorset Downs ⩘¹ 42 50.47 N 2.30 W
North Downs ⩘¹ 42 51.20 N 0.10 E
North Dum Dum 126 22.38 N 88.23 E
North Eagle Butte 198 45.02 N 101.15 W
North East, Md., U.S. 208 39.36 N 75.56 W
North East, Pa., U.S. 214 42.12 N 79.50 W
North-East □⁵ 156 21.00 S 27.30 E
Northeast Cape 180 63.18 N 168.42 W
Northeast Cape ▸ 180 63.17 N 168.45 W
Northeast Cape Fear ≃ 192 34.11 N 77.57 W
Northeast Creek ≃ 284b 39.18 N 76.29 W
North Eastern □⁴ 154 1.00 N 40.15 E
Northeastern University ⅴ² 283 42.20 N 71.05 W
North Eastham 207 41.51 N 69.59 W
Northeast Henrietta 210 43.04 N 77.36 W
Northeast Islands II 175c 7.36 N 151.57 E
North Easton 207 42.04 N 71.06 W
Northeast Pass 𝔲 175c 7.30 N 151.59 E
North East Point ▸, Ba. 238 21.20 N 73.01 W
North East Point ▸, Ba. 238 22.43 N 73.50 W
North East Point ▸, Kiribati 174o 1.57 N 157.16 W
Northeast Point ▸, St. Vin. 241h 13.03 N 61.13 W
Northeast Providence Channel 𝔲 238 25.40 N 77.09 W
North Edwards 228 35.01 N 117.44 W
North Egremont 207 42.11 N 73.26 W
Northeim 52 51.42 N 10.00 E
North Elkhorn Creek ≃ 218 38.13 N 84.48 W
North Elm Creek ≃ 222 30.53 N 97.00 W
North English 190 41.30 N 92.04 W
Northern □⁴, Ghana 150 9.30 N 1.00 W
Northern □⁴, Malaŵi 154 11.00 S 34.00 E
Northern □⁴, S.L. 150 9.15 N 11.45 W
Northern □⁴, Zam. 154 11.00 S 31.00 E
Northern □⁵, Pap. N. Gui. 164 9.00 S 148.30 E
Northern □⁵, Ug. 154 2.50 N 32.45 E
Northern Arm 186 49.10 N 55.23 W
Northern Cheyenne Indian Reservation ✦⁴ 202 45.31 N 106.45 W
Northern Circārs ⩘² 122 18.00 N 83.15 E
Northern Cook Islands II 14 10.00 S 161.00 W
Northern Division □⁵ 175g 16.30 S 179.30 E
Northern Dvina → Severnaja Dvina ≃ 24 64.32 N 40.30 E
Northern Indian Lake @ 176 57.20 N 97.20 W
Northern Ireland □⁸ 48 54.40 N 6.45 W
Northern Light Lake @ 190 48.15 N 90.38 W
Northern Mariana Islands □² 14 16.00 N 149.00 E
Northern Samar □⁴ 116 12.30 N 124.30 E
Northern Territory □⁸ 160 20.00 S 134.00 E
North Esk ≃, Scot., U.K. 46 56.44 N 2.28 W
North Esk ≃, Scot., U.K. 46 55.54 N 3.04 W
North Essendon 274b 37.45 S 144.54 E
North Evans 210 42.42 N 78.56 W
Northey Island I 260 51.44 N 0.43 E
North Fabius ≃ 194 39.54 N 91.30 W
North Fairfield 214 41.06 N 82.36 W
North Fair Oaks 282 37.28 N 122.12 W
North Falmouth 207 41.38 N 70.37 W
North Ferriby 44 53.43 N 0.30 W
Northfield, B.C., Can. 224 49.11 N 123.59 W
Northfield, Ct., U.S. 207 41.41 N 73.06 W
Northfield, Il., U.S. 278 42.05 N 87.46 W
Northfield, Ma., U.S. 207 42.41 N 72.27 W
Northfield, Mn., U.S. 190 44.27 N 93.09 W
Northfield, N.J., U.S. 208 39.22 N 74.33 W
Northfield, Oh., U.S. 214 41.20 N 81.32 W
Northfield, Vt., U.S. 188 44.09 N 72.39 W
Northfield Airport ✈ 279a 41.17 N 81.31 W
Northfield Center 279a 41.19 N 81.32 W
Northfield Park Race Track ◆ 279a 41.21 N 81.31 W
Northfield Village 279a 41.21 N 81.31 W
Northfield Woods 278 42.05 N 87.52 W
North Fiji Basin ✦¹ 14 16.00 S 174.00 E
North Fillmore 228 34.24 N 118.56 W
North Fitzroy 274b 37.47 S 144.59 E
Northfleet 42 51.27 N 0.21 E
North Flinders Range ⩘ 166 31.00 S 139.00 E
North Fond du Lac 190 43.48 N 88.29 W
Northford 207 41.23 N 72.47 W
North Foreland ▸ 42 51.23 N 1.27 E
North Fork 226 37.13 N 119.30 W
North Fork ≃ 194 36.13 N 92.17 W
North Fork Lake @¹ 226 38.56 N 121.00 W
North Fork Reservoir @¹ 224 45.13 N 122.15 W
North Fork Village 218 39.21 N 83.02 W
North Fort Myers 220 26.40 N 81.52 W
North Freedom 190 43.27 N 89.52 W
North Frisian Islands II 24 54.50 N 8.12 E
Northgate 216 43.01 N 85.36 W
Northgate ✦⁹ 282 38.00 N 122.33 W
North Georgetown 214 40.51 N 80.59 W
North Glanford 212 43.11 N 79.54 W
North Glen Ellyn 278 41.54 N 88.04 W
Northglenn 200 39.53 N 104.59 W
North Gower 212 45.08 N 75.43 W
North Grafton 207 42.14 N 71.42 W
North Granby 207 41.59 N 72.49 W
North Grand Island Bridge ✦⁵ 284a 43.04 N 78.59 W
North Great River 276 40.44 N 73.10 W
North Greece 212 43.15 N 77.44 W
North Grosvenordale 207 41.59 N 71.53 W
North Grove 216 40.37 N 85.58 W
North Gulfport 194 30.24 N 89.06 W
North Hadley 207 42.23 N 72.36 W
North Haledon 276 40.57 N 74.11 W
North Hampton 218 39.59 N 83.56 W
North Hanover 283 42.08 N 70.52 W
North Harbour ⊂ 269f 14.36 N 120.57 E
North Harbour ⊂ 274a 33.49 S 151.17 E
North Haven 207 41.23 N 72.51 W
North Head ▸, Austl. 274a 33.49 S 151.18 E
North Head ▸, N.Z. 172 36.25 S 174.03 E
North Henderson 192 36.21 N 78.22 W
North Henik Lake @ 176 61.45 N 97.40 W
North Hero 188 44.49 N 73.17 W
North Highlands 226 38.41 N 121.22 W
North Hill 42 50.34 N 4.25 W
North Hills, De., U.S. 285 39.46 N 75.30 W
North Hills, Il., U.S. 278 42.18 N 88.01 W
North Hills, N.Y., U.S. 276 40.47 N 73.41 W
North Hinksey 42 51.45 N 1.16 W
North Hogan Creek ≃ 218 39.03 N 84.54 W
North Hollywood ✦⁸ 280 34.10 N 118.23 W
North Holmwood 260 51.13 N 0.20 W
North Honcut Creek ≃ 226 39.19 N 121.36 W
North Hoosick 210 42.56 N 73.21 W
North Hornell 210 42.21 N 77.40 W
North Horr 154 3.19 N 37.04 E
North Houston 222 29.54 N 95.31 W
Northiam 42 50.59 N 0.36 E
North Industry 214 40.44 N 81.22 W
North Irwin 279b 40.20 N 79.43 W
North Island I, India 122 10.08 N 72.20 E
North Island I, Kenya 154 4.04 N 36.03 E
North Island I, N.Z. 172 39.00 S 176.00 E
North Island Naval Air Station ✈ 228 32.42 N 117.12 W
North Islet I 116 8.56 N 120.02 E
North Jackson 214 41.06 N 80.52 W
North Java 210 42.41 N 78.20 W
North Judson 216 41.12 N 86.46 W
North Kenai 180 60.44 N 151.19 W
North Kingstown 207 41.38 N 71.25 W
North Kingsville 214 41.54 N 80.42 W
North Knife Lake @ 176 58.05 N 97.05 W
North Knob ⋏ 210 41.43 N 75.33 W
North Korea → Korea, North □¹ 98 40.00 N 127.00 E
North La Junta 198 37.59 N 103.31 W
North Lake 210 43.09 N 88.22 W
North Lake @, N.Y., U.S. 276 41.09 N 73.41 W
North Lake @, Tx., U.S. 222 32.57 N 96.58 W
North Lakhimpur 120 27.14 N 94.07 E
Northland ✦⁹ 281 42.27 N 83.13 W
North Landing ≃ 208 36.31 N 76.01 W
North Laramie ≃ 198 42.08 N 104.56 W
North Las Vegas 204 36.11 N 115.07 W
North La Veta Pass ⋊ 200 37.37 N 105.11 W
North Lawrence 214 40.51 N 81.38 W
Northleach 42 51.51 N 1.50 W
North Lewisburg 218 40.13 N 83.33 W
North Liberty 216 41.32 N 86.25 W
North Lima 214 40.56 N 80.39 W
North Lindenhurst 276 40.42 N 73.22 W
North Line Island I 276 40.38 N 73.29 W
Northline Terrace 222 29.55 N 95.25 W
North Little Rock 194 34.46 N 92.16 W
North Llano ≃ 196 30.30 N 99.46 W
North Logan 202 41.46 N 111.48 W
North Loma Linda 228 34.02 N 117.05 W
North Loon Mountain ⋏ 202 45.07 N 115.52 W
North Loup 198 41.29 N 98.46 W
North Loup ≃ 198 41.17 N 98.23 W
North Luangwa National Park ◆ 154 11.50 S 32.15 E
North Luconia Shoals ✦² 108 5.40 N 112.35 E
North Macmillan ≃ 180 63.03 N 133.18 W
North Madison 214 41.48 N 81.03 W
North Magnetic Pole ◆ 16 77.19 N 101.49 W
North Malosmadulu Atoll I¹ 122 5.35 N 72.55 E
North Mamm Peak ⋏ 200 39.23 N 107.52 W
North Manchester 216 41.00 N 85.46 W
North Manitou Island I 190 45.06 N 86.01 W
North Mankato 190 44.10 N 94.02 W
North Manly 274a 33.46 S 151.16 E
North Maroota 170 33.29 S 150.56 E
North Marshfield 283 42.08 N 70.46 W
North Marysville 224 48.07 N 122.09 W
North Massapequa 276 40.42 N 73.27 W
Northmead, Austl. 274a 33.47 S 151.00 E
Northmead, S. Afr. 273d 26.10 S 28.20 E
North Merrick 276 40.41 N 73.33 W
North Miami 220 25.53 N 80.11 W
North Miami Beach 220 25.55 N 80.09 W
North Middleboro 207 41.56 N 70.58 W
North Milk ≃ 202 49.08 N 112.23 W
North Mokelumne ≃ 226 38.08 N 121.35 W
North Moose Lake @ 184 54.08 N 100.13 W
North Moreau Creek ≃ 194 38.30 N 92.18 W
North Muskegon 216 43.15 N 86.16 W
North Myrtle Beach 192 33.49 N 78.40 W
North Nahanni ≃ 180 62.05 N 124.30 W
North Naples 220 26.13 N 81.47 W
North Narrabeen 274a 33.42 S 151.18 E
North Nemah ≃ 224 46.30 N 123.53 W
North New Hyde Park 276 40.44 N 73.41 W
North New River Canal ≅ 220 26.05 N 80.12 W
North Newton 198 38.04 N 97.21 W
North Niles 216 41.52 N 86.15 W
North Norwich 210 42.37 N 75.31 W
North Oaks 222 30.22 N 97.41 W
North Ockendon ✦⁸ 260 51.32 N 0.18 E
North Ogden 200 41.18 N 111.57 W
North Olmsted 214 41.24 N 81.55 W
Northolt Aerodrome ✈ 260 51.33 N 0.23 W
Northome 190 47.52 N 94.16 W
Northop 262 53.12 N 3.08 W
North Ore Creek ≃ 281 42.43 N 83.47 W
North Orwell 210 41.55 N 76.19 W
North Ossetia → Severnaja Osetija □³ 84 43.00 N 44.15 E
Northowram 262 53.44 N 1.50 W
North Oxford 207 42.09 N 71.52 W
North Palisade ⋏ 204 37.06 N 118.31 W
North Palm Beach 220 26.49 N 80.04 W
North Para ≃ 168b 34.36 S 138.45 E
North Park ✦⁸ 278 41.59 N 87.43 W
North Park ◆ 279b 40.36 N 80.00 W
North Park Lake @ 279b 40.36 N 80.00 W
North Parramatta 274a 33.48 S 151.00 E
North Pass 𝔲 175c 7.41 N 151.48 E
North Patchogue 276 40.47 N 73.00 W
North Peak ⋏, Ak., U.S. 180 62.34 N 162.23 W
North Peak ⋏, Ca., U.S. 282 37.33 N 122.28 W
North Pease ≃ 196 34.15 N 100.07 W
North Pelham, N.H., U.S. 283 42.46 N 71.21 W
North Pelham, N.Y., U.S. 276 40.55 N 73.48 W
North Pembroke 207 42.05 N 70.47 W
North Pender Island I 224 48.49 N 123.17 W
North Perry 214 41.47 N 81.07 W
North Petherton 42 51.06 N 3.01 W
North Philadelphia ✦⁸ 285 39.58 N 75.09 W
North Philadelphia Airport ✈ 285 40.05 N 75.01 W
North Pine ≃ 171a 27.17 S 153.01 E
North Pine Grove 214 41.24 N 79.13 W
North Piney Creek ≃ 200 42.31 N 110.05 W
North Pitcher 210 42.37 N 75.49 W
North Plainfield 210 40.37 N 74.25 W
North Plains 224 45.35 N 122.59 W
North Plains ≃ 200 34.40 N 108.15 W
North Platte 198 41.07 N 100.45 W
North Platte ≃ 178 41.07 N 100.42 W
North Pleasureville 218 38.22 N 85.07 W
North Plympton 283 41.59 N 70.48 W
North Point, H.K. 271d 22.17 N 114.12 E
Northpoint, Pa., U.S. 214 40.54 N 79.08 W
North Point ▸, Barb. 241g 13.20 N 59.36 W
North Point ▸, Md., U.S. 284b 39.12 N 76.27 W
North Point ▸, Mi., U.S. 190 45.02 N 83.16 W
North Pole 180 64.45 N 147.21 W
North Pole ◆ 16 90.00 N 0.00
Northport, Al., U.S. 194 33.13 N 87.34 W
North Port, Fl., U.S. 220 27.03 N 82.15 W
Northport, Mi., U.S. 190 45.07 N 85.37 W
Northport, N.Y., U.S. 210 40.53 N 73.20 W
Northport, Wa., U.S. 202 48.54 N 117.46 W
North Portal 184 49.00 N 102.33 W
Northport Bay ⊂ 276 40.55 N 73.23 W
Northport Harbor ⊂ 276 40.53 N 73.22 W
North Powder 202 45.01 N 117.55 W
North Pownal 207 42.47 N 73.15 W
North Prairie 216 42.56 N 88.24 W
North Providence 207 41.50 N 71.25 W
North Puyallup 224 47.12 N 122.17 W
North Queensferry 46 56.01 N 3.25 W
North Quincy 219 39.58 N 91.24 W
North Raccoon ≃ 198 41.50 N 94.08 W
North Raisin ≃ 206 45.09 N 74.43 W
North Ram ≃ 182 52.16 N 115.38 W
North Randall 279a 41.27 N 81.31 W
North Reading 207 42.34 N 71.04 W
North Reservoir @¹ 283 42.28 N 71.07 W
North Richland Hills 222 32.50 N 97.13 W
North Richmond 282 37.57 N 122.22 W
Northridge, Oh., U.S. 218 39.59 N 83.46 W
Northridge, Oh., U.S. 218 39.48 N 84.11 W
Northridge ✦⁸ 280 34.14 N 118.33 W
Northridge Fashion Center ✦⁹ 280 34.13 N 118.33 W
North Ridge Village 218 39.57 N 86.09 W
North Ridgeville 214 41.23 N 82.01 W
North Rim 200 36.12 N 112.03 W
North River ⊂ 208 37.25 N 76.15 W
North Riverside 278 41.50 N 87.49 W
North Riverside Park Mall ✦⁹ 278 41.51 N 87.49 W
North Robinson 214 40.48 N 82.51 W
North Rocks 274a 33.46 S 151.02 E
North Ronaldsay I 46 59.22 N 2.26 W
North Ronaldsay Firth 𝔲 46 59.20 N 2.25 W
North Rose 210 43.11 N 76.53 W
North Royalton 214 41.18 N 81.43 W
North Rustico 186 46.27 N 63.19 W
North Ryde 274a 33.48 S 151.07 E
North Salem 214 40.09 N 81.33 W
North Salt Lake 200 40.50 N 111.54 W
North San Juan 226 39.22 N 121.06 W
North Santiam ≃ 224 44.41 N 123.00 W
North Saskatchewan ≃ 176 53.15 N 105.05 W
North Saugeen ≃ 212 44.19 N 81.17 W
North Scituate, Ma., U.S. 207 42.13 N 70.47 W
North Scituate, R.I., U.S. 207 41.49 N 71.35 W
North Sea ⵖ² 22 56.00 N 3.00 E
North Seaton Colliery 44 55.11 N 1.32 W
North Sentinel Island I 110 11.33 N 92.15 E
North Shafter 226 35.31 N 119.13 W
North Shields 44 55.01 N 1.27 W
Norths Highland ⩘¹ 9 66.40 S 126.00 E
North Shoal Lake @ 184 50.29 N 97.40 W
North Shore 216 42.16 N 88.23 W
Northshore ✦⁸ 283 42.32 N 70.57 W
North Shore Channel ≅ 278 42.05 N 87.41 W
North Shores 216 41.50 N 83.25 W
North Shoshone Peak ⋏ 204 39.09 N 117.29 W
North Siberian Lowland → Severo-Sibirskaja nizmennost' ≃ 74 73.00 N 100.00 E
Northside 174h 2.47 S 171.43 W
North Singa 126 23.16 N 89.30 E
North Sioux City 198 42.31 N 96.28 W
North Skunk ≃ 190 41.15 N 92.02 W
North Somercotes 44 53.28 N 0.08 E
North Sound 𝔲, Antig. 240c 17.07 N 61.45 W
North Sound 𝔲, Ire. 48 53.11 N 9.43 W
North Sound 𝔲, Scot., U.K. 46 59.18 N 2.46 W
North Spicer Island I 176 68.30 N 78.55 W
North Spirit Lake @ 184 52.30 N 92.53 W
North Spot I 236 16.15 N 88.11 W
North Springfield, Pa., U.S. 214 41.59 N 80.26 W
North Springfield, Va., U.S. 284c 38.48 N 77.12 W
North Stamford Reservoir @¹ 276 41.08 N 73.32 W
North Star, De., U.S. 285 39.46 N 75.43 W
North Star, Oh., U.S. 216 40.19 N 84.34 W
North Sterling Reservoir @¹ 198 40.47 N 103.17 W
North Stradbroke Island I 171a 27.35 S 153.28 E
North Sudbury 283 42.24 N 71.24 W
North Sulphur ≃ 196 33.23 N 95.18 W
North Sunday Creek ≃ 202 46.27 N 105.54 W
North Sunderland 44 55.34 N 1.39 W
North Swansea 207 41.46 N 71.15 W
North Sydenham ≃ 214 42.35 N 82.23 W
North Sydney, Austl. 274a 33.50 S 151.13 E
North Sydney, N.S., Can. 186 46.13 N 60.15 W
North Syracuse 210 43.08 N 76.07 W
North Tamborine 171a 27.56 S 153.11 E
North Taranaki Bight ⊂³ 172 38.42 S 174.15 E
North Tarrytown 276 41.05 N 73.51 W
North Tawton 42 50.48 N 3.53 W
North Tea Lake @ 190 45.56 N 79.03 W
North Terre Haute 194 39.31 N 87.21 W
North Tewksbury 283 42.38 N 71.14 W
North Thames ≃ 212 42.59 N 81.16 W
North Thompson ≃ 182 50.41 N 120.21 W
North Thoresby 44 53.28 N 0.03 W
North Tidworth 42 51.16 N 1.40 W
North Toe ≃ 192 36.00 N 82.16 W
North Tolsta 46 58.20 N 6.13 W
North Tonawanda 210 43.02 N 78.51 W
North Towanda 210 41.47 N 76.28 W
North Troy 206 44.59 N 72.24 W
North Truro 207 42.02 N 70.05 W
North Tule Draw V 196 34.30 N 101.36 W
North Tunica 194 34.42 N 90.23 W
North Turlock 226 37.31 N 120.51 W
North Turramurra 274a 33.43 S 151.09 E
North Twin Lake @ 186 49.16 N 55.56 W
North Tyne ≃ 44 54.59 N 2.08 W
North Ubian Island I 116 6.09 N 120.27 E
North Uist I 46 57.36 N 7.18 W
Northumberland 210 40.53 N 76.47 W
Northumberland □⁶, On., Can. 212 44.10 N 78.00 W
Northumberland □⁶, Eng., U.K. 44 55.15 N 2.05 W
Northumberland □⁶, Pa., U.S. 210 40.49 N 76.39 W
Northumberland □⁶, Va., U.S. 208 37.50 N 76.25 W
Northumberland Isles II 166 21.40 S 150.00 E
Northumberland National Park ◆ 44 55.15 N 2.20 W
Northumberland Strait 𝔲 186 46.00 N 63.30 W
North Umpqua ≃ 202 43.16 N 123.27 W
North Uxbridge 207 42.05 N 71.38 W
Northvale 276 41.00 N 73.57 W
North Valley Hills ⩘² 285 40.02 N 75.40 W
North Valley Stream 276 40.41 N 73.42 W
North Vancouver 224 49.19 N 123.04 W
North Vandergrift 279b 40.36 N 79.34 W
North Vernon 218 39.00 N 85.37 W
North Versailles 279b 40.22 N 79.48 W
North Vietnam → Vietnam □¹ 108 16.00 N 108.00 E
Northville, Mi., U.S. 216 42.25 N 83.29 W
Northville, N.Y., U.S. 210 43.13 N 74.10 W
Northville Downs ◆ 281 42.26 N 83.29 W
Northvue 214 40.54 N 79.56 W
North Wabasca Lake @ 182 56.00 N 113.55 W
North Wales 208 40.12 N 75.16 W
Northwall 46 59.16 N 2.17 W
North Walsham 42 52.50 N 1.24 E
North Wantagh 276 40.41 N 73.30 W
North Warren 214 41.52 N 79.09 W
North Washington, Pa., U.S. 214 41.03 N 79.49 W
North Washington, Pa., U.S. 279b 40.32 N 79.36 W
North Watuppa Pond @ 207 41.42 N 71.06 W
Northway 180 62.58 N 141.56 W
North Weald Bassett 42 51.43 N 0.10 E
North Webster 216 41.19 N 85.41 W
North Weissport 210 40.50 N 75.41 W
Northwest ≃ 208 36.31 N 76.05 W
North West Cape ▸, Austl. 162 21.45 S 114.10 E
Northwest Cape ▸, Ak., U.S. 180 63.46 N 171.45 W
Northwest Cape ▸, Fl., U.S. 220 25.13 N 81.11 W
North Westchester 207 41.34 N 72.24 W
North Western 210 43.20 N 75.22 W
North-Western □⁴ 154 13.00 S 25.00 E
Northwestern University ⅴ², Il., U.S. 278 42.04 N 87.40 W
Northwestern University (Chicago Campus) ⅴ², Il., U.S. 278 41.54 N 87.37 W
Northwest Frontier □⁴ 120 34.30 N 72.00 E
Northwest Gander ≃ 186 48.50 N 55.00 W
Northwest Harbor ⊂ 284b 39.16 N 76.35 W
Northwest Head ▸ 116 10.08 N 118.45 E
Northwest Miramichi ≃ 186 46.58 N 65.35 W
Northwest Pacific Basin ✦¹ 6 40.00 N 155.00 E
North West Point ▸ 174o 2.02 N 157.29 W
Northwest Providence Channel 𝔲 238 26.10 N 78.20 W
North West River 176 53.32 N 60.08 W
Northwest Territories □⁴ 176 70.00 N 100.00 W
North Weymouth 283 42.15 N 70.57 W
Northwich 44 53.16 N 2.32 W
North Wichita ≃ 196 33.43 N 99.29 W
North Wilbraham 207 42.09 N 72.25 W
North Wildwood 208 39.00 N 74.47 W
North Wilkesboro 192 36.09 N 81.08 W
North Willow Creek ≃ 202 46.51 N 107.54 W
North Wilmington 283 42.34 N 71.09 W
North Windham, Ct., U.S. 207 41.44 N 72.09 W
North Windham, Me., U.S. 188 43.50 N 70.26 W
Northwold 42 52.33 N 0.35 E
Northwood, Eng., U.K. 42 50.44 N 1.19 W
Northwood, Ia., U.S. 190 43.26 N 93.13 W
Northwood, Mi., U.S. 216 42.19 N 85.38 W
Northwood, N.D., U.S. 198 47.44 N 97.33 W
Northwood, Oh., U.S. 214 41.36 N 83.28 W
Northwood ✦⁸ 260 51.37 N 0.25 W
North Woodslee 281 42.13 N 82.43 W
Northwood Village 284c 39.02 N 77.01 W
North Yamhill ≃ 224 45.13 N 123.08 W
North Yelta 168b 34.03 S 137.37 E
North York 212 43.46 N 79.25 W
North York Moors ⩘² 44 54.24 N 0.53 W
North York Moors National Park ◆ 44 54.23 N 0.50 W
North Yorkshire □⁶ 44 54.15 N 1.30 W
North Yuba ≃ 226 39.22 N 121.08 W
North Zulch 222 30.55 N 96.07 W
Norton, N.B., Can. 186 45.38 N 65.42 W
Norton, Eng., U.K. 44 54.09 N 0.47 W
Norton, Eng., U.K. 262 53.20 N 2.40 W
Norton, Ks., U.S. 198 39.50 N 99.53 W
Norton, Ma., U.S. 207 41.58 N 71.11 W
Norton, Oh., U.S. 214 41.01 N 81.39 W
Norton, Vt., U.S. 206 45.00 N 71.47 W
Norton, Va., U.S. 192 36.56 N 82.37 W
Norton, Zimb. 154 17.53 S 30.42 E
Norton Air Force Base ■ 228 34.06 N 117.14 W
Norton Basin ⊂ 276 40.36 N 73.47 W
Norton Bay ⊂ 180 64.45 N 161.15 W
Norton Creek ≃ 281 42.34 N 83.34 W
Norton Fitzwarren 42 51.02 N 3.09 W
Norton Grove 207 42.00 N 71.12 W
Norton Heath 260 51.43 N 0.19 E
Norton Hill 210 42.25 N 74.04 W
Norton Pond @ 206 44.56 N 71.51 W
Norton Reservoir @¹ 283 41.59 N 71.12 W
Norton Shores 216 43.10 N 86.15 W
Norton Sound 𝔲 180 63.50 N 164.00 W
Nortonville, On., Can. 275b 43.43 N 79.44 W
Nortonville, Ks., U.S. 198 39.25 N 95.20 W
Nortorf, Dtsch. 30 54.10 N 9.50 E
Nortorf, Dtsch. 52 53.55 N 9.16 E
Nort-sur-Erdre 32 47.26 N 1.30 W
Noruega, Mar de → Norwegian Sea ⵖ² 10 70.00 N 2.00 E
Noruega → Norway □¹ 24 62.00 N 10.00 E
Norumbega Reservoir @¹ 283 42.20 N 71.18 W
Nørup 41 55.43 N 9.19 E
Norval 212 43.39 N 79.51 W
Norvalspont 158 30.38 S 25.27 E
Norvège → Norway □¹ 24 62.00 N 10.00 E
Norvegia, Cape ▸ 9 71.25 S 12.18 W
Norvell 216 42.10 N 84.11 W
Norvelt 214 40.12 N 79.32 W
Norvin Green State Forest ◆ 276 41.03 N 74.20 W
Norwalk, Ca., U.S. 228 33.54 N 118.04 W
Norwalk, Ct., U.S. 207 41.07 N 73.24 W
Norwalk, Ia., U.S. 190 41.28 N 93.40 W
Norwalk, Oh., U.S. 214 41.14 N 82.36 W
Norwalk ≃ 207 41.06 N 73.25 W
Norwalk Harbor ⊂ 207 41.06 N 73.24 W
Norwalk Islands II 276 41.03 N 73.25 W
Norway, In., U.S. 216 40.47 N 86.46 W
Norway, Ia., U.S. 190 41.54 N 91.55 W
Norway, Me., U.S. 188 44.12 N 70.32 W
Norway, Mi., U.S. 190 45.47 N 87.54 W
Norway (Norge) □¹, Europe 22 62.00 N 10.00 E
Norway (Norge) □¹, Europe 24 62.00 N 10.00 E
Norway Bay ⊂ 176 71.08 N 104.35 W
Norway House 184 53.59 N 97.50 W
Norway Lake @ 212 45.20 N 76.43 W
Norwegen → Norway □¹ 24 62.00 N 10.00 E
Norwegian Basin ✦¹ 10 68.00 N 2.00 W
Norwegian Sea ⵖ² 10 70.00 N 2.00 E
Norwegian Trench ✦¹ 10 59.00 N 4.30 E
Norwell 283 42.09 N 70.47 W
Norwich, On., Can. 212 42.59 N 80.36 W
Norwich, Eng., U.K. 42 52.38 N 1.18 E
Norwich, Ct., U.S. 207 41.32 N 72.05 W
Norwich, Ks., U.S. 198 37.27 N 97.50 W
Norwich, N.Y., U.S. 210 42.31 N 75.31 W
Norwich Airport ✈ 42 52.41 N 1.15 E
Norwin Heights 279b 40.20 N 79.44 W
Norwood, On., Can. 212 44.23 N 77.59 W
Norwood, Co., U.S. 200 38.07 N 108.17 W
Norwood, Ma., U.S. 207 42.11 N 71.12 W
Norwood, Mn., U.S. 190 44.46 N 93.55 W
Norwood, N.J., U.S. 276 40.59 N 73.57 W
Norwood, N.Y., U.S. 188 44.45 N 74.59 W
Norwood, N.C., U.S. 192 35.13 N 80.07 W
Norwood, Oh., U.S. 218 39.10 N 84.27 W
Norwood, Pa., U.S. 285 39.53 N 75.17 W
Norwood ✦⁸ 273d 26.10 S 28.04 E
Norwood Memorial Airport ✈ 283 42.11 N 71.10 W
Norwood Park ✦⁸ 278 41.59 N 87.48 W
Norwood Pond @ 283 42.35 N 70.52 W
Norwoodville 190 41.39 N 93.33 W
Noryang 98 34.56 N 127.52 E
Nosaka 94 35.39 N 140.34 E
Nosappu-misaki ▸ 92a 43.23 N 145.49 E
Nosate 266b 45.33 N 8.43 E
Nosbonsing, Lake @ 190 46.12 N 79.13 W
Nose 96 34.58 N 135.24 E
Nose ✦⁸ 270 34.49 N 135.09 E
Nose Creek ≃ 182 54.52 N 119.38 W
Noshiro 92 40.12 N 140.02 E
Noska ≃ 86 58.53 N 68.40 E
Nosop (Nossob) ≃ 156 26.55 S 20.37 E
Nosova 86 59.30 N 63.13 E
Nosovaja, Ross. 24 68.15 N 54.35 E
Nosovaja, Ross. 80 57.15 N 45.35 E
Nosovaja ≃ 78 50.55 N 31.35 E
Nosovo, Ross. 76 57.07 N 27.50 E
Nosovo, Ross. 83 47.16 N 38.40 E
Nosovščina 24 62.56 N 37.03 E
Nosratābād 128 29.54 N 59.59 E
Noss, Isle of I 46a 60.09 N 1.01 W
Nossa Senhora da Aparecida 256 22.02 S 42.48 W
Nossa Senhora das Dores 250 10.29 S 37.13 W
Nossa Senhora do Amparo 256 22.22 S 44.05 W
Nossa Senhora do Livramento 248 15.48 S 56.22 W
Nossa Senhora do Ó ✦⁸ 287b 23.30 S 46.41 W
Nossebro 26 58.11 N 12.43 E
Nossen 54 51.03 N 13.17 E
Nossentiner Heide ⩘ 54 53.35 N 12.25 E
Noss Head ▸ 46 58.28 N 3.04 W
Nossob 156 22.18 S 17.10 E
Nossob (Nosop) ≃ 156 26.55 S 20.37 E
Nossombougou 150 13.06 N 7.56 W
Nošul' 24 60.09 N 49.28 E
Nosy Varika 157b 20.35 S 48.32 E
Notasulga 194 32.33 N 85.40 W
Notch Cliff 284b 39.27 N 76.31 W
Notch Hill 182 50.52 N 119.28 W
Notch Peak ⋏ 200 39.08 N 113.24 W
Noteć ≃ 30 52.44 N 15.26 E
Notigi Lake @ 184 55.57 N 99.18 W
Notikewin ≃ 176 57.15 N 117.08 W
Noto, It. 70 36.53 N 15.04 E
Noto, Nihon 92 37.18 N 137.09 E
Noto, Golfo di ⊂ 70 36.50 N 15.12 E
Noto, Val di ⩘¹ 70 37.05 N 14.35 E
Noto Antica ⊥ 70 36.59 N 15.02 E
Notodden 26 59.34 N 9.17 E
Notogawa 94 35.10 N 136.10 E
Noto-hantō ▸¹ 92 37.20 N 137.00 E
Noto-hantō-kokutei-kōen ◆ 94 37.10 N 136.50 E
Noto-jima 94 37.08 N 137.00 E
Noto-jima I 94 37.07 N 137.00 E
Nōtori-dake ⋏ 94 35.37 N 138.15 E
Notoro-ko @ 92a 44.05 N 144.10 E
Notozero, ozero @ 24 66.28 N 32.05 E
Notre-Dame 186 46.19 N 64.43 W
Notre-Dame ⅴ¹ 261 48.51 N 2.21 E
Notre-Dame, Bois ◆ 261 48.45 N 2.35 E
Notre-Dame, Monts ⩘ 186 48.10 N 68.00 W
Notre-Dame, Ruisseau ≃ 275a 45.41 N 73.26 W
Notre Dame Bay ⊂ 186 49.45 N 55.15 W
Notre-Dame-de-Bellecombe 62 45.48 N 6.31 E
Notre-Dame-de-Lorette ⅴ¹ 50 50.25 N 2.42 E
Notre-Dame-de-Lourdes 184 49.32 N 98.33 W
Notre-Dame-de-Pierreville 206 46.06 N 72.53 W
Notre-Dame-des-Victoires ✦⁸ 275a 45.35 N 73.34 W
Notre-Dame-du-Haut ⅴ¹ 58 47.43 N 6.37 E
Notre-Dame-du-Laus 188 46.05 N 75.37 W
Notre-Dame-du-Nord 190 47.36 N 79.30 W
Notrees 196 31.55 N 102.45 W
Notreure ≃ 50 47.41 N 2.36 E
Notsu 96 33.02 N 131.42 E
Notsuharu 96 33.09 N 131.32 E
Nottawa 216 41.55 N 85.27 W
Nottawa Creek ≃ 216 42.01 N 85.24 W
Nottawasaga ≃ 212 44.32 N 80.01 W
Nottawasaga Bay ⊂ 212 44.35 N 80.15 W
Nottaway ≃ 176 51.22 N 79.55 W
Nottingham, Eng., U.K. 42 52.58 N 1.10 W
Nottingham, Pa., U.S. 208 39.45 N 76.01 W
Nottingham, Pa., U.S. 285 40.07 N 74.58 W
Nottingham Island I 176 63.20 N 77.55 W
Nottingham Park 278 41.46 N 87.48 W
Nottingham Road 158 29.22 S 30.02 E
Nottinghamshire □⁶ 44 53.00 N 1.00 W
Notting Hill 274b 37.54 S 145.08 E
Nottleben 54 50.58 N 10.50 E
Nottoway 192 37.08 N 78.05 W
Nottoway ≃ 192 36.33 N 76.55 W
Nottuln 52 51.55 N 7.22 E
Notukeu Creek ≃ 184 49.55 N 106.30 W
Nouâdhibou 148 20.54 N 17.04 W
Nouâdhibou, Râs ▸ 148 20.46 N 17.03 W
Nouakchott 150 18.06 N 15.57 W
Nouâmghâr 150 19.22 N 16.31 W
Nouan-le-Fuzelier 50 47.32 N 2.02 E
Nouans-les-Fontaines 50 47.08 N 1.18 E
Nouméa 175f 22.16 S 166.27 E
Noun ≃ 152 4.55 N 11.06 E
Nouna 150 12.44 N 3.52 W
Nounsley 260 51.46 N 0.36 E
Noupoort 158 31.10 S 24.57 E
Nous 158 28.44 S 19.52 E
Nouveau Brunswick → New Brunswick □⁴ 186 46.30 N 66.15 W
Nouveau Mexique → New Mexico □³ 178 34.30 N 106.00 W
Nouveau-Québec, Cratère du ⊜⁶ 176 61.17 N 73.40 W
Nouvelle 186 48.08 N 66.19 W
Nouvelle ≃ 186 48.07 N 66.18 W
Nouvelle-Calédonie I (New Caledonia) 175f 21.30 S 165.30 E
Nouvelle-Calédonie → New Caledonia □² 175f 21.30 S 165.30 E
Nouvelle Écosse → Nova Scotia □⁴ 186 45.00 N 63.00 W
Nouvelle-France, Cap de ▸ 176 62.27 N 73.42 W
Nouvelle Galles du Sud → New South Wales □³ 166 33.00 S 146.00 E
Nouvelle-Orléans → New Orleans 194 29.58 N 90.07 W
Nouvelles-Hébrides → Vanuatu □¹ 175f 16.00 S 167.00 E
Nouvelle Zélande → New Zealand □¹ 172 41.00 S 174.00 E
Nouvelle Zemble → Novaja Zemľa II 72 74.00 N 57.00 E
Nouvion-en-Ponthieu 50 50.12 N 1.47 E
Nouvion-sur-Meuse 56 49.42 N 4.48 E
Nouzonville 56 49.49 N 4.45 E
Nova, Magy. 61 46.41 N 16.41 E
Nova, Oh., U.S. 214 41.02 N 82.18 W
Nova América 255 15.01 S 49.56 W
Nova Andradina 255 22.10 S 53.15 W
Novabad, Taj. 85 39.01 N 70.09 E
Novabad, Taj. 85 38.37 N 68.45 E
Nová Baňa 30 48.26 N 18.39 E
Nová Bystřice 61 49.01 N 15.06 E
Nova Cachoeirinha ✦⁸ 287b 23.28 S 46.40 W
Nova Caipemba 152 7.26 S 14.38 E
Novacella ⅴ¹ 64 46.44 N 11.39 E
Nova Era 255 19.45 S 43.03 W
Nova Esperança 255 23.08 S 52.13 W
Novafeltria 66 43.53 N 12.17 E
Nova Friburgo 256 22.16 S 42.32 W
Nova Goa → Panaji 122 15.29 N 73.50 E
Nova Gorica 64 45.57 N 13.39 E
Nova Gradiška 36 45.16 N 17.23 E
Nova Granada 255 20.29 S 49.19 W
Nova Iguaçu 256 22.45 S 43.27 W
Nova Iguaçu □⁷ 287a 22.45 S 43.29 W
Novaja, Ross. 82 55.13 N 38.54 E
Novaja, Ross. 265b 55.48 N 38.03 E
Novaja ✦⁸ 265a 60.02 N 30.28 E
Novaja Astrachan' 83 49.07 N 38.36 E
Novaja Belaja 78 49.46 N 39.11 E
Novaja Belokoroviči 78 51.07 N 28.02 E
Novaja Binaradka 80 53.48 N 49.56 E
Novaja Borovaja 78 50.42 N 28.39 E
Novaja Čigla 78 51.13 N 40.28 E
Novaja Derevn'a, Ross. 82 54.01 N 38.53 E
Novaja Derevn'a, Ross. 88 57.15 N 103.08 E
Novaja Ivanovka 78 45.55 N 29.05 E
Novaja Janisol' 83 47.17 N 37.16 E
Novaja Kachovka 78 46.45 N 33.23 E
Novaja Kalitva 78 50.06 N 40.01 E
Novaja Kazanka 80 48.57 N 49.36 E
Novaja Kazmaska 80 57.29 N 53.31 E
Novaja Kruša 78 50.16 N 41.16 E
Novaja Ladoga 76 60.05 N 32.16 E
Novaja L'al'a 86 59.03 N 60.36 E
Novaja Majačka 78 46.36 N 33.14 E
Novaja Maluksa 76 59.39 N 31.21 E
Novaja Malykla 80 54.13 N 49.57 E
Novaja Mojgora 82 54.27 N 37.21 E
Novaja Odessa 78 47.19 N 31.47 E
Novaja Porubežka 80 51.45 N 49.40 E
Novaja Praga 78 48.33 N 32.54 E
Novaja Ropša 265a 59.45 N 29.53 E
Novaja Sibir', ostrov I 74 75.00 N 149.00 E
Novaja Sloboda 78 51.23 N 34.08 E
Novaja Slobodka 82 54.56 N 36.55 E
Novaja Šul'ba 86 50.33 N 81.20 E
Novaja Uda 88 54.07 N 103.53 E
Novaja Ušica 78 48.49 N 27.16 E
Novaja Usman' 78 51.37 N 39.24 E
Novaja Vodolaga 78 49.43 N 35.52 E
Novaja Zburjevka 78 46.28 N 32.24 E
Novaja Zemľa II 72 74.00 N 57.00 E

	English	Deutsch	Español	Français	Português
≃	River	Fluß	Río	Rivière	Rio
≅	Canal	Kanal	Canal	Canal	Canal
V	Waterfall, Rapids	Wasserfall, Stromschnellen	Cascada, Rápidos	Chute d'eau, Rapides	Cascata, Rápidos
𝔲	Strait	Meeresstraße	Estrecho	Détroit	Estreito
⊂	Bay, Gulf	Bucht, Golf	Bahía, Golfo	Baie, Golfe	Baía, Golfo
@	Lake, Lakes	See, Seen	Lago, Lagos	Lac, Lacs	Lago, Lagos
≋	Swamp	Sumpf	Pantano	Marais	Pântano
⌗	Ice Features, Glacier	Eis- und Gletscherformen	Accidentes Glaciales	Formes glaciaires	Acidentes glaciares
ⵖ	Other Hydrographic Features	Andere Hydrographische Objekte	Otros Elementos Hidrográficos	Autres données hydrographiques	Outros acidentes hidrográficos

	English	Deutsch	Español	Français	Português
✦	Submarine Features	Untermeerische Objekte	Accidentes Submarinos	Formes de relief sous-marin	Acidentes submarinos
□	Political Unit	Politische Einheit	Unidad Política	Entité politique	Unidade política
ⅴ	Cultural Institution	Kulturelle Institution	Institución Cultural	Institution culturelle	Instituição cultural
⊥	Historical Site	Historische Stätte	Sitio Histórico	Site historique	Sitio histórico
◆	Recreational Site	Erholungs- und Ferienort	Sitio de Recreo	Centre de loisirs	Area de Lazer
✈	Airport	Flughafen	Aeropuerto	Aéroport	Aeroporto
■	Military Installation	Militäranlage	Instalación Militar	Installation militaire	Instalação militar
✦	Miscellaneous	Verschiedenes	Misceláneo	Divers	Diversos

Name	Page	Lat.°′	Long.°′
Nováky	**30**	48.43 N	18.34 E
Nova Lamego	**150**	12.19 N	14.11 W
Novale (Rauth)	**64**	46.24 N	11.30 E
Novalesa	**62**	45.11 N	7.01 E
Novaliches Reservoir ⊜[1]	**269f**	14.43 N	121.05 E
Nova Lima	**255**	19.59 S	43.51 W
Nova Lisboa → Huambo	**152**	12.44 S	15.47 E
Nova Lusitânia	**156**	19.54 S	34.35 E
Nova Mambone	**156**	20.59 S	35.01 E
Nova Milanese	**266b**	45.35 N	9.12 E
Nova Nabúri	**154**	16.46 S	38.57 E
Nova Odessa	**256**	23.09 S	46.51 W
Nova Olinda	**250**	7.06 S	39.40 W
Nova Olinda do Norte	**246**	3.45 S	59.03 W
Nová Paka	**30**	50.29 N	15.31 E
Nova Ponente (Deutschnofen)	**64**	46.25 N	11.25 E
Nova Ponte	**255**	19.08 S	47.41 W
Nova Prata	**252**	28.47 S	51.36 W
Novar	**212**	45.27 N	79.15 W
Novara	**62**	45.28 N	8.38 E
Novara □[4]	**62**	45.40 N	8.30 E
Novara di Sicilia	**70**	38.01 N	15.08 E
Nová Role	**54**	50.15 N	12.47 E
Nova Roma	**255**	13.51 S	46.57 W
Nova Russas	**250**	4.42 S	40.34 W
Nova Scotia □[4], Can.	**176**	45.00 N	63.00 W
Nova Scotia □[4], Can.	**186**	45.00 N	63.00 W
Nova Siri	**68**	40.09 N	16.32 E
Nova Sofala	**156**	20.09 S	34.42 E
Nova Soure	**250**	11.14 S	38.29 W
Novate Mezzola	**58**	46.15 N	9.27 E
Novate Milanese	**266b**	45.32 N	9.08 E
Nova Timboteua	**250**	1.12 S	47.24 W
Novato	**226**	38.06 N	122.34 W
Novato Creek ≃	**282**	38.06 N	122.29 W
Nova Vandúzi	**156**	18.57 S	33.16 E
Nova Varoš	**38**	43.28 N	19.48 E
Nova Venécia	**255**	18.43 S	40.24 W
Nova Viçosa	**255**	17.53 S	39.22 W
Nova Vida	**248**	10.11 S	62.47 W
Nova Vida, Cachoeira L	**248**	9.25 S	63.36 W
Nova Zagora	**38**	42.29 N	26.01 E
Nove	**64**	45.43 N	11.40 E
Nové Hrady	**61**	48.47 N	14.37 E
Novelda	**34**	38.23 N	0.46 W
Novellara	**64**	44.51 N	10.44 E
Novelty	**219**	40.00 N	92.12 W
Nové Město	**30**	50.21 N	16.09 E
Nové Město nad Váhom	**30**	48.46 N	17.49 E
Nové Město na Moravě	**30**	49.34 N	16.04 E
Nové Mlýny, údolní nádrž ⊜[1]	**61**	48.54 N	16.34 E
Noventa di Piave	**64**	45.39 N	12.31 E
Noventa Padovana	**64**	45.24 N	11.58 E
Noventa Vicentina	**64**	45.17 N	11.32 E
Noves	**62**	43.52 N	4.54 E
Nové Sedlo	**54**	50.10 N	12.42 E
Nové Strašecí	**54**	50.07 N	13.53 E
Nové Údoli	**60**	48.48 N	13.48 E
Nové Zámky	**30**	47.59 N	18.11 E
Novgorod	**76**	58.31 N	31.17 E
Novgorodka	**78**	48.21 N	32.39 E
Novgorod Oblast' □[4]	**76**	58.15 N	33.00 E
Novgorod-Severskij	**78**	51.59 N	33.16 E
Novgorodskoje	**83**	48.20 N	37.50 E
Novi	**216**	42.28 N	83.28 W
Novi Bečej	**38**	45.36 N	20.08 E
Novi Beograd	**38**	44.49 N	20.27 E
Novice	**196**	31.59 N	99.37 W
Novičicha	**86**	52.13 N	81.24 E
Novi di Modena	**64**	44.54 N	10.54 E
Novigrad, Hrv.	**36**	45.19 N	13.34 E
Novigrad, Hrv.	**36**	44.11 N	15.33 E
Novikovo, Ross.	**86**	58.15 N	80.39 E
Novikovo, Ross.	**89**	46.23 N	143.20 E
Novi Ligure	**62**	44.46 N	8.47 E
Noville	**56**	50.40 N	5.23 E
Novi Lyon Drain ≊	**281**	42.30 N	83.38 W
Novinger	**194**	40.13 N	92.42 W
Novinka	**76**	59.49 N	33.20 E
Novion-Porcien	**50**	49.36 N	4.25 E
Novi Pazar, Blg.	**38**	43.21 N	27.12 E
Novi Pazar, Jugo.	**38**	43.08 N	20.31 E
Novi Sad	**38**	45.15 N	19.50 E
Novi Vinodolski	**36**	45.08 N	14.48 E
Novka	**76**	55.27 N	30.24 E
Novki	**80**	56.22 N	41.06 E
Novl'anka	**80**	55.48 N	41.44 E
Novlenskoje	**76**	59.37 N	39.20 E
Novo ≃, Bra.	**248**	4.55 S	70.33 W
Novo ≃, Bra.	**250**	4.30 S	53.50 W
Novo ≃, Bra.	**250**	6.22 S	55.42 W
Novo ≃, Bra.	**256**	21.23 S	42.44 W
Novo, Lago ⊜	**250**	1.30 N	50.40 W
Novoachtyrka	**83**	48.55 N	38.49 E
Nôvo Acôrdo	**255**	13.10 S	46.48 W
Novoajdar	**83**	48.57 N	39.00 E
Novoaleksandrovka, Kaz.	**86**	51.47 N	68.49 E
Novoaleksandrovka, Ross.	**80**	51.56 N	52.26 E
Novoaleksandrovka, Ukr.	**83**	48.17 N	39.37 E
Novoaleksandrovka, Ukr.	**83**	49.08 N	39.17 E
Novoaleksandrovo	**265b**	55.59 N	37.33 E
Novoaleksandrovsk	**80**	45.29 N	41.16 E
Novoaleksejevka, Kaz.	**86**	52.47 N	74.54 E
Novoaleksejevka, Kaz.	**86**	50.08 N	55.39 E
Novoaleksejevka, Kaz.	**86**	52.56 N	64.41 E
Novoaleksejevka, Ukr.	**78**	46.06 N	32.30 E
Novoaleksejevka, Ukr.	**78**	46.13 N	34.39 E
Novoaltajsk	**86**	53.24 N	83.58 E
Novoamvrosijevskoje	**83**	47.49 N	38.29 E
Novoanninskij	**80**	50.32 N	42.41 E
Novoarchangel'sk	**78**	48.39 N	30.48 E
Novoarchangel'skoje	**265b**	55.55 N	37.33 E
Novo Aripuanã	**246**	5.08 S	60.22 W
Novoasbest	**86**	57.44 N	60.45 E
Novoazovsk	**83**	47.08 N	38.05 E
Novobachmutovka	**83**	48.15 N	37.48 E
Novobatajsk	**83**	46.54 N	39.47 E
Novobelaja	**78**	49.49 N	39.18 E
Novobessergenovka	**83**	47.11 N	38.51 E
Novobogatinskoje	**80**	47.22 N	51.11 E
Novobogdanovka	**78**	47.06 N	35.29 E
Novobogordskoje	**80**	53.11 N	53.56 E
Novoborovaja	**83**	49.15 N	38.33 E
Novo Brasil	**255**	16.11 S	50.38 W
Novobratcevskij	**82**	55.51 N	37.23 E
Novoburejskij	**89**	49.49 N	129.54 E
Novočeboksarsk	**80**	56.08 N	47.30 E
Novo Čeremšansk	**80**	54.21 N	50.10 E
Novočerkassk	**83**	47.25 N	40.06 E
Novočernorečenskij	**86**	56.16 N	91.06 E
Novocharitonovo	**82**	55.35 N	38.30 E
Novocherkassk → Novočerkassk	**83**	47.25 N	40.06 E
Novochop'orsk	**80**	51.07 N	41.37 E
Novochop'orskij	**80**	51.06 N	41.33 E
Novochovrino ◆[8]	**265b**	55.52 N	37.30 E
Novociml'anskaja	**80**	47.59 N	42.17 E
Novo Cruzeiro	**255**	17.29 S	41.53 W
Novodanilovka	**78**	46.38 N	35.00 E
Novoderev'ankov-Skaja	**78**	46.19 N	38.45 E
Novoderkul	**83**	49.08 N	39.38 E
Novodevičje	**80**	53.37 N	48.52 E
Novodolinka	**86**	51.12 N	72.33 E
Novodolinskij	**86**	49.44 N	72.45 E
Novodoroninskoje	**88**	51.08 N	112.08 E
Novodružesk	**83**	48.58 N	38.21 E
Novodubovoje	**76**	52.19 N	39.13 E
Novodugino	**76**	55.38 N	34.18 E
Novodvinsk	**24**	64.26 N	40.47 E
Novodžerelijevskaja	**78**	45.46 N	38.41 E
Novoekonomičeskoje	**83**	48.18 N	37.15 E
Novofetinino	**82**	56.14 N	39.17 E
Novogaritovo	**80**	52.47 N	40.07 E
Novogirejevo ◆[8]	**265b**	55.45 N	37.49 E
Novogorbovo	**82**	55.43 N	36.29 E
Novogornyj	**86**	55.37 N	60.47 E
Novograd-Volynskij	**78**	50.36 N	27.36 E
Novogrigorjevka	**78**	46.24 N	34.59 E
Novogrigorjevskaja	**80**	49.26 N	43.37 E
Novogrodovka	**83**	48.13 N	37.20 E
Novogroznenskij	**84**	43.15 N	46.15 E
Novogrudok	**76**	53.36 N	25.50 E
Novogupalovka	**78**	48.02 N	35.26 E
Novo Hamburgo	**252**	29.41 S	51.08 W
Novo Horizonte	**255**	21.28 S	49.13 W
Novoignatjevka	**83**	47.38 N	37.41 E
Novoiljinsk	**88**	51.42 N	108.41 E
Novoiljinskij	**86**	57.54 N	55.30 E
Novoivanovka, Kaz.	**85**	43.08 N	71.26 E
Novoivanovka, Ukr.	**78**	49.44 N	33.28 E
Novoivanovka, Ukr.	**83**	47.41 N	38.23 E
Novoivanovskoje	**265b**	55.43 N	37.22 E
Novoizborsk	**76**	57.50 N	27.59 E
Novojampol'	**89**	52.55 N	127.38 E
Novojamskoje	**76**	52.14 N	34.28 E
Novoje, Ross.	**82**	55.38 N	38.55 E
Novoje, Ross.	**86**	58.53 N	68.40 E
Novoje Alechnovo	**82**	56.02 N	36.49 E
Novojegorjevskoje	**86**	51.46 N	80.53 E
Novojekaterinovka	**83**	47.43 N	38.07 E
Novoje Koval'ovo	**265a**	59.59 N	30.34 E
Novoje Leušino	**80**	56.48 N	40.32 E
Novojel'n'a	**76**	53.28 N	25.35 E
Novojenisejsk	**86**	58.16 N	92.24 E
Novoje Pavšino	**82**	54.15 N	37.07 E
Novoje Zarečje	**76**	57.43 N	34.22 E
Novokačalinsk	**89**	45.06 N	132.01 E
Novokadinsk	**88**	54.46 N	101.24 E
Novokamala	**88**	55.58 N	94.58 E
Novokarasuk	**86**	56.16 N	71.46 E
Novokaširovo	**80**	54.58 N	52.32 E
Novokaširsk	**82**	54.51 N	38.15 E
Novokazalinsk	**86**	45.50 N	62.10 E
Novokijevskij	**80**	50.27 N	43.08 E
Novokorsunskaja	**78**	45.38 N	39.09 E
Novokrasn'anka	**83**	49.08 N	38.18 E
Novokrasnoje	**78**	48.01 N	31.21 E
Novokručininskij	**88**	51.46 N	113.48 E
Novokubanka	**86**	51.40 N	70.44 E
Novokujbyševsk	**80**	53.07 N	49.58 E
Novokurovka	**89**	48.51 N	134.20 E
Novokuzneck	**86**	53.45 N	87.06 E
Novokuznetsk → Novokuzneck	**86**	53.45 N	87.06 E
Novolakskoje	**84**	43.07 N	46.29 E
Novolazarevskaja ⊍[3]	**9**	70.45 S	11.50 E
Novoleuškovskaja	**78**	45.59 N	39.58 E
Novoli	**68**	40.23 N	18.03 E
Novolimarevka	**83**	49.17 N	39.36 E
Novolukoml'	**76**	54.40 N	29.08 E
Novol'vovsk	**76**	53.55 N	38.47 E
Novomalorossijskaja	**78**	45.38 N	39.53 E
Novomansurkino	**80**	53.52 N	51.52 E
Novomargaritovka	**83**	46.54 N	38.50 E
Novomariinka	**88**	55.27 N	96.01 E
Novomarkovka	**86**	51.44 N	72.17 E
Novomel'nikov	**84**	43.56 N	45.09 E
Novomelovatka	**78**	50.27 N	40.46 E
Novomelovoje	**78**	51.23 N	38.13 E
Novo Mesto	**36**	45.48 N	15.10 E
Novomichajlovka, Ross.	**86**	55.13 N	81.57 E
Novomichajlovka, Ukr.	**78**	47.19 N	36.04 E
Novomichajlovka, Ukr.	**83**	47.51 N	37.29 E
Novomichajlovskij	**78**	44.15 N	38.51 E
Novomichajlovskoje	**82**	55.25 N	37.10 E
Novominskaja	**78**	46.19 N	38.57 E
Novomirgorod	**78**	48.47 N	31.39 E
Novomoskovsk, Ross.	**82**	54.05 N	38.13 E
Novomoskovsk, Ukr.	**78**	48.37 N	35.12 E
Novomyšastovskaja	**78**	45.12 N	38.35 E
Novonagajevo	**80**	55.56 N	54.15 E
Novonikolajevka, Kaz.	**85**	42.26 N	70.28 E
Novonikolajevka, Ross.	**83**	46.59 N	39.36 E
Novonikolajevka, Ukr.	**78**	47.59 N	35.55 E
Novonikolajevka, Ukr.	**78**	46.13 N	32.45 E
Novonikolajevskij	**80**	50.58 N	42.22 E
Novonikolayevsk → Novosibirsk	**86**	55.02 N	82.55 E
Novonikol'skoje, Ross.	**76**	59.25 N	33.13 E
Novonikol'skoje, Ross.	**80**	49.09 N	45.00 E
Novonikol'skoje, Ross.	**86**	59.46 N	79.12 E
Novonikol'skoje, Ross.	**265b**	55.50 N	37.15 E
Novonikol'skoje, Ukr.	**83**	49.21 N	39.51 E
Novoomel'kovo	**83**	49.08 N	39.05 E
Novo Oriente	**250**	5.32 S	40.42 W
Novoorsk	**86**	51.23 N	58.58 E
Novopavlovka	**88**	51.13 N	109.14 E
Novopavlovskaja	**84**	43.58 N	43.38 E
Novopavlovskoje	**88**	50.56 N	111.35 E
Novopetrovo	**86**	57.11 N	69.10 E
Novopetrovskoje	**82**	55.59 N	36.28 E
Novopiscovo	**76**	57.19 N	41.54 E
Novopodrezkovo	**82**	55.57 N	37.21 E
Novopokrovka, Kaz.	**86**	53.43 N	67.45 E
Novopokrovka, Kaz.	**86**	50.41 N	80.28 E
Novopokrovka, Kyrg.	**85**	42.52 N	74.45 E
Novopokrovka, Ross.	**89**	45.52 N	134.28 E
Novopokrovka, Ukr.	**78**	48.03 N	34.37 E
Novopokrovskoje	**80**	51.35 N	43.36 E
Novopolevodino	**80**	51.46 N	47.29 E
Novopolock	**76**	55.31 N	28.38 E
Novopskov	**83**	49.33 N	39.05 E
Novorajčichinsk	**89**	49.47 N	129.38 E
Novor'ažsk	**80**	53.44 N	40.07 E
Novorepnoje	**80**	51.06 N	48.24 E
Novorossijka	**85**	42.44 N	76.07 E
Novorossijsk	**78**	44.45 N	37.45 E
Novorossijskoje	**86**	50.13 N	58.00 E
Novorossiysk → Novorossijsk	**78**	44.45 N	37.45 E
Novorossoš'	**83**	49.32 N	39.15 E
Novorudnyj	**86**	51.30 N	58.10 E
Novorybinka	**86**	51.51 N	71.14 E
Novorybnoje	**74**	72.50 N	105.50 E
Novoržev	**76**	57.02 N	29.20 E
Novošachtinsk	**83**	47.47 N	39.56 E
Novosaratovka	**265a**	59.50 N	30.32 E
Novoščerbinovskaja	**78**	46.28 N	38.38 E
Novosel'e	**86**	54.10 N	76.53 E
Novoselenginsk	**88**	51.06 N	106.37 E
Novoselica	**78**	48.14 N	26.17 E
Novoselickoje	**84**	44.45 N	43.26 E
Novoseliščе	**78**	49.48 N	25.03 E
Novoselje	**265a**	59.48 N	30.05 E
Novoselki, Ross.	**82**	55.08 N	37.33 E
Novoselki, Ross.	**82**	54.49 N	38.55 E
Novosel'nyj	**86**	50.00 N	54.38 E
Novoselovka Pervaja	**83**	48.12 N	37.31 E
Novoselovo	**82**	56.04 N	39.04 E
Novosel'skoje	**78**	45.20 N	28.33 E
Novosemejkino	**80**	53.23 N	50.22 E
Novosergijevka, Ross.	**80**	52.06 N	53.39 E
Novosergijevka, Ross.	**265a**	59.54 N	30.34 E
Novoseslavino	**80**	53.21 N	40.26 E
Novošešminsk	**80**	55.04 N	51.15 E
Novoshakhtinsk → Novošachtinsk	**83**	47.47 N	39.56 E
Novosibirsk	**86**	55.02 N	82.55 E
Novosibirskije ostrova II	**74**	75.00 N	142.00 E
Novosibirsk Oblast' □[4]	**86**	55.00 N	80.00 E
Novosibirskoje vodochranilišče ⊜[1]	**86**	54.35 N	82.35 E
Novosil'	**76**	52.58 N	37.03 E
Novosil'skoje	**78**	51.56 N	38.31 E
Novosokol'niki	**76**	56.21 N	30.10 E
Novos'olki, Bela.	**76**	52.02 N	24.21 E
Novos'olki, Bela.	**76**	52.24 N	28.33 E
Novos'olki, Ross.	**76**	56.01 N	33.37 E
Novos'olki, Ross.	**80**	55.48 N	42.41 E
Novos'olki, Ross.	**80**	54.50 N	39.46 E
Novos'olki, Ross.	**265a**	59.42 N	30.17 E
Novos'olovka	**83**	49.04 N	37.42 E
Novos'olovo, Ross.	**86**	55.04 N	91.07 E
Novos'olovo, Ross.	**88**	56.04 N	107.42 E
Novos'olovskoje	**78**	45.26 N	33.34 E
Novospasovka	**83**	47.42 N	39.04 E
Novospasskoje	**80**	53.08 N	47.45 E
Novostrel'covka	**83**	49.20 N	39.55 E
Novostrojevo	**76**	54.27 N	21.50 E
Novosvetlovka	**83**	48.30 N	39.30 E
Novosysojevka	**89**	44.14 N	133.22 E
Novotavolžanka	**78**	50.22 N	36.50 E
Novotitarovskaja	**78**	45.14 N	39.00 E
Novotroick, Ross.	**86**	56.11 N	78.41 E
Novotroick, Ross.	**86**	51.12 N	58.20 E
Novotroickoje, Kaz.	**85**	43.42 N	73.46 E
Novotroickoje, Ross.	**80**	58.28 N	47.06 E
Novotroickoje, Ukr.	**78**	46.22 N	34.20 E
Novotroickoje, Ukr.	**83**	47.43 N	37.35 E
Novo-Troitsk → Novotroick	**86**	51.12 N	58.20 E
Novotulka, Ross.	**80**	52.38 N	48.45 E
Novotulka, Ross.	**80**	50.50 N	47.34 E
Novotul'skij	**82**	54.10 N	37.43 E
Novoukolovo	**78**	51.02 N	38.25 E
Novoukrainka	**78**	48.19 N	31.32 E
Novouljanovsk	**80**	54.08 N	48.24 E
Novoural'sk	**86**	51.15 N	57.16 E
Novouzensk	**80**	50.28 N	48.08 E
Novovaršavka	**86**	54.11 N	74.42 E
Novovasiljevka, Ukr.	**78**	46.51 N	36.46 E
Novovasiljevka, Ukr.	**78**	46.48 N	35.44 E
Novov'atsk	**80**	58.29 N	49.44 E
Novov'azniki	**80**	56.12 N	42.10 E
Novovolynsk	**78**	50.50 N	24.05 E
Novovoroncovka	**78**	47.29 N	33.54 E
Novovoronežskij	**78**	51.16 N	39.11 E
Novovoskresenovka	**85**	42.50 N	73.32 E
Novovoskresenskoje	**78**	47.21 N	33.37 E
Novozacharkino	**80**	52.11 N	48.29 E
Novozagorje	**82**	55.39 N	38.38 E
Novozavidovskij	**82**	56.33 N	36.26 E
Novožilovskaja	**24**	64.50 N	51.20 E
Novozizevka	**80**	50.48 N	49.08 E
Novozybkov	**76**	52.32 N	31.56 E
Novska	**36**	45.21 N	16.59 E
Nový Bohumín	**30**	49.56 N	18.20 E
Nový Bor	**54**	50.45 N	14.33 E
Novyj	**86**	55.39 N	86.39 E
Novyj Afon	**84**	43.06 N	40.48 E
Novyj Bor	**24**	66.43 N	52.16 E
Novyj Bug	**78**	47.41 N	32.30 E
Novyj Bujan	**80**	53.41 N	50.04 E
Novyj Bykov	**78**	50.36 N	31.39 E
Novyj Donbass ◆[8]	**83**	48.05 N	38.46 E
Novyj Dvor	**76**	52.50 N	24.21 E
Novyje Ajbesi	**80**	54.49 N	47.02 E
Novyje Aneny	**78**	46.52 N	29.14 E
Novyje Basy	**78**	50.53 N	34.51 E
Novyje Burasy	**80**	52.08 N	46.06 E
Novyje Denisoviči	**76**	54.12 N	29.13 E
Novyje Gorki	**80**	56.42 N	41.06 E
Novyje Maty	**80**	55.15 N	54.04 E
Novyje Salty	**80**	54.06 N	53.26 E
Novyje Senžary	**78**	49.21 N	34.19 E
Novyje Z'atcy	**80**	57.27 N	52.36 E
Nový Jičín	**30**	49.36 N	18.00 E
Novyj Jaryčev	**78**	49.55 N	24.18 E
Novyj Jegorlyk	**80**	46.24 N	41.54 E
Novyj Karačaj	**84**	43.49 N	41.56 E
Novyj Karamass	**80**	56.11 N	48.58 E
Novyj Kiner	**80**	56.24 N	49.44 E
Novyj Multan	**80**	57.09 N	52.19 E
Novyj Nekouz	**76**	57.54 N	38.04 E
Novyj Oskol	**78**	50.46 N	37.53 E
Novyj Pogost	**76**	55.30 N	27.29 E
Novyj Port	**74**	67.40 N	72.52 E
Novyj Put'	**85**	43.29 N	73.52 E
Novyj Ropsk	**76**	52.18 N	32.19 E
Novyj Stan	**82**	56.18 N	37.00 E
Novyj Svet	**83**	47.48 N	38.00 E
Novyj Tap	**86**	57.04 N	67.49 E
Novyj Terek ≃	**84**	43.37 N	47.25 E
Novyj Tevriz	**86**	59.04 N	78.08 E
Novyj Uzen	**72**	43.18 N	52.48 E
Novyj Vas'ugan	**86**	58.34 N	76.29 E
Novy Torjal	**80**	57.00 N	48.44 E
Nowa Dęba	**30**	50.26 N	21.46 E
Nowaja Semlja → Novaja Zeml'a II	**72**	74.00 N	57.00 E
Nowa Ruda	**30**	50.35 N	16.31 E
Nowa Sól (Neusalz)	**30**	51.48 N	15.44 E
Nowata	**196**	36.42 N	95.38 W
Nowater Creek ≃	**202**	43.57 N	108.00 W
Nowbarān	**128**	35.08 N	48.42 E
Nowe	**30**	53.40 N	18.43 E
Nowe Miasto Lubawskie	**30**	53.27 N	19.35 E
Nowe Miasto nad Pilicą	**30**	51.38 N	20.35 E
Nowendoc	**166**	31.32 S	151.43 E
Nowe Warpno	**30**	53.44 N	14.16 E
Nowfel low Shātow	**128**	34.23 N	50.32 E
Nowgong	**124**	25.04 N	79.27 E
Nowingi	**166**	34.36 S	142.14 E
Nowitna ≃	**180**	65.55 N	154.17 W
Nowogard	**30**	53.40 N	15.08 E
Nowogród	**30**	53.15 N	21.53 E
Nowogrodziec	**30**	51.12 N	15.25 E
Nowokusnezk → Novokuzneck	**86**	53.45 N	87.06 E
Nowood ≃	**202**	44.17 N	107.58 W
Nowosibirsk → Novosibirsk	**86**	55.02 N	82.55 E
Nowra	**170**	34.53 S	150.36 E
Nowrangapur	**122**	19.14 N	82.33 E
Nowshāk ∧	**123**	36.26 N	71.50 E
Nowshera	**123**	34.01 N	71.59 E
Nowy Dwór Gdański	**30**	54.13 N	19.06 E
Nowy Dwór Mazowiecki	**30**	52.26 N	20.43 E
Nowy Sącz	**30**	49.38 N	20.42 E
Nowy Sącz □[4]	**30**	49.30 N	20.15 E
Nowy Staw	**30**	54.09 N	19.00 E
Nowy Targ	**30**	49.29 N	20.02 E
Nowy Tomyśl	**30**	52.20 N	16.07 E
Now Zād	**120**	32.24 N	64.28 E
Noxapater	**194**	32.59 N	89.03 W
Noxe ≃	**50**	48.33 N	3.35 E
Noxen	**210**	41.25 N	76.03 W
Noxon	**202**	48.00 N	115.47 W
Noxon Reservoir ⊜[1]	**202**	47.54 N	115.40 W
Noxubee ≃	**194**	32.50 N	88.10 W
Noy ≃	**110**	17.05 N	105.02 E
Noya	**34**	42.47 N	8.53 W
Noya ≃	**152**	0.58 N	9.48 E
Noyant	**50**	47.31 N	0.08 E
Noye ≃	**50**	49.51 N	2.20 E
Noyelles-sur Mer	**50**	50.11 N	1.43 E
Noyers	**50**	47.42 N	4.00 E
Noyers, Ruisseau des ≃	**275a**	45.21 N	73.22 W
Noyes Island I	**182**	55.30 N	133.40 W
Noyon	**50**	49.35 N	3.00 E
Nožaj-Jurt	**84**	43.05 N	46.24 E
Nozawa-onsen	**94**	36.55 N	138.27 E
Nozay, Fr.	**32**	47.34 N	1.38 W
Nozay, Fr.	**261**	48.40 N	2.14 E
Nozeroy	**58**	46.47 N	6.02 E
Nozori-dam ◆[6]	**94**	36.43 N	138.39 E
Nozori-ko ⊜	**94**	36.42 N	138.39 E
Nozuta	**268**	35.35 N	139.27 E
Nqamakwe	**158**	32.12 S	27.56 E
Nqutu	**158**	28.13 S	30.32 E
N'Riquinha	**152**	15.45 S	21.42 E
N'Rougas	**158**	29.07 S	21.09 E
Nsa, Oued en V	**148**	32.28 N	5.24 E
Nsaba	**150**	5.39 N	0.45 W
Nsah	**152**	2.22 S	15.19 E
Nsang	**152**	2.02 N	10.56 E
Nsanje	**154**	16.55 S	35.12 E
Nsawam	**150**	5.50 N	0.20 W
Nsefu Game Reserve ◆[4]	**154**	13.07 S	32.10 E
Nsele ≃	**152**	4.14 S	15.33 E
Nseleni	**158**	28.33 S	31.39 E
Nsok	**152**	1.08 N	11.16 E
Nsoko	**158**	27.02 S	31.57 E
Nsontin	**152**	3.09 S	18.00 E
Nsouélé	**273b**	4.12 S	15.11 E
Nsukka	**150**	6.52 N	7.24 E
Nsuta	**150**	5.17 N	1.58 W
Ntakat	**150**	16.49 N	11.43 W
Ntambanana	**158**	28.36 S	31.45 E
Ntandembele	**152**	2.11 S	17.08 E
Ntcheu	**154**	14.49 S	34.38 E
Ntem ≃	**152**	2.15 N	9.45 E
Ntoum	**152**	0.23 N	9.47 E
Ntsama	**152**	0.32 S	14.38 E
N'Tsaoueni	**157a**	11.27 S	43.18 E
Ntui	**152**	4.27 N	11.38 E
Ntumba	**154**	8.20 S	32.05 E
Ntusi	**154**	0.03 N	31.13 E
Ntwetwe Pan ≚	**156**	20.30 S	25.20 E
Nuala	**154**	13.27 S	28.16 E
Nuanchitang	**104**	41.02 N	120.41 E
Nuanetsi ≃	**156**	22.40 S	31.50 E
Nuangola	**210**	41.09 N	75.58 W
Nuanli	**102**	23.26 N	100.51 E
Nuannuan	**269d**	25.06 N	121.44 E
Nuanshui	**100**	28.53 N	117.51 E
Nuanzhouying	**100**	25.22 N	117.22 E
Nuasjärvi ⊜	**26**	64.10 N	28.05 E
Nuatabu	**174t**	1.33 N	172.59 E
Nuatja	**150**	6.57 N	1.10 E
Nu'aymah	**132**	32.38 N	36.10 E
Nūbah	**142**	30.29 N	31.33 E
Nūbah, Jibāl an- ∧∧	**140**	11.00 N	30.45 E
Nūbārīyah, Tur'at an- ≊	**142**	30.43 N	30.46 E
Nubian Desert ◆[2]	**140**	20.30 N	33.00 E
Ñuble ≃	**252**	36.39 S	72.27 W
Nubra ≃	**123**	34.39 N	77.36 E
Nucet	**38**	46.28 N	22.35 E
Nucetto	**62**	44.20 N	8.04 E
Nucha → Šeki	**84**	41.12 N	47.12 E
Nuchatlitz Inlet ⊂	**182**	49.45 N	126.55 W
N'uchča	**24**	63.27 N	46.28 E
Nuch'ŏn-ni	**98**	38.14 N	126.16 E
Nucla	**200**	38.16 N	108.32 W
Núcleo Colonial São Bento	**287a**	22.44 S	43.18 W
N'učpas	**24**	60.51 N	51.18 E
Nucuray ≃	**246**	5.02 S	75.34 W
Nuda, Monte la ∧	**64**	44.17 N	10.15 E
Nudaybah	**142**	30.59 N	30.22 E
Nudol' ≃	**82**	56.07 N	36.42 E
Nudol'-Šarino	**82**	56.06 N	36.31 E
Nudow	**264a**	52.20 N	13.10 E
Nueces ≃	**196**	27.50 N	97.30 W
Nueces Plains ≚	**196**	28.30 N	99.15 W
Nueltin Lake ⊜	**176**	60.20 N	99.50 W
Nuenen	**52**	51.29 N	5.33 E
Nü'er ≃	**98**	40.57 N	121.19 E
Nü'erhe	**104**	41.04 N	121.00 E
Nuestra Señora de Talavera	**252**	25.26 S	63.48 W
Nueva, Isla I	**254**	55.13 S	66.30 W
Nueva Antioquia	**246**	6.05 N	69.26 W
Nueva Asunción □[5]	**248**	21.00 S	61.00 W
Nueva Atzacoalco ◆[8]	**286a**	19.29 N	99.05 W
Nueva Brunswick → New Brunswick □[4]	**186**	46.30 N	66.15 W
Nueva Caledonia → New Caledonia □[2]	**175f**	21.30 S	165.30 E
Nueva Chicago ◆[8]	**288**	34.40 S	58.30 W
Nueva Ciudad Guerrero	**232**	26.35 N	99.15 W
Nueva Concepción	**236**	14.08 N	89.18 W
Nueva Cuadrilla	**234**	18.04 N	101.33 W
Nueva Ecija □[4]	**116**	15.35 N	121.00 E
Nueva Escocia → Nova Scotia □[4]	**186**	45.00 N	63.00 W
Nueva Esparta □[3]	**246**	11.00 N	64.00 W
Nueva Francia	**252**	28.11 S	64.12 W
Nueva Galia	**252**	35.07 S	65.15 W
Nueva Germania	**252**	23.54 S	56.45 W
Nueva Gerona	**240p**	21.53 N	82.48 W
Nueva Guinea, Isla → New Guinea I	**164**	5.00 S	140.00 E
Nueva Hébridas → Vanuatu □[1]	**175f**	16.00 S	167.00 E
Nueva Helvecia	**258**	34.19 S	57.13 W
Nueva Imperial	**252**	38.44 S	72.57 W
Nueva Italia de Ruiz	**234**	19.01 N	102.06 W
Nueva Loja	**246**	0.06 N	76.52 W
Nueva Lubecka	**254**	44.32 S	70.24 W
Nueva Ocotepeque	**236**	14.24 N	89.13 W
Nueva Palmira	**258**	33.53 S	58.25 W
Nueva Paz	**240p**	22.46 N	81.45 W
Nueva Pompeya ◆[8]	**288**	34.39 S	58.25 W
Nueva Rosita	**232**	27.57 N	101.13 W
Nueva San Salvador	**236**	13.41 N	89.17 W
Nueva Segovia □[5]	**236**	13.40 N	86.10 W
Nueva Siberia, Islas → Novosibirskije ostrova II	**74**	75.00 N	142.00 E
Nueva Venecia	**236**	14.03 N	91.33 W
Nueva Vizcaya □[4]	**116**	16.25 N	121.10 E
Nueva Zelandia → New Zealand □[1]	**172**	41.00 S	174.00 E
Nueva Zembla, Isla de → Novaja Zeml'a II	**72**	74.00 N	57.00 E
Nueve, Canal Numero ≊	**252**	36.11 S	57.18 W
Nueve de Julio	**252**	35.27 S	60.52 W
Nuevitas	**240p**	21.33 N	77.16 W
Nuevitas, Bahía de ⊂	**240p**	21.30 N	77.12 W
Nuevo	**228**	33.48 N	117.09 W
Nuevo, Bajo ✣[4]	**238**	15.55 N	78.30 W
Nuevo, Cayo I	**232**	21.51 N	92.05 W
Nuevo, Golfo ⊂	**254**	42.42 S	64.36 W
Nuevo Berlín	**252**	32.59 S	58.03 W
Nuevo Camarón	**196**	27.05 N	99.55 W
Nuevo Casas Grandes	**232**	30.25 N	107.55 W
Nuevo Chagres	**236**	9.14 N	80.05 W
Nuevo Delicias	**232**	26.15 N	102.50 W
Nuevo Laredo	**232**	27.30 N	99.31 W
Nuevo Léon	**204**	32.20 N	115.12 W
Nuevo León □[3]	**232**	25.40 N	100.00 W
Nuevo Morelos	**234**	17.31 N	95.02 W
Nuevo Necaxa	**234**	20.13 N	98.00 W
Nuevo Poblado el Oro	**196**	26.50 N	101.19 W
Nuevo Primero de Mayo	**196**	26.01 N	98.02 W
Nuevo Progreso	**232**	18.38 N	92.18 W
Nuevo Rocafuerte	**246**	0.56 S	75.24 W
Nuevo Saucillo	**196**	27.20 N	104.54 W
Nufcor	**273d**	26.17 S	27.44 E
Nugaal □[4]	**144**	8.30 N	49.00 E
Nugaaleed, Dooxo V	**144**	8.35 N	48.35 E
Nugget Point ›	**172**	46.27 S	169.49 E
Nûgssuaq ›[1]	**176**	70.25 N	52.30 W
Nugu ⊜[1]	**122**	11.58 N	76.28 E
Nuguria Islands II	**14**	3.20 S	154.45 E
Nūh	**124**	28.07 N	77.01 E
Nūh, Rās ›	**128**	25.05 N	62.24 E
Nuhaka	**172**	39.03 S	177.45 E
Nuhaydāt as-Sūd, Jabal an- ∧	**142**	28.01 N	32.21 E
Nuhūd, Jabal an- ∧	**140**	14.50 N	29.53 E
Nui I[1]	**14**	7.15 S	177.10 E
Nuia	**76**	58.04 N	25.33 E
Nuits-Saint-Georges	**58**	47.08 N	4.57 E
Nuits-sur-Armançon	**50**	47.44 N	4.12 E
N'uja	**74**	60.32 N	116.14 E
N'uja ≃	**74**	60.32 N	116.20 E
Nujiang	**102**	29.58 N	97.25 E
N'uk, ozero ⊜	**24**	64.27 N	31.45 E
Nuka Island I	**180**	59.21 N	150.42 W
Nukan	**175c**	7.23 N	151.53 E
Nukata	**94**	34.55 N	137.17 E
Nukatl', chrebet ∧∧	**84**	42.15 N	46.35 E
Nukey Bluff ⊥[4]	**166**	32.33 S	135.40 E
Nukhayb	**128**	32.02 N	42.15 E
Nukhaylah ⊤[4]	**140**	19.03 N	26.19 E
Nukhaylah, Wādī an- V	**132**	31.27 N	35.49 E
Nukiki	**175e**	6.46 S	156.28 E
N'uksenica	**24**	60.25 N	44.13 E
Nuku'alofa	**174w**	21.08 S	175.12 W
Nukufetau I[1]	**14**	8.00 S	178.22 E
Nukuhu	**164**	5.35 S	149.25 E
Nukulaelae I[1]	**14**	9.23 S	179.52 E
Nukumanu Islands II	**14**	4.30 S	159.30 E
Nukunonu I	**14**	9.12 S	171.54 W
Nukunuku	**174w**	21.08 S	175.18 W
Nukuoro I[1]	**14**	3.51 N	154.58 E
Nukus	**72**	42.50 N	59.29 E
Nul	**175f**	16.49 S	168.24 E
Nulato	**180**	64.43 N	158.06 W
Nullagine	**162**	21.53 S	120.06 E
Nullagine ≃	**162**	20.43 S	120.33 E
Nullarbor	**162**	31.26 S	130.55 E
Nullarbor National Park ♣	**162**	31.30 S	130.30 E
Nullarbor Plain ≚	**162**	31.00 S	129.00 E
Nulltown	**218**	39.35 N	85.10 W
Nul'vand	**85**	38.16 N	70.32 E
Nulvi	**71**	40.47 N	8.45 E
Num, Mios I	**164**	1.30 S	135.13 E
Numabin Bay ⊂	**184**	56.30 N	103.08 W
Numakuma	**96**	34.23 N	133.20 E
Numan	**146**	9.28 N	12.02 E
Numana	**66**	43.31 N	13.37 E
Numancia	**116**	9.52 N	125.58 E
Numancia ⊥	**34**	41.48 N	2.25 W
Numansdorp	**52**	51.44 N	4.26 E
Numara I	**122**	6.26 N	73.03 E
Numata, Nihon	**92a**	43.48 N	141.57 E
Numata, Nihon	**94**	36.38 N	139.03 E
Numata, Nihon	**96**	34.27 N	132.24 E
Numatinna ≃	**140**	7.14 N	27.37 E
Numazu	**94**	35.06 N	138.52 E
Numbargulme, Mount ∧	**164**	14.56 S	145.03 E
Number 5 Mine	**214**	41.08 N	80.11 W
Numedal V	**26**	60.06 N	9.06 E
Numeralla	**171b**	36.11 S	149.20 E
Numeralla ≃	**171b**	36.06 S	149.11 E
Numfoor, Pulau I	**164**	1.03 S	134.54 E
Numidia	**210**	40.53 N	76.24 W
Numila	**229b**	21.54 N	159.33 W
Nu Mine	**214**	40.48 N	79.18 W
Numto	**74**	63.40 N	71.20 E
Numurkah	**166**	36.06 S	145.26 E
Nun ≃[1]	**150**	4.20 N	6.00 E
Nun'amo	**180**	65.37 N	170.40 W
Nunapitchuk	**180**	60.54 N	162.29 W
Nunawading	**169**	37.49 S	145.10 E
Nünchritz	**54**	51.18 N	13.23 E
Nunda	**210**	42.34 N	77.56 W
Nundah	**171a**	27.24 S	153.04 E
Nundu	**154**	3.49 S	29.05 E
Nuneaton	**42**	52.32 N	1.28 W
Núñes, Isla I	**254**	53.31 S	73.48 W
Núñez ◆[8]	**288**	34.33 S	58.27 W
Nunez ≃	**150**	10.36 N	14.40 W
Nungarin	**162**	31.11 S	118.06 E
Nungesser Lake ⊜	**184**	51.28 N	93.35 W
Nungwe	**154**	2.46 S	32.01 E
Nunica	**216**	43.04 N	86.04 W
Nunivak Island I	**180**	60.00 N	166.30 W
Nunjiang	**89**	49.10 N	125.11 E
Nunjikompita	**162**	32.16 S	134.19 E
Nunkini	**232**	20.20 N	90.11 W
Nunkun ∧	**123**	33.59 N	76.01 E
Nunligran	**180**	64.48 N	175.24 W
Nunnelly	**194**	35.51 N	87.28 W
Ñuñoa	**286e**	33.28 S	70.36 W
Nunshan	**89**	48.59 N	125.14 E
Nunspeet	**52**	52.23 N	5.46 E
Nuomin ≃	**89**	48.06 N	124.26 E
Nuomin Dashan ∧	**89**	50.15 N	122.46 E
Nuon ≃	**150**	6.30 N	8.36 W
Nuoro	**71**	40.19 N	9.20 E
Nuoro □[4]	**71**	40.10 N	9.20 E
Nuqruș, Jabal ∧	**140**	24.49 N	34.36 E
Nuquí	**246**	5.42 N	77.17 W
Nura	**86**	48.53 N	62.20 E
Nura ≃	**86**	50.30 N	69.59 E
Nurallao	**71**	39.47 N	9.05 E
Nuraminis	**71**	39.26 N	9.01 E
Nuratau, chrebet ∧∧	**85**	40.20 N	67.15 E
Nuraxi, Nuraghe su ⊥	**71**	39.42 N	9.00 E
N'urba	**74**	63.17 N	118.20 E
Nürburg	**56**	50.21 N	6.57 E
Nürburgring ♣	**56**	50.21 N	6.58 E
Nur Dağları ∧∧	**130**	36.45 N	36.20 E
Nure ≃	**62**	45.03 N	9.49 E
Nurek	**85**	38.23 N	69.19 E
Nurekskoje vodochranilišče ⊜[1]	**85**	38.30 N	69.30 E
Nuremberg	**210**	40.56 N	76.10 W
Nuremberg → Nürnberg	**60**	49.27 N	11.04 E
Nürenbei	**107**	30.11 N	106.04 E
Nūrestān □[9]	**123**	35.30 N	70.45 E
Nurettin	**130**	39.14 N	42.25 E
Nurhak	**130**	37.58 N	37.25 E
Nuria, Monte ∧	**66**	42.21 N	13.05 E
Nuriootpa	**168b**	34.29 S	139.00 E
Nurlat	**80**	54.26 N	50.46 E
Nurlaty	**80**	55.37 N	48.18 E
Nūrmahal	**123**	31.06 N	75.36 E
Nurmes	**26**	63.33 N	29.07 E
Nurmijärvi	**26**	60.28 N	24.48 E
Nūrnagar	**126**	22.20 N	89.03 E
Nürnberg	**60**	49.27 N	11.04 E
Nürnberg, Flughafen ⊠	**60**	49.30 N	11.06 E
Nūrpur, India	**123**	31.10 N	76.29 E
Nūrpur, India	**123**	32.18 N	75.54 E
Nurpur, India	**126**	22.13 N	88.05 E
Nūrpur, Pāk.	**123**	31.53 N	71.54 E
Nurrari Lakes ⊜	**162**	29.01 S	130.05 E
Nurri	**71**	39.43 N	9.14 E
Nurri, Mount ∧[2]	**166**	31.42 S	146.02 E
Nursery	**222**	28.56 N	97.06 W
Nürtingen	**56**	48.38 N	9.20 E
Nus	**62**	45.45 N	7.28 E
Nūsah	**144**	14.00 N	46.43 E
Nusa Tenggara Barat □[4]	**115b**	8.50 S	117.30 E
Nusa Tenggara Timur □[4]	**112**	9.30 S	122.00 E
Nusaybin	**130**	37.03 N	41.13 E
Nușayrīyah, Jabal an- ∧∧	**130**	35.30 N	36.12 E
Nusco	**68**	40.53 N	15.05 E
Nushagak ≃	**180**	59.00 N	158.30 W
Nushagak Bay ⊂	**180**	58.40 N	158.40 W
Nushagak Peninsula ›[1]	**180**	58.30 N	159.00 W
Nu Shan ∧∧	**102**	27.00 N	99.00 E
Nüshan Hu ⊜	**100**	32.57 N	118.03 E
Nu-shima I	**96**	34.10 N	134.50 E
Nushki	**120**	29.33 N	66.01 E
Nusplingen	**58**	48.08 N	8.53 E
Nušpoly	**82**	56.39 N	37.44 E
Nussdorf ◆[8]	**264b**	48.15 N	16.22 E
Nussdorf am Attersee	**64**	47.53 N	13.31 E
Nuta ≃	**96**	34.23 N	133.04 E
Nutauge, laguna ⊂	**180**	67.55 N	176.45 W
Nutepel'men, Ross.	**180**	67.26 N	174.56 W
Nutepelmen, Ross.	**180**	65.31 N	178.30 W
Nutfield	**260**	51.14 N	0.07 W
Nuth	**56**	50.55 N	5.54 E
Nuthe ≃, Dtsch.	**54**	51.58 N	11.53 E
Nuthe ≃, Dtsch.	**54**	52.23 N	13.04 E
Nut Lake Indian Reserve ◆[4]	**184**	52.20 N	103.30 W
Nutley	**210**	40.49 N	74.09 W
Nutrioso	**200**	33.57 N	109.12 W
Nut Swamp Brook ≃	**276**	40.21 N	74.06 W
Nuttby Mountain ∧[2]	**186**	45.33 N	63.13 W
Nutter Fort	**188**	39.15 N	80.19 W
Nutting Lake	**207**	42.32 N	71.16 W
Nutting Lake ⊜	**283**	42.32 N	71.16 W
Nutwood	**219**	39.05 N	90.39 W
Nutwood Downs	**164**	15.49 S	134.10 E
Nutzotin Mountains ∧∧	**180**	62.10 N	141.40 W
Nu'ūmīyah, Wādī an- V	**142**	29.31 N	31.17 E
Nuupere, Pointe ›	**174s**	17.36 S	149.47 W
Nu'uuli	**174u**	14.18 S	170.42 W
N'uvčim	**24**	61.22 N	50.42 E
Nuwākoṭ	**124**	28.08 N	83.53 E
Nuwaybi' al-Muzayyinah	**140**	28.58 N	34.39 E
Nuwerus	**158**	31.08 S	18.24 E
Nuweveldberge ∧∧	**158**	32.13 S	22.10 E
Nuxis	**71**	39.09 N	8.44 E
Nuyakuk Lake ⊜	**180**	60.00 N	158.40 W
Nuyts, Point ›	**162**	35.04 S	116.37 E
Nuyts Archipelago II	**162**	32.35 S	133.17 E
Nūzvīd	**122**	16.47 N	80.51 E
N'Vinda	**152**	13.04 S	18.57 E
Nwa	**152**	6.30 N	11.00 E
Nxainxai	**156**	19.50 S	21.13 E
Nxai Pan National Park ♣	**156**	19.45 S	24.50 E
Nxaunxau	**156**	18.19 S	21.04 E
Nyaake	**150**	4.52 N	7.37 W
Nyabéssan	**152**	2.24 N	10.24 E
Nyabing	**162**	33.32 S	118.09 E
Nyac	**180**	61.01 N	159.57 W
Nyack	**210**	41.05 N	73.55 W
Nyack Beach State Park ♣	**276**	41.07 N	73.55 W
Nyadiri ≃	**154**	16.44 S	32.33 E
Nyahanga	**154**	2.23 S	33.33 E
Nyahua	**154**	5.24 S	33.19 E
Nyahururu Falls	**154**	0.02 N	36.22 E
Nyah West	**166**	35.11 S	143.22 E
Nyainqêntanglha Feng ∧	**124**	30.22 N	90.35 E
Nyainqêntanglha Shan ∧∧	**120**	30.00 N	90.00 E
Nyainrong	**120**	32.09 N	92.11 E
Nyakabindi	**154**	2.38 S	33.59 E
Nyakakiri	**154**	2.15 S	31.28 E
Nyakanazi	**154**	3.00 S	31.15 E
Nyakrom	**150**	5.37 N	0.48 W
Nyakulenga	**152**	13.03 S	23.29 E
Nyala	**140**	12.03 N	24.53 E
Nyalam	**120**	28.11 N	85.58 E
Nyalas	**114**	2.26 N	102.28 E
Nyamandhlovu	**154**	19.50 S	28.16 E
Nyamina	**150**	13.19 N	6.59 W
Nyamlell	**140**	9.07 N	26.58 E
Nyamougo	**154**	1.29 S	34.33 E
Nyamtumbo	**154**	10.29 S	36.02 E
Nyamwage	**154**	8.08 S	39.00 E
Nyandekwa	**154**	3.55 S	32.30 E
Nyanding, Khawr V	**140**	8.40 N	32.41 E
Nyang ≃	**124**	29.25 N	94.22 E
Nyanga □[4]	**152**	3.00 S	11.00 E
Nyanga ≃	**152**	2.58 S	10.15 E
Nyanga, Lake ⊜	**162**	29.57 S	126.10 E
Nyangana	**156**	18.00 S	20.41 E
Nyangui ∧	**154**	17.53 S	32.44 E
Nyanji Mission	**154**	14.23 S	31.48 E
Nyanza □[4]	**154**	0.30 S	34.30 E
Nyanza-Lac	**154**	4.21 S	29.36 E
Nyasa, Lake (Lake Malawi) ⊜	**154**	12.00 S	34.30 E
Nyaunglebin	**110**	17.57 N	96.44 E
Nyavikungu	**154**	11.26 S	25.54 E
Nyazura	**154**	18.43 S	32.10 E
Nyazvidzi ≃	**154**	20.00 S	32.17 E
Nybergsund	**26**	61.15 N	12.19 E
Nyborg	**41**	55.19 N	10.48 E
Nybro	**26**	56.45 N	15.54 E
Nyda	**74**	66.36 N	72.54 E
Nyêmo	**124**	29.25 N	90.08 E
Nyengo Swamp ≋	**152**	14.51 S	22.07 E
Nyeri	**154**	0.25 S	36.57 E
Nyerol	**140**	8.41 N	32.02 E
Nyfer ≃	**42**	52.02 N	4.50 W
Nygčigen, mys ›	**180**	65.05 N	172.06 W
Nyhammar	**40**	60.17 N	14.58 E
Nyhyttan	**40**	59.40 N	14.48 E
Nyiel	**140**	6.06 N	31.13 E
Nyika National Park ♣	**154**	10.48 S	33.48 E
Nyika Plateau ∧∧[1]	**154**	10.40 S	33.50 E
Nyimba	**154**	14.35 S	30.52 E
Nyingchi	**120**	29.32 N	94.25 E
Nyíradony	**30**	47.41 N	21.55 E
Nyírbátor	**30**	47.50 N	22.08 E
Nyíregyháza	**30**	47.59 N	21.43 E
Nykøbing, Dan.	**26**	56.48 N	8.52 E
Nykøbing, Dan.	**41**	55.55 N	11.41 E
Nykøbing, Dan.	**41**	54.46 N	11.53 E
Nyköping	**40**	58.45 N	17.00 E
Nykroppa	**40**	59.38 N	14.18 E
Nykvarn	**40**	59.11 N	17.26 E
Nyland	**26**	63.00 N	17.46 E
Nyland Acres	**228**	34.14 N	119.09 W
Nylga, Ross.	**80**	56.46 N	52.22 E
Nylga, Ross.	**89**	51.38 N	127.35 E
Nylstroom	**156**	24.42 S	28.20 E
Nymagee	**166**	32.04 S	146.20 E
Nymboida ≃	**166**	29.39 S	152.30 E
Nymburk	**30**	50.11 N	15.03 E
Nymphenburg ◆[8]	**60**	48.09 N	11.30 E
Nynäshamn	**40**	58.54 N	17.57 E
Nyngan	**166**	31.34 S	147.11 E
Nyoma	**120**	33.11 N	78.38 E
Nyon	**58**	46.23 N	6.14 E
Nyong ≃	**152**	3.17 N	9.54 E
Nyons	**62**	44.22 N	5.08 E
Nyord I	**41**	55.03 N	12.13 E
Nyou	**150**	12.46 N	1.56 W
Nýřany	**60**	49.43 N	13.12 E
Nyrov	**24**	60.42 N	56.40 E
Nýrsko	**60**	49.18 N	13.09 E
Nyš	**89**	51.31 N	142.46 E
Nysa, Pol.	**30**	50.29 N	17.20 E
Nyša, Ross.	**80**	56.23 N	51.51 E
Nysa Kłodzka ≃	**30**	50.49 N	17.50 E
Nysa Łużycka (Neisse) (Nisa) ≃	**30**	52.04 N	14.46 E
Nyslott → Savonlinna	**26**	61.52 N	28.53 E
Nysø	**41**	55.08 N	12.02 E
Nyssa	**202**	43.52 N	116.59 W

ENGLISH — Name, Page, Lat.°′, Long.°′ · DEUTSCH — Name, Seite, Breite°′, Länge°′ E = Ost

Symbols in the index entries represent the broad categories identified in the key at the right. Symbols with superior numbers (∧∧[1]) identify subcategories (see complete key on page *I · 1).*

Symbole im Register stellen die rechts im Schlüssel erklärten Kategorien dar. Symbole mit hochgestellten Ziffern (∧∧[1]) bezeichnen Unterabteilungen einer Kategorie (vgl. vollständiger Schlüssel auf Seite *I · 1).*

Los símbolos incluídos en el texto del índice representan las grandes categorias identificadas con la clave a la derecha. Los símbolos con numeros en su parte superior (∧∧[1]) identifican las subcategorías (véase la clave completa en la página *I · 1).*

Les symboles de l'index représentent les catégories indiquées dans la légende à droite. Les symboles suivis d'un indice (∧∧[1]) représentent des sous-catégories (voir légende complète à la page *I · 1).*

Os símbolos incluídos no texto do índice representam as grandes categorias identificadas com a chave à direita. Os símbolos com números em sua parte superior (∧∧[1]) identificam as subcategorias (veja-se a chave completa à página *I · 1).*

∧ Mountain	Berg	Montaña	Montagne	Montanha
∧∧ Mountains	Gebirge	Montañas	Montagnes	Montanhas
)(Pass	Paß	Paso	Col	Passo
V Valley, Canyon	Tal, Cañon	Valle, Cañón	Vallée, Canyon	Vale, Canhão
≚ Plain	Ebene	Llano	Plaine	Planície
› Cape	Kap	Cabo	Cap	Cabo
I Island	Insel	Isla	Île	Ilha
II Islands	Inseln	Islas	Îles	Ilhas
⊥ Other Topographic Features	Andere Topographische Objekte	Otros Elementos Topográficos	Autres données topographiques	Outros acidentes topográficos

ESPAÑOL · FRANÇAIS · PORTUGUÊS

Nombre / Nom / Nome	Página / Page	Lat.°′	Long.°′ W = Oeste / Ouest
Nysted	41	54.40 N	11.45 E
Nytva	86	57.56 N	55.20 E
Nyūdō-zaki ≻	92	40.00 N	139.42 E
Nyugati Pályaudvar ✦[5]	264c	47.31 N	19.04 E
Nyūkawa	94	36.10 N	137.19 E
Nyumba ya Mungu Dam ✦[6]	154	3.51 S	37.28 E
Nyungwe	154	10.16 S	34.07 E
Nyunzu	154	5.57 S	28.01 E
Nyuri	120	27.42 N	92.13 E
Nyūzen	94	36.56 N	137.30 E
Nyvång	41	56.08 N	12.54 E
Nyvrovo	89	54.19 N	142.36 E
Nzaba	273b	4.06 S	15.16 E
Nzébéla	150	8.05 N	9.06 W
Nzega	154	4.13 S	33.11 E
Nzéla	152	1.25 S	12.39 E
Nzérékoré	150	7.45 N	8.49 W
N'zeto	152	7.14 S	12.52 E
Nzheleledam ⊚[1]	156	22.44 S	30.06 E
Nzi ≃	150	5.57 N	4.50 W
Nzima	154	3.03 S	32.48 E
Nziro	152	3.17 N	24.06 E
Nzo ≃	150	6.16 N	7.03 W
Nzoia ≃	154	0.03 N	33.57 E
Nzubuka	154	4.45 S	32.50 E
Nzwani (Anjouan) I	157a	12.15 S	44.25 E
O			
Oa, Mull of ≻	46	55.35 N	6.20 W
Oacoma	198	43.47 N	99.23 W
Oadby	42	52.36 N	1.04 W
Oad Street	260	51.20 N	0.41 E
Oahe, Lake ⊚[1]	198	45.30 N	100.25 W
Oahe Dam ✦[6]	198	44.21 N	100.23 W
Oahu I	229c	21.30 N	158.00 W
Oak ≃	184	49.51 N	100.28 W
O-Akan-dake ʌ	92a	43.27 N	144.10 E
Oakbank, Austl.	162	33.03 S	140.35 E
Oakbank, Austl.	168b	34.59 S	138.51 E
Oak Bay	224	48.27 N	123.18 W
Oak Beach	276	40.38 N	73.17 W
Oak Bluffs	207	41.27 N	70.33 W
Oakboro	192	35.13 N	80.19 W
Oak Brook	278	41.49 N	87.55 W
Oakbrook Center ✦[9]	278	41.52 N	87.57 W
Oakbrook Terrace	278	41.52 N	87.58 W
Oakburn	184	50.35 N	100.32 W
Oak City, N.C., U.S.	192	35.57 N	77.18 W
Oak City, Ut,. U.S.	200	39.22 N	112.20 W
Oak Creek, Co., U.S.	200	40.16 N	106.57 W
Oak Creek, Wi., U.S.	216	42.53 N	87.55 W
Oak Creek ≃, U.S.	198	45.39 N	100.31 W
Oak Creek ≃, Az., U.S.	200	34.41 N	111.56 W
Oak Creek ≃, Co., U.S.	200	40.25 N	106.50 W
Oak Creek ≃, Ks., U.S.	198	39.29 N	98.28 W
Oak Creek ≃, N.D., U.S.	198	48.38 N	100.24 W
Oak Creek ≃, Tx., U.S.	196	31.48 N	100.13 W
Oakdale, Ca., U.S.	226	37.46 N	120.50 W
Oakdale, Ct., U.S.	207	41.27 N	72.09 W
Oakdale, Il., U.S.	219	38.16 N	89.30 W
Oakdale, La., U.S.	194	30.48 N	92.39 W
Oakdale, Ma., U.S.	207	42.23 N	71.47 W
Oakdale, Ne., U.S.	198	42.04 N	97.58 W
Oakdale, N.J., U.S.	285	39.59 N	74.49 W
Oakdale, N.Y., U.S.	210	40.44 N	73.08 W
Oakdale, Pa., U.S.	214	40.23 N	80.11 W
Oakdale, Tn., U.S.	192	35.59 N	84.33 W
Oakdale Woods	278	41.56 N	87.58 W
Oakengates	42	52.42 N	2.28 W
Oakes	198	46.08 N	98.05 W
Oakesdale	202	47.07 N	117.14 W
Oakey	171a	27.26 S	151.43 E
Oakeys Brook ≃	276	40.25 N	74.30 W
Oakfield, Me., U.S.	188	46.05 N	68.09 W
Oakfield, N.Y., U.S.	210	43.03 N	78.16 W
Oakfield, Wi., U.S.	190	43.41 N	88.32 W
Oakford, Il., U.S.	219	40.06 N	89.58 W
Oakford, In., U.S.	216	40.25 N	86.06 W
Oakford, Pa., U.S.	208	40.09 N	74.58 W
Oak Forest	216	41.36 N	87.44 W
Oakgrove, Eng., U.K.	262	53.13 N	2.07 W
Oak Grove, La., U.S.	194	32.51 N	91.23 W
Oak Grove, Or., U.S.	224	45.25 N	122.38 W
Oak Hall	208	37.56 N	75.33 W
Oakham	42	52.40 N	0.43 W
Oak Harbor, Oh., U.S.	214	41.30 N	83.09 W
Oak Harbor, Wa., U.S.	224	48.17 N	122.38 W
Oak Hill, De., U.S.	285	39.44 N	75.36 W
Oak Hill, Fl., U.S.	220	28.51 N	80.51 W
Oak Hill, Mi., U.S.	190	44.13 N	86.18 W
Oak Hill, N.Y., U.S.	210	42.25 N	74.09 W
Oak Hill, Oh., U.S.	188	38.54 N	82.34 W
Oak Hill, W.V., U.S.	188	37.58 N	81.08 W
Oakhurst, Ca., U.S.	226	37.19 N	119.40 W
Oakhurst, N.J., U.S.	208	40.16 N	74.01 W
Oakhurst, Tx., U.S.	222	30.44 N	95.19 W
Oak Island I, N.S., Can.	186	44.31 N	64.18 W
Oak Island I, N.Y., U.S.	276	40.39 N	73.18 W
Oak Knolls	204	34.51 N	120.27 W
Oak Lake	184	49.47 N	100.38 W
Oak Lake ⊚, Mb., Can.	184	49.40 N	100.45 W
Oak Lake ⊚, On., Can.	184	50.26 N	93.50 W
Oak Lake ⊚, On., Can.	212	44.36 N	77.55 W
Oakland, On., Can.	214	42.09 N	82.36 W
Oakland, Ca., U.S.	226	37.48 N	122.16 W
Oakland, Ca., U.S.	282	37.48 N	122.16 W
Oakland, Fl., U.S.	220	28.33 N	81.38 W
Oakland, Il., U.S.	194	39.39 N	88.01 W
Oakland, Ia., U.S.	198	41.18 N	95.23 W
Oakland, Me., U.S.	188	44.32 N	69.43 W
Oakland, Md., U.S.	188	39.24 N	79.24 W
Oakland, Md., U.S.	284c	38.51 N	76.55 W
Oakland, Ms., U.S.	194	34.03 N	89.54 W
Oakland, Ne., U.S.	198	41.50 N	96.28 W
Oakland, N.J., U.S.	210	41.00 N	74.15 W
Oakland, Or., U.S.	202	43.25 N	123.17 W
Oakland, Pa., U.S.	210	41.57 N	75.36 W
Oakland, Pa., U.S.	214	40.59 N	80.22 W
Oakland, Tx., U.S.	222	29.36 N	96.50 W
Oakland □[6]	216	42.40 N	83.23 W
Oakland ✦[8]	279b	40.26 N	79.58 W
Oakland-Alameda County Coliseum ♠	282	37.45 N	122.12 W
Oakland Army Base ■	282	37.49 N	122.19 W
Oakland Beach	214	41.37 N	80.18 W
Oakland City	194	38.20 N	87.20 W
Oakland Gardens ✦[8]	276	40.45 N	73.45 W
Oakland Mall ✦[9]	281	42.32 N	83.07 W
Oakland Park	220	26.10 N	80.07 W
Oakland-Pontiac Airport ⊠	281	42.40 N	83.24 W
Oaklands	168b	35.00 S	137.41 E
Oaklands ✦[8]	273d	26.09 S	28.04 E
Oakland Southwest Airport ⊠	281	42.30 N	83.37 W
Oakland University ♁[2]	281	42.41 N	83.13 W
Oak Lane Manor	285	39.47 N	75.32 W
Oak Lawn, Il., U.S.	216	41.43 N	87.45 W
Oaklawn, Ks., U.S.	198	37.36 N	97.17 W
Oaklawn, Md., U.S.	284c	38.47 N	76.57 W
Oakleigh	169	37.54 S	145.06 E
Oakleigh South	274b	37.56 S	145.05 E
Oakley, Eng., U.K.	42	51.15 N	1.11 W
Oakley, Scot., U.K.	46	56.04 N	3.33 W
Oakley, Ca., U.S.	226	37.58 N	121.43 W
Oakley, Id., U.S.	202	42.14 N	113.52 W
Oakley, Il., U.S.	219	39.53 N	88.48 W
Oakley, Ks., U.S.	198	39.08 N	100.51 W
Oakley Park	216	42.34 N	83.30 W
Oaklyn	285	39.54 N	75.05 W
Oakman	194	33.42 N	87.23 W
Oakmont	214	40.31 N	79.50 W
Oak Mountain State Park ♠	194	33.22 N	86.41 W
Oakmulgee Creek ≃	194	32.28 N	87.09 W
Oak Neck ≻[1]	276	40.54 N	73.34 W
Oak Neck Point ≻	276	40.55 N	73.34 W
Oakohay Creek ≃	194	31.44 N	89.25 W
Oak Orchard Creek ≃	210	43.22 N	78.12 W
Oak Orchard Swamp ≋	210	43.07 N	78.18 W
Oakover ≃	162	20.43 S	120.33 E
Oak Park, Austl.	274b	37.43 S	144.55 E
Oak Park, Ca., U.S.	228	34.11 N	118.45 W
Oak Park, Il., U.S.	216	41.53 N	87.47 W
Oak Park, Mi., U.S.	216	42.27 N	83.10 W
Oak Park, Pa., U.S.	285	40.15 N	75.18 W
Oak Point	184	50.30 N	98.00 W
Oakridge, Ca., U.S.	226	38.03 N	121.20 W
Oak Ridge, N.J., U.S.	210	41.03 N	74.29 W
Oakridge, Or., U.S.	202	43.44 N	122.27 W
Oak Ridge, Pa., U.S.	214	41.00 N	79.18 W
Oak Ridge, Tn., U.S.	192	36.00 N	84.16 W
Oak Ridge Lake	276	41.00 N	74.32 W
Oak Ridge National Laboratory ♁[3]	192	36.00 N	84.15 W
Oak Ridge Reservoir ⊚[1]	276	41.03 N	74.30 W
Oaks	285	40.08 N	81.28 W
Oaks Corners	210	42.56 N	77.01 W
Oak Shades	276	40.26 N	74.13 W
Oakton	284c	38.52 N	77.18 W
Oaktown	194	38.52 N	87.26 W
Oakura	172	39.07 S	173.57 E
Oak Valley, N.J., U.S.	208	39.48 N	75.09 W
Oak Valley, Va., U.S.	284c	38.54 N	77.18 W
Oak View, Ca., U.S.	228	34.24 N	119.18 W
Oak View, Md., U.S.	284c	39.01 N	76.59 W
Oakview, N.J., U.S.	285	39.51 N	75.09 W
Oakview Beach	212	44.29 N	80.03 W
Oakville, Mb., Can.	184	49.56 N	97.58 W
Oakville, On., Can.	212	43.27 N	79.41 W
Oakville, Ct., U.S.	207	41.35 N	73.05 W
Oakville, In., U.S.	218	40.05 N	85.23 W
Oakville, Mo., U.S.	219	38.28 N	90.18 W
Oakville, Wa., U.S.	224	46.50 N	123.13 W
Oakwood, On., Can.	212	44.20 N	78.53 W
Oakwood, N.J., U.S.	285	39.52 N	74.50 W
Oakwood, Oh., U.S.	214	41.23 N	81.29 W
Oakwood, Oh., U.S.	216	41.05 N	84.22 W
Oakwood, Oh., U.S.	218	39.44 N	84.10 W
Oakwood, Tx., U.S.	222	31.35 N	95.50 W
Oakwood Beach	208	39.33 N	75.31 W
Oakwood Park ♠	279a	41.26 N	82.06 W
Oamaru	172	45.06 S	170.58 E
Ōamishirasato	94	35.31 N	140.19 E
Ōana	268	35.45 N	140.04 E
Oancea	38	45.55 N	28.06 E
Ōarai	94	36.18 N	140.34 E
Oaro	172	42.31 S	173.30 E
Ōasa	96	34.46 N	132.28 E
Oat Creek ≃	226	38.50 N	121.56 W
Oates Coast ⊥[2]	9	70.00 S	160.00 E
Oatka Creek ≃	210	43.01 N	77.44 W
Oatlands	166	42.18 S	147.21 E
Oatley	274a	33.59 S	151.05 E
Oatley Park ♠	274a	33.59 S	151.04 E
Oatman	200	35.01 N	114.22 W
Oaxaca □[3]	234	17.00 N	96.30 W
Oaxaca [de Juárez]	234	17.03 N	96.43 W
Ob' ≃	72	66.45 N	69.30 E
Oba ≃	190	48.55 N	84.17 W
Obaba	152	2.00 S	16.10 E
Obabika Lake ⊚	190	47.05 N	80.17 W
Obala	152	4.10 N	11.32 E
Oba Lake ⊚	190	48.38 N	84.18 W
Obama, Nihon	92	32.43 N	130.13 E
Obama, Nihon	94	35.30 N	135.45 E
Obama-wan ⊂	94	35.30 N	135.42 E
Oban, Austl.	166	21.14 S	139.03 E
Oban, Nig.	150	5.17 N	8.35 E
Oban, Scot., U.K.	46	56.25 N	5.29 W
Obanazawa	92	38.36 N	140.24 E
Obando	269f	14.43 N	120.56 E
Oban Hills ⋏[2]	150	5.35 N	8.35 E
Obara	94	35.15 N	137.18 E
Obata	94	34.30 N	136.40 E
Ob' Bay ⊂	9	70.35 S	163.22 E
Obbo	144	3.36 N	38.54 E
Obbola	26	63.42 N	20.19 E
Občuga	76	54.30 N	29.22 E
Obdach	61	47.04 N	14.41 E
Obed	182	53.33 N	117.12 W
Obed ≃	192	36.04 N	84.39 W
Obeliai	76	55.56 N	25.48 E
Obelisk ʌ	172	45.20 S	169.12 E
Oberá	252	27.29 S	55.08 W
Oberägeri	58	47.08 N	8.37 E
Oberalppass)(	58	46.39 N	8.40 E
Oberalpstock ʌ	58	46.44 N	8.46 E
Oberammergau	64	47.35 N	11.04 E
Oberau	64	47.33 N	11.08 E
Oberaudorf	64	47.39 N	12.10 E
Oberbauer	263	51.17 N	7.26 E
Oberbayern □[5]	60	48.15 N	11.45 E
Oberbieber	56	50.28 N	7.29 E
Oberbonsfeld	263	51.22 N	7.08 E
Oberbrügge	263	51.11 N	7.34 E
Obercunnersdorf	54	51.02 N	14.40 E
Oberdiessbach	58	46.51 N	7.38 E
Oberdolling	60	48.50 N	11.35 E
Oberdorla	54	51.10 N	10.25 E
Oberdrauburg	64	46.45 N	12.58 E
Oberelfringhausen	263	51.20 N	7.11 E
Ober Engadin V	58	46.37 N	9.58 E
Oberengstringen	58	47.25 N	8.28 E
Oberer See → Superior, Lake ⊚	190	48.00 N	88.00 W
Oberfranken □[5]	60	49.50 N	11.20 E
Obergeis	56	50.54 N	9.35 E
Ober-Grafendorf	61	48.09 N	15.33 E
Obergum	52	53.20 N	6.31 E
Obergünzburg	58	47.51 N	10.25 E
Obergurgl	64	46.52 N	11.01 E
Obergurig	54	51.07 N	14.24 E
Oberhaan	263	51.13 N	7.02 E
Oberhaching	60	48.02 N	11.37 E
Oberharmersbach	58	48.22 N	8.07 E
Oberhaslach	58	48.33 N	7.20 E
Oberhausen	56	51.28 N	6.50 E
Oberhof	54	50.41 N	10.44 E
Oberhofen	58	46.44 N	7.40 E
Oberinntal V	64	47.13 N	10.45 E
Oberjettingen	56	48.34 N	8.46 E
Oberjoch	58	47.31 N	10.23 E
Ober-Kassel ✦[8]	263	51.14 N	6.46 E
Oberkirch	58	48.31 N	8.05 E
Oberkirchbach	264b	48.17 N	16.12 E
Oberkirchen	56	51.09 N	8.22 E
Oberkochen	56	48.47 N	10.06 E
Oberkotzau	54	50.16 N	11.56 E
Oberlaa ✦[8]	264b	48.08 N	16.24 E
Oberlaapark ♠	264b	48.08 N	16.25 E
Oberlausitz □[9]	54	51.15 N	14.30 E
Oberlin, Ks., U.S.	198	39.49 N	100.31 W
Oberlin, La., U.S.	194	30.37 N	92.45 W
Oberlin, Oh., U.S.	214	41.17 N	82.13 W
Oberlin, Pa., U.S.	208	40.14 N	76.49 W
Oberloisdorf	61	47.27 N	16.30 E
Oberlungwitz	54	50.47 N	12.44 E
Obermarchtal	58	48.14 N	9.34 E
Obermeiser	56	51.26 N	9.19 E
Obermieming	64	47.18 N	10.59 E
Obermodern	56	48.51 N	7.32 E
Obermoschel	56	49.44 N	7.46 E
Obermühl	61	48.27 N	13.55 E
Obermünstertal	58	47.52 N	7.49 E
Obernai	58	48.28 N	7.29 E
Obernbeck	52	52.12 N	8.41 E
Obernberg am Inn	60	48.19 N	13.20 E
Obernburg am Main	56	49.50 N	9.08 E
Oberndorf	52	53.45 N	9.08 E
Oberndorf am Neckar	58	48.18 N	8.34 E
Oberndorf bei Salzburg	64	47.57 N	12.56 E
Oberndorf in Tirol	64	47.30 N	12.23 E
Oberne	171b	35.24 S	147.50 E
Oberne Hill ʌ[2]	171b	35.26 S	147.53 E
Obernhausen	56	50.29 N	9.56 E
Obernkirchen	52	52.16 N	9.07 E
Obernzell	60	48.34 N	13.39 E
Oberoderwitz	54	50.58 N	14.42 E
Oberon	170	33.43 S	149.52 E
Oberösterreich □[3]	30	48.15 N	14.00 E
Oberpfalz □[5]	60	49.30 N	12.10 E
Oberpleis	56	50.43 N	7.16 E
Oberpullendorf	61	47.31 N	16.31 E
Ober-Ramstadt	56	49.49 N	8.44 E
Oberried	58	46.44 N	7.58 E
Oberriet	58	47.19 N	9.33 E
Oberrimsingen	58	47.59 N	7.40 E
Oberröblingen	54	51.26 N	11.18 E
Ober Sankt Veit ✦[8]	264b	48.11 N	16.16 E
Oberscheidental	56	49.30 N	9.09 E
Oberscheinfeld	56	49.42 N	10.26 E
Oberscheld	56	50.44 N	8.20 E
Oberschleissheim	60	48.15 N	11.34 E
Oberschöneweide ✦[8]	264a	52.28 N	13.31 E
Oberseebach	56	48.58 N	7.59 E
Obersickte	54	52.13 N	10.38 E
Oberspier	54	51.19 N	10.51 E
Oberstadtfeld	56	50.10 N	6.46 E
Oberstaufen	58	47.33 N	10.01 E
Oberstdorf	58	47.24 N	10.16 E
Obersteinbach	56	49.02 N	7.41 E
Oberstreu	56	50.24 N	10.17 E
Obersuhl	56	50.56 N	10.02 E
Obersulm	56	49.08 N	9.27 E
Obertheres	56	50.01 N	10.26 E
Obertilliach	64	46.42 N	12.37 E
Obertin	78	48.42 N	25.11 E
Obertraubling	60	48.58 N	12.10 E
Obertraun	64	47.33 N	13.41 E
Obertrum	64	47.56 N	13.05 E
Obertrumer See ⊚	60	47.58 N	13.06 E
Obertürken	60	48.19 N	12.50 E
Oberueckersee ⊚	54	53.12 N	13.52 E
Oberursel	56	50.11 N	8.35 E
Oberuzwil	58	47.26 N	9.08 E
Obervellach	64	46.56 N	13.12 E
Oberviechtach	60	49.28 N	12.25 E
Obervolta → Burkina Faso □[1]	150	13.00 N	1.30 W
Oberwald	58	46.32 N	8.21 E
Oberwart	61	47.17 N	16.13 E
Oberweissbach	54	50.35 N	11.08 E
Oberwengern	263	51.23 N	7.22 E
Oberwesel	56	50.06 N	7.43 E
Oberwiesenthal	54	50.25 N	12.59 E
Oberwolfach	58	48.19 N	8.12 E
Oberwölz Stadt	61	47.13 N	14.17 E
Oberzeiring	61	47.15 N	14.29 E
Obetz	218	39.52 N	82.57 W
Obey, East Fork ≃	192	36.27 N	85.07 W
Obey, West Fork ≃	192	36.27 N	85.09 W
Obgruiten	263	51.13 N	7.01 E
Obhausen	54	51.23 N	11.39 E
Obi	150	8.22 N	8.46 E
Obi, Kepulauan II	164	1.30 S	127.45 E
Obi, Pulau I	164	1.30 S	127.45 E
Obi, Selat ⋓	164	0.52 S	127.33 E
Obiaruku	150	5.51 N	6.09 E
Obichingou ≃	85	38.53 N	70.01 E
Obichody	78	51.02 N	28.59 E
Óbidos	250	1.55 S	55.31 W
Obi-Garm	85	38.43 N	69.42 E
Obihiro	92a	42.55 N	143.12 E
Obikanda	85	39.10 N	67.10 E
Obilatu, Pulau I	108	1.25 S	127.20 E
Obil'noje	80	47.31 N	44.25 E
Obing	60	48.00 N	12.24 E
Obion	194	36.15 N	89.11 W
Obion ≃	194	35.55 N	89.39 W
Obion, Middle Fork ≃	194	36.13 N	88.56 W
Obion, Rutherford Fork ≃	194	36.17 N	89.01 W
Obion, South Fork ≃	194	36.17 N	89.03 W
Obion Creek ≃	194	36.35 N	89.11 W
Obiou, Grande Tête de l' ʌ	62	44.46 N	5.50 E
Obira	92a	44.00 N	141.35 E
Obitočnaja kosa ≻[2]	78	46.33 N	36.13 E
Obitočnyj zaliv ⊂	78	46.35 N	36.00 E
Obitsu ≃	94	35.24 N	139.54 E
Objačevo	24	60.20 N	49.34 E
Oblačnaja, gora ʌ	89	43.45 N	134.10 E
Öblarn	61	47.27 N	13.59 E
Oblastnaja	80	56.59 N	52.37 E
Oblivskaja	80	48.32 N	42.30 E
Oblong	194	39.00 N	87.54 W
Oblučje	89	49.03 N	131.04 E
Obninsk	82	55.05 N	36.37 E
Obnora ≃	76	58.14 N	40.58 E
Obnova	38	43.26 N	24.59 E
Obo	154	5.24 N	26.30 E
Obobogorap	158	27.18 S	20.04 E
Obock	144	11.59 N	43.16 E
Obojan'	78	51.13 N	36.16 E
Ō-boke ♠	96	33.55 N	133.46 E
Obokote	154	0.52 S	26.19 E
Obol'	76	55.22 N	29.17 E
Obol' ≃	76	55.24 N	29.02 E
Oboldino	265b	55.53 N	37.56 E
Obolon'	78	49.36 N	32.52 E
Oborniki	30	52.39 N	16.51 E
Obot	144	4.30 N	37.20 E
Obouya	152	0.56 S	15.43 E
Oboz'orskij	24	63.28 N	40.18 E
Obra ≃	30	52.36 N	15.28 E
Obrazcovo-Travino	80	45.58 N	48.02 E
Obree, Mount ʌ	164	9.30 S	148.05 E
Obrenovac	38	44.39 N	20.12 E
O'Brien	202	42.04 N	123.42 W
O'Brien Coulee V	202	48.38 N	110.22 W
Obrighoven-Lackhausen	52	51.40 N	6.38 E
Obrovac	36	44.12 N	15.41 E
Obrovo	76	52.30 N	25.34 E
Obručeva, gora ʌ	88	53.36 N	113.52 E
Obručevka	85	42.30 N	69.05 E
Obruk	130	38.10 N	33.12 E
Obryta	54	53.13 N	14.59 E
Obryvistoje	89	48.46 N	144.40 E
Obša ≃	76	55.55 N	32.32 E
Obšarovka	80	53.07 N	48.52 E
Obščij Syrt ʌ	80	52.00 N	51.30 E
Observation Peak ʌ	204	40.46 N	120.10 W
Observatoire, Caye de l' I	160	21.25 S	158.50 E
Observatorio Cerro Tololo ♁[3]	252	30.05 S	71.00 W
Observatory Inlet ⊂	182	55.10 N	129.54 W
Obskaja guba ⊂	72	69.00 N	73.00 E
Obsteig	64	47.18 N	10.56 E
Obtovo	78	51.37 N	33.13 E
Ob' Trench ✢[1]	14	33.00 S	98.00 E
Ōbu	94	35.00 N	136.58 E
Obu ✦[8]	270	34.44 N	135.09 E
Obuasi	150	6.14 N	1.39 W
Obubra	150	6.05 N	8.21 E
Obuchov	78	50.08 N	30.37 E
Obuchova	76	56.06 N	32.22 E
Obuchoviči	78	51.00 N	29.46 E
Obuchovka	86	46.13 N	81.05 E
Obuchovo, Ross.	82	55.50 N	38.16 E
Obuchovo, Ross.	82	56.09 N	36.55 E
Óbuda ✦[8]	264c	47.33 N	19.02 E
Óbudai-sziget I	264c	47.33 N	19.04 E
Obudu	150	6.40 N	9.09 E
Obuse	94	36.42 N	138.19 E
Obushkong Lake ⊚	190	47.42 N	80.48 W
Obuškovo	82	55.47 N	37.02 E
Obu-tōge)(	270	34.44 N	135.10 E
Obva ≃	86	58.32 N	55.18 E
Obvinsk	86	58.29 N	54.51 E
Obwalden □[3]	58	46.50 N	8.14 E
Obžericha	80	57.11 N	42.58 E
Očakov	78	46.37 N	31.33 E
Očakovo ✦[8]	265b	55.41 N	37.27 E
Ocala	192	29.11 N	82.08 W
Ocallí	248	6.09 S	78.18 W
Očamčira	84	42.44 N	41.28 E
Ocamo ≃	246	2.48 N	65.14 W
Ocampo, Méx.	232	28.11 N	108.23 W
Ocampo, Méx.	232	27.20 N	102.21 W
Ocampo, Méx.	234	22.50 N	99.20 W
Ocampo, Méx.	234	21.39 N	101.30 W
Ocaña, Col.	246	8.15 N	73.20 W
Ocaña, Esp.	34	39.56 N	3.31 W
Ocate Creek ≃	196	36.17 N	104.30 W
Occaquan ≃	208	38.40 N	77.14 W
Occaquan Reservoir ⊚[1]	208	38.43 N	77.22 W
Očchamuri	84	41.52 N	41.50 E
Occhieppo Inferiore	62	45.33 N	8.01 E
Occhiobello	64	44.55 N	11.35 E
Occidental, Cordillera ⋏, Col.	246	5.00 N	76.00 W
Occidental, Cordillera ⋏, Perú	248	10.00 S	77.00 W
Occidental College ♁[2]	280	34.08 N	118.13 W
Occidental de Zapata, Ciénaga ≋	240p	22.25 N	81.20 W
Occimiano	62	45.03 N	8.30 E
Occoquan	208	38.41 N	77.15 W
Occoquan Bay ⊂	208	38.37 N	77.13 W
Ocean □[6]	208	39.58 N	74.12 W
Oceana	192	37.41 N	81.37 W
Oceana Naval Air Station ■	208	36.50 N	76.02 W
Ocean Bay Park	276	40.39 N	73.08 W
Ocean Beach	276	40.38 N	73.18 W
Ocean Bluff	207	42.05 N	70.39 W
Ocean Breeze Park	220	27.15 N	80.14 W
Ocean Cape ≻	180	59.30 N	139.45 W
Ocean City, Md., U.S.	208	38.20 N	75.05 W
Ocean City, N.J., U.S.	208	39.16 N	74.34 W
Ocean City, Wa., U.S.	224	47.04 N	124.09 W
Ocean Falls	182	52.21 N	127.40 W
Ocean Gate	208	39.55 N	74.08 W
Ocean Grove, Austl.	169	38.16 S	144.32 E
Ocean Grove, Ma., U.S.	207	41.43 N	71.12 W
Ocean Heights	207	41.24 N	70.33 W
Ocean Island → Banaba I	174d	0.52 S	169.35 E
Ocean Lake ⊚[1]	202	43.11 N	108.36 W
Oceano	204	35.06 N	120.37 W
Ocean Park, B.C., Can.	224	49.02 N	122.53 W
Ocean Park, Wa., U.S.	224	46.29 N	124.02 W
Ocean Park ♠	271d	22.15 N	114.09 E
Ocean Port	276	40.19 N	74.00 W
Ocean Shores	224	47.01 N	124.09 W
Oceanside, Ca., U.S.	228	33.11 N	117.22 W
Oceanside, N.Y., U.S.	210	40.38 N	73.38 W
Ocean Springs	194	30.24 N	88.49 W
Ocean View, De., U.S.	208	38.32 N	75.05 W
Ocean View, N.J., U.S.	208	39.10 N	74.44 W
Oceanville	208	39.28 N	74.27 W
Oceola	214	40.51 N	83.06 W
Očer	80	57.53 N	54.42 E
Očeretino	83	48.14 N	37.36 E
O. C. Fisher Lake ⊚[1]	196	31.30 N	100.30 W
Ocha	89	53.34 N	142.56 E
Ochagavía, Canal ≊	286e	33.30 S	70.49 W
Ochanomizu Women's University ♁[2]	268	35.43 N	139.44 E
Ochansk	86	57.43 N	55.23 E
Ochapowace Indian Reserve ✦[4]	184	50.30 N	102.24 W
Ocheyedan	198	43.24 N	95.32 W
Ocheyedan ≃	198	43.08 N	95.09 W
Ochi, Nihon	96	33.32 N	133.15 E
Ōchi, Nihon	96	35.04 N	132.36 E
Ōchi, Nihon	96	34.16 N	134.18 E
Ochiai	96	35.01 N	133.45 E
Ochiai ✦[8]	268	35.43 N	139.42 E
O'Chiese Indian Reserve ✦[4]	182	52.50 N	115.28 W
Ochil Hills ⋏[2]	46	56.14 N	3.40 W
Ochiltree	44	55.28 N	4.23 W
Ōchise ≃	94	35.03 N	137.46 E
Ochlocknee	192	30.58 N	84.03 W
Ochlockonee ≃	192	29.58 N	84.21 W
Ochoco Creek ≃	202	44.19 N	120.53 W
Ochoco Mountains ⋏	202	44.30 N	120.35 W
Ochopee	220	25.54 N	81.18 W
Ocho Rios	241q	18.25 N	77.07 W
Ochota ≃	74	59.20 N	143.04 E
Ochotsk	74	59.23 N	143.18 E
Ochotskisches Meer → Okhotsk, Sea of ⊤[2]	74	53.00 N	150.00 E
Ochotskoje more → Okhotsk, Sea of ⊤[2]	74	53.00 N	150.00 E
Ochre River	184	51.03 N	99.47 W
Ochsenfurt	56	49.40 N	10.03 E
Ochsenhausen	58	48.04 N	9.56 E
Ochsenwerder ✦[8]	52	53.28 N	10.05 E
Ochta ≃	265a	59.57 N	30.24 E
Ochtrup	52	52.13 N	7.11 E
Ochvat	76	56.46 N	32.27 E
Oci ≃	152	15.14 S	15.16 E
Ocilla	192	31.35 N	83.15 W
Ock ≃	42	51.39 N	1.17 W
Ockelbo	26	60.53 N	16.43 E
Öckerö	26	57.43 N	11.39 E
Ockham	260	51.18 N	0.27 W
Ockholm	41	54.40 N	8.49 E
Ockies	158	31.31 S	21.41 E
Ocklawaha, Lake ⊚[1]	192	29.30 N	81.50 W
Ocmulgee ≃	192	31.58 N	82.32 W
Ocmulgee National Monument ♠	192	32.43 N	83.38 W
Ocna Mureș	38	46.23 N	23.51 E
Ocoa, Bahía de ⊂	238	18.22 N	70.39 W
Ocoee	220	28.34 N	81.32 W
Ocoee (Toccoa) ≃	192	35.12 N	84.40 W
Ocoña	248	16.26 S	73.07 W
Ocoña ≃	248	16.28 S	73.07 W
Oconee	219	39.17 N	89.07 W
Oconee ≃	192	31.58 N	82.32 W
Oconee, Lake ⊚[1]	192	33.30 N	83.15 W
Ocongate	248	13.38 S	71.24 W
O'Connell	170	33.32 S	149.44 E
Oconomowoc	216	43.06 N	88.29 W
Oconomowoc ≃	216	43.07 N	88.37 W
Oconomowoc Lake	216	42.37 N	88.28 W
Oconomowoc Lake ⊚	216	43.06 N	88.27 W
Oconto	190	44.53 N	87.51 W
Oconto ≃	190	44.53 N	87.50 W
Oconto, North Branch ≃	190	45.00 N	88.23 W
Oconto Falls	190	44.52 N	88.08 W
Ocós	236	14.31 N	92.11 W
Ocosingo	232	16.54 N	92.07 W
Ocotal	236	13.38 N	86.29 W
Ocotepec	234	17.13 N	93.09 W
Ocotepeque □[5]	236	14.30 N	89.00 W
Ocotlán	234	20.21 N	102.46 W
Ocotlán de Morelos	234	16.48 N	96.40 W
Ocoyoacac	234	19.16 N	99.26 W
Ocozocoautla [de Espinosa]	234	16.46 N	93.22 W
Ocracoke	192	35.06 N	75.58 W
Ocracoke Island I	192	35.09 N	75.53 W
Ocre, Monte ʌ	66	42.15 N	13.26 E
Ocros	248	10.24 S	77.24 W
Octoraro Creek ≃	208	39.39 N	76.09 W
Octoraro Creek, East Branch ≃	208	39.49 N	76.02 W
Octoraro Creek, West Branch ≃	208	39.49 N	76.05 W
Octoraro Lake ⊚[1]	208	39.48 N	76.02 W
Ocú	236	7.57 N	80.47 W
Ocuilán de Arteaga	234	18.58 N	99.25 W
Ocumare del Tuy	246	10.07 N	66.46 W
Ocuri	248	18.50 S	65.50 W
Ocussi	112	9.12 S	124.21 E
Oda, Ghana	150	5.55 N	0.59 W
Oda, Nihon	96	33.34 N	132.48 E
Ōda, Nihon	96	35.11 N	132.30 E
Oda ≃	96	34.37 N	133.44 E
Oda, Jabal ʌ	140	20.21 N	36.39 E
Ŏdaejin	98	41.34 N	129.40 E
Odae-san Kukrip Kongwŏn ♠	98	37.46 N	128.37 E
Ōdai	94	34.24 N	136.25 E
Ōdaigahara-zan ʌ	92	34.11 N	136.05 E
Odaka	92	37.34 N	141.00 E
Ödåkra	41	56.06 N	12.44 E
Odanakumadona	156	20.53 S	24.45 E
Ōdate	92	40.16 N	140.34 E
Odawara	94	35.15 N	139.10 E
Odayeri ✦[8]	267b	41.14 N	28.51 E
Odda	26	60.04 N	6.33 E
Odden	41	55.58 N	11.22 E
Odder	41	55.58 N	10.10 E
Oddville	218	38.27 N	84.15 W
Odebolt	198	42.18 N	95.15 W
Ödeby	40	59.24 N	15.25 E
Odei ≃	184	56.06 N	96.55 W
Odeleite, Ribeira de ≃	34	37.21 N	7.27 W
Odell, Il., U.S.	216	41.00 N	88.31 W
Odell, Ne., U.S.	198	40.03 N	96.48 W
Odell, Or., U.S.	224	45.37 N	121.32 W
Odell, Tx., U.S.	196	34.21 N	99.25 W
Odell Lake ⊚	202	43.34 N	122.00 W
Odelzhausen	60	48.19 N	11.12 E
Odem	196	27.57 N	97.34 W
Odemira	34	37.36 N	8.38 W
Ödemiș	130	38.13 N	27.59 E
Ödenburg → Sopron	61	47.41 N	16.36 E
Odendaalsrus	158	27.48 S	26.45 E
Odenkirchen ✦[8]	263	51.08 N	6.27 E
Odensbacken	40	59.10 N	15.32 E
Odense	41	55.24 N	10.23 E
Odense ≃	41	55.26 N	10.26 E
Odense Fjord ⊂	41	55.30 N	10.34 E
Odenthal	56	51.02 N	7.07 E
Odenton	208	39.05 N	76.42 W
Odenwald ⋏	56	49.40 N	9.00 E
Oder ≃, Dtsch.	52	51.40 N	10.06 E
Oder (Odra) ≃, Europe	30	53.32 N	14.38 E
Oderberg	54	52.52 N	14.02 E
Oderbruch ✦[1]	54	52.40 N	14.15 E
Oderen	58	47.55 N	6.59 E
Oderhaff (Zalew Szczeciński) ⊂	54	53.46 N	14.14 E
Oder-Havel-Kanal ≊	54	52.52 N	14.02 E
Oder-Spree-Kanal ≊	54	52.23 N	13.41 E
Odertalsperre ✦[6]	54	51.38 N	10.30 E
Oderzo	64	45.47 N	12.29 E
Odesa → Odessa	78	46.28 N	30.44 E
Ödeshög	26	58.14 N	14.39 E
Odessa, On., Can.	212	44.17 N	76.43 W
Odessa, Ukr.	78	46.28 N	30.44 E
Odessa, De., U.S.	208	39.27 N	75.39 W
Odessa, Fl., U.S.	220	28.11 N	82.35 W
Odessa, Mo., U.S.	194	38.59 N	93.57 W
Odessa, N.Y., U.S.	210	42.20 N	76.47 W
Odessa, Tx., U.S.	196	31.50 N	102.22 W
Odessa, Wa., U.S.	202	47.20 N	118.41 W
Odessa □[4]	78	47.30 N	30.00 E
Odessa Lake ⊚	212	44.19 N	76.41 W
Odesskoje	86	54.13 N	72.58 E
Odiakwe	156	20.01 S	25.17 E
Odib, Wādī V	140	22.38 N	36.06 E
Odiel ≃	34	37.10 N	6.54 W
Odienné	150	9.30 N	7.34 W
Odiham	42	51.15 N	0.57 W
Odin	219	38.37 N	89.03 W
Odin, Mount ʌ	182	50.33 N	118.08 W
Odincovo, Ross.	82	54.40 N	38.00 E
Odincovo, Ross.	82	55.41 N	37.17 E
Odiongan	116	12.24 N	121.59 E
Odiongan Bay ⊂	116	12.25 N	121.58 E
Odivelas	266c	38.47 N	9.11 W
Odobești	38	45.45 N	27.04 E
Odojev	76	53.56 N	36.41 E
Odolanów	30	51.35 N	17.39 E
Ōdomari-chosuichi ⊚	96	34.43 N	132.18 E
Odon	194	38.50 N	86.59 W
Ŏdŏngk	110	11.48 N	104.45 E
O'Donnell	196	32.57 N	101.49 W
O'Donnell ≃	162	18.22 S	126.36 E
Odoorn	52	52.51 N	6.51 E
Odorheiu Secuiesc	38	46.18 N	25.18 E
Odra (Oder) ≃	30	53.32 N	14.38 E
Odra Port	54	53.52 N	14.14 E
Odrinhas	266c	38.53 N	9.22 W
Odrzywół	30	51.32 N	20.33 E
Ødsted	41	55.39 N	9.25 E
Odum	192	31.39 N	82.01 W
Odžaci	38	45.30 N	19.16 E
Odzala, Parc National d' ♠	152	1.00 S	15.00 E
Odzi	154	18.58 S	32.23 E
Odzi ≃	154	19.45 S	32.24 E
Odziba	152	3.35 S	15.31 E
Ōe	96	35.23 N	135.09 E
Oebisfelde	54	52.25 N	10.59 E
Oedelem	50	51.10 N	3.20 E
Oederan	54	50.52 N	13.09 E
Oeding	52	51.56 N	6.49 E
Oedt	56	51.19 N	6.22 E
Oegstgeest	52	52.10 N	4.29 E
Oeiras, Bra.	250	7.01 S	42.08 W
Oeiras, Port.	266c	38.41 N	9.21 W
Oeiras do Pará	250	1.58 S	49.51 W
Oelde	52	51.49 N	8.08 E
Oelemari ≃	250	3.13 N	54.09 W
Oella	284b	39.16 N	76.47 W
Oelsig	54	51.41 N	13.22 E
Oelsnitz, Dtsch.	54	50.24 N	12.10 E
Oelsnitz, Dtsch.	54	50.43 N	12.41 E
Oels → Oleśnica	30	51.13 N	17.23 E
Oelwein	190	42.40 N	91.54 W
Oenpelli	164	12.20 S	133.04 E
Oensingen	58	47.17 N	7.44 E
Oepping	60	48.36 N	13.56 E
Oeraro-do I	98	34.27 N	127.30 E
Oer-Erkenschwick	52	51.39 N	7.15 E
Oerlinghausen	52	51.57 N	8.39 E
Oermten	263	51.29 N	6.27 E
Oesede	52	52.12 N	8.04 E
Oespel ✦[8]	263	51.30 N	7.23 E
Oeste, Canal del ≊	266a	40.32 N	3.42 W
Oeste, Parque del ♠	266a	40.26 N	3.44 W
Oesterdam ✦[5]	52	51.29 N	4.15 E
Oestrich	263	51.22 N	7.38 E
Oestrich ✦[8]	263	51.34 N	7.22 E
Oestrum ✦[8]	263	51.25 N	6.40 E
Ōetaka-yama ʌ	96	35.04 N	132.26 E
Oettingen in Bayern	56	48.57 N	10.36 E
Oetz	64	47.12 N	10.54 E
Oeuf ≃	50	48.11 N	2.21 E
Oeventrop	56	51.23 N	8.08 E
Oeversee	41	54.42 N	9.26 E
Ōe-yama ʌ	96	35.27 N	135.07 E
Oeyŏn-do I	98	36.14 N	126.05 E
Of	130	40.57 N	40.18 E
O'Fallon, Il., U.S.	219	38.35 N	89.54 W
O'Fallon, Mo., U.S.	219	38.48 N	90.41 W
O'Fallon Creek ≃	198	46.50 N	105.09 W
Ofanto ≃	68	41.22 N	16.13 E
Ofaqim	132	31.17 N	34.37 E
Ofenpass → Fuorn, Pass dal)(	58	46.37 N	10.15 E
Offa	150	8.09 N	4.44 E
Offaly □[6]	48	53.20 N	7.30 W
Offanengo	62	45.22 N	9.44 E
Offemont	58	47.40 N	6.53 E
Offenbach	56	50.08 N	8.47 E
Offenburg	58	48.28 N	7.57 E
Offendorf	58	48.43 N	7.55 E
Offerdal	26	63.28 N	14.00 E
Offham	260	51.17 N	0.23 E
Officer	274b	38.04 S	145.25 E
Officer Creek ≃	162	27.45 S	132.24 E
Offida	66	42.56 N	13.41 E
Offingen	58	48.29 N	10.21 E
Offranville	50	49.52 N	1.03 E
Offutt Air Force Base ■	198	41.08 N	95.56 W
Oficina Alemania	252	25.10 S	69.55 W
Oficina Alianza	248	20.46 S	69.42 W
Oficina Chile	252	25.09 S	69.54 W
Oficina Pedro de Valdivia	252	22.36 S	69.40 W
Oficina Victoria	248	20.44 S	69.42 W
Ofin	273a	6.33 N	3.30 E
Öflingen	58	47.35 N	7.55 E
Ofotfjorden ⊂[2]	24	68.23 N	16.10 E
Oftringen	58	47.19 N	7.56 E
Ofu	174y	14.10 S	169.42 W
Ofu I	174y	14.11 S	169.42 W
Ōfukuroshinden	268	35.53 N	139.27 E
Ōfuna	268	35.21 N	139.32 E
Ōfunato	92	39.04 N	141.43 E
Oga	92	39.53 N	139.51 E
Ogaden ✦[1]	144	8.00 N	44.00 E
Oga-hantō ≻[1]	92	39.55 N	139.50 E
Ōgaki, Nihon	94	35.21 N	136.37 E
Ōgaki, Nihon	96	34.06 N	132.30 E
Ogallala	198	41.07 N	101.43 W
Ogan ≃	112	3.01 S	104.44 E
Ogano	94	36.01 N	139.00 E
Ogasa	94	34.41 N	138.06 E
Ogasawara-guntō (Bonin Islands) II	14	27.00 N	142.10 E
Ōgata, Nihon	94	37.13 N	138.20 E
Ōgata, Nihon	96	33.01 N	133.01 E
Ogata, Nihon	96	32.58 N	131.29 E
Ōga-tō ʌ	94	36.13 N	138.06 E
Ogatsu	92	38.31 N	141.28 E
Ogawa, Nihon	92	32.35 N	130.43 E
Ogawa, Nihon	94	36.10 N	140.21 E
Ogawa, Nihon	94	36.37 N	137.58 E
Ogawa, Nihon	94	36.03 N	139.16 E
Ogawa, Nihon	94	36.45 N	140.08 E
Ogawa, Nihon	268	35.44 N	139.28 E
Ogawara-ko ⊚	92	40.47 N	141.20 E
Ogbomosho	150	8.08 N	4.15 E
Ogden, Ia., U.S.	190	42.02 N	94.01 W
Ogden, Ks., U.S.	198	39.06 N	96.42 W
Ogden, Pa., U.S.	208	39.49 N	75.27 W
Ogden, Ut,. U.S.	200	41.13 N	111.58 W
Ogden, Mount ʌ	180	58.26 N	133.23 W
Ogden Dunes	216	41.38 N	87.12 W
Ogden Island I	212	44.52 N	75.12 W
Ogden Reservoir ⊚[1]	262	53.42 N	2.22 W
Ogdensburg, N.J., U.S.	210	41.04 N	74.35 W
Ogdensburg, N.Y., U.S.	212	44.41 N	75.29 W
Ogeechee ≃	192	31.51 N	81.06 W
Ōge-jima I	96	34.12 N	134.38 E
Ogema	184	49.35 N	104.55 W
Oggersheim	56	49.29 N	8.22 E
Oghi Fort	123	34.31 N	73.01 E
Ogibalovo	76	60.34 N	39.40 E
Ogidaki Mountain ʌ[2]	190	46.58 N	83.58 W
Ogies	158	26.02 S	29.04 E
Ogi-jima I	96	34.26 N	134.04 E
Ogijo	273a	6.42 N	3.31 E
Ogilvie, Austl.	162	28.09 S	114.38 E
Ogilvie, Mn., U.S.	190	45.49 N	93.25 W
Ogilvie ≃	180	65.52 N	137.16 W
Ogilvie Mountains ⋏	180	65.00 N	139.30 W
Ogilville	218	39.08 N	86.01 W
Ōgimi	174m	26.42 N	128.07 E
Ōgino-sen ʌ	96	35.26 N	134.26 E
Ogle □[6]	216	42.01 N	89.20 W
Oglesby, Il., U.S.	216	41.17 N	89.03 W
Oglesby, Tx., U.S.	222	31.25 N	97.31 W
Oglethorpe	192	32.17 N	84.03 W
Ogliastra ✦[1]	71	39.56 N	9.37 E
Ogliastro Cilento	68	40.21 N	15.03 E
Oglio ≃	64	45.02 N	10.39 E
Ogmore	166	22.37 S	149.40 E
Ogmore ≃	42	51.28 N	3.38 W
Ogmore Vale	42	51.38 N	3.31 W
Ogni	86	51.54 N	83.31 E
Ognica	54	53.07 N	14.27 E
Ognon ≃	58	47.20 N	5.29 E
Ogn'ov Jar	86	58.23 N	76.29 E
Ogn'ovka	86	49.36 N	83.25 E
Ōgo	94	36.25 N	139.10 E
Ōgo ✦[8]	270	34.49 N	135.06 E
Ōgo ≃	270	34.47 N	135.04 E
Ogoamas, Bulu ʌ	112	0.40 N	120.12 E
Ogōchi-dam ✦[6]	94	35.47 N	139.04 E
Ogodža	89	52.44 N	132.31 E
Ogoja	150	6.40 N	8.48 E
Ogoki ≃	176	51.38 N	85.57 W
'Ogol, Khaṭṭ el V	150	20.01 N	15.29 W
Ogooué ≃	152	0.49 S	9.00 E
Ogooué-Ivindo □[4]	152	1.00 N	13.00 E
Ogooué-Lolo □[4]	152	1.00 S	12.30 E
Ogooué-Maritime □[4]	152	2.00 S	9.30 E
Ogōri, Nihon	96	33.22 N	130.32 E
Ogōri, Nihon	96	34.06 N	131.24 E
Ogorodnoje	78	45.53 N	28.50 E
Ogose	94	35.58 N	139.18 E
Ogosta ≃	38	43.45 N	23.51 E
Ogou ≃	150	7.50 N	1.19 E
Ogoyo	273a	6.26 N	3.29 E
Ogr	140	12.02 N	27.06 E
Ogre	76	56.51 N	24.36 E
Ogre ≃	76	56.48 N	24.36 E
Ogrodzieniec	30	50.27 N	19.31 E
Ogrosen	54	51.42 N	14.02 E
Ōguchi	94	35.20 N	136.55 E
Ŏgu-dong	98	38.57 N	126.56 E
Ogudu	273a	6.34 N	3.24 E
Ogulin	36	45.16 N	15.14 E
Ogun □[3]	150	6.45 N	3.25 E
Ogun ≃	150	6.36 N	3.27 E
Ogun Forest Reserve ♠	273a	6.37 N	3.26 E
Oguni, Nihon	92	38.04 N	139.45 E
Oguni, Nihon	96	33.07 N	131.04 E

≃	River	Fluß	Río	Rivière	Rio
≊	Canal	Kanal	Canal	Canal	Canal
⌞	Waterfall, Rapids	Wasserfall, Stromschnellen	Cascada, Rápidos	Chute d'eau, Rapides	Cascata, Rápidos
⋓	Strait	Meeresstraße	Estrecho	Détroit	Estreito
⊂	Bay, Gulf	Bucht, Golf	Bahía, Golfo	Baie, Golfe	Baía, Golfo
⊚	Lake, Lakes	See, Seen	Lago, Lagos	Lac, Lacs	Lago, Lagos
≋	Swamp	Sumpf	Pantano	Marais	Pântano
⊞	Ice Features, Glacier	Eis- und Gletscherformen	Accidentes Glaciales	Formes glaciaires	Acidentes glaciares
⊤	Other Hydrographic Features	Andere Hydrographische Objekte	Otros Elementos Hidrográficos	Autres données hydrographiques	Outros acidentes hidrográficos
✢	Submarine Features	Untermeerische Objekte	Accidentes Submarinos	Formes de relief sous-marin	Acidentes submarinos
□	Political Unit	Politische Einheit	Unidad Politica	Entité politique	Unidade política
♁	Cultural Institution	Kulturelle Institution	Institución Cultural	Institution culturelle	Instituição cultural
⊥	Historical Site	Historische Stätte	Sitio Histórico	Site historique	Sítio histórico
♠	Recreational Site	Erholungs- und Ferienort	Sitio de Recreo	Centre de loisirs	Area de Lazer
⊠	Airport	Flughafen	Aeropuerto	Aéroport	Aeroporto
■	Military Installation	Militäranlage	Instalación Militar	Installation militaire	Instalação militar
✦	Miscellaneous	Verschiedenes	Misceláneo	Divers	Diversos

ENGLISH Name	Page	Lat.°′	Long.°′	DEUTSCH Name	Seite	Breite°′	Länge°′ E = Ost

Ogunlogun 273a 6.41 N 3.28 E
Ogunquit 188 43.14 N 70.35 W
Ogura-san ʌ 94 36.02 N 138.37 E
Ogurčinskij, ostrov I 128 38.55 N 53.02 E
Oguta 150 5.44 N 6.44 E
Oğuz, Tür. 130 39.32 N 38.51 E
Oğuz, Tür. 130 37.49 N 41.22 E
Oğuzeli 130 36.59 N 37.30 E
Ogwashi-Uku 150 6.10 N 6.31 E
Ohakune 172 39.25 S 175.24 E
Ohanapecosh ≐ 224 46.38 N 121.37 W
Ohanet 148 28.45 N 8.55 E
Ohār 124 27.21 N 84.37 E
Ōhara, Nihon 94 35.15 N 140.23 E
Ōhara, Nihon 96 35.07 N 134.20 E
Ōharano ◈[8] 270 34.58 N 135.40 E
Ōhara-tunnel ◈[5] 94 35.12 N 137.50 E
Ōhata 92 41.24 N 141.10 E
Ōhatake 268 35.57 N 139.46 E
Ohau, Lake ⊜ 172 44.15 S 169.51 E
Ohaupo 172 37.55 S 175.19 E
Ohey 56 50.26 N 5.08 E
O'Higgins, Cabo › 174z 27.05 S 109.15 W
O'Higgins, Cerro ʌ 254 48.48 S 73.11 W
O'Higgins, Lago (Lago San Martín) ⊜ 254 49.00 S 72.40 W
Ohingaiti 172 39.52 S 175.43 E
Ohio 190 41.34 N 89.28 W
Ohio □[6], In., U.S. 218 38.57 N 84.51 W
Ohio □[6], W.V., U.S. 214 40.09 N 80.35 W
Ohio □[3], U.S. 178 40.15 N 82.45 W
Ohio □[3], U.S. 188 40.15 N 82.45 W
Ohio ≐ 178 36.59 N 89.08 W
Ohio Brush Creek ≐ 218 38.41 N 83.27 W
Ohio Brush Creek, Baker Fork ≐ 218 39.02 N 83.26 W
Ohio Brush Creek, Little West Fork ≐ 218 38.58 N 83.34 W
Ohio Brush Creek, West Fork ≐ 218 38.56 N 83.28 W
Ohio Canal ≊ 279a 41.26 N 81.40 W
Ohio Caverns ±[5] 216 40.14 N 83.43 W
Ohio City 216 40.46 N 84.36 W
Ohio Peak ʌ 200 38.49 N 107.07 W
Ohiopyle State Park ♦ 188 39.50 N 79.31 W
Ohioville, N.Y., U.S. 210 41.45 N 74.03 W
Ohioville, Pa., U.S. 214 40.40 N 80.29 W
Ōhira 94 36.20 N 139.42 E
Ōhira-yama ʌ 96 34.20 N 133.57 E
Ōhito 94 35.01 N 138.56 E
Ohlau → Oława 30 50.57 N 17.17 E
Ohligs ◈[8] 263 51.09 N 7.00 E
Ohlman 219 39.21 N 89.13 W
Ohlsdorf 64 47.57 N 13.47 E
Ohm ≐ 56 50.51 N 8.48 E
Ōho 94 36.08 N 140.06 E
Ohoitom 164 5.56 S 132.41 E
'Ohonua 174w 21.20 S 174.57 W
Ohoopee ≐ 192 31.54 N 82.07 W
Ōhori 268 35.20 N 139.52 E
Ohorn 54 51.10 N 14.02 E
Ohra Stausee ⊜[1] 54 50.46 N 10.42 E
Ohrdruf 54 50.50 N 10.44 E
Ohre ≐, Dtsch. 54 52.18 N 11.47 E
Ohře (Eger) ≐, Europe 54 50.32 N 14.08 E
Ohrid 38 41.07 N 20.47 E
Ohrid, Lake ⊜ 38 41.02 N 20.43 E
Ohrigstad 156 24.49 S 30.33 E
Öhringen 56 49.12 N 9.29 E
Ohrnberg 56 49.15 N 9.27 E
Ohuira, Bahía c 232 25.38 N 108.58 W
Ohura 172 38.50 S 174.59 E
Ōi, Nihon 96 35.28 N 135.37 E
Ōi, Nihon 268 35.51 N 139.30 E
Oi ◈[8] 268 35.35 N 139.45 E
Ōi ≐, Nihon 94 34.46 N 138.18 E
Ōi ≐, Nihon 96 35.01 N 135.39 E
Oiapoque 250 3.50 N 51.50 W
Oiapoque (Oyapock) ≐ 250 4.08 N 51.40 W
Oies, Île aux I 186 47.07 N 70.30 W
Ōigawa 94 34.48 N 138.17 E
Oignies 50 50.28 N 2.59 E
Oil Center 196 32.29 N 103.15 W
Oil City, La., U.S. 194 32.44 N 93.58 W
Oil City, Pa., U.S. 214 41.26 N 79.42 W
Oil Creek ≐ 214 41.26 N 79.42 W
Oil Creek State Park ♦ 214 41.33 N 79.40 W
Oildale 226 35.25 N 119.01 W
Oilmont 182 48.44 N 111.50 W
Oil Springs 214 42.47 N 82.07 W
Oilton, Ok., U.S. 196 36.05 N 96.35 W
Oilton, Tx., U.S. 196 27.33 N 98.59 W
Oil Trough 194 35.37 N 91.27 W
Oinville-sur-Montcient 261 49.02 N 1.51 E
Oir, Beinn an ʌ 46 55.54 N 6.00 W
Oirschot 52 51.30 N 5.18 E
Oise □[5] 50 49.30 N 2.30 E
Oise ≐ 50 49.00 N 2.04 E
Oise à l'Aisne, Canal de l' ≊ 50 49.36 N 3.11 E
Oisemont 50 49.57 N 1.46 E
Ōiso, Nihon 94 35.18 N 139.19 E
Ōiso, Nihon 270 34.33 N 135.01 E
Oissel 50 49.20 N 1.06 E
Oissery 261 49.04 N 2.49 E
Oisterwijk 52 51.35 N 5.12 E
Oistins 241g 13.04 N 59.32 W
Ōita 96 33.14 N 131.36 E
Ōita □[5] 96 33.15 N 131.30 E
Ōita ≐ 96 33.15 N 131.37 E
Oiticica 250 5.03 S 41.05 W
Oituz, Pasul)(38 46.03 N 26.23 E
Ōiwa 270 34.53 N 135.33 E
Oiyung 124 29.39 N 89.46 E
Ōizumi, Nihon 94 36.15 N 139.25 E
Ōizumi, Nihon 94 35.52 N 138.23 E
Oizuruga-dake ʌ 94 36.18 N 136.47 E
Öja I 40 58.45 N 17.52 E
Oja ≐ 86 53.26 N 91.55 E
Ojai 228 34.26 N 119.14 W
Öjaren ⊜ 40 60.43 N 16.50 E
Ojat' ≐ 76 60.31 N 33.00 E
Ojcowski Park Narodowy ♦ 30 50.15 N 19.50 E
Öje 26 60.49 N 13.51 E
Ojgon nuur ⊜ 88 49.10 N 96.36 E
Ojgor 86 49.10 N 89.17 E
Ōji 96 34.35 N 135.42 E
Ōjima 94 36.15 N 139.20 E
Ojinaga 232 29.34 N 104.25 W
Ojiya 92 37.18 N 138.48 E
Ojm'akon 74 63.28 N 142.49 E
Ojocaliente 234 22.34 N 102.15 W
Ojo de la Casa 200 31.23 N 106.32 W
Ojo del Carrizo 232 29.58 N 105.16 W
Ojo de Liebre, Laguna c 232 27.45 N 114.15 W
Ojok 88 52.35 N 104.27 E
Ojos del Salado, Nevado ʌ 252 27.06 S 68.32 W
Ojos Negros 232 31.52 N 116.16 W
Ojota 273a 6.35 N 3.23 E
Ojtal, Kaz. 85 42.55 N 73.17 E
Ojtal, Kyrg. 85 40.24 N 74.06 E
Oju 150 6.53 N 8.26 E
Ojuelos de Jalisco 234 21.52 N 101.35 W
Ojus 220 25.57 N 80.09 W
Oka 150 7.29 N 5.49 E
Oka ≐, Ross. 80 56.20 N 43.59 E
Oka ≐, Ross. 88 55.15 N 102.10 E
Okaba 164 8.06 S 139.42 E
Okabe, Nihon 94 36.12 N 139.15 E
Okabe, Nihon 94 34.55 N 138.17 E
Okagaki 96 33.50 N 130.38 E
Okahandja 156 21.59 S 16.58 E
Okahandja □[5] 156 21.30 S 17.00 E
Okahukura 172 38.47 S 175.13 E
Okahumpka 220 28.45 N 81.54 W
Okaihau 172 35.19 S 173.47 E
Okalataka 152 0.20 S 14.59 E
Okaloacoochee Slough ≐ 220 26.16 N 81.17 W
Okamoto 270 34.59 N 135.58 E
Okamoto ◈[8] 270 34.44 N 135.16 E
Okanagan (Okanogan) ≐ 182 48.06 N 119.43 W
Okanagan Centre 182 50.03 N 119.27 W
Okanagan Falls 182 49.21 N 119.34 W
Okanagan Indian Reserve ◈[4] 182 50.21 N 119.17 W
Okanagan Lake ⊜ 182 50.00 N 119.28 W
Okanagan Landing 182 50.14 N 119.22 W
Okanagan Mountain Provincial Park ♦ 182 49.45 N 119.40 W
Okanagan Range (Okanogan Range) ⋏ 182 49.00 N 120.00 W
Okanogan 202 48.21 N 119.34 W
Okanogan □[6] 224 48.39 N 120.41 W
Okanogan (Okanagan) ≐ 182 48.06 N 119.43 W
Okanogan Range (Okanagan Range) ⋏ 182 49.00 N 120.00 W
Okapilco Creek ≐ 192 30.45 N 83.30 W
Okaputa 156 20.09 S 16.56 E
Okāra 123 30.49 N 73.27 E
Okarche 196 35.44 N 97.58 W
Okarito 172 43.14 S 170.11 E
Okasaki 270 34.46 N 135.52 E
Okatibbee Reservoir ⊜[1] 194 32.30 N 88.47 W
Okato 172 39.12 S 173.53 E
Okauchee 216 43.06 N 88.26 W
Okauchee Lake ⊜ 216 43.07 N 88.26 W
Okaukuejo 156 19.10 S 15.54 E
Okavango (Cubango) ≐ 138 18.50 S 22.25 E
Okavango Delta ≚[2] 156 18.45 S 22.45 E
Ōkawa, Nihon 92 33.12 N 130.23 E
Ōkawa, Nihon 94 35.05 N 138.15 E
Ōkawa, Nihon 96 33.47 N 133.26 E
Ōkawachi 96 35.04 N 134.45 E
Ōkawado 268 35.56 N 139.50 E
Okawville 219 38.26 N 89.33 W
Okaya 94 36.03 N 138.03 E
Okayama 96 34.39 N 133.55 E
Okayama □[5] 96 35.00 N 134.00 E
Okazaki 94 34.57 N 137.10 E
Okch'ŏn 98 36.20 N 127.34 E
Oke-Aro 273a 6.41 N 3.19 E
Okeechobee 220 27.14 N 80.49 W
Okeechobee □[6] 220 27.25 N 80.52 W
Okeechobee, Lake ⊜ 220 26.55 N 80.45 W
O'Keefe Centre ʋ 275b 43.37 N 79.22 W
Okeene 196 36.06 N 98.19 W
Okefenokee Swamp ⩩ 192 30.42 N 82.20 W
Okegawa 94 36.00 N 139.35 E
Okehampton 42 50.44 N 4.00 W
Okeigbo 150 7.09 N 4.43 E
Okemah 196 35.25 N 96.18 W
Okement ≐ 42 50.50 N 4.01 W
Okemos 216 42.43 N 84.25 W
Okene 150 7.33 N 6.15 E
Oke-Ode 150 8.33 N 5.02 E
Oke Ogbe 273a 6.24 N 3.23 E
Oker 52 51.54 N 10.29 E
Oker ≐ 54 52.30 N 10.22 E
Okere ≐ 154 2.07 N 33.55 E
Okhaldunggā 124 27.19 N 86.30 E
Okhla ◈[8] 272a 28.34 N 77.18 E
Okhotsk, Sea of (Ochotskoje more) ⊤[2] 74 53.00 N 150.00 E
Okhotsk Basin ✢[1] 12 53.00 N 148.00 E
Okiep 156 29.39 S 17.53 E
Okinawa 174m 26.20 N 127.50 E
Okinawa □[5] 93b 26.31 N 127.59 E
Okinawa-jima I 174m 26.30 N 128.00 E
Okinawa-shotō II 93b 26.40 N 128.00 E
Okino-Daitō-jima I 90 24.28 N 131.11 E
Okino-Erabu-shima I 93b 27.22 N 128.35 E
Okino-Kl'uči 88 50.36 N 107.06 E
Okino-shima I, Nihon 94 35.12 N 136.04 E
Okino-shima I, Nihon 96 34.07 N 135.06 E
Okino-Tori-shima (Parece Vela) I 90 20.25 N 136.00 E
Oki-shotō II 92 36.15 N 133.15 E
Okitipupa 150 6.29 N 4.46 E
Okitsu-zaki › 96 33.09 N 133.14 E
Okkang-ni 98 40.18 N 124.42 E
Okkerbil' ≐ 265a 59.56 N 30.26 E
Okladnevo 76 58.36 N 33.39 E
Oklahoma, Pa., U.S. 214 41.07 N 78.44 W
Oklahoma, Pa., U.S. 279b 40.35 N 79.35 W
Oklahoma □[3], U.S. 178 35.30 N 98.00 W
Oklahoma □[3], U.S. 196 35.30 N 98.00 W
Oklahoma City 196 35.28 N 97.30 W
Oklawaha 220 29.02 N 81.55 W
Oklawaha ≐, Fl., U.S. 192 29.28 N 81.41 W
Oklawaha ≐, Fl., U.S. 220 29.03 N 81.52 W
Oklee 198 47.50 N 95.51 W
Okmulgee 196 35.37 N 95.57 W
Oknica 78 48.24 N 27.29 E
Okno 78 48.34 N 25.58 E
Oko, Wādī V 140 21.15 N 35.56 E
Okobojo Creek ≐ 198 44.38 N 100.28 W
Okok ≐ 154 2.06 N 33.53 E
Okoka 152 2.57 S 23.27 E
Okola 152 4.01 N 11.23 E
Okollo 154 2.40 N 31.08 E
Okolo 152 3.46 S 23.55 E
Okolona, Ar., U.S. 194 33.59 N 93.20 W
Okolona, Ky., U.S. 194 38.08 N 85.41 W
Okolona, Ms., U.S. 194 34.00 N 88.45 W
Okombahe 156 21.23 S 15.22 E
Okondja 152 0.41 S 13.47 E
Okonek 30 53.33 N 16.50 E
Okonešnikovo 86 54.50 N 75.05 E
Okotoks 182 50.44 N 113.59 W
Okoyo 152 1.28 S 15.04 E
Okpara ≐ 150 7.40 N 2.35 E
Okrika 150 4.47 N 7.04 E
Oksbøl 26 55.38 N 8.17 E
Okskij Zapovednik ◈[4] 80 54.45 N 40.45 E
Oksko-Donskaja ravnina ≚ 80 53.00 N 40.30 E
Oksovskij 24 62.37 N 39.55 E
Oksskolten ʌ 24 65.59 N 14.15 E
Oksu ≐, Asia 85 40.12 N 69.16 E
Oksu ≐, Taj. 120 38.09 N 73.57 E
Okt'abr', Kaz. 85 43.41 N 77.12 E
Okt'abr', Kaz. 86 45.45 N 61.34 E
Okt'abr', Ross. 76 57.50 N 37.26 E
Okt'abr'sk, Kaz. 86 49.28 N 57.25 E
Okt'abr'sk, Ross. 80 53.11 N 48.40 E
Okt'abr'skij, Bela. 76 52.38 N 28.53 E
Okt'abr'skij, Kaz. 86 52.35 N 62.40 E
Okt'abr'skij, Kaz. 86 49.38 N 83.35 E
Okt'abr'skij, Ross. 24 59.29 N 48.50 E
Okt'abr'skij, Ross. 24 61.04 N 43.08 E
Okt'abr'skij, Ross. 76 53.47 N 39.29 E
Okt'abr'skij, Ross. 78 44.56 N 39.00 E
Okt'abr'skij, Ross. 78 50.26 N 36.22 E
Okt'abr'skij, Ross. 80 54.28 N 53.28 E
Okt'abr'skij, Ross. 80 56.17 N 44.12 E
Okt'abr'skij, Ross. 80 57.08 N 40.20 E
Okt'abr'skij, Ross. 80 58.19 N 44.19 E
Okt'abr'skij, Ross. 80 56.35 N 53.58 E
Okt'abr'skij, Ross. 80 47.58 N 43.38 E
Okt'abr'skij, Ross. 82 55.37 N 37.58 E
Okt'abr'skij, Ross. 82 54.14 N 38.54 E
Okt'abr'skij, Ross. 83 47.28 N 40.04 E
Okt'abr'skij, Ross. 86 56.31 N 57.12 E
Okt'abr'skij, Ross. 88 50.04 N 118.04 E
Okt'abr'skij, Ross. 88 56.05 N 99.26 E
Okt'abr'skij, Ross. 89 53.01 N 128.37 E
Okt'abr'skij, Ross. 89 49.02 N 140.11 E
Okt'abr'skij, Taj. 85 38.33 N 68.22 E
Okt'abr'skoje, Kaz. 86 52.07 N 65.40 E
Okt'abr'skoje, Ross. 74 62.28 N 66.03 E
Okt'abr'skoje, Ross. 76 52.18 N 39.44 E
Okt'abr'skoje, Ross. 80 45.37 N 42.49 E
Okt'abr'skoje, Ross. 80 52.54 N 46.30 E
Okt'abr'skoje, Ross. 86 52.20 N 55.30 E
Okt'abr'skoje, Ross. 86 54.26 N 62.44 E
Okt'abr'skoje, Ukr. 78 48.38 N 33.04 E
Okt'abr'skoje, Ukr. 78 45.18 N 34.09 E
Okt'abr'skoje, Ukr. 83 48.28 N 37.22 E
Okt'abr'skoj Revol'ucii, ostrov I 74 79.30 N 97.00 E
Ok Tedi 164 5.44 S 141.09 E
Oktember'an 84 40.09 N 44.02 E
Oktong-ni 98 38.27 N 127.07 E
Oktwin 110 18.49 N 96.26 E
Oktyabr'skiy → Okt'abr'skij 80 54.28 N 53.28 E
Oku, Nihon 96 34.40 N 134.05 E
Oku, Nihon 174m 26.50 N 128.17 E
Ōkubo, Nihon 268 35.21 N 139.56 E
Ōkubo, Nihon 270 34.41 N 134.57 E
Ōkubo ◈[8] 268 35.24 N 139.35 E
Okučani 36 45.16 N 17.12 E
Ōkuchi, Nihon 92 32.04 N 130.37 E
Okuchi, Nihon 94 36.17 N 136.39 E
Okuku ≐ 172 43.16 S 172.28 E
Okulovka 76 58.26 N 33.18 E
Okumi 84 42.43 N 41.45 E
Okundi 150 6.22 N 8.44 E
Okun'ov Nos 24 66.15 N 52.28 E
Ōkura-yama ʌ 96 35.08 N 133.22 E
Okusawa ◈[8] 268 35.36 N 139.40 E
Okushiri 92a 42.10 N 139.31 E
Okushiri-tō I 92a 42.10 N 139.27 E
Ōkusu-yama ʌ[2] 268 35.15 N 139.38 E
Okuta 150 9.14 N 3.15 E
Okutadami Dam ◈[6] 94 37.09 N 139.15 E
Okutama 94 35.47 N 139.02 E
Okutama-ko ⊜ 94 35.47 N 139.02 E
Okutsu 96 35.14 N 133.56 E
Ōkuwa 94 35.41 N 137.40 E
Okwa (Chapman's) ≐ 156 22.30 S 23.00 E
Okwoga 150 7.01 N 7.50 E
Olá, Pan. 236 8.25 N 80.39 W
Ola, Ross. 74 59.35 N 151.17 E
Ola, Ar., U.S. 194 35.01 N 93.13 W
Ola ≐ 76 52.41 N 29.39 E
Ólafsfjörður 24a 66.06 N 18.38 W
Olambwe Valley Game Reserve ◈[4] 154 0.37 S 34.15 E
Olancha 204 36.16 N 118.00 W
Olancha Peak ʌ 204 36.16 N 118.07 W
Olanchito 236 15.30 N 86.35 W
Olancho □[5] 236 14.45 N 86.00 W
Öland I 26 56.45 N 16.38 E
Olandsån ≐ 40 60.20 N 18.14 E
Olango Island I 116 10.16 N 124.03 E
Olanta 192 33.56 N 79.55 W
Olar 192 33.10 N 81.11 W
Olarevo 76 59.22 N 40.04 E
Olaria, Bra. 256 21.52 S 43.56 W
Olaria, Bra. 287a 22.41 S 43.08 W
Olaria ◈[8] 287a 22.52 S 43.15 W
Olary 166 32.17 S 140.19 E
Olascoaga 252 35.12 S 60.36 W
Olasore 273a 6.40 N 3.17 E
Olathe, Co., U.S. 200 38.36 N 107.58 W
Olathe, Ks., U.S. 198 38.52 N 94.49 W
Olavarría 252 36.54 S 60.17 W
Olavinlinna ⊥ 26 61.52 N 29.00 E
Oława 30 50.57 N 17.17 E
Olbernhau 54 50.39 N 13.20 E
Olbersdorf 54 50.52 N 14.46 E
Olbersleben 54 51.09 N 11.20 E
Olbia 71 40.55 N 9.31 E
Olbia, Golfo di c 71 40.55 N 9.39 E
Ølby Lyng 41 55.29 N 12.09 E
Olca, Volcán ʌ[1] 248 20.57 S 68.30 W
Ol'chi 80 53.53 N 41.28 E
Olching 60 48.12 N 11.20 E
Ol'chon, ostrov I 88 53.09 N 107.24 E
Ol'chovaja ≐, Ross. 80 48.47 N 40.51 E
Ol'chovaja ≐, Ukr. 83 48.35 N 39.17 E
Ol'chovatka, Ross. 78 50.18 N 39.17 E
Ol'chovatka, Ukr. 83 48.15 N 38.25 E
Ol'chovka, Ross. 80 49.52 N 44.34 E
Ol'chovka, Ross. 86 56.22 N 63.46 E
Ol'chovoje 83 48.40 N 39.34 E
Olcott 210 43.20 N 78.42 W
Old ≐, Ca., U.S. 226 38.04 N 121.35 W
Old ≐, Tx., U.S. 222 30.25 N 96.19 W
Old Bahama Channel ʮ 238 22.30 N 78.50 W
Old Bedford ≐ 42 52.35 N 0.20 E
Old Bennington 210 42.52 N 73.12 W
Old Bethpage 276 40.45 N 73.27 W
Old Bethpage Village ⊥ 276 40.47 N 73.28 W
Old Brazoria 222 29.04 N 95.34 W
Old Bridge 276 40.24 N 74.21 W
Old Brookville 276 40.49 N 73.36 W
Oldbury 42 52.30 N 2.00 W
Old Cairo → Mişr al-Qadīmah ◈[8] 273c 30.00 N 31.14 E
Oldcastle 48 53.46 N 7.10 W
Old Colwyn 44 53.18 N 3.43 W
Old Cork 166 22.56 S 141.52 E
Old Creek Estates 284c 38.50 N 77.16 W
Old Crow 180 67.35 N 139.50 W
Old Crow ≐ 180 67.35 N 139.50 W
Oldeani 154 3.21 S 35.33 E
Oldebroek 52 52.26 N 5.54 E
Old Economy ⊥ 279b 40.36 N 80.14 W
Olden, Nor. 26 61.50 N 6.49 E
Olden, Tx., U.S. 196 32.25 N 98.45 W
Oldenbrok 52 53.17 N 8.23 E
Oldenburg, Dtsch. 52 53.08 N 8.13 E
Oldenburg, In., U.S. 218 39.20 N 85.12 W
Oldenburg □[9] 52 53.00 N 8.00 E
Oldenburg in Holstein 54 54.17 N 10.52 E
Oldendorf 52 53.35 N 9.14 E
Oldenstadt 52 52.58 N 10.35 E
Oldenswort 41 54.22 N 8.56 E
Oldenzaal 52 52.19 N 6.56 E
Oldersum 52 53.20 N 7.20 E
Old Faithful Geyser ⊤[4] 202 44.30 N 110.45 W
Old Farm 284c 39.03 N 77.09 W
Old Field 276 40.57 N 73.08 W
Old Field Point › 276 40.58 N 73.07 W
Old Forge, N.Y., U.S. 188 43.42 N 74.58 W
Old Forge, Pa., U.S. 210 41.22 N 75.44 W
Old Forge Village 276 40.49 N 74.29 W
Old Fort 214 41.15 N 83.09 W
Old Fort Erie ⊥ 284a 42.53 N 78.56 W
Old Fort Henry ⊥ 212 44.14 N 76.28 W
Old Fort Mountain ʌ 182 55.05 N 126.30 W
Old Fort Niagara ⊥ 284a 43.16 N 79.03 W
Old Fort Parker State Historic Site ⊥ 222 31.34 N 96.34 W
Old Fort Point › 240b 25.03 N 77.29 W
Old Greenwich 276 41.02 N 73.34 W
Oldham, Eng., U.K. 44 53.33 N 2.07 W
Oldham, S.D., U.S. 198 44.13 N 97.18 W
Oldham □[6] 218 38.23 N 85.27 W
Oldham □[8] 262 53.34 N 2.03 W
Oldham Pines 283 42.05 N 70.50 W
Oldham Pond ⊜ 283 42.03 N 70.51 W
Oldham Village 207 42.04 N 70.49 W
Old Harbor 180 57.12 N 153.19 W
Old Harbour 241q 17.56 N 77.07 W
Old Hickory Lake ⊜[1] 194 36.18 N 86.30 W
Old Howe ≐ 44 53.57 N 0.21 W
Oldisleben 54 51.18 N 11.10 E
Old Lyme 207 41.18 N 72.19 W
Old Malden ◈[8] 260 51.23 N 0.15 W
Oldman ≐ 182 49.56 N 111.42 W
Old Man House ⊥ 224 47.43 N 122.34 W
Old Man Mountain ʌ 186 49.08 N 57.43 W
Old Manor 276 40.24 N 74.11 W
Oldmans Creek ≐ 208 39.47 N 75.27 W
Oldmeldrum 46 57.20 N 2.20 W
Old Mkushi 154 14.22 S 29.22 E
Old Monroe 219 38.55 N 90.44 W
Old Mystic 207 41.23 N 71.57 W
Old Nene ≐ 42 52.40 N 0.10 E
Old North Bridge ⊥ 283 42.28 N 71.21 W
Old North Church ʋ[1] 283 42.22 N 71.03 W
Old Ocean 222 29.05 N 95.45 W
Ol Doinyo Sapuk National Park ♦ 154 1.09 S 37.12 E
Ol'doj ≐ 89 53.33 N 123.21 E
Old Orchard ◈[9] 278 42.04 N 87.45 W
Old Orchard Beach 188 43.31 N 70.22 W
Old Perlican 186 48.05 N 53.01 W
Old Place Creek ≐ 276 40.38 N 74.12 W
Old Point Comfort › 208 37.00 N 76.19 W
Old Rhodes Key I 220 25.22 N 80.14 W
Old Ripley 219 38.54 N 89.34 W
Old Road Bay c 284b 39.12 N 76.27 W
Old Road Bluff › 240c 16.59 N 61.50 W
Old Round Rock 222 30.31 N 97.42 W
Olds 182 51.47 N 114.06 W
Old Saybrook 207 41.17 N 72.22 W
Oldsmar 220 28.02 N 82.39 W
Old Speck Mountain ʌ 188 44.34 N 70.57 W
Old Sturbridge Village ⊥ 207 42.07 N 72.07 W
Old Swamp ≐ 283 42.11 N 70.57 W
Old Swedes Church ʋ[1] 285 39.44 N 75.32 W
Old Tampa Bay c 220 27.56 N 82.35 W
Old Tappan 276 41.00 N 73.59 W
Old Tate 156 21.22 S 27.46 E
Old Town 188 44.56 N 68.38 W
Old Trafford Cricket Ground ♦ 262 53.28 N 2.17 W
Old Trap 192 36.15 N 76.02 W
Olduvai Gorge V 154 2.58 S 35.22 E
Old Westbury 276 40.47 N 73.37 W
Old Westbury Gardens ♦ 276 40.46 N 73.36 W
Oldwick 210 40.40 N 74.44 W
Old Windsor 260 51.28 N 0.35 W
Old Wives Lake ⊜ 184 50.06 N 106.00 W
Old Woman Creek ≐ 198 43.19 N 104.21 W
Öldzijt, Mong. 88 48.07 N 102.34 E
Öldzijt, Mong. 102 45.18 N 106.12 E
Old Zoinsville 208 40.29 N 75.31 W
Olean 210 42.04 N 78.25 W
Olean Creek ≐ 210 42.04 N 78.25 W
O'Leary 186 46.42 N 64.13 W
Olecko 30 54.03 N 22.30 E
Olegário Maciel 256 22.19 S 45.35 W
Oleggio 62 45.36 N 8.38 E
Olekma → Ol'okma ≐ 74 60.22 N 120.42 E
Olema 24 64.30 N 46.08 E
Olen, Bel. 56 51.09 N 4.51 E
Ølen, Nor. 26 59.36 N 5.48 E
Ölen ⊜ 40 59.13 N 14.31 E
Olenegorsk 24 68.09 N 33.15 E
Olenevka 78 45.23 N 32.32 E
Olenica 24 66.29 N 35.20 E
Olenij, ostrov I 74 72.25 N 77.45 E
Olenino 76 56.12 N 33.29 E
Olenja Rečka 86 52.48 N 93.14 E
Olen'kovo 82 54.34 N 38.06 E
Olen'ok 74 68.33 N 112.18 E
Olen'ok ≐ 74 73.00 N 119.55 E
Olen'okskij zaliv c 74 73.20 N 121.00 E
Olentangy ≐ 214 39.58 N 83.06 W
Olenty 80 50.02 N 52.07 E
Olenty ≐ 80 49.50 N 52.03 E
Oleopolis 214 41.27 N 79.37 W
Oléron, Île d' I 32 45.56 N 1.15 W
Olesko 78 49.58 N 24.53 E
Olešná 60 49.46 N 13.48 E
Oleśnica 30 51.13 N 17.23 E
Olesno 30 50.53 N 18.25 E
Olevano Romano 66 41.52 N 13.02 E
Olevano sul Tusciano 68 40.40 N 15.01 E
Olevsk 78 51.13 N 27.39 E
Oley 208 40.23 N 75.47 W
Olfen 52 51.42 N 7.23 E
Ol'ga, Ross. 89 43.45 N 135.18 E
Olga, Wa., U.S. 224 48.37 N 122.50 W
Olga, Mount ʌ, Austl. 162 25.19 S 130.46 E
Olga, Mount ʌ, Vt., U.S. 207 42.51 N 72.48 W
Olgiata 267a 42.02 N 12.22 E
Olgiate Comasco 62 45.48 N 8.58 E
Olgiate Olona 62 45.38 N 8.53 E
Ölgij, Mong. 86 48.56 N 89.57 E
Ölgij, Mong. 86 48.59 N 92.01 E
Olginate 62 45.48 N 9.24 E
Ol'ginka, Ross. 78 44.14 N 38.53 E
Ol'ginka, Ukr. 83 47.42 N 37.31 E
Ol'gino 89 52.53 N 125.47 E
Ol'gino ◈[8] 265a 60.00 N 30.09 E
Ol'ginskaja, Ross. 78 45.57 N 38.34 E
Ol'ginskaja, Ross. 83 47.11 N 39.56 E
Ølgod 26 55.49 N 8.37 E
Ol'gopol' 78 48.12 N 29.29 E
Ol'govo 82 56.16 N 37.21 E
Olhão 34 37.02 N 7.50 W
Olho d'Água das Cunhãs 250 4.43 S 44.34 W
Olho d'Água das Flores 250 9.33 S 37.17 W
Oli ≐ 150 9.45 N 4.38 E
Olib, Otok I 36 44.22 N 14.48 E
Oliden 258 35.11 S 57.57 W
Oliena 71 40.16 N 9.24 E
Olifants (Rio dos Elefantes) ≐, Afr. 156 24.10 S 32.40 E
Olifants ≐, Namibia 156 25.30 S 19.30 E
Olifants ≐, S. Afr. 158 31.42 S 18.12 E
Olifants ≐, S. Afr. 158 33.41 S 21.42 E
Olifants ≐, S. Afr. 158 29.39 S 21.10 E
Olifantshoek 158 27.57 S 22.42 E
Olifantsrivierberge ⋏ 158 32.40 S 19.00 E
Oliki 265a 59.46 N 29.55 E
Olimarao I[1] 108 7.41 N 145.52 E
Olimbía ⊥ 38 37.38 N 21.41 E
Ólimbos 38 35.44 N 27.11 E
Ólimbos ʌ 130 34.56 N 32.52 E
Ólimbos, Óros ʌ 38 40.05 N 22.21 E
Olímpia 255 20.44 S 48.54 W
Olímpico, Estadio ♦ 286a 19.20 N 99.12 W
Olímpio Noronha 256 22.04 S 45.16 W
Olimpo → Ólimbos, Óros ʌ 38 40.05 N 22.21 E
Olin 190 41.59 N 91.08 W
Olinalá 234 17.50 N 98.51 W
Olinda, Austl. 170 32.50 S 150.08 E
Olinda, Austl. 274b 37.51 S 145.22 E
Olinda, Bra. 250 8.01 S 34.51 W
Olinda, Bra. 256 22.49 S 43.25 W
Olinda, Mount ʌ 274b 37.52 S 145.21 E
Olinda Creek ≐ 274b 37.41 S 145.21 E
Olindina 250 11.22 S 38.21 W
Olinsk 88 52.24 N 116.13 E
Olio 166 21.54 S 143.13 E
Olišovka 78 51.13 N 31.18 E
Olite 34 42.29 N 1.39 W
Oliva, Arg. 252 32.03 S 63.34 W
Oliva, Esp. 34 38.55 N 0.07 W
Oliva de la Frontera 34 38.16 N 6.55 W
Olivais ◈[8] 266c 38.46 N 9.06 E
Olival Basto 266c 38.47 N 9.10 W
Olivares, Cerro de ʌ 252 30.18 S 69.55 W
Olive Branch 194 34.57 N 89.49 W
Olivebridge 210 41.55 N 74.13 W
Olive Hill 218 38.18 N 83.10 W
Olivehurst 226 39.05 N 121.33 W
Oliveira 255 20.41 S 44.49 W
Oliveira dos Brejinhos 255 12.19 S 42.54 W
Oliveira Fortes 256 21.20 S 43.27 W
Olivelifuri I 122 5.17 N 73.35 E
Olive Mount ◈[8] 262 53.24 N 2.55 W
Olivença 154 11.47 S 35.13 E
Olivenza 34 38.41 N 7.06 W
Oliver 182 49.11 N 119.33 W
Olivera 258 34.38 S 59.15 W
Oliver Creek ≐ 222 33.06 N 97.17 W
Oliver Ditch ≊ 216 41.00 N 87.10 W
Oliverea 210 42.04 N 74.28 W
Oliver Estates 284c 38.59 N 77.18 W
Oliveri 70 38.07 N 15.03 E
Oliver Lake ⊜ 184 56.56 N 103.22 W
Oliver Springs 192 36.02 N 84.20 W
Olivet, Fr. 50 47.52 N 1.54 E
Olivet, Mi., U.S. 216 42.26 N 84.55 W
Olivet, S.D., U.S. 198 43.14 N 97.40 W
Oliveto Citra 68 40.41 N 15.14 E
Oliveto Lucano 68 40.32 N 16.11 E
Olivette 219 38.39 N 90.22 W
Olivia 198 44.46 N 94.59 W
Olivine Range ⋏ 172 44.18 S 168.30 E
Olivo 116 10.52 N 123.53 E
Olivo ≐ 70 37.22 N 14.15 E
Olivone 58 46.32 N 8.57 E
Olivos ◈[8] 258 34.32 S 58.29 W
Öljaren ⊜ 40 59.08 N 16.02 E
Olji Moron ≐ 89 44.16 N 121.42 E
Olla 194 31.54 N 92.14 W
Ollagüe 248 21.14 S 68.16 W
Ollagüe, Volcán ʌ[1] 248 21.18 S 68.12 W
Ollainville 261 48.35 N 2.13 E
Ollantaitambo 248 13.16 S 72.16 W
Ollatrim ≐ 48 52.52 N 8.13 W
Ollei 175b 7.43 N 134.37 E
Ollerton 262 53.17 N 2.20 W
Ollerup 41 55.04 N 10.30 E
Olliergues 62 45.40 N 3.38 E
Ollioules 62 43.08 N 5.51 E
Ollomont 62 45.50 N 7.22 E
Ollon 58 46.18 N 7.00 E
Olloua 152 0.56 S 14.34 E
Olmedillo de Roa 34 41.47 N 3.56 W
Olmedo, Esp. 34 41.23 N 4.41 W
Olmedo, It. 71 40.39 N 8.23 E
Olmo al Brembo 58 45.58 N 9.39 E
Olmos 248 5.59 S 79.46 W
Olmsted 214 41.24 N 81.44 W
Olmsted Falls 279a 41.22 N 81.54 W
Olmütz → Olomouc 30 49.36 N 17.16 E
Olney, Eng., U.K. 42 52.09 N 0.42 W
Olney, Il., U.S. 194 38.43 N 88.05 W
Olney, Md., U.S. 208 39.09 N 77.04 W
Olney, Mo., U.S. 219 39.05 N 91.15 W
Olney, Mt., U.S. 182 48.32 N 114.34 W
Olney, Tx., U.S. 196 33.22 N 98.45 W
Olney ◈[8] 285 40.02 N 75.08 W
Oloči 89 51.21 N 119.55 E
Olofström 26 56.16 N 14.30 E
Oloj ≐ 74 66.29 N 159.29 E
Ol'okma ≐ 74 60.22 N 120.42 E
Ol'okminsk 74 60.24 N 120.24 E
Ol'okminskij Stanovik ⋏ 88 54.30 N 120.00 E
Olokui ʌ 229a 21.08 N 156.51 W
Olomane ≐ 186 50.14 N 60.37 W
Olombo 152 1.18 S 15.53 E
Olomega, Laguna ⊜ 236 13.19 N 88.04 W
Olomouc 30 49.36 N 17.16 E
Olona ≐ 62 45.06 N 9.21 E
Olonec 24 61.00 N 32.57 E
Olongapo 116 14.50 N 120.16 E
Olonki 88 52.54 N 103.45 E
Olorgasailie National Monument ♦ 154 1.40 S 36.22 E
Oloron, Gave d' ≐ 32 43.33 N 1.05 W
Oloron-Sainte-Marie 32 43.12 N 0.36 W
Olosega 174y 14.11 S 169.39 W
Olosega I 174y 14.11 S 169.39 W
Olot 34 42.11 N 2.29 E
Olov'annaja, Ross. 88 50.56 N 115.35 E
Olov'annaja, Ross. 180 66.10 N 178.59 W
Oloví 54 50.11 N 12.33 E
Olpe, Dtsch. 56 51.02 N 7.52 E
Olpe, Ks., U.S. 198 38.15 N 96.10 W
Olperer ʌ 64 47.03 N 11.39 E
Olsabach ≐ 61 46.56 N 14.25 E
Ol'šana, Ukr. 78 49.13 N 31.13 E
Ol'šana, Ukr. 78 49.47 N 37.46 E
Ol'šana, Ukr. 78 50.48 N 34.02 E
Ol'šanka, Ross. 78 51.46 N 35.25 E
Ol'šanka, Ukr. 78 48.14 N 30.52 E
Ol'šany, Bela. 78 52.05 N 27.20 E
Olšany, Česko. 60 49.24 N 13.38 E
Ol'šany, Ukr. 78 50.03 N 35.53 E
Olsberg 56 51.21 N 8.29 E
Ølsemagle 41 55.30 N 12.10 E
Olshammar 40 58.45 N 14.48 E
Olst 52 52.20 N 6.06 E
Ølstykke 41 55.47 N 12.11 E
Olsufjevo 76 53.36 N 33.40 E
Olsztyn (Allenstein) 30 53.48 N 20.29 E
Olsztyn □[4] 30 53.50 N 20.40 E
Olsztynek 30 53.36 N 20.17 E
Olt □[6] 38 44.20 N 24.30 E
Olt ≐ 38 43.43 N 24.51 E
Olta 252 30.37 S 66.16 W
Olten 58 47.21 N 7.54 E
Olteni 38 44.10 N 25.18 E
Oltenița 38 44.05 N 26.39 E
Olteț ≐ 38 44.14 N 24.27 E
Olton 196 34.11 N 102.08 W
Oltre il Colle 64 45.54 N 9.46 E
Oltu 130 40.33 N 41.59 E
Oltu ≐ 130 40.49 N 41.40 E
Oluan Pi › 100 21.54 N 120.51 E
Olukonda 156 18.03 S 16.00 E
Olur 130 40.50 N 42.08 E
Olustee, Fl., U.S. 192 30.12 N 82.26 W
Olustee, Ok., U.S. 196 34.32 N 99.25 W
Olustee Creek ≐ 192 29.57 N 82.32 W
Oluta 234 17.55 N 94.54 W
Olutanga (Suba Nipa) 116 7.26 N 122.54 E
Olutanga Island I 116 7.22 N 122.52 E
Olutayan Island I 116 11.39 N 122.50 E
Olute 273a 6.28 N 3.16 E
Ol'utorskij, mys › 74 59.55 N 170.27 E
Ol'utorskij zaliv c 74 60.15 N 168.30 E
Oluwo 273a 6.42 N 3.18 E
Olvenstedt 54 52.09 N 11.34 E
Olvera 34 36.56 N 5.16 W
Olychovatka 78 50.12 N 37.31 E
Olyka 78 50.42 N 25.51 E
Olym 78 51.42 N 38.10 E
Olympe, Mont → Ólimbos, Óros ʌ 38 40.05 N 22.21 E
Olympia 224 47.02 N 122.53 W
Olympia Fields 216 41.32 N 87.42 W
Olympia Heights 220 25.43 N 80.21 W
Olympia → Olimbía ⊥ 38 37.38 N 21.41 E
Olympia Park ♦ 273d 26.15 S 28.26 E
Olympia-Stadion ♦ 264a 52.31 N 13.14 E
Olympic Mountains ⋏ 224 47.50 N 123.45 W
Olympic National Park ♦ 224 47.48 N 123.30 W
Olympic Valley 226 39.13 N 120.14 W
Olympic View 224 47.43 N 122.45 W
Olympieion ⊥ 267c 37.58 N 23.44 E
Olympique, Stade ♦ 275a 45.33 N 73.33 W
Olymp → Ólimbos, Óros ʌ 38 40.05 N 22.21 E
Olympus, Mount ʌ 224 47.48 N 123.43 W
Olympus, Mount ʌ[2] 192 38.03 N 83.39 W
Olympus, Mount → Ólimbos, Óros ʌ 38 40.05 N 22.21 E
Olyphant 210 41.28 N 75.36 W
Olzai 71 40.11 N 9.09 E
Ol'zony 88 52.57 N 105.15 E
Om ≐, Pap. N. Gui. 164 5.09 S 142.22 E
Om' ≐, Ross. 86 54.59 N 73.22 E
Ōma 92 41.32 N 140.55 E
Ōmachi, Nihon 94 36.30 N 137.52 E
Ōmachi, Nihon 270 34.28 N 135.25 E
Omaezaki 94 34.35 N 138.13 E
Omae-zaki › 94 34.36 N 138.14 E
Ōmagari 92 39.27 N 140.29 E
Omagh, On., Can. 275b 43.30 N 79.49 W
Omagh, N. Ire., U.K. 48 54.36 N 7.18 W
Ōmagi 268 35.52 N 139.42 E
Omaguas 246 4.08 S 73.15 W
Omaha, Ne., U.S. 198 41.15 N 95.56 W
Omaha, Tx., U.S. 222 33.11 N 94.45 W
Omaha Indian Reservation ◈[4] 198 42.08 N 96.22 W
Omak 202 48.24 N 119.31 W
Omakau 172 45.05 S 169.36 E
Omak Lake ⊜ 202 48.16 N 119.23 W
Omalo 84 42.23 N 45.38 E
Ōmama 94 36.26 N 139.17 E
Oman ('Umān) □[1] 118 22.00 N 58.00 E
Oman, Gulf of c 118 24.30 N 58.30 E
Omapere, Lake ⊜ 172 35.21 S 173.47 E
Omar 192 37.45 N 81.59 W
Omarama 172 44.29 S 169.58 E
Omaruru 156 21.28 S 15.56 E
Omaruru □[5] 156 21.00 S 16.00 E
Omaruru ≐ 156 22.07 S 14.15 E
Omas 248 12.31 S 76.17 W
Omatako ʌ 156 21.07 S 16.43 E
Omatako ≐ 156 17.59 S 20.30 E
Omate 248 16.41 S 70.59 W
Omatena 115b 9.53 S 119.47 E
Ōma-zaki › 92 41.32 N 140.55 E
Ombai, Selat ʮ 112 8.30 S 125.00 E
Ombella-Mpoko □[5] 152 5.00 N 18.00 E
Omberg ʌ[2] 26 58.20 N 14.39 E
Ombersley 42 52.17 N 2.13 W
Ombombo 156 18.43 S 13.53 E
Omboué 152 1.34 S 9.15 E
Ombrone ≐ 66 42.39 N 11.00 E
Ombúes de Lavalle 258 33.55 S 57.47 W
Ombutosu ʌ 156 21.22 S 16.50 E
Ombwe 154 4.22 S 25.35 E
Omčak 74 61.38 N 147.55 E
Omčaly 128 40.47 N 53.43 E
Omdraaisvlei 158 30.08 S 23.08 E
Omdurman → Umm Durmān 140 15.38 N 32.30 E
Ōme 94 35.47 N 139.15 E
Omega, Ga., U.S. 192 31.20 N 83.35 W
Omega, Oh., U.S. 218 39.09 N 82.55 W
Omegna 62 45.53 N 8.24 E
Omel'nik 78 49.12 N 33.32 E
Omemee 212 44.18 N 78.33 W
Omeo 166 37.06 S 147.36 E
Ömerköy 130 39.48 N 28.03 E
Ömerli 130 37.24 N 40.58 E
Ömerli Barajı ⊜[1] 130 41.00 N 29.20 E
Omerville 206 45.17 N 72.07 W
Ometepe, Isla de I 236 11.30 N 85.35 W
Ometepec 234 16.41 N 98.25 W
Ometepec ≐ 234 16.30 N 98.45 W
Om Hajer 144 14.24 N 36.46 E
Omi, Nihon 94 36.27 N 138.03 E
Ōmi, Nihon 94 37.01 N 137.48 E
Ōmi, Nihon 94 35.20 N 136.24 E
Omigawa 94 35.51 N 140.37 E
Ōmi-hachiman 94 35.08 N 136.06 E
Ōminato → Mutsu 92 41.17 N 141.10 E
Omineca ≐ 182 56.05 N 124.30 W
Omineca Mountains ⋏ 182 56.00 N 125.00 W
Omin-ni ◈[8] 271b 37.27 N 127.01 E
Ōmino 270 34.32 N 135.33 E
Omišalj 36 45.13 N 14.34 E
Ōmi-shima I, Nihon 96 34.25 N 131.13 E
Omi-shima I, Nihon 96 34.15 N 133.00 E
Omitara 156 22.18 S 18.01 E
Omitlán ≐ 234 17.06 N 99.34 W
Ōmiya, Nihon 94 36.33 N 140.25 E
Ōmiya, Nihon 94 35.54 N 139.38 E
Ōmiya, Nihon 96 35.35 N 135.06 E
Ōmiya-daichi ⋏[1] 268 35.56 N 139.38 E
Ōmiya Park Race Track ♦ 268 35.55 N 139.38 E
Øm Kloster ⊥ 41 56.03 N 9.45 E
Ommaney, Cape › 180 56.10 N 134.39 W
Ommanney Bay c 176 73.07 N 100.11 W
Omme ≐ 41 55.53 N 8.40 E
Ommen 52 52.32 N 6.25 E
Ömnödelger 88 47.52 N 109.55 E
Ömnögov' 86 49.06 N 91.43 E
Ömnögov' □[4] 102 43.00 N 104.00 E
Omø I 41 55.09 N 11.10 E
Omo ≐ 144 43.10 N 35.59 E
Omoa, Bahía de c 236 15.45 N 88.10 W
Omodeo, Lago ⊜ 71 40.08 N 8.55 E
Omogo 96 33.41 N 133.02 E
Omoi ≐ 94 36.09 N 139.41 E
Omoko 150 5.20 N 6.39 E
Omole 273a 6.38 N 3.22 E
Omoloj ≐ 74 71.10 N 132.08 E
Omolon ≐ 74 68.42 N 158.36 E
Omo National Park ♦ 144 6.00 N 35.45 E
Omono ≐ 92 39.46 N 140.03 E
Omont 56 49.36 N 4.44 E
Omo Ranch 226 38.35 N 120.35 W
Ōmori ◈[8] 268 35.34 N 139.44 E
Omotegō 94 37.03 N 140.18 E
Omoy 152 1.21 S 13.09 E
Omrel'kaj ≐ 180 68.34 N 170.30 E
Omro 190 44.02 N 88.44 W
Omsino 80 58.36 N 50.28 E
Omsk 86 55.00 N 73.24 E
Omsk Oblast' □[4] 86 56.00 N 73.00 E
Omsukčan 74 62.32 N 155.48 E
O-mu, Mya. 110 22.58 N 99.18 E
Ōmu, Nihon 92a 44.34 N 142.58 E
Omu-Aran 150 8.09 N 5.07 E
Ōmuda → Ōmuta 96 33.02 N 130.27 E
Omul, Vîrful ʌ 38 45.26 N 25.26 E
Omulew ≐ 30 53.05 N 21.32 E
Ōmura 92 32.54 N 129.57 E
Ōmura-wan c 92 32.57 N 129.52 E
Ōmuro 268 35.54 N 139.58 E
Omurtag 38 43.06 N 26.25 E
Ōmuta 96 33.02 N 130.27 E
Omutinskij 86 56.31 N 67.41 E
Omutninsk 86 58.40 N 52.12 E
Ŏmyŏnbo 98 41.16 N 127.36 E
On 110 21.40 N 106.35 E
Ona, Nor. 26 62.52 N 6.34 E
Ona, Fl., U.S. 220 27.28 N 81.55 W
Ona ≐ 86 52.34 N 89.50 E
Onabas 232 28.35 N 109.34 W
Ona → Bir'usa ≐ 88 57.43 N 95.24 E
Onadikondo 152 3.52 S 24.10 E
Onaga 198 39.29 N 96.10 W
Onagawa 92 38.26 N 141.27 E
Onahama 94 36.57 N 140.54 E
Onalaska, Tx., U.S. 222 30.48 N 95.07 W
Onalaska, Wa., U.S. 224 46.34 N 122.43 W
Onamia 190 46.04 N 93.40 W
Onancock 208 37.42 N 75.44 W
Onangué, Lac ⊜ 152 0.57 S 10.04 E
Onaping ≐ 190 46.37 N 81.18 W
Onaping Lake ⊜ 190 47.00 N 81.30 W
Onarga 216 40.42 N 88.00 W
Ōnari 268 35.55 N 139.37 E
Onatchiway, Lac ⊜ 186 49.00 N 71.03 W
Onawa 198 42.01 N 96.05 W

Symbols in the index entries represent the broad categories identified in the key at the right. Symbols with superior numbers (⋏[1]) identify subcategories (see complete key on page *I · 1).*

Symbole im Register stellen die rechts im Schlüssel erklärten Kategorien dar. Symbole mit hochgestellten Ziffern (⋏[1]) bezeichnen Unterabteilungen einer Kategorie (vgl. vollständiger Schlüssel auf Seite *I · 1).*

Los símbolos incluídos en el texto del índice representan las grandes categorías identificadas con la clave a la derecha. Los símbolos con numeros en su parte superior (⋏[1]) identifican las subcategorías (véase la clave completa en la página *I · 1).*

Les symboles de l'index représentent les catégories indiquées dans la légende à droite. Les symboles suivis d'un indice (⋏[1]) représentent des sous-catégories (voir légende complète à la page *I · 1).*

Os símbolos incluídos no texto do índice representam as grandes categorias identificadas com a chave à direita. Os símbolos com números em sua parte superior (⋏[1]) identificam as subcategorias (veja-se a chave completa à página *I · 1).*

ʌ Mountain	Berg	Montaña	Montagne	Montanha
⋏ Mountains	Gebirge	Montañas	Montagnes	Montanhas
)(Pass	Paß	Paso	Col	Passo
V Valley, Canyon	Tal, Cañon	Valle, Cañón	Vallée, Canyon	Vale, Canhão
≚ Plain	Ebene	Llano	Plaine	Planície
› Cape	Kap	Cabo	Cap	Cabo
I Island	Insel	Isla	Île	Ilha
II Islands	Inseln	Islas	Îles	Ilhas
± Other Topographic Features	Andere Topographische Objekte	Otros Elementos Topográficos	Autres données topographiques	Outros acidentes topográficos

ESPAÑOL

Nombre	Página	Lat.°′	Long.°′ W = Oeste
Onaway	190	45.21 N	84.13 W
Oncativo	252	31.55 S	63.40 W
Once, Canal Numero ≊	252	36.09 S	58.36 W
Onchāi	272b	22.57 N	88.19 E
Onchan	44	54.11 N	4.27 W
Onch'ŏn-dong	98	40.51 N	129.07 E
Oncócua	152	16.34 S	13.28 E
Onda, Esp.	34	39.58 N	0.15 W
Onda, India	126	23.08 N	87.12 E
Ondangwa	156	17.55 S	16.00 E
Ondas, Rio de ≃	255	12.08 S	45.00 W
Ondava ≃	30	48.27 N	21.48 E
Onderdijk	52	52.45 N	5.07 E
Onderstedorings	158	30.13 S	20.37 E
Ondjiva	152	17.03 S	15.47 E
Ondo, Nig.	150	7.04 N	4.47 E
Ondo, Nihon	96	34.11 N	132.32 E
Ondo □ 3	150	7.00 N	5.15 E
Ondo-ōhashi ⊷ 5	96	34.12 N	132.33 E
Öndörchaan	88	47.19 N	110.39 E
Öndörchangaj	88	49.20 N	94.50 E
Öndör-Önc	102	45.51 N	103.11 E
Öndöršireet	88	47.27 N	104.50 E
Öndör-Ulaan	88	48.03 N	100.30 E
Ondozero, ozero ⊜	24	63.48 N	33.20 E
O'Neals	226	37.08 N	119.42 W
One Arrow Indian Reserve ⊷ 4	184	52.48 N	106.03 W
Oneco, Ct., U.S.	207	41.41 N	71.48 W
Oneco, Fl., U.S.	220	27.26 N	82.32 W
Onega	24	63.55 N	38.05 E
Onega ≃	24	63.58 N	37.55 E
Onega, Lake → Onežskoje ozero ⊜	24	61.30 N	35.45 E
Oneglia	62	43.53 N	8.02 E
One Hundred and Two ≃	194	39.44 N	94.43 W
One Hundred and Two, West Fork ≃	194	40.26 N	94.49 W
One Hundred Fifty Mile House	182	52.06 N	121.55 W
One Hundred Mile House	182	51.39 N	121.18 W
Oneida, Il., U.S.	190	41.04 N	90.13 W
Oneida, Ky., U.S.	192	37.16 N	83.38 W
Oneida, N.Y., U.S.	210	43.05 N	75.39 W
Oneida, Oh., U.S.	218	39.28 N	84.23 W
Oneida, Pa., U.S.	210	40.54 N	76.08 W
Oneida, Tn., U.S.	192	36.29 N	84.30 W
Oneida □ 6	210	43.10 N	75.20 W
Oneida ≃	210	43.12 N	76.17 W
Oneida Castle	210	43.05 N	75.40 W
Oneida County Airport ⊠	210	43.09 N	75.23 W
Oneida Creek ≃	210	43.10 N	75.44 W
Oneida Indian Reservation ⊷ 4	190	44.30 N	88.10 W
Oneida Indian Reserve ⊷ 4	214	42.49 N	81.24 W
Oneida Lake ⊜	210	43.13 N	76.00 W
O'Neil Forebay ⊜ 1	226	37.05 N	121.03 W
O'Neill	198	42.27 N	98.38 W
Onekama	190	44.21 N	86.12 W
Onekotan, ostrov I	74	49.25 N	154.45 E
Onema	152	4.33 S	24.31 E
Onemen, zaliv ⊂	180	64.45 N	176.35 E
Oneonta, Al., U.S.	194	33.56 N	86.28 W
Oneonta, N.Y., U.S.	210	42.27 N	75.03 W
Oneroa I	174k	21.15 S	159.43 W
One Tree Hill	168b	34.43 S	138.46 E
One Tree Hill ∧ 2	274b	37.52 S	145.19 E
One Tree Hill Lookout ♠	169	36.48 S	144.18 E
Onevai I	174w	21.05 S	175.07 W
Onex	58	46.10 N	6.06 E
Onežskaja guba ⊂	24	64.20 N	36.30 E
Onežskij poluostrov ≻ 1	24	64.35 N	38.00 E
Onežskoje ozero (Lake Onega) ⊜	24	61.30 N	35.45 E
Onga ≃	96	33.54 N	130.39 E
Ongaonga	172	39.55 S	176.25 E
Ongarue	172	38.43 S	175.17 E
Ong Con, Cu Lao I	269c	10.45 N	106.50 E
Ongea Levu I	175g	19.08 S	178.24 W
Ongeluks ≃	158	32.24 S	19.46 E
Ongers ≃	158	31.04 S	23.13 E
Ongerup	162	33.58 S	118.29 E
Ongijn ≃	102	44.30 N	103.40 E
Ongjin	98	37.57 N	125.21 E
Ongoka	154	1.23 S	26.02 E
Ongole	122	15.31 N	80.04 E
Ongon	102	45.21 N	113.09 E
Ongudaj	86	50.45 N	86.09 E
Oni	84	42.34 N	43.27 E
Onich	46	56.42 N	5.13 W
Onida	198	44.42 N	100.03 W
Onifai	71	40.24 N	9.39 E
Oniferi	71	40.16 N	9.10 E
Onigajō-yama ∧	96	33.07 N	132.41 E
Onilahy ≃	157b	23.34 S	43.45 E
Onin, Jazirah ≻ 1	164	2.50 S	132.05 E
Onion Creek ≃	222	30.12 N	97.35 W
Onion Peak ∧	224	45.49 N	123.53 W
Onishi	94	36.09 N	139.04 E
Onistagane, Lac ⊜	186	50.42 N	71.19 W
Onitsha	150	6.09 N	6.47 E
Onji	270	34.37 N	135.38 E
Onjuku	94	35.11 N	140.22 E
Onkaparinga ≃	168b	35.10 S	138.28 E
Onkivesi ⊜	26	63.18 N	27.18 E
Onko	152	4.07 S	19.59 E
Onley	208	37.41 N	75.42 W
Onna	174m	26.30 N	127.51 E
Onnaing	50	50.23 N	3.36 E
Onno	58	45.55 N	9.17 E
Onny ≃	42	52.23 N	2.45 W
Ōno, Nihon	94	35.59 N	136.29 E
Ōno, Nihon	94	35.28 N	136.38 E
Ōno, Nihon	96	34.18 N	132.17 E
Ono, Nihon	96	34.51 N	134.56 E
Ōno, Nihon	96	33.02 N	131.30 E
Ono, Nihon	270	34.57 N	135.14 E
Ono, Pa., U.S.	208	40.24 N	76.32 W
Ono I	175g	18.55 S	178.29 E
Ōno ≃	96	33.15 N	131.43 E
Onochoj	88	51.58 N	108.01 E
Onoda	96	33.59 N	131.11 E
Ōno-dam ⊷ 6	96	35.15 N	135.27 E
Onogami	94	36.33 N	138.56 E
Ōnohara	96	34.05 N	133.40 E
Ono-I-Lau I	14	20.39 S	178.42 W
Ōnojō	96	33.32 N	130.28 E
Onolimbu	114	1.03 N	97.53 E
Ōnomi	96	33.21 N	133.09 E
Onomichi	96	34.25 N	133.12 E
Onon	88	49.08 N	112.38 E
Onon ≃	88	51.42 N	115.50 E
Onondaga, Mi., U.S.	216	42.26 N	84.33 W
Onondaga, N.Y., U.S.	210	43.00 N	76.11 W
Onondaga □ 6	210	43.03 N	76.09 W
Onondaga Creek ≃	210	43.04 N	76.11 W
Onondaga Indian Reservation ⊷ 4	210	42.55 N	76.09 W
Onor	89	50.11 N	142.40 E
Onota Lake ⊜	207	42.28 N	73.17 W
Onoto	246	9.36 N	65.12 W
Onotoa I 1	14	1.52 S	175.34 E
Onoway	182	53.42 N	114.12 W
Ons, Isla de I	34	42.23 N	8.56 W
Onsbjerg	41	55.51 N	10.35 E
Onseepkans	158	28.46 S	19.14 E
Onsen	96	35.33 N	134.29 E
Onset	207	41.44 N	70.39 W
Onslow	162	21.39 S	115.06 E
Onslow Bay ⊂	192	34.20 N	77.20 W
Onslow Village	260	51.14 N	0.36 W
Onsted	216	42.00 N	84.11 W

FRANÇAIS

Nom	Page	Lat.°′	Long.°′ W = Ouest
Onstmettingen	58	48.17 N	9.00 E
Onstwedde	52	53.02 N	7.02 E
On-take ∧	92	31.35 N	130.39 E
Ontake-san ∧	94	35.53 N	137.29 E
Ontario, Ca., U.S.	228	34.03 N	117.39 W
Ontario, In., U.S.	216	41.43 N	85.23 W
Ontario, N.Y., U.S.	210	43.13 N	77.17 W
Ontario, Oh., U.S.	214	40.45 N	82.35 W
Ontario, Or., U.S.	202	44.01 N	116.57 W
Ontario □ 6	210	42.54 N	77.17 W
Ontario □ 4	176	51.00 N	85.00 W
Ontario, Lake ⊜	212	43.45 N	78.00 W
Ontario Agricultural Museum ⊌	212	43.30 N	79.56 W
Ontario Center	210	43.14 N	77.19 W
Ontario International Airport ⊠	228	34.04 N	117.36 W
Ontario Place ♠	275b	43.38 N	79.25 W
Ontario Science Centre ⊌	275b	43.43 N	79.21 W
Ontelaunee, Lake ⊜	208	40.27 N	75.55 W
Ontinyent (Onteniente)	34	38.49 N	0.37 W
Ontojärvi ⊜	26	64.08 N	29.09 E
Ontonagon	190	46.52 N	89.18 W
Ontonagon ≃	190	46.52 N	89.20 W
Ontonagon, East Branch ≃	190	46.42 N	89.11 W
Ontonagon, Middle Branch ≃	190	46.42 N	89.10 W
Ontonagon, West Branch ≃	190	46.42 N	89.11 W
Ontong Java I 1	175e	5.20 S	159.30 E
Onufrijevka	78	48.54 N	33.26 E
Onufrijevo	82	55.51 N	36.31 E
Ōnuma	268	35.32 N	139.25 E
Onverwacht	250	5.36 N	55.12 W
Onward	216	40.42 N	86.12 W
Ŏnyang, Taehan	98	36.47 N	127.00 E
Ŏnyang, Taehan	98	35.34 N	129.07 E
Onzain	50	47.30 N	1.11 E
Onzo ≃	152	8.12 S	13.16 E
Oobagooma	162	16.46 S	123.59 E
Oodnadatta	162	27.33 S	135.28 E
Ood Weyne	144	9.25 N	45.04 E
Ōoka	94	36.30 N	137.59 E
Ooldea	162	30.27 S	131.50 E
Oolitic	218	38.54 N	86.31 W
Oologah	196	36.26 N	95.42 W
Oologah Lake ⊜ 1	196	36.33 N	95.36 W
Ooma	174d	0.53 S	169.36 E
Oombergen	50	50.54 N	3.50 E
Oona River	182	53.57 N	130.18 W
Ooratippra	162	22.00 S	136.00 E
Ooratippra Creek ≃	162	21.55 S	136.05 E
Oorlogskloof ≃	158	31.52 S	19.01 E
Oos	56	48.47 N	8.11 E
Oos-Londen → East London	158	33.00 S	27.55 E
Oostakker	50	51.06 N	3.46 E
Oostburg, Ned.	52	51.20 N	3.30 E
Oostburg, Wi., U.S.	190	43.37 N	87.47 W
Oost-Cappel	50	50.55 N	2.36 E
Oostduinkerke	50	51.07 N	2.41 E
Oostelijk Flevoland ⊷ 1	52	52.30 N	5.45 E
Oostende (Ostende)	50	51.13 N	2.55 E
Oosterbeek	52	52.00 N	5.50 E
Oosterend	52	53.05 N	4.52 E
Oosterhout	52	51.38 N	4.51 E
Oosterschelde ⊂	52	51.30 N	4.00 E
Oosterscheldedam ⊷ 6	52	51.38 N	3.42 E
Oosterwolde	52	52.59 N	6.17 E
Oosterzele	50	50.57 N	3.48 E
Oosthuizen	52	52.35 N	5.00 E
Oostkamp	50	51.09 N	3.14 E
Oostmahorn	52	53.24 N	6.09 E
Oostmalle	56	51.18 N	4.44 E
Oostpunt ≻	241s	12.02 N	68.45 W
Oostrozebeke	50	50.55 N	3.20 E
Oost-Souburg	52	51.27 N	3.35 E
Oost-Vlaanderen □ 4	50	51.00 N	3.45 E
Oostvleteren	50	50.56 N	2.44 E
Oost-Vlieland	52	53.17 N	5.04 E
Oostvoorne	52	51.55 N	4.06 E
Ootmarsum	52	52.25 N	6.54 E
Ootsa Lake	182	53.47 N	126.03 W
Ootsa Lake ⊜	182	53.49 N	126.18 W
Ootsi	156	25.02 S	25.45 E
Ootua, Mont ∧	174x	9.47 S	138.58 W
Opaka	38	43.27 N	26.10 E
Opala	152	0.37 S	24.21 E
Opalaca, Cordillera ⩘	236	14.30 N	88.20 W
Opal Cliffs	226	36.57 N	121.57 W
Opale, Côte d' ⫠ 2	50	50.40 N	1.35 E
Opalenica	30	52.19 N	16.23 E
Opalicha	265b	55.49 N	37.15 E
Opa-Locka	220	25.54 N	80.15 W
Opari	154	3.56 N	32.03 E
Oparino	24	59.52 N	48.17 E
Opasatica, Lac ⊜	190	48.05 N	79.18 W
Opasatika Lake ⊜	190	49.04 N	83.08 W
Opasquia	184	53.16 N	93.35 W
Opasquia Lake ⊜	184	53.18 N	93.34 W
Opatija	36	45.21 N	14.19 E
Opatów	30	50.49 N	21.26 E
Opava	30	49.56 N	17.54 E
Opava ≃	30	49.50 N	18.13 E
Opečenskij Posad	76	58.16 N	34.07 E
Opeepeesway Lake ⊜	190	47.38 N	82.14 W
Opeilu	273a	6.42 N	3.18 E
Opelika	194	32.38 N	85.22 W
Opelousas	194	30.32 N	92.04 W
Open Bay ⊂	164	4.50 S	151.20 E
Open Door	258	34.30 S	59.05 W
Opeongo ≃	190	45.30 N	77.57 W
Opeongo Lake ⊜	190	45.42 N	78.23 W
Opequon Creek ≃	188	39.35 N	77.52 W
Opfikon	58	47.26 N	8.35 E
Ophain-Bois-Seigneur-Isaac	50	50.40 N	4.21 E
Ophasselt	50	50.49 N	3.53 E
Opheim	202	48.51 N	106.24 W
Opherdicke	263	51.29 N	7.38 E
Opheusden	52	51.56 N	5.38 E
Ophir, Ak., U.S.	180	63.10 N	156.31 W
Ophir, Or., U.S.	202	42.33 N	124.22 W
Ophirton ⊷ 8	273d	26.14 S	28.01 E
Ophthalmia Range ⩘	162	23.17 S	119.30 E
Opi	66	41.47 N	13.50 E
Opienge	154	0.12 N	27.30 E
Opihikao	229d	19.25 N	154.53 W
Opinaca ≃	176	52.15 N	78.02 W
Opinan	46	57.43 N	5.47 W
Opinicon Lake ⊜	212	44.33 N	76.20 W
Opiscotéo, Lac ⊜	176	53.10 N	68.10 W
Opladen	56	51.04 N	7.00 E
Opmeer	52	52.43 N	4.56 E
Opobo	150	4.34 N	7.27 E
Opobo Town	150	4.30 N	7.30 E
Opočka	76	56.43 N	28.38 E
Opoczno	30	51.23 N	20.17 E
Opol	116	8.31 N	124.34 E
Opole (Oppeln)	30	50.41 N	17.55 E
Opole □ 4	30	50.30 N	17.45 E
Opole Lubelskie	30	51.09 N	21.58 E
Opon → Lapu-Lapu	116	10.19 N	123.57 E
Opononо, Lake ⊜	156	18.08 S	15.45 E
Opopeo	234	19.24 N	101.36 W
Oporto → Porto	34	41.11 N	8.36 W
Opošn'a	78	49.58 N	34.37 E
Opotiki	172	38.00 S	177.17 E
Opp	194	31.16 N	86.15 W
Oppach	54	51.03 N	14.30 E
Oppdal	26	62.36 N	9.40 E
Oppelhain	54	51.33 N	13.35 E

PORTUGUÊS

Nome	Página	Lat.°′	Long.°′ W = Oeste
Oppeln → Opole	30	50.41 N	17.55 E
Oppenau	58	48.28 N	8.10 E
Oppenberg	61	47.29 N	14.16 E
Oppenheim, Dtsch.	56	49.51 N	8.21 E
Oppenheim, N.Y., U.S.	210	43.04 N	74.42 W
Oppenheim Park ♠	284a	43.06 N	78.54 W
Oppenhuizen	52	53.00 N	5.42 E
Oppido Lucano	68	40.47 N	16.00 E
Oppido Mamertina	68	38.16 N	16.00 E
Oppio	66	44.03 N	10.50 E
Oppland □ 6	26	61.10 N	9.40 E
Opportunity, Mt., U.S.	202	46.07 N	112.49 W
Opportunity, Wa., U.S.	202	47.39 N	117.14 W
Oppum ⊷ 8	263	51.19 N	6.37 E
Opsa	76	55.32 N	26.47 E
Opsaheden	40	60.28 N	13.59 E
Optic Lake	184	54.46 N	101.13 W
Optima Lake ⊜ 1	196	36.40 N	101.10 W
Opua	172	35.19 S	174.07 E
Opunake	172	39.27 S	173.51 E
Opunohu, Baie d' ⊂	174s	17.30 S	149.51 W
Opuwo	152	18.03 S	13.45 E
Opwijk	50	50.58 N	4.11 E
Oquawka	190	40.55 N	90.56 W
Oquendo, Perú	286d	11.58 S	77.08 W
Oquendo, Pil.	116	12.08 N	124.32 E
O'Quinn	222	29.50 N	96.58 W
Or' ≃	86	51.12 N	58.30 E
Or, Côte d' ∧	58	47.10 N	4.50 E
Or, Étang d' ⊜	261	48.38 N	1.51 E
Ora (Auer), It.	64	46.21 N	11.18 E
Ora, Lībiyā	146	28.33 N	19.24 E
Ōra, Nihon	174m	26.33 N	128.02 E
Ora Banda	162	30.22 S	121.04 E
Oracle	200	32.36 N	110.46 W
Oradea	38	47.03 N	21.57 E
Oradell	276	40.57 N	74.02 W
Oradell Reservoir ⊜ 1	276	40.58 N	74.01 W
Öræfajökull ⍓	24a	64.03 N	16.38 W
Orahovica	38	45.31 N	17.53 E
Orai	124	25.59 N	79.28 E
Oraibi Wash V	200	35.26 N	110.49 W
Oraison	62	43.55 N	5.55 E
Oran	194	37.05 N	89.39 W
Oran, Sebkha d' ⊜	34	35.32 N	0.48 W
Orange, Austl.	166	33.17 S	149.06 E
Orange, Fr.	62	44.08 N	4.48 E
Orange, Ca., U.S.	228	33.47 N	117.51 W
Orange, Ct., U.S.	207	41.16 N	73.01 W
Orange, Ma., U.S.	207	42.35 N	72.18 W
Orange, N.J., U.S.	276	40.46 N	74.13 W
Orange, Oh., U.S.	279a	41.26 N	81.29 W
Orange, Tx., U.S.	194	30.05 N	93.44 W
Orange, Va., U.S.	188	38.14 N	78.06 W
Orange □ 6, Ca., U.S.	228	33.43 N	117.54 W
Orange □ 6, Fl., U.S.	220	28.32 N	81.16 W
Orange □ 6, In., U.S.	218	38.33 N	86.28 W
Orange □ 6, N.Y., U.S.	210	41.24 N	74.20 W
Orange (Oranje) ≃	156	28.41 S	16.28 E
Orange, Cabo ≻	250	4.24 N	51.33 W
Orange Bowl ♠	220	25.46 N	80.14 W
Orangeburg, Ky., U.S.	218	38.35 N	83.39 W
Orangeburg, N.Y., U.S.	210	41.03 N	73.57 W
Orangeburg, S.C., U.S.	192	33.29 N	80.51 W
Orange City, Fl., U.S.	220	28.57 N	81.17 W
Orange City, Ia., U.S.	198	43.00 N	96.03 W
Orange County Airport ⊠	228	33.40 N	117.51 W
Orange Cove	226	36.37 N	119.19 W
Orange Free State (Oranje-Vrystaat) □ 4	158	28.30 S	27.00 E
Orange Grove	196	27.57 N	97.56 W
Orange Grove ⊷ 8	273d	26.10 S	28.05 E
Orange Lake, Fl., U.S.	192	29.25 N	82.13 W
Orange Lake, N.Y., U.S.	210	41.33 N	74.06 W
Orange Lake ⊜	192	29.29 N	82.10 W
Orangemouth → Oranjemund	156	28.38 S	16.24 E
Orange Park	192	30.09 N	81.42 W
Orange Park Acres	280	33.48 N	117.47 W
Orange Reservoir ⊜ 1	276	40.46 N	74.17 W
Orangevale	226	38.40 N	121.13 W
Orangeville, On., Can.	212	43.55 N	80.06 W
Orangeville, Oh., U.S.	214	41.20 N	80.31 W
Orangeville, Pa., U.S.	210	41.05 N	76.25 W
Orangeville, Ut,. U.S.	200	39.13 N	111.03 W
Orange Walk	232	18.06 N	88.33 W
Orango Grande I	150	11.10 N	16.08 W
Orani, It.	71	40.15 N	9.11 E
Orani, Pil.	116	14.49 N	120.32 E
Oranienbaum	54	51.48 N	12.24 E
Oranienburg	54	52.45 N	13.14 E
Oranje	52	52.55 N	6.28 E
Oranjefontein	156	23.25 S	27.41 E
Oranje Gebergte ⩘	250	3.00 N	55.05 W
Oranjemund	156	28.38 S	16.24 E
Oranje → Orange ≃	156	28.41 S	16.28 E
Oranjerivier	158	29.40 S	24.12 E
Oranjestad	241s	12.33 N	70.06 W
Oranjeville	158	27.00 S	28.15 E
Oranki	80	55.53 N	43.44 E
Oranmore	48	53.16 N	8.54 W
Ŏran-ni	98	34.22 N	126.29 E
Oran → Wahran	148	35.43 N	0.43 W
Oranžerei	80	45.50 N	47.36 E
Or 'Aqiva	132	32.30 N	34.55 E
Orarak	140	6.15 N	32.23 E
Orari ≃	172	44.15 S	171.25 E
Oras	116	12.09 N	125.26 E
Oras ≃	116	12.08 N	125.26 E
Oras Bay ⊂	116	12.07 N	125.28 E
Orăștie	38	45.50 N	23.12 E
Orașul Stalin → Brașov	38	45.39 N	25.37 E
Oratório, Ribeirão do ≃	287b	23.37 S	46.32 W
Oratov	78	49.12 N	29.32 E
Oravais (Oravainen)	26	63.18 N	22.23 E
Oravița	38	45.02 N	21.41 E
Orawia	172	46.03 S	167.49 E
Orb ≃	32	43.15 N	3.18 E
Orba ≃	62	44.53 N	8.37 E
Orba Co ⊜	120	34.32 N	81.03 E
Orbassano	62	45.01 N	7.32 E
Orbe	58	46.43 N	6.32 E
Orbe ≃	58	46.47 N	6.39 E
Orbec-en-Auge	50	49.01 N	0.25 E
Orbetello	66	42.27 N	11.13 E
Orbetello, Laguna di ⊂	66	42.27 N	11.14 E
Orbey	58	48.08 N	7.10 E
Orbieu ≃	32	43.14 N	2.54 E
Orbigny	50	47.12 N	1.14 E
Órbigo ≃	34	41.58 N	5.40 W
Orbiquet ≃	50	49.09 N	0.14 E
Orbisonia	214	40.15 N	77.54 W
Orbost	166	37.42 S	148.27 E
Örbyhus	40	60.14 N	17.42 E
Orcadas ⊌ 3	9	60.45 S	44.43 W
Orcadas, Islas → Orkney Islands II	46	59.00 N	3.00 W
Orcadas del Sur, Islas → South Orkney Islands II	9	60.35 S	45.30 W
Orcades du Sud, Îles → South Orkney Islands II	9	60.35 S	45.30 W
Orcas	224	48.36 N	122.57 W
Orcas Island I	224	48.39 N	122.55 W
Orcemont	261	48.35 N	1.49 E
Orcera	34	38.19 N	2.39 W
Orchamps	58	47.09 N	5.40 E
Orchard, Ne., U.S.	198	42.20 N	98.14 W
Orchard, Tx., U.S.	222	29.36 N	95.58 W
Orchard City	200	38.49 N	107.58 W
Orchard Hills, Austl.	274a	33.47 S	150.43 E
Orchard Hills, Pa., U.S.	279b	40.35 N	79.32 W
Orchard Homes	202	46.51 N	114.02 W
Orchard Island	216	40.28 N	83.53 W
Orchard Lake ⊜	281	42.35 N	83.22 W
Orchard Lake Village	281	42.35 N	83.21 W
Orchard Mesa	200	39.02 N	108.33 W
Orchard Park	210	42.46 N	78.44 W
Orchard Park Airport ⊠	284a	42.48 N	78.45 W
Orchard Peak ∧	226	35.44 N	120.08 W
Orchards	224	45.40 N	122.33 W
Orchard Valley	200	41.05 N	104.48 W
Orchard View	285	40.04 N	74.53 W
Orchej	78	47.23 N	28.48 E
Orchha	124	25.21 N	78.39 E
Orchies	50	50.28 N	3.14 E
Orchon	88	49.09 N	105.21 E
Orchon ≃	88	50.21 N	106.05 E
Orchon Tuul	88	48.58 N	104.59 E
Orcia ≃	66	42.58 N	11.21 E
Orcières	62	44.41 N	6.20 E
Orčik ≃	78	49.10 N	35.04 E
Orco ≃	62	45.10 N	7.52 E
Ord	198	41.36 N	98.55 W
Ord ≃	160	15.30 S	128.21 E
Ord, Mount ∧	162	17.20 S	125.34 E
Orda	86	57.12 N	56.54 E
Ordenes	34	43.04 N	8.24 W
Orderville	200	37.16 N	112.38 W
Ordesa, Parque Nacional de ♠	34	42.39 N	0.02 E
Ord Mountain ∧	204	34.40 N	116.49 W
Ord Mountains ⩘	228	34.42 N	117.10 W
Ordoqui	252	35.54 S	61.10 W
Ord River	162	17.23 S	128.51 E
Ordu	130	41.00 N	37.53 E
Ordu □ 4	130	40.45 N	37.30 E
Ordubad	84	38.56 N	46.02 E
Ordway	198	38.13 N	103.45 W
Ordynskoje	86	54.22 N	81.56 E
Ordzhonikidze → Jenakijevo	83	48.14 N	38.13 E
Ordzhonikidze → Vladikavkaz, Ross.	84	43.03 N	44.40 E
Ordžhonikidze → Vladikavkaz, Ross.	84	43.03 N	44.40 E
Ordžonikidze, Azer.	84	40.53 N	47.23 E
Ordžonikidze, Kaz.	86	52.28 N	61.46 E
Ordžonikidze, Ukr.	78	47.40 N	34.04 E
Ordžonikidze, Ukr.	78	44.57 N	35.22 E
Ordžonikidzeabad	85	38.34 N	69.01 E
Ordžonikidzevskaja	84	43.18 N	45.03 E
Ordžonikidzevskij, Ross.	84	43.51 N	41.54 E
Ordžonikidzevskij, Ross.	86	54.46 N	88.59 E
Ore	150	6.44 N	4.52 E
Ore ≃	46	56.10 N	3.15 W
Öreälven ≃	26	63.32 N	19.44 E
Oreana	219	39.56 N	88.51 W
Örebro	40	59.17 N	15.13 E
Örebro Län □ 6	40	59.30 N	15.00 E
Orechov	78	47.34 N	35.47 E
Orechovka, Ross.	80	52.56 N	48.14 E
Orechovka, Ukr.	83	48.17 N	39.13 E
Orechovo	80	58.28 N	41.58 E
Orechovo-Zujevo	82	55.49 N	38.59 E
Orechovsk	76	54.41 N	30.30 E
Orechov'skij ⊷ 8	83	48.01 N	38.42 E
Ore City	222	32.48 N	94.43 W
Oredež	76	58.49 N	30.20 E
Oredež ≃	76	58.49 N	30.00 E
Orefield	208	40.38 N	75.35 W
Oregon, Il., U.S.	190	42.00 N	89.19 W
Oregon, Mo., U.S.	194	39.59 N	95.08 W
Oregon, Oh., U.S.	214	41.38 N	83.29 W
Oregon, Wi., U.S.	216	42.55 N	89.23 W
Oregon □ 3, U.S.	178	44.00 N	121.00 W
Oregon □ 3, U.S.	202	44.00 N	121.00 W
Oregon Caves National Monument ♠	202	42.06 N	123.24 W
Oregon City	224	45.21 N	122.36 W
Oregon Creek ≃	226	39.23 N	121.05 W
Oregon Dunes National Recreation Area ♠	202	43.45 N	124.12 W
Oregon House	226	39.21 N	121.17 W
Öregrund	40	60.20 N	18.26 E
Öregrundsgrepen ⊂	40	60.27 N	18.18 E
Orehoved	41	54.57 N	11.52 E
Orekhovo-Zuyevo → Orechovo-Zujevo	82	55.49 N	38.59 E
Orel	76	52.59 N	36.05 E
Orel', ozero ⊜	89	53.30 N	139.42 E
Oreland	285	40.07 N	75.10 W
Orellana	248	6.54 S	75.04 W
Orellana, Embalse de ⊜ 1	34	39.00 N	5.25 W
Orel Oblast' □ 4	76	53.00 N	36.20 E
Orem	200	40.17 N	111.41 W
Ören	130	37.02 N	27.57 E
Orenburg	86	51.54 N	55.06 E
Orenburg Oblast' □ 4	86	52.30 N	54.00 E
Örencik	130	39.16 N	29.33 E
Oreng, Indon.	114	4.33 N	96.49 E
Oreng, Indon.	114	4.03 N	97.28 E
Orense, Arg.	252	38.40 S	59.47 W
Orense, Esp.	34	42.20 N	7.51 W
Orense □ 4	34	42.15 N	7.30 W
Örenşehir	130	39.00 N	36.39 E
Orepuki	172	46.17 S	167.44 E
Oreški	82	55.43 N	36.21 E
Oressa ≃	76	52.33 N	28.45 E
Orestes	216	40.16 N	85.43 W
Orestes Pereyra	232	26.31 N	105.40 W
Orestiás	38	41.30 N	26.31 E
Orestimba Creek ≃	226	37.25 N	121.00 W
Øresund → The Sound ⊔	41	55.50 N	12.40 E
Oreti ≃	172	46.28 S	168.17 E
Oreto ≃	70	38.06 N	13.24 E
Orewa	172	36.34 S	174.42 E
Oreye	56	50.44 N	5.22 E
Orfanoú, Kólpos ⊂	38	40.40 N	23.50 E
Orford, Eng., U.K.	42	52.06 N	1.31 E
Orford, Eng., U.K.	262	53.25 N	2.35 W
Orford, Mont ∧	206	45.19 N	72.15 W
Orford Ness ≻	42	52.05 N	1.34 E
Orfordville	190	42.37 N	89.15 W
Organ Needle ∧	200	32.21 N	106.33 W
Organ Pipe Cactus National Monument ♠	200	32.00 N	112.55 W
Órgãos, Serra dos ⩘	256	22.22 S	42.45 W
Orgaz	34	39.39 N	3.54 W
Orge ≃	50	48.42 N	2.24 E
Orgelet	58	46.31 N	5.37 E
Orgères-en-Beauce	50	48.09 N	1.42 E
Orgerus	261	48.50 N	1.42 E
Orgeval	50	48.55 N	1.59 E
Orgeval ≃	261	49.00 N	1.54 E
Orgiano	64	45.21 N	11.28 E
Orgnac, Aven d' ⫠ 5	62	44.19 N	4.27 E
Orgnac-l'Aven	62	44.19 N	4.27 E
Orgof	144	3.03 N	41.44 E
Orgon	62	43.47 N	5.02 E
Orgosolo	71	40.12 N	9.21 E
Orgtrud	80	56.12 N	40.37 E
Orgūn	120	32.51 N	69.07 E
Orhaneli	130	39.54 N	29.00 E
Orhangazi	130	40.30 N	29.18 E
Orhanlar	130	39.54 N	27.37 E
Oria, It.	68	40.30 N	17.38 E
Oria, Zaïre	154	3.17 N	30.41 E
Orica	236	14.41 N	86.56 W
Oriçanga, Rio do ≃	256	22.18 S	47.03 W
Orichuna ≃	246	7.25 N	68.58 W
Oriči	80	58.24 N	49.05 E
Orick	204	41.17 N	124.03 W
Oricola	66	42.02 N	13.02 E
Orient, Ia., U.S.	198	41.12 N	94.24 W
Orient, N.Y., U.S.	207	41.08 N	72.18 W
Orient, Oh., U.S.	218	39.48 N	83.09 W
Orient, Wa., U.S.	182	48.53 N	118.13 W
Oriental, Méx.	234	19.22 N	97.37 W
Oriental, N.C., U.S.	192	35.01 N	76.41 W
Oriental, Cordillera ⩘, Col.	246	6.00 N	73.00 W
Oriental, Cordillera ⩘, Perú	248	11.00 S	74.00 W
Oriental, Pico ∧	286c	10.32 N	66.50 W
Oriental de Zapata, Ciénaga ≋	240p	22.15 N	80.50 W
Oriental Park	214	42.09 N	79.22 W
Oriente	252	38.44 S	60.37 W
Orientos	166	28.05 S	141.14 E
Origgio	266b	45.36 N	9.01 E
Origny-en-Thiérache	50	49.54 N	4.01 E
Origny-Sainte-Benoite	50	49.50 N	3.30 E
Orillia	212	44.37 N	79.25 W
Orimattila	26	60.48 N	25.45 E
Orinda	226	37.52 N	122.10 W
Orinduik	246	4.42 N	60.01 W
Orini	172	37.34 S	175.18 E
Orinin	78	48.46 N	26.24 E
Orinoco ≃	246	8.37 N	62.15 W
Orinoco, Delta del ⩧ 2	246	9.15 N	61.30 W
Oriola (Orihuela)	34	38.05 N	0.57 W
Oriole, Md., U.S.	208	38.10 N	75.48 W
Oriole, Pa., U.S.	210	41.08 N	77.13 W
Oriole Park ♠	284b	39.18 N	76.37 W
Oriolo	68	40.03 N	16.27 E
Oriomo	164	8.50 S	143.15 E
Orion, Pil.	116	14.37 N	120.34 E
Orion, Il., U.S.	190	41.21 N	90.22 W
Oripää	26	60.51 N	22.41 E
Oriskany	210	43.09 N	75.19 W
Oriskany Battlefield State Historic Site ⊥	210	43.11 N	75.23 W
Oriskany Creek ≃	210	43.10 N	75.20 W
Oriskany Falls	210	42.56 N	75.27 W
Orissa □ 3	118	20.00 N	84.00 E
Orissaare	76	58.34 N	23.05 E
Orissa Coast Canal ≊	126	21.51 N	87.41 E
Oristano	71	39.54 N	8.36 E
Oristano □ 4	71	39.55 N	8.40 E
Oristano, Golfo di ⊂	71	39.50 N	8.29 E
Öriszentpéter	61	46.51 N	16.25 E
Orituco ≃	246	8.45 N	67.27 W
Orivesi	26	61.41 N	24.21 E
Orivesi ⊜	26	62.16 N	29.24 E
Oriximiná	250	1.45 S	55.52 W
Orizaba	234	18.51 N	97.06 W
Orizaba, Pico de (Volcán Citlatépetl) ∧ 1	234	19.01 N	97.16 W
Orizona	255	17.03 S	48.18 W
Orjahovo	38	43.45 N	23.57 E
Ørje	26	59.29 N	11.39 E
Orjen ∧	38	42.30 N	18.38 E
Orjiva	34	36.54 N	3.25 W
Ork, Ness of ≻	46	59.05 N	2.48 W
Orkanger	26	63.19 N	9.52 E
Örkelljunga	41	56.17 N	13.17 E
Orken	263	51.06 N	6.34 E
Orkla ≃	26	63.18 N	9.50 E
Orkney, Sk., Can.	184	49.08 N	107.55 W
Orkney, S. Afr.	158	27.00 S	26.39 E
Orkney □ 4	46	59.00 N	3.00 W
Orkney Islands II	46	59.00 N	3.00 W
Orl'a	76	53.30 N	24.59 E
Orla ≃	54	50.46 N	11.31 E
Orlamünde	54	50.47 N	11.31 E
Orland, Ca., U.S.	204	39.44 N	122.11 W
Orland, In., U.S.	216	41.43 N	85.10 W
Orlândia	255	20.43 S	47.53 W
Orland Lake ⊜	278	41.38 N	87.52 W
Orlando, S. Afr.	273d	26.14 S	27.55 E
Orlando, Fl., U.S.	220	28.32 N	81.22 W
Orlando, Capo d' ≻	70	38.10 N	14.45 E
Orlando Dam ⊜ 1	273d	26.16 S	27.56 E
Orlando International Airport ⊠	220	28.26 N	81.19 W
Orlando Naval Training Center ■	220	28.34 N	81.20 W
Orlando West Extension	273d	26.15 S	27.54 E
Orland Park	216	41.37 N	87.51 W
Orland Square ⊷ 9	278	41.36 N	87.51 W
Orléanais □ 9	50	47.50 N	2.00 E
Orléans, On., Can.	212	45.28 N	75.31 W
Orléans, Fr.	50	47.55 N	1.54 E
Orleans, Ca., U.S.	204	41.18 N	123.32 W
Orleans, In., U.S.	218	38.39 N	86.27 W
Orleans, Ma., U.S.	207	41.47 N	69.59 W
Orleans, Ne., U.S.	198	40.07 N	99.27 W
Orleans, Vt., U.S.	188	44.48 N	72.12 W
Orleans □ 6, N.Y., U.S.	210	43.15 N	78.12 W
Orleans □ 6, Vt., U.S.	206	44.57 N	72.12 W
Orléans, Canal d' ≊	50	47.54 N	1.55 E
Orléans, Île d' I	186	46.55 N	70.58 W
Orléansville → Ech Cheliff	148	36.10 N	1.20 E
Orlik, Kaz.	80	48.17 N	51.32 E
Orlik, Ross.	88	52.30 N	99.55 E
Orlinaja, gora ∧	180	62.35 N	178.30 E
Orlinga	88	56.03 N	105.53 E
Orlinga ≃	88	56.03 N	105.53 E
Orlov	80	58.33 N	48.50 E
Orlová	30	49.50 N	18.24 E
Orlov Gaj	80	50.57 N	48.12 E
Orlovista	220	28.32 N	81.28 W
Orlovka, Ross.	78	51.02 N	40.32 E
Orlovka, Ross.	86	59.03 N	85.59 E
Orlovka, Ukr.	78	51.54 N	32.47 E
Orlovka, Ukr.	78	45.40 N	33.21 E
Orlovka, Ukr.	83	48.10 N	37.39 E
Orlovka ≃	86	58.40 N	86.08 E
Orlovo, Ross.	78	51.45 N	39.35 E
Orlovo, Ross.	265b	55.38 N	37.23 E
Orlovskij	80	46.52 N	42.03 E
Orlu	150	5.47 N	7.02 E
Orly	261	48.45 N	2.24 E
Ormanlı	130	41.10 N	31.39 E
Ormāra	128	25.12 N	64.38 E
Ormāra, Rās ≻	128	25.09 N	64.35 E
Orme, Rivière à l' ≃	275a	45.27 N	73.56 W
Ormea	62	44.09 N	7.54 E
Ormesby	44	54.33 N	1.11 W
Ormesby Saint Margaret	42	52.40 N	1.42 E
Ormiston	184	49.45 N	105.22 W
Ormoc	116	11.00 N	124.37 E
Ormoc Bay ⊂	116	10.58 N	124.35 E
Ormond	274b	37.54 S	145.03 E
Ormond Beach	192	29.17 N	81.03 W
Ormož	61	46.25 N	16.09 E
Ormsby	214	41.48 N	78.33 W
Ormsby □ 6	226	39.11 N	119.46 W
Ormsjön ⊜	26	64.23 N	16.03 E
Ormskirk	44	53.35 N	2.54 W
Ormstown	206	45.08 N	74.00 W
Ormtjernkampen Nasjonalpark ♠	26	61.12 N	9.48 E
Ornain ≃	56	48.46 N	4.47 E
Ornans	58	47.06 N	6.09 E
Ornäs	40	60.31 N	15.32 E
Ornavasso	58	45.58 N	8.24 E
Orne □ 5	32	48.40 N	0.05 E
Orne ≃, Fr.	32	49.19 N	0.14 W
Orne ≃, Fr.	50	48.08 N	0.11 E
Orne ≃, Fr.	56	49.17 N	6.11 E
Ornes	26	61.18 N	7.22 E
Orneta	30	54.08 N	20.08 E
Ornö I	40	59.04 N	18.24 E
Örnsköldsvik	26	63.18 N	18.43 E
Oro	98	40.02 N	127.26 E
Orø I	41	55.46 N	11.49 E
Orobie, Alpi ⩘	64	46.00 N	10.00 E
Oročanskij Golec, gora ∧	88	53.29 N	114.18 E
Oročen	74	58.28 N	125.26 E
Orocovis	240m	18.14 N	66.23 W
Orocué	246	4.48 N	71.20 W
Orocuina	236	13.26 N	87.06 W
Orodara	150	10.59 N	4.55 W
Orofino	202	46.28 N	116.15 W
Orogen Zizhiqi	89	50.34 N	123.40 E
Örög nuur ⊜, Mong.	86	50.10 N	91.00 E
Orog nuur ⊜, Mong.	102	45.03 N	100.42 E
Oro Grande	228	34.35 N	117.20 W
Orohena, Mont ∧	174s	17.37 S	149.28 W
Orok, Oldoinyo ∧	154	2.29 S	36.46 E
Oroku	174m	26.12 N	127.39 E
Or'ol	86	59.21 N	56.35 E
Or'ol' ≃	78	48.30 N	34.54 E
Oroluk I 1	14	7.32 N	155.18 E
Oromocto	186	45.51 N	66.29 W
Oromocto Lake ⊜	186	45.36 N	67.00 W
Oron, Nig.	150	4.48 N	8.14 E
Oron, Ross.	88	57.11 N	116.28 E
Oron, ozero ⊜	88	57.06 N	116.30 E
Orona I 1	14	4.29 S	172.10 W
Oron-la-Ville	58	46.34 N	6.50 E
Orono, On., Can.	212	43.59 N	78.37 W
Orono, Me., U.S.	188	44.52 N	68.40 W
Oronoque ≃	246	2.45 N	57.25 W
Oronsay I	46	56.01 N	6.16 W
Orontes → Asi ≃	130	36.02 N	35.58 E
Oropa, Santuario di ⊌ 1	62	45.38 N	7.58 E
Oropeo	234	18.50 N	101.48 W
Oroquieta	116	8.29 N	123.48 E
Orós	250	6.15 S	38.55 W
Orós, Açude ⊜ 1	250	6.15 S	39.05 W
Orosei	71	40.23 N	9.42 E
Orosei, Golfo di ⊂	71	40.15 N	9.44 E
Orosháza	30	46.34 N	20.40 E
Orosi	226	36.33 N	119.17 W
Orosí, Volcán ∧ 1	236	10.59 N	85.29 W
Oroszlány	30	47.30 N	18.19 E
Orotelli	71	40.18 N	9.07 E
Orote Peninsula ≻ 1	174p	13.26 N	144.38 E
Oroville, Ca., U.S.	226	39.30 N	121.33 W
Oroville, Wa., U.S.	202	48.56 N	119.26 W
Oroville, Lake ⊜ 1	204	39.32 N	121.25 W
Orowoc Creek ≃	276	40.43 N	73.13 W
Orpheus Island I	166	18.37 S	146.30 E
Orphin	261	48.35 N	1.47 E
Orpierre	62	44.19 N	5.41 E
Orpington ⊷ 8	260	51.23 N	0.06 E
Orrefors	26	56.50 N	15.45 E
Orrell	44	53.32 N	2.42 W
Orrick	194	39.12 N	94.07 W
Orrin	198	48.05 N	100.09 W
Orrin, Glen V	46	57.30 N	4.46 W
Orrin Reservoir ⊜ 1	46	57.30 N	4.45 W
Òrrius	266d	41.33 N	2.21 E
Orr Lake ⊜, Mb., Can.	184	56.07 N	97.11 W
Orr Lake ⊜, On., Can.	212	44.37 N	79.47 W
Orroroo	166	32.44 S	138.37 E
Orrs Island	188	43.45 N	69.58 W
Orrtanna	208	39.51 N	77.22 W
Orrville, Al., U.S.	194	32.18 N	87.14 W
Orrville, Oh., U.S.	214	40.50 N	81.45 W
Orrville, Pa., U.S.	279b	40.33 N	79.47 W
Orša, Bela.	76	54.30 N	30.24 E
Orsa, Sve.	26	61.07 N	14.37 E
Orša ≃	82	56.48 N	36.11 E
Orsago	64	45.56 N	12.25 E
Orsan	62	44.08 N	4.40 E
Oršanka	80	56.55 N	47.53 E
Orsara di Puglia	68	41.17 N	15.16 E
Orsasjön ⊜	26	61.07 N	14.34 E
Orsay	50	48.48 N	2.11 E
Orsett	260	51.31 N	0.22 E
Orsières	58	46.02 N	7.09 E
Orsjön ⊜	26	61.35 N	16.20 E
Orsk	86	51.12 N	58.34 E
Örskär I	40	60.31 N	18.23 E
Ørslev	41	55.02 N	11.59 E
Orsogna	66	42.13 N	14.17 E
Orsomarso	68	39.48 N	15.55 E
Orson	210	41.49 N	75.27 W
Orșova	38	44.42 N	22.24 E
Ørsta	26	62.12 N	6.09 E
Ørsted	41	55.20 N	10.04 E
Örsundaån ≃	40	59.44 N	17.21 E
Örsundsbro	40	59.44 N	17.18 E
Orta	130	40.38 N	33.06 E
Orta, Lago d' ⊜	62	45.49 N	8.24 E
Ortaca	130	36.49 N	28.47 E
Ortakent	130	37.02 N	27.21 E
Ortaklar	130	37.53 N	27.30 E
Ortaköy, Tür.	130	40.17 N	35.16 E
Ortaköy, Tür.	130	38.44 N	34.03 E
Ortaköy, Tür.	130	38.00 N	34.23 E
Ortaköy, Tür.	130	40.27 N	38.02 E
Ortaköy ⊷ 8	267b	41.03 N	29.01 E
Orta Nova	68	41.19 N	15.42 E
Orta San Giulio	62	45.48 N	8.25 E
Orte	66	42.27 N	12.23 E
Ortega	246	3.56 N	75.13 W
Ortegal, Cabo ≻	34	43.45 N	7.53 W
Orteguaza ≃	246	0.43 N	75.16 W
Ortelsburg → Szczytno	30	53.34 N	21.00 E
Ortenberg, Dtsch.	56	50.21 N	9.02 E
Ortenberg, Dtsch.	58	48.27 N	7.58 E
Ortenburg	60	48.33 N	13.14 E
Orth	54	54.27 N	11.03 E
Orthez	32	43.29 N	0.46 W
Orthon ≃	248	10.50 S	66.04 W
Ortigalita Creek ≃	226	36.57 N	120.52 W
Ortigalita Peak ∧	226	36.48 N	120.55 W
Ortigara, Monte ∧	64	46.00 N	11.29 E
Ortigueira	34	43.41 N	7.51 W
Ortigueira, Ría de ⊂ 1	34	43.42 N	7.51 W
Orting	224	47.05 N	122.12 W
Ortisei (Sankt Ulrich)	64	46.34 N	11.40 E
Ortiz, Méx.	232	28.17 N	110.43 W
Ortiz, Ven.	246	9.37 N	67.17 W
Ortles (Otler) ∧	64	46.31 N	10.33 E
Ortles ⩘	64	46.30 N	10.40 E
Örtofta	41	55.47 N	13.14 E
Ortolo ≃	71	41.30 N	8.55 E
Ortona	66	42.21 N	14.24 E
Ortona Lock ⊷ 5	220	26.47 N	81.18 W
Orton Park ♠	275b	43.46 N	79.12 W
Ortonura	85	41.29 N	76.12 E
Ortonville, Mi., U.S.	216	42.51 N	83.26 W
Ortonville, Mn., U.S.	198	45.18 N	96.26 W
Ortonville State Recreation Area ♠	216	42.52 N	83.26 W
Ortoterek	85	41.56 N	71.21 E
Orto-Tokoj	85	42.21 N	76.01 E
Ortovero	62	44.03 N	8.07 E
Ortrand	54	51.22 N	13.45 E

≃ River	Fluß	Río	Rivière	Rio
≊ Canal	Kanal	Canal	Canal	Canal
⌞ Waterfall, Rapids	Wasserfall, Stromschnellen	Cascada, Rápidos	Chute d'eau, Rapides	Cascata, Rápidos
⊔ Strait	Meeresstraße	Estrecho	Détroit	Estreito
⊂ Bay, Gulf	Bucht, Golf	Bahía, Golfo	Baie, Golfe	Baía, Golfo
⊜ Lake, Lakes	See, Seen	Lago, Lagos	Lac, Lacs	Lago, Lagos
≋ Swamp	Sumpf	Pantano	Marais	Pântano
⍓ Ice Features, Glacier	Eis- und Gletscherformen	Accidentes Glaciales	Formes glaciaires	Acidentes glaciares
⊤ Other Hydrographic Features	Andere Hydrographische Objekte	Otros Elementos Hidrográficos	Autres données hydrographiques	Outros acidentes hidrográficos

✦ Submarine Features	Untermeerische Objekte	Accidentes Submarinos	Formes de relief sous-marin	Acidentes submarinos
□ Political Unit	Politische Einheit	Unidad Politica	Entité politique	Unidade política
⊌ Cultural Institution	Kulturelle Institution	Institución Cultural	Institution culturelle	Instituição cultural
⊥ Historical Site	Historische Stätte	Sitio Histórico	Site historique	Sitio histórico
♠ Recreational Site	Erholungs- und Ferienort	Sitio de Recreo	Centre de loisirs	Area de Lazer
⊠ Airport	Flughafen	Aeropuerto	Aéroport	Aeroporto
■ Military Installation	Militäranlage	Instalación Militar	Installation militaire	Instalação militar
⊷ Miscellaneous	Verschiedenes	Misceláneo	Divers	Diversos

Örträsk 26 64.08 N 18.59 E
Ortueri 71 40.02 N 8.59 E
Ortúzar, Canal ≊ 286e 33.33 S 70.47 W
Örtze ≃ 52 52.40 N 9.57 E
Oruanui 172 38.35 S 176.02 E
Oruba 273a 6.35 N 3.25 E
Orudjevo 82 56.26 N 37.32 E
Orūmīyeh (Reẕā'īyeh) 128 37.33 N 45.04 E
Orūmīyeh, Daryācheh-ye (Lake Urmia) ⊜ 128 37.40 N 45.30 E
Orune 71 40.24 N 9.22 E
Oruro 248 17.59 S 67.09 W
Oruro □5 248 18.40 S 67.30 W
Or'us-Mijele ≃ 88 58.35 N 121.30 E
Orust I 26 58.10 N 11.38 E
Orūzgān (Qala-i-Hazār Qadam) 120 32.56 N 66.38 E
Orūzgān □4 120 33.15 N 66.00 E
Orval, Abbaye d' ♦1 56 49.38 N 5.22 E
Orvanne ≃ 50 48.22 N 2.50 E
Orvieto 66 42.43 N 12.07 E
Orvilla 208 40.16 N 75.17 W
Orvilliers 261 48.52 N 1.39 E
Orvin ≃ 50 48.28 N 3.23 E
Orvinio 66 42.08 N 12.56 E
Orviston 214 41.06 N 77.45 W
Orvyn, gora ∧ 180 65.14 N 175.20 W
Orwell, On., Can. 214 42.46 N 81.02 W
Orwell, N.Y., U.S. 212 43.35 N 76.00 W
Orwell, Oh., U.S. 214 41.32 N 80.52 W
Orwell ≃ 42 51.57 N 1.17 E
Orwigsburg 208 40.39 N 76.06 W
Orwin 208 40.35 N 76.31 W
Orxon ≃ 88 49.00 N 117.41 E
Or Yehuda 132 32.01 N 34.51 E
Oryu-dong ✦8 271b 37.29 N 126.51 E
Oržev 78 50.45 N 26.07 E
Orževka 80 52.43 N 42.55 E
Oržica 78 49.48 N 32.42 E
Orzinuovi 62 45.24 N 9.55 E
Orzyc ≃ 30 52.47 N 21.13 E
Orzysz 30 53.49 N 21.56 E
Oš, Kyrg. 85 40.33 N 72.48 E
Os, Nor. 26 62.30 N 11.12 E
Oš □4 85 40.00 N 72.30 E
Ōsa, Nihon 96 35.05 N 133.34 E
Osa, Ross. 86 57.17 N 55.26 E
Osa, Ross. 88 53.24 N 103.53 E
Oša ≃ 86 57.13 N 73.41 E
Osa, Península de ≻1 236 8.34 N 83.31 W
Osage, Ia., U.S. 190 43.17 N 92.48 W
Osage, Mo., U.S. 219 38.25 N 92.02 W
Osage, N.J., U.S. 285 39.51 N 75.01 W
Osage, Wy., U.S. 198 43.58 N 104.25 W
Osage □6 219 38.27 N 91.50 W
Osage ≃ 194 38.35 N 91.57 W
Osage Beach 194 38.09 N 92.37 W
Osage City 198 38.38 N 95.49 W
Osaka, Nihon 94 35.57 N 137.16 E
Ōsaka, Nihon 96 34.40 N 135.30 E
Ōsaka, Nihon 270 34.40 N 135.30 E
Ōsaka □5 96 34.30 N 135.30 E
Osaka Castle ⊥ 270 34.41 N 135.32 E
Ōsaka-heiya ≚ 270 34.43 N 135.30 E
Ōsaka International Airport ⊠ 270 34.47 N 135.26 E
Ōsaka-kō c 270 34.38 N 135.26 E
Ōsaka-kokusai-kūkō ⊠ 96 34.47 N 135.26 E
Osakarovka 86 50.32 N 72.39 E
Ōsaka-tōge)(270 34.56 N 135.18 E
Osaka University ♦2 270 34.42 N 135.30 E
Ōsaka-wan c 96 34.30 N 135.18 E
Ōsakiga-hana ≻ 96 35.11 N 132.25 E
Ōsaki-Kami-jima I 96 34.14 N 132.54 E
Osakis 198 45.52 N 95.09 W
Ōsaki-Shimo-jima I 96 34.10 N 132.50 E
Osâm ≃ 38 43.42 N 24.51 E
Osan 98 37.11 N 127.04 E
Osanovo 82 54.12 N 38.41 E
Osasco 256 23.32 S 46.46 W
Osasco □7 287b 23.32 S 46.46 W
Ōsawano 94 36.34 N 137.12 E
Osawatomie 198 38.29 N 94.57 W
Ōsa-yama ∧ 96 34.45 N 132.12 E
Osbaldeston 262 53.47 N 2.32 W
Osborne, Ks., U.S. 198 39.26 N 98.41 W
Osborne, Pa., U.S. 279b 40.32 N 80.10 W
Osburger Hochwald ✦3 56 49.40 N 6.50 E
Osburn 202 47.30 N 115.59 W
Osby 26 56.22 N 13.59 E
Osbyholm 41 55.51 N 13.36 E
Oscar Peak ∧ 182 54.51 N 129.07 W
Oscarville 180 60.43 N 161.46 W
Oscawana Lake 210 41.23 N 73.52 W
Osceola, Ar., U.S. 194 35.42 N 89.58 W
Osceola, In., U.S. 216 41.39 N 86.04 W
Osceola, Ia., U.S. 190 41.02 N 93.45 W
Osceola, Mo., U.S. 194 38.02 N 93.42 W
Osceola, Ne., U.S. 198 41.10 N 97.32 W
Osceola, Pa., U.S. 210 41.59 N 77.21 W
Osceola, Tx., U.S. 222 32.08 N 97.14 W
Osceola, Wi., U.S. 190 45.19 N 92.42 W
Osceola □6 220 28.00 N 81.15 W
Osceola Mills 214 40.51 N 78.16 W
Oščepkovo 86 56.29 N 70.42 E
Oschatz 54 51.17 N 13.07 E
Oschersleben 54 52.01 N 11.13 E
Oschiri 71 40.43 N 9.06 E
Oscoda 190 44.26 N 83.20 W
Öse ≃ 263 51.26 N 7.49 E
Osečenka 76 57.33 N 34.48 E
Osečina 38 44.23 N 19.36 E
Osejevskaja 82 55.53 N 38.10 E
Ošejkino 82 56.15 N 35.54 E
Osek 54 50.37 N 13.40 E
Ösel → Saaremaa I 76 58.25 N 22.30 E
Osen 24 64.17 N 10.30 E
Osetrovo 88 56.47 N 105.47 E
Ōse-zaki ≻ 94 35.02 N 138.47 E
Osgood, In., U.S. 218 39.07 N 85.17 W
Osgood, Oh., U.S. 216 40.20 N 84.30 W
Osgoode 212 45.08 N 75.36 W
Oshamambe 92a 42.30 N 140.22 E
O'Shanassy ≃ 166 18.59 S 138.46 E
O'Shaughnessy Dam ✦6 226 37.57 N 119.47 W
O'Shaughnessy Reservoir ⊜1 214 40.12 N 83.09 W
Oshawa 212 43.54 N 78.51 W
Oshawa Creek ≃ 212 43.52 N 78.49 W
Oshibe ✦8 270 34.45 N 135.04 E
Oshigambo 156 17.47 S 16.05 E
Oshika, Nihon 92 38.16 N 141.32 E
Ōshika, Nihon 94 35.34 N 138.02 E
Oshika-hantō ≻1 92 38.20 N 141.30 E
Oshikango 156 17.25 S 15.56 E
Ōshima, Nihon 92 33.03 N 129.33 E
Ōshima, Nihon 94 37.07 N 138.30 E
Ōshima, Nihon 94 34.45 N 139.22 E
Ōshima, Nihon 96 33.55 N 132.15 E
Ō-shima I, Nihon 92a 41.30 N 139.22 E
Ō-shima I, Nihon 94 34.43 N 139.23 E
Ō-shima I, Nihon 94 36.15 N 136.07 E
Ō-shima I, Nihon 96 33.54 N 130.26 E
Ō-shima I, Nihon 96 34.30 N 131.25 E
Ō-shima I, Nihon 96 34.00 N 133.22 E
Ō-shima I, Nihon 96 34.09 N 133.04 E
Ō-shima I, Nihon 96 33.38 N 134.30 E
Oshima-hantō ≻1 92a 42.00 N 140.30 E
Oshimizu 94 36.49 N 136.46 E
Oshino 94 35.28 N 138.51 E
Oshivre ✦8 272c 19.09 N 72.51 E
Oshkosh, Ne., U.S. 198 41.24 N 102.20 W
Oshkosh, Wi., U.S. 190 44.01 N 88.32 W
Oshnovīyeh 128 37.02 N 45.06 E
Oshodi 273a 6.34 N 3.21 E
Oshoek 158 26.13 S 30.59 E
Oshogbo 150 7.47 N 4.34 E
Osh → Oš 85 40.33 N 72.48 E
Oshtemo 216 42.15 N 85.41 W
Oshtorān Kūh ∧ 128 33.20 N 49.16 E
Oshtorīnān 128 34.01 N 48.38 E
Oshwe 152 3.24 S 19.30 E
Osi 150 8.08 N 5.14 E
Osica de Jos 38 44.15 N 24.17 E
Osich'ŏn-ni 98 41.25 N 128.16 E
Osiek 30 50.31 N 21.28 E
Osiglia 62 44.17 N 8.12 E
Osijek 38 45.33 N 18.41 E
Osilinka ≃ 182 56.05 N 124.29 W
Osilo 71 40.45 N 8.40 E
Osimo 66 43.29 N 13.29 E
Osini 71 39.50 N 9.29 E
Osinki 80 52.51 N 49.30 E
Osinniki, Ross. 80 58.03 N 47.02 E
Osinniki, Ross. 86 53.37 N 87.21 E
Osinovka, Ross. 88 50.34 N 109.27 E
Osinovka, Ross. 88 56.19 N 101.56 E
Osinovka, Ukr. 83 49.34 N 39.05 E
Osinovskij chrebet ⋀ 180 67.10 N 175.00 E
Osinów Dolny 54 52.48 N 14.10 E
Osintorf 76 54.42 N 30.39 E
Osio Sotto 62 45.36 N 9.35 E
Osipaonica 38 44.33 N 21.04 E
Osipenko 78 46.54 N 36.49 E
Osipenko → Berd'ansk 78 46.45 N 36.49 E
Osipoviči 76 53.18 N 28.38 E
Osipovo Selo 76 56.51 N 30.30 E
Osire 156 20.59 S 17.19 E
Osivān 120 26.43 N 72.55 E
Oskaloosa, Ia., U.S. 190 41.17 N 92.38 W
Oskaloosa, Ks., U.S. 198 39.12 N 95.18 W
Oskar-Fredriksborg 40 59.24 N 18.26 E
Oskarshamn 26 57.16 N 16.26 E
Oskarström 26 56.48 N 12.58 E
Os'kino 78 51.14 N 39.02 E
Oskol ≃ 78 49.06 N 37.25 E
Oskolkovo 24 67.58 N 53.42 E
Oskū 128 37.55 N 46.06 E
Oskuj 76 59.17 N 32.05 E
Oskuja ≃ 76 59.14 N 31.54 E
Osl'anka, gora ∧ 86 59.10 N 58.33 E
Oslava ≃ 61 49.05 N 16.22 E
Ösling ✦1 56 49.55 N 6.00 E
Oslo 26 59.55 N 10.45 E
Oslob 116 9.31 N 123.26 E
Oslofjorden c2 26 59.20 N 10.35 E
Os'ma ≃, Ross. 76 54.55 N 33.24 E
Ošma ≃, Ross. 80 57.52 N 47.45 E
Osmānābād 122 18.10 N 76.02 E
Osmancık 130 40.59 N 34.49 E
Osmaneli 130 40.22 N 30.01 E
Osmaniye 130 37.05 N 36.14 E
Osmanpaşa 130 39.38 N 34.58 E
Ošm'anskaja vozvyšennost' ⋀1 76 54.20 N 26.00 E
Ošm'any 76 54.25 N 25.56 E
Osmeña 116 10.11 N 125.31 E
Osmington 42 50.38 N 2.22 W
Os'mino 76 59.01 N 29.06 E
Osminog, gora ∧ 180 67.54 N 176.50 E
Ösmo 40 58.59 N 17.54 E
Osmond 198 42.21 N 97.35 W
Osmore ≃ 248 17.33 S 71.12 W
Osmoy 261 48.52 N 1.43 E
Osmussaar I 76 59.18 N 23.22 E
Osnabrück 52 52.16 N 8.02 E
Ośno 30 52.28 N 14.50 E
Osny 261 49.04 N 2.04 E
Oso 224 48.16 N 121.56 W
Oso ≃ 154 1.09 S 27.22 E
Oso, Gran Lago del → Great Bear Lake ⊜ 176 66.00 N 120.00 W
Ošoba 85 40.44 N 70.26 E
Osogna 58 46.18 N 9.00 E
Osoppo 64 46.15 N 13.05 E
Osorakan-zan ∧ 96 34.36 N 132.08 E
Osore-yama ∧ 92 41.18 N 141.05 E
Osorio, Quebrada ≃ 286c 10.36 N 66.56 W
Osório Fonseca 250 3.40 S 58.13 W
Osorno, Chile 254 40.34 S 73.09 W
Osorno, Esp. 34 42.24 N 4.22 W
Osorno, Volcán ∧1 254 41.06 S 72.30 W
Osorun 273a 6.33 N 3.29 E
Os'otr ≃ 82 54.58 N 38.46 E
Osoyoos 182 49.02 N 119.28 W
Osoyoos Indian Reserve ✦4 182 49.08 N 119.30 W
Osoyoos Lake ⊜ 182 49.00 N 119.26 W
Osøyra 26 60.11 N 5.28 E
Ospedaletti 62 43.48 N 7.43 E
Ospedaletto, It. 64 46.17 N 13.07 E
Ospedaletto, It. 64 46.03 N 11.33 E
Ospino 246 9.18 N 69.27 W
Ospitale di Cadore 64 46.20 N 12.19 E
Ospitaletto 64 45.33 N 10.04 E
Osprey 220 27.11 N 82.29 W
Osprey Reef ✢2 164 13.55 S 146.38 E
Ospwagan Lake ⊜ 184 55.35 N 98.03 W
Oss 52 51.46 N 5.31 E
Ossa, Mount ∧ 166 41.54 S 146.01 E
Ossabaw Island I 192 31.47 N 81.06 W
Osse ≃, Fr. 32 44.07 N 0.17 E
Osse ≃, Nig. 150 6.10 N 5.20 E
Ossenberg 263 51.34 N 6.35 E
Ossendrecht 52 51.24 N 4.19 E
Osseo, Mi., U.S. 216 41.53 N 84.33 W
Osseo, Wi., U.S. 190 44.34 N 91.13 W
Ossett 44 53.41 N 1.35 W
Ossi 71 40.40 N 8.35 E
Ossiacher See ⊜ 64 46.40 N 13.55 E
Ossian, In., U.S. 216 40.52 N 85.09 W
Ossian, Ia., U.S. 190 43.08 N 91.45 W
Ossian, Loch ⊜ 46 56.46 N 4.38 W
Ossining 210 41.09 N 73.51 W
Ossipee 188 43.41 N 71.07 W
Ossjøen ⊜ 26 61.13 N 11.53 E
Ossling 54 51.21 N 14.09 E
Ossona 266b 45.30 N 8.54 E
Ossora 74 59.20 N 163.13 E
Ossum-Bösinghoven 263 51.18 N 6.39 E
Ošta 24 60.49 N 35.32 E
Ostaboningue, Lac ⊜ 190 47.09 N 78.53 W
Östanå, Sve. 40 59.33 N 18.35 E
Östanå, Sve. 40 60.38 N 16.48 E
Östanbyn 40 60.39 N 16.48 E
Ostankino ✦8 265b 55.49 N 37.37 E
Östansjö 40 59.03 N 14.59 E
Ostapje 78 49.33 N 33.46 E
Ostaškov 76 57.09 N 33.06 E
Ostašovo 82 55.52 N 35.52 E
Ostbevern 52 52.02 N 7.50 E
Østbirk 41 55.58 N 9.46 E
Ostbüren 263 51.31 N 7.46 E
Østby 26 61.15 N 12.32 E
Ostchinesisches Meer → East China Sea ⊤2 90 30.00 N 126.00 E
Oste ≃ 52 53.51 N 8.59 E
Osted 41 55.34 N 11.58 E
Osteen 220 28.50 N 81.09 W
Ostellato 66 44.45 N 11.56 E
Ostende → Oostende 50 51.13 N 2.55 E
Ostenfelde 52 51.52 N 8.04 E
Oster ≃ 60 48.43 N 13.29 E
Osterath 56 51.16 N 6.37 E
Osterbönen 263 51.37 N 7.48 E
Osterburg, Dtsch. 54 52.47 N 11.44 E
Osterburg, Pa., U.S. 214 40.16 N 78.31 W
Osterburken 56 49.26 N 9.26 E
Österbybruk 40 60.12 N 17.54 E
Österbymo 26 57.50 N 15.16 E
Ostercappeln 52 52.20 N 8.13 E
Österdalälven ≃ 26 60.33 N 15.08 E
Østerdalen V 26 61.15 N 11.10 E
Österfärnebo 40 60.18 N 16.48 E
Osterfeld 54 51.05 N 11.56 E
Osterfeld ✦8 263 51.30 N 6.53 E
Östergötland □9 26 58.24 N 15.34 E
Östergötlands Län □6 26 58.25 N 15.45 E
Österhaninge 40 59.08 N 18.12 E
Osterhofen 60 48.42 N 13.01 E
Øster Højst 41 55.00 N 9.03 E
Osterholz-Scharmbeck 52 53.14 N 8.47 E
Osterley Park ♠ 260 51.30 N 0.21 W
Österlövsta 40 60.26 N 17.47 E
Ostermundigen 58 46.58 N 7.29 E
Osternienburg 54 51.48 N 12.01 E
Osterode 52 51.44 N 10.11 E
Osterode → Ostróda 30 53.43 N 19.59 E
Osterøya I 26 60.33 N 5.35 E
Österreich → Austria □1 30 47.20 N 13.20 E
Österreichisches Freilichtmuseum ♦ 61 47.10 N 15.19 E
Osterrönfeld 41 54.17 N 9.41 E
Östersjön → Baltic Sea ⊤2 24 57.00 N 19.00 E
Österskär 40 59.28 N 18.18 E
Östersund 26 63.11 N 14.39 E
Östervåla 40 60.11 N 17.11 E
Osterville 207 41.37 N 70.23 W
Osterwick 52 52.01 N 7.13 E
Osterwieck 54 51.58 N 10.42 E
Ostfeld ✦8 263 51.40 N 7.45 E
Østfold □6 26 59.20 N 11.30 E
Ostfriesische Inseln II 52 53.44 N 7.25 E
Ostfriesland □9 52 53.20 N 7.40 E
Ost-Ghats → Eastern Ghāts ⋀ 122 14.00 N 78.50 E
Östhammar 40 60.16 N 18.22 E
Ostheim vor der Rhön 56 50.27 N 10.14 E
Osthofen 56 49.42 N 8.19 E
Ostia, Bonifica di ✦1 267a 41.46 N 12.18 E
Ostia Antica ⊥ 66 41.45 N 12.16 E
Ostiano 64 45.13 N 10.15 E
Ostiglia 64 45.04 N 11.08 E
Ostki 78 51.16 N 27.22 E
Östliche Sierra Madre → Madre Oriental, Sierra ⋀ 232 22.00 N 99.30 W
Östmark 26 60.17 N 12.45 E
Ost'or, Ross. 76 54.01 N 32.48 E
Ost'or, Ukr. 78 50.57 N 30.53 E
Ost'or ≃, Europe 76 53.47 N 31.46 E
Ost'or ≃, Ukr. 78 50.56 N 30.52 E
Ostpeene ≃ 54 53.43 N 12.46 E
Ostra 66 43.37 N 13.09 E
Östraby 41 55.46 N 13.41 E
Ostrach 58 47.57 N 9.23 E
Ostrach ≃ 58 48.04 N 9.24 E
Östra Grevie 41 55.28 N 13.08 E
Östra Husby 40 58.35 N 16.33 E
Östra Laxsjön ⊜ 40 58.54 N 14.42 E
Östra Ljungby 41 56.11 N 13.04 E
Ostrander 214 40.15 N 83.12 W
Östra Ringsjön ⊜ 41 55.52 N 13.32 E
Ostrau 54 51.12 N 13.09 E
Ostrau → Ostrava 30 49.50 N 18.17 E
Ostrava 30 49.50 N 18.17 E
Ostra Vetere 66 43.36 N 13.03 E
Ostrhauderfehn 52 53.08 N 7.37 E
Östrich 263 51.40 N 6.55 E
Ostricourt 50 50.27 N 3.02 E
Östringen 56 49.13 N 8.43 E
Ostritz 54 51.01 N 14.56 E
Ostróda 30 53.43 N 19.59 E
Ostrog 78 50.20 N 26.31 E
Ostrogožsk 78 50.52 N 39.05 E
Ostrokonje 76 59.52 N 42.02 E
Ostrołęka 30 53.06 N 21.34 E
Ostrołęka □4 30 53.00 N 21.30 E
Ostroróg 30 52.39 N 16.27 E
Ostrošickij Gorodok 76 54.04 N 27.42 E
Ostrov, Bela. 76 52.53 N 25.59 E
Ostrov, Česko. 54 50.17 N 12.57 E
Ostrov, Rom. 38 44.06 N 27.22 E
Ostrov, Ross. 76 60.34 N 37.55 E
Ostrov, Ross. 76 57.20 N 28.22 E
Ostrov, Ross. 265b 55.35 N 37.51 E
Ostrov I 30 47.55 N 17.35 E
Ostrov'anskij 80 46.45 N 42.13 E
Ostrovec 76 54.37 N 25.57 E
Ostrovki 265a 59.48 N 30.50 E
Ostrovno 76 55.08 N 29.53 E
Ostrovskaja 80 50.26 N 44.27 E
Ostrovskoje 80 57.48 N 42.15 E
Ostrov-Zalit 76 58.01 N 28.04 E
Ostrowiec Świętokrzyski 30 50.57 N 21.23 E
Ostrów Lubelski 30 51.30 N 22.52 E
Ostrów Mazowiecka 30 52.49 N 21.54 E
Ostrów Wielkopolski 30 51.39 N 17.49 E
Ostryna 76 53.44 N 24.32 E
Ostrzeszów 30 51.25 N 17.57 E
Ostseebad Ahrenshoop 54 54.23 N 12.25 E
Ostseebad Boltenhagen 54 54.00 N 11.12 E
Ostseebad Dierhagen 41 54.17 N 12.22 E
Ostseebad Graal-Müritz 54 54.15 N 12.12 E
Ostseebad Nienhagen 54 54.09 N 11.58 E
Ostseebad Rerik 54 54.06 N 11.37 E
Ostseebad Wustrow 54 54.21 N 12.23 E
Ostsee → Baltic Sea ⊤2 24 57.00 N 19.00 E
Ost-Sümmern 263 51.26 N 7.44 E
Osttirol □9 64 46.55 N 12.30 E
Ostúa ≃ 236 14.17 N 89.33 W
Ostuacán 234 17.25 N 93.18 W
Ostula 234 18.30 N 103.28 W
Ostuni 68 40.44 N 17.35 E
Ostwald 58 48.33 N 7.43 E
Osu 98 35.31 N 127.18 E
Osuga 76 56.02 N 34.18 E
Osuga ≃ 76 57.16 N 34.49 E
Ōsuka 94 34.41 N 137.59 E
O'Sullivan, Lac ⊜ 190 47.37 N 76.05 W
Osum ≃ 38 40.48 N 19.52 E
Ōsumi 270 34.50 N 135.45 E
Ōsumi-hantō ≻1 92 31.20 N 130.55 E
Ōsumi-kaikyō ⋃ 92 31.00 N 131.00 E
Ōsumi-shotō II 93b 30.30 N 130.00 E
Osuna 34 37.14 N 5.07 W
Osupugo ∧ 154 1.40 N 35.49 E
Osvaldo Cruz 255 21.47 S 50.50 W
Osveja 76 56.01 N 28.06 E
Osvejskoje, ozero ⊜ 76 56.03 N 28.08 E
Ošvor 24 66.58 N 62.53 E
Oswaldtwistle 44 53.43 N 2.26 W
Oswaldtwistle Moor ✦3 262 53.43 N 2.23 W
Oswald West State Park ♠ 224 45.45 N 123.58 W
Oswayo 214 41.55 N 78.01 W
Oswayo Creek ≃ 210 42.02 N 78.21 W
Oswegatchie ≃ 188 44.42 N 75.30 W
Oswegatchie, Middle Branch ≃ 212 44.07 N 75.19 W
Oswegatchie, West Branch ≃ 188 44.18 N 75.20 W
Oswego, Il., U.S. 216 41.40 N 88.21 W
Oswego, In., U.S. 216 41.19 N 85.47 W
Oswego, Ks., U.S. 198 37.10 N 95.06 W
Oswego, N.Y., U.S. 212 43.27 N 76.30 W
Oswego □6 212 43.22 N 76.15 W
Oswego ≃, N.J., U.S. 208 39.40 N 74.32 W
Oswego ≃, N.Y., U.S. 212 43.28 N 76.31 W
Oswestry 42 52.52 N 3.04 W
Oświęcim 30 50.03 N 19.12 E
Osyka 194 31.00 N 90.28 W
Ota, Nihon 94 35.58 N 136.04 E
Ōta, Nihon 94 36.18 N 139.22 E
Ōta, Nihon 96 33.31 N 131.33 E
Ōta ✦8 268 35.34 N 139.43 E
Ōta ≃, Nihon 94 34.40 N 137.54 E
Ōta ≃, Nihon 96 34.22 N 132.25 E
Otago Peninsula ≻1 172 45.52 S 170.40 E
Otahuhu 172 36.57 S 174.51 E
Ōtake 96 34.12 N 132.13 E
Otaki, N.Z. 172 40.45 S 175.09 E
Ōtaki, Nihon 94 35.17 N 140.15 E
Ōtaki, Nihon 94 35.57 N 138.56 E
Ōtaki, Nihon 94 35.48 N 137.33 E
Ōtaki ≃ 94 35.49 N 137.40 E
Ōtaki-yama ∧ 96 34.07 N 134.08 E
Ōta-Koizumi-hikojō ♠ 94 36.16 N 139.24 E
Otane 172 39.53 S 176.38 E
Otanmäki 26 64.07 N 27.06 E
Otar 85 43.33 N 75.13 E
Otari 94 36.46 N 137.54 E
Otaru 92a 43.13 N 141.00 E
Otatara 172 46.26 S 168.18 E
Otatitlán 234 18.12 N 96.02 W
Otautau 172 46.09 S 168.00 E
Otava 26 61.39 N 27.04 E
Otava ≃ 30 49.27 N 14.12 E
Otavalo 246 0.14 N 78.16 W
Otavi 156 19.39 S 17.20 E
Ōtawara 94 36.52 N 140.02 E
Otawa-yama ∧ 270 34.28 N 135.53 E
Otay 228 32.35 N 117.03 W
Otchinjau 152 16.30 S 13.57 E
Oteapan 234 18.00 N 94.39 W
Otego 210 42.23 N 75.10 W
Otego Creek ≃ 210 42.25 N 75.07 W
Otélé 152 3.35 N 11.15 E
Otematata 172 44.37 S 170.16 E
Oteotea 175e 9.05 S 161.11 E
Otepää 76 58.03 N 26.30 E
Oteros ≃ 232 26.55 N 108.22 W
Otford, Austl. 170 34.12 S 151.01 E
Otford, Eng., U.K. 42 51.19 N 0.12 E
Otgon 88 47.11 N 97.33 E
Otgon Tenger uul ∧ 88 47.36 N 97.36 E
Otham 260 51.15 N 0.35 E
Othello 202 46.49 N 119.10 W
Othery 42 51.05 N 2.53 W
Othfresen 52 52.00 N 10.23 E
Óthiris, Óros ⋀ 38 39.02 N 22.37 E
Othis 261 49.04 N 2.41 E
Othonoí I 38 39.50 N 19.26 E
Oti ≃ 150 8.40 N 0.13 E
Otibanda 164 7.15 S 146.30 E
Otinapa 232 24.11 N 105.02 W
Otira 172 42.50 S 171.33 E
Otis, Co., U.S. 198 40.08 N 102.57 W
Otis, In., U.S. 216 41.36 N 86.54 W
Otis, Ks., U.S. 198 38.32 N 99.03 W
Otis, Ma., U.S. 207 42.11 N 73.05 W
Otisco 218 38.32 N 85.40 W
Otisco Lake ⊜ 210 42.52 N 76.18 W
Otish, Monts ⋀ 176 52.22 N 70.30 W
Otis Reservoir ⊜1 207 42.09 N 73.02 W
Otisville 210 41.28 N 74.32 W
Otjassy 80 53.14 N 41.39 E
Otjikondo 156 19.50 S 15.23 E
Otjimbingue 156 22.19 S 16.10 E
Otjinene 156 21.13 S 18.42 E
Otjiwarongo 156 20.29 S 16.36 E
Otjiwarongo □5 156 20.45 S 16.30 E
Otjozondjou ≃ 156 20.18 S 20.50 E
Otley 44 53.54 N 1.41 W
Otmanlı 130 41.52 N 34.37 E
Otm'ok, pereval)(85 42.20 N 73.10 E
Otmuchów 30 50.28 N 17.10 E
Otnes 26 61.45 N 11.14 E
Otnice 61 49.05 N 16.49 E
Ōtō 96 33.41 N 135.35 E
Otočac 36 44.52 N 15.14 E
Otog Qi 102 39.08 N 108.00 E
Ōtomi 175d 24.19 N 123.54 E
Oton 116 10.42 N 122.29 E
Otonabee ≃ 212 44.08 N 78.14 W
Otoque, Isla I 236 8.36 N 79.36 W
Ōtori-kita 270 34.33 N 135.27 E
Otorma 80 53.32 N 42.32 E
Otoro ≃ 236 15.00 N 88.16 W
Otorohanga 172 38.11 S 175.12 E
Otoskwin ≃ 176 52.13 N 88.06 W
Otowa 94 34.51 N 137.18 E
Otowa-yama ∧ 270 34.58 N 135.51 E
Otowa-yama-tunnel ✦5 94 34.58 N 135.51 E
Ōtoyo 96 33.46 N 133.40 E
Otra ≃ 26 58.09 N 8.00 E
Otradnaja 84 44.23 N 41.31 E
Otradnoje 265a 59.47 N 30.49 E
Otradnyj 80 53.22 N 51.21 E
Otranto 68 40.09 N 18.30 E
Otranto, Capo d' ≻ 68 40.06 N 18.31 E
Otranto, Strait of ⋃ 38 40.00 N 19.00 E
Otricoli 66 42.25 N 12.29 E
Otrokovice 30 49.13 N 17.31 E
Ötscher ∧ 61 47.52 N 15.12 E
Otsego 216 42.27 N 85.41 W
Otsego □6 210 42.42 N 74.56 W
Otsego Lake ⊜ 210 42.45 N 74.52 W
Otselic ≃ 210 42.20 N 75.58 W
Ōtsu, Nihon 96 35.00 N 135.52 E
Ōtsu, Nihon 268 35.16 N 139.42 E
Ōtsu ≃ 270 34.30 N 135.24 E
Ōtsuchi 92 39.21 N 141.54 E
Ōtsuki 94 35.36 N 138.57 E
Ōtsu-shima I 96 34.00 N 131.42 E
Otta, Nig. 150 6.42 N 3.10 E
Otta, Nor. 26 61.46 N 9.32 E
Otta ≃ 26 61.46 N 9.31 E
Ottakring ✦8 264b 48.12 N 16.19 E
Ottana 71 40.14 N 9.02 E
Otta Pass ⋃ 175c 7.09 N 151.53 E
Ottarnic Pond ⊜ 283 42.46 N 71.25 W
Ottati 68 40.28 N 15.19 E
Ottavia ✦8 267a 41.58 N 12.24 E
Ottaviano 68 40.51 N 14.28 E
Ottawa, On., Can. 212 45.25 N 75.42 W
Ottawa, Il., U.S. 216 41.20 N 88.50 W
Ottawa, Ks., U.S. 198 38.36 N 95.16 W
Ottawa, Oh., U.S. 216 41.01 N 84.02 W
Ottawa □6, Mi., U.S. 216 42.57 N 86.02 W
Ottawa □6, Oh., U.S. 214 41.31 N 82.56 W
Ottawa ≃, Can. 176 45.20 N 73.58 W
Ottawa ≃, Oh., U.S. 214 41.44 N 83.28 W
Ottawa ≃, Oh., U.S. 216 41.00 N 84.15 W
Ottawa-Carleton □6 212 45.15 N 75.45 W
Ottawa Hills 214 41.39 N 83.38 W
Ottawa International Airport ⊠ 212 45.19 N 75.40 W
Ottawa Islands II 176 59.30 N 80.10 W
Ottbergen 52 51.42 N 9.18 E
Ottenby 26 56.14 N 16.25 E
Ottendorf-Okrilla 54 51.11 N 13.50 E
Ottenhöfen 58 48.34 N 8.09 E
Ottenschlag 61 48.25 N 15.13 E
Ottensheim 61 48.20 N 14.11 E
Ottenstein Stausee ⊜1 61 48.37 N 15.17 E
Otter ≃ 42 50.46 N 3.17 W
Otterbach ≃ 56 49.07 N 8.21 E
Otterbäcken 40 58.57 N 14.02 E
Otterbein 216 40.29 N 87.06 W
Otterburn 44 55.14 N 2.10 W
Otterburne 184 49.30 N 97.03 W
Otterburn Park 206 45.33 N 73.13 W
Otter Creek 192 29.19 N 82.46 W
Otter Creek ≃, On., Can. 212 44.06 N 81.07 W

ENGLISH | **DEUTSCH**

Name | Page | Lat.°′ | Long.°′ — Name | Seite | Breite°′ | Länge°′ E = Ost

Otter Creek ≃, Il., U.S. 219 39.18 N 90.07 W
Otter Creek ≃, In., U.S. 218 38.58 N 85.37 W
Otter Creek ≃, Ia., U.S. 190 41.20 N 93.30 W
Otter Creek ≃, Mo., U.S. 219 39.31 N 91.51 W
Otter Creek ≃, Mt., U.S. 202 45.36 N 106.17 W
Otter Creek ≃, N.Y., U.S. 212 43.43 N 75.23 W
Otter Creek ≃, Ut., U.S. 200 38.10 N 112.02 W
Otter Creek ≃, Vt., U.S. 188 44.13 N 73.17 W
Otter Creek Reservoir ⊜1 200 38.12 N 111.59 W
Otterhöfen 56 48.33 N 8.12 E
Otter-Lake, P.Q., Can. 188 45.51 N 76.26 W
Otter Lake, Mi., U.S. 190 43.13 N 83.28 W
Otter Lake ⊜, On., Can. 212 45.17 N 79.56 W
Otter Lake ⊜, On., Can. 212 44.47 N 76.07 W
Otter Lake ⊜, Sk., Can. 184 55.35 N 104.39 W
Otter Lake ⊜1 219 39.26 N 89.54 W
Otterlo 52 52.06 N 5.45 E
Otterndorf 52 53.48 N 8.53 E
Otterøya I 26 62.42 N 6.48 E
Otter River 207 42.35 N 72.03 W
Ottersberg 52 53.06 N 9.08 E
Ottershaw 260 51.22 N 0.32 W
Ottersleben ✦8 54 52.05 N 11.34 E
Otter Tail ≃ 198 46.16 N 96.36 W
Otter Tail Lake ⊜ 198 46.23 N 95.40 W
Otterup 41 55.31 N 10.24 E
Otterville, On., Can. 212 42.55 N 80.36 W
Otterville, Il., U.S. 219 39.03 N 90.24 W
Otterville, Mo., U.S. 194 38.41 N 93.00 W
Ottery ≃ 42 50.39 N 4.20 W
Ottery Saint Mary 42 50.45 N 3.17 W
Ottignies 56 50.40 N 4.34 E
Ottine 222 29.36 N 97.35 W
Ottleben 54 52.05 N 11.07 E
Ottmarsbocholt 52 51.49 N 7.32 E
Ottnang 60 48.06 N 13.40 E
Ottnaren ⊜ 40 60.29 N 16.37 E
Otto, N.Y., U.S. 210 42.21 N 78.50 W
Otto, Tx., U.S. 222 31.27 N 96.49 W
Ottobeuren 58 47.56 N 10.18 E
Ottobeuren, Klosterkirche ♦1 58 47.56 N 10.18 E
Ottobiano 62 45.09 N 8.50 E
Ottobrunn 60 48.04 N 11.40 E
Ottone 62 44.37 N 9.20 E
Ottoschwanden 58 48.12 N 7.52 E
Ottosdal 158 26.58 S 26.00 E
Ottoshoop 156 25.45 S 25.59 E
Ottoville 216 40.55 N 84.20 W
Ottuk, Kyrg. 85 41.38 N 75.51 E
Ottuk, Kyrg. 85 42.18 N 76.18 E
Ottumwa 190 41.00 N 92.22 W
Ottweiler 56 49.24 N 7.09 E
Otty Lake ⊜ 212 44.50 N 76.13 W
Otu 150 8.14 N 3.24 E
Otukpa 150 7.09 N 7.41 E
Otumpa 252 27.19 S 62.13 W
Otun 273a 6.42 N 3.22 E
Otu → Ōtsu 96 35.00 N 135.52 E
Otuquis, Bañados de ≋ 248 19.20 S 58.30 W
Oturkpo 150 7.14 N 8.08 E
Otway, Bahía ⋃ 254 53.20 S 74.00 W
Otway, Cape ≻ 166 38.52 S 143.31 E
Otway, Seno c 254 53.05 S 71.30 W
Otway Range ⋀ 169 38.30 S 143.50 E
Otwock 30 52.07 N 21.16 E
Otyn'a 78 48.44 N 24.51 E
Ötztal V 64 47.05 N 10.55 E
Ötztaler Ache ≃ 64 47.14 N 10.50 E
Ötztaler Alpen (Alpi Venoste) ⋀ 64 46.45 N 10.55 E
Ou ≃, Lao 110 20.04 N 102.13 E
Ou ≃, Zhg. 100 28.01 N 120.44 E
Ou ≃, Zhg. 100 26.02 N 113.09 E
Oua ≃ 152 0.43 N 12.55 E
Ouachita ≃ 194 31.38 N 91.49 W
Ouachita, Lake ⊜1 194 34.40 N 93.25 W
Ouachita Mountains ⋀ 194 34.40 N 94.25 W
Ouaco 175f 20.50 S 164.29 E
Ouadâne 148 20.56 N 11.37 W
Ouadda 152 8.04 N 22.24 E
Ouaddaï □5 146 13.00 N 21.00 E
Ouadey, Ouadi el V 146 13.34 N 18.03 E
Ouagadougou 150 12.22 N 1.31 W
Ouahigouya 150 13.35 N 2.25 W
Ouahran → Wahran 148 35.43 N 0.43 W
Ouaka □5 152 6.00 N 21.00 E
Ouaka ≃ 152 4.59 N 19.56 E
Oualâta 150 17.18 N 7.02 W
Oualâta, Dahr ⊥4 150 17.48 N 7.24 W
Oualé ≃ 150 10.52 N 0.51 E
Oualidia 148 32.44 N 9.08 W
Ouallam 150 14.19 N 2.05 E
Ouallene 148 24.37 N 1.14 E
Oualto 150 9.01 N 10.06 W
Ouanary 250 4.13 N 51.40 W
Ouanda Djallé 146 8.54 N 22.48 E
Ouandago 146 7.10 N 18.42 E
Ouandja ≃ 146 9.35 N 21.43 E
Ouandja-Vakaga, Réserve de la ✦4 146 9.00 N 21.30 E
Ouango 152 4.19 N 22.33 E
Ouangolodougou 150 9.58 N 5.09 W
Ouaninou 150 8.11 N 7.51 W
Ouanne ≃ 50 47.57 N 2.47 E
Ouan Taredert 148 27.33 N 9.32 E
Ouaquaga 210 42.08 N 75.39 W
Ouara ≃ 154 5.05 N 24.26 E
Ouarâne ✦1 134 21.00 N 10.30 W
Ouararda, Passe de)(148 21.01 N 13.03 W
Ouareau ≃ 206 45.56 N 73.25 W
Ouareau, Lac ⊜1 206 46.17 N 74.09 W
Ouargaye 150 11.32 N 0.01 E
Ouarkoye 150 12.05 N 3.40 W
Ouarkziz, Jbel ⋀ 148 28.50 N 9.00 W
Ouarsenis, Djebel ∧ 34 35.53 N 1.38 E
Ouarville 50 48.21 N 1.46 E
Ouarzazate 148 30.57 N 6.50 W
Ouarzazate □4 148 30.55 N 6.45 W
Ouassoulou ≃ 150 11.35 N 8.11 W
Ouatcha 150 13.22 N 9.18 E
Oubangui (Ubangi) ≃ 152 0.30 S 17.42 E
Ouche ≃ 58 47.06 N 5.16 E
Oucques 50 47.49 N 1.18 E
Ōuda 94 34.28 N 135.56 E
Oudaze Lake ⊜ 212 45.27 N 79.11 W
Oud-Beijerland 52 51.49 N 4.25 E
Ouddorp 52 51.18 N 3.56 E
Oude IJssel (Issel) ≃ 52 52.00 N 6.10 E
Oudenaarde 50 50.51 N 3.36 E
Oudenbosch 52 51.35 N 4.31 E
Oudenburg 50 51.11 N 3.00 E
Oude-Pekela 52 53.04 N 6.58 E
Oude Rijn ≃ 52 52.05 N 4.20 E
Oudeschild 52 53.02 N 4.50 E
Oude-Tonge 52 51.41 N 4.12 E
Oudewater 52 52.02 N 4.52 E
Oud-Gastel 52 51.35 N 4.27 E
Oudjda → Oujda 148 34.41 N 1.45 W
Oud-Loosdrecht 52 52.13 N 5.04 E
Oudtshoorn 158 33.35 S 22.14 E
Oudyoumoudi 150 14.04 N 0.28 W
Oued Athmenia 34 36.15 N 6.17 E
Oued Cheham 36 36.23 N 7.46 E
Oued edh Dheheb, Khlij c 148 23.45 N 15.47 W
Oued Fodda 34 36.11 N 1.32 E
Oued Meliz 36 36.27 N 8.34 E
Oued Rhiou 34 35.58 N 0.55 E
Oued Tlelat 34 35.34 N 0.27 W
Oued Zarga 36 36.40 N 9.25 E
Oued-Zem 148 32.55 N 6.33 W
Ouellé 150 7.18 N 4.01 W
Ouémé □5 150 7.00 N 2.35 E
Ouémé ≃ 150 6.29 N 2.32 E
Ouen, Île I 175f 22.26 S 166.49 E
Ouenkoro 150 13.23 N 3.50 W
Ouenza, Djebel ∧ 36 35.57 N 8.05 E
Ouenzé ✦8 273b 4.14 S 15.17 E
Ouessa 150 11.03 N 2.47 W
Ouessant, Île d' (Ushant) I 32 48.28 N 5.05 W
Ouesso 152 1.37 N 16.04 E
Ouest □4 152 5.23 N 10.45 E
Ouest, Pointe de l' ≻ 186 49.52 N 64.31 W
Ouest, Rivière de l' ≃ 206 45.39 N 74.21 W
Ouezzane 148 34.52 N 5.35 W
Ouffet 56 50.26 N 5.28 E
Ouganda → Uganda □1 154 1.00 N 32.00 E
Ougarou 150 12.09 N 0.56 E
Oughter, Lough ⊜ 48 54.00 N 7.30 W
Oughterard 48 53.25 N 9.17 W
Oughtibridge 44 53.26 N 1.33 W
Ouham □5 152 7.00 N 18.00 E
Ouham ≃ 136 9.18 N 18.14 E
Ouham-Pendé □5 152 7.00 N 16.00 E
Ouidah 150 6.22 N 2.05 E
Ouidi 146 14.07 N 12.58 E
Ouimet Canyon V 190 48.47 N 88.40 W
Oujda 148 34.41 N 1.45 W
Oujda □4 148 34.05 N 2.10 W
Oulad Naïl, Monts des ⋀ 148 34.33 N 3.28 E
Oulainen 26 64.16 N 24.48 E
Oulangan kansallispuisto ♠ 24 66.12 N 29.30 E
Oulchy-le-Château 50 49.12 N 3.21 E
Oule ≃ 62 44.25 N 5.21 E
Ouled Agla 34 35.58 N 4.45 E
Ouleout Creek ≃ 210 42.20 N 75.18 W
Oulins 50 48.52 N 1.28 E
Oullins 62 45.43 N 4.48 E
Oulou, Bahr ≃ 146 9.48 N 21.32 E
Oulton Broad 42 52.31 N 1.42 E
Oulu 26 65.01 N 25.28 E
Oulujärvi ⊜ 26 64.20 N 27.15 E
Oulujoki ≃ 26 65.01 N 25.25 E
Oulun lääni □4 24 65.00 N 27.00 E
Oulx 62 45.02 N 6.50 E
Oumba 152 4.55 N 19.04 E
Oum-Chalouba 146 15.48 N 20.46 E
Oumé 150 6.23 N 5.25 W
Oum El Bouagui 148 35.53 N 7.07 E
Oum El Bouagui □5 148 35.50 N 7.15 E
Oum er Rbia, Oued ≃ 148 33.19 N 8.21 W
Oum-Hadjer 146 13.18 N 19.41 E
Oum Hadjer, Ouadi V 146 16.38 N 20.14 E
Oumiao 102 31.55 N 112.09 E
Oumm ed Droûs Guebli, Sebkhet ⊜ 148 24.03 N 11.45 W
Oumm ed Droûs Telli, Sebkhet ⊜ 148 24.20 N 11.30 W
Ounâne, Bîr ⊤4 148 21.28 N 3.56 W
Ounara 148 31.33 N 9.28 W
Ounasjoki ≃ 24 66.30 N 25.45 E
Oundle 42 52.29 N 0.29 W
Ounianga Kébir 146 19.04 N 20.29 E
Ouolossébougou 150 12.00 N 7.55 W
Our ≃ 56 49.53 N 6.18 E
Ouragahio 150 6.19 N 5.56 W
Ōura-wan c 174m 26.32 N 128.04 E
Ouray 200 38.01 N 107.40 W
Ouray, Mount ∧ 200 38.25 N 106.14 W
Ource ≃ 58 48.06 N 4.23 E
Ourcq ≃ 50 49.01 N 3.01 E
Ourcq, Canal de l' ≊ 50 48.51 N 2.22 E
Ourém 250 1.33 S 47.06 W
Ouri 146 21.34 N 19.13 E
Ouri, Tarso ∧ 146 21.25 N 18.56 E
Ouricuri 250 7.53 S 40.05 W
Ourimbah 170 33.22 S 151.23 E
Ourinhos 255 22.59 S 49.52 W
Ourique 34 37.39 N 8.13 W
Ournie 171b 35.56 S 147.51 E
Ouro, Paraná do ≃ 248 8.29 S 70.30 W
Ouro, Ponta do ≻ 158 26.51 S 32.54 E
Ouro Branco 250 6.42 S 36.57 W
Ouro Fino 256 22.17 S 46.22 W
Ouro Preto 255 20.23 S 43.30 W
Ouro Preto ≃ 248 11.02 S 65.13 W
Ouroufa, Vallée d' V 150 14.42 N 7.00 E
Ours, Grand Lac de l' → Great Bear Lake ⊜ 176 66.00 N 120.00 W
Oursi 150 14.41 N 0.27 W
Ourthe ≃ 56 50.38 N 5.35 E
Ourthe Occidentale ≃ 56 50.08 N 5.41 E
Ourthe Orientale ≃ 56 50.08 N 5.41 E
Ourville-en-Caux 50 49.44 N 0.36 E
Ōu-sammyaku ⋀ 92 38.45 N 140.50 E
Ouse ≃, On., Can. 212 44.17 N 78.03 W
Ouse ≃, Eng., U.K. 42 50.47 N 0.03 E
Ouse ≃, Eng., U.K. 44 53.42 N 0.41 W
Oust ≃ 32 47.39 N 2.06 W
Outaouais, Rivière des → Ottawa ≃ 176 45.20 N 73.58 W
Outardes, Baie aux c 186 49.02 N 68.30 W
Outardes, Rivière aux ≃ 176 49.04 N 68.28 W
Outardes Est, Rivière aux ≃ 206 45.06 N 74.04 W
Outardes Quatre, Réservoir ⊜1 186 49.50 N 68.58 W
Outardes Trois, Barrage ✦6 186 49.34 N 68.48 W
Outarville 50 48.13 N 2.01 E
Outcalt 276 40.23 N 74.24 W
Outeniekwaberge ⋀ 158 33.53 S 22.35 E
Outerbridge Crossing ✦5 276 40.31 N 74.15 W
Outer Harbour 168b 34.47 S 138.30 E
Outer Hebrides II 46 57.45 N 7.00 W
Outer Island I 190 47.03 N 90.30 W
Outer Santa Barbara Passage ⋃ 228 33.10 N 118.30 W
Outer Sister Island I 166 39.39 S 148.00 E
Outjo 156 20.08 S 16.08 E
Outjo □5 156 19.30 S 15.30 E
Outlane 262 53.39 N 1.53 W
Outlet Bay c 208 37.22 N 75.49 W
Outlook, Sk., Can. 184 51.30 N 107.03 W
Outlook, Mt., U.S. 198 48.53 N 104.46 W
Outokumpu 26 62.44 N 29.01 E
Outpost Mountain ∧ 180 69.08 N 151.12 W
Outreau 50 50.42 N 1.35 E
Outremont 206 45.31 N 73.38 W
Outside Canal ≊ 226 37.13 N 121.02 W
Out Skerries II 46a 60.25 N 0.42 W
Outwell 42 52.37 N 0.14 E
Ouvéa I 175f 20.30 S 166.35 E
Ouvéa, Lagon d' c 175f 20.33 S 166.27 E
Ouvèze ≃ 62 43.59 N 4.51 E
Ouvidor 255 18.14 S 47.50 W
Ouye, Forêt de l' ♠ 261 48.32 N 2.00 E
Ouyen 166 35.04 S 142.20 E
Ouzinkie 180 57.55 N 152.30 W
Ouzouer-le-Marché 50 47.55 N 1.32 E

Symbols in the index entries represent the broad categories identified in the key at the right. Symbols with superior numbers (⋀1) identify subcategories (see complete key on page *I · 1)*.

Symbole im Register stellen die rechts im Schlüssel erklärten Kategorien dar. Symbole mit hochgestellten Ziffern (⋀1) bezeichnen Unterabteilungen einer Kategorie (vgl. vollständiger Schlüssel auf Seite *I · 1)*.

Los símbolos incluídos en el texto del índice representan las grandes categorias identificadas con la clave a la derecha. Los símbolos con numeros en su parte superior (⋀1) identifican las subcategorias (véase la clave completa en la página *I · 1)*.

Les symboles de l'index représentent les catégories indiquées dans la légende à droite. Les symboles suivis d'un indice (⋀1) représentent des sous-catégories (voir légende complète à la page *I · 1)*.

Os símbolos incluídos no texto do índice representam as grandes categorias identificadas com a chave à direita. Os símbolos com números em sua parte superior (⋀1) identificam as subcategorias (veja-se a chave completa à página *I · 1)*.

∧ Mountain	Berg	Montaña	Montagne	Montanha
⋀ Mountains	Gebirge	Montañas	Montagnes	Montanhas
)(Pass	Paß	Paso	Col	Passo
V Valley, Canyon	Tal, Cañon	Valle, Cañón	Vallée, Canyon	Vale, Canhão
≚ Plain	Ebene	Llano	Plaine	Planície
≻ Cape	Kap	Cabo	Cap	Cabo
I Island	Insel	Isla	Île	Ilha
II Islands	Inseln	Islas	Îles	Ilhas
⊥ Other Topographic Features	Andere Topographische Objekte	Otros Elementos Topográficos	Autres données topographiques	Outros acidentes topográficos

ESPAÑOL — Nombre | Página | Lat.°′ | Long.°′ W = Oeste
FRANÇAIS — Nom | Page | Lat.°′ | Long.°′ W = Ouest
PORTUGUÊS — Nome | Página | Lat.°′ | Long.°′ W = Oeste

Ouzouer-sur-Loire 50 47.46 N 2.29 E
Ouzzal, Oued i-n- ✓ 148 21.35 N 2.00 E
Ovabağ 130 37.43 N 39.59 E
Ovacık, Tür. 130 41.05 N 32.55 E
Ovacık, Tür. 130 39.22 N 39.13 E
Ovada 62 44.38 N 8.38 E
Ovakent 130 38.06 N 28.02 E
Oval 210 41.09 N 77.11 W
Ovalau I 175g 17.40 S 178.48 E
Ovalle 252 30.36 S 71.12 W
Ovamboland □9 156 17.45 S 16.30 E
Ovana, Cerro ʌ 246 4.38 N 66.57 W
Ovar 34 40.52 N 8.38 W
Ovaro 64 46.29 N 12.52 E
Ovčinino 82 56.02 N 39.03 E
Ovcyno 265a 59.48 N 30.37 E
Övedskloster 41 55.41 N 13.38 E
Ovejas 246 9.32 N 75.14 W
Ovelgönne 52 53.20 N 8.25 E
Ovenden 262 53.44 N 1.53 W
Oveng 152 2.25 N 12.16 E
Overath 56 50.55 N 7.14 E
Overberge 263 51.37 N 7.41 E
Overbrook 198 38.46 N 95.33 W
Overbrook ✦8, Pa., U.S. 279b 40.24 N 79.59 W
Overbrook ✦8, Pa., U.S. 285 39.58 N 75.16 W
Overdinkel 52 52.14 N 7.01 E
Overflakkee I 52 51.45 N 4.10 E
Overflowing ≐ 184 53.10 N 101.05 W
Overhalla 24 64.30 N 11.57 E
Overijse 56 50.46 N 4.32 E
Overijssel □4 52 52.25 N 6.30 E
Over Jerstal 41 55.12 N 9.18 E
Överkalix 24 66.21 N 22.56 E
Overland 219 38.42 N 90.21 W
Overland Park 198 38.58 N 94.40 W
Overlea 208 39.22 N 76.31 W
Overloon 52 51.35 N 5.57 E
Övermark (Ylimarkku) 26 62.38 N 21.30 E
Overpeck Creek ≐ 276 40.51 N 74.02 W
Overpelt 56 51.13 N 5.25 E
Overseal 42 52.44 N 1.34 W
Overstrand 42 52.56 N 1.20 E
Overton, Eng., U.K. 42 51.15 N 1.15 W
Overton, Ne., U.S. 198 40.44 N 99.32 W
Overton, Nv., U.S. 204 36.32 N 114.26 W
Overton, Tx., U.S. 222 32.16 N 94.58 W
Overton Arm c 204 36.20 N 114.25 W
Övertorneå 24 66.23 N 23.40 E
Överum 26 57.59 N 16.19 E
Over Wallop 42 51.09 N 1.35 W
Ovett 194 31.29 N 89.01 W
Ovid, Mi., U.S. 216 43.00 N 84.22 W
Ovid, N.Y., U.S. 210 42.40 N 76.49 W
Ovidiopol' 78 46.17 N 30.27 E
Oviedo, Esp. 34 43.22 N 5.50 W
Oviedo, Fl., U.S. 220 28.40 N 81.13 W
Oviglio 62 44.52 N 8.29 E
Oviken 26 62.59 N 14.24 E
Oviksfjällen ʌ 26 63.02 N 13.51 E
Ovilla 222 32.32 N 96.53 W
Ovindoli 66 42.08 N 13.31 E
Ovinišče 76 58.22 N 37.02 E
Ovino 76 59.41 N 33.11 E
Oviši 76 57.34 N 21.45 E
Övörchangaj □4 102 46.00 N 102.30 E
Øvre Anarjokka Nasjonalpark ♦ 24 69.00 N 25.00 E
Øvre Årdal 26 61.19 N 7.48 E
Øvre Dividal Nasjonalpark ♦ 24 68.39 N 19.45 E
Øvre Pasvik Nasjonalpark ♦ 24 69.06 N 28.55 E
Øvre Rendal 26 61.53 N 11.05 E
Övre Vättern ⊜ 40 59.52 N 15.40 E
Ovruč 78 51.21 N 28.49 E
Ovs'anikovo 76 60.09 N 45.16 E
Ovs'anka, Ross. 86 55.57 N 92.33 E
Ovs'anka, Ross. 89 53.35 N 126.57 E
Ovs'annikovo 82 56.54 N 37.33 E
Ovstug 76 53.24 N 33.52 E
Owada 268 35.49 N 139.33 E
Owaka 172 46.27 S 169.40 E
Owambo □5 156 18.00 S 16.00 E
Owambo ≐ 156 18.45 S 17.03 E
Owando 152 0.29 S 15.55 E
Owaneco 219 39.29 N 89.12 W
Owariashi 94 35.12 N 137.02 E
Owasco 210 42.51 N 76.28 W
Owasco Inlet ≐ 210 42.45 N 76.28 W
Owasco Lake ⊜ 210 42.52 N 76.32 W
Owasco Outlet ≐ 210 43.04 N 76.39 W
Owase 92 34.04 N 136.12 E
Owasso 196 36.16 N 95.51 W
Owatonna 190 44.05 N 93.13 W
Owbeh 128 34.22 N 63.10 E
Owe 272c 19.04 N 73.04 E
Owego 210 42.06 N 76.15 W
Owego Creek, East Branch ≐ 210 42.10 N 76.15 W
Owego Creek, West Branch ≐ 210 42.10 N 76.15 W
Owel, Lough ⊜ 48 53.34 N 7.25 W
Owen, Austl. 168b 34.16 S 138.33 E
Owen, Dtsch. 56 48.35 N 9.27 E
Owen, In., U.S. 218 38.27 N 85.34 W
Owen, Wi., U.S. 190 44.57 N 90.33 W
Owen □6 218 38.33 N 84.49 W
Owen, Mount ʌ 172 41.33 S 172.32 E
Owenboy ≐ 48 51.48 N 8.18 W
Owendo 152 0.17 N 9.30 E
Owenea ≐ 48 54.47 N 8.26 W
Owen Falls Dam ✦6 154 0.27 N 33.11 E
Owen Fracture Zone ✦ 12 12.00 N 58.00 E
Owenkillew ≐ 48 54.44 N 7.18 W
Owenmore ≐ 48 54.07 N 9.50 W
Owen River 172 41.39 S 172.27 E
Owens ≐ 204 36.31 N 117.57 W
Owensboro 194 37.46 N 87.06 W
Owens Creek ≐, Ca., U.S. 226 37.13 N 120.42 W
Owens Creek ≐, Md., U.S. 208 39.33 N 77.20 W
Owens Lake ⊜ 204 36.25 N 117.56 W
Owen Sound 212 44.34 N 80.56 W
Owen Sound c 212 44.40 N 80.55 W
Owen Stanley Range ʌ 164 9.20 S 147.55 E
Owensville, In., U.S. 194 38.16 N 87.41 W
Owensville, Mo., U.S. 219 38.20 N 91.30 W
Owensville, Oh., U.S. 218 39.07 N 84.08 W
Owenton, Ky., U.S. 218 38.32 N 84.50 W
Owenton, Va., U.S. 208 37.53 N 77.06 W
Owentown 222 32.26 N 95.12 W
Owerri 150 5.29 N 7.02 E
Owhango 172 39.00 S 175.23 E
Owikeno Lake ⊜ 182 51.41 N 127.00 W
Owings 208 38.43 N 76.36 W
Owings Mills 284b 39.25 N 76.46 W
Owingsville 188 38.08 N 83.45 W
Owl ≐, Ab., Can. 182 54.54 N 111.57 W
Owl ≐, Mb., Can. 176 57.51 N 92.44 W
Owl Creek ≐, U.S. 198 44.41 N 103.29 W
Owl Creek ≐, Mt., U.S. 202 45.18 N 107.21 W
Owl Creek ≐, Wy., U.S. 202 43.41 N 108.11 W
Owl Creek, South Fork ≐ 202 43.43 N 108.32 W
Owl Creek Mountains ʌ 202 43.30 N 108.35 W
Owo 150 7.15 N 5.37 E
Oworonsoki 273a 6.33 N 3.24 E
Owosso 216 42.59 N 84.10 W
Owuru ≐ 273a 6.39 N 3.27 E
Owyhee 204 41.56 N 116.05 W
Owyhee ≐ 202 43.46 N 117.02 W
Owyhee, Lake ⊜1 202 43.28 N 117.20 W
Owyhee, South Fork ≐ 202 42.26 N 116.53 W
Oxapampa 248 10.34 S 75.24 W
Öxarfjördur c 24a 66.15 N 16.45 W
Oxbow, Sk., Can. 184 49.14 N 102.11 W
Oxbow, Mi., U.S. 281 42.38 N 83.28 W
Oxbow, N.Y., U.S. 212 44.17 N 75.37 W
Oxbow Lake ⊜ 281 42.38 N 83.28 W
Ox Creek ≐ 198 48.37 N 100.17 W
Oxelösund 40 58.40 N 17.06 E
Oxford, N.S., Can. 186 45.44 N 63.52 W
Oxford, N.Z. 172 43.18 S 172.11 E
Oxford, Eng., U.K. 42 51.46 N 1.15 W
Oxford, Al., U.S. 194 33.36 N 85.50 W
Oxford, Ct., U.S. 207 41.26 N 73.07 W
Oxford, Fl., U.S. 220 28.55 N 82.02 W
Oxford, In., U.S. 216 40.31 N 87.14 W
Oxford, Ia., U.S. 190 41.43 N 91.47 W
Oxford, Ks., U.S. 198 37.16 N 97.10 W
Oxford, Ky., U.S. 218 38.16 N 84.30 W
Oxford, Me., U.S. 188 44.07 N 70.29 W
Oxford, Md., U.S. 208 38.41 N 76.10 W
Oxford, Ma., U.S. 207 42.07 N 71.51 W
Oxford, Mi., U.S. 216 42.49 N 83.15 W
Oxford, Ms., U.S. 194 34.21 N 89.31 W
Oxford, Ne., U.S. 198 40.15 N 99.38 W
Oxford, N.J., U.S. 210 40.48 N 74.59 W
Oxford, N.Y., U.S. 210 42.26 N 75.35 W
Oxford, N.C., U.S. 192 36.18 N 78.35 W
Oxford, Oh., U.S. 218 39.30 N 84.44 W
Oxford, Pa., U.S. 208 39.47 N 75.58 W
Oxford, Wi., U.S. 190 43.46 N 89.34 W
Oxford □6 212 43.08 N 80.50 W
Oxford Falls 274a 33.44 S 151.15 E
Oxford House 184 54.56 N 95.16 W
Oxford House Indian Reserve ✦4 184 54.54 N 95.15 W
Oxford Junction 190 41.59 N 90.57 W
Oxford Lake ⊜ 184 54.51 N 95.37 W
Oxford Peak ʌ 202 42.16 N 112.06 W
Oxfordshire □6 42 51.50 N 1.15 W
Oxford Valley Mall ✦9 285 40.11 N 74.53 W
Oxhey 260 51.39 N 0.23 W
Oxie 41 55.33 N 13.04 E
Oxkutzcab 232 20.18 N 89.25 W
Oxley 166 34.12 S 144.06 E
Oxley Creek ≐ 171a 27.32 S 153.00 E
Oxnard 228 34.11 N 119.10 W
Oxnard Beach 228 34.09 N 119.13 W
Oxon Hill 284c 38.48 N 76.59 W
Oxon Run ≐ 284c 38.49 N 77.00 W
Ox Pasture Brook ≐ 283 42.45 N 70.54 W
Oxshott 260 51.20 N 0.21 W
Oxted 42 51.16 N 0.01 W
Oxtongue ≐ 212 45.19 N 79.01 W
Oxtongue Lake ⊜ 212 45.22 N 78.55 W
Oxus — Amu Darya ≐ 72 43.40 N 59.01 E
Oy 58 47.38 N 10.28 E
Oya, Malay. 112 2.52 N 111.53 E
Ōya, Nihon 96 35.20 N 134.40 E
Oya ≐ 112 2.52 N 111.52 E
Oyabe 94 36.40 N 136.52 E
Oyabe ≐ 94 36.48 N 137.04 E
Ōya-ji ✦1 94 36.38 N 139.48 E
Ōya-yama ʌ2 270 34.48 N 135.51 E
Oyali 130 37.14 N 41.45 E
Oyama, B.C., Can. 182 50.07 N 119.22 W
Oyama, Nihon 94 35.21 N 139.00 E
Ōyama, Nihon 94 36.18 N 139.48 E
Ōyama, Nihon 94 36.36 N 137.18 E
Ōyama, Nihon 268 35.36 N 139.22 E
Ōyamada 94 34.46 N 136.13 E
Oyamazaki 270 34.54 N 135.42 E
Oyameyo, Volcán ʌ1 286a 19.10 N 99.11 W
Oyan 152 0.02 N 10.17 E
Oyano 92 32.35 N 130.26 E
Oyapock (Oiapoque) ≐ 250 4.08 N 51.40 W
Oyashirazu ♦ 94 36.59 N 137.40 E
Oybin 54 50.50 N 14.44 E
Oye-et-Pallet 58 46.51 N 6.20 E
Oyem 152 1.37 N 11.35 E
Oyen 184 51.22 N 110.28 W
Øyeren ⊜ 26 59.48 N 11.14 E
Oykel ≐ 46 57.56 N 4.25 W
Oykel Bridge 46 57.58 N 4.43 W
Oymyakon — Ojm'akon 74 63.28 N 142.49 E
Oyo, Congo 152 0.01 N 15.54 E
Oyo, Nig. 150 7.51 N 3.56 E
Oyo □3 150 8.00 N 3.50 E
Oyo 115a 7.57 S 110.22 E
Oyodo 96 34.23 N 135.48 E
Oyodo ✦8 270 34.43 N 135.30 E
Ōyodo ≐ 92 31.53 N 131.28 E
Oyón 248 10.39 S 76.47 W
Oyonnax 58 46.15 N 5.40 E
Oyorogi-san ʌ 96 35.05 N 132.51 E
Oyotún 248 6.51 S 79.19 W
Oyster 208 37.17 N 75.55 W
Oyster Bay 210 40.51 N 73.31 W
Oyster Bay c 276 40.55 N 73.30 W
Oyster Bay Cove 276 40.52 N 73.31 W
Oyster Bay Harbor c 276 40.53 N 73.32 W
Oyster Creek 222 29.00 N 95.20 W
Oyster Creek ≐ 222 28.59 N 95.18 W
Oyster Point ʌ 282 37.50 N 121.52 W
Oyster Point > 168b 34.55 S 137.48 E
Oyster Rock I2 272c 18.54 N 72.50 E
Oysterville 202 46.33 N 124.02 W
Øystese 26 60.23 N 6.13 E
Oyten 52 53.04 N 9.01 E
Ozaki 268 35.59 N 139.51 E
Ozamiz 116 8.08 N 123.50 E
Ozanne ≐ 50 48.11 N 1.22 E
Ozariči 76 52.28 N 29.16 E
Ozark, Al., U.S. 194 31.27 N 85.38 W
Ozark, Ar., U.S. 194 35.29 N 93.49 W
Ozark, Mo., U.S. 194 37.01 N 93.12 W
Ozark National Scenic Riverways ♦ 194 37.10 N 91.10 W
Ozark Plateau ʌ1 194 37.00 N 93.00 W
Ozark Reservoir ⊜1 194 35.35 N 94.00 W
Ozarks, Lake of the ⊜1 194 38.10 N 92.50 W
Ozaukee □6 216 44.14 N 88.00 W
Ozbourn Seamount ✦3 14 26.00 S 174.50 W
Ózd 30 48.14 N 20.18 E
Ozd'atiči 76 54.06 N 28.50 E
Oze ≐ 96 34.12 N 132.14 E
Ozeblin ʌ 36 44.35 N 15.53 E
Ozek 86 46.35 N 40.41 E
Ozereckoje 82 56.04 N 37.23 E
Ozerelje 82 54.48 N 38.17 E
Ozerel'ki 82 55.51 N 38.52 E
Ozerišče 76 54.48 N 33.13 E
Ozerki, Ross. 80 51.13 N 53.56 E
Ozerki, Ross. 80 51.32 N 45.16 E
Ozerki, Ross. 80 52.01 N 45.29 E
Ozerki, Ross. 86 53.38 N 83.44 E
Ozerki, Ross. 265a 59.54 N 30.44 E
Ozerna ≐ 82 55.34 N 36.08 E
Ozerninskoje vodochranilišče ⊜1 82 55.45 N 36.15 E
Ozernoje 78 50.11 N 28.42 E
Ozernovskij 74 51.30 N 156.31 E
Ozernyj 180 66.24 N 179.06 W
Ozero 80 56.58 N 44.43 E
Ozery 82 54.51 N 38.34 E
Ozette Lake ⊜ 224 48.06 N 124.38 W
Ozgoryš 85 41.15 N 74.45 E
Ozieri 71 40.35 N 9.00 E
Ozimek 30 50.41 N 18.13 E
Ozinki 80 51.12 N 49.45 E
Ozogino, ozero ⊜ 74 69.16 N 146.36 E
Ozoir-la-Ferrière 261 48.46 N 2.40 E
Ozona, Fl., U.S. 220 28.04 N 82.46 W
Ozona, Tx., U.S. 196 30.42 N 101.12 W
Ozone Park ✦8 276 40.40 N 73.51 W
Ozorków 30 51.58 N 19.19 E
Oz'ornaja, Kaz. 86 53.25 N 63.15 E
Oz'ornaja, Ross. 86 51.08 N 60.50 E
Oz'ornoje, Ross. 80 51.46 N 51.28 E
Oz'ornoje, Ross. 80 51.41 N 44.55 E
Oz'ornoje, Ross. 86 56.48 N 71.15 E
Oz'ornyj 80 57.10 N 40.59 E
Oz'orsk, Ross. 76 54.25 N 22.01 E
Oz'orsk, Ukr. 78 51.43 N 26.24 E
Oz'orskij 89 46.36 N 143.08 E
Oz'ory 76 53.43 N 24.11 E
Ozouer-le-Voulgis 261 48.40 N 2.47 E
Özpınar 130 37.57 N 42.16 E
Ōzu, Nihon 92 32.52 N 130.52 E
Ōzu, Nihon 96 33.30 N 132.33 E
Ozubulu 150 5.57 N 6.51 E
Ozuluama 234 21.40 N 97.51 W
Ozumba 234 19.03 N 98.48 W
Ozurgeti 84 41.56 N 42.00 E

P

Pâ 150 11.33 N 3.15 W
Paagoumène 175f 20.29 S 164.11 E
Paal 56 51.02 N 5.11 E
Paama □8 175f 16.28 S 168.18 E
Paama I 175f 16.28 S 168.14 E
Paar ≐ 60 48.45 N 11.33 E
Paardekraal Monument ⊥ 273d 26.06 S 27.47 E
Paaren 264a 52.39 N 12.59 E
Paarl 158 33.45 S 18.56 E
Paasbach ≐ 263 51.25 N 7.11 E
Paauilo 229d 20.02 N 155.22 W
Pabarabuk 164 6.05 S 144.05 E
Pabbay I, Scot., U.K. 46 56.51 N 7.35 W
Pabbay I, Scot., U.K. 46 57.46 N 7.15 W
Pabbi 123 34.01 N 71.47 E
Pabbiring, Kepulauan II 112 4.55 S 119.25 E
Pabean 112 6.50 S 115.19 E
Pabellón, Punta > 254 43.14 S 74.23 W
Pabellón de Arteaga 234 22.10 N 102.21 W
Pabellones, Ensenada c 232 24.27 N 107.36 W
Pabianice 30 51.40 N 19.22 E
Pabillonis 71 39.35 N 8.43 E
Pablo 202 47.36 N 114.07 W
Pābna 124 24.00 N 89.15 E
Pabo 154 3.00 N 32.09 E
Pabradė 76 54.59 N 25.44 E
Paca 115b 8.29 S 120.11 E
Pacaás Novas, Parque Nacional ♦ 248 11.10 S 63.30 W
Pacaás Novos ≐ 248 10.51 S 65.20 W
Pacaás Novos, Serra dos ʌ 248 10.45 S 64.15 W
Pacaembu 255 21.34 S 51.17 W
Pacaembu, Estádio do ✦ 287b 23.33 S 46.39 W
Pacajá ≐ 250 1.56 S 50.50 W
Pacajus 250 4.10 S 38.28 W
Pacaltsdorp 158 34.00 S 22.28 E
Pacaraima, Sierra de — Pakaraima Mountains ʌ 246 5.30 N 60.40 W
Pacarán 248 12.52 S 76.03 W
Pacaraos 248 11.11 S 76.44 W
Pacasmayo 248 7.24 S 79.34 W
Pacatuba 250 3.58 S 38.37 W
Pace, Fl., U.S. 194 30.35 N 87.09 W
Pace, Ms., U.S. 194 33.47 N 90.51 W
Paceco 70 37.59 N 12.33 E
Pačelma, Ross. 80 53.15 N 43.21 E
Pačelma, Ross. 80 53.20 N 43.20 E
Pacet 115a 6.45 S 107.03 E
Pachača 74 60.34 N 169.03 E
Pachacamac ⊥ 248 12.14 S 76.52 W
Pachamba 126 24.12 N 86.16 E
Pachaug Pond ⊜ 207 41.34 N 71.54 W
Pacheco 226 37.59 N 122.04 W
Pacheco, Isla I 254 52.17 S 74.45 W
Pacheco Creek ≐ 226 36.58 N 121.28 W
Pacheco Pass)(226 37.03 N 121.13 W
Pāchh Elāsin 126 24.08 N 89.54 E
Pachino 70 36.43 N 15.05 E
Pachitea ≐ 248 8.46 S 74.32 W
Pachiza 248 7.16 S 76.46 W
Pachkoli ✦8 272c 19.08 N 72.54 E
Pachmarhi 124 22.28 N 78.26 E
Pacho 246 5.08 N 74.10 W
Pachomovo 82 54.38 N 37.33 E
Pachor 124 23.42 N 76.44 E
Pāchora 122 20.40 N 75.21 E
Pachotnyj Ugol 80 52.58 N 41.56 E
Pachra ≐ 82 55.32 N 37.59 E
Pachtaabad 85 38.28 N 68.10 E
Pachuca [de Soto] 234 20.07 N 98.44 W
Paciência ✦8 256 22.55 S 43.38 W
Pacific, B.C., Can. 182 54.46 N 128.17 W
Pacific, Mo., U.S. 219 38.28 N 90.44 W
Pacific, Wa., U.S. 224 47.15 N 122.14 W
Pacific □6 224 46.30 N 123.39 W
Pacifica 226 37.37 N 122.29 W
Pacific-Antarctic Ridge ✦3 6 62.00 S 157.00 W
Pacific Beach 224 47.12 N 124.12 W
Pacific City 224 45.12 N 123.57 W
Pacific Creek ≐ 200 42.08 N 109.24 W
Pacific Gardens 226 37.58 N 121.20 W
Pacific Grove 226 36.38 N 121.56 W
Pacific Islands, Trust Territory of the — Palau □2 14 5.00 N 137.00 E
Pacific Missile Test Center ■ 228 34.07 N 119.07 W
Pacífico, Océano — Pacific Ocean ⊤1 6 10.00 S 150.00 W
Pacific Ocean ⊤1 4 10.00 S 150.00 W
Pacific Ocean ⊤1 6 10.00 S 150.00 W
Pacifico Mountain ʌ 228 34.23 N 118.02 W
Pacific Palisades ✦8 280 34.03 N 118.32 W
Pacific Ranges ʌ 182 50.45 N 125.30 W
Pacific Rim National Park ♦ 182 48.45 N 125.40 W
Pacifique, Océan — Pacific Ocean ⊤1 6 10.00 S 150.00 W
Pacijan Island I 116 10.39 N 124.20 E
Pacinan, Tanjung > 115a 7.36 S 114.02 E
Paciran 115a 6.52 S 112.20 E
Pacitan 115a 8.12 S 111.07 E
Pack 61 46.58 N 14.59 E
Packanack Lake ⊜ 276 40.56 N 74.15 W
Packard Mountain ʌ2 207 42.28 N 72.21 W
Packevei-Duna ≐1 264c 47.19 N 19.02 E
Pack Monadnock Mountain ʌ 207 42.52 N 71.52 W
Packsattel)(61 46.58 N 14.58 E
Packwood 224 46.36 N 121.40 W
Packwood Lake ⊜ 224 46.35 N 121.34 W
Pacllón 248 10.18 S 77.07 W
Pacock Brook ≐ 276 41.05 N 74.31 W
Paço de Arcos 266c 38.42 N 9.17 W
Paço do Lumiar 250 2.31 S 44.07 W
Pacohuaras ≐ 248 10.04 S 65.46 W
Pacoima ✦8 280 34.16 N 118.26 W
Pacolet ≐ 192 34.50 N 81.27 W
Pacolet Mills 192 34.55 N 81.44 W
Pacora 246 9.05 N 79.17 W
Pacov 30 49.28 N 15.00 E
Pacsa 30 46.43 N 17.01 E
Pacquet 186 49.59 N 55.53 W
Pacuare ≐ 236 10.14 N 83.17 W
Pacuí ≐ 255 16.46 S 45.01 W
Pacuneiro ≐ 255 13.02 S 53.25 W
Pacy-sur-Eure 50 49.01 N 1.23 E
Paczków 30 50.27 N 17.00 E
Padada 116 6.42 N 125.22 E
Padada ≐ 116 6.42 N 125.23 E
Padaido, Kepulauan II 164 1.15 S 136.30 E
Padam 123 33.28 N 76.53 E
Padamarang, Pulau I 112 4.07 S 121.24 E
Padamo ≐ 246 2.54 N 65.17 W
Padampur 120 20.59 N 83.04 E
Padang, Indon. 112 1.39 S 108.55 E
Padang, Indon. 112 2.59 N 105.40 E
Padang, Indon. 112 6.11 S 120.26 E
Padang, Indon. 112 0.57 S 100.21 E
Padang, Pulau I 114 1.10 N 102.20 E
Padang Besar 114 6.40 N 100.19 E
Padangbetuah 112 3.39 S 102.13 E
Padang Endau 114 2.40 N 103.37 E
Padangpanjang 112 0.27 S 100.25 E
Padangsidempuan 114 1.22 N 99.16 E
Padangtiji 114 5.22 N 95.50 E
Padangtikar, Pulau I 112 0.50 S 109.32 E
Padang Tungku 114 4.14 N 101.59 E
Padany 24 63.17 N 33.22 E
Padas 115a 7.25 S 111.32 E
Padas ≐ 112 5.14 N 115.34 E
Padasjoki 26 61.21 N 25.17 E
Padauari ≐ 246 0.15 S 64.05 W
Padborg 41 54.49 N 9.22 E
Padcaya 248 21.52 S 64.48 W
Paddington ✦8 260 51.31 N 0.10 W
Paddington Station ✦5 260 51.31 N 0.11 W
Paddle ≐ 182 54.05 N 114.15 W
Paddle Prairie 176 57.57 N 117.29 W
Paddock Lake 216 42.34 N 88.06 W
Paddock Wood 42 51.11 N 0.23 E
Padea 38 44.01 N 23.52 E
Padea-besar I 112 3.30 S 123.05 E
Padeghar 272c 18.58 N 73.03 E
Paden City 188 39.36 N 80.56 W
Paderborn 52 51.43 N 8.45 E
Paderno Dugnano 266b 45.34 N 9.10 E
Paderno Ponchielli 64 45.14 N 9.55 E
Padghe 272c 19.03 N 73.07 E
Padibe 154 3.28 N 32.50 E
Padiham 44 53.49 N 2.19 W
Padilla 248 19.19 S 64.20 W
Padilla Bay c 224 48.35 N 122.32 W
Padjelanta Nationalpark ♦ 24 67.28 N 16.41 E
Padle 272c 19.09 N 73.03 E
Padloping Island I 176 67.07 N 62.35 W
Padma — Ganges ≐ 124 23.22 N 90.32 E
Padola 64 46.36 N 12.28 E
Padoue — Padova 64 45.25 N 11.53 E
Padova 64 45.25 N 11.53 E
Padova □4 64 45.21 N 11.49 E
Padovka 80 52.28 N 49.31 E
Pādra 120 22.14 N 73.05 E
Padrão, Ponta do > 152 6.03 S 12.18 E
Padrauna 124 26.55 N 83.59 E
Padre Bernardo 255 15.21 S 48.30 W
Padre Brito 256 21.18 S 43.59 W
Padre Burgos 116 10.02 N 125.01 E
Padre Island I 196 27.00 N 97.15 W
Padre Island National Seashore ♦ 196 27.00 N 97.25 W
Padre Miguel ✦8 287a 22.53 S 43.26 W
Padre Paraíso 255 17.06 S 41.31 W
Padria 71 40.24 N 8.38 E
Padrón 34 42.44 N 8.40 W
Padrone, Cape > 158 33.46 S 26.30 E
Padrt' 60 49.40 N 13.46 E
Padstow, Austl. 274a 33.57 S 151.02 E
Padstow, Eng., U.K. 42 50.33 N 4.56 W
Padua — Padova 64 45.25 N 11.53 E
Paducah, Ky., U.S. 194 37.05 N 88.36 W
Paducah, Tx., U.S. 196 34.00 N 100.18 W
Padula 68 40.20 N 15.39 E
Paduli 68 41.10 N 14.53 E
Padunskaja 86 55.02 N 85.02 E
Paea 174s 17.41 S 149.35 W
Paedun 98 35.03 N 128.21 E
Paekakariki 172 40.59 S 174.57 E
Paektu-san ʌ 98 42.00 N 128.03 E
Paengaroa 172 37.49 S 176.25 E
Paengnyŏng-do I 98 37.57 N 124.40 E
Paerdegat Basin c 276 40.37 N 73.54 W
Paeroa 172 37.23 S 175.40 E
Paesana 62 44.41 N 7.16 E
Paese 64 45.40 N 12.10 E
Paestum ⊥ 68 40.25 N 15.00 E
Paete 116 14.23 N 121.29 E
Páez ≐ 246 2.28 N 75.34 W
Pafúri 156 22.27 S 31.21 E
Pag 36 44.27 N 15.04 E
Pag, Otok I 36 44.30 N 15.00 E
Paga 150 10.58 N 1.06 W
Pagadenbaru 115a 6.28 S 107.46 E
Pagadian 116 7.49 N 123.25 E
Pagadian Bay c 116 7.48 N 123.31 E
Pagai Selatan, Pulau I 112 3.00 S 100.20 E
Pagai Utara, Pulau I 112 2.42 S 100.07 E
Pagalungan 116 7.04 N 124.41 E
Pagan 110 21.10 N 94.51 E
Pagan I 108 18.07 N 145.46 E
Pagancillo 252 29.34 S 68.03 W
Paganella ʌ 64 46.08 N 11.02 E
Pagani 68 40.45 N 14.37 E
Paganica 66 42.21 N 13.28 E
Paganico 66 42.55 N 11.25 E
Pagaralam 112 4.01 S 103.16 E
Pagasitikós Kólpos c 38 39.15 N 22.51 E
Pagatan 112 3.36 S 115.56 E
Pagato ≐ 184 55.49 N 102.05 W
Pagato Lake ⊜ 184 56.08 N 102.30 W
Pagbilao 116 13.58 N 121.41 E
Pagbilao Grande Island I 116 13.55 N 121.46 E
Pagdanan Bay c 116 10.31 N 119.15 E
Page, Az., U.S. 200 36.54 N 111.28 W
Page, N.D., U.S. 198 47.09 N 97.34 W
Page Field ⊠ 220 26.35 N 81.52 W
Pagėgiai 76 55.09 N 21.54 E
Pageland 192 34.46 N 80.23 W
Page Manor 218 39.45 N 84.06 W
Pager ≐ 154 3.09 N 32.30 E
Pagerdewa 112 3.46 S 105.18 E
Paget, Mount ʌ 244 54.26 S 36.33 W
Paghmān 120 34.36 N 68.57 E
Paglia ≐ 66 42.42 N 12.11 E
Pagliara 70 37.59 N 15.22 E
Paglieta 66 42.10 N 14.30 E
Pagliete, Bonifica delle ✦1 267a 41.53 N 12.12 E
Pagny-sur-Moselle 56 48.59 N 6.01 E
Pago Bay c 174p 13.25 N 144.48 E
Pagoda Peak ʌ 200 40.10 N 107.20 W
Pagoda Point > 110 15.57 N 94.15 E
Pagon, Bukit ʌ 112 4.18 N 115.19 E
Pago Pago 174u 14.16 S 170.42 W
Pago Pago Harbor c 174u 14.17 S 170.40 W
Pago Pago International Airport ⊠ 174u 14.20 S 170.43 W
Pagosa Springs 200 37.16 N 107.00 W
Pagote 272c 18.54 N 72.59 E
Pagouda 150 9.45 N 1.19 E
Pagri 124 27.44 N 89.09 E
Pagsangahan 116 13.13 N 122.33 E
Pagsanjan 116 14.15 N 121.25 E
Paguate 200 35.08 N 107.22 W
Pagudpud 116 18.34 N 120.47 E
Pagueras, Torrente de ≐ 266d 41.28 N 1.58 E
Paguyaman ≐ 112 0.31 N 122.38 E
Pagwi 164 4.03 S 143.02 E
Pah ≐ 84 39.08 N 39.40 E
Pahādi ✦8 272c 19.10 N 72.51 E
Pahala 229d 19.12 N 155.28 W
Pahalgam 123 34.02 N 75.20 E
Pahang □3 114 3.30 N 102.45 E
Pahang ≐ 114 3.32 N 103.28 E
Pahara, Laguna c 236 14.18 N 83.15 W
Pahāsu 124 28.11 N 78.03 E
Pahau Point > 229b 21.49 N 160.15 W
Pahi 114 5.28 N 102.13 E
Pahia Point > 172 46.19 S 167.41 E
Pahiatua 172 40.27 S 175.50 E
Pahlād Garhi 272a 28.40 N 77.21 E
Pahlavī — Bandar-e Anzalī 128 37.28 N 49.27 E
Pahlevī — Bandar-e Anzalī 128 37.28 N 49.27 E
Pahoa 229d 19.29 N 154.57 W
Pahokee 220 26.49 N 80.39 W
Pahrump 204 36.12 N 115.58 W
Pahsimeroi ≐ 202 44.41 N 114.03 W
Pahuatlán de Valle 234 20.17 N 98.09 W
Pahvant Range ʌ 200 38.45 N 112.15 W
Pai 110 19.19 N 98.27 E
Pai ≐ 110 19.09 N 97.33 E
Pai, Ilha do I 287a 22.59 S 43.05 W
Paia 229d 20.54 N 156.22 W
Paianía 267c 37.57 N 23.51 E
Paicines 226 36.44 N 121.17 W
Paico 248 14.02 S 73.39 W
Paide 76 58.54 N 25.33 E
Paidorzu, Monte ʌ 71 40.30 N 9.05 E
Paifangchang 107 30.31 N 106.38 E
Paige 222 30.13 N 97.07 W
Paignton 42 50.26 N 3.34 W
Paiguano 252 30.01 S 70.32 W
Paihia 172 35.17 S 174.05 E
Paiho 100 23.21 N 120.25 E
Paiján 248 7.44 S 79.19 W
Päijänne ⊜ 26 61.35 N 25.30 E
Paikgācha 126 22.35 N 89.20 E
Paikü Co ⊜ 124 28.48 N 85.36 E
Pail 123 32.38 N 72.27 E
Paila ≐ 248 16.02 S 64.12 W
Paila, Sierra la ʌ 196 25.50 N 101.30 W
Pailin 110 12.51 N 102.36 E
Pailitas 246 8.58 N 73.38 W
Paillaco 254 40.04 S 72.53 W
Pailolo Channel 밀 229a 21.05 N 156.42 W
Pailoutou 106 30.56 N 121.16 E
Pailoutun 104 40.44 N 122.49 E
Paimboeuf 32 47.17 N 2.02 W
Paimio 26 60.27 N 22.42 E
Paimpol 32 48.46 N 3.03 W
Painan 112 1.21 S 100.34 E
Paincourt 214 42.23 N 82.17 W
Painesdale 190 47.02 N 88.40 W
Painesville 214 41.43 N 81.14 W
Painscastle 42 52.07 N 3.12 W
Painshawfield 44 54.56 N 1.54 W
Painswick 42 51.48 N 2.11 W
Paint ≐ 190 45.58 N 88.15 W
Paint Creek ≐, Mi., U.S. 281 42.06 N 83.36 W
Paint Creek ≐, Oh., U.S. 218 39.18 N 82.56 W
Paint Creek ≐, Pa., U.S. 214 41.10 N 79.28 W
Paint Creek ≐, Tx., U.S. 196 30.18 N 99.54 W
Paint Creek, East Fork ≐ 218 39.32 N 83.25 W
Paint Creek, North Fork ≐ 218 39.18 N 83.02 W
Paint Creek Lake ⊜1 218 39.15 N 83.22 W
Painted Desert ✦2 200 36.00 N 111.20 W
Painted Post 210 42.09 N 77.05 W
Painted Rock Reservoir ⊜1 200 33.00 N 112.50 W
Painter 208 37.35 N 75.47 W
Painter Creek ≐ 218 40.05 N 84.21 W
Paintertown 279b 40.21 N 79.42 W
Paint Lake ⊜ 184 55.28 N 97.57 W
Paint Rock 196 31.30 N 99.55 W
Paint Rock ≐ 194 34.28 N 86.28 W
Paintsville 192 37.48 N 82.48 W
Paiolinho 256 21.52 S 45.54 W
Pai Pobre, Morro do ʌ 287b 23.40 S 46.55 W
Paisco 64 46.04 N 10.17 E
Paisha 100 23.40 N 119.35 E
Paisley, Austl. 274b 37.51 S 144.51 E
Paisley, On., Can. 212 44.18 N 81.16 W
Paisley, Scot., U.K. 46 55.50 N 4.26 W
Paisley, Fl., U.S. 220 28.59 N 81.32 W
Paisley, Or., U.S. 202 42.41 N 120.32 W
Paita, N. Cal. 175f 22.08 S 166.22 E
Paita, Perú 248 5.06 S 81.07 W
Paita, Bahía de c 248 5.04 S 81.05 W
Paitan 100 23.31 N 113.46 E
Paitan ≐ 110 22.35 N 117.30 E
Paitan, Teluk c 116 6.45 N 117.20 E
Paiton 115a 7.43 S 113.30 E
Paiva 256 21.18 S 43.25 W
Paiva ≐ 34 41.04 N 8.16 W
Paizhou 100 30.13 N 113.56 E
Paj 24 61.13 N 34.24 E
Pajala 24 67.11 N 23.22 E
Paján 246 1.34 S 80.25 W
Pajapan 234 18.15 N 94.42 W
Pajares, Puerto de)(34 43.00 N 5.46 W
Pajaro 226 36.54 N 121.39 W
Pajaro ≐ 226 36.51 N 121.48 W
Pájaros Point > 240m 18.31 N 64.18 W
Paj-Choj ʌ2 72 69.00 N 63.00 E
Pajdugina ≐ 86 58.50 N 81.47 E
Pajęczno 30 51.09 N 19.00 E
Pajeú ≐ 250 8.55 S 38.42 W
Pajiangkou 100 23.46 N 113.14 E
Pajjer, gora ʌ 24 66.42 N 64.25 E
Pajtug 85 40.53 N 72.15 E
Pak ≐ 110 21.05 N 102.31 E
Páka, Magy. 30 46.36 N 16.39 E
Paka, Malay. 114 4.39 N 103.26 E
Paka ≐ 114 4.40 N 103.27 E
Pākāla 122 13.28 N 79.07 E
Pakaraima Mountains ʌ 246 5.30 N 60.40 W
Pākaur 124 24.38 N 87.51 E
Pak Ban 110 21.14 N 102.28 E
Pakch'ŏn 98 39.45 N 125.35 E
Pak Chong 110 14.42 N 101.25 E
Pakeng 140 6.55 N 30.40 E
Pakenham, Austl. 169 38.05 S 145.29 E
Pakenham, On., Can. 212 45.18 N 76.17 W
Pākhāl ⊜1 122 17.57 N 79.59 E
Pákhi 267c 37.59 N 23.22 E
Pákhi I 267c 37.58 N 23.22 E
Pákhna 130 34.46 N 32.48 E
Pakhoi — Beihai 102 21.29 N 109.05 E
Pakin I 174 7.04 N 157.48 E
Pakipaki 172 39.41 S 176.48 E
Pakistan (Pākistān) □1, Asia 118 30.00 N 70.00 E
Pakistan (Pākistān) □1, Asia 120 30.00 N 70.00 E
Pakistan, East — Bangladesh □1 120 24.00 N 90.00 E
Pak Kong 271d 22.23 N 114.15 E
Pak Kret 269a 13.55 N 100.30 E
Pak Kwo Chau I 271d 22.16 N 114.20 E
Paklenica Nacionalni Park ♦ 36 44.21 N 15.23 E
Pakokku 110 21.20 N 95.05 E
Pakość 30 52.49 N 18.05 E
Pakouabo 150 7.10 N 5.48 W
Pakowki Lake ⊜ 184 49.22 N 110.57 W
Pākpattan 123 30.21 N 73.24 E
Pak Phanang 110 8.21 N 100.12 E
Pak Phayun 110 7.21 N 100.19 E
Pak Phraek 110 8.13 N 100.12 E
Pakrac 36 45.26 N 17.12 E
Pākrāganj 126 24.00 N 90.41 E
Pakruojis 76 55.58 N 23.52 E
Paks 30 46.39 N 18.53 E
Pak Sane — Muang Pakxan 110 18.22 N 103.39 E
Pāksey 126 24.05 N 89.03 E
Pak Thong Chai 110 14.43 N 102.01 E
Paktīā □4 120 33.30 N 69.30 E
Paktīkā □4 120 32.30 N 68.45 E
Pākundia 126 24.20 N 90.42 E
P'akupur ≐ 74 65.00 N 77.48 E
Pakwach 154 2.28 N 31.30 E
Pakwash Lake ⊜ 184 50.45 N 93.30 W
Pakxé 110 15.07 N 105.47 E
Pala, Mya. 110 12.51 N 98.40 E
Pala, Tchad 146 9.22 N 14.54 E
Pala, Ca., U.S. 228 33.22 N 117.05 W
Palaau State Park ♦ 229a 21.11 N 157.00 W
Palabek 154 3.26 N 32.34 E
Palacca Point > 238 21.15 N 73.26 W
Palace of Auburn Hills ♦ 281 42.41 N 83.14 W
Palacios 196 28.42 N 96.13 W
Palacios ≐ 248 16.36 S 64.18 W
Paladru 62 45.28 N 5.33 E
Palagano 64 44.20 N 10.39 E
Palagianello 68 40.37 N 16.58 E
Palagiano 68 40.35 N 17.02 E
Palagonia 70 37.19 N 14.45 E
Palagruža, Otoci II 36 42.24 N 16.15 E
Palai 122 9.44 N 76.41 E
Palai, Punta ʌ 71 40.20 N 8.55 E
Palaia 66 43.36 N 10.46 E
Palaiá Epídhavros 38 37.38 N 23.09 E
Palaiá Psará 38 38.46 N 25.36 E
Palaikhóri 130 34.55 N 33.05 E
Pala Indian Reservation ✦4 228 33.21 N 117.04 W
Palaiokhóra 38 35.14 N 23.41 E
Palaión Fáliron 267c 37.55 N 23.41 E
Palaiseau 50 48.43 N 2.15 E
Pālakollu 122 16.32 N 81.44 E
Pālam ✦8 272a 28.35 N 77.05 E
Palam Airport ⊠ 123 28.35 N 77.07 E
Palamás 38 39.28 N 22.05 E
Palamós 34 41.51 N 3.08 E
Pālampur 123 32.07 N 76.32 E
Palamuse 76 58.41 N 26.35 E
Palamut 130 38.59 N 27.41 E
Palana 74 59.07 N 159.58 E
Palanan, Mount ʌ 116 17.03 N 122.15 E
Palanan Bay c 116 17.09 N 122.27 E
Palanan Point > 116 17.09 N 122.30 E
Palanas 116 12.09 N 123.55 E
Palandöken Dağları ʌ 130 39.47 N 41.15 E
Pālang 126 23.13 N 90.21 E
Pālang ≐1 126 23.15 N 90.21 E
Palanga 76 55.55 N 21.03 E
Palangkaraya 112 2.16 S 113.56 E
Palani 122 10.28 N 77.32 E
Pālanpur 120 24.10 N 72.26 E
Palanquinos 34 42.27 N 5.31 W
Palanzano 64 44.26 N 10.11 E
Palaoa Point > 229a 20.44 N 156.58 W
Palapag 116 12.33 N 125.07 E
Palapye 156 22.37 S 27.06 E
Pālār ≐ 122 12.28 N 80.10 E
Palasan Island I 116 14.52 N 122.03 E
Palas de Rei 34 42.52 N 7.52 W
Palāshdānga 126 23.24 N 87.22 E
Palāśpol 126 22.43 N 89.05 E
Palāsthali 126 23.51 N 87.03 E
Palata 66 41.53 N 14.47 E
Palatcy 86 49.09 N 83.43 E
Palatine 216 42.06 N 88.02 W
Palatine Bridge 210 42.55 N 74.35 W
Palatka, Ross. 74 60.06 N 150.54 E
Palatka, Fl., U.S. 192 29.38 N 81.38 W
Palau, It. 71 41.11 N 9.23 E
Palau, Méx. 196 27.54 N 101.26 W
Palau (Belau) □2, Oc. 14 5.00 N 137.00 E
Palau (Belau) □2, Oc. 175b 7.30 N 134.30 E
Palauig 116 15.26 N 119.54 E
Palaui Island I 116 18.33 N 122.08 E
Palau Islands II 175b 7.30 N 134.30 E
Palauk 110 13.16 N 98.38 E
Pal'avaam ≐ 180 68.50 N 170.45 E
Pal'avaamskij chrebet ʌ 180 68.20 N 177.00 E
Palavas-les-Flots 62 43.32 N 3.56 E
Palaw 110 12.58 N 98.39 E
Palawai Basin ≐1 229a 20.47 N 156.55 W
Palawan □4 116 10.00 N 118.50 E
Palawan I 116 9.30 N 118.30 E
Palawan Passage 밀 116 10.00 N 118.00 E
Palayan 116 15.33 N 121.06 E
Pālayankottai 122 8.43 N 77.44 E
Palazzo Adriano 70 37.41 N 13.23 E
Palazzolo Acreide 70 37.04 N 14.54 E
Palazzolo dello Stella 64 45.48 N 13.05 E
Palazzolo sull'Oglio 62 45.36 N 9.53 E
Palazzolo Vercellese 62 45.11 N 8.14 E
Palazzo San Gervasio 68 40.56 N 16.00 E
Palazzuolo sul Senio 66 44.07 N 11.33 E
P'albong-san ʌ 98 40.16 N 127.57 E
Palca, Bol. 248 16.34 S 67.59 W
Palca, Perú 248 11.21 S 75.31 W
Palcamayo 248 11.18 S 75.46 W
Pal'co 76 53.17 N 34.56 E
Paldi 224 48.48 N 123.51 W
Paldiski 76 59.20 N 24.06 E
Pāldor ʌ 124 28.16 N 85.11 E
Palech 80 56.48 N 41.51 E
Palel 120 24.27 N 94.02 E
Paleleh 112 1.04 N 121.57 E
Palembang 112 2.55 S 104.45 E
Palena 66 41.59 N 14.08 E
Palena ≐ 254 43.50 S 72.59 W
Palena, Lago (Lago General Vintter) ⊜ 254 43.55 S 71.40 W
Palencia 34 42.01 N 4.32 W
Palencia □4 34 42.25 N 4.35 W
Palen Lake ⊜ 204 33.46 N 115.12 W
Palenque 232 17.31 N 91.58 W
Palenque ⊥ 232 17.30 N 92.00 W
Palenque, Punta > 238 18.14 N 70.09 W
Palenville 210 42.10 N 74.01 W
Paleparto, Monte ʌ 68 39.28 N 16.34 E
Palermo, Col. 246 2.54 N 75.26 W
Palermo, It. 70 38.07 N 13.21 E
Palermo, Ca., U.S. 226 39.26 N 121.33 W
Palermo, Ur. 252 33.48 S 55.59 W
Palermo □4 70 37.49 N 13.35 E
Palermo ✦8 288 34.35 S 58.25 W
Palermo, Golfo di c 70 38.08 N 13.26 E
Palese, Aeroporto di ⊠ 68 41.10 N 16.47 E
Palestina, Bra. 255 20.23 S 49.25 W
Palestina, Méx. 196 29.10 N 100.55 W
Palestine, Ar., U.S. 194 34.58 N 90.54 W
Palestine, Il., U.S. 194 39.00 N 87.36 W
Palestine, Oh., U.S. 218 40.03 N 84.45 W
Palestine, Tx., U.S. 222 31.45 N 95.37 W
Palestine □9 132 32.00 N 35.15 E
Palestine, Lake ⊜1 222 32.06 N 95.27 W
Palestrina 66 41.50 N 12.53 E
Paletwa 110 21.18 N 92.51 E
Palézieux 58 46.33 N 6.50 E
Palfau 61 47.42 N 14.48 E
Pālghāt 122 10.47 N 76.39 E

Symbol	English	Deutsch	Español	Français	Português
≐	River	Fluß	Río	Rivière	Rio
	Canal	Kanal	Canal	Canal	Canal
	Waterfall, Rapids	Wasserfall, Stromschnellen	Cascada, Rápidos	Chute d'eau, Rapides	Cascata, Rápidos
밀	Strait	Meeresstraße	Estrecho	Détroit	Estreito
c	Bay, Gulf	Bucht, Golf	Bahía, Golfo	Baie, Golfe	Baía, Golfo
⊜	Lake, Lakes	See, Seen	Lago, Lagos	Lac, Lacs	Lago, Lagos
	Swamp	Sumpf	Pantano	Marais	Pântano
	Ice Features, Glacier	Eis- und Gletscherformen	Accidentes Glaciales	Formes glaciaires	Acidentes glaciares
	Other Hydrographic Features	Andere Hydrographische Objekte	Otros Elementos Hidrográficos	Autres données hydrographiques	Outros acidentes hidrográficos

Symbol	English	Deutsch	Español	Français	Português
✦	Submarine Features	Untermeerische Objekte	Accidentes Submarinos	Formes de relief sous-marin	Acidentes submarinos
□	Political Unit	Politische Einheit	Unidad Política	Entité politique	Unidade política
	Cultural Institution	Kulturelle Institution	Institución Cultural	Institution culturelle	Instituição cultural
⊥	Historical Site	Historische Stätte	Sitio Histórico	Site historique	Sítio histórico
♦	Recreational Site	Erholungs- und Ferienort	Sitio de Recreo	Centre de loisirs	Área de Lazer
⊠	Airport	Flughafen	Aeropuerto	Aéroport	Aeroporto
■	Military Installation	Militäranlage	Instalación Militar	Installation militaire	Instalação militar
✦	Miscellaneous	Verschiedenes	Misceláneo	Divers	Diversos

Palgrave, Mount ʌ 162 23.22 S 115.58 E
Palgrave Point › 156 20.45 S 13.20 E
Palhais 266c 38.37 N 9.03 W
Palhano 250 4.44 S 37.57 W
Palhano ≃ 250 4.33 S 37.42 W
Pāli, India 120 25.46 N 73.20 E
Pali, India 124 25.51 N 76.33 E
Paliano 66 41.48 N 13.03 E
Palikea ʌ 229c 21.26 N 158.06 W
Palima 112 4.20 S 120.22 E
Palimanan 115a 6.42 S 108.26 E
Palimbang 116 6.12 N 124.12 E
Palimé 150 6.54 N 0.38 E
Palín 236 14.24 N 90.42 W
Palinges 32 46.33 N 4.13 E
Palinuro 68 40.02 N 15.17 E
Palinuro, Capo › 68 40.02 N 15.16 E
Palisade, Co., U.S. 200 39.06 N 108.21 W
Palisade, Ne., U.S. 198 40.20 N 101.06 W
Palisades, Id., U.S. 202 43.21 N 111.13 W
Palisades, N.Y., U.S. 276 41.01 N 73.55 W
Palisades Amusement Park ♦ 276 40.50 N 73.59 W
Palisades Interstate Park ♦ 210 40.56 N 73.55 W
Palisades Park, Mi., U.S. 216 42.18 N 86.19 W
Palisades Park, N.J., U.S. 276 40.50 N 73.59 W
Palisades Reservoir ⊜[1] 202 43.15 N 111.05 W
Paliseul 56 49.54 N 5.08 E
Pālitāna 120 21.31 N 71.50 E
Palivere 76 58.59 N 23.52 E
Palizada 232 18.15 N 92.05 W
Palizzi 68 37.58 N 15.59 E
Paljakka ʌ[2] 26 64.41 N 28.08 E
Pälkäne 26 61.20 N 24.16 E
Palk Bay c 122 9.30 N 79.15 E
Palkino, Ross. 76 57.32 N 28.01 E
Palkino, Ross. 80 58.15 N 42.56 E
Pālkonda 122 18.36 N 83.45 E
Pālkonda Range ⩘ 122 14.05 N 79.05 E
Palk Strait ⊔ 122 10.00 N 79.45 E
Palla Bianca (Weisskugel) ʌ 64 46.48 N 10.44 E
Pallagorio 68 39.18 N 16.54 E
Pallamana 168b 35.02 S 139.12 E
Pallasca 248 8.15 S 78.01 W
Pallas Grean 48 52.33 N 8.22 W
Pallaskenry 48 52.39 N 8.52 W
Pallas-Ounastunturin kansallispuisto ♦ 24 68.06 N 24.00 E
Pallasovka 80 50.03 N 46.53 E
Pallastunturi ʌ 24 68.06 N 24.00 E
Pallejà 266d 41.25 N 2.00 E
Pallës, Bishti i › 38 41.24 N 19.24 E
Palling 182 54.21 N 125.55 W
Pallíni 267c 38.00 N 23.53 E
Pallinup ≃ 162 34.29 S 118.54 E
Pallisa 154 1.10 N 33.42 E
Palliser, Cape › 172 41.37 S 175.17 E
Palliser Bay c 172 41.25 S 175.05 E
Pallu 123 28.56 N 74.13 E
Palluau 32 46.48 N 1.37 W
Palma, Bra. 255 21.22 S 42.19 W
Palma, Moç. 154 10.46 S 40.29 E
P'al'ma, Ross. 24 62.26 N 35.53 E
Palma ≃ 255 12.33 S 47.52 W
Palma, Badia de c 34 39.27 N 2.35 E
Palmácia 250 4.08 S 38.50 W
Palma del Río 34 37.42 N 5.17 W
Palma [de Mallorca] 34 39.34 N 2.39 E
Palma di Montechiaro 70 37.11 N 13.46 E
Palmahim 132 31.56 N 34.42 E
Palma Pegada 234 22.42 N 101.48 W
Palmar ≃ 246 10.10 N 71.50 W
Palmar, Lago Artificial del ⊜[1] 252 33.05 S 57.10 W
Palmar Camp 232 16.26 N 88.53 W
Palmar de Cariaco 286c 10.34 N 66.55 W
Palmar de los Sepúlveda 232 25.43 N 107.55 W
Palmar de Varela 246 10.45 N 74.45 W
Palmarejo 240m 18.03 N 67.05 W
Palmares, Bra. 250 8.41 S 35.36 W
Palmares, C.R. 236 10.03 N 84.26 W
Palmares, C.R. 236 9.21 N 83.40 W
Palmares do Sul 252 30.16 S 50.31 W
Palmaria, Isola I 62 44.02 N 9.51 E
Palmarito 246 7.37 N 70.10 W
Palmarola, Isola I 66 40.56 N 12.51 E
Palmar Sur 236 8.58 N 83.29 W
Palmas, Bra. 252 26.30 S 52.00 W
Palmas, Méx. 234 22.49 N 103.57 W
Palmas, Golfo di c 71 39.02 N 8.31 E
Palmas, Ilha das I, Bra. 287a 23.02 S 43.12 W
Palmas, Ilha das I, Bra. 287a 23.04 S 43.31 W
Palmas Bellas 236 9.14 N 80.05 W
Palmas de Monte Alto 255 14.16 S 43.10 W
Palma Sola 220 27.31 N 82.38 W
Palma Soriano 240p 20.13 N 76.00 W
Palm Bay 220 28.02 N 80.35 W
Palm Beach, Austl. 170 33.36 S 151.19 E
Palm Beach, Austl. 171a 28.08 S 153.28 E
Palm Beach, Fl., U.S. 220 26.42 N 80.02 W
Palm Beach □[6] 220 26.38 N 80.27 W
Palm Beach Gardens 220 26.49 N 80.06 W
Palm Beach International Airport ⊠ 220 26.41 N 80.05 W
Palm City 220 27.09 N 80.16 W
Palmdale, Ca., U.S. 228 34.34 N 118.06 W
Palmdale, Fl., U.S. 220 26.56 N 81.18 W
Palmdale, Pa., U.S. 208 40.18 N 76.37 W
Palmdale, Lake ⊜[1] 228 34.33 N 118.07 W
Palm Desert 204 33.43 N 116.23 W
Palmeira, Bra. 252 25.25 S 50.00 W
Palmeira, C.V. 150a 16.46 N 22.59 W
Palmeira das Missões 252 27.55 S 53.17 W
Palmeira d'Oeste 255 20.23 S 50.47 W
Palmeira dos Índios 250 9.25 S 36.37 W
Palmeirais 250 5.58 S 43.04 W
Palmeiral 256 21.38 S 46.31 W
Palmeiras 255 12.31 S 41.34 W
Palmeiras ≃, Bra. 250 12.22 S 47.08 W
Palmeiras ≃, Bra. 255 15.25 S 51.10 W
Palmeirina 250 8.56 S 36.17 W
Palmeirinhas, Ponta das › 152 9.05 S 13.00 E
Palmela ≃ 256 21.38 S 45.23 W
Palmelo 255 17.20 S 48.27 W
Palmer, Austl. 168b 34.51 S 139.10 E
Palmer, P.R. 240m 18.22 N 65.46 W
Palmer, Ak., U.S. 180 61.36 N 149.07 W
Palmer, Il., U.S. 219 39.27 N 89.24 W
Palmer, Ma., U.S. 207 42.09 N 72.19 W
Palmer, Ms., U.S. 194 31.16 N 89.15 W
Palmer, Ne., U.S. 198 41.13 N 98.15 W
Palmer, Tn., U.S. 194 35.21 N 85.34 W
Palmer, Tx., U.S. 222 32.26 N 96.40 W
Palmer ≃, Austl. 162 24.46 S 133.25 E
Palmer ≃, Austl. 164 15.34 S 142.26 E
Palmer ≃, P.Q., Can. 206 46.19 N 71.27 W
Palmer ◆[3] 9 64.46 S 64.03 W
Palmerah ●[8] 269e 6.12 S 106.47 E
Palmer Heights 208 40.42 N 75.16 W
Palmer Lake 200 38.52 N 104.48 W
Palmer Land ●[1] 9 71.30 S 65.00 W
Palmer Mill Brook ≃ 283 41.58 N 70.52 W
Palmer Park 284c 38.55 N 76.52 W
Palmer Park ♦ 281 42.26 N 83.07 W
Palmerston, On., Can. 212 43.50 N 80.51 W
Palmerston, N.Z. 172 45.29 S 170.43 E
Palmerston I[1] 14 18.04 S 163.10 W
Palmerston, Cape › 166 21.32 S 149.29 E
Palmerston Lake ⊜ 212 45.01 N 76.50 W
Palmerston North 172 40.21 S 175.37 E
Palmerton 210 40.48 N 75.36 W
Palmerville 164 15.59 S 144.05 E
Palmetto, Fl., U.S. 220 27.31 N 82.34 W
Palmetto, Ga., U.S. 192 33.31 N 84.40 W
Palmetto, La., U.S. 194 30.43 N 91.54 W
Palmford 158 27.11 S 29.42 E
Palm Harbor 220 28.04 N 82.45 W
Palmi 68 38.21 N 15.51 E
Palminópolis 255 16.47 S 50.08 W
Palmira, Arg. 252 33.03 S 68.34 W
Palmira, Col. 246 3.32 N 76.16 W
Palmira, Cuba 240p 22.14 N 80.23 W
Palmira, Ec. 246 2.05 S 78.43 W
Palmira, Méx. 196 28.58 N 100.47 W
Palmitas 252 33.31 S 57.49 W
Palmitos 252 27.05 S 53.08 W
Palmnicken → Jantarnyj 76 54.52 N 19.57 E
Palmoli 66 41.56 N 14.32 E
Palm River 220 27.56 N 82.23 W
Palms ●[8] 280 34.02 N 118.25 W
Palm Shores 220 28.11 N 80.35 W
Palm Springs, Ca., U.S. 204 33.49 N 116.32 W
Palm Springs, Fl., U.S. 220 26.39 N 80.06 W
Palmyra, Il., U.S. 219 39.26 N 89.59 W
Palmyra, In., U.S. 218 38.24 N 86.06 W
Palmyra, Mi., U.S. 216 41.52 N 83.56 W
Palmyra, Mo., U.S. 219 39.47 N 91.31 W
Palmyra, N.J., U.S. 208 40.00 N 75.01 W
Palmyra, N.Y., U.S. 210 43.03 N 77.14 W
Palmyra, Oh., U.S. 214 41.07 N 81.02 W
Palmyra, Pa., U.S. 208 40.18 N 76.35 W
Palmyra, Va., U.S. 192 37.51 N 78.15 W
Palmyra, Wi., U.S. 216 42.52 N 88.35 W
Palmyra ⊥ 130 34.33 N 38.17 E
Palmyra Atoll I[1] 14 5.52 N 162.06 W
Palmyra → Tudmur 130 34.33 N 38.17 E
Palo, It. 66 41.56 N 12.06 E
Palo, Pil. 116 11.10 N 124.59 E
Palo Alto, Méx. 196 26.32 N 99.45 W
Palo Alto, Ca., U.S. 226 37.26 N 122.08 W
Palo Alto, Pa., U.S. 208 40.41 N 76.11 W
Palo Alto Airport ⊠ 282 37.28 N 122.07 W
Palo Blanco, Méx. 196 26.45 N 101.32 W
Palo Blanco, P.R. 240m 18.26 N 66.39 W
Palo Blanco Creek ≃ 196 27.10 N 97.52 W
Paločka 86 58.25 N 84.32 E
Palo del Colle 68 41.03 N 16.42 E
Palo Duro Canyon State Park ♦ 196 34.55 N 101.42 W
Palo Duro Creek ≃, U.S. 196 36.39 N 100.58 W
Palo Duro Creek ≃, Tx., U.S. 196 35.00 N 101.55 W
Paloe, Pulau I 115b 8.20 S 121.43 E
Paloemeu ≃ 250 3.21 N 55.26 W
Palo Flechado Pass)(200 36.25 N 105.20 W
Paloh, Indon. 112 1.43 N 109.18 E
Paloh, Malay. 112 2.25 N 111.15 E
Paloh, Malay. 114 2.11 N 103.12 E
Paloich, Sūd. 140 6.45 N 30.08 E
Paloich, Sūd. 140 10.28 N 32.32 E
Palojoensuu 24 68.17 N 23.05 E
Paloma Creek ≃ 226 36.15 N 121.26 W
Palomares Creek ≃ 282 37.42 N 122.02 W
Palomar Mountain ʌ 204 33.22 N 116.50 W
Palomar Mountain State Park ♦ 228 33.19 N 116.53 W
Palomar Park 282 37.29 N 122.16 W
Palomas 196 28.43 N 103.45 W
Palomas Viejo 232 31.44 N 107.37 W
Palombara Sabina 66 42.04 N 12.46 E
Palominos, Isla I 240m 18.21 N 65.34 W
Palomonte 68 40.40 N 15.17 E
Palompon 116 11.03 N 124.23 E
Palo Negro 246 10.11 N 67.33 W
Palo Pinto 196 32.46 N 98.18 W
Palo Pinto Reservoir ⊜[1] 196 32.38 N 98.18 W
Palopo 112 3.00 S 120.12 E
Palora ≃ 246 1.51 S 77.49 W
Palos 240p 22.48 N 81.44 W
Palos, Cabo de › 34 37.38 N 0.41 W
Palo Santo 252 25.34 S 59.21 W
Palos de la Frontera 34 37.14 N 6.53 W
Palos Gardens 278 41.40 N 87.48 W
Palos Heights 216 41.40 N 87.47 W
Palos Hills 278 41.41 N 87.49 W
Palos Hills ♦ 278 41.42 N 87.53 W
Palos → Palos de la Frontera 34 37.14 N 6.53 W
Palos Park 278 41.40 N 87.49 W
Palos Verdes Estates 228 33.48 N 118.23 W
Palos Verdes Hills ⩘[2] 280 33.46 N 118.21 W
Palos Verdes Point › 228 33.47 N 118.26 W
Palotai-sziget I 264c 47.35 N 19.05 E
Paloúkia 267c 37.58 N 23.31 E
Palouse 202 46.54 N 117.04 W
Palouse ≃ 202 46.35 N 118.13 W
Palouse, South Fork ≃ 202 46.53 N 117.22 W
Palo Verde 204 33.25 N 114.43 W
Palo Verde, Parque Nacional ♦ 236 10.15 N 85.10 W
P'alovskoje vodochranilišče ⊜[1] 82 56.03 N 37.40 E
Palpa 248 14.32 S 75.11 W
Palpalá 252 24.15 S 65.12 W
Pålsboda 40 59.04 N 15.20 E
Pālsit 126 23.12 N 88.03 E
Paltamo 26 64.25 N 27.50 E
Paltenbach ≃ 61 47.34 N 14.20 E
Palu, Indon. 112 0.53 S 119.53 E
Palu, Tür. 130 38.42 N 39.57 E
Palu ≃ 112 0.52 S 119.51 E
Palu, Teluk c 112 0.40 S 119.45 E
Paluan 116 13.25 N 120.28 E
Paluan Bay c 116 13.23 N 120.25 E
Palù del Fersina 64 46.08 N 11.21 E
Paludi 68 39.32 N 16.41 E
Paluga 24 65.16 N 45.11 E
Paluke 150 5.02 N 8.06 W
Paluška ʌ 61 48.45 N 14.24 E
Paluxy ≃ 196 32.15 N 97.43 W
Paluzza 64 46.32 N 13.01 E
Palvantaš 85 40.34 N 72.12 E
Palvār, Kūh-e ʌ 128 30.04 N 57.28 E
Palvart 128 38.11 N 64.34 E
Palwal 124 28.09 N 77.20 E
Pal-Waukee Airport ⊠ 278 42.07 N 87.54 W
Pam 175f 20.16 S 164.19 E
Pama 150 11.15 N 0.42 E
Pama ≃ 152 4.23 N 18.27 E
Pamaluan 112 1.04 S 116.39 E
Pamanukan 115a 6.16 S 107.49 E
Pamarayan 115a 6.16 S 106.17 E
Pam'ati 0103 Borcov 86 56.13 N 92.20 E
Pam'atnaja 86 56.01 N 65.42 E
Pam'at' Parižskoj Kommuny 80 56.06 N 44.31 E
Pāmban Channel ⊔ 122 9.17 N 79.10 E
Pāmban Island I 122 9.15 N 79.20 E
Pambeguwa 150 10.40 N 8.19 E
Pambuhan 116 13.59 N 123.05 E
Pambuhan ≃ 116 12.34 N 124.55 E
Pambujan 116 12.34 N 124.56 E
Pamekasan 115a 7.10 S 113.28 E
Pamenang 112 2.07 S 102.31 E
Pameungpeuk 115a 7.38 S 107.43 E
Pamiers 32 43.07 N 1.36 E
Pamir ⩘ 118 38.00 N 73.00 E
Pamlico ≃ 192 35.20 N 76.30 W
Pamlico Sound ⊔ 192 35.20 N 75.55 W
Pamotan 115a 6.46 S 111.29 E
Pampa 196 35.32 N 100.57 W
Pampã ≃ 255 17.43 S 40.36 W
Pampa ●[1] 252 35.00 S 63.00 W
Pampa Almirón 252 26.42 S 59.08 W
Pampacolca 248 15.43 S 72.33 W
Pampa del Castillo 254 45.48 S 68.05 W
Pampa del Chañar 252 30.11 S 68.43 W
Pampa del Indio 252 26.02 S 59.55 W
Pampa del Infierno 252 26.31 S 61.10 W
Pampa de los Guanacos 252 26.14 S 61.51 W
Pampa Grande 248 18.05 S 64.06 W
Pampana ≃ 150 8.24 N 12.00 W
Pampanga □[4] 116 15.05 N 120.40 E
Pampanga ≃ 116 14.47 N 120.39 E
Pampanua 112 4.14 S 120.08 E
Pamparato 62 44.17 N 7.55 E
Pampas 248 12.24 S 74.54 W
Pampas ≃ 248 13.23 S 73.15 W
Pampas del Heath, Santuario Nacional ♦ 248 12.40 S 68.15 W
Pampeluna → Pamplona 34 42.49 N 1.38 W
Pamphylia □[9] 130 37.00 N 31.00 E
Pamplico 192 33.59 N 79.34 W
Pamplona, Col. 246 7.23 N 72.39 W
Pamplona, Esp. 34 42.49 N 1.38 W
Pampoenpoort 158 31.03 S 22.40 E
Pampow 54 53.32 N 14.15 E
Pāmpur 123 34.01 N 74.56 E
Pamukkale (Hierapolis) ⊥ 130 37.58 N 29.19 E
Pamukova 130 40.31 N 30.09 E
Pamunkey ≃ 208 37.32 N 76.48 W
Pana 219 39.23 N 89.04 W
Panabá 232 21.17 N 88.16 W
Panabo 116 7.19 N 125.42 E
Panaca 204 37.47 N 114.23 W
Panacan 116 9.16 N 118.25 E
Panacea 192 30.02 N 84.23 W
Panache, Lake ⊜ 190 46.15 N 81.20 W
Panadura 122 6.43 N 79.54 E
Panaeati Island I 164 10.40 S 152.20 E
Panāgar 124 23.18 N 79.59 E
Panagjurište 38 42.30 N 24.11 E
Panagtaran Point › 116 9.41 N 118.45 E
Panahan 112 1.44 S 111.49 E
Panaitan, Pulau I 115a 6.36 S 105.12 E
Panaitan, Selat ⊔ 115a 6.40 S 105.16 E
Panaji (Panjim) 122 15.29 N 73.50 E
Pānākua 272b 22.23 N 88.21 E
Panamá, Bra. 255 18.11 S 49.21 W
Panamá, Pan. 236 8.58 N 79.32 W
Panama, Il., U.S. 219 39.02 N 89.32 W
Panama, N.Y., U.S. 214 42.04 N 79.29 W
Panama, Ok., U.S. 194 35.10 N 94.40 W
Panamá □[4] 236 8.48 N 79.55 W
Panama (Panamá) □[1], N.A. 230 9.00 N 80.00 W
Panama (Panamá) □[1], N.A. 246 9.00 N 80.00 W
Panamá, Bahía de c 246 8.50 N 79.20 W
Panamá, Canal de ≊ 236 9.20 N 79.55 W
Panamá, Golfo de c 246 8.00 N 79.30 W
Panamá, Istmo de ⊥[3] 246 9.00 N 80.00 W
Panama Basin ✢[1] 18 5.00 N 83.30 W
Panama City 194 30.09 N 85.39 W
Panamá Vieja ⊥ 236 9.00 N 79.29 W
Panambi 252 28.18 S 53.30 W
Panamint Range ⩘ 204 36.30 N 117.20 W
Panamint Valley V 204 36.15 N 117.20 W
Pan'an 100 29.06 N 120.27 E
Panao, Perú 248 9.49 S 76.00 W
Pan'ao, Zhg. 107 30.09 N 103.37 E
Panaon Island I 116 10.03 N 125.13 E
Panarea, Isola I 70 38.38 N 15.04 E
Panaro ≃ 64 44.55 N 11.25 E
Panarukan 115a 7.42 S 113.56 E
Panasoffkee, Lake ⊜ 220 28.47 N 82.08 W
Panatinane Island I 164 11.15 S 153.10 E
Panay I 116 11.15 N 122.30 E
Panay ≃ 116 11.35 N 122.43 E
Panay Gulf c 116 10.15 N 122.15 E
Panayía 38 39.56 N 25.20 E
Panay Island I 116 13.58 N 124.20 E
Pancalieri 62 44.50 N 7.35 E
Pancas 266c 38.48 N 8.55 W
Pančevo, Jugo. 38 44.52 N 20.39 E
Pančevo, Ukr. 78 48.44 N 31.51 E
Panchagarh 124 26.20 N 88.34 E
Pānchāl 126 23.15 N 87.18 E
Pānchet Hill ʌ[2] 126 23.37 N 86.47 E
Pānchet Reservoir ⊜[1] 126 23.40 N 86.45 E
Pānchghara 272b 22.44 N 88.16 E
Panchgram 126 24.12 N 88.01 E
Panch'iao 269d 25.01 N 121.27 E
Panchla 126 22.32 N 88.09 E
Panchor 114 2.10 N 102.43 E
Pancho Simón ≃ 286b 23.03 N 82.21 W
Pānchur 272b 22.32 N 88.16 E
Pānchuria 272b 22.33 N 88.29 E
Panciu 38 45.55 N 27.05 E
Panda 156 24.02 S 34.45 E
Pandakan 115a 7.39 S 112.41 E
Pandamatenga 156 18.35 S 25.42 E
Pandan, Malay. 112 3.09 N 113.22 E
Pandan, Pil. 116 14.03 N 124.10 E
Pandan, Pil. 116 11.43 N 122.06 E
Pandan, Selat ⊔ 271c 1.15 N 103.44 E
Pandanan Island I 116 8.17 N 117.13 E
Pandan Bay c 116 11.43 N 122.04 E
Pandan Reservoir ⊜[1] 271c 1.19 N 103.44 E
Pandaria 124 22.14 N 81.25 E
Pandarochan Bay c 116 12.12 N 121.10 E
Pandasan 112 6.28 N 116.32 E
Pan de Azúcar 252 34.48 S 55.14 W
Pan de Azucar, Cerro ʌ 286e 33.19 S 70.42 W
Pan de Azucar Island I 116 11.17 N 123.10 E
Pandegelang 115a 6.18 S 106.06 E
Pandėlys 76 56.01 N 25.13 E
Pāndharkawada 122 20.01 N 78.32 E
Pandharpur 122 17.40 N 75.20 E
Pāndhurna 122 21.36 N 78.31 E
Pandian 98 36.38 N 116.27 E
Pandino 62 45.24 N 9.33 E
Pando 252 34.43 S 55.57 W
Pando □[5] 248 11.20 S 67.40 W
Pando, Cerro ʌ 236 8.55 N 82.43 W
Pandora 216 40.56 N 83.57 W
Pandu 152 5.01 N 19.16 E
Pandua, India 124 25.08 N 88.10 E
Pāndua, India 126 23.05 N 88.17 E
P'andž (Panj) ≃ 120 37.06 N 68.20 E
Panebianco ≃ 70 37.24 N 15.04 E
Panelas 250 8.40 S 36.01 W
Paneveggio 64 46.18 N 11.44 E
Panevėžys 76 55.44 N 24.21 E
Panfang 100 27.54 N 115.57 E
Panfilov 86 44.10 N 80.01 E
Panfilovo 80 50.26 N 42.55 E
Pāng ≃ 110 20.58 N 98.30 E
Panga 154 1.51 N 26.25 E
Pangala 152 3.19 S 14.34 E
Pangalanes, Canal des ≊ 157b 22.40 S 47.50 E
Pangandaran 115a 7.41 S 108.39 E
Pangani 154 5.26 S 38.58 E
Pangani ≃ 154 5.26 S 38.58 E
Panganiran 116 13.02 N 123.26 E
Pangantocan 116 7.50 N 124.49 E
Panganuran 116 7.24 N 122.03 E
Pangasinan □[4] 116 16.00 N 120.20 E
Pangbourne 42 51.29 N 1.05 W
Pangburn 194 35.25 N 91.50 W
Pange 56 49.05 N 6.22 E
Pangfou → Bengbu 100 32.58 N 117.24 E
Pangga, Tanjung › 115b 8.55 S 116.02 E
Panggezhuang, Zhg. 105 39.16 N 115.49 E
Panggezhuang, Zhg. 105 39.38 N 116.19 E
Panghkam 110 23.53 N 97.37 E
Pangi 154 3.11 S 26.38 E
Pangian 112 1.06 S 119.24 E
Pangjiabu 105 40.36 N 115.27 E
Pangkah 115a 6.58 S 109.10 E
Pangkajene 112 4.50 S 119.32 E
Pangkalanbrandan 114 4.01 N 98.17 E
Pangkalanbuun 112 2.41 S 111.37 E
Pangkalansusu 114 4.06 N 98.14 E
Pangkalaseang, Tanjung › 112 0.42 S 123.26 E
Pangkalpinang 112 2.08 S 106.08 E
Pangkatan 114 2.09 N 100.00 E
Pangke 114 1.01 N 103.10 E
Pangkor, Pulau I 114 4.13 N 100.33 E
Panglao 116 9.35 N 123.45 E
Panglao Island I 116 9.35 N 123.48 E
Pangman 184 49.39 N 104.38 W
Pangnirtung 176 66.08 N 65.44 W
Pango Aluquém 152 8.43 S 14.27 E
Pangŏjin 98 35.29 N 129.26 E
Pangong Tso ⊜ 120 33.45 N 78.43 E
Pangp'u → Bengbu 100 32.58 N 117.24 E
Pāngsa 126 23.47 N 89.25 E
Pangtara 110 20.57 N 96.40 E
Pangubatan 116 6.57 N 125.47 E
Panguil Bay c 116 8.01 N 123.43 E
Panguipulli 254 39.38 S 72.20 W
Panguipulli, Lago ⊜ 254 39.43 S 72.13 W
Panguiranan 116 12.04 N 123.19 E
Panguitch 200 37.49 N 112.26 W
Pangururan 114 2.37 N 98.42 E
Pangutaran 116 6.18 N 120.35 E
Pangutaran Group II 116 6.15 N 120.30 E
Pangutaran Island I 116 6.18 N 120.34 E
Pangutaran Passage ⊔ 116 6.13 N 120.30 E
Pangzidian 107 30.38 N 105.04 E
Panhandle 196 35.20 N 101.22 W
Paniai, Danau ⊜ 164 3.50 S 136.15 E
Pania-Mutombo 152 5.11 S 23.51 E
Paniau ʌ 229b 21.57 N 160.05 W
Panié, Mont ʌ 175f 20.36 S 164.46 E
Pānihāti 126 22.42 N 88.22 E
Panika 80 50.59 N 50.11 E
Panindícuaro 234 19.59 N 101.46 W
Panino, Ross. 76 56.25 N 34.34 E
Panino, Ross. 78 51.38 N 40.08 E
Panino-Nesterovo 82 55.23 N 38.11 E
Panīpāt 124 29.23 N 76.58 E
Paniqui 116 15.40 N 120.35 E
Panissières 62 45.47 N 4.20 E
Panitan 116 11.28 N 122.46 E
Panitian 116 9.05 N 118.05 E
Panj (P'andž) ≃ 120 37.06 N 68.20 E
Panjāb 120 34.22 N 67.01 E
Panjang 115a 5.28 S 105.18 E
Panjang, Pulau I 112 2.44 N 108.55 E
Panjang, Selat ⊔ 114 0.40 N 102.30 E
Panje 272c 18.54 N 72.57 E
Panjgūr 128 26.58 N 64.06 E
Panji 114 2.34 N 97.50 E
Panjiapie 100 32.54 N 120.42 E
Panjiatun 104 41.04 N 121.38 E
Panjim → Panaji 122 15.29 N 73.50 E
Pānjkora ≃ 123 34.39 N 71.44 E
Panjnad ≃ 123 28.57 N 70.30 E
Panjpāi 120 29.55 N 66.30 E
Panjshār ≃ 120 34.38 N 69.42 E
Pankakoski 26 63.19 N 30.09 E
Panke ≃ 264a 52.32 N 13.22 E
Panker 54 54.20 N 10.34 E
Pānkhāli 126 22.37 N 89.31 E
Pankof, Cape › 180 54.40 N 163.04 W
Pankow ●[8] 54 52.34 N 13.25 E
Pankratovo 76 59.10 N 43.30 E
Pankshin 150 9.20 N 9.24 E
Panlong, Zhg. 100 25.52 N 114.52 E
Panlong, Zhg. 106 31.58 N 121.35 E
Panlong, Zhg. 106 31.11 N 121.16 E
Panlong (Lo) ≃ 110 21.18 N 105.25 E
Panlongzhen 107 29.31 N 105.17 E
P'anmunjŏm 98 37.57 N 126.40 E
Panna 124 24.43 N 80.12 E
Pannawonica 162 21.44 S 116.22 E
Panni 68 41.13 N 15.16 E
Panningen 52 51.20 N 5.59 E
Pannonhalma ◆[1] 30 47.28 N 17.50 E
Panoche Creek ≃ 226 36.44 N 120.31 W
Panola 194 31.58 N 86.23 W
Panola □[6] 222 32.07 N 94.30 W
Páno Lévkara 130 34.52 N 33.18 E
Panopah 112 1.56 S 111.11 E
Páno Panayiá 130 34.55 N 32.38 E
Páno Plátres 130 34.53 N 32.52 E
Panora 198 41.41 N 94.21 W
Panorama 255 21.21 S 51.51 W
Pánormos 38 37.38 N 25.02 E
Panovo, Ross. 24 59.48 N 46.27 E
Panovo, Ross. 88 58.58 N 101.58 E
P'anp'yŏng-ni 98 40.28 N 125.49 E
Panruti 122 11.46 N 79.33 E
Pansfelde 54 51.39 N 11.16 E
Panshan 104 41.12 N 122.04 E
Panshanger Aerodrome ⊠ 260 51.48 N 0.08 W
Pansik, Rápido ↳ 236 14.30 N 85.15 W
Pansionat 265b 55.59 N 37.41 E
Pānskura 126 22.25 N 87.42 E
Pantabañgan 116 15.50 N 121.09 E
Pantajevka 78 48.41 N 32.53 E
Pantalica, Necropoli di ⊥ 70 37.08 N 15.01 E
Pantanal Matogrossense, Parque Nacional do ♦ 248 17.35 S 57.40 W
Pantanaw 110 16.59 N 95.28 E
Pântano 256 22.23 S 46.01 W
Pântano, Ribeirão do ≃ 256 22.15 S 45.59 W
Pantar, Pulau I 112 8.25 S 124.07 E
Pantelejmonovka 83 48.12 N 37.59 E
Pantelleria 70 36.50 N 11.57 E
Pantelleria, Isola di I 70 36.47 N 12.00 E
Panteón Nacional ⊥ 286c 10.31 N 66.55 W
Pantepec ≃ 234 20.56 N 97.44 W
Pantha 110 23.49 N 94.33 E
Pantheon ⊥ 267a 41.55 N 12.29 E
Panther Creek ≃, Id., U.S. 202 45.19 N 114.24 W
Panther Creek ≃, Ky., U.S. 194 37.45 N 87.19 W
Panther Creek, South Fork ≃ 194 37.42 N 87.05 W
Panther Lake 210 43.19 N 75.54 W
Pantin 50 48.54 N 2.24 E
Pantitlán ●[8] 286a 19.25 N 99.05 W
Panto, Tanjung › 115a 6.51 S 105.54 E
Panton, Mount ʌ[2] 162 17.21 S 129.13 E
Pantonlabu 114 5.08 N 97.28 E
Pantry Brook ≃ 283 42.24 N 71.22 W
Panu 152 3.48 S 19.07 E
Pánuco 234 22.03 N 98.10 W
Pánuco ≃ 234 22.16 N 97.47 W
Panuke Lake ⊜ 186 44.48 N 64.07 W
Panukulan 116 14.56 N 121.49 E
Pānuria 126 23.49 N 86.58 E
Pan'utino 78 48.56 N 36.17 E
Panvel 122 18.59 N 73.06 E
Panvel ≃ 272c 19.01 N 73.04 W
Panvel Creek ≃ 272c 18.59 N 73.00 E
Panwāri 124 25.27 N 79.29 E
Panxi 106 30.35 N 119.20 E
Panxian 102 25.50 N 104.36 E
Panxidu 98 35.39 N 115.52 E

ENGLISH

Name	Page	Lat.°′	Long.°′

Panyabungan 114 0.51 N 99.33 E
Panyam 150 9.25 N 9.13 E
Panyang 140 10.04 N 29.58 E
Panyčevo 86 57.05 N 81.49 E
Panyu 100 22.57 N 113.20 E
Panzerstausee ⊜[1] 263 51.11 N 7.16 E
Panzhuang 105 39.20 N 117.28 E
Panzi 152 7.13 S 17.58 E
Panzós 236 15.24 N 89.40 W
Pao ≃, Thai 110 16.13 N 103.43 E
Pao ≃, Ven. 246 8.06 N 64.17 W
Pao ≃, Ven. 246 8.33 N 68.01 W
Paochi → Baoji 102 34.23 N 107.09 E
Pão de Açúcar 250 9.45 S 37.26 W
Pão de Açúcar (Sugar Loaf) ʌ 287a 22.57 S 43.09 W
Paoki → Baoji 102 34.23 N 107.09 E
Paola, It. 68 39.22 N 16.03 E
Paola, Ks., U.S. 198 38.34 N 94.52 W
Paoli, In., U.S. 218 38.33 N 86.28 W
Paoli, Pa., U.S. 208 40.02 N 75.28 W
Paoli, Wi., U.S. 216 42.56 N 89.32 W
Paonia 200 38.52 N 107.35 W
Pāonta Sāhib 124 30.27 N 77.37 E
Paopao 174s 17.31 S 149.49 W
Paoshenmiao 98 41.12 N 118.17 E
Paotai Yingzi 98 41.48 N 115.12 E
Paoting → Baoding 105 38.52 N 115.29 E
Paotow → Baotou 102 40.40 N 109.59 E
Paoua 152 7.15 N 16.26 E
Paoying → Baoying 100 33.16 N 119.20 E
P'aozero, ozero ⊜ 24 66.05 N 30.58 E
Paozi 104 42.13 N 122.19 E
Pap 85 40.53 N 71.07 E
Pápa 30 47.19 N 17.28 E
Papa, Sound of ⊔ 46a 60.18 N 1.41 W
Papagaio 250 6.01 S 45.21 W
Papagaio ≃, Bra. 246 1.53 S 62.35 W
Papagaio ≃, Bra. 248 12.56 S 58.18 W
Papagayo ≃ 234 16.46 N 99.43 W
Papagayo, Golfo de c 236 10.42 N 85.50 W
Papago Indian Reservation ●[4] 200 32.20 N 112.00 W
Papaikou 229d 19.47 N 155.05 W
Papakating Creek ≃ 276 41.11 N 74.38 W
Papakura 172 37.04 S 174.57 E
Papalia 112 5.58 S 124.01 E
Papaloapan ≃ 234 18.42 N 95.38 W
Papanoa 234 17.21 N 101.02 W
Papantla [de Olarte] 234 20.27 N 97.19 W
Papar, Indon. 115a 7.41 S 112.04 E
Papar, Malay. 112 5.44 N 115.56 E
Papara, Poly. fr. 174s 17.44 S 149.21 W
Papara, Sol.Is. 175e 7.02 S 156.48 E
Paparoa 172 36.06 S 174.14 E
Paparoa National Park ♦ 172 42.05 S 171.25 E
Paparoa Range ⩘ 172 42.00 S 171.35 E
Papasidero 68 39.52 N 15.54 E
Papa Stour I 46a 60.20 N 1.42 W
Papatoetoe 172 36.58 S 174.52 E
Papawai Point › 229a 20.47 N 156.33 W
Papa Westray I 46 59.21 N 2.54 W
Papeari 174s 17.45 S 149.21 W
Papeete 174s 17.32 S 149.34 W
Papelón 286c 10.27 N 66.47 W
Papenburg 52 53.05 N 7.23 E
Papendrecht 52 51.50 N 4.40 E
Papenoo 174s 17.30 S 149.25 W
Papenoo ≃ 174s 17.30 S 149.25 W
Papetoai 174s 17.29 S 149.52 W
Papey I 24a 64.37 N 14.11 W
Paphlagonia □[9] 130 41.10 N 32.45 E
Paphos → Néa Páfos 130 34.45 N 32.25 E
Papilė 76 56.09 N 22.48 E
Papillion 198 41.09 N 96.02 W
Papineau 216 40.58 N 87.43 W
Papineau □[6] 206 45.50 N 75.00 W
Papineau, Lac ⊜ 206 45.48 N 74.46 W
Papineau Creek ≃ 212 45.13 N 77.43 W
Papineau-Labelle, Réserve ♦ 188 45.55 N 75.20 W
Papineau Lake ⊜ 212 45.20 N 77.50 W
Papineauville 206 45.37 N 75.01 W
Paposo 252 25.01 S 70.28 W
Papouasie Nouvelle-Guinée → Papua New Guinea □[1] 164 6.00 S 150.00 E
Papozze 64 44.59 N 12.02 E
Pappenheim, Dtsch. 54 50.47 N 10.27 E
Pappenheim, Dtsch. 56 48.56 N 10.58 E
Paps of Jura ⩘ 46 55.55 N 6.00 W
Papua, Gulf of c 164 8.30 S 145.00 E
Papua Neuguinea → Papua New Guinea □[1] 164 6.00 S 150.00 E
Papua New Guinea □[1] 164 6.00 S 147.00 E
Papuasia Nueva Guinea → Papua New Guinea □[1] 164 6.00 S 150.00 E
Papucaia 256 22.37 S 42.44 W
Papudo 252 32.31 S 71.27 W
Papulovo 24 60.34 N 48.00 E
Papun 110 18.04 N 97.27 E
Papunáua ≃ 246 2.09 N 70.32 W
Papunya 162 23.16 S 131.54 E
Papurí ≃ 246 0.36 N 69.11 W
Paquequer ≃ 256 22.12 S 42.54 W
Paquequer, Serra do ⩘ 256 22.12 S 42.40 W
Paquera 236 9.50 N 84.56 W
Paquetá, Ilha de I 287a 22.46 S 43.06 W
Par 42 50.21 N 4.43 W
Pará □[3] 250 4.00 S 53.00 W
Para □[5] 250 5.30 N 55.15 W
Pará ≃, Bra. 250 1.30 S 48.55 W
Pará ≃, Bra. 255 19.13 S 45.07 W
Para ≃, Ross. 80 54.23 N 40.52 E
Pará, Ilha do I 250 0.18 S 51.15 W
Para, Pulau I 112 3.05 N 125.30 E
Parabel' 86 58.43 N 81.31 E
Parabel' ≃ 86 58.44 N 81.35 E
Pará → Belém 250 1.27 S 48.29 W
Parabiago 62 45.33 N 8.57 E
Parabita 68 40.03 N 18.08 E
Paraburdoo 162 23.14 S 117.48 E
Paracale 116 14.17 N 122.48 E
Paracambi 256 22.37 S 43.43 W
Paracari ≃ 250 4.36 S 57.47 W
Paracas, Bahía de c 248 13.50 S 76.17 W
Paracas, Península de ›[1] 248 13.48 S 76.24 W
Paracatu 255 17.13 S 46.52 W
Paracatu ≃, Bra. 255 16.30 S 45.04 W
Paracatu ≃, Bra. 255 16.35 S 45.06 W
Paracel Islands → Xisha Qundao II 108 16.30 N 112.15 E
Parachilna 166 31.08 S 138.23 E
Pārachinār 120 33.54 N 70.06 E
Paracho de Verduzco 234 19.39 N 102.04 W
Parachute 200 39.27 N 108.03 W
Paraćin 38 43.52 N 21.24 E
Parácuaro 234 20.09 N 100.46 W
Paracuellos de Jarama 266a 40.30 N 3.32 W
Paracuru 250 3.24 S 39.04 W
Parád 30 47.55 N 20.02 E
Parada, Punta › 248 15.22 S 75.12 W
Paradas 34 37.18 N 5.30 W
Paradino 76 53.59 N 31.51 E

DEUTSCH

Name	Seite	Breite°′	Länge°′ E = Ost

Paradise, Guy. 246 6.45 N 58.00 W
Paradise, Ca., U.S. 204 39.44 N 121.38 W
Paradise, Mt., U.S. 202 47.23 N 114.48 W
Paradise, Nv., U.S. 204 36.09 N 115.10 W
Paradise, Pa., U.S. 208 40.01 N 76.08 W
Paradise, Tx., U.S. 222 33.09 N 97.41 W
Paradise Hill, Sk., Can. 184 53.32 N 109.28 W
Paradise Hill, Ak., U.S. 180 62.25 N 160.03 W
Paradise Island I 240b 25.05 N 77.19 W
Paradise Mountain ʌ 171a 27.45 S 152.02 E
Paradise Valley, Az., U.S. 200 33.31 N 111.56 W
Paradise Valley, Nv., U.S. 204 41.29 N 117.32 W
Parado 115b 8.45 S 118.36 E
Parado ≃ 250 10.17 S 55.39 W
Pāradwīp 120 20.16 N 86.37 E
Parafield 168b 34.47 S 138.38 E
Parafijevka 78 50.53 N 32.38 E
Paragačaj 84 39.07 N 45.56 E
Paragon 218 39.23 N 86.33 W
Paragonah 200 37.53 N 112.46 W
Paragould 194 36.03 N 90.30 W
Paraguá ≃, Bol. 248 13.34 S 61.53 W
Paragua ≃, Ven. 246 6.55 N 62.55 W
Paraguaçu 256 21.33 S 45.44 W
Paraguaçu ≃ 255 12.45 S 38.54 W
Paraguaçu Paulista 255 22.25 S 50.34 W
Paraguaipoa 246 11.21 N 71.57 W
Paraguaná, Península de ›[1] 246 11.55 N 70.00 W
Paraguarí 252 25.38 S 57.09 W
Paraguarí □[5] 252 26.00 S 57.10 W
Paraguay □[1], S.A. 244 23.00 S 58.00 W
Paraguay □[1], S.A. 252 23.00 S 58.00 W
Paraguay (Paraguai) ≃ 18 27.18 S 58.38 W
Parahyba → João Pessoa 250 7.07 S 34.52 W
Parai, Represa do ⊜[1] 256 23.20 S 45.35 W
Paraíba □[3] 250 7.15 S 36.30 W
Paraíba do Sul 256 22.09 S 43.17 W
Paraíba do Sul ≃ 255 21.37 S 41.03 W
Paraibano 250 6.30 S 44.01 W
Paraibuna 256 23.23 S 45.39 W
Paraibuna ≃, Bra. 256 22.06 S 43.08 W
Paraibuna ≃, Bra. 256 23.22 S 45.40 W
Paraibuna, Represa do ⊜[1] 256 23.25 S 45.30 W
Paraíso, Bra. 255 19.03 S 52.59 W
Paraíso, Bra. 256 22.19 S 45.42 W
Paraíso, C.R. 236 9.50 N 83.51 W
Paraíso, Méx. 234 18.24 N 93.14 W
Paraiso, Pan. 236 9.02 N 79.38 W
Paraíso do Norte 255 23.13 S 52.38 W
Paraíso Garcia 256 21.32 S 43.53 W
Paraíso Novillero 234 18.16 N 95.59 W
Paraisópolis 256 22.33 S 45.47 W
Paraitinga ≃, Bra. 256 23.34 S 46.02 W
Paraitinga ≃, Bra. 256 23.22 S 45.40 W
Parakan 115a 7.17 S 110.06 E
Parakou 150 9.21 N 2.37 E
Paralía Aspropírgos 267c 38.02 N 23.35 E
Paralímni 130 35.02 N 33.59 E
Parama Island I 164 9.00 S 143.25 E
Paramakkudi 122 9.33 N 78.36 E
Paramaribo 250 5.50 N 55.10 W
Parambu 250 6.13 S 40.43 W
Paramillo, Parque Nacional ♦ 246 7.15 N 76.15 W
Paramirim 255 13.26 S 42.15 W
Paramirim ≃ 250 11.34 S 43.18 W
Paramithiá 38 39.28 N 20.30 E
Paramonga 248 10.40 S 77.50 W
Paramoti 250 4.06 S 39.15 W
Paramount 228 33.53 N 118.09 W
Paramus 210 40.56 N 74.04 W
Paramušir, ostrov I 74 50.25 N 155.50 E
Paramus Park ●[9] 276 40.57 N 74.04 W
Paran, Nahal (Wādī al-Jirāfī) V 132 30.24 N 35.10 E
Paraná, Arg. 252 31.44 S 60.32 W
Paranã, Bra. 255 12.33 S 47.52 W
Paraná □[3] 252 24.00 S 51.00 W
Paranã ≃, Bra. 255 12.30 S 48.14 W
Paraná ≃, S.A. 18 33.43 S 59.15 W
Paraná, Pico ʌ 252 25.16 S 48.48 W
Paranabi 256 23.54 S 45.14 W
Paraná Bravo ≃[1] 258 33.53 S 58.27 W
Paranacito ≃ 258 33.44 S 58.33 W
Paraná de las Palmas ≃[1] 258 34.18 S 58.33 W
Paranaguá 252 25.31 S 48.30 W
Paranaguá, Baía de c 252 25.29 S 48.33 W
Paraná Guazú ≃[1] 258 34.00 S 58.25 W
Paranaíba 255 19.40 S 51.11 W
Paranaíba ≃ 255 20.07 S 51.05 W
Paranaidji 250 6.33 S 47.27 W
Paranaíta ≃ 250 9.28 S 56.43 W
Paranam 250 5.37 N 55.06 W
Paraná Miní ≃[1] 258 34.13 S 58.25 W
Paranapanema ≃ 255 22.40 S 53.09 W
Paranapiacaba 256 23.47 S 46.19 W
Paranapiacaba, Serra do ⩘ 252 24.20 S 49.00 W
Parañaque 269f 14.30 N 120.59 E
Paranavaí 255 23.04 S 52.28 W
Parang, Pil. 116 7.23 N 124.16 E
Parang, Pil. 116 5.55 N 120.54 E
Parang, Pulau I 115a 5.45 S 110.14 E
Paran'ga 80 56.43 N 49.24 E
Paranhos 255 23.55 S 55.25 W
Paranjang 98 37.08 N 126.55 E
Paranoá, Lago do ⊜ 255 15.48 S 47.50 W
Párao de Masa, Puerto de)(34 42.38 N 3.46 W
Paraopeba 255 19.18 S 44.25 W
Parapara 246 9.44 N 67.18 W
Paraparaumu 172 40.55 S 175.01 E
Paraparaumu Beach 172 40.54 S 174.59 E
Parapayè 58 45.55 N 7.32 E
Parapetí ≃ 248 18.58 S 62.21 W
Parara 112 2.37 S 120.07 E
Parás, Méx. 196 26.30 N 99.31 W
Paras, Perú 248 13.30 S 74.35 W
Parasan 116 8.05 N 123.33 E
Parāsī 124 27.32 N 83.40 E
Parāsia 124 22.12 N 78.46 E
Parasida 126 23.46 N 87.20 E
Parasnāth 124 23.59 N 86.02 E
Paratei 256 23.14 S 46.00 W
Parateí ≃ 256 23.12 S 46.00 W
Parati 256 23.13 S 44.43 W
Paratico 64 45.39 N 9.57 E
Parati-Mirim 256 23.14 S 44.38 W
Paratinga 255 12.42 S 43.10 W
Paratoo 166 32.42 S 139.22 E
Parauapebas ≃ 250 5.35 S 49.41 W
Parauari ≃ 250 4.36 S 57.47 W
Paraúna 255 17.02 S 50.26 W
Paravani, ozero ⊜ 84 41.26 N 43.48 E
Para Wirra Recreation Park ♦ 168b 34.43 S 138.50 E
Paray-le-Monial 32 46.27 N 4.07 E
Parbakalan 114 2.38 N 98.27 E
Pārbati ≃ 124 25.51 N 76.36 E
Pārbatipur 124 25.39 N 88.55 E
Parbhani 122 19.16 N 76.47 E
Parbig 86 57.14 N 81.24 E
Parbig ≃ 86 57.37 N 82.18 E
Parbold 262 53.36 N 2.46 W
Parburuan 114 1.52 N 99.55 E
Parchen 54 52.21 N 12.05 E
Parchim 54 53.25 N 11.51 E
Parchment 216 42.19 N 85.34 W
Parchomenko 83 48.34 N 39.43 E
Parchomovka 78 50.08 N 35.01 E
Parcines (Partschins) 64 46.41 N 11.04 E
Parczew 30 51.39 N 22.54 E

Symbols in the index entries represent the broad categories identified in the key at the right. Symbols with superior numbers (⩘[1]) identify subcategories (see complete key on page I · 1).

Symbole im Register stellen die rechts im Schlüssel erklärten Kategorien dar. Symbole mit hochgestellten Ziffern (⩘[1]) bezeichnen Unterabteilungen einer Kategorie (vgl. vollständiger Schlüssel auf Seite I · 1).

Los símbolos incluídos en el texto del índice representan las grandes categorias identificadas con la clave a la derecha. Los símbolos con numeros en su parte superior (⩘[1]) identifican las subcategorías (véase la clave completa en la página I · 1).

Les symboles de l'index représentent les catégories indiquées dans la légende à droite. Les symboles suivis d'un indice (⩘[1]) représentent des sous-catégories (voir légende complète à la page I · 1).

Os símbolos incluídos no texto do índice representam as grandes categorias identificadas com a chave à direita. Os símbolos com números em sua parte superior (⩘[1]) identificam as subcategorias (veja-se a chave completa à página I · 1).

	English	Deutsch	Español	Français	Português
ʌ	Mountain	Berg	Montaña	Montagne	Montanha
⩘	Mountains	Gebirge	Montañas	Montagnes	Montanhas
)(	Pass	Paß	Paso	Col	Passo
V	Valley, Canyon	Tal, Cañon	Valle, Cañón	Vallée, Canyon	Vale, Canhão
≍	Plain	Ebene	Llano	Plaine	Planície
›	Cape	Kap	Cabo	Cap	Cabo
I	Island	Insel	Isla	Île	Ilha
II	Islands	Inseln	Islas	Îles	Ilhas
⊥	Other Topographic Features	Andere Topographische Objekte	Otros Elementos Topográficos	Autres données topographiques	Outros acidentes topográficos

ESPAÑOL · FRANÇAIS · PORTUGUÊS

Nombre / Nom / Nome	Página / Page	Lat.°′	Long.°′ W = Oeste / Ouest
Pardee Reservoir ⊜ [1]	226	38.16 N	120.51 W
Pardeeville	190	43.32 N	89.18 W
Pardes Hanna-Karkur	132	32.28 N	34.58 E
Pārdi	122	20.31 N	72.57 E
Parding	120	32.52 N	88.39 E
Pardo ≃, Bra.	250	5.21 S	52.53 W
Pardo ≃, Bra.	252	29.59 S	52.23 W
Pardo ≃, Bra.	255	15.48 S	44.48 W
Pardo ≃, Bra.	255	20.10 S	48.38 W
Pardo ≃, Bra.	255	22.55 S	49.58 W
Pardo ≃, Bra.	255	15.39 S	38.57 W
Pardo ≃, Bra.	255	21.46 S	52.09 W
Pardo ≃, Bra.	256	23.32 S	45.30 W
Pardo ≃, Bra.	256	21.25 S	42.39 W
Pardomuan	114	2.06 N	98.20 E
Pardubice	30	50.02 N	15.47 E
Pare	115a	7.46 S	112.11 E
Parece Vela → Okino-Tori-shima I	90	20.25 N	136.00 E
Parecis	248	14.09 S	56.56 W
Parecis ≃	248	12.56 S	56.43 W
Parecis, Chapada dos ⋏	248	13.00 S	60.00 W
Parede	266c	38.41 N	9.21 W
Paredes de Nava	34	42.09 N	4.41 W
Paredón	232	25.56 N	100.58 W
Parelhas	250	6.41 S	36.39 W
Parelheiros ◆ [8]	256	23.51 S	46.44 W
Pareloup, Lac de ⊜	32	44.15 N	2.45 E
Paremata	172	41.07 S	174.52 E
Parempei I	174r	7.01 N	158.15 E
Paren'	74	62.28 N	163.05 E
Paren' ≃	74	62.25 N	163.10 E
Parengarenga Harbour ⊂	172	34.31 S	172.57 E
Parent	176	47.55 N	74.37 W
Parent, Lac ⊜	190	48.38 N	77.03 W
Parentis-en-Born	32	44.21 N	1.05 W
Pareora	172	44.30 S	171.12 E
Parepare	112	4.01 S	119.38 E
Parera	252	35.08 S	64.32 W
Parets del Vallès	266d	41.34 N	2.14 E
Parey	54	52.22 N	11.59 E
Parfenjevo, Ross.	24	61.21 N	42.43 E
Parfenjevo, Ross.	80	58.29 N	43.25 E
Parfentevo	82	55.06 N	38.49 E
Parfino	76	57.58 N	31.41 E
Parforce-Heide ◆ [3]	264a	52.22 N	13.10 E
Párga	38	39.17 N	20.23 E
Pārgaon	272c	18.59 N	73.05 E
Pargarutan	114	1.28 N	99.20 E
Pargas (Parainen)	26	60.18 N	22.18 E
Pargey Creek ≃	285	39.49 N	75.18 W
Pargny-sur-Saulx	56	48.46 N	4.50 E
Pargolovo ◆ [8]	265a	60.04 N	30.18 E
Parham	240c	17.05 N	61.46 W
Parhebangan	114	2.15 N	98.45 E
Pari ◆ [8]	287b	23.32 S	46.37 W
Paria ≃	200	36.52 N	111.36 W
Paria, Gulf of ⊂	246	10.20 N	62.00 W
Paria, Península de ≻ [1]	241r	10.40 N	62.10 W
Pariaguán	246	8.51 N	64.43 W
Pariaman	112	0.38 S	100.08 E
Pariamanu ≃	248	12.26 S	69.16 W
Pariči	76	52.48 N	29.25 E
Paricutín ∧ [1]	234	19.28 N	102.15 W
Parida, Isla I	236	8.07 N	82.20 W
Pariette Draw V	200	40.02 N	109.45 W
Parigi, Indon.	112	0.48 S	120.10 E
Parigi, Indon.	115a	6.12 S	106.22 E
Parigné-L'Évêque	50	47.56 N	0.22 E
Parika	246	6.52 N	58.25 W
Parikkala	26	61.33 N	29.30 E
Parima ≃	246	3.34 N	63.47 W
Parima, Sierra ⋏	246	2.30 N	64.00 W
Pariñas, Punta ≻	246	4.40 S	81.20 W
Parîngu Mare, Vîrful ∧	38	45.22 N	23.33 E
Parintins	250	2.36 S	56.44 W
Paripiranga	250	10.41 S	37.52 W
Pariquera-Açu	252	24.43 S	47.53 W
Paris, On., Can.	212	43.12 N	80.23 W
Paris, Fr.	50	48.52 N	2.20 E
Paris, Fr.	261	48.52 N	2.20 E
Paris, Ar., U.S.	194	35.17 N	93.43 W
Paris, Id., U.S.	202	42.13 N	111.24 W
Paris, Il., U.S.	194	39.36 N	87.41 W
Paris, Ky., U.S.	218	38.12 N	84.15 W
Paris, Me., U.S.	188	44.15 N	70.30 W
Paris, Mo., U.S.	219	39.28 N	92.00 W
Paris, Oh., U.S.	214	40.48 N	81.10 W
Paris, Pa., U.S.	214	40.24 N	80.31 W
Paris, Tn., U.S.	194	36.18 N	88.19 W
Paris, Tx., U.S.	196	33.39 N	95.33 W
Paris □ [5]	261	48.52 N	2.20 E
Paris, Port de ⊂	261	48.57 N	2.17 E
Parish	210	43.24 N	76.07 W
Parisien de Pantin, Cimetière ◆	261	48.54 N	2.23 E
Parisienne, Ile I	190	46.41 N	84.44 W
Paris-le-Bourget, Aéroport de ⊠	50	49.00 N	2.25 E
Parismina	236	10.12 N	83.38 W
Parismina ≃	236	10.19 N	83.21 W
Paris-Orly, Aéroport de ⊠	50	48.43 N	2.22 E
Paris-Plage, Aéroport ⊠	50	50.31 N	1.38 E
Parit	112	3.10 S	104.38 E
Parita, Bahía de ⊂	236	8.08 N	80.24 W
Parit Bunga	114	2.04 N	102.33 E
Parit Buntar	114	5.07 N	100.30 E
Pariti	112	10.01 S	123.43 E
Parit Jawa	114	1.57 N	102.39 E
Parižskaja Kommuna ◆ [8]	83	48.26 N	38.49 E
Park ≃	198	48.28 N	97.09 W
Park, North Branch ≃	198	48.26 N	97.27 W
Park, South Branch ≃	198	48.26 N	97.27 W
Parka	154	4.31 N	27.20 E
Parkano	26	62.01 N	23.01 E
Parkany	78	46.49 N	29.31 E
Parkchester	285	40.00 N	75.35 W
Park City, Il., U.S.	216	42.21 N	87.53 W
Park City, Ks., U.S.	198	37.48 N	97.19 W
Park City, Mt., U.S.	202	45.37 N	108.55 W
Park City, Ut,. U.S.	200	40.38 N	111.29 W
Park Creek ≃	285	40.13 N	75.08 W
Parkdale, P.E., Can.	186	46.15 N	63.07 W
Parkdale, Mo., U.S.	219	38.29 N	90.32 W
Parkdale, Or., U.S.	224	45.31 N	121.35 W
Parkdene	273d	26.14 S	28.16 E
Parkent	85	41.18 N	69.40 E
Parker, Az., U.S.	200	34.09 N	114.17 W
Parker, Co., U.S.	198	39.31 N	104.45 W
Parker, Fl., U.S.	194	30.07 N	85.36 W
Parker, Pa., U.S.	214	41.05 N	79.41 W
Parker, S.D., U.S.	198	43.23 N	97.08 W
Parker □ [6]	222	32.48 N	97.42 W
Parker ≃	207	42.45 N	70.49 W
Parker, Cape ≻	176	75.04 N	79.40 W
Parker, Lake ⊜	220	28.04 N	81.56 W
Parker City	218	40.11 N	85.12 W
Parker Dam	204	34.17 N	114.08 W
Parker Dam ◆ [6]	200	34.18 N	114.10 W
Parker Ford	285	40.12 N	75.35 W
Parker Peak ∧	198	43.24 N	103.41 W
Parker Range	162	31.38 S	119.35 E
Parker River National Wildlife Refuge ◆ [4]	283	42.45 N	70.48 W
Parkersburg, Il., U.S.	194	38.36 N	88.03 W
Parkersburg, Ia., U.S.	190	42.34 N	92.47 W
Parkersburg, W.V., U.S.	188	39.16 N	81.33 W
Parkers Creek ≃	285	40.00 N	74.53 W
Parkers Prairie	198	46.09 N	95.19 W
Parkerville	168a	31.53 S	116.09 E
Parker Volcano ∧ [1]	116	6.07 N	124.54 E
Parkes	166	33.08 S	148.11 E
Parkesburg	208	39.57 N	75.55 W
Park Falls	190	45.56 N	90.26 W
Park Forest	216	41.28 N	87.38 W
Parkgate, Eng., U.K.	262	53.18 N	3.05 W
Parkgate, Eng., U.K.	262	53.16 N	2.20 W
Park Hall	208	38.13 N	76.25 W
Parkhill, On., Can.	190	43.09 N	81.41 W
Parkhill, Pa., U.S.	214	40.22 N	78.52 W
Parkhill Gardens	273d	26.14 S	28.11 E
Parkin	194	35.15 N	90.34 W
Park Lake	216	42.48 N	84.27 W
Parkland, Pa., U.S.	285	40.09 N	74.56 W
Parkland, Wa., U.S.	224	47.09 N	122.25 W
Parklawn	284c	38.50 N	77.09 W
Park Layne	218	39.53 N	84.03 W
Parklea	274a	33.44 S	150.57 E
Parkman	214	41.22 N	81.03 W
Park Meadows	279b	40.18 N	79.44 W
Park Orchards	274b	37.46 S	145.13 E
Park Plateau ⋏ [1]	198	37.15 N	104.45 W
Park Range ⋏	200	40.40 N	106.40 W
Park Rapids	198	46.55 N	95.03 W
Park Ridge, Il., U.S.	216	42.00 N	87.50 W
Park Ridge, N.J., U.S.	276	41.02 N	74.02 W
Park Ridge Farms	285	40.10 N	74.42 W
Park River	198	48.23 N	97.44 W
Parkrose	224	45.33 N	122.33 W
Park Rynie	158	30.25 S	30.35 E
Parks	180	57.38 N	154.00 W
Parks Creek ≃	212	44.17 N	77.21 W
Park Shore Resort	216	41.55 N	85.59 W
Parkside, Md., U.S.	284c	39.02 N	77.06 W
Parkside, Pa., U.S.	285	39.52 N	75.23 W
Parksley	208	37.46 N	75.39 W
Park Station ◆ [5]	273d	26.12 S	28.03 E
Parkstein	60	49.44 N	12.04 E
Parkstetten	60	48.55 N	12.36 E
Parkston	198	43.23 N	97.59 W
Parksville, B.C., Can.	182	49.19 N	124.19 W
Parksville, N.Y., U.S.	210	41.51 N	74.45 W
Parktown ◆ [8]	273d	26.11 S	28.03 E
Parktown North ◆ [8]	273d	26.09 S	28.02 E
Parkview	279b	40.30 N	79.56 W
Parkville, Md., U.S.	208	39.22 N	76.32 W
Parkville, Mo., U.S.	194	39.11 N	94.40 W
Parkwater	202	47.40 N	117.19 W
Parkway, Ca., U.S.	226	38.29 N	121.27 W
Parkway, Mo., U.S.	219	38.20 N	90.57 W
Parkwood	284c	39.01 N	77.05 W
Parla	34	40.14 N	3.46 W
Parlākimidi	122	18.47 N	84.06 E
Parle, Lac qui ⊜	198	45.07 N	96.00 W
Parli	122	18.51 N	76.32 E
Parliament, Houses of ⊌	260	51.30 N	0.07 W
Parlier	226	36.36 N	119.31 W
Parma, It.	64	44.48 N	10.20 E
Parma, Id., U.S.	202	43.47 N	116.56 W
Parma, Mi., U.S.	216	42.15 N	84.35 W
Parma, Mo., U.S.	194	36.36 N	89.48 W
Parma, Oh., U.S.	214	41.24 N	81.43 W
Parma □ [4]	64	44.40 N	10.10 E
Parma ≃	64	44.56 N	10.26 E
Parma Heights	214	41.23 N	81.45 W
Parmain	261	49.07 N	2.12 E
Parmatown Mall ◆ [9]	279a	41.23 N	81.44 W
Parnaguá	250	10.13 S	44.38 W
Parnahyba → Parnaíba	250	2.54 S	41.47 W
Parnaíba	250	2.54 S	41.47 W
Parnaíba ≃	250	3.00 S	41.50 W
Parnaìbinha ≃	250	9.17 S	45.55 W
Parnamirim	250	8.05 S	39.34 W
Parnarama	250	5.41 S	43.06 W
Parnassós ∧	38	38.32 N	22.35 E
Parnassus	172	42.43 S	173.18 E
Parndorf	61	47.59 N	16.51 E
Parnell	216	40.14 N	88.42 W
Párnis ∧	38	38.11 N	23.42 E
Párnis Óros ⋏	267c	38.07 N	23.41 E
Parnon ⋏	38	37.18 N	22.35 E
Pärnu	76	58.24 N	24.32 E
Pärnu ≃	76	58.23 N	24.29 E
Pärnu-Jaagupi	76	58.37 N	24.30 E
Pärnu laht ⊂	76	58.15 N	24.25 E
Paro	124	27.26 N	89.25 E
Pārola	120	20.53 N	75.07 E
Paromaj	89	52.50 N	143.02 E
Paroo	162	26.16 S	119.46 E
Paroo ≃	166	31.28 S	143.32 E
Parorā	272b	22.48 N	88.09 E
Páros	38	37.04 N	25.08 E
Páros I	38	37.08 N	25.12 E
Parow	158	33.53 S	18.37 E
Parowan	200	37.50 N	112.49 W
Parpaillon ⋏	62	44.30 N	6.40 E
Parpan	58	46.46 N	9.33 E
Parr	216	41.02 N	87.13 W
Parral, Chile	252	36.09 S	71.50 W
Parral, Oh., U.S.	214	40.33 N	81.30 W
Parral ≃	232	27.39 N	105.07 W
Parral → Hidalgo del Parral	232	26.56 N	105.40 W
Parramatta	170	33.49 S	151.00 E
Parramatta ≃	274a	33.51 S	151.14 E
Parramatta Park ♠	274a	33.49 S	151.00 E
Parramore Island I	208	37.32 N	75.38 W
Parras de la Fuente	232	25.25 N	102.11 W
Parrett ≃	42	51.13 N	3.01 W
Parrish, Al., U.S.	194	33.43 N	87.17 W
Parrish, Fl., U.S.	220	27.35 N	82.25 W
Parris Island Marine Corps Recruit Depot ■	192	32.21 N	80.41 W
Parrita	236	9.30 N	84.19 W
Parrita ≃	236	9.29 N	84.19 W
Parrsboro	186	45.24 N	64.20 W
Parry, Cape ≻	176	70.08 N	124.24 W
Parry, Mount ∧	182	52.53 N	128.45 W
Parry Bay ⊂	176	68.07 N	82.00 W
Parry Channel ʊ	16	74.20 N	98.00 W
Parry Island I	212	45.18 N	80.10 W
Parry Island Indian Reserve ◆ [4]	212	45.18 N	80.10 W
Parry Peninsula ≻ [1]	180	69.45 N	124.30 W
Parry Sound	212	45.21 N	80.02 W
Parry Sound □ [6]	212	45.25 N	79.55 W
Parry Sound ʊ	212	45.21 N	80.06 W
Parryville	208	40.49 N	75.40 W
Parsberg	60	49.09 N	11.43 E
Parsdorf	60	48.09 N	11.47 E
Parseier Spitze ∧	58	47.10 N	10.28 E
Parsęta ≃	30	54.12 N	15.33 E
Parshād	120	24.11 N	73.42 E
Parshall	198	47.57 N	102.08 W
Parshallville	281	42.41 N	83.46 W
Paršino	88	59.10 N	111.48 E
Parsippany	210	40.51 N	74.25 W
Parsippany, Lake ⊜	276	40.51 N	74.26 W
Parsnāth ∧	124	23.53 N	86.08 E
Parsnip ≃	182	55.10 N	123.00 W
Parsoburan	114	2.19 N	99.20 E
Parsonage Island I	276	40.37 N	73.37 W
Parsons, Ks., U.S.	198	37.20 N	95.15 W
Parsons, Tn., U.S.	194	35.38 N	88.07 W
Parsons, W.V., U.S.	188	39.05 N	79.40 W
Parsons, Mount ∧ [2]	164	13.33 S	135.09 E
Parson's Pond	186	50.02 N	57.43 W
Parsons Pond ⊜	186	50.00 N	57.35 W
Parsons Range ⋏	164	13.30 S	135.15 E
Parsteiner See ⊜	54	52.55 N	13.59 E
Pärsti	76	58.25 N	25.32 E
Partābpur	124	23.29 N	83.13 E
Partanna	70	37.43 N	12.53 E
Partāppur	126	21.48 N	86.44 E
Partenen	58	46.58 N	10.03 E
Parthala	272a	28.36 N	77.24 E
Parthe ≃	54	51.22 N	12.21 E
Parthenay	32	46.39 N	0.15 W
Partington	262	53.25 N	2.26 W
Partinico	70	38.03 N	13.07 E
Partizansk	89	43.08 N	133.09 E
Partizánske	30	48.39 N	18.23 E
Partizanskoje	86	55.30 N	94.24 E
Parton	44	54.34 N	3.35 W
Partridge, Point ≻	224	48.13 N	122.46 W
Partridge Creek ≃	212	44.44 N	77.13 W
Partridge Crop Lake ⊜	184	55.38 N	97.27 W
Partridge Point ≻	186	50.09 N	56.10 W
Partry	48	53.41 N	9.19 W
Partschins → Parcines	64	46.41 N	11.04 E
Paru ≃, Bra.	250	1.33 S	52.38 W
Parú ≃, Ven.	246	4.20 N	66.27 W
Parubcan	116	13.43 N	123.45 E
Paru de Este ≃	250	1.10 N	54.40 W
Paru de Oeste ≃	250	1.30 S	56.00 W
Parung	115a	6.25 S	106.42 E
Pårup, Dan.	41	55.24 N	10.20 E
Pårup, Dan.	41	56.08 N	9.21 E
Parūr	122	10.09 N	76.14 E
Paruro	248	13.46 S	71.51 W
Parutino	78	46.43 N	31.53 E
Parvān □ [4]	120	35.15 N	69.30 E
Pārvatīpuram	122	18.47 N	83.26 E
Parvin State Park ♠	208	39.30 N	75.09 W
Pârvomaj	38	42.06 N	25.13 E
Paryang	120	30.11 N	83.09 E
Påryd	26	56.34 N	15.55 E
Parys	158	27.04 S	27.16 E
Paša ≃	76	60.29 N	32.55 E
Paşabahçe ◆ [8]	267b	41.06 N	29.05 E
Pasacao	116	13.31 N	123.03 E
Pasaco	236	13.59 N	90.12 W
Pasadena, Nf., Can.	186	49.01 N	57.36 W
Pasadena, Ca., U.S.	228	34.08 N	118.08 W
Pasadena, Md., U.S.	208	39.06 N	76.34 W
Pasadena, Tx., U.S.	222	29.41 N	95.12 W
Pasado, Cabo ≻	246	0.22 S	80.30 W
Pasaje	246	3.20 S	79.49 W
Pasaje ≃	252	25.35 S	63.57 W
Pasaje Talavera ≃ [1]	258	33.53 S	58.55 W
Pa Sak ≃	110	14.21 N	100.35 E
Paşaköy	130	35.09 N	33.36 E
Pasaleng Bay ⊂	116	18.36 N	120.56 E
Paşalimanı Adası I	130	40.28 N	27.37 E
Pasān	124	22.51 N	82.12 E
Pasanauri	84	42.21 N	44.41 E
Pasangkayu	112	1.10 S	119.20 E
Pasarbantal	112	2.45 S	101.20 E
Pasarseluma	112	4.09 S	102.32 E
Pasar Senen Station ◆ [5]	269e	6.10 S	106.50 E
Pasarsorkam	114	1.53 N	98.34 E
Pasarwajo	112	5.29 S	122.50 E
Pasatiempo	226	37.02 N	122.02 W
Pasaunda	272a	28.42 N	77.21 E
Pasawng	110	18.52 N	97.18 E
Pasay	269f	14.33 N	121.00 E
Pasayten ≃	224	49.08 N	120.35 W
Pasayten, Middle Fork ≃	224	48.53 N	120.37 W
Pasayten, West Fork ≃	224	48.53 N	120.37 W
Pascack Brook ≃	276	40.59 N	73.59 W
Pascagama, Lac ⊜	190	48.34 N	75.36 W
Pascagoula	194	30.21 N	88.33 W
Pascagoula ≃	194	30.21 N	88.34 W
Pascalis, Lac ⊜	190	48.16 N	77.24 W
Paşcani	38	47.15 N	26.44 E
Pasching	61	48.15 N	14.12 E
Pasco	202	46.13 N	119.05 W
Pasco □ [5]	248	10.30 S	75.15 W
Pasco □ [6]	220	28.20 N	82.27 W
Pascoag	207	41.57 N	71.42 W
Pascoe Vale	274b	37.44 S	144.56 E
Pascua ≃	254	48.13 S	73.22 W
Pascua, Isla de (Easter Island) (Rapa Nui) I	174z	27.07 S	109.22 W
Pas-de-Calais □ [5]	50	50.30 N	2.20 E
Pas-en-Artois	50	50.09 N	2.30 E
Pasewalk	54	53.30 N	14.00 E
Pashmāl	123	35.26 N	72.36 E
Pasian di Prato	64	46.03 N	13.11 E
Pasiano di Pordenone	64	45.51 N	12.37 E
Pasig	116	14.33 N	121.05 E
Pasig ≃	269f	14.36 N	120.58 E
Pāsighāt	120	28.04 N	95.20 E
Pašija	86	58.26 N	58.16 E
P'asina ≃	74	73.50 N	87.10 E
Pasinler (Hasankale)	130	39.59 N	41.41 E
Pašino	86	55.11 N	83.00 E
P'asino, ozero ⊜	74	69.45 N	87.45 E
P'asinskij zaliv ⊂	74	74.00 N	86.00 E
Pasirganting	112	2.02 S	100.53 E
Pasir Gudang	271c	1.27 N	103.53 E
Pasirian	115a	8.13 S	113.06 E
Pasir Mas	114	6.02 N	102.08 E
Pasir Panjang	271c	1.17 N	103.47 E
Pasirpengarayan	114	0.51 N	100.16 E
Pasir Puteh, Malay.	114	5.50 N	102.24 E
Pasir Puteh, Malay.	271c	1.26 N	103.56 E
Påskallavik	26	57.10 N	16.27 E
Paskeville	168b	34.02 S	137.54 E
Paškovo, Ross.	80	53.39 N	42.25 E
Paškovo, Ross.	89	48.54 N	130.42 E
Paškovskij	78	45.02 N	39.06 E
Pasłęk	30	54.05 N	19.39 E
Pasłęka ≃	30	54.26 N	19.45 E
Pasley, Cape ≻	162	33.57 S	123.31 E
Pasley Bay ⊂	176	70.40 N	96.27 W
Pašman, Otok I	36	43.58 N	15.21 E
Pasmore ≃	166	31.07 S	139.48 E
Pašn'a	24	63.21 N	56.28 E
Pasni	128	25.16 N	63.28 E
Paso de Indios	254	43.52 S	69.06 W
Paso del Cerro	252	31.29 S	55.50 W
Paso del Macho	234	18.58 N	96.43 W
Paso de los Libres	252	29.43 S	57.05 W
Paso de los Toros	252	32.49 S	56.31 W
Paso del Rey	288	34.39 S	58.46 W
Paso del Toro	234	19.02 N	96.07 W
Paso de Ovejas	234	19.17 N	96.26 W
Paso de Patria	252	27.13 S	58.35 W
Paso de San Antonio	196	29.05 N	103.55 W
Paso Hondo	232	15.49 N	92.02 W
Paso Limay	254	40.33 S	70.26 W
Pasorapa	248	18.16 S	64.37 W
Paso Robles	226	35.37 N	120.41 W
Paso Seco	240m	17.59 N	66.23 W
Paso Severino, Embalse ⊜ [1]	258	34.15 S	56.18 W
Pašozero	76	60.02 N	34.37 E
Pasqua Indian Reserve ◆ [4]	184	50.45 N	104.02 W
Pasque Island I	207	41.27 N	70.50 W
Pasquel, Punta ≻	232	25.30 N	111.01 W
Pasquia Hills ⋏ [2]	184	53.13 N	102.37 W
Pasquotank □ [6]	208	36.26 N	76.26 W
Pasquotank ≃	192	36.10 N	76.03 W
Pasrūr	123	32.16 N	74.40 E
Passadumkeag	188	45.11 N	68.37 W
Passadumkeag Mountain ∧ [2]	188	45.10 N	68.20 W
Passage East	48	52.13 N	6.59 W
Passagem Franca	250	6.10 S	43.47 W
Passage Point ≻	176	73.29 N	115.17 W
Passage West	48	51.52 N	8.20 W
Passaic	210	40.51 N	74.07 W
Passaic □ [6]	210	40.55 N	74.10 W
Passaic ≃	276	40.43 N	74.07 W
Passamaquoddy Bay ⊂	186	45.06 N	66.59 W
Passa Quatro	256	22.23 S	44.58 W
Passa Três	256	22.42 S	44.00 W
Passau	60	48.35 N	13.28 E
Passa Vinte	256	22.13 S	44.15 W
Pass Creek ≃	198	43.45 N	101.28 W
Passero, Capo ≻	70	36.40 N	15.09 E
Passignano sul Trasimeno	66	43.11 N	12.08 E
Passirio (Passer) ≃	64	46.41 N	11.10 E
Pass Island	186	47.29 N	56.11 W
Paššskij Perevoz	76	60.24 N	32.59 E
Passo Corese	66	42.09 N	12.39 E
Passo Fundo	252	28.15 S	52.24 W
Passopisciaro	70	37.52 N	15.02 E
Passo Real, Reprêsa do ⊜ [1]	252	28.55 S	53.10 W
Passos	255	20.43 S	46.37 W
Passow	54	53.08 N	14.06 E
Passy	58	45.55 N	6.41 E
Passy ◆ [8]	261	48.52 N	2.17 E
Pastaza □ [4]	246	1.45 S	76.50 W
Pastaza ≃	246	4.50 S	76.25 W
Pastecho ≃	182	56.07 N	114.15 W
Pasteur, Lac ⊜	186	50.13 N	66.58 W
Pastillo	240m	17.59 N	66.29 W
Pasto	246	1.13 N	77.17 W
Pastol Bay ⊂	180	63.07 N	163.15 W
Pastora Peak ∧	200	36.47 N	109.10 W
Pastoria Creek ≃	228	35.01 N	118.51 W
Pastos Bons	250	6.36 S	44.05 W
Pastrana	34	40.25 N	2.55 W
Pastrengo	64	45.29 N	10.48 E
Pašukovo	82	55.55 N	38.16 E
Pasuquin	116	18.20 N	120.37 E
Pasuruan	115a	7.38 S	112.54 E
Pasvalys	76	56.04 N	24.24 E
Pásztó	30	47.55 N	19.42 E
Pata	116	5.51 N	121.10 E
Patacamaya	248	17.14 S	67.55 W
Pātāchārkuchi	120	26.31 N	91.16 E
Patagonia	200	31.32 N	110.45 W
Patagonia ◆ [1]	254	44.00 S	68.00 W
Pataha Creek ≃	202	46.31 N	117.59 W
Pata Island I	116	5.49 N	121.10 E
Pātan, India	120	23.50 N	72.07 E
Pātan, India	124	23.18 N	79.42 E
Patapsco	208	39.32 N	76.53 W
Patapsco ≃	208	39.09 N	76.27 W
Patapsco, Cooks Branch ≃	284b	39.27 N	76.53 W
Patapsco, Davis Branch ≃	284b	39.19 N	76.51 W
Patapsco, North Branch ≃	208	39.21 N	76.53 W
Patapsco, Rockburn Branch ≃	284b	39.14 N	76.43 W
Patapsco, Soapstone Branch ≃	284b	39.13 N	76.43 W
Patapsco, South Branch ≃	208	39.21 N	76.53 W
Patapsco River Neck ≻ [1]	284b	39.14 N	76.27 W
Patapsco Valley State Park ♠	208	39.20 N	76.55 W
Patargān, Daqq-e ≋	128	33.30 N	60.40 E
Pataudi	124	28.19 N	76.47 E
Pataula Creek ≃	192	31.46 N	85.02 W
Patay	50	48.03 N	1.42 E
Pataz	248	7.44 S	77.37 W
Patchewollock	166	35.23 S	142.11 E
Patchogue	210	40.45 N	73.00 W
Patchogue Bay ⊂	276	40.44 N	73.01 W
Patchway	42	51.32 N	2.34 W
Pat Cleburne, Lake ⊜ [1]	222	32.25 N	97.30 W
Pate	154	2.08 S	41.00 E
Patea	172	39.45 S	174.28 E
Patea ≃	172	39.46 S	174.29 E
Patearoa	172	45.16 S	170.03 E
Pategi	150	8.44 N	5.44 E
Pate Island I	154	2.07 S	41.03 E
Pateley Bridge	44	54.05 N	1.45 W
Patel Nagar ◆ [8]	272a	28.39 N	77.10 E
Patensie	158	33.46 S	24.49 E
Patéras Óros ∧	267c	38.07 N	23.25 E
Patergassen	64	46.49 N	13.52 E
Paterna	34	39.30 N	0.26 W
Paternal ◆ [8]	288	34.36 S	58.28 W
Paternion	64	46.43 N	13.38 E
Paternò	70	37.34 N	14.54 E
Pateros, Pil.	269f	14.33 N	121.04 E
Pateros, Wa., U.S.	202	48.03 N	119.54 W
Patersdorf	60	49.01 N	12.59 E
Paterson, Austl.	170	32.36 S	151.37 E
Paterson, S. Afr.	158	33.26 S	25.58 E
Paterson, N.J., U.S.	210	40.55 N	74.10 W
Paterson ≃	170	32.43 S	151.39 E
Paterson, Cape ≻	169	38.40 S	145.36 E
Paterson Inlet ⊂	172	46.55 S	168.03 E
Paterswolde	52	53.08 N	6.35 E
Pātghāti	126	22.53 N	89.55 E
Pathalgaon	124	22.34 N	83.28 E
Pathānkot	123	32.17 N	75.39 E
Pathānkot Airport ⊠	123	32.15 N	75.37 E
Pātharghāra	272b	22.34 N	88.35 E
Patharia	124	23.54 N	79.12 E
Pathein (Bassein)	110	16.47 N	94.44 E
Pathfinder Reservoir ⊜ [1]	200	42.30 N	106.50 W
Pathfinder Seamount ✤ [3]	16	50.55 N	143.15 W
Pathiong	140	6.46 N	30.54 E
Pathiu	110	10.42 N	99.19 E
Path of Condie	46	56.15 N	3.30 W
Pāthrāil	126	24.12 N	89.56 E
Pathro ≃	126	24.12 N	86.48 E
Pathum Thani	110	14.01 N	100.32 E
Pati, Indon.	112	0.33 S	111.19 E
Pati, Indon.	115a	6.45 S	111.01 E
Patía	246	2.04 N	77.04 W
Patía ≃	246	2.13 N	78.40 W
Patiāla	123	30.19 N	76.24 E
Patiāla ∧	123	32.32 N	72.11 E
P'atichatki	78	48.24 N	33.42 E
Pati do Alferes	256	22.25 S	43.25 W
P'atigorsk	84	44.03 N	43.04 E
Pātihāl	272b	22.39 N	88.08 E
Patikul	116	6.04 N	121.06 E
Patillas	240m	18.00 N	66.01 W
P'atimar	80	49.31 N	50.32 E
Patinti, Selat ʊ	164	0.30 S	127.45 E
Patipāda	272c	19.04 N	73.05 E
Pati Point ≻	174p	13.36 N	144.57 E
Pātiram	124	25.19 N	88.45 E
Patire, Convento del ⊌ [1]	68	39.34 N	16.35 E
Pătîrlagele	38	45.19 N	26.22 E
Pativilca	248	10.42 S	77.47 W
Pativilca ≃	248	10.44 S	77.48 W
Pātkai Range ⋏	120	27.00 N	96.00 E
Pat Mayse Reservoir ⊜ [1]	196	33.40 N	95.35 W
Pátmos I	38	37.20 N	26.33 E
Patna, India	124	25.36 N	85.07 E
Patna, India	126	21.56 N	87.52 E
Pātna, India	272b	22.59 N	88.18 E
Patna, Scot., U.K.	44	55.21 N	4.30 W
Patnāgarh	122	20.43 N	83.09 E
Patnanongan Island I	116	14.48 N	122.11 E
P'atnica, Ross.	82	54.46 N	38.09 E
P'atnica, Ross.	82	56.05 N	36.48 E
P'atnickoje, Ross.	78	50.25 N	37.51 E
P'atnickoje, Ross.	82	54.20 N	35.53 E
Pātnoli	272c	18.57 N	73.05 E
Patnoñgon	116	10.55 N	122.00 E
Patnos	84	39.14 N	42.52 E
Pato Branco	252	26.13 S	52.40 W
Patoka	219	38.45 N	89.05 W
Patoka ≃	194	38.25 N	87.44 W
Patoka Lake ⊜ [1]	194	38.20 N	86.40 W
Patokino	82	56.27 N	39.06 E
Patomskoje nagorje ⋏ [1]	88	59.00 N	115.00 E
Paton, Île I	275a	45.31 N	73.45 W
Patonga	154	2.46 N	33.18 E
Patos	250	7.01 S	37.16 W
Patos, Lagoa dos ⊂	252	31.06 S	51.15 W
Patos, Río de los ≃	252	31.18 S	69.25 W
Patos, Rio dos ≃	248	13.33 S	56.29 W
Patos de Minas	255	18.35 S	46.32 W
Patos Island I	224	48.47 N	122.56 W
P'atovskij	82	54.41 N	36.04 E
Patquía	252	30.03 S	66.53 W
Pátrai	38	38.15 N	21.44 E
Patraïkós Kólpos ⊂	38	38.14 N	21.15 E
Pātrasāer	124	23.13 N	87.31 E
Patras → Pátrai	38	38.15 N	21.44 E
Patricio Lynch, Isla I	254	48.37 S	75.26 W
Patrick Air Force Base ■	220	28.15 N	80.36 W
Patrick Henry International Airport ⊠	208	37.08 N	76.30 W
Patrick Point ≻	214	42.35 N	81.28 W
Patrington	44	53.41 N	0.02 W
Patriot	218	38.50 N	84.49 W
Patrocínio	255	18.57 S	46.59 W
Patrocínio Paulista	255	20.38 S	47.17 W
Patsaliga Creek ≃	194	31.22 N	86.31 W
Patscherkofel ∧	64	47.13 N	11.28 E
Pattada	71	40.35 N	9.06 E
Pattani	110	6.52 N	101.16 E
Pattani ≃	110	6.53 N	101.16 E
Patten	188	45.59 N	68.26 W
Pattenburg	210	40.38 N	75.01 W
Pattensen	52	52.15 N	9.46 E
Pattenville	283	42.35 N	71.14 W
Patterdale	44	54.32 N	2.56 W
Patterson, Ca., U.S.	226	37.28 N	121.07 W
Patterson, Ga., U.S.	192	31.23 N	82.08 W
Patterson, Il., U.S.	219	39.29 N	90.29 W
Patterson, La., U.S.	194	29.41 N	91.18 W
Patterson, N.Y., U.S.	210	41.30 N	73.36 W
Patterson, Oh., U.S.	216	40.47 N	83.32 W
Patterson ≃	274b	38.05 S	145.07 E
Patterson, Mount ∧	180	64.04 N	134.39 W
Patterson Creek ≃	188	39.34 N	78.44 W
Patterson Gardens	216	41.56 N	83.25 W
Patterson Heights	214	40.45 N	80.19 W
Patterson Island I	190	48.39 N	87.00 W
Patterson Park ♠	284b	39.17 N	76.35 W
Pattersonville	210	42.53 N	74.05 W
Patti, India	123	31.17 N	74.51 E
Patti, India	124	25.55 N	82.12 E
Patti, It.	70	38.08 N	14.58 E
Patti, Golfo di ⊂	36	38.12 N	15.05 E
Pattison, Ms., U.S.	194	31.53 N	90.53 W
Pattison, Tx., U.S.	222	29.49 N	95.60 W
Pattoki	123	31.01 N	73.51 E
Patton	214	40.37 N	78.39 W
Patton, Cape ≻	169	38.42 S	143.50 E
Patton Park ♠	281	42.19 N	83.10 W
Pattonsburg	194	40.02 N	94.08 W
Patton Seamounts ✤ [3]	16	54.20 N	149.30 W
Pattscheid ◆ [8]	263	51.05 N	7.03 E
Pattukkottai	122	10.26 N	79.19 E
Pattullo, Mount ∧	180	56.14 N	129.39 W
Patu	250	6.06 S	37.38 W
Pātua	126	22.06 N	90.23 E
Patuākhāli	124	22.21 N	90.21 E
Patuca ≃	236	15.50 N	84.17 W
Patuca, Punta ≻	236	15.51 N	84.18 W
Patuha, Gunung ∧	115a	7.10 S	107.23 E
Pātul	272b	22.45 N	88.10 E
Patul, Cerro ∧	246	2.40 S	79.03 W
Pātuli	126	23.33 N	88.15 E
Patulul	236	14.25 N	91.10 W
Patumahoe	172	37.11 S	174.50 E
Pātūr	122	20.27 N	76.56 E
Patusi	164	2.10 S	147.10 E
Patutu ∧	172	39.15 S	175.51 E
Patuxent ≃	208	38.18 N	76.25 W
Patuxent, Western Branch ≃	208	38.47 N	76.43 W
Patuxent River Naval Air Test Center ■	208	38.17 N	76.25 W
Patuxent Wildlife Research Center ⊌ [3]	284c	39.03 N	76.48 W
Patvinsuon kansallispuisto ♠	24	63.10 N	30.55 E
Patwāri	272a	28.35 N	77.27 E
Pátzcuaro	234	19.31 N	101.36 W
Pátzcuaro, Lago de ⊜	234	19.35 N	101.35 W
Patzicía	236	14.38 N	90.56 W
Patzig	54	54.28 N	13.24 E
Patzún	236	14.41 N	91.01 W
Pau	32	43.18 N	0.22 W
Pau, Gave de ≃	32	43.33 N	1.12 W
Pau Brasil	255	15.27 S	39.39 W
Paucarbamba	248	12.25 S	74.36 W
Paucarpata	248	16.26 S	71.30 W
Paucartambo	248	13.18 S	71.40 W
Paudash Lake ⊜	212	44.58 N	78.04 W
Pau dos Ferros	250	6.07 S	38.10 W
Pauh	112	2.08 S	102.48 E
Pauhunri ∧	124	27.58 N	88.50 E
Pauini	248	7.40 S	66.58 W
Pauini ≃, Bra.	246	1.42 S	62.50 W
Pauini ≃, Bra.	248	7.47 S	67.05 W
Pauk	110	21.27 N	94.27 E
Pauksa Taung ∧	110	19.55 N	94.18 E
Paul	202	42.36 N	113.46 W
Paul, Lac à ⊜	186	49.52 N	70.46 W
Paula Lima	256	21.35 S	43.29 W
Paularo	64	46.32 N	13.07 E
Paulaya ≃	236	15.51 N	85.06 W
Paulding, Ms., U.S.	194	32.01 N	89.02 W
Paulding, Oh., U.S.	216	41.08 N	84.34 W
Paulding □ [6]	216	41.08 N	84.35 W
Paulding Bay ⊂	9	66.35 S	123.00 E
Paulhan	32	43.32 N	3.27 E
Paulicéia	255	21.17 S	51.51 W
Paulilatino	71	40.05 N	8.46 E
Paulina Peak ∧	202	43.41 N	121.15 W
Pauline, Mount ∧	182	53.33 N	119.54 W
Paulinenaue	54	52.40 N	12.43 E
Paulínia	256	22.45 S	47.10 W
Paulino Neves	250	2.43 S	42.33 W
Paulins Kill	210	41.03 N	74.49 W
Paulins Kill ≃	210	40.55 N	75.05 W
Paulinzella ⊥	54	50.42 N	11.06 E
Paulis → Isiro	154	2.47 N	27.37 E
Paulistana	250	8.09 S	41.09 W
Paulistas	255	18.25 S	42.52 W
Paullina	198	42.58 N	95.41 W
Paull Lake ⊜	184	56.08 N	104.50 W
Paullo	62	45.25 N	9.24 E
Paulo Afonso	250	9.21 S	38.14 W
Paulo Afonso, Cachoeira de ⌊	250	9.24 S	38.13 W
Paulo de Faria	255	20.02 S	49.24 W
Pauloff Harbor (Pavlof Harbor)	180	54.27 N	162.42 W
Paulpietersburg	158	27.30 S	30.51 E
Paul Roux	158	28.18 S	27.59 E
Paul-Sauvé, Parc ♠	275a	45.28 N	74.02 W
Paulsboro	208	39.49 N	75.14 W
Pauls Cross Roads	208	37.52 N	76.53 W
Paul Seamount ✤ [3]	14	23.26 N	172.36 W
Paulstown → Whitehall	48	52.41 N	7.01 W
Pauls Valley	196	34.44 N	97.13 W
Paulton, Eng., U.K.	42	51.18 N	2.30 W
Paulton, Pa., U.S.	279b	40.34 N	79.34 W
Pauma Indian Reservation ◆ [4]	228	33.22 N	116.58 W
Pāunān	272b	22.57 N	88.17 E
Paung	110	16.37 N	97.28 E
Paungbyin	110	24.16 N	94.49 E
Paungde	110	18.29 N	95.30 E
Paunggyi	110	17.19 N	96.11 E
Paup	164	3.15 S	142.35 E
Paupack	210	41.24 N	75.14 W
Pauri	124	30.09 N	78.47 E
Pausa, Dtsch.	54	50.35 N	12.00 E
Pausa, Perú	248	15.16 S	73.20 W
Pausania	36	40.55 N	9.06 E
Pausin	264a	52.38 N	13.03 E
Paute	246	2.47 S	78.50 W
Paute ≃	246	2.46 S	78.16 W
Pauto ≃	246	5.09 N	70.55 W
Pautou → Baotou	102	40.40 N	109.59 E
Pauwalu Point ≻	229a	20.52 N	156.08 W
Pauwela	229a	20.56 N	156.19 W
Pauwela Point ≻	229a	20.57 N	156.19 W
Pavai ◆ [8]	272c	19.07 N	72.55 E
Pavai Lake ⊜	272c	19.07 N	72.55 E
Pavda	86	59.15 N	59.30 E
Pāveh	128	35.03 N	46.22 E
Pavel'cevo	82	56.15 N	36.26 E
Pavelec	76	53.50 N	39.16 E
Pavelec Station ◆ [5]	265b	55.44 N	37.38 E
Pavia	62	45.10 N	9.10 E
Pavia □ [4]	62	45.07 N	9.08 E
Pavia, Naviglio di ≊	266b	45.27 N	9.11 E
Pavia di Udine	64	45.59 N	13.17 E
Pavilion, B.C., Can.	182	50.52 N	121.50 W
Pavilion, N.Y., U.S.	210	42.52 N	78.01 W
Pavilion Key I	220	25.42 N	81.22 W
Pavillion	200	43.14 N	108.41 W
Pavilly	50	49.34 N	0.58 E
Pāvilosta	76	56.53 N	21.14 E
Pavino	24	59.07 N	46.07 E
Pavione, Monte ∧	64	46.07 N	11.50 E
Pavlice	61	48.59 N	15.53 E
Pavlikeni	38	43.14 N	25.18 E
Pavliščevo, Ross.	82	55.11 N	35.59 E
Pavliščevo, Ross.	82	55.34 N	35.59 E
Pavlodar	86	52.18 N	76.57 E
Pavlodar □ [8]	86	52.00 N	76.00 E
Pavlof Bay ⊂	180	55.30 N	161.32 W
Pavlof Volcano ∧ [1]	180	55.24 N	161.52 W
Pavlograd	78	48.32 N	35.53 E
Pavlogradka	86	54.12 N	73.33 E
Pavlopol'	83	47.16 N	37.47 E
Pavlovka, Ross.	80	52.41 N	47.09 E
Pavlovka, Ross.	86	55.25 N	56.33 E
Pavlovka, Ross.	86	51.55 N	54.47 E
Pavlovka, Ukr.	78	47.45 N	37.14 E
Pavlovka, Ukr.	83	48.08 N	39.33 E
Pavlovka, Ukr.	83	49.36 N	38.42 E
Pavlovo, Ross.	76	60.05 N	45.17 E
Pavlovo, Ross.	80	55.58 N	43.04 E
Pavlovo, Ross.	265a	59.56 N	30.40 E
Pavlovo, Ross.	265a	59.49 N	30.54 E
Pavlovsk, Ross.	76	59.41 N	30.27 E
Pavlovsk, Ross.	78	50.27 N	40.08 E
Pavlovsk, Ross.	86	53.20 N	82.59 E
Pavlovskaja	78	46.08 N	39.48 E
Pavlovskaja Sloboda	82	55.49 N	37.05 E
Pavlovskij, Kaz.	86	52.32 N	63.06 E
Pavlovskij, Ross.	80	57.50 N	54.51 E
Pavlovskij Posad	82	55.47 N	38.40 E
Pavlyš	78	48.55 N	33.21 E
Pavne	272c	19.05 N	73.01 E
Pavo	192	31.02 N	84.04 W
Pavón, Arg.	258	34.23 S	59.03 W
Pavón, Col.	246	3.37 N	72.15 W
Pavón, Arroyo ≃	258	34.30 S	57.05 W
Pavona	267a	41.43 N	12.37 E
Pavonia	214	40.49 N	82.26 W
Pavšino	265b	55.49 N	37.21 E
Pavšozero	76	60.38 N	35.34 E
Pavullo nel Frignano	64	44.20 N	10.50 E
Pavuna, Arroio ≃	287a	22.58 S	43.23 W
Pavuvu Island I	175e	9.03 S	159.06 E
Pavy	76	58.03 N	29.30 E
Pawai, Pulau I	271c	1.12 N	103.43 E
Pawan ≃	112	1.51 S	109.57 E
Pawāyān	124	28.04 N	80.06 E
Pawcatuck	207	41.22 N	71.50 W
Paw Creek	192	35.16 N	80.56 W
Päwesin	54	52.31 N	12.42 E
Pawhuska	196	36.40 N	96.20 W
Pawling	210	41.33 N	73.36 W
Pawn ≃	110	18.53 N	97.19 E
Pawnee, Il., U.S.	219	39.35 N	89.34 W
Pawnee, Ok., U.S.	196	36.20 N	96.48 W
Pawnee ≃	198	38.10 N	99.06 W
Pawnee City	198	40.06 N	96.09 W
Pawnee Creek ≃	198	40.34 N	103.14 W
Pawnee Rock	198	38.15 N	98.58 W
Pawni	122	20.47 N	79.38 E
Pawota	110	17.46 N	97.17 E
Paw Paw, Il., U.S.	216	41.41 N	88.59 W
Paw Paw, Mi., U.S.	216	42.13 N	85.53 W
Paw Paw, W.V., U.S.	188	39.31 N	78.27 W
Paw Paw ≃	216	42.07 N	86.29 W
Paw Paw Creek ≃	216	40.52 N	85.58 W
Paw Paw Lake	216	42.12 N	86.15 W
Paw Paw Lake ⊜	216	42.12 N	86.16 W
Pawtucket	207	41.52 N	71.22 W
Pawtucket Falls ⌊	207	42.39 N	71.20 W
Paxoí I	38	39.12 N	20.12 E
Paxson	180	63.02 N	145.30 W
Paxton, Austl.	170	32.54 S	151.16 E
Paxton, Il., U.S.	216	40.27 N	88.05 W
Paxton, Ma., U.S.	207	42.18 N	71.55 W
Paxton, Ne., U.S.	198	41.07 N	101.21 W
Paxtonia	208	40.19 N	76.48 W
Paxtonville	208	40.46 N	77.05 W
Paya	236	15.37 N	85.17 W
Paya Besar	114	3.47 N	103.16 E
Payadapu	114	3.05 N	97.23 E
Payāgpur	124	27.25 N	81.48 E
Payagyi	110	17.29 N	96.32 E
Payakumbuh	112	0.14 S	100.38 E
Paya Lebar	271c	1.22 N	103.53 E
Paya Lebar Airport ⊠	271c	1.21 N	103.54 E
Payamlı	130	37.01 N	38.35 E
Payangan	115b	8.26 S	115.15 E
Payas, Cerro ∧	236	15.50 N	85.00 W
Payerne	58	46.49 N	6.56 E
Payeti	115b	9.41 S	120.20 E
Payette	202	44.04 N	116.55 W
Payette ≃	202	44.05 N	116.57 W
Payette, Middle Fork ≃	202	44.05 N	116.07 W
Payette, North Fork ≃	202	44.05 N	116.07 W
Payette, South Fork ≃	202	44.06 N	116.00 W
Payette Lake ⊜ [1]	202	44.57 N	116.05 W
Paylampur	272b	22.47 N	88.16 E
Payne	216	41.04 N	84.43 W
Payne ≃	206	45.14 N	75.08 W
Payne, Lac ⊜	176	59.25 N	74.00 W
Payne Bay ⊂	176	60.00 N	70.00 W
Payneham	168b	34.53 S	138.38 E
Paynes Creek ≃	204	40.16 N	122.11 W
Paynes Find	162	29.15 S	117.41 E
Paynesville, S. Afr.	273d	26.14 S	28.28 E
Paynesville, Mn., U.S.	198	45.22 N	94.42 W
Paynesville, Mo., U.S.	219	39.16 N	90.54 W
Paynetown State Recreation Area ♠	218	39.05 N	86.27 W
Paynton	184	53.01 N	108.56 W
Paysandú	252	32.19 S	58.05 W
Pays-Bas → Netherlands □ [1]	30	52.15 N	5.30 E
Payson, Az., U.S.	200	34.13 N	111.19 W
Payson, Il., U.S.	219	39.49 N	91.14 W

Symbol	English	Deutsch	Español	Français	Português
≃	River	Fluß	Río	Rivière	Rio
≊	Canal	Kanal	Canal	Canal	Canal
⌊	Waterfall, Rapids	Wasserfall, Stromschnellen	Cascada, Rápidos	Chute d'eau, Rapides	Cascata, Rápidos
ʊ	Strait	Meeresstraße	Estrecho	Détroit	Estreito
⊂	Bay, Gulf	Bucht, Golf	Bahía, Golfo	Baie, Golfe	Baía, Golfo
⊜	Lake, Lakes	See, Seen	Lago, Lagos	Lac, Lacs	Lago, Lagos
≋	Swamp	Sumpf	Pantano	Marais	Pântano
⍓	Ice Features, Glacier	Eis- und Gletscherformen	Accidentes Glaciales	Formes glaciaires	Acidentes glaciares
⍒	Other Hydrographic Features	Andere Hydrographische Objekte	Otros Elementos Hidrográficos	Autres données hydrographiques	Outros acidentes hidrográficos
✤	Submarine Features	Untermeerische Objekte	Accidentes Submarinos	Formes de relief sous-marin	Acidentes submarinos
□	Political Unit	Politische Einheit	Unidad Politica	Entité politique	Unidade política
⊌	Cultural Institution	Kulturelle Institution	Institución Cultural	Institution culturelle	Instituição cultural
⊥	Historical Site	Historische Stätte	Sitio Histórico	Site historique	Sitio histórico
♠	Recreational Site	Erholungs- und Ferienort	Sitio de Recreo	Centre de loisirs	Area de Lazer
⊠	Airport	Flughafen	Aeropuerto	Aéroport	Aeroporto
■	Military Installation	Militäranlage	Instalación Militar	Installation militaire	Instalação militar
◆	Miscellaneous	Verschiedenes	Misceláneo	Divers	Diversos

Payson, Ut., U.S. 200 40.02 N 111.43 W
Payún, Cerro ∧ 252 36.30 S 69.18 W
Paz ≐ 236 13.45 N 90.08 W
Paz, Cañada de la ≐ 288 34.53 S 58.38 W
Paz, Rio da ≐ 250 9.14 S 52.01 W
Pazar, Tür. 130 40.17 N 36.18 E
Pazar, Tür. 130 41.11 N 40.53 E
Pazarbaşı > 130 41.10 N 30.11 E
Pazarcık 130 37.31 N 37.19 E
Pazardžik 38 42.12 N 24.20 E
Pazarköy, Tür. 130 40.55 N 32.11 E
Pazarköy, Tür. 130 39.51 N 27.24 E
Pazarören 130 38.41 N 36.11 E
Pazaryeri, Tür. 130 38.05 N 28.14 E
Pazaryeri, Tür. 130 40.00 N 29.54 E
Paz de Ariporo 246 5.53 N 71.54 W
Paz de Río 246 5.59 N 72.47 W
Pazifischer Ozean — Pacific Ocean ≂[1] 6 10.00 S 150.00 W
P'ažijeva Sel'ga 24 61.29 N 34.29 E
Pazin 36 45.14 N 13.56 E
Pazña 248 18.36 S 66.55 W
Paznaun V 58 47.03 N 10.20 E
Pčevža 76 59.23 N 32.20 E
Pčevža ≐ 76 59.21 N 31.54 E
Pchery 54 50.10 N 14.08 E
Pe 110 13.28 N 98.31 E
Pea 174w 21.10 S 175.14 W
Pea ≐ 194 31.01 N 85.51 W
Peabody, Ks., U.S. 198 38.10 N 97.06 W
Peabody, Ma., U.S. 207 42.31 N 70.55 W
Peace ≐, Can. 176 59.00 N 111.25 W
Peace ≐, Fl., U.S. 220 26.55 N 82.05 W
Peace Arch ⊥ 224 49.00 N 122.45 W
Peace Bridge ✈[5] 284a 42.54 N 78.55 W
Peace Canyon Dam ✈[6] 182 55.59 N 121.59 W
Peace Dale 207 41.27 N 71.29 W
Peacehaven 42 50.47 N 0.01 E
Peace River 182 56.14 N 117.17 W
Peach Creek 188 37.52 N 81.59 W
Peach Creek ≐, Tx., U.S. 222 30.07 N 95.10 W
Peach Creek ≐, Tx., U.S. 222 29.24 N 97.19 W
Peach Creek, Sandy Fork ≐ 222 29.34 N 97.19 W
Peachdale 158 26.30 S 24.42 E
Peachland 182 49.46 N 119.44 W
Peach Orchard 192 33.28 N 82.04 W
Peach Springs 200 35.31 N 113.25 W
Peacock Hills ⋀[2] 176 66.05 N 110.45 W
Peacock Point >, On., Can. 212 42.47 N 79.59 W
Peacock Point >, Wake I. 174a 19.16 N 166.37 E
Peacock Sound ꭥ 9 72.55 S 100.00 W
Pea Hill Branch ≐ 284c 38.45 N 76.57 W
Peak Charles National Park ◆ 162 32.55 S 121.06 E
Peak Crossing 171a 27.47 S 152.44 E
Peak Dale 262 53.17 N 1.52 W
Peak District National Park ◆ 44 53.17 N 1.45 W
Peak Downs 166 22.12 S 148.10 E
Peake Creek ≐ 162 28.05 S 136.07 E
Peaked Mountain ∧ 186 46.34 N 68.49 W
Peak Forest 262 53.19 N 1.50 W
Peak Forest Canal ≚ 262 53.29 N 2.06 W
Peak Hill, Austl. 162 25.38 S 118.43 E
Peak Hill, Austl. 166 32.44 S 148.12 E
Peakhurst 274a 33.58 S 151.04 E
Peakview 171b 36.04 S 149.24 E
Peäldoajvi ∧ 24 69.11 N 26.36 E
Peale, Mount ∧ 200 38.26 N 109.14 W
Peale Island I 174a 19.19 N 166.35 E
Peapack Brook ≐ 276 40.41 N 74.39 W
Pearblossom 228 34.30 N 117.55 W
Pearce 200 31.54 N 109.49 W
Pearce, Royal Australian Air Force Station ■ 168a 31.41 S 116.01 E
Pearce Point > 164 14.25 S 129.21 E
Peard Bay ⊂ 180 70.51 N 159.10 W
Pea Ridge ∧ 218 38.25 N 83.36 W
Pea Ridge National Military Park ◆ 194 36.29 N 94.06 W
Pearisburg 192 37.19 N 80.44 W
Pearl, Il., U.S. 194 39.28 N 90.38 W
Pearl, Ms., U.S. 194 32.16 N 90.07 W
Pearl ≐ 194 30.11 N 89.32 W
Pearl, Lake ⊜ 283 42.04 N 71.21 W
Pearland 222 29.33 N 95.17 W
Pearl and Hermes Atoll I[1] 14 27.55 N 175.45 W
Pearl Bank ✈[4] 116 5.49 N 119.42 E
Pearl Beach 214 42.37 N 82.35 W
Pearl City 229c 21.23 N 157.58 W
Pearl Creek ≐ 198 44.15 N 98.08 W
Pearl Harbor ⊂ 229c 21.22 N 157.58 W
Pearl Harbor Naval Station ■ 229c 21.21 N 157.57 W
Pearl Peak ∧ 204 40.14 N 115.32 W
Pearl River, La., U.S. 194 30.22 N 89.44 W
Pearl River, N.Y., U.S. 210 41.03 N 74.01 W
Pearns Point > 240c 17.05 N 61.54 W
Pearsall 196 28.53 N 99.05 W
Pearse Island I 182 54.51 N 130.21 W
Pearsoll Peak ∧ 202 42.18 N 123.50 W
Pearson 192 31.17 N 82.51 W
Pearson Lake ⊜ 184 56.15 N 97.15 W
Pearston 158 32.35 S 25.08 E
Peary Land ✈[1] 16 83.00 N 35.00 W
Pease ≐ 196 34.12 N 99.07 W
Pease Air Force Base ■ 188 43.06 N 70.49 W
Peasedown Saint John 42 51.19 N 2.27 W
Peaster 222 32.52 N 97.52 W
Peat Inn 46 56.17 N 2.53 W
Pebane 154 17.10 S 38.08 E
Pebas 246 3.20 S 71.49 W
Pebble Beach 226 36.34 N 121.57 W
Pebble Island I 254 51.18 S 59.35 W
Peć 38 42.40 N 20.19 E
Pecan Bayou ≐ 196 31.28 N 98.43 W
Pecangakan 115a 6.41 S 110.42 E
Pecan Gap 196 33.26 N 95.51 W
Peçanha 255 18.33 S 42.34 W
Peças, Ilha das I 252 25.26 S 48.19 W
Pecatonica 190 42.18 N 89.21 W
Pecatonica ≐ 190 42.27 N 89.05 W
Pecatu 115b 8.50 S 115.07 E
Peccioli 66 43.33 N 10.43 E
Pécel 264c 47.29 N 19.21 E
Pečenegi 78 49.52 N 36.55 E
Pečenek 130 40.25 N 32.19 E
Pečenežin 78 48.32 N 24.54 E
Pečenga 24 69.33 N 31.07 E
Pečerniki 82 54.39 N 39.14 E
Pečernikovskije Vyselki 82 54.10 N 39.10 E
Pechanga Indian Reservation ✈[4] 228 33.27 N 117.04 W
Peche Island I 281 42.21 N 82.56 W
Pechincha ✈[8] 287a 22.56 S 43.21 W
Pechora — Pečora ≐ 24 68.13 N 54.15 E
Pechorskoje 265b 55.35 N 38.03 E
Pechra-Jakovlevskaja 265b 55.48 N 37.58 E
Pechra-Pokrovskoje 265b 55.50 N 37.57 E
Pechu 84 43.24 N 40.49 E
Peči 80 54.48 N 44.19 E
Pecica 38 46.10 N 21.05 E
Pečicy 82 55.36 N 38.27 E
Pecixe, Ilha de I 150 11.50 N 16.05 W
Peck 190 43.15 N 82.49 W
Peck Bay ⊂ 208 39.16 N 74.37 W
Peck-Berge ⋀[2] 264a 52.36 N 13.34 E
Peckeloh 52 52.01 N 8.07 E
Peckelsheim 52 51.36 N 9.07 E
Pecket Well 262 53.46 N 2.00 W
Peck Lake ⊜ 210 43.07 N 74.25 W
Peckman ≐ 276 40.53 N 74.13 W
Peconic ≐ 207 40.55 N 72.37 W
Pečora, Ross. 24 65.10 N 57.11 E
Pečora, Ukr. 78 48.52 N 28.42 E
Pečora ≐ 24 68.13 N 54.15 E
Pecora, Capo > 71 39.27 N 8.23 E
Pecoraro, Monte ∧ 68 38.32 N 16.20 E
Pečoro-Ilyčskij Zapovednik ✈[4] 24 62.20 N 59.00 E
Pečorskaja guba ⊂ 24 68.40 N 54.45 E
Pečorskoje more ≂[2] 24 70.00 N 54.00 E
Pečory 76 57.49 N 27.36 E
Pecos, N.M., U.S. 200 35.34 N 105.40 W
Pecos, Tx., U.S. 196 31.25 N 103.29 W
Pecos ≐ 178 29.42 N 101.22 W
Pecos National Monument ◆ 200 35.26 N 105.56 W
Pecos Plains ≚ 196 33.20 N 104.30 W
Pecq 50 50.41 N 3.20 E
Pecquencourt 50 50.23 N 3.13 E
Pecqueuse 261 48.39 N 2.03 E
Pécs 30 46.05 N 18.13 E
Pedana 122 16.16 N 81.10 E
Pedas 114 2.37 N 102.04 E
Pedasí 246 7.32 N 80.02 W
Pedaso 66 43.06 N 13.50 E
Peddāpuram 122 17.05 N 82.08 E
Pedder, Lake ⊜[1] 166 42.54 S 146.12 E
Peddie 158 33.12 S 27.07 E
Peddocks Island I 283 42.17 N 70.56 W
Pededze ≐ 76 56.56 N 26.54 E
Pedernales, Arg. 252 35.15 S 59.39 W
Pedernales, Méx. 234 19.08 N 101.28 W
Pedernales, Rep. Dom. 238 18.02 N 71.45 W
Pedernales, Ven. 246 9.58 N 62.16 W
Pedernales ≐ 196 30.26 N 98.04 W
Pedernales, Salar de ≚ 252 26.15 S 69.10 W
Pedernales Falls State Park ◆ 196 30.20 N 98.14 W
Pederobba 64 45.53 N 11.58 E
Pedersborg 41 55.27 N 11.34 E
Pederstrup 41 54.54 N 11.16 E
Pedesina 58 46.05 N 9.33 E
Pedhoulás 130 34.58 N 32.50 E
Pedja ≐ 76 58.25 N 26.11 E
Pedley 228 33.59 N 117.28 W
Pé do Morro 256 22.20 S 44.57 W
Pedra 250 8.30 S 36.57 W
Pedra Azul 255 16.01 S 41.16 W
Pedra Bela 256 22.47 S 46.27 W
Pedra Branca 250 5.27 S 39.43 W
Pedra de Guaratiba ✈[8] 287a 23.00 S 43.39 W
Pedra Grande, Recifes da ✈[2] 255 17.45 S 38.58 W
Pedra Lume 150a 16.46 N 22.54 W
Pedralva 256 22.14 S 45.28 W
Pedras 250 2.48 S 57.16 W
Pedras, Rio das ≐ 287a 22.51 S 43.01 W
Pedras de Fogo 250 7.23 S 35.07 W
Pedras Selada 256 22.21 S 44.26 W
Pedras Negras 248 12.51 S 62.54 W
Pedras Salgadas 34 41.32 N 7.36 W
Pedraza 246 10.11 N 74.55 W
Pedregal, Pan. 236 8.22 N 82.26 W
Pedregal, Ven. 246 11.01 N 70.08 W
Pedregulho 255 20.16 S 47.29 W
Pedreira 256 22.43 S 46.55 W
Pedreira ≐ 250 0.12 N 50.47 W
Pedreiras 250 4.34 S 44.39 W
Pedriceña 232 25.06 N 103.47 W
Pedricktown 208 39.46 N 75.24 W
Pedrinhas 250 11.12 S 37.41 W
Pedro, Point > 122 9.50 N 80.14 E
Pedro Afonso 250 8.59 S 48.11 W
Pedro Antonio de los Santos 234 21.36 N 98.58 W
Pedro Avelino 250 5.31 S 36.23 W
Pedro Bay 180 59.47 N 154.07 W
Pedro Betancourt 240p 22.44 N 81.17 W
Pedro Cays II 238 17.00 N 77.50 W
Pedro de Olla, Cerro ∧ 234 17.07 N 97.40 W
Pedro do Rio 256 22.20 S 43.09 W
Pedrógão Grande 34 39.55 N 8.09 W
Pedro Gomes 255 18.04 S 54.32 W
Pedro II 250 4.25 S 41.28 W
Pedro II, Ilha I 246 1.10 N 66.40 W
Pedro Juan Caballero 252 22.34 S 55.37 W
Pedro Leopoldo 255 19.38 S 44.03 W
Pedro Luro 252 39.29 S 62.41 W
Pedro Muñoz 34 39.24 N 2.58 W
Pedro Osório 252 31.51 S 52.45 W
Pedro R. Fernández 252 28.45 S 58.39 W
Pedro Teixeira 256 21.43 S 43.44 W
Pedro Velho 250 6.26 S 35.14 W
Peebinga 166 34.56 S 140.55 E
Peebles, Scot., U.K. 46 55.39 N 3.12 W
Peebles, Oh., U.S. 218 38.56 N 83.24 W
Peedamullah 162 21.50 S 115.38 E
Pee Dee ≐ 192 34.43 N 79.52 W
Peekaboo Mountain ∧[2] 188 45.45 N 67.53 W
Peekskill 210 41.17 N 73.55 W
Peel, Austl. 170 33.19 S 149.38 E
Peel, I. of Man 44 54.13 N 4.40 W
Peel ⊂[6] 212 43.45 N 79.47 W
Peel ≐ 180 67.37 N 134.40 W
Peel Channel ≐[1] 180 68.13 N 135.00 W
Peel Fell ∧ 44 55.17 N 2.35 W
Peel Inlet ⊂ 168a 32.35 S 115.44 E
Peel Island I 171a 27.30 S 153.22 E
Pe Ell 224 46.34 N 123.17 W
Peel Point > 176 73.22 N 114.35 W
Peel Sound ꭥ 176 73.15 N 96.30 W
Peene ≐ 54 54.09 N 13.46 E
Peenemünde 54 54.08 N 13.46 E
Peepeekisis Indian Reserve ✈[4] 184 50.52 N 103.24 W
Peer 56 51.08 N 5.28 E
Peerless 202 48.46 N 105.49 W
Peers 182 53.40 N 116.00 W
Peesane 184 52.52 N 103.36 W
Peetz 198 40.57 N 103.06 W
Peetzsee ⊜ 264a 52.26 N 13.50 E
Pefferlaw 212 44.19 N 79.12 W
Pefferlaw Brook ≐ 212 44.15 N 79.13 W
Pegasus, Port ⊂ 172 47.12 S 167.41 E
Pegasus Bay ⊂ 172 43.20 S 173.00 E
Pegau 54 51.10 N 12.14 E
Pegli 62 44.26 N 8.48 E
Peglia, Monte ∧ 66 42.49 N 12.13 E
Pegnitz 60 49.45 N 11.33 E
Pegnitz ≐ 60 49.29 N 11.00 E
Pego 34 38.51 N 0.07 W
Pegolotte 64 45.12 N 12.02 E
Pegswood 44 55.11 N 1.38 W
Pegtymel' ≐ 180 69.25 N 174.35 E
Pegtymel'skij chrebet ∧ 180 68.30 N 177.00 E
Pegu ≐ 110 16.47 N 96.13 E
Pegu — Bago 110 17.20 N 96.29 E
Pegueros 234 20.57 N 102.40 W
Peguis Indian Reserve ✈[4] 184 51.20 N 97.35 W
Pegu Yoma ⋀ 110 19.00 N 95.50 E
Pegwell Bay ⊂ 42 51.18 N 1.26 E
Pegyš 24 63.26 N 50.30 E
Pehčevo 38 41.46 N 22.54 E
Pehladpur ✈[8] 272a 28.35 N 77.06 E
Pehlivanköy 130 41.21 N 26.55 E
Pehowa 124 29.59 N 76.35 E
Pehuajó 252 35.48 S 61.53 W
Pehula 26 61.17 N 22.42 E
Peian — Bei'an 89 48.16 N 126.36 E
Peiching — Beijing 105 39.55 N 116.25 E
Peigan Indian Reserve ✈[4] 182 49.35 N 113.40 W
Peihai — Beihai 102 21.29 N 109.05 E
Peij 52 51.06 N 5.53 E
Peijiatun 98 39.19 N 121.41 E
Peikang 100 23.34 N 120.18 E
Peikang ≐ 100 23.31 N 120.08 E
Peikant'ang Tao I 100 26.13 N 119.59 E
Peilstein im Mühlviertel 60 48.37 N 13.53 E
Peinan 100 22.47 N 121.07 E
Peinan ≐ 100 22.46 N 121.10 E
Peine 52 52.19 N 10.13 E
Peine, Pointe à > 240d 15.23 N 61.15 W
Peinnechaung I 110 19.59 N 93.04 E
Peio 64 46.22 N 10.40 E
Peip'ing — Beijing 105 39.55 N 116.25 E
Peipsi järv (Čudskoje ozero) ⊜ 76 58.45 N 27.25 E
Peipus, Lake — Čudskoje ozero ⊜ 76 58.45 N 27.25 E
Peïra-Cava 62 43.56 N 7.22 E
Peirce, Cape > 180 58.35 N 161.47 W
Peisey-Nancroix 62 45.33 N 6.45 E
Peissenberg 64 47.48 N 11.04 E
Peissenberg ∧, Dtsch. 60 47.48 N 11.01 E
Peissenberg ∧, Dtsch. 64 47.48 N 11.01 E
Peiting 58 47.47 N 10.55 E
Peit'ou ✈[8] 269d 25.08 N 121.30 E
Peitz 54 51.51 N 14.24 E
Peixe 255 12.03 S 48.32 W
Peixe, Rio do ≐, Bra. 255 14.06 S 50.51 W
Peixe, Rio do ≐, Bra. 255 21.31 S 51.58 W
Peixe, Rio do ≐, Bra. 256 21.55 S 43.21 W
Peixe, Rio do ≐, Bra. 256 23.24 S 45.28 W
Peixe, Rio do ≐, Bra. 256 22.23 S 46.51 W
Peixe, Rio do ≐, Bra. 256 23.12 S 46.06 W
Peixe, Rio do ≐, Bra. 256 21.38 S 45.11 W
Peixe-Boi 250 1.12 S 47.18 W
Peixes, Rio dos ≐ 250 10.42 S 57.56 W
Peixian (Yunhe), Zhg. 98 34.21 N 117.59 E
Peixian, Zhg. 98 34.44 N 116.59 E
Peixoto, Represa de ⊜[1] 255 20.10 S 47.20 W
Peixoto de Azevedo ≐ 250 10.06 S 55.31 W
Peiziyan 98 35.07 N 115.01 E
Pejantan, Pulau I 112 0.07 N 107.14 E
Pejelagartero 234 18.04 N 93.45 W
Pek ≐ 38 44.46 N 21.33 E
Pekalongan 115a 6.53 S 109.40 E
Pekan 114 3.30 N 103.25 E
Pekanbaru 112 0.32 N 101.27 E
Pekanheran 112 0.21 S 102.26 E
Pekin, Il., U.S. 190 40.34 N 89.38 W
Pekin, In., U.S. 218 38.29 N 86.01 W
Pekin, N.Y., U.S. 284a 43.10 N 78.53 W
Pekin, Oh., U.S. 214 40.43 N 81.07 W
Pékin — Beijing 105 39.55 N 116.25 E
Peking — Beijing 105 39.55 N 116.25 E
Peking National Library ◆ 271a 39.56 N 116.22 E
Peking Railway Station ✈[4] 271a 39.54 N 116.26 E
Peking University ◆[2] 271a 39.59 N 116.19 E
Peking Zoo ◆ 271a 39.56 N 116.19 E
Peklino 76 53.33 N 33.32 E
Pekša ≐ 80 55.53 N 39.40 E
Pektubajevo 80 57.02 N 48.23 E
Pekul'nej, chrebet ⋀ 180 66.00 N 175.00 E
Pekul'nejskoje, ozero ⊜ 180 62.40 N 177.00 E
Péla 150 7.37 N 9.07 W
Pelabuhandagang 112 1.08 S 103.05 E
Pelabuhan Kelang 114 3.00 N 101.24 E
Pelabuhanratu 115a 6.59 S 106.33 E
Pelabuhanratu, Teluk ⊂ 115a 7.03 S 106.27 E
Pel'a-Chovanskaja 80 54.36 N 44.56 E
Pelado, Volcán ∧[1] 286a 19.09 N 99.13 W
Pelagejevka 83 48.06 N 38.36 E
Pelagie, Isole II 70a 35.40 N 12.40 E
Pelago 66 43.46 N 11.30 E
Pelahatchie 194 32.18 N 89.47 W
Pelaihari 112 3.48 S 114.45 E
Pelalawan 112 0.27 N 102.05 E
Pelat, Mont ∧ 62 44.16 N 6.42 E
Pelawan 114 2.47 N 102.55 E
Pełczyce 30 53.03 N 15.18 E
Pélé, Mont ∧ 152 3.15 S 11.14 E
Peleaga, Vîrful ∧ 38 45.22 N 22.54 E
Pelechuco 248 14.48 S 69.04 W
Peleduj 74 59.36 N 112.45 E
Pelée, Montagne ∧ 240e 14.48 N 61.10 W
Pelee, Point > 214 41.54 N 82.30 W
Pelee Island I 214 41.46 N 82.39 W
Pelee Passage ꭥ 214 41.52 N 82.37 W
Pelekech ∧ 154 3.48 N 35.04 E
Peleliu I 175b 7.01 N 134.15 E
Peleng, Pulau I 112 1.20 S 123.10 E
Peleng, Selat ꭥ 112 1.10 S 122.45 E
Pelenija 78 47.53 N 27.50 E
Pelf, Monte ∧ 64 46.14 N 12.12 E
Pelham, On., Can. 212 43.02 N 79.17 W
Pelham, Al., U.S. 194 33.17 N 86.48 W
Pelham, Ga., U.S. 192 31.07 N 84.09 W
Pelham, Ma., U.S. 207 42.23 N 72.24 W
Pelham, N.H., U.S. 207 42.44 N 71.19 W
Pelham, N.Y., U.S. 276 40.54 N 73.48 W
Pelham Bay ⊂ 276 40.52 N 73.47 W
Pelham Bay Park ◆ 276 40.52 N 73.49 W
Pelham Manor 276 40.53 N 73.48 W
Pelhřimov 30 49.26 N 15.13 E
Pelican 180 57.57 N 136.14 W
Pelican ≐ 184 46.17 N 96.08 W
Pelican, Punta > 200 31.19 N 113.43 W
Pelican Bay ⊂ 184 52.45 N 100.20 W
Pelican Island I, Mo., U.S. 219 38.52 N 90.18 W
Pelican Island I, Tx., U.S. 222 29.20 N 94.48 W
Pelican Lagoon ⊂ 168b 35.50 S 137.47 E
Pelican Lake 190 45.30 N 89.10 W
Pelican Lake ⊜, Ab., Can. 182 55.47 N 113.15 W
Pelican Lake ⊜, Mb., Can. 184 53.50 N 96.08 W
Pelican Lake ⊜, Mb., Can. 184 52.30 N 100.20 W
Pelican Lake ⊜, Mb., Can. 184 49.20 N 99.35 W
Pelican Lake ⊜, Sk., Can. 184 55.08 N 103.00 W
Pelican Lake ⊜, Sk., Can. 184 50.32 N 106.00 W
Pelican Lake ⊜, Mn., U.S. 190 48.05 N 92.54 W
Pelican Lake ⊜, S.D., U.S. 198 44.52 N 97.11 W
Pelican Mountain ∧ 182 55.35 N 113.40 W
Pelican Narrows 184 55.10 N 102.56 W
Pelican Point > 168b 34.48 S 138.29 E
Pelican Rapids, Mb., Can. 184 52.45 N 100.42 W
Pelican Rapids, Mn., U.S. 198 46.34 N 96.04 W
Pelileo 246 1.19 S 78.32 W
Pelister ∧ 38 41.00 N 21.12 E
Pelješac, Poluotok >[1] 36 42.58 N 17.20 E
Pelkosenniemi 24 67.07 N 27.30 E
Pelkum, Dtsch. 52 51.39 N 7.46 E
Pelkum, Dtsch. 263 51.40 N 7.24 E
Pella, S. Afr. 158 29.01 S 19.06 E
Pella, Ia., U.S. 190 41.24 N 92.54 W
Pélla ⊥ 38 40.45 N 22.33 E
Pellaro 68 38.01 N 15.39 E
Pell City 194 33.35 N 86.17 W
Pellecchia, Monte ∧ 66 42.07 N 12.52 E
Pellegrini 252 36.16 S 63.09 W
Pellegrini, Lago ⊜ 252 38.40 S 68.00 W
Pellegrino, Cozzo ∧ 68 39.45 N 16.03 E
Pellegrino, Monte ∧ 70 38.10 N 13.21 E
Pellegrino Parmense 64 44.44 N 9.55 E
Pellendorf 264b 48.06 N 16.27 E
Peller, Monte ∧ 64 46.18 N 10.57 E
Pellestrina, Litorale di ⊥[2] 64 45.16 N 12.18 E
Pelletier Lake ⊜ 184 56.30 N 97.00 W
Pellice ≐ 62 44.50 N 7.38 E
Pellingen 56 49.40 N 6.40 E
Pell Lake 216 42.32 N 88.21 W
Pello 24 66.47 N 24.00 E
Pellston 190 45.33 N 84.47 W
Pellworm I 30 54.31 N 8.38 E
Pelly 184 51.52 N 101.55 W
Pelly ≐ 180 62.47 N 137.19 W
Pelly Bay ⊂ 176 68.53 N 89.51 W
Pelly Crossing 180 62.50 N 136.35 W
Pelly Lake ⊜ 176 65.59 N 101.12 W
Pelly Mountains ⋀ 180 62.00 N 133.00 W
Pelón, Cerro ∧ 234 20.05 N 99.55 W
Peloncillo Mountains ⋀ 200 32.15 N 109.00 W
Pelopónnisos >[1] 38 37.30 N 22.00 E
Peloritani, Monti ⋀ 70 38.03 N 15.20 E
Pelotas 252 31.46 S 52.20 W
Pelotas ≐ 252 27.28 S 51.55 W
Pelplin 30 53.56 N 18.42 E
Pelque ≐ 254 51.03 S 70.58 W
Pelsin 54 53.48 N 13.40 E
Pelusium Bay — Ţīnah, Khalīj aţ- ⊂ 140 31.08 N 32.40 E
Pel'ušn'a 76 58.56 N 32.52 E
Pélussin 62 45.25 N 4.41 E
Pelvo d'Elva ∧ 62 44.33 N 9.15 E
Pelym 86 59.38 N 63.05 E
Pemadumcook Lake ⊜ 188 45.40 N 68.55 W
Pemalang 115a 6.54 S 109.22 E
Pemalang, Ujung > 115a 6.47 S 109.29 E
Pemali ≐ 115a 6.47 S 109.01 E
Pemangkat 112 1.10 N 108.58 E
Pematang 112 0.12 S 102.04 E
Pematangsiantar 114 2.57 N 99.03 E
Pematangtanahjawa 114 2.53 N 99.12 E
Pemba, Moç. 154 12.58 S 40.30 E
Pemba, Zam. 154 16.31 S 27.22 E
Pemba I 154 5.10 S 39.48 E
Pemba Channel ꭥ 154 5.10 S 39.20 E
Pembansan, Pegunungan ⋀ 115a 7.13 S 108.45 E
Pemberton, Austl. 162 34.28 S 116.01 E
Pemberton, B.C., Can. 182 50.20 N 122.48 W
Pemberton, Eng., U.K. 262 53.32 N 2.41 W
Pemberton, N.J., U.S. 208 39.58 N 74.41 W
Pemberton, Oh., U.S. 218 40.18 N 84.02 W
Pemberton Airport ✈ 285 39.59 N 74.41 W
Pemberton Heights 285 39.58 N 74.41 W
Pemberville 214 41.24 N 83.27 W
Pembina 198 48.57 N 97.14 W
Pembina ≐, Ab., Can. 182 54.45 N 114.15 W
Pembina ≐, N.A. 184 48.57 N 97.14 W
Pembina Hills ⋀[2] 198 49.10 N 98.25 W
Pembine 190 45.38 N 87.59 W
Pembrey 42 51.42 N 4.16 W
Pembroke, On., Can. 190 45.49 N 77.07 W
Pembroke, Wales, U.K. 42 51.41 N 4.55 W
Pembroke, Ga., U.S. 192 32.08 N 81.37 W
Pembroke, Ky., U.S. 194 36.46 N 87.21 W
Pembroke, Me., U.S. 188 44.57 N 67.09 W
Pembroke, N.Y., U.S. 210 43.00 N 78.27 W
Pembroke, N.C., U.S. 192 34.40 N 79.11 W
Pembroke, Va., U.S. 192 37.19 N 80.38 W
Pembroke, Cape > 176 62.56 N 81.55 W
Pembroke Castle ⊥ 42 51.41 N 4.56 W
Pembroke Dock 42 51.42 N 4.56 W
Pembroke Pines 220 26.00 N 80.13 W
Pembrokeshire Coast National Park ◆ 42 51.47 N 5.06 W
Pembuang 112 2.34 S 112.19 E
Pembuang ≐ 112 3.24 S 112.33 E
Pembury 42 51.09 N 0.19 E
Pemfling 60 49.16 N 12.37 E
Pemichigamau Lake ⊜ 184 56.16 N 99.33 W
Pemigewasset ≐ 188 43.26 N 71.40 W
Pemmican Portage 184 53.56 N 102.17 W
Pemuco 252 36.58 S 72.06 W
Pemynoos Indian Reserve ✈[4] 182 50.29 N 121.15 W
Pemzašen 84 40.35 N 43.57 E
Pena, Parque da ◆ 266c 38.47 N 9.23 W
Peña Barroza 248 22.10 S 67.25 W
Peña Blanca 236 8.27 N 81.40 W
Peñafiel, Esp. 34 41.36 N 4.07 W
Penafiel, Port. 34 41.12 N 8.17 W
Pen'agino 265b 55.50 N 37.21 E
Peña Gorda, Cerro ∧ 234 20.44 N 104.50 W
Peña Grande ✈[8] 266a 40.29 N 3.44 W
Pen'aksa 80 56.22 N 44.56 E
Peñalara ∧ 34 40.51 N 3.57 W
Peñalolén 286e 33.29 S 70.32 W
Pena-Lunanga 154 4.16 S 28.10 E
Penalva 250 3.18 S 45.10 W
Penambulai, Pulau I 164 6.24 S 134.48 E
Penang — George Town 114 5.25 N 100.20 E
Penanjung, Teluk ⊂ 115a 7.45 S 108.37 E
Penápolis 255 21.24 S 50.04 W
Peñaranda de Bracamonte 34 40.54 N 5.12 W
Pen Argyl 210 40.52 N 75.15 W
Penaron 114 4.38 N 97.40 E
Peñarroya-Pueblonuevo 34 38.18 N 5.16 W
Penarth 42 51.27 N 3.11 W
Peñas, Cabo de > 34 43.39 N 5.51 W
Penas, Golfo de ⊂ 254 47.22 S 74.50 W
Penasco 200 36.10 N 105.41 W
Peñasco, Rio ≐ 196 32.45 N 104.19 W
Penataquit Creek ≐ 276 40.43 N 73.14 W
Penbrook 208 40.16 N 76.50 W
Pencader 42 52.01 N 4.16 W
Pencahue 252 35.24 S 71.49 W
Pence 190 46.25 N 90.16 W
Pen Centre ✈[9] 284a 43.08 N 79.14 W
Penchard 261 48.59 N 2.52 E
Penck Trough V 9 73.00 S 2.45 W
Penco 252 36.44 S 72.59 W
Pencoed 42 51.32 N 3.30 W
Pendang, Indon. 112 1.28 S 114.51 E
Pendang, Malay. 114 6.00 N 100.28 E
Pendé ≐ 146 7.55 N 16.36 E
Pendéli 267c 38.03 N 23.52 E
Pendelikón Óros ∧ 267c 38.06 N 23.54 E
Pendembu, S.L. 150 8.06 N 10.42 W
Pendembu, S.L. 150 9.06 N 12.12 W
Pendências 250 5.15 S 36.43 W
Pendeng 114 4.06 N 97.36 E
Pender 198 42.06 N 96.42 W
Pender Bay ⊂ 162 16.45 S 122.42 E
Pendhar 272c 19.04 N 73.06 E
Pendik 267b 40.53 N 29.13 E
Pendjari ≐ 150 10.54 N 0.51 E
Pendjari, Parc National de la ◆ 150 11.20 N 1.15 E
Pendlebury 262 53.31 N 2.20 W
Pendle Hill 274a 33.48 S 150.57 E
Pendle Hill ∧[2] 44 53.52 N 2.17 W
Pendleton, In., U.S. 218 39.59 N 85.44 W
Pendleton, N.Y., U.S. 284a 43.05 N 78.44 W
Pendleton, Or., U.S. 202 45.40 N 118.47 W
Pendleton, S.C., U.S. 192 34.39 N 82.47 W
Pendleton ⊂[6] 218 38.42 N 84.22 W
Pendolo 112 2.05 S 120.42 E
Pendopo 112 3.17 S 103.52 E
Pend Oreille ≐ 202 49.04 N 117.37 W
Pend Oreille, Lake ⊜ 202 48.10 N 116.11 W
Pend Oreille, Mount ∧ 202 48.25 N 116.10 W
Pendotiba ≐ 287a 22.53 S 43.02 W
Pendžikent 85 39.29 N 67.35 E
Penebel 115b 8.25 S 115.09 E
Penedo 250 10.17 S 36.36 W
Penedono 34 40.59 N 7.24 W
Penela 34 40.02 N 8.23 W
Penelope 222 31.52 N 96.56 W
Penetang Harbour ⊂ 212 44.47 N 79.57 W
Penetanguishene 212 44.47 N 79.55 W
Penfield, Il., U.S. 216 40.18 N 87.57 W
Penfield, N.Y., U.S. 210 43.07 N 77.28 W
Penfield, Oh., U.S. 214 41.10 N 82.08 W
Penfield, Pa., U.S. 214 41.13 N 78.34 W
Penganga ≐ 122 19.53 N 79.09 E
Pengastulan 115b 8.11 S 114.55 E
Peng Chau I 271d 22.17 N 114.02 E
P'engchia Yü I 100 25.38 N 122.04 E
Penge, S. Afr. 156 24.22 S 30.13 E
Penge, Zaïre 154 5.31 S 24.37 E
Penge ✈[8] 260 51.25 N 0.04 W
Penggong 106 30.27 N 119.57 E
Penggongmiao 100 26.07 N 113.34 E
Penghu 100 25.24 N 118.11 E
P'enghu Ch'üntao (Pescadores) II 100 23.30 N 119.30 E
P'enghu Shuitao ꭥ 100 23.30 N 119.50 E
Pengiki, Pulau I 112 0.15 N 108.03 E
Pengjiachang 107 30.36 N 103.53 E
Pengjialouzi 104 41.56 N 123.40 E
Pengjiawan 100 32.16 N 114.04 E
Pengjiawu 105 39.41 N 117.10 E
Pengkalan Baharu 114 4.28 N 100.38 E
Pengkou 100 25.32 N 116.42 E
Penglai (Dengzhou) 98 37.48 N 120.42 E
Penglaizhen 107 30.36 N 105.14 E
Penglang 106 31.23 N 121.05 E
Pengnan 107 30.25 N 105.53 E
Pengpu — Bengbu 100 32.58 N 117.24 E
Pengshan 107 30.13 N 103.52 E
Pengshi 100 30.28 N 113.06 E
Pengshui 102 29.18 N 108.09 E
Penguin 166 41.07 S 146.04 E
Pengwaluote Shan ∧ 120 33.30 N 86.35 E
Pengxi 102 30.49 N 105.40 E
Pengxian 102 31.00 N 103.50 E
Pengze 100 29.53 N 116.33 E
Pengzhai 100 24.23 N 115.06 E
Pengzhuangzi 105 40.06 N 114.51 E
Penha 252 26.46 S 48.39 W
Penha ✈[8] 287a 22.49 S 43.17 W
Penha de França ✈[8] 287b 23.32 S 46.32 W
Penha Longa, Bra. 256 22.04 S 43.05 W
Penhalonga, Zimb. 154 18.54 S 32.40 E
Penhold 182 52.08 N 113.52 W
Penhold, Canadian Forces Base ■ 182 52.12 N 113.53 W
Penhorn Creek ≐ 276 40.45 N 74.05 W
Penhsi — Benxi 104 41.18 N 123.45 E
Peniche 34 39.21 N 9.23 W
Penicuik 46 55.50 N 3.14 W
Penida, Nusa I 115b 8.44 S 115.32 E
Penig 54 50.56 N 12.41 E
Peningo Neck >[1] 276 40.57 N 73.41 W
Peninjai 112 1.26 S 101.50 E
Peninsula Lake ⊜ 212 45.20 N 79.05 W
Peninsula State Park ◆ 190 45.09 N 87.14 W
Peñíscola 34 40.21 N 0.25 E
Penistone 44 53.32 N 1.37 W
Penitas 196 26.17 N 98.27 W
Penitencia Creek ≐ 282 37.27 N 121.55 W
Penitente, Serra do ⋀[2] 250 8.45 S 46.20 W
Penjamillo [de Degollado] 234 20.06 N 101.54 W
Pénjamo 234 20.26 N 101.44 W
Penketh 262 53.23 N 2.40 W
Penki — Benxi 104 41.18 N 123.45 E
Penkino 82 54.50 N 38.53 E
Penkridge 42 52.44 N 2.07 W
Penkun 54 53.17 N 14.14 E
Pen Lake ⊜ 212 45.28 N 78.23 W
Penllyn 285 40.10 N 75.15 W
Penmaenmawr 44 53.16 N 3.54 W
Penmarc'h, Pointe de > 32 47.48 N 4.22 W
Penn 279b 40.20 N 79.38 W
Penna, Punta della > 66 42.10 N 14.43 E
Pennabilli 66 43.49 N 12.16 E
Penn Acres 285 39.40 N 75.34 W
Pennant Hills 274a 33.45 S 151.04 E
Pennant Hills Park ◆ 274a 33.45 S 151.06 E
Pennant Point > 186 44.26 N 63.39 W
Pennant Station 184 50.33 N 108.12 W
Pennask Lake ⊜ 182 50.00 N 120.05 W
Pennask Mountain ∧ 182 49.53 N 120.07 W
Penn Brook ≐ 283 42.44 N 70.59 W
Penn Cove ⊂ 224 48.14 N 122.41 W
Penn Cove Park 224 48.14 N 122.41 W
Penndel 285 40.09 N 74.55 W
Penne 66 42.27 N 13.55 E
Penne, Punta > 68 40.41 N 17.56 E
Penne-d'Agenais 32 44.23 N 0.49 E
Pennedepie 50 49.25 N 0.11 E
Pennel Creek ≐ 198 46.34 N 104.52 W
Penneru ≐ 122 14.35 N 80.10 E
Pennes (Pens) 64 46.47 N 11.25 E
Pennes, Val di V 64 46.47 N 11.25 E
Penneshaw 168b 35.44 S 137.56 E
Penngrove 226 38.18 N 122.40 W
Penn Hills 214 40.28 N 79.51 W
Penn Hills Center ✈[9] 279b 40.28 N 79.50 W
Pennines ⋀ 44 54.10 N 2.05 W
Pennines, Alpes ⋀ 58 46.05 N 7.50 E
Penningby 40 59.41 N 18.40 E
Penningby slott ⊥ 40 59.41 N 18.40 E
Pennington, N.J., U.S. 208 40.19 N 74.47 W
Pennington, Tx., U.S. 222 31.11 N 95.14 W
Pennington ≐[1] 150 4.45 N 5.35 E
Pennington Gap 192 36.45 N 83.01 W
Penninino, Monte ∧ 66 43.06 N 12.53 E
Penn Run 214 40.37 N 79.01 W
Pennsauken 208 39.58 N 75.03 W
Pennsauken Creek ≐ 285 39.59 N 75.03 W
Pennsauken Creek, North Branch ≐ 285 39.58 N 75.01 W
Pennsauken Creek, South Branch ≐ 285 39.58 N 75.01 W
Pennsboro 188 39.17 N 80.58 W
Penns Brook ≐ 276 40.30 N 74.32 W
Pennsburg 208 40.23 N 75.29 W
Pennsbury Heights 285 40.12 N 74.49 W
Pennsbury Manor ⊥ 285 40.08 N 74.46 W
Penn's Cave ≐[5] 208 40.53 N 77.36 W
Penns Creek 210 40.52 N 77.04 W
Penns Creek ≐ 210 40.48 N 76.51 W
Pennsdale 210 41.15 N 76.48 W
Penns Grove 208 39.43 N 75.28 W
Pennside 208 40.20 N 75.53 W
Penns Neck 276 40.20 N 74.38 W
Pennsuco 220 25.53 N 80.22 W
Pennsville 208 39.39 N 75.31 W
Penns Woods 279b 40.21 N 79.46 W
Pennsylvania □[3], U.S. 178 40.45 N 77.30 W
Pennsylvania □[3], U.S. 188 40.45 N 77.30 W
Pennsylvania, University of ◆[2] 285 39.57 N 75.12 W
Pennsylvania Canal ≚ 285 40.13 N 74.47 W
Pennsylvania Station ✈[5] 276 40.45 N 74.00 W
Penn Valley, Ca., U.S. 226 39.12 N 121.11 W
Penn Valley, Pa., U.S. 285 40.01 N 75.16 W
Penn Valley Terrace 285 40.11 N 74.47 W
Pennville 216 40.29 N 85.08 W
Penn Wynne 285 39.59 N 75.16 W
Penny 182 53.50 N 121.17 W
Penn Yan 210 42.39 N 77.03 W
Pennycutaway ≐ 184 56.43 N 92.44 W
Penny Hill 285 39.46 N 75.30 W
Penny Ice Cap ⌂ 176 67.10 N 66.00 W
Pennypack Creek ≐ 285 40.02 N 75.00 W
Pennypack Park ◆ 285 40.04 N 75.03 W
Penny Strait ꭥ 176 76.30 N 97.00 W
Peno 76 56.55 N 32.45 E
Penobscot 210 41.10 N 75.52 W
Penobscot ≐ 188 44.30 N 68.50 W
Penobscot, East Branch ≐ 186 45.35 N 68.32 W
Penobscot, West Branch ≐ 188 45.35 N 68.32 W
Penobscot Bay ⊂ 188 44.15 N 68.52 W
Peno Creek ≐ 219 39.32 N 91.16 W
Pen'ok 86 55.30 N 81.34 E
Penola 166 37.23 S 140.50 E
Peñoles 196 25.39 N 104.38 W
Peñón Blanco 232 24.47 N 104.02 W
Penong 162 31.55 S 133.01 E
Penonomé 236 8.31 N 80.22 W
Penrhyn I[1] 14 9.00 S 158.00 W
Penrhyn Bay 44 53.19 N 3.45 W
Penrhyndeudraeth 42 52.56 N 4.04 W
Penrith, Austl. 170 33.45 S 150.42 E
Penrith, Eng., U.K. 44 54.40 N 2.44 W
Penryn, Eng., U.K. 42 50.09 N 5.06 W
Penryn, Ca., U.S. 226 38.51 N 121.10 W
Penryn, Pa., U.S. 208 40.12 N 76.22 W
Pensacola 194 30.25 N 87.13 W
Pensacola Bay ⊂ 194 30.25 N 87.06 W
Pensacola Mountains ⋀ 9 83.45 S 55.00 W
Pensacola Naval Air Station ■ 194 30.21 N 87.19 W
Pensacola Seamount ✈[3] 14 18.17 N 157.20 W
Pensaukee ≐ 190 44.49 N 87.55 W
Pensby 262 53.21 N 3.06 W
Pense 184 50.25 N 105.00 W
Penshaw 44 54.53 N 1.29 W
Pensiangan 112 4.33 N 116.19 E
Pensilva 42 50.30 N 4.25 W
Pensilvania 246 5.31 N 75.05 W
Pens — Pennes 64 46.47 N 11.25 E
Pentagna 256 22.09 S 43.45 W
Pentagon ✈ 284c 38.52 N 77.03 W
Pentagon Mountain ∧ 202 47.56 N 113.07 W
Pentecost □[8] 175f 15.45 S 168.12 E
Pentecoste 250 3.48 S 39.17 W
Pentecôte I 175f 15.42 S 168.10 E
Pentecôte ≐ 186 49.47 N 67.10 W
Pentecôte, Lac ⊜ 186 49.53 N 67.20 W
Penticton 182 49.30 N 119.35 W
Penticton Indian Reserve ✈[4] 182 49.30 N 119.40 W
Pentire Point > 42 50.36 N 4.55 W
Pentland 166 20.32 S 145.24 E
Pentland Firth ꭥ 46 58.44 N 3.07 W
Pentland Hills ⋀[2] 46 55.48 N 3.23 W
Pentraeth 44 53.17 N 4.12 W
Pentre Halkyn 262 53.15 N 3.12 W
Pentucket, Lake ⊜ 283 42.47 N 71.05 W
Pentucket Pond ⊜ 283 42.44 N 71.00 W
Pentwater 190 43.46 N 86.25 W
Penuba 112 0.20 S 104.28 E
Peñuelas 240m 18.03 N 66.43 W
Penuguan 112 2.27 S 104.31 E
Penukonda 122 14.05 N 77.35 E
Penunjok, Tanjong > 114 4.22 N 103.29 E
Pènwegon 110 18.13 N 96.34 E
Penwell 196 31.44 N 102.35 W
Peny 78 51.04 N 35.54 E
Penyagolosa ∧ 34 40.13 N 0.21 W
Penyal d'Ifac ◆ 34 38.38 N 0.05 E
Penyengat 114 0.54 N 102.20 E
Pen-y-Ghent ∧ 44 54.09 N 2.14 W
Penygroes, Wales, U.K. 42 51.49 N 4.02 W
Penygroes, Wales, U.K. 44 53.04 N 4.17 W
Penyu, Kepulauan II 164 5.22 S 127.46 E
Penyu, Teluk ⊂ 115a 7.45 S 109.15 E
Penza 80 53.13 N 45.00 E
Penzance 42 50.07 N 5.33 W
Penza Oblast' □[4] 80 53.00 N 45.00 E
Penzberg 64 47.45 N 11.23 E
Penžina ≐ 74 62.28 N 165.18 E
Penzing ✈[8] 264b 48.12 N 16.18 E
Penzino 80 52.07 N 50.27 E
Penžinskaja guba ⊂ 74 61.00 N 162.00 E
Penžinskij chrebet ⋀ 74 62.30 N 167.00 E
Penzlin 54 53.30 N 13.05 E
Péone 62 44.07 N 6.54 E
Peoples Creek ≐ 202 48.24 N 108.19 W
Peoples Ditch ≚ 226 36.15 N 119.41 W
Peoria, Az., U.S. 200 33.34 N 112.14 W
Peoria, Il., U.S. 190 40.41 N 89.35 W
Peoria, Oh., U.S. 216 40.19 N 83.27 W
Peoria Heights 190 40.44 N 89.34 W
Peotillos 234 22.30 N 100.37 W
Peotone 216 41.19 N 87.47 W
Peover Eye ≐ 262 53.15 N 2.31 W
Peover Heath 262 53.15 N 2.19 W
Pepa 154 7.42 S 29.47 E
Pepacton Reservoir ⊜[1] 210 42.06 N 74.54 W
Pepaw ≐ 184 52.40 N 102.23 W
Pepel 150 8.35 N 13.03 W
Peper 140 7.04 N 33.00 E
Pepin 190 44.26 N 92.08 W
Pepin, Lake ⊜ 190 44.30 N 92.15 W
Pepinster 56 50.34 N 5.49 E
Péplos 130 40.58 N 26.16 E
Pepperell 207 42.40 N 71.35 W
Pepper Park State Recreation Area ◆ 220 27.30 N 80.18 W
Pepper Pike 279a 41.28 N 81.27 W
Peqi'in Hadasha 132 32.59 N 35.20 E
Peqin 38 41.03 N 19.45 E
Pequannock 210 40.57 N 74.17 W
Pequannock ≐ 276 40.58 N 74.17 W
Pequanticut Brook ≐ 283 42.01 N 71.08 W
Pequea Creek ≐ 208 39.53 N 76.22 W
Pequeno ≐ 287a 22.55 S 43.25 W
Pequeri 256 21.50 S 43.06 W
Pequest ≐ 210 40.50 N 75.05 W
Pequez 208 39.53 N 76.22 W
Pequizeiro 250 8.32 S 48.58 W
Pequop Mountains ⋀ 204 40.45 N 114.40 W
Pequot Lakes 190 46.36 N 94.18 W
Perabumulih 112 3.27 S 104.15 E
Perak □[3] 114 5.00 N 101.00 E
Perak ≐ 114 3.58 N 100.53 E
Perak, Kuala ⊂ 114 4.00 N 100.47 E
Peralba, Monte ∧ 64 46.37 N 12.43 E
Perales de Alfambra 34 40.38 N 1.00 W
Perales del Rio 266a 40.19 N 3.38 W
Peralillo 252 34.29 S 71.29 W
Peralta 200 34.50 N 106.41 W
Pérama 267c 37.58 N 23.34 E
Perambalur 122 11.14 N 78.53 E

Symbols in the index entries represent the broad categories identified in the key at the right. Symbols with superior numbers (⋀[1]) identify subcategories (see complete key on page I · 1).

Symbole im Register stellen die rechts im Schlüssel erklärten Kategorien dar. Symbole mit hochgestellten Ziffern (⋀[1]) bezeichnen Unterabteilungen einer Kategorie (vgl. vollständiger Schlüssel auf Seite I · 1).

Los símbolos incluídos en el texto del índice representan las grandes categorías identificadas con la clave a la derecha. Los símbolos con numeros en su parte superior (⋀[1]) identifican las subcategorías (véase la clave completa en la página I · 1).

Les symboles de l'index représentent les catégories indiquées dans la légende à droite. Les symboles suivis d'un indice (⋀[1]) représentent des sous-catégories (voir légende complète à la page I · 1).

Os símbolos incluídos no texto do índice representam as grandes categorias identificadas com a chave à direita. Os símbolos com números em sua parte superior (⋀[1]) identificam as subcategorias (veja-se a chave completa à página I · 1).

∧	Mountain	Berg	Montaña	Montagne	Montanha
⋀	Mountains	Gebirge	Montañas	Montagnes	Montanhas
✕	Pass	Paß	Paso	Col	Passo
V	Valley, Canyon	Tal, Cañon	Valle, Cañón	Vallée, Canyon	Vale, Canhão
≚	Plain	Ebene	Llano	Plaine	Planície
>	Cape	Kap	Cabo	Cap	Cabo
I	Island	Insel	Isla	Île	Ilha
II	Islands	Inseln	Islas	Îles	Ilhas
⊥	Other Topographic Features	Andere Topographische Objekte	Otros Elementos Topográficos	Autres données topographiques	Outros acidentes topográficos

ESPAÑOL

Nombre	Página	Lat.°′	Long.°′ W = Oeste
Perämeri (Bottenviken) ⊂	26	65.00 N	23.00 E
Peranāmbattu	122	12.56 N	78.43 E
Peraní, Ákra ›	267c	37.54 N	23.31 E
Perarolo di Cadore	64	46.24 N	12.21 E
Peräseinäjoki	26	62.34 N	23.04 E
Percé	186	48.31 N	64.13 W
Percée, Pointe ∧	58	45.57 N	6.33 E
Perch ≃	212	44.00 N	76.05 W
Perchas	240m	18.19 N	66.59 W
Perchau	61	47.06 N	14.27 E
Perchauer Sattel)(	61	47.07 N	14.27 E
Perche, Collines du ⋏ [2]	50	48.25 N	0.40 E
Perche Creek ≃	194	38.49 N	92.24 W
Perch Lake ⊜	212	44.07 N	75.54 W
Perchtoldsdorf	61	48.07 N	16.17 E
Perchuškovo	265b	55.41 N	37.10 E
Percival Lakes ⊜	162	21.25 S	125.00 E
Percy Creek ≃	212	44.15 N	77.49 W
Percy Isles II	166	21.39 S	150.16 E
Percy Lake ⊜	212	45.13 N	78.22 W
Percy Reach ⊜	212	44.15 N	77.45 W
Perdagangan-tomuon	114	3.09 N	99.20 E
Perdasdefogu	71	39.41 N	9.26 E
Perdeberg	158	28.59 S	25.05 E
Perdekop	158	27.13 S	29.38 E
Perdices, Arroyo de las ≃	288	34.41 S	58.22 W
Perdida ≃	250	9.13 S	47.59 W
Perdido	194	31.00 N	87.37 W
Perdido ≃, Bra.	248	22.10 S	57.33 W
Perdido ≃, U.S.	194	30.29 N	87.26 W
Perdido, Arroyo ≃	254	42.55 S	67.00 W
Perdido, Arroyo del ≃	258	33.37 S	57.23 W
Perdido, Cuchilla del ⋏ [2]	258	33.43 S	57.17 W
Perdido, Monte ∧	34	42.40 N	0.05 E
Perdido Bay ⊂	194	30.21 N	87.27 W
Perdifumo	68	40.16 N	15.01 E
Perdix	208	40.22 N	76.57 W
Perdizes	255	19.21 S	47.17 W
Perdreauville	261	48.58 N	1.38 E
Perdu, Lac ⊜	186	50.44 N	70.14 W
Perdue	184	52.04 N	107.32 W
Perebrody	78	51.43 N	27.00 E
Perečin	78	48.44 N	22.26 E
Peredel	76	55.12 N	35.41 E
Peredel'cy	82	55.36 N	37.21 E
Peredelkino	265b	55.39 N	37.21 E
Peregino	76	57.27 N	31.21 E
Pereginskoje	78	48.49 N	24.12 E
Peregonovka	78	48.32 N	30.31 E
Pereira	246	4.49 N	75.43 W
Pereira Barreto	255	20.38 S	51.07 W
Pereiro	250	6.03 S	38.28 W
Perejaslav-Chmel'nickij	78	50.06 N	31.30 E
Perejaslavka	89	47.58 N	135.06 E
Perejaslavskaja	78	45.51 N	39.02 E
Perejezdnoje	83	48.47 N	38.04 E
Perejež'na	24	59.43 N	48.12 E
Perekopnoje	80	51.13 N	48.04 E
Perekopovka	78	50.37 N	33.25 E
Perekopskaja	80	49.21 N	43.20 E
Père-Lachaise, Cimetière du ◆	261	48.51 N	2.25 E
Perelazovskij	80	49.09 N	42.33 E
Perelazy	76	53.02 N	31.28 E
Perelesinskij	78	51.44 N	40.07 E
Perel'ub	80	51.52 N	50.22 E
Pere Marquette ≃	190	43.57 N	86.27 W
Pere Marquette, Big South Branch ≃	190	43.56 N	86.10 W
Pere Marquette State Park ♦	219	39.00 N	90.30 W
Perem'otnoje	80	51.11 N	50.49 E
Peremyšl'	82	54.16 N	36.10 E
Peremyšl'any	78	49.41 N	24.33 E
Perené ≃	248	11.09 S	74.18 W
Perenjori	162	29.26 S	116.17 E
Pereputje	92a	46.17 N	141.54 E
Pererov	78	52.04 N	28.00 E
Pereščepino	78	49.01 N	35.22 E
Pereščepnoje	80	50.32 N	45.06 E
Pereslavl'-Zalesskij	82	56.44 N	38.51 E
Peresypkino Pervoje	80	52.55 N	42.55 E
Peretrusovo	82	56.51 N	36.53 E
Pereval'sk	83	48.26 N	38.47 E
Perevoz, Ross.	80	55.36 N	44.32 E
Perevoz, Ross.	88	59.00 N	116.57 E
Perevoz, Ross.	265a	59.43 N	30.47 E
Pereyra, Arroyo ≃	288	34.47 S	58.08 W
Pereyra, Punta ›	258	34.14 S	58.04 W
Pérez	252	33.00 S	60.46 W
Perfugas	71	40.50 N	8.53 E
Perg	61	48.15 N	14.37 E
Pergamino	252	33.53 S	60.35 W
Pergamum ⊥	130	39.10 N	27.13 E
Pergau ≃	114	5.23 N	102.02 E
Pergine Valdarno	66	43.28 N	11.41 E
Pergine Valsugana	64	46.04 N	11.14 E
Pergola	66	43.34 N	12.50 E
Pergusa, Lago di ⊜	70	37.31 N	14.18 E
Perham	198	46.35 N	95.34 W
Perho	26	63.13 N	24.25 E
Peri	64	45.39 N	10.54 E
Peri ≃	130	38.50 N	39.35 E
Peribán de Ramos	234	19.32 N	102.28 W
Péribonca ≃	176	48.45 N	72.05 W
Péribonca, Lac ⊜	186	50.04 N	71.15 W
Perico, Arg.	252	24.23 S	65.06 W
Perico, Cuba	240p	22.46 N	81.01 W
Pericos	232	25.03 N	107.42 W
Pericumã ≃	250	2.17 S	44.42 W
Peridot	200	33.18 N	110.27 W
Périers	32	49.11 N	1.25 W
Perigiraja	112	0.16 S	103.30 E
Périgord □ [9]	32	45.20 N	1.00 E
Perigoso, Canal ⩌	250	0.05 N	49.40 W
Périgueux	32	45.11 N	0.43 E
Perijá, Serranía De ⋏	246	10.00 N	73.00 W
Perim → Barīm I	144	12.39 N	43.25 E
Peri-Mirim	250	2.38 S	44.54 W
Perinaldo	62	43.52 N	7.40 E
Peringat	114	6.02 N	102.17 E
Periprava	38	45.24 N	29.32 E
Perisher Valley ♦	171b	36.23 S	145.24 E
Peristérion	267c	38.01 N	23.42 E
Perito	68	40.18 N	15.09 E
Perito Moreno	254	46.36 S	70.56 W
Peritoró	250	4.20 S	44.18 W
Perivale ◆ [8]	260	51.32 N	0.19 W
Periyakulam	122	10.07 N	77.33 E
Periyār ≃	122	10.11 N	76.13 E
Perkasie	208	40.22 N	75.17 W
Perkins	196	35.58 N	97.02 W
Perkinsfield	212	44.42 N	79.57 W
Perkins Observatory ⊍ [3]	214	40.14 N	83.02 W
Perkinston	194	30.46 N	89.08 W
Perkinsville, In., U.S.	218	40.09 N	85.52 W
Perkinsville, N.Y., U.S.	210	42.32 N	77.38 W
Perkiomen Creek ≃	208	40.07 N	75.28 W
Perkiomen Creek, East Branch ≃	208	40.15 N	75.27 W
Perkiomen Junction	285	40.06 N	75.28 W
Perkiomen Valley Airport ⊠	285	40.12 N	75.25 W
Perl	56	49.28 N	6.36 E
Perlas, Archipiélago de las II	246	8.25 N	79.00 W
Perlas, Laguna de ⊂	236	12.30 N	83.40 W
Perlas, Punta de ›	236	12.23 N	83.30 W
Perleberg	54	53.04 N	11.51 E
Perlez	38	45.12 N	20.24 E
Perlis □ [3]	114	6.30 N	100.15 E

FRANÇAIS

Nom	Page	Lat.°′	Long.°′ W = Ouest
Perl'ovka	78	51.51 N	38.51 E
Perm'	86	58.00 N	56.15 E
Permanente Creek ≃	282	37.25 N	122.05 W
Permas	24	59.20 N	45.34 E
Përmet	38	40.14 N	20.21 E
Permisi	80	54.06 N	45.48 E
Perm' Oblast' □ [4]	86	58.00 N	58.00 E
Pernambuco □ [3]	250	8.00 S	37.00 W
Pernambuco → Recife	250	8.03 S	34.54 W
Pernate	266b	45.27 N	8.41 E
Pernatty Lagoon ⊜	166	31.31 S	137.14 E
Pernay	50	47.27 N	0.30 E
Pernegg an der Mur	61	47.22 N	15.21 E
Pernes-les-Fontaines	62	44.00 N	5.03 E
Pernik	38	42.36 N	23.02 E
Pernink	54	50.20 N	12.45 E
Perniö	26	60.12 N	23.08 E
Pernitz	61	47.54 N	15.58 E
Pernovo	82	55.58 N	39.10 E
Pero	266b	45.31 N	9.05 E
Peroba, Ribeirão do ≃	287b	23.27 S	46.22 W
Pérols, Étang de ⊂	62	43.33 N	3.56 E
Peron, Cape ›	168a	32.17 S	115.41 E
Péronne	50	49.56 N	2.56 E
Peron Peninsula › [1]	162	25.55 S	113.30 E
Pero Pinheiro	266c	38.51 N	9.20 W
Perosa Argentina	62	44.58 N	7.10 E
Perote	234	19.34 N	97.14 W
Peroto	248	14.50 S	64.31 W
Pérouges	58	45.54 N	5.11 E
Peroulaz	62	45.42 N	7.19 E
Pérou → Peru □ [1]	242	10.00 S	76.00 W
Perovo ◆ [8]	265b	55.44 N	37.46 E
Perow	182	54.31 N	126.26 W
Perpendicular, Point ›	170	35.06 S	150.48 E
Perpignan	32	42.41 N	2.53 E
Perranporth	42	50.20 N	5.09 W
Perrault Falls	184	50.19 N	93.11 W
Perray ≃	261	48.31 N	1.42 E
Perrero	62	44.56 N	7.05 E
Perriers-sur-Andelle	50	49.25 N	1.22 E
Perrignier	58	46.18 N	6.27 E
Perrigny	58	46.40 N	5.35 E
Perrin	196	33.02 N	98.04 W
Perrine	220	25.36 N	80.21 W
Perrineville	208	40.13 N	74.26 W
Perris	228	33.46 N	117.13 W
Perris, Lake ⊜ [1]	228	33.50 N	117.10 W
Perro, Laguna del ⊜	200	34.40 N	105.57 W
Perro, Punta del ›	34	36.45 N	6.25 W
Perros, Bahía de ⊂	240p	22.25 N	78.30 W
Perros-Guirec	32	48.49 N	3.27 W
Perrot, Île I	206	45.22 N	73.57 W
Perry, Fl., U.S.	192	30.07 N	83.34 W
Perry, Ga., U.S.	192	32.27 N	83.43 W
Perry, Il., U.S.	219	39.47 N	90.45 W
Perry, Ia., U.S.	190	41.50 N	94.06 W
Perry, Ks., U.S.	198	39.04 N	95.23 W
Perry, Me., U.S.	186	44.58 N	67.04 W
Perry, Mi., U.S.	216	42.49 N	84.13 W
Perry, Mo., U.S.	219	39.25 N	91.40 W
Perry, N.Y., U.S.	210	42.42 N	78.00 W
Perry, Oh., U.S.	214	41.45 N	81.08 W
Perry, Ok., U.S.	196	36.17 N	97.17 W
Perry, Tx., U.S.	222	31.25 N	96.55 W
Perry, Ut,. U.S.	200	41.27 N	112.02 W
Perry □ [6]	208	40.25 N	77.11 W
Perrydale	224	45.02 N	123.15 W
Perry Hall	208	39.24 N	76.27 W
Perry Heights	214	40.47 N	81.28 W
Perry-Jōriku-kinenhi ⊥	94	35.14 N	139.43 E
Perry Lake ⊜ [1]	198	39.20 N	95.30 W
Perryman	208	39.28 N	76.12 W
Perrymont	279b	40.33 N	80.02 W
Perryopolis	214	40.05 N	79.45 W
Perry Park	218	38.33 N	85.00 W
Perry Point	208	39.33 N	76.04 W
Perrysburg, N.Y., U.S.	210	42.27 N	79.00 W
Perrysburg, Oh., U.S.	214	41.33 N	83.37 W
Perry's Landing Monument ⊥	268	35.13 N	139.43 E
Perry's Victory and International Peace Memorial ⊥	214	41.33 N	82.50 W
Perrysville, Oh., U.S.	214	40.39 N	82.18 W
Perrysville, Pa., U.S.	279b	40.32 N	80.01 W
Perryton	196	36.24 N	100.48 W
Perryville, Ak., U.S.	180	55.54 N	159.10 W
Perryville, Ar., U.S.	194	35.00 N	92.48 W
Perryville, Ky., U.S.	192	37.39 N	84.57 W
Perryville, Md., U.S.	208	39.33 N	76.04 W
Perryville, Mo., U.S.	194	37.43 N	89.51 W
Perryville, N.Y., U.S.	210	43.01 N	75.48 W
Peršaj	76	54.02 N	26.41 E
Persan	50	49.09 N	2.16 E
Perșani, Munții ⋏	38	45.40 N	25.15 E
Persberg	40	59.45 N	14.15 E
Perschling ≃	61	48.20 N	15.58 E
Perşembe	130	41.04 N	37.46 E
Persepolis → Takht-e Jamshīd ⊥	128	29.57 N	52.52 E
Perseverance, Mount ∧	171a	27.25 S	152.10 E
Perseverancia	248	14.44 S	62.48 W
Pershagen	40	59.10 N	17.39 E
Pershing	218	39.49 N	84.53 W
Pershore	42	52.07 N	2.05 W
Pershyttan	40	59.30 N	15.00 E
Persia	198	41.34 N	95.34 W
Persia → Iran □ [1]	128	32.00 N	53.00 E
Persian Gulf (Arabian Gulf) ⊂	128	27.00 N	51.00 E
Pérsico, Golfo → Persian Gulf ⊂	128	27.00 N	51.00 E
Persimmon Creek ≃	194	31.31 N	86.50 W
Persique, Golfe → Persian Gulf ⊂	128	27.00 N	51.00 E
Persischer Golf → Persian Gulf ⊂	128	27.00 N	51.00 E
Peršotravensk, Ukr.	78	50.12 N	27.39 E
Peršotravensk, Ukr.	78	48.22 N	36.24 E
Peršotravnevoje, Ukr.	78	51.24 N	28.53 E
Peršotravnevoje, Ukr.	83	47.03 N	37.18 E
Perštejn	54	50.23 N	13.08 E
Perstorp	41	56.08 N	13.23 E
Pertandangan, Tanjung ›	114	2.41 N	100.14 E
Pertek	130	38.50 N	39.22 E
Perth, Austl.	168a	31.56 S	115.50 E
Perth, On., Can.	212	44.54 N	76.15 W
Perth, Scot., U.K.	46	56.24 N	3.28 W
Perth, N.Y., U.S.	210	43.03 N	74.12 W
Perth □ [6]	212	43.30 N	81.05 W
Perth Amboy	210	40.30 N	74.15 W
Perth-Andover	186	46.45 N	67.42 W
Perth Basin ✣ [1]	14	28.30 S	110.00 E
Perthes	58	48.39 N	4.49 E
Perth International Airport ⊠	168a	31.57 S	115.58 E
Perthois ◆ [1]	58	48.40 N	4.45 E
Pertokar	144	16.59 N	37.28 E
Pertominsk	24	64.47 N	38.25 E
Pertovo	80	54.22 N	41.31 E
Pertuis	62	43.41 N	5.30 E
Pertusato, Capo ›	71	41.21 N	9.10 E
Peru, Il., U.S.	216	41.19 N	89.07 W
Peru, In., U.S.	216	40.45 N	86.04 W
Peru, Ne., U.S.	198	40.28 N	95.44 W
Peru, N.Y., U.S.	188	44.34 N	73.31 W
Peru (Perú) □ [1], S.A.	242	10.00 S	76.00 W
Peru (Perú) □ [1], S.A.	248	10.00 S	76.00 W
Peruaçu ≃	255	15.11 S	44.07 W
Peru Basin ✣ [1]	18	15.00 S	85.00 W
Peruc	54	50.19 N	13.59 E

PORTUGUÊS

Nome	Página	Lat.°′	Long.°′ W = Oeste
Perućac, Jezero ⊜ [1]	38	43.55 N	19.10 E
Peru-Chile Trench ✣ [1]	18	20.00 S	73.00 W
Perugia	66	43.08 N	12.22 E
Perugia □ [4]	66	43.03 N	12.33 E
Perugorría	252	29.20 S	58.37 W
Peruíbe	252	24.19 S	47.00 W
Peruípe ≃	255	17.43 S	39.16 W
Perumalpār I [1]	122	11.10 N	72.04 E
Peruque Creek ≃	219	38.53 N	90.39 W
Perus ◆ [8]	256	23.25 S	46.45 W
Perušić	36	44.39 N	15.23 E
Péruwelz	50	50.31 N	3.35 E
Pervaja Maja	86	48.55 N	67.25 E
Pervari	128	37.54 N	42.36 E
Pervenchères	50	48.26 N	0.26 E
Pervesinka	80	52.13 N	43.15 E
Pervijze	50	51.05 N	2.47 E
Pervoavgustovskij	76	52.14 N	35.03 E
Pervoje Pole	180	63.05 N	179.19 E
Pervomajka, Kaz.	86	51.17 N	70.08 E
Pervomajka, Ukr.	83	49.09 N	37.58 E
Pervomajka ◆ [8]	83	48.17 N	39.50 E
Pervomajsk, Ross.	80	54.53 N	43.49 E
Pervomajsk, Ross.	88	58.02 N	94.05 E
Pervomajsk, Ukr.	78	48.04 N	30.52 E
Pervomajsk, Ukr.	83	48.37 N	38.35 E
Pervomajsk, Ukr.	83	49.05 N	39.37 E
Pervomajskij, Bela.	76	53.54 N	25.23 E
Pervomajskij, Kyrg.	85	42.51 N	74.04 E
Pervomajskij, Ross.	76	54.04 N	32.29 E
Pervomajskij, Ross.	80	53.22 N	51.38 E
Pervomajskij, Ross.	80	51.22 N	48.54 E
Pervomajskij, Ross.	80	53.15 N	40.18 E
Pervomajskij, Ross.	82	55.57 N	37.52 E
Pervomajskij, Ross.	82	54.03 N	37.32 E
Pervomajskij, Ross.	82	55.32 N	37.09 E
Pervomajskij, Ross.	86	54.52 N	61.08 E
Pervomajskij, Ross.	86	53.41 N	55.57 E
Pervomajskij, Ross.	86	59.29 N	61.24 E
Pervomajskij, Ross.	86	51.32 N	55.06 E
Pervomajskij, Ross.	88	51.44 N	115.39 E
Pervomajskij, Ukr.	78	49.24 N	36.12 E
Pervomajskij, Ukr.	83	47.58 N	38.47 E
Pervomajskoje, Kaz.	85	42.05 N	69.53 E
Pervomajskoje, Ross.	76	52.56 N	33.36 E
Pervomajskoje, Ross.	80	55.05 N	47.22 E
Pervomajskoje, Ross.	80	46.21 N	43.37 E
Pervomajskoje, Ross.	80	50.56 N	46.46 E
Pervomajskoje, Ross.	80	48.50 N	41.14 E
Pervomajskoje, Ross.	80	46.03 N	42.13 E
Pervomajskoje, Ross.	80	51.28 N	47.37 E
Pervomajskoje, Ross.	86	53.45 N	84.08 E
Pervomajskoje, Ross.	86	57.06 N	86.12 E
Pervomajskoje, Ukr.	78	45.43 N	33.51 E
Pervoural'sk	86	56.54 N	59.58 E
Pervušino	80	58.02 N	41.56 E
Pervyj Kuril'skij proliv ⩌	74	50.50 N	156.36 E
Perwenitz	264a	52.40 N	13.01 E
Pes'	76	58.55 N	34.19 E
Pes' ≃	76	59.08 N	35.18 E
Pesa ≃	66	43.44 N	11.01 E
Pes'akov, ostrov I	24	68.47 N	57.35 E
Pesangrohan ≃	269e	6.11 S	106.45 E
Pesaro	66	43.54 N	12.55 E
Pesaro e Urbino □ [4]	66	43.40 N	12.38 E
Pesca	246	5.33 N	73.03 W
Pescadero	226	37.15 N	122.22 W
Pescadero Creek ≃, Ca., U.S.	226	36.42 N	121.17 W
Pescadero Creek ≃, Ca., U.S.	226	37.16 N	122.25 W
Pescadores, Punta ›, Méx.	232	23.46 N	109.43 W
Pescadores, Punta ›, Perú	248	16.21 S	73.15 W
Pescadores → P'enghu Ch'üntao II	100	23.30 N	119.30 E
Pescaglia	66	43.58 N	10.25 E
Pesčanaja	78	48.08 N	29.44 E
Pesčanka, Ross.	80	51.18 N	43.40 E
Pesčanka, Ukr.	78	48.12 N	28.53 E
Pesčanoje, Kaz.	86	53.01 N	76.19 E
Pesčanoje, Ross.	24	62.09 N	35.48 E
Pesčanoje, Ukr.	78	49.44 N	31.50 E
Pesčanoje, Ukr.	83	49.34 N	37.51 E
Pesčanokopskoje	80	46.12 N	41.04 E
Pescantina	64	45.29 N	10.51 E
Pesčanyj	83	47.02 N	37.28 E
Pesčanyje, ostrova II	83	46.52 N	38.17 E
Pescara	66	42.28 N	14.13 E
Pescara □ [4]	66	42.20 N	13.57 E
Pescara ≃	66	42.28 N	14.13 E
Pescasseroli	66	41.48 N	13.47 E
Pesch	263	51.11 N	6.32 E
Pesch, Schloss ⊥	263	51.18 N	6.39 E
Peschici	68	41.57 N	16.01 E
Peschiera del Garda	64	45.26 N	10.42 E
Peschio, Monte ∧	267a	41.43 N	12.46 E
Pescia	66	43.54 N	10.41 E
Pescina	66	42.02 N	13.39 E
Pescocostanzo	66	41.53 N	14.04 E
Pescolanciano	66	41.41 N	14.20 E
Pescopagano	68	40.50 N	15.24 E
Pescorocchiano	66	42.12 N	13.09 E
Pesco Sannita	68	41.14 N	14.49 E
Pesé	236	7.54 N	80.37 W
Pesek, Pulau I	271c	1.17 N	103.41 E
Peseux	58	46.59 N	6.53 E
Peshastin	224	47.34 N	120.36 W
Peshastin Creek ≃	224	47.33 N	120.35 W
Peshāwar	123	34.01 N	71.33 E
Peshīn Jān	128	33.25 N	61.28 E
Peshkopi	38	41.41 N	20.26 E
Peshtigo	190	45.03 N	87.44 W
Peshtigo ≃	190	44.58 N	87.40 W
Pesio ≃	62	44.28 N	7.53 E
Pesjane	82	56.01 N	38.48 E
Peski, Bela.	76	53.21 N	24.38 E
Peski, Ross.	80	51.16 N	42.27 E
Peski, Ross.	82	55.13 N	38.46 E
Peški, Ross.	82	56.08 N	37.04 E
Peski, Ukr.	78	50.23 N	33.27 E
Peski, Ukr.	83	49.26 N	38.59 E
Peski-Rad'kovskije	83	49.17 N	37.36 E
Peskovatskoje	82	54.03 N	36.16 E
Peskovka, Ross.	86	59.04 N	52.22 E
Peskovka, Ukr.	78	50.42 N	29.38 E
Peškovo	83	47.02 N	39.24 E
Peškovo Grecovo	82	54.26 N	37.36 E
Peškovskoje	86	53.45 N	62.23 E
Pesmes	58	47.17 N	5.34 E
Pesnica	61	46.36 N	15.41 E
Pesnica ≃	61	46.24 N	16.05 E
Pešnoj, poluostrov › [2]	80	46.52 N	51.42 E
Pesočenskij	82	54.10 N	36.06 E
Pesočin	78	49.57 N	36.06 E
Pesočn'a	80	54.07 N	40.50 E
Pesočnoje, Bela.	76	53.20 N	27.06 E
Pesočnoje, Ross.	80	58.01 N	39.10 E
Pesočnyj	76	60.07 N	30.08 E
Peso da Régua	34	41.10 N	7.47 W
Pespire	236	13.35 N	87.22 W
Pesqueira	250	8.22 S	36.42 W
Pesquería	196	25.47 N	100.03 W
Pesquería ≃	196	25.54 N	99.11 W
Pessac	32	44.48 N	0.38 W
Pessin	54	52.38 N	12.40 E
Pessinetto	62	45.17 N	7.24 E
Pest □ [6]	30	47.25 N	19.20 E
Pest'aki	80	56.43 N	42.40 E
Peštera	38	42.02 N	24.18 E
Pesterzsébet ◆ [8]	264c	47.26 N	19.07 E
Pesthidegkút ◆ [8]	264c	47.34 N	18.58 E
Pestimre ◆ [8]	264c	47.24 N	19.12 E
Pestlőrinc ◆ [8]	264c	47.26 N	19.12 E
Pestovo, Ross.	76	58.36 N	35.48 E
Pestovo, Ross.	80	57.12 N	46.44 E

Pestovskoje vodochranilišče ⊜ [1]	82	56.06 N	37.40 E
Pestravka	80	52.24 N	49.58 E
Pestrecy	80	55.46 N	49.39 E
Pestrikovo	82	55.05 N	38.53 E
Pestújhely ◆ [8]	264c	47.32 N	19.07 E
Petacalco, Bahía ⊂	234	17.57 N	102.05 W
Petaḥ Tiqwa	132	32.05 N	34.53 E
Petäjävesi	26	62.15 N	25.12 E
Petal	194	31.20 N	89.15 W
Petalcingo	232	17.17 N	92.27 W
Petaling Jaya	114	3.05 N	101.39 E
Petalión, Kólpos ⊂	38	37.59 N	24.02 E
Petaluma	226	38.13 N	122.38 W
Petaluma ≃	226	38.06 N	122.30 W
Pétange	56	49.34 N	5.52 E
Petare	246	10.29 N	66.49 W
Petatlán	234	17.31 N	101.16 W
Petauke	154	14.15 S	31.20 E
Petawawa	190	45.54 N	77.17 W
Petawawa ≃	190	45.55 N	77.15 W
Pété	146	10.58 N	14.30 E
Petegem	50	50.58 N	3.32 E
Petén □ [5]	236	16.15 N	89.50 W
Petén Itzá, Lago ⊜	232	16.59 N	89.50 W
Petenwell Lake ⊜ [1]	190	44.10 N	89.57 W
Peter and Paul Fortress ⊥	265a	59.57 N	30.19 E
Peterboro	210	42.58 N	75.41 W
Peterborough, Austl.	166	32.58 S	138.50 E
Peterborough, On., Can.	212	44.18 N	78.19 W
Peterborough, Eng., U.K.	42	52.35 N	0.15 W
Peterborough, N.H., U.S.	188	42.52 N	71.57 W
Peterborough □ [6]	212	44.33 N	78.15 W
Peterculter	46	57.05 N	2.16 W
Peterhead	46	57.30 N	1.49 W
Peter Hill ∧	46	56.58 N	2.42 W
Peter I Island I	9	68.47 S	90.35 W
Peter Island I	240m	18.22 N	64.35 W
Peter Lake ⊜, N.T., Can.	176	63.08 N	92.48 W
Peter Lake ⊜, Sk., Can.	184	57.15 N	103.53 W
Peterlee	44	54.46 N	1.19 W
Peter Lougheed Provincial Park ♦	182	50.45 N	115.15 W
Peterman	194	31.35 N	87.15 W
Petermann Ranges ⋏	162	25.00 S	129.46 E
Petermann Reserve ◆ [4]	162	25.00 S	130.15 E
Peter Pond Lake ⊜	184	55.55 N	108.44 W
Peter Pond Lake Indian Reserve ◆ [4]	184	55.55 N	109.00 W
Petersberg	56	50.33 N	9.43 E
Peters Brook ≃	276	40.33 N	74.37 W
Petersburg, Ak., U.S.	180	56.49 N	132.57 W
Petersburg, Il., U.S.	219	40.00 N	89.50 W
Petersburg, In., U.S.	194	38.29 N	87.16 W
Petersburg, Mi., U.S.	216	41.54 N	83.42 W
Petersburg, Ne., U.S.	198	41.51 N	98.04 W
Petersburg, N.J., U.S.	208	39.15 N	74.43 W
Petersburg, N.Y., U.S.	210	42.44 N	73.20 W
Petersburg, Oh., U.S.	214	40.54 N	80.31 W
Petersburg, Pa., U.S.	214	40.34 N	78.03 W
Petersburg, Tn., U.S.	194	35.19 N	86.38 W
Petersburg, Tx., U.S.	196	33.52 N	101.36 W
Petersburg, Va., U.S.	208	37.13 N	77.24 W
Petersburg, W.V., U.S.	188	38.59 N	79.07 W
Petersburg National Battlefield ♦	208	37.14 N	77.22 W
Peters Canyon Reservoir ⊜ [1]	280	33.47 N	117.45 W
Peters Creek ≃, Ca., U.S.	282	37.15 N	122.13 W
Peters Creek ≃, Pa., U.S.	279b	40.18 N	79.52 W
Peters Creek, Piney Fork ≃	279b	40.16 N	79.58 W
Petersdorf	54	54.29 N	11.04 E
Petersfield, S. Afr.	273d	26.14 S	28.26 E
Petersfield, Eng., U.K.	42	51.00 N	0.56 W
Petershagen, Dtsch.	52	52.23 N	8.58 E
Petershagen, Dtsch.	54	52.24 N	14.20 E
Petershagen bei Berlin	54	52.31 N	13.46 E
Petersham, Austl.	274a	33.54 S	151.09 E
Petersham, Ma., U.S.	207	42.29 N	72.11 W
Peters Hill ∧ [2]	168b	34.11 S	138.50 E
Peterson	198	42.55 N	95.20 W
Peterson Air Force Base ■	198	38.49 N	104.42 W
Peters Pond ⊜	283	42.43 N	71.16 W
Peterswald Hill ∧ [2]	162	26.43 S	123.39 E
Peter the Great Bay → Petra Velikogo, zaliv ⊂	89	42.40 N	132.00 E
Peter the Great Monument ⊥	265a	59.56 N	30.18 E
Pétervására	30	48.01 N	20.06 E
Petilia Policastro	68	39.07 N	16.47 E
Pétionville	238	18.31 N	72.17 W
Petit	273d	26.06 S	28.22 E
Petit Bois Island I	194	30.12 N	88.26 W
Petit-Bourg	241o	16.12 N	61.36 W
Petit-Canal	241o	16.23 N	61.29 W
Petitcodiac	186	45.56 N	65.10 W
Petitcodiac ≃	186	45.50 N	64.33 W
Petit Cul-de-Sac Marin ⊂	241o	16.12 N	61.33 W
Petite Nation, Rivière de la ≃	206	45.35 N	75.06 W
Petite Rivière du Chêne ≃	206	46.34 N	72.02 W
Petite Rivière Noire, Piton de la ∧	157c	20.24 S	57.24 E
Petite Rivière Rouge ≃	206	45.45 N	75.00 W
Petites-Anses	241o	15.51 N	61.39 W
Petite Sauldre ≃	50	47.27 N	2.05 E
Petite Terre, Îles de la II	241o	16.10 N	61.07 W
Petit Forte	186	47.24 N	54.40 W
Petit-Fort-Philippe	50	51.00 N	2.07 E
Petit-Goâve	238	18.26 N	72.52 W
Petit Jean ≃	194	35.10 N	92.56 W
Petit Jean State Park ♦	194	35.06 N	92.57 W
Petit Loango	152	2.16 S	9.35 E
Petit Loango, Parc National du ♦	152	2.15 S	9.36 E
Petit Mécatina, Île du I	186	50.33 N	59.20 W
Petit Morin ≃	50	48.56 N	3.07 E
Petitot ≃	176	60.14 N	123.29 W
Petit Piton ∧	241f	13.50 N	61.04 W
Petit Rhône ≃	62	43.27 N	4.24 E
Petit-Saint-Bernard, Col du)(	62	45.41 N	6.53 E
Petitsikapau Lake ⊜	176	54.45 N	66.25 W
Petkeljärven kansallispuisto ♦	24	62.35 N	31.12 E
Petkus	54	51.59 N	13.21 E
Petlād	120	22.28 N	72.48 E
Petlalcingo	234	18.05 N	97.54 W
Peto	232	20.08 N	88.55 W
Petoh	114	2.53 N	103.15 E
Petone	172	41.13 S	174.52 E
Petorca	252	32.15 S	70.56 W
Petoskey	190	45.22 N	84.57 W
Petownikip Lake ⊜	184	52.56 N	92.02 W
Petra → Baṭrā ⊥	132	30.20 N	35.26 E
Petralia Soprana	70	37.47 N	14.06 E

Petralia Sottana	70	37.48 N	14.05 E
Petras, Mount ∧	9	75.52 S	128.38 W
Petra Velikogo, zaliv (Peter the Great Bay) ⊂	89	42.40 N	132.00 E
Petre, Point ›	212	43.50 N	77.09 W
Petrecovo	24	61.18 N	57.07 E
Petrella, Monte ∧	66	41.18 N	13.40 E
Petrella Salto	66	42.18 N	13.04 E
Petrella Tifernina	66	41.41 N	14.42 E
Petrič	38	41.24 N	23.13 E
Petrie	171a	27.16 S	152.59 E
Petrified Forest National Park ♦	200	34.55 N	109.49 W
Petrikov	76	52.08 N	28.30 E
Petrikovka	78	48.43 N	34.37 E
Petrila	38	45.27 N	23.25 E
Petrinja	36	45.26 N	16.17 E
Petriščevo, Ross.	82	54.37 N	36.57 E
Petriščevo, Ross.	82	55.30 N	36.18 E
Petrítis, Ákra ›	267c	37.56 N	23.24 E
Petrodvorec	76	59.53 N	29.54 E
Petroglyphs Provincial Park ♦	212	44.33 N	77.53 W
Petrogrado-Doneckoje ◆ [8]	83	48.42 N	38.41 E
Petrograd → Sankt-Peterburg	76	59.55 N	30.15 E
Petrohué	254	41.08 S	72.25 W
Petrolândia	250	9.05 S	38.18 W
Petrólea	246	8.30 N	72.35 W
Petroleum	216	40.36 N	85.09 W
Petrolia, On., Can.	214	42.52 N	82.09 W
Petrolia, Pa., U.S.	214	41.01 N	79.43 W
Petrolia, Tx., U.S.	196	34.01 N	98.14 W
Petrolina	250	9.24 S	40.30 W
Petrolina de Goiás	255	16.06 S	49.20 W
Petronà	68	39.03 N	16.45 E
Petrona, Punta ›	240m	17.56 N	66.23 W
Petronila Creek ≃	196	27.32 N	97.32 W
Petropavlovka, Ross.	78	50.06 N	40.54 E
Petropavlovka, Ross.	88	50.38 N	105.19 E
Petropavlovka, Ukr.	78	48.27 N	36.26 E
Petropavlovka, Ukr.	83	49.43 N	37.42 E
Petropavlovsk, Kaz.	86	54.54 N	69.06 E
Petropavlovsk, Ross.	86	56.20 N	57.09 E
Petropavlovsk-Kamčatskij	74	53.01 N	158.39 E
Petropavlovskoje, Ross.	86	52.04 N	84.08 E
Petropavlovskoje, Ross.	88	58.13 N	108.59 E
Petrópolis	256	22.31 S	43.10 W
Petros	192	36.05 N	84.26 W
Petroșani	38	45.25 N	23.22 E
Petrosino	70	37.43 N	12.29 E
Petro-Slav'anka	265a	59.48 N	30.31 E
Petroso, Monte ∧	66	41.44 N	13.55 E
Petroúpolis	267c	38.03 N	23.41 E
Petrovac	38	44.22 N	21.27 E
Petrovgrad → Zrenjanin	38	45.23 N	20.24 E
Petrovka, Ross.	80	53.13 N	51.58 E
Petrovka, Ukr.	78	46.54 N	30.44 E
Petrovka, Ukr.	83	48.48 N	39.16 E
Petrovka, Ukr.	83	48.53 N	39.52 E
Petrovo, Ross.	76	58.22 N	35.09 E
Petrovo, Ross.	82	55.00 N	38.08 E
Petrovo, Ross.	88	54.30 N	105.15 E
Petrovo, Ukr.	78	48.20 N	33.16 E
Petrovo-Dal'neje	265b	55.45 N	37.11 E
Petrovo-Krasnoselje ◆ [8]	83	48.18 N	38.52 E
Petrovsk	80	52.19 N	45.23 E
Petrovskaja	78	45.25 N	37.57 E
Petrovskij, Ross.	80	56.39 N	40.19 E
Petrovskij, Ross.	80	50.45 N	41.59 E
Petrovskij, Ross.	82	54.29 N	36.59 E
Petrovskoje, Ross.	80	52.39 N	40.15 E
Petrovskoje, Ross.	80	57.01 N	39.16 E
Petrovskoje, Ross.	82	55.27 N	38.21 E
Petrovskoje, Ross.	82	55.32 N	36.59 E
Petrovskoje, Ross.	265b	55.36 N	37.53 E
Petrovskoje, Ukr.	78	49.10 N	36.54 E
Petrovskoje, Ukr.	83	48.18 N	38.52 E
Petrovsko-Razumovskoje ◆ [8]	265b	55.50 N	37.34 E
Petrovsk-Zabajkal'skij	88	51.17 N	108.50 E
Petrov Val	80	50.09 N	45.12 E
Petrozavodsk	24	61.47 N	34.20 E
Petrozsény → Petroșani	38	45.25 N	23.22 E
Petrun'	24	66.28 N	60.43 E
Petrusburg	158	29.08 S	25.27 E
Petrušino	265a	59.48 N	30.50 E
Petrus Steyn	158	27.38 S	28.08 E
Petrusville	158	30.05 S	24.41 E
Petschora → Pečora ≃	24	68.13 N	54.15 E
Petten	52	52.45 N	4.39 E
Pettenbach	61	47.57 N	14.01 E
Petteril ≃	44	54.54 N	2.55 W
Petticoat Creek ≃	275b	43.48 N	79.06 W
Pettigoe	48	54.33 N	7.50 W
Pettinascura, Monte ∧	68	39.22 N	16.37 E
Pettineo	70	37.58 N	14.17 E
Pettisville	216	41.31 N	84.13 W
Pettnau	64	47.18 N	11.08 E
Pettneu am Arlberg	58	47.09 N	10.20 E
Pettus	196	28.37 N	97.48 W
Petty Harbour	186	47.28 N	52.43 W
Petty Island I	285	39.58 N	75.07 W
Petua	272b	22.25 N	88.27 E
Petuchovo	86	55.06 N	67.58 E
Petuški	80	55.55 N	39.28 E
Petworth	42	50.59 N	0.38 W
Petzow	264a	52.21 N	12.56 E
Peudada	114	5.12 N	96.35 E
Peuerbach	60	48.20 N	13.46 E
Peuetsagoe, Gunung ∧	114	4.55 N	96.20 E
Peureulak	114	4.48 N	97.53 E
Peureulak ≃	114	4.54 N	97.53 E
Peureulak, Ujung ›	114	4.54 N	97.54 E
Peusangan ≃	114	5.16 N	96.51 E
Peusangan, Ujung ›	114	5.16 N	96.50 E
Pevek	74	69.42 N	170.17 E
Pevely	219	38.17 N	90.23 W
Pevensey	42	50.49 N	0.20 E
Pevensey Levels ⩩	42	50.50 N	0.20 E
Peveragno	62	44.20 N	7.37 E
Pewamo	216	43.00 N	84.50 W
Pewaukee	216	43.04 N	88.15 W
Pewaukee Lake ⊜	216	43.04 N	88.19 W
Pewee Valley	218	38.18 N	85.29 W
Pews Creek ≃	276	40.27 N	74.06 W
Pewsey	42	51.21 N	1.46 W
Pewsey, Vale of V	42	51.20 N	1.48 W
Péyia	130	34.53 N	32.23 E
Peyrolles-en-Provence	62	43.39 N	5.35 E
Peyruis	62	44.02 N	5.56 E
Peza ≃	24	65.36 N	44.35 E
Pezas	86	54.39 N	87.46 E
Pezawa Taung ∧	110	19.33 N	94.31 E
Pézenas	32	43.27 N	3.25 E
Peženga	76	59.10 N	44.16 E
Pezinok	30	48.18 N	17.17 E
Pezu	123	32.19 N	70.44 E
Pezzana	62	45.16 N	8.29 E
Pfäfers	58	46.59 N	9.30 E
Pfaffenhausen	58	48.07 N	10.27 E
Pfaffenhofen an der Ilm	60	48.31 N	11.30 E
Pfaffenhoffen	56	48.51 N	7.37 E
Pfaffenöden ∧ [2]	264b	48.04 N	16.33 E
Pfäffikersee ⊜	58	47.21 N	8.48 E
Pfäffikon	58	47.22 N	8.47 E
Pfaffnau	58	47.14 N	7.54 E

Pfaffstätten	264b	48.01 N	16.16 E
Pfalzdorf	52	51.42 N	6.11 E
Pfalzel	56	49.47 N	6.41 E
Pfänder ∧	58	47.30 N	9.47 E
Pfarrkirchen	60	48.27 N	12.56 E
Pfarrweisach	56	50.09 N	10.44 E
Pfastatt	58	47.47 N	7.18 E
Pfatter	60	48.58 N	12.23 E
Pfaueninsel, Schloss ⊥	264a	52.26 N	13.07 E
Pfeddersheim	56	49.38 N	8.16 E
Pfeffenhausen	60	48.40 N	11.58 E
Pfeiffer-Big Sur State Park ♦	226	36.15 N	121.47 W
Pferderennbahn ♦	263	51.31 N	7.32 E
Pflugerville	222	30.26 N	97.37 W
Pforzen	58	47.55 N	10.37 E
Pforzheim	56	48.54 N	8.42 E
Pfreimd ≃	60	49.29 N	12.11 E
Pfrimm ≃	56	49.39 N	8.22 E
Pfronten	58	47.34 N	10.33 E
Pfuhl	58	48.24 N	10.02 E
Pfullendorf	58	47.55 N	9.15 E
Pfullingen	58	48.28 N	9.13 E
Pfunds	58	46.58 N	10.33 E
Pfungstadt	56	49.48 N	8.36 E
Pfyn	58	47.36 N	8.57 E
Pha-an	110	16.53 N	97.38 E
Phachi ≃	110	13.56 N	99.24 E
Phaéton, Port ⊂	174s	17.44 S	149.21 W
Phagwāra	123	31.14 N	75.46 E
Phala	156	23.45 S	26.57 E
Phalaborwa	156	23.55 S	31.13 E
Phalanx	214	41.15 N	80.58 W
Phalempin	50	50.31 N	3.01 E
Phālia	123	32.26 N	73.35 E
Phalodi	120	27.08 N	72.22 E
Phalsbourg	56	48.46 N	7.16 E
Phalta	126	22.17 N	88.07 E
Phaltan	122	17.59 N	74.26 E
Phalti	272b	22.46 N	88.34 E
Phan	110	19.28 N	99.43 E
Phanat Nikhom	110	13.27 N	101.11 E
Phangan, Ko I	110	9.45 N	100.04 E
Phang Hoei, Khao ∧	110	15.15 N	101.23 E
Phangnga	110	8.28 N	98.32 E
Phaniang ≃	110	16.49 N	102.24 E
Phanom Dongrak, Thiu Khao ⋏	110	14.25 N	103.30 E
Phanom Thuan	110	14.07 N	99.42 E
Phan Rang	110	11.34 N	108.59 E
Phan Thiet	110	10.56 N	108.06 E
Phan Thong	110	13.28 N	101.06 E
Phantom Lake	216	42.52 N	88.21 W
Pharenda	124	27.06 N	83.17 E
Phariāro	120	27.12 N	68.59 E
Pharr	196	26.11 N	98.11 W
Phasi Charoen	269a	13.43 N	100.26 E
Phasi Charoen, Khlong ≡	269a	13.44 N	100.30 E
Phat Diem	110	20.06 N	106.06 E
Phato	110	9.48 N	98.48 E
Phatthalung	110	7.37 N	100.05 E
Phayao	110	19.10 N	99.55 E
Pheasant Creek ≃	184	50.35 N	103.28 W
Pheba	194	33.35 N	88.56 W
Phelan	228	34.25 N	117.34 W
Phelps, N.Y., U.S.	210	42.57 N	77.03 W
Phelps, Tx., U.S.	222	30.42 N	95.27 W
Phelps, Wi., U.S.	190	46.03 N	89.05 W
Phelps Lake ⊜	192	35.46 N	76.27 W
Phenix City	192	32.28 N	85.00 W
Phepane ≃	156	25.50 S	22.45 E
Phet Buri ≃	110	13.13 N	99.59 E
Phetchabun	110	16.25 N	101.08 E
Phetchabun, Thiu Khao ⋏	110	16.20 N	100.55 E
Phetchaburi	110	13.06 N	99.57 E
Phibun Mangsahan	110	15.14 N	105.14 E
Phichai	110	17.17 N	100.05 E
Phichit	110	16.26 N	100.22 E
Philadelphia, S. Afr.	158	33.40 S	18.36 E
Philadelphia, Il., U.S.	219	39.58 N	90.07 W
Philadelphia, Ms., U.S.	194	32.46 N	89.07 W
Philadelphia, Mo., U.S.	219	39.50 N	91.44 W
Philadelphia, N.Y., U.S.	212	44.09 N	75.42 W
Philadelphia, Pa., U.S.	208	39.57 N	75.09 W
Philadelphia, Pa., U.S.	285	39.57 N	75.09 W
Philadelphia, Tn., U.S.	192	35.40 N	84.24 W
Philadelphia □ [6]	285	39.57 N	75.07 W
Philadelphia International Airport ⊠	208	39.53 N	75.14 W
Philadelphia Museum of Art ⊍	285	39.58 N	75.11 W
Philadelphia Naval Shipyard ■	285	39.53 N	75.11 W
Philadelphia Park Race Track ♦	285	40.07 N	74.57 W
Philae ⊥	140	24.01 N	32.53 E
Phil Campbell	194	34.21 N	87.42 W
Philip	198	44.02 N	101.39 W
Philipp	194	33.45 N	90.12 W
Philippeville	50	50.12 N	4.32 E
Philippeville → Skikda	148	36.50 N	6.58 E
Philippi	188	39.09 N	80.02 W
Philippi, Lake ⊜	166	24.22 S	139.00 E
Philippine Basin ✣ [1]	14	17.00 N	132.00 E
Philippine International Convention Center ♦	269f	14.32 N	120.59 E
Philippinen → Philippines □ [1]	116	13.00 N	122.00 E
Philippines (Pilipinas) □ [1], Asia	108	13.00 N	122.00 E
Philippines (Pilipinas) □ [1], Asia	116	13.00 N	122.00 E
Philippines, University of the ⊍ [2]	269f	14.39 N	121.04 E
Philippine Sea ⊤ [2]	14	20.00 N	135.00 E
Philippine Trench ✣ [1]	14	9.00 N	127.00 E
Philippolis	158	30.19 S	25.13 E
Philippopolis → Plovdiv	38	42.09 N	24.45 E
Philippsreut	60	48.52 N	13.41 E
Philippsthal	264a	52.20 N	13.09 E
Philipsburg, P.Q., Can.	206	45.02 N	73.05 W
Philipsburg, Ned. Ant.	238	17.59 N	63.10 W
Philipsburg, Mt., U.S.	202	46.19 N	113.17 W
Philipsburg, Pa., U.S.	214	40.53 N	78.13 W
Philipsburg Manor ⊥	276	41.05 N	73.52 W
Philipse Manor Hall State Historic Site ⊥	276	40.56 N	73.54 W
Philip Smith Mountains ⋏	180	68.30 N	148.00 W
Philipstown	158	30.26 S	24.29 E
Phillaur	123	31.01 N	75.47 E
Phillip Island I	169	38.29 S	145.14 E
Phillips, Me., U.S.	188	44.49 N	70.20 W
Phillips, Tx., U.S.	196	35.41 N	101.21 W
Phillips, Wi., U.S.	190	45.41 N	90.24 W
Phillipsburg, Ga., U.S.	192	31.34 N	83.31 W
Phillipsburg, Ks., U.S.	198	39.45 N	99.19 W
Phillipsburg, N.J., U.S.	210	40.41 N	75.11 W
Philmont	210	42.14 N	73.39 W
Philo, Il., U.S.	194	40.01 N	88.09 W
Philo, Oh., U.S.	188	39.51 N	81.54 W
Philomath	202	44.32 N	123.21 W

	English	Deutsch	Español	Français	Português
≃	River	Fluß	Río	Rivière	Rio
≡	Canal	Kanal	Canal	Canal	Canal
⅃	Waterfall, Rapids	Wasserfall, Stromschnellen	Cascada, Rápidos	Chute d'eau, Rapides	Cascata, Rápidos
⩌	Strait	Meeresstraße	Estrecho	Détroit	Estreito
⊂	Bay, Gulf	Bucht, Golf	Bahía, Golfo	Baie, Golfe	Baía, Golfo
⊜	Lake, Lakes	See, Seen	Lago, Lagos	Lac, Lacs	Lago, Lagos
⩩	Swamp	Sumpf	Pantano	Marais	Pântano
⊓	Ice Features, Glacier	Eis- und Gletscherformen	Accidentes Glaciales	Formes glaciaires	Acidentes glaciares
⊤	Other Hydrographic Features	Andere Hydrographische Objekte	Otros Elementos Hidrográficos	Autres données hydrographiques	Outros acidentes hidrográficos
✣	Submarine Features	Untermeerische Objekte	Accidentes Submarinos	Formes de relief sous-marin	Acidentes submarinos
□	Political Unit	Politische Einheit	Unidad Politica	Entité politique	Unidade política
⊍	Cultural Institution	Kulturelle Institution	Institución Cultural	Institution culturelle	Instituição cultural
⊥	Historical Site	Historische Stätte	Sitio Histórico	Site historique	Sitio histórico
♦	Recreational Site	Erholungs- und Ferienort	Sitio de Recreo	Centre de loisirs	Area de Lazer
⊠	Airport	Flughafen	Aeropuerto	Aéroport	Aeroporto
■	Military Installation	Militäranlage	Instalación Militar	Installation militaire	Instalação militar
◆	Miscellaneous	Verschiedenes	Misceláneo	Divers	Diversos

Name	Page	Lat.°′	Long.°′
Philpots Island I	176	74.48 N	80.00 W
Phimai	110	15.13 N	102.30 E
Phinga	272b	22.41 N	88.25 E
Phitsanulok	110	16.50 N	100.15 E
Phnom Penh → Phnum Pénh	110	11.33 N	104.55 E
Phnum Pénh	110	11.33 N	104.55 E
Phnum Tbêng Méanchey	110	13.49 N	104.58 E
Pho ≃	124	27.41 N	89.53 E
Phoenicia	210	42.05 N	74.18 W
Phoenix, Az., U.S.	200	33.26 N	112.04 W
Phoenix, Il., U.S.	278	41.36 N	87.38 W
Phoenix, Md., U.S.	208	39.30 N	76.36 W
Phoenix, N.Y., U.S.	210	43.13 N	76.18 W
Phoenix Islands II	14	4.00 S	172.00 W
Phoenix Lake ⊜[1]	282	37.57 N	122.35 W
Phoenix Park ♦	281	42.24 N	83.27 W
Phoenixville	208	40.07 N	75.30 W
Phon	110	15.49 N	102.36 E
Phong ≃	110	16.23 N	102.56 E
Phôngsali	110	21.41 N	102.06 E
Phong Tho	110	22.32 N	103.21 E
Phon Phisai	110	18.01 N	103.05 E
Phosphate Hill	166	21.52 S	139.51 E
Phrae	110	18.09 N	100.08 E
Phra Khanong -•-[8]	269a	13.42 N	100.35 E
Phra Nakhon → Krung Thep	110	13.45 N	100.31 E
Phra Nakhon Si Ayutthaya	110	14.21 N	100.33 E
Phran Kratai	110	16.40 N	99.36 E
Phrao	110	19.22 N	99.13 E
Phra Pradaeng	269a	13.40 N	100.32 E
Phra Rop, Khao ∧	110	13.11 N	99.31 E
Phrom Phiram	110	17.02 N	100.12 E
Phrygia □[9]	130	39.00 N	30.00 E
Phsar Réam	110	10.30 N	103.37 E
Phu Cat	110	14.01 N	109.03 E
Phu Huu, Viet	110	18.58 N	105.31 E
Phu Huu, Viet	269c	10.43 N	106.47 E
Phuket	110	7.53 N	98.24 E
Phuket, Ko I	110	8.00 N	98.22 E
Phularwān	123	32.22 N	73.00 E
Phulbari	126	21.52 N	88.08 E
Phulbāria	126	23.22 N	89.50 E
Phuljhuri	126	22.12 N	90.04 E
Phulkusma	126	22.43 N	86.52 E
Phu Loc	110	16.16 N	107.53 E
Phūlpur	124	25.33 N	82.06 E
Phulra	123	34.20 N	73.03 E
Phultala	126	22.59 N	89.28 E
Phu Ly	110	20.32 N	105.56 E
Phum Duang ≃	110	9.10 N	99.20 E
Phumĭ Bâ Kham	110	13.51 N	107.22 E
Phumĭ Banam	110	11.19 N	105.18 E
Phumĭ Béng	110	13.05 N	104.18 E
Phumĭ Châmbák	110	11.14 N	104.49 E
Phumĭ Chângho Ândêng	110	12.39 N	104.35 E
Phumĭ Chhuk	110	10.50 N	104.28 E
Phumĭ Chruŏy Slêng	110	13.14 N	105.57 E
Phumĭ Dăk Dăm	110	12.20 N	107.21 E
Phumĭ Kâmpóng Srâlau	110	14.05 N	105.46 E
Phumĭ Kâmpóng Trâbâk	110	13.06 N	105.14 E
Phumĭ Kântuŏt Sâmraông	110	14.12 N	104.37 E
Phumĭ Kaôh Kért	110	13.47 N	104.32 E
Phumĭ Kaôh Kŏng	110	11.26 N	103.11 E
Phumĭ Khpôb	110	11.02 N	105.12 E
Phumĭ Krêk	110	11.46 N	105.56 E
Phumĭ Lvéa Kraôm	110	13.21 N	102.54 E
Phumĭ Moŭng	110	13.45 N	103.33 E
Phumĭ Narŭng	110	13.53 N	105.34 E
Phumĭ Phnum Srâlau	110	11.03 N	103.42 E
Phumĭ Prêk Kák	110	12.15 N	105.32 E
Phumĭ Prêk Sândêk	110	11.51 N	105.22 E
Phumĭ Prey Toch	110	12.54 N	103.23 E
Phumĭ Puŏk Chăs	110	13.26 N	103.44 E
Phumĭ Rôluŏs Chăs	110	13.19 N	104.00 E
Phumĭ Sâmraông	110	14.11 N	103.31 E
Phumĭ Spœ Tbong	110	12.20 N	105.19 E
Phumĭ Srê Kôkir	110	13.08 N	106.04 E
Phumĭ Srê Rônéam	110	12.16 N	106.25 E
Phumĭ Tbêng	110	13.35 N	104.55 E
Phumĭ Thalabârĭvăt	110	13.33 N	105.57 E
Phumĭ Thmâ Pôk	110	13.57 N	103.04 E
Phumĭ Tnaôt	110	12.56 N	104.34 E
Phumĭ Tœk Choŭ	110	13.36 N	103.24 E
Phu My	110	14.10 N	109.03 E
Phung Hiep	110	9.49 N	105.50 E
Phuntsholing	124	26.53 N	89.23 E
Phuoc Binh	110	11.50 N	106.58 E
Phuoc Khanh	269c	10.40 N	106.48 E
Phuoc Long	110	9.26 N	105.28 E
Phuoc Long Xa	269c	10.49 N	106.46 E
Phuoc Luong	269c	10.45 N	106.48 E
Phu Quoc	110	10.13 N	103.58 E
Phu Quoc, Dao I	110	10.12 N	104.00 E
Phurphura	272b	22.44 N	88.08 E
Phu Tho	110	21.24 N	105.13 E
Phu Tho Hoa	269c	10.46 N	106.38 E
Phu Tho Race Track ♦	269c	10.46 N	106.40 E
Phutthaisong	110	15.32 N	103.01 E
Phu Vang	110	16.31 N	107.37 E
Phu Yen	110	21.16 N	104.39 E
Pi ≃	100	32.26 N	116.34 E
Pia	154	4.00 N	26.17 E
Piaanu Pass ⋓	175c	7.20 N	151.26 E
Piabas	250	1.12 S	46.54 W
Piabetá	256	22.37 S	43.10 W
Piabonha ≃	256	22.07 S	43.08 W
Piaçabuçu	250	10.24 S	36.25 W
Piacatuba	256	21.29 S	42.47 W
Piacenza	62	45.01 N	9.40 E
Piacenza □[4]	62	44.53 N	9.35 E
Piacouadie, Lac ⊜	186	51.16 N	70.54 W
Piadena	64	45.08 N	10.22 E
Piaggine	68	40.21 N	15.23 E
Piako ≃	172	37.12 S	175.30 E
Pialba	166	25.17 S	152.51 E
Piāli ≃	272b	22.23 N	88.35 E
Piana	36	42.14 N	8.38 E
Piana, Isola I	71	40.58 N	8.13 E
Piana Crixia	62	44.29 N	8.18 E
Piana degli Albanesi	70	38.00 N	13.17 E
Piana degli Albanesi, Lago di ⊜	70	37.58 N	13.18 E
Piana Mwanga	154	7.40 S	28.10 E
Piancastagnaio	66	42.51 N	11.41 E
Piancó	250	7.12 S	37.57 W
Pian Creek ≃	166	30.02 S	148.12 E
Pian di Sco	66	43.38 N	11.33 E
Pianella	66	42.24 N	14.02 E
Pianello Val Tidone	62	44.57 N	9.24 E
Pianezza	62	45.06 N	7.33 E
Pianguan	102	39.24 N	111.30 E
Pianjiaojie	102	26.01 N	100.32 E
Piankatank ≃	208	37.32 N	76.18 W
Pianling	104	41.24 N	123.58 E
Piano	64	45.46 N	11.08 E
Piano d'Arta	64	46.29 N	13.01 E
Piano del Voglio	66	44.10 N	11.13 E
Pianoro	64	44.22 N	11.20 E
Pianosa, Isola I, It.	36	42.35 N	10.04 E
Pianosa, Isola I, It.	66	42.13 N	15.45 E
Pianosinatico	66	44.07 N	10.44 E
Pianottoli-Caldarello, Fr.	71	41.29 N	9.03 E
Pianottoli-Caldarello, Fr.	71	41.29 N	9.03 E
Pians	58	47.08 N	10.30 E
Piapot	184	49.59 N	109.07 W
Piapot Indian Reserve -•-[4]	184	50.45 N	104.26 W
Piasa	219	39.07 N	90.07 W
Piasa Creek ≃	219	38.56 N	90.17 W
Piaseczno	30	52.05 N	21.01 E
Piashti, Lac ⊜	186	50.29 N	62.52 W
Piaski	30	51.08 N	22.51 E
Piat	116	17.48 N	121.29 E
Piatã	255	13.09 S	41.48 W
Piatra-Neamț	38	46.56 N	26.22 E
Piatra Olt	38	44.24 N	24.16 E
Piatt □[6]	219	40.00 N	88.35 W
Piau	256	21.31 S	43.19 W
Piauí □[3]	250	7.00 S	43.00 W
Piauí ≃, Bra.	250	6.38 S	42.42 W
Piauí ≃, Bra.	255	16.41 S	41.53 W
Piauí, Morro do ∧	255	14.59 S	47.31 W
Piaus ≃	255	12.27 S	49.32 W
Piave ≃	64	45.32 N	12.44 E
Piawaning	162	30.51 S	116.22 E
Piaxtla ≃	232	23.42 N	106.49 W
Piazza Armerina	70	37.23 N	14.22 E
Piazzi, Isla I	254	51.45 S	74.05 W
Piazzola sul Brenta	64	45.32 N	11.47 E
Piberegg	61	47.05 N	15.05 E
Pibor ≃	140	8.26 N	33.13 E
Pibor Post	140	6.48 N	33.08 E
Pibroch	182	54.16 N	113.52 W
Pic ≃	190	48.36 N	86.18 W
Pica	248	20.30 S	69.21 W
Picacho	200	32.42 N	111.29 W
Picacho, Cerro del ∧	286a	19.35 N	99.08 W
Pičajevo	80	53.15 N	42.12 E
Picanoc ≃	190	46.05 N	76.03 W
Picardie □[9]	50	49.45 N	2.50 E
Picatinny Arsenal ■	276	40.57 N	74.33 W
Picatinny Lake ⊜	276	40.57 N	74.33 W
Picayune	194	30.31 N	89.40 W
Piccadilly	186	48.34 N	58.55 W
Piccadilly Station -•-[5]	262	53.28 N	2.14 W
Piccione	66	43.11 N	12.31 E
Piccolo, Mar (Taranto) ⊤[2]	68	40.29 N	17.16 E
Piccotts End	260	51.46 N	0.28 W
Pic de Tio ∧	150	8.52 N	8.54 W
Piceance Creek ≃	200	40.05 N	108.14 W
Picentini, Monti ∧	68	40.45 N	15.00 E
Picerno	68	40.38 N	15.38 E
Pičeury	80	54.19 N	45.50 E
Pīch ≃	123	34.52 N	71.09 E
Pichana ≃	246	3.31 S	71.43 W
Pichanal	252	23.19 S	64.13 W
Picheng	106	32.07 N	119.42 E
Picher	196	36.59 N	94.49 W
Pichhor	124	25.58 N	78.24 E
Pichilemu	252	34.23 S	72.00 W
Pichileufú, Arroyo ≃	254	40.35 S	70.39 W
Pichimá	246	4.24 N	77.21 W
Pichi-Mahuída	252	38.50 S	64.57 W
Pichincha □[4]	246	0.10 S	78.40 W
Pichis ≃	248	9.59 S	74.59 W
Pichl bei Wels	60	48.11 N	13.54 E
Pichor	124	25.11 N	78.11 E
Pichtovka	86	56.00 N	82.42 E
Pichucalco	234	17.31 N	93.09 W
Picinguaba	256	23.22 S	44.50 W
Picinisco	66	41.39 N	13.52 E
Pic Island I	190	48.43 N	86.38 W
Pickardville	182	54.03 N	113.53 W
Pickaway □[6]	218	39.36 N	82.57 W
Pickens, Ms., U.S.	194	32.53 N	89.58 W
Pickens, S.C., U.S.	192	34.53 N	82.42 W
Pickens, W.V., U.S.	188	38.39 N	80.12 W
Pickensville	194	33.14 N	88.16 W
Pickerel ≃	190	45.55 N	80.50 W
Pickerel Lake ⊜	184	52.36 N	99.30 W
Pickering, On., Can.	212	43.52 N	79.02 W
Pickering, Eng., U.K.	44	54.14 N	0.46 W
Pickering, Vale of V	44	54.12 N	0.45 W
Pickering Beach	212	43.50 N	78.59 W
Pickering Brook	168a	32.03 S	116.08 E
Pickering Creek ≃	285	40.08 N	75.30 W
Pickering Creek Reservoir ⊜[1]	285	40.07 N	75.30 W
Pickett, Lake ⊜	220	28.36 N	81.07 W
Pickford	190	46.09 N	84.21 W
Pičkir'ajevo	80	54.12 N	42.27 E
Pickle Crow	176	51.30 N	90.04 W
Pickmere	262	53.17 N	2.28 W
Pick Mere ⊜	262	53.17 N	2.29 W
Pickstown	198	43.04 N	98.31 W
Pickton	222	33.02 N	95.24 W
Pickwick Lake ⊜[1]	194	34.55 N	88.10 W
Pickwick Landing Dam -•-[6]	194	35.00 N	88.21 W
Picnic Point >	274b	37.57 S	145.00 E
Pico	66	41.27 N	13.34 E
Pico ∧	150a	14.56 N	24.21 W
Pico I	148a	38.28 N	28.20 W
Pico, Ponta do ∧	148a	38.28 N	28.25 W
Pico da Neblina, Parque Nacional ♦	246	0.30 N	66.00 W
Pico de Orizaba, Parque Nacional ♦	234	19.05 N	97.16 W
Pico Rivera	228	33.58 N	118.05 W
Picos	250	7.05 S	41.28 W
Picota	248	6.55 S	76.20 W
Pico Truncado	254	46.48 S	67.58 W
Picquigny	50	49.57 N	2.09 E
Picton, Austl.	170	34.11 S	150.36 E
Picton, On., Can.	212	44.00 N	77.08 W
Picton, N.Z.	172	41.18 S	174.01 E
Picton, Eng., U.K.	262	53.14 N	2.51 W
Picton, Isla I	254	55.02 S	66.57 W
Picton Bay ⊂	212	44.03 N	77.08 W
Picton Junction	168a	33.21 S	115.41 E
Pictou	186	45.41 N	62.43 W
Pictou Island I	186	45.50 N	62.34 W
Picture Butte	182	49.53 N	112.47 W
Pictured Rocks National Lakeshore ♦	190	46.35 N	86.20 W
Picture Rocks	210	41.17 N	76.43 W
Picúa, Punta >	240m	18.25 N	65.46 W
Picuí	250	6.31 S	36.21 W
Picunda	84	43.12 N	40.21 E
Picún Leufú	254	39.31 S	69.15 W
Picún Leufú, Arroyo ≃	254	39.31 S	69.08 W
Picuris Indian Reservation -•-[4]	200	36.12 N	105.42 W
Pidálion, Akrotírion >	130	34.56 N	34.05 E
Pidarak	128	25.51 N	63.14 E
Piddle ≃	42	50.42 N	2.04 W
Piddletrenthide	42	50.48 N	2.25 W
Pide Adası I	267b	40.53 N	29.04 E
Pidie, Ujung >	114	5.30 N	95.53 E
Piding	64	47.46 N	12.55 E
Pidurutalagala ∧	122	7.00 N	80.46 E
Piedade	287a	22.41 S	43.05 W
Piedade -•-[8]	287a	22.53 S	43.19 W
Piedade do Baruel	287b	23.37 S	46.18 W
Piedade do Rio Grande	256	21.28 S	44.12 W
Piedecuesta	246	6.59 N	73.03 W
Piedicavallo	62	45.42 N	7.57 E
Piedicroce	32	42.23 N	9.23 E
Piediluco	66	42.32 N	12.45 E
Piedimonte Etneo	70	37.48 N	15.12 E
Piedimonte Matese	68	41.21 N	14.22 E
Piedimonte San Germano	66	41.30 N	13.45 E
Piedimulera	58	46.01 N	8.16 E
Piè di Ripa	66	43.15 N	13.29 E
Piedmont, Al., U.S.	194	33.55 N	85.36 W
Piedmont, Ca., U.S.	226	37.49 N	122.13 W
Piedmont, Mo., U.S.	194	37.09 N	90.41 W
Piedmont, Oh., U.S.	214	40.11 N	81.12 W
Piedmont, S.C., U.S.	192	34.54 N	82.21 W
Piedmont Lake ⊜[1]	214	40.08 N	81.11 W
Piedra, C.R.	236	9.29 N	83.40 W
Piedra, Ca., U.S.	226	36.48 N	119.22 W
Piedra ≃	200	37.01 N	107.24 W
Piedra, Cerro ∧	252	37.41 S	73.07 W
Piedra Azul, Quebrada ≃	286c	10.36 N	66.57 W
Piedrabuena	34	39.02 N	4.10 W
Piedra del Águila	254	40.03 S	70.05 W
Piedra del Águila, Embalse ⊜[1]	254	40.30 S	70.20 W
Piedrafita, Puerto de)(	34	42.40 N	7.01 W
Piedrahita	34	40.28 N	5.19 W
Piedra Roja	236	8.38 N	81.48 W
Piedras, Arroyo de las ≃	288	34.43 S	58.19 W
Piedras, Punta >, Arg.	258	35.25 S	57.08 W
Piedras, Punta >, Ven.	246	10.40 N	61.40 W
Piedras Blancas	252	31.11 S	59.56 W
Piedras Blancas, Point >	226	35.40 N	121.17 W
Piedras Coloradas	252	32.23 S	57.36 W
Piedras Negras, Guat.	232	17.11 N	91.15 W
Piedras Negras, Méx.	232	28.42 N	100.31 W
Piedras Negras ⊥	232	17.12 N	91.15 W
Piedra Sola	252	32.04 S	56.21 W
Piegaro	66	42.58 N	12.05 E
Pie Island I	190	48.15 N	89.05 W
Pieksämäki	26	62.18 N	27.08 E
Piéla	150	12.42 N	0.08 W
Pielach ≃	61	48.15 N	15.22 E
Pielavesi	26	63.14 N	26.45 E
Pielavesi ⊜	26	63.18 N	26.35 E
Pielinen ⊜	26	63.15 N	29.40 E
Pieljekaise Nationalpark ♦	24	66.18 N	16.58 E
Piemonte □[4]	62	45.00 N	8.00 E
Pienaarsrivier	156	25.15 S	28.18 E
Piendamó	246	2.38 N	76.30 W
Pieniężno	30	54.15 N	20.08 E
Pieniński Park Narodowy ♦	30	49.25 N	20.25 E
Pieni-Salpausselkä ∧	26	61.08 N	27.20 E
Piennes	56	49.19 N	5.47 E
Pieńsk	30	51.15 N	15.03 E
Pienza	66	43.04 N	11.41 E
Pierce, Co., U.S.	200	40.38 N	104.45 W
Pierce, Fl., U.S.	220	27.50 N	81.58 W
Pierce, Id., U.S.	202	46.29 N	115.47 W
Pierce, Ne., U.S.	198	42.11 N	97.31 W
Pierce, Tx., U.S.	222	29.14 N	96.12 W
Pierce □[6]	224	47.04 N	122.07 W
Pierce, Lake ⊜	220	27.58 N	81.31 W
Pierce City	194	36.56 N	94.00 W
Pierce Lake ⊜, Can.	184	54.10 N	92.56 W
Pierce Lake ⊜, Sk., Can.	184	54.30 N	109.42 W
Pierceton	216	41.12 N	85.42 W
Piermont	210	41.03 N	73.55 W
Pierowall	46	59.20 N	2.59 W
Pierpont, Oh., U.S.	214	41.45 N	80.34 W
Pierpont, S.D., U.S.	198	45.29 N	97.49 W
Pierre	198	44.22 N	100.21 W
Pierre, Bayou ≃, La., U.S.	194	31.51 N	93.06 W
Pierre, Bayou ≃, Ms., U.S.	194	31.55 N	91.11 W
Pierre-Buffière	32	45.42 N	1.21 E
Pierreclos	58	46.20 N	4.41 E
Pierre-de-Bresse	58	46.53 N	5.15 E
Pierrefeu-du-Var	62	43.13 N	6.08 E
Pierrefitte-sur-Aire	56	48.54 N	5.20 E
Pierrefitte-sur-Sauldre	50	47.30 N	2.09 E
Pierrefitte-sur-Seine	261	48.58 N	2.22 E
Pierrefonds, P.Q., Can.	206	45.29 N	73.52 W
Pierrefonds, Fr.	50	49.21 N	2.59 E
Pierrefontaine-les-Varans	58	47.13 N	6.33 E
Pierrelatte	62	44.23 N	4.42 E
Pierrelaye	261	49.01 N	2.09 E
Pierre Part	194	29.57 N	91.12 W
Pierre Pertuis, Col de)(	58	47.12 N	7.11 E
Pierrepont Manor	212	43.44 N	76.04 W
Pierre-sur-Haut ∧	62	45.39 N	3.49 E
Pierreville, P.Q., Can.	206	46.04 N	72.49 W
Pierreville, Trin.	241r	10.18 N	61.01 W
Pierron	219	38.47 N	89.36 W
Pierron, Lac ⊜	206	46.53 N	74.20 W
Pierry	50	49.01 N	3.56 E
Pierson	192	29.14 N	81.27 W
Piersonville	285	40.10 N	74.42 W
Pierz	190	45.58 N	94.06 W
Piesendorf	64	47.17 N	12.43 E
Piešt'any	30	48.36 N	17.50 E
Piesting ≃	61	48.02 N	16.30 E
Pietarsaari → Jakobstad	26	63.40 N	22.42 E
Pieterburen	52	53.24 N	6.27 E
Pieterlen	58	47.11 N	7.20 E
Pietermaritzburg	158	29.37 S	30.16 E
Pietersburg	156	23.54 S	29.25 E
Pietrabbondante	66	41.45 N	14.23 E
Pietracamela	66	42.31 N	13.33 E
Pietracatella	66	41.35 N	14.52 E
Pietra del Pertusillo, Lago di ⊜	68	40.17 N	15.58 E
Pietragalla	68	40.45 N	15.53 E
Pietra Ligure	62	44.09 N	8.17 E
Pietralunga	66	43.26 N	12.26 E
Pietramala	66	44.10 N	11.20 E
Pietramelara	68	41.16 N	14.11 E
Pietramontecorvino	68	41.32 N	15.07 E
Pietrapaola	68	39.29 N	16.49 E
Pietrapertosa	68	40.31 N	16.04 E
Pietraperzia	70	37.25 N	14.08 E
Pietrasanta	64	43.57 N	10.14 E
Pietrelcina	68	41.12 N	14.51 E
Piet Retief	158	27.01 S	30.50 E
Pietrosu, Vîrful ∧, Rom.	38	47.36 N	24.38 E
Pietrosu, Vîrful ∧, Rom.	38	47.08 N	25.11 E
Pieve	64	45.46 N	10.45 E
Pieve d'Alpago	64	46.10 N	12.21 E
Pieve del Cairo	62	45.03 N	8.48 E
Pieve di Cadore	64	46.26 N	12.22 E
Pieve di Cento	64	44.43 N	11.18 E
Pieve di Soligo	64	45.53 N	12.10 E
Pieve di Teco	62	44.03 N	7.56 E
Pieve Fosciana	64	44.08 N	10.25 E
Pievepelago	64	44.12 N	10.37 E
Pieve Porto Morone	62	45.07 N	9.26 E
Pieve Santo Stefano	66	43.40 N	12.02 E
Piffard	210	42.50 N	77.51 W
Pigari	80	51.24 N	49.42 E
Pigeon, Mi., U.S.	190	43.49 N	83.16 W
Pigeon, Pa., U.S.	214	41.32 N	79.03 W
Pigeon ≃, Mb., Can.	184	52.15 N	97.00 W
Pigeon ≃, On., Can.	212	44.22 N	78.31 W
Pigeon ≃, N.A.	190	48.00 N	89.34 W
Pigeon ≃, U.S.	192	36.00 N	83.11 W
Pigeon ≃, U.S.	216	41.46 N	85.47 W
Pigeon ≃, Mi., U.S.	190	43.56 N	83.17 W
Pigeon ≃, Mi., U.S.	190	45.27 N	84.33 W
Pigeon ≃, Mi., U.S.	216	42.54 N	86.11 W
Pigeon Bay ⊂	214	42.01 N	82.40 W
Pigeon Cove	207	42.40 N	70.38 W
Pigeon Creek ≃, Al., U.S.	194	31.20 N	86.42 W
Pigeon Creek ≃, In., U.S.	194	37.59 N	87.35 W
Pigeon Creek ≃, In., U.S.	216	41.41 N	85.17 W
Pigeon Creek ≃, Pa., U.S.	279b	40.12 N	79.55 W
Pigeon Creek ≃, Pa., U.S.	285	40.12 N	75.35 W
Pigeon Forge	192	35.47 N	83.33 W
Pigeon Lake ⊜, Ab., Can.	182	53.00 N	114.00 W
Pigeon Lake ⊜, On., Can.	212	44.30 N	78.30 W
Pigeon Run ≃	285	40.06 N	75.35 W
Pigeon Swamp ≡	276	40.23 N	74.29 W
Pigezhuang	105	39.39 N	116.15 E
Pigg ≃	192	37.00 N	79.29 W
Piggott	194	36.22 N	90.11 W
Piggs Peak	158	25.38 S	31.15 E
Pigkawagan	116	7.12 N	124.32 E
Piglio	66	41.49 N	13.08 E
Pigna	62	43.56 N	7.40 E
Pignans	62	43.18 N	6.13 E
Pignataro Maggiore	68	41.11 N	14.10 E
Pignola	68	40.34 N	15.47 E
Pigs, Bay of → Cochinos, Bahía de ⊂	240p	22.07 N	81.10 W
Pigüé	252	37.37 S	62.25 W
Pigŭm-do I	98	34.45 N	125.55 E
Pihama	172	39.30 S	173.56 E
Piha Passage ⋓	174w	21.07 S	175.05 W
Pihāri	124	27.38 N	80.12 E
Pihlajavesi ⊜	26	61.45 N	28.50 E
Pihlava	26	61.33 N	21.36 E
Pihtipudas	26	63.23 N	25.34 E
Pihuamo	234	19.15 N	103.23 W
P'ihyŏn	98	40.01 N	124.37 E
Piikkiö	26	60.26 N	22.31 E
Piippola	26	64.10 N	25.58 E
Pijijiapan	234	15.42 N	93.14 W
Pijnacker	52	52.02 N	4.27 E
Pijol, Pico ∧	236	15.06 N	87.35 W
Pikal'ovo	76	59.31 N	34.06 E
Pikangikum	184	51.49 N	94.00 W
Pikangikum Lake ⊜	184	51.48 N	94.00 W
Pike	210	42.33 N	78.09 W
Pike □[6], Il., U.S.	219	39.36 N	90.48 W
Pike □[6], Mo., U.S.	219	39.21 N	91.10 W
Pike □[6], Oh., U.S.	218	39.05 N	83.06 W
Pike □[6], Pa., U.S.	210	41.19 N	74.48 W
Pike ≃, N.A.	206	45.04 N	73.06 W
Pike ≃, Wi., U.S.	190	45.26 N	87.52 W
Pike, North Branch ≃	190	45.30 N	88.01 W
Pike, South Branch ≃	190	45.30 N	88.01 W
Pike Creek ≃, On., Can.	281	42.19 N	82.51 W
Pike Creek ≃, De., U.S.	285	39.42 N	75.42 W
Pike Lake ⊜	212	44.46 N	76.21 W
Pikelot I	14	8.05 N	147.38 E
Pike Lowe ∧[2]	262	53.42 N	2.34 W
Pike Run ≃	276	40.25 N	74.38 W
Pikes Peak	218	39.08 N	86.09 W
Pikes Peak ∧	200	38.51 N	105.03 W
Pikes Rocks ∧[2]	214	41.56 N	79.24 W
Pikesville	208	39.22 N	76.43 W
Piketberg	158	32.54 S	18.46 E
Piketon	218	39.04 N	83.00 W
Piketown	208	40.23 N	76.45 W
Pikeville, Ky., U.S.	192	37.28 N	82.31 W
Pikeville, Tn., U.S.	194	35.36 N	85.11 W
Pikkola	265a	59.42 N	30.08 E
Pikou	98	39.24 N	122.20 E
Pikounda	152	0.33 N	16.42 E
Pikwitonei	184	55.35 N	97.09 W
Pila, Arg.	252	36.01 S	58.08 W
Pila, It.	62	45.41 N	7.18 E
Piła (Schneidemühl), Pol.	30	53.10 N	16.44 E
Piła □[4]	30	53.15 N	16.30 E
Pilanesberg ∧	156	25.14 S	27.04 E
Pilanesberg Game Reserve -•-[4]	156	25.15 S	27.05 E
Pilão Arcado	250	9.56 S	42.29 W
Pilar, Arg.	252	31.41 S	63.54 W
Pilar, Arg.	252	31.27 S	61.15 W
Pilar, Arg.	258	34.27 S	58.54 W
Pilar, Bra.	250	9.36 S	35.56 W
Pilar, Bra.	287a	22.42 S	43.19 W
Pilar, Para.	252	26.52 S	58.23 W
Pilar, Pil.	116	11.29 N	123.00 E
Pilar, Pil.	116	9.52 N	126.06 E
Pilar □[5]	288	34.28 S	58.52 W
Pilar Bay ⊂	116	11.34 N	123.00 E
Pilarcitos Creek ≃	282	37.28 N	122.27 W
Pilarcitos Lake ⊜	282	37.33 N	122.25 W
Pilar de Goiás	255	14.41 S	49.27 W
Pilar do Sul	255	23.49 S	47.42 W
Pilares	196	30.24 N	104.52 W
Pilas Group II	116	6.45 N	121.35 E
Pilas Island I	116	6.38 N	121.37 E
Pilatus ∧	58	46.59 N	8.15 E
Pilawa	30	51.58 N	21.31 E
Pilaya ≃	248	20.55 S	64.04 W
Pilcher Park ♦	278	41.32 N	88.01 W
Pilchuck ≃	224	47.55 N	122.02 W
Pilchuck Creek ≃	224	48.12 N	122.13 W
Pilcomayo ≃	18	25.21 S	57.42 W
Pilcomayo, Brazo Norte ≃	252	24.56 S	58.16 W
Pilcomayo, Brazo Sur ≃	252	24.56 S	58.16 W
Pil'dozero	24	65.43 N	33.28 E
Piles Creek ≃	276	40.37 N	74.12 W
Pilga	162	21.29 S	119.25 E
Pilger	198	42.00 N	97.03 W
Pilgrim Gardens	285	39.57 N	75.19 W
Pilgrim Memorial Monument ⊥	207	42.04 N	70.12 W
Pilgrims Hatch	260	51.38 N	0.17 E
Pilgrim's Rest	156	24.55 S	30.44 E
Pil'gyn	180	69.18 N	179.08 E
Pili	116	13.33 N	123.16 E
Pīlībhīt	124	28.38 N	79.48 E
Pilica ≃	30	51.52 N	21.17 E
Pilipinas → Philippines □[1]	116	13.00 N	122.00 E
Pilis ⋏	264c	47.37 N	18.59 E
Pilisborosjenő	264c	47.36 N	19.00 E
Pilkhua	124	28.43 N	77.39 E
Pillaro	246	1.10 S	78.32 W
Pillar Point >	282	37.30 N	122.30 W
Pillar Point >[1]	212	43.59 N	76.09 W
Pillau → Baltijsk	76	54.39 N	19.55 E
Pilley's Island	186	49.31 N	55.44 W
Pilliga	166	30.21 S	148.54 E
Pillings Pond ⊜	283	42.32 N	71.02 W
Pillnitz -•-[8]	54	51.00 N	13.52 E
Pillon, Col du)(	58	46.22 N	7.13 E
Pillow	208	40.38 N	76.48 W
Pillsbury Sound ⋓	240m	18.20 N	64.49 W
Pil'na	80	55.33 N	45.55 E
Pílos	38	36.55 N	21.43 E
Pilot ∧	166	36.45 S	148.13 E
Pilot Butte	184	50.28 N	104.25 W
Pilot Grove	194	38.52 N	92.54 W
Pilot Hill	226	38.50 N	121.02 W
Pilot Knob	194	37.37 N	90.38 W
Pilot Knob ∧, Ar., U.S.	194	35.42 N	93.57 W
Pilot Knob ∧, Id., U.S.	202	45.54 N	115.42 W
Pilot Mound	184	49.16 N	98.55 W
Pilot Mountain	192	36.23 N	80.28 W
Pilot Peak ∧, Nv., U.S.	204	38.21 N	117.58 W
Pilot Peak ∧, Nv., U.S.	204	41.02 N	114.06 W
Pilot Peak ∧, Wy., U.S.	202	44.58 N	109.53 W
Pilot Point, Ak., U.S.	180	57.34 N	157.35 W
Pilot Point, Tx., U.S.	196	33.23 N	96.57 W
Pilot Rock	202	45.29 N	118.49 W
Pilot Rock ∧	200	35.09 N	109.53 W
Pilot Station	180	61.56 N	162.54 W
Pilottown	194	29.10 N	89.15 W
Pilpah Range ⋏	166	20.23 S	138.34 E
Pilsen → Plzeň	60	49.45 N	13.23 E
Pilsensee ⊜	60	48.01 N	11.11 E
Pilsum	52	53.29 N	7.04 E

ENGLISH

Name	Page	Lat.°′	Long.°′
Piltene	76	57.13 N	21.40 E
Pilu ≃	110	19.33 N	97.24 E
Piluchang	107	29.13 N	105.37 E
Pil'ugino	80	53.25 N	52.26 E
Pilusi	106	32.05 N	120.05 E
Pilzno	30	49.59 N	21.17 E
Pim ≃	74	61.18 N	71.57 E
Pima	200	32.53 N	109.49 W
Pimah	110	15.36 N	107.25 E
Pimba	166	31.15 S	136.47 E
Pimelles	50	47.50 N	4.10 E
Pimenta Bueno ≃	248	11.39 S	61.11 W
Pimenteira, Vereda ≃	250	9.58 S	42.46 W
Pimenteiras	250	6.14 S	41.25 W
Pimentel, Bra.	250	3.43 S	45.30 W
Pimentel, Perú	248	6.50 S	79.57 W
Pimlico Race Course ♦	284b	39.21 N	76.40 W
Pimmit Hills	284c	38.54 N	77.12 W
Pimmit Run ≃	284c	38.55 N	77.07 W
Pimu-Lendo	152	1.46 N	20.54 E
Pimville -•-[8]	273d	26.16 S	27.54 E
Pina	34	41.29 N	0.32 W
Pina ≃	76	52.10 N	26.14 E
Pinacanauan ≃	116	17.37 N	121.44 E
Pináculo, Cerro ∧	254	50.45 S	72.16 W
Pinalón, Cerro ∧	236	15.05 N	89.55 W
Pinamalayan	116	13.02 N	121.29 E
Pinang □[3]	114	5.20 N	100.20 E
Pinang, Pulau I	114	5.23 N	100.15 E
Pinangah	112	5.12 N	116.50 E
Pinang → George Town	114	5.25 N	100.20 E
Pınarbaşı, Tür.	130	41.36 N	33.07 E
Pınarbaşı, Tür.	130	38.44 N	36.24 E
Pinar del Río	240p	22.25 N	83.42 W
Pinar del Río □[4]	240p	22.30 N	83.45 W
Pinardville	188	42.59 N	71.30 W
Pınarhisar	130	41.37 N	27.30 E
Pınarlar	130	38.53 N	39.29 E
Pinas, Arg.	252	31.09 S	65.29 W
Piñas, Ec.	246	3.42 S	79.42 W
Piñas, Cerro ∧	236	15.25 N	85.47 W
Pinatubo, Mount ∧	116	15.08 N	120.21 E
Pinazo, Arroyo ≃	288	34.24 S	58.48 W
Pinchbeck	42	52.48 N	0.09 W
Pincher Creek	182	49.29 N	113.57 W
Pinchi Lake ⊜	182	54.35 N	124.20 W
Pinckney	216	42.27 N	83.56 W
Pinckney State Recreation Area ♦	216	42.25 N	84.04 W
Pinckneyville	194	38.04 N	89.22 W
Pinconning	190	43.51 N	83.57 W
Pincourt	206	45.23 N	74.00 W
Pinčuga	86	58.23 N	96.59 E
Pińczów	30	50.32 N	20.35 E
Pindaíba, Ribeirão ≃	255	14.18 S	51.45 W
Pindale	110	21.11 N	95.51 E
Pindamonhangaba	256	22.55 S	45.28 W
Pindar	162	28.29 S	115.48 E
Pindaré ≃	250	3.17 S	44.47 W
Pindaré-Mirim	250	3.37 S	45.21 W
Pind Dādan Khān	123	32.35 N	73.03 E
Pinde → Píndhos Óros ⋏	38	39.49 N	21.14 E
Pinder Point >	192	26.28 N	78.39 W
Píndhos Óros ⋏	38	39.49 N	21.14 E
Pindi Bhattiān	123	31.54 N	73.16 E
Pindiga	146	9.59 N	10.54 E
Pindi Gheb	123	33.14 N	72.16 E
Pindobaçu	250	10.44 S	40.21 W
Pindo → Píndhos Óros ⋏	38	39.49 N	21.14 E
Pindorama de Goiás	250	10.55 S	47.40 W
Pinduši	24	62.56 N	34.35 E
Pindus Mountains → Píndhos Óros ⋏	38	39.49 N	21.14 E
Pindwāra	120	24.48 N	73.04 E
Pine ≃, B.C., Can.	182	56.08 N	120.41 W
Pine ≃, Mb., Can.	184	52.00 N	100.09 W
Pine ≃, On., Can.	212	44.20 N	79.52 W
Pine ≃, Mi., U.S.	190	46.03 N	84.40 W
Pine ≃, Mi., U.S.	190	44.26 N	83.21 W
Pine ≃, Mi., U.S.	190	44.15 N	85.55 W
Pine ≃, Mi., U.S.	190	43.35 N	84.08 W
Pine ≃, Mi., U.S.	214	42.49 N	82.29 W
Pine ≃, Wi., U.S.	190	44.08 N	88.54 W
Pine ≃, Wi., U.S.	190	45.50 N	88.08 W
Pine ≃, Wi., U.S.	190	43.12 N	90.18 W
Pine Apple	194	31.52 N	86.59 W
Pine Banks Park ♦	283	42.26 N	71.04 W
Pine Barrens -•-[1]	208	39.48 N	74.35 W
Pine Beach	206	45.32 N	73.57 W
Pine Bluff	194	34.13 N	92.00 W
Pine Bluffs	198	41.10 N	104.04 W
Pine Brook	276	40.52 N	74.20 W
Pine Brook ≃, U.S.	276	41.04 N	74.05 W
Pine Brook ≃, Ma., U.S.	283	42.00 N	70.47 W
Pine Brook ≃, N.J., U.S.	276	40.19 N	74.20 W
Pine Bush	210	41.36 N	74.17 W
Pine Castle	220	28.28 N	81.22 W
Pine City, Mn., U.S.	190	45.49 N	92.58 W
Pine City, N.Y., U.S.	210	42.02 N	76.52 W
Pinecliff Lake ⊜	276	41.08 N	74.23 W
Pinecraft	220	27.19 N	82.30 W
Pine Creek	164	13.49 S	131.49 E
Pine Creek ≃, Ab., Can.	182	54.56 N	112.31 W
Pine Creek ≃, Ca., U.S.	204	40.40 N	120.46 W
Pine Creek ≃, Ca., U.S.	282	37.58 N	122.02 W
Pine Creek ≃, Nv., U.S.	204	40.36 N	116.10 W
Pine Creek ≃, Pa., U.S.	210	41.10 N	77.16 W
Pine Creek ≃, Pa., U.S.	279b	40.30 N	79.57 W
Pine Creek ≃, Pa., U.S.	285	40.05 N	75.37 W
Pine Creek, West Branch ≃	210	41.43 N	77.38 W
Pine Creek Indian Reserve -•-[4]	184	52.03 N	100.14 W
Pine Creek Lake ⊜[1]	196	34.05 N	95.05 W
Pine Creek Point >	276	41.07 N	73.16 W
Pine Crest, Fl., U.S.	220	28.01 N	82.32 W
Pinecrest, Va., U.S.	208	38.50 N	77.09 W
Pinecrest Lake ⊜	226	38.12 N	119.58 W
Pine Crest Point >	284a	42.52 N	79.11 W
Pinedale, Ca., U.S.	226	36.50 N	119.48 W
Pinedale, Wy., U.S.	200	42.52 N	109.51 W
Pine Falls	184	50.35 N	96.15 W
Pine Flat Lake ⊜[1]	226	36.52 N	119.18 W
Pinega	24	64.42 N	43.19 E
Pinega ≃	24	64.08 N	41.54 E
Pine Glen	212	45.19 N	75.43 W
Pine Grove, On., Can.	275b	43.48 N	79.35 W
Pine Grove, Ca., U.S.	226	38.25 N	120.39 W
Pine Grove, Fl., U.S.	220	28.16 N	81.11 W
Pine Grove, N.J., U.S.	285	39.53 N	74.52 W
Pine Grove, Pa., U.S.	208	40.32 N	76.23 W
Pine Grove, W.V., U.S.	188	39.33 N	80.40 W
Pine Grove Mills	214	40.44 N	77.53 W
Pine Hill, Austl.	166	23.39 S	146.58 E
Pine Hill, Al., U.S.	194	31.58 N	87.35 W
Pine Hill, N.J., U.S.	208	39.47 N	74.59 W
Pine Hill, N.Y., U.S.	210	42.08 N	74.29 W
Pinehill, Tx., U.S.	222	32.06 N	94.36 W
Pine Hills	220	28.33 N	81.27 W
Pinehouse Lake	184	55.31 N	106.36 W
Pinehouse Lake ⊜	184	55.32 N	106.35 W
Pinehurst, Ga., U.S.	192	32.11 N	83.45 W
Pinehurst, Id., U.S.	202	45.15 N	116.20 W
Pinehurst, Ma., U.S.	207	42.31 N	71.13 W
Pinehurst, N.Y., U.S.	284a	42.44 N	78.57 W

DEUTSCH

Name	Seite	Breite°′	Länge°′ E = Ost
Pinehurst, N.C., U.S.	192	35.11 N	79.28 W
Pinehurst, Tx., U.S.	222	30.10 N	95.41 W
Pinehurst Lake ⊜	182	54.39 N	111.25 W
Pine Island, Mn., U.S.	190	44.12 N	92.38 W
Pine Island, N.Y., U.S.	210	41.17 N	74.27 W
Pine Island I	220	26.35 N	82.06 W
Pine Island Bay ⊂	9	74.50 S	102.05 W
Pine Island Bayou ≃	194	30.10 N	94.07 W
Pine Island Creek ≃	283	42.47 N	70.48 W
Pine Island Dam -•-[6]	214	40.08 N	80.43 W
Pine Island Sound ⋓	220	26.33 N	82.10 W
Pine Lake, In., U.S.	216	41.38 N	86.45 W
Pine Lake, Ma., U.S.	283	42.23 N	71.27 W
Pine Lake ⊜, On., Can.	212	44.57 N	79.27 W
Pine Lake ⊜, Mi., U.S.	281	42.35 N	83.20 W
Pine Lake ⊜, N.Y., U.S.	210	43.12 N	74.31 W
Pineland	194	31.14 N	93.58 W
Pine Lawn	219	38.41 N	90.16 W
Pinellas □[6]	220	27.53 N	82.43 W
Pinellas, Point >	220	27.42 N	82.38 W
Pinellas Park	220	27.50 N	82.41 W
Pine Marsh ≡	276	40.37 N	73.34 W
Pine Meadow Lake ⊜	276	41.11 N	74.07 W
Pine Mountain ∧, U.S.	192	36.55 N	83.20 W
Pine Mountain ∧, Ca., U.S.	226	35.41 N	121.05 W
Pine Mountain ∧, Ca., U.S.	280	34.13 N	117.54 W
Pine Mountain ∧, Ct., U.S.	207	41.58 N	72.56 W
Pine Mountain ∧, Ga., U.S.	192	32.51 N	84.47 W
Pine Mountain ∧, Or., U.S.	202	43.47 N	120.54 W
Pine Mountain ∧, Wy., U.S.	200	41.02 N	109.01 W
Pine Nut Mountains ⋏	226	39.00 N	119.25 W
Pine Orchard Meadows	284b	39.17 N	76.52 W
Pine Pass)(	182	55.22 N	122.40 W
Pine Plains	210	41.59 N	73.40 W
Pine Point, Austl.	168b	34.34 S	137.52 E
Pine Point, N.T., Can.	176	61.01 N	114.15 W
Pine Point Park ♦	275b	43.43 N	79.33 W
Pine Portage Dam -•-[6]	176	49.18 N	88.19 W
Pine Prairie	194	30.47 N	92.25 W
Piner	218	38.50 N	84.32 W
Pine Rest	283	42.23 N	71.26 W
Pine Ridge, Pa., U.S.	285	39.55 N	75.22 W
Pine Ridge, S.D., U.S.	198	43.01 N	102.33 W
Pine Ridge, Va., U.S.	284c	38.52 N	77.14 W
Pine Ridge ∧	198	42.40 N	103.00 W
Pine Ridge Estates	276	41.02 N	73.41 W
Pine Ridge Indian Reservation -•-[4]	198	43.25 N	102.21 W
Pine River, Mb., Can.	184	51.47 N	100.32 W
Pine River, Mn., U.S.	190	46.43 N	94.24 W
Piñero	258	34.32 S	58.45 W
Pinerolo	62	44.53 N	7.21 E
Piñeros, Isla I	240m	18.15 N	65.35 W
Pinerovka	80	51.34 N	43.04 E
Pine Run ≃	279b	40.37 N	79.35 W
Pines ≃	283	42.27 N	70.58 W
Pines, Isle of → Juventud, Isla de la I	240p	21.40 N	82.50 W
Pines, Lake o' the ⊜[1]	222	32.46 N	94.35 W
Pines, Point of >	283	42.26 N	70.58 W
Pine Shores	220	27.17 N	82.32 W
Pines Lake ⊜	276	41.00 N	74.16 W
Pines Run ≃	285	39.50 N	75.05 W
Pine Swamp Knob ∧	188	39.33 N	79.31 W
Pineto	66	42.36 N	14.04 E
Pinetop	200	34.07 N	109.56 W
Pinetops	192	35.47 N	77.38 W
Pinetown	158	29.52 S	30.46 E
Pine Tree Hill ∧	114	3.43 N	101.42 E
Pine Valley, Md., U.S.	284b	39.26 N	76.39 W
Pine Valley, N.Y., U.S.	210	42.14 N	76.51 W
Pine Valley V	204	38.25 N	113.40 W
Pine Village	216	40.27 N	87.15 W
Pineville, Ky., U.S.	192	36.45 N	83.41 W
Pineville, La., U.S.	194	31.19 N	92.26 W
Pineville, Mo., U.S.	194	36.35 N	94.23 W
Pineville, N.C., U.S.	192	35.04 N	80.53 W
Pineville, Pa., U.S.	208	40.18 N	75.00 W
Pineville, W.V., U.S.	192	37.34 N	81.32 W
Pinewood, Fl., U.S.	220	25.53 N	80.14 W
Pinewood, S.C., U.S.	192	33.44 N	80.27 W
Piney	50	48.22 N	4.20 E
Piney ≃	194	35.49 N	87.33 W
Piney Branch ≃	284c	38.56 N	77.18 W
Piney Creek ≃, Tx., U.S.	222	31.03 N	94.34 W
Piney Creek ≃, Wy., U.S.	202	44.34 N	106.32 W
Piney Fork	214	40.15 N	80.50 W
Piney Point	222	29.46 N	95.31 W
Piney Point >	208	38.08 N	76.32 W
Piney Run ≃	284c	38.58 N	77.17 W
Piney Woods	194	32.03 N	89.59 W
Pinfold	262	53.36 N	2.55 W
Ping ≃, Thai	110	15.42 N	100.09 E
Ping ≃, Zhg.	100	25.59 N	115.07 E
Pinga	154	1.01 S	28.42 E
Ping'an, Zhg.	89	45.20 N	123.42 E
Ping'an, Zhg.	104	41.11 N	123.26 E
Ping'an, Zhg.	107	30.36 N	104.42 E
Ping'anbu	98	41.45 N	116.13 E
Ping'ancheng	105	40.03 N	117.48 E
Ping'andi	104	42.34 N	121.52 E
Pingaring	162	32.45 S	118.37 E
Pingba, Zhg.	100	31.19 N	113.18 E
Pingba, Zhg.	102	26.22 N	106.09 E
Pingchang	102	31.35 N	107.03 E
Pingchao	106	32.07 N	120.45 E
Pingding	98	37.48 N	113.37 E
Pingdingpu	104	42.22 N	123.55 E
Pingdingshan, Zhg.	98	41.26 N	124.45 E
Pingdingshan, Zhg.	100	33.45 N	113.17 E
Pingding Shan ∧	89	46.38 N	128.27 E
Pingdu	98	36.47 N	119.54 E
Pingelap I[1]	14	6.13 N	160.42 E
Pingelly	162	32.32 S	117.05 E
Pingfang, Zhg.	100	30.07 N	113.48 E
Pingfang, Zhg.	104	41.17 N	120.40 E
Pingfang, Zhg.	104	41.28 N	120.48 E
Pingfang, Zhg.	104	42.14 N	120.38 E
Pingfang, Zhg.	104	42.27 N	120.38 E
Pingfang, Zhg.	271a	39.56 N	116.33 E
Pingfangdu	104	41.45 N	121.12 E
Pingfangzi	104	41.31 N	121.21 E
Pinggau	61	47.27 N	16.04 E
Pinggu	105	40.09 N	117.07 E
Pingguo	102	23.19 N	107.39 E
Pinghai, Zhg.	100	25.14 N	119.15 E
Pinghai, Zhg.	100	22.39 N	114.53 E
Pinghe, Zhg.	100	24.25 N	117.22 E
Pinghe, Zhg.	102	22.51 N	102.30 E
Pinghe ≃	100	24.25 N	116.36 E
P'inghsiang → Pingxiang	102	22.09 N	106.43 E
Pinghu, Zhg.	100	26.46 N	118.48 E
Pinghu, Zhg.	100	30.56 N	115.22 E
Pinghu, Zhg.	100	22.42 N	114.08 E
Pinghu, Zhg.	106	30.42 N	121.01 E
Pingjiang	100	28.44 N	113.34 E
Pingjing	105	39.20 N	116.06 E
Pinglan	100	22.22 N	113.27 E
Pingle, Zhg.	102	24.37 N	110.40 E
Pingle, Zhg.	102	24.31 N	106.59 E
Pingli	102	32.19 N	109.21 E
Pingliang	102	35.32 N	106.41 E

Symbols in the index entries represent the broad categories identified in the key at the right. Symbols with superior numbers (⋏[1]) identify subcategories (see complete key on page *I · 1)*.

Symbole im Register stellen die rechts im Schlüssel erklärten Kategorien dar. Symbole mit hochgestellten Ziffern (⋏[1]) bezeichnen Unterabteilungen einer Kategorie (vgl. vollständiger Schlüssel auf Seite *I · 1)*.

Los símbolos incluídos en el texto del índice representan las grandes categorias identificadas con la clave a la derecha. Los símbolos con numeros en su parte superior (⋏[1]) identifican las subcategorías (véase la clave completa en la página *I · 1)*.

Les symboles de l'index représentent les catégories indiquées dans la légende à droite. Les symboles suivis d'un indice (⋏[1]) représentent des sous-catégories (voir légende complète à la page *I · 1)*.

Os símbolos incluídos no texto do índice representam as grandes categorias identificadas com a chave à direita. Os símbolos com números em sua parte superior (⋏[1]) identificam as subcategorias (veja-se a chave completa à página *I · 1)*.

∧	Mountain	Berg	Montaña	Montagne	Montanha
⋏	Mountains	Gebirge	Montañas	Montagnes	Montanhas
)(	Pass	Paß	Paso	Col	Passo
V	Valley, Canyon	Tal, Cañon	Valle, Cañón	Vallée, Canyon	Vale, Canhão
≃	Plain	Ebene	Llano	Plaine	Planície
>	Cape	Kap	Cabo	Cap	Cabo
I	Island	Insel	Isla	Île	Ilha
II	Islands	Inseln	Islas	Îles	Ilhas
≗	Other Topographic Features	Andere Topographische Objekte	Otros Elementos Topográficos	Autres données topographiques	Outros acidentes topográficos

ESPAÑOL — Nombre | Página | Lat.°′ | Long.°′ W = Oeste
FRANÇAIS — Nom | Page | Lat.°′ | Long.°′ W = Ouest
PORTUGUÊS — Nome | Página | Lat.°′ | Long.°′ W = Oeste

Nombre / Nom / Nome	Página / Page	Lat.°′	Long.°′
Pinglidian	98	37.17 N	119.59 E
Pingling	100	23.39 N	114.23 E
Pinglucheng	102	39.50 N	112.19 E
Pingluo	102	38.57 N	106.35 E
Pingluopu	104	41.56 N	123.20 E
Pingnan, Zhg.	100	26.56 N	119.02 E
Pingnan, Zhg.	102	23.30 N	110.30 E
Pingqiao	100	33.24 N	119.13 E
Pingquan	98	40.59 N	118.34 E
Pingrup	162	33.32 S	118.31 E
Ping Shan, H.K.	271d	22.27 N	114.00 E
Pingshan, Zhg.	100	25.36 N	117.52 E
Pingshan, Zhg.	100	23.26 N	113.15 E
Pingshan, Zhg.	100	22.43 N	114.22 E
Pingshan, Zhg.	102	38.15 N	114.10 E
Pingshang	98	35.11 N	119.07 E
Pingshi, Zhg.	100	32.32 N	113.03 E
Pingshi, Zhg.	100	25.20 N	113.02 E
Pingshui	100	29.53 N	120.38 E
Pingtaizi	105	40.44 N	116.25 E
Pingtan, Zhg.	100	25.31 N	119.47 E
Pingtan, Zhg.	100	23.04 N	114.38 E
Pingtan, Zhg.	107	29.38 N	105.16 E
Pingtan, Zhg.	107	29.50 N	105.56 E
Pingtan Dao I	100	25.33 N	119.48 E
Pingtang	102	25.50 N	107.19 E
Pingtian	100	25.19 N	113.31 E
P'ingtung	100	22.40 N	120.29 E
Pingües, Cayos II	240p	20.47 N	78.15 W
Pingwang	106	30.59 N	120.38 E
Pingwu	102	32.29 N	104.37 E
Pingxiang, Zhg.	100	27.38 N	113.50 E
Pingxiang, Zhg.	102	22.09 N	106.43 E
Pingyang, Zhg.	89	48.13 N	124.23 E
Pingyang, Zhg.	100	27.41 N	120.33 E
Pingyao, Zhg.	102	37.16 N	112.09 E
Pingyao, Zhg.	106	30.24 N	119.58 E
Pingyi	98	35.34 N	117.37 E
Pingyin	98	36.19 N	116.22 E
Pingyu	100	32.57 N	114.41 E
Pingyuan, Zhg.	98	37.11 N	116.25 E
Pingyuan, Zhg.	100	24.36 N	115.54 E
Pingzhai	102	24.07 N	104.22 E
Pingzhuang	98	42.03 N	119.22 E
Pinhal	256	22.12 S	46.45 W
Pinhal, Ribeirão do ≃	256	22.42 S	46.42 W
Pinhal Novo	34	38.38 N	8.55 W
Pinhalzinho	256	22.46 S	46.36 W
Pinhão	250	10.34 S	37.44 W
Pinheiral	256	22.31 S	43.59 W
Pinheirinhos	256	22.26 S	44.59 W
Pinheiro	250	2.31 S	45.05 W
Pinheiro de Loures	266c	38.50 N	9.12 W
Pinheiro Machado	252	31.34 S	53.23 W
Pinheiros, Bra.	255	18.21 S	40.14 W
Pinheiros, Bra.	256	22.32 S	44.54 W
Pinheiros ≃	287b	23.32 S	46.44 W
Pinhel	34	40.46 N	7.04 W
Pinhoe	42	50.44 N	3.27 W
Pinhuã ≃	248	6.21 S	65.00 W
Pini, Pulau I	110	0.08 N	98.40 E
Pinillos	246	8.55 N	74.28 W
Piniós ≃	38	39.54 N	22.45 E
Pinitos, Sierra de ∧	200	31.08 N	110.50 W
Pinjar, Lake ⊜	168a	31.38 S	115.49 E
Pinjarra	168a	32.37 S	115.53 E
Pinjor Garden ♦	123	30.47 N	76.47 E
Pinka ≃	61	47.00 N	16.35 E
Pinkafeld	61	47.22 N	16.07 E
Pinkiang — Harbin	89	45.45 N	126.41 E
Pinlaung	110	20.08 N	96.47 E
Pinlebu	110	24.05 N	95.21 E
Pinn ≃	260	51.31 N	0.29 W
Pinnacle ∧, N.Z.	172	41.49 S	173.17 E
Pinnacle ∧, N.Y., U.S.	188	43.13 N	74.23 W
Pinnacle ∧, Va., U.S.	188	39.08 N	78.26 W
Pinnacle Buttes ∧	202	43.44 N	109.57 W
Pinnacle Island I	180	60.12 N	172.46 W
Pinnacle Peak ∧	224	46.45 N	121.43 W
Pinnacles National Monument ♦	226	36.28 N	121.19 W
Pinnaroo	166	35.16 S	140.55 E
Pinneberg	52	53.40 N	9.47 E
Pinner ♦[8]	260	51.36 N	0.23 W
Pino, Sierra del ∧	196	28.15 N	103.03 W
Pin Oak Creek ≃	222	31.57 N	96.28 W
Pinocchio	66	43.35 N	13.30 E
Pinochle Peak ∧	224	45.43 N	123.36 W
Pinole	226	38.00 N	122.17 W
Pinole Creek ≃	282	38.01 N	122.18 W
Pinole Point ›	282	38.01 N	122.22 W
Pinole Ridge ∧	282	37.59 N	122.15 W
Pinos	234	22.18 N	101.34 W
Pinos, Mount ∧	228	34.50 N	119.09 W
Pinos, Point ›	226	36.38 N	121.56 W
Pinos-Puente	34	37.15 N	3.45 W
Pinotepa de Don Luis	234	16.25 N	97.55 W
Pinrang	112	3.48 S	119.38 E
Pins, Île de — Juventud, Isla de la I	240p	21.40 N	82.50 W
Pins, Île des I	175f	22.37 S	167.30 E
Pins, Pointe aux ›	214	42.15 N	81.51 W
Pins, Rivière des ≃	206	46.01 N	72.03 W
Pinsk	76	52.07 N	26.04 E
Pinson	194	33.41 N	86.41 W
Pinsot	62	45.21 N	6.06 E
Pinta, Isla I	246a	0.35 N	90.44 W
Pintada Arroyo V	196	34.53 N	104.39 W
Pintado	258	33.50 S	56.18 W
Pintado ≃	252	13.33 S	50.16 W
Pintado, Arroyo de ≃	258	34.08 S	56.14 W
Pintado, Cuchilla del ∧[2]	258	34.12 S	56.25 W
Pintados	248	20.37 S	69.38 W
Pintados, Salar de ≃	248	20.30 S	69.42 W
Pintasan	112	5.26 N	117.43 E
Pinteus	266c	38.52 N	9.09 W
Pintlala Creek ≃	194	32.21 N	86.30 W
Pinto Butte ∧	184	49.22 N	107.25 W
Pinto Creek ≃, Ab., Can.	182	53.51 N	117.35 W
Pinto Creek ≃, Sk., Can.	184	49.40 N	106.42 W
Pintos, Arroyo de ≃	258	33.55 S	56.51 W
Pintos Negreiros	256	22.18 S	45.13 W
Pintoyacu ≃, Ec.	246	2.07 S	76.03 W
Pintoyacu ≃, Perú	246	3.35 S	73.55 W
Pinturas ≃	254	46.35 S	70.18 W
Pintuyan	116	9.57 N	125.15 E
Pin'ug	24	60.15 N	47.48 E
Pinukpuk	116	17.35 N	121.22 E
Pinwherry	44	55.09 N	4.50 W
Pinxton	44	53.06 N	1.19 W
Pinzano al Tagliamento	64	46.11 N	12.57 E
Pinzgau V	64	47.15 N	12.40 E
Pinzón, Isla I	246a	0.36 S	90.40 W
Piobbico	66	43.35 N	12.31 E
Pioche	204	37.55 N	114.27 W
Pio IX	250	6.50 S	40.37 W
Piolenc	62	44.11 N	4.46 E
Piombino	66	42.55 N	10.32 E
Piombino, Canale di ⊻	66	42.53 N	10.30 E
Pioneer, Austl.	162	31.48 S	121.43 E
Pioneer, Ca., U.S.	226	38.25 N	120.33 W
Pioneer, Oh., U.S.	216	41.40 N	84.33 W
Pioneer Mine	182	50.46 N	122.46 W
Pioneer Mountains ∧	202	45.40 N	113.00 W
Pioneer Park ♦	273d	26.14 S	28.04 E
Pioner, ostrov I	74	79.50 N	92.30 E
Pionerskij	76	54.57 N	20.20 E
Pionierbivak	164	2.16 S	138.02 E
Pionki	30	51.30 N	21.27 E
Pio Pico State Historical Monument ♦	280	33.59 N	118.04 W
Piopio	172	38.28 S	175.01 E
Pioppo	70	38.03 N	13.14 E
Piora, Mount ∧	164	6.45 S	146.00 E
Pioraco	66	43.11 N	12.59 E
Piorini ≃	246	3.23 S	63.30 W
Piorini, Lago ⊜	246	3.34 S	63.15 W
Piotrków Trybunalski	30	51.25 N	19.42 E
Piotrków Trybunalski □[4]	30	51.30 N	19.45 E
Piotta	58	46.31 N	8.40 E
Pio V. Corpus (Limbujan)	116	11.53 N	124.03 E
Piove di Sacco	64	45.18 N	12.02 E
Piovene-Rocchette	64	45.45 N	11.25 E
Pio XII	250	3.53 S	45.17 W
Pipa	107	29.07 N	105.05 E
Pipalkoti	124	30.26 N	79.27 E
Pipanaco, Salar de ≃	252	28.07 S	66.25 W
Pīpār	120	26.23 N	73.32 E
Piparia	124	22.45 N	78.21 E
Pīpār Road	120	26.27 N	73.27 E
Pipas	152	14.56 S	12.12 E
Pipe Creek ≃, In., U.S.	194	40.08 N	85.52 W
Pipe Creek ≃, In., U.S.	216	40.45 N	86.13 W
Pipe Creek ≃, In., U.S.	218	39.26 N	85.06 W
Piper City	216	40.45 N	88.11 W
Pipe Spring National Monument ♦	200	36.43 N	112.33 W
Pipestem Creek ≃	198	46.54 N	98.43 W
Pipestem State Park ♦	192	37.32 N	81.00 W
Pipestone	198	44.00 N	96.19 W
Pipestone ≃	176	52.53 N	89.23 W
Pipestone Creek ≃, Can.	184	49.42 N	100.45 W
Pipestone Creek ≃, Mi., U.S.	216	42.04 N	86.24 W
Pipestone National Monument ♦	198	44.00 N	96.18 W
Pipi ≃	146	7.27 N	22.48 E
Pipinas	258	35.32 S	57.20 W
Piping Brook ≃	276	41.08 N	73.37 W
Pipiriki	172	39.29 S	175.03 E
Piplān	123	32.17 N	71.21 E
Piplūn	126	23.21 N	88.07 E
Pipmuacan, Réservoir ⊜[1]	186	49.35 N	70.30 W
Pipri	124	23.58 N	82.40 E
Pipriac	28	47.49 N	1.57 W
Piqiang	85	40.20 N	77.38 E
Piqiao	106	31.34 N	119.27 E
Piqua	218	40.08 N	84.14 W
Piquet Carneiro	250	5.48 S	39.25 W
Piquete	256	22.36 S	45.11 W
Piquete, Ribeirão ≃	256	22.36 S	45.01 W
Piquiri ≃, Bra.	248	17.18 S	56.44 W
Piquiri ≃, Bra.	248	17.39 S	55.09 W
Piquiri ≃, Bra.	252	24.03 S	54.14 W
Pira	150	8.30 N	1.44 E
Piracaia	256	23.03 S	46.21 W
Piracanjuba	255	17.18 S	49.01 W
Piracanjuba ≃	255	18.14 S	48.42 W
Piracão ≃	287a	23.02 S	43.36 W
Piracicaba	256	22.43 S	47.38 W
Piracicaba ≃	256	22.36 S	48.19 W
Piraçununga	255	21.59 S	47.25 W
Piracuruca	250	3.56 S	41.42 W
Pirae	174s	17.32 S	149.33 W
Piraeus — Peiraiévs	38	37.57 N	23.38 E
Pirahmet	130	38.11 N	39.51 E
Piraí	256	22.38 S	43.54 W
Piraí ≃	256	22.28 S	43.50 W
Piraí do Sul	252	24.31 S	49.56 W
Piraiévs (Piraeus)	38	37.57 N	23.38 E
Piraino	70	38.10 N	14.52 E
Piraju	255	23.12 S	49.23 W
Pirajuba	255	19.54 S	48.42 W
Pirajuçara, Ribeirão ≃	287b	23.34 S	46.43 W
Pirajuí	255	21.59 S	49.29 W
Pirakata	126	22.34 N	87.11 E
Piramida, gora ∧	88	54.15 N	95.45 E
Piramidal'nyj, pik ∧	85	39.34 N	69.57 E
Pirámide de Cuicuilco ⊥	286a	19.18 N	99.11 W
Pirámide de Santa Cecilia ⊥	286a	19.33 N	99.09 W
Pirámide de Tenayuca ⊥	286a	19.32 N	99.11 W
Piram Island I	120	21.36 N	72.41 E
Piran	36	45.32 N	13.34 E
Piraña, Arroyo ≃	288	34.24 S	58.30 W
Piranè	252	25.43 S	59.06 W
Piranga	255	20.41 S	43.18 W
Pirangaí	256	22.34 S	44.37 W
Piranguçu	256	22.31 S	45.30 W
Piranguinho	256	22.24 S	45.32 W
Piranhas	255	16.31 S	51.51 W
Piranhas ≃, Bra.	250	5.15 S	36.45 W
Piranhas ≃, Bra.	250	8.40 S	49.28 W
Piranhas ≃, Bra.	255	5.56 S	48.15 W
Piranji ≃	250	4.23 S	37.48 W
Pīrān Shahr	128	36.41 N	45.08 E
Pirapemas	250	3.43 S	44.14 W
Pirapetinga ≃	256	21.37 S	42.32 W
Pirapetinga, Ribeirão ≃	256	21.49 S	43.36 W
Pirapó ≃	255	22.30 S	52.01 W
Pirapora	255	17.21 S	44.56 W
Pirapora do Bom Jesus	256	23.24 S	47.00 W
Pirapora do Bom Jesus □[7]	287b	23.24 S	46.56 W
Piraputanga	255	20.26 S	55.32 W
Piraquara	252	25.26 S	49.04 W
Piraquê ≃	287a	23.01 S	43.37 W
Pirarajá	252	33.44 S	54.45 W
Pirata, Monte ∧[2]	240m	18.06 N	65.33 W
Pirate Creek ≃	282	37.33 N	121.52 W
Pir'atin	78	50.15 N	32.30 E
Piratinga ≃	255	15.41 S	46.07 W
Piratini	252	31.27 S	53.06 W
Piratini ≃	252	28.06 S	55.27 W
Piratininga	287a	22.57 S	43.04 W
Piratininga, Lagoa C	256	22.57 S	43.05 W
Piratuba	252	27.27 S	51.48 W
Piratuba, Lago C	250	1.37 N	50.10 W
Piratucu ≃	250	1.59 S	56.58 W
Piraúba	256	21.17 S	43.02 W
Piraube, Lac ⊜	186	50.33 N	71.42 W
Piray ≃	248	16.32 S	63.45 W
Piraziz	130	40.58 N	38.08 E
Pirbright	260	51.18 N	0.39 W
Pirdop	38	42.42 N	24.11 E
Pirenópolis	255	15.51 S	48.57 W
Pires, Ribeirão ≃	287b	23.43 S	46.25 W
Pires do Rio	255	17.18 S	48.17 W
Pirgos	38	37.41 N	21.28 E
Piriá	250	1.40 S	50.02 W
Piriápolis	252	34.54 S	55.17 W
Piribebuy	252	25.29 S	57.03 W
Pirin ∧	38	41.40 N	23.30 E
Piringçı ♦[8]	267b	41.10 N	28.50 E
Pirineos — Pyrenees ∧	34	42.40 N	1.00 E
Piripiri	250	4.16 S	41.47 W
Piritiba	250	11.44 S	40.34 W
Píritu, Ven.	246	11.22 N	69.08 W
Píritu, Ven.	246	9.23 N	69.12 W
Pirituba ♦[8]	287b	23.29 S	46.44 W
Pirk	52	50.38 N	12.11 E
Pīr Mahal	123	30.46 N	72.26 E
Pirmasens	56	49.12 N	7.36 E
Pirna	54	50.58 N	13.56 E
Piroči	82	55.04 N	38.57 E
Pirogovka	78	51.54 N	33.18 E
Pirogovskij	265b	55.59 N	37.44 E
Pirogovskoje vodochranilišče ⊜[1]	82	55.58 N	37.40 E
Pirojpur	126	22.34 N	89.59 E
Pirón ≃	34	41.23 N	4.31 W
Pirongia	172	38.00 S	175.12 E
Pirot	38	43.09 N	22.35 E
Pirovano	252	36.30 S	61.34 W
Pirovskoje	86	57.37 N	92.16 E
Pīr Panjāl Range ∧	123	33.37 N	74.32 E
Pirpirituba	250	6.46 S	35.30 W
Pirreşit Tepe ∧	84	38.56 N	43.55 E
Pirsagat	84	39.54 N	49.24 E
Pirsagat ≃	84	39.53 N	49.19 E
Pirtleville	200	31.22 N	109.34 W
Piru, Indon.	164	3.04 S	128.12 E
Piru, Ca., U.S.	228	34.25 N	118.48 W
Piru, Lake ⊜[1]	228	34.30 N	118.45 W
Piru, Teluk C	164	3.10 S	128.08 E
Piru Creek ≃	228	34.23 N	118.47 W
Pisa	66	43.43 N	10.23 E
Pisa □[4]	66	43.25 N	10.43 E
Pisa ∧[2]	26	63.13 N	28.18 E
Pisa ≃	30	53.15 N	21.52 E
Pisa, Certosa di ♦[1]	66	43.45 N	10.31 E
Pisa, Mount ∧	172	44.52 S	169.11 E
Pisagua	248	19.36 S	70.13 W
Pisam-bong ∧	98	40.41 N	126.34 E
Pisang, Pulau I	164	1.23 S	128.55 E
Pisarevka	78	49.53 N	40.12 E
Pisarve	272c	19.06 N	73.05 E
Pisau, Tanjong ›	116	6.04 N	118.03 E
Piščalje	80	58.14 N	48.42 E
Piscasaw Creek ≃	216	42.16 N	88.49 W
Piscataway	210	40.29 N	74.23 W
Piscataway Creek ≃, Md., U.S.	208	38.42 N	77.02 W
Piscataway Creek ≃, Va., U.S.	208	37.54 N	76.50 W
Pischia	38	45.55 N	21.20 E
Pisciotta	68	40.06 N	15.14 E
Pisco	248	13.42 S	76.13 W
Pisco ≃	248	13.42 S	76.15 W
Piscolt	38	47.35 N	22.18 E
Piscovo	80	57.11 N	40.32 E
Piseco Lake ⊜	210	43.23 N	74.36 W
Písek	49	49.19 N	14.10 E
Pisek	198	48.18 N	97.42 W
Pisgah, Md., U.S.	208	38.32 N	77.08 W
Pisgah, Oh., U.S.	218	39.19 N	84.22 W
Pisgah Forest	192	35.15 N	82.42 W
Pishan	120	37.37 N	78.18 E
Pishīn	120	30.35 N	67.00 E
Pishīn Lora (Lowrah) ≃	120	29.09 N	64.55 E
Pisidia □[9]	130	37.30 N	31.00 E
Pisinemo	200	32.02 N	112.18 W
Pising	112	5.05 S	121.54 E
Pis'mennoje	78	48.13 N	35.48 E
Pismo Beach	226	35.08 N	120.38 W
Pišnur	80	57.47 N	47.24 E
Piso, Lake ⊜	150	6.48 N	11.17 W
Pisogne	64	45.48 N	10.06 E
Pisqui ≃	248	7.45 S	75.01 W
Pissila	150	13.10 N	0.49 W
Pissos	32	44.19 N	0.47 W
Pistakee Highlands	216	42.25 N	88.11 W
Pistakee Lake ⊜	216	42.23 N	88.12 W
Pisticci	68	40.23 N	16.34 E
Pistoia	66	43.55 N	10.54 E
Pistoia □[4]	66	43.58 N	10.50 E
Pistolet Bay C	186	51.32 N	55.50 W
Pistuk Peak ∧	180	59.43 N	159.42 W
Pisuerga ≃	34	41.33 N	4.52 W
Pisz	30	53.38 N	21.49 E
Pit ≃	204	40.45 N	122.22 W
Pit, North Fork ≃	204	41.28 N	120.33 W
Pit, South Fork ≃	204	41.28 N	120.33 W
Pita	150	11.05 N	12.24 W
Pital	248	2.16 N	75.49 W
Pitalito	246	1.51 N	76.02 W
Pitampura Kālan ♦[8]	272a	28.42 N	77.08 E
Pitanga	252	24.46 S	51.44 W
Pitangueiras	255	21.02 S	48.13 W
Pitangueiras, Ribeirão das ≃	256	21.27 S	44.27 W
Pitangui	255	19.40 S	44.54 W
Pitcairn	279b	40.24 N	79.46 W
Pitcairn □[2], Oc.	6	25.04 S	130.05 W
Pitcairn □[2], Oc.	174e	25.04 S	130.05 W
Pitcher	210	42.35 N	75.52 W
Pitch Place	260	51.16 N	0.36 W
Piteå	26	65.20 N	21.30 E
Piteälven ≃	24	65.14 N	21.32 E
Piteglio	66	44.01 N	10.46 E
Pitelino	80	54.34 N	41.49 E
Piterka	80	50.42 N	47.27 E
Pitești	38	44.52 N	24.52 E
Pithapuram	122	17.07 N	82.16 E
Pithara	162	30.24 S	116.40 E
Pithiviers	50	48.10 N	2.15 E
Pithorāgarh	124	29.35 N	80.13 E
Piti, Lagoa ⊜	158	26.34 S	32.53 E
Pitigliano	66	42.38 N	11.40 E
Pitim	80	53.12 N	42.21 E
Pitinga ≃	246	1.32 S	59.49 W
Pitiquito	232	30.42 N	112.02 W
Pitjantjatjara Lands ♦[4]	162	27.00 S	130.30 E
Pitk'aranta	24	61.34 N	31.27 E
Pitkas Point	180	62.02 N	163.17 W
Pitlochry	46	56.43 N	3.45 W
Pitman	208	39.43 N	75.07 W
Pitman Airport ⊠	285	39.45 N	75.08 W
Pitmedden	46	57.20 N	2.11 W
Pitner Ditch ≃	216	41.14 N	86.53 W
Pitogo	116	10.08 N	124.33 E
Pitomača	36	45.57 N	17.14 E
Pitou, Zhg.	100	25.01 N	114.35 E
Pitou, Zhg.	100	23.44 N	116.05 E
Pitou, Zhg.	100	24.26 N	114.22 E
Pitrufquén	254	38.59 S	72.39 W
Pitsea	260	51.34 N	0.31 E
Pitseng	158	28.58 S	28.16 E
Pitsford Reservoir ⊜[1]	42	52.20 N	0.52 W
Pitt ≃	224	49.12 N	122.47 W
Pitt, Mount ∧	174c	29.01 S	167.56 E
Pittem	50	51.00 N	3.16 E
Pitten	61	47.44 N	16.14 E
Pittenweem	46	56.12 N	2.44 W
Pitt Island I	122	10.50 N	72.38 E
Pitt Island I	182	53.35 N	129.45 W
Pitt Lake ⊜	182	49.25 N	122.32 W
Pittsboro, In., U.S.	218	39.51 N	86.28 W
Pittsboro, Ms., U.S.	194	33.56 N	89.20 W
Pittsboro, N.C., U.S.	192	35.43 N	79.10 W
Pittsburg, Ca., U.S.	226	38.01 N	121.53 W
Pittsburg, In., U.S.	216	40.37 N	86.42 W
Pittsburg, Ks., U.S.	198	37.24 N	94.42 W
Pittsburg, N.H., U.S.	206	45.03 N	71.23 W
Pittsburg, Tx., U.S.	222	33.00 N	94.57 W
Pittsburgh, Pa., U.S.	214	40.26 N	79.59 W
Pittsburgh, Pa., U.S.	279b	40.26 N	79.59 W
Pittsburgh, University of ♦[2]	279b	40.27 N	79.58 W
Pittsburgh-Monroeville Airport ⊠	279b	40.27 N	79.46 W
Pittsfield, Il., U.S.	219	39.36 N	90.48 W
Pittsfield, Me., U.S.	188	44.46 N	69.22 W
Pittsfield, Ma., U.S.	207	42.27 N	73.14 W
Pittsfield, N.H., U.S.	188	43.18 N	71.19 W
Pittsfield, Pa., U.S.	214	41.50 N	79.23 W
Pittsford, Mi., U.S.	216	41.52 N	84.28 W
Pittsford, N.Y., U.S.	210	43.05 N	77.31 W
Pitt Stadium ♦	279b	40.27 N	79.58 W
Pittston	210	41.19 N	75.47 W
Pittsview	194	32.11 N	85.09 W
Pittsville	208	38.23 N	75.24 W
Pittsworth	166	27.43 S	151.38 E
Pitt Water C	170	33.37 S	151.18 E
Pituil	252	28.34 S	67.27 W
Pitumarca	248	13.59 S	71.25 W
Pituri Creek ≃	166	22.58 S	138.50 E
Pitzbach ≃	64	47.13 N	10.46 E
Pitztal V	64	47.07 N	10.47 E
Pium	250	10.27 S	49.11 W
Pium ≃	250	10.12 S	49.57 W
Piura	248	5.12 S	80.38 W
Piura □[5]	248	5.10 S	80.00 W
Piura ≃	248	5.32 S	80.53 W
Piute Peak ∧	204	35.27 N	118.24 W
Piute Reservoir ⊜[1]	200	38.17 N	112.12 W
Piva ≃	38	43.21 N	18.51 E
Pivan'	89	50.29 N	137.06 E
Piverone	62	45.27 N	8.00 E
Pivijay	246	10.28 N	74.37 W
Piwniczna	30	49.27 N	20.42 E
Pixian	102	30.49 N	103.49 E
Pixley	226	35.58 N	119.17 W
Pižanka	80	57.28 N	48.33 E
Pižma	80	57.52 N	47.06 E
Pižma ≃	80	57.37 N	48.58 E
Pizzighettone	62	45.11 N	9.47 E
Pizzillo, Monte ∧	70	37.48 N	15.01 E
Pizzo	68	38.44 N	16.10 E
Pizzoferrato	66	41.55 N	14.14 E
Pizzoli	66	42.26 N	13.18 E
Pizzone	66	41.40 N	14.02 E
Pjalka	24	66.43 N	40.59 E
Pjana ≃	80	55.40 N	45.57 E
Pjöngjang — P'yŏngyang	98	39.01 N	125.45 E
P. K. le Rouxdam ⊜[1]	158	30.12 S	24.54 E
Placanica	68	38.25 N	16.27 E
Place Bonaventure ♦[9]	275a	45.30 N	73.34 W
Placentia, Nf., Can.	186	47.14 N	53.58 W
Placentia, Ca., U.S.	228	33.52 N	117.52 W
Placentia Bay C	186	47.15 N	54.30 W
Placer, Pil.	116	11.52 N	123.55 E
Placer, Pil.	116	9.39 N	125.36 E
Placer □[6]	226	38.54 N	121.04 W
Placeres del Oro ≃	234	18.27 N	100.57 W
Placeres de Picacho	234	23.11 N	105.42 W
Placerville	226	38.43 N	120.47 W
Placetas	240p	22.19 N	79.40 W
Place Versailles ♦[9]	275a	45.35 N	73.32 W
Plachino	76	54.28 N	39.20 E
Plachtejevka	78	46.07 N	29.43 E
Placid, Lake ⊜	220	27.14 N	81.22 W
Placida	220	26.49 N	82.15 W
Plácido de Castro	248	10.20 S	67.11 W
Plácido Rosas	252	32.45 S	53.44 W
Placita de Morelos	234	18.31 N	103.42 W
Plačkovica ∧	38	41.45 N	22.35 E
Plaffeien	58	46.44 N	7.17 E
Plages, Lac des ⊜	206	45.59 N	74.54 W
Plage-Sainte-Cécile	50	50.34 N	1.35 E
Plailly	261	49.06 N	2.35 E
Plai Mat ≃	110	15.22 N	102.45 E
Plain	224	47.46 N	120.39 W
Plain City, Oh., U.S.	218	40.06 N	83.16 W
Plain City, Ut., U.S.	200	41.17 N	112.05 W
Plain Dealing	194	32.54 N	93.41 W
Plaines, Île aux I	275a	45.21 N	73.50 W
Plainfield, Ct., U.S.	207	41.40 N	71.54 W
Plainfield, Il., U.S.	216	41.37 N	88.12 W
Plainfield, In., U.S.	218	39.42 N	86.23 W
Plainfield, Ma., U.S.	207	42.30 N	72.55 W
Plainfield, N.J., U.S.	210	40.37 N	74.26 W
Plainfield, Oh., U.S.	214	40.13 N	81.43 W
Plainfield, Pa., U.S.	208	40.12 N	77.17 W
Plainfield, Wi., U.S.	190	44.12 N	89.29 W
Plainfield Heights	216	43.01 N	85.37 W
Plains, Ga., U.S.	192	32.02 N	84.23 W
Plains, Ks., U.S.	198	37.15 N	100.35 W
Plains, Mt., U.S.	202	47.27 N	114.52 W
Plains, Tx., U.S.	196	33.11 N	102.50 W
Plainsboro	208	40.20 N	74.36 W
Plainview, Ca., U.S.	226	36.08 N	119.08 W
Plainview, Il., U.S.	219	39.10 N	89.59 W
Plainview, Mn., U.S.	190	44.09 N	92.10 W
Plainview, Ne., U.S.	198	42.20 N	97.47 W
Plainview, N.Y., U.S.	210	40.46 N	73.28 W
Plainview, Tx., U.S.	196	34.11 N	101.42 W
Plainville, Ct., U.S.	207	41.40 N	72.51 W
Plainville, Il., U.S.	219	39.47 N	91.11 W
Plainville, In., U.S.	194	38.48 N	87.09 W
Plainville, Ks., U.S.	198	39.14 N	99.17 W
Plainville, Ma., U.S.	207	42.00 N	71.20 W
Plainville, N.Y., U.S.	210	43.10 N	76.27 W
Plainwell	216	42.26 N	85.38 W
Plaisance, Baie de C	186	47.18 N	61.53 W
Plaisir	261	48.49 N	1.57 E
Plaistow	207	42.50 N	71.05 W
Plaksino	76	56.11 N	30.42 E
Plamondon	182	54.51 N	112.19 W
Plampang	115b	8.48 S	117.48 E
Planá	60	49.52 N	12.44 E
Plana, Illa I	34	38.10 N	0.28 W
Planada	226	37.18 N	120.19 W
Planalto, Bra.	252	27.20 S	53.03 W
Planalto, Bra.	255	14.39 S	40.29 W
Planches	50	48.42 N	0.22 E
Plandome	276	40.48 N	73.42 W
Plandome Heights	276	40.48 N	73.42 W
Plandome Manor	276	40.49 N	73.42 W
Plan-d'Orgon	62	43.48 N	5.00 E
Plane ≃	54	52.23 N	12.30 E
Planegg	60	48.06 N	11.25 E
Planerskoje	78	44.57 N	35.14 E
Planeta Rica	246	8.25 N	75.36 W
Plangeross	64	46.59 N	10.52 E
Plankenfels	60	49.53 N	11.20 E
Plankinton	198	43.42 N	98.29 W
Plano, Il., U.S.	216	41.39 N	88.32 W
Plano, Tx., U.S.	222	33.01 N	96.41 W
Plansee ⊜	64	47.28 N	10.48 E
Plantagenet	206	45.32 N	75.00 W
Plantation, Fl., U.S.	220	26.07 N	80.14 W
Plantation, Fl., U.S.	220	24.58 N	80.33 W
Plantation, Ky., U.S.	218	38.17 N	85.36 W
Plantation Key I	220	24.58 N	80.33 W
Plant City	220	28.01 N	82.06 W
Plantersville, Al., U.S.	194	32.39 N	86.55 W
Plantersville, Ms., U.S.	194	34.12 N	88.39 W
Plantersville, Tx., U.S.	222	30.20 N	95.52 W
Planting Fields Arboretum State Park ♦	276	40.52 N	73.33 W
Plantsite	200	33.03 N	109.19 W
Plantsville	207	41.35 N	72.53 W
Plaquemine	194	30.17 N	91.14 W
Plaridel, Pil.	116	10.32 N	124.46 E
Plaridel, Pil.	116	8.37 N	123.43 E
Plasencia	34	40.02 N	6.05 W
Plaški	36	45.05 N	15.22 E
Plassenburg ⊥	60	50.06 N	11.28 E
Plassey	126	23.47 N	88.15 E
Plast	86	54.22 N	60.50 E
Plaster Rock	186	46.54 N	67.24 W
Plastovo	82	54.17 N	37.03 E
Plastun	89	44.45 N	136.19 E
Plastunovskaja	78	45.18 N	39.16 E
Plasy	60	49.56 N	13.24 E
Plata, Isla de la I	246	1.16 S	81.06 W
Plata, Río de la C[1]	258	35.00 S	57.00 W
Plata, Río de la ≃	240m	18.29 N	66.15 W
Platani ≃	70	37.24 N	13.16 E
Platania	68	39.00 N	16.19 E
Plátanos	288	34.47 S	58.11 W
Plátanos, Arroyo ≃	288	34.45 S	58.10 W
Plate, Île I	275a	45.22 N	73.48 W
Platea	214	41.57 N	80.20 W
Plateau □[3]	150	8.45 N	8.30 E
Plateau Creek ≃	200	39.11 N	108.18 W
Plateaux □[5]	152	2.15 S	15.30 E
Platì	68	38.13 N	16.03 E
Platinum	180	59.01 N	161.49 W
Platnirovskaja	78	45.23 N	39.23 E
Plato	246	9.47 N	74.47 W
Platono-Petrovka	83	46.59 N	39.28 E
Platonovka	80	52.43 N	41.57 E
Platón Sánchez	234	21.17 N	98.22 W
Platovo	83	48.05 N	39.53 E
Platrand	158	27.08 S	29.29 E
Platt	260	51.17 N	0.20 E
Platta	58	46.40 N	8.51 E
Platte	198	43.23 N	98.50 W
Platte ≃, U.S.	194	39.16 N	94.50 W
Platte ≃, Mn., U.S.	190	45.47 N	94.17 W
Platte ≃, Ne., U.S.	198	41.04 N	95.53 W
Platte ≃, Wi., U.S.	190	42.37 N	90.40 W
Platte Center	198	41.32 N	97.29 W
Platte City	194	39.22 N	94.46 W
Platte Creek ≃	198	43.19 N	99.00 W
Platte Island I	138	5.52 S	55.23 E
Plattekill	210	41.37 N	74.05 W
Platteville, Co., U.S.	200	40.12 N	104.49 W
Platteville, Wi., U.S.	190	42.44 N	90.28 W
Platt Hall ⊥	262	53.27 N	2.14 W
Plattling	60	48.47 N	12.53 E
Plattsburg	194	39.33 N	94.26 W
Plattsburgh	188	44.41 N	73.27 W
Plattsburgh Air Force Base ■	188	44.40 N	73.28 W
Plattsmouth	198	41.00 N	95.52 W
Plattsville	212	43.18 N	80.37 W
Platveld	156	19.58 S	17.07 E
Plau	54	53.27 N	12.16 E
Plaue, Dtsch.	54	52.24 N	12.25 E
Plaue, Dtsch.	54	50.47 N	10.54 E
Plauen	54	50.30 N	12.08 E
Plauer See ⊜	54	53.30 N	12.20 E
Plav	38	42.36 N	19.56 E
Plave	64	46.02 N	13.36 E
Pļaviņas	76	56.37 N	25.43 E
Plavsk	76	53.43 N	37.18 E
Plaxtol	260	51.15 N	0.18 E
Playa Azul	234	17.59 N	102.24 W
Playa Baracoa	286b	23.03 N	82.35 W
Playa Bonita	236	9.39 N	84.27 W
Playa de Fajardo	240m	18.20 N	65.38 W
Playa de Guayanés	240m	18.04 N	65.49 W
Playa de Guayanilla	240m	18.01 N	66.46 W
Playa del Carmen	232	20.36 N	87.06 W
Playa del Rey ♦[8]	280	33.58 N	118.26 W
Playa de Naguabo	240m	18.12 N	65.43 W
Playa de Ponce	240m	17.59 N	66.37 W
Playa Noriega, Laguna ⊜	232	29.10 N	111.50 W
Playas Lake ⊜	200	31.50 N	108.34 W
Playa Vicente	234	17.50 N	95.49 W
Play Cu	110	13.59 N	108.00 E
Playford ≃	162	19.03 S	135.35 E
Playgreen Lake ⊜	184	54.00 N	98.10 W
Playland ♦	276	40.58 N	73.41 W
Plaza	198	48.01 N	101.57 W
Plaza at Mid Island ♦[9]	276	40.46 N	73.32 W
Plaza de Caisán	236	8.46 N	82.45 W
Plaza de Mayo ♦	288	34.36 S	58.23 W
Plaza de Toros ♦	266a	40.26 N	3.39 W
Plaza de Toros Las Arenas ♦	266d	41.23 N	2.09 E
Plaza de Toros Monumental ♦	266d	41.24 N	2.11 E
Plaza Huincul	252	38.55 S	69.09 W
Plaza Park	285	40.04 N	75.43 W
Plazas de Soberanía en el Norte de África — Spanish North Africa □[2]	34	35.53 N	5.19 W
Pleasant	275b	43.41 N	79.49 W
Pleasant, Lake ⊜[1]	200	33.53 N	112.16 W
Pleasant, Mount ∧	192	37.44 N	79.10 W
Pleasant, Mount ∧[2]	186	45.26 N	66.49 W
Pleasant Bay C	186	46.49 N	60.48 W
Pleasantdale, Sk., Can.	184	52.35 N	104.30 W
Pleasantdale, N.Y., U.S.	210	42.47 N	73.40 W
Pleasant Gap	214	40.52 N	77.44 W
Pleasant Garden	192	35.57 N	79.45 W
Pleasant Grove, Ca., U.S.	226	38.49 N	121.29 W
Pleasant Grove, Ut., U.S.	200	40.21 N	111.44 W
Pleasant Grove Creek ≃	226	38.48 N	121.32 W
Pleasant Hill, Ca., U.S.	226	37.56 N	122.03 W
Pleasant Hill, Il., U.S.	219	39.26 N	90.52 W
Pleasant Hill, La., U.S.	194	31.49 N	93.31 W
Pleasant Hill, Mo., U.S.	194	38.47 N	94.16 W
Pleasant Hill, N.C., U.S.	208	36.32 N	77.32 W
Pleasant Hill, Oh., U.S.	218	40.03 N	84.20 W
Pleasant Hill Lake ⊜[1]	214	40.38 N	82.21 W
Pleasant Hills	279b	40.20 N	79.57 W
Pleasant Lake, In., U.S.	216	41.34 N	85.00 W
Pleasant Lake, Mi., U.S.	216	42.23 N	84.22 W
Pleasant Lake ⊜	216	42.13 N	83.56 W
Pleasant Mills	218	40.47 N	84.51 W
Pleasant Mount	210	41.44 N	75.26 W
Pleasanton, Ca., U.S.	226	37.39 N	121.52 W
Pleasanton, Ks., U.S.	198	38.10 N	94.42 W
Pleasanton, Tx., U.S.	196	28.58 N	98.28 W
Pleasanton Ridge ∧	282	37.40 N	121.55 W
Pleasant Plains, Il., U.S.	219	39.52 N	89.55 W
Pleasant Plains, N.J., U.S.	208	40.00 N	74.13 W
Pleasant Point	172	44.16 S	171.08 E
Pleasant Prairie	216	42.33 N	87.57 W
Pleasant Ridge	281	42.31 N	83.10 W
Pleasant Unity	214	40.15 N	79.28 W
Pleasant Valley, N.Y., U.S.	210	41.44 N	73.49 W
Pleasant Valley, Oh., U.S.	218	39.22 N	83.03 W
Pleasant Valley, Pa., U.S.	279b	40.31 N	75.18 W
Pleasantville, Ia., U.S.	190	41.23 N	93.16 W
Pleasantville, Md., U.S.	284b	39.11 N	76.38 W
Pleasantville, N.J., U.S.	208	39.23 N	74.31 W
Pleasantville, N.Y., U.S.	210	41.07 N	73.47 W
Pleasantville, Pa., U.S.	214	41.35 N	79.34 W
Pleasington	262	53.44 N	2.34 W
Pleasure Beach	207	41.18 N	72.08 W
Pleasure Ridge Park	218	38.09 N	85.51 W
Pleasureville	218	38.33 N	85.04 W
Pléaux	32	45.08 N	2.14 E
Plechanovo	82	54.14 N	37.33 E
Plechanovskoje	76	52.39 N	39.50 E
Plechovo	78	51.07 N	35.18 E
Plechý (Plöckenstein) ∧	60	48.46 N	13.51 E
Pledger	222	29.11 N	95.55 W
Pleebo	150	4.35 N	7.40 W
Pleiku — Play Cu	110	13.59 N	108.00 E
Pleinfeld	56	49.06 N	10.59 E
Pleissa	54	50.50 N	12.46 E
Pleisse ≃	54	51.20 N	12.22 E
Pléneuf	32	48.36 N	2.33 W
Plenty	184	51.47 N	108.36 W
Plenty ≃, Austl.	162	23.25 S	136.31 E
Plenty ≃, Austl.	274b	37.45 S	145.07 E
Plenty, Bay of C	172	37.40 S	177.00 E
Plentywood	198	48.46 N	104.33 W
Plered	115a	6.38 S	107.23 E
Pleščejevo, ozero ⊜	82	56.46 N	38.47 E
Pleščenicy	76	54.25 N	27.50 E
Pleseck	24	62.43 N	40.20 E
Plešivka	82	54.23 N	37.09 E
Plesna ≃	54	50.07 N	12.28 E
Pless	58	48.05 N	10.08 E
Plessa	54	51.28 N	13.37 E
Plessisville	206	46.14 N	71.47 W
Pless — Pszczyna	30	49.59 N	18.57 E
Pleszew	30	51.54 N	17.48 E
Pletenevka	82	54.31 N	36.06 E
Pleternica	38	45.17 N	17.48 E
Plétipi, Lac ⊜	176	51.44 N	70.06 W
Plet'onyj Tašlyk	78	48.29 N	31.40 E
Plettenberg	56	51.13 N	7.52 E
Plettenbergbaai	158	34.03 S	23.22 E
Pleurs	50	48.41 N	3.52 E
Pleven	38	43.25 N	24.37 E
Plevna, Mo., U.S.	219	39.58 N	92.05 W
Plevna, Mt., U.S.	198	46.25 N	104.31 W
Pleyben	32	48.14 N	3.58 W
Pleystein	60	49.39 N	12.25 E
Pliening	60	48.12 N	11.48 E
Pliezhausen	56	48.33 N	9.12 E
Plimmerton	172	41.05 S	174.52 E
Plimoth Plantation ⊥	207	41.57 N	70.38 W
Plintovka	265a	60.01 N	30.46 E
Pliski	78	51.07 N	32.24 E
Pliskov	78	49.23 N	29.18 E
Pliszka ≃	54	52.14 N	14.42 E
Plitvička Jezera Nacionalni Park ♦	36	44.53 N	15.38 E
Plješevica ∧	36	44.40 N	15.45 E
Pljevlja	38	43.21 N	19.21 E
Ploaghe	71	40.40 N	8.45 E
Plochingen	56	48.42 N	9.25 E
Płock	30	52.33 N	19.43 E
Płock □[4]	30	52.25 N	19.45 E
Plöckenpass)(	64	46.36 N	12.58 E
Plöckenstein (Plechý) ∧	60	48.46 N	13.51 E
Plockton	46	57.20 N	5.39 W
Pločno ∧	36	43.36 N	17.34 E
Plodorodnoje	80	46.44 N	41.06 E
Ploegsteert	50	50.43 N	2.53 E
Ploërmel	32	47.56 N	2.24 W
Ploești — Ploiești	38	44.56 N	26.02 E
Plogastel-Saint-Germain	28	47.59 N	4.16 W
Ploiești	38	44.56 N	26.02 E
Plomárion	38	38.59 N	26.22 E
Plomb du Cantal ∧	32	45.03 N	2.46 E
Plombières-les-Bains	58	47.58 N	6.29 E
Plombières-lès-Dijon	58	47.20 N	4.58 E
Plomer	258	34.48 S	59.02 W
Plomer, Point ›	166	31.19 S	152.58 E
Plön	54	54.09 N	10.25 E
Plonge, Lac la ⊜	184	55.08 N	107.25 W
Płońsk	30	52.38 N	20.23 E
Pl'os	80	57.27 N	41.31 E
Plose, Cima delle ∧	64	46.42 N	11.44 E
Ploskij	78	46.17 N	40.15 E
Ploskoje	76	52.45 N	38.21 E
Ploskoš'	76	56.46 N	31.16 E
Pl'oso	76	59.47 N	35.43 E
Plotbišče	80	56.50 N	50.35 E
Plotina	83	48.33 N	40.05 E
Plotnica	76	52.03 N	26.39 E
Plottier	252	38.58 S	68.14 W
Płoty	30	53.49 N	15.16 E
Plötz	54	51.38 N	11.56 E
Plouay	32	47.55 N	3.20 W
Ploučnice ≃	54	50.47 N	14.13 E
Ploudalmézeau	32	48.32 N	4.39 W
Plouguenast	32	48.17 N	2.43 W
Plouha	32	48.41 N	2.56 W
Plovdiv	38	42.09 N	24.45 E
Plover ≃	190	44.29 N	89.35 W
Plover Islands II	180	71.15 N	155.30 W
Pluckemin	276	40.39 N	74.39 W
Plum, Pa., U.S.	214	40.31 N	79.45 W
Plum, Pa., U.S.	214	41.35 N	79.51 W
Plum, Tx., U.S.	222	29.56 N	96.58 W
Pluma Hidalgo	234	15.55 N	96.25 W
Plumas	184	50.25 N	99.02 W
Plumbridge	48	54.46 N	7.15 W
Plum Brook ≃	281	42.34 N	82.58 W
Plum Creek ≃, Il., U.S.	278	41.33 N	87.29 W
Plum Creek ≃, Ne., U.S.	198	41.52 N	96.44 W
Plum Creek ≃, Oh., U.S.	279a	41.18 N	82.09 W
Plum Creek ≃, Pa., U.S.	279b	40.31 N	79.51 W
Plum Creek ≃, S.D., U.S.	198	44.13 N	100.43 W
Plum Creek ≃, Tx., U.S.	196	29.38 N	97.36 W
Plum Creek, Clear Fork ≃	222	29.45 N	97.37 W
Plumerville	194	35.09 N	92.38 W
Plum Grove	222	30.15 N	95.05 W
Plum Grove Estates	278	42.04 N	88.02 W
Plum Island	283	42.49 N	70.59 W
Plum Island I, Ma., U.S.	207	42.45 N	70.48 W
Plum Island I, N.Y., U.S.	207	41.11 N	72.12 W
Plum Island Airport ⊠	283	42.48 N	70.50 W
Plum Island Sound ⊻	283	42.45 N	70.48 W
Plum Island State Park ♠	283	42.42 N	70.47 W
Plumley	262	53.17 N	2.25 W
Plummer	202	47.20 N	116.53 W
Plummers Landing	218	38.19 N	83.33 W
Plumper Sound ⊻	224	48.47 N	123.13 W
Plum Point ›	276	40.50 N	40.43 W
Plumpton	274a	33.45 S	150.50 E
Plumridge Lakes ⊜	162	29.30 S	125.25 E
Plum Run ≃	279b	40.15 N	80.13 W
Plumsteadville	208	40.23 N	75.09 W
Plumtree	154	20.30 S	27.50 E
Plumville	214	40.48 N	79.11 W
Plumwood	218	40.01 N	83.23 W
Plungė	76	55.55 N	21.51 E
Pl'uskovo	76	52.46 N	33.49 E
Pl'ussa	76	58.26 N	29.21 E
Pl'ussa ≃	76	59.19 N	28.11 E
Plutarco Elías Calles, Presa ⊜[1]	232	29.10 N	109.40 W
Pluvigner	32	47.46 N	3.01 E
Plym ≃	42	50.22 N	4.07 W
Plymouth, Monts.	238	16.42 N	62.13 W
Plymouth, Trin.	241r	11.13 N	60.47 W
Plymouth, Eng., U.K.	42	50.23 N	4.10 W
Plymouth, Ca., U.S.	226	38.29 N	120.51 W
Plymouth, Ct., U.S.	207	41.40 N	73.03 W
Plymouth, Il., U.S.	194	40.17 N	90.55 W
Plymouth, In., U.S.	216	41.20 N	86.18 W
Plymouth, Ma., U.S.	207	41.57 N	70.40 W
Plymouth, Mi., U.S.	216	42.22 N	83.28 W
Plymouth, Ne., U.S.	198	40.18 N	96.59 W
Plymouth, N.H., U.S.	188	43.45 N	71.41 W
Plymouth, N.Y., U.S.	210	42.37 N	75.36 W
Plymouth, N.C., U.S.	192	35.52 N	76.44 W
Plymouth, Oh., U.S.	214	41.00 N	82.40 W
Plymouth, Pa., U.S.	210	41.14 N	75.56 W
Plymouth, Wi., U.S.	190	43.44 N	87.58 W
Plymouth □[6]	207	41.58 N	70.41 W
Plymouth ≃	283	42.12 N	70.54 W
Plymouth Airport ⊠	42	50.25 N	4.06 W
Plymouth Bay C	207	41.57 N	70.37 W
Plymouth Harbor C	283	41.58 N	70.39 W
Plymouth Meeting	285	40.06 N	75.16 W

Symbol	English	Deutsch	Español	Français	Português
≃	River	Fluß	Río	Rivière	Rio
≡	Canal	Kanal	Canal	Canal	Canal
L	Waterfall, Rapids	Wasserfall, Stromschnellen	Cascada, Rápidos	Chute d'eau, Rapides	Cascata, Rápidos
⊻	Strait	Meeresstraße	Estrecho	Détroit	Estreito
C	Bay, Gulf	Bucht, Golf	Bahía, Golfo	Baie, Golfe	Baía, Golfo
⊜	Lake, Lakes	See, Seen	Lago, Lagos	Lac, Lacs	Lago, Lagos
≚	Swamp	Sumpf	Pantano	Marais	Pântano
⁂	Ice Features, Glacier	Eis- und Gletscherformen	Accidentes Glaciales	Formes glaciaires	Acidentes glaciares
⊤	Other Hydrographic Features	Andere Hydrographische Objekte	Otros Elementos Hidrográficos	Autres données hydrographiques	Outros acidentes hidrográficos
✦	Submarine Features	Untermeerische Objekte	Accidentes Submarinos	Formes de relief sous-marin	Acidentes submarinos
□	Political Unit	Politische Einheit	Unidad Politica	Entité politique	Unidade política
♦	Cultural Institution	Kulturelle Institution	Institución Cultural	Institution culturelle	Instituição cultural
⊥	Historical Site	Historische Stätte	Sitio Histórico	Site historique	Sitio histórico
♠	Recreational Site	Erholungs- und Ferienort	Sitio de Recreo	Centre de loisirs	Area de Lazer
⊠	Airport	Flughafen	Aeropuerto	Aéroport	Aeroporto
■	Military Installation	Militäranlage	Instalación Militar	Installation militaire	Instalação militar
♦	Miscellaneous	Verschiedenes	Misceláneo	Divers	Diversos

ENGLISH / DEUTSCH

Name	Page (Seite)	Lat.°′ (Breite°′)	Long.°′ (Länge°′ E = Ost)
Plymouth Meeting Mall ◆[9]	285	40.07 N	75.17 W
Plymouth Rock ⊥	207	41.57 N	70.39 W
Plymouth Valley	285	40.07 N	75.23 W
Plympton, Eng., U.K.	42	50.23 N	4.03 W
Plympton, Ma., U.S.	207	41.57 N	70.48 W
Plymptonville	214	41.03 N	78.28 W
Plymstock	42	50.22 N	4.04 W
Plynlimon ∧	42	52.28 N	3.47 W
Plzeň	60	49.45 N	13.23 E
Pniewy	30	52.31 N	16.15 E
Pô	150	11.10 N	1.09 W
Po ≃, It.	36	44.57 N	12.04 E
Po ≃, Zhg.	100	28.57 N	116.39 E
Po, Foci del ≃[1]	64	44.52 N	12.30 E
Pô, Parc National de ♦	150	11.30 N	1.15 W
Poá	256	23.32 S	46.20 W
Poá ≃	287b	23.37 S	46.45 W
Poana ≃	250	0.56 N	57.03 W
Poarta Orientală, Pasul)(	38	45.06 N	22.18 E
Poás, Volcán ∧[1]	236	10.11 N	84.13 W
Pobé, Bénin	150	6.58 N	2.41 E
Pobé, Burkina	150	13.53 N	1.45 W
Pobeda, gora ∧	74	65.12 N	146.12 E
Pobeda Ice Island I	9	64.30 S	97.00 E
Pobedino	74	49.51 N	142.49 E
Pobedy, pik ∧	72	42.02 N	80.05 E
Pobershau	54	50.38 N	13.13 E
Poběžovice	60	49.31 N	12.48 E
Poblado Cerro Gordo	240m	18.29 N	66.20 W
Poblado Jacaguas	240m	18.03 N	66.32 W
Poblado Medianía Alta	240m	18.26 N	65.50 W
Poblado Sábalos	240m	18.11 N	67.09 W
Poblado Santana	240m	18.27 N	66.40 W
Poblet	258	35.04 S	57.57 W
Pocahontas, Ar., U.S.	194	36.15 N	90.58 W
Pocahontas, Il., U.S.	219	38.49 N	89.32 W
Pocahontas, Ia., U.S.	198	42.44 N	94.40 W
Pocahontas State Park ♦	208	37.23 N	77.34 W
Počajev	78	50.01 N	25.31 E
Pocantico Hills	276	41.06 N	73.50 W
Pocantico Lake ⊜	276	41.07 N	73.50 W
Poção	250	8.11 S	36.42 W
Pocasset	207	41.41 N	70.37 W
Pocatalico ≃	188	38.29 N	81.49 W
Pocatello	202	42.52 N	112.26 W
Počep	76	52.56 N	33.27 E
Počepy	76	53.17 N	31.20 E
Pocé-sur-Cisse	50	47.26 N	0.59 E
Pöchlarn	61	48.12 N	15.13 E
Pochvistnevo	80	53.38 N	52.08 E
Pocinhos, Bra.	250	7.04 S	36.03 W
Pocinhos, Bra.	256	21.56 S	46.25 W
Počinki	80	54.42 N	44.51 E
Počinnaja Sopka	76	58.25 N	34.22 E
Počinok	76	54.25 N	32.27 E
Pocitos, Salar ≚	252	24.30 S	67.03 W
Pockau	54	50.40 N	13.27 E
Pocking	60	48.24 N	13.19 E
Pocklington	44	53.56 N	0.46 W
Pocoata	248	18.41 S	66.11 W
Poço da Cruz, Açude ⊜[1]	250	8.30 S	37.35 W
Poço do Bispo ◆[8]	266c	38.44 N	9.06 W
Poções	255	14.31 S	40.21 W
Poço Fundo	256	21.48 S	45.58 W
Poço Fundo, Cachoeira do ⌊	256	22.10 S	44.13 W
Pocol	64	46.31 N	12.07 E
Pocola	194	35.13 N	94.28 W
Pocomoke ≃	208	37.58 N	75.39 W
Pocomoke City	208	38.04 N	75.34 W
Pocomoke Sound ⊍	208	37.52 N	75.49 W
Pocona	248	17.39 S	65.24 W
Poconé	248	16.15 S	56.37 W
Pocono International Raceway ♦	210	41.03 N	75.31 W
Pocono Lake	210	41.06 N	75.31 W
Pocono Manor	210	41.06 N	75.22 W
Pocono Mountains ⋏[2]	210	41.10 N	75.20 W
Pocono Pines	210	41.05 N	75.29 W
Pocono Summit	210	41.07 N	75.25 W
Pocopson	285	39.54 N	75.37 W
Pocopson Creek ≃	285	39.54 N	75.37 W
Poço Redondo	250	9.49 S	37.41 W
Poços de Caldas	256	21.48 S	46.34 W
Poço Verde	250	10.42 S	38.11 W
Pocrane	255	19.37 S	41.37 W
Pocrí	236	8.16 N	80.33 W
Podbel'skaja	80	53.37 N	51.50 E
Podberezje, Ross.	76	56.57 N	30.38 E
Podberezje, Ross.	82	56.46 N	37.10 E
Podbořany	54	50.11 N	13.25 E
Podborki	82	54.11 N	35.56 E
Podborovje	76	59.30 N	35.02 E
Podbuž	78	49.22 N	23.15 E
Podbužje	76	53.30 N	34.56 E
Podčerje	24	63.57 N	57.34 E
Podchožeje	82	54.19 N	38.34 E
Podčinnyj	80	50.52 N	45.13 E
Poddębice	30	51.53 N	18.58 E
Poddemjur	24	64.05 N	53.26 E
Poddolgoje	76	53.12 N	38.04 E
Poddorje	76	57.28 N	31.07 E
Poděbrady	30	50.08 N	15.07 E
Po della Donzella ≃	64	44.48 N	12.25 E
Po delle Tolle ≃	64	44.50 N	12.28 E
Podensac	32	44.39 N	0.22 W
Podenzano	62	44.57 N	9.41 E
Podersdorf am See	61	47.51 N	16.50 E
Podgajcy	78	49.16 N	25.08 E
Podgorenskij	78	50.24 N	39.39 E
Podgorica	38	42.26 N	19.14 E
Podgornaja	78	50.28 N	41.10 E
Podgornoje, Kaz.	85	42.55 N	72.25 E
Podgornoje, Ross.	78	51.43 N	39.07 E
Podgornoje, Ross.	78	50.27 N	39.37 E
Podgornoje, Ross.	80	46.33 N	43.07 E
Podgornoje, Ross.	86	57.47 N	82.36 E
Podgorodnaja	78	48.07 N	30.51 E
Podgorodnoje	78	48.34 N	35.08 E
Podhůří	60	49.28 N	13.40 E
Podi	112	1.08 S	121.16 E
Po di Goro ≃	64	44.48 N	12.27 E
Po di Volano ≃	64	44.49 N	12.15 E
Podjom-Michajlovka	80	52.49 N	50.32 E
Podjuchy ◆[8]	54	53.20 N	14.36 E
Podkamen'	78	49.57 N	25.19 E
Podkamennaja Tunguska	74	61.36 N	90.09 E
Podkamennaja Tunguska ≃	74	61.36 N	90.18 E
Podkoren	64	46.30 N	13.45 E
Podkumok ≃	84	44.14 N	43.36 E
Podlasie ◆[1]	30	52.30 N	23.00 E
Podlesnoje, Ross.	80	51.50 N	47.03 E
Podlesnoje, Ukr.	78	48.47 N	32.15 E
Podlopatki	88	50.55 N	107.05 E
Podmošje	82	56.23 N	37.24 E
Podol'sk	82	55.26 N	37.33 E
Podol'skaja vozvyšennost' ⋏[1]	78	49.00 N	27.00 E
Podor, Maur.	150	16.40 N	15.00 W
Podor, Sén.	150	16.40 N	14.57 W
Podora	24	62.22 N	54.19 E
Podosinovec	24	60.17 N	47.04 E
Podoz'orskij	80	57.14 N	40.20 E
Podporožje	24	60.53 N	34.07 E
Podravina ◆[1]	36	45.40 N	17.40 E
Podravska Slatina	38	45.42 N	17.42 E
Podrezčicha	24	59.22 N	51.28 E
Podstepnyj	80	51.08 N	51.28 E
Podsvilje	76	55.09 N	27.58 E
Podt'osovo	88	58.36 N	92.06 E
Pod'uga	24	61.06 N	40.53 E
Podujevo	38	42.55 N	21.11 E
Poduškino	265b	55.43 N	37.17 E
Podu Turcului	38	46.12 N	27.23 E
Podvoločisk	78	49.33 N	26.09 E
Podymachino	88	56.59 N	106.11 E
Podyvotje	78	52.03 N	34.08 E
Poe	216	40.56 N	85.05 W
Poechos, Embalse ⊜[1]	246	4.40 S	80.30 W
Poel I	54	54.00 N	11.26 E
Poeldijk	52	52.01 N	4.12 E
Poelela, Lagoa ⊜	156	24.38 S	35.00 E
Poelkapelle	50	50.55 N	2.57 E
Poestenkill	210	42.41 N	73.34 W
Poesten Kill ≃	210	42.43 N	73.42 W
Poetto	71	39.12 N	9.10 E
Pofadder	158	29.10 S	19.22 E
Pogamasing Lake ⊜	190	46.57 N	81.50 W
Pogan, Zhg.	100	28.18 N	116.46 E
Pogan, Zhg.	100	27.40 N	116.46 E
Pogăniș ≃	38	45.41 N	21.22 E
Pogar	76	52.33 N	33.16 E
Poge, Cape >	207	41.25 N	70.27 W
Poggendorf	54	54.03 N	13.07 E
Poggiardo	68	40.03 N	18.23 E
Poggibonsi	66	43.28 N	11.09 E
Poggio	64	44.30 N	10.00 E
Poggio Berni	66	44.02 N	12.24 E
Poggio Bustone	66	42.30 N	12.53 E
Poggio Imperiale	68	41.49 N	15.22 E
Poggiomarino	68	40.48 N	14.32 E
Poggio Mirteto	66	42.16 N	12.41 E
Poggio Moiano	66	42.12 N	12.53 E
Poggioreale	70	37.47 N	13.01 E
Poggio Renatico	64	44.46 N	11.29 E
Poggiorsini	68	40.55 N	16.15 E
Poggio Rusco	64	44.59 N	11.07 E
Poggio Sannita	66	41.47 N	14.25 E
Pöggstall	61	48.19 N	15.12 E
Pogibi	89	52.12 N	141.42 E
Pogil-to I	98	34.09 N	126.33 E
Pogliano	266b	45.32 N	8.59 E
Pogny	56	48.52 N	4.29 E
Pogoanele	38	44.54 N	27.00 E
Pogodajev	80	51.37 N	51.04 E
Pogoniani	38	40.00 N	20.25 E
Pogoreloje Gorodišče	76	56.08 N	34.56 E
Pogoso	152	6.46 S	17.12 E
Pogost, Bela.	76	53.51 N	29.09 E
Pogost, Bela.	76	52.51 N	27.39 E
Pogost, Ross.	80	57.39 N	42.33 E
Pogost, Ross.	82	56.52 N	39.04 E
Pogožeje	78	51.36 N	37.16 E
Pogradec	38	40.54 N	20.39 E
Po Grande ≃	64	44.57 N	12.26 E
Pograničnoje	80	50.32 N	48.38 E
Pograničnyj, Ross.	80	46.57 N	45.46 E
Pograničnyj, Ross.	89	44.25 N	131.24 E
Pogrebišče	78	49.29 N	29.16 E
Pogromni Volcano ∧[1]	180	54.33 N	164.45 W
Pogromnoje	80	52.35 N	52.32 E
Pogruznaja	80	54.14 N	50.29 E
Poh	112	0.46 S	122.49 E
P'ohang	98	36.03 N	129.20 E
Pohatcong Creek ≃	210	40.37 N	75.11 W
Pohénégamook	186	47.31 N	69.16 W
Pohick Creek ≃	284c	38.46 N	77.14 W
Pohick Creek, Rabbit Branch ≃	284c	38.48 N	77.17 W
Pohick Creek, Sideburn Branch ≃	284c	38.48 N	77.17 W
Pohjanmaa ◆[1]	26	64.00 N	25.00 E
Pohjois-Karjalan lääni □[4]	24	63.00 N	30.00 E
Pöhl, Talsperre ◆[6]	54	50.33 N	12.12 E
Pöhla	54	50.31 N	12.49 E
Pöhlde	52	51.37 N	10.18 E
Pohl-Göns	56	50.28 N	8.39 E
Pohlheim	56	50.34 N	8.45 E
Pohnpei I	174r	6.55 N	158.15 E
Pohořelice	61	48.59 N	16.32 E
Pohorje ⋏	36	46.30 N	15.20 E
Pohri	124	25.32 N	77.21 E
Pohsien → Boxian	100	33.53 N	115.45 E
Pohue Bay c	229d	19.00 N	155.48 W
Poiana Mare	38	43.55 N	23.04 E
Poiana Ruscă, Munții ⋏	38	45.41 N	22.30 E
Pöide	76	58.31 N	23.03 E
Poigny-la-Forêt	261	48.41 N	1.45 E
Poim	80	53.01 N	43.11 E
Poinsett, Cape >	9	65.42 S	113.18 E
Poinsett, Lake ⊜, Fl., U.S.	220	28.20 N	80.50 W
Poinsett, Lake ⊜, S.D., U.S.	198	44.34 N	97.05 W
Point	222	32.56 N	95.52 W
Point Arena	204	38.54 N	123.41 W
Point Au Fer Island I	194	29.15 N	91.15 W
Point Baker	180	56.21 N	133.37 W
Pointblank	222	30.45 N	95.13 W
Point Chautauqua	214	42.14 N	79.28 W
Point Comfort	196	28.41 N	96.33 W
Point Cook	274b	37.56 S	144.45 E
Point Cook Royal Australian Air Force Station ■	169	37.56 S	144.45 E
Point du Jour, Ruisseau du ≃	206	45.50 N	73.25 W
Pointe-à-la-Frégate	186	49.12 N	64.55 W
Pointe-à-la-Garde	186	48.05 N	66.32 W
Pointe a la Hache	194	29.34 N	89.47 W
Pointe-à-Maurier	186	50.20 N	59.48 W
Pointe-à-Pitre	241o	16.14 N	61.32 W
Pointe-à-Pitre-le Raizet, Aéroport de ⊠	241o	16.17 N	61.32 W
Pointe-au-Chêne	206	45.38 N	74.45 W
Pointe Aux Peaux Farms	216	41.57 N	83.16 W
Pointe-aux-Trembles	206	45.39 N	73.30 W
Pointe-Calumet	275a	45.30 N	73.58 W
Pointe-Claire	206	45.26 N	73.50 W
Pointe-des-Cascades	275a	45.20 N	73.58 W
Pointe-des-Galets → Le Port	157c	20.55 S	55.18 E
Pointe-du-Moulin	275a	45.22 N	73.52 W
Point Edward	214	43.00 N	82.24 W
Pointe-Noire, Congo	152	4.48 S	11.51 E
Pointe-Noire, Guad.	241o	16.14 N	61.47 W
Point Enterprise	222	31.40 N	96.26 W
Pointers	208	39.35 N	75.26 W
Point Fortin	241r	10.11 N	61.41 W
Point Hope	180	68.21 N	166.41 W
Point Imperial ∧	200	36.16 N	111.58 W
Point Independence	207	41.44 N	70.39 W
Point Lake ⊜	176	65.15 N	113.04 W
Point Leamington	186	49.20 N	55.24 W
Point Lookout, Md., U.S.	208	38.02 N	76.19 W
Point Lookout, N.Y., U.S.	276	40.35 N	73.35 W
Point Marion	188	39.44 N	79.53 W
Point McLeay	168b	35.32 S	139.06 E
Point Nepean National Park ♦	169	38.25 S	144.45 E
Point of Rocks	208	39.16 N	77.32 W
Point O'Woods	276	40.39 N	73.08 W
Point Pass	168b	34.05 S	139.03 E
Point Pelee National Park ♦	214	41.57 N	82.30 W
Point Peninsula >[1]	212	44.01 N	76.15 W
Point Pleasant, Md., U.S.	284b	39.11 N	76.35 W
Point Pleasant, N.J., U.S.	208	40.04 N	74.04 W
Point Pleasant, Oh., U.S.	218	38.54 N	84.14 W
Point Pleasant, Pa., U.S.	208	40.25 N	75.04 W
Point Pleasant, W.V., U.S.	188	38.50 N	82.08 W
Point Pleasant Beach	208	40.05 N	74.02 W
Point Reyes National Seashore ♦	204	38.00 N	122.58 W
Point Roberts	224	48.59 N	123.04 W
Point Salines International Airport ⊠	241k	12.01 N	61.47 W
Point Samson	162	20.36 S	117.12 E
Point Sapin	186	46.58 N	64.50 W
Point View Reservoir ⊜[1]	276	40.58 N	74.15 W
Point Whiteshed	180	60.28 N	145.57 W
Poirino	62	44.55 N	7.51 E
Poisevo	80	55.32 N	53.30 E
Poison Creek ≃	202	43.15 N	108.09 W
Poison Spider Creek ≃	200	42.46 N	106.31 W
Poisson Blanc, Réservoir du ⊜[1]	188	46.00 N	75.45 W
Poissonnier Point >	162	19.57 S	119.11 E
Poissons	58	48.25 N	5.13 E
Poissy	50	48.56 N	2.03 E
Poitiers	32	46.35 N	0.20 E
Poitou □[9]	32	46.20 N	0.30 W
Poix	50	49.47 N	1.59 E
Poix-Terron	56	49.39 N	4.39 E
Pojarkovo	89	49.38 N	128.38 E
Pojma ≃	88	56.54 N	97.48 E
Pojo	248	17.45 S	64.49 W
Pojoaque Valley	200	35.59 N	106.00 W
Pojuca	255	12.21 S	38.20 W
Pojuca ≃	255	12.34 S	38.03 W
Pokagon State Park ♦	216	41.43 N	85.01 W
Pokaran	120	26.55 N	71.55 E
Pokataroo	166	29.35 S	148.42 E
Pokatejeva	88	56.59 N	97.25 E
Pokatilovka, Kaz.	80	51.06 N	51.53 E
Pokatilovka, Kaz.	86	45.23 N	80.10 E
Poke Run ≃	279b	40.30 N	79.33 W
Pokharā	124	28.14 N	83.59 E
Pokharia	126	23.55 N	86.37 E
Poko, Sūd.	140	5.38 N	31.50 E
Poko, Zaïre	154	3.09 N	26.53 E
Pokoinu	174k	21.12 S	159.49 W
Pokojnoje	84	44.48 N	44.16 E
Pokok Sena	114	6.10 N	100.32 E
Pokol'ubiči	76	52.30 N	31.02 E
Pokrov	82	55.55 N	39.10 E
Pokrovka, Kaz.	86	49.28 N	81.28 E
Pokrovka, Kaz.	86	54.17 N	68.15 E
Pokrovka, Kyrg.	85	42.20 N	78.01 E
Pokrovka, Kyrg.	85	42.45 N	71.36 E
Pokrovka, Ross.	80	48.22 N	46.04 E
Pokrovka, Ross.	80	53.47 N	53.19 E
Pokrovka, Ross.	89	43.57 N	131.39 E
Pokrovo-Kirejevo	83	47.38 N	38.16 E
Pokrovsk	74	61.29 N	129.06 E
Pokrovskaja Arčada	80	52.56 N	44.13 E
Pokrovskij	78	46.32 N	31.38 E
Pokrovskoje, Ross.	76	52.38 N	36.51 E
Pokrovskoje, Ross.	80	54.04 N	43.37 E
Pokrovskoje, Ross.	80	53.54 N	40.26 E
Pokrovskoje, Ross.	82	56.25 N	37.03 E
Pokrovskoje, Ross.	82	55.53 N	36.19 E
Pokrovskoje, Ross.	83	47.25 N	38.54 E
Pokrovskoje, Ross.	86	57.14 N	66.48 E
Pokrovskoje, Ross.	265a	59.44 N	30.46 E
Pokrovskoje, Ukr.	78	49.44 N	38.13 E
Pokrovskoje, Ukr.	78	47.59 N	36.14 E
Pokrovskoje, Ukr.	83	48.37 N	38.09 E
Pokrovskoje ◆[8]	265b	55.37 N	37.37 E
Pokrovsko-Strešnevo ◆[8]	265b	55.49 N	37.29 E
Pokrovsk-Ural'skij	86	60.10 N	59.49 E
Pokur	74	61.02 N	75.26 E
Pola, Pil.	116	13.09 N	121.26 E
Pola, Ross.	76	57.56 N	31.50 E
Pola ≃	76	58.04 N	31.37 E
Pola Bay c	116	13.10 N	121.28 E
Polacca	200	35.50 N	110.22 W
Polacca Wash V	200	35.22 N	110.50 W
Pola de Laviana	34	43.15 N	5.34 W
Pola de Lena	34	43.10 N	5.49 W
Pola de Siero	34	43.23 N	5.40 W
Polān	128	25.35 N	61.12 E
Polanco	252	33.54 S	55.09 W
Poland, Kiribati	174o	1.59 N	157.32 W
Poland, N.Y., U.S.	210	43.13 N	75.03 W
Poland, Oh., U.S.	214	41.01 N	80.37 W
Poland (Polska) □[1], Europe	22	52.00 N	19.00 E
Poland (Polska) □[1], Europe	30	52.00 N	19.00 E
Polangui	116	13.17 N	123.29 E
Polanów	30	54.08 N	16.39 E
Polapare ≃	115b	9.43 S	119.06 E
Pola → Pula	64	44.52 N	13.50 E
Pol'arnik	180	67.03 N	178.53 W
Pol'arnyj, Ross.	24	69.12 N	33.22 E
Pol'arnyj, Ross.	74	69.10 N	178.48 E
Pol'arnyj Ural ⋏	24	66.55 N	64.30 E
Polatlı	130	39.36 N	32.09 E
Polba	272b	22.57 N	88.18 E
Polbain	46	58.02 N	5.23 W
Polbeth	46	55.52 N	3.33 W
Polch	56	50.18 N	7.18 E
Polcirkeln	24	66.34 N	21.05 E
Polcura	252	37.17 S	71.43 W
Połczyn Zdrój	30	53.46 N	16.06 E
Polden Hills ⋏[2]	42	51.08 N	2.50 W
Poldnevica	80	58.37 N	46.38 E
Pol'dorak	85	39.25 N	69.56 E
Poleang	112	4.42 S	121.46 E
Polebridge	182	48.45 N	114.17 W
Polecat Creek ≃	196	36.00 N	95.57 W
Poledník ∧	60	49.04 N	13.24 E
Polee, Pulau I	164	2.12 S	130.15 E
Polegate	42	50.49 N	0.15 E
Pol-e Khomrī	120	35.56 N	68.43 E
Pole Moor	262	53.39 N	1.54 W
Polenezköy ◆[8]	267b	41.07 N	29.12 E
Polen → Poland □[1]	30	52.00 N	19.00 E
Pol-e Safīd	128	36.06 N	53.01 E
Polesden Lacey ⊥	260	51.15 N	0.22 W
Polesella	64	44.58 N	11.45 E
Polesine □[9]	64	45.00 N	11.45 E
Polesine Parmense	64	45.01 N	10.04 E
Polesje	76	53.05 N	31.17 E
Polesje ◆[1]	72	52.00 N	27.00 E
Polessk [Labiau]	76	54.52 N	21.05 E
Polesskoje	78	51.14 N	29.22 E
Polesworth	42	52.37 N	1.36 W
Polevaja	78	51.37 N	36.30 E
Polevskoj	86	56.26 N	60.11 E
Polewali	112	3.25 S	119.20 E
Pol-e Žahāb	128	34.28 N	45.52 E
Polgár	30	47.52 N	21.08 E
Polgooth	42	50.19 N	4.48 W
Pŏlgyo	98	34.52 N	127.21 E
Poli, Cam.	146	8.29 N	13.15 E
Poli, Zhg.	98	35.57 N	118.17 E
Poli, Zhg.	98	35.43 N	119.47 E
Polia	68	38.45 N	16.19 E
Políaigos I	38	36.46 N	24.38 E
Policastro, Golfo di c	68	40.00 N	15.30 E
Policastro Bussentino	68	40.09 N	15.32 E
Police	30	53.35 N	14.33 E
Polička	30	49.43 N	16.16 E
Policoro	68	40.13 N	16.41 E
Polignac	62	45.04 N	3.52 E
Polignano a Mare	68	41.00 N	17.13 E
Poligny	58	46.50 N	5.43 E
Polihale State Park ♦	229b	22.05 N	159.45 W
Políkastron	38	41.00 N	22.34 E
Polikhnítos	38	39.05 N	26.11 E
Polillo	116	14.43 N	121.56 E
Polillo Island I	116	14.50 N	121.57 E
Polillo Islands II	116	14.50 N	122.05 E
Polillo Strait ⊍	116	14.44 N	121.51 E
Polinesia Francesa → French Polynesia □[2]	14	15.00 S	140.00 W
Polinik ∧	64	46.54 N	13.09 E
Polinyà de Vallès	266d	41.33 N	2.10 E
Pólis	130	35.02 N	32.25 E
Polist' ≃	76	58.06 N	31.31 E
Polistena	68	38.25 N	16.05 E
Politécnico Nacional, Instituto ⊎[2]	286a	19.30 N	99.08 W
Politotdel'skoje	83	47.33 N	39.05 E
Pölitz → Police	30	53.35 N	14.33 E
Polivanovo	80	53.36 N	47.23 E
Políyiros	38	40.23 N	23.27 E
Polizzi Generosa	70	37.49 N	14.00 E
Polizzo, Monte ∧	70	37.52 N	12.47 E
Polk, Ne., U.S.	198	41.04 N	97.47 W
Polk, Oh., U.S.	214	40.57 N	82.13 W
Polk, Pa., U.S.	214	41.22 N	79.55 W
Polk □[6], Fl., U.S.	220	28.01 N	81.37 W
Polk □[6], Or., U.S.	224	45.00 N	123.23 W
Polk □[6], Tx., U.S.	222	30.45 N	94.48 W
Polk City	220	28.10 N	81.49 W
Pol'kino	74	71.10 N	99.13 E
Polkton	192	35.00 N	80.12 W
Polla	68	40.30 N	15.30 E
Pollāchi	122	10.40 N	77.01 E
Pollanten	60	49.09 N	11.28 E
Pöllau	61	47.18 N	15.51 E
Pöllauberg	61	47.19 N	15.52 E
Polleben	54	51.34 N	11.36 E
Pollenfeld	60	48.57 N	11.12 E
Pollenza	66	43.16 N	13.21 E
Pollica	68	40.11 N	15.03 E
Pollina	70	37.59 N	14.09 E
Polling	64	47.48 N	11.09 E
Pollino, Monte ∧	68	39.55 N	16.11 E
Polloc Harbor c	116	7.23 N	124.12 E
Pollock, La., U.S.	194	31.31 N	92.24 W
Pollock, S.D., U.S.	198	45.54 N	100.17 W
Pollock Pines	226	38.46 N	120.34 W
Pollock Run ≃	279b	40.14 N	79.47 W
Pollok	222	31.27 N	94.52 W
Pollutri	66	42.08 N	14.35 E
Pollux ∧	172	44.14 S	168.53 E
Polmak	24	70.04 N	28.00 E
Polmont	46	55.59 N	3.42 W
Polná	30	49.29 N	15.43 E
Polnaja ≃	83	48.54 N	39.50 E
Pol'noje-Jaltunovo	80	53.59 N	41.52 E
Polnovo-Seliger	76	57.32 N	32.55 E
Polo, Il., U.S.	190	41.59 N	89.34 W
Polo, Mo., U.S.	194	39.33 N	94.02 W
Polochic ≃	236	15.28 N	89.22 W
Polock, Bela.	76	55.31 N	28.46 E
Polock, Ross.	86	52.46 N	59.42 E
Pologi	78	47.29 N	36.15 E
Pologne → Poland □[1]	30	52.00 N	19.00 E
Pologoje Zajmišče	80	48.29 N	45.57 E
Pologrudovo	86	57.07 N	74.13 E
Polom, Ross.	24	59.13 N	50.50 E
Polom, Ross.	80	57.47 N	53.29 E
Polo Magnético del Sur → South Magnetic Pole ◆	9	65.18 S	139.30 E
Pölömäki ∧[2]	26	63.21 N	27.03 E
Polomet' ≃	76	57.41 N	32.12 E
Polomolo	116	6.14 N	125.03 E
Polonia, Arroyo ≃	258	34.10 S	57.15 W
Polonia → Poland □[1]	30	52.00 N	19.00 E
Polonio, Cabo >	252	34.24 S	53.46 W
Polonnaruwa	122	7.56 N	81.00 E
Polonnaruwa ⊥	122	7.56 N	81.00 E
Polonnoje	78	50.07 N	27.30 E
Pološkovo	82	54.08 N	35.53 E
Polo Sur → South Pole ◆	9	90.00 S	0.00
Polotn'anyj	82	54.45 N	36.00 E
Polotsk → Polock	76	55.31 N	28.46 E
Polovinkino	83	49.14 N	38.55 E
Polovinnoje, Ross.	86	54.43 N	63.50 E
Polovinnoje, Ross.	86	53.46 N	79.15 E
Polovo	76	57.03 N	32.27 E
Polperro	42	50.19 N	4.31 W
Polruan	42	50.19 N	4.36 W
Pöls	61	47.13 N	14.35 E
Pölsbach ≃	61	47.11 N	14.45 E
Polska → Poland □[1]	30	52.00 N	19.00 E
Polski Trâmbeš	38	43.22 N	25.38 E
Polson	202	47.41 N	114.09 W
Polster ∧	61	47.32 N	14.58 E
Polsum	52	51.37 N	7.03 E
Poltava	78	49.35 N	34.34 E
Poltava □[4]	78	49.45 N	34.00 E
Poltavka	86	54.22 N	71.45 E
Poltevy Pen'ki	80	54.35 N	42.06 E
Poltimore	188	45.47 N	75.43 W
Põltsamaa	76	58.38 N	25.58 E
Põltsamaa ≃	76	58.27 N	26.09 E
Poludino	86	54.51 N	69.55 E
Poluj ≃	74	66.31 N	66.33 E
Polunočnoje	72	60.52 N	60.25 E
Polur	122	12.30 N	79.08 E
Polur'adinki	82	54.51 N	38.41 E
Poluškino	265b	55.41 N	38.05 E
Pol'ustrovo ◆[8]	265a	59.58 N	30.25 E
Põlva	76	58.03 N	27.03 E
Polvaredas	258	35.35 S	59.30 W
Polverigi	66	43.31 N	13.23 E
Polvijärvi	26	62.51 N	29.22 E
Polvilho	287b	23.23 S	46.50 W
Polvoranca	266a	40.19 N	3.48 W
Polynesia II	14	4.00 S	156.00 W
Polynesian Cultural Center ⊎	229c	21.39 N	157.55 W
Polynésie française → French Polynesia □[2]	14	15.00 S	140.00 W
Polynnoje	80	46.51 N	46.56 E
Polysajevo	86	54.35 N	86.14 E
Pölzig	54	50.57 N	12.11 E
Poma, Lago ⊜[1]	70	37.55 N	13.06 E
Pomabamba	248	8.50 S	77.28 W
Pomacanchi	248	14.02 S	71.34 W
Pomahaka ≃	172	46.09 S	169.34 E
Pomarance	66	43.18 N	10.52 E
Pomarico	68	40.31 N	16.33 E
Pomarkku	26	61.42 N	22.00 E
Pomata	248	16.16 S	69.18 W
Pomáz	264c	47.39 N	19.02 E
Pomba ≃	256	21.24 S	42.32 W
Pombais, Ribeira de ≃	266c	38.48 N	9.07 W
Pombal, Bra.	250	6.46 S	37.47 W
Pombal, Port.	34	39.55 N	8.38 W
Pombia	266b	45.39 N	8.38 E
Pomellen	54	53.20 N	14.23 E
Pomene	156	22.53 S	35.33 E
Pomerania □[9]	30	54.00 N	16.00 E
Pomeranian Bay c	54	54.00 N	14.15 E
Pomerene	200	31.59 N	110.17 W
Pomerode	252	26.45 S	49.11 W
Pomeroon ≃	246	7.37 N	58.45 W
Pomeroon-Supenaam □[4]	246	7.20 N	58.50 W
Pomeroy, S. Afr.	158	28.33 S	30.26 E
Pomeroy, N. Ire., U.K.	48	54.36 N	6.55 W
Pomeroy, Ia., U.S.	198	42.33 N	94.41 W
Pomeroy, Oh., U.S.	188	39.01 N	82.02 W
Pomeroy, Pa., U.S.	208	39.58 N	75.53 W
Pomeroy, Wa., U.S.	202	46.28 N	117.36 W
Pomezia	66	41.40 N	12.30 E
Pomfret, S. Afr.	156	25.50 S	23.32 E
Pomfret, Ct., U.S.	207	41.53 N	71.57 W
Pomfret, Md., U.S.	208	38.34 N	77.01 W
Pomi	38	47.42 N	23.19 E
Pomigliano	66	40.54 N	14.23 E
Pominovo	82	55.26 N	39.11 E
Pomio	164	5.30 S	151.30 E
Pommard	58	47.01 N	4.47 E
Pomme de Terre ≃, Mn., U.S.	198	45.10 N	96.05 W
Pomme de Terre ≃, Mo., U.S.	194	38.11 N	93.24 W
Pomme de Terre Lake ⊜[1]	194	37.51 N	93.19 W
Pommera	50	50.10 N	2.26 E
Pommern → Pomerania □[9]	30	54.00 N	16.00 E
Pommersche Bucht → Pomeranian Bay c	54	54.00 N	14.15 E
Pommersfelden	56	49.46 N	10.49 E
Pomona, Namibia	156	27.09 S	15.18 E
Pomona, Ca., U.S.	228	34.03 N	117.45 W
Pomona, Ks., U.S.	198	38.36 N	95.27 W
Pomona, N.J., U.S.	208	39.28 N	74.34 W
Pomona, N.Y., U.S.	276	41.10 N	74.02 W
Pomona College ⊎[2]	280	34.06 N	117.44 W
Pomona Estates	273d	26.06 S	28.15 E
Pomona Lake ⊜[1]	198	38.40 N	95.35 W
Pomona Park	192	29.30 N	81.35 W
Pomongo	152	5.00 S	19.08 E
Pomor'any	78	49.38 N	24.56 E
Pomorie	38	42.33 N	27.39 E
Pomorskij proliv ⊍	24	68.30 N	50.00 E
Pomorze → Pomerania □[9]	30	54.00 N	16.00 E
Pomošnaja	78	48.14 N	31.26 E
Pomozdino	24	62.12 N	54.06 E
Pompano Beach	220	26.14 N	80.07 W
Pompano Beach Highlands	220	26.16 N	80.06 W
Pompei	68	40.45 N	14.30 E
Pompei ⊥	68	40.45 N	14.30 E
Pompéia	255	22.08 S	50.10 W
Pompejevka	89	48.23 N	130.46 E
Pompeston Creek ≃	285	40.01 N	75.01 W
Pompéu	255	19.12 S	44.59 W
Pompey, Fr.	56	48.46 N	6.07 E
Pompey, N.Y., U.S.	210	42.54 N	76.01 W
Pomponio Creek ≃	282	37.18 N	122.25 W
Pomponio State Beach ♦	282	37.17 N	122.24 W
Pomponne	261	48.53 N	2.41 E
Pompon-yama ∧	270	34.56 N	135.37 E
Pomposa	66	44.49 N	12.11 E
Pomposa, Abbazia di ⊎[1]	64	44.49 N	12.11 E
Pompton ≃	276	40.54 N	74.16 W
Pompton Lakes	210	41.00 N	74.17 W
Pompton Lakes ⊜	276	41.00 N	74.17 W
Pompton Plains	276	40.58 N	74.18 W
Pomquet	186	45.38 N	61.51 W
Pomssen	54	51.14 N	12.37 E
Ponape → Pohnpei I	174r	6.55 N	158.15 E
Ponask Lake ⊜	184	54.00 N	92.41 W
Ponass Lakes ⊜	184	52.18 N	103.58 W
Ponazyrevo	80	58.21 N	46.19 E
Ponca	198	42.33 N	96.42 W
Ponca City	196	36.42 N	97.05 W
Ponca Creek ≃	198	42.48 N	98.05 W
Ponce	240m	18.01 N	66.37 W
Ponce, Aeropuerto ⊠	240m	18.01 N	66.34 W
Ponce de Leon	194	30.43 N	85.56 W
Ponce de Leon Bay c	220	25.21 N	81.07 W
Ponce de Leon Inlet c	192	29.04 N	80.55 W
Poncé-sur-le-Loir	50	47.46 N	0.40 E
Poncha Pass)(	200	38.25 N	106.05 W
Ponchatoula	194	30.26 N	90.26 W
Poncin	58	46.05 N	5.24 E
Poncitlán	234	20.22 N	102.55 W
Pond ≃	194	37.32 N	87.21 W
Pond Brook ≃, N.J., U.S.	276	41.02 N	74.15 W
Pond Brook ≃, Oh., U.S.	279a	41.17 N	81.24 W
Pondcreek	196	36.40 N	97.48 W
Pond Creek ≃, U.S.	196	36.40 N	97.33 W
Pond Creek ≃, Tx., U.S.	222	31.02 N	96.46 W
Pond Eddy	210	41.27 N	74.49 W
Ponder	222	33.11 N	97.17 W
Pondera Coulee V	202	48.16 N	111.03 W
Ponders End ◆[8]	260	51.39 N	0.03 W
Pondicherry	122	11.56 N	79.53 E
Pondicherry □[8]	122	11.56 N	79.50 E
Pond Inlet	176	72.41 N	78.00 W
Pond Inlet c	176	72.46 N	77.00 W
Pondok Tanjong	114	5.00 N	100.44 E
Pondoland □[9]	158	31.10 S	29.30 E
Pondosa	204	41.12 N	121.41 W
Pond Run ≃	285	40.13 N	74.44 W
Poneas Island I	116	9.55 N	125.57 E
Ponente, Capo >	70a	35.31 N	12.31 E
Ponente, Riviera di ⩲[2]	62	44.10 N	8.20 E
Ponérihouen	175f	21.05 S	165.24 E
Poneto	216	40.39 N	85.13 W
Ponežukaj	78	44.53 N	39.22 E
Ponferrada	34	42.33 N	6.35 W
Pong	110	19.10 N	100.17 E
Pongani	164	9.05 S	148.35 E
Pongara, Pointe >	152	0.21 N	9.21 E
Pongaroa	172	40.33 S	176.11 E
Pongau V	64	47.21 N	13.14 E
Pong Dam ◆[6]	123	31.59 N	75.57 E
Ponghyŏn	98	37.49 N	125.36 E
Pongo ≃	140	8.42 N	27.40 E
Pongolo ≃	158	26.57 S	32.17 E
Pon'goma	24	65.21 N	34.25 E
Pong Tamale	150	9.41 N	0.49 W
Ponhook Lake ⊜	186	44.19 N	64.53 W
Poni ≃	208	38.07 N	77.26 W
Poniatowa	30	51.11 N	22.05 E
Poniec	30	51.47 N	16.50 E
Ponil Creek ≃	196	36.29 N	104.48 W
Poninka	78	50.12 N	27.32 E
Ponino	80	58.16 N	52.49 E
Ponitz, Dtsch.	54	50.51 N	12.25 E
Pönitz, Dtsch.	54	54.03 N	10.40 E
Ponizovje	76	55.17 N	31.04 E
Ponkapog Pond ⊜	283	42.12 N	71.06 W
Pônley	110	12.26 N	104.27 E
Ponnaiyār ≃	122	11.46 N	79.47 E
Ponnāni	122	10.46 N	75.54 E
Ponnūru Nidubrolu	122	16.04 N	80.34 E
Pono	164	6.22 S	134.36 E
Ponoj	24	67.05 N	41.07 E
Ponoj ≃	24	66.59 N	41.17 E
Ponoka	182	52.42 N	113.35 W
Ponomar'ovka, Ross.	80	53.19 N	54.08 E
Ponomar'ovka, Ross.	86	56.08 N	82.23 E
Ponornica	78	51.43 N	32.49 E
Ponorogo	115a	7.52 S	111.27 E
Ponpāj	272b	22.56 N	88.15 E
Pons	32	45.35 N	0.33 W
Ponsacco	66	43.37 N	10.38 E
Ponson Island I	116	10.46 N	124.32 E
Ponsul ≃	34	39.40 N	7.31 W
Pont	62	45.34 N	7.07 E
Pont-à-Celles	50	50.30 N	4.21 E
Ponta Delgada	148a	37.44 N	25.40 W
Ponta Delgada □[5]	148a	37.40 N	25.30 W
Ponta de Pedras	250	1.23 S	48.52 W
Ponta Grossa	252	25.05 S	50.09 W
Pontalete	256	21.27 S	45.40 W
Pontalina	255	17.31 S	49.27 W
Pontallier-sur-Saône	58	47.18 N	5.25 E
Pont-à-Marcq	50	50.31 N	3.07 E
Pont-à-Mousson	56	48.54 N	6.04 E
Ponta Negra	256	22.57 S	35.10 W
Pontão	34	39.55 N	8.22 W
Ponta Porã	255	22.32 S	55.43 W
Pontardawe	42	51.44 N	3.51 W
Pontardulais	42	51.43 N	4.03 W
Pontarlier	58	46.54 N	6.22 E
Pontas de Pedra	250	7.38 S	34.48 W
Pontassieve	66	43.46 N	11.26 E
Pontaubert	50	47.29 N	3.52 E
Pont-Audemer	50	49.21 N	0.31 E
Pontault-Combault	261	48.47 N	2.36 E
Pontaumur	32	45.52 N	2.40 E
Pont-Aven	32	47.51 N	3.45 W
Pontbriand	206	46.09 N	71.15 W
Pont Canavese	62	45.25 N	7.36 E
Pontcarré	261	48.48 N	2.42 E
Pontcharra	62	45.26 N	6.01 E
Pontchartrain	261	48.48 N	1.54 E
Pontchartrain, Lake ⊜	194	30.10 N	90.10 W
Pontchâteau	32	47.26 N	2.05 W
Pont-Croix	32	48.02 N	4.29 W
Pont-d'Ain	58	46.03 N	5.20 E
Pont d'Arc ♦	62	44.23 N	4.26 E
Pont-de-Bonne	56	50.27 N	5.17 E
Pont-de-Chéruy	62	45.45 N	5.11 E
Pont-de-l'Arche	50	49.18 N	1.10 E
Pont-de-Pany	58	47.18 N	4.49 E
Pont-de-Poitte	58	46.35 N	5.41 E
Pont-de-Roide	58	47.23 N	6.46 E
Pont-de-Ruan	50	47.15 N	0.35 E
Pont-de-Salars	32	44.17 N	2.44 E
Pont-de-Vaux	58	46.26 N	4.56 E
Pont-de-Veyle	58	46.16 N	4.53 E
Ponte a Elsa	66	43.41 N	10.54 E
Ponte Alta do Bom Jesus	255	12.06 S	46.29 W
Ponte Alta do Norte	250	10.45 S	47.34 W
Ponte a Moriano	66	43.54 N	10.31 E
Ponteareas	34	42.11 N	8.30 W
Pontebba	64	46.30 N	13.18 E
Ponte Branca	255	16.27 S	52.40 W
Ponte Caffaro	64	45.50 N	10.32 E
Pontecagnano	68	40.39 N	14.52 E
Ponte Caldelas	34	42.23 N	8.30 W
Pontecchio Marconi	64	44.25 N	11.15 E
Pontecchio Polesine	64	45.01 N	11.49 E
Pontecorvo	66	41.27 N	13.40 E
Pontecurone	62	44.57 N	8.56 E
Ponte da Barca	34	41.48 N	8.25 W
Ponte d'Arbia	66	43.10 N	11.28 E
Ponte delle Arche	64	46.02 N	10.52 E
Ponte dell'Olio	62	44.52 N	9.39 E
Pontedera	66	43.40 N	10.38 E
Ponte de Sor	34	39.15 N	8.01 W
Pontedeume	34	43.24 N	8.10 W
Ponte di Barbarano	64	45.23 N	11.34 E
Ponte di Legno	64	46.16 N	10.31 E
Ponte di Nava	62	44.08 N	7.53 E
Ponte di Piave	64	45.43 N	12.28 E
Ponte do Lima	34	41.46 N	8.35 W
Ponte do Púngoè	156	19.30 S	34.32 E
Pontefract	44	53.42 N	1.18 W
Ponte Galeria ◆[8]	267a	41.49 N	12.21 E
Ponte Gardena (Waidbruck)	64	46.36 N	11.32 E
Ponte Ghiereto	66	43.59 N	11.15 E
Pontegrande	58	45.59 N	8.09 E
Ponte in Valtellina	64	46.12 N	9.59 E
Ponteix	184	49.45 N	107.29 W
Pontelagoscuro	64	44.53 N	11.36 E
Ponteland	44	55.03 N	1.44 W
Pontelandolfo	68	41.17 N	14.41 E
Pontelongo	64	45.15 N	12.02 E
Ponte nell'Alpi	64	46.11 N	12.16 E
Ponte Nova	255	20.24 S	42.54 W
Pont-en-Royans	62	45.04 N	5.21 E
Ponte Nuovo	66	43.01 N	12.28 E
Pontenure	62	44.59 N	9.47 E
Pontepetri	66	44.02 N	10.53 E
Ponte ricci oli	66	43.26 N	12.38 E
Ponte Rocchetta	64	46.14 N	11.04 E
Ponterwyd	42	52.25 N	3.50 W
Ponte San Giovanni	66	43.05 N	12.26 E
Ponte San Pietro	62	45.42 N	9.35 E
Pontesbury	42	52.39 N	2.54 W
Ponte Selva	64	45.52 N	9.54 E
Ponte Serrada	252	26.52 S	51.58 W
Pontestura	62	45.08 N	8.20 E
Ponte Tresa	58	45.58 N	8.52 E
Pontevedra, Arg.	258	34.45 S	58.42 W
Pontevedra, Esp.	34	42.26 N	8.38 W
Pontevedra, Pil.	116	10.22 N	122.52 E
Pontevedra □[4]	34	42.30 N	8.40 W
Pontevedra, Ría de c[1]	34	42.22 N	8.45 W
Ponte Vedra Beach	192	30.14 N	81.23 W
Pont-Évêque	62	45.32 N	4.55 E
Pontevico	64	45.16 N	10.05 E
Pontfaverger-Moronvilliers	50	49.18 N	4.19 E
Pontgibaud	32	45.50 N	2.52 E
Ponthévrard	261	48.33 N	1.55 E
Ponthierry	261	48.32 N	2.33 E
Ponthierville → Ubundu	154	0.21 S	25.29 E
Pontiac, Il., U.S.	216	40.52 N	88.37 W
Pontiac, Mi., U.S.	216	42.38 N	83.17 W
Pontiac □[6]	212	46.30 N	77.00 W
Pontiac Lake	281	42.40 N	83.28 W
Pontiac Lake ⊜	281	42.40 N	83.28 W
Pontiac Lake State Recreation Area ♦	216	42.41 N	83.28 W
Pontiac Mall ◆[9]	281	42.39 N	83.20 W
Pontiac State Recreation Area ♦	281	42.41 N	83.28 W
Pontianak	112	0.02 S	109.20 E
Pontian Kechil	114	1.29 N	103.23 E
Pontida	62	45.43 N	9.30 E
Pontigny	50	47.55 N	3.43 E
Pontinha ◆[8]	266c	38.46 N	9.11 W
Pontinia	66	41.24 N	13.02 E
Pontivy	32	48.04 N	2.59 W
Pont-l'Abbé	32	47.52 N	4.13 W
Pont-lès-Moulins	58	47.19 N	6.22 E
Pont-l'Évêque	50	49.18 N	0.11 E
Pontlevoy	50	47.23 N	1.15 E
Pontoise	50	49.03 N	2.06 E
Pontoise-Cormeilles-en-Vexin, Aérodrome ⊠	261	49.06 N	2.02 E
Ponton Creek ≃	162	31.10 S	124.25 E
Pontonnyj	265a	59.47 N	30.38 E
Pontoon Beach	219	38.43 N	90.04 W
Pontorson	32	48.33 N	1.31 W
Pontotoc, Ms., U.S.	194	34.14 N	88.59 W
Pontotoc, Tx., U.S.	196	30.54 N	98.59 W
Pontremoli	62	44.22 N	9.53 E
Pont-Remy	50	50.03 N	1.55 E
Pontresina	58	46.28 N	9.53 E
Pontrhydfendigaid	42	52.17 N	3.51 W
Pont-Rouge	206	46.45 N	71.42 W
Pont-Royal	62	43.43 N	5.11 E
Ponts	34	41.55 N	1.12 E
Pont-Sainte-Marie	50	48.19 N	4.06 E
Pont-Sainte-Maxence	50	49.18 N	2.36 E
Pont-Saint-Esprit	62	44.15 N	4.39 E
Pont-Saint-Martin	62	45.36 N	7.48 E
Pont-Scorff	28	47.50 N	3.24 W
Ponts Quentin, Ruisseau des ≃	261	48.44 N	1.48 E
Pont-sur-Yonne	50	48.17 N	3.12 E
Pontuda, Ilha I	287a	23.02 S	43.18 W
Pontus □[9]	130	40.15 N	38.00 E
Pontvallain	50	47.45 N	0.12 E
Pont-Viau ◆[8]	275a	45.34 N	73.41 W
Pontyberem	42	51.17 N	4.09 W
Pontycymer	42	51.37 N	3.34 W
Pontypool	42	51.43 N	3.02 W
Pontypridd	42	51.37 N	3.22 W

Symbols in the index entries represent the broad categories identified in the key at the right. Symbols with superior numbers (⋏[1]) identify subcategories (see complete key on page *I · 1).*

Symbole im Register stellen die rechts im Schlüssel erklärten Kategorien dar. Symbole mit hochgestellten Ziffern (⋏[1]) bezeichnen Unterabteilungen einer Kategorie (vgl. vollständiger Schlüssel auf Seite *I · 1).*

Los símbolos incluídos en el texto del índice representan las grandes categorias identificadas con la clave a la derecha. Los símbolos con numeros en su parte superior (⋏[1]) identifican las subcategorías (véase la clave completa en la página *I · 1).*

Les symboles de l'index représentent les catégories indiquées dans la légende à droite. Les symboles suivis d'un indice (⋏[1]) représentent des sous-catégories (voir légende complète à la page *I · 1).*

Os símbolos incluídos no texto do índice representam as grandes categorias identificadas com a chave à direita. Os símbolos com números em sua parte superior (⋏[1]) identificam as subcategorias (veja-se a chave completa à página *I · 1).*

	English	Deutsch	Español	Français	Português
∧	Mountain	Berg	Montaña	Montagne	Montanha
⋏	Mountains	Gebirge	Montañas	Montagnes	Montanhas
)(	Pass	Paß	Paso	Col	Passo
V	Valley, Canyon	Tal, Cañon	Valle, Cañón	Vallée, Canyon	Vale, Canhão
≚	Plain	Ebene	Llano	Plaine	Planície
>	Cape	Kap	Cabo	Cap	Cabo
I	Island	Insel	Isla	Île	Ilha
II	Islands	Inseln	Islas	Îles	Ilhas
⩲	Other Topographic Features	Andere Topographische Objekte	Otros Elementos Topográficos	Autres données topographiques	Outros acidentes topográficos

ESPAÑOL — Nombre | Página | Lat.°′ | Long.°′ W = Oeste
FRANÇAIS — Nom | Page | Lat.°′ | Long.°′ W = Ouest
PORTUGUÊS — Nome | Página | Lat.°′ | Long.°′ W = Oeste

Name	Page	Lat.°′	Long.°′
Pony	**202**	45.39 N	111.53 W
Ponyri	**76**	52.19 N	36.20 E
Ponza	**66**	40.54 N	12.58 E
Ponza, Isola di I	**66**	40.55 N	12.57 E
Ponziane, Isole II	**66**	40.55 N	12.57 E
Ponzone	**62**	44.35 N	8.27 E
Poochera	**162**	32.43 S	134.51 E
Pool □[5]	**152**	3.30 S	15.00 E
Poole	**42**	50.43 N	1.59 W
Poole, Mount ∧	**166**	29.37 S	141.46 E
Poole Bay c	**42**	50.42 N	1.52 W
Pooler	**192**	32.06 N	81.14 W
Poole's Cavern ⩟[5]	**262**	53.14 N	1.56 W
Pooles Island I	**208**	39.17 N	76.16 W
Poolesville	**208**	39.08 N	77.25 W
Poolewe	**46**	57.45 N	5.37 W
Pooley Island I	**182**	52.44 N	128.16 W
Pool's Cove	**186**	47.41 N	55.26 W
Poolville	**222**	32.58 N	97.52 W
Poona → Pune	**122**	18.32 N	73.52 E
Pooncarie	**166**	33.23 S	142.34 E
Poondinna, Mount ∧	**162**	27.20 S	129.59 E
Poopo	**248**	18.23 S	66.59 W
Poopó, Lago ⊜	**248**	18.45 S	67.07 W
Pooraka	**168b**	34.50 S	138.37 E
Poor Knights Islands II	**172**	35.30 S	174.45 E
Poor Man Indian Reserve ◆[4]	**184**	51.30 N	104.23 W
Poor Meadow Brook ≃	**283**	42.01 N	70.55 W
Poortjie	**158**	30.13 S	22.44 E
Poowong	**169**	38.21 S	145.46 E
Popa, Isla I	**236**	9.11 N	82.07 W
Popasnaja	**83**	48.37 N	38.20 E
Popasnoje	**78**	48.48 N	35.31 E
Popayán	**246**	2.27 N	76.36 W
Pope	**194**	34.12 N	89.56 W
Pope Creek ≃	**226**	38.37 N	122.17 W
Popel'n'a	**78**	49.57 N	29.27 E
Popel'nastoje	**78**	48.39 N	33.43 E
Poperečnoje	**88**	52.23 N	110.42 E
Poperinge	**50**	50.51 N	2.43 E
Popești	**38**	47.14 N	22.25 E
Popești-Leordeni	**38**	44.23 N	26.10 E
Pope Valley	**226**	38.37 N	122.26 W
Popham Bay c	**176**	64.10 N	65.10 W
Popigaj	**74**	71.55 N	110.47 E
Popigaj ≃	**74**	72.54 N	106.36 E
Popiltah Lake ⊜	**166**	33.10 S	141.43 E
Popinci	**38**	42.25 N	24.17 E
Popki	**80**	50.11 N	44.30 E
Popkum	**224**	49.12 N	121.44 W
Poplar, Ca., U.S.	**226**	36.03 N	119.08 W
Poplar, Mt., U.S.	**198**	48.06 N	105.11 W
Poplar, Wi., U.S.	**190**	46.35 N	91.47 W
Poplar ◆[8]	**260**	51.31 N	0.01 W
Poplar ≃, Can.	**184**	53.00 N	97.24 W
Poplar ≃, N.A.	**198**	48.05 N	105.11 W
Poplar ≃, Mn., U.S.	**198**	47.51 N	96.04 W
Poplar, West Fork ≃	**198**	48.31 N	105.22 W
Poplar Bluff	**194**	36.45 N	90.23 W
Poplar Grove	**216**	42.22 N	88.49 W
Poplar Heights	**284c**	38.53 N	77.12 W
Poplar Hill	**184**	52.05 N	94.18 W
Poplar Mountain ∧	**194**	36.43 N	85.03 W
Poplar Point	**184**	50.04 N	97.57 W
Poplar Ridge	**210**	42.44 N	76.37 W
Poplar Springs	**208**	39.21 N	77.06 W
Poplarville	**194**	30.50 N	89.32 W
Poplevinskij	**76**	53.41 N	39.33 E
Popocatépetl, Volcán ∧[1]	**234**	19.02 N	98.38 W
Popof Island I	**180**	55.17 N	160.25 W
Popoh	**115a**	8.15 S	111.48 E
Popokabaka	**152**	5.42 S	16.35 E
Popoli	**66**	42.10 N	13.50 E
Popondetta	**164**	8.46 S	148.14 E
Popova	**89**	42.58 N	131.42 E
Popovka, Ross.	**76**	60.08 N	39.21 E
Popovka, Ross.	**80**	49.14 N	41.12 E
Popovkino	**82**	56.07 N	36.01 E
Popovo	**38**	43.21 N	26.13 E
Poppberg ∧	**60**	49.25 N	11.35 E
Poppel	**56**	51.27 N	5.02 E
Poppenbüttel ◆[8]	**52**	53.39 N	10.04 E
Poppenhausen	**56**	50.06 N	10.08 E
Poppi	**66**	43.43 N	11.46 E
Popple ≃	**190**	45.50 N	88.21 W
Poprad	**30**	49.03 N	20.18 E
Poprad ≃	**30**	49.38 N	20.42 E
Popricani	**38**	47.18 N	27.31 E
Pŏpsŏng	**98**	35.22 N	126.27 E
Pŏptong	**98**	38.59 N	127.05 E
Poptún	**236**	16.21 N	89.26 W
Populonia	**66**	42.59 N	10.29 E
Poputnaja	**84**	44.31 N	41.27 E
Poquessing Creek ≃	**285**	40.03 N	74.58 W
Poquetanuck	**207**	41.29 N	72.02 W
Poquonock	**207**	41.54 N	72.40 W
Poquonock Bridge	**207**	41.20 N	72.01 W
Poquoson	**208**	37.07 N	76.21 W
Poquoson ≃	**208**	37.10 N	76.24 W
Poquott	**276**	40.57 N	73.05 W
Porādaha	**126**	23.51 N	89.01 E
Porādiha	**126**	21.33 N	86.26 E
Porāli Nai ≃	**120**	25.58 N	66.26 E
Poranga	**250**	4.44 S	40.55 W
Porangahau	**172**	40.18 S	176.37 E
Porangatu	**255**	13.26 S	49.10 W
Porbandar	**120**	21.38 N	69.36 E
Porce ≃	**246**	7.28 N	74.53 W
Porchaman	**128**	33.08 N	63.51 E
Porcher Island I	**182**	53.57 N	130.30 W
Porcheville	**261**	48.58 N	1.47 E
Porchov	**76**	57.46 N	29.34 E
Porcia	**64**	45.57 N	12.36 E
Porciúncula	**255**	20.58 S	42.02 W
Porco	**248**	19.50 S	65.59 W
Porcos, Rio dos ≃	**255**	12.42 S	45.07 W
Porcuna	**34**	37.52 N	4.11 W
Porcupine ≃	**180**	66.35 N	145.15 W
Porcupine Brook ≃	**283**	42.46 N	71.13 W
Porcupine Creek ≃	**202**	48.07 N	106.20 W
Porcupine Creek, Middle Fork ≃	**202**	48.31 N	106.30 W
Porcupine Creek, West Fork ≃	**202**	48.31 N	106.30 W
Porcupine Dome ∧	**180**	65.31 N	145.31 W
Porcupine Hills ⋏[2]	**184**	52.30 N	101.45 W
Porcupine Mountains State Park ♦	**190**	46.47 N	89.50 W
Pordenone	**64**	45.57 N	12.39 E
Pordenone □[4]	**64**	46.00 N	12.45 E
Pordim	**38**	43.23 N	24.51 E
Poreč	**36**	45.13 N	13.37 E
Porecatu	**255**	22.43 S	51.24 W
Porečje, Bela.	**76**	53.55 N	24.07 E
Porečje, Ross.	**76**	55.43 N	35.33 E
Porečje, Ross.	**76**	56.06 N	30.29 E
Porečje-Rybnoje	**80**	57.06 N	39.23 E
Poreckoje	**80**	55.12 N	46.20 E
Porez	**80**	57.40 N	51.10 E
Pori	**26**	61.29 N	21.47 E
Poricy Brook ≃	**276**	40.21 N	74.05 W
Poringland	**42**	52.33 N	1.21 E
Porirua	**172**	41.08 S	174.51 E
Porjaguba	**24**	66.47 N	33.45 E
Porkkala	**26**	59.59 N	24.26 E
Porlamar	**246**	10.57 N	63.51 W
Porlezza	**58**	46.03 N	9.07 E
Porlock	**42**	51.14 N	3.36 W
Porma ≃	**34**	42.29 N	5.28 W
Pornassio	**62**	44.04 N	7.52 E
Pörnbach	**60**	48.37 N	11.28 E
Pornic	**32**	47.07 N	2.06 W
Poro ∧	**154**	1.14 N	36.37 E
Porog, Ross.	**24**	63.50 N	38.29 E
Porog, Ross.	**76**	59.16 N	33.24 E
Porogi	**265a**	59.46 N	30.47 E
Poro Island I	**116**	10.40 N	124.27 E
Porokylä	**26**	63.33 N	29.06 E
Poroma	**248**	18.29 S	65.30 W
Poronaj ≃	**89**	49.14 N	143.06 E
Poronajsk	**89**	49.14 N	143.04 E
Porong	**115a**	7.32 S	112.41 E
Porong ≃	**115a**	7.32 S	112.51 E
Poropotank ≃	**208**	37.27 N	76.42 W
Poroškovo	**78**	48.41 N	22.45 E
Porosozero	**24**	62.43 N	32.42 E
Poroto Mountains ⋏	**154**	9.00 S	33.45 E
Porozovo	**76**	52.56 N	24.22 E
Porožskij	**88**	56.04 N	101.46 E
Porpoise Bay c	**9**	66.30 S	128.30 E
Porpoise Channel ʮ	**276**	40.55 N	73.09 W
Porquerolles	**62**	43.00 N	6.12 E
Porquerolles, Île de I	**62**	43.00 N	6.13 E
Porrentruy	**58**	47.25 N	7.05 E
Porretta Terme	**64**	44.09 N	10.59 E
Porsangen c[2]	**24**	70.58 N	27.00 E
Porsangerhalvøya >[1]	**24**	70.50 N	25.00 E
Porsea	**114**	2.27 N	99.09 E
Porsgrunn	**26**	59.09 N	9.40 E
Porsuk ≃	**130**	39.42 N	31.59 E
Portachuelo	**248**	17.21 S	63.24 W
Portacloy	**48**	54.19 N	9.48 W
Port Adelaide	**168b**	34.51 S	138.30 E
Portadown	**48**	54.26 N	6.27 W
Portaferry	**48**	54.23 N	5.33 W
Portage, In., U.S.	**216**	41.34 N	87.10 W
Portage, Mi., U.S.	**216**	42.12 N	85.34 W
Portage, Oh., U.S.	**216**	41.20 N	83.39 W
Portage, Pa., U.S.	**214**	40.23 N	78.40 W
Portage, Ut,. U.S.	**200**	41.58 N	112.14 W
Portage, Wi., U.S.	**190**	43.32 N	89.27 W
Portage □[6]	**214**	41.09 N	81.15 W
Portage ≃, Mi., U.S.	**216**	41.57 N	85.38 W
Portage ≃, Oh., U.S.	**214**	41.31 N	83.05 W
Portage, East Branch ≃	**216**	41.17 N	83.31 W
Portage, Middle Branch ≃	**216**	41.22 N	83.28 W
Portage, North Branch ≃	**216**	41.25 N	83.27 W
Portage, South Branch ≃	**216**	41.22 N	83.30 W
Portage Bay c	**184**	51.33 N	98.50 W
Portage Des Sioux	**219**	38.55 N	90.20 W
Portage Lake ⊜, Mi., U.S.	**190**	47.04 N	88.30 W
Portage Lake ⊜, Mi., U.S.	**216**	42.03 N	85.31 W
Portage Lake ⊜, Mi., U.S.	**216**	42.25 N	83.54 W
Portage Lakes	**214**	40.59 N	81.32 W
Portage Lakes ⊜	**214**	40.59 N	81.32 W
Portage Lakes State Park ♦	**214**	40.57 N	81.32 W
Portage-la-Prairie	**184**	49.59 N	98.18 W
Portage Park ◆[8]	**278**	41.57 N	87.46 W
Portageville, Mo., U.S.	**194**	36.25 N	89.41 W
Portageville, N.Y., U.S.	**210**	42.34 N	78.02 W
Portal, Ga., U.S.	**192**	32.32 N	81.55 W
Portal, N.D., U.S.	**198**	48.59 N	102.32 W
Port Alberni	**224**	49.14 N	124.48 W
Portal del Infierno ⌊	**236**	14.22 N	85.38 W
Portalegre, Bra.	**250**	6.02 S	38.00 W
Portalegre, Port.	**34**	39.17 N	7.26 W
Portales	**196**	34.11 N	103.20 W
Port Alexander	**180**	56.15 N	134.39 W
Port Alfred (Kowie)	**158**	33.36 S	26.55 E
Port Alice	**182**	50.23 N	127.27 W
Port Allegany	**214**	41.48 N	78.16 W
Port Allen	**194**	30.27 N	91.12 W
Port Alma, Austl.	**166**	23.35 S	150.51 E
Port Alma, On., Can.	**214**	42.11 N	82.15 W
Port Alsworth	**180**	60.12 N	154.20 W
Port Angeles	**224**	48.07 N	123.25 W
Port Angeles Harbor c	**224**	48.07 N	123.24 W
Port Anson	**186**	49.32 N	55.50 W
Port Antonio	**241q**	18.11 N	76.28 W
Port Aransas	**196**	27.50 N	97.04 W
Portarlington, Austl.	**169**	38.07 S	144.39 E
Portarlington, Ire.	**48**	53.10 N	7.11 W
Port Arthur, Austl.	**166**	43.09 S	147.51 E
Port Arthur, Tx., U.S.	**194**	29.53 N	93.55 W
Port Arthur → Lüshun	**98**	38.48 N	121.16 E
Port Arthur → Thunder Bay	**190**	48.23 N	89.15 W
Port Ashton	**180**	60.04 N	148.01 W
Port Askaig	**46**	55.51 N	6.07 W
Port Augusta	**166**	32.30 S	137.46 E
Port au Port	**186**	48.33 N	58.44 W
Port au Port Bay c	**186**	48.40 N	58.45 W
Port au Port Peninsula >[1]	**186**	48.35 N	59.00 W
Port-au-Prince	**238**	18.32 N	72.20 W
Port-au-Prince, Baie de c	**238**	18.40 N	72.30 W
Port Austin	**190**	44.02 N	82.59 W
Port-aux-Basques → Channel-Port-aux-Basques	**186**	47.34 N	59.09 W
Portavogie	**48**	54.27 N	5.27 W
Porta Westfalica	**52**	52.14 N	8.55 E
Porta Westfalica ♦	**52**	52.14 N	8.55 E
Port Bannatyne	**46**	55.52 N	5.05 W
Port Barre	**194**	30.33 N	91.57 W
Port Bell	**154**	0.17 N	32.39 E
Port-Bergé	**157b**	15.33 S	47.40 E
Port Blair	**110**	11.40 N	92.45 E
Port Blakely	**224**	47.37 N	122.28 W
Port Blandford	**186**	48.21 N	54.10 W
Port Bolivar	**222**	29.23 N	94.46 W
Port Borden	**186**	46.15 N	63.42 W
Port-Bouët	**150**	5.15 N	3.58 W
Port Broughton	**166**	33.36 S	137.56 E
Port Burwell	**212**	42.39 N	80.49 W
Port Byron, Il., U.S.	**190**	41.36 N	90.20 W
Port Byron, N.Y., U.S.	**210**	43.02 N	76.37 W
Port Campbell	**169**	38.37 S	143.00 E
Port Campbell National Park ♦	**169**	38.38 S	142.55 E
Port Canning	**126**	22.18 N	88.40 E
Port Carbon	**208**	40.42 N	76.10 W
Port Carling	**212**	45.07 N	79.35 W
Port-Cartier	**186**	50.01 N	66.52 W
Port-Cartier Sept-Îles, Réserve ♦	**186**	50.35 N	67.10 W
Port Chalmers	**172**	45.49 S	170.37 E
Port Charlotte	**220**	26.58 N	82.05 W
Port Chester	**210**	41.00 N	73.39 W
Port Chester Harbor c	**276**	40.59 N	73.40 W
Port Chicago	**226**	38.03 N	122.01 W
Port Clements	**182**	53.42 N	132.11 W
Port Clinton, Austl.	**168b**	34.14 S	138.01 E
Port Clinton, Oh., U.S.	**214**	41.30 N	82.56 W
Port Clinton, Pa., U.S.	**208**	40.35 N	76.02 W
Port Clyde	**188**	43.55 N	69.15 W
Port Colborne	**212**	42.53 N	79.14 W
Port Colden	**210**	40.45 N	74.57 W
Port Columbus International Airport ⊠	**218**	40.00 N	82.53 W
Port Coquitlam	**224**	49.16 N	122.46 W
Port Costa	**226**	38.03 N	122.11 W
Port Crane	**210**	42.10 N	75.50 W
Port Credit	**212**	43.33 N	79.35 W
Port-Cros	**62**	43.00 N	6.23 E
Port-Cros, Île de I	**62**	43.00 N	6.24 E
Port-Cros, Parc National de ♦	**62**	43.01 N	6.24 E
Port-Daniel, Réserve ♦	**186**	48.18 N	64.55 W
Port-de-Bouc	**62**	43.24 N	4.59 E
Port-de-Paix	**238**	19.57 N	72.50 W
Port Deposit	**208**	39.36 N	76.06 W
Port Dickinson	**210**	42.08 N	75.53 W
Port Dickson	**114**	2.31 N	101.48 E
Porte Crayon, Mount ∧	**188**	38.56 N	79.27 W
Port Edward, B.C., Can.	**182**	54.14 N	130.18 W
Port Edward, S. Afr.	**158**	31.02 S	30.13 E
Port Edwards	**190**	44.21 N	89.51 W
Port Edward → Weihai	**98**	37.28 N	122.07 E
Portegolpe	**236**	10.20 N	85.46 W
Porteiras	**250**	7.31 S	39.07 W
Porteirinha	**255**	15.44 S	43.02 W
Portel, Bra.	**250**	1.57 S	50.49 W
Portel, Port.	**34**	38.18 N	7.42 W
Portela, Aeroporto da ⊠	**266c**	38.46 N	9.08 W
Port Elgin, N.B., Can.	**186**	46.03 N	64.05 W
Port Elgin, On., Can.	**190**	44.26 N	81.24 W
Port Elizabeth, St. Vin.	**241h**	13.03 N	61.13 W
Port Elizabeth, S. Afr.	**158**	33.58 S	25.40 E
Port Elizabeth, N.J., U.S.	**208**	39.18 N	74.58 W
Port Ellen	**46**	55.39 N	6.12 W
Port Elliot	**168b**	35.32 S	138.41 E
Port-en-Bessin	**32**	49.21 N	0.45 W
Porter, In., U.S.	**216**	41.36 N	87.04 W
Porter, Ok., U.S.	**196**	35.52 N	95.31 W
Porter, Tx., U.S.	**222**	30.06 N	95.14 W
Porter, Wa., U.S.	**224**	46.56 N	123.18 W
Porter □[6]	**216**	41.28 N	87.04 W
Port'Ercole	**66**	42.23 N	11.12 E
Porter Corners	**210**	43.09 N	73.53 W
Porter Creek ≃	**279a**	41.41 N	81.56 W
Port Erin	**44**	54.06 N	4.44 W
Porter Lake ⊜	**184**	56.21 N	107.20 W
Porter Point >	**241h**	13.23 N	61.11 W
Porter Springs	**222**	31.16 N	95.36 W
Porters Retreat	**170**	34.00 S	149.48 E
Porters Run ≃	**279b**	40.27 N	79.33 W
Portersville	**214**	40.56 N	80.09 W
Porterville, S. Afr.	**158**	33.00 S	19.00 E
Porterville, Ca., U.S.	**204**	36.03 N	119.00 W
Porterville, Ms., U.S.	**194**	32.41 N	88.28 W
Portes-lés-Valence	**62**	44.52 N	4.53 E
Port Essington	**182**	54.09 N	129.57 W
Portete, Bahía c	**246**	12.13 N	71.55 W
Port-Étienne → Nouâdhibou	**148**	20.54 N	17.04 W
Port Ewen	**210**	41.54 N	73.58 W
Port-Eynon	**42**	51.33 N	4.13 W
Port-Eynon Point >	**42**	51.32 N	4.12 W
Portezuelo	**234**	20.25 N	102.31 W
Port Fairy	**166**	38.23 S	142.14 E
Port Fitzroy	**172**	36.10 S	175.21 E
Port Gamble	**224**	47.51 N	122.34 W
Port Gamble Indian Reservation ◆[4]	**224**	47.53 N	122.34 W
Port Gentil	**152**	0.43 S	8.47 E
Port Germein	**166**	33.01 S	138.00 E
Port Gibson, Ms., U.S.	**194**	31.57 N	90.59 W
Port Gibson, N.Y., U.S.	**210**	43.02 N	77.09 W
Port Glasgow	**46**	55.57 N	4.41 W
Portglenone	**48**	54.52 N	6.29 W
Port Graham	**180**	59.21 N	151.50 W
Port Greville	**186**	45.24 N	64.33 W
Porth	**42**	51.38 N	3.25 W
Port Hacking	**274a**	34.04 S	151.08 E
Port Hacking Point >	**170**	34.05 S	151.10 E
Port Hammond	**224**	49.13 N	122.39 W
Port Harcourt	**150**	4.43 N	7.05 E
Port Hardy	**182**	50.43 N	127.29 W
Port Hawkesbury	**186**	45.37 N	61.21 W
Porthcawl	**42**	51.29 N	3.43 W
Port Hedland	**162**	20.19 S	118.34 E
Port Heiden	**180**	56.55 N	158.41 W
Port Henry	**188**	44.02 N	73.27 W
Port Hill	**186**	46.35 N	63.53 W
Porthleven	**42**	50.05 N	5.19 W
Porthmadog	**42**	52.55 N	4.08 W
Porth Neigwl c	**42**	52.48 N	4.34 W
Port Hood	**186**	46.01 N	61.32 W
Port Hope, On., Can.	**212**	43.57 N	78.18 W
Port Hope, Mi., U.S.	**190**	43.56 N	82.42 W
Port Howe	**238**	24.15 N	75.21 W
Port Hueneme	**228**	34.08 N	119.11 W
Port Hughes	**168b**	34.04 S	137.32 E
Port Huron	**214**	42.58 N	82.25 W
Portici	**68**	40.49 N	14.20 E
Portico di Romagna	**66**	44.01 N	11.47 E
Portigliola	**68**	38.14 N	16.13 E
Port-Iljič	**84**	38.53 N	48.48 E
Portimão	**34**	37.08 N	8.32 W
Portinho, Rio do ≃	**287a**	23.03 S	43.35 W
Port Isaac	**42**	50.35 N	4.49 W
Port Isabel	**196**	26.04 N	97.12 W
Portishead	**42**	51.30 N	2.46 W
Port Jefferson, N.Y., U.S.	**210**	40.56 N	73.03 W
Port Jefferson, Oh., U.S.	**216**	40.19 N	84.05 W
Port Jefferson Harbor c	**276**	40.58 N	73.05 W
Port Jefferson Station	**210**	40.55 N	73.02 W
Port Jervis	**210**	41.22 N	74.41 W
Port Julia	**168b**	34.40 S	137.52 E
Port-Katon	**83**	46.52 N	38.46 E
Port Kembla	**170**	34.29 S	150.54 E
Port Kennedy	**285**	40.06 N	75.25 W
Port Kenny	**162**	33.10 S	134.42 E
Portknockie	**46**	57.41 N	2.51 W
Port Láirge → Waterford	**48**	52.15 N	7.06 W
Port Lambton	**214**	42.39 N	82.30 W
Portland, Austl.	**166**	38.21 S	141.36 E
Portland, Austl.	**170**	33.22 S	150.00 E
Portland, N.Z.	**172**	35.48 S	174.19 E
Portland, Ar., U.S.	**194**	33.14 N	91.30 W
Portland, Ct., U.S.	**207**	41.34 N	72.38 W
Portland, In., U.S.	**216**	40.26 N	84.58 W
Portland, Me., U.S.	**188**	43.39 N	70.15 W
Portland, Mi., U.S.	**216**	42.52 N	84.54 W
Portland, Mo., U.S.	**219**	38.42 N	91.43 W
Portland, N.Y., U.S.	**214**	42.22 N	79.28 W
Portland, N.D., U.S.	**198**	47.29 N	97.22 W
Portland, Or., U.S.	**224**	45.31 N	122.40 W
Portland, Pa., U.S.	**210**	40.55 N	75.06 W
Portland, Tn., U.S.	**194**	36.34 N	86.30 W
Portland, Tx., U.S.	**196**	27.52 N	97.19 W
Portland, Wi., U.S.	**216**	43.12 N	88.58 W
Portland, Bill of >	**42**	50.31 N	2.27 W
Portland, Cape >	**166**	40.45 S	147.57 E
Portland, Isle of I	**42**	50.33 N	2.27 W
Portland Bay c	**166**	38.19 S	141.47 E
Portland Bight c[3]	**241q**	17.53 N	77.08 W
Portland Canal c	**182**	55.10 N	130.08 W
Portland Creek Pond ⊜	**186**	50.12 N	57.34 W
Portland Inlet c	**182**	54.50 N	130.15 W
Portland International Airport ⊠	**224**	45.35 N	122.36 W
Portland Island I	**172**	39.17 S	177.52 E
Portland Mills	**214**	41.23 N	78.50 W
Portland Point >	**241q**	17.42 N	77.11 W
Portlandville	**210**	42.32 N	74.58 W
Port Laoise (Maryborough)	**48**	53.02 N	7.17 W
Port Lavaca	**196**	28.36 N	96.37 W
Portlaw	**48**	52.17 N	7.19 W
Port → Le Port	**157c**	20.55 S	55.18 E
Port-Lesney	**58**	47.00 N	5.49 E
Portlethen	**46**	57.03 N	2.06 W
Port Leyden	**212**	43.35 N	75.21 W
Port Lincoln	**166**	34.44 S	135.52 E
Port Lions	**180**	57.52 N	152.53 W
Portlock Reefs ✢[2]	**164**	9.30 S	144.45 E
Port Logan	**44**	54.43 N	4.56 W
Port Loko	**150**	8.46 N	12.47 W
Port-Louis, Fr.	**32**	47.43 N	3.21 W
Port-Louis, Guad.	**241o**	16.25 N	61.32 W
Port Louis, Maus.	**157c**	20.10 S	57.30 E
Port Ludlow	**224**	47.55 N	122.40 W
Port-Lyautey → Kenitra	**148**	34.16 N	6.40 W
Port MacDonnell	**166**	38.03 S	140.42 E
Port Macquarie	**166**	31.26 S	152.55 E
Port Madison Indian Reservation ◆[4]	**224**	47.45 N	122.35 W
Portmahomack	**46**	57.49 N	3.50 W
Port Maitland, N.S., Can.	**186**	43.59 N	66.09 W
Port Maitland, On., Can.	**214**	42.52 N	79.34 W
Port Maria	**241q**	18.22 N	76.54 W
Portmarnock	**48**	53.25 N	6.08 W
Port Matilda	**214**	40.48 N	78.03 W
Port Mayaca	**220**	27.08 N	80.12 W
Port McNeill	**182**	50.35 N	127.06 W
Port McNicoll	**212**	44.45 N	79.49 W
Port Melbourne	**274b**	37.51 S	144.56 E
Port Mellon	**182**	49.32 N	123.29 W
Port-Menier	**186**	49.48 N	64.20 W
Port Moller	**180**	55.59 N	160.34 W
Port Monmouth	**276**	40.25 N	74.05 W
Port Moody	**224**	49.17 N	122.51 W
Port Morant	**241q**	17.54 N	76.19 W
Portmore	**241q**	17.58 N	76.53 W
Port Moresby	**164**	9.30 S	147.10 E
Port Moresby □[5]	**164**	9.30 S	147.10 E
Port Morien	**186**	46.08 N	59.52 W
Port Morris	**276**	40.54 N	74.41 W
Port Mouton	**186**	43.56 N	64.51 W
Port Murray	**210**	40.47 N	74.54 W
Portnaguran	**46**	58.17 N	6.13 W
Portnahaven	**46**	55.41 N	6.31 W
Port Neches	**194**	29.59 N	93.57 W
Port Neill	**166**	34.07 S	136.20 E
Port Nelson	**184**	57.03 N	92.36 W
Portneuf	**206**	46.42 N	71.53 W
Portneuf □[6]	**206**	46.45 N	72.00 W
Portneuf ≃, P.Q., Can.	**186**	48.38 N	69.05 W
Portneuf ≃, P.Q., Can.	**206**	46.42 N	71.53 W
Portneuf ≃, Id., U.S.	**202**	42.58 N	112.35 W
Portneuf, Lac ⊜	**186**	49.08 N	70.18 W
Portneuf-Station	**206**	46.43 N	71.54 W
Portneuf-sur-Mer	**186**	48.37 N	69.06 W
Port Neville	**182**	50.29 N	126.05 W
Port Noarlunga	**168b**	35.09 S	138.28 E
Port Nolloth	**156**	29.17 S	16.51 E
Port Norris	**208**	39.14 N	75.02 W
Porto, Bra.	**250**	3.54 S	42.42 W
Porto, Port.	**34**	41.11 N	8.36 W
Porto, Bonifica di ◆[1]	**267a**	41.48 N	12.16 E
Porto Acre	**248**	9.34 S	67.31 W
Porto Alegre, Bra.	**252**	30.04 S	51.11 W
Porto Alegre, S. Tom./P.	**152**	0.02 N	6.32 E
Porto Amboim	**152**	10.44 S	13.44 E
Porto Azzurro	**66**	42.46 N	10.24 E
Portobello	**46**	55.58 N	3.07 W
Porto Belo, Bra.	**252**	27.10 S	48.33 W
Portobelo, Pan.	**236**	9.33 N	79.39 W
Porto Calvo	**250**	9.04 S	35.24 W
Porto Ceresio	**58**	45.54 N	8.55 E
Port O'Connor	**196**	28.27 N	96.24 W
Porto das Caixas	**256**	22.42 S	42.53 W
Porto d'Ascoli	**66**	42.55 N	13.53 E
Porto das Flôres	**256**	22.05 S	43.34 W
Porto das Gabarras	**250**	3.07 S	44.34 W
Pôrto de Mós	**34**	39.36 N	8.39 W
Porto de Moz	**250**	1.45 S	52.14 W
Porto de Pedras	**250**	9.10 S	35.17 W
Porto di Potenza Picena	**66**	43.21 N	13.42 E
Porto di Traiano, Necropoli del ⊥	**267a**	41.46 N	12.16 E
Porto dos Gaúchos	**250**	11.29 S	57.22 W
Porto Empedocle	**70**	37.17 N	13.32 E
Porto Esperança	**248**	19.37 S	57.27 W
Porto Esperidião	**248**	15.51 S	58.28 W
Porto Farina	**36**	37.10 N	10.12 E
Porto Feliz	**255**	23.13 S	47.32 W
Portoferraio	**66**	42.49 N	10.19 E
Porto Ferreira	**255**	21.51 S	47.28 W
Portofino	**62**	44.18 N	9.12 E
Port of Ness	**46**	58.29 N	6.13 W
Porto Franco	**250**	6.20 S	47.24 W
Port of Spain	**241r**	10.39 N	61.31 W
Porto Garibaldi	**66**	44.41 N	12.14 E
Porto Grande	**250**	0.42 N	51.24 W
Portogruaro	**64**	45.47 N	12.50 E
Porto Inglês	**150a**	15.08 N	23.13 W
Portola	**204**	39.48 N	120.28 W
Portola State Park ♦	**226**	37.15 N	122.13 W
Portola Valley	**226**	37.23 N	122.13 W
Porto Lucena	**252**	27.51 S	55.01 W
Pörtom (Pirttikylä)	**26**	62.42 N	21.37 E
Portomaggiore	**64**	44.42 N	11.48 E
Porto Maurizio	**62**	43.52 N	8.01 E
Porto Mendes	**252**	24.30 S	54.20 W
Porto Murtinho	**248**	21.42 S	57.52 W
Porto Nacional	**250**	10.42 S	48.25 W
Porto-Novo, Bénin	**150**	6.29 N	2.37 E
Porto Novo, Bra.	**256**	23.40 S	45.28 W
Porto Novo, India	**122**	11.29 N	79.46 E
Porto Novo Creek c	**273a**	6.26 N	3.20 E
Portopalo, It.	**70**	36.41 N	15.08 E
Porto Palo, It.	**70**	37.34 N	12.54 E
Port Orange	**192**	29.06 N	80.59 W
Port Orchard	**224**	47.32 N	122.38 W
Porto Real	**256**	22.25 S	44.20 W
Porto Real do Colégio	**250**	10.11 S	36.49 W
Porto Recanati	**66**	43.26 N	13.40 E
Port Orford	**202**	42.44 N	124.29 W
Porto Rico	**152**	6.08 S	12.30 E
Porto Rico → Puerto Rico □[2]	**240m**	18.15 N	66.30 W
Portorož	**64**	45.31 N	13.36 E
Porto Salvo	**266c**	38.43 N	9.18 W
Porto San Giorgio	**66**	43.11 N	13.48 E
Porto Santana	**250**	0.03 S	51.11 W
Porto Sant'Elpidio	**66**	43.15 N	13.45 E
Porto Santo I	**148**	33.04 N	16.20 W
Porto Santo Stefano	**66**	42.26 N	11.07 E
Porto São José	**255**	22.43 S	53.10 W
Portoscuso	**71**	39.12 N	8.23 E
Porto Seguro, Bra.	**255**	16.26 S	39.05 W
Porto-Séguro, Togo	**150**	6.12 N	1.29 E
Porto Torres	**71**	40.50 N	8.24 E
Porto União	**252**	26.15 S	51.05 W
Porto Válter	**248**	8.15 S	72.45 W
Porto Valtravaglia	**58**	45.58 N	8.41 E
Porto-Vecchio	**36**	41.35 N	9.16 E
Porto Velho	**248**	8.46 S	63.54 W
Porto Velho do Cunha	**256**	21.50 S	42.32 W
Portovenere	**62**	44.03 N	9.51 E
Portoviejo	**246**	1.03 S	80.27 W
Portpatrick, Scot., U.K.	**44**	54.51 N	5.07 W
Port Patrick, Vanuatu	**175f**	20.08 S	169.47 E
Port Penn	**208**	39.31 N	75.34 W
Port Perry	**212**	44.06 N	78.57 W
Port Phillip Bay c	**169**	38.07 S	144.48 E
Port Pirie	**166**	33.11 S	138.01 E
Port Providence	**285**	40.08 N	75.30 W
Portraine	**48**	53.30 N	6.07 W
Port Reading	**276**	40.33 N	74.15 W
Portree	**46**	57.24 N	6.12 W
Port Renfrew	**224**	48.33 N	124.25 W
Port Republic	**208**	39.31 N	74.29 W
Port Rexton	**186**	48.23 N	53.20 W
Port Richey	**220**	28.16 N	82.43 W
Port Richmond	**208**	37.33 N	76.49 W
Port Robinson	**284a**	43.02 N	79.13 W
Port Rowan	**214**	42.37 N	80.28 W
Port Royal, Jam.	**241q**	17.56 N	76.51 W
Port Royal, Ky., U.S.	**218**	38.33 N	85.04 W
Port Royal, Pa., U.S.	**208**	40.32 N	77.23 W
Port Royal, S.C., U.S.	**192**	32.22 N	80.41 W
Port Royal, Va., U.S.	**208**	38.10 N	77.11 W
Port-Royal-des-Champs, Abbaye de ♆[1]	**261**	48.45 N	2.01 E
Port Royal National Historic Park ♦	**186**	44.44 N	65.40 W
Portrush	**48**	55.12 N	6.40 W
Port Said → Būr Saʿīd	**142**	31.16 N	32.18 E
Port-Sainte-Marie	**32**	44.15 N	0.24 E
Port Saint Joe	**192**	29.49 N	85.18 W
Port Saint Johns	**158**	31.38 S	29.33 E
Port-Saint-Louis	**62**	43.23 N	4.48 E
Port Saint Lucie	**220**	27.20 N	80.20 W
Port Saint Mary	**44**	54.05 N	4.43 W
Port-Saint-Servan	**186**	51.19 N	58.02 W
Port Salerno	**220**	27.08 N	80.12 W
Portsalon	**48**	55.13 N	7.37 W
Port Sanilac	**190**	43.25 N	82.32 W
Port Saunders	**186**	50.39 N	57.18 W
Pörtschach	**61**	46.37 N	14.08 E
Portsea	**169**	38.19 S	144.43 E
Port Seton	**46**	55.58 N	2.57 W
Port Shepstone	**158**	30.46 S	30.22 E
Portslade	**42**	50.50 N	0.11 W
Portsmouth, Dom.	**240d**	15.35 N	61.28 W
Portsmouth, Eng., U.K.	**42**	50.48 N	1.05 W
Portsmouth, N.H., U.S.	**188**	43.04 N	70.45 W
Portsmouth, Oh., U.S.	**218**	38.43 N	82.59 W
Portsmouth, R.I., U.S.	**207**	41.36 N	71.15 W
Portsmouth, Va., U.S.	**208**	36.50 N	76.17 W
Portsmouth Naval Shipyard ■	**188**	43.05 N	70.45 W
Portsoy	**46**	57.41 N	2.41 W
Port Stanley	**214**	42.40 N	81.13 W
Port Stanley → Stanley	**254**	51.42 S	57.51 W
Portstewart	**48**	55.11 N	6.43 W
Port Sudan → Būr Sūdān	**140**	19.37 N	37.14 E
Port Sulphur	**194**	29.28 N	89.41 W
Port Sunlight	**262**	53.21 N	2.59 W
Port-sur-Saône	**58**	47.41 N	6.03 E
Port Talbot	**42**	51.36 N	3.47 W
Port Taufiq → Būr Tawfīq	**128**	29.57 N	32.34 E
Porttipahdan tekojärvi ⊜[1]	**24**	68.08 N	26.40 E
Port Tobacco River c	**208**	38.27 N	77.02 W
Port Townsend	**224**	48.07 N	122.45 W
Port Trevorton	**208**	40.42 N	76.52 W
Portugal □[1], Europe	**22**	39.30 N	8.00 W
Portugal □[1], Europe	**34**	39.30 N	8.00 W
Portugal, Cachoeira ⌊	**248**	9.55 S	64.16 W
Portugal Cove South	**186**	46.42 N	53.15 W
Portugalete	**34**	43.19 N	3.01 W
Portuguesa □[3]	**246**	9.10 N	69.15 W
Portuguesa ≃	**246**	7.57 N	67.32 W
Portuguese Guinea → Guinea-Bissau □[1]	**150**	12.00 N	15.00 W
Portumna	**48**	53.06 N	8.13 W
Port Union, Nf., Can.	**186**	48.30 N	53.05 W
Port Union, On., Can.	**275b**	43.47 N	79.08 W
Port-Vendres	**32**	42.31 N	3.07 E
Port Victoria → Victoria	**138**	4.38 S	55.27 E
Port Vila	**175f**	17.44 S	168.19 E
Portville	**210**	42.02 N	78.20 W
Port Vincent	**168b**	34.47 S	137.51 E
Port-Vladimir	**24**	69.25 N	33.06 E
Port Vue	**279b**	40.20 N	79.52 W
Port Waikato	**172**	37.23 S	174.44 E
Port Wakefield, Austl.	**168b**	34.11 S	138.09 E
Port Wakefield, Ak., U.S.	**180**	58.03 N	153.03 W
Port Washington, B.C., Can.	**224**	48.49 N	123.19 W
Port Washington, N.Y., U.S.	**210**	40.49 N	73.41 W
Port Washington, Oh., U.S.	**214**	40.27 N	81.37 W
Port Washington, Wi., U.S.	**190**	43.23 N	87.52 W
Port Weld	**114**	4.50 N	100.38 E
Port Welshpool	**169**	38.42 S	146.28 E
Port Wentworth	**192**	32.08 N	81.09 W
Port William, Scot., U.K.	**44**	54.46 N	4.35 W
Port William, Oh., U.S.	**218**	39.33 N	83.47 W
Port Wing	**190**	46.46 N	91.23 W
Porum	**196**	35.21 N	95.15 W
Porus	**241q**	18.02 N	77.25 W
Porvenir, Chile	**254**	53.18 S	70.22 W
Porvenir, Méx.	**232**	31.15 N	105.51 W
Porvoo (Borgå)	**26**	60.24 N	25.40 E
Porvoonjoki ≃	**26**	60.23 N	25.40 E
Porz	**56**	50.53 N	7.03 E
Porzdni	**80**	57.00 N	42.33 E
Porzuna	**34**	39.09 N	4.09 W
Posada	**71**	40.38 N	9.43 E
Posada ≃	**71**	40.39 N	9.45 E
Posadas, Arg.	**252**	27.23 S	55.53 W
Posadas, Esp.	**34**	37.48 N	5.06 W
Posavina V	**36**	45.10 N	17.20 E
Pošcharv	**85**	38.24 N	71.10 E
Poschiavino ≃	**58**	46.12 N	10.10 E
Poschiavo	**58**	46.18 N	10.04 E
Pošechon'e	**76**	58.30 N	39.07 E
Posen, Il., U.S.	**278**	41.37 N	87.40 W
Posen, Mi., U.S.	**190**	45.15 N	83.41 W
Posen → Poznań	**30**	52.25 N	16.55 E
Poseritz	**54**	54.18 N	13.16 E
Posesión, Bahía c	**254**	52.17 S	69.14 W
Posevnaja	**86**	54.18 N	83.20 E
Poshan → Boshan	**98**	36.29 N	117.50 E
Poshiwu	**106**	30.22 N	119.36 E
Posieux	**58**	46.46 N	7.06 E
Posina	**64**	45.47 N	11.15 E
Pösing	**60**	49.14 N	12.33 E
Posio	**26**	66.06 N	28.09 E
Positano	**68**	40.38 N	14.29 E
Posjet	**89**	42.39 N	130.50 E
Poso	**112**	1.23 S	120.44 E
Poso, Danau ⊜	**112**	1.52 S	120.35 E
Poso, Teluk c	**112**	1.15 S	120.55 E
Poso Creek ≃	**226**	35.41 N	119.22 W
Posof	**130**	41.31 N	42.42 E
Pos'olki	**80**	53.08 N	46.29 E
Pos'olok	**265a**	59.43 N	30.12 E
Posŏng	**98**	34.47 N	127.04 E
Posooy, Mount ∧	**116**	17.21 N	120.48 E
Pospelicha	**86**	51.57 N	81.46 E
Possagno	**64**	45.51 N	11.51 E
Posse, Bra.	**255**	14.05 S	46.22 W
Posse, Bra.	**256**	22.16 S	43.06 W
Possel	**152**	5.01 N	19.15 E
Possendorf	**54**	50.57 N	13.42 E
Posses	**256**	21.43 S	46.08 W
Possession Islands II	**9**	71.27 S	171.08 E
Possession Sound ʮ	**224**	48.00 N	122.20 W
Possidhonia ⊥	**38**	37.40 N	24.00 E
Pössneck	**54**	50.42 N	11.37 E
Possruck (Kozjak) ⋏	**61**	46.37 N	15.28 E
Possum Kingdom Lake ⊜[1]	**196**	32.55 N	98.28 W
Post	**196**	33.11 N	101.22 W
Posta	**66**	42.31 N	13.06 E
Postal (Burgstall)	**64**	46.36 N	11.11 E
Postau	**60**	48.39 N	12.20 E
Postavy	**76**	55.07 N	26.50 E
Postbauer	**60**	49.19 N	11.21 E
Post Creek ≃	**210**	42.09 N	77.02 W
Poste-de-la-Baleine	**176**	55.17 N	77.45 W
Postelle	**192**	35.02 N	84.22 W
Poste Ramartina	**157b**	19.38 S	45.58 E
Posterholt	**52**	51.07 N	6.03 E
Post Falls	**202**	47.43 N	116.57 W
Postiglione	**68**	40.33 N	15.13 E
Postmasburg	**158**	28.18 S	23.05 E
Postojna	**36**	45.47 N	14.13 E
Postojnska jama ⩟[7]	**36**	45.47 N	14.12 E
Postoloprty	**54**	50.20 N	13.40 E
P'ostraja Dresva	**74**	61.34 N	156.41 E
Postrevalle	**248**	18.29 S	63.51 W
Postsee ⊜	**54**	54.13 N	10.13 E
Poststadion ♦	**264a**	52.32 N	13.21 E
Postville	**190**	43.05 N	91.34 W
Pota	**115b**	8.20 S	120.46 E
Potaizi	**104**	41.34 N	121.08 E
Potake Pond ⊜	**276**	41.08 N	74.13 W
Pótam	**232**	27.36 N	110.23 W
Potanino	**76**	60.16 N	32.47 E
Potaro ≃	**246**	5.22 N	58.54 W
Potaro Landing	**246**	5.23 N	59.08 W
Potaro-Siparuni □[4]	**246**	5.00 N	59.30 W
Potato Creek ≃, Ga., U.S.	**192**	32.47 N	84.21 W
Potato Creek ≃, Pa., U.S.	**214**	41.53 N	78.23 W
Potawatomie Woods ♦	**278**	42.08 N	87.53 W
Potchefstroom	**158**	26.46 S	27.01 E
Poté	**255**	17.49 S	41.49 W
Poteau	**194**	35.03 N	94.37 W
Poteau ≃	**194**	35.23 N	94.26 W
Poteet	**196**	29.02 N	98.34 W
Potengi ≃	**250**	5.47 S	35.16 W
Pötenitz	**54**	53.57 N	10.58 E
Pötenitzer Wiek c	**54**	53.55 N	10.55 E
Potenji	**250**	7.06 S	40.00 W
Potenza	**68**	40.38 N	15.49 E
Potenza □[4]	**68**	40.30 N	15.50 E
Potenza ≃	**66**	43.25 N	13.40 E
Potenza Picena	**66**	43.22 N	13.37 E
Poteriteri, Lake ⊜	**172**	46.06 S	167.08 E
Potes	**34**	43.09 N	4.37 W
Potfontein	**158**	30.12 S	24.08 E
Potgietersrus	**156**	24.15 S	28.55 E
Poth	**196**	29.04 N	98.05 W
Potholes Reservoir ⊜[1]	**202**	47.01 N	119.19 W
Poti	**84**	42.09 N	41.40 E
Poti ≃	**250**	5.02 S	42.50 W
Potic Creek ≃	**210**	42.16 N	73.55 W
Potijevka	**78**	50.37 N	28.58 E
Potiraguá	**255**	15.36 S	39.53 W
Potirendaba	**255**	21.08 S	49.08 W
Potiskum	**146**	11.43 N	11.05 E
Potlatch	**202**	46.55 N	116.53 W
Potlatch ≃	**202**	46.28 N	116.46 W
Po Toi Island I	**271d**	22.10 N	114.15 E
Po Toi Island Group II	**271d**	22.11 N	114.16 E
Potol Point >	**116**	11.56 N	121.57 E
Potomac, Il., U.S.	**216**	40.18 N	87.48 W
Potomac, Md., U.S.	**284c**	39.01 N	77.12 W
Potomac ≃	**188**	38.00 N	76.18 W
Potomac, South Branch ≃	**188**	39.31 N	78.35 W
Potomac, South Branch, North Fork ≃	**188**	38.59 N	79.11 W
Potomac, South Branch, South Fork ≃	**188**	39.04 N	78.59 W
Potomac Creek ≃	**208**	38.21 N	77.18 W
Potomac Creek, Long Branch ≃	**208**	38.23 N	77.29 W
Potomac Heights	**208**	38.36 N	77.08 W
Poto-Poto ◆[8]	**273b**	4.15 S	15.18 E
Potosí, Bol.	**248**	19.35 S	65.45 W
Potosi, Mo., U.S.	**194**	37.56 N	90.47 W
Potosí □[5]	**248**	20.40 S	67.00 W
Pototan	**116**	10.55 N	122.40 E
Potrerillos, Chile	**252**	26.26 S	69.29 W
Potrerillos, Hond.	**236**	15.11 N	87.58 W
Potrerillos Arriba	**236**	8.41 N	82.30 W
Potrero	**236**	10.28 N	85.47 W
Potrero ◆[8]	**282**	37.48 N	122.24 W
Potrero de Gallegos	**234**	22.38 N	103.41 W
Potrero del Llano	**196**	29.12 N	104.28 W
Potrero Grande	**236**	9.00 N	83.11 W
Potrite	**248**	61.32 S	16.10 W
Potro, Cerro del ∧	**252**	28.24 S	69.39 W
Potsdam, Dtsch.	**54**	52.24 N	13.04 E
Potsdam, N.Y., U.S.	**188**	44.40 N	74.58 W
Potsdam, Oh., U.S.	**218**	39.58 N	84.25 W
Potsdam, Staatsforst ♦	**264a**	52.26 N	13.04 E
Potshausen	**52**	53.11 N	7.37 E
Pott, Île I	**175f**	19.35 S	163.36 E
Pottawatomie Creek ≃	**198**	38.29 N	94.55 W
Pottawatomi Indian Reservation ◆[4]	**198**	39.20 N	95.50 W
Pottendorf	**61**	47.55 N	16.23 E
Potten End	**260**	51.46 N	0.31 W
Pottenhofen	**61**	48.46 N	16.33 E
Pottenstein	**60**	49.46 N	11.25 E
Potter	**198**	41.13 N	103.18 W
Potter □[6]	**214**	41.47 N	78.01 W
Potter Hollow	**210**	42.25 N	74.13 W
Potter Lake	**216**	42.50 N	88.21 W
Potter Point >	**274a**	34.03 S	151.13 E
Potters Bar	**42**	51.42 N	0.11 W
Potters Mills	**208**	40.48 N	77.32 W
Potter Street	**260**	51.46 N	0.08 E
Pottersville	**276**	40.42 N	74.43 W
Potterville	**216**	42.38 N	84.45 W
Pöttmes	**60**	48.35 N	11.06 E
Potton	**42**	52.08 N	0.14 W
Potts Camp	**194**	34.38 N	89.18 W
Potts Creek ≃	**192**	37.45 N	80.00 W
Potts Grove	**210**	41.00 N	76.48 W
Potts Hill Reservoirs ⊜[1]	**274a**	33.54 S	151.02 E
Pott Shrigley	**262**	53.19 N	2.05 W
Pottstown	**208**	40.14 N	75.39 W
Pottstown Landing	**285**	40.14 N	75.40 W
Pottstown Limerick Airport ⊠	**285**	40.14 N	75.34 W
Pottstown Municipal Airport ⊠	**285**	40.16 N	75.40 W
Pottsville	**208**	40.41 N	76.11 W
Potwin	**198**	37.56 N	97.01 W
Pötzleinsdorf ◆[8]	**264b**	48.15 N	16.19 E
Pötzleinsdorfer Park ♦	**264b**	48.14 N	16.18 E
P'otzu	**100**	23.28 N	120.14 E
Pouancé	**32**	47.44 N	1.11 W
Pouce-Coupe	**182**	55.43 N	120.08 W
Pouce Coupé ≃	**182**	56.08 N	119.52 W
Pouch	**54**	51.37 N	12.24 E
Pouch Cove	**186**	47.46 N	52.46 W

Symbol	English	Deutsch	Español	Français	Português
≃	River	Fluß	Río	Rivière	Rio
≅	Canal	Kanal	Canal	Canal	Canal
⌊	Waterfall, Rapids	Wasserfall, Stromschnellen	Cascada, Rápidos	Chute d'eau, Rapides	Cascata, Rápidos
ʮ	Strait	Meeresstraße	Estrecho	Détroit	Estreito
c	Bay, Gulf	Bucht, Golf	Bahía, Golfo	Baie, Golfe	Baía, Golfo
⊜	Lake, Lakes	See, Seen	Lago, Lagos	Lac, Lacs	Lago, Lagos
≣	Swamp	Sumpf	Pantano	Marais	Pântano
⍓	Ice Features, Glacier	Eis- und Gletscherformen	Accidentes Glaciales	Formes glaciaires	Acidentes glaciares
⊤	Other Hydrographic Features	Andere Hydrographische Objekte	Otros Elementos Hidrográficos	Autres données hydrographiques	Outros acidentes hidrográficos
✢	Submarine Features	Untermeerische Objekte	Accidentes Submarinos	Formes de relief sous-marin	Acidentes submarinos
□	Political Unit	Politische Einheit	Unidad Politica	Entité politique	Unidade política
♆	Cultural Institution	Kulturelle Institution	Institución Cultural	Institution culturelle	Instituição cultural
⊥	Historical Site	Historische Stätte	Sitio Histórico	Site historique	Sitio histórico
♦	Recreational Site	Erholungs- und Ferienort	Sitio de Recreo	Centre de loisirs	Area de Lazer
⊠	Airport	Flughafen	Aeropuerto	Aéroport	Aeroporto
■	Military Installation	Militäranlage	Instalación Militar	Installation militaire	Instalação militar
◆	Miscellaneous	Verschiedenes	Misceláneo	Divers	Diversos

Pouembout 175f 21.08 S 164.53 E
Poughkeepsie 210 41.42 N 73.55 W
Poughquag 210 41.37 N 73.41 W
Pouilly-en-Auxois 58 47.16 N 4.33 E
Pouilly-sur-Loire 50 47.17 N 2.57 E
Pouilly-sur-Meuse 56 49.32 N 5.07 E
Poulain, Étang ⊜ 261 48.43 N 1.44 E
Poulan 192 31.30 N 83.47 W
Poulaphouca Reservoir ⊜¹ 48 53.08 N 6.31 W
Poulin-de-Courval, Lac ⊜ 186 48.52 N 70.27 W
Poulsbo 224 47.44 N 122.38 W
Poulter, Lac ⊜ 190 47.07 N 76.45 W
Poultney 188 43.31 N 73.14 W
Poulton-le-Fylde 44 53.51 N 2.59 W
Poum 175f 20.14 S 164.02 E
Poŭn 98 36.29 N 127.43 E
Pound 192 37.07 N 82.36 W
Poundmaker Indian Reserve ◆⁴ 184 52.51 N 109.00 W
Poundstock 42 50.46 N 4.33 W
Pouoanuu, Mont ∧ 174x 9.49 S 139.07 W
Pourri, Mont ∧ 62 45.32 N 6.53 E
Poursi-Saint-Rémy 56 49.41 N 5.05 E
Pourville-sur-Mer 50 49.55 N 1.02 E
Pouso Alegre 256 22.13 S 45.56 W
Pouso Alto 256 22.11 S 44.58 W
Pouso Redondo 252 27.15 S 49.57 W
Pouso Sêco 256 22.41 S 44.10 W
Pouss 146 10.51 N 15.03 E
Poutasi 175a 14.01 S 171.41 W
Poŭthĭsăt 110 12.32 N 103.55 E
Poŭthĭsăt ≃ 110 12.41 N 104.09 E
Pouxeux 58 48.06 N 6.34 E
Pouzauges 32 46.47 N 0.50 W
Považská Bystrica 30 49.08 N 18.27 E
Povenec 24 62.51 N 34.45 E
Poverello, Monte ∧ 70 38.05 N 15.22 E
Poverennyj 80 46.45 N 43.12 E
Poverty Bay c 172 38.42 S 177.58 E
Povetkino 82 54.20 N 38.23 E
Poviglio 64 44.51 N 10.32 E
Povljen ∧ 38 43.55 N 19.30 E
Póvoa, Mouchão da I 266c 38.51 N 9.03 W
Povoação 148a 37.45 N 25.15 W
Póvoa de Santa Iria 266c 38.52 N 9.04 W
Póvoa de Santo Adrião 266c 38.48 N 9.10 W
Póvoa de Varzim 34 41.23 N 8.46 W
Povorino 80 51.12 N 42.14 E
Povorotnyj, mys > 89 42.42 N 133.02 E
Povorsk 78 51.16 N 25.07 E
Povrly 54 50.40 N 14.10 E
Povungnituk 176 60.02 N 77.10 W
Povungnituk, Rivière de ≃ 176 60.03 N 77.15 W
Powassan 190 46.05 N 79.22 W
Poway 228 32.57 N 117.02 W
Powder ≃, U.S. 178 46.44 N 105.26 W
Powder ≃, Or., U.S. 202 44.45 N 117.03 W
Powder, Dry Fork ≃ 200 43.47 N 106.15 W
Powder, Middle Fork ≃ 200 43.42 N 106.33 W
Powder, North Fork ≃ 202 43.42 N 106.33 W
Powder, Red Fork ≃ 202 43.39 N 106.47 W
Powder, South Fork ≃ 202 43.40 N 106.30 W
Powder Horn Lake ⊜ 278 41.38 N 87.32 W
Powderly, Ky., U.S. 194 37.09 N 87.10 W
Powderly, Tx., U.S. 196 33.49 N 95.31 W
Powdermaker Ditch ≃ 279a 41.30 N 82.02 W
Powder Mill Village 284c 39.03 N 76.57 W
Powder River Pass x 200 44.09 N 107.04 W
Powell, Oh., U.S. 214 40.09 N 83.05 W
Powell, Pa., U.S. 210 41.42 N 76.31 W
Powell, Tx., U.S. 222 32.07 N 96.20 W
Powell, Wy., U.S. 202 44.45 N 108.45 W
Powell ≃ 192 36.29 N 83.42 W
Powell, Lake ⊜¹ 200 37.25 N 110.45 W
Powell, Mount ∧ 200 39.46 N 106.20 W
Powell Creek ≃, Austl. 166 25.02 S 143.40 E
Powell Creek ≃, Oh., U.S. 216 41.17 N 84.21 W
Powellhurst 224 45.30 N 122.32 W
Powell Lake ⊜ 182 50.11 N 124.24 W
Powell River 182 49.52 N 124.33 W
Powells Valley 208 40.26 N 76.56 W
Powellton 188 38.05 N 81.19 W
Powellville 208 38.19 N 75.22 W
Powers, Mi., U.S. 190 45.41 N 87.31 W
Powers, Or., U.S. 202 42.53 N 124.04 W
Powers Lake, N.D., U.S. 198 48.33 N 102.38 W
Powers Lake, Wi., U.S. 216 42.33 N 88.17 W
Powers Lookout ◆ 169 36.50 S 146.22 E
Powhatan, La., U.S. 194 31.52 N 93.12 W
Powhatan, Va., U.S. 192 37.32 N 77.55 W
Powhatan Mill 284b 39.20 N 76.43 W
Powhatan Point 188 39.51 N 80.48 W
Powis, Vale of V 42 52.38 N 3.08 W
Powissett Brook ≃ 283 42.16 N 71.14 W
Powlett ≃ 169 38.35 S 145.32 E
Pownal 210 42.45 N 73.14 W
Powys □⁶ 42 52.17 N 3.20 W
Poxoréo 255 15.50 S 54.23 W
Poya 175f 21.19 S 165.07 E
Poyang Hu ⊜ 100 29.00 N 116.25 E
Poyan Reservoir ⊜¹ 271c 1.23 N 103.40 E
Poyen 194 34.19 N 92.38 W
Poygan, Lake ⊜ 190 44.09 N 88.50 W
Poyle 260 51.28 N 0.31 W
Poynette 190 43.23 N 89.24 W
Poynor 222 32.04 N 95.36 W
Poynton 44 53.21 N 2.07 W
Poyntz Pass 48 54.18 N 6.23 W
Poyraz ◆⁸ 267b 41.12 N 29.07 E
Poyraz Burnu > 267b 41.12 N 29.08 E
Poysdorf 61 48.40 N 16.38 E
Pozantı 130 37.25 N 34.52 E
Požarevac 38 44.37 N 21.11 E
Poza Rica 234 20.33 N 97.27 W
Požarskoje 89 46.16 N 134.04 E
Pozdějovka 89 50.36 N 128.56 E
Požega 38 43.50 N 20.02 E
Poznań 30 52.25 N 16.55 E
Poznań □⁴ 30 52.20 N 16.55 E
Pozo Alcón 34 37.42 N 2.56 W
Pozo Almonte 248 20.16 S 69.48 W
Pozoblanco 34 38.22 N 4.51 W
Pozo-Cañada 34 38.48 N 1.45 W
Pozo Colorado 252 23.28 S 58.51 W
Pozo del Molle 252 32.02 S 62.55 W
Pozo del Tigre 252 24.54 S 60.19 W
Pozo Hondo 252 27.10 S 64.30 W
Pozos, Punta > 254 47.57 S 65.47 W
Pozsony → Bratislava 30 48.09 N 17.07 E
Pozuelo de Alarcón, Esp. 34 40.26 N 3.49 W
Pozuelo de Alarcón, Esp. 266a 40.26 N 3.49 W
Pozuelos 246 10.11 N 64.39 W
Pozuelos, Laguna ⊜ 252 22.22 S 66.01 W
Pozuzo 248 10.04 S 75.32 W
Pozuzo ≃ 248 9.52 S 75.12 W
Požva 86 59.05 N 56.05 E
Pozzallo 70 36.43 N 14.51 E
Pozzillo, Lago di ⊜ 70 37.40 N 14.35 E
Pozzolo Formigaro 62 44.48 N 8.47 E
Pozzomaggiore 71 40.24 N 8.39 E
Pozzuoli 68 40.49 N 14.07 E
Pozzuolo del Friuli 64 45.59 N 13.12 E
Pra ≃, Ghana 150 5.01 N 1.37 W
Pra ≃, Ross. 80 54.45 N 41.01 E
Prabuty 30 53.46 N 19.10 E
Praça Cruzeiro 256 22.43 S 42.38 W
Praça Sêca ◆⁸ 287a 22.54 S 43.21 W
Prachatice 30 49.01 N 14.00 E
Prachin Buri 110 14.03 N 101.22 E
Prachuap Khiri Khan 110 11.49 N 99.48 E
Prackenbach 60 49.06 N 12.50 E
Pracuí ≃ 250 2.26 S 51.19 W
Pracupí ≃ 250 2.06 S 51.30 W
Pradelles 62 44.46 N 3.53 E
Pradera 246 3.25 N 76.15 W
Prades 32 42.37 N 2.26 E
Pradleves 62 44.25 N 7.17 E
Prado 255 17.21 S 39.13 W
Prado, Museo del ◆ 266a 40.25 N 3.41 W
Prado Dam ◆⁶ 280 33.54 N 117.39 W
Prado Flood Control Basin ⊜¹ 280 33.54 N 117.38 W
Prados 255 21.03 S 44.05 W
Pr'adovka 78 48.55 N 34.41 E
Prads 62 44.13 N 6.27 E
Præstø 41 55.07 N 12.03 E
Praga → Praha 54 50.05 N 14.26 E
Pragelato 62 45.01 N 6.57 E
Pragersko 61 46.23 N 15.40 E
Praglia, Monastero di ◆¹ 64 45.23 N 11.45 E
Prag → Praha 54 50.05 N 14.26 E
Prägraten 61 47.01 N 12.23 E
Prague, Ne., U.S. 198 41.18 N 96.48 W
Prague, Ok., U.S. 196 35.29 N 96.41 W
Prague → Praha 54 50.05 N 14.26 E
Praha (Prague) 54 50.05 N 14.26 E
Praha ∧ 60 49.40 N 13.49 E
Prahova □⁶ 38 45.00 N 26.00 E
Prahova ≃ 38 44.43 N 26.27 E
Prahran 274b 37.51 S 144.59 E
Praia 150a 14.55 N 23.31 W
Praia a Mare 68 39.54 N 15.47 E
Praia da Cruz Quebrada 266c 38.42 N 9.14 W
Praia da Enseada 256 23.29 S 45.05 W
Praia das Maçãs 266c 38.50 N 9.28 W
Praia da Vitória 148a 38.44 N 27.04 W
Praia de Araçatiba 256 23.15 S 44.21 W
Praia Funda, Ponta da > 287a 23.05 S 43.33 W
Praia Grande, Bra. 252 29.12 S 49.57 W
Praia Grande, Bra. 256 24.01 S 46.25 W
Praiano 68 40.37 N 14.32 E
Praikalogu 115b 9.45 S 119.25 E
Prainha 250 1.48 S 53.29 W
Prainha Nova 248 7.16 S 60.23 W
Prairie 166 20.52 S 144.36 E
Prairie ≃, Mi., U.S. 216 41.55 N 85.38 W
Prairie ≃, Mn., U.S. 190 47.18 N 93.29 W
Prairie ≃, Wi., U.S. 190 45.10 N 89.42 W
Prairie City, Il., U.S. 190 40.37 N 90.28 W
Prairie City, Ia., U.S. 190 41.35 N 93.14 W
Prairie City, Or., U.S. 202 44.27 N 118.42 W
Prairie Creek ≃, Fl., U.S. 220 26.59 N 81.56 W
Prairie Creek ≃, Il., U.S. 216 41.21 N 88.12 W
Prairie Creek ≃, Il., U.S. 216 40.55 N 87.49 W
Prairie Creek ≃, Il., U.S. 278 41.36 N 87.40 W
Prairie Creek ≃, Mi., U.S. 216 42.59 N 85.01 W
Prairie Creek ≃, Ne., U.S. 198 41.22 N 97.32 W
Prairie Creek Reservoir ⊜¹ 218 40.08 N 85.17 W
Prairie Dog Creek ≃ 198 40.00 N 99.23 W
Prairie du Chien 190 43.03 N 91.08 W
Prairie du Sac 190 43.17 N 89.43 W
Prairie Elk Creek ≃ 198 48.00 N 105.51 W
Prairie Grove 194 35.58 N 94.19 W
Prairie Hill 222 31.39 N 96.47 W
Prairie Lea 222 29.44 N 97.45 W
Prairie River 184 52.52 N 103.00 W
Prairies, Coteau des ∧¹ 198 44.30 N 96.45 W
Prairies, Lake of the ⊜¹ 184 51.05 N 101.25 W
Prairies, Rivière des ≃ 275a 45.42 N 73.29 W
Prairie View, Il., U.S. 278 42.12 N 87.57 W
Prairie View, Tx., U.S. 222 30.05 N 95.59 W
Prairie Village 198 38.59 N 94.38 W
Prajekan 115a 7.47 S 113.59 E
Prakhon Chai 110 14.37 N 103.05 E
Pralboino 64 45.16 N 10.13 E
Prali 62 44.54 N 7.03 E
Pralls Island I 276 40.37 N 74.12 W
Pralognan-la-Vanoise 62 45.23 N 6.43 E
Pram 60 48.14 N 13.37 E
Pram ≃ 60 48.28 N 13.26 E
Pramaggiore, Monte ∧ 64 46.22 N 12.33 E
Prambachkirchen 60 48.19 N 13.55 E
Prambanan 115a 7.45 S 110.30 E
Pr'amicyno 78 51.39 N 35.56 E
Pramort 54 54.26 N 12.55 E
Prampram 150 5.42 N 0.07 E
Pran Buri 110 12.23 N 99.55 E
Pran Buri ≃ 110 12.24 N 100.00 E
Prang 150 7.59 N 0.53 W
Prangli I 76 59.38 N 25.02 E
Prānhita ≃ 122 18.49 N 79.55 E
Pranzo 64 45.55 N 10.48 E
Prapa, Khlong ≃ 269a 13.46 N 100.32 E
Prapat 114 2.40 N 98.56 E
Praraye 58 45.55 N 7.32 E
Prärien → Great Plains ≍ 16 42.00 N 100.00 W
Praskoveja 84 44.43 N 44.12 E
Praskovejevka 83 44.48 N 38.00 E
Praslin, Lac ⊜ 186 50.03 N 69.48 W
Praslin Island I 138 4.19 S 55.44 E
Prasonísi, Ákra > 38 35.42 N 27.46 E
Praszka 30 51.04 N 18.26 E
Prat, Isla I 254 48.15 S 75.00 W
Prata, Bra. 250 7.41 S 37.06 W
Prata, Bra. 255 19.18 S 48.55 W
Prata, Bra. 287a 22.45 S 43.25 W
Prata, Rio da ≃, Bra. 255 17.28 S 46.35 W
Prata, Rio da ≃, Bra. 255 18.49 S 49.54 W
Prata, Rio da ≃, Bra. 287a 22.56 S 43.34 W
Pratāpgarh, India 120 24.02 N 74.47 E
Pratāpgarh, India 124 25.54 N 81.58 E
Pratāpnagar 124 22.23 N 89.13 E
Pratápolis 255 20.45 S 46.52 W
Pratas Island → Tungsha Tao I 90 20.42 N 116.43 E
Pratau 54 51.50 N 12.38 E
Pratella 68 41.24 N 14.11 E
Prater ◆ 264b 48.12 N 16.25 E
Prathet Thai → Thailand □¹ 110 15.00 N 100.00 E
Pratinha 255 19.46 S 46.24 W
Prato 66 43.53 N 11.06 E
Prato allo Stelvio 64 46.37 N 10.35 E
Pratola Peligna 66 42.06 N 13.52 E
Pratola Serra 68 40.59 N 14.51 E
Pratolino 66 43.52 N 11.18 E
Pratomagno ∧ 66 43.39 N 11.39 E
Pratt 198 37.38 N 98.44 W
Pratteln 58 47.31 N 7.42 E
Prättigau V 58 46.55 N 9.45 E
Pratt's Bottom ◆⁸ 260 51.20 N 0.07 E
Prattsburg 210 42.31 N 77.17 W
Prattsville 210 42.18 N 74.26 W
Prattville 194 32.27 N 86.27 W
Pratudão ≃ 255 13.56 S 44.55 W
Prauthoy 58 47.40 N 5.17 E
Pravaja Mama ≃ 88 57.10 N 111.54 E
Pravda 89 47.00 N 142.01 E
Pravdinsk, Ross. 76 54.27 N 21.01 E
Pravdinsk, Ross. 80 56.32 N 43.34 E
Pravdinskij 82 56.04 N 37.51 E
Pravia 34 43.29 N 6.07 W
Prawet Buri Rom, Khlong ≃ 269a 13.42 N 100.35 E
Prawle Point > 42 50.13 N 3.42 W
Praya 115b 8.42 S 116.17 E
Pr'aža 24 61.42 N 33.35 E
Praz-sur-Arly 62 45.50 N 6.34 E
Prazzo 62 44.29 N 7.03 E
Preakness Brook ≃ 276 40.54 N 74.15 W
Preakness Mountain ∧ 276 40.58 N 74.13 W
Preakness Valley Park ◆ 276 40.55 N 74.14 W
Preble, In., U.S. 216 40.50 N 85.01 W
Preble, N.Y., U.S. 210 42.44 N 76.09 W
Preble □⁶ 218 39.45 N 84.38 W
Preci 66 42.53 N 13.02 E
Prečistoje, Ross. 76 55.41 N 34.56 E
Prečistoje, Ross. 76 55.31 N 32.22 E
Prečistoje, Ross. 80 58.27 N 40.19 E
Précy-sous-Thil 50 47.23 N 4.19 E
Précy-sur-Marne 261 48.56 N 2.47 E
Précy-sur-Oise 50 49.12 N 2.22 E
Preda 58 46.36 N 9.46 E
Predappio 66 44.06 N 11.58 E
Predazzo 64 46.19 N 11.36 E
Predeal 38 45.30 N 25.35 E
Prédecelle ≃ 261 48.35 N 2.07 E
Předenice 60 49.37 N 13.24 E
Predești 38 44.21 N 23.36 E
Predgornoje 86 47.10 N 81.00 E
Predigtstuhl ∧ 61 48.48 N 15.22 E
Předín 61 49.12 N 15.40 E
Predivinsk 86 57.04 N 93.27 E
Predlitz [-Turrach] 64 47.04 N 13.55 E
Predmostnoje 78 45.57 N 34.37 E
Predoi (Prettau) 64 47.02 N 12.06 E
Predore 64 45.41 N 10.01 E
Preeceville 184 51.58 N 102.40 W
Pré-en-Pail 32 48.27 N 0.12 W
Preesall 44 53.55 N 2.58 W
Preetz 54 54.14 N 10.16 E
Pregarten 61 48.21 N 14.32 E
Pregel → Pregol'a ≃ 76 54.41 N 20.22 E
Pregnana 266b 45.31 N 9.00 E
Pregol'a ≃ 76 54.41 N 20.22 E
Pregonero 246 8.01 N 71.46 W
Pregos 256 21.46 S 42.54 W
Pregradnaja 84 43.58 N 41.12 E
Pregradnoje 80 45.49 N 41.45 E
Preguiças ≃ 250 2.45 S 42.44 W
Preila 76 55.22 N 21.04 E
Preiļi 76 56.18 N 26.43 E
Preissac, Lac ⊜ 190 48.20 N 78.20 W
Prekestolen ◆ 26 59.00 N 6.01 E
Preko 36 44.05 N 15.11 E
Prekomurje ◆¹ 61 46.40 N 16.10 E
Prêk Poŭthĭ 110 11.51 N 105.07 E
Prelate 184 50.51 N 109.23 W
Přelouč 30 50.02 N 15.34 E
Premana 58 46.03 N 9.25 E
Prembun 115a 7.43 S 109.48 E
Prémery 32 47.10 N 3.20 E
Premià de Dalt 266d 41.31 N 2.21 E
Premià de Mar 266d 41.29 N 2.21 E
Premnitz 54 52.32 N 12.19 E
Prémont, P.Q., Can. 206 46.22 N 73.03 W
Premont, Tx., U.S. 196 27.21 N 98.07 W
Prémontré 50 49.33 N 3.24 E
Premosello 58 46.00 N 8.20 E
Premuda, Otok I 36 44.20 N 14.37 E
Prenestini, Monti ∧ 66 41.50 N 13.00 E
Prenjas 38 41.04 N 20.32 E
Prentice 190 45.32 N 90.17 W
Prentiss 194 31.35 N 89.52 W
Prenton 262 53.22 N 3.03 W
Prenzlau 54 53.19 N 13.52 E
Prenzlauer Berg ◆⁸ 264a 52.32 N 13.26 E
Preobraženije 89 42.57 N 133.55 E
Preobraženka 83 49.32 N 38.10 E
Preobraženovka 89 48.04 N 131.55 E
Preparis Island I 110 14.52 N 93.41 E
Preparis North Channel ≍ 110 15.27 N 94.05 E
Preparis South Channel ≍ 110 14.40 N 94.00 E
Přerov 30 49.27 N 17.27 E
Prerow 54 54.26 N 12.35 E
Pré-Saint-Didier 62 45.46 N 6.59 E
Presanella, Cima ∧ 64 46.13 N 10.40 E
Prescot 44 53.26 N 2.48 W
Prescott, On., Can. 212 44.43 N 75.31 W
Prescott, Az., U.S. 200 34.32 N 112.28 W
Prescott, Ar., U.S. 194 33.48 N 93.22 W
Prescott, Or., U.S. 224 46.02 N 122.53 W
Prescott, Wi., U.S. 190 44.44 N 92.48 W
Prescott and Russell □⁶ 206 45.25 N 75.00 W
Prescott Island I 176 73.01 N 96.50 W
Preševo 38 42.18 N 21.39 E
Presho 198 43.54 N 100.03 W
Presicce 68 39.54 N 18.16 E
Presidencia de la Plaza 252 27.01 S 59.51 W
Presidencia Roca 252 26.08 S 59.36 W
Presidencia Roque Sáenz Peña 252 26.47 S 60.27 W
Presidente Costa e Silva, Ponte ◆⁵ 287a 22.53 S 43.10 W
Presidente Derqui 258 34.29 S 58.51 W
Presidente Dutra 250 5.15 S 44.30 W
Presidente Epitácio 255 21.46 S 52.06 W
Presidente Getúlio 252 27.03 S 49.37 W
Presidente Hayes □⁵ 252 24.00 S 59.00 W
Presidente Nicolás Avellaneda, Parque ◆ 288 34.39 S 58.29 W
Presidente Olegário 255 18.25 S 46.25 W
Presidente Prudente 255 22.07 S 51.22 W
Presidente Ríos, Lago ⊜ 254 46.28 S 74.25 W
Presidente Roosevelt, Estação ◆⁵ 287b 23.33 S 46.36 W
Presidente Venceslau 255 21.52 S 51.50 W
Presidential Heights 279b 40.34 N 80.03 W
President Roxas 116 11.26 N 122.56 E
Presidio 196 29.33 N 104.22 W
Presidio ≃ 234 23.06 N 106.17 W
Presidio of San Francisco ◆ 226 37.48 N 122.28 W
Presles 50 50.23 N 4.35 E
Presles-en-Brie 261 48.43 N 2.45 E
Presnogor'kovka 86 54.35 N 65.08 E
Presnovka 86 54.40 N 67.09 E
Presolana, Passo della x 64 45.55 N 10.06 E
Prešov 30 49.00 N 21.15 E
Prespa, Lake ⊜ 38 40.55 N 21.00 E
Prespansko Jezero → Prespa, Lake ⊜ 38 40.55 N 21.00 E
Presque Isle 186 46.40 N 68.00 W
Presque Isle ≻¹ 214 42.09 N 80.06 W
Presque Isle ≃ 190 46.43 N 89.59 W
Presque Isle State Park ◆ 214 42.09 N 80.06 W
Presqu'ile Bay c 212 44.01 N 77.43 W
Presqu'ile Peninsula ≻¹ 212 44.00 N 77.41 W
Presqu'ile Provincial Park ◆ 212 44.00 N 77.42 W
Pressana 64 45.17 N 11.24 E
Pressath 60 49.46 N 11.56 E
Pressbaum 61 48.11 N 16.05 E
Pressburg → Bratislava 30 48.09 N 17.07 E
Pressel 54 51.34 N 12.41 E
Prestatyn 44 53.20 N 3.24 W
Prestbury 262 53.17 N 2.09 W
Prestea 150 5.27 N 2.08 W
Presteigne 42 52.17 N 3.00 W
Přeštice 60 49.34 N 13.20 E
Presto 279b 40.23 N 80.07 W
Preston, Austl. 169 37.45 S 145.01 E
Preston, Eng., U.K. 42 50.39 N 2.25 W
Preston, Eng., U.K. 44 53.46 N 0.12 W
Preston, Eng., U.K. 44 53.46 N 2.42 W
Preston, Ga., U.S. 192 32.03 N 84.32 W
Preston, Id., U.S. 202 42.05 N 111.52 W
Preston, Ia., U.S. 190 42.03 N 90.24 W
Preston, Ks., U.S. 198 37.45 N 98.33 W
Preston, Md., U.S. 208 38.42 N 75.54 W
Preston, Mn., U.S. 190 43.40 N 92.04 W
Preston, Wa., U.S. 224 47.31 N 121.55 W
Preston □⁸ 262 53.48 N 2.42 W
Preston ≃, Austl. 168a 33.20 S 115.40 E
Preston ≃, P.Q., Can. 206 46.05 N 75.04 W
Preston, Cape > 162 20.51 S 116.12 E
Preston, Lac ⊜ 206 46.05 N 75.04 W
Preston, Lake ⊜, Austl. 168a 32.59 S 115.42 E
Preston, Lake ⊜, Fl., U.S. 220 28.18 N 81.08 W
Preston Airport ≋ 276 40.22 N 74.15 W
Preston Brook 262 53.19 N 2.39 W
Preston Brook Canal Tunnel ◆⁵ 262 53.19 N 2.38 W
Preston Heights 216 41.28 N 88.08 W
Preston Hollow 210 42.27 N 74.13 W
Preston North End Football Ground ◆ 262 53.47 N 2.42 W
Prestonpans 46 55.57 N 3.00 W
Preston Peak ∧ 204 41.50 N 123.37 W
Prestonsburg 192 37.39 N 82.46 W
Prestrud Inlet c 9 78.18 S 156.00 W
Preststranda 26 59.06 N 9.04 E
Prestville 182 55.44 N 118.37 W
Prestwich 44 53.32 N 2.17 W
Prestwick 46 55.29 N 4.37 W
Prestwick Airport ≋ 46 55.30 N 4.36 W
Preto ≃, Bra. 246 1.41 S 63.48 W
Preto ≃, Bra. 248 8.03 S 62.54 W
Preto ≃, Bra. 250 11.21 S 43.52 W
Preto ≃, Bra. 250 3.32 S 43.46 W
Preto ≃, Bra. 255 13.37 S 48.06 W
Preto ≃, Bra. 255 17.00 S 46.12 W
Preto ≃, Bra. 255 18.44 S 50.23 W
Preto ≃, Bra. 255 20.08 S 49.38 W
Preto ≃, Bra. 256 22.14 S 43.07 W
Preto ≃, Bra. 256 22.01 S 43.20 W
Preto do Igapó-açu ≃ 246 4.26 S 59.48 W
Pretoria 158 25.45 S 28.10 E
Pretoriusvlei 158 28.30 S 22.59 E
Prettau → Predoi 64 47.02 N 12.06 E
Prettin 54 51.39 N 12.55 E
Prettyboy Reservoir ⊜¹ 208 39.38 N 76.45 W
Pretty Prairie 198 37.46 N 98.01 W
Pretzfeld 60 49.45 N 11.11 E
Pretzier 54 52.49 N 11.15 E
Pretzsch 54 51.42 N 12.48 E
Preussisch Eylau → Bagrationovsk 76 54.23 N 20.39 E
Preussisch-Oldendorf 52 52.18 N 8.30 E
Preussisch-Ströhen 52 52.29 N 8.40 E
Prevalje 61 46.32 N 14.55 E
Préveza 38 38.57 N 20.44 E
Prévost 206 45.52 N 74.05 W
Prevost Island I 224 48.50 N 123.22 W
Prey Lvéa 110 11.10 N 104.57 E
Prey Nôb 110 10.38 N 103.47 E
Prey Vêng 110 11.29 N 105.19 E
Prezza, Monte ∧ 66 42.02 N 13.49 E
Priaral'skije Karakumy ◆² 86 47.00 N 63.30 E
Priargunsk 88 50.27 N 119.00 E
Priay 58 46.00 N 5.17 E
Priazovskaja vozvyšennost' ∧¹ 83 47.30 N 37.30 E
Priazovskoje 78 46.43 N 35.38 E
Pribilof Islands II 180 57.00 N 170.00 W
Priboj 38 43.35 N 19.31 E
Příbram 30 49.42 N 14.01 E
Pribylovo 76 60.26 N 28.40 E
Priccio, Cozzo ∧ 70 37.01 N 14.46 E
Price, Austl. 168b 34.17 S 138.00 E
Price, Tx., U.S. 222 32.08 N 94.57 W
Price, Ut., U.S. 200 39.35 N 110.48 W
Price ≃ 200 39.10 N 110.06 W
Price, Cape > 110 13.34 N 93.03 E
Price Bend c 276 40.55 N 73.24 W
Price Island I 182 52.23 N 128.36 W
Prichard 194 30.44 N 88.04 W
Prickly Point > 241k 11.59 N 61.45 W
Pričornomorskaja nizmennost' ≍ 78 47.00 N 33.00 E
Priddy 196 31.40 N 98.31 W
Pridneprovskaja nizmennost' ≍ 78 50.00 N 32.00 E
Pridneprovskaja vozvyšennost' ∧¹ 78 49.00 N 32.00 E
Priego 34 40.27 N 2.18 W
Priego de Córdoba 34 37.26 N 4.11 W
Priekule, Lat. 76 56.26 N 21.35 E
Priekulė, Liet. 76 55.33 N 21.19 E
Prienai 76 54.38 N 23.57 E
Prien am Chiemsee 64 47.51 N 12.20 E
Prieros 54 52.13 N 13.46 E
Prieska 158 29.40 S 22.42 E
Priest ≃ 202 48.11 N 116.53 W
Priestewitz 54 51.15 N 13.30 E
Priest Island I 46 57.58 N 5.30 W
Priest Lake ⊜ 202 48.34 N 116.52 W
Priestley, Mount ∧ 182 55.13 N 128.53 W
Priest Rapids Lake ⊜¹ 202 46.45 N 119.55 W
Priest River 202 48.10 N 116.53 W
Prieta, Loma ∧ 226 37.07 N 121.51 W
Prieta, Peña ∧ 34 43.01 N 4.44 W
Prieto ≃ 240m 18.15 N 66.54 W
Prieto Diaz 116 13.02 N 124.12 E
Prievidza 30 48.47 N 18.37 E
Prignitz ◆¹ 54 53.05 N 12.15 E
Priiskovyj, Ross. 86 54.39 N 88.42 E
Priiskovyj, Ross. 88 51.57 N 116.39 E
Prijedor 36 44.59 N 16.43 E
Prijepolje 38 43.23 N 19.39 E
Prijutnoje 80 46.06 N 43.31 E
Prijutovo 80 53.54 N 53.56 E
Prikaspijskaja nizmennost' ≍ 80 48.00 N 52.00 E
Prikolotnoje 78 50.09 N 37.21 E
Prikro 150 7.39 N 3.59 W
Prilep 38 41.20 N 21.33 E
Prilepy 82 54.03 N 37.42 E
Prilly 58 46.32 N 6.36 E
Priluki, Ross. 76 59.16 N 39.53 E
Priluki, Ross. 82 54.51 N 37.53 E
Priluki, Ukr. 78 50.36 N 32.24 E
Prima Porta ◆⁸ 267a 42.00 N 12.29 E
Primavera 250 0.56 S 47.06 W
Přimda 60 49.41 N 12.41 E
Primeira Cruz 250 2.30 S 43.26 W
Primeiro de Maio 255 22.48 S 51.01 W
Primera 196 26.14 N 97.43 W
Primero ≃ 252 31.00 S 63.12 W
Primero de Mayo 196 27.12 N 101.15 W
Primghar 198 43.05 N 95.37 W
Primolano 64 45.58 N 11.42 E
Primorje [Warnicken] 76 54.57 N 20.02 E
Primorka 83 47.10 N 39.03 E
Primorsk, Azer. 84 40.35 N 49.46 E
Primorsk, Ross. 76 60.22 N 28.36 E
Primorsk, Ross. 80 49.16 N 45.03 E
Primorsk, Ukr. 78 46.44 N 36.20 E

ENGLISH — Name | Page | Lat.°′ | Long.°′

Primorskij, Ross. 89 43.07 N 131.38 E
Primorskij, Ukr. 78 45.07 N 35.29 E
Primorskij chrebet ∧ 88 52.30 N 106.00 E
Primorskij Kraj □⁸ 89 45.25 N 135.25 E
Primorsko-Achtarsk 78 46.03 N 38.11 E
Primorskoje 83 47.11 N 37.42 E
Primos 285 39.55 N 75.18 W
Primrose, S. Afr. 273d 26.12 S 28.10 E
Primrose, Pa., U.S. 210 40.42 N 76.17 W
Primrose, Pa., U.S. 279b 40.21 N 80.16 W
Primrose Brook ≃ 276 40.43 N 74.31 W
Primrose Lake ⊜ 184 54.55 N 109.45 W
Prims ≃ 56 49.20 N 6.44 E
Primstal 56 49.32 N 6.58 E
Prince, Lake ⊜¹ 208 36.48 N 76.38 W
Prince Albert, On., Can. 212 44.05 N 78.58 W
Prince Albert, Sk., Can. 184 53.12 N 105.46 W
Prince Albert, S. Afr. 158 33.13 S 22.02 E
Prince Albert Mountains ∧ 9 76.00 S 161.30 E
Prince Albert National Park ◆ 184 54.00 N 106.25 W
Prince Albert Road 158 33.01 S 21.40 E
Prince Albert Sound ≍ 176 70.25 N 115.00 W
Prince Alexander Mountains ∧ 164 3.30 S 142.50 E
Prince Alfred Hamlet 158 33.18 S 19.20 E
Prince Charles Island I 176 67.50 N 76.00 W
Prince Charles Mountains ∧ 9 72.00 S 67.00 E
Prince-de-Galles, Île du → Prince of Wales Island I, Austl. 164 10.40 S 142.10 E
Prince-de-Galles, Île du → Prince of Wales Island I, N.T., Can. 176 72.40 N 99.00 W
Prince Edward □⁶ 212 44.00 N 77.15 W
Prince Edward Bay c 212 43.57 N 76.57 W
Prince Edward Island □⁴, Can. 176 46.20 N 63.20 W
Prince Edward Island □⁴, Can. 186 46.20 N 63.20 W
Prince Edward Island National Park ◆ 186 46.31 N 63.26 W
Prince Edward Islands II 6 46.35 S 37.56 E
Prince Edward Park ◆ 274a 34.02 S 151.03 E
Prince Edward Point > 212 43.56 N 76.52 W
Prince Frederick 208 38.32 N 76.35 W
Prince Gallitzin State Park ◆ 214 40.40 N 78.32 W
Prince George, B.C., Can. 182 53.55 N 122.45 W
Prince George, Va., U.S. 208 37.13 N 77.17 W
Prince George □⁶ 208 37.13 N 77.10 W
Prince Georges □⁶ 208 38.49 N 76.45 W
Prince Georges Plaza ◆⁹ 284c 38.58 N 76.57 W
Prince Leopold Island I 176 74.02 N 89.55 W
Prince of Wales, Cape > 180 65.40 N 168.05 W
Prince of Wales Island I, Austl. 164 10.40 S 142.10 E
Prince of Wales Island I, N.T., Can. 176 72.40 N 99.00 W
Prince of Wales Island I, Ak., U.S. 180 55.47 N 132.50 W
Prince of Wales Strait ≍ 176 73.00 N 117.00 W
Prince Olav Coast ≐² 9 68.30 S 42.30 E
Prince Patrick Island I 176 76.45 N 119.30 W
Prince Regent ≃ 164 15.28 S 125.05 E
Prince Regent Inlet c 176 73.00 N 90.30 W
Prince Regent Nature Reserve ◆ 164 15.30 S 125.30 E
Prince Rupert 182 54.19 N 130.19 W
Prince Rupert Bay c 240d 15.34 N 61.29 W
Prince Rupert Bluff Point > 240d 15.35 N 61.29 W
Princesa, Puerto c 116 9.45 N 118.43 E
Princesa Astrid, Costa → Princess Astrid Coast ≐² 9 70.45 S 12.30 E
Princesa Carlota, Bahía → Princess Charlotte Bay c 164 14.25 S 144.00 E
Princesa Isabel 250 7.44 S 38.00 W
Princesa Marta, Costa → Princess Martha Coast ≐² 9 72.00 S 7.30 W
Princesa Ragnhild, Costa → Princess Ragnhild Coast ≐² 9 70.15 S 27.30 E
Princes Bay c 276 40.31 N 74.12 W
Princes Risborough 44 51.44 N 0.51 W
Princess Anne 208 38.12 N 75.41 W
Princess Astrid Coast ≐² 9 70.45 S 12.30 E
Princess Charlotte Bay c 164 14.25 S 144.00 E
Princess Martha Coast ≐² 9 72.00 S 7.30 W
Princess Ragnhild Coast ≐² 9 70.15 S 27.30 E
Princess Ranges ∧ 162 26.08 S 121.55 E
Princess Royal Channel ≍ 182 53.10 N 128.37 W
Princess Royal Island I 182 52.57 N 128.49 W
Princes Town 241r 10.16 N 61.23 W
Princeton, B.C., Can. 182 49.27 N 120.31 W
Princeton, Nf., Can. 186 48.25 N 53.36 W
Princeton, On., Can. 212 43.10 N 80.32 W
Princeton, Ca., U.S. 226 39.24 N 122.00 W
Princeton, Fl., U.S. 220 25.32 N 80.24 W
Princeton, Il., U.S. 190 41.22 N 89.27 W
Princeton, In., U.S. 194 38.21 N 87.34 W
Princeton, Ky., U.S. 194 37.06 N 87.52 W
Princeton, Me., U.S. 188 45.13 N 67.34 W
Princeton, Mi., U.S. 190 46.17 N 87.28 W
Princeton, Mn., U.S. 190 45.34 N 93.34 W
Princeton, Mo., U.S. 194 40.24 N 93.34 W
Princeton, N.J., U.S. 208 40.20 N 74.39 W
Princeton, N.C., U.S. 192 35.27 N 78.09 W
Princeton, Tx., U.S. 222 33.11 N 96.30 W
Princeton, W.V., U.S. 192 37.21 N 81.06 W
Princeton, Wi., U.S. 190 43.51 N 89.07 W
Princeton Airfield ≋ 276 40.24 N 74.39 W
Princeton Battlefield Park ◆ 276 40.20 N 74.41 W
Princeton Junction 208 40.19 N 74.37 W
Princeton Township 208 40.22 N 74.40 W
Princeton University ◆² 276 40.21 N 74.39 W
Princetown 42 50.33 N 4.00 W
Princeville, P.Q., Can. 206 46.10 N 71.53 W
Princeville, Il., U.S. 190 40.56 N 89.45 W
Princeville, N.C., U.S. 192 35.53 N 77.31 W
Prince William □⁶ 208 38.42 N 77.27 W
Prince William Forest Park ◆ 208 38.36 N 77.23 W
Prince William Sound ≍ 180 60.40 N 147.00 W
Príncipe I 152 1.37 N 7.25 E
Príncipe Alberto, Montes → Prince Albert Mountains ∧ 9 76.00 S 161.30 E

DEUTSCH — Name | Seite | Breite°′ | Länge°′ E = Ost

Príncipe Carlos, Montes → Prince Charles Mountains ∧ 9 72.00 S 67.00 E
Principe Channel ≍ 182 53.28 N 130.00 W
Príncipe da Beira 248 12.25 S 64.25 W
Príncipe de Gales, Isla → Prince of Wales Island I, Austl. 164 10.40 S 142.10 E
Príncipe de Gales, Isla → Prince of Wales Island I, N.T., Can. 176 72.40 N 99.00 W
Príncipe Eduardo, Isla → Prince Edward Island □⁴ 186 46.20 N 63.20 E
Príncipe Olav, Costa → Prince Olav Coast ≐² 9 68.30 S 42.30 E
Príncipe Patricio, Isla → Prince Patrick Island I 16 76.45 N 119.30 W
Prineville 202 44.18 N 120.51 W
Prineville Reservoir ⊜¹ 202 44.08 N 120.42 W
Prineville Southeast 202 44.17 N 120.53 W
Pringgabaja 115b 8.34 S 116.37 E
Pringsewu 112 5.24 S 104.55 E
Pringy 261 48.31 N 2.34 E
Prinsenbeek 52 51.36 N 4.42 E
Prinses Margrietkanaal ≍ 52 53.10 N 5.55 E
Prinshof 158 32.06 S 20.53 E
Prinzapolka 236 13.24 N 83.34 W
Prinzapolka ≃ 236 13.24 N 83.34 W
Prinzessin Astrid-Küste → Princess Astrid Coast ≐² 9 70.45 S 12.30 E
Prinzessin Charlotte Bucht → Princess Charlotte Bay c 164 14.25 S 144.00 E
Prinzessin Martha-Küste → Princess Martha Coast ≐² 9 72.00 S 7.30 W
Prinzessin Ragnhild-Küste → Princess Ragnhild Coast ≐² 9 70.15 S 27.30 E
Priobskoje plato ∧¹ 86 52.40 N 83.00 E
Priooksko-Terrasnyj Zapovednik ◆⁴ 82 54.51 N 37.36 E
Priolo Gargallo 70 37.09 N 15.11 E
Prior, Cabo > 34 43.34 N 8.19 W
Priort 264a 52.31 N 12.58 E
Priozernyj 80 47.23 N 45.14 E
Prioz'ornyj 86 47.50 N 84.13 E
Prioz'orsk 24 61.02 N 30.04 E
Prip'at' ≃ 78 51.21 N 30.09 E
Pripet Marshes → Polesje ◆¹ 72 52.00 N 27.00 E
Pripet → Prip'at' ≃ 78 51.21 N 30.09 E
Pripol'arnyj Ural ∧ 24 65.00 N 60.00 E
Priputni 78 50.57 N 32.14 E
Prirečje 88 55.07 N 101.03 E
Prirečnyj 80 51.03 N 52.26 E
Přísečnice 54 50.27 N 13.06 E
Priselje 76 55.09 N 32.49 E
Prišib, Azer. 84 39.08 N 48.36 E
Prišib, Ukr. 78 47.16 N 35.21 E
Prislon 82 56.48 N 37.16 E
Pristan'-Prževal'sk 85 42.34 N 78.18 E
Pristen', Ross. 78 51.15 N 36.41 E
Pristen', Ukr. 78 49.36 N 37.38 E
Priština 38 42.39 N 21.10 E
Pritchett 198 37.22 N 102.51 W
Přítluky 61 48.51 N 16.46 E
Pritzerbe 54 52.30 N 12.27 E
Pritzier 54 53.22 N 11.04 E
Pritzwalk 54 53.09 N 12.10 E
Privas 62 44.44 N 4.36 E
Priverno 66 41.28 N 13.11 E
Privetnoje 78 44.50 N 34.41 E
Privodino 24 61.05 N 46.28 E
Privokzal'nyj, Ross. 82 55.59 N 35.56 E
Privokzal'nyj, Ross. 86 58.53 N 60.43 E
Privol'je, Ukr. 83 49.01 N 38.18 E
Privol'je, Ukr. 83 48.52 N 37.16 E
Privol'naja 83 46.09 N 38.42 E
Privol'n'anskij ◆⁸ 83 48.41 N 38.28 E
Privol'noje, Ross. 80 50.57 N 46.06 E
Privol'noje, Ukr. 78 47.29 N 32.17 E
Privolžje 80 52.52 N 48.33 E
Privolžsk 80 57.23 N 41.17 E
Privolžskaja vozvyšennost' ∧¹ 80 52.00 N 46.00 E
Privolžskij, Ross. 80 46.24 N 48.00 E
Privolžskij, Ross. 80 51.24 N 46.02 E
Privolžskoje 80 51.06 N 45.57 E
Prizren 38 42.12 N 20.44 E
Prizzi 70 37.43 N 13.26 E
Prizzi, Lago di ⊜ 70 37.44 N 13.25 E
Prnjavor 36 44.52 N 17.40 E
Probolinggo 115a 7.45 S 113.13 E
Proboštov 54 50.39 N 13.50 E
Probstzella 54 50.32 N 11.22 E
Probus 42 50.17 N 4.57 W
Procchio 66 42.47 N 10.15 E
Prochladnoje 86 48.30 N 82.41 E
Prochladnyj 84 43.46 N 44.00 E
Prochorkino 86 59.34 N 79.26 E
Prochorovka 82 54.07 N 38.11 E
Prochowice 30 51.17 N 16.22 E
Procida 68 40.46 N 14.02 E
Procida, Isola di I 68 40.45 N 14.01 E
Procter 182 49.37 N 116.57 W
Proctor, Mn., U.S. 190 46.44 N 92.13 W
Proctor, Vt., U.S. 188 43.39 N 73.02 W
Proctor Brook ≃ 283 42.32 N 70.54 W
Proctor Lake ⊜ 228 35.07 N 118.21 W
Proctor Lake ⊜¹ 196 32.02 N 98.32 W
Proddatūr 122 14.44 N 78.33 E
Proença-a-Nova 34 39.45 N 7.55 W
Profen 54 51.07 N 12.13 E
Pro Football Hall of Fame ◆ 214 40.49 N 81.25 W
Prognoj 83 46.45 N 39.51 E
Progreso, Méx. 196 27.28 N 100.59 W
Progreso, Méx. 232 21.17 N 89.40 W
Progreso, Méx. 234 23.48 N 103.18 W
Progreso, Méx. 234 20.15 N 99.12 W
Progreso, Ur. 258 34.40 S 56.13 W
Progress, Ross. 89 49.42 N 129.39 E
Progress, Or., U.S. 224 45.28 N 122.47 W
Progress, Pa., U.S. 208 40.18 N 76.34 W
Project City 204 40.41 N 122.21 W
Prokopjeva 88 58.03 N 100.39 E
Prokopjevsk 86 53.53 N 86.45 E
Prokopyevsk → Prokopjevsk 86 53.53 N 86.45 E
Prokuplje 38 43.14 N 21.36 E
Prokuševo 76 59.55 N 34.56 E
Proletarij 86 56.19 N 69.46 E
Proletarij 76 58.26 N 31.44 E
Proletarsk, Ross. 80 46.42 N 41.44 E
Proletarsk, Taj. 85 40.10 N 69.30 E
Proletarsk, Ukr. 78 48.56 N 38.23 E
Proletarsk ◆⁸ 83 48.56 N 38.23 E
Proletarskij, Ross. 78 50.47 N 35.48 E
Proletarskij, Ross. 82 55.01 N 37.23 E
Proletarskij ◆⁸ 83 48.08 N 39.18 E
Prolysovo 76 52.54 N 34.09 E
Prome (Pyè) 110 18.49 N 95.13 E
Promised Land State Park ◆ 210 41.18 N 75.11 W
Promissão 255 21.32 S 49.52 W

Symbols in the index entries represent the broad categories identified in the key at the right. Symbols with superior numbers (∧¹) identify subcategories (see complete key on page I · 1).

Symbole im Register stellen die rechts im Schlüssel identifizierten Kategorien dar. Symbole mit hochgestellten Ziffern (∧¹) bezeichnen Unterabteilungen einer Kategorie (vgl. vollständiger Schlüssel auf Seite I · 1).

Los símbolos incluidos en el texto del índice representan las grandes categorías identificadas con la clave a la derecha. Los símbolos con numeros en su parte superior (∧¹) identifican las subcategorías (véase la clave completa en la página I · 1).

Les symboles de l'index représentent les catégories indiquées dans la légende à droite. Les symboles suivis d'un indice (∧¹) représentent des sous-catégories (voir légende complète à la page I · 1).

Os símbolos incluídos no texto do índice representam as grandes categorias identificadas com a chave à direita. Os símbolos com números em sua parte superior (∧¹) identificam as subcategorias (veja-se a chave completa à página I · 1).

∧ Mountain	Berg	Montaña	Montagne	Montanha
∧∧ Mountains	Gebirge	Montañas	Montagnes	Montanhas
x Pass	Paß	Paso	Col	Passo
V Valley, Canyon	Tal, Cañon	Valle, Cañón	Vallée, Canyon	Vale, Canhão
≍ Plain	Ebene	Llano	Plaine	Planície
> Cape	Kap	Cabo	Cap	Cabo
I Island	Insel	Isla	Île	Ilha
II Islands	Inseln	Islas	Îles	Ilhas
◆ Other Topographic Features	Andere Topographische Objekte	Otros Elementos Topográficos	Autres données topographiques	Outros acidentes topográficos

ESPAÑOL · FRANÇAIS · PORTUGUÊS

Nombre / Nom / Nome	Página / Page	Lat.°′	Long.°′ W = Oeste / W = Ouest
Promitorio	267a	42.03 N	12.39 E
Promontogno	58	46.21 N	9.34 E
Prompton	210	41.35 N	75.19 W
Prompton Lake ⊜[1]	210	41.36 N	75.20 W
Prompton Lake State Park ◆	210	41.37 N	75.22 W
Promyšlennaja	86	54.55 N	85.40 E
Promyšlennovskij	86	55.29 N	86.12 E
Promyšlennyj	24	67.35 N	63.55 E
Promyslovka	80	45.44 N	47.10 E
Pron'a ≃, Bela.	76	53.25 N	31.01 E
Pron'a ≃, Ross.	80	54.21 N	40.24 E
Pron'a Gorodišče	82	54.15 N	38.43 E
Pronin	80	49.12 N	42.11 E
Pronsfeld	56	50.10 N	6.20 E
Pronsk	76	54.07 N	39.37 E
Prony, Baie du c	175f	22.22 S	166.53 E
Prophet ≃	176	58.45 N	122.45 W
Prophetstown	190	41.40 N	89.56 W
Propriá	250	10.13 S	36.51 W
Propriano	36	41.40 N	8.55 E
Prorer Wiek c	54	54.27 N	13.38 E
Prorva	86	46.03 N	53.15 E
Proryvnoje	86	54.23 N	64.26 E
Pros'anaja	78	48.07 N	36.23 E
Pros'anov	78	49.42 N	35.47 E
Prösen	54	51.25 N	13.30 E
Proserpine	166	20.24 S	148.34 E
Prosigk	54	51.42 N	12.03 E
Proskurov → Chmel'nickij	78	49.25 N	27.00 E
Prosna ≃	30	52.10 N	17.39 E
Prosnica	80	58.26 N	50.15 E
Prosotsáni	38	41.10 N	23.59 E
Prospect, Austl.	168b	34.54 S	138.35 E
Prospect, Austl.	274a	33.48 S	150.56 E
Prospect, Ct., U.S.	207	41.30 N	72.58 W
Prospect, N.Y., U.S.	210	43.18 N	75.09 W
Prospect, Oh., U.S.	214	40.27 N	83.11 W
Prospect, Pa., U.S.	214	40.54 N	80.03 W
Prospect Bay c	208	38.56 N	76.14 W
Prospect Creek ≃	274a	33.55 S	150.59 E
Prospect Heights	278	42.05 N	87.56 W
Prospect Hill	168b	35.13 S	138.44 E
Prospect Hill ∧[2], Ma., U.S.	207	41.21 N	70.45 W
Prospect Hill ∧[2], Ma., U.S.	283	42.23 N	71.15 W
Prospect Hill Park ◆	283	42.23 N	71.15 W
Prospect Park, N.J., U.S.	276	40.56 N	74.10 W
Prospect Park, Pa., U.S.	214	41.31 N	78.13 W
Prospect Park, Pa., U.S.	285	39.53 N	75.18 W
Prospect Park ◆	276	40.40 N	73.58 W
Prospect Park Lake ⊜	276	40.39 N	73.57 W
Prospect Plains	276	40.19 N	74.28 W
Prospect Point	276	40.58 N	74.38 W
Prospect Point ›	276	40.52 N	73.43 W
Prospect Reservoir ⊜[1]	274a	33.49 S	150.54 E
Prospectville	285	40.13 N	75.11 W
Prosper	222	33.14 N	96.48 W
Prosperi Airport ⊠	278	41.33 N	87.47 W
Prosperidad	116	8.34 N	125.52 E
Prosser	202	46.12 N	119.46 W
Prosser Creek Reservoir ⊜[1]	226	39.22 N	120.08 W
Prostějov	30	49.29 N	17.07 E
Prostki	30	53.43 N	22.26 E
Proston	166	26.10 S	151.36 E
Proszowice	30	50.12 N	20.18 E
Protasovo, Ross.	82	54.48 N	38.35 E
Protasovo, Ross.	82	54.11 N	37.00 E
Protasovo, Ross.	82	56.08 N	37.36 E
Protasy	76	52.47 N	29.05 E
Protea	273d	26.17 S	27.51 E
Protection	198	37.12 N	99.29 W
Protection Island I	224	48.07 N	122.55 W
Protem	158	34.16 S	20.05 E
Protivín	61	49.12 N	14.13 E
Protoka ≃	78	45.43 N	37.46 E
Protva	82	55.01 N	36.41 E
Protva ≃	82	54.51 N	37.16 E
Protville	36	36.54 N	10.01 E
Prötzel	54	52.38 N	13.59 E
Proud Lake State Recreation Area ◆	281	42.34 N	83.33 W
Proulxville	206	46.40 N	72.30 W
Provadija	38	43.11 N	27.26 E
Provencal	194	31.39 N	93.12 W
Provence □[9]	62	44.00 N	6 00 E
Provence, Alpes de ⋏	62	43.40 N	6.00 E
Provenchères-sur-Fave	58	48.19 N	7.05 E
Providence, Ky., U.S.	194	37.23 N	87.45 W
Providence, R.I., U.S.	207	41.49 N	71.24 W
Providence, Ut,. U.S.	200	41.42 N	111.48 W
Providence □[6]	207	41.52 N	71.36 W
Providence ≃	207	41.43 N	71.21 W
Providence Forge	208	37.26 N	77.02 W
Providence Island I	138	9.14 S	51.02 E
Providência, Bra.	256	21.40 S	42.35 W
Providencia, Chile	286e	33.26 S	70.37 W
Providencia, Méx.	196	27.06 N	103.32 W
Providencia, Isla de I	236	13.21 N	81.22 W
Providenciales I	238	21.47 N	72.17 W
Providenija	180	64.23 N	173.18 W
Providenija, buchta c	180	64.30 N	173.20 W
Provincetown	207	42.03 N	70.10 W
Provins	50	48.33 N	3.18 E
Provo	200	40.14 N	111.39 W
Provo ≃	200	40.14 N	111.44 W
Provost	184	52.21 N	110.16 W
Provost, Lac ⊜	206	46.22 N	74.00 W
Prozor	36	43.49 N	17.37 E
Pru ≃	150	7.58 N	0.53 W
Prud'anka	78	50.14 N	36.09 E
Prudence Island I	207	41.37 N	71.19 W
Prudentópolis	252	25.12 S	50.57 W
Prudentov	80	49.39 N	46.19 E
Prudhoe	44	54.58 N	1.51 W
Prudhoe Bay c	180	70.20 N	148.20 W
Prudhoe Island I	166	21.19 S	149.40 E
Prudišči	82	54.24 N	38.26 E
Prudki	82	54.46 N	36.29 E
Prudnik	30	50.19 N	17.34 E
Prudy	76	53.47 N	26.32 E
Pruggern	64	47.25 N	13.52 E
Prüm	56	50.12 N	6.25 E
Prüm ≃	56	49.49 N	6.28 E
Pruna, Punta sa ∧	71	40.11 N	9.26 E
Prunay-le-Temple	261	48.52 N	1.40 E
Prunay-sous-Ablis	261	48.32 N	1.48 E
Prunedale	226	36.47 N	121.40 W
Prunéřov	54	50.25 N	13.16 E
Prunières	62	44.33 N	6.20 E
Prunn, Schloss ⊥	60	48.57 N	11.44 E
Pruszków	30	52.11 N	20.48 E
Prut ≃	78	45.30 N	28.12 E
Pruth → Prut ≃	78	45.30 N	28.12 E
Prutting	64	47.53 N	12.11 E
Prutz	58	47.05 N	10.40 E
Pružany	76	52.33 N	24.28 E
Prydz Bay c	9	69.00 S	76.00 E
Pryor	196	36.19 N	95.19 W
Pryor Creek ≃	202	45.54 N	108.19 W
Pryor Mountain ∧[2]	222	31.43 N	95.12 W
Prysor ≃	42	52.56 N	4.00 W
Przasnysz	30	53.01 N	20.55 E
Przedbórz	30	51.06 N	19.53 E
Przemków	30	51.32 N	15.48 E
Przemocze	54	53.27 N	14.55 E
Przemyśl	30	49.47 N	22.47 E
Przemyśl □[4]	30	50.00 N	22.40 E
Przeworsk	30	50.05 N	22.29 E
Przewóz	54	51.29 N	14.59 E
Przybiernów	54	53.46 N	14.46 E
Przysucha	30	51.22 N	20.38 E
Pšagar	85	39.58 N	68.08 E
Psakhná	38	38.35 N	23.38 E
Psará I	38	38.35 N	25.37 E
Psárion	38	37.20 N	21.51 E
Psebaj	84	44.07 N	40.47 E
Pšecha ≃	78	44.47 N	39.48 E
Psekups ≃	78	45.00 N	39.09 E
Pselec	78	51.17 N	36.32 E
Psikhikón	267c	38.01 N	23.46 E
Pšiš ≃	78	45.01 N	39.18 E
Pšiš, gora ∧	84	43.24 N	41.12 E
Psittália I	267c	37.56 N	23.35 E
Pskem	85	41.56 N	70.22 E
Pskem ≃	85	41.38 N	70.01 E
Pskent	85	40.54 N	69.20 E
Pskov	76	57.50 N	28.20 E
Pskov Oblast' □[4]	76	57.00 N	29.00 E
Pskovskoje ozero ⊜	76	58.00 N	28.00 E
Pskowsee → Pskovskoje ozero ⊜	76	58.00 N	28.00 E
Ps'ol ≃	78	49.02 N	33.33 E
Pšov	54	50.10 N	13.29 E
Pszczyna	30	49.59 N	18.57 E
Ptarmigan, Cape ›	176	71.04 N	118.07 W
Ptič'	76	52.09 N	28.52 E
Ptič' ≃	76	52.09 N	28.52 E
Ptolemaís	38	40.31 N	21.41 E
Ptolemais ⊥	146	32.43 N	20.57 E
Ptuj	61	46.25 N	15.52 E
Pu ≃, Zhg.	104	41.21 N	122.47 E
Pu ≃, Zhg.	107	30.25 N	103.49 E
Puah, Pulau I	112	0.30 S	122.34 E
Puakonikai	174d	0.52 S	169.36 E
Puamau, Baie c	174x	9.46 S	138.52 W
Puán, Arg.	252	37.33 S	62.43 W
Puan, Taehan	98	35.45 N	126.44 E
Pubāil	126	23.56 N	90.29 E
Pubnico	186	43.42 N	65.47 W
Pucallpa	248	8.23 S	74.32 W
Pucara	248	18.43 S	64.11 W
Pucarani	248	16.23 S	68.30 W
Puccha ≃	248	9.05 S	76.54 W
Puccia, Serra di ∧	70	37.44 N	13.56 E
Puce	214	42.18 N	82.47 W
Puces ≃	281	42.18 N	82.47 W
Pučevejem ≃	180	68.48 N	170.30 E
Pučež	80	56.59 N	43.11 E
Puchberg am Schneeberg	61	47.47 N	15.54 E
Pucheng, Zhg.	100	27.55 N	118.31 E
Pucheng, Zhg.	102	34.59 N	109.29 E
Pucheta	252	29.54 S	57.34 W
Puchheim	60	48.09 N	11.20 E
Púchov	30	49.08 N	18.20 E
Puchoviči	76	53.32 N	28.15 E
Pucioasa	38	45.04 N	25.26 E
Pucio Point ›	116	11.46 N	121.51 E
Pučišća	36	43.21 N	16.44 E
Puck	30	54.44 N	18.27 E
Puckapunyal	169	37.01 S	145.03 E
Pucketa Creek ≃	279b	40.33 N	79.45 W
Pudahuel	286e	33.26 S	70.46 W
Pudding ≃	224	45.18 N	122.43 W
Puddingstone Reservoir ⊜[1]	280	34.05 N	117.48 W
Puddington	262	53.15 N	3.00 W
Puddletown	42	50.45 N	2.21 W
Pūdeh Tal ≃	128	31.03 N	62.15 E
Pudem	80	58.18 N	52.10 E
Pudi	102	27.58 N	99.05 E
Pudimoe	158	27.26 S	24.44 E
Puding	102	26.21 N	105.40 E
Pudino	86	57.34 N	79.24 E
Pudops Dam ✦[6]	186	48.09 N	56.50 W
Pudož	24	61.48 N	36.32 E
Pudsey	44	53.48 N	1.40 W
Pudu ≃	102	26.19 N	102.45 E
Puduari ≃	246	2.08 S	61.15 W
Puduhe	102	25.39 N	102.39 E
Pudukkottai	122	10.23 N	78.49 E
Puebla □[3]	234	18.50 N	98.00 W
Puebla de Alcocer	34	38.59 N	5.15 W
Puebla de Don Fadrique	34	37.58 N	2.26 W
Puebla de Don Rodrigo	34	39.05 N	4.37 W
Puebla de Sanabria	34	42.03 N	6.38 W
Puebla de Trives	34	42.20 N	7.15 W
Puebla [de Zaragoza]	234	19.03 N	98.12 W
Pueblito de Ponce	240m	18.26 N	66.58 W
Pueblo	198	38.15 N	104.36 W
Pueblo Libertador	252	30.13 S	59.23 W
Pueblo Libre	286d	12.05 S	77.04 W
Pueblo Mountain ∧	202	42.06 N	118.39 W
Pueblo Nuevo, Col.	246	8.31 N	75.15 W
Pueblo Nuevo, Méx.	234	20.31 N	101.22 W
Pueblo Nuevo, Nic.	236	13.23 N	86.29 W
Pueblo Nuevo, P.R.	240m	18.28 N	66.51 W
Pueblo Nuevo, Ur.	258	34.26 S	56.29 W
Pueblo Nuevo, Ven.	246	11.58 N	69.55 W
Pueblo Nuevo ✦[8]	266a	40.26 N	3.39 W
Pueblo Nuevo Tiquisate	236	14.17 N	91.22 W
Pueblo of Acoma	200	35.03 N	107.35 W
Pueblo Reservoir ⊜[1]	198	38.15 N	104.45 W
Puebloviejo, Ec.	246	1.34 S	79.30 W
Pueblo Viejo, Méx.	234	17.33 N	100.05 W
Pueblo Viejo, Méx.	234	16.14 N	94.39 W
Pueblo Viejo, Laguna c	234	22.10 N	97.53 W
Pueblo Yaqui	232	27.19 N	110.01 W
Puelches	252	38.09 S	65.55 W
Puente Alto	252	33.37 S	70.35 W
Puente de Arganda	266a	40.19 N	3.31 W
Puente de Ixtla	234	18.37 N	99.20 W
Puente-Genil	34	37.23 N	4.47 W
Puente Hills ⋏[2]	280	34.00 N	117.55 W
Puente Hills Mall ✦[9]	280	33.59 N	117.56 W
Puente la Reina	34	42.40 N	1.49 W
Puente Negro	196	27.55 N	101.01 W
Puente Nuevo, Embalse de ⊜[1]	34	38.00 N	5.00 W
Puente Piedra	286d	11.57 S	77.05 W
Pueo Point ›	229b	21.54 N	160.04 W
Pu'er	102	23.07 N	101.00 E
Puerca, Punta ›	240m	18.14 N	65.36 W
Puerco ≃	200	34.53 N	110.07 W
Puerco, Rio ≃	200	34.22 N	106.50 W
Pu'erdu	102	28.08 N	104.24 E
Puerto Acosta	248	15.32 S	69.15 W
Puerto Adela	252	24.33 S	54.22 W
Puerto Aisén	254	45.24 S	72.42 W
Puerto Alegre	248	13.53 S	61.36 W
Puerto Ángel	234	15.40 N	96.29 W
Puerto Arista	234	15.56 N	93.48 W
Puerto Armuelles	236	8.17 N	82.52 W
Puerto Asís	246	0.30 N	76.31 W
Puerto Ayacucho	246	5.40 N	67.35 W
Puerto Ayora, Ec.	246a	0.45 S	90.19 W
Puerto Ayora, Ec.	246a	0.45 S	90.19 W
Puerto Bahía Negra	248	20.15 S	58.12 W
Puerto Baquerizo Moreno	246a	0.54 S	89.36 W
Puerto Barrios	236	15.43 N	88.36 W
Puerto Bermejo	252	26.56 S	58.30 W
Puerto Bermúdez	248	10.20 S	74.54 W
Puerto Berrío	246	6.29 N	74.24 W
Puerto Bolívar, Col.	246	12.15 N	71.58 W
Puerto Bolívar, Ec.	246	3.16 S	79.59 W
Puerto Boyacá	246	5.45 N	74.39 W
Puerto Busch	248	20.02 S	57.55 W
Puerto Cabello	246	10.28 N	68.01 W
Puerto Cabezas	236	14.02 N	83.23 W
Puerto Carreño	246	6.12 N	67.22 W
Puerto Casado	252	22.20 S	57.55 W
Puerto Castilla	236	16.01 N	86.01 W
Puerto Chicama	248	7.42 S	79.27 W
Puerto Colombia	246	10.59 N	74.58 W
Puerto Constanza	258	33.50 S	59.03 W
Puerto Cortés	236	15.48 N	87.56 W
Puerto Cumarebo	246	11.29 N	69.21 W
Puerto de Eten	248	6.54 S	79.52 W
Puerto Delicia	252	26.12 S	54.35 W
Puerto de Lomas	248	15.34 S	74.50 W
Puerto Delón	236	14.22 N	85.53 W
Puerto del Rosario	148	28.30 N	13.52 W
Puerto Deseado	254	47.45 S	65.54 W
Puerto El Triunfo	236	13.17 N	88.33 W
Puerto Escondido	234	15.50 N	97.10 W
Puerto Espãna → Port of Spain	241r	10.39 N	61.31 W
Puerto Esperanza	252	26.01 S	54.39 W
Puerto Felipe, Bahía → Port Phillip Bay c	169	38.07 S	144.48 E
Puerto Fonciere	252	22.29 S	57.48 W
Puerto Francisco de Orellana	246	0.28 S	76.58 W
Puerto Gonzalo Moreno	248	11.06 S	66.10 W
Puerto Guaraní	248	21.18 S	57.55 W
Puerto Heath	248	12.30 S	68.40 W
Puerto Iguazú	252	25.34 S	54.34 W
Puerto Inca	248	9.22 S	74.58 W
Puerto Ingeniero Ibáñez	254	46.18 S	71.56 W
Puerto Inírida	246	3.53 N	67.52 W
Puerto Jiménez	236	8.33 N	83.19 W
Puerto Juárez	232	21.11 N	86.49 W
Puerto la Cruz	246	10.13 N	64.38 W
Puerto la Plata, Zona Nacional □[5]	288	34.52 S	57.52 W
Puerto Leda	248	20.41 S	58.02 W
Puerto Leguízamo	246	0.12 S	74.46 W
Puerto Lempira	236	15.13 N	83.47 W
Puerto Libertad, Arg.	252	25.55 S	54.36 W
Puerto Libertad, Méx.	232	29.55 N	112.43 W
Puerto Limón, Col.	246	3.23 N	73.30 W
Puerto Limón, C.R.	236	10.00 N	83.02 W
Puertollano	34	38.41 N	4.07 W
Puerto Lobos	254	42.00 S	65.06 W
Puerto López	246	4.05 N	72.58 W
Puerto Madero	236	14.44 N	92.25 W
Puerto Madryn	254	42.46 S	65.03 W
Puerto Maldonado	248	12.36 S	69.11 W
Puerto Manatí	240p	21.22 N	76.50 W
Puerto Mihanovich	248	20.52 S	57.59 W
Puerto Montt	254	41.28 S	72.57 W
Puerto Morazán	236	12.51 N	87.11 W
Puerto Morelos	232	20.50 N	86.52 W
Puerto Nariño	246	4.56 N	67.48 W
Puerto Natales	254	51.44 S	72.31 W
Puerto Nuevo, Punta ›	240m	18.30 N	66.24 W
Puerto Octay	254	40.58 S	72.54 W
Puerto Ordaz → Ciudad Guayana	246	8.22 N	62.40 W
Puerto Padre	240p	21.12 N	76.36 W
Puerto Páez	246	6.13 N	67.28 W
Puerto Palmer, Pico ∧	196	27.08 N	101.47 W
Puerto Peñasco	232	31.20 N	113.33 W
Puerto Pilón	236	9.22 N	79.48 W
Puerto Pinasco	252	22.43 S	57.50 W
Puerto Pirámide	254	42.34 S	64.17 W
Puerto Piray	252	26.28 S	54.42 W
Puerto Píritu	246	10.04 N	65.03 W
Puerto Plata	238	19.48 N	70.41 W
Puerto Portillo	248	9.46 S	72.45 W
Puerto Princesa, Pil.	116	9.44 N	118.44 E
Puerto Princesa, Pil.	116	10.06 N	125.29 E
Puerto Real, Esp.	34	36.32 N	6.11 W
Puerto Real, P.R.	240m	18.05 N	67.11 W
Puerto Rico, Arg.	252	26.48 S	55.02 W
Puerto Rico, Bol.	248	11.05 S	67.38 W
Puerto Rico, Col.	246	1.54 N	75.10 W
Puerto Rico □[2], N.A.	230	18.15 N	66.30 W
Puerto Rico □[2], N.A.	240m	18.15 N	66.30 W
Puerto Rico Trench ✣[1]	16	20.00 N	66.00 W
Puerto Rondón	246	6.17 N	71.06 W
Puerto Saavedra	252	38.47 S	73.24 W
Puerto Salgar	246	5.28 N	74.39 W
Puerto Sandino	236	12.12 N	86.46 W
Puerto San José	236	13.55 N	90.49 W
Puerto San Julián	254	49.18 S	67.43 W
Puerto Santa Cruz	254	50.01 S	68.31 W
Puerto Sastre	252	22.06 S	57.59 W
Puerto Siles	248	12.48 S	65.05 W
Puerto Suarez	248	18.57 S	57.51 W
Puerto Supe	248	10.49 S	77.45 W
Puerto Tejada	246	3.14 N	76.24 W
Puerto Tolosa	246	0.59 S	74.09 W
Puerto Umbría	246	0.52 N	76.33 W
Puerto Vallarta	234	20.37 N	105.15 W
Puerto Varas	254	41.19 S	72.59 W
Puerto Victoria, Arg.	252	26.20 S	54.39 W
Puerto Victoria, Perú	248	9.54 S	74.58 W
Puerto Viejo, C.R.	236	10.26 N	83.59 W
Puerto Viejo, C.R.	236	9.39 N	82.45 W
Puerto Villamil	246a	0.56 S	91.01 W
Puerto Villamizar	246	8.19 N	72.26 W
Puerto Villarroel	248	16.50 S	64.47 W
Puerto Visser	254	45.24 S	67.08 W
Puerto Wilches	246	7.21 N	73.54 W
Puerto Williams	254	54.56 S	67.37 W
Puerto Ybapobó	252	23.42 S	57.12 W
Pueyrredón, Lago (Lago Cochrane) ⊜	254	47.20 S	72.00 W
Puffendorf	56	50.56 N	6.13 E
Puffing Billy Railroad Station ✦[5]	274b	37.55 S	145.21 E
Pugačov	80	52.01 N	48.50 E
Pugač'ovo	80	56.35 N	53.02 E
Puge, Tan.	154	4.45 S	33.07 E
Puge, Zhg.	102	27.28 N	102.31 E
Puget, Cape ›	180	59.52 N	148.26 W
Puget Island I	224	46.10 N	123.23 W
Puget Sound ⋓	224	47.50 N	122.30 W
Puget Sound Naval Shipyard ▪	224	47.33 N	122.38 W
Puget-sur-Argens	62	43.27 N	6.41 E
Puget-Théniers	62	43.57 N	6.54 E
Puget-Ville	62	43.17 N	6.08 E
Pugh Mountain ∧	224	48.08 N	121.22 W
Pughtown	285	40.10 N	75.40 W
Puglia □[4]	68	41.15 N	16.15 E
Pugong-ni	271b	37.43 N	126.58 E
Pugŏ-ri	98	42.01 N	129.59 E
Pugwash	186	45.51 N	63.40 W
Puhe	104	41.57 N	123.36 E
Puhi	229b	21.58 N	159.23 W
Puhja	76	58.20 N	26.19 E
Puhos	26	62.05 N	29.54 E
Puhosjärvi ⊜	26	65.19 N	27.55 E
Puica	248	15.04 S	72.42 W
Puiești	38	46.25 N	27.33 E
Puigcerdá	34	42.26 N	1.56 E
Puigmal ∧	34	42.23 N	2.07 E
Puimoisson	62	43.52 N	6.08 E
Puinahua, Canal de ≃[1]	248	5.20 S	74.13 W
Puinān	272b	22.56 N	88.13 E
Puir	89	53.10 N	141.25 E
Puisaye, Collines de la ⋏[2]	50	47.40 N	3.15 E
Puiseaux	50	48.12 N	2.28 E
Puiseaux ≃	50	48.00 N	2.44 E
Puiseux-en-France	261	49.04 N	2.29 E
Puiseux-Pontoise	261	49.03 N	2.01 E
Puisieux	50	50.07 N	2.42 E
Puits ≃	50	48.31 N	4.15 E
Pujada Bay c	116	6.51 N	126.14 E
Pujehun	150	7.21 N	11.42 W
Puji, Zhg.	100	27.59 N	113.25 E
Puji, Zhg.	100	29.58 N	112.32 E
Pujiang, Zhg.	100	29.28 N	119.53 E
Pujiang, Zhg.	107	30.12 N	103.30 E
Pujilí	246	0.57 S	78.41 W
Pujon	115a	7.50 S	112.28 E
Pujun	112	1.20 S	114.20 E
Pujut	114	1.25 N	100.39 E
Pujut, Tanjung ›	115a	5.52 S	106.02 E
Pukaki, Lake ⊜	172	44.07 S	170.10 E
Pukalani	229a	20.50 N	156.20 W
Pukaskwa ≃	190	48.00 N	85.53 W
Pukaskwa National Park ◆	190	48.20 N	85.50 W
Pukch'ang	98	39.36 N	126.17 E
Pukchin	98	40.10 N	125.43 E
Pukch'ŏn	98	36.13 N	126.45 E
Pukch'ŏng	98	40.15 N	128.20 E
Pukë	38	42.03 N	19.54 E
Pukeashun Mountain ∧	182	51.12 N	119.14 W
Pukekohe	172	37.12 S	174.55 E
Puketeraki Range ⋏	172	42.58 S	172.12 E
Puketoi Range ⋏	172	40.30 S	176.05 E
Pukeuri Junction	172	45.02 S	171.02 E
Pukhan-gang ≃	98	37.31 N	127.18 E
Pŭkhan-san ∧	271b	37.41 N	127.00 E
Pukhrāyān	124	26.14 N	79.51 E
Pukoo	229d	21.04 N	156.48 W
Pukou, Zhg.	100	26.16 N	119.35 E
Pukou, Zhg.	106	32.07 N	118.43 E
Puksoozero	24	62.38 N	40.36 E
Puksubaek-san ∧	98	40.42 N	127.44 E
Puktae-ch'ŏn ≃	98	40.28 N	129.00 E
Pula, Hrv.	36	44.52 N	13.50 E
Pula, It.	71	39.01 N	9.00 E
Pulacayo	248	20.25 S	66.41 W
Pulandian Wan c	98	39.18 N	121.35 E
Pulanduta Point ›	116	11.54 N	123.10 E
Pulangi ≃	116	7.18 N	124.50 E
Pulangpisau	112	2.46 S	114.14 E
Pulap I[1]	14	7.35 N	149.24 E
Púlar, Cerro ∧	252	24.11 S	68.04 W
Pulaski, In., U.S.	216	40.59 N	86.40 W
Pulaski, Mi., U.S.	216	42.07 N	84.40 W
Pulaski, N.Y., U.S.	212	43.34 N	76.07 W
Pulaski, Oh., U.S.	216	41.30 N	84.26 W
Pulaski, Pa., U.S.	214	41.07 N	80.26 W
Pulaski, Tn., U.S.	194	35.11 N	87.01 W
Pulaski, Va., U.S.	192	37.02 N	80.46 W
Pulaski, Wi., U.S.	190	44.40 N	88.14 W
Pulaski □[6]	216	41.03 N	86.36 W
Pulau ≃	164	5.50 S	138.15 E
Pulaukida	112	2.44 S	102.34 E
Pulaukijang	112	0.42 S	103.12 E
Pulaumerak, Indon.	115a	5.56 S	106.00 E
Pulaumerak, Indon.	115a	5.56 S	106.00 E
Pulauraja	114	2.42 N	99.37 E
Puławy	30	51.25 N	21.57 E
Pulborough	42	50.58 N	0.30 W
Pul'chakim	85	38.10 N	67.21 E
Pulehu Gulch V	229a	20.50 N	156.28 W
Pulfero	64	46.11 N	13.29 E
Pulga	123	31.59 N	77.26 E
Pulgaon	122	20.44 N	78.20 E
Pulham Market	42	52.26 N	1.14 E
Pulheim	56	51.00 N	6.47 E
Puli	100	23.58 N	120.57 E
Pulicat	122	13.25 N	80.19 E
Pulicat Lake c	122	13.40 N	80.10 E
Pulichatum	128	35.57 N	61.07 E
Puliciano	66	43.23 N	11.51 E
Puliyangudi	122	9.10 N	77.25 E
Pulj → Pula	64	44.52 N	13.50 E
Pulkau	61	48.42 N	15.51 E
Pulkau ≃	61	48.43 N	16.21 E
Pulkkila	26	64.16 N	25.52 E
Pulkovo ✦[8]	265a	59.46 N	30.20 E
Pullman, Mi., U.S.	216	42.29 N	86.05 W
Pullman, Wa., U.S.	202	46.43 N	117.10 W
Pullman ✦[8]	278	41.43 N	87.36 W
Púllo	248	15.14 S	73.50 W
Pully	58	46.31 N	6.39 E
Pul'mo	78	51.31 N	23.47 E
Pulo ⊥	68	41.12 N	16.34 E
Pulo Anna I	108	4.40 N	131.58 E
Pulog, Mount ∧	116	16.36 N	120.54 E
Pulogadung ✦[8]	269e	6.11 S	106.54 E
Pulon'ga	24	66.17 N	40.02 E
Púlpito do Sul	152	15.46 S	12.00 E
Pulsano	68	40.23 N	17.22 E
Pulsen	54	51.23 N	13.26 E
Pulsnitz	54	51.11 N	14.01 E
Pulsnitz ≃	54	51.27 N	13.30 E
Pulteney	210	42.31 N	77.10 W
Pultneyville	210	43.17 N	77.11 W
Pułtusk	30	52.43 N	21.05 E
Pulü, Zhg.	107	29.50 N	106.11 E
Pulu, Zhg.	120	36.11 N	81.30 E
Pulupandan	116	10.31 N	122.48 E
Pulur	130	40.10 N	39.53 E
Pulusuk I	14	6.42 N	149.19 E
Pulversheim	58	47.51 N	7.18 E
Puma Yumco ⊜	124	28.35 N	90.20 E
Pumbi	152	3.26 N	22.11 E
Pumei	102	23.28 N	105.15 E
Pumphrey	284b	39.13 N	76.38 W
Pumpkin Buttes ∧	200	43.44 N	105.54 W
Pumpkin Center	228	35.18 N	119.05 W
Pumpkin Creek ≃, Mt., U.S.	198	46.15 N	105.45 W
Pumpkin Creek ≃, Ne., U.S.	198	41.38 N	103.01 W
Pumsaint	42	52.03 N	3.58 W
Pumsi	80	57.12 N	51.39 E
Puná, Isla I	246	2.50 S	80.08 W
Punaauia	174s	17.38 S	149.36 W
Punaauia, Pointe de ›	174s	17.38 S	149.36 W
Punakha	124	27.37 N	89.52 E
Punaluu	229c	21.35 N	157.53 W
Punan, Indon.	112	1.20 N	115.34 E
Punan, Indon.	112	3.24 N	116.16 E
Punan, Zhg.	100	24.39 N	117.41 E
Punata	248	17.32 S	65.50 W
Pūnch	123	33.46 N	74.06 E
Pūnch ≃	123	33.12 N	73.40 E
Puncha	126	23.10 N	86.39 E
Punchaw	182	53.28 N	123.13 W
Punchbowl	274a	33.56 S	151.03 E
Pundaguitan	116	6.22 N	126.10 E
Punda Maria	156	22.40 S	31.05 E
Pünderich	56	50.02 N	7.08 E
Pūndri	124	29.45 N	76.33 E
Punduga	76	60.08 N	40.12 E
Pune (Poona)	122	18.32 N	73.52 E
P'ungam-ni	98	37.43 N	128.11 E
Pungan	85	40.45 N	70.49 E
Punganūru	122	13.22 N	78.35 E
Pungarancho ≃	234	18.47 N	100.41 W
Pungești	38	46.42 N	27.20 E
Punggol	271c	1.25 N	103.55 E
Punggol ≃	271c	1.25 N	103.54 E
Pungki	114	4.17 N	96.13 E
Pungo ≃	192	35.23 N	76.33 W
Pungo Andongo	152	9.40 S	15.35 E
Púngoè ≃	154	19.50 S	34.48 E
P'ungsan, C.M.I.K.	98	40.47 N	128.10 E
P'ungsan, C.M.I.K.	98	38.28 N	125.01 E
P'ungsong-ni	98	39.56 N	127.11 E
Punia	154	1.28 S	26.27 E
Punilla, Sierra de la ⋏	252	28.55 S	69.00 W
Puning	100	23.18 N	116.12 E
Punitaqui	252	30.50 S	71.16 W
Punjab □[3]	123	31.00 N	75.30 E
Punjab □[4]	120	31.00 N	72.00 E
Punkaharju ◆	26	61.47 N	29.20 E
Punkalaidun	26	61.07 N	23.06 E
Punnichy	184	51.23 N	104.18 W
Puno	248	15.50 S	70.02 W
Puno □[5]	248	15.00 S	70.00 W
Punta, Castillo de la ⊥	286b	23.09 N	82.21 W
Punta, Cerro de ∧	240m	18.10 N	66.36 W
Punta Alegre	240p	22.23 N	78.49 W
Punta Alta	254	38.53 S	62.05 W
Punta Arenas	254	53.09 S	70.55 W
Punta Banda, Cabo ›	232	31.45 N	116.45 W
Punta Brava ✦[8]	286b	23.01 N	82.30 W
Punta Cardón	246	11.38 N	70.14 W
Punta Colnett	232	31.05 N	116.05 W
Punta de Agua Creek (Tramperos Creek) ≃	196	35.32 N	102.27 W
Punta de Bombón	248	17.11 S	71.48 W
Punta de Díaz	252	28.03 S	70.37 W
Punta del Cobre	252	27.30 S	70.16 W
Punta del Este	252	34.58 S	54.57 W
Punta Delgada	254	42.46 S	63.38 W
Punta de los Llanos	252	30.09 S	66.33 W
Punta de Mata	246	9.43 N	63.38 W
Punta de Piedras	246	10.54 N	64.06 W
Punta Flecha	116	7.23 N	123.25 E
Punta Gorda, Belize	232	16.07 N	88.48 W
Punta Gorda, Nic.	236	11.31 N	83.47 W
Punta Gorda, Fl., U.S.	220	26.55 N	82.02 W
Punta Gorda ≃	236	11.30 N	83.47 W
Punta Gorda, Bahía de c	236	11.15 N	83.45 W
Punta Negra, Salar de ⩸	252	24.35 S	69.00 W
Punta Prieta	232	28.58 N	114.17 W
Punta Raisi, Aeroporto di ⊠	70	38.11 N	13.06 E
Puntarenas	236	9.58 N	84.50 W
Puntarenas □[4]	236	9.00 N	83.15 W
Punta Santiago	240m	18.10 N	65.45 W
Puntas del Sauce	258	33.51 S	57.01 W
Punto Fijo	246	11.42 N	70.13 W
Puntzi Lake ⊜	182	52.12 N	124.02 W
Punung	115a	8.08 S	111.01 E
Punxsutawney	214	40.56 N	78.58 W
Puolanka	26	64.52 N	27.40 E
Puolo Point ›	229b	21.54 N	159.36 W
Puper	164	0.10 S	131.18 E
Pup'yŏng	271b	37.30 N	126.43 E
Puqi, Zhg.	100	28.11 N	121.01 E
Puqi, Zhg.	100	29.43 N	113.53 E
Puqian, Zhg.	100	23.34 N	114.38 E
Puqian, Zhg.	102	20.03 N	110.36 E
Puquio	248	14.42 S	74.08 W
Pur ≃	74	67.31 N	77.55 E
Purabiya Plain ⩸	124	25.50 N	82.30 E
Puracé, Volcán ∧[1]	246	2.21 N	76.23 W
Purandarpur	126	23.51 N	87.36 E
Pūranpur	124	28.31 N	80.09 E
Purari ≃	164	7.25 S	145.05 E
Purba	114	2.54 N	98.42 E
Purbashthāli	126	23.28 N	88.21 E
Purbeck, Isle of I	42	50.38 N	2.00 W
Purbolinggo	115a	7.24 S	109.22 E
Purcell	196	35.00 N	97.21 W
Purcell Mountains ⋏	182	50.00 N	116.30 W
Purcellville	188	39.08 N	77.42 W
Purchase	276	41.02 N	73.43 W
Purchena	34	37.21 N	2.22 W
Purdon	222	31.57 N	96.37 W
Purdoški	80	54.40 N	43.32 E
Purdy	194	36.49 N	93.55 W
Purech	80	56.39 N	43.05 E
Pureora ∧	172	38.33 S	175.38 E
Purépero	234	19.55 N	102.01 W
Purfleet	42	51.29 N	0.15 E
Purga	171a	27.43 S	152.44 E
Purga Creek ≃	171a	27.42 S	152.45 E
Purgatoire ≃	198	38.04 N	103.10 W
Purgatory Brook ≃	283	42.11 N	71.11 W
Pürgg	61	47.32 N	14.04 E
Purgstall an der Erlauf	61	48.03 N	15.08 E
Puri	120	19.48 N	85.51 E
Purial, Sierra del ⋏	240p	20.12 N	74.42 W
Purificación, Col.	246	3.51 N	74.55 W
Purificación, Méx.	234	19.43 N	104.38 W
Purificación ≃, Méx.	232	23.58 N	98.42 W
Purificación ≃, Méx.	234	19.18 N	104.54 W
Purikari neem ›	76	59.40 N	25.43 E
Purísima	196	29.09 N	100.46 W
Purísima, Sierra de la ⋏	196	26.30 N	101.44 W
Purisima Creek ≃	282	37.24 N	122.26 W
Purísima de Bustos	234	21.02 N	101.52 W
Purkersdorf	61	48.12 N	16.11 E
Purleigh	260	51.41 N	0.40 E
Purley	222	33.05 N	95.16 W
Purley ✦[8]	260	51.20 N	0.07 W
Purling	210	42.17 N	74.00 W
Purmerend	52	52.31 N	4.57 E
Pūrna ≃, India	122	19.07 N	77.02 E
Pūrna ≃, India	122	21.05 N	76.00 E
Pūrnia	124	25.47 N	87.31 E
Puronga	76	60.09 N	40.54 E
Purranque	254	40.55 S	73.10 W
Purrorumba Hill ∧	171b	35.10 S	149.23 E
Purros	156	18.38 S	12.59 E
Purrumbete, Lake ⊜	169	38.17 S	143.14 E
Pursat → Poŭthĭsăt	110	12.32 N	103.55 E
Purton	42	51.36 N	1.52 W
Puruándiro	234	20.05 N	101.30 W
Puruarán	234	19.06 N	101.32 W
Puruí ≃	246	1.40 S	68.08 W
Purukcahu	112	0.35 S	114.35 E
Puruliya	126	23.20 N	86.22 E
Puruni ≃	246	6.00 N	59.12 W
Purus (Purús) ≃	242	3.42 S	61.28 W
Puruvesi ⊜	26	61.50 N	29.27 E
Purvis	194	31.08 N	89.24 W
Purwakarta	115a	6.34 S	107.26 E
Purwantoro	115a	7.51 S	111.15 E
Purwareja	115a	7.28 S	109.25 E
Purwodadi, Indon.	115a	7.49 S	110.00 E
Purwodadi, Indon.	115a	7.05 S	110.54 E
Purwokerto	115a	7.25 S	109.14 E
Purworejo	115a	7.43 S	110.01 E
Pusa	112	1.36 N	111.17 E
Pusad	122	19.54 N	77.35 E
Pusan	98	35.06 N	129.03 E
Pusan □[4]	98	35.10 N	129.05 E
Pūsa Road	124	25.59 N	85.41 E
Pusat Gayo, Pegunungan ⋏	114	4.15 N	97.05 E
Puščino	82	54.50 N	37.36 E
Pusgo Point ›	116	13.31 N	122.38 E
Pushang	98	36.08 N	119.42 E
Pushkar	120	26.30 N	74.33 E
Pushkin Airport ⊠	265a	59.41 N	30.21 E
Pushkin Drama Theatre ✿	265a	59.56 N	30.21 E
Pushkin → Puškin	76	59.43 N	30.25 E
Pushthrough	186	47.39 N	56.10 W
Puškar'ovka	78	48.40 N	34.16 E
Puskiakiwenin Indian Reserve ✦[4]	184	53.57 N	110.26 W
Puškin	76	59.43 N	30.25 E
Puškino, Azer.	84	39.27 N	48.33 E
Puškino, Ross.	80	51.14 N	46.59 E
Puškino, Ross.	82	56.01 N	37.51 E
Puškino, Ross.	82	56.36 N	35.46 E
Puškinskij	265a	59.43 N	30.18 E
Puškinskije Gory	76	57.01 N	28.54 E
Puskwaskau ≃	182	55.29 N	118.10 W
Puslinch Lake ⊜	212	43.25 N	80.16 W
Pusŏng-ni	98	40.19 N	127.19 E
Püspökladány	30	47.19 N	21.07 E
Pussay	50	48.21 N	2.00 E
Püssi	76	59.24 N	27.01 E
Pustertal V	64	46.45 N	12.20 E
Pustin'	76	59.54 N	35.32 E
Pustomyty	78	49.42 N	23.56 E
Pustoš'	76	60.07 N	42.45 E
Pustoška	76	56.20 N	29.22 E
Pustozersk	24	67.33 N	52.27 E
Pusur ≃[1]	126	21.45 N	89.30 E
Puszczykowo	30	52.17 N	16.52 E
Putaendo	252	32.38 S	70.44 W
Putah Creek ≃	226	38.33 N	121.42 W
Putai	100	23.23 N	120.09 E
Putana, Volcán ∧[1]	252	22.43 S	67.54 W
Putang ≃	269e	6.13 S	106.54 E
Putangqiao	106	31.34 N	118.59 E
Putao	102	27.21 N	97.24 E
Putaruru	172	38.03 S	175.47 E
Put'atin	89	42.52 N	132.25 E
Put'atino	80	54.10 N	41.07 E
Putbus	54	54.21 N	13.28 E
Puteaux	261	48.53 N	2.14 E
Puteran, Pulau I	115a	7.05 S	114.00 E
Putfontein Landbouhoewes	273d	26.08 S	28.24 E
Putgarten	54	54.40 N	13.25 E
Puth Kalān ✦[8]	272a	28.43 N	77.05 E
Putian, Zhg.	100	25.26 N	119.01 E
Putian, Zhg.	100	29.16 N	114.58 E
Putifigari	71	40.34 N	8.27 E
Putignano	68	40.51 N	17.07 E
Putila	78	48.01 N	25.03 E
Putilkovo	265b	55.52 N	37.23 E
Putina	248	14.55 S	69.52 W
Put-in-Bay	214	41.39 N	82.49 W
Putincevo	86	49.50 N	84.22 E
Puting, Tanjung ›	112	3.31 S	111.46 E
Putivl'	78	51.21 N	33.52 E
Putla de Guerrero	234	17.02 N	97.56 W
Putlitz	54	53.15 N	12.02 E
Putnam, Ct., U.S.	207	41.54 N	71.54 W
Putnam, Tx., U.S.	196	32.22 N	99.12 W
Putnam □[6], N.Y., U.S.	210	41.26 N	73.41 W
Putnam □[6], Oh., U.S.	216	41.01 N	84.03 W
Putnam Lake	210	41.28 N	73.35 W
Putnam Lake ⊜	276	41.05 N	73.38 W
Putnam Valley	210	41.20 N	73.52 W
Putnamville Reservoir ⊜[1]	283	42.36 N	70.57 W
Putney, Ga., U.S.	192	31.29 N	84.07 W
Putney, Vt., U.S.	188	42.58 N	72.31 W
Putney ✦[8]	260	51.28 N	0.13 W
Putney Island I	126	21.42 N	89.20 E
Puto	175e	5.41 S	154.43 E
Putorana, plato ⋏[1]	74	69.00 N	95.00 E
Putorino	172	39.08 S	177.00 E
Putre	248	18.12 S	69.35 W
Putri Narrows ⋓	271c	1.27 N	103.42 E
Putsonderwater	158	29.09 S	21.51 E
Pütt	263	51.11 N	6.59 E
Puttalam	122	8.02 N	79.49 E
Puttalam Lagoon c	122	8.07 N	79.47 E
Putte, Bel.	56	51.04 N	4.38 E
Putte, Ned.	52	51.22 N	4.23 E
Puttelange-lès-Farschviller	56	49.03 N	6.56 E
Putten	52	52.15 N	5.36 E
Putten I	52	51.50 N	4.15 E
Puttgarden	41	54.30 N	11.13 E
Püttlingen	56	49.17 N	6.53 E
Puttūr	122	13.27 N	79.33 E
Putty	170	32.57 S	150.40 E
Putty Creek ≃	170	33.05 S	150.37 E
Putú	252	35.13 S	72.17 W
Putumayo □[8]	246	0.30 N	76.00 W
Putumayo (Içá) ≃	246	3.07 S	67.58 W
Putuo	100	29.58 N	122.17 E
Putu Range ⋏	150	5.30 N	8.10 W
Pütürge	130	38.12 N	38.53 E
Putussibau	112	0.50 N	112.56 E
Putzkau	54	51.06 N	14.13 E
Putzu Idu	71	40.02 N	8.25 E
Pu'uhonua o Honaunau National Historical Park ◆	229d	19.25 N	155.54 W
Puu Kaaumakua ∧	229c	21.30 N	157.54 W
Puu Keahiakahoe ∧	229c	21.23 N	157.49 W
Puukohola Heiau National Historic Site ⊥	229d	20.00 N	155.46 W
Puukolii	229a	20.56 N	156.40 W
Puu Kukui ∧	229a	20.52 N	156.35 W
Puula ⊜	26	61.50 N	26.42 E
Puumala	26	61.32 N	28.11 E
Puunene	229a	20.51 N	156.27 W
Pu'upu'a	175a	13.34 S	172.09 W
Puurmani	76	58.34 N	26.17 E
Puurs	50	51.05 N	4.17 E
Puuwai	229b	21.54 N	160.12 W
Puxi	100	25.10 N	119.08 E
Puxian	102	36.30 N	111.02 E
Puxico	194	36.56 N	90.09 W
Puxingchang	107	30.41 N	105.06 E
Puyallup	224	47.11 N	122.17 W
Puyallup ≃	224	47.15 N	122.24 W
Puyang	98	35.42 N	114.59 E
Puyang ≃	100	30.05 N	120.11 E
Puyango (Tumbes) ≃	246	3.30 S	80.27 W
Puy-de-Dôme □[5]	32	45.45 N	3.05 E
Puyehue	254	40.40 S	72.37 W
Puyehue, Volcán ∧[1]	254	40.35 S	72.08 W
Puylaurens	32	43.34 N	2.01 E
Puy-l'Évêque	32	44.30 N	1.08 E
Puyloubier	62	43.31 N	5.41 E
Puymorens, Col de)(	32	42.30 N	1.50 E
Puyo, Ec.	246	1.28 S	77.59 W
Puyŏ, Taehan	98	36.18 N	126.54 E
Puysegur Point ›	172	46.09 S	166.36 E
Puyuan	106	30.41 N	120.38 E
Puyuguapi, Canal ⋓	254	44.45 S	72.48 W
Puyun-dong	98	41.55 N	129.30 E
Pūzak, Hāmūn-e ⊜	128	31.30 N	61.45 E
Puzhen	106	32.09 N	118.41 E
Puzzle Creek ≃	162	17.58 S	135.41 E
Puzzle Lake ⊜, On., Can.	212	44.36 N	76.58 W
Puzzle Lake ⊜, Fl., U.S.	220	28.41 N	81.02 W
Pwalagu	150	10.35 N	0.50 W
Pwani □[4]	154	7.00 S	39.00 E
Pweto	154	8.28 S	28.54 E
Pwinbyu	110	20.22 N	94.40 E
Pwllheli	42	52.53 N	4.25 W
Pyalo	110	19.09 N	95.11 E
Pyalong	169	37.07 S	144.54 E
Pyamalaw ≃[1]	110	15.49 N	94.42 E
Pyapon	110	16.17 N	95.41 E
Pyatigorsk → P'atigorsk	84	44.03 N	43.04 E
Pyawbwe	110	20.35 N	96.04 E
Pyaye	110	19.15 N	95.06 E
Pyčas	80	56.29 N	52.28 E
Pye Islands II	180	59.22 N	150.25 W
Pygmalion Point ›	110	6.45 N	93.49 E
Pyhäjärvi ⊜, Europe	26	61.53 N	30.00 E
Pyhäjärvi ⊜, Suomi	26	63.35 N	25.57 E
Pyhäjärvi ⊜, Suomi	26	62.46 N	25.30 E
Pyhäjärvi ⊜, Suomi	26	61.28 N	23.35 E
Pyhäjärvi ⊜, Suomi	26	61.00 N	22.18 E
Pyhäjoki	26	64.28 N	24.14 E
Pyhäjoki ≃	26	64.28 N	24.13 E
Pyhämaa I	26	60.57 N	21.20 E
Pyhän-Häkin kansallispuisto ◆	26	62.52 N	25.30 E
Pyhäsalmi	26	63.41 N	25.59 E
Pyhäselkä	26	62.26 N	29.58 E
Pyhäselkä ⊜	26	62.26 N	29.58 E
Pyhätunturi ∧	24	67.01 N	27.09 E
Pyhätunturin kansallispuisto ◆	24	67.01 N	27.10 E
Pyhra	61	48.10 N	15.41 E
Pyhtää (Pyttis)	26	60.29 N	26.32 E
Pyinbongyi	110	17.34 N	96.34 E
Pyingaing	110	23.09 N	94.51 E
Pyinkayaing	110	15.58 N	94.24 E

≃	River	Fluß	Río	Rivière	Rio
≊	Canal	Kanal	Canal	Canal	Canal
⌊	Waterfall, Rapids	Wasserfall, Stromschnellen	Cascada, Rápidos	Chute d'eau, Rapides	Cascata, Rápidos
⋓	Strait	Meeresstraße	Estrecho	Détroit	Estreito
c	Bay, Gulf	Bucht, Golf	Bahía, Golfo	Baie, Golfe	Baía, Golfo
⊜	Lake, Lakes	See, Seen	Lago, Lagos	Lac, Lacs	Lago, Lagos
⩸	Swamp	Sumpf	Pantano	Marais	Pântano
⊓	Ice Features, Glacier	Eis- und Gletscherformen	Accidentes Glaciales	Formes glaciaires	Acidentes glaciares
⫪	Other Hydrographic Features	Andere Hydrographische Objekte	Otros Elementos Hidrográficos	Autres données hydrographiques	Outros acidentes hidrográficos
✣	Submarine Features	Untermeerische Objekte	Accidentes Submarinos	Formes de relief sous-marin	Acidentes submarinos
□	Political Unit	Politische Einheit	Unidad Politica	Entité politique	Unidade política
✿	Cultural Institution	Kulturelle Institution	Institución Cultural	Institution culturelle	Institução cultural
⊥	Historical Site	Historische Stätte	Sitio Histórico	Site historique	Sitio histórico
◆	Recreational Site	Erholungs- und Ferienort	Sitio de Recreo	Centre de loisirs	Area de Lazer
⊠	Airport	Flughafen	Aeropuerto	Aéroport	Aeroporto
▪	Military Installation	Militäranlage	Instalación Militar	Installation militaire	Instalação militar
✦	Miscellaneous	Verschiedenes	Misceláneo	Divers	Diversos

ENGLISH / DEUTSCH

Name	Page	Lat.°′	Long.°′
Pyinmana	110	19.44 N	96.13 E
Pyle	42	51.32 N	3.42 W
Pylos → Pílos	38	36.55 N	21.43 E
Pymatuning Creek ≃	214	41.18 N	80.27 W
Pymatuning Reservoir ⊜[1]	214	41.37 N	80.30 W
Pymatuning State Park ♦, Oh., U.S.	214	41.38 N	80.33 W
Pymatuning State Park ♦, Pa., U.S.	214	41.30 N	80.27 W
Pymble	274a	33.45 S	151.09 E
Pyngopil'gyn, laguna ⊂	180	67.24 N	175.10 W
Pyŏktong	98	40.35 N	125.20 E
Pyŏlch'ang-ni	98	39.17 N	126.26 E
P'yŏngan Namdo □[4]	98	39.20 N	126.00 E
P'yŏngan Pukdo □[4]	98	40.10 N	125.20 E
P'yŏngch'ang	98	37.23 N	128.22 E
P'yŏngdong-ni	98	37.10 N	128.02 E
P'yŏnggang	98	38.26 N	127.16 E
P'yonghae	98	36.46 N	129.28 E
P'yŏngsan	98	38.19 N	126.23 E
P'yŏngt'aek	98	37.00 N	127.05 E
P'yŏngyang	98	39.01 N	125.45 E
P'yŏngyang □[4]	98	39.05 N	125.50 E
Pyŏrha-ri	98	40.48 N	126.32 E
Pyote	196	31.32 N	103.08 W
Pyramid Head ›	228	32.49 N	118.21 W
Pyramid Lake ⊜	204	40.00 N	119.35 W
Pyramid Lake ⊜[1]	228	34.39 N	118.47 W
Pyramid Lake Indian Reservation ◆[4]	204	40.20 N	119.35 W
Pyramid Peak ∧, Ca., U.S.	226	38.50 N	120.19 W
Pyramid Peak ∧, Wa., U.S.	224	47.07 N	121.24 W
Pyramid Peak ∧, Wy., U.S.	200	43.27 N	110.28 W
Pyramid Point ›	174h	2.52 S	171.37 W
Pyramids of Giza → Jīzah, Ahrāmāt al- ⊥	142	29.59 N	31.08 E
Pyrenäen → Pyrenees ⋆	34	42.40 N	1.00 E
Pyrenees ⋆	34	42.40 N	1.00 E
Pyrénées-Atlantiques □[5]	32	43.15 N	0.50 W
Pyrénées Occident, Parc National des ♦	32	42.48 N	0.08 W
Pyrénées-Orientales □[5]	32	42.30 N	2.20 E
Pyre Peak ∧	180	52.20 N	172.31 W
Pyrford	260	51.19 N	0.30 W
Pyrgi ⊥	66	42.01 N	11.58 E
Pyrgos → Pírgos	38	37.41 N	21.28 E
Pyrkanajjan, gora ∧	180	69.14 N	175.50 E
Pyrkino	80	53.29 N	45.07 E
Pyrmont	216	40.28 N	86.41 W
Pyrzyce	30	53.10 N	14.55 E
Pyšma	86	56.56 N	63.13 E
Pyšma ≃	86	57.08 N	66.18 E
Pytalovo	76	57.04 N	27.56 E
Pythonga, Lac ⊜	190	46.23 N	76.25 W
Pyu	110	18.29 N	96.26 E
Pyuntaza	110	17.52 N	96.44 E
Pyūthān	124	28.06 N	82.54 E
Pyvésa ≃	76	56.06 N	24.27 E
Pyzdry	30	52.11 N	17.41 E
Q			
Qabāṭīyah	132	32.25 N	35.17 E
Qabbāsīn	130	36.25 N	37.34 E
Qabb Ilyās	132	33.48 N	35.49 E
Qabr Hūd	144	16.08 N	49.37 E
Qacentina (Constantine)	148	36.22 N	6.37 E
Qacentina □[5]	148	36.20 N	6.40 E
Qaddīs Anṭūn, Dayr al- (Monastery of Saint Anthony) ʊ[1]	142	28.55 N	32.21 E
Qaddīs Būlus, Dayr al- (Monastery of Saint Paul) ʊ[1]	142	28.52 N	32.33 E
Qāderābād	128	30.17 N	53.16 E
Qādiān	123	31.49 N	75.23 E
Qā'emshahr	128	36.28 N	52.53 E
Qā'en	128	33.44 N	59.11 E
Qāfilah	142	31.04 N	30.16 E
Qagan	88	49.14 N	118.08 E
Qagan Nur ⊜, Zhg.	98	41.23 N	113.55 E
Qagan Nur ⊜, Zhg.	102	43.37 N	114.40 E
Qahā	142	30.17 N	31.12 E
Qahar Youyi Zhongqi	102	41.09 N	112.38 E
Qahbûna	142	30.48 N	31.54 E
Qaidam ≃	102	36.39 N	96.20 E
Qaidam Pendi ≚[1]	120	37.00 N	95.00 E
Qakar	120	36.32 N	80.43 E
Qala' an-Naḥl	140	13.38 N	34.57 E
Qalabshū	142	31.26 N	31.19 E
Qalamshāh	142	29.10 N	30.50 E
Qalandīyah	132	31.50 N	35.14 E
Qalandūl	142	27.49 N	30.50 E
Qalāt	120	32.07 N	66.54 E
Qal'at ash-Shaqīf (Beaufort Castle) ⊥	132	33.19 N	35.32 E
Qal'at Bīshah	144	20.01 N	42.36 E
Qal'at Ṣāliḥ	128	31.31 N	47.16 E
Qal'at Sukkar	128	31.51 N	46.05 E
Qal'eh Shahr	120	35.33 N	65.34 E
Qal'eh-ye Deh-e Bārez	128	27.26 N	57.12 E
Qal'eh-ye Now, Afg.	120	35.27 N	67.08 E
Qal'eh-ye Now, Afg.	128	34.59 N	63.08 E
Qal'eh-ye Panjeh	123	37.00 N	72.36 E
Qal'eh-ye Sarkārī	120	35.54 N	67.17 E
Qallābāt, Sūd.	140	12.43 N	23.26 E
Qallābāt, Sūd.	140	12.58 N	36.09 E
Qallīn	142	31.03 N	30.51 E
Qalqīlīya	132	32.11 N	34.58 E
Qalyūb	142	30.11 N	31.12 E
Qamar, Ghubbat al- ⊂	118	16.00 N	52.30 E
Qamata	158	32.00 S	27.21 E
Qamdo	102	31.11 N	97.15 E
Qamīnis	146	31.39 N	20.03 E
Qamr-ud-dīn Kārez	120	31.39 N	68.25 E
Qamṣar	128	33.45 N	51.26 E
Qanā, Ar. Su.	128	27.47 N	41.25 E
Qānā, Lubnān	132	33.13 N	35.18 E
Qanāyah	132	33.01 N	36.11 E
Qandahār	120	31.32 N	65.30 E
Qandahār □[4]	120	31.00 N	65.45 E
Qandala	144	11.28 N	49.52 E
Qanṭarah, Jabal ∧[2]	142	30.09 N	30.15 E
Qantur	140	9.45 N	25.52 E
Qārah, Ar. Su.	128	29.52 N	40.15 E
Qārah, Sūrīy.	130	34.09 N	36.44 E
Qarah Bāgh	128	34.56 N	61.46 E
Qarak	85	38.23 N	76.58 E
Qarāvol	120	37.14 N	68.46 E
Qardho	144	9.30 N	49.05 E
Qareh ≃	128	34.52 N	51.25 E
Qareh Sū ≃	128	39.27 N	47.23 E
Qareh Ẕīā' od Dīn	84	38.54 N	45.02 E
Qarqan ≃	90	39.25 N	88.20 E
Qarqīn	120	37.25 N	66.03 E
Qarṭabā	130	34.06 N	35.51 E
Qārūn, Birkat (Lake Moeris) ⊜	142	29.28 N	30.40 E
Qaryat al-Qaddāḥīyah	146	31.22 N	15.14 E
Qaryat al-Zuwaytīnah	146	30.58 N	20.07 E
Qaṣa-e Qand	128	26.12 N	60.45 E
Qāsh, Nahr al- (Gash) ≃	140	16.48 N	35.51 E
Qashqeh, Kūh-e ∧	128	28.23 N	55.18 E
Qāsim	132	32.59 N	36.05 E
Qāsimwāla	123	30.09 N	73.50 E
Qaṣr ad-Dayr, Jabal ∧	132	30.48 N	35.34 E
Qaṣr al-Azraq ⊥	132	31.53 N	36.49 E
Qasr al-Dubārā (Garden City) ◆[8]	273c	30.02 N	31.14 E
Qaṣr al-Farāfirah	140	27.03 N	27.58 E
Qaṣr al-Jibālī	142	29.20 N	30.38 E
Qaṣr al-Kharānah ⊥	132	31.44 N	36.28 E
Qaṣr al-Mushāsh ⊥	132	31.49 N	36.19 E
Qaṣr al-Mushattā ⊥	132	31.44 N	36.01 E
Qaṣr al Qarābūllī	146	32.45 N	13.43 E
Qaṣr 'Amrah ⊥	132	31.48 N	36.35 E
Qaṣr aṭ-Ṭūbah ⊥	132	31.20 N	36.34 E
Qaṣr Baghdād	142	30.44 N	30.53 E
Qaṣr Bū-Hādī	146	31.03 N	16.40 E
Qaṣr Ḍab'ah ⊥	132	31.36 N	36.03 E
Qaṣr-e Fīrūzeh	267d	35.40 N	51.32 E
Qasr el-Boukhari	148	35.51 N	2.52 E
Qaṣr-e Shīrīn	128	34.31 N	45.35 E
Qaṣr Qārūn	142	29.25 N	30.25 E
Qa'ṭabah	144	13.51 N	44.42 E
Qaṭanā	132	33.26 N	36.05 E
Qatar (Qaṭar) □[1], Asia	118	25.00 N	51.10 E
Qatar (Qaṭar) □[1], Asia	128	25.00 N	51.10 E
Qaṭia, Bi'r ⊤[4]	142	30.58 N	32.45 E
Qaṭmah	130	36.36 N	36.57 E
Qaṭrānī, Jabal ∧[2]	142	29.41 N	30.35 E
Qattāntyah, Ghurd al- ⩡[8]	142	29.50 N	30.17 E
Qattara Depression → Qaṭṭārah, Munkhafaḍ al- ⩡[7]	140	30.00 N	27.30 E
Qaṭṭārah, Munkhafaḍ al- (Qattara Depression) ⩡[7]	140	30.00 N	27.30 E
Qaṭṭīnah, Buḥayrat ⊜[1]	130	34.39 N	36.34 E
Qawz Rajab	140	16.04 N	35.34 E
Qāy	142	29.09 N	30.57 E
Qayṭah	132	33.04 N	36.08 E
Qāzigund	123	33.38 N	75.09 E
Qazvīn	128	36.16 N	50.00 E
Qeh	102	42.18 N	100.59 E
Qena → Qinā	140	26.10 N	32.43 E
Qeqertaq I	176	71.55 N	55.30 W
Qesari, Ḥorbat (Cæsarea) ⊥	132	32.30 N	34.53 E
Qeshm	128	26.58 N	56.16 E
Qeshm, Jazīreh-ye I	128	26.45 N	55.45 E
Qetura	132	29.58 N	35.03 E
Qeydār	128	36.07 N	48.35 E
Qeyṣār	120	35.41 N	64.17 E
Qezel Owzan ≃	128	36.45 N	49.22 E
Qezel Qeshlāq	84	39.08 N	45.21 E
Qi ≃, Zhg.	98	35.30 N	114.17 E
Qi ≃, Zhg.	100	30.09 N	115.20 E
Qi ≃, Zhg.	107	30.38 N	105.26 E
Qi ≃, Zhg.	107	29.15 N	106.24 E
Qiakemake	85	40.05 N	75.24 E
Qian ≃	102	23.25 N	110.10 E
Qian'an, Zhg.	89	45.00 N	124.01 E
Qian'an, Zhg.	98	39.59 N	118.40 E
Qiancaijiatun	104	41.14 N	121.38 E
Qiandiwu	105	39.16 N	116.38 E
Qiandong	100	23.41 N	116.55 E
Qiandun	106	31.16 N	121.00 E
Qianertaizi	104	42.04 N	122.42 E
Qianfang	100	28.32 N	116.13 E
Qian Gorlos	89	45.08 N	124.47 E
Qiangzilu	105	40.26 N	117.13 E
Qianhonghepu	104	41.23 N	123.07 E
Qianhuang	106	31.36 N	119.58 E
Qianji	100	33.55 N	118.56 E
Qianjiadian	89	43.42 N	122.35 E
Qianjiang, Zhg.	100	30.25 N	112.51 E
Qianjiang, Zhg.	102	23.37 N	109.00 E
Qianjian'gangzi	104	41.34 N	122.26 E
Qianjiangtai	104	41.46 N	122.03 E
Qianjiaqiao	106	30.53 N	121.31 E
Qianjiaying	105	39.35 N	118.21 E
Qianjiazhuang	106	32.16 N	120.17 E
Qianjing	106	31.33 N	121.15 E
Qianjinmiao	100	25.09 N	118.20 E
Qiankeng	106	30.43 N	119.47 E
Qiankoutou	105	39.42 N	117.01 E
Qianlijiazhuang	105	39.25 N	118.17 E
Qianluanshanzi	104	42.17 N	122.27 E
Qianmajiagushanzi	104	42.23 N	123.33 E
Qianmintun	104	41.49 N	123.15 E
Qianning	102	30.30 N	101.31 E
Qianpai	102	22.22 N	111.11 E
Qianqi	100	27.20 N	120.20 E
Qianqianjianglugou	104	41.59 N	120.58 E
Qiansandaoliangzi	104	42.06 N	120.44 E
Qianshahezi	104	41.46 N	123.01 E
Qianshan, Zhg.	100	30.38 N	116.33 E
Qianshan, Zhg.	106	31.06 N	120.24 E
Qian Shan ⋆	104	40.52 N	123.25 E
Qianshuangshanzi	104	41.22 N	121.13 E
Qiansuo	100	28.44 N	121.27 E
Qiantang ≃	106	30.23 N	120.33 E
Qiantangzhen	107	30.12 N	106.18 E
Qianwei, Zhg.	98	40.12 N	120.06 E
Qianwei, Zhg.	107	29.12 N	103.57 E
Qianxi, Zhg.	102	26.57 N	106.00 E
Qianxi, Zhg.	105	40.09 N	118.19 E
Qianxiatazi	104	42.23 N	123.53 E
Qianyamen	104	42.04 N	121.26 E
Qianyang	102	27.11 N	110.04 E
Qianyaopu	104	42.02 N	123.37 E
Qi'anzhen	106	32.11 N	121.03 E
Qianzhou	106	31.42 N	120.13 E
Qiaodun	100	27.29 N	120.18 E
Qiaoershan ⋆	102	31.48 N	99.10 E
Qiaogou	100	32.26 N	115.45 E
Qiaohengjin	102	29.30 N	99.50 E
Qiaojia	102	26.57 N	102.52 E
Qiaojiang	269b	31.15 N	121.19 E
Qiaokou	100	25.55 N	113.10 E
Qiaolima	120	34.35 N	81.00 E
Qiaolin	100	31.57 N	118.32 E
Qiaomu	98	39.34 N	114.27 E
Qiaopurikebazha	85	38.48 N	76.19 E
Qiaoqi	106	31.49 N	120.18 E
Qiaoshe	100	28.48 N	115.58 E
Qiaosi	106	30.21 N	120.18 E
Qiaotou, Zhg.	100	33.05 N	112.46 E
Qiaotou, Zhg.	102	28.17 N	99.22 E
Qiaotou, Zhg.	104	41.13 N	123.44 E
Qiaotou, Zhg.	106	32.11 N	119.14 E
Qiaotou, Zhg.	107	29.18 N	104.39 E
Qiaotoucun	106	30.36 N	119.08 E
Qiaotouji	100	31.45 N	117.34 E
Qiaotoupu	106	30.33 N	118.50 E
Qiaotouyi	100	28.24 N	112.58 E
Qiaotouzhen	106	30.49 N	119.13 E
Qiaowan	102	40.36 N	96.55 E
Qiaowei	102	22.51 N	109.50 E
Qiaoxia	106	31.09 N	119.35 E
Qiaoxiajie	100	28.10 N	120.34 E
Qiaozhen	106	31.39 N	121.24 E
Qibao	106	31.09 N	121.20 E
Qibyā	132	31.59 N	35.01 E
Qichun	100	30.17 N	115.26 E
Qiddīsah Kātrīnā, Dayr al- (Monastery of Saint Catherine) ʊ[1]	140	28.29 N	34.01 E
Qidong, Zhg.	102	26.44 N	112.04 E
Qidong, Zhg.	106	31.49 N	121.40 E
Qidu	100	30.16 N	117.46 E
Qiemo	120	38.08 N	85.32 E
Qiesanglinzi	104	41.42 N	123.30 E
Qieshikou	271a	39.59 N	116.24 E
Qiezixi	107	29.25 N	106.30 E
Qifosi	107	29.27 N	105.58 E
Qifṭ (Coptos)	140	26.00 N	32.49 E
Qigong	102	28.38 N	100.38 E
Qigongtai	104	41.50 N	123.08 E
Qihe (Yancheng)	98	36.48 N	116.44 E
Qiji	98	37.16 N	115.21 E
Qijiadian	89	46.48 N	125.36 E
Qijian	107	30.14 N	106.09 E
Qijiang	107	29.02 N	106.39 E
Qijiapuzi	104	40.54 N	122.31 E
Qijiawan	100	30.53 N	114.13 E
Qijiawopeng	104	41.02 N	121.26 E
Qijiazi	104	41.54 N	122.58 E
Qika	89	50.35 N	119.16 E
Qikou	98	38.35 N	117.31 E
Qila Abdullāh	120	30.43 N	66.38 E
Qila Dīdār Singh	123	32.08 N	74.01 E
Qilaguganni Shan ∧	124	28.46 N	87.38 E
Qila Lādgasht	128	27.54 N	62.57 E
Qila Saifullāh	120	30.43 N	68.21 E
Qila Sobha Singh	123	32.14 N	74.46 E
Qilian	102	38.05 N	100.12 E
Qilian Shan ∧	102	39.12 N	98.35 E
Qilian Shan ⋆	102	39.06 N	98.40 E
Qili Hai ≡	105	39.19 N	117.33 E
Qilihe, Zhg.	104	41.21 N	121.16 E
Qilihe, Zhg.	104	41.30 N	121.15 E
Qilihezi	104	40.56 N	121.02 E
Qiling	100	24.05 N	115.27 E
Qilingzicun	104	41.05 N	123.06 E
Qilinmen	106	32.04 N	118.55 E
Qilinzhen	106	31.56 N	121.21 E
Qiliping	100	31.27 N	114.39 E
Qiliqiao	106	31.35 N	120.48 E
Qilizhen, Zhg.	102	35.43 N	108.59 E
Qilizhen, Zhg.	106	32.19 N	121.05 E
Qilṭ, 'Ayn al- ⊤[4]	132	31.50 N	35.23 E
Qimafang	98	40.08 N	114.31 E
Qiman al-'Arūs	142	29.18 N	31.10 E
Qimen, Zhg.	100	29.52 N	117.42 E
Qimen, Zhg.	100	25.18 N	113.15 E
Qimoudi	105	39.35 N	115.32 E
Qimu Jiao ›	98	37.46 N	120.12 E
Qin ≃, Zhg.	100	23.58 N	115.47 E
Qin ≃, Zhg.	100	26.16 N	115.52 E
Qin ≃, Zhg.	102	35.01 N	113.25 E
Qinā	140	26.10 N	32.43 E
Qinā, Wādī V, Miṣr	140	26.12 N	32.44 E
Qinā, Wādī V, Miṣr	142	29.39 N	31.53 E
Qincaigou	104	40.38 N	120.37 E
Qing ≃, Zhg.	98	42.26 N	123.50 E
Qing ≃, Zhg.	102	30.22 N	111.20 E
Qing'an	89	46.52 N	127.30 E
Qingbaikou	105	40.01 N	115.50 E
Qingcaoge	100	30.50 N	116.46 E
Qingcheng	98	37.12 N	117.40 E
Qingchengzi	104	40.44 N	123.36 E
Qingchuan	102	32.36 N	105.09 E
Qingcungang	106	30.56 N	121.34 E
Qingdao (Tsingtao)	98	36.06 N	120.19 E
Qingdian	105	39.51 N	117.22 E
Qingduizi, Zhg.	98	39.50 N	123.18 E
Qingduizi, Zhg.	104	41.28 N	121.53 E
Qingfeng	98	35.54 N	115.07 E
Qingfengtuo	98	40.59 N	116.04 E
Qingfu	102	28.29 N	104.35 E
Qinggang	89	46.43 N	126.07 E
Qingguang	105	39.11 N	117.02 E
Qingguji	98	34.45 N	115.47 E
Qinghai (Tsinghai) □[4]	90	36.00 N	96.00 E
Qinghai Hu ⊜	102	36.50 N	100.20 E
Qinghai Nanshan ⋆	102	37.06 N	99.05 E
Qinghe, Zhg.	86	46.36 N	90.39 E
Qinghe, Zhg.	98	40.02 N	122.35 E
Qinghe, Zhg.	104	42.32 N	124.09 E
Qinghe, Zhg.	105	40.01 N	116.20 E
Qinghecheng	104	41.28 N	124.15 E
Qinghechengzi	104	41.44 N	121.25 E
Qinghemen	104	41.45 N	121.25 E
Qinghezhen	98	37.16 N	117.39 E
Qinghu	100	28.40 N	118.34 E
Qinghua	100	29.24 N	117.46 E
Qinghuayuan	105	40.00 N	116.19 E
Qinghuazhen	100	32.55 N	112.19 E
Qingjian	102	37.10 N	110.00 E
Qingjiang, Zhg.	100	28.05 N	115.29 E
Qingjiang, Zhg.	100	28.16 N	121.06 E
Qingjiang, Zhg.	100	33.35 N	119.02 E
Qingjiang, Zhg.	107	29.17 N	105.34 E
Qingjujie	107	30.42 N	106.07 E
Qinglian	100	24.27 N	112.45 E
Qingliu	100	26.12 N	116.52 E
Qingliuzhen	107	29.56 N	105.19 E
Qinglong, Zhg.	98	40.24 N	118.54 E
Qinglong, Zhg.	100	25.28 N	114.28 E
Qinglong, Zhg.	102	25.50 N	105.10 E
Qinglong ≃, Zhg.	98	39.51 N	118.51 E
Qinglong ≃, Zhg.	105	39.35 N	117.46 E
Qinglongchang, Zhg.	107	28.50 N	106.31 E
Qinglongchang, Zhg.	107	29.51 N	105.40 E
Qinglongchang, Zhg.	107	30.20 N	103.51 E
Qinglonggang	106	31.51 N	121.15 E
Qinglongguan	107	30.25 N	104.48 E
Qinglongji	98	34.05 N	116.37 E
Qinglongwan ≃	105	39.19 N	117.32 E
Qingmuguan	107	29.41 N	106.18 E
Qingningsi	106	31.16 N	121.33 E
Qingping, Zhg.	98	36.47 N	116.06 E
Qingping, Zhg.	107	29.00 N	106.21 E
Qingping, Zhg.	107	30.14 N	106.12 E
Qingpu	106	31.09 N	121.06 E
Qingshan, Zhg.	100	31.33 N	116.22 E
Qingshan, Zhg.	100	30.38 N	114.23 E
Qingshan, Zhg.	106	30.15 N	119.52 E
Qingshan, Zhg.	106	30.36 N	119.41 E
Qingshan, Zhg.	106	30.43 N	120.03 E
Qingshanpu	100	29.27 N	114.01 E
Qingshen	107	29.50 N	103.50 E
Qingshui, Zhg.	102	34.42 N	106.21 E
Qingshui, Zhg.	102	39.23 N	99.09 E
Qingshui, Zhg.	107	30.10 N	104.03 E
Qingshui ≃, Zhg.	102	37.30 N	105.30 E
Qingshui ≃, Zhg.	102	27.08 N	109.36 E
Qingshuihe	86	44.12 N	80.45 E
Qingshuijian	105	39.59 N	115.58 E
Qingshuilang Shan ⋆	102	26.15 N	99.35 E
Qingshuixi	102	29.09 N	103.55 E
Qingtan	100	31.48 N	112.48 E
Qingtang, Zhg.	100	26.28 N	115.48 E
Qingtang, Zhg.	100	24.14 N	113.51 E
Qingtian	100	28.10 N	120.17 E
Qingtong	107	29.28 N	103.27 E
Qingtongxia	102	37.53 N	105.54 E
Qingtuosi	98	35.29 N	118.20 E
Qingtuozi, Zhg.	104	41.05 N	121.28 E
Qingtuozi, Zhg.	105	39.08 N	117.45 E
Qingxi, Zhg.	89	49.19 N	127.10 E
Qingxi, Zhg.	100	31.40 N	118.00 E
Qingxi, Zhg.	107	30.40 N	106.14 E
Qingxian	98	38.34 N	116.46 E
Qingxizhen	107	29.09 N	103.55 E
Qingyang, Zhg.	89	45.20 N	128.47 E
Qingyang, Zhg.	100	30.38 N	117.48 E
Qingyang, Zhg.	102	36.06 N	107.47 E
Qingyangzhen	106	31.46 N	120.15 E
Qingyi ≃	107	29.34 N	103.42 E
Qingyuan, Zhg.	98	42.13 N	124.56 E
Qingyuan, Zhg.	100	27.38 N	119.04 E
Qingyuan, Zhg.	100	23.42 N	113.02 E
Qingyuan → Baoding	105	38.52 N	115.29 E
Qingyun (Xiejiaji)	98	37.52 N	117.21 E
Qingyunbao	104	42.34 N	123.50 E
Qingyundian	105	39.38 N	116.29 E
Qing Zang Gaoyuan ⋆[1]	12	33.00 N	92.00 E
Qingzhen, Zhg.	102	26.29 N	106.22 E
Qingzhen, Zhg.	106	30.45 N	120.30 E
Qingzhou	100	23.39 N	116.57 E
Qinhuai ≃	106	32.01 N	118.50 E
Qinhuangdao (Chinwangtao)	98	39.56 N	119.36 E
Qinjia	89	46.47 N	127.00 E
Qinlan	100	32.37 N	119.08 E
Qin Ling (Tsinlingshan) ⋆	102	34.00 N	108.00 E
Qinnan	100	33.16 N	119.55 E
Qinshui	102	35.41 N	112.11 E
Qintong	100	32.39 N	120.08 E
Qinxian	102	36.48 N	112.41 E
Qinyang	102	35.06 N	112.57 E
Qinyuan	102	36.30 N	112.15 E
Qinzhou	102	21.59 N	108.36 E
Qionghai (Jiaji)	110	19.20 N	110.30 E
Qionglai	107	30.25 N	103.27 E
Qionglaishan ⋆	102	31.21 N	102.50 E
Qionglong Shan ∧	106	31.15 N	120.25 E
Qiongzhong, Zhg.	90	19.02 N	109.49 E
Qiongzhong, Zhg.	110	19.04 N	109.48 E
Qiongzhou Haixia Ս	102	20.10 N	110.15 E
Qipandi	105	39.46 N	115.12 E
Qipanshan	98	42.05 N	117.30 E
Qiqian	89	52.12 N	120.49 E
Qiqihar (Tsitsihar)	89	47.19 N	123.55 E
Qira	120	37.00 N	80.47 E
Qir'awn, Buḥayrat al- ⊜[1]	132	33.34 N	35.42 E
Qiryat	132	32.49 N	35.06 E
Qiryat 'Anavim	132	31.48 N	35.07 E
Qiryat Ata	132	32.48 N	35.06 E
Qiryat Bialik	132	32.50 N	35.05 E
Qiryat Gat	132	31.36 N	34.46 E
Qiryat Ḥayyim	132	32.49 N	35.04 E
Qiryat Mal'akhi	132	31.44 N	34.44 E
Qiryat Motzkin	132	32.50 N	35.04 E
Qiryat Ono	132	32.04 N	34.51 E
Qiryat Shemona	132	33.13 N	35.34 E
Qiryat Tiv'on	132	32.43 N	35.08 E
Qiryat Yam	132	32.51 N	35.04 E
Qirzah, Wādī V	146	30.56 N	14.31 E
Qiseqi Shan ∧	89	48.37 N	122.32 E
Qishn	144	15.26 N	51.40 E
Qishon ≃	132	32.49 N	35.02 E
Qishrān I	144	20.14 N	40.05 E
Qishudang	107	29.13 N	104.39 E
Qishuyan	106	31.44 N	120.04 E
Qiṣrāyā	130	34.53 N	36.26 E
Qitai	86	44.01 N	89.28 E
Qitaihe	89	45.48 N	130.53 E
Qitaizi	104	41.33 N	122.11 E
Qitamu	89	44.22 N	126.20 E
Qitangzhen	107	29.47 N	106.16 E
Qiting	100	31.02 N	114.44 E
Qitingqiao	106	31.26 N	119.52 E
Qitou	100	24.54 N	117.29 E
Qiubei	102	24.07 N	104.12 E
Qiuchang	107	28.59 N	104.42 E
Qiuji	100	33.51 N	118.01 E
Qiujia	106	31.49 N	121.51 E
Qiujiatun	104	41.20 N	121.00 E
Qiujin	100	29.10 N	115.42 E
Qiuxi ≃	107	29.58 N	104.40 E
Qiuxizhen	107	29.56 N	104.41 E
Qiweigang	106	32.01 N	119.59 E
Qixia	98	37.17 N	120.48 E
Qixian (Zhaoge), Zhg.	98	35.38 N	114.11 E
Qixian, Zhg.	100	34.33 N	114.47 E
Qixianji	100	33.28 N	117.01 E
Qixiashan	106	32.10 N	118.57 E
Qi Xia Si ʊ[1]	106	32.12 N	118.58 E
Qixingqiao	106	30.49 N	120.51 E
Qiyahe	89	53.02 N	120.33 E
Qiyang	102	26.29 N	111.43 E
Qiyi	100	32.30 N	112.54 E
Qiying	102	36.38 N	106.25 E
Qizhou	100	30.04 N	115.20 E
Qizil Jilga	120	35.21 N	78.52 E
Qizil Langar	120	35.13 N	77.59 E
Qnadsa	148	31.48 N	2.26 W
Qogir Feng (K2) ∧	123	35.53 N	76.30 E
Qolhak ◆[8]	267d	35.47 N	51.26 E
Qom	128	34.39 N	50.54 E
Qom ≃	128	34.48 N	51.02 E
Qomolangma Feng → Everest, Mount ∧	124	27.59 N	86.56 E
Qomsheh	128	32.01 N	51.52 E
Qondūz ≃	120	37.00 N	68.16 E
Qorveh	128	35.10 N	47.48 E
Qoṭbābād	128	28.42 N	53.34 E
Qoṭūr	128	38.28 N	44.25 E
Qu ≃, Zhg.	100	29.12 N	119.27 E
Qu ≃, Zhg.	102	30.01 N	106.24 E
Quabbin Reservoir ⊜[1]	207	42.22 N	72.18 W
Quaddick Reservoir ⊜[1]	207	41.57 N	71.49 W
Quadra Island I	182	50.08 N	125.16 W
Quadraro ◆[8]	267a	41.51 N	12.33 E
Quadrath-Ichendorf	56	50.56 N	6.41 E
Quadros, Lagoa dos ⊂	252	29.42 S	50.05 W
Quāidābād	123	32.20 N	71.52 E
Quail Lake ⊜[1]	228	34.47 N	118.45 W
Quail Valley	228	33.43 N	117.15 W
Quairading	162	32.01 S	117.25 E
Quakake	210	40.51 N	76.02 W
Quakenbrück	52	52.40 N	7.57 E
Quaker Hill, Ct., U.S.	207	41.22 N	72.06 W
Quaker Hill, N.Y., U.S.	210	41.35 N	73.33 W
Quakers Hill	170	33.43 S	150.53 E
Quakers Knob ∧[2]	214	40.21 N	80.24 W
Quaker Street	210	42.44 N	74.11 W
Quakertown, N.J., U.S.	210	40.33 N	74.56 W
Quakertown, Pa., U.S.	208	40.26 N	75.20 W
Qualicum Beach	182	49.21 N	124.27 W
Quambatook	166	35.51 S	143.31 E
Quanah	196	34.17 N	99.44 W
Quanbao Shan ∧	102	34.09 N	111.29 E
Quangang	100	28.10 N	115.34 E
Quang Ngai	110	15.07 N	108.48 E
Quang Trach	110	17.45 N	106.27 E
Quanjiang	100	27.43 N	113.59 E
Quanjiao	100	32.06 N	118.16 E
Quan Long → Ca Mau	110	9.11 N	105.08 E
Quanmian	104	42.02 N	122.13 E
Quannan	100	24.44 N	114.31 E
Quannapowitt, Lake ⊜	283	42.31 N	71.05 W
Quanshang	100	26.25 N	116.55 E
Quanshengpu	104	41.59 N	123.22 E
Quanshui	104	41.18 N	124.11 E
Quanshuitou	105	40.24 N	116.39 E
Quantico, Md., U.S.	208	38.22 N	75.44 W
Quantico, Va., U.S.	208	38.31 N	77.17 W
Quantico Marine Corps Air Station ■	208	38.31 N	77.19 W
Quantock Hills ⋆[2]	42	51.07 N	3.10 W
Quantou	89	42.52 N	124.07 E
Quanxishi	100	26.51 N	112.45 E
Quanyanhezi	104	40.52 N	123.26 E
Quanzhou (Chuanchou)	100	24.54 N	118.35 E
Quanzhou Gang ⊂	100	24.52 N	118.37 E
Qu'Appelle	184	50.33 N	103.52 W
Qu'Appelle ≃	184	50.25 N	101.20 W
Qu'Appelle Dam ◆[6]	184	51.00 N	106.25 W
Quaraí	252	30.23 S	56.27 W
Quaraí ≃	252	30.12 S	57.36 W
Quaregnon	50	50.26 N	3.51 E
Quarles, Pegunungan ⋆	112	2.55 S	119.30 E
Quarrata	66	43.51 N	10.58 E
Quarré-les-Tombes	50	47.22 N	3.59 E
Quarry	222	30.18 N	96.30 W
Quarry Heights	276	41.04 N	73.45 W
Quarryville, Ct., U.S.	207	41.51 N	72.25 W
Quarryville, Pa., U.S.	208	39.53 N	76.09 W
Quartu Sant'Elena	71	39.14 N	9.11 E
Quartz Hill	228	34.39 N	118.13 W
Quartz Lake ⊜	176	70.55 N	80.33 W
Quartz Mountain ∧	202	43.10 N	122.40 W
Quartzsite	200	33.39 N	114.13 W
Quatis	256	22.25 S	44.16 W
Quatre, Isle à I	241h	12.57 N	61.15 W
Quatsino Sound Ս	182	50.25 N	127.55 W
Qubei	124	28.18 N	86.53 E
Qūchān	128	37.06 N	58.30 E
Quchijie	102	28.03 N	111.53 E
Qudaym	130	35.03 N	38.25 E
Qudi	98	37.06 N	117.15 E
Qudsia Gardens ♦	272a	28.40 N	77.13 E
Quê ≃	152	14.45 S	14.45 E
Queanbeyan	171b	35.21 S	149.14 E
Queanbeyan ≃	171b	35.20 S	149.14 E
Québec	206	46.49 N	71.14 W
Québec □[6]	206	46.50 N	71.20 W
Québec □[4]	176	52.00 N	72.00 W
Quebec Airport ⊠	206	46.47 N	71.23 W
Quebec House ⊥	260	51.14 N	0.05 E
Quebeck	194	35.49 N	85.34 W
Quebra-Anzol ≃	255	19.09 S	47.38 W
Quebra-Cangalha, Serra do ⋆	256	22.55 S	45.10 W
Quebracho	252	31.57 S	57.53 W
Quebrada Seca	240m	18.14 N	65.40 W
Quebradillas	240m	18.29 N	66.56 W
Quebrangulo	250	9.20 S	36.29 W
Quecholac	234	18.57 N	97.40 W
Quechultenango	234	17.25 N	99.13 W
Quecreek	214	40.06 N	79.05 W
Quedal, Cabo ›	254	40.59 S	73.59 W
Quedas	156	19.30 S	33.29 E
Quedlinburg	54	51.48 N	11.09 E
Queen	214	40.16 N	78.31 W
Queen Alexandra Range ⋆	9	84.00 S	168.00 E
Queen Alia International Airport ⊠	132	31.44 N	35.59 E
Queen Anne	208	38.55 N	75.57 W
Queen Anne Creek ≃	285	40.08 N	74.53 W
Queen Annes □[6]	208	39.03 N	76.04 W
Queen Bess, Mount ∧	182	51.16 N	124.34 W
Queenborough	42	51.26 N	0.45 E
Queen Charlotte	182	53.16 N	132.05 W
Queen Charlotte Bay ⊂	254	51.50 S	60.40 W
Queen Charlotte Islands II	182	53.00 N	132.00 W
Queen Charlotte Mountains ⋆	182	53.00 N	132.00 W
Queen Charlotte Sound Ս	182	51.30 N	129.30 W
Queen Charlotte Strait Ս	182	50.50 N	127.25 W
Queen City, Mo., U.S.	194	40.24 N	92.34 W
Queen City, Tx., U.S.	194	33.08 N	94.09 W
Queen Elizabeth II Reservoir ⊜[1]	260	51.23 N	0.24 W
Queen Elizabeth Islands II	16	78.00 N	95.00 W
Queen Fabiola Mountains ⋆	9	71.30 S	35.40 E
Queen Mary ◆	280	33.45 N	118.12 W
Queen Mary Coast ⩡[2]	9	67.00 S	96.00 E
Queen Mary Reservoir ⊜[1]	260	51.25 N	0.28 W
Queen Maud Gulf ⊂	176	68.25 N	102.30 W
Queen Maud Land ◆[1]	9	72.30 S	12.00 E
Queen Maud Mountains ⋆	9	86.00 S	160.00 W
Queens □[6]	210	40.34 N	73.52 W
Queensbury	44	53.46 N	1.50 W
Queens Channel Ս, Austl.	164	14.46 S	129.24 E
Queens Channel Ս, N.T., Can.	176	76.11 N	96.00 W
Queenscliff	169	38.16 S	144.40 E
Queensferry, Scot., U.K.	46	55.59 N	3.25 W
Queensferry, Wales, U.K.	44	53.12 N	3.01 W
Queensland □[3]	160	22.00 S	145.00 E
Queensland Plateau ✦[3]	14	17.00 S	150.00 E
Queens Park ♦, Austl.	274a	33.54 S	151.16 E
Queens Park ♦, On., Can.	275b	43.40 N	79.24 W
Queens Park ♦, Eng., U.K.	262	53.35 N	2.27 W
Queen's Park ♦, Eng., U.K.	262	53.44 N	2.28 W
Queensport	186	45.20 N	61.16 W
Queens Sound Ս	182	51.55 N	128.11 W
Queenston	284a	43.10 N	79.03 W
Queenston Chippawa Power Canal ≋	284a	43.08 N	79.03 W
Queenstown, Austl.	166	42.05 S	145.33 E
Queenstown, Guy.	246	7.12 N	58.29 W
Queenstown, N.Z.	172	45.02 S	168.40 E
Queenstown, S. Afr.	158	31.52 S	26.52 E
Queenstown, Md., U.S.	208	38.59 N	76.09 W
Queenstown → Cobh	48	51.51 N	8.17 W
Queensville	212	44.08 N	79.28 W
Queen Victoria Park ♦	284a	43.05 N	79.05 W
Que'er'ao I	100	28.48 N	121.51 E
Queerhe	104	40.57 N	121.35 E
Queets	224	47.32 N	124.19 W
Queets ≃	224	47.33 N	124.21 W
Queguay Grande ≃	252	32.09 S	58.09 W
Queich ≃	56	49.14 N	8.23 E
Queige	62	45.43 N	6.28 E
Queimada, Ilha I	250	0.10 S	50.50 W
Queimada Nova	250	8.35 S	41.25 W
Queimadas	250	10.58 S	39.38 W
Queimados	256	22.42 S	43.34 W
Queiros, Cap ›	175f	14.55 S	167.01 E
Quela	152	9.16 S	17.02 E
Quelimane	156	17.53 S	36.51 E
Quelizhen	106	30.54 N	121.26 E
Quelle	52	52.00 N	8.29 E
Quellendorf	54	51.45 N	12.07 E
Quellón	254	43.07 S	73.37 W
Quelo	152	6.27 S	12.48 E
Quelpart Island → Cheju-do I	90	33.20 N	126.30 E
Queluz, Bra.	256	22.32 S	44.46 W
Queluz, Port.	266c	38.45 N	9.15 W
Queluz → Conselheiro Lafaiete	255	20.40 S	43.48 W
Quemado, N.M., U.S.	200	34.20 N	108.29 W
Quemado, Tx., U.S.	196	28.56 N	100.38 W
Quemado, Punta de ›	240p	20.13 N	74.08 W
Quemado de Güines	240p	22.48 N	80.15 W
Quemahoning Reservoir ⊜[1]	214	40.09 N	78.57 W
Quembo ≃	152	14.57 S	20.22 E
Quemchi	254	42.09 S	73.29 W
Quemoy → Chinmen Tao I	100	24.27 N	118.23 E
Quemú Quemú	252	36.03 S	63.33 W
Quend	50	50.19 N	1.38 E
Quend Plage	50	50.19 N	1.33 E
Queñi, Nevado de ∧	254	40.14 S	71.49 W
Quenouilles, Lac aux ⊜	206	46.10 N	74.23 W
Quentin	208	40.17 N	76.26 W
Quepos	236	9.27 N	84.09 W
Quepos, Punta ›	236	9.23 N	84.10 W
Quequén	252	38.32 S	58.42 W
Querary ≃	246	1.04 N	69.51 W
Quercianella	66	43.27 N	10.22 E
Quercy □[9]	32	44.30 N	1.25 E
Querecotillo	248	4.50 S	80.40 W
Querenburg ◆[8]	263	51.27 N	7.16 E
Querenhorst	54	52.20 N	10.57 E
Querétaro	234	20.36 N	100.23 W
Querétaro □[3]	234	21.00 N	99.55 W
Querfurt	54	51.23 N	11.36 E
Quero	64	45.55 N	11.56 E
Querobabi	232	30.03 N	111.01 W
Quesada, C.R.	236	10.19 N	84.26 W
Quesada, Esp.	34	37.51 N	3.04 W
Queset Brook ≃	283	42.02 N	71.04 W
Queshan	100	32.48 N	114.01 E
Quesnel	182	52.59 N	122.30 W
Quesnel ≃	182	53.00 N	122.30 W
Quesnel Lake ⊜	182	52.32 N	121.05 W
Quesnoy	50	50.43 N	3.00 E
Que Son	110	15.40 N	108.14 E
Questa	200	36.42 N	105.35 W
Questembert	32	47.40 N	2.27 W
Quetico Lake ⊜	190	48.34 N	91.52 W
Quetico Provincial Park ♦	190	48.30 N	91.30 W
Quetta	120	30.12 N	67.00 E
Quettehou	32	49.36 N	1.18 W
Quetzala ≃	234	16.35 N	98.30 W
Quetzaltenango	236	14.50 N	91.31 W
Quetzaltenango □[5]	236	14.45 N	91.40 W
Quevedo	246	1.02 S	79.29 W
Quezaltepeque, El Sal.	236	13.50 N	89.17 W
Quezaltepeque, Guat.	236	14.38 N	89.27 W
Quezon, Pil.	116	15.34 N	120.49 E
Quezon, Pil.	116	14.01 N	122.11 E
Quezon □[4]	116	13.58 N	122.02 E
Quezon City	116	14.38 N	121.03 E
Quezon Memorial ⊥	269f	14.39 N	121.03 E
Qufu	98	35.36 N	117.02 E
Qugou, Zhg.	102	36.10 N	100.56 E
Qugou, Zhg.	105	39.17 N	116.15 E
Quibala	152	10.46 S	14.59 E
Quibaxi	152	8.29 S	14.36 E
Quibdó	246	5.42 N	76.40 W
Quiberon	32	47.29 N	3.07 W
Quiberville	50	49.54 N	0.55 E
Quíbor	246	9.56 N	69.37 W
Quibray Bay ⊂	274a	34.01 S	151.11 E
Quibú ≃	286b	23.05 N	82.27 W
Quiçama, Parque Nacional de ♦	152	9.45 S	13.30 E
Qui Chau	110	19.33 N	105.06 E
Quiches	248	8.25 S	77.27 W
Quickborn	52	53.44 N	9.53 E
Quiculungo	152	8.31 S	15.19 E
Quidapil Point ›	116	6.49 N	123.57 E
Quidnessett	207	41.37 N	71.27 W
Quidnick	207	41.41 N	71.32 W
Quiechapa ≃	234	16.37 N	95.59 W
Quien Sabe Creek ≃	226	36.43 N	121.09 W
Quiévrain	50	50.24 N	3.41 E
Quiévy	50	50.10 N	3.25 E
Quiindy	252	25.58 S	57.16 W
Quila	232	24.23 N	107.13 W
Quilalí	236	13.34 N	86.02 W
Quilates, Cap ›	34	35.20 N	3.45 W
Quilcene	224	47.49 N	122.52 W
Quilenda	152	10.33 S	14.22 E
Quilengues	152	14.05 S	14.04 E
Quileute Indian Reservation ◆[4]	224	47.55 N	124.38 W
Quilicura	286e	33.22 S	70.45 W
Quilimarí	252	32.07 S	71.30 W
Quilino	252	30.12 S	64.29 W
Quillabamba	248	12.49 S	72.43 W
Quillacollo	248	17.26 S	66.17 W
Quillagua	248	21.39 S	69.33 W
Quillan	32	42.52 N	2.11 E
Quillebeuf-sur-Seine	50	49.29 N	0.31 E
Quill Lake	184	52.05 N	104.15 W
Quillota	252	32.53 S	71.16 W
Quilmes	258	34.44 S	58.16 W
Quilmes □[5]	288	34.44 S	58.16 W
Quilmes, Aeródromo ⊠	288	34.42 S	58.15 W
Quilombo ≃	256	23.52 S	46.21 W
Quilon	122	8.53 N	76.36 E
Quilotosa Wash V	200	32.56 N	112.46 W
Quilpie	166	26.37 S	144.15 E
Quilpué	252	33.03 S	71.27 W
Quilty	48	52.47 N	9.26 W
Quimarí, Alto de ∧	246	8.07 N	76.23 W
Quimbango	152	11.01 S	17.26 E
Quimbaya	246	4.38 N	75.47 W
Quimbele	152	6.28 S	16.13 E
Quimbo	152	13.59 S	16.05 E
Quimbonge	152	8.36 S	18.30 E
Quimbumbe	152	7.50 S	14.03 E
Quimby	198	42.37 N	95.38 W
Quime	248	17.02 S	67.15 W
Quimichis	234	22.21 N	105.32 W
Quimilí	252	27.38 S	62.25 W
Quimper	32	48.00 N	4.06 W
Quimperlé	32	47.52 N	3.33 W
Quinalasag Island I	116	13.56 N	123.38 E
Quinault	224	47.28 N	123.50 W
Quinault ≃	224	47.23 N	124.18 W
Quinault, North Fork ≃	224	47.32 N	123.40 W
Quinault Indian Reservation ◆[4]	224	47.24 N	124.10 W
Quinault Lake ⊜	224	47.28 N	123.52 W
Quinby Inlet ⊂	208	37.28 N	75.40 W
Quincampoix	50	49.32 N	1.11 E
Quince Mil	248	13.16 S	70.38 W
Quinches	248	12.13 S	76.05 W
Quincy, Ca., U.S.	204	39.56 N	120.56 W
Quincy, Fl., U.S.	192	30.35 N	84.35 W
Quincy, Il., U.S.	219	39.56 N	91.24 W
Quincy, Ky., U.S.	218	38.37 N	83.07 W
Quincy, Ma., U.S.	207	42.15 N	71.00 W
Quincy, Mi., U.S.	216	41.56 N	84.53 W
Quincy, Oh., U.S.	216	40.17 N	83.58 W
Quincy, Or., U.S.	224	46.08 N	123.09 W
Quincy, Pa., U.S.	208	39.48 N	77.35 W
Quincy, Wa., U.S.	202	47.14 N	119.51 W
Quincy Bay ⊂	283	42.17 N	70.58 W
Quincy-sous-Sénart	261	48.40 N	2.33 E
Quincy-Voisins	261	48.54 N	2.53 E
Quindanning	168a	33.03 S	116.34 E
Quindío □[5]	246	4.30 N	75.40 W
Quinebaug	207	42.01 N	71.57 W
Quinebaug ≃	207	41.33 N	72.03 W
Quines	252	32.13 S	65.48 W
Quinga	154	15.49 S	40.15 E
Quingey	58	47.06 N	5.53 E
Quingyi ≃	100	31.12 N	118.29 E
Quinhagak	180	59.45 N	161.43 W
Qui Nhon	110	13.46 N	109.14 E
Quiniluban Islands II	116	11.27 N	120.48 E
Quinjenje	152	12.49 S	14.55 E
Quinlan	222	32.55 N	96.08 W
Quinn ≃	204	40.52 N	119.03 W
Quiñones, Arroyo de los ≃	266a	40.33 N	3.34 W
Quinson	62	43.42 N	6.02 E
Quinta da Boa Vista ♦	287a	22.54 S	43.15 W
Quintanar de la Orden	34	39.34 N	3.03 W
Quintana Roo □[3]	232	19.40 N	88.30 W
Quinta Normal	286e	33.27 S	70.42 W
Quinta Normal de Agricultura ʊ[2]	286e	33.27 S	70.42 W
Quinte, Bay of ⊂	212	44.07 N	77.15 W
Quinter	198	39.04 N	100.13 W
Quintero	252	32.47 S	71.32 W
Quintette Mountain ∧	182	54.52 N	120.53 W
Quintin	32	48.24 N	2.55 W

Column headings (Deutsch): Name · Seite · Breite°′ · Länge°′ E = Ost

Symbols in the index entries represent the broad categories identified in the key at the right. Symbols with superior numbers (⋆[1]) identify subcategories (see complete key on page *I · 1*).

Symbole im Register stellen die rechts im Schlüssel erklärten Kategorien dar. Symbole mit hochgestellten Ziffern (⋆[1]) bezeichnen Unterabteilungen einer Kategorie (vgl. vollständiger Schlüssel auf Seite *I · 1*).

Los símbolos incluídos en el texto del índice representan las grandes categorias identificadas con la clave a la derecha. Los símbolos con numeros en su parte superior (⋆[1]) identifican las subcategorías (véase la clave completa en la página *I · 1*).

Les symboles de l'index représentent les catégories indiquées dans la légende à droite. Les symboles suivis d'un indice (⋆[1]) représentent des sous-catégories (voir légende complète à la page *I · 1*).

Os símbolos incluídos no texto do índice representam as grandes categorias identificadas com a chave à direita. Os símbolos com números em sua parte superior (⋆[1]) identificam as subcategorias (veja-se a chave completa à página *I · 1*).

English	Deutsch	Español	Français	Português
∧ Mountain	Berg	Montaña	Montagne	Montanha
⋆ Mountains	Gebirge	Montañas	Montagnes	Montanhas
)(Pass	Paß	Paso	Col	Passo
V Valley, Canyon	Tal, Cañon	Valle, Cañón	Vallée, Canyon	Vale, Canhão
≚ Plain	Ebene	Llano	Plaine	Planície
› Cape	Kap	Cabo	Cap	Cabo
I Island	Insel	Isla	Île	Ilha
II Islands	Inseln	Islas	Îles	Ilhas
⩡ Other Topographic Features	Andere Topographische Objekte	Otros Elementos Topográficos	Autres données topographiques	Outros acidentes topográficos

ESPAÑOL

Nombre	Página	Lat.°′	Long.°′ W = Oeste
Quintino Sella, Canale ≊	266b	45.29 N	8.38 E
Quinto	34	41.25 N	0.29 W
Quinto ≃	252	34.14 S	64.10 W
Quinto Creek ≃	226	37.11 N	121.02 W
Quinto de Noviembre, Presa ◆[6]	236	13.59 N	88.44 W
Quinton, Sk., Can.	184	51.23 N	104.24 W
Quinton, N.J., U.S.	208	39.32 N	75.24 W
Quinton, Ok., U.S.	196	35.07 N	95.22 W
Quinto Romano ◆[8]	266b	45.29 N	9.05 E
Quinzano d'Oglio	64	45.19 N	10.00 E
Quinzáu	152	6.51 S	12.46 E
Quinze, Lac des ⊜	190	47.35 N	79.05 W
Quionga	154	10.37 S	40.30 E
Quipapá	250	8.50 S	36.02 W
Quipar ≃	34	38.14 N	1.36 W
Quipeio	152	12.26 S	15.30 E
Quipemba	152	7.12 S	15.06 E
Quipit ≃	116	8.04 N	122.29 E
Quipungo	152	14.51 S	14.30 E
Quiquive ≃	248	14.39 S	67.38 W
Quirauk Mountain ∧	208	39.42 N	77.31 W
Quiriguá ⊥	236	15.17 N	89.04 W
Quirihue	252	36.17 S	72.32 W
Quirima	152	10.48 S	18.09 E
Quirimba, Ilha I	154	12.20 S	40.36 E
Quirimbo	152	10.36 S	14.12 E
Quirindi	166	31.31 S	150.41 E
Quirino □[4]	116	16.25 N	121.35 E
Quirinópolis	255	18.32 S	50.30 W
Quiriquire	246	9.59 N	63.13 W
Quiriri ≃	152	15.13 S	18.47 E
Quiririm	256	23.02 S	45.38 W
Quirke Lake ⊜	190	46.28 N	82.33 W
Quiroga, Esp.	34	42.29 N	7.16 W
Quiroga, Méx.	234	19.40 N	101.32 W
Quirós	252	28.47 S	65.07 W
Quirpon Island I	186	51.35 N	55.25 W
Quirra, Salto di ◆[1]	71	39.35 N	9.33 E
Quissac	62	43.55 N	4.00 E
Quissanga	154	12.25 S	40.29 E
Quissico	156	24.42 S	34.44 E
Quissongo	152	10.01 S	15.07 E
Quistello	64	45.00 N	10.59 E
Quitapa	152	10.23 S	18.14 E
Quitaque	196	34.22 N	101.04 W
Quitasueño ✧[4]	236	14.20 N	81.15 W
Quiterajo	154	11.48 S	40.25 E
Quitilipi	252	26.52 S	60.13 W
Quitman, Ga., U.S.	192	30.47 N	83.33 W
Quitman, Ms., U.S.	194	32.02 N	88.43 W
Quitman, Tx., U.S.	222	32.47 N	95.27 W
Quitman, Lake ⊜[1]	222	32.52 N	95.27 W
Quito	246	0.13 S	78.30 W
Quitzdorf, Speicherbecken ⊜[1]	54	51.17 N	14.45 E
Quivilla	248	9.32 S	76.41 W
Quixadá	250	4.58 S	39.01 W
Quixeramobim	250	5.12 S	39.17 W
Quixeré	250	5.05 S	37.59 W
Quixico	152	7.59 S	14.25 E
Quixinge	152	9.52 S	14.23 E
Quixito ≃	246	4.29 S	70.18 W
Quizenga	152	9.21 S	15.28 E
Qujiadian	89	43.13 N	123.53 E
Qujiang, Zhg.	100	28.15 N	115.45 E
Qujiang, Zhg.	100	24.41 N	113.35 E
Qujiang, Zhg.	100	24.48 N	113.17 E
Qujing	102	25.32 N	103.41 E
Qujiu	102	22.28 N	107.40 E
Qukou	105	39.46 N	117.07 E
Qulay'ah, Ra's al- ›	128	28.53 N	48.18 E
Qulin	194	36.35 N	90.14 W
Qulubbā	142	27.45 N	30.50 E
Qulūd, Jabal ∧[2]	140	11.41 N	29.31 E
Qulūṣanā	142	28.21 N	30.44 E
Qulzum, Baḥr al- ⊂	142	29.55 N	32.31 E
Qumar ≃, Zhg.	90	34.42 N	94.50 E
Qumar ≃, Zhg.	120	34.39 N	95.00 E
Qumarlêb	102	34.35 N	95.27 E
Qumbu	158	31.10 S	28.48 E
Qumrān, Khirbat ⊥	132	31.44 N	35.27 E
Qunayfidhah, Nafūd ≛[8]	128	24.45 N	45.30 E
Qunbush Al-Ḥamrā'	142	29.00 N	30.59 E
Qungtag	120	29.59 N	87.33 E
Qunshen'guan	105	39.49 N	117.59 E
Quobba, Point ›	162	24.23 S	113.24 E
Quoich ≃	176	64.00 N	93.30 W
Quoich, Loch ⊜	46	57.04 N	5.17 W
Quoile ≃	48	54.21 N	5.42 W
Quoin Point ›	158	34.46 S	19.37 E
Quonochontaug	207	41.21 N	71.43 W
Quorn	166	32.21 S	138.03 E
Quorndon	42	52.45 N	1.09 W
Quoxo ≃	156	22.16 S	24.02 E
Qurayyah, Wādī V	132	30.26 N	34.01 E
Qurayyāt	128	23.17 N	58.55 E
Qurdūd	140	10.17 N	29.56 E
Qurrāṣah	140	14.38 N	32.12 E
Qurūn Ḥarhash ∧[2]	142	28.09 N	31.42 E
Qūṣ	140	25.55 N	32.45 E
Quṣayr ad-Daffah ⊥	146	30.20 N	23.57 E
Qūshchī	128	37.59 N	45.03 E
Qushui	107	30.41 N	106.02 E
Qutang	100	32.30 N	120.21 E
Qutbapur ◆[8]	272a	28.35 N	77.01 E
Qutb Minar ʋ[1]	272a	28.32 N	77.11 E
Qutdligssat	176	70.04 N	53.01 W
Quthing	158	30.30 S	27.36 E
Quṭūr	142	30.59 N	30.57 E
Quwaysinā	142	30.34 N	31.09 E
Quxi, Zhg.	100	28.00 N	120.31 E
Quxi, Zhg.	100	23.36 N	116.26 E
Quxia	106	32.06 N	120.09 E
Quxian, Zhg.	100	28.58 N	118.52 E
Quxian, Zhg.	102	30.51 N	106.59 E
Quxingji	98	34.52 N	114.39 E
Quxiong	102	31.09 N	96.00 E
Qüxü	120	29.22 N	90.43 E
Quyang	98	38.34 N	114.42 E
Qūyjāq-e-Bālā	84	39.16 N	47.07 E
Quyon	188	45.31 N	76.14 W
Quyquyó	252	26.14 S	57.01 W
Quzaymah, Jabal ∧	132	30.34 N	36.21 E
Quzhou	98	36.46 N	114.57 E
Quzong	102	30.08 N	96.00 E
R			
Råå	41	56.00 N	12.44 E
Raab	60	48.21 N	13.39 E
Raab (Rába) ≃	30	47.42 N	17.38 E
Raab → Győr	30	47.42 N	17.38 E
Raabs an der Thaya	61	48.51 N	15.30 E
Raadt ◆[8]	263	51.24 N	6.56 E
Raahe	26	64.41 N	24.29 E
Rääkkylä	26	62.19 N	29.37 E
Raalte	52	52.24 N	6.16 E
Raamsdonksveer	52	51.42 N	4.56 E
Ra'ananna	132	32.11 N	34.53 E
Raas, Pulau I	115a	7.09 S	114.32 E
Raasay I	46	57.23 N	6.04 W
Raasay, Sound of ʯ	46	57.27 N	6.06 W
Raasdorf	264b	48.15 N	16.34 E
Raasiku	76	59.22 N	25.11 E
Rab	36	44.46 N	14.46 E
Rab, Otok I	36	44.47 N	14.45 E
Raba	115b	8.27 S	118.46 E
Rába (Raab) ≃, Europe	30	47.42 N	17.38 E
Raba ≃, Pol.	30	50.09 N	20.30 E
Rabaable	144	8.17 N	48.18 E
Rabaçal ≃	34	41.30 N	7.12 W

FRANÇAIS

Nom	Page	Lat.°′	Long.°′ W = Ouest
Rábade	34	43.07 N	7.37 W
Rábahidvég	61	47.04 N	16.45 E
Rabai	154	3.58 S	39.37 E
Rabak	140	13.09 N	32.44 E
Rabal	164	6.22 S	134.52 E
Rabaraba	164	10.00 S	149.50 E
Rabat, Magreb	148	34.02 N	6.51 W
Rabat, Malta	36	35.52 N	14.25 E
Rabat (Victoria), Malta	36	36.02 N	14.14 E
Rabat □[4]	148	33.57 N	6.50 W
Rabaul	164	4.12 S	152.12 E
Rabbit ≃	216	42.38 N	86.06 W
Rabbit, Lac ⊜	190	47.30 N	78.22 W
Rabbit Creek ≃, S.D., U.S.	198	45.13 N	102.10 W
Rabbit Creek ≃, Tx., U.S.	222	32.26 N	94.47 W
Rabbit Ears Pass)(	200	40.23 N	106.37 W
Rabbit Lake ⊜, On., Can.	190	47.00 N	79.37 W
Rabbit Lake ⊜, Ca., U.S.	228	34.27 N	117.01 W
Rabbs Creek ≃	222	29.59 N	96.55 W
Rábca ≃	61	47.43 N	17.17 E
R'abcevo	76	54.39 N	32.19 E
Rabeira, Ponta da ›	287a	22.49 S	43.10 W
Rabenau	54	50.57 N	13.38 E
Rabette, Ruisseau la ≃	261	48.35 N	2.00 E
Rābi', Ash-Shallāl ar- (Fourth Cataract) ∟	140	18.47 N	32.03 E
Rābigh	128	22.48 N	39.01 E
Rabinal	236	15.06 N	90.27 W
Rabiusa ≃	58	46.48 N	9.20 E
Rabka	30	49.36 N	19.56 E
Rabkavi Banhatti	122	16.28 N	75.06 E
Rabnābād Channel ʯ	126	21.50 N	90.19 E
Rabnābād Islands II	126	21.58 N	90.24 E
Rabočeostrovsk	24	64.59 N	34.48 E
Rabočij	86	59.07 N	79.00 E
Rabong, Gunong ∧	114	4.48 N	102.07 E
Rabotki	80	56.03 N	44.38 E
R'abovskij	80	50.01 N	41.53 E
Rabun Bald ∧	192	34.58 N	83.18 W
Rabwāh	123	31.44 N	72.50 E
Raby	262	53.19 N	3.02 W
Rabyānah ⍑[4]	146	24.15 N	22.00 E
Rabyānah, Ṣaḥrā' ◆[2]	146	24.30 N	21.00 E
Racale	68	39.57 N	18.06 E
Racalmuto	70	37.24 N	13.44 E
Răcari	38	44.38 N	25.45 E
Racconigi	62	44.46 N	7.46 E
Raccoon ≃	194	41.35 N	93.37 W
Raccoon Creek ≃, N.J., U.S.	208	39.48 N	75.23 W
Raccoon Creek ≃, Oh., U.S.	188	38.43 N	82.11 W
Raccoon Creek ≃, Oh., U.S.	214	40.02 N	82.24 W
Raccoon Creek ≃, Pa., U.S.	214	40.38 N	80.22 W
Raccoon Creek ≃, Pa., U.S.	285	39.48 N	75.23 W
Raccoon Creek ≃, Va., U.S.	208	36.48 N	77.10 W
Raccoon Creek, South Branch ≃	285	39.44 N	75.15 W
Raccoon Creek State Park ♠	214	40.30 N	80.27 W
Raccoon Island I	285	39.49 N	75.22 W
Raccuia	70	38.03 N	14.54 E
Race, Cape ›	186	46.40 N	53.10 W
Raceland	194	29.43 N	90.35 W
Race Point ›	207	42.04 N	70.14 W
Racette, Lac ⊜	206	46.34 N	74.03 W
Racette, Ruisseau ≃	206	46.36 N	74.04 W
Raceview	273d	26.17 S	28.08 E
Rach'a	76	60.05 N	30.49 E
Rach Gia	110	10.01 N	105.05 E
Rach Gia, Vinh ⊂	110	10.00 N	105.00 E
Rachmanovka, Ross.	80	51.57 N	49.29 E
Rachmanovka, Ukr.	78	47.48 N	33.13 E
Rachmanovo	82	55.44 N	38.37 E
Rachny Lesovyje	78	48.47 N	28.29 E
Rachov	78	48.03 N	24.12 E
Raciąż	30	52.47 N	20.06 E
Racibórz (Ratibor)	30	50.06 N	18.13 E
Racine, Pa., U.S.	214	40.49 N	80.20 W
Racine, Wi., U.S.	216	42.43 N	87.46 W
Racine □[6]	216	42.45 N	88.05 W
Racines	64	46.52 N	11.18 E
Račinskij chrebet ⋏	84	42.30 N	43.30 E
Rackerby	226	39.26 N	121.20 W
Ráckeve	30	47.10 N	18.56 E
Rackwick	46	58.52 N	3.23 W
R'ad	76	57.56 N	35.04 E
Råda	40	60.00 N	13.36 E
Radama, Nosy II	157b	14.00 S	47.47 E
Radama, Presqu'île ›[1]	157b	14.16 S	47.53 E
Rådasjön ⊜	40	59.58 N	13.38 E
Radaur	124	30.02 N	77.09 E
Rădăuți	38	47.51 N	25.55 E
Radbuza ≃	60	49.46 N	13.24 E
Radčenskoje	78	49.48 N	40.32 E
Radcliff	194	37.50 N	85.56 W
Radcliffe	44	53.34 N	2.20 W
Radcliffe on Trent	42	52.57 N	1.03 W
Radda in Chianti	66	43.29 N	11.22 E
Raddusa	70	37.28 N	14.32 E
Råde	26	59.21 N	10.51 E
Radebaugh	279b	40.19 N	79.35 W
Radeberg	54	51.07 N	13.55 E
Radebeul	54	51.06 N	13.40 E
Radeburg	54	51.13 N	13.43 E
Radeče	36	46.04 N	15.11 E
Radechov	78	50.18 N	24.37 E
Radegast	54	51.39 N	12.05 E
Radenci	61	46.38 N	16.03 E
Radenthein	64	46.48 N	13.43 E
Radevormwald	56	51.12 N	7.21 E
Radford	192	37.07 N	80.34 W
Rādhānagar, India	126	23.09 N	87.19 E
Rādhānagar, India	272b	22.27 N	88.28 E
Rādhanpur	120	23.50 N	71.36 E
Radici, Foce delle)(	64	44.12 N	10.31 E
Radicofani	66	42.54 N	11.46 E
Radicondoli	66	43.16 N	11.02 E
Rădinești	38	44.48 N	23.46 E
Radiščevo	80	52.51 N	47.53 E
Radisson	184	52.27 N	107.23 W
Radiumbad Brambach	54	50.13 N	12.19 E
Radium Hot Springs	182	50.38 N	116.03 W
Rad'kovka	78	51.06 N	36.58 E
Radlett	42	51.42 N	0.20 W
Radlett Aerodrome ⊠	260	51.43 N	0.19 W
Radley Run ≃	285	39.54 N	75.37 W
Radlje ob Dravi	61	46.37 N	15.13 E
Rådmansö ›[1]	40	59.45 N	18.55 E
Radnevo	38	42.18 N	25.56 E
Radnice	60	49.51 N	13.37 E
Radnor, Oh., U.S.	214	40.23 N	83.09 W
Radnor, Pa., U.S.	285	40.02 N	75.21 W
Radnor Forest ∧	42	52.18 N	3.10 W
Radnor Mere ⊜	262	53.17 N	2.14 W
Radofinnikovo	76	59.09 N	30.55 E
Radogošča	76	59.47 N	34.51 E
Radoj'a	78	47.44 N	28.09 E
Radolfzell	58	47.44 N	8.58 E
Radom, Pol.	30	51.25 N	21.10 E
Radom, Il., U.S.	219	38.17 N	89.12 W
Radom □[4]	30	51.25 N	21.15 E
Radomicko	54	52.10 N	14.58 E
Radomir	38	42.33 N	22.58 E
Radomka	78	51.56 N	32.32 E
Radomka ≃	30	51.43 N	21.26 E
Radomsko	30	51.05 N	19.25 E

PORTUGUÊS

Nome	Página	Lat.°′	Long.°′ W = Oeste
Radomyšl'	78	50.30 N	29.14 E
Radomyśl Wielki	30	50.12 N	21.16 E
Radošice	60	49.33 N	13.39 E
Radoškoviči	76	54.09 N	27.14 E
Radotin	30	50.00 N	14.22 E
Radovicy	80	55.06 N	39.32 E
Radoviš	38	41.38 N	22.28 E
Radovljica	36	46.21 N	14.11 E
Radstadt	64	47.23 N	13.27 E
Radstädter Tauern)(	64	47.15 N	13.34 E
Radstock	42	51.18 N	2.28 W
Radstock, Cape ›	162	33.12 S	134.20 E
Raduha ∧	61	46.25 N	14.45 E
Radul'	78	51.49 N	30.42 E
Radun'	76	54.03 N	25.00 E
Radušnoje	78	47.49 N	33.29 E
Radutino	76	52.39 N	33.57 E
Radvaniči	76	52.02 N	24.02 E
Radviliškis	76	55.50 N	23.31 E
Radville	184	49.27 N	104.17 W
Radway	182	54.04 N	112.57 W
Radykovskoje	80	45.56 N	41.57 E
Radymno	30	49.57 N	22.48 E
Radyr	42	51.31 N	3.15 W
Radziejów	30	52.38 N	18.32 E
Radzyń Chełmiński	30	53.24 N	18.56 E
Radzyń Podlaski	30	51.48 N	22.38 E
Rae	176	62.50 N	116.03 W
Rae ≃	176	67.55 N	115.30 W
Rāe Bareli	124	26.13 N	81.14 E
Raeford	192	34.58 N	79.13 W
Rae Isthmus ≛[3]	176	66.55 N	86.10 W
Rāenda	126	22.18 N	89.51 E
Raeren	56	50.41 N	6.07 E
Raesfeld	52	51.46 N	6.50 E
Raeside, Lake ⊜	162	29.30 S	122.00 E
Rae Strait ʯ	176	68.45 N	95.00 W
Raetihi	172	39.26 S	175.17 E
Rafaela	252	31.16 S	61.29 W
Rafael Calzada	258	34.48 S	58.22 W
Rafael Castillo	288	34.43 S	58.37 W
Rafael Perazza	258	34.32 S	56.47 W
Rafaḥ	132	31.18 N	34.15 E
Rafaï	152	4.58 N	23.56 E
Rafalovka	78	51.22 N	25.52 E
Raffadali	70	37.24 N	13.32 E
Raffelberg, Rennbahn ♠	263	51.26 N	6.50 E
Raffili Mission	140	6.53 N	27.58 E
Rafḥā'	128	29.42 N	43.30 E
Rafinesque, Mount ∧[2]	210	42.47 N	73.37 W
Rafsanjān	128	30.24 N	56.01 E
Raft ≃	202	42.37 N	113.15 W
Raft River Mountains ⋏	200	41.55 N	113.25 W
Rafz	58	47.37 N	8.32 E
Raga	140	8.28 N	25.41 E
Ragada	64	46.10 N	10.38 E
Ragang, Mount ∧	116	7.43 N	124.32 E
Ragay	116	13.49 N	122.47 E
Ragay Gulf ⊂	116	13.30 N	122.45 E
Rågeleje	41	56.06 N	12.10 E
Rägelin	54	53.01 N	12.38 E
Ragewitz	54	51.14 N	12.51 E
Ragged, Mount ∧	162	33.27 S	123.25 E
Ragged Island I	238	22.12 N	75.44 W
Ragged Island Range II	238	22.40 N	75.54 W
Ragged Lake ⊜	212	45.28 N	78.38 W
Ragged Top Mountain ∧	200	41.27 N	105.20 W
Raghabpur	272b	22.25 N	88.21 E
Rāghogarh	124	24.27 N	77.12 E
Raghumāthbāri	126	22.22 N	87.47 E
Raghunāthpur, Bngl.	126	23.12 N	89.31 E
Raghunāthpur, India	126	23.33 N	86.40 E
Raglan, Austl.	170	33.26 S	149.36 E
Raglan, N.Z.	172	37.48 S	174.53 E
Raglan, Wales, U.K.	42	51.47 N	2.51 W
Ragland	194	33.44 N	86.09 W
Ragnitz	61	46.50 N	15.35 E
Rago Nasjonalpark ♠	24	67.26 N	16.00 E
Ragow	264a	52.17 N	13.33 E
Ragozino	86	59.15 N	77.52 E
Rågsveden	40	60.29 N	14.05 E
Raguda, Ghubbet ⊂	144	10.45 N	46.34 E
Raguhn	54	51.42 N	12.17 E
Raguli	80	45.38 N	43.42 E
Ragusa	70	36.55 N	14.44 E
Ragusa □[4]	70	36.55 N	14.36 E
Ragusa → Dubrovnik	38	42.38 N	18.07 E
Raguva	76	55.34 N	24.36 E
Raha	112	4.51 S	122.43 E
Rahad, Nahr ar- (Rahad) ≃	140	14.28 N	33.31 E
Rahad al-Bardī	140	11.18 N	23.53 E
Rahad Game Reserve ◆[4]	140	13.06 N	35.05 E
Rahaṭ, Ḥarrat ≛[9]	144	22.20 N	40.05 E
Rahatgaon	124	22.15 N	77.14 E
Rāhatgarh	124	23.47 N	78.22 E
Raḥbah	130	34.30 N	36.09 E
Rahden	52	52.26 N	8.36 E
Rahimatpur	122	17.36 N	74.12 E
Rahīm Ki Bāzār	120	24.19 N	69.09 E
Rahīmyār Khān	120	28.25 N	70.18 E
Rahlstedt ◆[8]	52	53.36 N	10.09 E
Rahm	263	51.26 N	6.26 E
Rahm ◆[8], Dtsch.	263	51.32 N	7.23 E
Rahm ◆[8], Dtsch.	263	51.21 N	6.47 E
Rahmer See ⊜	264a	52.45 N	13.25 E
Rahns	285	40.12 N	75.27 W
Rahnsdorf ◆[8]	264a	52.26 N	13.42 E
Rāhon	123	31.03 N	76.07 E
Rahotu	172	39.20 S	173.48 E
Rahouia	34	35.32 N	1.01 E
Rāhwāli	123	32.15 N	74.10 E
Rahway	210	40.36 N	74.16 W
Rahway ≃	276	40.35 N	74.12 W
Rahway, East Branch ≃	276	40.42 N	74.18 W
Rahway, Robinsons Branch ≃	276	40.37 N	74.17 W
Rahway, South Branch ≃	276	40.36 N	74.17 W
Rahway, West Branch ≃	276	40.42 N	74.18 W
Rahway River Parkway ♠	276	40.41 N	74.19 W
Raiano	66	42.06 N	13.49 E
Raiatea I	14	16.50 S	151.25 W
Rāichūr	122	16.12 N	77.22 E
Raidak ≃	124	26.22 N	89.45 E
Rāidighi	126	22.00 N	88.26 E
Raiding	61	47.34 N	16.32 E
Raiford	192	30.03 N	82.14 W
Raiganj	124	25.37 N	88.07 E
Raigarh	122	21.54 N	83.24 E
Raijua, Pulau I	112	10.37 S	121.36 E
Rāikot	123	30.39 N	75.36 E
Railroad	208	39.46 N	76.42 W
Railroad Canyon Reservoir ⊜[1]	228	33.42 N	117.16 W
Railroad Creek ≃	224	48.12 N	120.36 W
Rail Road Flat	226	38.20 N	120.30 W
Railroad Valley V	204	38.25 N	115.40 W
Railton	166	41.21 S	146.25 E
Raimangal ≃	126	21.47 N	89.08 E
Rain	56	48.41 N	10.55 E
Rainbach im Innkreis	60	48.27 N	13.32 E
Rainbow	228	33.24 N	117.10 W
Rainbow Bridge ◆[5]	284a	43.05 N	79.04 W
Rainbow Bridge National Monument ♠	200	37.06 N	110.57 W
Rainbow Falls ∟	182	52.23 N	119.59 W
Rainbow Lakes	276	40.52 N	74.28 W
Rainbow Park ♠	278	41.46 N	87.33 W
Rainbow Shores	212	43.37 N	76.12 W
Rainelle	188	37.58 N	80.46 W
Rainford	44	53.30 N	2.48 W
Rainham	42	51.23 N	0.36 E
Rainham ◆[8]	260	51.31 N	0.12 E
Rainhill	262	53.26 N	2.46 W
Rainhill Stoops	262	53.24 N	2.45 W
Rainier, Or., U.S.	224	46.05 N	122.56 W
Rainier, Wa., U.S.	224	46.53 N	122.41 W
Rainier, Mount ∧	224	46.52 N	121.46 W
Rainow	262	53.17 N	2.04 W
Rains □[6]	222	32.50 N	95.47 W
Rainsboro	218	39.13 N	83.25 W
Rainsford Island I	283	42.18 N	70.57 W
Rains → Riva di Tures	64	46.57 N	12.04 E
Rainworth	44	53.07 N	1.08 W
Rainy ≃, N.A.	184	48.50 N	94.41 W
Rainy ≃, Mi., U.S.	190	45.27 N	84.13 W
Rainy Lake ⊜, On., Can.	212	45.32 N	79.30 W
Rainy Lake ⊜, N.A.	184	48.42 N	93.10 W
Rainy Pass)(	224	48.32 N	120.39 W
Rainy River	190	48.43 N	94.34 W
Rāipur, Bngl.	126	23.03 N	90.46 E
Raipur, India	122	21.14 N	81.38 E
Raipur, India	124	30.19 N	78.06 E
Raipur, India	126	22.48 N	86.57 E
Raipur, India	272a	28.32 N	77.20 E
Raipur, India	272b	22.24 N	88.09 E
Rāipura	126	23.59 N	90.53 E
Raipur Uplands ⋏[1]	122	21.00 N	82.20 E
Rairākhol	120	21.04 N	84.21 E
Ra'īs	128	23.34 N	38.36 E
Raisdorf	54	54.17 N	10.16 E
Raisen	124	23.20 N	77.48 E
Ráisi, Punta ›	70	38.11 N	13.06 E
Raisin	226	36.36 N	119.54 W
Raisin ≃, On., Can.	206	45.08 N	74.29 W
Raisin ≃, Mi., U.S.	216	41.53 N	83.20 W
Rāisinghnagar	123	29.32 N	73.27 E
Raismes	50	50.23 N	3.29 E
Raita	126	24.07 N	88.57 E
Raitenbuch	60	49.01 N	11.08 E
Raití	236	14.35 N	85.02 W
Raivavae I	14	23.52 S	147.40 W
Rāiwind	123	31.15 N	74.13 E
Raizeux	261	48.37 N	1.41 E
Raja, Gili I	115a	7.14 S	113.47 E
Raja, Ujung ›	114	3.45 N	96.33 E
Rājābāri	126	23.23 N	90.28 E
Rajabasa	112	5.25 S	104.24 E
Rājābhāt Khāwa	124	26.37 N	89.32 E
Rājābhita	126	23.52 N	86.20 E
Rājahmundry	122	16.59 N	81.47 E
Rajāj	140	10.55 N	24.43 E
Rāja Jang	123	31.13 N	74.16 E
Raja-Jooseppi	24	68.28 N	28.21 E
Rājākhera	124	26.55 N	78.11 E
Rājaldesar	120	28.02 N	74.28 E
Raj-Aleksandrovka	83	48.48 N	37.51 E
Rājāluka	126	22.09 N	86.38 E
Rajamäki	26	60.32 N	24.45 E
Rājampet	122	14.11 N	79.10 E
Rajang ≃	112	2.04 N	111.12 E
Rājanpur	120	29.06 N	70.19 E
Rājapālaiyam	122	9.27 N	77.34 E
Rājāpur, Bngl.	126	22.34 N	90.09 E
Rājāpur, India	122	16.40 N	73.31 E
Rājāpur, India	124	25.23 N	81.09 E
Rājāpur, India	272b	22.39 N	88.11 E
Rājapur Canal ≊	272b	22.30 N	88.07 E
Rājasthān □[3]	120	27.00 N	74.00 E
Rājauri	123	33.23 N	74.18 E
Rājbāri, Bngl.	124	23.46 N	89.39 E
Rājbāri, India	126	22.25 N	88.48 E
Raj Bhavan ʋ	272b	22.34 N	88.21 E
Rājbirāj	124	26.32 N	86.44 E
Rajčichinsk	89	49.46 N	129.25 E
Rājendrapur	126	24.06 N	90.27 E
Rajevskij	86	54.04 N	54.56 E
Rāj Gangpur	124	22.11 N	84.36 E
Rājganj ≃[1]	126	22.21 N	90.16 E
Rājgarh, India	123	28.38 N	75.23 E
Rājgarh, India	124	23.56 N	76.58 E
Rājgarh, India	124	27.14 N	76.38 E
Rajghat ʋ[1]	272a	28.39 N	77.15 E
Rājgīr	124	25.02 N	85.25 E
Rajgorod	80	48.26 N	44.55 E
Rajgorodka, Ukr.	83	49.22 N	37.57 E
Rajgorodka, Ukr.	83	48.50 N	39.04 E
Rajgorodok, Kaz.	80	48.48 N	52.53 E
Rajgorodok, Ukr.	83	48.54 N	37.43 E
Rajgród	30	53.44 N	22.42 E
Rājhāt	272b	22.56 N	88.21 E
Rajhrad	61	49.05 N	16.37 E
Rājibpur	272b	22.49 N	88.34 E
Rajik	112	2.36 S	105.56 E
Rajka	61	48.02 N	17.11 E
Rājkot	120	22.18 N	70.47 E
Rajkuzi	265a	59.47 N	29.57 E
Rājmahāl	124	25.03 N	87.50 E
Rājmahāl Hills ⋏[2]	124	24.40 N	87.25 E
Rājnagar	126	23.57 N	87.19 E
Rāj Nāndgaon	120	21.06 N	81.02 E
Rajokri ◆[8]	272a	28.31 N	77.07 E
Rājpipla	120	21.47 N	73.34 E
Rājpur, India	120	21.56 N	75.08 E
Rājpur, India	126	22.25 N	88.25 E
Rājpur, India	272a	28.44 N	77.22 E
Rājpur ◆[8]	272a	28.41 N	77.12 E
Rājpura	124	30.29 N	76.36 E
Rājshāhi	124	24.22 N	88.36 E
Rājshāhi □[5]	124	25.15 N	89.15 E
Rajskoje	83	48.34 N	37.25 E
Rājula	122	21.03 N	71.26 E
Raka	124	29.26 N	85.50 E
Raka ≃	124	29.24 N	87.58 E
Rakaia	172	43.45 S	172.01 E
Rakaia ≃	172	43.56 S	172.13 E
Rakamaz	30	48.08 N	21.30 E
Rakaposhi ∧	123	36.10 N	74.30 E
Rakata, Pulau I	115a	6.10 S	105.26 E
Rakha La)(	124	27.53 N	87.34 E
Rakhawt, Wādī V	144	17.40 N	51.40 E
Rakhine □[8]	110	19.00 N	94.15 E
Rakhneh	128	31.39 N	59.13 E
Rakhni	120	30.03 N	69.55 E
Rakhshān ≃	128	27.10 N	63.25 E
Rākīn	132	31.14 N	35.42 E
Rakitnoje, Ross.	78	50.51 N	35.50 E
Rakitnoje, Ross.	89	45.36 N	134.17 E
Rakitnoje, Ukr.	78	49.42 N	30.27 E
Rakitnoje, Ukr.	78	51.17 N	27.14 E
Rakke	76	58.59 N	26.15 E
Rakkestad	26	59.26 N	11.21 E
Rakoniewice	30	52.10 N	16.16 E
Rakops	156	21.00 S	24.32 E
Rákoscsaba ◆[8]	264c	47.29 N	19.17 E
Rákoshegy ◆[8]	264c	47.28 N	19.14 E
Rákoskeresztúr ◆[8]	264c	47.29 N	19.15 E
Rákoskert ◆[8]	264c	47.28 N	19.19 E
Rákosliget ◆[8]	264c	47.30 N	19.16 E
Rákospalota ◆[8]	264c	47.34 N	19.08 E
Rákos-patak ≃	264c	47.33 N	19.04 E
Rákosszentmihály ◆[8]	264c	47.32 N	19.11 E
Rakovnická plošina ⋏[1]	54	50.08 N	13.47 E
Rakovník	54	50.05 N	13.43 E
Rakovski	38	42.18 N	24.58 E
Rakša	80	53.33 N	41.37 E
Raksakiny	86	60.37 N	73.52 E
Rakuša	80	47.03 N	52.47 E
Råkvåg	26	63.46 N	10.05 E
Rakvere	76	59.22 N	26.20 E
Rakwa	164	2.42 S	134.30 E
Raleigh, Nf., Can.	186	51.34 N	55.44 W
Raleigh, Ms., U.S.	194	32.02 N	89.31 W
Raleigh, N.C., U.S.	192	35.46 N	78.38 W
Raleigh Hills	224	45.29 N	122.45 W
Raleighvallen Voltz Berg, Natuurreservaat ♠, Sur.	246	4.45 N	56.05 W
Raleighvallen Voltz Berg, Natuurreservaat ♠, Sur.	250	4.50 N	55.10 W
Ralik Chain II	14	8.00 N	167.00 E
Ralls	196	33.40 N	101.23 W
Ralls □[6]	219	39.34 N	91.30 W
Ralsko ∧	54	50.42 N	14.47 E
Ralston, Ne., U.S.	198	41.12 N	96.02 W
Ralston, Pa., U.S.	210	41.31 N	76.57 W
Ram ≃	182	52.23 N	115.25 W
Rama, Nic.	236	12.09 N	84.15 W
Rama, Yis.	132	32.56 N	35.22 E
Rama ≃	236	12.08 N	84.13 W
Ramacca	70	37.23 N	14.42 E
Rāmachandrapuram	122	16.51 N	82.01 E
Ramādah	144	13.38 N	43.56 E
Ramah	200	35.07 N	108.29 W
Ramah Indian Reservation ◆[4]	200	34.50 N	108.25 W
Rama Indian Reserve ◆[4]	212	44.41 N	79.15 W
Ramales de la Victoria	34	43.15 N	3.27 W
Rām Allāh	132	31.54 N	35.12 E
Rāman	123	29.58 N	74.58 E
Rāmanagaram	122	12.43 N	77.18 E
Rāmanāthapuram	122	9.23 N	78.50 E
Ramanāthpur	272b	22.41 N	88.14 E
Ramanbāti	272b	22.47 N	88.08 E
Rāmānuj Ganj	124	23.48 N	83.42 E
Ramapo	276	41.08 N	74.10 W
Ramapo ≃	276	40.58 N	74.17 W
Ramapo Lake ⊜	276	41.02 N	74.16 W
Ramapo Mountains ⋏	276	41.08 N	74.12 W
Ramapo Valley Airport ⊠	276	41.06 N	74.02 W
Ramas, Cape ›	122	15.07 N	73.55 E
Ramasaig	46	57.24 N	6.44 W
Ramasucha	76	52.46 N	33.33 E
Ramat Gan	132	32.05 N	34.49 E
Ramat HaSharon	132	32.09 N	34.50 E
Ramat HaShofét	132	32.37 N	35.06 E
Ramathlabama	156	25.40 S	25.35 E
Ramatuelle	62	43.13 N	6.37 E
Rama VI Bridge ◆[5]	269a	13.48 N	100.31 E
Rāmban	123	33.15 N	75.15 E
Rambervillers	58	48.21 N	6.38 E
Rambi I	175g	16.30 S	179.59 E
Rambipuji	115a	8.13 S	113.36 E
Rambleton Acres	208	39.39 N	75.38 W
Ramblewood	285	39.55 N	74.56 W
Rambouillet	50	48.39 N	1.50 E
Rambouillet, Château de ⊥	261	48.39 N	1.49 E
Rambouillet, Forêt de ♠	261	48.40 N	1.50 E
Rambutyo Island I	164	2.20 S	147.50 E
Rām Dās	123	31.58 N	74.54 E
Rāmdia	126	23.42 N	89.32 E
Rāmdurg	122	15.57 N	75.18 E
Ramea	186	47.31 N	57.23 W
Ramea Islands II	186	47.31 N	57.21 W
Rāmechhāp	124	27.20 N	86.05 E
Rame Head ›, Transkei	158	31.48 S	29.22 E
Rame Head ›, Eng., U.K.	42	50.19 N	4.13 W
Rämen ⊜	40	60.18 N	15.10 E
Ramenje, Ross.	76	60.17 N	43.46 E
Ramenje, Ross.	82	56.34 N	37.13 E
Ramenka ◆[8]	265b	55.41 N	37.30 E
Ramenskoje	82	55.34 N	38.14 E
Ramer	194	32.03 N	86.13 W
Ramerupt	50	48.31 N	4.18 E
Rameški	76	57.21 N	36.03 E
Rāmeswaram	122	9.17 N	79.18 E
Ramey	214	40.48 N	78.24 W
Rāmganj	126	23.06 N	90.51 E
Rāmgarh, Bngl.	120	22.59 N	91.44 E
Rāmgarh, India	120	27.22 N	70.30 E
Rāmgarh, India	120	27.15 N	75.11 E
Rāmgarh, India	124	23.38 N	85.31 E
Rāmgarh, India	124	24.34 N	87.15 E
Rāmgarh, India	126	22.42 N	87.04 E
Rāmgarh Hills ⋏[2]	124	22.50 N	83.10 E
Ram Head ›	240m	18.18 N	64.42 W
Rāmhormoz	128	31.16 N	49.36 E
Ramingining	164	12.19 S	135.03 E
Ramingstein	64	47.04 N	13.50 E
Ramírez, Méx.	196	27.20 N	100.58 W
Ramírez, Méx.	196	25.57 N	97.46 W
Ramiriquí	246	5.24 N	73.20 W
Ramis ≃	144	7.59 N	41.34 E
Rāmjībanpur	126	22.50 N	87.37 E
Rāmkānāli	126	23.35 N	86.45 E
Raml, Qārat ar- ∧[2]	142	30.02 N	30.39 E
Ramla	132	31.55 N	34.52 E
Ramlu ∧	144	13.24 N	41.51 E
Ramm, Jabal ∧	132	29.35 N	35.24 E
Rämmen	40	60.07 N	14.08 E
Rāmnagar, India	123	32.49 N	75.19 E
Rāmnagar, India	124	25.17 N	83.02 E
Rāmnagar, India	124	29.24 N	79.07 E
Rāmnagar, India	126	21.41 N	87.33 E
Rāmnagar, India	272b	22.23 N	88.19 E
Ramnäs	40	59.46 N	16.12 E
Ramo	144	6.42 N	41.23 E
Ramon'	78	51.54 N	39.20 E
Ramon, Har ∧	132	30.30 N	34.38 E
Ramon, Makhtésh ≛[7]	132	30.36 N	34.49 E
Ramon, Naḥal V	132	30.36 N	34.55 E
Ramona, Ca., U.S.	228	33.02 N	116.52 W
Ramona, Ok., U.S.	196	36.31 N	95.55 W
Ramona, S.D., U.S.	198	44.07 N	97.12 W
Ramor, Lough ⊜	48	53.49 N	7.05 W
Ramos	234	22.50 N	101.55 W
Ramos ◆[8]	287a	22.51 S	43.15 W
Ramos ≃[1]	150	5.08 N	5.22 E
Ramosch	58	46.50 N	10.22 E
Ramos Island I	116	8.06 N	117.02 E
Ramos Mejía	258	34.38 S	58.34 W
Ramot	132	32.46 N	35.40 E
Ramotswa	156	24.56 S	25.50 E
Rāmpāl	126	22.34 N	89.39 E
Rampart	180	65.30 N	150.11 W
Ramparts ≃	180	66.11 N	129.03 W
Rampillon	50	48.33 N	3.04 E
Rampside	44	54.05 N	3.10 W
Rāmpur, India	120	31.27 N	77.38 E
Rāmpur, India	123	29.49 N	77.27 E
Rāmpur, India	124	28.49 N	79.02 E
Rāmpura	120	24.28 N	75.26 E
Rāmpura Phūl	123	30.17 N	75.14 E
Rampur Boalia → Rājshāhi	124	24.22 N	88.36 E
Rāmpur Hāt	126	24.10 N	87.47 E
Ramrath	263	51.06 N	6.41 E
Ramree Island I	110	19.06 N	93.48 E
Rāmsāgar	126	23.05 N	87.17 E
Ramsau	64	47.36 N	12.54 E
Ramsay Range ⋏	162	18.31 S	127.03 E
Ramsbeck	56	51.18 N	8.24 E
Ramsberg	40	59.46 N	15.17 E
Ramsbottom	44	53.40 N	2.19 W
Ramsden Bellhouse	260	51.37 N	0.29 E
Ramsden Heath	260	51.38 N	0.28 E
Ramsdorf	52	51.54 N	6.55 E
Ramsele	26	63.33 N	16.29 E
Ramsenthal	60	50.01 N	11.35 E
Ramseur	192	35.44 N	79.39 W
Ramsey, I. of Man	44	54.20 N	4.21 W
Ramsey, Eng., U.K.	42	51.56 N	1.14 E
Ramsey, Eng., U.K.	42	52.27 N	0.07 W
Ramsey, Il., U.S.	219	39.08 N	89.06 W
Ramsey, N.J., U.S.	210	41.03 N	74.08 W
Ramsey Bay ⊂	44	54.20 N	4.20 W
Ramsey Brook ≃	276	41.02 N	74.08 W
Ramsey Creek ≃	219	39.03 N	89.04 W
Ramsey Island I	42	51.52 N	5.10 W
Ramsey Lake ⊜	190	47.15 N	82.16 W
Ramsey Lake State Park ♠	219	39.10 N	89.08 W
Ramsgate, Austl.	274a	33.59 S	151.08 E
Ramsgate, S. Afr.	158	30.55 S	30.20 E
Ramsgate, Eng., U.K.	42	51.20 N	1.25 E
Rāmshai	124	26.44 N	88.51 E
Rāmshīr	128	30.54 N	49.24 E
Ramshorn Peak ∧	202	45.09 N	111.06 W
Rämshyttan	40	60.18 N	15.13 E
Ramsjö	26	62.11 N	15.39 E
Ramsloh	52	53.06 N	7.40 E
Ramstein	56	49.27 N	7.33 E
Rāmtek	120	21.24 N	79.20 E
Rāmu, Bngl.	120	21.25 N	92.07 E
Ramu, Kenya	154	3.56 N	41.13 E
Ramu ≃	164	4.02 S	144.41 E
Ramuševo	76	57.50 N	31.37 E
Ramvik	26	62.49 N	17.51 E
Ramville, Îlet I	240e	14.42 N	60.53 W
Ramygala	76	55.31 N	24.18 E
Ramzaj	80	53.18 N	44.44 E
Rānāghāt	126	23.11 N	88.35 E
Rana Kao, Volcán ∧[1]	174z	27.11 S	109.27 W
Ranalt	64	47.02 N	11.13 E
Rāna Pratāp Sāgar ⊜[1]	120	24.50 N	75.35 E
Rånäs	40	59.48 N	18.17 E
Ranau	112	5.58 N	116.41 E
Ranau, Danau ⊜	112	4.50 S	103.55 E
Ranbīrsinghpura	123	32.38 N	74.44 E
Ranburne	194	33.31 N	85.20 W
Rancabali	115a	7.08 S	107.21 E
Rancagua	252	34.10 S	70.45 W
Rancah	115a	7.12 S	108.30 E
Rance ≃	32	48.31 N	1.59 W
Rancevo, Ross.	76	56.56 N	34.03 E
Rancevo, Ross.	76	56.40 N	33.02 E
Rancharia	255	22.15 S	50.55 W
Rancheria	180	60.05 N	130.40 W
Ranchería ≃	246	11.34 N	72.54 W
Rancheria Rock ∧	202	44.53 N	120.08 W
Ranches of Taos	200	36.22 N	105.37 W
Ranchester	202	44.54 N	107.09 W
Rānchi	124	23.21 N	85.20 E
Ranchillos	252	26.57 S	65.03 W
Rānchi Plateau ⋏[1]	124	23.20 N	84.50 E
Ranch Lake ⊜	184	52.30 N	104.46 W
Rancho Colorado, Presa de ⊜[1]	286a	19.29 N	99.17 W
Rancho Cordova	226	38.35 N	121.18 W
Rancho Del Mar	226	38.10 N	122.15 W
Rancho Nuevo, Méx.	196	26.22 N	99.54 W
Rancho Nuevo, Méx.	234	23.12 N	97.48 W
Rancho Palos Verdes	228	33.45 N	118.24 W
Rancho Rinconado	226	37.18 N	122.01 W
Rancho Santa Fe	228	33.01 N	117.12 W
Rancho Veloz	240p	22.53 N	80.23 W
Ranchuelo	240p	22.23 N	80.09 W
Ranco, Lago ⊜	254	40.14 S	72.24 W
Rancocas	208	40.00 N	74.52 W
Rancocas Creek ≃	285	40.02 N	74.59 W
Rancocas Creek, North Branch ≃	208	40.00 N	74.52 W
Rancocas Creek, South Branch ≃	208	40.00 N	74.52 W
Rancocas Creek, Southwest Branch ≃	285	39.57 N	74.48 W
Rancocas Heights	285	39.59 N	74.51 W
Rancocas State Park ♠	285	40.00 N	74.50 W
Rancocas Woods	285	39.59 N	74.51 W
Rancul	252	35.03 S	64.42 W
Rand	166	35.36 S	146.35 E
Rand (Germiston) Airport ⊠	273d	26.15 S	28.09 E
Randa	58	46.07 N	7.47 E
Randall Lake ⊜	216	41.57 N	85.02 W
Randall Park Mall ◆[9]	279a	41.26 N	81.32 W
Randalls Island I	276	40.48 N	73.55 W
Randallstown	284b	39.22 N	76.48 W
Randalstown	48	54.45 N	6.19 W
Randan	32	46.01 N	3.21 E
Rāndaveswar	126	23.43 N	87.17 E
Randazzo	70	37.53 N	14.57 E
Randbøl	41	55.42 N	9.16 E
Randburg	273d	26.06 S	27.59 E
Randers	26	56.28 N	10.03 E
Randfontein	158	26.11 S	27.42 E
Randfontein □[5]	273d	26.13 S	27.40 E
Randgate	273d	26.11 S	27.41 E
Randhurst ◆[9]	278	42.05 N	87.56 W
Randle	224	46.32 N	121.57 W
Randleman	192	35.49 N	79.48 W
Randlett	196	34.10 N	98.27 W
Randolph, Az., U.S.	200	32.55 N	111.30 W
Randolph, Me., U.S.	188	44.13 N	69.46 W
Randolph, Ma., U.S.	207	42.09 N	71.02 W
Randolph, Ne., U.S.	198	42.22 N	97.21 W
Randolph, N.Y., U.S.	210	42.09 N	78.58 W
Randolph, Oh., U.S.	214	41.01 N	81.14 W
Randolph, Ut,. U.S.	200	41.39 N	111.10 W
Randolph, Vt., U.S.	188	43.55 N	72.39 W
Randolph, Wi., U.S.	190	43.32 N	89.00 W
Randolph □[6], In., U.S.	218	40.10 N	85.00 W
Randolph □[6], Mo., U.S.	219	39.22 N	92.20 W
Randolph Air Force Base ■	196	29.32 N	98.16 W
Randolph Hills	284c	39.03 N	77.05 W
Randolph Village	284c	38.53 N	76.52 W
Random Island I	186	48.08 N	53.45 W
Random Lake	190	43.33 N	87.57 W
Randow ≃	54	53.41 N	14.04 E
Randowaya	164	1.52 S	136.31 E
Randowbruch ⩸	54	53.15 N	14.10 E
Randsburg	228	35.22 N	117.39 W
Randse Afrikaanse Universiteit ʋ[2]	273d	26.11 S	27.50 E
Randsfjorden ⊜	26	60.25 N	10.24 E
Rand Stadium ♠	273d	26.14 S	28.03 E
Randublatung	115a	7.12 S	111.23 E
Randudongkal	115a	7.06 S	109.19 E
Randwick	170	33.55 S	151.15 E
Randwick Racecourse ♠	274a	33.54 S	151.14 E
Råneå	26	65.52 N	22.18 E
Ranelagh	258	34.48 S	58.12 W
Rāner	123	28.53 N	73.17 E
Ranérou	150	15.18 N	13.58 W
Rāneswar	126	24.02 N	87.25 E
Raneue	114	5.03 N	95.20 E
Ranford	168a	32.48 S	116.31 E
Ranfurly, N.Z.	172	45.08 S	170.06 E
Ranfurly, Scot., U.K.	46	55.52 N	4.33 W
Rangae	114	6.17 N	101.44 E
Rāngāmāti	120	22.38 N	92.12 E
Rangantemiang	112	0.35 S	113.19 E
Rangas, Tanjung ›	112	2.38 S	118.49 E
Rangasa, Tanjung ›	112	3.33 S	118.56 E
Rangaunu Bay ⊂	172	34.50 S	173.15 E
Range Creek ≃	200	39.18 N	110.04 W
Range Indian Reserve ◆[4]	182	49.09 N	119.50 W
Rangeley	188	44.57 N	70.38 W
Rangely	200	40.05 N	108.48 W
Ranger	196	32.28 N	98.40 W
Ranger Lake ⊜	190	46.54 N	83.35 W
Rangersdorf	64	46.51 N	12.58 E
Ranghe	100	33.43 N	112.51 E
Rangia	120	26.28 N	91.38 E
Rangiora	172	43.18 S	172.36 E

≃	River	Fluß	Río	Rivière	Rio
≊	Canal	Kanal	Canal	Canal	Canal
∟	Waterfall, Rapids	Wasserfall, Stromschnellen	Cascada, Rápidos	Chute d'eau, Rapides	Cascata, Rápidos
ʯ	Strait	Meeresstraße	Estrecho	Détroit	Estreito
⊂	Bay, Gulf	Bucht, Golf	Bahía, Golfo	Baie, Golfe	Baía, Golfo
⊜	Lake, Lakes	See, Seen	Lago, Lagos	Lac, Lacs	Lago, Lagos
⩸	Swamp	Sumpf	Pantano	Marais	Pântano
⍓	Ice Features, Glacier	Eis- und Gletscherformen	Accidentes Glaciales	Formes glaciaires	Acidentes glaciares
⍑	Other Hydrographic Features	Andere Hydrographische Objekte	Otros Elementos Hidrográficos	Autres données hydrographiques	Outros acidentes hidrográficos

✧	Submarine Features	Untermeerische Objekte	Accidentes Submarinos	Formes de relief sous-marin	Acidentes submarinos
□	Political Unit	Politische Einheit	Unidad Politica	Entité politique	Unidade política
ʋ	Cultural Institution	Kulturelle Institution	Institución Cultural	Institution culturelle	Institução cultural
⊥	Historical Site	Historische Stätte	Sitio Histórico	Site historique	Sitio histórico
♠	Recreational Site	Erholungs- und Ferienort	Sitio de Recreo	Centre de loisirs	Area de Lazer
⊠	Airport	Flughafen	Aeropuerto	Aéroport	Aeroporto
■	Military Installation	Militäranlage	Instalación Militar	Installation militaire	Instalação militar
◆	Miscellaneous	Verschiedenes	Misceláneo	Divers	Diversos

Name	Page	Lat.°′	Long.°′
Rangitaiki ≃	172	37.54 S	176.53 E
Rangitata ≃	172	44.12 S	171.30 E
Rangitikei ≃	172	40.18 S	175.14 E
Rangitukia	172	37.46 S	178.27 E
Rangkasbitung	115a	6.21 S	106.15 E
Rangkul'	85	38.29 N	74.22 E
Rangoon ≃	110	16.29 N	96.21 E
Rangoon → Yangon	110	16.47 N	96.10 E
Rangpo	124	27.11 N	88.32 E
Rangpur, Bngl.	124	25.45 N	89.15 E
Rangpur, Pāk.	123	30.31 N	71.34 E
Rangpuri ⊥	272a	28.33 N	77.08 E
Rangsang, Pulau I	114	1.00 N	102.55 E
Rangsdorf	54	52.17 N	13.25 E
Rangsdorfer See ⊜	264a	52.17 N	13.24 E
Ranguana Cay I	236	16.20 N	88.09 W
Ranguana Entrance ʯ	236	16.19 N	88.09 W
Rangun → Yangon	110	16.47 N	96.10 E
Ranholas	266c	38.47 N	9.22 W
Rānībāndh	126	22.52 N	86.47 E
Rānībennur	122	14.37 N	75.37 E
Rānīganj	126	23.37 N	87.08 E
Rānikhet	124	29.39 N	79.25 E
Ranino	80	52.58 N	40.15 E
Ranis	54	50.39 N	11.34 E
Rānīwāra	120	24.45 N	72.13 E
Rāniyah	128	36.15 N	44.53 E
Rankamhaeng National Park ♠	110	17.10 N	99.58 E
Ranken ≃	166	20.31 S	137.36 E
Ranken Store	166	19.35 S	136.55 E
Rankin, Il., U.S.	216	40.27 N	87.53 W
Rankin, Mi., U.S.	216	42.55 N	83.46 W
Rankin, Pa., U.S.	279b	40.24 N	79.52 W
Rankin, Tx., U.S.	196	31.13 N	101.56 W
Rankin Inlet	176	62.45 N	92.10 W
Rankins Springs	166	33.50 S	146.16 E
Rankūs	132	33.45 N	36.23 E
Rankweil	58	47.17 N	9.39 E
Ranlo	192	35.17 N	81.07 W
Ranneje	80	51.29 N	52.37 E
Rannersdorf	264b	48.08 N	16.28 E
Rannoch, Loch ⊜	46	56.41 N	4.20 W
Rannoch Moor ◆[3]	46	56.38 N	4.40 W
Rann of Kutch → Kutch, Rann of ◆[1]	120	24.05 N	70.10 E
Ranobe ≃	157b	17.10 S	44.08 E
Ranohira	157b	22.29 S	45.24 E
Ranomafana, Madag.	157b	18.57 S	48.50 E
Ranomafana, Madag.	157b	24.36 S	46.58 E
Ranomena	157b	23.25 S	47.17 E
Ranong	110	9.58 N	98.38 E
Ranongga Island I	175e	8.05 S	156.34 E
Ranopiso	157b	25.03 S	46.40 E
Ranot	110	7.46 N	100.19 E
Ranotsara Nord	157b	22.48 S	46.36 E
Rānsai	272c	18.53 N	73.05 E
Ransäter	40	59.46 N	13.26 E
Ransiki	164	1.30 S	134.10 E
Ransom, Il., U.S.	216	41.09 N	88.39 W
Ransom, Ks., U.S.	198	38.38 N	99.56 W
Ransom, Pa., U.S.	210	41.24 N	75.50 W
Ransom Creek ≃	284a	43.04 N	78.45 W
Ransomville	210	43.14 N	78.54 W
Ranson	188	39.17 N	77.51 W
Ransta	40	59.48 N	16.38 E
Ranstadt	56	50.21 N	8.59 E
Rantabe	157b	15.42 S	49.39 E
Rantasalmi	26	62.04 N	28.18 E
Rantau, Indon.	112	2.56 S	115.09 E
Rantau, Malay.	114	2.35 N	101.58 E
Rantaukampar	114	1.24 N	100.59 E
Rantaupanjang, Indon.	112	1.51 S	102.19 E
Rantaupanjang, Indon.	112	1.16 S	101.49 E
Rantaupanjang, Indon.	114	0.58 N	99.13 E
Rantauprapat	114	2.06 N	99.50 E
Rantekombola, Bulu ∧	112	3.21 S	120.01 E
Ranten	61	47.09 N	14.05 E
Rantepao	112	2.59 S	119.54 E
Rantigny	50	49.20 N	2.26 E
Rantoul	216	40.09 N	88.20 W
Rantsila	26	64.31 N	25.39 E
Rantzau	54	54.15 N	10.30 E
Ranua	26	65.55 N	26.32 E
Rānvād	272c	18.53 N	72.55 E
Ranwanalenaus	156	19.35 S	22.47 E
Råö	26	57.24 N	11.56 E
Rao'er	100	28.48 N	117.40 E
Raohe	89	46.47 N	134.00 E
Raon-L'Étape	58	48.24 N	6.51 E
Raon-sur-Plaine	58	48.31 N	7.06 E
Raoping	100	23.43 N	117.01 E
Raoui, 'Erg er ◆[2]	148	29.17 N	2.20 W
Raoul	192	34.27 N	83.36 W
Raoul Island I	14	29.16 S	177.54 W
Raoyang	98	38.16 N	115.44 E
Raoyang ≃	104	41.50 N	122.35 E
Raoyanghe	104	41.46 N	122.26 E
Rapa I	14	27.36 S	144.20 W
Rapa, Ponta do >	252	27.22 S	48.26 W
Rapallo	62	44.21 N	9.14 E
Rapang	112	3.50 S	119.48 E
Rāpar	120	23.34 N	70.38 E
Raparo, Monte ∧	68	40.12 N	15.59 E
Rapatovo	80	55.04 N	54.37 E
Rāpch ≃	128	25.28 N	59.21 E
Rapel ≃	252	33.55 S	71.51 W
Rapel, Embalse ⊜[1]	252	34.12 S	71.30 W
Rapelli	252	26.24 S	64.29 W
Raphoe	48	54.52 N	7.36 W
Rapid ≃, Mi., U.S.	190	45.55 N	86.58 W
Rapid ≃, Mn., U.S.	198	48.42 N	94.26 W
Rapid ≃, Wa., U.S.	224	47.48 N	121.18 W
Rapidan ≃	188	38.22 N	77.37 W
Rapid Bay	168b	35.32 S	138.12 E
Rapid City, Mb., Can.	184	50.08 N	100.02 W
Rapid City, Mi., U.S.	190	44.50 N	85.16 W
Rapid City, S.D., U.S.	198	44.04 N	103.13 W
Rapid Creek ≃	198	43.54 N	102.37 W
Rapide Taureau, Barrage du ◆[6]	206	46.52 N	73.39 W
Rapid River	190	45.55 N	86.58 W
Räpina	76	58.06 N	27.27 E
Rapkan	85	40.22 N	70.40 E
Rapla	76	59.01 N	24.47 E
Rapness	46	59.14 N	2.51 W
Rapolano Terme	66	43.17 N	11.36 E
Rapolla	68	40.58 N	15.41 E
Rapone	68	40.51 N	15.30 E
Raposo ∧[2]	266c	38.40 N	9.11 W
Rappahannock ≃	208	37.34 N	76.18 W
Rappbodestausee ⊜[1]	54	51.44 N	10.53 E
Rappenlochschlucht ∟	58	47.23 N	9.47 E
Rappottenstein	61	48.31 N	15.05 E
Rāptī □[8]	124	28.15 N	82.30 E
Rāpti (Raptī) ≃, Asia	124	26.18 N	83.41 E
Rāptī ≃, Nepāl	124	27.33 N	84.07 E
Rapulo ≃	248	13.43 S	65.32 W
Rapu-Rapu	116	13.11 N	124.08 E
Rapu Rapu Island I	116	13.12 N	124.09 E
Raqabah, Khashm ar- ∧[2]	142	28.18 N	31.43 E
Raquette ≃	206	45.00 N	74.42 W
Raraka I[1]	14	16.10 S	144.54 W
Rara National Park ♠	124	29.35 N	82.05 E
Rārh Plains ≃	126	23.13 N	87.20 E
Rāribahāl	126	24.05 N	87.21 E
Raritan	210	40.34 N	74.38 W
Raritan ≃	208	40.29 N	74.17 W
Raritan, North Branch ≃	210	40.33 N	74.41 W
Raritan, South Branch ≃	210	40.33 N	74.41 W
Raritan Bay c	208	40.28 N	74.12 W
Raroïa I	14	16.01 S	142.27 W
Raron	58	46.19 N	7.48 E
Rarotonga I	174k	21.14 S	159.46 W
Rarotonga International Airport ⊠	174k	21.12 S	159.49 W
Rarz	85	39.23 N	68.44 E
Rasa, Ilha I	287a	23.04 S	43.09 W
Rasa, Punta >, Arg.	252	36.17 S	56.47 W
Rasa, Punta >, Arg.	254	40.51 S	62.19 W
Rašaant	88	49.07 N	101.25 E
Rasa de Guaratiba, Ilha I	256	23.05 S	43.34 W
Rasa Island I	116	9.14 N	118.27 E
Ra's al-'Ayn	130	36.51 N	40.04 E
Ra's al-Barr	142	31.31 N	31.50 E
Ra's al-Khalīj	142	31.15 N	31.39 E
Ra's al-Khaymah	128	25.47 N	55.57 E
Ra's al-Unūf	146	30.31 N	18.34 E
Ra's al-Ushsh ◆[8]	142	31.08 N	32.18 E
Ra's an-Naqb, Miṣr	132	29.36 N	34.51 E
Ra's an-Naqb, Urd.	132	30.00 N	35.29 E
Rasawi	164	2.04 S	134.01 E
Ra's Ba'labakk	130	34.15 N	36.25 E
Rasbo	40	59.57 N	17.53 E
Raschau	54	50.32 N	12.50 E
Ras Dashen Terara ∧	144	13.16 N	38.24 E
Rasdorf	56	50.43 N	9.53 E
Raseborg	26	59.59 N	23.39 E
Raseiniai	76	55.24 N	23.07 E
Râs el Aïoun	36	35.30 N	8.18 E
Ras el Ma, Alg.	148	34.31 N	0.46 W
Râs el Mâ, Mali	150	16.37 N	4.28 W
Ras el Oued	34	35.57 N	5.03 E
Rasen-Antholz → Anterselva di Sopra	64	46.52 N	12.08 E
Raševka	78	50.14 N	33.54 E
Rashād	140	11.51 N	31.04 E
Rāshayyā	132	33.30 N	35.51 E
Rashīd (Rosetta)	142	31.24 N	30.25 E
Rashīd, Far' (Rosetta Branch) ≃	142	31.30 N	30.21 E
Rashīd, Maṣabb (Rosetta Mouth) ≃[1]	142	31.30 N	30.20 E
Rashīd Qal'eh	120	31.31 N	67.31 E
Rashin → Najin	98	42.15 N	130.18 E
Rasht	128	37.16 N	49.36 E
Rashtrapati Bhawan ☗	272a	28.37 N	77.12 E
Rasina ≃	38	43.37 N	21.22 E
Rāsipuram	122	11.28 N	78.10 E
Rasi Salai	110	15.20 N	104.09 E
Rāsk	128	26.13 N	61.25 E
Raška	38	43.17 N	20.37 E
Rask Mølle	41	55.52 N	9.37 E
Rās Koh ∧	128	28.50 N	65.12 E
Raškov	78	47.57 N	28.50 E
Raskunda	126	22.48 N	87.26 E
Rasm al-Arwām, Sabkhat ⊜	130	35.53 N	37.40 E
R'asna	76	54.01 N	31.12 E
R'asnopol'	78	47.04 N	31.12 E
Raso, Cabo >	266c	38.43 N	9.29 W
Raso, Ilhéu I	150a	16.37 N	24.36 W
Rasocolmo, Capo >	70	38.18 N	15.31 E
Rason Lake ⊜	162	28.46 S	124.20 E
Raspberry Peak ∧	194	34.23 N	94.01 W
Raspopinskaja	80	49.24 N	42.52 E
Rasra	124	25.51 N	83.51 E
Rass Jebel	36	37.13 N	10.09 E
Rasskazovka	265b	55.38 N	37.20 E
Rasskazovo	80	52.40 N	41.53 E
Rassua, ostrov I	74	47.45 N	153.01 E
Rassudovo	82	55.29 N	36.54 E
Rassvet, Ross.	84	43.58 N	46.44 E
Rassvet, Ross.	84	43.58 N	46.44 E
Rassvet, Ross.	86	57.02 N	91.34 E
Rassvet, Ross.	88	57.02 N	91.34 E
Rassypnaja	80	51.35 N	53.37 E
Rassypnoje	83	48.08 N	38.34 E
Rast	38	43.53 N	23.17 E
Rastälven ≃	40	59.37 N	14.56 E
Ra's Tannūrah	128	26.42 N	50.06 E
Rastatt	56	48.51 N	8.12 E
Rastavica ≃	78	49.44 N	30.01 E
Rastede	52	53.15 N	8.11 E
Rastegai'sa ∧	24	70.00 N	26.18 E
Rastenberg	54	51.10 N	11.25 E
Rastenburg → Kętrzyn	30	54.06 N	21.23 E
Rastorf	54	54.16 N	10.19 E
Rastorgujevo	82	55.33 N	37.41 E
Rastovcy	82	56.39 N	37.35 E
Rastunovo	82	55.16 N	37.50 E
Rasu, Monte ∧	71	40.25 N	9.00 E
Rasūl	123	32.42 N	73.34 E
Rasūlnagar	123	32.20 N	73.47 E
Rasulpur	272a	28.37 N	77.22 E
Rasulpur ◆[8]	272a	28.42 N	77.01 E
Rasun di sopra	64	46.48 N	12.03 E
Rasun di sotto	64	46.47 N	12.02 E
Rasura	58	46.06 N	9.33 E
Råsvalen ⊜	40	59.40 N	15.10 E
Răsvani	38	44.25 N	26.53 E
Rat ≃, Mb., Can.	184	49.35 N	97.08 W
Rat ≃, Mb., Can.	184	55.41 N	99.04 W
Ratahan	112	1.04 N	124.48 E
Ratak Chain II	14	9.00 N	171.00 E
Ratangarh	120	28.05 N	74.36 E
Ratanpur, India	126	23.07 N	87.04 E
Ratanpur, India	272b	22.50 N	88.14 E
Rätansbyn	26	62.29 N	14.32 E
Rat Burana	269a	13.41 N	100.30 E
Ratčino, Ross.	80	53.02 N	39.55 E
Ratčino, Ross.	82	55.16 N	38.39 E
Ratcliff	222	31.24 N	95.08 W
Rateče	64	46.30 N	13.43 E
Ratekau	54	53.57 N	10.44 E
Rāth	124	25.35 N	79.34 E
Rath ◆[8]	263	51.17 N	6.49 E
Rathangan	48	53.12 N	6.59 W
Rathbone	210	42.08 N	77.19 W
Rathbun Lake ⊜	212	44.47 N	78.12 W
Rathbun Lake ⊜[1]	190	40.54 N	93.05 W
Rathcoole	48	53.16 N	6.28 W
Rathcormack	48	52.05 N	8.17 W
Rathdowney, Austl.	171a	28.12 S	152.52 E
Rathdowney, Ire.	48	52.50 N	7.34 W
Rathdrum, Ire.	48	52.56 N	6.13 W
Rathdrum, Id., U.S.	202	47.48 N	116.53 W
Rathebur	54	53.44 N	13.46 E
Ratheim	52	51.04 N	6.10 E
Rathen	46	57.38 N	2.02 W
Rathenow	54	52.36 N	12.20 E
Rathfriland	48	54.14 N	6.10 W
Rathkeale	48	52.32 N	8.56 W
Rathlin Island I	48	55.18 N	6.13 W
Rathlin Sound ʯ	48	55.15 N	6.15 W
Ráth Luirc (Charleville)	48	52.21 N	8.41 W
Rathmecke	263	51.15 N	7.38 E
Rathmelton	48	55.02 N	7.38 W
Rathmore	48	52.03 N	9.13 W
Rathmullan	48	55.06 N	7.33 W
Rathnew	48	53.00 N	6.05 W
Ratho	46	55.55 N	3.22 W
Rathowen	48	53.40 N	7.31 W
Rathstock	54	52.31 N	14.32 E
Rathwell	184	49.40 N	98.32 W
Ratibor → Racibórz	30	50.06 N	18.13 E
Raticosa, Passo della)(	66	44.10 N	11.20 E
Rätikon ⋏	58	47.03 N	9.40 E
Ratingen	56	51.18 N	6.51 E
Ratisbon → Regensburg	60	49.01 N	12.06 E
Rätische Alpen → Rhaetian Alps ⋏	58	46.30 N	10.00 E
Rat Island I	181a	51.55 N	178.20 E
Rat Islands II	181a	51.40 N	178.30 E
Rat'kovo	82	56.01 N	38.38 E
Rat Lake ⊜	184	56.10 N	99.40 W
Ratlām	120	23.19 N	75.04 E
Ratmanova, ostrov I	180	65.46 N	169.02 W
Ratnāgiri	122	16.59 N	73.18 E
Ratnapura	122	6.41 N	80.24 E
Ratno	78	51.40 N	24.31 E
Ratodero	120	27.48 N	68.18 E
Ratomka	76	53.56 N	27.21 E
Raton	196	36.54 N	104.26 W
Raton Pass)(	196	36.59 N	104.29 W
Ratqah, Wādī ar- V	130	34.25 N	40.55 E
Ratt ≃	224	47.27 N	124.21 W
Rattanaburi	110	15.19 N	103.51 E
Rattaphum	110	7.08 N	100.16 E
Ratten	61	47.29 N	15.43 E
Rattlesnake	202	46.56 N	113.59 W
Rattlesnake Creek ≃, Ks., U.S.	198	38.13 N	98.22 W
Rattlesnake Creek ≃, Oh., U.S.	218	39.16 N	83.23 W
Rattlesnake Creek ≃, Or., U.S.	202	42.44 N	117.47 W
Rattlesnake Creek ≃, Wa., U.S.	224	46.45 N	120.55 W
Rattlesnake Creek ≃, Wa., U.S.	224	45.48 N	121.29 W
Rattlesnake Mountain ∧	207	41.42 N	72.50 W
Rattlesnake Peak ∧	280	34.16 N	117.47 W
Rattling Brook	186	49.38 N	56.10 W
Rattling Run ≃	279b	40.33 N	79.32 W
Rattray	46	56.35 N	3.19 W
Rattray Head >	46	57.37 N	1.49 W
Rattu	123	35.08 N	74.48 E
Rättvik	26	60.53 N	15.06 E
Ratz, Mount ∧	180	57.23 N	132.19 W
Ratzeburg	54	53.42 N	10.46 E
Ratzeburger See ⊜	54	53.45 N	10.47 E
Rätzlingen	54	52.23 N	11.08 E
Rau	112	0.34 N	100.01 E
Raub, Malay.	114	3.48 N	101.52 E
Raub, In., U.S.	216	40.44 N	87.29 W
Raubsville	208	40.38 N	75.12 W
Rauch	252	36.46 S	59.06 W
Raucheck ∧	64	47.30 N	13.14 E
Rauchenwarth	264b	48.05 N	16.32 E
Rauchtown	210	41.07 N	77.14 W
Raucourt-et-Flaba	56	49.36 N	4.57 E
Rauen	54	52.20 N	14.01 E
Rauenstein	54	50.24 N	11.03 E
Raufarhöfn	24a	66.30 N	15.57 W
Raufoss	26	60.43 N	10.37 E
Rauhe Ebrach ≃	56	49.50 N	10.56 E
Raukumara Range ⋏	172	37.47 S	178.02 E
Raul Soares	255	20.05 S	42.22 W
Rauma	26	61.08 N	21.30 E
Rauma ≃	26	62.33 N	7.43 E
Raumünzach	56	48.38 N	8.21 E
Rauna	76	57.20 N	25.43 E
Raunds	42	52.21 N	0.33 W
Raung, Gunung ∧	115a	8.08 S	114.03 E
Raunheim	56	50.01 N	8.28 E
Raupal'an	180	65.28 N	171.59 W
Raurimu	172	39.07 S	175.24 E
Rauris	64	47.13 N	13.00 E
Raurkela	124	22.13 N	84.53 E
Rauschenberg	56	50.53 N	8.55 E
Rausu	92a	44.01 N	145.12 E
Rautalampi	26	62.38 N	26.50 E
Rāutara	272b	22.51 N	88.28 E
Rautavaara	26	63.29 N	28.18 E
Ravahere I[1]	14	18.14 S	142.09 W
Ravalgaon	122	20.38 N	74.25 E
Ravanica, Manastir ☗[1]	38	43.58 N	21.26 E
Ravānsar	128	34.43 N	46.40 E
Ravanusa	70	37.16 N	13.58 E
Rāvar	128	31.15 N	56.53 E
Ravarano	64	44.35 N	10.04 E
Ravarino	64	44.44 N	11.06 E
Rava-Russkaja	78	50.14 N	23.37 E
Ravascletto	64	46.32 N	12.57 E
Ravat	85	39.54 N	70.12 E
Ravello	68	40.39 N	14.37 E
Ravelo	248	18.48 S	65.32 W
Raven	192	37.05 N	81.51 W
Ravena	210	42.28 N	73.49 W
Ravenglass	44	54.21 N	3.24 W
Raven Lake ⊜	212	45.13 N	78.51 W
Ravenna, It.	66	44.25 N	12.12 E
Ravenna, Ky., U.S.	192	37.41 N	83.57 W
Ravenna, Mi., U.S.	216	43.11 N	85.56 W
Ravenna, Ne., U.S.	198	41.01 N	98.54 W
Ravenna, Oh., U.S.	214	41.09 N	81.14 W
Ravenna □[4]	66	44.25 N	11.59 E
Ravensbourne	171a	27.22 S	152.10 E
Ravensbourne National Park ♠	171a	27.21 S	152.15 E
Ravensburg	58	47.47 N	9.37 E
Ravenscrag	184	49.30 N	109.05 W
Ravensdale	224	47.21 N	121.58 W
Ravenshoe	166	17.37 S	145.29 E
Ravensthorpe	162	33.35 S	120.02 E
Ravenswood, S. Afr.	273d	26.11 S	28.15 E
Ravenswood, Mi., U.S.	216	42.45 N	84.36 W
Ravenswood, W.V., U.S.	188	38.56 N	81.45 W
Ravenswood Park ♠	283	42.36 N	70.42 W
Ravenswood Point >	282	37.30 N	122.08 W
Ravensworth	284c	38.48 N	77.13 W
Rāver	120	21.15 N	76.02 E
Ravernet ≃	48	54.30 N	6.04 W
Rāvi ≃	123	30.35 N	71.49 E
Ravières	50	47.45 N	4.17 E
Ravine	208	40.34 N	76.24 W
Ravine Lake ⊜[1]	276	40.43 N	74.38 W
Ravinia Park ♠	278	42.09 N	87.46 W
Ravna Gora	36	45.23 N	14.57 E
Ravne	61	46.33 N	14.58 E
Ravnina	128	37.57 N	62.40 E
Ravsted	41	55.01 N	9.08 E
Rāwah	128	34.28 N	41.55 E
Rawaki I[1]	14	3.43 S	170.43 W
Rāwala Kot	123	33.52 N	73.46 E
Rāwalpindi	123	33.36 N	73.04 E
Rawa Mazowiecka	30	51.46 N	20.16 E
Rāwāndūz	128	36.37 N	44.31 E
Rawang	114	3.19 N	101.35 E
Rawas ≃	112	2.42 S	103.24 E
Rāwatsar	123	29.17 N	74.23 E
Rawāwiṣ, Wādī V	146	30.26 N	15.24 E
Rawḍah ⊜	130	35.15 N	41.05 E
Rawḍah, Wādī ar- V	130	34.22 N	37.21 E
Rawd al-Faraj ◆[8]	273c	30.05 N	31.14 E
Rawḍaw, Jazīrat ar- I	273c	30.01 N	31.13 E
Rawdon	206	46.03 N	73.43 W
Rawene	172	35.24 S	173.30 E
Rawḥah	144	19.28 N	41.48 E
Rawhide Creek ≃	198	42.06 N	104.20 W
Rawhide Lake ⊜	190	46.39 N	82.37 W
Rawhide Mountain ∧	204	38.17 N	116.25 W
Rawi	112	2.07 S	113.56 E
Rawi, Ko I	114	6.33 N	99.14 E
Rawicz	30	51.37 N	16.52 E
Rawlinna	162	31.01 S	125.20 E
Rawlins	200	41.47 N	107.14 W
Rawlinson, Mount ∧	162	25.58 S	127.28 E
Rawlinson Range ⋏	162	24.51 S	128.00 E
Rawmarsh	44	53.27 N	1.21 W
Rawreth	260	51.37 N	0.35 E
Rawson, Arg.	252	34.36 S	60.04 W
Rawson, Arg.	254	43.18 S	65.06 W
Rawson, Oh., U.S.	216	40.57 N	83.47 W
Rawsonville	158	33.41 S	19.20 E
Rawtenstall	44	53.42 N	2.18 W
Rawu	102	29.30 N	96.45 E
Rax ⋏	61	47.42 N	15.43 E
Raxāul	124	26.59 N	84.51 E
Ray, Il., U.S.	219	40.12 N	90.29 W
Ray, In., U.S.	216	41.45 N	84.53 W
Ray, N.D., U.S.	198	48.20 N	103.09 W
Ray ≃	42	51.48 N	1.15 W
Ray, Cape >	186	47.40 N	59.18 W
Raya	112	1.05 N	118.32 E
Raya, Bukit ∧	112	0.40 S	112.41 E
Raya, Gunong ∧	114	6.22 N	99.49 E
Raya, Pulau I	114	4.52 N	95.22 E
Rāyachoti	122	14.03 N	78.45 E
Rāyadurg	122	14.42 N	76.52 E
Rāyagarha	122	19.10 N	83.25 E
Rayburn	222	30.25 N	94.56 W
Rayen, Dtsch.	263	51.28 N	6.32 E
Rāyen, Īrān	128	29.34 N	57.26 E
Ray Hubbard, Lake ⊜[1]	222	32.53 N	96.35 W
Rāyikhah I	128	26.12 N	36.21 E
Rayland	214	40.11 N	80.41 W
Rayleigh	42	51.36 N	0.36 E
Raymond, Ab., Can.	182	49.27 N	112.39 W
Raymond, Ca., U.S.	226	37.13 N	119.54 W
Raymond, Il., U.S.	219	39.19 N	89.34 W
Raymond, Mn., U.S.	198	45.00 N	95.14 W
Raymond, Ms., U.S.	194	32.15 N	90.25 W
Raymond, Oh., U.S.	216	40.20 N	83.28 W
Raymond, Wa., U.S.	224	46.41 N	123.43 W
Raymond Terrace	170	32.46 S	151.44 E
Raymondville	196	26.29 N	97.47 W
Raymore	184	51.25 N	104.31 W
Ray Mountains ⋏	180	65.45 N	151.30 W
Rāyna	126	23.05 N	87.54 E
Rayne	194	30.14 N	92.16 W
Raynham	207	41.56 N	71.04 W
Raynham Dog Track ♠	283	41.59 N	71.04 W
Rayón, Méx.	232	29.43 N	110.35 W
Rayón, Méx.	234	17.12 N	93.00 W
Rayón, Méx.	234	21.51 N	99.40 W
Rayones	232	25.01 N	100.05 W
Rayong	110	12.40 N	101.17 E
Rāypur	272b	22.25 N	88.31 E
Rayrah ⊤[4]	140	15.21 N	34.41 E
Rayse Creek ≃	219	38.13 N	89.00 W
Raystown Lake ⊜[1]	214	40.20 N	78.05 W
Rayton	158	25.45 S	28.32 E
Raytown	194	39.00 N	94.27 W
Rayville	194	32.28 N	91.45 W
Raywood	222	30.02 N	94.40 W
Raz, Pointe du >	32	48.02 N	4.44 W
Raza, Punta >	234	21.02 N	105.20 W
Razan, Īrān	128	35.23 N	49.02 E
R'azan', Ross.	80	54.38 N	39.44 E
R'azancevo	82	56.42 N	39.12 E
Ražanj	38	43.40 N	21.33 E
R'azan' Oblast' □[4]	76	54.30 N	40.30 E
R'azanovo	82	55.29 N	37.31 E
Razbegaj	265a	59.47 N	29.56 E
Războeni	38	47.05 N	26.32 E
Razdan	84	40.30 N	44.46 E
Razdan ≃	84	39.58 N	44.27 E
Razdel'naja	78	46.51 N	30.05 E
Razdolinsk	86	58.25 N	94.38 E
Razdolje	88	52.27 N	103.13 E
Razdol'noje, Ross.	89	43.30 N	131.52 E
Razdol'noje, Ukr.	78	45.47 N	33.29 E
Razdol'noje, Ukr.	83	47.37 N	38.01 E
Razdol'nyj	80	46.38 N	42.57 E
Razdorskaja	78	47.33 N	40.38 E
Razdory, Ross.	265b	55.45 N	37.18 E
Razdory, Ukr.	78	48.21 N	35.42 E
R'aženoje	83	47.31 N	38.52 E
Raževo	86	56.09 N	68.25 E
Razgrad	38	43.32 N	26.31 E
Razim, Lacul ⊜	38	44.54 N	28.57 E
Razlog	38	41.53 N	23.28 E
Razmachnino	88	51.47 N	115.28 E
Razmitelevo	265a	59.54 N	30.41 E
Rāznas - ezers ⊜	76	56.20 N	27.27 E
Raznočinovka	80	46.37 N	47.57 E
Raznomojka	86	52.29 N	55.52 E
Razorback Mountain ∧	182	51.35 N	124.42 W
R'ažsk	80	53.43 N	40.04 E
Razvil'noje	80	46.14 N	41.18 E
Razzoli, Isola I	71	41.18 N	9.21 E
Ré, Île de I	32	46.12 N	1.25 W
Rea ≃	42	52.18 N	2.32 W
Read	262	53.49 N	2.21 W
Reading, Eng., U.K.	42	51.28 N	0.59 W
Reading, Il., U.S.	216	41.05 N	88.51 W
Reading, Ks., U.S.	198	38.31 N	95.57 W
Reading, Ma., U.S.	207	42.31 N	71.05 W
Reading, Mi., U.S.	216	41.50 N	84.44 W
Reading, Oh., U.S.	218	39.13 N	84.26 W
Reading, Pa., U.S.	208	40.20 N	75.55 W
Reading Center	210	42.26 N	76.56 W
Reading Station ◆[5]	285	39.57 N	75.10 W
Readington	210	40.34 N	74.44 W
Readlyn	190	42.42 N	92.13 W
Readsboro	207	42.46 N	72.56 W
Readstown	190	43.26 N	90.45 W
Reagan	222	31.13 N	96.47 W
Real	116	14.40 N	121.36 E
Real ≃	250	11.27 S	37.22 W
Real, Cordillera ⋏	248	19.00 S	66.30 W
Real, Estero ≃	236	12.55 N	87.23 W
Real del Padre	252	34.50 S	67.46 W
Real de San Carlos	258	34.26 S	57.53 W
Realengo ◆[8]	256	22.53 S	43.25 W
Real Felipe, Museo Histórico del ⊥	286d	12.04 S	77.09 W
Realicó	252	35.02 S	64.15 W
Realitos	196	27.27 N	98.32 W
Realmonte	70	37.18 N	13.28 E
Reamstown	208	40.12 N	76.07 W
Reana del Roiale	64	46.12 N	13.13 E
Reardan	202	47.40 N	117.52 W
Reata	232	26.08 N	101.05 W
Reatini, Monti ⋏	66	42.28 N	13.00 E
Réau	261	48.37 N	2.38 E
Reay	46	58.33 N	3.47 W
Reay Forest ◆[3]	46	58.19 N	4.47 W
Rebecca, Lake ⊜	162	29.53 S	122.10 E
Rebecq-Rognon	50	50.40 N	4.08 E
Rebeida, Wādī V	140	20.45 N	34.06 E
Rebel Hill	285	40.04 N	75.20 W
Rebersburg	210	40.57 N	77.27 W
Rebi	164	6.23 S	134.06 E
Rebiana Sand Sea → Rabyānah, Ṣaḥrā' ◆[2]	146	24.20 N	20.37 E
Rebild Bakker ♠	26	56.50 N	9.51 E
Reboly	24	63.50 N	30.47 E
Rebouças	252	25.36 S	50.42 W
Rebouças, Túnel ◆[5]	287a	22.56 S	43.14 W
Rebricha	86	53.05 N	82.20 E
Rebun-tō I	92a	45.23 N	141.02 E
Recalde	252	36.39 S	61.05 W
Recanati	66	43.24 N	13.32 E
Rečane	76	56.25 N	31.39 E
Recco	62	44.22 N	9.09 E
Recey-sur-Ource	58	47.47 N	4.52 E
Rēchah Lām	120	34.58 N	70.51 E
Rechberghausen	56	48.44 N	9.38 E
Recherche, Archipelago of the II	162	34.05 S	122.45 E
Recherche, Cape >	175e	10.11 S	161.19 E
Réchicourt-le-Château	58	48.40 N	6.51 E
Rechlin	54	53.21 N	12.43 E
Rechna Doāb ⋏[1]	123	31.35 N	73.30 E
Rechnitz	61	47.18 N	16.27 E
Rečica, Bela.	76	52.22 N	30.25 E
Rečica, Bela.	78	51.52 N	26.48 E
Recife	250	8.03 S	34.54 W
Recife, Kaap >	158	34.02 S	25.44 E
Recinto	252	36.48 S	71.44 W
Recke	52	52.22 N	7.43 E
Rečki	78	51.07 N	34.30 E
Recklinghausen	52	51.36 N	7.13 E
Recknitz ≃	54	54.14 N	12.28 E
Recoaro Terme	64	45.42 N	11.13 E
Recogne	56	49.55 N	5.22 E
Recoleta	286e	33.23 S	70.38 W
Recologne	58	47.16 N	5.50 E
Reconquista	252	29.09 S	59.39 W
Reconquista, Río de la ≃	288	34.25 S	58.35 W
Recovery Glacier ⊓	9	81.10 S	28.00 W
Recreio	255	21.32 S	42.28 W
Recreo	252	29.16 S	65.04 W
Rector	194	36.15 N	90.17 W
Rectorville	218	38.34 N	83.39 W
Recuay	248	9.43 S	77.28 W
Recz	30	53.16 N	15.33 E
Red (Hong) (Yuan) ≃, Asia	110	20.17 N	106.34 E
Red ≃, N.A.	178	50.24 N	96.48 W
Red ≃, U.S.	178	31.00 N	91.40 W
Red ≃, U.S.	194	36.32 N	87.22 W
Red ≃, Ky., U.S.	192	37.51 N	84.05 W
Red ≃, N.M., U.S.	200	36.39 N	105.42 W
Red ≃, Wi., U.S.	190	44.49 N	88.38 W
Red, Elm Fork ≃	196	34.53 N	99.19 W
Red, North Fork ≃	196	34.24 N	99.14 W
Red, Prairie Dog Town Fork ≃	196	34.35 N	99.58 W
Red, Salt Fork ≃	196	34.27 N	99.22 W
Red, South Fork ≃	194	36.41 N	86.56 W
Red, West Fork ≃	194	36.32 N	87.21 W
Reda	30	54.37 N	18.21 E
Redang, Pulau I	114	5.47 N	103.00 E
Redange	56	49.46 N	5.54 E
Redang Panjang	114	5.07 N	100.47 E
Red Bank, N.J., U.S.	208	40.20 N	74.03 W
Red Bank, Tn., U.S.	194	35.07 N	85.17 W
Red Bank Battle Monument ⊥	285	39.52 N	75.11 W
Redbank Creek ≃	214	40.58 N	79.33 W
Red Banks	194	34.49 N	89.33 W
Red Bay, Nf., Can.	186	51.44 N	56.25 W
Red Bay, Al., U.S.	194	34.26 N	88.08 W
Redbay, Fl., U.S.	194	30.35 N	85.56 W
Red Bay c	48	55.04 N	6.02 W
Redberry Lake ⊜	184	52.40 N	107.10 W
Redbird	214	41.48 N	81.06 W
Red Bluff	204	40.10 N	122.14 W
Red Bluff Reservoir ⊜[1]	196	31.57 N	103.56 W
Red Boiling Springs	194	36.31 N	85.50 W
Redbourn	42	51.48 N	0.24 W
Redbridge ◆[8]	42	51.34 N	0.05 E
Red Bud	219	38.12 N	89.59 W
Red Canyon V	198	43.18 N	103.49 W
Redcar	44	54.37 N	1.04 W
Red Cedar ≃, Mi., U.S.	216	42.43 N	84.33 W
Red Cedar ≃, Wi., U.S.	190	44.42 N	91.53 W
Red Cedar Lake ⊜	190	46.45 N	79.54 W
Red Clay Creek ≃	285	39.43 N	75.39 W
Red Clay Creek, East Branch ≃	285	39.49 N	75.42 W
Red Clay Creek, West Branch ≃	285	39.49 N	75.42 W
Redcliff, Ab., Can.	184	50.05 N	110.47 W
Red Cliff, Co., U.S.	200	39.31 N	106.22 W
Redcliff, Zimb.	154	19.02 S	29.50 E
Redcliffe	171a	27.14 S	153.07 E
Redcliffe, Mount ∧	162	28.25 S	121.32 E
Red Cliff Indian Reservation ◆[4]	190	46.50 N	90.47 W
Red Cliffs	166	34.19 S	142.11 E
Red Cloud	198	40.05 N	98.31 W
Red Creek	210	43.14 N	76.43 W
Red Creek ≃	194	30.41 N	88.40 W
Red Cross Lake ⊜	184	55.05 N	92.55 W
Red Deer	182	52.16 N	113.48 W
Red Deer ≃, Can.	176	50.56 N	109.54 W
Red Deer ≃, Can.	184	52.53 N	101.01 W
Red Deer Creek ≃	196	35.56 N	100.24 W
Red Deer Lake ⊜, Ab., Can.	182	52.43 N	113.02 W
Red Deer Lake ⊜, Mb., Can.	184	52.56 N	101.20 W
Reddersburg	158	29.38 S	26.07 E
Red Devil	180	61.46 N	157.18 W
Red Dial	44	54.48 N	3.10 W
Reddick	216	41.06 N	88.15 W
Redding, Ca., U.S.	204	40.35 N	122.23 W
Redding, Ct., U.S.	207	41.18 N	73.23 W
Redding Ridge	207	41.18 N	73.21 W
Reddish	262	53.26 N	2.09 W
Redditch	42	52.19 N	1.56 W
Rede ≃	44	55.08 N	2.13 W
Redefin	54	53.21 N	11.11 E
Redelinghuys	158	32.30 S	18.33 E
Redenção	250	4.13 S	38.43 W
Redenção da Serra	256	23.16 S	45.33 W
Redesdale V	44	55.17 N	2.16 W
Redes Mere ⊜	262	53.15 N	2.14 W
Redeye ≃	198	46.26 N	94.49 W
Redfield, Ia., U.S.	198	41.35 N	94.11 W
Redfield, N.Y., U.S.	212	43.32 N	75.49 W
Redfield, S.D., U.S.	198	44.52 N	98.31 W
Redfish Lake ⊜	202	44.07 N	114.56 W
Redford	196	29.47 N	104.10 W
Redford ◆[8]	281	42.25 N	83.16 W
Redford Township	216	42.25 N	83.16 W
Red Fox Forest	284c	38.49 N	77.15 W
Redhead	241r	10.47 N	60.57 W
Red Hill, Austl.	162	21.59 S	116.03 E
Redhill, Eng., U.K.	42	51.14 N	0.11 W
Red Hill, Ca., U.S.	280	33.45 N	117.48 W
Red Hill, Pa., U.S.	208	40.22 N	75.29 W
Red Hill ∧	172	41.38 S	173.04 E
Redhill Aerodrome ⊠	260	51.12 N	0.07 W
Red Hill Branch ≃	284b	39.14 N	76.51 W
Red Hook	210	41.59 N	73.52 W
Redhouse Creek ≃	284b	39.18 N	76.31 W
Rédics	61	46.36 N	16.30 E
Red Indian Lake ⊜	186	48.40 N	56.50 W
Redinger Lake ⊜[1]	226	37.09 N	119.26 W
Redington Beach	220	27.49 N	82.49 W
Redington Shores	220	27.50 N	82.50 W
Red Island I	186	47.23 N	54.11 W
Redja ≃	76	58.05 N	31.33 E
Redkey	216	40.21 N	85.09 W
Redkino	82	56.38 N	36.17 E
Red Lake, On., Can.	184	51.03 N	93.49 W
Redlake, Mn., U.S.	198	47.53 N	95.01 W
Red Lake ⊜, On., Can.	184	51.01 N	94.05 W
Red Lake ⊜, Az., U.S.	200	35.40 N	114.04 W
Red Lake ⊜, S.D., U.S.	198	43.44 N	99.13 W
Red Lake ⊜[1]	222	31.40 N	95.58 W
Red Lake ≃	198	47.55 N	97.01 W
Red Lake Falls	198	47.52 N	96.16 W
Red Lake Indian Reservation ◆[4]	198	48.05 N	95.05 W
Red Lake Road	184	49.58 N	93.22 W
Redland, Scot., U.K.	46	59.05 N	3.05 W
Redland, Tx., U.S.	222	31.25 N	94.43 W
Redland Bay	171a	27.37 S	153.18 E
Redlands, S. Afr.	158	29.52 S	22.57 E
Redlands, Ca., U.S.	228	34.04 N	117.10 W
Redlands, Co., U.S.	200	39.04 N	108.38 W
Red Level	194	31.24 N	86.36 W
Red Lick	194	31.47 N	90.58 W
Redlin	54	53.22 N	12.11 E
Red Lion, Pa., U.S.	208	39.54 N	76.36 W
Red Lion, Pa., U.S.	285	39.53 N	75.41 W
Red Lion Airport ⊠	285	39.54 N	74.45 W

Name	Seite	Breite°′	Länge°′ E = Ost
Red Lodge	202	45.11 N	109.14 W
Red Mill	206	46.25 N	72.28 W
Redmond, Or., U.S.	202	44.16 N	121.10 W
Redmond, Ut,. U.S.	200	39.00 N	111.51 W
Redmond, Wa., U.S.	224	47.40 N	122.07 W
Red Mountain	228	35.21 N	117.36 W
Red Mountain ∧, Ca., U.S.	204	41.35 N	123.06 W
Red Mountain ∧, Ca., U.S.	228	35.21 N	117.36 W
Red Mountain ∧, Mt., U.S.	202	47.07 N	112.44 W
Red Mountain Pass)(	200	37.54 N	107.43 W
Rednitz ≃	56	49.28 N	10.59 E
Red Oak, Ia., U.S.	198	41.00 N	95.13 W
Red Oak, Ok., U.S.	196	34.57 N	95.04 W
Red Oak, Tx., U.S.	222	32.31 N	96.48 W
Red Oak Creek ≃	222	32.28 N	96.30 W
Red Oaks Mill	210	41.40 N	73.53 W
Redon	32	47.39 N	2.05 W
Redonda I	238	16.55 N	62.19 W
Redonda, Ilha I	256	23.04 S	43.12 W
Redonda, Isla I	241r	9.52 N	61.35 W
Redonda Islands II	182	50.13 N	124.48 W
Redondela	34	42.17 N	8.36 W
Redondo, Port.	34	38.39 N	7.33 W
Redondo, Wa., U.S.	224	47.20 N	122.19 W
Redondo, Mount ∧	116	10.21 N	125.38 E
Redondo Beach	228	33.50 N	118.23 W
Redondo Beach State Park ♠	280	33.50 N	118.24 W
Redoubt, Mount ∧	224	48.57 N	121.18 W
Redoubt Volcano ∧[1]	180	60.29 N	152.45 W
Red Pass	182	52.59 N	118.59 W
Red Pheasant Indian Reserve ◆[4]	184	52.30 N	108.07 W
Red Pine Lake ⊜	212	45.12 N	78.42 W
Red Point >	170	34.29 S	150.55 E
Red Rock, B.C., Can.	182	53.39 N	122.41 W
Red Rock, On., Can.	190	48.58 N	88.15 W
Red Rock, Tx., U.S.	222	29.58 N	97.27 W
Red Rock I	282	37.56 N	122.26 W
Red Rock ≃	202	44.59 N	112.52 W
Red Rock, Lake ⊜[1]	190	41.30 N	93.02 W
Red Rock Canyon State Park ♠	228	35.23 N	118.00 W
Red Rock Creek ≃	196	36.36 N	97.03 W
Red Rocks Point >	162	32.13 S	127.32 E
Red Root Creek ≃	276	40.30 N	74.19 W
Red Run ≃, Md., U.S.	284b	39.24 N	76.47 W
Red Run ≃, Mi., U.S.	281	42.34 N	82.58 W
Redruth	42	50.13 N	5.14 W
Red Sea ⊤[2]	136	20.00 N	38.00 E
Red Springs	192	34.48 N	79.11 W
Redstone	182	52.08 N	123.42 W
Redstone ≃, N.T., Can.	180	64.17 N	124.33 W
Redstone ≃, On., Can.	190	48.27 N	81.03 W
Redstone Arsenal ■	194	34.38 N	86.38 W
Redstone Creek ≃	198	44.04 N	98.05 W
Redstone Lake ⊜	212	45.11 N	78.32 W
Red Sucker ≃	184	55.19 N	92.31 W
Red Sucker Lake ⊜	184	54.09 N	93.40 W
Reduction	279b	40.11 N	79.46 W
Redut	80	47.22 N	51.53 E
Redvers	184	49.33 N	101.39 W
Redwater	182	53.57 N	113.06 W
Redwater ≃	198	48.03 N	105.13 W
Red Wharf Bay c	44	53.18 N	4.10 W
Redwillow ≃	182	55.04 N	119.21 W
Red Willow Creek ≃	198	40.13 N	100.29 W
Red Wing	190	44.33 N	92.32 W
Redwood	212	44.18 N	75.48 W
Redwood ≃	198	44.34 N	95.05 W
Redwood City	226	37.29 N	122.14 W
Redwood Creek ≃, Ca., U.S.	204	41.18 N	124.05 W
Redwood Creek ≃, Ca., U.S.	226	38.18 N	122.18 W
Redwood Creek ≃, Ca., U.S.	282	37.31 N	122.12 W
Redwood Creek ≃, Ca., U.S.	282	37.52 N	122.35 W
Redwood Estates	226	37.10 N	121.59 W
Redwood Falls	198	44.32 N	95.07 W
Redwood National Park ♠	204	41.30 N	124.05 W
Redwood Point >	282	37.32 N	122.12 W
Redwood Regional Park ♠	282	37.38 N	122.10 W
Redwood Terrace	282	37.19 N	122.18 W
Redwood Valley	204	39.15 N	123.12 W
Ree, Lough ⊜	48	53.35 N	8.00 W
Reed City	190	43.52 N	85.30 W
Reeder	198	46.06 N	102.56 W
Reeders	210	41.01 N	75.20 W
Reed Lake ⊜, Mb., Can.	184	54.37 N	100.30 W
Reed Lake ⊜, Sk., Can.	184	50.24 N	107.05 W
Reedley	226	36.35 N	119.26 W
Reedsburg, Oh., U.S.	214	40.49 N	82.07 W
Reedsburg, Wi., U.S.	190	43.31 N	90.00 W
Reeds Peak ∧	200	33.09 N	107.51 W
Reedsport	202	43.42 N	124.05 W
Reedsville, Pa., U.S.	208	40.39 N	77.35 W
Reedsville, Wi., U.S.	190	44.09 N	87.57 W
Reedurban	214	40.47 N	81.26 W
Reedville	208	37.50 N	76.16 W
Reedy Creek ≃	220	28.04 N	81.21 W
Reedy Creek Swamp ≡	220	28.17 N	81.31 W
Reedy Lake ⊜	220	27.44 N	81.22 W
Reefton	172	42.07 S	171.52 E
Reelfoot Lake ⊜	194	36.25 N	89.22 W
Reepham	42	52.46 N	1.07 E
Reersø >[1]	41	55.31 N	11.06 E
Rees	52	51.45 N	6.23 E
Reese	190	43.27 N	83.41 W
Reese ≃	204	40.39 N	116.54 W
Reese Air Force Base ■	196	33.36 N	102.02 W
Reeseville	190	43.18 N	88.50 W
Reesville	218	39.29 N	83.41 W
Reetz	54	53.11 N	11.52 E
Refaa, Djebel ∧	34	35.34 N	5.52 E
Refahiye	130	39.54 N	38.46 E
Reform	194	33.22 N	88.00 W
Reforma de Pineda	234	16.24 N	94.28 W
Refton	208	39.57 N	76.14 W
Refuge Cove	182	50.07 N	124.50 W
Refugio	196	28.18 N	97.16 W
Refugio, Isla I	254	43.58 S	73.12 W
Refugio Creek ≃	282	38.01 N	122.17 W
Rega ≃	30	54.10 N	15.18 E
Regaïa	34	35.38 N	5.46 W
Regalbuto	70	37.39 N	14.38 E
Regau	64	47.59 N	13.41 E
Regen	60	48.59 N	13.07 E
Regen ≃	60	49.01 N	12.06 E
Regência	255	19.36 S	39.49 W
Regency Estates	284c	39.03 N	77.10 W
Regeneração	250	6.15 S	42.41 W
Regensburg	60	49.01 N	12.06 E
Regensdorf	58	47.26 N	8.28 E
Regenstauf	60	49.08 N	12.08 E
Regent, Austl.	274b	37.44 S	145.00 E
Regent, N.D., U.S.	198	46.25 N	102.33 W
Regent Park	284c	39.03 N	77.10 W
Regents Park	274a	33.53 S	151.02 E
Regents Park ◆[8]	273d	26.15 S	28.04 E
Regent's Park ♠	260	51.32 N	0.09 W
Regentville	274a	33.47 S	150.40 E
Reggane	148	26.42 N	0.10 E
Regge ≃	52	52.21 N	6.22 E
Reggello	66	43.41 N	11.32 E
Reggio di Calabria	68	38.07 N	15.39 E
Reggio di Calabria □[4]	68	38.10 N	16.00 E

Symbols in the index entries represent the broad categories identified in the key at the right. Symbols with superior numbers (⋏[1]) identify subcategories (see complete key on page *I · 1*).

Symbole im Register stellen die rechts im Schlüssel erklärten Kategorien dar. Symbole mit hochgestellten Ziffern (⋏[1]) bezeichnen Unterabteilungen einer Kategorie (vgl. vollständiger Schlüssel auf Seite *I · 1*).

Los símbolos incluidos en el texto del índice representan las grandes categorías identificadas con la clave a la derecha. Los símbolos con números en su parte superior (⋏[1]) identifican las subcategorías (véase la clave completa en la página *I · 1*).

Les symboles de l'index représentent les catégories indiquées dans la légende à droite. Les symboles suivis d'un indice (⋏[1]) représentent des sous-catégories (voir légende complète à la page *I · 1*).

Os símbolos incluídos no texto do índice representam as grandes categorias identificadas com a chave à direita. Os símbolos com números em sua parte superior (⋏[1]) identificam as subcategorias (veja-se a chave completa à página *I · 1*).

∧ Mountain	Berg	Montaña	Montagne	Montanha
⋏ Mountains	Gebirge	Montañas	Montagnes	Montanhas
)(Pass	Paß	Paso	Col	Passo
V Valley, Canyon	Tal, Cañon	Valle, Cañón	Vallée, Canyon	Vale, Canhão
≃ Plain	Ebene	Llano	Plaine	Planície
> Cape	Kap	Cabo	Cap	Cabo
I Island	Insel	Isla	Île	Ilha
II Islands	Inseln	Islas	Îles	Ilhas
◆ Other Topographic Features	Andere Topographische Objekte	Otros Elementos Topográficos	Autres données topographiques	Outros acidentes topográficos

ESPAÑOL Nombre / FRANÇAIS Nom / PORTUGUÊS Nome	Página / Page / Página	Lat.°′	Long.°′ W = Oeste / W = Ouest / W = Oeste
Reggiolo	64	44.55 N	10.48 E
Reggio nell'Emilia	64	44.43 N	10.36 E
Reggio nell'Emilia □[4]	64	44.37 N	10.37 E
Regharen ⊖	40	58.54 N	15.46 E
Reghin	38	46.47 N	24.42 E
Regina, Sk., Can.	184	50.25 N	104.39 W
Régina, Guy. fr.	250	4.19 N	52.08 W
Regina, S. Afr.	158	27.02 S	26.30 E
Regina Beach	184	50.47 N	105.00 W
Regina Elena, Canale ≅	266b	45.41 N	8.39 E
Región Metropolitana □[4]	252	33.30 S	70.30 W
Regis-Breitingen	54	51.05 N	12.26 E
Registro	252	24.30 S	47.50 W
Registro do Araguaia	255	15.44 S	51.50 W
Regiwar	120	25.57 N	65.44 E
Regla ◆[8]	286b	23.08 N	82.20 W
Regnéville	32	49.01 N	1.33 W
Regnitz ≃	56	49.54 N	10.49 E
Rego Park ◆[8]	276	40.44 N	73.52 W
Regozero	24	65.28 N	31.10 E
Regresso, Cachoeira do ∟	250	0.58 S	54.51 W
Regstrup	41	55.40 N	11.37 E
Reguengos de Monsaraz	34	38.25 N	7.32 W
Reh	263	51.22 N	7.33 E
Rehau	54	50.15 N	12.02 E
Rehbach ≃	56	49.27 N	8.27 E
Rehberg	54	52.43 N	12.10 E
Rehberge ⋏[2]	264a	52.35 N	13.11 E
Rehberge, Volkspark ♠	264a	52.33 N	13.20 E
Rehburg	52	52.28 N	9.13 E
Rehden	52	52.37 N	8.29 E
Rehe	56	50.38 N	8.07 E
Rehefeld-Zaunhaus	54	50.43 N	13.42 E
Rehfelde	54	52.30 N	13.54 E
Rehli	124	23.38 N	79.05 E
Rehme	52	52.12 N	8.49 E
Rehna	54	53.47 N	11.03 E
Rehoboth, Namibia	156	23.18 S	17.03 E
Rehoboth, Namibia	156	17.53 S	15.04 E
Rehoboth □[5]	156	23.30 S	17.00 E
Rehoboth Bay c	208	38.40 N	75.06 W
Rehoboth Beach	208	38.43 N	75.04 W
Rehoboth Seamount ✦[3]	16	37.30 N	59.50 W
Réhon	56	49.30 N	5.45 E
Rehovot	132	31.54 N	34.49 E
Rehti	124	22.44 N	77.26 E
Reiche Ebrach ≃	56	49.49 N	10.58 E
Reiche Liesing ≃	264b	48.08 N	16.16 E
Reichelsheim	56	49.43 N	8.50 E
Reichenau, Dtsch.	58	47.41 N	9.03 E
Reichenau, Schw.	58	46.49 N	9.24 E
Reichenau an der Rax	61	47.42 N	15.50 E
Reichenbach, Dtsch.	54	51.08 N	14.48 E
Reichenbach, Dtsch.	54	50.37 N	12.18 E
Reichenbach, Schw.	58	46.38 N	7.42 E
Reichenbach → Dzierżoniów	30	50.44 N	16.39 E
Reichenberg → Liberec	30	50.46 N	15.03 E
Reichenhofen	58	47.50 N	9.58 E
Reichensachsen	56	51.09 N	9.59 E
Reichen Spitze ∧	64	47.09 N	12.07 E
Reichertshausen	60	48.28 N	11.31 E
Reichertsheim	60	48.12 N	12.17 E
Reichertshofen	60	48.40 N	11.28 E
Reichraming	61	47.53 N	14.27 E
Reichsbrücke ◆[5]	264b	48.14 N	16.25 E
Reichshoffen	56	48.56 N	7.40 E
Reid	162	30.49 S	128.26 E
Reid, Mount ∧, Austl.	162	17.58 S	130.38 E
Reid, Mount ∧, Ak., U.S.	182	55.42 N	131.15 W
Reid Lake ⊖[1]	184	50.02 N	108.05 W
Reidsville, Ga., U.S.	192	32.05 N	82.07 W
Reidsville, N.C., U.S.	192	36.21 N	79.39 W
Reiffton	208	40.19 N	75.53 W
Reigate	42	51.14 N	0.13 W
Reigate and Banstead □[8]	260	51.17 N	0.12 W
Reignac-sur-Indre	50	47.13 N	0.55 E
Reignier	58	46.08 N	6.16 E
Reigoldswil	58	47.24 N	7.41 E
Reihoku	92	32.31 N	130.02 E
Reillanne	62	43.53 N	5.40 E
Reims	50	49.15 N	4.02 E
Reims, Montagne de ⋏[2]	50	49.08 N	4.00 E
Reina Alejandra → Queen Alexandra Range ⋏	9	84.00 S	168.00 E
Reina Carlota, Estrecho de la → Queen Charlotte Sound ʮ	182	51.30 N	129.30 W
Reinach, Schw.	58	47.30 N	7.35 E
Reinach, Schw.	58	47.15 N	8.11 E
Reina Fabiola → Queen Fabiola Mountains ⋏	9	71.30 S	35.40 E
Reina Maria, Costa de la → Queen Mary Coast ⩡[2]	9	67.00 S	96.00 E
Reina Maud, Tierras de la → Queen Maud Land ◆[1]	9	72.30 S	12.00 E
Reinbeck	190	42.19 N	92.35 W
Reinbek	52	53.31 N	10.14 E
Reinberg	54	54.12 N	13.15 E
Reindeer ≃	184	55.36 N	103.11 W
Reindeer Island I	184	52.25 N	98.00 W
Reindeer Lake ⊖	176	57.15 N	102.40 W
Reindeer Station	180	68.42 N	134.06 W
Reine Charlotte, Détroit de la → Queen Charlotte Sound ʮ	182	51.30 N	129.30 W
Reinerton	208	40.36 N	76.34 W
Reinfeld	52	53.49 N	10.28 E
Reinga, Cape ›	172	34.25 S	172.41 E
Reinhardswald ◆[3]	52	51.30 N	9.30 E
Reinhardtsdorf	54	50.53 N	14.11 E
Reinheim	56	49.49 N	8.50 E
Reinickendorf ◆[8]	264a	52.35 N	13.21 E
Reinosa	34	43.00 N	4.08 W
Reino Unido → United Kingdom □[1]	28	54.00 N	2.00 W
Reinsdorf, Dtsch.	54	50.42 N	12.33 E
Reinsdorf, Dtsch.	54	51.54 N	12.37 E
Reinshagen ◆[8]	263	51.10 N	7.09 E
Reinstorf	54	53.50 N	11.38 E
Reis	130	38.16 N	31.35 E
Reisach	64	46.39 N	13.09 E
Reisaelva ≃	24	69.48 N	21.00 E
Reischach	60	48.17 N	12.44 E
Reisdorf	56	49.53 N	6.15 E
Reisdorf, Camp ■	273b	4.21 S	15.15 E
Reisholz ◆[8]	263	51.11 N	6.52 E
Reisjärvi	26	63.37 N	24.54 E
Reiss	46	58.28 N	3.10 W
Reisterstown	208	39.28 N	76.49 W
Reisterstown Road Plaza ◆[9]	284b	39.02 N	76.42 W
Reitano	70	37.58 N	14.20 E
Reitdiep ≅	52	53.20 N	6.18 E
Reith bei Seefeld	64	47.18 N	11.12 E
Reit im Winkl	64	47.40 N	12.28 E
Reitz	158	27.53 S	28.31 E
Reitzenhain	54	50.33 N	13.13 E
Reivilo	158	27.36 S	24.08 E
Rejinagar	126	23.53 N	88.15 E
Rejmyra	40	58.50 N	15.55 E
Rejowiec Fabryczny	30	51.08 N	23.13 E
Rejštejn	60	49.09 N	13.31 E
Rekarne	40	59.26 N	16.20 E
Rekarne □[9]	40	59.17 N	16.25 E
Reken	52	51.50 N	7.02 E
Rekjoāti	272b	22.37 N	88.28 E
Reliance, N.T., Can.	176	62.42 N	109.08 W
Reliance, Wy., U.S.	200	41.40 N	109.11 W
Relief Reservoir ⊖[1]	226	38.16 N	119.44 W
Religione, Punta ›	70	36.42 N	14.46 E
Reliz Creek ≃	226	36.19 N	121.18 W
Rellingen	52	53.39 N	9.49 E
Rellinghausen ◆[8]	263	51.25 N	7.04 E
Reloncaví, Seno c	254	41.40 S	72.35 W
Remada	148	32.19 N	10.24 E
Remagen	56	50.34 N	7.13 E
Rémalard	50	48.26 N	0.47 E
Remanso	250	9.37 S	42.07 W
Remarde ≃	261	48.35 N	2.15 E
Remarkable, Mount ∧	162	32.48 S	138.10 E
Rembang	115a	6.42 S	111.20 E
Rembau	114	2.35 N	102.06 E
Rembia	114	2.20 N	102.13 E
Remchi	34	35.04 N	1.26 W
Remecó	252	37.38 S	63.39 W
Remedios, Col.	246	7.02 N	74.41 W
Remedios, Cuba	240p	22.30 N	79.33 W
Remedios, Pan.	236	8.14 N	81.51 W
Remedios, Punta ›	236	13.31 N	89.49 W
Remedios, Santuario de los ⊍[1]	286a	19.28 N	99.15 W
Remedios de Escalada ◆[8]	258	34.43 S	58.23 W
Remels	52	53.18 N	7.44 E
Remennicy	82	56.43 N	36.36 E
Remer	190	47.03 N	93.54 W
Remeshk	128	26.50 N	58.49 E
Remhoogte	158	29.33 S	23.01 E
Remich	56	49.33 N	6.22 E
Remich Airport ⊠	279b	40.36 N	79.49 W
Rémigny, Lac ⊖	190	47.51 N	79.12 W
Rémilly	56	49.01 N	6.24 E
Reminderville	214	41.20 N	81.23 W
Remington, In., U.S.	216	40.45 N	87.09 W
Remington, Va., U.S.	188	38.32 N	77.48 W
Rémire	250	4.53 N	52.17 W
Remiremont	58	48.01 N	6.35 E
Remo □[8]	273a	6.42 N	3.29 E
Remolá, Estany del c	266d	41.17 N	2.04 E
Remollon	62	44.28 N	6.10 E
Remontnoje	80	46.33 N	43.39 E
Remoray	58	46.46 N	6.14 E
Remoulins	62	43.56 N	4.34 E
Removka ◆[8]	83	47.59 N	38.43 E
Rempang, Pulau I	114	0.51 N	104.10 E
Remptendorf	54	50.31 N	11.39 E
Rems ≃	56	48.52 N	9.16 E
Remscheid	56	51.11 N	7.11 E
Remscheider-Stausee ⊖[1]	263	51.10 N	7.14 E
Remsen, Ia., U.S.	198	42.48 N	95.58 W
Remsen, N.Y., U.S.	210	43.19 N	75.11 W
Remsfeld	56	51.00 N	9.29 E
Remuna	126	21.33 N	86.54 E
Remus	190	43.36 N	85.09 W
Rémuzat	62	44.24 N	5.21 E
Rena	26	61.08 N	11.22 E
Renaix → Ronse	50	50.45 N	3.36 E
Renāla Khurd	123	30.53 N	73.36 E
Rena Point ›	116	16.10 N	119.45 E
Renard Islands II	164	10.50 S	153.05 E
Renata	182	49.26 N	118.06 W
Renaud Island I	9	65.40 S	66.00 W
Renca	286e	33.24 S	70.44 W
Renca, Cerro ∧	286e	33.23 S	70.43 W
Rencēni	76	57.44 N	25.26 E
Renchen	56	48.35 N	8.01 E
Rencontre East	186	47.38 N	55.12 W
Rencun	98	36.19 N	113.50 E
Renda, Ityo.	144	14.30 N	39.53 E
Renda, Lat.	76	57.09 N	22.22 E
Rende	68	39.19 N	16.11 E
Rendena, Valle V	58	46.08 N	10.42 E
Rend Lake ⊖[1]	194	38.05 N	88.58 W
Rendova Island I	175e	8.32 S	157.20 E
Rendsburg	41	54.18 N	9.40 E
Renens	58	46.32 N	6.35 E
Renesse	52	51.44 N	3.46 E
Renews	186	46.56 N	52.56 W
Renfrew, On., Can.	212	45.28 N	76.41 W
Renfrew, Scot., U.K.	46	55.53 N	4.24 W
Renfrew, Pa., U.S.	214	40.46 N	79.58 W
Renfrew □[6]	212	45.25 N	77.05 W
Rengam	114	1.53 N	103.24 E
Ren'gang	106	32.01 N	120.50 E
Rengasdengklok	115a	6.09 S	107.17 E
Rengat	112	0.24 S	102.33 E
Rengel	115a	7.04 S	112.00 E
Rengen ⊖	26	64.05 N	14.03 E
Rengezhuang	105	39.45 N	118.10 E
Rengit	114	1.41 N	103.09 E
Rengkang	112	1.07 N	112.10 E
Rengo	252	34.25 S	70.52 W
Rengsdorf	56	50.30 N	7.29 E
Reng Tlāng ∧	120	21.59 N	92.36 E
Renhe, Zhg.	100	33.32 N	114.02 E
Renhe, Zhg.	100	27.41 N	115.15 E
Renhechang	107	30.30 N	105.56 E
Renheji	100	31.56 N	115.07 E
Renhua	100	25.06 N	113.44 E
Renhuai	102	27.48 N	106.18 E
Reni	78	45.27 N	28.17 E
Renick	188	37.59 N	80.21 W
Renish Point ›	46	57.44 N	6.59 W
Renjiawopeng	104	41.27 N	122.18 E
Renjiaxu	106	30.49 N	121.00 E
Renju	100	24.51 N	115.54 E
Renko	26	60.54 N	24.17 E
Renkum	52	51.58 N	5.45 E
Renliuchang	107	29.13 N	106.39 E
Renlong	107	30.32 N	105.47 E
Renmark	166	34.11 S	140.45 E
Renmei	100	25.50 N	117.56 E
Renmin	89	46.37 N	125.32 E
Renna, Monte ∧	70	36.52 N	14.41 E
Rennau	54	52.17 N	10.55 E
Renne, Lac du → Reindeer Lake ⊖	176	57.15 N	102.40 W
Renne, Rivière le ≃	206	45.41 N	72.39 W
Rennell I	160	11.40 S	160.10 E
Rennell, Islas II	254	52.00 S	74.00 W
Rennell Sound ʮ	182	53.25 N	132.40 W
Renner	222	32.59 N	96.47 W
Rennerdale	279b	40.24 N	80.08 W
Rennerod	56	50.36 N	8.04 E
Renner Springs	162	18.20 S	133.48 E
Rennertshofen	60	48.45 N	11.02 E
Rennes	32	48.05 N	1.41 W
Rennick Bay c	9	70.18 S	161.45 E
Rennick Glacier ⊓	9	70.30 S	161.45 E
Rennie	184	49.51 N	95.33 W
Rennie's Mill	271d	22.18 N	114.15 E
Renningen	56	48.46 N	8.56 E
Renntier-See → Reindeer Lake ⊖	176	57.15 N	102.40 W
Rennweg	64	47.01 N	13.37 E
Reno, Nv., U.S.	226	39.31 N	119.48 W
Reno, Pa., U.S.	214	41.25 N	79.45 W
Reno, Tx., U.S.	222	32.56 N	97.05 W
Reno ≃	64	44.37 N	12.16 E
Reno Beach	214	41.40 N	83.15 W
Reno Hill ∧	200	42.35 N	106.03 W
Reno International Airport ⊠	226	39.30 N	119.46 W
Renoster ≃	158	31.37 S	20.37 E
Renous	186	46.49 N	65.48 W
Renous ≃	186	46.50 N	65.50 W
Renovo	214	41.19 N	77.45 W
Renqiao	100	33.27 N	117.16 E
Renqiu	98	38.43 N	116.05 E
Rens	41	54.54 N	9.06 E
Renshan	100	22.50 N	114.48 E
Renshou, Zhg.	100	27.08 N	117.51 E
Renshou, Zhg.	107	30.00 N	104.08 E
Rensjön	24	68.05 N	19.49 E
Rensselaer, In., U.S.	216	40.56 N	87.09 W
Rensselaer, Mo., U.S.	219	39.40 N	91.33 W
Rensselaer, N.Y., U.S.	210	42.38 N	73.44 W
Rensselaer □[6]	210	42.43 N	73.40 W
Rensselaer Falls	212	44.35 N	75.19 W
Rensselaerville	210	42.30 N	74.08 W
Rentería	34	43.19 N	1.54 W
Rentfort ◆[8]	263	51.35 N	6.57 E
Renton	224	47.28 N	122.12 W
Rentuo	107	29.14 N	106.23 E
Rentweinsdorf	56	50.04 N	10.47 E
Renun ≃	114	3.05 N	97.55 E
Renville	198	44.47 N	95.12 W
Renwez	56	49.50 N	4.36 E
Renwick, N.Z.	172	41.30 S	173.50 E
Renwick, Ia., U.S.	190	42.49 N	93.58 W
Renyichang	107	29.29 N	105.28 E
Renziehalusen Park ♠	279b	40.21 N	79.50 W
Réo, Burkina	150	12.19 N	2.28 W
Reo, Indon.	115b	8.19 S	120.30 E
Reola ◆[8]	272a	28.34 N	76.59 E
Repartimento ≃	250	6.06 S	50.40 W
Repaupo	285	39.48 N	75.18 W
Repbäcken	40	60.31 N	15.20 E
Répce ≃	30	47.41 N	17.03 E
Repentigny	206	45.44 N	73.28 W
Repetek	128	38.34 N	63.11 E
Repino	76	60.10 N	29.52 E
Repjovka, Ross.	78	51.05 N	38.39 E
Repjovka, Ross.	80	53.09 N	48.06 E
Repki	78	51.48 N	31.05 E
Repolka	76	59.16 N	29.34 E
Repolovo	86	60.40 N	69.50 E
Reporoa	172	38.26 S	176.21 E
Reposaari	26	61.37 N	21.27 E
Repton	194	31.24 N	87.14 W
Republic, Ks., U.S.	198	39.55 N	97.49 W
Republic, Mi., U.S.	190	46.24 N	87.58 W
Republic, Mo., U.S.	194	37.07 N	93.28 W
Republic, Oh., U.S.	214	41.07 N	83.00 W
Republic, Wa., U.S.	202	48.38 N	118.44 W
República Centroafricana → Central African Republic □[1]	136	7.00 N	21.00 E
Republic Airport ⊠	276	40.44 N	73.25 W
Republican ≃	198	39.03 N	96.48 W
Republican, North Fork ≃	198	40.01 N	101.59 W
Republican, South Fork ≃	198	40.03 N	101.31 W
Republic Observatory ⊍[3]	273d	26.11 S	28.05 E
Republic Steel Corporation ⊍[3]	279a	41.28 N	81.40 W
République centrafricaine → Central African Republic □[1]	136	7.00 N	21.00 E
Repueblo de Oriente	196	25.51 N	99.39 W
Repulse Bay	176	66.32 N	86.15 W
Repulse Bay c	166	20.36 S	148.43 E
Repvåg	24	70.45 N	25.41 E
Requena, Esp.	34	39.29 N	1.06 W
Requena, Perú	248	4.58 S	73.50 W
Réquista	32	44.02 N	2.32 E
Rère ≃	50	47.22 N	1.50 E
Reriutaba	250	4.10 S	40.35 W
Reşadiye	130	40.24 N	37.21 E
Reşadiye ◆[8]	267b	41.05 N	29.15 E
Reşadiye Yarımadası ›[1]	130	36.40 N	27.45 E
Resang, Tanjong ›	114	2.35 N	103.51 E
Resarö	40	59.26 N	18.20 E
Rescalda	266b	45.38 N	8.56 E
Rescaldina	266b	45.37 N	8.57 E
Reschenpass (Passo di Resia))(	64	46.50 N	10.30 E
Rescue	208	36.59 N	76.33 W
Research	274b	37.42 S	145.11 E
Reseda ◆[8]	280	34.12 N	118.31 W
Resen	38	41.05 N	21.00 E
Resende	256	22.28 S	44.27 W
Reserva	252	24.38 S	50.52 W
Reserva, Parque de la ♠	286d	12.04 S	77.02 W
Reserve, La., U.S.	194	30.03 N	90.33 W
Reserve, N.M., U.S.	200	33.42 N	108.45 W
Reserve Township	279b	40.29 N	79.59 W
Reservoir	274b	37.43 S	145.00 E
Reservoir Pond ⊖	283	42.10 N	71.07 W
Rešetilovka	78	49.34 N	34.04 E
Rešetnikovo	82	56.27 N	36.34 E
Reshui	98	42.09 N	119.18 E
Reshuitang	102	24.10 N	103.09 E
Resia, Passo di (Reschenpass))(	64	46.50 N	10.30 E
Resipol, Beinn ∧	46	56.43 N	5.39 W
Resistencia	252	27.27 S	58.59 W
Reșița	38	45.17 N	21.53 E
Resiutta	64	46.23 N	13.13 E
Resko	30	53.47 N	15.25 E
Rešma	80	57.24 N	42.34 E
Rešn'ovka	78	49.47 N	27.25 E
Resolute	176	74.41 N	94.54 W
Resolution Island I, N.T., Can.	176	61.30 N	65.00 W
Resolution Island I, N.Z.	172	45.40 S	166.40 E
Resolven	42	51.42 N	3.42 W
Resort, Loch c	46	58.03 N	7.06 W
Rešoty	76	57.09 N	28.30 E
Resplandes	250	6.17 S	45.13 W
Resplendor	255	19.20 S	41.15 W
Ressa ≃	76	54.45 N	35.10 E
Ressaca, Ribeirão da ≃	287b	23.38 S	46.51 W
Resse ◆[8]	263	51.34 N	7.07 E
Resseta ≃	76	53.49 N	35.15 E
Ressons-sur-Matz	50	49.33 N	2.45 E
Resta ≃	76	53.36 N	30.56 E
Resthaven	216	41.16 N	88.09 W
Restigouche (Ristigouche) ≃	186	48.04 N	66.20 W
Restín, Punta ›	246	4.17 S	81.15 W
Restinga	34	35.42 N	5.23 W
Restinga Seca	252	29.49 S	53.23 W
Reston, Mb., Can.	184	49.35 N	101.02 W
Reston, Scot., U.K.	46	55.51 N	2.11 W
Reston, Va., U.S.	208	38.58 N	77.20 W
Restoule Lake ⊖	190	46.03 N	79.47 W
Restrepo, Col.	246	4.15 N	73.33 W
Restrepo, Col.	246	3.48 N	76.31 W
Resuttano	70	37.41 N	14.02 E
Retalhuleu	236	14.32 N	91.41 W
Retalhuleu □[5]	236	14.20 N	91.50 W
Retamosa	252	33.35 S	54.44 W
Retem, Oued er V	148	33.30 N	5.45 E
Řetenice	54	50.38 N	13.46 E
Retezat, Parcul Național ♠	38	45.20 N	22.50 E
Retezatului, Munții ⋏	38	45.25 N	23.00 E
Rethel	50	49.31 N	4.22 E
Rethem	52	52.45 N	9.23 E
Réthimnon	38	35.22 N	24.29 E
Retiche, Alpi → Rhaetian Alps ⋏	58	46.30 N	10.00 E
Retie	56	51.16 N	5.04 E
Retiers	28	47.55 N	1.23 W
Retiro, Estacion ◆[5]	288	34.36 S	58.22 W
Retiro, Parque del ♠	266a	40.25 N	3.41 W
Retournac	62	45.12 N	4.02 E
Retreat	222	32.03 N	96.29 W
Retreat ≃	170	34.07 S	149.38 E
Retsof	210	42.50 N	77.53 W
Rettenberg	58	47.35 N	10.17 E
Rettendon	260	51.39 N	0.33 E
Rettendon Place	260	51.38 N	0.34 E
Rettichovka	89	44.10 N	132.47 E
Rettin	54	54.06 N	10.53 E
Return Creek ≃	226	37.56 N	119.28 W
Retz	61	48.45 N	15.57 E
Retzow	54	52.37 N	12.41 E
Reuden	54	52.04 N	12.18 E
Reungeut	114	4.34 N	96.22 E
Reunion (Réunion) □[2], Afr.	138	21.06 S	55.36 E
Reunion (Réunion) □[2], Afr.	157c	21.06 S	55.36 E
Reus	34	41.09 N	1.07 E
Reuschenberg	263	51.10 N	6.42 E
Reusel	52	51.21 N	5.22 E
Reusrath	263	51.06 N	6.57 E
Reuss ≃	58	47.28 N	8.14 E
Reut ≃	78	47.15 N	29.09 E
Reuterstadt Stavenhagen	54	53.42 N	12.53 E
Reutlingen	58	48.29 N	9.11 E
Reutov	82	55.46 N	37.52 E
Reutte	58	47.29 N	10.43 E
Reuver	52	51.17 N	6.05 E
Revadim	132	31.46 N	34.48 E
Rev'akino	82	54.22 N	37.40 E
Reval → Tallinn	76	59.25 N	24.45 E
Revda, Ross.	24	67.58 N	34.32 E
Revda, Ross.	86	56.48 N	59.57 E
Réveillon, Ruisseau le ≃	261	48.42 N	2.30 E
Revel	62	45.11 N	5.52 E
Revelganj	124	25.47 N	84.40 E
Revelstoke	182	50.59 N	118.12 W
Reventazón	248	6.10 S	80.58 W
Reventazón ≃	236	10.17 N	83.24 W
Revere, It.	64	45.03 N	11.08 E
Revere, Ma., U.S.	207	42.24 N	71.00 W
Revere, Pa., U.S.	208	40.31 N	75.10 W
Revere Beach ⩡[2]	283	42.25 N	70.59 W
Revermont ⋏[2]	58	46.27 N	5.25 E
Revesby	274a	33.57 S	151.01 E
Revest-du-Bion	62	44.05 N	5.33 E
Révia	154	13.23 S	36.31 E
Reviga	38	44.42 N	27.06 E
Revigny-sur-Ornain	56	48.50 N	4.59 E
Revilla del Campo	34	42.13 N	3.32 W
Revillagigedo, Islas II	232	19.00 N	111.30 W
Revillagigedo Channel ʮ	182	55.10 N	131.13 W
Revillagigedo Island I	182	55.35 N	131.23 W
Revillo	198	45.01 N	96.34 W
Revin	56	49.56 N	4.38 E
Revloc	214	40.29 N	78.45 W
Řevnićov	54	50.08 N	13.45 E
Revò	64	46.23 N	11.03 E
Revol'ucii, pik ∧	85	38.31 N	72.21 E
Revolución Mexicana	234	16.03 N	93.04 W
Revolution, Museum of the ⊍	265b	55.46 N	37.36 E
Revsundssjön ⊖	26	62.49 N	15.17 E
Revúboè ≃	154	16.13 S	33.37 E
Revuè ≃	156	19.49 S	34.00 E
Rew	214	41.54 N	78.32 W
Rewa	124	24.32 N	81.18 E
Rewa ≃	246	3.53 N	58.45 W
Rewāri	124	28.11 N	76.37 E
Rewataya, Taka ✦[2]	112	6.05 S	118.55 E
Rex, Mount ∧	9	74.57 S	76.00 W
Rexburg	202	43.49 N	111.47 W
Rexdale ◆[8]	275b	43.43 N	79.35 W
Rexford, Ks., U.S.	198	39.28 N	100.44 W
Rexford, Mt., U.S.	202	48.52 N	115.13 W
Rexhame	283	42.06 N	70.40 W
Rexton	186	46.39 N	64.52 W
Rexville	210	42.05 N	77.40 W
Rey, Arroyo del ≃	288	34.46 S	58.27 W
Rey, Embalse del ⊖[1]	266a	40.18 N	3.32 W
Rey, Estrecho del → King Sound ʮ	162	17.00 S	123.30 E
Rey, Isla del I	246	8.22 N	78.55 W
Rey, Laguna del ⊖	196	27.01 N	103.26 W
Rey Bouba	146	8.40 N	14.11 E
Reyes	248	14.19 S	67.23 W
Reyes, Point ›	204	38.00 N	123.01 W
Reyes Peak ∧	228	34.38 N	119.17 W
Reyhanlı	130	36.18 N	36.32 E
Rey Jorge, Estrecho → King George Sound ʮ	162	35.03 S	117.57 E
Rey Jorge, Isla → King George Island I	9	62.00 S	58.15 W
Reykjanes ›[1]	24a	63.49 N	22.43 W
Reykjanes Ridge ✦[3]	10	62.00 N	27.00 W
Reykjavík	24a	64.09 N	21.51 W
Reynella	168b	35.06 S	138.32 E
Reyno	194	36.21 N	90.45 W
Reynolds, Ga., U.S.	192	32.33 N	84.05 W
Reynolds, In., U.S.	216	40.44 N	86.52 W
Reynolds, N.D., U.S.	198	47.57 N	97.45 W
Reynolds Channel ʮ	276	40.36 N	73.40 W
Reynolds Creek ≃, Austl.	171a	27.56 S	152.36 E
Reynolds Creek ≃, On., Can.	212	43.00 N	80.58 W
Reynoldsville	214	41.05 N	78.53 W
Reynosa	232	26.07 N	98.18 W
Reyssouze ≃	58	46.27 N	4.54 E
Režž	86	57.23 N	61.24 E
Rež ≃	86	57.54 N	62.18 E
Reza, gora (Kūh-e Rīzeh) ∧	128	37.47 N	58.05 E
Rezé	32	47.12 N	1.34 W
Rēzekne	76	56.30 N	27.19 E
Rēzekne ≃	76	56.46 N	26.58 E
Rezeny	78	46.46 N	28.54 E
Rezina	78	47.44 N	28.58 E
Rezino	86	55.51 N	75.18 E
Rezovo	38	41.59 N	28.02 E
Rezovska (Mutlu) ≃	38	41.59 N	28.01 E
Rezvānshahr	128	37.33 N	49.09 E
Rezzato	64	45.31 N	10.19 E
Rezzoaglio	62	44.32 N	9.23 E
Rezzonico	58	46.04 N	9.16 E
Rhade	52	53.19 N	9.07 E
Rhadeswood Reservoir ⊖[1]	262	53.29 N	1.56 W
Rhaetian Alps (Rätische Alpen) (Alpi Retiche) ⋏	58	46.30 N	10.00 E
Rhallamane, Sebkha de ⁝	148	23.41 N	9.50 W
Rhame	198	46.13 N	103.39 W
Rharbi, Île I	148	34.39 N	11.03 E
Rharbi, Zahrez ⊖	148	34.50 N	2.50 E
Rhauderfehn	52	53.08 N	7.35 E
Rhaunen	56	49.52 N	7.20 E
Rhayader	42	52.18 N	3.30 W
Rhea Creek ≃	202	45.30 N	119.46 W
Rheda-Wiedenbrück	52	51.50 N	8.18 E
Rhede, Dtsch.	52	53.03 N	7.16 E
Rhede, Dtsch.	52	51.50 N	6.11 E
Rheden	52	52.01 N	6.02 E
Rheems	208	40.08 N	76.34 W
Rheem Valley	226	37.52 N	122.07 W
Rheidol ≃	42	52.25 N	4.05 W
Rheims → Reims	50	49.15 N	4.02 E
Rhein	184	51.22 N	102.10 W
Rheinau	56	48.41 N	7.56 E
Rheinbach	56	50.37 N	6.57 E
Rheinberg	52	51.33 N	6.35 E
Rheinböllen	56	50.00 N	7.40 E
Rheinbrohl	56	50.30 N	7.19 E
Rheinbrücke ◆[5]	263	51.12 N	6.44 E
Rheindürkheim	56	49.42 N	8.21 E
Rheine	52	52.17 N	7.26 E
Rheineck	58	47.28 N	9.35 E
Rheinen	263	51.27 N	7.38 E
Rheinfall ∟	58	47.41 N	8.38 E
Rheinfelden, Dtsch.	58	47.33 N	7.47 E
Rheinfelden, Schw.	58	47.33 N	7.48 E
Rheinhausen	56	51.24 N	6.44 E
Rhein-Herne-Kanal ≅	263	51.27 N	6.47 E
Rheinhessen-Pfalz □[5]	56	49.30 N	8.00 E
Rheinkamp	52	51.30 N	6.37 E
Rheinland-Pfalz □[3]	56	50.00 N	7.00 E
Rhein → Rhine ≃	30	51.52 N	6.02 E
Rheinsberg	54	53.06 N	12.53 E
Rheinstadion ♠	263	51.16 N	6.44 E
Rheinstein, Burg ⊥	56	50.00 N	7.50 E
Rheinwald V	58	46.32 N	9.17 E
Rheinwaldhorn ∧	58	46.30 N	9.02 E
Rheirs, Oued V	148	30.39 N	4.26 W
Rhêmes-Notre-Dame	62	45.34 N	7.07 E
Rhenen	52	51.57 N	5.34 E
Rhens	56	50.17 N	7.37 E
Rheurdt	263	51.27 N	6.28 E
Rheydt	56	51.10 N	6.25 E
Rheydt, Schloss ⊥	263	51.11 N	6.29 E
Rhin ≃	54	52.59 N	12.55 E
Rhinau	58	48.19 N	7.42 E
Rhine	192	31.59 N	83.12 W
Rhine (Rhein) (Rhin) ≃	30	51.52 N	6.02 E
Rhinebeck	210	41.55 N	73.54 W
Rhinecliff	210	41.55 N	73.57 W
Rhineland	219	38.43 N	91.31 W
Rhinelander	190	45.38 N	89.24 W
Rhin Kanal ≅	54	52.47 N	12.24 E
Rhinluch ⁝	54	52.50 N	12.50 E
Rhinns of Kells ⋏	44	55.07 N	4.22 W
Rhinns Point ›	46	55.40 N	6.30 W
Rhino Camp	154	2.58 N	31.24 E
Rhinow	54	52.45 N	12.20 E
Rhin → Rhine ≃	30	51.52 N	6.02 E
Rhiou, Oued ≃	34	36.00 N	0.55 E
Rhir, Cap ›	148	30.38 N	9.55 W
Rhis, Oued ≃	34	35.14 N	3.57 W
Rhiw ≃	42	52.36 N	3.11 W
Rho	62	45.32 N	9.02 E
Rhode Island □[3], U.S.	178	41.40 N	71.30 W
Rhode Island □[3], U.S.	207	41.40 N	71.30 W
Rhode Island I	207	41.33 N	71.15 W
Rhode Island Sound ʮ	207	41.25 N	71.15 W
Rhoden	52	51.28 N	9.00 E
Rhodes, Austl.	274a	33.50 S	151.05 E
Rhodes, S. Afr.	158	30.47 S	27.59 E
Rhodes, Eng., U.K.	262	53.33 N	2.14 W
Rhodesia → Zimbabwe □[1]	154	20.00 S	30.00 E
Rhodes Inyanga National Park ♠	154	18.12 S	32.45 E
Rhodes Matopos National Park ♠	154	20.33 S	28.20 E
Rhodes Park ♠	273d	26.12 S	28.06 E
Rhodes Peak ∧	202	46.41 N	114.47 W
Rhodes → Ródhos	38	36.26 N	28.13 E
Rhodes → Ródhos I	38	36.10 N	28.00 E
Rhodes' Tomb ⊥	154	20.30 S	28.30 E
Rhododendron	224	45.20 N	121.55 W
Rhododendron State Park ♠	207	42.47 N	72.12 W
Rhodon	261	48.43 N	2.04 E
Rhodon, Ruisseau le ≃	261	48.42 N	2.04 E
Rhodope Mountains (Rodopi) (Orosirá Rodhópis) ⋏	38	41.30 N	24.30 E
Rhodt	56	49.16 N	8.07 E
Rhome	222	33.03 N	97.28 W
Rhondda	42	51.40 N	3.27 W
Rhône □[5]	32	45.55 N	4.40 E
Rhône ≃	32	43.20 N	4.50 E
Rhône à Sète, Canal du ≅	62	43.25 N	3.42 E
Rhône au Rhin, Canal du ≅	58	47.06 N	5.19 E
Rhoose	42	51.24 N	3.20 W
Rhosesmor	262	53.12 N	3.10 W
Rhosllanerchrugog	44	53.00 N	3.03 W
Rhosneigr	44	53.14 N	4.31 W
Rhos-on-Sea	44	53.19 N	3.45 W
Rhossili	42	51.34 N	4.17 W
Rhourde-El-Baguel	148	31.24 N	6.57 E
Rhuddlan	44	53.18 N	3.27 W
Rhue ≃	32	45.23 N	2.29 E
Rhum I	46	57.00 N	6.20 W
Rhum, Sound of ʮ	46	56.56 N	6.14 W
Rhyl	44	53.19 N	3.29 W
Rhymney	42	51.46 N	3.18 W
Rhymney ≃	42	51.28 N	3.10 W
Rhynie	46	57.19 N	2.50 W
Riaba	152	3.23 N	8.46 E
Riace	68	38.25 N	16.29 E
Riachão	250	7.22 S	46.37 W
Riachão do Dantas	250	11.04 S	37.44 W
Riachão do Jacuípe	250	11.48 S	39.21 W
Riacho de Santana	255	13.37 S	42.57 W
Riacho Grande	256	23.48 S	46.35 W
Riachos, Islas de los II	254	40.10 S	62.08 W
Riachuelo, Bra.	250	10.44 S	37.11 W
Riachuelo, Chile	254	40.49 S	73.21 W
Riachuelo, Ur.	258	34.28 S	57.43 W
Riachuelo ≃	288	34.38 S	58.22 W
Riachuelo, Arroyo ≃	258	34.27 S	57.44 W
Rialma	255	15.18 S	49.34 W
Rialto, Bra.	256	22.35 S	44.16 W
Rialto, Ca., U.S.	228	34.06 N	117.22 W
Riamkanan, Waduk ⊖[1]	112	3.30 S	115.05 E
Rianápolis	255	15.29 S	49.28 W
Riāng	120	27.32 N	92.56 E
Riangnom	140	9.55 N	30.01 E
Riaño	34	42.58 N	5.01 W
Rians	62	43.37 N	5.45 E
Riánsares ≃	34	39.32 N	3.18 W
Riāsi	123	33.05 N	74.50 E
Riau □[4]	112	1.00 N	102.00 E
Riau, Kepulauan II	112	1.00 N	104.30 E
Riaz	58	46.38 N	7.04 E
Riaza	34	41.17 N	3.28 W
Riaza ≃	34	41.42 N	3.55 W
Ribadavia	34	42.17 N	8.08 W
Ribadeo	34	43.32 N	7.02 W
Ribadesella	34	43.28 N	5.04 W
Ribas de Jarama	266a	40.23 N	3.31 W
Ribas do Rio Pardo	255	20.27 S	53.46 W
Ribauè	154	14.57 S	38.17 E
Ribble ≃	44	53.44 N	2.50 W
Ribbleton	262	53.46 N	2.40 W
Ribble Valley □[8]	262	53.48 N	2.31 W
Ribbon Fall ∟	226	37.44 N	119.39 W
Ribchester	262	53.49 N	2.32 W
Ribe	41	55.21 N	8.46 E
Ribe □[6]	41	55.35 N	8.50 E
Ribe ≃	41	55.21 N	8.40 E
Ribeauvillé	58	48.12 N	7.19 E
Ribécourt	50	49.31 N	2.55 E
Ribeira	252	24.40 S	49.01 W
Ribeira do Iguape ≃	252	24.40 S	47.24 W
Ribeira do Pombal	250	10.50 S	38.32 W
Ribeira Grande, C.V.	150a	17.11 N	25.04 W
Ribeira Grande, Port.	148a	37.49 N	25.31 W
Ribeirão	250	8.31 S	35.23 W
Ribeirão das Lajes, Reprêsa do ⊖[1]	256	22.45 S	43.55 W
Ribeirão de São Joaquim	256	22.17 S	44.11 W
Ribeirão do Pinhal	255	23.24 S	50.18 W
Ribeirão Pires	256	23.43 S	46.25 W
Ribeirão Preto	255	21.10 S	47.48 W
Ribeirão Vermelho	255	21.11 S	45.03 W
Ribeirãozinho	255	16.27 S	52.35 W
Ribeiro Gonçalves	250	7.32 S	45.14 W
Ribeiro Junqueira	256	21.28 S	42.31 W
Ribeiros	256	21.59 S	45.35 W
Ribemont	50	49.48 N	3.28 E
Ribera	70	37.30 N	13.16 E
Ribérac	32	45.15 N	0.20 E
Riberalta	248	10.59 S	66.06 W
Riberão Pires □[7]	287b	23.43 S	46.21 W
Ribiers	62	44.14 N	5.52 E
Rib Lake	190	45.19 N	90.12 W
Ribnica, Slo.	36	45.44 N	14.44 E
Ribnica, Slo.	61	46.32 N	15.16 E
Ribnitz-Damgarten	54	54.15 N	12.28 E
Ribstone Creek ≃	184	52.51 N	110.05 W
Ricadi	68	38.37 N	15.52 E
Ricarda, Estany de la c	266d	41.18 N	2.07 E
Ricardo Flores Magón	232	29.58 N	106.58 W
Ricaurte	246	1.13 N	77.59 W
Riccall	44	53.50 N	1.04 W
Riccarton	172	43.32 S	172.36 E
Riccia	66	41.29 N	14.50 E
Riccione	66	43.59 N	12.39 E
Rice	222	32.15 N	96.30 W
Rice Creek ≃	216	42.16 N	84.57 W
Rice Lake	190	45.30 N	91.44 W
Rice Lake ⊖, On., Can.	190	47.42 N	82.08 W
Rice Lake ⊖, On., Can.	212	44.08 N	78.13 W
Rice Lake Indian Reserve ◆[4]	212	44.10 N	78.12 W
Riceville, Ia., U.S.	190	43.22 N	92.33 W
Riceville, Pa., U.S.	214	41.47 N	79.48 W
Riceville, Tn., U.S.	192	35.23 N	84.41 W
Rich, Cape ›	212	44.43 N	80.38 W
Richan	184	49.59 N	92.49 W
Richard B. Russell Lake ⊖[1]	192	34.05 N	82.39 W
Richard Collinson Inlet c	176	72.45 N	113.45 W
Richards	222	30.32 N	95.51 W
Richard's Bay	158	28.47 S	32.06 E
Richard's Bay c	158	28.50 S	32.02 E
Richards-Gebaur Air Force Base ■	194	38.51 N	94.33 W
Richard's Harbour	186	47.37 N	56.24 W
Richards Island I	180	69.20 N	134.30 W
Richardson	222	32.56 N	96.43 W
Richardson ≃	176	58.30 N	111.30 W
Richardson, Mount ∧	162	28.49 S	119.59 E
Richardson Bay c	282	37.52 N	122.29 W
Richardson Mountains ⋏, Can.	180	67.15 N	136.30 W
Richardson Mountains ⋏, N.Z.	172	44.45 S	168.31 E
Richardson Park	285	39.44 N	75.35 W
Richardsville	214	41.14 N	79.01 W
Richard-Toll	150	16.28 N	15.41 W
Richardton	198	46.53 N	102.18 W
Rîchât, Guelb er ∧[2]	148	21.07 N	11.24 W
Richboro	208	40.13 N	75.01 W
Richburg	210	42.05 N	78.09 W
Riche, Pointe ›	186	50.42 N	57.25 W
Richebourg	261	48.49 N	1.38 E
Richelieu, P.Q., Can.	206	45.27 N	73.15 W
Richelieu, Fr.	32	47.01 N	0.19 E
Richelieu □[6]	206	45.55 N	73.00 W
Richelieu ≃	206	46.03 N	73.07 W
Richer	184	49.39 N	96.28 W
Richey	198	47.38 N	105.04 W
Richfield, Id., U.S.	202	43.02 N	114.09 W
Richfield, Mn., U.S.	190	44.53 N	93.16 W
Richfield, Oh., U.S.	214	41.14 N	81.39 W
Richfield, Pa., U.S.	208	40.41 N	77.07 W
Richfield, Ut,. U.S.	200	38.46 N	112.05 W
Richfield Springs	210	42.51 N	74.59 W
Richford, N.Y., U.S.	210	42.21 N	76.12 W
Richford, Vt., U.S.	206	44.59 N	72.40 W
Rich Fountain	219	38.24 N	91.53 W
Richgrove	226	35.48 N	119.07 W
Richhill, N. Ire., U.K.	48	54.23 N	6.33 W
Rich Hill, Mo., U.S.	194	38.05 N	94.12 W
Richibucto	186	46.41 N	64.52 W
Richisau	58	47.02 N	8.54 E
Richland, Ga., U.S.	192	32.05 N	84.40 W
Richland, Mi., U.S.	216	42.22 N	85.27 W
Richland, Mo., U.S.	194	37.51 N	92.24 W
Richland, N.J., U.S.	208	39.29 N	74.52 W
Richland, N.Y., U.S.	212	43.34 N	76.03 W
Richland, Pa., U.S.	208	40.21 N	76.16 W
Richland, Tx., U.S.	222	31.56 N	96.26 W
Richland, Tx., U.S.	222	32.57 N	95.49 W
Richland, Wa., U.S.	202	46.17 N	119.17 W
Richland □[6]	214	40.46 N	82.31 W
Richland Center	190	43.20 N	90.23 W
Richland Creek ≃, Il., U.S.	219	38.14 N	89.54 W
Richland Creek ≃, Tn., U.S.	194	35.02 N	86.55 W
Richland Creek ≃, Tx., U.S.	222	31.58 N	96.03 W
Richlands, N.C., U.S.	192	34.53 N	77.32 W
Richlands, Va., U.S.	192	37.05 N	81.47 W
Richland Springs	196	31.16 N	98.57 W
Richmond, Austl.	166	20.44 S	143.08 E
Richmond, Austl.	170	33.36 S	150.46 E
Richmond, Austl.	274b	37.49 S	145.00 E
Richmond, B.C., Can.	224	49.09 N	123.06 W
Richmond, On., Can.	212	45.11 N	75.50 W
Richmond, P.Q., Can.	206	45.40 N	72.09 W
Richmond, N.Z.	172	41.20 S	173.11 E
Richmond, S. Afr.	158	31.23 S	23.56 E
Richmond, S. Afr.	158	29.54 S	30.08 E
Richmond, Eng., U.K.	44	54.24 N	1.44 W
Richmond, Ca., U.S.	226	37.56 N	122.20 W
Richmond, Il., U.S.	216	42.28 N	88.18 W
Richmond, In., U.S.	218	39.49 N	84.53 W
Richmond, Ks., U.S.	198	38.24 N	95.15 W
Richmond, Ky., U.S.	192	37.44 N	84.17 W
Richmond, Me., U.S.	188	44.05 N	69.47 W
Richmond, Ma., U.S.	207	42.22 N	73.22 W
Richmond, Mi., U.S.	214	42.48 N	82.45 W
Richmond, Mn., U.S.	190	45.27 N	94.31 W
Richmond, Mo., U.S.	194	39.16 N	93.58 W
Richmond, Oh., U.S.	214	40.26 N	80.46 W
Richmond, Tx., U.S.	222	29.34 N	95.45 W
Richmond, Ut,. U.S.	200	41.55 N	111.48 W
Richmond, Vt., U.S.	188	44.24 N	72.59 W
Richmond, Va., U.S.	208	37.33 N	77.27 W
Richmond □[6], P.Q., Can.	206	45.40 N	72.00 W
Richmond □[6], N.Y., U.S.	210	40.38 N	74.05 W
Richmond □[6], Va., U.S.	208	37.32 N	77.28 W
Richmond ◆[8], Eng., U.K.	42	51.28 N	0.18 W
Richmond ◆[8], Ca., U.S.	282	37.46 N	122.29 W
Richmond ◆[8], Pa., U.S.	285	39.59 N	75.06 W
Richmond, Mount ∧	172	41.29 S	173.24 E
Richmond, Point ›	282	37.55 N	122.23 W
Richmond Beach	224	47.46 N	122.23 W
Richmond Creek ≃	276	40.34 N	74.11 W

Symbol	English	Deutsch	Español	Français	Português
≃	River	Fluß	Río	Rivière	Rio
≅	Canal	Kanal	Canal	Canal	Canal
∟	Waterfall, Rapids	Wasserfall, Stromschnellen	Cascada, Rápidos	Chute d'eau, Rapides	Cascata, Rápidos
ʮ	Strait	Meeresstraße	Estrecho	Détroit	Estreito
c	Bay, Gulf	Bucht, Golf	Bahía, Golfo	Baie, Golfe	Baía, Golfo
⊖	Lake, Lakes	See, Seen	Lago, Lagos	Lac, Lacs	Lago, Lagos
⁝	Swamp	Sumpf	Pantano	Marais	Pântano
⊓	Ice Features, Glacier	Eis- und Gletscherformen	Accidentes Glaciales	Formes glaciaires	Acidentes glaciares
⊤	Other Hydrographic Features	Andere Hydrographische Objekte	Otros Elementos Hidrográficos	Autres données hydrographiques	Outros acidentes hidrográficos
✦	Submarine Features	Untermeerische Objekte	Accidentes Submarinos	Formes de relief sous-marin	Acidentes submarinos
□	Political Unit	Politische Einheit	Unidad Politica	Entité politique	Unidade política
⊍	Cultural Institution	Kulturelle Institution	Institución Cultural	Institution culturelle	Institução cultural
⊥	Historical Site	Historische Stätte	Sitio Histórico	Site historique	Sitio histórico
♠	Recreational Site	Erholungs- und Ferienort	Sitio de Recreo	Centre de loisirs	Area de Lazer
⊠	Airport	Flughafen	Aeropuerto	Aéroport	Aeroporto
■	Military Installation	Militäranlage	Instalación Militar	Installation militaire	Instalação militar
◆	Miscellaneous	Verschiedenes	Misceláneo	Divers	Diversos

ENGLISH — DEUTSCH

Name	Page (Seite)	Lat.°′ (Breite°′)	Long.°′ (Länge°′ E = Ost)
Richmond Heights, Fl., U.S.	220	25.37 N	80.22 W
Richmond Heights, Mo., U.S.	219	38.37 N	90.19 W
Richmond Heights, Oh., U.S.	214	41.33 N	81.30 W
Richmond Highlands	224	47.45 N	122.20 W
Richmond Hill, On., Can.	212	43.52 N	79.27 W
Richmond Hill, Ga., U.S.	192	31.56 N	81.18 W
Richmond Hill ⊸[8]	276	40.42 N	73.49 W
Richmond International Airport ⊠	208	37.30 N	77.19 W
Richmond Mall ⊸[9]	279a	41.32 N	81.30 W
Richmond National Battlefield Park ♠	208	37.25 N	77.23 W
Richmond Park ♠	260	51.26 N	0.16 W
Richmond Peak ∧	241h	13.17 N	61.13 W
Richmond Range ⋏	172	41.27 S	173.30 E
Richmond Royal Australian Air Force Base ■	170	33.37 S	150.48 E
Richmond-San Rafael Bridge ⊸[5]	282	37.56 N	122.27 W
Richmondtown Restoration ⊥	276	40.34 N	74.09 W
Richmond Valley ⊸[8]	276	40.31 N	74.13 W
Richmondville	210	42.38 N	74.33 W
Richrath	263	51.08 N	6.56 E
Rich Square	192	36.16 N	77.17 W
Rich Stadium ♠	284a	42.57 N	78.47 W
Richtenberg	54	54.12 N	12.53 E
Richterswil	58	47.13 N	8.42 E
Richton	194	31.20 N	88.56 W
Richton Park	216	41.29 N	87.42 W
Richvale, On., Can.	212	43.51 N	79.26 W
Richvale, Ca., U.S.	226	39.30 N	121.45 W
Richview	219	38.23 N	89.11 W
Richville, N.Y., U.S.	212	44.25 N	75.23 E
Richville, Oh., U.S.	214	40.45 N	81.27 W
Richwood, N.J., U.S.	285	39.43 N	75.10 W
Richwood, Oh., U.S.	214	40.25 N	83.17 W
Richwood, W.V., U.S.	188	38.13 N	80.32 W
Richwood Village	222	29.04 N	95.25 W
Ricinskij zapovednik ♠	84	43.25 N	40.30 E
Rickenbacker Air Force Base ■	218	39.48 N	82.56 W
Rickenpass)(	58	47.14 N	9.02 E
Ricken Tunnel ⊸[5]	58	47.12 N	9.05 E
Ricketts Glen State Park ♠	210	41.20 N	76.18 W
Ricketts Point >	274b	38.00 S	145.02 E
Rickleån ≃	26	64.05 N	20.56 E
Rickling	54	54.01 N	10.13 E
Rickmansworth	42	51.39 N	0.29 W
Rico	200	37.41 N	108.01 W
Ricoa ≃	241s	11.30 N	69.12 W
Ricobayo, Embalse de ⊜[1]	34	41.30 N	5.55 W
Ricupe	152	14.37 S	21.25 E
Ridā'	144	14.38 N	44.54 E
Ridanna (Ridnaun)	64	46.55 N	11.15 E
Riddarhyttan	40	59.48 N	15.33 E
Ridderkerk	52	51.52 N	4.36 E
Riddes	58	46.10 N	7.13 E
Riddle	202	42.57 N	123.21 W
Riddle Mountain ∧	202	43.07 N	118.30 W
Riddlesburg	214	40.10 N	78.15 W
Riddlewood	285	39.54 N	75.26 W
Riddon, Loch ⊂	46	55.58 N	5.12 W
Rideau ≃	212	45.27 N	75.42 W
Ridge, Eng., U.K.	260	51.41 N	0.15 W
Ridge, N.Y., U.S.	207	40.54 N	72.53 W
Ridge, Tx., U.S.	222	31.09 N	96.19 W
Ridge Acres	276	40.41 N	74.32 W
Ridgecrest, Ca., U.S.	204	35.37 N	117.40 W
Ridgecrest, Wa., U.S.	224	47.45 N	122.21 W
Ridgedale	184	53.04 N	104.09 W
Ridge Farm	194	39.53 N	87.39 W
Ridgefield, Ct., U.S.	207	41.16 N	73.29 W
Ridgefield, Il., U.S.	216	42.16 N	88.22 W
Ridgefield, N.J., U.S.	210	40.50 N	74.00 W
Ridgefield, Wa., U.S.	224	45.48 N	122.44 W
Ridgefield Park	276	40.51 N	74.01 W
Ridgeland, Ms., U.S.	194	32.25 N	90.07 W
Ridgeland, S.C., U.S.	192	32.28 N	80.58 W
Ridgely, Md., U.S.	208	38.56 N	75.53 W
Ridgely, Tn., U.S.	194	36.15 N	89.29 W
Ridge Manor	220	28.31 N	82.10 W
Ridgemont	210	43.13 N	77.43 W
Ridgetown	214	42.26 N	81.54 W
Ridgeville, Mb., Can.	184	49.04 N	97.01 W
Ridgeville, In., U.S.	216	40.17 N	85.01 W
Ridgeville, S.C., U.S.	192	33.05 N	80.18 W
Ridgeville Corners	216	41.26 N	84.15 W
Ridgeway, On., Can.	284a	42.53 N	79.03 W
Ridgeway, Mi., U.S.	216	41.59 N	83.51 W
Ridgeway, Mo., U.S.	194	40.22 N	93.56 W
Ridgeway, N.J., U.S.	208	40.01 N	74.17 W
Ridgeway, Oh., U.S.	216	40.30 N	83.34 W
Ridgeway, Tx., U.S.	222	33.11 N	95.46 W
Ridgeway, Wi., U.S.	190	43.00 N	89.59 W
Ridgeway Ditch ≊	279a	41.25 N	82.05 W
Ridgewood	210	40.58 N	74.07 W
Ridgewood ⊸[8]	276	40.42 N	73.53 W
Ridgewood Farm	285	39.57 N	75.34 W
Ridgewood Reservoir ⊜[1]	276	40.41 N	73.53 W
Ridgway, Co., U.S.	200	38.09 N	107.46 W
Ridgway, Il., U.S.	194	37.47 N	88.15 W
Ridgway, Pa., U.S.	214	41.25 N	78.43 W
Riding Mountain ∧	184	50.37 N	99.37 W
Riding Mountain National Park ♠	184	50.55 N	100.25 W
Riḍīwajār	124	27.57 N	83.26 E
Ridley Creek ≃	285	39.51 N	75.21 W
Ridley Creek State Park ♠	285	39.57 N	75.27 W
Ridley Park	285	39.52 N	75.19 W
Ridnaun → Ridanna	64	46.55 N	11.15 E
Riebeek-Kasteel	158	33.23 S	18.53 E
Riebeek-Oos	158	33.10 S	26.10 E
Riebeek-Wes	158	33.21 S	18.52 E
Riecawr, Loch ⊜	44	55.13 N	4.27 W
Riedau	60	48.18 N	13.38 E
Riedelbach	56	50.18 N	8.23 E
Rieden	60	49.19 N	11.57 E
Riedenburg	60	48.58 N	11.41 E
Rieder	54	51.44 N	11.10 E
Riederalp	58	46.23 N	8.01 E
Riedern	56	49.40 N	9.23 E
Ried im Innkreis	60	48.13 N	13.30 E
Ried im Oberinntal	58	47.03 N	10.39 E
Riedisheim	58	47.45 N	7.22 E
Riedlingen	58	48.09 N	9.28 E
Riedstadt	56	49.50 N	8.30 E
Riegel	58	48.09 N	7.45 E
Riegelsville, N.J., U.S.	210	40.49 N	74.52 W
Riegelsville, Pa., U.S.	208	40.36 N	75.12 W
Riegelwood	192	34.20 N	78.15 W
Riegersburg	61	47.00 N	15.56 E
Riegersburg, Schloss ⊥	61	47.01 N	15.56 E
Riegersdorf	64	46.33 N	13.47 E
Riehen	58	47.35 N	7.39 E
Rieka → Rijeka	36	45.20 N	14.27 E
Rielasingen	58	47.44 N	8.50 E
Riemke ⊸[8]	263	51.30 N	7.13 E
Riemst	56	50.48 N	5.36 E
Rieneck	56	50.05 N	9.38 E
Rienza (Rienz) ≃	64	46.43 N	11.39 E
Rienzi	194	34.45 N	88.31 W
Riesa	54	51.18 N	13.17 E
Riesco, Isla I	254	53.00 S	72.30 W
Rieseby	41	54.32 N	9.48 E
Riesel	222	31.28 N	96.56 W
Riesenbeck	52	52.16 N	7.37 E
Riese Pio X	64	45.44 N	11.55 E
Riesi	70	37.17 N	14.05 E
Riestedt	54	51.29 N	11.21 E
Riet ≃, S. Afr.	158	31.20 S	20.17 E
Riet ≃, S. Afr.	158	29.00 S	23.54 E
Rietavas	76	55.44 N	21.56 E
Rietberg	52	51.47 N	8.25 E
Rietbron	158	32.54 S	23.10 E
Rietfontein	156	21.58 S	20.58 E
Riethuiskraal	158	34.20 S	21.22 E
Rieti	66	42.24 N	12.51 E
Rieti □[4]	66	42.18 N	12.52 E
Rietschen	54	51.23 N	14.47 E
Rietspruit ≃, S. Afr.	273d	26.06 S	27.39 E
Rietspruit ≃, S. Afr.	273d	26.19 S	28.18 E
Rietvlei	158	30.29 S	29.51 E
Rietzer See ⊜	54	52.22 N	12.39 E
Rievaulx Abbey ʊ[1]	44	54.16 N	1.07 W
Riez	62	43.49 N	6.06 E
Riezlern	58	47.21 N	10.11 E
Rif ⋏	148	35.00 N	4.00 W
Riffe Lake ⊜[1]	224	46.30 N	122.20 W
Rifflart	273b	4.25 S	15.21 E
Rifiano (Riffian)	64	46.42 N	11.11 E
Rifle	200	39.32 N	107.46 W
Rifle ≃	190	44.00 N	83.49 W
Rifstangi >	24a	66.35 N	16.10 W
Rifton	210	41.50 N	74.03 W
Rift Valley □[4]	154	0.30 N	36.00 E
Rift Valley V	10	3.00 S	29.00 E
Rift Valley Lakes National Park ♠	144	7.30 N	38.30 E
Rīga, Lat.	76	56.57 N	24.06 E
Riga, Ross.	88	56.36 N	106.17 E
Riga, Mi., U.S.	216	41.49 N	83.50 W
Riga, Gulf of (Rīgas jūras līcis) (Riia laht) ⊂	76	57.30 N	23.35 E
Riga, Mount ∧	162	21.59 S	116.25 E
Rigacikun	150	10.40 N	7.28 E
Rigaih	114	4.40 N	95.34 E
Rīgān	128	28.37 N	58.58 E
Rīgas jūras līcis → Riga, Gulf of ⊂	76	57.30 N	23.35 E
Rīga Station ⊸[5]	265b	55.48 N	37.38 E
Rigaud	206	45.29 N	74.18 W
Rigaud ≃	206	45.29 N	74.18 W
Rigby	202	43.40 N	111.54 W
Rīgestān ⊸[1]	128	31.00 N	65.00 E
Riggins	202	45.25 N	116.18 W
Riggisberg	58	46.48 N	7.29 E
Riggston	219	39.42 N	90.25 W
Righedo, Passo del)(	64	44.27 N	9.55 E
Rigi ∧	58	47.05 N	8.30 E
Rignano Flaminio	66	42.12 N	12.29 E
Rignano Garganico	68	41.40 N	15.35 E
Rignano sull'Arno	66	43.43 N	11.27 E
Rigney	58	47.23 N	6.11 E
Rigney Bluff	210	43.19 N	77.38 W
Rigny-Ussé	50	47.15 N	0.18 E
Rigo	164	9.47 S	147.34 E
Rigolet	176	54.20 N	58.35 W
Rig-Rig	146	14.16 N	14.21 E
Rigside	46	55.36 N	3.47 W
Riguldi	76	59.08 N	23.33 E
Rīḥ, Jazīrat ar- I	140	18.10 N	38.27 E
Rihāb	132	32.19 N	36.06 E
Rihand ≃	124	24.33 N	82.59 E
Rihand Dam ⊸[6]	124	24.05 N	82.45 E
Riihimäki	26	60.45 N	24.46 E
Riiser-Larsen Peninsula >[1]	9	68.55 S	34.00 E
Rijau	150	11.07 N	5.14 E
Riječki Zaljev ⊂	36	45.15 N	14.25 E
Rijeka	36	45.20 N	14.27 E
Rijen	52	51.35 N	4.55 E
Rijkevorsel	56	51.21 N	4.46 E
Rijksdorp	52	52.09 N	4.25 E
Rijn → Rhine ≃	30	51.52 N	6.02 E
Rijnsburg	52	52.12 N	4.27 E
Rijssel → Lille	50	50.38 N	3.04 E
Rijssen	52	52.18 N	6.30 E
Rijswijk	52	52.04 N	4.20 E
Rikers Island I	276	40.47 N	73.53 W
Rikers Island Channel ʮ	276	40.47 N	73.52 W
Rikkavesi ⊜	26	62.50 N	28.44 E
Riksgränsen	24	68.24 N	18.12 E
Rikuchū-kaigan-kokuritsu-kōen ♠	92	39.25 N	141.57 E
Rikuzen-takata	92	39.01 N	141.38 E
Rila ⋏	38	42.08 N	23.33 E
Riley	198	39.17 N	96.49 W
Riley, Mount ∧	200	31.55 N	107.07 W
Riley, Point >	168b	33.53 S	137.36 E
Riley Creek ≃	216	41.02 N	84.00 W
Riley Lake ⊜	212	44.50 N	79.11 W
Rileys Range ⋏	170	34.21 S	150.10 E
Rilievo	70	37.55 N	12.33 E
Rillieux	62	45.49 N	4.54 E
Rillington	44	54.09 N	0.42 W
Rillito	200	32.24 N	111.09 W
Rillton	214	40.17 N	79.44 W
Rilly-la-Montagne	50	49.10 N	4.03 E
Rilski manastir ʊ[1]	38	42.08 N	23.20 E
Rima ≃	150	13.04 N	5.10 E
Rímac	286d	12.03 S	77.03 W
Rímac ≃	248	12.02 S	77.09 W
Rimachi, Laguna ⊜	246	4.25 S	76.43 W
Rimāḥ, Jabal ar- ∧	132	32.19 N	36.52 E
Rima San Giuseppe	62	45.52 N	8.00 E
Rimatara I	14	22.38 S	152.51 W
Rimavská Sobota	30	48.23 N	20.02 E
Rimbey	182	52.38 N	114.14 W
Rimbo	40	59.45 N	18.22 E
Rimé, Ouadi V	146	14.02 N	18.03 E
Rimersburg	214	41.02 N	79.30 W
Rimforsa	26	58.08 N	15.40 E
Rimi	150	12.58 N	7.43 E
Rimini	66	44.04 N	12.34 E
Rîmna ≃	38	45.39 N	27.19 E
Rîmnicu Sărat	38	45.23 N	27.03 E
Rîmnicu Vîlcea	38	45.06 N	24.22 E
Rimo Glacier ⊓	123	35.25 N	77.30 E
Rimogne	56	49.50 N	4.33 E
Rimouski	186	48.26 N	68.33 W
Rimouski ≃	186	48.27 N	68.32 W
Rimouski, Réserve ♠	186	48.03 N	68.15 W
Rimpar	56	49.51 N	9.57 E
Rimrock Lake ⊜[1]	224	46.38 N	121.12 W
Rimsko-Korsakovka	80	51.34 N	48.31 E
Rinbung	124	29.21 N	89.57 E
Rinca	115b	8.37 S	119.48 E
Rinca, Pulau I	115b	8.41 S	119.42 E
Rinchnach	60	48.57 N	13.12 E
Rinčin Lchumbe	88	51.07 N	99.40 E
Rincón, C.R.	236	8.42 N	83.29 W
Rincón, P.R.	240m	18.20 N	67.15 W
Rincon, Ga., U.S.	192	32.17 N	81.14 W
Rincon, N.M., U.S.	200	32.40 N	107.03 W
Rincón, Bahía de ⊂	240m	17.58 N	66.20 W
Rinconada	252	22.26 S	66.10 W
Rinconada, Hipódromo de la ♠	286c	10.26 N	66.56 W
Rincón de la Vieja, Parque Nacional ♠	236	10.48 N	85.18 W
Rincón del Bonete, Lago Artificial de ⊜[1]	252	32.45 S	56.00 W
Rincón del Ocote, Cerro ∧	236	13.36 N	87.10 W
Rincón de Romos	234	22.14 N	102.18 W
Rincon Indian Reservation ⊸[4]	228	33.15 N	116.57 W
Rincon Valley	226	38.28 N	122.39 W
Rindal	26	63.03 N	9.13 E
Rindown Castle ⊥	48	53.32 N	7.59 W
Rīngas	120	27.21 N	75.34 E
Ringdove	175f	16.38 S	168.09 E
Ringe	41	55.14 N	10.29 E
Ringebu	26	61.31 N	10.10 E
Ringenwalde	54	53.03 N	13.42 E
Ringertown	279b	40.25 N	79.36 W
Ringford	44	54.54 N	4.03 W
Ringgau ⊸[1]	56	51.04 N	10.04 E
Ringgit, Gunung ∧	115a	7.43 S	113.50 E
Ringgold, Ga., U.S.	192	34.54 N	85.06 W
Ringgold, La., U.S.	194	32.19 N	93.16 W
Ringgold, Pa., U.S.	214	41.00 N	79.10 W
Ringgold Isles II	175g	16.15 S	179.25 W
Ringim	150	12.08 N	9.10 E
Ringkøbing	26	56.05 N	8.15 E
Ringkøbing □[6]	41	56.10 N	8.50 E
Ringkøbing Fjord ⊂[2]	26	56.00 N	8.15 E
Ringlet	114	4.25 N	101.23 E
Ringling	196	34.10 N	97.35 W
Ringling Museums ʊ	220	27.23 N	82.34 W
Ringmer	42	50.53 N	0.04 E
Ringoes	208	40.26 N	74.52 W
Rings Island	283	42.49 N	70.52 W
Ringsted, Dan.	41	55.27 N	11.49 E
Ringsted, Ia., U.S.	198	43.17 N	94.30 W
Ringtown	210	40.51 N	76.14 W
Ringvassøy I	24	69.55 N	19.15 E
Ringville	48	52.02 N	7.34 W
Ringwood, Austl.	169	37.49 S	145.14 E
Ringwood, Eng., U.K.	42	50.51 N	1.47 W
Ringwood, N.J., U.S.	210	41.06 N	74.14 W
Ringwood Manor ⊥	276	41.08 N	74.15 W
Ringwood North	274b	37.48 S	145.14 E
Ringwood State Park ♠	210	41.08 N	74.16 W
Riñihue	254	39.49 S	72.27 W
Riñihue, Lago ⊜	254	39.50 S	72.18 W
Rinjani, Gunung ∧	115b	8.24 S	116.28 E
Rinkenæs	41	54.54 N	9.34 E
Rinkerode	52	51.50 N	7.41 E
Rinnes, Ben ∧	46	57.23 N	3.15 W
Rinnthal	56	49.13 N	7.55 E
Rín → Rhine ≃	30	51.52 N	6.02 E
Rinsumageest	52	53.18 N	5.57 E
Rinteln	52	52.11 N	9.04 E
Rinxent	50	50.48 N	1.44 E
Rio, Fl., U.S.	220	27.13 N	80.14 W
Rio, Wi., U.S.	190	43.26 N	89.14 W
Rio Azul	252	25.43 S	50.47 W
Riobamba	246	1.40 S	78.38 W
Río Blanco, Chile	252	32.55 S	70.19 W
Río Blanco (Tenango de Rio Blanco), Méx.	234	18.50 N	97.09 W
Rio Bonito	256	22.43 S	42.37 W
Rio Bonito ⊸[8]	287b	23.43 S	46.41 W
Rio Branco, Bra.	248	9.58 S	67.48 W
Río Branco, Ur.	252	32.34 S	53.25 W
Río Bravo, Méx.	196	28.17 N	100.55 W
Río Bravo, Méx.	232	25.59 N	98.06 W
Rio Brilhante	255	21.48 S	54.33 W
Río Bueno	254	40.19 S	72.58 W
Río Caribe	246	10.42 N	63.07 W
Rio Casca	255	20.13 S	42.39 W
Río Cauto	240p	20.33 N	76.55 W
Río Ceballos	252	31.10 S	64.20 W
Río Chico, Arg.	254	41.43 S	70.30 W
Río Chico, Ven.	246	10.18 N	65.59 W
Rio Claro, Bra.	255	22.24 S	47.33 W
Rio Claro, Bra.	256	22.43 S	44.09 W
Rio Claro, Trin.	241r	10.18 N	61.11 W
Rio Claro, Reprêsa do ⊜[1]	256	23.39 S	45.54 W
Río Colorado	252	39.01 S	64.05 W
Rio Comprido ⊸[8]	287a	22.55 S	43.12 W
Río Cuarto	252	33.08 S	64.21 W
Rio das Flores	256	22.10 S	43.35 W
Rio das Pedras	156	23.12 S	35.23 E
Rio de Contas	255	13.36 S	41.48 W
Rio de Janeiro, Bra.	256	22.54 S	43.14 W
Rio de Janeiro, Bra.	287a	22.54 S	43.14 W
Rio de Janeiro □[3]	255	22.00 S	42.30 W
Rio de Janeiro □[7]	287a	22.55 S	43.30 W
Río de Jesús	236	7.59 N	81.10 W
Rio Dell	204	40.29 N	124.06 W
Rio de Mouro	266c	38.46 N	9.20 W
Río de Oro	246	8.17 N	73.23 W
Rio do Prado	255	16.35 S	40.34 W
Rio do Sul	252	27.13 S	49.39 W
Rio Douro	287a	22.39 S	43.32 W
Rio Espera	255	20.51 S	43.29 W
Río Gallegos	254	51.38 S	69.13 W
Río Grande, Arg.	254	53.47 S	67.42 W
Rio Grande, Bra.	252	32.02 S	52.05 W
Río Grande, Méx.	234	15.59 N	97.27 W
Río Grande, Méx.	234	23.50 N	103.02 W
Río Grande, Nic.	236	12.53 N	86.32 W
Río Grande, P.R.	240m	18.23 N	65.50 W
Rio Grande, N.J., U.S.	208	39.00 N	74.52 W
Río Grande, Ven.	286c	10.35 N	66.57 W
Rio Grande, Ponte do ⊸[5]	287b	23.46 S	46.31 W
Rio Grande City	196	26.22 N	98.49 W
Rio Grande Da Serra, Bra.	256	23.44 S	46.24 W
Rio Grande da Serra, Bra.	287b	23.44 S	46.24 W
Rio Grande da Serra □[7]	287b	23.45 S	46.23 W
Rio Grande do Norte □[3]	250	5.45 S	36.00 W
Rio Grande do Sul □[3]	252	30.00 S	54.00 W
Rio Grande do Sul → Rio Grande	252	32.02 S	52.05 W
Rio Grande → Grande, Rio ≃	178	25.57 N	97.09 W
Riograndina	256	22.11 S	42.30 W
Ríohacha	246	11.33 N	72.55 W
Río Hato	236	8.23 N	80.10 W
Río Hondo, Méx.	286a	19.25 N	99.16 W
Rio Hondo, Tx., U.S.	196	26.14 N	97.34 W
Rioja	248	6.05 S	77.09 W
Rio Jaguari, Reservatório do ⊜[1]	256	22.55 S	46.25 W
Río Jueyes	240m	18.01 N	66.20 W
Riola	64	44.16 N	11.04 E
Río Lagartos	232	21.36 N	88.10 W
Riolândia	255	19.59 S	49.40 W
Rio Largo	250	9.29 S	35.51 W
Riola Sardo	71	39.59 N	8.32 E
Rio Linda	226	38.41 N	121.26 W
Riolo Terme	66	44.16 N	11.43 E
Río Luján	258	34.17 S	58.54 W
Riom	32	45.54 N	3.07 E
Riomaggiore	62	44.06 N	9.44 E
Rio Marina	66	42.49 N	10.25 E
Río Mayo	254	45.41 S	70.16 W
Rio Mulatos	248	19.42 S	66.47 W
Río Muni □[4]	152	1.30 N	10.30 E
Riondel	182	49.46 N	116.52 W
Rio Negro, Bra.	252	26.06 S	49.48 W
Rio Negro, Bra.	255	19.27 S	54.58 W
Río Negro, Chile	254	40.47 S	73.14 W
Ríonegro, Col.	246	6.09 N	75.22 W
Ríonegro, Col.	246	7.16 N	73.09 W
Río Negro □[4]	254	40.00 S	67.00 W
Rio Negro, Pantanal do ≡	248	19.00 S	56.00 W
Rionero in Vulture	68	40.56 N	15.41 E
Rionero Sannitico	66	41.42 N	14.08 E
Rioni ≃	84	42.08 N	41.39 E
Rio Novo	256	21.29 S	43.08 W
Rio Novo do Sul	255	20.52 S	40.56 W
Riópar	34	38.30 N	2.27 W
Rio Pardo	252	29.59 S	52.22 W
Rio Pardo de Minas	255	15.37 S	42.33 W
Río Pico	254	44.13 S	71.21 W
Río Piedras, Arg.	252	25.18 S	64.54 W
Río Piedras, P.R.	240m	18.24 N	66.03 W
Río Pilcomayo, Parque Nacional ♠	252	25.10 S	58.00 W
Rio Piracicaba	255	19.55 S	43.11 W
Rio Pomba	256	21.17 S	43.11 W
Rio Prêto	256	22.06 S	43.50 W
Rio Prêto → São José do Rio Prêto	256	22.10 S	42.57 W
Rio Rancho	200	35.14 N	106.38 W
Rio Real	250	11.28 S	37.56 W
Rio Saliceto	64	44.49 N	10.49 E
Río San Juan □[5]	236	11.10 N	84.30 W
Río Segundo	252	31.40 S	63.55 W
Ríosucio, Col.	246	5.25 N	75.42 W
Ríosucio, Col.	246	7.27 N	77.07 W
Río Tercero	252	32.11 S	64.06 W
Rio Tinto	250	6.48 S	35.05 W
Riotord	62	45.14 N	4.24 E
Rio Tuba	116	8.30 N	117.25 E
Riou, Île de I	62	43.11 N	5.24 E
Rioveggio	64	44.17 N	11.14 E
Rio Verde, Bra.	255	17.43 S	50.56 W
Ríoverde, Méx.	234	21.56 N	99.59 W
Rio Verde de Mato Grosso	255	18.56 S	54.52 W
Rio Vermelho	255	18.18 S	43.00 W
Rio Vista, Ca., U.S.	226	38.09 N	121.41 W
Rio Vista, Tx., U.S.	222	32.14 N	97.23 W
Rioz	58	47.25 N	6.04 E
Riozinho ≃, Bra.	246	2.55 S	67.07 W
Riozinho ≃, Bra.	250	7.06 S	51.40 W
Riozinho ≃, Bra.	250	10.22 S	49.50 W
Riozinho ≃, Bra.	250	8.25 S	45.43 W
Říp ∧	54	50.24 N	14.18 E
Ripacandida	68	40.55 N	15.43 E
Ripalti, Punta dei >	66	42.42 N	10.25 E
Ripatransone	66	43.00 N	13.46 E
Ripley, Eng., U.K.	44	53.03 N	1.24 W
Ripley, Eng., U.K.	260	51.18 N	0.29 W
Ripley, Il., U.S.	219	40.01 N	90.38 W
Ripley, In., U.S.	216	41.06 N	86.39 W
Ripley, Ms., U.S.	194	34.43 N	88.57 W
Ripley, N.Y., U.S.	214	42.16 N	79.42 W
Ripley, Oh., U.S.	218	38.44 N	83.50 W
Ripley, Tn., U.S.	194	35.44 N	89.31 W
Ripley, W.V., U.S.	188	38.49 N	81.42 W
Ripley □[6]	218	39.04 N	85.15 W
Ripoll	34	42.12 N	2.12 E
Ripoll ≃	266d	41.29 N	2.12 E
Ripollet	266d	41.30 N	2.10 E
Ripon, P.Q., Can.	206	45.47 N	75.06 W
Ripon, Eng., U.K.	44	54.08 N	1.31 W
Ripon, Ca., U.S.	226	37.44 N	121.07 W
Ripon, Wi., U.S.	190	43.50 N	88.50 W
Riposto	70	37.44 N	15.12 E
Rippling Ridge	284b	39.11 N	76.37 W
Ripponden	44	53.41 N	1.57 W
Rippowam ≃	276	41.03 N	73.33 W
Riquewihr	58	48.10 N	7.18 E
Ririba, Laga ≃	154	3.34 N	37.15 E
Ririe	202	43.37 N	111.46 W
Risālpur Cantonment	123	34.04 N	72.00 E
Risaralda □[5]	246	5.00 N	76.00 W
Risasi	154	0.25 S	25.44 E
Risbäck	26	64.42 N	15.32 E
Risca	42	51.37 N	3.07 W
Rischenau	52	51.53 N	9.17 E
Riscle	32	43.40 N	0.05 W
Risco, Ilha do I	246	3.07 S	58.19 W
Rishā', Wādī ar- V	128	25.33 N	44.05 E
Rīshahr	128	28.55 N	50.50 E
Rishīkesh	124	30.07 N	78.19 E
Rishiri-Rebun-Sarobetsu-kokuritsu-kōen ♠	92a	45.10 N	141.35 E
Rishiri-suidō ʮ	92a	45.10 N	141.25 E
Rishiri-tō I	92a	45.11 N	141.15 E
Rishiri-zan ∧	92a	45.11 N	141.15 E
Rishmayyā	132	33.44 N	35.36 E
Rishon LeẔiyyon	132	31.58 N	34.48 E
Rishpon	132	32.12 N	34.49 E
Rishra	272b	22.43 N	88.21 E
Rishrāsh, Wādī V	142	29.29 N	31.16 E
Rishton	262	53.46 N	2.25 W
Rishworth	262	53.40 N	1.57 W
Rishworth Moor ⊸[3]	262	53.39 N	2.01 W
Risinge	40	58.42 N	15.51 E
Rising Star	196	32.05 N	98.57 W
Rising Sun, In., U.S.	218	38.56 N	84.51 W
Rising Sun, Md., U.S.	208	39.41 N	76.03 W
Risingsun, Oh., U.S.	214	41.16 N	83.25 W
Risle ≃	50	49.26 N	0.23 E
Risnjak ∧	36	45.26 N	14.37 E
Rîşnov	38	45.36 N	25.28 E
Risø	41	55.42 N	12.06 E
Rison, Ar., U.S.	194	33.57 N	92.11 W
Rison, Md., U.S.	208	38.32 N	77.10 W
Risør	26	58.43 N	9.14 E
Ris-Orangis	50	48.39 N	2.25 E
Riss ≃	58	48.17 N	9.49 E
Rissani	148	31.23 N	4.09 W
Risskov ⊸[8]	41	56.11 N	10.14 E
Risstissen	58	48.16 N	9.49 E
Risti	76	58.59 N	24.03 E
Ristigouche (Restigouche) ≃	186	48.04 N	66.20 W
Ristiina	26	61.30 N	27.16 E
Ristijärvi	26	64.30 N	28.13 E
Ristinge	41	54.50 N	10.38 E
Ristna	76	58.56 N	22.05 E
Risum-Lindholm	41	54.45 N	8.53 E
Rita Blanca Creek ≃	196	35.40 N	102.29 W
Ritchie, S. Afr.	158	29.02 S	24.38 E
Ritchie, Md., U.S.	284c	38.52 N	76.52 W
Ritchie Branch ≃	284c	38.53 N	76.52 W
Rithāla ⊸[8]	272a	28.43 N	77.06 E
Ritidian Point >	174p	13.39 N	144.51 E
Ritscher Upland ⋏[1]	9	73.20 S	9.30 W
Ritsumeikan University ʊ[2]	270	35.01 N	135.46 E
Ritsurin-kōen ♠	96	34.21 N	134.02 E
Ritta Island I	220	26.44 N	80.48 W
Ritter, Mount ∧	226	37.42 N	119.12 W
Ritterhude	52	53.11 N	8.45 E
Rittersgrün	54	50.29 N	12.47 E
Rittman	214	40.58 N	81.46 W
Rittō	94	35.01 N	136.00 E
Ritzleben	54	52.50 N	11.21 E
Ritzville	202	47.07 N	118.22 W
Riu	120	28.19 N	95.03 E
Riva	208	38.57 N	76.35 W
Rivadavia, Arg.	252	35.28 S	62.57 W
Rivadavia, Arg.	252	33.11 S	68.28 W
Rivadavia, Arg.	252	24.11 S	62.53 W
Rivadavia, Arg.	252	31.33 S	68.37 W
Rivadavia, Chile	252	29.58 S	70.34 W
Riva del Garda	64	45.53 N	10.50 E
Riva del Sole	66	42.46 N	10.52 E
Riva di Tures (Rain)	64	46.57 N	12.04 E
Rivanazzano	62	44.56 N	9.01 E
Rivanna ≃	192	37.45 N	78.10 W
Rivare	216	40.49 N	84.50 W
Rivarolo Canavese	62	45.19 N	7.43 E
Rivarolo Mantovano	64	45.04 N	10.26 E
Rivas	236	11.26 N	85.50 W
Rivas □[5]	236	11.25 N	85.50 W
Rivasdale	273d	26.17 S	27.56 E
Rīvash	128	35.26 N	58.26 E
Rivas-Vaciamadrid	266a	40.20 N	3.31 W
Riva Trigoso	62	44.16 N	9.26 E
Rive, Île de la I	273b	4.21 S	15.26 E
Rive d'Arcano	64	46.08 N	13.02 E
Rive-de-Gier	62	45.32 N	4.37 E
Rivello	68	40.04 N	15.45 E
Rivera, Arg.	252	37.12 S	63.14 W
Rivera, Col.	246	2.47 N	75.15 W
Rivera, Ur.	252	30.54 S	55.31 W
Riverbank	226	37.44 N	120.56 W
River Cess	150	5.28 N	9.32 W
Riverdale, Ca., U.S.	226	36.25 N	119.51 W
Riverdale, Il., U.S.	278	41.38 N	87.37 W
Riverdale, Md., U.S.	284c	38.57 N	76.55 W
Riverdale, N.J., U.S.	276	40.59 N	74.18 W
Riverdale, N.D., U.S.	198	47.29 N	101.22 W
Riverdale, Or., U.S.	224	45.27 N	122.41 W
Riverdale ⊸[8]	276	40.54 N	73.54 W
Riverdale Heights	284c	38.58 N	76.55 W
Riverdale Park ♠	275b	43.40 N	79.21 W
River Drive Park	212	44.08 N	79.31 W
River Edge, N.J., U.S.	276	40.55 N	74.02 W
River Edge, Oh., U.S.	279a	41.25 N	81.51 W
River Falls, Al., U.S.	194	31.21 N	86.32 W
River Falls, Wi., U.S.	190	44.51 N	92.37 W
River Forest	278	41.53 N	87.48 W
Rivergaro	62	44.55 N	9.36 E
River Grove	278	41.55 N	87.50 W
Riverhaven	216	41.05 N	85.02 W
Riverhead, Eng., U.K.	260	51.17 N	0.10 E
Riverhead, N.Y., U.S.	207	40.55 N	72.39 W
River Hébert	186	45.42 N	64.23 W
River Hill	279b	40.12 N	79.54 W
River Hills	216	43.10 N	87.55 W
Riverhurst	184	50.53 N	106.52 W
Riverina ⊸[1]	166	35.30 S	145.30 E
River John	186	45.45 N	63.03 W
River Jordan	224	48.25 N	124.03 W
Riverlea	214	40.05 N	83.02 W
River Lea Navigation ≊	260	51.32 N	0.02 W
River Meadow Brook ≃	283	42.38 N	71.17 W
Rivermont	192	35.13 N	77.38 W
Rivero, Isla I	254	45.37 S	74.20 W
River Oaks	284c	38.57 N	77.11 W
River of Ponds	186	50.32 N	57.24 W
River Pines, Ca., U.S.	226	38.33 N	120.45 W
River Pines, Ma., U.S.	207	42.33 N	71.17 W
River Plaza	208	40.21 N	74.05 W
River Ridge Estates	284c	38.47 N	77.00 W
River Road	202	44.03 N	123.05 W
River Rouge	216	42.16 N	83.08 W
River Rouge Park ♠	281	42.22 N	83.15 W
Rivers	184	50.02 N	100.12 W
Rivers □[3]	150	4.30 N	6.30 E
Rivers, Lake of the ⊜	184	49.45 N	105.45 W
Riversdale, N.Z.	172	45.54 S	168.45 E
Riversdale, S. Afr.	158	34.07 S	21.15 E
Riverside, Ca., U.S.	228	33.57 N	117.23 W
Riverside, Ct., U.S.	276	41.02 N	73.35 W
Riverside, Il., U.S.	278	41.50 N	87.49 W
Riverside, Ia., U.S.	190	41.28 N	91.34 W
Riverside, Mi., U.S.	216	42.11 N	86.23 W
Riverside, Mi., U.S.	216	42.17 N	84.29 W
Riverside, N.J., U.S.	208	40.01 N	74.57 W
Riverside, N.Y., U.S.	210	42.55 N	73.40 W
Riverside, N.Y., U.S.	210	42.08 N	77.01 W
Riverside, Pa., U.S.	210	40.57 N	76.38 W
Riverside, Tx., U.S.	222	30.57 N	95.24 W
Riverside, Wa., U.S.	182	48.30 N	119.30 W
Riverside □[6]	228	33.45 N	117.10 W
Riverside ⊸[8]	281	42.20 N	82.57 W
Riverside International Raceway ♠	228	33.57 N	117.17 W
Riverside Manors	284a	43.11 N	79.03 W
Riverside Park ♠, Mi., U.S.	281	42.22 N	83.26 W
Riverside Park ♠, N.Y., U.S.	284a	42.57 N	78.54 W
Rivers Inlet	182	51.41 N	127.15 W
Rivers Inlet ⊂	182	51.39 N	127.30 W
Riversleigh	166	19.02 S	138.44 E
Riverstone	170	33.40 S	150.52 E
Riverton, Austl.	168b	34.09 S	138.45 E
Riverton, Mb., Can.	184	50.59 N	96.59 W
Riverton, N.Z.	172	46.21 S	168.01 E
Riverton, Il., U.S.	219	39.51 N	89.33 W
Riverton, Ne., U.S.	198	40.05 N	98.45 W
Riverton, N.J., U.S.	208	40.00 N	75.00 W
Riverton, Ut,. U.S.	200	40.31 N	111.56 W
Riverton, Va., U.S.	188	38.56 N	78.11 W
Riverton, Wy., U.S.	200	43.01 N	108.22 W
Riverton Heights	224	47.28 N	122.18 W
River Vale	276	40.59 N	74.00 W
Riverview, S. Afr.	158	28.27 S	32.10 E
River View, Al., U.S.	194	32.47 N	85.08 W
Riverview, Fl., U.S.	220	27.51 N	82.19 W
Riverview, Ks., U.S.	198	37.47 N	97.22 W
Riverview, Mi., U.S.	216	42.10 N	83.10 W
Riverview Park ♠	279b	40.29 N	80.01 W
Riverwood, Austl.	274a	33.57 S	151.03 E
Riverwood, In., U.S.	218	40.06 N	85.58 W
Riverwoods	278	42.10 N	87.54 W
Rives, Fr.	62	45.21 N	5.30 E
Rives, Tn., U.S.	194	36.21 N	89.02 W
Rivesaltes	32	42.46 N	2.52 E
Rives Junction	216	42.23 N	84.27 W
Rive Sud, Canal de la ≊	275a	45.25 N	73.41 W
Rivesville	188	39.31 N	80.07 W
Riviera, Az., U.S.	204	35.04 N	114.35 W
Riviera, Tx., U.S.	196	27.18 N	97.49 W
Riviera V	58	46.15 N	8.58 E
Riviera Beach, Fl., U.S.	220	26.46 N	80.03 W
Riviera Beach, Md., U.S.	208	39.10 N	76.30 W
Rivière-à-Claude	186	49.13 N	65.54 W
Rivière-au-Tonnerre	186	50.16 N	64.47 W
Rivière-Bleue	186	47.26 N	69.03 W
Rivière-Bois-Clair	206	46.34 N	71.50 W
Rivière-de-la-Chaloupe	186	49.08 N	62.32 W
Rivière-des-Prairies ⊸[8]	275a	45.39 N	73.33 W
Rivière-du-Loup	186	47.50 N	69.32 W
Rivière du Rempart	157c	20.06 S	57.41 E
Rivière-Matane	186	48.39 N	67.20 W
Rivière-Mékinac	206	46.47 N	72.48 W
Rivière-Pentecôte	186	49.47 N	67.10 W
Rivière-Pilote	240e	14.29 N	60.54 W
Rivière-Salée	240e	14.32 N	60.59 W
Rivière-Verte	186	47.19 N	68.09 W
Riviersonderend	158	34.09 S	19.55 E
Rivignano	64	45.52 N	13.03 E
Rivington	262	53.37 N	2.34 W
Rivington Reservoirs ⊜[1]	262	53.37 N	2.34 W
Rivisondoli	66	41.52 N	14.04 E
Rivoli	62	45.04 N	7.31 E
Rivoli Bay ⊂	166	37.32 S	140.04 E
Rivolta d'Adda	62	45.28 N	9.31 E
Rivoltella	64	45.27 N	10.33 E
Riwaka	172	41.05 S	173.00 E
Rixford	214	41.55 N	78.30 W
Rixheim	58	47.46 N	7.24 E
Riyadh → Ar-Riyāḍ	128	24.38 N	46.43 E
Rīyāq	132	33.51 N	36.00 E
Rizal	116	15.43 N	121.06 E
Rizal □[4]	116	14.35 N	121.10 E
Rizal Memorial Stadium ♠	269f	14.34 N	120.59 E
Rizal → Pasay	269f	14.33 N	121.00 E
Rize	130	41.02 N	40.31 E
Rize □[4]	130	40.55 N	40.55 E
Rīzeh, Kūh-e (gora Reza) ∧	128	37.47 N	58.05 E
Rizhao	98	35.27 N	119.29 E
Rizziconi	68	38.25 N	15.57 E
Rizzuto, Capo >	68	38.54 N	17.06 E
Rjukan	26	59.52 N	8.34 E
Rkîz, Lac ⊜	150	16.50 N	15.19 W
Rô	175f	21.22 S	167.50 E
Roa, Esp.	34	41.42 N	3.55 W
Roa, Nor.	26	60.17 N	10.37 E
Roa, Zaïre	154	3.49 N	24.56 E
Roachdale	194	39.50 N	86.48 W
Roade	42	52.09 N	0.53 W
Roadford Reservoir ⊜[1]	42	50.43 N	4.13 W
Roadhead	44	55.04 N	2.46 W
Roadknight, Point >	169	38.26 S	144.11 E
Roadside	158	27.31 S	28.52 E
Road Town	240m	18.27 N	64.37 W
Roag, East Loch ⊂	46	58.14 N	6.48 W
Roag, West Loch ⊂	46	58.13 N	6.53 W
Roaming Rock, Lake ⊜[1]	214	41.38 N	80.49 W
Roaming Shores	214	41.39 N	80.49 W
Roana	64	45.52 N	11.28 E
Roan Cliffs ⊥[4]	200	39.20 N	109.40 W
Roan Creek ≃	200	39.20 N	108.13 W
Roan Fell ∧	44	55.13 N	2.52 W
Roan Mountain	192	36.11 N	82.04 W
Roann	216	40.54 N	85.55 W
Roanne	32	46.02 N	4.04 E
Roanoke, Al., U.S.	194	33.09 N	85.22 W
Roanoke, Il., U.S.	190	40.47 N	89.11 W
Roanoke, In., U.S.	216	40.57 N	85.22 W
Roanoke, Tx., U.S.	222	33.01 N	97.14 W
Roanoke, Va., U.S.	192	37.16 N	79.56 W
Roanoke (Staunton) ≃	192	35.56 N	76.43 W
Roanoke Island I	192	35.53 N	75.39 W
Roanoke Rapids	192	36.27 N	77.39 W
Roanoke Rapids Dam ⊸[6]	192	36.24 N	77.40 W
Roan Plateau ⋏[1]	200	39.30 N	109.40 W
Roans Prairie	222	30.35 N	95.57 W
Roaring ≃	224	45.13 N	122.12 W
Roaring Branch	210	41.34 N	76.57 W
Roaring Brook ≃	212	43.44 N	75.24 W
Roaring Fork ≃	200	39.33 N	107.20 W
Roaring River Slough ≃	282	38.05 N	121.55 W
Roaring Run ≃	279b	40.33 N	79.32 W
Roaring Spring	214	40.20 N	78.23 W
Roaring Springs	196	33.54 N	100.52 W
Roaringwater Bay ⊂	48	51.31 N	9.26 W
Roatán	236	16.18 N	86.35 W
Roatán, Isla de I	236	16.23 N	86.30 W
Robâa Oued Yahia	36	36.05 N	9.35 E
Robāṭ Karīm	128	35.28 N	51.05 E
Robbeneiland I	158	33.49 S	18.22 E
Robbers Cave State Park ♠	196	35.01 N	95.27 W
Robbins, Ca., U.S.	226	38.53 N	121.42 W
Robbins, Il., U.S.	216	41.38 N	87.42 W
Robbins, N.C., U.S.	192	35.26 N	79.35 W
Robbins, Tn., U.S.	192	36.21 N	84.35 W
Robbins Airport ⊠	283	42.34 N	70.58 W
Robbins Ditch ≊	216	41.21 N	86.43 W
Robbins Island I	166	40.41 S	144.57 E
Robbins Pond ⊜	283	42.00 N	70.55 W
Robbins Rest	276	40.39 N	73.10 W
Robbinsville, N.J., U.S.	208	40.13 N	74.37 W
Robbinsville, N.C., U.S.	192	35.19 N	83.48 W
Robbio	62	45.17 N	8.35 E
Robe, Austl.	166	37.11 S	139.45 E
Robe, Ityo.	144	7.52 N	39.38 E
Robe ≃, Austl.	162	21.19 S	115.40 E
Robe ≃, Ire.	48	53.37 N	9.16 W
Robe, Mount ∧[2]	166	31.40 S	141.20 E
Robecchetto con Induno	266b	45.32 N	8.46 E
Robecco d'Oglio	64	45.15 N	10.04 E
Robecco sul Naviglio	266b	45.26 N	8.53 E
Röbel	54	53.23 N	12.35 E
Robeline	194	31.41 N	93.18 W
Röberget ∧[2]	40	59.45 N	14.54 E
Robersonville	192	35.49 N	77.15 W
Robert, Havre du ⊂	240e	14.40 N	60.55 W
Roberta	192	32.43 N	84.00 W
Roberta Mills	192	35.22 N	80.38 W
Robert E. Lee Memorial Park ♠	284b	39.23 N	76.39 W
Robert E. Lee's Birthplace ⊥	208	38.10 N	76.49 W
Robert-Espagne	56	48.45 N	5.02 E
Robert F. Kennedy Memorial Stadium ♠	284c	38.53 N	76.58 W
Robert H. Treman State Park ♠	210	42.24 N	76.35 W
Robert Lee	196	31.54 N	100.29 W
Robert Louis Stevenson Memorial State Park ♠	226	38.40 N	122.36 W
Robert Louis Stevenson's Tomb ⊥	175a	13.50 S	171.44 W
Robert Morse College ʊ[2]	279b	40.31 N	80.12 W
Robert Moses State Park ♠	210	40.37 N	73.16 W
Robert Mueller Municipal Airport ⊠	222	30.18 N	97.42 W
Roberto Payró	258	35.10 S	57.39 W
Robert Point >	168a	32.31 S	115.42 E
Roberts, Id., U.S.	202	43.43 N	112.07 W
Roberts, Il., U.S.	216	40.37 N	88.11 W
Roberts, Mt., U.S.	202	45.21 N	109.10 W
Roberts, Mount ∧	171a	28.13 S	152.28 E
Roberts, Point >	224	49.00 N	123.06 W
Robert's Arm	186	49.29 N	55.49 W
Robertsbridge	42	50.59 N	0.29 E
Roberts Canyon V	280	34.11 N	117.54 W
Roberts Creek Mountain ∧	204	39.52 N	116.18 W
Robertsdale, Al., U.S.	194	30.33 N	87.42 W
Robertsdale, Pa., U.S.	214	40.11 N	78.06 W
Robertsfield	150	6.15 N	10.24 W
Robertsfors	26	64.11 N	20.51 E
Robertsganj	124	24.42 N	83.04 E
Robertsham ⊸[8]	273d	26.15 S	28.00 E
Robertsholm	40	60.35 N	76.16 E
Robert S. Kerr Lake ⊜[1]	194	35.25 N	95.00 W
Roberts Mountain ∧	180	60.03 N	166.16 W
Robertson, Austl.	170	34.35 S	150.35 E
Robertson, S. Afr.	158	33.46 S	19.50 E
Robertson □[6], Ky., U.S.	218	38.32 N	84.04 W
Robertson □[6], Tx., U.S.	222	31.00 N	96.30 W
Robertson, Lac ⊜	186	51.00 N	59.10 W
Robertson Bay ⊂	9	71.25 S	170.00 E
Robertson Range ⋏	162	23.10 S	121.00 E
Robertsonville	206	46.09 N	71.13 W
Roberts Park	278	41.44 N	87.49 W
Roberts Peak ∧	182	52.57 N	120.32 W
Robertsport	150	6.45 N	11.22 W
Robertstown	168b	34.00 S	139.05 E
Robertsville	214	40.46 N	81.11 W
Robertville	56	50.27 N	6.07 E
Roberval	176	48.31 N	72.13 W
Robin Hood's Bay	44	54.25 N	0.33 W
Robins Air Force Base ■	192	32.38 N	83.35 W
Robins Island I	207	40.58 N	72.28 W
Robinson, Il., U.S.	194	39.00 N	87.44 W
Robinson, Tx., U.S.	222	31.28 N	97.06 W
Robinson ≃	164	16.03 S	137.16 E
Robinson, Lake ⊜[1]	192	34.26 N	80.10 W
Robinson Brook ≃	283	43.02 N	71.13 W
Robinson Creek ≃	226	38.16 N	119.15 W
Róbinson Crusoe, Isla (Isla Más a Tierra) I	244	33.38 S	78.52 W
Robinson Gorge National Park ♠	166	25.15 S	149.10 E
Robinson Lake ⊜	222	29.35 N	94.36 W
Robinson Lake Aerodrome ⊠	273d	26.08 S	27.42 E
Robinson Pond ⊜	283	42.48 N	71.23 W

Symbols in the index entries represent the broad categories identified in the key at the right. Symbols with superior numbers (⋏[1]) identify subcategories (see complete key on page *I · 1).*

Symbole im Register stellen die rechts im Schlüssel erklärten Kategorien dar. Symbole mit hochgestellten Ziffern (⋏[1]) bezeichnen Unterabteilungen einer Kategorie (vgl. vollständiger Schlüssel auf Seite *I · 1).*

Los símbolos incluídos en el texto del índice representan las grandes categorias identificadas con la clave a la derecha. Los símbolos con numeros en su parte superior (⋏[1]) identifican las subcategorías (véase la clave completa en la página *I · 1).*

Les symboles de l'index représentent les catégories indiquées dans la légende à droite. Les symboles suivis d'un indice (⋏[1]) représentent des sous-catégories (voir légende complète à la page *I · 1).*

Os símbolos incluídos no texto do índice representam as grandes categorias identificadas com a chave à direita. Os símbolos com números em sua parte superior (⋏[1]) identificam as subcategorias (veja-se a chave completa à página *I · 1).*

∧	Mountain	Berg	Montaña	Montagne	Montanha
⋏	Mountains	Gebirge	Montañas	Montagnes	Montanhas
)(	Pass	Paß	Paso	Col	Passo
V	Valley, Canyon	Tal, Cañon	Valle, Cañón	Vallée, Canyon	Vale, Canhão
≚	Plain	Ebene	Llano	Plaine	Planície
>	Cape	Kap	Cabo	Cap	Cabo
I	Island	Insel	Isla	Île	Ilha
II	Islands	Inseln	Islas	Îles	Ilhas
⊥	Other Topographic Features	Andere Topographische Objekte	Otros Elementos Topográficos	Autres données topographiques	Outros acidentes topográficos

ESPAÑOL — Nombre | Página | Lat.°′ | Long.°′ W = Oeste
FRANÇAIS — Nom | Page | Lat.°′ | Long.°′ W = Ouest
PORTUGUÊS — Nome | Página | Lat.°′ | Long.°′ W = Oeste

Nombre / Nom / Nome	Página / Page	Lat.°′	Long.°′
Robinson Range ⩘	162	25.45 S	119.00 E
Robinson Run ≃	279b	40.23 N	80.06 W
Robinson Run, North Branch ≃	279b	40.23 N	80.11 W
Robinsons	186	48.15 N	58.48 W
Robinvale	166	34.36 S	142.46 E
Robleda	34	40.23 N	6.36 W
Robledo	34	38.46 N	2.26 W
Roblin	184	51.14 N	101.21 W
Röblingen	54	51.28 N	11.40 E
Roboré	248	18.20 S	59.45 W
Röbrinken	40	58.36 N	15.53 E
Rob Roy Island I	175e	7.25 S	157.35 E
Robson, Mount ∧	182	53.07 N	119.09 W
Robstown	196	27.47 N	97.40 W
Roby, Eng., U.K.	262	53.25 N	2.51 W
Roby, Il., U.S.	219	39.44 N	89.24 W
Roby, Tx., U.S.	196	32.44 N	100.22 W
Roby Mill	262	53.34 N	2.44 W
Roca, Cabo da ≻	34	38.47 N	9.30 W
Roçado	250	6.40 S	44.19 W
Rocafuerte	246	0.55 S	80.28 W
Roça Grande	256	21.36 S	42.58 W
Rocanville	184	50.24 N	101.43 W
Roca Partida, Isla I	232	19.01 N	112.02 W
Roca Partida, Punta ≻	234	18.42 N	95.10 W
Rocas, Atol das I [1]	250	3.52 S	33.59 W
Roccabernarda	68	39.08 N	16.52 E
Roccacasale	66	42.07 N	13.53 E
Roccadaspide	68	40.26 N	15.12 E
Rocca di Cambio	66	42.14 N	13.29 E
Rocca di Mezzo	66	42.12 N	13.31 E
Rocca di Neto	68	39.11 N	17.00 E
Rocca di Papa	66	41.46 N	12.42 E
Roccafluvione	66	42.51 N	13.29 E
Roccagloriosa	68	40.06 N	15.26 E
Roccalbegna	66	42.47 N	11.30 E
Roccalumera	70	37.58 N	15.24 E
Rocca Massima	66	41.41 N	12.55 E
Roccamena	70	37.50 N	13.09 E
Roccamonfina	68	41.17 N	13.59 E
Roccanova	68	40.13 N	16.12 E
Roccapalumba	70	37.48 N	13.39 E
Rocca Pia	66	41.56 N	13.59 E
Rocca Pietore	64	46.26 N	11.59 E
Roccaprebalza	64	44.31 N	9.57 E
Rocca Priora	267a	41.48 N	12.45 E
Roccaraso	66	41.51 N	14.05 E
Rocca San Casciano	66	44.03 N	11.50 E
Rocca Santa Maria	66	42.41 N	13.30 E
Roccasecca	66	41.33 N	13.40 E
Roccasecca dei Volsci	66	41.29 N	13.13 E
Roccastrada	66	43.00 N	11.10 E
Roccavione	62	44.19 N	7.29 E
Roccavivara	66	41.50 N	14.36 E
Roccelito, Monte ∧	70	37.50 N	13.47 E
Roccella Ionica	68	38.19 N	16.24 E
Roccella Valdemone	70	37.56 N	15.00 E
Rocchetta Sant'Antonio	68	41.06 N	15.27 E
Rocciamelone ∧	62	45.12 N	7.05 E
Ročegda	24	62.42 N	43.23 E
Roch ≃	44	53.34 N	2.18 W
Rocha, Bra.	256	21.28 S	45.49 W
Rocha, Ur.	252	34.29 S	54.20 W
Rocha Miranda ➛ [8]	287a	22.52 S	43.22 W
Rocha Sobrinho	287a	22.47 S	43.25 W
Rochdale, Eng., U.K.	44	53.38 N	2.09 W
Rochdale, Ma., U.S.	207	42.11 N	71.54 W
Rochdale, N.Y., U.S.	210	41.43 N	73.50 W
Rochdale □ [8]	262	53.37 N	2.08 W
Rochdale Canal ≊	262	53.43 N	1.54 W
Roche	42	50.24 N	4.48 W
Rochebrune, Pic de ∧	62	44.49 N	6.51 E
Rochechouart	32	45.50 N	0.50 E
Rochedinho	255	20.14 S	54.33 W
Rochedo	255	19.57 S	54.52 W
Rochedo de Minas	256	21.38 S	43.01 W
Rochefort, Bel.	56	50.10 N	5.13 E
Rochefort, Fr.	32	45.57 N	0.58 W
Rochefort-en-Yvelines	50	48.35 N	1.59 E
Rochefort-Montagne	32	45.41 N	2.48 E
Rochefort-sur-Nenon	58	47.07 N	5.34 E
Roche Harbor	224	48.36 N	123.08 W
Rochehaut	56	49.51 N	5.00 E
Roche-la-Molière	62	45.26 N	4.19 E
Roche-lez-Beaupré	58	47.17 N	6.07 E
Rochelle, Ga., U.S.	192	31.57 N	83.27 W
Rochelle, Il., U.S.	216	41.55 N	89.04 W
Rochelle, Tx., U.S.	196	31.13 N	99.13 W
Rochelle Park	276	40.54 N	74.04 W
Rochemaure	62	44.35 N	4.42 E
Roche-Percée	184	49.03 N	102.45 W
Rochepot, Château de la ⊥	58	46.57 N	4.40 E
Rocher Fendu, Rapides du ∟	275a	45.19 N	73.57 W
Rochester, Austl.	166	36.22 S	144.42 E
Rochester, Eng., U.K.	42	51.24 N	0.30 E
Rochester, Eng., U.K.	44	55.16 N	2.16 W
Rochester, Il., U.S.	219	39.45 N	89.32 W
Rochester, In., U.S.	216	41.03 N	86.12 W
Rochester, Ma., U.S.	207	41.43 N	70.49 W
Rochester, Mi., U.S.	214	42.40 N	83.08 W
Rochester, Mn., U.S.	190	44.01 N	92.28 W
Rochester, N.H., U.S.	188	43.18 N	70.58 W
Rochester, N.Y., U.S.	210	43.09 N	77.36 W
Rochester, Oh., U.S.	214	41.07 N	82.18 W
Rochester, Pa., U.S.	214	40.42 N	80.17 W
Rochester, Tx., U.S.	196	33.19 N	99.51 W
Rochester, Wa., U.S.	224	46.49 N	123.05 W
Rochester, Wi., U.S.	216	42.44 N	88.13 W
Rochester City Airport ⊠	260	51.21 N	0.30 E
Rochester Hills	214	42.40 N	83.09 W
Rochester Mills	214	40.49 N	78.59 W
Rochester-Monroe County Airport ⊠	210	43.07 N	77.40 W
Rochester-Utica State Recreation Area ♠	214	42.39 N	83.04 W
Rochetaillée	62	45.25 N	4.27 E
Rocheuses → Rocky Mountains ⩘	16	48.00 N	116.00 W
Rochford	42	51.36 N	0.43 E
Rochford □ [8]	260	51.36 N	0.39 E
Rochfortbridge	48	53.23 N	7.17 W
Rochlitz	54	51.03 N	12.47 E
Rochon, Lac ◎	206	46.43 N	75.14 W
Rock	190	46.04 N	87.09 W
Rock □ [6]	216	42.41 N	89.05 W
Rock ≃, U.S.	190	41.29 N	90.37 W
Rock ≃, U.S.	198	43.05 N	96.27 W
Rockall I	22	57.35 N	13.48 W
Rockall Rise ✣ [3]	10	59.00 N	14.00 W
Rockanje	52	51.53 N	4.05 E
Rockaway, N.J., U.S.	210	40.54 N	74.30 W
Rockaway, Or., U.S.	224	45.36 N	123.56 W
Rockaway ≃	210	40.51 N	74.21 W
Rockaway Inlet c	276	40.34 N	73.55 W
Rockaway Neck	276	40.51 N	74.21 W
Rockaway Park ➛ [8]	276	40.35 N	73.50 W
Rockaway Point ➛ [8]	276	40.33 N	73.55 W
Rockaway Point ≻	276	40.33 N	73.56 W
Rockaways' Playland ♠	276	40.35 N	73.49 W
Rockbank	274b	37.43 S	144.39 E
Rock Bay	182	50.20 N	125.29 W
Rockbridge	219	39.16 N	90.12 W
Rock Bridge State Park ♠	219	38.53 N	92.19 W
Rock Brook ≃	276	40.25 N	74.40 W
Rock Candy Mountain ∧	224	47.01 N	123.07 W
Rockcastle ≃	192	36.58 N	84.21 W
Rock City Falls	210	43.04 N	73.55 W
Rockcliffe Park	212	45.27 N	75.41 W
Rockcorry	48	54.07 N	7.01 W
Rock Creek, B.C., Can.	182	49.06 N	118.58 W
Rock Creek, Oh., U.S.	214	41.39 N	80.51 W
Rock Creek ≃, N.A.	202	48.25 N	107.05 W
Rock Creek ≃, U.S.	208	39.43 N	77.13 W
Rock Creek ≃, U.S.	284c	38.54 N	77.04 W
Rock Creek ≃, Ca., U.S.	226	37.55 N	120.58 W
Rock Creek ≃, Co., U.S.	198	40.20 N	102.31 W
Rock Creek ≃, Il., U.S.	216	41.12 N	87.59 W
Rock Creek ≃, In., U.S.	216	40.42 N	86.35 W
Rock Creek ≃, In., U.S.	216	40.49 N	85.23 W
Rock Creek ≃, Mt., U.S.	202	45.31 N	108.49 W
Rock Creek ≃, Mt., U.S.	202	46.43 N	113.40 W
Rock Creek ≃, Nv., U.S.	204	40.39 N	116.54 W
Rock Creek ≃, Or., U.S.	202	45.34 N	120.25 W
Rock Creek ≃, Or., U.S.	202	42.39 N	119.08 W
Rock Creek ≃, Or., U.S.	224	45.51 N	123.12 W
Rock Creek ≃, S.D., U.S.	198	43.44 N	97.58 W
Rock Creek ≃, Ut,. U.S.	200	40.17 N	110.30 W
Rock Creek ≃, Wa., U.S.	202	46.55 N	117.56 W
Rock Creek ≃, Wa., U.S.	202	45.42 N	120.29 W
Rock Creek ≃, Wy., U.S.	200	41.54 N	106.08 W
Rock Creek Butte ∧	202	44.49 N	118.07 W
Rock Creek Hills	284c	39.01 N	77.04 W
Rock Creek Park ♠	284c	38.58 N	77.03 W
Rock Cut State Park ♠	216	42.20 N	89.00 W
Rockdale, Austl.	170	33.57 S	151.08 E
Rockdale, Il., U.S.	216	41.30 N	88.06 W
Rockdale, Md., U.S.	284b	39.21 N	76.45 W
Rockdale, Pa., U.S.	285	39.53 N	75.26 W
Rockdale, Tx., U.S.	222	30.39 N	97.00 W
Rockdale, W.V., U.S.	214	40.18 N	80.35 W
Rockefeller Center ⱱ	276	40.45 N	74.00 W
Rockefeller Park ♠	279a	41.32 N	81.38 W
Rockefeller Plateau ⩘ [1]	9	80.00 S	135.00 W
Rockenhausen	56	49.38 N	7.49 E
Rockensüss	56	51.03 N	9.50 E
Rockfall	207	41.31 N	72.41 W
Rock Falls	190	41.46 N	89.41 W
Rock Ferry	262	53.22 N	3.00 W
Rockfield	216	40.38 N	86.34 W
Rock Flat	171b	36.21 S	149.12 E
Rock Flat Creek ≃	171b	36.07 S	149.12 E
Rockford, Al., U.S.	194	32.53 N	86.13 W
Rockford, Il., U.S.	216	42.16 N	89.05 W
Rockford, In., U.S.	218	38.59 N	85.54 W
Rockford, Ia., U.S.	190	43.03 N	92.56 W
Rockford, Mi., U.S.	190	43.07 N	85.33 W
Rockford, Oh., U.S.	216	40.41 N	84.38 W
Rockford, Tn., U.S.	192	35.49 N	83.56 W
Rock Forest	206	45.20 N	71.59 W
Rockglen, Sk., Can.	184	49.10 N	105.57 W
Rock Glen, N.Y., U.S.	210	42.41 N	78.07 W
Rock Hall	208	39.08 N	76.14 W
Rockhammar	40	59.32 N	15.26 E
Rockhampton	166	23.23 S	150.31 E
Rockhampton Downs	162	18.57 S	135.01 E
Rock Hill, N.Y., U.S.	210	41.38 N	74.36 W
Rock Hill, S.C., U.S.	192	34.55 N	81.01 W
Rockhill Furnace	214	40.15 N	77.54 W
Rockingham, Austl.	168a	32.17 S	115.44 E
Rockingham, N.C., U.S.	192	34.56 N	79.46 W
Rockingham □ [6]	207	42.50 N	71.15 W
Rockingham Bay c	166	18.10 S	146.05 E
Rockingham Forest ➛ [3]	42	52.30 N	0.37 W
Rockingham State Historic Site ⊥	276	40.24 N	74.37 W
Rock Island, P.Q., Can.	206	45.01 N	72.06 W
Rock Island, Il., U.S.	190	41.30 N	90.34 W
Rock Island, Tx., U.S.	222	29.32 N	96.35 W
Rocklake	198	48.47 N	99.15 W
Rock Lake ◎, Mb., Can.	184	49.11 N	99.12 W
Rock Lake ◎, On., Can.	212	45.30 N	78.23 W
Rock Lake ◎, Il., U.S.	278	41.40 N	88.03 W
Rock Lake ◎, N.D., U.S.	198	48.50 N	99.10 W
Rock Lake ◎, Wi., U.S.	216	43.04 N	88.56 W
Rockland, On., Can.	188	45.33 N	75.17 W
Rockland, De., U.S.	285	39.47 N	75.34 W
Rockland, Id., U.S.	202	42.34 N	112.52 W
Rockland, Me., U.S.	188	44.06 N	69.06 W
Rockland, Ma., U.S.	207	42.07 N	70.55 W
Rockland, Mi., U.S.	190	46.44 N	89.10 W
Rockland, N.Y., U.S.	210	41.58 N	74.54 W
Rockland □ [6]	210	41.09 N	73.59 W
Rockland Lake	276	41.09 N	73.55 W
Rockland Lake ◎	276	41.08 N	73.55 W
Rockland Lake State Park ♠	276	41.08 N	73.55 W
Rocklands Reservoir ◎ [1]	166	37.15 S	142.00 E
Rockledge, Fl., U.S.	220	28.21 N	80.43 W
Rockledge, Pa., U.S.	285	40.03 N	75.05 W
Rockleigh	276	41.00 N	73.55 W
Rocklin	226	38.47 N	121.14 W
Rockmart	192	34.00 N	85.02 W
Rock Meadow Brook ≃	283	42.16 N	71.13 W
Rock of Cashel ⊥	48	52.31 N	7.53 W
Rock Point	208	38.16 N	76.50 W
Rock Point Provincial Park ♠	212	42.51 N	79.33 W
Rock Pond ◎	283	42.44 N	71.00 W
Rockport, Il., U.S.	219	39.32 N	91.00 W
Rockport, Ky., U.S.	194	37.20 N	86.59 W
Rockport, Me., U.S.	188	44.11 N	69.04 W
Rockport, Ma., U.S.	207	42.39 N	70.37 W
Rock Port, Mo., U.S.	194	40.24 N	95.30 W
Rockport, Tx., U.S.	196	28.01 N	97.03 W
Rock Rapids	198	43.25 N	96.10 W
Rock River	200	41.44 N	105.58 W
Rock Run	208	39.59 N	75.50 W
Rock Run ≃	284c	38.58 N	77.11 W
Rock Sound	238	24.54 N	76.12 W
Rocksprings, Tx., U.S.	196	30.00 N	100.12 W
Rock Springs, Wy., U.S.	200	41.35 N	109.12 W
Rockstone	246	5.59 N	58.33 W
Rock Stream	210	42.28 N	76.56 W
Rockton, Il., U.S.	216	42.27 N	89.04 W
Rockton, Pa., U.S.	214	41.05 N	78.39 W
Rock Valley	198	43.12 N	96.17 W
Rockville, N.Z.	172	40.44 S	172.38 E
Rockville, Ct., U.S.	207	41.52 N	72.27 W
Rockville, In., U.S.	194	39.45 N	87.13 W
Rockville, Md., U.S.	208	39.05 N	77.09 W
Rockville, Ma., U.S.	283	42.08 N	71.21 W
Rockville, Pa., U.S.	208	40.20 N	76.54 W
Rockville, R.I., U.S.	207	41.27 N	71.30 W
Rockville Centre	210	40.39 N	73.38 W
Rockwall	222	32.55 N	96.27 W
Rockwall □ [6]	222	32.55 N	96.23 W
Rockwell, Ia., U.S.	190	42.59 N	93.11 W
Rockwell, N.C., U.S.	192	35.33 N	80.24 W
Rockwell, Lake ◎	214	41.12 N	81.19 W
Rockwell City	198	42.23 N	94.38 W
Rockwell International Corporation ⱱ [3]	280	33.52 N	117.51 W
Rockwood, On., Can.	212	43.37 N	80.08 W
Rockwood, Me., U.S.	188	45.41 N	69.44 W
Rockwood, Mi., U.S.	216	42.04 N	83.14 W
Rockwood, Or., U.S.	224	45.31 N	122.28 W
Rockwood, Pa., U.S.	188	39.54 N	79.09 W
Rockwood, Tn., U.S.	192	35.51 N	84.41 W
Rockwood Lake ◎	276	41.06 N	73.38 W
Rockwood Lake Brook ≃	276	41.03 N	73.36 W
Rocky	196	35.09 N	99.03 W
Rocky ≃, Ab., Can.	182	53.08 N	117.59 W
Rocky ≃, Mi., U.S.	216	41.57 N	85.39 W
Rocky ≃, N.C., U.S.	192	35.37 N	79.09 W
Rocky ≃, Oh., U.S.	214	41.30 N	81.49 W
Rocky, East Branch ≃	279a	41.24 N	81.53 W
Rocky, West Branch ≃	214	41.24 N	81.53 W
Rocky Arroyo ∨	196	32.32 N	104.21 W
Rocky Boy's Indian Reservation ➛ [4]	202	48.18 N	109.45 W
Rocky Branch ≃	284c	38.53 N	77.19 W
Rocky Cape National Park ♠	166	40.56 S	145.35 E
Rocky Comfort Creek ≃	192	32.59 N	82.25 W
Rocky Coulee ∨	202	47.10 N	119.16 W
Rocky Creek ≃	192	35.53 N	80.47 W
Rockyford, Ab., Can.	182	51.13 N	113.08 W
Rocky Ford, Co., U.S.	198	38.06 N	103.43 W
Rocky Ford Creek ≃	216	41.19 N	83.37 W
Rocky Fork Lake ◎	218	39.11 N	83.28 W
Rocky Fork State Park ♠	218	39.11 N	83.30 W
Rocky Gorge Reservoir ◎ [1]	208	39.07 N	77.54 W
Rocky Grove	214	41.25 N	79.49 W
Rocky Gully	162	34.30 S	116.48 E
Rocky Harbour	186	49.36 N	57.55 W
Rocky Harbour c	271d	22.20 N	114.19 E
Rocky Hill, Ct., U.S.	207	41.40 N	72.39 W
Rocky Hill, N.J., U.S.	276	40.24 N	74.38 W
Rocky Island Lake ◎ [1]	190	46.56 N	83.04 W
Rocky Lake ◎	184	54.08 N	101.30 W
Rocky Mount, N.C., U.S.	192	35.57 N	77.48 W
Rocky Mount, Va., U.S.	192	36.59 N	79.53 W
Rocky Mountain ∧	202	47.49 N	112.49 W
Rocky Mountain House	182	52.22 N	114.55 W
Rocky Mountain National Park ♠	200	40.19 N	105.42 W
Rocky Mountains ⩘	16	48.00 N	116.00 W
Rocky Point, N.Y., U.S.	207	40.57 N	72.56 W
Rocky Point, Wa., U.S.	224	47.35 N	122.41 W
Rocky Point ≻, Ba.	192	26.00 N	77.25 W
Rocky Point ≻, Ire.	48	54.42 N	8.48 W
Rocky Point ≻, Namibia	156	19.03 S	12.30 E
Rocky Point ≻, Norf. I.	174c	29.03 S	167.55 E
Rocky Point ≻, Ak., U.S.	180	64.25 N	163.10 W
Rocky Point ≻, Ma., U.S.	207	41.57 N	70.35 W
Rocky Point ≻, N.Y., U.S.	276	40.55 N	73.32 W
Rocky Ridge	214	41.32 N	83.13 W
Rocky Ridge ∧	282	37.48 N	122.03 W
Rocky River	214	41.28 N	81.50 W
Rocky River Reservation ♠	279a	41.27 N	81.50 W
Rocky Run ≃, N.D., U.S.	198	47.38 N	99.02 W
Rocky Run ≃, Pa., U.S.	285	39.54 N	75.28 W
Rocky Run ≃, Va., U.S.	284c	38.58 N	77.15 W
Rocky Saugeen ≃	212	44.13 N	80.53 W
Rocky Top ∧	202	44.47 N	122.17 W
Roclenge-sur-Geer	56	50.45 N	5.36 E
Rocosas, Montañas → Rocky Mountains ⩘	16	48.00 N	116.00 W
Rocquencourt	261	48.50 N	2.07 E
Rocroi	50	49.55 N	4.31 E
Roda	192	36.58 N	82.49 W
Roda ≃	54	50.52 N	11.44 E
Rodach	56	50.20 N	10.46 E
Rodach ≃	56	50.08 N	10.52 E
Rodakovo	83	48.33 N	39.02 E
Rodalben	56	49.14 N	7.38 E
Rodalquilar	34	37.40 N	2.08 W
Rodas	240p	22.20 N	80.33 W
Rodas → Ródhos I	38	36.10 N	28.00 E
Rodaun ➛ [8]	264b	48.08 N	16.16 E
Rødberg	26	60.16 N	8.58 E
Rødby	41	54.42 N	11.24 E
Rødbyhavn	41	54.39 N	11.21 E
Roddickton	186	50.52 N	56.08 W
Rødding	41	55.23 N	9.06 E
Rodeiro	256	21.12 S	42.52 W
Rødekro	41	55.04 N	9.21 E
Rodel	46	57.41 N	7.05 W
Roden	52	53.07 N	6.26 E
Roden ≃	42	52.43 N	2.36 W
Rodenberg	52	52.18 N	9.21 E
Rodenkirchen, Dtsch.	52	53.24 N	8.26 E
Rodenkirchen, Dtsch.	56	50.54 N	6.59 E
Rödentel	54	50.17 N	11.01 E
Rodeo, Arg.	252	30.12 S	69.06 W
Rodeo, Méx.	232	25.11 N	104.34 W
Rodeo, Ca., U.S.	226	38.01 N	122.15 W
Rodeo, N.M., U.S.	200	31.50 N	109.01 W
Rodeo Lagoon c	282	37.50 N	122.31 W
Röderau	54	51.19 N	13.19 E
Roderick ≃	162	26.57 S	116.13 E
Roderick Island I	182	52.40 N	128.22 W
Rödermark	56	49.59 N	8.50 E
Rodewisch	54	50.32 N	12.24 E
Rodez	32	44.21 N	2.35 E
Rodgau	56	50.02 N	8.54 E
Rodheim-Bieber	56	50.37 N	8.35 E
Rodhópis, Orosirá → Rhodope Mountains ⩘	38	41.30 N	24.30 E
Ródhos (Rhodes)	38	36.26 N	28.13 E
Ródhos (Rhodes) I	38	36.10 N	28.00 E
Rodi Garganico	68	41.55 N	15.53 E
Roding	60	49.12 N	12.32 E
Roding ≃	42	51.31 N	0.06 E
Rodinka	80	57.24 N	43.34 E
Rodino, Ross.	76	58.57 N	44.59 E
Rodino, Ross.	86	52.30 N	80.15 E
Rodionovo-Nesvetajskaja	83	47.36 N	39.42 E
Rodman	180	57.28 N	135.21 W
Rodman Naval Station ■	236	8.56 N	79.36 W
Rodn'a	76	56.22 N	34.55 E
Rodnei, Munții ⩘	38	47.35 N	24.40 E
Rodney, On., Can.	214	42.34 N	81.41 W
Rodney, Ms., U.S.	194	31.51 N	91.11 W
Rodney, Cape ≻, N.Z.	172	36.17 S	174.49 E
Rodney, Cape ≻, Ak., U.S.	180	64.39 N	166.24 W
Rodney Bay c	241f	14.05 N	60.58 W
Rodney Village	208	39.07 N	75.31 W
Rodničok	80	51.26 N	42.54 E
Rodniki, Ross.	80	57.06 N	41.44 E
Rodniki, Ross.	265b	55.39 N	38.04 E
Rodnikovskij	86	50.39 N	57.12 E
Rodolfo, Lago → Rudolf, Lake ◎	144	3.30 N	36.05 E
Rodonit, Kep i ≻	38	41.35 N	19.27 E
Rodostov	76	51.58 N	24.57 E
Rødovre	41	55.41 N	12.29 E
Rodrigo de Freitas, Lagoa c	287a	22.58 S	43.13 W
Rodrigues I	12	19.42 S	63.25 E
Rodríguez, Méx.	196	27.10 N	100.01 W
Rodríguez, Ur.	258	34.23 S	56.33 W
Rodríguez, Arroyo ≃	288	34.52 S	58.02 W
Roduco	208	36.27 N	76.48 W
Rødven	26	62.38 N	7.33 E
Rødvig	41	55.15 N	12.23 E
Roe ≃	48	55.07 N	6.59 W
Roebling	208	40.06 N	74.47 W
Roebourne	162	20.47 S	117.09 E
Roebuck Bay c	162	18.04 S	122.17 E
Roehampton ➛ [8]	260	51.27 N	0.14 W
Roe Island I	282	38.04 N	122.02 W
Roeland Park	198	39.02 N	94.37 W
Roelands	168a	33.18 S	115.50 E
Roeliff Jansen Kill ≃	210	42.11 N	73.52 W
Roelofarendsveen	52	52.12 N	4.38 E
Roelofskamp	158	26.10 S	24.24 E
Roen, Monte ∧	64	46.22 N	11.11 E
Roer (Rur) ≃	56	51.12 N	5.59 E
Roermond	52	51.12 N	6.00 E
Roesbrugge-Haringe	50	50.55 N	2.37 E
Roeselare (Roulers)	50	50.57 N	3.08 E
Roesinger, Lake ◎	224	47.58 N	121.55 W
Roessleville	210	42.41 N	73.48 W
Roes Welcome Sound ɥ	176	64.00 N	88.00 W
Roetgen	56	50.39 N	6.12 E
Rœulx	50	50.30 N	4.06 E
Roff	196	34.37 N	96.50 W
Röfors	40	58.57 N	14.37 E
Rofrano	68	40.12 N	15.25 E
Rogačevo	82	56.26 N	37.10 E
Rogačov	76	53.05 N	30.03 E
Rogačovka	78	51.30 N	39.34 E
Rogagua, Laguna ◎	248	13.43 S	66.54 W
Rogaguado, Laguna ◎	248	12.52 S	65.43 W
Rogaland □ [6]	26	59.00 N	6.15 E
Rogalik	83	48.56 N	40.03 E
Rogan'	78	49.54 N	36.29 E
Rogans Hill	274a	33.44 S	151.01 E
Rogan's Seat ∧	44	54.25 N	2.07 W
Rogart	46	58.00 N	4.08 W
Rogäsen	54	52.19 N	12.20 E
Rogaška Slatina	36	46.14 N	15.38 E
Rogatica	38	43.48 N	19.00 E
Rogatin	78	49.25 N	24.37 E
Rogätz	54	52.19 N	11.46 E
Rogen ◎	26	62.19 N	12.23 E
Roger, Lac ◎	190	47.50 N	78.51 W
Roger Island I	283	42.43 N	70.50 W
Rogers, Ar., U.S.	194	36.19 N	94.07 W
Rogers, Ct., U.S.	207	41.50 N	71.54 W
Rogers, Oh., U.S.	214	40.48 N	80.38 W
Rogers, Tx., U.S.	222	30.55 N	97.13 W
Rogers, Mount ∧	192	36.39 N	81.33 W
Rogers City	190	45.25 N	83.49 W
Rogers Lake ◎	228	34.52 N	117.51 W
Rogers Park ➛ [8]	278	42.01 N	87.40 W
Rogers Pass)(	182	51.17 N	117.31 W
Rogersville, N.B., Can.	186	46.44 N	65.26 W
Rogersville, Al., U.S.	194	34.49 N	87.17 W
Rogersville, Tn., U.S.	192	36.24 N	83.00 W
Roggeveldberge ⩘	158	32.17 S	20.08 E
Roggewein, Cabo ≻	174z	27.07 S	109.15 W
Roggiano Gravina	68	39.37 N	16.09 E
Roghudi	68	38.03 N	15.55 E
Rogliano, Fr.	62	42.57 N	9.25 E
Rogliano, It.	68	39.11 N	16.20 E
Rognac	62	43.29 N	5.14 E
Rognedino	76	53.48 N	33.33 E
Rögnitz ≃	54	53.19 N	10.57 E
Rognon ≃	58	48.23 N	5.10 E
Rogny	50	47.45 N	2.53 E
Rogojampi	115a	8.19 S	114.17 E
Rogovatoje	78	51.14 N	38.22 E
Rogovo	82	55.13 N	37.05 E
Rogovskaja	78	45.44 N	38.44 E
Rogovskoje	80	58.33 N	50.43 E
Rogožkino	83	47.10 N	39.21 E
Rogoźno	30	52.46 N	17.00 E
Rogozov	78	50.14 N	31.03 E
Rogue ≃, Mi., U.S.	190	43.04 N	85.35 W
Rogue ≃, Or., U.S.	202	42.26 N	124.25 W
Rogue River	202	42.26 N	123.10 W
Rohdenhaus	263	51.18 N	7.01 E
Rohilkhand Plains ⌒	124	28.20 N	79.30 E
Rohinjan	272c	19.06 N	73.04 E
Rohitpur	126	23.42 N	90.19 E
Rohl ≃	140	6.22 N	29.46 E
Röhlinghausen ➛ [8]	263	51.36 N	7.14 E
Rohnert Park	226	38.20 N	122.42 W
Rohr	60	48.46 N	11.58 E
Rohrbach in Oberösterreich	60	48.34 N	13.59 E
Rohrbach-lès-Bitche	56	49.03 N	7.16 E
Rohrbeck	264a	52.32 N	13.02 E
Rohrberg	54	52.42 N	11.02 E
Röhrenfurth	56	51.09 N	9.32 E
Rohri	120	27.41 N	68.54 E
Röhrsdorf	54	50.51 N	12.50 E
Rohtak	123	28.54 N	76.34 E
Rohunta, Laguna c	236	15.12 N	83.30 W
Roi, Île du → King Island I	166	39.50 S	144.00 E
Roia (Roya) ≃	62	43.48 N	7.35 E
Roi Et	110	16.03 N	103.40 E
Roi Georges, Îles du II	14	14.32 S	145.08 W
Roi Léopold, Monts du → King Leopold Ranges ⩘	160	17.30 S	125.45 E
Roine ◎	26	61.24 N	24.06 E
Roinville	261	48.32 N	2.03 E
Roisel	50	49.57 N	3.06 E
Roissy	261	48.47 N	2.39 E
Roissy-en-France	261	49.00 N	2.31 E
Roitzsch	54	51.34 N	12.16 E
Roja, Lat.	76	57.30 N	22.49 E
Roja, Ukr.	83	47.59 N	37.20 E
Rojas	252	34.12 S	60.44 W
Rojl'anka	78	46.17 N	29.46 E
Rojo, Cabo ≻, Méx.	234	21.33 N	97.20 W
Rojo, Cabo ≻, P.R.	240m	17.56 N	67.11 W
Rojo, Mar → Red Sea ⊤ [2]	136	20.00 N	38.00 E
Rojo → Red ≃	178	31.00 N	91.40 W
Rokan	112	0.34 N	100.25 E
Rokan ≃	114	2.00 N	100.52 E
Rokan-kanan ≃	114	1.23 N	100.56 E
Rokan-kiri ≃	114	1.23 N	100.56 E
Röke	41	56.14 N	13.30 E
Rokeby National Park ♠	164	13.40 S	142.55 E
Rokel ≃	150	8.33 N	12.48 W
Rokewood	169	37.54 S	143.43 E
Rokewood Junction	169	37.51 S	143.41 E
Rokhah	120	35.16 N	69.28 E
Rokiškis	76	55.58 N	25.35 E
Rokkō-san ∧	96	34.46 N	135.16 E
Rokkō-sanchi ⩘	270	34.45 N	135.13 E
Roklum	54	52.04 N	10.44 E
Rokuan kansallispuisto ♠	26	64.32 N	26.33 E
Rokugō	94	35.29 N	138.27 E
Rokugō ➛ [8]	268	35.33 N	139.43 E
Rokusei	94	36.58 N	136.52 E
Rokycany	60	49.45 N	13.36 E
Rokytná ≃	61	49.05 N	16.22 E
Rolampont	58	47.57 N	5.16 E
Roland, Mb., Can.	184	49.25 N	97.55 W
Roland, Ar., U.S.	194	34.54 N	92.29 W
Roland, Ia., U.S.	190	42.09 N	93.30 W
Roland, Lake ◎ [1]	284b	39.23 N	76.38 W
Roland C. Nickerson State Park ♠	207	41.46 N	70.03 W
Rolândia	255	23.18 S	51.22 W
Roland Park ➛ [8]	284b	39.22 N	76.39 W
Roland Run ≃	284b	39.23 N	76.39 W
Rolava ≃	54	50.15 N	12.51 E
Røldal	26	59.49 N	6.48 E
Roldán	252	32.54 S	60.54 W
Roldanillo	246	4.24 N	76.09 W
Rolde	52	52.58 N	6.38 E
Roldskov ➛ [3]	26	56.48 N	9.50 E
Rolette	198	48.39 N	99.50 W
Roleystone	168a	32.08 S	116.04 E
Rolfe	198	42.48 N	94.31 W
Roll, Az., U.S.	200	32.45 N	113.59 W
Roll, In., U.S.	216	40.33 N	85.23 W
Rolla, B.C., Can.	182	55.54 N	120.09 W
Rolla, Ks., U.S.	198	37.07 N	101.07 W
Rolla, Mo., U.S.	194	37.57 N	91.46 W
Rolla, N.D., U.S.	198	48.51 N	99.37 W
Rolle	58	46.28 N	6.20 E
Rolle, Passo di)(	64	46.18 N	11.47 E
Rolleboise	261	49.01 N	1.36 E
Rolleston, Austl.	166	24.28 S	148.37 E
Rolleston, N.Z.	172	43.35 S	172.23 E
Rolling Acres	284b	39.17 N	76.52 W
Rollingbay	224	47.39 N	122.30 W
Rolling Fork	194	32.54 N	90.52 W
Rolling Fork ≃	194	37.55 N	85.50 W
Rolling Hills	280	33.46 N	118.21 W
Rolling Hills Estates	280	33.47 N	118.21 W
Rolling Meadows	216	42.05 N	88.00 W
Rolling Prairie	216	41.40 N	86.37 W
Rolling River Indian Reserve ➛ [4]	184	50.27 N	100.00 W
Rollingstone	166	19.03 S	146.24 E
Rollingwood	226	37.57 N	122.20 W
Rollins	182	47.54 N	114.11 W
Rollins Reservoir ◎ [1]	226	39.08 N	120.57 W
Rolvsøya I	24	71.00 N	24.00 E
Roma, Austl.	166	26.35 S	148.47 E
Roma (Rome), It.	66	41.54 N	12.29 E
Roma (Rome), It.	267a	41.54 N	12.29 E
Roma, Leso.	158	29.27 S	27.45 E
Roma, Tx., U.S.	196	26.25 N	99.01 W
Roma □ [4]	66	41.58 N	12.40 E
Romagna □ [9]	64	44.30 N	12.15 E
Romagnano Sesia	62	45.38 N	8.23 E
Romagne-sous-Montfaucon	56	49.20 N	5.05 E
Romain, Cape ≻	192	33.00 N	79.22 W
Romaine ≃	176	50.18 N	63.47 W
Romainmôtier	58	46.42 N	6.29 E
Romainville	261	48.53 N	2.26 E
Romakloster	26	57.31 N	18.27 E
Roman	38	46.55 N	26.56 E
Roman ≃	42	51.51 N	0.57 E
Romanche ≃	62	45.05 N	5.43 E
Romanche Gap ✣ [1]	10	0.10 S	18.15 W
Romang, Pulau I	164	7.35 S	127.26 E
Romang, Selat ɥ	164	7.30 S	127.00 E
Romania (România) □ [1], Europe	22	46.00 N	25.30 E
Romania (România) □ [1], Europe	38	46.00 N	25.30 E
Roman-Koš, gora ∧	78	44.37 N	34.15 E
Romankovcy	78	48.29 N	27.13 E
Roman Nose Mountain ∧	202	43.55 N	123.44 W
Romano, Cape ≻	220	25.50 N	81.41 W
Romano, Cayo I	240p	22.04 N	77.50 W
Romano Banco	266b	45.25 N	9.06 E
Romano di Lombardia	62	45.31 N	9.45 E
Romanova	88	57.04 N	103.24 E
Romanovka, Ross.	80	51.24 N	47.23 E
Romanovka, Ross.	80	51.45 N	42.45 E
Romanovka, Ross.	80	49.47 N	45.05 E
Romanovka, Ross.	86	54.38 N	76.03 E
Romanovka, Ross.	88	53.14 N	112.46 E
Romanovka, Ross.	265a	60.03 N	30.42 E
Romanovo, Ross.	82	56.39 N	39.14 E
Romanovo, Ross.	86	53.58 N	80.30 E
Romanovo, Ross.	86	52.37 N	81.14 E
Romanovo, Ross.	86	59.09 N	61.30 E
Romans d'Isonzo	64	45.53 N	13.26 E
Romanshorn	58	47.34 N	9.22 E
Romans-sur-Isère	62	45.03 N	5.03 E
Romansville	285	39.57 N	75.45 W
Romanzof Mountains ⩘	180	69.00 N	144.00 W
Romaški	80	50.13 N	46.41 E
Romaškino	80	52.29 N	51.48 E
Romaškovo	265b	55.44 N	37.20 E
Romayor	222	30.27 N	94.50 W
Rombari	154	4.33 N	31.02 E
Romblon	116	12.35 N	122.15 E
Romblon □ [4]	116	12.30 N	122.10 E
Romblon Island I	116	12.33 N	122.17 E
Romblon Passage ɥ	116	12.27 N	122.12 E
Rombo, Ilhéus do II	150a	14.58 N	24.40 W
Rome, Ga., U.S.	192	34.15 N	85.09 W
Rome, Il., U.S.	190	40.53 N	89.30 W
Rome, Ms., U.S.	194	33.57 N	90.28 W
Rome, N.Y., U.S.	210	43.12 N	75.27 W
Rome, Oh., U.S.	214	41.36 N	80.52 W
Rome, Pa., U.S.	210	41.51 N	76.21 W
Rome, Wi., U.S.	216	42.58 N	88.38 W
Rome City	216	41.29 N	85.22 W
Romeleåsen ⩘ [2]	41	55.34 N	13.33 E
Romenay	58	46.30 N	5.04 E
Romeno	64	46.24 N	11.07 E
Romentino	62	45.28 N	8.42 E
Romeo	214	42.48 N	83.00 W
Romeoville	216	41.38 N	88.05 W
Römerberg	56	49.17 N	8.24 E
Romero, Isla I	258	33.48 S	59.20 W
Rome → Roma	66	41.54 N	12.29 E
Rometan	128	39.56 N	64.23 E
Rometta	70	38.10 N	15.25 E
Romfartuna	40	59.44 N	16.35 E
Romford ➛ [8]	260	51.35 N	0.11 E
Römhild	54	50.24 N	10.32 E
Romiley	262	53.25 N	2.05 W
Romilly, Mount ∧ [2]	162	20.27 S	126.34 E
Romilly-sur-Seine	50	48.31 N	3.43 E
Romit	85	38.44 N	69.17 E
Romit, zapovednik ♠	85	38.52 N	69.20 E
Romita	234	20.52 N	101.31 W
Romitorio	267a	42.01 N	12.39 E
Rommani	148	34.34 N	6.37 W
Romme	40	60.26 N	15.30 E
Rommerskirchen	56	51.02 N	6.40 E
Romney, In., U.S.	216	40.14 N	86.54 W
Romney, W.V., U.S.	188	39.20 N	78.45 W
Romney Marsh ≡	42	51.03 N	0.55 E
Romny, Ross.	89	50.44 N	129.15 E
Romny, Ukr.	78	50.45 N	33.30 E
Rømø I	26	55.08 N	8.31 E
Romodan	78	49.59 N	33.19 E
Romodanovo	80	54.26 N	45.20 E
Romoland	228	33.45 N	117.10 W
Romont	58	46.42 N	6.55 E
Romorantin-Lanthenay	50	47.22 N	1.45 E
Rompin, Malay.	114	2.42 N	102.31 E
Rompin, Malay.	114	2.48 N	103.29 E
Rompin ≃	114	2.49 N	103.29 E
Romrod	56	50.43 N	9.13 E
Rom → Roma	66	41.54 N	12.29 E
Romsdalen ∨	26	62.15 N	8.05 E
Romsdalsfjorden c [2]	26	62.39 N	7.15 E
Romsey, Austl.	169	37.21 S	144.45 E
Romsey, Eng., U.K.	42	50.59 N	1.30 W
Romsø I	41	55.31 N	10.48 E
Romulus, Mi., U.S.	216	42.13 N	83.23 W
Romulus, N.Y., U.S.	210	42.45 N	76.50 W
Røn, Nor.	26	61.03 N	9.03 E
Ron, Viet	110	17.53 N	106.27 E
Ron, Mui ≻	110	18.07 N	106.27 E
Rona, Schw.	58	46.34 N	9.38 E
Rona, Zaïre	154	2.14 N	30.52 E
Rona I, Scot., U.K.	46	57.34 N	5.59 W
Rona I, Scot., U.K.	46	59.07 N	5.49 W
Ronald	224	47.14 N	121.01 W
Ronan	202	47.31 N	114.06 W
Ronas Hill ∧ [2]	46a	60.31 N	1.28 W
Ronas Voe c	46a	60.32 N	1.29 W
Ronay I	46	57.29 N	7.11 W
Roncade	64	45.38 N	12.22 E
Roncador, Cayos de ✣ [4]	236	13.32 N	80.03 W
Roncador, Serra do ⩘ [1]	242	12.00 S	52.00 W
Roncador Reef ✣ [2]	175e	6.13 S	159.22 E
Roncegno	64	46.03 N	11.25 E
Roncesvalles	34	43.01 N	1.19 W
Ronceverte	192	37.44 N	80.27 W
Ronchamp	58	47.42 N	6.39 E
Ronchi dei Legionari	64	45.50 N	13.30 E
Ronchin	50	50.36 N	3.06 E
Ronchis	64	45.49 N	13.00 E
Ronciglione	66	42.17 N	12.13 E
Ronco	58	46.08 N	8.44 E
Ronco Canavese	62	45.30 N	7.32 E
Roncofreddo	66	44.02 N	12.20 E
Roncone	64	45.59 N	10.40 E
Ronco Scrivia	62	44.37 N	8.59 E
Roncq	50	50.45 N	3.07 E
Rond, Sommet ∧	206	45.05 N	72.33 W
Ronda	34	36.44 N	5.10 W
Ronda, Serranía de ⩘	34	36.44 N	5.03 W
Rondane ∧	26	61.55 N	9.45 E
Rondane Nasjonal Park ♠	26	61.50 N	9.50 E
Rønde	41	56.18 N	10.29 E
Ronde, Pointe ≻	240d	15.33 N	61.29 W
Rondeau Harbour c	214	42.18 N	81.53 W
Rondeau Provincial Park ♠	214	42.16 N	81.51 W
Rondebult	273d	26.18 S	28.14 E
Ronde Island I	241k	12.18 N	61.35 W
Rondissone	62	45.15 N	7.58 E
Rondon	255	23.23 S	52.48 W
Rondônia □ [3]	248	11.00 S	63.00 W
Rondonópolis	255	16.28 S	54.38 W
Rondout	278	42.17 N	87.53 W
Rondout Creek ≃	210	41.55 N	73.53 W
Rondout Reservoir ◎ [1]	210	41.50 N	74.29 W
Rone ≃	50	50.46 N	3.27 E
Ronehamn	26	57.10 N	18.29 E
Rong ≃	102	24.32 N	109.15 E
Ronga	80	56.43 N	48.32 E
Rongai	154	0.10 S	35.51 E
Rong'an	102	25.10 N	109.20 E
Rongbaca	102	31.48 N	99.40 E
Rongchang	107	29.24 N	105.36 E
Rongcheng, Zhg.	98	37.08 N	122.23 E
Rongcheng, Zhg.	105	39.03 N	115.52 E
Rongding	107	28.57 N	103.40 E
Ronge, Lac la ◎	184	55.10 N	105.00 W
Rongelap I [1]	14	11.20 N	166.50 E
Rongjiang	102	25.52 N	108.37 E
Rongkop	115a	8.10 S	110.45 E
Rongola	158	27.22 S	31.37 E
Rongotea	172	40.18 S	175.25 E
Rõngu	76	58.09 N	26.15 E
Rongui, Ilha I	154	10.50 S	40.40 E
Rongwanshi	100	28.10 N	112.57 E
Rongxian, Zhg.	102	22.50 N	110.38 E
Rongxian, Zhg.	107	29.28 N	104.25 E
Ronkiti Harbor c	174r	6.48 N	158.10 E
Ronkonkoma	276	40.48 N	73.06 W
Ronkonkoma, Lake ◎	276	40.50 N	73.07 W
Rønne	26	55.06 N	14.42 E
Rönne ≃	41	56.16 N	12.50 E
Ronneburg	54	50.51 N	12.10 E
Ronneby	26	56.12 N	15.18 E
Ronne Entrance c	9	72.30 S	74.00 W
Ronne Ice Shelf ⊓	9	78.30 S	61.00 W
Ronnenberg	52	52.20 N	9.40 E
Rönneshytta	40	58.56 N	15.02 E
Rönninge	40	59.12 N	17.44 E
Ronroni	175e	9.37 S	159.58 E
Rönsahl	263	51.07 N	7.30 E
Ronsdorf ➛ [8]	263	51.14 N	7.12 E
Ronse (Renaix-Gleiche)	50	50.45 N	3.36 E
Röntgenmuseum ⱱ	263	51.12 N	7.16 E
Ronuro ≃	255	11.56 S	53.33 W
Roodepoort □ [5]	273d	26.10 S	27.52 E
Roodepoort-Maraisburg	158	26.11 S	27.54 E
Roodeschool	52	53.25 N	6.45 E
Roodhouse	219	39.29 N	90.22 W
Roof Butte ∧	200	36.28 N	109.05 W
Rooiberge ∧	158	28.27 S	28.26 E
Rooiboklaagte ≃	156	20.50 S	21.00 E
Rooidam	158	28.07 S	21.15 E
Rooilyf	158	28.49 S	21.57 E
Rooiwal	158	27.18 S	27.32 E
Rooks Creek ≃	216	40.57 N	88.44 W
Rookwood Cemetery ➛	274a	33.53 S	151.04 E
Roon, Pulau I	164	2.23 S	134.33 E
Rooniu, Mont ∧	174s	17.49 S	149.12 W
Roordahuizum	52	53.06 N	5.46 E
Roorkee	124	29.52 N	77.53 E
Roosboom	158	28.36 S	29.44 E
Roosendaal	52	51.32 N	4.28 E
Roosevelt, Az., U.S.	200	33.40 N	111.08 W
Roosevelt, Mn., U.S.	198	48.48 N	95.05 W
Roosevelt, N.J., U.S.	208	40.13 N	74.28 W
Roosevelt, N.Y., U.S.	276	40.40 N	73.35 W
Roosevelt, Ok., U.S.	196	34.50 N	99.01 W
Roosevelt, Ut,. U.S.	200	40.17 N	109.59 W
Roosevelt ≃	248	7.35 S	60.20 W
Roosevelt Beach	210	43.19 N	78.52 W
Roosevelt Campobello International Park ♠	186	44.52 N	66.58 W
Roosevelt Field ➛ [9]	276	40.45 N	73.37 W
Roosevelt Island I	9	79.30 S	162.00 W
Roosevelt Park	216	43.11 N	86.15 W
Roosevelt Park ♠	276	40.33 N	74.21 W
Roosevelt Raceway ♠	276	40.44 N	73.36 W
Roosevelt Roads Naval Station ■	240m	18.15 N	65.38 W
Roosevelt Terrace	226	38.08 N	122.16 W
Root	58	47.07 N	8.23 E
Root ≃, N.T., Can.	180	62.50 N	123.40 W
Root ≃, Mn., U.S.	190	43.46 N	91.15 W
Root ≃, Wi., U.S.	216	42.44 N	87.47 W
Root, North Branch ≃	190	43.49 N	92.10 W
Root, South Branch ≃	190	43.44 N	91.58 W
Root Lake ◎	184	54.04 N	101.24 W
Rootstown	214	41.05 N	81.14 W
Rooty Hill	170	33.46 S	150.50 E
Ropang	115b	8.52 S	117.29 E
Ropaži	76	57.08 N	24.30 E
Ropča	24	63.02 N	52.16 E
Ropczyce	30	50.03 N	21.37 E

Symbol	English	Deutsch	Español	Français	Português
≃	River	Fluß	Río	Rivière	Rio
≊	Canal	Kanal	Canal	Canal	Canal
∟	Waterfall, Rapids	Wasserfall, Stromschnellen	Cascada, Rápidos	Chute d'eau, Rapides	Cascata, Rápidos
ɥ	Strait	Meeresstraße	Estrecho	Détroit	Estreito
c	Bay, Gulf	Bucht, Golf	Bahía, Golfo	Baie, Golfe	Baía, Golfo
◎	Lake, Lakes	See, Seen	Lago, Lagos	Lac, Lacs	Lago, Lagos
≡	Swamp	Sumpf	Pantano	Marais	Pântano
⊓	Ice Features, Glacier	Eis- und Gletscherformen	Accidentes Glaciales	Formes glaciaires	Acidentes glaciares
⊤	Other Hydrographic Features	Andere Hydrographische Objekte	Otros Elementos Hidrográficos	Autres données hydrographiques	Outros acidentes hidrográficos
✣	Submarine Features	Untermeerische Objekte	Accidentes Submarinos	Formes de relief sous-marin	Acidentes submarinos
□	Political Unit	Politische Einheit	Unidad Politica	Entité politique	Unidade política
ⱱ	Cultural Institution	Kulturelle Institution	Institución Cultural	Institution culturelle	Instituição cultural
⊥	Historical Site	Historische Stätte	Sitio Histórico	Site historique	Sitio histórico
♠	Recreational Site	Erholungs- und Ferienort	Sitio de Recreo	Centre de loisirs	Area de Lazer
⊠	Airport	Flughafen	Aeropuerto	Aéroport	Aeroporto
■	Military Installation	Militäranlage	Instalación Militar	Installation militaire	Instalação militar
➛	Miscellaneous	Verschiedenes	Misceláneo	Divers	Diversos

ENGLISH — Name Page Lat.°′ Long.°′ | DEUTSCH — Name Seite Breite°′ Länge°′ E = Ost

Roper 192 35.52 N 76.36 W
Roper ≃ 164 14.43 S 135.27 E
Roper Bar 164 14.44 S 134.44 E
Roper Valley 164 14.56 S 134.00 E
Ropes Creek ≃ 274a 33.43 S 150.47 E
Ropesville 196 33.26 N 102.09 W
Roppe 58 47.40 N 6.55 E
Ropša 265a 59.44 N 29.52 E
Roque 250 3.01 S 45.23 W
Roquebillière 62 44.01 N 7.18 E
Roquebrune-Cap-Martin 62 43.46 N 7.28 E
Roquebrune-sur-Argens 62 43.26 N 6.38 E
Roquefavour, Aqueduc de ≊1 62 43.31 N 5.19 E
Roquefort 32 44.02 N 0.19 W
Roquemaure 62 44.03 N 4.47 E
Roque Pérez 258 35.25 S 59.20 W
Roquestéron 62 43.52 N 7.00 E
Roquevaire 62 43.21 N 5.36 E
Rora Head > 46 58.52 N 3.25 W
Roraima □3 246 1.00 N 61.00 W
Roraima, Mount ∧ 246 5.12 N 60.44 W
Rörbäcksnäs 26 61.08 N 12.49 E
Roreto Chisone 62 44.59 N 7.06 E
Rorey Lake ⊜ 180 66.55 N 128.25 W
Rorke Lake ⊜ 184 54.33 N 92.30 W
Rorke's Drift ⊥ 158 28.20 S 30.32 E
Rorketon 184 51.26 N 99.32 W
Røros 26 62.35 N 11.20 E
Rorschach 58 47.29 N 9.30 E
Rørvig 41 55.57 N 11.46 E
Rørvik 24 64.51 N 11.14 E
Ros' ≃ 78 49.39 N 31.35 E
Rosà, It. 64 45.43 N 11.45 E
Rosa, Zam. 154 9.38 S 31.21 E
Rosa, Cap > 36 36.58 N 8.14 E
Rosa, Lake ⊜ 238 21.00 N 73.30 W
Rosa, Monte ∧ 58 45.55 N 7.53 E
Rosairinho 266c 38.40 N 9.01 W
Rošal' 80 55.40 N 39.51 E
Rosales, Méx. 232 28.12 N 105.33 W
Rosales, Pil. 116 15.54 N 120.38 E
Rosalia 202 47.14 N 117.22 W
Rosalie, Lake ⊜ 220 27.58 N 81.28 W
Rosalind Bank ⊹4 238 16.30 N 80.30 W
Rosamond, Ca., U.S. 228 34.51 N 118.09 W
Rosamond, Il., U.S. 219 39.23 N 89.10 W
Rosamond Lake ⊜ 228 34.50 N 118.04 W
Rosamorada 234 22.08 N 105.12 W
Rosana 255 22.33 S 53.00 W
Rosander, Mount ∧ 224 48.46 N 124.42 W
Rosanky 222 29.56 N 97.18 W
Rosanna 274b 37.45 S 145.04 E
Rosans 62 44.23 N 5.28 E
Rosario, Arg. 252 32.57 S 60.40 W
Rosário, Bra. 250 2.57 S 44.14 W
Rosario, Méx. 232 27.37 N 109.16 W
Rosario, Méx. 234 23.00 N 105.52 W
Rosario, Para. 252 24.27 S 57.03 W
Rosario, Pil. 116 13.51 N 121.12 E
Rosario, Pil. 116 16.14 N 120.29 E
Rosario, Ur. 258 34.19 S 57.21 W
Rosario, Ven. 246 10.19 N 72.19 W
Rosario ≃, Arg. 252 24.50 S 65.43 W
Rosario ≃, Ur. 258 34.26 S 57.21 W
Rosario, Bahía ⊂ 232 29.52 N 115.45 W
Rosario, Cayo el I 240p 21.38 N 81.53 W
Rosario, Islas del II 246 10.10 N 75.46 W
Rosario Bank ⊹2 238 18.30 N 84.05 W
Rosario de Arriba 232 30.01 N 115.40 W
Rosario de la Frontera 252 25.48 S 64.58 W
Rosario de Lerma 252 24.59 S 65.35 W
Rosario del Tala 252 32.18 S 59.09 W
Rosário de Minas 256 21.43 S 43.38 W
Rosário do Sul 252 30.15 S 54.55 W
Rosário Oeste 248 14.50 S 56.25 W
Rosario Strait ⊔ 224 48.30 N 122.45 W
Rosarito, Méx. 204 32.20 N 117.02 W
Rosarito, Méx. 232 26.27 N 111.38 W
Rosarito, Embalse de ⊜1 34 40.05 N 5.15 W
Rosarno 68 38.29 N 15.59 E
Rosas 196 26.09 N 103.27 W
Rosazza 62 45.41 N 7.58 E
Rošča 82 54.47 N 36.51 E
Roščino 76 60.15 N 29.37 E
Rosciolo 66 42.07 N 13.20 E
Roscoe, Il., U.S. 216 42.25 N 89.01 W
Roscoe, N.Y., U.S. 210 41.55 N 74.54 W
Roscoe, Pa., U.S. 214 40.04 N 79.51 W
Roscoe, S.D., U.S. 198 45.26 N 99.20 W
Roscoe, Tx., U.S. 196 32.26 N 100.32 W
Roscoe ≃ 180 69.40 N 120.57 W
Roscoe Village ⊥ 214 40.18 N 81.54 W
Roscoff 32 48.44 N 3.59 E
Roscommon, Ire. 48 53.38 N 8.11 W
Roscommon, Mi., U.S. 190 44.29 N 84.35 W
Roscommon □6 48 53.45 N 8.15 W
Roscrea 48 52.57 N 7.47 W
Rosdorf 52 51.30 N 9.53 E
Rose, It. 68 39.24 N 16.17 E
Rose, N.Y., U.S. 210 43.09 N 76.53 W
Rose, Monte ∧ 70 37.39 N 13.25 E
Rose, Mount ∧ 226 39.21 N 119.55 W
Rose, Pointe de la > 240e 14.40 N 60.53 W
Roseau, Dom. 240d 15.18 N 61.24 W
Roseau, Mn., U.S. 198 48.50 N 95.45 W
Roseau ≃, Dom. 240d 15.18 N 61.24 W
Roseau ≃, N.A. 198 49.08 N 97.15 W
Roseau ≃, St. Luc. 241f 13.58 N 61.02 W
Rosebank ⬥8 273d 26.09 S 28.02 E
Rosebank Station 275b 43.47 N 79.07 W
Roseberry Lakes ⊜ 184 52.40 N 92.30 W
Roseberth 166 25.47 S 139.37 E
Rosebery 166 41.46 S 145.32 E
Rosebery ⬥8 274a 33.55 S 151.12 E
Rose-Blanche 186 47.37 N 58.41 W
Roseboom 210 42.45 N 74.47 W
Roseboro 192 34.57 N 78.30 W
Rose Bowl ♦ 280 34.10 N 118.09 W
Rosebud, Austl. 169 38.21 S 144.54 E
Rosebud, Mo., U.S. 219 38.23 N 91.24 W
Rosebud, Mt., U.S. 202 46.16 N 106.26 W
Rose Bud, Pa., U.S. 214 40.45 N 78.33 W
Rosebud, S.D., U.S. 198 43.13 N 100.51 W
Rosebud, Tx., U.S. 222 31.04 N 96.58 W
Rosebud ≃ 182 51.25 N 112.37 W
Rosebud Creek ≃ 202 46.16 N 106.28 W
Rosebud Indian Reservation ⬥4 198 43.25 N 100.28 W
Roseburg 202 43.13 N 123.20 W
Rosebush 190 43.41 N 84.46 W
Rose City 190 44.25 N 84.07 W
Rose Creek ≃, U.S. 198 40.04 N 97.07 W
Rose Creek ≃, Ca., U.S. 226 38.07 N 120.24 W
Rosecroft Raceway ♦ 284c 38.48 N 76.58 W
Rosedale, Austl. 166 24.38 S 151.55 E
Rosedale, Ab., Can. 182 51.25 N 112.38 W
Rosedale, B.C., Can. 224 49.11 N 121.48 W
Rosedale, In., U.S. 194 39.37 N 87.17 W
Rosedale, La., U.S. 194 30.27 N 91.27 W
Rosedale, Md., U.S. 284b 39.19 N 76.30 W
Rosedale, Ms., U.S. 194 33.51 N 91.01 W
Rosedale ⬥8, On., Can. 275b 43.41 N 79.22 W
Rosedale ⬥8, N.Y., U.S. 276 40.39 N 73.45 W
Rosedale Estates 284c 38.47 N 76.58 W
Rosedale Hills 218 39.42 N 86.07 W
Rosedene 158 32.01 S 22.07 E
Rosehall 246 6.16 N 57.21 W
Rosehearty 46 57.42 N 2.07 W
Rose-Hill, Maus. 157c 20.14 S 57.27 E
Rose Hill, N.C., U.S. 192 34.49 N 78.01 W
Rose Hill, Va., U.S. 192 36.40 N 83.22 W
Rose Hill, Wa., U.S. 224 47.42 N 122.10 W
Rosehill Cemetery ⬥ 278 41.59 N 87.41 W
Rosehill Racecourse ♦ 274a 33.49 S 151.02 E
Rose Hills Memorial Park ⬥ 280 34.01 N 118.02 W
Roseira 256 22.54 S 45.18 W
Rose Island I, Am. Sam. 14 14.32 S 168.08 W
Rose Island I, Ba. 192 25.06 N 77.14 W
Rose Lake 182 54.24 N 126.02 W
Roseland, Ca., U.S. 226 38.30 N 122.55 W
Roseland, In., U.S. 216 41.42 N 86.15 W
Roseland, La., U.S. 194 30.45 N 90.30 W
Roseland, N.J., U.S. 276 40.49 N 74.17 W
Roseland, Oh., U.S. 214 40.47 N 82.32 W
Roseland ⬥8 278 41.42 N 87.38 W
Roselawn 216 41.09 N 87.19 W
Roselle, Il., U.S. 216 41.59 N 88.04 W
Roselle, N.J., U.S. 276 40.39 N 74.15 W
Roselle Field ⊠ 278 41.59 N 88.06 W
Rosellen 263 51.08 N 6.43 E
Roselle Park 276 40.39 N 74.15 W
Rosellerheide 263 51.07 N 6.44 E
Rose Lodge 224 45.01 N 123.52 W
Rosemary 182 50.46 N 112.05 W
Rosemary Brook ≃ 283 42.19 N 71.15 W
Rosemead 280 34.04 N 118.04 W
Rosemère 206 45.38 N 73.48 W
Rosemont, Ca., U.S. 226 38.34 N 121.20 W
Rosemont, Il., U.S. 278 41.59 N 87.52 W
Rosemont, Ky., U.S. 218 38.01 N 84.32 W
Rosemont, Oh., U.S. 214 41.03 N 80.53 W
Rosemont, Pa., U.S. 285 40.01 N 75.19 W
Rosemont Horizon ♦ 278 42.00 N 87.53 W
Rosenberg 222 29.33 N 95.48 W
Rosendaël 50 51.02 N 2.24 E
Rosendal, Nor. 26 59.59 N 6.01 E
Rosendal, S. Afr. 158 28.30 S 27.55 E
Rosendale 210 41.51 N 74.05 W
Roseneath 273d 26.17 S 28.11 E
Rosenfeld 58 48.17 N 8.43 E
Rosengarten 52 53.23 N 9.54 E
Rosenhayn 208 39.28 N 75.07 W
Rosenheim 64 47.51 N 12.07 E
Rosenhügel ⬥8 263 51.10 N 7.12 E
Rosenthal, Dtsch. 54 50.51 N 14.04 E
Rosenthal, Dtsch. 56 50.58 N 8.52 E
Rosenthal ⬥8 264a 52.36 N 13.23 E
Rose Peak ∧ 200 33.26 N 109.22 W
Rosepine 194 30.55 N 93.17 W
Rose Point > 182 54.13 N 131.35 W
Rosersberg 40 59.35 N 17.53 E
Rosersberg ⊥ 40 59.34 N 17.50 E
Roses, Golf de ⊂ 34 42.10 N 3.15 E
Roseto 210 40.52 N 75.12 W
Roseto Capo Spulico 68 39.59 N 16.36 E
Roseto degli Abruzzi 66 42.41 N 14.01 E
Roseto Valfortore 68 41.22 N 15.06 E
Rosetown 184 51.33 N 108.00 W
Rose Tree 285 39.56 N 75.23 W
Rose Tree Park ♦ 285 39.56 N 75.24 W
Rosetta Branch → Rashīd, Far' ≃ 142 31.30 N 30.21 E
Rosetta Mouth → Rashīd, Maşabb ≃1 142 31.30 N 30.20 E
Rosetta → Rashīd 142 31.24 N 30.25 E
Rosettenville ⬥8 273d 26.15 S 28.03 E
Rosevale 171a 27.51 S 152.29 E
Rose Valley, Sk., Can. 184 52.18 N 103.50 W
Rose Valley, Pa., U.S. 285 39.53 N 75.23 W
Rose Valley, Pa., U.S. 285 40.10 N 75.13 W
Rose Valley, Wa., U.S. 224 46.06 N 122.50 W
Roseville, Austl. 274a 33.47 S 151.11 E
Roseville, Ca., U.S. 226 38.45 N 121.17 W
Roseville, Il., U.S. 190 40.43 N 90.39 W
Roseville, Mi., U.S. 214 42.29 N 82.56 W
Roseville, Mn., U.S. 190 45.00 N 93.09 W
Roseville, Oh., U.S. 188 39.48 N 82.04 W
Roseville, Pa., U.S. 210 41.51 N 76.57 W
Roseville Park 285 39.42 N 75.43 W
Rosewood, Austl. 171a 27.39 S 152.35 E
Rosewood, Austl. 171b 35.41 S 147.52 E
Rosewood, Oh., U.S. 216 40.13 N 83.58 W
Rosewood Heights 219 38.53 N 90.05 W
Roseworthy 168b 34.32 S 138.44 E
Roshage > 26 57.07 N 8.38 E
Roshanara Gardens ♦ 272a 28.40 N 77.12 E
Rosharon 222 29.21 N 95.28 W
Rosheim 58 48.30 N 7.28 E
Rosherville Dam ⊜1 273d 26.14 S 28.07 E
Rosh Ha'Ayin 132 32.06 N 34.57 E
Rosholt, S.D., U.S. 198 45.52 N 96.43 W
Rosholt, Wi., U.S. 190 44.37 N 89.18 W
Rosh Pinna 132 32.58 N 35.32 E
Rosica ≃ 38 43.15 N 25.42 E
Rosice 30 49.11 N 16.23 E
Rosiclare 194 37.25 N 88.20 W
Rosières-aux-Salines 58 48.36 N 6.20 E
Rosières-en-Santerre 50 49.49 N 2.43 E
Rosiers, Rivière des ≃ 206 45.59 N 72.07 W
Rosignano Marittimo 66 43.24 N 10.28 E
Rosignano Solvay 66 43.23 N 10.26 E
Rosignol 246 6.17 N 57.32 W
Roşiori de Vede 38 44.07 N 25.00 E
Rositz 54 51.01 N 12.22 E
Roskilde 41 55.39 N 12.05 E
Roskilde □6 41 55.30 N 12.05 E
Roskilde Fjord ⊂ 41 55.56 N 12.00 E
Roskow 54 52.28 N 12.42 E
Roslagen □9 40 59.30 N 18.40 E
Roslags-Bro 40 59.50 N 18.44 E
Rosl'akovo 24 69.03 N 33.09 E
Rosl'atino 76 59.46 N 44.15 E
Roslavl' 76 53.57 N 32.52 E
Roslev 26 56.42 N 8.59 E
Roslindale ⬥8 283 42.18 N 71.07 W
Roslyn, N.Y., U.S. 276 40.48 N 73.39 W
Roslyn, Pa., U.S. 208 40.07 N 75.08 W
Roslyn, Pa., U.S. 285 39.57 N 75.36 W
Roslyn, Wa., U.S. 224 47.13 N 120.59 W
Roslyn Estates 276 40.47 N 73.40 W
Roslyn Harbor 276 40.49 N 73.38 W
Roslyn Heights 276 40.47 N 73.38 W
Rosmalen 52 51.43 N 5.22 E
Rosman 192 35.08 N 82.49 W
Rosmead 158 31.29 S 25.08 E
Ros Mhic Thriúin → New Ross 48 52.24 N 6.56 W
Røsnæs >1 41 55.44 N 10.59 E
Rosne, Ruisseau le ≃ 261 48.58 N 2.25 E
Rosneath 46 56.01 N 4.49 W
Rosny-sous-Bois 261 48.53 N 2.29 E
Rosny-sur-Seine 50 49.00 N 1.38 E
Rosolina 64 45.05 N 12.15 E
Rosolini 70 36.49 N 14.57 E
Rošore 85 38.20 N 72.19 E
Rosporden 32 47.58 N 3.50 W
Rösrath 56 50.54 N 7.11 E
Ross, Austl. 166 42.02 S 147.29 E
Ross', Bela. 76 53.17 N 24.24 E
Ross, N.Z. 172 42.54 S 170.49 E
Ross, Ca., U.S. 226 37.55 N 122.32 W
Ross, In., U.S. 278 41.32 N 87.23 W
Ross, Oh., U.S. 218 39.19 N 84.39 W
Ross □6 218 39.20 N 83.06 W
Ross ≃ 180 61.59 N 132.26 W
Ross, Cape > 116 10.56 N 119.13 E
Ross, Mount ∧ 172 41.28 S 175.21 E
Ross, Point > 174c 29.04 S 167.56 E
Ross, Pointe > 275a 45.21 N 73.48 W
Rossa 58 46.22 N 9.08 E
Rossach 56 50.09 N 10.56 E
Rossano 68 39.35 N 16.39 E
Rossasna 76 54.39 N 30.53 E
Rossau 54 52.47 N 11.38 E
Rossbach 54 51.15 N 11.53 E
Ross Behy 48 52.02 N 9.58 W
Ross-Béthio 150 16.16 N 16.08 W
Rossburg 216 40.17 N 84.38 W
Rossburn 184 50.40 N 100.52 W
Ross Carbery 48 51.35 N 9.01 W
Rosscott Manor 285 39.39 N 75.44 W
Ross Dam ⬥6 224 48.44 N 121.04 W
Rossdorf 56 49.51 N 8.45 E
Rosseau 212 45.16 N 79.39 W
Rosseau, Lake ⊜ 212 45.10 N 79.35 W
Rossel, Cap > 175f 20.23 S 166.36 E
Rossell y Rius 252 33.11 S 55.42 W
Rossen ⊜ 40 60.19 N 16.26 E
Rossendale □8 262 53.43 N 2.14 W
Rosser 222 32.28 N 96.27 W
Rosses Bay ⊂ 48 55.02 N 8.27 W
Rosses Point 48 54.18 N 8.33 W
Rossford 214 41.37 N 83.33 W
Ross Fork Creek ≃ 202 47.05 N 109.43 W
Rosshaupten 58 47.39 N 10.43 E
Rosshyttan 40 60.04 N 16.21 E
Ross Ice Shelf ⊟ 9 81.30 S 175.00 W
Rossiglione 62 44.34 N 8.40 E
Rossignol, Lake ⊜ 186 44.10 N 65.10 W
Rossija → Russia □1 72 60.00 N 80.00 E
Rössing 156 22.31 S 14.52 E
Rossio, Estação do ⬥5 266c 38.43 N 9.09 W
Ross Island I, Ant. 9 77.30 S 168.00 E
Ross Island I, Mb., Can. 184 54.14 N 97.45 W
Rossiter 214 40.53 N 78.55 W
Rossitten → Rybačij 76 55.09 N 20.51 E
Rossiya → Russia □1 72 60.00 N 80.00 E
Rossla 54 51.28 N 11.04 E
Ross Lake ⊜1 224 48.53 N 121.04 W
Ross Lake National Recreation Area ♦ 224 48.45 N 121.00 W
Rossland 182 49.05 N 117.48 W
Rosslare 48 52.17 N 6.23 W
Rosslare Harbour 48 52.15 N 6.22 W
Rosslau 54 51.53 N 12.14 E
Rosslea 48 54.14 N 7.11 W
Rossleben 54 51.17 N 11.25 E
Rosslyn Farms 279b 40.26 N 80.05 W
Rossmoor 280 33.47 N 118.05 W
Rossmore 274a 33.57 S 150.46 E
Rossmoyne 208 40.13 N 76.57 W
Rosso 150 16.30 N 15.49 W
Rossön 26 63.55 N 16.21 E
Ross-on-Wye 42 51.55 N 2.35 W
Rossony 76 55.53 N 28.49 E
Rossoš', Ross. 78 51.08 N 38.29 E
Rossoš', Ross. 78 50.12 N 39.34 E
Rossouw 158 31.09 S 27.18 E
Ross R. Barnett Reservoir ⊜1 194 32.30 N 90.00 W
Ross River 180 61.59 N 132.27 W
Ross-Schelfeis → Ross Ice Shelf ⊟ 9 81.30 S 175.00 W
Ross Sea ⊤2 9 76.00 S 175.00 W
Rosstal 56 49.25 N 10.52 E
Rosston 218 40.03 N 86.17 W
Rossu, Capu > 36 42.14 N 8.33 E
Røssvatnet ⊜ 24 65.45 N 14.00 E
Rossville, Ga., U.S. 192 34.58 N 85.17 W
Rossville, Il., U.S. 216 40.22 N 87.40 W
Rossville, In., U.S. 216 40.25 N 86.35 W
Rossville, Ks., U.S. 198 39.08 N 95.57 W
Rossville, Md., U.S. 284b 39.20 N 76.29 W
Rosswein 54 51.03 N 13.10 E
Røst II 24 67.28 N 11.59 E
Rostāg 120 37.07 N 69.49 E
Röstånga 41 56.00 N 13.17 E
Rosthern 184 52.40 N 106.17 W
Rostherne 262 53.21 N 2.23 W
Rostherne Mere ⊜ 262 53.21 N 2.23 W
Roštkala 120 37.16 N 71.49 E
Rostock 54 54.05 N 12.07 E
Rostov 80 57.11 N 39.25 E
Rostov-na-Donu 83 47.14 N 39.42 E
Rostov Oblast' □4 78 48.00 N 40.00 E
Rostrataville 158 26.49 S 25.39 E
Rostraver Airport ⊠ 279b 40.13 N 79.50 W
Rostrevor 48 54.06 N 6.12 W
Rosvinskoje 24 66.32 N 52.26 E
Roswell, Ga., U.S. 192 34.01 N 84.21 W
Roswell, N.M., U.S. 196 33.23 N 104.31 W
Roswell, Oh., U.S. 214 40.28 N 81.21 W
Rosyth 46 56.03 N 3.26 W
Rot ≃ 58 48.19 N 9.54 E
Rota 34 36.37 N 6.21 W
Rota I 108 14.10 N 145.12 E
Rot am See 56 49.15 N 10.01 E
Rotan 196 32.51 N 100.27 W
Rotanda 156 19.33 S 32.50 E
Rotary Island I 285 40.14 N 74.49 W
Rotbach ≃ 263 51.34 N 6.41 E
Rotberg 264a 52.21 N 13.31 E
Rote-Erde, Stadion ♦ 263 51.30 N 7.27 E
Rotenburg 52 53.06 N 9.24 E
Rotenburg an der Fulda 56 51.00 N 9.45 E
Roter Main ≃ 54 50.04 N 11.24 E
Rotes Meer → Red Sea ⊤2 136 20.00 N 38.00 E
Roth, Dtsch. 56 50.46 N 7.42 E
Roth, Dtsch. 60 49.15 N 11.06 E
Roth ≃ 58 48.27 N 10.10 E
Rötha 54 51.12 N 12.25 E
Rothaargebirge ⩘ 56 51.05 N 8.15 E
Rothbury 44 55.19 N 1.55 W
Rothbury Forest ⬥3 44 55.18 N 1.54 W
Rothemühl 54 53.36 N 13.49 E
Röthenbach, Dtsch. 58 47.37 N 9.59 E
Röthenbach, Schw. 58 46.51 N 7.45 E
Röthenbach an der Pegnitz 60 49.29 N 11.15 E
Rothenburg 54 51.20 N 14.58 E
Rothenburg ob der Tauber 56 49.23 N 10.10 E
Rothenkirchen 54 50.33 N 12.30 E
Rothenschirmbach 54 51.27 N 11.33 E
Rothenstein ∧2 263 51.07 N 7.41 E
Rother ≃, Eng., U.K. 42 50.54 N 0.42 E
Rother ≃, Eng., U.K. 42 50.57 N 0.32 W
Rothera ⊛3 9 67.34 S 68.08 W
Rotherham, N.Z. 172 42.42 S 172.57 E
Rotherham, Eng., U.K. 44 53.26 N 1.20 W
Rothes 46 57.31 N 3.13 W
Rothesay, N.B., Can. 186 45.23 N 66.00 W
Rothesay, Scot., U.K. 46 55.51 N 5.03 W
Rothneusiedl ⬥8 264b 48.08 N 16.23 E
Rothrist 58 47.19 N 7.53 E
Rothsay, Austl. 162 29.17 S 116.53 E
Rothsay, Mn., U.S. 198 46.28 N 96.16 W
Rothschild 190 44.53 N 89.37 W
Rothsville 208 40.09 N 76.15 W
Rothwell, N.B., Can. 186 46.04 N 66.04 W
Rothwell, Eng., U.K. 42 52.25 N 0.48 W
Rothwell, Eng., U.K. 44 53.46 N 1.29 W
Roti, Pulau I 112 10.45 S 123.10 E
Roti, Selat ⊔ 112 10.25 S 123.25 E
Roto 166 33.03 S 145.28 E
Rotoiti, Lake ⊜, N.Z. 172 41.50 S 172.50 E
Rotoiti, Lake ⊜, N.Z. 172 38.02 S 176.25 E
Rotomanu 172 42.39 S 171.32 E
Rotonda 68 39.57 N 16.02 E
Rotondella 68 40.10 N 16.32 E
Rotondo, Monte ∧ 36 42.13 N 9.03 E
Rotoroa, Lake ⊜ 172 41.52 S 172.38 E
Rotorua 172 38.09 S 176.15 E
Rotorua, Lake ⊜ 172 38.05 S 176.16 E
Rotowaro 172 37.36 S 175.05 E
Rott 64 47.54 N 10.59 E
Rott ≃ 60 48.27 N 13.26 E
Rottach-Egern 64 47.41 N 11.46 E
Rott am Inn 64 47.59 N 12.07 E
Röttenbach 60 49.09 N 11.02 E
Rottenbach-Tremersdorf 56 50.21 N 10.56 E
Rottenbuch 64 47.44 N 10.58 E
Rottenburg am Neckar 58 48.28 N 8.56 E
Rottenburg an der Laaber 60 48.42 N 12.02 E
Rottenmann 61 47.31 N 14.22 E
Rotterdam, Ned. 52 51.55 N 4.28 E
Rotterdam, N.Y., U.S. 210 42.48 N 73.59 W
Rotterdam, Luchthaven ⊠ 52 51.58 N 4.30 E
Rotterdam Junction 210 42.52 N 74.03 W
Rotthalmünster 60 48.21 N 13.12 E
Rotthausen ⬥8 263 51.30 N 7.05 E
Rottingdean 42 50.48 N 0.04 W
Röttingen 56 49.30 N 9.58 E
Rottleberode 54 51.31 N 10.57 E
Rottnest Island I 168a 32.00 S 115.30 E
Rottofreno 62 45.03 N 9.34 E
Rottum 263 51.36 N 7.42 E
Rottumeroog I 52 53.33 N 6.35 E
Rottumerplaat I 52 53.32 N 6.30 E
Rottweil 58 48.10 N 8.37 E
Rotuma I 14 12.30 S 177.05 E
Rotwand ∧ 64 47.39 N 11.56 E
Rötz 60 49.21 N 12.32 E
Roubaix 50 50.42 N 3.10 E
Roubideau Creek ≃ 200 38.44 N 108.10 W
Roubidoux Creek ≃ 194 37.51 N 92.13 W
Roubion ≃ 62 44.31 N 4.42 E
Rouceux 58 48.22 N 5.41 E
Roudnice [nad Labem] 54 50.22 N 14.16 E
Rouen 50 49.26 N 1.05 E
Rougé 32 47.47 N 1.27 W
Rouge ≃, On., Can. 212 43.48 N 79.07 W
Rouge ≃, P.Q., Can. 206 45.39 N 74.42 W
Rouge ≃, P.Q., Can. 206 45.33 N 74.20 W
Rouge, Bell Branch ≃ 281 42.23 N 83.16 W
Rouge, Lac ⊜ 206 46.56 N 74.38 W
Rouge, Mer → Red Sea ⊤2 136 20.00 N 38.00 E
Rouge, River ≃ 281 42.17 N 83.06 W
Rougeau, Forêt de ♦ 261 48.35 N 2.30 E
Rougemont, Fr. 58 47.29 N 6.21 E
Rougemont, Schw. 58 46.29 N 7.12 E
Rougemont-le-Château 58 47.44 N 6.58 E
Rouge → Red ≃ 178 31.00 N 91.40 W
Rough ≃ 194 37.29 N 87.08 W
Rough And Ready 226 39.14 N 121.08 W
Rough River Lake ⊜1 194 37.40 N 86.25 W
Rouiba 34 36.44 N 3.17 E
Rouillac 32 45.47 N 0.04 W
Rouillon 261 48.33 N 2.00 E
Roulans 58 47.19 N 6.14 E
Rouleau 184 50.11 N 104.55 W
Roulers → Roeselare 50 50.57 N 3.08 E
Roulette 214 41.46 N 78.09 W
Roumanie → Romania □1 38 46.00 N 25.30 E
Round Harbour 186 49.51 N 55.40 W
Roundhead 216 40.34 N 83.50 W
Round Hill Head > 166 24.10 S 151.53 E
Round Hill Regional Park ♦ 279b 40.15 N 79.51 W
Round Knowe ∧2 48 55.08 N 6.55 W
Round Lake, Il., U.S. 278 42.21 N 88.05 W
Round Lake, Mn., U.S. 198 43.32 N 95.28 W
Round Lake, N.Y., U.S. 210 42.56 N 73.47 W
Round Lake ⊜, Nf., Can. 186 51.08 N 56.33 W
Round Lake ⊜, On., Can. 190 45.38 N 77.32 W
Round Lake ⊜, On., Can. 212 44.30 N 77.52 W
Round Lake ⊜, On., Can. 212 45.28 N 79.24 W
Round Lake ⊜, Sk., Can. 184 50.33 N 102.23 W
Round Lake ⊜, Il., U.S. 278 42.22 N 88.05 W
Round Lake ⊜, Mi., U.S. 216 41.58 N 84.17 W
Round Lake Beach 216 42.22 N 88.05 W
Round Lake Park 216 42.21 N 88.04 W
Round Mound ∧2 198 38.55 N 99.39 W
Round Mountain 204 38.42 N 117.04 W
Round Mountain ∧, Austl. 166 30.27 S 152.14 E
Round Mountain ∧, Austl. 171b 36.15 S 148.34 E
Round Pond ⊜, Nf., Can. 186 48.10 N 56.00 W
Round Pond ⊜, Ma., U.S. 283 42.36 N 70.49 W
Round Rock 222 30.30 N 97.40 W
Roundstone 48 53.23 N 9.53 W
Round Top 210 42.16 N 74.02 W
Round Top ∧2 208 40.30 N 76.42 W
Round Top Regional Park ♦ 282 37.51 N 122.12 W
Roundup 202 46.26 N 108.32 W
Round Valley Indian Reservation ⬥4 204 39.50 N 123.20 W
Round Valley Reservoir ⊜1 210 40.36 N 74.50 W
Roundwood 48 53.04 N 6.13 W
Roura 250 4.44 N 52.20 W
Rourkela → Raurkela 124 22.13 N 84.53 E
Rousay I 46 59.10 N 3.02 W
Rouse Hill 274a 33.41 S 150.56 E
Rouses Point 206 45.00 N 73.22 W
Rouseville 214 41.28 N 79.41 W
Rousies 50 50.16 N 4.00 E
Rousseau, Lake ⊜1 220 29.02 N 82.32 W
Rousset, Col de)(62 44.50 N 5.24 E
Roussigny 261 48.39 N 2.06 E
Roussillon, Fr. 62 45.22 N 4.49 E
Roussillon, Fr. 62 43.54 N 5.17 E
Roussillon □9 32 42.30 N 2.30 E
Roussy-le-Village 56 49.27 N 6.10 E
Routhierville 186 48.11 N 67.09 W
Routot 50 49.23 N 0.44 E
Rouveen 52 52.36 N 6.11 E
Rouvignies 50 50.20 N 3.26 E
Rouville □6 206 45.23 N 73.04 W
Rouvray 50 47.25 N 4.06 E
Rouvray, Lac ⊜ 186 49.18 N 70.49 W
Rouxville 158 30.29 S 26.46 E
Rouyn 190 48.15 N 79.01 W
Rouzerville 208 39.44 N 77.32 W
Rovaniemi 24 66.34 N 25.48 E
Rovasenda 62 45.32 N 8.19 E
Rovato 64 45.34 N 10.00 E
Rovbickskaja 76 52.40 N 24.05 E
Rove, Tunnel du ⬥5 62 43.22 N 5.17 E
Rovegno 62 44.35 N 9.17 E
Rovellasca 62 45.40 N 9.03 E
Rovello Porro 62 45.39 N 9.02 E
Roven'ki, Ross. 78 49.56 N 38.54 E
Roven'ki, Ukr. 83 48.05 N 39.21 E
Rovenskaja Sloboda 76 52.13 N 30.19 E
Roverbella 64 45.16 N 10.46 E
Rovere 66 42.10 N 13.31 E
Roverè della Luna 64 46.15 N 11.10 E
Roveredo 58 46.14 N 9.08 E
Rovereto 64 45.53 N 11.02 E
Roverè Veronese 64 45.36 N 11.03 E
Rövershagen 54 54.10 N 12.15 E
Roversi 252 27.35 S 61.57 W
Roverud 26 60.15 N 12.03 E
Roviano 66 42.01 N 13.00 E
Rovigo 64 45.04 N 11.47 E
Rovigo □4 64 45.02 N 11.50 E
Rovinj 36 45.05 N 13.38 E
Rovira 246 4.14 N 75.14 W
Rovno 78 50.37 N 26.15 E
Rovno □4 78 51.00 N 26.30 E
Rovnoje, Kyrg. 85 42.53 N 73.32 E
Rovnoje, Ross. 80 50.47 N 46.05 E
Rovnoje, Ukr. 78 48.15 N 31.45 E
Rovubu (Ruvubu) ≃ 154 2.23 S 30.47 E
Rovuma (Ruvuma) ≃ 154 10.29 S 40.28 E
Rów 54 52.58 N 14.45 E
Rowan □6 218 38.17 N 83.26 W
Rowan Lake ⊜ 184 49.18 N 93.32 W
Rowanty Creek ≃ 208 36.58 N 77.21 W
Rowena, Austl. 166 29.49 S 148.54 E
Rowena, Tx., U.S. 196 31.39 N 100.03 W
Rowe Park ♦ 273a 6.30 N 3.23 E
Rowhill 273d 26.14 S 28.26 E
Rowland, N.C., U.S. 192 34.32 N 79.17 W
Rowland, Pa., U.S. 210 41.28 N 75.03 W
Rowland Flat 168b 34.35 S 138.56 E
Rowland Heights 280 33.58 N 117.54 W
Rowlands Gill 44 54.54 N 1.45 W
Rowlesburg 188 39.20 N 79.40 W
Rowlett 222 32.54 N 96.33 W
Rowlett, Isla I 254 44.48 S 74.25 W
Rowlett Creek ≃ 222 32.49 N 96.31 W
Rowley 207 42.43 N 70.52 W
Rowley ≃, N.T., Can. 176 70.16 N 77.45 W
Rowley ≃, Ma., U.S. 283 42.43 N 70.49 W
Rowley Island I 176 69.08 N 78.50 W
Rowley Shoals ⊹2 162 17.30 S 119.00 E
Rowntree Mill Park ♦ 275b 43.45 N 79.35 W
Rowsburg 214 40.52 N 82.10 W
Rowville 274b 37.56 S 145.14 E
Roxa, Ilha I 150 11.15 N 15.40 W
Roxana 219 38.50 N 90.04 W
Roxas, Pil. 108 11.35 N 122.45 E
Roxas, Pil. 116 17.08 N 121.36 E
Roxas, Pil. 116 12.35 N 121.31 E
Roxas, Pil. 116 10.20 N 119.21 E
Roxas (Capiz), Pil. 116 11.35 N 122.45 E
Roxboro, P.Q., Can. 275a 45.31 N 73.48 W
Roxboro, N.C., U.S. 192 36.23 N 78.58 W
Roxborough 241r 11.15 N 60.35 W
Roxborough ⬥8 285 40.02 N 75.13 W
Roxburgh, N.Z. 172 45.32 S 169.19 E
Roxburgh, Scot., U.K. 46 55.34 N 2.30 W
Roxbury, Ct., U.S. 207 41.33 N 73.18 W
Roxbury, N.Y., U.S. 210 42.17 N 74.33 W
Roxbury, Pa., U.S. 214 40.07 N 77.40 W
Roxbury, Va., U.S. 208 37.28 N 77.09 W
Roxbury ⬥8, Ma., U.S. 283 42.20 N 71.06 W
Roxbury ⬥8, N.Y., U.S. 276 40.34 N 73.54 W
Roxby Downs 162 30.43 S 136.46 E
Roxel 52 51.57 N 7.32 E
Roxen ⊜ 26 58.30 N 15.41 E
Roxie 194 31.30 N 91.04 W
Roxo, Cap > 150 12.20 N 16.43 W
Roxton 196 33.33 N 95.44 W
Roxton Pond (Sainte-Pudentienne) 206 45.29 N 72.40 W
Roxwell 260 51.45 N 0.23 E
Roy, N.M., U.S. 196 35.56 N 104.11 W
Roy, Ut,. U.S. 200 41.09 N 112.01 W
Roy, Wa., U.S. 224 47.00 N 122.32 W
Roya (Roia) ≃ 62 43.48 N 7.35 E
Royal 198 43.03 N 95.17 W
Royal Albert Hall ⊛ 260 51.30 N 0.11 W
Royal Australian Naval College ⊛2 170 35.07 S 150.42 E
Royal Bangkok Sports Club ♦ 269a 13.44 N 100.33 E
Royal Botanic Gardens ♦, Austl. 274a 33.52 S 151.13 E
Royal Botanic Gardens ♦, Austl. 274b 37.50 S 144.59 E
Royal Canal ≊ 48 53.21 N 6.15 W
Royal Center 216 40.51 N 86.29 W
Royal Chitwan National Park ♦ 124 27.30 N 84.30 E
Royal City 202 46.54 N 119.38 W
Royale, Isle I 190 48.00 N 89.00 W
Royal Gorge V 200 38.17 N 105.45 W
Royal Island I 192 25.31 N 76.51 W
Royalla 171b 35.31 S 149.09 E
Royal Leamington Spa 42 52.18 N 1.31 W
Royal Natal National Park ♦ 158 28.45 S 28.57 E
Royal National Park ♦ 170 34.10 S 151.05 E
Royal Naval College ■ 260 51.29 N 0.01 W
Royal Oak, B.C., Can. 224 48.30 N 123.23 W
Royal Oak, Md., U.S. 208 38.44 N 76.10 W
Royal Oak, Mi., U.S. 216 42.29 N 83.08 W
Royal Oak Township 281 42.27 N 83.10 W
Royal Ontario Museum ⊛ 275b 43.40 N 79.24 W
Royal Palms State Beach ♦ 280 33.44 N 118.19 W
Royal Park ♦ 274b 37.47 S 144.57 E
Royal Roads ⊂ 224 48.26 N 123.26 W
Royalton, In., U.S. 218 39.56 N 86.21 W
Royalton, Mn., U.S. 190 45.49 N 94.17 W
Royalton, Pa., U.S. 208 40.11 N 76.44 W
Royal Tunbridge Wells 42 51.08 N 0.16 E
Royal Turf Club ♦ 269a 13.46 N 100.32 E
Royan 32 45.37 N 1.01 W
Royaume-Uni → United Kingdom □1 28 54.00 N 2.00 W
Roybon 62 45.15 N 5.15 E
Royce Brook ≃ 276 40.32 N 70.35 W
Roydon, Eng., U.K. 42 51.46 N 0.03 E
Roydon, Eng., U.K. 42 52.50 N 0.32 E
Roye 50 49.42 N 2.48 E
Royersford 208 40.11 N 75.32 W
Royerton 216 40.15 N 85.21 W
Roy Hill 162 22.38 S 119.57 E
Royse City 222 32.58 N 96.19 W
Royston, Eng., U.K. 42 52.03 N 0.01 W
Royston, Eng., U.K. 44 53.37 N 1.27 W
Royston, Ga., U.S. 192 34.17 N 83.06 W
Royton 44 53.34 N 2.08 W
Rožaj 38 42.50 N 20.10 E
Różan 30 52.53 N 21.25 E
Rozay-en-Brie 50 48.41 N 2.58 E
Roždestvenka, Kaz. 86 50.52 N 71.22 E
Roždestvenka, Ross. 86 55.21 N 77.29 E
Roždestvenka, Ross. 86 55.42 N 70.00 E
Roždestveno, Ross. 76 57.44 N 37.57 E
Roždestveno, Ross. 80 53.15 N 50.04 E
Roždestveno, Ross. 82 56.51 N 36.33 E
Roždestveno, Ross. 82 55.57 N 36.23 E
Roždestvenskaja Chava 78 51.38 N 39.40 E
Roždestvenskoje, Ross. 80 58.09 N 45.35 E
Roždestvenskoje, Ross. 80 52.47 N 42.10 E
Roždestvenskoje, Ross. 80 51.14 N 42.10 E
Roždestvo 76 57.36 N 33.48 E
Rozel 43b 49.14 N 2.03 W
Rozelle 274a 33.52 S 151.10 E
Roželov 60 49.33 N 13.48 E
Rozewie, Przylądek > 30 54.51 N 18.21 E
Rozhnof, Cape > 180 55.58 N 160.58 W
Rožišče 78 50.54 N 25.15 E
Rožki 80 56.41 N 50.31 E
Rožkov 80 51.39 N 52.19 E
Rožmberk ⊜ 61 49.04 N 14.47 E
Rožmberk nad Vltavou 61 48.39 N 14.22 E
Rožmitál pod Třemšínem 60 49.36 N 13.52 E
Rožn'atov 78 48.56 N 24.09 E
Rožňava 30 48.40 N 20.32 E
Roznov 38 46.50 N 26.31 E
Rožnov pod Radhoštěm 30 49.28 N 18.10 E
Rożnów 30 49.46 N 20.42 E
Rozovka 78 47.23 N 37.04 E
Rozoy-sur-Serre 50 49.43 N 4.08 E
Roztocze ⩘2 30 50.30 N 23.20 E
Roztoky 54 50.09 N 14.22 E
Rozzano 62 45.20 N 9.06 E
Rrëshen 38 41.47 N 19.54 E
Rrogozhinë 38 41.05 N 19.40 E
Rtiščevo 80 52.16 N 43.47 E
Ru ≃ 100 32.43 N 115.01 E
Ru, Tanjong > 114 2.50 N 101.17 E
Ruabon 42 52.59 N 3.02 W
Ruacaná 152 17.25 S 14.12 E
Ruacana Falls ⌊ 152 17.22 S 14.12 E
Ruaha National Park ♦ 154 7.30 S 34.40 E
Ruahine Range ⩘ 172 40.00 S 176.06 E
Ruahmi, Ra's > 142 28.44 N 32.50 E
Ruanda 154 10.33 S 34.57 E
Ruanda → Rwanda □1 154 2.00 S 30.00 E
Ruango 164 5.35 S 150.10 E
Ruapehu, Mount ∧ 172 39.17 S 175.34 E
Ruapuke Island I 172 46.47 S 168.30 E
Ruatahuna 172 38.33 S 176.57 E
Ruatapu 172 42.48 S 170.53 E
Ruathair, Loch an ⊜ 46 58.18 N 3.56 W
Ruatoria 172 37.53 S 178.20 E
Ruawai 172 36.08 S 174.02 E
Rub' al Khali → Ar-Rub' al-Khālī ⬥2 118 20.00 N 51.00 E
Rubanovka 78 47.00 N 34.10 E
Rubbestadneset 26 59.49 N 5.17 E
Rubcovsk 86 51.33 N 81.10 E
Rubcy 83 49.12 N 37.33 E
Rubeho Mountains ⩘ 154 6.55 S 36.30 E
Rubel' 78 51.58 N 27.04 E
Rübeland 54 51.45 N 10.50 E
Rubelles 261 48.34 N 2.41 E
Rubery ⬥8 42 52.24 N 2.00 W
Rubeshibe 92a 43.47 N 143.38 E
Rubežka 80 51.26 N 51.59 E
Rubežnoje 83 49.01 N 38.23 E
Rubí, Esp. 266d 41.29 N 2.02 E
Rubi, Zaïre 154 2.49 N 25.14 E
Rubí ≃, Esp. 266d 41.26 N 2.00 E
Rubi ≃, Zaïre 152 2.48 N 23.54 E
Rubiana 62 45.08 N 7.23 E
Rubiataba 255 15.08 S 49.48 W
Rubicon ≃ 226 39.00 N 120.44 W
Rubicone ≃ 66 44.08 N 12.28 E
Rubidoux 228 33.59 N 117.24 W
Rubiera 64 44.39 N 10.45 E
Rubim 255 16.23 S 40.32 W
Rubino 150 6.04 N 4.18 W
Rubio 246 7.43 N 72.22 W
Rubio Woods ♦ 278 41.38 N 87.46 W
Rubl'ovka 78 49.15 N 33.19 E
Rubl'ovo 82 55.47 N 37.21 E
Ruboani 140 8.06 N 30.45 E
Rubona 154 0.33 N 30.10 E
Rubondo Island I 154 2.20 S 31.52 E
Rubondo Island National Park ♦ 154 2.20 S 31.52 E
Rubtsovsk → Rubcovsk 86 51.33 N 81.10 E
Ruby, Ak., U.S. 180 64.44 N 155.30 W
Ruby, N.Y., U.S. 210 42.01 N 74.01 W
Ruby ≃ 202 45.34 N 112.21 W
Ruby Creek ≃ 224 48.43 N 120.59 W
Ruby Dome ∧ 204 40.37 N 115.28 W
Ruby Lake ⊞ 204 40.10 N 115.30 W
Ruby Mountains ⩘ 204 40.25 N 115.35 W
Ruby Valley V 204 40.30 N 115.15 W
Rucava 76 56.09 N 21.10 E
Ruchan' 76 53.33 N 32.48 E
Ruche 261 49.02 N 2.27 E
Rucheng 100 25.34 N 113.41 E
Ruciane-Nida 30 53.39 N 21.35 E
Ručji ⬥8 265a 60.01 N 30.24 E
Ručjuvom 24 66.42 N 61.08 E
Rucphen 52 51.32 N 4.34 E
Ruda 64 45.50 N 13.24 E
Rudall 166 33.41 S 136.16 E
Rudall ≃ 162 22.16 S 122.47 E
Rudall River National Park ♦ 162 22.25 S 122.40 E
Ruda Śląska 30 50.18 N 18.51 E
Rudauli 124 26.45 N 81.45 E
Ruḍaymat al-Liwā' 132 33.01 N 36.35 E
Rūdbār, Afg. 128 30.09 N 62.36 E
Rūdbār, Īrān 128 36.48 N 49.24 E
Rudbøl 41 54.54 N 8.45 E
Ruddervoorde 50 51.06 N 3.12 E
Ruddiman Terrace 216 43.12 N 86.17 W
Rudelsburg ⊥ 54 51.07 N 11.43 E
Ruden I 54 54.12 N 13.46 E
Rudensk 76 53.36 N 27.52 E
Rüdersdorf, Dtsch. 54 52.29 N 13.47 E
Rudersdorf, Öst. 61 47.03 N 16.07 E
Rüdersdorf, Forst ⬥3 264a 52.26 N 13.50 E
Rüdesheim am Rhein 56 49.59 N 7.56 E
Rudeville 276 41.09 N 74.33 W
Rudewa 154 10.06 S 34.39 E
Rudge Ramos 287b 23.41 S 46.34 W
Rūdiškės 76 54.31 N 24.50 E
Rudki 78 49.39 N 23.29 E
Rudkino 78 51.27 N 39.01 E
Rudkøbing 41 54.56 N 10.43 E
Rudn'a, Ross. 76 54.57 N 31.06 E
Rudn'a, Ross. 80 50.48 N 44.33 E
Rudnaja Pristan' 89 44.22 N 135.48 E
Rudnevka ≃ 265b 55.43 N 37.56 E
Rudnevo 82 54.44 N 38.09 E
Rudnica 78 48.15 N 28.55 E
Rudničnyj, Kaz. 86 44.40 N 78.55 E
Rudničnyj, Ross. 24 59.38 N 52.27 E
Rudničnyj, Ross. 86 56.08 N 86.12 E
Rudničnyj, Ross. 86 59.42 N 60.18 E
Rudnik 30 50.28 N 22.15 E
Rüdnitz 54 52.43 N 13.37 E
Rudnyj, Kaz. 86 52.57 N 63.07 E
Rudnyj, Ross. 89 44.21 N 134.58 E
Rudo 38 43.37 N 19.22 E
Rudolf, Lake (Lake Turkana) ⊜ 144 3.30 N 36.00 E
Rudolfov 61 48.59 N 14.34 E
Rudolph 216 41.17 N 83.40 W
Rudolstadt 54 50.43 N 11.20 E
Rudong, Zhg. 102 21.39 N 111.23 E
Rudong, Zhg. 106 32.19 N 121.12 E
Rudovka, Ross. 80 53.07 N 42.23 E
Rudovka, Ukr. 83 49.24 N 38.27 E
Rudow ⬥8 264a 52.25 N 13.30 E
Rudrón ≃ 34 42.47 N 3.45 W
Rūdsar 128 37.08 N 50.18 E
Ruds Vedby 41 55.33 N 11.23 E
Rudyard, Mi., U.S. 190 46.13 N 84.36 W
Rudyard, Mt., U.S. 202 48.33 N 110.33 W
Rudyerd Bay ⊂ 182 55.35 N 130.44 W
Rue, Fr. 50 50.16 N 1.40 E
Rue, Schw. 58 46.37 N 6.50 E
Ruecas ≃ 34 39.00 N 5.55 W
Rueil-Malmaison 261 48.53 N 2.11 E
Ruen ∧ 38 42.10 N 22.31 E
Ruenya (Luenha) ≃ 154 16.24 S 33.48 E

Symbols in the index entries represent the broad categories identified in the key at the right. Symbols with superior numbers (⩘1) identify subcategories (see complete key on page *I · 1*).

Symbole im Register stellen die rechts im Schlüssel erklärten Kategorien dar. Symbole mit hochgestellten Ziffern (⩘1) bezeichnen Unterabteilungen einer Kategorie (vgl. vollständiger Schlüssel auf Seite *I · 1*).

Los símbolos incluídos en el texto del índice representan las grandes categorias identificadas con la clave a la derecha. Los símbolos con numeros en su parte superior (⩘1) identifican las subcategorías (véase la clave completa en la página *I · 1*).

Les symboles de l'index représentent les catégories indiquées dans la légende à droite. Les symboles suivis d'un indice (⩘1) représentent des sous-catégories (voir légende complète à la page *I · 1*).

Os símbolos incluídos no texto do índice representam as grandes categorias identificadas com a chave à direita. Os símbolos com números em sua parte superior (⩘1) identificam as subcategorias (veja-se a chave completa à página *I · 1*).

∧	Mountain	Berg	Montaña	Montagne	Montanha
⩘	Mountains	Gebirge	Montañas	Montagnes	Montanhas
)(	Pass	Paß	Paso	Col	Passo
V	Valley, Canyon	Tal, Cañon	Valle, Cañón	Vallée, Canyon	Vale, Canhão
≚	Plain	Ebene	Llano	Plaine	Planície
>	Cape	Kap	Cabo	Cap	Cabo
I	Island	Insel	Isla	Île	Ilha
II	Islands	Inseln	Islas	Îles	Ilhas
⊥	Other Topographic Features	Andere Topographische Objekte	Otros Elementos Topográficos	Autres données topographiques	Outros acidentes topográficos

ESPAÑOL — FRANÇAIS — PORTUGUÊS

Nombre / Nom / Nome	Página / Page	Lat.°′	Long.°′ W = Oeste / W = Ouest
Rufā'ah	140	14.46 N	33.22 E
Ruffano	68	39.59 N	18.15 E
Ruffec	32	46.01 N	0.12 E
Ruffieu	58	46.00 N	5.40 E
Ruffieux	62	45.51 N	5.50 E
Ruffin	192	33.00 N	80.48 W
Ruffle Bar I	276	40.36 N	46.51 W
Rufford	262	53.38 N	2.49 W
Rufford Old Hall ⊥	262	53.38 N	2.49 W
Ruffs Dale	279b	40.10 N	79.37 W
Rufidschi			
→ Rufiji ≃	154	8.00 S	39.20 E
Rufiji ≃	154	8.00 S	39.20 E
Rufina	66	43.49 N	11.29 E
Rufino	252	34.16 S	62.42 W
Rufisque	150	14.43 N	17.17 W
Rufunsa	154	15.05 S	29.40 E
Rufus	224	45.41 N	120.44 W
Rufus, Mount ∧	168b	34.20 S	139.07 E
Rugāji	76	57.00 N	27.08 E
Rugao	100	32.25 N	120.36 E
Rugby, Eng., U.K.	42	52.23 N	1.15 W
Rugby, N.D., U.S.	198	48.22 N	99.59 W
Rugeley	42	52.46 N	1.55 W
Rügen I	54	54.25 N	13.24 E
Rüggeberg	263	51.16 N	7.22 E
Rugged Mountain ∧	182	50.02 N	126.41 W
Ruggles Beach	214	41.22 N	82.29 W
Rugles	50	48.49 N	0.42 E
Rugufu ≃	154	5.10 S	30.14 E
Ruguj	76	59.28 N	32.50 E
Ruḥama	132	31.30 N	34.42 E
Ruhea	124	26.10 N	88.25 E
Ruhengeri	154	1.30 S	29.38 E
Ruhla	54	50.53 N	10.22 E
Ruhland	54	51.27 N	13.52 E
Ruhlsdorf	264a	52.23 N	13.16 E
Ruhmannsfelden	60	48.59 N	12.59 E
Ruhner Berge ⋏ [2]	54	53.17 N	11.55 E
Ruhnu saar I	76	57.48 N	23.15 E
Ruhpolding	64	47.45 N	12.38 E
Ruhr ≃	52	51.27 N	6.44 E
Ruhrort ◆ [8]	263	51.26 N	6.45 E
Ruhr-Universität ʋ [2]	263	51.27 N	7.16 E
Ruhstorf an der Rott	60	48.26 N	13.20 E
Ruhudji ≃	154	8.52 S	36.01 E
Ruhuhu ≃	154	10.31 S	34.34 E
Ruhunu National Park ♠	122	6.30 N	81.30 E
Rui'an	100	27.49 N	120.38 E
Ruichang	100	29.41 N	115.40 E
Ruicheng	102	34.45 N	110.45 E
Ruidoso	200	33.19 N	105.40 W
Ruidoso, Rio ≃	200	33.23 N	105.16 W
Ruidoso Downs	200	33.19 N	105.36 W
Ruifeng Sha I	106	31.25 N	121.36 E
Ruihong	100	28.45 N	116.23 E
Ruijin	100	25.50 N	116.00 E
Ruinen	52	52.46 N	6.22 E
Ruiselede	50	51.03 N	3.24 E
Ruislip ◆ [8]	260	51.34 N	0.25 W
Ruivo, Pico ∧	148	32.45 N	16.56 W
Ruiz	234	21.57 N	105.09 W
Ruiz, Nevado del ∧ [1]	246	4.54 N	75.18 W
Ruiz de Montoya	252	26.59 S	55.03 W
Rūjiena	76	57.54 N	25.21 E
Rujm ar-Rashīd, Jabal ∧	132	31.53 N	36.18 E
Rujm aṣ-Ṣakhrī	132	31.02 N	35.43 E
Rukan-shō ✢ [2]	174m	26.06 N	127.32 E
Ruki ≃	152	0.05 N	18.17 E
Rukni	126	23.33 N	86.33 E
Rukungiri	154	0.48 S	29.55 E
Rukwa □ [4]	154	7.00 S	31.30 E
Rukwa, Lake ⊜	154	8.00 S	32.25 E
Rule	196	33.11 N	99.53 W
Rule Creek ≃	198	38.02 N	103.02 W
Ruleville	194	33.43 N	90.33 W
Rulle	52	52.20 N	8.04 E
Rully	58	46.52 N	4.45 E
Rulo	198	40.03 N	95.25 W
Rülzheim	56	49.09 N	8.16 E
Rum	61	47.08 N	16.51 E
Rum ≃	190	45.11 N	93.23 W
Ruma	38	45.00 N	19.49 E
Rumaat	164	5.49 S	132.48 E
Rumāh	128	25.34 N	47.09 E
Rumahtinggih	164	6.23 S	140.17 E
Rum'ancevo, Ross.	82	55.38 N	37.26 E
Rum'ancevo, Ross.	82	55.58 N	36.32 E
Rum'ancevo ◆ [8]	83	48.21 N	38.06 E
Rumänien			
→ Romania □ [1]	38	46.00 N	25.30 E
Rumaysh	132	33.05 N	35.22 E
Rumbek	140	6.48 N	29.41 E
Rumbeke	50	50.56 N	3.10 E
Rumberpon, Pulau I	164	1.50 S	134.15 E
Rumbling Bridge	46	56.10 N	3.35 W
Rumburk	54	50.57 N	14.32 E
Rum Cay I	238	23.40 N	74.53 W
Rumelange	56	49.28 N	6.02 E
Rumelifeneri ◆ [8]	267b	41.14 N	29.06 E
Rumelihisarı ◆ [8]	267b	41.05 N	29.03 E
Rumelihisarı ⊥	267b	41.05 N	29.02 E
Rumelikavağı ◆ [8]	267b	41.11 N	29.04 E
Rumford	188	44.33 N	70.33 W
Rumford ≃	283	41.58 N	71.11 W
Rumia	30	54.35 N	18.25 E
Rumigny	50	49.48 N	4.16 E
Rumilly	62	45.52 N	5.57 E
R'uminskoje	82	56.31 N	38.47 E
Rum Jungle	164	13.01 S	131.00 E
R'umki	265a	59.47 N	30.02 E
Rümlang	58	47.27 N	8.32 E
Rummah, Wādī ar- ∨	128	26.12 N	44.04 E
Rummānah	142	31.01 N	32.40 E
Rummānah, Bi'r ar- ⍑ [4]	142	31.00 N	32.40 E
Rummel	214	40.13 N	78.48 W
Rummelsburg ◆ [8]	264a	52.30 N	13.29 E
Rummenohl ◆ [8]	263	51.17 N	7.32 E
Rumney	42	51.31 N	3.07 W
Rumoi	92a	43.56 N	141.39 E
Rumont	56	48.50 N	5.17 E
Rumphi	154	11.01 S	33.52 E
Rump Mountain ∧	188	45.12 N	71.04 W
Rumson	208	40.22 N	73.59 W
Rumst	50	51.05 N	4.25 E
Rumula	164	16.35 S	145.20 E
Rumung I	174q	9.37 N	138.10 E
Rumuruti	154	0.16 N	36.32 E
Runan	100	33.01 N	114.22 E
Runanga	172	42.24 S	171.16 E
Runaway, Cape ›	172	37.32 S	177.59 E
Runazi	154	2.47 S	31.28 E
Runcorn ◆ [8]	44	53.20 N	2.44 W
Rundeng	114	2.39 N	97.52 E
Rundēni	76	56.16 N	27.50 E
Rundu	156	17.52 S	19.43 E
Rundvik	26	63.32 N	19.26 E
Runere	154	3.06 S	33.16 E
Rŭng, Kaôh I	110	10.44 N	103.14 E
Rungāni	120	26.38 N	65.43 E
Runge	222	28.52 N	97.42 W
Rungis	261	48.45 N	2.21 E
Rungis-Halles, Marché de ʋ	261	48.46 N	2.21 E
Rungsted	41	55.53 N	12.33 E
Rungus Point ›	116	13.43 N	123.58 E
Rungwa, Tan.	154	7.21 S	31.40 E
Rungwa, Tan.	154	6.57 S	33.31 E
Rungwa ≃	154	7.36 S	31.50 E
Rungwa Game Reserve ◆ [4]	154	7.00 S	34.10 E
Rungwe	154	9.10 S	33.36 E
Runhällen	40	60.02 N	16.49 E
Runheji	100	32.30 N	116.05 E
Runkel	56	50.24 N	8.10 E
Runmarö I	40	59.17 N	18.46 E
Runn ⊜	40	60.33 N	15.40 E
Runnemede	285	39.51 N	75.04 W
Running Springs	228	34.12 N	117.07 W
Running Water Draw ∨	196	33.58 N	101.30 W
Runnymede □ [8]	260	51.24 N	0.32 W
Runnymede ⊥	42	51.26 N	0.34 W
Rünthe	263	51.39 N	7.39 E
Runwell	260	51.37 N	0.32 E
Ruo ≃, Afr.	154	16.33 S	35.09 E
Ruo ≃, Zhg.	102	41.00 N	100.10 E
Ruo'ergai	102	33.16 N	102.55 E
Ruoheng	100	28.24 N	121.31 E
Ruokolahti	26	61.17 N	28.50 E
Ruoms	62	44.27 N	4.21 E
Ruoqiang	90	38.30 N	88.05 E
Ruoti	68	40.43 N	15.41 E
Ruovesi	26	61.59 N	24.05 E
Ruoxi	100	29.18 N	115.20 E
Rupanco	254	40.46 S	72.42 W
Rupanco, Lago ⊜	254	40.49 S	72.28 W
Rupari	168b	35.37 S	139.09 E
Rupat, Pulau I	114	1.50 N	101.35 E
Rupat, Selat ⩋	114	1.50 N	101.25 E
Rupdia	126	23.08 N	89.18 E
Rupea	38	46.02 N	25.13 E
Rupert, Id., U.S.	202	42.37 N	113.40 W
Rupert, Vt., U.S.	210	43.15 N	73.13 W
Rupert, W.V., U.S.	188	37.57 N	80.41 W
Rupert, Rivière de ≃	176	51.29 N	78.45 W
Rupert Creek ≃	166	20.53 S	142.23 E
Rupganj	126	23.48 N	90.31 E
Rūpnagar	123	30.59 N	76.31 E
Rūpnārāyan ≃	126	22.13 N	88.03 E
Ruponda	154	10.15 S	38.42 E
Ruppertenrod	56	50.37 N	9.05 E
Ruppiner See ⊜	54	52.48 N	12.50 E
Rupprechtseck ∧	61	47.14 N	14.00 E
Rupt de Mad ≃	56	49.01 N	6.02 E
Rupt-sur-Moselle	58	47.56 N	6.40 E
Rupununi ≃	246	4.03 N	58.34 W
Ruqqād, Wādī ar- ∨	132	32.44 N	35.46 E
Rur (Roer) ≃	56	51.12 N	5.59 E
Rural Hall	192	36.14 N	80.17 W
Rural Retreat	192	36.53 N	81.16 W
Rural Ridge	279b	40.35 N	79.50 W
Rural Valley	214	40.48 N	79.18 W
Rurberg	56	50.37 N	6.22 E
Ruri-kei ♠	96	35.03 N	135.26 E
Rurrenabaque	248	14.28 S	67.34 W
Rurstausee ⊜ [1]	56	50.36 N	6.22 E
Rurutu I	14	22.26 S	151.20 W
Rusambo	154	16.35 S	32.12 E
Rušan	120	37.58 N	71.30 E
Rusanov	78	50.29 N	31.09 E
Rusanovka	78	50.32 N	33.44 E
Rusape	154	18.32 S	32.07 E
Rusavkina-Popovščina	265b	55.42 N	38.04 E
Ruṣayriṣ, Khazzān ar- ⊜ [1]	140	11.40 N	34.20 E
Ruschuk			
→ Ruse	38	43.50 N	25.57 E
Ruscom ≃	214	42.18 N	82.38 W
Ruscom Station	214	42.13 N	82.39 W
Ruse, Blg.	38	43.50 N	25.57 E
Ruše, Slo.	61	46.32 N	15.31 E
Rusera	124	25.45 N	86.02 E
Rush, Ire.	48	53.32 N	6.06 W
Rush, N.Y., U.S.	210	42.59 N	77.39 W
Rush, Pa., U.S.	210	41.47 N	76.03 W
Rush □ [6]	218	39.37 N	85.27 W
Rush ≃, N.D., U.S.	198	47.00 N	96.54 W
Rush ≃, Wi., U.S.	190	44.34 N	92.19 W
Rushan (Xiacun)	98	36.54 N	121.29 E
Rush Center	198	38.27 N	99.18 W
Rush City	190	45.41 N	92.57 W
Rush Creek ≃, Co., U.S.	198	38.22 N	102.32 W
Rush Creek ≃, Ne., U.S.	198	41.27 N	102.32 W
Rush Creek ≃, N.Y., U.S.	284a	42.00 N	78.52 W
Rush Creek ≃, Oh., U.S.	188	39.38 N	82.33 W
Rush Creek ≃, Oh., U.S.	214	40.34 N	83.20 W
Rush Creek ≃, Ok., U.S.	196	34.42 N	97.10 W
Rushden	42	52.17 N	0.36 W
Rushford, Mn., U.S.	190	43.48 N	91.45 W
Rushford, N.Y., U.S.	210	42.23 N	78.15 W
Rush Hill	219	39.13 N	91.43 W
Rush Lake ⊜, On., Can.	190	47.48 N	82.12 W
Rush Lake ⊜, Wi., U.S.	190	43.56 N	88.49 W
Rushland	285	40.15 N	75.02 W
Rushmore	198	43.37 N	95.48 W
Rusholme ◆ [8]	262	53.27 N	2.12 W
Rush Springs	196	34.46 N	97.57 W
Rushsylvania	216	40.27 N	83.40 W
Rushville, Il., U.S.	219	40.07 N	90.33 W
Rushville, In., U.S.	218	39.36 N	85.26 W
Rushville, Ne., U.S.	198	42.43 N	102.27 W
Rushville, N.Y., U.S.	210	42.45 N	77.13 W
Rusinga Island I	154	0.24 S	34.10 E
Rusizi (Ruzizi) ≃	154	3.16 S	29.14 E
Rusk	222	31.47 N	95.09 W
Rusk □ [6]	222	32.10 N	94.50 W
Rusken ⊜	26	57.17 N	14.20 E
Ruskin, B.C., Can.	224	49.12 N	122.28 W
Ruskin, Fl., U.S.	220	27.43 N	82.26 W
Ruskington	44	53.02 N	0.23 W
Rusnė	76	55.18 N	21.22 E
Rušons ⊜	76	56.11 N	27.02 E
Rusovce	61	48.04 N	17.10 E
Russa	272b	22.29 N	88.21 E
Russas	250	4.56 S	37.58 W
Russbach ≃	61	48.10 N	16.58 E
Russee	41	54.18 N	10.04 E
Russell, Mb., Can.	184	50.47 N	101.15 W
Russell, On., Can.	212	45.15 N	75.22 W
Russell, N.Z.	172	35.16 S	174.07 E
Russell, Ia., U.S.	190	40.58 N	93.11 W
Russell, Ks., U.S.	198	38.53 N	98.51 W
Russell, Ky., U.S.	188	38.31 N	82.41 W
Russell, Ma., U.S.	207	42.11 N	72.51 W
Russell, Mn., U.S.	198	44.19 N	95.57 W
Russell, Pa., U.S.	214	41.56 N	79.08 W
Russell, Cape ›	176	75.15 N	117.35 W
Russell, Mount ∧	180	62.48 N	151.52 W
Russell Cave National Monument ♠	194	34.54 N	85.48 W
Russell Creek ≃	194	37.14 N	85.30 W
Russell Gardens	276	40.47 N	73.43 W
Russell Island I	176	73.55 N	98.25 W
Russell Islands II	175e	9.04 S	159.12 E
Russellkonda	120	19.56 N	84.35 E
Russell Lake ⊜	184	56.15 N	101.30 W
Russell Range ⋏	162	33.24 S	123.28 E
Russells Point	216	40.28 N	83.54 W
Russell Springs	194	37.03 N	85.05 W
Russellton	214	40.37 N	79.50 W
Russellville, Al., U.S.	194	34.30 N	87.43 W
Russellville, Ar., U.S.	194	35.16 N	93.08 W
Russellville, Ky., U.S.	194	36.50 N	86.53 W
Russellville, Mo., U.S.	194	38.30 N	92.26 W
Russellville, Oh., U.S.	218	38.51 N	83.47 W
Russellville, Or., U.S.	224	45.31 N	122.33 W
Rüsselsheim	56	50.00 N	8.25 E
Russi	66	44.22 N	12.02 E
Russia	216	40.14 N	84.24 W
Russia □ [1], Europe	72	60.00 N	80.00 E
Russia □ [1], Europe	74	60.00 N	100.00 E
Russian ≃	204	38.27 N	123.08 W
Russian Mission	180	61.47 N	161.19 W
Russiaville	216	40.25 N	86.16 W
Russka	76	58.59 N	28.30 E
Russkaja Bujlovka	78	50.22 N	40.03 E
Russkaja Gavan'	74	76.10 N	62.35 E
Russkaja Pol'ana	86	53.47 N	73.53 E
Russkaja Talovka	80	49.59 N	49.05 E
Russkaja Žuravka	80	50.21 N	40.33 E
Russkij	89	43.03 N	131.50 E
Russkij, ostrov I	74	77.00 N	96.00 E
Russkij Aktaš	80	55.02 N	52.07 E
Russkij Brod	76	52.36 N	37.22 E
Russkij Kameškir	80	52.52 N	46.06 E
Russkij Turek	80	57.03 N	50.13 E
Russkij Vožoj	80	56.57 N	53.22 E
Russkij Zavorot, mys ›	24	68.58 N	54.34 E
Russkoje	83	47.45 N	38.56 E
Russkoje-Dobrino	80	54.22 N	52.28 E
Russko-Vysockoje	265a	59.42 N	29.56 E
Rust, Dtsch.	58	48.16 N	7.43 E
Rust, Öst.	61	47.48 N	16.41 E
Rustajskij	80	56.31 N	44.49 E
Rustam	123	34.21 N	72.17 E
Rustavi	84	41.33 N	45.02 E
Rustburg	192	37.16 N	79.06 W
Rustenburg	158	25.37 S	27.08 E
Rustfontein	158	30.28 S	29.17 E
Rustic Canyon ∨	280	34.04 N	118.31 W
Rustig	158	27.22 S	27.09 E
Rustington	42	50.48 N	0.31 W
Ruston, La., U.S.	194	32.31 N	92.38 W
Ruston, Wa., U.S.	224	47.17 N	122.30 W
Rusville	273d	26.10 S	28.18 E
Rutana	154	3.55 S	30.00 E
Rutčenkovo	83	47.57 N	37.44 E
Rute	34	37.19 N	4.22 W
Rütenbrock	52	52.50 N	7.10 E
Ruteng	115b	8.36 S	120.27 E
Rutenga	154	21.08 S	30.45 E
Rutersville	222	29.57 N	96.48 W
Rutgers University ʋ [2], N.J., U.S.	276	40.30 N	74.27 W
Rutgers University (Newark) ʋ [2], N.J., U.S.	276	40.44 N	74.10 W
Rutgers University (Camden) ʋ [2], N.J., U.S.	285	39.56 N	75.07 W
Ruth, Ms., U.S.	194	31.22 N	90.18 W
Ruth, Nv., U.S.	204	39.16 N	114.59 W
Rüthen	52	51.29 N	8.25 E
Rutherford, Ca., U.S.	226	38.28 N	122.25 W
Rutherford, N.J., U.S.	210	40.49 N	74.06 W
Rutherford, Tn., U.S.	194	36.07 N	88.59 W
Rutherfordton	192	35.22 N	81.57 W
Rutherglen, Scot., U.K.	46	55.50 N	4.12 W
Ruther Glen, Va., U.S.	208	37.56 N	77.27 W
Ruthin	44	53.07 N	3.18 W
Ruthton	198	44.10 N	96.06 W
Ruthven, On., Can.	214	42.03 N	82.40 W
Ruthven, Ia., U.S.	198	43.07 N	94.53 W
Rüti	58	47.16 N	8.51 E
Rutigliano	68	41.01 N	17.00 E
Rutino	68	40.18 N	15.04 E
Rutka ≃	80	56.22 N	46.38 E
Rutland, B.C., Can.	182	49.53 N	119.24 W
Rutland, Fl., U.S.	220	28.51 N	82.13 W
Rutland, Il., U.S.	216	40.59 N	89.03 W
Rutland, Ma., U.S.	207	42.22 N	71.56 W
Rutland, N.D., U.S.	198	46.03 N	97.30 W
Rutland, Vt., U.S.	188	43.36 N	72.58 W
Rutland □ [6]	210	43.21 N	73.15 W
Rutland Island I	110	11.25 N	92.40 E
Rutland State Park ♠	207	42.23 N	72.01 W
Rutland Water ⊜ [1]	42	52.39 N	0.38 W
Rutledge, Ga., U.S.	192	33.37 N	83.36 W
Rutledge, Pa., U.S.	285	39.54 N	75.20 W
Rutledge, Tn., U.S.	192	36.16 N	83.30 W
Rutog	120	33.28 N	79.40 E
Rutshuru	154	1.11 S	29.27 E
Rüttenscheid ◆ [8]	263	51.26 N	7.00 E
Rutter	190	46.06 N	80.40 W
Rutul	84	41.33 N	47.25 E
Ruukki	26	64.40 N	25.06 E
Ruurlo	52	52.05 N	6.26 E
Ruvo del Monte	68	40.51 N	15.32 E
Ruvo di Puglia	68	41.07 N	16.29 E
Ruvu	154	6.48 S	38.39 E
Ruvu ≃	154	6.23 S	38.52 E
Ruvubu (Rovubu) ≃	154	2.23 S	30.47 E
Ruvuma □ [4]	154	11.00 S	36.00 E
Ruvuma (Rovuma) ≃	154	10.29 S	40.28 E
Ruwayān, Wādī ar- ⩱ [7]	142	29.07 N	30.10 E
Ruwaybah ⍑ [4]	140	15.39 N	28.45 E
Ruwayfī, Jabal ar- ∧	132	31.12 N	36.00 E
Ruwenzori National Park ♠	154	0.15 S	30.00 E
Ruwenzori Range ⋏	154	0.23 N	29.54 E
Ruwer	56	49.47 N	6.43 E
Ruwer ≃	56	49.47 N	6.42 E
Ruya (Luia) ≃	154	16.34 S	33.12 E
Ruyang	100	34.10 N	112.26 E
Ruy Barbosa	255	12.18 S	40.27 W
Ruyigi	154	3.29 S	30.15 E
Ruyton-Eleven-Towns	42	52.48 N	2.54 W
Ruza	82	55.42 N	36.12 E
Ruza ≃	82	55.38 N	36.17 E
Ruzajevka, Kaz.	86	52.49 N	66.57 E
Ruzajevka, Ross.	80	54.04 N	44.57 E
Ružany	76	52.52 N	24.53 E
Ružičnaja	78	49.24 N	26.58 E
Ružin	78	49.43 N	29.14 E
Ruzizi (Rusizi) ≃	154	3.16 S	29.14 E
Ružomberok	30	49.06 N	19.18 E
Ruzskoje vodochranilišče ⊜ [1]	82	55.47 N	36.00 E
Ruzyně ⊠	54	50.06 N	14.17 E
Ruzzah, Jabal ∧ [2]	142	30.01 N	30.26 E
Rwamagana	154	1.57 S	30.34 E
Rwanda □ [1], Afr.	138	2.00 S	30.00 E
Rwanda □ [1], Afr.	154	2.00 S	30.00 E
Rwashamaire	154	0.49 S	30.08 E
Ry	41	56.05 N	9.46 E
Ryal Fold	262	53.41 N	2.30 W
Ryan	196	34.01 N	97.57 W
Ryan ≃	182	50.25 N	122.43 W
Ryan, Loch ⊂	44	54.58 N	5.02 W
Ryan Peak ∧	202	43.54 N	114.25 W
Ryans Creek ≃	169	36.43 S	146.12 E
Ryarsh	260	51.19 N	0.24 E
Ryazan'			
→ R'azan'	80	54.38 N	39.44 E
Rybačij	76	55.09 N	20.51 E
Rybačij, poluostrov › [1]	24	69.42 N	32.36 E
Rybačje	86	46.27 N	81.32 E
Rybackaja ◆ [8]	265a	60.00 N	30.30 E
Rybackoje ◆ [8]	265a	59.50 N	30.30 E
Rybakovka	78	46.37 N	31.20 E
Rybinsk	76	58.03 N	38.52 E
Rybinsker Stausee			
→ Rybinskoje vodochranilišče ⊜ [1]	76	58.30 N	38.25 E
Rybinskije Budy	78	51.13 N	35.57 E
Rybinskoje	86	55.47 N	94.47 E
Rybinskoje vodochranilišče ⊜ [1]	76	58.30 N	38.25 E
Rybkino	80	54.15 N	43.46 E
Rybnaja Sloboda	80	55.28 N	50.09 E
Rybnica	78	47.45 N	29.01 E
Rybnik	30	50.06 N	18.32 E
Rybnoje, Ross.	76	54.44 N	39.30 E
Rybnoje, Ross.	86	58.08 N	94.30 E
Rybnovsk	89	53.12 N	141.50 E
Ryburn ≃	262	53.43 N	1.54 W
Rybuška	80	51.17 N	45.26 E
Rychwał	30	52.05 N	18.09 E
Ryčkovo	86	58.09 N	61.43 E
Rycroft	182	55.45 N	118.43 W
Ryd	26	56.28 N	14.41 E
Rydaholm	26	56.59 N	14.16 E
Rydal, Austl.	170	33.29 S	150.02 E
Rydal, Pa., U.S.	285	40.06 N	75.06 W
Rydalmere	274a	33.49 S	151.02 E
Rydbo	40	59.28 N	18.11 E
Ryde, Austl.	170	33.49 S	151.06 E
Ryde, Eng., U.K.	42	50.44 N	1.10 W
Ryder	198	47.55 N	101.40 W
Ryder's Hill ∧ [2]	42	50.31 N	3.53 W
Ryderwood	224	46.22 N	123.02 W
Rydsgård	41	55.28 N	13.35 E
Rydzyna	30	51.48 N	16.40 E
Rye, Austl.	169	38.23 S	144.49 E
Rye, Eng., U.K.	42	50.57 N	0.44 E
Rye, N.Y., U.S.	210	40.58 N	73.41 W
Rye, Tx., U.S.	222	30.27 N	94.46 W
Rye ≃	44	54.10 N	0.45 W
Ryegate	202	46.17 N	109.15 W
Rye Hills-Rye Brook	276	41.00 N	73.41 W
Rye Lake ⊜	276	41.04 N	73.43 W
Ryeosu			
→ Yŏsu	98	34.46 N	127.44 E
Rye Patch Reservoir ⊜ [1]	204	40.38 N	118.18 W
Ryer Island I	282	38.05 N	122.01 W
Ryes	32	49.19 N	0.37 W
Ryfoss	26	61.09 N	8.49 E
Ryfylke ◆ [1]	26	59.30 N	5.30 E
Rygge	26	59.23 N	10.43 E
Rygnestad	26	59.16 N	7.29 E
Ryhope	44	54.52 N	1.21 W
Rykaartspos	158	26.32 S	26.39 E
Ryker Lake ⊜	276	41.03 N	74.33 W
Rykerts	182	49.00 N	116.35 W
Ryki	30	51.39 N	21.56 E
Rykonec	76	59.33 N	36.34 E
Ryley	182	53.17 N	112.26 W
Rylovići	76	52.31 N	32.04 E
Ryl'sk	78	51.36 N	34.43 E
Rylstone	170	32.48 S	149.58 E
Rymanów	30	49.34 N	21.53 E
Rýmařov	30	49.56 N	17.16 E
Ryn	30	53.56 N	21.33 E
Rynfield	273d	26.09 S	28.20 E
Rynok	80	45.39 N	47.34 E
Ryn-Peski ◆ [2]	80	48.24 N	49.00 E
Ryō	270	34.44 N	135.55 E
Ryōhaku-sanchi ⋏	94	36.09 N	136.45 E
Ryojun			
→ Lüshun	98	38.48 N	121.16 E
Ryōkami	94	36.00 N	138.58 E
Ryōke	268	35.58 N	139.33 E
Ryōnan	96	33.15 N	133.55 E
Ryōtsu	92	38.05 N	138.26 E
Rypin	30	53.05 N	19.25 E
Ryškany	78	47.58 N	27.32 E
Ryslinge	41	55.15 N	10.33 E
Rysy ∧	30	49.12 N	20.04 E
Ryton	44	54.59 N	1.46 W
Ryton ≃	44	53.25 N	1.00 W
Ryton-on-Dunsmore	42	52.22 N	1.26 W
Ryūga-do ⩱ [5]	96	33.39 N	133.45 E
Ryūgasaki	94	35.54 N	140.11 E
Ryūjin	96	33.53 N	135.29 E
Ryukyu Islands			
→ Nansei-shotō II	90	26.30 N	128.00 E
Ryukyu Trench ✢ [1]	12	24.45 N	128.00 E
Ryūmon-dake ∧	270	34.26 N	135.53 E
Ryūō, Nihon	94	35.04 N	136.07 E
Ryūō, Nihon	94	35.39 N	138.30 E
Ryūsen	270	34.28 N	135.37 E
Ryūyō	94	34.40 N	137.48 E
Ržaksa	80	52.09 N	42.02 E
Ržanica	76	53.26 N	33.55 E
Ržava	78	51.14 N	36.43 E
Rzepin	30	52.22 N	14.50 E
Rzeszów	30	50.03 N	22.00 E
Rzeszów □ [4]	30	50.00 N	22.00 E
Ržev	76	56.16 N	34.20 E
Ržiščov	78	49.58 N	31.03 E
Ržovka ◆ [8]	265a	59.58 N	30.30 E
S			
Sa	110	18.34 N	100.45 E
Sa ≃	105	40.22 N	117.58 E
Saa	152	4.22 N	11.27 E
Sa'ad	132	31.28 N	34.32 E
Sa'ādatābād	128	30.06 N	53.08 E
Sääksjärvi ⊜	26	61.24 N	22.24 E
Saal	54	54.19 N	12.29 E
Saalach ≃	64	47.51 N	13.00 E
Saal an der Donau	60	48.54 N	11.56 E
Saal an der Saale	56	50.19 N	10.21 E
Saalbach	64	47.23 N	12.38 E
Saalburg	54	50.30 N	11.43 E
Saaldorf	54	50.27 N	11.41 E
Saale ≃	54	51.57 N	11.55 E
Saaler Bodden ⊂	54	54.20 N	12.28 E
Saales	58	48.21 N	7.07 E
Saaletalsperre ◆ [6]	54	50.30 N	11.35 E
Saalfeld	54	50.39 N	11.22 E
Saalfelden	64	47.25 N	12.51 E
Šaamar	88	50.08 N	106.10 E
Saâne ≃, Fr.	50	49.54 N	0.56 E
Saane ≃, Schw.	58	46.59 N	7.16 E
Saanen	58	46.29 N	7.16 E
Saanenmöser	58	46.31 N	7.18 E
Saanich Inlet ⊂	224	48.38 N	123.30 W
Saar (Sarre) ≃	56	49.42 N	6.34 E
Saarbrücken	56	49.14 N	6.59 E
Saarburg	56	49.36 N	6.33 E
Sääre	76	57.56 N	22.02 E
Saarelouis			
→ Saarlouis	56	49.21 N	6.45 E
Saaremaa I	76	58.25 N	22.30 E
Saarijärvi	26	62.43 N	25.16 E
Saaristomeren kansallispuisto ♠	26	59.50 N	21.50 E
Saarland □ [3]	56	49.20 N	7.00 E
Saarlautern			
→ Saarlouis	56	49.21 N	6.45 E
Saarlouis	56	49.21 N	6.45 E
Saarmund	264a	52.19 N	13.07 E
Saarn ◆ [8]	263	51.24 N	6.53 E
Saarnberg ◆ [8]	263	51.25 N	6.53 E
Saar			
→ Saarland □ [3]	56	49.20 N	7.00 E
Saas Almagell	58	46.07 N	7.58 E
Saas Fee	58	46.07 N	7.55 E
Saas Grund	58	46.08 N	7.56 E
Saastal ∨	58	46.10 N	7.56 E
Saatly	84	39.56 N	48.23 E
Saavedra	252	37.45 S	62.22 W
Saba I	238	17.38 N	63.10 W
Saba ≃, Nihon	96	34.02 N	131.30 E
Saba ≃, Ross.	76	59.08 N	29.00 E
Sabā', Wādī al- ∨	128	28.35 N	36.35 E
Saba Bank ✢ [2]	238	17.30 N	63.30 W
Šabac	38	44.45 N	19.42 E
Sabadell	34	41.33 N	2.06 E
Sabae	94	35.57 N	136.11 E
Sab'ah	142	30.15 N	32.33 E
Sabah □ [3]	112	5.20 N	117.10 E
Sabajevo	80	53.59 N	45.43 E
Sabak, Cape ›	181a	52.20 N	173.45 E
Sabak Bernam	114	3.46 N	100.59 E
Sabal	112	0.59 S	123.14 E
Sabalān ∧	128	38.15 N	47.48 E
Sabalana, Kepulauan II	112	6.45 S	118.50 E
Sabalgarh	124	26.15 N	77.24 E
Sabaluka Game Reserve ◆ [4]	140	16.18 N	32.40 E
Sabana	240m	18.20 N	65.44 W
Sabana, Archipiélago de II	240p	23.00 N	80.00 W
Sabana de La Mar	238	19.04 N	69.23 W
Sabana de Mendoza	246	9.26 N	70.46 W
Sabanagrande, Hond.	236	13.50 N	87.15 W
Sabana Grande, P.R.	240m	18.05 N	66.58 W
Sabanalamar, Ensenada ⊂	240p	21.36 N	78.44 W
Sabanalarga	246	10.38 N	74.55 W
Sabana Llana	240m	18.02 N	66.15 W
Sabancuy	232	18.58 N	91.11 W
Sabaneta, Rep. Dom.	238	19.30 N	71.21 W
Sabaneta, Ven.	246	8.46 N	69.56 W
Sabaneta, Puntan ›	174n	15.17 N	145.49 E
Sābang, India	126	22.11 N	87.36 E
Sabang (Dampelas), Indon.	112	0.11 N	119.51 E
Sabang, Indon.	114	5.55 N	95.19 E
Sabanillas	232	25.08 N	101.44 W
Šabanovo	82	55.38 N	38.43 E
Şabanözü	130	40.29 N	33.18 E
Sabará	255	19.54 S	43.48 W
Sabarei	154	4.20 N	36.55 E
Sābari ≃	122	17.34 N	81.15 E
Sābarmati ≃	120	22.18 N	72.22 E
Sabasṭīyah (Samaria)	132	32.17 N	35.12 E
Sab'atayn, Ramlat as- ⩱ [8]	144	15.30 N	46.10 E
Sabathu	123	30.59 N	76.59 E
Sabatini, Monti ⋏	66	42.10 N	12.15 E
Sabato ≃	66	41.08 N	14.45 E
Sabaudia	66	41.18 N	13.01 E
Sabaudia, Lago di ⊂	66	41.16 N	13.02 E
Sabaúna	256	23.29 S	46.05 W
Saba Wanak	144	10.33 N	44.08 E
Sabaya	248	19.01 S	68.23 W
Şabāyā, Jabal I	144	18.35 N	41.03 E
Sabažo	84	42.14 N	41.48 E
Sabbioneta	64	45.00 N	10.39 E
Sabe	272c	19.11 N	73.02 E
Šabel'kovka	83	48.45 N	37.29 E
Šabel'sk	83	46.51 N	38.29 E
Şāberī, Hāmūn-e ⊜	128	31.30 N	61.20 E
Sabetha	198	39.54 N	95.48 W
Sabhā, Lībiyā	146	27.03 N	14.26 E
Şabḥā, Urd.	132	32.20 N	36.30 E
Sābhār	126	23.51 N	90.15 E
Sabi (Save) ≃, Afr.	156	21.00 S	35.02 E
Sabi ≃, Nihon	94	36.48 N	140.04 E
Sabicy	76	58.50 N	29.18 E
Sabidana, Jabal ∧	140	18.04 N	36.50 E
Sabie	156	25.10 S	30.48 E
Sábiè ≃	156	25.19 S	32.18 E
Sabile	76	57.03 N	22.35 E
Sabillasville	208	39.42 N	77.27 W
Sabina	218	39.29 N	83.38 W
Sabina □ [9]	36	42.15 N	12.42 E
Sabinal	196	29.19 N	99.27 W
Sabinal ≃	196	29.06 N	99.27 W
Sabinal, Cayo I	240p	21.40 N	77.18 W
Sabiñánigo	34	42.31 N	0.22 W
Sabinas	232	27.51 N	101.07 W
Sabinas ≃, Méx.	232	27.37 N	100.42 W
Sabinas ≃, Méx.	232	26.51 N	99.34 W
Sabinas ≃, Méx.	234	22.59 N	98.58 W
Sabinas Hidalgo	232	26.30 N	100.10 W
Sabine ≃	178	30.00 N	93.45 W
Sabine, Mount ∧	169	38.38 S	143.44 E
Sabine, South Fork ≃	222	32.52 N	96.10 W
Sabine Bay ⊂	176	75.35 N	109.30 W
Sabine Lake ⊜	194	29.50 N	93.50 W
Sabine Pass ⊂	194	29.44 N	93.52 W
Sabine Peninsula › [1]	176	76.20 N	109.30 W
Sabini, Monti ⋏	66	42.13 N	12.50 E
Sabinópolis	255	18.40 S	43.06 W
Sabinov	30	49.06 N	21.06 E
Sabinsville	210	41.52 N	77.31 W
Sabir, Jabal ∧	144	13.30 N	44.03 E
Sabirabad	84	40.01 N	48.29 E
Šabla	38	43.32 N	28.32 E
Sabl'a, gora ∧	24	64.48 N	58.50 E
Sablayan	116	12.50 N	120.46 E
Sable, Anse au ⊂	275a	45.21 N	73.56 W
Sable, Cape ›	186	43.25 N	65.35 W
Sable, Cape › [1]	220	25.12 N	81.05 W
Sable, Île de I	160	19.15 S	159.56 E
Sable, Rivière du ≃	176	55.30 N	68.21 W
Sable Island I	186	43.55 N	59.50 W
Sables, Lac aux ⊜	206	46.53 N	72.22 W
Sables, River aux ≃	190	46.13 N	82.04 W
Sablé-sur-Sarthe	32	47.50 N	0.20 W
Sablinskoje	84	44.31 N	43.14 E
Sablūkah, Ash-Shallāl as- (Sixth Cataract) ⌞	140	16.20 N	32.42 E
Šablykino	76	52.51 N	35.12 E
Šabo, Centraf.	152	7.50 N	17.49 E
Šabo, Ukr.	78	46.08 N	30.23 E
Saboeiro	250	6.32 S	39.54 W
Sabogal ≃	236	10.55 N	84.43 W
Sāboli ◆ [8]	272a	28.43 N	77.18 E
Sabonkafi	150	14.38 N	8.45 E
Sabor ≃	34	41.10 N	7.07 W
Sabou	150	12.04 N	2.14 W
Sabourin, Lac ⊜	190	47.58 N	77.41 W
Sabra, Tanjung ›	164	2.17 S	132.19 E
Şabrātah	146	32.47 N	12.29 E
Sabres	32	44.09 N	0.44 W
Sabrevois	206	45.12 N	73.14 W
Sabrina Coast ⩱ [2]	9	67.00 S	119.30 E
Sabuda, Pulau I	164	2.38 S	131.36 E
Sabugal	34	40.21 N	7.05 W
Sabugo	266c	38.49 N	9.18 W
Sabuka	273b	4.27 S	15.10 E
Sabula	190	42.04 N	90.10 W
Sabunči	84	40.26 N	49.56 E
Sabuncu	130	39.33 N	30.12 E
Saburovo	265b	55.53 N	37.16 E
Saburovo ◆ [8]	265b	55.38 N	37.42 E
Şabyā	144	17.09 N	42.37 E
Sabyin	110	19.06 N	94.11 E
Sabyndy	86	50.53 N	70.33 E
Sabzevār	128	36.13 N	57.42 E
Sac ≃	194	38.01 N	93.43 W
Sacaba	248	17.23 S	66.02 W
Sacaca	248	18.05 S	66.26 W
Sacacomie, Lac ⊜	206	46.31 N	73.14 W
Sacagawea ≃	202	47.27 N	107.58 W
Sacajawea Peak ∧	202	45.15 N	117.17 W
Sacanche	248	7.05 S	76.44 W
Sacandaga ≃	210	43.19 N	73.50 W
Sacandaga, West Branch ≃	210	43.22 N	74.17 W
Sacandica	152	5.58 S	15.56 E
Sacaola	152	12.57 S	22.25 E
Sacariúna ≃	248	12.52 S	57.22 W
Sacaton	200	33.04 N	111.44 W
Sacavém	266c	38.47 N	9.06 W
Sačchere	84	42.21 N	43.23 E
Sac City	198	42.25 N	94.59 W
Sacco ≃	66	41.31 N	13.32 E
Sacedón	34	40.29 N	2.43 W
Săcele	38	45.37 N	25.42 E
Şaç Geçidi)(	130	39.54 N	42.22 E
Šacha ≃	82	56.45 N	39.10 E
Sachalin, ostrov (Sakhalin) I	89	51.00 N	143.00 E
Sachalin Oblast' □ [4]	89	51.00 N	143.00 E
Sachalinskij zaliv ⊂	89	53.45 N	141.30 E
Šachand	85	40.54 N	71.28 E
Sachayoj	252	26.41 S	61.50 W
Šachbuz	84	39.25 N	45.34 E
Šachdagskij chrebet ⋏	84	40.24 N	45.35 E
Saché	50	47.14 N	0.33 E
Šache ≃	84	43.47 N	39.27 E
Sachicapa	152	10.21 S	19.59 E
Sachigo ≃	176	55.06 N	88.58 W
Sachigo Lake ⊜	184	53.49 N	92.08 W
Sachimbo	152	9.14 S	20.16 E
Sachnovščina	78	49.08 N	35.53 E
Šachovskaja	76	56.02 N	35.29 E
Sachrang	64	47.41 N	12.15 E
Šachrichan	85	40.44 N	72.03 E
Šachrinau	85	38.34 N	68.20 E
Šachrisabz	72	39.03 N	66.50 E
Šachristan	85	39.47 N	68.49 E
Šachristan, pereval)(	85	39.33 N	68.33 E
Šachrovka	80	58.34 N	52.12 E
Sachse	222	32.59 N	96.36 W
Sachseln	58	46.52 N	8.15 E
Sachsen □ [3]	30	51.00 N	13.00 E
Sachsen □ [9]	30	52.45 N	9.30 E
Sachsen-Anhalt □ [3]	30	52.00 N	11.30 E
Sachsenbrunn	54	50.27 N	10.56 E
Sachsenburg	64	46.50 N	13.21 E
Sachsenhagen	52	52.24 N	9.16 E
Sachsenhausen, Dtsch.	54	52.47 N	13.14 E
Sachsenhausen, Dtsch.	56	51.15 N	9.00 E
Sachs Harbour	176	72.00 N	125.00 W
Sächsische Schweiz ◆ [1]	54	50.55 N	14.10 E
Šachterskij	180	64.42 N	177.40 E
Šachtinsk	86	49.40 N	72.37 E
Šachtnoje	83	47.57 N	38.17 E
Šacht'orsk, Ross.	89	49.11 N	142.07 E
Šacht'orsk, Ukr.	83	48.03 N	38.28 E
Šacht'orskij ◆ [8]	83	48.09 N	39.08 E
Šachty	83	47.42 N	40.13 E
Šachunja	80	57.40 N	46.37 E
Sachy	56	49.40 N	5.08 E
Sacile	64	45.57 N	12.30 E
Šack, Bela.	76	53.25 N	27.41 E
Šack, Ross.	80	54.01 N	41.43 E
Šack, Ukr.	78	51.31 N	23.57 E
Sackets Harbor	212	43.56 N	76.07 W
Sackville	186	45.54 N	64.22 W
Saclay	261	48.44 N	2.10 E
Saclay, Étang de ⊜	261	48.45 N	2.10 E
Saco, Me., U.S.	188	43.30 N	70.26 W
Saco, Mt., U.S.	202	48.27 N	107.20 W
Saco ≃	188	43.27 N	70.22 W
Saco Bay ⊂	188	43.30 N	70.15 W
Sacol Island I	116	6.58 N	122.13 E
Sacotes	266c	38.48 N	9.20 W
Sacra, Isola I	267a	41.45 N	12.15 E
Sacra Família do Tinguá	256	22.29 S	43.36 W
Sacramento, Bra.	255	19.53 S	47.27 W
Sacramento, Ca., U.S.	226	38.34 N	121.29 W
Sacramento □ [6]	226	38.35 N	121.30 W
Sacramento ≃, Ca., U.S.	204	38.03 N	121.56 W
Sacramento ≃, N.M., U.S.	200	32.16 N	105.31 W
Sacramento, Pampa del ⩨	248	8.00 S	75.50 W
Sacramento Metropolitan Airport ⊠	226	38.42 N	121.37 W
Sacramento Mountains ⋏	200	32.45 N	105.30 W
Sacramento River Deep Water Ship Channel ≊	226	38.15 N	121.40 W
Sacramento South	226	38.32 N	121.26 W
Sacramento Valley ∨	204	39.15 N	122.00 W
Sacramento Wash ∨	200	34.43 N	114.28 W
Sacre ≃	248	12.56 S	58.18 W
Sacré-Cœur ʋ [1]	261	48.53 N	2.21 E
Sacred Heart	198	44.47 N	95.21 W
Sacriston	44	54.49 N	1.37 W
Sacro, Monte ∧	68	40.13 N	15.20 E
Sacro Monte ʋ [1]	62	45.49 N	8.15 E
Sacrow ◆ [8]	264a	52.26 N	13.06 E
Sacrower See ⊜	264a	52.27 N	13.06 E
Săcueni	38	47.21 N	22.06 E
Sacul	222	31.50 N	94.56 W
Sacupana	246	8.35 N	61.39 W
Sada, Esp.	34	43.21 N	8.15 W
Sada, Nihon	96	35.15 N	132.43 E
Sádaba	34	42.17 N	1.16 W
Sadābād, India	124	27.27 N	78.03 E
Sa'dābād, Īrān	128	29.23 N	51.07 E
Sa'dābād, Īrān	128	34.51 N	50.36 E
Şadad	130	34.18 N	36.56 E
Şa'dah	144	16.52 N	43.37 E
Sadaik Taung ∧	110	15.09 N	98.12 E
Sadali	71	39.49 N	9.16 E
Sada-misaki ›	96	33.20 N	132.01 E
Sada-misaki-hantō › [1]	96	33.26 N	132.13 E
Sadamitsu	96	34.02 N	134.04 E
Sadane ≃	115a	6.01 S	106.37 E
Sadang ≃	112	3.43 S	119.27 E
Sadanga	116	17.09 N	121.02 E
Sadani	154	6.03 S	38.47 E
Sadao	110	6.38 N	100.26 E
Sadarpur, Bngl.	126	23.28 N	90.02 E
Sādarpur, India	272a	28.33 N	77.21 E
Sadčikovka	86	53.01 N	63.27 E
Sadda	120	33.42 N	70.20 E
Saddle ≃	276	40.52 N	74.07 W
Saddleback, Mount ∧	168a	32.58 S	116.28 E
Saddle Brook	276	40.54 N	74.06 W
Saddlebunch Keys II	220	24.37 N	81.37 W
Saddle Lake Indian Reserve ◆ [4]	182	54.00 N	111.40 W
Saddle Mountain ∧, Co., U.S.	200	38.50 N	105.28 W
Saddle Mountain ∧, Or., U.S.	224	45.58 N	123.41 W
Saddle Mountains ⋏	202	46.50 N	119.55 W
Saddle Mountain State Park ♠	224	45.58 N	123.41 W
Saddle Peak ∧	110	13.09 N	93.01 E
Saddle River	276	40.54 N	74.05 W
Saddle Rock	276	40.48 N	73.45 W
Saddleworth, Austl.	168b	34.05 S	138.47 E
Saddleworth, Eng., U.K.	262	53.33 N	1.59 W
Saddleworth Moor ◆ [3]	262	53.33 N	1.57 W
Sa Dec	110	10.18 N	105.46 E
Sadelkow	54	53.36 N	13.26 E
Sādhaura	124	30.23 N	77.13 E
Sādhuhāti	126	23.34 N	89.01 E
Sadieville	218	38.23 N	84.32 W
Sadiola	150	13.53 N	11.42 W
Sādiqābād	120	28.18 N	70.08 E
Sadiya	120	27.50 N	95.40 E
Sa'dīyah, Wādī ∨	144	20.35 N	39.38 E
Sa'dīyāt, Ra's as- ›	132	33.41 N	35.25 E
Sadler Lake ⊜	184	55.17 N	103.45 W
Sado I	92	38.00 N	138.25 E
Sado ≃	34	38.29 N	8.55 W
Sado-kaikyō ⩋	92	37.50 N	138.40 E
Sadon	84	42.51 N	44.00 E
Sadovoje, Ross.	80	46.56 N	44.23 E
Sadovoje, Ross.	80	47.46 N	44.30 E
Sadovoje Pervoje	78	51.33 N	40.29 E
Sadowara	92	32.02 N	131.26 E
Sādri	120	25.11 N	73.26 E
Šadrina	89	51.33 N	130.22 E
Šadrino	86	55.52 N	91.06 E
Šadrinsk	86	56.05 N	63.38 E
Sadsburyville	208	39.59 N	75.53 W
Sādulpur	123	28.38 N	75.24 E
Sädvaluspen	24	66.24 N	16.51 E
Sæby, Dan.	26	57.20 N	10.32 E
Sæby, Dan.	41	55.33 N	11.19 E
Saegertown	214	41.43 N	80.09 W
Sae Islands II	164	0.45 S	145.15 E
Saeki, Nihon	96	34.22 N	132.11 E
Saeki, Nihon	96	34.51 N	134.06 E
Saeki			
→ Saiki	96	32.57 N	131.54 E
Saengil-to I	98	34.19 N	126.59 E
Saerbeck	52	52.10 N	7.38 E

≃ River	Fluß	Río	Rivière	Rio
≊ Canal	Kanal	Canal	Canal	Canal
⌞ Waterfall, Rapids	Wasserfall, Stromschnellen	Cascada, Rápidos	Chute d'eau, Rapides	Cascata, Rápidos
⩋ Strait	Meeresstraße	Estrecho	Détroit	Estreito
⊂ Bay, Gulf	Bucht, Golf	Bahía, Golfo	Baie, Golfe	Baía, Golfo
⊜ Lake, Lakes	See, Seen	Lago, Lagos	Lac, Lacs	Lago, Lagos
⩨ Swamp	Sumpf	Pantano	Marais	Pântano
⍓ Ice Features, Glacier	Eis- und Gletscherformen	Accidentes Glaciales	Formes glaciaires	Acidentes glaciares
⍑ Other Hydrographic Features	Andere Hydrographische Objekte	Otros Elementos Hidrográficos	Autres données hydrographiques	Outros acidentes hidrográficos

✢ Submarine Features	Untermeerische Objekte	Accidentes Submarinos	Formes de relief sous-marin	Acidentes submarinos
□ Political Unit	Politische Einheit	Unidad Politica	Entité politique	Unidade política
ʋ Cultural Institution	Kulturelle Institution	Institución Cultural	Institution culturelle	Institução cultural
⊥ Historical Site	Historische Stätte	Sitio Histórico	Site historique	Sitio histórico
♠ Recreational Site	Erholungs- und Ferienort	Sitio de Recreo	Centre de loisirs	Area de Lazer
⊠ Airport	Flughafen	Aeropuerto	Aéroport	Aeroporto
■ Military Installation	Militäranlage	Instalación Militar	Installation militaire	Instalação militar
◆ Miscellaneous	Verschiedenes	Misceláneo	Divers	Diversos

Name	Page	Lat.°′	Long.°′
Saerluojia Hu ⊜	120	33.55 N	86.55 E
Særslev, Dan.	41	55.31 N	10.11 E
Særslev, Dan.	41	55.43 N	11.23 E
Saeul	56	49.44 N	5.59 E
Ṣafā, Tulūl aṣ- ∧[1]	132	33.02 N	37.12 E
Safad → Ẓefat	132	32.58 N	35.30 E
Safājah, Jazīrat I	140	26.45 N	33.59 E
Safakulevo	86	54.59 N	62.33 E
Ṣafānīyah	142	28.49 N	30.48 E
Safdar Jang Airport ⊠	272a	28.37 N	77.13 E
Safdar Jang's Tomb ⊥	272a	28.36 N	77.13 E
Safed Koh Range ⩘	123	33.58 N	70.25 E
Safe Harbor Dam ◈[6]	208	39.59 N	76.28 W
Safenbach ≃	61	47.06 N	16.05 E
Safety Bay	168a	32.18 S	115.43 E
Safety Harbor	220	27.59 N	82.41 W
Säffle	26	59.08 N	12.56 E
Safford	200	32.50 N	109.42 W
Saffron Walden	42	52.01 N	0.15 E
Safi	148	32.20 N	9.17 W
Safi □[4]	148	32.05 N	9.00 W
Safia	164	9.35 S	148.40 E
Ṣafīābād	128	36.45 N	57.58 E
Safīd ≃	120	36.44 N	65.38 E
Safīd Kūh, Selseleh-ye ⩘	128	34.30 N	63.30 E
Safidon	124	29.25 N	76.40 E
Safiental V	58	46.40 N	9.18 E
Safioune, Sebkhet ⩸	148	32.16 N	5.27 E
Safipur	126	23.01 N	90.22 E
Ṣāfītā	130	34.49 N	36.07 E
Safonovo, Ross.	24	65.42 N	47.39 E
Safonovo, Ross.	76	55.06 N	33.15 E
Safonovo, Ross.	82	55.33 N	38.17 E
Safrakköyü ◈[8]	267b	41.00 N	28.47 E
Safranbolu	130	41.15 N	32.45 E
Ṣafṭ al-ʿInab	142	30.49 N	30.41 E
Ṣafṭ al-Khammār	142	28.02 N	30.42 E
Ṣafṭ al-Laban	273c	30.02 N	31.10 E
Ṣafṭ al-Mulūk	142	30.49 N	30.41 E
Ṣafṭ Rāshīn	142	28.58 N	30.55 E
Ṣafṭ Turāb	142	30.54 N	31.07 E
Ṣafwān	128	30.07 N	47.43 E
Saga, Kaz.	86	50.23 N	64.15 E
Saga, Kaz.	86	49.25 N	55.17 E
Saga, Nihon	92	33.15 N	130.18 E
Saga, Nihon	96	33.05 N	133.06 E
Saga, Zhg.	120	29.30 N	85.22 E
Saga □[5]	96	33.21 N	130.28 E
Sagaba	152	11.17 S	23.07 E
Sagae	92	38.22 N	140.17 E
Sagaing	110	21.52 N	95.59 E
Sagaing □[8]	110	24.00 N	95.00 E
Sagak, Cape ≻	180	52.48 N	169.08 W
Ṣagalaherang	115a	6.40 S	107.39 E
Šagalakasa	80	46.54 N	50.43 E
Sagamāthā □[8]	124	27.15 N	86.45 E
Sagami ≃	94	35.19 N	139.22 E
Sagamihara	94	35.34 N	139.23 E
Sagamihara-daichi ⩘[1]	268	35.27 N	139.27 E
Sagamiko	94	35.37 N	139.12 E
Sagami-ko ⊜	94	35.35 N	139.16 E
Sagami-nada c	94	35.00 N	139.30 E
Sagami-wan c	94	35.15 N	139.25 E
Sagamore, Ma., U.S.	207	41.46 N	70.31 W
Sagamore, Pa., U.S.	214	40.46 N	79.13 W
Sagamore Beach	207	41.47 N	70.31 W
Sagamore Hill National Historic Site ⊥	276	40.53 N	73.30 W
Ṣagamore Hills	279a	41.02 N	81.26 W
Šagan ≃, Kaz.	86	50.37 N	79.15 E
Sagån ≃, Sve.	40	59.35 N	16.54 E
Saganaga Lake ⊜	190	48.14 N	90.52 W
Saganashkee Slough ≃	278	41.41 N	87.53 W
Saganash Lake ⊜	190	49.04 N	82.35 W
Saganoseki	96	33.15 N	131.53 E
Ṣaganthit Kyun I	110	11.56 N	98.29 E
Šagany, ozero ⊜	78	45.43 N	29.53 E
Sagan → Żagań	30	51.37 N	15.19 E
Sagaon	272c	19.12 N	73.06 E
Sāgar, India	122	14.10 N	75.02 E
Sāgar, India	124	23.50 N	78.43 E
Sagara	94	34.41 N	138.12 E
Sagaranten	115a	7.13 S	106.52 E
Sagard	54	54.31 N	13.33 E
Sāgardīghi	126	24.17 N	88.06 E
Sagaredžo	84	41.44 N	45.20 E
Sāgar Island I	126	21.43 N	88.06 E
Sagarmatha → Everest, Mount ∧	124	27.59 N	86.56 E
Sagarmatha National Park ♦	124	27.50 N	86.45 E
Sāgar Plateau ⩘[1]	124	23.30 N	78.30 E
Sagavanirktok ≃	180	70.20 N	148.00 W
Sagay	116	10.57 N	123.25 E
Sage, Mount ∧	240m	18.25 N	64.39 W
Sage Creek ≃, N.A.	202	48.58 N	110.06 W
Sage Creek ≃, U.S.	202	44.50 N	108.26 W
Sage Creek ≃, Mt., U.S.	202	47.16 N	109.43 W
Sage Creek ≃, Mt., U.S.	202	48.20 N	110.03 W
Sagemace Bay c	184	51.49 N	100.03 W
Sagerton	196	33.05 N	99.58 W
Saggaubach ≃	61	46.43 N	15.24 E
Sag Harbor	207	40.59 N	72.17 W
Ṣaghbīn	132	33.37 N	35.42 E
Ṣaghīr, Al-Baḥr aṣ- ≋	142	31.09 N	31.56 E
Sagil	86	50.20 N	91.40 E
Saginaw, Mi., U.S.	190	43.25 N	83.56 W
Saginaw, Tx., U.S.	222	32.52 N	97.22 W
Saginaw ≃	190	43.39 N	83.51 W
Saginaw Bay c	190	43.50 N	83.40 W
Sagiz, Kaz.	80	47.31 N	53.16 E
Sagiz, Kaz.	86	48.12 N	54.56 E
Sagiz ≃	86	47.32 N	53.20 E
Sağkaya	130	37.11 N	35.41 E
Sagleipie	150	7.00 N	8.52 W
Ṣaglek Bay c	176	58.35 N	63.00 W
Šaglyteniz, ozero ⊜	86	54.08 N	69.52 E
Šagonar	86	51.32 N	92.48 E
Sagra ∧	34	37.57 N	2.34 W
Sagrado	64	45.52 N	13.29 E
Sagres	34	37.00 N	8.56 W
Sag Sag	164	5.35 S	148.20 E
Sagsaj	86	48.54 N	89.37 E
Sagsajn ≃	102	44.50 N	96.26 E
Sagu, Indon.	112	8.15 S	123.13 E
Ṣagu, Rom.	38	46.03 N	21.17 E
Saguache	200	38.05 N	106.05 W
Saguache Creek ≃	200	37.52 N	105.51 W
Sagua de Tánamo	240p	20.35 N	75.14 W
Sagua la Chica ≃	240p	22.45 N	79.39 W
Sagua la Grande	240p	22.49 N	80.05 W
Saguaro National Monument ♦	200	32.12 N	110.38 W
Saguenay ≃	176	48.08 N	69.44 W
Saguna	272b	22.59 N	88.29 E
Sagunay Lake	216	41.43 N	86.34 W
Sagunovka	78	49.17 N	32.23 E
Sagunt	34	39.41 N	0.16 W
Saguny	78	50.36 N	39.43 E
Sagutjevo	76	52.28 N	33.28 E
Sāgwāra	120	23.41 N	74.01 E
Sagy	261	49.03 N	1.57 E
Sa'gya	120	28.55 N	88.05 E
Sagyndyk, mys ≻	84	44.02 N	50.52 E
Sah	150	15.38 N	4.03 W
Saḥāb	132	31.53 N	36.00 E
Sahaba	140	18.55 N	30.28 E
Sahagún, Col.	246	8.57 N	75.27 W
Sahagún, Esp.	34	42.22 N	5.02 W
Saḥam	132	32.42 N	35.47 E
Saḥam al-Jawlān	132	32.46 N	35.56 E
Sahana Ambodipont	157b	14.37 S	50.11 E
Sahand, Kūh-e ∧	128	37.44 N	46.27 E
Sahara ◈[2]	10	26.00 N	13.00 E
Sahāranpur	124	29.58 N	77.33 E
Sahara Occidentale → Western Sahara □[2]	148	24.30 N	13.00 W
Sahara Occidental → Western Sahara □[2]	148	24.30 N	13.00 W
Saharsa	124	25.53 N	86.36 E
Sahasinaka	157b	21.49 S	47.49 E
Sahasrail	126	23.19 N	89.43 E
Sahaswān	124	28.05 N	78.45 E
Sahel, Canal du ≋	150	13.44 N	6.05 W
Sahel, Oued ≃	34	36.26 N	4.33 E
Sahel → Sudan ◈[1]	134	10.00 N	20.00 E
Sāhibabad	272a	28.40 N	77.22 E
Sahibābad ◈[8]	272a	28.45 N	77.05 E
Sāhibganj	124	25.15 N	87.39 E
Sāhibi ≃	124	28.29 N	76.44 E
Ṣahin	130	41.01 N	26.50 E
Sāhīwāl, Pāk.	123	30.40 N	73.06 E
Sāhīwāl, Pāk.	123	31.58 N	72.20 E
Sahlenburg	52	53.52 N	8.38 E
Ṣaḥneh	128	34.29 N	47.41 E
Ṣaḥrā', Bi'r ⊤[4]	140	22.52 N	28.37 E
Ṣahrajat al-Kubrā wa Kafr Jirjis Yūsuf	142	30.38 N	31.17 E
Sahtlam	224	48.48 N	123.54 W
Sahuaripa	232	29.03 N	109.14 W
Sahuarita	200	31.57 N	110.58 W
Sahuayo de José María Morelos	234	20.04 N	102.43 W
Sahul Shelf ✣[4]	14	12.30 S	125.00 E
Sa Huynh	110	14.40 N	109.04 E
Ṣahwat al-Qamḥ	132	32.36 N	36.23 E
Šahy	30	48.05 N	18.57 E
Saï	150	13.50 N	5.00 W
Sai ≃, India	124	25.39 N	82.47 E
Sai ≃, Nihon	94	36.36 N	136.35 E
Sai ≃, Nihon	94	36.37 N	138.14 E
Saibai Island I	164	9.24 S	142.40 E
Sai Buri	110	6.42 N	101.37 E
Sai Buri ≃	110	6.43 N	101.39 E
Saïda	148	34.50 N	0.09 E
Saïda □[5]	148	33.00 N	0.30 W
Saidābād, Bngl.	126	24.18 N	89.43 E
Saʿīdābād, Īrān	267d	35.40 N	51.11 E
Saidaiji	96	34.39 N	134.02 E
Saïdia	148	35.04 N	2.15 W
Saʿīdīyeh	128	36.26 N	48.48 E
Saido	268	35.52 N	139.41 E
Saidor	164	5.35 S	146.30 E
Saidpur, Bngl.	124	25.47 N	88.54 E
Saidpur, India	124	25.33 N	83.11 E
Saidu	123	34.45 N	72.21 E
Saigawa	96	33.39 N	130.57 E
Saignelégier	58	47.15 N	7.00 E
Saignon	62	43.52 N	5.26 E
Saigō	92	36.12 N	133.20 E
Sai Gon ≃	269c	10.45 N	106.45 E
Saigon → Thanh Pho Ho Chi Minh	269c	10.45 N	106.40 E
Saihaku	96	35.20 N	133.20 E
Saihan Toroi	102	41.41 N	100.26 E
Saijō, Nihon	96	33.55 N	133.11 E
Saijō, Nihon	96	34.56 N	133.07 E
Saijō ≃	96	34.48 N	132.51 E
Saikai-kokuritsu-kōen ♦	92	33.12 N	129.22 E
Sai Keng	271d	22.26 N	114.16 E
Saiki	96	32.57 N	131.54 E
Saiki-wan c	96	33.00 N	131.58 E
Sai Kung	271d	22.23 N	114.15 E
Saileati	85	38.57 N	74.45 E
Sailkupa	126	23.41 N	89.15 E
Saillans	62	44.42 N	5.11 E
Sailly	261	49.02 N	1.48 E
Sailmouille, Ruisseau ≃	261	48.37 N	2.17 E
Sailolof	164	1.15 S	130.46 E
Sailor Creek ≃	202	42.56 N	115.29 W
Ṣail-sous-Couzan	62	45.44 N	3.57 E
Šaim	86	60.21 N	64.14 E
Saima	98	41.00 N	124.14 E
Saimaa ⊜	26	61.15 N	28.15 E
Saimaa Canal ≋	26	61.05 N	28.18 E
Saimbeyli	130	38.00 N	36.06 E
Saín Alto	234	23.35 N	103.15 W
Saindak	128	29.17 N	61.34 E
Ṣāʾīn Dezh	128	36.40 N	46.33 E
Sainghin-en-Weppes	50	50.33 N	2.54 E
Sainjang	98	39.15 N	125.51 E
Sainō-ha'iji ⊥	96	35.29 N	133.39 E
Sains-du-Nord	50	50.06 N	4.00 E
Sains-en-Gohelle	50	50.27 N	2.41 E
Sains-Richaumont	50	49.49 N	3.42 E
Saint Abb's Head ≻	46	55.54 N	2.09 W
Sainte-Adèle	206	45.57 N	74.07 W
Sainte-Adresse	50	49.30 N	0.05 E
Saint-Adrien	206	45.49 N	71.43 W
Saint-Affrique	32	43.57 N	2.53 E
Saint-Agapit	206	46.34 N	71.27 W
Saint Agatha	212	43.26 N	80.36 W
Sainte-Agathe, Mb., Can.	184	49.34 N	97.10 W
Sainte-Agathe, Fr.	62	45.49 N	3.37 E
Sainte-Agathe [-de-Lotbinière]	206	46.23 N	71.24 W
Sainte-Agathe-des-Monts	206	46.03 N	74.17 W
Sainte-Agnès, Fr.	62	43.48 N	7.28 E
Saint Agnes, Eng., U.K.	42	50.18 N	5.13 W
Saint Agnes I	42a	49.54 N	6.20 W
Saint-Agrève	62	45.01 N	4.24 E
Saint-Aignan	50	47.16 N	1.23 E
Saint-Aimé (Massueville)	206	45.55 N	72.56 W
Saint Albans, Austl.	169	37.44 S	144.48 E
Saint Albans, Austl.	170	33.17 S	150.59 E
Saint Alban's, Nf., Can.	186	47.52 N	55.51 W
Saint Albans, Eng., U.K.	42	51.46 N	0.21 W
Saint Albans, Mo., U.S.	219	38.35 N	90.46 W
Saint Albans, Vt., U.S.	188	44.48 N	73.05 W
Saint Albans, W.V., U.S.	188	38.23 N	81.50 W
Saint Albans □[8]	260	51.45 N	0.20 W
Saint Albans ◈[8]	276	40.42 N	73.46 W
Saint Albans, Cape ≻	168b	35.49 S	138.07 E
Saint Albans Cathedral ✝[1]	260	51.45 N	0.20 W
Saint Albert, Ab., Can.	182	53.38 N	113.38 W
Saint-Albert, P.Q., Can.	206	46.00 N	72.05 W
Saint Aldhelm's Head ≻	42	50.34 N	2.04 W
Saint-Alexandre-de-Kamouraska	186	47.41 N	69.38 W
Saint-Alexis-des-Monts	206	46.28 N	73.08 W
Saint-Amable	275a	45.39 N	73.18 W
Saint-Amand	56	48.49 N	4.36 E
Saint-Amand-en-Puisaye	50	47.31 N	3.04 E
Saint-Amand-les-Eaux	50	50.26 N	3.26 E
Saint-Amand-Longpré	50	47.41 N	1.01 E
Saint-Amand-Montrond	32	46.44 N	2.30 E
Saint-Amant-Roche-Savine	62	45.34 N	3.38 E
Saint-Amarin	58	47.53 N	7.01 E
Saint-Ambroix	62	44.15 N	4.11 E
Sainte-Amélie	184	50.59 N	99.21 W
Saint-Amour	58	46.26 N	5.21 E
Saint-André	157c	20.57 S	55.39 E
Saint-André, Cap ≻	157b	16.11 S	44.27 E
Saint-André, Ruisseau ≃	275a	45.22 N	73.29 W
Saint-André-Avellin	206	45.43 N	75.03 W
Saint-André-de-l'Eure	50	48.54 N	1.17 E
Saint-André-de-Valborgne	62	44.09 N	3.41 E
St.-André-Est	206	45.34 N	74.20 W
Saint-André-les-Alpes	62	43.58 N	6.30 E
Saint-André-les-Vergers	50	48.17 N	4.03 E
Saint Andrew	241g	13.15 N	59.33 W
Saint Andrew, Mount ∧	241h	13.11 N	61.13 W
Saint Andrew Lakes ⊜	212	44.36 N	76.40 W
Saint Andrews, N.B., Can.	186	45.05 N	67.03 W
Saint Andrews, Scot., U.K.	46	56.20 N	2.48 W
Saint Andrews, S.C., U.S.	192	32.46 N	79.59 W
Saint Andrews Bay c	46	56.22 N	2.50 W
Saint Andrew's Cathedral ✝[1]	271c	1.18 N	103.51 E
Saint Andrews Channel Ц	186	46.03 N	60.38 W
Saint Ann	219	38.43 N	90.22 W
Sainte-Anne, Guad.	241o	16.14 N	61.23 W
Saint Anne, Guernsey	43b	49.42 N	2.12 W
Sainte-Anne, Mart.	240e	14.26 N	60.53 W
Saint Anne, Il., U.S.	216	41.01 N	87.42 W
Sainte-Anne ≃	206	46.33 N	72.12 W
Saint Anne, Cathedral of ✝[1]	273b	4.18 S	15.19 E
Sainte Anne, Lac ⊜, Ab., Can.	182	53.43 N	114.27 W
Sainte-Anne, Lac ⊜, P.Q., Can.	186	50.05 N	67.50 W
Sainte-Anne-de-Beaupré	186	47.02 N	70.56 W
Sainte-Anne-de-Bellevue	275a	45.24 N	73.57 W
Sainte-Anne-de-la-Pérade	206	46.35 N	72.12 W
Sainte-Anne-de-Madawaska	186	47.15 N	68.02 W
Sainte-Anne-des-Chênes	184	49.40 N	96.40 W
Sainte-Anne-des-Monts	186	49.08 N	66.30 W
Sainte-Anne-des-Plaines	206	46.46 N	73.48 W
Saint Anne of the Congo ✝[1]	273b	4.16 S	15.17 E
Saint Anne's	44	53.45 N	3.02 W
Saint Ann's Bay	241q	18.26 N	77.08 W
Saint Anns Bay c	186	46.20 N	60.30 W
Saint Ann's Head ≻	42	51.41 N	5.10 W
Saint-Anselme	186	46.37 N	70.58 W
Saint Ansgar	190	43.22 N	92.55 W
Saint-Anthème	62	45.31 N	3.55 E
Saint Anthony, N.B., Can.	186	46.22 N	64.45 W
Saint Anthony, Nf., Can.	186	51.22 N	55.35 W
Saint Anthony, Id., U.S.	202	43.57 N	111.40 W
Saint-Antoine, P.Q., Can.	206	45.46 N	73.59 W
Saint-Antoine, Fr.	62	45.10 N	5.13 E
Saint-Antonin	32	44.09 N	1.45 E
Saint-Apollinaire (Francoeur)	206	46.37 N	71.31 W
Saint Arnaud, Austl.	166	36.37 S	143.15 E
Saint Arnaud, N.Z.	172	41.48 S	172.50 E
Saint-Arnoult, Forêt de ♦	261	48.35 N	1.55 E
Saint-Arnoult-en-Yvelines	50	48.34 N	1.56 E
Saint Arvans	42	51.40 N	2.41 W
Saint Asaph	44	53.16 N	3.26 W
Saint-Astier	32	45.09 N	0.32 E
Saint Athan	42	51.24 N	3.25 W
Saint-Auban	62	43.51 N	6.44 E
Saint-Aubert, Mont ∧[2]	50	50.39 N	3.24 E
Saint Aubert Island I	219	38.40 N	91.52 W
Saint-Aubin, Fr.	50	49.53 N	0.53 E
Saint-Aubin, Fr.	58	47.02 N	5.20 E
Saint Aubin, Jersey	43b	49.11 N	2.10 W
Saint-Aubin, Schw.	58	46.54 N	6.47 E
Saint-Aubin-d'Aubigné	32	48.15 N	1.36 W
Saint-Aubin-lès-Elbeuf	50	49.18 N	1.01 E
Saint-Aubin-sur-Aire	58	48.42 N	5.27 E
Saint-Augustin	157b	23.33 S	43.46 E
Saint-Augustin ≃	176	51.14 N	58.41 W
Saint-Augustin-Deux-Montagnes	275a	45.38 N	73.59 W
Saint Augustine	192	29.53 N	81.18 W
Saint-Augustin Nord-Ouest ≃	186	51.16 N	58.42 W
Saint-Augustin-Saguenay	186	51.14 N	58.39 W
Saint-Aulaye	32	45.12 N	0.08 E
Saint Austell	42	50.20 N	4.48 W
Saint-Avertin	50	47.22 N	0.44 E
Saint-Avold	56	49.06 N	6.42 E
Saint-Ay	50	47.51 N	1.45 E
Saint-Aygulf	62	43.23 N	6.44 E
Saint Barbe	186	51.12 N	56.46 W
Saint Barnabas Chapel ✝[1]	174c	29.02 S	167.55 E
Saint-Barthélemy I	238	17.54 N	62.50 W
Saint-Basile	186	47.21 N	68.14 W
Saint-Basile-de-Portneuf	206	46.45 N	71.49 W
Saint-Basile-le-Grand	206	45.32 N	73.17 W
Saint Bathans, Mount ∧	172	44.44 S	169.46 E
Sainte-Baume, Chaîne de la ⩘	62	43.20 N	5.45 E
Saint-Béat	32	42.55 N	0.42 E
Saint Bees	44	54.30 N	3.37 W
Saint Bees Head ≻	44	54.32 N	3.38 W
Saint Benedict	214	40.38 N	78.44 W
Saint-Benoît, Fr.	261	48.40 N	1.55 E
Saint-Benoît, Réu.	157c	21.02 S	55.43 E
Saint-Benoît-du-Sault	32	46.27 N	1.23 E
Saint-Benoît-en-Woëvre	56	48.59 N	5.47 E
Saint Bernard	218	39.10 N	84.29 W
Saint-Bernard, Île I	275a	45.23 N	73.45 W
Saint-Bernard-de-Dorchester	206	46.30 N	71.08 W
Saint-Béron	62	45.30 N	5.43 E
Saint-Blaise, P.Q., Can.	206	45.13 N	73.17 W
Saint-Blaise, Schw.	58	47.01 N	6.59 E
Saint-Blaise-la-Roche	58	48.24 N	7.10 E
Saint Blaize, Cape ≻	158	34.11 S	22.10 E
Saint Blazey	42	50.22 N	4.43 W
Saint-Blin	58	48.16 N	5.25 E
Saint-Bonaventure, P.Q., Can.	206	45.58 N	72.41 W
Saint Bonaventure, N.Y., U.S.	210	42.05 N	78.28 W
Saint-Boniface-de-Shawinigan	206	46.30 N	72.49 W
Saint-Bonnet	62	44.41 N	6.05 E
Saint-Bonnet-de-Joux	58	46.29 N	4.27 E
Saint-Bonnet-le-Château	62	45.25 N	4.04 E
Saint-Bonnet-le-Froid	62	45.09 N	4.27 E
Saint Boswells	46	55.34 N	2.39 W
Saint Brendan's	186	48.52 N	53.40 W
Saint-Brice-sous-Forêt	261	49.00 N	2.21 E
Saint Bride, Mount ∧	182	51.30 N	115.57 W
Saint Bride's	186	46.55 N	54.10 W
Saint Brides Bay c	42	51.48 N	5.15 W
Saint Bride's Major	42	51.28 N	3.38 W
Saint-Brieuc	32	48.31 N	2.47 W
Saint-Brieux	184	52.38 N	104.52 W
Saint-Broing-Les-Moines, Fr.	58	47.41 N	4.50 E
Saint-Broing-les-Moines, Fr.	58	48.32 N	6.36 E
Saint-Bruno	206	45.32 N	73.21 W
Saint-Bruno, Mont ∧[2]	275a	45.33 N	73.19 W
Saint-Calais	50	47.55 N	0.45 E
Saint-Calixte-de-Kilkenny	206	45.57 N	73.51 W
Saint-Cannat	62	43.37 N	5.18 E
Saint-Casimir	206	46.40 N	72.08 W
Saint-Cassien, Lac de ⊜[1]	62	43.35 N	6.48 E
Saint Catharines	212	43.10 N	79.15 W
Saint Catharines Airport ⊠	284a	43.11 N	79.10 W
Saint Catherine	220	28.37 N	82.08 W
Saint Catherine, Monastery of → Qiddīsah Kātrīnā, Dayr al- ✝[1]	140	28.29 N	34.01 E
Saint Catherine, Mount ∧	241k	12.10 N	61.40 W
Sainte-Catherine-de-Fierbois	50	47.09 N	0.39 E
Saint Catherines Island I	192	31.38 N	81.10 W
Saint Catherine's Point ≻	42	50.34 N	1.15 W
Saint-Célestin (Annaville)	206	46.13 N	72.26 W
Saint-Céré	32	44.52 N	1.53 E
Saint-Cergue	58	46.27 N	6.09 E
Saint-Césaire	206	45.25 N	73.00 W
Saint-Cézaire-sur-Siagne	62	43.39 N	6.48 E
Saint-Chamas	62	43.33 N	5.02 E
Saint-Chamond	62	45.28 N	4.30 E
Saint-Chaptes	62	43.58 N	4.17 E
Saint Charles, Ar., U.S.	194	34.22 N	91.08 W
Saint Charles, Id., U.S.	202	42.06 N	111.23 W
Saint Charles, Il., U.S.	216	41.54 N	88.18 W
Saint Charles, Md., U.S.	208	38.36 N	76.56 W
Saint Charles, Mi., U.S.	190	43.17 N	84.08 W
Saint Charles, Mn., U.S.	190	43.58 N	92.03 W
Saint Charles, Mo., U.S.	219	38.47 N	90.28 W
Saint Charles □[6]	219	38.47 N	90.43 W
Saint-Charles ≃	275a	45.40 N	73.27 W
Saint-Charles, Lac ⊜	206	46.55 N	71.23 W
Saint-Charles-de-Drummond	206	45.54 N	72.28 W
Saint Charles Mesa	198	38.15 N	104.32 W
Saint-Charles-sur-Richelieu	206	45.41 N	73.11 W
Saint-Chef	62	45.38 N	5.22 E
Saint-Chély-d'Apcher	32	44.48 N	3.17 E
Saint-Chéron	261	48.33 N	2.07 E
Saint-Christophe-en-Bazelle	50	47.11 N	1.43 E
Saint-Christophe-Nevis → Saint Kitts and Nevis □[1]	238	17.20 N	62.45 W
Saint Christopher (Saint Kitts) I	238	17.20 N	62.45 W
Saint Christopher-Nevis → Saint Kitts and Nevis □[1]	238	17.20 N	62.45 W
Saint-Chrysostome	206	45.06 N	73.46 W
Saint-Ciers-sur-Gironde	32	45.18 N	0.37 W
Saint Clair, Mi., U.S.	214	42.48 N	82.29 W
Saint Clair, Mo., U.S.	219	38.20 N	90.58 W
Saint Clair, Pa., U.S.	208	40.43 N	76.11 W
Saint Clair, Pa., U.S.	279b	40.16 N	79.33 W
Saint Clair □[6], Il., U.S.	219	38.31 N	90.00 W
Saint Clair □[6], Mi., U.S.	214	42.50 N	82.42 W
Saint Clair ≃	214	42.37 N	82.31 W
Saint Clair, Lake ⊜	214	42.25 N	82.41 W
Saint Clair Beach	281	42.19 N	82.51 W
Saint Clair Flats	214	42.32 N	82.37 W
Saint Clair Flats ≚	281	42.35 N	82.36 W
Saint Clair Flats Canal ≋	214	42.20 N	82.58 W
Saint Clair Flats State Wildlife Area ◈[4]	281	42.36 N	82.40 W
Saint Clair Haven	214	42.34 N	82.47 W
Saint Clair Shores	214	42.29 N	82.53 W
Saint-Clair-sur-Epte	50	49.12 N	1.41 E
Saint Clairsville, Oh., U.S.	214	40.04 N	80.54 W
Saint Clairsville, Pa., U.S.	214	40.09 N	78.31 W
Saint Clair Tunnel ◈[5]	214	42.57 N	82.25 W
Saint-Claud	32	45.53 N	0.23 E
Saint-Claude, Mb., Can.	184	49.40 N	98.22 W
Saint-Claude, Fr.	58	46.23 N	5.52 E
Saint-Claude, Guad.	241o	16.02 N	61.42 W
Saint-Claude, Ruisseau ≃	275a	45.25 N	73.28 W
Saint Clears	42	51.50 N	4.30 W
Saint Clements	212	43.31 N	80.39 W
Saint Clements Bay c	208	38.17 N	76.42 W
Sainte-Clothilde	206	45.59 N	72.14 W
Sainte-Clotilde-de-Châteauguay	206	45.10 N	73.41 W
Saint-Cloud, Fr.	50	48.50 N	2.11 E
Saint Cloud, Fl., U.S.	220	28.14 N	81.16 W
Saint Cloud, Mn., U.S.	190	45.33 N	94.09 W
Saint-Cloud, Parc de ♦	261	48.50 N	2.13 E
Saint-Colomban-des-Villards	62	45.18 N	6.14 E
Sainte-Colombe	58	47.52 N	4.32 E
Saint Columb Major	42	50.26 N	4.56 W
Saint Combs	46	57.39 N	1.54 W
Saint-Constant	206	45.22 N	73.37 W
Saint-Cosme-en-Vairais	50	48.16 N	0.28 E
Sainte-Croix, P.Q., Can.	206	46.38 N	71.44 W
Sainte-Croix, Schw.	58	46.49 N	6.31 E
Saint Croix I	241n	17.45 N	64.45 W
Saint Croix ≃, N.A.	186	45.10 N	67.10 W
Saint Croix ≃, U.S.	190	44.45 N	92.49 W
Sainte-Croix-aux-Mines	58	48.16 N	7.13 E
Saint Croix Falls	190	45.24 N	92.38 W
Saint Croix Island I	158	33.48 S	25.45 E
Saint Croix Island National Monument ♦	188	45.08 N	67.08 W
Saint Croix National Scenic Riverway ♦	190	46.00 N	92.25 W
Saint Croix State Park ♦	190	46.00 N	92.40 W
Sainte-Croix-Vallée-Francaise	62	44.11 N	3.44 E
Saint-Cuthbert	206	46.09 N	73.14 W
Saint-Cyprien	32	44.52 N	1.02 E
Saint-Cyrille-de-Wendover	206	45.56 N	72.26 W
Saint-Cyr-L'École	50	48.48 N	2.04 E
Saint-Cyr-l'École, Aérodrome de ⊠	261	48.49 N	2.04 E
Saint Cyr Range ⩘	180	61.10 N	131.10 W
Sainte-Cyr-sous-Dourdan	261	48.34 N	2.02 E
Saint-Cyr-sur-Loire	50	47.24 N	0.40 E
Saint-Cyr-sur-Mer	62	43.11 N	5.43 E
Saint-Dalmas-de-Tende	62	44.03 N	7.35 E
Saint-Damien-de-Brandon	206	46.20 N	73.29 W
Saint David, Az., U.S.	200	31.54 N	110.12 W
Saint David, Il., U.S.	190	40.29 N	90.02 W
Saint David's, Nf., Can.	186	48.12 N	58.52 W
Saint Davids, On., Can.	284a	43.10 N	79.06 W
Saint David's, Wales, U.K.	42	51.54 N	5.16 W
Saint Davids, Pa., U.S.	285	40.02 N	75.22 W
Saint David's Cathedral ✝[1]	42	51.54 N	5.16 W
Saint David's Head ≻	42	51.55 N	5.19 W
Saint David's Island I	240a	32.22 N	64.39 W
Saint Day	42	50.14 N	5.11 W
Saint-Denis, Fr.	50	48.56 N	2.22 E
Saint-Denis, Réu.	157c	20.52 S	55.28 E
Saint-Denis, Basilique ✝[1]	261	48.56 N	2.22 E
Saint-Denis-de-l'Hôtel	50	47.52 N	2.07 E
Saint-Denis-en-Bugey	58	45.57 N	5.20 E
Saint-Denis-Rivière-Richelieu	206	45.47 N	73.09 W
Saint Dennis	42	50.23 N	4.53 W
Saint-Didier-en-Velay	62	45.18 N	4.17 E
Saint-Didier-les-Bains	62	44.00 N	5.07 E
Saint-Dié	58	48.17 N	6.57 E
Saint-Disdier	62	44.44 N	5.54 E
Saint-Dizier	58	48.38 N	4.57 E
Saint Dogmaels	42	52.05 N	4.40 W
Saint-Donat-de-Montcalm	206	46.19 N	74.13 W
Saint-Donat-sur-l'Herbasse	62	45.07 N	5.00 E
Sainte-Dorothée ◈[8]	275a	45.32 N	73.49 W
Saint-Dyé-sur-Loire	50	47.39 N	1.29 E
Saint-Édouard-de-Maskinongé	206	46.20 N	73.09 W
Saint Edward	198	41.34 N	97.52 W
Saint-Égrève	62	45.14 N	5.41 E
Saint Eleanor's	186	46.25 N	63.49 W
Saint Elias, Cape ≻	180	59.52 N	144.30 W
Saint Elias, Mount ∧	180	60.18 N	140.55 W
Saint Elias Mountains ⩘	180	60.30 N	139.30 W
Saint-Élie	250	4.50 N	53.17 W
Saint Elmo	219	39.01 N	88.50 W
Saint-Éloi	186	48.02 N	69.14 W
Saint-Émile-de-Montcalm	206	46.06 N	74.00 W
Saint-Émile-de-Québec	206	46.52 N	71.20 W
Saint-Émile-de-Suffolk	206	45.56 N	74.55 W
Sainte-Enimie	32	44.22 N	3.26 E
Saint-Épain	50	47.08 N	0.32 E
Saint-Esprit ≃	206	45.52 N	73.27 W
Saint-Étienne	62	45.26 N	4.24 E
Saint-Étienne-de-Lugdarès	62	44.39 N	3.57 E
Saint-Étienne-de-Saint-Geoirs	62	45.20 N	5.21 E
Saint-Étienne-des-Grès	206	46.26 N	72.46 W
Saint-Étienne-de-Tinée	62	44.15 N	6.55 E
Saint-Étienne-du-Rouvray	50	49.23 N	1.06 E
Saint-Étienne-en-Dévoluy	62	44.42 N	5.56 E
Saint-Étienne-le-Laus	62	44.30 N	6.10 E
Saint-Étienne-les-Orgues	62	44.03 N	5.47 E
Saint-Étienne-lès-Remiremont	58	48.02 N	6.37 E
Saint-Eugène	206	45.30 N	74.28 W
Saint-Eustache	206	45.34 N	73.54 W
Saint-Evroult-Notre-Dame-du-Bois	50	48.48 N	0.28 E
Saint-Fabien	186	48.18 N	68.52 W
Saint Faith's	158	30.30 S	30.12 E
Saint-Fargeau	50	47.38 N	3.04 E
Saint-Fargeau-Ponthierry	261	48.33 N	2.32 E
Saint-Félicien, P.Q., Can.	176	48.39 N	72.26 W
Saint-Félicien, Fr.	62	45.05 N	4.38 E
Sainte-Félicité	186	48.54 N	67.20 W
Saint-Félix	62	45.48 N	5.58 E
Saint-Félix-de-Kingsey	206	45.48 N	72.12 W
Saint-Félix-de-Valois	206	46.10 N	73.26 W
Saint-Ferdinand (Bernierville)	206	46.06 N	71.34 W
Saintfield	48	54.28 N	5.50 W
Saint Fillans	46	56.23 N	4.07 W
Saint-Firmin	62	44.47 N	6.02 E
Saint-Firmin-sur-Loire	50	47.37 N	2.44 E
Saint-Flavien	206	46.31 N	71.36 W
Saint-Florent	36	42.41 N	9.18 E
Saint-Florentin	50	48.00 N	3.44 E
Saint-Florent-sur-Cher	32	46.59 N	2.15 E
Saint-Floris, Parc National ♦	146	9.40 N	21.35 E
Saint-Flour	32	45.02 N	3.05 E
Saint-Fons	62	45.42 N	4.52 E
Saint-Fortunat	206	45.58 N	71.36 W
Sainte-Foy	206	46.47 N	71.17 W
Sainte-Foy-la-Grande	32	44.50 N	0.13 E
Sainte-Foy-l'Argentière	62	45.42 N	4.28 E
Sainte-Foy-lès-Lyon	62	45.44 N	4.48 E
Sainte-Foy-Tarentaise	62	45.35 N	6.53 E
Saint Francis, Ks., U.S.	198	39.46 N	101.47 W
Saint Francis, S.D., U.S.	198	43.08 N	100.54 W
Saint Francis, Wi., U.S.	216	42.58 N	87.52 W
Saint Francis ≃, N.A.	186	47.10 N	68.57 W
Saint Francis ≃, U.S.	194	34.38 N	90.35 W
Saint Francis, Cape ≻, Nf., Can.	186	47.50 N	52.47 W
Saint Francis, Cape ≻, S. Afr.	158	34.14 S	24.49 E
Saint Francis, Lake ⊜	206	45.08 N	74.25 W
Saint Francis Bay c	158	34.35 S	25.10 E
Saint Francisville	194	30.46 N	91.22 W
Saint-François	241o	16.15 N	61.17 W
Saint-François ≃	206	46.07 N	72.55 W
Saint-François, Lac ⊜	206	45.55 N	71.10 W
Saint-François de Boundji	152	1.03 S	15.22 E
Saint-François-de-Laval ◈[8]	275a	45.40 N	73.34 W
Saint-François-du-Lac	206	46.04 N	72.50 W
Saint Francois Mountains ⩘[2]	194	37.30 N	90.35 W
Saint-François-sur-Bugeon	62	45.24 N	6.21 E
Saint-Front	62	44.59 N	4.08 E
Saint-Gabriel	206	46.17 N	73.23 W
Saint-Gabriel-de-Gaspé	186	48.31 N	64.32 W
Saint-Gabriel-de-Rimouski	186	48.25 N	68.10 W
Saint-Gall → Sankt Gallen	58	47.25 N	9.23 E
Saint-Galmier	62	45.35 N	4.19 E
Sainte-Gauburge-Sainte-Colombe	50	48.42 N	0.26 E
Saint-Gaudens	32	43.07 N	0.44 E
Saint-Gaudens National Historic Site ⊥	188	43.29 N	72.19 W
Saint-Gaultier	32	46.38 N	1.25 E
Saint-Gély-du-Fesc	62	43.42 N	3.48 E
Saint-Genest-Lerpt	62	45.27 N	4.20 E
Saint-Genest-Malifaux	62	45.20 N	4.25 E
Sainte-Geneviève, P.Q., Can.	275a	45.29 N	73.52 W
Sainte Genevieve, Mo., U.S.	194	37.59 N	90.03 W
Sainte-Geneviève-de-Batiscan	206	46.32 N	72.20 W
Sainte-Geneviève-des-Bois	50	48.38 N	2.20 E
Saint-Gengoux-le-National	58	46.37 N	4.39 E
Saint-Genis-de-Saintonge	32	45.29 N	0.34 W
Saint-Genis-Laval	62	45.41 N	4.48 E
Saint-Genis-Pouilly	58	46.15 N	6.01 E
Saint-Genix-sur-Guiers	62	45.36 N	5.38 E
Saint-Geoire-en-Valdaine	62	45.27 N	5.38 E
Saint George, Austl.	166	28.02 S	148.35 E
Saint George, Ber.	240a	32.22 N	64.40 W
Saint George, N.B., Can.	186	45.08 N	66.49 W
Saint George, On., Can.	212	43.15 N	80.15 W
Saint George, Pa., U.S.	214	41.15 N	79.47 W
Saint George, S.C., U.S.	192	33.11 N	80.34 W
Saint George, Ut,. U.S.	200	37.06 N	113.34 W
Saint George ◈[8]	276	40.39 N	74.05 W
Saint George, Cape ≻, Nf., Can.	186	48.27 N	59.15 W
Saint George, Cape ≻, Pap. N. Gui.	164	4.52 S	152.52 E
Saint George, Cape ≻, Fl., U.S.	192	29.35 N	85.04 W
Saint George, Point ≻	204	41.47 N	124.15 W
Saint George Island, Ak., U.S.	180	56.36 N	169.32 W
Saint George Island, Md., U.S.	208	38.07 N	76.29 W
Saint George Island I, Ak., U.S.	180	56.35 N	169.35 W
Saint George Island I, Fl., U.S.	192	29.39 N	84.55 W
Saint George's, Nf., Can.	186	48.26 N	58.29 W
Saint-Georges, P.Q., Can.	188	46.07 N	70.40 W
Saint-Georges, P.Q., Can.	206	46.37 N	72.40 W
Saint-Georges, Fr.	58	48.40 N	6.56 E
Saint George's, Gren.	241k	12.03 N	61.45 W
Saint-Georges, Guy. fr.	250	3.54 N	51.48 W
Saint Georges, De., U.S.	208	39.33 N	75.39 W
Saint Georges Basin c	170	35.07 S	150.36 E
Saint George's Bay c, Nf., Can.	186	48.20 N	59.00 W
Saint Georges Bay c, N.S., Can.	186	45.50 N	61.45 W
Saint George's Channel Ц, Europe	28	52.00 N	6.00 W
Saint George's Channel Ц, Pap. N. Gui.	164	4.30 S	152.30 E
Saint-Georges-de-Reneins	58	46.04 N	4.43 E
Saint-Georges-de-Windsor	206	45.42 N	71.50 W
Saint-Georges-en-Couzan	62	45.42 N	3.56 E
Saint Georges Head ≻	170	35.12 S	150.42 E
Saint George's Island I	240a	32.22 N	64.40 W
Saint George Sound Ц	192	29.47 N	84.42 W
Saint-Gérard, Bel.	56	50.21 N	4.45 E
Saint-Gérard, P.Q., Can.	206	45.46 N	71.25 W
Saint-Germain	32	48.54 N	2.05 E
Saint-Germain ≃	206	45.55 N	72.30 W
Saint-Germain, Forêt de ♦	261	48.55 N	2.05 E
Saint-Germain-de-Calberte	62	44.13 N	3.48 E
Saint-Germain-de-Grantham	206	45.50 N	72.34 W
Saint-Germain-de-Joux	58	46.11 N	5.44 E
Saint-Germain-des-Champs	50	47.25 N	3.55 E
Saint-Germain-du-Bois	58	46.45 N	5.15 E
Saint-Germain-du-Plain	58	46.42 N	4.58 E
Saint-Germain-en-Laye	50	48.54 N	2.05 E
Saint-Germain-en-Laye, Château de ⊥	261	48.54 N	2.06 E
Saint-Germain-Laval	62	45.50 N	4.01 E
Saint-Germain-Laxis	261	48.35 N	2.43 E
Saint-Germain-Lembron	32	45.28 N	3.14 E
Saint-Germain-lès-Arlay	58	46.46 N	5.34 E
Saint-Germain-lès-Corbeil	261	48.37 N	2.29 E
Saint-Germain-l'Herm	32	45.28 N	3.33 E
Saint-Germain-sur-Morin	261	48.53 N	2.51 E
Saint Germans	42	50.24 N	4.18 W
Saint-Germer-de-Fly	50	49.27 N	1.47 E
Saint-Gervais-d'Auvergne	32	46.02 N	2.49 E
Saint-Gervais-les-Bains	62	45.54 N	6.43 E
Saint-Gervasy	62	43.53 N	4.29 E
Saint-Géry	32	44.29 N	1.35 E
Saint-Gilles, Bel.	50	50.49 N	4.20 E
Saint-Gilles, P.Q., Can.	206	46.31 N	71.22 W
Saint-Gilles, Fr.	62	43.41 N	4.26 E
Saint-Gilles-Croix-de-Vie	32	46.42 N	1.57 W
Saint-Gingolph	58	46.24 N	6.52 E
Saint-Girons	32	42.59 N	1.09 E
Saint-Gobain	50	49.36 N	3.23 E
Saint Gotthard Pass → San Gottardo, Passo del)(	58	46.33 N	8.34 E
Saint Govan's Head ≻	42	51.36 N	4.55 W
Saint-Gratien	261	48.58 N	2.17 E
Saint-Grégoire (Larochelle)	206	46.16 N	72.30 W
Saint Gregory, Mount ∧	186	49.19 N	58.13 W
Saint-Guénolé	32	47.49 N	4.20 W
Saint-Guillaume-d'Upton	206	45.53 N	72.46 W

Symbols in the index entries represent the broad categories identified in the key at the right. Symbols with superior numbers (⩘[1]) identify subcategories (see complete key on page *I · 1*).

Symbole im Register stellen die rechts im Schlüssel erklärten Kategorien dar. Symbole mit hochgestellten Ziffern (⩘[1]) bezeichnen Unterabteilungen einer Kategorie (vgl. vollständiger Schlüssel auf Seite *I · 1*).

Los símbolos incluídos en el texto del índice representan las grandes categorias identificadas con la clave a la derecha. Los símbolos con numeros en su parte superior (⩘[1]) identifican las subcategorías (véase la clave completa en la página *I · 1*).

Les symboles de l'index représentent les catégories indiquées dans la légende à droite. Les symboles suivis d'un indice (⩘[1]) représentent des sous-catégories (voir légende complète à la page *I · 1*).

Os símbolos incluídos no texto do índice representam as grandes categorias identificadas com a chave à direita. Os símbolos com números em sua parte superior (⩘[1]) identificam as subcategorias (veja-se a chave completa à página *I · 1*).

∧ Mountain	Berg	Montaña	Montagne	Montanha
⩘ Mountains	Gebirge	Montañas	Montagnes	Montanhas
)(Pass	Paß	Paso	Col	Passo
V Valley, Canyon	Tal, Cañon	Valle, Cañón	Vallée, Canyon	Vale, Canhão
≚ Plain	Ebene	Llano	Plaine	Planície
≻ Cape	Kap	Cabo	Cap	Cabo
I Island	Insel	Isla	Île	Ilha
II Islands	Inseln	Islas	Îles	Ilhas
♦ Other Topographic Features	Andere Topographische Objekte	Otros Elementos Topográficos	Autres données topographiques	Outros acidentes topográficos

ESPAÑOL — Nombre · Página · Lat.°′ · Long.°′ W = Oeste
FRANÇAIS — Nom · Page · Lat.°′ · Long.°′ W = Ouest
PORTUGUÊS — Nome · Página · Lat.°′ · Long.°′ W = Oeste

Saint-Héand 62 45.31 N 4.22 E
Saint Helena 226 38.30 N 122.28 W
Saint Helena □² 10 15.57 S 5.42 W
Saint Helena, Mount ^ 226 38.40 N 122.38 W
Saint Helena Sound ⌇ 192 32.27 N 80.25 W
Sainte-Hélène, Île I 275a 45.31 N 73.32 W
Sainte-Hélène-de-Bagot 206 45.44 N 72.44 W
Saint Helens, Austl. 166 41.20 S 148.15 E
Saint Helens, Eng., U.K. 42 50.42 N 1.06 W
Saint Helens, Eng., U.K. 44 53.28 N 2.44 W
Saint Helens, Or., U.S. 224 45.51 N 122.48 W
Saint Helens □⁸ 262 53.28 N 2.45 W
Saint Helens, Mount ^¹ 224 46.12 N 122.11 W
Saint Helens Canal ≅ 262 53.27 N 2.42 W
Saint Helier 43b 49.11 N 2.06 W
Saint Henry 216 40.25 N 84.38 W
Sainte-Hermine 32 46.33 N 1.04 W
Saint-Hilaire-du-Harcouët 32 48.35 N 1.06 W
Saint-Hilarion 261 48.37 N 1.44 E
Saint-Hippolyte, Fr. 58 47.19 N 6.49 E
Saint-Hippolyte, Fr. 62 43.38 N 4.45 E
Saint-Hippolyte-de-Kilkenny 206 45.56 N 74.01 W
Saint-Hippolyte-du-Fort 62 43.58 N 3.51 E
Saint-Honorat, Mont ^ 62 44.05 N 6.46 E
Saint-Hubert, Bel. 56 50.01 N 5.23 E
Saint-Hubert, P.Q., Can. 206 45.30 N 73.25 W
Saint-Hubert, Étang de ⊜ 261 48.43 N 1.51 E
Saint-Hubert-le-Roi 261 48.43 N 1.52 E
Saint-Hugues 206 45.48 N 72.52 W
Saint-Hyacinthe 206 45.37 N 72.57 W
Saint-Hyacinthe □⁶ 206 45.40 N 73.05 W
Saint-Ignace, N.B., Can. 186 46.42 N 65.05 W
Saint Ignace, Mi., U.S. 190 45.52 N 84.43 W
Saint Ignace Island I 190 48.48 N 87.55 W
Saint Ignatius, Guy. 246 3.20 N 59.47 W
Saint Ignatius, Mt., U.S. 202 47.19 N 114.05 W
Saint-Imier 58 47.09 N 7.00 E
Saint-Imier, Vallon de V 58 47.10 N 7.00 E
Saint-Isidore 186 47.33 N 65.03 W
Saint-Isidore-d'Auckland 206 45.16 N 71.31 W
Saint-Isidore-de-Laprairie 275a 45.18 N 73.41 W
Saint Ives, Austl. 274a 33.44 S 151.10 E
Saint Ives, Eng., U.K. 32 50.12 N 5.29 W
Saint Ives, Eng., U.K. 42 52.20 N 0.05 W
Saint Ives Bay c 42 50.14 N 5.28 W
Saint Jacob 219 38.43 N 89.46 W
Saint Jacobs 212 43.32 N 80.33 W
Saint-Jacques 206 45.57 N 73.34 W
Saint-Jacques ≐ 275a 45.26 N 73.29 W
Saint James, Il., U.S. 219 38.57 N 88.51 W
Saint James, Mi., U.S. 190 45.45 N 85.30 W
Saint James, Mn., U.S. 198 43.58 N 94.37 W
Saint James, Mo., U.S. 194 37.59 N 91.36 W
Saint James, N.Y., U.S. 210 40.52 N 73.09 W
Saint James, Cape > 182 51.56 N 131.01 W
Saint James City 220 26.29 N 82.04 W
Saint James Islands II 240m 18.19 N 64.50 W
Saint-Janvier 275a 45.43 N 73.56 W
Saint-Jean □⁶ 206 45.15 N 73.20 W
Saint-Jean ≐, P.Q., Can. 186 48.46 N 64.26 W
Saint-Jean ≐, P.Q., Can. 186 50.17 N 64.20 W
Saint-Jean, Île I 275a 45.41 N 73.39 W
Saint-Jean, Lac ⊜ 176 48.35 N 72.05 W
Saint-Jean, Rapides de ⌊ 275a 45.19 N 73.15 W
Saint-Jean Airport ⊠ 275a 45.18 N 73.17 W
Saint-Jean-aux-Bois 50 49.21 N 2.55 E
Saint-Jean-Baptiste 184 49.16 N 97.21 W
Saint-Jean-Baptiste-de-Rouville 206 45.31 N 73.07 W
Saint-Jean-Cap-Ferrat 62 43.41 N 7.20 E
Saint-Jean-d'Angély 32 45.57 N 0.31 W
Saint-Jean-d'Assé 50 48.09 N 0.07 E
Saint-Jean-de-Bournay 62 45.29 N 5.08 E
Saint-Jean-de-Braye 50 47.54 N 1.58 E
Saint-Jean-de-la-Ruelle 50 47.55 N 1.52 E
Saint-Jean-de-Losne 58 47.06 N 5.15 E
Saint-Jean-de-Luz 32 43.23 N 1.40 W
Saint-Jean-de-Maurienne 62 45.17 N 6.21 E
Saint-Jean-de-Monts 32 46.48 N 2.03 W
Saint-Jean-des-Piles 206 46.41 N 72.45 W
Saint-Jean-du-Gard 62 44.06 N 3.53 E
Saint-Jean-en-Royans 62 45.01 N 5.18 E
Saint-Jean-Pied-de-Port 32 43.10 N 1.14 W
Saint-Jean-Port-Joli 186 47.13 N 70.16 W
Saint-Jean-Soleymieux 62 45.30 N 4.02 E
Saint-Jean-sur-Richelieu 206 45.19 N 73.16 W
Saint-Jeoire 58 46.09 N 6.28 E
Saint-Jérôme 206 45.47 N 74.00 W
Saint Jo 196 33.41 N 97.31 W
Saint Joachim 214 42.16 N 82.38 W
Saint Joe 216 41.18 N 84.54 W
Saint Joe ≐ 202 47.21 N 116.42 W
Saint John, N.B., Can. 186 45.16 N 66.03 W
Saint John, Jersey 43b 49.15 N 2.08 W
Saint John, In., U.S. 216 41.27 N 87.28 W
Saint John, Ks., U.S. 198 38.00 N 98.45 W
Saint John, N.D., U.S. 198 48.56 N 99.42 W
Saint John, Wa., U.S. 202 47.05 N 117.34 W
Saint John I 240m 18.20 N 64.45 W
Saint John ≐, Liber. 150 6.40 N 9.10 W
Saint John ≐, N.A. 186 45.15 N 66.04 W
Saint John, Cape > 186 50.00 N 55.32 W
Saint John, Lake ⊜, Nf., Can. 186 48.23 N 54.41 W
Saint John, Lake ⊜, On., Can. 212 44.41 N 79.20 W
Saint John Bay c 186 50.54 N 57.08 W
Saint John Island I 186 50.49 N 57.14 W
Saint John's, Antig. 240c 17.06 N 61.51 W
Saint John's, Nf., Can. 186 47.34 N 52.43 W
Saint John's, I. of Man 44 54.13 N 4.38 W
Saint Johns, Az., U.S. 200 34.30 N 109.21 W
Saint Johns, Mi., U.S. 216 43.00 N 84.33 W
Saint Johns, Mo., U.S. 219 38.42 N 90.20 W
Saint Johns, Oh., U.S. 216 40.33 N 84.05 W
Saint Johns ≐, Ca., U.S. 226 36.25 N 119.25 W
Saint Johns ≐, Fl., U.S. 192 30.24 N 81.24 W
Saint Johnsburg 210 43.05 N 78.53 W
Saint Johnsbury 188 44.25 N 72.00 W
Saint Johns Creek ≐ 219 38.34 N 91.01 W
Saint John's Jerusalem ⊥ 260 51.25 N 0.14 E
Saint Johns Marsh ⊞ 220 27.45 N 80.40 W
Saint John's Point > 48 54.13 N 5.40 W
Saint Johns → Saint-Jean-sur-Richelieu 206 45.19 N 73.16 W
Saint John's University ᵾ² 276 40.43 N 73.48 W
Saint Johnsville 210 42.59 N 74.41 W
Saint Joseph, N.B., Can. 186 45.59 N 64.34 W
Saint Joseph, Dom. 240d 15.26 N 61.26 W
Saint Joseph, Mart. 240e 14.40 N 61.03 W
Saint-Joseph, N. Cal. 175f 20.27 S 166.36 E
Saint-Joseph, Réu. 157c 21.22 S 55.36 E
Saint Joseph, Il., U.S. 194 40.06 N 88.02 W
Saint Joseph, La., U.S. 194 31.55 N 91.14 W
Saint Joseph, Mi., U.S. 216 42.05 N 86.29 W
Saint Joseph, Mn., U.S. 190 45.33 N 94.19 W
Saint Joseph, Mo., U.S. 194 39.46 N 94.50 W
Saint Joseph, Tn., U.S. 194 35.02 N 87.30 W
Saint Joseph □⁶, In., U.S. 216 41.41 N 86.15 W
Saint Joseph □⁶, Mi., U.S. 216 41.55 N 85.31 W
Saint Joseph ≐, U.S. 216 42.07 N 86.29 W
Saint Joseph ≐, U.S. 216 41.05 N 85.08 W
Saint Joseph, East Branch ≐ 216 41.39 N 84.34 W
Saint-Joseph, Île I 275a 45.41 N 73.42 W
Saint-Joseph, Lac ⊜ 206 46.54 N 71.38 W
Saint Joseph, Lake ⊜ 176 51.05 N 90.35 W
Saint Joseph, West Branch ≐ 216 41.39 N 84.34 W
Saint Joseph Bay c 192 29.47 N 85.21 W
Saint Joseph Channel ⌇ 190 46.19 N 84.04 W
Saint-Joseph-d'Alma → Alma 186 48.33 N 71.39 W
Saint-Joseph-de-Beauce 186 46.18 N 70.53 W
Saint-Joseph-de-Mékinac 206 46.55 N 72.42 W
Saint-Joseph-de-Sorel 206 46.02 N 73.07 W
Saint-Joseph-du-Lac 275a 45.32 N 74.00 W
Saint Joseph Island I 190 46.13 N 83.57 W
Saint Joseph's University ᵾ² 285 40.00 N 75.14 W
Saint-Jouin-Bruneval 50 49.39 N 0.10 E
Saint-Jovite 206 46.07 N 74.36 W
Sainte-Julie 206 45.35 N 73.19 W
Saint-Julien 58 46.23 N 5.27 E
Saint-Julien-Chapteuil 62 45.02 N 4.04 E
Saint-Julien-du-Sault 50 48.02 N 3.18 E
Saint-Julien-du-Verdon 62 43.55 N 6.32 E
Saint-Julien-en-Beauchêne 62 44.37 N 5.42 E
Saint-Julien-en-Born 32 44.04 N 1.14 W
Saint-Julien-en-Genevois 58 46.08 N 6.05 E
Saint-Julien-en-Jarez 62 45.28 N 4.31 E
Saint-Julien-les-Villas 50 48.16 N 4.06 E
Saint-Julien-Molin-Molette 62 45.19 N 4.37 E
Sainte-Julienne 206 45.58 N 73.43 W
Saint-Junien 32 45.53 N 0.54 E
Saint Just, P.R. 240m 18.23 N 66.00 W
Saint Just, Eng., U.K. 42 50.07 N 5.42 W
Saint-Just-en-Chaussée 50 49.30 N 2.26 E
Saint-Just-en-Chevalet 32 45.55 N 3.50 E
Sainte-Justine 206 46.15 N 73.05 W
Saint-Just-Malmont 62 45.20 N 4.19 E
Saint-Just-sur-Loire 62 45.29 N 4.16 E
Saint Keverne 42 50.03 N 5.06 W
Saint Kilda, Austl. 168b 34.44 S 138.32 E
Saint Kilda, Austl. 169 37.52 S 144.59 E
Saint Kilda, N.Z. 172 45.54 S 170.30 E
Saint Kilda I 28 57.49 N 8.36 W
Saint Kitts 168b 34.21 S 139.04 E
Saint Kitts and Nevis □¹, N.A. 230 17.20 N 62.45 W
Saint Kitts and Nevis □¹, N.A. 238 17.20 N 62.45 W
Saint Kitts → Saint Christopher I 238 17.20 N 62.45 W
Saint-Lambert, P.Q., Can. 206 45.30 N 73.30 W
Saint-Lambert, Fr. 261 48.44 N 2.01 E
Saint Landry 194 30.50 N 92.15 W
Saint-Laurent, Mb., Can. 184 50.24 N 97.56 W
Saint-Laurent, P.Q., Can. 206 45.30 N 73.40 W
Saint-Laurent, Fr. 58 48.09 N 6.27 E
Saint-Laurent-Blangy 50 50.18 N 2.48 E
Saint-Laurent-de-Chamousset 62 45.44 N 4.28 E
Saint-Laurent-du-Maroni 250 5.30 N 54.02 W
Saint-Laurent-du-Maroni □⁸ 250 4.00 N 53.30 W
Saint-Laurent-du-Pont 62 45.23 N 5.44 E
Saint-Laurent-du-Var 62 43.40 N 7.11 E
Saint-Laurent-en-Caux 50 49.45 N 0.53 E
Saint-Laurent-en-Grandvaux 58 46.35 N 5.57 E
Saint-Laurent-et-Benon 32 45.09 N 0.49 W
Saint-Laurent-les-Bains 62 44.37 N 3.58 E
Saint-Laurent → Saint Lawrence ≐ 176 49.30 N 67.00 W
Saint-Laurent-sur-Saône 58 46.18 N 4.50 E
Saint Lawrence, Austl. 166 22.21 S 149.31 E
Saint Lawrence, Nf., Can. 186 46.55 N 55.24 W
Saint Lawrence □⁶ 212 44.30 N 75.27 W
Saint Lawrence ≐ 176 49.30 N 67.00 W
Saint Lawrence, Cape > 186 47.03 N 60.37 W
Saint Lawrence, Gulf of c 186 48.00 N 62.00 W
Saint Lawrence, Lake ⊜ 206 44.56 N 75.04 W
Saint Lawrence Island I 180 63.30 N 170.30 W
Saint Lawrence Islands National Park ♦ 212 44.18 N 76.08 W
Saint Lawrence Seaway ≅ 275a 45.43 N 73.25 W
Saint-Lazare 184 50.26 N 101.16 W
Saint-Lazare, Gare ◆⁵ 261 48.53 N 2.20 E
Saint-Léandre 186 48.44 N 67.36 W
Saint-Léger-en-Yvelines 261 48.43 N 1.46 E
Saint-Léger-sur-Dheune 58 46.51 N 4.38 E
Saint Leo 220 28.20 N 82.15 W
Saint Leon 218 39.17 N 84.57 W
Saint-Léonard, N.B., Can. 186 47.10 N 67.56 W
Saint-Léonard, P.Q., Can. 206 45.35 N 73.35 W
Saint Leonard, Md., U.S. 208 38.28 N 76.30 W
Saint-Léonard-d'Aston 206 46.06 N 72.22 W
Saint-Léonard-de-Noblat 32 45.50 N 1.29 E
Saint Leonards, Eng., U.K. 42 50.49 N 1.51 W
Saint Leonards, Eng., U.K. 42 50.51 N 0.34 E
Saint-Leu-d'Esserent 50 49.13 N 2.25 E
Saint-Leu-la-Forêt 50 49.01 N 2.15 E
Saint-Liboire 206 45.39 N 72.46 W
Saint-Lô 32 49.07 N 1.05 W
Saint-Louis, Sk., Can. 184 52.56 N 105.49 W
Saint-Louis, Fr. 58 47.35 N 7.34 E
Saint-Louis, Guad. 241o 15.57 N 61.19 W
Saint-Louis, Réu. 157c 21.16 S 55.25 E
Saint-Louis, Sén. 150 16.02 N 16.30 W
Saint Louis, Mi., U.S. 190 43.24 N 84.36 W
Saint Louis, Mo., U.S. 219 38.37 N 90.11 W
Saint Louis, Tx., U.S. 222 32.18 N 95.20 W
Saint-Louis □⁴ 150 16.00 N 14.30 W
Saint Louis □⁶ 219 38.39 N 90.25 W
Saint-Louis ≐, P.Q., Can. 275a 45.19 N 73.53 W
Saint Louis ≐, U.S. 190 46.45 N 92.06 W
Saint-Louis, Lac ⊜ 206 45.24 N 73.48 W
Saint-Louis, Pointe > 275a 45.19 N 73.53 W
Saint Louis Crossing 218 39.19 N 85.51 W
Saint-Louis-de-Champlain 206 46.25 N 72.36 W
Saint-Louis-de-Kent 186 46.44 N 64.58 W
Saint Louis Park 190 44.56 N 93.20 W
Saint Louisville 214 40.10 N 82.25 W
Saint-Loup-sur-Aujon 58 47.53 N 5.05 E
Saint-Loup-sur-Semouse 58 47.53 N 6.16 E
Saint-Luc, P.Q., Can. 206 45.22 N 73.18 W
Saint-Luc, Schw. 58 46.13 N 7.36 E
Sainte-Luce 240e 14.28 N 60.56 W
Saint Lucia □¹, N.A. 230 13.53 N 60.58 W
Saint Lucia □¹, N.A. 241f 13.53 N 60.58 W
Saint Lucia, Cape > 158 28.25 S 32.25 E
Saint Lucia, Lake ⊜ 158 28.05 S 32.26 E
Saint Lucia Channel ⌇ 238 14.09 N 60.57 W
Saint Lucia Estuary 158 28.22 S 32.25 E
Saint Lucia Game Reserve ♦⁴ 158 28.10 S 32.28 E
Sainte-Lucie, Fr. 36 41.42 N 9.22 E
Saint Lucie □⁶ 220 27.29 N 80.20 W
Saint Lucie Canal ≅ 220 27.10 N 80.15 W
Saint Lucie Inlet c 220 27.10 N 80.10 W
Saint Lucie Lock ◆⁵ 220 27.07 N 80.17 W
Saint-Lucien 261 48.39 N 1.38 E
Saint-Lupicin 58 46.24 N 5.47 E
Saint-Magnance 50 47.27 N 4.04 E
Saint Magnus Bay c 46a 60.24 N 1.34 W
Saint Magnus Cathedral ᵾ¹ 46 58.58 N 2.57 W
Saint-Malo, P.Q., Can. 206 45.12 N 71.30 W
Saint-Malo, Fr. 32 48.39 N 2.01 W
Saint-Malo, Golfe de c 32 48.45 N 2.00 W
Saint-Mamert-du-Gard 62 43.53 N 4.12 E
Saint-Mammès 50 48.23 N 2.49 E
Saint-Mandé 261 48.50 N 2.25 E
Saint-Mandrier-sur-Mer 62 43.04 N 5.56 E
Saint-Marc 238 19.07 N 72.42 W
Saint-Marc, Canal de ⌇ 238 18.50 N 72.45 W
Saint-Marc-des-Carrières 206 46.41 N 72.03 W
Saint-Marcel 58 46.47 N 4.54 E
Saint-Marcellin 62 45.09 N 5.19 E
Saint-Marcelline-de-Kildare 206 46.07 N 73.36 W
Saint-Marc-sur-Richelieu 275a 45.41 N 73.12 W
Saint-Mard 261 49.02 N 2.42 E
Saint Margaret Bay c 186 51.01 N 56.58 W
Saint Margaret's at Cliffe 42 51.09 N 1.24 E
Saint Margarets Bay c 186 44.35 N 64.00 W
Saint Margaret's Hope 46 58.49 N 2.57 W
Sainte-Marguerite ≐ 176 50.09 N 66.36 W
Sainte-Marguerite, Baie c 186 50.06 N 66.36 W
Sainte-Marguerite-sur-Mer 50 49.55 N 0.57 E
Sainte-Marie 240e 14.47 N 61.00 W
Sainte-Marie, Cap > 157b 25.36 S 45.08 E
Sainte-Marie-aux-Mines (Markirch) 58 48.15 N 7.11 E
Saint Maries 202 47.18 N 116.33 W
Saint Maries ≐ 202 47.19 N 116.33 W
Saint-Marin → San Marino □¹ 66 43.56 N 12.25 E
Saint Marks, S. Afr. 158 32.01 S 27.22 E
Saint Marks, Fl., U.S. 192 30.09 N 84.12 W
Saint Marks ≐ 192 30.08 N 84.12 W
Sainte-Marthe-de-Gaspé 186 49.12 N 66.10 W
Sainte-Marthe-sur-le-Lac 275a 45.32 N 73.56 W
Saint-Martin (Sint Maarten) I 238 18.04 N 63.04 W
Saint-Martin, Cap > 240e 14.52 N 61.13 W
Saint Martin, Lake ⊜ 184 51.37 N 98.29 W
Saint-Martin-Boulogne 50 50.43 N 1.38 E
Saint-Martin-d'Ardèche 62 44.18 N 4.35 E
Saint-Martin-d'Auxigny 50 47.12 N 2.25 E
Saint-Martin-de-Belleville 62 45.23 N 6.30 E
Saint-Martin-de-Bossenay 50 48.26 N 3.41 E
Saint-Martin-de-Bréthencourt 261 48.31 N 1.56 E
Saint-Martin-de-Crau 62 43.38 N 4.49 E
Saint-Martin-de-Londres 62 43.47 N 3.44 E
Saint-Martin-de-Nigelles 261 48.37 N 1.37 E
Saint-Martin-d'Entraunes 62 44.08 N 6.46 E
Saint-Martin-des-Champs 261 48.53 N 1.43 E
Saint-Martin-de-Valamas 62 44.56 N 4.22 E
Saint-Martin-d'Hères 62 45.10 N 5.46 E
Saint-Martin-du-Puy 50 47.20 N 3.52 E
Saint-Martin-du-Tertre 261 49.06 N 2.21 E
Saint-Martin-du-Var 62 43.49 N 7.12 E
Sainte-Martine 206 45.15 N 73.48 W
Saint-Martin-en-Bresse 58 46.49 N 5.04 E
Saint-Martin-la-Garenne 261 49.02 N 1.41 E
Saint-Martin-la-Plaine 62 45.32 N 4.36 E
Saint Martins, N.B., Can. 186 45.21 N 65.32 W
Saint Martin's, Eng., U.K. 42 52.55 N 2.59 W
Saint Martin's I 42a 49.58 N 6.20 W
Saint Martins Keys II 220 28.47 N 82.44 W
Saint-Martin-Vésubie 62 44.04 N 7.15 E
Saint Martinville 194 30.07 N 91.49 W
Saint Mary 194 37.52 N 89.58 W
Saint Mary ≐, B.C., Can. 182 49.37 N 115.38 W
Saint Mary ≐, N.A. 182 49.37 N 112.52 W
Saint Mary, Cape > 150 13.28 N 16.40 W
Saint Mary, Mount ^ 164 8.10 S 147.00 E
Saint Mary Bourne 42 51.16 N 1.24 W
Saint Mary Cray ◆⁸ 260 51.23 N 0.07 E
Saint Mary Lake ⊜ 202 48.40 N 113.30 W
Saint Marylebone ◆⁸ 260 51.31 N 0.10 W
Saint Mary of the Lake Seminary ᵾ² 278 42.17 N 88.00 W
Saint Mary Peak ^ 166 31.30 S 138.33 E
Saint Mary Reservoir ⊜¹ 182 49.19 N 113.12 W
Saint Marys, Austl. 166 41.35 S 148.10 E
Saint Marys, Austl. 170 33.47 S 150.47 E
Saint Mary's, Nf., Can. 186 46.55 N 53.34 W
Saint Mary's, On., Can. 212 43.16 N 81.08 W
Saint Marys, Ak., U.S. 180 62.04 N 163.10 W
Saint Marys, Ga., U.S. 192 30.43 N 81.32 W
Saint Marys, Ks., U.S. 198 39.11 N 96.04 W
Saint Marys, Oh., U.S. 216 40.32 N 84.23 W
Saint Marys, Pa., U.S. 214 41.25 N 78.33 W
Saint Marys, W.V., U.S. 188 39.23 N 81.12 W
Saint Marys □⁶ 208 38.17 N 76.38 W
Saint Mary's I 42a 49.55 N 6.18 W
Saint Marys ≐, N.S., Can. 186 45.02 N 61.54 W
Saint Marys ≐, N.A. 190 45.58 N 83.54 W
Saint Marys ≐, U.S. 192 30.43 N 81.27 W
Saint Marys ≐, U.S. 216 41.05 N 85.08 W
Saint Marys ≐, Md., U.S. 208 38.06 N 76.26 W
Saint Mary's, Cape >, Nf., Can. 186 46.49 N 54.12 W
Saint Marys, Cape >, N.S., Can. 186 44.05 N 66.13 W
Saint Marys, North Prong ≐ 192 30.22 N 82.06 W
Saint Marys, South Prong ≐ 192 30.22 N 82.06 W
Saint Mary's Bay 42 51.00 N 0.58 E
Saint Mary's Bay c, Nf., Can. 186 46.50 N 53.47 W
Saint Marys Bay c, N.S., Can. 186 44.25 N 66.10 W
Saint Marys City 208 38.11 N 76.26 W
Saint Mary's Hoo 260 51.28 N 0.36 E
Saint Marys Lake ⊜ 278 42.17 N 87.59 W
Saint Mary's Marshes ⊞ 260 51.28 N 0.35 E
Saint-Mathieu 32 45.42 N 0.46 E
Saint-Mathieu, Pointe de > 32 48.20 N 4.46 W
Saint-Mathieu-de-Laprairie 275a 45.19 N 73.31 W
Saint Matthew Island I 180 60.30 N 172.45 W
Saint Matthews, Ky., U.S. 218 38.15 N 85.39 W
Saint Matthews, S.C., U.S. 192 33.39 N 80.46 W
Saint Matthias Group II 164 1.30 S 149.40 E
Saint-Maur-des-Fossés 50 48.48 N 2.30 E
Sainte-Maure-de-Touraine 32 47.07 N 0.37 E
Saint-Maurice, Fr. 261 48.49 N 2.25 E
Saint-Maurice, Schw. 58 46.13 N 7.00 E
Saint-Maurice □⁶ 206 46.35 N 73.00 W
Saint-Maurice ≐ 176 46.21 N 72.31 W
Saint-Maurice, Parc de ♦ 206 46.52 N 73.10 W
Saint-Maurice-de-Montagne 58 46.34 N 5.50 E
Saint-Maurice-Montcouronne 261 48.35 N 2.07 E
Saint Mawes 42 50.09 N 5.01 W
Saint Mawgan 42 50.28 N 4.58 W
Saint-Max 58 48.42 N 6.13 E
Sainte-Maxime 62 43.18 N 6.38 E
Saint-Maximin-la-Sainte-Baume 62 43.27 N 5.52 E
Saint-Méen-le-Grand 32 48.11 N 2.12 W
Saint Meinrad 194 38.10 N 86.48 W
Sainte-Menehould 56 49.05 N 4.54 E
Saint-Menges 56 49.44 N 4.56 E
Sainte-Mère-Église 32 49.25 N 1.19 W
Saint Merryn 42 50.31 N 4.58 W
Saint-Méry 261 48.35 N 2.50 E
Saint-Mesme 261 48.32 N 1.58 E
Saint-Mesmes 261 48.59 N 2.42 E
Saint Michael, Ak., U.S. 180 63.29 N 162.02 W
Saint Michael, Pa., U.S. 214 40.20 N 78.46 W
Saint Michaels 208 38.47 N 76.13 W
Saint-Michel, Fr. 50 49.55 N 4.08 E
Saint-Michel, Fr. 62 45.13 N 6.28 E
Saint-Michel ◆⁸ 275a 45.35 N 73.35 W
Saint-Michel-de-Napierville 206 45.14 N 73.34 W
Saint-Michel-des-Saints 206 46.41 N 73.55 W
Saint-Michel-sur-Meurthe 58 48.19 N 6.54 E
Saint-Michel-sur-Orge 261 48.38 N 2.18 E
Saint-Mihiel 56 48.54 N 5.33 E
Saint Monance 46 56.12 N 2.46 W
Sainte-Monique-des-Deux-Montagnes 275a 45.40 N 74.00 W
Sainte-Montaine 50 47.29 N 2.19 E
Saint-Moritz → Sankt Moritz 58 46.30 N 9.50 E
Saint-Narcisse 206 46.34 N 72.28 W
Saint-Nazaire 32 47.17 N 2.12 W
Saint-Nazaire-en-Royans 62 45.04 N 5.15 E
Saint-Nazaire-le-Désert 62 44.34 N 5.17 E
Saint Nazianz 190 44.00 N 87.55 W
Saint Neots 42 52.14 N 0.17 W
Saint-Nicéphore 206 45.50 N 72.25 W
Saint-Nicolas, Bel. 56 50.38 N 5.32 E
Saint-Nicolas, P.Q., Can. 206 46.42 N 71.24 W
Saint-Nicolas-aux-Bois 50 49.36 N 3.25 E
Saint-Nicolas-d'Aliermont 50 49.53 N 1.13 E
Saint-Nicolas → Sint-Niklaas 50 51.10 N 4.08 E
Saint-Nizier-du-Moucherotte 62 45.10 N 5.38 E
Saint-Nom-la-Bretèche 261 48.51 N 2.01 E
Saint Nora Lake ⊜ 212 45.08 N 78.49 W
Saint-Norbert-d'Arthabaska 206 46.07 N 71.50 W
Sainte-Odile ᵾ¹ 58 48.26 N 7.24 E
Saint-Omer 50 50.45 N 2.15 E
Saintonge □⁹ 32 45.30 N 0.30 W
Saint-Ouen, Fr. 50 50.02 N 2.03 E
Saint-Ouen, Fr. 261 48.54 N 2.20 E
Saint-Ouen-l'Aumône 50 49.03 N 2.06 E
Saint-Pacôme 186 47.24 N 69.57 W
Saint-Pamphile 186 46.58 N 69.47 W
Saint Pancras ◆⁸ 260 51.32 N 0.07 W
Saint Paris 218 40.07 N 83.57 W
Saint-Pascal 186 47.32 N 69.49 W
Saint-Paterne 50 48.24 N 0.07 E
Saint-Pathus 261 49.04 N 2.48 E
Saint-Patrice, Lac ⊜ 190 46.22 N 77.20 W
Saint Paul, Ab., Can. 182 53.59 N 111.17 W
Saint-Paul, Fr. 62 43.42 N 7.07 E
Saint-Paul, Fr. 62 44.31 N 6.45 E
Saint-Paul, Réu. 157c 21.00 S 55.16 E
Saint Paul, In., U.S. 218 39.25 N 85.28 W
Saint Paul, Ks., U.S. 198 37.31 N 95.10 W
Saint Paul, Mn., U.S. 190 44.57 N 93.05 W
Saint Paul, Ne., U.S. 198 41.13 N 98.27 W
Saint Paul, Or., U.S. 224 45.12 N 122.58 W
Saint Paul, Va., U.S. 192 36.54 N 82.18 W
Saint-Paul ≐, Can. 176 51.26 N 57.40 W
Saint Paul ≐, Liber. 150 6.23 N 10.48 W
Saint Paul, Cape > 150 5.49 N 0.57 E
Saint-Paul, Île I 6 38.43 S 77.29 E
Saint-Paul, Lac ⊜ 206 46.18 N 72.29 W
Saint Paul Bay c 116 10.14 N 118.54 E
Saint-Paul-de-Chester (Chesterville) 206 45.57 N 71.49 W
Saint-Paul-en-Jarez 62 45.29 N 4.35 E
Saint-Paul-et-Valmalle 62 43.38 N 3.40 E
Saint-Paulien 62 45.08 N 3.49 E
Saint-Paulin 206 46.25 N 73.01 W
Saint Paul Island 180 57.07 N 170.17 W
Saint Paul Island I, N.S., Can. 186 47.15 N 60.10 W
Saint Paul Island I, Ak., U.S. 180 57.10 N 170.15 W
Saint Pauls 192 34.48 N 78.58 W
Saint Paul's Cathedral ᵾ¹ 260 51.31 N 0.06 W
Saint Paul's Cray ◆⁸ 260 51.24 N 0.07 E
Saint Pauls Inlet c 186 49.50 N 57.45 W
Saint Paul's Point > 174e 25.04 S 130.05 W
Saint-Paul-Trois-Châteaux 62 44.21 N 4.46 E
Saint-Péravy-la-Colombe 50 48.00 N 1.42 E
Saint-Péray 62 44.57 N 4.50 E
Saint-Père 50 47.28 N 3.46 E
Saint Peter, Il., U.S. 219 38.52 N 88.51 W
Saint Peter, Mn., U.S. 190 44.19 N 93.57 W
Saint Peter, Lake ⊜ 212 45.18 N 78.02 W
Saint Peter Island I 162 32.17 S 133.35 E
Saint Peter Port 43b 49.27 N 2.32 W
Saint Peters, N.S., Can. 186 45.40 N 60.52 W
Saint Peters, Mo., U.S. 219 38.48 N 90.37 W
Saint Peters, Pa., U.S. 285 40.11 N 75.44 W
Saint Peters Bay 186 46.25 N 62.35 W
Saint Petersburg, Fl., U.S. 220 27.46 N 82.40 W
Saint Petersburg, Pa., U.S. 214 41.10 N 79.37 W
Saint Petersburg Beach 220 27.43 N 82.44 W
Saint Petersburg → Sankt-Peterburg 76 59.55 N 30.15 E
Saint Peter's College ᵾ² 276 40.44 N 74.05 W
Saint-Philippe-d'Argenteuil 206 45.37 N 74.25 W
Saint-Philippe-de-Laprairie 275a 45.21 N 73.28 W
Saint-Pie 206 45.30 N 72.54 W
Saint-Pierre, P.Q., Can. 275a 45.27 N 73.39 W
Saint-Pierre, Fr. 62 45.40 N 3.45 E
Saint-Pierre, It. 62 45.42 N 7.14 E
Saint-Pierre, Mart. 240e 14.45 N 61.11 W
Saint-Pierre, Réu. 157c 21.19 S 55.29 E
Saint-Pierre, St. P./M. 186 46.47 N 56.11 W
Saint-Pierre I 186 46.47 N 56.11 W
Saint-Pierre ≐ 275a 45.23 N 73.34 W
Saint-Pierre, Lac ⊜, P.Q., Can. 186 50.08 N 68.26 W
Saint-Pierre, Lac ⊜, P.Q., Can. 206 46.12 N 72.52 W
Saint Pierre and Miquelon (Saint-Pierre-et-Miquelon) □², N.A. 176 46.55 N 56.20 W
Saint Pierre and Miquelon (Saint-Pierre-et-Miquelon) □², N.A. 186 46.55 N 56.20 W
Saint-Pierre-d'Albigny 62 45.34 N 6.09 E
Saint-Pierre-de-Bœuf 62 45.22 N 4.45 E
Saint-Pierre-de-Broughton 206 46.15 N 71.12 W
Saint-Pierre-de-Chartreuse 62 45.20 N 5.49 E
Saint-Pierre-des-Corps 50 47.23 N 0.44 E
Saint-Pierre-de-Vacquière 62 43.52 N 4.13 E
Saint-Pierre-du-Vauvray 50 49.14 N 1.13 E
Saint-Pierre-Église 32 49.40 N 1.24 W
Saint-Pierre-en-Port 50 49.48 N 0.29 E
Saint-Pierre-et-Miquelon → Saint Pierre and Miquelon □² 186 46.55 N 56.20 W
Saint Pierre Island I 138 9.19 S 50.43 E
Saint Pierre-Jolys 184 49.26 N 96.59 W
Saint-Pierre-le-Moûtier 32 46.48 N 3.07 E
Saint-Pierre-lès-Elbeuf 50 49.16 N 1.03 E
Saint-Pierre-sur-Dives 28 49.01 N 0.02 W
Saint-Pierreville 62 44.49 N 4.29 E
Saint-Point, Lac de ⊜ 58 46.49 N 6.19 E
Saint-Pol-de-Léon 32 48.41 N 3.59 W
Saint-Pol-sur-Mer 50 51.02 N 2.21 E
Saint-Pol-sur-Ternoise 50 50.23 N 2.20 E
Saint-Polycarpe 206 45.18 N 74.18 W
Saint-Pons 32 43.29 N 2.46 E
Saint-Pourçain-sur-Sioule 32 46.19 N 3.17 E
Saint-Prex 58 46.29 N 6.28 E
Saint-Priest 62 45.42 N 4.57 E
Saint-Priest-en-Jarez 62 45.28 N 4.22 E
Saint-Prix 261 49.01 N 2.16 E
Saint-Prosper-de-Dorchester 188 46.13 N 70.29 W
Saint-Quentin, N.B., Can. 186 47.30 N 67.23 W
Saint-Quentin, Fr. 50 49.51 N 3.17 E
Saint-Quentin, Canal de ≅ 50 49.36 N 3.11 E
Saint-Quentin, Étang de ⊜ 261 48.47 N 2.01 E
Saint-Rambert-d'Albon 62 45.17 N 4.49 E
Saint-Rambert-en-Bugey 62 45.57 N 5.26 E
Saint-Rambert-sur-Loire 62 45.30 N 4.15 E
Saint-Raphaël 62 43.25 N 6.46 E
Saint-Raymond 206 46.54 N 71.50 W
Saint-Rédempter-de-Lévis 206 46.42 N 71.17 W
Saint Regis 202 47.17 N 115.06 W
Saint-Régis ≐, P.Q., Can. 275a 45.14 N 73.34 W
Saint Regis ≐, N.A. 188 45.00 N 74.39 W
Saint Regis ≐, Mt., U.S. 202 47.18 N 115.05 W
Saint Regis, West Branch ≐ 188 44.47 N 74.46 W
Saint Regis Falls 188 44.40 N 74.32 W
Saint Regis Indian Reservation ◆⁴ 206 44.58 N 74.39 W
Saint-Rémi 206 45.16 N 73.37 W
Saint-Rémi-d'Amherst 206 46.01 N 74.46 W
Saint-Rémy (lès-Chevreuse), Fr. 50 48.42 N 2.05 E
Saint-Rémy, Fr. 58 46.46 N 4.50 E
Saint Remy, N.Y., U.S. 210 41.54 N 74.01 W
Saint-Rémy-de-Provence 62 43.47 N 4.50 E
Saint-Rémy-en-Bouzemont 58 48.38 N 4.39 E
Saint-Rémy-lès-Chevreuse 261 48.42 N 2.05 E
Saint-Rémy-l'Honoré 261 48.45 N 1.53 E
Saint-Rémy-sur-Avre 50 48.46 N 1.15 E
Saint-Renan 32 48.26 N 4.37 W
Saint-Révérien 50 47.13 N 3.30 E
Saint-Rhémy 62 45.50 N 7.11 E
Saint-Riquier 50 50.08 N 1.57 E
Saint Robert 194 37.50 N 92.09 W
Saint-Roch-de-l'Achigan 206 45.51 N 73.36 W
Saint-Romain-de-Colbosc 50 49.32 N 0.22 E
Saint-Romain-le-Puy 62 45.33 N 4.07 E
Saint-Romans 62 45.07 N 5.19 E
Saint-Romuald 206 46.45 N 71.14 W
Sainte-Rosalie 206 45.38 N 72.54 W
Sainte-Rose 241o 16.20 N 61.42 W
Sainte-Rose ◆⁸ 275a 45.36 N 73.47 W
Sainte-Rose-du-Lac 184 51.03 N 99.32 W
Saintry-sur-Seine 261 48.36 N 2.30 E
Saintes, Bel. 50 50.42 N 4.10 E
Saintes, Fr. 32 45.45 N 0.38 W
Saint-Saëns 50 49.40 N 1.17 E
Saint Sampson 43b 49.29 N 2.31 W
Saint-Saturnin-d'Apt 62 43.56 N 5.23 E
Saint-Sauveur, Fr. 50 47.37 N 3.12 E
Saint-Sauveur, Fr. 58 47.48 N 6.23 E
Saint-Sauveur-des-Monts 206 45.52 N 74.10 W
Saint-Sauveur-sur-Tinée 62 44.05 N 7.06 E
Saint-Savin 32 46.34 N 0.52 E
Sainte-Savine 50 48.18 N 4.03 E
Saint-Savinien 32 45.53 N 0.41 W
Saint Saviour 43b 49.11 N 2.06 W
Saint Sebastian Bay c 158 34.25 S 21.00 E
Saint-Sébastien 206 45.07 N 73.09 W
Saint-Sébastien, Cap > 157b 12.26 S 48.44 E
Saint-Seine-l'Abbaye 58 47.26 N 4.47 E
Saint-Séverin 56 50.32 N 5.25 E
Saint Shotts 186 46.38 N 53.35 W
Sainte-Sigolène 62 45.14 N 4.15 E
Saint-Siméon 186 47.50 N 69.53 W
Saint-Simon 50 49.45 N 3.10 E
Saint Simons Island 192 31.09 N 81.22 W
Saint Simons Island I 192 31.14 N 81.21 W
Saint-Sixte ≐ 206 45.39 N 75.08 W
Saintes-Maries, Golfe des c 62 43.25 N 4.31 E
Saintes-Maries-de-la-Mer 62 43.27 N 4.26 E
Sainte-Sophie-de-Mégantic 206 46.09 N 71.42 W
Saint-Soupplets 261 49.02 N 2.48 E
Saint Stanislas Bay c 174o 1.53 N 157.30 W
Saint-Stanislas-de-Kosta 206 45.11 N 74.08 W
Saint Stephen, N.B., Can. 186 45.12 N 67.17 W
Saint Stephen, S.C., U.S. 192 33.24 N 79.55 W
Saint-Sulpice-de-Favières 261 48.33 N 2.11 E
Saint-Sulpice-les-Feuilles 32 46.19 N 1.22 E
Sainte-Suzanne 58 47.30 N 6.46 E
Saint-Sylvestre 206 46.22 N 71.14 W
Saint-Symphorien, Fr. 32 44.26 N 0.30 W
Saint-Symphorien, Fr. 261 48.31 N 1.46 E
Saint-Symphorien-d'Ozon 62 45.38 N 4.52 E
Saint-Symphorien-sur-Coise 62 45.38 N 4.27 E
Sainte-Thècle 206 46.49 N 72.31 W
Saint-Théodore-d'Acton 206 45.41 N 72.35 W
Sainte-Thérèse 206 45.38 N 73.51 W
Sainte-Thérèse, Île I, P.Q., Can. 275a 45.22 N 73.15 W
Sainte-Thérèse, Île I, P.Q., Can. 275a 45.41 N 73.28 W
Saint-Thibault-des-Vignes 261 48.52 N 2.41 E
Saint Thomas, On., Can. 212 42.47 N 81.12 W
Saint Thomas, Mo., U.S. 219 38.22 N 92.13 W
Saint Thomas, N.D., U.S. 198 48.37 N 97.26 W
Saint Thomas I 240m 18.21 N 64.55 W
Saint Thomas → Charlotte Amalie 240m 18.21 N 64.56 W
Sainte-Timothée 206 45.18 N 74.02 W
Sainte-Tite 206 46.44 N 72.34 W
Saint-Tite-des-Caps 186 47.08 N 70.47 W
Saint-Trivier-de-Courtes 58 46.28 N 5.05 E
Saint-Trivier-sur-Moignans 58 46.04 N 4.54 E
Saint-Tropez 62 43.16 N 6.38 E
Saint Tudy 42 50.33 N 4.43 W
Sainte-Tulle 62 43.47 N 5.46 E
Saint-Ubald 206 46.45 N 72.16 W
Saint-Urbain-de-Charlevoix 186 47.33 N 70.32 W
Saint-Ursanne 58 47.22 N 7.10 E
Saint-Uze 62 45.11 N 4.52 E
Saint-Valérien 50 48.11 N 3.06 E
Saint-Valéry-en-Caux 50 49.52 N 0.44 E
Saint-Valéry-sur-Somme 50 50.11 N 1.38 E
Saint-Vallier, Fr. 58 46.38 N 4.22 E
Saint-Vallier, Fr. 62 45.10 N 4.49 E
Saint-Vallier-de-Thiey 62 43.42 N 6.51 E
Saint-Varent 32 46.53 N 0.14 W
Saint-Venant 50 50.37 N 2.33 E
Saint-Véran 62 44.42 N 6.52 E
Sainte-Victoire, Montagne ^ 62 43.32 N 5.39 E
Saint-Victoret 62 43.25 N 5.14 E
Saint Vincent 198 48.58 N 97.13 W
Saint Vincent I 241h 13.15 N 61.12 W
Saint-Vincent, Baie de c 175f 22.00 S 166.05 E
Saint-Vincent, Cap > 157b 21.57 S 43.16 E
Saint Vincent, Cape > 166 43.18 S 145.50 E
Saint Vincent, Cape → São Vicente, Cabo de > 34 37.01 N 9.00 W
Saint Vincent, Gulf c 168b 35.00 S 138.05 E
Saint Vincent and the Grenadines □¹, N.A. 230 13.15 N 61.12 W
Saint Vincent and the Grenadines □¹, N.A. 241h 13.15 N 61.12 W
Saint-Vincent-de-Paul ◆⁸ 275a 45.37 N 73.39 W
Saint-Vincent-de-Tyrosse 32 43.40 N 1.18 W
Saint Vincent Passage ⌇ 238 13.30 N 61.00 W
Saint Vincent's 186 46.48 N 53.38 W

≐ River	Fluß	Río	Rivière	Rio
≅ Canal	Kanal	Canal	Canal	Canal
⌊ Waterfall, Rapids	Wasserfall, Stromschnellen	Cascada, Rápidos	Chute d'eau, Rapides	Cascata, Rápidos
⌇ Strait	Meeresstraße	Estrecho	Détroit	Estreito
c Bay, Gulf	Bucht, Golf	Bahía, Golfo	Baie, Golfe	Baía, Golfo
⊜ Lake, Lakes	See, Seen	Lago, Lagos	Lac, Lacs	Lago, Lagos
⊞ Swamp	Sumpf	Pantano	Marais	Pântano
Ice Features, Glacier	Eis- und Gletscherformen	Accidentes Glaciales	Formes glaciaires	Acidentes glaciares
Other Hydrographic Features	Andere Hydrographische Objekte	Otros Elementos Hidrográficos	Autres données hydrographiques	Outros acidentes hidrográficos

◆ Submarine Features	Untermeerische Objekte	Accidentes Submarinos	Formes de relief sous-marin	Acidentes submarinos
□ Political Unit	Politische Einheit	Unidad Política	Entité politique	Unidade política
ᵾ Cultural Institution	Kulturelle Institution	Institución Cultural	Institution culturelle	Instituição cultural
⊥ Historical Site	Historische Stätte	Sitio Histórico	Site historique	Sítio histórico
♦ Recreational Site	Erholungs- und Ferienort	Sitio de Recreo	Centre de loisirs	Área de Lazer
⊠ Airport	Flughafen	Aeropuerto	Aéroport	Aeroporto
■ Military Installation	Militäranlage	Instalación Militar	Installation militaire	Instalação militar
◆ Miscellaneous	Verschiedenes	Misceláneo	Divers	Diversos

Name	Page	Lat.°'	Long.°'
Saint-Vit	58	47.11 N	5.49 E
Saint-Vith	56	50.17 N	6.08 E
Saint-Vivien-de-Médoc	32	45.26 N	1.02 W
Saint-Vrain	261	48.33 N	2.20 E
Saint Walburg	184	53.39 N	109.12 W
Saint-Wandrille-Rançon	50	49.32 N	0.46 E
Saint-Wenceslas ≃	206	46.18 N	72.23 W
Saint Williams	212	42.40 N	80.25 W
Saint-Witz	261	49.05 N	2.34 E
Saint-Yrieix-la-Perche	32	45.31 N	1.12 E
Saint-Yvon	186	49.10 N	64.48 W
Saint-Zacharie	62	43.23 N	5.43 E
Saint-Zénon	206	46.33 N	73.49 W
Sāinthiya	126	23.57 N	87.40 E
Saipan I	174n	15.12 N	145.45 E
Saipan Channel ʊ	174n	15.05 N	145.41 E
Saipan International Airport ⊠	174n	15.07 N	145.43 E
Saiqi	100	27.00 N	119.43 E
Saishu-to → Cheju-do I	90	33.20 N	126.30 E
Saita	96	34.08 N	133.49 E
Saita ≃	96	34.08 N	133.38 E
Saitama □[5]	94	36.00 N	139.30 E
Saitama University ⊍[2]	268	35.52 N	139.36 E
Saito	92	32.06 N	131.24 E
Saiwai ⬥[8]	268	35.33 N	139.41 E
Saiwa Swamp National Park ♣	154	1.06 N	35.12 E
Saiyidān ⬥[8]	272a	28.40 N	77.05 E
Sai Yok	110	14.07 N	99.08 E
Sajak	86	47.02 N	77.22 E
Sajam	164	0.53 S	132.41 E
Sajama	248	18.07 S	69.00 W
Sajama, Nevado ∧	248	18.06 S	68.54 W
Sajanogorsk	86	53.08 N	91.29 E
Sajano-Šušenskoje vodochranilišče ⊜[1]	86	52.20 N	92.25 E
Sajan → Sayan Mountains ⋏	88	52.45 N	96.00 E
Sajantuj	88	51.44 N	107.30 E
Sajasan	84	43.03 N	46.17 E
Sajat	128	38.47 N	63.53 E
Sajchan	88	48.40 N	102.39 E
Sajchandulaan	102	44.40 N	109.01 E
Sajchan-Ovoo	102	45.27 N	103.54 E
Sajchin	80	48.50 N	46.47 E
Sajen	115a	7.40 S	112.31 E
Šajgino	80	57.46 N	46.51 E
Sajīd I	144	16.52 N	41.50 E
Šajmak'	120	37.27 N	74.44 E
Sajnšand	102	44.52 N	110.09 E
Sajó (Slaná) ≃	30	47.56 N	21.08 E
Sajószentpéter	30	48.13 N	20.44 E
Sajram	85	42.18 N	69.45 E
Sajukino	80	52.47 N	41.59 E
Sājūr (Bağırsak) ≃	130	36.40 N	38.05 E
Sak ≃	158	30.02 S	20.40 E
Saka, Kenya	154	0.09 S	39.20 E
Saka, Nihon	96	34.20 N	132.31 E
Sakado	94	35.57 N	139.24 E
Sakae, Nihon	94	35.50 N	140.15 E
Sakae, Nihon	94	36.58 N	138.35 E
Sa Kaeo	110	13.49 N	102.04 E
Sakahogi	94	35.26 N	136.59 E
Sakai, Nihon	94	36.10 N	136.14 E
Sakai, Nihon	94	36.16 N	139.15 E
Sakai, Nihon	94	36.06 N	139.48 E
Sakai, Nihon	96	34.35 N	135.28 E
Sakai, Nihon	268	35.25 N	139.22 E
Sakai ≃	94	35.18 N	139.29 E
Sakaide	96	34.19 N	133.52 E
Sakaigawa	94	35.35 N	138.37 E
Sakaiminato	96	35.33 N	133.15 E
Sakākah	128	29.59 N	40.06 E
Sakakawea, Lake ⊜[1]	198	47.50 N	102.20 W
Sakaki	94	36.28 N	138.11 E
Sakakita	94	36.25 N	138.01 E
Sakala, Pulau I	112	6.54 S	116.15 E
Sakami ≃	176	53.40 N	76.40 W
Sakami, Lac ⊜	176	53.15 N	76.45 W
Sakania	154	12.45 S	28.34 E
Sakar	128	38.56 N	63.45 E
Sakar ⋏	38	41.59 N	26.16 E
Sakaraha	157b	22.55 S	44.32 E
Sakar-Čaga	128	37.38 N	61.40 E
Sakar Island I	164	5.25 S	148.05 E
Sakartvelo → Georgia □[1]	22	42.00 N	44.00 E
Sakarya □[4]	130	40.45 N	30.35 E
Sakarya ≃	130	41.07 N	30.39 E
Sakashita	94	35.34 N	137.32 E
Sakassou	150	7.27 N	5.18 W
Sakata	92	38.55 N	139.50 E
Sakauchi	94	35.36 N	136.25 E
Sakawa	96	33.30 N	133.17 E
Sakawa ≃	94	35.15 N	139.11 E
Sakchu	98	40.23 N	125.01 E
Sakesar	123	32.33 N	71.56 E
Sakété	150	6.43 N	2.40 E
Sakhā	142	31.05 N	30.57 E
Sakhalin → Sachalin, ostrov I	89	51.00 N	143.00 E
Sākhar	120	32.57 N	65.32 E
Sakhi Sarwar	120	29.59 N	70.18 E
Sakhnin	132	32.52 N	35.17 E
Şakhrīyāt, Jabal aş- ∧	132	31.01 N	36.21 E
Sakht Sar	128	36.53 N	50.41 E
Saki	78	45.09 N	33.35 E
Şāki ⬥[8]	272c	19.06 N	72.53 E
Šakiai	76	54.57 N	23.03 E
Sākib	132	32.17 N	35.49 E
Sakiet Sidi Youssef	36	36.13 N	8.22 E
Sakijang Bendera, Pulau I	271c	1.13 N	103.51 E
Sakijang Pelepah, Pulau I	271c	1.13 N	103.52 E
Sakishima-shotō II	175d	24.46 N	124.00 E
Sakito	92	33.02 N	129.32 E
Sakkara → Şaqqārah	142	29.51 N	31.13 E
Sakmara ≃	86	51.46 N	55.01 E
Sako	270	34.53 N	135.47 E
Sakon Nakhon	110	17.10 N	104.09 E
Sakonnet	207	41.28 N	71.12 W
Sakonnet Point >	207	41.27 N	71.12 W
Sakoyra	150	14.17 N	1.24 E
Sakra, Pulau I	271c	1.16 N	103.42 E
Sakrand	120	26.08 N	68.16 E
Sakrivier	158	30.54 S	20.28 E
Sakrow-Paretzer Kanal ≅	264a	52.28 N	12.55 E
Saks	194	33.42 N	85.52 W
Saksagan' ≃	78	47.53 N	33.18 E
Saksauldala ⬥[2]	86	44.30 N	73.00 E
Sakskøbing	41	54.48 N	11.39 E
Sakti	124	22.02 N	82.58 E
Saku, Nihon	94	36.09 N	138.30 E
Saku, Nihon	94	36.13 N	138.29 E
Sakubva	154	19.00 S	32.10 E
Sakugi	96	34.52 N	132.43 E
Sakuma	94	35.05 N	137.48 E
Sakuma-dam ⬥[6]	94	35.05 N	137.47 E
Sakuma-ko ⊜[1]	94	35.08 N	137.47 E
Sakura	94	35.43 N	140.14 E
Sakura ≃	94	36.05 N	140.14 E
Sakurae	96	34.57 N	132.20 E
Sakurai	96	34.30 N	135.51 E
Sakura-tōge)(	270	34.36 N	135.53 E
Saku-shima I	94	34.43 N	137.03 E
Sakutō	96	35.01 N	134.14 E
Sakwaso Lake ⊜	184	53.01 N	91.55 W
Säkylä	26	61.02 N	22.20 E
Sakyō ⬥[8]	270	35.02 N	135.48 E
Sal I	150a	16.45 N	22.55 W
Sal ≃	80	47.31 N	40.45 E
Sal, Cay I	238	23.42 N	80.24 W
Sal, Ponta do >	266c	38.41 N	9.22 W
Sal, Punta >	236	15.53 N	87.37 W
Šal'a, Ross.	86	57.15 N	58.43 E
Šal'a, Slov.	30	48.09 N	17.52 E
Sala, Sve.	40	59.55 N	16.36 E
Sala, Ouadi V	146	17.00 N	20.53 E
Sala Baganza	64	44.43 N	10.14 E
Salabangka, Kepulauan II	112	3.02 S	122.25 E
Salaberry, Île de I	206	45.17 N	74.07 W
Salaberry-de-Valleyfield	206	45.15 N	74.08 W
Salaca ≃	76	57.45 N	24.21 E
Salacgrīva	76	57.45 N	24.21 E
Sala Consilina	68	40.24 N	15.36 E
Salada, Laguna ⊜, Arg.	258	35.17 S	59.24 W
Salada, Laguna ⊜, Méx.	232	32.20 N	115.40 W
Saladas	252	28.15 S	58.38 W
Saladillo	252	35.38 S	59.46 W
Saladillo ≃, Arg.	252	29.05 S	63.25 W
Saladillo ≃, Arg.	252	33.25 S	63.02 W
Saladillo, Arroyo ≃	258	35.33 S	59.04 W
Saladillo de Rodríguez, Arroyo ≃	258	35.29 S	59.01 W
Saladillo Dulce, Arroyo ≃	252	31.25 S	60.33 W
Salado, Arg.	252	28.18 S	67.15 W
Salado, Tx., U.S.	222	30.57 N	97.32 W
Salado ≃, Arg.	252	29.13 S	66.34 W
Salado ≃, Arg.	252	38.49 S	64.57 W
Salado ≃, Arg.	252	31.42 S	60.44 W
Salado ≃, Arg.	252	35.44 S	57.21 W
Salado ≃, Cuba	240p	20.36 N	76.56 W
Salado ≃, Méx.	232	26.52 N	99.19 W
Salado ≃, Méx.	234	17.55 N	96.58 W
Salado ≃, Méx.	234	18.44 N	103.36 W
Salado, Arroyo ≃, Arg.	254	41.37 S	65.02 W
Salado, Arroyo ≃, Arg.	254	40.35 S	66.33 W
Salado, Rio ≃	200	34.16 N	106.52 W
Salado Creek ≃, Tx., U.S.	196	29.14 N	98.25 W
Salado Creek ≃, Tx., U.S.	222	30.59 N	97.25 W
Salaga	150	8.33 N	0.31 W
Salagle	144	1.50 N	42.17 E
Sālah	132	32.38 N	36.46 E
Şalāh ad-Dīn □[4]	128	34.15 N	43.55 E
Salahin	144	2.57 N	46.26 E
Sala'ilua	175a	13.41 S	172.34 W
Salair	86	54.13 N	85.47 E
Salairskij kr'až ∧	86	54.15 N	85.30 E
Sălaj □[6]	38	47.15 N	23.00 E
Salak	114	2.34 N	98.20 E
Salak, Gunung ∧	115a	6.42 S	106.44 E
Šalakas	76	55.35 N	26.08 E
Šalakuša	24	62.15 N	40.17 E
Salal	146	14.51 N	17.13 E
Salala, Chile	252	30.41 S	71.32 W
Salala, Liber.	150	6.40 N	10.05 W
Salālah, Sūd.	140	21.19 N	36.13 E
Şalālah, 'Umān	118	17.00 N	54.06 E
Salamá, Guat.	236	15.06 N	90.16 W
Salamá, Hond.	236	14.50 N	86.36 W
Salamajärven kansallispuisto ♣	26	63.20 N	24.40 E
Salaman	115a	7.35 S	110.08 E
Salamanca, Chile	252	31.47 S	70.58 W
Salamanca, Esp.	34	40.58 N	5.39 W
Salamanca, Méx.	234	20.34 N	101.12 W
Salamanca, Perú	248	15.31 S	72.50 W
Salamanca, Perú	286d	12.05 S	77.00 W
Salamanca, N.Y., U.S.	210	42.09 N	78.42 W
Salamanca □[4]	34	40.45 N	6.00 W
Salamanga	158	26.28 S	32.39 E
Salamat □[5]	146	11.00 N	20.30 E
Salamat, Bahr ≃	146	9.27 N	18.06 E
Salāmbek	120	28.18 N	65.09 E
Salamina	246	5.25 N	75.29 W
Salamínos, Órmos ⊂	267c	37.56 N	23.27 E
Salamís	38	37.59 N	23.28 E
Salamís I	38	37.54 N	23.26 E
Salamis ⊥	130	35.10 N	33.54 E
Salamīyah	130	35.01 N	37.03 E
Salām Khān	120	31.47 N	66.45 E
Salamonia	216	40.23 N	84.52 W
Salamonie ≃	216	40.50 N	85.43 W
Salamonie Lake ⊜[1]	216	40.46 N	85.37 W
Salāmūn	142	31.04 N	31.28 E
Salandra	68	40.31 N	16.19 E
Sālang, Tūnel-e ⬥[5]	120	35.19 N	69.02 E
Salani	175a	14.00 S	171.33 W
Salantai	76	56.04 N	21.32 E
Salaparuta	70	37.47 N	13.00 E
Salaquí	246	7.18 N	77.33 W
Salaquí ≃	246	7.27 N	77.07 W
Salāqūs	142	28.44 N	30.50 E
Salar	85	41.21 N	69.22 E
Salara	64	44.59 N	11.25 E
Salard	38	47.13 N	22.03 E
Salarjovo	265b	55.37 N	37.26 E
Salas	248	6.16 S	79.37 W
Salas de los Infantes	34	42.01 N	3.17 W
Salat ≃	32	43.10 N	0.58 E
Salatiga	115a	7.19 S	110.30 E
Salauš	80	55.59 N	52.53 E
Salavat	86	53.21 N	55.55 E
Salavaux	58	46.55 N	7.02 E
Salaverry	248	8.14 S	78.58 W
Salavina	252	28.48 S	63.25 W
Salawati I	164	1.07 S	130.52 E
Salawe	154	3.19 S	32.52 E
Salay	116	8.52 N	124.47 E
Salāya	120	22.19 N	69.35 E
Sala y Gómez, Isla I	18	26.28 S	105.28 W
Sala y Gomez Ridge ⌖[3]	18	25.00 S	98.00 W
Salazgor'	80	54.07 N	43.09 E
Salba	88	53.14 N	92.36 E
Salbani	126	22.38 N	87.20 E
Salbohed	40	59.55 N	16.19 E
Salbosjön ⊜	40	59.50 N	14.54 E
Salbris	50	47.26 N	2.03 E
Šalbuzdag, gora ∧	84	41.19 N	47.48 E
Salcajá	236	14.53 N	91.27 W
Salccantay, Nevado ∧	248	13.20 S	72.33 W
Salcedo, Pil.	116	11.09 N	125.40 E
Salcedo, Rep. Dom.	238	19.23 N	70.25 W
Salcha ≃	180	64.29 N	147.00 W
Salching	60	48.49 N	12.34 E
Salcia	38	43.57 N	24.56 E
Šalčininkai	76	54.18 N	25.23 E
Salcombe	42	50.13 N	3.47 W
Salda ≃	86	58.48 N	61.20 E
Šaldaj	86	51.56 N	78.48 E
Saldaña	34	42.31 N	4.44 W
Saldaña ≃	246	4.01 N	74.52 W
Saldanha	158	33.00 S	17.56 E
Saldanhabaai ⊂	158	33.04 S	18.00 E
Šaldež	80	56.52 N	44.46 E
Saldungaray	252	38.12 S	61.47 W
Saldus	76	56.40 N	22.30 E
Sale, Austl.	166	38.06 S	147.04 E
Sale, It.	62	44.59 N	8.48 E
Salé, Magreb	148	34.04 N	6.50 W
Sale, Eng., U.K.	44	53.26 N	2.19 W
Salebabu, Pulau I	108	3.55 N	126.40 E
Salechard	74	66.33 N	66.40 E
Sale Creek	194	35.22 N	85.06 W
Salée, Rivière ʊ	241o	16.17 N	61.33 W
Saleh, Teluk ⊂	115b	8.34 S	117.57 E
Salelologa	175a	13.44 S	172.10 W
Salem, On., Can.	212	43.42 N	80.27 W
Salem, Dtsch.	58	47.46 N	9.16 E
Salem, India	122	11.39 N	78.10 E
Salem, S. Afr.	158	33.28 S	26.29 E
Salem, Sve.	40	59.13 N	17.44 E
Salem, Ar., U.S.	194	36.22 N	91.49 W
Salem, Il., U.S.	219	38.37 N	88.56 W
Salem, In., U.S.	218	38.03 N	86.15 W
Salem, Ia., U.S.	190	40.51 N	91.37 W
Salem, Ky., U.S.	194	37.15 N	88.14 W
Salem, Ma., U.S.	207	42.31 N	70.53 W
Salem, Mi., U.S.	281	42.24 N	83.34 W
Salem, Mo., U.S.	194	37.38 N	91.32 W
Salem, N.H., U.S.	207	42.47 N	71.12 W
Salem, N.J., U.S.	208	39.34 N	75.28 W
Salem, N.Y., U.S.	210	43.10 N	73.19 W
Salem, Oh., U.S.	214	40.54 N	80.51 W
Salem, Or., U.S.	224	44.56 N	123.02 W
Salem, S.D., U.S.	198	43.43 N	97.23 W
Salem, Ut,. U.S.	200	40.03 N	111.40 W
Salem, Va., U.S.	192	37.17 N	80.03 W
Salem, W.V., U.S.	188	39.16 N	80.33 W
Salem, Wi., U.S.	216	42.33 N	88.06 W
Salem □[6]	208	39.34 N	75.20 W
Salem ≃	208	39.34 N	75.31 W
Salem Airfield ⊠	281	42.25 N	83.34 W
Sale Marasino	64	45.43 N	10.06 E
Salem Canal ≅	285	39.41 N	75.31 W
Salem Depot	283	42.47 N	71.12 W
Salem Harbor ⊂	283	42.31 N	70.53 W
Salem Heights	214	40.54 N	80.53 W
Salemi	70	37.49 N	12.48 E
Salem Maritime National Historic Site ⊥	207	42.31 N	70.53 W
Salem State College ⊍[2]	283	42.30 N	70.54 W
Salem Upland ⋏[1]	194	37.25 N	91.30 W
Sälen, Sve.	26	61.10 N	13.16 E
Salen, Scot., U.K.	46	56.31 N	5.57 W
Salen, Scot., U.K.	46	56.43 N	5.47 W
Salentina, Penisola >[1]	68	40.25 N	18.00 E
Salentine, Murge ⬥[1]	68	40.02 N	18.13 E
Salento	68	40.15 N	15.11 E
Salernes	62	43.33 N	6.14 E
Salerno	68	40.41 N	14.47 E
Salerno □[4]	68	40.27 N	15.16 E
Salerno, Golfo di ⊂	68	40.32 N	14.42 E
Salers	32	45.08 N	2.30 E
Salesbury	262	53.47 N	2.30 W
Salesópolis	256	23.32 S	45.51 W
Salève, Mont ∧	58	46.07 N	6.10 E
Salford	44	53.28 N	2.18 W
Salford □[8]	262	53.28 N	2.23 W
Salfords	260	51.12 N	0.10 W
Šalgačova	24	62.19 N	39.35 E
Salgado	250	11.02 S	37.28 W
Salgan	80	55.14 N	45.30 E
Salgar	246	5.58 N	75.59 W
Šalgija	86	47.35 N	70.36 E
Salgir ≃	78	45.38 N	35.01 E
Salgótarján	30	48.07 N	19.48 E
Salgueiro	250	8.04 S	39.06 W
Salher ∧	122	20.43 N	73.56 E
Sali, Alg.	148	26.58 N	0.01 W
Šali, Hrv.	36	43.56 N	15.10 E
Šali, Ross.	80	55.41 N	49.40 E
Šali, Ross.	84	43.08 N	45.54 E
Salí ≃	252	27.33 S	64.57 W
Salice Salentino	68	40.23 N	17.58 E
Salice Terme	62	44.55 N	9.01 E
Salici, Monte ∧	70	37.44 N	14.38 E
Salida, Ca., U.S.	226	37.42 N	121.05 W
Salida, Co., U.S.	200	38.32 N	105.59 W
Salies-de-Béarn	32	43.29 N	0.55 W
Şalīf	144	15.18 N	42.40 E
Salignac-Eyvignes	32	44.59 N	1.19 E
Salihli	130	38.29 N	28.09 E
Şālikha	126	23.18 N	89.22 E
Šalikovo	82	55.30 N	36.13 E
Salim	140	12.52 N	28.40 E
Salima	154	13.47 S	34.26 E
Salīmah, Wāḥat ⊤[4]	140	21.22 N	29.19 E
Salimani	157a	11.47 S	43.17 E
Salimbatu	112	2.57 N	117.21 E
Salimgarh Fort ⊥	272a	28.40 N	77.14 E
Salimi	152	9.24 S	23.35 E
Salin	110	20.35 N	94.39 E
Salina, Ks., U.S.	198	38.50 N	97.36 W
Salina, Ok., U.S.	196	36.17 N	95.09 W
Salina, Pa., U.S.	214	40.31 N	79.30 W
Salina, Ut,. U.S.	200	38.57 N	111.51 W
Salina, Canale di ≅	70	38.32 N	14.54 E
Salina, Isola I	70	38.34 N	14.50 E
Salina Cruz	234	16.10 N	95.12 W
Salina Point >	238	22.13 N	74.18 W
Salinas, Bra.	255	16.10 S	42.17 W
Salinas, Ec.	246	2.13 S	80.58 W
Salinas, P.R.	240m	17.59 N	66.18 W
Salinas, Ca., U.S.	226	36.40 N	121.39 W
Salinas ≃, Bra.	255	16.37 S	42.18 W
Salinas (Chixoy) ≃, N.A.	232	16.28 N	90.33 W
Salinas ≃, Ca., U.S.	226	36.45 N	121.48 W
Salinas, Pampa de las ≍	252	31.58 S	66.42 W
Salinas, Ponta das >	152	12.50 S	12.56 E
Salinas, Sierra de ⋏	226	36.18 N	121.20 W
Salinas de Garci Mendoza	248	19.38 S	67.43 W
Salinas de Hidalgo	234	22.38 N	101.43 W
Salinas del Rey	196	27.38 N	102.24 W
Salinas Municipal Airport ⊠	226	36.40 N	121.40 W
Salinas National Monument ♣	200	34.05 N	106.14 W
Salinas Valley V	226	36.15 N	121.15 W
Salinas Victoria	196	25.53 N	100.19 W
Salin-de-Giraud	62	43.25 N	4.44 E
Salindres	62	44.10 N	4.10 E
Saline, La., U.S.	194	32.09 N	92.58 W
Saline, Mi., U.S.	216	42.10 N	83.46 W
Saline ≃, Ar., U.S.	194	33.44 N	93.58 W
Saline ≃, Ar., U.S.	194	33.10 N	92.08 W
Saline ≃, Il., U.S.	194	37.35 N	88.08 W
Saline ≃, Ks., U.S.	198	38.51 N	97.30 W
Saline ≃, Mi., U.S.	216	41.59 N	83.37 W
Saline, North Fork ≃	194	37.44 N	88.19 W
Saline Bayou ≃	194	31.45 N	92.58 W
Saline di Volterra	66	43.22 N	10.49 E
Saline Lake ⊜[1]	194	31.55 N	92.55 W
Salines, Point >	241k	12.00 N	61.48 W
Salines, Pointe des >	240e	14.24 N	60.53 W
Salineville	214	40.37 N	80.51 W
Salingyi	110	21.58 N	95.03 E
Salinópolis	250	0.37 S	47.20 W
Šalinskoje	86	55.43 N	93.46 E
Salins-les-Bains	58	46.57 N	5.53 E
Salins-les-Thermes	62	45.28 N	6.32 E
Salipolo	112	3.45 S	119.29 E
Salisbury, Austl.	168b	34.46 S	138.38 E
Salisbury, Dom.	240d	15.26 N	61.27 W
Salisbury, Eng., U.K.	42	51.05 N	1.48 W
Salisbury, Ct., U.S.	207	41.59 N	73.25 W
Salisbury, Md., U.S.	208	38.21 N	75.35 W
Salisbury, Ma., U.S.	207	42.50 N	70.51 W
Salisbury, Mo., U.S.	194	39.25 N	92.48 W
Salisbury, N.C., U.S.	192	35.40 N	80.28 W
Salisbury, Pa., U.S.	188	39.45 N	79.04 W
Salisbury Cathedral ⊍[1]	42	51.05 N	1.48 W
Salisbury Center	210	43.09 N	74.47 W
Salisbury Hall ⊥	260	51.43 N	0.16 W
Salisbury → Harare	154	17.50 S	31.03 E
Salisbury Island I, Austl.	162	34.21 S	123.32 E
Salisbury Island I, N.T., Can.	176	63.30 N	77.00 W
Salisbury Mills	210	41.26 N	74.08 W
Salisbury Plain ≍	42	51.12 N	1.55 W
Salisbury Plain ≃	283	42.02 N	70.58 W
Salish Mountains ⋏	202	48.15 N	114.45 W
Salito ≃	70	37.29 N	13.46 E
Salitpa	194	31.37 N	88.01 W
Salitre ≃	250	9.29 S	40.39 W
Salix	214	40.18 N	78.46 W
Şaljany	84	39.34 N	48.58 E
Šalkar, Kaz.	80	48.03 N	48.56 E
Šalkar, Kaz.	80	50.32 N	51.51 E
Šalkar, ozero ⊜	80	50.33 N	51.40 E
Šalkar-Jega-Kara, ozero ⊜	86	50.45 N	60.54 E
Salkehatchie ≃	192	32.37 N	80.53 W
Şalkhad	132	32.29 N	36.43 E
Salkhia	272b	22.35 N	88.21 E
Salkum	224	46.31 N	122.37 W
Salla	24	66.50 N	28.40 E
Salladasburg	210	41.17 N	77.14 W
Sallagriffon	62	43.53 N	6.54 E
Sallanches	58	45.56 N	6.38 E
Salland ⬥[1]	52	52.20 N	6.20 E
Salles-Curan	32	44.11 N	2.47 E
Salles-sous-Bois	62	44.27 N	4.56 E
Sallgast	54	51.35 N	13.51 E
Salling ⬥[1]	26	56.40 N	9.00 E
Salliqueló	252	36.45 S	62.56 W
Sallisaw	196	35.27 N	94.47 W
Sallisaw Creek ≃	194	35.23 N	94.52 W
Salluit	176	62.14 N	75.38 W
Sallūm	140	19.23 N	37.06 E
Sallūm, Khalīj as- ⊂	146	31.41 N	25.21 E
Salm ≃, Bel.	56	50.22 N	5.52 E
Salm ≃, Dtsch.	56	49.51 N	6.51 E
Salmās	128	38.11 N	44.47 E
Salmchâteau	56	50.16 N	5.54 E
Salme	76	58.10 N	22.15 E
Salmi	24	61.22 N	31.53 E
Salmo	182	49.12 N	117.17 W
Salmon	202	45.10 N	113.53 W
Salmon ≃, B.C., Can.	182	54.05 N	122.34 W
Salmon ≃, N.B., Can.	186	46.06 N	65.56 W
Salmon ≃, On., Can.	212	44.11 N	77.15 W
Salmon ≃, N.A.	188	45.02 N	74.31 W
Salmon ≃, Ct., U.S.	207	41.29 N	72.29 W
Salmon ≃, Id., U.S.	202	45.51 N	116.46 W
Salmon ≃, N.Y., U.S.	212	43.35 N	76.12 W
Salmon ≃, Or., U.S.	224	45.03 N	124.00 W
Salmon ≃, Or., U.S.	224	45.22 N	122.02 W
Salmon, East Fork ≃	202	44.16 N	114.19 W
Salmon, Middle Fork ≃	202	45.18 N	114.36 W
Salmon, North Branch ≃	212	43.32 N	75.48 W
Salmon, South Fork ≃	202	45.23 N	115.31 W
Salmon Arm	182	50.42 N	119.16 W
Salmon-Bay	186	51.26 N	57.36 W
Salmon Creek ≃, N.Y., U.S.	210	43.16 N	77.02 W
Salmon Creek ≃, N.Y., U.S.	210	43.19 N	77.43 W
Salmon Creek ≃, Wa., U.S.	224	45.44 N	122.45 W
Salmon Creek ≃, Wa., U.S.	224	46.26 N	122.52 W
Salmon Falls Creek ≃	202	42.43 N	114.51 W
Salmon Falls Creek Reservoir ⊜[1]	202	42.08 N	114.45 W
Salmon Gums	162	32.59 S	121.38 E
Salmon Lake ⊜	212	44.49 N	78.28 W
Salmon Mountain ∧	188	45.14 N	71.08 W
Salmon Mountains ⋏	204	41.00 N	123.00 W
Salmon Peak ∧	196	29.28 N	100.10 W
Salmon Point >	212	43.52 N	77.14 W
Salmon River Mountains ⋏	202	44.45 N	115.30 W
Salmon River Reservoir ⊜[1]	212	43.32 N	75.52 W
Salmon Valley	182	54.05 N	122.41 W
Salmyš ≃	86	52.01 N	55.21 E
Sal'nica	78	49.44 N	28.02 E
Salo, Centraf.	152	3.12 N	16.07 E
Salò, It.	64	45.36 N	10.31 E
Salo, Suomi	26	60.23 N	23.08 E
Salobel'ak	80	57.07 N	48.05 E
Salobra ≃	248	20.12 S	56.29 W
Salomatino	80	50.01 N	44.50 E
Salome	200	33.46 N	113.36 W
Salomon, Cap >	240e	14.30 N	61.06 W
Salomon, Îles → Solomon Islands □[1]	175e	8.00 S	159.00 E
Salomón, Islas → Solomon Islands □[1]	175e	8.00 S	159.00 E
Salomone, Monte ∧	267a	41.47 N	12.44 E
Salomon-Inseln → Solomon Islands □[1]	175e	8.00 S	159.00 E
Salon ≃	58	47.32 N	5.41 E
Salona	210	41.05 N	77.28 W
Salon-de-Provence	62	43.38 N	5.06 E
Salonga ≃	152	0.10 S	19.50 E
Salonga, Parc National de la ♣	152	1.45 S	21.20 E
Salonika → Thessaloníki	38	40.38 N	22.56 E
Salonta	38	46.48 N	21.40 E
Salor ≃, Esp.	34	39.39 N	7.03 W
Salor ≃, Esp.	34	39.42 N	6.28 W
Salorno (Salurn)	64	46.14 N	11.13 E
Saloslovo	265b	55.42 N	37.09 E
Saloum ≃	150	13.50 N	16.45 W
Šalovka ≃	265b	55.47 N	38.12 E
Salpausselkä ∧	26	61.00 N	26.30 E
Şalpazarı	130	40.59 N	39.10 E
Şalqīn	130	36.08 N	36.27 E
Sal Rei	150a	16.11 N	22.55 W
Salsacate	252	31.19 S	65.05 W
Salsette Island I	272c	19.10 N	72.53 E
Salsilgo, Qawz ⊥[8]	140	10.49 N	22.54 E
Salsipuedes, Canal ʊ	232	28.37 N	113.00 W
Salsipuedes, Punta >, C.R.	236	8.28 N	83.37 W
Salsipuedes, Punta >, Méx.	232	32.05 N	116.53 W
Šal'sk	80	46.28 N	41.33 E
Šal'skij	24	61.48 N	35.58 E
Sal'sko-Manyčskaja gr'ada ∧	80	46.40 N	42.30 E
Salso ≃	70	37.06 N	13.57 E
Salsomaggiore Terme	64	44.49 N	9.59 E
Salt ≃, U.S.	202	43.08 N	111.02 W
Salt ≃, Az., U.S.	200	33.23 N	112.18 W
Salt ≃, Ky., U.S.	194	38.00 N	85.57 W
Salt ≃, Mi., U.S.	281	42.39 N	82.47 W
Salt ≃, Mo., U.S.	219	39.28 N	91.04 W
Salt, Elk Fork ≃	219	39.28 N	91.53 W
Salt, Middle Fork ≃	219	39.28 N	91.49 W
Salt, North Fork ≃	219	39.30 N	91.47 W
Salt, South Fork ≃	219	39.28 N	91.49 W
Salta	252	24.47 S	65.25 W
Salta □[4]	252	25.00 S	64.30 W
Saltaim, ozero ⊜	86	56.10 N	71.45 E
Saltair	224	48.57 N	123.46 W
Saltaire	276	40.39 N	73.12 W
Saltanovka	76	52.47 N	34.17 E
Saltara	66	43.45 N	12.54 E
Salt Ash, Austl.	170	32.47 S	151.55 E
Saltash, Eng., U.K.	42	50.24 N	4.12 W
Saltbæk Vig ⊂	41	55.43 N	11.12 E
Salt Basin ⊜	196	31.50 N	105.00 W
Saltburn-by-the-Sea	44	54.35 N	0.58 W
Salt Cay I	240b	25.06 N	77.18 W
Saltcoats, Sk., Can.	184	51.03 N	102.12 W
Saltcoats, Scot., U.K.	46	55.38 N	4.47 W
Salt Creek ≃, On., Can.	275b	43.48 N	79.42 W
Salt Creek ≃, Ca., U.S.	204	36.15 N	116.49 W
Salt Creek ≃, Il., U.S.	194	40.08 N	89.50 W
Salt Creek ≃, Il., U.S.	278	41.49 N	87.50 W
Salt Creek ≃, In., U.S.	216	41.37 N	87.09 W
Salt Creek ≃, In., U.S.	218	38.50 N	86.32 W
Salt Creek ≃, In., U.S.	218	39.27 N	85.09 W
Salt Creek ≃, Ks., U.S.	198	39.06 N	97.44 W
Salt Creek ≃, N.M., U.S.	196	33.35 N	104.23 W
Salt Creek ≃, Ok., U.S.	196	36.32 N	96.43 W
Salt Creek ≃, Or., U.S.	202	43.43 N	122.26 W
Salt Creek ≃, Or., U.S.	224	45.09 N	123.13 W
Salt Creek ≃, Wy., U.S.	202	43.41 N	106.20 W
Salt Creek, Middle Fork ≃	218	39.04 N	86.15 W
Salt Creek, North Fork ≃, Il., U.S.	216	40.13 N	88.50 W
Salt Creek, North Fork ≃, In., U.S.	218	39.08 N	86.21 W
Salt Creek, West Branch ≃	278	42.02 N	88.01 W
Salt Creek South Fork ≃	218	39.02 N	86.16 W
Salt Draw V	196	31.19 N	103.28 W
Saltee Islands II	48	52.07 N	6.36 W
Salten	41	56.05 N	9.35 E
Saltfleet	44	53.25 N	0.11 E
Saltford	42	51.24 N	2.27 W
Salt Fork Lake ⊜[1]	214	41.07 N	81.30 W
Salt Fork State Park ♣	214	40.06 N	81.29 W
Saltholm I	41	55.38 N	12.46 E
Saltillo, Méx.	232	25.25 N	101.00 W
Saltillo, Ms., U.S.	194	34.22 N	88.40 W
Saltillo, Pa., U.S.	214	40.13 N	78.01 W
Saltillo, Tn., U.S.	194	35.22 N	88.12 W
Saltillo, Tx., U.S.	222	33.11 N	95.20 W
Salt Island I	240m	18.23 N	64.31 W
Salt Lake	158	29.16 S	24.00 E
Salt Lake ⊜	196	34.05 N	103.05 W
Salt Lake City	200	40.45 N	111.53 W
Salto, Arg.	252	34.17 S	60.15 W
Salto, Ur.	252	31.23 S	57.58 W
Salto ≃	66	42.23 N	12.54 E
Salto, Lago del ⊜	66	42.15 N	13.02 E
Salto da Divisa	255	16.00 S	39.57 W
Salto de las Rosas	252	34.43 S	68.14 W
Salto del Fraile >	286d	12.11 S	77.03 W
Salto del Guairá	252	24.03 S	54.17 W
Salto Grande	255	22.54 S	49.59 W
Salto Grande, Embalse ⊜[1]	252	31.00 S	57.55 W
Salton City	204	33.19 N	115.59 W
Salton Sea ⊜	204	33.19 N	115.50 W
Salton Sea State Recreation Area ♣	204	33.29 N	115.53 W
Saltonstall, Lake ⊜	283	42.47 N	71.04 W
Sāltora	126	23.32 N	86.56 E
Saltoro Range ⋏	123	35.17 N	77.03 E
Salto Santiago, Represa de ⊜[1]	252	25.40 S	52.30 W
Salt Pan Creek ≃	274a	33.59 S	151.02 E
Saltpeter Creek ⊂	284b	39.20 N	76.22 W
Salt Point	210	41.44 N	73.42 W
Saltpond	150	5.12 N	1.04 W
Salt Range ⋏	123	32.40 N	72.35 E
Salt River Indian Reservation ⬥[4]	200	33.31 N	111.48 W
Saltsburg	214	40.29 N	79.27 W
Saltsjöbaden	40	59.17 N	18.18 E
Salt Slough ≃	226	37.18 N	120.54 W
Saltspring Island I	224	48.47 N	123.30 W
Salt Springs Reservoir ⊜[1]	226	38.30 N	120.11 W
Saltville	192	36.52 N	81.45 W
Salt Wells Creek ≃	200	41.39 N	108.59 W
Saltykovka, Ross.	80	52.07 N	44.05 E
Saltykovka, Ross.	265b	55.46 N	37.55 E
Saluda, S.C., U.S.	192	34.00 N	81.46 W
Saluda, Va., U.S.	208	37.36 N	76.35 W
Saluda ≃	192	34.00 N	81.04 W
Saludecio	66	43.52 N	12.40 E
Saluën → Salween ≃	12	16.31 N	97.37 E
Salue Timpaus, Selat ʊ	112	1.55 S	124.00 E
Salug	116	8.07 N	122.47 E
Saluggia	62	45.14 N	8.00 E
Sālūmbar	120	24.08 N	74.03 E
Salunga	208	40.06 N	76.26 W
Saluping Island I	116	6.20 N	122.02 E
Salūq 'Atīq	130	36.36 N	39.07 E
Sālūr	122	18.32 N	83.13 E
Salurn → Salorno	64	46.14 N	11.13 E
Salussola	62	45.27 N	8.07 E
Salutaris	256	22.10 S	43.17 W
Saluzzo	62	44.39 N	7.29 E
Salvación, Bahía ⊂	254	50.55 S	75.05 W
Salvado, Mount ∧	162	25.15 S	121.01 E
Salvador, Bra.	255	12.59 S	38.31 W
Salvador, Pil.	116	7.54 N	123.50 E
Salvador, Ca., U.S.	226	38.20 N	122.18 W
Salvador, El → El Salvador □[1]	236	13.50 N	88.55 W
Salvador, Lake ⊜	194	29.45 N	90.15 W
Salvador Island I	116	15.31 N	119.55 E
Salvador María	258	35.18 S	59.10 W
Salvador Mazza	252	22.04 S	63.43 W
Salvage	186	48.41 N	53.38 W
Salvail ≃	206	45.49 N	72.58 W
Salvaterra	250	0.46 S	48.31 W
Salvaterra de Magos	34	39.01 N	8.48 W
Salvatierra	234	20.13 N	100.53 W
Salve	68	39.51 N	18.17 E
Salviac	32	44.41 N	1.16 E
Salwā, Dawḥat ⊂	128	25.30 N	50.40 E
Salwā Baḥrī	140	24.44 N	32.56 E
Salween ≃	12	16.31 N	97.37 E
Salyān	124	28.22 N	82.10 E
Salyer	204	40.53 N	123.35 W
Şalyersville	192	37.45 N	83.04 W
Šalygino	78	51.34 N	34.07 E
Salza ≃, Dtsch.	54	51.23 N	11.50 E
Salza ≃, Öst.	61	47.40 N	14.43 E
Salzach ≃	30	48.12 N	12.56 E
Salza Irpina	68	40.55 N	14.53 E
Salzbergen	52	52.19 N	7.20 E
Salzböde ≃	56	50.40 N	8.42 E
Salzbrunn	156	24.23 S	18.00 E
Salzburg	64	47.48 N	13.02 E
Salzburg □[3]	64	47.25 N	13.15 E
Salzgitter	54	52.10 N	10.25 E
Salzgitter-Bad ⬥[8]	52	52.04 N	10.23 E
Salzgitter-Barum ⬥[8]	52	52.07 N	10.25 E
Salzgitter-Immendorf ⬥[8]	52	52.09 N	10.26 E
Salzgitter-Lebenstedt ⬥[8]	52	52.09 N	10.20 E
Salzgitter-Thiede ⬥[8]	52	52.11 N	10.29 E
Salzgitter-Watenstedt ⬥[8]	54	52.06 N	10.22 E
Salzhaff ⊂	54	54.06 N	11.36 E
Salzhausen	52	53.13 N	10.09 E
Salzhemmendorf	52	52.04 N	9.35 E
Salzkammergut ⬥[1]	64	47.45 N	13.30 E
Salzkotten	52	51.40 N	8.36 E
Salzmünde	54	51.31 N	11.49 E
Salzwedel	54	52.51 N	11.09 E
Sam, Gabon	152	0.58 N	11.16 E
Sām, India	120	26.50 N	70.31 E
Samā	132	32.28 N	36.14 E
Sama ≃	248	18.10 S	70.40 W
Sam A. Baker State Park ♣	194	37.16 N	90.34 W
Samacá	246	5.29 N	73.29 W
Samacimbo	152	13.33 S	16.59 E
Sama [de Langreo]	34	43.18 N	5.41 W
Samādūn	142	30.20 N	30.57 E
Samagaltaj	88	50.36 N	95.03 E
Samah	146	28.12 N	19.09 E
Samāika ⬥[8]	272a	28.32 N	77.05 E
Samaipata	248	18.09 S	63.52 W
Samal (Peñaplata)	116	7.05 N	125.42 E
Samalá ≃	236	14.11 N	91.47 W
Samalanga	114	5.13 N	96.22 E
Şamalayuca	200	31.21 N	106.28 W
Šamaldy-Saj	85	41.12 N	72.11 E
Samales Group II	116	6.00 N	121.45 E
Samalga Pass ʊ	180	52.48 N	169.25 W
Samal Island I	116	7.03 N	125.44 E
Sāmalkot	122	17.03 N	82.11 E
Samālūt	142	28.18 N	30.42 E
Samambaia ≃	255	22.45 S	53.21 W
Samāna, India	124	30.09 N	76.12 E
Samaná, Rep. Dom.	238	19.13 N	69.19 W
Samaná, Bahía de ⊂	238	19.10 N	69.25 W
Samaná, Cabo >	238	19.18 N	69.09 W
Samana Cay I	238	23.06 N	73.42 W
Samandağı	130	36.07 N	35.56 E
Samandıra	130	40.59 N	29.13 E
Samandıra ≃	267b	40.59 N	29.15 E
Samangān	120	36.16 N	68.01 E
Samangān □[4]	120	36.15 N	67.40 E
Samangwa	152	4.24 S	24.10 E
Samani	92a	42.07 N	142.56 E
Samaniego	246	1.20 N	77.35 W
Samanlı Dağları ⋏	130	40.36 N	29.30 E
Samannūd	142	30.58 N	31.15 E
Samar	132	29.49 N	35.01 E
Samar □[4]	116	11.50 N	125.00 E
Samar I	116	12.00 N	125.00 E
Samara	80	53.12 N	50.09 E
Samara ≃, Ross.	80	53.10 N	50.04 E
Samara ≃, Ukr.	78	48.27 N	35.07 E
Samarai	164	10.37 S	150.40 E
Samara Oblast' □[4]	80	53.30 N	50.30 E
Samarate	62	45.38 N	8.47 E
Samarga	89	47.17 N	138.48 E
Samarga ≃	89	47.15 N	138.46 E
Samaria, Id., U.S.	202	42.07 N	112.20 W
Samaria, Mi., U.S.	216	41.48 N	83.35 W
Samaria (As-Sāmirah) □[9]	132	32.15 N	35.10 E
Samaria, Mount ∧	169	36.52 S	146.03 E
Samaria Gorge → Farángi Samariás V	38	35.18 N	24.00 E
Samariapo	246	5.15 N	67.48 W
Samarinda	112	0.30 S	117.09 E
Samarka	89	44.44 N	134.13 E
Samarkand	85	39.40 N	66.48 E
Samarkand □[4]	85	39.40 N	67.15 E
Sāmarrā'	128	34.12 N	43.52 E
Samar Sea ⊤[2]	116	12.15 N	124.15 E
Samarskoje, Kaz.	86	49.00 N	83.23 E
Samarskoje, Ross.	83	46.56 N	39.41 E
Şamarskoje, Ross.	86	52.02 N	58.10 E
Šamary	86	57.21 N	58.14 E
Samasata	123	29.21 N	71.33 E
Samassi	71	39.29 N	8.54 E
Samastīpur	124	25.51 N	85.47 E
Samatya ⬥[8]	267b	41.00 N	28.56 E
Samaúna	248	7.50 S	60.02 W
Samawāri	120	28.34 N	66.46 E
Samba, Centraf.	152	6.49 N	21.12 E
Samba, India	123	32.34 N	75.07 E
Samba, Zaïre	152	0.14 N	21.19 E
Samba, Zaïre	154	4.38 S	26.22 E
Samba Caju	152	8.46 S	15.24 E
Sambaetiba	256	22.41 S	42.48 W
Sambaíba	250	7.08 S	45.21 W
Sambalpur	120	21.27 N	83.58 E
Sambar, Tanjung >	112	2.59 S	110.19 E
Sambas	112	1.20 N	109.15 E
Sambava	157b	14.16 S	50.10 E
Sambawizi	154	18.21 S	26.16 E
Şambayat	130	37.41 N	38.03 E
Šambāza	120	31.49 N	69.20 E
Sambek, Ross.	83	47.20 N	39.01 E
Sambek, Ross.	83	47.45 N	39.48 E
Sambek ≃	83	47.16 N	39.01 E
Sambesi → Zambezi ≃	138	18.55 S	36.04 E
Sambhal	124	28.35 N	78.33 E
Sāmbhar	120	26.55 N	75.12 E
Sāmbhar Lake ⊜	120	26.58 N	75.05 E
Sambiase	68	38.58 N	16.17 E
Sambia → Zambia □[1]	154	14.30 S	27.30 E
Sambit, Pulau I	112	1.46 N	119.03 E
Sambito ≃	250	5.40 S	42.10 W
Sambo	152	12.57 S	16.05 E
Samboan	116	9.32 N	123.18 E
Samboja	112	1.02 S	117.02 E
Sambolabbo	152	7.05 N	11.59 E
Sâmbor, Kâm.	110	12.46 N	105.58 E
Sambor, Ukr.	78	49.32 N	23.11 E
Samborombón ≃	252	35.43 S	57.20 W
Samborombón, Bahía ⊂	252	36.00 S	57.12 W
Samborondón	246	1.57 S	79.44 W
Sambre ≃	32	50.28 N	4.52 E
Sambre à l'Oise, Canal de la ≅	50	49.39 N	3.20 E
Sambreville	56	50.26 N	4.37 E
Sambriāl	123	32.28 N	74.21 E
Sambú ≃	246	8.05 N	78.18 W
Sambuca di Sicilia	70	37.39 N	13.07 E
Sambuca Pistoiese	66	44.06 N	11.00 E
Sambughetti, Monte ∧	70	37.50 N	14.22 E
Sambungo	152	8.39 S	20.43 E
Sambusu	156	17.50 S	19.20 E
Samch'ŏk	98	37.27 N	129.10 E
Sam Chom, Khao ∧	110	8.07 N	99.26 E
Samch'ŏnp'o	98	34.57 N	128.03 E
Samdžir, gora ∧	88	52.32 N	93.53 E
Same	154	4.04 S	37.44 E
Same ≃	94	36.54 N	140.49 E
Samedan	58	46.33 N	9.52 E
Samegawa	94	37.02 N	140.31 E
Sāmen	128	34.12 N	48.42 E
Samene, Oued V	148	26.49 N	7.08 E
Samer	50	50.38 N	1.45 E
Sameru Dando ∧	124	27.02 N	90.20 E
Samet'	80	57.49 N	40.44 E
Samford	171a	27.23 S	152.53 E
Samfya	154	11.21 S	29.32 E
Samga	98	35.25 N	128.05 E
Samho	98	39.56 N	127.53 E
Saminka ≃	265b	55.45 N	37.17 E
Samiria ≃	246	4.42 S	74.13 W
Samish	224	48.35 N	122.33 W
Samish ≃	224	48.38 N	122.29 W
Samish Bay ⊂	224	48.36 N	122.28 W
Samish Lake ⊜	224	48.39 N	122.24 W
Samj	132	32.27 N	36.30 E
Şamka	110	20.09 N	96.57 E
Šamkir	84	40.50 N	46.02 E
Samlesbury	262	53.46 N	2.38 W
Samlesbury Aerodrome ⊠	262	53.47 N	2.34 W
Samlesbury Bottoms	262	53.45 N	2.34 W
Samlesbury Higher Hall ⊥	262	53.46 N	2.34 W
Şamlı	130	39.48 N	27.51 E
Sammamish, Lake ⊜	224	47.36 N	122.06 W
Sammichele di Bari	68	40.53 N	16.57 E
Samnangjin	98	35.23 N	128.50 E
Samnaun	58	46.56 N	10.22 E

Column headings: ENGLISH — Name, Page, Lat.°', Long.°'; DEUTSCH — Name, Seite, Breite°', Länge°' E = Ost

Symbols in the index entries represent the broad categories identified in the key at the right. Symbols with superior numbers (⋏[1]) identify subcategories (see complete key on page I · 1).

Symbole im Register stellen die rechts im Schlüssel erklärten Kategorien dar. Symbole mit hochgestellten Ziffern (⋏[1]) bezeichnen Unterabteilungen einer Kategorie (vgl. vollständiger Schlüssel auf Seite I · 1).

Los símbolos incluídos en el texto del índice representan las grandes categorias identificadas con la clave a la derecha. Los símbolos con numeros en su parte superior (⋏[1]) identifican las subcategorías (véase la clave completa en la página I · 1).

Les symboles de l'index représentent les catégories indiquées dans la légende à droite. Les symboles suivis d'un indice (⋏[1]) représentent des sous-catégories (voir légende complète à la page I · 1).

Os símbolos incluídos no texto do índice representam as grandes categorias identificadas com a chave à direita. Os símbolos com números em sua parte superior (⋏[1]) identificam as subcategorias (veja-se a chave completa à página I · 1).

Symbol	English	Deutsch	Español	Français	Português
∧	Mountain	Berg	Montaña	Montagne	Montanha
⋏	Mountains	Gebirge	Montañas	Montagnes	Montanhas
)(	Pass	Paß	Paso	Col	Passo
V	Valley, Canyon	Tal, Cañon	Valle, Cañón	Vallée, Canyon	Vale, Canhão
≍	Plain	Ebene	Llano	Plaine	Planície
>	Cape	Kap	Cabo	Cap	Cabo
I	Island	Insel	Isla	Île	Ilha
II	Islands	Inseln	Islas	Îles	Ilhas
⊥	Other Topographic Features	Andere Topographische Objekte	Otros Elementos Topográficos	Autres données topographiques	Outros acidentes topográficos

ESPAÑOL: Nombre · Página · Lat.°′ · Long.°′ W = Oeste
FRANÇAIS: Nom · Page · Lat.°′ · Long.°′ W = Ouest
PORTUGUÊS: Nome · Página · Lat.°′ · Long.°′ W = Oeste

Samnaungruppe ^ 58 47.00 N 10.25 E
San Ngao 110 17.15 N 99.01 E
Samnū 146 27.17 N 14.53 E
Samnye 98 35.55 N 127.05 E
Samo 164 3.58 S 152.51 E
Samoa americane — American Samoa □² 175a 14.20 S 170.00 W
Samoa — American Samoa □² 175a 14.20 S 170.00 W
Samoa Basin ✦¹ 14 16.00 S 166.00 W
Samoa i Sisifo — Western Samoa □¹ 175a 13.55 S 172.00 W
Samoa Islands II 175a 14.00 S 171.00 W
Samo Alto 252 30.25 S 70.58 W
Samoa Occidentales — Western Samoa □¹ 175a 13.55 S 172.00 W
Samoa Occidental — Western Samoa □¹ 175a 13.55 S 172.00 W
Samoa — Western Samoa □¹ 175a 13.55 S 172.00 W
Samobor 36 45.48 N 15.43 E
Samoded 24 63.38 N 40.29 E
Samoëns 58 46.05 N 6.44 E
Samofalovka 80 48.57 N 44.13 E
Samoggia ≃ 64 44.41 N 11.15 E
Samojlovka 80 51.12 N 43.43 E
Samokov 38 42.20 N 23.33 E
Samolaco 58 46.15 N 9.21 E
Samora ≃ 266c 38.50 N 8.57 W
Sámos 38 37.45 N 27.00 E
Sámos I 38 37.48 N 26.44 E
Samosdelka 80 46.02 N 47.53 E
Samoset 220 27.28 N 82.32 W
Samosir, Pulau I 114 2.35 N 98.50 E
Samotevići 76 53.13 N 31.50 E
Samothrace — Samothráki I 38 40.30 N 25.32 E
Samothráki 38 40.28 N 25.31 E
Samothráki I 38 40.30 N 25.32 E
Samouco 266c 38.43 N 9.00 W
Šamovo 76 54.12 N 31.22 E
Samovol'no-Ivanovka 80 52.33 N 50.53 E
S'amozero 24 61.54 N 33.18 E
Sampacho 252 33.23 S 64.43 W
Sampaga 112 2.19 S 119.07 E
Sampaio Correia 256 22.52 S 42.36 W
Sampalan 115b 8.41 S 115.34 E
Sampanahan 112 2.38 S 116.11 E
Sampang 115a 7.12 S 113.14 E
Sampara ≃ 112 3.49 S 122.28 E
Sampawams Creek ≃ 276 40.41 N 73.19 W
Sam Pervyj 86 45.28 N 56.06 E
Sampéyre 62 44.34 N 7.11 E
Sampford Peverell 42 50.56 N 3.22 W
Sampieri 70 36.43 N 14.44 E
Sampit 112 2.32 S 112.57 E
Sampit ≃ 112 2.44 S 112.54 E
Sampit, Teluk ⊂ 112 3.05 S 113.03 E
Sampolawa 112 5.36 S 122.43 E
Sampson 279b 40.10 N 79.53 W
Sampson State Park ♦ 210 42.44 N 76.55 W
Sampués 246 9.11 N 75.23 W
Sampur 80 52.19 N 41.37 E
Sampwe 154 9.20 S 27.26 E
Samrajevka 78 49.46 N 29.44 E
Samrāla 123 30.51 N 76.11 E
Sam Rayburn Reservoir ⊜¹ 194 31.27 N 94.37 W
Samre 144 13.07 N 39.10 E
Samreboi 150 5.36 N 2.34 W
Samro, ozero ⊜ 76 58.57 N 28.49 E
Samrong, Khlong ≚ 269a 13.39 N 100.34 E
Sams ≃ 224 47.38 N 124.01 W
Samsang 120 30.31 N 82.37 E
Samsø I 41 55.52 N 10.37 E
Samsø Bælt Ʉ 41 55.48 N 10.47 E
Samson, Al., U.S. 194 31.06 N 86.02 W
Sam Son, Viet 110 19.44 N 105.54 E
Samson I 42a 49.56 N 6.22 W
Samson Indian Reserve ✦⁴ 182 52.48 N 113.10 W
Samsonovka 85 42.44 N 70.32 E
Samsonvale, Lake ⊜¹ 171a 27.15 S 152.55 E
Samsonville 210 41.53 N 74.18 W
Sams Point ∧ 210 41.40 N 74.22 W
Samsu 98 41.19 N 127.59 E
Samsun 130 41.17 N 36.20 E
Samsun □⁴ 130 41.15 N 36.00 E
Samsun Körfezi ⊂ 130 41.18 N 36.21 E
Samtens 54 54.21 N 13.17 E
Samthar 124 25.51 N 78.55 E
Samtown 194 31.16 N 92.26 W
Samtredia 84 42.10 N 42.20 E
Samu 112 2.01 S 115.57 E
Samūdragarh 126 23.21 N 88.20 E
Samuel, Mount ∧ 162 19.41 S 134.09 E
Samuel P. Taylor State Park ♦ 226 38.01 N 122.44 W
Samugheo 71 39.57 N 8.56 E
Samuhú 252 27.31 S 60.24 W
Samui, Ko I 110 9.30 N 100.00 E
Samukawa 94 35.22 N 139.23 E
Samundri 123 31.04 N 72.58 E
Samur ≃ 84 41.53 N 48.32 E
Samur-Apšeronskij kanal ≚ 84 41.38 N 48.25 E
Samurskij chrebet ^ 84 41.35 N 47.35 E
Samus' 86 56.46 N 84.44 E
Samusele 152 10.06 S 24.05 E
Samut Prakan 110 13.36 N 100.36 E
Samut Prakan □⁴ 269a 13.35 N 100.35 E
Samut Sakhon 110 13.32 N 100.17 E
Samut Songkhram 110 13.24 N 100.00 E
Samuyi Shankou)(124 29.55 N 84.46 E
S'amža 76 60.01 N 41.02 E
San 150 13.18 N 4.54 W
San (Xan) ≃, Asia 110 13.32 N 105.58 E
San ≃, Europe 30 50.44 N 21.50 E
San ≃, Zhg. 100 33.02 N 119.21 E
Saña, Perú 248 6.55 S 79.35 W
Ṣan'ā', Yaman 144 15.23 N 44.12 E
Ṣana ≃, Bos. 36 45.03 N 16.23 E
Šan'a ≃, Ross. 82 54.41 N 35.55 E
Sanaag □⁴ 144 10.30 N 47.45 E
Sanaba 150 12.25 N 3.49 W
Sanab[illegible] 150 15.06 N 10.55 W
Ṣan[illegible] 142 27.30 N 30.47 E
Sanada 94 36.27 N 138.20 E
Sanae ᵿ³ 9 70.30 S 2.30 W
Sanafā 142 30.47 N 31.21 E
Ṣanāfīr I 128 27.55 N 34.40 E
Sanaga ≃ 152 3.35 N 9.38 E
Sanage-yama ∧ 94 35.12 N 137.10 E
Sanagōchi 96 33.59 N 134.28 E
San Agustín, Arg. 252 38.01 S 58.21 W
San Agustín, Arg. 252 31.59 S 64.23 W
San Agustín, Bol. 248 21.05 S 67.45 W
San Agustín, Col. 246 1.53 N 76.16 W
San Agustín, Méx. 200 31.31 N 106.15 W
San Agustín, Pil. 116 16.30 N 121.45 E
San Agustín, Pil. 116 12.25 N 120.59 E
San Agustín, Cape ≻ 116 6.16 N 126.11 E
San Agustín, Plains of ≚ 200 33.50 N 108.00 W
San Agustín Atenango 234 17.38 N 97.59 W
San Agustín de Valle Fértil 252 30.38 S 67.27 W
San Agustín Loxicha 234 16.01 N 96.38 W
San Agustín Tlaxiaca 234 20.07 N 98.53 W
Sanak Islands II 180 54.25 N 162.35 W
San Alberto 196 27.30 N 101.20 W
San Alejo 236 13.26 N 87.58 W
Sān al-Hajar, Birkat ⊜ 142 31.03 N 31.54 E
Sān al-Hajar al-Qiblīyah 142 30.58 N 31.52 E
Sanalona, Presa ⊜¹ 232 24.53 N 107.00 W
San Ambrosio, Isla I 244 26.21 S 79.52 W
Sanam Chai, Khlong ≚ 269a 13.38 N 100.27 E
Sanana 112 2.04 S 125.58 E
Sanana, Pulau I 112 2.12 S 125.55 E
Sānand 120 22.59 N 72.23 E
Sanandaj 128 35.19 N 47.00 E
Sanandita 248 21.40 S 63.35 W
San Andreas 226 38.11 N 120.40 W
San Andreas Fault V 282 37.25 N 122.15 W
San Andreas Lake ⊜ 282 37.36 N 122.26 W
San Andrés, Col. 236 12.35 N 81.42 W
San Andrés, Col. 246 6.49 N 72.52 W
San Andrés, Méx. 232 27.14 N 114.14 W
San Andrés, Pan. 236 8.36 N 82.44 W
San Andrés, Isla de I 236 12.32 N 81.42 W
San Andrés, Laguna ⊂ 234 22.40 N 97.52 W
San Andrés Calpan 234 19.06 N 98.27 W
San Andrés Cohamiata 234 22.12 N 104.03 W
San Andrés de Giles 258 34.27 S 59.27 W
San Andres Mountains ^ 200 32.55 N 106.45 W
San Andres Point ≻ 116 13.34 N 121.52 E
San Andrés Sajcabajá 236 15.13 N 90.55 W
San Andrés Timilpan 234 19.52 N 99.45 W
San Andrés Tototlepec ✦⁸ 286a 19.15 N 99.10 W
San Andrés Tuxtla 234 18.27 N 95.13 W
San Andrés y Providencia □⁸ 238 12.30 N 81.45 W
Sananduva 252 27.57 S 51.48 W
San Angelo 196 31.27 N 100.26 W
San Angel — Villa Obregón ✦⁸ 286a 19.21 N 99.12 W
San Anselmo 226 37.58 N 122.33 W
San Antero 246 9.23 N 75.46 W
San Antonio, Arg. 252 28.57 S 65.20 W
San Antonio, Arg. 252 28.56 S 65.06 W
San Antonio, Belize 236 16.15 N 89.02 W
San Antonio, Chile 252 27.53 S 70.03 W
San Antonio, Chile 252 33.35 S 71.38 W
San Antonio, Col. 246 3.55 N 75.28 W
San Antonio, C.R. 236 10.12 N 85.26 W
San Antonio, N. Mar. Is. 174n 15.08 N 145.43 E
San Antonio, Perú 248 6.22 S 76.21 W
San Antonio, Pil. 116 12.25 N 124.17 E
San Antonio, Pil. 116 14.57 N 120.05 E
San Antonio, P.R. 240m 18.30 N 67.07 W
San Antonio, Fl., U.S. 220 28.20 N 82.16 W
San Antonio, N.M., U.S. 200 35.06 N 106.22 W
San Antonio, Tx., U.S. 196 29.25 N 98.29 W
San Antonio, Ur. 252 31.22 S 57.48 W
San Antonio, Ur. 258 34.27 S 56.05 W
San Antonio □⁷ 286b 22.55 N 82.29 W
San Antonio ≃, Méx. 196 29.13 N 103.47 W
San Antonio ≃, Méx. 232 31.00 N 116.15 W
San Antonio ≃, Ca., U.S. 226 35.52 N 120.48 W
San Antonio ≃, Tx., U.S. 196 28.30 N 96.50 W
San Antonio ≃¹ 288 34.24 S 58.31 W
San Antonio, Cabo ≻ 252 36.40 S 56.42 W
San Antonio, Cabo de ≻ 240p 21.52 N 84.57 W
San Antonio, Lake ⊜¹ 226 35.55 N 121.00 W
San Antonio, Mount ∧ 228 34.17 N 117.39 W
San Antonio, Punta ≻, Méx. 232 29.46 N 115.42 W
San Antonio, Punta ≻, Méx. 232 26.31 N 111.28 W
San Antonio, Río ≃ 200 37.11 N 105.55 W
San Antonio Bay ⊂, Pil. 116 8.38 N 117.35 E
San Antonio Bay ⊂, Tx., U.S. 196 28.20 N 96.45 W
San Antonio Canyon V 280 34.12 N 117.40 W
San Antonio Creek ≃ 226 38.09 N 122.33 W
San Antonio Dam ✦⁶ 280 34.09 N 117.41 W
San Antonio de Areco 258 34.15 S 59.28 W
San Antonio de Galipán 286c 10.33 N 66.53 W
San Antonio de los Baños 240p 22.53 N 82.30 W
San Antonio de los Cobres 252 24.11 S 66.21 W
San Antonio del Táchira 246 7.50 N 72.27 W
San Antonio de Padua, Arg. 258 34.40 S 58.42 W
San Antonio de Padua, Méx. 234 22.35 N 104.30 W
San Antonio de Padua, Mission ᵿ¹ 226 36.01 N 121.15 W
San Antonio de Tamanaco 246 9.41 N 66.03 W
San Antonio El Bravo 232 30.10 N 104.42 W
San Antonio Eloxochitlán 234 18.11 N 96.52 W
San Antonio Heights 228 34.10 N 117.40 W
San Antonio Mountain ∧ 200 36.52 N 106.02 W
San Antonio Nogalar 234 23.04 N 98.22 W
San Antonio Oeste 254 40.44 S 64.56 W
San Antonio Reservoir ⊜¹ 226 37.35 N 121.50 W
San Antonio Someyucan 286a 19.27 N 99.16 W
San Antonio Suchitepéquez 236 14.32 N 91.25 W
San Antonio Tecómitl ✦⁸ 286a 19.13 N 98.59 W
San Antonio Ticino 266b 45.35 N 8.46 E
San Ardo 226 36.01 N 120.54 W
Sanaroa Island I 164 9.35 S 151.00 E
Sanary-sur-Mer 62 43.07 N 5.48 E
Sanatoga 285 40.15 N 75.36 W
Sanatoga Creek ≃ 285 40.14 N 75.36 W
Sanatorium 194 31.53 N 89.46 W
San Augustine 194 31.31 N 94.06 W
San Augustin Pass)(200 32.26 N 106.34 W
Sanaur 123 30.18 N 76.27 E
Sanaw 144 17.50 N 51.00 E
Sanāwad 120 22.11 N 76.04 E
Sanāwān 123 30.19 N 70.59 E
Sanbao, Zhg. 102 43.00 N 93.19 E
Sanbao, Zhg. 105 40.20 N 116.02 E
Sanbaoyingzi 104 41.34 N 120.56 E
San Bartolomeo in Galdo 68 41.24 N 15.01 E
San Basilio 71 39.32 N 9.11 E
San Benedetto, Alpe di ^ 66 43.53 N 11.43 E
San Benedetto del Tronto 66 42.57 N 13.53 E
San Benedetto in Alpe 66 43.59 N 11.41 E
San Benedetto Po 64 45.02 N 10.55 E
San Benedicto, Isla I 232 19.18 N 110.49 W
San Benigno Canavese 62 45.13 N 7.46 E
San Benito, Bol. 248 17.31 S 65.55 W
San Benito, Guat. 232 16.55 N 89.54 W
San Benito, Perú 248 7.26 S 78.56 W
San Benito, Tx., U.S. 196 26.07 N 97.37 W
San Benito □⁶ 226 36.51 N 121.24 W
San Benito ≃ 226 36.53 N 121.34 W
San Benito Mountain ∧ 226 36.22 N 120.38 W
San Bernard ≃ 222 28.52 N 95.27 W
San Bernardino, Schw. 58 46.28 N 9.12 E
San Bernardino, Ca., U.S. 228 34.07 N 117.18 W
San Bernardino □⁶ 228 34.40 N 117.17 W
San Bernardino, Passo del)(58 46.30 N 9.11 E
San Bernardino Mountains ^ 204 34.10 N 116.45 W
San Bernardino National Forest ♦ 280 34.12 N 117.38 W
San Bernardino Strait Ʉ 116 12.32 N 124.10 E
San Bernardo, Arg. 252 27.17 S 60.42 W
San Bernardo, Chile 252 33.36 S 70.43 W
San Bernardo, Méx. 232 25.59 N 105.33 W
San Bernardo, Isla I 236 11.32 N 85.06 W
San Bernardo, Islas de II 246 9.45 N 75.50 W
San Bernardo del Viento 246 9.21 N 75.57 W
Sanbe-yama ∧ 96 35.08 N 132.37 E
San Biagio 66 44.35 N 11.52 E
San Biagio di Callalta 64 45.41 N 12.22 E
San Biagio Platani 70 37.31 N 13.32 E
San Biagio Saracinisco 66 41.37 N 13.55 E
San Blas, Méx. 232 26.05 N 108.46 W
San Blas, Méx. 234 21.31 N 105.16 W
San Blas, Cape ≻ 192 29.40 N 85.22 W
San Blas, Golfo de ⊂ 246 9.30 N 79.00 W
San Blas, Serranía de ^ 246 9.18 N 79.00 W
San Blas de los Sauces 252 28.24 S 67.05 W
San Bonifacio 64 45.24 N 11.16 E
San Borja 248 14.49 S 66.51 W
Sanborn, Ia., U.S. 198 43.10 N 95.39 W
Sanborn, Mn., U.S. 198 44.12 N 95.07 W
Sanborn, N.Y., U.S. 210 43.08 N 78.53 W
Sanborn, N.D., U.S. 198 46.56 N 98.13 W
San Bovio 266b 45.28 N 9.19 E
San Bruno 226 37.37 N 122.24 W
San Bruno, Point ≻ 282 37.39 N 122.22 W
San Bruno Mountain ∧ 282 37.42 N 122.25 W
Sanbu 94 35.39 N 140.23 E
San Buenaventura, Bol. 248 14.28 S 67.35 W
San Buenaventura, Méx. 232 27.05 N 101.32 W
San Buenaventura — Ventura 228 34.17 N 119.18 W
San Buono 66 41.59 N 14.34 E
San Calogero 68 38.34 N 16.01 E
San Calogero, Monte ∧ 70 37.57 N 13.44 E
San Candido (Innichen) 64 46.44 N 12.17 E
Sancang 100 32.45 N 120.43 E
San Carlo 58 46.25 N 8.32 E
San Carlos, Arg. 252 27.45 S 55.54 W
San Carlos, Arg. 252 33.46 S 69.02 W
San Carlos, Arg. 252 25.56 S 65.56 W
San Carlos, Chile 252 36.25 S 71.58 W
San Carlos, Chile 286e 33.36 S 70.35 W
San Carlos, Méx. 232 29.01 N 100.51 W
San Carlos, Méx. 232 24.35 N 98.56 W
San Carlos, Nic. 236 11.07 N 84.47 W
San Carlos, Pan. 236 8.29 N 79.57 W
San Carlos, Para. 252 22.16 S 57.18 W
San Carlos, Pil. 116 15.55 N 120.20 E
San Carlos, Pil. 116 10.30 N 123.25 E
San Carlos, Az., U.S. 200 33.20 N 110.27 W
San Carlos, Ca., U.S. 226 37.29 N 122.15 W
San Carlos, Ur. 252 34.48 S 54.55 W
San Carlos, Ven. 246 9.40 N 68.36 W
San Carlos ≃, C.R. 236 10.47 N 84.12 W
San Carlos ≃, Az., U.S. 200 33.16 N 110.27 W
San Carlos ≃, Ven. 246 9.07 N 68.25 W
San Carlos, Riacho ≃ 252 22.51 S 57.51 W
San Carlos Airport ≋ 282 37.31 N 122.15 W
San Carlos Bay ⊂ 220 26.28 N 82.03 W
San Carlos Borromeo, Mission ᵿ¹ 226 36.34 N 121.55 W
San Carlos Centro 252 31.44 S 61.06 W
San Carlos de Bariloche 254 41.09 S 71.18 W
San Carlos de Bolívar 252 36.15 S 61.06 W
San Carlos de Chena 286e 33.35 S 70.44 W
San Carlos de Guaroa 246 3.44 N 73.14 W
San Carlos del Zulia 246 9.01 N 71.55 W
San Carlos de Río Negro 246 1.55 N 67.04 W
San Carlos Indian Reservation ✦⁴ 200 33.23 N 110.09 W
San Carlos Reservoir ⊜¹ 200 33.13 N 110.24 W
San Carlos Viejo, Canal ≚ 286e 33.25 S 70.38 W
San Carpoforo Creek ≃ 226 35.47 N 121.19 W
San Casciano dei Bagni 66 42.52 N 11.53 E
San Casciano in Val di Pesa 66 43.39 N 11.11 E
San Cataldo, It. 68 40.23 N 18.17 E
San Cataldo, It. 70 37.29 N 13.59 E
San Cayetano 252 38.20 S 59.37 W
Sancergues 50 47.09 N 2.55 E
Sancerre 50 47.20 N 2.51 E
Sancerrois, Collines du ^² 50 47.25 N 2.45 E
San Cesario di Lecce 68 40.18 N 18.10 E
San Cesario sul Panaro 64 44.34 N 11.02 E
Sancey-le-Grand 58 47.18 N 6.35 E
Sancha, Zhg. 105 40.27 N 116.26 E
Sancha, Zhg. 106 31.52 N 119.06 E
Sancha ≃ 102 26.55 N 106.06 E
Sanchaba 107 30.19 N 114.03 E
Sanchahe 89 44.59 N 126.04 E
Sanchakou 105 39.47 N 117.19 E
Sanchang 106 31.54 N 121.15 E
Sanchazi 104 41.07 N 124.15 E
Sanchazicun 104 42.03 N 123.59 E
Sanchenglong 89 44.02 N 120.58 E
Sanchez 238 19.14 N 69.36 W
Sánchez Creek ≃ 222 32.36 N 97.50 W
Sánchez Magallanes 234 18.18 N 93.52 W
Sānchi 124 23.29 N 77.44 E
Sanchih 100 25.16 N 121.30 E
San Chirico Raparo 68 40.11 N 16.05 E
Sanch'ŏng 98 35.25 N 127.52 E
Sanchung 269d 25.04 N 121.30 E
Sanch'ungch'iao 269d 25.12 N 121.35 E
San Cipirello 70 37.58 N 13.10 E
San Cipriano Picentino 68 40.43 N 14.52 E
San Ciro de Acosta 234 21.38 N 99.49 W
San Clemente, Esp. 34 39.24 N 2.26 W
San Clemente, Ca., U.S. 228 33.25 N 117.36 W
San Clemente, Arroyo de ≃ 266d 41.20 N 2.00 E
San Clemente, Cerro ∧ 254 46.36 S 73.20 W
San Clemente a Casauria ᵿ¹ 66 42.14 N 13.55 E
San Clemente Island I 228 32.54 N 118.29 W
Sancoins 32 46.50 N 2.55 E
San Colombano al Lambro 62 45.11 N 9.29 E
San Cono 70 37.17 N 14.22 E
Sancoso Point ≻ 116 8.15 N 126.27 E
San Cosme 252 27.22 S 58.31 W
San Cosmo Albanese 68 39.35 N 16.25 E
San Costantino Albanese 68 40.02 N 16.18 E
San Cristóbal, Arg. 252 30.19 S 61.14 W
San Cristóbal, Cuba 240p 22.43 N 83.03 W
San Cristóbal, Rep. Dom. 238 18.25 N 70.06 W
San Cristóbal, Ven. 246 7.46 N 72.14 W
San Cristobal I 175e 10.36 S 161.45 E
San Cristóbal, Bahía ⊂ 232 27.23 N 114.38 W
San Cristóbal, Cerro ∧, Chile 286e 33.25 S 70.39 W
San Cristóbal, Cerro ∧, Perú 286d 12.02 S 77.01 W
San Cristóbal, Isla I 246a 0.50 S 89.26 W
San Cristóbal, Nevis — Saint Kitts and Nevis □¹ 238 17.20 N 62.45 W
San Cristóbal, Volcán ∧¹ 236 12.42 N 87.01 W
San Cristóbal de la Barranca 234 21.03 N 103.26 W
San Cristóbal de la Laguna 148 28.29 N 16.19 W
San Cristóbal de las Casas 234 16.45 N 92.38 W
San Cristóbal Totonicapán 236 14.55 N 91.26 W
San Cristobal Trench ✦¹ 14 11.15 S 162.45 E
San Cristóbal Verapaz 236 15.23 N 90.24 W
San Cristobal Wash V 200 32.47 N 113.44 W
San Croce, Monte ∧ 66 41.17 N 13.58 E
Sancti Spíritus 240p 21.56 N 79.27 W
Sancti Spíritus □⁴ 240p 22.00 N 79.20 W
San Cugat, Riera de ≃ 266d 41.29 N 2.11 E
Sančursk 80 56.57 N 47.15 E
Sancy, Puy de ∧ 32 45.32 N 2.49 E
Sand, Dtsch. 56 48.32 N 7.55 E
Sand, Nor. 26 59.29 N 6.15 E
Sand ≃, Ab., Can. 184 54.22 N 111.05 W
Sand ≃, S. Afr. 156 22.25 S 30.05 E
Sand ≃, S. Afr. 158 28.05 S 26.25 E
Sanda, Nihon 96 34.53 N 135.14 E
Sanda, Nihon 268 35.28 N 139.21 E
Sandafā al-Fa'r 142 28.32 N 30.40 E
Sandai 112 1.15 S 110.31 E
Sanda Island I 44 55.18 N 5.34 W
Sandakan 112 5.50 N 118.07 E
Sandakan, Pelabuhan ⊂ 116 5.45 N 118.05 E
Sandal, Baie du ⊂ 175f 20.50 S 167.05 E
San Damián 248 12.02 S 76.24 W
San Damiano d'Asti 62 44.50 N 8.04 E
San Damiano Macra 62 44.29 N 7.16 E
Sāndān 110 12.42 N 106.01 E
Sandan, Chāh ⊤⁴ 128 28.59 N 63.27 E
Sandane 26 61.46 N 6.13 E
San Daniele del Friuli 64 46.09 N 13.00 E
Sandan-kyō ♦ 96 34.38 N 132.13 E
Sandanski 38 41.34 N 23.17 E
Sandaogang 89 46.08 N 130.05 E
Sandaogou, Zhg. 104 41.39 N 121.45 E
Sandaogou, Zhg. 105 39.33 N 115.27 E
Sandaohe 86 44.21 N 85.37 E
Sandaoliangzi 104 41.20 N 122.07 E
Sandaolingzi 104 40.58 N 124.08 E
Sandaozhen 89 47.25 N 126.25 E
Sandaré 150 14.42 N 10.18 W
Sandared 26 57.43 N 12.47 E
Sandarne 26 61.16 N 17.10 E
Sand Arroyo V 196 37.29 N 101.29 W
Sandatal 80 46.16 N 41.46 E
Sandau 54 52.47 N 12.02 E
Sanday I 46 59.15 N 2.35 W
Sanday Sound ⊂ 46 59.11 N 2.31 W
Sandbach 44 53.09 N 2.22 W
Sandbank 44 55.59 N 4.58 W
Sandbanks Provincial Park ♦ 212 43.55 N 77.17 W
Sandbochum ✦⁸ 263 51.40 N 7.41 E
Sand City 226 36.37 N 121.51 W
Sand Coulee 202 47.23 N 111.10 W
Sand Coulee Creek ≃ 202 47.27 N 111.18 W
Sand Creek ≃, U.S. 200 41.13 N 105.43 W
Sand Creek ≃, In., U.S. 218 39.03 N 85.51 W
Sand Creek ≃, Ks., U.S. 198 37.26 N 98.12 W
Sand Creek ≃, Mn., U.S. 190 45.56 N 92.39 W
Sand Creek ≃, Mt., U.S. 202 47.18 N 106.45 W
Sand Creek ≃, S.D., U.S. 198 44.02 N 98.05 W
Sand Creek ≃, Wy., U.S. 200 43.27 N 105.26 W
Sand Creek ≃, Wy., U.S. 200 41.02 N 107.52 W
Sand Creek ≃, Wy., U.S. 202 44.16 N 107.55 W
Sand Cut 220 26.56 N 80.35 W
Sande, Dtsch. 52 51.45 N 8.39 E
Sande, Dtsch. 52 53.30 N 8.01 E
Sandefjord 26 59.08 N 10.14 E
San Demetrio Corone 68 39.34 N 16.22 E
San Demetrio ne'Vestini 66 42.17 N 13.34 E
Sanders, Az., U.S. 200 35.12 N 109.19 W
Sanders, Ky., U.S. 218 38.39 N 84.56 W
Sandersdorf, Dtsch. 54 51.37 N 12.15 E
Sandersdorf, Dtsch. 60 48.54 N 11.37 E
Sandersleben 54 51.40 N 11.34 E
Sanderson 196 30.08 N 102.23 W
Sanderstead ✦⁸ 260 51.20 N 0.05 W
Sanderston 168b 34.46 S 139.13 E
Sandersville, Ga., U.S. 192 32.58 N 82.48 W
Sandersville, Ms., U.S. 194 31.47 N 89.01 W
Sandeshkhali 126 22.22 N 88.53 E
Sandesneben 52 53.41 N 10.30 E
Sandfly Lake ⊜ 184 55.45 N 106.05 W
Sand Fork 188 38.54 N 80.45 W
Sandgate, Austl. 171a 27.20 S 153.05 E
Sandgate, Eng., U.K. 42 51.05 N 1.08 E
Sandhammaren ≻ 26 55.23 N 14.12 E
Sandhamn 40 59.17 N 18.55 E
Sandhead 44 54.48 N 4.58 W
Sandheuwel 158 31.46 S 20.48 E
Sandhill, On., Can. 275b 43.50 N 79.49 W
Sand Hill, Ma., U.S. 207 42.13 N 70.44 W
Sand Hill ∧² 210 42.31 N 77.37 W
Sand Hill ≃ 198 47.36 N 96.52 W
Sand Hills ^² 198 42.10 N 101.00 W
Sandhorst 52 53.29 N 7.29 E
Sandhurst 42 51.19 N 0.48 W
Sāndi 124 27.18 N 79.57 E
Sandia 248 14.17 S 69.26 W
Sandia Crest ∧ 200 35.13 N 106.27 W
Sandia Indian Reservation ✦⁴ 200 35.15 N 106.30 W
Sandian 100 30.56 N 114.48 E
San Diego, Ca., U.S. 228 32.42 N 117.09 W
San Diego, Tx., U.S. 196 27.45 N 98.14 W
San Diego □⁶ 228 33.00 N 117.05 W
San Diego ≃, Cuba 240p 22.20 N 83.16 W
San Diego ≃, Ca., U.S. 204 32.46 N 117.13 W
San Diego, Cabo ≻ 254 54.38 S 65.07 W
San Diego Aqueduct ≚¹ 228 32.55 N 116.55 W
San Diego Bay ⊂ 228 32.37 N 117.07 W
San Diego Creek ≃ 196 27.47 N 98.03 W
San Diego de Alcala, Mission ᵿ¹ 228 32.48 N 117.06 W
San Diego de la Unión 234 21.28 N 100.52 W
San Diego Naval Training Center ■ 228 32.44 N 117.13 W
San Dieguito ≃ 228 32.58 N 117.16 W
Sandies Creek ≃ 222 29.06 N 97.20 W
Sandıklı 130 38.28 N 30.17 E
Sandīla 124 27.05 N 80.31 E
Sandilands 168b 34.31 S 137.46 E
Sandilands Village 240b 25.02 N 77.18 W
San Dimas 228 34.06 N 117.48 W
San Dimas Canyon V 280 34.10 N 117.46 W
San Dimas Reservoir ⊜¹ 280 34.09 N 117.43 W
San Dionisio, Nic. 236 12.45 N 85.51 W
San Dionisio, Pil. 116 11.16 N 123.06 E
Sand Island I, Mid. Is. 174g 28.12 N 177.23 W
Sand Island I, Hi., U.S. 229c 21.18 N 157.53 W
Sand Islet I 174g 28.16 N 177.23 W
Sandiway 262 53.14 N 2.36 W
Sand Key I 220 27.53 N 82.51 W
Sandkrug 54 52.53 N 13.52 E
Sandl 61 48.33 N 14.38 E
Sand Lake 210 42.38 N 73.32 W
Sand Lake ⊜, On., Can. 184 50.05 N 94.39 W
Sand Lake ⊜, On., Can. 212 44.34 N 76.15 W
Sand Lake ⊜, On., Can. 212 44.56 N 77.02 W
Sandling ∧ 64 47.39 N 13.43 E
Sandnes 26 58.51 N 5.44 E
Sandness 46a 60.17 N 1.38 W
Sandoa 152 9.41 S 22.52 E
Sandogora 80 58.12 N 40.59 E
Sandomierz 30 50.41 N 21.45 E
San Domingo Creek ≃ 226 38.07 N 120.40 W
San Domino, Isola I 66 42.07 N 15.29 E
Sandon 260 51.43 N 0.32 E
Sandoná 246 1.17 N 77.28 W
San Donaci 68 40.27 N 17.55 E
San Donà di Piave 64 45.38 N 12.34 E
San Donato di Lecce 68 40.15 N 18.10 E
San Donato di Ninea 68 39.42 N 16.03 E
San Donato Milanese 62 45.24 N 9.16 E
San Donato Val di Comino 66 41.42 N 13.49 E
Sandongo 152 15.30 S 21.28 E
San Dorligo della Valle 64 45.36 N 13.51 E
Sandouping 102 30.48 N 110.49 E
Sandoval 219 38.36 N 89.06 W
Sandovalina 255 22.27 S 51.44 W
Sandover ≃ 162 21.43 S 136.32 E
Sandovo 76 58.28 N 36.25 E
Sandoway 110 18.28 N 94.22 E
Sandown 42 50.39 N 1.09 W
Sandown Park Racecourse ♦, Austl. 274b 37.57 S 145.10 E
Sandown Park Race Course ♦, Eng., U.K. 260 51.22 N 0.22 W
Sand Point, Ak., U.S. 180 55.20 N 160.30 W
Sandpoint, Id., U.S. 202 48.16 N 116.33 W
Sandrancourt 261 49.02 N 1.39 E
Sandray I 46 56.53 N 7.30 W
Sandridge, Eng., U.K. 260 51.47 N 0.18 W
Sand Ridge, N.Y., U.S. 210 43.15 N 76.14 W
Sandrigo 64 45.39 N 11.36 E
Sandringham, Austl. 166 24.05 S 139.04 E
Sandringham, Austl. 169 37.57 S 145.00 E
Sandringham, Eng., U.K. 42 52.50 N 0.30 E
Sandringham ✦⁸ 273d 26.09 S 28.07 E
Sandringham House ⊥ 42 52.50 N 0.30 E
Sand River Valley 158 28.28 S 29.33 E
Sandrovka 78 48.57 N 35.46 E
Sands Key I 220 25.30 N 80.11 W
Sandslån 26 63.01 N 17.47 E
Sandspit 182 53.14 N 131.50 W
Sands Point 276 40.51 N 73.43 W
Sands Point ≻ 276 40.52 N 73.44 W
Sand Springs, Ok., U.S. 196 36.08 N 96.06 W
Sand Springs, Tx., U.S. 196 32.15 N 101.22 W
Sandspruit 158 27.18 S 29.48 E
Sandspruit ≃ 273d 26.07 S 28.03 E
Sandstedt 52 53.21 N 8.31 E
Sandston 208 37.31 N 77.18 W
Sandstone, Austl. 162 27.59 S 119.17 E
Sandstone, Mn., U.S. 190 46.07 N 92.52 W
Sandstone Creek ≃ 216 42.23 N 84.33 W
Sandu, Zhg. 100 29.46 N 120.12 E
Sandu, Zhg. 100 26.02 N 113.16 E
Sandu, Zhg. 100 29.12 N 114.40 E
Sandu, Zhg. 102 25.59 N 107.52 E
Sanduan 104 41.10 N 121.27 E
Sandu Ao ⊂ 100 26.35 N 119.50 E
Sandugan Point ≻ 116 9.18 N 123.26 E
Sandumba 152 13.45 S 17.29 E
Sandun, Zhg. 106 31.52 N 121.50 E
Sandun, Zhg. 106 30.19 N 120.05 E
Sanduo 100 32.49 N 119.42 E
Sandusky, In., U.S. 218 39.25 N 85.29 W
Sandusky, Mi., U.S. 190 43.25 N 82.49 W
Sandusky, N.Y., U.S. 210 42.35 N 78.23 W
Sandusky, Oh., U.S. 214 41.26 N 82.42 W
Sandusky □⁶ 214 41.21 N 83.07 W
Sandusky ≃ 214 41.27 N 83.00 W
Sandusky Bay ⊂ 214 41.27 N 82.52 W
Sand uul ∧ 102 43.27 N 104.04 E
Sandvig 26 55.17 N 14.47 E
Sandvika 26 59.54 N 10.31 E
Sandviken 40 60.37 N 16.46 E
Sandweiler 56 49.37 N 6.13 E
Sandwich, Eng., U.K. 42 51.17 N 1.20 E
Sandwich, Il., U.S. 216 41.38 N 88.37 W
Sandwich, Ma., U.S. 207 41.45 N 70.29 W
Sandwich Bay ⊂, Nf., Can. 176 53.35 N 57.15 W
Sandwich Bay ⊂, Namibia 156 23.22 S 14.30 E
Sandwich del Sur, Islas — South Sandwich Islands II 18 57.45 S 26.30 W
Sandwick, B.C., Can. 182 49.42 N 124.59 W
Sandwick, Scot., U.K. 46a 60.00 N 1.15 W
Sand Wick ⊂ 46a 60.42 N 0.52 W
Sandwip 124 22.29 N 91.26 E
Sandwīp Channel Ʉ 124 22.30 N 91.35 E
Sandwīp Island I 124 22.30 N 91.25 E
Sandy, Eng., U.K. 42 52.08 N 0.18 W
Sandy, Or., U.S. 224 45.23 N 122.15 W
Sandy, Pa., U.S. 214 41.07 N 78.47 W
Sandy, Ut., U.S. 200 40.35 N 111.53 W
Sandy ≃, Me., U.S. 188 44.45 N 69.52 W
Sandy ≃, Or., U.S. 224 45.34 N 122.24 W
Sandy ≃, Va., U.S. 192 36.35 N 79.25 W
Sandy Bay ⊂, Nic. 236 14.28 N 83.16 W
Sandy Bay ⊂, Ma., U.S. 283 42.40 N 70.37 W
Sandy Bay Indian Reserve ✦⁴ 184 50.33 N 98.40 W
Sandy Bay Mountain ∧ 188 45.47 N 70.25 W
Sandy Beach 210 43.04 N 78.55 W
Sandy Branch ≃ 284c 39.03 N 77.16 W
Sandy Cape ≻, Austl. 166 41.25 S 144.45 E
Sandy Cape ≻, Austl. 166 24.42 S 153.17 E
Sandy Creek 212 43.38 N 76.05 W
Sandy Creek ≃, Austl. 166 32.10 S 144.39 E
Sandy Creek ≃, U.S. 196 34.25 N 99.35 W
Sandy Creek ≃, U.S. 196 36.50 N 98.10 W
Sandy Creek ≃, Il., U.S. 219 39.34 N 90.35 W
Sandy Creek ≃, N.Y., U.S. 212 43.44 N 76.15 W
Sandy Creek ≃, N.Y., U.S. 212 43.20 N 77.55 W
Sandy Creek ≃, N.C., U.S. 192 36.08 N 78.02 W
Sandy Creek ≃, Oh., U.S. 214 40.38 N 81.26 W
Sandy Creek ≃, Pa., U.S. 214 41.18 N 79.51 W
Sandy Creek ≃, Tx., U.S. 196 30.34 N 98.26 W
Sandy Creek ≃, Tx., U.S. 222 29.02 N 96.33 W
Sandy Creek, East Branch ≃ 210 43.17 N 78.03 W
Sandy Creek, North Branch ≃ 212 43.51 N 75.58 W
Sandy Creek, West Branch ≃ 210 43.17 N 78.03 W
Sandy Desert ✦² 128 28.40 N 62.30 E
Sandy Hook, Ct., U.S. 207 41.25 N 73.16 W
Sandy Hook, Ky., U.S. 192 38.05 N 83.07 W
Sandy Hook, Ms., U.S. 194 31.02 N 89.48 W
Sandy Hook ≻² 208 40.27 N 74.00 W
Sandy Hook Bay ⊂ 276 40.26 N 74.03 W
Sandykači 128 36.33 N 62.34 E
Sandy Key I 220 25.02 N 81.01 W
Sandy Lake 214 41.20 N 80.04 W
Sandy Lake ⊜, Nf., Can. 186 49.16 N 57.00 W
Sandy Lake ⊜, On., Can. 184 53.02 N 93.00 W
Sandy Lake ⊜, On., Can. 212 44.33 N 78.24 W
Sandy Lick Creek ≃ 214 41.09 N 79.05 W
Sandy Point ≻, Austl. 168b 34.16 S 138.09 E
Sandy Point ≻, Trin. 241r 11.09 N 60.50 W
Sandy Point ≻, R.I., U.S. 207 41.14 N 71.35 W
Sandy Point Town 238 17.22 N 62.50 W
Sandy Pond ⊜ 283 42.26 N 71.19 W
Sandy Ridge 214 40.49 N 78.14 W
Sandy Springs 192 33.55 N 84.22 W
Sandyville, Md., U.S. 208 39.31 N 76.55 W
Sandyville, Oh., U.S. 214 40.38 N 81.23 W
Sandžak ✦¹ 38 43.10 N 19.30 E
San Eladio 258 34.46 S 59.11 W
San Elizario 200 31.35 N 106.16 W
San Emigdio Creek ≃ 228 35.02 N 119.11 W
San Emilio 116 17.14 N 120.37 E
Sanen ≃ 115a 8.23 S 113.37 E
San Enrique 252 35.47 S 60.22 W
San Estanislao 252 24.39 S 56.26 W
San Esteban 236 15.17 N 85.52 W
San Esteban, Isla I 232 28.42 N 112.36 W
San Esteban de Gormaz 34 41.35 N 3.12 W
San Fele 68 40.49 N 15.32 E
San Felice (Sankt Felix) 64 46.30 N 11.08 E
San Felice Circeo 66 41.14 N 13.05 E
San Felice sul Panaro 64 44.50 N 11.08 E
San Felipe, Chile 252 32.45 S 70.44 W
San Felipe, Col. 246 1.55 N 67.06 W
San Felipe, Méx. 232 31.00 N 114.52 W
San Felipe, Méx. 234 21.29 N 101.13 W
San Felipe, Pil. 116 15.04 N 120.04 E
San Felipe, Tx., U.S. 222 29.48 N 96.06 W
San Felipe, Ven. 246 10.20 N 68.44 W
San Felipe, Castillo de ⊥ 236 15.39 N 89.01 W
San Felipe, Cayos de II 240p 21.58 N 83.30 W
San Felipe Aztatán 234 22.23 N 105.24 W
San Felipe Creek ≃ 204 33.09 N 115.46 W
San Felipe de Vichayal 248 4.52 S 81.05 W
San Felipe Indian Reservation ✦⁴ 200 35.26 N 106.26 W
San Felipe Jalapa de Díaz 234 18.04 N 96.32 W
San Felipe Nuevo Mercurio 232 24.22 N 102.06 W
San Felipe Pueblo 200 35.27 N 106.28 W
San Félix ≃ 236 8.10 N 81.51 W
San Félix, Isla I 244 26.17 S 80.05 W
San Ferdinando di Puglia 68 41.18 N 16.04 E
San Fermín 196 26.20 N 104.49 W
San Fernando, Arg. 258 34.26 S 58.34 W
San Fernando, Chile 252 34.35 S 71.00 W
San Fernando, Esp. 34 36.28 N 6.12 W
San Fernando, Méx. 196 28.32 N 100.54 W
San Fernando, Méx. 200 31.16 N 110.36 W
San Fernando, Méx. 232 24.50 N 98.10 W
San Fernando, Méx. 234 16.52 N 93.13 W
San Fernando, Pil. 116 16.37 N 120.19 E
San Fernando, Pil. 116 12.30 N 123.46 E
San Fernando, Pil. 116 15.01 N 120.41 E
San Fernando, Trin. 241r 10.17 N 61.28 W
San Fernando, Ca., U.S. 228 34.16 N 118.26 W
San Fernando, Ven. 246 7.54 N 67.28 W
San Fernando □⁵ 288 34.28 S 58.34 W
San Fernando, Aeródromo ≋ 288 34.27 S 58.35 W
San Fernando Airport ≋ 280 34.17 N 118.25 W
San Fernando Creek ≃ 196 27.28 N 97.46 W
San Fernando de Atabapo 246 4.03 N 67.42 W
San Fernando de Henares 266a 40.26 N 3.32 W
San Fernando del Valle de Catamarca 252 28.28 S 65.47 W
San Fernando Mission ᵿ¹ 280 34.16 N 118.28 W
San Fernando Point ≻ 116 16.38 N 120.17 E
San Fernando Valley V 280 34.13 N 118.27 W
San Fili 68 39.20 N 16.09 E
San Filippo del Mela 70 38.10 N 15.17 E
Sånfjället ∧ 26 62.17 N 13.32 E
Sånfjällets Nationalpark ♦ 26 62.20 N 13.40 E
San Floriano 64 46.02 N 12.18 E
Sanford, Co., U.S. 200 37.15 N 105.54 W
Sanford, Fl., U.S. 220 28.48 N 81.16 W
Sanford, Me., U.S. 188 43.26 N 70.46 W
Sanford, Mi., U.S. 190 43.40 N 84.22 W
Sanford, N.C., U.S. 192 35.28 N 79.10 W
Sanford, Tx., U.S. 196 35.42 N 101.32 W
Sanford ≃ 162 27.22 S 115.53 E
Sanford, Mount ∧ 180 62.13 N 144.09 W
San Francesco, Convento ᵿ¹, It. 66 42.28 N 12.45 E
San Francesco, Convento ᵿ¹, It. 267a 42.03 N 12.46 E
San Francisco, Arg. 252 31.26 S 62.05 W

Symbol	English	Deutsch	Español	Français	Português
≃	River	Fluß	Río	Rivière	Rio
≚	Canal	Kanal	Canal	Canal	Canal
⌊	Waterfall, Rapids	Wasserfall, Stromschnellen	Cascada, Rápidos	Chute d'eau, Rapides	Cascata, Rápidos
Ʉ	Strait	Meeresstraße	Estrecho	Détroit	Estreito
⊂	Bay, Gulf	Bucht, Golf	Bahía, Golfo	Baie, Golfe	Baía, Golfo
⊜	Lake, Lakes	See, Seen	Lago, Lagos	Lac, Lacs	Lago, Lagos
≝	Swamp	Sumpf	Pantano	Marais	Pântano
✱	Ice Features, Glacier	Eis- und Gletscherformen	Accidentes Glaciales	Formes glaciaires	Acidentes glaciares
⊤	Other Hydrographic Features	Andere Hydrographische Objekte	Otros Elementos Hidrográficos	Autres données hydrographiques	Outros acidentes hidrográficos

Symbol	English	Deutsch	Español	Français	Português
✦	Submarine Features	Untermeerische Objekte	Accidentes Submarinos	Formes de relief sous-marin	Acidentes submarinos
□	Political Unit	Politische Einheit	Unidad Política	Entité politique	Unidade política
ᵿ	Cultural Institution	Kulturelle Institution	Institución Cultural	Institution culturelle	Instituição cultural
⊥	Historical Site	Historische Stätte	Sitio Histórico	Site historique	Sitio histórico
♦	Recreational Site	Erholungs- und Ferienort	Sitio de Recreo	Centre de loisirs	Área de Lazer
≋	Airport	Flughafen	Aeropuerto	Aéroport	Aeroporto
■	Military Installation	Militäranlage	Instalación Militar	Installation militaire	Instalação militar
✦	Miscellaneous	Verschiedenes	Misceláneo	Divers	Diversos

San Francisco, Col. 246 1.11 N 76.53 W
San Francisco, C.R. 236 9.49 N 85.15 W
San Francisco, El Sal. 236 13.42 N 88.06 W
San Francisco, Pan. 236 8.15 N 80.58 W
San Francisco, Pil. 116 8.30 N 125.56 E
San Francisco, Pil. 116 10.04 N 125.09 E
San Francisco, Ca., U.S. 226 37.46 N 122.25 W
San Francisco, Ca., U.S. 282 37.46 N 122.25 W
San Francisco □[6] 226 37.45 N 122.22 W
San Francisco ≐, Arg. 252 23.16 S 64.03 W
San Francisco ≐, U.S. 200 32.59 N 109.22 W
San Francisco, Arroyo ≐ 288 34.43 S 58.19 W
San Francisco, Paso de ӿ 252 26.53 S 68.19 W
San Francisco, University of ⊕[2] 282 37.46 N 122.26 W
San Francisco Bay c 226 37.43 N 122.17 W
San Francisco Creek ≐ 196 29.53 N 102.19 W
San Francisco Culhuacán ✦[8] 286a 19.20 N 99.08 W
San Francisco de Borja 232 27.53 N 106.41 W
San Francisco de Horizonte 196 25.56 N 103.26 W
San Francisco de Lajas 234 23.07 N 105.07 W
San Francisco de la Paz 236 14.55 N 86.14 W
San Francisco del Chañar 252 29.47 S 63.56 W
San Francisco del Monte de Oro 252 32.36 S 66.08 W
San Francisco del Oro 232 26.52 N 105.51 W
San Francisco del Rincón 234 21.01 N 101.51 W
San Francisco de Macoris 238 19.18 N 70.15 W
San Francisco de Mostazal 252 33.59 S 70.43 W
San Francisco el Grande, Iglesia de ⊕[1] 266a 40.25 N 3.43 W
San Francisco International Airport ≋ 226 37.37 N 122.23 W
San Francisco Ixhuatán 234 16.22 N 94.29 W
San Francisco Libre 236 12.30 N 86.18 W
San Francisco Maritime National Historical Park ♦ 282 37.48 N 122.27 W
San Francisco-Oakland Bay Bridge ✦[5] 282 37.48 N 122.22 W
San Francisco → São Francisco ≐ 242 10.30 S 36.24 W
San Francisco State Fish and Game Refuge ✦[4] 282 37.35 N 122.25 W
San Francisco State University ⊕[2] 282 37.43 N 122.28 W
San Francisco Tlalcilalcalpa 234 19.18 N 99.46 W
San Francisco Tlaltenco ✦[8] 286a 19.17 N 99.01 W
San Francisco Zoological Gardens ♦ 282 37.44 N 122.30 W
San Francisquito Creek ≐ 282 37.28 N 122.07 W
San Franco, Cerro ʌ 236 15.25 N 87.18 W
San Fratello 70 38.01 N 14.36 E
San Fratello ≐ 70 38.02 N 14.34 E
Sanga, Ang. 152 11.07 S 15.22 E
Sanga, Burkina 150 11.10 N 0.10 E
Sanga, Mali 150 14.28 N 3.19 W
Sanga, Zaïre 154 7.02 S 28.21 E
San Gabriel, Ec. 246 0.36 N 77.49 W
San Gabriel, Ca., U.S. 228 34.05 N 118.06 W
San Gabriel ≐, Ca., U.S. 280 33.45 N 118.07 W
San Gabriel ≐, Tx., U.S. 222 30.46 N 97.01 W
San Gabriel, Isla I 258 34.28 S 57.54 W
San Gabriel, North Fork ≐, Ca., U.S. 280 34.15 N 117.52 W
San Gabriel, North Fork ≐, Tx., U.S. 196 30.38 N 97.41 W
San Gabriel, South Fork ≐ 196 30.38 N 97.41 W
San Gabriel Arcangel, Mission ⊕[1] 280 34.06 N 118.06 W
San Gabriel Chilac 234 18.19 N 97.21 W
San Gabriel Dam ✦[6] 280 34.13 N 117.52 W
San Gabriel Mountains ⩓ 228 34.20 N 118.00 W
San Gabriel Peak ʌ 280 34.15 N 118.06 W
San Gabriel Reservoir ⊜[1] 228 34.13 N 117.51 W
Sangačal, mys › 84 40.07 N 49.30 E
San Galgano, Abbazia di ⊕[1] 66 43.10 N 11.10 E
Sangaly 24 61.08 N 43.19 E
Sangamankanda Point › 122 7.01 N 81.52 E
Sangamner 122 19.34 N 74.13 E
Sangamon □[6] 219 39.47 N 89.40 W
Sangamon ≐ 194 40.07 N 90.20 W
Sangamon, South Fork ≐ 219 39.48 N 89.32 W
Sanga Puitã 255 22.40 S 55.36 W
Sangar 74 63.55 N 127.31 E
Sangar Sarāy 120 34.24 N 70.38 E
Sangasanga-dalam 112 0.40 S 117.14 E
Sanga Sanga Island I 116 5.04 N 119.47 E
Sangat 123 30.05 N 74.50 E
Sangatte 50 50.56 N 1.45 E
San Gavino Monreale 71 39.33 N 8.47 E
Sangay ʌ[1] 246 2.00 S 78.20 W
Sangay, Parque Nacional ♦ 246 1.50 S 78.20 W
Sangayán, Isla I 248 13.51 S 76.28 W
Sang Bast 128 35.59 N 59.46 E
Sangbé 152 6.03 N 12.28 E
Sangchris Lake ⊜[1] 219 39.35 N 89.30 W
Sangchris Lake State Park ♦ 219 39.38 N 89.28 W
Sangchungshih 100 25.04 N 121.29 E
Sangeang, Pulau I 115b 8.12 S 119.04 E
Sang-e Māsheh 120 33.08 N 67.27 E
San Gemini 66 42.37 N 12.33 E
San Genesio Atesino 64 46.32 N 11.20 E
Sangenjaya ✦[8] 268 35.38 N 139.40 E
Sanger, Ca., U.S. 226 36.42 N 119.33 W
Sanger, Tx., U.S. 196 33.21 N 97.10 W
Sangerhausen 54 51.28 N 11.17 E
San Germán 240m 18.05 N 67.03 W
San Germano Vercellese 62 45.21 N 8.15 E
San Geronimo 226 38.01 N 122.39 W
San Gerónimo, Arroyo ≐ 258 33.57 S 56.05 W
Sangerville 188 45.09 N 69.21 W
Sanggan ≐ 90 40.21 N 115.21 E
Sanggar, Teluk c 115b 8.20 S 118.18 E
Sanggau 112 0.08 N 110.36 E
Sangge-ri ✦[8] 271b 37.41 N 127.05 E
Sanggin Dalai 102 38.11 N 105.17 E
Sanggona 112 3.52 S 121.46 E
Sangha □[5], Centraf. 152 3.35 N 16.20 E
Sangha □[5], Congo 152 1.00 N 15.30 E
Sangha ≐ 152 1.13 S 16.49 E
Sanghar 120 26.02 N 68.57 E
San Giacomo (Sankt Jakob in Pfitsch) 64 46.57 N 11.36 E
San Giacomo Filippo 58 46.20 N 9.21 E
Sangihe, Kepulauan II 112 3.00 N 125.30 E
Sangihe, Pulau I 112 3.35 N 125.32 E
Sangijn dalaj nuur ⊜ 88 49.17 N 99.00 E
San Gil 246 6.33 N 73.08 W
Sangilen, chrebet ⩓ 88 50.18 N 96.30 E
San Gimignano 66 43.28 N 11.02 E
San Ginesio 66 43.06 N 13.19 E
San Gion 58 46.38 N 8.50 E
San Giorgio 68 40.51 N 14.23 E
San Giorgio Canavese 62 45.20 N 7.48 E
San Giorgio della Richinvelda 64 46.03 N 12.52 E
San Giorgio del Sannio 68 41.04 N 14.51 E
San Giorgio di Lomellina 62 45.10 N 8.47 E
San Giorgio di Nogaro 64 45.50 N 13.13 E
San Giorgio di Piano 64 44.39 N 11.22 E
San Giorgio Ionico 68 40.27 N 17.23 E
San Giorgio la Molara 68 41.16 N 14.55 E
San Giorgio Lucano 68 40.07 N 16.23 E
San Giorgio Monferrato 62 45.07 N 8.23 E
San Giorgio Morgeto 68 38.23 N 16.06 E
San Giorgio Piacentino 62 44.57 N 9.44 E
San Giorgio su Legnano 266b 45.34 N 8.55 E
San Giovanni (Sankt Johann) 64 46.38 N 11.44 E
San Giovanni al Timavo (Sankt Johann in Ahrn) 64 46.58 N 11.57 E
San Giovanni a Piro 68 40.03 N 15.27 E
San Giovanni-Bianco 58 45.52 N 9.39 E
San Giovanni d'Asso 66 43.09 N 11.35 E
San Giovanni Gemini 70 37.38 N 13.39 E
San Giovanni Ilarione 64 45.30 N 11.15 E
San Giovanni in Croce 64 45.05 N 10.22 E
San Giovanni in Fiore 68 39.15 N 16.42 E
San Giovanni in Laterano ⊕[1] 267a 41.53 N 12.30 E
San Giovanni in Persiceto 64 44.38 N 11.11 E
San Giovanni la Punta 70 37.35 N 15.07 E
San Giovanni Lupatoto 64 45.23 N 11.03 E
San Giovanni Rotondo 68 41.42 N 15.44 E
San Giovanni Suergiu 71 39.07 N 8.31 E
San Giovanni Valdarno 66 43.34 N 11.32 E
San Giuliano, Lago di ⊜ 68 40.37 N 16.30 E
San Giuliano Milanese 266b 45.24 N 9.17 E
San Giuliano Terme 66 43.46 N 10.26 E
San Giuseppe, It. 62 44.22 N 8.18 E
San Giuseppe, It. 70 37.58 N 13.11 E
San Giuseppe Vesuviano 68 40.50 N 14.30 E
San Giustino 66 43.33 N 12.10 E
San Giusto, Aeroporto di ≋ 66 43.11 N 10.21 E
San Giusto Canavese 62 45.19 N 7.49 E
Sangju 98 36.26 N 128.09 E
Sangkapura 115a 5.52 S 112.40 E
Sângkê ≐ 110 13.13 N 103.41 E
Sangkhai 110 14.39 N 103.52 E
Sangkulirang 112 0.59 N 117.58 E
Sāngla 123 31.43 N 73.23 E
Sangley Point › 269f 14.30 N 120.55 E
Sāngli 122 16.52 N 74.34 E
Sanglin 100 27.54 N 114.46 E
Sangluoshu 98 37.31 N 117.43 E
Sangmélima 152 2.56 N 11.59 E
Sangngagqoiling 120 28.33 N 93.00 E
Sangnyŏng-ni 98 38.14 N 126.54 E
Sango 270 34.36 N 135.42 E
San Godenzo 66 43.55 N 11.37 E
Sāngole 122 17.26 N 75.12 E
Sangolquí 246 0.19 S 78.27 W
San Gorgonio Mountain ʌ 204 34.06 N 116.50 W
San Gottardo, Passo del ӿ 58 46.33 N 8.34 E
Sangou 98 41.02 N 118.11 E
Sangre de Cristo Mountains ⩓ 200 37.30 N 105.15 W
San Gregorio, Arg. 252 34.19 S 62.02 W
San Gregorio, It. 66 42.19 N 13.29 E
San Gregorio, Ca., U.S. 226 37.19 N 122.23 W
San Gregorio, Ur. 252 32.37 S 55.40 W
San Gregorio, Ur. 258 33.57 S 56.45 W
San Gregorio ✦[8] 286a 19.15 N 99.03 W
San Gregorio, Arroyo ≐ 258 33.59 S 56.50 W
San Gregorio Creek ≐ 282 37.19 N 122.25 W
San Gregorio Magno 68 40.39 N 15.24 E
San Gregorio State Beach ♦ 282 37.19 N 122.24 W
Sangre Grande 241r 10.35 N 61.07 W
Sangro ≐ 66 42.14 N 14.32 E
Sangrūr 123 30.14 N 75.50 E
Sangsang 120 29.25 N 86.40 E
Sangshuyuan 86 42.23 N 88.30 E
Sangsues, Lac aux ⊜ 190 46.29 N 77.57 W
Sangtuda 85 38.04 N 69.04 E
Sanguandian 100 31.19 N 118.05 E
Sanguang 106 31.47 N 121.16 E
Sanguanmiao 100 32.25 N 114.04 E
Sanguanyingzi 104 41.39 N 120.44 E
Sangudo 182 53.53 N 114.54 W
Sangue, Rio do ≐ 248 11.01 S 58.39 W
Sangüesa 34 42.35 N 1.17 W
Sanguinetto 64 45.11 N 11.09 E
Sanguliu 104 40.45 N 124.14 E
Sangurli 272c 18.56 N 73.07 E
Sangutane ≐ 156 24.07 S 33.47 E
Sangvor, Taj. 85 38.47 N 71.12 E
Sangvor, Taj. 85 38.53 N 71.06 E
Sangwa 154 5.30 S 26.00 E
Sangya 120 30.52 N 91.40 E
Sangyuanbao 105 40.15 N 115.32 E
Sangyuanpu 104 31.37 N 118.53 E
Sangyuanzhen 107 30.30 N 103.26 E
Sangzhi 102 29.18 N 110.02 E
Sangzidian 98 36.46 N 116.55 E
Sanhe, Zhg. 100 24.24 N 116.34 E
Sanhe, Zhg. 105 39.59 N 117.04 E
Sanhechang, Zhg. 102 31.22 N 106.48 E
Sanhechang, Zhg. 107 30.04 N 105.01 E
Sanhecun 98 42.28 N 129.39 E
Sanheji 100 32.42 N 117.55 E
Sanhekou 106 31.50 N 120.08 E
Sanhetun 104 42.38 N 123.38 E
Sanhezhan 104 41.08 N 121.28 E
Sanhezhen 100 31.30 N 117.14 E
Sanhezhuang 105 40.04 N 116.18 E
San Hipólito, Punta › 232 26.59 N 113.59 W
Sanhsient'ai I 100 23.08 N 121.25 E
Sanhsing 100 24.40 N 121.39 E
Sanhu 100 30.06 N 113.41 E
Sanhui, Zhg. 107 30.06 N 106.36 E
Sanhui, Zhg. 107 29.57 N 105.53 E
Sanhūr 142 29.35 N 30.46 E
Sanhūr al-Madīnah 142 31.07 N 30.44 E
Sani 100 24.25 N 120.46 E
Sanibel 220 26.26 N 82.01 W
Sanibel Island I 220 26.27 N 82.06 W
Sānī Bheri ≐ 124 28.42 N 82.16 E
San Ignacio, Arg. 252 27.16 S 55.32 W
San Ignacio, C.R. 236 9.48 N 84.09 W
San Ignacio, Hond. 236 14.38 N 87.02 W
San Ignacio, Méx. 232 27.27 N 112.51 W
San Ignacio, Méx. 234 23.12 N 100.12 W
San Ignacio, Méx. 234 23.55 N 106.25 W
San Ignacio, Para. 252 26.52 S 57.03 W
San Ignacio, Perú 248 5.08 S 78.59 W
San Ignacio, Isla I 232 25.25 N 108.54 W
San Ignacio, Laguna ⊜ 232 26.54 N 113.13 W
San Ignacio de Moxo 248 14.53 S 65.36 W
San Ignacio de Velasco 248 16.23 S 60.59 W
San Ildefonso, Cape › 116 16.02 N 121.59 E
San Ildefonso, Cerro ʌ 236 15.31 N 88.17 W
San Ildefonso Indian Reservation ✦[4] 200 35.53 N 106.08 W
San Ildefonso o La Granja 34 40.54 N 4.00 W
San Ildefonso Peninsula ›[1] 116 16.10 N 122.05 E
San Ildefonso Villa Alta 234 17.21 N 96.09 W
San'in-kaigan-kokuritsu-kōen ♦ 96 35.38 N 134.38 E
Sanino 265a 59.50 N 29.54 E
Sanin Pass ӿ 158 29.34 S 29.19 E
San Isidro, Arg. 252 28.27 S 65.44 W
San Isidro, Arg. 258 34.27 S 58.30 W
San Isidro, C.R. 236 9.22 N 83.42 W
San Isidro, Méx. 200 31.31 N 106.18 W
San Isidro, Nic. 236 12.56 N 86.12 W
San Isidro, Perú 286d 12.07 S 77.03 W
San Isidro, Pil. 116 11.24 N 124.21 E
San Isidro, Tx., U.S. 196 26.42 N 98.27 W
San Isidro □[5] 288 34.29 S 58.33 W
San Isidro el Real, Catedral de ⊕[1] 266a 40.25 N 3.42 W
Sanitaria Springs 210 42.09 N 75.46 W
Sanitatas 156 18.11 S 12.47 E
Sanitz 54 54.04 N 12.22 E
San Jacinto, Col. 246 9.50 N 75.08 W
San Jacinto, Méx. 196 25.29 N 103.44 W
San Jacinto, Pil. 116 12.34 N 123.44 E
San Jacinto, Ca., U.S. 228 33.47 N 116.57 W
San Jacinto □[6] 222 30.35 N 95.10 W
San Jacinto ≐, Ca., U.S. 228 33.43 N 117.16 W
San Jacinto ≐, Tx., U.S. 222 29.46 N 95.05 W
San Jacinto, East Fork ≐ 222 30.05 N 95.09 W
San Jacinto, West Fork ≐ 222 30.02 N 95.15 W
San Jacinto Monument ⊥ 222 29.45 N 95.01 W
San Jacinto Peak ʌ 204 33.49 N 116.41 W
San Jacinto Valley V 228 33.50 N 117.05 W
Sanjahā 142 30.50 N 31.38 E
San Javier, Arg. 252 27.53 S 55.08 W
San Javier, Arg. 252 30.35 S 59.57 W
San Javier, Bol. 248 14.34 S 64.42 W
San Javier, Bol. 248 16.20 S 62.38 W
San Javier, Méx. 196 26.16 N 99.27 W
San Javier, Ur. 252 32.41 S 58.08 W
San Javier ≐ 252 31.30 S 60.20 W
San Javier de Loncomilla 252 35.35 S 71.45 W
Sanjbāwī 120 30.17 N 68.21 E
Sanje 154 0.46 S 31.30 E
San Jeronimito 234 17.33 N 101.20 W
San Jerónimo, Guat. 236 15.03 N 90.12 W
San Jerónimo, Méx. 234 17.08 N 100.28 W
San Jerónimo Norte 252 31.33 S 61.05 W
Sanjiadian, Zhg. 105 40.09 N 116.36 E
Sanjiadian, Zhg. 105 39.22 N 115.58 E
Sanjiadian, Zhg. 105 39.58 N 116.06 E
Sanjiang, Zhg. 102 25.42 N 109.23 E
Sanjiang, Zhg. 107 29.33 N 104.03 E
Sanjiangzhen 107 30.31 N 103.48 E
Sanjiaocheng 102 36.47 N 104.40 E
Sanjiaopao 104 41.22 N 122.17 E
Sanjiaoshancun 104 40.42 N 122.26 E
Sanjiazhen 107 30.17 N 105.32 E
Sanjiazi, Zhg. 104 41.53 N 121.42 E
Sanjiazi, Zhg. 104 40.42 N 123.16 E
Sanjiazi, Zhg. 104 42.02 N 122.20 E
Sanjiazi, Zhg. 104 40.54 N 121.59 E
Sanjiazi, Zhg. 104 42.33 N 121.38 E
Sanjiaziyingzi 104 41.52 N 120.49 E
Sanjie, Zhg. 100 32.35 N 118.08 E
Sanjie, Zhg. 102 25.01 N 101.02 E
Sanjō 92 37.37 N 138.57 E
San Joaquín, Bol. 248 13.04 S 64.49 W
San Joaquín, Chile 286e 33.30 S 70.37 W
San Joaquín, Para. 252 24.57 S 56.07 W
San Joaquin, Pil. 116 10.35 N 122.08 E
San Joaquin, Ca., U.S. 226 36.36 N 120.11 W
San Joaquin □[6] 226 37.57 N 121.17 W
San Joaquín ≐, Bol. 248 13.08 S 63.41 W
San Joaquin ≐, Ca., U.S. 226 38.03 N 121.50 W
San Joaquin, Middle Fork ≐ 226 37.32 N 119.11 W
San Joaquin, North Fork ≐ 226 37.32 N 119.11 W
San Joaquin, South Fork ≐ 226 37.26 N 119.14 W
San Joaquin Valley V 204 36.50 N 120.10 W
San Jon 196 35.06 N 103.19 W
San Jorge, Arg. 252 31.54 S 61.52 W
San Jorge, El Sal. 236 13.25 N 88.21 W
San Jorge, Nic. 236 11.27 N 85.48 W
San Jorge ≐ 246 9.07 N 74.44 W
San Jorge, Bahía de c 200 31.12 N 113.15 W
San Jorge, Cabo › 254 45.47 S 67.21 W
San Jorge, Canal de → Saint George's Channel ų 28 52.00 N 6.00 W
San Jorge, Golfo c 254 46.00 S 67.00 W
San Jorge Island I 175e 8.27 S 159.35 E
San José, Arg. 252 27.46 S 55.47 W
San José, C.R. 236 9.56 N 84.05 W
San José, Méx. 196 28.16 N 100.15 W
San Jose, N. Mar. Is. 174n 15.09 N 145.43 E
San José, Para. 252 25.33 S 56.45 W
San José, Pil. 116 12.27 N 121.03 E
San Jose, Pil. 116 10.45 N 121.56 E
San Jose, Pil. 116 15.48 N 121.00 E
San Jose, Ca., U.S. 226 37.20 N 121.53 W
San Jose, Ca., U.S. 282 37.20 N 121.53 W
San Jose, Il., U.S. 194 40.18 N 89.36 W
San Jose, N.M., U.S. 200 35.23 N 105.28 W
San José, Ven. 286c 10.34 N 66.57 W
San José □[4] 236 9.40 N 84.00 W
San José □[5] 258 34.15 S 56.45 W
San José □[7] 286b 22.57 N 82.14 W
San Jose ≐, B.C., Can. 182 52.14 N 122.15 W
San José ≐, Ur. 258 34.38 S 56.29 W
San José, Arroyo ≐ 282 38.03 N 122.30 W
San José, Golfo c 254 42.20 S 64.18 W
San José, Isla I, Méx. 232 25.00 N 110.38 W
San José, Isla I, Pan. 236 8.15 N 79.07 W
San José, Laguna c 240m 18.25 N 66.01 W
San Jose, Mission ⊕[1] 282 37.32 N 121.55 W
San Jose, Rio ≐ 200 34.52 N 107.01 W
San Jose Arena ♦ 282 37.20 N 121.54 W
San José Ayuquila 234 17.58 N 97.57 W
San José Batuc 232 29.15 N 109.44 W
San José Buena Vista 236 13.49 N 90.19 W
San Jose Creek ≐ 280 34.01 N 118.03 W
San José de Aura 196 27.34 N 101.23 W
San José de Bácum 232 27.32 N 110.09 W
San Jose de Buan 116 12.02 N 125.01 E
San José de Chiquitos 248 17.51 S 60.47 W
San José de Copán 236 14.54 N 88.44 W
San José de Feliciano 252 30.23 S 58.45 W
San José de Galipán 286c 10.35 N 66.54 W
San José de Galipán, Quebrada ≐ 286c 10.37 N 66.54 W
San José de Gracia 234 20.40 N 102.35 W
San José de Guanipa 246 8.54 N 64.09 W
San José de Guaribe 246 9.52 N 65.48 W
San José de Iturbide 234 21.00 N 100.23 W
San José de Jáchal 252 30.14 S 68.45 W
San José de la Esquina 252 33.06 S 61.42 W
San José de la Parilla 234 23.44 N 104.07 W
San José de la Popa 196 26.10 N 100.47 W
San José de las Flores 234 17.20 N 95.24 W
San José de las Lajas 240p 22.58 N 82.09 W
San José de las Raíces 232 24.35 N 100.14 W
San José del Cabo 232 23.03 N 109.41 W
San José del Guaviare 246 2.35 N 72.38 W
San José de Llanetes 234 22.55 N 103.16 W
San José de los Molinos 248 13.57 S 75.41 W
San José de Lourdes 234 23.18 N 103.01 W
San José del Valle 234 23.20 N 98.24 W
San José de Mayo 258 34.20 S 56.42 W
San José de Ocuné 246 4.15 N 70.20 W
San José de Sisa 248 6.37 S 76.39 W
San José de Tiznados 246 9.23 N 67.33 W
San Jose Hills ⩓[2] 280 34.04 N 117.49 W
San Jose Island I 196 28.10 N 96.45 W
San Jose Municipal Airport ≋ 226 37.22 N 121.56 W
San Jose State University ⊕[2] 282 37.20 N 121.53 W
San Juan, Arg. 252 31.32 S 68.31 W
San Juan, Guat. 236 15.52 N 88.53 W
San Juan, Méx. 196 29.34 N 104.36 W
San Juan, Perú 248 15.21 S 75.10 W
San Juan, Pil. 116 13.50 N 121.24 E
San Juan, Pil. 116 16.40 N 120.20 E
San Juan, Pil. 116 8.25 N 126.20 E
San Juan, P.R. 240m 18.28 N 66.07 W
San Juan □[4] 252 31.00 S 69.00 W
San Juan □[6] 224 48.34 N 122.59 W
San Juan ≐, Arg. 252 32.17 S 67.22 W
San Juan ≐, B.C., Can. 182 48.34 N 124.24 W
San Juan ≐, Col. 246 4.03 N 77.27 W
San Juan ≐, Méx. 232 26.22 N 98.51 W
San Juan ≐, Méx. 234 18.36 N 95.40 W
San Juan ≐, Méx. 234 17.59 N 99.47 W
San Juan ≐, N.A. 236 10.56 N 83.42 W
San Juan ≐, Perú 248 13.27 S 76.11 W
San Juan ≐, Pil. 269f 14.35 N 121.01 E
San Juan ≐, S.A. 246 1.11 N 78.33 W
San Juan ≐, U.S. 200 37.18 N 110.28 W
San Juan ≐, Ur. 258 34.17 S 57.58 W
San Juan ≐, Ven. 246 10.14 N 62.38 W
San Juan, Bahía de c 240m 18.27 N 66.07 W
San Juan, Cabezas de › 240m 18.23 N 65.37 W
San Juan, Cabo ›, Arg. 254 54.44 S 63.44 W
San Juan, Cabo ›, Gui. Ecu. 152 1.08 N 9.23 E
San Juan, Embalse de ⊜[1] 34 40.30 N 4.15 W
San Juan, Pasaje de ų 240m 18.24 N 65.37 W
San Juan, Pico ʌ 240p 21.59 N 80.09 W
San Juan, Port c 224 48.34 N 124.27 W
San Juan, Punta › 174z 27.03 S 109.22 W
San Juan Basin ≡[1] 200 36.15 N 108.20 W
San Juan Bautista, Méx. 196 26.58 N 101.24 W
San Juan Bautista, Para. 252 26.38 S 57.10 W
San Juan Bautista, Ca., U.S. 226 36.51 N 121.32 W
San Juan Bautista State Historical Park ♦ 226 36.51 N 121.31 W
San Juan Capistrano 228 33.30 N 117.39 W
San Juan Capistrano Mission ⊕[1] 228 33.31 N 117.40 W
San Juan Cotzal 236 15.26 N 91.01 W
San Juan Creek ≐, Ca., U.S. 226 35.40 N 120.22 W
San Juan Creek ≐, Ca., U.S. 228 33.28 N 117.41 W
San Juan de Abajo 234 20.48 N 105.13 W
San Juan de Aragón, Bosque ♦ 286a 19.28 N 99.04 W
San Juan de Aragón, Zoológico de ♦ 286a 19.28 N 99.05 W
San Juan de Colón 246 8.02 N 72.16 W
San Juan de Dios 286c 10.35 N 66.55 W
San Juan de Guadalupe 232 24.38 N 102.44 W
San Juan [de la Maguana] 238 18.48 N 71.14 W
San Juan de la Vega 234 20.38 N 100.46 W
San Juan del Cesar 246 10.46 N 73.01 W
San Juan del Monte 269f 14.36 N 121.02 E
San Juan del Norte 236 10.55 N 83.42 W
San Juan del Oro ≐ 248 21.02 S 65.19 W
San Juan de los Cayos 246 11.10 N 68.25 W
San Juan de los Lagos 234 21.15 N 102.18 W
San Juan de los Lagos ≐ 234 21.18 N 102.33 W
San Juan de los Morros 246 9.55 N 67.21 W
San Juan del Río, Méx. 232 24.47 N 104.27 W
San Juan del Río, Méx. 234 20.23 N 100.00 W
San Juan del Salado 234 23.18 N 101.56 W
San Juan del Sur 236 11.15 N 85.52 W
San Juan de Lurigancho 286d 11.59 S 77.01 W
San Juan de Micay ≐ 246 3.05 N 77.32 W
San Juan de Miraflores 286d 12.11 S 76.57 W
San Juan de Payara 246 7.39 N 67.36 W
San Juan de Sabinas 196 27.55 N 101.18 W
San Juan Evangelista 234 17.54 N 95.08 W
San Juan Guichicovi 234 16.58 N 95.06 W
San Juanico 232 26.15 N 112.24 W
San Juanillo 236 10.02 N 85.44 W
San Juan Indian Reservation ✦[4] 200 36.03 N 106.04 W
San Juan Island I 224 48.32 N 123.05 W
San Juan Island National Historical Park ♦ 224 48.28 N 123.00 W
San Juan Islands II 224 48.36 N 122.50 W
San Juanito, Isla I 234 21.43 N 106.38 W
San Juan Ixcaquixtla 234 18.27 N 97.49 W
San Juan Ixtayopan ✦[8] 286a 19.14 N 99.00 W
San Juan Lachao 234 16.14 N 97.09 W
San Juan Mazatlán 234 17.02 N 95.25 W
San Juan Mountains ⩓ 200 37.35 N 107.10 W
San Juan Nepomuceno, Col. 246 9.57 N 75.05 W

ENGLISH Name	Page	Lat.°′	Long.°′

San Juan Nepomuceno, Para. 252 26.06 S 55.58 W
San Juan Peyotán 234 22.24 N 104.21 W
San Juan Quiahije 234 16.17 N 97.20 W
San Juan Sacatepéquez 236 14.43 N 90.39 W
San Juan Teita 234 17.05 N 97.25 W
San Juan y Martínez 240p 22.16 N 83.50 W
San Julián, Méx. 234 21.01 N 102.10 W
San Julian, Pil. 116 11.45 N 125.27 E
San Julián, Quebrada ≐ 286c 10.37 N 66.51 W
San Justo, Arg. 252 30.47 S 60.35 W
San Justo, Arg. 258 34.40 S 58.33 W
San Justo, Aeródromo ≋ 288 34.44 S 58.36 W
Sankanbiaiwa ʌ 150 8.56 N 10.48 W
Sankarani ≐ 150 12.01 N 8.19 W
Sankarankovil 122 9.10 N 77.33 E
Sankarpur 272b 22.51 N 88.27 E
Sānkdaha 126 22.46 N 89.10 E
Sankeng 100 23.36 N 112.48 E
Sankertown 214 40.28 N 78.35 W
Sankeshu 104 42.38 N 122.25 E
Sankeshwar 122 16.16 N 74.29 E
Sankey Brook ≐ 262 53.22 N 2.38 W
Sankh ≐ 124 22.15 N 84.48 E
Sankheda 120 22.10 N 73.35 E
Sānkosh ≐ 124 26.48 N 89.56 E
Sānkra 120 21.18 N 82.39 E
Sānkrāil 272b 22.34 N 88.14 E
Sankt Aegyd am Neuwalde 61 47.52 N 15.35 E
Sankt Andrä 61 46.46 N 14.49 E
Sankt Andrä [-vor dem Hagenthale] 61 48.19 N 16.13 E
Sankt Andreasberg 54 51.43 N 10.31 E
Sankt Anton am Arlberg 58 47.08 N 10.16 E
Sankt Antönien 58 46.58 N 9.49 E
Sankt Augustin 56 50.40 N 7.16 E
Sankt Bartholomä ⊕[1] 64 47.32 N 12.58 E
Sankt Blasien 58 47.46 N 8.07 E
Sankt Christopher-Nevis → Saint Kitts and Nevis □[1] 238 17.20 N 62.45 W
Sankt Egidien 54 50.47 N 12.36 E
Sankt Florian ⊕[1] 61 48.12 N 14.23 E
Sankt Gallen, Öst. 61 47.41 N 14.37 E
Sankt Gallen, Schw. 58 47.25 N 9.23 E
Sankt Gallen □[3] 58 47.10 N 9.08 E
Sankt Gallenkirch 58 47.01 N 9.59 E
Sankt Georgen, Dtsch. 58 48.07 N 8.20 E
Sankt Georgen, Dtsch. 58 47.59 N 7.47 E
Sankt Georgen, Öst. 61 46.43 N 14.55 E
Sankt Georgen im Attergau 64 47.56 N 13.29 E
Sankt Gertraud → Santa Gertrude 64 46.29 N 10.53 E
Sankt Gertrud ✦[8] 54 53.52 N 10.47 E
Sankt Gilgen 64 47.46 N 13.22 E
Sankt Goar 56 50.09 N 7.43 E
Sankt Goarshausen 56 50.09 N 7.44 E
Sankt Helena → Saint Helena □[2] 8 15.57 S 5.42 W
Sankt Hubert 56 51.23 N 6.26 E
Sankt Ingbert 56 49.17 N 7.06 E
Sankt Jakob im Lesachtal 64 46.41 N 12.56 E
Sankt Jakob im Rosental 61 46.33 N 14.03 E
Sankt Jakob in Defereggen 64 46.55 N 12.20 E
Sankt Jakob → San Giacomo 64 46.57 N 11.36 E
Sankt Johann am Tauern 61 47.22 N 14.29 E
Sankt Johann im Pongau 64 47.21 N 13.12 E
Sankt Johann im Walde 64 46.54 N 12.37 E
Sankt Johann in Tirol 64 47.31 N 12.26 E
Sankt Johann → San Giovanni 64 46.38 N 11.44 E
Sankt Kanzian 61 46.37 N 14.34 E
Sankt Leonhard am Forst 61 48.09 N 15.17 E
Sankt Leonhard im Pitztal 64 47.04 N 10.51 E
Sankt Leonhard → San Leonardo 64 46.49 N 11.15 E
Sankt Lorenz ✦[8] 52 53.51 N 10.40 E
Sankt Lorenzen im Lesachtal 64 46.42 N 12.47 E
Sankt Lorenzen → San Lorenzo di Sebato 64 46.47 N 11.54 E
Sankt Lorenz-Golf → Saint Lawrence, Gulf of c 186 48.00 N 62.00 W
Sankt Lorenz-Insel → Saint Lawrence Island I 180 63.30 N 170.30 W
Sankt Lorenz → Saint Lawrence ≐ 176 49.30 N 67.00 W
Sankt Mang 58 47.44 N 10.21 E
Sankt Margarethen an der Raab 61 47.03 N 15.45 E
Sankt Märgen 58 48.00 N 8.05 E
Sankt Margrethen 58 47.27 N 9.36 E
Sankt Martin 64 47.28 N 13.23 E
Sankt Martin an der Raab 61 46.55 N 16.08 E
Sankt Martin in Gsies → San Martino in Casies 64 46.49 N 12.14 E
Sankt Mauritz 52 51.57 N 7.39 E
Sankt Michael im Lungau 64 47.06 N 13.38 E
Sankt Michael in Obersteiermark 61 47.20 N 15.01 E
Sankt Michel → Mikkeli 26 61.41 N 27.15 E
Sankt Moritz 58 46.30 N 9.50 E
Sankt Niklaus 58 46.11 N 7.48 E
Sankt Niklaus → San Nicolò d'Ultimo 64 46.30 N 10.55 E
Sankt Oswald 60 48.54 N 13.25 E
Sankt Paul im Lavanttal 61 46.42 N 14.52 E
Sankt Peter, Dtsch. 30 54.18 N 8.38 E
Sankt Peter, Dtsch. 58 48.01 N 8.01 E
Sankt Peter ⊕[1] 263 51.37 N 7.12 E
Sankt Peter am Kammersberg 61 47.11 N 14.11 E
Sankt Peter am Ottersbach 61 46.48 N 15.45 E
Sankt-Peterburg (Saint Petersburg), Ross. 76 59.55 N 30.15 E
Sankt-Peterburg (Saint Petersburg), Ross. 265a 59.55 N 30.15 E
Sankt-Peterburg, Gorod □[7] 265a 59.55 N 30.15 E
Sankt Peter in der Au 61 48.03 N 14.37 E
Sankt Pölten 61 48.12 N 15.37 E
Sankt-Quirinus-Dom ⊕[1] 263 51.12 N 6.42 E
Sankt Stefan an der Gail 64 46.37 N 13.31 E
Sankt Stefan im Rosental 61 46.54 N 15.42 E
Sankt Ulrich → Ortisei 64 46.34 N 11.40 E

DEUTSCH Name	Seite	Breite°′	Länge°′ E = Ost

Sankt Valentin 61 48.10 N 14.32 E
Sankt Veit an der Glan 61 46.46 N 14.21 E
Sankt Veit an der Gölsen 61 48.03 N 15.40 E
Sankt Veit im Pongau 64 47.20 N 13.09 E
Sankt-Viktors-Dom ⊕[1] 263 51.40 N 6.27 E
Sankt Vincent → Saint Vincent and the Grenadines □[1] 241h 13.15 N 61.12 W
Sankt Wallburg → Santa Valburga 64 46.33 N 11.00 E
Sankt Wendel 56 49.28 N 7.10 E
Sankt-Willibrodi-Dom ⊕[1] 263 51.40 N 6.37 E
Sankt Wolfgang im Salzkammergut 64 47.44 N 13.27 E
Sankuru ≐ 152 4.17 S 20.25 E
San Lázaro 252 22.10 S 57.55 W
San Lázaro, Cabo › 232 24.48 N 112.19 W
San Lazaro Race Track ♦ 269f 14.37 N 120.59 E
San Lazzaro di Savena 64 44.28 N 11.25 E
San Leandro 226 37.43 N 122.09 W
San Leandro Creek ≐ 282 37.45 N 122.12 W
San Leo 66 43.54 N 12.21 E
San Leon 222 29.29 N 94.55 W
San Leonardo (Sankt Leonhard), It. 64 46.49 N 11.15 E
San Leonardo, Méx. 196 27.28 N 104.55 W
San Leonardo ≐ 70 37.59 N 13.41 E
San Leone 70 37.16 N 13.35 E
Sanlicheng 100 31.48 N 114.12 E
Sanlidian 100 30.48 N 118.15 E
Sanlifan 100 30.51 N 115.15 E
Sanlintang 106 31.08 N 121.29 E
Sanlipu 106 31.46 N 119.03 E
Sanliuji 100 32.08 N 116.19 E
Şanlıurfa 130 37.08 N 38.46 E
Şanlıurfa □[4] 130 37.20 N 39.15 E
San Lope 246 6.12 N 71.56 W
San Lorenzo, Arg. 252 28.08 S 58.46 W
San Lorenzo, Arg. 252 32.45 S 60.44 W
San Lorenzo, Bol. 248 21.26 S 64.47 W
San Lorenzo, Ec. 246 1.17 N 78.50 W
San Lorenzo, Hond. 236 13.25 N 87.27 W
San Lorenzo, It. 70 38.01 N 15.50 E
San Lorenzo, Méx. 196 25.37 N 97.35 W
San Lorenzo, Méx. 232 25.32 N 102.11 W
San Lorenzo, Nic. 236 12.23 N 85.40 W
San Lorenzo, P.R. 240m 18.11 N 65.58 W
San Lorenzo, Ca., U.S. 226 37.40 N 122.07 W
San Lorenzo, Ven. 246 9.47 N 71.04 W
San Lorenzo ≐, Méx. 232 24.15 N 107.24 W
San Lorenzo ≐, Ca., U.S. 226 36.58 N 122.01 W
San Lorenzo, Bahía de c 236 13.19 N 87.30 W
San Lorenzo, Cabo › 246 1.04 S 80.56 W
San Lorenzo, Golfo del → Saint Lawrence, Gulf of c 186 48.00 N 62.00 W
San Lorenzo, Isla I, Méx. 232 28.38 N 112.51 W
San Lorenzo, Isla I, Perú 248 12.05 S 77.15 W
San Lorenzo, Monte (Cerro Cochrane) ʌ 254 47.37 S 72.19 W
San Lorenzo Bellizzi 68 39.53 N 16.20 E
San Lorenzo Creek ≐, Ca., U.S. 226 36.12 N 120.38 W
San Lorenzo Creek ≐, Ca., U.S. 282 37.39 N 122.09 W
San Lorenzo de El Escorial 34 40.35 N 4.09 W
San Lorenzo de la Parrilla 34 39.51 N 2.22 W
San Lorenzo del Vallo 68 39.40 N 16.18 E
San Lorenzo di Sebato (Sankt Lorenzen) 64 46.47 N 11.54 E
San Lorenzo in Campo 66 43.36 N 12.56 E
San Lorenzo Nuovo 66 42.41 N 11.54 E
San Lorenzo → Saint Lawrence ≐ 176 49.30 N 67.00 W
San Lorenzo Tezonco ✦[8] 286a 19.18 N 99.04 W
San Luca 68 38.09 N 16.04 E
Sanlúcar de Barrameda 34 36.47 N 6.21 W
Sanlúcar la Mayor 34 37.23 N 6.12 W
San Lucas, Bol. 248 20.06 S 65.07 W
San Lucas, Ec. 246 3.45 S 79.15 W
San Lucas, Méx. 232 22.53 N 109.54 W
San Lucas, Ca., U.S. 226 36.08 N 121.01 W
San Lucas, Cabo › 232 22.52 N 109.53 W
San Luis, Arg. 252 33.18 S 66.21 W
San Luis, Cuba 240p 20.12 N 75.51 W
San Luis, Cuba 240p 22.17 N 83.46 W
San Luis, Guat. 236 16.14 N 89.27 W
San Luis, Perú 286d 12.04 S 77.00 W
San Luis, Az., U.S. 200 32.04 N 111.57 W
San Luis, Co., U.S. 200 37.12 N 105.25 W
San Luis, Ven. 246 11.07 N 69.42 W
San Luis □[4] 252 34.00 S 66.00 W
San Luis ✦[8] 286b 23.05 N 82.20 W
San Luis ≐ 234 17.13 N 100.55 W
San Luis, Arroyo ≐ 258 34.10 S 57.44 W
San Luís, Laguna ⊜ 248 13.45 S 64.00 W
San Luis, Sierra de ⩓ 252 32.40 S 65.50 W
San Luis Acatlán 234 16.48 N 98.45 W
San Luis Creek ≐ 200 37.42 N 105.44 W
San Luis de la Loma 234 17.18 N 100.55 W
San Luis de la Paz 234 21.18 N 100.31 W
San Luis del Cordero 232 25.26 N 104.18 W
San Luis del Palmar 252 27.31 S 58.34 W
San Luis Gonzaga 232 24.55 N 111.16 W
San Luis Gonzaga, Bahía c 232 29.48 N 114.22 W
San Luis Jilotepeque 236 14.39 N 89.44 W
San Luis Obispo 226 35.16 N 120.39 W
San Luis Obispo □[6] 226 35.30 N 120.30 W
San Luis Pass c 222 29.05 N 95.08 W
San Luis Peak ʌ 200 37.59 N 106.56 W
San Luis Potosí 234 22.09 N 100.59 W
San Luis Potosí □[3] 234 22.30 N 100.30 W
San Luis Reservoir ⊜[1] 226 37.07 N 121.05 W
San Luis Rey 228 33.14 N 117.20 W
San Luis Rey ≐ 204 33.12 N 117.24 W
San Luis Rey, Mission ⊕[1] 228 33.14 N 117.20 W
San Luis Río Colorado 232 32.29 N 114.48 W
San Luis Soyatlán 234 20.12 N 103.18 W
San Luis State Recreation Area ♦ 226 37.04 N 121.05 W
San Luis Valley V 200 37.25 N 106.00 W
Sanluri 71 39.34 N 8.54 E
San Macario 266b 45.36 N 8.47 E
Sanmaiden 270 34.34 N 135.51 E
San Mamete 58 46.02 N 9.04 E
San Mango d'aquino 68 39.03 N 16.11 E
San Manuel, Arg. 252 37.47 S 58.50 W
San Manuel, Méx. 234 17.37 N 93.24 W
San Manuel, Az., U.S. 200 32.35 N 110.37 W
San Marcelino 116 14.58 N 120.09 E
San Marcello Pistoiese 66 44.03 N 10.47 E
San Marcial ≐ 232 28.04 N 110.44 W

Symbols in the index entries represent the broad categories identified in the key at the right. Symbols with superior numbers (⩓[1]) identify subcategories (see complete key on page I · 1).

Symbole im Register stellen die rechts im Schlüssel erklärten Kategorien dar. Symbole mit hochgestellten Ziffern (⩓[1]) bezeichnen Unterabteilungen einer Kategorie (vgl. vollständiger Schlüssel auf Seite I · 1).

Los símbolos incluídos en el texto del índice representan las grandes categorias identificadas con la clave a la derecha. Los símbolos con numeros en su parte superior (⩓[1]) identifican las subcategorías (véase la clave completa en la página I · 1).

Les symboles de l'index représentent les catégories indiquées dans la légende à droite. Les symboles suivis d'un indice (⩓[1]) représentent des sous-catégories (voir légende complète à la page I · 1).

Os símbolos incluídos no texto do índice representam as grandes categorias identificadas com a chave à direita. Os símbolos com números em sua parte superior (⩓[1]) identificam as subcategorias (veja-se a chave completa à página I · 1).

ʌ Mountain	Berg	Montaña	Montagne	Montanha
⩓ Mountains	Gebirge	Montañas	Montagnes	Montanhas
ӿ Pass	Paß	Paso	Col	Passo
V Valley, Canyon	Tal, Cañon	Valle, Cañón	Vallée, Canyon	Vale, Canhão
≡ Plain	Ebene	Llano	Plaine	Planície
› Cape	Kap	Cabo	Cap	Cabo
I Island	Insel	Isla	Île	Ilha
II Islands	Inseln	Islas	Îles	Ilhas
± Other Topographic Features	Andere Topographische Objekte	Otros Elementos Topográficos	Autres données topographiques	Outros acidentes topográficos

ESPAÑOL · FRANÇAIS · PORTUGUÊS

Nombre / Nom / Nome	Página / Page	Lat.°′	Long.°′ W = Oeste / W = Ouest
San Marco, Capo ›, It.	70	37.30 N	13.01 E
San Marco, Capo ›, It.	71	39.51 N	8.26 E
San Marco Argentano	68	39.33 N	16.07 E
San Marco dei Cavoti	68	41.18 N	14.53 E
San Marco in Lamis	68	41.43 N	15.38 E
San Marco la Catola	68	41.31 N	15.00 E
San Marcos, Chile	252	30.56 S	71.03 W
San Marcos, Col.	246	8.39 N	75.08 W
San Marcos, C.R.	236	9.40 N	84.01 W
San Marcos, El Sal.	236	13.39 N	89.11 W
San Marcos, Guat.	236	14.58 N	91.48 W
San Marcos, Hond.	236	14.24 N	88.56 W
San Marcos, Hond.	236	15.17 N	88.23 W
San Marcos, Méx.	234	16.48 N	99.21 W
San Marcos, Méx.	234	20.02 N	99.20 W
San Marcos, Méx.	234	20.47 N	104.11 W
San Marcos, Ca., U.S.	228	33.08 N	117.09 W
San Marcos, Tx., U.S.	196	29.52 N	97.56 W
San Marcos □[5]	236	15.00 N	91.55 W
San Marcos ≃	196	29.29 N	97.28 W
San Marcos, Isla I	232	27.13 N	112.06 W
San Marcos, Laguna ⊜	234	20.17 N	103.33 W
San Marcos, Universidad Nacional de ʊ[2]	286d	12.04 S	77.05 W
San Marcos Arteaga	234	17.45 N	97.58 W
San Marcos de Colón	236	13.26 N	86.48 W
San Marino, S. Mar.	66	43.55 N	12.28 E
San Marino, Ca., U.S.	280	34.07 N	118.06 W
San Marino □[1], Europe	22	43.56 N	12.25 E
San Marino □[1], Europe	66	43.56 N	12.25 E
San Martín, Arg.	252	29.14 S	65.46 W
San Martín, Arg.	252	33.04 S	68.28 W
San Martín, Col.	246	3.42 N	73.42 W
San Martin, Ca., U.S.	226	37.05 N	121.37 W
San Martín, Ur.	258	33.45 S	57.37 W
San Martín □[5]	248	7.00 S	76.50 W
San Martín ≃, Bol.	248	13.08 S	63.43 W
San Martín ≃, Bol.	248	11.50 S	67.16 W
San Martín ʊ[3]	9	68.07 S	67.08 W
San Martín, Arroyo ≃	258	33.49 S	57.44 W
San Martín, Cuchilla ⋏[2]	258	33.45 S	57.54 W
San Martín, Lago (Lago O'Higgins) ⊜	254	49.00 S	72.40 W
San Martín, Volcán ∧[1]	234	18.33 N	95.12 W
San Martín de Bolaños	234	21.29 N	103.58 W
San Martín [de las Pirámides]	234	19.42 N	98.50 W
San Martín de las Vacas	196	25.30 N	101.20 W
San Martín de los Andes	254	40.10 S	71.21 W
San Martin de Porras	286d	12.04 S	77.04 W
San Martín de Valdeiglesias	34	40.21 N	4.24 W
San Martín → General San Martín	258	34.34 S	58.32 W
San Martín Hidalgo	234	20.27 N	103.57 W
San Martino, It.	62	45.27 N	8.47 E
San Martino (Sankt Martin), It.	64	46.47 N	11.13 E
San Martino, It.	64	45.25 N	10.35 E
San Martino Buon Albergo	64	45.25 N	11.05 E
San Martino d'agri	68	40.14 N	16.04 E
San Martino di Castrozza	64	46.16 N	11.48 E
San Martino di Lupari	64	45.39 N	11.51 E
San Martino in Badia (Saint Martin)	64	46.41 N	11.52 E
San Martino in Casies (Sankt Martin in Gsies)	64	46.49 N	12.14 E
San Martino in Rio	64	44.44 N	10.48 E
San Martino Valle Caudina	68	41.01 N	14.39 E
San Martín Peras	234	17.19 N	98.15 W
San Marzano di San Giuseppe	68	40.27 N	17.30 E
San Marzano sul Sarno	66	40.46 N	14.35 E
San Mateo, Méx.	234	22.59 N	103.30 W
San Mateo, Pil.	269f	14.42 N	121.07 E
San Mateo, Ca., U.S.	226	37.33 N	122.19 W
San Mateo, Fl., U.S.	192	29.36 N	81.35 W
San Mateo, N.M., U.S.	200	35.19 N	107.38 W
San Mateo, Ven.	246	9.45 N	64.33 W
San Mateo □[6]	226	37.25 N	122.20 W
San Mateo Atenco	234	19.16 N	99.32 W
San Mateo Bridge ◆[5]	282	37.36 N	122.13 W
San Mateo Canyon V	228	33.23 N	117.36 W
San Mateo Creek ≃	282	37.34 N	122.18 W
San Mateo del Mar	234	16.12 N	95.00 W
San Mateo Ixtatán	236	15.50 N	91.29 W
San Mateo Memorial Park ♦	282	37.17 N	122.18 W
San Mateo Point ›	228	33.23 N	117.36 W
San Mateo Tecoloapan	286a	19.34 N	99.14 W
San Matías	248	16.22 S	58.24 W
San Matías, Golfo ⊂	254	41.30 S	64.15 W
San Mauro Castelverde	70	37.55 N	14.11 E
San Mauro Forte	68	40.29 N	16.15 E
San Mauro la Bruca	68	40.07 N	15.17 E
San Mauro Marchesato	68	39.06 N	16.56 E
San Mauro Torinese	62	45.06 N	7.46 E
San Medi, Arroyo de ≃	266d	41.28 N	2.06 E
Sanmen	100	29.06 N	121.24 E
San Menaio	68	41.56 N	15.58 E
Sanmen Wan ⊂	100	29.08 N	121.44 E
Sanmenxia (Shanxian)	102	34.45 N	111.05 E
San Michele, Sacra di ʊ[1]	62	45.11 N	7.21 E
San Michele all'Adige	64	46.12 N	11.08 E
San Michele al Tagliamento	64	45.46 N	12.59 E
San Michele di Ganzaria	70	37.17 N	14.26 E
San Michele Mondovì	62	44.23 N	7.54 E
San Michele Salentino	68	40.38 N	17.37 E
San Miguel, Arg.	252	28.00 S	57.36 W
San Miguel, Bol.	248	16.42 S	61.01 W
San Miguel, Chile	286e	33.30 S	70.40 W
San Miguel, Ec.	246	1.44 S	79.01 W
San Miguel, El Sal.	236	13.29 N	88.11 W
San Miguel, Esp.	148	28.05 N	16.37 W
San Miguel, Méx.	232	29.10 N	101.28 W
San Miguel, Méx.	234	23.23 N	98.10 W
San Miguel, Pan.	246	8.27 N	78.56 W
San Miguel, Perú	248	13.01 S	73.58 W
San Miguel, Perú	286d	12.06 S	77.07 W
San Miguel, Pil.	116	15.09 N	120.59 E
San Miguel, Ca., U.S.	226	35.45 N	120.41 W
San Miguel ≃, Bol.	248	13.52 S	63.56 W
San Miguel (Cuilco) ≃, N.A.	236	15.56 N	92.10 W
San Miguel ≃, S.A.	246	0.08 N	75.51 W
San Miguel ≃, S.A.	248	19.15 S	59.20 W
San Miguel ≃, Co., U.S.	200	38.23 N	108.48 W
San Miguel, Cerro ∧[2]	248	19.19 S	60.36 W
San Miguel, Golfo de ⊂	246	8.22 N	78.17 W
San Miguel, Volcán de ∧[1]	236	13.26 N	88.16 W
San Miguel Arcángel, Mission ʊ[1]	226	35.44 N	120.42 W
San Miguel Bay ⊂	116	13.50 N	123.10 E
San Miguel Chimalapa	234	16.43 N	94.41 W
San Miguel Creek ≃	196	28.30 N	98.25 W
San Miguel de Allende	234	20.55 N	100.45 W
San Miguel de Cruces	232	24.25 N	105.51 W
San Miguel del Monte	258	35.27 S	58.48 W
San Miguel de Pallaques	248	7.00 S	78.51 W
San Miguel de Salcedo	246	1.02 S	78.34 W
San Miguel de Tucumán	252	26.49 S	65.13 W
San Miguel El Alto	234	21.01 N	102.21 W
San Miguel El Grande	234	17.02 N	97.37 W
San Miguel → General Sarmiento	258	34.33 S	58.43 W
San Miguel Island I, Pil.	116	13.23 N	123.48 E
San Miguel Island I, Ca., U.S.	204	34.02 N	120.22 W
San Miguel Islands II	116	7.45 N	118.28 E
San Miguelito	236	11.24 N	84.54 W
San Miguel Ixtahuacán	236	15.15 N	91.45 W
San Miguel Mountain ∧	228	32.42 N	116.56 W
San Miguel Sola de Vega	234	16.31 N	96.59 W
San Miguel Talea de Castro	234	17.22 N	96.15 W
San Miguel Tecuixiapan	234	17.58 N	99.27 W
San Miguel Tenango	234	16.16 N	95.36 W
San Miguel Totolapan	234	18.08 N	100.23 W
Sanming	100	26.14 N	117.36 E
San Miniato	66	43.41 N	10.51 E
San Murezzan → Sankt Moritz	58	46.30 N	9.50 E
Sannahed	40	59.06 N	15.09 E
Sannan	96	35.04 N	135.02 E
Sannār	140	13.33 N	33.38 E
San Narciso, Pil.	116	13.34 N	122.34 E
San Narciso, Pil.	116	15.01 N	120.05 E
Sannazzaro de'Burgondi	62	45.06 N	8.54 E
Sannicandro di Bari	68	41.00 N	16.48 E
Sannicandro Garganico	68	41.50 N	15.34 E
Sannicola	68	40.05 N	18.04 E
San Nicola, Isola I	66	42.07 N	15.30 E
San Nicola, Monte ∧	68	38.35 N	16.24 E
San Nicola Arcella	68	39.51 N	15.48 E
San Nicola da Crissa	68	38.40 N	16.17 E
San Nicolás, Cuba	240p	22.47 N	81.55 W
San Nicolás, Esp.	148	27.59 N	15.46 W
San Nicolás, Hond.	236	15.00 N	88.45 W
San Nicolás, Méx.	234	16.26 N	98.32 W
San Nicolás, Perú	248	15.13 S	75.12 W
San Nicolas, Pil.	116	18.09 N	120.38 E
San Nicolás ≃	234	19.40 N	105.14 W
San Nicolás de los Arroyos	252	33.20 S	60.13 W
San Nicolás de los Garza	196	25.45 N	100.18 W
San Nicolas Island I	204	33.15 N	119.31 W
San Nicolò di Comelico	64	46.35 N	12.31 E
San Nicolò d'Ultimo (Sankt Nikolaus)	64	46.30 N	10.55 E
San Nicolò Ferrarese	64	44.42 N	11.42 E
San Nicolò Gerrei	71	39.30 N	9.18 E
Sannieshof	158	26.30 S	25.47 E
Sannikova, proliv ʮ	74	74.30 N	140.00 E
Ṣannīn, Jabal ∧	132	33.57 N	35.52 E
Sannio, Monti del ⋏	66	41.30 N	14.45 E
Sanniquellie	150	7.22 N	8.43 W
Sannohe	92	40.22 N	141.15 E
Sannois	261	48.58 N	2.15 E
Sannūr, Wādī V	142	28.58 N	31.03 E
Sano	94	36.19 N	139.35 E
Sañogasta	252	29.18 S	67.36 W
Sanok	30	49.34 N	22.13 E
Sânon ≃	58	48.38 N	6.20 E
San Onofre	246	9.44 N	75.32 W
San Onofre Mountain ∧	228	33.22 N	117.30 W
San Pablo, Chile	254	40.24 S	73.01 W
San Pablo, Col.	246	1.40 N	77.00 W
San Pablo, Pil.	116	14.04 N	121.19 E
San Pablo, Pil.	116	7.40 N	123.27 E
San Pablo, Ca., U.S.	226	37.57 N	122.20 W
San Pablo ◆[8]	286a	19.11 N	99.04 W
San Pablo ≃, Bol.	248	14.52 S	63.42 W
San Pablo ≃, Méx.	234	18.32 N	96.01 W
San Pablo ≃, Pan.	236	7.51 N	81.10 W
San Pablo, Point ›	282	37.58 N	122.26 W
San Pablo Autopan	234	19.21 N	99.40 W
San Pablo Bay ⊂	226	38.06 N	122.22 W
San Pablo Creek ≃	282	37.58 N	122.30 W
San Pablo Huixtepec	234	16.50 N	96.46 W
San Pablo Reservoir ⊜[1]	282	37.56 N	122.15 W
San Pablo Ridge ∧	282	37.55 N	122.15 W
San Pablo Strait ʮ	282	37.58 N	122.26 W
San Pablo Villa de Mitla	234	16.55 N	96.24 W
Sanpāda	272c	19.04 N	73.01 E
San Pancrazio Salentino	68	40.25 N	17.50 E
San Paolo	64	46.29 N	11.15 E
San Paolo di Civitate	68	41.44 N	15.15 E
San Pascual	116	13.08 N	122.59 E
San Pasqual Indian Reservation ◆[4]	228	33.12 N	116.58 W
San Pedro, Arg.	252	33.40 S	59.40 W
San Pedro, Arg.	252	24.14 S	64.52 W
San Pedro, Arg.	252	27.57 S	65.10 W
San Pedro, Chile	252	21.57 S	68.34 W
San Pedro, Chile	252	33.54 S	71.28 W
San Pedro, Col.	246	9.24 N	75.04 W
San Pedro, C.R.	236	9.56 N	84.03 W
San Pédro, C. Iv.	150	4.44 N	6.37 W
San Pedro, Para.	252	24.07 S	56.59 W
San Pedro, Tx., U.S.	196	27.47 N	97.40 W
San Pedro, Ur.	258	34.21 S	57.51 W
San Pedro, Ven.	246	8.50 N	71.58 W
San Pedro □[5]	252	24.15 S	56.30 W
San Pedro ◆[8]	228	33.44 N	118.18 W
San Pedro ≃, Cuba	240p	21.09 N	78.30 W
San Pedro ≃, Méx.	232	30.56 N	108.08 W
San Pedro ≃, Méx.	234	21.45 N	105.30 W
San Pedro ≃, N.A.	200	32.59 N	110.47 W
San Pedro ≃, N.A.	232	17.45 N	91.25 W
San Pedro ≃, Ven.	286c	10.35 N	66.48 W
San Pedro, Arroyo ≃	258	34.21 S	57.56 W
San Pedro, Point ›, Ca., U.S.	282	37.35 N	122.31 W
San Pedro, Point ›, Ca., U.S.	282	37.59 N	122.27 W
San Pedro, Punta ›	252	25.30 S	70.38 W
San Pedro, Volcán ∧[1]	252	21.53 S	68.25 W
San Pedro Amuzgos	234	16.39 N	98.06 W
San Pedro Apóstol	234	16.44 N	96.44 W
San Pedro Ayampuc	236	14.47 N	90.27 W
San Pedro Bay ⊂, Pil.	116	11.11 N	125.05 E
San Pedro Bay ⊂, Ca., U.S.	228	33.45 N	118.11 W
San Pedro Breakwater ◆[5]	280	33.42 N	118.16 W
San Pedro Carchá	236	15.29 N	90.16 W
San Pedro Channel ʮ	228	33.35 N	118.25 W
San Pedro Creek ≃, Ca., U.S.	282	37.36 N	122.30 W
San Pedro Creek ≃, Tx., U.S.	222	31.34 N	95.14 W
San Pedro de Arriba	258	34.18 S	57.47 W
San Pedro de Atacama	252	22.55 S	68.13 W
San Pedro de Buena Vista	248	18.13 S	65.59 W
San Pedro de Curahuara	248	17.40 S	68.02 W
San Pedro de la Cueva	232	29.18 N	109.44 W
San Pedro de las Colonias	232	25.45 N	102.59 W
San Pedro del Gallo	232	25.33 N	104.18 W
San Pedro de Lloc	248	7.26 S	79.31 W
San Pedro del Norte	236	13.04 N	84.33 W
San Pedro del Paraná	252	26.46 S	56.15 W
San Pedro de Macorís	238	18.27 N	69.18 W
San Pedro El Alto	234	16.01 N	96.28 W
San Pedro Huamelula	234	16.02 N	95.40 W
San Pedro Jicayán	234	16.25 N	97.59 W
San Pedro Juchatengo	234	16.21 N	97.06 W
San Pedro Mártir ◆[8]	286a	19.16 N	99.10 W
San Pedro Mixtepec	234	16.00 N	97.07 W
San Pedro Peaks ⋏	200	36.07 N	106.49 W
San Pedro Pinula	236	14.40 N	89.51 W
San Pedro Pochutla	234	15.44 N	96.28 W
San Pedro Sacatepéquez	236	14.58 N	91.46 W
San Pedro Sula	236	15.27 N	88.02 W
San Pedro Tabasco	232	17.47 N	91.10 W
San Pedro Tapanatepec	234	16.21 N	94.12 W
San Pedro Tututepec	234	16.09 N	97.38 W
San Pedro Xalostoc	286a	19.32 N	99.05 W
San Pedro y Miquelón → Saint Pierre and Miquelon □[2]	186	46.55 N	56.20 W
San Pelayo	246	8.58 N	75.51 W
San Pellegrino	62	45.50 N	9.40 E
San Piero a Grado	66	43.41 N	10.21 E
San Piero in Bagno	66	43.51 N	11.58 E
San Pierre	216	41.12 N	86.53 W
San Pietro (Sankt Peter)	64	47.01 N	12.03 E
San Pietro, Isola di I	71	39.08 N	8.17 E
San Pietro a Maida	68	38.50 N	16.20 E
San Pietro di Cadore	64	46.34 N	12.35 E
San Pietro in Casale	64	44.42 N	11.24 E
San Pietro in Gu	64	45.37 N	11.40 E
San Pietro in Guarano	68	39.20 N	16.19 E
San Pietro in Palazzi	66	43.20 N	10.30 E
San Pietro in Vaticano ʊ[1]	267a	41.54 N	12.28 E
San Pietro Vara	62	44.20 N	9.35 E
San Pietro Vernotico	68	40.29 N	18.00 E
San Pitch ≃	200	39.03 N	111.51 W
Sanpoil ≃	202	47.53 N	118.41 W
San Policarpio	116	12.11 N	125.30 E
San Polo d'Enza	64	44.38 N	10.26 E
Sanpu	98	34.09 N	117.10 E
Sanqiao	106	30.35 N	119.58 E
San Quentin	282	37.56 N	122.29 W
San Quentin State Prison ʊ	282	37.56 N	122.28 W
Sanquhar	44	55.22 N	3.56 W
Sanquianga, Parque Nacional ♦	246	2.30 N	78.15 W
San Quintin	116	16.00 N	120.50 E
San Quintín, Cabo ›	232	30.21 N	116.00 W
San Quirico d'Orcia	66	43.03 N	11.36 E
Sanqutan	100	27.17 N	115.04 E
Sanquzhen	107	29.39 N	105.37 E
San Rafael, Arg.	252	34.36 S	68.20 W
San Rafael, Chile	252	35.19 S	71.32 W
San Rafael, Méx.	232	25.01 N	100.33 W
San Rafael, Méx.	234	20.12 N	96.51 W
San Rafael, Ca., U.S.	226	37.58 N	122.31 W
San Rafael, N.M., U.S.	200	35.06 N	107.52 W
San Rafael, Ven.	246	10.58 N	71.44 W
San Rafael ≃, Bol.	248	18.38 S	58.55 W
San Rafael ≃, Ut,. U.S.	200	38.47 N	110.07 W
San Rafael Bay ⊂	282	37.58 N	122.28 W
San Rafael de las Tortillas	196	26.49 N	99.32 W
San Rafael del Norte	236	13.12 N	86.06 W
San Rafael del Sur	236	11.51 N	86.27 W
San Rafael Desert ◆[2]	200	38.40 N	110.30 W
San Rafael Hills ⋏[2]	280	34.10 N	118.12 W
San Rafael Mountains ⋏	204	34.45 N	119.50 W
San Rafael Oriente	236	13.23 N	88.21 W
San Rafael Swell ⋏[1]	200	38.40 N	110.45 W
San Rafael Tasajera	236	13.16 N	88.52 W
San Ramón, Arg.	252	27.42 S	64.17 W
San Ramón, Bol.	248	13.17 S	64.43 W
San Ramón, C.R.	236	10.06 N	84.28 W
San Ramón, Hond.	236	14.41 N	84.43 W
San Ramón, Perú	248	11.08 S	75.20 W
San Ramon, Pil.	116	13.16 N	124.05 E
San Ramon, Ca., U.S.	282	37.47 N	121.59 W
San Ramón, Ur.	252	34.18 S	55.58 W
San Ramon Creek ≃	282	37.54 N	122.03 W
San Ramón de la Nueva Orán	252	23.08 S	64.20 W
San Ramon Valley V	282	37.46 N	121.58 W
Sanrao	100	23.59 N	116.50 E
San-rei ∧	96	33.50 N	133.59 E
San Remigio	116	11.05 N	123.56 E
San Remo, Austl.	169	38.31 S	145.22 E
San Remo, It.	62	43.49 N	7.46 E
San Remo, N.Y., U.S.	210	40.52 N	73.13 W
San Roberto	68	38.18 N	15.44 E
San Rodrigo ≃	196	28.54 N	100.37 W
San Román ≃	236	16.21 N	90.22 W
San Román, Cabo ›	246	12.12 N	70.00 W
San Roque, Arg.	252	28.34 S	58.43 W
San Roque, Arg.	252	30.17 S	68.41 W
San Roque, Esp.	34	36.13 N	5.24 W
San Roque, N. Mar. Is.	174n	15.15 N	145.47 E
San Roque, Pil.	269f	14.29 N	120.54 E
San Roque, Cabo → São Roque, Cabo de ›	250	5.29 S	35.16 W
San Roque, Punta ›	232	27.11 N	114.26 W
San Rosendo	252	37.16 S	72.43 W
San Rufo	68	40.26 N	15.28 E
San Saba	196	31.11 N	98.43 W
San Saba ≃	196	31.15 N	98.35 W
San Saep, Khlong ≅	269a	13.45 N	100.36 E
San Salvador, Arg.	252	29.16 S	57.31 W
San Salvador, Arg.	252	31.37 S	58.30 W
San Salvador, El Sal.	236	13.42 N	89.12 W
San Salvador (Watling Island) I	238	24.02 N	74.28 W
San Salvador ≃	258	33.37 S	58.06 W
San Salvador, Cuchilla ⋏[2]	258	33.56 S	57.45 W
San Salvador, Volcán de ∧[1]	236	13.44 N	89.17 W
San Salvador de Jujuy	252	24.11 S	65.18 W
San Salvador el Seco	234	19.08 N	97.39 W
San Salvatore, Monte ∧	70	37.50 N	14.03 E
San Salvatore Monferrato	62	44.59 N	8.34 E
San Salvatore Telesino	68	41.14 N	14.30 E
San Salvo	66	42.03 N	14.44 E
Sansanné-Mango	150	10.21 N	0.28 E
Sans Bois Creek ≃	196	35.20 N	94.50 W
San Sebastián, El Sal.	236	13.44 N	88.50 W
San Sebastián, Guat.	236	14.34 N	91.39 W
San Sebastián, Hond.	236	14.24 N	88.42 W
San Sebastián, Méx.	234	20.47 N	104.51 W
San Sebastián, P.R.	240m	18.20 N	66.59 W
San Sebastián, Bahía ⊂	254	53.12 S	68.20 W
San Sebastián de la Gomera	148	28.06 N	17.06 W
San Sebastián del Álamo	234	21.26 N	102.21 W
San Sebastián de los Reyes	266a	40.33 N	3.38 W
San Sebastián de Yalí	236	13.18 N	86.11 W
San Sebastián → Donostia	34	43.19 N	1.59 W
San Sebastiano	64	45.38 N	10.16 E
San Sebastiano Curone	62	44.47 N	9.04 E
San Sebastián Tecomaxtlahuaca	234	17.21 N	98.02 W
San Sebastián Zinacatepec	234	18.20 N	97.15 W
San Secondo Parmense	64	44.55 N	10.14 E
Sansepolcro	66	43.34 N	12.08 E
San Severino Lucano	68	40.01 N	16.08 E
San Severino Marche	66	43.13 N	13.10 E
San Severo	68	41.41 N	15.23 E
Sansha	100	26.58 N	120.12 E
Sanshengchang	89	44.51 N	120.21 E
Sanshierzhan	89	53.16 N	121.49 E
Sanshijia, Zhg.	98	41.44 N	119.15 E
Sanshijia, Zhg.	98	41.05 N	119.03 E
Sanshilibao	98	39.15 N	121.48 E
Sanshiling	106	30.51 N	119.29 E
Sanshisanzhan	89	53.10 N	121.27 E
Sanshui	100	23.11 N	112.53 E
San Sigismondo (Sankt Sigmund)	64	46.49 N	11.46 E
San Simeon	226	35.39 N	121.11 W
San Simon, Méx.	204	30.30 N	115.58 W
San Simon, Az., U.S.	200	32.16 N	109.13 W
San Simón ≃, Bol.	248	13.13 S	63.31 W
San Simon ≃, Az., U.S.	200	32.50 N	109.39 W
San Simon Wash V	200	31.45 N	112.25 W
San Siro ◆[8]	266b	45.29 N	9.07 E
Sanski Most	36	44.46 N	16.40 E
Sanso	150	11.43 N	6.51 W
San Solano	252	31.29 S	65.55 W
Sansom Park Village	222	32.48 N	97.24 W
Sanson	172	40.13 S	175.25 E
San Sosti	68	39.40 N	16.02 E
San Sperate	71	39.21 N	9.00 E
Sans Souci	274a	33.59 S	151.08 E
Sans-Souci ⊥	238	19.37 N	72.12 W
Sanssouci, Schloss ʊ	54	52.24 N	13.02 E
San Stefano Ticino	266b	45.29 N	8.55 E
Santa, Perú	248	8.59 S	78.36 W
Santa, Pil.	116	17.29 N	120.26 E
Santa ≃	248	8.58 S	78.39 W
Santa, Isla del I	248	9.02 S	78.40 W
Santa Adélia	255	21.16 S	48.48 W
Santa Albertina	255	20.02 S	50.44 W
Santa Amalia	34	39.01 N	6.01 W
Santa Ana, Arg.	252	27.22 S	55.34 W
Santa Ana, Bol.	248	13.45 S	65.35 W
Santa Ana, Bol.	248	18.43 S	58.44 W
Santa Ana, Col.	246	9.19 N	74.35 W
Santa Ana, Ec.	246	1.13 S	80.23 W
Santa Ana, El Sal.	236	13.59 N	89.34 W
Santa Ana, Méx.	232	24.04 N	100.30 W
Santa Ana, Méx.	232	30.33 N	111.07 W
Santa Ana, Ca., U.S.	228	33.44 N	117.52 W
Santa Ana, Ven.	246	9.19 N	64.39 W
Santa Ana ≃, Cuba	286b	23.04 N	82.32 W
Santa Ana ≃, Ca., U.S.	228	33.38 N	117.57 W
Santa Ana, Volcán de ∧[1]	236	13.50 N	89.38 W
Santa Ana Canyon V	280	33.53 N	117.43 W
Santa Ana de Chena	286e	33.34 S	70.47 W
Santa Ana del Alto Beni	248	15.31 S	67.30 W
Santa Ana Heights	228	33.39 N	117.54 W
Santa Ana Indian Reservation ◆[4]	200	35.28 N	106.37 W
Santa Ana Island I	175e	10.50 S	162.28 E
Santa Ana Maya	234	20.00 N	101.01 W
Santa Ana Mountains ⋏	228	33.45 N	117.35 W
Santa Ana Race Track ♦	269f	14.35 N	121.01 E
Santa Ana Tlacotenco ◆[8]	286a	19.10 N	98.59 W
Santa Anita	234	20.33 N	103.27 W
Santa Anita Canyon V	280	34.12 N	118.01 W
Santa Anita Park ♦	280	34.08 N	118.03 W
Santa Anna	196	31.44 N	99.19 W
Santa Apolonia	196	25.38 N	97.59 W
Santa Bárbara, Chile	252	37.40 S	72.01 W
Santa Barbara, Col.	246	5.53 N	75.35 W
Santa Bárbara, Hond.	236	14.53 N	88.14 W
Santa Bárbara, Méx.	232	26.48 N	105.49 W
Santa Bárbara, Méx.	234	18.52 N	101.07 W
Santa Barbara, Ca., U.S.	204	34.25 N	119.42 W
Santa Bárbara, Ven.	246	3.57 N	67.06 W
Santa Bárbara, Ven.	246	7.47 N	71.10 W
Santa Bárbara □[5]	236	15.10 N	88.20 W
Santa Barbara □[6]	228	33.28 N	119.02 W
Santa Bárbara ≃	248	16.58 S	61.39 W
Santa Bárbara, Morro de ∧	287a	22.57 S	43.28 W
Santa Bárbara, Túnel ◆[5]	287a	22.56 S	43.12 W
Santa Barbara Channel ʮ	204	34.15 N	119.55 W
Santa Bárbara do Monte Verde	256	21.58 S	43.42 W
Santa Bárbara do Sul	252	28.22 S	53.15 W
Santa Barbara do Tugúrio	256	21.15 S	43.35 W
Santa Barbara Island I	228	33.28 N	119.02 W
Santa Branca	256	23.24 S	45.53 W
Santa Branca, Represa ⊜[1]	256	23.20 S	45.50 W
Santaca	158	26.36 S	32.32 E
Santa Catalina, Arg.	252	21.57 S	66.04 W
Santa Catalina, Pil.	116	9.20 N	122.51 E
Santa Catalina, Ur.	258	33.49 S	57.29 W
Santa Catalina, Arroyo ≃	288	34.46 S	58.27 W
Santa Catalina, Gulf of ⊂	228	33.20 N	117.45 W
Santa Catalina, Isla I	232	25.40 N	110.47 W
Santa Catalina, Laguna ⊜	288	34.46 S	58.27 W
Santa Catalina Island I	228	33.23 N	118.24 W
Santa Catalina o Calovébora	236	8.47 N	81.20 W
Santa Catarina, Méx.	204	31.37 N	115.48 W
Santa Catarina, Méx.	232	25.41 N	100.28 W
Santa Catarina □[3]	252	27.00 S	50.00 W
Santa Catarina, Ilha de I	252	27.36 S	48.30 W
Santa Catarina Juquila	234	16.14 N	97.18 W
Santa Caterina di Pittinuri	71	40.06 N	8.30 E
Santa Caterina Valfurva	64	46.25 N	10.29 E
Santa Caterina Villarmosa	70	37.35 N	14.02 E
Santa Cecília	252	26.56 S	50.27 W
Santa Cesarea Terme	68	40.02 N	18.29 E
Santa Clara, Col.	246	2.43 S	69.43 W
Santa Clara, Cuba	240p	22.24 N	79.58 W
Santa Clara, Méx.	232	29.17 N	107.01 W
Santa Clara, Méx.	234	19.41 N	102.30 W
Santa Clara, Méx.	286a	19.34 N	99.04 W
Santa Clara, Ca., U.S.	226	37.20 N	121.56 W
Santa Clara, Ut,. U.S.	200	37.07 N	113.39 W
Santa Clara □[6]	226	37.20 N	121.53 W
Santa Clara ≃, Ca., U.S.	228	34.14 N	119.16 W
Santa Clara ≃, Ut,. U.S.	200	37.05 N	113.36 W
Santa Clara, Bahía de ⊂	240p	23.05 N	80.30 W
Santa Clara, University of ʊ[2]	282	37.21 N	121.56 W
Santa Clara de Olimar	252	32.55 S	54.58 W
Santa Clara Indian Reservation ◆[4]	200	35.59 N	106.10 W
Santa Clara Valley V	226	37.10 N	121.40 W
Santa Clarita	286d	12.00 S	77.01 W
Santa Clotilde	246	2.34 S	73.44 W
Santa Coloma de Cervelló	266d	41.22 N	2.01 E
Santa Coloma de Farners	34	41.52 N	2.40 E
Santa Coloma de Gramanet	266d	41.27 N	2.13 E
Santa Comba	34	43.02 N	8.49 W
Santa Comba Dão	34	40.24 N	8.08 W
Santa Cristina	64	46.34 N	11.43 E
Santa Cristina d'aspromonte	68	38.15 N	15.58 E
Santa Croce	64	46.05 N	12.18 E
Santa Croce, Capo ›	70	37.14 N	15.15 E
Santa Croce, Lago di ⊜	64	46.10 N	12.20 E
Santa Croce Camerina	70	36.50 N	14.31 E
Santa Croce del Sannio	68	41.23 N	14.43 E
Santa Croce di Magliano	66	41.42 N	14.59 E
Santa Croce Sull'Arno	66	43.42 N	10.47 E
Santa Cruz, Bra.	250	6.13 S	36.01 W
Santa Cruz, Bra.	255	19.56 S	40.09 W
Santa Cruz, Chile	252	34.38 S	71.22 W
Santa Cruz, C.R.	236	10.16 N	85.36 W
Santa Cruz, Méx.	200	31.14 N	110.35 W
Santa Cruz, Perú	248	6.37 S	78.57 W
Santa Cruz, Pil.	116	6.50 N	125.25 E
Santa Cruz, Pil.	116	14.17 N	121.25 E
Santa Cruz, Pil.	116	13.29 N	122.02 E
Santa Cruz, Pil.	116	13.04 N	120.43 E
Santa Cruz, Pil.	116	15.46 N	119.55 E
Santa Cruz (Tubajon), Pil.	116	10.19 N	125.33 E
Santa Cruz, Ca., U.S.	226	36.58 N	122.01 W
Santa Cruz, Ven.	246	8.25 N	71.39 W
Santa Cruz, Ven.	286c	10.26 N	67.01 W
Santa Cruz □[4]	254	49.00 S	70.00 W
Santa Cruz □[5]	248	17.30 S	61.30 W
Santa Cruz □[6]	226	36.58 N	122.01 W
Santa Cruz ◆[8], Bra.	256	22.56 S	43.41 W
Santa Cruz ◆[8], India	272c	19.05 N	72.50 E
Santa Cruz ≃, Arg.	254	50.08 S	68.20 W
Santa Cruz ≃, Cuba	286b	23.04 N	82.29 W
Santa Cruz ≃, N.A.	200	32.42 N	111.33 W
Santa Cruz, Ilha I	287a	22.52 S	43.07 W
Santa Cruz, Isla I	246a	0.38 S	90.23 W
Santa Cruz, Sierra de ⋏	236	15.40 N	89.15 W
Santa Cruz Basin ✢[1]	14	12.00 S	163.00 E
Santa Cruz Cabrália	255	16.17 S	39.02 W
Santa Cruz da Graciosa	148a	39.05 N	28.01 W
Santa Cruz das Flores	148a	39.27 N	31.07 W
Santa Cruz de Goiás	255	17.19 S	48.30 W
Santa Cruz de Juventino Rosas	234	20.39 N	101.00 W
Santa Cruz de la Palma	148	28.41 N	17.45 W
Santa Cruz de la Sierra	248	17.48 S	63.10 W
Santa Cruz de la Zarza	34	39.58 N	3.10 W
Santa Cruz del Quiché	236	15.02 N	91.08 W
Santa Cruz del Sur	240p	20.43 N	78.00 W
Santa Cruz de Mudela	34	38.38 N	3.28 W
Santa Cruz de Tenerife	148	28.27 N	16.14 W
Santa Cruz de Tenerife □[4], Esp.	34	28.20 N	16.50 W
Santa Cruz de Tenerife □[4], Esp.	148	28.15 N	17.00 W
Santa Cruz do Capibaribe	250	7.57 S	36.12 W
Santa Cruz do Piauí	250	7.09 S	41.48 W
Santa Cruz do Prata	256	21.12 S	46.45 W
Santa Cruz do Rio Pardo	255	22.55 S	49.37 W
Santa Cruz do Sul	252	29.43 S	52.26 W
Santa Cruz International Airport ⊠	272c	19.05 N	72.52 E
Santa Cruz Island I	204	34.01 N	119.45 W
Santa Cruz Islands II	14	11.00 S	166.15 E
Santa Cruz Meyehualco ◆[8]	286a	19.20 N	99.03 W
Santa Cruz Mountains ⋏	226	37.15 N	122.00 W
Santa Cruz Point ›	116	15.44 N	119.52 E
Santa Cruz Tacache de Mina	234	17.51 N	98.07 W
Santadi	71	39.05 N	8.43 E
Santa Domenica Talao	68	39.49 N	15.51 E
Santa Domenica Vittoria	70	37.55 N	14.58 E
Sant Adrià de Besòs	266d	41.25 N	2.14 E
Santa Elena, Arg.	252	30.57 S	59.48 W
Santa Elena, Ec.	246	2.14 S	80.51 W
Santa Elena, El Sal.	236	13.22 N	88.25 W
Santa Elena, Méx.	196	27.59 N	103.56 W
Santa Elena, Méx.	232	27.28 N	102.33 W
Santa Elena, Méx.	234	18.39 N	101.34 W
Santa Elena ≃	248	15.42 S	67.13 W
Santa Elena, Bahía de ⊂	246	2.06 S	80.53 W
Santa Elena, Golfo de ⊂	236	10.59 N	85.50 W
Santa Elena, Punta ›, C.R.	236	10.54 N	85.57 W
Santa Elena, Punta ›, Ec.	246	2.11 S	81.00 W
Santa Elena del Gomero	286e	33.29 S	70.46 W
Santa Elena de Uairén	246	4.37 N	61.08 W
Santa Elisabetta	70	37.26 N	13.33 E
Santa Eufemia	34	38.36 N	4.54 W
Santa Eugenia	34	42.33 N	9.00 W
Santa Eulalia, Esp.	34	40.34 N	1.19 W
Santa Eulalia, Guat.	236	15.45 N	91.29 W
Santa Eulària del Riu	34	38.59 N	1.31 E
Santa Fe, Arg.	252	31.38 S	60.42 W
Santa Fé, Bra.	255	15.40 S	51.16 W
Santa Fé, Bra.	255	23.01 S	51.48 W
Santa Fe, Esp.	34	37.11 N	3.43 W
Santa Fe, Hond.	236	15.55 N	86.05 W
Santa Fé, Pan.	236	8.31 N	81.05 W
Santa Fe, Pil.	116	11.09 N	123.47 E
Santa Fe, Pil.	116	16.10 N	120.57 E
Santa Fe, Pil.	116	12.10 N	122.00 E
Santa Fe, Mo., U.S.	219	39.22 N	91.49 W
Santa Fe, N.M., U.S.	200	35.41 N	105.56 W
Santa Fe □[4]	252	31.00 S	61.00 W
Santa Fé ◆[8]	286b	23.05 N	82.31 W
Santa Fe ≃, Fl., U.S.	192	29.53 N	82.53 W
Santa Fe ≃, N.M., U.S.	200	35.36 N	106.20 W
Santa Fé, Aeropuerto ⊠	286b	23.04 N	82.28 W
Santa Fe, Isla I	246a	0.49 S	90.04 W
Santa Fé, Ribeirão ≃	287b	23.24 S	46.48 W
Santa Fe Baldy ∧	200	35.50 N	105.46 W
Santa Fe Dam ◆[6]	280	34.07 N	117.58 W
Santa Fe de Bogotá	246	4.36 N	74.05 W
Santa Fe de Minas	255	16.42 S	45.26 W
Santa Fé do Sul	255	20.13 S	50.56 W
Santa Fe Flood Control Basin ≅[1]	280	34.07 N	117.58 W
Santa Fe Springs	280	33.56 N	118.04 W
Santa Filomena	250	9.07 S	45.56 W
Santa Fiora	66	42.50 N	11.35 E
Santa Flavia	70	38.05 N	13.31 E
Sant'Agata Bolognese	64	44.40 N	11.08 E
Sant'Agata de'Goti	68	41.05 N	14.30 E
Sant'Agata del Bianco	68	38.05 N	16.05 E
Sant'Agata di Militello	70	38.04 N	14.38 E
Sant'Agata di Puglia	68	41.09 N	15.23 E
Sant'Agata Feltria	66	43.52 N	12.12 E
Sant'Agata sul Santerno	66	44.26 N	11.51 E
Santa Gertrude (Sankt Gertraud)	64	46.29 N	10.53 E
Santa Gertrudis	196	26.09 N	98.44 W
Santa Giusta, Stagno di ⊜	71	39.52 N	8.35 E
Sant'Agostino	64	44.48 N	11.23 E
Sāntāhār	124	24.48 N	88.59 E
Santa Helena	250	2.14 S	45.18 W
Santa Helena de Goiás	255	17.43 S	50.35 W
Santai, Zhg.	85	39.14 N	77.42 E
Santai, Zhg.	86	44.35 N	81.18 E
Santai, Zhg.	102	31.10 N	105.02 E
Santai, Zhg.	104	41.56 N	123.11 E
Santai, Zhg.	104	41.48 N	121.53 E
Santai, Zhg.	105	38.58 N	115.49 E
Santa Inês	255	13.17 S	39.48 W
Santa Inés, Bahía ⊂	232	26.59 N	111.59 W
Santa Inés, Isla I	254	53.45 S	72.45 W
Santa Inés Ahuatempan	234	18.25 N	98.01 W
Santa Iria de Azóia	266c	38.51 N	9.05 W
Santa Isabel, Arg.	252	36.15 S	66.56 W
Santa Isabel, Arg.	252	33.54 S	61.42 W
Santa Isabel, Bra.	256	23.19 S	46.14 W
Santa Isabel, Ec.	246	3.21 S	79.19 W
Santa Isabel, Méx.	234	23.15 N	100.52 W
Santa Isabel, P.R.	240m	17.58 N	66.24 W
Santa Isabel I	175e	8.00 S	159.00 E
Santa Isabel ≃	236	15.59 N	90.00 W
Santa Isabel, Pico de ∧	152	3.35 N	8.46 E
Santa Isabel Creek ≃	196	27.39 N	99.38 W
Santa Isabel de Sihuas	248	16.20 S	72.06 W
Santa Isabel do Araguaia	250	6.07 S	48.19 W
Santa Isabel do Rio Prêto	256	22.14 S	44.05 W
Santa Isabel → Malabo	152	3.45 N	8.47 E
Santaizi	104	41.21 N	121.36 E
Santa Josefa	116	8.02 N	125.57 E
Santa Julia	286e	33.30 S	70.38 W
Santa Juliana	255	19.19 S	47.32 W
Sant'Alberto	66	44.32 N	12.09 E
Sant'Alfio	70	37.44 N	15.08 E
Sāntalpur	120	23.45 N	71.10 E
Santa Luce	66	43.28 N	10.34 E
Santa Lucía, Arg.	252	28.59 S	59.06 W
Santa Lucía, Arg.	252	31.32 S	68.29 W
Santa Lucía, Cuba	240p	21.02 N	76.00 W
Santa Lucía, Cuba	240p	22.40 N	83.58 W
Santa Lucia, It.	64	46.28 N	10.21 E
Santa Lucía, Ur.	258	34.27 S	56.24 W
Santa Lucía, Ven.	246	8.07 N	69.46 W
Santa Lucía ≃	258	34.48 S	56.22 W
Santa Lucía, Cabo → Saint Lucia, Cape ›	158	28.25 S	32.25 E
Santa Lucía, Cuchilla ⋏[2]	258	34.09 S	56.11 W
Santa Lucía Chico ≃	258	34.21 S	56.20 W
Santa Lucía Cotzumalguapa	236	14.20 N	91.01 W
Santa Lucia Creek ≃	226	36.13 N	121.30 W
Santa Lucia del Mela	70	38.09 N	15.17 E
Santa Lucia di Piave	64	45.51 N	12.17 E
Santa Lucia Range ⋏	226	36.00 N	121.20 W
Santa Lucía → Saint Lucia □[1]	241f	13.53 N	60.58 W
Santaluz	250	11.15 S	39.22 W
Santa Luzia, Bra.	250	6.53 S	36.56 W
Santa Luzia, Port.	34	37.44 N	8.24 W
Santa Luzia I	150a	16.46 N	24.45 W
Santa Magdalena	252	34.30 S	63.56 W
Santa-Manza, Golfu di ⊂	71	41.37 N	9.22 E
Santa Margarita	226	35.23 N	120.36 W
Santa Margarita ≃	228	33.14 N	117.25 W
Santa Margarita, Isla I	232	24.27 N	111.50 W
Santa Margarita Lake ⊜[1]	226	35.20 N	120.28 W
Santa Margarita Mountains ⋏	228	33.30 N	117.25 W
Santa Margherita di Belice	70	37.41 N	13.01 E
Santa Margherita Ligure	62	44.20 N	9.12 E
Santa María, Arg.	252	26.41 S	66.02 W
Santa Maria, Bra.	252	29.41 S	53.48 W
Santa Maria, C.V.	150a	16.36 N	22.54 W
Santa María, C.R.	236	9.39 N	83.57 W
Santa María, Méx.	196	28.02 N	101.38 W
Santa María, Pan.	236	8.07 N	80.40 W
Santa Maria, Pil.	116	17.22 N	120.29 E
Santa María, P.R.	240m	18.09 N	65.26 W
Santa Maria, Schw.	58	46.16 N	9.09 E
Santa Maria, Schw.	58	46.36 N	10.24 E
Santa Maria, Ca., U.S.	204	34.57 N	120.26 W
Santa Maria I, Port.	148a	36.58 N	25.06 W
Santa Maria I, Vanuatu	175f	14.15 S	167.30 E
Santa Maria ≃, Bra.	252	29.48 S	54.56 W
Santa Maria ≃, Bra.	252	21.50 S	54.53 W
Santa María ≃, Méx.	232	31.00 N	107.14 W
Santa María ≃, Méx.	234	21.48 N	99.10 W
Santa María ≃, Pan.	236	8.06 N	80.29 W
Santa Maria ≃, Az., U.S.	200	34.19 N	113.31 W
Santa María, Bahía ⊂	232	25.04 N	108.06 W

Symbol	English	Deutsch	Español	Français	Português
≃	River	Fluß	Río	Rivière	Rio
≅	Canal	Kanal	Canal	Canal	Canal
╰	Waterfall, Rapids	Wasserfall, Stromschnellen	Cascada, Rápidos	Chute d'eau, Rapides	Cascata, Rápidos
ʮ	Strait	Meeresstraße	Estrecho	Détroit	Estreito
⊂	Bay, Gulf	Bucht, Golf	Bahía, Golfo	Baie, Golfe	Baía, Golfo
⊜	Lake, Lakes	See, Seen	Lago, Lagos	Lac, Lacs	Lago, Lagos
⩩	Swamp	Sumpf	Pantano	Marais	Pântano
⊓	Ice Features, Glacier	Eis- und Gletscherformen	Accidentes Glaciales	Formes glaciaires	Acidentes glaciares
⩒	Other Hydrographic Features	Andere Hydrographische Objekte	Otros Elementos Hidrográficos	Autres données hydrographiques	Outros acidentes hidrográficos

Symbol	English	Deutsch	Español	Français	Português
✢	Submarine Features	Untermeerische Objekte	Accidentes Submarinos	Formes de relief sous-marin	Acidentes submarinos
□	Political Unit	Politische Einheit	Unidad Politica	Entité politique	Unidade política
ʊ	Cultural Institution	Kulturelle Institution	Institución Cultural	Institution culturelle	Institução cultural
⊥	Historical Site	Historische Stätte	Sitio Histórico	Site historique	Sitio histórico
♦	Recreational Site	Erholungs- und Ferienort	Sitio de Recreo	Centre de loisirs	Area de Lazer
⊠	Airport	Flughafen	Aeropuerto	Aéroport	Aeroporto
■	Military Installation	Militäranlage	Instalación Militar	Installation militaire	Instalação militar
◆	Miscellaneous	Verschiedenes	Misceláneo	Divers	Diversos

Name / Name	Page / Seite	Lat.°′ / Breite°′	Long.°′ / Länge°′ E = Ost
Santa María, Cabo ›	**252**	34.40 S	54.10 W
Santa Maria, Cabo de ›, Ang.	**152**	13.25 S	12.32 E
Santa Maria, Cabo de ›, Port.	**34**	36.58 N	7.54 W
Santa Maria, Cabo → Sainte-Marie, Cap ›	**157b**	25.36 S	45.08 E
Santa Maria, Cape ›	**238**	23.41 N	75.19 W
Santa María, Cayo I	**240p**	22.40 N	79.00 W
Santa María, Cerro ∧	**286d**	11.56 S	76.57 W
Santa Maria, Giogo di (Pass Umbrail))(	**64**	46.34 N	10.25 E
Santa María, Isla I, Chile	**252**	37.02 S	73.33 W
Santa María, Isla I, Ec.	**246a**	1.17 S	90.26 W
Santa Maria, Isola I	**71**	41.17 N	9.22 E
Santa María, Laguna de ⊜	**200**	31.07 N	107.16 W
Santa Maria, Ribeirão ≃	**250**	7.10 S	49.13 W
Santa María, Volcán ∧[1]	**236**	14.45 N	91.33 W
Santa María Ajoloapan	**234**	19.58 N	99.03 W
Santa Maria a Monte	**66**	43.42 N	10.42 E
Santa María Asunción Tlaxiaco	**234**	17.16 N	97.41 W
Santa Maria a Vico	**68**	41.02 N	14.29 E
Santa María Ayoquezco	**234**	16.41 N	96.50 W
Santa Maria Capua Vetere	**68**	41.05 N	14.15 E
Santa María Chimalapa	**234**	16.55 N	94.41 W
Santa María Colotepec	**234**	15.53 N	96.55 W
Santa Maria da Boa Vista	**250**	8.49 S	39.49 W
Santa Maria da Vitória	**255**	13.24 S	44.12 W
Santa Maria degli Angeli	**66**	43.03 N	12.34 E
Santa María de Huazamoto	**234**	22.30 N	104.30 W
Santa María de Ipire	**246**	8.49 N	65.19 W
Santa Maria de Itabira	**255**	19.27 S	43.08 W
Santa Maria del Cedro	**68**	39.45 N	15.50 E
Santa Maria della Versa	**62**	44.59 N	9.18 E
Santa Maria delle Grazie ʊ[1]	**266b**	45.27 N	9.10 E
Santa María del Oro	**232**	25.56 N	105.22 W
Santa María de los Ángeles	**234**	22.11 N	103.14 W
Santa María del Refugio	**234**	23.44 N	101.14 W
Santa María del Río	**234**	21.48 N	100.45 W
Santa María del Valle	**234**	20.54 N	102.22 W
Santa Mariá de Mohovano	**232**	26.42 N	103.39 W
Santa Maria di Galeria ◆[8]	**267a**	42.01 N	12.19 E
Santa Maria di Leuca, Capo ›	**68**	39.47 N	18.22 E
Santa Maria di Licodia	**70**	37.37 N	14.53 E
Santa Maria di Siponto ʊ[1]	**68**	41.40 N	15.51 E
Santa Maria do Suaçuí	**255**	18.12 S	42.25 W
Santa María Huazolotitlán	**234**	16.17 N	97.56 W
Santa María Jalapa del Marqués	**234**	16.30 N	95.28 W
Santa María la Real de Nieva	**34**	41.04 N	4.24 W
Santa Maria Madalena	**255**	21.57 S	42.01 W
Santa Maria Maggiore	**58**	46.08 N	8.28 E
Santa Maria Maggiore ʊ[1]	**267a**	41.53 N	12.30 E
Santa Maria Nuova	**66**	43.29 N	13.18 E
Santa-Maria-Siché	**36**	41.52 N	8.59 E
Santa María Tulpetlac	**286a**	19.34 N	99.03 W
Santa María Xadani	**234**	15.56 N	96.04 W
Santa María Zoquitlán	**234**	16.33 N	96.23 W
Santa Marinella	**66**	42.02 N	11.51 E
Santa Marta, Col.	**246**	11.15 N	74.13 W
Santa Marta, Guat.	**236**	13.58 N	91.18 W
Santa Marta, Cabo de ›, Ang.	**152**	13.52 S	12.25 E
Santa Marta, Cabo de ›, Moç.	**158**	26.05 S	32.58 E
Santa Marta, Cerro ∧	**234**	18.19 N	94.48 W
Santa Marta, Ciénaga Grande ⊂	**246**	10.50 N	74.25 W
Santa Marta Grande, Cabo de ›	**252**	28.38 S	48.45 W
Sant'Ambrogio	**64**	45.31 N	10.50 E
Santa Mónica, Méx.	**196**	28.12 N	100.37 W
Santa Monica, Ca., U.S.	**228**	34.01 N	118.29 W
Santa Mónica ◆[8]	**286c**	10.29 N	66.53 W
Santa Monica Bay ⊂	**228**	33.54 N	118.25 W
Santa Monica Beach State Park ♠	**280**	34.01 N	118.30 W
Santa Monica Mountains ⋏	**228**	34.05 N	118.40 W
Santa Monica Mountains National Recreation Area ♠	**228**	34.05 N	118.45 W
Santa Monica Municipal Airport ⊠	**280**	34.01 N	118.27 W
Santan	**112**	0.03 S	117.28 E
Santana	**255**	12.59 S	44.03 W
Santana ◆[8]	**287b**	23.29 S	46.38 W
Santana ≃	**255**	19.43 S	51.02 W
Santana, Coxilha de ⋏[2]	**252**	31.15 S	55.15 W
Santana, Ilha de I	**250**	2.18 S	43.41 W
Santana, Ribeirão ≃	**250**	9.47 S	50.13 W
Santana da Boa Vista	**252**	30.52 S	53.07 W
Santana da Vargem	**256**	21.15 S	45.30 W
Santana de Caldas	**256**	21.50 S	46.24 W
Santana de Cataguases	**256**	21.17 S	42.33 W
Santana de Parnaíba	**256**	23.27 S	46.55 W
Santana de Parnaíba □[7]	**287b**	23.27 S	46.54 W
Santana do Campestre	**256**	21.16 S	42.56 W
Santana do Capivari	**256**	22.14 S	44.56 W
Santana do Cariri	**250**	7.11 S	39.44 W
Santana do Deserto	**256**	21.57 S	43.11 W
Santana do Garambéu	**256**	21.36 S	44.06 W
Santana do Ipanema	**250**	9.22 S	37.14 W
Santana do Livramento	**252**	30.53 S	55.31 W
Santana do Matos	**250**	5.57 S	36.39 W
Santander, Col.	**246**	3.01 N	76.28 W
Santander, Esp.	**34**	43.28 N	3.48 W
Santander, Pil.	**116**	9.25 N	123.20 E
Santander □[5]	**246**	7.00 N	73.15 W
Santander Jiménez	**232**	24.13 N	98.28 W
Sant'andrea, Isola I	**68**	40.03 N	17.57 E
Sant'Andrea Frius	**71**	39.29 N	9.10 E
Sant Andreu de la Barca	**266d**	41.27 N	1.59 E
Santa Nella	**226**	37.03 N	121.02 W
Santanésia	**256**	22.30 S	43.49 W
Santang	**100**	28.44 N	116.32 E
Sant'Angelo, Castel ⊥	**267a**	41.55 N	12.28 E
Sant'Angelo, Monte ∧	**267a**	41.56 N	12.49 E
Sant'Angelo dei Lombardi	**68**	40.56 N	15.11 E
Sant'Angelo in Vado	**66**	43.40 N	12.25 E
Sant'Angelo Lodigiano	**62**	45.14 N	9.24 E
Sant'Angelo Muxard	**70**	37.28 N	13.32 E
Sant'Angelo Romano	**267a**	42.02 N	12.42 E
Santanghu	**102**	44.13 N	93.22 E
Santanilla, Islas II	**238**	17.25 N	83.55 W
Santa Ninfa	**70**	37.46 N	12.53 E
Sant'Antimo	**68**	40.56 N	14.14 E
Sant'antine, Nuraghe ⊥	**71**	40.29 N	8.46 E
Sant'Antioco	**71**	39.04 N	8.27 E
Sant'Antioco, Isola di I	**71**	39.02 N	8.25 E
Sant Antoni de Portmany	**34**	38.58 N	1.18 E
Sant'Antonio Abate	**68**	40.43 N	14.32 E
Sant'Antonio di Santadi	**71**	39.43 N	8.29 E
Sant'Antonio Morignone	**64**	46.24 N	10.21 E
Santanyi	**34**	39.22 N	3.07 E
Santa Panagia, Capo ›	**70**	37.07 N	15.18 E
Santa Paula	**228**	34.21 N	119.03 W
Santa Paula Creek ≃	**228**	34.21 N	119.03 W
Santa Perpètua de Mogoda	**266d**	41.32 N	2.11 E
Santapogue Creek ≃	**276**	40.40 N	73.21 W
Santa Pola, Cap de ›	**34**	38.12 N	0.31 W
Sant'Apollinare in Classe ʊ[1]	**66**	44.22 N	12.15 E
Santaquin	**200**	39.58 N	111.47 W
Santa Quitéria	**250**	4.20 S	40.10 W
Santa Quitéria do Maranhão	**250**	3.31 S	42.32 W
Sant'Arcangelo	**68**	40.15 N	16.17 E
Santarcangelo di Romagna	**66**	44.04 N	12.27 E
Sant'Arcangelo Trimonte	**68**	41.10 N	14.56 E
Santarém, Bra.	**250**	2.26 S	54.42 W
Santarém, Port.	**34**	39.14 N	8.41 W
Santarém □[5]	**266c**	38.50 N	8.56 W
Santaren Channel ⊔	**238**	24.00 N	79.30 W
Santa Rita, Bra.	**250**	7.08 S	34.58 W
Santa Rita, Bra.	**287a**	22.41 S	43.28 W
Santa Rita, Col.	**246**	0.33 N	73.58 W
Santa Rita, Hond.	**236**	15.09 N	87.53 W
Santa Rita, Méx.	**196**	27.29 N	100.33 W
Santa Rita, Méx.	**232**	28.34 N	111.42 W
Santa Rita, Pil.	**116**	11.27 N	124.56 E
Santa Rita, Mt., U.S.	**182**	48.42 N	112.19 W
Santa Rita, Ven.	**246**	10.32 N	71.32 W
Santa Rita, Punta ›	**258**	34.28 S	57.52 W
Santa Rita de Caldas	**256**	22.02 S	46.20 W
Santa Rita de Catuna	**252**	30.57 S	66.13 W
Santa Rita de Jacutinga	**256**	22.09 S	44.06 W
Santa Rita del Rucio	**234**	23.04 N	100.19 W
Santa Rita do Araguaia	**255**	17.20 S	53.12 W
Santa Rita do Ibitipoca	**256**	21.33 S	43.55 W
Santa Rita do Sapucaí	**256**	22.15 S	45.42 W
Santa Rita do Weil	**246**	3.29 S	69.19 W
Santa Rita Park	**226**	37.02 N	120.35 W
Santa Rosa, Arg.	**252**	36.37 S	64.17 W
Santa Rosa, Arg.	**252**	23.22 S	64.30 W
Santa Rosa, Bol.	**248**	14.10 S	66.53 W
Santa Rosa, Bol.	**248**	10.36 S	67.25 W
Santa Rosa, Bol.	**248**	17.07 S	63.35 W
Santa Rosa, Bra.	**252**	27.52 S	54.29 W
Santa Rosa, Bra.	**255**	15.01 S	47.13 W
Santa Rosa, Col.	**246**	2.31 N	68.13 W
Santa Rosa, C.R.	**236**	10.51 N	85.38 W
Santa Rosa, Ec.	**246**	3.27 S	79.58 W
Santa Rosa, Méx.	**204**	31.59 N	116.45 W
Santa Rosa, Méx.	**234**	22.18 N	104.24 W
Santa Rosa, Para.	**248**	21.46 S	61.43 W
Santa Rosa, Para.	**252**	26.52 S	56.49 W
Santa Rosa, Ca., U.S.	**226**	38.26 N	122.42 W
Santa Rosa, N.M., U.S.	**196**	34.56 N	104.40 W
Santa Rosa, Tx., U.S.	**196**	26.15 N	97.50 W
Santa Rosa, Ur.	**258**	34.30 S	56.03 W
Santa Rosa, Ven.	**246**	7.03 N	68.28 W
Santa Rosa, Ven.	**246**	8.26 N	69.24 W
Santa Rosa, Ven.	**286c**	10.30 N	66.46 W
Santa Rosa □[5]	**236**	14.10 N	90.18 W
Santa Rosa, Mount ∧[2]	**174p**	13.32 N	144.55 E
Santa Rosa, Parque Nacional ♠	**236**	10.50 N	85.45 W
Santa Rosa, Presa ⊜[1]	**234**	20.58 N	103.35 W
Santa Rosa Beach	**194**	30.23 N	86.13 W
Santa Rosa Creek ≃	**226**	35.34 N	121.06 W
Santa Rosa de Aguán	**236**	15.57 N	85.43 W
Santa Rosa de Amanadona	**246**	1.29 N	66.55 W
Santa Rosa [de Copán]	**236**	14.47 N	88.46 W
Santa Rosa de Huechuraba	**286e**	33.21 S	70.41 W
Santa Rosa del Conlara	**252**	32.20 S	65.12 W
Santa Rosa de Leales	**252**	27.09 S	65.15 W
Santa Rosa de Lima	**236**	13.37 N	87.53 W
Santa Rosa de Locobe	**286e**	33.26 S	70.33 W
Santa Rosa del Palmar	**248**	16.54 S	62.24 W
Santa Rosa de Osos	**246**	6.39 N	75.28 W
Santa Rosa de Río Primero	**252**	31.09 S	63.23 W
Santa Rosa de Sucumbíos	**246**	0.22 N	77.10 W
Santa Rosa de Viterbo	**246**	5.53 N	72.59 W
Santa Rosa Indian Reservation ◆[4]	**204**	33.35 N	116.35 W
Santa Rosa Island I, Ca., U.S.	**204**	33.58 N	120.06 W
Santa Rosa Island I, Fl., U.S.	**194**	30.22 N	86.55 W
Santa Rosa Jáuregui	**234**	20.44 N	100.27 W
Santa Rosalía, Méx.	**196**	26.08 N	98.59 W
Santa Rosalía, Méx.	**232**	27.19 N	112.17 W
Santa Rosalía, Ven.	**246**	9.02 N	69.01 W
Santa Rosa Range ⋏	**204**	41.35 N	117.40 W
Santa Rosa Wash V	**200**	33.00 N	112.00 W
Santa Rosita	**286d**	12.03 S	76.59 W
Sant'Arsenio	**68**	40.28 N	15.29 E
Šantarskije ostrova II	**74**	55.00 N	137.36 E
Santa Severa	**66**	42.02 N	11.57 E
Santa Severina	**68**	39.09 N	16.55 E
Santa Sofia	**66**	43.57 N	11.54 E
Santa Susana	**228**	34.16 N	118.43 W
Santa Susana Mountains ⋏	**228**	34.20 N	118.42 W
Santa Sylvina	**252**	27.49 S	61.09 W
Santa Tecla → Nueva San Salvador	**236**	13.41 N	89.17 W
Santa Teresa, Bra.	**255**	19.55 S	40.36 W
Santa Teresa, Méx.	**196**	29.34 N	104.39 W
Santa Teresa, Méx.	**200**	30.52 N	111.33 W
Santa Teresa, Méx.	**232**	25.17 N	97.51 W
Santa Teresa, Méx.	**234**	22.28 N	104.44 W
Santa Teresa ≃	**255**	11.47 S	48.37 W
Santa Teresa, Embalse de ⊜[1]	**34**	40.40 N	5.30 W
Santa Teresa de lo Ovalle	**286e**	33.23 S	70.47 W
Santa Teresa di Riva	**70**	37.57 N	15.22 E
Santa Teresa Gallura	**71**	41.14 N	9.11 E
Santa Tereza de Goiás	**255**	13.38 S	49.01 W
Santa Terezinha	**250**	10.28 S	50.31 W
Santa Valburga (Sankt Wallburg)	**64**	46.33 N	11.00 E
Santa Venerina	**70**	37.41 N	15.08 E
Santa Venetia	**226**	38.01 N	122.31 W
Santa Vitória	**255**	18.50 S	50.08 W
Santa Vitória do Palmar	**252**	33.31 S	53.21 W
Santa Vittoria, Monte ∧	**71**	39.45 N	9.18 E
Santa Vittoria in Matenano	**66**	43.01 N	13.29 E
Santa Ynez ≃	**204**	34.41 N	120.36 W
Santa Ynez Canyon V	**280**	34.04 N	118.34 W
Santa Ysabel Indian Reservation ◆[4]	**204**	33.11 N	116.41 W
Sant Bartomeu de la Quadra	**266d**	41.26 N	2.02 E
Sant Boi de Llobregat	**266d**	41.21 N	2.03 E
Sant Carles de la Ràpita	**34**	40.37 N	0.36 E
Sant Climent de Llobregat	**266d**	41.20 N	2.00 E
Sant Cugat del Vallès	**266d**	41.28 N	2.05 E
Santee	**228**	32.50 N	116.58 W
Santee ≃	**192**	33.14 N	79.28 W
Santee Dam ◆[6]	**192**	33.24 N	80.12 W
Santee Indian Reservation ◆[4]	**198**	42.45 N	97.50 W
Sant'Egidio alla Vibrata	**66**	42.49 N	13.42 E
Sant'Elena	**64**	45.12 N	11.43 E
Sant'Elia a Pianisi	**66**	41.38 N	14.52 E
Sant'Elia Fiumerapido	**66**	41.32 N	13.52 E
Sant'Elpidio a Mare	**66**	43.14 N	13.41 E
Santena	**62**	44.57 N	7.45 E
Santenay	**58**	46.55 N	4.41 E
Santeny	**261**	48.43 N	2.34 E
San Teodoro, It.	**70**	37.51 N	14.42 E
San Teodoro, It.	**71**	40.46 N	9.39 E
Santermo in Colle	**68**	40.48 N	16.45 E
Santerno ≃	**66**	44.34 N	11.58 E
Santerre □[9]	**50**	49.40 N	2.40 E
Sant'Eufemia, Golfo di ⊂	**68**	38.50 N	16.00 E
Sant'Eufemia a Maiella	**66**	42.07 N	14.02 E
Sant'Eufemia d'Aspromonte	**68**	38.16 N	15.52 E
Sant'Eufemia Lamezia	**68**	38.55 N	16.15 E
Sant Feliu de Guíxols	**34**	41.47 N	3.02 E
Sant Feliu de Llobregat	**266d**	41.23 N	2.03 E
Sant Fost de Campsentelles	**266d**	41.31 N	2.14 E
Sānthia, Bngl.	**126**	24.03 N	89.33 E
Santhià, It.	**62**	45.22 N	8.10 E
Santiago, Bol.	**248**	18.19 S	59.34 W
Santiago, Bra.	**252**	29.11 S	54.53 W
Santiago, Chile	**252**	33.27 S	70.40 W
Santiago, Chile	**286e**	33.27 S	70.40 W
Santiago, Méx.	**232**	23.28 N	109.43 W
Santiago, Pan.	**236**	8.06 N	80.59 W
Santiago, Para.	**252**	27.09 S	56.47 W
Santiago, Perú	**248**	14.11 S	75.44 W
Santiago, Pil.	**116**	16.41 N	121.33 E
Santiago I	**150a**	15.05 N	23.40 W
Santiago ≃, Arg.	**288**	34.50 S	57.57 W
Santiago ≃, Méx.	**232**	25.11 N	105.26 W
Santiago ≃, S.A.	**246**	4.27 S	77.38 W
Santiago, Cape ›	**116**	13.46 N	120.39 E
Santiago, Cerro ∧	**236**	8.33 N	81.44 W
Santiago, Isla I, Arg.	**288**	34.50 S	57.53 W
Santiago, Isla I, Ec.	**246a**	0.14 S	90.45 W
Santiago, Serranía de ⋏	**248**	18.25 S	59.25 W
Santiago Atitlán	**236**	14.38 N	91.14 W
Santiago Chazumba	**234**	18.12 N	97.40 W
Santiago Choapan	**234**	17.20 N	95.57 W
Santiago Creek ≃, Ca., U.S.	**228**	35.06 N	119.17 W
Santiago Creek ≃, Ca., U.S.	**228**	33.46 N	117.54 W
Santiago Dam ◆[6]	**280**	33.47 N	117.43 W
Santiago de Cao	**248**	7.58 S	79.15 W
Santiago de Chocorvos	**248**	13.50 S	75.16 W
Santiago de Chuco	**248**	8.09 S	78.11 W
Santiago de Compostela	**34**	42.53 N	8.33 W
Santiago de Cuba	**240p**	20.01 N	75.49 W
Santiago de Cuba □[4]	**240p**	20.10 N	75.55 W
Santiago de Huari	**248**	19.00 S	66.48 W
Santiago de Huata	**248**	16.06 S	68.53 W
Santiago de la Peña	**234**	20.57 N	97.24 W
Santiago de las Vegas ◆[8]	**286b**	22.58 N	82.23 W
Santiago del Estero	**252**	27.47 S	64.16 W
Santiago del Estero □[4]	**252**	28.00 S	63.30 W
Santiago [de los Caballeros]	**238**	19.27 N	70.42 W
Santiago de Machaca	**248**	17.05 S	69.16 W
Santiago de Méndez	**246**	2.43 S	78.19 W
Santiago de Surco	**286d**	12.09 S	77.01 W
Santiago do Cacém	**34**	38.01 N	8.42 W
Santiago Island I	**116**	16.24 N	119.56 E
Santiago Ixcuintla	**234**	21.49 N	105.13 W
Santiago Ixtayutla	**234**	16.33 N	97.39 W
Santiago Jamiltepec	**234**	16.17 N	97.49 W
Santiago Juxtlahuaca	**234**	17.20 N	98.01 W
Santiago Lachiguirí	**234**	16.41 N	95.32 W
Santiago Larre	**258**	35.34 S	59.10 W
Santiago Maravatío	**234**	20.10 N	101.00 W
Santiago Papasquiaro	**232**	25.03 N	105.25 W
Santiago Peak ∧, Ca., U.S.	**228**	33.42 N	117.32 W
Santiago Peak ∧, Tx., U.S.	**196**	29.47 N	103.25 W
Santiago Pinotepa Nacional	**234**	16.19 N	98.01 W
Santiago Reservoir ⊜[1]	**228**	33.47 N	117.43 W
Santiago → Santiago de Compostela	**34**	42.53 N	8.33 W
Santiago Tepalcatlapan ◆[8]	**286a**	19.15 N	99.08 W
Santiago Tulantepec	**234**	20.02 N	98.22 W
Santiago Tutla	**234**	17.10 N	95.26 W
Santiago Tuxtla	**234**	18.28 N	95.18 W
Santiago Vázquez	**258**	34.48 S	56.21 W
Santiago Yaveo	**234**	17.19 N	95.42 W
Santiago Zacatepec	**234**	17.11 N	95.51 W
Santiaguillo, Laguna ⊜	**232**	24.48 N	104.48 W
Santiam Pass)(	**202**	44.25 N	121.51 W
San Tian Zhu (Three Indian Temples) ʊ[1]	**106**	30.15 N	120.08 E
Santiao Chiao ›	**100**	25.02 N	121.59 E
Santiaoqiao	**106**	31.36 N	121.22 E
Santi Filippo e Giacomo	**70**	37.51 N	12.31 E
Santiguila	**150**	12.42 N	7.26 W
Sant'Ilario d'Enza	**64**	44.46 N	10.27 E
San Timoteo	**246**	9.48 N	71.04 W
San Timoteo Canyon V	**228**	34.04 N	117.17 W
Säntis ∧	**58**	47.15 N	9.21 E
Santissima Trinita di Saccargia ʊ[1]	**71**	40.41 N	8.42 E
Santissimo ◆[8]	**287a**	22.53 S	43.31 W
Santisteban del Puerto	**34**	38.15 N	3.12 W
Sant Joan de Labritja	**34**	39.05 N	1.30 E
Sant Joan Despí	**266d**	41.22 N	2.04 E
Sant Jordi, Golf de ⊂	**34**	40.53 N	1.00 E
Sant Just Desvern	**266d**	41.23 N	2.05 E
Sant Mateu del Maestrat	**34**	40.28 N	0.11 E
Santō, Nihon	**94**	35.21 N	136.22 E
Santō, Nihon	**96**	35.19 N	134.53 E
Santo, Tx., U.S.	**196**	32.36 N	98.13 W
Santo, Vanuatu	**175f**	15.32 S	167.08 E
Santo Aleixo	**256**	22.34 S	43.04 W
Santo Amaro, Bra.	**250**	2.33 S	43.14 W
Santo Amaro, Bra.	**255**	12.32 S	38.43 W
Santo Amaro ◆[8]	**287b**	23.39 S	46.42 W
Santo Amaro, Ilha de I	**256**	23.57 S	46.14 W
Santo Amaro das Brotas	**250**	10.47 S	37.04 W
Santo Anastácio	**255**	21.58 S	51.39 W
Santo André	**256**	23.40 S	46.31 W
Santo Ângelo	**252**	28.18 S	54.16 W
Santo Antão I	**150a**	17.05 N	25.10 W
Santo Antônio, Bra.	**250**	6.18 S	35.27 W
Santo António, S. Tom./P.	**152**	1.39 N	7.26 E
Santo Antônio ≃, Bra.	**250**	11.31 S	48.37 W
Santo Antônio ≃, Bra.	**255**	17.30 S	45.37 W
Santo Antônio ≃, Bra.	**287a**	22.42 S	43.37 W
Santo António, Ilha de I	**156**	21.58 S	35.28 E
Santo Antônio da Charneca	**266c**	38.37 N	9.02 W
Santo Antônio da Patrulha	**252**	29.50 S	50.32 W
Santo Antônio de Jesus	**255**	12.58 S	39.16 W
Santo Antônio de Pádua	**255**	21.32 S	42.11 W
Santo Antonio de Posse	**256**	22.36 S	46.55 W
Santo Antônio do Amparo	**255**	20.57 S	44.55 W
Santo Antônio do Aventureiro	**256**	21.45 S	42.49 W
Santo Antônio do Içá	**246**	3.05 S	67.57 W
Santo Antônio do Jardim	**256**	22.07 S	46.41 W
Santo Antônio do Leverger	**248**	15.52 S	56.05 W
Santo Antônio do Pinhal	**256**	22.47 S	45.41 W
Santo Antônio do Rio Verde	**255**	17.57 S	47.27 W
Santo Antônio do Sudoeste	**252**	26.02 S	53.44 W
Santo Augusto	**252**	27.51 S	53.47 W
Santo Corazón	**248**	17.59 S	58.51 W
Santo Domingo, Cuba	**240p**	22.35 N	80.15 W
Santo Domingo, Méx.	**196**	25.38 N	101.05 W
Santo Domingo, Méx.	**196**	25.48 N	104.28 W
Santo Domingo, Méx.	**232**	25.32 N	112.02 W
Santo Domingo, Nic.	**236**	12.16 N	85.05 W
Santo Domingo, Rep. Dom.	**238**	18.28 N	69.54 W
Santo Domingo ≃, Méx.	**234**	16.41 N	93.00 W
Santo Domingo ≃, Méx.	**234**	17.40 N	98.07 W
Santo Domingo ≃, Méx.	**234**	18.10 N	96.08 W
Santo Domingo ≃, Méx.	**236**	16.15 N	91.17 W
Santo Domingo, Arroyo ≃	**204**	30.43 N	116.03 W
Santo Domingo, Isla → Hispaniola I	**238**	19.00 N	71.00 W
Santo Domingo de la Calzada	**34**	42.26 N	2.57 W
Santo Domingo de los Colorados	**246**	0.15 S	79.09 W
Santo Domingo Indian Reservation ◆[4]	**200**	35.30 N	106.25 W
Santo Domingo Nuxaá	**234**	17.08 N	97.02 W
Santo Domingo Pueblo	**200**	35.30 N	106.21 W
Santo Domingo Tehuantepec	**234**	16.20 N	95.14 W
Santo Domingo Teojomulco	**234**	16.36 N	97.14 W
Santo Domingo Zanatepec	**234**	16.29 N	94.21 W
Santo Estêvão	**255**	12.26 S	39.13 W
Sant'Olcese	**62**	44.30 N	8.58 E
Santolea, Embalse de ⊜[1]	**34**	40.47 N	0.19 W
Santo / Malo □[8]	**175f**	15.20 S	166.55 E
San Tomé	**246**	8.58 N	64.08 W
San Tommaso	**66**	42.11 N	13.58 E
Sant'Omobono Imagna	**62**	45.48 N	9.32 E
Santoña	**34**	43.27 N	3.27 W
Santong ≃	**98**	42.39 N	126.03 E
Santo Nino Island I	**116**	11.55 N	124.27 E
Sant' Onofrio ◆[8]	**267a**	41.56 N	12.25 E
Santo Onofre ≃	**255**	12.34 S	43.12 W
Santop, Pic ∧	**175f**	18.39 S	169.03 E
Sant'Oreste	**66**	42.14 N	12.32 E
Santorini → Thíra I	**38**	36.24 N	25.29 E
Santorso	**64**	45.44 N	11.23 E
Santos	**256**	23.57 S	46.20 W
Santos, Arroyo de los ≃	**258**	35.28 S	57.29 W
Santos, Baía de ⊂	**256**	24.00 S	46.21 W
Santos Dumont	**256**	21.28 S	43.34 W
Santos Dumont, Aeroporto ⊠	**256**	22.55 S	43.10 W
Santoshpur	**272b**	22.40 N	88.10 E
Santo Stefano, Isola I	**66**	40.47 N	13.27 E
Santo Stefano Belbo	**62**	44.43 N	8.14 E
Santo Stefano d'Aveto	**62**	44.35 N	9.27 E
Santo Stefano di Cadore	**64**	46.33 N	12.32 E
Santo Stefano di Camastra	**70**	38.01 N	14.21 E
Santo Stefano di Magra	**64**	44.10 N	9.55 E
Santo Stefano Quisquina	**70**	37.37 N	13.29 E
Santo Stino di Livenza	**64**	45.44 N	12.41 E
Santos Tomás del Norte	**236**	13.11 N	86.56 W
Santo Tirso	**34**	41.21 N	8.28 W
Santo Tomás, Col.	**246**	10.46 N	74.45 W
Santo Tomás, Méx.	**232**	31.33 N	116.24 W
Santo Tomás, Nic.	**236**	12.04 N	85.05 W
Santo Tomás, Perú	**248**	6.36 S	77.48 W
Santo Tomás, Perú	**248**	14.29 S	72.06 W
Santo Tomas, Pil.	**116**	7.29 N	125.38 E
Santo Tomás ≃, Méx.	**204**	31.32 N	116.40 W
Santo Tomás ≃, Perú	**248**	13.47 S	72.09 W
Santo Tomás, Punta ›	**232**	31.34 N	116.42 W
Santo Tomas, University of ʊ[2]	**269f**	14.37 N	120.59 E
Santo Tomás, Volcán ∧[1]	**246a**	0.48 S	91.07 W
Santo Tomás y Principe → Sao Tome and Principe □[1]	**152**	1.00 N	7.00 E
Santo Tomé, Arg.	**252**	28.33 S	56.03 W
Santo Tomé, Arg.	**252**	31.40 S	60.46 W
Santo Tomé de Guayana → Ciudad Guayana	**246**	8.22 N	62.40 W
Sant' Pietro, Lago di ⊜	**68**	41.01 N	15.30 E
Santpoort	**52**	52.25 N	4.38 E
Sant Quirze de la Serra	**266d**	41.32 N	2.05 E
Santuanjiang	**106**	30.54 N	121.43 E
Santuario de Quillacas	**248**	19.14 S	66.58 W
Santu Lussurgiu	**71**	40.08 N	8.39 E
Santunying	**105**	40.14 N	118.12 E
Sant Vicenç dels Horts	**266d**	41.24 N	2.01 E
San Ubaldo	**236**	11.51 N	85.20 W
Sanuki	**268**	35.16 N	139.53 E
Sanuki-sammyaku ⋏	**96**	34.09 N	134.11 E
Şānūr	**132**	32.21 N	35.15 E
San Valentino in Abruzzo Citeriore	**66**	42.14 N	13.59 E
San Valentino Torio	**68**	40.48 N	14.36 E
San Venanzo	**66**	42.52 N	12.16 E
San Vendemiano	**64**	45.54 N	12.20 E
San Vicente, Arg.	**252**	28.30 S	64.09 W
San Vicente, Arg.	**258**	34.58 S	58.22 W
San Vicente, El Sal.	**236**	13.38 N	88.48 W
San Vicente □[5]	**288**	34.56 S	58.24 W
San Vicente, Cabo → São Vicente, Cabo de ›	**34**	37.01 N	9.00 W
San Vicente, Volcán de ∧[1]	**236**	13.36 N	88.51 W
San Vicente Creek ≃	**282**	37.32 N	122.31 W
San Vicente de Alcántara	**34**	39.21 N	7.08 W
San Vicente de Cañete	**248**	13.05 S	76.24 W
San Vicente de Chucurí	**246**	6.54 N	73.25 W
San Vicente de la Barquera	**34**	43.26 N	4.24 W
San Vicente del Caguán	**246**	2.07 N	74.46 W
San Vicente de Tagua-Tagua	**252**	34.26 S	71.05 W
San Vicente Mountain ∧	**280**	34.08 N	118.31 W
San Vicente Reservoir ⊜[1]	**228**	32.55 N	116.55 W
San Vicente → Saint Vincent and the Grenadines □[1]	**241h**	13.15 N	61.12 W
San Vicente Tancuayalab	**234**	21.44 N	98.34 W
San Vigilio	**64**	45.34 N	10.41 E
San Vigilio ʊ[1]	**64**	46.37 N	11.07 E
San Vincenzo	**66**	43.06 N	10.32 E
San Vito, C.R.	**236**	8.50 N	82.58 W
San Vito, It.	**71**	39.26 N	9.32 E
San Vito, Capo ›	**70**	38.11 N	12.44 E
San Vito, Serralta di ∧	**68**	38.46 N	16.22 E
San Vito al Tagliamento	**64**	45.54 N	12.52 E
San Vito Chietino	**66**	42.18 N	14.27 E
San Vito dei Normanni	**68**	40.39 N	17.42 E
San Vito lo Capo	**70**	38.10 N	12.45 E
San Vito Romano	**66**	41.53 N	12.59 E
San Vito sullo Ionio	**68**	38.43 N	16.25 E
Sanwa, Nihon	**94**	37.07 N	138.21 E
Sanwa, Nihon	**94**	36.12 N	139.49 E
Sanwa, Nihon	**96**	34.42 N	133.15 E
San Xavier Indian Reservation ◆[4]	**200**	32.05 N	111.08 W
Sanxi, Zhg.	**100**	30.22 N	118.25 E
Sanxi, Zhg.	**100**	27.42 N	120.04 E
Sanxing, Zhg.	**106**	31.47 N	121.35 E
Sanxing, Zhg.	**106**	31.58 N	121.07 E
Sanxingchang, Zhg.	**107**	30.19 N	104.09 E
Sanxingchang, Zhg.	**107**	30.32 N	104.38 E
Sanxingjie	**106**	32.06 N	121.01 E
Sanyang, Zhg.	**100**	28.37 N	116.15 E
Sanyang, Zhg.	**100**	31.20 N	113.10 E
Sanyang, Zhg.	**100**	27.57 N	114.22 E
Sanyangzhen	**106**	31.55 N	121.29 E
Sanyanjing	**104**	41.28 N	122.27 E
Sanyanqiao	**100**	28.39 N	113.43 E
Sanyati ≃	**154**	16.49 S	28.45 E
San Ygnacio	**196**	27.03 N	99.27 W
Sanyō, Nihon	**96**	34.45 N	134.01 E
Sanyō, Nihon	**96**	34.02 N	131.10 E
Sanyuan	**102**	34.35 N	108.54 E
Sanyuanpu	**98**	42.02 N	125.44 E
Sanyuhao	**98**	42.30 N	117.34 E
Sanyuzhen	**106**	32.08 N	121.19 E
Sanza	**68**	40.15 N	15.33 E
Sanzao Dao I	**100**	22.03 N	113.21 E
Sanza Pombo	**152**	7.19 S	15.59 E
Sanzar ≃	**85**	40.00 N	67.40 E
San Zeno di Montagna	**64**	45.37 N	10.43 E
Sanzha	**98**	41.44 N	114.39 E
Sanzhan, Zhg.	**89**	49.42 N	125.20 E
Sanzhan, Zhg.	**89**	49.36 N	126.38 E
Sanzuodian	**98**	41.36 N	118.49 E
São Benedito	**250**	4.03 S	40.53 W
São Benedito ≃	**250**	9.11 S	57.02 W
São Benedito das Areias	**256**	21.19 S	47.02 W
São Benedito do Rio Preto	**250**	3.20 S	43.35 W
São Bento	**250**	2.42 S	44.50 W
São Bento ≃	**256**	21.42 S	45.18 W
São Bento, Mosteiro de ʊ[1]	**287a**	22.54 S	43.11 W
São Bento Abade	**256**	21.35 S	45.04 W
São Bento de Caldas	**256**	22.08 S	46.18 W
São Bento do Norte	**250**	5.04 S	36.02 W
São Bento do Sapucaí	**256**	22.42 S	45.43 W
São Bento do Sul	**252**	26.15 S	49.23 W
São Bento do Una	**250**	8.32 S	36.22 W
São Bernardino	**287a**	22.40 S	43.26 W
São Bernardo	**250**	3.22 S	42.24 W
São Bernardo do Campo	**256**	23.42 S	46.33 W
São Bernardo do Campo □[7]	**287b**	23.44 S	46.33 W
São Borja	**252**	28.39 S	56.00 W
São Brás	**250**	10.05 S	36.55 W
São Brás de Alportel	**34**	37.09 N	7.53 W
Sâo Braz, Cabo de ›	**152**	9.59 S	13.19 E
São Caetano de Odivelas	**250**	0.45 S	48.02 W
São Caetano do Sul	**256**	23.36 S	46.34 W
São Caetano do Sul □[7]	**287b**	23.37 S	46.33 W
São Carlos	**255**	22.01 S	47.54 W
São Cristóvão	**250**	11.01 S	37.12 W
São Cristóvão ◆[8]	**287a**	22.54 S	43.14 W
Saodatun	**104**	42.02 N	123.31 E
São Domingos, Bra.	**252**	26.34 S	52.32 W
São Domingos, Bra.	**255**	13.24 S	46.19 W
São Domingos, Bra.	**256**	21.41 S	42.47 W
São Domingos, Gui.-B.	**150**	12.22 N	16.08 W
São Domingos ≃, Bra.	**248**	12.28 S	64.13 W
São Domingos ≃, Bra.	**255**	13.24 S	47.12 W
São Domingos ≃, Bra.	**255**	19.13 S	50.44 W
São Domingos ≃, Bra.	**255**	20.03 S	53.13 W
São Domingos da Bocaina	**256**	21.50 S	44.01 W
São Domingos do Capim	**250**	1.41 S	47.47 W
São Domingos do Maranhão	**250**	5.42 S	44.22 W
São Felipe	**255**	14.49 S	41.23 W
São Félix de Balsas	**250**	7.08 S	44.52 W
São Félix do Araguaia	**250**	11.36 S	50.39 W
São Félix do Piauí	**250**	5.56 S	42.07 W
São Filipe	**150a**	14.54 N	24.31 W
São Francisco	**255**	15.57 S	44.52 W
São Francisco ≃, Bra.	**242**	10.30 S	36.24 W
São Francisco ≃, Bra.	**255**	16.09 S	40.39 W
São Francisco ≃, Bra.	**256**	21.50 S	42.42 W
São Francisco ≃, Bra.	**287a**	22.57 S	43.20 W
São Francisco, Baía de ⊂	**252**	26.10 S	48.34 W
São Francisco, Ilha de I	**252**	26.18 S	48.37 W
São Francisco de Assis	**252**	29.33 S	55.08 W
São Francisco de Goiás	**255**	15.55 S	49.16 W
São Francisco de Paula	**252**	29.27 S	50.35 W
São Francisco do Croará	**287a**	22.42 S	43.08 W
São Francisco do Maranhão	**250**	6.15 S	42.52 W
São Francisco do Piauí	**250**	7.15 S	42.32 W
São Francisco do Sul	**252**	26.14 S	48.39 W
São Francisco Xavier	**256**	22.54 S	45.58 W
São Gabriel	**252**	30.20 S	54.19 W
São Gabriel da Palha	**255**	19.01 S	40.32 W
São Gabriel de Goiás	**255**	15.12 S	47.34 W
São Gonçalo, Bra.	**256**	21.36 S	46.19 W
São Gonçalo, Bra.	**256**	22.51 S	43.04 W
São Gonçalo □[7]	**287a**	22.48 S	43.01 W
São Gonçalo do Abaeté	**255**	18.20 S	45.49 W
São Gonçalo do Sapucaí	**256**	21.54 S	45.36 W
São Gonçalo dos Campos	**255**	12.25 S	38.58 W
Sao Hill	**154**	8.20 S	35.12 E
São Jerônimo	**252**	29.58 S	51.43 W
São Jerônimo, Serra de ⋏[1]	**255**	16.30 S	54.50 W
São Jerônimo da Serra	**255**	23.43 S	50.44 W
São João	**150**	11.32 N	15.26 W
São João ≃, Bra.	**255**	12.27 S	51.07 W
São João ≃, Bra.	**256**	22.33 S	42.29 W
São João da Barra	**255**	21.38 S	41.03 W
São João da Boa Vista	**256**	21.58 S	46.47 W
São João D'Aliança	**255**	14.42 S	47.32 W
São João da Madeira	**34**	40.54 N	8.30 W
São João da Mata	**256**	21.56 S	45.56 W
São João da Ponte	**255**	15.56 S	44.01 W
São João da Serra	**256**	21.28 S	43.27 W
São João das Lampas	**266c**	38.52 N	9.24 W
São João de Côrtes	**250**	2.12 S	44.32 W
São João del-Rei	**255**	21.09 S	44.16 W
São João de Meriti	**256**	22.48 S	43.22 W
São João de Meriti □[7]	**287a**	22.48 S	43.21 W
São João de Meriti ≃	**287a**	22.48 S	43.18 W
São João do Araguaia	**250**	5.23 S	48.46 W
São João do Jaguaribe	**250**	5.16 S	38.16 W
São João do Paraíso	**255**	15.19 S	42.01 W
São João do Piauí	**250**	8.21 S	42.15 W
São João do Sabugi	**250**	6.43 S	37.12 W
São João dos Patos	**250**	6.30 S	43.42 W
São João Evangelista	**255**	18.32 S	42.45 W
São João Nepomuceno	**256**	21.33 S	43.01 W
São João Novo	**256**	23.33 S	47.01 W
São Joaquim	**252**	28.18 S	49.56 W
São Joaquim, Parque Nacional de ♠	**252**	28.15 S	49.57 W
São Joaquim da Barra	**255**	20.35 S	47.53 W
São Jorge I	**148a**	38.38 N	28.03 W
São Jorge, Castelo de ⊥	**266c**	38.43 N	9.08 W
São José, Bra.	**252**	27.38 S	48.39 W
São José, Bra.	**256**	22.43 S	42.36 W
São José ≃, Bra.	**255**	19.10 S	40.12 W
São José ≃, Bra.	**287a**	22.39 S	43.27 W
São José, Ponta de ›	**152**	12.36 S	13.12 E
São José da Laje	**250**	9.01 S	36.03 W
São José de Anauá	**246**	1.00 N	61.23 W
São José de Encoge	**152**	7.38 S	14.41 E
São José de Mipibu	**250**	6.05 S	35.15 W
São José de Piranhas	**250**	7.07 S	38.30 W
São José do Alegre	**256**	22.19 S	45.32 W
São José do Barreiro	**256**	22.38 S	44.35 W
São José do Belmonte	**250**	7.52 S	38.46 W
São José do Campestre	**250**	6.18 S	35.42 W
São José do Cedro	**252**	26.30 S	53.30 W
São José do Egito	**250**	7.28 S	37.16 W
São José do Gurupi	**250**	1.36 S	46.13 W
São José do Norte	**252**	32.01 S	52.03 W
São José do Peixe	**250**	7.24 S	42.34 W
São José do Piriá	**250**	1.17 S	46.18 W
São José do Rio Parto	**256**	21.36 S	46.54 W
São José do Rio Preto, Bra.	**255**	20.48 S	49.23 W
São José do Rio Prêto, Bra.	**256**	22.10 S	42.57 W
São José dos Campos	**256**	23.11 S	45.53 W
São José dos Lopes	**256**	21.48 S	43.53 W
São José dos Pinhais	**252**	25.31 S	49.13 W
São José do Turvo	**256**	22.21 S	43.59 W
São Julião da Barra	**266c**	38.40 N	9.21 W
São Julião do Tojal	**266c**	38.51 N	9.08 W
São Leopoldo	**252**	29.46 S	51.09 W
São Lourenço	**256**	22.07 S	45.03 W
São Lourenço, Pantanal de ≋	**248**	17.30 S	56.30 W
São Lourenço da Serra	**256**	23.52 S	46.57 W
São Lourenço do Oeste	**252**	26.24 S	52.46 W
São Lourenço do Sul	**252**	31.22 S	51.58 W
São Luís	**250**	2.31 S	44.16 W
São Luís de Montes Belos	**255**	16.32 S	50.20 W
São Luís do Curu	**250**	3.40 S	39.14 W
São Luís Do Paraitinga	**256**	23.14 S	45.20 W
São Luís do Quitunde	**250**	9.20 S	35.33 W
São Luís Gonzaga	**252**	28.24 S	54.58 W
São Mamede	**250**	6.56 S	37.06 W
São Manuel	**255**	22.44 S	48.34 W
São Manuel ≃	**242**	7.21 S	58.03 W
São Manuel do Guaiaçu	**256**	21.20 S	42.51 W
São Marcos ≃	**255**	18.15 S	47.37 W
São Mateus, Bra.	**255**	18.44 S	39.51 W

Symbols in the index entries represent the broad categories identified in the key at the right. Symbols with superior numbers (⋏[1]) identify subcategories (see complete key on page *I · 1).*

Symbole im Register stellen die rechts im Schlüssel erklärten Kategorien dar. Symbole mit hochgestellten Ziffern (⋏[1]) bezeichnen Unterabteilungen einer Kategorie (vgl. vollständiger Schlüssel auf Seite *I · 1).*

Los símbolos incluídos en el texto del índice representan las grandes categorías identificadas con la clave a la derecha. Los símbolos con numeros en su parte superior (⋏[1]) identifican las subcategorías (véase la clave completa en la página *I · 1).*

Les symboles de l'index représentent les catégories indiquées dans la légende à droite. Les symboles suivis d'un indice (⋏[1]) représentent des sous-catégories (voir légende complète à la page *I · 1).*

Os símbolos incluídos no texto do índice representam as grandes categorias identificadas com a chave à direita. Os símbolos com números em sua parte superior (⋏[1]) identificam as subcategorias (veja-se a chave completa à página *I · 1).*

English	Deutsch	Español	Français	Português
∧ Mountain	Berg	Montaña	Montagne	Montanha
⋏ Mountains	Gebirge	Montañas	Montagnes	Montanhas
)(Pass	Paß	Paso	Col	Passo
V Valley, Canyon	Tal, Cañon	Valle, Cañón	Vallée, Canyon	Vale, Canhão
≚ Plain	Ebene	Llano	Plaine	Planície
› Cape	Kap	Cabo	Cap	Cabo
I Island	Insel	Isla	Île	Ilha
II Islands	Inseln	Islas	Îles	Ilhas
⊥ Other Topographic Features	Andere Topographische Objekte	Otros Elementos Topográficos	Autres données topographiques	Outros acidentes topográficos

ESPAÑOL — Nombre / Página / Lat.°′ / Long.°′ W = Oeste
FRANÇAIS — Nom / Page / Lat.°′ / Long.°′ W = Ouest
PORTUGUÊS — Nome / Página / Lat.°′ / Long.°′ W = Oeste

São Mateus, Bra. 256 22.49 S 43.23 W
São Mateus, Port. 148a 38.26 N 28.27 W
São Mateus, Braço Norte ≃ 255 18.37 S 40.05 W
São Mateus de Minas 256 22.42 S 46.03 W
São Mateus do Sul 252 25.52 S 50.23 W
São Miguel 250 6.13 S 38.30 W
São Miguel I 148a 37.47 N 25.30 W
São Miguel ≃ 255 16.26 S 41.00 W
São Miguel do Araguaia 255 13.19 S 50.13 W
São Miguel d'Oeste 252 26.45 S 53.34 W
São Miguel do Guamá 250 1.37 S 47.27 W
São Miguel dos Campos 250 9.47 S 36.05 W
São Miguel dos Macacos 250 1.11 S 50.28 W
São Miguel do Tapuio 250 5.30 S 41.20 W
São Miguel Paulista (Baquiriru) ✦8 256 23.30 S 46.26 W
Saona, Isla I 238 18.09 N 68.40 W
Saonara 64 45.22 N 11.59 E
Saône ≃ 58 45.44 N 4.50 E
Saône-et-Loire □5 32 46.42 N 4.45 E
Saonek 164 0.28 S 130.47 E
Saoner 120 21.23 N 78.54 E
São Nicolau I 150a 16.35 N 24.15 W
São Nicolau ≃ 250 5.45 S 42.02 W
São Paulo, Bra. 256 23.32 S 46.37 W
São Paulo, Bra. 287b 23.32 S 46.37 W
São Paulo □3 255 22.00 S 49.00 W
São Paulo □7 287b 23.33 S 46.38 W
São Paulo, Ribeirão de ≃ 256 22.16 S 46.37 W
São Paulo de Olivença 246 3.27 S 68.48 W
São Paulo do Potengi 250 5.55 S 35.45 W
São Pedro 255 19.53 S 51.55 W
São Pedro ≃ 255 16.30 S 41.17 W
São Pedro de Caldas 256 21.49 S 46.16 W
São Pedro de Viseu 250 2.33 S 49.33 W
São Pedro do Estoril 266c 38.42 N 9.22 W
São Pedro do Piauí 250 5.56 S 42.43 W
São Pedro do Sul, Bra. 252 29.37 S 54.10 W
São Pedro do Sul, Port. 34 40.45 N 8.04 W
São Rafael 250 5.47 S 36.55 W
São Raimundo das Mangabeiras 250 7.01 S 45.29 W
São Raimundo Nonato 250 9.01 S 42.42 W
Saorge 62 43.59 N 7.33 E
Saori 94 35.11 N 136.44 E
São Romão 255 16.22 S 45.04 W
São Roque, Bra. 256 23.06 S 44.42 W
São Roque, Bra. 256 23.32 S 47.08 W
São Roque, Cabo de ≻ 250 5.29 S 35.16 W
São Roque da Fartura 256 21.51 S 46.45 W
São Salvador → Salvador 255 12.59 S 38.31 W
São Sebastião 256 23.48 S 45.25 W
São Sebastião, Canal de ʊ 256 23.48 S 45.23 W
São Sebastião, Ilha de I 256 23.50 S 45.18 W
São Sebastião, Pico de ʌ 256 23.52 S 45.23 W
São Sebastião, Ponta ≻ 156 22.07 S 35.30 E
São Sebastião da Bela Vista 256 22.10 S 45.45 W
São Sebastião da Boa Vista 250 1.42 S 49.31 W
São Sebastião da Grama 256 21.43 S 46.49 W
São Sebastião da Vitória 256 21.14 S 44.25 W
São Sebastião do Barreado 256 22.04 S 43.38 W
São Sebastião do Maranhão 255 18.05 S 42.35 W
São Sebastião do Paraíso 255 20.55 S 47.00 W
São Sebastião do Rio Claro 255 15.45 S 51.30 W
São Sebastião do Rio Verde 256 22.13 S 44.58 W
São Sebastião dos Robertos 256 22.13 S 46.32 W
São Sebastião do Umbuzeiro 250 8.09 S 37.01 W
São Sepé 252 30.10 S 53.34 W
São Silvestre do Jacare22 256 23.23 S 46.01 W
São Simão, Bra. 255 18.56 S 50.30 W
São Simão, Bra. 255 21.30 S 47.33 W
São Simão, Represa de ⊜1 255 18.40 S 50.00 W
São Tiago 255 20.55 S 44.30 W
São Timóteo 255 13.51 S 42.11 W
São Tomé, Bra. 250 5.58 S 36.04 W
São Tomé, S. Tom./P. 152 0.20 N 6.44 E
São Tomé I 152 0.12 N 6.39 E
São Tomé ≃, Bra. 250 8.10 S 58.13 W
São Tomé ≃, Bra. 256 21.26 S 46.02 W
São Tomé, Cabo de ≻ 255 21.59 S 40.59 W
São Tomé, Pico de ʌ 152 0.16 N 6.33 E
Sao Tome and Principe (São Tomé e Principe) □1, Afr. 138 1.00 N 7.00 E
Sao Tome and Principe (São Tomé e Principe) □1, Afr. 152 1.00 N 7.00 E
São Tomé das Letras 256 21.43 S 44.59 W
Sao Tomé-et-Principe → Sao Tome and Principe □1 152 1.00 N 7.00 E
Saou 62 44.39 N 5.04 E
Saoura, Oued V 148 29.00 N 0.55 W
São Valério ≃ 250 11.20 S 48.28 W
São Vicente 256 23.58 S 46.23 W
São Vicente I 150a 16.50 N 25.00 W
São Vicente, Cabo de (Cape Saint Vincent) ≻ 34 37.01 N 9.00 W
São Vicente, Ribeirão ≃ 256 21.59 S 45.40 W
São Vicente de Minas 256 21.42 S 44.27 W
São Vicente Ferrer 250 7.35 S 35.30 W
Sa Pa 110 22.21 N 103.50 E
Sápai 38 41.02 N 25.41 E
Sapanca 130 40.41 N 30.16 E
Sapang Baho ≃ 269f 14.33 N 121.06 E
Sapao 116 10.01 N 126.02 E
Sapão ≃ 250 11.01 S 45.32 W
Saparua, Pulau I 164 3.34 S 128.40 E
Sapatgrām 124 26.20 N 90.08 E
Sapé, Bra. 250 7.06 S 35.13 W
Sape, Indon. 115b 8.34 S 118.59 E
Sapé ≃ 287a 22.52 S 43.02 W
Sape, Selat ʊ 115b 8.39 S 119.18 E
Sapele 150 5.54 N 5.41 E
Sapello ≃ 200 35.47 N 104.59 W
Sapelo Island I 192 31.28 N 81.15 W
Saperkino 80 54.05 N 51.38 E
Saphane 130 39.01 N 29.14 E
Sapian Bay c 116 11.33 N 122.37 E
Sapindji 152 9.39 S 23.12 E
Sapitwa ʌ 154 15.57 S 35.36 E
Šapki 76 59.36 N 31.14 E
Šapkina ≃ 24 66.44 N 52.25 E
Šapkino 80 51.42 N 42.24 E
Šapkovo, Ross. 76 55.47 N 33.20 E
Šapkovo, Ross. 82 54.34 N 39.10 E
Sa Pobla 34 39.46 N 3.01 E
Sapodilla Cays I 236 16.08 N 88.15 W
Saponara 70 38.11 N 15.26 E
Saponé 150 12.03 N 1.36 W
Sap'o-ri 98 40.49 N 129.31 E
Sap'ornaja 265a 59.46 N 30.41 E
Saporoschje → Zaporožje 78 47.50 N 35.10 E
Saposoa 248 6.56 S 76.48 W
Sapou 175c 7.18 N 151.53 E
Sapožok 80 53.56 N 40.41 E
Sappa Creek ≃ 198 40.07 N 99.38 W
Sappa Creek, Middle Fork ≃ 198 39.40 N 100.53 W
Sappa Creek, North Fork ≃ 198 39.47 N 100.35 W
Sappa Creek, South Fork ≃ 198 39.47 N 100.35 W
Sappada 64 46.34 N 12.41 E
Sapphire Mountains ⋏ 202 46.20 N 113.45 W
Sappho 224 48.04 N 124.16 W
Sappington 219 38.32 N 90.22 W
Sapporo 92a 43.03 N 141.21 E
Šapri 68 40.04 N 15.38 E
Šapša 76 60.34 N 34.01 E
Sap Songkhla, Thale c 110 7.13 N 100.30 E
Šapsugskaja 78 44.45 N 38.05 E
Šaptajev 86 47.55 N 67.28 E
Saptakośī ≃ 124 26.31 N 86.58 E
Sapta-ri 271b 37.43 N 126.44 E
Sapu 152 12.29 S 19.26 E
Sapucaí 256 22.19 S 46.42 W
Sapucaí ≃ 256 21.33 S 45.40 W
Sapucaia 256 22.00 S 42.54 W
Sapucaí-Mirim 256 22.44 S 45.45 W
Sapucaí-Mirim ≃ 256 22.12 S 45.53 W
Sapudi, Pulau I 115a 7.06 S 114.20 E
Sapulpa 196 35.59 N 96.06 W
Sapulu 115a 6.54 S 112.57 E
Sapuran 115a 7.28 S 109.58 E
Sapwe 154 10.57 S 28.10 E
Sāq, Jabal ʌ2 128 26.17 N 43.16 E
Sāqiat al-ʿAbd 140 20.48 N 30.19 E
Sāqiyat Makkī 142 30.00 N 31.13 E
Saqqārah 142 29.51 N 31.13 E
Saqqārah (Step Pyramid) ⊥ 142 29.52 N 31.13 E
Saqqez 128 36.14 N 46.16 E
Saquarema 256 22.56 S 42.30 W
Saquarema, Lagoa de c 256 22.55 S 42.33 W
Saquena 248 4.40 S 73.31 W
Saquish Neck ≻1 283 42.00 N 70.37 W
Saquisilí 246 0.51 S 78.40 W
Sāra, Bngl. 126 24.07 N 89.02 E
Sara, Burkina 150 11.43 N 3.50 W
Sara, Pil. 116 11.16 N 123.01 E
Sara, Ross. 80 54.38 N 46.46 E
Sarāb 128 37.56 N 47.32 E
Sarabia, Méx. 234 17.03 N 95.01 W
Sarabia, Méx. 234 20.31 N 101.05 W
Sarabia ≃ 234 17.11 N 94.56 W
Sarābiyūm 142 30.23 N 32.17 E
Saraburi 110 14.32 N 100.55 E
Saracena 68 39.46 N 16.09 E
Saraceno, Monte ʌ 66 41.27 N 14.44 E
Saracura ≃ 255 12.18 S 40.07 W
Saracuruna ≃ 287a 22.41 S 43.13 W
Saraféré 150 15.50 N 3.42 W
Saragosa 196 31.01 N 103.39 W
Saragossa → Zaragoza 34 41.38 N 0.53 W
Saraguay ✦8 275a 45.31 N 73.45 W
Saraguro 246 3.36 S 79.13 W
Sarai 80 53.44 N 41.00 E
Sarāi Alamgir 123 32.54 N 73.45 E
Saraikela 124 22.43 N 85.57 E
Sarāi Naurang 123 32.50 N 70.47 E
Saraipāli 120 21.20 N 83.00 E
Säräisniemi 26 64.27 N 26.47 E
Sarajas de Madrid ✦8 266a 40.28 N 3.35 W
Sarajčik 80 47.30 N 51.43 E
Sarajevo 38 43.52 N 18.25 E
Saraj-Gir 80 53.36 N 53.24 E
Saraji 166 22.21 S 148.18 E
Sarajskij 80 47.19 N 40.45 E
Sarakhs 128 36.32 N 61.11 E
Saraktaš 86 51.50 N 56.22 E
Sarala 86 54.52 N 89.14 E
Saraland 194 30.49 N 88.04 W
Šaraldaj 88 51.01 N 107.38 E
Saralžinskaja 80 49.12 N 48.55 E
Saramacca □5 250 5.40 N 55.40 W
Saramacca ≃ 250 5.51 N 55.53 W
Saramaguacán ≃ 240p 21.30 N 77.17 W
Saran, Fr. 50 47.57 N 1.53 E
Šaran', Kaz. 86 49.46 N 72.52 E
Šaran, Ross. 80 54.49 N 54.00 E
Saran, Gunung ʌ 112 0.25 S 111.18 E
Saranac 216 42.55 N 85.12 W
Saranac ≃ 188 44.42 N 73.27 W
Saranac Lake 188 44.19 N 74.07 W
Saranakan, gora ʌ 88 52.35 N 113.50 E
Saranap 226 37.53 N 122.06 W
Šaranbaš-Kn'azevo 80 54.58 N 54.09 E
Saranda 154 5.43 S 34.59 E
Sarandapótamos ≃ 267c 38.26 N 23.54 E
Sarandë 38 39.52 N 20.00 E
Sarandi 252 27.56 S 52.55 W
Sarandí ✦8 258 34.40 S 58.21 W
Sarandí del Yi 252 33.21 S 55.38 W
Sarandí Grande 258 33.44 S 56.20 W
Sarandira 256 21.50 S 43.11 W
Šaranga 80 57.11 N 46.34 E
Sarangani Bay c 116 5.57 N 125.11 E
Sarangani Island I 116 5.27 N 125.28 E
Sarangani Islands II 116 5.25 N 125.26 E
Sarangani Strait ʊ 116 5.31 N 125.23 E
Sārangarh 120 21.36 N 83.05 E
Sārangpur 124 23.34 N 76.28 E
Sārankhola 126 22.18 N 89.47 E
Saranley 144 2.22 N 42.17 E
Saranpaul' 24 64.14 N 60.53 E
Saransk 80 54.11 N 45.11 E
Sarantina, Valle V 64 46.35 N 11.25 E
Sara Peak ʌ 150 9.41 N 9.17 E
Saraphi 110 18.43 N 99.03 E
Sarapiquí ≃ 236 10.43 N 83.56 W
Šarapó ≃ 287a 22.46 S 43.37 W
Šarapovo, Ross. 80 55.17 N 44.42 E
Šarapovo, Ross. 82 55.11 N 37.16 E
Sarapuí ≃ 287a 22.46 S 43.24 W
Sarapuí, Canal de ≚ 287a 22.44 S 43.16 W
Sarapul 80 56.28 N 53.48 E
Sarapul'skaja vozvyšennost' ⋏1 80 56.15 N 53.30 E
Sarapul'skoje 89 48.52 N 135.59 E
Saraqib 130 35.52 N 36.48 E
Sarare 246 9.47 N 69.10 W
Sarare ≃ 246 7.18 N 70.41 W
Sarar Plain ≃ 144 9.25 N 46.17 E
Sara Sara, Nevado ʌ 248 15.19 S 73.27 W
Sarasota 220 27.20 N 82.31 W
Sarasota □6 220 27.10 N 82.21 W
Sarasota Bay c 220 27.23 N 82.39 W
Sarasota-Bradenton Airport ⊠ 220 27.24 N 82.33 W
Sarasota Springs 220 27.17 N 82.28 W
Saraswati ≃ 272b 22.59 N 88.22 E
Sarata 78 46.02 N 29.38 E
Sarath 126 24.14 N 86.50 E
Saratoga, Austl. 170 33.28 S 151.21 E
Saratoga, Ca., U.S. 226 37.15 N 122.01 W
Saratoga, In., U.S. 216 40.14 N 84.55 W
Saratoga, Tx., U.S. 222 30.17 N 94.31 W
Saratoga, Wy., U.S. 200 41.27 N 106.48 W
Saratoga □6 210 43.00 N 73.51 W
Saratoga Battlefield Monument ⊥ 210 43.05 N 75.36 W
Saratoga Creek ≃ 282 37.25 N 121.58 W
Saratoga Lake ⊜ 210 43.01 N 73.39 W
Saratoga National Historical Park ♦ 210 43.00 N 73.38 W
Saratoga Passage ʊ 224 48.10 N 122.30 W
Saratoga Spa State Park ♦ 210 43.03 N 73.50 W
Saratoga Springs 210 43.04 N 73.47 W
Šara-Togot 88 53.01 N 106.43 E
Saratok 112 1.44 N 111.20 E
Saratov 80 51.34 N 46.02 E
Saratovka 86 51.12 N 54.54 E
Saratov Oblast' □4 80 51.30 N 47.00 E
Saratovskoje vodochranilišče ⊜1 80 52.45 N 48.30 E
Saraurcu ʌ 246 0.06 S 77.55 W
Sarāvān, Īrān 128 27.15 N 62.40 E
Saravan, Lao 110 15.43 N 106.25 E
Sarawak □3 112 2.30 N 113.30 E
Saray 130 41.26 N 27.55 E
Saraya, Guinée 150 10.46 N 10.24 W
Saraya, Sén. 150 12.50 N 11.45 W
Sarāyān 128 33.51 N 58.31 E
Saraycık 130 40.57 N 35.08 E
Saraydüzü 130 41.20 N 34.52 E
Sarā-ye Aḥmadī 128 27.56 N 56.42 E
Sarayevo → Sarajevo 38 43.52 N 18.25 E
Sarayköy 130 37.55 N 28.58 E
Sarayönü 130 38.17 N 32.25 E
Sarbaj 80 53.39 N 51.34 E
Sarbāz 128 26.39 N 61.15 E
Sarbinowo 54 52.40 N 14.40 E
Sárbogárd 30 46.53 N 18.38 E
Sarca ≃ 64 45.52 N 10.52 E
Sarce ≃ 50 48.09 N 4.18 E
Sarcee Indian Reserve ✦4 182 50.58 N 114.06 W
Sarcelle, Passe de la ʊ 175f 22.29 S 167.12 E
Sarcelles 50 49.00 N 2.23 E
Sarche di Calavino 64 46.03 N 10.57 E
Sarcidano ✦1, It. 36 39.55 N 9.05 E
Sarcidano ✦1, It. 71 39.49 N 9.10 E
Šarčino 86 53.09 N 81.45 E
Sarclet 46 58.22 N 3.07 W
Sarcoxie 194 37.04 N 94.06 W
Sārda (Mahākālī) ≃ 124 27.22 N 81.23 E
Sard āb)(123 36.40 N 71.32 E
Sārda Canal ≚ 124 28.08 N 80.24 E
Sardagna 64 46.03 N 11.06 E
Sardah 124 24.18 N 88.44 E
Sardaq 128 34.48 N 58.07 E
Sardara 71 39.37 N 8.49 E
Sardār Chāh 128 27.58 N 64.50 E
Sardārpur 120 22.39 N 74.59 E
Sardārshahr 120 28.26 N 74.29 E
Sar Dasht, Īrān 128 36.09 N 45.28 E
Sar Dasht, Īrān 128 32.32 N 48.52 E
Sardegna □4 71 40.00 N 9.00 E
Sardegna (Sardinia) I 71 40.00 N 9.00 E
Sardeh Band 120 33.17 N 68.39 E
Sardhana 124 29.09 N 77.37 E
Sardiha 126 22.22 N 87.09 E
Sardinal 236 10.31 N 85.39 W
Sardinata 246 8.05 N 72.48 W
Sardinia, N.Y., U.S. 210 42.32 N 78.31 W
Sardinia, Oh., U.S. 218 39.00 N 83.48 W
Sardinia → Sardegna I 71 40.00 N 9.00 E
Sardinien → Sardegna I 71 40.00 N 9.00 E
Sardis, B.C., Can. 224 49.08 N 121.57 W
Sardis, Al., U.S. 194 32.17 N 86.59 W
Sardis, Ga., U.S. 192 32.58 N 81.45 W
Sardis, Ky., U.S. 218 38.31 N 83.57 W
Sardis, Ms., U.S. 194 34.26 N 89.55 W
Sardis, Pa., U.S. 279b 40.29 N 79.42 W
Sardis, Tn., U.S. 194 35.27 N 88.18 W
Sardis Lake ⊜1 194 34.27 N 89.43 W
Šardona, Piz ʌ 58 46.55 N 9.15 E
Šardonem' 24 63.56 N 44.37 E
Sarek ʌ 24 67.25 N 17.46 E
Sareks Nationalpark ♦ 24 67.15 N 17.30 E
Sārenga, India 126 22.46 N 87.02 E
Sārenga, India 272b 22.31 N 88.13 E
Sarentino (Sarnthein) 64 46.38 N 11.21 E
Sar-e Pol 120 36.14 N 65.55 E
Sarepta 194 32.53 N 93.26 W
Sarezzo 64 45.39 N 10.12 E
Sargans 58 47.03 N 9.26 E
Sargasso Sea ⊤2 8 30.00 N 50.00 W
Sargasso Sea ⊤2 8 30.00 N 50.00 W
Sargatskoje 86 55.37 N 73.30 E
Sargé-lès-le-Mans 50 48.02 N 0.14 E
Sargent, Ga., U.S. 192 33.25 N 84.52 W
Sargent, Ne., U.S. 198 41.38 N 99.22 W
Sargent Creek ≃ 226 35.57 N 120.52 W
Sargodha 123 32.05 N 72.40 E
Šargol'džin 88 52.21 N 114.42 E
Šargorod 78 48.44 N 28.05 E
Šargou ≃ 85 43.25 N 73.50 E
Šargul', ozero ⊜ 86 54.35 N 78.51 E
Šargun 85 38.37 N 67.53 E
Sarh 146 9.09 N 18.23 E
Sarhli, Djebel ʌ 34 36.06 N 0.40 E
Sārī 128 36.34 N 53.04 E
Saría I 38 35.50 N 27.15 E
Saribi, Tanjung ≻ 164 1.36 S 135.25 E
Sarıbuğday 130 40.35 N 35.35 E
Saric 232 31.08 N 111.23 W
Saricumbe 152 12.12 S 19.46 E
Sarigan I 108 16.42 N 145.47 E
Sarıgazi ✦8 267b 41.01 N 29.12 E
Sarıgöl 130 38.14 N 28.43 E
Sarıkamış 130 40.20 N 42.35 E
Sarıkaya, Tür. 130 38.47 N 32.15 E
Sarıkaya, Tür. 130 39.30 N 35.24 E
Sarikei 112 2.07 N 111.31 E
Sarıköy 130 40.12 N 27.36 E
Sarilhos Grandes 266c 38.41 N 8.58 W
Sarilhos Pequenos 266c 38.41 N 8.59 W
Sarim 154 0.23 S 40.58 E
Sarimbun, Pulau I 271c 1.26 N 103.41 E
Sarina 166 21.26 S 149.13 E
Sarine ≃ 58 46.54 N 7.14 E
Sariñena 34 41.48 N 0.10 W
Sarıoğlan 130 39.05 N 35.59 E
Saripul' 85 38.26 N 70.08 E
Sarīr 146 27.36 N 22.32 E
Sarısu 84 39.01 N 42.55 E
Sarita 196 27.13 N 97.47 W
Sariwŏn 98 38.31 N 125.44 E
Sarıyar Barajı ⊜1 130 40.02 N 31.40 E
Sarız 130 38.30 N 36.30 E
Šarja 80 58.24 N 45.30 E
Sarju (Babaī) ≃ 124 27.42 N 81.16 E
Sark I 43b 49.26 N 2.21 W
Sark ≃ 44 54.58 N 3.04 W
Sarkad 30 46.44 N 21.23 E
Šarkan 80 57.18 N 53.53 E
Sarkand 86 45.26 N 79.54 E
Şarkikaraağaç 130 38.04 N 31.23 E
Şarkışla 130 39.21 N 36.26 E
Šarkovščina 76 55.22 N 27.28 E
Şarköy 130 40.37 N 27.06 E
Sarlat-la-Canéda 32 44.53 N 1.13 E
Šarlauk 128 38.13 N 55.38 E
Sarles 198 48.56 N 98.59 W
Šarlyk 86 52.55 N 54.35 E
Sarmakovo 84 43.43 N 43.12 E
Sarmanovo 80 55.15 N 52.36 E
Sărmașu 38 46.46 N 24.11 E
Sarmathura 124 26.31 N 77.22 E
Sarmatskaja ≃ 83 47.20 N 38.48 E
Sármellék 30 46.44 N 17.10 E
Sarmi 164 1.51 S 138.44 E
Sarmiento 254 45.36 S 69.05 W
Sarmiento ≃ 288 34.25 S 58.35 W
Sarmiento de Gambia, Cerro ʌ 254 54.27 S 70.50 W
Sarmiento de Gamboa, Lago ⊜ 254 51.04 S 72.45 W
Särna 26 61.41 N 13.08 E
Sarna, ozero ⊜ 80 48.24 N 44.38 E
Sarnano 66 43.02 N 13.18 E
Sārnāth ⊥ 124 25.24 N 83.01 E
Sarnen 58 46.54 N 8.15 E
Sârnena gora ⋏ 38 42.35 N 25.10 E
Sarner See ⊜ 58 46.52 N 8.13 E
Sarnia 214 42.58 N 82.23 W
Sarnico 64 45.40 N 9.57 E
Sarno 68 40.49 N 14.37 E
Sarnow 54 53.45 N 13.37 E
Sarnowa 30 51.38 N 16.54 E
Sarnthein → Sarentino 64 46.38 N 11.21 E
Šarnutovskij 80 47.40 N 43.46 E
Sarny 78 51.21 N 26.36 E
Saroako 112 2.31 S 121.22 E
Šaroargun ≃ 84 43.02 N 45.44 E
Sarolangun 112 2.18 S 102.42 E
Saroma-ko ⊜ 92a 44.08 N 143.50 E
Saron 158 33.11 S 19.01 E
Saronikós Kólpos c 38 37.54 N 23.12 E
Saronno 62 45.38 N 9.02 E
Saros Körfezi c 130 40.30 N 26.20 E
Sárospatak 30 48.19 N 21.34 E
Šarovka 78 50.01 N 35.27 E
Sarowbī 120 34.36 N 69.43 E
Sarpa 80 47.07 N 45.29 E
Sarpa, ozero ⊜ 80 47.18 N 45.20 E
Šarpajevka 78 48.34 N 40.59 E
Sar Passage ʊ 175b 7.12 N 134.23 E
Sarpinskije ozera ⊜ 80 47.30 N 45.00 E
Šar Planina ⋏ 38 42.05 N 20.50 E
Sarpsborg 26 59.17 N 11.07 E
Sarpy Creek ≃ 202 46.15 N 107.09 W
Sárrabus ✦1 71 39.23 N 9.21 E
Sarralbe 56 49.00 N 7.01 E
Sarras 62 45.11 N 4.48 E
Sarrath, Oued V 36 35.59 N 8.23 E
Sarratt 260 51.41 N 0.29 W
Sarre 62 45.43 N 7.15 E
Sarre (Saar) ≃ 56 49.42 N 6.34 E
Sarre Blanche ≃ 56 48.41 N 7.01 E
Sarrebourg 58 48.44 N 7.03 E
Sarrebruck → Saarbrücken 56 49.14 N 6.59 E
Sarreguemines 56 49.06 N 7.03 E
Sarre Rouge ≃ 56 48.41 N 7.01 E
Sarre-Union 56 48.56 N 7.05 E
Sarria 34 42.47 N 7.24 W
Sarriá ✦8 266d 41.24 N 2.08 E
Sarro 150 13.43 N 5.15 W
Sarroch 71 39.04 N 9.00 E
Sars 86 56.33 N 57.07 E
Sarsfield 212 45.27 N 75.21 W
Sarsina 66 43.55 N 12.08 E
Sarsol 272c 19.02 N 73.01 E
Sarstedt 52 52.14 N 9.51 E
Sarstein ʌ 64 47.36 N 13.41 E
Sarstoon (Sarstún) ≃ 236 15.53 N 88.55 W
Sarstún (Sarstoon) ≃ 236 15.53 N 88.55 W
Sarsuna 272b 22.28 N 88.18 E
Sart 56 50.31 N 5.56 E
Sartang ≃ 74 67.44 N 133.12 E
Sarteano 66 42.59 N 11.52 E
Sartell 190 45.37 N 94.12 W
Sartène 36 41.36 N 8.59 E
Sarthe □5 32 48.00 N 0.05 E
Sarthe ≃ 32 47.30 N 0.32 W
Sartičala 84 41.43 N 45.10 E
Sartilly 32 48.45 N 1.27 W
Sartirana Lomellina 62 45.07 N 8.39 E
Sartlan, ozero ⊜ 86 55.00 N 78.35 E
Sartol'gen 80 48.57 N 47.03 E
Sartrouville 261 48.57 N 2.10 E
Saru 85 42.20 N 77.55 E
Sarufutsu 92a 45.16 N 142.12 E
Saruhanlı 130 38.44 N 27.34 E
Šarur, Azer. 84 39.33 N 44.58 E
Şarūr, ʿUmān 128 23.22 N 58.07 E
Šar Us ≃ 88 47.08 N 97.38 E
Saru-shima I 268 35.17 N 139.42 E
Sarvadyk 80 46.07 N 44.07 E
Sárvár 30 47.15 N 16.57 E
Sarver 214 40.44 N 79.45 W
Sarvestān 128 29.16 N 53.13 E
Sárvíz ≃ 30 46.24 N 18.41 E
Saryagač 85 41.27 N 69.10 E
Saryassija 85 38.25 N 67.57 E
Sarybarak 85 43.24 N 71.30 E
Sarybasat 86 46.38 N 60.27 E
Sarybulak, Kaz. 86 49.27 N 76.27 E
Sarybulak, Kyrg. 85 40.54 N 73.49 E
Saryč, mys ≻ 78 44.23 N 33.45 E
Sarychosor 85 38.32 N 69.49 E
Sarydala 85 41.11 N 70.27 E
Saryg-Sep 88 51.30 N 95.36 E
Sary-Išikotrau ✦2 86 45.30 N 76.00 E
Sarykamskoje ozero ⊜ 72 41.56 N 57.25 E
Sarykoby 85 43.44 N 72.35 E
Sarykol'skij chrebet ⋏ 120 38.00 N 74.30 E
Sarykomej 86 45.12 N 74.11 E
Sarykopa, ozero ⊜ 86 50.22 N 64.08 E
Sarymogol 85 39.55 N 72.47 E
Sarymoin, ozero ⊜ 86 51.36 N 64.30 E
Şaryozek 86 44.22 N 77.59 E
Šarypovo 86 55.33 N 89.12 E
Saryšagan 86 46.07 N 73.38 E
Sarysu 86 48.23 N 69.59 E
Sarysu ≃ 86 45.12 N 66.36 E
Sary-Taš 85 39.44 N 73.15 E
Sarytau 86 49.54 N 76.41 E
Saryžaz 72 42.55 N 79.38 E
Sarzana 64 44.07 N 9.58 E
Sarzanello, Fortezza di ⊥ 64 44.08 N 9.58 E
Sarzeau 32 47.32 N 2.46 W
S'as' ≃ 76 60.09 N 32.30 E
Saʿsaʿ, Sūrīy. 132 33.17 N 36.02 E
Sasa, Yis. 132 33.02 N 35.24 E
Sasabe 200 31.27 N 111.31 W
Sasabe ≃ 200 30.41 N 111.56 W
Sasabeneh 144 7.55 N 43.39 E
Sasaga-mine ʌ 96 33.49 N 133.17 E
Sasaginnigak Lake ⊜ 184 51.36 N 95.40 W
Sasago-tunnel ✦5 94 35.38 N 138.47 E
Sasaguri 96 33.37 N 130.32 E
Sasak 110 0.01 S 99.42 E
Sasakwa 196 34.56 N 96.31 W
Sasamungga 175e 7.02 S 156.47 E
Sasao 270 34.57 N 135.20 E
Sasar, Tanjung ≻ 115b 9.17 S 119.56 E
Sāsarām 124 24.57 N 84.02 E
Sasayama 96 35.04 N 135.13 E
Sasa-yama ʌ 96 33.03 N 132.40 E
Sasbach 58 48.08 N 7.37 E
Sasco Brook ≃ 276 41.07 N 73.18 W
Sásd 30 46.15 N 18.06 E
Sasebo 92 33.10 N 129.43 E
Sasebo Naval Base ■ 92 33.09 N 129.45 E
Saseenos 224 48.24 N 123.40 W
Saseginaga, Lac ⊜ 190 47.06 N 78.35 W
Sashalom ✦8 264c 47.31 N 19.11 E
Sas-hegy ʌ2 264c 47.23 N 19.18 E
Sashiki 174m 26.10 N 127.47 E
Sashima 94 36.08 N 139.51 E
Saskatchewan □4, Can. 176 54.00 N 105.00 W
Saskatchewan □4, Can. 184 54.00 N 105.00 W
Saskatchewan ≃ 184 53.12 N 99.16 W
Saskatoon 184 52.07 N 106.38 W
Saskylach 74 71.55 N 114.01 E
Saslaya, Cerro ʌ 238 13.45 N 85.03 W
Sasmik, Cape ≻ 180 51.36 N 177.55 W
Sāsni 124 27.43 N 78.05 E
Sasolburg 158 26.48 S 27.45 E
Sason 130 38.20 N 41.25 E
Sasovo 80 54.21 N 41.54 E
Saspamco 196 29.14 N 98.18 W
Saspul Gompa 123 34.15 N 77.09 E
Sassafras, Austl. 274b 37.52 S 145.21 E
Sassafras, Ky., U.S. 192 37.14 N 83.06 W
Sassafras ≃ 208 39.23 N 76.02 W
Sassafras Mountain ʌ 192 35.03 N 82.48 W
Sassafras Neck ≻1 208 39.25 N 75.55 W
Sassandra 150 4.58 N 6.05 W
Sassandra ≃ 150 4.58 N 6.05 W
Sassano 68 40.20 N 15.33 E
Sassari 71 40.44 N 8.33 E
Sassari □4 71 40.40 N 9.00 E
Sassbach ≃ 61 46.43 N 15.48 E
Sasse ≃ 62 44.15 N 5.55 E
Sassello 62 44.29 N 8.30 E
Sassenage 62 45.12 N 5.40 E
Sassenberg 52 51.59 N 8.02 E
Sassenheim 52 52.13 N 4.31 E
Sassnitz 54 54.31 N 13.38 E
Sassocorvaro 66 43.47 N 12.30 E
Sasso di Castalda 68 40.30 N 15.40 E
Sassoferrato 66 43.26 N 12.51 E
Sasso Marconi 64 44.24 N 11.15 E
S'as'stroj 76 60.08 N 32.34 E
Sassuolo 64 44.33 N 10.47 E
Sastobe 85 42.34 N 70.00 E
Sastown 150 4.40 N 8.26 W
Sastre 252 31.45 S 61.50 W
Sas van Gent 52 51.14 N 3.47 E
Sasyk, ozero ⊜ 78 45.12 N 33.31 E
Sasykkol', ozero ⊜ 86 46.35 N 81.00 E
Şasykoli 80 47.33 N 47.00 E
Šat ≃ 82 54.08 N 37.47 E
Satadougou 150 12.21 N 10.07 W
Satah Mountain ʌ 182 52.29 N 124.41 W
Şatakunta ✦1 26 61.30 N 23.00 E
Šatalovka 78 51.09 N 38.16 E
Šatalovo 76 54.20 N 32.27 E
Sata-misaki ≻ 92 30.59 N 130.40 E
Satāna 122 20.35 N 74.12 E
Satanov 78 49.15 N 26.16 E
Satanta 198 37.26 N 100.59 W
Sátão 34 40.44 N 7.44 W
Sātāra, India 122 17.41 N 73.59 E
Satara, S. Afr. 156 24.29 S 31.47 E
Sataua 175a 13.28 S 172.40 W
Sātbāria, Bngl. 126 23.52 N 89.26 E
Sātbāria, India 272b 22.25 N 88.33 E
Satélite 232 31.43 N 106.23 W
Satellite Beach 220 28.10 N 80.35 W
Satellite Channel ʊ 224 48.43 N 123.30 W
Satema 152 4.18 N 21.42 E
Satengar, Pulau I 112 7.31 S 117.17 E
Säter 40 60.21 N 15.45 E
Sātgāchia 126 23.16 N 88.08 E
Sātghara 272b 22.44 N 88.21 E
Saticoy 228 34.17 N 119.09 W
Satilla ≃ 192 30.59 N 81.28 W
Satilpa Creek ≃ 194 31.39 N 88.05 W
Satin 222 31.21 N 97.02 W
Satipo 248 11.16 S 74.37 W
Sátiro Dias 250 11.36 S 38.36 W
Satis 80 55.02 N 43.48 E
Satīt (Tekeze) ≃ 140 14.20 N 35.50 E
Satka 86 55.03 N 59.01 E
Satkānia 120 22.04 N 92.03 E
Sātkhira 124 22.43 N 89.06 E
Šatki 80 55.11 N 44.08 E
Satla Bīl ≕ 126 22.54 N 90.04 E
Satluj → Sutlej ≃ 120 29.23 N 71.02 E
Satna 124 24.35 N 80.50 E
Sato, Cañada de ≃ 288 34.35 S 58.38 W
Satomi 94 36.43 N 140.30 E
Sátoraljaújhely 30 48.24 N 21.39 E
Šatov 61 48.48 N 16.01 E
Šatovo 82 54.56 N 37.14 E
Satow 54 53.59 N 11.51 E
Sātpura Range ⋏ 122 22.00 N 78.00 E
Sätrabrunn 40 59.51 N 16.27 E
Satriano di Lucania 68 40.33 N 15.33 E
Šatrovo 86 56.31 N 64.38 E
Satrup 41 54.41 N 9.35 E
Satsop ≃ 224 47.03 N 123.30 W
Satsop, Middle Fork ≃ 224 47.05 N 123.30 W
Satsop, West Fork ≃ 224 47.02 N 123.32 W
Satsuma 194 30.51 N 88.03 W
Satsuma-hantō ≻1 92 31.25 N 130.25 E
Satsunan-shotō II 93b 29.00 N 130.00 E
Sattahip 110 12.40 N 100.54 E
Sāttānkulam 122 8.27 N 77.56 E
Satte 94 36.04 N 139.43 E
Sattel 58 47.05 N 8.42 E
Sattenapalle 122 16.24 N 80.11 E
Satthwa 110 17.46 N 94.30 E
Sattledt 61 48.04 N 14.03 E
Satui 112 3.47 S 115.27 E
Sātuli 272b 22.33 N 88.34 E
Satu Mare 38 47.48 N 22.53 E
Satu Mare □6 38 47.40 N 23.00 E
Satun 110 6.37 N 100.04 E
Šatura 80 55.34 N 39.32 E
Saturna 224 48.43 N 123.11 W
Saturna Island I 224 48.47 N 123.08 W
Saturnino M. Laspiur 252 31.42 S 62.29 W
Šaturtorf 76 55.34 N 39.26 E
Satus Creek ≃ 202 46.16 N 120.07 W
Satus Peak ʌ 224 46.15 N 120.45 W
Satyamangalam 122 11.31 N 77.15 E
Satzkorn 264a 52.29 N 12.59 E
Sau ≃ 269c 10.46 N 106.48 E
Saualpe ⋏ 61 46.55 N 14.40 E
Sauble ≃ 212 44.40 N 81.17 W
Sauce, Arg. 252 30.05 S 58.46 W
Sauce, Perú 248 6.44 S 76.10 W
Sauce, Ur. 258 34.39 S 56.04 W
Sauce, Arroyo ≃ 258 34.26 S 57.28 W
Sauce, Arroyo del ≃ 288 34.41 S 58.50 W
Sauce Corto, Arroyo ≃ 252 36.55 S 61.48 W
Saucier 194 30.38 N 89.08 W
Saucillo 232 28.01 N 105.17 W
Sauda 26 59.39 N 6.20 E
Saudade 256 21.56 S 43.03 W
Sauðárkrókur 24a 65.46 N 19.41 W
Saúde 250 10.56 S 40.24 W
Saúde ✦8 287b 23.37 S 46.37 W
Saudi Arabia (Al-ʿArabīyah as-Suʿūdīyah) □1 118 25.00 N 45.00 E
Saudi-Arabien → Saudi Arabia □1 118 25.00 N 45.00 E
Saudron 58 48.30 N 5.20 E
Sauer (Sûre) ≃, Europe 56 49.44 N 6.31 E
Sauer ≃, Europe 56 48.55 N 8.10 E
Sauerkohl-Berge ⋏2 264a 52.20 N 13.45 E
Sauerlach 64 47.58 N 11.38 E
Sauerland ✦1 52 51.10 N 8.00 E
Saueruiná ≃ 248 12.00 S 58.43 W
Sauê-Uiná ≃ 248 12.24 S 58.40 W
Saug ≃ 116 7.27 N 125.44 E
Saugatuck, Ct., U.S. 276 41.08 N 73.23 W
Saugatuck, Mi., U.S. 216 42.39 N 86.12 W
Saugatuck ≃ 276 41.07 N 73.22 W
Saugatuck Reservoir ⊜1 207 41.16 N 73.22 W
Saugeen ≃ 190 44.30 N 81.22 W
Saugeen Indian Reserve ✦4 212 44.33 N 81.18 W
Saugerties 210 42.04 N 73.57 W
Saughall 262 53.13 N 2.58 W
Saugor → Sāgar 124 23.50 N 78.43 E
Saugstad, Mount ʌ 182 52.15 N 126.31 W
Saugus, Ca., U.S. 228 34.24 N 118.32 W
Saugus, Ma., U.S. 207 42.27 N 71.00 W
Saugus ≃ 283 42.28 N 70.58 W
Saugus Iron Works National Historical Site ⊥ 283 42.28 N 71.01 W
Sauh, Tanjong ≻ 114 3.46 N 100.49 E
Saujil 252 28.11 S 66.14 W
Saujon 32 45.40 N 0.56 W
Sauk ≃, Mn., U.S. 198 45.36 N 94.10 W
Sauk ≃, Wa., U.S. 224 48.30 N 121.37 W
Sauk Centre 198 45.44 N 94.57 W
Sauk City 190 43.16 N 89.43 W
Sauk Rapids 190 45.35 N 94.09 W
Sauksaj ≃ 85 39.11 N 72.15 E
Sauk Village 216 41.29 N 87.34 W
Saukville 190 43.22 N 87.56 W
Şaül 250 3.37 N 53.12 W
Šaul'der 85 42.47 N 68.24 E
Sauldre ≃ 50 47.16 N 1.30 E
Sauldre, Canal de la ≚ 50 47.36 N 2.06 E
Saulgau 58 48.01 N 9.30 E
Saulgrub 64 47.40 N 11.01 E
Saulheim 56 49.51 N 8.09 E
Saulieu 50 47.16 N 4.14 E
Saulkrasti 76 57.17 N 24.25 E
Saulnot 58 47.34 N 6.38 E
Sault-au-Mouton 186 48.33 N 69.15 W
Sault au Récollet ✦8 275a 45.34 N 73.39 W
Sault aux Cochons, Rivière du ≃ 186 48.44 N 69.04 W
Sault-de-Vaucluse 62 44.05 N 5.25 E
Saulteaux ≃ 182 55.16 N 114.25 W
Saulteaux Indian Reserve ✦4 184 53.08 N 108.18 W
Sault-lès-Rethel 50 49.30 N 4.22 E
Sault Sainte Marie, On., Can. 190 46.31 N 84.20 W
Sault Sainte Marie, Mi., U.S. 190 46.29 N 84.20 W
Saulx ≃, Fr. 56 48.45 N 4.35 E
Saulx ≃, Fr. 261 48.41 N 2.19 E
Saulx-de-Vesoul 58 47.42 N 6.17 E
Saulx-les-Chartreux 261 48.42 N 2.16 E
Saulxures-sur-Moselotte 58 47.57 N 6.46 E
Şaum'ani 84 41.21 N 44.46 E
Šaum'anovsk 84 40.26 N 46.34 E
Saumarez Reef ✢2 166 21.50 S 153.40 E
Saumlaki 164 7.57 S 131.19 E
Saumon, Rivière au ≃ 206 45.41 N 71.27 W
Saumons, Rivíere aux ≃ 186 49.25 N 62.15 W
Saumur 32 47.16 N 0.05 W
Saundatti 122 15.47 N 75.07 E
Saundersfoot 42 51.43 N 4.43 W
Saunders Island I, Falk. Is. 254 51.20 S 60.10 W
Saunders Island I, S. Geor. 9 57.47 S 26.27 W
Saunders Point ʌ2 162 27.52 S 125.38 E
Saunderstown 207 41.30 N 71.25 W
Saunemin 216 40.54 N 88.24 W
Saupite 152 13.54 S 17.43 E
Sauquoit 210 43.00 N 75.16 W
Sauquoit Creek ≃ 210 43.08 N 75.16 W
Saura 84 44.14 N 50.50 E
Sauran 85 43.29 N 67.50 E
Saurimo 152 9.39 S 20.24 E
Saur-Mogila ⊥ 83 47.56 N 38.46 E
Sausalito 226 37.51 N 122.29 W
Sausar 120 21.39 N 78.47 E
Sauškin 80 49.30 N 43.32 E
Sausset-les-Pins 62 43.20 N 5.07 E
Saussy 58 47.28 N 4.57 E
Sausu 112 1.00 S 120.30 E
Saútar 152 11.06 S 18.27 E
Sauteurs 241k 12.14 N 61.38 W
Sauvas 62 44.19 N 4.09 E
Sauve 62 43.56 N 3.57 E
Sauveterre 62 44.02 N 4.48 E
Sauveterre-de-Béarn 34 43.24 N 0.56 W
Sauveterre-de-Guyenne 32 44.42 N 0.05 W
Sauvie Island I 224 45.41 N 122.49 W
Sauvo 26 60.21 N 22.42 E
Sauwald ✦3 60 48.28 N 13.40 E
Sauzal 200 31.37 N 106.18 W
Sauze di Cesana 62 44.56 N 6.51 E
Sauze d'Oulx 62 45.02 N 6.52 E
Sava, It. 68 40.24 N 17.34 E
S'ava, Ross. 80 58.01 N 46.22 E
Sava ≃ 38 44.50 N 20.26 E
Sävaån ≃ 40 59.45 N 17.24 E
Savage, Md., U.S. 208 39.08 N 76.49 W
Savage, Mt., U.S. 198 47.27 N 104.20 W
Savai'i I 175a 13.35 S 172.25 W
Savala ≃ 80 51.03 N 41.30 E
Savalen ⊜ 26 62.15 N 10.29 E
Savalou 150 7.56 N 1.58 E
Savana Island I 240m 18.20 N 65.05 W
Savana Passage ʊ 240m 18.21 N 65.04 W
Savane ≃ 186 51.08 N 71.26 W
Savanna, Il., U.S. 190 42.05 N 90.09 W
Savanna, Ok., U.S. 196 34.49 N 95.50 W
Savannah, Ga., U.S. 192 32.05 N 81.06 W
Savannah, Mo., U.S. 194 39.56 N 94.49 W
Savannah, N.Y., U.S. 210 43.04 N 76.45 W
Savannah, Oh., U.S. 214 40.57 N 82.21 W
Savannah, Tn., U.S. 194 35.13 N 88.14 W
Savannah ≃ 192 32.02 N 80.53 W
Savannah River Plant ⊍3 192 33.15 N 81.40 W
Savannah Sound 192 25.06 N 76.09 W
Savannakhét 110 16.33 N 104.45 E
Savanna-la-Mar 241q 18.13 N 78.08 W
Savanna Portage State Park ♦ 190 46.51 N 93.10 W
Sāvantvādi 122 15.54 N 73.49 E
Savanūr 122 14.58 N 75.21 E
Sävar 26 63.54 N 20.34 E
Savara ≃ 62 45.42 N 7.12 E
Savasse ≃ 62 45.03 N 5.02 E
Savaştepe 130 39.22 N 27.40 E
Savat 130 38.21 N 40.38 E
Savcılıbüyükoba 130 39.14 N 33.41 E
Savé 150 8.02 N 2.29 E
Save (Sabi) ≃, Afr. 156 21.00 S 35.02 E
Save ≃, Fr. 32 43.47 N 1.17 E
Sāveh 128 35.01 N 50.20 E
Savelli 68 39.19 N 16.47 E
Savelugu 150 9.37 N 0.49 W
Savenay 32 47.22 N 1.57 W
Săveni 38 47.57 N 26.52 E
Saverdun 32 43.14 N 1.35 E
Savernake Forest ✦3 42 51.24 N 1.38 W
Saverne 56 48.44 N 7.22 E
Savery Creek ≃ 200 41.01 N 107.27 W
Saviči, Bela. 76 52.25 N 29.03 E
Saviči, Bela. 78 51.37 N 30.17 E
Savick Brook ≃ 262 53.45 N 2.47 W
Savièse 58 46.16 N 7.20 E
Savigliano 62 44.38 N 7.40 E
Savignano Irpino 68 41.14 N 15.11 E
Savignano sul Panaro 64 44.29 N 11.02 E
Savignano sul Rubicone 66 44.05 N 12.24 E
Savignone 62 44.34 N 8.58 E
Savigny-lès-Beaune 58 47.04 N 4.49 E
Savigny-le-Temple 261 48.35 N 2.35 E

Symbol	English	Deutsch	Español	Français	Português
≃	River	Fluß	Río	Rivière	Rio
≚	Canal	Kanal	Canal	Canal	Canal
ʟ	Waterfall, Rapids	Wasserfall, Stromschnellen	Cascada, Rápidos	Chute d'eau, Rapides	Cascata, Rápidos
ʊ	Strait	Meeresstraße	Estrecho	Détroit	Estreito
c	Bay, Gulf	Bucht, Golf	Bahía, Golfo	Baie, Golfe	Baía, Golfo
⊜	Lake, Lakes	See, Seen	Lago, Lagos	Lac, Lacs	Lago, Lagos
≕	Swamp	Sumpf	Pantano	Marais	Pântano
⁂	Ice Features, Glacier	Eis- und Gletscherformen	Accidentes Glaciales	Formes glaciaires	Acidentes glaciares
⊤	Other Hydrographic Features	Andere Hydrographische Objekte	Otros Elementos Hidrográficos	Autres données hydrographiques	Outros acidentes hidrográficos
✢	Submarine Features	Untermeerische Objekte	Accidentes Submarinos	Formes de relief sous-marin	Acidentes submarinos
□	Political Unit	Politische Einheit	Unidad Política	Entité politique	Unidade política
⊍	Cultural Institution	Kulturelle Institution	Institución Cultural	Institution culturelle	Instituição cultural
⊥	Historical Site	Historische Stätte	Sitio Histórico	Site historique	Sítio histórico
♦	Recreational Site	Erholungs- und Ferienort	Sitio de Recreo	Centre de loisirs	Area de Lazer
⊠	Airport	Flughafen	Aeropuerto	Aéroport	Aeroporto
■	Military Installation	Militäranlage	Instalación Militar	Installation militaire	Instalação militar
✦	Miscellaneous	Verschiedenes	Misceláneo	Divers	Diversos

ENGLISH Name Page Lat.°′ Long.°′ — DEUTSCH Name Seite Breite°′ Länge°′ E = Ost

Savigny-sur-Braye 50 47.53 N 0.49 E
Savigny-sur-Orge 50 48.40 N 2.21 E
Savill Gardens ♦ 260 51.27 N 0.36 W
Savincy 78 49.24 N 37.04 E
Savines 62 44.32 N 6.24 E
Savinjske Alpe ⩘ 61 46.23 N 14.35 E
Savinka, Ross. 80 50.06 N 47.06 E
Savinka, Ross. 82 54.27 N 38.52 E
Savino 80 56.35 N 41.13 E
Savino-Borisovskaja 24 62.38 N 44.34 E
Savinsk 89 52.10 N 140.23 E
Savinskij 24 62.58 N 40.08 E
Savio 66 44.18 N 12.18 E
Savio ≃ 66 44.19 N 12.20 E
Saviore dell'Adamello 64 46.05 N 10.24 E
Savirşin 38 46.01 N 22.14 E
Savitaipale 26 61.12 N 27.42 E
Savnik 38 42.57 N 19.05 E
Savognin 58 46.36 N 9.36 E
Savoie □5 32 45.30 N 6.25 E
Savo Island I 175e 9.08 S 159.49 E
Savolaks ◆1 26 62.00 N 28.00 E
Sav'olovo 82 56.52 N 37.22 E
Sav'olovo Station ◆5 265b 55.48 N 37.35 E
Savona, B.C., Can. 182 50.45 N 120.50 W
Savona, It. 62 44.17 N 8.30 E
Savona, N.Y., U.S. 210 42.17 N 77.13 W
Savona □4 62 44.18 N 8.16 E
Savonlinna 26 61.52 N 28.53 E
Savonnières 50 47.21 N 0.33 E
Savonranta 26 62.11 N 29.12 E
Savoonga 180 63.42 N 170.27 W
Savory Creek ≃ 162 23.22 S 122.37 E
Savoureuse ≃ 58 47.31 N 6.51 E
Savoy 196 33.34 N 96.21 W
Savran' 78 48.09 N 30.04 E
Savruši 80 55.02 N 50.40 E
Sävsjö 26 57.25 N 14.40 E
S'avta 24 67.08 N 61.45 E
Savu Basin ◆1 14 9.15 S 123.15 E
Savudrija 64 45.30 N 13.30 E
Savur 130 37.33 N 40.53 E
Savusavu 175g 16.16 S 179.21 E
Savusavu Bay c 175g 16.45 S 179.15 E
Savu Sea
— Sawu, Laut ▼2 112 9.40 S 122.00 E
Savuto ≃ 68 39.02 N 16.06 E
Savvatejevka 88 52.20 N 103.39 E
Savvino, Ross. 82 55.43 N 36.48 E
Savvino, Ross. 82 56.33 N 37.47 E
Savvo-Borz'a 88 50.46 N 118.18 E
Sawāb, Wādī as- V 130 34.36 N 40.25 E
Sawabala Point ⩥ 164 10.10 S 151.15 E
Sawah 112 2.23 N 115.14 E
Sawahlunto 112 0.40 S 100.47 E
Sawai 164 2.58 S 129.09 E
Sawai, Teluk c 164 2.55 S 129.12 E
Sawāi Mādhopur 124 25.59 N 76.22 E
Sawākin 140 19.07 N 37.20 E
Sawal, Gunung ▲ 115a 7.12 S 108.16 E
Sawan, Indon. 115b 8.08 S 115.11 E
Sawan, Mya. 110 24.30 N 96.19 E
Sawang 114 0.45 N 103.21 E
Sawankhalok 110 17.19 N 99.50 E
Sawara 94 35.53 N 140.30 E
Sawata 92 38.00 N 138.16 E
Sawatch Range ⩘ 200 39.10 N 106.25 W
Sawbridgeworth 42 51.50 N 0.09 E
Sawdā', Jabal as- ⩘2 146 28.40 N 15.30 E
Sawdā', Qurnat as- ▲ 130 34.18 N 36.07 E
Sawdirī 140 14.25 N 29.05 E
Sawel Mountain ▲ 48 54.49 N 7.02 W
Sawhāj 140 26.33 N 31.42 E
Sawi 110 10.14 N 99.07 E
Sawin, Lac ⊜ 206 46.32 N 73.54 W
Sawknah 146 29.04 N 15.47 E
Sawl 142 29.21 N 31.14 E
Sawla 150 9.17 N 2.25 W
Saw Log Creek ≃ 198 38.07 N 99.42 W
Saw Mill ≃ 276 40.56 N 73.53 W
Sawmill Brook ≃, Ma., U.S. 283 42.34 N 70.46 W
Sawmill Brook ≃, N.J., U.S. 276 40.28 N 74.26 W
Sawmill Creek ≃, N.J., U.S. 276 40.46 N 74.05 W
Sawmill Creek ≃, Pa., U.S. 279b 40.10 N 79.58 W
Sawmill Pond Brook ≃ 276 41.10 N 74.23 W
Sawmill Run ≃ 285 40.07 N 75.21 W
Sawmills 154 19.31 S 28.02 E
Sawqirah, Ghubbat c 118 18.35 N 57.00 E
Sawston 42 52.07 N 0.10 E
Sawtayr ▼4 140 17.03 N 30.24 E
Sawtooth National Recreation Area ♦ 202 44.00 N 114.55 W
Sawtry 42 52.27 N 0.17 W
Sawu, Laut (Savu Sea) ▼2 112 9.40 S 122.00 E
Sawu, Pulau I 112 10.30 S 121.54 E
Sawyer, Mi., U.S. 216 41.53 N 86.35 W
Sawyer, N.D., U.S. 198 48.05 N 101.03 W
Sawyers Hill ⩘2 186 47.11 N 53.52 W
Sawyers Valley 168a 31.54 S 116.13 E
Sawyerville, P.Q., Can. 206 45.20 N 71.34 W
Sawyerville, Il., U.S. 219 39.05 N 89.48 W
Sawyerwood 214 41.02 N 81.27 W
Saxby ≃ 166 18.25 S 140.53 E
Saxdalen 40 60.09 N 14.57 E
Saxen ⊜ 40 59.46 N 14.25 E
Saxike 120 30.44 N 86.22 E
Saxilby 44 53.17 N 0.40 W
Saxis 208 37.55 N 75.43 W
Saxmundham 42 52.13 N 1.29 E
Saxon, Schw. 58 46.09 N 7.11 E
Saxon, Wi., U.S. 190 46.29 N 90.24 W
Saxonburg 214 40.45 N 79.49 W
Saxon Woods Park ♦ 276 40.59 N 73.45 W
Saxony
— Sachsen □9 30 52.45 N 9.30 E
Saxton 214 40.12 N 78.14 W
Say 150 13.07 N 2.21 E
Sāy, Jazīrat I 140 20.42 N 30.20 E
Saya de Malha Bank ◆4 12 10.30 S 61.30 E
Sayama, Nihon 94 35.51 N 139.24 E
Sayama, Nihon 270 34.31 N 135.34 E
Sayama-kyūryō ⩘2 268 35.47 N 139.24 E
Sayán 248 11.08 S 77.12 W
Sayan Mountains (Sajany) ⩘ 88 52.45 N 96.00 E
Sayansk 88 54.02 N 102.06 E
Sayaxché 232 16.31 N 90.10 W
Saybrook, Il., U.S. 216 40.25 N 88.31 W
Saybrook, Oh., U.S. 214 41.50 N 80.51 W
Saybrook Manor 207 41.17 N 72.23 W
Sayda, Dtsch. 54 50.43 N 13.25 E
Saydā (Sidon), Lubnān 132 33.33 N 35.22 E
Saydā □4 132 33.15 N 35.15 E
Saydnāyā 132 33.42 N 36.22 E
Sayghān 120 35.11 N 67.42 E
Sayhūt 144 15.12 N 51.14 E
Sayil ⊥ 232 20.16 N 89.42 W
Saylah 142 29.21 N 30.58 E
Saylorsburg 210 40.54 N 75.19 W
Saylorville Lake ⊜1 190 41.48 N 93.46 W
Saylūn, Khirbat (Shiloh) ⊥ 132 32.03 N 35.17 E
Säynätsalo 26 62.08 N 25.46 E
Sayō 96 35.00 N 134.22 E
Sayqal, Bahr ⊜ 132 33.40 N 37.06 E
Sayram Hu ⊜ 86 44.36 N 81.13 E
Sayre, Ok., U.S. 196 35.17 N 99.38 W
Sayre, Pa., U.S. 210 41.58 N 76.30 W
Sayreville 208 40.27 N 74.21 W
Sayula 234 19.52 N 103.37 W
Sayula, Laguna de ⊜ 234 20.03 N 103.31 W
Sayula de Alemán 234 17.52 N 94.57 W

Sayultepec 234 17.27 N 97.17 W
Sayville 210 40.44 N 73.04 W
Sayward 182 50.22 N 125.55 W
Saywūn 144 15.56 N 48.47 E
Saza 92 33.14 N 129.39 E
Sazanit I 38 40.30 N 19.16 E
Sazdy, Kaz. 80 46.57 N 49.19 E
Sazdy, Kaz. 86 47.22 N 61.48 E
Saze 62 43.56 N 4.41 E
Sažino 86 56.20 N 58.11 E
Sazlijka ≃ 38 42.02 N 25.52 E
Sazonovo 76 59.04 N 35.14 E
Šazud 120 37.43 N 72.11 E
Sazykul', ozero ⊜ 86 55.22 N 67.34 E
Sba 148 28.13 N 0.08 W
Sbeïtla 148 35.14 N 9.08 E
Sbiba 36 35.33 N 9.05 E
Scaddan 162 33.27 S 121.43 E
Scaër 32 48.02 N 3.42 W
Scafati 68 40.45 N 14.31 E
Scafell Pikes ▲ 44 54.27 N 3.12 W
Scaggsville 208 39.09 N 76.54 W
Scajaquada Creek ≃ 284a 42.56 N 78.53 W
Scala, Teatro alla ⊍ 266b 45.28 N 9.11 E
Scala Coeli 68 39.27 N 16.53 E
Scalasaig 46 56.04 N 6.11 W
Scalby 44 54.18 N 0.27 W
Scalea 68 39.49 N 15.48 E
Scaletta Zanclea 68 38.03 N 15.28 E
Scalloway 46a 60.08 N 1.18 W
Scalpay I, Scot., U.K. 46 57.17 N 5.59 W
Scalpay I, Scot., U.K. 46 57.52 N 6.40 W
Scalp Level 214 40.14 N 78.50 W
Scalp Mountain ▲2 48 55.04 N 7.24 W
Scammon 198 37.16 N 94.49 W
Scammon Bay 180 61.53 N 165.38 W
Scammon Bay c 180 61.53 N 165.54 W
Scammonden Water ⊜1 262 53.38 N 1.56 W
Scampton 44 53.18 N 0.34 W
Scandale 68 39.07 N 16.57 E
Scandia 198 39.47 N 97.47 W
Scandiano 64 44.36 N 10.43 E
Scandicci 66 43.45 N 11.11 E
Scanlon 190 46.42 N 92.25 W
Scanno 66 41.54 N 13.53 E
Scansano 66 42.41 N 11.20 E
Scantic ≃ 207 41.52 N 72.38 W
Scapa 182 51.52 N 111.59 W
Scapa Flow c 46 58.55 N 3.06 W
Scapegoat Mountain ▲ 202 47.19 N 112.50 W
Ščapino 74 55.19 N 159.25 E
Ščapov 80 51.01 N 51.11 E
Ščapovo 82 55.09 N 38.11 E
Scappoose 224 45.45 N 122.52 W
Ščar ≃ 76 53.13 N 25.46 E
Ščara ≃ 76 53.27 N 24.45 E
Scaramia, Capo ⩥ 70 36.47 N 14.29 E
Scarba I 46 56.11 N 5.43 W
Scarborough, Austl. 168a 31.54 S 115.45 E
Scarborough, On., Can. 212 43.47 N 79.15 W
Scarborough, Trin. 241r 11.11 N 60.44 W
Scarborough, Eng., U.K. 44 54.17 N 0.24 W
Scarborough Centre ◆9 275b 43.47 N 79.16 W
Scarborough Point ⩥ 171a 27.12 S 153.07 E
Scarborough Reef ◆2 116 15.08 N 117.46 E
Scardroy 46 57.31 N 4.59 W
Scargill 172 42.56 S 172.57 E
Scarinish 46 56.29 N 6.48 W
Scarisbrick 262 53.37 N 2.56 W
Ščarišoara 38 44.00 N 24.35 E
Scarlino 66 42.54 N 10.51 E
Scarp I 46 58.02 N 7.08 W
Scarpe ≃ 50 50.30 N 3.27 E
Scarperia 66 44.00 N 11.21 E
Scarper Peak ▲ 282 37.32 N 122.26 W
Scarriff 48 52.55 N 8.31 W
Scarsdale, Austl. 169 37.40 S 143.40 E
Scarsdale, N.Y., U.S. 210 40.59 N 73.49 W
Scartaglin 48 52.10 N 9.26 W
Scarth Hill 262 53.33 N 2.52 W
Sčastje 83 48.44 N 39.14 E
Scatarie Island I 186 46.00 N 59.44 W
Scatter Creek ≃ 224 46.48 N 123.06 W
Scauri, It. 66 41.15 N 13.42 E
Scauri, It. 70 36.45 N 11.58 E
Scavaig, Loch c 46 57.09 N 6.10 W
Scawfell Island I 166 20.52 S 149.36 E
Sceaux 50 48.47 N 2.17 E
Sceaux, Château de ⊥ 261 48.46 N 2.18 E
Ščedrin 76 52.53 N 29.33 E
Ščedrovka 83 49.30 N 40.13 E
Ščeglovo 265a 60.02 N 30.46 E
Ščeljajur 24 65.21 N 53.21 E
Ščelkan ≃ 80 50.47 N 43.33 E
Ščelkovo 76 55.55 N 38.00 E
Ščemilovo 265b 55.48 N 38.05 E
Ščena 64 46.41 N 11.12 E
Scenery Hill 214 40.05 N 80.04 W
Sčeptre 184 50.51 N 109.15 W
Ščerbakovo, Ross. 74 65.15 N 160.30 E
Ščerbakovo, Ross. 86 56.01 N 73.29 E
Ščerbakty 86 52.29 N 78.09 E
Ščerbinka 82 55.31 N 37.35 E
Ščerbinovka 83 48.26 N 37.50 E
Scey-sur-Saône-et-Saint-Albin 58 47.40 N 5.58 E
Schaale ≃ 54 53.21 N 10.49 E
Schaalsee ⊜ 54 53.35 N 10.57 E
Schaan 58 47.10 N 9.31 E
Schabs
— Sciaves 64 46.46 N 11.40 E
Schachendorf 61 47.16 N 16.26 E
Schaefferstown 208 40.17 N 76.17 W
Schaephuysen 263 51.26 N 6.29 E
Schaerbeek 50 50.51 N 4.23 E
Schafberg ▲ 64 47.47 N 13.26 E
Schäferberg ▲ 264a 52.25 N 13.08 E
Schaffhausen 58 47.42 N 8.38 E
Schaffhausen □3 58 47.40 N 8.35 E
Schafstädt 54 51.23 N 11.46 E
Schäftlarn 64 47.59 N 11.28 E
Schagen 52 52.46 N 4.47 E
Schaghticoke 210 42.54 N 73.35 W
Schalchen 60 48.07 N 13.10 E
Schale 52 52.26 N 7.37 E
Schalkau 54 50.24 N 11.00 E
Schalke ◆8 263 51.31 N 7.05 E
Schälker Heide ◆3 263 51.24 N 7.36 E
Schalksmühle 56 51.14 N 7.31 E
Schaller 198 42.29 N 95.17 W
Schanck, Cape ⩥ 169 38.30 S 144.53 E
S-Chanf 58 46.36 N 9.59 E
Schanfigg V 58 46.51 N 9.38 E
Schanghai
— Shanghai 106 31.14 N 121.28 E
Schangnau 58 46.50 N 7.52 E
Schapbach 58 48.22 N 8.18 E
Schapen 52 52.24 N 7.33 E
Šchaprode 54 54.31 N 13.10 E
Šchara, gora ▲ 84 43.00 N 43.06 E
Scharbeutz 54 54.03 N 10.44 E
Schardenberg 60 48.32 N 13.30 E
Schardenberg ▲2 263 51.27 N 6.28 E
Scharding 60 48.27 N 13.26 E
Scharhörn I 52 53.57 N 8.25 E
Schari
— Chari ≃ 146 12.58 N 14.31 E
Scharl 263 51.06 N 7.40 E
Scharmützelsee ⊜ 54 52.15 N 14.03 E
Scharnhorst ◆8 263 51.32 N 7.32 E
Scharnitz 64 47.23 N 11.15 E
Scharnitzer Klause ⟩⟨ 64 47.24 N 11.16 E
Scharrel 52 53.04 N 7.42 E

Scharzfeld 52 51.37 N 10.22 E
Schässburg
— Sighişoara 38 46.13 N 24.48 E
Schauinsland ▲ 58 47.55 N 7.54 E
Schaumburg 216 42.02 N 88.05 W
Schaut 84 43.43 N 42.32 E
Schebeli
— Shabeelle ≃ 144 0.12 S 42.45 E
Scheessel 52 53.10 N 9.29 E
Schefferville 176 54.48 N 66.50 W
Scheggia 66 43.24 N 12.40 E
Scheggino 66 42.43 N 12.50 E
Scheibbs 61 48.00 N 15.10 E
Scheiblingstein 264b 48.16 N 16.13 E
Scheidegg 58 47.35 N 9.51 E
Scheifling 61 47.09 N 14.24 E
Scheinfeld 56 49.40 N 10.27 E
Schelde (Escaut) ≃ 50 51.22 N 4.15 E
Schelklingen 58 48.22 N 9.44 E
Schell Creek Range ⩘ 204 39.10 N 114.40 W
Schellenberg ▲ 60 48.18 N 13.03 E
Schellsburg 214 40.03 N 78.39 W
Schelsen ◆8 263 51.09 N 6.31 E
Schenectady 210 42.48 N 73.56 W
Schenectady □6 210 42.47 N 73.53 W
Schenefeld 52 53.36 N 9.49 E
Schenevus 210 42.32 N 74.49 W
Schenevus Creek ≃ 210 42.33 N 74.50 W
Schenkendorf 264a 52.16 N 13.35 E
Schenkenzell 58 48.19 N 8.22 E
Schenklengsfeld 56 50.49 N 9.50 E
Schenley 214 40.41 N 79.40 W
Schenley Park ♦ 279b 40.26 N 79.56 W
Schepsdorf-Lohne 52 52.30 N 7.16 E
Schererville 216 41.30 N 87.27 W
Scherfede 52 51.32 N 9.02 E
Scherlebeck 263 51.37 N 7.08 E
Schermbeck 52 51.41 N 6.52 E
Schermerhorn 52 52.36 N 4.52 E
Schermützelsee ⊜ 54 52.34 N 14.04 E
Scherpenheuvel 56 50.59 N 4.59 E
Scherpenzeel 52 52.05 N 5.30 E
Schertz 196 29.33 N 98.16 W
Schesch, Erg
— Chech, Erg ◆2 148 25.00 N 2.15 W
Schessitz 60 49.59 N 11.01 E
Schevelinger-Stausee ⊜1 263 51.08 N 7.26 E
Scheveningen ◆8 52 52.06 N 4.18 E
Schiedam 52 51.55 N 4.24 E
Schieder 52 51.55 N 9.09 E
Schiefbahn 56 51.14 N 6.31 E
Schiehallion ▲ 46 56.40 N 4.06 W
Schierke 54 51.46 N 10.40 E
Schierling 60 48.50 N 12.08 E
Schiermonnikoog 52 53.29 N 6.09 E
Schiermonnikoog I 52 53.28 N 6.15 E
Schiers 58 46.59 N 9.41 E
Schiessen 58 48.18 N 10.14 E
Schiffdorf 52 53.32 N 8.39 E
Schiffenensee ⊜ 58 46.50 N 7.10 E
Schifferstadt 56 49.23 N 8.22 E
Schiffsshebewerk ◆5 263 51.37 N 7.19 E
Schihkiatschwang
— Shijiazhuang 98 38.03 N 114.28 E
Schijndel 52 51.37 N 5.25 E
Schikoku
— Shikoku I 92 33.45 N 133.30 E
Schildau 54 51.27 N 12.56 E
Schilde 56 51.14 N 4.35 E
Schilde ≃ 54 53.26 N 10.53 E
Schildow 54 52.38 N 13.23 E
Schildwolde 52 53.14 N 6.49 E
Schiller Park 216 41.57 N 87.52 W
Schillingsfürst 56 49.17 N 10.15 E
Schillingstedt 54 51.14 N 11.11 E
Schilpario 64 46.01 N 10.09 E
Schiltach 58 48.17 N 8.20 E
Schiltigheim 58 48.36 N 7.45 E
Schimborn 56 50.03 N 9.11 E
Schimmert 56 50.55 N 5.50 E
Schinveld 56 50.57 N 5.59 E
Schinznach Bad 58 47.27 N 8.10 E
Schio 64 45.43 N 11.21 E
Schipbeek ≃ 52 52.14 N 6.09 E
Schiphol, Luchthaven ⊠ 52 52.17 N 4.40 E
Schipkau 54 51.31 N 13.53 E
Schirgiswalde 54 51.05 N 14.27 E
Schirmeck 58 48.29 N 7.13 E
Schirnding 54 50.05 N 12.13 E
Schisuoka
— Shizuoka 94 34.58 N 138.23 E
Schjetman Reef ▼2 14 15.10 N 178.40 W
Schkeuditz 54 51.24 N 12.13 E
Schkoder-See
— Scutari, Lake ⊜ 38 42.12 N 19.18 E
Schkölen 54 51.02 N 11.49 E
Schkopau 54 51.23 N 11.59 E
Schladen 54 52.01 N 10.32 E
Schladming 64 47.23 N 13.41 E
Schlanders
— Silandro 64 46.38 N 10.46 E
Schlangen 52 51.49 N 8.50 E
Schlangenbad 56 50.05 N 8.05 E
Schlänitz-See ⊜ 264a 52.27 N 12.57 E
Schlanstedt 54 52.00 N 11.02 E
Schlater 194 33.38 N 90.20 W
Schlegel Lake ⊜ 276 40.59 N 74.03 W
Schlei c 54 54.36 N 9.51 E
Schleiden 56 50.31 N 6.28 E
Schleife 54 51.32 N 14.32 E
Schleinitz Range ⩘ 164 3.10 S 151.40 E
Schleithal 58 48.59 N 8.02 E
Schleitheim 58 47.45 N 8.29 E
Schleiz 54 50.34 N 11.49 E
Schlema 54 50.40 N 12.40 E
Schlepzig 54 52.01 N 13.53 E
Schlesien
— Silesia □9 30 51.00 N 16.45 E
Schlesischer (Ost) Bahnhof ◆5 264a 52.30 N 13.26 E
Schleswig, Dtsch. 52 54.31 N 9.33 E
Schleswig, Ia., U.S. 198 42.09 N 95.26 W
Schleswig-Holstein □3 30 54.20 N 9.40 E
Schlettau 54 50.33 N 12.56 E
Schlettstadt
— Sélestat 58 48.16 N 7.27 E
Schleusingen 54 50.31 N 10.45 E
Schlieben 54 51.43 N 13.23 E
Schliengen 58 47.46 N 7.35 E
Schlieren 58 47.24 N 8.27 E
Schliersee 64 47.44 N 11.51 E
Schlitz 56 50.40 N 9.33 E
Schloss Holte 52 51.52 N 8.35 E
Schloss Neuhaus 52 51.44 N 8.43 E
Schlossvippach 54 51.06 N 11.08 E
Schloss Zeil 64 47.52 N 10.00 E
Schlotheim 54 51.14 N 10.39 E
Schluchsee 58 47.49 N 8.10 E
Schluchsee ⊜ 58 47.49 N 8.10 E
Schlucht, Col de la ⟩⟨ 58 48.04 N 7.02 E
Schlüchtern 56 50.20 N 9.31 E
Schluderns
— Sluderno 64 46.40 N 10.35 E
Schlüsselburg 52 52.29 N 9.04 E
Schlüsselfeld 56 49.45 N 10.37 E
Schlutup ◆8 54 53.53 N 10.48 E
Schmachtendorf ◆8 263 51.32 N 6.49 E
Schmallenberg 56 51.09 N 8.17 E
Schmalkalden 54 50.43 N 10.26 E
Schmallenberg 56 51.09 N 8.17 E
Schmalnau 56 50.27 N 9.47 E
Schmannewitz 54 51.24 N 12.58 E
Schmarsau 54 52.54 N 11.21 E
Schmelz 56 49.27 N 6.51 E
Schmidmühlen 60 49.16 N 11.56 E
Schmidt 56 50.39 N 6.25 E

Schmidtsdrif 158 28.41 S 24.02 E
Schmiedeberg 54 50.50 N 13.40 E
Schmiedefeld 54 50.37 N 10.49 E
Schmilka 54 50.53 N 14.14 E
Schmöckwitz ◆8 264a 52.23 N 13.39 E
Schmölln 54 50.53 N 12.20 E
Schmutter ≃ 58 48.42 N 10.46 E
Schnabelwaid 60 49.49 N 11.35 E
Schnackenburg 54 53.02 N 11.32 E
Schnait 58 48.47 N 9.23 E
Schnaitsee 60 48.04 N 12.22 E
Schnaittach 60 49.33 N 11.19 E
Schnaittenbach 60 49.33 N 12.01 E
Schnakenbek 52 53.23 N 10.30 E
Schnecksville 208 40.41 N 75.36 W
Schneealpe ⩘ 61 47.41 N 15.36 E
Schneeberg 54 50.36 N 12.38 E
Schneeberg ▲, Dtsch. 54 50.03 N 11.51 E
Schneeberg ▲, Öst. 61 47.47 N 15.47 E
Schneidemühl
— Piła 30 53.10 N 16.44 E
Schneider 216 41.11 N 87.26 W
Schneifel ⩘1 56 50.15 N 6.25 E
Schneverdingen 52 53.07 N 9.47 E
Schney 56 50.10 N 11.04 E
Schober Gruppe ⩘ 64 46.55 N 12.42 E
Schobüll 41 54.30 N 9.00 E
Schöckl ▲ 61 47.11 N 15.28 E
Schodn'a 82 55.51 N 37.25 E
Schodn'a ≃ 265b 55.50 N 37.25 E
Schœlcher 240e 14.37 N 61.06 W
Schoenbrunn Village State Memorial ⊥ 214 40.27 N 81.24 W
Schofield 190 44.54 N 89.36 W
Schofield Barracks ■ 229c 21.30 N 158.04 W
Schofields 274a 33.42 S 150.52 E
Schöftland 58 47.18 N 8.03 E
Schoharie 210 42.39 N 74.18 W
Schoharie □6 210 42.40 N 74.19 W
Schoharie Creek ≃ 210 42.57 N 74.18 W
Schoharie Reservoir ⊜1 210 42.22 N 74.26 W
Scholen 52 52.44 N 8.46 E
Scholes 44 53.49 N 1.25 W
Schollene 54 52.41 N 12.13 E
Schöllenen V 58 46.40 N 8.35 E
Schöller ◆8 263 51.14 N 7.01 E
Schöllkrippen 56 50.05 N 9.14 E
Schöllnach 60 48.45 N 13.11 E
Scholls 224 45.24 N 122.55 W
Scholven ◆8 263 51.36 N 7.01 E
Schomberg, On., Can. 212 44.00 N 79.41 W
Schömberg, Dtsch. 56 48.47 N 8.38 E
Schömberg, Dtsch. 58 48.13 N 8.46 E
Schonach 58 48.08 N 8.11 E
Schönaich 58 48.39 N 9.03 E
Schönau, Dtsch. 56 49.26 N 8.49 E
Schönau, Dtsch. 58 47.47 N 7.53 E
Schönau, Dtsch. 64 47.37 N 12.59 E
Schönau, Dtsch. 60 48.29 N 12.52 E
Schönbeck 54 53.34 N 13.34 E
Schönberg, Dtsch. 54 50.31 N 11.57 E
Schönberg, Dtsch. 54 50.11 N 12.19 E
Schönberg, Dtsch. 54 54.23 N 10.22 E
Schönberg, Dtsch. 54 53.50 N 11.38 E
Schönberg, Dtsch. 60 48.50 N 13.20 E
Schönberger Strand 54 54.25 N 10.24 E
Schönberg im Stubaital 64 47.11 N 11.25 E
Schönbrunn 54 50.32 N 10.53 E
Schönbrunn, Schloss ⊍ 264b 48.11 N 16.19 E
Schönbrunner Schlosspark ♦ 264b 48.11 N 16.19 E
Schondra ≃ 56 50.07 N 9.44 E
Schöneback, Dtsch. 54 53.03 N 12.13 E
Schönebeck, Dtsch. 54 52.01 N 11.44 E
Schönebeck ◆8 263 51.28 N 6.56 E
Schöneberg ◆8 264a 52.29 N 13.21 E
Schöneck, Dtsch. 54 50.23 N 12.20 E
Schöneck, Dtsch. 56 50.13 N 8.52 E
Schönecken 56 50.09 N 6.27 E
Schönefeld 264a 52.23 N 13.30 E
Schöneiche 54 52.28 N 13.41 E
Schönenwerd 58 47.22 N 8.00 E
Schönerlinde 264a 52.39 N 13.27 E
Schönewalde 54 51.49 N 13.13 E
Schönfeld 264a 52.41 N 13.44 E
Schönfliess 264a 52.39 N 13.20 E
Schongau 58 47.49 N 10.54 E
Schönhagen, Dtsch. 54 54.38 N 10.01 E
Schönhagen, Dtsch. 54 52.14 N 13.08 E
Schönhausen, Dtsch. 54 52.35 N 12.02 E
Schönhausen, Dtsch. 263 51.37 N 7.38 E
Schönheide 54 50.30 N 12.31 E
Schönholthausen 56 51.11 N 8.00 E
Schöningen 54 52.08 N 10.58 E
Schönkirchen 54 54.20 N 10.15 E
Schönmünzach 58 48.36 N 8.22 E
Schönnebeck ◆8 263 51.29 N 7.04 E
Schönningstedt 52 53.32 N 10.15 E
Schönow 54 52.40 N 13.32 E
Schönsee 60 49.31 N 12.33 E
Schönthal 60 49.21 N 12.36 E
Schönungen 56 50.03 N 10.18 E
Schönwald, Dtsch. 54 50.12 N 12.05 E
Schönwald, Dtsch. 58 48.06 N 8.11 E
Schönwalde, Dtsch. 54 54.11 N 10.45 E
Schönwalde, Dtsch. 54 52.40 N 13.26 E
Schönwalde, Dtsch. 54 52.37 N 13.07 E
Schönwies 58 47.11 N 10.39 E
Schoodic Lake ⊜ 188 45.21 N 68.54 W
Schoolcraft 216 42.06 N 85.38 W
Schoolhouse Run ≃ 285 40.13 N 75.27 W
Schoombee 158 31.28 S 25.30 E
Schoondijke 52 51.21 N 3.32 E
Schoonebeek 52 52.39 N 6.52 E
Schoonhoven 52 51.56 N 4.51 E
Schoorl 52 52.42 N 4.41 E
Schopfheim 58 47.39 N 7.49 E
Schopfloch 56 49.07 N 10.18 E
Schopp 56 49.21 N 7.41 E
Schöppenstedt 54 52.08 N 10.46 E
Schöppingen 52 52.05 N 7.14 E
Schorfheide 54 52.56 N 13.43 E
Schorfheide ◆3 54 52.55 N 13.35 E
Schörfling 64 47.56 N 13.36 E
Schorndorf 56 48.48 N 9.31 E
Schortens 52 53.31 N 7.56 E
Schoten 50 51.15 N 4.30 E
Schötmar 52 52.04 N 8.45 E
Schott 56 50.30 N 9.07 E
Schottland
— Scotland □8 28 57.00 N 4.00 W
Schouten, Kepulauan II 164 0.55 S 135.55 E
Schouten Island I 166 42.19 S 148.17 E
Schouten Islands II 164 3.30 S 144.40 E
Schouwen I 52 51.43 N 3.50 E
Schrader Creek ≃ 210 41.43 N 76.30 W
Schrader Range ⩘ 164 5.05 S 144.15 E
Schramberg 58 48.13 N 8.23 E
Schram City 219 39.09 N 89.27 W
Schrankogel ▲ 64 47.02 N 11.06 E
Schraplau 54 51.26 N 11.40 E
Schreiber 190 48.48 N 87.15 W
Schrems 61 48.47 N 15.04 E
Schrick 61 48.30 N 16.37 E
Schriever 194 29.44 N 90.48 W
Schrobenhausen 60 48.33 N 11.17 E
Schröcken 58 47.15 N 10.05 E
Schroffenstein ▲ 158 27.11 S 18.42 E
Schroon ≃ 210 43.50 N 73.46 W
Schroon Lake ⊜ 188 43.47 N 73.46 W
Schrozberg 56 49.20 N 9.59 E
Schruns 58 47.04 N 9.55 E
Schulenburg, Dtsch. 52 52.12 N 9.47 E
Schulenburg, Tx., U.S. 222 29.40 N 96.54 W
Schuls
— Scuol 58 46.48 N 10.18 E

Schultz Lake ⊜ 176 64.45 N 97.30 W
Schulzendorf 54 52.22 N 13.35 E
Schulzendorf 264a 52.29 N 13.47 E
Schumacher 190 48.28 N 81.18 W
Schüpfheim 58 46.57 N 8.01 E
Schüren ◆8 263 51.30 N 7.32 E
Schussen ≃ 58 47.37 N 9.32 E
Schussenried 58 48.00 N 9.40 E
Schüttenberg ▲2 61 48.05 N 16.44 E
Schutter ≃ 58 48.44 N 7.50 E
Schüttorf 52 52.19 N 7.13 E
Schuyler, Ne., U.S. 198 41.26 N 97.03 W
Schuyler, Va., U.S. 192 37.47 N 78.41 W
Schuyler □6, Il., U.S. 219 40.07 N 90.34 W
Schuyler □6, N.Y., U.S. 210 42.23 N 76.52 W
Schuyler Lake 210 42.47 N 75.02 W
Schuylerville 210 43.06 N 73.34 W
Schuylkill □6 210 40.41 N 76.12 W
Schuylkill ≃ 208 39.53 N 75.12 W
Schuylkill Canal ⊼ 285 40.14 N 75.42 W
Schuylkill Haven 208 40.37 N 76.10 W
Schwaan 54 53.56 N 12.06 E
Schwabach 60 49.20 N 11.01 E
Schwaben □5 58 48.15 N 10.30 E
Schwaben □9 30 48.10 N 9.25 E
Schwabing ◆8 60 48.10 N 11.34 E
Schwäbische Alb ⩘ 58 48.25 N 9.30 E
Schwäbisch Gmünd 56 48.48 N 9.47 E
Schwäbisch Hall 56 49.07 N 9.44 E
Schwabmünchen 58 48.11 N 10.45 E
Schwabstedt 41 54.23 N 9.11 E
Schwadorf 61 48.04 N 16.35 E
Schwafheim 263 51.25 N 6.39 E
Schwagstorf 52 52.31 N 7.45 E
Schwaigern 56 49.08 N 9.03 E
Schwalenberg 52 51.52 N 9.11 E
Schwalm ≃ 56 51.10 N 9.25 E
Schwalmstadt 56 50.55 N 9.11 E
Schwalmtal 56 51.13 N 6.16 E
Schwanden 58 47.00 N 9.04 E
Schwandorf 60 49.20 N 12.08 E
Schwanebeck, Dtsch. 54 52.37 N 13.32 E
Schwanebeck, Dtsch. 54 51.58 N 11.07 E
Schwanenstadt 60 48.03 N 13.46 E
Schwanenwerder ◆8 264a 52.27 N 13.10 E
Schwaner, Pegunungan ⩘ 112 0.40 S 112.40 E
Schwanewede 52 53.14 N 8.35 E
Schwangau 58 47.35 N 10.44 E
Schwansen ◆1 41 54.35 N 9.50 E
Schwante 264a 52.44 N 13.05 E
Schwarme 52 52.54 N 9.01 E
Schwarmstedt 52 52.40 N 9.37 E
Schwartau ≃ 54 53.56 N 10.41 E
Schwarza, Dtsch. 54 50.38 N 10.32 E
Schwarza, Dtsch. 54 50.41 N 11.19 E
Schwarza ≃, Dtsch. 54 50.41 N 11.19 E
Schwarza ≃, Öst. 61 47.43 N 16.13 E
Schwarzach, Dtsch. 60 48.55 N 12.49 E
Schwarzach, Öst. 58 47.27 N 9.45 E
Schwarzach ≃ 60 49.36 N 12.08 E
Schwarzach im Pongau 64 47.19 N 13.09 E
Schwarzbach ≃, Dtsch. 56 49.16 N 7.18 E
Schwarzbach ≃, Dtsch. 263 51.19 N 6.44 E
Schwarzburg 54 50.38 N 11.12 E
Schwarze Elster ≃ 54 51.49 N 12.51 E
Schwarzer Luber ≃ 60 49.00 N 12.03 E
Schwarzenbach am Wald 54 50.17 N 11.37 E
Schwarzenbach an der Saale 54 50.13 N 11.56 E
Schwarzenbek 54 53.30 N 10.29 E
Schwarzenberg 54 50.32 N 12.47 E
Schwarzenberg ◆8 263 51.24 N 6.42 E
Schwarzenberg Park ♦ 264b 48.14 N 16.15 E
Schwarzenborn 56 50.37 N 9.58 E
Schwarzenbruck 60 49.21 N 11.14 E
Schwarzenburg 58 46.49 N 7.21 E
Schwarzenfeld 60 49.23 N 12.08 E
Schwarzer Berg ▲2 263 51.41 N 7.12 E
Schwarzer Mann ▲ 56 50.15 N 6.21 E
Schwarzer Regen ≃ 60 49.10 N 12.50 E
Schwarzes Meer
— Black Sea ▼2 22 43.00 N 35.00 E
Schwarzheide 54 51.29 N 13.51 E
Schwarzkogel ▲ 61 47.25 N 15.25 E
Schwarzrand ⩘ 156 25.37 S 16.50 E
Schwarzriegel ▲ 60 49.14 N 12.56 E
Schwarzsee 58 46.40 N 7.20 E
Schwarzwald (Black Forest) ⩘ 58 48.00 N 8.15 E
Schwarzwälder Hochwald ⩘3 56 49.39 N 6.55 E
Schwatka Mountains ⩘ 180 67.25 N 157.00 W
Schwaz 64 47.20 N 11.42 E
Schwechat 61 48.08 N 16.29 E
Schwechat ≃ 61 48.08 N 16.34 E
Schwedeneck 41 54.27 N 10.05 E
Schweden
— Sweden □1 24 62.00 N 15.00 E
Schwedt 54 53.03 N 14.17 E
Schweez 54 53.53 N 12.24 E
Schwefflinghausen 263 51.16 N 7.25 E
Schwegenheim 56 49.16 N 8.20 E
Schwei 52 53.24 N 8.21 E
Schweich 56 49.49 N 6.45 E
Schweidnitz
— Świdnica 30 50.51 N 16.29 E
Schweighausen 58 48.13 N 7.57 E
Schweighouse-sur-Moder 56 48.49 N 7.44 E
Schweinfurt 56 50.03 N 10.14 E
Schweinitz 54 51.48 N 13.01 E
Schweinrich 54 53.10 N 12.37 E
Schweizer Nationalpark ♦ 58 46.38 N 10.11 E
Schweizer-Reneke 158 27.11 S 25.18 E
Schweiz
— Switzerland □1 58 47.00 N 8.00 E
Schwelm 56 51.17 N 7.17 E
Schwendi 58 48.10 N 9.58 E
Schwenke 263 51.11 N 7.26 E
Schwenksville 285 40.16 N 75.28 W
Schwepnitz 54 51.20 N 13.57 E
Schwerin, Dtsch. 54 53.38 N 11.25 E
Schwerin, Dtsch. 263 51.33 N 7.20 E
Schweriner See ⊜ 54 53.45 N 11.28 E
Schwertberg 61 48.16 N 14.35 E
Schwerte 56 51.26 N 7.34 E
Schwetzingen 56 49.23 N 8.34 E
Schweyen 56 49.23 N 7.28 E
Schwieberdingen 58 48.52 N 9.04 E
Schwielochsee ⊜ 54 52.03 N 14.12 E
Schwielowsee ⊜ 264a 52.20 N 12.57 E
Schwitten 263 51.27 N 7.48 E
Schwyz 58 47.02 N 8.40 E
Schwyz □3 58 47.05 N 8.40 E
Sciacca 70 37.31 N 13.03 E
Sciara 70 37.55 N 13.46 E
Sciaves (Schabs) 64 46.46 N 11.40 E
Scicli 70 36.47 N 14.42 E
Scie ≃ 50 49.55 N 1.02 E
Science and Industry, Museum of ⊍ 278 41.47 N 87.35 W
Sciez 58 46.20 N 6.23 E
Scigliano 68 39.08 N 16.19 E
Ščigry 78 51.53 N 36.55 E
Scilla 68 38.15 N 15.44 E
Scilly, Isles of II 42a 49.55 N 6.20 W
Ščinawa 30 51.25 N 16.27 E
Scio, N.Y., U.S. 210 42.10 N 77.59 W
Scio, Oh., U.S. 214 40.23 N 81.05 W
Scio, Or., U.S. 202 44.42 N 122.50 W
Scionzier 58 46.03 N 6.34 E

Sciota 210 40.56 N 75.19 W
Scioto □6 218 38.48 N 83.01 W
Scioto ≃ 188 38.44 N 83.01 W
Scioto Brush Creek ≃ 218 38.50 N 83.01 W
Scipio, In., U.S. 218 39.05 N 85.43 W
Scipio, Ut., U.S. 200 39.14 N 112.06 W
Scipio Center 210 42.47 N 76.34 W
Scippo Creek ≃ 218 39.31 N 82.59 W
Ščit ▲ 36 44.02 N 17.47 E
Ščitkoviči 76 53.13 N 27.59 E
Scituate 207 42.11 N 70.43 W
Scituate Reservoir ⊜1 207 41.47 N 71.36 W
Sclafani Bagni 70 37.49 N 13.51 E
Scobey 202 48.47 N 105.25 W
Scoffera, Passo della ⟩⟨ 62 44.29 N 9.07 E
Scofield Reservoir ⊜1 200 39.47 N 111.09 W
Scoglitti ◆8 70 36.53 N 14.26 E
Ščokino 76 54.01 N 37.31 E
Scole 42 52.22 N 1.10 E
Ščolkovo 82 55.55 N 38.00 E
Scoltenna ≃ 64 44.15 N 10.50 E
Scolt Head ⩥ 42 52.58 N 0.42 E
Scone 166 32.03 S 150.52 E
Scooba 194 32.49 N 88.28 W
Scopello 62 45.46 N 8.06 E
Scordia 70 37.18 N 14.51 E
Scoresby 274b 37.54 S 145.14 E
Scorrano, It. 66 42.35 N 13.49 E
Scorrano, It. 68 40.05 N 18.18 E
Ščors 78 51.49 N 31.59 E
Ščorsk 78 48.22 N 34.06 E
Scorzè 64 45.34 N 12.06 E
Scotch ≃ 206 45.27 N 74.59 W
Scotch Plains 210 40.39 N 74.23 W
Scotchtown 210 41.29 N 74.21 W
Scotia, Ne., U.S. 198 41.27 N 98.42 W
Scotia, N.Y., U.S. 210 42.49 N 73.57 W
Scotia Lake ⊜ 190 47.05 N 81.23 W
Scotian Shelf ◆4 16 44.00 N 62.00 W
Scotia Ridge ◆3 18 54.00 S 50.00 W
Scotia Sea ▼2 18 56.00 S 40.00 W
Scotland, On., Can. 212 43.01 N 80.22 W
Scotland, Pa., U.S. 208 39.58 N 77.35 W
Scotland, S.D., U.S. 198 43.08 N 97.43 W
Scotland, Tx., U.S. 196 33.40 N 98.28 W
Scotland □8 28 57.00 N 4.00 W
Scotland Neck 192 36.07 N 77.25 W
Scotland Run ≃ 285 39.39 N 75.03 W
Scotlandville 194 30.31 N 91.10 W
Ščot'ovo 83 48.09 N 39.04 E
Scotrun 210 41.04 N 75.19 W
Scotsburn 186 45.39 N 62.51 W
Scotstown 206 45.32 N 71.17 W
Scott, Sk., Can. 184 52.23 N 108.50 W
Scott, Ms., U.S. 194 33.35 N 91.04 W
Scott, Oh., U.S. 216 40.59 N 84.35 W
Scott □6, Il., U.S. 219 39.38 N 90.27 W
Scott □6, In., U.S. 218 38.41 N 85.46 W
Scott □6, Ky., U.S. 218 38.18 N 84.35 W
Scott ≃ 204 41.48 N 123.02 W
Scott, Cape ⩥ 182 50.47 N 128.26 W
Scott, Mount ▲, Ok., U.S. 196 34.44 N 98.32 W
Scott, Mount ▲, Or., U.S. 202 42.56 N 122.01 W
Scott Air Force Base ■ 219 38.32 N 89.52 W
Scott Base ⊍3 9 77.50 S 166.25 E
Scottburgh 158 30.19 S 30.40 E
Scott City, Ks., U.S. 198 38.28 N 100.54 W
Scott City, Mo., U.S. 194 37.13 N 89.31 W
Scott Cove c 276 41.03 N 73.28 W
Scott Creek ≃ 226 37.02 N 122.13 W
Scottdale, Mi., U.S. 216 42.03 N 86.27 W
Scottdale, Pa., U.S. 214 40.06 N 79.35 W
Scotter 44 53.29 N 0.40 W
Scott Haven 279b 40.15 N 79.47 W
Scott Island I, Ant. 9 67.24 S 179.55 W
Scott Island I, On., Can. 212 44.36 N 76.20 W
Scott Islands II 182 50.48 N 128.40 W
Scott Lake 220 25.56 N 80.13 W
Scott Lake ⊜ 202 44.11 N 115.47 W
Scott Mountain ▲ 202 44.21 N 112.50 W
Scott Peak ▲ 160 14.00 S 121.50 E
Scott Reef ▼2 284c 38.58 N 77.12 W
Scott Run ≃ 216 42.11 N 85.24 W
Scotts 198 41.52 N 103.40 W
Scottsbluff
Scotts Bluff National Monument ♦ 198 41.49 N 103.41 W
Scottsboro 194 34.40 N 86.02 W
Scottsburg, In., U.S. 218 38.41 N 85.46 W
Scottsburg, N.Y., U.S. 210 42.40 N 77.43 W
Scottsdale, Austl. 166 41.10 S 147.31 E
Scottsdale, Az., U.S. 200 33.30 N 111.53 W
Scotts Flat Reservoir ⊜1 226 39.17 N 120.55 W
Scotts Head ⩥ 240d 15.13 N 61.23 W
Scotts Hill 194 35.31 N 88.15 W
Scotts Level Branch ≃ 284b 39.22 N 76.45 W
Scottsmoor 220 28.46 N 80.53 W
Scotts Valley 226 37.03 N 122.00 W
Scottsville, Ky., U.S. 194 36.45 N 86.11 W
Scottsville, N.Y., U.S. 210 43.01 N 77.44 W
Scott Township 279b 40.23 N 80.11 W
Scottville, Il., U.S. 219 39.29 N 90.06 W
Scottville, Mi., U.S. 190 43.57 N 86.16 W
Scourie 46 58.20 N 5.08 W
Scout Lake 184 49.22 N 106.00 W
Scrabster 46 58.37 N 3.32 W
Scranton, Ia., U.S. 198 42.01 N 94.32 W
Scranton, N.Y., U.S. 210 42.44 N 78.50 W
Scranton, N.D., U.S. 198 46.08 N 103.08 W
Scranton, Pa., U.S. 210 41.24 N 75.39 W
Scremerston 44 55.44 N 1.59 W
Screven 192 31.29 N 82.01 W
Screw ≃ 164 3.55 S 142.50 E
Scribner 198 41.40 N 96.39 W
Scridain, Loch c 46 56.21 N 6.07 W
Scripps Institution of Oceanography ⊍3 228 32.52 N 117.15 W
Scrivia ≃ 62 45.03 N 8.54 E
Scroggins 222 32.58 N 95.11 W
Scrooby 44 53.25 N 1.01 W
Scrub Island I 240m 18.28 N 64.31 W
Ščučin 76 53.36 N 24.45 E
Ščučinsk 86 52.56 N 70.12 E
Ščučje, Ross. 78 51.45 N 40.29 E
Ščučje, Ross. 80 51.46 N 40.29 E
Ščučje, Ross. 86 55.17 N 63.59 E
Ščučje Ozero 86 56.28 N 56.38 E
Scugog ≃ 212 44.24 N 78.45 W
Scugog, Lake ⊜ 212 44.10 N 78.51 W
Scugog Indian Reserve ◆4 212 44.11 N 78.54 W
Scugog Island I 212 44.10 N 78.53 W
Ščukino 82 54.28 N 37.01 E
Scunthorpe 44 53.36 N 0.38 W
Scuol (Schuls) 58 46.48 N 10.18 E
Scuppernong ≃ 192 35.56 N 76.18 W
Ščurcola Marsicana 66 42.03 N 13.20 E
Ščurovo 82 55.03 N 38.49 E
Scurrival Point ⩥ 46 57.01 N 7.31 W
Scurry 222 32.31 N 96.23 W
Scutari, Lake ⊜ 38 42.12 N 19.18 E
Scutari
— Shkodër 38 42.05 N 19.30 E
Sè ◆8 287b 23.33 S 46.37 W
Seabeck 224 47.38 N 122.51 W
Sea Bird Island I 224 49.15 N 121.45 W
Seabird Island Indian Reserve ◆4 182 49.17 N 121.42 W
Seaboard 192 36.29 N 77.26 W
Sea Bright 276 40.21 N 73.58 W
Seabrook, Md., U.S. 284c 38.58 N 76.50 W
Seabrook, N.J., U.S. 208 39.30 N 75.13 W

Symbols in the index entries represent the broad categories identified in the key at the right. Symbols with superior numbers (⩘1) identify subcategories (see complete key on page I · 1).

Symbole im Register stellen die rechts im Schlüssel erklärten Kategorien dar. Symbole mit hochgestellten Ziffern (⩘1) bezeichnen Unterabteilungen einer Kategorie (vgl. vollständiger Schlüssel auf Seite I · 1).

Los símbolos incluídos en el texto del índice representan las grandes categorías identificadas con la clave a la derecha. Los símbolos con numeros en su parte superior (⩘1) identifican las subcategorías (véase la clave completa en la página I · 1).

Les symboles de l'index représentent les catégories indiquées dans la légende à droite. Les symboles suivis d'un indice (⩘1) représentent des sous-catégories (voir légende complète à la page I · 1).

Os símbolos incluídos no texto do índice representam as grandes categorias identificadas com a chave à direita. Os símbolos com números em sua parte superior (⩘1) identificam as subcategorias (veja-se a chave completa à página I · 1).

▲ Mountain	Berg	Montaña	Montagne	Montanha
⩘ Mountains	Gebirge	Montañas	Montagnes	Montanhas
⟩⟨ Pass	Paß	Paso	Col	Passo
V Valley, Canyon	Tal, Cañon	Valle, Cañón	Vallée, Canyon	Vale, Canhão
≃ Plain	Ebene	Llano	Plaine	Planície
⩥ Cape	Kap	Cabo	Cap	Cabo
I Island	Insel	Isla	Île	Ilha
II Islands	Inseln	Islas	Îles	Ilhas
◆ Other Topographic Features	Andere Topographische Objekte	Otros Elementos Topográficos	Autres données topographiques	Outros acidentes topográficos

ESPAÑOL — Nombre | Página | Lat.°′ | Long.°′ W = Oeste
FRANÇAIS — Nom | Page | Lat.°′ | Long.°′ W = Ouest
PORTUGUÊS — Nome | Página | Lat.°′ | Long.°′ W = Oeste

Seabrook, Tx., U.S. 222 29.33 N 95.01 W
Seabrook, Lake ⊜ 162 30.56 S 119.40 E
Sea Cliff 210 40.50 N 73.38 W
Seacock Swamp ≃ 208 36.48 N 76.51 W
Seacombe 262 53.25 N 3.01 W
Sea Dog Island I 276 40.36 N 73.35 W
Seadrift 196 28.30 N 96.47 W
Seaford, Eng., U.K. 42 50.46 N 0.06 E
Seaford, De., U.S. 208 38.38 N 75.36 W
Seaford, N.Y., U.S. 276 40.39 N 73.29 W
Seaford, Va., U.S. 208 37.11 N 76.26 W
Seaford Creek ≃ 276 40.38 N 73.29 W
Seaforth, Austl. 274a 33.48 S 151.15 E
Seaforth, On., Can. 190 43.33 N 81.24 W
Seaforth, Eng., U.K. 262 53.28 N 3.01 W
Seaforth, Loch ⊂ 46 57.54 N 6.40 W
Seafox Seamount ✣[3] 14 30.30 S 172.45 W
Seager Wheeler Lake ⊜ 184 54.27 N 103.30 W
Seagoville 222 32.38 N 96.32 W
Seagraves 196 32.56 N 102.33 W
Seaham 44 54.52 N 1.21 W
Seaholme 274b 37.52 S 144.50 E
Seahorse Breakers ✣[2] 112 5.30 N 112.37 E
Seahorse Point › 176 63.47 N 80.09 W
Seahouses 44 55.35 N 1.38 W
Seahurst 224 47.28 N 122.22 W
Sea Island I 224 49.12 N 123.10 W
Sea Islands II 192 31.20 N 81.20 W
Sea Isle City 208 39.09 N 74.41 W
Seal 260 51.17 N 0.14 E
Seal ≃ 176 59.04 N 94.48 W
Seal, Cape › 158 34.07 S 23.25 E
Sea Lake 166 35.30 S 142.51 E
Sealand 262 53.12 N 2.58 W
Sealark Channel ɯ 175e 9.18 S 160.20 E
Seal Bay ⊂ 9 71.40 S 12.25 W
Seal Beach 228 33.44 N 118.06 W
Seal Beach National Wildlife Refuge ◆[4] 280 33.45 N 118.03 W
Seal Cays II 238 21.10 N 71.38 W
Seal Cove, N.B., Can. 186 44.39 N 66.51 W
Seal Cove, Nf., Can. 186 49.56 N 56.23 W
Sealdah Railroad Station ◆[5] 272b 22.34 N 88.23 E
Seale 194 32.17 N 85.10 W
Sealevel 192 34.51 N 76.23 W
Seal Island I 186 43.25 N 66.01 W
Seal Islands II 282 38.03 N 122.03 W
Seal Lake ⊜ 176 54.18 N 61.40 W
Seal Rocks II[1] 282 37.47 N 122.31 W
Sealston 208 38.15 N 77.19 W
Sealy 222 29.46 N 96.09 W
Seaman 218 38.56 N 83.34 W
Seamer 44 54.14 N 0.26 W
Seanor 214 40.13 N 78.54 W
Seara 252 27.07 S 52.17 W
Searchlight 204 35.27 N 114.55 W
Searcy 194 35.15 N 91.44 W
Searles Lake ⊜ 204 35.43 N 117.20 W
Sears Lake ⊜ 281 42.35 N 83.39 W
Searsport 188 44.27 N 68.55 W
Sears Tower ☉ 278 41.53 N 87.38 W
Searsville Lake ⊜ 282 37.24 N 122.14 W
Seascale 44 54.24 N 3.29 W
Seashore State Park ♠ 208 36.54 N 76.02 W
Seaside, Ca., U.S. 226 36.36 N 121.51 W
Seaside, Or., U.S. 224 45.59 N 123.55 W
Seaside Park 208 39.55 N 74.04 W
Seaside Park ♠ 276 41.10 N 73.12 W
Seaton, Eng., U.K. 42 50.43 N 3.05 W
Seaton, Eng., U.K. 44 53.54 N 0.14 W
Seaton, Eng., U.K. 44 54.41 N 3.33 W
Seaton ≃ 42 50.22 N 4.22 W
Seaton Delaval 44 55.04 N 1.31 W
Seaton Sluice 44 55.05 N 1.28 W
Seat Pleasant 284c 38.53 N 76.54 W
Seattle 224 47.36 N 122.19 W
Seattle, Mount ʌ 180 60.06 N 139.11 W
Seattle Heights 224 47.48 N 122.20 W
Seattle-Tacoma International Airport ⊠ 224 47.27 N 122.18 W
Seatuck National Wildlife Refuge ◆[4] 276 40.43 N 73.13 W
Seaview, Eng., U.K. 42 50.43 N 1.06 W
Sea View, Ma., U.S. 283 42.08 N 70.42 W
Seaview, N.Y., U.S. 276 40.39 N 73.09 W
Seaview, Wa., U.S. 224 46.20 N 124.03 W
Seaward Kaikoura Range ⋀ 172 42.14 S 173.39 E
Seaward Roads ɯ 174g 28.13 N 177.25 W
Sea World ♠, Fl., U.S. 220 28.25 N 81.28 W
Sea World ♠, Oh., U.S. 214 41.21 N 81.23 W
Seba 112 10.29 S 121.50 E
Sébaco 236 12.51 N 86.06 W
Sebago Lake ⊜ 188 43.50 N 70.35 W
Se Bai ≃ 110 15.13 N 104.47 E
Sebakor, Teluk ⊂ 164 3.35 S 132.50 E
Şebakung 112 1.37 S 116.26 E
Šebalin 80 47.22 N 43.36 E
Šebalino, Ross. 80 48.16 N 43.21 E
Šebalino, Ross. 86 51.17 N 85.40 E
Sebanga 114 1.24 N 101.10 E
Sebangan, Teluk ⊂ 112 3.15 S 113.30 E
Sebangka, Pulau I 112 0.07 N 104.36 E
Sébaou, Oued ≃ 34 36.55 N 3.55 E
Sebarok, Pulau I 271c 1.13 N 103.48 E
Sebastian, Fl., U.S. 220 27.46 N 80.29 W
Sebastian, Tx., U.S. 196 26.20 N 97.47 W
Sebastian, Cape › 202 42.19 N 124.26 W
Sebastian Inlet ⊂ 220 27.51 N 80.26 W
Sebastián Vizcaíno, Bahía ⊂ 232 28.00 N 114.30 W
Sebastião de Lacerda 256 22.17 S 43.35 W
Sebastopol, Austl. 169 37.36 S 143.51 E
Sebastopol, Ca., U.S. 204 38.24 N 122.49 W
Sebastopol, Ms., U.S. 194 32.34 N 89.20 W
Sebatik, Pulau I 112 4.10 N 117.45 E
Sebba 150 13.26 N 0.32 E
Sebderat 144 15.26 N 36.40 E
Sébé ≃ 152 1.02 S 13.06 E
Sebec Lake ⊜ 188 45.18 N 69.18 W
Şebeka 198 46.38 N 95.05 W
Šebekino 78 50.25 N 36.56 E
Şébékoro 150 12.57 N 8.59 W
Šebelinka 78 49.27 N 36.30 E
Seben 130 40.24 N 31.34 E
Sebenico → Šibenik 36 43.44 N 15.54 E
Sebera, Punta ʌ 71 39.03 N 8.50 E
Seberi 252 27.29 S 53.24 W
Şeberida 112 0.43 S 102.31 E
Šeberta 88 54.40 N 99.54 E
Sebeş 38 45.58 N 23.34 E
Sebesi, Pulau I 115a 5.57 S 105.30 E
Sebes Körös (Crişul Repede) ≃ 38 46.55 N 20.59 E
Sebewaing 190 43.43 N 83.27 W
Sebež 76 56.17 N 28.29 E
Sebille Manor 281 42.39 N 82.49 W
Şebinkarahisar 130 40.18 N 38.26 E
Šebiş 38 46.23 N 22.08 E
Sebnitz 54 50.58 N 14.16 E
Sebou, Oued ≃ 148 34.15 N 6.40 W
Sebree 194 37.36 N 87.31 W
Sebrell 208 36.47 N 77.07 W
Sebring, Fl., U.S. 220 27.29 N 81.26 W
Sebring, Oh., U.S. 214 40.55 N 81.01 W
Sebringville 212 43.24 N 81.04 W
Sebuku 112 4.03 N 116.56 E
Sebuku, Pulau I, Indon. 112 3.30 S 116.22 E
Sebuku, Pulau I, Indon. 115a 5.53 S 105.31 E
Şebuku, Teluk ⊂ 112 4.00 N 118.26 E
Šebunino 89 46.27 N 141.51 E
Seč 60 49.36 N 13.30 E
Seca, Ilha I 287a 22.50 S 43.11 W
Secane 285 39.55 N 75.18 W
Secang 115a 7.23 S 110.15 E
Secas, Islas II 236 7.58 N 82.02 W
Secaucus 276 40.47 N 74.03 W
Secchia ≃ 64 45.04 N 11.00 E
Sečenovo 80 55.13 N 45.54 E
Secesh ≃ 202 45.02 N 115.43 W
Séchault 56 49.16 N 4.44 E
Şechelt 182 49.28 N 123.45 W
Šechman' 76 52.32 N 40.29 E
Sechura 248 5.33 S 80.51 W
Sechura, Bahía de ⊂ 248 5.42 S 81.00 W
Sechura, Desierto de ◆[2] 248 5.50 S 80.40 W
Seckach 56 49.26 N 9.20 E
Seckau 61 47.16 N 14.47 E
Seckau ☉[1] 61 47.16 N 14.47 E
Seckauer Alpen ⋀ 61 47.20 N 14.40 E
Seckauer Zinken ʌ 61 47.20 N 14.44 E
Seclantas 252 25.18 S 66.15 W
Seclin 50 50.33 N 3.02 E
Seco ≃, Arg. 252 23.08 S 63.57 W
Seco ≃, Arg. 254 48.34 S 67.02 W
Seco ≃, Esp. 266d 41.30 N 2.09 E
Seco, Arroyo ≃, Ca., U.S. 226 36.25 N 121.20 W
Seco, Arroyo ≃, Ca., U.S. 280 34.05 N 118.13 W
Seco Creek ≃, N.M., U.S. 200 32.59 N 107.18 W
Seco Creek ≃, Tx., U.S. 196 29.02 N 99.08 W
Seco Island I 116 11.19 N 121.40 E
Second ≃ 276 40.47 N 74.09 W
Second Cliff ⩡[4] 283 42.12 N 70.43 W
Second Han-gang Bridge ◆[5] 271b 37.34 N 126.54 E
Second Herring Brook ≃ 283 42.09 N 70.47 W
Second Lake ⊜ 206 45.09 N 71.10 W
Second Mountain ʌ 208 40.33 N 76.30 W
Second San Diego Aqueduct ≍[1] 228 32.41 N 117.01 W
Second Swamp ≃ 208 37.08 N 77.12 W
Second Valley 168b 35.33 S 138.14 E
Second Watchung Mountain ʌ 276 40.55 N 74.13 W
Sečovce 30 48.43 N 21.40 E
Sečovská Polianka 30 48.47 N 21.42 E
Secretário, Ribeirão do ≃ 256 22.14 S 43.25 W
Secretary 208 38.36 N 75.56 W
Secretary Island I 172 45.15 S 166.55 E
Section 194 34.34 N 85.59 W
Secubun Island I 116 5.06 N 120.18 E
Sécure ≃ 248 15.10 S 64.52 W
Security 198 38.45 N 104.44 W
Security Square ◆[9] 284b 39.19 N 76.45 W
Séd ≃ 30 47.00 N 18.31 E
Seda, Lat. 76 57.40 N 25.46 E
Seda, Liet. 76 56.10 N 22.04 E
Seda, Zhg. 102 32.20 N 100.41 E
Seda ≃ 76 57.47 N 25.15 E
Sedah 112 10.46 S 123.12 E
Sedalia, Ab., Can. 184 51.41 N 110.40 W
Sedalia, In., U.S. 216 40.25 N 86.31 W
Sedalia, Mo., U.S. 194 38.42 N 93.13 W
Sedalia, Oh., U.S. 218 39.44 N 83.29 W
Sedan, Austl. 168b 34.35 S 139.18 E
Sedan, Fr. 56 49.42 N 4.57 E
Sedan, Ks., U.S. 198 37.07 N 96.11 W
Sedanka, Cape › 180 53.49 N 166.06 W
Sedanka Island I 180 53.50 N 166.10 W
Sedano 34 42.43 N 3.45 W
Sedano, Tanjung › 115a 7.49 S 114.27 E
Sedanovo 88 56.58 N 101.22 E
Sedari, Tanjung › 115a 5.57 S 107.18 E
Sedayu 115a 6.59 S 112.33 E
Sedbergh 44 54.20 N 2.31 W
Sedco Hills 228 33.39 N 117.24 W
Seddin 54 52.16 N 13.01 E
Seddin-Berg ʌ[2] 264a 52.24 N 13.40 E
Seddinsee ⊜ 264a 52.23 N 13.41 E
Seddon 172 41.40 S 174.05 E
Seddonville 172 41.33 S 171.59 E
Sedé Boqér 132 30.52 N 34.47 E
Sedel'nikovo 86 56.57 N 75.18 E
Séderon 62 44.12 N 5.32 E
Sederot 132 31.31 N 34.35 E
Sedgefield, Eng., U.K. 44 54.39 N 1.26 W
Sedgefield, N.J., U.S. 276 40.51 N 74.28 W
Sedgefield, N.C., U.S. 192 35.10 N 80.51 W
Sedge Island I 276 40.21 N 73.59 W
Sedgewick 182 52.46 N 111.41 W
Sedgwick, Co., U.S. 198 40.56 N 102.31 W
Sedgwick, Ks., U.S. 198 37.55 N 97.25 W
Sedgwick, Mount ʌ 200 35.11 N 108.06 W
Sédhiou 150 12.44 N 15.33 W
Sedico 64 46.06 N 12.06 E
Sedilo 71 40.10 N 8.55 E
Sedini 71 40.51 N 8.49 E
Sedlčany 30 49.40 N 14.26 E
Sedley 208 36.46 N 76.59 W
Sedlice 60 49.23 N 13.56 E
Sedlitz 54 51.33 N 14.03 E
Sedlo ʌ 54 50.36 N 14.17 E
Şedn'ov 78 51.39 N 31.34 E
Šedok 84 44.13 N 40.52 E
Sedom (Sodom) ⊥ 132 31.04 N 35.23 E
Sedona 200 34.52 N 111.45 W
Sedot Yam 132 32.29 N 34.53 E
Sedova, pik ʌ 72 73.29 N 54.58 E
Sedovo 83 47.03 N 38.10 E
Sedovo-Vasiljevka 83 47.14 N 38.08 E
Sedrata 36 36.08 N 7.32 E
Sedriano 62 45.29 N 8.58 E
Sedrina 62 45.47 N 9.38 E
Sedro Woolley 224 48.30 N 122.14 W
Sedrun 58 46.41 N 8.46 E
Şedtim 24 66.25 N 56.20 E
Šeduva 76 55.46 N 23.46 E
Sędziszów 30 50.04 N 21.41 E
See 58 47.05 N 10.28 E
Seebad Ahlbeck 54 53.56 N 14.11 E
Seebad Bansin 54 53.57 N 14.07 E
Seebad Heringsdorf 54 53.56 N 14.08 E
Seeberg, Dtsch. 264a 52.33 N 13.41 E
Seeberg, Schw. 58 47.09 N 7.40 E
Seebergsattel)(61 47.38 N 15.18 E
Seeber Lake ⊜ 184 53.52 N 93.03 W
Seeboden 64 46.49 N 13.30 E
Seebruck 64 47.56 N 12.28 E
Seebrugg 58 47.49 N 8.13 E
Seeburg 264a 52.31 N 13.07 E
Seefeld, Dtsch. 52 53.27 N 8.21 E
Seefeld, Dtsch. 54 52.37 N 13.40 E
Seefeld in Tirol 64 47.20 N 11.11 E
Seefin ʌ[2] 48 52.18 N 8.32 W
Seeg 58 47.38 N 10.36 E
Seege ≃ 54 53.04 N 11.23 E
Seehausen, Dtsch. 54 52.53 N 11.45 E
Seehausen, Dtsch. 54 52.06 N 11.17 E
Seeheim 156 26.50 S 17.45 E
Seeheim-Jugenheim 56 49.45 N 8.38 E
Seehof 264a 52.24 N 13.17 E
Seeis 156 22.29 S 17.39 E
Seekaskootch Indian Reserve ◆[4] 184 53.43 N 109.55 W
Seekoegat 158 33.03 S 22.31 E
Seekoei ≃ 158 30.18 S 25.01 E
Seekonk 207 41.48 N 71.20 W
Seelbach 58 48.18 N 7.56 E
Seeley Lake 202 47.10 N 113.29 W
Seeleys Bay 212 44.29 N 76.14 W
Seelingstädt 54 50.46 N 12.14 E
Seelow 54 52.32 N 14.23 E
Seelyville, In., U.S. 194 39.29 N 87.16 W
Seelyville, Pa., U.S. 210 41.35 N 75.17 W
Seelze 52 52.24 N 9.35 E
Seemade 144 7.10 N 48.36 E
Seemalik Butte ʌ 180 60.09 N 167.08 W
Seemenbach ≃ 56 50.17 N 8.59 E
Seemore Downs 162 30.42 S 125.15 E
Seen 58 47.29 N 8.46 E
Seengen 58 47.19 N 8.13 E
Seeon 64 47.58 N 12.26 E
Seer Green 260 51.37 N 0.36 W
Seergu 102 32.00 N 103.33 E
Seerhausen 54 51.16 N 13.15 E
Sées 50 48.36 N 0.10 E
Seesen 52 51.53 N 10.10 E
Seeshaupt 64 47.49 N 11.18 E
Seest 41 55.29 N 9.27 E
Seetal 61 47.09 N 13.57 E
Seetaler Alpen ⋀ 61 47.05 N 14.35 E
Seevetal 52 53.23 N 9.59 E
Seewalchen am Attersee 64 47.57 N 13.35 E
Seewiesen 61 47.37 N 15.16 E
Seewinkel ◆[1] 61 47.48 N 16.49 E
Seewis 58 47.00 N 9.32 E
Séez 62 45.37 N 6.48 E
Seez ≃ 58 47.07 N 9.18 E
Şefaatli 130 39.31 N 34.46 E
Šefadu 150 8.39 N 10.59 W
Sefar ⊥ 148 24.27 N 9.16 E
Sefare 156 23.02 S 27.28 E
Seferihisar 130 38.11 N 26.51 E
Séféto 150 14.08 N 9.49 W
Seffern 56 50.04 N 6.30 E
Seffner 220 27.59 N 82.17 W
Sefīd ≃ 128 37.26 N 49.55 E
Sefīd Ābeh 128 30.56 N 60.35 E
Sefrou 148 33.50 N 4.50 W
Sefton, N.Z. 172 43.15 S 172.40 E
Sefton, Eng., U.K. 262 53.30 N 2.58 W
Sefton □[8] 262 53.34 N 3.14 W
Sefton, Mount ʌ 172 43.41 S 170.03 E
Sefton Park ♠ 262 53.23 N 2.56 W
Segag 144 7.40 N 42.50 E
Segaliud ≃ 116 5.43 N 117.55 E
Segama ≃ 112 5.27 N 118.48 E
Segamat 114 2.30 N 102.49 E
Segang 100 31.58 N 114.18 E
Segangane 34 35.09 N 3.00 W
Şegarcea 38 44.06 N 23.45 E
Šegarka ≃ 86 57.16 N 84.05 E
Segbana 150 10.56 N 3.42 E
Segbwema 150 8.00 N 10.57 W
Segen ≃ 144 4.49 N 36.57 E
Segera 164 8.15 S 143.30 E
Segeri 112 4.39 S 119.33 E
Segesta ⊥ 70 37.56 N 12.50 E
Segesvár → Sighişoara 38 46.13 N 24.48 E
Segeža 24 63.44 N 34.19 E
Seggiano 66 42.56 N 11.33 E
Seggueur, Oued es V 148 31.39 N 2.26 E
Šegmas 24 64.43 N 49.14 E
Segni 66 41.41 N 13.01 E
Segno 222 30.35 N 94.41 W
Segorbe 34 39.51 N 0.29 W
Ségou 150 13.27 N 6.16 W
Şégou □[4] 150 14.00 N 5.40 E
Šegovary 24 62.23 N 42.57 E
Segovia, Col. 246 7.07 N 74.42 W
Segovia, Esp. 34 40.57 N 4.07 W
Segovia □[4] 34 41.15 N 4.00 W
Segozero, ozero ⊜ 24 63.18 N 33.45 E
Segrate 266b 45.29 N 9.19 E
Segré 32 47.41 N 0.53 W
Segre ≃ 34 41.22 N 0.20 E
Seguam Island I 180 52.17 N 172.30 W
Seguam Pass ɯ 180 52.08 N 172.45 W
Séguédine 146 20.12 N 12.59 E
Séguéla, C. Iv. 150 7.57 N 6.40 W
Séguéla, Mali 150 14.07 N 6.44 W
Séguélon 150 9.25 N 7.09 W
Séguénéga 150 13.27 N 1.58 W
Seguí 252 31.57 S 60.08 W
Seguin 196 29.34 N 97.57 W
Seguin ≃ 212 45.21 N 80.01 W
Seguine Point › 276 40.31 N 74.12 W
Segula Island I 181a 52.01 N 178.07 E
Segundo 198 37.07 N 104.45 W
Segundo ≃ 252 31.21 S 62.59 W
Seguntur 112 1.54 N 117.47 E
Segura 34 39.50 N 6.59 W
Segura ≃ 34 38.06 N 0.38 W
Segura, Sierra de ⋀ 34 38.00 N 2.43 W
Sehāni Kalān 272a 28.41 N 77.25 E
Sehāni Khurd 272a 28.42 N 77.25 E
Sehāra Bāzār 126 23.06 N 87.49 E
Sehithwa 156 20.23 S 22.45 E
Sehlabathebe 158 29.53 S 29.05 E
Sehlabathebe National Park ♠ 158 29.53 S 29.06 E
Sehma 54 50.32 N 13.00 E
Sehnde 52 52.18 N 9.57 E
Sehnkwehn 150 5.13 N 9.12 W
Sehnkwehn ≃ 150 5.12 N 9.21 W
Sehore 124 23.12 N 77.05 E
Sehwān 120 26.26 N 67.52 E
Sehyŏn-ni 98 38.20 N 127.41 E
Seia 34 40.25 N 7.42 W
Seibert 198 39.18 N 102.52 W
Seibu 268 35.50 N 139.22 E
Seiches-sur-le-Loir 32 47.35 N 0.22 W
Seidan 96 34.19 N 134.45 E
Seidersville 210 40.35 N 75.23 W
Seiersberg 61 47.01 N 15.24 E
Seiffen 54 50.39 N 13.26 E
Seifhennersdorf 54 50.56 N 14.36 E
Seignelay 50 47.54 N 3.36 E
Seigneurial, Lac ⊜ 275a 45.33 N 73.20 W
Seika 270 34.46 N 135.48 E
Seikpyu 110 20.55 N 94.47 E
Seil I 46 56.18 N 5.39 W
Seiland I 24 70.25 N 23.15 E
Seilhac 32 45.22 N 1.42 E
Seiling 196 36.08 N 98.55 W
Seillans 62 43.38 N 6.38 E
Seille ≃, Fr. 56 49.07 N 6.11 E
Seille ≃, Fr. 58 46.31 N 4.56 E
Seilo 140 12.20 N 23.50 E
Seim → Şejm ≃ 78 51.27 N 32.34 E
Sein, Île de I 32 48.02 N 4.51 W
Seinaiji 94 35.30 N 137.42 E
Seinäjoki 26 62.47 N 22.50 E
Seine □[5] 50 48.50 N 2.10 E
Seine ≃, Mb., Can. 184 49.54 N 97.07 W
Seine ≃, On., Can. 190 48.40 N 92.49 W
Seine ≃, Fr. 32 49.26 N 0.26 E
Seine, Baie de la ⊂ 32 49.30 N 0.30 W
Seine-et-Marne □[5] 50 48.30 N 3.00 E
Seine-et-Oise □[5] 50 48.45 N 2.00 E
Seine-Maritime □[5] 50 49.45 N 1.00 E
Seine-Port 50 48.33 N 2.33 E
Seine-Saint-Denis □[5] 261 48.55 N 2.30 E
Seip Mound State Memorial ⊥ 218 39.15 N 83.13 W
Seipstown 208 40.35 N 75.40 W
Seis de Septiembre → Morón 258 34.39 S 58.37 W
Seishin → Ch'ŏngjin 98 41.47 N 129.50 E
Seitenstetten 61 48.02 N 14.39 E
Seitovka 80 46.43 N 48.03 E
Seitsemisen kansallispuisto ♠ 26 61.58 N 23.20 E
Seiwa 94 34.29 N 136.30 E
Seixal 34 38.38 N 9.06 W
Seixas, Ponta do › 250 7.09 S 34.47 W
Seiz 61 47.23 N 14.55 E
Seize Îles, Lac des ⊜ 206 45.54 N 74.28 W
Sejaka 112 3.34 S 116.12 E
Sejerø I 41 55.53 N 11.09 E
Sejerø Bugt ⊂ 41 55.50 N 11.15 E
Sejm ≃ 78 51.27 N 32.34 E
Şejmčan 74 62.53 N 152.26 E
Šejno 80 53.22 N 43.12 E
Sejny 30 54.07 N 23.20 E
Sejorong 115b 9.02 S 116.48 E
Sejs 41 56.09 N 9.36 E
Sekači 80 50.30 N 43.37 E
Sekadau 112 0.01 S 110.54 E
Sekake 158 29.58 S 28.27 E
Sekampung ≃ 115a 5.36 S 105.50 E
Sekayam ≃ 112 0.07 N 110.38 E
Sekayu 112 2.51 S 103.51 E
Seke, Ityo. 144 9.56 N 38.19 E
Seke, Tan. 154 3.20 S 33.31 E
Seke-Banza 152 5.20 S 13.16 E
Sekeladi 112 2.38 S 102.14 E
Sekenke 154 4.16 S 34.10 E
Şekerli 130 37.33 N 39.22 E
Šeki (Nucha), Azer. 84 41.12 N 47.12 E
Seki, Nihon 94 35.29 N 136.55 E
Seki, Nihon 94 34.51 N 136.24 E
Seki, Tür. 130 36.24 N 29.13 E
Sekidō-san ʌ 94 36.58 N 136.59 E
Sekigahara 94 35.22 N 136.28 E
Sekigane 96 35.22 N 133.46 E
Sekijō 94 36.14 N 139.55 E
Sekima 112 1.41 S 111.31 E
Sekinomiya 96 35.22 N 134.38 E
Sekiu 224 48.15 N 124.18 W
Sekiya 270 34.27 N 135.42 E
Sekiyado 94 36.06 N 139.47 E
Seki-zaki › 96 33.15 N 131.54 E
Sekoma 156 24.41 S 23.50 E
Sekondi-Takoradi 150 4.59 N 1.43 W
Sekota 144 12.38 N 39.03 E
Sekpiegu 150 9.33 N 0.02 W
Sekretaris ≃ 269e 6.10 S 106.47 E
Şekretarka 80 52.36 N 44.11 E
Šekšema 80 58.22 N 45.11 E
Šeksna 76 59.13 N 38.30 E
Sekudai 114 1.32 N 103.40 E
Sela ≃[1] 126 21.54 N 89.39 E
Şela, Ponta da › 256 23.54 S 45.27 W
Šelabolicha 86 53.25 N 82.37 E
Şela Dingay 144 9.59 N 39.33 E
Šelagskij, mys › 74 70.06 N 170.26 E
Selah 202 46.39 N 120.31 W
Şelai ≃ 114 2.13 N 103.26 E
Šelajevo 88 56.56 N 97.42 E
Şelama 114 5.13 N 100.42 E
Šelanger 80 56.13 N 48.16 E
Selangor □[3] 114 3.20 N 101.30 E
Selangor ≃ 114 3.20 N 101.15 E
Selaön I 40 59.24 N 17.12 E
Selaphum 110 16.02 N 103.57 E
Selargius 71 39.16 N 9.10 E
Selaru, Pulau I 164 8.09 S 131.00 E
Selatan, Tanjung › 112 4.10 S 114.38 E
Sel'atin 78 47.53 N 25.12 E
Selatpanjang 114 1.00 N 102.43 E
Selawik 180 66.37 N 160.03 W
Selawik ≃ 180 66.36 N 160.20 W
Selawik Lake ⊜ 180 66.30 N 160.40 W
Selayar, Pulau I 112 6.05 S 120.30 E
Selayar, Selat ɯ 112 5.42 S 120.28 E
Selb 54 50.10 N 12.08 E
Selbeck ◆[8] 263 51.22 N 6.52 E
Selbecke ◆[8] 263 51.20 N 7.28 E
Selbitz 54 50.19 N 11.44 E
Selborne 42 51.06 N 0.56 W
Selbu 26 63.13 N 11.02 E
Selbusjøen ⊜ 26 63.14 N 10.54 E
Selby, Austl. 274b 37.55 S 145.22 E
Selby, Eng., U.K. 44 53.48 N 1.04 W
Selby, S.D., U.S. 198 45.30 N 100.01 W
Selby ◆[8] 273d 26.13 S 28.02 E
Selbyville 208 38.27 N 75.13 W
Selchow 264a 52.21 N 13.28 E
Sel'co, Ross. 24 63.18 N 41.22 E
Sel'co, Ross. 76 53.22 N 34.06 E
Selcourt 273d 26.18 S 28.27 E
Selčuga ≃ 89 49.42 N 133.20 E
Selçuk 130 37.56 N 27.22 E
Sel'cy, Ross. 76 57.57 N 35.59 E
Sel'cy, Ross. 265a 59.57 N 30.43 E
Selden, Ks., U.S. 198 39.32 N 100.34 W
Selden, N.Y., U.S. 210 40.51 N 73.02 W
Seldovia 180 59.27 N 151.43 W
Sele ≃ 68 40.29 N 14.56 E
Sele, Piana del ⩦ 68 40.33 N 14.57 E
Sele, Selat ɯ 164 1.10 S 131.05 E
Sele, Tanjung › 164 1.26 S 130.55 E
Selebi Phikwe 156 22.00 S 27.50 E
Selec 76 52.33 N 33.35 E
Şelec-Cholopejev 76 53.23 N 30.24 E
Šelechov 88 52.13 N 104.08 E
Selečn'a 76 52.23 N 34.23 E
Selection Park 273d 26.18 S 28.27 E
Selegas 71 39.34 N 9.06 E
Selemadeg 115b 8.29 S 115.02 E
Selembao 273b 4.22 S 15.17 E
Selemdža ≃ 89 51.42 N 128.53 E
Şelemdžinsk 89 52.36 N 131.08 E
Šelemeti 80 57.27 N 48.07 E
Selendi 130 38.45 N 28.53 E
Selenduma 88 50.55 N 106.10 E
Selenga (Selenge) ≃ 88 52.16 N 106.16 E
Selenge, Mong. 88 49.25 N 103.59 E
Selenge, Zaïre 152 1.58 S 18.11 E
Selenge □[4] 88 49.30 N 106.30 E
Selenge (Selenga) ≃ 88 52.16 N 106.16 E
Selenginsk 88 52.06 N 107.01 E
Selenicë 38 40.32 N 19.38 E
Selenn'ach ≃ 74 67.48 N 144.54 E
Selent 54 54.17 N 10.26 E
Selenter See ⊜ 54 54.17 N 10.28 E
Sélestat (Schlettstadt) 58 48.16 N 7.27 E
Seletar ≃ 271c 1.25 N 103.52 E
Seletar, Pulau I 271c 1.27 N 103.52 E
Seletar Airport ⊠ 271c 1.16 N 103.53 E
Seletar Hills 271c 1.23 N 103.53 E
Seletar Reservoir ⊜[1] 271c 1.24 N 103.48 E
Selety ≃ 86 53.06 N 73.22 E
Seletyteniz, ozero ⊜ 86 53.15 N 73.15 E
Selezen'ovo, Ross. 26 60.45 N 28.39 E
Selezen'ovo, Ross. 76 59.12 N 42.18 E
Selezni, Ross. 76 55.39 N 31.29 E
Selezni, Ross. 80 52.48 N 41.15 E
Selezn'ovo 76 60.45 N 28.39 E
Self Defense Fleet Headquarters ■ 268 35.18 N 139.38 E
Selfoss 24a 63.56 N 20.57 W
Selfridge 198 46.02 N 100.55 W
Selfridge Air National Guard Base ■ 281 42.36 N 82.49 W
Selghar 272c 18.57 N 73.02 E
Sel'gon 89 49.36 N 135.26 E
Sélibaby 150 15.10 N 12.11 W
Şelichino 89 50.22 N 137.38 E
Šelichova, zaliv ⊂ 74 60.00 N 158.00 E
Šelichovo 88 55.42 N 97.41 E
Selidovo 83 48.08 N 37.18 E
Seligenthal 54 50.45 N 10.28 E
Seliger, ozero ⊜ 76 57.13 N 33.05 E
Seligman, Az., U.S. 200 35.19 N 112.52 W
Seligman, Mo., U.S. 194 36.31 N 93.56 W
Selim 114 3.51 N 101.29 E
Selimbau 112 0.37 N 112.08 E
Selimiye 130 37.24 N 27.40 E
Selim River 114 3.50 N 101.24 E
Selínia 267c 37.56 N 23.32 E
Selinsgrove 208 40.47 N 76.51 W
Selinunte ⊥, It. 36 37.35 N 12.49 E
Selinunte ⊥, It. 70 37.35 N 12.49 E
Seliščе, Ross. 24 64.58 N 46.18 E
Seliščе, Ross. 76 56.53 N 33.16 E
Selitrennoje 80 47.11 N 47.27 E
Selivanovskaja 80 48.52 N 41.42 E
Seližarovo 76 56.51 N 33.27 E
Selje 26 62.03 N 5.22 E
Seljord 26 59.29 N 8.37 E
Selkämeri (Bottenhavet) ⊂ 26 62.00 N 20.00 E
Selke ≃ 54 51.52 N 11.14 E
Selkirk, Mb., Can. 184 50.09 N 96.52 W
Selkirk, On., Can. 212 42.49 N 79.56 W
Selkirk, Scot., U.K. 46 55.33 N 2.50 W
Selkirk, N.Y., U.S. 210 42.32 N 73.48 W
Selkirk Mountains ⋀ 182 51.00 N 117.40 W
Selkirk Provincial Park ♠ 212 42.49 N 79.58 W
Selkirk Shores State Park ♠ 212 43.33 N 76.12 W
Šelkovka 82 55.32 N 36.22 E
Šelkovskaja 84 43.30 N 46.22 E
Sella 64 46.00 N 11.25 E
Sella, Monte ʌ 64 46.40 N 12.02 E
Sella, Paso di)(64 46.30 N 11.45 E
Sella di Corno 66 42.21 N 13.14 E
Sellano 66 42.54 N 12.55 E
Selle ≃ 50 49.54 N 2.17 E
Seller Lake ⊜ 184 55.00 N 94.32 W
Sellero 64 46.03 N 10.20 E
Sellers 192 34.17 N 79.28 W
Sellersburg 218 38.23 N 85.45 W
Sellersville 208 40.21 N 75.18 W
Selles-sur-Cher 50 47.16 N 1.33 E
Sellia Marina 68 38.55 N 16.45 E
Sellières 58 46.50 N 5.34 E
Sellin 54 54.22 N 13.41 E
Sells 200 31.54 N 111.52 W
Selly Oak ◆[8] 42 52.25 N 1.52 W
Selm 52 51.42 N 7.28 E
Selma, Al., U.S. 194 32.24 N 87.01 W
Selma, Ca., U.S. 226 36.34 N 119.36 W
Selma, In., U.S. 218 40.11 N 85.16 W
Selma, N.C., U.S. 192 35.32 N 78.17 W
Selman City 222 32.11 N 94.58 W
Selmer 194 35.10 N 88.35 W
Selmigerheide ◆[8] 263 51.38 N 7.47 E
Selmont 194 32.23 N 87.01 W
Selmsdorf 54 53.48 N 10.50 E
Şelommes 50 47.45 N 1.12 E
Šelon' ≃ 76 58.14 N 30.50 E
Seloncourt 58 47.28 N 6.52 E
Selong 115b 8.39 S 116.32 E
Şelongey 58 47.35 N 5.10 E
Šelopugino 88 51.39 N 117.33 E
Selouane 34 35.04 N 2.58 W
Selous, Mount ʌ 180 62.57 N 132.31 W
Selous Game Reserve ◆[4] 154 9.10 S 37.10 E
Selsdon ◆[8] 260 51.21 N 0.04 W
Selsey 42 50.44 N 0.48 W
Selsey Bill › 42 50.43 N 0.48 W
Selsingen 52 53.22 N 9.13 E
Selston 44 53.04 N 1.20 W
Selters 56 50.32 N 7.44 E
Selty 80 57.19 N 52.10 E
Seltz 56 48.53 N 8.06 E
Selu, Pulau I 164 7.32 S 130.54 E
Selva, Arg. 252 29.46 S 62.03 W
Selva, It. 64 46.33 N 11.46 E
Sel'vačevo 82 55.25 N 37.57 E
Selva di Cadore 64 46.27 N 12.02 E
Selvagens, Ilhas II 148 30.05 N 15.55 W
Selvas ◆[3] 242 5.00 S 68.00 W
Selvino 62 45.48 N 9.45 E
Selway ≃ 202 46.08 N 115.36 W
Selwyn 166 21.32 S 140.30 E
Selwyn, Mount ʌ 182 55.59 N 123.36 W
Selwyn, Passage ɯ 175f 16.03 S 168.12 E
Selwyn Lake ⊜ 176 59.55 N 104.35 W
Selwyn Mountains ⋀ 180 63.10 N 130.20 W
Selwyn Range ⋀ 166 21.35 S 140.35 E
Şelz ≃ 56 49.59 N 8.02 E
Šemacha, Azer. 84 40.38 N 48.39 E
Šemacha, Ross. 86 56.15 N 59.16 E
Semai, Pulau I 164 3.08 S 132.30 E
Semakau, Pulau I 271c 1.12 N 103.46 E
Seman ≃ 38 40.56 N 19.24 E
Semanggol 114 4.57 N 100.38 E
Şemangka, Teluk ⊂ 112 5.36 S 104.42 E
Šemanicha 80 57.18 N 45.24 E
Semans 184 51.25 N 104.44 W
Semanu 115a 8.00 S 110.39 E
Semarang 115a 6.58 S 110.25 E
Semaria 124 24.16 N 79.54 E
Sematan 112 1.48 N 109.46 E
Semau, Pulau I 112 10.13 S 123.22 E
Semayang, Kenohan ⊜ 112 0.14 S 116.28 E
Sembabule 154 0.05 S 31.27 E
Sembadel 62 45.16 N 3.41 E
Sembakung ≃ 112 3.47 N 117.30 E
Sembawang 271c 1.27 N 103.50 E
Sembé 152 1.39 N 14.36 E
Semberong ≃ 114 2.27 N 103.37 E
Semblançay 50 47.30 N 0.35 E
Sembo ≃ 152 7.42 S 13.01 E
Semcy 76 52.51 N 33.28 E
Şemdinli 128 37.18 N 44.35 E
Šemejkino 83 48.19 N 39.32 E
Semeliškės 76 54.40 N 24.40 E
Semenanjung Malaysia □[9] 114 4.00 N 102.00 E
Semendua 152 3.11 S 18.05 E
Semène ≃ 62 45.23 N 4.13 E
Semenicului, Munţii ⋀ 38 45.05 N 22.05 E
Semenyih 114 2.57 N 101.51 E
Semertak 89 52.57 N 132.34 E
Şemeru, Gunung ʌ 115a 8.06 S 112.55 E
Šemetovo 82 54.28 N 38.30 E
Semeževo 76 52.58 N 27.00 E
Semiahmoo Bay ⊂ 224 48.58 N 122.48 W
Semibalki 83 47.00 N 39.03 E
Semibratovo 80 57.18 N 39.32 E
Semibugry 80 46.11 N 48.16 E
Semichi Islands II 181a 52.42 N 174.00 E
Semides'atnoje 78 51.21 N 38.44 E
Semidi Islands II 180 56.07 N 156.44 W
Semigorsk 88 56.42 N 104.41 E
Semijarka 86 50.54 N 78.20 E
Semikarakorsk 80 47.31 N 40.48 E
Semilej 80 53.57 N 45.21 E
Semilovo 80 55.04 N 42.10 E
Semiluki 78 51.41 N 39.02 E
Semily 30 50.36 N 15.20 E
Seminara 68 38.20 N 15.52 E
Seminary 194 31.33 N 89.29 W
Seminoe Reservoir ⊜[1] 200 42.00 N 106.50 W
Seminoe State Park ♠ 202 42.05 N 106.55 W
Seminole, Fl., U.S. 220 27.50 N 82.47 W
Seminole, Ok., U.S. 196 35.13 N 96.40 W
Seminole, Tx., U.S. 196 32.43 N 102.38 W
Seminole □[6] 220 28.45 N 81.13 W
Seminole, Lake ⊜[1] 192 30.46 N 84.50 W
Seminole Draw V 196 32.27 N 102.20 W
Seminole Park 220 27.52 N 82.45 W
Seminskij chrebet ⋀ 86 51.05 N 85.50 E
Semiozerje 88 49.52 N 110.23 E
Semioz'ornoje 86 52.22 N 64.08 E
Semioz'ornyj 88 53.44 N 120.25 E
Semipalatinsk 86 50.28 N 80.13 E
Semipalatinsk □[8] 86 49.00 N 80.00 E
Semipolka 86 54.07 N 67.16 E
Semipolki 78 50.43 N 30.56 E
Semirara Island I 116 12.04 N 121.23 E
Semisopochnoi Island I 181a 52.00 N 179.35 E
Semitau 112 0.33 N 111.58 E
Semizbugy 86 50.12 N 74.48 E
Semizbugy, gora ʌ 86 50.10 N 74.56 E
Semjany 80 56.02 N 45.59 E
Semli Kalān 124 24.10 N 76.39 E
Seml'ovo 76 55.03 N 33.58 E
Semmens Lake ⊜ 184 55.03 N 94.11 W
Semmering 61 47.38 N 15.49 E
Semnān 128 35.33 N 53.24 E
Semnān □[4] 128 35.30 N 54.00 E
Şemois ≃ 56 49.53 N 4.45 E
Šemonaicha 86 50.39 N 81.54 E
Sem'ono-Aleksandrovka 78 51.03 N 40.12 E
Sem'onov 24 56.48 N 44.30 E
Sem'onovka, Kaz. 86 51.20 N 70.46 E
Sem'onovka, Kyrg. 85 42.43 N 77.32 E
Sem'onovka, Ukr. 78 52.10 N 32.35 E
Sem'onovka, Ukr. 78 49.36 N 33.10 E
Sem'onovskoje, Ross. 82 55.03 N 37.46 E
Sem'onovskoje, Ross. 82 55.18 N 38.21 E
Šemordan 80 56.11 N 50.26 E
Sempach 58 47.08 N 8.11 E
Sempacher See ⊜ 58 47.09 N 8.09 E
Sempang Mangayau, Tanjong › 112 7.02 N 116.45 E
Semple Lake ⊜ 184 55.02 N 95.38 W
Sempol 115a 8.01 S 114.08 E
Semporna 112 4.28 N 118.36 E
Sempu, Pulau I 115a 8.26 S 112.42 E
Semuda 112 2.51 S 112.58 E
Semuliki ≃ 154 1.14 N 30.28 E
Şemur-en-Auxois 50 47.29 N 4.20 E
Šemurša 80 54.53 N 47.32 E
Šemyšejka 80 52.54 N 45.24 E
Semža 24 66.09 N 44.08 E
Sên ≃ 110 12.32 N 104.28 E
Sena, Bol. 248 11.32 S 67.11 W
Sena, Moç. 154 17.27 S 35.00 E
Senador Amaral 256 22.35 S 46.11 W
Senador Canedo 255 16.43 S 49.05 W
Senador Côrtes 256 21.48 S 42.56 W
Senador Firmino 255 20.55 S 43.06 W
Senador Guiomard 248 10.14 S 67.36 W
Senador José Bento 256 22.10 S 46.10 W
Senador José Porfirio 250 2.39 S 51.55 W
Senador Pompeu 250 5.35 S 39.22 W
Senago 266b 45.35 N 9.07 E
Senahú 236 15.24 N 89.50 W
Senai 114 1.36 N 103.39 E
Senainville 261 48.30 N 1.37 E
Senaja 112 6.45 N 117.03 E
Senaki 84 42.17 N 42.04 E
Senale 64 46.31 N 11.06 E
Senales, Val di V 64 46.45 N 10.50 E
Sena Madureira 248 9.04 S 68.40 W
Senamaninik 114 0.45 N 100.47 E
Senanayake Samudra ⊜[1] 122 7.11 N 81.29 E
Senang, Pulau I 271c 1.11 N 103.44 E
Senanga 152 16.06 S 23.16 E
Sénart, Forêt de ♠ 261 48.40 N 2.30 E
Sénas 62 43.45 N 5.05 E
Sena → Seine ≃ 32 49.26 N 0.26 E
Senate 184 49.18 N 109.41 W
Senath 194 36.08 N 90.09 W
Şenatobia 194 34.37 N 89.58 W
Šenber 86 49.46 N 66.09 E
Šenbertal 86 48.43 N 60.20 E
Senča 78 50.16 N 33.20 E
Send 260 51.17 N 0.31 W
Sendafa 144 9.07 N 39.00 E
Sendai, Nihon 92 31.49 N 130.18 E
Sendai, Nihon 92 38.15 N 140.53 E
Sendai ≃, Nihon 92 31.51 N 130.12 E
Sendai ≃, Nihon 96 35.32 N 134.11 E
Sendai-heiya ⩦ 92 38.15 N 141.00 E
Sendelingsdrif 156 28.12 S 16.53 E
Senden, Dtsch. 52 51.51 N 7.29 E
Senden, Dtsch. 58 48.19 N 10.03 E
Sendenhorst 52 51.50 N 7.49 E
Sendhwa 120 21.41 N 75.06 E
Sêndo 102 31.42 N 95.16 E
Sendurjana 120 21.32 N 78.17 E
Senduruhan 112 1.00 S 110.46 E
Sene ≃ 150 7.30 N 0.33 W
Senebui, Tanjung › 114 2.17 N 101.03 E
Senec 30 48.14 N 17.24 E
Seneca, Il., U.S. 216 41.18 N 88.36 W
Seneca, Ks., U.S. 198 39.50 N 96.03 W
Seneca, Md., U.S. 284c 39.04 N 77.17 W
Seneca, Mo., U.S. 194 36.50 N 94.36 W
Seneca, Or., U.S. 202 44.08 N 118.58 W
Seneca, Pa., U.S. 214 41.23 N 79.42 W
Seneca, S.C., U.S. 192 34.41 N 82.57 W
Seneca □[6], N.Y., U.S. 210 42.54 N 76.52 W
Seneca □[6], Oh., U.S. 214 41.07 N 83.11 W
Seneca ≃ 210 43.12 N 76.17 W
Seneca, Mount ʌ 210 42.01 N 78.49 W
Seneca Castle 210 42.53 N 77.06 W
Seneca Caverns ⩡[5] 214 41.11 N 82.53 W
Seneca Creek ⊂ 284b 39.19 N 76.22 W
Seneca Creek ≃ 196 36.36 N 102.52 W
Seneca Falls 210 42.54 N 76.47 W
Seneca Lake ⊜ 210 42.40 N 76.57 W
Seneca Mall ◆[9] 284a 42.50 N 78.47 W
Seneca State Park ♠ 208 39.08 N 77.15 W
Senecaville Lake ⊜[1] 188 39.55 N 81.25 W
Seneffe 50 50.31 N 4.15 E
Senegal (Sénégal) □[1], Afr. 134 14.00 N 14.00 W
Senegal (Sénégal) □[1], Afr. 150 14.00 N 14.00 W
Sénégal ≃ 150 15.48 N 16.32 W
Seneghe 71 40.05 N 8.36 E
Senekal 158 28.19 S 27.36 E
Senerchia 68 40.44 N 15.12 E
Senetosa, Capu di › 71 41.33 N 8.47 E
Sénez 62 43.55 N 6.24 E
Senežskoje, ozero ⊜ 82 56.12 N 37.00 E
Senftenberg 54 51.31 N 14.00 E
Senga Hill 154 9.22 S 31.12 E
Sengbachstausee ⊜[1] 263 51.08 N 7.09 E
Şengejskij, ostrov I 24 68.27 N 51.05 E
Šengel'šij 86 48.33 N 57.28 E
Sengés 255 24.06 S 49.29 W
Senggarang 114 1.45 N 103.03 E
Sênggê ≃ 120 32.28 N 79.44 E
Senghenydd 42 51.36 N 3.16 W
Sengilej 80 53.58 N 48.46 E
Sengkamang 114 0.42 N 101.55 E
Sengsengebirge ⋀ 61 47.47 N 14.15 E
Senguer ≃ 254 45.32 S 68.54 W
Sengwa ≃ 154 17.07 S 28.05 E
Sengwarden 52 53.35 N 8.02 E
Senhāti 126 22.53 N 89.33 E
Senhor do Bonfim 250 10.27 S 40.11 W
Senica 30 48.41 N 17.22 E
Senigallia 66 43.43 N 13.13 E
Senirkent 130 38.07 N 30.33 E
Senise 68 40.09 N 16.18 E
Senj 36 44.59 N 14.54 E
Senja I 24 69.20 N 17.30 E
Senjitu 98 41.56 N 116.25 E
Senjō-san ʌ 96 35.26 N 133.36 E
Senkevičevka 78 50.32 N 25.02 E
Senkobo 154 17.38 S 25.58 E
Sen'kovo 83 49.31 N 37.43 E
Şenköy 130 36.05 N 36.05 E
Šenkursk 24 62.08 N 42.53 E
Senlac 184 52.29 N 109.41 W
Şenlikköy ◆[8] 267b 40.59 N 28.47 E
Šenlis 50 49.12 N 2.35 E
Senlisse 261 48.41 N 1.59 E

Symbol	English	Deutsch	Español	Français	Português
≃	River	Fluß	Río	Rivière	Rio
≍	Canal	Kanal	Canal	Canal	Canal
ʟ	Waterfall, Rapids	Wasserfall, Stromschnellen	Cascada, Rápidos	Chute d'eau, Rapides	Cascata, Rápidos
ɯ	Strait	Meeresstraße	Estrecho	Détroit	Estreito
⊂	Bay, Gulf	Bucht, Golf	Bahía, Golfo	Baie, Golfe	Baía, Golfo
⊜	Lake, Lakes	See, Seen	Lago, Lagos	Lac, Lacs	Lago, Lagos
⩦	Swamp	Sumpf	Pantano	Marais	Pântano
⊼	Ice Features, Glacier	Eis- und Gletscherformen	Accidentes Glaciales	Formes glaciaires	Acidentes glaciares
⊽	Other Hydrographic Features	Andere Hydrographische Objekte	Otros Elementos Hidrográficos	Autres données hydrographiques	Outros acidentes hidrográficos
✣	Submarine Features	Untermeerische Objekte	Accidentes Submarinos	Formes de relief sous-marin	Acidentes submarinos
□	Political Unit	Politische Einheit	Unidad Politica	Entité politique	Unidade política
☉	Cultural Institution	Kulturelle Institution	Institución Cultural	Institution culturelle	Institução cultural
⊥	Historical Site	Historische Stätte	Sitio Histórico	Site historique	Sitio histórico
♠	Recreational Site	Erholungs- und Ferienort	Sitio de Recreo	Centre de loisirs	Area de Lazer
⊠	Airport	Flughafen	Aeropuerto	Aéroport	Aeroporto
■	Military Installation	Militäranlage	Instalación Militar	Installation militaire	Instalação militar
◆	Miscellaneous	Verschiedenes	Misceláneo	Divers	Diversos

ENGLISH / DEUTSCH

Name	Page / Seite	Lat.°′ / Breite°′	Long.°′ / Länge°′ E = Ost
Senmonorom	110	12.27 N	107.12 E
Senn, Dahr ou ⏏[4]	150	18.30 N	11.00 W
Sennaja	78	45.15 N	37.01 E
Sennan	96	34.22 N	135.17 E
Senne(Zenne) ≃	50	51.04 N	4.26 E
Sennecey-le-Grand	58	46.39 N	4.52 E
Senne II → Sennestadt	52	51.59 N	8.37 E
Sennen	42	50.04 N	5.42 W
Sennestadt	52	51.59 N	8.37 E
Senneterre	190	48.23 N	77.15 W
Senneville	275a	45.27 N	73.57 W
Sennevoy-le-Bas	50	47.48 N	4.17 E
Senno	76	54.49 N	29.43 E
Sennoj, Ross.	80	52.11 N	46.57 E
Sennoj, Ross.	80	50.16 N	43.37 E
Sennokura-yama ʌ	94	36.49 N	138.50 E
Sennori	71	40.47 N	8.35 E
Sennwald	58	47.16 N	9.30 E
Sennybridge	42	51.57 N	3.34 W
Senoia	192	33.18 N	84.33 W
Senonches	50	48.33 N	1.02 E
Senones	58	48.24 N	6.59 E
Senorbì	71	39.32 N	9.08 E
Sénou	150	12.31 N	6.56 W
Sénouire ≃	62	45.16 N	3.25 E
Şenpazar	130	41.48 N	33.16 E
Šenqunyane ≃	158	30.03 S	28.10 E
Senqu → Orange ≃	156	28.41 S	16.28 E
Senriyama	270	34.47 N	135.30 E
Sens	50	48.12 N	3.17 E
Sense ≃	58	46.54 N	7.14 E
Sensée ≃	50	50.16 N	3.06 E
Sensée, Canal de la ≋	50	50.14 N	3.17 E
Sensuntepeque	236	13.52 N	88.38 W
Şenta	38	45.56 N	20.04 E
Šentala	80	54.27 N	51.29 E
Sentani, Danau ⊜	164	2.36 S	140.34 E
Sentarum, Danau ⊜	112	0.51 N	112.06 E
Sentas	86	49.19 N	82.28 E
Sentelek	86	51.13 N	83.44 E
Şentery	154	5.22 S	25.45 E
Šentilj	61	46.41 N	15.40 E
Sentinel	196	35.09 N	99.10 W
Sentinel Butte ʌ	198	46.53 N	103.50 W
Sentinel Peak ʌ	182	54.54 N	121.57 W
Sentinel Range ⩘	9	78.10 S	85.30 W
Şentino ≃	66	43.24 N	12.59 E
Šentjur	36	46.13 N	15.24 E
Sentolo	115a	7.50 S	110.13 E
Sentosa I	271c	1.15 N	103.50 E
Sento Sé	250	9.51 S	41.51 W
Sentsū-zan ʌ	96	35.09 N	133.11 E
Senyavin Islands II	14	6.55 N	158.00 E
Senye	152	1.34 N	9.50 E
Şenyurt	130	37.06 N	40.40 E
Šenzaki-wan c	96	34.24 N	131.15 E
Sen-zan ʌ	96	34.21 N	134.51 E
Senzig	54	52.17 N	13.39 E
Senzu-dake ʌ	270	34.57 N	135.52 E
Seo de Urgel	34	42.21 N	1.28 E
Seohāra	124	29.13 N	78.35 E
Seolag-san Kukrip Kongwŏn ♦	98	38.09 N	128.24 E
Seon	58	47.21 N	8.10 E
Seonāth ≃	122	21.44 N	82.28 E
Seoni	124	22.05 N	79.32 E
Seoni Mālwa	124	22.27 N	77.28 E
Seorīnārāyan	120	21.44 N	82.35 E
Seoul Bridge ◆[5]	271b	37.32 N	126.56 E
Seoul National University ʊ[2]	271b	37.28 N	126.57 E
Seoul → Sŏul	98	37.33 N	126.58 E
Seoul Stadium ♦	271b	37.35 N	127.02 E
Seoul Station ◆[5]	271b	37.34 N	126.58 E
Sepahat	114	1.34 N	101.53 E
Sepang	114	2.42 N	101.45 E
Sepanjang, Pulau I	112	7.10 S	115.50 E
Separation Creek ≃	200	41.59 N	107.28 W
Separation Point ›	172	40.47 S	173.00 E
Sepasu	112	0.43 N	117.35 E
Sepatini ≃	248	7.36 S	65.24 W
Sépeaux	50	47.57 N	3.14 E
Sepetiba ◆[8]	256	22.58 S	43.42 W
Şepetiba, Baía de c	256	23.00 S	43.48 W
Šepetovka	78	50.11 N	27.04 E
Sepi	175e	8.33 S	159.50 E
Sepik ≃	164	3.51 S	144.34 E
Sepino	66	41.24 N	14.37 E
Sep'o	98	38.39 N	127.22 E
Sępólno Krajeńskie	30	53.28 N	17.32 E
Sépone → Muang Xépôn	110	16.41 N	106.14 E
Sepopa	156	18.13 S	22.13 E
Sępopol	30	54.15 N	21.00 E
Sepoti ≃	248	6.43 S	61.38 W
Sepotuba ≃	248	15.56 S	57.39 W
Seppeltsfield	168b	34.30 S	138.54 E
Seppenrade	52	51.46 N	7.23 E
Sepphoris → Ẓippori	132	32.45 N	35.17 E
Seppois-le-Bas	58	47.33 N	7.10 E
Septeuil	261	48.54 N	1.41 E
Sept Frères, Lac des ⊜	206	46.20 N	75.10 W
Sept-Îles (Seven Islands)	186	50.12 N	66.23 W
Septvaux	50	49.34 N	3.23 E
Sepulga ≃	194	31.11 N	86.46 W
Sepúlveda	34	41.18 N	3.45 W
Sepulveda ◆[8]	280	34.13 N	118.28 W
Sepulveda Dam ◆[6]	280	34.10 N	118.29 W
Sepulveda Flood Control Basin ≚[1]	228	34.11 N	118.29 W
Seputih ≃	112	4.42 S	105.54 E
Sepyč	80	58.11 N	54.08 E
Sequals	64	46.10 N	12.50 E
Sequatchie ≃	192	35.02 N	85.38 W
Sequeros	34	40.31 N	6.01 W
Sequillo ≃	34	41.45 N	5.30 W
Sequim	224	48.04 N	123.06 W
Sequim Bay c	224	48.03 N	123.02 W
Sequoia National Park ♦	204	36.30 N	118.30 W
Sera	96	34.36 N	133.03 E
Şera, Pulau I	164	7.40 S	131.05 E
Šerabad	128	37.40 N	67.01 E
Serachs	128	36.32 N	61.13 E
Serafettin Dağları ⩘	130	39.05 N	41.10 E
Şerafimovič	80	49.36 N	42.43 E
Šeragul	88	54.29 N	100.56 E
Seraidi	36	36.55 N	7.41 E
Seraing	56	50.36 N	5.29 E
Seraja ≃	82	56.15 N	38.45 E
Seram (Ceram) I	164	3.00 S	129.00 E
Seram, Laut (Ceram Sea) ₸[2]	108	2.30 S	128.00 E
Serampore	126	22.45 N	88.21 E
Serang	115a	6.07 S	106.09 E
Serang ≃	115a	6.43 S	110.35 E
Serangoon	271c	1.22 N	103.54 E
Serangoon ≃	271c	1.24 N	103.56 E
Serangoon, Pulau I	271c	1.25 N	103.56 E
Serangoon Harbour c	271c	1.23 N	103.57 E
Serapo	66	41.13 N	13.34 E
Serasan, Pulau I	112	2.30 N	109.03 E
Serasan, Selat ⋓	112	2.20 N	109.00 E
Seravalle Sesia	62	45.41 N	8.19 E
Seravezza	64	43.59 N	10.13 E
Seraya, Pulau I	271c	1.16 N	103.43 E
Serayevo → Sarajevo	38	43.52 N	18.25 E
Şerayu ≃	115a	7.41 S	109.06 E
Šerbakul'	86	54.38 N	72.24 E
Serbeulangit, Pegunungan ⩘	114	3.45 N	97.50 E
Serbia → Srbija □[3]	38	44.00 N	21.00 E
Serchio ≃	64	43.47 N	10.16 E
Serdce-Kamen', mys ›	180	66.57 N	171.40 W
Serdež	80	57.17 N	48.17 E
Serditoje	83	48.02 N	38.24 E
Serdo	144	11.58 N	41.18 E
Serdoba ≃	80	52.34 N	44.01 E
Serdobsk	80	52.28 N	44.13 E
Séré'ama, Mont ʌ	175f	13.47 S	167.29 E
Serebr'anka, Ross.	86	57.13 N	70.42 E
Serebr'anka, Ross.	265b	55.45 N	37.55 E
Serebr'anka, Ukr.	83	48.55 N	38.08 E
Serebr'anka ≃	265b	55.47 N	37.42 E
Serebr'ansk	86	49.43 N	83.20 E
Serebr'anyj Bor ◆[8]	265b	55.48 N	37.25 E
Serebr'anyje Prudy	82	54.28 N	38.44 E
Serebrovo	88	55.24 N	97.52 E
Serechoviči	78	51.25 N	24.40 E
Sered'	30	48.17 N	17.44 E
Sereda, Ross.	76	55.54 N	35.31 E
Şereda, Ross.	80	58.00 N	40.27 E
Šeredar' ≃	82	55.56 N	39.04 E
Seredejskij	76	54.03 N	35.14 E
Seredīči	76	53.35 N	35.51 E
Seredina-Buda	78	52.11 N	34.01 E
Serednikovo, Ross.	80	55.15 N	39.40 E
Serednikovo, Ross.	265b	55.56 N	37.14 E
Seredn'ovo	265b	55.35 N	37.18 E
Seredžius	76	55.05 N	23.25 E
Şereflikoçhisar	130	38.56 N	33.33 E
Šereges	86	52.57 N	88.02 E
Seregno	62	45.39 N	9.12 E
Serein ≃	50	47.55 N	3.31 E
Şeremban	114	2.43 N	101.56 E
Šeremetjevka	80	55.23 N	51.32 E
Šeremetjevo, Aeroport ⊠	82	55.59 N	37.24 E
Šeremetjevskij	82	55.59 N	37.30 E
Seremuk ≃	164	1.36 S	131.46 E
Serena	216	41.29 N	88.44 W
Seren del Grappa	64	45.59 N	11.51 E
Serengeti National Park ♦	154	2.20 S	34.50 E
Serengeti Plain ≚	154	2.50 S	35.00 E
Serengka	112	1.40 S	110.40 E
Serenje	154	13.15 S	30.14 E
Şereno	256	21.19 S	42.39 W
Šereševo	76	52.33 N	24.13 E
Seret ≃	78	48.38 N	25.52 E
Serfaus	58	47.02 N	10.36 E
Ser'ga	86	57.46 N	56.52 E
Sergač	80	55.32 N	45.28 E
Sergeant	214	41.38 N	78.45 W
Sergeant Bluff	198	42.24 N	96.21 W
Sergeja Kirova, ostrova II	74	77.12 N	89.30 E
Sergejeviči	76	53.30 N	27.45 E
Sergejevka, Kaz.	86	53.51 N	67.25 E
Sergejevka, Kaz.	86	51.39 N	68.13 E
Sergejevka, Ross.	89	44.22 N	131.39 E
Sergejevka, Ross.	89	43.21 N	133.22 E
Sergejevka, Ukr.	83	48.40 N	37.22 E
Sergejevo	86	57.18 N	86.02 E
Sergen	130	41.42 N	27.42 E
Sergijevka	78	51.46 N	41.05 E
Sergijev Posad (Zagorsk)	82	56.18 N	38.08 E
Sergijevskaja, Ross.	76	60.16 N	43.54 E
Sergijevskaja, Ross.	80	50.16 N	43.47 E
Sergijevskij	80	51.56 N	51.54 E
Sergili	85	41.13 N	69.14 E
Sergines	50	48.20 N	3.15 E
Serginskij	72	62.30 N	65.38 E
Sergipe □[3]	250	10.30 S	37.30 W
Sergokala	84	42.27 N	47.40 E
Sergozero, ozero ⊜	24	66.47 N	36.42 E
Seria	112	4.39 N	114.23 E
Serian	112	1.10 N	110.34 E
Seriana, Valle V	64	45.55 N	9.55 E
Seriate	62	45.41 N	9.43 E
Seribu, Kepulauan II	115a	5.36 S	106.33 E
Seribudolok, Indon.	114	2.56 N	98.37 E
Seribudolok, Indon.	114	2.51 N	99.04 E
Sericho	154	1.05 N	39.05 E
Seridó ≃	250	6.12 S	37.10 W
Sérifontaine	50	49.21 N	1.46 E
Sérifos	38	37.09 N	24.31 E
Sérifos I	38	37.11 N	24.31 E
Sérignan-du-Comtat	62	44.11 N	4.51 E
Sérigny ≃	176	56.47 N	66.00 W
Serik	130	36.55 N	31.06 E
Seringat, Pulau I	271c	1.14 N	103.51 E
Serino	68	40.51 N	14.52 E
Serinyol	130	36.24 N	36.11 E
Serio ≃	62	45.16 N	9.45 E
Seritinga	256	21.54 S	44.30 W
Serjol	24	60.02 N	48.58 E
Serkhe, Cerro ʌ	248	17.22 S	69.22 W
Serkout, Djebel ʌ	148	23.30 N	6.48 E
Serkovo	82	54.28 N	38.46 E
Şerles ʌ	64	47.08 N	11.23 E
Šerlovaja Gora	88	50.34 N	116.15 E
Serm ◆[8]	263	51.21 N	6.42 E
Sermaise	261	48.32 N	2.05 E
Sermaises	50	48.18 N	2.12 E
Sermaize-les-Bains	56	48.47 N	4.55 E
Serman	80	53.34 N	46.22 E
Sermata, Pulau I	164	8.13 S	128.55 E
Sermide	64	45.00 N	11.18 E
Sermilik c[2]	176	65.37 N	38.03 W
Sermizelles	50	47.32 N	3.48 E
Şermoneta	66	41.33 N	12.59 E
Šerna ≃	82	55.51 N	38.34 E
Sernambetiba, Pontal de ›	287a	23.02 S	43.27 W
Sernambitiba	287a	22.41 S	42.59 W
Serniki	78	51.49 N	26.14 E
Sernovodsk	80	53.56 N	51.17 E
Sernur	80	56.56 N	49.09 E
Sernyy Zavod	128	39.59 N	58.50 E
Séro	150	14.48 N	11.04 W
Serodino	252	32.37 S	60.57 W
Ser'odka	76	58.10 N	28.12 E
Seroglazka	80	47.01 N	47.29 E
Ser'ogovo	24	62.20 N	50.36 E
Serooskerke	52	51.42 N	3.50 E
Seropédica	256	22.44 S	43.43 W
Serov	86	59.29 N	60.31 E
Serovo	85	40.27 N	71.12 E
Serowe	156	22.25 S	26.44 E
Ser'oža ≃	80	55.34 N	42.29 E
Serpa	34	37.56 N	7.36 W
Serpeddi, Punta ʌ	71	39.22 N	9.18 E
Serpejsk	76	54.20 N	34.59 E
Serpent, Rivière au ≃	186	49.33 N	71.14 W
Serpentine	168a	32.22 S	115.59 E
Serpentine ≃, Austl.	168a	32.33 S	115.46 E
Serpentine ≃, B.C., Can.	224	49.05 N	122.50 W
Serpentine Lakes ⊜	162	28.32 S	129.09 E
Serpentine National Park ♦	168a	32.22 S	116.01 E
Serpentine Reservoir ⊜[1]	168a	32.25 S	116.08 E
Serpent Mound State Memorial ⊥	218	39.02 N	83.26 W
Serpents Mouth ⋓	241r	10.00 N	62.00 W
Serpnevoje	78	46.18 N	29.02 E
Serpuchov	82	54.55 N	37.25 E
Serpukhov → Serpuchov	82	54.55 N	37.25 E
Serqo → Sark I	43b	49.26 N	2.21 W
Serra	255	20.07 S	40.18 W
Serra, Monte ʌ	66	43.46 N	10.33 E
Serra Branca	250	7.29 S	36.40 W
Serracapriola	68	41.48 N	15.09 E
Serrada	64	45.53 N	11.09 E
Serra da Canastra, Parque Nacional da ♦	255	20.10 S	46.40 W
Serra da Capivara, Parque Nacionl da ♦	250	8.40 S	42.15 W
Serra d'aiello	68	39.05 N	16.08 E
Serra de'Conti	66	43.33 N	13.02 E
Serra di Corvo, Lago di ⊜[1]	68	40.51 N	16.14 E
Serradifalco	70	37.27 N	13.53 E
Serra do Navio	250	0.59 N	52.03 W
Serra dos Aimorés	255	17.46 S	40.15 W
Serra do Salitre	255	19.06 S	46.41 W
Serra dos Órgãos, Parque Nacional da ♦	256	22.26 S	43.02 W
Sérrai	38	41.05 N	23.32 E
Serramanna	71	39.25 N	8.55 E
Serramazzoni	64	44.25 N	10.47 E
Serramonte Center ◆[9]	282	37.40 N	122.28 W
Serrana	255	21.14 S	47.36 W
Serrana, Cayo de ✤[4]	236	14.23 N	80.12 W
Serra Negra	256	22.36 S	46.42 W
Serra Negra do Norte	250	6.40 S	37.24 W
Serrânia	255	21.33 S	46.03 W
Serranilla, Cayo de ✤[4]	236	15.50 N	79.50 W
Serranópolis	255	18.16 S	52.00 W
Serranos	256	21.51 S	44.30 W
Serrara	68	40.42 N	13.54 E
Serra San Bruno	68	38.35 N	16.20 E
Serra San Quirico	66	43.27 N	13.01 E
Serrastretta	68	39.01 N	16.25 E
Serrat, Cap ›	36	37.14 N	9.13 E
Serra Talhada	250	7.59 S	38.18 W
Serravalle, It.	66	43.57 N	12.30 E
Serravalle, It.	66	42.47 N	13.01 E
Serravalle, S. Mar.	66	43.57 N	12.30 E
Serravalle all'Adige	64	45.49 N	11.01 E
Serravalle Scrivia	62	44.43 N	8.51 E
Serre	68	40.35 N	15.11 E
Serre ≃	50	49.41 N	3.23 E
Serrenti	71	39.29 N	8.58 E
Serre-Ponçon, Barrage de ◆[6]	62	44.33 N	6.30 E
Serre-Ponçon, Lac de ⊜[1]	62	44.30 N	6.17 E
Serres	62	44.26 N	5.43 E
Serrezuela	252	30.38 S	65.23 W
Serri	71	39.42 N	9.08 E
Serrières	62	45.19 N	4.45 E
Serrinha	250	11.39 S	39.00 W
Serriola, Bocca)(	66	43.31 N	12.21 E
Serris	261	48.51 N	2.47 E
Serrita	250	7.56 S	39.19 W
Serro	255	18.37 S	43.23 W
Şersale	68	39.01 N	16.44 E
Šerstin	76	52.39 N	31.03 E
Šerstobitovo	86	57.16 N	78.52 E
Sertã	34	39.48 N	8.06 W
Sertânia	250	8.05 S	37.16 W
Sertãozinho	256	22.19 S	46.03 W
Sertig-Dörfli	58	46.44 N	9.51 E
Sertung, Pulau I	115a	6.06 S	105.24 E
Seru	144	7.50 N	40.28 E
Şerua, Pulau I	164	6.18 S	130.01 E
Šerubaj-Nura ≃	86	49.54 N	72.31 E
Serui	164	1.53 S	136.14 E
Seruini ≃	248	7.42 S	66.42 W
Serule	156	21.58 S	27.20 E
Serutu, Pulau I	112	1.42 S	108.45 E
Seruwai	114	4.21 N	98.10 E
Sérvia	38	40.11 N	22.00 E
Servi Burnu ›	130	41.40 N	28.06 E
Servigliano	66	43.05 N	13.29 E
Servon	261	48.43 N	2.35 E
Servoz	58	45.56 N	6.46 E
Serwaru	112	8.10 S	127.42 E
Sêrxü	102	33.04 N	97.45 E
Seryševo	89	51.08 N	128.20 E
Şes, Muntele ⩘	38	47.05 N	22.30 E
Šešan	180	66.46 N	171.26 W
Sesayap ≃	112	3.36 N	117.15 E
Sesayap Lama	112	3.36 N	117.03 E
Sešča	76	53.45 N	33.23 E
Sese Islands II	154	0.20 S	32.20 E
Seseke ≃	263	51.37 N	7.32 E
Sesfontein	156	19.07 S	13.39 E
Sesheke	152	17.28 S	24.18 E
Seshu	105	39.33 N	115.37 E
Sesia ≃	62	45.05 N	8.37 E
Sesia, Val V	62	45.47 N	8.05 E
Sesibu	112	4.02 N	116.33 E
Sesimbra	34	38.26 N	9.06 W
Seskar, ostrov I	76	60.02 N	28.23 E
Şeskarö	26	65.44 N	23.44 E
Šešma ≃	80	55.27 N	51.05 E
Sesmarias ≃	256	22.28 S	44.27 W
Sesoko-jima I	174m	26.38 N	127.52 E
Sespe	228	34.23 N	118.58 W
Sespe Creek ≃	204	34.23 N	118.57 W
Sessa	152	13.56 S	20.38 E
Sessa Aurunca	68	41.14 N	13.56 E
Ses Salines, Cap de ›	34	39.16 N	3.03 E
Séssé	146	11.30 N	17.34 E
Sessenheim	56	48.48 N	7.59 E
Şesta Godano	62	44.17 N	9.40 E
Šestakovka	78	48.32 N	31.58 E
Šestakovo, Ross.	82	56.21 N	35.49 E
Šestakovo, Ross.	88	56.29 N	103.59 E
Şestao	34	43.18 N	3.00 W
Šestern'a	78	47.33 N	33.16 E
Sestino	66	43.42 N	12.18 E
Sesto (Sexten)	64	46.42 N	12.21 E
Sesto Calende	62	45.44 N	8.38 E
Sesto Fiorentino	66	43.50 N	11.12 E
Sestola	64	44.14 N	10.46 E
Sesto San Giovanni	62	45.32 N	9.14 E
Sestra ≃, Ross.	80	52.11 N	49.36 E
Sestra ≃, Ross.	82	56.43 N	37.14 E
Sestriere	62	44.57 N	6.53 E
Sestri Levante	62	44.16 N	9.24 E
Sestri Ponente	62	44.25 N	8.51 E
Sestroreck	76	60.06 N	29.58 E
Sestroreckij Razliv, ozero ⊜	265a	60.04 N	30.00 E
Şestu	71	39.18 N	9.05 E
Šešupe ≃	76	55.03 N	22.12 E
Šešurga	80	57.29 N	47.35 E
Šešuvis ≃	76	55.13 N	22.15 E
Šēta, Liet.	76	55.17 N	24.15 E
Seta, Nihon	270	34.58 N	135.55 E
Seta ≃	270	34.56 N	135.54 E
Setagaya ◆[8]	268	35.39 N	139.40 E
Setail ≃	115a	8.30 S	114.21 E
Setaka	96	33.09 N	130.28 E
Setana	92a	42.26 N	139.51 E
Setapak	114	3.11 N	101.42 E
Setauket	210	40.57 N	73.07 W
Sète	62	43.24 N	3.41 E
Sete Barras	252	24.23 S	47.55 W
Sete Cidades, Parque Nacional de ♦	250	3.50 S	41.40 W
Sete de Setembro ≃	255	12.56 S	52.51 W
Sete Lagoas	255	19.27 S	44.14 W
Sete Pontes	256	22.51 S	43.05 W
Sete Quedas, Cachoeira das ∟	250	9.27 S	56.41 W
Sete Quedas, Parque Nacional de ♦	252	24.02 S	54.12 W
Sete Rios ◆[8]	266c	38.45 N	9.10 W
Setesdal V	26	59.25 N	7.25 E
Seth Ward	196	34.13 N	101.42 W
Setī □[8]	124	29.15 N	81.00 E
Setī ≃	124	28.58 N	81.06 E
Setlagodi	158	26.16 S	25.06 E
Set Net, Punta ›	236	12.28 N	83.30 W
Seto, Nihon	94	35.14 N	137.06 E
Seto, Nihon	96	33.27 N	132.15 E
Seto, Nihon	96	34.44 N	134.02 E
Setoda	96	34.18 N	133.05 E
Seto-naikai ₸[2]	96	34.20 N	133.30 E
Seto-naikai-kokuritsu-kōen ♦	96	34.15 N	133.28 E
Seton Hall University ʊ[2]	276	40.45 N	74.15 W
Seton Lake ⊜	182	50.45 N	122.05 W
Seton Portage	182	50.43 N	122.18 W
Seto-saki ›	174m	26.51 N	128.18 E
Setouchi	93b	28.10 N	129.15 E
Seto-zaki ›	96	33.40 N	135.20 E
Setraki	78	49.23 N	40.49 E
Setta ≃	64	44.22 N	11.14 E
Settat	148	33.04 N	7.37 W
Settat □[4]	148	33.05 N	7.30 W
Sette Bagni ≃	267a	42.00 N	12.31 E
Setté Cama	152	2.32 S	9.45 E
Settecamini ◆[8]	267a	41.56 N	12.37 E
Sette-Daban, chrebet ⩘	74	62.00 N	138.00 E
Settee Lake ⊜	184	57.03 N	96.55 W
Settepani, Monte ʌ	62	44.15 N	8.12 E
Settimo Milanese	266b	45.29 N	9.03 E
Settimo San Pietro	71	39.17 N	9.11 E
Settimo Torinese	62	45.09 N	7.46 E
Settimo Vittone	62	45.33 N	7.50 E
Settingiano	68	38.55 N	16.31 E
Setting Lake ⊜	184	55.00 N	98.38 W
Settle	44	54.04 N	2.16 W
Settlement Point ›	169	38.25 S	145.25 E
Settlers	156	25.02 S	28.30 E
Settlers Cabin Regional Park ♦	279b	40.26 N	80.10 W
Settons, Lac des ⊜	50	41.11 N	4.04 E
Settsu	96	34.46 N	135.33 E
Setúbal	34	38.32 N	8.54 W
Setúbal □[5]	266c	38.37 N	9.00 W
Setúbal, Baía de c	34	38.27 N	8.53 W
Setun' ≃	265b	55.44 N	37.33 E
Seui	71	39.50 N	9.19 E
Seul, Lac ⊜	184	50.20 N	92.30 W
Seul Choix Point ›	190	45.56 N	85.52 W
Seulimeum	114	5.22 N	95.35 E
Seulo	71	39.52 N	9.14 E
Seúl → Sŏul	98	37.33 N	126.58 E
Seumanyam	114	3.45 N	96.38 E
Seurre	58	47.00 N	5.09 E
Seuzach	58	47.32 N	8.44 E
Sev ≃	76	52.24 N	34.10 E
Sevan	84	40.34 N	44.57 E
Sevan, ozero ⊜	84	40.20 N	45.20 E
Sévaré	150	14.32 N	4.06 W
Sevastopol'	78	44.36 N	33.32 E
Şevastopol'skij	86	53.08 N	65.44 E
Ševčenkovo, Ukr.	78	49.41 N	37.10 E
Ševčenkovo, Ukr.	78	45.33 N	29.20 E
Ševčenkovo, Ukr.	78	51.40 N	33.39 E
Ševčenkovo Vtoroje	78	47.29 N	36.08 E
Sevelen, Dtsch.	52	51.29 N	6.25 E
Şevelen, Schw.	58	47.07 N	9.29 E
Ševelevskaja	24	60.52 N	44.12 E
Ševelevskij Majdan	80	54.25 N	42.15 E
Seven ≃	44	54.11 N	0.52 W
Seven Caves ⏏[5]	218	39.13 N	83.23 W
Seven Creeks ≃	169	36.43 S	145.34 E
Seven Harbors	216	42.40 N	83.34 W
Sevenhill	168b	33.53 S	138.38 E
Seven Hills, Austl.	274a	33.46 S	150.57 E
Seven Hills, Oh., U.S.	214	41.23 N	81.40 W
Seven Islands → Sept-Îles	186	50.12 N	66.23 W
Seven Kings ◆[8]	260	51.34 N	0.05 E
Seven Mile	218	39.28 N	84.33 W
Seven Mile Beach National Park ♦	170	34.49 S	150.46 E
Sevenmile Bridge ◆[5]	220	24.41 N	81.11 W
Sevenmile Creek ≃	218	39.28 N	84.33 W
Sevenoaks, Eng., U.K.	42	51.16 N	0.12 E
Seven Oaks, Tx., U.S.	222	30.51 N	94.51 W
Sevenoaks □[8]	260	51.18 N	0.10 E
Sevenoaks Weald	260	51.14 N	0.12 E
Seven Palm Lake ⊜	220	25.12 N	80.44 W
Seven Persons	184	49.52 N	110.54 W
Seven Sisters	42	51.46 N	3.43 W
Seven Sisters Peaks ⩘	182	54.58 N	128.10 W
Seventy Mile House	182	51.18 N	121.24 W
Seven Valleys	208	39.51 N	76.46 W
Sévérac-le-Château	32	44.19 N	3.04 E
Severance Center ◆[9]	279a	41.31 N	81.33 W
Sever'anskij les ♦	83	48.55 N	38.00 E
Severka ≃	82	55.10 N	38.45 E
Severn, S. Afr.	158	26.36 S	22.52 E
Severn, Md., U.S.	208	39.08 N	76.41 W
Severn, N.C., U.S.	208	36.30 N	77.11 W
Severn, Va., U.S.	208	37.17 N	76.24 W
Severn ≃, On., Can.	176	56.02 N	87.36 W
Severn ≃, On., Can.	212	44.52 N	79.41 W
Severn ≃, U.K.	42	51.35 N	2.40 W
Severn, Mouth of the ≃	42	51.25 N	3.00 W
Severnaja Dvina ≃	24	64.32 N	40.30 E
Severnaja Osetija □[3]	84	43.00 N	44.15 E
Severnaja Sos'va ≃	72	64.10 N	65.28 E
Severnaja Zeml'a II	74	79.30 N	98.00 E
Severna Park	208	39.04 N	76.32 W
Severn Bridge ◆[5]	42	51.39 N	2.42 W
Severn Lake ⊜	184	53.54 N	90.48 W
Severnoje, Ross.	80	58.02 N	41.26 E
Severnoje, Ross.	80	54.06 N	52.32 E
Severnoje, Ross.	84	44.49 N	42.51 E
Severnoje, Ross.	86	56.21 N	78.23 E
Severnoje, Ukr.	83	48.04 N	38.44 E
Severn River c, Md., U.S.	208	38.58 N	76.28 W
Severn River c, Va., U.S.	208	37.19 N	76.25 W
Severn Tunnel ◆[5]	42	51.35 N	2.44 W
Severnyj, Ross.	24	67.38 N	64.06 E
Severnyj, Ross.	265b	55.56 N	37.33 E
Severnyje uvaly ⩘[2]	24	59.30 N	49.00 E
Severnyj Kommunar	80	58.23 N	54.02 E
Severnyj Prijut	84	43.16 N	41.51 E
Severnyj Ural ⩘	24	63.00 N	59.00 E
Severo-Bajkal'skoje nagorje ⩘[1]	88	57.00 N	111.00 E
Severočeský Kraj □[4]	30	50.30 N	14.00 E
Severodoneck	83	48.58 N	38.27 E
Severodvinsk	24	64.34 N	39.50 E
Severo-Dvinskij kanal ≋	76	59.45 N	38.22 E
Severo-Jenisejskij	74	60.22 N	93.01 E
Severo-Kazachstan □[8]	86	54.30 N	69.00 E
Severo-Kuril'sk	74	50.40 N	156.08 E
Severomoravský Kraj □[4]	30	49.45 N	17.50 E
Severomorsk	24	69.05 N	33.24 E
Severo-Mujskij chrebet ⩘	88	56.30 N	114.00 E
Severo-Sibirskaja nizmennost' ≚	74	73.00 N	100.00 E
Severoural'sk	86	60.09 N	59.57 E
Severo-Zadonsk	82	54.02 N	38.24 E
Severskaja	78	44.51 N	38.42 E
Severskij Donec ≃	72	47.35 N	40.54 E
Severskij Donec-Donbass, kanal ≋	83	48.55 N	37.45 E
Severucha	86	58.28 N	63.25 E
Severy	198	37.37 N	96.13 W
Seveso	62	45.39 N	9.09 E
Şeveso ≃	266b	45.30 N	9.12 E
Ševětin	61	49.06 N	14.35 E
Sevettijärvi	24	69.26 N	28.38 E
Sevier ≃	200	39.04 N	113.06 W
Sevier, East Fork ≃	200	38.14 N	112.12 W
Sevier Bridge Reservoir ⊜[1]	200	39.21 N	111.57 W
Sevier Desert ◆[2]	200	39.25 N	112.50 W
Sevier Lake ⊜	200	38.55 N	113.09 W
Sevierville	192	35.52 N	83.33 W
Sevilla, Col.	246	4.16 N	75.57 W
Sevilla (Seville), Esp.	34	37.23 N	5.59 W
Sevilla □[4]	34	37.25 N	5.35 W
Sevilla, Isla I	236	8.14 N	82.24 W
Seville, Fl., U.S.	192	29.19 N	81.29 W
Seville, Oh., U.S.	214	41.00 N	81.51 W
Seville → Sevilla	34	37.23 N	5.59 W
Sevir	130	39.12 N	38.13 E
Şevketiye	130	40.05 N	27.51 E
Ševli ≃	89	54.08 N	133.04 E
Sevlievo	38	43.01 N	25.06 E
Sevran	50	48.56 N	2.32 E
Sevrej	102	43.35 N	102.12 E
Sèvres	50	48.49 N	2.12 E
Sévrier	58	45.52 N	6.08 E
Şevsk	78	52.09 N	34.30 E
Ševykan	88	54.20 N	106.49 E
Sewa ≃	150	7.18 N	12.08 W
Sewanee	194	35.04 N	85.55 W
Sewāni	123	28.55 N	75.37 E
Seward, Ak., U.S.	180	60.06 N	149.26 W
Seward, Ne., U.S.	198	40.54 N	97.05 W
Seward, N.Y., U.S.	210	42.43 N	74.37 W
Seward, Pa., U.S.	214	40.25 N	79.01 W
Seward Glacier ⊓	180	60.22 N	140.15 W
Seward Peninsula ›[1]	180	65.00 N	164.00 W
Sewaren	276	40.33 N	74.15 W
Sewekow	54	53.15 N	12.39 E
Sewell, Chile	252	34.05 S	70.23 W
Sewell, N.J., U.S.	208	39.45 N	75.08 W
Sewen	58	47.48 N	6.54 E
Sewernaja-Semlja → Severnaja Zeml'a II	74	79.30 N	98.00 E
Seweweekspoort	158	33.22 S	21.25 E
Sewickley	214	40.32 N	80.11 W
Sewickley Creek ≃	279b	40.14 N	79.47 W
Sewickley Heights	279b	40.33 N	80.09 W
Sewickley Hills	279b	40.34 N	80.08 W
Sewri ◆[8]	272c	19.00 N	72.51 E
Sexcello	152	3.58 S	11.38 E
Sexsmith	182	55.21 N	118.47 W
Sexten → Sesto	64	46.42 N	12.21 E
Sextin ≃	232	25.44 N	105.14 W
Sexton	218	39.42 N	85.27 W
Sexton Island I	276	40.39 N	73.14 W
Seya ◆[8], Nihon	268	35.29 N	139.29 E
Seya ◆[8], Nihon	268	35.27 N	139.30 E
Seybaplaya	232	19.39 N	90.40 W
Seybothenreuth	60	49.54 N	11.43 E
Seybouse, Oued ≃	148	36.54 N	7.47 E
Seychellen → Seychelles □[1]	138	4.35 S	55.40 E
Seychelles □[1]	138	4.35 S	55.40 E
Seychelles Bank ✤[4]	12	4.45 S	55.30 E
Seyches	32	44.33 N	0.18 E
Seyda	54	51.53 N	12.53 E
Seydim	130	40.33 N	34.45 E
Seydişehir	130	37.25 N	31.51 E
Seyđisfjörđur	24a	65.16 N	14.00 W
Seyfe Gölü ⊜	130	39.13 N	34.23 E
Seyhan ≃	130	36.43 N	34.53 E
Seyhan Barajı ⊜[1]	130	37.05 N	35.15 E
Seyitgazi	130	39.27 N	30.43 E
Seylac	144	11.21 N	43.29 E
Seymour, Austl.	169	37.02 S	145.08 E
Seymour, Ciskei	158	32.33 S	26.46 E
Seymour, Ct., U.S.	207	41.23 N	73.04 W
Seymour, In., U.S.	218	38.57 N	85.53 W
Seymour, Ia., U.S.	190	40.40 N	93.07 W
Seymour, Mo., U.S.	194	37.08 N	92.46 W
Seymour, Tx., U.S.	196	33.35 N	99.15 W
Seymour, Wi., U.S.	190	44.30 N	88.19 W
Seymour ≃	182	51.05 N	126.50 W
Seymour Inlet c	182	51.03 N	127.10 W
Seymour Johnson Air Force Base ■	192	35.21 N	77.58 W
Seymour Range ⩘	224	48.40 N	124.00 W
Seymourville	194	30.27 N	91.29 W
Seyne	62	44.21 N	6.21 E
Seynod	58	45.53 N	6.05 E
Seyring	264b	48.20 N	16.29 E
Seyssel	58	45.57 N	5.49 E
Şeytan ≃	267b	41.06 N	28.59 E
Sežana	36	45.42 N	13.52 E
Sézanne	50	48.43 N	3.43 E
Şezela	158	30.24 S	30.42 E
Sežim	24	62.07 N	58.21 E
Sezimovo Ústí	30	49.23 N	14.42 E
Sezze	66	41.30 N	13.03 E
Sfax	148	34.44 N	10.46 E
Sfax □[8]	148	34.50 N	10.20 E
Sferracavallo ◆[8]	70	38.12 N	13.17 E
Sfîntu-Gheorghe	38	45.52 N	25.47 E
Sfîntu Gheorghe, Braţul ≃[1]	38	44.53 N	29.36 E
Sfîntu Gheorghe, Ostrovul I	38	45.07 N	29.22 E
Sfizef	148	35.14 N	0.15 W
Sforzesco, Castello ⊥	266b	45.28 N	9.11 E
's-Gravendeel	52	51.46 N	4.37 E
's-Gravenhage (The Hague)	52	52.06 N	4.18 E
's-Gravenzande	52	52.00 N	4.10 E
Sgritheall, Beinn ʌ	46	57.08 N	5.35 W
Sgurgola	66	41.40 N	13.09 E
Sha ≃, Zhg.	98	37.31 N	117.50 E
Sha ≃, Zhg.	100	26.35 N	118.02 E
Sha ≃, Zhg.	100	33.39 N	114.38 E
Sha ≃, Zhg.	104	41.21 N	123.07 E
Sha'alav, Har ʌ	132	30.04 N	35.06 E
Sha'alvim	132	31.52 N	34.59 E
Shaanxi (Shensi) □[4]	102	35.00 N	109.00 E
Sha'ar HaGolan	132	32.41 N	35.36 E
Sha'ar Menashe	132	32.27 N	35.01 E
Shab'ā	132	33.21 N	35.45 E
Shaba □[4]	154	8.00 S	27.00 E
Shābah	142	31.11 N	30.46 E
Shabakunk Creek ≃	285	40.15 N	74.43 W
Shabās al-Milḥ	142	31.12 N	30.39 E
Shabās ash-Shuhadā'	142	31.05 N	30.45 E
Shabās 'Umayr	142	31.06 N	30.48 E
Shabbona	216	41.46 N	88.52 W
Shabeellaha Dhexe □[4]	144	3.00 N	46.00 E
Shabeellaha Hoose □[4]	144	1.30 N	44.15 E
Shabeelle (Shebele) ≃	144	0.12 S	42.45 E
Shabestar	128	38.11 N	45.42 E
Shabomeka Lake ⊜	212	44.54 N	77.09 W
Shabotik ≃	190	48.50 N	85.34 W
Shabqadar	123	34.13 N	71.34 E
Shabrāmant	142	29.56 N	31.12 E
Shabshīr al-Ḥiṣṣah	142	30.52 N	31.04 E
Shabunda	154	2.42 S	27.20 E
Shabwah	144	15.22 N	47.01 E
Shache (Yarkand)	120	38.25 N	77.16 E
Shacheng	105	40.25 N	115.31 E
Shacheng Gang c	100	27.10 N	120.24 E
Shackan Indian Reserve ◆[4]	182	50.17 N	121.12 W
Shackleton Ice Shelf ⊓	9	66.00 S	100.00 E
Shackleton Range ⩘	9	80.40 S	26.00 W
Shādegān	128	30.40 N	48.38 E
Shade Gap	214	40.11 N	77.52 W
Shadehill Reservoir ⊜[1]	198	45.45 N	102.15 W
Shade Mountain ʌ	208	40.34 N	77.30 W
Shades Glen	210	41.11 N	75.42 W
Shadi	100	26.08 N	114.49 E
Shadian	98	35.30 N	114.26 E
Shading	102	31.20 N	94.40 E
Shadow Lake ⊜, On., Can.	212	44.43 N	78.48 W
Shadow Lake ⊜, Ma., U.S.	283	42.50 N	71.14 W
Shadow Lake ⊜, N.J., U.S.	276	40.21 N	74.06 W
Shado-Wood Village	214	40.35 N	79.12 W
Shadrinsk → Šadrinsk	86	56.05 N	63.38 E
Shadui	102	31.30 N	100.10 E
Shady Cove	202	42.04 N	122.36 W
Shady Grove, Fl., U.S.	192	30.17 N	83.37 W
Shady Grove, Tx., U.S.	222	32.48 N	97.01 W
Shady Hills	216	40.36 N	85.41 W
Shady Shores	222	33.10 N	97.02 W
Shadyside	188	39.58 N	80.45 W
Sha'f	132	32.38 N	36.51 E
Shafer, Lake ⊜	216	40.47 N	86.46 W
Shafer Butte ʌ	202	43.47 N	116.05 W
Shafir	132	31.42 N	34.44 E
Shaft	128	37.12 N	49.24 E
Shafter	226	35.30 N	119.16 W
Shaftesbury	42	51.01 N	2.12 W
Shafton	279b	40.20 N	79.42 W
Shaftsburg	216	42.48 N	84.18 W
Shaftsbury	210	43.00 N	73.11 W
Shafu	100	22.25 N	113.01 E
Shag ≃	172	45.29 S	170.49 E
Shagamu	150	6.51 N	3.39 E
Shageluk	180	62.36 N	159.32 W
Shag Rocks II[1]	244	53.33 S	42.02 W
Shaguotun	104	41.10 N	120.38 E
Shāhābād, India	122	17.08 N	76.56 E
Shāhābād, India	123	30.10 N	76.53 E
Shāhābād, India	124	27.39 N	79.57 E
Shāhābād, India	272c	19.01 N	73.02 E
Shāhābād, Īrān	128	37.32 N	56.54 E
Shāhābād, Īrān	267d	35.47 N	51.31 E
Shāhāda	120	21.28 N	74.18 E
Shah Alam	114	3.04 N	101.33 E
Shahbā'	132	32.51 N	36.37 E
Shāhbandar	120	24.10 N	67.54 E
Shāhbāz Kalāt	128	26.42 N	63.58 E
Shāhbāzpur ⋓	124	22.05 N	90.50 E
Shahdād, Namakzār-e ≚	128	30.30 N	58.30 E
Shāhdādkot	120	27.51 N	67.54 E
Shāhdādpur	120	25.56 N	68.37 E
Shāhdara, India	272a	28.30 N	77.25 E
Shāhdara, Pāk.	123	31.38 N	74.18 E
Shāhdara ◆[8]	272a	28.40 N	77.18 E
Shahdol	124	23.20 N	81.21 E
Shahe, Zhg.	98	36.56 N	114.30 E
Shahe, Zhg.	98	34.44 N	118.58 E
Shahe, Zhg.	98	37.01 N	119.43 E
Shahe, Zhg.	102	22.06 N	109.43 E
Shahedian	100	33.01 N	113.44 E
Shaheji	100	32.26 N	118.14 E
Shahepu	104	41.08 N	121.01 E
Shaheyi	98	39.53 N	118.31 E
Shaheying	104	40.50 N	120.46 E
Shahezhan	98	35.49 N	116.23 E
Shahezhen	105	40.08 N	116.15 E
Shahezi	89	46.05 N	129.20 E
Shāhganj	124	26.03 N	82.41 E
Shāhgarh, India	120	27.07 N	69.54 E
Shāhgarh, India	124	24.19 N	79.08 E
Shahḥāt	146	32.49 N	21.52 E
Shāhī Kowt	123	34.16 N	70.34 E
Shāhjahānpur	124	27.53 N	79.55 E
Shāh Jūy	120	32.31 N	67.25 E
Shāh Kot	123	31.34 N	73.29 E
Shāh Kūh ʌ	128	31.37 N	59.16 E
Shāhpur, India	122	16.42 N	76.50 E
Shāhpur, Pāk.	120	28.43 N	68.25 E
Shāhpur, Pāk.	123	32.17 N	72.26 E
Shāhpura, India	120	27.23 N	75.58 E
Shāhpura, India	120	25.38 N	74.56 E
Shāhpura, India	124	23.11 N	80.42 E
Shāhpur Chākar	120	26.09 N	68.39 E
Shahrak	120	34.06 N	64.18 E
Shahr-e Bābak	128	30.07 N	55.09 E
Shahr-e Kord	128	32.19 N	50.50 E
Shahr-e Monjān	120	36.02 N	70.46 E
Shahr-e Ṣafā	128	31.50 N	66.22 E
Shahrestān	120	34.22 N	66.47 E
Shāhrūd ≃	128	36.40 N	49.26 E
Shahryār	128	35.28 N	51.05 E
Shahu	100	30.11 N	113.39 E
Shāhzādpur	126	24.10 N	89.36 E
Shā'ib al-Banāt, Jabal ʌ	140	26.59 N	33.29 E
Shaighālu	120	31.11 N	68.49 E
Shaikou	100	27.19 N	117.35 E
Sha'īrah, Jabal ʌ[2]	132	30.06 N	34.17 E
Sha'īrah, Jabal ash- ⩘	132	29.31 N	34.29 E
Shājāpur	124	23.26 N	76.16 E
Shajian	100	24.46 N	117.38 E
Shajianzi	98	41.01 N	125.26 E
Shajiazhuang	106	32.13 N	120.53 E
Shajing	100	23.36 N	114.06 E
Shajingzi	102	37.42 N	105.09 E
Shakaga-dake ʌ	96	33.11 N	130.53 E
Shakaga-hana ›	96	34.25 N	134.14 E
Shakaga-take-tunnel ◆[5]	96	33.27 N	130.52 E
Shakardarra	123	33.14 N	71.30 E
Shakargarh	123	32.16 N	75.10 E
Shakarpura	272a	28.46 N	77.21 E
Shakarpur Khās ◆[8]	272a	28.38 N	77.17 E
Shakaskraal	158	29.26 S	31.14 E
Shakawe	156	18.23 S	21.50 E
Shakeng	98	42.13 N	116.35 E
Shaker Heights	214	41.28 N	81.32 W
Shaker Heights Park ♦	279a	41.29 N	81.33 W
Shakespeare	212	43.22 N	80.49 W
Shākhen	128	33.22 N	59.32 E
Shakhty → Šachty	83	47.42 N	40.13 E
Shaki	150	8.39 N	3.25 E
Shākir, Jazīrat I	140	27.30 N	33.59 E
Shakopee	190	44.47 N	93.31 W
Shakotan-hantō ›[1]	92a	43.20 N	140.30 E
Shakou	100	24.25 N	113.32 E
Shakshūk	142	29.28 N	30.42 E
Shaktoolik	180	64.20 N	161.09 W
Shakujii ◆[8]	268	35.45 N	139.37 E
Shakūrpur ◆[8]	272a	28.41 N	77.09 E
Shala, Lake ⊜	144	7.25 N	38.30 E
Shalalth	182	50.44 N	122.13 W
Shalatayn, Bi'r ₸[4]	140	23.08 N	35.36 E
Shaleitian Dao I	98	39.03 N	118.44 E
Shaler Mountains ⩘	176	72.35 N	110.45 W
Shaleshanto	156	19.09 S	23.58 E
Shalford	260	51.13 N	0.34 W
Shālimah	142	31.14 N	30.52 E
Shalimar Railroad Station ◆[5]	272b	22.33 N	88.19 E
Shaling, Zhg.	104	41.09 N	122.22 E
Shaling, Zhg.	104	41.20 N	123.01 E
Shalingpu	104	41.47 N	123.11 E
Shalingzi	105	40.42 N	114.55 E
Shaliuhe, Zhg.	102	36.28 N	98.57 E
Shaliuhe, Zhg.	105	39.53 N	117.56 E
Shallotte	192	33.58 N	78.23 W
Shallowater	196	33.41 N	101.59 W
Shallow Brook ≃	276	40.21 N	74.35 W
Shallow Lake	212	44.36 N	81.05 W
Shaluhe	89	51.08 N	126.00 E
Shaluli Shan ⩘	102	30.45 N	99.45 E
Shām, Bādiyat ash- (Syrian Desert) ◆[2]	128	32.00 N	40.00 E
Shām, Jabal ash- ʌ	128	23.13 N	57.16 E
Shama ≃	154	6.16 S	32.27 E
Shaman	85	38.50 N	75.36 E
Shamattawa	184	55.52 N	92.05 W
Shambe	140	7.07 N	30.46 E

Symbols in the index entries represent the broad categories identified in the key at the right. Symbols with superior numbers (⩘[1]) identify subcategories (see complete key on page *I · 1).*

Symbole im Register stellen die rechts im Schlüssel erklärten Kategorien dar. Symbole mit hochgestellten Ziffern (⩘[1]) bezeichnen Unterabteilungen einer Kategorie (vgl. vollständiger Schlüssel auf Seite *I · 1).*

Los símbolos incluídos en el texto del índice representan las grandes categorias identificadas con la clave a la derecha. Los símbolos con numeros en su parte superior (⩘[1]) identifican las subcategorías (véase la clave completa en la página *I · 1).*

Les symboles de l'index représentent les catégories indiquées dans la légende à droite. Les symboles suivis d'un indice (⩘[1]) représentent des sous-catégories (voir légende complète à la page *I · 1).*

Os símbolos incluídos no texto do índice representam as grandes categorias identificadas com a chave à direita. Os símbolos com números em sua parte superior (⩘[1]) identificam as subcategorias (veja-se a chave completa à página *I · 1).*

ʌ Mountain	Berg	Montaña	Montagne	Montanha
⩘ Mountains	Gebirge	Montañas	Montagnes	Montanhas
)(Pass	Paß	Paso	Col	Passo
V Valley, Canyon	Tal, Cañon	Valle, Cañón	Vallée, Canyon	Vale, Canhão
≚ Plain	Ebene	Llano	Plaine	Planície
› Cape	Kap	Cabo	Cap	Cabo
I Island	Insel	Isla	Île	Ilha
II Islands	Inseln	Islas	Îles	Ilhas
⏏ Other Topographic Features	Andere Topographische Objekte	Otros Elementos Topográficos	Autres données topographiques	Outros acidentes topográficos

ESPAÑOL Nombre	Página	Lat.°′	Long.°′ W = Oeste
FRANÇAIS Nom	Page	Lat.°′	Long.°′ W = Ouest
PORTUGUÊS Nome	Página	Lat.°′	Long.°′ W = Oeste

Shambi 152 1.49 S 22.39 E
Shambu 144 9.40 N 37.03 E
Shambuanda 152 6.38 S 20.13 E
Shām Churasi 123 31.30 N 75.45 E
Shamei 100 24.32 N 118.25 E
Shamepūr ✦8 272a 28.45 N 77.09 E
Shamīl 128 27.30 N 56.53 E
Shāmli 124 29.27 N 77.19 E
Shammākh 132 30.30 N 35.30 E
Shamokin 208 40.47 N 76.33 W
Shamona Creek ≃ 285 40.02 N 75.43 W
Shamrock, Fl., U.S. 192 29.38 N 83.08 W
Shamrock, Tx., U.S. 196 35.12 N 100.14 W
Shamsābād 124 27.01 N 78.08 E
Shamsher 272a 28.44 N 77.24 E
Shamva 154 17.18 S 31.34 E
Shan □3 110 22.00 N 98.00 E
Shanbiao 98 35.28 N 113.57 E
Shancheng 102 37.01 N 107.00 E
Shanchengzhen 98 42.23 N 125.26 E
Shandaken 210 42.07 N 74.23 W
Shandan 102 38.45 N 101.15 E
Shandatgyi 110 19.37 N 94.43 E
Shandī 140 16.42 N 33.26 E
Shandian ≃ 98 42.23 N 116.21 E
Shandianhe 98 42.22 N 116.15 E
Shandīd 142 30.55 N 30.40 E
Shandon 226 35.39 N 120.22 W
Shandong 107 29.31 N 106.25 E
Shandong (Shantung) □4 98 36.00 N 118.00 E
Shandong Bandao (Shantung Peninsula) ≻1 98 37.00 N 121.00 E
Shaner 279b 40.17 N 79.47 W
Shanesville 214 40.31 N 81.39 W
Shangalume 154 10.49 S 26.34 E
Shangani 154 19.47 S 29.22 E
Shangani ≃ 154 18.41 S 27.10 E
Shang'ao 106 30.41 N 119.25 E
Shangba 106 32.11 N 118.46 E
Shangbahe 100 30.40 N 115.05 E
Shangbai 106 30.29 N 119.58 E
Shangbancheng 105 40.50 N 118.03 E
Shangbatang 102 32.46 N 96.20 E
Shangcai 100 33.16 N 114.15 E
Shangcang 105 39.54 N 117.23 E
Shangchen 106 30.07 N 119.53 E
Shangcheng 100 31.48 N 115.24 E
Shangchewan 100 29.48 N 113.01 E
Shangch'iu → Shangqiu 98 34.27 N 115.42 E
Shangchuan Dao I 102 21.42 N 112.47 E
Shangdang 106 32.06 N 119.24 E
Shangdayangqi 89 51.07 N 124.02 E
Shangdian 100 34.07 N 112.23 E
Shangdianmiao 106 30.56 N 120.51 E
Shangdouying 105 40.36 N 115.33 E
Shangdu 98 41.29 N 113.34 E
Shangduichunshi 104 41.00 N 123.02 E
Shangdundu 100 27.56 N 116.15 E
Shangfu 100 28.40 N 114.59 E
Shanggaixin 102 23.25 N 100.02 E
Shanggan 100 25.56 N 119.22 E
Shanggang 100 33.30 N 120.04 E
Shanggangzi 104 42.26 N 123.03 E
Shanggao 100 28.18 N 114.54 E
Shanggecun 106 31.49 N 119.07 E
Shanggu 98 40.47 N 118.28 E
Shangguanying 98 41.18 N 117.07 E
Shanghai, Va., U.S. 208 37.37 N 76.47 W
Shanghai, Zhg. 106 31.14 N 121.28 E
Shanghai, Zhg. 106 31.07 N 121.22 E
Shanghai, Zhg. 269b 31.14 N 121.28 E
Shanghailingao 104 41.57 N 120.55 E
Shanghai Museum ᵾ 269b 31.13 N 121.28 E
Shanghai Shi (Shanghai Shih) □7 106 31.10 N 121.30 E
Shanghai Station ✦5 269b 31.15 N 121.28 E
Shanghang 100 25.06 N 116.25 E
Shanghe 98 37.19 N 117.07 E
Shanghekou 98 40.26 N 124.47 E
Shanghetou 105 39.12 N 116.59 E
Shanghewantun 104 41.42 N 123.23 E
Shang Hu ⊜ 106 31.39 N 120.41 E
Shanghuang 106 31.33 N 119.34 E
Shanghuangqi 98 41.29 N 116.31 E
Shanghucun 105 40.45 N 115.45 E
Shangjao → Shangrao 100 28.26 N 117.58 E
Shangjiafen 104 41.18 N 121.10 E
Shangjiahe 98 41.51 N 124.28 E
Shangjiaodao 100 29.00 N 119.54 E
Shangjiatai 104 40.53 N 123.35 E
Shangjie 100 27.06 N 116.06 E
Shangjin 102 33.09 N 110.03 E
Shangjiuwu 100 33.59 N 113.01 E
Shangkasa 120 33.45 N 80.12 E
Shangkou 98 36.59 N 118.53 E
Shanglanjiagou 104 40.52 N 120.37 E
Shanglin, Zhg. 98 38.19 N 116.05 E
Shanglin, Zhg. 102 23.28 N 108.33 E
Shanglin, Zhg. 104 41.31 N 122.14 E
Shanglishi 100 27.52 N 113.46 E
Shangliuhezicun 104 41.28 N 123.32 E
Shangliulinzi 104 41.02 N 123.13 E
Shangmagushan 104 41.41 N 124.10 E
Shangmatai 105 39.22 N 117.15 E
Shangmatun 104 40.57 N 123.22 E
Shangmingdian 106 31.12 N 120.57 E
Shangmingju 105 39.41 N 115.12 E
Shangnan 102 33.31 N 110.45 E
Shangpandaoling 104 41.42 N 121.14 E
Shangpeibu 106 31.28 N 119.13 E
Shangping, Zhg. 100 25.57 N 117.33 E
Shangping, Zhg. 100 24.43 N 115.27 E
Shangping, Zhg. 100 24.29 N 114.38 E
Shangpuzi 104 41.37 N 121.35 E
Shangqianbu 106 30.27 N 120.04 E
Shangqiao 100 31.02 N 117.42 E
Shangqing, Zhg. 100 25.53 N 118.36 E
Shangqing, Zhg. 100 28.02 N 117.00 E
Shangqingshuicun 105 39.56 N 115.38 E
Shangqiu (Zhuji), Zhg. 98 34.27 N 115.42 E
Shangqiu, Zhg. 98 34.23 N 115.37 E
Shangrao 100 28.26 N 117.58 E
Shangshe 102 38.15 N 113.20 E
Shangshibatai 104 42.02 N 120.51 E
Shangshui 100 33.33 N 114.34 E
Shangsi 102 22.09 N 107.57 E
Shangtan 106 30.27 N 118.42 E
Shangtang 100 33.23 N 118.02 E
Shan Guan ⋈ 100 27.30 N 117.06 E
Shangweiniuchang 104 40.54 N 120.44 E
Shangxian 102 33.51 N 109.54 E
Shangxingzhen 106 31.32 N 119.15 E
Shangxinhe 106 32.02 N 118.43 E
Shangxinqiu 104 42.27 N 121.37 E
Shangyangbao 98 42.30 N 124.14 E
Shangyangcun 106 30.48 N 118.40 E
Shangye 98 35.26 N 117.59 E
Shangyi (Nanhaoqian) 98 41.04 N 114.03 E
Shangying 89 44.10 N 127.17 E
Shangyinkou 102 32.52 N 103.04 E
Shangyou 100 25.51 N 114.30 E
Shangyou ≃ 100 25.49 N 114.50 E
Shangyou Shuiku ⊜1 100 25.52 N 114.21 E
Shangyu 100 30.02 N 120.54 E
Shangyuan 104 41.39 N 120.55 E
Shangyun 102 23.01 N 99.50 E
Shangzhai 98 39.13 N 114.17 E
Shangzhaoshugou 104 42.12 N 121.58 E
Shangzhazi 105 40.52 N 117.42 E
Shangzhenzhuang 105 40.20 N 117.06 E
Shangzhi 89 45.13 N 127.59 E
Shangzhuangtai 105 39.41 N 115.25 E
Shanhaiguan 98 40.01 N 119.44 E
Shanhaikwan → Shanhaiguan 98 40.01 N 119.44 E
Shanhecun 89 45.38 N 128.27 E
Shanhetun 89 44.44 N 127.12 E
Shanjiazhuang 105 38.52 N 115.45 E
Shanklin 42 50.38 N 1.10 W
Shankou, Zhg. 100 26.40 N 117.46 E
Shankou, Zhg. 100 28.58 N 115.12 E
Shankou, Zhg. 100 28.48 N 114.29 E
Shankou, Zhg. 102 21.38 N 109.43 E
Shanlenggang 102 28.33 N 103.23 E
Shanli 100 29.52 N 117.21 E
Shanlian 106 30.42 N 120.19 E
Shanmenjie 106 30.40 N 118.52 E
Shanmulong 102 24.39 N 98.05 E
Shannanguan 100 31.36 N 116.52 E
Shannock 207 41.26 N 71.38 W
Shannon, Ire. 48 52.43 N 8.53 W
Shannon, N.Z. 172 40.33 S 175.25 E
Shannon, S. Afr. 158 29.08 S 26.18 E
Shannon, Ga., U.S. 192 34.20 N 85.04 W
Shannon, Il., U.S. 190 42.09 N 89.44 W
Shannon, Ms., U.S. 194 34.06 N 88.42 W
Shannon ≃ 48 52.36 N 9.41 W
Shannon, Lake ⊜ 224 48.37 N 121.42 W
Shannon, Mouth of the ≃1 48 52.30 N 9.50 W
Shannon Airport ⊠ 48 52.41 N 8.55 W
Shannons Flat 171b 35.54 S 148.58 E
Shannontown 192 33.53 N 80.21 W
Shannonville 212 44.12 N 77.13 W
Shanpo 100 30.06 N 114.20 E
Shanrendong 89 46.50 N 123.08 E
Shanrenqiao 106 31.16 N 120.27 E
Shanshan 86 42.52 N 90.10 E
Shanshenmiao 105 40.45 N 117.11 E
Shanshūr 142 30.21 N 31.00 E
Shansi → Shanxi □4 102 37.00 N 112.00 E
Shanting 98 35.09 N 117.29 E
Shāntipur 126 23.15 N 88.26 E
Shantou (Swatow) 100 23.23 N 116.41 E
Shantung Peninsula → Shandong Bandao ≻1 98 37.00 N 121.00 E
Shantung → Shandong □4 98 36.00 N 118.00 E
Shanty Bay 212 44.25 N 79.36 W
Shanwa 154 3.10 S 33.46 E
Shanwei 100 22.47 N 115.21 E
Shanxi (Shansi) □4 102 37.00 N 112.00 E
Shanxian 98 34.48 N 116.03 E
Shanxian → Sanmenxia 102 34.45 N 111.05 E
Shanxiawu 100 28.52 N 113.52 E
Shanxu 102 22.21 N 107.58 E
Shanyang, Zhg. 100 26.43 N 119.13 E
Shanyang, Zhg. 102 33.35 N 109.49 E
Shanyang, Zhg. 106 31.19 N 120.16 E
Shanyao 100 25.13 N 118.55 E
Shanyaqiao 106 31.15 N 119.25 E
Shanyin 102 39.33 N 112.50 E
Shanzhangjiafen 105 40.37 N 116.44 E
Shanzui 105 40.48 N 118.13 E
Shanzuizi 104 41.55 N 120.30 E
Shaobo 100 32.30 N 119.32 E
Shaodenggao 104 42.13 N 121.47 E
Shaodian, Zhg. 98 34.08 N 118.25 E
Shaodian, Zhg. 100 33.10 N 114.18 E
Shaoguan 100 24.50 N 113.37 E
Shaogudian 98 36.57 N 115.32 E
Shaoguyingzi 104 41.33 N 120.27 E
Shaohing → Shaoxing 100 30.00 N 120.35 E
Shaohsing → Shaoxing 100 30.00 N 120.35 E
Shaojiaolou 106 31.05 N 121.32 E
Shaokuan → Shaoguan 100 24.50 N 113.37 E
Shaowu 100 27.20 N 117.28 E
Shaoxing 100 30.00 N 120.35 E
Shaoyang, Zhg. 102 27.15 N 111.28 E
Shaoyang, Zhg. 102 27.00 N 111.18 E
Shaoyun 107 29.30 N 105.57 E
Shaozihe 98 40.13 N 123.33 E
Shap 44 54.32 N 2.41 W
Shapinsay I 46 59.03 N 2.53 W
Shāpūr ≃ 128 29.39 N 51.03 E
Shaq'ah, Ra's ash- ≻ 130 34.19 N 35.41 E
Shaqqā 132 32.53 N 36.42 E
Shaqq al-Ju'ayfir, Wādī ∨ 140 15.16 N 26.00 E
Shaqrā', Ar. Su. 128 25.15 N 45.15 E
Shaqrā, Lubnān 132 33.12 N 35.28 E
Shaqrā', Sūrīy. 132 32.54 N 36.14 E
Shaqrā', Yaman 144 13.21 N 45.42 E
Shaquan 86 44.33 N 83.25 E
Shaquzhen 107 30.33 N 103.45 E
Sharafābād 272a 28.36 N 77.23 E
Sharafkhāneh 128 38.11 N 45.29 E
Sharan Jogīzai 120 31.02 N 68.33 E
Sharatin Mountain ∧ 180 57.49 N 152.41 W
Sharbatāt, Ra's ash- ≻ 118 17.56 N 56.21 E
Sharbīn, Jabal ∧ 132 33.43 N 36.21 E
Sharbot Lake 212 44.46 N 76.41 W
Sharbot Lake ⊜ 212 44.46 N 76.41 W
Share 150 8.50 N 4.56 E
Shari 92a 43.55 N 144.50 E
Shari-dake ∧ 92a 43.46 N 144.43 E
Sharīṭah, Ra's ≻ 128 26.23 N 56.23 E
Shark ≃ 220 25.21 N 81.05 W
Shark Bay ᑕ 162 25.30 S 113.30 E
Shark Point ≻, Austl. 274a 33.55 S 151.17 E
Shark Point ≻, Fl., U.S. 220 25.23 N 81.09 W
Shark River Hills 208 40.12 N 74.03 W
Sharktooth Mountain ∧ 180 58.35 N 127.57 W
Sharm ash-Shaykh 140 27.51 N 34.17 E
Sharnbrook 42 52.13 N 0.32 W
Sharnūb 142 31.01 N 30.35 E
Sharon, On., Can. 214 42.53 N 81.22 W
Sharon, Ct., U.S. 207 41.52 N 73.28 W
Sharon, Ma., U.S. 207 42.07 N 71.10 W
Sharon, N.D., U.S. 198 47.35 N 97.53 W
Sharon, Pa., U.S. 214 41.13 N 80.29 W
Sharon, Tn., U.S. 194 36.14 N 88.49 W
Sharon, Wi., U.S. 216 42.30 N 88.43 W
Sharon Center 214 41.06 N 81.44 W
Sharon Hill 285 39.54 N 75.16 W
Sharon Park 218 39.23 N 84.35 W
Sharon Springs, Ks., U.S. 198 38.53 N 101.45 W
Sharon Springs, N.Y., U.S. 210 42.48 N 74.37 W
Sharon Valley 207 41.53 N 73.29 W
Sharonville 218 39.16 N 84.24 W
Sharpe, Lake ⊜1 198 44.05 N 99.55 W
Sharpe Lake ⊜ 184 54.24 N 93.30 W
Sharpes 220 28.25 N 80.45 W
Sharp Island I 271d 22.22 N 114.17 E
Sharpley 285 39.48 N 75.33 W
Sharp Park ♦ 282 37.37 N 122.29 W
Sharp Peak ∧ 116 5.58 N 125.31 E
Sharpsburg, Il., U.S. 219 39.37 N 89.21 W
Sharpsburg, Ky., U.S. 218 38.12 N 83.55 W
Sharpsburg, Pa., U.S. 279b 40.29 N 79.55 W
Sharps Hill 279b 40.30 N 79.56 W
Sharps Run ≃ 285 39.54 N 74.49 W
Sharpsville, In., U.S. 216 40.22 N 86.05 W
Sharpsville, Pa., U.S. 214 41.15 N 80.28 W
Sharptown, Md., U.S. 208 38.32 N 75.43 W
Sharptown, N.J., U.S. 285 39.39 N 75.21 W
Sharqī, Al-Jabal ash- (Anti-Lebanon) ⊀ 132 33.35 N 36.00 E
Sharqīyah, Aṣ-Ṣaḥrā' ash- (Arabian Desert) ✦2 140 28.00 N 32.00 E
Sharqpur 123 31.28 N 74.06 E
Sharshar, Jabal ∧2 140 23.52 N 30.20 E
Shartlesville 208 40.31 N 76.06 W
Shārūnah 142 28.36 N 30.51 E
Shārūnah, Wādī ∨ 142 28.36 N 30.52 E
Shasha 144 6.20 N 35.57 E
Shashe ≃ 156 22.14 S 29.20 E
Shashemene 144 7.12 N 38.43 E
Shashi 102 30.19 N 112.14 E
Shashibu 100 25.48 N 114.54 E
Shasi → Shashi 102 30.19 N 112.14 E
Shasta 204 40.36 N 122.29 W
Shasta ≃ 204 41.50 N 122.35 W
Shasta, Mount ∧1 204 41.20 N 122.20 W
Shasta Lake ⊜1 204 40.50 N 122.25 W
Shatangjiang 106 31.25 N 120.01 E
Shaṭānūf 142 30.14 N 31.04 E
Shatawī 140 14.39 N 32.06 E
Shāṭi', Wādī ash- ∨ 146 27.30 N 13.15 E
Shatian, Zhg. 100 25.53 N 113.44 E
Shatian, Zhg. 100 23.59 N 113.56 E
Shatila 132 33.51 N 35.30 E
Sha Tin 271d 22.23 N 114.11 E
Shatt al-Arab → Arab, Shatt al- ≃ 128 29.57 N 48.34 E
Shattuck 196 36.16 N 99.52 W
Shatuji 98 35.18 N 115.45 E
Shatuosi 102 31.20 N 108.51 E
Shauck 214 40.37 N 82.40 W
Shaunavon 184 49.40 N 108.25 W
Shaver Lake 226 37.09 N 119.18 W
Shaver Lake ⊜1 226 37.08 N 119.17 W
Shavertown 210 41.19 N 75.55 W
Shavé Ẓiyyon 132 32.59 N 35.05 E
Shavington 44 53.04 N 2.27 W
Shaw, Eng., U.K. 44 53.34 N 2.05 W
Shaw, Ms., U.S. 194 33.36 N 90.46 W
Shaw ≃ 162 20.20 S 119.17 E
Shaw Air Force Base ■ 192 33.58 N 80.29 W
Shawan, Zhg. 86 44.34 N 85.48 E
Shawan, Zhg. 100 27.52 N 119.28 E
Shawan, Zhg. 107 29.25 N 103.33 E
Shawanaga Inlet ᑕ 190 45.32 N 80.24 W
Shawangunk Kill ≃ 210 41.41 N 74.10 W
Shawangunk Mountains ⊀ 210 41.35 N 74.30 W
Shawano 190 44.46 N 88.36 W
Shawbury 42 52.47 N 2.39 W
Shaw Creek ≃ 192 33.34 N 81.30 W
Shawforth 262 53.41 N 2.10 W
Shawhan 218 38.18 N 84.16 W
Shawinigan 206 46.33 N 72.45 W
Shawinigan ≃ 206 46.32 N 72.46 W
Shawinigan, Lac ⊜ 206 46.41 N 73.10 W
Shawinigan Falls → Shawinigan 206 46.33 N 72.45 W
Shawinigan-Sud 206 46.31 N 72.45 W
Shaw Island I 224 48.34 N 122.57 W
Shawmarī, Wādī ash- ∨ 132 30.21 N 36.25 E
Shawmere ≃ 190 48.20 N 82.28 W
Shawnee, Ks., U.S. 198 39.02 N 94.43 W
Shawnee, Oh., U.S. 188 39.36 N 82.12 W
Shawnee, Ok., U.S. 196 35.19 N 96.55 W
Shawnee, Lake ⊜ 276 40.58 N 74.35 W
Shawnee Hills 214 40.07 N 83.09 W
Shawnee On Delaware 210 41.01 N 75.07 W
Shawnee State Park ♦ 218 38.43 N 83.10 W
Shawneetown 194 37.42 N 88.11 W
Shawnī 142 30.45 N 30.55 E
Shawnigan Lake 224 48.38 N 123.35 W
Shawnigan Lake ⊜ 224 48.37 N 123.37 W
Shawo, Som. 144 3.26 N 45.21 E
Shawo, Zhg. 98 34.28 N 114.37 E
Shawo, Zhg. 100 31.44 N 115.08 E
Shawo, Zhg. 100 28.52 N 114.47 E
Shawsheen ≃ 283 42.42 N 71.08 W
Shawsheen Village 283 42.40 N 71.09 W
Shawtown 279b 40.20 N 79.42 W
Shawville 188 45.36 N 76.30 W
Shaxi, Zhg. 100 28.34 N 118.06 E
Shaxi, Zhg. 100 26.53 N 115.34 E
Shaxi, Zhg. 100 24.38 N 113.42 E
Shaxi, Zhg. 106 31.34 N 121.04 E
Shaxian 100 26.24 N 117.47 E
Shaxikou 100 26.33 N 118.02 E
Shaximiao 107 29.57 N 106.19 E
Shayang 100 30.42 N 112.33 E
Shaybārā I 128 25.27 N 36.48 E
Shay Gap 162 20.25 S 120.03 E
Shaykh, Jabal ash- (Mount Hermon) ∧ 132 33.26 N 35.51 E
Shaykh, Wādī ash- ∨ 142 28.48 N 30.55 E
Shaykh Al-Ḥadīd 130 36.30 N 36.35 E
Shaykh Miskīn 132 32.49 N 36.09 E
Shaykh Sa'd 128 32.34 N 46.17 E
Shaykh 'Uthmān 144 12.52 N 44.59 E
Shayuan 100 27.45 N 120.38 E
Shazhen 98 36.23 N 115.47 E
Shazhou 106 31.52 N 120.32 E
Shazihe 102 32.12 N 106.42 E
Shchekino → Ščokino 76 54.01 N 37.31 E
Shchelkovo → Ščolkovo 76 55.55 N 38.00 E
Shcherbakov → Rybinsk 76 58.03 N 38.52 E
She ≃ 100 30.41 N 114.32 E
Sheaf ≃ 44 53.23 N 1.26 W
Shea Island I 276 41.03 N 73.24 W
Sheakleyville 214 41.27 N 80.13 W
Shea Stadium ♦ 276 40.45 N 73.51 W
Shebele 144 9.43 N 42.43 E
Shebele (Shabeelle) ≃ 144 0.12 S 42.45 E
Sheberghān 120 36.41 N 65.45 E
Shebeshekong ≃ 212 45.26 N 80.19 W
Sheboygan 190 43.45 N 87.42 W
Sheboygan ≃ 190 43.45 N 87.42 W
Sheboygan Falls 190 43.43 N 87.48 W
Shebu 100 27.40 N 112.48 E
Shechem ⊥ 132 32.13 N 35.15 E
Shechem → Nābulus 132 32.13 N 35.16 E
Shecheng 102 37.14 N 113.05 E
Shedd Canyon ∨ 226 35.39 N 120.26 W
Shedden 214 42.44 N 81.21 W
Shediac 186 46.13 N 64.32 W
Shedin Peak ∧ 182 55.55 N 127.32 W
Sheekh 144 9.56 N 45.11 E
Sheelin, Lough ⊜ 48 53.48 N 7.22 W
Sheenjek ≃ 180 66.45 N 144.33 W
Sheep ≃ 182 50.44 N 113.51 W
Sheep Creek ≃, Ab., Can. 182 54.04 N 119.00 W
Sheep Creek ≃, U.S. 202 42.27 N 115.36 W
Sheep Creek ≃, Ut., U.S. 200 40.55 N 109.39 W
Sheep Creek ≃, Wy., U.S. 200 42.03 N 106.04 W
Sheep Haven ᑕ 48 55.10 N 7.52 W
Sheepmoor 158 26.42 S 30.13 E
Sheep Mountain ∧, Az., U.S. 200 32.32 N 114.14 W
Sheep Mountain ∧, Wy., U.S. 200 43.33 N 110.32 W
Sheep Peak ∧ 196 31.14 N 104.59 W
Sheepranch 226 38.13 N 120.28 W
Sheep Range ⊀ 204 36.45 N 115.05 W
Sheepshead Bay ✦8 276 40.35 N 73.56 W
's-Heerenberg 52 51.53 N 6.15 E
's-Heerenhoek 52 51.27 N 3.46 E
Sheerness 42 51.27 N 0.45 E
Sheet Harbour 186 44.55 N 62.32 W
Shefar'am 132 32.48 N 35.10 E
Sheffield, N.Z. 172 43.23 S 172.01 E
Sheffield, Eng., U.K. 44 53.23 N 1.28 W
Sheffield, Al., U.S. 194 34.45 N 87.41 W
Sheffield, Il., U.S. 190 41.21 N 89.44 W
Sheffield, Ia., U.S. 190 42.53 N 93.12 W
Sheffield, Ma., U.S. 207 42.06 N 73.21 W
Sheffield, Oh., U.S. 214 41.25 N 82.05 W
Sheffield, Pa., U.S. 214 41.42 N 79.02 W
Sheffield, Tx., U.S. 196 30.41 N 101.49 W
Sheffield Island I 276 41.03 N 73.25 W
Sheffield Island Harbor ᑕ 276 41.03 N 73.25 W
Sheffield Lake 214 41.29 N 82.06 W
Sheffield Lake ⊜ 186 49.20 N 56.35 W
Shefford 42 52.02 N 0.20 W
Shefford □6 206 45.25 N 72.30 W
Shefu 100 26.11 N 115.22 E
Shegangshi 100 28.32 N 113.36 E
Shegaon 122 20.47 N 76.41 E
Sheho 184 51.38 N 103.12 W
Shehong 102 30.56 N 105.22 E
Shehongmiao 107 30.44 N 106.03 E
Shehy Mountains ⊀ 48 51.48 N 9.15 W
Sheikh Hasan 144 12.04 N 35.53 E
Sheikhpura 124 25.09 N 85.51 E
Shekatika 186 51.17 N 58.20 W
Shekhūpura 123 31.42 N 73.59 E
Sheki → Šeki 84 41.12 N 47.12 E
Shekki → Zhongshan 100 22.31 N 113.22 E
Shek Kong 271d 22.26 N 114.06 E
Shek Kong Airfield ⊠ 271d 22.27 N 114.05 E
Shek Kwu Chau I 271d 22.12 N 113.59 E
Shekou 100 30.44 N 114.20 E
Shek Uk Shan ∧ 271d 22.27 N 114.18 E
Shelagyote Peak ∧ 182 55.58 N 127.12 W
Shelbina 219 39.41 N 92.02 W
Shelbourne 169 36.52 S 144.01 E
Shelburn 194 39.11 N 87.24 W
Shelburne, N.S., Can. 186 43.46 N 65.19 W
Shelburne, On., Can. 212 44.04 N 80.12 W
Shelburne Bay ᑕ 164 11.49 S 143.00 E
Shelburne Falls 207 42.36 N 72.44 W
Shelby, In., U.S. 216 41.11 N 87.20 W
Shelby, Ia., U.S. 198 41.30 N 95.27 W
Shelby, Mi., U.S. 190 43.36 N 86.21 W
Shelby, Ms., U.S. 194 33.57 N 90.46 W
Shelby, Mt., U.S. 202 48.30 N 111.51 W
Shelby, Ne., U.S. 198 41.11 N 97.25 W
Shelby, N.C., U.S. 192 35.17 N 81.32 W
Shelby, Oh., U.S. 214 40.52 N 82.39 W
Shelby □6, Il., U.S. 219 39.24 N 88.48 W
Shelby □6, In., U.S. 218 39.31 N 85.47 W
Shelby □6, Ky., U.S. 218 38.15 N 85.13 W
Shelby □6, Mo., U.S. 219 39.49 N 92.03 W
Shelby □6, Oh., U.S. 216 40.17 N 84.09 W
Shelby Village 281 42.38 N 83.04 W
Shelbyville, Il., U.S. 219 39.24 N 88.47 W
Shelbyville, In., U.S. 218 39.31 N 85.46 W
Shelbyville, Ky., U.S. 218 38.12 N 85.13 W
Shelbyville, Mo., U.S. 219 39.48 N 92.02 W
Shelbyville, Tn., U.S. 194 35.29 N 86.27 W
Shelbyville, Lake ⊜1 219 39.30 N 88.40 W
Sheldon, Il., U.S. 216 40.46 N 87.33 W
Sheldon, Ia., U.S. 198 43.10 N 95.51 W
Sheldon, Mi., U.S. 216 42.17 N 83.28 W
Sheldon, Mo., U.S. 194 37.39 N 94.17 W
Sheldon, Tx., U.S. 222 29.52 N 95.08 W
Sheldon Brook ≃ 276 41.03 N 73.52 W
Sheldon Creek ≃ 212 44.07 N 79.53 W
Sheldon Point 180 62.32 N 164.52 W
Sheldon Reservoir ⊜1 222 29.52 N 95.10 W
Sheldonville 283 42.02 N 71.23 W
Sheldrake ≃ 276 40.57 N 73.44 W
Sheldrake Lake ⊜, On., Can. 212 44.49 N 77.16 W
Sheldrake Lake ⊜, N.Y., U.S. 276 40.57 N 73.46 W
Shelikof Strait ʮ 180 57.30 N 155.00 W
Shell ≃ 184 50.58 N 101.24 W
Shell, Loch ᑕ 46 58.00 N 6.30 W
Shellbrook 184 53.13 N 106.24 W
Shell Brook ≃ 184 53.21 N 106.00 W
Shell Creek ≃, U.S. 200 40.56 N 108.37 W
Shell Creek ≃, Ne., U.S. 198 41.27 N 96.58 W
Shell Creek ≃, N.D., U.S. 198 47.59 N 102.17 W
Shell Creek ≃, Wy., U.S. 202 44.31 N 108.03 W
Shellen 146 9.54 N 12.00 E
Shelley, B.C., Can. 182 54.00 N 122.37 W
Shelley, Id., U.S. 202 43.22 N 112.07 W
Shellharbour 170 34.35 S 150.52 E
Shell Lake, Sk., Can. 184 53.18 N 107.04 W
Shell Lake, Wi., U.S. 190 45.44 N 91.55 W
Shell Lakes ⊜ 162 29.21 S 127.25 E
Shellman 192 31.45 N 84.36 W
Shellmouth Dam ✦6 184 50.58 N 101.25 W
Shellow Bowells 260 51.45 N 0.20 E
Shell Rock 190 42.42 N 92.34 W
Shell Rock ≃ 190 42.38 N 92.30 W
Shellrock Peak ∧ 224 46.43 N 121.14 W
Shellsburg 190 42.05 N 91.52 W
Shelocta 214 40.39 N 79.18 W
Shelter, Port ᑕ 271d 22.21 N 114.17 E
Shelter Island 207 41.04 N 72.20 W
Shelter Island I, H.K. 271d 22.20 N 114.17 E
Shelter Island I, N.Y., U.S. 207 41.04 N 72.20 W
Shelter Island Heights 207 41.05 N 72.21 W
Shelter Island Sound ʮ 207 41.03 N 72.22 W
Shelton, Ct., U.S. 207 41.18 N 73.05 W
Shelton, Ne., U.S. 198 40.47 N 98.44 W
Shelton, Wa., U.S. 224 47.13 N 123.06 W
Shemanker ≃ 150 8.12 N 9.45 E
Shemogue 186 46.09 N 64.11 W
Shemya Station 181a 52.43 N 174.05 E
Shenandoah, Ia., U.S. 198 40.45 N 95.22 W
Shenandoah, Pa., U.S. 208 40.49 N 76.12 W
Shenandoah, Va., U.S. 188 38.29 N 78.37 W
Shenandoah ≃ 188 39.19 N 77.44 W
Shenandoah, North Fork ≃ 188 38.57 N 78.12 W
Shenandoah, South Fork ≃ 188 38.57 N 78.12 W
Shenandoah Heights 210 40.49 N 76.12 W
Shenandoah National Park ♦ 188 38.48 N 78.12 W
Shenango 214 41.23 N 80.24 W
Shenango ≃ 214 40.57 N 80.23 W
Shenango River Lake ⊜1 214 41.22 N 80.28 W
Shenchi 102 39.09 N 112.19 E
Shencottah 122 8.58 N 77.16 E
Shencun 106 31.04 N 118.51 E
Shendam 150 8.53 N 9.32 E
Shendang 106 30.34 N 120.49 E
Shending Shan ∧ 89 46.38 N 133.28 E
Shenduncun 106 30.48 N 120.25 E
Shenfield 260 51.38 N 0.19 E
Shengang, Zhg. 100 27.20 N 116.18 E
Shengang, Zhg. 106 31.54 N 120.08 E
Shenge 150 7.55 N 12.57 W
Shengfang 105 39.04 N 116.42 E
Shenggongjing 106 31.07 N 119.48 E
Shenghongqing 100 30.12 N 114.56 E
Shengjiachi 107 30.28 N 105.03 E
Shengjiaqiao 106 31.27 N 121.24 E
Shengjiatun 104 41.14 N 121.22 E
Shengjin'gao 104 42.04 N 120.43 E
Shengou 100 34.08 N 113.13 E
Shengqing 104 41.34 N 121.36 E
Shengshan 106 30.50 N 120.15 E
Shengshui 98 35.45 N 119.39 E
Shengshuihezi 98 42.27 N 125.59 E
Shengsi Liedao II 100 30.42 N 122.20 E
Shengtian 100 27.14 N 113.06 E
Shengxian 100 29.36 N 120.48 E
Shengze 106 30.55 N 120.39 E
Shengzigou 104 41.35 N 124.04 E
Shenhu 100 24.38 N 118.39 E
Shenipsit Lake ⊜ 207 41.53 N 72.26 W
Shenji 98 34.47 N 115.09 E
Shenjia 89 46.06 N 126.46 E
Shenjiadian 89 46.35 N 130.38 E
Shenjiatai 104 41.22 N 120.50 E
Shenjiawan 106 31.43 N 121.19 E
Shenjiazhuang 106 32.18 N 120.26 E
Shenjing, Zhg. 102 21.59 N 112.28 E
Shenjing, Zhg. 105 40.24 N 114.49 E
Shenjingzi 104 41.47 N 123.41 E
Shenk'eng 269d 25.00 N 121.36 E
Shenkou 100 28.42 N 116.02 E
Shenley 260 51.41 N 0.17 W
Shenmu 102 38.56 N 110.19 E
Shennan 105 38.59 N 114.56 E
Shenorock 210 41.20 N 73.44 W
Shenqiu 100 33.24 N 115.02 E
Shenquan 100 22.59 N 116.20 E
Shenquan Gang ᑕ 100 22.54 N 116.18 E
Shensi → Shaanxi □4 102 35.00 N 109.00 E
Shenton, Mount ∧ 162 28.00 S 123.22 E
Shentuan 98 35.30 N 119.17 E
Shenxian, Zhg. 98 38.01 N 115.33 E
Shenxian, Zhg. 98 36.15 N 115.41 E
Shenxing 105 39.02 N 115.19 E
Shenyang (Mukden) 104 41.48 N 123.27 E
Shenze 98 38.11 N 115.11 E
Shenzhen 100 22.34 N 114.07 E
Sheoganj 120 25.09 N 73.04 E
Sheokhāla 126 22.46 N 88.10 E
Sheopur 124 25.40 N 76.42 E
Shepard 182 50.57 N 113.55 W
Shepard Island I 9 74.25 S 132.30 W
Shepards Brook ≃ 283 42.08 N 71.25 W
Shepaug ≃ 207 41.28 N 73.19 W
Shepherd, Mi., U.S. 190 43.31 N 84.41 W
Shepherd, Tx., U.S. 222 30.30 N 95.01 W
Shepherd □8 175f 17.05 S 168.25 E
Shepherd, Îles II 175f 16.55 S 168.36 E
Shepherdstown 188 39.25 N 77.48 W
Shepherdsville 194 37.59 N 85.42 W
Sheppard Air Force Base ■ 196 33.58 N 98.30 W
Sheppard Peak ∧ 180 57.41 N 132.37 W
Sheppard Pond ⊜ 276 41.08 N 74.13 W
Shepparton 166 36.23 S 145.25 E
Shepperd, Lake ⊜ 162 29.55 S 123.09 E
Shepperton 260 51.24 N 0.27 W
Sheppey, Isle of I 42 51.24 N 0.50 E
Sheppler Hill ∧2 279b 40.09 N 79.49 W
Sheppton 210 40.53 N 76.07 W
Shepshed 42 52.47 N 1.18 W
Shepton Mallet 42 51.12 N 2.33 W
Shepway 260 51.15 N 0.33 E
Sheqi 100 33.03 N 112.57 E
Sherab 140 10.43 N 24.47 E
Sherada 144 7.21 N 36.32 E
Sheraden ✦8 279b 40.28 N 80.05 W
Sherard, Cape ≻ 176 74.36 N 80.25 W
Sherborn 283 42.14 N 71.22 W
Sherborne 42 50.57 N 2.31 W
Sherborne Lake ⊜ 212 45.11 N 78.47 W
Sherborne Saint John 42 51.18 N 1.07 W
Sherbro ≃ 150 7.45 N 12.55 W
Sherbro Island I 150 7.45 N 12.55 W
Sherbrooke, N.S., Can. 186 45.08 N 61.59 W
Sherbrooke, P.Q., Can. 206 45.25 N 71.54 W
Sherbrooke □6 206 45.25 N 71.55 W
Sherbrooke Lake ⊜ 186 44.40 N 64.35 W
Sherburn 198 43.39 N 94.43 W
Sherburne 210 42.40 N 75.29 W
Sherburne Reef ⊹2 164 3.20 S 148.00 E
Sherburn in Elmet 44 53.48 N 1.15 W
Shercock 48 54.00 N 6.54 W
Shere 260 51.13 N 0.28 W
Sheridan, Ar., U.S. 194 34.18 N 92.24 W
Sheridan, Ca., U.S. 226 38.59 N 121.22 W
Sheridan, Il., U.S. 216 41.32 N 88.41 W
Sheridan, In., U.S. 218 40.08 N 86.13 W
Sheridan, Mt., U.S. 202 45.27 N 112.11 W
Sheridan, Or., U.S. 202 45.05 N 123.23 W
Sheridan, Pa., U.S. 208 40.21 N 76.14 W
Sheridan, Tx., U.S. 222 29.29 N 96.40 W
Sheridan, Wy., U.S. 202 44.47 N 106.57 W
Sheridan, Mount ∧ 202 44.16 N 110.32 W
Sheridan Park ♦ 284a 42.59 N 78.54 W
Sheringa 162 33.51 S 135.15 E
Sheringham 42 52.57 N 1.12 E
Sherkston 284a 42.53 N 79.08 W
Sherlock ≃ 162 20.44 S 117.35 E
Sherman, Ct., U.S. 207 41.34 N 73.29 W
Sherman, Il., U.S. 219 39.54 N 89.36 W
Sherman, Ky., U.S. 218 38.44 N 84.36 W
Sherman, Ms., U.S. 194 34.21 N 88.50 W
Sherman, N.Y., U.S. 214 42.09 N 79.35 W
Sherman, Tx., U.S. 196 33.38 N 96.36 W
Sherman □6 224 45.25 N 120.49 W
Sherman Creek ≃ 208 40.23 N 77.02 W
Sherman Mills 188 45.52 N 68.23 W
Sherman Mountain ∧ 194 36.01 N 93.17 W
Sherman Oaks ✦8 280 34.09 N 118.26 W
Sherman Reservoir ⊜1 198 41.20 N 98.55 W
Sherman Station 188 45.53 N 68.25 W
Sherpur, Bngl. 124 24.41 N 89.25 E
Sherpur, Bngl. 124 25.01 N 90.01 E
Sher Qila 123 36.06 N 74.03 E
Sherrard 190 41.19 N 90.31 W
Sherridon 184 55.07 N 101.05 W
Sherrill 210 43.04 N 75.35 W
Sherrodsville 214 40.29 N 81.14 W
Sher Shāh 123 30.06 N 71.21 E
Shertallai 122 9.42 N 76.20 E
's-Hertogenbosch 52 51.41 N 5.19 E
Sherway Centre ✦9 275b 43.37 N 79.33 W
Sherwood, On., Can. 275b 43.50 N 79.31 W
Sherwood, P.E., Can. 186 46.17 N 63.08 W
Sherwood, Ar., U.S. 194 34.48 N 92.13 W
Sherwood, Md., U.S. 208 38.36 N 76.19 W
Sherwood, Mi., U.S. 216 42.00 N 85.14 W
Sherwood, N.D., U.S. 198 48.57 N 101.37 W
Sherwood, Oh., U.S. 216 41.17 N 84.33 W
Sherwood, Or., U.S. 224 45.21 N 122.50 W
Sherwood, Tn., U.S. 194 35.04 N 85.55 W
Sherwood, Lake ⊜ 281 42.36 N 83.33 W
Sherwood Forest, Ca., U.S. 226 37.57 N 122.17 W
Sherwood Forest, Md., U.S. 284c 39.05 N 77.01 W
Sherwood Forest ✦3 44 53.08 N 1.08 W
Sherwood Island State Park ♦ 276 41.07 N 73.20 W
Sherwood Manor 207 42.01 N 72.38 W
Sherwood Park, Ab., Can. 182 53.31 N 113.19 W
Sherwood Park, De., U.S. 285 39.44 N 75.39 W
Sherwood Park, N.Y., U.S. 210 42.36 N 73.43 W
Sherwood Park ♦ 275b 43.43 N 79.24 W
Sherwood Point ≻ 276 41.07 N 73.20 W
Sherwood Shores 196 30.36 N 98.22 W
She Shan ∧2 106 31.06 N 121.11 E
Sheshea ≃ 248 9.36 S 74.10 W
Shesh Gāv 120 33.45 N 68.33 E
Shet Bandar 272c 18.58 N 72.56 E
Shetek, Lake ⊜ 198 44.08 N 95.42 W
Shetland □4 46a 60.30 N 1.15 W
Shetland del Sur, Islas → South Shetland Islands II 9 62.00 S 58.00 W
Shetland Islands II 46a 60.30 N 1.15 W
Shetou 106 31.39 N 119.27 E
Shetrunji ≃ 120 21.19 N 72.07 E
Shetucket ≃ 207 41.31 N 72.05 W
Sheva 272c 18.56 N 72.57 E
Sheva Nhava 272c 18.58 N 72.58 E
Shevaroy Hills ⊀2 122 11.50 N 78.16 E
Shevington 262 53.34 N 2.42 W
Shevington Moor 262 53.35 N 2.41 W
Shewa □4 144 9.00 N 39.00 E
Shewa Gimira 144 7.00 N 35.50 E
Shexian, Zhg. 98 36.33 N 113.40 E
Shexian, Zhg. 100 29.53 N 118.26 E
Sheyang, Zhg. 100 33.20 N 119.38 E
Sheyang, Zhg. 100 33.46 N 120.18 E
Sheyenne 198 47.49 N 99.07 W
Sheyenne ≃ 198 47.05 N 96.50 W
Sheykhābād 120 34.05 N 68.45 E
Shey-Phoksundo National Park ♦ 124 29.30 N 82.45 E
Shezhu 106 31.19 N 119.16 E
Shḥīm 132 33.37 N 35.29 E
Shi ≃, Zhg. 100 32.18 N 114.31 E
Shi ≃, Zhg. 100 32.32 N 115.52 E
Shiant, Sound of ʮ 46 57.55 N 6.25 W
Shiant Islands II 46 57.53 N 6.21 W
Shiawassee □6 216 42.56 N 84.09 W
Shiawassee ≃ 216 43.06 N 84.10 W
Shiawassee, South Branch ≃ 216 42.49 N 83.56 W
Shiba 100 32.45 N 118.07 E
Shiba ≃ 268 35.47 N 139.44 E
Shibadu 102 28.01 N 110.51 E
Shibakawa 94 35.13 N 138.33 E
Shibām 144 15.56 N 48.38 E
Shiban 107 30.18 N 104.28 E
Shibanxi 107 29.17 N 103.51 E
Shibaocheng 102 39.48 N 96.10 E
Shibarni 140 14.50 N 24.25 E
Shibasaki 268 35.39 N 139.34 E
Shibata 92 37.57 N 139.20 E
Shibayama 94 35.41 N 140.25 E
Shibayama-gata ⊜ 94 36.21 N 136.23 E
Shibden Hall ⊥ 262 53.44 N 1.51 W
Shibecha 92a 43.17 N 144.36 E
Shibetsu, Nihon 92a 43.40 N 145.08 E
Shibetsu, Nihon 92a 44.10 N 142.23 E
Shibi 100 26.43 N 120.02 E
Shibīn al-Kawm 142 30.33 N 31.01 E
Shibīn al-Qanāṭir 142 30.19 N 31.19 E
Shibing 102 26.50 N 108.04 E
Shibishan 100 29.21 N 116.45 E
Shiblanjah 142 30.28 N 31.16 E
Shibu 98 36.45 N 119.27 E
Shibukawa 94 36.29 N 139.00 E
Shibure-yama ∧ 270 34.45 N 135.05 E
Shibushi 92 31.28 N 131.07 E
Shibutsu-san ∧ 94 36.54 N 139.11 E
Shibuya ✦8 268 35.40 N 139.42 E
Shibuzi 98 36.09 N 119.06 E
Shicha 100 28.24 N 115.50 E
Shichangyu 104 41.12 N 123.14 E
Shicheng, Zhg. 98 40.39 N 124.17 E
Shicheng, Zhg. 100 25.18 N 119.21 E
Shicheng, Zhg. 100 26.22 N 116.22 E
Shicheng Dao I 98 39.31 N 123.02 E
Shichisō 94 35.33 N 137.07 E
Shickley 198 40.25 N 97.43 W
Shickshinny 210 41.09 N 76.09 W
Shidai 100 30.20 N 117.56 E
Shidao 98 36.53 N 122.23 E
Shideng 102 26.44 N 99.11 E
Shidler 196 36.46 N 96.39 W
Shido 96 34.19 N 134.10 E
Shidong, Zhg. 107 28.59 N 105.27 E
Shidong, Zhg. 107 30.25 N 105.20 E
Shidongzigou 105 40.41 N 118.23 E
Shiel, Loch ⊜ 46 56.47 N 5.35 W
Shiel Bridge 46 57.12 N 5.25 W
Shieldaig 46 57.31 N 5.39 W
Shieldhill 46 55.58 N 3.46 W
Shields ≃ 202 45.43 N 110.28 W
Shiercun 106 30.31 N 119.34 E
Shi'er Shan ∧ 100 29.18 N 118.08 E
Shi'erwei 106 32.15 N 119.14 E
Shifang 100 25.01 N 116.14 E
Shifnal 42 52.40 N 2.21 W
Shifo 107 29.58 N 103.50 E
Shifobao 104 41.28 N 121.27 E
Shifochang 107 30.19 N 105.07 E
Shifodian 100 32.06 N 115.46 E
Shifosi 104 42.08 N 123.20 E
Shifoya 98 40.12 N 123.10 E
Shiga, Nihon 94 36.20 N 137.59 E
Shiga, Nihon 94 35.09 N 135.55 E
Shiga □5 96 35.15 N 136.00 E
Shigaib 140 15.01 N 23.36 E
Shigang, Zhg. 100 32.13 N 120.58 E
Shigang, Zhg. 106 32.14 N 121.00 E
Shigangmen 269b 31.21 N 121.17 E
Shigaopu 107 30.16 N 104.01 E
Shigar ≃, Asia 123 34.39 N 75.51 E
Shigar ≃, Pāk. 123 34.39 N 75.51 E
Shigaraki 94 34.52 N 136.03 E
Shigaraki-gū ᵾ1 94 34.54 N 136.04 E
Shigenobu 96 33.48 N 132.50 E
Shigenobu ≃ 96 33.48 N 132.41 E
Shigezhuang, Zhg. 105 38.57 N 116.19 E
Shigezhuang, Zhg. 105 38.59 N 115.36 E
Shigezhuang, Zhg. 105 39.18 N 116.53 E
Shigouyi 102 37.44 N 106.26 E
Shigu, Zhg. 100 29.27 N 117.14 E
Shigu, Zhg. 102 26.50 N 99.55 E
Shiguaigou 102 40.42 N 110.20 E
Shiguantun 104 41.38 N 123.39 E
Shigulingyu 105 40.38 N 116.54 E
Shīḥān ∧ 132 31.23 N 35.44 E
Shihchiachuang → Shijiazhuang 98 38.03 N 114.28 E
Shihch'i → Zhongshan 100 22.31 N 113.22 E
Shihe 98 39.19 N 121.52 E
Shihengyuanyu 106 31.50 N 121.45 E
Shihezi 86 44.18 N 86.02 E
Shihkiachwang → Shijiazhuang 98 38.03 N 114.28 E
Shihlin ✦8 269d 25.06 N 121.31 E
Shihti 269d 25.02 N 121.44 E
Shihting 269d 24.59 N 121.39 E
Shihu, Zhg. 98 41.29 N 126.18 E
Shihu, Zhg. 105 40.04 N 117.17 E
Shihuajie 102 32.20 N 111.25 E
Shihudang 106 30.58 N 121.07 E
Shihuixi 107 29.02 N 105.04 E
Shihuiyaozi 104 42.08 N 123.47 E
Shihuxia 105 40.48 N 117.22 E
Shiida 96 33.39 N 131.04 E
Shijiaba 107 30.18 N 104.46 E
Shijiagangzi 104 42.19 N 123.34 E
Shijiagou 104 42.27 N 123.28 E
Shijiao 100 23.36 N 112.59 E
Shijiaqiao, Zhg. 106 32.18 N 119.26 E
Shijiaqiao, Zhg. 106 30.46 N 120.06 E
Shijiawu 105 39.21 N 116.15 E
Shijiaxiang 107 29.38 N 104.59 E
Shijiayaozhuang 106 32.13 N 120.29 E
Shijiazhai, Zhg. 98 38.56 N 114.18 E
Shijiazhai, Zhg. 269b 31.23 N 121.30 E
Shijiazhen 106 31.51 N 121.10 E
Shijiazhuang 98 38.03 N 114.28 E
Shijiazi, Zhg. 104 42.07 N 122.18 E
Shijiazi, Zhg. 104 42.39 N 122.06 E
Shijiedu 106 30.57 N 119.13 E
Shijing, Zhg. 98 35.30 N 118.57 E
Shijing, Zhg. 100 24.40 N 118.24 E
Shijing, Zhg. 105 39.54 N 114.58 E

≃ River	Fluß	Río	Rivière	Rio
⌅ Canal	Kanal	Canal	Canal	Canal
ᒪ Waterfall, Rapids	Wasserfall, Stromschnellen	Cascada, Rápidos	Chute d'eau, Rapides	Cascata, Rápidos
ʮ Strait	Meeresstraße	Estrecho	Détroit	Estreito
ᑕ Bay, Gulf	Bucht, Golf	Bahía, Golfo	Baie, Golfe	Baía, Golfo
⊜ Lake, Lakes	See, Seen	Lago, Lagos	Lac, Lacs	Lago, Lagos
☷ Swamp	Sumpf	Pantano	Marais	Pântano
⩍ Ice Features, Glacier	Eis- und Gletscherformen	Accidentes Glaciales	Formes glaciaires	Acidentes glaciares
⍑ Other Hydrographic Features	Andere Hydrographische Objekte	Otros Elementos Hidrográficos	Autres données hydrographiques	Outros acidentes hidrográficos

⊹ Submarine Features	Untermeerische Objekte	Accidentes Submarinos	Formes de relief sous-marin	Acidentes submarinos
□ Political Unit	Politische Einheit	Unidad Politica	Entité politique	Unidade política
ᵾ Cultural Institution	Kulturelle Institution	Institución Cultural	Institution culturelle	Institução cultural
⊥ Historical Site	Historische Stätte	Sitio Histórico	Site historique	Sitio histórico
♦ Recreational Site	Erholungs- und Ferienort	Sitio de Recreo	Centre de loisirs	Area de Lazer
⊠ Airport	Flughafen	Aeropuerto	Aéroport	Aeroporto
■ Military Installation	Militäranlage	Instalación Militar	Installation militaire	Instalação militar
✦ Miscellaneous	Verschiedenes	Misceláneo	Divers	Diversos

Name	Page	Lat.°′	Long.°′
Shijingshan	**105**	39.56 N	116.07 E
Shijiu Hu ⊜	**106**	31.28 N	118.53 E
Shijiusuo	**98**	35.24 N	119.29 E
Shijiu Tuo I	**98**	39.11 N	118.56 E
Shijōnawate	**270**	34.45 N	135.39 E
Shijūmagari-tōge)(	**96**	35.11 N	133.32 E
Shika	**94**	37.01 N	136.47 E
Shikami-yama ∧	**270**	34.47 N	135.10 E
Shikano	**96**	35.28 N	134.04 E
Shikārpur, India	**122**	14.16 N	75.21 E
Shikārpur, India	**124**	28.17 N	78.01 E
Shikārpur, Pāk.	**120**	27.57 N	68.38 E
Shikatsu	**94**	35.14 N	136.53 E
Shikengkong ∧	**100**	24.56 N	113.00 E
Shikewusumiao	**102**	40.13 N	108.52 E
Shiki	**94**	35.50 N	139.35 E
Shikishima	**94**	35.41 N	138.32 E
Shikohābād	**124**	27.06 N	78.36 E
Shikoku I	**92**	33.45 N	133.30 E
Shikoku-sanchi ⋏	**96**	33.47 N	133.30 E
Shikoma	**268**	35.11 N	139.56 E
Shikotsu-ko ⊜	**92a**	42.45 N	141.20 E
Shikotsu-Tōya-kokuritsu-kōen ♠	**92a**	42.47 N	141.00 E
Shikuang	**106**	31.54 N	121.24 E
Shil	**272c**	19.09 N	73.03 E
Shilabo	**144**	6.05 N	44.48 E
Shilbottle	**44**	55.23 N	1.42 W
Shildon	**44**	54.38 N	1.39 W
Shiliangji	**100**	33.54 N	115.14 E
Shilibao	**105**	39.55 N	116.29 E
Shiliguri	**124**	26.42 N	88.26 E
Shilihe	**104**	41.31 N	123.22 E
Shiling	**106**	30.26 N	119.35 E
Shilipeng	**106**	31.14 N	119.35 E
Shilipu, Zhg.	**105**	39.29 N	116.18 E
Shilipu, Zhg.	**105**	39.11 N	115.59 E
Shilipu, Zhg.	**105**	40.15 N	117.58 E
Shiliuban	**100**	24.08 N	117.33 E
Shillelagh	**48**	52.45 N	6.32 W
Shillingstone	**42**	50.54 N	2.14 W
Shillington	**208**	40.18 N	75.57 W
Shillong	**120**	25.34 N	91.53 E
Shilo, Canadian Forces Base ■	**184**	49.49 N	99.38 W
Shiloh, Il., U.S.	**219**	38.34 N	89.54 W
Shiloh, N.J., U.S.	**208**	39.27 N	75.17 W
Shiloh, Oh., U.S.	**214**	40.58 N	82.36 W
Shiloh, Oh., U.S.	**218**	39.49 N	84.13 W
Shiloh, Oh., U.S.	**218**	39.49 N	84.13 W
Shiloh, Pa., U.S.	**208**	39.59 N	76.49 W
Shiloh National Military Park ♠	**194**	35.06 N	88.21 W
Shiloh → Saylūn, Khirbat ⊥	**132**	32.03 N	35.17 E
Shilong, Zhg.	**100**	23.07 N	113.48 E
Shilong, Zhg.	**102**	23.54 N	109.40 E
Shilong, Zhg.	**107**	30.15 N	106.34 E
Shilou	**100**	22.58 N	113.29 E
Shima, Nihon	**92**	34.13 N	136.51 E
Shima, Nihon	**270**	34.59 N	135.20 E
Shima, Zhg.	**100**	24.27 N	117.49 E
Shima, Zhg.	**107**	29.38 N	105.50 E
Shimabara	**92**	32.47 N	130.22 E
Shimachang, Zhg.	**107**	28.59 N	105.55 E
Shimachang, Zhg.	**107**	29.03 N	105.36 E
Shimada, Nihon	**94**	34.49 N	138.11 E
Shimada, Nihon	**268**	35.59 N	139.25 E
Shimagahara	**94**	34.46 N	136.03 E
Shima-hantō ≻[1]	**94**	34.26 N	136.33 E
Shimamiao	**106**	32.08 N	119.20 E
Shimamoto	**96**	34.53 N	135.40 E
Shimane □[5]	**96**	35.00 N	132.30 E
Shimane-hantō ≻[1]	**96**	35.30 N	133.00 E
Shimantan	**100**	33.17 N	113.28 E
Shimanto ≃	**96**	32.56 N	133.00 E
Shimata ≃	**96**	33.57 N	131.55 E
Shimber Berris ∧	**144**	10.44 N	47.15 E
Shimei	**106**	32.14 N	120.10 E
Shimen, Zhg.	**98**	39.44 N	118.52 E
Shimen, Zhg.	**102**	29.28 N	111.17 E
Shimen, Zhg.	**105**	40.06 N	117.42 E
Shimen, Zhg.	**106**	30.37 N	120.26 E
Shimen, Zhg.	**107**	29.36 N	106.27 E
Shimen, Zhg.	**107**	29.09 N	106.02 E
Shimencun, Zhg.	**106**	31.21 N	119.34 E
Shimencun, Zhg.	**106**	30.23 N	119.41 E
Shimendong	**100**	28.16 N	120.07 E
Shimengou	**104**	40.40 N	123.43 E
Shimenjie	**100**	29.34 N	116.44 E
Shimenlou	**100**	28.58 N	114.51 E
Shimenying	**105**	39.54 N	116.05 E
Shimenzi	**89**	48.30 N	121.31 E
Shimian	**102**	29.18 N	102.22 E
Shimiaozi	**104**	40.39 N	123.31 E
Shimizu, Nihon	**92**	35.01 N	138.29 E
Shimizu, Nihon	**92a**	43.01 N	142.53 E
Shimizu, Nihon	**94**	36.02 N	136.09 E
Shimizu, Nihon	**94**	35.01 N	138.29 E
Shimizu, Nihon	**96**	34.05 N	135.26 E
Shimizu → Tosa-shimizu	**92**	32.46 N	132.57 E
Shimizu-tunnel ◆[5]	**94**	36.52 N	138.55 E
Shimla	**123**	31.06 N	77.10 E
Shimminato	**94**	36.47 N	137.04 E
Shimobe	**94**	35.27 N	138.29 E
Shimoda	**94**	34.40 N	138.57 E
Shimodate	**94**	36.18 N	139.59 E
Shimofusa	**94**	35.52 N	140.21 E
Shimofusa-daichi ⋏[1]	**268**	35.45 N	139.58 E
Shimofusa-kōkūkichi, Kaijō-jieitai- ■	**94**	35.50 N	140.05 E
Shimofusa Naval Air Base ■	**268**	35.48 N	140.01 E
Shimoga	**122**	13.55 N	75.34 E
Shimogawara	**268**	35.56 N	139.21 E
Shimogōri	**268**	35.21 N	140.03 E
Shimogyō ◆[8]	**270**	34.59 N	135.45 E
Shimohōya	**268**	35.45 N	139.34 E
Shimoichi	**96**	34.22 N	135.47 E
Shimoigusa ◆[8]	**268**	35.43 N	139.37 E
Shimoji	**175d**	24.45 N	125.16 E
Shimoji-jima I	**175d**	24.49 N	125.09 E
Shimojō	**94**	35.24 N	137.47 E
Shimokawa	**92a**	44.18 N	142.39 E
Shimokita-hantō ≻[1]	**92**	41.15 N	141.00 E
Shimomatsu	**270**	34.27 N	135.23 E
Shimomizo	**268**	35.31 N	139.23 E
Shimoni	**154**	4.39 S	39.23 E
Shimoniikura	**268**	35.47 N	139.38 E
Shimonita	**94**	36.13 N	138.47 E
Shimonoseki	**96**	33.57 N	130.57 E
Shimookudomi	**268**	35.53 N	139.26 E
Shimoryūzu-zaki ≻	**96**	33.30 N	133.34 E
Shimosakamoto	**270**	35.03 N	135.53 E
Shimosuwa	**94**	36.04 N	138.05 E
Shimotajiri	**270**	34.57 N	135.28 E
Shimotomi	**268**	35.50 N	139.29 E
Shimotsu	**96**	34.10 N	135.08 E-
Shimotsuchidana	**268**	35.24 N	139.27 E
Shimotsui	**96**	34.26 N	133.47 E
Shimotsuma	**94**	36.11 N	139.58 E
Shimotsuruma	**268**	35.29 N	139.28 E
Shimoya	**268**	35.23 N	139.21 E
Shimoyama	**94**	35.02 N	137.19 E
Shimoyugi	**268**	35.38 N	139.23 E
Shimura ◆[8]	**268**	35.46 N	139.41 E
Shin, Loch ⊜	**46**	58.06 N	4.34 W
Shinagawa ◆[8]	**268**	35.37 N	139.45 E
Shinan	**102**	22.43 N	109.54 E
Shinano	**94**	36.48 N	138.13 E
Shinano ≃	**92**	37.56 N	139.03 E
Shinarā	**142**	28.47 N	30.46 E
Shināṣ	**128**	24.46 N	56.28 E
Shinawari	**123**	33.32 N	70.48 E
Shinbārī	**273c**	30.07 N	31.09 E
Shīndand	**128**	33.18 N	62.08 E
Shindenbaru-kichi, Kōkū-jieitai- ■	**92**	32.04 N	131.30 E
Shindo	**268**	35.21 N	139.21 E
Shiner	**222**	29.25 N	97.10 W
Shingbwiyang	**110**	26.41 N	96.13 E
Shingishū → Sinŭiju	**98**	40.05 N	124.24 E
Shinglehouse	**214**	41.57 N	78.11 W
Shingle Springs	**226**	38.40 N	120.56 W
Shing Mun Reservoir ⊜[1]	**271d**	22.23 N	114.08 E
Shingo	**96**	34.59 N	133.23 E
Shingū, Nihon	**92**	33.44 N	135.59 E
Shingū, Nihon	**96**	34.55 N	134.33 E
Shingū, Nihon	**96**	33.56 N	133.38 E
Shingwidzi	**156**	23.05 S	31.25 E
Shingwidzi (Singuédeze) ≃	**156**	23.53 S	32.17 E
Shinichi	**96**	34.33 N	133.16 E
Shining Tor ∧	**262**	53.16 N	2.01 W
Shinīrah	**132**	32.22 N	36.45 E
Shinji	**96**	35.24 N	132.54 E
Shinji-ko ⊜	**96**	35.27 N	132.58 E
Shinjō, Nihon	**92**	38.46 N	140.18 E
Shinjō, Nihon	**270**	34.30 N	135.44 E
Shinjuku ◆[8]	**268**	35.41 N	139.42 E
Shinkawa	**94**	35.09 N	136.50 E
Shīnkay	**120**	31.57 N	67.26 E
Shinkolobwe	**154**	11.02 S	26.35 E
Shinmachi	**94**	36.16 N	139.07 E
Shinminato ≃	**270**	34.38 N	135.09 E
Shinnārah, Minqār ≗[4]	**142**	28.52 N	30.38 E
Shinnayō	**96**	34.04 N	131.47 E
Shinnecock Bay ⊂	**207**	40.52 N	72.28 W
Shinnel Water ≃	**44**	55.13 N	3.49 W
Shinness	**46**	58.05 N	4.28 W
Shinnston	**188**	39.23 N	80.18 W
Shino-jima I	**94**	34.39 N	137.00 E
Shinsai-bashi ◆[8]	**270**	34.40 N	135.31 E
Shinshār	**130**	34.36 N	36.44 E
Shinshiro	**94**	34.54 N	137.30 E
Shinshū-shinmachi	**94**	36.34 N	138.01 E
Shintone	**94**	35.50 N	140.20 E
Shinyanga	**154**	3.40 S	33.26 E
Shinyanga □[4]	**154**	3.45 S	33.00 E
Shin-yōdo ≃[1]	**270**	34.41 N	135.26 E
Shio	**94**	36.52 N	136.48 E
Shiobara	**94**	36.58 N	139.49 E
Shiocton	**190**	44.26 N	88.34 W
Shiogama	**92**	38.19 N	141.01 E
Shiojiri	**94**	36.06 N	137.58 E
Shiojiri-tōge)(	**94**	36.05 N	138.02 E
Shiomi-dake ∧	**94**	35.34 N	138.12 E
Shionoe	**96**	34.10 N	134.05 E
Shiono-misaki ≻	**92**	33.26 N	135.45 E
Shioya	**94**	36.46 N	139.51 E
Shioya ◆[8]	**270**	34.38 N	135.06 E
Shioya-zaki ≻, Nihon	**92**	33.26 N	135.45 E
Shioya-zaki ≻, Nihon	**94**	36.59 N	140.59 E
Shiozawa	**94**	37.02 N	138.51 E
Shipai, Zhg.	**100**	23.08 N	113.21 E
Shipai, Zhg.	**106**	31.30 N	120.55 E
Shipanpu	**107**	30.28 N	104.23 E
Shipantuo	**107**	30.25 N	106.13 E
Ship Bottom	**208**	39.38 N	74.10 W
Shipbourne	**260**	51.15 N	0.17 E
Ship Cove	**186**	47.06 N	54.05 W
Shipdham	**42**	52.37 N	0.53 E
Shiping, Zhg.	**102**	28.20 N	107.42 E
Shiping, Zhg.	**102**	23.47 N	102.30 E
Shipley	**44**	53.50 N	1.47 W
Shipman, Il., U.S.	**219**	39.07 N	90.03 W
Shipman, Va., U.S.	**192**	37.43 N	78.50 W
Shippan Point ≻	**276**	41.01 N	73.32 W
Shippegan	**186**	47.45 N	64.42 W
Shippensburg	**208**	40.03 N	77.31 W
Shippenville	**214**	41.15 N	79.28 W
Shippingport	**214**	40.38 N	80.25 W
Shippō	**94**	35.10 N	136.48 E
Shiprock	**200**	36.47 N	108.41 W
Ship Rock ∧	**200**	36.42 N	108.50 W
Shipshaw ≃	**186**	48.27 N	71.12 W
Shipshewana	**216**	41.40 N	85.34 W
Shipston-on-Stour	**42**	52.04 N	1.37 W
Shipton-under-Wychwood	**42**	51.51 N	1.35 W
Shipu, Zhg.	**100**	29.13 N	121.55 E
Shipu, Zhg.	**106**	31.15 N	121.03 E
Shiqian	**102**	27.31 N	108.20 E
Shiqiao, Zhg.	**100**	33.12 N	112.36 E
Shiqiao, Zhg.	**100**	26.58 N	114.23 E
Shiqiao, Zhg.	**106**	30.30 N	119.11 E
Shiqiao, Zhg.	**107**	30.25 N	104.31 E
Shiqiaopu	**107**	30.05 N	105.23 E
Shiqiaozi	**104**	41.27 N	123.43 E
Shiqi → Zhongshan	**100**	22.31 N	113.22 E
Shiqma ≃	**132**	31.36 N	34.30 E
Shiquan, Zhg.	**102**	33.03 N	108.17 E
Shiquan, Zhg.	**106**	30.30 N	120.48 E
Shirahama, Nihon	**94**	34.54 N	139.54 E
Shirahama, Nihon	**96**	33.40 N	135.20 E
Shirahata-yama ∧	**96**	34.54 N	134.23 E
Shiraitono-taki ⌊	**94**	35.18 N	138.38 E
Shirakami-misaki ≻	**92a**	41.24 N	140.12 E
Shirakawa, Nihon	**94**	37.07 N	140.13 E
Shirakawa, Nihon	**94**	35.35 N	137.12 E
Shirakawa, Nihon	**94**	36.16 N	136.54 E
Shirakawa-no-seki-ato ⊥	**94**	37.03 N	140.15 E
Shirakawa-tōge ∧[2]	**270**	34.42 N	135.07 E
Shirako	**94**	35.26 N	140.23 E
Shirākol	**126**	22.18 N	88.16 E
Shirakura-yama ∧	**94**	35.00 N	137.46 E
Shirama-yama ∧	**96**	34.01 N	135.23 E
Shiramine	**94**	36.10 N	136.37 E
Shirane	**94**	35.38 N	138.28 E
Shirane-san ∧, Nihon	**94**	36.38 N	138.32 E
Shirane-san ∧, Nihon	**94**	36.48 N	139.22 E
Shirane-san (Kita-dake) ∧, Nihon	**94**	35.40 N	138.15 E
Shiranuka	**92a**	42.57 N	144.05 E
Shiraoi	**92a**	42.33 N	141.21 E
Shiraoka	**94**	36.01 N	139.40 E
Shiraone	**272c**	19.03 N	73.01 E
Shirasawa	**94**	36.40 N	139.08 E
Shirati	**154**	1.08 S	33.59 E
Shīrāz	**128**	29.36 N	52.32 E
Shirbīn	**142**	31.11 N	31.32 E
Shirdley Hill	**262**	53.36 N	2.58 W
Shire (Chire) ≃	**154**	17.42 S	35.19 E
Shirebrook	**44**	53.12 N	1.13 W
Shiremanstown	**208**	40.13 N	76.57 W
Shiretoko-hantō ≻[1]	**92a**	44.00 N	145.00 E
Shiretoko-kokuritsu-kōen ♠	**92a**	44.08 N	145.10 E
Shiretoko-misaki ≻	**92a**	44.14 N	145.17 E
Shīrīn ≃	**120**	36.49 N	65.01 E
Shīr Kūh ∧	**128**	31.34 N	54.04 E
Shirland	**216**	42.27 N	89.12 W
Shirley, B.C., Can.	**224**	48.23 N	123.54 W
Shirley, Il., U.S.	**216**	40.24 N	89.04 W
Shirley, In., U.S.	**218**	39.53 N	85.34 W
Shirley, Ma., U.S.	**207**	42.32 N	71.39 W
Shirley Plantation ⊥	**208**	37.21 N	77.15 W
Shirleysburg	**214**	40.18 N	77.53 W
Shiro	**222**	30.37 N	95.53 W
Shiroi	**94**	35.48 N	140.04 E
Shiroishi	**92**	38.00 N	140.37 E
Shirokawa	**96**	33.23 N	132.46 E
Shirone	**92**	37.46 N	139.01 E
Shirotori, Nihon	**94**	35.53 N	136.52 E
Shirotori, Nihon	**96**	34.15 N	134.20 E
Shirouma-dake ∧	**94**	36.45 N	137.46 E
Shiroyama	**94**	35.35 N	139.19 E
Shiro-yama ∧	**270**	34.38 N	135.53 E
Shirpur	**120**	21.21 N	74.53 E
Shirrell Heath	**42**	50.55 N	1.12 W
Shirshābah	**142**	30.47 N	31.10 E
Shīrvān	**128**	37.24 N	57.55 E
Shisaka-jima I	**96**	34.07 N	133.11 E
Shisanling	**105**	40.19 N	116.16 E
Shi San Ling (Ming Tombs) ⊥	**105**	40.19 N	116.13 E
Shisanzhan	**89**	51.21 N	125.43 E
Shisha Hai ⊜	**271a**	39.57 N	116.22 E
Shishaldin Volcano ∧[1]	**180**	54.45 N	163.57 W
Shishan	**104**	41.16 N	121.30 E
Shishi	**100**	24.48 N	118.38 E
Shishikui	**96**	33.34 N	134.18 E
Shishi Shan ∧	**100**	24.44 N	117.54 E
Shishmaref	**180**	66.14 N	166.09 W
Shishmaref Inlet ⊂	**180**	66.07 N	165.50 W
Shishou	**102**	29.43 N	112.19 E
Shisht al-Anʿām	**142**	30.52 N	30.44 E
Shisiazhan	**89**	51.36 N	125.42 E
Shisixian	**104**	40.53 N	122.59 E
Shisler Point ≻	**284a**	42.52 N	79.08 W
Shisui	**94**	35.43 N	140.16 E
Shitai	**100**	30.13 N	117.27 E
Shitan, Zhg.	**100**	27.44 N	112.42 E
Shitan, Zhg.	**100**	23.10 N	113.47 E
Shitang, Zhg.	**100**	28.16 N	121.36 E
Shitang, Zhg.	**102**	25.38 N	110.50 E
Shitangwan	**106**	31.40 N	120.13 E
Shitara	**94**	35.05 N	137.35 E
Shithāthah	**128**	32.33 N	43.29 E
Shiting, Zhg.	**100**	27.36 N	113.16 E
Shiting, Zhg.	**105**	39.31 N	115.41 E
Shitoufangzi	**89**	48.38 N	126.08 E
Shitougouzi	**89**	49.19 N	125.55 E
Shitoumiao	**102**	41.41 N	106.50 E
Shitoumiaozi	**104**	41.38 N	121.26 E
Shitoushan	**105**	40.27 N	116.13 E
Shitoushuangmiao	**98**	41.28 N	118.55 E
Shituan	**107**	30.09 N	105.01 E
Shitunwei	**104**	41.07 N	121.31 E
Shiv	**120**	26.11 N	71.15 E
Shivalya	**126**	23.50 N	89.47 E
Shively	**218**	38.12 N	85.49 W
Shivering, Mount ∧	**170**	34.08 S	150.02 E
Shivpuri	**124**	25.26 N	77.39 E
Shivta, Ḥorvot (Subeita) ⊥	**132**	30.53 N	34.38 E
Shivwits Plateau ⋏[1]	**200**	36.15 N	113.40 W
Shiwaku-shotō II	**96**	34.20 N	133.45 E
Shiwan, Zhg.	**100**	27.17 N	112.57 E
Shiwan, Zhg.	**100**	28.12 N	113.49 E
Shiwan, Zhg.	**100**	23.01 N	113.04 E
Shiwan, Zhg.	**102**	37.35 N	109.01 E
Shiwenchang	**104**	41.43 N	123.54 E
Shiwu	**89**	43.48 N	124.13 E
Shixi, Zhg.	**100**	28.16 N	117.45 E
Shixi, Zhg.	**100**	28.16 N	115.36 E
Shixia	**105**	40.20 N	114.59 E
Shixian	**89**	43.05 N	129.47 E
Shixiancun	**106**	31.12 N	120.29 E
Shixiechang	**107**	29.51 N	106.41 E
Shixing	**100**	24.58 N	114.03 E
Shixun	**100**	24.44 N	118.11 E
Shiyachang	**107**	30.27 N	106.31 E
Shiyan, Zhg.	**102**	32.38 N	110.44 E
Shiyan, Zhg.	**107**	30.22 N	104.27 E
Shiyangchang, Zhg.	**107**	29.56 N	105.37 E
Shiyangchang, Zhg.	**107**	30.42 N	105.57 E
Shiyanqiao	**107**	29.19 N	105.22 E
Shiyiwei	**106**	31.59 N	120.43 E
Shiyizhan	**89**	51.13 N	125.52 E
Shiyu	**107**	29.46 N	106.06 E
Shizhangzi	**98**	40.24 N	119.48 E
Shizheng	**100**	24.32 N	115.50 E
Shizhenjie	**100**	28.51 N	116.56 E
Shizhong, Zhg.	**100**	24.57 N	117.06 E
Shizhong, Zhg.	**106**	30.44 N	120.16 E
Shizhongtan	**107**	30.26 N	104.35 E
Shizhu, Zhg.	**100**	28.48 N	120.06 E
Shizhu, Zhg.	**102**	29.56 N	108.09 E
Shizhuang	**106**	32.08 N	120.31 E
Shizhuangzi, Zhg.	**104**	42.24 N	122.53 E
Shizhuangzi, Zhg.	**105**	40.38 N	116.59 E
Shizhuzi	**104**	41.18 N	121.35 E
Shizichang	**107**	29.32 N	106.14 E
Shizigu	**105**	39.23 N	118.08 E
Shizikou	**100**	24.12 N	113.38 E
Shizilin	**106**	31.26 N	121.25 E
Shizipo	**105**	40.21 N	115.07 E
Shizipu	**106**	30.59 N	119.07 E
Shizuchi-kokutei-kōen ♠	**96**	33.45 N	133.08 E
Shizugawa	**92**	38.40 N	141.27 E
Shizui, Zhg.	**89**	43.08 N	126.06 E
Shizui, Zhg.	**98**	38.52 N	113.42 E
Shizuma ≃	**96**	35.12 N	132.28 E
Shizunai	**92a**	42.20 N	142.22 E
Shizuoka	**94**	34.58 N	138.23 E
Shizuoka □[5]	**94**	35.00 N	138.00 E
Shkodër	**38**	42.05 N	19.30 E
Shkumbin ≃	**38**	41.01 N	19.26 E
Shō ≃	**94**	36.47 N	137.04 E
Shoal ≃	**194**	30.41 N	86.39 W
Shoal Cape ≻	**162**	33.53 S	121.07 E
Shoal Creek ≃, U.S.	**194**	37.05 N	94.42 W
Shoal Creek ≃, U.S.	**194**	34.50 N	87.33 W
Shoal Creek ≃, U.S.	**194**	40.28 N	92.42 W
Shoal Creek ≃, Il., U.S.	**219**	38.28 N	89.35 W
Shoal Creek ≃, Mo., U.S.	**194**	39.44 N	93.32 W
Shoal Creek, East Fork ≃	**219**	38.51 N	89.30 W
Shoal Creek, Middle Fork ≃	**219**	39.05 N	89.33 W
Shoal Creek, West Fork ≃	**219**	39.05 N	89.33 W
Shoal Harbour	**186**	48.11 N	53.59 W
Shoalhaven ≃	**170**	34.52 S	150.44 E
Shoalhaven Bight ⊂[3]	**170**	34.52 S	150.47 E
Shoal Lake	**184**	50.26 N	100.34 W
Shoal Lake ⊜	**184**	49.32 N	95.00 W
Shoal Point ≻	**276**	41.08 N	73.15 W
Shoals	**194**	38.39 N	86.47 W
Shoals, Bay of ⊂	**168b**	35.37 S	137.37 E
Shoalwater Bay ⊂	**166**	22.02 S	150.25 E
Shōbara	**96**	34.51 N	133.01 E
Shōboku	**96**	35.06 N	134.07 E
Shobonier	**219**	38.52 N	89.05 W
Shōbu	**94**	36.04 N	139.36 E
Shōdai	**270**	34.51 N	135.42 E
Shōdo-shima I	**96**	34.30 N	134.17 E
Shoeburyness	**42**	51.32 N	0.48 E
Shoe Cove	**186**	49.55 N	55.33 W
Shoemakersville	**208**	40.30 N	75.58 W
Shōgawa	**94**	36.34 N	136.59 E
Shogunle	**273a**	6.35 N	3.21 E
Shohola	**210**	41.28 N	74.55 W
Shohola Creek ≃	**210**	41.28 N	74.55 W
Shokambetsu-dake ∧	**92a**	43.43 N	141.31 E
Shokan	**210**	41.58 N	74.13 W
Shōkawa	**94**	36.02 N	136.57 E
Sholingnur	**122**	13.07 N	79.25 E
Shomera	**132**	33.05 N	35.17 E
Shomolu	**273a**	6.32 N	3.23 E
Shōmyō-no-taki ⌊	**94**	36.35 N	137.24 E
Shona, Eilean I	**46**	56.47 N	5.52 W
Shōnai	**96**	33.11 N	131.26 E
Shōnai ≃	**94**	35.04 N	136.50 E
Shōnan	**268**	35.50 N	140.02 E
Shongum	**276**	40.50 N	74.33 W
Shongum Lake ⊜	**276**	40.51 N	74.32 W
Shongwe	**158**	27.24 S	32.25 E
Shōō	**96**	35.02 N	134.08 E
Shooters Hill	**170**	33.54 S	149.52 E
Shooters Island I	**276**	40.39 N	74.10 W
Shopiere	**216**	42.34 N	88.57 W
Shoranūr	**122**	10.46 N	76.17 E
Shorāpur	**122**	16.31 N	76.45 E
Shoreacres, B.C., Can.	**182**	49.26 N	117.32 W
Shore Acres, Ca., U.S.	**226**	38.02 N	121.58 W
Shore Acres, Ma., U.S.	**207**	42.12 N	70.44 W
Shore Acres, N.J., U.S.	**208**	40.01 N	74.06 W
Shoreacres, Tx., U.S.	**222**	29.37 N	95.01 W
Shoreditch ◆[8]	**260**	51.32 N	0.05 W
Shoreham, Austl.	**169**	38.25 S	145.03 E
Shoreham, Eng., U.K.	**260**	51.20 N	0.11 E
Shoreham, Mi., U.S.	**216**	42.03 N	86.30 W
Shoreham-by-Sea	**42**	50.49 N	0.16 W
Shorewood, Il., U.S.	**216**	41.32 N	88.12 W
Shorewood, Wi., U.S.	**216**	43.05 N	87.53 W
Shorewood Hills	**216**	43.04 N	89.26 W
Shorkot	**123**	30.50 N	72.04 E
Shorkot Road	**123**	30.47 N	72.15 E
Shorne	**260**	51.25 N	0.26 E
Short Acres	**226**	36.21 N	119.38 W
Short Beach	**207**	41.15 N	72.50 W
Short Creek	**214**	40.11 N	80.55 W
Shortland Islands II	**175e**	6.55 S	155.53 E
Short Mountain ∧	**192**	36.23 N	83.10 W
Shortsville	**210**	42.57 N	77.13 W
Shoshone	**202**	42.56 N	114.24 W
Shoshone ≃	**202**	44.52 N	108.11 W
Shoshone, North Fork ≃	**202**	44.29 N	109.18 W
Shoshone, South Fork ≃	**202**	44.27 N	109.14 W
Shoshone Basin ≚[1]	**202**	43.05 N	108.05 W
Shoshone Lake ⊜	**202**	44.22 N	110.43 W
Shoshone Mountains ⋏	**204**	39.00 N	117.30 W
Shoshone Peak ∧	**204**	36.56 N	116.16 W
Shoshone Range ⋏	**204**	40.20 N	116.50 W
Shoshong	**156**	22.59 S	26.30 E
Shoshoni	**200**	43.14 N	108.06 W
Shostka → Šostka	**78**	51.52 N	33.30 E
Shotley Gate	**42**	51.58 N	1.15 E
Shotton	**262**	53.12 N	3.02 W
Shotton Colliery	**44**	54.44 N	1.20 W
Shotts	**46**	55.49 N	3.48 W
Shotwick	**262**	53.14 N	2.59 W
Shou'anzhen	**107**	30.16 N	103.37 E
Shouchang	**100**	29.22 N	119.13 E
Shoufeng	**100**	23.52 N	121.30 E
Shouguang	**98**	36.53 N	118.42 E
Shouning	**100**	27.27 N	119.30 E
Shournagh ≃	**48**	51.53 N	8.35 W
Shoushan	**104**	41.12 N	123.03 E
Shouwangfen	**105**	40.35 N	117.48 E
Shouxian	**100**	32.35 N	116.47 E
Shouyang	**102**	37.59 N	113.09 E
Shōwa, Nihon	**94**	36.37 N	139.04 E
Shōwa, Nihon	**96**	34.43 N	133.39 E
Showell	**208**	38.23 N	75.12 W
Show Low	**200**	34.15 N	110.01 W
Shqipëri → Albania □[1]	**38**	41.00 N	20.00 E
Shreve	**214**	40.40 N	82.01 W
Shreveport	**194**	32.30 N	93.44 W
Shrevewood	**284c**	38.53 N	77.13 W
Shrewsbury, Eng., U.K.	**42**	52.43 N	2.45 W
Shrewsbury, Ma., U.S.	**207**	42.17 N	71.42 W
Shrewsbury, N.J., U.S.	**208**	40.19 N	74.03 W
Shrewsbury, Pa., U.S.	**208**	39.46 N	76.40 W
Shrewsbury River ⊂	**276**	40.21 N	74.00 W
Shrewton	**42**	51.12 N	1.55 W
Shri Dūngargarh	**120**	28.05 N	74.00 E
Shri Mohangarh	**120**	27.17 N	71.14 E
Shriner Mountain ∧	**210**	40.56 N	77.20 W
Shrīrangapattana	**122**	12.25 N	76.42 E
Shrivenham	**42**	51.36 N	1.39 W
Shropshire □[6]	**42**	52.40 N	2.40 W
Shropshire Union Canal ≋	**262**	53.17 N	2.53 W
Shrub Oak	**210**	41.20 N	73.49 W
Shrule	**48**	53.30 N	9.08 W
Shu ≃	**98**	34.07 N	118.30 E
Shuajingsi	**102**	32.00 N	103.05 E
Shuanfeng Shan ∧	**107**	29.26 N	105.47 E
Shuang ≃	**269d**	25.00 N	121.31 E
Shuangbai	**102**	24.54 N	101.32 E
Shuangcheng	**89**	45.21 N	126.17 E
Shuangchengzi	**105**	40.11 N	118.03 E
Shuangdian	**100**	32.23 N	120.51 E
Shuangdun	**106**	32.13 N	121.08 E
Shuangfeng, Zhg.	**102**	27.24 N	112.05 E
Shuangfeng, Zhg.	**106**	31.31 N	121.01 E
Shuangfeng, Zhg.	**106**	31.31 N	121.02 E
Shuangfeng Shan ∧	**100**	24.28 N	114.43 E
Shuangfengyi	**107**	29.27 N	105.09 E
Shuangfu	**105**	39.48 N	117.44 E
Shuangfuchang, Zhg.	**107**	29.41 N	103.31 E
Shuangfuchang, Zhg.	**107**	30.08 N	103.32 E
Shuanggang, Zhg.	**89**	45.07 N	122.59 E
Shuanggang, Zhg.	**100**	28.11 N	117.30 E
Shuanggetun	**89**	48.58 N	129.57 E
Shuanggou, Zhg.	**98**	34.03 N	117.37 E
Shuanggou, Zhg.	**100**	32.12 N	112.21 E
Shuanggou, Zhg.	**100**	33.16 N	118.10 E
Shuanggufen	**107**	29.38 N	104.11 E
Shuanghe, Zhg.	**100**	31.33 N	116.46 E
Shuanghe, Zhg.	**100**	31.41 N	112.46 E
Shuanghe, Zhg.	**107**	29.40 N	104.48 E
Shuanghe, Zhg.	**107**	30.07 N	105.10 E
Shuanghe, Zhg.	**107**	30.15 N	104.44 E
Shuanghechang, Zhg.	**107**	28.51 N	104.51 E
Shuanghechang, Zhg.	**107**	29.25 N	106.17 E
Shuanghechang, Zhg.	**107**	29.12 N	105.43 E
Shuanghechang, Zhg.	**107**	29.18 N	105.36 E
Shuang-hsi	**269d**	25.01 N	121.39 E
Shuangji ≃	**100**	34.05 N	114.24 E
Shuangjiang, Zhg.	**100**	26.48 N	116.28 E
Shuangjiang, Zhg.	**102**	23.37 N	99.41 E
Shuangjiang, Zhg.	**107**	30.13 N	105.45 E
Shuangjiangqiao	**102**	25.19 N	98.51 E
Shuangjianji	**100**	33.12 N	116.40 E
Shuangjingzi	**104**	42.28 N	123.42 E
Shuangkou	**105**	39.15 N	117.02 E
Shuangliao	**89**	43.31 N	123.30 E
Shuanglin	**106**	30.47 N	120.19 E
Shuanglingzi, Zhg.	**104**	40.54 N	124.10 E
Shuanglingzi, Zhg.	**104**	40.50 N	123.06 E
Shuangliu	**107**	30.34 N	103.55 E
Shuangliushu	**100**	31.56 N	115.12 E
Shuanglongtai	**104**	40.56 N	122.39 E
Shuangmiao, Zhg.	**100**	28.24 N	120.45 E
Shuangmiao, Zhg.	**100**	32.09 N	116.52 E
Shuangmiaozi, Zhg.	**104**	42.25 N	122.17 E
Shuangmiaozi, Zhg.	**104**	42.02 N	121.52 E
Shuangpai	**110**	25.57 N	111.32 E
Shuangpaishi	**106**	31.24 N	118.59 E
Shuangqiao, Zhg.	**100**	32.29 N	116.41 E
Shuangqiao, Zhg.	**105**	39.54 N	116.37 E
Shuangqiao, Zhg.	**106**	30.59 N	118.47 E
Shuangshanzi	**98**	40.21 N	119.08 E
Shuangshipu	**107**	29.14 N	104.42 E
Shuangshiqiao, Zhg.	**107**	29.22 N	105.51 E
Shuangshiqiao, Zhg.	**107**	29.23 N	104.29 E
Shuangshu	**105**	39.34 N	117.01 E
Shuangshutai	**89**	43.50 N	121.15 E
Shuangtaizi, Zhg.	**104**	41.34 N	121.12 E
Shuangtaizi, Zhg.	**104**	42.21 N	124.10 E
Shuangtaizi, Zhg.	**104**	42.25 N	123.11 E
Shuangtaizi, Zhg.	**104**	41.00 N	122.34 E
Shuangtaizi, Zhg.	**104**	41.11 N	121.14 E
Shuangtaizi ≃	**104**	40.59 N	121.51 E
Shuangtaizihe Kou ≃[1]	**104**	40.55 N	121.50 E
Shuangtang, Zhg.	**100**	28.01 N	116.44 E
Shuangtang, Zhg.	**105**	39.03 N	116.17 E
Shuangtang, Zhg.	**105**	38.53 N	116.54 E
Shuangtangdian	**106**	30.59 N	118.51 E
Shuangtuo	**105**	39.14 N	117.20 E
Shuangtuozhen	**105**	39.29 N	118.23 E
Shuangxi, Zhg.	**100**	27.01 N	119.03 E
Shuangxi, Zhg.	**106**	30.24 N	119.50 E
Shuangyang	**89**	43.32 N	125.42 E
Shuangyangdian	**104**	41.07 N	121.16 E
Shuangyaocun	**105**	38.55 N	117.03 E
Shuangyashan	**89**	46.37 N	131.22 E
Shuʿayb, Wādī V	**132**	31.54 N	35.38 E
Shuʿayt, Wādī V	**144**	18.15 N	52.00 E
Shubenacadie ≃	**186**	45.20 N	63.30 W
Shublik Mountains ⋏	**180**	69.31 N	145.40 W
Shubrā al-Khaymah	**142**	30.06 N	31.15 E
Shubrā Bābil	**142**	30.54 N	31.11 E
Shubrā Khalfūn	**142**	30.29 N	31.05 E
Shubrā Khīt	**142**	31.02 N	30.43 E
Shubuta	**194**	31.51 N	88.41 W
Shucheng	**100**	31.27 N	116.57 E
Shufu	**85**	39.27 N	75.52 E
Shufuka Shan ∧	**89**	50.28 N	123.10 E
Shugudali	**89**	52.47 N	124.02 E
Shuheyingzi	**104**	42.18 N	122.16 E
Shuhezhen	**106**	31.35 N	121.35 E
Shūhō	**96**	34.13 N	131.18 E
Shuhong	**100**	28.39 N	120.09 E
Shuibatang	**102**	28.39 N	107.03 E
Shuibei, Zhg.	**100**	28.04 N	115.01 E
Shuibei, Zhg.	**106**	31.40 N	119.39 E
Shuichaoyang	**100**	26.22 N	117.57 E
Shuicheng	**102**	26.41 N	104.50 E
Shuidao	**98**	37.10 N	121.33 E
Shuidiangou	**89**	47.43 N	122.40 E
Shuidong, Zhg.	**106**	31.23 N	119.37 E
Shuidong, Zhg.	**106**	30.47 N	118.57 E
Shuidongjie	**106**	31.07 N	119.33 E
Shuiduixia	**106**	30.17 N	118.50 E
Shuihai	**100**	33.02 N	120.26 E
Shuihouling	**100**	30.43 N	116.26 E
Shuiji	**100**	27.26 N	118.20 E
Shuijiahuangdi	**104**	42.14 N	123.28 E
Shuijian	**105**	40.09 N	115.58 E
Shuijing	**102**	26.10 N	99.09 E
Shuijingtang	**102**	28.50 N	108.11 E
Shuikou, Zhg.	**100**	26.18 N	113.46 E
Shuikou, Zhg.	**100**	26.59 N	117.41 E
Shuikou, Zhg.	**100**	26.22 N	118.44 E
Shuikou, Zhg.	**100**	24.00 N	115.55 E
Shuikou, Zhg.	**102**	25.54 N	109.06 E
Shuikou, Zhg.	**107**	29.29 N	103.42 E
Shuikouchang	**107**	29.33 N	103.40 E
Shuikouguan	**102**	22.30 N	106.34 E
Shuikoushan	**102**	26.30 N	112.30 E
Shuikouxu	**100**	25.09 N	114.28 E
Shuiliandong	**98**	42.12 N	125.09 E
Shuimenzi	**98**	39.36 N	122.19 E
Shuimingqiao	**106**	31.03 N	119.09 E
Shuimoqipan	**85**	39.51 N	76.42 E
Shuiquan'gou	**104**	41.58 N	121.50 E
Shuiquanzi, Zhg.	**104**	42.15 N	121.32 E
Shuiquanzi, Zhg.	**104**	40.53 N	121.05 E
Shuitangzi	**102**	29.18 N	101.10 E
Shuiting	**100**	29.10 N	119.14 E
Shuitou, Zhg.	**100**	24.43 N	118.25 E
Shuitou, Zhg.	**100**	23.53 N	113.37 E
Shuitou, Zhg.	**100**	27.38 N	120.16 E
Shuitouwei	**100**	26.06 N	115.28 E
Shuituzhen	**107**	29.47 N	106.31 E
Shuiyang	**106**	31.14 N	118.47 E
Shuiyang ≃	**106**	31.14 N	118.48 E
Shuiye	**98**	36.08 N	114.07 E
Shuizhai	**98**	36.54 N	117.24 E
Shuizhuyang	**100**	26.59 N	119.13 E
Shujāābād	**123**	29.53 N	71.18 E
Shujālpur	**124**	23.24 N	76.43 E
Shujiawazi	**104**	42.20 N	121.57 E
Shuksan, Mount ∧	**224**	48.50 N	121.36 W
Shulan	**89**	44.27 N	126.57 E
Shulaps Peak ∧	**182**	50.57 N	122.31 W
Shule	**85**	39.23 N	76.06 E
Shule ≃	**102**	40.50 N	94.10 E
Shūlgareh	**120**	36.19 N	66.53 E
Shullsburg	**190**	42.34 N	90.13 W
Shulu (Xinji)	**98**	37.54 N	115.13 E
Shumagin Islands II	**180**	55.07 N	159.45 W
Shumatuscacant ≃	**283**	42.03 N	70.51 W
Shumen → Šumen	**38**	43.16 N	26.55 E
Shūnah, Wādī ash- V	**142**	29.38 N	32.13 E
Shun'an	**100**	30.57 N	117.57 E
Shūnat Nimrīn	**132**	31.54 N	35.37 E
Shunayn, Sabkhat ⊜	**146**	30.30 N	21.00 E
Shunchang	**100**	26.50 N	117.48 E
Shunde	**100**	22.50 N	113.14 E
Shundian	**100**	34.15 N	113.20 E
Shundianqiao	**106**	31.24 N	120.41 E
Shunge	**102**	37.25 N	95.27 E
Shungnak	**180**	66.53 N	157.02 W
Shunhechang	**107**	29.57 N	104.42 E
Shunlongchang	**107**	30.04 N	103.27 E
Shunshanpu	**104**	42.08 N	122.21 E
Shuntianhu	**100**	24.08 N	114.48 E
Shunyi	**105**	40.08 N	116.38 E
Shuoduzong	**102**	30.48 N	95.47 E
Shuojiaji	**100**	33.42 N	119.44 E
Shuping	**107**	29.19 N	104.43 E
Shupiyan	**123**	33.43 N	74.50 E
Shuqayyiqah, Nafūd ≗[8]	**128**	25.45 N	43.55 E
Shuqualak	**194**	32.58 N	88.34 W
Shūr ≃, Īrān	**128**	31.45 N	55.15 E
Shūr ≃, Īrān	**128**	30.57 N	57.42 E
Shūr ≃, Īrān	**128**	35.57 N	56.24 E
Shūr ≃, Īrān	**128**	34.38 N	51.46 E
Shuri	**174m**	26.13 N	127.43 E
Shurkhua	**110**	22.15 N	93.38 E
Shurugwi	**154**	19.40 S	30.00 E
Shūsf	**128**	31.48 N	60.01 E
Shūsh	**128**	32.11 N	48.15 E
Shushan	**210**	43.05 N	73.21 W
Shushan Hu ⊜	**98**	35.36 N	116.27 E
Shūshtar	**128**	32.03 N	48.51 E
Shuswap ≃	**182**	50.50 N	119.00 W
Shuswap Lake ⊜	**182**	50.57 N	119.15 W
Shuṭab	**142**	27.08 N	31.14 E
Shutendōji-yama ∧	**96**	33.06 N	130.54 E
Shuteye Peak ∧	**226**	37.21 N	119.25 W
Shutlingsloe ∧	**262**	53.13 N	2.02 W
Shūtō	**96**	34.05 N	132.05 E
Shuwak	**140**	14.23 N	35.52 E
Shuwaykah	**132**	32.20 N	35.02 E
Shuya	**174m**	26.40 N	128.06 E
Shuyak Island I	**180**	58.35 N	152.30 W
Shuyang	**98**	34.08 N	118.47 E
Shuya → Šuja	**24**	61.55 N	34.12 E
Shuyūkh Fawqānī	**130**	36.46 N	38.03 E
Shuzenji	**94**	34.58 N	138.56 E
Shwangliao → Liaoyuan	**89**	42.54 N	125.07 E
Shwebo	**110**	22.34 N	95.42 E
Shwegun	**110**	17.09 N	97.39 E
Shwegyin	**110**	17.55 N	96.53 E
Shweli (Longchuan) ≃	**102**	23.56 N	96.17 E
Shwenyaung	**110**	20.46 N	96.57 E
Shyamdih	**126**	23.47 N	86.56 E
Shyok	**120**	34.11 N	78.08 E
Shyok ≃	**120**	35.13 N	75.53 E
Si ≃	**98**	35.11 N	116.42 E
Sia	**164**	6.49 S	134.19 E
Siabu	**114**	1.01 N	99.29 E
Siachen Glacier ⊓	**123**	35.30 N	77.00 E
Sīād Kuh, Kavīr-e ≚	**128**	32.40 N	53.52 E
Siagne ≃	**62**	43.32 N	6.57 E
Siāhān Range ⋏	**128**	27.25 N	64.30 E
Sīāh Kūh, Selseleh-ye ⋏	**128**	34.00 N	64.00 E
Siak ≃	**114**	1.13 N	102.09 E
Siak Kecil ≃	**114**	1.16 N	102.08 E
Siak Sri Indrapura	**114**	0.46 N	102.04 E
Sialang	**114**	1.31 N	99.27 E
Sialejevskaja P'atina	**80**	53.49 N	44.32 E
Siālkot	**123**	32.30 N	74.31 E
Sialsūk	**120**	23.24 N	92.45 E
Siam, Gulf of → Thailand, Gulf of ⊂	**110**	10.00 N	101.00 E
Siamanna	**71**	39.55 N	8.46 E
Siam → Thailand □[1]	**110**	15.00 N	100.00 E
Si'an	**106**	30.54 N	119.39 E
Siangtan → Xiangtan	**100**	27.51 N	112.54 E
Sianhala	**150**	10.03 N	6.51 W
Sianów	**30**	54.15 N	16.16 E
Siantan, Pulau I	**112**	3.10 N	106.15 E
Sian → Xi'an	**102**	34.15 N	108.52 E
Sianzhuang	**100**	33.05 N	119.13 E
Siapa ≃	**246**	2.07 N	66.28 W
Siargao Island I	**116**	9.53 N	126.02 E
Siari	**123**	34.56 N	76.44 E
Siasconset	**207**	41.15 N	69.58 W
Siasi	**116**	5.33 N	120.49 E
Siasi Island I	**116**	5.33 N	120.51 E
Šiaškotan, ostrov I	**74**	48.49 N	154.06 E
Siátista	**38**	40.16 N	21.33 E
Siaton	**116**	9.04 N	123.02 E
Siaton ≃	**116**	9.02 N	123.02 E
Siaton Point ≻	**116**	9.03 N	123.01 E
Siau, Pulau I	**112**	2.42 N	125.24 E
Siaugues-Saint-Romain	**62**	45.06 N	3.38 E
Šiauliai	**76**	55.56 N	23.19 E
Siazan'	**84**	41.05 N	49.06 E
Sibago Island I	**116**	6.45 N	122.24 E
Sibāʿī, Jabal as- ∧	**140**	25.43 N	34.09 E
Sibaj	**86**	52.42 N	58.39 E
Sibalom	**116**	10.47 N	122.01 E
Sibanicú	**240p**	21.14 N	77.31 W
Sibao	**100**	25.55 N	116.42 E
Sibari, Piana di ≚	**68**	39.45 N	16.25 E
Sibasa	**156**	22.53 S	30.33 E
Sibati	**86**	47.12 N	88.15 E
Sibayi ⊜	**158**	27.20 S	32.40 E
Sibay Island I	**116**	11.51 N	121.29 E
Sibbald	**184**	51.23 N	110.09 W
Sibbald Point Provincial Park ♠	**212**	44.19 N	79.19 W
Šibbe	**85**	39.53 N	72.05 E
Sibbo	**26**	60.22 N	25.16 E
Sibchar	**126**	23.21 N	90.09 E
Šibenik	**36**	43.44 N	15.54 E
Siberia Occidental, Llanura de → Zapadno-Sibirskaja ravnina ≚	**72**	60.00 N	75.00 E
Siberia → Sibir' ◆[1]	**74**	65.00 N	110.00 E
Sibérie Occidental, Dépression de la → Zapadno-Sibirskaja ravnina ≚	**72**	60.00 N	75.00 E
Siberut, Pulau I	**108**	1.20 S	98.55 E
Sibi	**120**	29.33 N	67.53 E
Sibiči	**89**	46.04 N	135.22 E
Sibidiri	**164**	9.00 S	142.15 E
Sibigo	**114**	2.51 N	95.55 E
Sibillini, Monti ⋏	**66**	42.54 N	13.13 E
Sibir' (Siberia) ◆[1]	**74**	65.00 N	110.00 E
Sibir'akova, ostrov I	**74**	72.50 N	79.00 E
Sibircevo	**89**	44.12 N	132.26 E
Sibiti	**152**	3.41 S	13.21 E
Sibiti ≃	**154**	3.49 S	34.46 E
Sibiu	**38**	45.48 N	24.09 E
Sibiu □[6]	**38**	46.00 N	24.15 E
Sible Hedingham	**42**	51.58 N	0.35 E
Sibley, Il., U.S.	**216**	40.35 N	88.23 W
Sibley, Ia., U.S.	**198**	43.23 N	95.45 W
Sibley, La., U.S.	**194**	32.33 N	93.18 W
Sibley, Ms., U.S.	**194**	31.22 N	91.23 W
Sibley Peninsula ≻[1]	**190**	48.25 N	88.45 W
Sibley Provincial Park ♠	**190**	48.25 N	88.49 W
Siboa	**112**	0.30 N	120.02 E
Sibochi	**107**	28.50 N	104.32 E
Sibolga	**114**	1.45 N	98.48 E
Siborang	**114**	1.08 N	99.26 E
Siborongborong	**114**	2.13 N	98.59 E
Sibpur, Bngl.	**124**	24.02 N	90.44 E
Sibpur, India	**272b**	22.24 N	88.33 E
Sibpur, India	**272b**	22.34 N	88.19 E
Sibsa ≃[1]	**126**	22.01 N	89.30 E
Sibsāgar	**120**	26.59 N	94.39 E
Sibu	**112**	2.18 N	111.49 E
Sibu, Pulau I	**114**	2.13 N	104.04 E
Sibuatan, Gunung ∧	**114**	2.56 N	98.24 E
Sibuguey ≃	**116**	7.38 N	122.48 E
Sibuguey Bay ⊂	**116**	7.30 N	122.40 E
Sibut	**152**	5.44 N	19.05 E
Sibuti	**112**	4.03 N	113.48 E
Sibutu Island I	**112**	4.46 N	119.29 E
Sibutu Passage ʊ	**112**	4.50 N	119.35 E
Sibuyan Island I	**116**	12.25 N	122.34 E
Sibuyan Sea ⊤[2]	**116**	12.50 N	122.40 E
Siby	**150**	12.23 N	8.20 W
Sibyŏn	**98**	38.19 N	126.41 E
Sicamous	**182**	50.50 N	119.00 W
Sicapoo, Mount ∧	**116**	18.01 N	120.56 E
Siccus ≃	**166**	31.26 S	139.30 E
Sichakou	**98**	41.39 N	116.26 E
Šichany	**80**	52.07 N	47.13 E
Sichifulo ≃	**154**	17.26 S	25.02 E
Si Chon	**110**	9.00 N	99.54 E
Sichote-Alin' ⋏	**89**	48.00 N	138.00 E
Sichote-Alinskij zapovednik ♠	**89**	45.15 N	136.15 E
Šichtovo	**76**	55.43 N	32.18 E
Sichuan (Szechwan) □[4]	**102**	31.00 N	105.00 E
Sichuan Pendi ≚[1]	**102**	30.00 N	105.00 E
Sichuanzhai	**102**	23.02 N	101.44 E
Sicié, Cap ≻	**62**	43.03 N	5.51 E
Sicignano degli Alburni	**68**	40.34 N	15.18 E
Sicilia □[4]	**36**	37.30 N	14.00 E
Sicilia (Sicily) I	**70**	37.30 N	14.00 E
Sicilia, Isla de → Sicilia I	**70**	37.30 N	14.00 E
Sicily, Strait of ʊ	**36**	37.20 N	11.20 E
Sicily Island	**194**	31.50 N	91.39 W
Sicily → Sicilia I	**70**	37.30 N	14.00 E
Sickingmühle	**263**	51.42 N	7.07 E
Sicklerville	**208**	39.43 N	74.58 W
Sicogon Island I	**116**	11.27 N	123.16 E
Sico Tinto ≃	**236**	15.58 N	84.58 W
Sicuani	**248**	14.16 S	71.13 W
Siculiana	**70**	37.20 N	13.25 E
Sicun	**106**	31.55 N	119.18 E
Šid	**38**	45.08 N	19.13 E
Sīdah, Qārat ∧[2]	**142**	30.16 N	29.58 E
Sidamo □[4]	**144**	5.00 N	39.00 E
Sidao	**271a**	39.51 N	116.26 E
Sidaohe	**105**	40.24 N	117.17 E
Sidareja	**115a**	7.29 S	108.47 E
Sidas	**112**	0.24 N	109.46 E
Sidcup ◆[8]	**260**	51.25 N	0.06 E
Siddeburen	**52**	53.25 N	6.52 E
Siddhapur	**120**	23.55 N	72.23 E
Siddinghausen	**263**	51.32 N	7.48 E
Siddington	**262**	53.14 N	2.14 W
Siddipet	**122**	18.06 N	78.51 E
Sideia Island I	**164**	10.35 S	150.50 E
Sidel'kino	**80**	54.32 N	51.08 E
Sidéradougou	**150**	10.40 N	4.15 W
Siderno	**68**	38.16 N	16.18 E
Siderópolis	**252**	28.35 S	49.26 W
Šiderty ≃, Kaz.	**80**	50.10 N	52.20 E
Šiderty ≃, Kaz.	**86**	52.32 N	74.50 E
Sidhauli	**124**	27.17 N	80.50 E
Sídheros, Ákra ≻	**38**	35.19 N	26.19 E

Symbols in the index entries represent the broad categories identified in the key at the right. Symbols with superior numbers (⋏[1]) identify subcategories (see complete key on page *I · 1).*

Symbole im Register stellen die rechts im Schlüssel erklärten Kategorien dar. Symbole mit hochgestellten Ziffern (⋏[1]) bezeichnen Unterabteilungen einer Kategorie (vgl. vollständiger Schlüssel auf Seite *I · 1).*

Los símbolos incluídos en el texto del índice representan las grandes categorias identificadas con la clave a la derecha. Los símbolos con numeros en su parte superior (⋏[1]) identifican las subcategorías (véase la clave completa en la página *I · 1).*

Les symboles de l'index représentent les catégories indiquées dans la légende à droite. Les symboles suivis d'un indice (⋏[1]) représentent des sous-catégories (voir légende complète à la page *I · 1).*

Os símbolos incluídos no texto do índice representam as grandes categorias identificadas com a chave à direita. Os símbolos com números em sua parte superior (⋏[1]) identificam as subcategorias (veja-se a chave completa à página *I · 1).*

∧	Mountain	Berg	Montaña	Montagne	Montanha
⋏	Mountains	Gebirge	Montañas	Montagnes	Montanhas
)(	Pass	Paß	Paso	Col	Passo
V	Valley, Canyon	Tal, Cañon	Valle, Cañón	Vallée, Canyon	Vale, Canhão
≚	Plain	Ebene	Llano	Plaine	Planície
≻	Cape	Kap	Cabo	Cap	Cabo
I	Island	Insel	Isla	Île	Ilha
II	Islands	Inseln	Islas	Îles	Ilhas
≗	Other Topographic Features	Andere Topographische Objekte	Otros Elementos Topográficos	Autres données topographiques	Outros acidentes topográficos

ESPAÑOL — Nombre / Página / Lat.°′ / Long.°′ W = Oeste
FRANÇAIS — Nom / Page / Lat.°′ / Long.°′ W = Ouest
PORTUGUÊS — Nome / Página / Lat.°′ / Long.°′ W = Oeste

Sidhi 124 24.25 N 81.53 E
Sidhirókastron 38 41.14 N 23.22 E
Sīdī ʿAbd ar-Raḥmān 140 30.58 N 29.44 E
Sidi Aïch 34 36.37 N 4.42 E
Sidi Aïssa 148 35.53 N 3.48 E
Sidi Akacha 34 36.28 N 1.18 E
Sidi Ali 34 36.06 N 0.25 E
Sidi Ali, Oued V 148 34.07 N 2.05 W
Sidi Ali Ben Nasrallah 36 35.15 N 9.50 E
Sīdī Barrānī 140 31.36 N 25.55 E
Sidi bel Abbès 148 35.13 N 0.10 W
Sidi Bel Abbes □[5] 148 35.00 N 1.00 W
Sidi Bennour 148 32.30 N 8.30 W
Sidi Bou Zid 148 35.02 N 9.30 E
Sidi Bou Zid □[8] 148 35.00 N 9.15 E
Sidi Daoud 36 37.00 N 10.55 E
Sidi el Hani, Sebkhet ⊜ 36 35.33 N 10.25 E
Sīdī Ghāzī 142 31.12 N 31.03 E
Sīdī Ḥunaysh 140 31.10 N 27.37 E
Sidi Ifni 148 29.24 N 10.12 W
Sidi Kacem 148 34.15 N 5.39 W
Sidikalang 114 2.45 N 98.19 E
Sidimo 144 2.27 N 41.58 E
Sidi Mohammed Ben Ali 34 36.09 N 0.51 E
Sidi Moussa, Oued V 148 26.58 N 3.54 E
Sidi Okba 148 34.48 N 5.54 E
Sīdī Sālim 142 31.17 N 30.48 E
Sidi Slimane 148 34.15 N 5.49 W
Sidi Smaïl 148 32.49 N 8.30 W
Sidlaghatta 122 13.23 N 77.52 E
Sidlaw Hills ⩘[2] 46 56.30 N 3.10 W
Sidley, Mount ∧ 9 77.02 S 126.00 W
Sidli 124 26.33 N 90.28 E
Sidman 214 40.20 N 78.45 W
Sidmouth 42 50.41 N 3.15 W
Sidnaw 190 46.30 N 88.42 W
Sidney, B.C., Can. 224 48.39 N 123.24 W
Sidney, Il., U.S. 194 40.01 N 88.04 W
Sidney, In., U.S. 216 41.06 N 85.45 W
Sidney, Ia., U.S. 198 40.44 N 95.38 W
Sidney, Mt., U.S. 198 47.43 N 104.09 W
Sidney, Ne., U.S. 198 41.08 N 102.58 W
Sidney, N.Y., U.S. 210 42.18 N 75.23 W
Sidney, Oh., U.S. 216 40.17 N 84.09 W
Sidney Center 210 42.17 N 75.15 W
Sidney Island I 224 48.37 N 123.18 W
Sidney Lanier, Lake ⊜[1] 192 34.15 N 83.57 W
Sido 150 11.40 N 7.36 W
Sidoan 112 0.16 N 120.12 E
Sidoarjo 115a 7.27 S 112.43 E
Sidon 194 33.24 N 90.12 W
Sidon → Ṣaydā 132 33.33 N 35.22 E
Sidorovo 76 58.48 N 40.58 E
Sidory 80 50.08 N 43.19 E
Sidr, Ra's as- › 142 29.36 N 32.40 E
Sidr, Wādī V 142 29.40 N 32.41 E
Sidra, Gulf of → Surt, Khalīj ⊂ 146 31.30 N 18.00 E
Sidrolândia 255 20.55 S 54.58 W
Sidu, Zhg. 100 23.48 N 117.18 E
Sidu, Zhg. 100 24.12 N 115.15 E
Siduan 106 30.59 N 121.48 E
Siebengebirge ⩘[2] 56 50.40 N 7.14 E
Siebenlehn 54 51.01 N 13.18 E
Sieber 52 51.42 N 10.25 E
Siebnen 58 47.11 N 8.54 E
Siedenbollentin 54 53.44 N 13.23 E
Siedenburg 52 52.41 N 8.56 E
Siedlce 30 52.11 N 22.16 E
Siedlce □[4] 30 52.15 N 22.00 E
Sieg ≃ 56 50.45 N 7.05 E
Siegburg 56 50.47 N 7.12 E
Siegen 56 50.52 N 8.02 E
Siegenburg 60 48.45 N 11.51 E
Siegendorf im Burgenland 61 47.47 N 16.33 E
Siegenfeld 264b 48.02 N 16.10 E
Sieghartskirchen 61 48.15 N 16.01 E
Siegler Springs 226 38.54 N 122.39 W
Siegsdorf 64 47.46 N 12.39 E
Sielbeck 54 54.11 N 10.37 E
Sielenbach 60 48.24 N 11.10 E
Siemens, Cape › 164 1.21 S 149.34 E
Siemensstadt ✦[8] 264a 52.32 N 13.17 E
Siemianowice Śląskie 30 50.19 N 19.01 E
Siemiatycze 30 52.26 N 22.53 E
Siĕmpang 110 14.07 N 106.23 E
Siĕmréab 110 13.22 N 103.51 E
Siems-Dänischburg ✦[8] 54 53.55 N 10.44 E
Siena 66 43.19 N 11.21 E
Siena □[4] 66 43.13 N 11.24 E
Sieniawa 30 50.11 N 22.36 E
Sienna → Siena 66 43.19 N 11.21 E
Sienyang → Xianyang 102 34.22 N 108.42 E
Sieradz 30 51.36 N 18.45 E
Sieradz □[4] 30 51.40 N 18.45 E
Sieraków 30 52.39 N 16.04 E
Sierck-les-Bains 56 49.26 N 6.21 E
Sierksdorf 54 54.04 N 10.46 E
Sierning 61 48.03 N 14.19 E
Sierpc 30 52.52 N 19.41 E
Si'erpu 104 40.47 N 120.41 E
Sierra □[6] 226 39.30 N 120.30 W
Sierra Blanca 200 31.11 N 105.21 W
Sierra Blanca Peak ∧ 200 33.23 N 105.48 W
Sierra-Bullones 116 9.51 N 124.20 E
Sierra Chica 252 36.50 S 60.13 W
Sierra City 226 39.33 N 120.37 W
Sierra Colorada 254 40.35 S 67.48 W
Sierra de Agua 232 17.32 N 88.54 W
Sierra de Outes 34 42.51 N 8.54 W
Sierra Gorda 252 22.54 S 69.19 W
Sierra Leona → Sierra Leone □[1] 150 8.30 N 11.30 W
Sierra Leone □[1], Afr. 134 8.30 N 11.30 W
Sierra Leone □[1], Afr. 150 8.30 N 11.30 W
Sierra Leone Basin ✢[1] 10 5.00 N 17.00 W
Sierra Leone Rise ✢[3] 10 5.30 N 21.00 W
Sierra Madre 228 34.09 N 118.03 W
Sierra Mojada 196 27.17 N 103.42 W
Sierra Nevada, Parque Nacional ♦ 246 8.36 N 70.50 W
Sierra Peak ∧ 280 33.51 N 117.39 W
Sierra San Pedro Mártir, Parque Nacional ♦ 204 31.00 N 115.30 W
Sierras Bayas 252 36.57 S 60.09 W
Sierraville 226 39.35 N 120.21 W
Sierra Vista 200 31.33 N 110.18 W
Sierre 58 46.18 N 7.32 E
Siersleben 54 51.36 N 11.32 E
Siesta Key 220 27.19 N 82.34 W
Siesta Key I 220 27.16 N 82.33 W
Siete Puntas ≃ 252 23.34 S 57.20 W
Siethen 264a 52.17 N 13.13 E
Siethener See ⊜ 264a 52.17 N 13.12 E
Sietow 54 53.26 N 12.35 E
Sieve ≃ 66 43.46 N 11.26 E
Sievering ✦[8] 264b 48.15 N 16.20 E
Siezenheim 64 47.48 N 12.59 E
Sifahandra 114 1.30 N 97.21 E
Sifangtai, Zhg. 89 46.55 N 127.00 E
Sifangtai, Zhg. 104 41.33 N 121.19 E
Sifangtai, Zhg. 104 41.02 N 122.46 E
Sifangtai, Zhg. 104 41.35 N 122.57 E
Sifen 100 27.32 N 113.30 E
Sifeni 144 12.16 N 40.21 E
Sifentoudun 106 32.18 N 121.21 E
Siffu ≃ 116 17.12 N 121.48 E
Sifié 150 7.59 N 6.55 W
Sífnos I 38 36.59 N 24.40 E
Sifón Villanueva 196 27.17 N 100.17 W
Sifton 184 51.21 N 100.07 W
Sig, Alg. 34 35.32 N 0.11 W
Sig, Ross. 24 65.35 N 34.13 E
Si Galangang 114 1.15 N 99.20 E
Šigali 80 55.33 N 48.02 E
Sigean 32 43.02 N 2.59 E
Sigel 214 41.17 N 79.07 W
Sigep 110 1.02 S 98.49 E
Siggebohyttan 40 59.37 N 15.01 E
Sighetu Marmației 38 47.56 N 23.54 E
Sighișoara 38 46.13 N 24.48 E
Sighty Crag ∧ 44 55.07 N 2.37 W
Sigillo 66 43.20 N 12.44 E
Sigiriya 122 7.57 N 80.45 E
Siglan 74 59.02 N 152.25 E
Siglerville 208 40.44 N 77.31 W
Sigli 114 5.23 N 95.57 E
Sigli, Cap › 34 36.54 N 4.46 E
Sigloy 50 47.50 N 2.14 E
Siglufjörður 24a 66.10 N 18.56 W
Sigmaringen 58 48.05 N 9.13 E
Sigmaringendorf 58 48.04 N 9.15 E
Signa 66 43.47 N 11.05 E
Signachi 84 41.37 N 45.54 E
Signalberg ∧ 60 49.28 N 12.32 E
Signal Hill, Ca., U.S. 280 33.47 N 118.09 W
Signal Hill, Il., U.S. 219 38.34 N 90.05 W
Signal Hill National Historic Park ♦ 186 47.35 N 52.40 W
Signal Mountain 194 35.07 N 85.20 W
Signal Mountain ∧ 188 44.12 N 72.20 W
Signal Peak ∧ 200 37.19 N 113.29 W
Signau 58 46.55 N 7.43 E
Signes 62 43.18 N 5.52 E
Signy ʊ[3] 9 60.43 S 45.36 W
Signy-l'Abbaye 50 49.42 N 4.25 E
Signy-Le-Petit 50 49.54 N 4.17 E
Šigony 80 53.23 N 48.42 E
Sigourney 190 41.20 N 92.12 W
Sigre ≃ 236 15.49 N 84.38 W
Sigriswil 58 46.43 N 7.42 E
Sígsig 246 3.01 S 78.45 W
Sigtuna 40 59.37 N 17.43 E
Siguanea, Ensenada de la ⊂ 240p 21.38 N 83.05 W
Siguatepeque 236 14.32 N 87.49 W
Siguel ≃ 116 5.58 N 125.06 E
Sigüenza 34 41.04 N 2.38 W
Sigües 34 42.38 N 1.00 W
Siguiri 150 11.25 N 9.10 W
Sigulda 76 57.09 N 24.51 E
Sigurd 200 38.50 N 111.58 W
Siguri Falls ∟ 154 8.31 S 37.23 E
Sihabuhabu, Dolok ∧ 114 2.10 N 99.21 E
Sihai 105 40.33 N 116.24 E
Sihala → Sri Lanka □[1] 122 7.00 N 81.00 E
Sihanoukville → Kâmpóng Saôm 110 10.38 N 103.30 E
Sihecun 105 39.56 N 117.07 E
Sihepeng 114 1.06 N 99.27 E
Sihl ≃ 58 47.23 N 8.32 E
Sihlepu 158 27.42 S 32.06 E
Sihlsee ⊜ 58 47.07 N 8.47 E
Sihong 100 33.28 N 118.11 E
Sihor 120 21.42 N 71.58 E
Sihorā 124 23.29 N 80.07 E
Sihu 98 34.38 N 117.59 E
Sihuas 248 8.34 S 77.37 W
Sihuas ≃ 248 16.37 S 72.19 W
Sihui 102 23.19 N 112.40 E
Şihŭng ✦[8] 271b 37.28 N 126.54 E
Šiiči 76 52.15 N 29.14 E
Siikajoki ≃ 26 64.50 N 24.44 E
Siilinjärvi 26 63.05 N 27.40 E
Siʿīr 132 31.35 N 35.09 E
Siirt 130 37.56 N 41.57 E
Siirt □[4] 128 38.00 N 42.00 E
Sija 24 63.38 N 41.38 E
Sijā ≃ 124 29.08 N 81.35 E
Sijbekarspel 52 52.43 N 4.59 E
Sijiaba 106 32.02 N 121.18 E
Sijianfang 104 42.29 N 122.17 E
Sijiao Shan I 100 30.41 N 122.28 E
Sijiazi 98 41.47 N 120.06 E
Sijing 106 31.07 N 121.16 E
Sijunjung 112 0.42 S 100.58 E
Sijupu 107 30.02 N 106.18 E
Sik 114 5.49 N 100.44 E
Sika 115b 8.45 S 122.12 E
Sikalongo 154 16.46 S 27.07 E
Sikandarābād 124 28.27 N 77.42 E
Sikandarpur, India 272a 28.42 N 77.21 E
Sikandarpur, India 272b 22.57 N 88.12 E
Sikandra 124 24.57 N 86.02 E
Sikandra Rao 124 27.42 N 78.24 E
Sikanni Chief ≃ 176 58.20 N 121.50 W
Sikao 110 7.34 N 99.21 E
Sīkar 120 27.37 N 75.09 E
Sikarpur 272b 22.36 N 88.32 E
Sikasso 150 11.19 N 5.40 W
Sikasso □[4] 150 10.55 N 7.00 W
Sikéai 38 36.46 N 22.56 E
Sikelenge 152 14.50 S 24.14 E
Sikeli 112 5.16 S 121.48 E
Sikensi 150 5.40 N 4.34 W
Sikeshu 86 44.25 N 84.14 E
Sikeston 194 36.52 N 89.35 W
Sikfors 40 59.48 N 14.35 E
Si Khiu 110 14.53 N 101.44 E
Sikiá 38 40.02 N 23.56 E
Sikiang → Xi ≃ 102 22.25 N 113.23 E
Sikijang 114 4.22 N 98.02 E
Siking → Xi'an 102 34.15 N 108.52 E
Síkinos 38 36.39 N 25.06 E
Síkinos I 38 36.39 N 25.06 E
Sikión ⊥ 38 37.59 N 22.44 E
Sikkim □[3] 124 27.35 N 88.35 E
Siklós ⊥ 30 45.52 N 18.28 E
Sikonge 154 5.38 S 32.46 E
Şikosi 156 17.59 S 23.19 E
Šikotan, ostrov (Shikotan-tō) I 92a 43.47 N 146.45 E
Sikrod 272a 28.43 N 77.11 E
Sikt'ach 74 69.55 N 125.02 E
Sikuati 112 6.53 N 116.40 E
Sikutu 112 0.53 N 120.37 E
Sil ≃ 34 42.27 N 7.43 W
Šila 86 56.33 N 93.02 E
Silacayoapan 234 17.30 N 98.09 W
Sila Grande ⩘ 68 39.22 N 16.30 E
Sila Greca ⩘ 68 39.30 N 16.30 E
Silai ≃ 126 22.41 N 87.46 E
Şilalahi 114 2.48 N 98.32 E
Šilalė 76 55.28 N 22.12 E
Silam, Gunong ∧ 116 4.58 N 118.10 E
Silāmpur ✦[8] 272a 28.40 N 77.16 E
Silandro (Schlanders) 64 46.38 N 10.46 E
Silang 116 14.14 N 120.58 E
Silangcheng 98 42.19 N 115.43 E
Silanus 71 40.17 N 8.53 E
Silao 234 20.56 N 101.26 W
Sila Piccola ⩘ 68 39.05 N 16.35 E
Silas 194 31.45 N 88.19 W
Silat 112 0.21 N 111.47 E
Sīlat az-Zahr 132 32.19 N 35.11 E
Silau ≃ 114 2.58 N 99.48 E
Silaut 112 2.22 S 101.08 E
Silaw Aihagam, Gunung ∧ 114 5.25 N 95.40 E
Silay 116 10.48 N 122.58 E
Silay, Mount ∧ 116 10.47 N 123.14 E
Silba 36 44.23 N 14.42 E
Silbertal 58 47.05 N 9.59 E
Silchar 120 24.49 N 92.48 E
Silda, India 126 22.37 N 86.49 E
Šil'da, Ross. 86 51.46 N 59.45 E
Şile 130 41.11 N 29.36 E
Šile ≃ 64 45.33 N 12.27 E
Şileby 42 52.43 N 1.06 W
Šilega 24 64.03 N 44.01 E
Silenrieux 50 50.14 N 4.24 E
Silent Lake ⊜ 212 44.55 N 78.04 W
Silent Lake Provincial Park ♦ 212 44.54 N 78.05 W
Siler City 192 35.43 N 79.27 W
Sileru ≃ 122 17.47 N 81.24 E
Silesia □[9] 30 51.00 N 16.45 E
Silet 148 22.44 N 4.37 E
Siletz 202 44.43 N 123.55 W
Siletz ≃ 202 44.54 N 124.00 W
Silex 219 39.07 N 91.03 W
Silgaḍhī 124 29.16 N 80.59 E
Silghāt 120 26.37 N 92.56 E
Silhouette I 138 4.29 S 55.14 E
Siliana 148 36.05 N 9.22 E
Siliana □[8] 148 36.00 N 9.20 E
Siliana, Oued ≃ 36 36.33 N 9.25 E
Silifke 130 36.22 N 33.56 E
Şilijiang 105 39.43 N 117.28 E
Šilikty 86 47.10 N 84.32 E
Silingan, Mount ∧ 116 7.46 N 122.30 E
Siling Co ⊜ 120 31.50 N 89.00 E
Siliqua 71 39.18 N 8.48 E
Silistra 38 44.07 N 27.16 E
Şilivri 130 41.04 N 28.15 E
Šiljak ∧ 38 43.45 N 21.50 E
Siljan ⊜ 26 60.50 N 14.45 E
Siljansnäs 26 60.45 N 14.42 E
Šilka 88 51.51 N 116.02 E
Šilka ≃ 74 53.22 N 121.32 E
Silkāripāra 126 24.14 N 87.28 E
Silkeborg 41 56.10 N 9.34 E
Silkworth 210 41.16 N 76.05 W
Sill ≃ 64 47.16 N 11.25 E
Sillamäe 76 59.24 N 27.45 E
Sillānwāli 123 31.50 N 72.33 E
Sillaro ≃ 66 44.34 N 11.51 E
Sille 130 37.56 N 32.26 E
Sillem Island I 176 70.55 N 71.30 W
Sillen ⊜ 40 58.59 N 17.22 E
Sillenstede 52 53.34 N 7.59 E
Sillery, P.Q., Can. 206 46.46 N 71.15 W
Sillery, Fr. 50 49.12 N 4.08 E
Silli 150 11.36 N 2.30 W
Sillian 64 46.45 N 12.25 E
Sillil 144 10.59 N 43.26 E
Sillon de Talbert ›[1] 32 48.53 N 3.05 W
Silloth 44 54.52 N 3.23 W
Sillustani ⊥ 248 15.45 S 70.05 W
Şilly-le-Long 261 49.06 N 2.48 E
Šil'naja Balka 80 50.34 N 49.01 E
Silnice 60 48.54 N 13.44 E
Siloam Springs 194 36.11 N 94.32 W
Siloam Springs State Park ♦ 219 39.53 N 90.54 W
Şilogui 110 1.14 S 99.00 E
Šilovići 76 55.24 N 32.33 E
Šilovka 80 54.03 N 48.40 E
Šilovo, Ross. 76 55.00 N 33.46 E
Šilovo, Ross. 80 54.19 N 40.53 E
Silowana Plains ≡ 152 17.00 S 23.15 E
Silphuh 126 23.44 N 86.22 E
Silsbee 194 30.20 N 94.10 W
Silsby Lake ⊜ 184 55.29 N 95.46 W
Silschede 263 51.21 N 7.19 E
Silsden 44 53.55 N 1.55 W
Sils im Engadin 58 46.22 N 9.46 E
Silton 184 50.48 N 104.55 W
Siluas 112 1.17 N 109.51 E
Şiluko 150 6.31 N 5.09 E
Šilutė 76 55.21 N 21.29 E
Silvacane, Abbaye de ʊ[1] 62 43.44 N 5.20 E
Silvan (Miyafarkin) 130 38.08 N 41.01 E
Silvana 224 48.12 N 122.15 W
Sīlvāneh 128 37.25 N 44.51 E
Silvânia 255 16.42 S 48.38 W
Silvano d'Orba 62 44.41 N 8.40 E
Silvan Reservoir ⊜[1] 169 37.50 S 145.25 E
Silvaplana 58 46.26 N 9.47 E
Silvassa 122 20.17 N 73.00 E
Silveiras 256 22.40 S 44.52 W
Silver 196 32.04 N 100.40 W
Silverado 228 33.45 N 117.35 W
Silver Bank ✢[2] 238 20.30 N 69.45 W
Silver Bank Passage ʉ 238 20.45 N 70.15 W
Silver Bay 190 47.17 N 91.15 W
Silver Bell 200 32.23 N 111.29 W
Silver City, N.M., U.S. 200 32.46 N 108.16 W
Silver City, N.C., U.S. 192 35.00 N 79.12 W
Silver Creek, Ms., U.S. 194 31.36 N 89.59 W
Silver Creek, Ne., U.S. 198 41.18 N 97.39 W
Silver Creek, N.Y., U.S. 214 42.32 N 79.10 W
Silver Creek ≃, Az., U.S. 200 34.44 N 110.02 W
Silver Creek ≃, Ca., U.S. 226 38.47 N 120.35 W
Silver Creek ≃, Ca., U.S. 226 36.36 N 120.41 W
Silver Creek ≃, Il., U.S. 219 38.20 N 89.52 W
Silver Creek ≃, Il., U.S. 278 41.54 N 87.50 W
Silver Creek ≃, In., U.S. 218 38.17 N 85.47 W
Silver Creek ≃, In., U.S. 218 39.36 N 84.59 W
Silver Creek ≃, Ky., U.S. 192 37.48 N 84.30 W
Silver Creek ≃, Mi., U.S. 281 42.06 N 83.17 E
Silver Creek ≃, Or., U.S. 202 43.16 N 119.13 W
Silver Creek ≃, Wa., U.S. 224 46.32 N 121.55 W
Silver Creek, Muddy Fork ≃ 218 38.25 N 86.44 W
Silver Creek, South Fork ≃ 226 38.49 N 120.27 W
Silverdale, B.C., Can. 224 49.09 N 122.24 W
Silverdale, N.Z. 172 36.37 S 174.40 E
Silverdale, Eng., U.K. 44 54.10 N 2.49 W
Silverdale, Pa., U.S. 208 40.21 N 75.16 W
Silverdale, Wa., U.S. 224 47.38 N 122.41 W
Silverdalen 26 57.32 N 15.44 E
Silverdome ♦ 281 42.39 N 83.15 W
Silver End 42 51.51 N 0.37 E
Silver Falls State Park ♦ 202 44.48 N 122.50 W
Silverfields 273d 26.07 S 27.49 E
Silver Fork ≃ 219 39.06 N 92.21 W
Silver Grove 218 39.02 N 84.23 W
Silver Hill 284c 38.50 N 76.56 W
Silverhope Creek ≃ 224 49.18 N 121.27 W
Silver Lake, Ca., U.S. 226 38.38 N 120.07 W
Silver Lake, In., U.S. 216 41.04 N 85.53 W
Silver Lake, Ks., U.S. 198 39.06 N 95.51 W
Silver Lake, Ma., U.S. 207 42.34 N 71.11 W
Silver Lake, Mn., U.S. 190 44.54 N 94.11 W
Silver Lake, Oh., U.S. 214 41.09 N 81.27 W
Silver Lake, Or., U.S. 202 43.07 N 121.02 W
Silverlake, Wa., U.S. 224 46.17 N 122.48 W
Silver Lake, Wi., U.S. 216 42.32 N 88.09 W
Silver Lake ⊜, Ca., U.S. 226 38.39 N 120.07 W
Silver Lake ⊜, De., U.S. 208 39.11 N 75.32 W
Silver Lake ⊜, Ma., U.S. 283 42.01 N 70.48 W
Silver Lake ⊜, N.Y., U.S. 210 42.42 N 78.02 W
Silver Lake ⊜, N.Y., U.S. 276 41.03 N 73.45 W
Silver Lake ⊜, Or., U.S. 202 43.22 N 119.24 W
Silver Lake ⊜, Or., U.S. 202 43.06 N 120.53 W
Silver Lake ⊜, Wa., U.S. 224 46.17 N 122.47 W
Silver Lake ⊜, Wa., U.S. 224 48.58 N 122.04 W
Silver Lake Park ♦ 276 41.03 N 73.45 W
Silver Lake Reservoir ⊜[1], Ca., U.S. 280 34.06 N 118.16 W
Silver Lake Reservoir ⊜[1], N.Y., U.S. 276 40.37 N 74.06 W
Silvermine ≃ 276 41.08 N 73.26 W
Silver Mine Bay ⊂ 271d 22.16 N 114.00 E
Silvermine Brook ≃ 276 41.08 N 73.27 W
Silvermine Mountains ⩘ 48 52.45 N 8.15 W
Silvermines 48 52.47 N 8.13 W
Silver Mountain ∧ 280 34.12 N 117.52 W
Silver Peak ∧ 228 33.28 N 118.35 W
Silver Peak Range ⩘ 204 37.35 N 117.45 W
Silver Spring, Md., U.S. 208 38.59 N 77.01 W
Silver Spring, Pa., U.S. 208 40.04 N 76.26 W
Silver Springs, Nv., U.S. 226 39.24 N 119.13 W
Silver Springs, N.Y., U.S. 210 42.39 N 78.05 W
Silver Springs State Park ♦ 216 41.38 N 88.32 W
Silver Star Mountain ∧ 224 48.33 N 120.35 W
Silver Star Provincial Park ♦ 182 50.22 N 119.05 W
Silverstone 42 52.05 N 1.02 W
Silver Streams 158 28.20 S 23.33 E
Silverthrone Mountain ∧ 182 51.31 N 126.06 W
Silvertip Mountain ∧ 202 47.47 N 113.15 W
Silverton, Austl. 166 31.53 S 141.13 E
Silverton, B.C., Can. 182 49.57 N 117.21 W
Silverton, Eng., U.K. 42 50.48 N 3.28 W
Silverton, Co., U.S. 200 37.48 N 107.39 W
Silverton, N.J., U.S. 208 40.00 N 74.08 W
Silverton, Oh., U.S. 218 39.12 N 84.24 W
Silverton, Or., U.S. 224 45.00 N 122.46 W
Silverton, Tx., U.S. 196 34.28 N 101.19 W
Silverwood Lake ⊜[1] 228 34.18 N 117.19 W
Silves 34 37.11 N 8.26 W
Silvi 66 42.34 N 14.05 E
Silvia 246 2.37 N 76.21 W
Silvianópolis 256 22.02 S 45.50 W
Silvícola 164 8.39 S 126.59 E
Silvies ≃ 202 43.22 N 118.48 W
Silview 285 39.42 N 75.37 W
Silvolde 52 51.54 N 6.53 E
Silvretta Gruppe ⩘ 58 46.50 N 10.10 E
Sim 86 54.59 N 57.41 E
Sim, Cap › 148 31.23 N 9.51 W
Sima, Comores 157a 12.11 S 44.17 E
Sima, Ross. 80 56.41 N 39.33 E
Simaltala 124 24.43 N 86.33 E
Simanggang 112 1.15 N 111.26 E
Simangumban 114 1.42 N 99.10 E
Şimanoviči 76 53.05 N 28.38 E
Šimanovsk 89 52.00 N 127.42 E
Simao 102 22.50 N 101.00 E
Simão Dias 250 10.44 S 37.49 W
Simão Pereira 256 21.58 S 43.19 W
Simara Island I 116 12.48 N 122.03 E
Simard, Lac ⊜ 190 47.37 N 78.41 W
Simaria Kalān 124 24.04 N 84.56 E
Simatang, Pulau I 112 1.04 N 120.23 E
Simav 130 39.05 N 28.59 E
Simav ≃ 130 40.23 N 28.31 E
Simav Gölü ⊜ 130 39.09 N 28.55 E
Simaxis 71 39.56 N 8.41 E
Simba, Kenya 154 2.10 S 37.36 E
Simba, Tan. 154 1.44 S 34.13 E
Simba, Zaïre 152 0.36 N 22.55 E
Simbach 60 48.34 N 12.45 E
Simbach am Inn 60 48.16 N 13.01 E
Simbario 68 38.37 N 16.20 E
Simberi Island I 164 2.40 S 152.00 E
Simbirsk → Uljanovsk 80 54.20 N 48.24 E
Simbo, Tan. 154 4.53 S 29.44 E
Simbo, Tan. 154 4.40 S 33.27 E
Simbo Island I 175e 8.17 S 156.33 E
Simbruini, Monti ⩘ 66 41.55 N 13.15 E
Simcoe 212 42.50 N 80.18 W
Simcoe □[6] 212 44.25 N 79.50 W
Simcoe, Lake ⊜ 212 44.20 N 79.20 W
Simcoe Creek ≃ 224 46.22 N 120.36 W
Simcoe Island I 212 44.10 N 76.31 W
Simcoe Point › 275b 43.49 N 79.01 W
Simdega 124 22.37 N 84.31 E
Simeiz 78 44.26 N 34.01 E
Simen 104 40.44 N 123.49 E
Simeng 107 29.56 N 103.44 E
Simen Mountains National Park ♦ 144 13.08 N 38.15 E
Simenti 150 13.00 N 13.25 W
Simeri ≃ 68 38.52 N 16.43 E
Simeria 38 45.51 N 23.01 E
Simeto ≃ 70 37.24 N 15.06 E
Simeulue, Pulau I 114 2.33 N 96.05 E
Simferopol' 78 44.57 N 34.06 E
Sími 38 36.36 N 27.50 E
Sími I 38 36.35 N 27.52 E
Simi, Arroyo ≃ 228 34.16 N 118.39 W
Simiane 62 43.25 N 5.26 E
Simianshan 107 28.49 N 105.09 E
Simikoṭ 124 29.58 N 81.50 E
Similkameen ≃ 182 48.56 N 119.26 W
Simingchang 107 29.02 N 105.45 E
Simiri 150 14.08 N 2.08 E
Simisa Island I 116 5.57 N 121.35 E
Simití 246 7.58 N 73.57 W
Simi Valley 228 34.16 N 118.47 W
Simiyu ≃ 154 2.33 S 33.25 E
Simizu → Shimizu 94 35.01 N 138.29 E
Simla, India 272b 22.47 N 88.16 E
Simla, India 272b 22.54 N 88.22 E
Simla, Co., U.S. 198 39.08 N 104.05 W
Simla ✦[8] 272b 22.35 N 88.22 E
Simlāpāl 126 22.55 N 87.05 E
Şimleu Silvaniei 38 47.14 N 22.48 E
Simlipālgarh 126 21.51 N 86.23 E
Simme ≃ 58 46.41 N 7.38 E
Simmelsdorf 60 49.36 N 11.21 E
Simmental V 58 46.37 N 7.25 E
Simmerath 56 50.36 N 6.18 E
Simmerberg 58 47.35 N 9.56 E
Simmering ✦[8] 264b 48.11 N 16.25 E
Simmern 56 49.59 N 7.31 E
Simmesport 194 30.59 N 91.48 W
Simmie 184 49.57 N 108.06 W
Simmons Island I 282 38.06 N 121.58 W
Simmons Point › 282 38.03 N 121.56 W
Simmonswood Moss ✦[3] 262 53.30 N 2.50 W
Simms 202 47.29 N 111.55 W
Simnas 76 54.24 N 23.39 E
Simoca 252 27.16 S 65.21 W
Simões 250 7.36 S 40.49 W
Simojärvi ⊜ 26 66.06 N 27.03 E
Simojoki ≃ 26 65.37 N 25.03 E
Simojovel 234 17.12 N 92.38 W
Simon, Lac ⊜, P.Q., Can. 206 46.10 N 74.45 W
Simon, Lac ⊜, P.Q., Can. 206 45.58 N 75.05 W
Simón Bolívar, Aeropuerto Internacional ⊠ 286c 10.37 N 66.59 W
Simoneti 84 42.14 N 42.52 E
Simonette ≃ 182 55.07 N 118.00 W
Simonhouse Lake ⊜ 184 54.30 N 101.10 W
Simonicha 80 56.31 N 53.50 E
Simoniči 78 51.53 N 28.04 E
Simonoseki → Shimonoseki 96 33.57 N 130.57 E
Simonsbath 42 51.09 N 3.45 W
Simonson Brook ≃ 276 40.26 N 74.37 W
Simonstone 262 53.48 N 2.20 W
Simonstorp 40 58.47 N 16.09 E
Simon's Town 158 34.14 S 18.26 E
Simonton Lake 216 41.44 N 85.59 W
Simoom Sound 182 50.45 N 126.29 W
Šimorskoje 80 55.19 N 42.02 E
Simpang, Indon. 112 1.16 S 104.05 E
Simpang, Indon. 112 1.03 S 110.06 E
Simpang, Indon. 112 0.09 N 103.15 E
Simpangampat 114 2.55 N 99.43 E
Simpang Empat 114 6.20 N 100.11 E
Simpang-kanan ≃ 114 2.21 N 97.51 E
Simpang-kiri ≃ 114 2.21 N 97.51 E
Simpang Rengam 114 1.50 N 103.19 E
Simpangtiga 114 2.23 N 99.47 E
Simpangulim 114 5.06 N 97.32 E
Simpele 26 61.26 N 29.22 E
Simplício Mendes 250 7.51 S 41.54 W
Simplon Pass)(58 46.15 N 8.02 E
Simplon Tunnel ✦[5] 58 46.15 N 8.05 E
Simpnäs 40 59.52 N 19.04 E
Simp'o-ri 98 38.36 N 127.41 E
Simpson, La., U.S. 194 31.14 N 93.00 W
Simpson, Pa., U.S. 210 41.35 N 75.29 W
Simpson ≃ 254 45.25 S 72.32 W
Simpson, Isla I 254 45.53 S 73.48 W
Simpson Desert ✦[2] 162 25.00 S 137.00 E
Simpson Desert National Park ♦ 162 25.40 S 138.15 E
Simpson Island I 190 48.48 N 87.40 W
Simpson Lake ⊜ 180 68.10 N 126.35 W
Simpson Peak ∧ 180 59.44 N 131.27 W
Simpson Peninsula ›[1] 176 68.34 N 88.45 W
Simpsons Gap National Park ♦ 162 23.40 S 133.45 E
Simpson Strait ʉ 176 68.27 N 97.45 W
Simpsonville, Ky., U.S. 218 38.13 N 85.21 W
Simpsonville, Md., U.S. 208 39.11 N 76.52 W
Simpsonville, S.C., U.S. 192 34.44 N 82.15 W
Simrishamn 26 55.33 N 14.20 E
Sims 216 40.30 N 85.51 W
Şimsbury 207 41.52 N 72.48 W
Šimsk 76 58.13 N 30.43 E
Simssee ⊜ 64 47.52 N 12.14 E
Simunjan 112 1.23 N 110.45 E
Simurāli 126 23.03 N 88.30 E
Simušir, ostrov I 74 46.58 N 152.02 E
Sīnāʾ □[4] 142 30.15 N 32.40 E
Sīna ≃ 122 17.22 N 75.54 E
Sīnāʾ, Shibh Jazīrat (Sinai Peninsula) ›[1] 140 29.30 N 34.00 E
Sinabang 114 2.29 N 96.23 E
Sinabelkirchen 61 47.06 N 15.50 E
Sinabung, Gunung ∧ 114 3.10 N 98.24 E
Sinadhago 144 5.22 N 46.20 E
Sinagra 70 38.05 N 14.51 E
Sinai, Mount ∧ 241k 12.04 N 61.42 W
Sinai, Mount → Mūsā, Jabal ∧ 140 28.32 N 33.59 E
Sinaia 38 45.21 N 25.33 E
Sinai Peninsula → Sīnāʾ, Shibh Jazīrat ›[1] 140 29.30 N 34.00 E
Sin'aja ≃, Europe 76 57.10 N 28.31 E
Sin'aja ≃, Ross. 74 61.06 N 126.50 E
Sinajana 174p 13.28 N 144.45 E
Sinako, Mount ∧ 116 7.30 N 125.17 E
Sinaloa □[3] 232 25.00 N 107.30 W
Sinaloa ≃ 232 25.18 N 108.30 W
Sinalunga 66 43.12 N 11.44 E
Sinamaica 246 11.05 N 71.51 W
Sinamary ≃ 250 5.27 N 53.00 W
Sinan, Tür. 130 37.52 N 41.00 E
Sinan, Zhg. 102 27.54 N 108.18 E
Sinanju 98 39.36 N 125.36 E
Sinanpaşa 130 38.45 N 30.15 E
Sīnarū 142 29.22 N 30.45 E
Sinatle 84 42.28 N 43.04 E
Sin'avka, Bela. 76 52.58 N 26.29 E
Sin'avka, Ross. 83 47.17 N 39.17 E
Sīnāwin 146 31.02 N 10.36 E
Sinbad Creek ≃ 282 37.35 N 121.53 W
Sinbaungwe 110 19.43 N 95.10 E
Sinbo 110 24.46 N 97.03 E
Sinbokchang 98 41.01 N 128.54 E
Sincan, Tür. 130 39.28 N 37.54 E
Sincan, Tür. 130 39.59 N 32.26 E
Sincé 246 9.15 N 75.09 W
Sincelejo 246 9.18 N 75.24 W
Sinch'ang, C.M.I.K. 98 40.07 N 128.28 E
Sinch'ang, C.M.I.K. 98 40.19 N 125.27 E
Sinch'ŏn 98 38.22 N 125.28 E
Sinch'ŏn-ni 271b 37.27 N 126.48 E
Sinclair 200 41.46 N 107.06 W
Sinclair, Lake ⊜[1] 192 33.11 N 83.16 W
Sinclair, Point › 162 32.06 S 133.00 E
Sinclair Island I 224 48.37 N 122.40 W
Sinclair Mills 182 54.02 N 121.41 W
Sinclair's Bay ⊂ 46 58.30 N 3.07 W
Sinclairville 214 42.15 N 79.15 W
Sind □[4] 120 25.30 N 69.00 E
Sind ≃ 124 26.26 N 79.13 E
Sinda 89 48.57 N 136.18 E
Sindal 26 57.28 N 10.13 E
Sindangan 116 8.14 N 123.00 E
Sindangan ≃ 116 8.13 N 123.00 E
Sindangan Bay ⊂ 116 8.11 N 122.50 E
Sindangan Point › 116 8.10 N 122.40 E
Sindangbarang 115a 7.27 S 107.08 E
Sindara 152 1.02 S 10.40 E
Sindari 120 25.35 N 71.55 E
Sindelfingen 56 48.42 N 9.00 E
Sindèr 150 14.29 N 1.22 E
Sindhnūr 122 15.47 N 76.46 E
Sindhulī Māḍhi 124 27.16 N 85.58 E
Sindi 76 58.24 N 24.40 E
Sindia 71 40.18 N 8.39 E
Sindingale 110 18.17 N 94.25 E
Sındıran 130 39.17 N 32.41 E
Sındırgı 130 39.14 N 28.10 E
Sindiyūn 142 30.15 N 31.12 E
Sin-do I 98 39.48 N 124.14 E
Sindŏk 98 36.47 N 126.10 E
Sindor 24 62.50 N 51.57 E
Sindou 150 10.40 N 5.10 W
Sindri 126 23.45 N 86.42 E
Sind Sāgar Doāb ⩘[1] 123 31.30 N 71.30 E
Sine V 150 14.10 N 16.28 W
Sinegorje 24 59.42 N 50.40 E
Sinegorsk 89 47.10 N 142.30 E
Şinegorskij 78 48.00 N 40.53 E
Šine-Ider 88 48.56 N 99.33 E
Sinekçi 130 40.16 N 27.24 E
Sinekli 130 41.14 N 28.12 E
Sinel'nikovo 78 48.20 N 35.31 E
Sinendé 150 10.21 N 2.23 E
Sinen'kije 80 51.15 N 45.46 E
Sinepuxent Bay ⊂ 208 38.16 N 75.09 W
Sines 34 37.57 N 8.52 W
Sines, Cabo de › 34 37.57 N 8.53 W
Sinevir 78 48.30 N 23.38 E
Sinevka 78 50.33 N 34.06 E
Sinewit, Mount ∧ 164 4.40 S 152.00 E
Sinez'orki 76 53.02 N 34.26 E
Sinfra 150 6.37 N 5.55 W
Singair 126 23.49 N 90.08 E
Singako 146 9.50 N 19.29 E
Singal 123 36.06 N 73.53 E
Singalamwe 156 17.41 S 23.23 E
Singālila ∧ 124 27.13 N 88.01 E
Singālila Range ⩘ 124 27.25 N 88.05 E
Singaparna 115a 7.21 S 108.06 E
Singapore, Sing. 114 1.17 N 103.51 E
Singapore, Sing. 271c 1.17 N 103.51 E
Singapore □[1], Asia 108 1.22 N 103.48 E
Singapore □[1], Asia 114 1.22 N 103.48 E
Singapore I 271c 1.23 N 103.48 E
Singapore ≃ 271c 1.17 N 103.51 E
Singapore, National University of ʊ[2] 271c 1.18 N 103.46 E
Singapore Station ✦[5] 271c 1.17 N 103.50 E
Singapore Strait ʉ 112 1.15 N 104.00 E
Singapour → Singapore □[1] 114 1.22 N 103.48 E
Singapur → Singapore 114 1.17 N 103.51 E
Singapur → Singapore □[1] 114 1.22 N 103.48 E
Singaraja 115b 8.07 S 115.06 E
Singarka ≃ 265a 59.53 N 29.54 E
Singāti 126 22.44 N 89.43 E
Singatoka 175g 18.08 S 177.30 E
Sing Buri 110 14.53 N 100.25 E
Singe 272b 22.57 N 88.26 E
Singen (Hohentwiel) 58 47.46 N 8.50 E
Singer 194 30.39 N 93.24 W
Singhi 126 23.37 N 87.48 E
Singida 154 4.49 S 34.45 E
Singida □[4] 154 5.30 S 34.30 E
Singing, India 102 28.59 N 94.50 E
Singing, India 120 28.53 N 94.47 E
Singing Tower ♦ 220 27.57 N 81.34 W
Singkaling Hkāmti 110 26.00 N 95.42 E
Singkang 112 4.08 S 120.01 E
Singkawang 112 0.54 N 109.00 E
Singkep, Pulau I 112 0.30 S 104.25 E
Singkil 114 2.17 N 97.49 E
Singkuang 114 1.03 N 98.56 E
Singleton, Austl. 170 32.34 S 151.10 E
Singleton, Eng., U.K. 42 50.55 N 0.46 W
Singleton, Mount ∧, Austl. 162 29.28 S 117.18 E
Singleton, Mount ∧, Austl. 162 22.00 S 130.49 E
Singleton Ditch ≅ 216 41.10 N 87.37 W
Singlewell or Ifield 260 51.25 N 0.23 E
Singö 40 60.10 N 18.44 E
Singö I 40 60.11 N 18.46 E
Singora → Songkhla 110 7.12 N 100.36 E
Şingorkai 164 5.55 S 146.55 E
Šingoža 86 47.45 N 80.40 E
Singpāra 272b 22.40 N 88.31 E
Singrāmau 124 25.57 N 82.23 E
Singuédeze (Shingwidzi) ≃ 156 23.53 S 32.17 E
Singur 126 22.49 N 88.14 E
Sin'gye 98 38.36 N 126.30 E
Sinhai → Lianyungang 98 34.39 N 119.16 E
Sinh Ho 110 22.22 N 103.14 E
Sinhŭng 98 40.11 N 127.34 E
Siniaka-Minia, Réserve de ■ 146 10.30 N 18.00 E
Sinicha 83 49.31 N 37.34 E
Sinička ≃ 265b 55.50 N 37.19 E
Sinije gory ⩘[2] 80 51.10 N 49.25 E
Sinije Lip'agi 78 51.23 N 38.29 E
Siniloan 116 14.25 N 121.27 E
Sining → Xining 102 36.38 N 101.55 E
Siniscola 71 40.34 N 9.41 E
Sinj 36 43.42 N 16.38 E
Sinjah 140 13.09 N 33.56 E
Sinjai 112 5.07 S 120.15 E
Sinjang-ni 98 39.04 N 127.46 E
Sinjār 128 36.19 N 41.52 E
Sinjār, Jabal ⩘ 130 36.25 N 41.40 E
Sinji-do I 98 34.20 N 126.50 E
Sinkan 110 24.08 N 97.01 E
Sinkāt 140 18.50 N 36.50 E
Sinkiang → Xinjiang Uygur Zizhiqu □[4] 90 40.00 N 85.00 E
Sinking ≃ 48 53.37 N 8.52 W
Sinking Creek ≃ 210 40.51 N 77.34 W
Sinking Spring, Oh., U.S. 218 39.04 N 83.23 W
Sinking Spring, Pa., U.S. 208 40.19 N 76.02 W
Şin'kok-ni 271b 37.37 N 126.46 E
Šinkovo, Ross. 76 56.03 N 31.31 E
Sin'kovo, Ross. 82 56.26 N 36.04 E
Sin'kovo, Ross. 82 54.37 N 38.56 E
Sin'kovo, Ross. 82 56.23 N 37.19 E
Sinks Canyon State Park ♦ 200 42.45 N 108.50 W
Sin-le-Noble 50 50.22 N 3.07 E
Sinmak 98 38.25 N 126.14 E
Sinmi-do I 98 39.33 N 124.53 E
Sinn ≃ 56 50.03 N 9.42 E
Sinnahwā 142 30.25 N 31.21 E
Sínnai 71 39.18 N 9.12 E
Sinnamahoning 214 41.19 N 78.06 W
Sinnamary 250 5.23 N 52.57 W
Sinnar 122 19.51 N 74.00 E
Sinnemahoning Creek ≃ 210 41.15 N 77.54 W
Sinnemahoning Creek, Bennett Branch ≃ 210 41.20 N 78.08 W
Sinnemahoning Creek, Driftwood Branch ≃ 210 41.20 N 78.08 W
Sinnemahoning Creek, First Fork ≃ 210 41.19 N 78.05 W
Sinnersdorf 56 51.01 N 6.49 E
Sinnes 26 58.56 N 6.50 E
Sinni ≃ 68 40.09 N 16.42 E
Sînnicolau Mare 38 46.05 N 20.38 E
Sinntal 56 50.18 N 9.38 E
Sinnūris 142 29.25 N 30.52 E
Sinnyŏng 98 36.04 N 128.46 E
Sino, Pedra do ∧ 256 22.30 S 43.03 W
Sinoie, Lacul ⊜ 38 44.38 N 28.53 E
Sinop, Bra. 250 11.55 S 55.35 W
Sinop, Tür. 130 42.01 N 35.09 E
Sinop □[4] 130 41.40 N 34.50 E
Sinop Burnu › 130 42.02 N 35.12 E
Sinp'a 98 41.24 N 127.46 E
Sinp'o 98 40.03 N 128.12 E
Sins 58 47.11 N 8.23 E
Sinsang 98 39.38 N 127.25 E
Sinsen 263 51.40 N 7.11 E
Sinsheim 56 49.15 N 8.53 E
Sinsiang → Xinxiang 98 35.20 N 113.51 E
Sinsin 56 50.17 N 5.15 E
Sinsi-ri 98 39.59 N 124.58 E
Sinskoje 74 61.08 N 126.48 E
Sinspelt 56 49.58 N 6.19 E
Sint-Amandsberg 50 51.04 N 3.45 E
Sintana 38 46.21 N 21.30 E
Sint-Andries 50 51.12 N 3.10 E
Sintang 112 0.04 N 111.30 E
Sint Annaland 52 51.36 N 4.06 E
Sint Annaparochie 52 53.16 N 5.39 E
Sint Anthonis 52 51.37 N 5.52 E
Sint Christoffelberg ∧[2] 241s 12.20 N 69.08 W

≃	River	Fluß	Río	Rivière	Rio
≅	Canal	Kanal	Canal	Canal	Canal
∟	Waterfall, Rapids	Wasserfall, Stromschnellen	Cascada, Rápidos	Chute d'eau, Rapides	Cascata, Rápidos
ʉ	Strait	Meeresstraße	Estrecho	Détroit	Estreito
⊂	Bay, Gulf	Bucht, Golf	Bahía, Golfo	Baie, Golfe	Baía, Golfo
⊜	Lake, Lakes	See, Seen	Lago, Lagos	Lac, Lacs	Lago, Lagos
≡	Swamp	Sumpf	Pantano	Marais	Pântano
⊓	Ice Features, Glacier	Eis- und Gletscherformen	Accidentes Glaciales	Formes glaciaires	Acidentes glaciares
⊤	Other Hydrographic Features	Andere Hydrographische Objekte	Otros Elementos Hidrográficos	Autres données hydrographiques	Outros acidentes hidrográficos

✢	Submarine Features	Untermeerische Objekte	Accidentes Submarinos	Formes de relief sous-marin	Acidentes submarinos
□	Political Unit	Politische Einheit	Unidad Politica	Entité politique	Unidade política
ʊ	Cultural Institution	Kulturelle Institution	Institución Cultural	Institution culturelle	Instituição cultural
⊥	Historical Site	Historische Stätte	Sitio Histórico	Site historique	Sitio histórico
♦	Recreational Site	Erholungs- und Ferienort	Sitio de Recreo	Centre de loisirs	Area de Lazer
⊠	Airport	Flughafen	Aeropuerto	Aéroport	Aeroporto
■	Military Installation	Militäranlage	Instalación Militar	Installation militaire	Instalação militar
✦	Miscellaneous	Verschiedenes	Misceláneo	Divers	Diversos

Name / Name	Page / Seite	Lat.°′ / Breite°′	Long.°′ / Länge°′ E = Ost
Sint-Denijs-Westrem	50	51.01 N	3.40 E
Sint Eustatius I	238	17.30 N	62.59 W
Sint-Gillis-Waas	50	51.13 N	4.08 E
Sint Helenabaai ⊂	158	32.43 S	18.05 E
Sint-Joris-Weert	56	50.48 N	4.39 E
Sint-Joris-Winge	56	50.55 N	4.52 E
Sint-Katelijne-Waver	56	51.04 N	4.32 E
Sint-Kruis, Bel.	50	51.13 N	3.15 E
Sint Kruis, Ned. Ant.	241s	12.18 N	69.08 W
Sint-Lenaarts	56	51.21 N	4.41 E
Sint Maarten	52	52.46 N	4.44 E
Sint Maarten (Saint-Martin) I	238	18.04 N	63.04 W
Sint Maartensdijk	52	51.33 N	4.05 E
Sint-Michiels	50	51.11 N	3.12 E
Sint Michielsgestel	52	51.38 N	5.21 E
Sint Nicolaas	241s	12.27 N	69.52 W
Sint-Niklaas (Saint-Nicolas)	50	51.10 N	4.08 E
Sint-Oedenrode	52	51.34 N	5.27 E
Sinton	196	28.02 N	97.30 W
Sintong	114	1.31 N	100.58 E
Sint Pancras	52	52.39 N	4.46 E
Sint-Pieters-Leeuw	50	50.47 N	4.14 E
Sintra	34	38.48 N	9.23 W
Sintra, Serra de ⩘[2]	266c	38.47 N	9.25 W
Sintra Granjo do Marquez, Aeroporto ⊠	266c	38.49 N	9.20 W
Sint-Truiden	56	50.48 N	5.12 E
Sint Willebrord	52	51.33 N	4.35 E
Sinú ≃	246	9.24 N	75.49 W
Sin'ucha ≃, Ross.	84	44.45 N	40.58 E
Sin'ucha ≃, Ukr.	78	48.03 N	30.51 E
Sin'uga	88	57.45 N	115.13 E
Sinŭiju	98	40.05 N	124.24 E
Sinujif	144	8.33 N	48.59 E
Sinŭp, C.M.I.K.	98	39.54 N	126.47 E
Sinŭp, Taehan	98	37.54 N	127.12 E
Sinwŏn-ni	98	38.13 N	125.44 E
Sinzig	56	50.32 N	7.15 E
Sinzing	60	49.00 N	12.02 E
Sió ≃, Magy.	30	46.20 N	18.55 E
Sio ≃, Togo	150	6.17 N	1.13 E
Siocon	116	7.42 N	122.08 E
Siófok	30	46.54 N	18.04 E
Sioma	152	16.39 S	23.30 E
Sioma Ngweze National Park ♦	152	17.15 S	23.20 E
Sion (Sitten)	58	46.14 N	7.21 E
Sionascaig, Loch ⊜	46	58.04 N	5.11 W
Sion Mills	48	54.47 N	7.29 W
Sioule ≃	32	46.22 N	3.19 E
Sioux Center	198	43.04 N	96.10 W
Sioux City	198	42.30 N	96.24 W
Sioux Falls	198	43.33 N	96.42 W
Sioux Lookout	184	50.06 N	91.55 W
Sioux Narrows	184	49.25 N	94.06 W
Sioux Rapids	198	42.53 N	95.09 W
Sipalay	116	9.45 N	122.24 E
Sipalay ≃	116	9.46 N	122.24 E
Sipaliwini □[5]	250	4.00 N	56.00 W
Sipaliwini ≃	250	2.22 N	56.50 W
Sipaozi	104	41.26 N	122.13 E
Sipapo ≃	246	5.03 N	67.48 W
Siparia	241r	10.08 N	61.30 W
Šipčenski prohod)(	38	42.46 N	25.19 E
Şipek	130	40.14 N	41.29 E
Sipes	220	28.48 N	81.14 W
Sipesville	214	40.06 N	79.06 W
Šipicyno, Ross.	24	61.17 N	46.28 E
Šipicyno, Ross.	86	56.04 N	77.18 E
Šipilovo	82	54.49 N	37.32 E
Siping	89	43.12 N	124.20 E
Sipingjie	98	42.31 N	125.08 E
Sipirok	114	1.37 N	99.16 E
Sipitang	112	5.05 N	115.33 E
Sipiwesk	184	55.27 N	97.24 W
Sipiwesk Lake ⊜	184	55.05 N	97.35 W
Siple ᵿ[3]	9	75.56 S	84.15 W
Siple, Mount ʌ	9	73.15 S	126.06 W
Siple Coast ⍊[2]	9	82.00 S	153.00 W
Sipocot	116	13.46 N	122.58 E
Sipofaneni	158	26.41 S	31.41 E
Sipot	114	4.31 N	96.02 E
Şipoteny	78	47.18 N	28.11 E
Šipovatoje	78	49.56 N	37.24 E
Sipplingen	58	47.47 N	9.05 E
Si Prachan	110	14.37 N	100.09 E
Sipsey ≃	194	33.00 N	88.10 W
Sipsey Creek ≃	194	33.53 N	88.17 W
Sipu	98	40.48 N	113.43 E
Sipul	164	5.50 S	148.45 E
Šipunovo	86	52.13 N	82.17 E
Šipunskij, mys ›	74	53.06 N	160.02 E
Sipupus	114	1.25 N	99.31 E
Sipura, Pulau I	112	2.12 S	99.40 E
Siqian, Zhg.	100	22.31 N	112.52 E
Siqian, Zhg.	100	24.40 N	114.06 E
Siqueira Campos	255	23.42 S	49.50 W
Siquia ≃	236	12.09 N	84.13 W
Siquijor	116	9.13 N	123.30 E
Siquijor □[4]	116	9.11 N	123.34 E
Siquijor Island I	116	9.11 N	123.34 E
Siquirres	236	10.06 N	83.30 W
Siquisique	246	10.34 N	69.42 W
Sīra, India	122	13.45 N	76.54 E
Sira, Nor.	26	58.25 N	6.38 E
Šira, Ross.	86	54.29 N	89.56 E
Sira ≃	26	58.17 N	6.24 E
Si Racha	110	13.10 N	100.56 E
Siracuas	248	21.03 S	61.46 W
Siracusa (Syracuse)	70	37.04 N	15.17 E
Siracusa □[4]	70	37.03 N	15.00 E
Sir Adam Beck II Reservoir ⊜[1]	284a	43.08 N	79.04 W
Sirāhā	124	26.39 N	86.12 E
Šir'aj	80	49.34 N	44.07 E
Šir'ajevo	78	47.23 N	30.13 E
Sirājganj	124	24.27 N	89.43 E
Sir Alexander, Mount ʌ	182	53.56 N	120.23 W
Sirāmpur	126	24.08 N	86.20 E
Şiran	130	40.12 N	39.08 E
Sirasso	150	9.16 N	6.06 W
Sirault	50	50.30 N	3.47 E
Siraway	116	7.34 N	122.08 E
Sirba ≃	150	13.46 N	1.40 E
Şīr Banī Yās I	128	24.19 N	52.37 E
Sir Colin Mackenzie Wildlife Sanctuary ◆[4]	169	37.40 S	145.32 E
Sirdalsvatn ⊜	26	58.33 N	6.41 E
Sīrdān	128	36.39 N	49.12 E
Sirdar	182	49.15 N	116.37 W
Širdkoje	78	48.08 N	34.49 E
Sir Douglas, Mount ʌ	182	50.44 N	115.20 W
Sire	144	9.00 N	36.55 E
Sir Edward Pellew Group II	164	15.40 S	136.48 E
Širega	76	60.10 N	41.15 E
Sireniki	180	64.25 N	173.57 W
Sirente, Monte ʌ	66	42.09 N	13.36 E
Siret	38	47.57 N	26.04 E
Siret ≃	38	45.24 N	28.01 E
Sirevåg	26	58.30 N	5.47 E
Sir Francis Drake, Mount ʌ	182	50.48 N	124.47 W
Sir Francis Drake Channel ʉ	240m	18.25 N	64.30 W
Sirghāyā	132	33.48 N	36.09 E
Sirḥān, Wādī as- V	128	30.30 N	38.00 E
Sirhind	124	30.39 N	76.23 E
Sirhind Canal ≋	123	30.47 N	76.01 E
Siria → Syria □[1]	128	35.00 N	38.00 E
Sirik, Tanjong ›	112	2.46 N	111.19 E
Sirikit Reservoir ⊜[1]	110	17.50 N	100.30 E
Sírina I	130	36.21 N	26.42 E
Širinguši	80	53.51 N	42.46 E
Sirino, Monte ʌ	68	40.08 N	15.50 E
Siriya-zaki ›	92	41.26 N	141.28 E
Sir James MacBrien, Mount ʌ	180	62.07 N	127.41 W
Sīrjān	128	29.27 N	55.40 E
Sir Joseph Banks Group II	166	34.32 S	136.17 E
Sirkābād	126	23.16 N	86.12 E
Sirkeli	130	40.09 N	32.52 E
Sirmaur	124	24.51 N	81.23 E
Sirmione	64	45.30 N	10.36 E
Širmovka	78	49.34 N	29.06 E
Sirnach	58	47.28 N	9.00 E
Şırnak □[4]	128	37.30 N	42.30 E
Siro, Jabal ʌ	140	14.23 N	24.23 E
Sirohi	120	24.54 N	72.51 E
Širokaja Pad'	89	50.14 N	142.09 E
Širokij	89	49.45 N	129.30 E
Širokij Bujerak	80	52.07 N	47.46 E
Širokino	83	47.06 N	37.49 E
Širokoje, Ukr.	78	47.41 N	33.14 E
Širokoje, Ukr.	83	47.58 N	38.13 E
Širokolanovka	78	47.10 N	31.24 E
Širokovo	88	55.27 N	99.23 E
Sirolo	66	43.32 N	13.37 E
Sirombu	114	0.57 N	97.25 E
Sironj	124	24.06 N	77.42 E
Síros I	38	37.26 N	24.54 E
Síros → Ermoúpolis	38	37.26 N	24.56 E
Sirotino, Bela.	76	55.23 N	29.37 E
Sirotino, Ukr.	83	48.55 N	38.31 E
Sirotinskaja	80	49.16 N	43.39 E
Siroua, Jebel ʌ	148	30.41 N	7.37 W
Sırpsındığı	130	41.46 N	26.29 E
Sirrah, Nafūd as- ⍊[8]	128	23.05 N	44.25 E
Sīrrī, Jazīreh-ye I	128	25.55 N	54.32 E
Sirsa, India	123	29.32 N	75.01 E
Sirsa, India	126	22.14 N	86.38 E
Sirsāganj	124	27.03 N	78.42 E
Sirs al-Layyānah	142	30.26 N	30.58 E
Sir Sandford, Mount ʌ	182	51.40 N	117.52 W
Sirsi	122	14.37 N	74.51 E
Sirsilla	122	18.23 N	78.50 E
Sirsinā, Mişr	142	30.36 N	30.54 E
Sirsinā, Mişr	142	29.24 N	30.58 E
Sirsiri	154	4.24 N	31.53 E
Sir Thomas, Mount ʌ	162	27.10 S	129.45 E
Siruma	116	14.00 N	123.15 E
Sirupa ≃	232	29.10 N	108.35 W
Şirvan	130	38.02 N	42.00 E
Sīrvān (Diyālā) ≃	128	33.14 N	44.31 E
Širvanskaja ravnina ≚	84	40.15 N	48.00 E
Širvintos	76	55.03 N	24.57 E
Sir Wilfrid Laurier, Mount ʌ	182	52.47 N	119.45 W
Sir Wilfrid Laurier's Birthplace National Historic Site ⊥	206	45.51 N	73.45 W
Sirykrabet ⊥	86	44.07 N	62.35 E
Sís ≃, Guat.	236	14.09 N	91.39 W
Šiš ≃, Ross.	86	57.19 N	73.23 E
Sisa, Mount ʌ	164	6.08 S	142.45 E
Sisaba ʌ	154	6.09 S	29.48 E
Sisaiya Thāna	124	27.35 N	81.20 E
Sisak	36	45.29 N	16.23 E
Si Sa Ket	110	15.07 N	104.20 E
Šišaki	78	49.53 N	34.00 E
Šišakovo	76	60.02 N	41.30 E
Si Satchanalai	110	17.31 N	99.46 E
Šišchid (Kyzyl-Chem) ≃	88	51.21 N	96.58 E
Šiševka	76	58.52 N	38.52 E
Sishangcun	105	40.16 N	116.33 E
Sishen	158	27.55 S	22.59 E
Sishili	106	32.09 N	120.45 E
Sishilijie	100	29.08 N	116.44 E
Sishilipu	105	40.12 N	118.08 E
Sishuang Liedao II	100	26.42 N	120.24 E
Sishui	98	35.39 N	117.15 E
Sisian	84	39.32 N	46.02 E
Sisib Lake ⊜	184	52.35 N	99.22 W
Šišicy	76	53.13 N	27.32 E
Sisikon	58	46.57 N	8.42 E
Sisim ≃	88	55.09 N	91.54 E
Sisipuk Lake ⊜	184	55.45 N	101.50 W
Šiškejevo	80	54.12 N	44.45 E
Šiškino	88	52.18 N	113.35 E
Siskiyou Mountains ⩘	204	41.55 N	123.15 W
Siskiyou Pass)(	202	42.03 N	122.36 W
Şişli ◆[8]	267b	41.04 N	28.59 E
Šišlovo	82	54.14 N	38.33 E
Sison	116	9.40 N	125.31 E
Sisŏphŏn	110	13.35 N	102.59 E
Sisquoc ≃	204	34.54 N	120.18 W
Sissa ≃	115b	8.29 S	121.18 E
Sissach	58	47.28 N	7.49 E
Sissano	164	3.00 S	142.05 E
Sisséla	150	10.49 N	10.37 W
Sisseton	198	45.39 N	97.02 W
Sisseton Indian Reservation ◆[4]	198	45.40 N	97.02 W
Sissili ≃	150	10.16 N	1.15 W
Sisson Branch Reservoir ⊜[1]	186	47.16 N	67.20 W
Sissonne	50	49.34 N	3.54 E
Sissonville	188	38.31 N	81.37 W
Sīstān ◆[1]	128	30.30 N	62.00 E
Sīstān va Balūchestān □[4]	128	28.30 N	60.30 E
Sister Bay	190	45.11 N	87.07 W
Sister Lakes	216	42.05 N	86.12 W
Sisteron	62	44.12 N	5.56 E
Sisters	202	44.17 N	121.32 W
Sistersville	188	39.33 N	80.59 W
Sistig	56	50.29 N	6.30 E
Sisto ≃	66	41.18 N	13.10 E
Sistranda	26	63.43 N	8.50 E
Sit' ≃, Ross.	76	59.59 N	40.10 E
Sit' ≃, Ross.	76	58.16 N	37.54 E
Sitabamba	248	8.02 S	77.44 W
Sitai, Zhg.	85	39.23 N	77.56 E
Sitai, Zhg.	98	41.16 N	114.23 E
Sitaizi, Zhg.	104	42.29 N	123.20 E
Sitaizi, Zhg.	104	41.17 N	122.16 E
Sitaizui	105	40.49 N	115.20 E
Sitakili	150	13.07 N	11.14 W
Sitalike	154	6.38 S	31.08 E
Sitalkuchi	124	26.10 N	89.11 E
Sītāmarhi	124	26.36 N	85.29 E
Sitampiky	157b	16.41 S	46.06 E
Si Tangkay	112	4.40 N	119.24 E
Sītāpur	124	27.34 N	80.41 E
Sītāpur Branch ≋	124	28.10 N	80.25 E
Sitārāmpur	126	23.43 N	86.53 E
Siteki	158	26.32 S	31.58 E
Sites	226	39.19 N	122.20 W
Si Thep ⊥	110	15.30 N	101.10 E
Sithoniá	38	35.12 N	26.07 E
Sithoniá ›[1]	38	40.10 N	23.47 E
Sitidgi Lake ⊜	180	68.32 N	132.42 W
Sítio D'Abadia	255	14.48 S	46.16 W
Sítio Novo	250	5.51 S	46.43 W
Sitka	180	57.03 N	135.02 W
Sitkalidak Island I	180	57.10 N	153.14 W
Sitka National Historical Park ♦	180	57.05 N	135.15 W
Sitka Point ›	180	57.00 N	135.49 W
Sitka Sound ʉ	180	57.00 N	135.30 W
Sitkinak Island I	180	56.35 N	154.12 W
Sitkinak Strait ʉ	180	56.39 N	154.06 W
Šitkino	88	56.23 N	98.21 E
Sitkovcy	78	48.54 N	29.12 E
Sitna ≃	38	47.37 N	27.08 E
Sitn'a-Ščelkanovo	82	54.58 N	37.59 E
Sitnica ≃	38	42.45 N	21.01 E
Sitniki	80	56.27 N	44.06 E
Sitnikovo	86	56.23 N	67.53 E
Sitobela	158	26.53 S	31.36 E
Sitona	144	14.28 N	37.27 E
Sitrah	128	26.09 N	50.38 E
Sitrah ⊤[4]	140	28.42 N	26.54 E
Sittard	56	51.00 N	5.53 E
Sittendorf	264b	48.05 N	16.10 E
Sittensen	52	53.17 N	9.30 E
Sitten → Sion	58	46.14 N	7.21 E
Sitter ≃	58	47.29 N	9.14 E
Sittingbourne	42	51.21 N	0.44 E
Sittoung ≃	110	17.10 N	96.58 E
Sittwe (Akyab)	110	20.09 N	92.54 E
Situ	105	39.20 N	115.39 E
Situbondo	115a	7.42 S	114.00 E
Siufaalele Point ›	174y	14.17 S	169.29 W
Si'ufage	174y	14.14 S	169.32 W
Siulakderas	112	1.55 S	101.18 E
Siu Lek Yuen	271d	22.23 N	114.12 E
Siumbatu	112	2.45 S	122.03 E
Siumpu, Pulau I	112	5.40 S	122.31 E
Siuna	236	13.44 N	84.46 W
Siurgus Donigala	71	39.35 N	9.12 E
Siuri	126	23.55 N	87.32 E
Siusi (Seis)	64	46.32 N	11.34 E
Siuslaw ≃	202	44.01 N	124.08 W
Siva ≃	80	56.48 N	53.55 E
Sivaganga	122	9.52 N	78.29 E
Sivakāsi	122	9.27 N	77.49 E
Sivaki	89	52.39 N	126.45 E
Sīvand ≃	128	29.51 N	52.46 E
Sivas	130	39.45 N	37.02 E
Sivas □[4]	130	39.30 N	37.15 E
Sivaš ʉ	78	46.00 N	34.30 E
Sivaslı	130	38.30 N	29.42 E
Sivašskoje	78	46.23 N	34.34 E
Sivé	150	15.42 N	13.12 W
Šiveluč, vulkan ʌ[1]	74	56.39 N	161.18 E
Siverek	130	37.45 N	39.19 E
Siverskij	76	59.21 N	30.05 E
Sivkovo	82	55.26 N	35.53 E
Sivomaskinskij	24	66.40 N	62.35 E
Sivri Ada I	267b	40.54 N	28.59 E
Sivrice	130	38.27 N	39.19 E
Sivrihisar	130	39.27 N	31.34 E
Sivry-Courtry	261	48.32 N	2.45 E
Sivry-sur-Meuse	56	49.19 N	5.16 E
Sīwah	140	29.12 N	25.31 E
Sīwah, Wāḥat ⊤[4]	140	29.12 N	25.31 E
Siwalik Range ⩘	120	31.00 N	78.00 E
Siwān	124	26.13 N	84.22 E
Siwang ≃	107	29.25 N	103.50 E
Sixaola ≃	236	9.34 N	82.34 W
Six Flags Great America ♦	216	42.21 N	87.55 W
Six Flags over Mid-America ♦	219	38.31 N	90.40 W
Six Flags Over Texas ♦	222	32.45 N	97.05 W
Six-Fours-la-Plage	62	43.06 N	5.51 E
Sixian	100	33.30 N	117.56 E
Sixitou	100	27.31 N	119.57 E
Six Mile Creek ≃, On., Can.	284a	43.15 N	79.10 W
Sixmile Creek ≃, Ky., U.S.	218	38.26 N	84.58 W
Sixmile Creek ≃, N.Y., U.S.	284a	43.17 N	78.58 W
Sixmilecross	48	54.34 N	7.08 W
Six Mile Lake ⊜	212	44.55 N	79.45 W
Sixmile Run ≃	276	40.28 N	74.35 W
Six Mile Water ≃	48	54.42 N	6.14 W
Six Nations Indian Reserve ◆[4]	212	43.03 N	80.07 W
Sixshooter Draw V	196	30.51 N	102.33 W
Sixteen Mile Creek ≃, On., Can.	275b	43.27 N	79.40 W
Sixteenmile Creek ≃, Mt., U.S.	202	46.06 N	111.23 W
Sixth Cataract → Sablūkah, Ash-Shallāl as- ʟ	140	16.20 N	32.42 E
Siyāl, Jazā'ir II	140	22.47 N	36.12 E
Siyāna	124	28.38 N	78.03 E
Siyang	100	33.43 N	118.41 E
Si Yat ≃	110	13.42 N	101.26 E
Siyeteb	140	18.00 N	35.01 E
Siz'absk	24	65.05 N	53.49 E
Sizaja	88	58.07 N	100.38 E
Sizhijian	98	42.25 N	114.36 E
Siziano	62	45.20 N	9.12 E
Sizilien → Sicilia I	70	37.30 N	14.00 E
Siziman	89	50.43 N	140.26 E
Siziwang Qi	102	41.33 N	111.31 E
Sizun	32	48.24 N	4.05 W
Sizuoka → Shizuoka	94	34.58 N	138.23 E
Sjælland I	41	55.30 N	11.45 E
Sjællands Odde ›[1]	41	55.58 N	11.22 E
Själevad	26	63.18 N	18.36 E
Sjanovo	82	54.59 N	37.25 E
Sjenica	38	43.16 N	20.00 E
Sjeništa ʌ	38	43.42 N	18.37 E
Sjoa ≃	26	61.41 N	9.33 E
Sjöbo	41	55.38 N	13.42 E
Sjøholt	26	62.29 N	6.48 E
Sjösa	40	58.46 N	17.04 E
Sjötorp	40	58.50 N	13.59 E
Skaby	264a	52.19 N	13.51 E
Skaby-Berge ⩘[2]	264a	52.19 N	13.49 E
Skåde	41	56.06 N	10.13 E
Skadovsk	78	46.08 N	32.54 E
Skælskør	41	55.15 N	11.19 E
Skærbæk, Dan.	41	55.31 N	9.38 E
Skærbæk, Dan.	41	55.09 N	8.46 E
Skævinge	41	55.55 N	12.10 E
Skaftafell National Park ♦	24a	64.15 N	17.00 W
Skaftung	26	62.07 N	21.22 E
Skagafjörður ⊂	24a	65.55 N	19.35 W
Skagen	26	57.44 N	10.36 E
Skagern ⊜	40	58.59 N	14.17 E
Skagerrak ʉ	26	57.45 N	9.00 E
Skagersvik	40	58.58 N	14.06 E
Skaggs Creek ≃	194	36.54 N	86.04 W
Skagit □[6]	224	48.29 N	121.45 W
Skagit ≃	224	48.20 N	122.25 W
Skagit Bay ⊂	224	48.19 N	122.24 W
Skagway	180	59.28 N	135.19 W
Skaidi	24	70.25 N	24.30 E
Skaistkalne	76	56.23 N	24.39 E
Skála Oropoú	38	38.20 N	23.46 E
Skala-Podol'skaja	78	48.51 N	26.12 E
Skalat	78	49.26 N	25.59 E
Skalbmierz	30	50.19 N	20.25 E
Skälderviken	41	56.17 N	12.50 E
Skälderviken ⊂	41	56.18 N	12.38 E
Skalica	30	48.51 N	17.14 E
Skalino	76	58.32 N	40.13 E
Skalistaja, gora ʌ	84	42.48 N	45.08 E
Skalistyj, gora ʌ	180	68.12 N	178.10 E
Skalistyj chrebet ⩘	84	43.15 N	43.00 E
Skalistyj Golec, gora ʌ	88	56.24 N	119.12 E
Skalka ⊜	24	66.50 N	18.46 E
Skalka, údolní nádrž ⊜[1]	54	50.06 N	12.19 E
Skalná	54	50.07 N	12.23 E
Skal'nyj	86	58.22 N	57.59 E
Skamania	224	45.37 N	122.02 W
Skamania □[6]	224	45.58 N	121.53 W
Skamlingsbanke ʌ[2]	41	55.25 N	9.34 E
Skamokawa	224	46.16 N	123.27 W
Skanderborg	41	56.02 N	9.56 E
Skanderborg Sø ⊜	41	56.01 N	9.56 E
Skåne □[9]	41	55.59 N	13.30 E
Skaneateles	210	42.56 N	76.25 W
Skaneateles Falls	210	43.00 N	76.27 W
Skaneateles Lake ⊜	210	42.53 N	76.24 W
Skånevik	26	59.44 N	5.59 E
Skänninge	26	58.24 N	15.05 E
Skanör	26	55.25 N	12.52 E
Skara	26	58.22 N	13.25 E
Skaraborgs Län □[6]	26	58.20 N	13.30 E
Skaramagás	267c	38.01 N	23.36 E
Skärblacka	40	58.34 N	15.54 E
Skarð	24a	64.03 N	19.50 W
Skardhø ʌ	26	62.30 N	8.45 E
Skārdu	123	35.18 N	75.37 E
Skärhamn	26	58.00 N	11.33 E
Skarhult	41	55.49 N	13.23 E
Skarnes	26	60.15 N	11.41 E
Skärplinge	40	60.28 N	17.46 E
Skarszewy	30	54.05 N	18.27 E
Skårup	41	55.05 N	10.42 E
Skaryszew	30	51.19 N	21.15 E
Skarżysko-Kamienna	30	51.08 N	20.53 E
Skášov	60	49.31 N	13.26 E
Skate Creek ≃	224	46.37 N	121.41 W
Skattkärr	40	59.25 N	13.41 E
Skaudvilė	76	55.24 N	22.35 E
Skaugum	26	59.51 N	10.26 E
Skawina	30	49.59 N	19.49 E
Skebobruk	40	59.58 N	18.36 E
Skebokvarn	40	59.04 N	16.42 E
Skedviken ⊜	40	59.46 N	18.16 E
Skedvisjön ⊜	40	59.35 N	15.40 E
Skeena ≃	182	54.09 N	130.02 W
Skeena Crossing	182	55.06 N	127.49 W
Skeena Mountains ⩘	176	57.00 N	128.30 W
Skeen Peak ʌ	222	32.59 N	97.48 W
Skegness	44	53.10 N	0.21 E
Skegrie	41	55.24 N	13.04 E
Skei	26	61.38 N	6.30 E
Skeikampen	26	61.20 N	10.07 E
Skelde	41	54.51 N	9.44 E
Skeleton Coast ⍊[2]	156	19.15 S	12.30 E
Skeleton Coast Park ♦	156	19.25 S	12.55 E
Skeleton Creek ≃	196	35.58 N	97.25 W
Skeleton Lake ⊜	212	45.15 N	79.27 W
Skellefteå	26	64.46 N	20.57 E
Skellefteälven ≃	26	64.42 N	21.06 E
Skelleftehamn	26	64.41 N	21.14 E
Skellig Rocks II[1]	48	51.48 N	10.31 W
Skellytown	196	35.34 N	101.11 W
Skelmersdale	44	53.33 N	2.48 W
Skelmorlie	46	55.51 N	4.53 W
Skelton, Eng., U.K.	44	54.33 N	0.59 W
Skelton, Eng., U.K.	44	54.43 N	2.51 W
Skene	26	57.29 N	12.38 E
Skene, Mount ʌ	169	37.25 S	146.23 E
Skepptuna	40	59.43 N	18.05 E
Skerne ≃	44	54.29 N	1.34 W
Skerpioensdrif	158	31.05 S	21.33 E
Skerries	48	53.35 N	6.07 W
Skerryvore I[2]	46	56.19 N	7.07 W
Skewen	42	51.40 N	3.51 W
Skhíza I	38	36.44 N	21.46 E
Ski	26	59.43 N	10.50 E
Skíathos	38	39.10 N	23.29 E
Skíathos I	38	39.10 N	23.28 E
Skiatook	196	36.22 N	96.00 W
Skibbereen	48	51.33 N	9.15 W
Skibby	41	55.45 N	11.58 E
Skibotn	24	69.24 N	20.16 E
Skiddaw ʌ	44	54.38 N	3.08 W
Skidegate	182	53.15 N	132.00 W
Skidegate Inlet ⊂	182	53.14 N	132.00 W
Skidel'	76	53.34 N	24.15 E
Skidmore	196	28.15 N	97.41 W
Skien	26	59.12 N	9.36 E
Skierniewice	30	51.58 N	20.08 E
Skierniewice □[4]	30	52.10 N	20.15 E
Skiftet ʉ	26	60.15 N	21.05 E
Skihist Mountain ʌ	182	50.11 N	121.54 W
Skikda (Philippeville)	148	36.50 N	6.58 E
Skikda □[5]	148	36.45 N	7.00 E
Skilak Lake ⊜	180	60.25 N	150.25 W
Skillet Fork ≃	194	38.08 N	88.07 W
Skillingaryd	26	57.26 N	14.05 E
Skillman	276	40.25 N	74.42 W
Škin'	82	55.11 N	38.30 E
Skinnastaður	24a	66.07 N	16.24 W
Skinner Reservoir ⊜[1]	228	33.35 N	117.03 W
Skinnskatteberg	40	59.50 N	15.41 E
Skippack	285	40.14 N	75.24 W
Skippack Creek ≃	285	40.09 N	75.27 W
Skippack Creek, West Branch ≃	285	40.14 N	75.23 W
Skippers	208	36.37 N	77.38 W
Skipskop	158	34.33 S	20.25 E
Skipton, Austl.	169	37.41 S	143.22 E
Skipton, Eng., U.K.	44	53.58 N	2.01 W
Skirfare ≃	44	54.07 N	2.01 W
Skirmish Point ›	171a	27.05 S	153.13 E
Skíros	38	38.53 N	24.33 E
Skíros I	38	38.53 N	24.32 E
Skivarp	41	55.25 N	13.34 E
Skive	26	56.34 N	9.02 E
Skjálfandafljót ≃	24a	65.57 N	17.38 W
Skjálfandi ⊂	24a	66.08 N	17.38 W
Skjeberg	26	59.14 N	11.12 E
Skjern	26	55.57 N	8.30 E
Skjern ≃	41	55.57 N	8.40 E
Sklad	74	71.55 N	123.33 E
Šklov	76	54.13 N	30.18 E
Skniga ≃	82	54.53 N	37.24 E
Skobeleva, pik ʌ	85	39.49 N	72.44 E
Skoby	40	60.02 N	18.01 E
Škocjanske jame ⍊[7]	36	45.40 N	14.00 E
Skodborg	41	55.25 N	9.09 E
Skodsborg	41	55.49 N	12.34 E
Skoenmakerskop	158	34.02 S	25.33 E
Škofije	64	45.34 N	13.48 E
Škofja Loka	36	46.10 N	14.18 E
Skoganvarre	24	69.47 N	25.06 E
Skoghall	40	59.19 N	13.26 E
Skogstorp	40	59.20 N	16.28 E
Skokholm Island I	42	51.42 N	5.16 W
Skoki	30	52.41 N	17.10 E
Skokie	216	42.02 N	87.44 W
Skokie ≃	216	42.05 N	87.46 W
Skokie Lagoons ⊂	278	42.07 N	87.47 W
Skokloster ⊥	40	59.42 N	17.37 E
Skokomish, North Fork ≃	224	47.18 N	123.14 W
Skokomish, South Fork ≃	224	47.18 N	123.14 W
Skokomish Indian Reservation ◆[4]	224	47.21 N	123.12 W
Sköldinge	40	59.02 N	16.26 E
Skole	78	49.02 N	23.29 E
Sköllersta	40	59.09 N	15.20 E
Skolsta	40	59.40 N	17.14 E
Skolwin	54	53.32 N	14.35 E
Skomer Island I	42	51.44 N	5.17 W
Skomoroški, Ross.	82	54.05 N	36.57 E
Skomoroški, Ukr.	78	49.20 N	29.26 E
Skón	110	12.04 N	105.04 E
Skookumchuck ≃	224	46.41 N	123.00 W
Skookumchuck Reservoir ⊜[1]	224	47.47 N	122.42 W
Skoonspruit ≃	158	27.00 S	26.38 E
Skootamatta ≃	212	44.32 N	77.20 W
Skootamatta Lake ⊜	212	44.50 N	77.15 W
Skópelos, Ellás	38	39.02 N	26.26 E
Skópelos, Ellás	38	39.07 N	23.43 E
Skópelos I	38	39.10 N	23.40 E
Skopin	76	53.51 N	39.33 E
Skopje	38	41.59 N	21.26 E
Skórcz	30	53.48 N	18.32 E
Skorodnoje, Bela.	78	51.38 N	28.49 E
Skorodnoje, Ross.	78	51.05 N	37.14 E
Skørping	26	56.50 N	9.53 E
Skotfoss	26	59.12 N	9.30 E
Skotovataja	83	48.13 N	37.54 E
Škotovo	89	43.20 N	132.21 E
Skotterud	26	59.59 N	12.07 E
Skovby	41	54.53 N	10.00 E
Skövde	26	58.24 N	13.50 E
Skovlund	41	55.44 N	8.43 E
Skovorodino	89	53.59 N	123.55 E
Skowhegan	188	44.45 N	69.43 W
Skownan	184	51.57 N	99.36 W
Skradin	36	43.49 N	15.56 E
Skreen	48	54.15 N	8.45 W
Skreia	26	60.39 N	10.56 E
Skriplivka	76	57.32 N	30.38 E
Skrīveri	76	56.39 N	25.08 E
Skromberga	41	56.00 N	12.58 E
Skrudaliena	76	55.49 N	26.43 E
Skrunda	76	56.41 N	22.01 E
Skruv	26	56.41 N	15.22 E
Skrydstrup	41	55.14 N	9.15 E
Skudeneshavn	26	59.09 N	5.17 E
Skukuza	156	25.01 S	31.38 E
Skuleberget ʌ[2]	26	63.05 N	18.21 E
Skulforp	26	58.21 N	13.49 E
Skull	48	51.32 N	9.33 W
Skull Creek ≃	222	29.32 N	96.24 W
Skull Valley	200	34.30 N	112.41 W
Skull Valley Indian Reservation ◆[4]	200	40.24 N	112.45 W
Skultuna	40	59.43 N	16.25 E
Skuna ≃	194	33.54 N	89.41 W
Skunk ≃	190	40.42 N	91.07 W
Škunovka	86	50.45 N	55.27 E
Skuodas	76	56.16 N	21.32 E
Škuratovskij	82	54.07 N	37.36 E
Škurinskaja	78	46.35 N	39.22 E
Skurišenskaja	80	49.52 N	42.57 E
Skurup	41	55.28 N	13.30 E
Skutskär	40	60.38 N	17.25 E
Skvira	78	49.44 N	29.40 E
Skwentna	180	61.58 N	151.11 W
Skwentna ≃	180	62.00 N	151.08 W
Skwierzyna	30	52.36 N	15.30 E
Skye, Island of I	46	57.18 N	6.15 W
Sky Harbor Airport ⊠	278	42.09 N	87.51 W
Skykomish	224	47.42 N	121.21 W
Skykomish ≃	224	47.50 N	122.03 W
Skykomish, North Fork ≃	224	47.47 N	121.33 W
Skykomish, South Fork ≃	224	47.47 N	121.33 W
Sky Lake	220	28.28 N	81.24 W
Sky Lake ⊜	212	44.48 N	81.15 W
Skyland, Nv., U.S.	226	39.01 N	119.56 W
Skyland, N.C., U.S.	192	35.29 N	82.31 W
Skylight	218	38.25 N	85.31 W
Skyline	284c	38.50 N	76.54 W
Skyline Lakes ⊜	276	41.04 N	74.16 W
Skyllberg	40	58.57 N	14.59 E
Skyring, Península ›[1]	254	45.58 S	74.53 W
Skyring, Seno ʉ	254	52.35 S	72.00 W
Sky Sailing Airport ⊠	282	37.30 N	121.58 W
Skytop	210	41.14 N	75.15 W
Skyttorp	40	60.05 N	17.44 E
Skyway	224	47.29 N	122.14 W
Slackhall	262	53.20 N	1.53 W
Slackwood	208	40.15 N	74.44 W
Slade Green ◆[8]	260	51.28 N	0.12 E
Sladkij	80	46.10 N	42.17 E
Sladkovo	86	55.32 N	70.20 E
Slagelse	41	55.24 N	11.22 E
Slagnäs	24	65.34 N	18.05 E
Slagovišči	76	53.57 N	35.54 E
Slaithwaite	262	53.37 N	1.53 W
Slamannan	46	55.56 N	3.50 W
Slamet, Gunung ʌ	115a	7.14 S	109.12 E
Slaná (Sajó) ≃	30	47.56 N	21.08 E
Slancy	76	59.06 N	28.04 E
Slaney ≃	48	52.21 N	6.30 W
Slangerup	41	55.51 N	12.11 E
Slănic	38	45.15 N	25.57 E
Slănic Moldova	38	46.13 N	26.26 E
Slano	36	42.47 N	17.54 E
Slanské vrchy ⩘	30	48.50 N	21.30 E
Slaný	54	50.11 N	14.04 E
Šlapanice	30	49.10 N	16.44 E
Slaščevskaja	80	49.52 N	42.21 E
Śląsk → Silesia □[9]	30	51.00 N	16.45 E
Slastucha	80	51.57 N	44.32 E
Slate Bottom Creek ≃	284a	42.53 N	78.45 W
Slate Creek ≃, Ks., U.S.	198	37.08 N	97.09 W
Slate Creek ≃, Pa., U.S.	279b	40.28 N	79.32 W
Slatedale	208	40.45 N	75.40 W
Slate Hill	210	41.23 N	74.29 W
Slater, Ia., U.S.	190	41.52 N	93.40 W
Slater, Mo., U.S.	194	39.13 N	93.04 W
Slater Creek ≃	200	40.59 N	107.23 W
Slatersville	207	42.00 N	71.34 W
Slaterville Springs	210	42.24 N	76.21 W
Slatina	38	44.26 N	24.22 E
Slatington	208	40.44 N	75.36 W
Slatino	78	50.12 N	36.11 E
Slaton	196	33.26 N	101.38 W
Slattocks	262	53.35 N	2.10 W
Slaughter	194	30.43 N	91.08 W
Slaung	115a	8.02 S	111.24 E
Slautnoje	74	63.00 N	167.59 E
Slava	89	52.08 N	129.24 E
Slav'anka, Ross.	89	42.53 N	131.21 E
Slav'anka, Ukr.	78	48.24 N	36.43 E
Slav'anka, Uzb.	85	40.40 N	68.32 E
Slav'anka ≃	265a	59.50 N	30.32 E
Slav'anogorsk	83	49.02 N	37.31 E
Slav'anoserbsk	83	48.42 N	38.59 E
Slav'ansk	83	48.52 N	37.37 E
Slav'ansk-na-Kubani	78	45.15 N	38.08 E
Slave ≃	176	61.18 N	113.39 W
Slave Coast ⍊[2]	150	6.25 N	3.00 E
Slave Lake	182	55.17 N	114.46 W
Slavgorod, Bela.	76	53.27 N	31.00 E
Slavgorod, Ross.	86	53.00 N	78.40 E
Slavgorod, Ukr.	78	48.06 N	35.31 E
Slavgorod, Ukr.	78	50.36 N	35.21 E
Slavitino	82	56.41 N	39.13 E
Slavkino	80	52.58 N	47.11 E
Slavkoviči	76	57.39 N	29.05 E
Slavkovský les ⩘	54	50.07 N	12.45 E
Slavkov u Brna	61	49.09 N	16.52 E
Slavnoje	76	54.18 N	29.27 E
Slavonia → Slavonija □[9]	36	45.00 N	18.00 E
Slavonice	61	49.00 N	15.21 E
Slavonija □[9]	36	45.00 N	18.00 E
Slavonska Požega	36	45.20 N	17.41 E
Slavonski Brod	38	45.10 N	18.01 E
Slavsk	76	55.03 N	21.41 E
Slavskoje	78	48.49 N	23.24 E
Slavuta	78	50.18 N	26.52 E
Sława	30	51.53 N	16.04 E
Slawi	115a	6.59 S	109.08 E
Sławno	30	54.22 N	16.40 E
Slayton	198	43.59 N	95.45 W
Slea ≃	44	53.03 N	0.12 W
Sleaford	42	53.00 N	0.24 W
Slea Head ›	48	52.06 N	10.27 W
Sleat, Point of ›	46	57.01 N	6.02 W
Sleat, Sound of ʉ	46	57.06 N	5.49 W
Sledge	194	34.25 N	90.13 W
Sledge Island I	180	64.29 N	166.13 W
Sled Lake ⊜	184	54.27 N	107.25 W
Sledmere	44	54.04 N	0.35 W
Slednevo	82	56.25 N	38.36 E
Sled'uki	76	53.35 N	30.22 E
Sleen	52	52.46 N	6.48 E
Sleeping Bear Dunes National Lakeshore ♦	190	44.50 N	86.08 W
Sleeping Giant State Park ♦	207	41.25 N	72.53 W
Sleepy Eye	198	44.17 N	94.43 W
Sleepy Hollow, Ca., U.S.	226	38.00 N	122.34 W
Sleepy Hollow, Ca., U.S.	280	33.57 N	117.47 W
Sleepy Hollow, Il., U.S.	216	42.06 N	88.24 W
Sleetmute	180	61.42 N	157.11 W
Sleidinge	50	51.08 N	3.41 E
Sleights	44	54.27 N	0.40 W
Sleman	115a	7.42 S	110.20 E
Slepino	76	59.11 N	29.02 E
Ślesin	30	52.23 N	18.19 E
Slessor Glacier ⊓	9	79.50 S	28.30 W
Slickville	214	40.27 N	79.31 W
Slidell	194	30.16 N	89.46 W
Slide Mountain ʌ	210	42.00 N	74.23 W
Sliderock Mountain ʌ	202	46.35 N	113.33 W
Sliedrecht	52	51.49 N	4.45 E
Slieve Aughty Mountains ⩘	48	53.05 N	8.35 W
Slieve Bloom Mountains ⩘	48	53.05 N	7.35 W
Slievekimalta ʌ	48	52.45 N	8.16 W
Slievenamon ʌ	48	52.25 N	7.34 W
Sligeach → Sligo	48	54.17 N	8.28 W
Sligo (Sligeach), Ire.	48	54.17 N	8.28 W
Sligo, Pa., U.S.	214	41.06 N	79.29 W
Sligo □[6]	48	54.10 N	8.40 W
Sligo Bay ⊂	48	54.20 N	8.40 W
Sligo Creek ≃	284c	38.57 N	76.58 W
Slikkerveer	52	51.53 N	4.37 E
Slingebeek ≃	52	51.56 N	6.17 E
Slinger	190	43.20 N	88.17 W
Šlino, ozero ⊜	76	57.40 N	33.23 E
Slioch ʌ	46	57.41 N	5.22 W
Slippery Rock	214	41.03 N	80.03 W
Slippery Rock Creek ≃	214	40.51 N	80.15 W
Šlissel'burg	265a	59.57 N	31.02 E
Slite	26	57.43 N	18.48 E
Slīteres Rezervāts ♦	76	57.38 N	22.25 E
Sliven	38	42.40 N	26.19 E
Slivnica	38	42.51 N	23.02 E
Sloan, Ia., U.S.	198	42.13 N	96.13 W
Sloan, Nv., U.S.	204	35.56 N	115.12 W
Sloan, N.Y., U.S.	210	42.53 N	78.47 W
Sloan Peak ʌ	224	48.03 N	121.20 W
Sloansville	210	42.46 N	74.20 W
Sloatsburg	210	41.09 N	74.11 W
Sloboda, Bela.	76	53.58 N	28.08 E
Sloboda, Ross.	76	55.30 N	31.51 E
Sloboda, Ross.	78	51.09 N	40.17 E
Sloboda, Ukr.	78	51.11 N	33.37 E
Slobodka, Bela.	76	55.41 N	27.11 E
Slobodka, Ross.	82	54.22 N	37.33 E
Slobodka, Ukr.	78	47.53 N	29.21 E
Slobodskoj	86	58.42 N	50.12 E
Slobodzeja	78	46.44 N	29.43 E
Slobodzeja-Mare	78	45.34 N	28.12 E
Slobozia, Rom.	38	43.51 N	25.54 E
Slobozia, Rom.	38	44.34 N	27.23 E
Slocan	182	49.46 N	117.28 W
Slocan Lake ⊜	182	49.56 N	117.22 W
Slochteren	52	53.12 N	6.47 E
Slocomb	194	31.06 N	85.35 W
Slocum	207	41.32 N	71.31 W
Slocum Mountain ʌ	228	35.18 N	117.13 W
Słomniki	30	50.15 N	20.06 E
Slonim	76	53.06 N	25.19 E
Slonovka	78	50.39 N	37.45 E
Słońsk	54	52.35 N	14.50 E
Sloop Channel ʉ	276	40.36 N	73.31 W
Sloping Hills	276	40.42 N	74.34 W
Slosh Indian Reserve ◆[4]	182	50.44 N	122.13 W
Sloten	52	52.54 N	5.38 E
Sloten ◆[8]	52	52.21 N	4.48 E
Slotermeer ⊜	52	52.55 N	5.40 E
Slough	42	51.31 N	0.36 W
Slough □[8]	260	51.32 N	0.35 W
Slough Brook ≃	276	40.45 N	74.21 W
Sloughhouse	226	38.30 N	121.12 W
Slovakia □[1], Europe	22	48.30 N	20.00 E
Slovakia (Slovenská Republika) □[1], Europe	30	48.30 N	20.00 E
Slovakia → Slovensko □[9]	30	48.50 N	20.00 E
Slovan	214	40.21 N	80.23 W
Slovečna ≃	78	51.41 N	29.41 E
Slovečno	78	51.23 N	28.21 E
Slovenia □[1], Europe	22	46.15 N	15.10 E
Slovenia (Slovenija) □[1], Europe	36	46.15 N	15.10 E
Slovenija → Slovenia □[1]	36	46.15 N	15.10 E
Slovenj Gradec	61	46.31 N	15.05 E
Slovenska Bistrica	61	46.23 N	15.34 E
Slovenske Gorice ⩘[2]	61	46.35 N	15.55 E
Slovenské rudohorie ⩘	30	48.45 N	20.00 E
Slovensko □[9]	30	48.50 N	20.00 E
Slovinka	80	58.02 N	43.07 E
Slowakei → Slovensko □[9]	30	48.50 N	20.00 E
Słowiński Park Narodowy ♦	30	54.40 N	17.25 E
Słubice	54	52.20 N	14.32 E
Sluč' ≃, Bela.	76	52.08 N	27.31 E
Sluč' ≃, Ukr.	78	51.37 N	26.38 E
Sluck	76	53.01 N	27.33 E
Sl'ud'anka	88	51.38 N	103.42 E
Sluderno (Schluderns)	64	46.40 N	10.35 E
Sludy	76	58.52 N	36.52 E
Sluis	52	51.18 N	3.24 E
Sluiskil	52	51.16 N	3.50 E
Šluknov	54	51.00 N	14.27 E
Slunj	36	45.07 N	15.35 E
Słupca	30	52.19 N	17.52 E
Słupia ≃	30	54.35 N	16.50 E
Słupsk (Stolp)	30	54.28 N	17.01 E
Słupsk □[4]	30	54.10 N	17.15 E
Slurry	156	25.49 S	25.52 E
Šl'uz-Mokr'aki	86	59.17 N	88.50 E
Sly, Oued ≃	34	36.04 N	1.08 E
Smachtino	82	54.51 N	36.25 E
Smackover	194	33.21 N	92.43 W
Smackover Creek ≃	194	33.22 N	92.24 W
Småland □[9]	26	57.20 N	15.00 E
Smålandsfarvandet ʉ	41	55.05 N	11.20 E
Smålandsstenar	26	57.10 N	13.24 E
Smalininkai	76	55.05 N	22.35 E
Smallbridge	262	53.38 N	2.08 W
Smalleytown	276	40.39 N	74.28 W
Smallwood	210	41.40 N	74.49 W
Smallwood Reservoir ⊜[1]	176	54.05 N	64.30 W
Smallwood State Park ♦	208	38.33 N	77.12 W
Smara	148	26.44 N	11.41 W
Smartt Syndicate Dam ⊜[1]	158	30.40 S	23.18 E
Smartville	226	39.12 N	121.18 W
Smeaton	184	53.30 N	104.49 W
Smeaton Bay ⊂	182	55.20 N	130.50 W
Smečno	54	50.10 N	14.03 E
Smedby	40	58.33 N	16.16 E
Smědeč	61	48.56 N	14.09 E
Smederevo	38	44.40 N	20.56 E
Smederevska Palanka	38	44.22 N	20.58 E
Smedjebacken	40	60.08 N	15.25 E
Smela	78	49.14 N	31.53 E
Smeloje	78	50.55 N	33.36 E
Šmel'ovka	80	54.47 N	49.11 E
Smelt Brook ≃, Ma., U.S.	283	42.13 N	70.58 W
Smelt Brook ≃, Ma., U.S.	283	42.00 N	70.43 W
Smelt Pond ⊜	283	41.58 N	70.43 W
Smeralda, Costa ⍊[2]	71	41.04 N	9.30 E
Smerwick Harbour ⊂	48	52.12 N	10.24 W
Smethport	214	41.48 N	78.26 W
Smethwick	42	52.30 N	1.58 W
Smicksburg	214	40.52 N	79.10 W
Smidovič	89	48.36 N	133.49 E

Symbols in the index entries represent the broad categories identified in the key at the right. Symbols with superior numbers (⩘[1]) identify subcategories (see complete key on page *I · 1).*

Symbole im Register stellen die rechts im Schlüssel erklärten Kategorien dar. Symbole mit hochgestellten Ziffern (⩘[1]) bezeichnen Unterabteilungen einer Kategorie (vgl. vollständiger Schlüssel auf Seite *I · 1).*

Los símbolos incluídos en el texto del índice representan las grandes categorias identificadas con la clave a la derecha. Los símbolos con numeros en su parte superior (⩘[1]) identifican las subcategorías (véase la clave completa en la página *I · 1).*

Les symboles de l'index représentent les catégories indiquées dans la légende à droite. Les symboles suivis d'un indice (⩘[1]) représentent des sous-catégories (voir légende complète à la page *I · 1).*

Os símbolos incluídos no texto do índice representam as grandes categorias identificadas com a chave à direita. Os símbolos com números em sua parte superior (⩘[1]) identificam as subcategorias (veja-se a chave completa à página *I · 1).*

ʌ Mountain	Berg	Montaña	Montagne	Montanha
⩘ Mountains	Gebirge	Montañas	Montagnes	Montanhas
)(Pass	Paß	Paso	Col	Passo
V Valley, Canyon	Tal, Cañon	Valle, Cañón	Vallée, Canyon	Vale, Canhão
≚ Plain	Ebene	Llano	Plaine	Planície
› Cape	Kap	Cabo	Cap	Cabo
I Island	Insel	Isla	Île	Ilha
II Islands	Inseln	Islas	Îles	Ilhas
⍊ Other Topographic Features	Andere Topographische Objekte	Otros Elementos Topográficos	Autres données topographiques	Outros acidentes topográficos

ESPAÑOL

Nombre	Página	Lat.°′	Long.°′ W = Oeste
Šmidta, mys ›	180	68.56 N	179.30 W
Šmidta, ostrov I	74	81.08 N	90.48 E
Šmidta, poluostrov ›[1]	89	54.10 N	142.40 E
Šmidta → Mys Šmidta	180	68.56 N	179.26 W
Śmigiel	30	52.01 N	16.32 E
Smilde	52	52.56 N	5.27 E
Smile	218	38.15 N	83.29 W
Smiley, Sk., Can.	184	51.37 N	109.29 W
Smiley, Tx., U.S.	222	29.16 N	97.38 W
Smiloviči	76	53.45 N	28.01 E
Smiltene	76	57.26 N	25.56 E
Smirnovskij	86	54.31 N	69.25 E
Smirnych	89	49.43 N	142.38 E
Smite ≃	44	53.04 N	0.48 W
Smith	182	55.10 N	114.02 W
Smith □[6]	222	32.20 N	95.15 W
Smith ≃, U.S.	192	36.29 N	79.45 W
Smith ≃, Ca., U.S.	204	41.56 N	124.12 W
Smith ≃, Mt., U.S.	202	47.25 N	111.29 W
Smith ≃, Or., U.S.	202	43.43 N	124.05 W
Smith, Cape ›	190	45.48 N	81.35 W
Smith Arm ⊂	180	66.15 N	124.00 W
Smith Bay ⊂	180	70.51 N	154.25 W
Smithboro, Il., U.S.	219	38.54 N	89.20 W
Smithboro, N.Y., U.S.	210	42.02 N	76.24 W
Smith Canyon V	198	37.46 N	103.26 W
Smith Center	198	39.46 N	98.47 W
Smith Creek ≃, S.D., U.S.	198	43.58 N	99.20 W
Smith Creek ≃, Wa., U.S.	224	46.45 N	123.53 W
Smithdale	279b	40.14 N	79.48 W
Smithers, B.C., Can.	182	54.47 N	127.10 W
Smithers, W.V., U.S.	188	38.10 N	81.18 W
Smithers Lake ◎[1]	222	29.29 N	95.38 W
Smithfield, Austl.	168b	34.41 S	138.41 E
Smithfield, Austl.	274a	33.51 S	150.57 E
Smithfield, On., Can.	212	44.04 N	77.41 W
Smithfield, S. Afr.	158	30.09 S	26.30 E
Smithfield, Eng., U.K.	44	54.59 N	2.52 W
Smithfield, N.C., U.S.	192	35.30 N	78.20 W
Smithfield, Oh., U.S.	214	40.16 N	80.46 W
Smithfield, Pa., U.S.	214	39.48 N	79.48 W
Smithfield, Ut,. U.S.	200	41.50 N	111.49 W
Smithfield, Va., U.S.	208	36.58 N	76.37 W
Smithflat	226	38.44 N	120.45 W
Smith Haven Mall ◆[9]	276	40.52 N	73.08 W
Smithills Hall ⊥	262	53.36 N	2.27 W
Smith Island I, Ant.	9	62.59 S	62.32 W
Smith Island I, N.C., U.S.	192	33.52 N	77.59 W
Smith Island I, Va., U.S.	208	37.10 N	75.51 W
Smith Island I, Wa., U.S.	224	48.19 N	122.50 W
Smith Island II	208	38.01 N	76.02 W
Smithland	194	37.08 N	88.24 W
Smithmill	214	40.46 N	78.25 W
Smith Mountain ∧	280	34.17 N	117.52 W
Smith Mountain Lake ◎[1]	192	37.10 N	79.40 W
Smith Peak ∧	202	48.50 N	116.39 W
Smith Peninsula ›[1]	9	74.25 S	61.15 W
Smith Point	222	29.27 N	94.45 W
Smith Point ›, N.S., Can.	186	45.51 N	63.25 W
Smith Point ›, Tx., U.S.	222	29.32 N	94.46 W
Smith Point ›, Va., U.S.	208	37.53 N	76.14 W
Smithport	214	40.50 N	78.52 W
Smith River	204	41.55 N	124.08 W
Smiths	194	32.32 N	85.05 W
Smithsburg	208	39.39 N	77.34 W
Smiths Creek	214	42.55 N	82.36 W
Smiths Falls	212	44.54 N	76.01 W
Smiths Fork ≃	202	41.23 N	110.12 W
Smiths Grove	194	37.03 N	86.12 W
Smiths Mills	276	41.01 N	74.22 W
Smith Sound ɰ	182	51.18 N	127.48 W
Smithton, Austl.	166	40.51 S	145.07 E
Smithton, Il., U.S.	219	38.24 N	89.59 W
Smithton, Mo., U.S.	194	38.40 N	93.05 W
Smithton, Pa., U.S.	279b	40.09 N	79.44 W
Smithtown	210	40.52 N	73.13 W
Smithtown Bay ⊂	276	40.57 N	73.12 W
Smith Valley	218	39.36 N	86.12 W
Smithville, On., Can.	212	43.06 N	79.33 W
Smithville, Ga., U.S.	192	31.54 N	84.15 W
Smithville, In., U.S.	218	39.04 N	86.30 W
Smithville, Ms., U.S.	194	34.04 N	88.23 W
Smithville, Mo., U.S.	194	39.23 N	94.34 W
Smithville, N.J., U.S.	208	39.59 N	74.44 W
Smithville, N.J., U.S.	285	39.29 N	74.27 W
Smithville, Oh., U.S.	214	40.51 N	81.51 W
Smithville, Tn., U.S.	194	35.57 N	85.48 W
Smithville, Tx., U.S.	222	30.00 N	97.09 W
Smithville Flats	210	42.24 N	75.49 W
Smithville Lake ◎[1]	194	39.25 N	94.30 W
Smögen	26	58.21 N	11.13 E
Smoke Creek ≃, Mt., U.S.	198	48.18 N	104.41 W
Smoke Creek ≃, N.Y., U.S.	284a	42.49 N	78.52 W
Smoke Creek, South Branch ≃	284a	42.49 N	78.49 W
Smoke Creek Desert ◆[2]	204	40.30 N	119.40 W
Smoke Lake ◎	212	45.32 N	78.41 W
Smokeless	214	40.24 N	76.02 W
Smokerun	214	40.48 N	78.26 W
Smoketown	208	40.02 N	76.12 W
Smokey, Cape ›	186	46.38 N	60.21 W
Smokey Dome ∧	202	43.29 N	114.56 W
Smoky ≃	182	56.10 N	117.21 W
Smoky Bay	162	32.22 S	133.56 E
Smoky Cape ›	166	30.56 S	153.05 E
Smoky Hill ≃	198	39.03 N	96.48 W
Smoky Hill, North Fork ≃	198	38.55 N	101.17 W
Smoky Lake	182	54.07 N	112.28 W
Smøla I	24	63.24 N	8.00 E
Smol'anica	76	52.42 N	24.38 E
Smol'aninovo	89	43.19 N	132.28 E
Smol'any	76	54.36 N	30.04 E
Smolensk	76	54.47 N	32.03 E
Smolenskaja vozvyšennost' ⋏[1]	76	54.30 N	33.00 E
Smolensk Oblast' □[4]	76	55.00 N	33.00 E
Smolenskoje	86	52.20 N	85.05 E
Smoleviči	76	54.02 N	28.05 E
Smólikas ∧	38	40.06 N	20.52 E
Smoljan	38	41.35 N	24.41 E
Smolny ♥	265a	59.57 N	30.24 E
Smolovka	76	55.33 N	30.13 E
Smoot	200	42.37 N	110.54 W
Smoothstone ≃	184	55.20 N	106.39 W
Smoothstone Lake ◎	184	54.40 N	106.50 W
Smorgon'	76	54.29 N	26.24 E
Smorodovka	76	57.08 N	29.52 E
Smotrič	78	48.56 N	26.34 E
Smotrič ≃	78	48.34 N	26.38 E
Smuškovoje	80	47.20 N	45.55 E
Smyčka	82	56.04 N	35.56 E
Smygehamn	41	55.21 N	13.22 E
Smygehuk ›	41	55.21 N	13.23 E
Smyley Island I	9	72.55 S	78.00 W
Smyrna, De., U.S.	208	39.17 N	75.36 W
Smyrna, Ga., U.S.	192	33.53 N	84.30 W
Smyrna, N.Y., U.S.	210	42.41 N	75.34 W
Smyrna, Tn., U.S.	194	35.58 N	86.31 W
Smyrna ≃	208	39.22 N	75.31 W
Smyrna → İzmir	130	38.25 N	27.09 E
Smyšl'ajevka	80	53.15 N	50.22 E
Smyth, Canal ɰ	254	52.15 S	73.40 W
Smythe, Mount ∧	176	57.54 N	124.53 W

FRANÇAIS

Nom	Page	Lat.°′	Long.°′ W = Ouest
Smythe Park ♠	275b	43.41 N	79.30 W
Smythesdale	169	37.38 S	143.41 E
Sn'adin	78	52.04 N	28.19 E
Snæfell ∧, Ísland	24a	64.48 N	15.32 W
Snaefell ∧, I. of Man	44	54.16 N	4.27 W
Snæfellness ›[1]	24a	64.50 N	23.00 W
Snag	180	62.24 N	140.22 W
Snaght, Slieve ∧	48	55.12 N	7.20 W
Snagost'	78	51.21 N	34.54 E
Snahapish ≃	224	47.38 N	124.11 W
Snaith	44	53.41 N	1.02 W
Sn'ajevo	80	52.34 N	46.11 E
Snake ≃, Yk., Can.	180	65.58 N	134.10 W
Snake ≃, U.S.	202	46.12 N	119.02 W
Snake ≃, Ca., U.S.	226	39.07 N	121.43 W
Snake ≃, Mn., U.S.	190	45.49 N	92.46 W
Snake ≃, Mn., U.S.	198	48.26 N	97.07 W
Snake ≃, Ne., U.S.	198	42.47 N	100.48 W
Snake Bight ⊂[3]	220	25.10 N	80.50 W
Snake Brook ≃	283	42.18 N	71.22 W
Snake Creek ≃, Mt., U.S.	202	48.32 N	108.53 W
Snake Creek ≃, Ne., U.S.	198	42.01 N	102.45 W
Snake Creek ≃, S.D., U.S.	198	44.58 N	98.29 W
Snake Creek, South Fork ≃	198	45.02 N	98.36 W
Snake Creek Canal ≍	220	25.57 N	80.11 W
Snake Indian ≃	182	53.11 N	118.00 W
Snake Range ⋏	204	39.00 N	114.15 W
Snake Rapids ㄴ	212	45.14 N	77.20 W
Snake River Plain ≚	202	43.00 N	113.00 W
Snake Valley	169	37.37 S	143.35 E
Snake Valley V	204	39.20 N	113.55 W
Snape	42	52.11 N	1.30 E
Snaptun	41	55.49 N	10.04 E
Snares Islands II	9	48.00 S	166.30 E
Snasahögarna ∧	26	63.13 N	12.21 E
Sn'atyn	78	48.28 N	25.34 E
Snay Pôl	110	11.40 N	105.13 E
Sneads	192	30.42 N	84.55 W
Snedsted	26	56.54 N	8.32 E
Sneedville	192	36.31 N	83.13 W
Sneek	52	53.02 N	5.40 E
Sneekermeer ◎	52	53.02 N	5.45 E
Snee-osh-Beach	224	48.24 N	122.33 W
Sneeuberg ∧	158	32.25 S	19.12 E
Sneeuberg ⋏	158	31.46 S	24.20 E
Snekkersten	41	56.00 N	12.36 E
Snelgrove	275b	43.44 N	79.49 W
Snelling	204	37.31 N	120.26 W
Snettisham	42	52.53 N	0.30 E
Snežnaja ≃	88	51.28 N	104.38 E
Snežnik ∧	36	45.35 N	14.27 E
Snežnoje	83	48.01 N	38.46 E
Śniardwy, Jezioro ◎	30	53.46 N	21.44 E
Snicarte	219	40.07 N	90.14 W
Snicarte Island I	219	40.08 N	90.12 W
Snigir'ovka	78	47.06 N	32.47 E
Snina	30	48.59 N	22.07 E
Snipe Keys II	220	24.40 N	81.38 W
Snipe Lake ◎	182	55.07 N	116.46 W
Snizort, Loch ⊂	46	57.34 N	6.28 W
Snøde	41	55.05 N	10.55 E
Snodland	42	51.20 N	0.27 E
Snoghøj	41	55.31 N	9.43 E
Snøhetta ∧	26	62.20 N	9.17 E
Snohomish	224	47.54 N	122.05 W
Snohomish □[6]	224	48.02 N	121.41 W
Snohomish ≃	224	48.01 N	122.13 W
Snønipa ∧	26	61.42 N	6.41 E
Snook	222	30.29 N	96.28 W
Snoqualmie	224	47.31 N	121.49 W
Snoqualmie ≃	224	47.50 N	122.03 W
Snoqualmie, Middle Fork ≃	224	47.31 N	121.46 W
Snoqualmie, North Fork ≃	224	47.31 N	121.46 W
Snoqualmie, South Fork ≃	224	47.31 N	121.46 W
Snoqualmie Falls	224	47.32 N	121.49 W
Snoqualmie Mountain ∧	224	47.27 N	121.25 W
Snoqualmie Pass)(	224	47.25 N	121.25 W
Snøtinden ∧	24	66.38 N	14.00 E
Snov	76	53.13 N	26.24 E
Snov ≃	78	51.45 N	31.45 E
Snover	190	43.27 N	82.58 W
Snowbird Lake ◎	176	60.41 N	103.00 W
Snow Canyon State Park ♠	200	37.11 N	113.42 W
Snow Creek ≃	224	47.59 N	122.53 W
Snowden, Sk., Can.	184	53.30 N	104.41 W
Snowden, Pa., U.S.	279b	40.16 N	79.58 W
Snowden Oaks	284c	39.04 N	76.52 W
Snowdenville	285	40.11 N	75.36 W
Snowdon ∧	44	53.04 N	4.05 W
Snowdonia National Park ♠	28	53.00 N	3.57 W
Snowdoun	194	32.14 N	86.17 W
Snowdrift	176	62.23 N	110.47 W
Snowflake	200	34.30 N	110.04 W
Snow Hill, Md., U.S.	208	38.10 N	75.23 W
Snow Hill, N.C., U.S.	192	35.27 N	77.40 W
Snowking Mountain ∧	224	48.24 N	121.17 W
Snow Lake	184	54.53 N	100.02 W
Snow Lakes ◎	224	47.29 N	120.45 W
Snowmass Mountain ∧	200	39.07 N	107.04 W
Snow Mountain ∧	226	39.23 N	122.45 W
Snow Peak ∧	202	48.35 N	118.29 W
Snows Brook ≃	283	42.47 N	71.06 W
Snow Shoe	214	41.02 N	77.57 W
Snowshoe Butte ∧	224	47.13 N	121.22 W
Snowshoe Peak ∧	202	48.13 N	115.41 W
Snowtown	166	33.47 S	138.13 E
Snow Water Lake ◎	204	41.07 N	115.00 W
Snowy ≃	166	37.48 S	148.32 E
Snowy Mountain ∧	188	43.42 N	74.23 W
Snowy Mountains ⋏	166	36.30 S	148.20 E
Snowyside Peak ∧	202	43.57 N	114.58 W
Snubba Range ⋏	171b	35.40 S	148.10 E
Snuŏl	110	12.04 N	106.26 E
Snyder, Ok., U.S.	196	34.39 N	98.57 W
Snyder, Tx., U.S.	196	32.43 N	100.55 W
Snyder □[6]	210	40.47 N	77.03 W
Snydertown	210	40.53 N	76.40 W
Soacha	246	4.35 N	74.13 W
Soahany	157b	18.42 S	44.13 E
Soaker, Mount ∧	172	45.23 S	167.15 E
Soalala	157b	16.06 S	45.20 E
Soalara	157b	23.36 S	43.44 E
Soaloka	157b	18.32 S	45.15 E
Sŏam	98	38.01 N	126.43 E
Soamanonga	157b	23.52 S	44.47 E
Soān ≃	123	33.01 N	71.44 E
Soan-do I	98	34.09 N	126.39 E
Soanierana Ivongo	157b	16.55 S	49.35 E
Soanindrariny	157b	19.54 S	47.14 E
Soap Creek ≃	190	40.55 N	92.14 W
Soap Lake	202	47.23 N	119.29 W
Soasiu → Tidore	108	0.40 N	127.26 E
Soatá	246	6.20 N	72.41 W
Soavina	157b	20.23 S	46.56 E
Soavinandriana	157b	19.09 S	46.45 E
Soay I	46	57.08 N	6.14 W
Soazza	58	46.22 N	9.13 E
Sob ≃	78	48.42 N	29.17 E
Sobaek-sanmaek ⋏	98	36.00 N	128.00 E
Sobat ≃	140	9.22 N	31.33 E
Sobernheim	56	49.47 N	7.38 E
Soběšice	60	49.12 N	13.41 E
Soběslav	30	49.15 N	14.44 E
Sobger ≃	164	3.44 S	140.20 E
Sobič	78	51.52 N	33.14 E
Sobinka	80	55.59 N	40.01 E

PORTUGUÊS

Nome	Página	Lat.°′	Long.°′ W = Oeste
Soboba Indian Reservation ◆[4]	228	33.47 N	116.54 W
Soboko	140	6.49 N	24.50 E
Sobolekovo	80	55.39 N	51.53 E
Sobolev	80	51.56 N	51.43 E
Sobolevka	78	48.36 N	29.30 E
Sobolevo	82	55.31 N	38.43 E
Sobolino	88	53.23 N	119.42 E
Sobótka	30	50.55 N	16.45 E
Sobradinho	252	29.24 S	53.03 W
Sobradinho, Reprêsa de ◎[1]	250	9.40 S	42.00 W
Sobrado	34	41.02 N	8.16 W
Sobral	250	3.42 S	40.21 W
Sobrance	30	48.45 N	22.11 E
Sobrante Ridge ∧	282	37.58 N	122.15 W
Sobrarbe ◆[1]	34	42.22 N	0.10 E
Sobue	94	35.15 N	136.43 E
Søby	41	54.56 N	10.16 E
Soča	64	46.20 N	13.39 E
Soča (Isonzo) ≃	64	45.47 N	13.32 E
Socaire	252	23.36 S	67.51 W
Socchieve	64	46.25 N	12.52 E
Soc Giang	110	22.54 N	106.01 E
Socgorodok	78	50.11 N	38.09 E
Soch	85	39.57 N	71.08 E
Soch ≃	85	40.20 N	71.02 E
Sochaczew	30	52.14 N	20.14 E
Sochaux	58	47.31 N	6.50 E
Soch'e → Shache	120	38.25 N	77.16 E
Sochi → Soči	84	43.35 N	39.45 E
Sŏch'ŏn	98	36.05 N	126.41 E
Sochondo	88	51.49 N	112.32 E
Sochondo, gora ∧	88	49.44 N	111.05 E
Soch'ŏng-do I	98	37.46 N	124.45 E
Sochor, gora ∧	88	51.18 N	105.15 E
Soči	84	43.35 N	39.45 E
Social Circle	192	33.39 N	83.43 W
Social Security Administration ♥	284b	39.19 N	76.44 W
Sociedade Hípica Paulista ♠	287b	23.36 S	46.41 W
Société, Îles de la (Society Islands) II	14	17.00 S	150.00 W
Society Hill	192	34.30 N	79.51 W
Society Islands → Société, Îles de la II	14	17.00 S	150.00 W
Society Ridge ✦[3]	14	17.00 S	151.00 W
Soco ≃	238	18.27 N	69.12 W
Socoltenango	232	16.13 N	92.15 W
Socompa, Paso)(	252	24.27 S	68.18 W
Soconusco, Sierra de → Madre, Sierra ⋏	236	15.20 N	92.20 W
Socorro, Bra.	256	22.36 S	46.32 W
Socorro, Col.	246	6.29 N	73.16 W
Socorro, Pil.	116	9.37 N	125.58 E
Socorro, N.M., U.S.	200	34.03 N	106.53 W
Socorro, Tx., U.S.	200	31.39 N	106.18 W
Socorro ◆[8]	287b	23.39 S	46.42 W
Socorro, Isla I	232	18.45 N	110.58 W
Socota	248	6.18 S	78.44 W
Socotora, Isla → Suquṭrā I	118	12.30 N	54.00 E
Socotra → Suquṭrā I	118	12.30 N	54.00 E
Soc Trang	110	9.36 N	105.58 E
Socuéllamos	34	39.17 N	2.48 W
Soda Creek	182	52.21 N	122.18 W
Soda Creek ≃	226	38.48 N	122.29 W
Soda Lake ◎, Ca., U.S.	204	35.08 N	116.04 W
Soda Lake ◎, Ca., U.S.	226	35.15 N	119.53 W
Sodankylä	24	67.29 N	26.32 E
Soda Springs	202	42.39 N	111.36 W
Soddy-Daisy	194	35.16 N	85.10 W
Sodegaura	94	35.26 N	139.57 E
Söderälgen ◎	40	59.43 N	14.35 E
Söderåsen ⋏[2]	41	56.04 N	13.05 E
Söderbärke	40	60.05 N	15.33 E
Söderby-Karl	40	59.53 N	18.41 E
Söderfors	40	60.23 N	17.14 E
Söderhamn	26	61.18 N	17.03 E
Söderköping	26	58.29 N	16.18 E
Södermanland □[9]	41	59.12 N	16.49 E
Södermanlands Län □[6]	40	59.15 N	16.40 E
Södernmanland □[9]	40	59.12 N	16.49 E
Söderslätt □[9]	41	55.29 N	13.15 E
Södertälje	40	59.12 N	17.37 E
Södertörn ›[1]	40	59.05 N	18.00 E
Sodhra	123	32.28 N	74.11 E
Sodingen ◆[8]	263	51.32 N	7.15 E
Sodium	158	30.11 S	23.09 E
Sodo	144	6.52 N	37.47 E
Sodom → Sedom ⊥	132	31.04 N	35.23 E
Sodpur	272b	22.39 N	88.23 E
Södra Björkfjärden ⊂	40	59.18 N	17.32 E
Södra Hörken ◎	40	60.02 N	15.02 E
Södra Kvarken ɰ	26	60.15 N	19.05 E
Södra Råda	40	59.01 N	14.10 E
Södra Sandby	41	55.43 N	13.20 E
Södra Vi	26	57.45 N	15.48 E
Sodražica	36	45.46 N	14.38 E
Sodus	210	43.14 N	77.03 W
Sodus Bay ⊂	210	43.15 N	76.58 W
Sodus Creek ≃	210	43.13 N	76.56 W
Sodus Point	210	43.16 N	76.59 W
Sŏdu-su ≃	98	42.05 N	129.00 E
Sodwalls	170	33.31 S	149.59 E
Sodwana Bay National Park ♠	158	27.30 S	32.39 E
Soe	112	9.52 S	124.17 E
Soeda	96	33.34 N	130.52 E
Soekmekaar	156	23.28 S	29.58 E
Soela väin ɰ	76	58.40 N	22.35 E
Soerabaja → Surabaya	115a	7.15 S	112.45 E
Soest, Dtsch.	52	51.34 N	8.07 E
Soest, Ned.	52	52.09 N	5.18 E
Soestdijk	52	52.11 N	5.18 E
Soestdijk, Paleis ♥	52	52.12 N	5.15 E
Soeste ≃	52	53.10 N	7.44 E
Soesterberg	52	52.07 N	5.17 E
Soeurs, Île des I	275a	45.28 N	73.33 W
Sofádhes	38	39.20 N	22.06 E
Sofala	170	33.05 S	149.42 E
Sofala □[5]	156	19.00 S	35.00 E
Sofia ≃	157b	15.27 S	47.23 E
Sofia → Sofija	38	42.41 N	23.19 E
Sofiero	41	56.05 N	12.39 E
Sofija (Sofia)	38	42.41 N	23.19 E
Sofijevka, Ukr.	78	46.33 N	34.03 E
Sofijevka, Ukr.	78	48.04 N	33.52 E
Sofijevskij	83	48.12 N	38.52 E
Sofijsk, Ross.	89	51.34 N	139.52 E
Sofijsk, Ross.	89	52.15 N	133.58 E
Sofjanga	24	65.52 N	31.15 E
Sofje-Kondratjevka	83	48.18 N	38.12 E
Sofjino	82	55.30 N	38.11 E
Sofrino	82	56.09 N	37.56 E
Sofronovo	76	59.48 N	36.54 E
Sogakofe	150	6.00 N	0.36 E
Sogamoso	246	5.43 N	72.56 W
Sogamoso ≃	246	7.13 N	73.56 W
Soğanlı ≃	130	41.11 N	32.38 E
Soğanlı Geçidi)(	130	40.33 N	40.16 E
Soğanlıköy ◆[8]	267b	40.55 N	29.12 E
Sogcho → Sokch'o	98	38.12 N	128.36 E
Sogda	89	50.24 N	132.12 E
Sögel	52	52.50 N	7.31 E
Sogen	164	9.25 S	147.25 E
Sogliano al Rubicone	66	44.00 N	12.18 E

Sognafjorden ⊂[2]	26	61.06 N	5.10 E
Søgne	26	58.05 N	7.49 E
Sogne Fjord → Sognafjorden ⊂[2]	26	61.06 N	5.10 E
Sogn og Fjordane □[6]	26	61.30 N	6.50 E
Sogod, Pil.	116	10.45 N	124.00 E
Sogod, Pil.	116	10.23 N	124.59 E
Sogod Bay ⊂	116	10.15 N	125.02 E
Sogo Nur ◎	102	42.18 N	101.08 E
Sogoža ≃	76	58.28 N	39.06 E
Sogri-san Kukrip Kongwŏn ♠	98	36.33 N	127.52 E
Soğuksu Milli Parkı ♠	130	40.25 N	32.35 E
Söğüt	130	40.00 N	30.11 E
Söğütalan	130	40.03 N	28.34 E
Söğüt Gölü ◎	130	37.03 N	29.53 E
Söğütlü	130	40.54 N	30.29 E
Sog Xian	120	31.50 N	93.45 E
Sohāgpur, India	124	23.19 N	81.21 E
Sohāgpur, India	124	22.42 N	78.12 E
Sohāg → Sawhāj	140	26.33 N	31.42 E
Soham	42	52.20 N	0.20 E
Sohano	175e	5.27 S	154.40 E
Soharkha	272a	28.35 N	77.24 E
Soheit-Tinlot	56	50.29 N	5.22 E
Sohland	54	51.02 N	14.25 E
Söhlde	52	52.11 N	10.14 E
Sohna	124	28.15 N	77.04 E
Sŏhŭng	98	38.27 N	126.10 E
Sŏhwa-ri	98	38.15 N	128.13 E
Soignies (Zinnik)	50	50.35 N	4.04 E
Soignolles-en-Brie	261	48.39 N	2.42 E
Soin	150	12.47 N	3.49 W
Soindres	261	48.57 N	1.40 E
Soini	26	62.52 N	24.13 E
Sointula	182	50.38 N	127.01 W
Soira ∧	144	14.45 N	39.32 E
Soisalo ∧	26	62.40 N	28.10 E
Soissons	50	49.22 N	3.20 E
Soisy-sous-Montmorency	261	48.59 N	2.18 E
Soisy-sur-Seine	261	48.39 N	2.27 E
Sōja	96	34.40 N	133.45 E
Sojana	24	65.48 N	43.20 E
Sojat	120	25.55 N	73.40 E
Šojda	24	61.11 N	37.40 E
Sojiji Temple ♥[1]	268	35.31 N	139.41 E
Sojītra	120	22.33 N	72.43 E
Šojna	24	67.52 N	44.08 E
Sŏjosŏn-man ⊂	98	39.20 N	124.50 E
Sojoton Point ›	116	9.58 N	122.27 E
Sok ≃	80	53.24 N	50.08 E
Sōka, Nihon	94	35.49 N	139.48 E
Soka, Taehan	271b	37.30 N	126.48 E
Sokal'	78	50.29 N	24.17 E
Šokal'skogo, proliv ɰ	74	79.00 N	100.25 E
Sokch'o	98	38.12 N	128.36 E
Söke	130	37.45 N	27.24 E
Sokehs Passage ɰ	174r	7.01 N	158.11 E
Sokele	154	9.55 S	24.36 E
Sokhós	38	40.49 N	23.21 E
Sokir'any	78	48.27 N	27.25 E
Sokirincy	78	50.42 N	32.46 E
Sokna	26	60.14 N	9.54 E
Sokodé	150	8.59 N	1.08 E
Sokol, Ross.	74	72.24 N	126.48 E
Sokol, Ross.	76	59.28 N	40.10 E
Sokol, Ross.	89	47.14 N	142.45 E
Sokol ∧	60	49.03 N	13.31 E
Sokólka, Pol.	30	53.25 N	23.31 E
Sokolka, Ross.	80	55.34 N	51.30 E
Sokol'niki ◆[8]	265b	55.48 N	37.41 E
Sokolniki Park ♠	265b	55.48 N	37.41 E
Sokol'nikovo	82	55.21 N	35.49 E
Sokolo	150	14.44 N	6.08 W
Sokologornoje	78	46.29 N	34.58 E
Sokolov	54	50.09 N	12.40 E
Sokolova-Gora	78	50.19 N	28.36 E
Sokolova Pustyn'	82	54.51 N	38.03 E
Sokolovka	86	55.06 N	69.12 E
Sokolovo, Ross.	24	65.21 N	56.57 E
Sokolovo, Ross.	76	52.55 N	34.39 E
Sokolovo, Ross.	80	52.49 N	42.26 E
Sokolovo, Ross.	82	56.02 N	36.55 E
Sokolovo, Ross.	86	52.33 N	84.46 E
Sokolovo-Kundr'učenskij	83	47.50 N	39.57 E
Sokołów	30	50.14 N	22.07 E
Sokołów Podlaski	30	52.25 N	22.15 E
Sokol'skoje	80	57.08 N	43.13 E
Sokone	150	13.53 N	16.22 W
Sokoto	150	13.04 N	5.16 E
Sokoto □[3]	150	12.05 N	5.30 E
Sokoto ≃	150	11.20 N	4.10 E
Šokpar	85	43.49 N	74.21 E
Sŏkp'o-ri	98	37.46 N	125.27 E
Sokrutovka	80	47.54 N	46.33 E
Šokša	76	58.24 N	42.27 E
Soksa-ri	98	40.40 N	127.17 E
Sokskije jary ⋏[2]	80	54.10 N	51.30 E
Sŏk-to I	98	38.40 N	125.00 E
Sokuluk	85	42.52 N	74.18 E
Sokur, Ross.	80	52.01 N	45.48 E
Sokur, Ross.	86	55.13 N	83.13 E
Sol', Slov.	30	48.56 N	21.36 E
Sol', Ukr.	83	48.43 N	38.02 E
Sol, Costa del ⊥[2]	34	36.40 N	4.00 W
Sola, Nor.	26	58.53 N	5.36 E
Sola, Vanuatu	175f	13.53 S	167.33 E
Sola, Zaïre	154	5.09 S	27.06 E
Soła ≃	30	50.04 N	19.13 E
Solacolu	38	44.23 N	26.34 E
Solai	154	0.02 N	36.09 E
Šolaksaj	86	51.45 N	64.48 E
Solan	123	30.55 N	77.07 E
Solana	220	26.56 N	82.01 W
Solana Beach	228	32.59 N	117.16 W
Solander, Cape ›	274a	34.01 S	151.14 E
Solander Island I	172	46.34 S	166.53 E
Solânea	250	6.45 S	35.39 W
Solangāri	272b	22.36 N	88.27 E
Sol'anka ≃	80	50.10 N	51.20 E
Solano	116	16.31 N	121.11 E
Solano □[6]	226	38.15 N	121.52 W
Solāpur	122	17.41 N	75.55 E
Solar, Morro ∧[2]	286d	12.11 S	77.02 W
Solarino	70	37.06 N	15.07 E
Solaro	266b	45.37 N	9.05 E
Solaro, Monte ∧	68	40.33 N	14.13 E
Solberg	26	63.47 N	17.38 E
Solbiate Arno	62	45.42 N	8.48 E
Solbiate Olona	266b	45.39 N	8.53 E
Solca, Arg.	252	30.46 S	66.28 W
Solca, Rom.	38	47.42 N	25.50 E
Solčava	61	46.25 N	14.41 E
Sol'cy	76	58.08 N	30.20 E
Solda Gölü ◎	130	37.33 N	29.42 E
Soldatskaja	84	43.48 N	43.49 E
Soldatskoje	85	40.52 N	68.56 E
Soldatsko-Stepnoje	80	49.32 N	45.30 E
Sölde ◆[8]	263	51.31 N	7.35 E
Sol de Julio	252	29.33 S	63.27 W
Sölden	64	46.58 N	11.00 E
Sölderholz ◆[8]	263	51.29 N	7.35 E
Soldier Creek ≃	198	39.04 N	95.39 W
Soldier Field ♠	278	41.52 N	87.37 W
Soldier Key I	220	25.35 N	80.10 W
Soldier Point ›	240c	17.02 N	61.41 W
Soldier Pond	186	47.09 N	68.34 W
Soldiers Grove	190	43.23 N	90.46 W
Soldotna	180	60.29 N	151.04 W
Sole, Val di V	64	46.20 N	10.45 E
Solebury	208	40.23 N	75.02 W
Solec Kujawski	30	53.06 N	18.14 E
Soledad, Col.	246	10.55 N	74.46 W
Soledad, Ca., U.S.	226	36.25 N	121.19 W
Soledad, Ven.	246	8.10 N	63.34 W

Soledad, Cerro ∧	196	26.29 N	103.23 W
Soledad de Doblado	234	19.03 N	96.25 W
Soledad Díez Gutiérrez	234	22.12 N	100.57 W
Soledade	252	28.50 S	52.30 W
Soledade de Minas	256	22.04 S	45.03 W
Soledad Pass)(	228	34.30 N	118.07 W
Soleduck ≃	224	47.55 N	124.35 W
Solemar	256	24.05 S	46.36 W
Solen	198	46.23 N	100.47 W
Sølen ∧	26	61.55 N	11.30 E
Solenoje	80	46.14 N	42.32 E
Solentiname, Archipiélago de II	236	11.10 N	85.00 W
Solenzara	36	41.51 N	9.23 E
Solenzo	150	12.11 N	4.05 W
Solero	62	44.55 N	8.30 E
Solers	261	48.40 N	2.43 E
Solesmes	50	50.11 N	3.30 E
Soleure → Solothurn	58	47.13 N	7.32 E
Solferino	64	45.23 N	10.34 E
Solginskij	24	61.05 N	41.19 E
Solgne	56	48.58 N	6.18 E
Solgonskij kr'až ∧	86	55.30 N	91.00 E
Solhan	130	38.58 N	41.03 E
Solheim, Nor.	26	60.53 N	5.27 E
Solheim, S. Afr.	273d	26.11 S	28.10 E
Soliera	64	44.45 N	10.55 E
Soligalič	76	59.05 N	42.17 E
Solignac-sur-Loire	62	44.58 N	3.53 E
Soligny-la-Trappe	50	48.37 N	0.32 E
Soligorsk	76	52.48 N	27.32 E
Solihull	42	52.25 N	1.45 W
Solikamsk	86	59.39 N	56.47 E
Solila	157b	21.25 S	46.37 E
Sol'-Ileck	86	51.10 N	54.59 E
Soliman	148	36.42 N	10.30 E
Solimões → Amazon ≃	242	0.10 S	49.00 W
Solin ≃	50	48.02 N	2.43 E
Solingen	56	51.10 N	7.05 E
Solís, Arg.	258	34.18 S	59.20 W
Solís, Ur.	252	34.36 S	55.29 W
Solís, Presa ◎[1]	234	20.05 N	100.36 W
Soliseño	196	26.01 N	97.48 W
Söll	64	47.30 N	12.11 E
Šollar	84	41.40 N	48.38 E
Sollas	46	57.39 N	7.21 W
Sollefteå	26	63.10 N	17.16 E
Sollenau	61	47.53 N	16.15 E
Sollentuna	40	59.28 N	17.54 E
Sóller	34	39.46 N	2.42 E
Søllerød	41	55.49 N	12.31 E
Sollerön I	26	60.55 N	14.37 E
Søllested	41	54.49 N	11.17 E
Solliès-Pont	62	43.11 N	6.03 E
Solling ⋏	52	51.45 N	9.35 E
Söllingen	54	52.05 N	10.55 E
Solln ◆[8]	60	48.05 N	11.31 E
Sollom	262	53.40 N	2.50 W
Sollstedt	54	51.25 N	10.31 E
Solms	56	50.32 N	8.24 E
Solna	40	59.22 N	18.01 E
Solncedar	78	44.34 N	38.01 E
Solncevo	265b	55.39 N	37.24 E
Solnečnogorsk	82	56.11 N	36.59 E
Solnhofen	56	48.53 N	10.59 E
Solo ≃	115a	6.47 S	112.33 E
Šolochovskij	80	48.18 N	41.03 E
Solodča	80	49.39 N	44.17 E
Solodniki	80	48.25 N	45.16 E
Solofra	68	40.50 N	14.51 E
Sologne ◆[1]	50	47.50 N	2.00 E
Šologoncy	74	66.13 N	114.14 E
Solok	112	0.48 S	100.39 E
Sololá, Guat.	236	14.46 N	91.11 W
Sololá, Som.	144	0.07 N	41.31 E
Sololá □[5]	236	14.40 N	91.15 W
Solomennikova	86	58.20 N	89.02 E
Solomennoje	24	61.51 N	34.19 E
Solomon, Az., U.S.	200	32.48 N	109.37 W
Solomon, Ks., U.S.	198	38.55 N	97.22 W
Solomon ≃	198	38.54 N	97.22 W
Solomon, North Fork ≃	198	39.29 N	98.26 W
Solomon, South Fork ≃	198	39.29 N	98.26 W
Solomon Basin ✦[1]	14	7.00 S	152.00 E
Solomon Islands □[1]	175e	8.00 S	159.00 E
Solomon Islands II	175e	8.00 S	159.00 E
Solomons	208	38.20 N	76.28 W
Solomon Sea ⍑[2]	14	8.00 S	155.00 E
Solomon's Pools → Sulaymān, Birak ⊥	132	31.41 N	35.10 E
Solon, Ia., U.S.	190	41.48 N	91.29 W
Solon, Me., U.S.	188	44.56 N	69.51 W
Solon, Oh., U.S.	214	41.23 N	81.26 W
Solon, Zhg.	89	46.36 N	121.13 E
Solonešnoje	86	51.40 N	84.21 E
Solonka	80	50.13 N	41.28 E
Sol'onoje, Ross.	84	44.03 N	40.53 E
Sol'onoje, Ukr.	78	48.13 N	34.52 E
Sol'onoje, Ukr.	83	49.18 N	37.39 E
Sol'onoje, ozero ◎	86	55.20 N	70.05 E
Sol'onoje Ozero	78	45.53 N	34.27 E
Sol'onoje Zajmišče	80	47.56 N	46.07 E
Solonópole	250	5.44 S	39.01 W
Solon Springs	190	46.21 N	91.49 W
Solopaca	68	41.11 N	14.33 E
Solor, Kepulauan II	112	8.25 S	123.30 E
Solor, Pulau I	112	8.27 S	123.05 E
Solo → Surakarta	115a	7.35 S	110.50 E
Solotča	80	54.48 N	39.51 E
Solothurn	58	47.13 N	7.32 E
Solothurn □[3]	58	47.25 N	7.35 E
Solotobe	86	44.38 N	66.05 E
Solotvin	78	48.42 N	24.25 E
Solotvina	78	47.57 N	23.52 E
Soloveckije ostrova II	24	65.07 N	35.53 E
Solovjovka	76	60.46 N	30.09 E
Solovjovsk, Ross.	88	49.55 N	115.42 E
Solovjovsk, Ross.	89	54.14 N	124.26 E
Solre-le-Château	50	50.10 N	4.05 E
Solre-sur-Sambre	50	50.18 N	4.08 E
Solrød Strand	41	55.32 N	12.14 E
Solsona	34	41.59 N	1.31 E
Solt	30	46.48 N	19.00 E
Šolta, Otok I	36	43.23 N	16.15 E
Soltānābād	128	36.23 N	58.02 E
Soltau	52	52.59 N	9.49 E
Solton	86	52.50 N	86.28 E
Solunto ⊥	70	38.06 N	13.32 E
Solus, Mount ∧	168a	32.28 S	116.13 E
Solutré-Pouilly	58	46.18 N	4.43 E
Solva	42	51.52 N	5.11 W
Solva ≃	42	51.52 N	5.17 W
Solvang	204	34.36 N	120.08 W
Solvarbo	40	60.24 N	15.40 E
Solvay	210	43.03 N	76.12 W
Sölvesborg	26	56.03 N	14.33 E
Sol'vyčegodsk	24	61.21 N	46.52 E
Solway Firth ⊂[1]	44	54.50 N	3.35 W
Solwezi	154	12.11 S	26.25 E
Soly	76	54.31 N	26.11 E
Solymár	264c	47.36 N	18.56 E
Solza	24	64.33 N	39.29 E
Sōma, Nihon	92	37.48 N	140.57 E
Soma, Tür.	130	39.10 N	27.36 E
Somabula	154	19.41 S	29.41 E
Sōmahara-chūtonchi, Rikujō-jieitai- ■	94	36.23 N	138.58 E
Somain	50	50.22 N	3.17 E
Somalia (Somaliya) □[1], Afr.	136	6.00 N	48.00 E
Somalia (Somaliya) □[1], Afr.	144	6.00 N	48.00 E

Somali Basin ✦[1]	12	0.00	52.00 E
Somalie → Somalia □[1]	144	6.00 N	48.00 E
Somaliland → Somalia □[1]	144	6.00 N	48.00 E
Somali Republic → Somalia □[1]	144	6.00 N	48.00 E
Somaliya → Somalia □[1]	144	6.00 N	48.00 E
Somalomo	152	3.23 N	12.44 E
Sŏman	98	41.20 N	128.54 E
Somanga	154	8.24 S	39.17 E
Sombernon	58	47.18 N	4.42 E
Sombo	152	8.42 S	20.57 E
Sombor	38	45.46 N	19.07 E
Sombra	214	42.43 N	82.29 W
Sombrerete	234	23.38 N	103.39 W
Sombreretillo	196	26.19 N	99.58 W
Sombrero I	238	18.36 N	63.26 W
Sombrero Channel ɰ	110	7.41 N	93.35 E
Sombrio	252	29.07 S	49.40 W
Sombrio, Lagoa do ⊂	252	29.12 S	49.42 W
Şomcuta-Mare	38	47.31 N	23.29 E
Somdari	120	25.49 N	72.35 E
Somenos	224	48.49 N	123.44 W
Somercotes	44	53.04 N	1.22 W
Somerdale, N.J., U.S.	208	39.50 N	75.01 W
Somerdale, Oh., U.S.	214	40.34 N	81.22 W
Someren	52	51.24 N	5.44 E
Somero	26	60.37 N	23.32 E
Sõmerpalu	76	57.51 N	26.48 E
Somers, Austl.	169	38.24 S	145.10 E
Somers, Ct., U.S.	207	41.59 N	72.26 W
Somers, Mt., U.S.	202	48.04 N	114.13 W
Somers, Wi., U.S.	216	42.38 N	87.54 W
Somersby	170	33.25 S	151.17 E
Somerset, Austl.	166	41.03 S	145.49 E
Somerset, Mb., Can.	184	49.24 N	98.39 W
Somerset, Co., U.S.	200	38.55 N	107.28 W
Somerset, Ky., U.S.	192	37.05 N	84.36 W
Somerset, Md., U.S.	284c	38.58 N	77.05 W
Somerset, Ma., U.S.	207	41.46 N	71.07 W
Somerset, N.J., U.S.	208	40.44 N	74.34 W
Somerset, Oh., U.S.	188	39.48 N	82.17 W
Somerset, Pa., U.S.	188	40.00 N	79.04 W
Somerset, Tx., U.S.	196	29.13 N	98.40 W
Somerset, Wi., U.S.	190	45.07 N	92.40 W
Somerset □[6], Eng., U.K.	42	51.08 N	3.00 W
Somerset □[6], Md., U.S.	208	38.12 N	75.41 W
Somerset □[6], N.J., U.S.	208	40.34 N	74.37 W
Somerset □[6], Pa., U.S.	214	40.09 N	79.00 W
Somerset Airport ⊠	276	40.37 N	74.40 W
Somerset Center	216	42.03 N	84.25 W
Somerset East	158	32.42 S	25.35 E
Somerset Hills Airport ⊠	276	40.41 N	74.32 W
Somerset Island I, Ber.	240a	32.17 N	64.52 W
Somerset Island I, N.T., Can.	176	73.15 N	93.30 W
Somerset Reservoir ◎[1]	171a	27.03 S	152.35 E
Somerset West	158	34.08 S	18.50 E
Somersham	42	52.23 N	0.01 E
Somers Point	208	39.19 N	74.35 W
Somersworth	188	43.15 N	70.51 W
Somerton, Eng., U.K.	42	51.03 N	2.44 W
Somerton, Az., U.S.	200	32.35 N	114.42 W
Somerton ◆[8]	285	40.06 N	75.01 W
Somerton Creek ≃	208	36.32 N	76.55 W
Somervell □[6]	222	32.15 N	97.45 W
Somerville, Austl.	169	38.13 S	145.10 E
Somerville, Ma., U.S.	207	42.23 N	71.06 W
Somerville, N.J., U.S.	210	40.34 N	74.36 W
Somerville, Oh., U.S.	218	39.33 N	84.38 W
Somerville, Tn., U.S.	194	35.14 N	89.21 W
Somerville, Tx., U.S.	222	30.20 N	96.31 W
Somerville Lake ◎[1]	222	30.18 N	96.40 W
Someș (Szamos) ≃	38	48.07 N	22.22 E
Someșu Cald ≃	38	46.44 N	23.22 E
Someșul Mare ≃	38	47.12 N	24.12 E
Someșul Mic ≃	38	47.09 N	23.55 E
Someșul Rece ≃	38	46.44 N	23.22 E
Somino	76	59.21 N	34.52 E
Somis	228	34.16 N	119.00 W
Sŏmjin-gang ≃	98	34.58 N	127.46 E
Somma	66	42.40 N	12.44 E
Sommacampagna	64	45.24 N	10.50 E
Somma Lombardo, It.	62	45.41 N	8.42 E
Somma Lombardo, It.	266b	45.41 N	8.42 E
Sommariva	166	26.24 S	146.36 E
Sommariva del Bosco	62	44.46 N	7.47 E
Sommatino	70	37.20 N	13.59 E
Somme □[5]	50	49.55 N	2.30 E
Somme ≃, Fr.	50	49.01 N	4.12 E
Somme ≃, Fr.	50	50.11 N	1.39 E
Somme, Baie de la ⊂	50	50.14 N	1.33 E
Somme, Canal de la ≍	50	49.55 N	2.43 E
Sommedieue	56	49.05 N	5.28 E
Sommelsdijk	52	51.45 N	4.09 E
Sommen ◎	26	58.01 N	15.15 E
Sommepy-Tahure	56	49.15 N	4.33 E
Sommerberg ◆[8]	263	51.27 N	7.32 E
Sömmerda	54	51.10 N	11.07 E
Sommersdorf	54	53.17 N	14.11 E
Sommersted	41	55.19 N	9.19 E
Sommesous	50	48.44 N	4.12 E
Somme Woods ♠	278	42.09 N	87.49 W
Somnitel'nyj	89	52.12 N	139.04 E
Somo ≃	190	45.29 N	89.48 W
Somogy □[6]	30	46.25 N	17.35 E
Somonauk	216	41.38 N	88.40 W
Somonauk Creek ≃	216	41.32 N	88.41 W
Somosierra, Puerto de)(	34	41.09 N	3.35 W
Somosomo	175g	16.46 S	179.58 W
Somosomo Strait ɰ	175g	16.47 S	179.58 E
Somotillo	236	13.02 N	86.55 W
Somoto	236	13.28 N	86.35 W
Somovo, Ross.	76	52.53 N	34.58 E
Somovo, Ross.	78	51.44 N	39.23 E
Sompeta	122	18.56 N	84.36 E
Somplago	64	46.21 N	13.04 E
Sompolno	30	52.24 N	18.31 E
Somport, Puerto de)(	34	42.48 N	0.31 W
Sompuis	50	48.41 N	4.23 E
Somuncurá, Meseta de ⋏[1]	254	41.30 S	67.15 W
Şomvix	58	46.44 N	8.56 E
Šomyškol'	86	46.30 N	59.53 E
Son, Ned.	52	51.31 N	5.30 E
Son, Nor.	26	59.31 N	10.42 E
Son ≃	124	25.42 N	84.52 E
Soná	236	8.01 N	81.19 W
Sona-Bata	152	4.54 S	15.09 E
Sonādugi	126	22.47 N	90.40 E
Sonaguera	236	15.38 N	86.20 W
Sonahula	124	25.05 N	87.09 E
Sonāmarg	123	34.18 N	75.18 E
Sonāmukhi	126	23.18 N	87.25 E
Sonāpur	126	23.42 N	89.30 E
Sonar	164	2.33 S	133.00 E
Sonār ≃	124	24.24 N	79.56 E
Sonari	272c	18.52 N	72.59 E
Sonarpur	272b	22.26 N	88.25 E
Sonātikri	272b	22.57 N	88.20 E
Sonceboz	58	47.11 N	7.11 E
Sonchamp	261	48.35 N	1.53 E
Sŏnch'ŏn	98	39.48 N	124.55 E
Soncino	62	45.24 N	9.52 E
Sondags ≃, S. Afr.	158	28.43 S	30.16 E
Sondags ≃, S. Afr.	158	33.44 S	25.51 E

Symbol	English	Deutsch	Español	Français	Português
≃	River	Fluß	Río	Rivière	Rio
≍	Canal	Kanal	Canal	Canal	Canal
ㄴ	Waterfall, Rapids	Wasserfall, Stromschnellen	Cascada, Rápidos	Chute d'eau, Rapides	Cascata, Rápidos
ɰ	Strait	Meeresstraße	Estrecho	Détroit	Estreito
⊂	Bay, Gulf	Bucht, Golf	Bahía, Golfo	Baie, Golfe	Baía, Golfo
◎	Lake, Lakes	See, Seen	Lago, Lagos	Lac, Lacs	Lago, Lagos
≡	Swamp	Sumpf	Pantano	Marais	Pântano
⌂	Ice Features, Glacier	Eis- und Gletscherformen	Accidentes Glaciales	Formes glaciaires	Acidentes glaciares
⍑	Other Hydrographic Features	Andere Hydrographische Objekte	Otros Elementos Hidrográficos	Autres données hydrographiques	Outros acidentes hidrográficos
✦	Submarine Features	Untermeerische Objekte	Accidentes Submarinos	Formes de relief sous-marin	Acidentes submarinos
□	Political Unit	Politische Einheit	Unidad Politica	Entité politique	Unidade política
♥	Cultural Institution	Kulturelle Institution	Institución Cultural	Institution culturelle	Institução cultural
⊥	Historical Site	Historische Stätte	Sitio Histórico	Site historique	Sitio histórico
♠	Recreational Site	Erholungs- und Ferienort	Sitio de Recreo	Centre de loisirs	Area de Lazer
⊠	Airport	Flughafen	Aeropuerto	Aéroport	Aeroporto
■	Military Installation	Militäranlage	Instalación Militar	Installation militaire	Instalação militar
◆	Miscellaneous	Verschiedenes	Misceláneo	Divers	Diversos

Sondalo 64 46.20 N 10.19 E
Sønderå ≃ 41 54.53 N 8.59 E
Sønderborg 41 54.55 N 9.47 E
Sønderby 41 55.47 N 10.01 E
Sønder Felding 41 55.57 N 8.47 E
Sønderhav 41 54.51 N 9.30 E
Sønderjylland □⁶ 41 55.10 N 9.15 E
Sønder Nærå 41 55.18 N 10.30 E
Sønder Omme 41 55.50 N 8.54 E
Sondershausen 54 51.22 N 10.52 E
Søndersø 41 55.29 N 10.16 E
Sondi 114 2.58 N 98.52 E
Søndre Strømfjord 176 66.59 N 50.40 W
Søndre Strømfjord c² 176 66.30 N 52.15 W
Sondrio 64 46.10 N 9.52 E
Sondrio □⁴ 58 46.10 N 10.03 E
Sonduga 76 60.08 N 41.55 E
Sone ≃ 126 21.34 N 86.54 E
Sonepur 120 20.50 N 83.55 E
Sonestown 210 41.21 N 76.33 W
Song, Malay. 112 2.01 N 112.33 E
Song, Nig. 146 9.50 N 12.38 E
Song, Thai 110 18.28 N 100.11 E
Song ≃ 100 27.02 N 118.18 E
Song'ao 100 29.36 N 121.41 E
Songbahutun 104 41.28 N 121.11 E
Song Bay Hap, Cua c 110 8.46 N 104.52 E
Songbu 100 31.05 N 114.48 E
Sŏngbyŏn-ni 98 38.03 N 125.18 E
Song Cau 110 13.27 N 109.13 E
Sŏng-ch'ŏn-gang ≃ 98 39.48 N 127.35 E
Songcun 106 30.26 N 119.43 E
Songe 26 58.41 N 9.00 E
Songea 154 10.41 S 35.39 E
Songeons 50 49.33 N 1.52 E
Songgaizhen 107 29.03 N 105.54 E
Songgang 100 22.49 N 113.51 E
Songgato ≃ 164 3.26 S 140.22 E
Songhe 100 31.10 N 113.20 E
Songhua ≃ 89 47.44 N 132.32 E
Songhuahu ⊜ 89 43.20 N 127.07 E
Songhuajiang 89 44.46 N 125.54 E
Songhwa 98 38.21 N 125.08 E
Songino 88 48.54 N 95.54 E
Sŏngjang-ni 98 41.02 N 126.50 E
Songjiachang 107 28.47 N 104.55 E
Songjiang 106 31.01 N 121.14 E
Songjiangzhen 98 42.12 N 126.56 E
Songjiapu 107 29.38 N 104.42 E
Songjiaying 105 40.38 N 115.14 E
Sŏngjin — Kimch'aek 98 40.41 N 129.12 E
Songjŏng 98 35.10 N 126.46 E
Songju 98 35.55 N 128.16 E
Songkan 102 28.27 N 106.50 E
Songkhla 110 7.12 N 100.36 E
Songkhram ≃ 110 17.39 N 104.28 E
Songkou, Zhg. 100 25.48 N 118.36 E
Songkou, Zhg. 100 24.32 N 116.24 E
Songlinba 100 24.00 N 115.59 E
Songlindian 105 39.25 N 115.54 E
Songling 89 48.02 N 121.12 E
Song Ling ∧ 98 41.10 N 120.09 E
Songmen 100 28.19 N 121.34 E
Songming 102 25.24 N 102.59 E
Sŏngmo-do I 98 37.42 N 126.18 E
Songnae-ri 98 39.28 N 126.59 E
Sŏngnam 98 37.26 N 127.08 E
Sŏng-ni 98 39.38 N 127.06 E
Songnim 98 38.44 N 125.38 E
Songo 152 7.22 S 14.51 E
Songololo 152 5.42 S 14.02 E
Songot ∧ 154 3.59 N 34.28 E
Songpan 102 32.40 N 103.24 E
Song Phi Nong 110 14.13 N 100.03 E
Sŏngsa-ri 271b 37.38 N 126.52 E
Songshancun 104 41.02 N 121.09 E
Songshu 98 39.50 N 122.06 E
Songshugou 105 41.02 N 117.49 E
Songtangmiao 106 31.08 N 119.16 E
Songtao 102 28.06 N 109.05 E
Songtun 98 39.54 N 123.56 E
Songuj 24 68.47 N 33.00 E
Songu-ri 98 37.49 N 127.09 E
Songwe, Zaïre 154 3.24 S 26.16 E
Songwe, Zaïre 154 12.25 S 29.40 E
Songwe ≃ 154 9.43 S 33.56 E
Songxi, Zhg. 100 27.33 N 118.46 E
Songxi, Zhg. 100 26.16 N 116.59 E
Songxia, Zhg. 100 25.44 N 119.36 E
Songxia, Zhg. 100 30.07 N 120.51 E
Songxian 102 34.10 N 112.05 E
Songyan 98 37.13 N 113.43 E
Songyin 106 30.54 N 121.13 E
Songyin ≃ 100 28.18 N 119.44 E
Songzhangzi 98 41.13 N 119.08 E
Songzhuang 106 32.06 N 121.17 E
Son Ha 110 15.03 N 108.34 E
Soni, Ehi ∧ 146 20.49 N 17.23 E
Sonico 64 46.10 N 10.21 E
Sonid Youqi 102 42.44 N 112.40 E
Sonid Zuoqi 102 43.58 N 113.59 E
Sonīpat 124 28.59 N 77.01 E
Sonkach 124 22.59 N 76.21 E
Sonk'ol', ozero ⊜ 85 41.50 N 75.08 E
Sonkovo 76 57.47 N 37.09 E
Son La 110 21.19 N 103.54 E
Sonmiāni 120 25.26 N 66.36 E
Sonmiāni Bay c 120 25.15 N 66.30 E
Sonnberg ∧ 264b 48.20 N 16.15 E
Sonneberg 54 50.22 N 11.10 E
Sonnefeld 56 50.13 N 11.08 E
Sonnen 60 48.41 N 13.43 E
Sonnenberg ∧² 61 47.52 N 16.28 E
Sonnewalde 54 51.42 N 13.38 E
Sonning Common 42 51.31 N 0.59 W
Sonningdale 184 52.24 N 107.40 W
Sonnino 66 41.25 N 13.14 E
Sonntagberg 61 47.59 N 14.45 E
Sono 270 34.48 N 135.55 E
Sono, Rio do ≃, Bra. 250 8.58 S 48.11 W
Sono, Rio do ≃, Bra. 255 17.02 S 45.32 W
Sonobe 96 35.06 N 135.28 E
Sonogno 58 46.21 N 8.47 E
Sonoita Creek ≃ 200 31.30 N 110.58 W
Sonoma 226 38.17 N 122.27 W
Sonoma □⁶ 226 38.26 N 122.35 W
Sonoma Creek ≃ 226 38.10 N 122.24 W
Sonoma Mountains ∧ 226 38.17 N 122.35 W
Sonoma Peak ∧ 204 40.52 N 117.36 W
Sonoma State Historical Park ♦ 226 38.18 N 122.28 W
Sononder 158 29.43 S 21.51 E
Sonop 158 25.39 S 27.42 E
Sonora, Ca., U.S. 226 37.59 N 120.22 W
Sonora, Tx., U.S. 196 30.34 N 100.38 W
Sonora □³ 232 29.20 N 110.40 W
Sonora ≃ 232 28.48 N 111.33 W
Sonoran Desert ✦² 16 30.00 N 113.00 W
Sonora Pass ⅹ 226 38.19 N 119.37 W
Sonostrov 24 66.09 N 34.10 E
Sonoyta 232 31.51 N 112.50 W
Sonoyta ≃ 200 31.16 N 113.26 W
Sonpăr Hills ∧² 124 24.20 N 82.15 E
Sonqor 128 34.47 N 47.36 E
Sonsan 98 36.16 N 128.17 E
Sonsbeck 52 51.37 N 6.22 E
Sonseca 34 39.42 N 3.57 W
Sonskyn 158 30.47 S 26.28 E
Sonsón 246 5.42 N 75.18 W
Sonsonate 236 13.43 N 89.44 W
Sonsorol Islands II 108 5.20 N 132.13 E
Sonstorp 40 58.45 N 15.36 E
Sonstraal 158 27.07 S 22.28 E
Sontag 194 31.39 N 90.12 W
Son Tay 110 21.08 N 105.30 E
Sonthofen 58 47.31 N 10.17 E
Sontra 56 51.04 N 9.56 E
Sonwān 124 27.40 N 81.45 E

Sonyea 210 42.41 N 77.50 W
Soochow — Suzhou 106 31.18 N 120.37 E
Sooke 224 48.23 N 123.43 W
Sooke ≃ 224 48.23 N 123.42 W
Sooke Basin c 224 48.23 N 123.40 W
Sooke Lake ⊜ 224 48.33 N 123.42 W
Sooner Lake ⊜¹ 196 36.26 N 97.02 W
Soonwald ∧ 56 49.55 N 7.40 E
Soo — Sault Sainte Marie 190 46.29 N 84.20 W
Sooyaac 144 0.03 N 42.17 E
Sopa Sopa Head › 164 1.58 S 146.35 E
Sopchoppy 192 30.03 N 84.29 W
Soperton 192 32.22 N 82.35 W
Sop Hao 110 20.33 N 104.27 E
Sophia 192 37.42 N 81.15 W
Sopki 76 57.06 N 30.55 E
Sopockin 76 53.50 N 23.39 E
Sopot 30 54.28 N 18.34 E
Sop Pong 110 22.04 N 102.03 E
Sop Prap 110 17.53 N 99.20 E
Soprabolzano 64 46.32 N 11.24 E
Sopron 61 47.41 N 16.36 E
Sopronhorpács 61 47.29 N 16.44 E
Sopronkövesd 61 47.33 N 16.45 E
Šoptykol' 86 51.16 N 75.45 E
Sopur 123 34.18 N 74.28 E
Sŏp'yŏng-ni 98 35.01 N 127.24 E
Soquel 226 36.59 N 121.57 W
Soquel Creek ≃ 226 36.58 N 121.57 W
Sor, Ribeira de ≃ 34 39.00 N 8.17 W
Sør-Aurdal 30 ...
Sora 66 41.43 N 13.37 E
Sorada 122 19.45 N 84.26 E
Sorae-san ∧ 271b 37.27 N 126.47 E
Soraga 64 46.22 N 11.39 E
Soragna 64 44.56 N 10.07 E
Söråker 26 62.31 N 17.30 E
Sorano 66 42.41 N 11.43 E
Šorapani 84 42.05 N 43.05 E
Soras 248 14.07 S 73.37 W
Sorata 248 15.47 S 68.40 W
Soratte, Monte ∧ 66 42.15 N 12.30 E
Sorau — Żary 30 51.38 N 15.09 E
Soraya 248 14.10 S 73.19 W
Sorbas 34 37.07 N 2.07 W
Sorbas, gora ∧ 86 47.25 N 84.12 E
Sorbhog 120 26.30 N 90.52 E
Sorbie 44 54.48 N 4.26 W
Sorbo ≃ 85 38.45 N 69.20 E
Sorbolo 64 44.51 N 10.28 E
Sorbonne ☉² 261 48.51 N 2.21 E
Sorcier, Lac au ⊜ 206 46.42 N 73.24 W
Sorcievolo 32 45.34 N 7.59 E
Sore 32 44.20 N 0.35 W
Sorel 206 46.02 N 73.07 W
Sorell 166 42.47 S 147.33 E
Sorell, Cape › 166 42.12 S 145.10 E
Sorel Point › 43b 49.16 N 2.10 W
Sørenberg 58 46.50 N 8.03 E
Sorento 219 39.00 N 89.34 W
Soreq ≃ 132 31.56 N 34.42 E
Soresina 64 45.17 N 9.51 E
Sörfjärden c 40 59.24 N 16.50 E
Sørfjorden c² 26 60.24 N 6.40 E
Sørfold 24 67.28 N 15.22 E
Sörforsa 26 61.40 N 17.00 E
Sorge ≃ 41 54.21 N 9.25 E
Sorgono 71 40.01 N 9.06 E
Sorgues 62 44.00 N 4.52 E
Sorgun 130 39.49 N 35.11 E
Sori 62 44.22 N 9.06 E
Soria 34 41.46 N 2.28 W
Soria □⁴ 34 41.35 N 2.35 W
Soriano 252 33.24 S 58.19 W
Soriano □⁵ 258 33.45 S 57.45 W
Soriano Calabro 68 38.36 N 16.14 E
Soriano nel Cimino 66 42.25 N 12.14 E
Sorico 58 46.10 N 9.22 E
Sorido 164 1.09 S 136.03 E
Sørli-do I 98 34.26 N 127.48 E
Sørli 26 64.15 N 13.45 E
Sormonne ≃ 56 49.46 N 4.40 E
Sorn 46 55.30 N 4.18 W
Sorne ≃ 58 47.22 N 7.22 E
Sorø, Dan. 41 55.26 N 11.34 E
Soro, India 120 21.17 N 86.40 E
Soro, Monte ∧ 70 37.56 N 14.42 E
Sorocaba 255 23.29 S 47.27 W
Sorocabuçu ≃ 256 23.38 S 47.13 W
Soročinka 80 47.30 N 51.44 E
Soročinsk 80 52.26 N 53.10 E
Soročkino 86 57.02 N 68.52 E
Sorocco 240m 18.22 N 65.38 W
Sorok 88 52.20 N 100.12 E
Sorok ≃ 61 47.07 N 16.50 E
Soroka 78 48.09 N 28.17 E
Sorokino, Ross. 86 53.45 N 84.58 E
Sorokino, Ross. 86 54.13 N 91.31 E
Sorokošíči 78 51.12 N 30.35 E
Sorokšár ✦⁸ 264c 47.24 N 19.07 E
Sorol I¹ 108 8.08 N 140.23 E
Soron 124 27.53 N 78.45 E
Sorong 164 0.53 S 131.15 E
Sororó ≃ 250 5.24 S 49.07 W
Sorot' ≃ 76 57.04 N 28.50 E
Soroti 154 1.43 N 33.37 E
Soroyskije 86 59.53 N 71.34 E
Sørøya I 24 70.36 N 22.46 E
Sorpestausee ⊜¹ 56 51.20 N 7.56 E
Sorraia ≃ 34 38.56 N 8.53 W
Sorrento, Austl. 169 38.20 S 144.45 E
Sorrento, It. 68 40.37 N 14.22 E
Sorrento, Fl., U.S. 220 28.48 N 81.33 W
Sorrento, La., U.S. 194 30.11 N 90.51 W
Sorris Sorris 156 20.57 S 14.50 E
Sør Rondane Mountains ∧ 9 72.00 S 25.00 E
Sorsakoski 26 62.27 N 27.39 E
Sorsatunturi ∧ 24 67.24 N 29.38 E
Sorsele 24 65.30 N 17.30 E
Sorsk 86 54.01 N 90.12 E
Sorso 71 40.48 N 8.34 E
Sorsogon 116 12.58 N 124.00 E
Sorsogon □⁴ 116 12.50 N 123.55 E
Sorsogon Bay c 116 12.55 N 123.56 E
Sörstafors 40 59.35 N 16.13 E
Sorsu 85 40.17 N 70.48 E
Sort 34 42.24 N 1.08 E
Sortandy 86 51.42 N 71.00 E
Sortat 46 58.33 N 3.13 W
Sortavala 26 61.42 N 30.41 E
Sortino 70 37.09 N 15.02 E
Sortland 24 68.40 N 15.20 E
Sør-Trøndelag □⁶ 26 63.00 N 10.40 E
Sorunda 40 59.01 N 17.48 E
Sörup 41 54.43 N 9.40 E
Sörve neem › 76 57.54 N 22.03 E
Sörvik 40 60.11 N 15.09 E
Sorviži 80 58.52 N 49.33 E
Sosa, Dtsch. 54 50.30 N 12.39 E
Sosa, Taehan 271b 37.29 N 126.47 E
Šoša ≃ 82 56.31 N 36.05 E
Sosan 98 36.47 N 126.26 E
Sósdala 41 56.02 N 13.40 E
Sos del Rey Católico 34 42.30 N 1.13 W
Sosedka 80 53.10 N 42.36 E
Sosedno 76 58.14 N 28.42 E
Sosenka ≃, Ross. 265b 55.35 N 37.23 E
Sosenka ≃, Ross. 265b 55.47 N 37.42 E
Sosenki 265b 55.34 N 37.26 E
Sosetalsperre ✦⁶ 52 51.44 N 10.20 E
Soshigaya ✦⁸ 268 35.39 N 139.36 E
Sosjöfjällen ∧ 26 63.53 N 13.15 E
Soška 24 62.42 N 50.40 E
Soskovo 76 52.45 N 35.23 E
Sosna ≃ 76 52.45 N 38.55 E
Sosneado, Cerro ∧ 252 34.45 S 69.59 W
Sosnica 78 51.32 N 32.28 E

Sosnicy 76 57.38 N 30.25 E
Sosnogorsk 24 63.37 N 53.51 E
Sosnovaja Maza 80 52.30 N 47.53 E
Sosnovaja Pol'ana ✦⁸ 265a 59.50 N 30.09 E
Sosnovec 24 64.26 N 34.27 E
Sosnovica 76 60.21 N 40.50 E
Sosnovka, Kaz. 86 51.36 N 79.28 E
Sosnovka, Kyrg. 85 42.40 N 73.55 E
Sosnovka, Ross. 24 66.30 N 40.32 E
Sosnovka, Ross. 80 56.13 N 47.13 E
Sosnovka, Ross. 80 52.26 N 43.29 E
Sosnovka, Ross. 80 57.48 N 51.43 E
Sosnovka, Ross. 80 56.17 N 51.17 E
Sosnovka, Ross. 80 53.14 N 41.22 E
Sosnovka, Ross. 80 57.16 N 53.31 E
Sosnovka, Ross. 80 54.06 N 46.38 E
Sosnovka, Ross. 82 54.31 N 38.08 E
Sosnovka, Ross. 82 54.54 N 38.41 E
Sosnovka, Ross. 86 59.10 N 81.18 E
Sosnovka, Ross. 88 54.09 N 109.35 E
Sosnovo, Ross. 76 52.32 N 30.15 E
Sosnovo, Ross. 86 56.42 N 54.35 E
Sosnovoborsk 80 53.18 N 46.16 E
Sosnovoje 78 50.49 N 27.00 E
Sosnovo-Oz'orskoje 88 52.31 N 111.30 E
Sosnovskij 86 54.36 N 73.10 E
Sosnovskoje 80 55.48 N 43.10 E
Sosnovyj Bor, Bela. 76 52.32 N 29.36 E
Sosnovyj Bor, Ross. 76 59.55 N 29.07 E
Sosnovyj Bor, Ross. 86 57.07 N 55.03 E
Sosnovyj Solonec 80 53.17 N 49.33 E
Sosnowiec 30 50.18 N 19.08 E
Soso 194 31.45 N 89.16 W
Sosok 112 0.17 N 110.14 E
Šošolinski 62 43.53 N 7.27 E
Sospirolo 64 46.09 N 12.04 E
Sossusvlei ⊜ 156 24.40 S 15.23 E
Šoštanj 61 46.23 N 15.03 E
Šostka 78 51.52 N 33.30 E
Sosura 98 42.16 N 130.37 E
Sos'va, Ross. 72 63.40 N 62.06 E
Sos'va, Ross. 86 59.10 N 61.50 E
Sos'va ≃ 86 59.32 N 62.20 E
Sosyka ≃ 78 46.35 N 39.05 E
Sot' ≃ 80 58.00 N 40.39 E
Sota ≃ 150 11.52 N 3.24 E
Sotik 154 0.41 S 35.21 E
Sotkamo 26 64.08 N 28.25 E
Sotnicyno 80 54.17 N 41.49 E
Soto de Aldovea 266a 40.26 N 3.27 W
Soto de Pajares 266a 40.17 N 3.32 W
Soto la Marina 234 23.46 N 98.13 W
Soto la Marina ≃ 234 23.45 N 97.45 W
Soto la Marina, Barra I 232 24.10 N 97.43 W
Sotomayor 248 19.18 S 65.03 W
Sotonera, Embalse de ⊜¹ 34 42.05 N 0.48 W
Sotouboua 150 8.34 N 0.59 E
Sotta, Fr. 71 41.32 N 9.12 E
Sotta, Fr. 71 41.32 N 9.12 E
Sottens 58 46.39 N 6.44 E
Sottern ⊜ 40 59.02 N 15.29 E
Sotteville 50 49.25 N 1.06 E
Sottile, Punta › 70a 35.30 N 12.38 E
Sottomarina 64 45.13 N 12.17 E
Sottrum 52 53.06 N 9.14 E
Sottunga I 26 60.08 N 20.40 E
Souain-Perthes-lès-Hurlus 56 49.11 N 4.32 E
Souanké 152 2.05 N 14.03 E
Soubakaniédougou 150 10.28 N 5.01 W
Soubré 150 5.47 N 6.36 W
Soudan 166 20.05 S 137.00 E
Soudan — Sudan □¹ 140 15.00 N 30.00 E
Soude ≃ 50 48.52 N 4.10 E
Soudersburg 208 40.01 N 76.09 W
Souderton 208 40.18 N 75.19 W
Souesmes 50 47.27 N 2.10 E
Soufflay 152 2.01 N 14.54 E
Soufflenheim 56 48.50 N 7.58 E
Soufflot, Lac ⊜ 190 47.24 N 78.31 W
Souflion 38 41.12 N 26.18 E
Soufrière 241f 13.52 N 61.04 W
Soufrière ∧, Guad. 241o 16.03 N 61.40 W
Soufrière ∧, St. Vin. 241h 13.20 N 61.11 W
Soufrière Bay c, Dom. 240d 15.14 N 61.22 W
Soufrière Bay c, St. Luc. 241f 13.51 N 61.04 W
Sougahatchee Creek ≃ 194 32.38 N 85.50 W
Sougne-Remouchamps 56 50.29 N 5.40 E
Souguer 148 35.12 N 1.30 E
Souhegan ≃ 188 42.51 N 71.29 W
Souillac 32 44.54 N 1.29 E
Souilly 56 49.01 N 5.17 E
Souk-el-Arba-des-Beni-Hassan 34 35.16 N 5.20 W
Souk-Khemis-du-Sahel 34 35.17 N 6.05 W
Souk Larbat Gharb 148 34.43 N 6.01 W
Sŏul (Seoul), Taehan 98 37.33 N 126.58 E
Sŏul (Seoul), Taehan 271b 37.33 N 126.58 E
Sŏul □⁴ 98 37.34 N 127.00 E
Soulac-sur-Mer 32 45.31 N 1.07 W
Soulaines-Dhuys 58 48.22 N 4.44 E
Soulanges □⁶ 206 45.20 N 74.15 W
Soulanges, Canal de ≍ 275a 45.20 N 73.58 W
Soulougou 150 13.01 N 0.23 E
Soulsbyville 226 37.59 N 120.16 W
Soultzeren 58 48.04 N 7.06 E
Soultz-Haut-Rhin 58 47.53 N 7.14 E
Soultzmatt 58 47.58 N 7.14 E
Soultz-sous-Forêts 56 48.56 N 7.53 E
Soummam, Oued ≃ 34 36.45 N 5.04 E
Sound Beach 210 40.57 N 72.58 W
Sounding Creek ≃ 184 52.06 N 110.28 W
Sounding Lake ⊜ 184 52.08 N 110.29 W
Sound View Park ♦ 276 40.49 N 73.52 W
Soúnion, Ákra › 38 37.39 N 24.02 E
Soup Harbour c 212 43.51 N 77.11 W
Souppes-sur-Loing 50 48.11 N 2.44 E
Souq Ahras 148 36.23 N 8.00 E
Souris, Man., Can. 184 49.38 N 100.15 W
Souris, P.E., Can. 186 46.21 N 62.15 W
Souris ≃ 198 49.39 N 99.34 W
Sourlake 194 30.09 N 94.25 W
Sourland Mountain ∧² 208 40.29 N 74.43 W
Sourou ≃ 150 12.45 N 3.25 W
Souroukaha 150 8.13 N 5.08 W
Souš 54 50.32 N 13.24 E
Sous, Oued V 148 30.27 N 9.31 W
Sousa 250 6.45 S 38.14 W
Sousânia 255 16.11 S 49.05 W
Sousas 256 22.52 S 46.59 W
Sous-le-Vent, Îles — Leeward Islands II 238 17.00 N 63.00 W
Sousse 148 35.49 N 10.38 E
Sousse □⁸ 148 35.40 N 10.30 E
Sout ≃, S. Afr. 158 31.35 S 18.24 E
Sout ≃, S. Afr. 158 28.56 S 20.42 E
Sout ≃, S. Afr. 158 33.03 S 23.28 E
South ≃, Ia., U.S. 190 41.29 N 93.20 W
South ≃, Ma., U.S. 283 42.10 N 70.43 W
South ≃, Mo., U.S. 219 39.52 N 91.26 W
South ≃, N.J., U.S. 208 40.29 N 74.23 W
South ≃, N.C., U.S. 192 34.20 N 78.03 W
South ≃, Va., U.S. 192 37.46 N 79.23 W
South ≃, Va., U.S. 208 38.02 N 77.23 W

South Acton 207 42.27 N 71.27 W
South Africa (Suid-Afrika) □¹, Afr. 138 30.00 S 26.00 E
South Africa (Suid-Afrika) □¹, Afr. 156 30.00 S 26.00 E
Southall ✦⁸ 260 51.31 N 0.23 W
South Alligator ≃ 164 12.15 S 132.24 E
Southam 42 52.15 N 1.23 W
South Amboy 208 40.28 N 74.17 W
South America ✦¹ 4 15.00 S 60.00 W
South America ✦¹ 18 15.00 S 60.00 W
South Amherst, Ma., U.S. 207 42.20 N 72.30 W
South Amherst, Oh., U.S. 214 41.22 N 82.14 W
Southampton, N.S., Can. 186 45.35 N 64.15 W
Southampton, On., Can. 212 44.29 N 81.23 W
Southampton, Eng., U.K. 42 50.55 N 1.25 W
Southampton, Ma., U.S. 207 42.13 N 72.43 W
Southampton, N.Y., U.S. 207 40.53 N 72.23 W
Southampton, Pa., U.S. 285 40.10 N 75.02 W
Southampton □⁶ 208 36.42 N 77.05 W
Southampton (Eastleigh) Airport ⊠ 42 50.57 N 1.21 W
Southampton, Cape › 176 62.09 N 83.40 W
Southampton Island I 176 64.20 N 84.40 W
South Andaman I 110 11.45 N 92.45 E
South Anna ≃ 192 37.48 N 77.25 W
South Apopka 220 28.39 N 81.31 W
Southard 208 40.08 N 74.14 W
Southards Pond ⊜ 276 40.43 N 73.20 W
South Ashburnham 207 42.36 N 71.56 W
South Aulatsivik Island I 176 56.45 N 61.30 W
South Australia □³ 162 30.00 S 135.00 E
South Australian Basin ✦¹ 14 38.00 S 126.00 E
Southaven 194 34.59 N 90.02 W
South Bald Mountain ∧ 200 40.45 N 105.41 W
South Baldy ∧ 200 33.59 N 107.11 W
South Banda Basin ✦¹ 14 6.30 S 127.30 E
Southbank 182 54.02 N 125.46 W
South Barre 207 42.23 N 72.05 W
South Barrington 278 42.06 N 88.07 W
South Barrule ∧² 44 54.12 N 4.40 W
South Bass Island I 214 41.39 N 82.49 W
South Bay 220 26.39 N 80.42 W
South Bay c, Mb., Can. 184 56.43 N 99.00 W
South Bay c, N.T., Can. 176 63.58 N 83.30 W
South Bay c, On., Can. 190 45.38 N 81.50 W
South Bay c, On., Can. 212 43.55 N 77.03 W
South Bay c, On., Can. 212 44.52 N 79.47 W
South Bay c, Fl., U.S. 220 26.42 N 80.45 W
South Bay c, Va., U.S. 208 37.14 N 75.52 W
South Bay c, Wa., U.S. 224 46.53 N 124.04 W
South Baymouth 190 45.33 N 82.01 W
South Beach ♦ 276 40.35 N 74.05 W
South Beacon Mountain ∧ 210 41.29 N 73.57 W
South Bedias Creek ≃ 222 30.54 N 95.42 W
South Bellingham 207 42.03 N 71.28 W
South Belmar 208 40.10 N 74.02 W
South Beloit 216 42.29 N 89.02 W
South Bend, In., U.S. 216 41.41 N 86.15 W
South Bend, Wa., U.S. 224 46.40 N 123.48 W
South Benfleet 42 51.33 N 0.34 E
South Bentinck Arm c 182 52.15 N 126.50 W
South Bethlehem 214 41.00 N 79.20 W
South Bihar Plains ≍ 124 25.15 N 84.30 E
South Bloomfield 218 39.43 N 82.59 W
Southborough, Eng., U.K. 42 51.10 N 0.15 E
Southborough, Ma., U.S. 207 42.18 N 71.31 W
South Bosque ≃ 222 31.29 N 97.16 W
South Boston 192 36.41 N 78.54 W
South Boston ✦⁸ 283 42.20 N 71.03 W
South Bound Brook 276 40.33 N 74.32 W
South Bradenton 220 27.27 N 82.35 W
South Branch, Nf., Can. 186 47.55 N 59.02 W
South Branch, N.J., U.S. 276 40.33 N 74.42 W
South Brent 42 50.25 N 3.50 W
Southbridge, N.Z. 172 43.49 S 172.15 E
Southbridge, Ma., U.S. 207 42.04 N 72.02 W
South Britain 207 41.28 N 73.15 W
Southbrook, Austl. 171a 27.41 S 151.43 E
Southbrook, N.Z. 172 43.20 S 172.36 E
South Brook ≃ 285 39.52 N 75.44 W
South Brookfield 186 44.23 N 64.58 W
South Brooklyn ✦⁸ 276 40.41 N 73.59 W
South Bruny Island I 166 43.23 S 147.17 E
South Buganda □⁵ 154 0.30 S 31.35 E
South Burlington 188 44.28 N 73.10 W
Southbury 207 41.28 N 73.12 W
South Butler 210 43.08 N 76.46 W
South Byfield 283 42.44 N 70.54 W
South Byron 210 43.03 N 78.04 W
South Cairo 210 42.17 N 73.57 W
South Canaan 210 41.30 N 75.25 W
South Cape › 175g 17.01 S 179.55 E
South Carolina □³, U.S. 178 34.00 N 81.00 W
South Carolina □³, U.S. 192 34.00 N 81.00 W
South Carver 207 41.50 N 70.44 W
South Castor ≃ 212 45.15 N 75.23 W
South Cave 44 53.46 N 0.35 W
South Cerney 42 51.40 N 1.56 W
South Chagrin Reservation ♦ 279a 41.25 N 81.25 W
South Channel ⅹ, Pil. 116 14.20 N 120.37 E
South Channel ⅹ, Mi., U.S. 190 45.38 N 84.32 W
South Channel ≃¹ 281 42.32 N 82.40 W
South Chaplin 207 41.46 N 72.07 W
South Charleston, Oh., U.S. 218 39.49 N 83.38 W
South Charleston, W.V., U.S. 188 38.22 N 81.41 W
South Chatham 207 41.40 N 70.01 W
South Chelmsford 283 42.34 N 71.23 W
South Chicago ✦⁸ 278 41.44 N 87.33 W
South China Basin ✦¹ 12 15.00 N 115.00 E
South China Sea ᵖ² 108 10.00 N 113.00 E
South Cle Elum 224 47.11 N 120.56 W
South Coast Botanic Garden ♦ 280 33.47 N 118.21 W
South Coatesville 208 39.58 N 75.49 W
South Coffeyville 196 36.59 N 95.37 W
South Concho ≃ 196 31.21 N 100.28 W
South Corinth 210 43.12 N 73.51 W
South Corning 210 42.07 N 77.02 W
South Cotabato □⁴ 116 6.15 N 125.00 E
South Creek ≃ 170 33.36 S 150.50 E
South Crest 273d 26.15 S 28.07 E
South Dakota □³, U.S. 178 44.15 N 100.00 W

South Dakota □³, U.S. 198 44.15 N 100.00 W
South Dandalup ≃ 168a 32.35 S 115.53 E
South Dandalup Dam ✦⁶ 168a 32.38 S 116.04 E
South Darenth 260 51.24 N 0.15 E
South Dartmouth 207 41.35 N 70.56 W
South Dayton 210 42.21 N 79.03 W
South Deerfield 207 42.28 N 72.36 W
South Dennis, Ma., U.S. 207 41.41 N 70.09 W
South Dennis, N.J., U.S. 208 39.10 N 74.49 W
South Dorset 210 43.13 N 73.04 W
South Dorset Downs ∧¹ 42 50.40 N 2.25 W
South Dos Palos 226 36.57 N 120.39 W
South Downs ∧¹ 42 50.55 N 0.25 W
South Dum Dum 126 22.37 N 88.25 E
South Duxbury 207 42.01 N 70.41 W
South East □⁵ 156 25.00 S 25.45 E
Southeast Asia Treaty Organization Headquarters ☉ 269a 13.45 N 100.31 E
South East Cape ›, Austl. 166 43.39 S 146.50 E
Southeast Cape ›, Ak., U.S. 180 62.55 N 169.42 W
Southeast Indian Ridge ✦³ 6 50.00 S 110.00 E
South Easton 207 42.02 N 71.04 W
Southeast Pacific Basin ✦¹ 6 60.00 S 115.00 W
South East Point ›, Austl. 166 39.00 S 146.20 E
South East Point ›, Kiribati 174o 1.40 N 157.10 W
South Egg Harbor 208 39.31 N 74.39 W
South Egremont 207 42.09 N 73.25 W
South Elgin 216 41.59 N 88.17 W
South Elkhorn Creek ≃ 218 38.13 N 84.48 W
South El Monte 280 34.03 N 118.02 W
Southend 46 55.20 N 5.38 W
Southend Municipal Airport ⊠ 42 51.34 N 0.41 E
Southend-on-Sea 42 51.33 N 0.43 E
Southend-on-Sea □⁸ 260 51.33 N 0.41 E
Southend Pier ✦⁵ 260 51.31 N 0.44 E
Southern English ≃ 190 41.30 N 91.56 W
Southern □⁴, Malawi 154 15.30 S 35.00 E
Southern □⁴, S.L. 150 8.00 N 12.15 W
Southern □⁴, Zam. 154 16.30 S 27.00 E
Southern □⁵, Bots. 156 24.45 S 24.00 E
Southern □⁵, Ug. 154 0.30 S 30.30 E
Southern Alps ∧ 172 43.30 S 170.30 E
Southern California, University of ☉² 280 34.02 N 118.17 W
Southern Cook Islands II 14 20.00 S 159.00 W
Southern Cross 162 31.13 S 119.19 E
Southern Ghāts ∧ 122 9.30 N 77.00 E
Southern Highlands □⁵ 164 6.00 S 143.30 E
Southern Indian Lake ⊜ 176 57.10 N 98.40 W
Southern Leyte □⁴ 116 10.50 N 124.55 E
Southern Lueti ≃ 152 16.14 S 23.13 E
Southern Pines 192 35.10 N 79.23 W
Southern Ute Indian Reservation ✦⁴ 200 37.05 N 107.45 W
Southern View 219 39.46 N 89.39 W
Southern Yemen — Yemen □¹ 144 15.00 N 47.00 E
Southery 42 52.32 N 0.23 E
South Esk ≃, Austl. 166 41.25 S 147.08 E
South Esk ≃, Scot., U.K. 46 56.42 N 2.32 W
South Esk ≃, Scot., U.K. 46 55.53 N 3.04 W
Southesk Tablelands ∧¹ 162 20.50 S 126.40 E
South Essex 207 42.38 N 70.46 W
South Euclid 214 41.31 N 81.31 W
Southey 184 50.56 N 104.30 W
South Fabius ≃ 219 39.54 N 91.30 W
South Fallsburg 210 41.42 N 74.37 W
South Farmbridge 260 51.38 N 0.41 E
South Farmingdale 276 40.43 N 73.26 W
Southfield, Ma., U.S. 207 42.06 N 73.18 W
Southfield, Mi., U.S. 216 42.28 N 83.13 W
Southfields 210 41.15 N 74.11 W
South Fiji Basin ✦¹ 14 26.00 S 175.00 E
Southfleet 260 51.25 N 0.19 E
South Floral Park 276 40.43 N 73.42 W
South Foreland › 42 51.09 N 1.23 E
South Fork, Co., U.S. 200 37.40 N 106.37 W
South Fork, Pa., U.S. 214 40.22 N 78.47 W
South Fort George 182 53.54 N 122.45 W
South Forty Foot Drain ≍ 42 52.56 N 0.15 W
South Fox Island I 190 45.25 N 85.50 W
South Fulton 194 36.30 N 88.52 W
South Gate, Ca., U.S. 228 33.57 N 118.12 W
Southgate, Fl., U.S. 220 27.18 N 82.32 W
Southgate, Mi., U.S. 216 42.12 N 83.11 W
Southgate, Wa., U.S. 224 47.10 N 122.30 W
Southgate ✦⁸ 260 51.38 N 0.08 W
Southgate U.S.A. ✦⁹ 279a 41.25 N 81.32 W
South Georgia I 244 54.15 S 36.45 W
South Georgia and the South Sandwich Islands □² 244 54.00 S 38.00 W
South Gibson 210 41.44 N 75.38 W
South Glamorgan □⁶ 42 51.30 N 3.25 W
South Glastonbury 207 41.40 N 72.35 W
South Glens Falls 210 43.17 N 73.38 W
South Grafton 207 42.11 N 71.42 W
South Grand ≃ 194 38.18 N 93.28 W
South Grand Island Bridge ✦⁵ 284a 43.00 N 78.56 W
South Green 260 51.37 N 0.26 E
South Greensburg 214 40.17 N 79.33 W
South Hackensack 276 40.51 N 74.02 W
South Hadley, Ma., U.S. 188 42.15 N 72.34 W
South Hadley, Ma., U.S. 207 42.15 N 72.34 W
South Hadley Falls 207 42.13 N 72.36 W
South Hamilton 207 42.36 N 70.52 W
South Hams ≃ 42 50.22 N 3.50 W
South Hanningfield 260 51.39 N 0.31 E
South Hanover 283 42.05 N 70.51 W
South Harbor c 269f 14.33 N 120.58 E
South Harpswell 188 43.43 N 70.01 W
South Hartford 210 43.21 N 73.25 W
South Harwich 207 41.40 N 70.02 W
South Hātia Island I 124 22.19 N 91.07 E
South Haven, In., U.S. 216 41.32 N 87.08 W
South Haven, Ks., U.S. 198 37.03 N 97.24 W
South Haven, Mi., U.S. 216 42.24 N 86.16 W
South Hayling 42 50.47 N 0.59 W
South Head ›, Austl. 274a 33.50 S 151.17 E
South Head ›, N.Z. 172 36.26 S 174.14 E
South Heart ≃ 182 55.34 N 116.11 W
South Heights 279b 40.35 N 80.14 W
South Hempstead 276 40.41 N 73.37 W
South Henderson 192 36.17 N 78.25 W
South Henik Lake ⊜ 176 61.30 N 97.30 W
South Hero 188 44.38 N 73.18 W
South Hetton 44 54.48 N 1.24 W
South Hill, N.Y., U.S. 210 42.25 N 76.33 W
South Hill, Va., U.S. 192 36.43 N 78.07 W
South Hills ✦⁸ 273d 26.15 S 28.05 E
South Hills Village ✦⁹ 279b 40.21 N 80.03 W

South Hingham 207 42.11 N 70.52 W
South Hogan Creek ≃ 218 39.03 N 84.54 W
South Holland 216 41.36 N 87.36 W
South Holston Lake ⊜¹ 192 36.35 N 82.00 W
South Honcut Creek ≃ 226 39.19 N 121.35 W
South Honshu Ridge ✦³ 14 24.00 N 142.00 E
South Hopkinton 207 41.24 N 71.45 W
South Horr 154 2.06 N 36.55 E
South Houston 222 29.39 N 95.14 W
South Huntington 276 40.49 N 73.23 W
South Indian Basin ✦¹ 6 60.00 S 120.00 E
South Indian Lake 184 56.46 N 98.57 W
Southington, Ct., U.S. 207 41.35 N 72.52 W
Southington, Oh., U.S. 214 41.19 N 80.57 W
South International Falls 190 48.35 N 93.23 W
South Ionia 216 42.57 N 85.04 W
South Island I, India 122 10.03 N 72.17 E
South Island I, Kenya 154 2.38 N 36.36 E
South Island I, Micron. 175c 6.59 N 151.59 E
South Island I, N.Z. 172 43.00 S 171.00 E
South Islet I 116 8.44 N 119.49 E
South Jacksonville 219 39.42 N 90.13 W
South Kemptville Creek ≃ 212 44.54 N 75.41 W
South Kenosha 216 42.32 N 87.50 W
South Kent 207 41.40 N 73.28 W
South Kirkby 44 53.34 N 1.20 W
South Konkan Hills ∧² 122 17.00 N 73.30 E
South Korea — Korea, South □¹ 98 36.30 N 128.00 E
South Ladder Creek ≃ 198 38.41 N 101.34 W
South Laguna 228 33.30 N 117.45 W
Southlake 222 32.57 N 97.09 W
South Lake ⊜, On., Can. 212 44.26 N 76.13 W
South Lake ⊜, Fl., U.S. 220 28.37 N 80.52 W
South Lake Tahoe 226 38.56 N 119.58 W
South Lancaster 207 42.26 N 71.41 W
Southland, Ky., U.S. 218 38.01 N 84.31 W
Southland, Mi., U.S. 216 42.13 N 84.24 W
Southland, Tx., U.S. 196 33.22 N 101.33 W
Southland ✦⁹ 282 37.39 N 122.06 W
South Laurel 284c 39.05 N 76.52 W
Southlawn, Il., U.S. 219 39.45 N 89.37 W
Southlawn, Md., U.S. 284c 38.48 N 76.59 W
South Layhill 284c 39.04 N 77.03 W
South Lebanon 218 39.22 N 84.12 W
South Lee 207 42.16 N 73.16 W
South Lima 210 42.51 N 77.41 W
South Line Island I 276 40.37 N 73.30 W
South Llano ≃ 196 30.30 N 99.46 W
South Lockport 284a 43.09 N 78.42 W
South Lorain 279a 41.27 N 82.08 W
South Loup ≃ 198 41.04 N 98.40 W
South Luangwa National Park ♦ 154 12.50 S 31.45 E
South Luconia Shoals ✦² 112 5.00 N 112.42 E
South Lynnfield 283 42.31 N 71.00 W
South Lyon 216 42.27 N 83.39 W
South Macmillan ≃ 180 63.03 N 133.18 W
South Magnetic Pole ✦ 9 65.18 S 139.30 E
South Malosmadulu Atoll I¹ 122 5.10 N 72.58 E
South Manitou Island I 190 45.01 N 86.07 W
South Marsh Island I 208 38.06 N 76.02 W
South Medford 202 42.18 N 122.50 W
South Media 285 39.54 N 75.23 W
South Melbourne 274b 37.50 S 144.57 E
South Merrimack 207 42.48 N 71.33 W
South Miami 220 25.42 N 80.17 W
South Miami Heights 220 25.35 N 80.22 W
South Middleboro 207 41.49 N 70.49 W
South Milford 216 41.31 N 85.16 W
South Mills 192 36.26 N 76.19 W
South Milwaukee 216 42.54 N 87.51 W
South Mimms 260 51.42 N 0.14 W
Southminster 42 51.40 N 0.50 E
South Modesto 226 37.38 N 120.58 W
South Mokelumne ≃ 226 38.08 N 121.35 W
South Molton 42 51.01 N 3.50 W
South Monroe 216 41.54 N 83.25 W
Southmont 214 40.18 N 78.56 W
South Montrose 210 41.48 N 75.53 W
South Moose Lake ⊜ 184 53.46 N 100.08 W
South Mountain 208 39.51 N 77.29 W
South Mountain ∧, U.S. 208 39.40 N 77.30 W
South Mountain ∧, Id., U.S. 202 42.44 N 116.54 W
South Mountain Reservation ♦ 276 40.45 N 74.18 W
South Mount Vernon 214 40.23 N 82.23 W
South Nahanni ≃ 176 61.03 N 123.20 W
South Naknek 180 58.43 N 157.00 W
South Nation ≃ 188 45.34 N 75.06 W
South Negril Point › 241q 18.15 N 78.22 W
South New Berlin 210 42.31 N 75.23 W
South New Castle 214 40.58 N 80.21 W
South New River Canal ≍ 220 26.04 N 80.12 W
South Norfolk — Chesapeake 208 36.43 N 76.15 W
South Normanton 44 53.06 N 1.20 W
South Norwalk Reservoir ⊜¹ 276 41.11 N 73.27 W
South Norwood ✦⁸ 260 51.24 N 0.04 W
South Nutfield 260 51.14 N 0.08 W
South Nyack 276 41.04 N 73.55 W
South Ockendon 260 51.32 N 0.18 E
South Ogden 200 41.11 N 111.58 W
Southold 207 41.03 N 72.25 W
South Onondaga 210 42.56 N 76.13 W
South Orange 276 40.47 N 74.15 W
South Orkney Islands II 9 60.35 S 45.30 W
South Oroville 226 39.30 N 121.33 W
South Ossetia — Yugo Osetija □⁹ 84 42.20 N 44.00 E
South Otselic 210 42.38 N 75.46 W
Southowram 262 53.43 N 1.50 W
South Oxhey 260 51.38 N 0.23 W
South Oyster Bay c 276 40.38 N 73.28 W
South Palo Duro Creek ≃ 196 36.06 N 101.29 W
South Para ≃ 168b 34.36 S 138.45 E
South Para Reservoir ⊜¹ 168b 34.42 S 138.52 E
South Paris 188 44.13 N 70.30 W
South Park 216 41.44 N 88.17 W
South Park ♦, N.Y., U.S. 284a 42.50 N 78.50 W
South Park ♦, Pa., U.S. 279b 40.19 N 80.01 W
South Pasadena, Ca., U.S. 280 34.06 N 118.08 W
South Pasadena, Fl., U.S. 220 27.46 N 82.43 W
South Pass ⅹ 200 42.22 N 108.55 W
South Pass ⅹ 175c 7.14 N 151.52 E
South Passage ⅹ, Austl. 171a 27.22 S 153.26 E
South Passage ⅹ, Oh., U.S. 214 41.35 N 82.45 W
South Patrick Shores 220 28.12 N 80.35 W
South Pekin 190 40.29 N 89.39 W
South Pender 224 48.45 N 123.14 W

Symbols in the index entries represent the broad categories identified in the key at the right. Symbols with superior numbers (∧¹) identify subcategories (see complete key on page I · 1).

Symbole im Register stellen die rechts im Schlüssel erklärten Kategorien dar. Symbole mit hochgestellten Ziffern (∧¹) bezeichnen Unterabteilungen einer Kategorie (vgl. vollständiger Schlüssel auf Seite I · 1).

Los símbolos incluídos en el texto del índice representan las grandes categorias identificadas con la clave a la derecha. Los símbolos con numeros en su parte superior (∧¹) identifican las subcategorias (véase la clave completa en la página I · 1).

Les symboles de l'index représentent les catégories indiquées dans la légende à droite. Les symboles suivis d'un indice (∧¹) représentent des sous-catégories (voir légende complète à la page I · 1).

Os símbolos incluídos no texto do índice representam as grandes categorias identificadas com a chave à direita. Os símbolos com números em sua parte superior (∧¹) identificam as subcategorias (veja-se a chave completa à página I · 1).

Symbol	ENGLISH	DEUTSCH			
∧	Mountain	Berg	Montaña	Montagne	Montanha
∧	Mountains	Gebirge	Montañas	Montagnes	Montanhas
ⅹ	Pass	Paß	Paso	Col	Passo
V	Valley, Canyon	Tal, Cañon	Valle, Cañón	Vallée, Canyon	Vale, Canhão
≍	Plain	Ebene	Llano	Plaine	Planície
›	Cape	Kap	Cabo	Cap	Cabo
I	Island	Insel	Isla	Île	Ilha
II	Islands	Inseln	Islas	Îles	Ilhas
✦	Other Topographic Features	Andere Topographische Objekte	Otros Elementos Topográficos	Autres données topographiques	Outros acidentes topográficos

ESPAÑOL — Nombre / Página / Lat.°′ / Long.°′ W = Oeste
FRANÇAIS — Nom / Page / Lat.°′ / Long.°′ W = Ouest
PORTUGUÊS — Nome / Página / Lat.°′ / Long.°′ W = Oeste

South Pender Island I 224 48.45 N 123.10 W
South Perth 168a 31.59 S 115.52 E
South Petherton 42 50.58 N 2.49 W
South Philadelphia ◆8 285 39.56 N 75.10 W
South Philipsburg 214 40.53 N 78.13 W
South Pittsburg 194 35.00 N 85.42 W
South Plainfield 210 40.34 N 74.24 W
South Platte ≃ 178 41.07 N 100.42 W
South Platte, North Fork ≃ 200 39.25 N 105.10 W
South Point >, Barb. 241g 13.02 N 59.31 W
South Point >, Pil. 116 10.24 N 122.30 E
South Pole ◆ 9 90.00 S 0.00
South Porcupine 190 48.28 N 81.13 W
Southport, Austl. 166 43.25 S 146.59 E
Southport, Austl. 171a 27.58 S 153.25 E
Southport, Eng., U.K. 44 53.39 N 3.01 W
Southport, Ct., U.S. 207 41.08 N 73.17 W
Southport, Fl., U.S. 194 30.17 N 85.38 W
Southport, In., U.S. 218 39.39 N 86.07 W
Southport, N.Y., U.S. 210 42.03 N 76.49 W
Southport, N.C., U.S. 192 33.55 N 78.01 W
South Portland 188 43.38 N 70.14 W
South Portsmouth 218 38.43 N 83.00 W
South Pottstown 208 40.14 N 75.39 W
South Prairie Creek ≃ 224 47.08 N 122.10 W
South Raisin ≃ 206 45.08 N 74.35 W
South Range 190 47.04 N 88.38 W
South Renovo 214 41.19 N 77.44 W
South Reservoir ◎1 283 42.27 N 71.07 W
South Ribble □8 262 53.45 N 2.42 W
South River, On., Can. 190 45.50 N 79.23 W
South River, N.J., U.S. 208 40.26 N 74.23 W
South River ᴄ 208 38.57 N 76.29 W
South Rockwood 216 42.04 N 83.16 W
South Ronaldsay I 46 58.46 N 2.58 W
South Roxana 219 38.50 N 90.04 W
South Royalston 207 42.37 N 72.08 W
South Rukuru ≃ 154 10.46 S 34.14 E
South Russell 214 41.25 N 81.21 W
South Salmara 124 25.55 N 90.01 E
South Sand Bluff > 158 31.19 S 30.01 E
South Sandwich Islands II 18 57.45 S 26.30 W
South Sandwich Trench ✦1 18 56.30 S 25.00 W
South Sandy Creek ≃ 212 43.43 N 76.12 W
South San Francisco 226 37.39 N 122.24 W
South San Gabriel 280 34.03 N 118.05 W
South San Jose Hills 280 34.01 N 117.55 W
South San Ramon Creek ≃ 282 37.42 N 121.55 W
South Santiam ≃ 202 44.41 N 123.00 W
South Saskatchewan ≃ 184 53.15 N 105.05 W
South Saugeen ≃ 212 44.08 N 81.02 W
South Seaville 208 39.10 N 74.45 W
South Setauket 210 40.54 N 73.06 W
South Shafter 226 35.28 N 119.17 W
South Shetland Islands II 9 62.00 S 58.00 W
South Shields 44 55.00 N 1.25 W
South Shore 218 38.43 N 82.59 W
South Shore ◆8 278 41.46 N 87.35 W
South Shore Mall ◆9 276 40.44 N 73.15 W
South Shore Plaza ◆9 283 42.13 N 71.01 W
Southside 174h 2.49 S 171.43 W
South Side ◆8 279b 40.26 N 79.58 W
Southside Place 222 29.42 N 95.26 W
South Sioux City 198 42.28 N 96.24 W
South Skunk ≃ 190 41.15 N 92.02 W
South Slocan 182 49.28 N 117.32 W
South Solon 218 39.44 N 83.36 W
South Sound ʮ 48 53.02 N 9.28 W
South Spicer Island I 176 68.06 N 79.13 W
South Standard 219 39.21 N 89.47 W
South Station ◆5 283 42.21 N 71.04 W
South Sterling 210 41.17 N 75.21 W
South Stony Brook 276 40.53 N 73.07 W
South Stradbroke Island I 171a 27.51 S 153.25 E
South Streator 216 40.39 N 88.23 W
South Suburban → Behāla 126 22.31 N 88.19 E
South Sulphur ≃ 196 33.23 N 95.18 W
South Sunday Creek ≃ 202 46.27 N 105.54 W
South Superior 200 41.45 N 108.57 W
South Swansea 207 41.43 N 71.12 W
South Taranaki Bight ᴄ3 172 39.40 S 174.10 E
South Tasman Rise ✦3 6 49.00 S 148.00 E
South Temple 208 40.24 N 75.55 W
South Thompson ≃ 182 50.41 N 120.21 W
South Toms River 208 39.56 N 74.12 W
South Torrington 198 42.02 N 104.10 W
South Towanda 210 41.45 N 76.27 W
South Tucson 200 32.11 N 110.58 W
South Turkeyfoot Creek ≃ 216 41.25 N 83.58 W
South Turlock 226 37.29 N 120.51 W
South Twillingate Island I 186 49.37 N 54.47 W
South Tyne ≃ 44 54.59 N 2.08 W
South Ubian 116 5.11 N 120.30 E
South Uist I 46 57.15 N 7.21 W
South Umpqua ≃ 202 43.20 N 123.25 W
South Valley 210 42.42 N 74.43 W
South Valley Hills ⋏2 285 40.00 N 75.40 W
South Valley Stream 276 40.38 N 73.44 W
South Venice 220 27.03 N 82.25 W
South Ventana Cone ∧ 204 36.17 N 121.38 W
South Vestal 210 42.01 N 76.00 W
South Vietnam → Vietnam □1 108 16.00 N 108.00 E
Southview 214 40.20 N 80.16 W
Southview Apartments 284c 38.50 N 77.00 W
South Wabasca Lake ◎ 182 55.54 N 113.45 W
South Wales 210 42.43 N 78.35 W
South Walpole 283 42.06 N 71.15 W
Southwark ◆8 260 51.30 N 0.06 W
South Warren Reservoir ◎1 168b 34.43 S 138.55 E
Southwater 42 51.01 N 0.21 W
South Waverly 210 41.59 N 76.32 W
South Weald 260 51.37 N 0.16 E
Southwell 44 53.05 N 0.58 W
South Wellfleet 207 41.55 N 69.59 W
South Wellington 224 49.06 N 123.53 W
Southwest 214 40.12 N 79.32 W
South West Bay ᴄ 240b 25.00 N 77.32 W
Southwest Branch ≃ 284c 38.53 N 76.48 W
South Westbury 276 40.45 N 73.35 W
South West Cape >, Austl. 166 43.34 S 146.02 E
South West Cape >, N.Z. 172 47.17 S 167.28 E
Southwest Cape >, Ak., U.S. 180 63.18 N 171.27 W
Southwest Cape >, Vir. Is., U.S. 241n 17.41 N 64.54 W
Southwest Channel ʮ 220 27.34 N 82.45 W
South West City 194 36.30 N 94.36 W
South Westerlo 210 42.27 N 74.02 W
Southwest Greensburg 214 40.17 N 79.33 W
Southwest Harbor 188 44.16 N 68.19 W
Southwest Indian Ridge ✦3 6 30.00 S 60.00 E
Southwest Miramichi ≃ 186 46.58 N 65.35 W
Southwest Museum ʊ 280 34.06 N 118.13 W
Southwest National Park ♠ 166 43.15 S 146.15 E
Southwest Pacific Basin ✦1 6 40.00 S 150.00 W
Southwest Point >, Ba. 238 25.51 N 77.13 W
South West Point >, Kiribati 174o 1.52 N 157.33 W
Southwest Point >, Pap. N. Gui. 164 2.14 S 146.34 E
South Weymouth 283 42.10 N 70.57 W
South Weymouth Naval Air Station ■ 207 42.09 N 70.57 W
South Whitley 216 41.05 N 85.37 W
South Whittier 280 33.57 N 118.02 W
South Wichita ≃ 196 33.43 N 99.29 W
Southwick, Eng., U.K. 42 50.50 N 0.13 W
Southwick, Ma., U.S. 207 42.03 N 72.46 W
South Williamson 192 37.40 N 82.17 W
South Williamsport 210 41.13 N 76.59 W
South Wilmington 216 41.10 N 88.16 W
South Windham 188 43.44 N 70.25 W
South Windsor 207 41.49 N 72.37 W
Southwold 42 52.20 N 1.40 E
Southwood 210 42.59 N 76.08 W
Southwood Acres 207 41.59 N 72.32 W
South Woodham Ferrers 42 51.39 N 0.37 E
South Woodslee 214 42.14 N 82.43 W
South Woodstock 207 41.56 N 71.57 W
Southworth 224 47.31 N 122.30 W
South Yadkin ≃ 192 35.45 N 80.27 W
South Yamhill ≃ 224 45.13 N 123.08 W
South Yarmouth 207 41.40 N 70.11 W
South Yarra 274b 37.51 S 145.00 E
South Yorkshire □6 44 53.30 N 1.15 W
South Yuba ≃ 226 39.17 N 121.12 W
South Zeal 42 50.44 N 3.54 W
Soutpan 158 28.43 S 26.04 E
Soutpansberg ⋏ 156 22.55 S 29.30 E
Souttouf, Adrar ⋏ 148 22.15 N 15.40 W
Souvigny 32 46.32 N 3.11 E
Souzy-la-Briche 261 48.32 N 2.09 E
Sovata 38 46.35 N 25.04 E
Soverato 68 38.41 N 16.33 E
Sovere 64 45.49 N 10.01 E
Sovereign Hill Historical Park ⊥ 169 37.37 S 143.51 E
Sovereign Mountain ∧ 180 62.08 N 148.36 W
Soveria Mannelli 68 39.05 N 16.22 E
Sövestad 41 55.30 N 13.47 E
Sovetašen 84 40.06 N 44.33 E
Sovetka 83 47.30 N 39.15 E
Sovetsk, Ross. 76 55.05 N 21.53 E
Sovetsk, Ross. 76 53.56 N 37.39 E
Sovetsk, Ross. 80 57.37 N 48.58 E
Sovetskaja, Ross. 80 49.00 N 42.07 E
Sovetskaja, Ross. 84 44.46 N 41.11 E
Sovetskaja, Ross. 84 44.02 N 44.03 E
Sovetskaja Gavan' 89 48.58 N 140.18 E
Sovetskich Oficerov, pik ∧ 85 38.26 N 73.18 E
Sovetskij, Ross. 76 60.32 N 28.41 E
Sovetskij, Ross. 80 56.46 N 48.32 E
Sovetskij, Ross. 86 51.04 N 56.29 E
Sovetskij, Taj. 85 40.11 N 71.19 E
Sovetskij, Taj. 85 38.02 N 69.35 E
Sovetskij, Ukr. 78 45.20 N 34.56 E
Sovetskoje, Kaz. 85 42.17 N 70.15 E
Sovetskoje, Ross. 78 50.21 N 39.01 E
Sovetskoje, Ross. 80 51.27 N 46.44 E
Sovetskoje, Ross. 84 42.52 N 45.41 E
Şovetskoje, Ross. 84 43.19 N 43.36 E
Šovgenovskij 78 45.02 N 40.14 E
Sovicille 66 43.17 N 11.13 E
Sovico 266b 45.39 N 9.16 E
Søvik 26 62.33 N 6.18 E
Søvind 41 55.54 N 10.01 E
Sovpolje 24 65.18 N 43.55 E
Sow ≃ 42 52.48 N 2.00 W
Sowa Pan ≚ 156 20.45 S 26.00 E
Sowek 164 0.49 S 135.30 E
Sowerby, Eng., U.K. 44 54.13 N 1.21 W
Sowerby, Eng., U.K. 262 53.42 N 1.56 W
Sowerby Bridge 44 53.43 N 1.54 W
Soweto 158 26.14 S 27.54 E
Sowjetisches Ehrenmal ⊥ 264a 52.29 N 13.28 E
Soy 56 50.17 N 5.31 E
Sōya-kaikyō → La Perouse Strait ʮ 89 45.45 N 142.00 E
Sōya-misaki > 92a 45.31 N 141.56 E
Soyang-chŏsuji ◎1 98 37.56 N 127.53 E
Soyapango 236 13.42 N 89.09 W
Soyers Lake ◎ 212 45.02 N 78.37 W
Soyet 124 24.12 N 76.10 E
Soyland Moor ◆3 262 53.40 N 2.02 W
Soyo 152 6.07 S 12.18 E
Soyons 62 44.53 N 4.51 E
Sož ≃, Europe 78 51.57 N 30.48 E
Soz' ≃, Ross. 82 56.48 N 36.44 E
Şozimskij 24 59.44 N 52.16 E
Šožma 24 61.56 N 40.15 E
Sozopol 38 42.25 N 27.42 E
Sozzago 266b 45.24 N 8.43 E
Spa 56 50.30 N 5.52 E
Spaatz Island I 9 73.12 S 75.00 W
Space Needle ʊ 224 47.38 N 122.23 W
Space Obelisk ⊥ 265b 55.49 N 37.38 E
Spadafora 70 38.13 N 15.22 E
Spada Lake ◎1 224 47.57 N 121.40 W
Spaden 52 53.34 N 8.38 E
Spahl 56 50.39 N 9.55 E
Spaichingen 58 48.04 N 8.44 E
Spain (España) □1, Europe 22 40.00 N 4.00 W
Spain (España) □1, Europe 34 40.00 N 4.00 W
Spakenburg 52 52.15 N 5.23 E
Spalato → Split 36 43.31 N 16.27 E
Spalding, Austl. 166 33.30 S 138.37 E
Spalding, Sk., Can. 184 52.20 N 104.30 W
Spalding, Eng., U.K. 42 52.47 N 0.10 W
Spalding, Mo., U.S. 219 39.38 N 91.32 W
Spalding, Ne., U.S. 198 41.41 N 98.21 W
Spalt 56 49.10 N 10.55 E
Spam Island I 174h 2.48 S 171.43 W
Spanaway 224 47.06 N 122.26 W
Spandau ◆8 54 52.33 N 13.12 E
Spandau, Berliner Forst ◆3 264a 52.35 N 13.11 E
Spandau, Berliner Forst ♠ 264a 52.35 N 13.10 E
Spang 41 54.56 N 9.50 E
Spangenberg 56 51.07 N 9.40 E
Spangler 214 40.38 N 78.46 W
Spaniard's Bay 186 47.37 N 53.17 W
Spanien → Spain □1 34 40.00 N 4.00 W
Spanish 190 46.12 N 82.21 W
Spanish ≃ 190 46.11 N 82.19 W
Spanish Camp 222 29.23 N 96.10 W
Spanish Fork 200 40.06 N 111.39 W
Spanish Lake 219 38.47 N 90.12 W
Spanish North Africa □2, Afr. 34 35.53 N 5.19 W
Spanish North Africa □2, Afr. 134 35.53 N 5.19 W
Spanish Peak ∧ 202 44.24 N 119.46 W
Spanish Point > 240a 32.18 N 64.48 W
Spanish Sahara → Western Sahara □2 134 24.30 N 13.00 W
Spanish Town, Br. Vir. Is. 240m 18.27 N 64.26 W
Spanish Town, Jam. 241q 17.59 N 76.57 W
Spannberg 61 48.27 N 16.44 E
Sparagio, Monte ∧ 70 38.03 N 12.46 E
Sparbach 264b 48.04 N 16.11 E
Spargi, Isola I 71 41.14 N 9.21 E
Sparkford 42 51.02 N 2.34 W
Sparkill 276 41.02 N 73.56 W
Sparkle Lake 210 41.18 N 73.47 W
Sparkman 194 33.55 N 92.50 W
Sparks, Ga., U.S. 192 31.10 N 83.26 W
Sparks, Nv., U.S. 226 39.32 N 119.45 W
Sparland 190 41.02 N 89.26 W
Sparlingville 214 42.58 N 82.30 W
Sparneck 54 50.09 N 11.50 E
Sparreholm 40 59.04 N 16.49 E
Sparrow Bush 210 41.23 N 74.43 W
Sparrow Lake ◎ 212 44.49 N 79.24 W
Sparrowpit 262 53.19 N 1.52 W
Sparrows Point 208 39.13 N 76.28 W
Sparrows Point > 284b 39.12 N 76.30 W
Sparta, On., Can. 212 42.42 N 81.05 W
Sparta, Ga., U.S. 192 33.16 N 82.58 W
Sparta, Il., U.S. 194 38.07 N 89.42 W
Sparta, Ky., U.S. 218 38.40 N 84.54 W
Sparta, Mi., U.S. 190 43.09 N 85.42 W
Sparta, N.J., U.S. 210 41.02 N 74.38 W
Sparta, N.C., U.S. 192 36.30 N 81.07 W
Sparta, Oh., U.S. 214 40.24 N 82.42 W
Sparta, Tn., U.S. 194 35.55 N 85.27 W
Sparta, Wi., U.S. 190 43.56 N 90.48 W
Sparta Brook ≃ 276 41.08 N 73.52 W
Spartak Garden ♠ 265a 59.51 N 30.30 E
Sparta Lake 210 41.03 N 74.34 W
Spartanburg, In., U.S. 218 40.03 N 84.51 W
Spartanburg, S.C., U.S. 192 34.56 N 81.55 W
Spartansburg 214 41.49 N 79.41 W
Sparta → Spárti 38 37.05 N 22.27 E
Spartel, Cap > 34 35.48 N 5.56 W
Spárti (Sparta) 38 37.05 N 22.27 E
Spartivento, Capo >, It. 68 37.55 N 16.04 E
Spartivento, Capo >, It. 71 38.53 N 8.50 E
Spas-Demensk 76 54.25 N 34.01 E
Spas-Klepiki 80 55.08 N 40.13 E
Spass 82 55.55 N 35.55 E
Spassk-Dal'nij 89 44.37 N 132.48 E
Spasskij 86 53.42 N 59.12 E
Spasskij Zavod 86 49.32 N 73.17 E
Spasskoje, Ross. 76 53.06 N 36.24 E
Spasskoje, Ross. 80 55.52 N 45.42 E
Spasskoje, Ross. 82 54.05 N 38.28 E
Spassk-R'azanskij 80 54.24 N 40.23 E
Spas-Zaulok 82 56.29 N 36.34 E
Spáta 267c 38.00 N 21.31 E
Spátha, Ákra > 38 35.42 N 23.44 E
Spaulding 219 39.52 N 89.32 W
Spaulding, Lake ◎1 226 39.20 N 120.37 W
Speaks 222 29.15 N 96.42 W
Spean, Glen V 46 56.53 N 4.45 W
Spean Bridge 46 56.53 N 4.54 W
Spear, Cape > 186 47.32 N 52.32 W
Spearfish 198 44.29 N 103.51 W
Spearman 196 36.11 N 101.11 W
Spearsville 218 39.21 N 86.11 W
Spearville 198 37.51 N 99.45 W
Spearwood 168a 32.07 S 115.47 E
Speas Artemidos (Rock Tombs) ⊥ 142 27.54 N 30.52 E
Specchia 68 39.57 N 18.18 E
Spechtsbrunn 54 50.30 N 11.14 E
Spectacle Island I 283 42.19 N 70.59 W
Spectrum ♠ 285 39.54 N 75.10 W
Spectrum Range ⋏ 180 57.30 N 130.40 W
Spednic Lake ◎ 186 45.36 N 67.35 W
Speed 218 38.24 N 85.45 W
Speed ≃ 212 43.23 N 80.22 W
Speedway 218 39.48 N 86.16 W
Speicher 58 47.24 N 9.27 E
Speichersee ◎ 60 48.13 N 11.45 E
Speightstown 241g 13.15 N 59.39 W
Speigletown 210 42.48 N 73.38 W
Speikkogel ∧ 61 47.14 N 15.03 E
Speinshart 60 49.47 N 11.49 E
Speising ◆8 264b 48.10 N 16.17 E
Speke ◆8 262 53.21 N 2.51 W
Speke Gulf ᴄ 154 2.20 S 33.15 E
Speke Hall ⊥ 262 53.20 N 2.52 W
Speldorf ◆8 263 51.25 N 6.52 E
Spellen 263 51.37 N 6.37 E
Spello 66 42.59 N 12.40 E
Spelthorne □8 260 51.25 N 0.28 W
Spelve, Loch ᴄ 46 56.22 N 5.46 W
Spenard 180 61.11 N 149.55 W
Spence Bay 176 69.32 N 93.31 W
Spencer, In., U.S. 194 39.17 N 86.45 W
Spencer, Ia., U.S. 198 43.08 N 95.08 W
Spencer, Ma., U.S. 207 42.14 N 71.59 W
Spencer, Ne., U.S. 198 42.52 N 98.42 W
Spencer, N.Y., U.S. 210 42.12 N 76.29 W
Spencer, N.C., U.S. 192 35.41 N 80.26 W
Spencer, Oh., U.S. 214 41.06 N 82.07 W
Spencer, S.D., U.S. 198 43.43 N 97.35 W
Spencer, Tn., U.S. 194 35.44 N 85.28 W
Spencer, W.V., U.S. 188 38.48 N 81.21 W
Spencer, Wi., U.S. 190 44.45 N 90.17 W
Spencer, Cape >, Austl. 166 35.18 S 136.53 E
Spencer, Cape >, N.B., Can. 186 45.12 N 65.55 W
Spencer, Cape >, Ak., U.S. 180 58.14 N 136.40 W
Spencer, Mount ∧ 224 49.03 N 124.38 W
Spencer, Point > 180 65.18 N 166.50 W
Spencer Brook ≃ 283 42.28 N 71.22 W
Spencer Creek ≃, On., Can. 212 43.17 N 79.54 W
Spencer Creek ≃, Mo., U.S. 219 39.33 N 91.20 W
Spencer Field ⊠ 281 42.31 N 83.33 W
Spencer Gulf ᴄ 166 34.00 S 137.00 E
Spencer Lake ◎ 224 47.16 N 122.57 W
Spencerport 210 43.11 N 77.48 W
Spencertown 210 42.20 N 73.33 W
Spencerville, On., Can. 212 44.51 N 75.33 W
Spencerville, In., U.S. 216 41.16 N 84.55 W
Spencerville, Md., U.S. 208 39.06 N 76.58 W
Spencerville, Oh., U.S. 216 40.42 N 84.21 W
Spences Bridge 182 50.25 N 121.21 W
Spenge 52 52.08 N 8.28 E
Spennymoor 44 54.42 N 1.35 W
Spenser Mountains ⋏ 172 42.15 S 172.30 E
Sperenberg 54 52.08 N 13.22 E
Sperillen ◎ 26 60.28 N 10.03 E
Sperling 224 49.08 N 122.33 W
Sperlinga 70 37.46 N 14.21 E
Sperlonga 66 41.15 N 13.26 E
Spermaceti Cove ᴄ 276 40.26 N 73.59 W
Sperone, Capo > 71 38.57 N 8.25 E
Sperrin Mountains ⋏ 48 54.50 N 7.05 W
Sperry Creek ≃ 279a 41.29 N 81.53 W
Sperry Rand Corporation ʊ3 276 40.45 N 73.42 W
Sperryville 188 38.39 N 78.13 W
Spessart ◆1 56 50.10 N 9.20 E
Spesutie Island I 208 39.27 N 76.05 W
Spétsai I 38 37.16 N 23.08 E
Spevakovka 83 49.03 N 38.54 E
Spexard 52 51.52 N 8.24 E
Spey ≃ 46 57.40 N 3.06 W
Spey Bay ᴄ 46 57.41 N 3.00 W
Speyer 56 49.19 N 8.26 E
Speyerbach ≃ 56 49.19 N 8.27 E
Speyside 241r 11.18 N 60.32 W
Spezia → La Spezia 62 44.07 N 9.50 E
Spezzano Albanese 68 39.40 N 16.19 E
Spezzano della Sila 68 39.18 N 16.20 E
Sphinx → Abū al-Hawl ⊥ 142 29.59 N 31.08 E
Spiazzo 64 46.07 N 10.40 E
Spiceland 218 39.50 N 85.26 W
Spicer 198 45.13 N 94.56 W
Spicer Creek ≃ 284a 43.02 N 78.53 W
Spicer Meadow Reservoir ◎1 226 38.23 N 119.59 W
Spicheren 56 49.12 N 6.58 E
Spickard 194 40.14 N 93.35 W
Spicket ≃ 283 42.42 N 71.09 W
Spieka 52 53.45 N 8.35 E
Spiekeroog I 52 53.46 N 7.42 E
Spiess Seamount ✦3 8 54.40 S 0.15 E
Spiez 58 46.41 N 7.39 E
Şpijkenisse 52 51.21 N 4.20 E
Špikov 78 48.46 N 28.35 E
Spilamberto 64 44.32 N 11.01 E
Spilimbergo 64 46.07 N 12.54 E
Spilinga 68 38.37 N 15.54 E
Spillersboda 40 59.42 N 18.51 E
Spillimacheen ≃ 182 50.55 N 116.20 W
Spillville 190 43.12 N 91.57 W
Spilsby 44 53.11 N 0.06 E
Spinazzola 68 40.58 N 16.06 E
Spīn Būldak 120 31.01 N 66.24 E
Spincourt 56 49.20 N 5.40 E
Spindale 192 35.21 N 81.55 W
Spindoli 66 43.12 N 12.54 E
Spinea-Orgnano 64 45.29 N 12.10 E
Spinetta Marengo 62 44.53 N 8.41 E
Spinnerstown 208 40.26 N 75.26 W
Spinoso 68 40.16 N 15.58 E
Spires → Speyer 56 49.19 N 8.26 E
Spirit Lake, Id., U.S. 202 47.57 N 116.52 W
Spirit Lake, Ia., U.S. 198 43.25 N 95.06 W
Spirit Lake ◎ 224 46.16 N 122.08 W
Spirit River 182 55.47 N 118.50 W
Spiritwood 184 53.22 N 107.31 W
Spiro 194 35.14 N 94.37 W
Spirovo 76 57.26 N 34.59 E
Spišská Nová Ves 30 48.57 N 20.34 E
Spitak 84 40.51 N 44.16 E
Spital am Pyhrn 61 47.39 N 14.20 E
Spithead ʮ 42 50.45 N 1.05 W
Spit Point > 162 20.02 S 119.00 E
Spitsbergen I 12 78.45 N 16.00 E
Spitsbergen Bank ✦4 12 76.00 N 23.00 E
Spittal an der Drau 64 46.48 N 13.30 E
Spittal of Glenshee 46 56.48 N 3.28 W
Spitz 61 48.22 N 15.25 E
Spitzbergen und Jan Mayen → Svalbard □2 12 78.00 N 20.00 E
Spitzer Berg ∧2 264a 52.38 N 13.35 E
Spixworth 42 52.40 N 1.20 E
Spjelkavik 26 62.28 N 6.23 E
Splavnucha 80 51.05 N 45.22 E
Splendora 222 30.14 N 95.10 W
Split 36 43.31 N 16.27 E
Split, Cape > 186 45.20 N 64.30 W
Split Lake ◎ 184 56.08 N 96.15 W
Splitrock Reservoir ◎1 276 40.58 N 74.27 W
Spluga, Passo della (Splügenpass))(58 46.30 N 9.20 E
Splügen 58 46.33 N 9.20 E
Splügenpass (Passo della Spluga))(58 46.30 N 9.20 E
Spodsbjerg 41 54.56 N 10.50 E
Şpofford 196 29.11 N 100.25 W
Špogi 76 56.05 N 26.44 E
Spokane 202 47.39 N 117.25 W
Spokane ≃ 202 47.54 N 118.20 W
Spokane, Mount ∧ 202 47.55 N 117.07 W
Spokane Indian Reservation ◆4 202 47.55 N 118.00 W
Şpokojnaja 84 44.15 N 41.25 E
Špola 78 49.01 N 31.24 E
Spoleto 66 42.44 N 12.44 E
Spoltore 66 42.27 N 14.08 E
Spondigna 64 46.38 N 10.37 E
Spondon 42 52.54 N 1.25 W
Sponds Hill ∧2 262 53.19 N 2.03 W
Spóng 110 13.27 N 105.34 E
Spoon ≃ 194 40.18 N 90.04 W
Spooner 190 45.49 N 91.53 W
Spořice 54 50.26 N 13.25 E
Spornitz 54 53.24 N 11.43 E
Spornoje 74 62.20 N 151.03 E
Sporovo 76 52.25 N 25.20 E
Spørring 41 56.18 N 10.09 E
Sportforum ♠ 264a 52.33 N 13.29 E
Sport Hill 207 41.14 N 73.16 W
Sporting Hill 208 40.09 N 76.26 W
Sportsman's Park Race Track ♠ 278 41.50 N 87.46 W
Spotorno 62 44.14 N 8.25 E
Spot Pond ◎ 283 42.27 N 71.06 W
Spotswood, Austl. 274b 37.50 S 144.53 E
Spotswood, N.J., U.S. 208 40.23 N 74.23 W
Spotsylvania 208 38.12 N 77.35 W
Spotsylvania □6 208 38.15 N 77.30 W
Spotsylvania Court House Battlefield ⊥ 208 38.15 N 77.35 W
Sprague, Mb., Can. 184 49.02 N 95.38 W
Sprague, Wa., U.S. 202 47.18 N 117.58 W
Sprague ≃ 202 42.34 N 121.51 W
Sprague, North Fork ≃ 202 42.26 N 121.07 W
Sprague, South Fork ≃ 202 42.26 N 121.07 W
Spragueville 207 41.53 N 71.32 W
Sprain Ridge Park ♠ 276 40.59 N 73.51 W
Sprankle Mills 214 41.00 N 79.07 W
Spratly Islands II 108 10.00 N 114.00 E
Spratt Point > 212 44.36 N 80.01 W
Spray 202 44.50 N 119.47 W
Spray Lakes Reservoir ◎1 182 50.55 N 115.20 W
Spreča ≃ 38 44.45 N 18.06 E
Spreckels 226 36.36 N 121.34 W
Spreckelsville 229a 20.53 N 156.24 W
Spree ≃ 54 52.32 N 13.13 E
Spreenhagen 54 52.20 N 13.52 E
Spreeufontein 158 33.22 S 20.45 E
Spreewald ◆1 54 51.50 N 14.05 E
Spremberg 54 51.34 N 14.22 E
Sprendlingen 56 49.51 N 7.59 E
Spresiano 64 45.46 N 12.16 E
Spring 222 30.04 N 95.25 W
Spring ≃, U.S. 194 36.52 N 94.44 W
Spring ≃, Ar., U.S. 194 36.08 N 91.05 W
Spring, North Fork ≃ 194 37.18 N 94.21 W
Spring, South Fork ≃ 194 36.19 N 91.30 W
Spring Arbor 216 42.12 N 84.33 W
Spring Bay ᴄ 200 41.40 N 112.50 W
Springbok 156 29.43 S 17.55 E
Springboro, Oh., U.S. 218 39.33 N 84.14 W
Springboro, Pa., U.S. 214 41.48 N 80.22 W
Spring Branch ≃ 284b 39.26 N 76.35 W
Springbrook, On., Can. 275b 43.39 N 79.47 W
Springbrook, Md., U.S. 284c 39.03 N 77.00 W
Spring Brook, N.Y., U.S. 210 42.49 N 78.40 W
Spring Brook ≃ 278 41.58 N 87.59 W
Springbrook Forest 284c 39.03 N 77.01 W
Springburn 172 43.40 S 171.28 E
Spring City, Pa., U.S. 208 40.10 N 75.32 W
Spring City, Tn., U.S. 192 35.41 N 84.51 W
Spring City, Ut,. U.S. 200 39.28 N 111.29 W
Spring Coulee V 198 48.31 N 100.54 W
Spring Creek, N.Z. 172 41.28 S 173.58 E
Spring Creek, Pa., U.S. 214 41.53 N 79.32 W
Spring Creek ≃, Austl. 166 24.12 S 140.58 E
Spring Creek ≃, U.S. 198 40.30 N 101.21 W
Spring Creek ≃, Ga., U.S. 192 30.54 N 84.45 W
Spring Creek ≃, Il., U.S. 216 40.49 N 87.50 W
Spring Creek ≃, Il., U.S. 219 39.52 N 89.37 W
Spring Creek ≃, Il., U.S. 278 41.32 N 88.04 W
Spring Creek ≃, Mo., U.S. 219 38.21 N 91.10 W
Spring Creek ≃, Nv., U.S. 204 39.55 N 117.50 W
Spring Creek ≃, N.D., U.S. 198 47.15 N 101.48 W
Spring Creek ≃, Pa., U.S. 214 41.24 N 78.57 W
Spring Creek ≃, Pa., U.S. 214 40.56 N 77.47 W
Spring Creek ≃, S.D., U.S. 198 45.54 N 100.18 W
Spring Creek ≃, S.D., U.S. 198 43.52 N 102.42 W
Spring Creek ≃, Tx., U.S. 222 30.02 N 95.16 W
Springdale, Nf., Can. 186 49.30 N 56.04 W
Springdale, Ar., U.S. 194 36.11 N 94.07 W
Springdale, Oh., U.S. 218 39.17 N 84.28 W
Springdale, Pa., U.S. 214 40.32 N 79.47 W
Springdale, S.C., U.S. 192 33.57 N 81.06 W
Springdale, Ut,. U.S. 200 37.11 N 112.59 W
Springdale, Wa., U.S. 202 48.03 N 117.44 W
Spring Dale, W.V., U.S. 192 37.52 N 80.48 W
Springe 52 52.12 N 9.32 E
Springer 196 36.21 N 104.35 W
Springers Brook ≃ 285 39.44 N 74.41 W
Springerville 200 34.08 N 109.17 W
Springfield, N.S., Can. 186 44.38 N 64.52 W
Springfield, On., Can. 212 42.50 N 80.56 W
Springfield, N.Z. 172 43.20 S 171.55 E
Springfield, S. Afr. 158 29.02 S 22.53 E
Springfield, Co., U.S. 198 37.24 N 102.36 W
Springfield, Fl., U.S. 194 30.09 N 85.36 W
Springfield, Ga., U.S. 192 32.22 N 81.18 W
Springfield, Il., U.S. 219 39.48 N 89.38 W
Springfield, Ky., U.S. 194 37.41 N 85.13 W
Springfield, Ma., U.S. 207 42.06 N 72.35 W
Springfield, Mi., U.S. 216 42.19 N 85.14 W
Springfield, Mn., U.S. 198 44.14 N 94.58 W
Springfield, Mo., U.S. 194 37.12 N 93.17 W
Springfield, N.J., U.S. 276 40.43 N 74.18 W
Springfield, Oh., U.S. 218 39.55 N 83.48 W
Springfield, Or., U.S. 202 44.02 N 123.01 W
Springfield, Pa., U.S. 285 39.55 N 75.19 W
Springfield, S.C., U.S. 192 33.29 N 81.16 W
Springfield, S.D., U.S. 198 42.51 N 97.53 W
Springfield, Tn., U.S. 194 36.30 N 86.53 W
Springfield, Vt., U.S. 188 43.17 N 72.28 W
Springfield, Va., U.S. 284c 38.45 N 77.13 W
Springfield, Lake ◎1 219 39.44 N 89.36 W
Springfield Center 210 42.50 N 74.53 W
Springfield Estates 284c 38.47 N 77.11 W
Springfield Lake ◎ 285 40.11 N 75.00 W
Springfield Lake ◎1 222 31.36 N 96.33 W
Springfield Mall ◆9 284c 38.46 N 77.11 W
Springfield Plateau ⋏1 194 37.10 N 93.30 W
Springfontein 158 30.19 S 25.36 E
Spring Garden 246 6.59 N 58.31 W
Spring Garden Brook ≃ 276 40.46 N 74.23 W
Spring Garden Township 208 39.57 N 76.44 W
Spring Glen, N.Y., U.S. 210 41.40 N 74.26 W
Spring Glen, Pa., U.S. 208 40.38 N 76.37 W
Spring Glen, Ut,. U.S. 200 39.39 N 110.51 W
Spring Green 190 43.10 N 90.04 W
Spring Grove, Il., U.S. 216 42.26 N 88.13 W
Spring Grove, Mn., U.S. 190 43.33 N 91.38 W
Spring Grove, Pa., U.S. 208 39.52 N 76.51 W
Springhill, N.S., Can. 186 45.39 N 64.03 W
Spring Hill, Ca., U.S. 226 39.15 N 121.03 W
Spring Hill, Fl., U.S. 220 28.33 N 82.27 W
Springhill, La., U.S. 194 33.00 N 93.28 W
Spring Hill, Pa., U.S. 214 40.23 N 78.40 W
Spring Hill, Tn., U.S. 194 35.45 N 86.55 W
Spring Hill, Tx., U.S. 222 32.34 N 94.48 W
Springhills 216 40.16 N 83.22 W
Spring Hope 192 35.56 N 78.06 W
Springhouse, B.C., Can. 182 51.55 N 122.07 W
Spring House, Pa., U.S. 285 40.11 N 75.14 W
Spring Lake, Mi., U.S. 216 43.04 N 86.11 W
Spring Lake, N.J., U.S. 208 40.09 N 74.01 W
Spring Lake, N.C., U.S. 192 35.10 N 78.58 W
Spring Lake ◎, Mi., U.S. 216 43.06 N 86.11 W
Spring Lake ◎, N.J., U.S. 276 40.35 N 74.25 W
Spring Lake Heights 208 40.09 N 74.01 W
Spring Mill, Oh., U.S. 214 40.54 N 82.36 W
Spring Mill, Pa., U.S. 285 40.04 N 75.17 W
Spring Mill Reservoir ◎1 262 53.39 N 2.13 W
Spring Mills 210 40.51 N 77.34 W
Spring Mill State Park ♠ 218 38.43 N 86.25 W
Spring Mount 208 40.17 N 75.28 W
Spring Mountains ⋏ 204 36.10 N 115.40 W
Spring Pond ◎ 283 42.30 N 70.57 W
Springport, In., U.S. 218 40.03 N 85.24 W
Springport, Mi., U.S. 216 42.22 N 84.41 W
Spring Run 214 40.09 N 83.47 W
Springs 158 26.13 S 28.25 E
Springs □5 273d 26.14 S 28.30 E
Springs Aerodrome ⊠ 273d 26.15 S 28.24 E
Springside 285 40.04 N 74.51 W
Springs Junction 172 42.19 S 172.11 E
Springsure 166 24.07 S 148.05 E
Springton 168b 34.43 S 139.05 E
Springtown 222 32.58 N 97.41 W
Springvale, Austl. 162 17.48 S 127.41 E
Springvale, Austl. 166 23.33 S 140.42 E
Springvale, Austl. 169 37.57 S 145.09 E
Springvale, Me., U.S. 188 43.28 N 70.47 W
Springvale South 274b 37.58 S 145.09 E
Spring Valley, Ca., U.S. 228 32.44 N 116.59 W
Spring Valley, Il., U.S. 190 41.19 N 89.11 W
Spring Valley, Mn., U.S. 190 43.41 N 92.23 W
Spring Valley, N.Y., U.S. 210 41.06 N 74.02 W
Spring Valley, Oh., U.S. 218 39.36 N 84.00 W
Spring Valley, Tx., U.S. 222 29.47 N 95.31 W
Spring Valley, Wi., U.S. 190 44.50 N 92.14 W
Spring Valley V 204 39.15 N 114.25 W
Spring Valley Creek ≃ 204 39.20 N 114.25 W
Springview 198 42.49 N 99.44 W
Springville, Al., U.S. 194 33.46 N 86.28 W
Springville, Ca., U.S. 204 36.08 N 118.49 W
Springville, Ia., U.S. 190 42.03 N 91.26 W
Springville, N.J., U.S. 285 39.56 N 74.52 W
Springville, N.Y., U.S. 210 42.30 N 78.40 W
Springville, Pa., U.S. 210 41.42 N 75.55 W
Springville, Ut,. U.S. 200 40.09 N 111.36 W
Springwater 210 42.38 N 77.35 W
Springwood 170 33.42 S 150.33 E
Sprint ≃ 44 54.22 N 2.45 W
Sprite Creek ≃ 210 43.08 N 74.44 W
Sproat Lake ◎ 182 49.16 N 125.03 W
Sprockhövel 56 51.22 N 7.15 E
Sprogels Run ≃ 285 40.14 N 75.37 W
Sprogø I 41 55.20 N 10.58 E
Sprötze 52 53.18 N 9.49 E
Sproul 214 40.16 N 78.28 W
Sprout Brook ≃ 276 40.54 N 74.05 W
Spruce ≃ 184 53.15 N 105.43 W
Spruce Brook 186 48.45 N 58.11 W
Spruce Creek 214 40.37 N 78.08 W
Spruce Creek ≃ 210 43.07 N 74.46 W
Spruce Grove 182 53.32 N 113.55 W
Spruce Knob ∧ 188 38.42 N 79.32 W
Spruce Knob-Seneca Rocks National Recreation Area ♠ 188 38.50 N 79.20 W
Spruce Lake 184 53.32 N 109.05 W
Spruce Mountain ∧, Az., U.S. 200 34.28 N 112.24 W
Spruce Mountain ∧, Nv., U.S. 204 40.33 N 114.49 W
Spruce Pine, Al., U.S. 194 34.23 N 87.43 W
Spruce Pine, N.C., U.S. 192 35.54 N 82.03 W
Spruce Run Reservoir ◎1 210 40.40 N 74.57 W
Spruce Run State Park ♠ 210 40.40 N 74.56 W
Spruce Woods Provincial Park ♠ 184 49.42 N 99.05 W
Spry 208 39.55 N 76.41 W
Spry Lake ◎ 212 44.44 N 81.15 W
Spulico, Capo > 68 39.58 N 16.39 E
Spur 196 33.28 N 100.51 W
Spurfield 182 55.13 N 114.16 W
Spurger 194 30.42 N 94.11 W
Spurn Head > 44 53.34 N 0.07 E
Spurr, Mount ∧ 180 61.18 N 152.15 W
Sputendorf 264a 52.20 N 13.13 E
Spuzzum 182 49.41 N 121.25 W
Spy Hill 184 50.36 N 101.41 W
Spy Pond ◎ 283 42.24 N 71.09 W
Squally Channel ʮ 182 53.10 N 129.15 W
Squamish 182 49.42 N 123.09 W
Squamish ≃ 182 49.45 N 123.09 W
Squam Lake ◎ 188 43.45 N 71.32 W
Square Butte Creek ≃ 198 46.55 N 100.55 W
Square Lake ◎ 186 47.03 N 68.20 W
Squatec 186 47.53 N 68.43 W
Squaw Cap Mountain ∧ 186 47.53 N 66.53 W
Squaw Creek ≃, Id., U.S. 202 43.51 N 116.22 W
Squaw Creek ≃, Il., U.S. 278 42.21 N 88.07 W
Squaw Creek ≃, Or., U.S. 202 44.27 N 121.20 W
Squaw Creek Lake ◎1 222 32.19 N 97.47 W
Squaw Harbor 180 55.11 N 160.30 W
Squaw Hill ∧ 200 41.48 N 105.02 W
Squaw Island I 284a 42.56 N 78.54 W
Squaw Peak ∧, Ca., U.S. 226 39.11 N 120.16 W
Squaw Peak ∧, Mt., U.S. 202 47.10 N 114.21 W
Squaw Rapids 184 53.41 N 103.20 W
Squaw Rapids Dam ◆6 184 53.40 N 103.25 W
Squaw Run ≃ 279b 40.29 N 79.52 W
Squaw Valley State Recreation Area ♠ 226 39.12 N 120.15 W
Squibnocket Point > 207 41.18 N 70.47 W
Squilax 182 50.52 N 119.35 W
Squillace 68 38.47 N 16.31 E
Squillace, Golfo di ᴄ 68 38.50 N 16.50 E
Squinzano 68 40.26 N 18.03 E
Squire 192 37.14 N 81.36 W
Squires, Mount ∧ 162 26.12 S 127.28 E
Squirrel ≃ 180 66.57 N 160.27 W
Squirrel Hill ◆8 279b 40.26 N 79.55 W
Squirrel Hill Tunnel ◆5 279b 40.26 N 79.55 W
Squirrel's Heath ◆8 260 51.35 N 0.13 E
Şragen 115a 7.26 S 111.02 E
Šramkovka 78 50.10 N 32.05 E
Srbija (Serbia) □3 38 44.00 N 21.00 E
Srbobran 38 45.33 N 19.48 E
Srê Âmběl 110 11.07 N 103.46 E
Sredinnyj chrebet ⋏ 74 56.00 N 158.00 E
Sredna Gora ⋏ 38 42.30 N 25.00 E
Sredn'aja Achtuba 80 48.43 N 44.52 E
Sredn'aja Mokla ≃ 88 55.01 N 119.37 E
Sredn'aja Nanaki, gora ∧ 89 52.26 N 132.50 E
Sredn'aja Ol'okma 88 55.26 N 120.33 E
Srednegorje 76 60.34 N 29.25 E
Sredneje Kujto, ozero ◎ 24 65.08 N 31.15 E
Srednekolymsk 74 67.27 N 153.41 E
Srednerusskaja vozvyšennost' ⋏1 72 52.00 N 38.00 E
Srednesibirskoje ploskogorje ⋏1 74 65.00 N 105.00 E
Srednij Ikorec 78 51.05 N 39.45 E
Srednij Kalar 88 55.51 N 117.24 E
Srednij Ural ⋏ 86 58.00 N 59.00 E
Srednij Urgal 89 51.09 N 132.59 E
Srednij Vas'ugan 86 59.16 N 78.15 E
Srednyj 83 48.09 N 39.50 E
Srê Khtŭm 110 12.10 N 106.52 E
Śrem 30 52.08 N 17.01 E
Srê Moăt 110 13.18 N 107.10 E
Sremska Mitrovica 38 44.58 N 19.37 E
Sremski Karlovci 38 45.12 N 19.57 E
Srêng ≃ 110 13.21 N 103.27 E
Srêpôk ≃ 110 13.33 N 106.16 E
Sretensk 88 52.15 N 117.43 E
Sretenskoje 88 56.28 N 96.25 E
Srīdharpur 126 23.04 N 89.25 E
Sri Hargobindpur 123 31.41 N 75.39 E
Sri Jayawardenepura (Kotte) 122 6.54 N 79.54 E
Srīkākulam 122 18.18 N 83.54 E
Sri Kālahasti 122 13.45 N 79.43 E
Sri Lanka □1, Asia 118 7.00 N 81.00 E
Sri Lanka □1, Asia 122 7.00 N 81.00 E
Srīnagar, Bngl. 126 23.32 N 90.18 E
Srīnagar, India 123 34.05 N 74.49 E
Srīnagar, India 124 30.13 N 78.47 E
Srīnagar Airport ⊠ 123 34.00 N 74.52 E
Srīpur, Bngl. 126 24.12 N 90.29 E
Srīpur, Bngl. 126 23.36 N 89.24 E
Srīrampur, India 122 19.34 N 74.34 E
Srirāmpur, India 272b 22.49 N 88.29 E
Srīrangam 122 10.52 N 78.41 E
Srīvardhan 122 18.02 N 73.01 E
Srīvilliputtūr 122 9.31 N 77.38 E
Środa Śląska 30 51.10 N 16.36 E
Środa Wielkopolski 30 52.14 N 17.17 E
Srpska Crnja 38 45.43 N 20.42 E
Ssangmun-ni ◆8 271b 37.39 N 127.02 E

≃ River — Fluß — Río — Rivière — Rio
≊ Canal — Kanal — Canal — Canal — Canal
ʟ Waterfall, Rapids — Wasserfall, Stromschnellen — Cascada, Rápidos — Chute d'eau, Rapides — Cascata, Rápidos
ʮ Strait — Meeresstraße — Estrecho — Détroit — Estreito
ᴄ Bay, Gulf — Bucht, Golf — Bahía, Golfo — Baie, Golfe — Baía, Golfo
◎ Lake, Lakes — See, Seen — Lago, Lagos — Lac, Lacs — Lago, Lagos
≚ Swamp — Sumpf — Pantano — Marais — Pântano
⍓ Ice Features, Glacier — Eis- und Gletscherformen — Accidentes Glaciales — Formes glaciaires — Acidentes glaciares
〒 Other Hydrographic Features — Andere Hydrographische Objekte — Otros Elementos Hidrográficos — Autres données hydrographiques — Outros acidentes hidrográficos

✦ Submarine Features — Untermeerische Objekte — Accidentes Submarinos — Formes de relief sous-marin — Acidentes submarinos
□ Political Unit — Politische Einheit — Unidad Politica — Entité politique — Unidade política
ʊ Cultural Institution — Kulturelle Institution — Institución Cultural — Institution culturelle — Instituição cultural
⊥ Historical Site — Historische Stätte — Sitio Histórico — Site historique — Sitio histórico
♠ Recreational Site — Erholungs- und Ferienort — Sitio de Recreo — Centre de loisirs — Area de Lazer
⊠ Airport — Flughafen — Aeropuerto — Aéroport — Aeroporto
■ Military Installation — Militäranlage — Instalación Militar — Installation militaire — Instalação militar
◆ Miscellaneous — Verschiedenes — Misceláneo — Divers — Diversos

Name	Page	Lat.°′	Long.°′
Ssuchunghsi	100	22.06 N	120.44 E
Ssup'ing → Siping	89	43.12 N	124.20 E
Staaken ◆[8]	264a	52.32 N	13.08 E
Staaten ≃	164	16.24 S	141.17 E
Staaten River National Park ♦	164	16.40 S	143.00 E
Staatsburg	210	41.50 N	73.55 W
Staatz	61	48.40 N	16.29 E
Stabbursdalen Nasjonalpark ♦	24	70.06 N	24.30 E
Staberhuk ›	54	54.24 N	11.19 E
Stabroek	50	51.20 N	4.22 E
Stachanov	83	48.34 N	38.40 E
Stachy	60	49.06 N	13.40 E
Stack, Loch ⊜	46	58.20 N	4.55 W
Stack Skerry I[2]	46	59.01 N	4.31 W
Stacksteads	262	53.41 N	2.13 W
Stacyville	190	43.26 N	92.46 W
Stad-Delden	52	52.16 N	6.42 E
Stade	52	53.36 N	9.28 E
Staden, Bel.	50	50.59 N	3.01 E
Staden, Dtsch.	56	50.20 N	8.54 E
Städjan ʌ	26	61.55 N	12.52 E
Stadl an der Mur	61	47.05 N	13.58 E
Stadlandet ›[1]	26	62.07 N	5.18 E
Stadlau ◆[8]	264b	48.14 N	16.28 E
Stadl-Paura	64	48.05 N	13.53 E
Stadskanaal	52	53.00 N	6.55 E
Stadtallendorf	56	50.50 N	9.01 E
Stadtbergen	58	48.22 N	10.50 E
Stadthagen	52	52.19 N	9.13 E
Stadtilm	54	50.47 N	11.05 E
Städtische Rahmede	263	51.17 N	7.40 E
Stadtkyll	56	50.21 N	6.32 E
Stadtlauringen	56	50.11 N	10.22 E
Stadtlengsfeld	56	50.47 N	10.07 E
Stadtlohn	52	51.59 N	6.55 E
Stadtoldendorf	52	51.53 N	9.37 E
Stadtprozelten	56	49.47 N	9.25 E
Stadtroda	54	50.51 N	11.44 E
Stadtsteinach	54	50.09 N	11.30 E
Stadt Wehlen	54	50.58 N	14.02 E
Stadum	41	54.44 N	9.03 E
Stäfa	58	47.15 N	8.44 E
Staffa I	46	56.25 N	6.20 W
Staffanstorp	41	55.38 N	13.13 E
Staffelberg ʌ	56	50.06 N	11.02 E
Staffelde	264a	52.44 N	13.00 E
Staffelsee ⊜	64	47.42 N	11.10 E
Staffelstein	56	50.06 N	11.00 E
Staffin	46	57.37 N	6.12 W
Staffora ≃	62	45.04 N	9.01 E
Stafford, Eng., U.K.	42	52.48 N	2.07 W
Stafford, Ct., U.S.	207	41.59 N	72.17 W
Stafford, Ks., U.S.	198	37.57 N	98.36 W
Stafford, N.Y., U.S.	210	42.59 N	78.04 W
Stafford, Tx., U.S.	222	29.37 N	95.34 W
Stafford, Va., U.S.	208	38.25 N	77.24 W
Stafford □[6]	208	38.25 N	77.30 W
Staffordshire □[6]	28	52.50 N	2.00 W
Stafford Springs	207	41.57 N	72.18 W
Staffordsville	188	37.49 N	82.50 W
Staffordville	207	41.59 N	72.15 W
Stagen	112	3.18 S	116.10 E
Stag Pond ⊜	276	40.59 N	74.42 W
Stahl-Berg ʌ[2]	264a	52.21 N	13.46 E
Stahlbrode	54	54.14 N	13.17 E
Stahle	52	51.50 N	9.25 E
Stahnsdorf	54	52.23 N	13.13 E
Stahringen	58	47.47 N	8.58 E
Staicele	76	57.50 N	24.45 E
Staines	42	51.26 N	0.31 W
Staines Reservoirs ⊜[1]	260	51.27 N	0.30 W
Stainforth	44	53.36 N	1.01 W
Staining	44	53.49 N	2.59 W
Stainland	262	53.40 N	1.53 W
Stainmore Forest ◆[3]	44	54.30 N	2.10 W
Stains	261	48.57 N	2.23 E
Stainz	61	46.54 N	15.16 E
Stairtown	222	29.43 N	97.44 W
Stajki	78	50.05 N	30.54 E
Staked Plain → Estacado, Llano ⌣	196	33.30 N	102.40 W
Stäket	40	59.28 N	17.48 E
Stakroge	41	55.53 N	8.51 E
Stalać	38	43.40 N	21.25 E
Stalbridge	42	50.58 N	2.23 W
Stalden	58	46.14 N	7.52 E
Stalettì	68	38.46 N	16.32 E
Stalham	42	52.47 N	1.31 E
Stalheim	26	60.50 N	6.40 E
Stalhofen	61	47.05 N	15.16 E
Stalinabad → Dušanbe	85	38.35 N	68.48 E
Stalin → Brașov	38	45.39 N	25.37 E
Stalingrad → Volgograd	80	48.44 N	44.25 E
Stalin → Kuçovë	38	40.48 N	19.54 E
Stalino → Doneck	83	48.00 N	37.48 E
Stalinogorsk → Novomoskovsk	82	54.05 N	38.13 E
Stalinsk → Novokuzneck	86	53.45 N	87.06 E
Stalin → Varna	38	43.13 N	27.55 E
Stallarholmen	40	59.22 N	17.12 E
Ställberg	40	59.59 N	14.55 E
Ställdalen	40	59.56 N	14.56 E
Stallwang	60	49.03 N	12.40 E
Stalowa Wola	30	50.35 N	22.02 E
Stalybridge	44	53.29 N	2.03 W
Stambaugh	190	46.04 N	88.37 W
Stamford, Austl.	166	21.16 S	143.49 E
Stamford, Eng., U.K.	42	52.39 N	0.29 W
Stamford, Ct., U.S.	207	41.03 N	73.32 W
Stamford, N.Y., U.S.	210	42.24 N	74.36 W
Stamford, Tx., U.S.	196	32.56 N	99.48 W
Stamford, Vt., U.S.	207	42.45 N	73.04 W
Stamford, Lake ⊜[1]	196	33.05 N	99.35 W
Stamford Bridge	44	53.59 N	0.55 W
Stamford Brige Stadium ♦	260	51.29 N	0.11 W
Stamford Harbor c	276	41.02 N	73.32 W
Stamford Museum ʋ	276	41.07 N	73.33 W
Stammbach	54	50.09 N	11.41 E
Stammersdorf ◆[8]	264b	48.18 N	16.25 E
Stammham	60	48.15 N	12.53 E
Stammheim, Dtsch.	56	48.41 N	8.46 E
Stammheim, Schw.	58	47.38 N	8.47 E
Stampede Reservoir ⊜[1]	226	39.29 N	120.07 W
Stamping Ground	218	38.16 N	84.41 W
Stampriet	156	24.20 S	18.28 E
Stamps	194	33.21 N	93.29 W
Stams	64	47.16 N	10.59 E
Stanaford	188	37.48 N	81.09 W
Stanardsville	188	38.17 N	78.26 W
Stanberry	194	40.13 N	94.32 W
Stanborough	260	51.47 N	0.13 W
Stancija-Gorčakovo	85	40.25 N	71.45 E
Stancionno-Ojašinskij	86	55.28 N	83.53 E
Standard, Ab., Can.	182	51.07 N	112.59 W
Standard, Ak., U.S.	180	64.47 N	148.32 W
Standard, Ca., U.S.	226	37.59 N	120.20 W
Standard, Pa., U.S.	214	40.10 N	79.32 W
Standard Oil Company Refinery ʋ[3]	282	37.57 N	122.24 W
Standard Shaft	279b	40.10 N	79.32 W
Standedge Canal Tunnel ◆[5]	262	53.34 N	2.00 W
Standedge Railway Tunnel ◆[5]	262	53.34 N	2.00 W
Standerton	158	26.58 S	29.07 E
Standiford Field ⊠	218	38.11 N	85.44 W
Standing Rock Indian Reservation ◆[4]	198	45.50 N	101.10 W
Standing Stone Creek ≃	214	40.30 N	78.00 W
Standing Stones ⊥	46	58.12 N	6.48 W
Standish, Eng., U.K.	44	53.36 N	2.41 W
Standish, Mi., U.S.	190	43.58 N	83.57 W
Standish Monument ⊥	283	42.01 N	70.41 W
Standon	42	51.53 N	0.02 E
Stanfield, Az., U.S.	200	32.52 N	111.57 W
Stanfield, Or., U.S.	202	45.46 N	119.12 W
Stanford, S. Afr.	158	34.26 S	19.29 E
Stanford, Ca., U.S.	226	37.25 N	122.08 W
Stanford, Ky., U.S.	192	37.31 N	84.39 W
Stanford, Mt., U.S.	202	47.09 N	110.13 W
Stanford Center ◆[9]	282	37.27 N	122.10 W
Stanford Heights	210	42.46 N	73.53 W
Stanford le Hope	42	51.31 N	0.26 E
Stanford Linear Accelerator ʋ[3]	282	37.25 N	122.12 W
Stanford Rivers	260	51.41 N	0.13 E
Stanford University ʋ[2]	282	37.26 N	122.10 W
Stanfordville	210	41.52 N	73.43 W
Stånga	26	57.17 N	18.28 E
Stångån ≃	26	58.27 N	15.37 E
Stångby	41	55.46 N	13.10 E
Stange	26	60.43 N	11.11 E
Stanger	158	29.27 S	31.14 E
Stanghella	64	45.08 N	11.45 E
Stanhope, Eng., U.K.	44	54.45 N	2.01 W
Stanhope, Ia., U.S.	190	42.17 N	93.47 W
Stanhope, N.J., U.S.	210	40.54 N	74.42 W
Staničnо-Luganskoje	83	48.39 N	39.30 E
Stanislaus □[6]	226	37.39 N	121.00 W
Stanislaus ≃	226	37.40 N	121.14 W
Stanislaus, Clark Fork ≃	226	38.22 N	119.52 W
Stanislaus, Middle Fork ≃	226	38.09 N	120.21 W
Stanislaus, North Fork ≃	226	38.09 N	120.21 W
Stanislaus, South Fork ≃	226	38.04 N	120.25 W
Stanislav	78	46.34 N	32.09 E
Stanislavčik	78	48.58 N	28.07 E
Stanislav → Ivano-Frankovsk	78	48.55 N	24.43 E
Stanisławów → Ivano-Frankovsk	78	48.55 N	24.43 E
Stanke Dimitrov	38	42.16 N	23.07 E
Staňkov	60	49.34 N	13.04 E
Stanley, Austl.	166	40.46 S	145.18 E
Stanley, N.B., Can.	186	46.17 N	66.44 W
Stanley, Falk. Is.	254	51.42 S	57.51 W
Stanley, H.K.	271d	22.13 N	114.12 E
Stanley, Eng., U.K.	44	54.52 N	1.42 W
Stanley, Scot., U.K.	46	56.28 N	3.27 W
Stanley, N.Y., U.S.	210	42.49 N	77.06 W
Stanley, N.C., U.S.	192	35.21 N	81.05 W
Stanley, N.D., U.S.	198	48.19 N	102.23 W
Stanley, Va., U.S.	188	38.34 N	78.30 W
Stanley, Wi., U.S.	190	44.57 N	90.56 W
Stanley ≃	171a	27.09 S	152.32 E
Stanley, Mont ʌ[2]	273b	4.19 S	15.15 E
Stanley Bay c	271d	22.12 N	114.12 E
Stanley Falls ⌙	154	0.30 N	25.12 E
Stanley Mills	275b	43.46 N	79.44 W
Stanley Mound ʌ	271d	22.14 N	114.12 E
Stanley Park ♦, B.C., Can.	224	49.19 N	123.09 W
Stanley Park ♦, Eng., U.K.	262	53.26 N	2.57 W
Stanley Park ♦, Eng., U.K.	262	53.49 N	3.02 W
Stanley Reservoir ⊜[1]	122	11.54 N	77.50 E
Stanleyville → Kisangani	154	0.30 N	25.12 E
Stanlow	44	53.17 N	2.52 W
Stanmore ◆[8]	260	51.37 N	0.19 W
Stannards	210	42.05 N	77.55 W
Stannington	44	55.06 N	1.40 W
Stanovoj chrebet ϰ	74	56.20 N	126.00 E
Stanovoje nagorje (Stanovoy Mountains) ϰ	88	56.00 N	114.00 E
Stanovoj Kolodez'	76	52.51 N	36.16 E
Stanovoy Mountains → Stanovoje nagorje ϰ	88	56.00 N	114.00 E
Stans	58	46.57 N	8.22 E
Stansbury	168b	34.55 S	137.47 E
Stansmore Range ϰ	162	21.23 S	128.33 E
Stansstad	58	46.59 N	8.20 E
Stanstead	206	45.01 N	72.05 W
Stanstead □[6]	206	45.10 N	72.00 W
Stanstead Abbots	42	51.47 N	0.01 E
Stansted	260	51.20 N	0.18 E
Stansted Mountfitchet	42	51.54 N	0.12 E
Stanthorpe	166	28.39 S	151.57 E
Stanton, Eng., U.K.	42	52.19 N	0.53 E
Stanton, Ca., U.S.	228	33.48 N	117.59 W
Stanton, De., U.S.	208	39.43 N	75.37 W
Stanton, Ia., U.S.	198	41.05 N	95.11 W
Stanton, Ky., U.S.	192	37.50 N	83.51 W
Stanton, Mi., U.S.	190	43.17 N	85.04 W
Stanton, Mo., U.S.	219	38.16 N	91.06 W
Stanton, Ne., U.S.	198	41.57 N	97.13 W
Stanton, N.D., U.S.	198	47.19 N	101.22 W
Stanton, Tn., U.S.	194	35.27 N	89.24 W
Stanton, Tx., U.S.	196	32.07 N	101.47 W
Stantonsburg	192	35.36 N	77.49 W
Stanwell	260	51.27 N	0.29 W
Stanwell Moor	260	51.28 N	0.30 W
Stanwood	224	48.14 N	122.22 W
Stanwyck Estates	285	39.42 N	75.33 W
Stanzach	58	47.23 N	10.34 E
Stanz im Mürztal	61	47.28 N	15.30 E
Stapelburg	54	51.53 N	10.40 E
Stapelfeld	52	53.36 N	10.13 E
Staphorst	52	52.37 N	6.12 E
Stapleford	42	52.56 N	1.16 W
Stapleford Abbotts	260	51.38 N	0.10 E
Stapleford Aerodrome ⊠	260	51.39 N	0.08 E
Stapleford Tawney	260	51.40 N	0.11 E
Staplehurst	42	51.10 N	0.33 E
Staples	198	46.21 N	94.47 W
Stapleton, Al., U.S.	194	30.44 N	87.47 W
Stapleton, Ne., U.S.	198	41.28 N	100.30 W
Stąporków	30	51.09 N	20.34 E
Star', Ross.	76	53.37 N	34.09 E
Star, Ms., U.S.	194	32.05 N	90.02 W
Star, N.C., U.S.	192	35.24 N	79.47 W
Stará Boleslav	54	50.12 N	14.42 E
Starachowice	30	51.03 N	21.04 E
Stara Fužina	64	46.17 N	13.54 E
Staraja	265a	59.55 N	30.38 E
Staraja Belica, Bela.	76	54.42 N	29.38 E
Staraja Belica, Ross.	78	51.59 N	35.13 E
Staraja Belogorka	80	52.05 N	53.17 E
Staraja Derevn'a ◆[8]	265a	59.59 N	30.15 E
Staraja Duginka	82	54.20 N	38.45 E
Staraja Kriuša	78	50.12 N	41.09 E
Staraja Kulatka	80	52.43 N	47.37 E
Staraja Kupavna	82	55.48 N	38.10 E
Staraja Majačka	78	46.30 N	33.11 E
Staraja Majna	80	54.36 N	48.57 E
Staraja Poltavka	80	50.28 N	46.28 E
Staraja Porubežka	80	52.03 N	49.11 E
Staraja Račejka	80	53.22 N	48.03 E
Staraja Rudn'a	76	52.50 N	30.17 E
Staraja Russa	76	58.00 N	31.23 E
Staraja Ruza	82	55.39 N	36.20 E
Staraja Sachča	80	54.25 N	49.58 E
Staraja Sin'ava	78	49.36 N	27.37 E
Staraja Sitn'a	82	54.56 N	38.09 E
Staraja Terizmorga	80	54.16 N	44.32 E
Staraja Toropa	76	56.17 N	31.40 E
Staraja Ušica	78	48.35 N	27.07 E
Staraja Veduga	78	51.48 N	38.31 E
Staraja Vičuga	80	57.16 N	41.53 E
Staraja Vyževka	78	51.27 N	24.24 E
Staranzano	64	45.49 N	13.30 E
Stara Pazova	38	44.59 N	20.10 E
Stara Planina (Balkan Mountains) ϰ	38	42.45 N	25.00 E
Stará Role	54	50.14 N	12.47 E
Starav, Ben ʌ	46	56.32 N	5.03 W
Stará Voda	60	50.00 N	12.36 E
Stara Zagora	38	42.25 N	25.38 E
Starbejevo	265b	55.55 N	37.28 E
Starbrick	214	41.50 N	79.12 W
Starbuck, Mb., Can.	184	49.46 N	97.36 W
Starbuck, Mn., U.S.	198	45.36 N	95.31 W
Starbuck, Wa., U.S.	202	46.31 N	118.07 W
Starbuck I	14	5.37 S	155.53 W
Starčenkovo	78	47.17 N	36.59 E
Star City, Sk., Can.	184	52.53 N	104.21 W
Star City, Ar., U.S.	194	33.56 N	91.50 W
Star City, In., U.S.	216	40.58 N	86.33 W
Starcross	42	50.38 N	3.27 W
Stare Czarnowo	54	53.16 N	14.45 E
Staré Sedliště	60	49.45 N	12.42 E
Starford	214	40.42 N	78.58 W
Stargard Szczeciński (Stargard in Pommern)	30	53.20 N	15.02 E
Stargo	200	33.04 N	109.21 W
Star Harbour c	175e	10.47 S	162.18 E
Stari Bar	38	42.06 N	19.08 E
Starica, Ross.	76	56.30 N	34.56 E
Starica, Ross.	76	59.04 N	29.30 E
Starica, Ross.	80	48.13 N	45.56 E
Stari Grad	36	43.11 N	16.36 E
Starij R'ad	76	58.05 N	34.54 E
Starina	76	59.37 N	44.42 E
Stari Vlah ◆[1]	38	43.35 N	20.15 E
Star Junction	214	40.04 N	79.46 W
Stark □[6]	214	40.48 N	81.22 W
Starke	192	29.56 N	82.06 W
Starke □[6]	216	41.18 N	86.37 W
Starkey	210	42.32 N	76.56 W
Starkville	194	33.27 N	88.49 W
Star Lake	224	47.22 N	122.18 W
Star Mountains ϰ	164	5.05 S	141.05 E
Starnberg	60	48.00 N	11.20 E
Starnberger See ⊜	64	47.55 N	11.18 E
Starnikovo	82	55.22 N	38.24 E
Staroalejskoje	86	51.00 N	82.01 E
Starobačaty	86	54.14 N	86.07 E
Starobaltačevo	86	56.01 N	55.56 E
Starobel'sk	83	49.16 N	38.56 E
Starobeševo	83	47.44 N	38.03 E
Starobin	76	52.44 N	27.28 E
Staročerkasskaja	83	47.15 N	40.03 E
Starocuruchajtuj	88	50.12 N	119.15 E
Staroderev'ankov-Skaja	78	46.08 N	38.58 E
Starodub	76	52.35 N	32.46 E
Starod'umejevo	80	55.16 N	54.22 E
Starogan'kino	80	53.55 N	52.15 E
Starogard Gdański	30	53.59 N	18.33 E
Staroignatjevka	83	47.32 N	37.47 E
Staroje	76	59.16 N	40.40 E
Staroje Bajsarovo	80	55.31 N	53.54 E
Staroje Drožžanoje	80	54.44 N	47.34 E
Staroje Ibrajkino	80	54.52 N	51.02 E
Staroje Jaškino	80	52.49 N	52.57 E
Staroje Jermakovo	80	54.04 N	51.59 E
Staroje Oleničevo	80	45.34 N	47.11 E
Staroje Rachino	76	58.08 N	32.39 E
Staroje Šajgovo	80	54.18 N	44.26 E
Staroje Šajmurzino	80	54.45 N	47.58 E
Staroje Selo	76	55.14 N	29.54 E
Staroje Sindrovo	80	54.25 N	44.06 E
Staroje Slavkino	80	52.34 N	45.08 E
Staroje Ustje	80	53.28 N	41.51 E
Starojurjevo	80	53.21 N	40.42 E
Starokazačje	78	46.21 N	29.59 E
Starokonstantinov	78	49.46 N	27.13 E
Starokuručevo	80	55.09 N	54.04 E
Starolaspa	83	47.34 N	37.59 E
Staroleuškovskaja	78	45.59 N	39.44 E
Staromichajlovka	83	47.58 N	37.36 E
Starominskaja	78	46.31 N	39.04 E
Staromlinovka	78	47.42 N	36.49 E
Staromušta	80	55.49 N	54.14 E
Staronikolajevo	82	55.37 N	36.16 E
Staro-Podgorodneje	82	54.46 N	38.57 E
Staropokrovka	85	42.50 N	75.18 E
Staroščerbinovskaja	78	46.37 N	38.40 E
Staroseslavino	80	53.12 N	40.25 E
Starošešminsk	80	55.22 N	51.15 E
Starosiedle	54	51.50 N	14.50 E
Starosoldatskoje	86	56.12 N	72.37 E
Starosubchangulovo	86	53.06 N	57.26 E
Starotimoškino	24	53.43 N	47.32 E
Starotitarovskaja	78	45.14 N	37.09 E
Staroutkinsk	86	57.14 N	59.20 E
Staroverovka	78	49.33 N	35.42 E
Starožilovo	80	54.14 N	39.55 E
Starožil'sk	80	56.34 N	47.17 E
Star Peak ʌ	204	40.32 N	118.10 W
Starr	214	41.32 N	79.22 W
Starrucca	210	41.54 N	75.28 W
Start Bay c	42	50.17 N	3.36 W
Start Point ›	42	50.13 N	3.38 W
Startup	224	47.52 N	121.44 W
Starvation Reservoir ⊜[1]	200	40.15 N	110.30 W
Starved Rock State Park ♦	216	41.19 N	88.58 W
Staryj Ajbesi	80	54.57 N	47.03 E
Staryj-Ajdar	83	48.43 N	39.11 E
Staryj Bagr'až	80	54.54 N	51.39 E
Staryj Bir'uz'ak	84	44.47 N	46.54 E
Staryj Bol'ševik	265b	55.57 N	37.47 E
Staryj Čartorijsk	78	51.15 N	25.54 E
Staryj Chop'or	80	51.30 N	42.58 E
Staryj Čindant	88	50.33 N	115.33 E
Staryje Burasy	80	52.16 N	46.09 E
Staryje Dorogi	76	53.02 N	28.16 E
Staryje Maty	80	55.14 N	53.55 E
Staryje Popel'uchi	78	48.18 N	28.55 E
Staryje Senžary	78	49.25 N	34.27 E
Staryje Turdaki	80	53.55 N	45.29 E
Staryje Z'atcy	80	57.21 N	52.39 E
Staryj Kazangal	80	50.15 N	47.39 E
Staryj Kistruss	80	54.28 N	40.34 E
Staryj Krym, Ukr.	78	45.03 N	35.05 E
Staryj Krym, Ukr.	83	47.10 N	37.30 E
Staryj Lesken	84	43.20 N	43.55 E
Staryj Medved'	76	58.18 N	30.30 E
Staryj Merčik	78	49.58 N	35.46 E
Staryj Oskol	78	51.19 N	37.51 E
Staryj Sambor	78	49.27 N	22.59 E
Staryj Terek ≃	84	44.00 N	47.24 E
Staryj Tukšum	80	53.42 N	48.33 E
Starý Plzenec	60	49.42 N	13.28 E
Stary Sącz	30	49.34 N	20.38 E
Stassfurt	54	51.51 N	11.34 E
Staszów	30	50.34 N	21.20 E
State Center	190	42.01 N	93.09 W
State College	214	40.47 N	77.51 W
State Fair Grounds ♦	284b	39.27 N	76.38 W
Stateline, Ca., U.S.	226	38.57 N	119.57 W
State Line, Ms., U.S.	194	31.26 N	88.28 W
Stateline, Nv., U.S.	204	38.58 N	119.56 W
Staten Island I	276	40.35 N	74.09 W
Staten Island Mall ◆[9]	276	40.35 N	74.10 W
Statenville	192	30.42 N	83.01 W
State Park Place	219	38.40 N	90.03 W
State Road	192	36.19 N	80.52 W
Statesboro	192	32.26 N	81.47 W
Statesville	192	35.46 N	80.53 W
Stateville Correctional Center ʋ	278	41.35 N	88.06 W
Station Peak	162	21.10 S	118.11 E
Statte	68	40.34 N	17.12 E
Statue of Liberty National Monument ♦	210	40.41 N	74.03 W
Staubbachfall ⌙	58	46.35 N	7.55 E
Staufen	58	47.53 N	7.44 E
Staufenberg	56	50.40 N	8.43 E
Staughton Vale	169	37.51 S	144.17 E
Staunton, Il., U.S.	219	39.00 N	89.47 W
Staunton, Va., U.S.	188	38.08 N	79.04 W
Staunton → Roanoke ≃	192	35.56 N	76.43 W
Stavanger	26	58.58 N	5.45 E
Stave ≃	224	49.10 N	122.26 W
Stave Lake ⊜	182	49.15 N	122.21 W
Staveley	44	53.16 N	1.20 W
Stavelot	56	50.23 N	5.56 E
Stavely, Ab., Can.	182	50.10 N	113.38 W
Stavely, Eng., U.K.	44	54.22 N	2.49 W
Staveren	52	52.53 N	5.22 E
Stavern	26	59.00 N	10.02 E
Stavišče	78	49.23 N	30.12 E
Stavnoje	78	48.59 N	22.40 E
Stavropol'	72	45.02 N	41.59 E
Stavropol' Kraj □[8]	84	44.38 N	43.30 E
Stavropol → Toljatti	80	53.31 N	49.26 E
Stavrovo	80	56.08 N	40.00 E
Stavsnäs	40	59.17 N	18.41 E
Stawell	166	37.04 S	142.46 E
Stawell ≃	166	20.38 S	142.55 E
Stawiski	30	53.23 N	22.09 E
Stawiszyn	30	51.55 N	18.07 E
Staxigoe	46	58.28 N	3.04 W
Stayner	212	44.25 N	80.05 W
Stayton	202	44.48 N	122.47 W
Stazzema	64	43.59 N	10.19 E
Steamboat	226	39.22 N	119.44 W
Steamboat Creek ≃	226	39.31 N	119.42 W
Steamboat Mountain ʌ	200	41.58 N	108.58 W
Steamboat Slough ≃	226	38.11 N	121.40 W
Steamboat Springs	200	40.29 N	106.49 W
Steamburg	210	42.07 N	78.54 W
Stearns	192	36.41 N	84.28 W
Stearns Pond ⊜	283	42.37 N	71.04 W
Stębark	30	53.30 N	20.08 E
Stebbins	180	63.32 N	162.18 W
Stebl'ov	78	49.24 N	31.06 E
Stechow	54	52.38 N	12.28 E
Steckborn	58	47.40 N	8.55 E
Stederdorf	52	52.21 N	10.15 E
Stedten	54	51.26 N	11.41 E
Stedum	52	53.18 N	6.41 E
Steeg	58	47.14 N	10.17 E
Steel ≃	190	48.46 N	86.54 W
Steel City	210	40.38 N	75.20 W
Steele, Mo., U.S.	194	36.05 N	89.49 W
Steele, N.D., U.S.	198	46.51 N	99.54 W
Steele ◆[8]	263	51.27 N	7.05 E
Steele, Mount ʌ	200	41.50 N	107.00 W
Steele Creek ≃, Tx., U.S.	222	31.13 N	96.19 W
Steele Creek ≃, Tx., U.S.	222	32.01 N	97.28 W
Steeles Corners	275b	43.48 N	79.25 W
Steeleville	194	38.00 N	89.39 W
Steelhead	224	49.13 N	122.19 W
Steel's Drift	158	27.21 S	29.30 E
Steels Point ›	174c	29.02 S	168.00 E
Steels Run ≃	279b	40.25 N	79.38 W
Steelton, N.Y., U.S.	284a	42.47 N	78.49 W
Steelton, Pa., U.S.	208	40.14 N	76.50 W
Steelville	194	37.58 N	91.21 W
Steenbergen	52	51.35 N	4.19 E
Steenburg Lake ⊜	212	44.50 N	77.41 W
Steenderen	52	52.04 N	6.11 E
Steens Mountain ϰ	202	42.35 N	118.40 W
Steenvoorde	50	50.48 N	2.35 E
Steenwijk	52	52.47 N	6.08 E
Steepbank ≃	184	57.01 N	111.28 W
Steephill Lake ⊜	184	55.58 N	103.08 W
Steep Holm I	42	51.21 N	3.07 W
Steeping ≃	44	53.06 N	0.18 E
Steeple Claydon	42	51.56 N	0.59 W
Steep Point ›	162	26.08 S	113.08 E
Steep Rock	184	51.26 N	98.48 W
Stefanie, Lake (Chew Bahir) ⊜	144	4.40 N	36.50 E
Stefansson Island I	176	73.20 N	105.45 W
Ştefan Vodă	38	44.19 N	27.19 E
Steffisburg	58	46.47 N	7.39 E
Steg	58	47.21 N	8.56 E
Stegalovka	76	52.24 N	38.19 E
Stege	41	54.59 N	12.18 E
Stegeborg	26	58.26 N	16.35 E
Stege Bugt c	41	55.01 N	12.05 E
Stegelitz	54	53.08 N	13.51 E
Steger	216	41.28 N	87.38 W
Stegersbach	61	47.10 N	16.10 E
Steglitz ◆[8]	264a	52.28 N	13.19 E
Stehag	41	55.54 N	13.23 E
Stehekin	224	48.18 N	120.39 W
Stehekin ≃	224	48.21 N	120.40 W
Steiermark □[3]	30	47.10 N	15.10 E
Steigerwald ϰ	56	49.40 N	10.20 E
Steigra	54	51.18 N	11.39 E
Steilacoom	224	47.10 N	122.36 W
Steimbke	52	52.40 N	9.22 E
Stein, Dtsch.	60	49.25 N	11.01 E
Stein, Ned.	56	50.57 N	5.46 E
Stein, Schw.	58	47.33 N	7.58 E
Steina	54	51.12 N	14.01 E
Steinach, Dtsch.	54	50.25 N	11.10 E
Steinach, Dtsch.	58	48.18 N	8.04 E
Steinach, Öst.	64	47.05 N	11.28 E
Steinach ≃	56	50.11 N	11.12 E
Steinamanger → Szombathely	61	47.14 N	16.38 E
Stein am Rhein	58	47.40 N	8.51 E
Steinau	56	50.23 N	9.27 E
Steinbach, Mb., Can.	184	49.32 N	96.41 W
Steinbach, Dtsch.	56	48.43 N	8.10 E
Steinbach-Hallenberg	54	50.42 N	10.34 E
Steinberg ʌ[2]	263	51.05 N	7.27 E
Steinberger Slough ≃	282	37.33 N	122.13 W
Steinbourg	56	48.46 N	7.25 E
Steindorf	61	46.42 N	14.01 E
Steinen	58	47.38 N	7.44 E
Steinernes Meer ϰ	64	47.30 N	12.58 E
Steinfeld, Dtsch.	52	52.35 N	8.12 E
Steinfeld, Dtsch.	54	50.22 N	10.44 E
Steinfeld, Öst.	64	46.45 N	13.15 E
Steinfort	56	49.40 N	5.55 E
Steinforth	263	51.09 N	6.32 E
Steinfurt	52	52.09 N	7.21 E
Steingaden	58	47.42 N	10.51 E
Steinhagen, Dtsch.	52	52.00 N	8.24 E
Steinhagen, Dtsch.	54	54.13 N	12.59 E
Steinhatchee ≃	192	29.40 N	83.24 W
Steinhausen	156	21.49 S	18.20 E
Steinhausen ʋ[1]	58	48.01 N	9.41 E
Steinheid	54	50.28 N	11.04 E
Steinheim, Dtsch.	52	51.52 N	9.05 E
Steinheim, Dtsch.	56	48.58 N	9.16 E
Steinheim, Dtsch.	58	48.01 N	10.09 E
Steinhöfel	54	52.24 N	14.10 E
Steinhöring	60	48.05 N	12.02 E
Steinhude	52	52.27 N	9.21 E
Steinhuder Meer ⊜	52	52.28 N	9.19 E
Steinkjer	26	64.01 N	11.30 E
Steinkopf	156	29.18 S	17.43 E
Steinloge	52	52.54 N	8.19 E
Stein-Neukirch	56	50.41 N	8.03 E
Steinpass)(	64	47.39 N	12.45 E
Steinsdorf	54	52.02 N	14.40 E
Steinshamn	26	62.47 N	6.29 E
Steinstücken ◆[8]	264a	52.23 N	13.08 E
Steinwiesen	54	50.17 N	11.28 E
Stekene	50	51.12 N	4.02 E
Stekl'anka	76	59.08 N	41.37 E
Steklino	76	56.51 N	32.10 E
Steksovo	80	55.17 N	43.25 E
Stella, It.	62	44.24 N	8.30 E
Stella, S. Afr.	158	26.38 S	24.48 E
Stella, Ne., U.S.	198	40.13 N	95.46 W
Stella Niagara	210	43.12 N	79.02 W
Stella-Plage	50	50.29 N	1.35 E
Stellaquo Indian Reserve ◆[4]	182	54.03 N	124.55 W
Stellarton	186	45.34 N	62.40 W
Stelle	52	53.23 N	10.06 E
Stellenbosch	158	33.58 S	18.50 E
Steller, Mount ʌ	180	60.30 N	143.02 W
Stelvio, Parco Nazionale dello ♦	58	46.30 N	10.40 E
Stelvio, Passo dello)(	58	46.32 N	10.27 E
Stemwede	52	52.25 N	8.27 E
Stenay	56	49.29 N	5.11 E
Stendal	54	52.36 N	11.51 E
Stende	76	57.09 N	22.33 E
Stenden	263	51.25 N	6.27 E
Stenhammar slott ⊥	40	59.03 N	16.31 E
Stenhouse Bay	166	35.17 S	136.56 E
Stenhousemuir	46	56.02 N	3.48 W
Stenico	64	46.03 N	10.51 E
Stenlille	41	55.32 N	11.36 E
Stenløse	41	55.46 N	12.12 E
Stenness, Loch of ⊜	46	59.00 N	3.15 W
Stenón	267c	37.58 N	22.20 E
Stenón Návstathmou ꭒ	267c	37.58 N	23.33 E
Stensätra	40	60.36 N	16.44 E
Stensele	24	65.05 N	17.09 E
Stenstorp	26	58.16 N	13.43 E
Stenstrup	41	55.07 N	10.31 E
Stentrop	263	51.30 N	7.49 E
Stenungsund	26	58.05 N	11.49 E
Stepan'	78	51.10 N	26.18 E
Stepanakert	84	39.49 N	46.44 E
Stepanavan	84	41.00 N	44.23 E
Stepancevo, Ross.	80	56.08 N	41.42 E
Stepancevo, Ross.	82	56.22 N	36.10 E
Stepancy	78	49.42 N	31.18 E
Stepano-Krynka	83	47.55 N	38.21 E
Stepanovka, Ross.	80	52.04 N	53.02 E
Stepanovka, Ross.	86	57.13 N	67.26 E
Stepanovka, Ukr.	78	50.58 N	34.37 E
Stepanovo	82	55.43 N	38.28 E
Stepanovskoje	265b	55.47 N	37.10 E
Stepan Razin	84	40.24 N	49.59 E
Stepanščino	82	55.15 N	38.30 E
Stepenitz ≃	54	53.48 N	11.10 E
Stephans-Dom ʋ[1]	264b	48.12 N	16.23 E
Stephanskirchen	64	47.51 N	12.11 E
Stephen	198	48.27 N	96.52 W
Stephen A. Forbes State Park ♦	219	38.44 N	88.46 W
Stephen F. Austin State Historic Park ♦	222	29.48 N	96.05 W
Stephens	194	33.24 N	93.04 W
Stephens, Cape ›	172	40.42 S	173.57 E
Stephens, Port c	166	32.45 S	152.05 E
Stephens City	188	39.05 N	78.13 W
Stephens Creek	166	31.50 S	141.30 E
Stephens Island I	182	54.10 N	130.45 W
Stephens Knob ʌ[2]	192	36.37 N	84.20 W
Stephens Lake ⊜[1]	184	56.26 N	95.07 W
Stephens Mills	210	42.23 N	77.38 W
Stephenson	190	45.24 N	87.36 W
Stephenson, Lake ⊜	222	29.35 N	94.40 W
Stephenson, Mount ʌ	9	69.49 S	69.43 W
Stephens Passage ꭒ	180	57.50 N	133.50 W
Stephentown	210	42.33 N	73.23 W
Stephentown Center	210	42.34 N	73.25 W
Stephenville, Nf., Can.	186	48.33 N	58.35 W
Stephenville, Tx., U.S.	196	32.13 N	98.12 W
Stephenville Crossing	186	48.30 N	58.26 W
Stepn'ak	86	52.50 N	70.50 E
Stepney ◆[8]	260	51.31 N	0.02 W
Stepnica	54	53.40 N	14.36 E
Stepnoj	80	48.56 N	45.36 E
Stepnoje, Ross.	80	51.24 N	46.52 E
Stepnoje, Ross.	84	44.17 N	44.36 E
Step Pyramid → Şaqqārah ⊥	142	29.52 N	31.14 E
Steps Point ›	174u	14.22 S	170.45 W
Steptoe Valley V	204	39.25 N	114.45 W
Stepurino	76	56.24 N	35.16 E
Sterdyń	30	52.35 N	22.18 E
Sterkaar	158	31.05 S	23.42 E
Sterkrade ◆[8]	263	51.31 N	6.51 E
Sterkspruit	158	30.32 S	27.22 E
Sterkstroom	158	31.32 S	26.32 E
Sterlibaševo	86	53.28 N	55.15 E
Sterling, S. Afr.	158	31.16 S	21.28 E
Sterling, Ak., U.S.	180	60.32 N	150.48 W
Sterling, Co., U.S.	198	40.37 N	103.12 W
Sterling, Ct., U.S.	207	41.42 N	71.49 W
Sterling, Il., U.S.	190	41.47 N	89.41 W
Sterling, Ks., U.S.	198	38.12 N	98.12 W
Sterling, Ma., U.S.	207	42.26 N	71.45 W
Sterling, Mi., U.S.	190	44.02 N	84.01 W
Sterling, Ne., U.S.	198	40.27 N	96.22 W
Sterling, N.Y., U.S.	210	43.20 N	76.39 W
Sterling, Oh., U.S.	214	40.58 N	81.51 W
Sterling, Ok., U.S.	196	34.45 N	98.10 W
Sterling, Va., U.S.	208	39.00 N	77.25 W
Sterling City	196	31.50 N	100.59 W
Sterling Creek ≃	210	43.20 N	76.42 W
Sterling Forest Lake ⊜	276	41.10 N	74.16 W
Sterling Heights	214	42.34 N	83.01 W
Sterling Junction	207	42.24 N	71.46 W
Sterling Park	282	37.41 N	122.26 W
Sterling Run	214	41.25 N	78.12 W
Sterlington	194	32.41 N	92.05 W
Sterlitamak	86	53.37 N	55.58 E
Şternberg	54	53.43 N	11.49 E
Šternberk	30	49.44 N	17.18 E
Şternstein ʌ	61	48.34 N	14.16 E
Šterovka	83	48.19 N	38.57 E
Sterup	41	54.44 N	9.44 E
Sterzing → Vipiteno	64	46.54 N	11.26 E
Şteszew	30	52.18 N	16.42 E
Štětí	54	50.25 N	14.23 E
Stetson Pond ⊜	283	42.02 N	70.50 W
Stetten am kalten Markt	58	48.07 N	9.04 E
Stettin → Szczecin	30	53.24 N	14.32 E
Stettler	182	52.19 N	112.43 W
Steuben □[6], In., U.S.	216	41.38 N	85.00 W
Steuben □[6], N.Y., U.S.	210	42.20 N	77.19 W
Steubenville	214	40.22 N	80.38 W
Stevenage	42	51.55 N	0.14 W
Stevens, N.J., U.S.	285	40.05 N	74.49 W
Stevens, Pa., U.S.	208	40.13 N	76.09 W
Stevens, Lake ⊜	224	48.01 N	122.05 W
Stevens, Mount ʌ	172	40.48 S	172.27 E
Stevens Creek ≃, Ca., U.S.	282	37.26 N	122.05 W
Stevens Creek ≃, S.C., U.S.	192	33.34 N	82.03 W
Stevens Creek Park ♦	282	37.17 N	122.04 W
Stevens Creek Reservoir ⊜[1]	282	37.17 N	122.05 W
Stevens Institute of Technology ʋ[2]	276	40.44 N	74.02 W
Stevenson, Al., U.S.	194	34.52 N	85.50 W
Stevenson, Md., U.S.	284b	39.25 N	76.43 W
Stevenson, Wa., U.S.	224	45.42 N	121.53 W
Stevenson Creek ≃	162	27.06 S	135.33 E
Stevenson Entrance ꭒ	180	58.45 N	152.20 W
Stevenson Lake ⊜	184	53.56 N	96.09 W
Stevens Pass)(	224	47.45 N	121.04 W
Stevens Peak ʌ	202	47.27 N	115.46 W
Stevens Point	190	44.31 N	89.34 W
Stevenston	46	55.39 N	4.45 W
Stevens Village	180	66.00 N	149.05 W
Stevensville, On., Can.	284a	42.57 N	79.04 W
Stevensville, Md., U.S.	208	38.58 N	76.18 W
Stevensville, Mi., U.S.	216	42.00 N	86.31 W
Stevensville, Mt., U.S.	202	46.30 N	114.05 W
Stevensville, Pa., U.S.	210	41.46 N	76.11 W
Stevinson	226	37.20 N	120.51 W
Stevns Klint ≗[4]	41	55.18 N	12.27 E
Steward	216	41.51 N	89.01 W
Stewardson	219	39.15 N	88.37 W
Stewart, B.C., Can.	182	55.56 N	129.59 W
Stewart, Mn., U.S.	190	44.43 N	94.29 W
Stewart ≃	180	63.18 N	139.25 W
Stewart, Cape ›	164	11.57 S	134.45 E
Stewart, Isla I	254	54.52 S	71.12 W
Stewart, Mount ʌ	166	20.12 S	145.29 E
Stewart Island I	172	47.00 S	167.50 E
Stewart Islands II	175e	8.25 S	162.52 E
Stewart Lake ⊜	219	40.09 N	90.16 W
Stewart Manor	276	40.43 N	73.41 W
Stewarton	46	55.41 N	4.31 W
Stewartstown, N. Ire., U.K.	48	54.35 N	6.41 W
Stewartstown, Pa., U.S.	208	39.45 N	76.35 W
Stewartsville, Mo., U.S.	194	39.45 N	94.29 W
Stewartsville, N.J., U.S.	208	40.41 N	75.06 W
Stewartsville, Pa., U.S.	279b	40.21 N	79.46 W
Stewart Valley	184	50.36 N	107.50 W
Stewartville	190	43.51 N	92.29 W
Stewiacke	186	45.08 N	63.21 W
Steyerberg	52	52.34 N	9.01 E
Steyning	42	50.53 N	0.20 W
Steynsburg	158	31.15 S	25.49 E
Steynsrus	158	27.58 S	27.33 E
Steyr	61	48.03 N	14.25 E
Steyr ≃	61	48.02 N	14.25 E
Steyregg	61	48.17 N	14.22 E
Steytlerville	158	33.21 S	24.21 E
Stežki	80	53.06 N	41.13 E
Stezzano	62	45.38 N	9.39 E
Sthal	126	24.12 N	89.44 E
Ştia	66	43.48 N	11.42 E
Štiavnické vrchy ϰ	30	48.40 N	18.45 E
Stickle Pond ⊜	276	40.59 N	74.25 W
Stickney, Eng., U.K.	44	53.05 N	0.01 E
Stickney, Il., U.S.	216	41.49 N	87.46 W
Stickney, S.D., U.S.	198	43.35 N	98.26 W
Stidsvig	41	56.12 N	13.08 E
Stiefingbach ≃	61	46.47 N	15.35 E
Stiege	54	51.40 N	10.53 E
Stiene	76	57.26 N	24.34 E
Stienitzfliess ≃	264a	52.33 N	13.43 E
Stienitz-See ⊜	264a	52.30 N	13.49 E
Stiens	52	53.15 N	5.45 E
Stiepel ◆[8]	263	51.25 N	7.15 E
Stif	148	36.09 N	5.26 E
Stif □[5]	148	36.15 N	5.10 E
Stiftskirche ʋ[1]	263	51.23 N	7.00 E
Stige	41	55.26 N	10.25 E
Stigler	196	35.15 N	95.07 W
Stigliano	68	40.24 N	16.14 E
Stigtomta	40	58.48 N	16.47 E
Stikine ≃	180	56.40 N	132.30 W
Stikine Ranges ϰ	180	58.45 N	130.00 W
Stiklestad	26	63.48 N	11.33 E
Stilbaai	158	34.24 S	21.26 E
Stiles	210	40.40 N	75.30 W
Stiles Pond ⊜	283	42.41 N	71.02 W
Stilesville	210	42.05 N	75.24 W
Stilfontein	158	26.50 S	26.50 E
Stilís	38	38.55 N	22.36 E
Still	148	34.20 N	5.51 E
Stillaguamish ≃	224	48.11 N	122.22 W
Stillaguamish, North Fork ≃	224	48.11 N	122.07 W
Stillaguamish, South Fork ≃	224	48.11 N	122.07 W
Stillhouse Hollow Lake ⊜[1]	222	31.00 N	97.35 W
Stilling	41	56.04 N	10.00 E
Stillman Valley	216	42.07 N	89.11 W
Stillmore	192	32.26 N	82.12 W
Still Pond	208	39.19 N	76.02 W
Still Run ≃	285	39.49 N	75.18 W
Stillwater, B.C., Can.	182	49.46 N	124.18 W
Stillwater, Mn., U.S.	190	45.03 N	92.48 W
Stillwater, N.J., U.S.	210	41.02 N	74.52 W
Stillwater, N.Y., U.S.	210	42.56 N	73.39 W
Stillwater, Oh., U.S.	214	40.20 N	81.18 W
Stillwater, Ok., U.S.	196	36.06 N	97.03 W
Stillwater, Pa., U.S.	210	41.09 N	76.22 W
Stillwater ≃, Mt., U.S.	202	45.38 N	109.17 W
Stillwater ≃, Oh., U.S.	218	39.47 N	84.12 W
Stillwater Creek ≃	214	40.25 N	81.22 W
Stillwater Range ϰ	204	39.50 N	118.15 W
Stillwell, Il., U.S.	219	40.13 N	91.11 W
Stillwell, Ok., U.S.	194	35.49 N	94.38 W
Stilo	68	38.29 N	16.28 E
Stilo, Punta ›	68	38.28 N	16.36 E
Stimberg ʌ[2]	263	51.40 N	7.15 E
Stimigliano	66	42.18 N	12.34 E
Stimson, Mount ʌ	202	48.31 N	113.36 W
Stînca-Costești, Lacul (vodochranilišče Kostešty-Stynka) ⊜[1]	38	47.55 N	27.10 E
Stinchar ≃	44	55.06 N	5.00 W
Stinear Nunataks ϰ	9	69.42 S	64.40 E
Stine Canal ≋	226	35.15 N	119.08 W
Stine Mountain ʌ	202	45.44 N	113.07 W
Stingray Point ›	208	37.33 N	76.18 W
Stînișoarei, Munții ϰ	38	47.10 N	26.00 E
Stinking Water Creek ≃	198	40.22 N	101.07 W
Stinnett	196	35.49 N	101.26 W
Stintino	71	40.56 N	8.13 E
Ştintonville	273d	26.14 S	28.13 E
Štip	38	41.44 N	22.12 E
Stiperstones ʌ	42	52.35 N	2.56 W
Stiring-Wendel	56	49.12 N	6.56 E
Stírka ʌ	60	49.24 N	13.34 E
Stirling, Austl.	162	21.44 S	133.45 E
Stirling, Austl.	168a	31.54 S	115.47 E
Stirling, Austl.	168b	35.00 S	138.43 E
Stirling, Ab., Can.	182	49.30 N	112.31 W
Stirling, On., Can.	212	44.18 N	77.33 W
Stirling, Scot., U.K.	46	56.07 N	3.57 W
Stirling, N.J., U.S.	210	40.40 N	74.29 W
Stirling, Mount ʌ	162	31.50 S	117.38 E
Stirling Castle ⊥	46	56.07 N	3.57 W
Stirling City	204	39.54 N	121.31 W
Stirling Range ϰ	162	34.23 S	117.50 E
Stirling Range National Park ♦	162	34.22 S	118.00 E
Stirling Reservoir ⊜[1]	168a	33.08 S	116.03 E
Stirrat	192	37.43 N	82.00 W
Ştissing Mountain ʌ	210	41.57 N	73.42 W
Štitary	61	48.56 N	15.51 E
Stittsville	212	45.15 N	75.55 W
Stittville	210	43.13 N	75.17 W
Stjärnhov	40	59.05 N	17.00 E
Stjärnsund, Sve.	40	60.26 N	16.12 E
Stjärnsund, Sve.	40	58.51 N	14.55 E
Stjernøya I	24	70.18 N	22.45 E
Stjørdalshalsen	26	63.28 N	10.56 E
Stöberhai ʌ	54	51.39 N	10.34 E
Stochod ≃	78	51.52 N	25.38 E

Symbols in the index entries represent the broad categories identified in the key at the right. Symbols with superior numbers (ϰ[1]) identify subcategories (see complete key on page *I · 1*).

Symbole im Register stellen die rechts im Schlüssel erklärten Kategorien dar. Symbole mit hochgestellten Ziffern (ϰ[1]) bezeichnen Unterabteilungen einer Kategorie (vgl. vollständiger Schlüssel auf Seite *I · 1*).

Los símbolos incluídos en el texto del índice representan las grandes categorias identificadas con la clave a la derecha. Los símbolos con numeros en su parte superior (ϰ[1]) identifican las subcategorías (véase la clave completa en la página *I · 1*).

Les symboles de l'index représentent les catégories indiquées dans la légende à droite. Les symboles suivis d'un indice (ϰ[1]) représentent des sous-catégories (voir légende complète à la page *I · 1*).

Os símbolos incluídos no texto do índice representam as grandes categorias identificadas com a chave à direita. Os símbolos com números em sua parte superior (ϰ[1]) identificam as subcategorias (veja-se a chave completa à página *I · 1*).

	English	Deutsch	Español	Français	Português
ʌ	Mountain	Berg	Montaña	Montagne	Montanha
ϰ	Mountains	Gebirge	Montañas	Montagnes	Montanhas
)(	Pass	Paß	Paso	Col	Passo
V	Valley, Canyon	Tal, Cañon	Valle, Cañón	Vallée, Canyon	Vale, Canhão
⌣	Plain	Ebene	Llano	Plaine	Planície
›	Cape	Kap	Cabo	Cap	Cabo
I	Island	Insel	Isla	Île	Ilha
II	Islands	Inseln	Islas	Îles	Ilhas
≗	Other Topographic Features	Andere Topographische Objekte	Otros Elementos Topográficos	Autres données topographiques	Outros acidentes topográficos

ESPAÑOL

Nombre	Página	Lat.°′	Long.°′ W = Oeste
Stock	260	51.40 N	0.27 E
Stock, Étang du ⊜	56	48.45 N	6.55 E
Stockach	58	47.51 N	9.00 E
Stöckalp	58	46.48 N	8.17 E
Stockamöllan	41	55.57 N	13.22 E
Stockbridge, Eng., U.K.	42	51.07 N	1.29 W
Stockbridge, Ga., U.S.	192	33.32 N	84.14 W
Stockbridge, Ma., U.S.	207	42.17 N	73.19 W
Stockbridge, Mi., U.S.	216	42.27 N	84.10 W
Stockbridge Bowl ⊜	207	42.20 N	73.19 W
Stockbridge Indian Reservation ◆[4]	190	44.52 N	88.53 W
Stockbury	260	51.20 N	0.39 E
Stockby	40	59.20 N	17.41 E
Stockdale, Oh., U.S.	218	38.57 N	82.51 W
Stockdale, Tx., U.S.	196	29.14 N	97.57 W
Stockelsdorf	52	53.54 N	10.38 E
Stöcken	54	53.00 N	10.40 E
Stockerau	61	48.23 N	16.13 E
Stockertown	208	40.45 N	75.15 W
Stockett	202	47.21 N	111.09 W
Stockheim	56	50.19 N	9.01 E
Stockholm, Sve.	40	59.20 N	18.03 E
Stockholm, Me., U.S.	186	47.02 N	68.08 W
Stockholm, N.J., U.S.	210	41.05 N	74.31 W
Stockholm, Lake ⊜	276	41.04 N	74.32 W
Stockholms Län □[6]	40	59.30 N	18.20 E
Stock Island	220	24.34 N	81.45 W
Stockland	216	40.37 N	87.36 W
Stockport, Eng., U.K.	44	53.25 N	2.10 W
Stockport, N.Y., U.S.	210	42.19 N	73.45 W
Stockport □[8]	262	53.23 N	2.08 W
Stocksbridge	44	53.27 N	1.34 W
Stockstadt	56	49.48 N	8.28 E
Stocksund	40	59.23 N	18.04 E
Stockton, Austl.	170	32.55 S	151.47 E
Stockton, Al., U.S.	194	30.59 N	87.51 W
Stockton, Ca., U.S.	226	37.57 N	121.17 W
Stockton, Il., U.S.	190	42.20 N	90.00 W
Stockton, Ks., U.S.	198	39.26 N	99.15 W
Stockton, Md., U.S.	208	38.03 N	75.24 W
Stockton, Mo., U.S.	194	37.41 N	93.47 W
Stockton, N.J., U.S.	208	40.24 N	74.58 W
Stockton, N.Y., U.S.	214	42.19 N	79.22 W
Stockton, Ut,. U.S.	200	40.27 N	112.21 W
Stockton Heath, Eng., U.K.	44	53.22 N	2.34 W
Stockton Heath, Eng., U.K.	262	53.22 N	2.34 W
Stockton Metropolitan Airport ⊠	226	37.54 N	121.15 W
Stockton-on-Tees	44	54.34 N	1.19 W
Stockton Plateau ⩘[1]	196	30.30 N	102.30 W
Stockton Reservoir ⊜[1]	194	37.40 N	93.45 W
Stockton Springs	188	44.29 N	68.51 W
Stockum, Dtsch.	52	51.40 N	7.42 E
Stockum, Dtsch.	263	51.28 N	7.22 E
Stockum, Dtsch.	263	51.32 N	7.47 E
Stockum, Dtsch.	263	51.36 N	6.39 E
Stockum ◆[8]	263	51.16 N	6.44 E
Stockville	198	40.31 N	100.22 W
Stockwell	216	40.17 N	86.46 W
Stockwell, Lake ⊜	285	39.51 N	74.47 W
Stoco Lake ⊜	212	44.28 N	77.18 W
Stoczek Łukowski	30	51.58 N	21.58 E
Stod	60	49.39 N	13.10 E
Stoddard Mountain ∧	228	34.42 N	117.07 W
Stöde	26	62.25 N	16.35 E
Stodoliči	78	51.44 N	28.30 E
Stodolišče	76	54.11 N	32.39 E
Stœng Tréng	110	13.31 N	105.58 E
Stoer	46	58.12 N	5.20 W
Stoer, Point of ›	46	58.15 N	5.21 W
Stoffberg	156	25.29 S	29.49 E
Stoj, gora ∧	78	48.37 N	23.11 E
Stojba	89	52.49 N	131.43 E
Stoke	260	51.27 N	0.37 E
Stoke ≃	206	45.35 N	71.58 W
Stoke, Monts ⩘	206	45.33 N	71.42 W
Stoke D'Abernon	260	51.19 N	0.23 W
Stokenchurch	42	51.40 N	0.55 W
Stoke Newington ◆[8]	260	51.34 N	0.05 W
Stoke-on-Trent	42	53.00 N	2.10 W
Stoke Poges	260	51.33 N	0.35 W
Stokes, Mount ∧	172	41.06 S	174.06 E
Stokes Inlet ⊂	162	33.50 S	121.08 E
Stokesley	44	54.28 N	1.11 W
Stokes Point ›	166	40.10 S	143.56 E
Stokes Range ⩘[2]	164	15.46 S	130.57 E
Stokkemarke	41	54.50 N	11.23 E
Stokksnes ›	24a	64.17 N	14.54 W
Stol ∧	38	44.13 N	22.14 E
Stolac	36	43.05 N	17.58 E
Stolbcy	76	53.29 N	26.44 E
Stolberg, Dtsch.	54	51.34 N	10.57 E
Stolberg, Dtsch.	56	50.46 N	6.13 E
Stolbišči	80	55.39 N	49.14 E
Stolboucha	86	49.59 N	84.30 E
Stolbovo	76	52.38 N	34.47 E
Stolbovoj, ostrov I	74	74.05 N	136.00 E
Stolbun	76	52.48 N	31.25 E
Stolby, zapovednik ♦	88	55.45 N	92.45 E
Stolin	78	51.53 N	26.51 E
Stollberg	54	50.42 N	12.47 E
Stöllet	26	60.24 N	13.16 E
Stol'noje	78	51.31 N	31.55 E
Stolpe	264a	52.40 N	13.16 E
Stolpen	54	51.05 N	14.04 E
Stolper Heide ◆[3]	264a	52.39 N	13.14 E
Stolpino	80	57.24 N	42.55 E
Stolp → Słupsk	30	54.28 N	17.01 E
Stolzenau	52	52.31 N	9.04 E
Ston	36	42.50 N	17.42 E
Stondon Massey	260	51.41 N	0.18 E
Stone, Eng., U.K.	42	52.54 N	2.10 W
Stone, Eng., U.K.	260	51.27 N	0.16 E
Stoneboro	214	41.20 N	80.06 W
Stone Canyon Reservoir ⊜[1]	280	34.07 N	118.28 W
Stone Corral Creek ≃	226	39.16 N	122.06 W
Stone Creek	214	40.24 N	81.34 W
Stonecutters Island I	271d	22.19 N	114.08 E
Stonefort	194	37.37 N	88.42 W
Stoneham, Ma., U.S.	283	42.28 N	71.06 W
Stoneham, Pa., U.S.	214	41.49 N	79.07 W
Stone Harbor	208	39.03 N	74.45 W
Stonehaven	46	56.57 N	2.12 W
Stonehenge	166	24.22 S	143.17 E
Stonehenge ⊥	42	51.11 N	1.49 W
Stonehill College ʋ[2]	283	42.03 N	71.05 W
Stonehouse, Eng., U.K.	42	51.45 N	2.17 W
Stonehouse, Scot., U.K.	46	55.43 N	4.00 W
Stone Indian Reserve ◆[4]	182	51.54 N	123.12 W
Stoneleigh	42	52.21 N	1.31 W
Stonelick Creek ≃	218	39.07 N	84.13 W
Stonelick State Park ♦	218	39.13 N	84.04 W
Stone Mountain	192	33.48 N	84.10 W
Stone Mountain ∧, Pa., U.S.	210	40.37 N	77.48 W
Stone Mountain ∧, Vt., U.S.	188	44.34 N	71.40 W
Stone Mountain Memorial State Park ♦	192	33.49 N	84.06 W
Stone Park	278	41.54 N	87.53 W
Stoner	182	53.36 N	122.40 W
Stoner Creek ≃	218	38.18 N	84.14 W
Stone Ridge	210	41.51 N	74.09 W

FRANÇAIS

Nom	Page	Lat.°′	Long.°′ W = Ouest
Stonerstown	214	40.13 N	78.16 W
Stones, East Fork ≃	194	35.59 N	86.27 W
Stones, West Fork ≃	194	35.59 N	86.27 W
Stones River National Battlefield ⊥	194	35.52 N	86.26 W
Stonestown ◆[9]	282	37.44 N	122.28 W
Stonevilla	279b	40.18 N	79.31 W
Stoneville	192	36.27 N	79.54 W
Stonewall, Mb., Can.	184	50.09 N	97.21 W
Stonewall, La., U.S.	194	32.16 N	93.49 W
Stonewall, Ms., U.S.	194	32.07 N	88.47 W
Stonewall, Ok., U.S.	196	34.39 N	96.31 W
Stonewall Manor	284c	38.53 N	77.14 W
Stoney Creek	212	43.13 N	79.46 W
Stoney Point ›	214	42.18 N	82.34 W
Stonington, Ct., U.S.	207	41.20 N	71.54 W
Stonington, Il., U.S.	219	39.38 N	89.11 W
Stonington, Me., U.S.	188	44.09 N	68.40 W
Stony ≃, Ak., U.S.	180	61.45 N	156.35 W
Stony ≃, Mn., U.S.	190	47.44 N	91.47 W
Stony Brook	210	40.55 N	73.08 W
Stony Brook ≃, Ct., U.S.	276	41.04 N	73.28 W
Stony Brook ≃, Ct., U.S.	276	41.08 N	73.22 W
Stony Brook ≃, Ma., U.S.	283	42.38 N	71.22 W
Stony Brook ≃, Ma., U.S.	283	42.22 N	71.16 W
Stony Brook ≃, N.J., U.S.	276	40.19 N	74.41 W
Stony Brook ≃, N.J., U.S.	276	40.56 N	74.26 W
Stony Brook Harbor ⊂	276	40.54 N	73.10 W
Stony Brook Reservation ♦	283	42.16 N	71.09 W
Stony Creek, Ct., U.S.	207	41.15 N	72.44 W
Stony Creek, Va., U.S.	208	36.56 N	77.24 W
Stony Creek ≃, Ca., U.S.	204	39.41 N	121.58 W
Stony Creek ≃, Il., U.S.	278	41.41 N	87.51 W
Stony Creek ≃, Mi., U.S.	216	41.57 N	83.18 W
Stony Creek ≃, Mi., U.S.	216	43.00 N	84.55 W
Stony Creek ≃, N.Y., U.S.	212	43.49 N	76.14 W
Stony Creek ≃, Pa., U.S.	285	40.07 N	75.21 W
Stony Creek ≃, Va., U.S.	208	36.56 N	77.23 W
Stony Creek, Middle Fork ≃	226	39.25 N	122.31 W
Stony Creek, North Fork ≃	226	39.22 N	122.37 W
Stony Creek, South Fork ≃	226	39.22 N	122.39 W
Stony Creek Indian Reserve ◆[4]	182	53.57 N	124.07 W
Stony Creek Mills	208	40.21 N	75.52 W
Stonyford	226	39.22 N	122.32 W
Stony Gorge Reservoir ⊜[1]	226	39.34 N	122.31 W
Stony Indian Reserve ◆[4]	182	51.10 N	114.55 W
Stony Island I, Mi., U.S.	281	42.07 N	83.08 W
Stony Island I, N.Y., U.S.	212	43.53 N	76.25 W
Stony Kill ≃	210	42.24 N	73.38 W
Stony Lake ⊜, Mb., Can.	176	58.51 N	98.35 W
Stony Lake ⊜, On., Can.	212	44.33 N	78.05 W
Stony Plain	182	53.32 N	114.00 W
Stony Plain Indian Reserve ◆[4]	182	53.30 N	113.45 W
Stony Point, Austl.	169	38.22 S	145.13 E
Stony Point, Mi., U.S.	216	41.57 N	83.16 W
Stony Point, N.Y., U.S.	210	41.13 N	73.59 W
Stony Point, N.C., U.S.	192	35.51 N	81.02 W
Stony Point ›	284a	42.50 N	78.52 W
Stony Point ›[1]	212	43.52 N	76.15 W
Stony Prairie	214	41.21 N	83.10 W
Stony Rapids	176	59.16 N	105.50 W
Stony Ridge	214	41.30 N	83.30 W
Stony River	180	61.47 N	156.41 W
Stony Run	284b	39.11 N	76.42 W
Stony Run ≃	285	40.09 N	75.32 W
Stony Stratford	42	52.04 N	0.52 W
Stoober Bach ≃	61	47.27 N	16.35 E
Stop ≃	283	42.10 N	71.19 W
Stopnica	30	50.27 N	20.57 E
Stoppenberg ◆[8]	263	51.29 N	7.02 E
Stör ≃	54	53.50 N	11.29 E
Storå	40	59.43 N	15.08 E
Storå ≃	26	56.19 N	8.19 E
Stora Alvaret ⩩	26	56.30 N	16.30 E
Stora Gla ⊜	26	59.30 N	12.30 E
Stora Kloten ⊜	40	59.52 N	15.16 E
Stora Le ⊜	26	59.05 N	11.53 E
Stora Lulevatten ⊜	24	67.10 N	19.16 E
Stora Mellösa	40	59.13 N	15.30 E
Stora Möja I, Sve.	26	59.26 N	18.55 E
Stora Möja I, Sve.	40	59.26 N	18.55 E
Stora Norn ⊜	40	60.14 N	15.42 E
Stora Sjöfallets Nationalpark ♦	24	67.44 N	18.16 E
Stora Skedvi	40	60.24 N	15.48 E
Stora Sundby	40	59.16 N	16.07 E
Storavan ⊜	24	65.40 N	18.15 E
Stora Vika	40	58.56 N	17.48 E
Storby	26	60.13 N	19.34 E
Stord I	26	59.53 N	5.25 E
Store Andst	41	55.29 N	9.14 E
Storebælt ʯ	41	55.30 N	11.00 E
Store Heddinge	41	55.19 N	12.25 E
Store Magleby	41	55.36 N	12.38 E
Store Merløse	41	55.33 N	11.40 E
Støren	26	63.02 N	10.18 E
Store Sotra I	26	60.18 N	5.05 E
Storeton	262	53.21 N	3.03 W
Storey □[6]	226	39.28 N	119.30 W
Storfjärden ⊜	40	60.30 N	17.23 E
Storfjorden ⊂[2]	26	62.25 N	6.30 E
Storfors	40	59.32 N	14.16 E
Störitzsee ⊜	264a	52.23 N	13.51 E
Störkanal ≅	54	53.36 N	11.30 E
Storkerson Bay ⊂	176	73.00 N	124.50 W
Storkerson Peninsula ›[1]	176	72.30 N	106.30 W
Storkow, Dtsch.	54	53.19 N	14.17 E
Storkow, Dtsch.	54	52.15 N	13.56 E
Storlien	26	63.19 N	12.06 E
Stormarn ◆[1]	52	53.45 N	10.20 E
Storm Bay ⊂	166	43.10 S	147.32 E
Stormberg ∧	158	30.57 S	26.41 E
Stormberge ⩘	158	31.27 S	26.55 E
Storm King Mountain ∧	224	46.39 N	122.10 W
Storm Lake	198	42.38 N	95.12 W
Storm Mountain ∧	180	59.37 N	150.35 W
Stormont-Dundas and Glengarry □[6]	206	45.10 N	75.00 W
Štormovo	83	49.06 N	38.55 E
Stormsrivier	158	33.59 S	23.52 E
Stormsvlei	158	34.05 S	20.06 E
Stormville	210	41.34 N	73.45 W
Stornara	68	41.17 N	15.46 E
Stornarella	68	41.15 N	15.44 E
Stornorrforsen	26	63.52 N	20.03 E
Stornoway	46	58.12 N	6.23 W
Storo	64	45.51 N	10.35 E
Storoževaja	84	43.53 N	41.27 E

PORTUGUÊS

Nome	Página	Lat.°′	Long.°′ W = Oeste
Storoževsk	24	61.57 N	52.16 E
Storožinec	78	48.10 N	25.43 E
Storrensjön ⊜	26	63.38 N	12.34 E
Storrington	42	50.55 N	0.28 W
Storrs	207	41.48 N	72.15 W
Storsjøen ⊜, Nor.	26	60.23 N	11.40 E
Storsjøen ⊜, Nor.	26	61.35 N	11.12 E
Storsjön ⊜, Sve.	26	62.48 N	13.07 E
Storsjön ⊜, Sve.	26	63.12 N	14.18 E
Storsjön ⊜, Sve.	40	60.34 N	16.44 E
Storsjön ⊜, Sve.	40	59.04 N	17.12 E
Storsteinsfjellet ∧	24	68.14 N	17.52 E
Storstrøm □[6]	41	55.00 N	11.55 E
Storstrømmen ʯ	41	54.58 N	11.55 E
Storstrømsbroen ◆[5]	41	54.58 N	11.50 E
Stort ≃	260	51.46 N	0.01 E
Storthoaks	184	49.22 N	101.38 W
Storuman	24	65.06 N	17.06 E
Storuman ⊜[1]	24	65.14 N	16.54 E
Storuman-See → Storavan ⊜	24	65.40 N	18.15 E
Storvarts gruve	26	62.38 N	11.31 E
Storvätteshågna ∧	26	62.07 N	12.27 E
Storvik	40	60.35 N	16.32 E
Storvindeln ⊜	24	65.43 N	17.05 E
Storvreta	40	59.58 N	17.42 E
Story	202	44.34 N	106.53 W
Story City	190	42.11 N	93.35 W
Stosch, Isla I	254	49.09 S	75.26 W
Stössen	54	51.06 N	11.55 E
Stotfold	42	52.01 N	0.14 W
Stotternheim	54	51.03 N	11.02 E
Stottville	210	42.17 N	73.44 W
Stouchsburg	208	40.23 N	76.14 W
Stough Park ♦	280	34.12 N	118.18 W
Stoughton, Sk., Can.	184	49.41 N	103.03 W
Stoughton, Eng., U.K.	260	51.15 N	0.35 W
Stoughton, Ma., U.S.	207	42.07 N	71.06 W
Stoughton, Wi., U.S.	216	42.55 N	89.13 W
Stoumont	56	50.25 N	5.48 E
Stoŭng ≃	110	12.50 N	104.19 E
Stour ≃, Eng., U.K.	42	51.52 N	1.16 E
Stour ≃, Eng., U.K.	42	50.43 N	1.46 W
Stour ≃, Eng., U.K.	42	51.18 N	1.22 E
Stour ≃, Eng., U.K.	42	52.20 N	2.15 W
Stourbridge	42	52.27 N	2.09 W
Stourport-on-Severn	42	52.21 N	2.16 W
Stout Lake ⊜	184	52.08 N	94.33 W
Stoutsville	219	39.33 N	91.51 W
Stover	194	38.26 N	92.59 W
Stow, Ma., U.S.	207	42.26 N	71.30 W
Stow, N.Y., U.S.	214	42.09 N	79.25 W
Stow, Oh., U.S.	214	41.10 N	81.27 W
Stowe, Pa., U.S.	208	40.15 N	75.40 W
Stowe, Vt., U.S.	188	44.27 N	72.41 W
Stowell	194	29.47 N	94.23 W
Stowe Township	279b	40.29 N	80.04 W
Stow Maries	260	51.40 N	0.39 E
Stowmarket	42	52.11 N	1.00 E
Stow-on-the-Wold	42	51.56 N	1.44 W
Stowupland	42	52.12 N	1.01 E
Stoyoma Mountain ∧	182	49.59 N	121.13 W
Stoystown	214	40.06 N	78.57 W
Stožec	60	48.51 N	13.50 E
Stra	64	45.25 N	12.00 E
Straach	54	51.57 N	12.35 E
Strabane, N. Ire., U.K.	48	54.49 N	7.27 W
Strabane, Pa., U.S.	214	40.15 N	80.11 W
Straberg	263	51.05 N	6.45 E
Strachan	46	57.01 N	2.32 W
Strachan Island I	164	9.00 S	142.10 E
Strachur	46	56.10 N	5.04 W
Stradbally	48	53.00 N	7.08 W
Stradbroke	42	52.19 N	1.16 E
Stradeč'	76	51.56 N	23.40 E
Stradella	62	45.05 N	9.18 E
Stradone	48	53.58 N	7.14 W
Stradovn'a, ozero ⊜	82	56.53 N	36.18 E
Straelen	56	51.27 N	6.16 E
Strafford	285	40.03 N	75.25 W
Straffordville	212	42.45 N	80.47 W
Strahan	166	42.09 S	145.19 E
Straight Creek ≃	218	38.46 N	83.55 W
Strakonice	60	49.16 N	13.55 E
Stralsund	54	54.19 N	13.05 E
Strambino	62	45.23 N	7.53 E
Strand	158	34.06 S	18.50 E
Stranda	26	62.19 N	6.54 E
Strande	54	54.26 N	10.12 E
Strandhill	48	54.17 N	8.36 W
Stranger Creek ≃	198	39.00 N	95.01 W
Strangford	48	54.22 N	5.34 W
Strangford Lough ⊜	48	54.28 N	5.35 W
Strängnäs	40	59.23 N	17.02 E
Strångsjö	40	58.54 N	16.12 E
Strangways ≃	164	14.52 S	133.50 E
Strangways, Mount ∧	162	23.02 S	133.51 E
Stranorlar	48	54.48 N	7.46 W
Stranraer	44	54.55 N	5.02 W
Strasbourg, Sk., Can.	184	51.04 N	104.57 W
Strasbourg, Fr.	58	48.35 N	7.45 E
Strasbourg, Aéroport ⊠	58	48.32 N	7.38 E
Strasburg, Dtsch.	54	53.30 N	13.44 E
Strasburg, Co., U.S.	198	39.44 N	104.20 W
Strasburg, N.D., U.S.	198	46.08 N	100.09 W
Strasburg, Oh., U.S.	214	40.35 N	81.31 W
Strasburg, Pa., U.S.	208	39.58 N	76.11 W
Strasburg, Va., U.S.	188	38.59 N	78.21 W
Straševiči	76	56.49 N	34.36 E
Strašín	60	49.08 N	13.38 E
Stråssa	40	59.45 N	15.13 E
Strassburg → Strasbourg	58	48.35 N	7.45 E
Strasshof an der Nordbahn	61	48.19 N	16.39 E
Strasskirchen	60	48.50 N	12.43 E
Strata Florida Abbey ʋ[1]	42	52.16 N	3.51 W
Stratford, On., Can.	212	43.22 N	80.57 W
Stratford, N.Z.	172	39.20 S	174.17 E
Stratford, Ca., U.S.	226	36.11 N	119.49 W
Stratford, Ct., U.S.	207	41.11 N	73.08 W
Stratford, De., U.S.	285	39.40 N	75.38 W
Stratford, Ia., U.S.	190	42.16 N	93.55 W
Stratford, N.J., U.S.	208	39.49 N	75.00 W
Stratford, N.Y., U.S.	210	43.11 N	74.42 W
Stratford, Ok., U.S.	196	34.47 N	96.57 W
Stratford, Tx., U.S.	196	36.20 N	102.04 W
Stratford, Wi., U.S.	190	44.48 N	90.04 W
Stratford Centre	206	45.47 N	71.16 W
Stratford Point ›	276	41.09 N	73.06 W
Stratford-upon-Avon	42	52.12 N	1.41 W
Strathalbyn	168b	35.16 S	138.54 E
Strathaven	46	55.40 N	4.04 W
Strathbogie Ranges ⩘	169	36.55 S	145.45 E
Strathclair	184	50.24 N	100.24 W
Strathclyde □[4]	46	56.00 N	5.15 W
Strathcona Provincial Park ♦	182	49.40 N	125.50 W
Strathdearn V	46	57.15 N	4.05 W
Strathdon	46	57.11 N	3.02 W
Strathearn V	46	56.18 N	3.45 W
Strathfield	170	33.52 S	151.06 E
Strathgordon	166	42.46 S	146.03 E
Strath Kanaird	46	57.59 N	5.11 W
Strathlorne	186	46.11 N	61.17 W
Strathminglo	46	56.16 N	3.16 W
Strathmoor ◆[8]	281	42.23 N	83.11 W
Strathmore, Ab., Can.	182	51.03 N	113.23 W
Strathmore, Ca., U.S.	204	36.08 N	119.03 W
Strathmore, N.J., U.S.	276	40.24 N	74.13 W
Strathmore V	46	56.39 N	3.00 W
Strathpeffer	46	57.35 N	4.33 W
Strathpine	171a	27.19 S	152.59 E
Strathroy	214	42.57 N	81.38 W
Strathy ≃	46	58.34 N	4.00 W
Strathy Point ›	46	58.35 N	4.02 W
Strattanville	214	41.12 N	79.19 W
Stratton, Eng., U.K.	42	50.50 N	4.31 W
Stratton, Eng., U.K.	42	51.44 N	1.59 W
Stratton, Co., U.S.	198	39.18 N	102.36 W
Stratton, Me., U.S.	188	45.08 N	70.26 W
Stratton, Ne., U.S.	198	40.08 N	101.13 W
Stratton, Oh., U.S.	214	40.32 N	80.38 W
Stratton Mountain ∧	188	43.05 N	72.56 W
Stratton Saint Margaret	42	51.35 N	1.45 W
Straubing	60	48.53 N	12.34 E
Strauch	263	51.09 N	6.56 E
Straumen	26	63.52 N	11.18 E
Straupitz	54	51.54 N	14.07 E
Strausberg	54	52.35 N	13.53 E
Straus-Berger Stadtforst ♦	264a	52.34 N	13.52 E
Strausberg-Vorstadt	264a	52.32 N	13.51 E
Straussberg	54	51.23 N	10.44 E
Straussee ⊜	264a	52.35 N	13.53 E
Straussfurt	54	51.09 N	10.59 E
Strausstown	208	40.30 N	76.11 W
Stravignano	66	43.05 N	12.49 E
Strawberry	226	38.13 N	118.35 W
Strawberry ≃, Ar., U.S.	194	35.53 N	91.13 W
Strawberry ≃, Ut,. U.S.	200	40.10 N	110.24 W
Strawberry Island I	284a	42.57 N	78.55 W
Strawberry Mountain ∧	202	44.19 N	118.43 W
Strawberry Point, Ca., U.S.	282	37.54 N	122.31 W
Strawberry Point, Ia., U.S.	190	42.41 N	91.32 W
Strawberry Point ›	283	42.15 N	70.46 W
Strawberry Reservoir ⊜[1]	200	40.11 N	111.08 W
Strawberry Valley	226	39.34 N	121.06 W
Strawbridge Lake ⊜	285	39.57 N	74.57 W
Strawn	196	32.33 N	98.29 W
Straw Pump	279b	40.19 N	79.40 W
Stráž	61	49.04 N	14.54 E
Strážnice	30	48.54 N	17.18 E
Strážov	60	49.18 N	13.15 E
Strážske	30	48.53 N	21.50 E
Streaky Bay	162	32.48 S	134.13 E
Streaky Bay ⊂	162	32.36 S	134.08 E
Streamwood	216	42.01 N	88.10 W
Streatham, Austl.	169	37.41 S	143.04 E
Streatham, B.C., Can.	182	53.52 N	126.12 W
Streatham ◆[8]	260	51.26 N	0.08 W
Streator	216	41.07 N	88.50 W
Strebersdorf ◆[8]	264b	48.18 N	16.23 E
Středočeský Kraj □[4]	30	49.55 N	14.30 E
Stredoslovenský Kraj □[4]	30	48.50 N	19.10 E
Street	42	51.07 N	2.42 W
Streeter	198	46.39 N	99.21 W
Streetman	222	31.53 N	96.19 W
Streetsboro	214	41.14 N	81.20 W
Streets Run ≃	279b	40.23 N	79.56 W
Streetsville	212	43.35 N	79.42 W
Strehaia	38	44.37 N	23.12 E
Strehla	54	51.21 N	13.13 E
Streitberg	60	49.49 N	11.13 E
Střela ≃	60	49.55 N	13.33 E
Strelasund ʯ	54	54.20 N	13.05 E
Strel'covka	83	49.18 N	39.52 E
Streleckaja Step', zapovednik ♦	83	49.16 N	40.05 E
Streleckije Vyselki	82	54.12 N	38.57 E
Strelica	78	51.37 N	38.55 E
Střelice	61	49.09 N	16.30 E
Strelitzalt	54	53.20 N	13.05 E
Strelka	86	58.05 N	93.01 E
Strelka ≃	265a	59.52 N	30.03 E
Strelka-Čun'a	74	61.45 N	102.48 E
Strelkovo	82	55.28 N	37.37 E
Strelkovoje	78	45.54 N	34.53 E
Strel'na, Ross.	24	66.06 N	38.40 E
Strel'na, Ross.	76	59.51 N	30.02 E
Strel'na ≃	24	66.04 N	38.39 E
Strel'skaja	24	59.28 N	47.47 E
Střelské Hoštice	60	49.18 N	13.46 E
Strem ≃	61	47.00 N	16.31 E
Strembo	64	46.09 N	10.44 E
Stremilovo	82	55.09 N	37.09 E
Strenči	76	57.37 N	25.41 E
Strengen	58	47.08 N	10.27 E
Strensall	44	54.03 N	1.02 W
Stresa	62	45.53 N	8.32 E
Strešen'	78	47.08 N	28.36 E
Strešin	76	52.43 N	30.05 E
Stretford	44	53.27 N	2.19 W
Stretton, Austl.	162	32.32 S	117.41 E
Stretton, Eng., U.K.	42	52.44 N	0.35 W
Stretton, Eng., U.K.	44	53.21 N	2.35 W
Streu ≃	56	50.21 N	10.16 E
Strib	41	55.32 N	9.47 E
Striberg	40	59.33 N	14.56 E
Stříbro	60	49.46 N	13.00 E
Strichen	46	57.34 N	2.05 W
Strickherdicke	263	51.29 N	7.43 E
Strickland ≃	164	6.00 S	142.05 E
Strigno	64	46.04 N	11.31 E
Strijen	52	51.45 N	4.33 E
Striker, Lake ⊜[1]	222	31.57 N	94.59 W
Strimón (Struma) ≃	38	40.47 N	23.51 E
Stringtown	218	40.05 N	86.29 W
Striven, Loch ⊂	46	55.58 N	5.09 W
Strižament, gora ∧	84	44.46 N	42.01 E
Strižavka	78	49.19 N	28.28 E
Striži	80	58.30 N	49.13 E
Strjama ≃	38	42.10 N	24.56 E
Strobel	252	32.03 S	60.37 W
Strobel, Lago ⊜	254	48.22 S	71.12 W
Strobl	64	47.43 N	13.29 E
Strobleton	214	41.22 N	79.25 W
Strøby	41	55.23 N	12.18 E
Stroeder	254	40.11 S	62.37 W
Strofádhes, Nísoi II	38	37.15 N	21.00 E
Strogino ◆[8]	265b	55.49 N	37.25 E
Strogonof Point ›	180	56.53 N	158.49 W
Stroh	216	41.34 N	85.11 W
Ströhen	52	52.32 N	8.41 E
Stroitel'	78	50.47 N	36.26 E
Strokestown	48	53.47 N	8.08 W
Strom ≃	54	53.15 N	13.50 E
Stroma I	46	58.41 N	3.08 W
Stromberg, Dtsch.	52	51.48 N	8.12 E
Stromberg, Dtsch.	56	49.57 N	7.46 E
Stromboli, Isola I	70	38.47 N	15.13 E
Strome	182	52.48 N	112.04 W
Stromeferry	46	57.21 N	5.34 W
Strömkendorf	54	53.58 N	11.29 E
Stromness	46	58.57 N	3.18 W
Strömsberg	40	60.24 N	17.35 E
Strömsbro	40	60.42 N	17.10 E
Strömsbruk	26	61.53 N	17.19 E
Stromsburg	198	41.06 N	97.35 W
Strömsholm	40	59.32 N	16.15 E
Strömsnäsbruk	26	56.33 N	13.43 E
Strömstad	26	58.56 N	11.10 E
Strömsund	26	63.51 N	15.35 E
Strömsvattudal ⊜	26	63.56 N	15.28 E
Stromyn'	82	56.03 N	38.29 E
Strong	194	33.06 N	92.20 W
Strong ≃	194	31.51 N	90.08 W
Strong City	198	38.23 N	96.32 W
Stronghurst	190	40.44 N	90.54 W
Strongoli	68	39.15 N	17.03 E
Strongs Creek ≃	276	40.40 N	73.22 W
Strongs Neck ›[1]	276	40.58 N	73.07 W
Strongstown	214	40.33 N	78.55 W
Strongsville	214	41.18 N	81.50 W
Strongsville Airport ⊠	279a	41.19 N	81.52 W
Stronsay I	46	59.07 N	2.37 W
Stronsay Firth ʯ	46	59.02 N	2.41 W
Stronsdorf	61	48.39 N	16.18 E
Strontian	46	56.41 N	5.34 W
Strood	42	51.24 N	0.28 E
Stropkov	30	49.12 N	21.40 E
Stropnice ≃	61	48.52 N	14.30 E
Stroppiana	62	45.14 N	8.27 E
Stroud, Austl.	166	32.20 S	151.56 E
Stroud, Eng., U.K.	42	51.45 N	2.12 W
Stroud, Ok., U.S.	196	35.44 N	96.39 W
Stroudsburg	210	40.59 N	75.11 W
Strövelstorp	41	56.09 N	12.49 E
Strubenvale	273d	26.16 S	28.28 E
Strücklingen	52	53.07 N	7.40 E
Struer	26	56.29 N	8.37 E
Struga	38	41.11 N	20.40 E
Strugi-Krasnyje	76	58.17 N	29.06 E
Struisbaai	158	34.49 S	20.04 E
Struisbult	273d	26.19 S	28.29 E
Strule ≃	48	54.43 N	7.25 W
Strum	190	44.32 N	91.23 W
Struma (Strimón) ≃	38	40.47 N	23.51 E
Strumble Head ›	42	52.02 N	5.04 W
Strumica	38	41.26 N	22.38 E
Strümp	263	51.17 N	6.40 E
Strunino	82	56.23 N	38.34 E
Strupna	82	54.43 N	38.48 E
Struthers	214	41.03 N	80.36 W
Struy	46	57.24 N	4.39 W
Strydenburg	158	29.58 S	23.40 E
Strydomsvlei	158	33.10 S	23.03 E
Strydpoort	158	27.00 S	25.58 E
Stryj	78	49.15 N	23.51 E
Stryj ≃	78	49.24 N	24.13 E
Stryker, Mt., U.S.	182	48.40 N	114.46 W
Stryker, Oh., U.S.	216	41.30 N	84.24 W
Strykersville	210	42.42 N	78.27 W
Stryków	30	51.55 N	19.37 E
Stryn	26	61.55 N	6.47 E
Strynø I	41	54.54 N	10.37 E
Strypa ≃	78	48.52 N	25.26 E
Strzegom	30	50.57 N	16.21 E
Strzegowo-Osada	30	52.55 N	20.18 E
Strzelce Krajeńskie	30	52.53 N	15.32 E
Strzelce Opolskie	30	50.31 N	18.19 E
Strzelecki Creek ≃	166	29.37 S	139.59 E
Strzelecki Desert ◆[2]	166	28.00 S	140.10 E
Strzeleckie, Mount ∧	162	21.10 S	133.53 E
Strzelecki National Park ♦	166	40.14 S	148.06 E
Strzelin	30	50.47 N	17.03 E
Strzelno	30	52.38 N	18.11 E
Strzyżów	30	49.52 N	21.47 E
Stuart, Fl., U.S.	220	27.11 N	80.15 W
Stuart, Ia., U.S.	198	41.30 N	94.19 W
Stuart, Ne., U.S.	198	42.35 N	99.08 W
Stuart, Va., U.S.	192	36.38 N	80.15 W
Stuart ≃	182	54.00 N	123.32 W
Stuart, Central Mount ∧	162	21.54 S	133.27 E
Stuart, Mount ∧	224	47.29 N	120.54 W
Stuart Channel ʯ	224	48.55 N	123.45 W
Stuart Island I, Ak., U.S.	180	63.35 N	162.30 W
Stuart Island I, Wa., U.S.	224	48.42 N	123.12 W
Stuart Lake ⊜	182	54.32 N	124.35 W
Stuart Mountains ⩘	172	45.00 S	167.37 E
Stuart Range ⩘	162	29.10 S	134.56 E
Stuarts Draft	192	38.01 N	79.02 W
Stubai V	64	47.06 N	11.19 E
Stubaier Alpen ⩘	64	47.10 N	11.05 E
Stubalpe ⩘	61	47.06 N	14.54 E
Stübbecken	263	51.23 N	7.36 E
Stubbekøbing	41	54.53 N	12.03 E
Stubbenfelde	54	54.02 N	14.01 E
Stubbenkammer	54	54.35 N	13.40 E
Stubbington	42	50.50 N	1.13 W
Stubbins	262	53.39 N	2.19 W
Stubenberg	61	47.14 N	15.48 E
Stubla ≃	78	50.50 N	26.04 E
Stubner Kogel ∧	64	47.07 N	13.06 E
Studená	61	49.11 N	15.17 E
Studenec	80	54.52 N	48.16 E
Studenica, Manastir ʋ[1]	38	43.21 N	20.35 E
Studen Kladenec, jazovir ⊜[1]	38	41.37 N	25.30 E
Studholme Junction	172	44.44 S	171.08 E
Studland	42	50.39 N	1.58 W
Studley	42	52.16 N	1.52 W
Stud'onoje, Ross.	80	51.36 N	53.10 E
Stud'onoje, Ross.	86	53.37 N	77.31 E
Stud'onok	78	51.42 N	34.07 E
Studsvik	40	58.46 N	17.23 E
Stugudal	26	62.54 N	11.52 E
Stugun	26	63.10 N	15.36 E
Stuhleck ∧	61	47.34 N	15.47 E
Stühlingen	58	47.44 N	8.26 E
Stuhlweissenburg → Székesfehérvár	30	47.12 N	18.25 E
Stuhr	52	53.01 N	8.45 E
Stuie	182	52.22 N	126.02 W
Stukely, Lac ⊜	206	45.22 N	72.15 W
Stukenbrock	52	51.54 N	8.39 E
Stull ≃	184	55.10 N	92.39 W
Stull Lake ⊜	184	54.23 N	92.34 W
Stülpe	54	52.02 N	13.19 E
Stumm	64	47.17 N	11.53 E
Stump Creek	214	41.01 N	78.50 W
Stump Creek ≃	276	40.28 N	74.16 W
Stumpf	263	51.06 N	7.13 E
Stump Lake ⊜	198	47.54 N	98.24 W
Stumsdorf	54	51.37 N	12.03 E
Stuorre Tjõure ∧	26	63.56 N	13.30 E
Stupart ≃	184	56.00 N	93.22 W
Stupava	61	48.17 N	17.02 E
Stupino	82	54.53 N	38.05 E
Stuppach	56	49.27 N	9.44 E
Stura di Ala ≃	62	45.18 N	7.24 E
Stura di Demonte ≃	62	44.40 N	7.53 E
Stura di Lanzo ≃	62	45.06 N	7.44 E
Stura di Val Grande ≃	62	45.18 N	7.24 E
Stura di Viù ≃	62	45.16 N	7.26 E
Sturbridge	207	42.06 N	72.04 W
Sturdee	162	31.52 S	132.23 E
Sturge Island I	9	67.27 S	164.18 E
Sturgeon, Mo., U.S.	219	39.14 N	92.16 W
Sturgeon, Pa., U.S.	279b	40.23 N	80.13 W
Sturgeon ≃, On., Can.	190	46.19 N	79.58 W
Sturgeon ≃, Sk., Can.	184	53.12 N	105.53 W
Sturgeon ≃, Mi., U.S.	190	45.24 N	84.38 W
Sturgeon ≃, Mi., U.S.	190	45.50 N	86.41 W
Sturgeon ≃, Mi., U.S.	190	47.02 N	88.30 W
Sturgeon Bay	190	44.50 N	87.22 W
Sturgeon Bay ⊂	184	52.00 N	97.50 W
Sturgeon Falls	190	46.22 N	79.55 W
Sturgeon Lake ⊜, Ab., Can.	182	55.06 N	117.30 W
Sturgeon Lake ⊜, On., Can.	184	55.25 N	90.55 W
Sturgeon Lake ⊜, On., Can.	212	44.28 N	78.42 W
Sturgeon Lake ⊜, Wa., U.S.	224	45.44 N	122.48 W
Sturgeon Lake Indian Reserve ◆[4], Ab., Can.	182	55.04 N	117.29 W
Sturgeon Lake Indian Reserve ◆[4], Sk., Can.	184	53.25 N	106.05 W
Sturgeon Landing	184	54.16 N	101.49 W
Sturgeon Point ›	212	42.42 N	79.03 W
Sturgis, Sk., Can.	184	51.58 N	102.32 W
Sturgis, Ky., U.S.	194	37.32 N	87.59 W
Sturgis, Mi., U.S.	216	41.47 N	85.25 W
Sturgis, Ms., U.S.	194	33.20 N	89.02 W
Sturgis, S.D., U.S.	198	44.24 N	103.30 W
Sturla	62	44.24 N	8.59 E
Sturminster Newton	42	50.50 N	2.19 W
Štúrovo	30	47.48 N	18.49 E
Sturry	42	51.18 N	1.07 E
Sturt, Mount ∧	166	29.33 S	141.42 E
Sturt Creek	162	19.10 S	128.10 E
Sturt Creek ≃	162	20.08 S	127.24 E
Sturtevant	216	42.41 N	87.53 W
Sturt National Park ♦	166	29.00 S	141.40 E
Sturt Stony Desert ◆[2]	166	28.30 S	141.00 E
Sturup flygplats ⊠	41	55.34 N	13.21 E
Stürzelberg	263	51.08 N	6.49 E
Stutterheim	158	32.33 S	27.28 E
Stuttgart, Dtsch.	56	48.46 N	9.11 E
Stuttgart, Ar., U.S.	194	34.30 N	91.33 W
Stuttgart □[5]	56	49.00 N	9.45 E
Stuttgart, Flughafen ⊠	56	48.41 N	9.12 E
Stützengrün	54	50.32 N	12.31 E
Stützerbach	54	50.38 N	10.51 E
Stuyvesant	210	42.24 N	73.47 W
Stuyvesant Falls	210	42.21 N	73.44 W
Stviga ≃	78	52.04 N	27.54 E
Styal	262	53.21 N	2.15 W
Stykkishólmur	24a	65.06 N	22.48 W
Styla	83	47.41 N	37.50 E
Styr' ≃	78	52.07 N	26.35 E
Styrum ◆[8]	263	51.27 N	6.51 E
Styx ≃, On., Can.	212	44.11 N	80.57 W
Styx ≃, Al., U.S.	194	30.31 N	87.27 W
Suaçuí Grande ≃	255	18.50 S	41.46 W
Suai	112	3.48 N	113.38 E
Suain	164	3.20 S	142.55 E
Suaita	246	6.07 N	73.27 W
Suakin Archipelago II	140	18.42 N	38.30 E
Sual	116	16.04 N	120.05 E
Suan	98	38.42 N	126.22 E
Suao, T'aiwan	100	24.36 N	121.51 E
Su'ao, Zhg.	100	25.38 N	119.42 E
Suapure ≃	246	6.25 N	66.23 W
Suaqui Grande	232	28.24 N	109.54 W
Suār	124	29.02 N	79.03 E
Suātala	124	23.09 N	79.02 E
Şuatima	114	4.13 N	96.04 E
Šubač	76	60.22 N	38.14 E
Subačius	76	55.46 N	24.47 E
Subah	115a	6.58 S	109.52 E
Subaio	256	22.30 S	42.50 W
Subang	115a	6.34 S	107.45 E
Subansiri ≃	120	26.48 N	93.50 E
Šubarkuduk	86	49.13 N	56.34 E
Subar Laut, Pulau I	271c	1.13 N	103.50 E
Subarnapur	272b	22.58 N	88.34 E
Subarnarekha ≃	120	21.34 N	87.24 E
Šubarši	86	48.35 N	57.12 E
Subashi	85	38.22 N	74.57 E
Subasio, Monte ∧	66	43.03 N	12.40 E
Subate	76	56.01 N	25.56 E
Subay', 'Urūq as- ◆[2]	144	22.15 N	43.05 E
Subbiano	66	43.34 N	11.52 E
Subbotino	86	53.04 N	91.55 E
Subchankulovo	80	54.34 N	53.49 E
Subei	102	39.27 N	95.03 E
Subeita → Shivta, Horvot ⊥	132	30.53 N	34.38 E
Suben	60	48.25 N	13.26 E
Subhepur	272a	28.45 N	77.16 E
Subi, Pulau I	112	2.55 N	108.50 E
Subiaco	66	41.55 N	13.06 E
Subic	116	14.53 N	120.14 E
Subic Bay ⊂	116	14.45 N	120.13 E
Subic Bay Naval Base (U.S.) ■	116	14.47 N	120.16 E
Subipur	272b	22.54 N	88.08 E
Subk al-Ahad	142	30.18 N	31.02 E
Sublette	198	37.28 N	100.50 W
Sublett Range ⩘	202	42.20 N	112.50 W
Sublime	222	29.29 N	96.48 W
Subotica	38	46.06 N	19.39 E
Suburban Airport ⊠	284c	39.05 N	76.50 W
Suburban Village	285	39.58 N	75.34 W
Suca	144	6.31 N	39.14 E
Sucarnoochee ≃	194	32.25 N	88.02 W
Succasunna	210	40.52 N	74.38 W
Succor Creek ≃	202	43.38 N	116.56 W
Suceava	38	47.39 N	26.19 E
Suceava □[6]	38	47.30 N	25.45 E
Suceava ≃	38	47.32 N	26.32 E
Sucha [Beskidzka]	30	49.44 N	19.36 E
Suchaja	88	52.32 N	107.06 E
Suchaja Volnovacha ≃	83	47.37 N	38.01 E
Suchań	30	53.17 N	15.19 E
Suchana	74	68.45 N	118.00 E
Suchang	107	30.34 N	103.34 E
Suchan → Partizansk	89	43.08 N	133.09 E
Süchbaatar	88	50.15 N	106.12 E
Süchbaatar □[4]	102	45.30 N	114.00 E
Suchdol ◆[8]	54	50.08 N	14.21 E
Suchdol nad Lužnicí	61	48.54 N	14.53 E
Suchedniów	30	51.03 N	20.51 E
Suchetgarh	123	32.34 N	74.40 E
Suchiapa	234	16.37 N	93.05 W
Suchiapa ≃	234	16.36 N	93.01 W
Súchil	234	23.38 N	103.55 W
Suchiniči	76	54.06 N	35.20 E
Suchitepéquez □[5]	236	14.25 N	91.20 W
Suchitlán	234	19.22 N	103.43 W
Suchitoto	236	13.56 N	89.02 W
Suchobezvodnoje	80	57.03 N	44.50 E
Suchoborka	24	59.06 N	49.58 E
Suchodol, Ross.	80	53.55 N	51.14 E
Suchodol, Ross.	82	54.27 N	37.22 E
Suchodol'skij	76	53.43 N	38.17 E
Suchodrev ≃	82	54.44 N	35.59 E
Suchoj	80	47.06 N	41.21 E
Suchoj Jelančik ≃	83	47.16 N	38.25 E
Suchoj Log	86	56.55 N	62.01 E
Suchoj Pit	86	58.48 N	92.49 E
Suchoj Sambek ≃	83	47.23 N	39.07 E
Suchoj Torec ≃	83	48.49 N	37.36 E
Suchona ≃	24	60.46 N	46.24 E
Suchorečka	80	52.49 N	52.27 E
Suchotinka	80	52.31 N	41.35 E
Suchou → Suzhou	106	31.18 N	120.37 E
Suchoverkovo	76	56.37 N	35.35 E
Suchov Pervyj	80	49.59 N	43.28 E
Süchow → Xuzhou	98	34.16 N	117.11 E
Süchteln	56	51.17 N	6.22 E
Suchumi	84	43.01 N	41.02 E
Sucio ≃	246	7.27 N	77.07 W
Suck ≃	48	53.16 N	8.03 W
Sucker Creek ≃	212	44.09 N	77.08 W
Sucker Creek Indian Reserve ◆[4]	182	55.28 N	116.10 W
Sucker Lake ⊜	212	44.46 N	78.16 W
Suckling, Mount ∧	164	9.45 S	148.55 E
Sucre, Arg.	258	34.30 S	59.07 W
Sucre, Bol.	248	19.02 S	65.17 W
Sucre, Col.	246	8.49 N	74.44 W
Sucre, Ec.	246	1.16 S	80.26 W
Sucre □[3]	246	10.25 N	63.30 W
Sucre □[5], Col.	246	9.00 N	75.00 W
Sucre □[5], Ven.	286c	10.25 N	66.50 W
Sucúa	246	2.28 S	78.10 W
Sucuaro	246	4.34 N	68.50 W
Sucumbíos □[4]	246	0.06 N	76.52 W
Sucunduri ≃	248	5.50 S	59.32 W
Sucuriju	250	1.39 N	49.57 W
Sucuriú ≃	255	20.47 S	51.38 W
Sucy-en-Brie	50	48.46 N	2.32 E
Sud, Canal du ʯ	238	18.40 N	73.05 W
Sud, Grand Récif ✤[2]	175f	23.00 S	167.02 E

≃	River	Fluß	Río	Rivière	Rio
≅	Canal	Kanal	Canal	Canal	Canal
∟	Waterfall, Rapids	Wasserfall, Stromschnellen	Cascada, Rápidos	Chute d'eau, Rapides	Cascata, Rápidos
ʯ	Strait	Meeresstraße	Estrecho	Détroit	Estreito
⊂	Bay, Gulf	Bucht, Golf	Bahía, Golfo	Baie, Golfe	Baía, Golfo
⊜	Lake, Lakes	See, Seen	Lago, Lagos	Lac, Lacs	Lago, Lagos
⩩	Swamp	Sumpf	Pantano	Marais	Pântano
◹	Ice Features, Glacier	Eis- und Gletscherformen	Accidentes Glaciales	Formes glaciaires	Acidentes glaciares
⍑	Other Hydrographic Features	Andere Hydrographische Objekte	Otros Elementos Hidrográficos	Autres données hydrographiques	Outros acidentes hidrográficos

✤	Submarine Features	Untermeerische Objekte	Accidentes Submarinos	Formes de relief sous-marin	Acidentes submarinos
□	Political Unit	Politische Einheit	Unidad Politica	Entité politique	Unidade política
ʋ	Cultural Institution	Kulturelle Institution	Institución Cultural	Institution culturelle	Instituição cultural
⊥	Historical Site	Historische Stätte	Sitio Histórico	Site historique	Sitio histórico
♦	Recreational Site	Erholungs- und Ferienort	Sitio de Recreo	Centre de loisirs	Area de Lazer
⊠	Airport	Flughafen	Aeropuerto	Aéroport	Aeroporto
■	Military Installation	Militäranlage	Instalación Militar	Installation militaire	Instalação militar
◆	Miscellaneous	Verschiedenes	Misceláneo	Divers	Diversos

ENGLISH / DEUTSCH

Name	Page (Seite)	Lat.°′ (Breite°′)	Long.°′ (Länge°′ E = Ost)
Sud, Pointe ›	157a	11.53 S	43.49 E
Sud, Rivière du ≃	206	45.08 N	73.15 W
Suda	76	59.09 N	37.33 E
Suda ≃	76	59.11 N	37.30 E
Südafrika → South Africa □[1]	156	30.00 S	26.00 E
Sudaj	76	58.58 N	43.08 E
Sudak	78	44.52 N	34.59 E
Südamerika → South America ≗[1]	18	15.00 S	60.00 W
Sudan	196	34.04 N	102.31 W
Sudan (As-Sūdān) □[1], Afr.	136	15.00 N	30.00 E
Sudan (As-Sūdān) □[1], Afr.	140	15.00 N	30.00 E
Sudan •[1]	10	10.00 N	20.00 E
Sudañez	248	19.06 S	64.44 W
Sudarsan	272b	22.59 N	88.17 E
Südbahnhof •[5]	264b	48.11 N	16.23 E
Sudberg •[8]	263	51.11 N	7.08 E
Sudbišči	76	52.57 N	37.39 E
Sud'bodarovka	80	52.19 N	54.07 E
Südbrookmerland	52	53.29 N	7.24 E
Sudbury, On., Can.	190	46.30 N	81.00 W
Sudbury, Eng., U.K.	42	52.02 N	0.44 E
Sudbury, Ma., U.S.	207	42.23 N	71.25 W
Sudbury ≃	283	42.28 N	71.22 W
Sudbury Center	283	42.23 N	71.25 W
Sudbury Reservoir ⊜[1]	207	42.19 N	71.31 W
Südchinesisches Meer → South China Sea ▿[2]	108	10.00 N	113.00 E
Sud Dakota → South Dakota □[3]	198	44.15 N	100.00 W
Sudd an-Na'ām, Jabal ∧	142	29.49 N	31.43 E
Sudd → As-Sudd •[1]	140	8.00 N	31.00 E
Suddie	246	7.07 N	58.29 W
Sude ≃	54	53.22 N	10.45 E
Süderbrarup	41	54.38 N	9.46 E
Süderlügum	41	54.52 N	8.55 E
Suderwich	263	51.37 N	7.15 E
Sudeten → Sudety ⋏	30	50.30 N	16.00 E
Sudety ⋏	30	50.30 N	16.00 E
Süd-Georgien → South Georgia I	244	54.15 S	36.45 W
Sudi	154	10.06 S	39.57 E
Sudislavl'	80	57.53 N	41.43 E
Südkamen	263	51.35 N	7.39 E
Süd-Korea → Korea, South □[1]	98	36.30 N	128.00 E
Sudlersville	208	39.11 N	75.51 W
Südlicher Bug → Južnyj Bug ≃	78	46.59 N	31.58 E
Südlicher Indianer-See → Southern Indian Lake ⊜	176	57.10 N	98.40 W
Sudnikovo	82	55.53 N	36.02 E
Sudogda	80	55.57 N	40.50 E
Sudomskaja vozvyšennost' ⋏[1]	76	57.25 N	29.25 E
Sudong, Pulau I	271c	1.13 N	103.44 E
Süd-Orkney-Inseln → South Orkney Islands II	9	60.35 S	45.30 W
Sudost' ≃	76	52.19 N	33.24 E
Sud-Ouest □[4]	152	5.10 N	9.00 E
Sud-Ouest, Pointe du ›	186	49.23 N	63.36 W
Sudovaja Višn'a	78	49.49 N	23.22 E
Südradde ≃	52	52.41 N	7.34 E
Süd-Sandwich-Inseln → South Sandwich Islands II	18	57.45 S	26.30 W
Süd-Shetland-Inseln → South Shetland Islands II	9	62.00 S	58.00 W
Sudūd	142	30.25 N	30.54 E
Südwest-Kap → South West Cape ›	166	43.34 S	146.02 E
Sudweyhe	52	52.59 N	8.53 E
Sudža	78	51.12 N	35.16 E
Sue	96	33.35 N	130.30 E
Sue ≃	140	7.41 N	28.03 E
Sueca	34	39.12 N	0.19 W
Suecia → Sweden □[1]	24	62.00 N	15.00 E
Sue Creek ⊂	284b	39.17 N	76.24 W
Suedberg	208	40.32 N	76.28 W
Suède → Sweden □[1]	24	62.00 N	15.00 E
Suemez Island I	182	55.17 N	133.21 W
Suèvres	50	47.40 N	1.28 E
Suez, Gulf of → Suways, Khalīj as- ⊂	140	29.00 N	32.50 E
Suez → As-Suways	142	29.58 N	32.33 E
Suez Canal → Suways, Qanāt as- ≊	142	29.55 N	32.33 E
Sūf	132	32.19 N	35.50 E
Ṣufaynah	128	23.09 N	40.32 E
Suffern	210	41.06 N	74.09 W
Suffern Park	276	41.07 N	74.07 W
Suffield, Ab., Can.	184	50.12 N	111.10 W
Suffield, Ct., U.S.	207	41.58 N	72.39 W
Suffield, Oh., U.S.	214	41.01 N	81.21 W
Suffield, Canadian Forces Base ■	184	50.15 N	111.10 W
Suffolk	208	36.43 N	76.35 W
Suffolk □[6], Eng., U.K.	42	52.10 N	1.00 E
Suffolk □[6], Ma., U.S.	207	42.21 N	71.04 W
Suffolk □[6], N.Y., U.S.	210	40.55 N	72.40 W
Suffolk, Ruisseau ≃	206	45.48 N	74.59 W
Suffolk Downs Race Track ♦	283	42.23 N	71.00 W
Ṣūfiān	128	38.17 N	45.59 E
Sufi-Kurgan	85	40.02 N	73.30 E
Sufu → Kashi	85	39.29 N	75.59 E
Suga-jima I	94	34.29 N	136.53 E
Sugana, Val V	64	46.00 N	11.40 E
Sugandha	272b	22.54 N	88.20 E
Sugandy	85	43.27 N	74.38 E
Sugano	268	35.44 N	139.56 E
Sugar ≃, U.S.	190	42.26 N	89.12 W
Sugar ≃, N.H., U.S.	188	43.24 N	72.24 W
Sugar ≃, N.Y., U.S.	212	43.31 N	75.19 W
Sugar City	202	43.52 N	111.44 W
Sugarcreek, Oh., U.S.	214	40.30 N	81.39 W
Sugarcreek, Pa., U.S.	214	41.25 N	79.52 W
Sugar Creek ≃, U.S.	216	40.47 N	87.45 W
Sugar Creek ≃, Il., U.S.	194	40.09 N	89.38 W
Sugar Creek ≃, Il., U.S.	219	38.28 N	89.37 W
Sugar Creek ≃, Il., U.S.	219	39.48 N	89.32 W
Sugar Creek ≃, In., U.S.	194	39.51 N	87.21 W
Sugar Creek ≃, In., U.S.	218	39.21 N	86.00 W
Sugar Creek ≃, Mi., U.S.	281	42.06 N	83.36 W
Sugar Creek ≃, N.Y., U.S.	210	42.38 N	77.09 W
Sugar Creek ≃, Oh., U.S.	214	40.31 N	81.28 W
Sugar Creek ≃, Oh., U.S.	216	40.57 N	84.11 W
Sugar Creek ≃, Oh., U.S.	218	39.27 N	83.25 W
Sugar Creek ≃, Ok., U.S.	196	35.05 N	98.10 W
Sugar Creek ≃, Pa., U.S.	210	41.47 N	76.27 W
Sugar Creek ≃, Wi., U.S.	216	42.43 N	88.19 W
Sugar Grove, Il., U.S.	216	41.45 N	88.27 W
Sugargrove, Pa., U.S.	214	41.59 N	79.21 W
Sugar Grove, Va., U.S.	192	36.46 N	81.24 W
Sugar Hill	192	34.06 N	84.02 W
Sugar Island I, On., Can.	212	44.26 N	77.17 W
Sugar Island I, Mi., U.S.	190	46.25 N	84.12 W
Sugar Land	222	29.37 N	95.38 W
Sugar Loaf	210	41.19 N	74.17 W
Sugarloaf ∧[2]	214	41.24 N	81.06 W
Sugarloaf Hill ∧[2]	274b	37.58 S	145.19 E
Sugarloaf Key I	220	24.40 N	81.32 W
Sugarloaf Mountain ∧, Ky., U.S.	218	38.13 N	83.32 W
Sugarloaf Mountain ∧, Me., U.S.	188	45.01 N	70.22 W
Sugar Loaf Mountain ∧, Md., U.S.	208	39.16 N	77.23 W
Sugar Loaf Mountain ∧, Ok., U.S.	194	35.02 N	94.28 W
Sugarloaf Mountain ∧[2]	220	28.39 N	81.44 W
Sugar Loaf → Pão de Açúcar ∧	287a	22.57 S	43.09 W
Sugarloaf Peak ∧	280	34.14 N	117.38 W
Sugarloaf Point ›, Austl.	166	32.26 S	152.33 E
Sugar Loaf Point ›, On., Can.	284a	42.52 N	79.17 W
Sugarloaf Reservoir ⊜[1]	169	37.41 S	145.18 E
Sugarloaf Ridge State Park ♦	226	38.26 N	122.29 W
Sugar Notch	210	41.11 N	75.55 W
Sugar Pine Point State Park ♦	226	39.03 N	120.07 W
Sugartown	285	40.00 N	75.31 W
Sugauli	124	26.46 N	84.44 E
Sugbai Passage ʉ	116	5.22 N	120.33 E
Sugbay	116	7.31 N	123.19 E
Sugbuhan Point ›	116	10.04 N	126.04 E
Suggi Lake ⊜	184	54.22 N	102.47 W
Suginami •[8]	268	35.42 N	139.38 E
Sugita •[8]	268	35.23 N	139.38 E
Sugito	94	36.02 N	139.44 E
Şuğla Gölü ⊜	130	37.20 N	32.02 E
Šugnou	85	38.35 N	70.20 E
Sugod	116	12.03 N	124.09 E
Sugoj ≃	74	64.15 N	154.29 E
Šugonovo	82	54.41 N	36.41 E
Šugozero	76	59.55 N	34.12 E
Šugurovo, Ross.	80	53.25 N	46.29 E
Šugurovo, Ross.	80	54.31 N	52.06 E
Sugut ≃	112	6.26 N	117.43 E
Suguta ≃	154	2.03 N	36.33 E
Suguti	154	1.44 S	33.39 E
Suhai Hu ⊜	102	38.50 N	94.00 E
Suhaitu	102	44.50 N	93.39 E
Ṣuḥār	128	24.22 N	56.45 E
Suheli Island I[1]	122	10.03 N	72.17 E
Suhl	54	50.37 N	10.41 E
Suhlendorf	54	52.55 N	10.46 E
Suhopolje	36	45.48 N	17.30 E
Suhr	58	47.22 N	8.05 E
Suhr ≃	58	47.25 N	8.04 E
Suhum	150	6.05 N	0.27 W
Şuhut	130	38.32 N	30.33 E
Šūi	120	28.37 N	69.19 E
Suiá-Miçu ≃	250	11.13 S	53.15 W
Suianzhan	89	53.07 N	125.20 E
Suiattle ≃	224	48.20 N	121.33 W
Suichang	100	28.34 N	119.14 E
Suichuan	100	26.26 N	114.32 E
Suichuan ≃	100	26.30 N	114.45 E
Suid Afrika → South Africa □[1]	156	30.00 S	26.00 E
Suide	102	37.32 N	110.12 E
Suiding	86	44.03 N	80.49 E
Suido-suigenchi ⊜[1]	270	34.54 N	135.17 E
Suidvaal	158	26.52 S	29.47 E
Suifenhe	89	44.24 N	131.10 E
Suifu	94	36.37 N	140.29 E
Suifu → Yibin	107	28.47 N	104.38 E
Suigō-kokutei-kōen ♦	94	36.05 N	140.20 E
Suigō-Tsukuba-kokutei-kōen ♦	94	36.00 N	140.20 E
Suihua	89	46.37 N	127.00 E
Suijiang	102	28.31 N	104.07 E
Suileng	89	47.18 N	127.10 E
Suining, Zhg.	100	33.54 N	117.56 E
Suining, Zhg.	102	26.21 N	110.00 E
Suining, Zhg.	107	30.31 N	105.34 E
Suipacha	252	34.45 S	59.41 W
Suiping	100	33.10 N	113.57 E
Suippe ≃	50	49.25 N	3.57 E
Suippes	56	49.08 N	4.32 E
Suir ≃	48	52.15 N	7.00 W
Suisse → Switzerland □[1]	58	47.00 N	8.00 E
Suisun Bay ⊂	226	38.06 N	122.00 W
Suisun City	226	38.14 N	122.02 W
Suisun Creek ≃	226	38.12 N	122.06 W
Suita	96	34.45 N	135.32 E
Suitland	284c	38.50 N	76.55 W
Suixi, Zhg.	100	33.56 N	116.46 E
Suixi, Zhg.	102	21.25 N	110.15 E
Suixian, Zhg.	98	34.26 N	115.05 E
Suixian, Zhg.	100	31.42 N	113.20 E
Suiyang, Zhg.	89	44.26 N	130.53 E
Suiyang, Zhg.	102	27.56 N	107.18 E
Suiyangdian	100	32.04 N	112.55 E
Suiza → Switzerland □[1]	58	47.00 N	8.00 E
Suize ≃	58	48.08 N	5.08 E
Suizhong	98	40.20 N	120.19 E
Šuja, Ross.	24	61.55 N	34.12 E
Šuja, Ross.	80	56.50 N	41.23 E
Šuja ≃, Ross.	24	61.54 N	34.15 E
Šuja ≃, Ross.	80	57.56 N	43.15 E
Sujānagar	126	23.57 N	89.25 E
Sujāngarh	120	27.42 N	74.28 E
Sujāwal	120	24.36 N	68.05 E
Suji	107	29.35 N	103.37 E
Sujiabu	100	31.38 N	116.22 E
Sujiaqiao	105	39.24 N	116.10 E
Sujiatun	104	41.40 N	123.22 E
Sujiawan	107	29.48 N	104.57 E
Sujiawu	105	39.17 N	115.55 E
Şujiazui	100	33.40 N	119.29 E
Šujskoje	76	59.22 N	40.59 E
Sujutkina Kosa, mys ›	84	44.13 N	47.15 E
Sukabihanawa	112	9.30 S	124.57 E
Sukabumi	115a	6.55 S	106.56 E
Sukadana, Indon.	112	1.15 S	109.57 E
Sukadana, Indon.	115a	5.05 S	105.33 E
Sukadana, Teluk ⊂	112	1.24 S	109.50 E
Sukagawa	92	37.17 N	140.23 E
Sukamandi	115a	6.20 S	107.39 E
Sukamara	112	2.43 S	111.11 E
Sukanegara	115a	7.06 S	107.07 E
Sukapura	115a	7.52 S	113.03 E
Sukaraja, Indon.	112	2.21 S	110.37 E
Sukaraja, Indon.	115a	7.27 S	108.12 E
Sukaraja, Indon.	115a	7.27 S	109.17 E
Sukarno, Pegunungan → Jaya, Puncak ∧	164	4.05 S	137.11 E
Sukau	112	5.32 N	118.17 E
Sukchar	272b	22.42 N	88.22 E
Sukch'ŏn	98	39.24 N	125.38 E
Sukematsu	270	34.31 N	135.26 E
Sukeva	26	63.52 N	27.26 E
Sukhnah, 'Ayn ▿[4]	142	29.35 N	32.15 E
Sukhothai	110	17.01 N	99.49 E
Sukhumi → Suchumi	84	43.01 N	41.02 E
Sukkertoppen (Maniitsoq)	176	65.25 N	52.53 W
Sukkozero	24	63.11 N	32.18 E
Sukkur	120	27.42 N	68.52 E
Sukkwan Island I	182	55.05 N	132.45 W
Suklāra	126	23.11 N	86.21 E
Sukmanovka	78	51.47 N	41.34 E
Sukodadi	115a	7.06 S	112.19 E
Sukoharjo	115a	7.41 S	110.50 E
Sukovo	82	54.54 N	38.19 E
Sukroml'a	76	56.53 N	34.44 E
Sukses	156	21.01 S	16.52 E
Suksun	86	57.07 N	57.24 E
Sukumo	92	32.56 N	132.44 E
Sukun, Pulau I	115b	8.07 S	122.08 E
Sukunka ≃	182	55.37 N	121.37 W
Sul, Baía ⊂	252	27.40 S	48.35 W
Sul, Canal do ʉ	250	0.10 S	49.30 W
Sula I	26	61.08 N	4.55 E
Sula ≃, Ross.	24	67.16 N	52.07 E
Sula ≃, Ukr.	78	49.40 N	32.41 E
Sula, Kepulauan II	112	1.52 S	125.22 E
Sulaco ≃	236	15.01 N	87.44 W
Sulaimān Khel	123	33.41 N	71.01 E
Sulaimān Range ⋏	120	30.30 N	70.10 E
Sulak, Ross.	80	51.52 N	48.21 E
Sulak, Ross.	84	43.16 N	47.32 E
Sulak ≃	84	43.20 N	47.34 E
Sulakyurt	130	40.10 N	33.44 E
Sulang	115a	6.48 S	111.23 E
Sulat	116	11.49 N	125.27 E
Sulauan Point ›	116	8.37 N	124.29 E
Sulawesi (Celebes) I	112	2.00 S	121.00 E
Sulawesi Selatan □[4]	112	3.30 S	120.00 E
Sulawesi Tengah □[4]	112	1.00 N	123.00 E
Sulawesi Tenggara □[4]	112	4.00 S	122.00 E
Sulawesi Utara □[4]	112	0.30 N	124.00 E
Sulaymān, Birak (Solomon's Pools) ⊥	132	31.41 N	35.10 E
Sulby	44	54.18 N	4.29 W
Sulcis •[1]	71	39.04 N	8.41 E
Suldalsvatnet ⊜	26	59.35 N	6.45 E
Sūldeh	128	36.34 N	52.01 E
Sulechów	30	52.06 N	15.37 E
Sulęcin	30	52.26 N	15.08 E
Suleja	86	55.09 N	58.50 E
Sulejów	30	51.22 N	19.53 E
Sulejówek	30	52.14 N	21.17 E
Sulen, Mount ∧	164	3.25 S	142.15 E
Sule Skerry I[2]	46	59.05 N	4.26 W
Suleymaniye Mosque ✝[1]	267b	41.00 N	28.57 E
Süleymanlı	130	37.54 N	36.50 E
Šülfeld	52	53.48 N	10.14 E
Šul'ginka	83	49.08 N	38.56 E
Šul'gino, Ross.	82	54.33 N	37.35 E
Sulğino, Ross.	82	55.50 N	35.55 E
Sulia	154	1.32 S	26.33 E
Suliki	112	0.06 S	100.27 E
Sulima	150	6.58 N	11.35 W
Sulin	83	48.54 N	40.07 E
Sulina	38	45.09 N	29.40 E
Sulina, Braţul ≃[1]	38	45.09 N	29.41 E
Sulincheer	102	42.41 N	109.20 E
Sulingen	52	52.41 N	8.47 E
Sulinskij	83	47.52 N	40.06 E
Sulitelma ∧	24	67.08 N	16.24 E
Sulkava	26	61.47 N	28.23 E
Sullana	248	4.53 S	80.41 W
Sullane ≃	48	51.53 N	8.56 W
Sulligent	194	33.54 N	88.08 W
Sullivan, Il., U.S.	194	39.35 N	88.36 W
Sullivan, In., U.S.	194	39.06 N	87.24 W
Sullivan, Mo., U.S.	219	38.12 N	91.09 W
Sullivan, Oh., U.S.	214	41.02 N	82.13 W
Sullivan, Wi., U.S.	216	43.00 N	88.35 W
Sullivan □[6], N.Y., U.S.	210	41.39 N	74.42 W
Sullivan □[6], Pa., U.S.	210	41.25 N	76.29 W
Sullivan Canyon V	280	34.03 N	118.30 W
Sullivan Creek ≃	226	37.53 N	120.25 W
Sullivan Lake ⊜	182	52.00 N	112.00 W
Sullivan Stadium ♦	283	42.05 N	71.16 W
Sullivanville	210	42.14 N	76.46 W
Sully-sur-Loire	50	47.46 N	2.22 E
Sulm ≃	61	46.45 N	15.34 E
Sulmona	66	42.03 N	13.55 E
Sulot' ≃	82	56.41 N	38.01 E
Sulphur, Yk., Can.	180	63.47 N	138.53 W
Sulphur, In., U.S.	218	38.14 N	86.28 W
Sulphur, Ky., U.S.	218	38.29 N	85.16 W
Sulphur, La., U.S.	194	30.14 N	93.22 W
Sulphur, Ok., U.S.	196	34.30 N	96.58 W
Sulphur ≃, Ab., Can.	182	53.50 N	119.10 W
Sulphur ≃, U.S.	194	33.07 N	93.52 W
Sulphur Creek ≃	198	44.46 N	102.25 W
Sulphur Draw V	196	33.12 N	102.17 W
Sulphur Springs, In., U.S.	218	40.00 N	85.26 W
Sulphur Springs, Oh., U.S.	214	40.52 N	82.52 W
Sulphur Springs, Tx., U.S.	222	33.08 N	95.36 W
Sulphur Springs Draw V	196	32.12 N	101.36 W
Sulphur Springs Valley V	200	31.50 N	109.50 W
Sulsul	144	5.06 N	44.55 E
Sultan	224	47.51 N	121.48 W
Sultan ≃	224	47.52 N	121.49 W
Sultana	226	36.33 N	119.20 W
Sultanahmet Mosque ✝[1]	267b	41.00 N	28.58 E
Sultan Alonto, Lake ⊜	116	7.53 N	124.15 E
Sultana Point ›	168b	35.08 S	137.45 E
Sulṭanatābād •[8]	267d	35.46 N	51.28 E
Sultançiftligi •[8]	267b	41.02 N	29.13 E
Sultandağı	130	38.32 N	31.14 E
Sultan Dağı ∧	130	38.58 N	27.26 E
Sultanhanı	130	38.15 N	33.33 E
Sultanhisar	130	37.53 N	28.10 E
Sultan Kudarat	116	7.17 N	124.16 E
Sultan Kudarat □[4]	116	6.20 N	124.20 E
Sultan Mosque ✝[1]	271c	1.18 N	103.52 E
Sultānpur, India	123	31.13 N	75.11 E
Sultānpur, India	124	26.16 N	82.04 E
Sultānpur Dabās •[8]	272a	28.46 N	77.03 E
Sultan sa Barongis	116	6.46 N	124.38 E
Sultan-Saly	83	47.21 N	39.35 E
Sulu	164	5.25 S	151.00 E
Sulu □[4]	116	6.00 N	121.00 E
Suluan Island I	116	10.46 N	125.57 E
Sulu Archipelago II	116	6.00 N	121.00 E
Sulu Basin ⊹[1]	12	8.00 N	121.30 E
Sulu Chi ⊜	124	30.12 N	86.20 E
Sülüklü	130	39.05 N	30.58 E
Sul'ukta	85	39.56 N	69.34 E
Sululta	144	9.10 N	38.48 E
Suluntah	146	32.36 N	21.43 E
Suluova (Suluca)	130	40.47 N	35.42 E
Sulūq	146	31.39 N	20.15 E
Sulusaj	85	38.50 N	67.05 E
Sulusaray	130	40.00 N	36.06 E
Sulu Sea ▿[2]	116	8.00 N	120.00 E
Suly	86	53.45 N	66.30 E
Sulz	58	48.18 N	7.51 E
Sulz am Neckar	58	48.21 N	8.37 E
Sulzano	64	45.41 N	10.05 E
Sulzbach	56	49.18 N	7.07 E
Sulzbach ≃	60	48.36 N	13.02 E
Sulzbach am Kocher	56	48.58 N	9.50 E
Sulzbach-Rosenberg	60	49.30 N	11.45 E
Sulzberger Bay ⊂	9	77.00 S	152.00 W
Sulzbrunn	58	47.41 N	10.20 E
Sulzburg	58	47.50 N	7.42 E
Sülze	52	52.46 N	10.02 E
Šum, Ross.	76	59.52 N	31.46 E
Šum, Ross.	88	54.51 N	95.18 E
Suma •[8]	270	34.39 N	135.08 E
Šum'ači	76	53.52 N	32.25 E
Šumadija •[1]	38	44.10 N	20.50 E
Sumalata	112	0.59 N	122.30 E
Sumallo ≃	224	49.14 N	121.05 W
Sumampa	252	29.22 S	63.28 W
Šumanaj	86	42.37 N	59.08 E
Sumangat, Tanjong ›	116	6.35 N	117.33 E
Sumano-ura ♦	96	34.38 N	135.08 E
Sūmār	128	33.52 N	45.39 E
Sumarokovo	82	55.46 N	35.55 E
Sumas	202	49.00 N	122.15 W
Sumas ≃	224	49.09 N	122.12 W
Sumatera (Sumatra) I	108	0.05 S	102.00 E
Sumatera Barat □[4]	112	0.30 S	100.30 E
Sumatera Selatan □[4]	112	3.00 S	104.00 E
Sumatera Utara □[4]	114	2.20 N	99.00 E
Sum'atino	82	55.00 N	36.21 E
Sumatou	107	30.28 N	104.03 E
Sumatra → Sumatera I	108	0.05 S	102.00 E
Sumava Resorts	216	41.10 N	87.26 W
Sumayḥ	140	12.43 N	30.50 E
Sumba I	115b	10.00 S	120.00 E
Sumba, Île I	152	1.44 N	19.32 E
Sumba, Selat ʉ	115b	9.05 S	120.00 E
Sumbar ≃	128	38.00 N	55.17 E
Sumbawa I	115b	8.40 S	118.00 E
Sumbawa Besar	115b	8.30 S	117.26 E
Sumbawanga	154	7.58 S	31.37 E
Sumbay	248	15.58 S	71.23 W
Sumbe	152	11.13 S	13.50 E
Sümber	90	46.21 N	108.20 E
Sumbilla	34	43.10 N	1.40 W
Sumbing, Gunung ∧	115a	7.23 S	110.04 E
Sumbu National Park ♦	154	8.50 S	30.25 E
Sumburgh Head ›	46a	59.53 N	1.20 W
Sumburgh Roost ʉ	46a	59.49 N	1.19 W
Šumbut	80	55.33 N	50.41 E
Sumbuya	150	7.39 N	11.58 W
Sumdo	120	35.01 N	78.41 E
Sumé	250	7.39 S	36.55 W
Sumedang	115a	6.52 S	107.55 E
Sümeg	30	46.59 N	17.17 E
Šumek	86	48.42 N	85.32 E
Šumen	38	43.16 N	26.55 E
Sumène	62	43.59 N	3.43 E
Sumenep	115a	7.01 S	113.52 E
Šumerl'a	80	55.30 N	46.26 E
Sumgait	84	40.36 N	49.38 E
Sumgait ≃	84	40.37 N	49.37 E
Šumicha	86	55.14 N	63.19 E
Sumida •[8]	268	35.42 N	139.48 E
Sumida ≃	268	35.40 N	139.47 E
Sumidouro	256	22.03 S	42.41 W
Sumilao	116	8.18 N	124.57 E
Šumilino	76	55.18 N	29.37 E
Šumilinskaja	80	49.58 N	41.26 E
Suminoe •[8]	270	34.36 N	135.28 E
Sumisu-jima I	90	31.27 N	140.03 E
Sumiswald	58	47.02 N	7.45 E
Sumiyoshi •[8]	270	34.36 N	135.31 E
Sumki	86	55.03 N	65.44 E
Sumkino	86	58.09 N	68.21 E
Sumlog ≃	116	6.53 N	126.02 E
Summer Bridge	44	54.03 N	1.41 W
Summerdale	208	40.18 N	76.56 W
Summerfield, Fl., U.S.	220	29.00 N	82.02 W
Summerfield, Mo., U.S.	219	38.17 N	91.49 W
Summerfield, N.C., U.S.	192	36.12 N	79.54 W
Summerford, Nf., Can.	186	49.29 N	54.47 W
Summerford, Oh., U.S.	218	39.55 N	83.29 W
Summerhill, Ire.	48	53.29 N	6.44 W
Summerhill, Pa., U.S.	214	40.22 N	78.46 W
Summer Island I	190	45.34 N	86.39 W
Summer Isles II	46	58.02 N	5.28 W
Summer Lake ⊜	202	42.50 N	120.45 W
Summerland	182	49.36 N	119.41 W
Summerland Reserve •[4]	169	38.31 S	145.10 E
Sümmern	56	51.25 N	7.43 E
Summer Palace ✝	265a	59.53 N	29.55 E
Summerseat	262	53.38 N	2.19 W
Summerside	186	46.24 N	63.47 W
Summersville, Mo., U.S.	194	37.10 N	91.39 W
Summersville, W.V., U.S.	188	38.16 N	80.51 W
Summerton	192	33.36 N	80.21 W
Summertown	194	35.26 N	87.18 W
Summerville, On., Can.	275b	43.37 N	79.34 W
Summerville, Ga., U.S.	192	34.28 N	85.20 W
Summerville, Pa., U.S.	214	41.06 N	79.11 W
Summerville, S.C., U.S.	192	33.00 N	80.11 W
Summit, Eng., U.K.	262	53.40 N	2.05 W
Summit, Ak., U.S.	180	63.20 N	149.08 W
Summit, Ca., U.S.	228	34.20 N	117.25 W
Summit, Il., U.S.	216	41.47 N	87.48 W
Summit, Ms., U.S.	194	31.17 N	90.28 W
Summit, N.J., U.S.	210	40.44 N	74.21 W
Summit, N.Y., U.S.	210	42.35 N	74.35 W
Summit, S.D., U.S.	198	45.18 N	97.02 W
Summit, Wa., U.S.	224	47.10 N	122.21 W
Summit □[6]	214	41.05 N	81.31 W
Summit Creek ≃	224	46.00 N	121.10 W
Summit Farms	284b	39.19 N	76.32 W
Summit Hill	210	40.49 N	75.52 W
Summit Lake	182	54.17 N	122.38 W
Summit Lake ⊜	224	47.04 N	123.07 W
Summit Mountain ∧	204	39.23 N	116.28 W
Summit Park	276	41.09 N	74.03 W
Summit Park Mall •[9]	284a	43.05 N	78.56 W
Summit Peak ∧	200	37.21 N	106.42 W
Summit Rock ∧	172	45.25 S	170.04 E
Summit Station	208	40.34 N	76.12 W
Summitville, In., U.S.	216	40.20 N	85.38 W
Summitville, N.Y., U.S.	210	41.37 N	74.27 W
Summitville, Oh., U.S.	214	40.41 N	80.53 W
Summt	264a	52.41 N	13.22 E
Summter See ⊜	264a	52.42 N	13.23 E
Šumná	61	48.56 N	15.52 E
Sumnal	120	35.45 N	78.40 E
Sumner, Ia., U.S.	190	42.50 N	92.05 W
Sumner, Ms., U.S.	194	33.58 N	90.22 W
Sumner, Wa., U.S.	224	47.12 N	122.14 W
Sumner, Lake ⊜	172	42.42 S	172.13 E
Sumner, Lake ⊜[1]	196	34.38 N	104.25 W
Sumner Lake State Park ♦	196	34.38 N	104.24 W
Sumner Strait ʉ	180	56.15 N	133.45 W
Sumoto	96	34.21 N	134.54 E
Sumpangbinangae	112	4.24 S	119.36 E
Šumperk	30	49.58 N	16.58 E
Sumpiuh	115a	7.37 S	109.21 E
Sumprabum	110	26.33 N	97.34 E
Sumpter	281	42.10 N	83.29 W
Sumrall	194	31.25 N	89.32 W
Sumsar	85	41.18 N	71.19 E
S'umsi	80	57.07 N	51.37 E
Šumskij	88	54.48 N	99.09 E
Sumskij Posad	24	64.15 N	35.25 E
Šumskoje	78	50.07 N	26.07 E
Šumšu, ostrov I	74	50.45 N	156.20 E
Sumter	192	33.55 N	80.20 W
Sumter □[6]	220	28.38 N	82.08 W
Sumusṭā al-Waqf	142	28.55 N	30.51 E
Sumy	78	50.55 N	34.45 E
Sumy □[4]	78	51.00 N	34.00 E
Sumzom	102	29.45 N	96.10 E
S'un' ≃, Ross.	80	55.44 N	54.16 E
Sun ≃, Mt., U.S.	202	47.30 N	111.19 W
Sun ≃, Zhg.	107	29.13 N	106.21 E
Suna, Kenya	154	1.05 S	34.26 E
Suna, Ross.	80	57.51 N	50.05 E
Suna ≃	24	62.08 N	34.12 E
Sunagawa	92a	43.29 N	141.55 E
Sun al-Heteimi ▿[4]	132	31.05 N	34.00 E
Sun' al-Menī'i ▿[4]	132	31.07 N	34.12 E
Sunām	123	30.08 N	75.48 E
Sunāmganj	120	25.04 N	91.24 E
Sunami	94	35.25 N	136.40 E
Sunan	98	39.13 N	125.41 E
Sunapee Lake ⊜	188	43.23 N	72.03 W
Sunart, Loch ⊂	46	56.41 N	5.43 W
Sunashinden	268	35.53 N	139.30 E
Sunbāṭ	142	30.48 N	31.12 E
Sunbright	192	36.14 N	84.40 W
Sunburst	202	48.52 N	111.54 W
Sunbury, Austl.	169	37.35 S	144.44 E
Sunbury, Eng., U.K.	260	51.25 N	0.26 W
Sunbury, N.C., U.S.	192	36.26 N	76.36 W
Sunbury, Oh., U.S.	214	40.14 N	82.51 W
Sunbury, Pa., U.S.	210	40.51 N	76.47 W
Sunchales	252	30.56 S	61.34 W
Sunch'ang	98	35.23 N	127.07 E
Sunchild Indian Reserve •[4]	182	52.43 N	115.24 W
Sünching	60	48.53 N	12.21 E
Suncho Corral	252	27.56 S	63.27 W
Sunch'ŏn, C.M.I.K.	98	39.26 N	125.54 E
Sunch'ŏn, Taehan	98	34.57 N	127.28 E
Sun City, Az., U.S.	200	33.35 N	112.16 W
Sun City, Ca., U.S.	228	33.42 N	117.11 W
Sun City, Fl., U.S.	220	27.40 N	82.28 W
Sun City Center	220	27.43 N	82.21 W
Suncook	188	43.07 N	71.27 W
Suncook ≃	188	43.08 N	71.28 W
Sunda, Selat (Sunda Strait) ʉ	112	6.00 S	105.45 E
Sundance	198	44.24 N	104.22 W
Sundar	112	4.54 N	115.12 E
Sundar ∧	124	28.26 N	84.20 E
Sundarbans •[1]	126	22.00 N	89.00 E
Sundargarh	124	22.07 N	84.02 E
Sundarnagar	123	31.32 N	76.53 E
Sunda Shelf ⊹[4]	14	5.00 N	107.00 E
Sunda Strait → Sunda, Selat ʉ	112	6.00 S	105.45 E
Sunday Creek ≃	169	37.02 S	145.05 E
Sundby, Dan.	41	54.42 N	11.48 E
Sundby, Sve.	40	59.23 N	17.03 E
Sundbyberg	40	59.22 N	17.58 E
Sundbyholm	40	59.27 N	16.37 E
Sundbyholm slott ⊥	40	59.27 N	16.37 E
Sunde	26	59.50 N	5.43 E
Sunderland, On., Can.	212	44.16 N	79.04 W
Sunderland, Eng., U.K.	44	54.55 N	1.23 W
Sunderland, Ma., U.S.	207	42.28 N	72.34 W
Sunderland, Vt., U.S.	210	43.06 N	73.06 W
Sundern	56	51.20 N	8.00 E
Sünderup	41	54.46 N	9.27 E
Sundhausen	54	50.56 N	10.40 E
Sundhouse	58	48.15 N	7.36 E
Sundi-Lutete	152	4.34 S	14.14 E
Sundown, Austl.	162	26.14 S	133.12 E
Sundown, N.Y., U.S.	210	41.53 N	74.28 W
Sundown, Tx., U.S.	196	33.27 N	102.29 W
Sundra	273d	26.11 S	28.33 E
Sundre	182	51.48 N	114.38 W
Sundridge, On., Can.	190	45.46 N	79.24 W
Sundridge, Eng., U.K.	260	51.17 N	0.08 E
Sunds	41	56.12 N	9.01 E
Sundsbruk	26	62.27 N	17.22 E
Sundsvall	26	62.23 N	17.18 E
Sundwig	263	51.23 N	7.47 E
Suneori	268	35.56 N	139.24 E
Sunfield	216	42.45 N	84.59 W
Sunfish Creek ≃	218	39.01 N	83.03 W
Sunflower	194	33.32 N	90.32 W
Sunflower, Mount ∧	198	39.04 N	102.01 W
Sungaianyar	112	2.55 S	116.18 E
Sungaiapit	114	1.09 N	102.10 E
Sungaibamban	114	3.26 N	99.09 E
Sungaibatu	112	0.48 N	110.45 E
Sungai Bayor	114	5.15 N	100.47 E
Sungaibuntu	115a	6.03 S	107.24 E
Sungaidareh	112	0.58 S	101.30 E
Sungaigerong	112	2.59 S	104.52 E
Sungaiguntung	112	0.18 N	103.37 E
Sungaikakap	112	0.04 S	109.10 E
Sungai Kolok	114	6.02 N	101.58 E
Sungailangsat	112	0.52 S	101.18 E
Sungai Lembing	114	3.55 N	103.02 E
Sungailiat	112	1.51 S	106.08 E
Sungailimau	112	0.31 S	100.03 E
Sungaimanasip	114	1.49 N	100.54 E
Sungainipah	114	0.57 N	98.57 E
Sungaipakning	114	1.20 N	102.09 E
Sungaipenuh	112	2.05 S	101.23 E
Sungaipenyu	112	0.16 N	109.04 E
Sungai Petani	114	5.39 N	100.30 E
Sungaipinang	112	0.48 S	114.04 E
Sungairampah	114	3.29 N	99.09 E
Sungairotan, Indon.	112	1.39 S	102.51 E
Sungairotan, Indon.	112	3.06 S	104.18 E
Sungaisalak	112	0.27 S	102.59 E
Sungaiselan	112	2.24 S	105.59 E
Sungai Siput	114	4.49 N	101.04 E
Sungaitampang	114	2.20 N	100.07 E
Sungaitiram	112	0.47 S	117.12 E
Šungaj	80	48.32 N	46.46 E
Sungari → Songhua ≃	89	47.44 N	132.32 E
Sungchiang → Songjiang	106	31.01 N	121.14 E
Sungezhuang	105	40.15 N	116.39 E
Sungguminasa	112	5.12 S	119.27 E
Sungi ≃	115b	8.38 S	115.06 E
Sungi Point ›	116	10.55 N	125.50 E
Sungkai	114	4.00 N	101.19 E
Sung Kong I	271d	22.11 N	114.17 E
Sung Noen	110	14.54 N	101.50 E
Sungsang	112	2.22 S	104.56 E
Sungshan Domestic Airport ⊠	269d	25.04 N	121.33 E
Sungurlu	130	40.10 N	34.23 E
Sunhezhen	105	40.03 N	116.31 E
Suni	71	40.17 N	8.33 E
Suning	98	38.25 N	115.50 E
Sunjiabu	106	30.55 N	118.54 E
Sunjiadizi	104	42.09 N	124.09 E
Sunjiagou	104	40.45 N	120.39 E
Sunjiajiang	105	40.10 N	115.32 E
Sunjiakanzi	104	40.42 N	123.02 E
Sunjiawan	104	41.59 N	121.42 E
Sunjiazhai	106	30.55 N	121.52 E
Sunjikāy	140	12.20 N	29.46 E
Sunkar, gora ∧	86	44.15 N	73.50 E
Sunken Meadow State Park ♦	207	40.54 N	73.16 W
Sunkośī ≃	124	26.55 N	87.09 E
Sunland •[8]	280	34.16 N	118.19 W
Sunland Park	200	32.15 N	106.45 W
Sunlight Creek ≃	202	44.47 N	109.23 W
Sunlongwan	104	41.19 N	122.57 E
Sunman	218	39.14 N	85.05 W
Sunnansjö	40	60.13 N	14.57 E
Sunndalsøra	26	62.40 N	8.33 E
Sunne	26	59.50 N	13.09 E
Sunnemo	40	59.53 N	13.43 E
Sunnersta	40	59.48 N	17.39 E
Sunnī, Khawr V	140	7.09 N	28.41 E
Sunningdale	260	51.24 N	0.38 W
Sunninghill	42	51.25 N	0.40 W
Sunnybrae	186	45.24 N	62.30 W
Sunny Corner	170	33.23 S	149.53 E
Sunny Crest	278	41.33 N	87.42 W
Sunnydale	224	47.28 N	122.20 W
Sunnyland	220	27.17 N	82.29 W
Sunnylvsfjorden ⊂[2]	26	62.17 N	7.01 E
Sunnymead	228	33.56 N	117.14 W
Sunnynook	182	51.17 N	111.40 W
Sunnyridge	273d	26.10 S	28.11 E
Sunnyside, Nf., Can.	186	47.51 N	53.55 W
Sunnyside, Ca., U.S.	226	32.40 N	117.01 W
Sunny Side, Tx., U.S.	222	29.54 N	96.04 W
Sunnyside, Ut,. U.S.	200	39.33 N	110.23 W
Sunnyside, Wa., U.S.	202	46.19 N	120.00 W
Sunnyside ⊥	276	41.03 N	73.52 W
Sunnyslope, Ab., Can.	182	51.40 N	113.32 W
Sunnyslope, Wa., U.S.	224	47.30 N	122.44 W
Sunnyvale, Ca., U.S.	226	37.22 N	122.02 W
Sunnyvale, Tx., U.S.	222	32.48 N	96.33 W
Sunol	282	37.36 N	121.53 W
Sunol Ridge ∧	282	37.38 N	121.56 W
Sun Prairie	216	43.11 N	89.12 W
Sunray	196	36.01 N	101.49 W
Sunrise, Ky., U.S.	218	38.33 N	84.14 W
Sunrise, Tx., U.S.	222	31.17 N	96.53 W
Sunrise, Wy., U.S.	200	42.19 N	104.42 W
Sunrise Heights	216	42.18 N	85.09 W
Sunrise Mall •[9]	276	40.41 N	73.26 W
Sunrise Manor	204	36.08 N	115.04 W
Sunrise Peak ∧	224	46.20 N	121.46 W
Sun River Terrace	216	41.06 N	87.45 W
Sunset, La., U.S.	194	30.24 N	92.04 W
Sunset, Tx., U.S.	196	33.27 N	97.46 W
Sunset •[8]	282	37.45 N	122.30 W
Sunset Bay	214	42.11 N	79.24 W
Sunset Beach, Ca., U.S.	280	33.43 N	118.04 W
Sunset Beach, Hi., U.S.	229c	21.40 N	158.02 W
Sunset Country •[1]	166	35.00 S	141.30 E
Sunset Crater National Monument ♦	200	35.18 N	111.21 W
Sunset Heights	196	31.53 N	102.22 W
Sunset Hill	276	40.26 N	74.35 W
Sunset Hills	279b	40.35 N	80.15 W
Sunset Peak ∧	280	34.13 N	117.42 W
Sunset Prairie	182	55.50 N	120.48 W
Sunset Valley	214	40.18 N	79.44 W
Sunshine, Austl.	166	37.47 S	144.50 E
Sunshine, Austl.	169	37.47 S	144.50 E
Sunshine, Ak., U.S.	180	62.10 N	150.04 W
Sunshine Island I	271d	22.16 N	114.03 E
Sunshine Point ›	281	42.36 N	82.47 W
Sunshine Skyway Bridge •[5]	220	27.37 N	82.39 W
Suntai ≃	146	8.05 N	10.04 E
Suntar	74	62.10 N	117.40 E
Suntar-Chajata, chrebet ⋏	74	62.00 N	143.00 E
Suntaug Lake ⊜	283	42.32 N	71.00 W
Süntel ⋏	52	52.12 N	9.25 E
Sun Temple ✝[1]	273c	29.55 N	31.11 E
Sunter •[8]	269e	6.09 S	106.50 E
Sunter, Kali ≊	269e	6.07 S	106.50 E
Sunti ≃	272b	22.37 N	88.34 E
Suntrana	180	63.51 N	148.51 W
Suntsar	128	25.31 N	62.00 E
Suntu	144	8.06 N	36.57 E
Sun Valley, Id., U.S.	202	43.41 N	114.21 W
Sun Valley, Nv., U.S.	226	39.34 N	119.47 W
Sun Valley •[8]	280	34.14 N	118.21 W
SunValley Center •[9]	282	37.58 N	122.03 W
Sun Village	228	34.35 N	118.03 W
Sunwapta ≃	182	52.32 N	117.41 W
Sunwi-do I	98	37.44 N	125.15 E
Sunwu	89	49.27 N	127.20 E
Sunwui → Jiangmen	100	22.35 N	113.05 E
Sunyani	150	7.20 N	2.20 W
Sunying	98	34.30 N	114.21 E
Sunža ≃	84	43.26 N	46.08 E
Sunženskij chrebet ⋏	84	43.21 N	45.00 E
Sun Zhong Shan Ling (Tomb of Sun Yat Sen) ⊥	106	32.10 N	118.56 E
Suojarvi	24	62.05 N	32.21 E
Suolahti	26	62.34 N	25.52 E
Suomenlahti → Finland, Gulf of ⊂	26	60.00 N	27.00 E
Suomenselkä ∧	26	63.59 N	27.00 E
Suomi → Finland □[1]	24	64.00 N	26.00 E
Suomussalmi	26	64.53 N	29.05 E
Suō-nada ▿[2]	96	33.50 N	131.30 E
Suonenjoki	26	62.37 N	27.08 E
Suontee ⊜	26	61.40 N	26.30 E
Suordach	74	66.43 N	132.04 E
Suoshu	106	31.57 N	119.00 E
Supachuy	248	19.29 S	64.31 W
Supamo ≃	246	6.48 N	61.50 W
Supaul	124	26.07 N	86.36 E
Supe	144	8.37 N	35.38 E
Superbe ≃	50	48.35 N	3.53 E
Superga, Basilica di ✝[1]	62	45.05 N	7.46 E
Superior, Az., U.S.	200	33.17 N	111.05 W
Superior, Mt., U.S.	202	47.11 N	114.53 W
Superior, Ne., U.S.	198	40.01 N	98.04 W
Superior, Wi., U.S.	190	46.43 N	92.06 W
Superior, Laguna ⊂	234	16.20 N	94.55 W
Superior, Lake ⊜	190	48.00 N	88.00 W
Superior Lake ⊜	228	35.15 N	117.02 W
Superior Valley V	228	35.16 N	117.00 W
Supersano	68	40.01 N	18.14 E
Supetar	36	43.23 N	16.33 E
Suphan Buri	110	14.28 N	100.07 E
Suphan Buri ≃	110	13.29 N	100.17 E
Süphan Dağı ∧	84	38.56 N	42.50 E
Supino	66	41.37 N	13.14 E
Supiori I	164	0.45 S	135.30 E
Sūpkhār	124	22.12 N	80.56 E
Supoj ≃	78	49.38 N	31.48 E
Suponevo	76	53.12 N	34.18 E
Supoqiao	107	30.40 N	103.59 E
Süpplingen	54	52.14 N	10.54 E
Supraśl	30	53.13 N	23.20 E
Supraśl ≃	30	53.04 N	22.56 E
Sup'ung	98	40.27 N	124.57 E
Sup'ung-chŏsuji ⊜[1]	98	40.30 N	125.05 E
Supur	126	23.01 N	86.52 E
Suputinskij zapovednik ♦	89	43.40 N	132.20 E
Sūq-'Abs	144	15.59 N	43.04 E
Sūq ash-Shuyūkh	128	30.53 N	46.28 E
Suq'at al-Jamal	140	12.48 N	27.42 E
Suqian	100	33.59 N	118.18 E
Suqiao, Zhg.	100	34.08 N	113.47 E
Suqiao, Zhg.	105	39.03 N	116.29 E
Sūq Suwayq	128	24.23 N	38.27 E
Suquamish	224	47.43 N	122.33 W
Suquṭrā (Socotra) I	118	12.30 N	54.00 E
Ṣūr (Tyre), Lubnān	132	33.16 N	35.11 E
Ṣūr, 'Umān	118	22.35 N	59.31 E
Sur, Cabo ›	174z	27.12 S	109.26 W
Sur, Campos de Hielo ⍓	254	49.10 S	73.30 W
Sur, Canal ʉ	288	34.37 S	58.15 W
Sur, Point ›	226	36.18 N	121.54 W
Sura	80	53.53 N	45.45 E
Sura •[8]	272b	22.33 N	88.25 E
Sura ≃	80	56.06 N	46.00 E
Sura, Cape ›	144	11.10 N	47.30 E

Symbols in the index entries represent the broad categories identified in the key at the right. Symbols with superior numbers (⋏[1]) identify subcategories (see complete key on page *I · 1).*

Symbole im Register stellen die rechts im Schlüssel erklärten Kategorien dar. Symbole mit hochgestellten Ziffern (⋏[1]) bezeichnen Unterabteilungen einer Kategorie (vgl. vollständiger Schlüssel auf Seite *I · 1).*

Los símbolos incluídos en el texto del índice representan las grandes categorias identificadas con la clave a la derecha. Los símbolos con numeros en su parte superior (⋏[1]) identifican las subcategorías (véase la clave completa en la página *I · 1).*

Les symboles de l'index représentent les catégories indiquées dans la légende à droite. Les symboles suivis d'un indice (⋏[1]) représentent des sous-catégories (voir légende complète à la page *I · 1).*

Os símbolos incluídos no texto do índice representam as grandes categorias identificadas com a chave à direita. Os símbolos com números em sua parte superior (⋏[1]) identificam as subcategorias (veja-se a chave completa à página *I · 1).*

Symbol	English	Deutsch	Español	Français	Português
∧	Mountain	Berg	Montaña	Montagne	Montanha
⋏	Mountains	Gebirge	Montañas	Montagnes	Montanhas
)(	Pass	Paß	Paso	Col	Passo
V	Valley, Canyon	Tal, Cañon	Valle, Cañón	Vallée, Canyon	Vale, Canhão
≚	Plain	Ebene	Llano	Plaine	Planície
›	Cape	Kap	Cabo	Cap	Cabo
I	Island	Insel	Isla	Île	Ilha
II	Islands	Inseln	Islas	Îles	Ilhas
≗	Other Topographic Features	Andere Topographische Objekte	Otros Elementos Topográficos	Autres données topographiques	Outros acidentes topográficos

ESPAÑOL · FRANÇAIS · PORTUGUÊS

Nombre / Nom / Nome	Página / Page / Página	Lat.°′	Long.°′ W = Oeste / W = Ouest / W = Oeste
Şūrāb, Pāk.	120	28.29 N	66.16 E
Šurab, Taj.	85	40.03 N	70.33 E
Surabaya	115a	7.15 S	112.45 E
S'urachi, Nuraghe ⊥	71	40.01 N	8.33 E
Şurad	142	30.59 N	30.54 E
Surag-san ∧	271b	37.42 N	127.04 E
Surahammar	40	59.43 N	16.13 E
Sūrak	128	25.43 N	58.48 E
Surakarta	115a	7.35 S	110.50 E
Suramana	112	0.50 S	119.33 E
Surami	84	42.01 N	43.34 E
Şūrān, Īrān	128	27.18 N	62.04 E
Šuran, Ross.	80	55.22 N	49.50 E
Şūrān, Sūrīy.	130	36.34 N	37.13 E
Şūrān, Sūrīy.	130	35.17 N	36.45 E
Şuran ≃	58	46.02 N	5.19 E
Šurany	30	48.06 N	18.14 E
Surar	144	7.27 N	40.57 E
Surat, Austl.	166	27.09 S	149.04 E
Sūrat, India	120	21.10 N	72.50 E
Sūratgarh	123	29.19 N	73.54 E
Surat Thani (Ban Don)	110	9.08 N	99.19 E
Surava	80	52.57 N	41.18 E
Suraž, Bela.	76	55.25 N	30.44 E
Suraż, Pol.	30	52.58 N	22.58 E
Suraž, Ross.	76	53.01 N	32.24 E
Surbiton ◆[8]	260	51.24 N	0.18 W
Surbo	68	40.24 N	18.08 E
Surbourg	56	48.55 N	7.51 E
Surchan	80	46.39 N	49.38 E
Surchandarja □[4]	85	38.00 N	67.30 E
Surchandarja ≃	85	37.58 N	67.50 E
Surchdara	85	38.37 N	69.55 E
Şurchob ≃	85	38.53 N	70.03 E
Šurči	85	37.59 N	67.47 E
Surco ≃	286d	12.13 S	77.03 W
Surdulica	38	42.41 N	22.10 E
Sûre (Sauer) ≃	56	49.44 N	6.31 E
Şureanu, Munţii ⩘	38	45.38 N	23.27 E
Šureksor, ozero ⊜	86	52.16 N	75.50 E
Surendorf	41	54.28 N	10.04 E
Surendranagar	120	22.42 N	71.41 E
Suresnes	261	48.52 N	2.14 E
Suretka	236	9.34 N	82.56 W
Surf City	208	39.39 N	74.09 W
Surfers Paradise	171a	28.00 S	153.26 E
Surfside, Fl., U.S.	220	25.52 N	80.07 W
Surfside, Tx., U.S.	222	28.57 N	95.17 W
Surgères	32	46.07 N	0.45 W
Surgidero	240p	22.41 N	82.18 W
Surgijn ≃	88	47.20 N	95.50 E
Surgoinsville	192	36.28 N	82.51 W
Sürgü	130	38.01 N	37.59 E
Sürgücü	130	37.35 N	40.44 E
Surgut	74	61.14 N	73.20 E
Surhuisterveen	52	53.10 N	6.10 E
Suri	164	7.10 S	143.55 E
Suria	272b	22.51 N	88.33 E
Suriāpet	122	17.09 N	79.37 E
Suribachi-yama ∧[2]	174f	24.45 N	141.17 E
Suribao ≃	116	11.33 N	125.28 E
Surigao	116	9.45 N	125.30 E
Surigao del Norte □[4]	116	9.35 N	125.36 E
Surigao del Sur □[4]	116	9.00 N	126.00 E
Surigao Strait ʯ	116	10.15 N	125.23 E
Surikova	86	56.59 N	91.31 E
Surin	110	14.53 N	103.29 E
Suriname □[1], S.A.	242	4.00 N	56.00 W
Suriname □[1], S.A.	250	4.00 N	56.00 W
Surinam → Suriname □[1]	250	4.00 N	56.00 W
Šurinda	88	55.13 N	113.23 E
Suring	190	44.59 N	88.22 W
Sūrīyah → Syria □[1]	128	35.00 N	38.00 E
S'urkum	89	50.08 N	140.31 E
S'urkum, mys ›	89	50.05 N	140.41 E
Šurma	80	56.58 N	50.21 E
Sūrmaq	128	31.03 N	52.48 E
Surmelin ≃	50	49.04 N	3.13 E
Surnadalsøra	26	62.59 N	8.39 E
Surodadi	115a	6.53 S	109.15 E
Surovaticha	80	55.45 N	43.56 E
Surovikino	80	48.36 N	42.51 E
Surovo	88	55.37 N	105.36 E
Surprise	200	33.37 N	112.19 W
Surprise, Lake ⊜	222	29.33 N	94.41 W
Surprise Valley V	204	41.35 N	120.05 W
Surquillo	286d	12.07 S	77.02 W
Surrency	192	31.43 N	82.11 W
Surrey	198	48.14 N	101.07 W
Surrey □[6]	42	51.10 N	0.20 W
Surrey, University of ʋ[2]	260	51.14 N	0.36 W
Surrey Heath □[8]	260	51.23 N	0.35 W
Surry	208	37.08 N	76.50 W
Surry □[6]	208	37.10 N	76.50 W
Sursee	58	47.10 N	8.06 E
Sursés V	58	46.34 N	9.38 E
Sursk	80	53.04 N	45.42 E
Surskij Majdan	80	55.01 N	46.32 E
Surskoje	80	54.30 N	46.44 E
Surt	146	31.12 N	16.35 E
Surt, Khalīj (Gulf of Sidra) c	146	31.30 N	18.00 E
Surtainville	28	49.25 N	1.50 W
Surtanāhu	120	26.22 N	70.00 E
Surte	26	57.49 N	12.01 E
Surtsey I	24a	63.16 N	20.32 W
Suru	164	6.50 S	144.45 E
Suru ≃	123	34.45 N	76.12 E
Surubiú ≃	250	3.58 S	48.52 W
Sürüç	130	36.58 N	38.24 E
Suruga-wan c	94	34.51 N	138.33 E
Suruí	256	22.40 S	43.07 W
Suruí ≃	287a	22.42 S	43.07 W
Surulangun	112	2.37 S	102.45 E
Suru-Lere ◆[8]	273a	6.31 N	3.22 E
Surumu ≃	246	3.22 N	60.19 W
Surveyor Creek ≃	198	40.20 N	102.38 W
Surveyor Point ›	168b	34.47 S	137.51 E
Survilliers	261	49.06 N	2.33 E
Surwold	52	53.00 N	7.30 E
Şury-le-Comtal	62	45.32 N	4.10 E
Šuryškary	74	65.54 N	65.22 E
Susa, It.	62	45.08 N	7.03 E
Susa, Nihon	96	34.37 N	131.36 E
Suså ≃	41	55.11 N	11.46 E
Susa, Valle di V	62	45.09 N	7.10 E
Sūsah	146	32.54 N	21.58 E
Susak, Otok I	36	44.31 N	14.18 E
Susaki	96	33.22 N	133.17 E
Susami	96	33.33 N	135.30 E
Susamyr	85	42.09 N	73.58 E
Susamyr ≃	85	42.08 N	74.03 E
Susamyrtau, chrebet ⩘	85	42.08 N	73.15 E
Susan	208	37.22 N	76.19 W
Susan ≃	204	40.19 N	120.17 W
Susan, Port c	224	48.10 N	122.25 W
Susana Knolls	228	34.16 N	118.41 W
Sūsangerd	128	31.34 N	48.11 E
Susanino, Ross.	76	59.30 N	30.22 E
Susanino, Ross.	80	58.09 N	41.36 E
Susanino, Ross.	89	52.47 N	140.06 E
Susano	256	23.32 S	46.20 W
Susano □[7]	287b	23.35 S	46.18 W
Şusanville	204	40.24 N	120.39 W
Šušary, Ross.	265a	59.46 N	30.21 E
Šušary, Ross.	265a	59.48 N	30.23 E
Susch	58	46.46 N	10.04 E
Susegana	64	45.51 N	12.15 E
Suşehri	130	40.11 N	38.06 E
Şüsel	54	54.04 N	10.43 E
Šušenskoje	86	53.19 N	91.58 E
Sušice	60	49.14 N	13.32 E
Susitna	180	61.33 N	150.31 W
Susitna ≃	180	61.16 N	150.30 W
Susleny	78	47.25 N	28.59 E
Suslonger	80	56.18 N	48.13 E
Sušn'aki Pervoje	86	57.53 N	88.47 E
Susobana ≃	94	36.37 N	138.11 E
Susoh	114	3.43 N	96.50 E
Susong	100	30.09 N	116.06 E
Susono	94	35.09 N	138.54 E
Suspiro del Moro, Puerto del)(	34	37.04 N	3.39 W
Susquehanna	210	41.56 N	75.36 W
Susquehanna □[6]	210	41.50 N	75.50 W
Susquehanna ≃	188	39.33 N	76.05 W
Susquehanna, West Branch ≃	210	40.53 N	76.47 W
Susquehanna State Park ♦	208	39.36 N	76.09 W
Susques	252	23.25 S	66.29 W
Sussa ≃	152	7.22 S	17.05 E
Süssen	56	48.41 N	9.45 E
Süssenbrunn ◆[8]	264b	48.17 N	16.30 E
Süsser See ⊜	54	51.30 N	11.40 E
Sussex, N.B., Can.	186	45.43 N	65.31 W
Sussex, N.J., U.S.	210	41.12 N	74.36 W
Sussex, Va., U.S.	208	36.54 N	77.16 W
Sussex, Wi., U.S.	216	43.08 N	88.13 W
Sussex □[6], De., U.S.	208	38.42 N	75.23 W
Sussex □[6], N.J., U.S.	210	41.08 N	74.41 W
Sussex □[6], Va., U.S.	208	36.50 N	77.15 W
Sussex, Vale of V	42	50.57 N	0.17 W
Sussex Inlet	170	35.11 S	150.36 E
Sussey	50	47.13 N	4.22 E
Sustenhorn ∧	58	46.42 N	8.28 E
Susten Pass)(	58	46.44 N	8.27 E
Şusteren	52	51.04 N	5.51 E
Šustikovo	82	55.17 N	35.59 E
Susu	174m	26.47 N	128.19 E
Susubona	175e	8.18 S	159.27 E
Susui	112	4.56 N	116.41 E
Susuman	74	62.47 N	148.10 E
Susurluk	130	39.54 N	28.10 E
Şusuzmüsellim	130	41.06 N	27.03 E
Šušvė ≃	76	55.10 N	23.49 E
Susz	30	53.44 N	19.20 E
Sutāhāta	126	22.08 N	88.07 E
Sutak	123	33.12 N	77.28 E
Sutama	94	35.47 N	138.25 E
Sut-Chol'	86	51.24 N	91.17 E
Sütçüler	130	37.30 N	30.59 E
Sutera	70	37.31 N	13.44 E
Sutersville	214	40.14 N	79.48 W
Suthat, Wat ʋ[1]	269a	13.45 N	100.30 E
Sutherland, Austl.	170	34.02 S	151.04 E
Sutherland, S. Afr.	158	32.24 S	20.40 E
Sutherland, Ia., U.S.	198	42.58 N	95.29 W
Sutherland, Ne., U.S.	198	41.09 N	101.07 W
Sutherland ≃	182	54.29 N	125.05 W
Sutherland, Lake ⊜	224	48.05 N	123.42 W
Sutherland Falls ∟	172	44.48 S	167.44 E
Sutherlands	168b	34.10 S	139.13 E
Sutherlin	202	43.23 N	123.18 W
Suthiāna	272a	28.31 N	77.26 E
Sutjeska Nacionalni Park ♦	38	43.22 N	18.45 E
Sutlej (Satluj) (Langqên) ≃	120	29.23 N	71.02 E
Sutri	66	42.14 N	12.13 E
Sutrio	64	46.31 N	12.59 E
Sutschou → Suzhou	106	31.18 N	120.37 E
Sütschou → Xuzhou	98	34.16 N	117.11 E
Sutter	226	39.10 N	121.45 W
Sutter □[6]	226	39.08 N	121.37 W
Sutter Buttes ∧	226	39.12 N	121.50 W
Sutter Bypass ≃	226	38.47 N	121.38 W
Sutter Creek	226	38.23 N	120.48 W
Sutter Creek ≃	226	38.22 N	120.59 W
Sutton, Austl.	171b	35.10 S	149.15 E
Sutton, P.Q., Can.	206	45.06 N	72.37 W
Sutton, Eng., U.K.	42	52.23 N	0.07 E
Sutton, Eng., U.K.	260	51.12 N	0.26 W
Sutton, Ak., U.S.	180	61.43 N	148.53 W
Sutton, Ma., U.S.	207	42.09 N	71.45 W
Sutton, Ne., U.S.	198	40.36 N	97.51 W
Sutton, W.V., U.S.	188	38.39 N	80.42 W
Sutton ◆[8]	42	51.22 N	0.12 W
Sutton, Monts ⩘	206	45.05 N	72.30 W
Sutton-at-Home	260	51.25 N	0.14 E
Sutton Bridge	42	52.46 N	0.12 E
Sutton Coldfield	42	52.34 N	1.48 W
Sutton Courtenay	42	51.39 N	1.17 W
Sutton Forest	170	34.35 S	150.19 E
Sutton in Ashfield	44	53.08 N	1.15 W
Sutton Lake ⊜[1]	188	38.40 N	80.40 W
Sutton Lane Ends	262	53.14 N	2.06 W
Sutton Leach	262	53.26 N	2.42 W
Sutton on Sea	44	53.19 N	0.17 E
Sutton on Trent	44	53.10 N	0.49 W
Sutton Park	276	40.49 N	74.42 W
Sutton Place ⊥	260	51.16 N	0.33 W
Suttons Bay	190	44.58 N	85.39 W
Sutton Scotney	42	51.10 N	1.21 W
Sutton Valence	42	51.12 N	0.36 E
Sutton Veny	42	51.11 N	2.08 W
Sutton Weaver	262	53.18 N	2.41 W
Sutton West	212	44.18 N	79.22 W
Suttor ≃	166	21.25 S	147.45 E
Suttrop	56	51.27 N	8.22 E
Suttsu	92a	42.48 N	140.14 E
Sutwik Island I	180	56.34 N	157.05 W
Suunduk ≃	86	51.46 N	58.46 E
Suurberge ⩘	158	33.18 S	25.32 E
Suurbraak	158	34.00 S	20.39 E
Suure-Jaani	76	58.33 N	25.28 E
Suur Munamägi ∧[2]	76	57.43 N	27.04 E
Suur Pakri I	76	59.20 N	23.55 E
Suva	175g	18.08 S	178.25 E
Şuvainiškis	76	56.10 N	25.17 E
Šuvalovo Oz'orki ◆[8]	265a	60.02 N	30.18 E
Suva Planina ⩘	38	43.10 N	22.10 E
Suvarlı	130	37.32 N	37.38 E
Şuvasvesi ⊜	26	62.39 N	28.12 E
Šuvel'an	84	40.30 N	50.09 E
Suvereto	66	43.05 N	10.40 E
Suvo	88	53.39 N	110.00 E
Suvorka	88	56.33 N	103.24 E
Suvorov	82	54.07 N	36.30 E
Suvorovo, Ross.	82	56.07 N	35.54 E
Suvorovo, Ukr.	78	45.34 N	28.59 E
Suwa, Erit.	144	14.17 N	41.06 E
Suwa, Nihon	94	36.02 N	138.08 E
Suwa-ko ⊜	94	36.05 N	138.05 E
Suwałki	30	54.07 N	22.56 E
Suwałki □[4]	30	54.10 N	22.15 E
Suwannaphum	110	15.33 N	103.47 E
Suwannee ≃	192	29.18 N	83.09 W
Suwannee Lake ⊜	184	56.08 N	100.10 W
Suwanose-jima I	93b	29.38 N	129.43 E
Suwanose-suidō ʯ	93b	29.32 N	129.40 E
Suwarrow I[1]	14	13.15 S	163.05 W
Suwaydah	130	35.46 N	39.38 E
Şuwaylih	132	32.02 N	35.50 E
Suways, Khalīj as- (Gulf of Suez) c	140	29.00 N	32.50 E
Suways, Qanāt as- (Suez Canal) ≊	142	29.55 N	32.33 E
Suwŏn	98	37.17 N	127.01 E
Suwon-dong	98	41.54 N	129.43 E
Suxi	100	29.25 N	120.07 E
Suxian	100	33.38 N	116.58 E
Suya	150	9.28 N	3.11 E
Suykbulak	86	49.48 N	80.50 E
Suyo	246	4.30 S	80.00 W
Suzak	86	44.07 N	68.28 E
Suzaka	94	36.39 N	138.19 E
Suzdal'	80	56.25 N	40.26 E
Suze ≃	58	47.08 N	7.14 E
Suze-la-Rousse	62	44.17 N	4.51 E
Suzhi	98	42.17 N	113.42 E
Suzhou (Soochow)	106	31.18 N	120.37 E
Suzhuang	105	40.04 N	116.44 E
Suzi ≃	98	41.55 N	124.17 E
Suzigou	98	40.25 N	123.25 E
S'uzikozero	24	61.48 N	37.20 E
Suz'omka	76	52.19 N	34.05 E
Suzu	92	37.25 N	137.17 E
Suzuka	94	34.51 N	136.35 E
Suzuka ≃	94	34.54 N	136.39 E
Suzuka-kokutei-kōen ♦	94	35.00 N	136.25 E
Suzuka-sammyaku ⩘	94	35.00 N	136.25 E
Suzuki	268	35.43 N	139.31 E
S'uz'um	80	58.02 N	47.32 E
Suzu-misaki ›	92	37.31 N	137.21 E
Suzun	86	53.47 N	82.19 E
Suzzara	64	45.00 N	10.45 E
Sværdborg	41	55.05 N	11.54 E
Sval'ava	78	48.33 N	22.59 E
Svalbard □[2]	12	78.00 N	20.00 E
Svalöv	41	55.55 N	13.06 E
Svaneholm	41	55.30 N	13.28 E
Svaneke	26	55.08 N	15.09 E
Svanetskij chrebet ⩘	84	42.55 N	42.42 E
Svängsta	26	56.16 N	14.46 E
Svanninge	41	55.07 N	10.15 E
Svanskog	26	59.11 N	12.33 E
Svapa ≃	78	51.44 N	34.56 E
Şvappavaara	24	67.39 N	21.04 E
Švarcevskij	82	54.06 N	37.59 E
Svärdsjö	26	60.45 N	15.55 E
Švaricha	80	57.33 N	49.37 E
Svartå	40	59.08 N	14.31 E
Svartälven ≃	40	59.19 N	14.35 E
Svartån ≃	40	59.37 N	16.33 E
Svarte	41	55.25 N	13.43 E
Svartenhuk ›[1]	176	71.55 N	55.00 W
Svärtinge	40	58.39 N	16.00 E
Svartisen ⊓	24	66.38 N	14.00 E
Svartlöga I	40	59.34 N	19.03 E
Svartsjölandet I	40	59.22 N	17.41 E
Svataj	74	67.57 N	151.54 E
Svatava	54	50.11 N	12.35 E
Svatava ≃	54	50.11 N	12.38 E
Sv'atica ≃	80	58.22 N	51.43 E
Sv'atogorskaja	83	49.04 N	37.32 E
Sv'atoj Nos, mys ›, Ross.	24	68.10 N	39.45 E
Sv'atoj Nos, mys ›, Ross.	74	72.52 N	140.42 E
Sv'atoj Nos, poluostrov ›[1]	88	53.40 N	108.50 E
Sv'atoslavka	80	51.20 N	43.26 E
Svatovo	83	49.23 N	38.13 E
Svay Chék	110	13.48 N	102.58 E
Svay Riĕng	110	11.05 N	105.48 E
Sveafallen ∟	40	59.10 N	14.22 E
Svebølle	41	55.38 N	11.20 E
Sveča	80	58.16 N	47.32 E
Svedala	41	55.30 N	13.14 E
Svėdasai	76	55.41 N	25.22 E
Sveg	26	62.02 N	14.21 E
Şvegssjön ⊜[1]	26	62.03 N	14.10 E
Švėkšna	76	55.31 N	21.37 E
Svelgen	26	61.47 N	5.15 E
Svelvik	26	59.37 N	10.24 E
Sven'	76	53.09 N	34.21 E
Švenčionėliai	76	55.10 N	26.00 E
Švenčionys	76	55.07 N	26.10 E
Svendborg	41	55.03 N	10.37 E
Svenljunga	26	57.30 N	13.07 E
Svennevad	40	59.01 N	15.22 E
Svensen	224	46.10 N	123.39 W
Svenstorp	41	55.46 N	13.15 E
Şvenstrup	26	56.59 N	9.52 E
Šventoji	76	56.02 N	21.05 E
Šventoji ≃	76	55.06 N	24.22 E
Sverbejevo	89	53.36 N	123.15 E
Sverdlovo, Ross.	80	51.16 N	44.34 E
Sverdlovo, Ross.	82	56.38 N	36.37 E
Sverdlovsk	83	48.05 N	39.40 E
Sverdlovsk → Jekaterinburg	86	56.51 N	60.36 E
Sverdrup, ostrov I	74	74.35 N	79.30 E
Sverige → Sweden □[1]	24	62.00 N	15.00 E
Şverkestaån ≃	40	59.28 N	15.28 E
Švermov	54	50.09 N	14.05 E
Svessa	78	51.57 N	33.54 E
Sveti Arhandjel Mihajlo ʋ[1]	38	42.07 N	21.28 E
Sveti Jovan Bigorski ʋ[1]	38	41.38 N	20.37 E
Svetiloviči	76	52.48 N	31.19 E
Sveti Nikole	38	41.52 N	21.58 E
Sveti Petar u Šumi	64	45.11 N	13.52 E
Svetlaja	89	46.33 N	138.18 E
Světlá nad Sázavou	30	49.40 N	15.25 E
Svetlanovo	83	48.42 N	38.28 E
Svetlogorsk, Bela.	76	52.38 N	29.42 E
Svetlogorsk, Ross.	76	54.57 N	20.10 E
Svetlograd	72	45.20 N	42.40 E
Svetloje	80	57.03 N	53.38 E
Svetlovodsk	78	49.04 N	33.15 E
Svetlyj, Ross.	76	54.41 N	20.08 E
Svetlyj, Ross.	86	50.47 N	60.53 E
Svetlyj, Ross.	88	58.26 N	115.55 E
Svetlyj Jar	80	48.29 N	44.46 E
Svetogorsk	24	61.07 N	28.51 E
Svetozarevo	38	43.58 N	21.16 E
Svežen'kaja	80	54.01 N	42.26 E
Şvidník	30	49.18 N	21.35 E
Švihov	60	49.29 N	13.17 E
Svijaga ≃	80	55.47 N	48.40 E
Svilajnac	38	44.14 N	21.13 E
Svilengrad	38	41.46 N	26.12 E
Svindal	26	58.30 N	7.28 E
Svinecea Mare, Vîrful ∧	38	44.48 N	22.09 E
Svinesund	26	59.06 N	11.16 E
Svinninge	41	55.43 N	11.28 E
Svir'	76	54.51 N	26.24 E
Svir' ≃	76	60.30 N	32.48 E
Svirica	76	60.29 N	32.51 E
Svirsk	88	53.04 N	103.21 E
Svir'stroj	76	60.48 N	33.43 E
Sviščovka	80	52.51 N	43.44 E
Svisloč', Bela.	76	53.02 N	24.06 E
Svisloč', Bela.	76	53.26 N	28.59 E
Svisloč' ≃	76	53.26 N	28.59 E
Svištov	38	43.37 N	25.20 E
Svistunovka	83	49.29 N	38.20 E
Svit	30	49.03 N	20.12 E
Svitava ≃	30	49.09 N	16.38 E
Svitávka	30	49.30 N	16.37 E
Svitavy	30	49.45 N	16.27 E
Svitino	82	54.54 N	35.49 E
Svoboda, Ross.	78	47.12 N	40.39 E
Svoboda, Ross.	78	51.58 N	36.17 E
Svobodnaja	89	46.48 N	143.23 E
Svobodnoje	83	47.32 N	37.34 E
Svobodnyj, Ross.	80	52.20 N	46.22 E
Svobodnyj, Ross.	89	51.24 N	128.08 E
Svobodnyj Port	78	46.20 N	31.51 E
Svoge	38	42.58 N	23.21 E
Svojna	82	54.09 N	36.39 E
Svol'na ≃	76	55.43 N	28.02 E
Svolvær	24	68.14 N	14.34 E
Svor	54	50.47 N	14.36 E
Svorkmo	26	63.10 N	9.45 E
Svratka ≃	61	49.11 N	16.38 E
Svržno	60	49.35 N	12.46 E
Svullrya	26	60.25 N	12.24 E
Swābi	123	34.07 N	72.28 E
Swadlincote	42	52.47 N	1.33 W
Swaffham	42	52.39 N	0.41 E
Swain	210	42.29 N	77.51 W
Swain Reefs ✣[2]	166	21.40 S	152.15 E
Swainsboro	192	32.35 N	82.20 W
Swains Island I[1]	14	11.03 S	171.05 W
Swakop ≃	156	22.38 S	14.36 E
Swakopmund	156	22.41 S	14.34 E
Swakopmund □[5]	156	23.00 S	15.00 E
Swale □[8]	260	51.21 N	0.41 E
Swale ≃	44	54.06 N	1.20 W
Swale Canyon V	224	45.49 N	121.05 W
Swale Creek ≃	224	45.49 N	121.05 W
Swaledale V	44	54.25 N	1.47 W
Swallowfield	218	38.21 N	84.51 W
Swalmen	52	51.15 N	6.02 E
Swamp City	222	32.29 N	94.56 W
Swampscott	207	42.28 N	70.55 W
Swan	222	32.26 N	95.22 W
Swan ≃, Austl.	168a	32.03 S	115.45 E
Swan ≃, Can.	184	52.30 N	100.47 W
Swan ≃, Ab., Can.	182	55.31 N	115.17 W
Swan ≃, Mn., U.S.	190	47.01 N	93.16 W
Swan ≃, Mt., U.S.	202	48.04 N	114.05 W
Swan Acres	279b	40.33 N	80.02 W
Swanage	42	50.37 N	1.58 W
Swan Bay c	169	38.14 S	144.40 E
Swan Creek ≃, Austl.	171a	28.08 S	152.13 E
Swan Creek ≃, Mi., U.S.	216	41.58 N	85.19 W
Swan Creek ≃, Mi., U.S.	216	41.58 N	83.17 W
Swan Creek ≃, Oh., U.S.	216	41.39 N	83.32 W
Swan Creek ≃, S.D., U.S.	198	45.19 N	100.15 W
Swan Creek, North Branch ≃	281	42.06 N	83.23 W
Swan Creek Point ›	281	42.40 N	82.39 W
Swanee → Suwannee ≃	192	29.18 N	83.09 W
Swan Hill	166	35.21 S	143.34 E
Swan Hills	182	54.43 N	115.24 W
Swan Hills ⩘[2]	182	54.48 N	115.52 W
Swanington	216	40.35 N	87.17 W
Swan Island I	169	38.15 S	144.41 E
Swan Islands → Santanilla, Islas II	238	17.25 N	83.55 W
Swank Creek ≃	224	47.07 N	120.45 W
Swan Lake, Mb., Can.	184	49.24 N	98.46 W
Swan Lake, Mt., U.S.	202	47.55 N	113.50 W
Swan Lake, N.Y., U.S.	210	41.45 N	74.47 W
Swan Lake ⊜, Mb., Can.	184	52.30 N	100.45 W
Swan Lake ⊜, On., Can.	184	54.17 N	91.12 W
Swan Lake ⊜, Il., U.S.	219	38.57 N	90.33 W
Swan Lake ⊜, Mn., U.S.	190	44.19 N	94.15 W
Swanland	44	53.44 N	0.29 W
Swanley	42	51.24 N	0.12 E
Swanlinbar	48	54.10 N	7.42 W
Swannanoa	192	35.36 N	82.23 W
Swannanoa, Lake ⊜	276	41.01 N	74.31 W
Swan Peak ∧	202	47.43 N	113.38 W
Swanquarter	192	35.24 N	76.20 W
Swan Range ⩘	202	47.50 N	113.40 W
Swan Reach	166	34.34 S	139.36 E
Swan River	184	52.06 N	101.16 W
Swansboro	192	34.41 N	77.07 W
Swanscombe	260	51.26 N	0.18 E
Swansea, Austl.	166	42.08 S	148.04 E
Swansea, Austl.	170	33.05 S	151.38 E
Swansea, Wales, U.K.	42	51.38 N	3.57 W
Swansea, Il., U.S.	219	38.32 N	89.59 W
Swansea, Ma., U.S.	207	41.44 N	71.11 W
Swansea, S.C., U.S.	192	33.44 N	81.05 W
Swansea ◆[8]	275b	43.38 N	79.28 W
Swansea Bay c	42	51.35 N	3.52 W
Swans Island I	188	44.10 N	68.25 W
Swanson Lake ⊜[1]	198	40.09 N	101.06 W
Swanton, Oh., U.S.	216	41.35 N	83.53 W
Swanton, Vt., U.S.	206	44.55 N	73.07 W
Swanville	190	45.54 N	94.38 W
Swanzey Center	207	42.49 N	72.10 W
Swarbacks Minn ʯ	46a	60.20 N	1.36 W
Swartberg	158	30.15 S	29.23 E
Swarthmore	208	39.54 N	75.21 W
Swarthmore College ʋ[2]	285	39.54 N	75.21 W
Swart-Kei ≃	158	32.09 S	27.24 E
Swart-Mfolozi ≃	158	28.22 S	31.58 E
Swartplaas	158	26.08 S	26.57 E
Swartruggens	156	25.40 S	26.42 E
Swartruggens ⩘	158	33.02 S	19.35 E
Swartswood Lake	210	41.04 N	74.51 W
Swartswood State Park ♦	210	41.05 N	74.50 W
Swartz Creek	216	42.57 N	83.49 W
Swarupkāti	126	22.45 N	90.06 E
Swarupnagar	126	22.49 N	88.52 E
Swarzędz	30	52.26 N	17.05 E
Swasey Peak ∧	200	39.23 N	113.19 W
Swasey Wash V	200	39.15 N	112.53 W
Swasiland → Swaziland □[1]	158	26.30 S	31.30 E
Swāt ≃	123	34.20 N	71.34 E
Swatara Creek ≃	208	40.11 N	76.44 W
Swa-Tenda	152	7.09 S	17.07 E
Swatow → Shantou	100	23.23 N	116.41 E
Swauger Creek ≃	226	38.16 N	119.16 W
Swauk Pass)(	224	47.21 N	120.40 W
Sway	42	50.47 N	1.37 W
Swayzee	216	40.30 N	85.49 W
Swaziland □[1], Afr.	138	26.30 S	31.30 E
Swaziland □[1], Afr.	158	26.30 S	31.30 E
Swea City	190	43.23 N	94.19 W
Swede Hill	279b	40.17 N	79.34 W
Swedeland	285	40.05 N	75.20 W
Sweden (Sverige) □[1], Europe	22	62.00 N	15.00 E
Sweden (Sverige) □[1], Europe	24	62.00 N	15.00 E
Sweden Valley	214	41.45 N	77.56 W
Swede Run ≃	285	40.02 N	74.58 W
Swedesboro	208	39.44 N	75.18 W
Swedesburg	285	40.06 N	75.20 W
Swedish Knoll ∧	200	39.16 N	111.26 W
Swedru	150	5.32 N	0.43 W
Sween, Loch c	46	55.59 N	5.39 W
Sweeney Plan	279b	40.11 N	79.48 W
Sweeny	222	29.02 N	95.41 W
Sweeny Park ♦	284a	43.02 N	78.52 W
Sweet Briar	192	37.33 N	79.04 W
Sweetgrass	182	49.00 N	111.57 W
Sweet Grass Creek ≃	202	45.47 N	109.47 W
Sweetgrass Hills ⩘[2]	202	48.55 N	111.30 W
Sweet Grass Indian Reserve ◆[4]	184	52.44 N	108.45 W
Sweetheart Abbey ʋ[1]	44	54.59 N	3.38 W
Sweet Home, Or., U.S.	202	44.23 N	122.44 W
Sweet Home, Tx., U.S.	222	29.21 N	97.04 W
Sweetsers	216	40.34 N	85.46 W
Sweet Springs	194	38.57 N	93.24 W
Sweet Valley	210	41.17 N	76.09 W
Sweetwater, Fl., U.S.	220	25.46 N	80.21 W
Sweet Water, Il., U.S.	219	40.03 N	89.42 W
Sweetwater, Tn., U.S.	192	35.36 N	84.27 W
Sweetwater, Tx., U.S.	196	32.28 N	100.24 W
Sweetwater ≃	200	42.31 N	107.02 W
Sweetwater Creek	220	27.59 N	82.33 W
Sweetwater Creek ≃, U.S.	196	35.18 N	99.57 W
Sweetwater Creek ≃, Tx., U.S.	196	32.40 N	100.06 W
Sweetwater Mountains ⩘	226	38.30 N	119.17 W
Swellendam	158	34.02 S	20.26 E
Swepsonville	192	36.01 N	79.21 W
Swerdlovsk → Jekaterinburg	86	56.51 N	60.36 E
Świdnica (Schweidnitz)	30	50.51 N	16.29 E
Świdnik	30	51.14 N	22.41 E
Świdwin	30	53.47 N	15.47 E
Świebodzice	30	50.52 N	16.19 E
Świebodzin	30	52.15 N	15.32 E
Świecie	30	53.25 N	18.28 E
Świerzawa	30	51.01 N	15.54 E
Świerzno	54	53.57 N	14.59 E
Święta	54	53.35 N	14.36 E
Świętokrzyskie, Góry ⩘	30	50.55 N	21.00 E
Świętokrzyski Park Narodowy ♦	30	50.55 N	21.00 E
Swift ≃, Eng., U.K.	42	52.23 N	1.16 W
Swift ≃, Ak., U.S.	180	61.53 N	156.18 W
Swift ≃, Ma., U.S.	207	42.12 N	72.22 W
Swift Creek ≃, Al., U.S.	194	32.25 N	86.38 W
Swift Creek ≃, N.C., U.S.	192	35.12 N	77.05 W
Swift Creek ≃, N.C., U.S.	192	35.57 N	77.35 W
Swift Creek ≃, Va., U.S.	208	37.17 N	77.15 W
Swift Current	184	50.17 N	107.50 W
Swift Current Creek ≃	184	50.40 N	107.44 W
Swifton	194	35.49 N	91.07 W
Swift Reservoir ⊜[1]	224	46.04 N	122.05 W
Swiftwater	210	41.06 N	75.20 W
Swilly ≃	48	54.57 N	7.42 W
Swilly, Lough c	48	55.10 N	7.38 W
Swimming ≃	276	40.21 N	74.05 W
Swimming River Reservoir ⊜[1]	276	40.19 N	74.07 W
Świna ≃[1]	54	53.55 N	14.17 E
Swinburne, Cape ›	176	71.14 N	98.34 W
Swinden Reservoirs ⊜[1]	262	53.48 N	2.10 W
Swindle Island I	182	52.32 N	128.35 W
Swindon	42	51.34 N	1.47 W
Swinemünde → Świnoujście	30	53.53 N	14.14 E
Swineshead	42	52.56 N	0.09 W
Swinford	48	53.57 N	8.57 W
Swinging Bridge Reservoir ⊜[1]	210	41.37 N	74.48 W
Swinomish Indian Reservation ◆[4]	224	48.25 N	122.33 W
Świnoujście (Swinemünde)	30	53.53 N	14.14 E
Swinton, Eng., U.K.	44	53.28 N	1.20 W
Swinton, Eng., U.K.	262	53.31 N	2.20 W
Swinton, Scot., U.K.	46	55.43 N	2.15 W
Swissvale	279b	40.25 N	79.52 W
Swisttal	56	50.40 N	6.54 E
Switzerland □[6]	218	38.45 N	85.04 W
Switzerland □[1], Europe	22	47.00 N	8.00 E
Switzerland □[1], Europe	58	47.00 N	8.00 E
Swona I	46	58.45 N	3.03 W
Swordfish Seamount ✣[3]	14	18.25 N	158.25 W
Swords	48	53.28 N	6.13 W
Swords Range ⩘	166	21.57 S	141.32 E
Swormville	284a	43.02 N	78.42 W
Sworton Heath	262	53.21 N	2.28 W
Swoyerville	210	41.18 N	75.52 W
Syalach	74	66.12 N	124.00 E
Syam	58	46.42 N	5.57 E
Syāmnagar	126	22.21 N	89.07 E
Syāmpur, India	126	22.18 N	88.02 E
Syampur, India	272b	22.29 N	88.13 E
Sybille Creek ≃	198	42.07 N	105.02 W
Syburg ◆[8]	263	51.25 N	7.29 E
Sycamore, Ga., U.S.	192	31.40 N	83.38 W
Sycamore, Il., U.S.	216	41.59 N	88.41 W
Sycamore, Oh., U.S.	214	40.56 N	83.10 W
Sycamore Creek ≃, Az., U.S.	200	33.38 N	111.40 W
Sycamore Creek ≃, Mi., U.S.	216	42.43 N	84.32 W
Sycamore Creek ≃, Oh., U.S.	214	40.59 N	83.12 W
Sycamore Creek ≃, Tx., U.S.	196	29.14 N	100.48 W
Sycamore Gardens	285	39.42 N	75.42 W
Sycamore Island I	279b	40.29 N	79.52 W
Sycamore Slough ≃	226	38.48 N	121.44 W
Sycan ≃	202	42.27 N	121.15 W
Sycaway	210	42.44 N	73.39 W
Syčova	86	57.35 N	69.20 E
Syčovka	76	55.50 N	34.17 E
Syców	30	51.19 N	17.43 E
Sydenham, Austl.	274b	37.42 S	144.46 E
Sydenham, On., Can.	212	44.25 N	76.36 W
Sydenham ◆[8], S. Afr.	273d	26.09 S	28.06 E
Sydenham ◆[8], Eng., U.K.	260	51.26 N	0.03 W
Sydenham ≃, On., Can.	190	42.33 N	82.25 W
Sydenham ≃, On., Can.	212	44.35 N	80.57 W
Sydenham Lake ⊜	212	44.25 N	76.35 W
Sydenham West	274b	37.41 S	144.39 E
Sydney, Austl.	170	33.52 S	151.13 E
Sydney, Austl.	274a	33.52 S	151.13 E
Sydney, N.S., Can.	186	46.09 N	60.11 W
Sydney, Fl., U.S.	220	27.58 N	82.12 W
Sydney, University of ʋ[2]	274a	33.53 S	151.11 E
Sydney Bay c, On., Can.	212	44.54 N	81.05 W
Sydney Bay c, Norf. I.	174c	29.04 S	167.57 E
Sydney Bay Bluff ⊥[4]	212	44.54 N	81.07 W
Sydney Harbour Bridge ◆[5]	170	33.52 S	151.12 E
Sydney Lake ⊜	184	50.40 N	94.24 W
Sydney Mines	186	46.14 N	60.14 W
Sydney Point ›	174d	0.53 S	169.36 E
Syferbult	158	26.00 S	27.20 E
Sygan	279b	40.21 N	80.08 W
Syke	52	52.54 N	8.49 E
Sykesville, Md., U.S.	208	39.22 N	76.58 W
Sykesville, Pa., U.S.	214	41.03 N	78.49 W
Sykkylven	26	62.24 N	6.35 E
Syktyvkar	24	61.40 N	50.46 E
Sylacauga	194	33.10 N	86.15 W
Sylarna ∧	26	63.02 N	12.13 E
Sylhet	120	24.54 N	91.52 E
Syloga	24	63.50 N	43.39 E
Sylt I	30	54.54 N	8.20 E
Sylva	192	35.22 N	83.13 W
Sylva ≃	86	57.39 N	56.54 E
Sylvan	224	45.30 N	122.41 W
Sylvan Beach	210	43.11 N	75.43 W
Sylvan Glen	285	40.11 N	75.42 W
Sylvan Grove	198	39.00 N	98.23 W
Sylvan Hills	194	34.50 N	92.13 W
Sylvania, Austl.	274a	34.01 S	151.07 E
Sylvania, Ga., U.S.	192	32.45 N	81.38 W
Sylvania, Oh., U.S.	214	41.43 N	83.42 W
Sylvania, Pa., U.S.	210	41.48 N	76.51 W
Sylvania Heights	274a	34.02 S	151.06 E
Sylvan Lake, Ab., Can.	182	52.19 N	114.05 W
Sylvan Lake, Il., U.S.	278	42.15 N	88.03 W
Sylvan Lake, Mi., U.S.	281	42.37 N	83.20 W
Sylvan Lake ⊜, Ab., Can.	182	52.21 N	114.10 W
Sylvan Lake ⊜, In., U.S.	216	41.29 N	85.20 W
Sylvan Lake ⊜, Mi., U.S.	281	42.37 N	83.20 W
Sylvan Pass)(	202	44.28 N	110.08 W
Sylvan Shores	220	28.49 N	81.41 W
Sylvensteinsee ⊜[1]	64	47.34 N	11.32 E
Sylvester, Ga., U.S.	192	31.31 N	83.50 W
Sylvester, Tx., U.S.	196	32.43 N	100.15 W
Sylvester, Mount ∧[2]	186	48.11 N	55.04 W
Sylvia	198	37.57 N	98.24 W
Sym	74	60.20 N	88.23 E
Symmes Creek ≃	188	38.26 N	82.27 W
Syn'a	24	65.22 N	57.42 E
Syndal	274b	37.53 S	145.09 E
Synkovo	82	55.21 N	37.38 E
Synnyr, chrebet ⩘	88	56.50 N	111.10 E
Syntul	80	55.00 N	41.18 E
Synžereja	78	47.38 N	28.09 E
Syon House ⊥	260	51.29 N	0.19 W
Syosset	210	40.49 N	73.30 W
Syowa ʋ[3]	9	69.00 S	39.35 E
Syracuse, In., U.S.	216	41.25 N	85.45 W
Syracuse, Ks., U.S.	198	37.58 N	101.45 W
Syracuse, Ne., U.S.	198	40.39 N	96.11 W
Syracuse, N.Y., U.S.	210	43.02 N	76.08 W
Syracuse Hancock International Airport ⊠, N.Y., U.S.	210	43.07 N	76.07 W
Syracuse Hancock International Airport ⊠, N.Y., U.S.	212	43.07 N	76.07 W
Syracuse → Siracusa	70	37.04 N	15.18 E
Syrčan	80	57.22 N	50.15 E
Syrdarja	85	40.52 N	68.38 E
Syrdarja □[4]	85	40.30 N	68.40 E
Syrdarja (Syr Darya) ≃	72	46.03 N	61.00 E
Syr-Darya → Syrdarja ≃	72	46.03 N	61.00 E
Syre	46	58.22 N	4.14 W
Syre ≃	56	49.42 N	6.29 E
Syria (Sūrīyah) □[1], Asia	118	35.00 N	38.00 E
Syria (Sūrīyah) □[1], Asia	128	35.00 N	38.00 E
Syriam	110	16.46 N	96.15 E
Syrian Desert → Shām, Bādiyat ash- ◆[2]	128	32.00 N	40.00 E
Syrien → Syria □[1]	128	35.00 N	38.00 E
Syrie → Syria □[1]	128	35.00 N	38.00 E
Syrskij	76	52.34 N	39.29 E
Sysert'	86	56.29 N	60.49 E
Sysmä	26	61.30 N	25.41 E
Sysola ≃	24	61.42 N	50.53 E
Sysslebäck	26	60.44 N	12.52 E
Syston	42	52.42 N	1.04 W
Systyg-Chem	88	52.40 N	95.30 E
Syt'kovo	76	56.31 N	34.01 E
Sytykanskij, porog ∟	88	57.49 N	118.33 E
Syukunoshō	270	34.50 N	135.32 E
Syväri ⊜	26	63.16 N	28.06 E
Syzran'	80	53.09 N	48.27 E
Syzran' ≃	80	53.04 N	48.26 E
Szabadka → Subotica	38	46.06 N	19.39 E
Szabolcs-Szatmár-Bereg □[6]	30	48.00 N	22.10 E
Szada	264c	47.38 N	19.19 E
Szamocin	30	53.02 N	17.08 E
Szamos (Someș) ≃	38	48.07 N	22.20 E
Szamotuły	30	52.37 N	16.35 E
Szarvas	30	46.52 N	20.34 E
Szatmárnémeti → Satu Mare	38	47.48 N	22.53 E
Százhalombatta	264c	47.20 N	18.56 E
Szczawnica	30	49.26 N	20.30 E
Szczecin (Stettin)	30	53.24 N	14.32 E
Szczecin □[4]	30	53.45 N	15.00 E
Szczecinek (Neustettin)	30	53.43 N	16.42 E
Szczeciński, Zalew (Oderhaff) c	54	53.46 N	14.14 E
Szczekociny	30	50.38 N	19.50 E
Szczuczyn	30	53.34 N	22.18 E
Szczytno	30	53.34 N	21.00 E
Szechwan Basin → Sichuan Pendi ⊻[1]	102	30.00 N	105.00 E
Szechwan → Sichuan □[4]	102	31.00 N	105.00 E
Szécsény	30	48.06 N	19.31 E
Szeged	30	46.15 N	20.09 E
Szeghalom	30	47.01 N	21.11 E
Székesfehérvár	30	47.12 N	18.25 E
Szekszárd	30	46.21 N	18.42 E
Szemenyecsörnye	61	46.30 N	16.37 E
Szentendre	30	47.40 N	19.05 E
Szentendrei-Duna ≃[1]	264c	47.36 N	19.05 E
Szentendrei-sziget I	264c	47.39 N	19.07 E
Szentes	30	46.39 N	20.16 E
Szentgotthárd	61	46.57 N	16.17 E
Szentpéterfa	61	47.06 N	16.29 E
Szeping → Siping	89	43.12 N	124.20 E
Szépművészeti Museum ʋ	264c	47.31 N	19.05 E
Szerencs	30	48.09 N	21.13 E
Szigethalom	264c	47.20 N	19.00 E
Szigetszentmiklós	264c	47.21 N	19.03 E
Szilas-patak ≃	264c	47.36 N	19.06 E
Szlichtyngowa	30	51.43 N	16.15 E
Szob	30	47.50 N	18.52 E
Szolnok	30	47.10 N	20.12 E
Szombathely	61	47.14 N	16.38 E
Szprotawa	30	51.34 N	15.33 E
Sztum	30	53.56 N	19.01 E
Szubin	30	53.00 N	17.44 E
Szydłowiec	30	51.14 N	20.51 E
Szypliszki	30	54.15 N	23.05 E
T			
Ta ≃	94	36.17 N	139.54 E
Taacyn ≃	102	45.09 N	101.27 E
Taal	116	13.53 N	120.55 E
Taal, Lake ⊜	116	13.55 N	121.00 E
Taalintehdas → Dalsbruk	26	60.02 N	22.31 E
Taan ≃	100	24.24 N	120.36 E
Taancan Point ›	116	10.00 N	125.01 E
Taavetti	26	60.55 N	27.34 E
Tabacal	252	23.16 S	64.15 W
Tabacal, Quebrada ≃	286c	10.31 N	67.02 W
Tabaco	116	13.23 N	123.44 E
Tabacundo	246	0.03 N	78.12 W
Tabai ≃	164	3.01 S	135.52 E
Tabalosos	248	6.21 S	76.41 W
Tabanan	115b	8.32 S	115.08 E
Tabango	116	11.19 N	124.22 E
Tabankulu	158	30.58 S	29.19 E
Tábara	34	41.49 N	5.57 W
Tabar Island I	164	2.55 S	152.05 E
Tabar Islands II	164	2.50 S	152.00 E
Tabarka	148	36.57 N	8.45 E
Tabarz	54	50.52 N	10.31 E
Ţabas	128	33.36 N	56.54 E
Tabasará ≃	236	8.00 N	81.39 W
Tabasco □[3]	232	18.15 N	93.00 W

	English	Deutsch	Español	Français	Português
≃	River	Fluß	Río	Rivière	Rio
≊	Canal	Kanal	Canal	Canal	Canal
∟	Waterfall, Rapids	Wasserfall, Stromschnellen	Cascada, Rápidos	Chute d'eau, Rapides	Cascata, Rápidos
ʯ	Strait	Meeresstraße	Estrecho	Détroit	Estreito
c	Bay, Gulf	Bucht, Golf	Bahía, Golfo	Baie, Golfe	Baía, Golfo
⊜	Lake, Lakes	See, Seen	Lago, Lagos	Lac, Lacs	Lago, Lagos
⩸	Swamp	Sumpf	Pantano	Marais	Pântano
⊓	Ice Features, Glacier	Eis- und Gletscherformen	Accidentes Glaciales	Formes glaciaires	Acidentes glaciares
⊤	Other Hydrographic Features	Andere Hydrographische Objekte	Otros Elementos Hidrográficos	Autres données hydrographiques	Outros acidentes hidrográficos
✣	Submarine Features	Untermeerische Objekte	Accidentes Submarinos	Formes de relief sous-marin	Acidentes submarinos
□	Political Unit	Politische Einheit	Unidad Política	Entité politique	Unidade política
ʋ	Cultural Institution	Kulturelle Institution	Institución Cultural	Institution culturelle	Instituição cultural
⊥	Historical Site	Historische Stätte	Sitio Histórico	Site historique	Sitio histórico
♦	Recreational Site	Erholungs- und Ferienort	Sitio de Recreo	Centre de loisirs	Area de Lazer
⊠	Airport	Flughafen	Aeropuerto	Aéroport	Aeroporto
■	Military Installation	Militäranlage	Instalación Militar	Installation militaire	Instalação militar
◆	Miscellaneous	Verschiedenes	Misceláneo	Divers	Diversos

Name	Page	Lat.	Long.
Tabas Masīnā	128	32.48 N	60.14 E
Tabat	86	52.57 N	90.43 E
Tabatinga ≐	255	17.24 S	43.18 W
Tabayama	94	35.47 N	138.55 E
Tabayin	110	22.42 N	95.19 E
Tabb	208	37.08 N	76.29 W
Tabei	98	39.44 N	122.29 E
Tabelbala	148	29.23 N	3.15 W
Tabelbala, Kahal ⊥[8]	148	28.30 N	2.00 W
Taber	182	49.47 N	112.08 W
Taberg, Sve.	26	57.41 N	14.05 E
Taberg, Sve.	40	59.50 N	14.08 E
Taberg, N.Y., U.S.	210	43.18 N	75.37 W
Tabernacle	285	39.50 N	74.42 W
Tabi	152	8.10 S	13.18 E
Tabiang	174d	0.52 S	169.35 E
Tabiano Terme	64	44.48 N	10.21 E
Tabira	250	7.35 S	37.33 W
Tabiteuea	174t	1.25 N	173.07 E
Tabiteuea I[1]	14	1.20 S	174.50 E
Tabla	150	13.46 N	3.01 E
Tabla, Cerro de la ∧	240m	18.03 N	66.08 W
Tablada	288	34.42 S	58.32 W
Tablas, Cabo ≻	252	31.51 S	71.34 W
Tablas Island I	116	12.24 N	122.02 E
Tablas Plateau ⋏[1]	116	9.43 N	122.43 E
Tablas Strait ꓷ	116	12.40 N	121.48 E
Tablat	34	36.24 N	3.19 E
Table Bay ⊂	158	33.53 S	18.27 E
Table Cape ≻	172	39.06 S	178.00 E
Tableland	162	17.17 S	127.00 E
Table Mountain ∧, Nf., Can.	186	47.43 N	59.13 W
Table Mountain ∧, S. Afr.	158	33.57 S	18.25 E
Table Mountain ∧, Az., U.S.	200	32.49 N	110.31 W
Table Rock	198	40.10 N	96.05 W
Table Rock Lake ⊜[1]	194	36.35 N	93.30 W
Tabletop ∧, Austl.	162	22.32 S	123.55 E
Table Top ∧, Az., U.S.	200	32.46 N	112.07 W
Tabletop Mountain ∧	171b	35.58 S	148.30 E
Tabley Mere ⊜	262	53.17 N	2.25 W
Tabligbo	150	6.35 N	1.30 E
Tablones	240m	18.15 N	65.45 W
Taboan ≐	116	17.57 N	122.11 E
Taboão, Ribeirão do ≐	287b	23.40 S	46.28 W
Taboão da Serra	256	23.38 S	46.46 W
Taboco ≐	248	19.53 S	55.58 W
Taboga	236	8.48 N	79.33 W
Tabogon	116	10.57 N	124.02 E
Tábor, Česko.	30	49.25 N	14.41 E
Tabor, Ross.	74	71.16 N	150.12 E
Tabor, Ia., U.S.	198	40.53 N	95.40 W
Tabor, N.J., U.S.	276	40.52 N	74.29 W
Tabor, S.D., U.S.	198	42.56 N	97.39 W
Tabor, Mount → Tavor, Har ∧	132	32.41 N	35.23 E
Tabora	154	5.01 S	32.48 E
Tabora □[4]	154	5.15 S	32.45 E
Tabor City	192	34.08 N	78.52 W
Tabory	86	58.31 N	64.33 E
Tabou	150	4.25 N	7.21 W
Tabrīz	128	38.05 N	46.18 E
Tábua, Riacho da ≐	250	9.12 S	44.25 W
Tabuaço	34	41.07 N	7.34 W
Tabuaeran I[1]	14	3.52 N	159.20 W
Tabuão	256	21.59 S	44.02 W
Tábuas	256	22.12 S	43.37 W
Tabu-dong	98	36.03 N	128.31 E
Tabuelan	116	10.49 N	123.52 E
Tabūk, Ar. Su.	128	28.23 N	36.35 E
Tabuk, Pil.	116	17.24 N	121.25 E
Tabuleiro	256	21.22 S	43.15 W
Tabuleiro do Norte	250	5.15 S	38.07 W
Tabuny	86	52.46 N	78.45 E
Tabuse	96	33.57 N	132.03 E
Tabuyung	114	0.51 N	99.00 E
Tabwémasana, Mont ∧	175f	15.20 S	166.44 E
Täby	40	59.30 N	18.03 E
Tacagua, Quebrada ≐	286c	10.37 N	67.02 W
Tacámbaro de Codallos	234	19.14 N	101.28 W
Tacaná	236	15.14 N	92.05 W
Tacaná, Volcán ∧[1]	236	15.08 N	92.06 W
Tacañitas	252	28.38 S	62.36 W
Tacaratu	250	9.06 S	38.10 W
Taceno	58	46.02 N	9.21 E
T'ačev	78	48.02 N	23.34 E
Taché, Lac ⊜	176	64.00 N	120.00 W
Tacheng (Qoqek)	86	46.45 N	82.57 E
Tacherting	60	48.05 N	12.34 E
Tachia	100	24.21 N	120.37 E
Tachia ≐	100	24.20 N	120.33 E
Tachiaochang Airport ⊠	107	32.01 N	118.47 E
Tachiataš	72	42.22 N	59.35 E
Tachibana, Nihon	96	33.11 N	130.36 E
Tachibana, Nihon	96	33.54 N	132.17 E
Tachie ≐	182	54.40 N	124.50 W
Tachikawa	94	35.42 N	139.25 E
Tachikawa Air Base ■	268	35.43 N	139.25 E
Tachinger See ⊜	60	47.58 N	12.45 E
Táchira □[3]	246	7.50 N	72.05 W
Tachoshui	100	24.20 N	121.44 E
Tachov	60	49.48 N	12.38 E
Tachta, Ross.	80	45.54 N	42.07 E
Tachta, Ross.	89	53.08 N	139.53 E
Tachta-Bazar	128	35.57 N	62.50 E
Tachtabrod	86	52.38 N	67.34 E
Tachtakupyr	86	43.02 N	60.17 E
Tachtamygda	89	54.06 N	123.34 E
Tacima	250	6.30 S	35.39 W
Tacina ≐	68	38.56 N	16.53 E
Tacinskij	80	48.13 N	41.17 E
Taciuã, Lago ≐	246	4.29 S	60.35 W
Tacloban	116	11.15 N	125.00 E
Taclobo	116	12.20 N	122.34 E
Tacna, Perú	248	18.01 S	70.15 W
Tacna, Az., U.S.	200	32.41 N	113.57 W
Tacna □[5]	248	17.40 S	70.20 W
Tacoignières	261	48.50 N	1.40 E
Tacoma	224	47.15 N	122.26 W
Tacoma Narrows Bridge ⊶[5]	224	47.16 N	122.33 W
Taconic	207	42.02 N	73.24 W
Taconic Range ⋏	210	42.30 N	73.20 W
Taconic State Park ♦	210	42.05 N	73.34 W
Tacony ⊶[8]	285	40.02 N	75.03 W
Tacony Creek ≐	285	40.01 N	75.06 W
Tacony Creek Park ♦	285	40.02 N	75.07 W
Tacony Palmyra Bridge ⊶[5]	285	40.01 N	75.02 W
Taco Pozo	252	25.37 S	63.17 W
Tacotalpa	234	17.36 N	92.49 W
Tacotalpa ≐	234	17.50 N	92.52 W
Tacuarembó	252	31.44 S	55.59 W
Tacuarembó ≐	252	32.25 S	55.29 W
Tacuarí ≐	252	32.46 S	53.18 W
Tacuatí	252	23.27 S	56.35 W
Tacuba ⊶[8]	286a	19.28 N	99.12 W
Tacubaya ⊶[8]	286a	19.25 N	99.12 W
Tacuparé, Cachoeira ∟	250	5.20 S	55.50 W
Tacurong	116	6.42 N	124.42 E
Tacuru, Bra.	252	23.43 N	55.02 W
Tacuru, Bra.	255	23.38 S	55.01 W
Tacurú, Laguna ⊜	258	34.58 S	58.25 W
Tacutu (Takutu) ≐	246	3.01 N	60.29 W
Tadain	270	34.52 N	135.24 E
Tadami	92	37.21 N	139.19 E
Tadaoka	270	34.29 N	135.24 E
Tadasuni	71	40.06 N	8.53 E
Tadcaster	44	53.53 N	1.16 W
Tademaït, Plateau du ⋏[1]	148	28.30 N	2.00 E
Tadenac Lake ⊜	212	45.03 N	79.56 W
Tādepallegūdem	122	16.50 N	81.30 E
Tadía, Ciénaga de ⊜	246	6.48 N	76.49 W
Tadine	175f	21.33 S	167.52 E
Tadio, Lagune ⊂	150	5.11 N	5.15 W
Tadjemout	148	25.37 N	3.48 E
Tadjenanet	34	36.08 N	5.59 E
Tadjeraout, Oued V	148	21.17 N	1.19 E
Tadjoura	144	11.47 N	42.54 E
Tadjoura, Golfe de ⊂	144	11.42 N	43.00 E
Tadley	42	51.21 N	1.08 W
Tado	94	35.08 N	136.38 E
Tadok	114	3.58 N	96.19 E
Tadotsu	96	34.16 N	133.45 E
Tadoule Lake ⊜	176	58.36 N	98.20 W
Tadoussac	186	48.09 N	69.43 W
Tādpatri	122	14.55 N	78.01 E
Taduno	112	1.55 S	123.05 E
Tadworth	42	51.17 N	0.14 W
Tadzhikistan → Tajikistan □[1]	72	39.00 N	71.00 E
Tadzhikstan → Tajikistan □[1]	72	39.00 N	71.00 E
Tadžikabad	85	39.07 N	70.50 E
T'aean	98	36.46 N	126.16 E
T'aebaek-san ∧	98	37.06 N	128.55 E
T'aebaek-sanmaek ⋏	98	37.40 N	128.50 E
Taebu-do I	98	37.15 N	126.35 E
Taech'ŏn	98	36.22 N	126.34 E
Taech'ŏng-do I	98	37.49 N	124.43 E
Taedong	98	39.05 N	125.31 E
Taedong-gang ≐	98	38.42 N	125.15 E
Taegu	98	35.52 N	128.35 E
Taegu □[4]	98	35.50 N	128.35 E
Taegwan	98	40.13 N	125.12 E
Taehan-Min'guk → Korea, South □[1]	98	36.30 N	128.00 E
Taehŭksan-do I	98	34.40 N	125.25 E
Taehŭng	98	40.06 N	126.56 E
Taehwajŏn	271b	37.36 N	126.52 E
T'aein	98	35.40 N	126.55 E
Taejin	98	36.34 N	129.24 E
Taejŏn	98	36.20 N	127.26 E
Taejujŏm	98	38.24 N	127.58 E
T'aemo-san ∧	271b	37.27 N	127.04 E
Taeng ≐	110	19.06 N	98.57 E
Taer	102	34.09 N	98.50 E
Ta'erwan	100	31.49 N	113.25 E
Taeryanghwa	98	41.14 N	129.42 E
Taf ≐	42	51.47 N	4.26 W
Tafahi I	14	15.51 S	173.43 W
Tafahnā al-'Azab	142	30.36 N	31.15 E
Tafalla	34	42.31 N	1.40 W
Tafanlieh	100	21.58 N	120.46 E
Ṭafas	132	32.44 N	36.04 E
Tafāsīkh, Ghurd at- ⊥[8]	142	29.43 N	29.45 E
Tafassasset, Oued (Oued Tafassâsset) V	148	20.56 N	10.12 E
Tafassâsset, Ténéré du ⊶[2]	146	21.00 N	11.00 E
Tafea □[8]	175f	19.30 S	169.00 E
Tafelbaai → Table Bay ⊂	158	33.53 S	18.27 E
Tafelberg ∧	250	3.55 N	56.10 W
Tafermaar	164	6.51 S	134.06 E
Taff ≐	42	51.27 N	3.09 W
Tafiré	150	9.04 N	5.10 W
Tafí Viejo	252	26.44 S	65.16 W
Taflan	130	41.25 N	36.09 E
Tafna, Oued ≐	34	35.17 N	1.30 W
Tafo	150	6.13 N	0.22 W
Tafraoute	148	29.40 N	8.58 W
Taft, Īrān	128	31.45 N	54.14 E
Taft, Pil.	116	11.54 N	125.25 E
Taft, Ca., U.S.	204	35.08 N	119.27 W
Taft, Fl., U.S.	220	28.23 N	81.24 W
Taft, Ok., U.S.	196	35.45 N	95.32 W
Taft, Tx., U.S.	196	27.58 N	97.23 W
Taftān, Kūh-e ∧	128	28.36 N	61.08 E
Tafton	210	41.25 N	75.11 W
Taga, Nihon	94	35.13 N	136.17 E
Taga, Nihon	270	34.49 N	135.49 E
Taga, W. Sam.	175a	13.46 S	172.28 W
Tagabukid	116	7.00 N	126.21 E
Taga Dzong	124	27.04 N	89.53 E
Tagagawik ≐	180	66.30 N	159.00 W
Tagaj	80	54.18 N	47.39 E
Tagajō	92	38.20 N	141.00 E
Tagan	86	54.57 N	77.18 E
Tagana-an	116	9.42 N	125.35 E
Taganrog	83	47.12 N	38.56 E
Taganrogskij zaliv ⊂	78	47.00 N	38.23 E
Tagant □[4]	150	18.20 N	11.30 W
Tagânt ⊶[1]	150	18.00 N	12.00 W
Tagapula Island I	116	12.04 N	124.12 E
Tågarp	41	55.56 N	12.57 E
Tagauayan Island I	116	10.58 N	121.13 E
Tagawa	96	33.38 N	130.49 E
Tagaytay	116	14.06 N	120.56 E
Tagbara	152	5.56 N	21.09 E
Tagbilaran	116	9.39 N	123.51 E
Tagdempt → Tihert	148	35.28 N	1.21 E
Tage	164	6.20 S	143.20 E
Tageren Canal ≡	174q	9.33 N	138.09 E
Taggia	62	43.52 N	7.51 E
Taghit	148	30.55 N	2.02 W
Taghkanic Creek ≐	210	42.13 N	73.45 W
Taghmon	48	52.18 N	6.39 W
Tagig	269f	14.32 N	121.04 E
Tagig ≐	269f	14.31 N	121.05 E
T'aginka	78	46.47 N	33.04 E
Tagish Lake ⊜	180	59.45 N	134.15 W
Tagliacozzo	66	42.04 N	13.14 E
Tagliamento ≐	64	45.38 N	13.06 E
Tagliata, Monte della ∧	64	44.34 N	9.48 E
Taglio di Po	64	45.00 N	12.12 E
Tagna	88	53.36 N	101.54 E
Tagna ≐	88	53.38 N	101.53 E
Tago	116	9.02 N	126.13 E
Tago ≐	116	9.01 N	126.14 E
Tagoloan	116	8.32 N	124.45 E
Tagolo Point ≻	116	8.44 N	123.23 E
Tagon Harbour ⊂	162	33.53 S	123.00 E
Tagounit	148	29.58 N	5.36 W
Tagourâret ⊤[4]	150	17.45 N	7.43 W
Tagow Bāy	120	35.42 N	66.03 E
Tagrina, Oued V	148	21.00 N	6.16 E
Taguatinga	255	12.25 S	46.26 W
Tagubanhan Island I	116	11.08 N	123.07 E
Tagudin	116	16.56 N	120.27 E
Taguedoufat V	150	14.50 N	7.42 E
Taguke	120	32.07 N	84.35 E
Tagul ≐	88	55.35 N	97.45 E
Tagula Island I	160	11.30 S	153.30 E
Tagum	116	7.28 N	125.48 E
T'agun	86	53.56 N	85.38 E
Tagun Bay ⊂	116	13.55 N	123.46 E
Tagus (Tejo) (Tajo) ≐	34	38.40 N	9.24 W
T'agyŏng-ni	98	38.04 N	126.03 E
Tah, Sebkha ⊜	148	27.45 N	12.42 W
Taha	89	47.33 N	124.14 E
Tahaa I	14	16.38 S	151.30 W
Tahakopa	172	46.31 S	169.23 E
Tahala	148	34.04 N	4.20 W
Tahan, Gunong ∧	114	4.38 N	102.14 E
Tahanaoute	148	31.24 N	7.54 W
Tahāneh-ye Ney Basteh	128	32.59 N	60.53 E
Tahara	94	34.40 N	137.16 E
Tahart	148	22.51 N	5.12 E
Tahat ∧	148	23.18 N	5.47 E
Taheke	172	35.27 S	173.39 E
Ṭāherī	128	27.42 N	52.21 E
Tahgong, Puntan ≻	174n	15.06 N	145.39 E
Tahifet	148	22.58 N	5.55 E
Tahiryuak Lake ⊜	176	70.56 N	112.20 W
Tahiti I	174s	17.37 S	149.27 W
Tahkuna neem ≻	76	59.07 N	22.36 E
Tāhlāb (Ṭālāb) ≐	128	28.09 N	62.45 E
Tahlequah	196	35.54 N	94.58 W
Ṭahmā wa Minshāt 'Abd as-Sayyid	142	29.38 N	31.14 E
Tahmoor	170	34.13 S	150.36 E
Tahneta Pass)(	180	61.53 N	147.20 W
Tahoe, Lake ⊜	226	39.07 N	120.03 W
Tahoe City	226	39.10 N	120.08 W
Tahoe Lake ⊜	176	70.15 N	108.45 W
Tahoe Paradise	226	38.52 N	120.01 W
Tahoe Valley	226	38.55 N	120.00 W
Tahoka	196	33.10 N	101.47 W
Taholah	224	47.20 N	124.17 W
Tahoua	150	14.54 N	5.16 E
Tahoua □[5]	150	16.00 N	5.00 E
Tahquamenon ≐	190	46.34 N	85.02 W
Tahquamenon Falls State Park ♦	190	46.29 N	85.05 W
Tahsi	100	24.57 N	121.53 E
Tahsis	182	49.55 N	126.39 W
Ṭahṭā	140	26.46 N	31.30 E
Tahtaköprü	130	39.57 N	29.39 E
Tahtsa Lake ⊜	182	53.42 N	127.26 W
Tahtsa Peak ∧	182	53.33 N	127.47 W
Tahu	100	24.26 N	120.52 E
Tahuamanu ≐	248	11.06 S	67.36 W
Tahuata I	174x	9.57 S	139.05 W
Tahulandang, Pulau I	112	2.20 N	125.25 E
Tahuna	112	3.37 N	125.29 E
Tahuofang ⊜[1]	104	41.55 N	124.07 E
Tahuya ≐	224	47.23 N	123.03 W
Ṭahwāy	142	30.22 N	30.52 E
Taï, C. Iv.	150	5.52 N	7.27 W
Tai, It.	64	46.25 N	12.20 E
Tai, Nihon	270	34.31 N	135.26 E
Tai ⊶[8]	270	34.45 N	135.00 E
Taiaçupebá	256	23.40 S	46.11 W
Tai'an, Zhg.	98	36.12 N	117.07 E
Tai'an, Zhg.	104	41.23 N	122.27 E
Tai'an, Zhg.	107	30.05 N	105.47 E
Tai'angang	106	31.43 N	121.40 E
Taiarapu, Presqu'île de ≻[1]	174s	17.47 S	149.14 W
Taibai	102	34.00 N	107.18 E
Taibai Shan ∧, Zhg.	98	39.19 N	114.11 E
Taibai Shan ∧, Zhg.	102	33.54 N	107.46 E
Taibilla, Sierra de ⋏	34	38.10 N	2.10 W
Taibon Agordino	64	46.18 N	12.00 E
Taibus Qi (Baochang)	98	41.56 N	115.22 E
Taicang	106	31.26 N	121.07 E
T'aichou → Taizhou	100	32.30 N	119.58 E
T'aichung	100	24.09 N	120.41 E
Taichu → T'aichung	100	24.09 N	120.41 E
Taicunzhen	106	31.27 N	119.03 E
Taiden → Taejŏn	98	36.20 N	127.26 E
Taiei	94	35.49 N	140.25 E
Taieri ≐	172	46.03 S	170.11 E
Taif → Aṭ-Ṭā'if	144	21.16 N	40.24 E
Taigu	102	37.28 N	112.30 E
Tai Hang	271d	22.17 N	114.11 E
Taihang Shan ⋏	102	38.00 N	114.00 E
Taihape	172	39.40 S	175.48 E
Taihe, Zhg.	100	33.11 N	115.36 E
Taihe, Zhg.	100	26.49 N	114.55 E
Taihe, Zhg.	107	30.10 N	105.56 E
Taihezhen, Zhg.	89	44.47 N	123.29 E
Taihezhen, Zhg.	107	30.07 N	103.50 E
Taihezhen, Zhg.	107	30.06 N	106.03 E
Taiho	174m	26.39 N	128.07 E
Taihoku → T'aipei	100	25.03 N	121.30 E
T'aihsi	100	23.42 N	120.11 E
T'aihsien → Taizhou	100	32.30 N	119.58 E
Taihu	100	30.26 N	116.16 E
Tai Hu ⊜	106	31.15 N	120.10 E
Taijiang	102	26.32 N	108.22 E
Taijimiao	98	40.55 N	113.46 E
Taijüan → Taiyuan	102	37.55 N	112.30 E
Taikang	98	34.04 N	114.50 E
Taikkyi	110	17.19 N	95.58 E
Taikou	102	31.53 N	111.07 E
Taiko-yama ∧	96	35.46 N	135.12 E
Taikyu → Taegu	98	35.52 N	128.35 E
Tailai	89	46.23 N	123.27 E
Tai Lam Chung	271d	22.22 N	114.01 E
Tai Lam Chung Reservoir ⊜[1]	271d	22.23 N	114.01 E
Tailem Bend	166	35.16 S	139.27 E
Tailfingen	58	48.15 N	9.01 E
Tai Long, H.K.	271d	22.13 N	113.59 E
Tai Long, H.K.	271d	22.25 N	114.22 E
Tai Long Bay ⊂	271d	22.24 N	114.24 E
Taima, Nihon	96	34.30 N	135.42 E
T'aima, T'aiwan	100	22.37 N	120.59 E
Taimba	74	60.18 N	98.58 E
Taimei	100	23.19 N	114.29 E
Tai Mong Tsai	271d	22.24 N	114.18 E
Tai Mo Shan ∧	271d	22.25 N	114.07 E
Taimyr-Halbinsel → Tajmyr, poluostrov ≻[1]	74	76.00 N	104.00 E
Tain	46	57.48 N	4.04 W
Tainaka	270	34.36 N	135.37 E
T'ainan	100	23.00 N	120.12 E
Taínaron, Ákra ≻	38	36.22 N	22.30 E
Taining	100	26.54 N	117.09 E
Tain-l'Hermitage	62	45.04 N	4.51 E
Tai O, H.K.	100	22.15 N	113.51 E
Taio, It.	64	46.20 N	11.04 E
Taiobeiras	255	15.49 S	42.14 W
Tai Pang Wan ⊂	100	22.30 N	114.24 E
T'aipei, T'aiwan	100	25.03 N	121.30 E
T'aipei, T'aiwan	269d	25.03 N	121.30 E
T'aipei □[6]	269d	25.00 N	121.40 E
Taipei Bridge ⊶[5]	269d	25.04 N	121.30 E
T'aipeihsien	100	25.00 N	121.27 E
Taipei Institute of Technology ⊍[2]	269d	25.02 N	121.32 E
Taipei New Park ♦	269d	25.03 N	121.31 E
T'aipei Shih □[7]	269d	25.05 N	121.33 E
Taiping, Malay.	114	4.51 N	100.44 E
Taiping, Zhg.	100	30.18 N	118.12 E
Taiping, Zhg.	100	22.49 N	113.41 E
Taiping, Zhg.	102	22.40 N	107.05 E
Taiping, Zhg.	107	30.24 N	103.37 E
Taipingchang, Zhg.	102	27.25 N	103.04 E
Taipingchang, Zhg.	107	29.33 N	103.33 E
Taipingchang, Zhg.	107	30.25 N	103.46 E
Taipingchang, Zhg.	107	29.53 N	106.04 E
Taipingchang, Zhg.	107	29.55 N	103.49 E
Taipingchang, Zhg.	107	30.10 N	106.21 E
Taipingchang, Zhg.	107	30.39 N	105.54 E
Taipingchuan, Zhg.	89	44.23 N	123.11 E
Taipingchuan, Zhg.	98	42.36 N	127.20 E
Taipingdian	102	32.08 N	111.45 E
Taipingkou	100	29.50 N	113.35 E
Taipingling	89	43.26 N	128.09 E
Taipingshan, Zhg.	98	40.34 N	122.25 E
Taipingshan, Zhg.	104	41.36 N	123.41 E
Taipingshao	98	40.54 N	125.08 E
Taipingsi	107	29.24 N	103.34 E
Taipingxigou	104	42.36 N	121.13 E
Taipingzhai	104	42.14 N	124.07 E
Taipingzhen, Zhg.	89	46.44 N	130.44 E
Taipingzhen, Zhg.	102	35.42 N	107.37 E
Taipingzhen, Zhg.	107	29.24 N	105.47 E
Taipingzhen, Zhg.	107	30.26 N	104.12 E
Taipingzhuang, Zhg.	104	42.38 N	123.45 E
Taipingzhuang, Zhg.	105	40.03 N	116.24 E
Taipingzhuang, Zhg.	105	40.08 N	117.36 E
Tai Po Hoi ⊂	271d	22.26 N	114.12 E
Tai Po Tsai	271d	22.21 N	114.15 E
Taipu	250	5.37 S	35.36 W
Taira	94	36.26 N	136.57 E
Taira → Iwaki	94	37.03 N	140.55 E
Tairetá	256	22.36 S	43.42 W
Tairiqiao	106	30.59 N	121.33 E
Tais	112	4.06 S	102.34 E
Taisen-zan ∧	96	33.06 N	131.17 E
Taisha	96	35.24 N	132.40 E
Taisha → Izumo	96	35.22 N	132.46 E
Taishaku-kyō ♦	96	34.53 N	133.13 E
Taishaku-zan ∧, Nihon	94	36.58 N	139.28 E
Taishaku-zan ∧, Nihon	270	34.47 N	135.07 E
Taishan, Zhg.	98	39.01 N	113.36 E
Taishan, Zhg.	102	22.16 N	112.44 E
Taishanchang	107	30.32 N	106.42 E
Taishi, Nihon	96	34.50 N	134.33 E
Taishi, Nihon	270	34.31 N	135.39 E
Taishō	96	33.12 N	132.58 E
Taishō ⊶[8]	270	34.38 N	135.27 E
Tai Shui Hang	271d	22.25 N	14.13 E
Taishun	100	27.33 N	119.43 E
Tai Tam Bay ⊂	271d	22.13 N	114.13 E
Taitao, Península de ≻[1]	254	46.30 S	74.25 W
Taitapu	172	43.40 S	172.33 E
Taitō ⊶[8]	268	35.43 N	139.47 E
Tai Tong	271d	22.25 N	114.01 E
Taitouying	98	40.02 N	119.12 E
Taitō-zaki ≻	94	35.18 N	140.25 E
T'aitung	100	22.45 N	121.09 E
Taivalkoski	26	65.34 N	28.15 E
Tai Wan	271d	22.10 N	114.15 E
Taiwan (T'aiwan) □[1], Asia	90	23.30 N	121.00 E
Taiwan (T'aiwan) □[1], Asia	100	23.30 N	121.00 E
T'aiwan I	100	23.30 N	121.00 E
Taiwan Strait ꓷ	100	24.00 N	119.00 E
Tai Wan Tau	271d	22.18 N	114.17 E
Taixi	100	24.42 N	116.56 E
Taixian	100	32.31 N	120.09 E
Taixing	106	32.11 N	120.01 E
Taixizhen	106	31.03 N	119.49 E
Taiyang	100	30.12 N	119.19 E
Taiyanggong	271a	39.58 N	116.25 E
Taíyetos Óros ⋏	38	37.16 N	22.12 E
Ṭaiyiba	132	32.16 N	35.01 E
Taiyuan	102	37.55 N	112.30 E
Taizhao	120	30.01 N	93.08 E
Taizhou	100	32.30 N	119.58 E
Taizhou Liedao II	100	28.30 N	121.53 E
Taizi ≐	98	41.00 N	122.26 E
Ta'izz	144	13.38 N	44.04 E
Tāj al-'Izz	142	30.57 N	31.35 E
Tajarḥī	146	24.21 N	14.28 E
Tajbola	24	68.26 N	33.19 E
Tajdakovo	82	54.29 N	37.32 E
Tajerouine	36	35.54 N	8.34 E
Tajetteret, Oued V	148	21.20 N	7.22 E
Tajga	86	56.04 N	85.37 E
Tajgonos, mys ≻	74	60.35 N	160.08 E
Tajgonos, poluostrov ≻[1]	74	61.20 N	161.00 E
Tajikistan □[1], Asia	72	39.00 N	71.00 E
Tajikistan □[1], Asia	85	39.00 N	71.00 E
Tajikstan → Tajikistan □[1]	72	39.00 N	71.00 E
Tajima	94	37.12 N	139.46 E
Tajimi	94	35.19 N	137.08 E
Tajique	200	34.45 N	106.17 W
Tajiri	270	34.24 N	135.18 E
Tajitos	232	30.58 N	112.18 W
Tajlakdžegen	86	43.54 N	60.29 E
Tajlakovy	86	59.20 N	74.04 E
Tāj Mahal ⊥	124	27.10 N	78.03 E
Tajmura ≐	72	63.46 N	98.01 E
Tajmyr, ozero ⊜	74	74.30 N	102.30 E
Tajmyr, poluostrov ≻[1]	74	76.00 N	104.00 E
Tajna	88	56.27 N	95.30 E
Tajninka	265b	55.54 N	37.45 E
Tajo → Tagus ≐	34	38.40 N	9.24 W
Tajožnyj, Ross.	86	56.09 N	94.29 E
Tajožnyj, Ross.	88	56.13 N	94.55 E
Tajpur, India	124	25.51 N	85.41 E
Tajpur, India	124	29.10 N	78.29 E
Tājpur, India	272b	22.44 N	88.16 E
Tajpur Khurd ⊶[8]	272a	28.35 N	77.03 E
Tajšet	88	55.57 N	98.00 E
Tajsojgan	80	48.19 N	53.29 E
Tajturka	88	52.51 N	103.28 E
Tajumulco, Volcán ∧[1]	236	15.02 N	91.55 W
Tajuña ≐	34	40.07 N	3.35 W
Tājūrā', Lībiyā	146	32.53 N	13.21 E
Tajura, Ross.	88	57.00 N	106.35 E
Tajura ≐	88	57.00 N	106.35 E
Tajžina	86	53.38 N	87.28 E
Tak	110	16.52 N	99.08 E
Takāb	128	36.24 N	47.07 E
Takabanare-jima I	174m	26.22 N	127.59 E
Takabara	150	11.50 N	11.30 W
Takachiho	92	32.42 N	131.18 E
Takachu	156	22.37 S	21.58 E
Takada → Bungo-takada	96	33.33 N	131.27 E
Takada → Yamato-takada	96	34.31 N	135.45 E
Takagi	268	35.56 N	139.35 E
Takahagi	94	36.43 N	140.43 E
Takahama, Nihon	94	34.55 N	136.59 E
Takahama, Nihon	94	37.00 N	136.46 E
Takahama, Nihon	96	35.29 N	135.33 E
Takahara ≐	94	36.28 N	137.15 E
Takahashi	96	34.47 N	133.37 E
Takahashi ≐	96	34.31 N	133.42 E
Takahe, Mount ∧	9	76.16 S	112.14 W
Takaido ⊶[8]	268	35.40 N	139.37 E
Takaishi	96	34.32 N	135.26 E
Takaka	172	40.51 S	172.48 E
Takakkaw Falls ∟	182	51.30 N	116.28 W
Takalaou	146	10.07 N	19.48 E
Takalar	112	5.28 S	119.24 E
Takamatsu, Nihon	94	36.46 N	136.43 E
Takamatsu, Nihon	96	34.20 N	134.03 E
Takami-shima I	96	34.19 N	133.41 E
Takamiya	96	34.47 N	132.44 E
Takami-yama ∧	94	34.25 N	136.05 E
Takamori	94	35.33 N	137.53 E
Takanabe	92	32.08 N	131.30 E
Takanawa-hantō ≻[1]	96	33.58 N	132.56 E
Takanawa-san ∧	96	33.56 N	132.51 E
Takane, Nihon	94	36.02 N	137.29 E
Takane, Nihon	94	35.50 N	138.25 E
Takanezawa	94	36.37 N	139.59 E
Takano	96	35.02 N	132.55 E
Takanosu	92	40.13 N	140.22 E
Takaoka	94	36.45 N	137.01 E
Takao → Kaohsiung	100	22.38 N	120.17 E
Takao-kokutei-kōen ♦	94	35.38 N	139.15 E
Takao-san ∧, Nihon	94	35.38 N	139.15 E
Takao-san ∧, Nihon	270	34.49 N	135.51 E
Takapau	172	40.02 S	176.21 E
Takapuna	172	36.47 S	174.47 E
Takara-jima I	93b	29.09 N	129.13 E
Takarazuka	270	34.49 N	135.21 E
Takasago	96	34.45 N	134.48 E
Takasaki	94	36.20 N	139.01 E
Takase	96	34.10 N	133.45 E
Takase ≐	94	36.28 N	137.52 E
Takashima, Nihon	92	32.39 N	129.45 E
Takashima, Nihon	94	35.18 N	136.01 E
Taka-shima I	96	34.50 N	131.50 E
Takashippu	174m	26.24 N	127.44 E
Takasu	94	35.57 N	136.53 E
Takata	96	33.06 N	130.28 E
Takata → Joetsu	94	37.06 N	138.15 E
Takata → Rikuzen-takata	92	39.01 N	141.38 E
Takatō	94	35.50 N	138.04 E
Takatomi	94	35.29 N	136.47 E
Takatori	96	34.27 N	135.48 E
Takatori-yama ∧	96	33.18 N	130.43 E
Takatori-yama ∧[2]	268	35.18 N	139.37 E
Takatsu ≐	96	34.42 N	131.49 E
Takatsuki, Nihon	94	35.28 N	136.14 E
Takatsuki, Nihon	96	34.51 N	135.37 E
Takaungu	154	3.41 S	39.51 E
Ta-kaw	110	21.36 N	98.56 E
Takayama, Nihon	94	36.08 N	137.15 E
Takayama, Nihon	94	36.37 N	138.57 E
Takayama, Nihon	94	36.40 N	138.21 E
Takayama, Nihon	270	34.45 N	135.44 E
Takayanagi, Nihon	94	37.13 N	138.38 E
Takayanagi, Nihon	268	35.25 N	139.57 E
Tak Bai	114	6.16 N	102.03 E
Takčijan	85	38.32 N	68.03 E
Takebe	96	34.52 N	133.54 E
Takefu	94	35.54 N	136.10 E
Takehara	96	34.21 N	132.55 E
Takeli	85	40.30 N	69.25 E
Takenake	120	34.11 N	81.20 E
Takengon	114	4.38 N	96.50 E
Takeno ≐	96	35.45 N	135.06 E
Takenotsuka ⊶[8]	268	35.48 N	139.48 E
Takeo	92	33.12 N	130.01 E
Takeoka	268	35.12 N	139.51 E
Tåkern ⊜	26	58.21 N	14.48 E
Takeshi	94	36.17 N	138.14 E
Take-shima I	93b	30.49 N	130.26 E
Take-shima (Tok-to) II	92	37.17 N	131.53 E
Tākestān	128	36.04 N	49.43 E
Taketa	96	32.58 N	131.24 E
Taketoyo	94	34.51 N	136.55 E
Takêv	110	10.59 N	104.47 E
Take-yama ∧[2]	268	35.13 N	139.39 E
Takhādīd ⊤[4]	128	29.59 N	44.30 E
Takhār □[4]	120	36.30 N	69.30 E
Takhatpur	124	22.09 N	81.52 E
Takhli	110	15.15 N	100.21 E
Ta Khoa	110	21.13 N	104.18 E
Takht-e Jamshīd ⊥	128	29.57 N	52.52 E
Takht-i-Bhāi	123	34.17 N	71.56 E
Tāki, India	126	22.36 N	88.55 E
Taki, Nihon	94	34.30 N	136.33 E
Taki, Nihon	96	35.16 N	132.38 E
Taki, Pap. N. Gui.	175e	6.29 S	155.50 E
Takijuk Lake ⊜	176	66.15 N	113.05 W
Takikawa	92a	43.33 N	141.54 E
Takino	96	34.56 N	134.58 E
Takipur	126	24.19 N	87.58 E
Takitimu Mountains ⋏	172	45.41 S	167.53 E
Takla Lake ⊜	182	55.25 N	125.53 W
Takla Landing	182	55.29 N	125.58 W
Takla Makan → Taklimakan Shamo ⊶[2]	90	39.00 N	83.00 E
Taklimakan Shamo ⊶[2]	90	39.00 N	83.00 E
Tako	94	35.44 N	140.28 E
Takob	85	38.50 N	68.57 E
Tako-bana ≻	96	35.36 N	133.06 E
Takolekaju, Pegunungan ⋏	112	2.00 S	121.00 E
Takoma Park	284c	38.58 N	77.00 W
Takoradi → Sekondi-Takoradi	150	4.59 N	1.43 W
Takotna	180	62.56 N	156.04 W
Takow → Kaohsiung	100	22.38 N	120.17 E
Takpochao, Okso ∧	174n	15.11 N	145.45 E
Takrouna	36	36.09 N	10.20 E
Taksimo	88	51.03 N	107.50 E
Taksino	82	56.19 N	36.10 E
Takslesluk Lake ⊜	180	61.04 N	162.55 W
Taksony	264c	47.20 N	19.04 E
Taku	92	33.17 N	130.08 E
Taku ≐	180	58.26 N	133.59 W
Takuan, Mount ∧	175e	6.27 S	155.36 E
Takua Pa	110	8.53 N	98.21 E
Taku Glacier ⩍	180	58.35 N	134.10 W
Takum	150	7.17 N	9.59 E
Takuma	96	34.13 N	133.40 E
Takundi	152	4.45 S	16.34 E
Takutea I	14	19.49 S	158.18 W
Takut Tangub Bay ⊂	116	6.33 N	122.15 E
Takutu (Tacutu) ≐	246	3.01 N	60.29 W
Takuu Islands II	14	4.45 S	157.00 E
Takysie Lake	182	53.54 N	125.53 W
Tāl	123	34.55 N	72.13 E
Tala, Bngl.	126	22.46 N	89.16 E
Tāla, India	124	23.43 N	81.02 E
Tala, Méx.	234	20.40 N	103.42 W
Talā, Miṣr	142	30.41 N	30.56 E
Tala, Ur.	252	34.21 S	55.46 W
Tala, Arroyo del ≐	258	33.37 S	56.34 W
Ṭālāb (Tāhlāb) ≐	128	28.09 N	62.45 E
Talacogon	116	8.28 N	125.46 E
Talaga	112	2.11 S	125.53 E
Talagang	123	32.55 N	72.25 E
Talagante	252	33.40 S	70.56 W
Talagou	104	41.37 N	120.32 E
Ta Lai	110	11.24 N	107.23 E
Talaimannar	122	9.05 N	79.44 E
Talāja	120	21.21 N	72.03 E
Talak ⊶[1]	150	18.20 N	6.00 E
Talakag	116	8.16 N	124.37 E
Talakan	89	49.38 N	133.18 E
Talakovka	83	47.10 N	37.43 E
Tālāla	120	21.02 N	70.32 E
Talalajevka	78	50.51 N	33.08 E
Talamanca, Cordillera de ⋏	236	9.30 N	83.40 W
Talamba	123	30.32 N	72.14 E
Talamone	66	42.33 N	11.08 E
Talana, It.	71	40.02 N	9.30 E
Talana, S. Afr.	158	28.10 S	30.15 E
Talandža	89	49.27 N	131.35 E
Talang, Gunung ∧	112	0.58 S	100.39 E
Talangbatu	112	4.06 S	105.29 E
Talangbetutu	112	2.53 S	104.41 E
Talangpadang	112	5.21 S	104.11 E
Talangrimbo	112	3.29 S	105.25 E
Talant	58	47.19 N	5.00 E
Talap	80	48.26 N	48.03 E
Talara	246	4.34 S	81.17 W
Talarrubias	34	39.02 N	5.14 W
Talas	85	42.32 N	72.14 E
Talas □[4]	85	42.30 N	72.00 E
Talas ≐	85	44.02 N	69.37 E
Talasea	164	5.20 S	150.05 E
Talasskij-Alatau, chrebet ⋏	85	42.10 N	72.00 E
Talatakoh, Pulau I	112	0.22 S	122.05 E
Tal'at al-Jamā'ah, Rujm ∧	132	30.23 N	35.30 E
Talata Mafara	150	12.35 N	6.04 E
Talaud, Kepulauan II	108	4.20 N	126.50 E
Talavera	116	15.35 N	120.55 E
Talavera de la Reina	34	39.57 N	4.50 W
Talawdī	140	10.38 N	30.23 E
Talayan	116	6.55 N	124.24 E
Tālbāndh	126	22.03 N	86.20 E
Talbingo	171b	35.34 S	148.18 E
Talbingo Reservoir ⊜[1]	171b	35.43 S	148.20 E
Talbot	169	37.11 S	143.43 E
Talbot ≐	212	44.28 N	79.10 W
Talbot, Cape ≻	164	13.48 S	126.43 E
Talbot Brook	168a	32.01 S	116.40 E
Talbot Brook ≐	168a	32.10 S	116.49 E
Talbot Islands II	164	9.15 S	142.08 E
Talbot Lake ⊜, Mb., Can.	184	54.00 N	99.55 W
Talbot Lake ⊜, On., Can.	212	44.42 N	78.51 W
Talbotton	192	32.40 N	84.32 W
Talbotville Royal	214	42.48 N	81.15 W
Talbragar ≐	166	32.12 S	148.37 E
Talca	252	35.26 S	71.40 W
Talcahuano	252	36.43 S	73.07 W
Tālcher	120	20.57 N	85.13 E
Talchichitle, Isla I	232	24.59 N	108.04 W
Talco	196	33.21 N	95.06 W
Talcottville	207	41.49 N	72.30 W
Talcy, Château de ⊥	50	47.46 N	1.27 E
Taldan	89	53.40 N	124.48 E
Tāldāngra	126	23.02 N	87.06 E
Taldom	82	56.44 N	37.32 E
Taldyapan, Kaz.	80	48.07 N	47.08 E
Taldyapan, Kaz.	80	49.46 N	50.14 E
Taldyk, pereval)(	85	39.47 N	73.11 E
Taldykuduk	80	50.09 N	49.33 E
Taldy-Kurgan	86	45.00 N	78.23 E
Taldy-Kurgan □[8]	86	45.30 N	78.30 E
Tale	150	9.26 N	1.07 W
Taleex	144	9.09 N	48.26 E
Talence	32	44.49 N	0.35 W
Talent	202	42.14 N	122.47 W
Tālesh	128	37.48 N	48.55 E
Taley	152	6.40 N	16.23 E
Talgar	85	43.18 N	77.18 E
Talgar, pik ∧	85	43.05 N	77.20 E
Talgarreg	42	52.08 N	4.18 W
Talgarth	42	52.00 N	3.15 W
Ṭalḥ, 'Ilw aṭ- ∧[2]	142	28.30 N	29.38 E
Talhār	120	24.53 N	68.49 E
Tali, Pointe de ≻	241o	15.56 N	61.12 W
Talia, Austl.	162	33.19 S	134.54 E
Talia, Méx.	196	25.44 N	102.26 W
Taliabu, Pulau I	112	1.48 S	124.48 E
Talian Dao I	98	39.03 N	122.52 E
Talibon	116	10.09 N	124.19 E
Talibong, Ko I	110	7.15 N	99.23 E
Talica, Ross.	76	58.44 N	41.34 E
Talica, Ross.	80	58.01 N	51.30 E
Talica, Ross.	86	57.00 N	63.43 E
Talickij Čamlyk	80	52.02 N	40.32 E
Talien → Dalian	98	38.53 N	121.35 E
Talihina	196	34.45 N	95.02 W
Tālīkota	122	16.29 N	76.19 E
Talikud Island I	116	6.56 N	125.42 E
Talim Island I	116	14.21 N	121.14 E
Talimuashili	85	39.08 N	77.03 E
Taling Chan	269a	13.46 N	100.27 E
Taliouine	148	30.36 N	7.49 W
Taliparamba	122	12.03 N	75.21 E
Tali Post	140	5.54 N	30.47 E
Talisay, Pil.	116	14.08 N	122.55 E
Talisay, Pil.	116	10.44 N	122.58 E
Talisay, Pil.	116	10.15 N	123.51 E
Talisayan	116	9.00 N	124.55 E
Talisei, Pulau I	112	1.51 N	125.05 E
Talish-Mikeyli	84	39.23 N	48.22 E
Talish Mountains (Kūhhā-ye Ṭavālesh ⋏	128	38.42 N	48.18 E
Talisker	46	57.17 N	6.27 W
Taliwang	115b	8.44 S	116.52 E
Tal'ka	76	53.22 N	28.21 E
Talkeetna	180	62.20 N	150.07 W
Talkeetna Mountains ⋏	180	62.10 N	148.15 W
Ṭalkhā	142	31.03 N	31.22 E
Talkheh ≐	128	37.52 N	45.53 E
Talladale	46	57.42 N	5.29 W
Talladega	194	33.26 N	86.06 W
Tall 'Afar	128	36.22 N	42.27 E
Tallaght	48	53.17 N	6.21 W
Tal Lah, India	126	22.19 N	87.18 E
Tallah, Miṣr	142	28.05 N	30.44 E
Tallahaga Creek ≐	194	32.55 N	88.58 W
Tallahala Creek ≐	194	31.12 N	89.05 W
Tallahassee	192	30.26 N	84.16 W
Tallahatchie ≐	194	33.33 N	90.10 W
Tall al-Abyaḍ	130	36.41 N	38.57 E
Tall al-'Amārnah (Akhetatem) ⊥	142	27.38 N	30.54 E
Tall al-Maskhūtah (Succotah) ⊥	142	30.33 N	32.07 E
Tall al-Muqayyar (Ur) ⊥	128	30.57 N	46.09 E
Tallanalla	168a	33.06 S	116.07 E
Tallangatta	166	36.13 S	147.15 E
Tallangatta Creek ≐	171b	36.15 S	147.13 E
Tallapoosa	194	33.44 N	85.17 W
Tallapoosa ≐	194	32.30 N	86.16 W
Tallard	62	44.28 N	6.03 E
Talla Reservoir ⊜[1]	46	55.29 N	3.24 W
Tall ar-Ratābah (Pithom) ⊥	142	30.32 N	32.06 E
Tall ar-Rub' (Mendes) ⊥	142	30.58 N	31.31 E
Tallassee	194	32.32 N	85.53 W
Tall as-Sulṭān ⊥	132	31.52 N	35.27 E
Tall Banī 'Umrān	142	27.40 N	30.54 E
Tall Basṭah (Bubastis) ⊥	142	30.34 N	31.31 E
Tällberg	26	60.49 N	15.00 E
Tall Bīsah	130	34.50 N	36.44 E
Tall-e Khosrow-ye Soflá	128	30.37 N	51.35 E
Talleyville	208	39.48 N	75.32 W
Tallinn	76	59.25 N	24.45 E
Tall Kalakh	130	34.40 N	36.15 E
Tall Kayf	128	36.29 N	43.08 E
Tall Kūjik	130	36.48 N	42.04 E
Tallmadge	214	41.06 N	81.27 W
Tallman	276	41.07 N	74.06 W
Tallman Mountain State Park ♦	276	41.01 N	73.54 W
Talloires	62	45.51 N	6.13 E
Tallong	170	34.44 S	150.05 E
Tallow	48	52.05 N	8.00 W
Tallowa Dam ⊶[6]	170	34.47 S	150.18 E
Tall Rāk	142	30.54 N	31.43 E
Tall Rif'at	130	36.28 N	37.06 E
Tall Salḥab	130	35.15 N	36.22 E
Tall Tamir	130	36.39 N	40.22 E
Tallula	219	39.56 N	89.56 W
Tallulah	194	32.24 N	91.11 W
Tally	80	53.08 N	53.04 E
Tally Ho	274b	37.52 S	145.09 E
Tālma	126	23.29 N	89.54 E
Talmage, Ca., U.S.	204	39.08 N	123.10 W
Talmage, Ne., U.S.	198	40.31 N	96.01 W
Talmage, Pa., U.S.	208	40.07 N	76.13 W
Talmalmo	171b	35.56 S	147.30 E
Talmas	50	50.02 N	2.20 E
Talmazy	78	46.38 N	29.40 E
Tal'menka	86	53.51 N	83.35 E
Talmine	46	58.31 N	4.26 W
Talmont	32	46.28 N	1.37 W
Tal'niki	88	52.47 N	102.24 E
Tal'noje	78	48.53 N	30.42 E
Talo ∧	144	10.44 N	37.55 E
Taloda	120	21.34 N	74.13 E
Talofofo	174p	13.21 N	144.45 E
Talofofo Bay ⊂	174p	13.20 N	144.46 E
Taloga	196	36.02 N	98.57 W
Taloje	88	55.24 N	95.40 E
Taloje Budrukh	272c	19.05 N	73.05 E
Talok	112	1.03 N	118.48 E
Talon, Lake ⊜	190	46.18 N	79.05 W
Talonan, Tano ≻	115b	9.07 S	117.02 E
Tāloqān	120	36.44 N	69.33 E
Taloro ≐	71	40.08 N	8.58 E
Talovaja	78	51.06 N	40.44 E
Talovka, Kaz.	80	50.25 N	47.35 E
Talovka, Ross.	80	49.58 N	45.01 E
Talovka, Ross.	84	44.14 N	46.36 E
Talovka, Ross.	86	51.27 N	81.54 E
Talovka, Ross.	86	57.10 N	93.09 E
Talovoje	83	48.18 N	39.40 E
Talpa	196	31.47 N	99.43 W
Talpa de Allende	234	20.23 N	104.51 W
Talquin, Lake ⊜[1]	192	30.26 N	84.33 W

Symbols in the index entries represent the broad categories identified in the key at the right. Symbols with superior numbers (⋏[1]) identify subcategories (see complete key on page *I · 1)*.

Symbole im Register stellen die rechts im Schlüssel erklärten Kategorien dar. Symbole mit hochgestellten Ziffern (⋏[1]) bezeichnen Unterabteilungen einer Kategorie (vgl. vollständiger Schlüssel auf Seite *I · 1)*.

Los símbolos incluídos en el texto del índice representan las grandes categorias identificadas con la clave a la derecha. Los símbolos con numeros en su parte superior (⋏[1]) identifican las subcategorías (véase la clave completa en la página *I · 1)*.

Les symboles de l'index représentent les catégories indiquées dans la légende à droite. Les symboles suivis d'un indice (⋏[1]) représentent des sous-catégories (voir légende complète à la page *I · 1)*.

Os símbolos incluídos no texto do índice representam as grandes categorias identificadas com a chave à direita. Os símbolos com números em sua parte superior (⋏[1]) identificam as subcategorias (veja-se a chave completa à página *I · 1)*.

	English	Deutsch	Español	Français	Português
∧	Mountain	Berg	Montaña	Montagne	Montanha
⋏	Mountains	Gebirge	Montañas	Montagnes	Montanhas
)(	Pass	Paß	Paso	Col	Passo
V	Valley, Canyon	Tal, Cañon	Valle, Cañón	Vallée, Canyon	Vale, Canhão
≐	Plain	Ebene	Llano	Plaine	Planície
≻	Cape	Kap	Cabo	Cap	Cabo
I	Island	Insel	Isla	Île	Ilha
II	Islands	Inseln	Islas	Îles	Ilhas
⊥	Other Topographic Features	Andere Topographische Objekte	Otros Elementos Topográficos	Autres données topographiques	Outros acidentes topográficos

ESPAÑOL / FRANÇAIS / PORTUGUÊS

Nombre / Nom / Nome	Página / Page	Lat.°′	Long.°′ W = Oeste / W = Ouest
Tālsa	272b	22.49 N	88.33 E
Talsarnau	42	52.54 N	4.03 W
Talsi	76	57.15 N	22.36 E
Talšik	86	53.42 N	71.53 E
Taltal	252	25.24 S	70.29 W
Taltapin Lake ⊜	182	54.19 N	125.20 W
Taltson ≃	176	61.23 N	112.45 W
Talu	112	0.14 N	99.59 E
Taludaa	112	0.20 N	123.28 E
Taluk	112	0.32 S	101.35 E
Talumphuk, Laem ≻	110	8.30 N	100.10 E
Taluti, Teluk c	164	3.21 S	129.45 E
Talvik'ul'a	24	68.45 N	29.19 E
Talwandi Bhāi	123	30.51 N	74.56 E
Talwood	166	28.30 S	149.30 E
Taly	78	49.51 N	40.04 E
Ṭalyā	142	30.16 N	31.00 E
Tal-y-bont	42	52.29 N	3.59 W
Tama, Arg.	252	30.31 S	66.32 W
Tama, Nihon	94	35.37 N	139.27 E
Tama, Ia., U.S.	190	41.58 N	92.34 W
Tama ≃	94	35.32 N	139.47 E
Tama Cemetery ◆	268	35.41 N	139.31 E
Tamacuarí, Pico ∧	246	1.15 N	64.45 W
Tamadjert	148	25.36 N	7.20 E
Tamagawa, Nihon	94	37.12 N	140.24 E
Tamagawa, Nihon	96	34.01 N	132.56 E
Tamagawa ◆[8]	268	35.37 N	139.39 E
Tamagawa-josui ≃	268	35.42 N	139.35 E
Tamakautonga	174v	19.05 S	169.55 W
Tamaki	94	34.29 N	136.38 E
Tāmākośī ≃	124	27.22 N	85.59 E
Tama-kyūryō ⋀[2]	268	35.35 N	139.30 E
Tamala, Austl.	162	26.42 S	113.45 E
Tamala, Ross.	80	52.33 N	43.16 E
Tamalameque	246	8.52 N	73.49 W
Tamalave, Sierra ⋀	234	22.45 N	99.15 W
Ṭamalāy	142	30.30 N	30.51 E
Tamale	150	9.25 N	0.50 W
Tamalea	112	2.29 S	119.19 E
Tamalpais, Mount ∧	226	37.56 N	122.35 W
Tamalpais Valley	226	37.53 N	122.32 W
Tamamura	94	36.18 N	139.07 E
Taman, Indon.	115a	7.25 S	112.41 E
Taman', Ross.	78	45.13 N	36.43 E
Tamana	92	32.55 N	130.33 E
Tamana I	14	2.29 S	175.59 E
Tamaná, Cerro ∧	246	5.02 N	76.17 W
Tamana, Mount ∧[2]	241r	10.28 N	61.12 W
Tamanaco ≃	246	9.25 N	65.23 W
Tamanan	115a	8.01 S	113.49 E
Tamanar	148	31.00 N	9.35 W
Tamandourirt, Oued V	150	19.39 N	2.04 W
Tamanduateí ≃	287b	23.36 S	46.35 W
Tamanhint	146	27.13 N	14.36 E
Tamani	150	13.20 N	6.50 W
Tamaniquá	246	2.38 S	65.44 W
Taman Negara ♠	114	4.43 N	102.23 E
Tamano	96	34.30 N	133.56 E
Tamanquaré, Ilha I	246	0.28 S	64.55 W
Tamanskij zaliv c	78	45.18 N	36.45 E
Tamanthi	110	25.19 N	95.18 E
Tamanusi	112	1.48 S	121.18 E
Tamapatz	234	21.35 N	99.09 W
Tamaqua	208	40.47 N	75.58 W
Tamar ≃, Austl.	166	41.04 S	146.47 E
Tamar ≃, Nepāl	124	26.55 N	87.10 E
Tamar ≃, Eng., U.K.	42	50.22 N	4.10 W
Támara	246	5.50 N	72.10 W
Tamarac ≃	198	48.29 N	97.07 W
Tamarack Lake ⊜[1]	214	41.35 N	80.05 W
Tamarite de Litera	34	41.52 N	0.26 E
Tamaroa	194	38.08 N	89.14 W
Tamarome	164	2.54 S	133.38 E
Tamarugal, Pampa del ≚	248	21.00 S	69.25 W
Tamashima	96	34.32 N	133.40 E
Tamási	30	46.38 N	18.18 E
Tamaské	150	14.49 N	5.39 E
Tamatsukuri	94	36.06 N	140.25 E
Tamaulipas □[3]	232	24.00 N	98.45 W
Tamaya ≃	248	8.31 S	74.13 W
Tamayu	96	35.25 N	133.01 E
Tama Zoological Park ♠	268	35.39 N	139.24 E
Tamazula	232	24.57 N	106.57 W
Tamazula de Gordiano	234	19.38 N	103.15 W
Tamazulapan del Progreso	234	17.41 N	97.34 W
Tamazunchale	234	21.16 N	98.47 W
Tamba	96	35.09 N	135.25 E
Tambach-Dietharz	54	50.48 N	10.36 E
Tambacounda	150	13.47 N	13.40 W
Tambacounda □[4]	150	14.00 N	13.00 W
Tamba Dabatou	150	11.48 N	10.40 W
Tambak	115a	5.45 S	112.37 E
Tambakboyo	115a	6.48 S	111.50 E
Tamba-kōchi ⋀[1]	92	35.20 N	135.30 E
Tambakrejo	115a	7.16 S	111.36 E
Tambalan	112	3.08 N	115.34 E
Tambangsawah	112	3.02 S	102.11 E
Tambara, Moç.	154	16.45 S	34.15 E
Tambara, Nihon	96	33.54 N	133.04 E
Tāmbaram	122	12.55 N	80.07 E
Tambaú ≃	256	21.34 S	47.05 W
Tambault, Île à I	275a	45.20 N	73.51 W
Tambea	112	4.12 S	121.36 E
Tambej	74	71.30 N	71.50 E
Tambelan, Kepulauan II	112	1.00 N	107.30 E
Tambelan Besar, Pulau I	112	0.58 N	107.34 E
Tambellup	162	34.02 S	117.39 E
Tamberías	252	31.28 S	69.25 W
Tambisan, Pulau I	116	5.27 N	119.10 E
Tambler	116	6.03 N	125.09 E
Tambo, Austl.	166	24.53 S	146.15 E
Tambo, Perú	248	12.56 S	74.01 W
Tambo ≃, Austl.	166	37.51 S	147.48 E
Tambo ≃, Perú	248	17.10 S	71.51 W
Tambo ≃, Perú	248	10.43 S	73.45 W
Tamboara	255	23.09 S	52.33 W
Tambo Grande	248	4.56 S	80.21 W
Tambohorano	157b	17.30 S	43.58 E
Tamboli	112	3.57 S	121.20 E
Tambolongang, Pulau I	112	6.36 S	120.24 E
Tambopata ≃	248	12.36 S	69.11 W
Tambor	236	9.43 N	85.01 W
Tambora, Gunung ∧	115b	8.14 S	117.55 E
Tamboril	250	4.50 S	40.20 W
Tamborine	171a	27.53 S	153.08 E
Tamborine Mountain ∧[2]	171a	27.55 S	153.10 E
Tamboritha, Mount ∧	166	37.28 S	146.41 E
Tamboryacu ≃	246	2.31 S	73.40 W
Tambov	80	52.43 N	41.25 E
Tambovka, Ross.	80	47.18 N	47.23 E
Tambovka, Ross.	89	50.06 N	128.04 E
Tambov Oblast' □[4]	80	52.45 N	41.30 E
Tambre ≃	34	42.49 N	8.53 W
Tambu	112	0.02 S	119.52 E
Tambu, Teluk c	112	0.02 N	119.45 E
Tambulian Point ≻	116	7.22 N	123.27 E
Tambunan	112	5.40 N	116.22 E
Tambura	140	5.36 N	27.28 E
Tamchaket	150	17.15 N	10.40 W
Tam Chuak, Laem ≻	110	8.33 N	98.12 E
Tamdhas	124	28.04 N	83.14 E
Tame	246	6.28 N	71.44 W
Tame ≃	262	53.25 N	2.09 W
Tameapa	232	25.39 N	107.22 W
Tamedda, Djebel ∧	148	32.48 N	0.05 E
Tâmega ≃	34	41.05 N	8.21 W
Tameghza	148	34.23 N	7.57 E
Tamel Aike	254	48.19 S	70.58 W
Tamelelt	148	31.50 N	7.29 W
Tamenghest	148	22.56 N	5.30 E
Tamenghest □[5]	148	25.00 N	5.00 E
Tamenghest, Oued V	148	22.10 N	0.10 E
Tamenuen	164	6.27 S	139.48 E
Tamerton Foliot	42	50.26 N	4.08 W
Tamesí ≃	234	22.13 N	97.52 W
Tameside □[8]	262	53.29 N	2.03 W
Tamga, Kyrg.	85	42.09 N	77.32 E
Tamga, Ross.	89	45.34 N	133.36 E
Tamgak, Monts ⋀	150	19.11 N	8.42 E
Tamgué, Massif du ⋀	150	12.00 N	12.18 W
Tamiahua	234	21.16 N	97.27 W
Tamiahua, Laguna de c	234	21.35 N	97.35 W
Tamiami Canal ≍	220	25.47 N	80.15 W
Tamiang ≃	114	4.25 N	98.16 E
Tamica	24	64.10 N	38.05 E
Tamil Harbor c	174q	9.30 N	138.09 E
Tamil Nādu □[3]	122	11.00 N	78.15 E
Tamiment	210	41.09 N	75.02 W
Tamina	222	30.11 N	96.26 W
Tamir	88	50.24 N	107.25 E
Tamiryn ≃	88	47.48 N	102.36 E
Tamiš (Timiș) ≃	38	44.51 N	20.39 E
Tamitatoala ≃	255	11.56 S	53.36 W
Ṭāmīyah	142	29.29 N	30.58 E
Tamkūhi	124	26.41 N	84.11 E
Tam Ky	110	15.34 N	108.29 E
Tamlūk	126	22.18 N	87.55 E
Tāmma	120	25.11 N	93.42 E
Tammaro ≃	68	41.09 N	14.50 E
Tammerfors → Tampere	26	61.30 N	23.45 E
Tammisaari → Ekenäs	26	59.58 N	23.26 E
Tamms	194	37.14 N	89.16 W
Ṭammūh	273c	29.56 N	31.16 E
Tāmna	126	23.15 N	86.21 E
Tämnarån ≃	40	60.31 N	17.39 E
Tämnaren ⊜	40	60.10 N	17.20 E
Tamnum	144	15.07 N	50.49 E
Tamon ◆[8]	270	34.39 N	135.04 E
Tampa, Ang.	152	15.30 S	13.27 E
Tampa, Fl., U.S.	220	27.56 N	82.27 W
Tampa Bay c	220	27.45 N	82.35 W
Tampa International Airport ⊠	220	27.59 N	82.32 W
Tampamachoco, Laguna c	234	21.00 N	97.21 W
Tampang	112	5.54 S	104.43 E
Tampaón ≃	234	21.59 N	98.36 W
Tamparan	116	8.27 N	117.13 E
Tampere	26	61.30 N	23.45 E
Tampico, Méx.	234	22.13 N	97.51 W
Tampico, Il., U.S.	190	41.37 N	89.47 W
Tampico, In., U.S.	218	38.48 N	85.58 W
Tampin	114	2.28 N	102.14 E
Tampiquito	234	23.52 N	98.14 W
Tampulonanjing, Gunung ∧	114	1.46 N	99.24 E
Tam Quan	110	14.35 N	109.03 E
Tamra	132	32.51 N	35.12 E
Tamrau, Pegunungan ⋀	164	0.30 S	132.27 E
Tamri	148	30.43 N	9.43 W
Tamsagbulag	88	47.14 N	117.21 E
Tamsalu	76	59.10 N	26.06 E
Tamshiyacu	246	4.05 S	72.58 W
Tamsweg	64	47.08 N	13.48 E
Tamu	110	24.13 N	94.18 E
Tamuín	234	21.59 N	98.45 W
Tamuk Island I	116	6.27 N	121.49 E
Tamuning	174p	13.29 N	144.46 E
Tamura	268	35.22 N	139.22 E
Tamusuke	85	38.03 N	76.53 E
Tamworth, Austl.	166	31.05 S	150.55 E
Tamworth, On., Can.	212	44.29 N	77.00 W
Tamworth, Eng., U.K.	42	52.39 N	1.40 W
Tamyang	98	35.21 N	126.58 E
Tan ≃	100	23.57 N	115.47 E
Tana, Chile	248	19.27 S	69.57 W
Tana, Nor.	24	70.28 N	28.18 E
Tana ≃, Cuba	240p	20.42 N	77.25 W
Tana (Teno) ≃, Europe	24	70.30 N	28.23 E
Tana ≃, Kenya	154	2.32 S	40.31 E
T'an'a ≃, Ross.	88	58.40 N	120.30 E
Tana, Lake ⊜	144	12.00 N	37.20 E
Tanabe, Nihon	96	34.49 N	135.46 E
Tanabe, Nihon	96	33.44 N	135.22 E
Tanabi	255	20.37 S	49.37 W
Tanacross	180	63.23 N	143.21 W
Tanafjorden c[2]	24	70.54 N	28.40 E
Tanaga Island I	180	51.50 N	178.00 W
Tanaga Volcano ∧[1]	180	51.53 N	178.09 W
Tanagro ≃	68	40.38 N	15.14 E
Tanaguarena	286c	10.37 N	66.49 W
Tanagura	94	37.02 N	140.23 E
Tanah, Tanjung ≻	115a	6.29 S	108.32 E
Tanahbala, Pulau I	110	0.25 S	98.25 E
Tanahgrogot	112	1.55 S	116.12 E
Tanahjampea, Pulau I	112	7.05 S	120.42 E
Tanahmasa, Pulau I	110	0.12 S	98.27 E
Tanahmerah, Indon.	112	3.41 N	117.31 E
Tanahmerah, Indon.	164	6.05 S	140.17 E
Tanah Merah, Malay.	114	5.48 N	102.09 E
Tanah Merah, Malay.	114	2.36 N	101.48 E
Tanahputih	114	1.41 N	101.03 E
Tanaka ◆[8]	270	34.42 N	134.59 E
Tanakeke, Pulau I	112	5.30 S	119.16 E
Tanakpur	124	29.05 N	80.07 E
Tan'am	128	23.09 N	56.29 E
Tanami	162	19.59 S	129.43 E
Tanami Desert ◆[2]	162	20.00 S	129.30 E
Ṭanān, Miṣr	142	30.15 N	31.14 E
Tan An, Viet	110	8.46 N	105.11 E
Tan An, Viet	110	10.32 N	106.25 E
Tanana	180	65.10 N	152.05 W
Tanana ≃	180	65.09 N	151.55 W
Tananarive → Antananarivo	157b	18.55 S	47.31 E
Tanapag	174n	15.14 N	145.45 E
Tanapag, Lagunan c	174n	15.14 N	145.44 E
Tanaro ≃	62	45.01 N	8.47 E
Tanārūt, Wādī V	146	30.08 N	9.59 E
Tanashi	94	35.44 N	139.33 E
Tanat ≃	42	52.46 N	3.07 W
Tanauan	116	11.07 N	125.01 E
Tanbar	166	25.50 S	141.55 E
Ṭanbidī	142	28.38 N	30.47 E
Tan Binh	269c	10.48 N	106.40 E
Tanbu, Zhg.	98	35.51 N	118.17 E
Tanbu, Zhg.	100	28.08 N	114.12 E
Tancarville	50	49.29 N	0.28 E
Tancarville, Canal de ≍	50	49.28 N	0.28 E
Tancha	174m	26.28 N	127.50 E
Tan Chau	110	10.48 N	105.15 E
Tancheng	98	34.37 N	118.23 E
Tanchoj	88	51.33 N	105.07 E
Tanch'ŏn	98	40.27 N	128.54 E
Tancítaro	234	19.20 N	102.22 W
Tancítaro, Pico de ∧	234	19.23 N	102.13 W
Tancochapa ≃	234	17.59 N	94.04 W
Tanda, C. Iv.	150	7.48 N	3.10 W
Tānda, India	123	31.42 N	75.38 E
Tānda, India	124	28.59 N	78.56 E
Tānda, India	124	26.33 N	82.39 E
Tānda, Pāk.	123	32.42 N	74.22 E
Tandag	116	9.04 N	126.12 E
Tandah	142	27.41 N	30.46 E
Tandai	154	19.36 S	32.48 E
Tandaj	80	47.33 N	51.30 E
Tandala	154	9.23 S	34.14 E
Tandaltī	140	13.01 N	31.52 E
Ţăndărei	38	44.38 N	27.40 E
Tandaué	152	17.00 S	18.06 E
Tandian	98	40.39 N	124.46 E
Tandil	252	37.19 S	59.09 W
Tandjilé □[5]	146	9.45 N	16.30 E
Tandjilé ≃	146	9.45 N	15.50 E
Tāndliānwāla	123	31.02 N	73.08 E
Tando Ādam	120	25.46 N	68.40 E
Tando Allāhyār	120	25.28 N	68.43 E
Tando Bāgo	120	24.47 N	68.58 E
Tando Muhammad Khān	120	25.08 N	68.32 E
Tandou Bougou	152	3.32 S	10.53 E
Tandou Lake ⊜	166	32.38 S	142.05 E
Tandovo, ozero ⊜	86	55.07 N	78.02 E
Tando Zinze	152	5.22 S	12.26 E
Tandragee	48	54.20 N	6.25 W
Tandridge	260	51.14 N	0.02 W
Tandridge □[8]	260	51.17 N	0.05 W
Tandslet	41	54.55 N	9.59 E
Tandubas	116	5.10 N	120.20 E
Tandubatu Island I	116	5.13 N	120.17 E
Tandula Tank ⊜[1]	122	20.40 N	81.12 E
Tandun	112	0.36 N	100.38 E
Tāndūr	122	17.14 N	77.35 E
Tanduy ≃	115a	7.41 S	108.47 E
Taneatua	172	38.04 S	177.01 E
Tanega-shima I	93b	30.40 N	131.00 E
Taneichi	92	40.26 N	141.43 E
Tan Emellel	148	27.30 N	9.45 E
Tanete	112	4.32 S	119.36 E
Taneum Creek ≃	224	47.10 N	120.40 W
Tanew ≃	30	50.31 N	22.16 E
Taneytown	208	39.39 N	77.10 W
Tanezrouft ◆[2]	148	24.00 N	0.45 W
Tanezzuft, Wādī V	146	25.51 N	10.19 E
Tanforan Park ◆[9]	282	37.38 N	122.25 W
Tang ≃, Zhg.	98	38.45 N	115.35 E
Tang ≃, Zhg.	100	32.09 N	112.25 E
Tang ≃, Zhg.	100	33.18 N	117.46 E
Tang ≃, Zhg.	104	41.15 N	123.21 E
Tang ≃, Zhg.	105	40.43 N	116.38 E
Tanga, Ross.	88	51.02 N	111.33 E
Tånga, Sve.	41	56.12 N	12.46 E
Tanga, Tan.	154	5.04 S	39.06 E
Tanga □[4]	154	5.00 S	38.15 E
Tangail	124	24.15 N	89.55 E
Tangainony	157b	22.42 S	47.45 E
Tanga Islands II	14	3.30 S	153.15 E
Tanga Langua ≻	241k	12.14 N	61.39 W
Tangalla	122	6.01 N	80.48 E
Tangamong Lake ⊜	212	44.43 N	77.51 W
Tangancícuaro [de Arista]	234	19.54 N	102.08 W
Tanganika, Lago → Tanganyika, Lake ⊜	154	6.00 S	29.30 E
Tanganjika-See → Tanganyika, Lake ⊜	154	6.00 S	29.30 E
Tanganyika, Lake ⊜	154	6.00 S	29.30 E
Tangarana ≃	246	3.02 S	75.08 W
Tangarare	175e	9.35 S	159.39 E
Tanga-shima I	96	34.40 N	134.35 E
Tangba	107	30.00 N	105.46 E
Tangchi	89	47.00 N	123.46 E
Tangchigou	104	41.04 N	124.11 E
Tangcun, Zhg.	100	29.50 N	118.54 E
Tangcun, Zhg.	100	25.26 N	113.10 E
Tangdaohe	98	40.38 N	118.58 E
Tanger (Tangier)	148	35.48 N	5.45 W
Tanger □[4]	148	35.35 N	5.50 W
Tanger ≃	54	52.33 N	11.59 E
Tangerang	115a	6.11 S	106.37 E
Tangerhütte	54	52.26 N	11.48 E
Tangerine	220	28.47 N	81.38 W
Tang'erli	105	39.09 N	116.43 E
Tangermünde	54	52.32 N	11.58 E
Tangfang, Zhg.	102	27.00 N	101.08 E
Tangfang, Zhg.	104	41.20 N	120.34 E
Tangfang, Zhg.	105	39.29 N	118.01 E
Tangfangqiao	106	31.45 N	120.50 E
Tangfeng	98	38.07 N	115.30 E
Tanggangzi	104	41.01 N	122.54 E
Tanggeasinua, Pegunungan ⋀	112	3.24 S	121.42 E
Tanggengtou	106	30.55 N	119.03 E
Tanggou	100	33.59 N	118.57 E
Tanggu	105	39.01 N	117.40 E
Tangguantun	98	38.43 N	116.55 E
Tanggul	115a	8.10 S	113.26 E
Tanggulashan (Tuotuoheyan)	120	34.05 N	92.45 E
Tanggula Shan ⋀	120	33.00 N	92.00 E
Tanggula Shankou)(	120	32.59 N	91.45 E
Tanggushiluke	120	38.45 N	80.55 E
Tanghe	100	32.43 N	112.48 E
Tanghekou	105	40.44 N	116.38 E
Tanghu	105	39.11 N	115.24 E
Tanghuang	106	31.41 N	119.25 E
Tangi	123	34.18 N	71.40 E
Tangier, N.S., Can.	186	44.48 N	62.42 W
Tangier, Va., U.S.	208	37.49 N	75.59 W
Tangier Island I	208	37.50 N	76.00 W
Tangier Sound ʮ	208	38.02 N	75.58 W
Tangier → Tanger	148	35.48 N	5.45 W
Tangijatuo	107	29.36 N	106.39 E
Tangipahoa ≃	194	30.20 N	90.18 W
Tangjia	100	22.23 N	113.36 E
Tangjiagou	100	30.48 N	117.28 E
Tangjiang	100	25.51 N	114.44 E
Tangjiapao	104	41.59 N	122.14 E
Tangjiaqiao	106	31.24 N	119.12 E
Tangjin	98	36.54 N	126.37 E
Tangjiqiaozhen	106	31.13 N	121.31 E
Tangkahan	112	1.36 S	113.52 E
Tangkak	114	2.16 N	102.33 E
Tangkou	100	30.06 N	118.11 E
Tanglad	115b	8.47 S	115.35 E
Tanglewood, Fl., U.S.	220	26.37 N	81.53 W
Tanglewood, Tx., U.S.	222	30.30 N	96.59 W
Tanglewood ♠	207	42.21 N	73.20 W
Tangling	100	26.14 N	119.24 E
Tanglitun	104	41.45 N	123.57 E
Tangmai	102	30.08 N	95.11 E
Tangmarg	123	34.02 N	74.26 E
Tangmazhai	104	41.10 N	122.44 E
Tang Nhon Phu	269c	10.50 N	106.47 E
Tang-ni	98	34.12 N	126.52 E
Tango	96	35.44 N	135.06 E
Tango-hantō ≻[1]	96	35.40 N	135.10 E
Tangowahine	172	35.52 S	173.56 E
Tangpu, Zhg.	100	29.51 N	120.47 E
Tangpu, Zhg.	100	28.28 N	114.58 E
Tangqi	106	30.29 N	120.11 E
Tangqiao	106	31.13 N	119.15 E
Tangra Yumco ⊜	120	31.00 N	86.20 E
Tangsanying	98	41.38 N	117.40 E
Tangschan → Tangshan	105	39.38 N	118.11 E
Tangse	114	5.01 N	95.55 E
Tangshan, Zhg.	105	40.10 N	116.22 E
Tangshan, Zhg.	105	39.38 N	118.11 E
Tangshan, Zhg.	106	32.05 N	119.03 E
Tang Shan ∧	106	32.03 N	119.02 E
Tangshi	106	31.33 N	120.51 E
Tangtou, Zhg.	98	35.16 N	118.35 E
Tangtou, Zhg.	102	27.42 N	108.17 E
Tangtou, Zhg.	106	31.38 N	120.19 E
Tangtouxia	100	22.50 N	114.06 E
Tangtse	120	34.02 N	78.11 E
Tanguá	256	22.44 S	42.43 W
Tangub	116	8.03 N	123.44 E
Tanguiéta	150	10.37 N	1.16 E
Tanguip Point ≻	116	7.43 N	126.32 E
Tanguj	88	55.23 N	100.58 E
Tangulbei	154	0.48 N	36.17 E
Tangusu, Telukan c	116	5.27 N	119.03 E
Tangwang ≃	89	46.40 N	129.54 E
Tangxi	100	29.04 N	119.23 E
Tangxian	98	38.45 N	114.58 E
Tangxianzhen	100	31.59 N	113.07 E
Tangyan	110	22.29 N	98.24 E
Tangyi	98	36.32 N	115.47 E
Tangyin, Zhg.	98	35.55 N	114.21 E
Tangyin, Zhg.	100	27.32 N	116.16 E
Tangyuan	89	46.42 N	129.55 E
Tangzha	106	32.05 N	120.49 E
Tanhuato	234	20.17 N	102.20 W
Taniantaweng Shan ⋀	102	30.00 N	98.00 E
Tanigami ◆[8]	270	34.46 N	135.10 E
Tanigawa-dake ∧	94	36.50 N	138.56 E
Tanigumi	94	35.31 N	136.36 E
Tanimbar, Kepulauan II	164	7.30 S	131.30 E
Taninges	58	46.07 N	6.36 E
Tanintharyi □[8]	110	12.00 N	99.00 E
Tanır	130	38.26 N	36.55 E
Tanis (Zoan) ⊥	142	30.57 N	31.53 E
Tanishpa ∧	120	31.10 N	68.24 E
Tanjay	116	9.31 N	123.09 E
Tanjiafang	98	36.41 N	118.36 E
Tanjiahe	100	31.58 N	113.56 E
Tanjiang	100	24.07 N	116.32 E
Tanjiaqiao	100	30.11 N	118.15 E
Tanjil ≃	169	38.08 S	146.17 E
Tanjong Dawai	114	5.41 N	100.22 E
Tanjong Malim	114	3.41 N	101.31 E
Tanjore → Thanjāvūr	122	10.48 N	79.09 E
Tanjung, Indon.	112	2.11 S	115.23 E
Tanjung, Indon.	115a	6.52 S	108.52 E
Tanjung, Indon.	115b	8.21 S	116.09 E
Tanjungbalai	114	2.58 N	99.48 E
Tanjungbatu, Indon.	112	0.45 N	117.26 E
Tanjungbatu, Indon.	112	2.17 N	118.05 E
Tanjungbatu, Indon.	112	0.38 N	103.26 E
Tanjungenim	112	3.45 S	103.48 E
Tanjungkarang-Telukbetung	115a	5.27 S	105.16 E
Tanjunglabu	112	2.57 S	106.54 E
Tanjungmedan, Indon.	114	1.26 N	100.34 E
Tanjungmedan, Indon.	114	2.06 N	100.14 E
Tanjungmengedar	114	2.39 N	100.01 E
Tanjungpandan	112	2.45 S	107.39 E
Tanjungpinang	112	0.55 N	104.27 E
Tanjungpriok ◆[8]	269e	6.06 S	106.53 E
Tanjungpura	114	3.54 N	98.26 E
Tanjungpusu	112	0.01 S	113.30 E
Tanjungraja	112	3.21 S	104.40 E
Tanjungredep	112	2.09 N	117.29 E
Tanjungsamak	114	0.52 N	103.03 E
Tanjungselor	112	2.51 N	117.22 E
Tanjungslamat	114	3.49 N	98.20 E
Tanjunguban	112	1.03 N	104.14 E
Tānk	120	32.13 N	70.23 E
Tan Kena	148	26.33 N	9.35 E
Tan Kien	269c	10.42 N	106.35 E
Tankou	100	25.48 N	114.50 E
Tankwa ≃	158	32.20 S	19.33 E
Tanlay	50	47.50 N	4.05 E
Tann	56	50.38 N	10.01 E
Tanna	54	50.30 N	11.51 E
Tanna I	175f	19.30 S	169.20 E
Tannan	96	35.05 N	135.10 E
Tännäs	26	62.27 N	12.40 E
Tanna-tunnel ◆[5]	94	35.06 N	139.00 E
Tannay	50	47.21 N	3.36 E
Tanne	54	51.41 N	10.42 E
Tannenberg → Stębark	30	53.30 N	20.08 E
Tannenbergsthal	54	50.26 N	12.27 E
Tanner	194	34.43 N	86.58 W
Tanner, Mount ∧	182	49.40 N	118.34 W
Tannersville, N.Y., U.S.	210	42.12 N	74.08 W
Tannersville, Pa., U.S.	210	41.03 N	75.18 W
Tännesberg	60	49.32 N	12.20 E
Tännforsen ⌞	26	63.27 N	12.44 E
Tannhausen	56	48.59 N	10.21 E
Tannheim	58	47.30 N	10.31 E
Tannila	26	65.29 N	25.59 E
Tannis Bugt c	26	57.40 N	10.15 E
Tannu-Ola, chrebet ⋀	74	51.00 N	94.00 E
Tannūrah, Ra's ≻	128	26.40 N	50.30 E
Tano, Nihon	96	33.26 N	134.00 E
Tano, Nihon	270	34.57 N	135.36 E
Tano ≃	150	5.07 N	2.56 W
Tanon Strait ʮ	116	10.20 N	123.30 E
Tânout	150	14.58 N	8.53 E
Tanpok ≃	250	3.27 N	54.00 W
Tanque de Dolores	234	23.40 N	101.10 W
Tanque Grande, Ribeirão ≃	287b	23.25 S	46.28 W
Tan Qui Dong	269c	10.44 N	106.42 E
Tanquinho	255	11.58 S	39.06 W
Tansania → Tanzania □[1]	154	6.00 S	35.00 E
T'an' Šan' → Tien Shan ⋀	90	42.00 N	80.00 E
Tansboro	285	39.46 N	74.55 W
Tānsen	124	27.52 N	83.33 E
Tanshui	100	25.10 N	121.26 E
Tanshui ≃	100	25.11 N	121.25 E
Tansilla	150	12.26 N	4.23 W
Tánsin, Isla de I	236	15.17 N	83.54 W
Tánsin, Laguna de c	236	15.19 N	83.58 W
Tan Son Nhut Airport ⊠	269c	10.49 N	106.40 E
Tansyk	86	47.20 N	79.52 E
Ṭanṭā	142	30.47 N	31.00 E
Tantabogue Creek ≃	222	31.00 N	95.21 W
Tan-Tan	148	28.26 N	11.06 W
Tan-Tan □[4]	148	28.05 N	11.00 W
Tantangara Reservoir ⊜[1]	171b	35.45 S	148.39 E
Tan Thoi Nhut	269c	10.50 N	106.36 E
Tan Thuan Dong	269c	10.45 N	106.44 E
Tāntipāra	126	23.54 N	87.22 E
Tantō	96	35.29 N	135.00 E
Tantonville	58	48.28 N	6.08 E
Tantou, Zhg.	100	29.07 N	121.09 E
Tantou, Zhg.	100	26.03 N	119.35 E
Tantou, Zhg.	100	26.53 N	115.26 E
Tantou Shan I	100	29.11 N	122.01 E
Tantoyuca	234	21.21 N	98.14 W
Tanuku	122	16.45 N	81.42 E
Tanuma	94	36.22 N	139.35 E
Tanumshede	26	58.44 N	11.19 E
Tanunda	168b	34.32 S	138.57 E
Tan'urer ≃	180	64.44 N	174.15 E
Tanushimaru	96	33.21 N	130.41 E
Tanvald	30	50.45 N	15.19 E
Tanwax Creek ≃	224	46.52 N	122.27 W
Tanworth-in-Arden	42	52.20 N	1.50 W
Tanxi	100	28.58 N	115.38 E
Tanxia	100	23.58 N	115.34 E
Tanxu Shan I	106	30.37 N	121.37 E
Tanyang	98	36.57 N	128.21 E
Tanyeri	130	39.37 N	39.50 E
Tanyi	98	35.14 N	118.09 E
Tanymas ≃	85	38.25 N	72.39 E
Tanzania □[1], Afr.	138	6.00 S	35.00 E
Tanzania □[1], Afr.	154	6.00 S	35.00 E
Tanzanie → Tanzania □[1]	154	6.00 S	35.00 E
Tanzawa-Ōyama-kokutei-kōen ♠	94	35.30 N	139.10 E
Tanzawa-san ∧	94	35.28 N	139.10 E
Tao ≃, Zhg.	100	25.56 N	115.06 E
Tao ≃, Zhg.	102	35.52 N	103.16 E
Tao, Ko I	110	10.05 N	99.52 E
Tao'an	89	45.22 N	122.47 E
Taochong	100	31.04 N	118.06 E
Taochuan	102	25.07 N	111.06 E
Taocun	98	37.10 N	121.05 E
Taodigou	105	40.52 N	116.14 E
Tao'er ≃	89	45.42 N	124.05 E
Taoerdeng	98	40.44 N	119.02 E
Taohe	105	39.12 N	116.50 E
Taohua	106	31.23 N	120.04 E
Taohuachiyingzi	104	42.18 N	121.06 E
Taohua Dao I	100	29.48 N	122.17 E
Taohuanbuligai	104	42.13 N	122.14 E
Taohuatu	104	41.40 N	120.40 E
Taohuayuan	106	30.34 N	118.42 E
Taohuazhen	105	40.04 N	114.59 E
Taojiagou	107	29.48 N	104.48 E
Taojiahe	100	30.55 N	115.56 E
Taojialiang	104	42.36 N	121.25 E
Taolahusu	98	42.34 N	116.48 E
Taolaizhao	89	44.51 N	125.57 E
Taolakepa	120	32.05 N	85.22 E
Taole	102	38.46 N	106.40 E
Taolin	98	34.30 N	118.30 E
Taoling	100	30.21 N	118.16 E
Taoluo	98	35.17 N	119.24 E
T'aonan → Tao'an	89	45.22 N	122.47 E
Taongi I[1]	14	14.37 N	168.58 E
Taormina	70	37.51 N	15.17 E
Taos, Mo., U.S.	219	38.30 N	92.04 W
Taos, N.M., U.S.	200	36.24 N	105.34 W
Taos Pueblo	200	36.26 N	105.32 W
Taoudenni	148	22.40 N	4.00 W
Taougrite	34	36.15 N	0.55 E
Taounate	148	34.25 N	4.39 W
Taounate □[4]	148	34.30 N	4.40 W
Taoura	36	36.09 N	8.03 E
Taourirt	148	34.25 N	2.53 W
Taourirt ∧	148	24.03 N	5.02 E
Taoussa	150	16.55 N	0.35 W
Taowu	106	31.47 N	118.46 E
Taoxi, Zhg.	100	31.33 N	117.00 E
Taoxi, Zhg.	100	25.18 N	116.05 E
Taoxi, Zhg.	100	28.44 N	119.36 E
Taoxiantun	104	41.39 N	123.27 E
Taoyuan, Zhg.	100	25.48 N	117.32 E
Taoyuan, Zhg.	102	28.46 N	111.20 E
Taozhu	100	28.50 N	121.31 E
Taozhuang	106	30.58 N	120.48 E
Tapa, Eesti	76	59.16 N	25.58 E
Tapa, India	123	30.19 N	75.21 E
Tapaan Island I	116	5.28 N	120.44 E
Tapacari	248	17.31 S	66.36 W
Tapachula	232	14.54 N	92.17 W
Tapaga, Cape ≻	175a	14.01 S	171.23 W
Tapah	114	4.11 N	101.16 E
Tapah Road	114	4.10 N	101.12 E
Tapaje ≃	246	2.44 N	78.07 W
Tapajós ≃	250	2.24 S	54.41 W
Tapaktuan	114	3.16 N	97.11 E
Tapalpa	234	19.57 N	103.46 W
Tapalqué	252	36.21 S	60.01 W
Tapan	112	2.10 S	101.04 E
Tapanahony ≃	250	4.22 N	54.27 W
Tapanui	172	45.57 S	169.16 E
Tapanuli, Teluk c	114	1.38 N	98.45 E
Tapasi	126	23.40 N	87.08 E
Tapauá	248	5.45 S	63.04 W
Tapauá ≃	248	5.40 S	64.21 W
Tapawera	172	41.24 S	172.49 E
Tapaz	116	11.16 N	122.32 E
Tapejara	252	28.04 S	52.00 W
Tapera	252	28.38 S	52.52 W
Taperas	248	17.54 S	60.23 W
Taperoá, Bra.	250	7.12 S	36.49 W
Taperoá, Bra.	255	13.31 S	39.06 W
Tapes	252	30.40 S	51.23 W
Tapeta	150	6.29 N	8.51 W
Taphan Hin	110	16.13 N	100.26 E
Taphoen ≃	110	14.07 N	99.25 E
Tāpi ≃, India	120	21.06 N	72.41 E
Ta Pi ≃, Thai	110	9.05 N	99.12 E
Tapiales	288	34.42 S	58.31 W
Tapiantana Channel ʮ	116	6.23 N	122.00 E
Tapiantana Group II	116	6.20 N	122.00 E
Tapiantana Island I	116	6.18 N	121.59 E
Tapiche ≃	248	4.59 S	73.51 W
Tapili	154	3.25 N	27.40 E
Tapilula	234	17.14 N	93.02 W
Taping (Daying) ≃	102	24.17 N	97.14 E
Tapini	164	8.20 S	147.00 E
Tapiraí	255	19.52 S	46.01 W
Tapirapé ≃	250	10.41 S	50.38 W
Tapiratiba	256	21.28 S	46.45 W
Tapis, Gunong ∧	114	4.03 N	102.54 E
Tapiutan Island I	116	11.12 N	119.16 E
Tapiwa	174d	0.52 S	169.35 E
Taplan National Park ♠	110	14.20 N	102.20 E
Tāplejungg	124	27.21 N	87.40 E
Tapoa ≃	150	12.36 N	2.29 E
Tapol	146	8.31 N	15.35 E
Tapolca	30	46.53 N	17.27 E
Tappahannock	208	37.55 N	76.51 W
Tappal	124	28.03 N	77.35 E
Tappan	210	41.01 N	73.56 W
Tappan, Lake ⊜[1]	276	41.01 N	73.59 W
Tappan Lake ⊜[1]	214	40.21 N	81.11 W
Tappan Zee c	276	41.06 N	73.53 W
Tappan Zee Bridge ◆[5]	276	41.04 N	73.54 W
Tappen	198	46.52 N	99.38 W
Tappernøje	41	55.10 N	11.59 E
Tappi-zaki ≻	92	41.15 N	140.21 E
Tappo	150	10.12 N	2.38 W
Tapps, Lake ⊜	224	47.13 N	122.09 W
Tapsiā ◆[8]	272b	22.32 N	88.22 E
Tapuaenuku ∧	172	42.00 S	173.40 E
Tapuio ≃	250	3.41 S	44.16 W
Tapul Group II	116	5.30 N	121.00 E
Tapul Island I	116	5.43 N	120.55 E
Tapun	110	18.22 N	95.27 E
Tapurucuara	246	0.24 S	65.02 W
Taputapu, Cape ≻	174u	14.19 S	170.50 W
Taqāṭu' Hayyā	140	18.20 N	36.22 E
Taqian	100	29.03 N	117.03 E
Taqiao, Zhg.	100	31.28 N	118.25 E
Taqiao, Zhg.	100	28.24 N	117.02 E
Ṭaqṭaq	128	35.53 N	44.35 E
Taquara	252	29.39 S	50.47 W
Taquara ◆[8]	287a	22.55 S	43.21 W
Taquara, Serra da ∧	256	22.12 S	43.53 W
Taquaras, Ponta das ≻	252	27.01 S	48.34 W
Taquari, Bra.	252	29.48 S	51.51 W
Taquari, Bra.	255	17.50 S	53.17 W
Taquari ≃, Bra.	248	19.15 S	57.17 W
Taquari ≃, Bra.	252	29.56 S	51.44 W
Taquari, Pantanal do ≡	248	18.20 S	56.30 W
Taquaritinga	255	21.24 S	48.30 W
Taquaruçu ≃, Bra.	248	20.30 S	55.49 W
Taquaruçu ≃, Bra.	255	21.35 S	52.07 W
Tar ≃, Kyrg.	85	40.38 N	73.26 E
Tar ≃, N.C., U.S.	192	35.33 N	77.05 W
Tara, Austl.	166	27.17 S	150.28 E
Tara, On., Can.	212	44.28 N	81.09 W
Tara, Ross.	86	56.54 N	74.22 E
Tara, Zam.	154	16.56 S	26.47 E
Tara ⋀	38	43.55 N	19.25 E
Tara ≃, Europe	38	43.21 N	18.51 E
Tara ≃, Ross.	86	56.42 N	74.36 E
Taraba ≃	146	8.30 N	10.15 E
Tarabine, Oued ti-n- V	148	20.50 N	7.25 E
Tarabuco	248	19.10 S	64.57 W
Ṭarābulus (Tripoli), Lībiyā	146	32.54 N	13.11 E
Ṭarābulus (Tripoli), Lubnān	130	34.26 N	35.51 E
Ṭarābulus (Tripolitania) □[9]	146	31.00 N	15.00 E
Tarabusi Creek ≃	281	42.24 N	83.19 W
Tarabya ◆[8]	267b	41.08 N	29.03 E
Tarach ≃	154	4.09 N	34.56 E
Taradale	172	39.32 S	176.51 E
Taragaj ≃	85	41.35 N	77.42 E
Tarāghin	146	25.59 N	14.26 E
Tarago	170	35.04 S	149.39 E
Tara Hills	282	38.00 N	122.19 W
Tarai ≚	124	26.35 N	86.40 E
Taraia	124	26.05 N	84.53 E
Taraira (Traíra) ≃	246	1.04 S	69.26 W
Tara Island I	116	12.17 N	120.22 E
Taraju	115a	7.27 S	107.59 E
Tarakan	112	3.18 N	117.38 E
Tarakan, Pulau I	112	3.21 N	117.36 E
Tarakanovka	82	55.07 N	35.44 E
Tārakeshwar	126	22.54 N	88.02 E
Taraklı	130	40.24 N	30.29 E
Taraklija, Mol.	78	45.54 N	28.38 E
Taraklija, Mol.	78	46.34 N	29.06 E
Taralga	170	34.24 S	149.49 E
Tarama	175d	24.40 N	124.41 E
Taramakau ≃	172	42.34 S	171.08 E
Taramana	112	8.10 S	124.51 E
Tarama-shima I	175d	24.39 N	124.42 E
Tarana	170	33.32 S	149.54 E
Tārānagar	123	28.41 N	75.02 E
Taranaki, Mount ∧	172	39.18 S	174.04 E
Tarancón	34	40.01 N	3.00 W
Tarandacuao	234	19.59 N	100.32 W
Taranga Island I	172	35.58 S	174.43 E
Tarangire National Park ♠	154	4.00 S	36.00 E
Tarangnan	116	11.54 N	124.45 E
Tarango, Presa ⊜[1]	286a	19.22 N	99.13 W
Taranovka	78	49.37 N	36.08 E
Taransay I	46	57.54 N	7.01 W
Taranta Peligna	66	42.01 N	14.10 E
Tarantine, Murge ◆[1]	68	40.22 N	17.40 E
Taranto	68	40.28 N	17.15 E
Taranto □[4]	68	40.37 N	17.15 E
Taranto, Golfo di c	68	40.10 N	17.20 E
Tarapacá	246	2.52 S	69.44 W
Tarapoto	248	6.30 S	76.25 W
Ṭaraq al-Hbâri ◆[1]	130	34.17 N	39.16 E
Ṭaraq an-Na'jah ◆[1]	130	34.16 N	39.53 E
Ṭaraq Sidâoui ◆[1]	130	34.33 N	39.54 E
Taraquá	246	0.06 N	68.28 W
Tarare	58	45.54 N	4.26 E
Tarariras	258	34.17 S	57.37 W
Tararua Range ⋀	172	40.46 S	175.23 E
Tarāsa Dwīp I	110	8.15 N	93.10 E
Tarašča	78	49.34 N	30.29 E
Tarascon, Fr.	32	42.51 N	1.36 E
Tarascon, Fr.	62	43.48 N	4.40 E
Tarasht ◆[8]	267d	35.42 N	51.21 E
Tarasovka, Ross.	83	49.28 N	40.05 E
Tarasovka, Ross.	265b	55.58 N	37.50 E
Tarasovka, Ukr.	83	48.21 N	37.33 E
Tarasovka, Ukr.	83	49.40 N	38.23 E
Tarasovo, Ross.	24	66.13 N	46.39 E
Tarasovo, Ross.	24	62.49 N	41.10 E
Tarasovo, Ross.	80	58.18 N	48.45 E
Tarasovo, Ross.	88	55.52 N	107.48 E
Tarasovskij	78	48.43 N	40.22 E
Tarasp	58	46.38 N	10.25 E
Tarat	148	26.13 N	9.18 E
Tarat, Oued V	148	26.09 N	9.20 E
Tarata, Bol.	248	17.37 S	66.01 W
Tarata, Perú	248	17.28 S	70.02 W
Taratai	174t	1.32 N	173.00 E
Taratakbuluh	112	0.23 N	101.27 E
Tāratanr	126	23.58 N	86.29 E
Tarauacá	248	8.10 S	70.46 W
Tarauacá ≃	248	7.19 S	70.15 W
Taravao, Baie de c	174s	17.43 S	149.17 W
Taravao, Isthme de ≗[3]	174s	17.43 S	149.19 W
Taravo ≃	36	41.42 N	8.49 E
Tarawa I[1]	174t	1.25 N	173.00 E
Tarawera	172	39.02 S	176.35 E
Tarawera, Lake ⊜	172	38.12 S	176.27 E
Tarawera, Mount ∧[1]	172	38.14 S	176.30 E
Tarazona	34	41.54 N	1.44 W
Tarazona de la Mancha	34	39.15 N	1.55 W
Tarba	144	0.48 N	42.39 E
Tårbæk	41	55.47 N	12.36 E
Tarbagataj, Ross.	88	51.30 N	107.22 E
Tarbagataj, Ross.	88	52.07 N	109.12 E
Tarbagataj, Ross.	88	51.12 N	109.05 E
Tarbagataj, chrebet ⋀	86	47.12 N	83.00 E
Tarbat Ness ≻	46	57.51 N	3.47 W
Tarbela	123	34.08 N	72.49 E
Tarbela Reservoir ⊜[1]	123	34.10 N	72.50 E
Tarbert, Ire.	48	52.32 N	9.23 W
Tarbert, Scot., U.K.	46	55.52 N	5.26 W
Tarbert, Scot., U.K.	46	57.54 N	6.49 W
Tarbert, East Loch c	46	57.52 N	6.45 W
Tarbert, Loch c	46	55.57 N	6.00 W
Tarbert, West Loch c, Scot., U.K.	46	57.55 N	6.54 W
Tarbert, West Loch c, Scot., U.K.	46	55.48 N	5.32 W
Tarbes	32	43.14 N	0.05 E
Tarbet	46	56.12 N	4.43 W
Tarbock Green	262	53.23 N	2.49 W
Tarbolton	46	55.31 N	4.29 W
Tarboro	192	35.53 N	77.32 W
Tarbū	146	26.02 N	15.10 E
Tarcăului, Munții ⋀	38	46.45 N	26.20 E
Tarcento	64	46.13 N	13.13 E
Tarchankut, mys ≻	78	45.21 N	32.30 E
Tarchov Cholm, gora ∧[2]	76	57.11 N	38.25 E
Tarchovka	265a	60.04 N	29.58 E
Tarcoola	162	30.41 S	134.33 E
Tarcoon	166	30.16 S	146.43 E
Tarcutta	171b	35.17 S	147.44 E
Tarcutta Creek ≃	171b	35.08 S	147.36 E
Tārdah	272b	22.27 N	88.31 E
Tardajos	34	42.21 N	3.49 W
Tardoki-Jani, gora ∧	89	48.55 N	138.04 E
Tardun	162	28.48 S	115.45 E
Taredo ◆[8]	272c	19.58 N	72.49 E
Taree	166	31.54 S	152.28 E
Tareja	74	73.20 N	90.37 E
Taremert-n-Akli, Oued V	148	25.49 N	5.17 E
Tärendö	24	67.10 N	22.38 E
Tarent, Golf von → Taranto, Golfo di c	68	40.10 N	17.20 E
Tarentaise V	62	45.30 N	6.30 E
Tarento, Golfo de → Taranto, Golfo di c	68	40.10 N	17.20 E
Tarentum	214	40.36 N	79.45 W
Tarf, Garaet et ⊜	148	35.40 N	7.10 E
Ṭarfā', Baṭn aṭ- ≡	128	23.50 N	51.27 E
Ṭarfā', Ra's aṭ- ≻	144	17.05 N	42.24 E
Ṭarfā', Wādī aṭ- V	142	28.25 N	30.50 E
Ṭarfāwī, Bi'r ⊤[4], Miṣr	140	22.55 N	28.53 E
Tarfawi, Bi'r ⊤[4], Sūd.	140	21.04 N	34.08 E
Tarfaya	148	27.58 N	12.55 W
Tarfside	46	56.54 N	2.50 W
Tarf Water ≃	44	54.55 N	4.35 W
Targa	124	22.27 N	84.40 E
Targan ≃	85	43.38 N	75.58 E
Target Rock National Wildlife Refuge ◆[4]	276	40.56 N	73.26 W
Targhee Pass)(	202	44.41 N	111.17 W
Targon	32	44.44 N	0.16 W
Târgovište	38	43.15 N	26.34 E
Targuist	148	34.57 N	4.18 W
Târgu-Mureș → Tîrgu Mureș	38	46.33 N	24.33 E
Tarhjijt	148	29.05 N	9.24 W
Tarhu	102	41.09 N	107.58 E
Tarhūnah	146	32.26 N	13.38 E
Tari	164	5.50 S	143.00 E
Tarialan	86	49.47 N	91.55 E
Tariat	88	48.06 N	99.32 E
Táriba	246	7.49 N	72.13 W

≃ River	Fluß	Río	Rivière	Rio
≍ Canal	Kanal	Canal	Canal	Canal
⌞ Waterfall, Rapids	Wasserfall, Stromschnellen	Cascada, Rápidos	Chute d'eau, Rapides	Cascata, Rápidos
ʮ Strait	Meeresstraße	Estrecho	Détroit	Estreito
c Bay, Gulf	Bucht, Golf	Bahía, Golfo	Baie, Golfe	Baía, Golfo
⊜ Lake, Lakes	See, Seen	Lago, Lagos	Lac, Lacs	Lago, Lagos
≡ Swamp	Sumpf	Pantano	Marais	Pântano
⍓ Ice Features, Glacier	Eis- und Gletscherformen	Accidentes Glaciales	Formes glaciaires	Acidentes glaciares
⊤ Other Hydrographic Features	Andere Hydrographische Objekte	Otros Elementos Hidrográficos	Autres données hydrographiques	Outros acidentes hidrográficos

✥ Submarine Features	Untermeerische Objekte	Accidentes Submarinos	Formes de relief sous-marin	Acidentes submarinos
□ Political Unit	Politische Einheit	Unidad Politica	Entité politique	Unidade política
✧ Cultural Institution	Kulturelle Institution	Institución Cultural	Institution culturelle	Instituição cultural
⊥ Historical Site	Historische Stätte	Sitio Histórico	Site historique	Sitio histórico
♠ Recreational Site	Erholungs- und Ferienort	Sitio de Recreo	Centre de loisirs	Area de Lazer
⊠ Airport	Flughafen	Aeropuerto	Aéroport	Aeroporto
■ Military Installation	Militäranlage	Instalación Militar	Installation militaire	Instalação militar
◆ Miscellaneous	Verschiedenes	Misceláneo	Divers	Diversos

Tarifa 34 36.01 N 5.36 W
Tarifa, Punta de ⋗ 34 36.00 N 5.37 W
Tariffville 207 41.54 N 72.45 W
Tarija 248 21.31 S 64.45 W
Tarija □5 248 21.30 S 64.40 W
Tarikere 122 13.43 N 75.49 E
Tariki 172 39.14 S 174.15 E
Tariku ≃ 164 3.04 S 138.09 E
Tarīm 144 16.03 N 48.59 E
Tarim ≃ 90 41.05 N 86.40 E
Tarimoro 234 20.17 N 100.45 W
Tarim Pendi ⌣1 90 39.00 N 83.00 E
Taring 114 3.50 N 97.33 E
Tarīn Kowt 120 32.52 N 65.38 E
Taritatu ≃ 164 2.54 S 138.27 E
Tarituba 256 23.02 S 44.36 W
Tarjannevesi ⊜ 26 62.07 N 24.03 E
Tarka 150 14.37 N 7.55 E
Tarka ≃ 158 32.18 S 26.08 E
Tarka, Vallée de V 150 14.00 N 6.00 E
Tarkastad 158 32.00 S 26.16 E
Tarkazy 80 53.52 N 53.39 E
Tarkhūrān 128 34.41 N 50.00 E
Tarki 84 42.56 N 47.30 E
Tarkiln 207 41.57 N 71.36 W
Tarkington Bayou ≃ 222 30.10 N 94.59 W
Tarkio 194 40.26 N 95.22 W
Tarkio ≃ 198 40.10 N 95.26 W
Tarko-Sale 74 64.55 N 77.49 E
Tarkwa 150 5.19 N 1.59 W
Tarlac 116 15.29 N 120.35 E
Tarlac □4 116 15.30 N 120.25 E
Tarlac ≃ 116 15.45 N 120.27 E
Tarland 46 57.08 N 2.52 W
Tarlee 168b 34.16 S 138.46 E
Tarleton 44 53.41 N 2.50 W
T'arlevo 265a 59.42 N 30.27 E
Tarlo ≃ 170 34.28 S 150.04 E
Tarlo River National Park ♦ 170 34.31 S 149.55 E
Tarlscough 262 53.37 N 2.52 W
Tarm 26 55.55 N 8.32 E
Tarma 248 11.25 S 75.42 W
Tarmstedt 52 53.13 N 9.04 E
Tarn □5 32 43.50 N 2.00 E
Tarn ≃ 32 44.05 N 1.06 E
Tarna ≃ 30 47.31 N 19.59 E
Tärnaby 24 65.43 N 15.16 E
Tarnak ≃ 120 31.26 N 65.31 E
Tarna Mare, Rom. 38 47.29 N 26.20 E
Tarna Mare, Rom. 38 48.04 N 23.12 E
Tårnby 41 55.38 N 12.36 E
Tarneit 274b 37.52 S 144.41 E
Tarn-et-Garonne □5 32 44.05 N 1.20 E
Tarnewitz 54 53.58 N 11.14 E
Tarnobrzeg 30 50.35 N 21.41 E
Tarnobrzeg □4 30 50.45 N 21.50 E
Tarnogród 30 50.23 N 22.45 E
Tarnogskij Gorodok 24 60.29 N 43.33 E
Tarnopol — Ternopol' 78 49.34 N 25.36 E
Tarnów, Pol. 30 50.01 N 21.00 E
Tarnów, Pol. 54 52.47 N 14.58 E
Tarnów □4 30 50.00 N 21.00 E
Tarnowskie Góry 30 50.27 N 18.52 E
Tärnsjö 40 60.09 N 16.56 E
Tarn Tāran 123 31.27 N 74.55 E
Taro ≃ 36 45.00 N 10.15 E
Taron 164 4.25 S 153.05 E
Tarong 166 26.46 S 151.51 E
Taronga Zoo ♦ 274a 33.51 S 151.15 E
Taroom 166 25.39 S 149.49 E
Tarouca 34 41.00 N 7.40 W
Taroudant 148 30.31 N 8.55 W
Ta Roun, Co ∧ 110 17.17 N 106.18 E
Tarp 41 54.40 N 9.23 E
Tarpey 226 36.47 N 119.41 W
Tarpon, Lake ⊜ 220 28.07 N 82.44 W
Tarpon Springs 220 28.08 N 82.45 W
Tarporley 44 53.09 N 2.40 W
Tarqui 246 1.35 S 75.15 W
Tarquinia 66 42.15 N 11.45 E
Tarqūmiyah 132 31.35 N 35.01 E
Tarra ≃ 246 9.05 N 72.30 W
Tarrabool Lake ⊜ 162 18.15 S 135.04 E
Tarrafal, C.V. 150a 16.58 N 25.19 W
Tarrafal, C.V. 150a 15.17 N 23.46 W
Tarragona 34 41.07 N 1.15 E
Tarragona □4 34 41.00 N 0.45 E
Tarraleah 166 42.18 S 146.27 E
Tarrant □6 222 32.47 N 97.18 W
Tarrant City 194 33.34 N 86.46 W
Tarrant Hinton 42 50.53 N 2.05 W
Tarrara Creek ≃ 208 36.33 N 77.10 W
Tarras 172 44.50 S 169.25 E
Tàrrega 34 41.39 N 1.09 E
Tarri 144 0.42 N 41.38 E
Tarrs 214 40.10 N 79.35 W
Tarrtown 214 40.51 N 79.31 W
Tarryall Creek ≃ 200 39.05 N 105.19 W
Tarrytown 210 41.04 N 73.51 W
Tarrytown Reservoir ⊜1 276 41.05 N 73.51 W
Tarsus 130 36.55 N 34.53 E
Tarta 128 40.02 N 52.46 E
Tartagal, Arg. 252 22.32 S 63.49 W
Tartagal, Arg. 252 28.40 S 59.52 W
Tartaro ≃ 64 45.02 N 11.30 E
Tartas ≃ 86 55.37 N 76.44 E
Tartu 76 58.23 N 26.43 E
Ṭarṭūs 130 34.53 N 35.53 E
Ṭarṭūs □8 130 35.00 N 36.00 E
Taruaçu 256 21.37 S 42.56 W
Tarui 94 35.22 N 136.32 E
Tarum ≃ 115a 5.59 S 107.03 E
Tarumi ◆8 270 34.38 N 135.03 E
Tarumirim 255 19.16 S 41.59 W
Tarumizu 92 31.29 N 130.42 E
Tarumovka 84 44.03 N 46.33 E
Tarusa 82 54.43 N 37.11 E
Tarusa ≃ 82 54.44 N 37.11 E
Ṭārūṭ 142 30.32 N 31.28 E
Tarutao, Ko I 114 6.35 N 99.40 E
Tarutino, Ross. 82 55.07 N 36.56 E
Tarutino, Ukr. 78 46.12 N 29.09 E
Tarutung 114 2.01 N 98.58 E
Tarvagatajn nuruu ∧ 88 48.20 N 99.00 E
Tarves 46 57.22 N 2.13 W
Tarvisio 64 46.30 N 13.35 E
Tarvo ≃ 248 14.47 S 61.03 W
Tarwin ≃ 169 38.42 S 145.50 E
Tarwin, East Branch ≃ 169 38.34 S 146.00 E
Tarwin, West Branch ≃ 169 38.34 S 146.00 E
Tarza 24 62.30 N 40.25 E
Tarzan 196 32.18 N 101.58 W
Tarzana ◆8 280 34.10 N 118.32 W
Tarzo 64 45.58 N 12.14 E
Tas 80 48.27 N 51.02 E
Tas ≃ 42 52.36 N 1.18 E
Taşağıl 130 36.55 N 31.14 E
Tašanta 86 49.43 N 89.11 E
Tasaral 86 46.20 N 73.58 E
Tašauz 72 41.50 N 59.58 E
Tašauz □8 128 40.15 N 59.00 E
Tasāwah 146 25.58 N 13.30 E
Tasbuget 86 44.48 N 65.33 E
Taschkent — Taškent 85 41.20 N 69.18 E
Taşçı 130 38.13 N 35.48 E
Taşdelen 130 38.51 N 38.31 E
Tasejeva ≃ 86 58.06 N 94.01 E
Tasejevo 86 57.12 N 94.54 E
Taseko ≃ 182 52.00 N 123.40 W
Taseko Lakes ⊜ 182 51.15 N 123.35 W
Taseko Mountain ∧ 182 51.14 N 123.28 W
Tašelan 88 51.45 N 108.55 E
Tasendjanet, Oued V 148 24.36 N 1.07 E
Tāsgaon 122 17.02 N 74.36 E
Tashan, Zhg. 104 40.48 N 122.39 E
Tashan, Zhg. 104 40.51 N 120.56 E
Tashi Gang Dzong 120 27.19 N 91.34 E
Tashimalike 85 39.06 N 75.41 E
Tashiyi 100 29.43 N 112.48 E
Tashk, Daryācheh-ye ⊜ 128 29.45 N 53.30 E
Tashkent — Taškent 85 41.20 N 69.18 E
Tāshkurghān — Kholm 120 36.42 N 67.41 E
Tashuik'u 269d 25.18 N 121.30 E
Tasikmalaya 115a 7.20 S 108.12 E
Tasīl 132 32.50 N 35.58 E
Tåsinge I 41 55.00 N 10.36 E
Tašir 84 41.07 N 44.17 E
Taširovo 82 55.25 N 36.39 E
Tasitan 85 39.17 N 76.07 E
Tåsjö 26 64.13 N 15.54 E
Tåsjön ⊜ 26 64.15 N 15.47 E
Taskajevo 86 55.06 N 78.36 E
Taşkent, Tür. 130 36.55 N 32.31 E
Taškent (Tashkent), Uzb. 85 41.20 N 69.18 E
Taškent □4 85 41.00 N 69.30 E
Taškepri 128 36.18 N 62.38 E
Taşkesen 130 39.43 N 41.29 E
Taskesken 86 47.15 N 80.44 E
Taşköprü 130 41.30 N 34.14 E
Taskul 164 2.35 S 150.25 E
Taš-Kumyr 85 41.21 N 72.14 E
Taškyja 86 40.16 N 74.19 E
Tašla 80 51.47 N 52.46 E
Taşlı ≃ 267b 41.03 N 28.56 E
Tasman, Mount ∧ 172 43.34 S 170.09 E
Tasman Basin ⌣1 6 43.00 S 158.00 E
Tasman Bay c 172 41.00 S 173.20 E
Tasmania □3 166 43.00 S 147.00 E
Tasmania I 166 42.00 S 147.00 E
Tasmanien — Tasmania I 166 42.00 S 147.00 E
Tasman Mountains ∧ 172 41.07 S 172.33 E
Tasman Peninsula ⋗1 166 43.05 S 147.50 E
Tasman Sea ⊤2 14 40.00 S 163.00 E
T'asmin ≃ 78 49.05 N 32.48 E
Tăşnad 38 47.29 N 22.35 E
Tasoba 80 47.42 N 49.52 E
Taşova 130 40.46 N 36.20 E
Tasrār Sharīf 123 33.52 N 74.46 E
Taşrumi 84 38.48 N 44.04 E
Tassajara Creek ≃ 282 37.41 N 121.53 W
Tassara 150 16.48 N 5.39 E
Tassdorf 264a 52.30 N 13.47 E
Tassialouc, Lac ⊜ 176 59.03 N 74.00 W
Tassin-la-Demi-Lune 62 45.46 N 4.47 E
Tasso Lake ⊜ 212 45.27 N 78.56 W
Tassu, Serra di lu ∧ 71 41.01 N 9.08 E
Taštagol 86 52.47 N 87.53 E
Tastiota 232 28.22 N 111.23 W
Tåstrup 41 55.39 N 12.19 E
Taštyp 86 52.48 N 89.54 E
Taşucu 130 36.19 N 33.53 E
Tasutkol'skoje vodochranilišče ⊜1 85 43.22 N 74.00 E
Tata, Magreb 148 29.44 N 7.56 W
Tata, Magy. 30 47.39 N 18.18 E
Tata □4 148 29.40 N 7.45 W
Tat'a, vulkan ∧1 92a 44.21 N 146.15 E
Tataa, Pointe ⋗ 174s 17.34 S 149.37 W
Tatabánya 30 47.34 N 18.26 E
Tatahuicapan 234 18.14 N 94.45 W
Tatal 80 47.17 N 46.16 E
Tatalin ≃ 102 37.30 N 95.28 E
Tata Mailau ∧ 112 8.55 S 125.30 E
Tatamy 208 40.44 N 75.15 W
Tataouine 148 32.56 N 10.27 E
Tata Raphael, Camp ■ 273b 4.18 S 15.17 E
Tatarbunary 78 45.49 N 29.36 E
Tatarija □3 80 55.00 N 51.00 E
Tatarinka 76 55.58 N 33.54 E
Tatarino 80 50.36 N 39.07 E
Tatarinovo, Ross. 82 55.13 N 37.56 E
Tatarinovo, Ross. 82 56.34 N 38.25 E
Tatarischer Sund — Tatarskij proliv ⊔ 89 50.00 N 141.15 E
Tatarka, Bela. 76 53.16 N 28.48 E
Tatarka, Ross. 86 53.58 N 75.05 E
Tatarlar 130 41.46 N 26.55 E
Tatarovo ◆8 265b 55.46 N 37.26 E
Tātārpur ◆8 272a 28.39 N 77.07 E
Tatarsk 86 55.13 N 75.58 E
Tatarskij Kandyz 80 54.07 N 53.07 E
Tatarskij proliv (Tatar Strait) ⊔ 89 50.00 N 141.15 E
Tatarskij Sajman 80 53.18 N 47.07 E
Tatarskoje-Maklakovo 80 55.48 N 45.34 E
Tatarstan — Tatarija □3 80 55.00 N 51.00 E
Tatar Strait — Tatarskij proliv ⊔ 89 50.00 N 141.15 E
Tatau ≃ 112 3.07 N 112.49 E
Tatau Island I 164 2.50 S 152.00 E
Tataurovo, Ross. 76 58.44 N 43.20 E
Tataurovo, Ross. 82 57.48 N 40.34 E
Tataurovo, Ross. 88 51.37 N 112.56 E
Tate 192 34.25 N 84.22 W
Tate ≃ 166 17.22 S 143.44 E
Tatebayashi 94 36.15 N 139.32 E
Tate Gallery ♥ 260 51.29 N 0.08 W
Tateishi-misaki ⋗ 94 35.46 N 136.01 E
Tateiwa 94 37.05 N 139.32 E
Tateiwa-chosuichi ⊜1 96 34.33 N 135.12 E
Tateshina 94 36.18 N 138.15 E
Tateyama, Nihon 94 34.59 N 139.52 E
Tateyama, Nihon 94 36.40 N 137.19 E
Tate-yama ∧ 94 36.35 N 137.37 E
Tathlina Lake ⊜ 176 60.32 N 117.32 W
Tathlīth, Wādī V 144 20.44 N 44.17 E
Tathong Point ⋗ 271d 22.14 N 114.17 E
Tathra 166 36.44 S 149.59 E
Tatikawa — Tachikawa 94 35.42 N 139.25 E
Tatiščevo, Ross. 80 51.40 N 45.35 E
Tatiščevo, Ross. 82 56.24 N 37.31 E
Tatitlek 180 60.52 N 146.41 W
Tatla Lake 182 51.55 N 124.36 W
Tatla Lake ⊜ 182 52.00 N 124.25 W
Tatlayoko Lake 182 51.39 N 124.24 W
Tatlayoko Lake ⊜ 182 51.30 N 124.25 W
Tatlow, Mount ∧ 182 51.23 N 123.52 W
Tatnam, Cape ⋗ 176 57.16 N 91.00 W
Tatomi 94 35.36 N 138.31 E
Tatoosh Island I 224 48.24 N 124.44 W
Tatrang 120 38.28 N 85.35 E
Tatranský národní park ♦ 30 49.10 N 20.05 E
Tatrzański Park Narodowy ♦ 30 49.15 N 20.00 E
Tatsfield 260 51.18 N 0.02 E
Tatsuno, Nihon 94 35.59 N 137.59 E
Tatsuno, Nihon 96 34.52 N 134.33 E
Tatsunokuchi 94 36.27 N 136.25 E
Tatsuruhama 94 37.04 N 136.53 E
Tatsuyama 94 34.58 N 137.49 E
Tatta 120 24.45 N 67.55 E
Tattenhall 44 53.06 N 2.46 W
Tatton Hall ⊥ 262 53.20 N 2.23 W
Tatton Mere ⊜ 262 53.19 N 2.22 W
Tatton Park ♦ 262 53.19 N 2.22 W
Tatty 85 43.12 N 73.19 E
Tatu ≃ 100 24.12 N 120.29 E
Tatupé ◆8 287b 23.32 S 46.34 W
Tatuk Lake ⊜ 182 53.32 N 124.15 W
Tatum, N.M., U.S. 196 33.15 N 103.19 W
Tatum, Tx., U.S. 222 32.19 N 94.31 W
Tat'ung — Datong 102 40.05 N 113.18 E
Tat'un Shan ∧ 269d 25.11 N 121.31 E
Tatvan 130 38.30 N 42.16 E
Tatzuli ≃ 100 24.08 N 121.39 E
Tau, Am. Sam. 174y 14.14 S 169.32 W
Tau, Kaz. 80 49.40 N 47.17 E
Tau, Nor. 26 59.04 N 5.54 E
Tau I 174y 14.15 S 169.30 W
Tauá 250 6.01 S 40.26 W
Taualap Pass ⊔ 175c 7.28 N 151.36 E
Taubaté 256 23.02 S 45.33 W
Tauber ≃ 56 49.46 N 9.31 E
Tauberbischofsheim 56 49.37 N 9.40 E
Taucha 54 51.23 N 12.30 E
Taučik 72 44.21 N 51.19 E
Tauern-Tunnel ◆5 64 47.05 N 13.05 E
Täuffelen 58 47.04 N 7.12 E
Taufkirchen 60 48.21 N 12.08 E
Taufstein ∧ 56 50.31 N 9.14 E
Taughannock Creek ≃ 210 42.33 N 76.36 W
Taughannock Falls State Park ♦ 210 42.32 N 76.35 W
Tauini ≃ 246 0.30 N 58.22 W
Taujskaja guba c 74 59.20 N 150.20 E
Taukum ◆2 86 44.50 N 75.30 E
Taulabé 236 14.38 N 87.58 W
Taulihawā 124 27.32 N 83.03 E
Taulov 41 55.33 N 9.37 E
Taumarunui 172 38.52 S 175.17 E
Taum Sauk Mountain ∧ 194 37.34 N 90.44 W
Taunay 248 20.18 S 56.05 W
Taunay, Cascatinha ⊔ 287a 22.57 S 43.17 W
Taung 158 27.33 S 24.47 E
Taungbon 110 15.25 N 97.50 E
Taungdwingyi 110 20.01 N 95.33 E
Taunggon 110 23.38 N 96.32 E
Taunggyi 110 20.47 N 97.02 E
Taungnyo Range ∧ 110 15.38 N 97.56 E
Taungup 110 18.51 N 94.14 E
Taungup Pass ⊔ 110 18.40 N 94.45 E
Taunsa 123 30.42 N 70.39 E
Taunsa Barrage ◆6 123 30.31 N 70.51 E
Taunton, Eng., U.K. 42 51.01 N 3.06 W
Taunton, Ma., U.S. 207 41.54 N 71.05 W
Taunton, N.Y., U.S. 210 43.01 N 76.13 W
Taunton ≃ 207 41.42 N 71.10 W
Taunton, Vale of V 42 51.02 N 3.08 W
Taunton Lake ⊜ 285 39.51 N 74.51 W
Taunton Lakes 285 39.51 N 74.51 W
Taunus ∧ 56 50.10 N 8.15 E
Taunusstein 56 50.08 N 8.08 E
Taupiri 172 37.37 S 175.11 E
Taupitz 61 47.33 N 14.00 E
Taupo 172 38.41 S 176.05 E
Taupo, Lake ⊜ 172 38.49 S 175.55 E
Tauragė 76 55.15 N 22.17 E
Taurak 86 51.35 N 85.01 E
Tauranga 172 37.42 S 176.10 E
Taurasi 68 41.00 N 14.57 E
Taureau, Réservoir ⊜1 206 46.46 N 73.50 W
Tauri ≃ 164 8.08 S 146.06 E
Taurianova 68 38.21 N 16.01 E
Tauripampa 248 12.35 S 76.07 W
Taurisano 68 39.57 N 18.13 E
Taurisma 248 15.10 S 72.51 W
Tauroa Point ⋗ 172 35.10 S 173.04 E
Taurovo 86 59.36 N 73.18 E
Taurus Mountains — Toros Dağları ∧ 130 37.00 N 33.00 E
Tauste 34 41.55 N 1.15 W
Tautira 174s 17.44 S 149.09 W
Tauxigny 50 47.13 N 0.50 E
Tauz 84 41.00 N 45.38 E
Tavaí 252 26.07 S 55.32 W
Tavajvaam ≃ 180 64.56 N 177.30 E
Tavajza 89 45.12 N 136.44 E
Tavālesh, Kūhhā-ye — Talish Mountains ∧ 128 38.42 N 48.18 E
Tavanasa 58 46.45 N 9.04 E
Tavannes 58 47.13 N 7.12 E
Tavant 50 47.07 N 0.23 E
Tavares, Bra. 250 7.38 S 37.54 W
Tavares, Fl., U.S. 220 28.48 N 81.43 W
Tavares, Ilha dos I 287a 22.49 S 43.06 W
Tavarnelle Val di Pesa 66 43.33 N 11.10 E
Tavas 130 37.34 N 29.04 E
Tavastehus — Hämeenlinna 26 61.00 N 24.27 E
Tavaux 58 47.02 N 5.24 E
Tavda 86 58.03 N 65.15 E
Tavda ≃ 86 57.47 N 67.18 E
Tave ≃ 62 44.07 N 4.42 E
Tavera ≃ 64 46.29 N 11.21 E
Taverham 42 52.41 N 1.12 E
Taverna 68 39.01 N 16.35 E
Tavern Creek ≃ 194 38.19 N 92.18 W
Tavernelle, It. 64 44.18 N 10.04 E
Tavernelle, It. 66 43.00 N 12.09 E
Tavernes 62 43.36 N 6.01 E
Tavernes de Valldigna 34 39.04 N 0.16 W
Tavernier 220 25.00 N 80.30 W
Tavernole sul Mella 64 45.45 N 10.14 E
Taverny 50 49.02 N 2.13 E
Taveta, Kenya 154 3.24 S 37.41 E
Taveta, Tan. 154 9.01 S 35.37 E
Taveuni I 175g 16.51 S 179.58 W
Taviano 68 39.59 N 18.05 E
Tavil'dara 85 38.43 N 70.28 E
Tavira 34 37.07 N 7.39 W
Tavistock, On., Can. 212 43.19 N 80.50 W
Tavistock, Eng., U.K. 42 50.33 N 4.08 W
Tavn-Gašun 80 46.01 N 45.55 E
Tavolara, Isola I 71 40.54 N 9.42 E
Tavoliere ◆1 68 41.35 N 15.25 E
Tavolžan 86 52.44 N 77.27 E
Tavor, Har (Mount Tabor) ∧ 132 32.41 N 35.23 E
Távora ≃ 34 41.09 N 7.35 W
Tavoy — Dawei 110 14.05 N 98.12 E
Tavoy Point ⋗ 110 13.32 N 98.10 E
Tavričanka 89 43.22 N 131.52 E
Tavričeskoje 86 54.35 N 73.38 E
Tavry 265a 59.55 N 30.42 E
Tavşanlı 130 39.33 N 29.30 E
Tavsalayihüseynan 130 38.38 N 40.32 E
Tavua 175g 17.27 S 177.51 E
Tavy ≃ 42 50.16 N 4.10 W
Taw ≃ 42 51.04 N 4.11 W
Tawa ≃ 124 22.48 N 77.48 E
Tawaeli 112 0.43 S 119.51 E
Tawakoni, Lake ⊜1 222 32.55 N 96.00 W
Tawara 270 34.27 N 135.57 E
Tawarada 268 35.19 N 140.04 E
Tawaramoto 96 34.33 N 135.48 E
Tawas City 190 44.16 N 83.30 W
Tawau 112 4.15 N 117.54 E
Tawd ≃ 262 53.33 N 2.51 W
Tāwī ≃ 123 32.40 N 74.41 E
Tawīlah, Juzur II 140 27.35 N 33.46 E
Tawi-Tawi □4 116 5.20 N 120.00 E
Tawi-Tawi Group II 116 5.10 N 120.15 E
Tawi-Tawi Island I 116 5.10 N 120.00 E
Tawkar 140 18.26 N 37.44 E
Tawu 100 22.22 N 120.54 E
Tāwūq 128 35.08 N 44.27 E
Tāwurghā' 146 32.00 N 15.08 E
Tawwah Banī Ibrāhīm 142 28.05 N 30.41 E
Taxco de Alarcón 234 18.33 N 99.36 W
Taxenbach 64 47.17 N 12.58 E
Taxi 89 49.26 N 126.08 E
Taxila 123 33.44 N 72.50 E
Taxisco 236 14.04 N 90.28 W
Taxkorgan Tajik Zizhixian 120 37.49 N 75.14 E
Taxusi 102 32.58 N 98.10 E
Tay ≃, On., Can. 212 44.53 N 76.07 W
Tay ≃, Yk., Can. 180 62.34 N 134.22 W
Tay ≃, Scot., U.K. 46 56.22 N 3.21 W
Tay, Firth of c1 46 56.26 N 3.00 W
Tay, Lake ⊜ 162 32.55 S 120.48 E
Tay, Loch ⊜ 46 56.31 N 4.10 W
Tayabamba 248 8.17 S 77.18 W
Tayabas 116 14.01 N 121.35 E
Tayabas Bay c 116 13.45 N 121.45 E
Tayan 112 0.02 S 110.07 E
Tayandu, Kepulauan II 164 5.30 S 132.15 E
Tayayi 105 39.25 N 115.03 E
Tayeegle 144 4.02 N 44.31 E
Taylor, B.C., Can. 182 56.10 N 120.41 W
Taylor, Az., U.S. 200 34.27 N 110.05 W
Taylor, Ar., U.S. 194 33.06 N 93.27 W
Taylor, Mi., U.S. 216 42.14 N 83.16 W
Taylor, Mo., U.S. 219 39.56 N 91.32 W
Taylor, Ne., U.S. 198 41.46 N 99.22 W
Taylor, Pa., U.S. 210 41.23 N 75.42 W
Taylor, Tx., U.S. 222 30.34 N 97.24 W
Taylor ≃ 200 38.40 N 106.51 W
Taylor, Mount ∧, N.Z. 172 43.30 S 171.19 E
Taylor, Mount ∧, N.M., U.S. 200 35.14 N 107.37 W
Taylor Creek ≃, On., Can. 275b 43.42 N 79.20 W
Taylor Creek ≃, Il., U.S. 219 39.13 N 90.18 W
Taylor Lake Village 222 29.36 N 95.03 W
Taylor Mountain ∧ 202 44.53 N 114.13 W
Taylor Mountains ∧ 180 60.50 N 157.20 W
Taylor Run ≃ 285 39.57 N 75.39 W
Taylors 192 34.55 N 82.17 W
Taylors Bush Park ♦ 275b 43.42 N 79.19 W
Taylors Island 208 38.28 N 76.17 W
Taylor Springs 219 39.08 N 89.30 W
Taylors Run ≃ 279b 40.11 N 79.57 W
Taylorstown 214 40.10 N 80.23 W
Taylorsville, In., U.S. 218 39.17 N 85.57 W
Taylorsville, Ky., U.S. 194 38.01 N 85.20 W
Taylorsville, Ms., U.S. 194 31.49 N 89.25 W
Taylorsville, N.C., U.S. 192 35.55 N 81.10 W
Taylorsville Dam ◆6 218 39.53 N 84.10 W
Taylortown, N.J., U.S. 276 40.56 N 74.24 W
Taylortown, Oh., U.S. 214 40.28 N 80.40 W
Taylortown Reservoir ⊜1 276 40.58 N 74.22 W
Taylorville 219 39.32 N 89.17 W
Taylorville, Lake ⊜1 219 39.30 N 89.15 W
Taymā' 128 27.38 N 38.29 E
Taymouth 186 46.11 N 66.37 W
Taymyr Peninsula — Tajmyr, poluostrov ⋗1 74 76.00 N 104.00 E
Tay Ninh 110 11.18 N 106.06 E
Taynuilt 46 56.25 N 5.14 W
Tayoltita 232 24.05 N 105.56 W
Tayport 46 56.27 N 2.53 W
Táyros 267c 37.58 N 23.42 E
Tayside □4 46 56.30 N 3.30 W
Taytay, Pil. 116 10.49 N 119.31 E
Taytay, Pil. 116 14.34 N 121.08 E
Taytay Bay c 116 10.45 N 119.30 E
Tayu 115a 6.32 S 111.02 E
Tayüan, T'aiwan 100 25.04 N 121.11 E
Tayuan, Zhg. 89 51.27 N 124.16 E
Tayyārah 140 13.12 N 30.47 E
Ṭayyebāt 128 34.44 N 60.45 E
Taz ≃ 72 67.32 N 78.40 E
Taza 148 34.16 N 4.01 W
Taza □4 148 34.05 N 3.45 W
Tazawa-ko ⊜ 92 39.43 N 140.40 E
Tazenakht 148 30.35 N 7.12 W
Tazewell, Tn., U.S. 192 36.27 N 83.34 W
Tazewell, Va., U.S. 192 37.06 N 81.31 W
Tazhuang 105 39.55 N 117.13 E
Tazicheng 89 46.35 N 123.06 E
Tazigou ≃ 104 41.44 N 121.30 E
Tazin ≃ 176 60.26 N 110.45 W
Tazin Lake ⊜ 176 59.47 N 109.03 W
T'ažinskij 86 56.07 N 88.31 E
Tāzirbū ⚲4 146 25.45 N 21.00 E
Tazishan 107 29.28 N 104.14 E
Tazlina 180 62.04 N 145.25 W
Tazlina Lake ⊜ 180 61.50 N 146.30 W
Tazoult-Lambese 34 35.29 N 6.15 E
Tazovskaja guba c 74 69.05 N 76.00 E
Tazovskij 74 67.28 N 78.42 E
Tazovskij poluostrov ⋗1 72 68.35 N 76.00 E
Tazrouk 148 23.25 N 6.16 E
Tazumal ⊥ 236 13.59 N 89.41 W
Tāzumuddin 126 22.29 N 90.53 E
Tazungdām 102 28.02 N 97.35 E
Tbessa 148 35.28 N 8.09 E
Tbessa □5 148 35.10 N 8.00 E
Tbilisi 84 41.43 N 44.49 E
Tbilisskaja 78 45.23 N 40.12 E
Tchad, Lac (Lake Chad) ⊜ 146 13.20 N 14.00 E
Tchad — Chad □1 146 15.00 N 19.00 E
Tchaguine Golo 146 10.03 N 16.19 E
Tchamba 150 9.02 N 1.25 E
Tch'ang-Cha — Changsha 100 28.12 N 112.58 E
Tchaourou 150 8.53 N 2.36 E
Tchefuncta ≃ 194 30.22 N 90.10 W
Tchékapika 152 1.17 S 16.11 E
Tcheljabinsk — Čel'abinsk 86 55.10 N 61.24 E
Tcheng-Tcheou — Zhengzhou 102 34.48 N 113.39 E
Tchentlo Lake ⊜ 182 55.11 N 125.00 W
Tchériba 150 12.16 N 3.05 W
Tchesinkut Lake ⊜ 182 54.05 N 125.40 W
Tchetti 150 7.50 N 1.40 E
Tchibanga 152 2.51 S 11.02 E
Tchigaï, Plateau du ⋆1 146 21.30 N 14.50 E
Tchikala-Tcholohanga 152 12.38 S 16.03 E
Tchin-Tabáradene 150 15.58 N 5.50 E
Tchitondi 152 4.33 S 12.08 E
Tchollirè 146 8.24 N 14.10 E
Tchong-K'ing — Chongqing 107 29.34 N 106.35 E
Tchořovice 54 49.27 N 13.48 E
Tchula 194 33.10 N 90.13 W
T.C. Steele State Memorial ⊥ 218 39.08 N 86.20 W
Tczew 30 54.06 N 18.48 E
Té ≃ 110 12.27 N 106.02 E
Te, Kinh ≃ 269c 10.45 N 106.42 E
Teá ≃ 246 0.30 S 65.09 W
Teaca 38 46.55 N 24.31 E
Teacapan 234 22.33 N 105.45 W
Tea Creek ≃ 284a 43.02 N 79.06 W
Teaehoa, Pointe ⋗ 174x 9.51 S 139.01 W
Teague 222 31.37 N 96.17 W
Teahupoo 174s 17.51 S 149.13 W
Te Anau 172 45.25 S 167.43 E
Te Anau, Lake ⊜ 172 45.12 S 167.48 E
Teanaway ≃ 224 47.10 N 120.50 W
Teanaway, Middle Fork ≃ 224 47.15 N 120.53 W
Teanaway, North Fork ≃ 224 47.22 N 120.53 W
Teaneck 276 40.53 N 74.00 W
Teangue 46 57.07 N 5.50 W
Teano 68 41.15 N 14.04 E
Teapa 234 17.33 N 92.57 W
Teapa ≃ 234 17.58 N 92.54 W
Te Araroa 172 37.38 S 178.22 E
Tearinibai 174t 1.35 N 172.58 E
Te Aroha 172 37.33 S 175.43 E
Teaticket 207 41.33 N 70.35 W
Tea Tree 162 22.11 S 133.17 E
Tea Tree Gully 168b 34.49 S 138.44 E
Te Atukura ∧ 174k 21.14 S 159.45 W
Te Awamutu 172 38.01 S 175.19 E
Teba, Esp. 34 36.58 N 4.56 W
Teba, Indon. 164 1.29 S 137.54 E
Tebakang 112 1.06 N 110.30 E
Tebas 256 21.35 S 42.44 W
Tebay 44 54.26 N 2.35 W
Tebbetts 219 38.37 N 91.57 W
Teberda 84 43.28 N 41.45 E
Teberdinskij zapovednik ♦ 84 43.20 N 41.45 E
Tebicuary ≃ 252 26.36 S 58.16 W
Tebicuary-Mí ≃ 252 26.26 S 56.51 W
Tebingbulan 112 3.03 S 103.44 E
Tebingtinggi, Indon. 112 0.36 N 101.36 E
Tebingtinggi, Indon. 112 3.36 S 103.05 E
Tebingtinggi, Indon. 114 3.20 N 99.09 E
Tebingtinggi, Pulau I 114 0.54 N 102.45 E
Tébourba 36 36.49 N 9.51 E
Téboursouk 148 36.28 N 9.15 E
Téboursouk, Monts de ∧ 36 36.30 N 9.10 E
Tebra ≃ 76 56.51 N 21.12 E
Tebstrup 41 55.59 N 9.53 E
Tebulosmta, gora ∧ 84 42.33 N 45.19 E
Tebza ≃ 80 58.23 N 41.19 E
Tecalitlán 234 19.26 N 103.15 W
Tecamachalco 234 18.53 N 97.44 W
Tecate 232 32.34 N 116.38 W
Tech ≃ 32 42.36 N 3.03 E
Teche, Bayou ≃ 194 29.43 N 91.13 W
Techendorf 64 46.43 N 13.17 E
Techiman 150 7.35 N 1.56 W
Techimentia 150 7.11 N 2.02 W
Techirghiol 38 44.03 N 28.36 E
Techlé 148 21.35 N 14.58 W
Techou — Dezhou 98 37.27 N 116.18 E
Techtin 76 53.51 N 29.44 E
Tecka 254 43.29 S 70.48 W
Tecka ≃ 254 42.37 S 70.25 W
Tecklenburg 52 52.13 N 7.48 E
Teckomatorp 41 55.52 N 13.05 E
Tecolote Creek ≃ 200 35.22 N 105.15 W
Tecolotlán 234 20.13 N 104.03 W
Tecolutla 234 20.29 N 97.00 W
Tecomán 234 18.55 N 103.53 W
Tecomate, Laguna c 234 16.35 N 99.25 W
Tecominoacán 234 17.53 N 93.37 W
Tecopa 204 35.50 N 116.13 W
Tecozautla 234 20.32 N 99.38 W
Tecpan ≃ 234 17.25 N 100.40 W
Tecpán de Galeana 234 17.15 N 100.41 W
Tecpán Guatemala 236 14.46 N 91.00 W
Tecpatan 234 17.08 N 93.18 W
Tecuala 234 22.23 N 105.27 W
Tecuamburro, Volcán ∧1 236 14.09 N 90.24 W
Tecuautzi, Cerro ∧ 286a 19.19 N 99.00 W
Tecuci 38 45.50 N 27.26 E
Tecumseh, On., Can. 214 42.19 N 82.54 W
Tecumseh, Mi., U.S. 216 42.00 N 83.56 W
Tecumseh, Ne., U.S. 198 40.22 N 96.11 W
Tecumseh, Ok., U.S. 196 35.15 N 96.56 W
Ted Ceidaar Dabole 144 4.24 N 43.55 E
Teddington ◆8 260 51.25 N 0.20 W
Tédji 146 11.46 N 21.19 E
Tedori ≃ 94 36.29 N 136.28 E
Tedrow 216 41.37 N 84.13 W
Tedžen 128 37.23 N 60.31 E
Tedžen (Harīrūd) ≃ 128 37.24 N 60.38 E
Tedženstroj 128 36.55 N 60.53 E
Teec Nos Pos 200 36.56 N 109.42 W
Teeli 86 51.07 N 90.14 E
Teels Marsh ≡ 204 38.12 N 118.21 W
Teen ⊜ 40 59.07 N 14.40 E
Teerijärvi — Terjärv 26 63.32 N 23.30 E
Tees ≃ 44 54.34 N 1.16 W
Tees Bay c 44 54.39 N 1.07 W
Teesdale V 44 54.38 N 2.07 W
Tees-Side Airport ✈ 44 54.31 N 1.25 W
Teesside — Middlesbrough 44 54.35 N 1.14 W
Teeswater 212 44.00 N 81.17 W
Teeswater ≃ 212 44.18 N 81.17 W
Tefé 250 3.22 S 64.42 W
Tefé ≃ 242 3.35 S 64.47 W
Tefé, Lago ⊜ 246 3.27 S 64.47 W
Tefenni 130 37.18 N 29.47 E
Tefft 216 41.12 N 86.58 W
Tefle 150 5.59 N 0.35 E
Tegal 115a 6.52 S 109.08 E
Tegalombo 115a 8.04 S 111.17 E
Tégama ⋆1 150 15.50 N 8.12 E
Tega-numa ⊜ 268 35.51 N 140.04 E
Tegel ◆8 264a 52.35 N 13.17 E
Tegel, Berliner Forst ◆3 264a 52.37 N 13.16 E
Tegelen 52 51.21 N 6.09 E
Tegeler See ⊜ 264a 52.35 N 13.15 E
Tegernsee 64 47.43 N 11.45 E
Tegernsee ⊜ 64 47.42 N 11.45 E
Teggiano 68 40.23 N 15.32 E
Teghra 124 25.29 N 85.57 E
Tegid, Llyn ⊜ 42 52.53 N 3.36 W
Tegina 150 10.05 N 6.14 E
Tegineneng 112 5.12 S 105.10 E
Tegistyk 85 44.02 N 68.22 E
Teglio 64 46.10 N 10.04 E
Tégua I 175f 13.15 S 166.37 E
Teguaida 254 41.02 S 73.26 W
Tegucigalpa 236 14.06 N 87.13 W
Tegul'det 86 57.19 N 88.10 E
Tehachapi 228 35.07 N 118.26 W
Tehachapi Creek ≃ 228 35.17 N 118.38 W
Tehachapi Mountains ∧ 228 35.00 N 118.40 W
Tehachapi Pass ⊔ 228 35.06 N 118.18 W
Tehamiyam 140 18.20 N 36.32 E
Te Hapua 172 34.31 S 172.54 E
Tehar ◆8 272a 28.38 N 77.07 E
Te Haroto 172 39.08 S 176.36 E
Tehata 126 23.43 N 88.32 E
Tehek Lake ⊜ 176 64.55 N 95.38 W
Teheran — Tehrān 128 35.40 N 51.26 E
Téhini 150 9.36 N 3.40 W
Tehoohaivei, Cap ⋗ 174x 9.49 S 138.54 W
Te Hope O Te Keho, Cap ⋗ 174x 10.02 S 139.06 W
Tehoru 164 3.23 S 129.30 E
Tehrān, Īrān 128 35.40 N 51.26 E
Tehrān, Īrān 267d 35.40 N 51.26 E
Tehrān □4 128 35.30 N 51.30 E
Tehrān, University of ♥2 267d 35.42 N 51.24 E
Tehran International Airport ✈ 267d 35.41 N 51.19 E
Tehrān Pārs ◆8 267d 35.44 N 51.32 E
Tehrathum 124 27.07 N 87.32 E
Tehri 124 30.23 N 78.29 E
Tehuacán 234 18.27 N 97.23 W
Tehuacana 222 31.44 N 96.33 W
Tehuacana Creek ≃, Tx., U.S. 222 31.31 N 97.02 W
Tehuacana Creek ≃, Tx., U.S. 222 31.50 N 95.59 W
Tehuantepec 234 16.20 N 95.14 W
Tehuantepec ≃ 234 16.10 N 95.07 W
Tehuantepec, Golfo de c 234 16.00 N 94.50 W
Tehuantepec, Istmo de ⋆3 234 17.00 N 95.00 W
Tehuantepec Ridge ⌣3 16 13.30 N 98.00 W
Tehuelches 254 46.56 S 67.27 W
Tehuipango 234 18.31 N 97.04 W
Tehuitzingo 234 18.21 N 98.17 W
Teiá 266d 41.30 N 2.19 E
Teichl ≃ 61 47.46 N 14.10 E
Teichröda 54 50.45 N 11.18 E
Teichwolframsdorf 54 50.43 N 12.14 E
Teide, Parque Nacional del ♦ 148 28.15 N 16.30 W
Teide, Pico de ∧ 148 28.16 N 16.38 W
Teifi ≃ 42 52.07 N 4.42 W
Teifiside ◆1 42 52.02 N 4.22 W
Teiga Plateau ⋆1 140 15.38 N 25.40 E
Teign ≃ 42 50.33 N 3.29 W
Teignmouth 42 50.33 N 3.30 W
Teise ≃ 260 51.13 N 0.25 E
Teisendorf 64 47.51 N 12.49 E
Teisnach 60 49.02 N 13.00 E
Teith ≃ 46 56.08 N 3.59 W
Teixeira 250 7.13 S 37.15 W
Teixeira Pinto 150 12.10 N 13.55 W
Teixeira Soares 252 25.22 S 50.27 W
Tejakula 115b 8.08 S 115.20 E
Tejamén 232 24.48 N 105.07 W
Tejkovo 80 56.52 N 40.34 E
Tejon Creek ≃ 228 35.08 N 118.53 W
Tejon Pass ⊔ 228 34.48 N 118.52 W
Tejo — Tagus ≃ 34 38.40 N 9.24 W
Tejupan, Punta ⋗ 234 18.20 N 103.32 W
Tejupilco de Hidalgo 234 18.54 N 100.09 W
Te Kaha 172 37.44 S 177.41 E
Tekai ≃ 114 4.14 N 102.23 E
Tékakwitha, Île I 275a 45.25 N 73.42 W
Tekam ≃ 114 3.52 N 102.27 E
Tekamah 198 41.46 N 96.13 W
Te Kao 172 34.39 S 172.57 E
Tekapo, Lake ⊜ 172 43.53 S 170.31 E
Te Karaka 172 38.28 S 177.52 E
Tekāri 124 24.56 N 84.50 E
Te Kauwhata 172 37.24 S 175.09 E
Tekax 232 20.12 N 89.17 W
Teke 130 41.04 N 29.39 E
Teke, ozero ⊜ 86 53.48 N 73.00 E
Teke Burnu ⋗ 130 38.05 N 26.36 E
Tekeli 86 44.48 N 78.57 E
Tekeli Dağı ∧ 130 40.09 N 37.28 E
Tekes 86 43.10 N 81.43 E
Tekes ≃ 86 43.36 N 82.32 E
Tekeze (Satīt) ≃ 140 14.20 N 35.50 E
Tekirdağ 130 40.59 N 27.31 E
Tekirdağ □4 130 41.00 N 27.30 E
Tekkali 122 18.37 N 84.14 E
Tekke 130 40.43 N 36.12 E
Tekke Burnu ⋗ 130 40.02 N 26.10 E
Tekkiraz 130 40.59 N 37.08 E
Tekman 130 39.38 N 41.31 E
Tekoa 202 47.13 N 117.04 W
Tekong, Pulau I 271c 1.24 N 104.03 E
Tekong Kechil, Pulau I 271c 1.25 N 104.01 E
Tekonsha 216 42.05 N 84.59 W
Te Kopuru 172 36.02 S 173.56 E
Tekouiat, Oued V 148 22.25 N 2.35 E
Tékro ⚲4 146 19.30 N 20.58 E
Tekstil'ščiki 82 55.57 N 37.49 E
Tekstil'ščiki ◆8 265b 55.42 N 37.44 E
Teku 112 0.46 S 123.26 E
Te Kuiti 172 38.20 S 175.10 E
Tekukor, Pulau I 271c 1.14 N 103.50 E
Tel ≃ 122 20.50 N 83.54 E
Tela, Hond. 236 15.44 N 87.27 W
Tela, India 272a 28.44 N 77.20 E
Tela, Bahía de c 236 15.48 N 87.30 W
Telaga 116 6.51 N 117.03 E
Telaga, Teluk c 114 2.10 N 98.00 E
Telaga-kulon 115a 6.58 S 108.18 E
Télagh 148 34.47 N 0.34 W
Telaopengsha Shan ∧ 120 30.33 N 86.25 E
Tel Ashqelon ⊥ 132 31.39 N 34.32 E
Telavåg 26 60.16 N 4.49 E
Telavi 84 41.55 N 45.28 E
Tel Aviv □5 132 32.05 N 34.48 E
Tel Aviv-Yafo 132 32.03 N 34.46 E
Telč 30 49.11 N 15.27 E
Tel'čje 76 53.21 N 36.20 E
Telde 148 28.00 N 15.25 W
Tele ≃, Afr. 158 30.26 S 27.33 E
Tele ≃, Zaïre 152 2.48 N 23.54 E
Telechany 76 52.31 N 25.51 E
Teleckoje, ozero ⊜ 86 51.35 N 87.40 E
Telefomin 164 5.10 S 141.35 E
Telegapulang 112 2.55 S 112.25 E
Telegino 80 52.55 N 44.34 E
Telegrafo, Pizzo ∧ 70 37.37 N 13.10 E
Telegraph Canyon V 280 33.55 N 117.45 W
Telegraph Cove 182 50.33 N 126.50 W
Telegraph Creek 180 57.55 N 131.10 W
Telêmaco Borba 252 24.20 S 50.40 W
Telemark □6 26 59.30 N 8.40 E
Telemba 88 52.43 N 113.16 E
Telembí ≃ 246 1.50 N 78.16 W
Telén 252 36.16 S 65.30 W
Telen ≃ 112 0.26 S 116.42 E
Teleneşty 78 47.30 N 28.22 E
Teleno ∧ 34 42.21 N 6.23 W
Teleorman □6 38 44.00 N 25.15 E
Teleorman ≃ 38 43.52 N 25.26 E
Téléphone, Île du I 273b 4.20 S 15.12 E
Telerig 38 43.51 N 27.40 E
Telertheba, Djebel ∧ 148 24.10 N 6.51 E
Telescope Peak ∧ 204 36.10 N 117.05 W
Telescope Point ⋗ 241k 12.08 N 61.36 W
Telese 68 41.13 N 14.32 E
Telesterion ⊥ 267c 38.02 N 23.32 E
Telferner 222 28.51 N 96.53 W
Telfes 64 47.10 N 11.22 E
Telford, Eng., U.K. 42 52.40 N 2.28 W
Telford, Pa., U.S. 208 40.19 N 75.19 W
Telfs 64 47.18 N 11.04 E
Telgte 52 51.59 N 7.47 E
Telica ≃ 236 14.43 N 86.08 W
Telica, Volcán ∧1 236 12.36 N 86.50 W
Telida 180 63.23 N 153.16 W
Télimélé 150 10.54 N 13.02 W
Telixtlahuaca 234 17.18 N 96.54 W
Telizi 265a 59.42 N 29.59 E
Teljo, Jabal ∧ 140 14.42 N 25.56 E
Telkwa 182 54.42 N 127.03 W
Telkwa ≃ 182 54.41 N 127.02 W
Tel Lakhish ⊥ 132 31.34 N 34.51 E
Tellaro ≃ 70 36.50 N 15.06 E
Tell City 194 37.57 N 86.46 W
Teller 180 65.16 N 166.22 W
Tellicherry 122 11.45 N 75.32 E
Tellico ≃ 192 35.36 N 84.13 W
Tellico Plains 192 35.21 N 84.17 W
Tellier 254 47.39 S 66.03 W
Tellier, Lac ⊜ 206 46.23 N 74.00 W
Tello 246 3.04 N 75.08 W
Telluride 200 37.56 N 107.48 W
Tel'ma 88 52.43 N 103.41 E
Tel'mana 83 48.30 N 39.18 E
Tel'manovo 83 47.24 N 38.02 E
Tel Megiddo (Armageddon) ⊥ 132 32.35 N 35.11 E
Telmen 88 48.38 N 97.37 E
Telmen nuur ⊜ 88 48.50 N 97.18 E
Tel Mond 132 32.15 N 34.56 E
Tel'novskij 89 49.22 N 142.05 E
Telo 110 0.03 N 98.16 E
Teloekbetoeng — Tanjungkarang-Telukbetung 115a 5.27 S 105.16 E
Telogia Creek ≃ 192 30.16 N 84.44 W
Telok Anson 114 4.02 N 101.01 E
Telok Datok 114 2.49 N 101.31 E
Teloloapan 234 18.21 N 99.51 W
Telpaneca 236 13.32 N 86.17 W
Telsen 254 42.24 S 66.57 W
Telsen, Arroyo ≃ 254 42.23 S 66.34 W
Telšiai 76 55.59 N 22.15 E

Symbols in the index entries represent the broad categories identified in the key at the right. Symbols with superior numbers (∧1) identify subcategories (see complete key on page I · 1).

Symbole im Register stellen die rechts im Schlüssel erklärten Kategorien dar. Symbole mit hochgestellten Ziffern (∧1) bezeichnen Unterabteilungen einer Kategorie (vgl. vollständiger Schlüssel auf Seite I · 1).

Los símbolos incluídos en el texto del índice representan las grandes categorías identificadas con la clave a la derecha. Los símbolos con numeros en su parte superior (∧1) identifican las subcategorías (véase la clave completa en la página I · 1).

Les symboles de l'index représentent les catégories indiquées dans la légende à droite. Les symboles suivis d'un indice (∧1) représentent des sous-catégories (voir légende complète à la page I · 1).

Os símbolos incluídos no texto do índice representam as grandes categorias identificadas com a chave à direita. Os símbolos com números em sua parte superior (∧1) identificam as subcategorias (veja-se a chave completa à página I · 1).

∧ Mountain	Berg	Montaña	Montagne	Montanha
∧ Mountains	Gebirge	Montañas	Montagnes	Montanhas
⊔ Pass	Paß	Paso	Col	Passo
V Valley, Canyon	Tal, Cañon	Valle, Cañón	Vallée, Canyon	Vale, Canhão
≡ Plain	Ebene	Llano	Plaine	Planície
⋗ Cape	Kap	Cabo	Cap	Cabo
I Island	Insel	Isla	Île	Ilha
II Islands	Inseln	Islas	Îles	Ilhas
⊥ Other Topographic Features	Andere Topographische Objekte	Otros Elementos Topográficos	Autres données topographiques	Outros acidentes topográficos

ESPAÑOL — Nombre | Página | Lat.°′ | Long.°′ W = Oeste

FRANÇAIS — Nom | Page | Lat.°′ | Long.°′ W = Ouest

PORTUGUÊS — Nome | Página | Lat.°′ | Long.°′ W = Oeste

Nombre / Nom / Nome	Página / Page	Lat.°′	Long.°′
Telti	71	40.52 N	9.21 E
Teltow	54	52.23 N	13.16 E
Teltow ◆[1]	264a	52.18 N	13.25 E
Teltower Hochfläche ⋏[1]	264a	52.22 N	13.20 E
Teltowkanal ≋	264a	52.26 N	13.35 E
Telukbatang	112	1.00 S	109.46 E
Telukbayur, Indon.	112	2.09 N	117.24 E
Telukbayur, Indon.	112	1.00 S	100.22 E
Telukbrombang	114	2.03 N	100.52 E
Telukbutun	112	4.13 N	108.12 E
Telukdalem	114	0.34 N	97.49 E
Teluklanjut	112	0.09 N	103.29 E
Teluklecak	114	1.51 N	101.44 E
Telukmerbau	114	2.04 N	100.38 E
Telukpambang	114	1.28 N	102.28 E
Teluk Punggur, Ujung ≻	112	3.53 S	102.17 E
Telumengtang Shan ∧	120	30.33 N	86.27 E
Teluša	76	53.03 N	29.31 E
Tem'	88	55.21 N	100.44 E
Tema	150	5.38 N	0.01 E
Temae	174s	17.29 S	149.46 W
Temagami, Lake ⊜	190	47.00 N	80.05 W
Temaju, Pulau I	112	0.29 N	108.52 E
Temalacacingo	234	17.52 N	98.41 W
Temalı Bendi ◆[6]	267b	41.04 N	29.06 E
Te Manga ∧	174k	21.13 S	159.45 W
Temangan Baharu	114	5.42 N	102.09 E
Temangga	112	0.27 N	111.21 E
Temanggung	115a	7.18 S	110.10 E
Temascal, Méx.	234	23.24 N	104.14 W
Temascal, Méx.	234	18.15 N	96.20 W
Tem'asovo	86	52.59 N	58.06 E
Temastián	234	21.53 N	103.28 W
Tematagi I[1]	14	21.41 S	140.40 W
Temax	232	21.09 N	88.56 W
Tembakul, Pulau I	271c	1.14 N	103.52 E
Tembe	154	0.16 S	28.14 E
Tembe ≏	158	26.03 S	32.26 E
Tembeling	114	4.04 N	102.19 E
Tembeling ≏	114	4.04 N	102.20 E
Tembenči ≏	74	64.36 N	99.58 E
Tembesi ≏	112	1.43 S	103.06 E
Tembilahan	112	0.19 S	103.09 E
Tembisa	158	25.58 S	28.14 E
Temblador	246	8.59 N	62.44 W
Tembleque	34	39.42 N	3.30 W
Temblor Range ⋏	226	35.20 N	119.55 W
Tembo Aluma	152	7.42 S	17.17 E
Tembuè	154	14.52 S	32.58 E
Tembuland □[9]	158	31.30 S	27.40 E
Teme ≏	42	52.09 N	2.18 W
Temecula	228	33.29 N	117.08 W
Temecula Creek ≏	228	33.28 N	117.08 W
Temelli	130	39.44 N	32.22 E
Temengor	114	5.19 N	101.22 E
Temengor, Tasek ⊜[1]	114	5.30 N	101.20 E
Temerin	38	45.24 N	19.53 E
Temerloh	114	3.27 N	102.25 E
Temescal Canyon V	280	34.04 N	118.32 W
Temescal Wash V	228	33.40 N	117.20 W
Temesvár → Timișoara	38	45.45 N	21.13 E
Temiang, Pulau I	112	0.19 N	104.23 E
Teminaabuan	164	1.26 S	132.01 E
Temir	86	49.08 N	57.06 E
Temir ≏	86	48.31 N	57.27 E
Temirgojevskaja	78	45.07 N	40.16 E
Temirlanovka	85	42.36 N	69.17 E
Temirtau, Kaz.	86	50.05 N	72.56 E
Temirtau, Ross.	86	53.08 N	87.28 E
Témiscamie, Lac ⊜	186	51.11 N	72.12 W
Témiscaming	190	46.43 N	79.06 W
Témiscouata, Lac ⊜	186	47.41 N	68.47 W
Temixco	234	18.50 N	99.14 W
Temnik ≏	88	51.00 N	106.18 E
Temnikov	80	54.38 N	43.12 E
Temnikovo	265b	55.43 N	38.01 E
Temo ≏	71	40.21 N	8.47 E
Temoaya	234	19.28 N	99.35 W
Temora	166	34.26 S	147.32 E
Temosachic	232	28.57 N	107.51 W
Tempe	200	33.24 N	111.54 W
Tempe, Danau ⊜	112	4.06 S	119.57 E
Tempelfelde	264a	52.43 N	13.43 E
Tempelhof ◆[8]	264a	52.28 N	13.23 E
Temperance	216	41.46 N	83.34 W
Temperanceville	208	37.53 N	75.32 W
Temperley ◆[8]	258	34.47 S	58.24 W
Tempest, Mount ∧[2]	171a	27.10 S	153.26 E
Tempilang	112	2.07 S	105.40 E
Tempino	112	1.44 S	103.29 E
Tempio di Clitunno ⊥	66	42.48 N	12.45 E
Tempio Pausania	71	40.54 N	9.06 E
Tempisque ≏	236	10.12 N	85.14 W
Temple, Ok., U.S.	196	34.16 N	98.14 W
Temple, Pa., U.S.	208	40.24 N	75.55 W
Temple, Tx., U.S.	222	31.05 N	97.20 W
Temple City	228	34.06 N	118.03 W
Templecombe	42	51.00 N	2.25 W
Temple Ewell	42	51.09 N	1.16 E
Temple Hills Park	284c	38.48 N	76.57 W
Templemore	48	52.48 N	7.50 W
Templers	168b	34.28 S	138.45 E
Temple Sowerby	44	54.39 N	2.35 W
Templestowe	169	37.45 S	145.07 E
Temple Terrace	220	28.02 N	82.23 W
Templeton, P.Q., Can.	212	45.29 N	75.36 W
Templeton, Ca., U.S.	226	35.33 N	120.42 W
Templeton, In., U.S.	216	40.31 N	87.12 W
Templeton, Ma., U.S.	207	42.33 N	72.04 W
Templeton, Pa., U.S.	214	40.55 N	79.27 W
Templeton ≏	166	21.14 S	138.13 E
Temple University ∪[2]	285	39.59 N	75.09 W
Templeuve	50	50.32 N	3.10 E
Templi, Valle dei ⊥	70	37.17 N	13.35 E
Templin	54	53.07 N	13.30 E
Templiner See ⊜	264a	52.22 N	13.01 E
Templo Island I	116	13.09 N	122.52 E
Tempoal ≏	234	21.47 N	98.27 W
Tempoal de Sánchez	234	21.31 N	98.23 W
Tempy	82	56.38 N	37.18 E
Temr'uk	78	45.17 N	37.23 E
Temr'ukskij zaliv ⊂	78	45.24 N	37.20 E
Temse	50	51.08 N	4.13 E
Temù	64	46.15 N	10.28 E
Temuco	252	38.44 S	72.36 W
Temuka	172	44.15 S	171.17 E
Temwen I	174r	6.52 N	158.19 E
Tena	246	0.59 S	77.49 W
Tenabo	232	20.03 N	90.14 W
Tenafly	210	40.55 N	73.57 W
Tenaha	194	31.57 N	94.15 W
Tenakee Springs	180	57.47 N	135.13 W
Tenakill Brook ≏	276	40.59 N	73.58 W
Tena Kourou ∧[2]	150	10.45 N	5.25 W
Tenāli	122	16.15 N	80.35 E
Tenamaxtlán	234	20.13 N	104.10 W
Tenancingo [de Degollado]	234	18.58 N	99.36 W
Tenango de Arista	234	19.07 N	99.33 W
Tenantongo, Presa ⊜[1]	286a	19.28 N	99.16 W
Tenasillahe Island I	224	46.14 N	123.27 W
Tenasserim	110	12.05 N	99.01 E
Tenay	58	45.55 N	5.30 E
Tenaya Creek ≏	226	37.44 N	119.35 W
Tenbury Wells	42	52.19 N	2.35 W
Tenby	42	51.41 N	4.43 W
Tence	62	45.07 N	4.17 E
Tench Island I	164	1.40 S	150.40 E
Tencin	62	45.19 N	5.58 E
Tenda, Colle di (Col de Tende))(	62	44.09 N	7.34 E
Tendaho	144	11.48 N	40.52 E
Tendai-san ∧	270	34.55 N	135.28 E
Tende	62	44.05 N	7.36 E
Tende, Col de (Colle di Tenda))(	62	44.09 N	7.34 E
Tende, Tunnel de ◆[5]	62	44.09 N	7.34 E
Ten Degree Channel ʮ	110	10.00 N	93.00 E
Tendeka	158	27.44 S	30.54 E
Tendō	92	38.21 N	140.22 E
Tendrara	148	33.04 N	1.59 W
Tendrovskaja kosa ≻[2]	78	46.12 N	31.50 E
Tendrovskij zaliv ⊂	78	46.15 N	31.55 E
Tendürek Dağı ∧	84	39.22 N	43.52 E
Ténenkou	150	14.28 N	4.55 W
Tenente Marques ≏	248	11.10 S	59.56 W
Tenente Portela	252	27.22 S	53.45 W
Ténéré ◆[2]	146	19.00 N	10.30 E
Ténéré, Erg du ⫠[8]	146	17.35 N	10.55 E
Tenerife I	148	28.19 N	16.34 W
Ténès	148	36.31 N	1.14 E
Ténès, Cap ≻	34	36.33 N	1.21 E
Tenexpa	234	17.11 N	100.43 W
Tenextepango	234	18.43 N	98.57 W
Teng ≏	110	19.52 N	97.45 E
Tengah, Kepulauan II	112	7.30 S	117.30 E
Teng'aopu	104	41.05 N	122.49 E
Tengchong	102	25.04 N	98.29 E
Tengeh Reservoir ⊜[1]	271c	1.21 N	103.39 E
Tengen	58	47.49 N	8.40 E
Tenggara, Nusa (Lesser Sunda Islands) II	108	9.00 S	120.00 E
Tenggarong	112	0.24 S	116.58 E
Tengger Shamo ◆[2]	102	38.00 N	104.40 E
Tenggol, Pulau I	114	4.48 N	103.38 E
Tenghilan	112	6.14 N	116.19 E
Tengi ≏	114	3.24 N	101.10 E
Tengiz, ozero ⊜	86	50.24 N	68.57 E
Tengjiabao	100	31.10 N	115.29 E
Tengqiao	110	18.22 N	109.46 E
Tengra	272b	22.48 N	88.32 E
Tengréla	150	10.29 N	6.24 W
Tengtian	100	27.04 N	115.40 E
Tengtiao (Na) ≏	110	22.05 N	103.09 E
Ten'guševo	80	54.46 N	42.44 E
Tengxian, Zhg.	98	35.08 N	117.10 E
Tengxian, Zhg.	102	23.21 N	110.53 E
Teniente Rodolfo Marsh ∪[3]	9	62.12 S	58.54 W
Tenigerbad	58	46.42 N	8.57 E
Tenino	224	46.51 N	122.51 W
Tenis, ozero ⊜	86	56.09 N	71.56 E
Teniya-zaki ≻	174m	26.33 N	128.09 E
Teniz, ozero ⊜	86	54.08 N	64.34 E
Tenjin ≏	96	35.30 N	133.53 E
Tenjo, Mount ∧[2]	174p	13.25 N	144.42 E
Tenkāsi	122	8.58 N	77.18 E
Tenke, Zaïre	154	10.35 S	26.07 E
Tenke, Zaïre	154	11.26 S	26.45 E
Tenkeli	74	70.01 N	140.58 E
Tenkergynpil'gyn, laguna ⊂	180	68.30 N	178.00 W
Ten'ki	80	55.26 N	49.00 E
Tenkiller Ferry Lake ⊜[1]	196	35.43 N	95.00 W
Tenkodogo	150	11.47 N	0.22 W
Tenmile ≏, Ma., U.S.	283	41.58 N	71.20 W
Tenmile ≏, N.Y., U.S.	210	41.40 N	73.31 W
Ten Mile Creek ≏, On., Can.	284a	43.07 N	79.11 W
Ten Mile Creek ≏, Ky., U.S.	218	38.43 N	84.46 W
Tenmile Creek ≏, Oh., U.S.	216	41.42 N	83.33 W
Tenmile Creek ≏, Pa., U.S.	188	40.08 N	80.22 W
Tenmile Creek ≏, Tx., U.S.	222	32.34 N	96.34 W
Ten Mile Lake ⊜	186	51.06 N	56.41 W
Tenmile Run ≏	276	40.27 N	74.35 W
Tenmile Wash V	200	32.52 N	113.28 W
Tenmoku-san ∧	94	35.52 N	139.03 E
Tenna ≏	66	43.14 N	13.47 E
Tennant Creek	162	19.40 S	134.10 E
Tennenbronn	58	48.11 N	8.20 E
Tennengau ◆[1]	64	47.40 N	13.15 E
Tennengebirge ⋏	64	47.30 N	13.15 E
Tennent	208	40.16 N	74.20 W
Tennent Pond ⊜	276	40.26 N	74.20 W
Tennessee □[3]	178	35.50 N	85.30 W
Tennessee ≏	178	37.04 N	88.33 W
Tennessee Colony	222	31.50 N	95.50 W
Tenneville	56	50.06 N	5.32 E
Tennille	192	32.56 N	82.48 W
Tenno	64	45.55 N	10.49 E
Tennōji ◆[8]	270	34.39 N	135.31 E
Teno	252	34.52 S	71.11 W
Teno (Tana) ≏	24	70.30 N	28.23 E
Tenom	112	5.08 N	115.57 E
Ténos, Pointe ≻	240e	14.48 N	61.00 W
Tenosique	232	17.29 N	91.26 W
Tenri	96	34.36 N	135.51 E
Tenryū, Nihon	94	35.16 N	137.51 E
Tenryū, Nihon	94	34.52 N	137.49 E
Tenryū ≏	94	34.39 N	137.47 E
Tensas ≏	194	31.38 N	91.49 W
Tensed	202	47.09 N	116.55 W
Tensift, Oued ≏	148	32.02 N	9.22 W
Ten Sleep	202	44.02 N	107.27 W
Tensta	40	60.02 N	17.40 E
Tente ◆[8]	263	51.18 N	7.14 E
Tenteksor ≡	80	47.18 N	53.24 E
Tentena	112	1.47 S	120.39 E
Tenterden	42	51.05 N	0.42 E
Tenterfield	166	29.03 S	152.01 E
Tent Hill	171a	27.36 S	152.14 E
Tenthill Creek ≏	171a	27.34 S	152.14 E
Ten Thousand Islands II	220	25.50 N	81.33 W
Tentolomatinan, Gunung ∧	112	0.56 N	121.48 E
Tentugal	250	1.19 S	46.59 W
Tentulia	272b	22.50 N	88.28 E
Teocaltiche	234	21.26 N	102.35 W
Teocelo	234	19.23 N	96.58 W
Teocuitatlán de Corona	234	20.07 N	103.24 W
Teodelina	252	34.11 S	61.32 W
Teófilo Cunha	287a	22.39 S	43.34 W
Teófilo Otoni	255	17.51 S	41.30 W
Teofipol'	78	49.50 N	26.25 E
Teohotepapa, Pointe ≻	174x	9.46 S	138.48 W
Teohotupa, Pointe ≻	174x	9.46 S	138.50 W
Teo Lakes ⊜	184	51.30 N	109.21 W
Teolo	64	45.21 N	11.40 E
Teomabal Island I	116	6.20 N	120.51 E
Teor	64	45.51 N	13.03 E
Teora	68	40.51 N	15.15 E
Teotihuacán ⊥	234	19.44 N	98.50 W
Teotitlán de Flores Magón	234	18.08 N	97.05 W
Teotitlán del Valle	234	17.02 N	96.30 W
Tepa, Ghana	150	7.00 N	2.10 W
Tepa, Indon.	164	7.52 S	129.31 E
Tepalcatepec	234	19.11 N	102.51 W
Tepalcingo	234	18.36 N	98.51 W
Tepa Point ≻	174v	19.07 S	169.56 W
Tepatitlán de Morelos	234	20.49 N	102.44 W
Tepatlaxco [de Hidalgo]	234	19.04 N	97.58 W
Tepe	130	37.48 N	40.47 E
Tepeaca	234	18.58 N	97.54 W
Tepeapulco	234	19.47 N	98.33 W
Tepebaşı	130	36.40 N	32.45 E
Tepechitlán	234	21.40 N	103.20 W
Tepeguaje	196	25.40 N	99.50 W
Tepeguajes	234	23.30 N	97.50 W
Tepehan	130	38.06 N	38.45 E
Tepehuanes	232	25.21 N	105.44 W
Tepehuanes ≏	232	25.10 N	105.25 W
Tepeji de Ocampo	234	19.54 N	99.21 W
Tepelenë	38	40.18 N	20.01 E
Tepelmeme de Morelos	234	17.51 N	97.21 W
Tepelská vrchovina ⋏[1]	60	50.00 N	13.00 E
Tepeören	130	41.04 N	35.30 E
Tepepan ◆[8]	286a	19.16 N	99.08 W
Tepe Saif	267d	35.36 N	51.18 E
Tepetiltic, Volcán ∧[1]	234	21.15 N	104.43 W
Tepetixtla	234	17.13 N	100.08 W
Tepetlixpa	234	19.02 N	98.49 W
Tepi	144	7.10 N	35.23 E
Tepic	234	21.30 N	104.54 W
Tepko	168b	34.58 S	139.11 E
Teplá	60	49.59 N	12.52 E
Teplá ≏	54	50.14 N	12.52 E
Teplice	54	50.39 N	13.48 E
Teplik	78	48.40 N	29.44 E
Teplitz → Teplice	54	50.39 N	13.48 E
Teplooz'orsk	89	49.00 N	131.48 E
Teplovka	80	51.33 N	51.33 E
Teplovo	80	55.25 N	42.56 E
Tepoca, Bahía ⊂	232	30.15 N	112.50 W
Tepoca, Punta ≻	232	29.55 N	112.46 W
Te Pohue	172	39.15 S	176.41 E
Tepopa, Cabo ≻	232	29.22 N	112.27 W
Te Puia	172	38.04 S	178.18 E
Te Puke	172	37.47 S	176.20 E
Tepuxtepec, Presa ⊜[1]	234	20.02 N	100.13 W
Tepuzhuacán	234	20.53 N	104.33 W
Tequila	234	20.54 N	103.47 W
Tequisquita Slough ≏	226	36.58 N	121.27 W
Tequixquitla	234	19.19 N	97.40 W
Tequma	132	31.27 N	34.35 E
Ter ≏, Esp.	34	42.01 N	3.12 E
Ter ≏, Ityo.	144	7.20 N	42.11 E
Ter ≏, Eng., U.K.	42	51.50 N	0.36 E
Téra	150	14.01 N	0.45 E
Tera ≏	34	41.54 N	5.44 W
Teradomari	92	37.38 N	138.46 E
Terai	94	36.26 N	136.30 E
Teraina I	14	4.43 N	160.24 W
Ter'ajevo	82	56.11 N	36.07 E
Terakhāda	126	22.56 N	89.40 E
Teralba	170	32.58 S	151.37 E
Teramo	66	42.39 N	13.42 E
Teramo □[6]	66	42.39 N	13.41 E
Terán	234	16.45 N	93.10 W
Terang	169	38.14 S	142.55 E
Teranum	114	3.44 N	101.49 E
Ter Apel	52	52.53 N	7.04 E
Teraruma	164	8.00 S	141.50 E
Teras	114	3.45 N	101.49 E
Teratak	112	0.46 S	110.32 E
Terborg	52	51.55 N	6.21 E
Terbuny	76	52.08 N	38.17 E
Tercan	130	39.47 N	40.24 E
Terceira I	148a	38.43 N	24.13 W
Tercero ≏	252	32.55 S	62.19 W
Tercero de Febrero, Parque ♠	288	34.34 S	58.25 W
Terdal	122	16.30 N	75.03 E
Terdoppio, Torrente ≏	266b	45.30 N	8.37 E
Terebovl'a	78	49.18 N	25.43 E
Terebuš	82	54.16 N	38.09 E
Terebutinec	76	59.01 N	33.39 E
Terechovka	76	52.13 N	31.27 E
Terechovo	82	55.50 N	35.45 E
Te Rehunga	172	40.13 S	176.01 E
Tereida	140	10.35 N	31.17 E
Terek, Kyrg.	85	40.01 N	73.33 E
Terek, Ross.	84	43.29 N	44.08 E
Terek ≏	84	43.44 N	46.33 E
Terekli-Mekteb	84	44.10 N	45.53 E
Terek-Saj	85	41.32 N	71.09 E
Terektinskij chrebet ⋏	86	50.30 N	86.00 E
Terekty	80	48.34 N	49.02 E
Terempa	112	3.14 N	106.14 E
Terence Bay	186	44.28 N	63.43 W
Teren'ga	80	53.42 N	48.24 E
Terengganu □[3]	114	5.00 N	103.00 E
Terengganu ≏	114	5.17 N	103.05 E
Terenino	76	54.31 N	33.35 E
Terenkuduk	80	48.24 N	47.11 E
Terenni ⊥	150	16.30 N	9.35 W
Terenos	255	20.26 S	54.50 W
Terensaj	86	51.36 N	59.31 E
Terenuzek	86	45.05 N	64.59 E
Teresina	250	5.05 S	42.49 W
Tereška ≏	80	51.48 N	46.26 E
Teresópolis	256	22.26 S	42.59 W
Terespol	30	52.05 N	23.36 E
Teresva	78	48.01 N	23.42 E
Terevaka, Cerro ∧	174z	27.05 S	109.23 W
Terezín	54	50.31 N	14.08 E
Tergauči	85	41.11 N	71.30 E
Tergnier	50	49.39 N	3.18 E
Tergun Daba Shan ⋏	102	38.25 N	95.55 E
Terhorne	52	53.02 N	5.46 E
Teriang	114	3.14 N	102.25 E
Teriang ≏	114	3.19 N	102.31 E
Teribe ≏	236	9.22 N	82.32 W
Terib'orka	24	69.08 N	35.08 E
Terihi I	174x	10.02 S	138.49 W
Terio	164	8.25 S	143.00 E
Terjärv (Teerijärvi)	26	63.32 N	23.30 E
Terlago	64	46.06 N	11.02 E
Terlano	64	46.32 N	11.15 E
Terlingua	196	29.19 N	103.37 W
Terlingua Creek ≏	196	29.10 N	103.36 W
Terlizzi	68	41.08 N	16.32 E
Termas de Río Hondo	252	27.29 S	64.52 W
Terme	130	41.12 N	36.59 E
Terme del Brennero (Brennerbad)	64	46.58 N	11.29 E
Terme di Stigliano	66	42.09 N	12.01 E
Terme di Suio	68	41.18 N	13.51 E
Terme di Valdieri	62	44.12 N	7.16 E
Termeno (Tramin)	64	46.20 N	11.14 E
Termez	72	37.14 N	67.16 E
Termignon	62	45.17 N	6.49 E
Terminal	258	34.09 S	57.31 W
Terminal Island I	280	33.45 N	118.15 W
Terminal Island Coast Guard Base ■	280	33.43 N	118.17 W
Termini Imerese	70	37.59 N	13.42 E
Termini Imerese, Golfo di ⊂	70	38.01 N	13.45 E
Terminillo, Monte ∧	66	42.28 N	13.00 E
Términos, Laguna de ⊂	232	18.37 N	91.33 W
Termit, Massif de ⋏	146	16.15 N	11.17 E
Termoli	66	42.00 N	15.00 E
Termonde → Dendermonde	50	51.02 N	4.07 E
Termsdorf	264a	52.16 N	13.07 E
Tern ≏	42	52.47 N	2.32 W
Ternate, Indon.	108	0.48 N	127.24 E
Ternate, Pil.	116	14.17 N	120.43 E
Ternberg	61	47.58 N	14.22 E
Ternej	89	45.03 N	136.37 E
Terneuzen	52	51.20 N	3.50 E
Terni	66	42.34 N	12.37 E
Terni □[4]	66	42.41 N	12.19 E
Ternitz	61	47.44 N	16.03 E
Ternoise ≏	50	50.23 N	2.01 E
Ternopol'	78	49.34 N	25.36 E
Ternopol' □[4]	78	49.30 N	25.30 E
Ternovatoje	78	47.50 N	36.09 E
Ternovka, Ross.	78	51.40 N	41.37 E
Ternovka, Ross.	80	53.09 N	45.02 E
Ternovka, Ross.	80	51.19 N	42.56 E
Ternovka, Ukr.	78	47.02 N	32.01 E
Ternovka, Ukr.	78	48.32 N	29.58 E
Ternovoje	80	51.03 N	43.43 E
Ternovskaja	78	45.53 N	40.24 E
Terolak	114	3.53 N	101.23 E
Terong	114	4.43 N	100.44 E
Terontola	66	43.13 N	12.02 E
Terpe	54	51.32 N	14.19 E
Terpenija, mys ≻	89	48.39 N	144.44 E
Terpenija, zaliv ⊂	89	49.00 N	143.30 E
Terra Alta	188	39.26 N	79.32 W
Terra Bella	204	35.58 N	119.03 W
Terrace	182	54.31 N	128.35 W
Terrace Bay	190	48.47 N	87.06 W
Terracina	66	41.17 N	13.15 E
Terra del Sole	66	44.11 N	11.57 E
Terral	196	33.53 N	97.56 W
Terralba	71	39.43 N	8.39 E
Terra Linda	226	38.01 N	122.32 W
Terra Nova Bay ⊂	9	74.45 S	164.30 E
Terranova da Sibari	68	39.39 N	16.20 E
Terranova di Pollino	68	39.59 N	16.18 E
Terranova di Sicilia → Gela	70	37.04 N	14.15 E
Terra Nova Lake ⊜	186	48.30 N	54.20 W
Terra Nova National Park ♠	186	48.37 N	53.56 W
Terranova → Newfoundland □[4]	176	52.00 N	56.00 W
Terranuova Bracciolini	66	43.33 N	11.35 E
Terra Rica	255	22.43 S	52.38 W
Terrarossa, Foce di)(	64	44.12 N	10.26 E
Terra Roxa	252	24.08 S	53.59 W
Terras, Pinhal do ◆[3]	266c	38.39 N	9.02 W
Terra Santa	250	2.06 S	56.29 W
Terrasini	70	38.09 N	13.05 E
Terrassa	34	41.34 N	2.01 E
Terrasse-Vaudreuil	206	45.24 N	73.59 W
Terrasson-la-Villedieu	32	45.08 N	1.18 E
Terravecchia	68	39.29 N	16.58 E
Terrebonne	206	45.42 N	73.38 W
Terrebonne □[6]	206	46.00 N	74.10 W
Terrebonne Bay ⊂	194	29.09 N	90.35 W
Terre Ceia	220	27.35 N	82.35 W
Terre-de-Bas	241o	15.51 N	61.39 W
Terre-de-Bas I	241o	15.52 N	61.38 W
Terre de Feu → Tierra del Fuego, Isla Grande de I	254	54.00 S	69.00 W
Terre-de-Haut	241o	15.58 N	61.35 W
Terre-de-Haut I	241o	15.52 N	61.35 W
Terre des Hommes ♠	275a	45.31 N	73.32 W
Terre Haute	194	39.28 N	87.24 W
Terre Hill	208	40.09 N	76.03 W
Terrell	222	32.44 N	96.16 W
Terrell, Lake ⊜	224	48.52 N	122.41 W
Terrell Hills	196	29.28 N	98.27 W
Terrenceville	186	47.40 N	54.44 W
Terre-Neuve → Newfoundland □[4]	176	52.00 N	56.00 W
Terre Noire Creek ≏	194	33.49 N	92.55 W
Terre Rouge Creek ≏	194	33.49 N	93.11 W
Terres australes et antarctiques françaises → French Southern and Antarctic Territories □[2]	6	49.30 S	69.30 E
Terrey Hills	170	33.41 S	151.14 E
Terrigal	170	33.27 S	151.27 E
Terrington Saint Clement	42	52.45 N	0.18 E
Territoires du Nord-Ouest → Northwest Territories □[4]	176	70.00 N	100.00 W
Territorio Antártico Británico → British Antarctic Territory □[2]	9	60.00 S	45.00 W
Territorio Británico del Océano Índico → British Indian Ocean Territory □[2]	12	7.00 S	72.00 E
Territorios del Noroeste → Northwest Territories □[4]	176	70.00 N	100.00 W
Terror Point ≻	182	53.10 N	129.56 W
Terrugem	266c	38.51 N	9.20 W
Terry, Ms., U.S.	194	32.05 N	90.17 W
Terry, Mt., U.S.	198	46.47 N	105.18 W
Terry Peak ∧	198	44.19 N	103.50 W
Terryville, Ct., U.S.	207	41.40 N	73.00 W
Terryville, N.Y., U.S.	210	40.54 N	73.03 W
Tersa, Ross.	80	52.05 N	47.32 E
Tersa, Ross.	80	50.53 N	43.48 E
Tersa ≏	80	50.46 N	44.40 E
Tersakan Gölü ⊜	130	38.35 N	33.06 E
Tersakkan ≏	86	51.15 N	67.10 E
Terschelling I	52	53.24 N	5.20 E
Tersiva, Punta ∧	62	45.37 N	7.28 E
Terskej-Alatau, chrebet ⋏	85	41.55 N	77.00 E
Terskij chrebet ⋏	84	43.32 N	45.00 E
Terslev	41	55.22 N	11.59 E
Tersløse	41	55.31 N	11.30 E
Tertenia	71	39.42 N	9.34 E
Terter	84	40.20 N	46.55 E
Terter ≏	84	40.35 N	47.22 E
Teru	123	36.11 N	72.45 E
Teruel, Col.	246	2.44 N	75.33 W
Teruel, Esp.	34	40.21 N	1.06 W
Teruel □[4]	34	40.35 N	0.45 W
Terujak	114	4.23 N	97.31 E
Tervakoski	26	60.48 N	24.37 E
Tervel	38	43.45 N	27.24 E
Tervola	26	66.05 N	24.48 E
Tervuren	56	50.49 N	4.31 E
Terwagne	56	50.27 N	5.20 E
Terwolde	52	52.16 N	6.06 E
Terzaghi Dam ◆[6]	182	50.49 N	122.12 W
Terzigno	68	40.48 N	14.29 E
Teržola	84	42.12 N	42.59 E
Tes	88	50.27 N	93.30 E
Tésa, Magy.	30	48.02 N	18.51 E
Teša, Ross.	80	55.30 N	42.50 E
Tesalia	246	2.29 N	75.44 W
Tešanj	38	44.37 N	18.00 E
Tes-Chem (Tesijn) ≏	88	50.28 N	93.04 E
Teschendorf	54	52.51 N	13.10 E
Tescott	198	39.00 N	97.52 W
Tesechoacán ≏	234	18.31 N	95.42 W
Teseney	144	15.07 N	36.41 E
Tesero	64	46.17 N	11.31 E
Teshekpuk Lake ⊜	180	70.35 N	153.30 W
Teshikaga	92a	43.29 N	144.28 E
Te-shima I, Nihon	96	34.29 N	134.05 E
Te-shima I, Nihon	96	34.24 N	133.40 E
Teshio	92a	44.53 N	141.44 E
Teshio ≏	92a	44.53 N	141.44 E
Teshio-sanchi ⋏	92a	44.15 N	142.05 E
Tešig	88	49.56 N	102.34 E
Tesijn (Tes-Chem) ≏	88	50.28 N	93.04 E
Tesimo (Tisens)	64	46.34 N	11.10 E
Teslić	38	44.37 N	17.51 E
Teslin	180	60.09 N	132.45 W
Teslin ≏	180	61.34 N	134.54 W
Teslin Lake ⊜	180	60.15 N	132.57 W
Tesouras ≏	255	14.36 S	50.51 W
Tesouro	255	16.04 S	53.34 W
Tesovo	82	55.34 N	36.05 E
Tesperhude	52	53.24 N	10.26 E
Tessa, Oued ≏	36	36.34 N	8.54 E
Tessa-Araral, Oued V	148	26.18 N	1.58 E
Tessala, Djebel ∧	34	35.17 N	0.48 W
Tessala, Monts du ⋏	34	35.25 N	0.45 W
Tessalit	150	20.12 N	1.00 E
Tessancourt-sur-Aubette	261	49.02 N	1.55 E
Tessaoua	150	13.45 N	7.59 E
Tessei	96	34.56 N	133.20 E
Tessenderlo	56	51.04 N	5.05 E
Tesserete	58	46.04 N	8.58 E
Tessin	54	54.01 N	12.28 E
Tessin → Ticino □[3]	58	46.20 N	8.45 E
Tessy-sur-Vire	32	48.58 N	1.04 W
Test ≏	42	50.55 N	1.29 W
Testa, Capo ≻	71	41.14 N	9.08 E
Teston, On., Can.	275b	43.52 N	79.32 W
Teston, Eng., U.K.	260	51.15 N	0.26 E
Testour	36	36.33 N	9.27 E
Tesuque	200	35.45 N	105.55 W
Têt ≏	32	42.44 N	3.02 E
Tetachuck Lake ⊜	182	53.20 N	125.50 W
Tetagouche ≏	186	47.38 N	65.41 W
Tetas, Punta ≻	252	23.31 S	70.38 W
Tetbury	42	51.39 N	2.10 W
Tete	154	16.13 S	33.35 E
Tete □[5]	154	15.15 S	32.40 E
Tété ≏	146	9.12 N	20.29 E
Tête-à-la-Baleine	186	50.41 N	59.20 W
Tête du Parmelan ∧	58	45.57 N	6.14 E
Tête-Jaune-Cache	182	52.57 N	119.26 W
Te Teko	172	38.02 S	176.48 E
Tetepare Island I	175e	8.43 S	157.33 E
Tétépisca, Lac ⊜	186	51.00 N	69.25 W
Teterboro	276	40.52 N	74.03 W
Teterboro Airport ⊠	276	40.51 N	74.04 W
Téterchen	56	49.14 N	6.34 E
Tetere ≏	88	59.30 N	105.00 E
Teterev ≏	78	51.01 N	30.05 E
Teterow	54	53.46 N	12.34 E
Teteven	38	42.55 N	24.16 E
Tetiaroa I[1]	14	17.05 S	149.32 W
Tetica ∧	34	37.15 N	2.25 W
Tetijev	78	49.23 N	29.41 E
Tetla	234	19.26 N	98.06 W
Tetlin	180	63.08 N	142.31 W
Tetlin Lake ⊜	180	63.05 N	142.45 W
Teton	202	43.53 N	111.40 W
Teton ≏, Id., U.S.	202	43.54 N	111.51 W
Teton ≏, Mt., U.S.	202	47.56 N	110.31 W
Tetonia	202	43.49 N	111.09 W
Teton Range ⋏	202	43.45 N	110.50 W
Tétouan	148	35.34 N	5.23 W
Tétouan □[4]	148	35.30 N	5.30 W
Tetovo	38	42.01 N	20.58 E
Tétreauville ◆[8]	275a	45.36 N	73.32 W
Tetri-Ckaro	84	41.34 N	44.28 E
Tetschen → Děčín	54	50.48 N	14.13 E
Tetsuta	96	34.56 N	133.28 E
Tettau	54	50.28 N	11.15 E
Tettens	52	53.38 N	7.53 E
Tettnang	58	47.40 N	9.35 E
Tetuán → Tétouan	148	35.34 N	5.23 W
Tetufera, Mont ∧	174s	17.40 S	149.26 W
Tetulbāria	126	21.58 N	90.03 E
Tetulia ≏[1]	126	22.15 N	90.37 E
Teturi	154	1.04 N	29.08 E
Tet'uši	80	54.57 N	48.50 E
Tet'ušskoje	80	54.18 N	48.03 E
Teublitz	60	49.13 N	12.05 E
Teuchern	54	51.07 N	12.01 E
Teuco ≏	252	25.38 S	60.12 W
Teufelshöhle ⫠[5]	60	49.45 N	11.25 E
Teufels-Insel → Diable, Île du I	250	5.17 N	52.35 W
Teufelsmoor ◆[3]	52	53.15 N	8.50 E
Teufen	58	47.23 N	9.23 E
Teufenbach	61	47.08 N	14.21 E
Teuhtli, Volcán ∧[1]	286a	19.14 N	99.01 W
Teulada	71	38.58 N	8.46 E
Teulada, Capo ≻	71	38.52 N	8.38 E
Teúl de González Ortega	234	21.28 N	103.29 W
Teulon	184	50.23 N	97.16 W
Teun, Pulau I	164	6.59 S	129.08 E
Teunom ≏	114	4.26 N	95.48 E
Teunz	60	49.29 N	12.23 E
Teupitz	54	52.08 N	13.36 E
Teureubangan-cut	114	3.12 N	97.18 E
Teuri-tō I	92a	44.25 N	141.19 E
Teuschnitz	54	50.24 N	11.23 E
Teutleben	54	50.57 N	10.33 E
Teutoburger Wald ◆[3]	52	52.10 N	8.15 E
Teutopolis	194	39.07 N	88.28 W
Teutschenthal	54	51.27 N	11.46 E
Teuva	26	62.29 N	21.44 E
Tevere ≏	66	41.44 N	12.14 E
Teverya (Tiberias)	132	32.47 N	35.32 E
Teviot ≏	44	55.36 N	2.26 W
Teviot Brook ≏	171a	27.51 S	152.57 E
Teviotdale V	44	55.25 N	2.50 W
Teviothead	44	55.21 N	2.56 W
Tevli	76	52.20 N	24.15 E
Tevriz	86	57.34 N	72.24 E
Te Waewae Bay ⊂	172	46.15 S	167.30 E
Tewah	112	1.05 S	113.42 E
Te Whaiti	172	38.35 S	176.47 E
Tewkesbury	42	51.59 N	2.09 W
Tewksbury	207	42.36 N	71.14 W
Tew-Mac Airport ⊠	283	42.36 N	71.12 W
Têwo	102	34.02 N	103.05 E
Texada Island I	182	49.40 N	124.24 W
Texana, Lake ⊜[1]	222	28.58 N	96.32 W
Texarkana, Ar., U.S.	194	33.26 N	94.02 W
Texarkana, Tx., U.S.	194	33.25 N	94.02 W
Texas, Austl.	166	28.51 S	151.11 E
Texas, Oh., U.S.	216	41.26 N	83.57 W
Texas □[3], U.S.	178	31.30 N	99.00 W
Texas □[3], U.S.	196	31.30 N	99.00 W
Texas City	222	29.23 N	94.54 W
Texcaltitlán	234	18.54 N	99.55 W
Texcoco, Lago de ⊜	234	19.30 N	99.00 W
Texel I	52	53.05 N	4.45 E
Texhoma	196	36.30 N	101.46 W
Texico	196	34.23 N	103.03 W
Texline	196	36.23 N	103.01 W
Texoma, Lake ⊜[1]	196	33.55 N	96.37 W
Teyateyaneng	158	29.07 S	27.34 E
Teyéa ⊥	38	37.29 N	22.24 E
Teylān	120	35.32 N	64.47 E
Teynham	42	51.20 N	0.50 E
Teywarah	120	33.21 N	64.25 E
Teza ≏	80	56.32 N	41.53 E
Teziutlán	234	19.49 N	97.21 W
Težler, gora ∧	84	40.42 N	44.37 E
Tezoatlán de Segura y Luna	234	17.42 N	97.49 W
Tezpur	120	26.37 N	92.48 E
Tezu	120	27.53 N	96.11 E
Tezzeron Lake ⊜	182	54.41 N	124.25 W
Tha ≏	110	20.07 N	100.36 E
Tha-anne ≏	176	60.31 N	94.37 W
Thabana-Ntlenyana ∧	158	29.28 S	29.16 E
Thaba Nchu	158	29.17 S	26.52 E
Thabankulu ∧	158	27.30 S	30.20 E
Thaba-Putsoa Range ⋏	158	29.45 S	27.55 E
Thabaung	110	17.02 N	94.48 E
Thabawleikkyi	110	12.01 N	99.12 E
Thabazimbi	156	24.41 S	27.21 E
Thabor, Mont ∧	62	45.07 N	6.34 E
Thabyu	110	15.36 N	98.29 E
Thacher Island I	207	42.38 N	70.35 W
Thādiq	128	25.18 N	45.52 E
Thagyettaw	110	13.45 N	98.09 E
Thai Binh	110	20.27 N	106.20 E
Thailand (Prathet Thai) □[1], Asia	108	15.00 N	100.00 E
Thailand (Prathet Thai) □[1], Asia	110	15.00 N	100.00 E
Thailand, Gulf of ⊂	110	10.00 N	101.00 E
Thaïlande → Thailand □[1]	110	15.00 N	100.00 E
Thailandia → Thailand □[1]	110	15.00 N	100.00 E
Thai Muang	110	8.24 N	98.16 E
Thai Nguyen	110	21.36 N	105.50 E
Thak	120	30.32 N	70.13 E
Thakhek → Muang Khammouan	110	17.24 N	104.48 E
Thākurdwāra	124	29.12 N	78.51 E
Thākurdwāri	272b	22.34 N	88.28 E
Thākurgaon	124	26.02 N	88.28 E
Thākurpukur	272b	22.28 N	88.19 E
Thākurvādi	272c	18.54 N	73.04 E
Thal, Dtsch.	54	50.55 N	10.23 E
Thal, Pāk.	123	33.22 N	70.33 E
Tha'l, Jabal ∧	140	14.13 N	24.14 E
Thala	36	35.35 N	8.40 E
Thalang	110	8.01 N	98.19 E
Thal-Assling	64	46.47 N	12.38 E
Thalāthah	142	30.35 N	32.20 E
Thal Desert ◆[2]	123	31.30 N	71.40 E
Thale	54	51.45 N	11.02 E
Thalfang	56	49.45 N	6.59 E
Thalgau	64	47.50 N	13.15 E
Thalheim	54	50.42 N	12.51 E
Thalheim bei Wels	61	48.09 N	14.02 E
Tha Li	110	17.37 N	101.25 E
Thalia	196	33.59 N	99.32 W
Thālith, Ash-Shallāl ath- (Third Cataract) ⌊	140	19.49 N	30.19 E
Thalitter	56	51.13 N	8.53 E
Thalkirch	58	46.38 N	9.16 E
Thallon	166	28.38 S	148.52 E
Thallwitz	54	51.26 N	12.40 E
Thalmah, Marsā ⊂	142	29.03 N	32.38 E
Thalmässing	60	49.05 N	11.13 E
Thalwil	58	47.17 N	8.34 E
Thamar, Jabal ∧	144	13.53 N	45.12 E
Thame	42	51.45 N	0.59 W
Thames	172	37.08 S	175.33 E
Thames ≏, On., Can.	190	42.19 N	82.27 W
Thames ≏, Eng., U.K.	42	51.28 N	0.43 E
Thames ≏, Ct., U.S.	207	41.18 N	72.05 W
Thames, Firth of ⊂	172	37.00 S	175.25 E
Thames Barrier ◆[6]	260	51.29 N	0.03 E
Thames Ditton	260	51.23 N	0.21 W
Thames Estuary ⊂[1]	260	51.30 N	0.40 W
Thamesford	212	43.04 N	81.00 W
Thames Haven	260	51.30 N	0.31 E
Thamesville	214	42.33 N	81.59 W
Thāmit, Wādī V	146	31.15 N	16.06 E
Thammasat University ∪[2]	269a	13.45 N	100.30 E
Thamūd, Bi'r ⊤[4]	144	17.17 N	49.56 E
Thāna, India	122	19.12 N	72.58 E
Thāna, Pāk.	128	28.55 N	63.45 E
Thāna Creek ⊂	272c	19.00 N	72.57 E
Thāna Gāzi	124	27.25 N	76.19 E
Thāna Kasba	124	25.13 N	77.20 E
Thanbyuzayat	110	15.58 N	97.44 E
Thandaung	110	19.04 N	96.41 E
Thānedārwāla	123	32.36 N	71.07 E
Thānesar	124	29.59 N	76.49 E
Thanet, Isle of I	42	51.22 N	1.20 E
Thanet Lake ⊜	212	44.47 N	77.46 W
Thang Binh	110	15.44 N	108.22 E
Thangoo	162	18.10 S	122.22 E
Thangool	166	24.29 S	150.35 E
Thanh Hoa	110	19.48 N	105.46 E
Thanh My Tay	269c	10.49 N	106.46 E
Thanh Pho Ho Chi Minh (Saigon), Viet	110	10.45 N	106.40 E
Thanh Pho Ho Chi Minh (Saigon), Viet	269c	10.45 N	106.40 E
Thanjāvūr	122	10.48 N	79.09 E
Thann	58	47.49 N	7.05 E
Thannhausen	58	48.17 N	10.28 E
Thāno Bula Khān	120	25.22 N	67.50 E
Than Uyen	110	22.00 N	103.54 E
Thaoge ≏	156	20.27 S	22.36 E
Thaon-les-Vosges	58	48.15 N	6.25 E
Tha Pla	110	17.48 N	100.32 E
Thap Than ≏	110	15.21 N	104.06 E
Tharabwin West	110	12.17 N	99.03 E
Tharād	120	24.24 N	71.38 E
Tharandt	54	50.59 N	13.35 E
't Harde	52	52.25 N	5.53 E
Thar Desert (Great Indian Desert) ◆[2]	120	27.00 N	71.00 E
Thargomindah	166	28.00 S	143.49 E
Thāri Pātan ∧	124	28.58 N	82.04 E
Thar Nhom	140	7.26 N	30.29 E
Tharptown	210	40.48 N	76.34 W
Tharr, Wüste → Thar Desert ◆[2]	120	27.00 N	71.00 E
Tharrawaddy	110	17.39 N	95.48 E
Tharrawaw	110	17.41 N	95.28 E
Tharros ⊥	71	39.52 N	8.26 E
Tharsuinn, Beinn ∧	46	57.47 N	4.21 W
Tharthār, Buḥayrat ath- ⊜	128	34.00 N	43.05 E
Tharthār, Wādī ath- V	128	33.59 N	43.12 E
Tharwa	171b	35.31 S	149.04 E
Tha Sala	110	8.40 N	99.56 E
Thásos	38	40.47 N	24.42 E
Thásos I	38	40.41 N	24.47 E
Thásos ⊥	38	40.46 N	24.33 E
Tha Tako	110	15.38 N	100.29 E
Thatcham	42	51.25 N	1.15 W
Thatch Cay I	240m	18.22 N	64.52 W
Thatcher	200	32.50 N	109.45 W
Thatch Island I	276	40.38 N	73.23 W
That Khe	110	22.16 N	106.28 E
Thaton	110	16.55 N	97.22 E
That Phanom	110	16.57 N	104.44 E
Thatto Heath	262	53.26 N	2.45 W
Tha Tum	110	15.19 N	103.41 E
Thau, Bassin de ⊂	32	43.23 N	3.36 E
Thaungdut	110	24.26 N	94.42 E
Thaungyin ≏	110	17.50 N	97.42 E
Tha Uthen	110	17.34 N	104.36 E
Thawville	216	40.41 N	88.07 W
Thaxted	42	51.57 N	0.20 E
Thaya (Dyje) ≏	61	48.37 N	16.56 E
Thayawthadangyi Kyun I	110	12.20 N	98.00 E
Thayer, Il., U.S.	219	39.32 N	89.46 W
Thayer, In., U.S.	216	41.10 N	87.20 W
Thayer, Ks., U.S.	198	37.29 N	95.28 W
Thayer, Mo., U.S.	194	36.31 N	91.32 W
Thayetchaung	110	13.52 N	98.16 E
Thayetmyo	110	19.19 N	95.11 E
Thayngen	58	47.45 N	8.42 E
Thazi	110	20.51 N	96.05 E
The Aldermen Islands II	172	36.58 S	176.05 E
Theale	42	51.27 N	1.04 W
Thealka	192	37.49 N	82.47 W
The Basin	274b	37.51 S	145.19 E
Thebes	194	37.13 N	89.28 W
Thebes ⊥	140	25.42 N	32.37 E
Thebes → Thívai	38	38.21 N	23.19 E
The Birket ≏	262	53.24 N	3.01 W
The Bluffs ⫠[4]	210	43.22 N	76.40 W
The Bourne ≏	260	51.22 N	0.29 W
The Calvados Chain II	164	11.10 S	152.40 E
The Camels Hump ∧	169	37.23 S	144.35 E
The Capital ∪	284c	38.53 N	77.00 W
The Cheviot ∧	44	55.28 N	2.09 W
The Citadel ⊥, Magy.	264c	47.29 N	19.03 E

Symbol	English	Deutsch	Español	Français	Português
≏	River	Fluß	Río	Rivière	Rio
≋	Canal	Kanal	Canal	Canal	Canal
⌊	Waterfall, Rapids	Wasserfall, Stromschnellen	Cascada, Rápidos	Chute d'eau, Rapides	Cascata, Rápidos
ʮ	Strait	Meeresstraße	Estrecho	Détroit	Estreito
⊂	Bay, Gulf	Bucht, Golf	Bahía, Golfo	Baie, Golfe	Baía, Golfo
⊜	Lake, Lakes	See, Seen	Lago, Lagos	Lac, Lacs	Lago, Lagos
≡	Swamp	Sumpf	Pantano	Marais	Pântano
⌸	Ice Features, Glacier	Eis- und Gletscherformen	Accidentes Glaciales	Formes glaciaires	Acidentes glaciares
⊤	Other Hydrographic Features	Andere Hydrographische Objekte	Otros Elementos Hidrográficos	Autres données hydrographiques	Outros acidentes hidrográficos

Symbol	English	Deutsch	Español	Français	Português
✥	Submarine Features	Untermeerische Objekte	Accidentes Submarinos	Formes de relief sous-marin	Acidentes submarinos
□	Political Unit	Politische Einheit	Unidad Politica	Entité politique	Unidade política
∪	Cultural Institution	Kulturelle Institution	Institución Cultural	Institution culturelle	Instituição cultural
⊥	Historical Site	Historische Stätte	Sitio Histórico	Site historique	Sitio histórico
♠	Recreational Site	Erholungs- und Ferienort	Sitio de Recreo	Centre de loisirs	Area de Lazer
⊠	Airport	Flughafen	Aeropuerto	Aéroport	Aeroporto
■	Military Installation	Militäranlage	Instalación Militar	Installation militaire	Instalação militar
◆	Miscellaneous	Verschiedenes	Misceláneo	Divers	Diversos

The Citadel ⊥, Mişr 273c 30.02 N 31.15 E
The Cloisters ⊍ 276 40.52 N 73.56 W
The Colony 222 33.05 N 96.52 W
The Coorong ⊂ 168b 35.40 S 139.15 E
The Coteau ⩘[2] 184 51.10 N 107.30 W
The Curragh ♦ 48 53.10 N 6.52 W
The Dalles 224 45.35 N 121.10 W
The Dalles Dam ◆[6] 224 45.37 N 121.08 W
The Deeps ⊂ 46a 60.09 N 1.23 W
Thedford 198 41.58 N 100.34 W
Thedinghausen 52 52.58 N 9.01 E
The Downs ⊤[3] 42 51.13 N 1.27 E
Theebine 166 25.57 S 152.33 E
The English Companys Islands II 164 11.50 S 136.32 E
The Entrance 170 33.21 S 151.30 E
Theessen 54 52.14 N 12.02 E
The Everglades ≡ 220 26.00 N 80.40 W
The Fens ◆[1] 42 52.38 N 0.02 E
The Fishing Lakes ⊜ 184 50.45 N 103.51 W
The Flash ⊜ 262 53.29 N 2.33 W
The Flat Tops ⩘ 200 40.00 N 107.10 W
The Forest of Nisene Marks State Park ♦ 226 37.03 N 121.53 W
The Glenkens ◆[1] 44 55.10 N 4.15 W
Thègon 110 18.39 N 95.25 E
The Granites 162 20.35 S 130.21 E
The Granites ∧ 162 20.35 S 130.20 E
The Graves II 283 42.22 N 70.52 W
The Grove 222 31.16 N 97.32 W
The Hague → 's-Gravenhage 52 52.06 N 4.18 E
The Heads › 202 42.44 N 124.31 W
The Hermitage ⊍ 265a 59.56 N 30.20 E
The Home Park ♦ 260 51.28 N 0.36 W
The Hunters Hills ⩘[2] 172 44.30 S 170.50 E
Theinkun 110 11.53 N 99.09 E
The Isles Lagoon ⊂ 174o 1.50 N 157.23 W
Theissen 54 51.05 N 12.06 E
Theiss → Tisa ≃ 38 45.15 N 20.17 E
The Key Indian Reserve ◆[4] 184 51.45 N 102.08 W
The Lake Fleet Islands II 212 44.18 N 76.07 W
The Lakes National Park ♦ 166 38.05 S 147.40 E
The Little Minch ꓤ 46 57.35 N 6.55 W
Thelon ≃ 176 64.16 N 96.05 W
The Long Mynd ∧ 42 52.35 N 2.48 W
The Lower Hope ≃[1] 260 51.28 N 0.28 E
Thelwall 262 53.23 N 2.32 W
The Lynd 166 18.56 S 144.30 E
Them 41 56.06 N 9.33 E
The Machars ◆[1] 44 54.50 N 4.33 W
The Mall in Columbia ◆[9] 284b 39.13 N 76.52 W
Themar 54 50.30 N 10.37 E
The Meadows Race Track ♦ 279b 40.13 N 80.12 W
The Mere ⊜ 262 53.20 N 2.24 W
Théméricourt 261 49.05 N 1.54 E
The Minch ꓤ 46 58.10 N 5.50 W
The Mumbles 42 51.34 N 4.00 W
Then 123 32.26 N 75.44 E
The Narrows ꓤ 276 40.37 N 74.03 W
The Navy Islands II 212 44.21 N 76.03 W
The Naze › 42 51.53 N 1.16 E
The Needles › 42 50.39 N 1.34 W
Thénezay 32 46.43 N 0.02 W
Thenia 148 36.43 N 3.34 E
Theniet el Hadd 148 35.47 N 2.01 E
The Oa ›[1] 46 55.37 N 6.16 W
The Oaks, Austl. 170 34.04 S 150.34 E
The Oaks, Ca., U.S. 226 39.13 N 121.05 W
Theodore, Austl. 166 24.57 S 150.05 E
Theodore, Sk., Can. 184 51.25 N 102.54 W
Theodore, Al., U.S. 194 30.32 N 88.10 W
Theodore Francis Green Airport ⊠ 207 41.44 N 71.26 W
Theodore Roosevelt Inaugural National Historical Site ⊥ 284a 42.54 N 78.52 W
Theodore Roosevelt Island I 284c 38.54 N 77.03 W
Theodore Roosevelt Lake ⊜[1] 200 33.42 N 111.07 W
Theodore Roosevelt National Park (South Unit) ♦, N.D., U.S. 198 46.55 N 103.26 W
Theodore Roosevelt National Park (North Unit) ♦, N.D., U.S. 198 47.34 N 103.24 W
Theodor-Heuss-Brücke ◆[5] 263 51.15 N 6.45 E
Theog 123 31.07 N 77.21 E
Theólogos 38 40.39 N 24.41 E
The Orchards 284b 39.18 N 76.50 W
Théoule-sur-Mer 62 43.31 N 6.57 E
The Oval ⊥ 260 51.29 N 0.07 W
The Pages II 168b 35.47 S 138.17 E
The Paps ∧ 48 52.00 N 9.17 W
The Pas 184 53.50 N 101.15 W
The Peak ∧ 192 36.24 N 81.39 W
Thepha 110 6.52 N 100.58 E
The Pinnacle ∧[2] 219 39.22 N 90.55 W
Thérain ≃ 50 49.15 N 2.27 E
The Rajah ∧ 182 53.15 N 118.31 W
The Rand → Witwatersrand ◆[1] 158 26.00 S 27.00 E
The Range 154 19.00 S 31.04 E
Theresa 212 44.12 N 75.47 W
Theresa Creek ≃ 166 23.26 S 148.09 E
Theresa Park 274a 34.01 S 150.39 E
Theresienstadt → Terezín 54 50.31 N 14.08 E
The Rhins ›[1] 44 54.50 N 5.00 W
The Rip ⊂ 169 38.17 S 144.37 E
Thermaïkós Kólpos ⊂ 38 40.23 N 22.47 E
Thermalito 226 39.31 N 121.36 W
Thermopílai ⊥ 38 38.48 N 22.33 E
Thermopolis 200 43.38 N 108.12 W
Thermopylae → Thermopílai ⊥ 38 38.48 N 22.33 E
The Road ⊂ 42a 49.56 N 6.20 W
The Rock 166 35.16 S 147.07 E
The Rockies ∧ 224 46.39 N 122.22 W
Theron Mountains ⩘ 9 79.05 S 28.15 W
The Rope ≗[4] 174e 25.04 S 130.05 W
Thérouanne 50 50.38 N 2.15 E
The Savannahs ⊜ 220 27.19 N 80.17 W
Theseion ⊥ 267c 37.58 N 23.43 E
Thesiger Bay ⊂ 176 71.30 N 124.05 W
The Sisters ∧[2] 162 26.17 S 126.40 E
The Slot → New Georgia Sound ꓤ 175e 8.00 S 158.10 E
The Sluice ≍ 262 53.41 N 2.57 W
The Sny ≃ 219 39.16 N 90.44 W
The Solent ꓤ 42 50.46 N 1.20 W
The Sound (Øresund) ꓤ 41 55.50 N 12.40 E
The Springs 207 40.52 N 72.32 W
Thesprotikón 38 39.15 N 20.47 E
Thessalía ◻[9] 38 39.30 N 22.00 E
Thessalon 190 46.15 N 83.34 W
Thessaloníki (Salonika) 38 40.38 N 22.56 E
Thessalonique → Thessaloníki 38 40.38 N 22.56 E
The Storr ∧ 46 57.31 N 6.12 W
The Swale ꓤ 42 51.22 N 0.56 E
Thet ≃ 42 52.24 N 0.45 E
The Tauride Palace ⊍ 265a 59.57 N 30.23 E
The Terraces ≗[4] 162 28.40 S 121.30 E
Thetford 42 52.25 N 0.45 E
Thetford-Mines 206 46.05 N 71.18 W
The Thorofare ꓤ 208 37.15 N 75.54 W
The Thumbs ∧ 172 43.36 S 170.44 E
Thetis Island 224 49.59 N 123.40 W
Thetis Island I 224 49.00 N 123.41 W
The Twelve Pins ∧ 48 53.31 N 9.50 W
The Twins ∧ 172 41.14 S 172.39 E
Theunissen 158 28.30 S 26.41 E
Theux 56 50.32 N 5.49 E
The Valley 238 18.13 N 63.04 W
Thevenard 162 32.09 S 133.38 E
Thevenard Island I 162 21.27 S 115.00 E
The Wash ⊂ 42 52.55 N 0.15 E
The Weald ◆[1] 42 51.05 N 0.05 E
The Whirlpool ≃ 284a 43.07 N 79.04 W
The Winehead ∧ 210 40.58 N 77.28 W
The Wolds ⩘[2] 44 53.20 N 0.10 W
The Woodlands 222 30.09 N 95.27 W
The Wrekin ∧[2] 42 52.41 N 2.34 W
Theydon Bois 260 51.40 N 0.06 E
Theys 62 45.18 N 6.00 E
Thiais 261 48.46 N 2.23 E
Thiant 50 50.18 N 3.27 E
Thiaucourt-Regniéville 56 48.57 N 5.52 E
Thibaudeau 184 57.05 N 94.08 W
Thiberville 50 49.08 N 0.27 E
Thibodaux 194 29.47 N 90.49 W
Thicket 222 30.24 N 94.38 W
Thicket Portage 184 55.19 N 97.42 W
Thiéblemont-Farémont 58 48.41 N 4.44 E
Thief ≃ 198 48.08 N 96.10 W
Thief Lake ⊜ 198 48.30 N 95.55 W
Thief River Falls 198 48.07 N 96.10 W
Thièle ≃ 58 47.03 N 7.05 E
Thiel Mountains ⩘ 9 85.15 S 91.00 W
Thielsen, Mount ∧ 202 43.09 N 122.04 W
Thiendorf 54 51.17 N 13.44 E
Thiene 64 45.42 N 11.29 E
Thiensville 216 43.14 N 87.58 W
Thier 263 51.05 N 7.22 E
Thiérache, Collines de la ⩘[2] 50 49.50 N 3.50 E
Thierhaupten 58 48.34 N 10.54 E
Thiers 62 45.51 N 3.34 E
Thiersheim 54 50.04 N 12.07 E
Thierville-sur-Meuse 56 49.10 N 5.21 E
Thiès 150 14.48 N 16.56 W
Thiès ◻[4] 150 14.45 N 16.50 W
Thiesi 71 40.31 N 8.43 E
Thiessow 54 54.16 N 13.43 E
Thieux 261 49.01 N 2.40 E
Thieveley Pike ∧[2] 262 53.45 N 2.12 W
Thika 154 1.03 S 37.05 E
Thikombia Island I 175g 15.44 S 179.55 W
Thilay 56 49.52 N 4.49 E
Thilenius, Cape › 164 1.35 S 149.57 E
Thimphu 124 27.28 N 89.39 E
Thines 62 44.29 N 4.03 E
Thingvallavatn ⊜ 24a 64.12 N 21.10 W
Thingvellir 24a 64.17 N 21.07 W
Thingvellir National Park ♦ 24a 64.17 N 21.06 W
Thio 175f 21.37 S 166.14 E
Thionville 56 49.22 N 6.10 E
Thiou 150 13.48 N 2.40 W
Thíra 38 36.25 N 25.26 E
Thíra I 38 36.24 N 25.29 E
Third ≃ 276 40.49 N 74.08 W
Third Cataract → Thālith, Ash-Shallāl ath- ⊥ 140 19.49 N 30.19 E
Third Cliff ⊥[4] 283 42.11 N 70.43 W
Third Creek ≃, Mo., U.S. 219 38.26 N 91.40 W
Third Creek ≃, N.C., U.S. 192 35.47 N 80.31 W
Third Han-gang Bridge ◆[5] 271b 37.32 N 127.00 E
Third Herring Brook ≃ 283 42.07 N 70.48 W
Third Lake ⊜ 206 45.14 N 71.12 W
Third Street Station ◆[5] 282 37.46 N 122.23 W
Thirlmere 170 34.12 S 150.34 E
Thirlmere ⊜ 44 54.33 N 3.04 W
Thirlmere Lakes National Park ♦ 170 34.14 S 150.32 E
Thiron 50 48.19 N 0.59 E
Thironne ≃ 50 48.17 N 1.15 E
Thirroul 170 34.19 S 150.56 E
Thirsk 44 54.14 N 1.20 W
Thirtieth Street Station ◆[5] 285 39.57 N 75.11 W
Thirtymile Creek ≃ 198 46.22 N 102.03 W
Thirtymile Point › 210 43.22 N 78.29 W
Thiruvārūr 122 10.46 N 79.39 E
Thisted 26 56.57 N 8.42 E
Thistilfjördur ⊂ 24a 66.20 N 15.25 W
Thistledown Race Track ♦ 279a 41.26 N 81.32 W
Thistle Island I 166 35.00 S 136.09 E
Thistletown ◆[8] 275b 43.44 N 79.33 W
Thithia Island I 175g 17.45 S 179.18 W
Thívai (Thebes) 38 38.21 N 23.19 E
Thiverval-Grignon 261 48.51 N 1.55 E
Thiviers 32 45.25 N 0.56 E
Thizy 32 46.02 N 4.19 E
Thjórsá ≃ 24a 63.47 N 20.48 W
Thlewiaza ≃ 176 60.28 N 94.45 W
Thoa ≃ 176 60.30 N 109.47 W
Tho Chu, Dao II 110 9.20 N 103.28 E
Thoen 110 17.36 N 99.12 E
Thohoyandou 156 23.00 S 30.29 E
Thoi Binh 110 9.21 N 105.05 E
Thoirette 58 46.16 N 5.32 E
Thoiry 261 48.52 N 1.48 E
Thoissey 58 46.10 N 4.48 E
Tholen 52 51.32 N 4.12 E
Tholen I 52 51.35 N 4.05 E
Tholey 56 49.29 N 7.02 E
Thollon 58 46.23 N 6.43 E
Thomas, Ok., U.S. 196 35.44 N 98.44 W
Thomas, Pa., U.S. 279b 40.15 N 80.06 W
Thomas, Wa., U.S. 224 47.21 N 122.13 W
Thomas, W.V., U.S. 188 39.08 N 79.29 W
Thomasboro 216 40.15 N 88.11 W
Thomas Creek ≃ 202 44.40 N 122.56 W
Thomas Hill Reservoir ⊜[1] 194 39.40 N 92.40 W
Thomas J. O'Brien Lock and Dam ◆[5] 278 41.39 N 87.35 W
Thomas Lake ⊜ 184 57.00 N 96.43 W
Thomas Mountains ⩘ 9 75.32 S 70.57 W
Thomas Point › 208 38.54 N 76.28 W
Thomaston, Al., U.S. 194 32.15 N 87.37 W
Thomaston, Ct., U.S. 207 41.40 N 73.04 W
Thomaston, Ga., U.S. 192 32.53 N 84.19 W
Thomaston, Me., U.S. 188 44.04 N 69.10 W
Thomaston, N.Y., U.S. 276 40.47 N 73.43 W
Thomaston, Tx., U.S. 222 29.00 N 97.09 W
Thomastown, Austl. 274b 37.41 S 145.01 E
Thomastown, Ire. 48 52.31 N 7.08 W
Thomasville, Al., U.S. 194 31.54 N 87.44 W
Thomasville, Ga., U.S. 192 30.50 N 83.58 W
Thomasville, N.C., U.S. 192 35.52 N 80.04 W
Thomasville, Pa., U.S. 208 39.56 N 76.51 W
Thomes Creek ≃ 204 39.59 N 122.06 W
Thom Lake ⊜ 184 55.24 N 96.08 W
Thomlinson, Mount ∧ 182 55.33 N 127.29 W
Thompson, Mb., Can. 184 55.45 N 97.45 W
Thompson, Ct., U.S. 207 41.57 N 71.51 W
Thompson, Ia., U.S. 190 43.22 N 93.46 W
Thompson, Mo., U.S. 219 39.11 N 91.59 W
Thompson, N.D., U.S. 198 47.46 N 97.06 W
Thompson, Oh., U.S. 214 41.41 N 81.03 W
Thompson, Pa., U.S. 210 41.52 N 75.31 W
Thompson ≃, B.C., Can. 182 50.15 N 121.33 W
Thompson ≃, U.S. 194 39.45 N 93.36 W
Thompson Creek ≃, U.S. 198 45.04 N 104.25 W
Thompson Creek ≃, Ms., U.S. 194 31.10 N 88.54 W
Thompson Falls 202 47.35 N 115.20 W
Thompson Island I 283 42.23 N 71.01 W
Thompson Pass)(180 61.08 N 145.45 W
Thompson Peak ∧ 204 41.00 N 123.03 W
Thompson Place 224 47.03 N 122.45 W
Thompson Ridge 210 41.34 N 74.20 W
Thompson Run ≃ 279b 40.24 N 79.50 W
Thompsons 222 29.30 N 95.36 W
Thompsons Creek ≃ 284a 43.03 N 79.08 W
Thompson Sound ꓤ 172 45.09 S 166.57 E
Thompsontown 208 40.33 N 77.14 W
Thompsonville 190 44.31 N 85.56 W
Thomsen ≃ 176 74.08 N 119.35 W
Thomson, Ga., U.S. 192 33.28 N 82.30 W
Thomson, Il., U.S. 190 41.58 N 90.06 W
Thomson, N.Y., U.S. 210 43.07 N 73.35 W
Thomson ≃, Austl. 166 25.11 S 142.53 E
Thomson ≃, Austl. 169 37.58 S 146.32 E
Thomson, Lake ⊜[1] 169 37.45 S 146.22 E
Thomson Lake ⊜[1] 184 49.45 N 106.35 W
Thon ≃ 50 49.53 N 3.55 E
Thon Buri 110 13.43 N 100.29 E
Thônes 62 45.53 N 6.20 E
Thong 260 51.24 N 0.24 E
Thong Hoe 271c 1.25 N 103.42 E
Thong Tay Hoi 269c 10.50 N 106.39 E
Thongwa 110 16.46 N 96.32 E
Thon Lac Nghiep 110 11.20 N 108.54 E
Thonnance-lès-Joinville 58 48.27 N 5.10 E
Thonon-les-Bains 58 46.22 N 6.29 E
Thonotosassa 220 28.03 N 82.18 W
Thonze 110 17.38 N 95.47 E
Thorah Island I 212 44.27 N 79.14 W
Thorame-Haute 62 44.06 N 6.33 E
Thorburn 186 45.34 N 62.33 W
Thoreau 200 35.24 N 108.13 W
Thorembais-les-Béguines 56 50.40 N 4.49 E
Thorenc 62 43.48 N 6.49 E
Thorens-Glières 58 45.59 N 6.15 E
Thorhild 182 54.10 N 113.07 W
Thorial 140 8.40 N 29.56 E
Thorigny-sur-Marne 261 48.53 N 2.42 E
Thorigny-sur-Oreuse 50 48.17 N 3.24 E
Thórisvatn ⊜ 24a 64.16 N 18.54 W
Thörl 61 47.31 N 15.13 E
Thorlákshöfn 24a 63.53 N 21.18 W
Thormanby 44 54.10 N 1.14 W
Thorn 52 51.10 N 5.50 E
Thornaby-on-Tees 44 54.34 N 1.18 W
Thornapple ≃, Mi., U.S. 216 42.56 N 85.28 W
Thornapple ≃, Wi., U.S. 190 45.28 N 91.16 W
Thornapple Lake ⊜ 216 42.37 N 85.11 W
Thornburg 279b 40.26 N 80.05 W
Thornbury, Austl. 274b 37.45 S 145.00 E
Thornbury, On., Can. 212 44.34 N 80.26 W
Thornbury, N.Z. 172 46.17 S 168.06 E
Thornbury, Eng., U.K. 42 51.37 N 2.32 W
Thorn Creek ≃ 278 41.36 N 87.35 W
Thorndale, On., Can. 212 43.06 N 81.08 W
Thorndale, Tx., U.S. 222 30.36 N 97.12 W
Thorndike 207 42.11 N 72.20 W
Thorndon 42 52.17 N 1.08 E
Thorne 44 53.37 N 0.58 W
Thorne ≃ 184 54.56 N 90.35 W
Thorne Bay 182 55.44 N 132.32 W
Thorney 42 52.37 N 0.07 W
Thorngumbald 44 53.43 N 0.10 W
Thornhill, On., Can. 275b 43.48 N 79.25 W
Thornhill, S. Afr. 273d 26.07 S 28.09 E
Thornhill, Scot., U.K. 44 55.15 N 3.46 W
Thornhurst 210 41.11 N 75.35 W
Thornleigh 274a 33.44 S 151.05 E
Thornton, Austl. 171a 27.49 S 152.23 E
Thornton, Eng., U.K. 44 53.53 N 3.02 W
Thornton, Eng., U.K. 262 53.30 N 3.00 W
Thornton, Eng., U.K. 262 53.47 N 1.51 W
Thornton, Scot., U.K. 46 56.10 N 3.09 W
Thornton, Ar., U.S. 194 33.46 N 92.29 W
Thornton, Ca., U.S. 226 38.14 N 121.25 W
Thornton, Co., U.S. 200 39.52 N 104.58 W
Thornton, Il., U.S. 278 41.35 N 87.37 W
Thornton, Pa., U.S. 285 39.54 N 75.32 W
Thornton, Tx., U.S. 222 31.24 N 96.34 W
Thornton Beach ♦ 282 37.42 N 122.30 W
Thornton Dale 44 54.14 N 0.43 W
Thornton Hough 262 53.19 N 3.03 W
Thornton-le-Moors 262 53.16 N 2.50 W
Thornton Moor Reservoir ⊜[1] 262 53.47 N 1.55 W
Thorntonville 196 31.34 N 102.55 W
Thorn → Toruń 30 53.02 N 18.35 E
Thornwood 210 41.07 N 73.46 W
Thornwood Common 260 51.43 N 0.08 E
Thorny Mountain ∧[2] 194 37.06 N 91.10 W
Thorofare 285 39.50 N 75.11 W
Thorold 212 43.07 N 79.12 W
Thorold South 284a 43.06 N 79.12 W
Thoronet, Abbaye du ⊍[1] 62 43.28 N 6.16 E
Thorp, Wa., U.S. 224 47.04 N 120.40 W
Thorp, Wi., U.S. 190 44.57 N 90.47 W
Thorpe 260 51.24 N 0.32 W
Thorpe-le-Soken 42 51.52 N 1.10 E
Thorp Spring 222 32.28 N 97.49 W
Thorsby, Ab., Can. 182 53.14 N 114.03 W
Thorsby, Al., U.S. 194 32.54 N 86.42 W
Thorshavn → Tórshavn 22 62.01 N 6.46 W
Thórshöfn 24a 66.13 N 15.17 W
Thorsø 41 56.18 N 9.48 E
Thorsteinson Lake ⊜ 184 57.15 N 97.30 W
Thot Not 110 10.16 N 105.32 E
Thouars 32 46.59 N 0.13 W
Thouin, Cape › 162 20.20 S 118.12 E
Thoune → Thun 58 46.45 N 7.37 E
Thourotte 50 49.29 N 2.53 E
Thousand Islands II 212 44.15 N 76.12 W
Thousand Islands International Bridge ◆[5] 212 44.20 N 75.58 W
Thousand Lake Mountain ∧ 200 38.25 N 111.29 W
Thousand Oaks 228 34.10 N 118.50 W
Thousand Ships Bay ⊂ 175e 8.25 S 159.40 E
Thousand Springs Creek ≃ 200 41.17 N 113.51 W
Thowa ≃ 154 1.33 S 40.03 E
Thowgla Creek ≃ 171b 36.10 S 147.57 E
Thrace ◻[9] 38 41.20 N 26.45 E
Thrakikón Pélagos ⊤[2] 38 40.15 N 24.28 E
Thrall 222 30.35 N 97.18 W
Thrapston 42 52.24 N 0.32 W
Thrasher Lake ⊜ 212 44.55 N 78.58 W
Thread Creek ≃ 216 43.01 N 83.42 W
Thredbo Village 171b 36.29 S 148.19 E
Three Bridges 208 40.31 N 74.47 W
Three Brothers ∧ 224 47.23 N 120.45 W
Three Brothers Mountain ∧ 224 49.10 N 120.46 W
Three Creek ≃ 208 36.47 N 77.10 W
Three Fathoms Cove ⊂ 271d 22.26 N 114.17 E
Three Fingered Jack ∧ 202 44.29 N 121.50 W
Three Fingers ∧ 224 48.10 N 121.41 W
Three Fools Creek ≃ 224 48.53 N 120.57 W
Three Forks 202 45.53 N 111.33 W
Three Hills 182 51.42 N 113.16 W
Three Hummock Island I 166 40.26 S 144.55 E
Three Kings Islands II 172 34.10 S 172.05 E
Three Lakes 190 45.47 N 89.09 W
Three M Airport ⊠ 285 40.08 N 74.51 W
Three Mile Bay 212 44.04 N 76.11 W
Three Mile Plains 186 44.58 N 64.07 W
Three Oaks 216 41.47 N 86.36 W
Three Pagodas Pass)(110 15.18 N 98.23 E
Threepoint Lake ⊜ 184 55.41 N 98.56 W
Three Points, Cape › 150 4.45 N 2.06 W
Three Rivers, Austl. 162 25.07 S 119.09 E
Three Rivers, Ma., U.S. 207 42.10 N 72.21 W
Three Rivers, Mi., U.S. 216 41.56 N 85.37 W
Three Rivers, Tx., U.S. 196 28.27 N 98.10 W
Three Rivers ◻[8] 260 51.40 N 0.27 W
Three Rivers → Trois-Rivières 206 46.21 N 72.33 W
Three Sisters 158 31.54 S 23.06 E
Three Sisters ∧ 202 44.10 N 121.46 W
Three Sisters Islands II 175e 10.10 S 161.57 E
Three Springs, Austl. 162 29.32 S 115.45 E
Three Springs, Pa., U.S. 214 40.12 N 77.59 W
Threlkeld 44 54.38 N 3.03 W
Throat ≃ 184 51.48 N 93.30 W
Throckmorton 196 33.10 N 99.10 W
Throgs Neck ◆[8] 276 40.49 N 73.49 W
Throgs Neck Bridge ◆[5] 276 40.48 N 73.48 W
Throgs Point › 276 40.48 N 73.48 W
Throop 210 41.27 N 75.36 W
Throssel, Lake ⊜ 162 27.27 S 124.16 E
Throssell Range ⩘ 162 22.03 S 121.43 E
Thrushel ≃ 42 50.39 N 4.15 W
Thruway Mall ◆[9] 284a 42.55 N 78.46 W
Thu, Cu Lao I 110 10.33 N 108.57 E
Thuan Chau 110 21.26 N 103.41 E
Thu Dau Mot 110 10.58 N 106.39 E
Thu Duc 269c 10.51 N 106.45 E
Thueyts 62 44.41 N 4.13 E
Thuilley-aux-Groseilles 58 48.34 N 5.58 E
Thuin 50 50.20 N 4.17 E
Thul 120 28.14 N 68.46 E
Thulaythiwāt, Tilāl ath- ∧ 132 30.58 N 36.40 E
Thulba ≃ 56 50.11 N 9.52 E
Thule 16 76.34 N 68.47 W
Thulī Bherī ≃ 124 28.42 N 82.16 E
Thum 54 50.40 N 12.57 E
Thumb Peak ∧ 116 9.48 N 118.36 E
Thumby 41 54.35 N 9.54 E
Thun 58 46.45 N 7.37 E
Thun Chang 110 19.25 N 100.53 E
Thunder Bay 190 48.23 N 89.15 W
Thunder Bay ⊂, On., Can. 190 48.24 N 89.00 W
Thunder Bay ⊂, On., Can. 212 44.48 N 80.03 W
Thunder Bay ⊂, Mi., U.S. 190 45.00 N 83.22 W
Thunder Bay ≃ 190 45.04 N 83.25 W
Thunder Bay, North Branch ≃ 190 45.08 N 83.35 W
Thunderbird, Lake ⊜[1] 196 35.15 N 97.20 W
Thunderbolt 192 32.02 N 81.03 W
Thunder Butte ∧ 198 45.19 N 101.53 W
Thunder Butte Creek ≃ 198 45.13 N 101.42 W
Thunder Creek ≃, Sk., Can. 184 50.23 N 105.32 W
Thunder Creek ≃, Wa., U.S. 224 48.40 N 121.05 W
Thunder Hills ⩘[2] 184 54.30 N 106.00 W
Thunder Mountain ∧[2] 216 42.16 N 86.20 W
Thundersley 260 51.34 N 0.35 E
Thunersee ⊜ 58 46.40 N 7.45 E
Thüngen 56 49.56 N 9.51 E
Thung Song 110 8.09 N 99.41 E
Thung Wa 110 7.06 N 99.46 E
Thur ≃, Fr. 58 48.05 N 7.23 E
Thur ≃, Schw. 58 47.36 N 8.35 E
Thurcroft 44 53.24 N 1.16 W
Thurgau ◻[3] 58 47.35 N 9.00 E
Thurgovie → Thurgau ◻[3] 58 47.35 N 9.00 E
Thüringen 58 47.12 N 9.45 E
Thüringen ◻[3] 30 51.00 N 11.00 E
Thüringer Wald ⩘ 30 50.40 N 10.50 E
Thürkow 54 53.50 N 12.33 E
Thurles 48 52.41 N 7.49 W
Thurmont 208 39.37 N 77.24 W
Thurn, Pass)(64 47.19 N 12.24 E
Thurnau 60 50.01 N 11.23 E
Thurnham 260 51.17 N 0.36 E
Thurnscoe 44 53.31 N 1.19 W
Thurnwald Range ⩘ 164 4.45 S 141.15 E
Thurø 41 55.03 N 10.40 E
Thurrock ◻[8] 260 51.30 N 0.21 E
Thursby 44 54.51 N 3.03 W
Thursday Island 164 10.35 S 142.13 E
Thurso, P.Q., Can. 206 45.36 N 75.15 W
Thurso, Scot., U.K. 46 58.35 N 3.32 W
Thurso ≃ 46 58.36 N 3.30 W
Thurstaston 262 53.21 N 3.08 W
Thurston 42 52.15 N 0.49 E
Thurston ◻[6] 224 46.59 N 122.42 W
Thurston Island I 9 72.20 S 99.00 W
Thusis 58 46.42 N 9.26 E
Thwaites Iceberg Tongue ⊓ 9 74.45 S 106.30 W
Thy ◆[1] 26 57.00 N 8.30 E
Thyborøn 26 56.42 N 8.13 E
Thylungra 166 26.04 S 143.28 E
Thyolo 154 16.10 S 35.10 E
Thyregod 41 55.54 N 9.16 E
Thysville → Mbanza-Ngungu 152 5.15 S 14.52 E
Tiadiaye 150 14.25 N 16.42 W
Tía Juana 246 10.16 N 71.22 W
Tian ≃ 105 40.42 N 116.33 E
Tiana, Esp. 266d 44.29 N 2.16 E
Tiana, It. 71 40.04 N 9.08 E
Tian'anmen Square ⊥ 271a 39.55 N 116.23 E
Tianbao 100 24.36 N 117.35 E
Tianchang 100 32.41 N 119.01 E
Tiancunpu 105 39.06 N 115.41 E
Tiandeng 102 23.09 N 107.10 E
Tiandong 102 23.36 N 107.08 E
Tian'e 102 25.01 N 107.20 E
Tianeti 84 42.07 N 44.59 E
Tianfanjie 100 29.20 N 116.50 E
Tiangang, Zhg. 89 43.24 N 125.54 E
Tiangang, Zhg. 89 43.55 N 127.00 E
Tiangongsi 105 39.14 N 115.53 E
Tianguá 250 3.44 S 40.59 W
Tianhe 100 27.01 N 114.30 E
Tianhekou 100 32.08 N 113.25 E
Tianhelong 89 43.56 N 120.39 E
Tianhuang 98 35.29 N 117.18 E
Tianjara, Mount ∧ 170 35.11 S 150.18 E
Tianjia, Zhg. 104 41.07 N 122.03 E
Tianjia, Zhg. 107 29.40 N 105.08 E
Tianjiaba 102 32.08 N 110.03 E
Tianjiatun 104 41.39 N 123.44 E
Tianjiawopu 104 42.28 N 122.38 E
Tianjiazhen 100 29.56 N 115.26 E
Tianjin (Tientsin) 105 39.08 N 117.12 E
Tianjing 106 31.27 N 120.46 E
Tianjin Shi (Tientsin Shih) ◻[7] 98 39.30 N 117.15 E
Tianjun 102 37.25 N 98.58 E
Tiankai 105 39.38 N 115.51 E
Tiankoura 150 10.46 N 3.16 W
Tiankoye 150 12.35 N 12.40 W
Tianlin, Zhg. 102 24.14 N 106.03 E
Tianlin, Zhg. 107 29.49 N 105.19 E
Tian Ling ∧ 89 44.22 N 129.52 E
Tianmashan 106 31.04 N 121.08 E
Tianmen 100 30.39 N 113.06 E
Tianmu Shan ⩘ 100 30.25 N 119.30 E
Tianpu 106 31.56 N 121.07 E
Tianqiaochang 104 40.52 N 121.02 E
Tianqiaoling 89 43.26 N 129.38 E
Tianquan 102 30.10 N 102.48 E
Tian Shan → Tien Shan ⩘ 90 42.00 N 80.00 E
Tianshenggang 106 32.03 N 120.45 E
Tianshifu 98 41.17 N 124.21 E
Tianshui 102 34.30 N 105.58 E
Tianshuijing, Zhg. 102 40.17 N 95.21 E
Tianshuijing, Zhg. 104 41.19 N 121.48 E
Tianshuituo 105 39.20 N 118.12 E
Tianshuizhan 104 41.00 N 123.34 E
Tiantai 100 29.09 N 121.02 E
Tiantang 102 22.32 N 111.55 E
Tiantou, Zhg. 100 28.48 N 120.39 E
Tiantou, Zhg. 100 26.19 N 115.57 E
Tianwangsi 106 31.45 N 119.12 E
Tianxin, Zhg. 100 27.53 N 113.06 E
Tianxin, Zhg. 100 28.11 N 114.35 E
Tianxin, Zhg. 102 27.21 N 111.00 E
Tianxingqiao 106 32.05 N 119.57 E
Tianxiyang 100 26.31 N 118.33 E
Tianyang 102 23.51 N 106.34 E
Tianyangping 107 29.11 N 105.16 E
Tianyar 115b 8.12 S 115.30 E
Tianzhen 98 40.28 N 114.06 E
Tianzhongying 100 33.13 N 115.22 E
Tianzhu, Zhg. 102 37.14 N 102.59 E
Tianzhu, Zhg. 102 26.50 N 109.00 E
Tianzhuang, Zhg. 100 25.43 N 113.40 E
Tianzhuang, Zhg. 105 39.25 N 117.54 E
Tianzhuangtai 104 40.50 N 122.08 E
Tiao ≃ 106 30.56 N 120.11 E
Tiaodengchang 107 30.47 N 106.22 E
Tiarel 174s 17.32 S 149.20 W
Tiarno 64 45.53 N 10.40 E
Tiaro 166 25.44 S 152.35 E
Tiassalé 150 5.54 N 4.50 W
Tiati ∧ 154 1.19 N 35.56 E
Ti'avea 175a 13.57 S 171.24 W
Tiawichi Creek ≃ 222 32.19 N 94.44 W
Tiba → Chiba 94 35.36 N 140.07 E
Tibaji 252 24.30 S 50.24 W
Tibaji ≃ 252 22.47 S 51.01 W
Tibari 154 5.01 N 31.43 E
Tibasti, Sarīr ◆[2] 146 24.00 N 17.00 E
Tibati 152 6.27 N 12.38 E
Tibbermore 46 56.22 N 3.32 W
Tibbie 194 31.21 N 88.14 W
Tibe 144 9.03 N 37.08 E
Tibel'ti 88 51.46 N 103.11 E
Tiberias, Lake → Kinneret, Yam ⊜ 132 32.48 N 35.35 E
Tiberias → Teverya 132 32.47 N 35.32 E
Tiberina, Val V 66 43.31 N 12.10 E
Tiber → Tevere ≃ 66 41.44 N 12.14 E
Tibesti ⩘ 146 21.30 N 17.30 E
Tibet, Lake ⊜ 220 28.27 N 81.31 W
Tibet, Plateau of → Qing Zang Gaoyuan ⩘[1] 12 33.00 N 92.00 E
Tibet → Xizang Zizhiqu ◻[4] 90 32.00 N 88.00 E
Tibiao 116 11.17 N 122.02 E
Tibiao Point › 116 11.18 N 122.02 E
Tibidabo ∧ 266d 41.25 N 2.07 E
Tibiri, Niger 150 13.06 N 4.00 E
Tibiri, Niger 150 13.34 N 7.04 E
Tibirke 41 56.03 N 12.07 E
Tiblawan 116 6.29 N 126.06 E
Tiblemont, Lac ⊜ 190 48.14 N 77.18 W
Tibnah 132 32.59 N 36.13 E
Tibnīn 132 33.12 N 35.25 E
Tibooburra 166 29.26 S 142.01 E
Tibro 26 58.26 N 14.10 E
Tiburon 226 37.52 N 122.27 W
Tiburón, Cabo › 246 8.42 N 77.24 W
Tiburón, Isla I 232 29.00 N 112.23 W
Tiburon Peninsula ›[1] 282 37.53 N 122.28 W
Tiča, jazovir ⊜[1] 38 43.05 N 26.45 E
Ticao Island I 116 12.31 N 123.42 E
Ticao Pass ꓤ 116 12.38 N 123.47 E
Tice 220 26.40 N 81.48 W
Tice Creek ≃ 282 37.53 N 122.03 W
Ticehurst 42 51.03 N 0.25 E
Tichigan 216 42.50 N 88.12 W
Tichigan Lake ⊜ 216 42.49 N 88.13 W
Tîchît 150 18.28 N 9.30 W
Tîchît, Dahr ≗[4] 150 18.30 N 9.25 W
Tichmenevo, Ross. 76 58.00 N 38.36 E
Tichmenevo, Ross. 89 49.12 N 142.54 E
Ticho 144 7.50 N 39.32 E
Tichon 24 59.23 N 46.38 E
Tichonova Pustyn' 82 54.38 N 36.09 E
Tichonoviči 78 51.56 N 32.09 E
Tichonovka 88 53.13 N 104.13 E
Tichookeanskij 89 43.00 N 132.24 E
Tichoreck 78 45.51 N 40.09 E
Tichtozero 24 65.35 N 30.27 E
Tichvin 76 59.39 N 33.31 E
Tichvinskaja gr'ada ∧ 76 59.30 N 34.30 E
Ticino ◻[3] 58 46.20 N 8.45 E
Ticino ≃ 36 45.09 N 9.14 E
Tickfaw 194 30.34 N 90.28 W
Tickfaw ≃ 194 30.20 N 90.28 W
Tickhill 44 53.26 N 1.06 W
Ticomán ◆[8] 286a 19.31 N 99.08 W
Ticonderoga 188 43.50 N 73.25 W
Ticul 232 20.24 N 89.32 W
Tīdah 142 31.15 N 30.50 E
Tidaholm 26 58.11 N 13.57 E
Tidan ≃ 40 58.42 N 13.58 E
Tiddim 110 23.23 N 93.39 E
Tide Lake ⊜ 184 50.33 N 111.20 W
Tideswell 44 53.16 N 1.46 W
Tidewater 208 37.51 N 76.42 W
Tidewater ◆[1] 208 37.45 N 77.00 W
Tidikelt ≚ 148 26.54 N 1.20 E
Tidioute 214 41.41 N 79.24 W
Tidirhine, Jebel ∧ 148 34.50 N 4.30 W
Tidjikja 150 18.33 N 11.25 W
Tidö 40 59.30 N 16.28 E
Tidone ≃ 62 45.04 N 9.32 E
Tidore 108 0.40 N 127.26 E
Tiébissou 150 7.10 N 5.13 W
Tiechang, Zhg. 98 41.44 N 126.11 E
Tiechang, Zhg. 100 24.10 N 115.30 E
Tiechang, Zhg. 102 26.34 N 103.58 E
Tiechang, Zhg. 105 40.04 N 118.12 E
Tiechangpu 107 29.29 N 104.20 E
Tiefenbach 60 49.26 N 12.35 E
Tiefenbroich 263 51.18 N 6.49 E
Tiefencastel 58 46.40 N 9.35 E
Tiefensee 54 52.41 N 13.50 E
Tiefo 107 29.45 N 104.33 E
T'iehling → Tieling 104 42.18 N 123.49 E
Tiekou 98 37.16 N 121.13 E
Tiel 52 51.54 N 5.25 E
Tieli 89 46.59 N 128.02 E
Tieling 104 42.18 N 123.49 E
Tielt 50 51.00 N 3.19 E
Tielutou 100 27.49 N 115.48 E
Tiémé 150 9.33 N 7.19 W
T'ienching → Tianjin 105 39.08 N 117.12 E
T'ienchung 100 23.52 N 120.35 E
Tienen 56 50.48 N 4.57 E
Tiengen 58 47.38 N 8.16 E
Tiénigboué 150 8.11 N 5.43 W
Tienko 150 10.14 N 7.29 W
Tien Shan ⩘ 90 42.00 N 80.00 E
T'ienshui → Tianshui 102 34.30 N 105.58 E
Tientsin → Tianjin 105 39.08 N 117.12 E
Tien Yen 110 21.20 N 107.24 E
Tiepido ≃ 64 44.37 N 10.59 E
Tie Plant 194 33.44 N 89.47 W
Tierga 34 41.37 N 1.36 W
Tiergarten ◆[8] 264a 52.31 N 13.21 E
Tiergarten ♦ 264a 52.31 N 13.21 E
Tieroko, Tarso ∧ 146 20.45 N 17.52 E
Tierp 40 60.20 N 17.30 E
Tierpark ♦ 264a 52.30 N 13.32 E
Tierra Amarilla, Chile 252 27.29 S 70.17 W
Tierra Amarilla, N.M., U.S. 200 36.42 N 106.32 W
Tierra Blanca, Méx. 196 27.12 N 104.53 W
Tierra Blanca, Méx. 234 18.25 N 96.20 W
Tierra Blanca Creek ≃ 196 34.58 N 101.55 W
Tierra Buena 226 39.09 N 121.40 W
Tierra Colorada, Méx. 234 17.10 N 99.35 W
Tierra Colorada, Méx. 234 17.56 N 92.39 W
Tierra Colorada, Bajo de la ≚[1] 254 42.52 S 66.48 W
Tierra de Campos ◆[1] 34 42.10 N 4.50 W
Tierra del Fuego ◻[8] 254 54.00 S 67.00 W
Tierra del Fuego, Isla Grande de I 254 54.00 S 69.00 W
Tierra del Fuego, Parque Nacional ♦ 254 54.39 S 68.30 W
Tierra del Norte → Severnaja Zeml'a II 74 79.30 N 98.00 E
Tierralta 246 8.11 N 76.04 W
Tierra Redonda Mountain ∧ 226 35.47 N 120.59 W
Tierras Australes y Antárticas Francesas → French Southern and Antarctic Territories ◻[2] 6 49.30 S 69.30 E
Tieshan 100 30.14 N 114.52 E
Tieshanguan 100 23.30 N 113.54 E
Tiétar ≃ 34 39.50 N 6.01 W
Tietê 255 23.07 S 47.43 W
Tietê ≃ 255 20.40 S 51.35 W
Tiéti 175f 20.57 S 165.19 E
Tieton 224 46.42 N 120.45 W
Tieton ≃ 224 46.45 N 120.45 W
Tieton, South Fork ≃ 224 46.38 N 121.08 W
Tietzow 264a 52.43 N 12.56 E
Tif 148 27.00 N 1.37 E
Tiffany Mountain ∧ 202 48.40 N 119.56 W
Tiffin 214 41.07 N 83.11 W
Tiffin ≃ 216 41.17 N 84.23 W
Tiflis → Tbilisi 84 41.43 N 44.49 E
Tifton 192 31.27 N 83.30 W
Tiftona 192 35.05 N 85.10 W
Tiga, Île I 175f 21.07 S 167.49 E
Tiga, Pulau I 112 5.43 N 115.39 E
Tigalda Island I 180 54.05 N 165.05 W
Tigapuluh, Pegunungan ⩘ 112 1.05 S 102.30 E
Tigard 224 45.25 N 122.46 W
Tigasaki → Chigasaki 94 35.19 N 139.24 E
Tigbauan 116 10.41 N 122.22 E
Tigeaux 261 48.50 N 2.54 E
Tiger Lake ⊜ 220 27.53 N 81.22 W
Tiger Stadium ♦ 281 42.20 N 83.04 W
Tigery 261 48.38 N 2.31 E
Tighennif 148 35.20 N 0.21 E
Tighvein ∧[2] 46 55.30 N 5.10 W
Tigil' 74 57.48 N 158.40 E
Tiglid 148 28.31 N 10.15 W
Tiglione ≃ 62 44.48 N 8.27 E
Tignale 64 45.44 N 10.44 E
Tignall 192 33.52 N 82.44 W
Tignère 152 7.22 N 12.39 E
Tignes 62 45.30 N 6.55 E
Tignish 186 46.57 N 64.02 W
Tignousti, Jebel ∧ 148 31.31 N 6.44 W
Tigoda ≃ 76 59.22 N 31.54 E
Tigray ◻[4] 144 13.40 N 40.00 E
Tigre, Arg. 258 34.25 S 58.34 W
Tigre, Col. 246 2.28 N 68.15 W
Tigre ◻[5] 288 34.24 S 58.37 W
Tigre ≃, Arg. 288 34.25 S 58.35 W
Tigre ≃, Méx. 234 22.43 N 97.51 W
Tigre ≃, Perú 246 4.26 S 74.05 W
Tigre ≃, Ven. 246 9.20 N 62.30 W
Tigre, Cerro ∧ 236 8.31 N 83.28 W
Tigre, Isla del I 258 34.47 S 56.23 W
Tigre, Punta del › 258 34.46 S 56.33 W
Tigres, Baía dos ⊂ 152 16.38 S 11.46 E
Tigre → Tigris ≃ 128 31.00 N 47.25 E
Tigris (Dicle) (Dijlah) ≃ 128 31.00 N 47.25 E
Tiguabos 240p 20.14 N 75.21 W
Tiguentourine 148 27.50 N 9.18 E
Tiguesmat ⩘[2] 148 24.54 N 8.14 W
Tigy 50 47.48 N 2.12 E
Tigyaing 110 23.46 N 96.08 E
Tigzert, Oued V 148 28.20 N 9.35 W
Tigzirt 34 36.54 N 4.08 E
Tīh, Jabal at- ⩘[1] 140 29.30 N 34.00 E
Tihāmah ≚ 128 26.00 N 36.30 E
Tihany ⊥ 30 46.54 N 17.53 E
Tihert 148 35.28 N 1.21 E
Tihert ◻[5] 148 35.00 N 1.45 E
Ṭihnāwī, Wādī aṭ- V 142 28.11 N 30.46 E
Tihuatlán 234 20.43 N 97.32 W
Tihua → Ürümqi 86 43.48 N 87.35 E
Tiilikkajärven kansallispuisto ♦ 26 63.38 N 28.20 E
Tijamuchi ≃ 248 14.10 S 64.58 W
Tijesno 36 43.48 N 15.39 E
Tījī 146 32.01 N 11.22 E
Tijuana 232 32.32 N 117.01 W
Tijuana ≃ 204 32.33 N 117.07 W
Tijuca ◆[8] 287a 22.56 S 43.14 W
Tijuca, Barra da ꓤ 287a 23.01 S 43.18 W
Tijuca, Lagoa da ⊂ 287a 22.59 S 43.20 W
Tijuca, Parque Nacional da ♦ 287a 22.58 S 43.15 W
Tijuca, Pico da ∧ 287a 22.56 S 43.17 W
Tijucas 252 27.14 S 48.38 W
Tijucas do Sul 252 25.55 S 49.12 W
Tijuco ≃ 255 18.40 S 50.05 W
Tikal ⊥ 232 17.20 N 89.39 W
Tīkamgarh 124 24.44 N 78.50 E
Tikaré 150 13.17 N 1.43 W
Tikchik Lakes ⊜ 180 60.07 N 158.35 W
Tikei, Île I 14 14.58 S 144.32 W
Tikhand ◆[8] 272a 28.31 N 77.17 E
Tikhoretsk → Tichoreck 78 45.51 N 40.09 E
Tikitiki 172 37.48 S 178.24 E
Tiko 152 4.05 N 9.22 E
Tikokino 172 39.49 S 176.27 E
Tikrīt 128 34.36 N 43.42 E
Tikša 24 64.07 N 32.27 E
Tikšeozero, ozero ⊜ 24 66.16 N 31.53 E
Tiksi 74 71.36 N 128.48 E
Tiku 112 0.24 S 99.56 E
Til 130 38.44 N 41.49 E
Tiladummati Atoll I[1] 122 6.50 N 73.05 E
Tilamuta 112 0.30 N 122.20 E
Tilarán 236 10.28 N 84.59 W

ENGLISH Name	Page	Lat.°′	Long.°′	DEUTSCH Name	Seite	Breite°′	Länge°′ E = Ost

Symbols in the index entries represent the broad categories identified in the key at the right. Symbols with superior numbers (⩘[1]) identify subcategories (see complete key on page *I · 1*).

Symbole im Register stellen die rechts im Schlüssel erklärten Kategorien dar. Symbole mit hochgestellten Ziffern (⩘[1]) bezeichnen Unterteilungen einer Kategorie (vgl. vollständiger Schlüssel auf Seite *I · 1*).

Los símbolos incluídos en el texto del índice representan las grandes categorias identificadas con la clave a la derecha. Los símbolos con numeros en su parte superior (⩘[1]) identifican las subcategorías (véase la clave completa en la página *I · 1*).

Les symboles de l'index représentent les catégories indiquées dans la légende à droite. Les symboles suivis d'un indice (⩘[1]) représentent des sous-catégories (voir légende complète à la page *I · 1*).

Os símbolos incluídos no texto do índice representam as grandes categorias identificadas com a chave à direita. Os símbolos com números em sua parte superior (⩘[1]) identificam as subcategorias (veja-se a chave completa à página *I · 1*).

∧ Mountain	Berg	Montaña	Montagne	Montanha
⩘ Mountains	Gebirge	Montañas	Montagnes	Montanhas
)(Pass	Paß	Paso	Col	Passo
V Valley, Canyon	Tal, Cañon	Valle, Cañón	Vallée, Canyon	Vale, Canhão
≚ Plain	Ebene	Llano	Plaine	Planície
› Cape	Kap	Cabo	Cap	Cabo
I Island	Insel	Isla	Île	Ilha
II Islands	Inseln	Islas	Îles	Ilhas
≗ Other Topographic Features	Andere Topographische Objekte	Otros Elementos Topográficos	Autres données topographiques	Outros acidentes topográficos

ESPAÑOL

Nombre	Página	Lat.°′	Long.°′ W = Oeste
Tilbalakan, Laguna c	236	15.30 N	84.17 W
Tilbānah	142	30.59 N	31.27 E
Tilburg	52	51.34 N	5.05 E
Tilbury, On., Can.	214	42.16 N	82.26 W
Tilbury, Eng., U.K.	42	51.28 N	0.23 E
Tilcara	252	23.34 S	65.22 W
Tilcha	166	29.36 S	140.54 E
Til-Châtel	58	47.31 N	5.10 E
Tilden, Il., U.S.	219	38.12 N	89.40 W
Tilden, Ne., U.S.	198	42.02 N	97.50 W
Tilden, Tx., U.S.	196	28.28 N	98.33 W
Tilden Lake ⊜	226	38.07 N	119.36 W
Tilden Woods	284c	39.03 N	77.09 W
Tilemsès	150	15.37 N	4.44 E
Tilemsi, Vallée du V	150	16.15 N	0.02 E
Tilff	56	50.34 N	5.35 E
Tilghman Island I	208	38.42 N	76.20 W
Tilhar	124	27.59 N	79.44 E
Tilia, Oued V	148	27.27 N	0.01 W
Tiligul ≃	78	47.04 N	30.57 E
Tiligulo-Berezanka	78	46.52 N	31.24 E
Tiligul'skij liman ⊜	78	46.48 N	31.08 E
Tiliktino	82	56.06 N	36.36 E
Tilimsen	148	34.52 N	1.15 W
Tilimsen □[5]	148	35.00 N	2.00 W
Tilin	110	21.42 N	94.04 E
Tilisarao	252	32.44 S	65.18 W
Till ≃, Eng., U.K.	44	55.41 N	2.12 W
Till ≃, Eng., U.K.	44	53.16 N	0.37 W
Tillaberi	150	14.13 N	1.27 E
Tillamook	202	45.27 N	123.50 W
Tillamook □[6]	224	45.25 N	123.39 W
Tillamook ≃	224	45.28 N	123.53 W
Tillamook Bay c	224	45.30 N	123.53 W
Tillamook Head >	224	45.57 N	124.00 W
Tillanchāng Dwīp I	110	8.30 N	93.37 E
Tillberga	40	59.41 N	16.37 E
Tille ≃	58	47.07 N	5.21 E
Tillery, Lake ⊜[1]	192	35.17 N	80.05 W
Tilley	182	50.27 N	111.39 W
Tilli	126	23.57 N	89.57 E
Tillia	150	16.08 N	4.47 E
Tillicoultry	46	56.09 N	3.45 W
Tillicum	224	47.08 N	122.33 W
Tillières-sur-Avre	50	48.46 N	1.04 E
Tilling Bourne ≃	260	51.13 N	0.34 W
Tillmans Corner	194	30.43 N	88.05 W
Tillson	210	41.49 N	74.04 W
Tillsonburg	212	42.51 N	80.44 W
Tillyfourie	46	57.11 N	2.35 W
Tilogne	150	15.58 N	13.36 W
Tilomar	112	9.21 S	125.08 E
Tílos I	38	36.25 N	27.25 E
Tilpa	166	30.57 S	144.24 E
Tilrhemt	148	33.10 N	3.21 E
Tilsit → Sovetsk	76	55.05 N	21.53 E
Tilt ≃	46	56.46 N	3.50 W
Tilton, Il., U.S.	194	40.05 N	87.38 W
Tilton, Ky., U.S.	218	38.22 N	83.45 W
Tilton, N.H., U.S.	188	43.26 N	71.35 W
Tilton ≃	224	46.33 N	122.33 W
Tiltonsville	214	40.10 N	80.41 W
Tilzapotla	234	18.29 N	99.16 W
Tim	78	51.37 N	37.07 E
Tim ≃	76	52.15 N	37.22 E
Ṭimā	140	26.54 N	31.26 E
Timah, Bukit ∧[2]	271c	1.21 N	103.47 E
Timahoe	48	53.20 N	6.49 W
Timaná	246	1.58 N	75.56 W
Timane ≃	248	20.34 S	59.15 W
Timanskij kr'až ∧	24	65.00 N	51.00 E
Timar	84	38.49 N	43.27 E
Timaricha	80	57.33 N	44.47 E
Timaru	172	44.24 S	171.15 E
Timaševo, Ross.	80	53.21 N	51.12 E
Timaševo, Ross.	82	55.08 N	36.29 E
Timaševsk	78	45.37 N	38.57 E
Timau, It.	64	46.35 N	13.00 E
Timau, Kenya	154	0.05 N	37.14 E
Timavo San Giovanni	64	45.48 N	13.37 E
Timay al-Amdīd	142	30.57 N	31.32 E
Timbákion	38	35.04 N	24.46 E
Timbalier Bay c	194	29.10 N	90.20 W
Timbaúba	250	7.31 S	35.19 W
Timbavati Game Reserve ◆[4]	156	24.27 S	31.27 E
Timbedgha	150	16.15 N	8.10 W
Timber	224	45.43 N	123.17 W
Timber Creek	164	15.39 S	130.29 E
Timber Creek ≃	198	44.49 N	98.17 W
Timber Lake, Il., U.S.	278	42.14 N	88.07 W
Timberlake, Oh., U.S.	214	41.41 N	81.25 W
Timber Lake, S.D., U.S.	198	45.26 N	101.04 W
Timber Run ≃	284b	39.27 N	76.52 W
Timber Trails	278	41.52 N	87.57 W
Timberview	284b	39.13 N	76.45 W
Timbío	246	2.20 N	76.40 W
Timbiras	250	4.15 S	43.57 W
Timblin	214	40.58 N	79.12 W
Timbó, Bra.	252	26.50 S	49.18 W
Timbo, Guinée	150	10.38 N	11.50 W
Timbo, Liber.	150	5.37 N	9.43 W
Timbó ≃	287a	22.52 S	43.16 W
Timboon	169	38.29 S	142.59 E
Timbuctoo	285	40.00 N	74.49 W
Timbuktu → Tombouctou	150	16.46 N	3.01 W
Timbun Mata, Pulau I	112	4.39 N	118.28 E
Timel'ga	86	58.53 N	76.42 E
Timelkam	60	48.00 N	13.36 E
Times Square ♠	276	40.45 N	74.00 W
Timétrine	150	19.27 N	0.26 W
Timétrine ⋏	150	19.20 N	0.42 W
Timeu Creek ≃	182	54.28 N	114.27 W
Timewell	219	40.00 N	90.52 W
Timgad ⊥	148	35.29 N	6.28 E
Timimoun	148	29.14 N	0.16 E
Timimoun, Sebkha de ⊜	148	29.00 N	0.05 E
Timinar	140	19.02 N	30.29 E
Timi Ouli, Ehi ∧	146	21.08 N	16.31 E
Timir'azevo	76	55.05 N	21.37 E
Timir'azevskij	86	56.29 N	84.54 E
Timirevo	82	55.08 N	39.10 E
Timirist, Râs >	150	19.23 N	16.32 W
Timiș □[6]	38	45.40 N	21.20 E
Timiș (Tamiš) ≃	38	44.51 N	20.39 E
Timiskaming, Lake ⊜	190	47.10 N	79.25 W
Timișoara	38	45.45 N	21.13 E
Timkoviči	76	53.03 N	27.00 E
Timkovo	82	55.56 N	38.37 E
Timmendorfer Strand	54	54.00 N	10.46 E
Timmernabben	26	56.58 N	16.26 E
Timmins	190	48.28 N	81.20 W
Timmonsville	192	34.08 N	79.56 W
Timms Hill ∧[2]	190	45.27 N	90.11 W
Timok ≃	38	44.13 N	22.40 E
Timon	250	5.06 S	42.49 W
Timonovo	82	56.13 N	37.02 E
Timor I	112	9.00 S	125.00 E
Timor Sea ⊤[2]	14	11.00 S	128.00 E
Timor Timur □[4]	112	8.35 S	126.00 E
Timor Trough ✢[1]	14	9.50 S	126.00 E
Timošino, Ross.	76	60.05 N	36.10 E
Timošino, Ross.	80	57.50 N	44.25 E
Timotes	246	8.59 N	70.44 W
Timothy Lake ⊜[1]	224	45.07 N	121.47 W
Timoudi	148	29.19 N	1.09 W
Timousserarène ≃	150	16.21 N	8.07 E
Timpanogos Cave National Monument ♠	200	40.18 N	111.52 W
Timpas Creek ≃	198	38.02 N	103.38 W
Timpaus, Pulau I	112	1.51 S	124.01 E
Timperley	262	53.24 N	2.19 W
Timpson	194	31.54 N	94.23 W
Timpton ≃	74	58.43 N	127.12 E
Timra	26	62.31 N	17.22 E

FRANÇAIS

Nom	Page	Lat.°′	Long.°′ W = Ouest
Timsāh, Buḥayrat at- (Lake Timsah) ⊜	142	30.34 N	32.17 E
Timsah, Lake → Timsāh, Buḥayrat at- ⊜	142	30.34 N	32.17 E
Timšer	24	62.06 N	54.40 E
Tims Ford Lake ⊜[1]	194	35.15 N	86.10 W
Timun	114	0.50 N	103.22 E
Timur	85	42.50 N	68.26 E
Timur, Banjaran ⋏	114	5.00 N	102.30 E
Timurni	124	22.22 N	77.22 E
Tīn, Ra's at- >	146	32.37 N	23.08 E
Tina ≃	158	31.18 S	29.14 E
Tinaca Point >	116	5.33 N	125.20 E
Tinaco	246	9.42 N	68.26 W
Tinaga Island I	116	14.28 N	122.56 E
Ṭīnah, Khalīj aṭ- c	140	31.08 N	32.40 E
Tinahely	48	52.48 N	6.28 W
Tinaja, Punta >	248	16.14 S	73.39 W
Tinalmud	116	13.36 N	122.53 E
Tinambac	116	13.49 N	123.19 E
Tinambung	112	3.31 S	119.01 E
Ti-n-Amzi V	150	18.20 N	4.32 E
Tinapagee	166	29.28 S	144.23 E
Tinaquillo	246	9.55 N	68.18 W
Tindari, Capo >	70	38.10 N	15.03 E
Tinderry Peak ∧	171b	35.42 S	149.16 E
Tindila	150	10.16 N	8.15 W
Tindis	126	21.35 N	86.44 E
Tindivanam	122	12.15 N	79.39 E
Tindouf	148	27.50 N	8.04 W
Tindouf, Hamada de ◆[1]	148	27.30 N	9.00 W
Tindouf, Sebkha de ≚	148	27.45 N	7.15 W
Tineba, Pegunungan ⋏	112	1.40 S	120.25 E
Tinée ≃	62	43.55 N	7.11 E
Tineg ≃	116	17.38 N	120.37 E
Tineo	34	43.20 N	6.25 W
Ting ≃	100	24.24 N	116.35 E
Tinga ∧	146	9.21 N	23.38 E
Tingambato	234	19.30 N	101.52 W
Tinggi, Pulau I	114	2.18 N	104.07 E
Tingha	166	29.57 S	151.13 E
Tinghert, Ḥamādat (Plateau du Tinghert) ⋏[1]	148	29.00 N	9.00 E
Tinghert, Plateau du (Ḥamādat Tinghert) ⋏[1]	148	29.00 N	9.00 E
Tinghsien → Dingxian	98	38.32 N	114.59 E
Tingkar ∧	116	5.20 N	117.06 E
Ting Kau	271d	22.22 N	114.05 E
Tingkawk Sakan	110	26.04 N	96.44 E
Tingkou	98	36.34 N	119.46 E
Tinglev	41	54.56 N	9.15 E
Tinglin	106	30.53 N	121.17 E
Tingliuhe	98	39.34 N	118.49 E
Tingloy	116	13.40 N	120.52 E
Tingmerkpuk Mountain ∧	180	68.34 N	162.28 W
Tingo de Saposoa	248	7.07 S	76.38 W
Tingo María	248	9.09 S	75.56 W
Tingo María, Parque Nacional ♠	248	9.15 S	76.05 W
Tingqian	100	30.10 N	115.54 E
Tingri, Zhg.	120	28.35 N	86.38 E
Tingri, Zhg.	120	28.38 N	87.04 E
Tingsiqiao	100	29.50 N	114.12 E
Tingsryd	26	56.32 N	14.59 E
Tingstäde	26	57.44 N	18.36 E
Tingsted	41	54.49 N	11.56 E
Tinguá	256	22.36 S	43.26 W
Tingüindín	234	19.45 N	102.29 W
Tinguiririca, Volcán ∧[1]	252	34.49 S	70.21 W
Tingvoll	26	62.54 N	8.12 E
Tingvollfjorden c[2]	26	62.50 N	8.11 E
Tingwick	206	45.50 N	71.58 W
Tingwon Group II	164	2.35 S	149.45 E
Tingzitou	106	30.12 N	119.46 E
Tinharé, Ilha de I	255	13.30 S	38.58 W
Tinh Bien	110	10.36 N	104.57 E
Tinian	174n	14.58 N	145.38 E
Tinian I	174n	15.00 N	145.38 E
Tinian Harbor c	174n	14.57 N	145.36 E
Tinié	150	14.20 N	1.28 W
Tiniguiban	116	11.22 N	119.30 E
Tinitian	116	10.04 N	119.12 E
Tinjar ≃	112	4.04 N	114.18 E
Tinjil, Pulau I	115a	6.58 S	105.47 E
Tinker Air Force Base ■	196	35.25 N	97.24 W
Tinkers Creek ≃, Md., U.S.	284c	38.46 N	76.57 W
Tinkers Creek ≃, Oh., U.S.	214	41.22 N	81.37 W
Tinkertown	283	42.01 N	70.44 W
Tinkisso ≃	150	11.21 N	9.10 W
Tinley Creek ≃	278	41.39 N	87.45 W
Tinley Creek Woods ♠	278	41.39 N	87.47 W
Tinley Park	216	41.34 N	87.47 W
Tinniswood, Mount ∧	182	50.19 N	123.50 W
Tinnoset	26	59.43 N	9.02 E
Tinnsjø ⊜	26	59.54 N	8.55 E
Tinogasta	252	28.04 S	67.34 W
Tinompo	112	2.09 S	121.17 E
Tínos	38	37.32 N	25.10 E
Tínos I	38	37.38 N	25.10 E
Tinquipaya	248	19.11 S	65.51 W
Tin Rerhoh, Tassili ⋏	150	19.40 N	4.00 E
Tinrhir	148	31.28 N	5.30 W
Tin Sam	271d	22.22 N	114.11 E
Tinskoj	88	56.10 N	96.55 E
Tinsley	194	32.43 N	90.27 W
Tinsukia	120	27.30 N	95.22 E
Tintagel, B.C., Can.	182	54.12 N	125.35 W
Tintagel, Eng., U.K.	42	50.40 N	4.45 W
Tintagel Head >	42	50.41 N	4.46 W
Tintaldra	171b	36.03 S	147.56 E
Tintas, Rio das ≃	287a	22.52 S	43.28 W
Tinte, Cerro ∧	248	22.40 S	67.02 W
Tintern Abbey ʋ[1]	42	51.41 N	2.40 W
Tintern Parva	42	51.42 N	2.40 W
Tintigny	56	49.41 N	5.31 E
Tintina	252	27.02 S	62.43 W
Tintinara	166	35.54 S	140.03 E
Tintioulé	150	10.13 N	9.12 W
Tinto ∧	46	55.36 N	3.39 W
Tinto ≃	34	37.12 N	6.55 W
Ti-n-Toumma ◆[1]	146	16.04 N	12.40 E
Tintwistle	262	53.28 N	1.58 W
Tinui	172	40.53 S	176.04 E
Tinwald	172	43.55 S	171.43 E
Ti-n-Zaouatene	150	19.55 N	2.52 E
Tinzap ≃	120	38.23 N	77.24 E
Tio	144	14.42 N	40.58 E
Tioga, Il., U.S.	219	40.13 N	91.21 W
Tioga, N.D., U.S.	198	48.23 N	102.56 W
Tioga, Pa., U.S.	210	41.55 N	77.08 W
Tioga □[6], N.Y., U.S.	210	42.06 N	76.16 W
Tioga □[6], Pa., U.S.	210	41.45 N	77.17 W
Tioga ◆[8]	285	40.00 N	75.10 W
Tioga ≃	210	42.09 N	77.05 W
Tioga Center	210	42.04 N	76.21 W
Tioga Pass)(	226	37.54 N	119.16 W
Tioga Terrace	210	42.03 N	76.07 W
Tiojala	24	61.10 N	23.52 E
Tioman, Pulau I	114	2.48 N	104.10 E
Tiona	214	41.45 N	79.03 W
Tione di Trento	64	46.02 N	10.43 E
Tionesta	214	41.30 N	79.27 W
Tionesta Creek ≃	214	41.28 N	79.22 W
Tionesta Lake ⊜[1]	214	41.28 N	79.28 W
Tioor, Pulau I	164	4.45 S	131.45 E
Tior	140	6.23 N	31.11 E
Tioro	112	4.41 S	122.36 E

PORTUGUÊS

Nome	Página	Lat.°′	Long.°′ W = Oeste
Tioro, Selat υ	112	4.40 S	122.20 E
Tioroniaradougou	150	9.21 N	5.38 W
Tioughnioga ≃	210	42.14 N	75.51 W
Tioughnioga, East Branch ≃	210	42.36 N	76.10 W
Tipasa	34	36.35 N	2.27 E
Tipitapa	236	12.12 N	86.06 W
Tipoca, Monter ∧[2]	250	3.34 N	51.20 W
Tipp City	218	39.57 N	84.10 W
Tippecanoe, In., U.S.	216	41.12 N	86.06 W
Tippecanoe, Oh., U.S.	214	40.16 N	81.17 W
Tippecanoe □[6]	216	40.25 N	86.53 W
Tippecanoe ≃	216	40.31 N	86.47 W
Tippecanoe, Lake ⊜	216	41.20 N	85.46 W
Tippecanoe Battlefield State Memorial ⊥	216	40.31 N	86.52 W
Tippecanoe River State Park ♠	216	41.07 N	86.36 W
Tipperary, Austl.	164	13.44 S	131.02 E
Tipperary, Ire.	48	52.29 N	8.10 W
Tipperary □[6]	48	52.40 N	8.20 W
Tipton, Eng., U.K.	42	52.32 N	2.05 W
Tipton, Ca., U.S.	226	36.03 N	119.18 W
Tipton, In., U.S.	216	40.16 N	86.02 W
Tipton, Ia., U.S.	190	41.46 N	91.07 W
Tipton, Mi., U.S.	216	42.01 N	84.04 W
Tipton, Mo., U.S.	194	38.39 N	92.46 W
Tipton, Ok., U.S.	196	34.30 N	99.08 W
Tipton, Pa., U.S.	214	40.38 N	78.18 W
Tipton □[6]	216	40.17 N	86.02 W
Tipton, Mount ∧	200	35.32 N	114.12 W
Tiptonville	194	36.22 N	89.28 W
Tip Top Mountain ∧	190	48.16 N	85.59 W
Tiptree	42	51.49 N	0.45 E
Tiptūr	122	13.16 N	76.29 E
Tiputini ≃	246	0.47 S	75.32 W
Tiquicheo	234	18.53 N	100.44 W
Tīra	132	32.14 N	34.57 E
Tira Chapéu, Morro ∧	256	22.45 S	44.39 W
Tiradentes	255	21.07 S	44.11 W
Tīrah, Baḥr ≅	142	31.03 N	31.15 E
Tīrān I	128	27.56 N	34.34 E
Tīrān, Maḍīq υ	140	27.58 N	34.28 E
Tiran, Strait of → Tīrān, Maḍīq υ	140	27.58 N	34.28 E
Tirana → Tiranë	38	41.20 N	19.50 E
Tiranë	38	41.20 N	19.50 E
Tirano	64	46.13 N	10.10 E
Tiraque	248	17.37 S	65.04 W
Tirari Desert ◆[2]	162	28.00 S	138.20 E
Tiraspol'	78	46.51 N	29.38 E
Tirat Karmel	132	32.46 N	34.58 E
Tirat Ẕevi	132	32.25 N	35.32 E
Tirau	172	37.59 S	175.45 E
Tire	130	38.04 N	27.45 E
Tirebolu	130	41.00 N	38.48 E
Tiree I	46	56.31 N	6.49 W
Tire Hill	214	40.16 N	78.55 W
Tires (Tiers), It.	64	46.28 N	11.31 E
Tires, Port.	266c	38.43 N	9.21 W
Tires ◆[1]	148	23.30 N	13.10 W
Tîrgoviște	38	44.56 N	25.27 E
Tîrgu Bujor	38	45.52 N	27.54 E
Tîrgu-Cărbunești	38	44.58 N	23.31 E
Tîrgu-Frumos	38	47.13 N	27.00 E
Tîrgu Jiu	38	45.02 N	23.17 E
Tîrgu-Lăpuș	38	47.27 N	23.52 E
Tîrgu Mureș	38	46.33 N	24.33 E
Tîrgu-Neamț	38	47.12 N	26.22 E
Tîrgu Ocna	38	46.15 N	26.37 E
Tîrgu Secuiesc	38	46.00 N	26.08 E
Tîrgusor	38	44.28 N	28.25 E
Tirhahart, Oued V	148	23.45 N	3.10 E
Tiria, Monte ∧	71	40.23 N	9.16 E
Tirich Mīr ∧	123	36.15 N	71.50 E
Tiriro	150	10.27 N	8.39 W
Tiris Zemmour □[4]	148	24.10 N	9.30 W
Tirl'anskij	86	54.14 N	58.35 E
Tirna ≃	122	18.04 N	76.57 E
Tîrnava Mare ≃	38	46.09 N	23.42 E
Tîrnava Mică ≃	38	46.11 N	23.55 E
Tîrnăveni	38	46.20 N	24.17 E
Tírnavos	38	39.45 N	22.17 E
Tirnovo → Veliko Târnovo	38	43.04 N	25.39 E
Tiro	214	40.54 N	82.46 W
Tirodi	120	21.41 N	79.42 E
Tirol □[3]	64	47.15 N	11.20 E
Tiroler Ache (Grossache) ≃	60	47.51 N	12.30 E
Tirolo (Tirol)	64	46.42 N	11.10 E
Tiros	255	19.00 S	45.58 W
Tiroungoulou	146	9.34 N	22.09 E
Tīr Pol	128	34.36 N	61.15 E
Tirrenia	66	43.38 N	10.17 E
Tirreno, Mare → Tyrrhenian Sea ⊤[2]	36	40.00 N	12.00 E
Tirry ≃	46	58.02 N	4.26 W
Tirsā, Miṣr	142	29.25 N	30.49 E
Tirsā, Miṣr	273c	29.58 N	31.12 E
Tirschenreuth	60	49.53 N	12.21 E
Tirso ≃	71	39.53 N	8.32 E
Tirsted	41	54.44 N	11.21 E
Tirstrup	41	56.18 N	10.42 E
Tīrthahalli	122	13.42 N	75.14 E
Tirua Point >	172	38.23 S	174.38 E
Tiruchchirāppalli	122	10.49 N	78.41 E
Tiruchengodu	122	11.23 N	77.56 E
Tirukkalukkunram	122	12.37 N	80.04 E
Tirukkovilūr	122	11.57 N	79.12 E
Tiruliai	76	55.47 N	23.22 E
Tirumangalam	122	9.50 N	77.59 E
Tirunelveli	122	8.44 N	77.42 E
Tirupati	122	13.39 N	79.25 E
Tiruppattūr, India	122	12.30 N	78.34 E
Tiruppattūr, India	122	10.08 N	78.37 E
Tiruppur	122	11.06 N	77.21 E
Tirūr	122	10.54 N	75.55 E
Tiruttani	122	13.11 N	79.38 E
Tirutturaippūndi	122	10.32 N	79.39 E
Tiruvalla	122	9.23 N	76.34 E
Tiruvallūr	122	13.09 N	79.55 E
Tiruvannāmalai	122	12.13 N	79.04 E
Tiruvettipuram	122	12.40 N	79.33 E
Tirūvottiyūr	122	13.09 N	80.18 E
Tiruvur	122	17.06 N	80.38 E
Tisa (Tisza) ≃	38	45.15 N	20.17 E
Tis'ah	142	30.02 N	32.35 E
Tisaiyanvilai	122	8.20 N	77.53 E
Tisaren ⊜	40	59.00 N	15.08 E
Tisbury	42	51.04 N	2.03 W
Tisdale	184	52.51 N	104.04 W
Tishomingo, Ms., U.S.	194	34.38 N	88.13 W
Tishomingo, Ok., U.S.	196	34.14 N	96.40 W
Tisisat Falls ᒐ	144	11.29 N	37.35 E
Ṭīsīyah	132	32.24 N	36.27 E
Tisjön ⊜	26	60.55 N	12.58 E
Tiskilwa	190	41.17 N	89.30 W
Tiskino	86	58.05 N	83.10 E
Tiškovka	78	48.29 N	30.56 E
Tiškovo, Ross.	80	46.02 N	48.36 E
Tiškovo, Ross.	82	56.05 N	37.44 E
Tisma	236	12.05 N	86.01 W
Tisnaren ⊜	40	58.57 N	15.57 E
Tišnevo	82	55.10 N	36.17 E
Tišnov	30	49.21 N	16.25 E
Tisovec	30	48.43 N	19.57 E
Tissa	146	7.26 N	10.16 E
Tissemsilt	148	35.35 N	1.50 E
Tissø ⊜	41	55.35 N	11.18 E
Tīsta ≃	124	25.23 N	89.43 E
Tisul'	86	55.45 N	88.19 E
Tisvildeleje	41	56.03 N	12.05 E
Tisza (Tisa) ≃	38	45.15 N	20.17 E

Nome	Página	Lat.°′	Long.°′ W = Oeste
Tiszaföldvár	30	46.59 N	20.15 E
Tiszafüred	30	47.37 N	20.46 E
Tiszavasvári	30	47.58 N	21.22 E
Tit	148	23.00 N	5.10 E
Titaf	148	27.26 N	0.13 W
Titāgarh	126	22.45 N	88.22 E
Titano, Monte ∧	66	43.55 N	12.28 E
Titao	150	13.46 N	2.04 W
Tit-Ary	74	71.58 N	127.01 E
Titel	38	45.12 N	20.18 E
Tithwāl	123	34.24 N	73.47 E
Titicaca, Lago ⊜	248	15.50 S	69.20 W
Titicus	207	41.18 N	73.30 W
Titi Karangan	114	5.31 N	100.37 E
Titikaveka	174k	21.15 S	159.45 W
Titilāgarh	122	20.18 N	83.09 E
Titisee-Neustadt	58	47.54 N	8.13 E
Titlis ∧	58	46.47 N	8.25 E
Tito	68	40.35 N	15.40 E
Titonka	190	43.14 N	94.02 W
Titou	100	29.52 N	112.42 E
Titova Korenica	36	44.45 N	15.43 E
Titovka	83	48.59 N	39.44 E
Titovo, Ross.	80	53.17 N	43.41 E
Titovo, Ross.	82	54.19 N	36.56 E
Titovo, Ross.	82	55.35 N	39.07 E
Titovo Velenje	61	46.22 N	15.07 E
Titov Veles	38	41.41 N	21.48 E
Titov vrh ∧	38	42.00 N	20.51 E
Titran	26	63.40 N	8.18 E
Tittabawassee ≃	190	43.23 N	83.59 W
Titteri ⋏	34	36.00 N	3.30 E
Titterstone Clee Hill ∧[2]	42	52.23 N	2.35 W
Titting	60	49.00 N	11.13 E
Tittling	60	48.44 N	13.23 E
Tittmoning	60	48.04 N	12.46 E
Titu	38	44.41 N	25.32 E
Titule	154	3.17 N	25.32 E
Titus □[6]	222	33.05 N	94.58 W
Titusville, Fl., U.S.	220	28.36 N	80.48 W
Titusville, N.J., U.S.	208	40.18 N	74.52 W
Titusville, Pa., U.S.	214	41.37 N	79.40 W
Titz	56	51.01 N	6.25 E
Tiu Chung Chau I	271d	22.20 N	114.19 E
Tiumpan Head >	46	58.16 N	6.09 W
Tiuni	120	30.57 N	77.51 E
Tiva ≃	154	2.20 S	38.48 E
Tivaouane	150	14.57 N	16.49 W
Tiveden ⋏[2]	40	58.45 N	14.40 E
Tiverton, Eng., U.K.	42	50.55 N	3.29 W
Tiverton, R.I., U.S.	207	41.37 N	71.12 W
Tivoli, Gren.	241k	12.10 N	61.37 W
Tivoli, It.	66	41.58 N	12.48 E
Tivoli, N.Y., U.S.	210	42.03 N	73.54 W
Tivoli, Tx., U.S.	196	28.27 N	96.53 W
Tivoli ♠	41	55.40 N	12.34 E
Ṭiwāl, Wādī V	146	10.22 N	22.43 E
Ṭiwāl al-'Abā ∧	130	36.20 N	39.22 E
Tiwi, Pil.	116	13.27 N	123.41 E
Ṭīwī, 'Umān	128	22.49 N	59.16 E
Tiwuronto	115b	8.48 S	120.09 E
Tixtla de Guerrero	234	17.35 N	99.26 W
Tiyās	130	34.33 N	37.40 E
Tiyo, Pegunungan ⋏	164	4.00 S	135.30 E
Tizapán ◆[8]	286a	19.20 N	99.13 W
Tizapán El Alto	234	20.10 N	103.04 W
Tizimín	232	21.10 N	88.10 W
Tizi-Ouzou	148	36.48 N	4.02 E
Tizi Ouzou □[5]	148	36.40 N	4.10 E
Tizmant ash-Sharqīyah	142	29.03 N	31.03 E
Tiznados ≃	246	8.16 N	67.47 W
Tiznit	148	29.43 N	9.44 W
Tiznit □[4]	148	29.40 N	9.45 W
Tizoc	196	25.41 N	101.59 W
Tjällmo	40	58.43 N	15.21 E
Tjeukemeer ⊜	52	52.54 N	5.50 E
Tjilatjap → Cilacap	115a	7.44 S	109.00 E
Tjirebon → Cirebon	115a	6.44 S	108.34 E
Tjolotjo	154	19.47 S	27.46 E
Tjøme I	26	59.07 N	10.24 E
Tjörn I	26	58.00 N	11.38 E
Tjörnarp	41	56.00 N	13.37 E
Tkibuli	84	42.21 N	42.59 E
Tkvarčeli	84	42.51 N	41.41 E
Tlachichuca	234	19.06 N	97.25 W
Tlacoapa	234	17.09 N	98.52 W
Tlacotalpan	234	18.37 N	95.40 W
Tlacotepec	234	17.46 N	99.59 W
Tlacuitapan	234	21.14 N	102.12 W
Tláhuac ◆[8]	286a	19.16 N	99.00 W
Tlahualilo de Zaragoza	232	26.07 N	103.27 W
Tlahuelilpan	234	20.08 N	99.14 W
Tlahuitoltepec	234	17.04 N	95.59 W
Tlajomulco de Zúñiga	234	20.28 N	103.27 W
Tlalchapa	234	18.24 N	100.28 W
Tlalcozotitlán	234	17.54 N	99.15 W
Tlalixtac de Cabrera	234	17.04 N	96.39 W
Tlalixtaquilla	234	17.21 N	98.28 W
Tlalnepantla	234	19.33 N	99.12 W
Tlalnepantla ≃	286a	19.31 N	99.16 W
Tlalpan ◆[8]	286a	19.17 N	99.10 W
Tlalpujahua	234	19.48 N	100.10 W
Tlaltenango de Sánchez Román	234	21.47 N	103.19 W
Tl'ančetamak	80	55.28 N	52.37 E
Tlapacoyan	234	19.58 N	97.13 W
Tlapa de Comonfort	234	17.33 N	98.33 W
Tlapaneco ≃	234	18.05 N	98.48 W
Tlapehuala	234	18.13 N	100.31 W
Tlapeng	156	23.15 S	21.49 E
Tlaquepaque	234	20.39 N	103.19 W
Tl'arata	84	42.07 N	46.22 E
Tlatlauquitepec	234	19.51 N	97.29 W
Tlaxcala □[3]	234	19.25 N	98.10 W
Tlaxcala [de Xicoténcatl]	234	19.19 N	98.14 W
Tlaxcoapan	234	20.05 N	99.13 W
Tlaxco [de Morelos]	234	19.37 N	98.07 W
Tlaxmalac	234	18.21 N	99.25 W
Tlazazalca	234	19.58 N	102.04 W
Tletat ed Douair	34	35.59 N	2.55 E
Tlētē Ouāte Gharbī, Jabal ∧	130	35.20 N	39.13 E
Tlevak Strait υ	182	55.03 N	132.58 W
Tlhakgameng	158	26.27 S	24.21 E
Tloch	84	42.38 N	46.28 E
Tlučiná	60	49.44 N	13.14 E
Tlumač	78	48.52 N	25.01 E
Tłuszcz	30	52.26 N	21.26 E
Tmassah	146	26.22 N	15.47 E
Tmīsān	146	27.32 N	13.19 E
Tnâot ≃	110	11.29 N	104.57 E
Tnekvejem ≃	180	65.50 N	177.31 E
Toa ≃	240p	20.23 N	74.32 W
Toa Alta	240m	18.23 N	66.15 W
Toab	46a	59.53 N	1.19 W
Toa Baja	240m	18.27 N	66.15 W
Toabré ≃	236	8.56 N	80.33 W
Toachi ≃	246	0.08 N	79.18 W
Toahayaná	232	26.08 N	107.44 W
Toamasina	157b	18.10 S	49.23 E
Toamasina □[4]	157b	18.00 S	48.40 E
Toandonggu	98	40.33 N	127.35 E
Toandos Peninsula >[1]	224	47.43 N	122.47 W
Toano, It.	64	44.23 N	10.34 E
Toano, Va., U.S.	208	37.22 N	76.48 W
Toano Draw V	204	41.27 N	114.35 W
Toano Range ⋏	204	40.50 N	114.20 W
Toast	192	36.30 N	80.37 W
Toa Vaca, Embalse ⊜[1]	240m	18.06 N	66.28 W
Toay	252	36.40 S	64.21 W
Toba, Mali	150	11.52 N	7.28 W
Toba, Nihon	94	34.29 N	136.51 E

Nome	Página	Lat.°′	Long.°′ W = Oeste
Toba, Zhg.	102	31.18 N	97.40 E
Toba ≃	182	50.30 N	124.15 W
Toba, Danau ⊜	114	2.35 N	98.50 E
Tobacco ≃	190	43.49 N	84.24 W
Tobacco Plains Indian Reserve ◆[4]	182	49.04 N	115.06 W
Tobacco Root Mountains ⋏	202	45.35 N	112.00 W
Tobago I	241r	11.15 N	60.40 W
Toba Inlet c	182	50.20 N	124.50 W
Toba Kākar Range ⋏	120	31.15 N	68.00 E
Tobalaba Eulogio Sánchez, Aeródromo ⊠	286e	33.27 S	70.33 W
Tobalai, Pulau I	164	1.37 S	128.20 E
Tobarra	34	38.35 N	1.41 W
Tobas	252	28.08 S	62.42 W
Tobašino	80	56.56 N	47.40 E
Toba Tek Singh	123	30.58 N	72.29 E
Tobe	96	33.44 N	132.47 E
Tobejuba, Isla I	246	9.20 N	60.52 W
Tobekuduk	86	49.50 N	54.15 E
Tobelo	108	1.44 N	128.01 E
Tobelombang	112	0.57 S	122.00 E
Tobercurry	48	54.03 N	8.43 W
Tobermorey	166	22.15 S	138.00 E
Tobermory, Austl.	166	27.17 S	143.41 E
Tobermory, On., Can.	190	45.15 N	81.40 W
Tobermory, Scot., U.K.	46	56.37 N	6.05 W
Toberonochy	46	56.13 N	5.38 W
Tōbetsu	92a	43.13 N	141.31 E
Tobi I	108	3.00 N	131.10 E
Tobias	198	40.25 N	97.20 W
Tobias Barreto	250	11.11 S	38.01 W
Tobiishi-bana >	174f	24.45 N	141.17 E
Tobin, Mount ∧	204	40.22 N	117.32 W
Tobin Lake ⊜, Austl.	162	21.45 S	125.49 E
Tobin Lake ⊜, Sk., Can.	184	53.40 N	103.35 W
Tobique ≃	186	46.46 N	67.42 W
Tobi-shima I	92	39.12 N	139.34 E
Toblach → Dobbiaco	64	46.44 N	12.14 E
Tobo, Indon.	164	3.34 S	130.11 E
Tobo, Sve.	40	60.16 N	17.39 E
Toboali	112	3.00 S	106.30 E
Tobol	86	52.40 N	62.39 E
Tobol ≃	86	58.10 N	68.12 E
Toboli	112	0.43 S	120.05 E
Tobol'sk	86	58.12 N	68.16 E
Tobong-san ∧	271b	37.42 N	127.01 E
Tobor	150	12.39 N	16.16 W
Toboso	116	10.43 N	123.31 E
Tobré	150	10.12 N	2.08 E
Tobruk → Ṭubruq	146	32.05 N	23.59 E
Tobseda	24	68.36 N	52.14 E
Tōbu	94	36.21 N	138.20 E
Toburdanovo	80	55.22 N	47.38 E
Toby, Mount ∧	207	42.29 N	72.32 W
Tobyhanna	210	41.10 N	75.25 W
Tobyhanna Creek ≃	210	41.07 N	75.39 W
Tobyhanna State Park ♠	210	41.13 N	75.25 W
Tobyš ≃	24	65.30 N	51.00 E
Toca Grande, Morro da ∧	287a	22.58 S	43.31 W
Tocantínia	250	9.33 S	48.22 W
Tocantinópolis	250	6.20 S	47.25 W
Tocantins □[3]	250	10.00 S	48.00 W
Tocantins ≃, Bra.	242	1.45 S	49.10 W
Tocantins ≃, Bra.	250	5.21 S	55.58 W
Tocantinzinho ≃	255	13.57 S	48.20 W
Toccoa	192	34.34 N	83.19 W
Toccoa (Ocoee) ≃	192	35.12 N	84.40 W
Toce ≃	58	45.56 N	8.29 E
Tochapan	234	18.54 N	97.37 W
Tochcha Lake ⊜	182	54.56 N	125.54 W
Tochigi	94	36.23 N	139.44 E
Tochigi □[5]	94	36.45 N	139.45 E
Tochimilco	234	18.54 N	98.34 W
Tochio	92	37.28 N	139.00 E
Tochoj	88	50.30 N	105.00 E
Tochta	24	62.14 N	48.48 E
Tochtamyš	120	37.50 N	74.39 E
Tockholes	262	53.42 N	2.31 W
Tockoje	80	52.32 N	52.45 E
Töcksfors	26	59.30 N	11.50 E
Točnik	60	49.27 N	13.19 E
Toco, Chile	252	22.05 S	69.35 W
Toco, Trin.	241r	10.50 N	60.57 W
Tocoa	236	15.41 N	86.03 W
Tócome ≃	286c	10.29 N	66.49 W
Toconao	252	23.11 S	68.01 W
Tocopilla	252	22.05 S	70.12 W
Tocos do Moji	256	22.22 S	46.06 W
Tocuco ≃	246	9.36 N	72.15 W
Tocumwal	166	35.49 S	145.34 E
Tocuyo ≃	246	11.03 N	68.23 W
Tocuyo de la Costa	246	11.02 N	68.23 W
Toda	94	35.48 N	139.41 E
Toda Bhīm	124	26.55 N	76.49 E
Todaiji Temple ʋ[1]	270	34.42 N	135.51 E
Todang-ni	271b	37.37 N	126.50 E
Toda Rāisingh	120	26.01 N	75.29 E
Todd	214	40.16 N	78.04 W
Todd ≃	162	24.52 S	135.48 E
Todd Estates	285	39.40 N	75.43 W
Todd Fork ≃	218	39.21 N	84.08 W
Todd Fork, East Fork ≃	218	39.24 N	84.00 W
Toddington	42	51.57 N	0.32 W
Todd Point >	284b	39.15 N	76.27 W
Toddville, Md., U.S.	208	38.17 N	76.04 W
Toddville, N.Y., U.S.	210	41.17 N	73.53 W
Todeli	112	1.40 S	124.29 E
Todenyang	154	4.32 N	35.56 E
Todi	66	42.47 N	12.24 E
Tödi ∧	58	46.49 N	8.56 E
Todmorden, Austl.	162	27.08 S	134.48 E
Todmorden, Eng., U.K.	44	53.43 N	2.05 W
Todoga-saki >	92	39.33 N	142.05 E
Todoromi	270	34.53 N	135.28 E
Todos Santos, Bol.	248	16.48 S	65.08 W
Todos Santos, Méx.	232	23.27 N	110.13 W
Todos Santos, Bahía c	232	31.48 N	116.42 W
Todro	154	3.21 N	30.14 E
Todtenhausen	52	52.20 N	8.56 E
Todtmoos	58	47.44 N	8.00 E
Todtmoos Au	58	47.42 N	7.58 E
Todtnau	58	47.50 N	7.56 E
Toe Head >	46	57.50 N	7.08 W
Tōei	94	35.04 N	137.41 E
T'oejo	98	39.54 N	127.46 E
Toéssé	150	11.50 N	1.16 W
Toetoes Bay c	172	46.38 S	168.43 E
Tofield	182	53.22 N	112.40 W
Tofino	182	49.09 N	125.54 W
Töfsingdalens Nationalpark ♠	26	62.09 N	12.30 E
Tofte	26	59.33 N	10.34 E
Toften ⊜	40	59.03 N	14.36 E
Tofterup	41	55.39 N	8.50 E
Toftlund	41	55.11 N	9.04 E
Toga	94	36.27 N	137.02 E
Toga I	175f	13.26 S	166.42 E
Togakushi	94	36.44 N	138.05 E
Togakushi-yama ∧	94	36.46 N	138.04 E
Toganas	80	50.49 N	52.02 E
Tōgane	94	35.33 N	140.22 E
Togauchi	96	34.34 N	132.13 E
Togdheer □[4]	144	9.00 N	46.00 E
Toggenburg V	58	47.15 N	9.10 E
Togho	152	6.01 N	17.26 E
Togi	94	37.08 N	136.44 E
Togiak	180	59.04 N	160.24 W
Togiak Bay c	180	59.00 N	160.30 W

Nome	Página	Lat.°′	Long.°′ W = Oeste
Togian, Kepulauan II	112	0.20 S	122.00 E
Togian, Pulau I	112	0.22 S	121.56 E
Töging am Inn	60	48.15 N	12.35 E
Togliatti → Toljatti	80	53.31 N	49.26 E
Togni	140	18.04 N	35.13 E
Tōgō, Nihon	94	35.05 N	137.03 E
Tōgō, Nihon	96	35.28 N	133.53 E
Togo □[1], Afr.	134	8.00 N	1.10 E
Togo □[1], Afr.	150	8.00 N	1.10 E
Togochale	144	9.33 N	43.18 E
Tōgō-ike ⊜	96	35.28 N	133.54 E
Togoron	116	12.35 N	123.37 E
Tögrög, Mong.	102	45.46 N	94.48 E
Tögrög, Mong.	102	45.32 N	102.59 E
Togtoh	102	40.22 N	111.11 E
Togučin	86	55.16 N	84.23 E
Togur	86	58.24 N	82.49 E
Togura	94	36.29 N	138.09 E
Toguzak ≃	86	54.06 N	62.50 E
Toguzbulak	85	42.06 N	76.44 E
Togwotee Pass)(	202	43.45 N	110.04 W
Tŏgyu-san ∧	98	35.46 N	127.40 E
Tŏgyu-san Kukrip Kongwŏn ♠	98	35.52 N	127.45 E
Togyz	86	47.34 N	60.33 E
Tōhaku	96	35.30 N	133.40 E
Tohakum Peak ∧	204	40.11 N	119.27 W
Tohāna	124	29.42 N	75.54 E
Tohiea, Mont ∧	174s	17.33 S	149.49 W
Tohma ≃	130	38.31 N	38.25 E
Toholampi	26	63.46 N	24.15 E
Tohopekaliga, Lake ⊜	220	28.12 N	81.23 W
Tohor, Tanjong >	114	1.51 N	102.42 E
T'ohyŏn-ni	98	39.53 N	124.52 E
Toi, Nihon	94	34.54 N	138.47 E
Toi, Niue	174v	18.57 S	169.51 W
Toijala	26	61.10 N	23.52 E
Toili	112	1.27 S	122.24 E
Toi-misaki >	92	31.20 N	131.22 E
Tōin	94	35.05 N	136.35 E
Toinya	140	6.17 N	29.44 E
Toi Sar	120	31.06 N	69.54 E
Toiyabe Range ⋏	204	39.10 N	117.10 W
Tojg	128	32.04 N	61.48 E
To-jima I	96	33.12 N	132.22 E
Tojo, Indon.	112	1.17 S	121.11 E
Tōjō, Nihon	96	34.53 N	133.16 E
Tōjō, Nihon	270	34.55 N	135.04 E
Tojtepa	85	41.03 N	69.22 E
Tōju-in ʋ[1]	94	35.19 N	136.04 E
Tok	180	63.19 N	142.59 W
Tok ≃	80	52.46 N	52.22 E
Tokaanu	172	38.58 S	175.46 E
Tokachi ≃	92a	42.44 N	143.42 E
Tokachi-dake ∧	92a	43.25 N	142.41 E
Tokachi-heiya ≚	92a	43.00 N	143.30 E
Tōkagi	268	35.42 N	139.56 E
Tokai, Malay.	114	6.01 N	100.24 E
Tōkai, Nihon	94	36.27 N	140.34 E
Tōkai, Nihon	94	35.00 N	136.53 E
Tokaj ≃	78	51.18 N	41.04 E
Tokala	112	1.47 S	121.43 E
Tōkamachi	94	37.08 N	138.46 E
Tokanui	172	46.34 S	168.56 E
Tokara-kaikyō υ	93b	30.10 N	130.10 E
Tokara-rettō II	93b	29.36 N	129.43 E
Tokarevka	86	50.08 N	73.12 E
Tokar Game Reserve ◆[4]	140	18.15 N	37.45 E
Tokar'ovka	80	51.59 N	41.09 E
Tokar'ovo, Ross.	76	55.17 N	35.04 E
Tokar'ovo, Ross.	265b	55.38 N	37.55 E
Tokashiki-jima I	93b	26.11 N	127.21 E
Tokat	130	40.19 N	36.34 E
Tokat □[4]	130	40.25 N	36.30 E
Tŏkchŏk-kundo II	98	37.14 N	126.07 E
Tŏkch'ŏn	98	39.46 N	126.19 E
Tokeland	224	46.42 N	123.58 W
Tokelau □[2]	14	9.00 S	171.45 W
Tokelau-Inseln → Tokelau □[2]	14	9.00 S	171.45 W
Tokeneke Brook ≃	276	41.03 N	73.28 W
Tŏkhŭng-ni	98	40.02 N	127.08 E
Toki	94	35.21 N	137.11 E
Toki ≃	94	35.12 N	136.52 E
Tokio → Tōkyō	94	35.42 N	139.46 E
Toki Point >	174a	19.19 N	166.35 E
Tokiwadaira	268	35.48 N	139.57 E
Tokke ⊜	26	59.01 N	9.15 E
Tokko	74	59.59 N	119.52 E
Tokko ≃	88	58.42 N	119.50 E
Toklar	130	38.26 N	36.01 E
Toklat ≃	180	64.27 N	150.17 W
Tokma	88	58.13 N	105.42 E
Tokmak, Kyrg.	85	42.55 N	75.18 E
Tokmak, Ukr.	78	47.15 N	35.43 E
Toko	172	39.20 S	174.24 E
Tököl	264c	47.19 N	18.58 E
Tokolimbu	112	2.48 S	121.34 E
Tokomaru	172	40.28 S	175.30 E
Tokomaru Bay	172	38.08 S	178.18 E
Tokoname	94	34.53 N	136.51 E
Toko Range ⋏	166	23.05 S	138.20 E
Tokoro ≃	92a	44.07 N	144.05 E
Tokoroa	172	38.14 S	175.52 E
Tokorozawa	94	35.47 N	139.28 E
Tokovskoje	78	47.38 N	33.59 E
Tokrau ≃	86	46.48 N	75.24 E
Toksook Bay	180	60.32 N	165.06 W
Toksovo	76	60.09 N	30.31 E
Tok-to (Take-shima) II	92	37.17 N	131.53 E
Toktogul	85	41.50 N	72.50 E
Toktogul'skoje vodochranilišče ⊜[1]	85	41.50 N	72.55 E
Toku Island I	14	18.10 S	174.11 W
Tokuji	96	34.11 N	131.40 E
Tokul Creek ≃	224	47.35 N	121.50 W
Tokung	112	0.18 S	114.28 E
Tokuno-shima I	93b	27.45 N	128.58 E
Tokur	89	53.10 N	132.53 E
Tokura	270	34.58 N	135.18 E
Tokura-tōge)(	96	35.17 N	134.31 E
Tokusaga-mine ∧	96	34.26 N	131.41 E
Tokushima	96	34.04 N	134.34 E
Tokushima □[5]	96	33.45 N	134.00 E
Tokuyama, Nihon	94	35.42 N	136.29 E
Tokuyama, Nihon	96	34.03 N	131.49 E
Tokwe ≃	154	21.09 S	31.30 E
Tōkyō, Nihon	94	35.42 N	139.46 E
Tōkyō, Nihon	268	35.42 N	139.46 E
Tōkyō □[5]	94	35.45 N	139.30 E
Tokyo Bay → Tōkyō-wan c	94	35.25 N	139.47 E
Tōkyō-daigaku-uchūkūkan-kenkyūsho ʋ[3]	92	31.17 N	131.05 E
Tokyo Disneyland ♠	268	35.37 N	139.53 E
Tōkyō-kō c	268	35.37 N	139.47 E
Tōkyō-kokusai-kūkō ⊠	94	35.45 N	140.21 E
Tokyo Station ◆[5]	268	35.41 N	139.46 E
Tokyo Tower ʋ	268	35.39 N	139.45 E
Tokyo University ʋ[2]	268	35.42 N	139.46 E
Tokyo University of Education ʋ[2]	268	35.43 N	139.44 E
Tōkyō-wan (Tokyo Bay) c	94	35.25 N	139.47 E
Tokzār	120	35.52 N	66.26 E
Tol I	175c	7.22 N	151.37 E
Tolaga Bay	172	38.22 S	178.18 E
Tolala	112	2.56 S	121.06 E
Tolang	114	1.56 N	99.26 E
Tolbert	52	53.10 N	6.21 E
Tolbo Nuur	86	48.25 N	90.17 E
Tolbuchino	80	57.51 N	40.03 E
Tolderol Point >	168b	35.22 S	139.10 E
Toldo, Pico del ∧	240p	20.30 N	74.54 W
Tole, Kaz.	85	42.40 N	70.08 E

≃ River	Fluß	Río	Rivière	Rio
≅ Canal	Kanal	Canal	Canal	Canal
ᒐ Waterfall, Rapids	Wasserfall, Stromschnellen	Cascada, Rápidos	Chute d'eau, Rapides	Cascata, Rápidos
υ Strait	Meeresstraße	Estrecho	Détroit	Estreito
c Bay, Gulf	Bucht, Golf	Bahía, Golfo	Baie, Golfe	Baía, Golfo
⊜ Lake, Lakes	See, Seen	Lago, Lagos	Lac, Lacs	Lago, Lagos
≚ Swamp	Sumpf	Pantano	Marais	Pântano
⌂ Ice Features, Glacier	Eis- und Gletscherformen	Accidentes Glaciales	Formes glaciaires	Acidentes glaciares
⊤ Other Hydrographic Features	Andere Hydrographische Objekte	Otros Elementos Hidrográficos	Autres données hydrographiques	Outros acidentes hidrográficos

✢ Submarine Features	Untermeerische Objekte	Accidentes Submarinos	Formes de relief sous-marin	Acidentes submarinos
□ Political Unit	Politische Einheit	Unidad Política	Entité politique	Unidade política
ʋ Cultural Institution	Kulturelle Institution	Institución Cultural	Institution culturelle	Instituição cultural
⊥ Historical Site	Historische Stätte	Sitio Histórico	Site historique	Sítio histórico
♠ Recreational Site	Erholungs- und Ferienort	Sitio de Recreo	Centre de loisirs	Area de Lazer
⊠ Airport	Flughafen	Aeropuerto	Aéroport	Aeroporto
■ Military Installation	Militäranlage	Instalación Militar	Installation militaire	Instalação militar
◆ Miscellaneous	Verschiedenes	Misceláneo	Divers	Diversos

Tolé, Pan. 236 8.14 N 81.41 W
Toledo, Bol. 248 18.10 S 67.25 W
Toledo, Bra. 252 24.44 S 53.45 W
Toledo, Bra. 256 22.44 S 46.23 W
Toledo, Col. 246 7.19 N 72.28 W
Toledo, Esp. 34 39.52 N 4.01 W
Toledo, Pil. 116 10.23 N 123.38 E
Toledo, Il., U.S. 194 39.16 N 88.14 W
Toledo, Ia., U.S. 190 41.59 N 92.34 W
Toledo, Oh., U.S. 214 41.39 N 83.33 W
Toledo, Or., U.S. 202 44.37 N 123.56 W
Toledo, Wa., U.S. 224 46.26 N 122.50 W
Toledo, Ur. 258 34.45 S 56.05 W
Toledo □4 34 39.45 N 4.00 W
Toledo □5 236 16.20 N 88.55 W
Toledo, Montes de ⅄ 34 39.33 N 4.20 W
Toledo Bend
Reservoir ⊜1 194 31.30 N 93.45 W
Toledo Express
Airport ⊠ 216 41.35 N 83.49 W
Tolentino 66 43.12 N 13.17 E
Tolfa 66 42.09 N 11.56 E
Tolfa, Monti della ⅄ 66 42.08 N 11.54 E
Tolga, Alg. 148 34.46 N 5.22 E
Tolga, Nor. 26 62.25 N 11.00 E
Toli 86 45.57 N 83.37 E
Toliara 157b 23.21 S 43.40 E
Toliara □4 157b 24.00 S 45.00 E
Tolima □5 246 3.45 N 75.15 W
Tolima, Nevado del ʌ 246 4.40 N 75.19 W
Tolimán, Méx. 234 19.36 N 103.55 W
Tolimán, Méx. 234 20.55 N 99.56 W
Tolitoli 112 1.02 N 120.49 E
Toljatti (Togliatti) 80 53.31 N 49.26 E
Tol'ka 74 64.02 N 81.55 E
Tolkmicko 30 54.20 N 19.31 E
Tolland 207 41.52 N 72.22 W
Tolland □6 207 41.52 N 72.22 W
Tollarp 26 55.56 N 13.59 E
Tollense ≃ 54 53.54 N 13.02 E
Tollensesee ⊜ 54 53.30 N 13.11 E
Tollesboro 218 38.33 N 83.34 W
Tollesbury 42 51.46 N 0.50 E
Tolleson 200 33.27 N 112.15 W
Tollhouse 226 37.01 N 119.23 W
Tolloche 252 25.30 S 63.32 W
Tølløse 41 55.37 N 11.45 E
Tollygunge ✈8 272b 22.30 N 88.21 E
Tolmači 76 57.26 N 35.41 E
Tolmačovo 76 58.52 N 29.55 E
Tolmezzo 64 46.24 N 13.01 E
Tolmin 36 46.11 N 13.44 E
Tolna 30 46.26 N 18.46 E
Tolna □6 30 46.30 N 18.35 E
Tolo 152 2.56 S 18.34 E
Tolo, Teluk ᴄ 112 2.00 S 122.30 E
Toloa, Houma ⲻ 174w 21.17 S 175.08 W
Toločin 76 54.25 N 29.42 E
Tolokiwa Island I 164 5.20 S 147.40 E
Tolomo 89 50.03 N 137.45 E
Tolong Bay ᴄ 116 9.20 N 122.49 E
Tolongoina 157b 21.33 S 47.31 E
Tolono 194 39.59 N 88.15 W
Tolosa 34 43.08 N 2.04 W
Tolosa, Aeródromo ⊠ 288 34.53 S 57.58 W
Tolovana ≃ 180 64.51 N 149.45 W
Tolpuddle 42 50.45 N 2.18 W
Tolsan-do I 98 34.38 N 127.45 E
Tol'skij Majdan 80 54.57 N 44.39 E
Tolsta Head ⲻ 46 58.20 N 6.10 W
Tolstoj, mys ⲻ 74 59.10 N 155.12 E
Tolstoje 78 48.50 N 25.44 E
Tolstopal'cevo 265b 55.38 N 37.13 E
Tolt, North Fork ≃ 224 47.42 N 121.49 W
Toltén 254 39.13 S 73.14 W
Toltén ≃ 254 39.15 S 73.14 W
Tolti 123 35.02 N 76.06 E
Toltry ʌ1 78 49.00 N 26.10 E
Tolt-Seattle Water
Supply Reservoir
⊜1 224 47.42 N 121.39 W
Tolú 246 9.31 N 75.35 W
Toluca 216 41.00 N 89.08 W
Toluca, Nevado de
ʌ1 234 19.08 N 99.44 W
Toluca [de Lerdo] 234 19.17 N 99.40 W
Tolvajarvi 24 62.17 N 31.27 E
Tolvdalselva ≃ 26 58.10 N 8.00 E
Tolve 68 40.42 N 16.01 E
Tolwa 140 6.38 N 32.37 E
Tolworth ✈8 260 51.23 N 0.17 W
Tolyatti
→ Toljatti 80 53.31 N 49.26 E
Tolybaj 86 50.31 N 62.19 E
Tom' ≃, Ross. 86 56.50 N 84.27 E
Tom' ≃, Ross. 89 51.00 N 127.54 E
Toma 150 12.46 N 2.53 W
Tomago 170 32.50 S 151.44 E
Tomah 190 43.58 N 90.30 W
Tomahawk 190 45.28 N 89.43 W
Tomakomai 92a 42.38 N 141.36 E
Tomakovka 78 47.48 N 34.44 E
Tomani 112 4.50 N 115.55 E
Tomanivi ʌ 175g 17.37 S 178.01 E
Tomar, Kaz. 86 49.24 N 75.03 E
Tomar, Port. 34 39.36 N 8.25 W
Tomari 89 47.47 N 142.03 E
Tomarovka 78 50.41 N 36.14 E
Tomarza 130 38.27 N 35.49 E
Tomás Barrón
(Eucaliptus) 248 17.35 S 67.31 W
Tomasboda ʌ2 40 59.24 N 14.58 E
Tomás Gomensoro 252 30.26 S 57.26 W
Tomašgorod 78 51.19 N 27.02 E
Tomasine ≃ 190 46.40 N 76.16 W
Tomás Jofré 258 34.43 S 59.19 W
Tomašov 61 48.09 N 17.16 E
Tomašpol' 78 48.33 N 28.31 E
Tomaszów Lubelski 30 50.28 N 23.25 E
Tomaszów
Mazowiecki 30 51.32 N 20.01 E
Tomatin 46 57.20 N 3.59 W
Tomatlán 234 19.56 N 105.15 W
Tomatlán ≃ 234 19.50 N 105.23 W
Tomave 248 20.06 S 66.35 W
Tomazina 255 23.46 S 49.58 W
Tomba di Nerone ✈8 267a 41.57 N 12.27 E
Tombadonkéa 150 11.00 N 14.23 W
Tombador, Serra do
ʌ1 248 12.00 S 57.40 W
Tomball 222 30.06 N 95.37 W
Tombe 140 5.49 N 31.41 E
Tombigbee ≃ 194 31.04 N 87.58 W
Tombo, Punta ⲻ 254 44.03 S 65.11 W
Tombôco 152 6.48 S 13.18 E
Tombolo 64 45.38 N 11.50 E
Tombos 255 20.55 S 42.02 W
Tombouctou
(Timbuktu) 150 16.46 N 3.01 W
Tombouctou □4 150 18.20 N 3.50 W
Tombs of the Caliphs
⊥ 273c 30.03 N 31.17 E
Tombstone 200 31.42 N 110.04 W
Tombstone Mountain
ʌ 180 64.25 N 138.30 W
Tombua 152 15.49 S 11.53 E
Tom Burke 156 23.05 S 28.00 E
Tomdoun 46 57.04 N 5.03 W
Tomé 252 36.37 S 72.57 W
Tomea, Pulau I 112 5.45 S 123.56 E
Tomé-Açu 250 2.25 S 48.09 W
Tömek 130 38.02 N 32.41 E
Tomelilla 26 55.33 N 13.57 E
Tomelloso 34 39.10 N 3.01 W
Tomerong 170 35.04 S 150.35 E
Tomhannock
Reservoir ⊜1 210 42.51 N 73.33 W
Tomi ≃ 152 5.07 N 19.19 E
Tomich 46 57.18 N 4.48 W
Tomichi Creek ≃ 200 38.31 N 106.58 W
Tomifobia ≃ 206 45.11 N 72.02 W
Tomiko Lake ⊜ 190 46.32 N 79.49 W
Tomilino 265b 55.39 N 37.57 E
Tomini 112 0.30 N 120.32 E
Tomini, Teluk ᴄ 112 0.20 S 121.00 E
Tominian 150 13.17 N 4.35 W
Tomintoul 46 57.14 N 3.22 W
Tomio ≃ 270 34.35 N 135.44 E
Tomioka 94 36.15 N 138.54 E
Tomisato 94 35.44 N 140.19 E
Tomiura 94 35.03 N 139.50 E
Tomiyama, Nihon 94 35.11 N 137.48 E
Tomiyama, Nihon 94 35.05 N 139.51 E
Tomizawa 94 35.14 N 138.29 E
T'omkino 76 55.05 N 35.01 E
Tomkins Cove 210 41.15 N 73.59 W
Tomkinson Ranges ⅄ 162 26.11 S 129.05 E
Tomkinsville 208 38.19 N 76.53 W
Tomlinson Run State
Park ◆ 214 40.33 N 80.34 W
Tommerup
Stationsby 41 55.19 N 10.13 E
Tommot 74 58.58 N 126.19 E
Tomnavoulin 46 57.18 N 3.19 W
T'omnyj 88 53.24 N 118.31 E
Tomo ≃ 246 5.20 N 67.48 W
Tomobe 94 36.20 N 140.20 E
Tomogashima-suidō
ʮ 96 34.17 N 135.00 E
Tomohon 112 1.19 N 124.49 E
Tömör Bulag 88 49.16 N 100.15 E
Tomori 174m 26.08 N 127.44 E
Tomori, Teluk ᴄ 112 1.58 S 121.28 E
Tompa 88 55.08 N 109.47 E
Tompkins, Nf., Can. 186 47.48 N 59.13 W
Tompkins, Sk., Can. 184 50.04 N 108.47 W
Tompkins □6 210 42.27 N 76.30 W
Tompkins County
Airport ⊠ 210 42.29 N 76.57 W
Tompkinsville 194 36.42 N 85.41 W
Tompo 112 0.56 N 120.20 E
Tom Price 162 22.41 S 117.43 E
Tom Price, Mount ʌ 162 22.39 S 117.40 E
Tomptokan 74 57.06 N 133.59 E
Tomra 26 62.35 N 6.56 E
Toms ≃ 208 39.57 N 74.07 W
Toms, Ridgeway
Branch ≃ 208 40.00 N 74.14 W
Toms Cove ᴄ 208 37.53 N 75.22 W
Toms Creek ≃ 208 39.38 N 77.17 W
Tomsk 86 56.30 N 84.58 E
Tomsk Oblast' □4 86 58.00 N 82.00 E
Toms River 208 39.58 N 74.12 W
Tom Steed Reservoir
⊜1 196 34.45 N 99.00 W
Tomtabacken ʌ2 26 57.30 N 14.28 E
Tomtök 130 36.41 N 34.22 E
Tomuzlovka ≃ 84 44.46 N 44.10 E
Ton 64 46.15 N 11.04 E
Tonadico 64 46.11 N 11.50 E
Tonaki-shima I 93b 26.21 N 127.09 E
Tonalá, Méx. 234 16.04 N 93.45 W
Tonalá, Méx. 234 20.37 N 103.14 W
Tonalá, Passo del ʮ 64 46.16 N 10.35 E
Tonami 94 36.38 N 136.54 E
Tonantins 246 2.47 S 67.47 W
Tonantins ≃ 246 2.47 S 67.47 W
Tonara 71 40.02 N 9.10 E
Tonasket 202 48.42 N 119.26 W
Tonate 250 4.55 N 52.22 W
Tonatico 234 18.47 N 99.41 W
Tonawanda, N.Y.,
U.S. 210 43.01 N 78.52 W
Tonawanda, N.Y.,
U.S. 210 42.59 N 78.52 W
Tonawanda Channel
≃1 284a 43.04 N 79.00 W
Tonawanda Creek ≃ 210 43.02 N 78.53 W
Tonawanda Indian
Reservation ✈4 210 43.05 N 78.27 W
Tonawanda Island I 284a 43.02 N 78.53 W
Tonbara 96 35.05 N 132.47 E
Tonbo 110 18.31 N 95.05 E
Tonbridge 42 51.12 N 0.16 E
Tonbridge and
Malling □8 260 51.16 N 0.20 E
Tonda 270 34.50 N 135.36 E
Tonda ≃ 96 33.38 N 135.24 E
Tondabayashi 96 34.30 N 135.36 E
Tondano 112 1.19 N 124.54 E
Tonder 41 54.56 N 8.54 E
Tondhre 272c 19.05 N 73.08 E
Tondi 122 9.44 N 79.01 E
Tondibi 150 16.39 N 0.14 W
Tondidji 150 13.06 N 10.20 W
Tondi Kiwindi 150 14.28 N 2.02 E
Tondoro 156 17.45 S 18.50 E
Tone, Nihon 94 36.42 N 139.13 E
Tone, Nihon 94 35.51 N 140.09 E
Tone ≃ 94 35.44 N 140.51 E
Tonekābon 128 36.49 N 50.53 E
Tone-unga ≅ 268 35.54 N 139.53 E
Tonež 78 51.49 N 27.48 E
Tonga, Cam. 152 4.58 N 10.42 E
Tonga, Süd. 140 9.28 N 31.03 E
Tonga □1 14 20.00 S 175.00 W
Tongaat 158 29.37 S 31.03 E
Tonga Islands II 14 20.00 S 175.00 W
Tong'an 100 24.46 N 118.08 E
Tonganoxie 198 39.06 N 95.05 W
Tong'anqiao 106 31.22 N 120.27 E
Tonga Ridge ✈3 14 21.00 S 175.00 W
Tongariro, Mount ʌ 172 39.08 S 175.38 E
Tongariro National
Park ◆ 172 39.15 S 175.30 E
Tongas 115a 7.44 S 113.06 E
Tongatapu □8 174w 21.10 S 175.10 W
Tongatapu I 174w 21.10 S 175.10 W
Tongatapu Group II 14 21.10 S 175.10 W
Tonga Trench ✈1 14 20.00 S 173.00 W
Tongbai, Zhg. 100 32.22 N 113.24 E
Tongbai, Zhg. 105 39.35 N 116.44 E
Tongbai Shan ʌ 100 32.20 N 113.14 E
Tongbai Shan ʌ 100 32.20 N 113.15 E
Tongbei 89 47.45 N 126.46 E
Tongcheng, Zhg. 100 31.03 N 116.58 E
Tongcheng, Zhg. 102 32.53 N 118.58 E
Tongcheng, Zhg. 100 29.11 N 113.49 E
Tongchengzhen 104 31.30 N 118.07 E
Tongchengzhuang 105 39.22 N 117.36 E
T'ongch'ŏn 98 38.54 N 127.54 E
Tongchuan 102 35.10 N 109.01 E
Tongdao 102 26.23 N 109.23 E
Tongde 102 35.17 N 100.42 E
Tongerbao 104 41.26 N 123.02 E
Tongeren 56 50.47 N 5.28 E
Tongerlo 56 51.07 N 4.54 E
Tonggou 98 41.53 N 125.46 E
Tonggu, Zhg. 100 28.33 N 114.22 E
Tonggu, Zhg. 100 21.53 N 112.55 E
Tongguan, Zhg. 102 34.35 N 110.15 E
Tongguan, Zhg. 100 28.29 N 112.48 E
Tongguan, Zhg. 102 34.38 N 110.20 E
Tongguan, Zhg. 102 23.18 N 101.23 E
Tongguanyi 107 29.20 N 106.23 E
Tonghai 102 24.07 N 102.49 E
Tonghaikou 100 30.14 N 113.08 E
Tonghe, Zhg. 89 45.59 N 128.45 E
Tonghe, Zhg. 102 32.56 N 112.45 E
Tongho-ri 98 35.49 N 127.54 E
Tonghua
(Kuaidamao), Zhg. 98 41.40 N 125.44 E
Tonghua, Zhg. 98 41.41 N 125.55 E
Tonghui ≃ 271a 39.53 N 116.21 E
Tongi 126 23.53 N 90.24 E
Tong Island I 100 26.55 N 120.05 E
Tongjiang, Zhg. 89 47.40 N 132.30 E
Tongjiang, Zhg. 102 31.58 N 107.14 E
Tongjiangchang 107 29.37 N 103.43 E
Tongjiangkou 104 42.37 N 123.41 E
Tongjing 100 31.47 N 118.33 E
Tongjosŏn-man ᴄ 98 39.30 N 128.00 E
Tongjuzhen 98 38.36 N 117.11 E
Tongken ≃ 89 46.31 N 126.22 E
Tongli 106 31.10 N 120.43 E
Tongliang 107 29.51 N 106.03 E
Tongliao 89 43.39 N 122.14 E
Tongling, Zhg. 100 30.53 N 117.46 E
Tongling, Zhg. 102 23.28 N 109.40 E
Tonglu 100 29.48 N 119.40 E
Tonglü Yunhe ≅ 106 32.04 N 121.40 E
Tongmang-ni 98 37.37 N 126.26 E
Tongmu, Zhg. 102 27.57 N 113.55 E
Tongmu, Zhg. 102 24.09 N 110.04 E
Tongnae 98 35.12 N 129.05 E
Tongnan 107 30.11 N 105.48 E
Tongno-gang ≃ 98 40.58 N 126.04 E
Tongo 166 30.30 S 143.45 E
Tongoa I 175f 16.54 S 168.34 E
Tongobory 157b 23.32 S 44.20 E
Tongololo Creek ≃ 162 22.06 S 121.08 E
Tongoy 252 30.15 S 71.30 W
Tongqin 100 28.52 N 119.56 E
Tongquansi 107 30.23 N 104.50 E
Tongquil Island I 116 6.02 N 121.51 E
Tongren, Zhg. 102 27.38 N 109.03 E
Tongren, Zhg. 102 35.32 N 101.54 E
Tongrengchang 107 30.02 N 106.42 E
Tongsa ≃ 124 26.52 N 90.57 E
Tongsa Dzong 124 27.31 N 90.30 E
Tongsan-ni 271b 37.38 N 126.53 E
Tongshan 100 29.38 N 114.29 E
Tongshi 98 35.26 N 117.43 E
Tongshuping 100 27.17 N 114.54 E
Tongta 110 21.20 N 99.16 E
Tongtai 100 32.38 N 120.47 E
Tongtian 107 28.56 N 105.17 E
Tongtian ≃ 102 33.25 N 96.32 E
Tongue 46 58.28 N 4.25 W
Tongue ≃, U.S. 202 46.24 N 105.52 W
Tongue ≃, N.D., U.S. 198 48.56 N 97.18 W
Tongue ≃, Tx., U.S. 196 34.07 N 100.25 W
Tongue, Kyle of ᴄ 46 58.30 N 4.26 W
Tongue of the Ocean
✈1 238 24.30 N 77.30 W
Tongue River
Reservoir ⊜1 202 45.06 N 106.47 W
Tongwei 102 35.07 N 105.27 E
Tongxi 107 29.59 N 106.08 E
Tongxian 105 39.55 N 116.39 E
Tongxianchang 107 30.14 N 105.24 E
Tongxiang 106 30.38 N 120.32 E
Tongxin 102 37.02 N 106.09 E
Tongxinchang 107 29.42 N 106.26 E
Tongxing 107 30.35 N 106.12 E
Tongxu 98 34.29 N 114.28 E
Tongyang-ni 98 39.08 N 126.52 E
Tongyang Yunhe ≅ 106 32.02 N 120.48 E
Tongyu 89 44.48 N 123.05 E
Tongyuan, Zhg. 100 28.04 N 116.08 E
Tongyuan, Zhg. 106 30.28 N 120.52 E
Tongyuanpu 104 40.49 N 123.54 E
Tongzhaipu 100 32.48 N 112.44 E
Tongzi 107 28.08 N 106.49 E
Tongzidixia 104 41.08 N 120.34 E
Tonica 216 41.12 N 89.04 W
Tonila 234 19.26 N 103.31 W
Tönisberg 263 51.25 N 6.30 E
Tönisheide 263 51.19 N 7.03 E
Tönisvorst 56 51.19 N 6.29 E
Tonj 140 7.17 N 28.45 E
Tonk 120 26.10 N 75.47 E
Tonkawa 196 36.40 N 97.18 W
Tonkin, Gulf of ᴄ 110 20.00 N 108.00 E
Tonkin
→ Bac Phan □9 110 22.00 N 105.00 E
Tonkino 80 57.23 N 46.28 E
Tonkou, Mont ʌ 150 7.27 N 7.39 W
Tônlé Sab, Bœng ⊜ 110 13.00 N 104.00 E
Tonle Sap
→ Tônlé Sab,
Bœng ⊜ 110 13.00 N 104.00 E
Tonnay-Boutonne 32 45.58 N 0.42 W
Tonneins 32 44.23 N 0.19 E
Tonner Canyon V 280 33.58 N 117.48 W
Tonnerre 50 47.51 N 3.58 E
Tönnet 40 60.14 N 13.30 E
Tönning 41 54.19 N 8.56 E
Tōno 92 39.19 N 141.32 E
Tonogaya 268 35.46 N 139.42 E
Tonopah 204 38.04 N 117.13 W
Tonoshō, Nihon 94 35.49 N 140.42 E
Tonoshō, Nihon 96 34.29 N 134.11 E
Tonosí 246 7.24 N 80.27 W
Tonota 156 21.29 S 27.29 E
Tonquish Creek ≃ 281 42.21 N 83.22 W
Tons ≃ 124 25.17 N 82.04 E
Tonšajevo 80 57.44 N 47.00 E
Tønsberg 26 59.17 N 10.25 E
Tönsholt 263 51.38 N 6.58 E
Tonstad 26 58.40 N 6.43 E
Tonto Creek ≃ 200 33.46 N 111.15 W
Tontogany 216 41.25 N 83.44 W
Tonto National
Monument ◆ 200 33.34 N 111.02 W
Tonya 130 40.53 N 39.16 E
Tonyandy 42 51.38 N 3.27 W
Tonyrefail 42 51.36 N 3.25 W
Toobeah 166 28.25 S 149.52 E
Toodyay 168a 31.33 S 116.28 E
Tooele 200 40.31 N 112.17 W
Toogoolawah 171a 27.06 S 152.23 E
Tool 222 32.16 N 96.10 W
Toolik ≃ 180 69.33 N 149.30 W
Tooma 171b 35.58 S 148.03 E
Tooma ≃ 171b 36.04 S 148.00 E
Tooma Reservoir ⊜1 171b 36.04 S 148.16 E
Toomebridge 48 54.45 N 6.27 W
Toompine 166 27.13 S 144.22 E
Toomsboro 192 32.49 N 83.04 W
Toomyvara 48 52.50 N 8.02 W
Toongabbie 274a 33.47 S 150.57 E
Toora 169 38.40 S 146.20 E
Toora-Chem 88 52.28 N 96.17 E
Toorak 274b 37.51 S 145.01 E
Toormakeady 48 53.39 N 9.24 W
Toorop Indian
Reserve ✈4 182 51.56 N 122.29 W
Toot Hill 260 51.42 N 0.12 E
Tootias 144 3.57 N 43.57 E
Tootie, Mount ʌ 170 33.28 S 150.30 E
Tootsi 76 58.34 N 24.47 E
Toowoomba 171a 27.33 S 151.57 E
Topanga 280 34.06 N 118.36 W
Topanga Canyon V 280 34.05 N 118.36 W
Topanga State Park
◆ 280 34.06 N 118.33 W
Topar 86 49.32 N 72.50 E
Topawa 200 31.48 N 111.49 W
Topaz Lake ⊜ 226 38.41 N 119.32 W
Topçam 130 40.01 N 33.55 E
Topchanchi 126 23.54 N 86.12 E
Topchin 54 52.10 N 13.34 E
Töpchin 86 52.49 N 83.10 E
Topčieka, In., U.S. 216 41.32 N 85.32 W
Topeka, Ks., U.S. 198 39.02 N 95.40 W
Töpen 54 50.23 N 11.52 E
Topia 234 25.13 N 106.34 W
Topilejo ✈8 286a 19.12 N 99.09 W
Topki 66 43.02 N 12.30 E
Topkanovo 82 54.43 N 38.29 E
Topkapı ✈8 267b 41.02 N 28.54 E
Topkapı Palace ⊥ 267b 41.00 N 28.59 E
Topki 86 55.16 N 85.36 E
Topko, gora ʌ 74 57.08 N 137.50 E
Topl'a ≃ 30 48.45 N 21.45 E
Topley 182 54.30 N 126.18 W
Toplica ≃ 38 43.13 N 21.49 E
Toplița 38 46.55 N 25.21 E
T'oploje, Ross. 76 53.13 N 38.53 E
T'oploje, Ross. 76 53.37 N 37.36 E
T'oploje, Ukr. 83 48.47 N 39.19 E
T'oplyj Stan 80 53.58 N 50.10 E
T'oplyj Stan ✈8 265b 55.37 N 37.30 E
Topo ≃ 286c 10.33 N 66.55 W
Topocalma, Punta ⲻ 252 34.08 S 72.01 W
Top of Hebers 262 53.34 N 2.12 W
Topo Infiernito ʌ 286c 10.35 N 66.26 W
Topol'čany 30 48.34 N 18.10 E
Topoli 80 47.59 N 51.36 E
Topolobampo 232 25.36 N 109.03 W
Topolog 38 44.53 N 28.22 E
Topolovățu Mare 38 45.46 N 21.37 E
Topolovgrad 38 42.05 N 26.20 E
Topororok 76 58.33 N 33.28 E
Topozero, ozero ⊜ 24 65.40 N 32.00 E
Toppenish 202 46.22 N 120.18 W
Toppenish Creek ≃ 202 46.20 N 120.11 W
Toppenish Ridge ʌ 224 46.18 N 120.40 W
Toppings 262 53.37 N 2.25 W
Toprakkale 130 37.06 N 36.07 E
Tops, Mount ʌ 162 21.50 S 134.00 E
Topsa 24 62.39 N 43.34 E
Topsfield 207 42.38 N 70.57 W
Topsham, Eng., U.K. 42 50.41 N 3.27 W
Topsham, Me., U.S. 188 43.55 N 69.58 W
Top Springs 164 16.38 S 131.50 E
Topton 208 40.30 N 75.42 W
Toquima Range ⅄ 204 38.45 N 116.55 W
Toquop Wash V 204 36.45 N 114.11 W
Tor 144 7.51 N 33.35 E
Torahime 94 35.25 N 136.16 E
Torano Castello 68 39.30 N 16.08 E
Torawitan, Tanjung ⲻ 112 1.46 N 124.58 E
Toraya 248 14.03 S 73.18 W
Torbali 130 38.10 N 27.21 E
Torbat-e Heydarīyeh 128 35.16 N 59.13 E
Torbat-e Jām 128 35.14 N 60.36 E
Torbay 186 47.40 N 52.44 W
Torbay □9 42 50.26 N 3.34 W
Tor Bay ᴄ 42 50.25 N 3.30 W
Torbejevo, Ross. 80 54.05 N 43.15 E
Torbejevo, Ross. 82 54.44 N 36.11 E
Torbert, Mount ʌ 180 61.25 N 152.20 W
Torbino 76 58.35 N 32.53 E
Torbole 64 45.52 N 10.52 E
Torbreck, Mount ʌ 169 37.21 S 145.57 E
Torbrook 186 44.55 N 64.59 W
Torch ≃ 184 53.50 N 103.05 W
Torchany 80 55.34 N 46.36 E
Torchiarolo 68 40.29 N 18.03 E
Torch Lake ⊜ 190 45.00 N 85.19 W
Torčin 78 50.46 N 24.59 E
Torcy 261 48.51 N 2.39 E
Torda
→ Turda 38 46.34 N 23.47 E
Tordera ≃ 34 41.39 N 2.47 E
Tordesillas 34 41.30 N 5.00 W
Tordino ≃ 66 42.44 N 13.59 E
Tor di Quinto ✈8 267a 41.56 N 12.28 E
Töre 26 65.54 N 22.39 E
Töreboda 40 58.43 N 14.08 E
Torej 88 50.33 N 104.50 E
Torekov 26 56.26 N 12.37 E
Toreno 34 42.42 N 6.30 W
Torez 83 48.01 N 38.37 E
Torfou 261 48.32 N 2.14 E
Torgau 54 51.34 N 13.00 E
Torgelow 54 53.37 N 14.00 E
Torgelower See ⊜ 54 53.34 N 12.47 E
Torghay 88 58.28 N 119.50 E
Torgun ≃ 80 50.15 N 46.18 E
Torhamn 26 56.05 N 15.50 E
Torhout 50 51.04 N 3.06 E
Toribulu 112 0.19 S 120.01 E
Toride 94 35.53 N 140.04 E
Torigakubi-misaki ⲻ 94 37.10 N 138.06 E
Torigoe 94 36.21 N 136.36 E
Torii-tōge ʮ 270 34.25 N 135.43 E
Torii-tōge ʮ 94 36.02 N 138.24 E
Toriki 265a 59.47 N 30.07 E
Torino (Turin) 62 45.03 N 7.40 E
Torino □4 62 45.08 N 7.22 E
Torino di Sangro
Marina 66 42.11 N 14.32 E
Toriō ≃ 34 42.35 N 5.34 W
Torit 255 16.20 S 45.40 W
Torit 154 4.24 N 32.34 E
Toritto 68 41.00 N 16.41 E
Toriya 94 36.59 N 136.54 E
Torjun 115a 7.10 S 113.13 E
Torkestān, Selseleh-
ye Band-e ⅄ 128 35.25 N 64.15 E
Torkoviči 76 58.52 N 30.20 E
Torlino 80 58.53 N 63.46 E
Torment, Point ⲻ 162 17.02 S 123.36 E
Tormentine, Cape ⲻ 186 46.07 N 63.47 W
Tormes ≃ 34 41.18 N 6.29 W
Tormestorp 41 56.07 N 13.44 E
Tormey 282 38.03 N 122.15 W
Tormini 64 45.36 N 10.29 E
Tormosin 80 48.12 N 42.42 E
Torna 34 42.33 N 9.04 E
Torna ≃ 122 18.16 N 73.37 E
Tornado Mountain ʌ 182 49.58 N 114.39 W
Tornal'a 30 48.27 N 20.20 E
Tornareccio 66 42.02 N 14.24 E
Tornberget ʌ2 40 59.08 N 18.01 E
Torne ≃ 44 53.36 N 0.44 W
Torneälven
(Tornionjoki) ≃ 24 65.48 N 24.08 E
Torne Brook ≃ 276 41.08 N 74.10 W
Tornesch 52 53.41 N 9.43 E
Torneträsk ⊜ 24 68.20 N 19.10 E
Torngat Mountains ⅄ 176 59.00 N 64.00 W
Tornillo 200 31.27 N 106.05 W
Tornillo Creek ≃ 196 29.11 N 103.00 W
Tornimparte 66 42.17 N 13.18 E
Torning 41 56.17 N 9.20 E
Tornio 26 65.51 N 24.08 E
Tornionjoki
(Torneälven) ≃ 24 65.48 N 24.08 E
Tornquist 252 38.06 S 62.14 W
Tornyosgorsk 88 50.50 N 31.14 E
T'orny, Ukr. 78 48.09 N 33.33 E
T'orny, Ukr. 78 50.59 N 33.59 E
T'orny, Ukr. 83 49.05 N 37.57 E
Tornyiszentmiklós 61 46.31 N 16.34 E
Toro 34 41.31 N 5.24 W
Torö I 40 58.50 N 17.50 E
Toro, Arroyo ≃ 288 34.27 S 58.52 W
Toro, Cañada del ≃ 286 35.16 S 59.05 W
Toro, Cerro ʌ 234 19.10 N 104.27 W
Toro, Lago del ⊜ 254 51.14 S 72.45 W
Toro, Punta ⲻ 252 33.47 S 71.49 W
Torobuku 112 4.25 S 122.26 E
Torodi 150 13.18 N 1.40 E
Toro-iseki ⊥ 94 34.57 N 138.24 E
Torok 146 10.03 N 14.33 E
Torokina 175e 6.14 S 155.03 E
Törökszentmiklós 30 47.11 N 20.25 E
Torola ≃ 236 13.52 N 88.30 W
Torom 89 54.32 N 135.50 E
Torom ≃ 89 54.24 N 135.44 E
Toroni, Nevado ʌ 248 19.43 S 68.41 W
Toronto, Austl. 170 33.01 S 151.36 E
Toronto, On., Can. 212 43.39 N 79.23 W
Toronto, On., Can. 275b 43.39 N 79.23 W
Toronto, On., Can. 275b 43.39 N 79.23 W
Toronto, Ks., U.S. 198 37.47 N 95.56 W
Toronto, Oh., U.S. 214 40.27 N 80.36 W
Toronto, S.D., U.S. 198 44.34 N 96.38 W
Toronto □6 275b 43.44 N 79.24 W
Toronto Canadian
Forces Base ■ 212 43.45 N 79.28 W
Toronto, University of
✈2 275b 43.40 N 79.24 W
Toronto Harbour ᴄ 275b 43.38 N 79.23 W
Toronto Island
Airport ⊠ 275b 43.38 N 79.24 W
Toronto Lake ⊜1 198 37.48 N 95.57 W
Toronto Reservoir ⊜1 210 41.38 N 74.51 W
Toronto Zoo, Metro ✈ 275b 43.49 N 79.11 W
Toro Peak ʌ 204 33.32 N 116.25 W
Toropec 76 56.30 N 31.38 E
Toropovo 82 54.21 N 36.07 E
Tororo 154 0.42 N 34.11 E
Toros (Acho), Plaza
de ◆ 286d 12.02 S 77.02 W
Toros Dağları (Taurus
Mountains) ⅄ 130 37.00 N 33.00 E
Torošino 76 57.56 N 28.36 E
Torosozero 24 62.30 N 38.10 E
Torotoro 248 18.07 S 65.46 W
Toroume ʌ2 174k 21.15 S 159.45 W
Torpa ⊥ 26 57.39 N 13.16 E
Torpè 71 40.38 N 9.40 E
Torphins 46 57.06 N 2.37 W
Tor Pignatara ✈8 267a 41.52 N 12.32 E
Torpo 26 60.40 N 8.43 E
Torpoint 42 50.22 N 4.11 W
Torpy ≃ 182 53.44 N 120.55 W
Torquay, Austl. 169 38.21 S 144.19 E
Torquay, Sk., Can. 184 49.08 N 103.31 W
Torquay, Eng., U.K. 42 50.28 N 3.30 W
Torquemada 34 42.02 N 4.19 W
Torraca 68 40.07 N 15.38 E
Torraccia, Fosso ≃ 267a 42.00 N 12.30 E
Torrance, Ca., U.S. 228 33.50 N 118.20 W
Torrance, Pa., U.S. 214 40.25 N 79.14 W
Torrance Lake ⊜ 212 57.04 N 98.12 W
Torrance Municipal
Airport ⊠ 280 33.48 N 118.20 W
Torrão 34 38.18 N 8.13 W
Torre Annunziata 68 40.45 N 14.27 E
Torre Baja 34 40.07 N 1.15 W
Torrebelvicino 64 45.43 N 11.18 E
Torre Beretti 62 45.04 N 8.40 E
Torreblanca 34 40.13 N 0.12 E
Torrebruna 66 41.52 N 14.33 E
Torrecilla ʌ 34 37.36 N 2.31 W
Torrecilla en
Cameros 34 42.16 N 2.37 W
Torre del Campo 34 37.46 N 3.53 W
Torre del Greco 68 40.47 N 14.22 E
Torre del Lago
Puccini 66 43.50 N 10.17 E
Torre de Moncorvo 34 41.10 N 7.03 W
Torre de'Passeri 66 42.14 N 13.56 E
Torre di Mosto 64 45.41 N 12.43 E
Torre di Santa Maria 64 46.14 N 9.51 E
Torredonjimeno 34 37.46 N 3.57 W
Torre Faro ✈8 70 38.16 N 15.39 E
Torre Gaia ✈8 267a 41.51 N 12.39 E
Torregrotta 70 38.11 N 15.21 E
Torrejon Air Base ■ 266a 40.28 N 3.28 W
Torrejoncillo 34 39.54 N 6.28 W
Torrejón de Ardoz 34 40.27 N 3.29 W
Torrejón-Tajo,
Embalse de ⊜1 34 39.50 N 5.50 W
Torrelaguna 34 40.50 N 3.32 W
Torrelavega 34 43.21 N 4.03 W
Torrellas, Riera de ≃ 266d 41.23 N 2.01 E
Torrelles de
Llobregat 266d 41.21 N 1.59 E
Torrelletes 266d 41.21 N 1.57 E
Torremaggiore 68 41.41 N 15.17 E
Torremolinos 34 36.37 N 4.30 W
Torrenieri 66 43.05 N 11.32 E
Torrens ≃ 168b 34.56 S 138.30 E
Torrens, Lake ⊜ 166 31.00 S 137.50 E
Torrens, Mount ʌ 168b 34.52 S 138.56 E
Torrens Creek 166 20.46 S 145.02 E
Torrens Creek ≃ 166 22.22 S 145.09 E
Torrens Island I 168b 34.48 S 138.32 E
Torrent, Arg. 252 28.05 S 58.06 W
Torrent, Esp. 34 39.26 N 0.28 W
Torreões 256 21.52 S 43.33 W
Torreón 232 25.33 N 103.26 W
Torre Orsaia 68 40.08 N 15.28 E
Torre Pedrera 66 44.06 N 12.31 E
Torre Pellice 62 44.49 N 7.13 E
Torreperogil 34 38.02 N 3.17 W
Torres, Arg. 258 34.26 S 59.08 W
Torres, Bra. 252 29.21 S 49.44 W
Torres, Arroyo ≃ 288 34.39 S 58.45 W
Torres, Îles II 175f 13.15 S 166.37 E
Torre Santa Susanna 68 40.28 N 17.44 E
Torresdale ✈8 285 40.03 N 75.00 W
Torres de Alcalá 34 35.10 N 4.16 W
Torres Martinez
Indian Reservation
✈4 204 33.35 N 116.02 W
Torres Novas 34 39.29 N 8.32 W
Torres Strait ʮ 164 10.25 S 142.10 E
Torres Vedras 34 39.06 N 9.16 W
Torretta 68 38.08 N 13.14 E
Torrette di Fano 66 43.47 N 13.07 E
Torrevella 34 37.59 N 0.41 W
Torricella 68 40.21 N 17.29 E
Torricella in Sabina 66 42.16 N 12.52 E
Torricella Peligna 66 42.01 N 14.15 E
Torricella Sicura 66 42.39 N 13.39 E
Torricelli Mountains ⅄ 164 3.25 S 142.20 E
Torridge ≃ 42 51.03 N 4.11 W
Torridon 46 57.33 N 5.31 W
Torridon, Loch ᴄ 46 57.35 N 5.46 W
Torriglia 62 44.31 N 9.10 E
Torrijos, Esp. 34 39.59 N 4.17 W
Torrijos, Pil. 116 13.19 N 122.05 E
Torrild 41 55.59 N 10.04 E
Torrimpietra ✈8 267a 41.56 N 12.12 E
Torrin 46 57.12 N 6.02 W
Torring 41 55.51 N 9.29 E
Torrington, Ct., U.S. 207 41.48 N 73.07 W
Torrington, Wy., U.S. 198 42.03 N 104.10 W
Torrinha 255 22.26 S 48.09 W
Torrita di Siena 66 43.10 N 11.46 E
Torröjen ⊜ 26 63.55 N 12.56 E
Torrox 34 36.46 N 3.58 W
Torrvarpen ⊜ 40 59.42 N 14.30 E
Torsåker 40 60.31 N 16.29 E
Tor Sapienza ✈8 267a 41.54 N 12.35 E
Torsås 26 56.24 N 16.00 E
Torsby ⊥ 26 60.08 N 13.00 E
Torsby 40 57.25 N 18.43 E
Tors Cove 186 47.13 N 52.51 W
Torshälla 40 59.25 N 16.28 E
Tórshavn 22 62.01 N 6.46 W
Torside Reservoir ⊜1 262 53.29 N 1.54 W
Torsö I 40 58.47 N 13.48 E
Torsö 40 58.41 N 13.38 E
Torteval 43b 49.27 N 2.38 W
Tortola 70 37.58 N 13.46 E
Tortola I 240m 18.27 N 64.36 W
Tórtolas, Cerro de
las ʌ 252 29.56 S 69.54 W
Tortoli 71 39.55 N 9.39 E
Tortona 62 44.54 N 8.52 E
Tortora 68 39.56 N 15.48 E
Tortoreto 66 42.48 N 13.55 E
Tortorici 70 38.02 N 14.49 E
Tortosa 34 40.48 N 0.31 E
Tortosa, Cap de ⲻ 34 40.43 N 0.55 E
Tortue ≃ 186 50.18 N 65.23 W
Tortue, Île de la I 238 20.04 N 72.49 W
Tortue, Rivière de la
≃ 206 45.24 N 73.32 W
Tortuguero ≃ 236 10.34 N 83.31 W
Tortuguero, Laguna
ᴄ 240m 18.28 N 66.26 W
Tortuguero, Parque
Nacional ◆ 236 10.25 N 83.55 W
Tortuguitas 288 34.28 S 58.46 W
Tortum 130 40.19 N 41.35 E
Toru ≃ 114 1.26 N 98.46 E
Toruaigyr 85 42.32 N 76.26 E
Torue 112 0.58 S 120.18 E
Torugart, pereval ʮ 130 40.33 N 75.20 E
Torul 130 40.35 N 39.18 E
Toruń 30 53.02 N 18.35 E
Toruń □4 30 53.20 N 19.00 E
Torunos 246 8.30 N 70.04 W
Torup, Sve. 26 56.58 N 13.05 E
Torup, Sve. 41 55.34 N 13.12 E
Tõrva 76 58.00 N 25.56 E
Tory 88 51.47 N 103.00 E
Tory Island I 48 55.16 N 8.14 W
Torysa ≃ 30 48.39 N 21.21 E
Tory Sound ʮ 48 55.14 N 8.14 W
Toržok 76 57.03 N 34.58 E
Torzym 30 52.20 N 15.04 E
Tosa, Nihon 96 33.29 N 133.25 E
Tosa, Nihon 96 33.44 N 133.32 E
T'oša ≃ 80 55.38 N 42.09 E
T'osan 98 38.18 N 126.43 E
Tosari 115a 7.53 S 112.54 E
Tosa-shimizu 92 32.46 N 132.57 E
Tosa-wan ᴄ 96 33.20 N 133.40 E
Tosayama 96 33.38 N 133.32 E
Tosa-yamada 96 33.36 N 133.41 E
Tosca 156 25.53 S 23.58 E
Toscaig 46 57.24 N 5.50 W
Toscana (Tuscany)
□4 36 43.25 N 11.00 E
Toscano ≃ 234 18.01 N 102.32 W
Toscolano 64 45.38 N 10.37 E
Tösens 58 47.01 N 10.36 E
Toses, Collada de ʮ 34 42.19 N 2.01 E
Tōshi-jima I 94 34.31 N 136.53 E
Toshima ✈8 268 35.44 N 139.43 E
To-shima I 94 34.31 N 139.17 E
Tōshō-gū ✈1 94 36.46 N 139.36 E
Tosi, Indon. 115b 9.35 S 118.57 E
Tosi, It. 66 43.45 N 11.31 E
Tosilei 144 1.25 N 41.24 E
Toškalykaja, gora ʌ 86 50.38 N 89.30 E
Toškovskij 83 48.46 N 38.34 E
Tosna ≃ 265a 59.46 N 30.46 E
Tosno 76 59.33 N 30.53 E
Toson Cengel 88 48.47 N 98.15 E
Toson Hu ⊜ 102 35.18 N 98.54 E
T'osovo 76 55.37 N 34.30 E
T'osovo-Netyl'skij 76 58.57 N 31.04 E
T'osovskij 76 58.48 N 30.52 E
Töss ≃ 58 47.33 N 8.33 E
Tossens 52 53.34 N 8.16 E
Tossicia 66 42.33 N 13.39 E
Tostado 252 29.14 S 61.46 W
Tõstamaa 76 58.20 N 24.00 E
Töstedt 52 53.17 N 9.42 E
Tosterön I 40 59.25 N 17.00 E
Tostu 85 41.34 N 71.34 E
Tost uul ʌ 102 43.15 N 100.30 E
Tosu 96 33.22 N 130.31 E
Tosya 130 41.01 N 34.02 E
Totagatic ≃ 190 46.05 N 92.11 W
Totak ⊜ 26 59.42 N 7.57 E
Totana 34 37.46 N 1.30 W
Totānāla 126 22.05 N 87.40 E
Totatiche 234 21.56 N 103.27 W
Totban 80 46.47 N 49.06 E
Toteng 156 20.22 S 22.58 E
Tôtes 50 49.41 N 1.03 E
Totes Gebirge ⅄ 30 47.42 N 13.55 E
T'otkino 78 51.17 N 34.16 E
Tot'ma 76 59.57 N 42.45 E
Totnes 42 50.25 N 3.41 W
Totness 250 5.53 N 56.19 W
Toto 152 7.08 S 14.16 E
Totonicapán 236 14.55 N 91.22 W
Totonicapán □5 236 15.00 N 91.20 W
Totopotomoy Creek
≃ 208 37.41 N 77.13 W
Totora, Bol. 248 17.42 S 65.09 W
Totora, Bol. 248 17.49 S 68.07 W
Totoras 252 32.35 S 61.11 W
Totos 248 13.31 S 74.30 W
Tototlán 234 20.33 N 102.48 W
Totowa 210 40.54 N 74.12 W
Totoya Island I 175g 18.57 S 179.50 W
Totson Mountain ʌ 180 64.26 N 157.15 W
Totsuka ✈8 268 35.24 N 139.32 E
Tottenham, Austl. 166 32.14 S 147.21 E
Tottenham, On., Can. 212 44.01 N 79.49 W
Tottenham ✈8 260 51.35 N 0.04 W
Tottenham Hotspur
Football Ground ◆ 260 51.36 N 0.04 W
Totten Inlet ᴄ 224 47.07 N 123.02 W
Tottenville ✈8 276 40.31 N 74.15 W
Totteridge ✈8 260 51.38 N 0.12 W
Tottington 44 53.37 N 2.20 W
Totton 42 50.56 N 1.29 W
Tottori 96 35.30 N 134.14 E
Tottori □5 96 35.30 N 134.00 E
Tottori-sakyū ʌ2 96 35.31 N 134.15 E
Totuskey Creek ≃ 208 37.52 N 76.45 W
Tou, Motu I 174k 21.11 S 159.48 W
Touba, C. Iv. 150 8.17 N 7.41 W
Touba, Sén. 150 14.51 N 15.53 W
Toubei 100 26.44 N 116.05 E
Toubéré Bafal 150 14.23 N 13.32 W
Toubkal, Jebel ʌ 148 31.05 N 7.55 W
Toubkal, Parc
National du ◆ 148 31.05 N 7.55 W
Touboro 146 13.59 N 12.18 E
Touboro 152 7.43 N 15.12 E
T'ouch'eng 100 24.52 N 121.49 E
Touchet ≃ 202 46.02 N 118.41 W
Touchwood Hills ʌ2 184 51.35 N 104.17 W
Touchwood Lake ⊜,
Ab., Can. 182 54.50 N 111.23 W
Touchwood Lake ⊜,
Mb., Can. 184 54.29 N 95.00 W
Toucy 50 47.44 N 3.18 E
Toudao ≃ 98 42.46 N 127.11 E
Toudaogou, Zhg. 98 42.46 N 129.12 E
Toudaogou, Zhg. 104 41.37 N 121.40 E
Toudaogou, Zhg. 105 40.58 N 117.59 E
Touët-sur-Var 62 43.57 N 7.00 E
Tougan 150 13.04 N 3.04 W
Touggourt 148 33.10 N 6.00 E
Toughkenamon 285 39.50 N 75.46 W
Tougouri 150 13.19 N 0.31 W
Tougué 150 11.27 N 11.41 W
Touho 175f 20.47 S 165.14 E
Touiel, Oued V 148 31.30 N 4.46 E
Touil, Oued V 148 35.30 N 2.33 E
Touisset 207 41.43 N 71.13 W
Toukanasi 100 29.22 N 119.06 E
Toukley 170 33.16 S 151.33 E
Toukoto 150 13.27 N 9.53 W
Toul 50 48.41 N 5.54 E
Touléplieu 150 6.35 N 8.25 W
Touliu 100 23.43 N 120.32 E
Toulnustouc ≃ 186 49.35 N 68.24 W
Toulnustouc Nord-Est
≃ 186 50.56 N 67.44 W
Toulon, Fr. 62 43.07 N 5.56 E
Toulon, Il., U.S. 190 41.05 N 89.51 W
Toulon Lake ⊜ 204 40.01 N 118.40 W
Toulon-sur-Arroux 32 46.42 N 4.08 E
Touloubre ≃ 62 43.33 N 5.02 E
Toulourenc ≃ 62 44.13 N 5.29 E
Toulouse 32 43.36 N 1.26 E
Toumen Shan I 100 28.41 N 121.46 E
Toumfafi 150 15.02 N 5.38 E
Toumodi 150 6.33 N 5.01 W
Tounan 100 23.41 N 120.28 E
Tounassine, Hamada
✈2 148 28.30 N 5.00 W
Toungo 146 8.07 N 12.03 E
Toungoo 110 18.56 N 96.26 E
Toupeng 106 30.19 N 120.31 E
Touques 50 49.22 N 0.06 E
Touques ≃ 50 49.22 N 0.06 E
Tour, Étang de la ⊜ 261 48.40 N 1.53 E
Toura, Monts du ⅄ 150 7.40 N 7.25 W
Touraine 188 45.34 N 75.47 W
Touraine □9 50 47.12 N 1.30 E
Tourakom 110 18.26 N 102.32 E
Tourane
→ Da Nang 108 16.04 N 108.13 E
Touraoine ≈4 148 24.37 N 11.23 W
Tourbe ≃ 56 49.10 N 4.52 E
Tourcoing 50 50.43 N 3.09 E
Touriñan, Cabo ⲻ 34 43.03 N 9.18 W

Symbols in the index entries represent the broad categories identified in the key at the right. Symbols with superior numbers (⅄1) identify subcategories (see complete key on page I · 1).

Symbole im Register stellen die rechts im Schlüssel erklärten Kategorien dar. Symbole mit hochgestellten Ziffern (⅄1) bezeichnen Unterabteilungen einer Kategorie (vgl. vollständiger Schlüssel auf Seite I · 1).

Los símbolos incluídos en el texto del índice representan las grandes categorías identificadas con la clave a la derecha. Los símbolos con números en su parte superior (⅄1) identifican las subcategorías (véase la clave completa en la página I · 1).

Les symboles de l'index représentent les catégories indiquées dans la légende à droite. Les symboles suivis d'un indice (⅄1) représentent des sous-catégories (voir légende complète à la page I · 1).

Os símbolos incluídos no texto do índice representam as grandes categorias identificadas com a chave à direita. Os símbolos com números em sua parte superior (⅄1) identificam as subcategorias (veja-se a chave completa à página I · 1).

	English	Deutsch	Español	Français	Português
ʌ	Mountain	Berg	Montaña	Montagne	Montanha
⅄	Mountains	Gebirge	Montañas	Montagnes	Montanhas
ʮ	Pass	Paß	Paso	Col	Passo
V	Valley, Canyon	Tal, Cañon	Valle, Cañón	Vallée, Canyon	Vale, Canhão
≐	Plain	Ebene	Llano	Plaine	Planície
ⲻ	Cape	Kap	Cabo	Cap	Cabo
I	Island	Insel	Isla	Île	Ilha
II	Islands	Inseln	Islas	Îles	Ilhas
✈	Other Topographic Features	Andere Topographische Objekte	Otros Elementos Topográficos	Autres données topographiques	Outros acidentes topográficos

ESPAÑOL · FRANÇAIS · PORTUGUÊS

Nombre / Nom / Nome	Página / Page	Lat.°′	Long.°′ W = Oeste / W = Ouest
Tournai	50	50.36 N	3.23 E
Tournan-en-Brie	50	48.44 N	2.46 E
Tourndo, Oued ∨	148	22.15 N	10.28 E
Tournesac ≃	50	47.15 N	4.12 E
Tournon	62	45.04 N	4.50 E
Tournus	58	46.34 N	4.54 E
Touros	250	5.12 S	35.28 W
Tou Rout	110	16.24 N	107.00 E
Tourouvre	50	48.35 N	0.40 E
Tourrette-Levens	62	43.47 N	7.16 E
Tours	50	47.23 N	0.41 E
Tours-sur-Marne	50	49.03 N	4.07 E
Tours-sur-Meymont	62	45.40 N	3.35 E
Tourteron	56	49.32 N	4.39 E
Tourves	62	43.24 N	5.56 E
Toury	50	48.12 N	1.56 E
Toussaint Creek ≃	214	41.35 N	83.04 W
Tousside, Pic ∧	146	21.02 N	16.25 E
Toussoro, Mont ∧	146	9.18 N	23.28 E
Toussus-le-Noble	261	48.45 N	2.07 E
Toussus-le-Noble, Aéroport de ⊠	261	48.45 N	2.10 E
Toustain	36	36.40 N	8.15 E
Toutai, Zhg.	89	45.40 N	124.50 E
Toutai, Zhg.	104	41.41 N	121.11 E
Toutaizi	104	42.19 N	122.49 E
Toutle	224	46.20 N	122.41 W
Toutle ≃	224	46.17 N	122.55 W
Toutle, North Fork ≃	224	46.23 N	122.34 W
Toutle, South Fork ≃	224	46.20 N	122.44 W
Toutle Mountain Range ⋏	224	46.20 N	122.30 W
Toutuohe	100	31.06 N	116.25 E
Touws ≃	158	33.45 S	21.11 E
Touwsrivier	158	33.20 S	20.00 E
Touzhan	89	49.27 N	119.41 E
Toužim	60	50.04 N	13.00 E
Töv □4	88	47.30 N	106.30 E
Tova	24	65.58 N	40.45 E
Tovar	246	8.20 N	71.46 W
Tovarkovo	82	54.42 N	35.57 E
Tovarkovskij	76	53.40 N	38.14 E
Tove ≃	42	52.05 N	0.38 W
Tovey	219	39.35 N	89.27 W
Tow	196	30.53 N	98.28 W
Tōwa	96	33.13 N	132.53 E
Towaco	210	40.55 N	74.20 W
Towada	92	40.37 N	141.13 E
Towada-Hachimantai-kokuritsu-kōen ♠	92	40.35 N	140.53 E
Towada-ko ⊜	92	40.28 N	140.55 E
Towai	172	35.29 S	174.08 E
Towamencin Creek ≃	285	40.13 N	75.23 W
Towanda, Il., U.S.	216	40.34 N	88.54 W
Towanda, Ks., U.S.	198	37.47 N	96.59 W
Towanda, Pa., U.S.	210	41.46 N	76.26 W
Towanda Creek ≃	210	41.45 N	76.26 W
Towan Head ≻	42	50.25 N	5.07 W
Towar Gardens	216	42.45 N	84.28 W
Towari	112	4.36 S	121.29 E
Towcester	42	52.08 N	1.00 W
Tower	190	47.48 N	92.16 W
Tower City, N.D., U.S.	198	46.55 N	97.40 W
Tower City, Pa., U.S.	208	40.35 N	76.33 W
Tower Hamlets ◆8	260	51.32 N	0.03 W
Tower Hill, Austl.	166	22.03 S	144.36 E
Tower Hill, Il., U.S.	219	39.23 N	88.57 W
Towerhill Creek ≃	166	22.29 S	144.39 E
Tower of London ⊥	260	51.30 N	0.05 W
Tower Peak ∧	226	38.09 N	119.33 W
Towers of Silence ʊ1	272c	18.58 N	72.48 E
Tower Soudan State Park ♠	190	47.50 N	92.15 W
Towla, Mount ∧	154	21.22 S	29.52 E
Tow Law	44	54.44 N	1.49 W
Towlī	84	39.11 N	47.32 E
Town ≃	283	42.00 N	70.57 W
Town and Country	202	47.42 N	117.23 W
Town Bank	208	39.00 N	74.56 W
Town Creek ≃, Al., U.S.	194	34.46 N	87.25 W
Town Creek ≃, Al., U.S.	194	34.24 N	86.11 W
Town Creek ≃, Oh., U.S.	216	41.05 N	84.25 W
Town Creek Manor	208	38.19 N	76.27 W
Towneley Hall ⊥	262	53.46 N	2.13 W
Towner	198	48.20 N	100.24 W
Town Estates	285	40.04 N	74.52 W
Town Hill ∧2	240a	32.19 N	64.44 W
Townline Tunnel ◆5	284a	42.57 N	79.15 W
Town of Niagara	284a	43.06 N	78.59 W
Town of Pines	216	41.41 N	86.58 W
Townsend, On., Can.	212	42.54 N	80.07 W
Townsend, De., U.S.	208	39.23 N	75.41 W
Townsend, Ma., U.S.	207	42.40 N	71.42 W
Townsend, Mt., U.S.	202	46.19 N	111.31 W
Townsend, Va., U.S.	208	37.11 N	75.57 W
Townsend, Mount ∧	171b	36.25 S	148.15 E
Townsend Island I	276	40.38 N	73.26 W
Townsends Inlet ⊂	208	39.07 N	74.43 W
Townshend Island I	166	22.15 S	150.30 E
Township Line Run ≃	279b	40.13 N	79.33 W
Townsville	166	19.16 S	146.48 E
Townville	214	41.41 N	79.53 W
Towrang	170	34.42 S	149.51 E
Towrang, Mount ∧	170	34.46 S	149.51 E
Towra Point ≻	274a	34.00 S	151.10 E
Towr Kham	123	34.08 N	71.05 E
Towrzī, Afg.	120	30.11 N	65.59 E
Towrzī, Afg.	128	32.38 N	65.53 E
Towson	208	39.24 N	76.36 W
Towson State College ʊ2	284b	39.24 N	76.37 W
Towuti, Danau ⊜	112	2.45 S	121.32 E
Toxkan (Aksaj) ≃, Asia	85	40.55 N	78.16 E
Toxkan ≃, Zhg.	90	41.08 N	80.11 E
Toyah	196	31.19 N	103.47 W
Toyah Creek ≃	196	31.18 N	103.27 W
Tōya-ko ⊜	92a	42.35 N	140.51 E
Toyama	94	36.41 N	137.13 E
Toyama □5	94	36.30 N	137.30 E
Toyama-heiya ≚	94	36.40 N	137.15 E
Toyama-wan ⊂	94	36.50 N	137.10 E
Toyapakeh	115b	8.41 S	115.29 E
Tōyo, Nihon	96	33.55 N	133.05 E
Tōyō, Nihon	96	33.30 N	134.16 E
Toyo ≃	94	34.47 N	137.20 E
Toyoake	94	35.03 N	137.01 E
Toyoda, Nihon	94	34.45 N	137.49 E
Toyoda, Nihon	268	35.39 N	139.23 E
Toyofuta	268	35.53 N	139.57 E
Toyohama	96	34.04 N	133.38 E
Toyohara	175d	24.15 N	123.48 E
Toyohashi	94	34.46 N	137.23 E
Toyohira	96	34.40 N	132.24 E
Toyokawa	94	34.49 N	137.24 E
Toyo-kawa-yōsui ≊	94	34.35 N	137.03 E
Toyonaka, Nihon	96	34.09 N	133.42 E
Toyonaka, Nihon	96	34.47 N	135.28 E
Toyone	94	35.09 N	137.43 E
Toyono	94	36.43 N	138.16 E
Toyooka, Nihon	94	35.33 N	137.54 E
Toyooka, Nihon	94	34.50 N	137.52 E
Toyooka, Nihon	96	35.32 N	134.50 E
Toyooka, Nihon	268	35.11 N	139.58 E
Toyosaka, Nihon	92	37.56 N	139.13 E
Toyosaka, Nihon	96	34.34 N	132.50 E
Toyosato	94	36.06 N	140.02 E
Toyoshina	94	36.18 N	137.54 E
Toyota, Nihon	94	35.05 N	137.09 E
Toyota, Nihon	94	36.46 N	138.19 E
Toyota, Nihon	96	34.12 N	131.04 E
Toyota-ko ⊜	96	34.14 N	131.08 E
Toyotomi	94	35.34 N	138.33 E
Toyotsu	96	33.40 N	130.58 E
Toyoura	96	34.08 N	130.58 E
Toy's Hill	260	51.14 N	0.06 E
Tozer, Mount ∧	164	12.45 S	143.13 E
Tozeur	148	33.55 N	8.08 E
Tozi, Mount ∧	180	65.41 N	150.58 W
Tozitna ≃	180	65.08 N	152.23 W
Tpig	84	41.47 N	47.36 E
Traar ◆8	263	51.23 N	6.36 E
Trabaria, Bocca)(	66	43.36 N	12.14 E
Traben-Trarbach	56	49.57 N	7.06 E
Trabia	70	37.59 N	13.39 E
Trabiju	255	22.03 S	48.18 W
Trabuco, Arroyo ≃	228	33.31 N	117.40 W
Trabzon	130	41.00 N	39.43 E
Trabzon □4	130	40.50 N	39.50 E
Tracadie	186	47.31 N	64.54 W
Trachselwald	58	47.01 N	7.45 E
Tra Cu	110	9.42 N	106.16 E
Tracy, P.Q., Can.	206	46.01 N	73.09 W
Tracy, Ca., U.S.	226	37.44 N	121.25 W
Tracy, Mn., U.S.	198	44.14 N	95.37 W
Tracy City	194	35.15 N	85.44 W
Tracyton	224	47.36 N	122.39 W
Tradate	62	45.43 N	8.54 E
Trade Lake ⊜	184	55.22 N	103.44 W
Tradewater ≃	194	37.31 N	88.03 W
Trading Bay ⊂	212	45.15 N	78.55 W
Tradinghouse Creek Reservoir ⊜1	222	31.35 N	96.55 W
Traditional Cultures, Museum of ʊ	269f	14.31 N	121.00 E
Trælleborg ⊥	41	55.23 N	11.17 E
Traer	190	42.11 N	92.27 W
Traessu, Monte ∧	71	40.28 N	8.40 E
Trafalgar, Austl.	169	38.12 S	146.09 E
Trafalgar, On., Can.	275b	43.29 N	79.43 W
Trafalgar, In., U.S.	218	39.24 N	86.09 W
Trafalgar, Cabo ≻	34	36.11 N	6.02 W
Trafaria	266c	38.40 N	9.14 W
Trafford	214	40.23 N	79.45 W
Trafford □8	262	53.24 N	2.21 W
Trafford, Lake ⊜	220	26.25 N	81.30 W
Trafford Park	262	53.28 N	2.20 W
Trafoi	64	46.33 N	10.31 E
Tragacete	34	40.21 N	1.51 W
Tragliata ◆8	267a	41.58 N	12.15 E
Tragwein	61	48.20 N	14.37 E
Traição, Córrego ≃	287b	23.36 S	46.41 W
Traid	34	40.40 N	1.49 W
Traiguén	252	38.15 S	72.41 W
Traiguén, Isla I	254	45.35 S	73.42 W
Trail	182	49.06 N	117.42 W
Trail Creek	216	41.41 N	86.51 W
Trailer Estates	220	27.24 N	82.34 W
Trail Ridge ∧	192	30.35 N	82.05 W
Traînel	50	48.25 N	3.27 E
Trainer	285	39.50 N	75.25 W
Traipu	250	9.58 S	37.01 W
Traíra (Taraira) ≃	246	1.04 S	69.26 W
Trairão ≃	250	7.20 S	51.14 W
Traíras ≃	255	14.07 S	48.31 W
Trairi	250	3.17 S	39.15 W
Traisen	61	48.02 N	15.37 E
Traisen ≃	61	48.22 N	15.46 E
Traiskirchen	61	48.01 N	16.18 E
Traismauer	61	48.21 N	15.44 E
Traîtres, Baie des ⊂	174x	9.50 S	139.02 W
Trajouce	266c	38.44 N	9.20 W
Trakai	76	54.38 N	24.56 E
Trakt	24	62.44 N	51.11 E
Träkvista	40	59.16 N	17.47 E
Tralee	48	52.16 N	9.42 W
Tralee Bay ⊂	48	52.15 N	9.59 W
Trá Lí → Tralee	48	52.16 N	9.42 W
Tramatza	71	40.00 N	8.39 E
Tramayes	58	46.18 N	4.36 E
Tramelan	58	47.13 N	7.06 E
Tra Mi	110	15.20 N	108.13 E
Tramin → Termeno	64	46.20 N	11.14 E
Trammel	192	37.00 N	82.17 W
Trammel Creek ≃	194	36.52 N	86.23 W
Tramonti di sopra	64	46.18 N	12.47 E
Tramore	48	52.10 N	7.10 W
Tramperos Creek (Punta de Agua Creek) ≃	196	35.32 N	102.27 W
Tramping Lake ⊜	184	52.08 N	108.49 W
Tramutola	68	40.19 N	15.47 E
Trân	38	42.50 N	22.39 E
Tranås	26	58.03 N	14.59 E
Trancão ≃	266c	38.48 N	9.06 W
Trancas	252	26.13 S	65.17 W
Trancoso	34	40.47 N	7.21 W
Trand	123	34.38 N	72.59 E
Tranderup	41	54.52 N	10.22 E
Tranebjerg	41	55.50 N	10.36 E
Tranekær	41	55.00 N	10.51 E
Tranemo	26	57.29 N	13.21 E
Tranent	46	55.57 N	2.58 W
Tränental	158	27.09 S	19.33 E
Trang	110	7.33 N	99.36 E
Trangahy	157b	19.07 S	44.43 E
Trangan, Pulau I	164	6.35 S	134.20 E
Trangie	166	32.02 S	147.59 E
Tran Grande ≃	116	6.43 N	124.01 E
Trängslet	26	61.25 N	13.40 E
Trani	68	41.17 N	16.26 E
Tranmere	262	53.23 N	3.01 W
Trannon ≃	42	52.31 N	3.25 W
Tranoroa	157b	24.42 S	45.04 E
Tranquebar	122	11.02 N	79.51 E
Tranqueras	252	31.12 S	55.45 W
Tranquility	218	38.58 N	83.32 W
Tranquillity	226	36.38 N	120.15 W
Transantarctic Mountains ⋏	9	85.00 S	175.00 W
Trans-en-Provence	62	43.30 N	6.29 E
Transfer	214	41.20 N	80.26 W
Transit Airpark ⊠	284a	43.06 N	78.44 W
Transkei □1, Afr.	138	31.20 S	29.00 E
Transkei □1, Afr.	158	31.20 S	29.00 E
Transquaking ≃	208	38.22 N	76.00 W
Transsylvanische Alpen → Carpații Meridionali ⋏	38	45.30 N	24.15 E
Transtrand	26	61.05 N	13.19 E
Transtrandsfjällen ∧	26	61.17 N	13.00 E
Transvaal □4	156	25.00 S	29.00 E
Transylvania □9	38	46.30 N	24.00 E
Transylvanian Alps → Carpații Meridionali ⋏	38	45.30 N	24.15 E
Tranters Creek ≃	192	35.33 N	77.05 W
Traona	58	46.09 N	9.31 E
Trapalcó, Salinas de ≚	254	39.45 S	66.45 W
Trapani	70	38.01 N	12.31 E
Trapani □4	70	37.50 N	12.40 E
Traphole Brook ≃	283	42.10 N	71.11 W
Trappe, Md., U.S.	208	38.39 N	76.03 W
Trappe, Pa., U.S.	208	40.12 N	75.29 W
Trappenkamp	54	54.03 N	10.16 E
Trapper Peak ∧	202	45.54 N	114.18 W
Trappes	50	48.47 N	2.00 E
Trappeto	70	38.04 N	13.03 E
Trapuá ≃	287b	23.36 S	46.17 W
Traralgon	169	38.12 S	146.32 E
Traralgon Creek ≃	169	38.10 S	146.31 E
Traras, Monts des ⋏	34	35.10 N	1.40 W
Trarza □4	150	17.45 N	15.45 W
Trârza ◆1	150	18.00 N	15.00 W
Trasacco	66	41.57 N	13.32 E
Trasadingen	58	47.40 N	8.26 E
Trascăului, Munții ⋏	38	46.23 N	23.33 E
Trasimeno, Lago ⊜	66	43.08 N	12.06 E
Trask ≃	224	45.28 N	123.53 W
Träslövsläge	26	57.04 N	12.16 E
Trasna	82	54.45 N	38.42 E
Trás-os-Montes □9	34	41.30 N	7.15 W
Trassem	56	49.34 N	6.31 E
Trâstenik	38	43.31 N	24.28 E
Trat	110	12.14 N	102.30 E
Tratalias	71	39.06 N	8.34 E
Tratzberg, Schloss ⊥	64	47.23 N	11.44 E
Trauchgau	58	47.38 N	10.49 E
Traun	61	48.13 N	14.14 E
Traun ≃, Dtsch.	60	48.00 N	12.32 E
Traun ≃, Öst.	30	48.16 N	14.22 E
Traunkirchen	64	47.50 N	13.47 E
Traunreut	64	47.56 N	12.35 E
Traunsee ⊜	64	47.51 N	13.48 E
Traunstein, Dtsch.	64	47.52 N	12.38 E
Traunstein, Öst.	61	48.26 N	15.07 E
Traunstein ∧	64	47.52 N	13.50 E
Trautenstein	54	51.41 N	10.43 E
Travagliato	64	45.31 N	10.05 E
Trave ≃	54	53.54 N	10.50 E
Travedona	62	45.48 N	8.40 E
Travellers Lake ⊜	166	33.18 S	142.00 E
Travemünde ◆8	54	53.57 N	10.52 E
Traver	226	36.27 N	119.29 W
Travers, Mount ∧	172	42.01 S	172.44 E
Travers, Val de ∨	58	46.57 N	6.38 E
Traverse, Lake ⊜	198	45.43 N	96.40 W
Traverse Bay ⊂	184	50.40 N	96.25 W
Traverse City	190	44.45 N	85.37 W
Traversella	62	45.30 N	7.45 E
Traverse Peak ∧	180	65.10 N	159.12 W
Traversetolo	64	44.38 N	10.23 E
Travers Reservoir ⊜1	182	50.14 N	112.51 W
Tra Vinh	110	9.56 N	106.20 E
Travis	222	31.08 N	97.00 W
Travis □6	222	30.18 N	97.40 W
Travis, Lake ⊜1	196	30.27 N	98.00 W
Travis Air Force Base ■	226	38.16 N	121.55 W
Travnik	36	44.14 N	17.40 E
Trawalla	169	37.26 S	143.29 E
Trawbreaga Bay ⊂	48	55.17 N	7.18 W
Trawick	222	31.46 N	94.45 W
Trawsfynydd	42	52.54 N	3.55 W
Trayning	162	31.07 S	117.48 E
Trazegnies	50	50.28 N	4.19 E
Trbovlje	36	46.10 N	15.03 E
Treadwell	210	42.21 N	75.03 W
Treales	262	53.47 N	2.51 W
Treasure Island	220	27.46 N	82.46 W
Treasure Island I	226	37.48 N	122.22 W
Treasure Island Naval Station ■	282	37.49 N	122.22 W
Trebatsch	54	52.05 N	14.09 E
Trebbia ≃	62	45.04 N	9.41 E
Trebbin	54	52.13 N	13.13 E
Třebechovice pod Orebem	30	50.12 N	16.00 E
Trebel	54	52.59 N	11.20 E
Trebel ≃	54	53.55 N	13.01 E
Trebelsee ⊜	54	52.28 N	12.47 E
Třebenice	54	50.29 N	14.00 E
Trebgast	60	50.04 N	11.33 E
Třebíč	30	49.13 N	15.53 E
Trebinje	38	42.43 N	18.20 E
Trebisacce	68	39.52 N	16.32 E
Trebišov	30	48.40 N	21.47 E
Trebitz	54	51.45 N	12.44 E
Trebizond → Trabzon	130	41.00 N	39.43 E
Trebjerg ∧2	41	55.10 N	10.14 E
Třebkov	60	49.22 N	14.04 E
Treble Mountain ∧	182	55.50 N	129.51 W
Treblinka	30	52.39 N	22.03 E
Třeboň	61	49.00 N	14.47 E
Třebouň ∧	60	50.01 N	12.59 E
Trebsen	54	51.17 N	12.45 E
Trebur	56	49.56 N	8.25 E
Trecastagni	70	37.37 N	15.05 E
Trecate	62	45.26 N	8.44 E
Trecchina	68	40.02 N	15.46 E
Trece Martires	116	14.16 N	120.50 E
Trecenta	64	45.02 N	11.28 E
Tred Avon River ⊂	208	38.42 N	76.08 W
Tredegar	42	51.47 N	3.16 W
Tredici Archi, Ponte ◆5	66	41.32 N	14.57 E
Treene ≃	41	54.22 N	9.05 E
Trees Mills	279b	40.23 N	80.13 W
Treffen	64	46.40 N	13.52 E
Treffort	58	46.16 N	5.22 E
Treffurt	56	51.08 N	10.14 E
Trèfle, Lac du ⊜	206	46.36 N	73.55 W
Tregaron	42	52.13 N	3.55 W
Tregnago	64	45.31 N	11.10 E
Tregosse Islets II	166	17.41 S	150.43 E
Tregubovo	76	58.59 N	31.33 E
Tréguier	32	48.47 N	3.14 W
Treharris	42	51.41 N	3.16 W
Treherne	184	49.38 N	98.41 W
Trehörningsjö	26	63.42 N	18.48 E
Treia, Dtsch.	41	54.30 N	9.17 E
Treia, It.	66	43.19 N	13.19 E
Treig, Loch ⊜	46	56.50 N	4.44 W
Treinta y Tres	252	33.14 S	54.23 W
Treis	56	50.10 N	7.17 E
Trekkopje	156	22.18 S	14.53 E
Trélazé	32	47.27 N	0.28 W
Trelde Næs ≻	41	55.37 N	9.52 E
Trelew	254	43.15 S	65.18 W
Trelleborg	41	55.22 N	13.10 E
Treloar	219	38.39 N	91.10 W
Tremadog	42	52.56 N	4.09 W
Tremadog Bay ⊂	42	52.52 N	4.15 W
Tremblant, Lac ⊜	206	46.15 N	74.38 W
Tremblant, Mont ∧	206	46.16 N	74.35 W
Tremblay, Hippodrome du ♠	261	48.50 N	2.29 E
Tremblay-lès-Gonesse	261	48.59 N	2.34 E
Trembleur Lake ⊜	182	54.51 N	125.07 W
Tremedal	255	14.58 S	41.24 W
Tremembé	256	22.58 S	45.33 W
Tremezzo	58	45.59 N	9.15 E
Tremino	88	56.42 N	98.04 E
Tremiti, Isole II	66	42.07 N	15.30 E
Tremo La)(	124	27.44 N	89.12 E
Tremont, Il., U.S.	190	40.31 N	89.29 W
Tremont, In., U.S.	216	41.39 N	87.02 W
Tremont, Pa., U.S.	208	40.37 N	76.23 W
Tremont ◆8	276	40.51 N	73.55 W
Tremont City	218	40.00 N	83.50 W
Tremonton	200	41.42 N	112.09 W
Třemošna	60	49.49 N	13.20 E
Třemošná ≃	60	49.52 N	13.32 E
Tremp	34	42.10 N	0.54 E
Trempealeau	190	44.00 N	91.26 W
Trempealeau ≃	190	44.02 N	91.32 W
Tremsbüttel	52	53.44 N	10.18 E
Trena	144	10.45 N	40.38 E
Trenčín	30	48.54 N	18.04 E
Trendelburg	52	51.34 N	9.25 E
Trenel	252	35.42 S	64.08 W
Trêng	110	12.49 N	102.54 E
Trenggalek	115a	8.03 S	111.43 E
Trenque Lauquen	252	35.58 S	62.42 W
Trent	54	54.31 N	13.15 E
Trent ≃, On., Can.	212	44.06 N	77.34 W
Trent ≃, Eng., U.K.	28	53.42 N	0.41 W
Trent ≃, N.C., U.S.	192	35.05 N	77.02 W
Trent, Vale of ∨	42	52.44 N	1.50 W
Trent and Mersey Canal ≊	262	53.19 N	2.39 W
Trente et un Milles, Lac des ⊜	188	46.12 N	75.49 W
Trentham	169	37.23 S	144.19 E
Trentino-Alto Adige □4	64	46.30 N	11.20 E
Trento	64	46.04 N	11.08 E
Trento □4	64	46.08 N	11.07 E
Trentola-Ducenta	68	40.59 N	14.10 E
Trenton, N.S., Can.	186	45.37 N	62.38 W
Trenton, On., Can.	212	44.06 N	77.35 W
Trenton, Fl., U.S.	192	29.36 N	82.49 W
Trenton, Ga., U.S.	192	34.52 N	85.30 W
Trenton, Il., U.S.	219	38.36 N	89.40 W
Trenton, Ky., U.S.	194	36.43 N	87.15 W
Trenton, Mi., U.S.	216	42.08 N	83.10 W
Trenton, Mo., U.S.	194	40.04 N	93.36 W
Trenton, Ne., U.S.	198	40.10 N	101.00 W
Trenton, N.J., U.S.	208	40.13 N	74.44 W
Trenton, N.C., U.S.	192	35.04 N	77.21 W
Trenton, Oh., U.S.	218	39.29 N	84.28 W
Trenton, Tn., U.S.	194	35.58 N	88.56 W
Trenton, Tx., U.S.	196	33.26 N	96.20 W
Trenton, Canadian Forces Base ■	190	44.07 N	77.33 W
Trenton Channel ≃1	281	42.06 N	83.11 W
Trent → Trento	64	46.04 N	11.08 E
Trentwood	202	47.42 N	117.13 W
Trepalade	64	45.34 N	12.24 E
Trepassey	186	46.44 N	53.22 W
Trepassey Bay ⊂	186	46.37 N	53.20 W
Treptow ◆8	54	52.29 N	13.29 E
Trepuzzi	68	40.24 N	18.05 E
Trequanda	66	43.11 N	11.40 E
Tresa ≃	58	46.00 N	8.43 E
Tres Algarrobos	252	35.12 S	62.46 W
Tres Árboles	252	32.24 S	56.43 W
Tres Arroyos	252	38.23 S	60.17 W
Tres Cerros	254	48.13 S	67.33 W
Treščevo	82	54.11 N	37.55 E
Tresckow	210	40.54 N	75.58 W
Tresco I	42a	49.57 N	6.19 W
Três Corações	256	21.42 S	45.16 W
Trescore Balneario	62	45.41 N	9.50 E
Três Coroas	252	29.32 S	50.48 W
Tres de Febrero □5	288	34.36 S	58.35 W
Tres de Febrero → Caseros	258	34.36 S	58.33 W
Três de Maio	252	27.47 S	54.14 W
Tresenda	64	46.10 N	10.05 E
Tres Esquinas	246	0.43 N	75.16 W
Três Fronteiras	255	20.13 S	50.55 W
Treshnish Isles II	46	56.30 N	6.24 W
Treshnish Point ≻	46	56.33 N	6.21 W
Tre Signori, Picco dei (Dreiherrnspitze) ∧	64	47.04 N	12.15 E
Três Ilhas	256	22.04 S	43.29 W
Tresinaro ≃	64	44.39 N	10.47 E
Tres Isletas	252	26.21 S	60.26 W
Treskino	80	52.40 N	44.40 E
Três Lagoas	255	20.48 S	51.43 W
Tres Lagos	254	49.37 S	71.30 W
Tres Lomas	252	36.27 S	62.51 W
Três Marias	255	18.12 S	45.14 W
Três Marias, Represa de ⊜1	255	18.12 S	45.15 W
Tres Montes, Golfo ⊂	254	46.54 S	75.00 W
Tres Montes, Península ≻1	254	46.50 S	75.30 W
Tres Montosas ∧	200	34.06 N	107.28 W
Tres Morros, Alto de ∧	246	7.08 N	76.11 W
Tresnuraghes	71	40.15 N	8.31 E
Tres Padres, Pico ∧	286a	19.35 N	99.08 W
Tres Palacios ≃	196	28.45 N	96.09 W
Tres Palos, Laguna ⊂	234	16.46 N	99.44 W
Três Passos	252	27.27 S	53.56 W
Tres Picos	234	15.52 N	93.32 W
Tres Picos, Cerro ∧, Arg.	252	38.09 S	61.57 W
Tres Picos, Cerro ∧, Méx.	234	16.12 N	93.37 W
Tres Pinos	226	36.48 N	121.19 W
Tres Pinos Creek ≃	226	36.47 N	121.21 W
Três Pontas	256	21.22 S	45.31 W
Três Pontas, Cabo das ≻	152	10.23 S	13.32 E
Tres Puntas, Cabo ≻, Arg.	254	47.06 S	65.53 W
Tres Puntas, Cabo ≻, Guat.	236	15.56 N	88.37 W
Três Ranchos	255	18.22 S	47.47 W
Tres Reyes Islands II	116	13.14 N	121.51 E
Três Rios, Bra.	256	22.07 S	43.12 W
Tres Ríos, C.R.	236	9.54 N	83.58 W
Tressancourt	261	48.55 N	2.00 E
Třešť	30	49.18 N	15.30 E
Tresta	46a	60.14 N	1.21 W
Tres Valles	234	18.15 N	96.08 W
Tres Vírgenes, Volcán de las ∧1	232	27.27 N	112.34 W
Tres Zapotes ⊥	234	18.28 N	95.24 W
Tret'akovskaja Galereja ʊ	265b	55.45 N	37.37 E
Tretet	114	4.40 N	96.51 E
Trets	62	43.27 N	5.41 E
Tretten	26	61.19 N	10.19 E
Treuchtlingen	56	48.57 N	10.54 E
Treuen	54	50.32 N	12.18 E
Treuenbrietzen	54	52.06 N	12.52 E
Treuhandgebiet Pazifische Inseln → Trust Territory of the Pacific Islands □2	14	5.00 N	137.00 E
Trevelín	254	43.04 S	71.28 W
Trèves → Trier	56	49.45 N	6.38 E
Trevi	66	42.52 N	12.45 E
Treviglio	62	45.31 N	9.35 E
Trevignano Romano	66	42.09 N	12.15 E
Treviño	34	42.44 N	2.45 W
Treviso	64	45.40 N	12.15 E
Treviso □4	64	45.50 N	12.13 E
Trevor	216	42.30 N	88.07 W
Trevorton	208	40.46 N	76.40 W
Trevose	208	40.08 N	74.58 W
Trevose Head ≻	42	50.33 N	5.01 W
Trevose Heights	285	40.09 N	74.59 W
Trévoux	58	45.56 N	4.46 E
Trexlertown	208	40.33 N	75.36 W
Trezevant	194	36.00 N	88.37 W
Trezzano sul Naviglio	266b	45.25 N	9.04 E
Trezzo sull'Adda	62	45.36 N	9.31 E
Trgovište	38	42.21 N	22.05 E
Trhomné	60	49.55 N	13.05 E
Trhové Sviny	61	48.51 N	14.39 E
Triabunna	166	42.30 S	147.55 E
Triadelphia Reservoir ⊜1	208	39.13 N	77.01 W
Trialeti	84	41.33 N	44.07 E
Trialetskij chrebet ⋏	84	41.45 N	43.50 E
Triana	66	42.47 N	11.33 E
Triánda	38	36.24 N	28.10 E
Triangle, Eng., U.K.	262	53.42 N	1.56 W
Triangle, Va., U.S.	208	38.32 N	77.20 W
Triangle Lake	210	42.32 N	74.13 W
Triangul'atorov, pik ∧	88	53.45 N	97.00 E
Triángulos, Arrecifes ✦2	232	20.57 N	92.16 W
Triaucourt-en-Argonne	56	48.59 N	5.04 E
Tribeni	126	22.59 N	88.24 E
Triberg	58	48.08 N	8.13 E
Tribes Hill	210	42.57 N	74.17 W
Tribobó	287a	22.52 S	43.01 W
Triborough Bridge ◆5	276	40.47 N	73.55 W
Tri Brata, porog ⌊	86	57.25 N	95.39 E
Tribsees	54	54.05 N	12.45 E
Tribugá, Ensenada de ⊂	246	5.45 N	77.20 W
Tribune, Sk., Can.	184	49.15 N	103.50 W
Tribune, Ks., U.S.	198	38.28 N	101.45 W
Tribune Channel ⋓	182	50.50 N	126.16 W
Tribuswinkel	264b	48.00 N	16.16 E
Tricarico	68	40.37 N	16.09 E
Tricase	68	39.56 N	18.22 E
Tricesimo	64	46.10 N	13.13 E
Trichardt	158	26.28 S	29.13 E
Trichiana	64	46.05 N	12.07 E
Trichinopoly → Tiruchchirāppalli	122	10.49 N	78.41 E
Trichūr	122	10.31 N	76.13 E
Tri Cities	222	32.09 N	95.56 W
Tricot	50	49.34 N	2.35 E
Tri County Supply Canal ≊	198	40.49 N	100.06 W
Trida	166	33.01 S	145.01 E
Trident Peak ∧	204	41.54 N	118.25 W
Triduby	78	48.06 N	30.24 E
Trieben	61	47.29 N	14.30 E
Triebes	54	50.41 N	12.01 E
Triel-sur-Seine	261	48.59 N	2.00 E
Trient → Trento	64	46.04 N	11.08 E
Triepkendorf	54	53.17 N	13.20 E
Trier	56	49.45 N	6.38 E
Trier □5	56	50.00 N	6.40 E
Triesen	58	47.06 N	9.31 E
Trieste (Triest)	64	45.40 N	13.46 E
Trieste □4	64	45.40 N	13.50 E
Trieste, Gulf of ⊂	64	45.40 N	13.35 E
Triesting ≃	61	48.05 N	16.24 E
Trieux ≃	56	49.20 N	5.56 E
Triftern	60	48.24 N	13.01 E
Trigal	248	18.17 S	64.08 W
Triggiano	68	41.04 N	16.55 E
Triglav ∧	64	46.23 N	13.50 E
Triglitz	54	53.12 N	12.05 E
Trigna, Pizzo ∧	70	37.58 N	13.34 E
Trigno ≃	66	42.04 N	14.48 E
Trigueros	34	37.23 N	6.50 W
Tríkala	38	39.34 N	21.46 E
Trikhonís, Límni ⊜	38	38.34 N	21.28 E
Trikora, Puncak (Wilhelmina Peak) ∧	164	4.15 S	138.45 E
Tri-Lakes	216	41.14 N	85.26 W
Trilbardou	261	48.57 N	2.48 E
Trilby	220	28.27 N	82.11 W
Trilesy	78	49.59 N	29.50 E
Trillick	48	54.27 N	7.30 W
Trilport	50	48.57 N	2.57 E
Trim	48	53.34 N	6.47 W
Triman	120	29.38 N	69.05 E
Trimbach	58	47.22 N	7.54 E
Trimble □6	218	38.37 N	85.20 W
Trim Creek ≃	216	41.10 N	87.38 W
Trimdon	44	54.42 N	1.25 W
Trimont	198	43.45 N	94.42 W
Trimonte	256	21.43 S	42.35 W
Trin	58	46.50 N	9.22 E
Trinchera Creek ≃	200	37.19 N	105.45 W
Trincheras, Méx.	196	25.37 N	101.55 W
Trincheras, Méx.	232	30.24 N	111.32 W
Trincomalee	122	8.34 N	81.14 E
Trincomali Channel ⋓	224	48.02 N	123.30 W
Trindade	255	16.40 S	49.30 W
Trindade I	244	20.31 S	29.19 W
Třinec	30	49.41 N	18.40 E
Tring	42	51.48 N	0.40 W
Trinidad, Bol.	248	14.47 S	64.47 W
Trinidad, Col.	246	5.25 N	71.40 W
Trinidad, Cuba	240p	21.48 N	79.59 W
Trinidad, Hond.	236	14.57 N	88.45 W
Trinidad, Co., U.S.	198	37.10 N	104.30 W
Trinidad, Tx., U.S.	222	32.08 N	96.05 W
Trinidad, Ur.	252	33.32 S	56.54 W
Trinidad I	241r	10.30 N	61.15 W
Trinidad ≃	234	17.49 N	95.09 W
Trinidad, Golfo ⊂	254	49.55 S	75.25 W
Trinidad, Isla I	252	39.08 S	61.58 W
Trinidad and Tobago □1, N.A.	230	11.00 N	61.00 W
Trinidad and Tobago □1, N.A.	241r	11.00 N	61.00 W
Trinità	62	44.30 N	7.45 E
Trinità, Lago della ⊜	70	37.43 N	12.46 E
Trinità d'agultu	71	40.59 N	8.54 E
Trinitapoli	68	41.21 N	16.05 E
Trinité, Havre de la ⊂	240e	14.44 N	60.58 W
Trinity, Nf., Can.	186	48.59 N	53.55 W
Trinity, Tx., U.S.	222	30.56 N	95.22 W
Trinity □6	222	31.07 N	95.10 W
Trinity ≃, Ca., U.S.	204	41.11 N	123.42 W
Trinity ≃, Tx., U.S.	222	29.47 N	94.42 W
Trinity, Clear Fork ≃	196	32.46 N	97.21 W
Trinity, East Fork ≃	222	32.30 N	96.30 W
Trinity, Elm Fork ≃	222	32.47 N	96.54 W
Trinity, South Fork ≃	204	40.54 N	123.35 W
Trinity, West Fork ≃	196	32.48 N	96.51 W
Trinity Bay ⊂, Nf., Can.	186	48.00 N	53.40 W
Trinity Bay ⊂, Tx., U.S.	222	29.40 N	94.45 W
Trinity Islands II	180	56.33 N	154.25 W
Trinity Mountain ∧	202	43.36 N	115.26 W
Trinity Mountains ⋏	204	41.00 N	122.30 W
Trinity Park ♠	275b	43.39 N	79.25 W
Trinity Peak ∧	204	40.14 N	118.45 W
Trinity Site ⊥	200	33.41 N	106.28 W
Trinkat Island I	110	8.05 N	93.30 E
Trinkitat	140	18.41 N	37.43 E
Trino	62	45.12 N	8.18 E
Trins	64	47.05 N	11.25 E
Trinway	214	40.08 N	82.00 W
Triolet	157c	20.03 S	57.32 E
Triolo ≃	66	41.40 N	15.34 E
Trion	192	34.32 N	85.18 W
Trionto ≃	68	39.37 N	16.45 E
Trionto, Capo ≻	68	39.37 N	16.45 E
Triora	62	43.59 N	7.46 E
Tripa ≃	114	3.53 N	96.23 E
Tripi	70	38.03 N	15.06 E
Triplett Creek ≃	218	38.10 N	83.27 W
Triplett Creek, North Fork ≃	218	38.10 N	83.31 W
Tripoli	190	42.48 N	92.15 W
Trípolis	38	37.31 N	22.21 E
Tripolis ⊥	130	37.58 N	28.59 E
Tripolis → Ṭarābulus	146	32.54 N	13.11 E
Tripolitania → Ṭarābulus □9	146	31.00 N	15.00 E
Tripoli → Ṭarābulus, Lībiyā	146	32.54 N	13.11 E
Tripoli → Ṭarābulus, Lubnān	130	34.26 N	35.51 E
Tripolje	78	50.07 N	30.46 E
Triponzo	66	42.50 N	12.56 E
Tripp	198	43.13 N	97.57 W
Trips Subdivision	281	42.34 N	83.25 W
Triptis	54	50.44 N	11.52 E
Tripura □3	120	24.00 N	92.00 E
Triquet, Lac ⊜	186	50.42 N	59.47 W
Trisanna ≃	58	47.07 N	10.30 E
Tristan da Cunha Group II	10	37.15 S	12.30 W
Tristan Island I	10	37.05 S	12.17 W
Tristán Suárez	258	34.53 S	58.34 W
Tristao, Îles II	150	10.53 N	14.58 W
Tristate Village	278	41.44 N	87.57 W
Triste	34	42.23 N	0.43 W
Triste, Golfo ⊂	246	10.40 N	68.10 W
Triśuli Gaṅggā ≃	124	27.49 N	84.47 E
Tri Ton	110	10.25 N	105.00 E
Tritriva	157b	22.46 S	46.07 E
Trittau	52	53.37 N	10.25 E
Trittenheim	56	49.49 N	6.54 E
Triuggio	266b	45.40 N	9.16 E
Triumph	194	29.20 N	89.28 W
Triunfo, Igarapé ≃	250	6.22 S	52.25 W
Trivandrum	122	8.29 N	76.55 E
Trivento	66	41.47 N	14.33 E
Trivero	62	45.40 N	8.10 E
Trivigno	68	40.35 N	15.59 E
Trnava	30	48.23 N	17.35 E
Trnovo → Veliko Târnovo	38	43.04 N	25.39 E
Tr'ochgolovyj Golec, gora ∧	88	53.22 N	107.03 E
Tr'ochizbenka	83	48.45 N	38.58 E
Tr'ochsv'atskoje	82	56.29 N	37.03 E
Trochtelfingen	58	48.18 N	9.14 E
Trochu	182	51.50 N	113.13 W
Troense	41	55.02 N	10.39 E
Trofa, Arroyo de ≃	266a	40.30 N	3.45 W
Trofaiach	61	47.25 N	15.00 E
Trofarello	62	44.59 N	7.44 E
Trögd ≻1	40	59.31 N	17.15 E
Trogen	58	47.24 N	9.28 E
Trogir	36	43.31 N	16.15 E
Troglav ∧	36	43.57 N	16.36 E
Tröglitz	54	51.04 N	12.11 E
Troia	68	41.22 N	15.18 E
Troica	76	54.24 N	40.14 E
Troice-Lykovo ◆8	265b	55.47 N	37.24 E
Troick, Ross.	86	54.06 N	61.35 E
Troick, Ross.	88	57.25 N	94.50 E
Troickaja	78	45.08 N	38.07 E
Troickij, Ross.	80	50.14 N	43.05 E
Troickij, Ross.	80	50.14 N	43.03 E
Troickij, Ross.	86	50.41 N	54.38 E
Troickij, Ross.	86	57.03 N	63.43 E
Troickij, Ross.	88	54.36 N	113.09 E
Troickije Rosl'ai	80	53.21 N	41.24 E
Troickij Sungur	80	53.17 N	47.37 E
Troickij Zavod	88	53.27 N	102.09 E
Troicko-Charcyzsk	83	47.58 N	38.16 E
Troickoje, Ross.	78	51.17 N	41.28 E
Troickoje, Ross.	80	46.26 N	44.15 E
Troickoje, Ross.	80	53.23 N	52.48 E
Troickoje, Ross.	80	53.06 N	52.32 E
Troickoje, Ross.	80	53.22 N	48.23 E
Troickoje, Ross.	82	55.23 N	37.25 E
Troickoje, Ross.	82	54.52 N	37.07 E
Troickoje, Ross.	83	47.22 N	38.53 E
Troickoje, Ross.	86	52.58 N	84.40 E
Troickoje, Ross.	86	59.07 N	58.25 E
Troickoje, Ross.	86	52.19 N	56.23 E
Troickoje, Ross.	89	49.27 N	136.36 E
Troickoje, Ukr.	78	47.38 N	30.19 E
Troickoje, Ukr.	78	49.55 N	38.19 E
Troickoje, Ukr.	83	48.32 N	38.23 E
Troicko-Pečorsk	24	62.44 N	56.06 E
Troina	70	37.47 N	14.36 E
Troina ≃	70	37.49 N	14.46 E
Troisdorf	56	50.49 N	7.08 E
Trois Fourches, Cap des ≻	148	35.26 N	2.58 W
Trois-Pistoles	186	48.07 N	69.10 W
Trois Pitons, Morne ∧	240d	15.22 N	61.20 W
Trois Ponts	56	50.22 N	5.52 E
Trois-Rivières, P.Q., Can.	206	46.21 N	72.33 W
Trois-Rivières, Guad.	241o	15.59 N	61.39 W
Trois-Rivières-Ouest	206	46.19 N	72.35 W
Troisvierges	56	50.08 N	6.00 E
Trojan	38	42.51 N	24.43 E
Trojanov	78	50.07 N	28.31 E
Trojanova Tabla ⊥	38	44.37 N	22.20 E
Trojanovka	78	51.20 N	25.17 E
Trojebratskij	86	54.28 N	66.01 E
Trojekurovo, Ross.	76	53.25 N	39.43 E
Trojekurovo, Ross.	76	53.00 N	38.58 E
Troldhede	41	55.59 N	8.45 E
Trolleholm	41	55.54 N	13.15 E
Trollhättan	26	58.16 N	12.18 E
Trollheimen ∧	26	62.51 N	9.05 E
Trombay ◆8	272c	19.02 N	72.57 E
Trombetas ≃	250	1.55 S	55.35 W
Tromelin, Île I	138	15.52 S	54.25 E
Tromello	62	45.12 N	8.52 E
Tromper Wiek ⊂	54	54.37 N	13.24 E
Trompia, Val ∨	64	45.44 N	10.12 E
Trompsburg	158	30.01 S	25.46 E
Troms □6	24	69.15 N	19.40 E
Tromsø	24	69.40 N	18.58 E
Trona	204	35.45 N	117.22 W
Tronador, Monte ∧	254	41.10 S	71.54 W
Troncoso	234	22.44 N	102.22 W
Trondheim	26	63.25 N	10.25 E
Trondheimsfjorden ⊂2	26	63.39 N	10.49 E
Trondheimsleia ⋓	26	63.30 N	9.00 E
Tronto ≃	66	42.54 N	13.55 E
Tronville-en-Barrois	56	48.43 N	5.17 E
Tronzano Vercellese	62	45.21 N	8.10 E
Troo	50	47.47 N	0.47 E
Troödos	130	34.55 N	32.53 E
Trooilapspan	158	28.40 S	21.25 E
Troon, Eng., U.K.	42	50.12 N	5.16 W
Troon, Scot., U.K.	46	55.32 N	4.40 W
Trooper	285	40.09 N	75.24 W
Troparevo	82	55.23 N	35.54 E
Tropar'ovo ◆8	265b	55.39 N	37.29 E
Tropas, Rio das ≃	250	6.07 S	57.28 W
Tropea	68	38.41 N	15.54 E
Trophy Mountain ∧	182	51.47 N	119.48 W
Tropic	200	37.37 N	112.04 W
Tropojë	38	42.24 N	20.10 E
Troppau → Opava	30	49.56 N	17.54 E
Trosa	40	58.54 N	17.33 E
Troškovo	80	57.19 N	46.05 E
Troškūnai	76	55.36 N	24.51 E
Trosna	76	52.26 N	35.46 E
Trossingen	58	48.04 N	8.38 E
Trostan ∧	48	55.03 N	6.09 W
Trost'anec, Ukr.	78	50.28 N	34.59 E
Trost'anec, Ukr.	78	48.31 N	29.12 E
Tröstau	60	50.01 N	11.57 E
Trostberg	60	48.01 N	12.32 E
Trostenskoje, ozero ⊜	82	55.52 N	36.29 E
Trotha ◆8	54	51.31 N	11.58 E
Trottiscliffe	260	51.19 N	0.21 E
Trotuș ≃	38	46.03 N	27.14 E
Trotwood	218	39.47 N	84.18 W
Troublesome Creek ≃	219	39.54 N	91.37 W
Troubridge Point ≻	168b	35.11 S	137.41 E
Trou-du-Nord	238	19.38 N	72.01 W
Troup	222	32.08 N	95.07 W
Troup Head ≻	46	57.41 N	2.18 W
Troupsburg	210	42.03 N	77.33 W
Trout	194	31.41 N	92.10 W
Trout ≃, N.T., Can.	176	61.19 N	119.51 W
Trout ≃, N.A.	206	45.05 N	74.10 W
Trout Brook ≃, Ma., U.S.	283	42.16 N	71.18 W
Trout Brook ≃, Ma., U.S.	283	42.39 N	71.16 W
Trout Creek, Mi., U.S.	190	46.28 N	89.00 W
Trout Creek, Mt., U.S.	182	47.50 N	115.35 W
Trout Creek, N.Y., U.S.	210	42.12 N	75.17 W
Trout Creek ≃, Az., U.S.	200	34.56 N	113.36 W
Trout Creek ≃, Or., U.S.	202	44.48 N	121.03 W
Trout Creek ≃, Or., U.S.	202	42.23 N	118.36 W
Trout Creek ≃, Pa., U.S.	285	40.07 N	75.24 W
Trout Creek ≃, Wa., U.S.	224	46.02 N	121.12 W
Trout Creek Pass)(	200	38.54 N	105.58 W
Troutdale	224	45.32 N	122.23 W
Trout Lake	224	45.59 N	121.31 W

English	Deutsch	Español	Français	Português
≃ River	Fluß	Río	Rivière	Rio
≊ Canal	Kanal	Canal	Canal	Canal
⌊ Waterfall, Rapids	Wasserfall, Stromschnellen	Cascada, Rápidos	Chute d'eau, Rapides	Cascata, Rápidos
⋓ Strait	Meeresstraße	Estrecho	Détroit	Estreito
⊂ Bay, Gulf	Bucht, Golf	Bahía, Golfo	Baie, Golfe	Baía, Golfo
⊜ Lake, Lakes	See, Seen	Lago, Lagos	Lac, Lacs	Lago, Lagos
≚ Swamp	Sumpf	Pantano	Marais	Pântano
⊠ Ice Features, Glacier	Eis- und Gletscherformen	Accidentes Glaciales	Formes glaciaires	Acidentes glaciares
⫪ Other Hydrographic Features	Andere Hydrographische Objekte	Otros Elementos Hidrográficos	Autres données hydrographiques	Outros acidentes hidrográficos

English	Deutsch	Español	Français	Português
✦ Submarine Features	Untermeerische Objekte	Accidentes Submarinos	Formes de relief sous-marin	Acidentes submarinos
□ Political Unit	Politische Einheit	Unidad Política	Entité politique	Unidade política
ʊ Cultural Institution	Kulturelle Institution	Institución Cultural	Institution culturelle	Institução cultural
⊥ Historical Site	Historische Stätte	Sitio Histórico	Site historique	Sitio histórico
♠ Recreational Site	Erholungs- und Ferienort	Sitio de Recreo	Centre de loisirs	Area de Lazer
⊠ Airport	Flughafen	Aeropuerto	Aéroport	Aeroporto
■ Military Installation	Militäranlage	Instalación Militar	Installation militaire	Instalação militar
◆ Miscellaneous	Verschiedenes	Misceláneo	Divers	Diversos

Name	Page	Lat.°′	Long.°′
Trout Lake ⊜, B.C., Can.	182	50.35 N	117.26 W
Trout Lake ⊜, N.T., Can.	176	60.35 N	121.10 W
Trout Lake ⊜, On., Can.	184	51.13 N	93.20 W
Trout Lake ⊜, On., Can.	190	46.18 N	79.20 W
Trout Lake ⊜, On., Can.	190	46.13 N	80.35 W
Trout Lake Creek ≃	224	46.00 N	121.30 W
Trout Peak ∧	202	44.36 N	109.32 W
Trout River	186	49.29 N	58.08 W
Trout Run	210	41.23 N	77.03 W
Troutville, Pa., U.S.	214	41.02 N	78.47 W
Troutville, Va., U.S.	192	37.25 N	79.52 W
Trouville-sur-Mer	50	49.22 N	0.05 E
Trowbridge	42	51.20 N	2.13 W
Troxelville	210	40.48 N	77.12 W
Troy, Al., U.S.	194	31.48 N	85.58 W
Troy, Id., U.S.	202	46.44 N	116.46 W
Troy, Il., U.S.	219	38.43 N	89.52 W
Troy, In., U.S.	194	37.59 N	86.47 W
Troy, Ks., U.S.	198	39.46 N	95.05 W
Troy, Mi., U.S.	214	42.34 N	83.09 W
Troy, Mo., U.S.	219	38.58 N	90.58 W
Troy, Mt., U.S.	202	48.27 N	115.53 W
Troy, N.H., U.S.	207	42.49 N	72.10 W
Troy, N.Y., U.S.	210	42.43 N	73.41 W
Troy, N.C., U.S.	192	35.21 N	79.53 W
Troy, Oh., U.S.	218	40.02 N	84.12 W
Troy, Pa., U.S.	210	41.47 N	76.47 W
Troy, Tn., U.S.	194	36.20 N	89.09 W
Troy, Tx., U.S.	222	31.12 N	97.18 W
Troy Brook ≃	276	40.50 N	74.22 W
Troyes	50	48.18 N	4.05 E
Troy Grove	216	41.28 N	89.05 W
Troy Hills	210	40.51 N	74.23 W
Troy Lake ⊜	204	34.49 N	116.33 W
Troy Meadows ≡	276	40.50 N	74.22 W
Troy Peak ∧	204	38.19 N	115.30 W
Troy → Truva ⊥	130	39.57 N	26.15 E
Trpanj	36	43.00 N	17.17 E
Trstená	30	49.22 N	19.37 E
Trstenik	38	43.37 N	21.00 E
Trst → Trieste	64	45.40 N	13.46 E
Truax	184	49.55 N	104.58 W
Trubč'ovsk	76	52.37 N	33.44 E
Trubetčino	76	52.53 N	39.33 E
Trubino, Ross.	82	54.58 N	36.42 E
Trubino, Ross.	82	55.59 N	38.08 E
Trub'ož ≃	82	56.44 N	38.51 E
Truchas	200	36.02 N	105.48 W
Truchas Peak ∧	200	35.58 N	105.39 W
Truchtersheim	58	48.40 N	7.36 E
Trucial States → United Arab Emirates □[1]	128	24.00 N	54.00 E
Truckee	226	39.19 N	120.10 W
Truckee ≃	204	39.51 N	119.24 W
Trucksville	210	41.18 N	75.56 W
Trud	76	57.37 N	33.58 E
Trudfront	80	45.56 N	47.41 E
Trudnovo	86	56.39 N	91.30 E
Trudovaja	83	48.21 N	38.04 E
Trudovoj	80	51.42 N	52.43 E
Trues Creek ≃	276	40.41 N	73.17 W
Truganina	274b	37.49 S	144.43 E
Truim ≃	46	57.02 N	4.10 W
Truite, Lac à la ⊜	190	47.16 N	78.17 W
Trujillo, Col.	246	4.10 N	76.19 W
Trujillo, Esp.	34	39.28 N	5.53 W
Trujillo, Hond.	236	15.55 N	86.00 W
Trujillo, Méx.	234	23.10 N	103.13 W
Trujillo, Perú	248	8.07 S	79.02 W
Trujillo, Ven.	246	9.22 N	70.26 W
Trujillo □[3]	246	9.25 N	70.30 W
Trujillo Alto	240m	18.22 N	66.01 W
Trujillo Creek ≃	196	35.28 N	102.52 W
Truk Islands II	175c	7.25 N	151.47 E
Truk Lagoon ⊂	175c	7.25 N	151.45 E
Trull Brook ≃	283	42.39 N	71.15 W
Truman	198	43.49 N	94.26 W
Trumann	194	35.40 N	90.30 W
Trumansburg	210	42.32 N	76.39 W
Trumbauersville	208	40.25 N	75.23 W
Trumbull	207	41.14 N	73.12 W
Trumbull □[6]	214	41.14 N	80.52 W
Trumbull, Mount ∧	200	36.25 N	113.10 W
Trumon	114	2.49 N	97.38 E
Trun, Fr.	50	48.51 N	0.02 E
Trun, Schw.	58	46.45 N	8.58 E
Trundle	166	32.55 S	147.43 E
Trung Luong	110	13.57 N	109.15 E
Trung Phan □[9]	110	15.00 N	108.00 E
Trunovskoje	80	45.29 N	42.08 E
Truro, Austl.	168b	34.25 S	139.07 E
Truro, N.S., Can.	186	45.22 N	63.16 W
Truro, Eng., U.K.	42	50.16 N	5.03 W
Truro, Ma., U.S.	207	41.59 N	70.03 W
Trusan ≃	112	4.58 N	115.11 E
Truscott	196	33.45 N	99.49 W
Trušeny	78	47.04 N	28.41 E
Trușești	38	47.46 N	27.01 E
Trusetal	54	50.47 N	10.25 E
Truskavec	78	49.16 N	23.33 E
Truslejka	80	53.54 N	46.24 E
Trus Madi, Gunong ∧	112	5.33 N	116.31 E
Trust Territory of the Pacific Islands □[2]	14	5.00 N	137.00 E
Truth or Consequences (Hot Springs)	200	33.07 N	107.15 W
Trutnov	30	50.34 N	15.55 E
Truva (Troy) ⊥	130	39.57 N	26.15 E
Truxall	279b	40.33 N	79.33 W
Truxton, Mo., U.S.	219	39.00 N	91.14 W
Truxton, N.Y., U.S.	210	42.43 N	76.02 W
Truxton Wash V	200	35.38 N	114.04 W
Truyère ≃	32	44.39 N	2.34 E
Trwyn Cilan ›	42	52.46 N	4.30 W
Tryon, Ne., U.S.	198	41.33 N	100.57 W
Tryon, N.C., U.S.	192	35.12 N	82.14 W
Tryonville	214	41.42 N	79.47 W
Trysil	26	61.19 N	12.16 E
Trysilelva (Klarälven) ≃	26	59.23 N	13.32 E
Tryškiai	76	56.04 N	22.35 E
Tryweryn ≃	42	52.55 N	3.35 W
Trzcianka	30	53.03 N	16.28 E
Trzciel	30	52.23 N	15.52 E
Trzcińsko-Zdrój	30	52.58 N	14.35 E
Trzebiatów	30	54.04 N	15.14 E
Trzebiel	54	51.37 N	14.50 E
Trzebież	30	53.42 N	14.31 E
Trzebinia	30	50.10 N	19.18 E
Trzebnica	30	51.19 N	17.03 E
Trzemeszno	30	52.35 N	17.50 E
Trzęsacz	54	54.05 N	14.58 E
Tržič	61	46.22 N	14.19 E
Tsacha Lake ⊜	182	53.05 N	124.40 W
Tsala Apopka Lake ⊜	220	28.52 N	82.20 W
Tsamkong → Zhanjiang	102	21.16 N	110.28 E
Tsandi	156	17.42 S	14.50 E
Tsangano	154	15.08 S	34.32 E
Ts'anghsien → Cangzhou	98	38.19 N	116.51 E
T'sangwu → Wuzhou	102	23.30 N	111.27 E
Ts'aot'un	100	23.59 N	120.41 E
Tsarabaria	157b	13.46 S	49.58 E
Tsaramandroso	157b	16.22 S	47.02 E
Tsaratanana	157b	16.47 S	47.39 E
Tsaratanana, Massif du ⋏	157b	14.00 S	49.00 E
Tsaraxaibis	158	27.25 S	19.22 E
Tsaritsyn → Volgograd	80	48.44 N	44.25 E
Tsau	156	20.12 S	22.22 E
Tsaukaib	156	26.37 S	15.31 E
Tsavo	154	2.59 S	38.28 E
Tsavo East National Park ♦	154	2.11 S	38.25 E
Tsavo West National Park ♦	154	2.55 S	37.55 E
Tsawwassen	224	49.01 N	123.06 W
Tsaydaychuz Peak ∧	182	53.02 N	126.35 W
Tsayta Lake ⊜	182	55.25 N	125.30 W
Tschad → Chad □[1]	146	15.00 N	19.00 E
Tschad-See → Chad, Lake ⊜	146	13.20 N	14.00 E
Tschagguns	58	47.05 N	9.54 E
Tschamut	58	46.40 N	8.42 E
Tschangscha → Changsha	100	28.12 N	112.58 E
Tschangtschun → Changchun	89	43.53 N	125.19 E
Tscheljuskin, Kap → Čel'uskin, mys ›	74	77.45 N	104.20 E
Tschengtu → Chengdu	107	30.39 N	104.04 E
Tschenstochau → Częstochowa	30	50.49 N	19.06 E
Tschernitz	54	51.35 N	14.37 E
Tscheschkaja-Bucht → Češskaja guba ⊂	24	67.30 N	46.30 E
Tschida, Lake ⊜[1]	198	46.36 N	101.54 W
Tschingtau → Qingdao	98	36.06 N	120.19 E
Tschittagong → Chittagong	120	22.20 N	91.50 E
Tschuktschen-Meer → Chukchi Sea ⊤[2]	16	69.00 N	171.00 W
Tschungking → Chongqing	107	29.34 N	106.35 E
Tsekanyani	156	19.52 S	26.39 E
Tsembeyi	158	31.36 S	27.03 E
Ts'engwen ≃	100	23.03 N	120.03 E
Tsenke ≃	273b	4.24 S	15.26 E
Tses	156	25.58 S	18.08 E
Tsévié	150	6.25 N	1.13 E
Tshabong	156	26.03 S	22.29 E
Tshabuta	152	7.47 S	23.16 E
Tshane	156	24.05 S	21.54 E
Tshaneni	158	26.00 S	31.47 E
Tshangalele, Lac ⊜	154	10.55 S	27.03 E
Tshangu ≃	273b	4.25 S	15.23 E
Tshela	152	4.59 S	12.56 E
Tshesebe	156	21.51 S	27.35 E
Tshibeke	154	2.44 S	28.36 E
Tshibinda	154	2.19 S	28.45 E
Tshibomba	152	9.02 S	22.34 E
Tshidilamolomo	156	25.50 S	24.41 E
Tshikapa	152	6.25 S	20.48 E
Tshilenge	152	6.15 S	23.46 E
Tshimbulu	152	6.29 S	22.51 E
Tshindjamba	152	10.54 S	22.41 E
Tshinota	152	7.01 S	20.57 E
Tshinsenda	154	12.18 S	27.58 E
Tshisuku	152	6.26 S	19.55 E
Tshitadi	152	6.45 S	21.45 E
Tshoa	152	5.34 S	12.41 E
Tshofa	154	5.14 S	25.15 E
Tshopo ≃	154	0.33 N	25.07 E
Tshuapa ≃	152	0.14 S	20.42 E
Tshukudu	156	22.30 S	23.22 E
Tshumbiri	152	2.39 S	16.14 E
Tshwaane	156	22.29 S	22.03 E
Tsiafajavona ∧	157b	19.21 S	47.15 E
Tsianaloka	157b	18.08 S	44.50 E
Tsiémé ≃	273b	4.15 S	15.18 E
Tsiga	152	1.32 S	10.11 E
Tsihombe	157b	25.18 S	45.29 E
Tsilmamo	144	6.01 N	35.17 E
Tsimanampetsotsa, Lac ⊜	157b	24.08 S	43.46 E
Tsimilofo	157b	24.59 S	45.10 E
Tsimpsean Indian Reserve ◆[4]	182	54.30 N	130.22 W
Tsinan → Jinan	98	36.40 N	116.57 E
Tsineng	158	27.06 S	23.04 E
Tsinghai → Qinghai □[4]	90	36.00 N	96.00 E
Tsingkiang → Qingjiang	100	33.35 N	119.02 E
Tsingtao → Qingdao	98	36.06 N	120.19 E
Tsing Yi I	271d	22.21 N	114.05 E
Tsingyuan → Baoding	105	38.52 N	115.29 E
Tsining → Jining	98	35.25 N	116.36 E
Tsinjoarivo	157b	19.37 S	47.40 E
Tsinjomitondraka	157b	15.36 S	47.08 E
Tsinling Shan → Qin Ling ⋏	102	34.00 N	108.00 E
Tsintsabis	156	18.45 S	17.51 E
Tsiribihina ≃	157b	19.42 S	44.31 E
Tsiroanomandidy	157b	18.46 S	46.02 E
Tsitondroina	157b	21.19 S	46.00 E
Tsitsihar → Qiqihar	89	47.19 N	123.55 E
Tsitsikama Forest and Coastal National Park ♦	158	33.57 S	23.53 E
Tsitsutl Peak ∧	182	52.44 N	125.47 W
Tsivory	157b	24.04 S	46.05 E
Tskhinvali → Cchinvali	84	42.13 N	43.56 E
Tsna → Cna ≃	80	54.32 N	42.05 E
Tsobis	156	19.27 S	17.30 E
Tsolo	158	31.18 S	28.37 E
Tsomo	158	32.00 S	27.42 E
Tsomo ≃	158	32.25 S	27.50 E
Tsoying	100	22.41 N	120.17 E
Tsu	94	34.43 N	136.31 E
Tsubakuro-dake ∧	94	36.24 N	137.42 E
Tsubame	92	37.39 N	138.56 E
Tsubata	94	36.40 N	136.44 E
Tsuboro-suigenchi ⊜[1]	270	34.24 N	135.54 E
Tsuchiura	94	36.05 N	140.12 E
Tsuchiyama	94	34.56 N	136.17 E
Tsuda, Nihon	96	34.17 N	134.15 E
Tsuda, Nihon	270	34.49 N	135.43 E
Tsuen Wan (Quanwan)	271d	22.22 N	114.07 E
Tsugaru-hantō ›[1]	92	41.00 N	140.30 E
Tsugaru-heiya ≚	92	40.49 N	140.27 E
Tsugaru-kaikyō ʊ	92a	41.35 N	141.00 E
Tsuge	94	34.37 N	135.57 E
Tsugu	94	35.10 N	137.37 E
Tsuha	174m	26.14 N	127.47 E
Tsuiki	96	33.40 N	131.03 E
Tsujidō	268	35.20 N	139.27 E
Tsukahara	268	35.18 N	139.58 E
Tsukechi	94	35.38 N	137.26 E
Tsuken-jima I	174m	26.15 N	127.57 E
Tsukigase	94	34.42 N	136.02 E
Tsukinowa-kofun ⊥	96	34.55 N	134.11 E
Tsukiyono	94	36.41 N	138.59 E
Tsukuba	94	36.13 N	140.06 E
Tsukuba-san ∧	94	36.13 N	140.06 E
Tsukude	94	34.59 N	137.25 E
Tsukui	94	35.35 N	139.16 E
Tsukumi	96	33.04 N	131.52 E
Tsukumono ◆[8]	270	34.50 N	135.11 E
Tsukushi-heiya ≚	96	33.20 N	130.30 E
Tsukushi-sanchi ⋏	92	33.30 N	130.30 E
Tsumagoi	94	36.31 N	138.32 E
Tsumeb	156	19.13 S	17.42 E
Tsumeb □[5]	156	19.00 S	17.30 E
Tsumeki-zaki ›	94	34.39 N	138.59 E
Tsumis Park	156	23.43 S	17.28 E
Tsumkwe	156	19.41 S	20.30 E
Tsuna	96	34.26 N	134.54 E
Tsunan	94	37.01 N	138.39 E
Tsunashima ◆[8]	268	35.32 N	139.38 E
Tsunekami-misaki ›	94	35.38 N	135.49 E
Tsuni → Zunyi	102	27.39 N	106.57 E
Tsuno-shima I	96	34.21 N	130.51 E
Tsuru	94	35.33 N	138.55 E
Tsuruga	94	35.39 N	136.04 E
Tsurugaoka-hachimangu Shrine ♦[1]	268	35.19 N	139.33 E
Tsurugashima	268	35.56 N	139.24 E
Tsuruga-wan ⊂	94	35.45 N	136.04 E
Tsurugi	94	36.27 N	136.38 E
Tsurugi-dake ∧	94	36.37 N	137.37 E
Tsurugi-san ∧	96	33.51 N	134.06 E
Tsurugi-san-kokutei-kōen ♦	96	33.50 N	134.06 E
Tsuruhara	270	34.26 N	135.20 E
Tsuruma	268	35.51 N	139.33 E
Tsurumi ◆[8]	268	35.30 N	139.41 E
Tsurumi ≃	94	35.29 N	139.41 E
Tsurumi-dake ∧	96	33.17 N	131.26 E
Tsuruoka	92	38.44 N	139.50 E
Tsushima, Nihon	94	35.10 N	136.43 E
Tsushima, Nihon	96	33.05 N	132.30 E
Tsushima II	92	34.30 N	129.22 E
Tsushima-kaikyō (Eastern Channel) ʊ	92	34.00 N	129.00 E
Tsuwano	96	34.28 N	131.46 E
Tsuyama	96	35.03 N	134.00 E
Tsuyazaki	96	33.47 N	130.28 E
Ttruchchendūr	122	8.29 N	78.07 E
Tua	152	3.38 S	16.36 E
Tua ≃	34	41.13 N	7.26 W
Tua, Tanjung ›	115a	5.54 S	105.44 E
Tua Chau	110	21.55 N	103.21 E
Tuakau	172	37.16 S	174.57 E
Tual	164	5.40 S	132.45 E
Tualatin	224	45.23 N	122.45 W
Tualatin ≃	224	45.20 N	122.39 W
Tuam	48	53.31 N	8.50 W
Tuamarina	172	41.26 S	173.57 E
Tuamotu, Îles (Tuamotu Archipelago) II	14	19.00 S	142.00 W
Tuamotu Ridge ✦[3]	14	17.00 S	145.00 W
Tuan, Tanjong ›	114	2.23 N	101.52 E
Tuanan	112	2.07 S	114.24 E
Tuanfeng	100	30.38 N	114.51 E
Tuan Giao	110	21.35 N	103.25 E
Tuangku, Pulau I	114	2.10 N	97.16 E
Tuanlin	98	39.35 N	119.15 E
Tuannian	107	29.55 N	106.03 E
Tuanpi	100	30.44 N	115.13 E
Tuanshan	98	40.02 N	123.34 E
Tuanwang	98	36.45 N	120.38 E
Tuanxi	102	27.28 N	107.08 E
Tuapa	174v	18.57 S	169.54 W
Tuapeka Mouth	172	46.01 S	169.31 E
Tuapse	84	44.07 N	39.05 E
Tuaran	112	6.11 N	116.14 E
Tuas	114	1.19 N	103.38 E
Tuasivi	175a	13.40 S	172.07 W
Tuasivi, Cape ›	175a	13.40 S	172.07 W
Tuatapere	172	46.08 S	167.41 E
Tuath, Loch ʊ	46	56.30 N	6.12 W
Tuba	88	57.24 N	102.48 E
Tuba ≃	86	53.57 N	91.31 E
Tubac	200	31.36 N	111.02 W
Tuba City	200	36.08 N	111.14 W
T'ub'ak-Čekurča	80	56.05 N	49.56 E
Tubalan Head ›	116	6.30 N	125.35 E
Tuban	115a	6.54 S	112.03 E
Tubarão	252	28.30 S	49.01 W
Ṭūbās	132	32.19 N	35.22 E
Tubau	112	3.08 N	113.42 E
Tubbataha Reefs ✦[2]	116	8.51 N	119.56 E
Tubbergen	52	52.25 N	6.46 E
Tubbs Island I	282	38.08 N	122.26 W
Ṭubhār	142	29.19 N	30.42 E
Tubig ≃	116	11.54 N	125.25 E
Tubigan Island I	116	6.26 N	120.47 E
Tubingantan Point ›	116	5.54 N	120.55 E
Tübingen	58	48.31 N	9.02 E
Tübingen □[5]	58	48.10 N	9.30 E
Tubinskij	86	52.53 N	58.13 E
Tubize	50	50.41 N	4.12 E
T'ub-Karagan, mys ›	84	44.39 N	50.18 E
T'ub-Karagan, poluostrov ›[1]	84	44.30 N	50.30 E
Tubli	116	13.56 N	124.09 E
Tubod	116	8.03 N	123.48 E
Tubre	64	46.39 N	10.27 E
Ṭubruq (Tobruk)	146	32.05 N	23.59 E
Tuburan, Pil.	116	10.44 N	123.49 W
Tuburan, Pil.	116	6.39 N	122.16 E
Tubusereia	164	9.33 S	147.18 E
Tubutama	200	30.53 N	111.29 W
Tucacas	246	10.48 N	68.19 W
Tucacas, Punta ›	246	10.50 N	68.14 W
Tucalota Creek ≃	228	33.32 N	117.10 W
Tucannon ≃	202	46.33 N	118.11 W
Tucano	250	10.58 S	38.48 W
Tucava ≃	248	18.37 S	58.59 W
T'uch'ang	100	24.35 N	121.29 E
Tucheim	54	52.17 N	12.11 E
Tüchen	54	53.04 N	12.05 E
T'uch'eng, T'aiwan	269d	24.59 N	121.26 E
Tucheng, Zhg.	98	38.53 N	121.15 E
Tucheng, Zhg.	102	28.12 N	105.58 E
Tuchengzi, Zhg.	98	41.20 N	116.29 E
Tuchengzi, Zhg.	98	40.29 N	124.24 E
Tuchengzi, Zhg.	104	42.27 N	122.44 E
Tuchengzicun	104	41.52 N	120.41 E
Tuchengziwuhao	98	40.56 N	113.58 E
Tuchlovice	54	50.06 N	14.00 E
Tuchola	30	53.35 N	17.50 E
Tuchów	30	49.54 N	21.03 E
T'uchtet	86	56.32 N	89.19 E
Tuckahoe, N.J., U.S.	208	39.17 N	74.45 W
Tuckahoe, N.Y., U.S.	276	40.57 N	73.49 W
Tuckahoe ≃	208	39.17 N	74.39 W
Tuckahoe Creek ≃	208	38.49 N	75.53 W
Tuckanarra	162	27.07 S	118.05 E
Tucker Heights	210	42.55 N	73.55 W
Tuckerman	194	35.43 N	91.11 W
Tuckernuck Island I	207	41.18 N	70.15 W
Tuckerton, N.J., U.S.	208	39.36 N	74.20 W
Tuckerton, Pa., U.S.	208	40.25 N	75.57 W
Tuckfield, Mount ∧	162	18.44 S	124.54 E
Tučkovo	82	55.36 N	36.28 E
Tucson	200	32.13 N	110.55 W
Tucumã ≃[1]	246	3.58 S	66.26 W
Tucumán □[4]	252	27.00 S	65.30 W
Tucumán → San Miguel de Tucumán	252	26.49 S	65.13 W
Tucumcari	196	35.10 N	103.43 W
Tucumcari Mountain ∧	196	35.08 N	103.42 W
Tucunuco	252	30.36 S	68.38 W
Tucupido	246	9.17 N	65.47 W
Tucupita	246	9.04 N	62.03 W
Tucuruí	250	3.42 S	49.27 W
Tucuruí, Reprêsa de ⊜[1]	250	4.40 S	49.20 W
Tucuruvi ◆[8]	287b	23.28 S	46.35 W
Tuczna	30	51.54 N	23.26 E
Tud ≃	42	52.38 N	1.15 E
Tudameda	112	10.52 S	122.55 E
Tudcum	252	30.14 S	69.15 W
Tudeå ≃	41	55.23 N	11.13 E
Tudela, Esp.	34	42.05 N	1.36 W
Tudela, Pil.	116	8.15 N	123.50 E
Tudela de Duero	34	41.35 N	4.35 W
Tudian	106	30.35 N	120.37 E
Tudichang	107	30.06 N	103.56 E
Tuditang	100	30.12 N	114.18 E
Tudmur (Palmyra)	130	34.33 N	38.17 E
Tudu	76	59.11 N	26.51 E
Tudweiliog	42	52.54 N	4.35 W
Tuela ≃	34	41.30 N	7.12 W
Tuen Mun	271d	22.24 N	113.58 E
Tuenno	64	46.20 N	11.01 E
Tueré ≃	250	2.48 S	50.59 W
Tuergate	85	40.28 N	75.21 E
Tufanbeyli	130	38.16 N	36.13 E
Tufānganj	124	26.19 N	89.40 E
Tuffé	50	48.07 N	0.31 E
Tufi	164	9.05 S	149.20 E
Tufo	68	41.00 N	14.47 E
Tufts University ♦[2]	283	42.24 N	71.07 W
Tufu Point ›	174y	14.13 S	169.32 W
Tugaske	184	50.53 N	106.16 W
Tugela	158	29.09 S	31.29 E
Tugela ≃	158	29.14 S	31.30 E
Tugela Falls ∟	158	28.45 S	28.58 E
Tugela Ferry	158	28.44 S	30.27 E
Tug Fork ≃	192	38.06 N	82.36 W
Tuggerah Lake ⊂	170	33.18 S	151.30 E
Tughlakābād ◆[8]	272a	28.31 N	77.16 E
Tugidak Island I	180	56.30 N	154.36 W
Tuğköyü	130	38.27 N	42.16 E
Tuglie	68	40.04 N	18.05 E
Tugnug Point ›	116	11.21 N	125.38 E
Tugolesskij Bor	80	55.33 N	39.49 E
Tugolukovo	80	51.56 N	41.40 E
Tugubun Point ›	116	7.00 N	126.27 E
Tuguegarao	116	17.37 N	121.44 E
Tugulym	86	57.04 N	64.39 E
Tugun	171a	28.09 S	153.30 E
Tugur	89	53.48 N	136.48 E
Tugur ≃	89	53.48 N	136.44 E
Tugurskij poluostrov ›[1]	89	54.00 N	137.24 E
Tuguša	88	55.57 N	96.26 E
Tugutuj	88	52.40 N	104.50 E
Tuhai ≃	98	37.55 N	118.05 E
Tuhepu	104	40.54 N	122.49 E
Tuhuangba	102	31.40 N	108.21 E
Tuibo	89	44.01 N	127.47 E
Tuichi ≃	248	14.36 S	67.35 W
Tuim	86	54.20 N	89.55 E
Tuineje	148	28.19 N	14.03 W
Tuira ≃	246	8.21 N	78.03 W
Tuirc, Beinn an ∧[2]	46	55.34 N	5.34 W
Tuitán	234	21.08 N	103.48 W
Tuitui	256	22.47 S	46.42 W
Tuj ≃	86	57.33 N	72.31 E
T'ujabuguz	85	40.58 N	69.15 E
Tujemojnak	86	49.20 N	62.55 E
Tuji-ri	98	41.31 N	127.12 E
Tujmazy	80	54.36 N	53.42 E
Tüjn Gol ≃	102	45.04 N	100.46 E
Tujunga ◆[8]	280	34.15 N	118.17 W
Tujunga Valley V	280	34.17 N	118.20 W
Tujunga Wash V	280	34.09 N	118.24 W
Tukaj	86	55.24 N	90.49 E
T'ukalinsk	86	55.52 N	72.12 E
Tukan	86	53.50 N	57.26 E
Tukan ≃	86	60.02 N	71.36 E
Tukangbesi, Kepulauan II	112	5.40 S	123.50 E
Tukayel	144	8.08 N	45.22 E
Ṭūkh, Miṣr	142	30.21 N	31.12 E
Ṭūkh, Miṣr	142	27.41 N	30.49 E
Ṭūkh al-Aqlām	142	30.52 N	31.26 E
Ṭūkh al-Khayl	142	28.06 N	30.40 E
Tukituki ≃	172	39.36 S	176.57 E
Tuk Méas	110	10.40 N	104.34 E
Tukolon'	88	55.24 N	107.42 E
Tukosméra, Mont ∧	175f	19.35 S	169.22 E
Tukpo	154	4.25 N	25.52 E
Tūkrah	146	32.32 N	20.34 E
Tuktoyaktuk	180	69.27 N	133.02 W
Tuktoyaktuk Peninsula ›[1]	180	69.45 N	131.20 W
Tukuj-Mekteb	84	44.20 N	45.11 E
Tukums	76	57.00 N	23.10 E
Tukuran	116	7.51 N	123.35 E
Tukuringra, chrebet ⋏	89	54.20 N	126.20 E
Tukuyu	154	9.15 S	33.39 E
T'uk'u Yüeh ∧	269d	25.02 N	121.38 E
Tukwila	224	47.28 N	122.15 W
Tula, Am. Sam.	174u	14.15 S	170.34 W
Tula, It.	71	40.44 N	8.59 E
Tula, Méx.	234	23.00 N	99.43 W
Tula, Nig.	146	9.50 N	11.28 E
Tula, Ross.	82	54.12 N	37.37 E
Tula ≃, Kenya	154	0.50 S	39.51 E
Tula ≃, Méx.	234	20.40 N	99.30 W
Tula ⊥	234	20.06 N	99.19 W
Tula de Allende	234	20.03 N	99.21 W
Tulaghi	175e	9.06 S	160.09 E
Tulagt Ar ≃	120	36.35 N	92.20 E
Tulai Nanshan ⋏	102	38.44 N	98.20 E
Tūlak	128	33.58 N	63.44 E
Tulalip Indian Reservation ◆[4]	224	48.06 N	122.15 W
Tulancingo	234	20.05 N	98.22 W
Tulangbawang ≃	112	4.24 S	105.52 E
Tula Oblast' □[4]	76	54.00 N	37.30 E
Tulaodian	104	41.13 N	121.27 E
T'ul'apsy	86	57.28 N	89.38 E
Tulare, Ca., U.S.	226	36.12 N	119.20 W
Tulare, S.D., U.S.	198	44.44 N	98.30 W
Tulare □[6]	226	36.20 N	119.18 W
Tulare Canal ≅	226	36.08 N	119.25 W
Tulare Lake Bed ⊜	226	36.03 N	119.49 W
Tulare Lake Canal ≅	226	36.04 N	119.39 W
Tularosa	200	33.04 N	106.01 W
Tularosa ≃	200	33.41 N	108.46 W
Tularosa Valley ≚[1]	200	32.45 N	106.10 W
Tulbagh	158	33.17 S	19.09 E
Tulbing	264b	48.16 N	16.09 E
Tulbinger Kogel ∧[2]	264b	48.17 N	16.09 E
Tulcán	246	0.48 N	77.43 W
Tulcea	38	45.11 N	28.48 E
Tulcea □[6]	38	45.00 N	29.00 E
Tul'čin	78	48.39 N	28.52 E
Tulcingo de Valle	234	18.03 N	98.26 W
Tule ≃, Nic.	236	11.20 N	84.52 W
Tule ≃, Ca., U.S.	226	36.03 N	119.50 W
Tule, North Branch ≃	226	36.06 N	119.22 W
Tule, South Branch ≃	226	36.05 N	119.29 W
Tule Canal ≅	226	38.37 N	121.35 W
Tule Creek ≃	196	34.40 N	101.14 W
T'ulek	85	41.56 N	75.41 E
Tulelake	204	41.57 N	121.29 W
Tule Lake Sump ⊜[1]	204	41.54 N	121.32 W
Tulemalu Lake ⊜	176	62.58 N	99.25 W
T'ulenij, mys ›	84	40.12 N	50.22 E
T'ulenij, ostrov I	84	44.28 N	47.30 E
Tule River Indian Reservation ◆[4]	204	36.02 N	118.42 W
Tulette	62	44.17 N	4.56 E
Tule Valley V	200	39.20 N	113.25 W
T'ul'gan	86	52.22 N	56.12 E
Tul'goviči	78	51.47 N	29.38 E
Tuli	154	21.59 S	29.15 E
Tuli ≃	154	21.48 S	29.04 E
Tulia	196	34.32 N	101.45 W
Tuliahan ≃	269f	14.41 N	120.58 E
Tulica ≃	82	54.12 N	37.37 E
Tulik Volcano ∧[1]	180	53.22 N	168.03 W
Tuling	100	25.11 N	118.50 E
Tuliszków	30	52.05 N	18.17 E
Ṭūlkarm	132	32.19 N	35.02 E
T'ul'kino	86	59.49 N	56.30 E
T'ul'kubas	85	42.28 N	70.02 E
Tulla	48	52.52 N	8.45 W
Tullahoma	194	35.21 N	86.12 W
Tullamarine	274b	37.41 S	144.52 E
Tullamarine International Airport ⊠, Austl.	169	37.40 S	144.50 E
Tullamarine International Airport ⊠, Austl.	274b	37.40 S	144.50 E
Tullamore, Austl.	166	32.38 S	147.34 E
Tullamore, On., Can.	275b	43.47 N	79.46 W
Tullamore, Ire.	48	53.16 N	7.30 W
Tullaroop Creek ≃	169	36.53 S	143.53 E
Tullaroop Reservoir ⊜[1]	169	37.07 S	143.52 E
Tull Bay ⊂	208	36.30 N	76.04 W
Tulle	32	45.16 N	1.46 E
Tullgarn	40	58.57 N	17.35 E
Tullibigeal	166	33.25 S	146.44 E
Tullinge	40	59.12 N	17.53 E
Tullins	62	45.18 N	5.29 E
Tulln	61	48.20 N	16.03 E
Tullner Feld ◆[1]	264b	48.19 N	16.10 E
Tulloch Reservoir ⊜[1]	226	37.53 N	120.35 W
Tullock Creek ≃	202	46.08 N	107.27 W
Tullos	194	31.49 N	92.19 W
Tullow	48	52.48 N	6.44 W
Tullus	140	11.03 N	24.33 E
Tully, Austl.	166	17.56 S	145.56 E
Tully, N.Y., U.S.	210	42.47 N	76.06 W
Tully Dam ◆[6]	207	42.39 N	72.11 W
Tullytown	208	40.09 N	74.49 W
Ṭulmaythah	146	32.43 N	20.57 E
Tuloma ≃	24	68.52 N	32.49 E
Tulpfontein	158	32.44 S	19.43 E
Tulsa	196	36.09 N	95.59 W
Tulsequah	176	58.35 N	133.35 W
Tulsī Lake ⊜	272c	19.11 N	72.55 E
Tulsīpur	124	28.07 N	82.18 E
Tulsk	48	53.47 N	8.16 W
Tul'skij	84	44.31 N	40.10 E
Tulstrup	41	56.07 N	9.46 E
Tultepec	234	19.41 N	99.08 W
Tultitlán	286a	19.39 N	99.09 W
Tuluá	246	4.06 N	76.11 W
Tuluksak	180	61.06 N	160.58 W
Tulum	232	20.13 N	87.28 W
Tulum ⊥	232	20.12 N	87.26 W
Tulumayo ≃	248	11.10 S	75.16 W
Tulun	88	54.35 N	100.33 E
Tulungagung	115a	8.04 S	111.54 E
Tulungselapan	112	3.15 S	105.19 E
Tuluran Island I	116	10.59 N	119.17 E
Tulu Welel ∧	144	8.53 N	34.47 E
Tulyehualco ◆[8]	286a	19.15 N	99.01 W
Tum	164	3.38 S	130.23 E
Tuma	80	55.09 N	40.34 E
Tuma ≃	236	13.03 N	84.44 W
Tumacacori National Monument ♦	200	31.25 N	111.01 W
Tumaco	246	1.49 N	78.46 W
Tumaco, Rada de ⊂	246	1.55 N	78.45 W
Tumak	80	46.14 N	48.31 E
Tumalykol'	86	48.21 N	60.03 E
Tuman'an	84	41.00 N	44.40 E
Tuman-gang (Tumen) ≃	98	42.18 N	130.41 E
Tumannaja, gora ∧	180	66.33 N	179.43 E
Tumanovo	76	55.25 N	34.39 E
Tumanšet ≃	88	55.53 N	97.30 E
Tumanskij	180	63.58 N	178.12 E
Tumany	74	60.56 N	155.56 E
Tumarbong	116	10.23 N	119.27 E
T'um'ati → Sklad	74	71.55 N	123.33 E
Tumatumari	246	5.22 N	59.00 W
Tumauini	116	17.17 N	121.49 E
Tumba	40	59.12 N	17.49 E
Tumba, Lac ⊜	152	0.48 S	18.03 E
Tumbarumba	171b	35.47 S	148.01 E
Tumbarumba Creek ≃	171b	35.58 S	148.03 E
Tumbes	246	3.34 S	80.28 W
Tumbes □[5]	246	3.50 N	80.30 W
Tumbes (Puyango) ≃	246	3.30 S	80.27 W
Tumbes, Punta ›	252	36.37 S	73.07 W
Tumbiscatio de Ruiz	234	18.31 N	102.21 W
Tumble Mountain ∧	202	45.19 N	110.02 W
Tumbler Ridge	182	55.07 N	120.55 W
Tumblong	171b	35.09 S	148.00 E
Tumbotino	80	55.59 N	43.02 E
Tumbur	154	4.20 N	31.34 E
Tumby Bay	166	34.22 S	136.06 E
Tumča ≃	24	66.36 N	30.48 E
Tŭmch'on-ni ◆[8]	271b	37.34 N	126.51 E
T'umen', Ross.	86	57.09 N	65.32 E
Tumen, Zhg.	98	42.58 N	129.49 E
Tumen (Tuman-gang) ≃	98	42.18 N	130.41 E
T'umen'-Aryk	86	44.02 N	67.01 E
T'umencevo	86	53.20 N	81.31 E
T'umenec, porog ∟	88	56.38 N	99.00 E
T'umen' Oblast' □[4]	86	58.00 N	69.00 E
Tumenpu	107	29.49 N	103.39 E
Tumenskoje	82	55.00 N	38.32 E
Tumenzi	102	37.43 N	103.09 E
Tumeremo	246	7.18 N	61.30 W
Tumiritinga	255	18.58 S	41.38 W
Tumkūr	122	13.21 N	77.05 E
Tummel ≃	46	56.38 N	3.40 W
Tumnin ≃	89	49.18 N	140.22 E
Tumon Bay ⊂	174p	13.31 N	144.48 E
Tumos ≃	156	22.55 S	14.37 E
Tumoteqi	102	40.52 N	111.28 E
Tumpang	115a	8.00 S	112.46 E
Tumpat	114	6.12 N	102.10 E
Tumsar	120	21.23 N	79.44 E
Tumtum	182	47.53 N	117.40 W
Tumu, Ghana	150	10.52 N	1.59 W
Tumu, Zhg.	105	40.23 N	115.36 E
Tumuc-Humac Mountains ⋏	250	2.20 N	55.00 W
Tumut	171b	35.18 S	148.13 E
Tumut ≃	171b	35.07 S	148.13 E
Tumut Pond Reservoir ⊜[1]	171b	35.59 S	148.25 E
Tumutuk	80	55.02 N	53.19 E
Tumwater	224	47.00 N	122.54 W
Tun ≃	110	17.25 N	98.42 E
Tuna Canyon V	280	34.03 N	118.36 W
Tunago Lake ⊜	180	66.18 N	125.50 W
Tuna-Hästberg	40	60.20 N	15.11 E
Tunapuna	241r	10.38 N	61.23 W
Tunari, Cerro ∧	248	17.18 S	66.22 W
Tunas Creek ≃	196	31.01 N	102.11 W
Tunas de Zaza	240p	21.38 N	79.33 W
Tūnat al-Jabal, Miṣr	142	27.46 N	30.44 E
Tūnat al-Jabal, Miṣr	142	28.13 N	30.43 E
Tunaydah	140	25.31 N	29.21 E
Tunbridge Wells → Royal Tunbridge Wells	42	51.08 N	0.16 E
Tunçbilek	130	39.37 N	29.29 E
Tunceli	130	39.07 N	39.32 E
Tunceli □[4]	130	39.10 N	39.30 E
Tunchang	110	19.28 N	110.08 E
T'unch'i → Tunxi	100	29.44 N	118.18 E
Tunda, Pulau I	115a	5.49 S	106.16 E
Tundazi ∧	154	17.33 S	28.05 E
Tündern	52	52.04 N	9.22 E
Tūndla	124	27.12 N	78.17 E
Tundubai ⊤[4]	140	18.31 N	28.33 E
Tunduru	154	11.07 S	37.21 E
Tundyk ≃	86	51.04 N	77.24 E
Tundža ≃	38	41.40 N	26.34 E
Tune	41	55.36 N	12.11 E
Tunesien → Tunisia □[1]	148	34.00 N	9.00 E
T'unež	82	54.37 N	38.29 E
Túnez → Tunis	148	36.48 N	10.11 E
Túnez → Tunisia □[1]	148	34.00 N	9.00 E
T'ung ≃	74	63.46 N	121.35 E
Tunga	150	8.00 N	9.19 E
Tunga ≃	122	14.00 N	75.41 E
Tungabhadra ≃	122	15.57 N	78.15 E
Tungabhadra Reservoir ⊜[1]	122	15.16 N	76.21 E
Tungaru	140	10.14 N	30.42 E
Tungauan Bay ⊂	116	7.28 N	122.21 E
Tungchi University ♦[2]	269b	31.18 N	121.29 E
Tungchi Yü I	100	23.15 N	119.40 E
T'ungchou → Tongxian	105	39.55 N	116.39 E
Tungch'üan Tao I	100	25.58 N	119.58 E
T'ungch'uan → Tongchuan	102	35.01 N	109.01 E
Tungelsta	40	59.06 N	18.02 E
Tung Hai → East China Sea ⊤[2]	90	30.00 N	126.00 E
Tungho	100	22.58 N	121.18 E
T'unghsien → Tongxian	105	39.55 N	116.39 E
T'unghua → Tonghua	98	41.41 N	125.55 E
Tunghwa → Tonghua	98	41.41 N	125.55 E
Tungir ≃	88	55.24 N	120.32 E
Tungirskij chrebet ⋏	88	54.40 N	119.40 E
Tungkal ≃	112	0.49 S	103.29 E
Tungkang	100	22.28 N	120.26 E
Tungkillo	168b	34.49 S	139.04 E
Tungku	112	5.01 N	118.53 E
Tungla	236	13.18 N	84.26 W
T'ungliao → Tongliao	89	43.39 N	122.14 E
Tung Lung Island I	271d	22.15 N	114.17 E
Tung O	271d	22.12 N	114.08 E
Tungokočen	88	53.33 N	115.36 E
Tungsha Tao (Pratas Island) I	90	20.42 N	116.43 E
Tungshih	100	24.15 N	120.49 E
Tungsten	180	61.57 N	128.16 W
Tungsunga, Jabal ∧	140	11.29 N	23.21 E
Tungting Tao I	100	24.10 N	118.14 E
Tungurahua □[4]	246	1.15 S	78.35 W
Tungurahua ∧[1]	246	1.27 S	78.26 W
Tungyin Tao I	100	26.22 N	120.30 E
Tuni	122	17.21 N	82.33 E
Tunia ≃	246	1.13 N	72.44 W
Tunica	194	34.41 N	90.22 W
Tunis	148	36.48 N	10.11 E
Tunis □[8]	148	36.50 N	10.15 E
Tunis, Golfe de ⊂	36	37.00 N	10.30 E
Tunis et Banlieue □[8]	36	36.48 N	10.10 E
Tunisia (Tunisie) □[1], Afr.	134	34.00 N	9.00 E
Tunisia (Tunisie) □[1], Afr.	148	34.00 N	9.00 E
Tunisie → Tunisia □[1]	148	34.00 N	9.00 E
Tunis Sud □[8]	148	36.30 N	10.00 E
Tūnis → Tunisia □[1]	148	34.00 N	9.00 E
Tunitas Creek ≃	282	37.21 N	122.24 W
Tunja	246	5.31 N	73.22 W
Tunjang	114	6.16 N	100.21 E
Tunka	88	51.45 N	102.32 E
Tunkás	232	20.54 N	88.45 W
Tunkhannock	210	41.32 N	75.56 W
Tunkhannock Creek ≃	210	41.32 N	75.57 W
Tunkhannock Creek, East Branch ≃	210	41.38 N	75.43 W
Tunliu	102	36.19 N	112.54 E
Tunnel	210	42.13 N	75.44 W
Tunnel Hill, Ga., U.S.	192	34.50 N	85.02 W
Tunnelhill, Pa., U.S.	214	40.29 N	78.33 W
Tunnelton, In., U.S.	218	38.46 N	86.21 W
Tunnelton, W.V., U.S.	188	39.23 N	79.44 W
Tunnsjøen ⊜	24	64.43 N	13.24 E
Tunø I	41	55.57 N	10.26 E
Tuntenhausen	64	47.56 N	12.01 E
Tuntum	250	5.14 S	44.39 W
Tuntutuliak	180	60.22 N	162.38 W
Tununak	180	60.35 N	165.16 W
Tunungayualok Island I	176	56.05 N	61.05 W
Tunuyán	252	33.34 S	69.01 W
Tunuyán ≃	252	34.03 S	66.45 W
Tunxi	100	29.44 N	118.18 E
Tuo ≃, Zhg.	100	33.16 N	117.45 E
Tuo ≃, Zhg.	102	28.57 N	105.27 E
Tuobalage	120	31.37 N	88.10 E
Tuobuja	74	62.00 N	122.02 E
Tuocheng	100	24.05 N	115.13 E
Tuoe Shan ∧	102	24.20 N	103.32 E
Tuoheji	100	33.26 N	117.26 E
Tuoj-Chaja	74	62.32 N	111.18 E
Tuoji Dao I	98	38.09 N	120.14 E
Tuokedingling	120	32.45 N	84.55 E
Tuokusidawan Ling ∧	120	37.14 N	85.47 E
Tuoli	105	39.46 N	116.01 E
Tuolumne	226	37.57 N	120.14 W
Tuolumne □[6]	226	37.59 N	120.23 W
Tuolumne ≃	226	37.36 N	121.10 W
Tuolumne, Lyell Fork ≃	226	37.53 N	119.23 W
Tuolumne, North Fork ≃	226	37.54 N	120.15 W
Tuolumne, South Fork ≃	226	37.50 N	120.03 W
Tuolunduo	89	50.35 N	120.05 E
Tuong Duong	110	19.16 N	104.27 E
Tuotuo ≃	120	34.15 N	93.11 E
Tuowu	102	28.58 N	102.13 E
T'up	85	42.44 N	78.22 E
Tupã	255	21.56 S	50.30 W
Tupaciguara	255	18.35 S	48.42 W
Tupana ≃	246	4.25 S	60.05 W
Tupanciretã	252	29.05 S	53.51 W
Tuparro ≃	246	5.13 N	67.50 W
Tupelo, Ms., U.S.	194	34.15 N	88.42 W
Tupelo, Ok., U.S.	196	34.36 N	96.25 W
Tupelo National Battlefield ⊥	194	34.13 N	88.44 W
Tupi	116	6.19 N	124.57 E
Tupičov	78	51.46 N	31.26 E
Tupik	88	54.26 N	119.57 E
Tupilac	116	7.40 N	122.30 E
Tupinambarana, Ilha I	246	3.00 S	58.00 W
Tupi Paulista	255	21.24 S	51.34 W
Tupiraçaba	255	14.29 S	48.34 W
Tupiza	248	21.27 S	65.43 W
Tuplice	30	51.41 N	14.50 E
Tupman	226	35.17 N	119.21 W
Tupper	182	55.31 N	120.02 W
Tupper Lake	188	44.13 N	74.29 W
Tupperville	214	42.36 N	82.16 W
Tupuai, Île I	14	23.18 S	149.30 W
Tupungato	252	33.22 S	69.08 W
Tupungato, Cerro ∧	252	33.22 S	69.47 W
Tuqiao, Zhg.	106	31.39 N	120.24 E
Tuqiao, Zhg.	106	31.56 N	119.03 E
Tuqiao, Zhg.	107	30.24 N	105.28 E
Tuqiaozhen	107	30.32 N	104.50 E
Tuquan	89	45.26 N	121.50 E
Túquerres	246	1.05 N	77.37 W
Tuquiaochang	107	29.47 N	106.01 E
Tura, India	124	25.31 N	90.13 E
Ṭurā, Miṣr	142	29.56 N	31.16 E
Tura, Ross.	74	64.17 N	100.15 E
Tura ≃, Ross.	86	57.12 N	66.56 E
Tura ≃, Ross.	88	51.36 N	114.09 E
Turabah	144	21.13 N	41.39 E
Turabah ⊤[4]	128	28.15 N	42.55 E
Turābah, 'Ayn at- ⊤[4]	132	31.36 N	35.25 E
Turāg ≃	126	23.45 N	90.21 E
Turaiyūr	122	11.10 N	78.37 E
Turakina	172	40.02 S	175.13 E
Turakina ≃	172	40.04 S	175.08 E
Turama ≃	164	6.50 S	143.05 E
Turambhe	272c	19.04 N	73.01 E
Turan, Ross.	88	51.38 N	101.40 E
Turan, Ross.	88	52.08 N	93.55 E
Turangi	172	39.00 S	175.49 E
Turano ≃	66	42.26 N	12.47 E

Symbols in the index entries represent the broad categories identified in the key at the right. Symbols with superior numbers (⋏[1]) identify subcategories (see complete key on page *I · 1).*

Symbole im Register stellen die rechts im Schlüssel erklärten Kategorien dar. Symbole mit hochgestellten Ziffern (⋏[1]) bezeichnen Unterabteilungen einer Kategorie (vgl. vollständiger Schlüssel auf Seite *I · 1).*

Los símbolos incluídos en el texto del índice representan las grandes categorias identificadas con la clave a la derecha. Los símbolos con numeros en su parte superior (⋏[1]) identifican las subcategorías (véase la clave completa en la página *I · 1).*

Les symboles de l'index représentent les catégories indiquées dans la légende à droite. Les symboles suivis d'un indice (⋏[1]) représentent des sous-catégories (voir légende complète à la page *I · 1).*

Os símbolos incluídos no texto do índice representam as grandes categorias identificadas com a chave à direita. Os símbolos com números em sua parte superior (⋏[1]) identificam as subcategorias (veja-se a chave completa à página *I · 1).*

Symbol	English	Deutsch	Español	Français	Português
∧	Mountain	Berg	Montaña	Montagne	Montanha
⋏	Mountains	Gebirge	Montañas	Montagnes	Montanhas
)(	Pass	Paß	Paso	Col	Passo
V	Valley, Canyon	Tal, Cañon	Valle, Cañón	Vallée, Canyon	Vale, Canhão
≚	Plain	Ebene	Llano	Plaine	Planície
›	Cape	Kap	Cabo	Cap	Cabo
I	Island	Insel	Isla	Île	Ilha
II	Islands	Inseln	Islas	Îles	Ilhas
⊥	Other Topographic Features	Andere Topographische Objekte	Otros Elementos Topográficos	Autres données topographiques	Outros acidentes topográficos

ESPAÑOL Nombre	Página	Lat.°′	Long.°′ W = Oeste

FRANÇAIS Nom	Page	Lat.°′	Long.°′ W = Ouest

PORTUGUÊS Nome	Página	Lat.°′	Long.°′ W = Oeste

Turanskaja nizmennost' ≚ 86 44.30 N 63.00 E
Turāq al-'Ilab ⋌[2] 130 33.55 N 38.18 E
Turate 266b 45.39 N 9.00 E
Tur'at Ghunaym 142 31.16 N 31.29 E
Turayf 128 31.44 N 38.33 E
Turbaco 246 10.20 N 75.25 W
Turbacz ∧ 30 49.33 N 20.08 E
Turbat 128 25.59 N 63.04 E
Turbenthal 58 47.27 N 8.51 E
Turbigo 62 45.32 N 8.44 E
Turbio ≏ 234 20.19 N 101.37 W
Turbo 246 8.06 N 76.43 W
Turbotville 210 41.06 N 76.46 W
Turbov 78 49.21 N 28.44 E
Turčasovo 24 63.06 N 39.12 E
Turchi, Balata dei ≻ 70 36.43 N 12.02 E
Turčiansky Svätý Martin
— Martin 30 49.05 N 18.55 E
Turckheim 58 48.05 N 7.17 E
Turda 38 46.34 N 23.47 E
Turdej 76 53.22 N 38.01 E
Turee Creek 162 23.37 S 118.39 E
Turee Creek ≏ 162 23.35 S 117.25 E
Turek 30 52.02 N 18.30 E
Turen 115a 8.10 S 112.41 E
Turenki 26 60.55 N 24.38 E
Turfan Depression
— Turpan Pendi ≛[7] 86 42.40 N 89.10 E
Turfan
— Turpan 86 42.56 N 89.10 E
Turffontein ◆[8] 273d 26.15 S 28.02 E
Turffontein Race Course ♦ 273d 26.14 S 28.03 E
Turgaj, Kaz. 86 49.38 N 63.28 E
Turgaj, Kaz. 86 51.46 N 72.44 E
Turgaj □[8] 86 50.00 N 65.20 E
Turgaj ≏ 86 48.01 N 62.45 E
Turgajskaja ložbina V 86 51.00 N 64.30 E
Turgajskoje plato ⋌[1] 86 51.00 N 64.00 E
Turgen', Kaz. 85 43.24 N 77.36 E
Türgen, Mong. 86 50.04 N 91.36 E
Turgen' ≏ 85 43.50 N 77.38 E
Turgenevka 88 53.02 N 105.41 E
Turgenevo 80 54.50 N 46.19 E
Turginovo 82 56.30 N 36.00 E
Turgojak 86 55.10 N 60.07 E
Turgoš 76 59.18 N 35.10 E
Turgovishte
— Tărgovište 38 43.15 N 26.34 E
Turgut, Tür. 130 38.37 N 31.49 E
Turgut, Tür. 130 37.22 N 28.02 E
Turgutlu 130 38.30 N 27.43 E
Turgwi ≏ 154 20.28 S 32.18 E
Turhal 130 40.24 N 36.06 E
Türi, Eesti 76 58.48 N 25.26 E
Turi, It. 68 40.55 N 17.01 E
Turia ≏ 34 39.27 N 0.19 W
Turiaçu 250 1.41 S 45.21 W
Turiaçu ≏ 250 1.36 S 45.19 W
Turiančajskij zapovednik ♦ 84 40.40 N 47.35 E
Turij Rog 89 45.14 N 131.58 E
Turijsk 78 51.07 N 24.31 E
Turilovka 83 49.06 N 40.13 E
Turimetta Head ≻ 274a 33.42 S 151.19 E
Turimiquire, Cerro ∧ 246 10.07 N 63.53 W
Turin, Ab., Can. 182 49.58 N 112.31 W
Turin, N.Y., U.S. 212 43.38 N 75.25 W
Turinge 40 59.12 N 17.27 E
Turinsk 86 58.03 N 63.42 E
Turinskaja Sloboda 86 57.37 N 64.25 E
Turin
— Torino 62 45.03 N 7.40 E
Turja ≏ 78 51.48 N 24.52 E
Turka, Ross. 88 52.57 N 108.13 E
Turka, Ukr. 78 49.10 N 23.02 E
Turka ≏ 88 52.56 N 108.13 E
Turkana, Lake
— Rudolf, Lake ⊜ 144 3.30 N 36.05 E
Türkei
— Turkey □[1] 22 39.00 N 35.00 E
Türkeli Adası I 130 40.30 N 27.30 E
Turkestan 85 43.18 N 68.15 E
Turkestanskij chrebet ⋌ 85 39.35 N 69.15 E
Turkestanskij kanal ≅ 85 42.44 N 69.00 E
Túrkeve 30 47.06 N 20.45 E
Turkey 196 34.23 N 100.53 W
Turkey (Türkiye) □[1], Asia 22 39.00 N 35.00 E
Turkey (Türkiye) □[1], Asia 130 39.00 N 35.00 E
Turkey ≏ 190 42.43 N 91.01 W
Turkey Branch ≏ 284c 38.52 N 76.48 W
Turkey City 214 41.11 N 79.37 W
Turkey Creek 164 17.02 S 128.12 E
Turkey Creek ≏, On., Can. 281 42.14 N 83.06 W
Turkey Creek ≏, U.S. 198 39.58 N 96.02 W
Turkey Creek ≏, In., U.S. 278 41.31 N 87.18 W
Turkey Creek ≏, Ia., U.S. 198 41.20 N 95.05 W
Turkey Creek ≏, Ks., U.S. 198 38.53 N 97.11 W
Turkey Creek ≏, Ne., U.S. 198 40.23 N 96.53 W
Turkey Creek ≏, Ok., U.S. 196 35.58 N 97.56 W
Turkey Creek ≏, Tx., U.S. 222 30.39 N 97.05 W
Turkey Island I 284c 38.58 N 77.12 W
Turkey Point ≻, On., Can. 212 42.40 N 80.21 W
Turkey Point ≻, Fl., U.S. 220 25.26 N 80.19 W
Turkey Point Provincial Park ♦ 212 42.40 N 80.22 W
Turkey Run State Park ♦ 194 39.54 N 87.13 W
Turkeytown 279b 40.12 N 79.44 W
Türkheim 58 48.03 N 10.38 E
Turki 80 51.59 N 43.16 E
Turkish Republic of Northern Cyprus
— Cyprus, North □[1] 130 35.15 N 33.40 E
Türkiye
— Turkey □[1] 22 39.00 N 35.00 E
Turkmān Deh 267d 35.40 N 51.36 E
Turkmenia
— Turkmenistan □[1] 72 40.00 N 60.00 E
Turkmenija
— Turkmenistan □[1] 72 40.00 N 60.00 E
Turkmenistan □[1], Asia 72 40.00 N 60.00 E
Turkmenistan □[1], Asia 128 39.00 N 60.00 E
Turkmeniya
— Turkmenistan □[1] 72 40.00 N 60.00 E
Turkmen-Kala 128 37.26 N 62.20 E
Turkmenskij zaliv c 128 38.54 N 53.48 E
Turk Mine 154 19.45 S 28.50 E
Türkoğlu 130 37.31 N 36.49 E
Turks and Caicos Islands □[2], N.A. 230 21.45 N 71.35 W
Turks and Caicos Islands □[2], N.A. 238 21.45 N 71.35 W
Turks Island Passage ⊔ 238 21.25 N 71.19 W
Turks Islands II 238 21.24 N 71.07 W
Turks-und Caicos-Inseln
— Turks and Caicos Islands □[2] 238 21.45 N 71.35 W
Turku (Åbo) 26 60.27 N 22.17 E
Turkwel ≏ 154 3.06 N 36.06 E
Turlan 85 43.36 N 69.03 E
Turley 196 36.14 N 95.58 W
Turlock 226 37.29 N 120.50 W
Turlock Lake ⊜[1] 226 42.17 N 73.21 W
Turmalina 255 17.17 S 42.45 W
Turmantas 76 55.42 N 26.27 E
Turmerito, Quebrada ≏ 286c 10.26 N 66.55 W
Turnagain ≏ 180 59.06 N 127.35 W
Turnagain, Cape ≻ 172 40.29 S 176.37 E
Turnagain Arm c 180 61.00 N 150.00 W
Turnagain Island I 164 9.34 S 142.18 E
Turnau 61 47.33 N 15.20 E
Turnbull, Mount ∧ 200 33.04 N 110.16 W
Turnbull, Mount ∧[2] 162 21.03 S 131.57 E
Turneffe Islands II 232 17.22 N 87.51 W
Turner, Austl. 162 17.50 S 128.17 E
Turner, Mt., U.S. 202 48.50 N 108.24 W
Turner, Or., U.S. 202 44.50 N 122.57 W
Turner ≏ 162 20.21 S 118.25 E
Turner Field ✈ 285 40.13 N 75.13 W
Turners Falls 207 42.36 N 72.33 W
Turners Peninsula ≻[1] 150 7.22 N 12.22 W
Turnersville, N.J., U.S. 285 39.46 N 75.03 W
Turnersville, Tx., U.S. 222 31.37 N 97.44 W
Turner Valley 182 50.40 N 114.17 W
Turnhout 56 51.19 N 4.57 E
Türnitz 61 47.57 N 15.30 E
Turnor Lake ⊜ 184 56.32 N 108.38 W
Turnov 30 50.35 N 15.10 E
Tŭrnovo
— Veliko Tărnovo 38 43.04 N 25.39 E
Turnpike Lake ⊜ 283 42.01 N 71.19 W
Turnu-Măgurele 38 43.45 N 24.53 E
Turnu Roşu, Pasul)(38 45.33 N 24.16 E
Turnu-Severin
— Drobeta-Turnu Severin 38 44.38 N 22.39 E
Turobin 30 50.50 N 22.45 E
Turočak 86 52.16 N 87.08 E
Turon 198 37.48 N 98.25 W
Turon ≏ 170 33.03 S 149.43 E
Turopin 78 51.00 N 24.27 E
Turopolje ≚ 36 45.40 N 16.05 E
Tuross ≏ 171b 36.09 S 149.39 E
Turov 76 52.04 N 27.44 E
Turovo 82 54.52 N 37.49 E
Turpan 86 42.56 N 89.10 E
Turpan Pendi (Turfan Depression) ≛[7] 86 42.40 N 89.10 E
Turques et Caicos, Îles
— Turks and Caicos Islands □[2] 238 21.45 N 71.35 W
Turquia
— Turkey □[1] 22 39.00 N 35.00 E
Turquie
— Turkey □[1] 22 39.00 N 35.00 E
Turquino, Pico ∧ 240p 19.59 N 76.50 W
Turrach 64 46.57 N 13.52 E
Turramurra 274a 33.44 S 151.08 E
Turrell 194 35.22 N 90.15 W
Turret Peak ∧ 200 34.15 N 111.53 W
Turriaco 64 45.49 N 13.26 E
Turrialba 236 9.54 N 83.41 W
Turrialba, Volcán ∧[1] 236 10.02 N 83.46 W
Turriers 62 44.24 N 6.10 E
Turriff 46 57.32 N 2.28 W
Turritano ◆[1] 71 40.45 N 8.35 E
Turrubares, Cerro ∧ 236 9.47 N 84.28 W
Tursi 68 40.15 N 16.28 E
Tursunzade 85 38.32 N 68.13 E
Turtas ≏ 86 59.06 N 68.52 E
Turtipar 124 26.10 N 83.54 E
Turtle ≏, Mb., Can. 184 51.07 N 99.39 W
Turtle ≏, On., Can. 184 48.51 N 92.45 W
Turtle, North Branch ≏ 198 47.57 N 97.35 W
Turtle Creek, N.B., Can. 186 45.58 N 64.53 W
Turtle Creek, Pa., U.S. 214 40.24 N 79.49 W
Turtle Creek ≏, Pa., U.S. 279b 40.23 N 79.51 W
Turtle Creek ≏, S.D., U.S. 198 44.55 N 98.29 W
Turtle Creek ≏, Wi., U.S. 216 42.29 N 89.03 W
Turtle-Flambeau Flowage ⊜[1] 190 46.05 N 90.11 W
Turtleford 184 53.23 N 108.56 W
Turtle Harbor Channel ⊔ 220 25.15 N 80.18 W
Turtle Islands II 150 7.37 N 13.02 W
Turtle Lake, N.D., U.S. 198 47.31 N 100.53 W
Turtle Lake, Wi., U.S. 190 45.23 N 92.08 W
Turtle Lake ⊜ 184 53.35 N 108.40 W
Turtle Mountain ∧[2] 184 49.00 N 100.15 W
Turtle Mountain Indian Reservation ◆[4] 198 48.51 N 99.45 W
Turtle Mountain Provincial Park ♦ 184 49.03 N 100.15 W
Turtmann 58 46.18 N 7.41 E
Turton and Entwistle Reservoir ⊜[1] 262 53.39 N 2.25 W
Turton Bottoms 262 53.38 N 2.24 W
Turton Moor ◆[3] 262 53.40 N 2.29 W
Turton Tower ◉[8] 262 53.38 N 2.25 W
Turu ≏ 74 64.38 N 100.00 E
Turua 172 37.14 S 175.34 E
Turuchan ≏ 74 65.56 N 87.42 E
Turuchansk 74 65.49 N 87.59 E
Turuntajevo, Ross. 86 56.38 N 85.58 E
Turuntajevo, Ross. 88 52.12 N 107.37 E
Turusele ∧ 71 40.09 N 9.34 E
Turvo 252 28.56 S 49.41 W
Turvo ≏, Bra. 255 17.46 S 50.12 W
Turvo ≏, Bra. 255 19.56 S 49.55 W
Turvo ≏, Bra. 256 22.04 S 45.42 W
Turvo ≏, Bra. 256 22.29 S 44.15 W
Turvo Grande ≏ 256 21.42 S 44.22 W
Turvolândia 256 21.47 S 45.47 W
Turvo Pequeno ≏ 256 21.42 S 44.22 W
Turyu-san ∧ 98 41.10 N 128.47 E
Turzovka 30 49.25 N 18.39 E
Tusa 70 37.59 N 14.14 E
Tusa ≏ 70 38.01 N 14.14 E
Tusas, Rio ≏ 200 36.23 N 106.03 W
Tuscaloosa 194 33.12 N 87.34 W
Tuscaloosa, Lake ⊜[1] 194 33.20 N 87.35 W
Tuscania 66 42.25 N 11.52 E
Tuscany
— Toscana □[4] 36 43.25 N 11.00 E
Tuscarawas 214 40.24 N 81.25 W
Tuscarawas □[6] 214 40.30 N 81.30 W
Tuscarawas ≏ 214 40.17 N 81.52 W
Tuscarora, N.Y., U.S. 210 42.38 N 77.52 W
Tuscarora, Pa., U.S. 208 40.46 N 76.02 W
Tuscarora Creek ≏, N.Y., U.S. 210 42.07 N 77.14 W
Tuscarora Creek ≏, Pa., U.S. 208 40.32 N 77.23 W
Tuscarora Creek, North Branch ≏ 210 42.05 N 77.18 W
Tuscarora Indian Reservation ◆[4] 210 43.09 N 78.57 W
Tuscarora Mountain ∧ 188 40.10 N 77.45 W
Tuscarora Mountains ∧ 204 41.00 N 116.20 W
Tuscarora State Park ♦ 208 40.48 N 76.01 W
Tuscarora Tunnel ◆[5] 214 40.05 N 77.50 W
Tuscola, Il., U.S. 194 39.47 N 88.16 W
Tuscola, Tx., U.S. 196 32.12 N 99.48 W
Tuscolo ⊥ 267a 41.48 N 12.42 E
Tuscumbia, Al., U.S. 194 34.43 N 87.42 W
Tuscumbia, Mo., U.S. 194 38.13 N 92.27 W
Tuse 41 55.43 N 11.37 E
Tushan 98 34.14 N 117.51 E
Tušino ◆[8] 265b 55.50 N 37.26 E
Tuskegee 194 32.25 N 85.41 W
Tusker Rock II[1] 42 51.27 N 3.40 W
Tussey Mountain ∧ 214 40.25 N 78.07 W
Tüssling 60 48.13 N 12.36 E
Tustin 228 33.44 N 117.49 W
Tustin Marine Corps Air Station (Helicopter) ■ 280 33.43 N 117.50 W
Tustumena Lake ⊜ 180 60.12 N 150.50 W
Tuszyn 30 51.37 N 19.34 E
Tut 130 37.48 N 37.55 E
Tuta 152 14.37 S 20.45 E
Tutaekuri ≏ 172 39.30 S 176.54 E
Tutaizi 104 41.01 N 122.38 E
Tutajev 80 57.53 N 39.32 E
Tutak 84 39.32 N 42.46 E
Tutang 100 29.21 N 116.24 E
Tutbury 42 52.51 N 1.41 W
Tuthills Creek ≏ 276 40.45 N 73.02 W
Tuticorin 122 8.47 N 78.08 E
Tutin 38 42.59 N 20.20 E
T'ut'kovo 82 54.37 N 38.32 E
Tutóia 250 2.45 S 42.16 W
Tutoko, Mount ∧ 172 44.36 S 168.00 E
Tutong 112 4.50 N 114.40 E
Tutova ≏ 38 46.06 N 27.32 E
Tutrakan 38 44.03 N 26.37 E
Tu
— Tsu 94 34.43 N 136.31 E
Tuttle, N.D., U.S. 198 47.08 N 99.59 W
Tuttle, Ok., U.S. 196 35.17 N 97.48 W
Tuttle Creek Lake ⊜[1] 198 39.22 N 96.40 W
Tuttlingen 58 47.59 N 8.49 E
Tutuala 112 8.24 S 127.15 E
Tutuban Station ◆[5] 269f 14.37 N 120.58 E
Tutu Bay c 116 5.55 N 121.12 E
Tutubu 154 5.30 S 32.41 E
Tutuí ≏ 250 2.39 S 54.10 W
Tutuila I 174u 14.18 S 170.42 W
Tutūn 142 29.09 N 30.46 E
Tütüncü 130 40.04 N 27.43 E
Tutupaca, Volcán ∧[1] 248 17.01 S 70.22 W
Tutura 88 54.46 N 105.15 E
Tututalak Mountain ∧ 180 67.46 N 161.10 W
Tutwiler 194 34.00 N 90.25 W
Tutzing 64 47.54 N 11.17 E
Tuul ≏ 88 48.57 N 104.48 E
Tuupovaara 26 62.29 N 30.36 E
Tuurun-Poorin lääni □[4] 26 61.20 N 22.30 E
Tuusniemi 26 62.49 N 28.30 E
Tuutapu, Cerro ∧ 174z 27.08 S 109.24 W
Tuva □[3] 72 52.00 N 95.00 E
T'uva-Guba 24 69.08 N 33.32 E
Tuvalu □[1] 14 8.00 S 178.00 E
Tuvutha Island I 175g 17.40 S 178.48 W
Tuwang 107 29.06 N 105.48 E
Tuwayq, Jabal ⋌ 118 23.00 N 46.00 E
Tuwayyil ash-Shihāq ∧[2] 132 30.36 N 36.08 E
Tuxedo Park, De., U.S. 285 39.43 N 75.37 W
Tuxedo Park, N.Y., U.S. 210 41.11 N 74.11 W
Tuxer Alpen ⋌ 64 47.10 N 11.45 E
Tuxford, Sk., Can. 184 50.35 N 105.35 W
Tuxford, Eng., U.K. 44 53.13 N 0.53 W
Tuxiaqiao 100 28.47 N 121.29 E
Tuxpan, Méx. 234 20.57 N 97.24 W
Tuxpan, Méx. 234 21.57 N 105.18 W
Tuxpan, Méx. 234 19.33 N 103.24 W
Tuxpan, Méx. 234 19.34 N 100.28 W
Tuxpan ≏ 234 20.58 N 97.18 W
Tuxsun 86 42.47 N 88.38 E
Tuxtepec 234 18.06 N 96.07 W
Tuxtla Gutiérrez 234 16.45 N 93.07 W
Tuy 34 42.03 N 8.38 W
Tuy ≏ 246 10.24 N 65.59 W
Tuy An 110 13.17 N 109.16 E
Tuyen Hoa 110 17.50 N 106.10 E
Tuyen Quang 110 21.49 N 105.13 E
Tuy Hoa 110 13.05 N 109.18 E
Tūysarkān 128 34.33 N 48.27 E
Tuyün
— Duyun 102 26.12 N 107.31 E
Tuyūr, Burj at- ∧[2] 140 20.55 N 27.55 E
Tuža 80 57.37 N 47.57 E
T'uzašu, pereval)(85 42.21 N 73.48 E
T'uzbel' 85 40.34 N 73.21 E
Tuzdykol', ozero ⊜ 80 49.36 N 52.20 E
Tuz Gölü ⊜ 130 38.45 N 33.25 E
Tuzigoot National Monument ◆ 200 34.49 N 112.01 W
Ṭūz Khurmātū 128 34.53 N 44.38 E
Tuzla, Bos. 38 44.32 N 18.41 E
Tuzla, Tür. 130 36.42 N 35.05 E
Tuzla ≏ 130 39.43 N 40.16 E
Tuzla Gölü ⊜ 130 39.02 N 35.50 E
Tuzlagözü 130 38.11 N 41.34 E
Tuzlov ≏ 83 47.23 N 40.08 E
Tuzluca 84 40.03 N 43.40 E
Tuzlukçu 130 38.28 N 31.38 E
Tuzly 78 45.52 N 30.05 E
Tuzuntla ≏ 234 18.51 N 100.44 W
Tvardica, Blg. 38 42.42 N 25.52 E
Tvardica, Mol. 78 46.09 N 28.57 E
Tvedestrand 26 58.37 N 8.55 E
Tveitsund 26 59.01 N 8.32 E
Tver' (Kalinin) 82 56.52 N 35.55 E
Tverca ≏ 76 56.52 N 35.55 E
Tver' Oblast' □[4] 76 57.00 N 34.00 E
Twain Harte 226 38.02 N 120.14 W
Twann 58 47.06 N 7.10 E
Twardogóra 30 51.22 N 17.28 E
Tweed 212 44.29 N 77.19 W
Tweed ≏ 44 55.46 N 2.00 W
Tweed ≏ 170 28.10 S 153.31 E
Tweeddale V 46 55.40 N 3.10 W
Tweede Exloërmond 52 52.55 N 6.58 E
Tweed Heads 171a 28.10 S 153.31 E
Tweedmouth 44 55.45 N 2.01 W
Tweedsmuir Provincial Park ♦ 182 52.55 N 126.05 W
Tweedy Mountain ∧ 202 45.29 N 112.58 W
Tweeling 158 27.38 S 28.31 E
Twee Rivieren 158 26.27 S 20.37 E
Tweespruit 158 29.11 S 27.01 E
Twello 52 52.14 N 6.06 E
Twelve Mile 216 40.52 N 86.13 W
Twelve Mile Creek ≏, On., Can. 212 43.11 N 79.16 W
Twelvemile Creek ≏, N.Y., U.S. 210 43.18 N 78.51 W
Twelvemile Island I 279b 40.32 N 79.51 W
Twelve Mile Lake ⊜, On., Can. 212 45.02 N 78.43 W
Twelve Mile Lake ⊜, Sk., Can. 184 49.29 N 106.14 W
Tweng 64 47.11 N 13.36 E
Twente ◆[1] 52 52.17 N 6.40 E
Twentekanaal ≅ 52 52.15 N 6.40 E
Twentieth Century Fox Studios ◆[3] 280 34.03 N 118.25 W
Twentyfive Mile Wash V 200 37.33 N 111.07 W
Twenty Mile Creek ≏ 212 43.10 N 79.22 W
Twentynine Palms 204 34.08 N 116.03 W
Twentynine Palms Marine Corps Center ■ 204 34.25 N 116.10 W
Tweya 152 0.54 S 19.05 E
Twickenham ◆[8] 260 51.27 N 0.20 W
Twilight Cove c 162 32.16 S 126.03 E
Twilight Park 210 42.11 N 74.05 W
Twillingate 186 49.39 N 54.46 W
Twimberg 61 46.55 N 14.50 E
Twin Beach 216 42.38 N 83.24 W
Twin Bridge Farm 285 39.57 N 75.33 W
Twin Bridges 202 45.32 N 112.19 W
Twin Butte Creek ≏ 198 38.46 N 100.56 W
Twin Buttes ∧ 202 44.20 N 122.15 W
Twin Buttes Reservoir ⊜[1] 196 31.20 N 100.35 W
Twin City 192 32.34 N 82.09 W
Twin Creek ≏ 218 39.33 N 84.21 W
Twin Falls 202 42.33 N 114.27 W
Twin Heads ⋌ 162 20.13 S 126.30 E
Twin Hills 180 59.23 N 159.58 W
Twin Lakes, Ca., U.S. 226 36.58 N 122.00 W
Twin Lakes, Ga., U.S. 192 30.42 N 83.12 W
Twin Lakes, In., U.S. 216 41.19 N 86.23 W
Twin Lakes, Mi., U.S. 216 42.02 N 86.04 W
Twin Lakes, Oh., U.S. 214 41.11 N 81.21 W
Twin Lakes, Pa., U.S. 210 41.24 N 74.54 W
Twin Lakes, Wi., U.S. 216 42.31 N 88.14 W
Twin Lakes ⊜, Ca., U.S. 226 38.09 N 119.21 W
Twin Lakes ⊜, Ct., U.S. 207 42.02 N 73.26 W
Twin Lakes ⊜, Wa., U.S. 224 47.55 N 120.51 W
Twin Oaks 208 39.51 N 75.26 W
Twin Peak Islands II 162 34.00 S 122.50 E
Twin Peaks 228 34.12 N 117.12 W
Twin Peaks ∧, Ca., U.S. 282 37.45 N 122.27 W
Twin Peaks ⋌, Id., U.S. 202 44.35 N 114.29 W
Twin Rocks, Or., U.S. 224 45.36 N 123.57 W
Twin Rocks, Pa., U.S. 214 40.29 N 78.51 W
Twinsburg 214 41.18 N 81.26 W
Twin Valley 198 47.15 N 96.15 W
Twisp 202 48.21 N 120.07 W
Twiss Green 262 53.27 N 2.32 W
Twist 52 52.38 N 7.03 E
Twiste ≏ 52 51.29 N 9.09 E
Twistringen 52 52.48 N 8.38 E
Twitchell Reservoir ⊜[1] 204 35.00 N 120.19 W
Twitya ≏ 180 64.10 N 128.12 W
Two, Channel ⊔ 220 24.50 N 80.45 W
Two Butte Creek ≏ 198 38.02 N 102.08 W
Twofold Bay c 166 37.06 S 149.55 E
Two Harbors 190 47.01 N 91.40 W
Two Hills 182 53.43 N 111.45 W
Two Lakes ⊜ 224 46.22 N 121.27 W
Two Medicine ≏ 202 48.29 N 112.14 W
Two Mile Creek ≏, On., Can. 284a 43.16 N 79.06 W
Twomile Creek ≏, N.Y., U.S. 284a 43.01 N 78.55 W
Twong 140 8.18 N 28.20 E
Two Penny Run ≏ 285 39.41 N 75.26 W
Two River Lake ⊜ 184 53.52 N 91.27 W
Two Rivers 190 44.09 N 87.34 W
Two Rivers Reservoir ⊜[1] 196 33.17 N 104.45 W
Two Thumb Range ⋌ 172 43.45 S 170.43 E
Two Wells 168b 34.36 S 138.30 E
Twrch ≏, Wales, U.K. 42 52.42 N 3.29 W
Twrch ≏, Wales, U.K. 42 51.46 N 3.46 W
Twyford, Eng., U.K. 42 51.29 N 0.53 W
Twyford, Eng., U.K. 42 51.01 N 1.19 W
Twymyn ≏ 42 52.38 N 3.44 W
Tyabb 169 38.16 S 145.11 E
Tybee Island 192 32.01 N 80.51 W
Tybju 24 60.37 N 50.20 E
Tychy 30 50.09 N 18.59 E
Tyczyn 30 49.58 N 22.02 E
Tydal 26 63.04 N 11.34 E
Tye 196 32.27 N 99.52 W
Tyende Creek ≏ 200 36.50 N 109.43 W
Tyendinaga Indian Reserve ◆[4] 212 44.11 N 77.07 W
Tyers ≏ 169 38.10 S 146.26 E
Tyfors 40 60.09 N 14.12 E
Tygarts Creek ≏ 218 38.43 N 82.57 W
Tygda 89 53.07 N 126.20 E
Tygda ≏ 89 52.35 N 127.55 E
Tygelsjö 41 55.31 N 13.00 E
Tygh Valley 224 45.14 N 121.10 W
Tyin ⊜ 26 61.17 N 8.13 E
Tyja ≏ 88 55.36 N 109.20 E
Tylden 158 32.07 S 27.05 E
Tyldesley 44 53.31 N 2.28 W
Tyler, Mn., U.S. 198 44.16 N 96.08 W
Tyler, Pa., U.S. 214 41.14 N 78.32 W
Tyler, Tx., U.S. 222 32.21 N 95.18 W
Tyler □[6] 222 30.47 N 94.32 W
Tyler, Lake ⊜ 222 32.13 N 95.10 W
Tyler East, Lake ⊜[1] 222 32.15 N 95.10 W
Tyler Park 284c 38.52 N 77.12 W
Tylersburg 214 41.23 N 79.19 W
Tyler State Park ♦, Pa., U.S. 208 40.14 N 74.59 W
Tyler State Park ♦, Tx., U.S. 222 32.29 N 95.14 W
Tylersville 210 41.00 N 77.25 W
Tylerton 208 37.58 N 76.01 W
Tylertown 194 31.06 N 90.08 W
Tylla 40 60.28 N 15.33 E
Tylösand 26 56.39 N 12.44 E
Tylöskog ⋌[2] 40 58.45 N 15.20 E
Tylovaj 80 57.30 N 53.47 E
Tym ≏, Ross. 74 59.25 N 80.04 E
Tym' ≏, Ross. 89 51.51 N 143.10 E
Tymna, laguna c 180 64.00 N 178.30 E
Tymochtee Creek ≏ 214 40.57 N 83.16 W
Tymovskoje 89 50.51 N 142.39 E
Tymsk 86 59.24 N 80.18 E
Tynagh 48 53.09 N 8.22 W
Tyndall 198 42.59 N 97.51 W
Tyndall Air Force Base ■ 194 30.04 N 85.35 W
Tyndaris ⊥ 70 38.09 N 15.03 E
Tyndinskij 74 55.10 N 124.43 E
Tyndrum 46 56.27 N 4.44 W
Tyne ≏, Eng., U.K. 44 55.01 N 1.26 W
Tyne ≏, Scot., U.K. 46 56.01 N 2.37 W
Tyne and Wear □[6] 44 54.55 N 1.35 W
Tynemouth 44 55.01 N 1.24 W
Tyner 216 41.24 N 86.24 W
Tyngsboro 283 42.40 N 71.25 W
Tyngsjö 40 60.18 N 13.53 E
Tynica 78 51.08 N 32.54 E
Týn nad Vltavou 30 49.14 N 14.26 E
Tynnelsö 40 59.25 N 17.06 E
Tynset 26 62.17 N 10.47 E
Tyonek 180 61.02 N 151.17 W
Typta 88 54.35 N 104.31 E
Tyr 89 52.57 N 139.48 E
Tyre 214 40.26 N 80.16 W
Tyresö 40 59.14 N 18.18 E
Tyre
— Şūr 132 33.16 N 35.11 E
Tyret' 88 53.41 N 102.19 E
Tyrgetuj 88 51.27 N 113.46 E
Tyrifjorden ⊜ 26 60.02 N 10.08 E
Tyringe 41 56.10 N 13.35 E
Tyringham 207 42.14 N 73.12 W
Tyrka 88 54.30 N 107.09 E
Tyrma 89 50.03 N 132.12 E
Tyrma ≏ 89 50.29 N 131.18 E
Tyrnovo 78 48.10 N 27.40 E
Tyrnyauz 84 43.23 N 42.56 E
Tyrone, Ky., U.S. 218 38.01 N 84.50 W
Tyrone, N.Y., U.S. 210 42.25 N 77.03 W
Tyrone, Ok., U.S. 196 36.57 N 101.03 W
Tyrone, Pa., U.S. 214 40.40 N 78.14 W
Tyrone Lake ⊜ 281 42.42 N 83.43 W
Tyrrell, Lake ⊜ 166 35.21 S 142.50 E
Tyrrellspass 48 53.23 N 7.22 W
Tyrrhenian Sea (Mare Tirreno) ≈[2] 36 40.00 N 12.00 E
Tyrrhenisches Meer
— Tyrrhenian Sea ≈[2] 36 40.00 N 12.00 E
Tysmenica 78 48.54 N 24.49 E
Tysnesøy I 26 60.00 N 5.35 E
Tysons Corner 284c 38.55 N 77.14 W
Tysons Corner Center ◆[9] 284c 38.55 N 77.13 W
Tysons Green 284c 38.55 N 77.15 W
Tysse 26 60.22 N 5.45 E
Tyssedal 26 60.07 N 6.34 E
Tysslingen ⊜ 40 59.19 N 15.02 E
Tystberga 40 58.52 N 17.15 E
Tystrup Sø ⊜ 41 55.22 N 11.35 E
Tytherington 262 53.17 N 2.08 W
Tytuvėnai 76 55.36 N 23.12 E
Ty Ty 192 31.28 N 83.38 W
Tyumen'
— T'umen' 86 57.09 N 65.32 E
Tyvrov 78 49.01 N 28.30 E
Tywa ≏ 54 53.13 N 14.29 E
Tywardreath 42 50.22 N 4.41 W
Tywi ≏ 42 51.46 N 4.22 W
Tywyn 42 52.35 N 4.05 W
Tzaneen 156 23.50 S 30.09 E
Tzekung
— Zigong 107 29.24 N 104.47 E
Tzeliutsing
— Zigong 107 29.24 N 104.47 E
Tzucacab 232 20.04 N 89.03 W
Tzukung
— Zigong 107 29.24 N 104.47 E
Tzupo
— Boshan 98 36.29 N 117.50 E
Tzupo
— Zibo 98 36.47 N 118.01 E

U

Uaboe 174b 0.31 S 166.55 E
Uac, Mount ∧ 116 12.12 N 123.40 E
Uaçá ≏ 250 4.13 N 51.32 W
Uagadugu
— Ouagadougou 150 12.22 N 1.31 W
Uamba 152 7.12 S 16.25 E
Uamba (Wamba) ≏, Afr. 152 3.56 S 17.12 E
Uamba ≏, Ang. 152 7.58 S 17.09 E
Uampochane 158 26.23 S 32.41 E
Uaoa Bay c 229a 20.56 N 156.16 W
Uaran
— Ouarâne ◆[1] 134 21.00 N 10.30 W
Uato-Lari 112 8.45 S 126.34 E
Uatumã ≏ 246 2.26 S 57.37 W
Uauá 250 9.50 S 39.28 W
Uaupés (Vaupés) ≏ 246 0.02 N 67.16 W
Uaxactún ⊥ 232 17.24 N 89.39 W
Ubá 255 21.07 S 42.56 W
Uba ≏ 86 50.15 N 81.45 E
Übach-Palenberg 56 50.55 N 6.07 E
Ubagan ≏ 86 54.24 N 64.45 E
Ubai 164 5.40 S 150.40 E
Ubaidullaganj 124 22.59 N 77.36 E
Ubaitaba 255 14.18 S 39.20 W
Ubajara 250 3.51 S 40.56 W
Ubajara, Parque Nacional de ♦ 250 3.47 S 40.56 W
Ubangi (Oubangui) ≏ 152 0.30 S 17.42 E
Ubatã 255 14.12 S 39.31 W
Ubaté 246 5.19 N 73.49 W
Ubatuba 256 23.26 S 45.04 W
Ubatuba, Baía de c 256 23.27 S 45.02 W
Ubauro 120 28.10 N 69.44 E
Ubay 116 10.03 N 124.28 E
Ubaye 62 44.28 N 6.22 E
Ubaye ≏ 62 44.28 N 6.18 E
Ubayyid, Wādī al- V 128 32.34 N 43.48 E
Ubby 41 55.37 N 11.13 E
Ube 96 33.56 N 131.15 E
Ubed' ≏ 78 51.27 N 32.29 E
Úbeda 34 38.01 N 3.22 W
Uberaba 255 19.45 S 47.55 W
Uberaba ≏ 255 20.07 S 48.31 W
Uberaba, Lagoa ⊜ 248 17.30 S 57.45 W
Überacker 60 48.11 N 12.52 E
Über dem Wind, Inseln
— Leeward Islands II 238 17.00 N 63.00 W
Uberlândia 255 18.56 S 48.18 W
Überlingen 58 47.46 N 9.10 E
Überlinger See c 58 47.45 N 9.09 E
Übersee 64 47.49 N 12.28 E
Ubiaja 150 6.38 N 6.21 E
Ubili 154 1.07 S 26.55 E
Ubin, Pulau I 271c 1.24 N 103.58 E
Ubinskoje 86 55.19 N 79.41 E
Ubinskoje, ozero ⊜ 86 55.30 N 80.05 E
Ubl'a 30 48.55 N 22.23 E
Ubly 190 43.42 N 82.55 W
Uboldo 266b 45.37 N 9.00 E
Ubombo 158 27.33 S 32.00 E
Ubondo 154 0.52 S 25.37 E
Ubon Ratchathani 110 15.14 N 104.54 E
Úborsko 60 49.20 N 13.09 E
Ubort' ≏ 78 52.06 N 28.28 E
Ubrique 34 36.41 N 5.27 W
Ubudiah, Masjid ◉[1] 114 4.46 N 100.56 E
Ubundu (Ponthierville) 154 0.21 S 25.29 E
Ubur-Tochtor 88 50.06 N 113.37 E
Uča ≏, Ross. 82 56.02 N 37.37 E
Uča ≏, Ross. 265b 55.56 N 37.57 E
Ucacha 252 33.02 S 63.31 W
Uč-Adži 128 38.05 N 62.48 E
Učaly 86 54.19 N 59.27 E
Učami 74 63.50 N 96.29 E
Učaral 86 46.10 N 80.56 E
Ucayali □[5] 248 9.00 S 74.00 W
Ucayali ≏ 242 4.30 S 73.27 W
Uccellina, Monti dell' ⋌ 66 42.38 N 11.05 E
Uccle 50 50.48 N 4.19 E
Uch 123 29.14 N 71.03 E
Uchab 156 19.47 S 17.42 E
Uchāna 124 29.28 N 76.10 E
Uchaud 62 43.45 N 4.16 E
Uchee Creek ≏ 192 32.18 N 84.57 W
Uchihara 94 36.22 N 140.21 E
Uchihata 270 34.25 N 135.27 E
Uchiko 96 33.33 N 132.39 E
Uchi Lake 184 51.05 N 92.35 W
Uchinada 94 36.39 N 136.39 E
Uchinomi 96 34.30 N 134.20 E
Uchinoura 92 31.16 N 131.05 E
Uchiumi 96 33.01 N 132.30 E
Uchiura-wan c 92a 42.20 N 140.40 E
Uchiza 248 8.29 S 76.23 W
Uchoa 255 20.56 S 49.13 W
Ucholovo 80 53.47 N 40.29 E
Uchra ≏ 80 58.20 N 39.00 E
Uchta, Ross. 24 61.12 N 38.32 E
Uchta, Ross. 24 63.33 N 53.38 E
Uchte 52 52.30 N 8.54 E
Uchte ≏ 54 52.46 N 11.45 E
Uchtoma 76 60.10 N 38.02 E
Uchtspringe 54 52.32 N 11.36 E
Učinskij Ryboučastok 86 60.02 N 65.10 E
Učinskoje vodochranilišče ⊜[1] 82 56.02 N 37.45 E
Uckange 56 49.18 N 6.09 E
Ückendorf ◆[8] 263 51.30 N 7.07 E
Uckermark ◆[1] 54 53.10 N 13.35 E
Uckfield 42 50.58 N 0.06 E
Üçköşe 130 40.13 N 41.00 E
Uckro 54 51.51 N 13.37 E
Učkupr'uk 85 40.33 N 71.04 E
Učkurgan 85 41.07 N 72.05 E
Ucluelet 182 48.57 N 125.33 W
Ucon 202 43.35 N 111.57 W
Üçpınar 130 37.08 N 32.16 E
Ucria 70 38.03 N 14.53 E
Üçtepeler ∧ 130 39.39 N 42.41 E
Učterek 85 41.45 N 73.12 E
Úcua ≏ 152 8.35 S 13.40 E
Učujevskij Majdan 80 54.33 N 44.30 E
Učur ≏ 74 58.48 N 130.35 E
Uda ≏, Ross. 88 51.47 N 107.33 E
Uda ≏, Ross. 88 56.05 N 99.34 E
Uda ≏, Ross. 89 54.42 N 135.14 E
Udagamandalam 122 11.24 N 76.42 E
Udaipur 120 24.35 N 73.41 E
Udaj ≏ 78 50.05 N 33.07 E
Udala 126 21.35 N 86.34 E
Udalguri 120 26.46 N 92.08 E
Udall 198 37.23 N 97.06 W
Udamalpet 122 10.35 N 77.15 E
Udankudi 122 8.26 N 78.01 E
Udaquiola 252 36.34 S 58.31 W
Udarnyj 89 49.07 N 142.09 E
Udaypur 124 26.56 N 86.31 E
Udbina 36 44.32 N 15.46 E
Udby 41 55.05 N 11.57 E
Uddeholm 40 60.01 N 13.37 E
Uddel 52 52.15 N 5.46 E
Uddevalla 26 58.21 N 11.55 E
Uddingston 46 55.50 N 4.06 W
Uddjaure ⊜ 24 65.55 N 17.49 E
Udel'naja 82 55.38 N 38.03 E
Udel'naja ◆[8] 265a 60.01 N 30.19 E
Uden 52 51.40 N 5.36 E
Udenhout 52 51.37 N 5.08 E
Uder 56 51.22 N 10.05 E
Üdersdorf 56 50.09 N 6.49 E
Udgīr 122 18.23 N 77.07 E
Udhampur 123 32.56 N 75.08 E
Udhruḥ 132 30.20 N 35.36 E
Udi 150 6.19 N 7.25 E
Udimskij 24 61.09 N 45.52 E
Udine 64 46.03 N 13.14 E
Udine □[4] 64 46.10 N 13.00 E
Udmurtia
— Udmurtija □[3] 80 57.00 N 53.00 E
Udmurtija □[3] 80 57.00 N 53.00 E
Udokan, chrebet ⋌ 88 56.20 N 118.10 E
Udoml'a 76 57.52 N 35.01 E
Udone-jima I 94 34.28 N 139.18 E
Udono 92 33.44 N 136.01 E
Udon Thani 110 17.26 N 102.46 E
Udor, Mount ∧ 162 23.30 S 131.01 E
Udot I 175c 7.23 N 151.43 E
Udskaja guba c 89 54.50 N 135.45 E
Udskoje 89 54.32 N 134.26 E
Udubo 146 11.57 N 10.38 E
Udupi 122 13.21 N 74.45 E
Udy 78 50.24 N 36.03 E
Udyl', ozero ⊜ 89 52.06 N 139.48 E
Udža 74 71.14 N 117.10 E
Udžary 84 40.31 N 47.39 E
Uebigau 54 51.35 N 13.18 E
Uebonti 112 0.55 S 121.38 E
Uebonti, Teluk c 112 0.50 S 121.45 E
Uecker ≏ 54 53.45 N 14.04 E
Ueckeritz 54 54.00 N 14.02 E
Ueckermünde 54 53.44 N 14.03 E
Ueckermünder Heide ◆[3] 54 53.40 N 14.10 E
Ueda 94 36.24 N 138.16 E
Uedem 52 51.40 N 6.16 E
Uedesheim 263 51.10 N 6.48 E
Uegō 268 35.13 N 139.56 E
Ueharu 175d 24.25 N 123.46 E
Uehlfeld 56 49.40 N 10.43 E
Uele ≏ 136 4.09 N 22.26 E
Uelen 180 66.10 N 169.48 W
Uel'kal' 180 65.32 N 179.17 W
Uelsen 52 52.30 N 6.53 E
Uelzen, Dtsch. 52 52.58 N 10.33 E
Uelzen, Dtsch. 263 51.33 N 7.44 E
Ueno, Nihon 94 36.05 N 138.47 E
Ueno, Nihon 94 34.45 N 136.08 E
Ueno, Nihon 270 34.53 N 135.14 E
Uenohara 94 35.37 N 139.07 E
Ueno Park ♦ 268 35.43 N 139.46 E
Uenoshiba 270 34.33 N 135.28 E
Uerdingen ◆[8] 263 51.21 N 6.39 E
Uere ≏ 154 3.42 N 25.24 E
Uetersen 52 53.41 N 9.39 E
Uettingen 56 49.48 N 9.43 E
Uetz 264a 52.28 N 12.56 E
Uetze 52 52.28 N 10.11 E
Ufa 86 54.44 N 55.56 E
Ufa ≏ 86 54.40 N 56.00 E
Ufala, Punta ≻ 70 38.22 N 14.59 E
Uffculme 42 50.54 N 3.20 W
Uffenheim 56 49.32 N 10.14 E
Ufita ≏ 68 41.09 N 14.56 E
Ufra 128 40.00 N 53.02 E
Uft'uga ≏ 76 59.46 N 39.21 E
Ugab ≏ 156 21.08 S 13.40 E
Ugak Bay c 180 57.25 N 152.45 W
Ugāle 76 57.16 N 22.02 E
Ugalla ≏ 154 5.08 S 30.42 E
Ugamskij chrebet ⋌ 85 42.00 N 70.20 E
Uganda □[1] 154 1.00 N 32.00 E
Uganik Island I 180 57.53 N 153.28 W
Ugârčin 38 43.06 N 24.25 E
Ugarit ⊥ 130 35.35 N 35.45 E
Ugashik 180 57.32 N 157.25 W
Ugashik Bay c 180 57.34 N 157.38 W
Ugatkyn ≏ 180 68.24 N 171.30 E
Ugento 68 39.56 N 18.10 E
Ugep 150 5.48 N 8.05 E
Ugerløse 41 55.35 N 11.40 E
Uggiano la Chiesa 68 40.06 N 18.27 E
Ughaybish 140 10.52 N 31.05 E
Ughelli 150 5.29 N 5.59 E
Ugie 158 31.10 S 28.13 E
Ugie ≏ 46 57.30 N 1.47 W
Ugíjar 34 36.57 N 3.03 W
Ugine 62 45.45 N 6.25 E
Uglegorsk, Ross. 89 49.02 N 142.03 E
Uglegorsk, Ukr. 83 48.19 N 38.17 E
Uglekamensk 89 43.13 N 133.11 E
Uglezavodsk 89 47.21 N 142.38 E
Uglič 76 57.32 N 38.19 E
Ugljan, Otok I 36 44.05 N 15.10 E
Uglovaja 80 57.01 N 52.57 E
Uglovka 76 58.14 N 33.31 E
Uglovoje 89 43.20 N 132.06 E
Uglovskoje 86 51.23 N 80.12 E
Ugly-Zavod 78 52.11 N 32.53 E
Ugnev 78 50.23 N 23.44 E
Ugodiči 80 57.10 N 39.30 E
Ugodskij Zavod 82 55.02 N 36.45 E
Ugol'naja, buchta c 180 63.00 N 179.20 E
Ugolnyy 180 62.58 N 179.17 E
Ugoma ∧ 154 4.00 S 28.45 E
Ugovizza 64 46.31 N 13.29 E
Ugra 76 54.47 N 34.17 E
Ugra ≏ 82 54.30 N 36.07 E
Ugrojedy 78 50.52 N 35.17 E
Ugr'umovo 82 55.09 N 37.40 E
Ugtaal Cajdam 88 48.17 N 105.25 E
Uguj 86 56.02 N 76.03 E
Uğurludağ 130 40.27 N 34.28 E
Ug'ut 85 41.24 N 74.50 E

Symbol	English	Deutsch	Español	Français	Português
≏	River	Fluß	Río	Rivière	Rio
≅	Canal	Kanal	Canal	Canal	Canal
L	Waterfall, Rapids	Wasserfall, Stromschnellen	Cascada, Rápidos	Chute d'eau, Rapides	Cascata, Rápidos
⊔	Strait	Meeresstraße	Estrecho	Détroit	Estreito
c	Bay, Gulf	Bucht, Golf	Bahía, Golfo	Baie, Golfe	Baía, Golfo
⊜	Lake, Lakes	See, Seen	Lago, Lagos	Lac, Lacs	Lago, Lagos
≡	Swamp	Sumpf	Pantano	Marais	Pântano
⊓	Ice Features, Glacier	Eis- und Gletscherformen	Accidentes Glaciales	Formes glaciaires	Acidentes glaciares
≈	Other Hydrographic Features	Andere Hydrographische Objekte	Otros Elementos Hidrográficos	Autres données hydrographiques	Outros acidentes hidrográficos

Symbol	English	Deutsch	Español	Français	Português
✣	Submarine Features	Untermeerische Objekte	Accidentes Submarinos	Formes de relief sous-marin	Acidentes submarinos
□	Political Unit	Politische Einheit	Unidad Politica	Entité politique	Unidade política
◉	Cultural Institution	Kulturelle Institution	Institución Cultural	Institution culturelle	Instituição cultural
⊥	Historical Site	Historische Stätte	Sitio Histórico	Site historique	Sitio histórico
♦	Recreational Site	Erholungs- und Ferienort	Sitio de Recreo	Centre de loisirs	Area de Lazer
✈	Airport	Flughafen	Aeropuerto	Aéroport	Aeroporto
■	Military Installation	Militäranlage	Instalación Militar	Installation militaire	Instalação militar
◆	Miscellaneous	Verschiedenes	Misceláneo	Divers	Diversos

Ugyak, Cape > 180 58.17 N 154.04 W
Uh (Už) ≃ 30 48.34 N 22.00 E
Uha-dong 98 40.41 N 125.38 E
Uhayjibah, Jabal al- ʌ 132 30.11 N 34.33 E
Uherčice 61 48.55 N 15.38 E
Uherské Hradiště 30 49.05 N 17.28 E
Uherský Brod 30 49.02 N 17.39 E
Uhingen 56 48.42 N 9.35 E
Úhlava ≃ 60 49.43 N 13.23 E
Uhlenhorst 156 23.45 S 17.55 E
Uhlingen 58 47.43 N 8.19 E
Uhlman Lake ⊜ 184 56.40 N 98.23 W
Uhlstädt 54 50.44 N 11.28 E
Uhrichsville 214 40.23 N 81.20 W
Uhyst, Dtsch. 54 51.11 N 14.13 E
Uhyst, Dtsch. 54 51.24 N 14.30 E
Uiche 152 12.03 S 21.02 E
Ui-do I 98 34.37 N 125.51 E
Uig 46 57.35 N 6.22 W
Uíge 152 7.37 S 15.03 E
Uíge □[5] 152 7.00 S 15.30 E
Ŭijŏngbu 98 37.44 N 127.03 E
Ŭiju 98 40.12 N 124.32 E
Uil 86 49.05 N 54.40 E
Uil ≃ 80 48.36 N 52.30 E
Uilpata, gora ʌ 84 42.48 N 43.48 E
Uimaharju 26 62.55 N 30.15 E
Uinebona ≃ 246 5.04 N 63.01 W
Uinskoje 86 56.53 N 56.35 E
Uinta ≃ 200 40.14 N 109.51 W
Uintah and Ouray Indian Reservation ◆[4] 200 40.20 N 110.20 W
Uinta Mountains ⋏ 200 40.45 N 110.05 W
Uiraúna 250 6.31 S 38.25 W
Uis 156 21.08 S 14.49 E
Ŭisŏng 98 36.22 N 128.41 E
Uitenhage 158 33.40 S 25.28 E
Uitgeest 52 52.32 N 4.43 E
Uithoorn 52 52.14 N 4.50 E
Uithuizen 52 53.24 N 6.40 E
Uithuizermeeden 52 53.24 N 6.42 E
Uitspanning 158 26.46 S 29.56 E
Uj ≃, Asia 86 54.17 N 64.58 E
Uj ≃, Ross. 86 57.06 N 74.12 E
Ujae I[1] 14 9.05 N 165.40 E
Ujaly 86 44.37 N 60.57 E
Ujandina ≃ 74 68.23 N 145.50 E
Ujar 86 55.48 N 94.20 E
Ujarrás ⊥ 236 9.51 N 83.50 W
Ujedinenija, ostrov I 72 77.28 N 82.28 E
Ujelang I[1] 14 9.49 N 160.55 E
Ujemskij 24 64.29 N 40.50 E
Újezd, Česko. 54 50.03 N 14.44 E
Újezd, Česko. 60 49.26 N 13.27 E
Újezd u Brna 61 49.06 N 16.45 E
Újfehértó 30 47.48 N 21.40 E
Ujgursaj 85 40.53 N 71.03 E
Ujhāni 124 28.01 N 79.01 E
Uji 96 34.53 N 135.48 E
Uji ≃ 96 34.53 N 135.42 E
Uji-guntō II 92 31.11 N 129.27 E
Ujiie 94 36.41 N 139.58 E
Ujiji 154 4.55 S 29.41 E
Uji-tawara 96 34.51 N 135.52 E
Uji-yamada → Ise 94 34.29 N 136.42 E
Ujjain 120 23.11 N 75.46 E
Újkér 61 47.28 N 16.49 E
'Ujmān 128 25.25 N 55.27 E
Újpest ◆[8] 264c 47.34 N 19.06 E
Ujście 30 53.04 N 16.43 E
Ujskoje 86 54.22 N 60.00 E
Ujum 85 38.22 N 70.51 E
Ujung 112 7.04 S 120.46 E
Ujungbatu 114 0.43 N 100.31 E
Ujungbatu, Pulau I 114 2.20 N 97.24 E
Ujungberung 115a 6.55 S 107.42 E
Ujunggading 110 0.16 N 99.33 E
Ujunggenteng 115a 7.22 S 106.24 E
Ujungkulon, Semenanjung >[1] 115a 6.45 S 105.20 E
Ujungkulon National Park ♦ 115a 6.40 S 105.20 E
Ujunglamuru 112 4.40 S 119.58 E
Ujungpandang (Makasar) 112 5.07 S 119.24 E
Újvidék → Novi Sad 38 45.15 N 19.50 E
Uk 88 55.04 N 98.52 E
Uka, Nihon 174m 26.48 N 128.14 E
Uka, Ross. 74 57.50 N 162.06 E
Ukamas 158 28.02 S 19.45 E
Ukara Island I 154 1.50 S 33.03 E
Ukerewe Island I 154 2.03 S 33.00 E
Ukhayḍir, Wādī V 132 30.55 N 37.01 E
Ukhra 126 23.39 N 87.14 E
Ukhrul 120 25.07 N 94.22 E
Ukhta → Uchta 24 63.33 N 53.38 E
Ukiah, Ca., U.S. 204 39.09 N 123.12 W
Ukiah, Or., U.S. 202 45.08 N 118.55 W
Ukibaru-jima I 174m 26.18 N 128.00 E
Ukiha 96 33.19 N 130.47 E
Uki Ni Masi Island I 175e 10.15 S 161.45 E
Ukmergė 76 55.15 N 24.45 E
Ukolnoi Island I 180 55.14 N 161.34 W
Ukraina → Ukraine □[1] 22 49.00 N 32.00 E
Ukraine □[1], Europe 22 49.00 N 32.00 E
Ukraine □[1], Europe 78 49.00 N 32.00 E
Ukrainka 86 54.39 N 71.20 E
Ukrainsk 83 48.06 N 37.18 E
Ukrina ≃ 36 45.05 N 17.56 E
Uks'anskoje 86 55.57 N 63.01 E
Uktuz 86 55.38 N 68.30 E
Uktym 24 62.38 N 48.52 E
Uku 152 11.24 S 14.15 E
Ukui 112 0.09 S 102.11 E
Ukurejskij 88 52.24 N 116.49 E
Ukuti 154 3.39 N 33.32 E
Ukyō ◆[8] 270 35.03 N 135.42 E
Ukyr 88 49.28 N 108.52 E
Ula, India 272b 22.43 N 88.33 E
Ula, Tür. 130 37.05 N 28.26 E
Ulaanbaatar 88 47.55 N 106.53 E
Ulaanbaatar □[8] 88 47.55 N 106.53 E
Ulaanbadrach 102 44.07 N 110.11 E
Ulaan Chus 86 49.02 N 89.23 E
Ulaangom 86 49.58 N 92.02 E
Ulaan nuur ⊜ 102 44.30 N 103.35 E
Ulaan Tajga ⋏ 88 50.45 N 98.30 E
Ula-Chuduk 80 47.39 N 45.34 E
Ulak Island I 181a 51.22 N 179.00 W
Ulakmedan 114 2.43 N 99.38 E
Ulamba 152 9.07 S 23.40 E
Ulamona 164 5.00 S 151.15 E
Ulan, Austl. 166 32.17 S 149.44 E
Ulan, Zhg. 102 36.59 N 98.26 E
Ulan Bator → Ulaanbaatar 88 47.55 N 106.53 E
Ulanbel' 86 44.48 N 71.10 E
Ulan Buh Shamo ◆[2] 102 40.00 N 106.30 E
Ulan-Burgasy, chrebet ⋏ 88 52.45 N 109.00 E
Ulan-Erge 80 46.19 N 44.53 E
Ulang ≃ 236 14.27 N 83.14 W
Ulanhot → Horqin Youyi Qianqi 89 46.05 N 122.05 E
Ulānia 126 22.12 N 90.29 E
Ulanov 78 49.42 N 28.08 E
Ulanovo 78 51.46 N 34.18 E
Ulanovskij 82 54.04 N 37.51 E
Ulanów 30 50.30 N 22.16 E
Ulansuhai Nur ⊜ 102 40.56 N 108.49 E
Ulan-Ude 88 51.50 N 107.37 E
Ulan Ul Hu ⊜ 120 34.45 N 90.25 E
Ulan-Ušotej 88 50.45 N 105.29 E
Ular, Pulau I 271c 1.14 N 103.45 E
Ulaş 130 39.27 N 37.03 E
Ul'ašovo 24 65.27 N 56.57 E
Ulatis Creek ≃ 226 38.18 N 121.00 W
Ul'atuj 88 51.09 N 116.14 E
Ulawa Island I 175e 9.46 S 161.57 E
Ulawun, Mount ʌ 164 5.03 S 151.20 E
Ulaya 154 7.04 S 36.54 E
Ułazów 30 50.17 N 23.00 E
Ul'ba 86 50.16 N 83.22 E
Ul'banskij zaliv c 89 53.45 N 137.50 E
Ulchin 98 36.59 N 129.23 E
Ul'chun-Partija 88 49.56 N 112.46 E
Ulcinj 38 41.55 N 19.11 E
Ulco 158 28.21 S 24.15 E
Ulcombe 260 51.12 N 0.39 E
Ulcumayo 248 11.01 S 75.55 W
Uldum 41 55.51 N 9.36 E
Uldz ≃ 88 49.56 N 115.31 E
Uleåborg → Oulu 26 65.01 N 25.28 E
Ulefoss 26 59.17 N 9.16 E
Ulen 198 47.04 N 96.15 W
Ulety 88 51.22 N 112.29 E
Ulfborg 26 56.16 N 8.20 E
Ulft 52 51.54 N 6.23 E
Ulgueira 266c 38.47 N 9.28 W
Ulhās ≃ 272c 19.13 N 73.01 E
Ulhāsnagar 122 19.13 N 73.07 E
Uliast 86 48.57 N 91.17 E
Uliastaj (Džavchlant) 88 47.45 N 96.49 E
Úlice 60 49.45 N 13.09 E
Ulindi ≃ 154 1.40 S 25.52 E
Ulingan 164 4.30 S 145.25 E
Ulithi I[1] 108 9.58 N 139.40 E
Ulja 74 58.51 N 141.50 E
Uljanino 82 55.21 N 38.26 E
Uljanovka, Ross. 76 59.38 N 30.46 E
Uljanovka, Ukr. 78 48.20 N 30.13 E
Uljanovka, Ukr. 78 50.58 N 34.18 E
Uljanovo, Ross. 76 53.43 N 35.32 E
Uljanovo, Uzb. 85 40.07 N 68.30 E
Uljanovsk 80 54.20 N 48.24 E
Uljanovsk Oblast' □[4] 80 53.30 N 47.30 E
Uljanovskoje, Kaz. 86 50.02 N 73.42 E
Uljanovskoje, Ross. 89 46.17 N 142.13 E
Uljuan tekojärvi ⊜ 26 64.19 N 25.57 E
Ul'kajak ≃ 86 48.54 N 62.00 E
Ul'kan 88 57.14 N 107.19 E
Ul'kan ≃ 88 55.53 N 107.45 E
Ul'ken-Karoj, ozero ⊜ 86 54.00 N 71.58 E
Ulla 76 55.14 N 29.15 E
Ulla ≃, Bela. 76 55.14 N 29.14 E
Ulla ≃, Esp. 34 42.39 N 8.44 W
Ulladulla 170 35.21 S 150.29 E
Ulladulla Head > 170 35.22 S 150.30 E
Ullāpāra 126 24.19 N 89.34 E
Ullapool 46 57.54 N 5.10 W
Ullastrell 266d 41.31 N 1.58 E
Üllendahl ◆[8] 263 51.19 N 7.18 E
Ullerslev 41 55.22 N 10.40 E
Ullervad 40 58.40 N 13.52 E
Ullin 194 37.17 N 89.11 W
Üllő 264c 47.23 N 19.21 E
Ullswater ⊜ 44 54.34 N 2.54 W
Ullučaj ≃ 84 42.18 N 48.08 E
Ullŭng-do I 92 37.29 N 130.52 E
Ullvettern ⊜ 40 59.27 N 14.16 E
Ullvi 40 59.42 N 16.37 E
Ulm, Dtsch. 58 48.24 N 10.00 E
Ulm, Mt., U.S. 202 47.25 N 111.30 W
Ulma 38 47.53 N 25.18 E
Ul'ma ≃ 89 51.54 N 129.18 E
Ulmarra 166 29.37 S 153.02 E
Ulmen 56 50.13 N 6.59 E
Ulmeni 38 45.04 N 26.39 E
Ulmer, Mount ʌ 9 77.35 S 86.09 W
Ulmeu-Meisereich 56 50.13 N 6.58 E
Ulongué 154 14.37 S 34.19 E
Ulpur 126 23.04 N 89.50 E
Ulricehamn 26 57.47 N 13.25 E
Ulrichskirchen 61 48.24 N 16.29 E
Ulrichstein 56 50.34 N 9.11 E
Ulrum 52 53.22 N 6.20 E
Ulsan 98 35.34 N 129.19 E
Ulsta 46a 60.30 N 1.09 W
Ulsteinvik 26 62.20 N 5.53 E
Ulster 210 41.51 N 76.30 W
Ulster □[6] 210 41.56 N 74.00 W
Ulster □[9] 48 54.35 N 7.00 W
Ulster ≃ 56 50.51 N 9.59 E
Ulster Canal ≍ 48 54.08 N 7.22 W
Ultimo, Val d' V 64 46.35 N 11.00 E
Ultraoriental, Cordillera (Serra do Divisor) ⋏ 248 8.20 S 73.30 W
Ulu, Indon. 112 2.45 N 125.24 E
Ulu, Ross. 74 60.19 N 127.24 E
Ulu, Sūd. 140 10.43 N 33.29 E
Ulúa ≃ 236 15.53 N 87.44 W
Ulubāria 126 22.28 N 88.06 E
Ulubat Gölü ⊜ 130 40.10 N 28.35 E
Ulubey, Tür. 130 38.25 N 29.18 E
Ulubey, Tür. 130 40.53 N 37.43 E
Uluborlu 130 38.05 N 30.28 E
Uluçınar 130 36.27 N 35.51 E
Uludağ ʌ 130 40.04 N 29.13 E
Uludāngar 272b 22.51 N 88.31 E
Uludere 128 37.27 N 42.51 E
Ulugan Bay c 116 10.07 N 118.47 E
Ulugqat 85 39.48 N 74.21 E
Uluinggalau ʌ 175g 16.54 S 179.59 E
Ulujul ≃ 86 57.46 N 85.30 E
Ulukışla, Kıbrıs 130 35.13 N 33.37 E
Ulukışla, Tür. 130 37.33 N 34.30 E
Ulul I 14 8.35 N 149.40 E
Ulu Laho, Bukit ʌ 114 5.43 N 101.27 E
Ulunchan 88 54.51 N 111.02 E
Ulundi 158 28.17 S 31.26 E
Ulunga 89 46.31 N 136.56 E
Ulungur ≃ 86 46.59 N 87.27 E
Ulungur Hu ⊜ 86 47.15 N 87.20 E
Ulurijskij Golec, gora ʌ 88 50.12 N 111.45 E
Uluru National Park ♦ 162 25.20 S 131.00 E
Ulus 130 41.35 N 32.39 E
Ulusara 126 24.16 N 90.36 E
Ulut ≃ 116 12.00 N 125.27 E
Ulutau 86 48.39 N 67.01 E
Ulutau, gora ʌ 86 48.39 N 66.56 E
Ulutau, gory ⋏ 86 49.00 N 67.00 E
Ulu Tiram 114 1.36 N 103.49 E
Ulu Yam 114 3.27 N 101.38 E
Ulva 272c 18.59 N 73.02 E
Ulva I 46 56.29 N 6.14 W
Ulvenhout 52 51.34 N 4.48 E
Ulverston 44 54.12 N 3.06 W
Ulverstone 166 41.09 S 146.10 E
Ulvöarna II 26 63.01 N 18.40 E
Ulvshale >[1] 41 55.02 N 12.16 E
Ulvshyttan 40 60.18 N 15.22 E
Ulvsund)(41 54.59 N 12.11 E
Ulyanovsk → Uljanovsk 80 54.20 N 48.24 E
Ulysses, Ks., U.S. 198 37.34 N 101.21 W
Ulysses, Ne., U.S. 198 41.04 N 97.12 W
Ulysses, Pa., U.S. 214 41.54 N 77.46 W
Uly-Žilanšik ≃ 86 48.51 N 63.47 E
Ulzë 38 41.41 N 19.54 E
Uma 89 52.36 N 120.37 E
Umag 36 45.25 N 13.32 E
Umaji 96 33.33 N 134.03 E
Umal'tinskij 89 51.56 N 133.36 E
Umán, Méx. 232 20.53 N 89.45 W
Uman', Ukr. 78 48.44 N 30.14 E
Uman I 175c 7.18 N 151.53 E
Umanak 176 70.40 N 52.07 W
Umanak Fjord c[2] 176 70.55 N 53.00 W
Umancevo 80 47.44 N 44.16 E
'Umān → Oman □[1] 118 22.00 N 58.00 E
Umargāon 122 20.12 N 72.45 E
Umari 250 6.38 S 38.42 W
Umari ≃ 248 7.05 S 64.34 W
'Umarī, Qā' al- ⊜ 132 31.42 N 36.57 E
Umaria 124 23.32 N 80.50 E
Umarizal 250 5.59 S 37.49 W
Umarkot 120 25.22 N 69.44 E
Umatac 174p 13.18 N 144.39 E
Umatilla, Fl., U.S. 220 28.55 N 81.39 W
Umatilla, Or., U.S. 202 45.55 N 119.20 W
Umatilla ≃ 202 45.55 N 119.20 W
Umatilla, Lake ⊜[1] 202 45.44 N 120.35 W
Umatilla Indian Reservation ◆[4] 202 45.41 N 118.31 W
Umayan ≃ 116 8.13 N 125.50 E
Umaze 270 34.57 N 135.03 E
Umba 24 66.41 N 34.15 E
Umbagog Lake ⊜ 188 44.45 N 71.05 W
Umbai 114 2.10 N 102.20 E
Umbaúba 250 11.22 S 37.39 W
Umbelasha ≃ 140 9.51 N 24.50 E
Umbertide 66 43.18 N 12.20 E
Umbogintwini 158 30.00 S 30.58 E
Umboi Island I 164 5.36 S 148.00 E
Umbrail, Pass (Giogo di Santa Maria))(64 46.34 N 10.25 E
Umbria □[4] 66 43.00 N 12.30 E
Umbriatico 68 39.21 N 16.55 E
Umbroli 272c 19.11 N 73.06 E
Umbukul 164 2.30 S 150.00 E
Umbuzero, ozero ⊜ 24 67.43 N 34.25 E
Ume ≃ 154 16.40 S 28.26 E
Umeå 26 63.50 N 20.15 E
Umeälven ≃ 24 63.47 N 20.16 E
Umedani 270 34.44 N 135.51 E
Umedpur 126 22.31 N 89.59 E
Umfolozi Game Reserve ◆[4] 158 28.19 S 31.50 E
Umfors 24 65.56 N 15.00 E
Umfreville Lake ⊜ 184 50.18 N 94.45 W
Umfuli ≃ 154 17.30 S 29.23 E
Umgungundhlovu ⊥ 158 28.27 S 31.28 E
Umguza 154 19.25 S 27.51 E
Umhausen 64 47.08 N 10.56 E
Umhlanga Rocks 158 29.43 S 31.06 E
Umi 96 33.34 N 130.30 E
Umingan 116 15.56 N 120.50 E
Umkomaas 158 30.15 S 30.42 E
Umm ad-Daraj, Jabal ʌ 132 32.19 N 35.48 E
Umm 'Ajārim ≗[8] 142 30.50 N 32.49 E
Umm al-Abīd 146 27.31 N 15.02 E
Umm al-'Arā'is, Wādī V 146 26.26 N 13.55 E
Umm al-Arānib 146 26.08 N 14.45 E
Umm al-Birak 128 23.25 N 39.13 E
Umm al-Ḥawāyā, Jabal ʌ 142 28.41 N 31.06 E
Umm al-Jimāl, Khirbat ⊥ 132 32.20 N 36.22 E
Umm al-Khashab 144 17.21 N 42.32 E
Umm al-Qaywayn 128 25.35 N 55.34 E
Umm al-Qiṭṭayn 132 32.19 N 36.38 E
Umm al-Quṣūr 142 27.23 N 30.54 E
Ummanz 54 54.28 N 13.10 E
Umm Artah, Wādī V 142 28.41 N 32.37 E
Umm as-Sa'd ⊥ 132 33.16 N 36.47 E
Umm Badr 140 14.14 N 27.57 E
Umm Balad, Wādī V 142 27.40 N 32.39 E
Umm Bayyū'd 140 12.05 N 31.40 E
Umm Bel 140 13.32 N 28.04 E
Umm Boim 140 11.43 N 25.57 E
Umm Dabbī 140 14.37 N 30.23 E
Umm Dam 140 13.45 N 30.59 E
Umm Dhibbān, Sūd. 140 14.14 N 29.37 E
Umm Dhibbān, Sūd. 140 15.26 N 32.51 E
Umm Digulgulaya 140 10.29 N 24.57 E
Umm Dīnār 142 30.12 N 31.04 E
Umm Durmān (Omdurman) 140 15.38 N 32.30 E
Umm el Faḥm 132 32.31 N 35.09 E
Ummeln 52 51.58 N 8.27 E
Ummendorf 54 52.09 N 11.11 E
Umm Habwah, Jabal ʌ[2] 142 27.23 N 31.29 E
Umm Ḥamāṭ 132 31.02 N 35.46 E
Umm Jamālah 140 11.27 N 28.12 E
Umm Kaddādah 140 13.36 N 26.42 E
Umm Khunān 273c 29.55 N 31.15 E
Umm Khushayb, Wādī V 142 30.24 N 32.43 E
Umm Kuwaykah 140 13.00 N 32.17 E
Umm Lajj 128 25.04 N 37.13 E
Umm Marahik, Jabal ʌ[2] 140 13.40 N 26.53 E
Umm Mirdi 140 18.59 N 33.32 E
Umm Mitmān ≗[8] 142 30.41 N 32.30 E
Umm Qantur 140 14.17 N 31.22 E
Umm Qaṣr 128 30.02 N 47.56 E
Umm Qurayn 140 9.58 N 28.55 E
Umm Quṣayr 132 31.40 N 35.53 E
Umm Raqm, Jabal ʌ 142 30.14 N 31.52 E
Umm Rīshah, Birkat ⊜ 142 30.21 N 30.22 E
Umm Rumaylah ⫧[4] 140 16.55 N 31.40 E
Umm Ruwābah 140 12.54 N 31.13 E
Umm Saggāt, Wādī V 140 15.15 N 23.12 E
Umm Saysabān, Jabal ʌ 132 29.45 N 35.10 E
Umm Sayyālah 140 14.25 N 31.10 E
Umm Shalīl 140 10.51 N 23.42 E
Umm Shanqah 140 13.14 N 27.14 E
Umm Shuṭūr 140 7.17 N 33.14 E
Umm Sidr, Wādī V 142 27.54 N 32.33 E
Umm Sughra ⫧[4] 140 15.03 N 27.12 E
Umm 'Umayd, Ra's ʌ 142 27.50 N 32.19 E
Umm 'Umayyid, Bi'r ⫧[4] 142 27.53 N 32.30 E
Umm 'Umayyid, Wādī V 142 27.37 N 32.41 E
Umm Urūmah I 128 25.46 N 36.32 E
Umm Walad 132 32.39 N 36.26 E
Umm Zaytah, Jabal ʌ[2] 142 29.49 N 32.16 E
Umnak 180 53.17 N 168.20 W
Umnak Island I 180 53.25 N 168.10 W
Umnak Pass)(180 53.20 N 167.45 W
Umnäs 24 65.24 N 16.10 E
Umniati 154 18.39 S 29.49 E
Umniati ≃ 154 17.30 S 29.23 E
Um'ot, Ross. 80 54.08 N 42.42 E
Um'ot, Ross. 80 52.31 N 42.58 E
Umpferstedt 54 50.59 N 11.25 E
Umpqua ≃ 202 43.42 N 124.03 W
Umpulo 152 12.38 S 17.42 E
'Umrān 144 15.50 N 43.56 E
'Umrānī, Wādī al- V 142 27.37 N 30.53 E
Umraniye 130 39.10 N 31.15 E
Umraniye ◆[8] 267b 41.01 N 29.05 E
Umred 122 20.51 N 79.20 E
Umreth 120 22.42 N 73.07 E
Umsini, Gunung ʌ 164 1.22 S 133.45 E
Ŭmsŏng 98 36.56 N 127.41 E
Umstead State Park ♦ 192 35.52 N 78.47 W
Umtanum Creek ≃ 224 46.52 N 120.35 W
Umtata 158 31.35 S 28.47 E
Umtentweni 158 30.42 S 30.28 E
Umuahia 150 5.33 N 7.29 E
Umuarama 255 23.45 S 53.20 W
Umurbey 130 40.14 N 26.36 E
Umurlu 130 37.50 N 27.58 E
Umzimkulu 158 30.16 S 29.56 E
Umzingwani ≃ 154 22.12 S 29.56 E
Umzinto 158 30.22 S 30.33 E
Una, Bra. 255 15.18 S 39.04 W
Una, India 120 20.49 N 71.02 E
Una, India 123 31.29 N 76.17 E
Una ≃ 36 45.16 N 16.55 E
Una, Mount ʌ 172 42.13 S 172.35 E
Una, Ribeirão ≃ 287b 23.31 S 46.18 W
Unac ≃ 36 44.30 N 16.09 E
Uña de Gato 196 25.58 N 99.41 W
Unadilla, Ga., U.S. 192 32.15 N 83.44 W
Unadilla, N.Y., U.S. 210 42.19 N 75.18 W
Unadilla ≃ 210 42.20 N 75.25 W
Unaí 255 16.23 S 46.53 W
Unakami 94 35.46 N 140.45 E
Unalakleet 180 63.53 N 160.47 W
Unalaska 180 53.52 N 166.32 W
Unalaska Island I 180 53.45 N 166.45 W
Unanderra 170 34.27 S 150.52 E
Unango 154 12.50 S 35.20 E
Únanov 61 48.54 N 16.04 E
Unao 124 25.35 N 78.36 E
Unare ≃ 246 10.03 N 65.14 W
Unauna, Pulau I 112 0.10 S 121.35 E
Unayyir, Ḥarrat al- ≗[9] 128 25.20 N 37.45 E
'Unayzah, Ar. Su. 128 26.06 N 43.56 E
'Unayzah, Urd. 132 30.29 N 35.48 E
'Unayzah, Jabal ʌ, Asia 128 32.12 N 39.18 E
'Unayzah, Jabal ʌ, Urd. 132 30.30 N 35.47 E
Unazuki 94 36.49 N 137.35 E
Uncasville 207 41.26 N 72.06 W
Unchahra 124 24.23 N 80.47 E
Ŭnch'ŏn 98 38.34 N 125.26 E
Uncia 248 18.27 S 66.37 W
Uncompahgre ≃ 200 38.45 N 108.06 W
Uncompahgre Peak ʌ 200 38.04 N 107.28 W
Uncompahgre Plateau ⋏[1] 200 38.30 N 108.25 W
Uncukul' 84 42.42 N 46.48 E
Uncular 130 40.28 N 41.28 E
Unda 88 51.42 N 116.56 E
Unda ≃ 88 51.25 N 116.05 E
Unden ⊜ 40 58.47 N 14.26 E
Undenäs 40 58.39 N 14.25 E
Underberg 158 29.50 S 29.22 E
Under River 260 51.15 N 0.14 E
Undersåker 26 63.20 N 13.23 E
Underwood, In., U.S. 218 38.36 N 85.46 W
Underwood, N.D., U.S. 198 47.27 N 101.08 W
Underwood, Wa., U.S. 224 45.43 N 121.31 W
Undløse 41 55.36 N 11.35 E
Undory 80 54.37 N 48.25 E
Undu, Tanjung > 115b 10.05 S 120.51 E
Undu Point > 175g 16.08 S 179.57 W
Undva nina > 76 58.32 N 21.55 E
Unea Island I 164 4.55 S 149.10 E
Uneča 76 52.50 N 32.40 E
Uneča ≃ 76 52.50 N 31.56 E
Uneiuxi ≃ 246 0.34 S 64.58 W
Úněšov 60 49.53 N 13.09 E
Unga Island I 180 55.15 N 160.45 W
Ungama Bay c 154 2.45 S 40.20 E
Ungaran 115a 7.07 S 110.24 E
Ungarie 166 33.38 S 146.58 E
Ungarn → Hungary □[1] 30 47.00 N 20.00 E
Ungava, Péninsule d' >[1] 176 60.00 N 74.00 W
Ungava Bay c 176 59.30 N 67.30 W
Ungch'ŏn 98 35.07 N 128.44 E
Ungen' 78 47.12 N 27.48 E
Unggi 98 42.20 N 130.24 E
Ungurkuj 88 50.27 N 106.58 E
Ungvár → Užgorod 78 48.37 N 22.18 E
Unhos 266c 38.50 N 9.07 W
Unhošť 54 50.04 N 14.08 E
Uni 80 57.46 N 51.30 E
União 250 4.35 S 42.52 W
União da Vitória 252 26.13 S 51.05 W
União dos Palmares 250 9.10 S 36.02 W
Unica 24 62.38 N 34.38 E
Unicoi 192 36.11 N 82.20 W
Unicorn Branch ≃ 208 39.15 N 75.52 W
Unidad Santa Fe ◆[8] 286a 19.23 N 99.15 W
Uniejów 30 51.58 N 18.49 E
Unieux 62 45.24 N 4.16 E
Unije, Otok I 36 44.38 N 14.15 E
Unimak Island I 180 54.50 N 164.00 W
Unimak Pass)(180 54.35 N 164.43 W
Unini ≃ 246 1.41 S 61.31 W
Unión, Arg. 252 35.09 S 65.57 W
Union, On., Can. 212 42.42 N 81.12 W
Unión, C.R. 236 8.36 N 83.03 W
Unión, Para. 252 24.48 S 56.33 W
Union, Il., U.S. 216 42.14 N 88.33 W
Union, Ia., U.S. 190 42.14 N 93.03 W
Union, Ky., U.S. 218 38.56 N 84.40 W
Union, La., U.S. 194 30.06 N 90.54 W
Union, Ms., U.S. 194 32.34 N 89.07 W
Union, Mo., U.S. 219 38.26 N 91.00 W
Union, N.J., U.S. 210 40.41 N 74.15 W
Union, Oh., U.S. 218 39.53 N 84.18 W
Union, Or., U.S. 202 45.12 N 117.51 W
Union, S.C., U.S. 192 34.42 N 81.37 W
Union, Wa., U.S. 224 47.21 N 123.06 W
Union, W.V., U.S. 192 37.35 N 80.32 W
Union □[6], In., U.S. 218 39.38 N 84.56 W
Union □[6], N.J., U.S. 208 40.40 N 74.11 W
Union □[6], Oh., U.S. 214 40.18 N 83.19 W
Union □[6], Pa., U.S. 210 40.58 N 76.54 W
Unión ◆[8] 258 34.53 S 56.08 W
Union Bay 182 49.35 N 124.53 W
Union Beach 208 40.26 N 74.10 W
Union Bridge 208 39.34 N 77.10 W
Union Center 210 42.09 N 76.04 W
Union City, Ca., U.S. 226 37.35 N 122.04 W
Union City, Ga., U.S. 192 33.35 N 84.32 W
Union City, In., U.S. 194 40.07 N 85.05 W
Union City, Mi., U.S. 216 42.04 N 85.09 W
Union City, N.J., U.S. 276 40.46 N 74.01 W
Union City, Oh., U.S. 216 40.11 N 84.48 W
Union City, Pa., U.S. 214 41.53 N 79.50 W
Union City, Tn., U.S. 194 36.25 N 89.03 W
Union City Dam ◆[6] 214 41.55 N 79.54 W
Uniondale, S. Afr. 158 33.40 S 23.08 E
Uniondale, In., U.S. 216 40.50 N 85.15 W
Uniondale, N.Y., U.S. 276 40.42 N 73.35 W
Union Dale, Pa., U.S. 210 41.43 N 75.30 W
Unión de Reyes 240p 22.48 N 81.32 W
Unión de San Antonio 234 21.06 N 101.58 W
Union des Émirats Arabes → United Arab Emirates □[1] 128 24.00 N 54.00 E
Unión de Tula 234 19.58 N 104.16 W
Union Flat Creek ≃ 202 46.50 N 117.59 W
Union Gap 202 46.33 N 120.28 W
Union Grove, Tx., U.S. 222 32.34 N 94.55 W
Union Grove, Wi., U.S. 216 42.41 N 88.03 W
Unión Hidalgo 234 16.28 N 94.50 W
Union Hill 210 43.13 N 77.23 W
Union Lake 216 42.36 N 83.26 W
Union Lake ⊜, Mi., U.S. 216 42.03 N 85.11 W
Union Lake ⊜, Mi., U.S. 281 42.37 N 83.26 W
Union Lake ⊜, N.J., U.S. 208 39.25 N 75.03 W
Union Mills 216 41.29 N 86.46 W
Union Park 220 28.30 N 81.15 W
Union Pier 216 41.49 N 86.41 W
Union Point 192 33.36 N 83.04 W
Unionport, In., U.S. 218 40.07 N 85.06 W
Unionport, Oh., U.S. 214 40.21 N 80.51 W
Union Seamount ◆[3] 16 49.35 N 132.45 W
Union Springs, Al., U.S. 194 32.08 N 85.42 W
Union Springs, N.Y., U.S. 210 42.50 N 76.41 W
Union Station ◆[5], On., Can. 275b 43.39 N 79.23 W

ENGLISH Name	Page	Lat.°'	Long.°'	DEUTSCH Name	Seite	Breite°'	Länge°' E = Ost

Union Station ◆[5], Ca., U.S. 280 34.04 N 118.14 W
Union Station ◆[5], D.C., U.S. 284c 38.54 N 77.00 W
Union Station ◆[5], Il., U.S. 278 41.53 N 87.38 W
Uniontown, Al., U.S. 194 32.26 N 87.30 W
Uniontown, Ky., U.S. 194 37.46 N 87.55 W
Uniontown, Md., U.S. 208 39.35 N 77.06 W
Uniontown, Oh., U.S. 214 40.58 N 81.24 W
Uniontown, Pa., U.S. 188 39.54 N 79.44 W
Union Valley Reservoir ⊜[1] 226 38.50 N 120.26 W
Union Village 207 41.59 N 71.32 W
Unionville, On., Can. 275b 43.52 N 79.18 W
Unionville, Ct., U.S. 207 41.45 N 72.53 W
Unionville, In., U.S. 218 39.14 N 86.25 W
Unionville, Mi., U.S. 190 43.39 N 83.27 W
Unionville, Mo., U.S. 194 40.28 N 93.00 W
Unionville, N.J., U.S. 285 40.01 N 74.46 W
Unionville, N.Y., U.S. 210 41.18 N 74.34 W
Unionville, Oh., U.S. 214 41.47 N 81.00 W
Unionville, Pa., U.S. 285 39.54 N 75.44 W
Unionville Center 214 40.08 N 83.21 W
Uniopolis 216 40.36 N 84.05 W
Unipouheos Indian Reserve ◆[4] 184 53.52 N 110.21 W
Unisan 116 13.51 N 121.59 E
United 214 40.13 N 79.29 W
United Arab Emirates (Al-Imārāt al-'Arabīyah al-Muttaḥidah) □[1], Asia 118 24.00 N 54.00 E
United Arab Emirates (Al-Imārāt al-'Arabīyah al-Muttaḥidah) □[1], Asia 128 24.00 N 54.00 E
United Arab Republic → Egypt □[1] 140 27.00 N 30.00 E
United Kingdom □[1], Europe 22 54.00 N 2.00 W
United Kingdom □[1], Europe 28 54.00 N 2.00 W
United Kingdom Sovereign Base Area ■ 130 35.00 N 33.45 E
United Nations Headquarters ʋ 276 40.45 N 73.58 W
United States □[1] 178 38.00 N 97.00 W
United States Air Force Academy ■ 200 39.00 N 104.55 W
United States Coast Guard Academy ■ 207 41.22 N 72.06 W
United States Merchant Marine Academy ʋ[2] 276 40.48 N 73.46 W
United States Military Academy ■ 210 41.23 N 73.58 W
United States Naval Academy ■ 208 38.59 N 76.30 W
United States Steel Corporation (Lorain Plant) ʋ[3], Oh., U.S. 279a 41.27 N 82.07 W
United States Steel Corporation ʋ[3], Pa., U.S. 279b 40.20 N 79.54 W
United States Steel Corporation ʋ[3], Pa., U.S. 279b 40.25 N 79.54 W
United States Steel Corporation Fairless Works ʋ[3] 285 40.09 N 74.45 W
Unity 184 52.27 N 109.10 W
Unity Reservoir ⊜[1] 279b 40.17 N 79.30 W
Universal City 196 29.32 N 98.17 W
Universal City ʋ[3] 280 34.09 N 118.21 W
Universal Mall ◆[9] 281 42.30 N 83.05 W
Università Degli Studi ʋ[2] 266b 45.28 N 9.14 E
Universitaria, Ciudad ʋ[2] 266d 41.23 N 2.08 E
University 194 34.21 N 89.32 W
University City 219 38.39 N 90.19 W
University Gardens 276 40.46 N 73.43 W
University Heights, Ca., U.S. 226 37.26 N 122.12 W
University Heights, Oh., U.S. 279a 41.29 N 81.32 W
University Park, Il., U.S. 216 41.36 N 87.39 W
University Park, Md., U.S. 284c 38.58 N 76.57 W
University Park, N.M., U.S. 200 32.06 N 106.39 W
University Park, Tx., U.S. 222 32.52 N 96.47 W
University Place 224 47.14 N 122.32 W
University View 218 40.00 N 83.03 W
Unjha 120 23.48 N 72.24 E
Unkel 56 50.35 N 7.13 E
Unken 64 47.39 N 12.43 E
Unkurda 86 55.48 N 59.24 E
Unley 168b 34.57 S 138.35 E
Unna 52 51.32 N 7.41 E
'Unnāb, Jabal al- ʌ 132 29.57 N 36.55 E
'Unnāb, Wādī al- V 132 30.11 N 36.39 E
Unnão 124 26.32 N 80.30 E
Uno, Canal Numero ≍ 252 36.17 S 57.08 W
Uno, Ilha I 150 11.12 N 16.15 W
Unoke 94 36.43 N 136.42 E
Ŭnp'a 98 38.26 N 125.45 E
Unpenji-san ʌ 96 34.02 N 133.44 E
Unqua Point > 276 40.39 N 73.26 W
Unquillo 252 31.14 S 64.19 W
Ŭnsan 98 39.25 N 126.01 E
Unseburg 54 51.56 N 11.30 E
Unserfrau → Madonna 64 46.43 N 10.52 E
Unsleben 56 50.22 N 10.15 E
Unst I 46a 60.45 N 0.53 W
Unstrut ≃ 54 51.10 N 11.48 E
Un't 88 49.07 N 102.50 E
Unten 174m 26.41 N 128.00 E
Unterägeri 58 47.08 N 8.35 E
Unterbach, Dtsch. 263 51.12 N 6.54 E
Unterbäch, Schw. 58 46.17 N 7.48 E
Unter dem Wind, Inseln → Windward Islands II 238 13.00 N 61.00 W
Unterelchingen 58 48.27 N 10.07 E
Unterföhring 60 48.12 N 11.38 E
Unterfranken □[5] 56 50.10 N 10.00 E
Untergermaringen 58 47.56 N 10.40 E
Unterglottertal 58 48.03 N 7.56 E
Untergriesbach 60 48.35 N 13.40 E
Untergröningen 56 48.55 N 9.53 E
Untergrüne 263 51.22 N 7.39 E
Unterhaching 60 48.04 N 11.38 E
Unterhausen 58 48.26 N 9.16 E
Unterinntal V 64 47.24 N 11.47 E
Unterjettenberg 64 47.41 N 12.49 E
Unterlaa ◆[8] 264b 48.08 N 16.25 E
Unterlüss 52 52.50 N 10.17 E
Untermauerbach 264b 48.14 N 16.12 E
Untermünkheim 56 49.09 N 9.44 E
Untermünstertal 58 47.51 N 7.46 E
Unteröwisheim 56 49.08 N 8.40 E
Unterrath ◆[8] 263 51.16 N 6.47 E
Unterschächen 58 46.52 N 8.47 E
Unterschwaningen 56 49.04 N 10.37 E
Unterseen 58 46.41 N 7.51 E
Untertauern 64 47.18 N 13.30 E
Unterterzen 58 47.07 N 9.15 E
Unterthingau 58 47.46 N 10.31 E
Unterueckersee ⊜ 54 53.17 N 13.51 E
Unteruhldingen 58 47.43 N 9.14 E
Unterwasser 58 47.12 N 9.19 E
Unterweissbach 54 50.37 N 11.10 E
Unterwellenborn 54 50.39 N 11.26 E
Unterwössen 64 47.44 N 12.27 E
Unterzeiring 61 47.15 N 14.31 E
Untraverket 40 60.25 N 17.18 E
Unuli Horog 120 35.06 N 91.51 E
Ünye 130 41.08 N 37.17 E
Unža 80 58.01 N 44.01 E
Unža ≃ 80 57.20 N 43.08 E
Unzen-Amakusa-kokuritsu-kōen ♦ 92 32.45 N 130.17 E
Unzen-dake ʌ 92 32.45 N 130.17 E
Unže-Pavinskaja 86 58.53 N 64.02 E
Uojan 88 56.07 N 111.38 E
Uono ≃ 94 37.15 N 138.53 E
Uo-shima I 96 34.11 N 133.19 E
Uozu 94 36.48 N 137.24 E
Upa ≃ 76 54.02 N 36.15 E
Upala 236 10.47 N 85.02 W
Upanema 250 5.38 S 37.15 W
Upano ≃ 246 2.45 S 78.12 W
Upata 246 8.01 N 62.24 W
Upatoi Creek ≃ 192 32.22 N 84.58 W
Upavon 42 51.18 N 1.49 W
Ŭpchŏ-ri 98 37.53 N 125.09 E
Upchurch 260 51.23 N 0.39 E
Upemba, Lac ⊜ 154 8.36 S 26.26 E
Upemba, Parc National de l' ♦ 154 9.10 S 26.35 E
Upernavik 176 72.47 N 56.10 W
Upgant-Schott 52 53.30 N 7.16 E
Uphal 140 6.58 N 34.16 E
Upham 198 48.34 N 100.43 W
Up Holland 262 53.33 N 2.44 W
Uphusen 52 53.01 N 8.58 E
Upi 116 6.57 N 124.09 E
Upía ≃ 246 4.18 N 72.45 W
Upington 158 28.25 S 21.15 E
Upire ≃ 246 11.27 N 68.58 W
Upland, Ca., U.S. 228 34.05 N 117.38 W
Upland, In., U.S. 216 40.28 N 85.29 W
Upland, Ne., U.S. 198 40.19 N 98.54 W
Upland, Pa., U.S. 285 39.51 N 75.23 W
Upleta 120 21.44 N 70.17 E
Upnuk Lake ⊜ 180 60.21 N 158.58 W
Upolu I 175a 13.55 S 171.45 W
Upolu Point > 229d 20.16 N 155.51 W
Uporovo 86 56.18 N 66.17 E
Upper □[4] 150 10.30 N 1.30 W
Upper Arlington 218 40.00 N 83.03 W
Upper Arrow Lake ⊜ 182 50.30 N 117.55 W
Upper Artichoke Reservoir ⊜[1] 283 42.48 N 70.57 W
Upper Bay c 276 40.41 N 74.03 W
Upper Beaconsfield 274b 38.01 S 145.25 E
Upper Berkshire Valley 276 40.56 N 74.35 W
Upper Beverley Lake ⊜ 212 44.37 N 76.05 W
Upper Black Eddy 210 40.35 N 75.07 W
Upper Blackville 186 46.39 N 65.52 W
Upper Brookville 276 40.51 N 73.34 W
Upper Canada Village ⊥ 206 44.57 N 75.03 W
Upper Castlereagh 274a 33.43 S 150.40 E
Upperco 208 39.33 N 76.50 W
Upper Coliban Reservoir ⊜[1] 169 37.18 S 144.23 E
Upper Crystal Springs Reservoir ⊜[1] 282 37.30 N 122.20 W
Upper Darby 208 39.55 N 75.16 W
Upper Demerara-Berbice □[4] 246 5.30 N 58.20 W
Upper des Lacs Lake ⊜[1] 198 48.50 N 102.07 W
Upper Egypt → Aṣ-Ṣa'īd □[9] 140 26.00 N 32.00 E
Upper End 262 53.17 N 1.52 W
Upper Erskine Lake ⊜ 276 41.06 N 74.15 W
Upper Fairmount 208 38.06 N 75.47 W
Upper Falls 284b 39.26 N 76.24 W
Upper Ferntree Gully 274b 37.54 S 145.19 E
Upper Fraser 182 54.07 N 121.56 W
Upper Ganga Canal ≍ 124 29.57 N 78.12 E
Upper Gap)(212 44.06 N 76.50 W
Upper Goose Lake ⊜ 184 51.44 N 92.44 W
Upper Greenwood Lake 276 41.10 N 74.22 W
Upper Greenwood Lake ⊜ 276 41.11 N 74.23 W
Upper Hat Creek 182 50.38 N 121.35 W
Upper Humber ≃ 186 49.10 N 57.28 W
Upper Hutt 172 41.08 S 175.04 E
Upper Iowa ≃ 190 43.29 N 91.14 W
Upper Island Cove 186 47.39 N 53.12 W
Upper Keechi Creek ≃ 222 31.23 N 95.42 W
Upper Klamath Lake ⊜ 202 42.23 N 122.55 W
Upper Lake 204 39.10 N 122.54 W
Upper Lake ⊜ 204 41.44 N 120.08 W
Upper Lehigh 210 41.02 N 75.55 W
Upper Liard 180 60.02 N 128.55 W
Upper Machodoc Creek ≃ 208 38.18 N 77.02 W
Upper Manitou Lake ⊜ 184 49.24 N 92.48 W
Upper Marlboro 208 38.48 N 76.45 W
Upper Matecumbe Key I 220 24.55 N 80.39 W
Upper Moutere 172 41.16 S 173.00 E
Upper Musquodoboit 186 45.08 N 62.57 W
Upper Mystic Lake ⊜ 283 42.27 N 71.09 W
Upper Nyack 210 41.07 N 73.55 W
Upper Peirce Reservoir ⊜[1] 271c 1.22 N 103.48 E
Upper Red Lake ⊜ 198 48.10 N 94.40 W
Upper Rideau Lake ⊜ 212 44.41 N 76.20 W
Upper River Rouge ≃ 281 42.23 N 83.16 W
Upper Saddle River 276 41.03 N 74.05 W
Upper Saint Clair 279b 40.21 N 80.05 W
Upper Sandusky 214 40.49 N 83.16 W
Upper San Leandro Reservoir ⊜[1] 226 37.47 N 122.07 W
Upper Sheila 186 47.28 N 64.56 W
Upper Straits Lake ⊜ 281 42.35 N 83.24 W
Upper Sumas 224 49.01 N 122.12 W
Upper Swan 168a 31.46 S 116.01 E
Upper Takaka 172 41.02 S 172.50 E
Upper Takutu-Upper Essequibo □[4] 246 3.00 N 59.00 W
Upper Tean 42 52.57 N 1.58 W
Upper Tooting ◆[8] 260 51.26 N 0.10 W
Upper Ugashik Lake ⊜ 180 57.40 N 156.43 W
Upper Volta → Burkina Faso □[1] 150 13.00 N 1.30 W
Upper Windigo Lake ⊜ 184 52.30 N 91.35 W
Upper Yarra Reservoir ⊜[1] 169 37.41 S 145.56 E
Upper Yosemite Fall ˪ 226 37.45 N 119.36 W
Uppingham 42 52.35 N 0.43 W
Uppland □[9] 40 59.59 N 17.48 E
Upplanda 40 60.14 N 17.44 E
Upplands Väsby 40 59.31 N 17.54 E
Uppsala 40 59.52 N 17.38 E
Uppsala Län □[6] 40 60.00 N 17.45 E
Upright, Cape > 180 60.17 N 172.15 W
Upsala → Uppsala 40 59.52 N 17.38 E
Upshi 120 33.50 N 77.49 E
Upshur □[6] 222 32.45 N 94.55 W
Upstart, Cape > 166 19.42 S 147.45 E
Upton, P.Q., Can. 206 45.39 N 72.41 W
Upton, Eng., U.K. 44 53.37 N 1.17 W

Symbols in the index entries represent the broad categories identified in the key at the right. Symbols with superior numbers (⋏[1]) identify subcategories (see complete key on page *I · 1).*

Symbole im Register stellen die rechts im Schlüssel erklärten Kategorien dar. Symbole mit hochgestellten Ziffern (⋏[1]) bezeichnen Unterabteilungen einer Kategorie (vgl. vollständiger Schlüssel auf Seite *I · 1).*

Los símbolos incluídos en el texto del índice representan las grandes categorias identificadas con la clave a la derecha. Los símbolos con numeros en su parte superior (⋏[1]) identifican las subcategorías (véase la clave completa en la página *I · 1).*

Les symboles de l'index représentent les catégories indiquées dans la légende à droite. Les symboles suivis d'un indice (⋏[1]) représentent des sous-catégories (voir légende complète à la page *I · 1).*

Os símbolos incluídos no texto do índice representam as grandes categorias identificadas com a chave à direita. Os símbolos com números em sua parte superior (⋏[1]) identificam as subcategorias (veja-se a chave completa à página *I · 1).*

	English	Deutsch	Español	Français	Português
ʌ	Mountain	Berg	Montaña	Montagne	Montanha
⋏	Mountains	Gebirge	Montañas	Montagnes	Montanhas
)(	Pass	Paß	Paso	Col	Passo
V	Valley, Canyon	Tal, Cañon	Valle, Cañón	Vallée, Canyon	Vale, Canhão
≚	Plain	Ebene	Llano	Plaine	Planície
>	Cape	Kap	Cabo	Cap	Cabo
I	Island	Insel	Isla	Île	Ilha
II	Islands	Inseln	Islas	Îles	Ilhas
≗	Other Topographic Features	Andere Topographische Objekte	Otros Elementos Topográficos	Autres données topographiques	Outros acidentes topográficos

ESPAÑOL

Nombre	Página	Lat. °'	Long. °' W = Oeste
Upton, Eng., U.K.	44	53.13 N	2.52 W
Upton, Eng., U.K.	260	51.30 N	0.35 W
Upton, Eng., U.K.	262	53.23 N	3.06 W
Upton, Ky., U.S.	194	37.27 N	85.53 W
Upton, Ma., U.S.	207	42.10 N	71.36 W
Upton, Wy., U.S.	198	44.05 N	104.37 W
Upton Hill ∧[2]	169	36.52 S	145.27 E
Upton upon Severn	42	52.04 N	2.13 W
Uptown ◆[8]	278	41.58 N	87.40 W
Upwell	42	52.36 N	0.12 E
Upwey	274b	37.54 S	145.20 E
Uquía, Cerro ∧	246	4.22 N	63.46 W
Urabá, Golfo de ⊂	246	8.25 N	76.53 W
Urachi	84	42.21 N	47.36 E
Uracoa	246	9.00 N	62.21 W
Urad	54	52.15 N	14.45 E
Uradome-kaigan ♠	96	35.35 N	134.21 E
Urad Zhonghou Lianheqi	102	41.42 N	108.49 E
Uraga	268	35.15 N	139.43 E
Uraga-kō ⊂	268	35.14 N	139.44 E
Uraga-suidō ʮ	94	35.13 N	139.45 E
Uragawara	94	37.09 N	138.26 E
Urahoro	92a	42.48 N	143.39 E
Uraj	86	60.08 N	64.48 E
Urakan	88	58.38 N	106.01 E
Urakawa	92a	42.09 N	142.47 E
Ural ≃	72	47.00 N	51.48 E
Uralla	166	30.39 S	151.30 E
Ural Mountains → Ural'skije gory ⩘	72	60.00 N	60.00 E
Uralo-Kl'uči	88	56.03 N	97.28 E
Uralovo	78	52.11 N	33.34 E
Ural'sk	80	51.14 N	51.22 E
Ural'sk □[4]	80	50.00 N	51.00 E
Ural'skij	80	51.36 N	51.40 E
Ural'skije gory (Ural Mountains) ⩘	72	60.00 N	60.00 E
Urambo	154	5.04 S	32.03 E
Uran	272c	18.52 N	72.56 E
Urana	166	35.20 S	146.16 E
Urandangi	166	21.36 S	138.18 E
Urandi	255	14.46 S	42.38 W
Urangan	166	25.18 S	152.54 E
Urania, Austl.	168b	34.31 S	137.36 E
Urania, La., U.S.	194	31.51 N	92.17 W
Uranium City	176	59.34 N	108.36 W
Uranquinty	171b	35.12 S	147.15 E
Urarey	162	27.26 S	122.18 E
Urariá, Paraná ≃[1]	246	3.03 S	57.43 W
Uraricaá ≃	246	3.20 N	61.56 W
Uraricoera	246	3.27 N	60.59 W
Uraricoera ≃	246	3.02 N	60.30 W
Uras	71	39.42 N	8.42 E
Urasaki	174m	26.40 N	127.53 E
Urasoe	174m	26.15 N	127.43 E
Ura-T'ube	85	39.55 N	68.59 E
Uravakonda	122	14.57 N	77.16 E
Uravan	200	38.22 N	108.44 W
Urawa	94	35.51 N	139.39 E
Urayasu	94	35.39 N	139.54 E
'Urayfan Nāqah, Jabal ∧	132	30.22 N	34.27 E
'Urayyiḍah, Bi'r ⊤[4]	142	29.00 N	31.58 E
Urazmetovo	86	53.49 N	55.25 E
Urazovka	80	55.24 N	45.38 E
Urazovo	78	50.07 N	38.04 E
Urbach	56	50.53 N	7.05 E
Urban	224	48.38 N	122.40 W
Urbana, Ar., U.S.	194	33.09 N	92.26 W
Urbana, Il., U.S.	194	40.06 N	88.12 W
Urbana, In., U.S.	216	40.53 N	85.47 W
Urbana, Mo., U.S.	194	37.50 N	93.10 W
Urbana, Oh., U.S.	218	40.06 N	83.45 W
Urbancrest	218	39.53 N	83.05 W
Urbandale, Ia., U.S.	190	41.37 N	93.42 W
Urbandale, Mi., U.S.	216	44.09 N	85.11 W
Urbania	66	43.40 N	12.31 E
Urbanna	208	37.38 N	76.34 W
Urbano Noris	240p	20.36 N	76.08 W
Urbano Santos	250	3.12 S	43.23 W
Urbe	62	44.29 N	8.36 E
Urbe, Aeroporto dell' ⊠	267a	41.57 N	12.30 E
Urbiña, Peña ∧	34	43.01 N	5.57 W
Urbino	66	43.43 N	12.38 E
Urbisaglia	66	43.12 N	13.23 E
Urcos	248	13.42 S	71.38 W
Urda	80	48.47 N	47.26 E
Urdaneta	116	15.59 N	120.34 E
Urdenbach ◆[8]	263	51.09 N	6.53 E
Urdinarrain	252	32.41 S	58.53 W
Urdoma	24	61.47 N	48.32 E
Urdžar	86	47.05 N	81.38 E
Uré	246	7.46 N	75.31 W
Ure ≃, Fr.	50	48.45 N	0.11 E
Ure ≃, Eng., U.K.	44	54.01 N	1.12 W
Urečje	76	52.57 N	27.54 E
Ūrein	142	30.58 N	30.42 E
Ureki	84	41.59 N	41.46 E
Ureliki	180	64.23 N	173.15 W
Uren'	80	57.28 N	45.49 E
Uren ⊜	40	58.59 N	16.44 E
Urén ≃	236	9.33 N	82.55 W
Ureña	246	7.55 N	72.28 W
Urenui	172	39.00 S	174.23 E
Uréparapara I	175f	13.32 S	167.20 E
Ures	232	29.26 N	110.24 W
Ureshino, Nihon	92	33.06 N	129.59 E
Ureshino, Nihon	94	34.37 N	136.29 E
Ureterp	52	53.05 N	6.10 E
Urewera National Park ♠	172	38.40 S	177.00 E
Urft ≃	56	50.35 N	6.30 E
Urga	86	43.35 N	58.30 E
Urgamal	88	48.29 N	94.20 E
Urga → Ulaanbaatar	88	47.55 N	106.53 E
Urgenč	72	41.33 N	60.38 E
Urgnano	62	45.35 N	9.41 E
Urgučenskij Golec, gora ∧	88	53.30 N	118.08 E
Ürgüp	130	38.38 N	34.56 E
Urgut	85	39.23 N	67.15 E
Urho	86	46.48 N	89.45 E
Urho Kekkosen kansallispuisto ♠	24	68.10 N	28.30 E
Uri, India	123	34.05 N	74.02 E
Uri, It.	71	40.38 N	8.29 E
Uri □[3]	58	46.50 N	8.40 E
Uriah	194	31.18 N	87.30 W
Uriangato	234	20.09 N	101.11 W
Uribante ≃	246	7.18 N	70.44 W
Uribe	246	3.13 N	74.24 W
Uribelarrea	258	35.09 S	58.54 W
Uribia	246	11.43 N	72.16 W
Urich	194	38.27 N	94.00 W
Urick ◆[8]	265a	59.50 N	30.11 E
Urickij	86	53.19 N	65.34 E
Urickoje	78	52.02 N	38.11 E
Urie ≃	46	57.19 N	2.30 W
Urimba	152	10.56 S	16.32 E
Urión ≃[1]	288	34.24 S	58.31 W
Urique	232	27.13 N	107.55 W
Urique ≃	232	26.29 N	107.58 W
Uri-Rotstock ∧	58	46.52 N	8.33 E
Urituyacu ≃	246	4.45 S	75.28 W
Uriuaná ≃	250	2.47 S	50.29 W
Urizura	94	36.30 N	140.27 E
Urjala	26	61.05 N	23.32 E
Urk	52	52.39 N	5.36 E
Urkan ≃	89	53.27 N	126.56 E
Urkarach	84	42.11 N	47.38 E
Urla	130	38.18 N	26.46 E
Urlaţi	38	44.59 N	26.14 E
Urlingford	48	52.42 N	7.35 W
Urlings	240c	17.02 N	61.52 W
Urluk	88	50.03 N	107.55 E
Urma	126	23.10 N	86.15 E
Urman, Ross.	86	54.52 N	56.52 E

FRANÇAIS

Nom	Page	Lat. °'	Long. °' W = Ouest
'Urmān, Sūrīy.	132	32.30 N	36.45 E
Urmary	80	55.42 N	47.57 E
Urmetan	85	39.27 N	68.17 E
Urmi ≃	89	48.44 N	134.16 E
Urmia, Lake → Orūmīyeh, Daryācheh-ye ⊜	128	37.40 N	45.30 E
Urmia → Orūmīyeh	128	37.33 N	45.04 E
Urmston	44	53.27 N	2.21 W
Urnäsch	58	47.19 N	9.17 E
Urnersee ⊜	58	46.55 N	8.37 E
Uroindo	248	21.41 S	64.41 W
Üröm	264c	47.36 N	19.01 E
Uromi	150	6.44 N	6.18 E
Uroševac	38	42.22 N	21.09 E
Uroyán, Montañas de ⩘	240m	18.14 N	67.02 W
Urožajnoje, Ross.	84	43.42 N	44.13 E
Urožajnoje, Ross.	84	44.47 N	44.55 E
Urquhart, Glen V	46	57.20 N	4.35 W
Urrao	246	6.20 N	76.11 W
Urr Water ≃	44	54.53 N	3.49 W
Ursa	219	40.04 N	91.22 W
Uršel'skij	80	55.41 N	40.13 E
Ursensollen	60	49.24 N	11.46 E
Ursk	86	54.27 N	85.24 E
Urspring	56	48.33 N	9.53 E
Ur → Tall al-Muqayyar ⊥	128	30.57 N	46.09 E
Urtazym	86	52.12 N	58.50 E
Urtigueira	252	24.12 S	50.55 W
Urt Moron	120	37.00 N	93.18 E
Uru ≃	255	15.24 S	49.36 W
Uruaçu	255	14.30 S	49.10 W
Uruana	255	15.30 S	49.41 W
Uruapan	204	31.38 N	116.15 W
Uruapan del Progreso	234	19.25 N	102.04 W
Urubamba	248	13.18 S	72.07 W
Urubamba ≃	248	10.44 S	73.45 W
Urubaxi ≃	246	0.31 S	64.50 W
Urubu ≃, Bra.	246	2.55 S	58.25 W
Urubu ≃, Bra.	250	10.51 S	49.47 W
Uruburetama	250	3.38 S	39.30 W
Urucará	250	2.32 S	57.45 W
Uruch ≃	84	43.28 N	44.06 E
Urucu ≃	246	4.11 S	63.36 W
Uruçuca	255	14.35 S	39.16 W
Uruçuí	250	7.14 S	44.33 W
Uruçuí, Serra da ⩘[2]	250	9.00 S	44.45 W
Urucuia ≃	255	16.08 S	45.05 W
Uruçui-preto ≃	250	7.20 S	44.38 W
Urucurituba	250	2.41 S	57.40 W
Urugi	94	35.16 N	137.42 E
Uruguaiana	252	29.45 S	57.05 W
Uruguay □[1], S.A.	244	33.00 S	56.00 W
Uruguay □[1], S.A.	252	33.00 S	56.00 W
Uruguay (Uruguai) ≃	252	34.12 S	58.18 W
Urugudejevskij Golec, gora ∧	88	51.25 N	102.09 E
Urul'ga	88	51.45 N	114.47 E
Urul'unguj ≃	88	50.24 N	119.08 E
Ur'um, ozero ⊜	86	54.33 N	78.30 E
Urumchi → Ürümqi	90	43.48 N	87.35 E
Ur'umkan ≃	88	52.35 N	120.08 E
Ürümqi	90	43.48 N	87.35 E
Urundel	252	23.33 S	64.25 W
Ur'ung-Chaja	74	72.48 N	113.23 E
Uruoca	250	3.20 S	40.32 W
Urup	84	43.52 N	41.09 E
Urup ≃	84	44.49 N	41.10 E
Urup, gora ∧	84	43.38 N	40.58 E
Urup, ostrov I	74	46.00 N	150.00 E
Urupá ≃	248	10.54 S	61.57 W
Urupadi ≃	250	3.51 S	57.21 W
Urupês	255	21.13 S	49.17 W
Ur'upino	88	52.46 N	120.00 E
Ur'upinsk	80	50.47 N	41.59 E
Ururicaia, Ilha I	250	1.30 S	52.05 W
Uruša	89	54.03 N	122.54 E
Urus-Martan	84	43.08 N	45.32 E
Urusovo	82	54.15 N	38.26 E
Urussanga	252	28.31 S	49.19 W
Urussu	80	54.36 N	53.24 E
Urutaí	255	17.28 S	48.12 W
Urutaí, Ilha I	250	1.07 S	51.17 W
Urutaú	252	25.42 S	63.04 W
Uruti	172	38.57 S	174.32 E
Uru Uru, Lago ⊜	248	18.10 S	67.10 W
Uruwira	154	6.27 S	31.21 E
Uryl'	86	49.15 N	86.20 E
Uryū-yama ∧	270	35.03 N	135.48 E
Uryv	78	51.07 N	39.10 E
Urzajbaš	80	54.43 N	54.23 E
Urziceni	38	44.43 N	26.38 E
Ürzig	56	49.59 N	7.01 E
Urzulei	71	40.06 N	9.30 E
Uržum	80	57.08 N	50.00 E
Us	261	49.06 N	1.58 E
Us ≃	86	52.07 N	92.15 E
Usa, Nihon	96	33.31 N	131.22 E
Usa, Ross.	86	54.03 N	88.45 E
Uša ≃, Bela.	76	54.00 N	28.55 E
Usa ≃, Ross.	24	65.57 N	56.55 E
Ušač' ≃	76	55.32 N	28.30 E
Ušači	76	55.11 N	28.37 E
Usada Island I	116	6.08 N	120.33 E
Usadel	54	53.26 N	13.11 E
Uşak	130	38.41 N	29.25 E
Uşak □[4]	130	38.35 N	29.20 E
Ušaki	76	59.29 N	30.59 E
Usakos	156	22.01 S	15.32 E
Ušakovka	83	48.48 N	39.48 E
Ušakovo, Ross.	86	56.22 N	75.41 E
Ušakovo, Ross.	89	51.55 N	126.34 E
Usambara Mountains ⩘	154	4.45 S	38.30 E
Usangu Flats ⩩	154	8.30 S	34.15 E
Usanovy	86	59.28 N	73.24 E
Ušaral	85	43.54 N	70.42 E
Usarp Mountains ⩘	9	71.10 S	160.00 E
Úšava	60	49.46 N	12.40 E
Usaymir, Wādī al- V	273c	30.04 N	31.23 E
Ušba, gora ∧	84	43.08 N	42.40 E
Ušbas ≃	85	43.55 N	69.39 E
Usborne, Mount ∧	254	51.41 S	58.50 W
Ušće	38	43.28 N	20.37 E
Uščerpje	76	52.43 N	31.53 E
Uscio	62	44.25 N	9.10 E
Usedom	54	53.52 N	13.55 E
Usedom (Uznam) I	54	54.00 N	14.00 E
Useldange	56	49.47 N	5.59 E
Usellus	71	39.48 N	8.51 E
Usen' ≃	80	54.44 N	53.38 E
'Usfān	144	21.55 N	39.21 E
Ushaa	152	14.55 S	23.18 E
Ushant → Ouessant, Île d' I	32	48.28 N	5.05 W
Ushashi	154	2.00 S	33.57 E
'Ushayrah	144	21.46 N	40.38 E
Ushetu	154	4.10 S	32.16 E
Ushibuka	92	32.11 N	130.01 E
Ushiku	94	35.58 N	140.08 E
Ushimado	96	34.37 N	134.10 E
Ushuaia	254	54.48 S	68.18 W
Usibelli	180	63.51 N	148.47 W
Ušica ≃	78	48.35 N	27.08 E
Usingen	56	50.20 N	8.32 E
Usini	71	40.40 N	8.32 E
Usinsk	24	65.58 N	56.39 E
Usisya	154	11.09 S	34.11 E
Usk, B.C., Can.	182	54.38 N	128.25 W
Usk, Wales, U.K.	42	51.43 N	2.54 W
Usk, Wa., U.S.	202	48.18 N	117.16 W
Usk ≃	42	51.36 N	2.58 W
Uškanij kr'až ∧	180	65.15 N	178.35 E

PORTUGUÊS

Nome	Página	Lat. °'	Long. °' W = Oeste
Uskedal	26	59.56 N	5.52 E
Usken ⊜	40	59.39 N	15.01 E
Uskovo	265b	55.56 N	37.19 E
Üsküb → Skopje	38	41.59 N	21.26 E
Uskumru ◆[8]	267b	41.12 N	29.01 E
Uslar	52	51.39 N	9.38 E
Úslava ≃	60	49.45 N	13.24 E
Usmajac	234	19.52 N	103.34 W
Usman', Ross.	76	52.02 N	39.44 E
Usman', Ross.	89	51.29 N	134.00 E
Usmanka	80	52.49 N	51.42 E
Usmānpur ◆[8]	272a	28.41 N	77.15 E
Usmas ezers ⊜	76	57.11 N	22.10 E
Usmat	85	39.44 N	67.40 E
Usmate Velate	62	45.39 N	9.21 E
Ušmunskij Golec, gora ∧	89	51.40 N	118.35 E
Usmyn'	76	55.52 N	31.09 E
Ušna ≃	80	55.43 N	42.12 E
Usoke	154	5.06 S	32.20 E
Usolje, Ross.	80	53.23 N	49.05 E
Usolje, Ross.	82	56.49 N	38.40 E
Usolje, Ross.	86	59.25 N	56.41 E
Usolje-Sibirskoje	88	52.47 N	103.38 E
Usolka ≃	86	57.47 N	94.35 E
Uson	116	12.13 N	123.47 E
Usoro	150	5.34 N	6.13 E
Usovo	265b	55.44 N	37.13 E
Uspallata	252	32.35 S	69.20 W
Uspanapa ≃	234	17.58 N	94.29 W
Uspenka, Kaz.	86	52.54 N	77.25 E
Uspenka, Ross.	80	50.38 N	41.28 E
Uspenka, Ukr.	83	47.43 N	38.42 E
Uspenka, Ukr.	83	48.23 N	39.10 E
Uspenovka	80	51.16 N	53.36 E
Uspenskij	86	48.42 N	72.40 E
Uspenskoje	82	55.43 N	37.04 E
Usri ≃	126	24.03 N	86.23 E
Uššaj	86	43.50 N	58.53 E
Ussassai	71	39.49 N	9.23 E
Usseglio	62	45.14 N	7.13 E
Ussel	32	45.33 N	2.18 E
Ussel ≃	56	48.44 N	11.04 E
Usshers Creek ≃	284a	43.03 N	79.02 W
Usson-en-Forez	62	45.23 N	3.56 E
Ussure	154	4.39 S	34.23 E
Ussuri (Wusuli) ≃	89	48.27 N	135.04 E
Ussurijsk	89	43.48 N	131.59 E
Ūst	123	36.56 N	72.53 E
Usta	80	57.26 N	45.40 E
Usta ≃	80	56.53 N	45.28 E
Ust'-Ajsk	86	56.07 N	57.40 E
Ustaoset	26	60.30 N	8.04 E
Ustaritz	32	43.24 N	1.27 W
Ust'-Bagar'ak	86	56.08 N	61.52 E
Ust'-Barguzin	88	53.27 N	108.59 E
Ust'-Belaja	74	65.30 N	173.20 E
Ust'-Bol'šereck	74	52.48 N	156.14 E
Ust'-B'ur'	86	53.49 N	90.15 E
Ust'-Buzulukskaja	80	50.12 N	42.10 E
Ust'-Bystr'anskaja	80	47.49 N	41.03 E
Ust'-Čaja	86	58.17 N	82.38 E
Ust'-Čaryšskaja Pristan'	86	52.24 N	83.39 E
Ust'-Čaun	74	68.47 N	170.30 E
Ust'-Choperskaja	80	49.36 N	42.24 E
Ust'-Čil'ma	24	65.27 N	52.06 E
Ust'-Čižapka	86	59.02 N	79.37 E
Ust'-Čorna	78	48.18 N	23.56 E
Ust'-Čornaja	88	52.57 N	119.02 E
Ust'-Dolyssy	76	56.09 N	29.39 E
Ust'-Doneckij	80	47.39 N	40.52 E
Ust'-Džegutinskaja	84	44.05 N	41.58 E
Úštěk	54	50.36 N	14.20 E
Ust'-Elegest	88	51.32 N	94.05 E
Uster	58	47.21 N	8.43 E
Ust'-Gr'aznucha	80	50.28 N	45.26 E
Ustica	70	38.42 N	13.11 E
Ustica, Isola di I	70	38.42 N	13.11 E
Ust'-Il'a	88	50.25 N	113.41 E
Ust'-Ilga	88	55.00 N	105.02 E
Ust'-Ilimsk	88	58.00 N	102.39 E
Ust'-Ilimskoje vodochranilišče ⊜[1]	88	57.00 N	102.15 E
Ustilug	78	50.51 N	24.09 E
Ust'-Ilyč	24	62.32 N	56.41 E
Ústí nad Labem	54	50.40 N	14.02 E
Ústí nad Orlicí	30	49.58 N	16.24 E
Ustinovka, Ukr.	78	47.57 N	32.32 E
Ustinovka, Ukr.	83	48.49 N	38.34 E
Ust'-Išim	86	57.44 N	71.10 E
Ust'-Izes	86	55.56 N	76.56 E
Ust'-Ižora	265a	59.48 N	30.36 E
Ustja ≃	24	61.30 N	42.36 E
Ust'-Javron'ga	24	63.25 N	44.21 E
Ustje, Ross.	76	60.49 N	32.49 E
Ustje, Ross.	76	59.38 N	39.43 E
Ustje, Ross.	80	57.47 N	39.47 E
Ustje, Ross.	82	55.16 N	36.20 E
Ustje, Ross.	86	57.46 N	94.42 E
Ustje-Kirovskoje	76	58.45 N	35.55 E
Ustka	30	54.35 N	16.50 E
Ust'-K'achta	88	50.32 N	106.16 E
Ust'-Kajtym	86	57.23 N	95.28 E
Ust'-Kalmanka	86	52.07 N	83.19 E
Ust'-Kamčatsk	74	56.15 N	162.30 E
Ust'-Kamenogorsk	86	49.58 N	82.38 E
Ust'-Kan, Ross.	86	50.57 N	84.45 E
Ust'-Kan, Ross.	86	56.31 N	93.48 E
Ust'-Karenga	88	54.26 N	116.30 E
Ust'-Karsk	88	52.43 N	118.48 E
Ust'-Katav	86	54.56 N	58.10 E
Ust'-Kemčug	86	57.13 N	90.30 E
Ust'-Kil'mez'	80	56.57 N	50.30 E
Ust'-Kišert'	86	57.22 N	57.15 E
Ust'-Koksa	86	50.18 N	85.36 E
Ust'-Kujda	74	70.01 N	135.36 E
Ust'-Kulom	24	61.42 N	53.40 E
Ust'-Kurd'um	80	51.39 N	46.12 E
Ust'-Kurenga	86	57.27 N	75.34 E
Ust'-Kut	88	56.46 N	105.40 E
Ust'-Labinsk	78	45.13 N	39.42 E
Ust'-Lubija	88	52.36 N	120.16 E
Ust'-Luga	76	59.40 N	28.15 E
Ust'-Lyža	24	65.44 N	56.36 E
Ust'-Maja	74	60.25 N	134.32 E
Ust'-Manja	72	62.11 N	60.20 E
Ust'-Naryk	86	54.20 N	87.25 E
Ust'-Nemda	80	57.03 N	50.22 E
Ust'-Nera	74	64.34 N	143.12 E
Ust'-Niman	89	51.23 N	132.42 E
Ust'-N'ukža	88	56.34 N	121.37 E
Uštobe	86	45.16 N	78.00 E
Ust'-Omčug	74	61.09 N	149.38 E
Ust'-Ordynskij	88	52.48 N	104.45 E
Ust'-Ordynskij Burjatskij Avtonomnyj Okrug □[8]	88	53.30 N	104.00 E
Ust'-Oz'ornaja	88	50.42 N	117.06 E
Ust'-Oz'ornoje	86	58.54 N	87.48 E
Ust'-Paden'ga	24	61.53 N	42.36 E
Ust'-Pečengskoje	76	59.47 N	42.37 E
Ust'-Pinega	24	64.11 N	41.56 E
Ust'-Pit	86	58.59 N	91.44 E
Ust'-Pogožje	80	49.28 N	44.38 E
Ustreka	76	58.38 N	34.33 E
Ust'-Reki	24	62.12 N	46.45 E
Ustroń	30	49.43 N	18.49 E
Ustrzyki Dolne	30	49.26 N	22.37 E
Ust'-Šara	76	60.13 N	33.57 E
Ust'-Ščerbedino	80	51.53 N	42.52 E
Ust'-Slav'anka ◆[8]	265a	59.50 N	30.32 E
Ust'-Šonoša	24	61.10 N	41.18 E
Ust'-Sumy	86	54.48 N	80.26 E
Ust'-Tara	86	56.41 N	74.39 E
Ust'-Tarka	86	55.34 N	75.42 E
Ust'-Tašino	89	51.07 N	129.35 E
Ust'-Tygda	89	52.35 N	127.53 E
Ust'-Tym	86	59.26 N	80.08 E
Ust'-Tyrma	89	50.29 N	131.18 E
Ust'uckoje	76	58.32 N	35.20 E
Ust'-Uda	88	54.10 N	103.03 E
Üstükran	130	39.16 N	41.17 E
Ust'-Ulagan	86	50.38 N	87.58 E
Ust'-Umal'ta	89	51.39 N	133.18 E
Ust'-Undurga	89	53.07 N	118.04 E
Ust'-Unja	24	61.48 N	57.48 E
Ust'-Urgal	89	51.09 N	132.33 E
Ust'urt, plato ⩘[1]	72	43.00 N	56.00 E
Ust'-Us	86	52.07 N	92.17 E
Ust'-Usa	24	65.59 N	56.54 E
Ust'-Uza	80	52.58 N	45.17 E
Ust'užna	76	58.51 N	36.26 E
Ust'-Vichoreva	88	56.47 N	101.24 E
Ust'-Voja	24	64.27 N	57.40 E
Ust'-Vyjskaja	24	62.57 N	46.41 E
Ust'-Vym'	24	62.14 N	50.24 E
Ust'-Zaza	88	53.10 N	111.40 E
Ust'-Žuja	88	58.48 N	118.12 E
Usu	86	44.27 N	84.37 E
Usuchčaj	84	41.25 N	47.53 E
Usuda	94	36.12 N	138.29 E
Usugli	88	52.39 N	115.16 E
Usui	96	33.34 N	130.42 E
Usuki	96	33.08 N	131.49 E
Usuki-wan ⊂	96	33.10 N	131.52 E
Usulután	236	13.21 N	88.27 W
Usumacinta ≃	232	18.24 N	92.38 W
Usumbura → Bujumbura	154	3.23 S	29.22 E
Ušumun	89	52.49 N	126.27 E
Ušur	80	57.47 N	52.58 E
Usuyŏng	98	34.35 N	126.18 E
Usu-zan ∧	92a	42.32 N	140.51 E
Usv'aty	76	55.45 N	30.45 E
Uta	71	39.17 N	8.57 E
Utah □[3], U.S.	178	39.30 N	111.30 W
Utah □[3], U.S.	200	39.30 N	111.30 W
Utah Lake ⊜	200	40.13 N	111.49 W
Utajärvi	26	64.45 N	26.23 E
Utamba	154	1.06 S	26.50 E
Utamboni ≃	152	1.00 N	9.48 E
Utan	115b	8.24 S	117.07 E
Utano	94	34.28 N	135.59 E
Utapi	156	17.31 S	15.08 E
Utashinai	92a	43.31 N	142.03 E
Utata	88	50.51 N	102.45 E
'Utaybah, Buḥayrat al- ⊜	132	33.32 N	36.37 E
Ute	198	42.03 N	95.42 W
Ute ≃	248	15.28 S	65.05 W
Ute Creek ≃	196	35.21 N	103.50 W
Utegi	154	1.20 S	34.35 E
Utelle	62	43.55 N	7.15 E
Utembo ≃	152	17.06 S	22.01 E
Ute Mountain Indian Reservation ◆[4]	200	37.10 N	108.35 W
Utena	76	55.30 N	25.36 E
Utengule	154	8.57 S	35.50 E
Ute Reservoir ⊜[1]	196	36.21 N	103.31 W
Úterský potok ≃	60	49.48 N	13.06 E
Utersum	30	54.43 N	8.24 E
Utete	154	7.59 S	38.47 E
Utevka	80	52.57 N	50.58 E
Utfort	263	51.28 N	6.38 E
Uthai Thani	110	15.22 N	100.03 E
Uthal	120	25.48 N	66.37 E
U Thong	110	14.22 N	99.54 E
Uthumphon Phisai	110	15.05 N	104.08 E
Utiariti	248	13.02 S	58.17 W
Utica, Il., U.S.	216	41.20 N	89.00 W
Utica, In., U.S.	218	38.20 N	85.39 W
Utica, Ks., U.S.	198	38.38 N	100.10 W
Utica, Mi., U.S.	214	42.37 N	83.02 W
Utica, Ms., U.S.	194	32.06 N	90.37 W
Utica, Ne., U.S.	198	40.54 N	97.21 W
Utica, N.Y., U.S.	210	43.06 N	75.13 W
Utica, Oh., U.S.	214	40.14 N	82.27 W
Utica, Pa., U.S.	214	41.26 N	79.58 W
Utica → Utique ⊥	36	37.03 N	10.03 E
Utiel	34	39.34 N	1.12 W
Utikoomak Lake Indian Reserve ◆[4]	182	55.57 N	115.30 W
Utikuma Lake ⊜	182	55.50 N	115.25 W
Utila	236	16.06 N	86.54 W
Utila, Isla de I	236	16.06 N	86.56 W
Utinga	287b	23.38 S	46.32 W
Utinga ≃	255	12.34 S	41.20 W
Utique	36	37.03 N	10.03 E
Utique ⊥	36	37.03 N	10.03 E
Utirik I[1]	14	11.15 N	169.48 E
Utlängan I	26	56.01 N	15.47 E
Utl'ukskij liman ⊂[1]	78	46.15 N	35.12 E
Ut'ma	86	57.35 N	71.45 E
Utmānzai	123	34.11 N	71.46 E
Uto	92	32.41 N	130.40 E
Utö I	40	58.56 N	18.16 E
Utokota	156	17.50 S	20.22 E
Utonde	152	1.56 N	9.49 E
Utopia, Austl.	162	22.14 S	134.33 E
Utopia, Tx., U.S.	196	29.37 N	99.32 W
Utorgoš	76	58.17 N	30.15 E
Utraula	124	27.19 N	82.25 E
Utrecht, Ned.	52	52.05 N	5.08 E
Utrecht, S. Afr.	158	27.38 S	30.20 E
Utrecht □[4]	52	52.05 N	5.08 E
Utrera	34	37.11 N	5.47 W
Utroja ≃	76	57.23 N	28.09 E
Utsaladdy	224	48.15 N	122.30 W
Utsira	26	59.18 N	4.54 E
Utsjoki	24	69.53 N	27.00 E
Utsumi	96	34.21 N	133.17 E
Utsunomiya	94	36.33 N	139.52 E
Utta	80	46.23 N	46.01 E
Uttamapālāiyam	122	9.48 N	77.20 E
Uttaradit	110	17.38 N	100.06 E
Uttarkāshi	120	30.44 N	78.27 E
Uttarpara-Kotrung	272b	22.40 N	88.21 E
Uttar Pradesh □[3]	120	27.00 N	80.00 E
Uttendorf, Öst.	60	48.09 N	13.07 E
Uttendorf, Öst.	64	47.17 N	12.34 E
Uttenweiler	58	48.09 N	9.36 E
Ütterlingsen	263	51.15 N	7.45 E
Utting	60	48.02 N	11.05 E
Uttlesford □[8]	260	51.47 N	0.19 E
Uttoxeter	42	52.54 N	1.51 W
Utu	154	1.45 S	27.54 E
Utuado	240m	18.16 N	66.42 W
Utukok ≃	180	70.04 N	162.18 W
Utulei	174u	14.17 S	170.40 W
Utunomiya → Utsunomiya	94	36.33 N	139.52 E
Utupua I	14	11.16 S	166.29 E
Utva ≃	86	51.28 N	52.40 E
Utzenstorf	58	47.08 N	7.33 E
Uudenmaan lääni □[4]	26	60.30 N	25.00 E
Uulu	76	58.17 N	24.35 E
Üür ≃	88	50.18 N	101.54 E
Uurainen	26	62.30 N	25.27 E
Uusikaarlepyy (Nykarleby)	26	63.32 N	22.32 E
Uusikaupunki (Nystad)	26	60.48 N	21.25 E
Uusimaa ◆[1]	26	60.30 N	25.00 E
Uvá, Bra.	255	15.53 S	50.25 W
Uva, Ross.	80	56.59 N	52.13 E
Uvá ≃	246	3.57 N	68.24 W
Uvalda	192	33.41 N	83.25 W
Uvalde	196	29.12 N	99.47 W
Úvaly	54	50.03 N	14.47 E
Uvån ≃	40	60.01 N	13.37 E
Uvaroviči	76	52.36 N	30.44 E
Uvarovka	76	55.32 N	35.37 E
Uvarovo	80	51.59 N	42.15 E
Uvas Creek ≃	226	36.58 N	121.33 W
Uvas Reservoir ⊜[1]	226	37.05 N	121.42 W
Uvat	86	59.09 N	68.54 E
'Uvda, Biq'at V	132	29.57 N	34.57 E
Uvdal	26	60.16 N	8.44 E
Uvel'skij	86	54.26 N	61.22 E
Uvernet	62	44.22 N	6.38 E
Uvero, Punta ›	241s	11.21 N	68.41 W
Uvinza	154	5.06 S	30.22 E
Uvira	154	3.24 S	29.08 E
Uvod' ≃	80	56.26 N	41.26 E
Uvongo Beach	158	30.51 S	30.23 E
Uvs □[4]	86	50.00 N	92.00 E
Uvs nuur ⊜	74	50.20 N	92.45 E
Uvworé ›	175f	18.47 S	169.16 E
Uwa	96	33.20 N	132.30 E
Uwajima	96	33.13 N	132.34 E
Uwa-kai ⊤[2]	96	33.15 N	132.15 E
'Uwaybid, Jabal ∧	142	30.06 N	32.09 E
Uwayl	140	8.46 N	27.24 E
'Uwaynāt	130	35.43 N	36.05 E
'Uwaynāt, Jabal al- ∧	140	21.54 N	24.58 E
'Uwayriḍ, Ḥarrat al- ⩦[9]	128	27.00 N	37.30 E
Uwchland	285	40.05 N	75.42 W
Uwi, Pulau I	112	1.05 N	107.24 E
Uxbridge, On., Can.	212	44.06 N	79.07 W
Uxbridge, Ma., U.S.	207	42.04 N	71.37 W
Uxbridge ◆[8]	260	51.33 N	0.29 W
Uxmal ⊥	232	20.22 N	89.46 W
Uyak Bay ⊂	180	57.36 N	153.57 W
Uyama	270	34.50 N	135.41 E
U-yin	110	22.53 N	95.13 E
Uyo	150	5.03 N	7.56 E
Uyu ≃	110	24.51 N	94.57 E
Uyuni	248	20.28 S	66.50 W
Uyuni, Salar de ⩩	248	20.20 S	67.42 W
Už (Uh) ≃, Europe	30	48.34 N	22.00 E
Už ≃, Ukr.	78	51.15 N	30.12 E
Uza ≃, Ross.	76	57.48 N	29.31 E
Uza ≃, Ross.	80	53.02 N	45.18 E
Užanicha	86	54.41 N	81.02 E
Uzas	86	57.04 N	76.55 E
Užava	76	57.14 N	21.27 E
'Uzaym, Nahr al- ≃	128	34.01 N	44.19 E
Uzbekistan □[1]	72	41.00 N	64.00 E
Uzboj ≃	128	39.30 N	55.00 E
Uzda	76	53.27 N	27.13 E
Uzdin	38	45.12 N	20.38 E
Uzerche	32	45.26 N	1.34 E
Uzès	62	44.01 N	4.25 E
Uzgen	85	40.46 N	73.18 E
Užgorod	78	48.37 N	22.18 E
Užice	38	43.51 N	19.51 E
Uzin	78	49.50 N	30.24 E
Uzkij Lug	88	50.42 N	108.01 E
Uzkoje ◆[8]	265b	55.37 N	37.32 E
Uzlovaja	76	53.59 N	38.10 E
Uzmorje	80	51.15 N	45.55 E
Uznach	58	47.14 N	9.00 E
Uznam (Usedom) I	54	54.00 N	14.00 E
Uzola ≃	80	56.32 N	43.38 E
Uz'ukovo	80	53.38 N	49.43 E
Üzümlü, Tür.	130	37.32 N	31.37 E
Üzümlü, Tür.	130	36.44 N	29.14 E
Uzun	85	38.22 N	68.03 E
Uzun Ada I	130	38.28 N	26.42 E
Uzunagač, Kaz.	85	43.13 N	76.20 E
Uzunagač, Kaz.	85	43.36 N	76.19 E
Uzunbulak	86	45.23 N	84.06 E
Uzunca ≃	267b	40.58 N	28.50 E
Uzunköprü	130	41.16 N	26.41 E
Uzunkuduk	85	40.33 N	67.11 E
Uzunkuyu	130	38.17 N	26.33 E
Uzunovo	82	54.32 N	38.37 E
Užur	86	55.20 N	89.50 E
Užventis	76	55.47 N	22.39 E

V

Vä	26	55.59 N	14.05 E
Vaajakoski	26	62.16 N	25.54 E
Vääksy	26	61.11 N	25.33 E
Vaal ≃	158	29.04 S	23.38 E
Vaala	26	64.26 N	26.48 E
Vaaldam ⊜[1]	158	26.55 S	28.12 E
Vaalhartsdam ⊜[1]	158	28.06 S	24.55 E
Vaalkop ∧	158	31.21 S	26.31 E
Vaals	56	50.56 N	6.01 E
Vaalserberg ∧[2]	56	50.45 N	6.01 E
Vaalwater	156	24.20 S	28.03 E
Vaasa (Vasa)	26	63.06 N	21.36 E
Vaasan lääni □[4]	26	63.00 N	23.00 E
Vaassen	52	52.17 N	5.57 E
Vabalninkas	76	55.58 N	24.45 E
Vabkent	128	40.02 N	64.30 E
Vác	30	47.47 N	19.08 E
Vaca, Bol.	248	19.54 S	63.48 W
Vača, Ross.	80	55.48 N	42.46 E
Vaca, Mount ∧	226	38.24 N	122.06 W
Vacacaí ≃	252	29.55 S	53.06 W
Vaca Key I	220	24.43 N	81.04 W
Vacaria	252	28.30 S	50.56 W
Vacaria ≃, Bra.	255	16.39 S	42.45 W
Vacaria ≃, Bra.	255	21.55 S	53.59 W
Vacas, Arroyo de las ≃	258	34.00 S	58.18 W
Vacaville	226	38.21 N	121.59 W
Vacca, Kaap ›	158	34.21 S	21.53 E
Vaccarès, Étang de ⊂	62	43.32 N	4.34 E
Vach ≃	74	60.45 N	76.45 E
Vacha	56	50.50 N	10.01 E
Vache, Île à I	238	18.05 N	73.38 W
Vaches, Île aux I	275a	45.41 N	73.40 W
Vaches, Rivière aux ≃	206	46.02 N	72.46 W
Vachrušev	89	48.59 N	142.58 E
Vachruševo	83	48.10 N	38.46 E
Vachš ≃	72	37.06 N	68.18 E
Vachšskij chrebet ⩘	85	38.35 N	69.45 E
Vachtan	80	57.58 N	46.42 E
Vači	84	42.05 N	47.13 E
Vacía Talega, Punta ›	240m	18.27 N	65.54 W
Vacoas	157c	20.18 S	57.29 E
Vad, Ross.	80	55.32 N	44.12 E
Vad, Sve.	40	60.02 N	15.39 E
Vad ≃	80	54.33 N	42.37 E
Väddö I	40	60.00 N	18.50 E
Vădeni	38	45.22 N	27.56 E
Vader	224	46.24 N	122.57 W
Vadheim	26	61.13 N	5.49 E
Vādi	272c	18.56 N	73.06 E
Vadino	76	55.16 N	33.16 E
Vadinsk	80	53.43 N	43.04 E
Vadnagar	120	23.47 N	72.38 E
Vadodara	122	22.18 N	73.12 E
Vado de Cedillos	200	31.05 N	105.50 W
Vado de Piedra	196	29.50 N	104.40 W
Vado Hondo	200	31.09 N	111.22 W
Vado Ligure	62	44.17 N	8.27 E
Vadret, Piz ∧	58	46.41 N	9.57 E
Vadsbro	40	58.58 N	16.36 E
Vadsø	24	70.05 N	29.46 E
Vadstena	26	58.27 N	14.54 E
Vaduz	58	47.09 N	9.31 E
Vadvetjåkko Nationalpark ♠	24	68.35 N	18.20 E
Væggerløse	41	54.42 N	11.56 E
Værøy I	24	67.40 N	12.39 E
Vaga ≃	24	62.48 N	42.56 E
Vagaj	86	57.56 N	69.01 E
Vagaj ≃	86	57.59 N	69.01 E
Vågåmo	26	61.53 N	9.06 E
Vaganski Vrh ∧	36	44.22 N	15.31 E
Vaggeryd	26	57.30 N	14.07 E
Vaghena Island I	175e	7.26 S	157.46 E
Vaglia	66	43.54 N	11.17 E
Vaglio Basilicata	68	40.40 N	15.55 E
Vagney	58	48.01 N	6.43 E
Vagnhärad	40	58.55 N	17.30 E
Vagues	258	34.19 S	59.26 W
Váh ≃	30	47.55 N	18.00 E
Vaiano	66	43.58 N	11.07 E
Vaich, Loch ⊜	46	57.43 N	4.46 W
Vaiden	194	33.19 N	89.44 W
Vaigai ≃	122	9.21 N	79.00 E
Vaigat ʮ	176	70.11 N	53.00 W
Vaihingen an der Enz	56	48.56 N	8.58 E
Vaijāpur	122	19.55 N	74.44 E
Vaikam	122	9.46 N	76.24 E
Väike-Maarja	76	59.08 N	26.15 E
Väike Pakri I	76	59.20 N	24.00 E
Vail, Co., U.S.	200	39.38 N	106.22 W
Vail, Ia., U.S.	198	42.03 N	95.11 W
Vaila I	46a	60.12 N	1.37 W
Vailala ≃	164	7.25 S	145.25 E
Vaileka	175g	17.23 S	178.09 E
Vail Lake ⊜[1]	228	33.29 N	116.58 W
Vailly-sur-Aisne	50	49.25 N	3.31 E
Vailly-sur-Sauldre	50	47.27 N	2.39 E
Vail Mills	210	43.03 N	74.13 W
Vailoatai	174u	14.22 S	170.47 W
Vail Point ›	212	44.43 N	80.45 W
Vails Gate	210	41.27 N	74.04 W
Vaimali	175f	16.34 S	168.11 E
Vaiņode	76	56.26 N	21.50 E
Vaippār ≃	122	9.01 N	78.17 E
Vair ≃	58	48.27 N	5.42 E
Vairano Scalo	68	41.20 N	14.08 E
Vairao	174s	17.47 S	149.17 W
Vaires-sur-Marne	261	48.52 N	2.39 E
Vaison-la-Romaine	62	44.14 N	5.04 E
Vaitahu	174x	9.56 S	139.06 W
Vaîte	58	47.35 N	5.44 E
Vaitogi	174u	14.21 S	170.44 W
Vaitown	150	6.52 N	10.52 W
Vaitupu I	14	7.28 S	178.41 E
Vaja ≃	80	57.27 N	46.00 E
Vajgač	72	70.25 N	58.46 E
Vajgač, ostrov I	72	70.00 N	59.30 E
Vajk'	84	39.40 N	45.30 E
Vakaga □[5]	146	10.00 N	22.30 E
Vakaga ≃	146	9.48 N	21.32 E
Vākhān ≃	120	37.00 N	72.40 E
Vākhān ◆[1]	120	37.00 N	73.00 E
Vaklan	272c	19.07 N	73.06 E
Vaksdal	26	60.29 N	5.44 E
Vala ≃	80	56.59 N	51.16 E
Valaam	24	61.23 N	30.57 E
Valaam, ostrov I	26	61.22 N	30.57 E
Vålådalen	26	63.10 N	12.57 E
Valadeces	196	26.14 N	98.40 W
Valadim	154	12.22 S	36.10 E
Valais (Wallis) □[3]	58	46.10 N	7.30 E
Val-Alain	206	46.24 N	71.45 W
Valamaz	80	57.32 N	52.05 E
Valandovo	38	41.19 N	22.34 E
Valangin	58	47.01 N	6.54 E
Valap	272c	19.03 N	73.08 E
Valare, Baie ⊂	174s	17.31 S	149.46 W
Valašské Klobouky	30	49.08 N	18.01 E
Valašské Meziříčí	30	49.28 N	17.58 E
Valatie	210	42.24 N	73.40 W
Vala Ull	272c	19.02 N	73.07 E
Val-Bélair	206	46.51 N	71.26 W
Valbella	58	46.45 N	9.33 E
Vålberg	26	59.24 N	13.12 E
Valbert	56	51.07 N	7.44 E
Valbo	40	60.40 N	17.04 E
Valbondione	64	46.02 N	10.00 E
Valbonnais	62	44.54 N	5.54 E
Valcanuta ◆[8]	267a	41.53 N	12.25 E
Vâlcĕdrâm	38	43.42 N	23.27 E
Valcheta	254	40.42 S	66.09 W
Valchetta ≃	267a	41.58 N	12.30 E
Valchiusella	62	45.32 N	7.42 E
Valcivières	62	45.35 N	3.48 E
Valcourt	206	45.29 N	72.18 W
Valdagno	64	45.39 N	11.18 E
Valdahon	58	47.09 N	6.21 E
Valdai Hills → Valdajskaja vozvyšennost' ⩘[2]	76	57.00 N	33.30 E
Valdaj, Ross.	24	63.26 N	35.30 E
Valdaj, Ross.	76	57.59 N	33.14 E
Valdajskaja vozvyšennost' ⩘[2]	24	57.00 N	33.30 E
Valdarno V	66	43.45 N	11.15 E
Valdavia ≃	34	42.24 N	4.16 W
Val-David	206	46.01 N	74.12 W
Valdebeba, Arroyo de ≃	266a	41.23 N	2.10 E
Valdeblore	62	44.04 N	7.12 E
Val-de-Cães	250	1.23 S	48.29 W
Valdecañas, Embalse de ⊜[1]	34	39.45 N	5.30 W
Valdelândia	255	15.11 S	50.02 W
Val-de-Marne □[5]	261	48.47 N	2.29 E
Valdemārpils	76	57.22 N	22.35 E
Valdemarsvik	26	58.12 N	16.36 E
Valdepeñas	34	38.46 N	3.23 W
Valderaduey ≃	34	41.31 N	5.42 W
Valderas	34	42.05 N	5.27 W
Valderice	70	38.03 N	12.38 E
Valderrama	116	11.00 N	122.08 E
Valderrobres	34	40.53 N	0.09 E
Valders	190	44.03 N	87.53 W
Valdés, Península ›[1]	254	42.30 S	64.00 W
Val-des-Bois	188	45.54 N	75.35 W
Valdese	192	35.44 N	81.33 W
Valdes Island I	224	49.04 N	123.38 W
Valdéz, Ec.	246	1.15 N	79.00 W
Valdez, Ak., U.S.	180	61.07 N	146.16 W
Valdieri	62	44.17 N	7.24 E
Val-d'Isère	62	45.27 N	6.59 E
Valdivia, Chile	254	39.48 S	73.14 W
Valdivia, Col.	246	7.11 N	75.27 W
Valdobbiadene	64	45.54 N	12.00 E
Valdoie	58	47.40 N	6.51 E
Val-d'Oise □[5]	50	49.10 N	2.10 E
Val-d'Or	190	48.07 N	77.47 W
Valdorf	52	52.09 N	8.51 E
Valdosta	192	30.49 N	83.16 W
Valdoviño	34	43.36 N	8.08 W
Valdres V	26	60.55 N	9.10 E
Valdurna (Durnholz)	64	46.44 N	11.26 E
Vale, Guernsey	43b	49.29 N	2.31 W
Vale, Or., U.S.	202	43.58 N	117.14 W
Valea lui Mihai	38	47.31 N	22.09 E
Vale de Lobos	266c	38.49 N	9.17 W
Valeene	218	38.26 N	86.24 W
Valeggio sul Mincio	64	45.21 N	10.44 E
Valehouse Reservoir ⊜[1]	262	53.29 N	1.57 W
Valemount	182	52.50 N	119.15 W
Valença, Bra.	255	13.22 S	39.05 W
Valença, Bra.	256	22.15 S	43.43 W
Valença, Port.	34	42.02 N	8.38 W
Valença do Piauí	250	6.24 S	41.45 W
Valençay	50	47.09 N	1.34 E
Valence	62	44.56 N	4.54 E
Valence → València	34	39.28 N	0.22 W
València, Esp.	34	39.28 N	0.22 W
Valencia, Hond.	236	14.47 N	85.18 W
Valencia, Pil.	116	7.57 N	125.03 E
Valencia, Ca., U.S.	228	34.26 N	118.36 W
Valencia, Pa., U.S.	214	40.40 N	79.59 W
Valencia, Ven.	246	10.11 N	68.00 W
València □[4]	34	39.30 N	0.45 W
València, Golf de ⊂	34	39.50 N	0.30 E
Valencia, Lago de ⊜	246	10.15 N	67.45 W
Valencia, Quebrada ≃	286c	10.30 N	66.46 W
Valencia de Alcántata	34	39.25 N	7.14 W
Valencia de Don Juan	34	42.18 N	5.31 W
Valencia Island I	48	51.52 N	10.20 W
Valenciennes	50	50.21 N	3.32 E

≃	River	Fluß	Río	Rivière	Rio
≊	Canal	Kanal	Canal	Canal	Canal
∟	Waterfall, Rapids	Wasserfall, Stromschnellen	Cascada, Rápidos	Chute d'eau, Rapides	Cascata, Rápidos
ʮ	Strait	Meeresstraße	Estrecho	Détroit	Estreito
⊂	Bay, Gulf	Bucht, Golf	Bahía, Golfo	Baie, Golfe	Baía, Golfo
⊜	Lake, Lakes	See, Seen	Lago, Lagos	Lac, Lacs	Lago, Lagos
⩩	Swamp	Sumpf	Pantano	Marais	Pântano
⍓	Ice Features, Glacier	Eis- und Gletscherformen	Accidentes Glaciales	Formes glaciaires	Acidentes glaciares
⊤	Other Hydrographic Features	Andere Hydrographische Objekte	Otros Elementos Hidrográficos	Autres données hydrographiques	Outros acidentes hidrográficos

✦	Submarine Features	Untermeerische Objekte	Accidentes Submarinos	Formes de relief sous-marin	Acidentes submarinos
□	Political Unit	Politische Einheit	Unidad Politica	Entité politique	Unidade política
♁	Cultural Institution	Kulturelle Institution	Institución Cultural	Institution culturelle	Instituição cultural
⊥	Historical Site	Historische Stätte	Sitio Histórico	Site historique	Sitio histórico
♠	Recreational Site	Erholungs- und Ferienort	Sitio de Recreo	Centre de loisirs	Area de Lazer
⊠	Airport	Flughafen	Aeropuerto	Aéroport	Aeroporto
■	Military Installation	Militäranlage	Instalación Militar	Installation militaire	Instalação militar
◆	Miscellaneous	Verschiedenes	Misceláneo	Divers	Diversos

ENGLISH — Name | Page | Lat.°' | Long.°'

DEUTSCH — Name | Seite | Breite°' | Länge°' E = Ost

Name	Page	Lat.°'	Long.°'
Vălenii de Munte	**38**	45.12 N	26.03 E
Valensole	**62**	43.50 N	5.59 E
Valentano	**66**	42.34 N	11.49 E
Valente	**250**	11.34 S	39.27 W
Valentigney	**58**	47.28 N	6.50 E
Valentin	**89**	43.08 N	134.17 E
Valentín Alsina ◂ [8]	**288**	34.40 S	58.25 W
Valentine, Ne., U.S.	**198**	42.52 N	100.33 W
Valentine, Tx., U.S.	**196**	30.34 N	104.29 W
Valentine Mountain ∧	**224**	48.32 N	123.56 W
Valentinovka	**265b**	55.55 N	37.56 E
Valenton	**261**	48.45 N	2.28 E
Valenza	**62**	45.01 N	8.38 E
Valenzano	**68**	41.02 N	16.53 E
Valenzuela	**269f**	14.42 N	120.58 E
Våler	**26**	60.40 N	11.50 E
Valera	**246**	9.19 N	70.37 W
Valérien, Mont ∧ [2]	**261**	48.53 N	2.13 E
Vale Royal □ [8]	**262**	53.17 N	2.37 W
Valets, Lac ⊜	**190**	48.32 N	76.30 W
Valette, La → Valletta	**36**	35.54 N	14.31 E
Valfabbrica	**66**	43.09 N	12.36 E
Valflaunès	**62**	43.48 N	3.52 E
Valfurva	**64**	46.27 N	10.25 E
Valfurva V	**64**	46.26 N	10.26 E
Valga	**76**	57.47 N	26.02 E
Valge ≃	**76**	59.35 N	25.42 E
Valgorge	**62**	44.35 N	4.07 E
Valgrisanche	**62**	45.38 N	7.04 E
Valguarnera Caropepe	**70**	37.30 N	14.23 E
Valhalla, S. Afr.	**158**	25.49 S	28.08 E
Valhalla, N.Y., U.S.	**210**	41.04 N	73.46 W
Valhalla, Lake ⊜	**276**	40.56 N	74.22 W
Valiente, Península › [1]	**236**	9.05 N	81.51 W
Valiente, Punta ›	**236**	9.11 N	81.55 W
Valier, Il., U.S.	**194**	38.01 N	89.03 W
Valier, Mt., U.S.	**202**	48.18 N	112.14 W
Valier, Pa., U.S.	**214**	40.55 N	79.03 W
Valili ∧	**175g**	16.39 S	179.10 E
Valinda	**280**	34.02 N	117.56 W
Valinhos	**256**	22.57 S	47.01 W
Valjevo	**38**	44.16 N	19.53 E
Valka	**76**	57.46 N	26.00 E
Valkeakoski	**26**	61.16 N	24.02 E
Valkenburg	**56**	50.52 N	5.50 E
Valkenswaard	**52**	51.21 N	5.28 E
V'alki, Ross.	**82**	55.39 N	38.05 E
Valki, Ukr.	**78**	49.50 N	35.37 E
Valkininkas	**76**	54.21 N	24.50 E
Valla	**40**	59.02 N	16.23 E
Valladares	**196**	26.53 N	100.37 W
Valladolid, Ec.	**246**	4.33 S	79.08 W
Valladolid, Esp.	**34**	41.39 N	4.43 W
Valladolid, Méx.	**232**	20.41 N	88.12 W
Valladolid □ [4]	**34**	41.40 N	4.50 W
Vallage ◂ [1]	**58**	48.24 N	5.00 E
Vallåkra	**41**	55.58 N	12.52 E
Vallarsa	**64**	45.47 N	11.07 E
Vallata	**68**	41.02 N	15.15 E
Vallauris	**62**	43.35 N	7.03 E
Vallco Fashion Park ◂ [9]	**282**	37.19 N	122.01 W
Valldal	**26**	62.20 N	7.21 E
Valldoreix	**266d**	41.28 N	2.04 E
Valle, Esp.	**34**	43.14 N	4.18 W
Valle, Lat.	**76**	56.30 N	24.44 E
Valle □ [5]	**236**	13.30 N	87.35 W
Valle, Arroyo ≃	**226**	37.39 N	121.54 W
Vallecas ◂ [8]	**266a**	40.23 N	3.37 W
Valle Castellana	**66**	42.44 N	13.29 E
Vallecillo	**196**	26.40 N	99.58 W
Vallecito	**226**	38.07 N	120.27 W
Vallecitos	**200**	36.05 N	106.20 W
Vallecitos Creek ≃	**282**	37.36 N	121.53 W
Vallecorsa	**66**	41.27 N	13.24 E
Valle Crucis Abbey ⌂ [1]	**42**	52.59 N	3.12 W
Valle d'Aosta □ [4]	**62**	45.45 N	7.25 E
Valle de Bravo	**234**	19.11 N	100.08 W
Valle de Guadalupe	**234**	21.00 N	102.37 W
Valle de Guanape	**246**	9.54 N	65.41 W
Valle de Juárez	**234**	19.53 N	102.51 W
Valle de la Pascua	**246**	9.13 N	66.00 W
Valle del Cauca □ [5]	**246**	3.45 N	76.30 W
Valle de Olivos	**232**	27.12 N	106.17 W
Valle de Santiago	**234**	20.23 N	101.12 W
Valle de Zaragoza	**232**	27.28 N	105.49 W
Valle di Cadore	**64**	46.24 N	12.20 E
Valle di Sotto	**64**	46.25 N	10.21 E
Valledolmo	**70**	37.45 N	13.49 E
Valledupar	**246**	10.29 N	73.15 W
Valle Edén	**252**	31.50 S	56.09 W
Vallefiorita	**68**	38.46 N	16.27 E
Vallegrande	**248**	18.29 S	64.06 W
Valle Hermoso, Arg.	**252**	31.07 S	64.29 W
Valle Hermoso, Méx.	**196**	25.39 N	97.52 W
Vallehermoso, Pil.	**116**	10.20 N	123.19 E
Vallejo	**226**	38.06 N	122.15 W
Valle Lomellina	**62**	45.09 N	8.40 E
Vallelunga Pratameno	**70**	37.41 N	13.50 E
Valle Mosso	**62**	45.38 N	8.09 E
Vällen ⊜	**40**	60.03 N	18.20 E
Vallenar	**252**	28.35 S	70.46 W
Vallendar	**56**	50.24 N	7.37 E
Vallensbæk	**41**	55.38 N	12.22 E
Vallentuna	**40**	59.32 N	18.05 E
Vallepietra	**66**	41.55 N	13.14 E
Valleraugue	**62**	44.05 N	3.38 E
Valle Redondo	**204**	32.31 N	116.46 W
Vallermosa	**71**	39.22 N	8.48 E
Vallerotonda	**66**	41.33 N	13.55 E
Valleroy	**56**	49.12 N	5.55 E
Valles Caldera ≛ [6]	**200**	35.52 N	106.33 W
Valles → Ciudad de Valles	**234**	21.59 N	99.01 W
Vallet	**32**	47.10 N	1.16 W
Valletta	**36**	35.54 N	14.31 E
Valley, Al., U.S.	**194**	32.49 N	85.10 W
Valley, Ne., U.S.	**198**	41.18 N	96.20 W
Valley, Wa., U.S.	**182**	48.10 N	117.43 W
Valley ≃	**184**	51.21 N	99.55 W
Valley Bend	**188**	38.46 N	79.56 W
Valley Center, Ca., U.S.	**228**	33.13 N	117.02 W
Valley Center, Ks., U.S.	**198**	37.50 N	97.22 W
Valley City, N.D., U.S.	**198**	46.55 N	97.59 W
Valley City, Oh., U.S.	**214**	41.14 N	81.56 W
Valley Cottage	**210**	41.07 N	73.57 W
Valley Creek ≃, Pa., U.S.	**285**	40.06 N	75.28 W
Valley Creek ≃, Pa., U.S.	**285**	39.58 N	75.40 W
Valley Creek ≃, Tx., U.S.	**196**	31.43 N	100.02 W
Valleydale	**280**	34.06 N	117.56 W
Valley Falls, Ks., U.S.	**198**	39.20 N	95.27 W
Valley Falls, N.Y., U.S.	**210**	42.54 N	73.34 W
Valley Falls, R.I., U.S.	**207**	41.54 N	71.23 W
Valley Farms	**200**	32.59 N	111.26 W
Valleyfield	**186**	49.08 N	53.37 W
Valley Forge	**208**	40.05 N	75.28 W
Valley Forge Estates	**285**	40.05 N	75.26 W
Valley Forge National Historical Park ♠	**208**	40.06 N	75.27 W
Valley Grove	**214**	40.05 N	80.34 W
Valley Head, Al., U.S.	**194**	34.34 N	85.36 W
Valley Head, W.V., U.S.	**188**	38.32 N	80.02 W
Valley Home	**226**	37.50 N	120.55 W
Valley Mede	**284b**	39.17 N	76.50 W
Valley Mills	**222**	31.39 N	97.28 W
Valley of Desolation National Monument ♠	**158**	32.17 S	24.30 E
Valley of Fire State Park ♠	**204**	36.26 N	114.30 W
Valley of the Kings ⊥	**140**	25.45 N	32.37 E
Valley Park	**219**	38.32 N	90.29 W
Valley Plaza ◂ [9]	**280**	34.11 N	118.24 W
Valley Springs, Ca., U.S.	**226**	38.12 N	120.50 W
Valley Springs, S.D., U.S.	**198**	43.34 N	96.28 W
Valley Station	**194**	38.06 N	85.52 W
Valley Stream	**210**	40.39 N	73.42 W
Valley Stream ≃	**276**	40.39 N	73.45 W
Valley Stream State Park ♠	**276**	40.41 N	73.42 W
Valleyview, Ab., Can.	**182**	55.04 N	117.17 W
Valley View, Il., U.S.	**216**	41.50 N	88.03 W
Valley View, Oh., U.S.	**279a**	41.23 N	81.37 W
Valley View, Pa., U.S.	**210**	40.38 N	76.32 W
Valley View, Tx., U.S.	**196**	33.29 N	97.10 W
Valley View Park	**228**	34.13 N	117.20 W
Vallgrund I	**26**	63.12 N	21.14 E
Valliant	**196**	34.00 N	95.05 W
Valli del Pasubio	**64**	45.41 N	11.15 E
Vallières	**58**	45.54 N	5.56 E
Vallimanca, Arroyo ≃	**252**	35.40 S	60.02 W
Vallio	**64**	45.38 N	10.23 E
Vallirana	**266d**	41.23 N	1.56 E
Vallø	**41**	55.24 N	12.15 E
Vallo della Lucania	**68**	40.14 N	15.17 E
Valloire	**62**	45.10 N	6.26 E
Vallombrosa	**64**	43.44 N	11.32 E
Vallonia	**218**	38.50 N	86.05 W
Vallon-Pont-d'Arc	**62**	44.24 N	4.24 E
Vallorbe	**58**	46.43 N	6.22 E
Vallorcine	**58**	46.02 N	6.56 E
Vallouise	**62**	44.51 N	6.29 E
Vallromanes	**266d**	41.32 N	2.18 E
Valls	**34**	41.17 N	1.15 E
Valluga ∧	**58**	47.09 N	10.12 E
Vallvidrera ◂ [8]	**266d**	41.25 N	2.07 E
Vallvidrera, Riera de ≃	**266d**	41.25 N	2.01 E
Val-Marie	**184**	49.14 N	107.44 W
Valmaseda	**34**	43.12 N	3.12 W
Valmeyer	**219**	38.17 N	90.18 W
Valmiera	**76**	57.33 N	25.24 E
Valmondois	**261**	49.06 N	2.12 E
Valmont	**50**	49.44 N	0.31 E
Valmontone	**66**	41.46 N	12.57 E
Valmy	**56**	49.05 N	4.46 E
Valognes	**32**	49.31 N	1.28 W
Valois	**210**	42.32 N	76.53 W
Valois, Baie de ⊂	**275a**	45.26 N	73.47 W
Valok	**78**	45.47 N	34.57 E
Valona → Vlorë	**38**	40.27 N	19.30 E
Valongo	**34**	41.11 N	8.30 W
Valoria la Buena	**34**	41.48 N	4.32 W
Vālpārai	**122**	10.22 N	76.58 E
Valparaíso, Bra.	**255**	21.13 S	50.51 W
Valparaíso, Chile	**252**	33.02 S	71.38 W
Valparaíso, Méx.	**234**	22.46 N	103.34 W
Valparaiso, Fl., U.S.	**194**	30.29 N	86.29 W
Valparaiso, In., U.S.	**216**	41.28 N	87.03 W
Valparaiso, Ne., U.S.	**198**	41.04 N	96.49 W
Valparaíso □ [4]	**252**	32.45 S	71.20 W
Valparaíso ≃	**234**	22.33 N	103.39 W
Valpelline V	**62**	45.50 N	7.25 E
Valpovo	**38**	45.39 N	18.26 E
Valprato Soana	**62**	45.31 N	7.33 E
Valréas	**62**	44.23 N	4.59 E
Valrico	**220**	27.57 N	82.16 W
Val Roveto V	**66**	41.52 N	13.30 E
Vals ≃	**158**	27.23 S	26.30 E
Vals, Tanjung ›	**164**	8.26 S	137.38 E
Val-Saint-Michel	**206**	46.52 N	71.27 W
Valsbaai ⊂	**158**	34.12 S	18.40 E
Valserine ≃	**58**	46.06 N	5.50 E
Valserrhein ≃	**58**	46.42 N	9.10 E
Valsertal V	**58**	46.37 N	9.10 E
Valsetz	**202**	44.50 N	123.39 W
Valsinni	**68**	40.10 N	16.26 E
Valsjöbyn	**26**	64.04 N	14.08 E
Valskog	**40**	59.27 N	15.57 E
Vals-les-Bains	**62**	44.40 N	4.22 E
Vals Platz	**58**	46.37 N	9.11 E
Vals-Près-le-Puy	**62**	45.01 N	3.52 E
Valstagna	**64**	45.51 N	11.39 E
Val-Suzon	**58**	47.25 N	4.54 E
Valtellina V	**64**	46.11 N	9.55 E
Valthermond	**52**	52.53 N	6.59 E
Valtice	**61**	48.44 N	16.45 E
Valtierrilla	**234**	20.32 N	101.08 W
Valtimo	**26**	63.40 N	28.48 E
Valtorta	**58**	45.59 N	9.32 E
Valtournanche	**62**	45.53 N	7.37 E
Valujec	**76**	52.46 N	33.23 E
Valujevka	**80**	46.44 N	43.43 E
Valujevo	**265b**	55.35 N	37.21 E
Valujki	**78**	50.13 N	38.08 E
Valvasone	**64**	45.59 N	12.52 E
Valverde	**148**	27.48 N	17.55 W
Valverde del Camino	**34**	37.34 N	6.45 W
Val Verde Park	**228**	34.27 N	118.40 W
Valyermo	**228**	34.26 N	117.50 W
Vamba ≃	**152**	7.27 S	14.17 E
Vamdrup	**41**	55.25 N	9.17 E
Våmhus	**26**	61.08 N	14.28 E
Vamizi, Ilha I	**154**	11.02 S	40.40 E
Vammala	**26**	61.20 N	22.54 E
Vamori Wash V	**200**	31.57 N	112.21 W
Van, Tür.	**128**	38.28 N	43.20 E
Van, Pa., U.S.	**214**	41.19 N	79.40 E
Van, Tx., U.S.	**222**	32.31 N	95.38 W
Van □ [4]	**128**	39.00 N	43.45 E
Vanajavesi ⊜	**26**	61.09 N	24.15 E
Vanak ◂ [8]	**267d**	35.45 N	51.23 E
Van Alstyne	**196**	33.25 N	96.34 W
Vanån ≃	**40**	60.31 N	14.14 E
Vananda	**182**	49.45 N	124.33 W
Vanapa ≃	**164**	9.05 S	147.10 E
Vanault-les-Dames	**56**	48.51 N	4.46 E
Vanavana I [1]	**14**	20.47 S	139.09 W
Vanavara	**74**	60.22 N	102.16 E
Van Buren, Ar., U.S.	**194**	35.26 N	94.20 W
Van Buren, In., U.S.	**216**	40.37 N	85.30 W
Van Buren, Me., U.S.	**186**	47.09 N	67.56 W
Van Buren, Mo., U.S.	**194**	36.59 N	91.00 W
Van Buren, Oh., U.S.	**216**	41.08 N	83.38 W
Van Buren □ [6]	**216**	42.14 N	86.04 W
Van Buren Point	**214**	42.27 N	79.25 W
Vanč	**85**	38.23 N	71.26 E
Vanč ≃	**85**	38.18 N	71.19 E
Vance Air Force Base ■	**196**	36.21 N	97.55 W
Vanceboro	**188**	45.33 N	67.25 W
Vanceburg	**218**	38.35 N	83.19 W
Vancleave	**194**	30.32 N	88.41 W
Van Cortlandt Park ♠	**276**	40.54 N	73.53 W
Van Cortlandtville	**210**	41.19 N	73.54 W
Vancouver, B.C., Can.	**224**	49.16 N	123.07 W
Vancouver, Wa., U.S.	**224**	45.38 N	122.39 W
Vancouver, Cape ›, Austl.	**162**	35.01 S	118.12 E
Vancouver, Cape ›, Ak., U.S.	**180**	60.33 N	165.27 W
Vancouver, Mount ∧	**180**	60.20 N	139.40 W
Vancouver International Airport ⊠	**224**	48.39 N	123.26 W
Vancouver Island I	**182**	49.45 N	126.00 W
Vancouver Island Ranges ⋏	**182**	49.25 N	125.25 W
Vancouver Lake ⊜	**224**	45.41 N	122.44 W
Van Daalen ≃	**164**	3.05 S	138.09 E
Vandalia, Il., U.S.	**219**	38.57 N	89.05 W
Vandalia, Mi., U.S.	**216**	41.55 N	85.55 W
Vandalia, Mo., U.S.	**219**	39.18 N	91.29 W
Vandalia, Oh., U.S.	**218**	39.53 N	84.11 W
Vandalia Lake ⊜ [1]	**219**	39.01 N	89.09 W
Vandam	**84**	40.57 N	47.57 E
Vandavāsi	**122**	12.30 N	79.37 E
Vandekerckhove Lake ⊜	**184**	57.02 N	101.25 W
Vandel	**41**	55.42 N	9.13 E
Vandenberg Air Force Base ■	**204**	34.43 N	120.33 W
Van den Bosch, Tanjung ›	**164**	4.06 S	132.55 E
Vandenesse	**58**	47.13 N	4.37 E
Vanderbijlpark	**158**	26.42 S	27.54 E
Vanderbilt, Mi., U.S.	**190**	45.08 N	84.39 W
Vanderbilt, Tx., U.S.	**196**	28.49 N	96.37 W
Vanderbilt Mansion National Historic Site ⊥	**210**	41.47 N	73.56 W
Vanderbilt Museum ⌂	**276**	40.54 N	73.22 W
Vandercook Lake	**216**	42.11 N	84.23 W
Vandergrift	**214**	40.36 N	79.33 W
Vanderhoof	**182**	54.01 N	124.01 W
Vanderlin Island I	**164**	15.44 S	137.02 E
Vandervoort	**194**	34.22 N	94.21 W
Van Diemen, Cape ›, Austl.	**164**	11.10 S	130.23 E
Van Diemen, Cape ›, Austl.	**164**	16.31 S	139.41 E
Van Diemen Gulf ⊂	**164**	11.50 S	132.00 E
Vandling	**210**	41.38 N	75.29 W
Vandoeuvre-lès-Nancy	**58**	48.39 N	6.11 E
Vandoies (Vintl)	**64**	46.49 N	11.43 E
Vändra	**76**	58.39 N	25.02 E
Van Duzen ≃	**204**	40.33 N	124.08 W
Vandúzi ≃	**154**	18.56 S	34.01 E
Vandykpark	**273d**	26.16 S	28.19 E
Vandžiogala	**76**	55.07 N	23.58 E
Vanegas	**234**	23.51 N	100.52 W
Vänern ⊜	**26**	58.55 N	13.30 E
Vänersborg	**26**	58.22 N	12.19 E
Van Etten	**210**	42.11 N	76.33 W
Vang, Mount ∧	**9**	73.56 S	68.39 W
Vanga	**154**	4.39 S	39.13 E
Vangaindrano	**157b**	23.21 S	47.36 E
Vängelälven ≃	**26**	63.41 N	16.25 E
Van Gölü ⊜	**128**	38.33 N	42.46 E
Vangsnes	**26**	61.11 N	6.38 E
Vanguard	**184**	49.55 N	107.20 W
Vangunu, Mount ∧	**175e**	8.42 S	158.00 E
Vangunu Island I	**175e**	8.38 S	158.00 E
Van Hook Arm ⊂	**198**	47.50 N	102.25 W
Van Horn	**196**	31.02 N	104.49 W
Van Horne	**190**	42.00 N	92.05 W
Van Hornesville	**210**	42.54 N	74.50 W
Vani	**84**	42.06 N	42.30 E
Vanier	**212**	45.26 N	75.40 W
Vanikolo I	**14**	11.39 S	166.54 E
Vaniköy ◂ [8]	**267b**	41.04 N	29.04 E
Vanimo	**164**	2.40 S	141.20 E
Vanino	**89**	49.05 N	140.15 E
Vānīvilāsa Sāgara ⊜ [1]	**122**	13.52 N	76.26 E
Vāniyambādi	**122**	12.41 N	78.37 E
Vankarem	**180**	67.51 N	175.50 W
Vankarem ≃	**180**	67.42 N	176.17 W
Vankarem, laguna ⊂	**180**	67.40 N	176.00 W
Vankaremskaja nizmennost' ≚	**180**	67.30 N	176.00 W
Van Kleef Aquarium ♠	**271c**	1.18 N	103.51 E
Vankleek Hill	**206**	45.31 N	74.39 W
Vanlay	**50**	48.02 N	4.01 E
Van Lear	**192**	37.46 N	82.45 W
Vanlue	**216**	40.58 N	83.28 W
Vanna I	**24**	70.09 N	19.51 E
Vännäs	**26**	63.55 N	19.45 E
Vanndale	**194**	35.18 N	90.46 W
Vanne ≃	**50**	48.12 N	3.16 E
Vanne et du Loing, Aqueduc de ≍ [1]	**261**	48.36 N	2.26 E
Vannes	**32**	47.39 N	2.46 W
Vannes-sur-Cosson	**50**	47.43 N	2.13 E
Van Ninh	**110**	12.42 N	109.14 E
Van Norman Lakes ⊜ [1]	**228**	34.18 N	118.28 W
Vannovka	**85**	42.32 N	70.21 E
Van Nuys ◂ [8]	**228**	34.11 N	118.26 W
Van Nuys Airport ⊠	**280**	34.12 N	118.29 W
Van Nuys-Sherman Oaks War Memorial Park ♠	**280**	34.10 N	118.27 W
Vanoi ≃	**64**	46.06 N	11.45 E
Vanoise, Massif de la ⋏	**62**	45.20 N	6.40 E
Vanoise, Parc National de la ♠	**62**	45.20 N	6.45 E
Van Ormer	**214**	40.41 N	78.30 W
Van Phong, Vung ⊂	**110**	12.33 N	109.18 E
Vanport	**214**	40.41 N	80.20 W
Van Reenen	**158**	28.22 S	29.24 E
Van Reenen's Plaats	**158**	30.55 S	21.14 E
Van Rees, Pegunungan ⋏	**164**	2.35 S	138.15 E
Vanrhynsdorp	**158**	31.36 S	18.44 E
Vanrook	**166**	16.57 S	141.57 E
Vanryndam ⊜ [1]	**273d**	26.09 S	28.21 E
Vansant	**192**	37.13 N	82.05 W
Van Saun Mill Brook ≃	**276**	40.55 N	74.03 W
Vansbro	**40**	60.31 N	14.13 E
Van Sciver Lake ⊜	**285**	40.09 N	74.48 W
Van Sickle Island I	**282**	38.04 N	121.53 W
Vansittart Island I	**176**	65.50 N	84.00 W
Vansjön ⊜	**40**	59.59 N	16.57 E
Vanskoje	**76**	58.56 N	36.52 E
Vanstadensrus	**158**	29.59 S	27.02 E
Vantaa (Vanda)	**26**	60.16 N	25.03 E
Vantaa ≃	**26**	60.13 N	24.59 E
Vanthali	**120**	21.29 N	70.20 E
Vanua Lava I	**175f**	13.48 S	167.28 E
Vanua Levu I	**175g**	16.33 S	179.15 E
Vanua Mbalavu Island I	**175g**	17.40 S	178.57 W
Vanuatu □ [1], Oc.	**14**	16.00 S	167.00 E
Vanuatu □ [1], Oc.	**175f**	16.00 S	167.00 E
Vanves	**261**	48.50 N	2.18 E
Van Vleck	**222**	29.01 N	95.53 W
Van Voorhis	**279b**	40.10 N	79.58 W
Van Wert	**216**	40.52 N	84.35 W
Van Wert □ [6]	**216**	40.52 N	84.35 W
Vanwyksdorp	**158**	33.46 S	21.28 E
Vanwyksvlei	**158**	30.18 S	21.49 E
Vanzaghello	**266b**	45.35 N	8.47 E
Vanzago	**266b**	45.32 N	9.00 E
Van Zandt □ [6]	**222**	32.35 N	95.50 W
Vanzylsrus	**158**	26.52 S	22.04 E
Vao	**175f**	22.39 S	167.32 E
Vapn'arka	**78**	48.32 N	28.44 E
Vaprio d'Adda	**62**	45.35 N	9.31 E
Vaqueros Creek ≃	**226**	36.16 N	121.20 W
Var □ [5]	**62**	43.30 N	6.20 E
Var ≃	**62**	43.39 N	7.12 E
Vara	**26**	58.16 N	12.57 E
Vara ≃	**64**	44.09 N	9.53 E
Varada ≃	**122**	14.55 N	75.40 E
Varadero	**240p**	23.09 N	81.16 W
Varades	**32**	47.23 N	1.02 W
Varages	**62**	43.36 N	5.58 E
Varaita ≃	**62**	44.49 N	7.36 E
Varaita, Valle V	**62**	44.35 N	7.10 E
Varakļāni	**76**	56.37 N	26.44 E
Varallo, It.	**62**	45.49 N	8.15 E
Varallo, It.	**266b**	45.40 N	8.38 E
Varāmīn	**128**	35.20 N	51.39 E
Vārānasi (Benares)	**124**	25.20 N	83.00 E
Varandej	**24**	68.48 N	58.00 E
Varangerfjorden ⊂ [2]	**24**	70.00 N	30.00 E
Varangerhalvøya › [1]	**24**	70.25 N	29.30 E
Varangéville	**56**	48.38 N	6.19 E
Varano, Lago Di ⊂	**68**	41.53 N	15.45 E
Varano de'Melegari	**64**	44.41 N	10.01 E
Varapodio	**68**	38.19 N	15.59 E
Varaždin	**36**	46.19 N	16.20 E
Varazze	**62**	44.22 N	8.34 E
Varberg	**26**	57.06 N	12.15 E
Varces	**62**	45.05 N	5.41 E
Varciche	**84**	42.08 N	42.43 E
Vardak □ [4]	**120**	34.15 N	68.00 E
Vardaman	**194**	33.52 N	89.10 W
Vardar (Axiós) ≃	**38**	40.35 N	22.50 E
Varde	**26**	55.38 N	8.29 E
Vardenik	**84**	40.08 N	45.27 E
Vardenis	**84**	40.11 N	45.43 E
Vardenskij chrebet ⋏	**84**	39.58 N	45.25 E
Vardhoúsia Óri ⋏	**38**	38.44 N	22.07 E
Vardø	**24**	70.21 N	31.02 E
Vardūj ≃	**123**	37.01 N	70.47 E
Varedo	**62**	45.36 N	9.09 E
Varegovo	**80**	57.47 N	39.17 E
Varel	**52**	53.22 N	8.10 E
Varela	**252**	34.07 S	66.27 W
Varėna	**76**	54.13 N	24.34 E
Varengeville-sur-Mer	**50**	49.55 N	0.59 E
Varenikovskaja	**78**	45.07 N	37.37 E
Varenna	**58**	46.01 N	9.17 E
Varenne ≃	**50**	49.53 N	1.08 E
Varennes	**206**	45.41 N	73.26 W
Varennes, Îles de II	**275a**	45.40 N	73.27 W
Varennes-en-Argonne	**56**	49.14 N	5.02 E
Varennes-Jarcy	**261**	48.41 N	2.34 E
Varennes-Saint-Sauveur	**58**	46.29 N	5.15 E
Varennes-sur-Allier	**32**	46.19 N	3.24 E
Varennes-sur-Amance	**58**	47.54 N	5.37 E
Varenovka	**83**	47.18 N	39.02 E
Vareš	**38**	44.09 N	18.19 E
Varese	**62**	45.48 N	8.48 E
Varese □ [4]	**62**	45.48 N	8.40 E
Varese, Lago di ⊜	**62**	45.49 N	8.45 E
Varese Ligure	**62**	44.22 N	9.37 E
Varèze ≃	**62**	45.25 N	4.45 E
Varfolomejevka	**80**	50.01 N	48.12 E
Vårgårda	**26**	58.02 N	12.48 E
Vargas □ [5]	**286c**	10.34 N	66.52 W
Vargaši	**86**	55.23 N	65.48 E
Vargem	**256**	22.53 S	46.25 W
Vargem, Riacho da ≃	**250**	8.42 S	39.09 W
Vargem Alegre	**256**	22.30 S	43.55 W
Vargem do Laje	**256**	22.08 S	44.49 W
Vargem Grande	**250**	3.33 S	43.56 W
Vargem Grande ◂ [8]	**287a**	22.59 S	43.29 W
Vargem Grande, Ribeirão da ≃	**256**	22.17 S	45.40 W
Vargem Grande do Sul	**256**	21.50 S	46.53 W
Vargem Grande Paulista	**256**	23.36 S	47.01 W
Varginha	**256**	21.33 S	45.26 W
Vargön	**26**	58.22 N	12.22 E
Varigotti	**62**	44.11 N	8.24 E
Väringen ⊜	**40**	59.26 N	15.23 E
Varirata National Park ♠	**164**	9.20 S	147.20 E
Varjão	**255**	17.03 S	49.37 W
Varkallai	**122**	8.40 N	76.50 E
Varkaus	**26**	62.19 N	27.55 E
Varkhān ≃	**128**	32.55 N	65.30 E
Varlamovo	**86**	54.38 N	60.40 E
Värmdölandet I	**40**	59.20 N	18.33 E
Värmeln ⊜	**26**	59.32 N	12.54 E
Värmland □ [9]	**26**	59.48 N	13.03 E
Värmlands Län □ [6]	**26**	59.45 N	13.15 E
Värmlandsnäs › [1]	**26**	59.00 N	13.10 E
Varna, Blg.	**38**	43.13 N	27.55 E
Varna (Vahrn), It.	**64**	46.44 N	11.38 E
Varna, Ross.	**86**	53.24 N	60.58 E
Varna, N.Y., U.S.	**210**	42.27 N	76.26 W
Värnamo	**26**	57.11 N	14.02 E
Varnavino	**80**	57.24 N	45.04 E
Varnenski zaliv ⊂	**38**	43.11 N	27.56 E
Varner-Hogg Plantation State Historic Park ♠	**222**	29.09 N	95.37 W
Varnhem	**26**	58.23 N	13.39 E
Varniai	**76**	55.45 N	22.22 E
Varnsdorf	**54**	50.52 N	14.40 E
Varnville	**192**	32.51 N	81.04 W
Värö	**26**	57.16 N	12.11 E
Városliget ♠	**264c**	47.31 N	19.06 E
Varpaisjärvi	**26**	63.22 N	27.45 E
Várpalota	**30**	47.12 N	18.09 E
Varpan ⊜	**40**	60.38 N	15.36 E
Varresbeck ◂ [8]	**263**	51.15 N	7.06 E
Vars, On., Can.	**212**	45.21 N	75.21 W
Vars, Fr.	**62**	44.37 N	6.41 E
Vars, Col de)(	**62**	44.32 N	6.42 E
Vârşec	**38**	43.12 N	23.17 E
Varsi	**62**	44.40 N	9.51 E
Varsinais-Suomi ◂ [1]	**26**	60.40 N	22.30 E
Värska	**76**	57.58 N	27.38 E
Varsovie → Warszawa	**30**	52.15 N	21.00 E
Varsseveld	**52**	51.57 N	6.28 E
Vårsta	**40**	59.10 N	17.48 E
Vartašen	**84**	41.06 N	47.28 E
Varto	**130**	39.10 N	41.28 E
V'artsil'a	**24**	62.11 N	30.41 E
Varty Lake ⊜	**212**	44.23 N	76.48 W
Varuna ≃	**124**	25.21 N	83.03 E
Varva	**78**	50.31 N	32.41 E
Varvarin	**38**	43.43 N	21.19 E
Varvarovka, Ukr.	**78**	48.42 N	36.02 E
Varvarovka, Ukr.	**78**	49.33 N	35.12 E
Varvarovka, Ukr.	**83**	49.05 N	38.24 E
Varysburg	**210**	42.46 N	78.19 W
Várzea	**256**	22.30 S	44.46 W
Várzea, Rio da ≃	**252**	27.13 S	53.19 W
Várzea Alegre	**250**	6.47 S	39.17 W
Várzea da Palma	**255**	17.36 S	44.44 W
Varzea de Sintra	**266c**	38.49 N	9.24 W
Várzea Grande	**248**	15.39 S	56.08 W
Varzeão	**252**	24.34 S	49.26 W
Várzea Paulista	**256**	23.12 S	46.50 W
Varzi, It.	**62**	44.49 N	9.12 E
Varzi, Ross.	**80**	56.03 N	52.50 E
Varzino	**24**	68.19 N	38.19 E
Varzo	**36**	46.12 N	8.15 E
Varzob	**85**	38.46 N	68.49 E
Varzob ≃	**85**	38.30 N	68.45 E
Varzuga	**24**	67.24 N	36.32 E
Varzy	**50**	47.22 N	3.23 E
Varzyk	**85**	41.07 N	71.14 E
Vas	**64**	45.56 N	11.56 E
Vas □ [6]	**61**	47.05 N	16.45 E
Vasai (Bassein)	**122**	19.21 N	72.48 E
Vasalemma	**76**	59.14 N	24.18 E
Vašana ≃	**82**	54.36 N	37.10 E
Vasar	**272c**	19.11 N	73.09 E
Vasa → Vaasa	**26**	63.06 N	21.36 E
Vascão, Ribeirão do ≃	**34**	37.31 N	7.31 W
Vaşcău	**38**	46.28 N	22.28 E
Väse	**40**	59.23 N	13.57 E
Vāshi	**272c**	19.04 N	72.59 E
Vashon	**224**	47.26 N	122.27 W
Vashon Heights	**224**	47.30 N	122.28 W
Vashon Island I	**224**	47.24 N	122.27 W
Vasilevići	**76**	52.14 N	29.49 E
Vasilija, mys ›	**180**	64.34 N	178.33 E
Vasiliká	**38**	40.28 N	23.08 E
Vasiliški	**76**	53.47 N	24.51 E
Vasiljevka, Bela.	**76**	52.15 N	31.31 E
Vasiljevka, Ross.	**89**	46.52 N	134.03 E
Vasiljevka, Ukr.	**78**	47.26 N	35.16 E
Vasiljevo, Ross.	**24**	60.46 N	38.59 E
Vasiljevo, Ross.	**80**	55.52 N	48.42 E
Vasiljevskij, ostrov I	**265a**	59.56 N	30.15 E
Vasiljevskij Moch	**76**	57.01 N	35.55 E
Vasiljevskoje, Ross.	**80**	56.56 N	41.40 E
Vasiljevskoje, Ross.	**80**	56.31 N	45.49 E
Vasiljevskoje, Ross.	**82**	55.00 N	37.25 E
Vasiljevskoje, Ross.	**82**	56.20 N	37.54 E
Vasil'kov	**78**	50.12 N	30.19 E
Vasil'kovka	**78**	48.13 N	36.02 E
Vasil'sursk	**80**	56.08 N	46.01 E
Vasis	**86**	57.22 N	74.44 E
Vaška ≃	**24**	64.53 N	45.47 E
Vaskelovo	**76**	60.22 N	30.22 E
Vaskess Bay ⊂	**174o**	1.51 N	157.31 W
Vaškovci	**78**	48.24 N	27.08 E
Vaškovcy	**78**	48.23 N	25.30 E
Vaslui	**38**	46.38 N	27.44 E
Vaslui □ [6]	**38**	46.30 N	27.45 E
Väsman ⊜	**40**	60.11 N	15.04 E
Vass	**192**	35.15 N	79.16 W
Vassako-Bolo, Réserve Naturelle Intégrale de la ◂ [4]	**146**	8.10 N	19.45 E
Vassar	**190**	43.22 N	83.35 W
Vassdalseggi ∧	**26**	59.46 N	7.10 E
Vassieux-en-Vercors	**62**	44.53 N	5.22 E
Vassouras	**256**	22.25 S	43.40 W
Vassy	**50**	47.34 N	4.10 E
Västanfors	**40**	59.59 N	15.49 E
Västerås	**40**	59.37 N	16.33 E
Västeråsfjärden ⊂	**40**	59.34 N	16.34 E
Västerbotten □ [9]	**26**	64.36 N	20.04 E
Västerbottens Län □ [6]	**24**	64.00 N	17.30 E
Västerby	**40**	60.19 N	15.55 E
Västerdalälven ≃	**40**	60.33 N	15.08 E
Västerfärnebo	**40**	59.57 N	16.17 E
Västergötland □ [9]	**26**	58.01 N	13.03 E
Västerhaninge	**40**	59.07 N	18.06 E
Västernorrlands Län □ [6]	**26**	63.00 N	17.30 E
Västervik	**26**	57.45 N	16.38 E
Västmanland □ [9]	**40**	59.38 N	15.15 E
Västmanlands Län □ [6]	**40**	59.45 N	16.20 E
Vasto	**66**	42.07 N	14.42 E
Västra Laxsjön ⊜	**40**	58.54 N	14.38 E
Västra Ringsjön ⊜	**41**	55.53 N	13.28 E
Västra Torup	**41**	56.09 N	13.29 E
Vastseliina	**76**	57.44 N	27.17 E
Vas'ugan ≃	**86**	59.07 N	80.46 E
Vas'uganje ≡	**86**	58.00 N	77.00 E
Vas'unino	**82**	55.15 N	37.01 E
Vašutino	**265b**	55.56 N	37.26 E
Vašutkiny ozera ⊜	**24**	68.06 N	61.18 E
Vasvár	**61**	47.03 N	16.49 E
Vát	**61**	47.17 N	16.47 E
Vața de Jos	**38**	46.10 N	22.35 E
Vatan	**32**	47.05 N	1.48 E
Vaternish Point ›	**46**	57.36 N	6.38 W
Vatersay I	**46**	56.55 N	7.32 W
Vaterstetten	**60**	48.07 N	11.47 E
Vathí	**38**	37.45 N	26.59 E
Vatican (Cité du) → Vatican City □ [1]	**267a**	41.54 N	12.27 E
Vatican City (Città del Vaticano) □ [1], Europe	**66**	41.54 N	12.27 E
Vatican City (Città del Vaticano) □ [1], Europe	**267a**	41.54 N	12.27 E
Vaticano, Capo ›	**68**	38.38 N	15.50 E
Vatikanstadt → Vatican City □ [1]	**66**	41.54 N	12.27 E
V'atka ≃	**80**	55.36 N	51.30 E
V'atka → Kirov	**80**	58.38 N	49.42 E
Vatlirchvin, gora ∧	**180**	68.08 N	179.52 W
Vatnajökull ⌓	**24a**	64.25 N	16.50 W
Vatneyri	**24a**	65.38 N	23.57 W
Vätö I	**40**	59.49 N	18.57 E
Vatoa Island I	**175g**	19.50 S	178.13 W
Vatoloha ∧	**157b**	17.52 S	47.48 E
Vatomandry	**157b**	19.20 S	48.59 E
Vatra Dornei	**38**	47.21 N	25.21 E
V'atskije Pol'any	**80**	56.14 N	51.04 E
V'atskij uval ⋏ [2]	**80**	57.20 N	49.10 E
V'atskoje, Ross.	**80**	57.52 N	40.16 E
V'atskoje, Ross.	**89**	48.44 N	135.43 E
Vattalkundu	**122**	10.10 N	77.46 E
Vättern ⊜	**26**	58.24 N	14.36 E
Vättersee → Vättern ⊜	**26**	58.24 N	14.36 E
Vattholma	**40**	60.01 N	17.44 E
Vättis	**58**	46.55 N	9.27 E
Vatu Ira Channel ⊔	**175g**	17.17 S	178.31 E
Vatukoula	**175g**	17.31 S	177.51 E
Vatulele I	**175g**	18.33 S	177.37 E
Vatulino	**82**	55.39 N	36.09 E
Vatutino	**78**	49.02 N	31.04 E
Vaubecourt	**56**	48.56 N	5.07 E
Vauclaix	**50**	47.14 N	3.49 E
Vauclin, Montagne du ∧	**240e**	14.33 N	60.53 W
Vaucluse	**274a**	33.51 S	151.17 E
Vaucluse □ [5]	**62**	44.00 N	5.10 E
Vaucluse, Fontaine de ⊥	**62**	43.55 N	5.08 E
Vaucluse, Plateau de ⋏ [1]	**62**	44.00 N	5.22 E
Vaucouleurs	**58**	48.36 N	5.40 E
Vaucouleurs ≃	**261**	48.59 N	1.44 E
Vaucresson	**261**	48.50 N	2.09 E
Vaud □ [3]	**58**	46.40 N	6.30 E
Vaudherland	**261**	49.00 N	2.29 E
Vaudoy-en-Brie	**50**	48.41 N	3.05 E
Vaudreuil (Saint-Michel-de-Vaudreuil)	**206**	45.24 N	74.01 W
Vaudreuil □ [6]	**206**	45.26 N	74.15 W
Vaudreuil, Baie de ⊂	**275a**	45.24 N	74.00 W
Vaufrey	**58**	47.21 N	6.55 E
Vaughan	**212**	43.47 N	79.36 W
Vaughn, N.M., U.S.	**200**	34.36 N	105.12 W
Vaughn, Wa., U.S.	**224**	47.21 N	122.46 W
Vaughnsville	**216**	40.53 N	84.09 W
Vaugneray	**62**	45.44 N	4.39 E
Vaugrigneuse	**261**	48.36 N	2.07 E
Vauhallan	**261**	48.44 N	2.12 E
Vaujours	**261**	48.56 N	2.35 E
Vaulovo	**82**	56.09 N	39.17 E
Vaulruz	**58**	46.37 N	6.59 E
Vaulx-en-Velin	**62**	45.47 N	4.56 E
Vaupés □ [8]	**246**	0.45 N	70.30 W
Vaupés (Uaupés) ≃	**246**	0.02 N	67.16 W
Vauréal	**261**	49.02 N	2.02 E
Vauréal, Chute ⌊	**186**	49.34 N	62.42 W
Vauvenargues	**62**	43.33 N	5.36 E
Vauvert	**62**	43.42 N	4.17 E
Vauvillers	**58**	47.55 N	6.06 E
Vauvise ≃	**50**	47.18 N	2.57 E
Vaux ≃	**50**	49.33 N	4.17 E
Vaux, Ru des ≃	**261**	48.42 N	2.00 E
Vauxhall	**182**	50.04 N	112.07 W
Vaux-le-Compte, Château de ⊥	**50**	48.35 N	2.42 E
Vaux-le-Pénil	**261**	48.32 N	2.41 E
Vaux-lès-Saint-Claude	**58**	46.22 N	5.44 E
Vaux-le-Vicomte, Château de ⊥	**261**	48.34 N	2.43 E
Vaux-Sous-Aubigny	**58**	47.39 N	5.17 E
Vaux-sur-Seine	**261**	49.00 N	1.58 E
Vavatenina	**157b**	17.28 S	49.12 E
Vava'u I	**14**	18.36 S	174.00 W
Vava'u Group II	**14**	18.40 S	174.00 W
Vavincourt	**56**	48.49 N	5.13 E
Vavoua	**150**	7.23 N	6.29 W
Vavož	**80**	56.47 N	51.55 E
Vavuniya	**122**	8.45 N	80.30 E
Vaxholm	**40**	59.24 N	18.20 E
Växjö	**26**	56.52 N	14.49 E
V'aža	**78**	49.16 N	41.01 E
Vaza-barris ≃	**250**	11.10 S	37.10 W
Vazante	**255**	18.00 S	46.54 W
Vazante Grande ≃	**248**	19.21 S	56.53 W
V'azemskij	**89**	47.32 N	134.48 E
Važgort	**24**	64.01 N	47.02 E
V'az'ma	**76**	55.13 N	34.18 E
V'az'ma ≃, Ross.	**76**	55.28 N	33.34 E
V'az'ma ≃, Ross.	**82**	56.29 N	35.49 E
V'azniki	**80**	56.15 N	42.10 E
Vazobe ∧	**157b**	18.25 S	47.18 E
V'azovaja	**80**	57.39 N	45.44 E
V'azovka, Ross.	**80**	48.19 N	45.36 E
V'azovka, Ross.	**80**	50.52 N	43.57 E
V'azovka, Ross.	**80**	51.48 N	45.47 E
V'azovka, Ross.	**80**	52.52 N	48.24 E
V'azovoje, Ross.	**78**	51.54 N	36.59 E
V'azovoje, Ross.	**78**	51.09 N	37.01 E
V'azovok	**78**	49.11 N	31.25 E
Vazuza ≃	**76**	56.10 N	34.35 E
Vazuzskoje vodochranilišče ⊜ [1]	**76**	56.00 N	34.28 E
V'azyn'	**76**	54.25 N	27.10 E
Vazzola	**64**	45.50 N	12.23 E
Veachland	**218**	38.12 N	85.11 W
Veado, Ilha do I	**287a**	22.57 S	43.06 W
Veazie	**188**	44.50 N	68.42 W
Veberöd	**41**	55.38 N	13.29 E
Veblen	**198**	45.51 N	97.17 W
Vecchiano	**66**	43.47 N	10.23 E
Vechelde	**52**	52.16 N	10.22 E
Vecht (Vechte) ≃	**52**	52.35 N	6.05 E
Vechta	**52**	52.43 N	8.16 E
Vechte (Vecht) ≃	**52**	52.35 N	6.05 E
Veckerhagen	**52**	51.30 N	9.35 E
Vecpiebalga	**76**	57.08 N	25.50 E
Vecsés	**30**	47.25 N	19.16 E
Vecumnieki	**76**	56.36 N	24.31 E
Vedado ◂ [8]	**286b**	23.08 N	82.24 W
Vedano al Lambro	**266b**	45.37 N	9.16 E
Vedano Olona	**62**	45.46 N	8.53 E
Vedāranniyam	**122**	10.22 N	79.51 E
Vedbæk	**41**	55.51 N	12.34 E
Vedder Crossing	**224**	49.06 N	121.57 W
Veddige	**26**	57.16 N	12.19 E
Vedea	**38**	44.47 N	24.37 E
Vedea ≃	**38**	43.43 N	25.32 E
Vedelago	**64**	45.41 N	12.01 E
Vedène	**62**	43.59 N	4.54 E
Vedeno	**84**	42.58 N	46.05 E
Vedeseta	**58**	45.53 N	9.32 E
Vedevåg	**40**	59.32 N	15.17 E
Vedi	**84**	39.56 N	44.42 E
Vedia	**252**	34.30 S	61.32 W
Vednoje	**76**	57.08 N	36.10 E
Vedomša	**82**	56.44 N	38.21 E
Vedrovo	**80**	57.33 N	42.52 E
Veedersburg	**194**	40.06 N	87.15 W
Veen	**263**	51.37 N	6.27 E
Veendam	**52**	53.06 N	6.58 E
Veenendaal	**52**	52.02 N	5.34 E
Veenhuizen	**52**	53.03 N	6.24 E
Veenoord	**52**	52.43 N	6.50 E
Veere	**52**	51.34 N	3.40 E
Veert	**52**	51.33 N	6.17 E
Vefsna ≃	**24**	65.50 N	13.12 E
Vega	**196**	35.15 N	102.26 W
Vega I	**24**	65.39 N	11.50 E
Vega, Arroyo de la ≃	**266a**	40.31 N	3.33 W
Vega Alta	**240m**	18.25 N	66.20 W
Vega Baja	**240m**	18.27 N	66.23 W
Vega Point ›	**181a**	51.49 N	177.16 E
Vegår ⊜	**26**	58.48 N	8.47 E
Vegesack ◂ [8]	**52**	53.10 N	8.37 E
Veghel	**52**	51.37 N	5.33 E
Veglie	**68**	40.20 N	17.58 E
Vegreville	**182**	53.30 N	112.03 W
Veguita	**200**	34.30 N	106.46 W
Vehār Lake ⊜	**272c**	19.09 N	72.55 E
Vehlefanz	**264a**	52.43 N	13.06 E
Vehnemoor ◂ [3]	**52**	53.05 N	8.00 E
Veigné	**50**	47.17 N	0.44 E
Veil, Loch ⊜	**46**	56.20 N	4.25 W
Veilsdorf	**54**	50.24 N	10.48 E
Veinte de Noviembre	**196**	25.47 N	97.33 W
Veinticinco de Agosto	**258**	34.24 S	56.25 W
Veinticinco de Mayo, Arg.	**252**	35.26 S	60.10 W
Veinticinco de Mayo, Arg.	**252**	34.35 S	68.33 W
Veinticinco de Mayo, Ur.	**258**	34.12 S	56.22 W
Veintiocho de Mayo	**246**	3.50 S	78.52 W
Veintiocho de Noviembre	**254**	51.39 S	72.18 W
Veintisiete de Abril	**236**	10.15 N	85.45 W
Veio ⊥	**66**	42.02 N	12.24 E
Veiros	**250**	2.05 S	52.10 W
Veisiejai	**76**	54.06 N	23.42 E
Veitsbronn	**56**	49.31 N	10.53 E
Veitsch	**61**	47.35 N	15.30 E
Veitschalpe ⋏	**61**	47.39 N	15.30 E
Veitshöchheim	**56**	49.50 N	9.52 E
Vejbystrand	**41**	56.19 N	12.45 E
Vejdelevka	**78**	50.09 N	38.27 E
Vejen	**41**	55.29 N	9.09 E
Vejer de la Frontera	**34**	36.15 N	5.58 W
Vejlby	**41**	56.12 N	10.13 E
Vejle	**41**	55.42 N	9.32 E
Vejle □ [6]	**41**	55.45 N	9.30 E
Vejle Fjord ⊂	**41**	55.40 N	9.50 E
Vejprty	**54**	50.30 N	13.02 E
Vejrhøj ∧ [2]	**41**	55.47 N	11.24 E
Vejrø I	**41**	55.02 N	11.22 E
Vekšor	**24**	60.33 N	49.26 E
Vel'a ≃	**82**	56.31 N	37.41 E
Vela Luka	**36**	42.58 N	16.43 E
Velapāda	**272c**	18.59 N	73.04 E
Velardeña	**232**	25.04 N	103.44 W
Velas	**148a**	38.41 N	28.13 W
Velas, Cabo ›	**236**	10.22 N	85.53 W
Velázquez	**252**	34.02 S	54.17 W
Velbert	**56**	51.20 N	7.02 E
Velburg	**60**	49.14 N	11.41 E
Velddrif	**158**	32.47 S	18.11 E
Velden, Dtsch.	**60**	49.37 N	11.31 E
Velden, Dtsch.	**60**	48.19 N	12.16 E
Velden, Öst.	**61**	46.37 N	14.03 E
Veldhoven	**52**	51.24 N	5.24 E
Velebit ⋏	**36**	44.38 N	15.03 E
Velebitski Kanal ⊔	**36**	45.00 N	14.50 E
Velegož	**82**	54.42 N	37.16 E
Veleka ≃	**38**	42.04 N	27.58 E
Velemín	**54**	50.33 N	13.59 E
Velen	**52**	51.53 N	6.59 E
Velencei-tó ⊜	**30**	47.12 N	18.35 E
Velesa ≃	**76**	56.03 N	31.58 E
Velešín	**61**	48.50 N	14.28 E
Velestínon	**38**	39.23 N	22.45 E
Velet'ma	**80**	55.20 N	42.25 E
Velevščina	**76**	54.44 N	28.35 E
Vélez	**246**	6.01 N	73.41 W
Velez de la Gomera, Peñón de I	**34**	35.11 N	4.21 W
Vélez-Málaga	**34**	36.47 N	4.06 W
Vélez Rubio	**34**	37.39 N	2.04 W
Velgast	**54**	54.16 N	12.48 E
Vel'gija	**76**	58.23 N	33.59 E
Velhas, Canal do ≍	**287a**	22.42 S	43.22 W
Velhas, Rio das ≃	**255**	17.13 S	44.49 W
Veličkovo	**82**	54.59 N	36.46 E
Velika Gorica	**36**	45.43 N	16.05 E
Velikaja, Ross.	**24**	59.13 N	49.04 E
Velikaja, Ross.	**180**	64.04 N	176.12 E
Velikaja ≃, Ross.	**74**	64.40 N	176.20 E
Velikaja ≃, Ross.	**76**	57.48 N	28.20 E
Velikaja Aleksandrovka	**78**	47.20 N	33.18 E
Velikaja Bagačka	**78**	49.47 N	33.43 E
Velikaja Beloz'orka	**78**	47.16 N	34.42 E
Velikaja Danilovka	**78**	50.04 N	36.19 E
Velikaja Dymerka	**78**	50.36 N	30.55 E
Velikaja Gluša	**78**	51.49 N	25.02 E
Velikaja Kema	**89**	45.30 N	137.12 E
Velikaja Kochnovka	**78**	49.07 N	33.27 E
Velikaja Korenicha	**78**	46.57 N	31.54 E
Velikaja Kosnica	**78**	48.09 N	28.27 E
Velikaja Lepeticha	**78**	47.11 N	33.56 E

Symbols in the index entries represent the broad categories identified in the key at the right. Symbols with superior numbers (⋏[1]) identify subcategories (see complete key on page *I · 1*).

Symbole im Register stellen die rechts im Schlüssel erklärten Kategorien dar. Symbole mit hochgestellten Ziffern (⋏[1]) bezeichnen Unterabteilungen einer Kategorie (vgl. vollständiger Schlüssel auf Seite *I · 1*).

Los símbolos incluídos en el texto del índice representan las grandes categorias identificadas con la clave a la derecha. Los símbolos con numeros en su parte superior (⋏[1]) identifican las subcategorías (véase la clave completa en la página *I · 1*).

Les symboles de l'index représentent les catégories indiquées dans la légende à droite. Les symboles suivis d'un indice (⋏[1]) représentent des sous-catégories (voir légende complète à la page *I · 1*).

Os símbolos incluídos no texto do índice representam as grandes categorias identificadas com a chave à direita. Os símbolos com números em sua parte superior (⋏[1]) identificam as subcategorias (veja-se a chave completa à página *I · 1*).

English	Deutsch	Español	Français	Português
∧ Mountain	Berg	Montaña	Montagne	Montanha
⋏ Mountains	Gebirge	Montañas	Montagnes	Montanhas
)(Pass	Paß	Paso	Col	Passo
V Valley, Canyon	Tal, Cañon	Valle, Cañón	Vallée, Canyon	Vale, Canhão
≚ Plain	Ebene	Llano	Plaine	Planície
› Cape	Kap	Cabo	Cap	Cabo
I Island	Insel	Isla	Île	Ilha
II Islands	Inseln	Islas	Îles	Ilhas
≛ Other Topographic Features	Andere Topographische Objekte	Otros Elementos Topográficos	Autres données topographiques	Outros acidentes topográficos

ESPAÑOL Nombre / FRANÇAIS Nom / PORTUGUÊS Nome	Página / Page	Lat.°′	Long.°′ W = Oeste / W = Ouest
Velikaja Michajlovka	78	47.04 N	29.52 E
Velikaja Novos'olka	78	47.50 N	36.50 E
Velikaja Pisarevka	78	50.26 N	35.28 E
Velikaja Rublevka	78	49.53 N	34.49 E
Velikaja Vradijevka	78	47.52 N	30.35 E
Velika Kapela ⋏	36	45.15 N	15.00 E
Velika Morava ≃	38	44.43 N	21.03 E
Velika Plana	38	44.20 N	21.04 E
Velike Lašče	36	45.50 N	14.38 E
Veliki Bečkerek → Zrenjanin	38	45.23 N	20.24 E
Velikij Ber'oznyj	78	48.53 N	22.27 E
Velikij Bor	78	52.02 N	29.56 E
Velikij Burluk	78	50.05 N	37.24 E
Velikij Byčkov	78	47.58 N	24.03 E
Velikij Chutor	78	49.52 N	32.06 E
Velikij Dvor	82	56.46 N	37.25 E
Velikije Borki	78	49.32 N	25.45 E
Velikije Dederkaly	78	50.02 N	26.07 E
Velikije Kopani	78	46.29 N	32.59 E
Velikije Korovincy	78	49.59 N	28.17 E
Velikije Krynki	78	49.27 N	33.29 E
Velikije Lučki	78	48.26 N	22.35 E
Velikije Luki	76	56.20 N	30.32 E
Velikije Mosty	78	50.14 N	24.06 E
Velikije Soročincy	78	50.03 N	33.56 E
Velikij Gluboček	78	49.37 N	25.32 E
Velikij Log	83	48.15 N	39.33 E
Velikij Ust'ug	24	60.48 N	46.18 E
Velikij Žvančik	78	48.46 N	26.59 E
Veliki kanal ≊	38	45.45 N	18.50 E
Veliki Stol (Hochstuhl) ∧	61	46.26 N	14.10 E
Veliki Vitorog ∧	36	44.07 N	17.03 E
Velikoanadol'skij les ♠	83	47.42 N	37.23 E
Velikoarch-angel'skoje	78	50.51 N	40.46 E
Velikockoje	83	49.21 N	40.02 E
Velikodolinskoje	78	46.21 N	30.35 E
Velikodvorskaja	76	60.18 N	41.58 E
Velikodvorskij	80	55.15 N	40.41 E
Veliko Gradište	38	44.45 N	21.32 E
Velikoje, Ross.	76	59.32 N	36.59 E
Velikoje, Ross.	80	57.21 N	39.47 E
Velikoje, ozero ⊜, Ross.	76	57.02 N	36.34 E
Velikoje, ozero ⊜, Ross.	80	55.13 N	40.10 E
Velikonda Hills ⋏[2]	122	14.45 N	79.10 E
Velikookt'abr'skij	76	57.26 N	33.49 E
Velikoploskoje	78	47.01 N	29.40 E
Velikorusskoje	86	54.39 N	74.38 E
Veliko Târnovo	38	43.04 N	25.39 E
Velikovisočnoje	24	67.16 N	52.01 E
Velikovo	76	59.18 N	42.08 E
Velilla de San Antonio	266a	40.22 N	3.29 W
Veli Lošinj	36	44.31 N	14.30 E
Velimče	78	51.36 N	24.44 E
Vélingara, Sén.	150	15.00 N	14.40 W
Vélingara, Sén.	150	13.09 N	14.07 W
Velingrad	38	42.04 N	24.00 E
Velino ≃	66	42.33 N	12.43 E
Velino, Monte ∧	66	42.09 N	13.23 E
Veliž	76	55.38 N	31.12 E
Veližany	86	57.34 N	65.49 E
Vélizy-Villacoublay	261	48.47 N	2.10 E
Veljaminovo, Ross.	82	55.12 N	37.52 E
Veljaminovo, Ross.	82	55.53 N	36.52 E
Velká Bíteš	30	49.17 N	16.13 E
Vel'ké Kapušany	30	48.33 N	22.04 E
Velké Meziříčí	30	49.21 N	16.00 E
Velké Němčie	61	48.59 N	16.40 E
Velké Pavlovice	61	48.54 N	16.49 E
Velký Bor	60	49.22 N	13.42 E
Velký Šenov	54	51.00 N	14.25 E
Vellach ≃	61	46.35 N	14.29 E
Vella Gulf ʮ	175e	8.00 S	156.50 E
Vella Lavella I	175e	7.45 S	156.40 E
Vellano	66	43.57 N	10.43 E
Vellār ≃	122	11.29 N	79.46 E
Vellberg	56	49.05 N	9.53 E
Vellechevreux-et-Courbenans	58	47.33 N	6.32 E
Velletri	66	41.41 N	12.47 E
Vellinge	41	55.28 N	13.01 E
Vellmar	56	51.21 N	9.28 E
Vellore, On., Can.	275b	43.50 N	79.34 W
Vellore, India	122	12.56 N	79.08 E
Velm	264b	48.03 N	16.27 E
Velma	196	34.27 N	97.40 W
Vel'maj ≃	180	67.26 N	175.28 W
Velmede	56	51.21 N	8.22 E
Velo d'Astico	64	45.43 N	11.23 E
Velp	52	52.00 N	5.59 E
Velp ≃	56	50.58 N	5.05 E
Velpke	54	52.24 N	10.56 E
Velsen	52	52.27 N	4.39 E
Vel'sk	24	61.05 N	42.05 E
Vel't	24	68.03 N	49.55 E
Velten	54	52.41 N	13.10 E
Veltheim	52	52.11 N	8.58 E
Veltrusy	54	50.14 N	14.18 E
Veluwe ◆[1]	52	52.12 N	5.45 E
Veluwemeer ⊜	52	52.22 N	5.38 E
Velva, It.	62	44.16 N	9.33 E
Velva, N.D., U.S.	198	48.03 N	100.55 W
Velvary	54	50.15 N	14.15 E
Vémars	261	49.04 N	2.34 E
Vemdalen	26	62.27 N	13.52 E
Vemmenæs	41	54.59 N	10.40 E
Ven I	41	55.54 N	12.41 E
Venachar, Loch ⊜	46	56.13 N	4.19 W
Venaco	36	42.14 N	9.10 E
Venadillo	246	4.43 N	74.55 W
Venado	234	22.56 N	101.05 W
Venado, Isla I	241r	10.00 N	62.25 W
Venado, Isla del I	236	11.57 N	83.44 W
Venado Tuerto	252	33.45 S	61.58 W
Venafiorita, Aeroporto di ⊠	71	40.53 N	9.30 E
Venafro	66	41.29 N	14.02 E
Venalzio	62	45.09 N	7.01 E
Venâncio Aires	252	29.36 S	52.11 W
Venango	214	41.46 N	80.07 W
Venango □[6]	214	41.24 N	79.50 W
Venanson	62	44.03 N	7.15 E
Venant	261	48.30 N	2.06 E
Venarey-les-Laumes	58	47.32 N	4.26 E
Venaria	62	45.08 N	7.38 E
Venasca	62	44.33 N	7.24 E
Venasque	62	43.59 N	5.09 E
Vence	62	43.43 N	7.07 E
Venceslau Brás	256	22.31 S	45.21 W
Venceslau Braz	255	23.51 S	49.48 W
Vencimont	56	50.02 N	4.55 E
Venda □[1], Afr.	138	23.00 S	30.30 E
Venda □[1], Afr.	156	23.00 S	30.30 E
Venda Nova	34	41.40 N	7.58 W
Vendargues	62	43.39 N	3.58 E
Vendas Novas	34	38.41 N	8.28 W
Vendée □[5]	32	46.40 N	1.20 W
Vendéen, Bocage ◆[1]	32	46.40 N	1.30 W
Vendel	40	60.10 N	17.36 E
Vendelsö	40	59.12 N	18.12 E
Vendeuvre-sur-Barse	58	48.14 N	4.28 E
Vendičany	78	48.37 N	27.48 E
Vendin-lès-Béthune	50	50.32 N	2.37 E
Vendin-le-Vieil	50	50.28 N	2.52 E
Vendôme	50	47.48 N	1.04 E
Vendsyssel ◆[1]	26	57.20 N	10.00 E
Venecia	236	10.22 N	84.17 W
Venecia → Venezia	64	45.27 N	12.21 E
Venedig → Venezia	64	45.27 N	12.21 E
Venedocia	216	40.44 N	84.25 W
Venedy	219	38.24 N	89.39 W
Veneta, Laguna ⊂	64	45.25 N	12.19 E
Venetia	214	40.15 N	80.03 W
Venetian Village	216	42.24 N	88.02 W
Venetie	180	67.01 N	146.25 W
Veneto □[4]	64	45.30 N	11.45 E
Venev	82	54.21 N	38.16 E
Venezia (Venice)	64	45.27 N	12.21 E
Venezia □[4]	64	45.35 N	12.34 E
Venezuela □[1], S.A.	242	8.00 N	66.00 W
Venezuela □[1], S.A.	246	8.00 N	66.00 W
Venezuela, Golfo de ⊂	246	11.30 N	71.00 W
Venezuelan Basin ✢[1]	16	15.00 N	68.00 W
Veng	41	56.07 N	9.53 E
Vengerovka	83	48.43 N	38.24 E
Vengerovo	86	55.41 N	76.45 E
Vengurla	122	15.52 N	73.38 E
Veniaminof, Mount ∧	180	56.13 N	159.18 W
Venice, Fl., U.S.	220	27.05 N	82.27 W
Venice, Il., U.S.	219	38.40 N	90.10 W
Venice, La., U.S.	194	29.16 N	89.21 W
Venice, Oh., U.S.	214	41.27 N	82.46 W
Venice, Pa., U.S.	279b	40.19 N	80.14 W
Venice ◆[8]	228	34.00 N	118.29 W
Venice, Gulf of ⊂	64	45.15 N	13.00 E
Venice Gardens	220	27.04 N	82.26 W
Venice → Venezia	64	45.27 N	12.21 E
Venise → Venezia	64	45.27 N	12.21 E
Vénissieux	62	45.41 N	4.53 E
Venjan	26	60.57 N	13.55 E
Venjansjön ⊜	26	60.54 N	14.00 E
Venkatagiri	122	13.58 N	79.35 E
Venlo	52	51.24 N	6.10 E
Vennesla	26	58.17 N	7.59 E
Vennhausen ◆[8]	263	51.13 N	6.51 E
Venosa	68	40.57 N	15.49 E
Vénosc	62	44.59 N	6.07 E
Venosta, Val ∨	64	46.40 N	10.35 E
Venoste, Alpi (Ötztaler Alpen) ⋏	64	46.45 N	10.55 E
Venray	52	51.32 N	5.59 E
Vent	64	46.52 N	10.56 E
Vent, Îles du → Windward Islands II	238	13.00 N	61.00 W
Venta ≃	76	57.24 N	21.33 E
Ventanas	246	1.23 S	79.25 W
Ventasso, Monte ∧	64	44.23 N	10.17 E
Ventersburg	158	28.09 S	27.08 E
Ventersdorp	158	26.17 S	26.48 E
Venterspos	273d	26.18 S	27.39 E
Venterstad	158	30.47 S	25.48 E
Venticano	68	41.05 N	14.50 E
Ventimiglia	62	43.47 N	7.36 E
Ventimiglia di Sicilia	70	37.55 N	13.34 E
Ventnor	42	50.36 N	1.11 W
Ventnor City	208	39.20 N	74.28 W
Ventotene	66	40.48 N	13.26 E
Ventotene, Isola I	66	40.47 N	13.25 E
Ventoux, Mont ∧	62	44.10 N	5.17 E
Ventry	48	52.08 N	10.22 W
Ventspils	76	57.24 N	21.36 E
Ventuari ≃	246	3.58 N	67.02 W
Ventura (San Buenaventura)	228	34.16 N	119.17 W
Ventura □[6]	228	34.30 N	119.00 W
Ventura ≃	228	34.16 N	119.18 W
Venturina	66	43.02 N	10.36 E
Venus, Fl., U.S.	220	27.04 N	81.21 W
Venus, Pa., U.S.	214	41.22 N	79.29 W
Venus, Tx., U.S.	222	32.26 N	97.06 W
Vénus, Pointe ≻	174s	17.29 S	149.29 W
Venus Bay ⊂	169	38.40 S	145.43 E
Venustiano Carranza, Méx.	232	16.21 N	92.33 W
Venustiano Carranza, Méx.	234	19.44 N	103.47 W
Venustiano Carranza, Méx.	234	20.31 N	97.38 W
Venustiano Carranza, Bahía ⊂	232	19.20 N	87.35 W
Venustiano Carranza, Presa ⊜[1]	232	27.30 N	100.40 W
Venzone	64	46.20 N	13.09 E
Véore ≃	62	44.49 N	4.49 E
Vép	61	47.14 N	16.44 E
Veprik	78	50.23 N	34.11 E
Vepsovskaja vozvyšennost' ⋏[1]	76	60.20 N	35.15 E
Ver ≃	42	51.42 N	0.20 W
Vera, Arg.	252	29.28 S	60.13 W
Vera, Esp.	34	37.15 N	1.52 W
Vera, Il., U.S.	219	39.02 N	89.07 W
Veracruz, Méx.	200	32.25 N	115.05 W
Vera Cruz, Pa., U.S.	208	40.30 N	75.30 W
Veracruz □[3]	234	19.20 N	96.40 W
Veracruz [Llave]	234	19.12 N	96.08 W
Veraguas □[4]	236	8.30 N	81.00 W
Verano Brianza	266b	45.41 N	9.14 E
Veranópolis	252	28.57 S	51.33 W
Verāval	120	20.54 N	70.22 E
Verba	78	50.17 N	25.37 E
Verbania	58	45.56 N	8.33 E
Verbank	210	41.44 N	73.43 W
Verbeek, Pegunungan ⋏	112	2.35 S	121.25 E
Verberg ◆[8]	263	51.22 N	6.36 E
Verberie	50	49.19 N	2.44 E
Verbicaro	68	39.45 N	15.55 E
Verbier	58	46.06 N	7.13 E
Verbilki	82	56.32 N	37.36 E
Verbinskij	83	47.53 N	40.02 E
Verbl'užka	78	48.23 N	32.54 E
Verbovskij	80	55.32 N	42.00 E
Vercelli	62	45.19 N	8.25 E
Vercelli □[4]	62	45.37 N	8.10 E
Vercel-Villedieu-le-Camp	58	47.11 N	6.24 E
Verch'aja Irmen'	86	54.35 N	82.14 E
Verchazovka	80	50.56 N	48.46 E
Vercheje Talyzino	80	55.06 N	45.49 E
Verchères	206	45.47 N	73.21 W
Verchères □[6]	206	45.45 N	73.20 W
Verchn'ačka	78	48.49 N	30.02 E
Verchn'aja Amga	74	59.30 N	126.08 E
Verchn'aja Angara ≃	88	55.42 N	109.54 E
Verchn'aja Balkarija	84	43.06 N	43.24 E
Verchn'aja Buzinovka	80	49.04 N	43.12 E
Verchn'aja Čebula	86	56.02 N	87.36 E
Verchn'aja Chava	78	51.50 N	39.56 E
Verchn'aja Chila	88	52.06 N	115.54 E
Verchn'aja Chortica	78	47.51 N	35.01 E
Verchn'aja Čuginka	83	48.55 N	39.39 E
Verchn'aja Dobrinka	80	50.46 N	45.03 E
Verchn'aja Gniluša	78	50.16 N	40.23 E
Verchn'aja Grajvoronka	78	51.41 N	37.46 E
Verchn'aja Inta	24	66.00 N	60.20 E
Verchn'aja Maza	80	52.58 N	47.56 E
Verchn'aja Orl'anka	80	53.44 N	51.04 E
Verchn'aja Pyšma	86	56.55 N	60.37 E
Verchn'aja Salda	86	58.02 N	60.33 E
Verchn'aja Serebr'akovka	80	47.21 N	42.14 E
Verchn'aja Sin'áčicha	86	57.59 N	61.40 E
Verchn'aja Sysert'	86	56.26 N	60.46 E
Verchn'aja Tajmyra ≃	74	74.15 N	99.48 E
Verchn'aja Tarka	86	56.37 N	77.30 E
Verchnaja Tereška	80	52.54 N	47.24 E
Verchn'aja Tišanka	78	51.19 N	40.32 E
Verchn'aja Tojma	24	62.13 N	45.00 E
Verchn'aja Troica	76	57.15 N	37.08 E
Verchn'aja Tura	86	58.22 N	59.49 E
Verchn'aja Zaimka	88	55.51 N	110.09 E
Verchn'aja Zima	88	53.48 N	101.47 E
Verchneaks'onovskij	80	48.21 N	42.38 E
Verchneangarskij chrebet ⋏	88	56.20 N	111.30 E
Verchne-Anikin	83	48.09 N	39.59 E
Verchnebakanskij	78	44.52 N	37.39 E
Verchneber'ozovskij	86	50.17 N	82.13 E
Verchnebuzanskij	80	46.38 N	48.02 E
Verchnecaricynskij	80	48.23 N	43.57 E
Verchnedneprovsk	78	48.39 N	34.21 E
Verchnedneprovskij	76	54.59 N	33.21 E
Verchneduvannyj	78	48.20 N	39.48 E
Verchnedvinsk	76	55.47 N	27.56 E
Verchneimbatskoje	74	63.11 N	87.58 E
Verchnejarkejevo	80	55.27 N	54.19 E
Verchneje	78	48.53 N	38.28 E
Verchneje ◆[8]	83	48.53 N	38.28 E
Verchneje Šachlovo	82	55.02 N	37.15 E
Verchneje Sinevidnoje	78	49.06 N	23.34 E
Verchnekarabachskij kanal ≊	84	39.44 N	47.57 E
Verchnemakejevka	78	49.10 N	41.03 E
Verchnemulomskoje vodochranilišče ⊜[1]	24	68.30 N	31.05 E
Verchnesadovoje	78	44.42 N	33.42 E
Verchnesjezžeje	80	52.44 N	51.15 E
Verchnespasskoje	80	52.39 N	41.47 E
Verchne-T'oploje	83	48.51 N	39.26 E
Verchnetulomskij	24	68.38 N	31.45 E
Verchneural'sk	86	53.53 N	59.13 E
Verchneusinskoje	86	52.14 N	93.01 E
Verchnevil'ujsk	74	63.27 N	120.18 E
Verchnevolynskoje	85	40.43 N	68.51 E
Verchnij Amyl	88	53.08 N	94.30 E
Verchnij Avz'an	86	53.32 N	57.33 E
Verchnij Balyklej	80	49.34 N	45.10 E
Verchnij Baskunčak	80	48.14 N	46.44 E
Verchnij Byk	78	50.43 N	41.14 E
Verchnije Dvoriki	82	56.28 N	38.22 E
Verchnije Kigi	86	55.25 N	58.37 E
Verchnije Korobki	80	50.19 N	44.38 E
Verchnije Lipki	80	49.38 N	43.51 E
Verchnije Tatyšly	86	56.17 N	55.52 E
Verchnij Ikorec	78	51.11 N	39.46 E
Verchnij Karačan	80	51.24 N	41.46 E
Verchnij Krasnyj Pereval	89	46.33 N	134.37 E
Verchnij Kužebar	86	53.22 N	93.15 E
Verchnij Landech	80	56.51 N	42.36 E
Verchnij Leb'ažinskij	80	46.45 N	47.50 E
Verchnij Lomov	80	53.28 N	43.34 E
Verchnij Lomovec	76	52.13 N	38.37 E
Verchnij Mamon	78	50.10 N	40.23 E
Verchnij Most	76	57.31 N	28.50 E
Verchnij Nejvinskij	86	57.17 N	60.09 E
Verchnij Petr'ak	86	57.29 N	77.30 E
Verchnij Rogačik	78	47.14 N	34.21 E
Verchnij Šergol'džin	88	50.12 N	108.20 E
Verchnij Tagil	86	57.22 N	59.56 E
Verchnij Takermen'	80	55.39 N	52.43 E
Verchnij Trojanov Val (Upper Trajan's Wall) ⊥	78	46.35 N	29.00 E
Verchnij Ufalej	86	56.04 N	60.14 E
Verchnij Ul'chun	88	49.34 N	112.32 E
Verchnij Uslon	80	55.47 N	48.57 E
Verchnij Zub, gora ∧	86	53.45 N	89.15 E
Verchnyje Nikul'asy	76	60.25 N	30.45 E
Verchnyj Jenisej (Ulug-Chem) ≃	88	51.47 N	92.00 E
Verchnyj Nagol'čik	83	48.05 N	39.06 E
Verchojansk	74	67.35 N	133.27 E
Verchojanskij chrebet ⋏	74	67.00 N	129.00 E
Vercholensk	88	54.06 N	105.35 E
Verchopuja	24	61.34 N	41.31 E
Verchošižemje	80	58.01 N	49.07 E
Verchososna	78	50.44 N	38.14 E
Verchoturje	86	58.52 N	60.48 E
Verchoturovo	86	58.22 N	95.21 E
Verchovažje	24	60.45 N	42.00 E
Verchovcevo	78	48.29 N	34.14 E
Verchovina	78	48.09 N	24.47 E
Verchovino	76	59.33 N	43.19 E
Verchovje	76	52.49 N	37.14 E
Verchovl'an'	82	55.03 N	38.21 E
Verchozim	80	52.56 N	46.23 E
Verchubinka	86	50.29 N	82.26 E
Verclause	62	44.23 N	5.26 E
Vercors ◆[1]	62	44.57 N	5.25 E
Verdalsøra	26	63.48 N	11.29 E
Verde ≃, Bra.	248	11.54 S	55.48 W
Verde ≃, Bra.	248	13.33 S	58.01 W
Verde ≃, Bra.	250	10.27 S	42.16 W
Verde ≃, Bra.	255	19.11 S	50.44 W
Verde ≃, Bra.	255	15.07 S	48.40 W
Verde ≃, Bra.	255	17.05 S	46.05 W
Verde ≃, Bra.	255	18.01 S	50.14 W
Verde ≃, Bra.	255	19.55 S	49.45 W
Verde ≃, Bra.	255	21.12 S	51.53 W
Verde ≃, Bra.	256	21.34 S	45.31 W
Verde ≃, Bra.	256	21.38 S	47.03 W
Verde ≃, Méx.	234	16.45 N	98.07 W
Verde ≃, Méx.	234	15.59 N	97.47 W
Verde ≃, Méx.	234	21.37 N	99.15 W
Verde ≃, Méx.	234	20.42 N	103.14 W
Verde ≃, Para.	252	23.09 S	57.37 W
Verde ≃, S.A.	248	13.59 S	60.24 W
Verde ≃, Az., U.S.	200	33.33 N	111.40 W
Verde, Arroyo ≃, Arg.	254	41.56 S	65.03 W
Verde, Arroyo ≃, Bol.	248	11.25 S	66.20 W
Verde, Cape ≻	238	22.50 N	74.52 W
Verde, Cerro ∧	234	20.30 N	104.36 W
Verde, Costa ♠[2]	71	39.34 N	8.28 E
Verde Grande ≃	255	14.35 S	43.53 W
Verde Island I	116	13.33 N	121.05 E
Verde Island Passage ʮ	116	13.34 N	120.51 E
Verdello	62	45.36 N	9.37 E
Verden, Dtsch.	52	52.55 N	9.13 E
Verden, Ok., U.S.	196	35.05 N	98.05 W
Verde Pequeno ≃	255	14.48 S	43.31 W
Verdesela, Pinhal da ♠	266c	38.37 N	9.08 W
Verdi	226	39.31 N	119.59 W
Verdigre	198	42.35 N	98.02 W
Verdigre Creek ≃	198	42.42 N	98.03 W
Verdigris ≃	196	35.48 N	95.19 W
Verdinho ≃	255	17.29 S	50.27 W
Verdon	198	40.08 N	95.42 W
Verdon ≃	62	43.43 N	5.46 E
Verdon, Canal du ≊	62	43.43 N	5.57 E
Verdoy	210	42.46 N	73.48 W
Verduga	76	58.46 N	29.12 E
Verdugo Mountains ⋏	280	34.13 N	118.18 W
Verdun, P.Q., Can.	206	45.27 N	73.34 W
Verdun, Fr.	32	43.52 N	1.14 E
Verdun-sur-le-Doubs	58	46.54 N	5.01 E
Verdun-sur-Meuse	56	49.10 N	5.23 E
Verdura ≃	70	37.28 N	13.12 E
Vereb'jo	76	58.41 N	32.42 E
Vereeniging	158	26.38 S	27.57 E
Veregin	184	51.35 N	102.05 W
Vereinigte Arabische Emirate → United Arab Emirates □[1]	128	24.00 N	54.00 E
Vereinigte Königreich → United Kingdom □[1]	28	54.00 N	2.00 W
Vereinigte Staaten → United States □[1]	178	38.00 N	97.00 W
Vereja, Ross.	82	55.46 N	39.06 E
Vereja, Ross.	82	55.21 N	36.11 E
Vereja, Ross.	265b	55.37 N	38.02 E
Veremejki	76	53.46 N	31.15 E
Vereščagino, Ross.	74	64.14 N	87.37 E
Vereščagino, Ross.	80	58.05 N	54.40 E
Veresegyház	264c	47.39 N	19.17 E
Veresoč'	78	51.19 N	31.46 E
Veretje	82	54.08 N	36.17 E
Véretz	50	47.22 N	0.48 E
Verga	285	39.52 N	75.10 W
Verga, Cap ≻	150	10.12 N	14.27 W
Vergara	252	32.56 S	53.57 W
Vergato	64	44.17 N	11.07 E
Vergel	196	25.39 N	103.32 W
Vergeletto	58	46.14 N	8.36 E
Vergemont Creek ≃	166	24.12 S	143.17 E
Vergennes	188	44.10 N	73.15 W
Verghereto	66	43.47 N	12.00 E
Vergiate	62	45.43 N	8.42 E
Vergons	62	43.55 N	6.35 E
Vergt	32	45.02 N	0.43 E
Vergulevka	83	48.24 N	38.32 E
Verigino	82	56.42 N	38.08 E
Verín	34	41.56 N	7.26 W
Veringenstadt	58	48.11 N	9.12 E
Verin Talin	84	40.23 N	43.53 E
Veriora	76	58.00 N	27.21 E
Veríssimo	255	19.42 S	48.18 W
Verkeerdevlei	158	28.48 S	26.48 E
Verkhneudinsk → Ulan-Ude	88	51.50 N	107.37 E
Verkhniy Ufaley → Verchnij Ufalej	86	56.04 N	60.14 E
Verkhnyaya Salda → Verchn'aja Salda	86	58.02 N	60.33 E
Verkhoyansk → Verchojansk	74	67.35 N	133.27 E
Verkykerskop	158	27.54 S	29.17 E
Verl (Senne I)	52	51.53 N	8.31 E
Vermaaklikheid	158	34.19 S	21.01 E
Vermaas	158	26.30 S	25.59 E
Vermand	50	49.52 N	3.09 E
Vermejo ≃	196	36.30 N	104.33 W
Vermelho ≃, Bra.	250	9.16 S	47.23 W
Vermelho ≃, Bra.	250	7.44 S	47.17 W
Vermelho ≃, Bra.	250	5.33 S	49.14 W
Vermelho ≃, Bra.	255	14.54 S	51.06 W
Vermenton	50	47.40 N	3.44 E
Vermette Lake ⊜	184	55.40 N	109.05 W
Vermezzo	266b	45.24 N	8.59 E
Vermiglio	64	46.18 N	10.42 E
Vermilion, Ab., Can.	182	53.22 N	110.51 W
Vermilion, Oh., U.S.	214	41.25 N	82.21 W
Vermilion □[6]	216	40.08 N	87.37 W
Vermilion ≃, Ab., Can.	184	53.44 N	110.18 W
Vermilion ≃, On., Can.	190	46.16 N	81.41 W
Vermilion ≃, Il., U.S.	216	41.19 N	89.04 W
Vermilion ≃, La., U.S.	194	29.46 N	92.09 W
Vermilion ≃, Mn., U.S.	190	48.16 N	92.30 W
Vermilion ≃, Oh., U.S.	214	41.26 N	82.22 W
Vermilion, Middle Fork ≃	216	40.12 N	87.45 W
Vermilion, North Fork ≃, Il., U.S.	216	40.49 N	88.30 W
Vermilion, North Fork ≃, Il., U.S.	216	40.13 N	87.39 W
Vermilion, South Fork ≃	216	40.49 N	88.30 W
Vermilion Bay	184	49.51 N	93.24 W
Vermilion Bay ⊂	194	29.40 N	92.00 W
Vermilion Lake ⊜, On., Can.	184	50.03 N	92.13 W
Vermilion Lake ⊜, Mn., U.S.	190	47.53 N	92.25 W
Vermilion Pass)(	182	51.14 N	116.03 W
Vermillion	198	42.46 N	96.55 W
Vermillion ≃	198	42.44 N	96.53 W
Vermillion, East Fork ≃	198	43.44 N	97.03 W
Vermillion, West Fork ≃	198	43.44 N	97.03 W
Vermillion Bluffs ♠[4]	200	40.50 N	108.30 W
Vermillion Creek ≃, U.S.	200	40.46 N	108.53 W
Vermillion Creek ≃, Ks., U.S.	198	39.12 N	96.13 W
Vermont, Austl.	274b	37.50 S	145.12 E
Vermont, Il., U.S.	194	40.17 N	90.25 W
Vermont □[3], U.S.	178	43.50 N	72.45 W
Vermont □[3], U.S.	188	43.50 N	72.45 W
Vermontville	216	42.37 N	85.01 W
Vernà, Pizzo di ∧	70	38.01 N	15.15 E
Vernaison	62	45.39 N	4.49 E
Vernal	200	40.27 N	109.31 W
Vernalis	226	37.37 N	121.17 W
Vernante	62	44.15 N	7.32 E
Vernayaz	58	46.08 N	7.02 E
Vernazza	62	44.08 N	9.41 E
Verndale	198	46.24 N	95.01 W
Verne	52	51.41 N	8.34 E
Verner	190	46.25 N	80.07 W
Verneuil	32	48.44 N	0.56 E
Verneuil-L'Étang	261	48.39 N	2.50 E
Verneuil-sur-Avre	50	48.44 N	0.56 E
Verneuil-sur-Seine	50	48.59 N	1.59 E
Verneukpan	158	30.00 S	21.00 E
Verneukpan ≌	158	30.00 S	21.10 E
Vernier	58	46.13 N	6.06 E
Verninge	41	55.18 N	10.13 E
Vernio	66	44.03 N	11.09 E
Vernole	68	40.17 N	18.18 E
Vernon, B.C., Can.	182	50.16 N	119.16 W
Vernon, On., Can.	212	45.10 N	75.28 W
Vernon, Fr.	50	49.05 N	1.29 E
Vernon, Al., U.S.	194	33.45 N	88.06 W
Vernon, Ca., U.S.	280	34.01 N	118.13 W
Vernon, Ct., U.S.	207	41.49 N	72.28 W
Vernon, Fl., U.S.	194	30.37 N	85.42 W
Vernon, Il., U.S.	219	38.48 N	89.05 W
Vernon, In., U.S.	218	38.59 N	85.36 W
Vernon, Mi., U.S.	216	42.56 N	84.02 W
Vernon, N.J., U.S.	210	41.11 N	74.29 W
Vernon, N.Y., U.S.	210	43.05 N	75.32 W
Vernon, Oh., U.S.	214	41.23 N	80.34 W
Vernon, Tx., U.S.	196	34.09 N	99.15 W
Vernon, Ut,. U.S.	200	40.05 N	112.25 W
Vernon, Lake ⊜	212	45.20 N	79.17 W
Vernon Dam ◆[6]	207	42.46 N	72.31 W
Vernon Hills	278	42.13 N	87.58 W
Vernonia	224	45.51 N	123.11 W
Vernon Lake ⊜[1]	194	31.15 N	93.25 W
Vernon River	186	46.12 N	62.50 W
Vernouillet	261	48.58 N	1.59 E
Vernoux-en-Vivarais	62	44.54 N	4.39 E
Verny	56	49.01 N	6.12 E
Vero ≃	34	42.00 N	0.10 E
Vero Beach	220	27.38 N	80.23 W
Véroia	38	40.31 N	22.12 E
Verolanuova	64	45.19 N	10.04 E
Verolavecchia	64	45.19 N	10.03 E
Veroli	66	41.41 N	13.25 E
Verona, On., Can.	212	44.29 N	76.42 W
Verona, It.	64	45.27 N	11.00 E
Verona, Ky., U.S.	218	38.49 N	84.39 W
Verona, Ms., U.S.	194	34.11 N	88.43 W
Verona, N.J., U.S.	276	40.49 N	74.14 W
Verona, N.Y., U.S.	210	43.08 N	75.34 W
Verona, Oh., U.S.	218	39.54 N	84.29 W
Verona, Pa., U.S.	279b	40.30 N	79.50 W
Verona, Wi., U.S.	216	42.59 N	89.31 W
Verona □[4]	64	45.25 N	11.02 E
Verona Beach	210	43.12 N	75.44 W
Verona Beach State Park ♠	210	43.14 N	75.44 W
Verona Park	216	42.21 N	85.09 W
Verónica	258	35.22 S	57.20 W
Verperluda, ostrov I	265a	59.59 N	30.01 E
Verplanck	210	41.15 N	73.58 W
Verran	166	33.51 S	136.18 E
Verrazano-Narrows Bridge ◆[5]	210	40.36 N	74.03 W
Verrès	62	45.40 N	7.42 E
Verrettes	238	19.03 N	72.28 W
Verrey-sous-Salmaise	58	47.26 N	4.40 E
Verrières, Bois de ♠	261	48.45 N	2.15 E
Verrières-le-Buisson	261	48.45 N	2.16 E
Versa ≃	62	44.54 N	8.16 E
Versailles, Fr.	50	48.48 N	2.08 E
Versailles, Il., U.S.	194	39.53 N	90.39 W
Versailles, In., U.S.	218	39.04 N	85.15 W
Versailles, Ky., U.S.	218	38.03 N	84.43 W
Versailles, Mo., U.S.	194	38.25 N	92.50 W
Versailles, N.Y., U.S.	210	42.31 N	78.59 W
Versailles, Oh., U.S.	216	40.13 N	84.29 W
Versailles, Pa., U.S.	279b	40.21 N	79.51 W
Versailles, Château de ⊥	261	48.48 N	2.07 E
Versailles, Parc de ♠	261	48.49 N	2.06 E
Versailles State Park ♠	218	39.04 N	85.13 W
Verse ≃	263	51.15 N	7.46 E
Versec → Vršac	38	45.07 N	21.18 E
Versestausee ⊜[1]	263	51.11 N	7.41 E
Versien	158	27.05 S	27.52 E
Veršina Tei	86	53.20 N	89.36 E
Veršino-Darasunskij	88	52.20 N	115.32 E
Veršino-Šachtaminskij	88	51.21 N	117.50 E
Versmold	52	52.02 N	8.09 E
Versoix	58	46.16 N	6.10 E
Ver-sur-Launette	261	49.06 N	2.41 E
Vert	261	48.57 N	1.41 E
Vert, Cap ≻	150	14.43 N	17.30 W
Vert'ačij	80	48.57 N	43.53 E
Verte, Île I, P.Q., Can.	186	48.02 N	69.26 W
Verte, Île I, P.Q., Can.	275a	45.34 N	73.30 W
Vertedero	240m	18.05 N	66.15 W
Verteillac	32	45.21 N	0.22 E
Vertientes	240p	21.16 N	78.09 W
Vertijevka	78	51.10 N	31.51 E
Vertkovo	82	56.07 N	36.25 E
Vert-le-Grand	261	48.34 N	2.22 E
Vert-le-Petit	261	48.33 N	2.22 E
Vertlinskoje	82	56.14 N	36.58 E
Vertou	32	47.10 N	1.29 W
Vertova	62	45.48 N	9.50 E
Vert-Saint-Denis	261	48.34 N	2.37 E
Vertus	50	48.54 N	4.00 E
Verucchio	66	43.59 N	12.25 E
Verulam	158	29.45 S	31.02 E
Verulamium ⊥	42	51.45 N	0.22 W
Verviers	56	50.35 N	5.52 E
Vervins	50	49.50 N	3.54 E
Verwall Gruppe ⋏	58	47.02 N	10.10 E
Verwood	42	50.53 N	1.52 W
Veryan	42	50.13 N	4.54 W
Verzasca ≃	58	46.09 N	8.52 E
Verzegnis	64	46.25 N	12.59 E
Verzenay	50	49.10 N	4.09 E
Verzino	68	39.19 N	16.51 E
Verzuolo	62	44.36 N	7.29 E
Verzy	50	49.09 N	4.10 E
Vesanto	26	62.56 N	26.25 E
Vesava ◆[8]	272c	19.08 N	72.48 E
Vescovato, Fr.	36	42.30 N	9.26 E
Vescovato, It.	64	45.10 N	10.10 E
Vescovo di Squillace, Roccelletta del ⊥	68	38.48 N	16.35 E
Vesdre ≃	56	50.37 N	5.37 E
Veseja	76	53.04 N	27.41 E
Veselí nad Lužnicí	30	49.11 N	14.43 E
Veselí nad Moravou	30	48.58 N	17.22 E
Veselinovo	78	47.21 N	31.14 E
Veselovskoje	86	54.00 N	78.43 E
Veselovskoje vodochranilišče ⊜[1]	80	47.00 N	41.18 E
Vésenaz	58	46.14 N	6.12 E
Vešenskaja	80	49.38 N	41.43 E
Vesgre ≃	50	48.48 N	1.36 E
Vesijärvi ⊜	26	61.06 N	25.32 E
Vesjegonsk	76	58.40 N	37.16 E
Veškajma, Ross.	80	54.04 N	47.02 E
Veškajma, Ross.	80	54.03 N	47.08 E
Veški	265b	55.56 N	37.37 E
Vesle ≃	50	49.23 N	3.38 E
Vešn'aki ◆[8]	265b	55.44 N	37.49 E
Ves'olaja Gora	83	48.43 N	39.16 E
Ves'olaja Rošča	86	53.47 N	76.22 E
Vesole, Monte ∧	68	40.24 N	15.10 E
Ves'oloje, Kaz.	85	43.19 N	77.06 E
Ves'oloje, Ross.	80	50.17 N	45.15 E
Ves'oloje, Ross.	83	47.10 N	38.45 E
Ves'oloje, Ukr.	78	47.01 N	34.55 E
Ves'olo-Voznesenka	83	47.09 N	38.20 E
Ves'olyj, Ross.	80	47.06 N	40.45 E
Ves'olyj, Ross.	83	47.20 N	39.18 E
Ves'olyje Terny	78	48.07 N	33.32 E
Ves'olyj Jar, Ross.	86	51.18 N	81.07 E
Ves'olyj Jar, Ross.	89	43.57 N	135.28 E
Ves'olyj Podol, Kaz.	86	53.31 N	65.54 E
Ves'olyj Podol, Ukr.	78	49.36 N	33.16 E
Ves'olyj Pos'olok ◆[8]	265a	59.54 N	30.28 E
Vesoul	58	47.38 N	6.10 E
Vespasiano	255	19.40 S	43.55 W
Vespolate	62	45.21 N	8.40 E
Vesta	236	9.43 N	83.03 W
Vest-Agder □[6]	26	58.30 N	7.10 E
Vestal	210	42.05 N	76.03 W
Vestal Center	210	42.02 N	76.01 W
Vestavia Hills	194	33.26 N	86.46 W
Vestbygd	26	58.06 N	6.35 E
Vesterålen II	24	68.45 N	15.00 E
Vester Egede	41	55.16 N	11.59 E
Vesterø Havn	26	57.18 N	10.56 E
Vester Skerninge	41	55.03 N	10.28 E
Vester Sottrup	41	54.57 N	9.43 E
Vestfjorden ⊂[2]	24	68.08 N	15.00 E
Vestfold □[6]	26	59.15 N	10.10 E
Vestmannaeyjar	24a	63.26 N	20.12 W
Vestone	64	45.42 N	10.24 E
Vestreno	58	46.06 N	9.18 E
Vestsjælland □[6]	41	55.35 N	11.30 E
Vestvågøya I	24	68.15 N	13.50 E
Vésubie ≃	62	43.52 N	7.12 E
Vesubio → Vesuvio ∧[1]	68	40.49 N	14.26 E
Vesuvio (Vesuvius) ∧[1]	68	40.49 N	14.26 E
Vesuvius Bay	224	48.53 N	123.35 W
Vesuvius → Vesuvio ∧[1]	68	40.49 N	14.26 E
Vesuv → Vesuvio ∧[1]	68	40.49 N	14.26 E
Veszprém	30	47.06 N	17.55 E
Veszprém □[6]	30	46.50 N	17.30 E
Vésztő	30	46.55 N	21.16 E
Vet ≃	158	27.40 S	25.40 E
Vetapālem	122	15.47 N	80.19 E
Vetčin	76	52.27 N	28.10 E
Veterans Stadium ♠	285	39.54 N	75.10 W
Vétheuil	50	49.04 N	1.42 E
Vetju	24	62.57 N	50.44 E
Vetka	76	52.33 N	31.10 E
Vetlanda	26	57.26 N	15.04 E
Vetl'anka	80	52.52 N	51.09 E
Vetluga	80	57.51 N	45.47 E
Vetluga ≃	80	56.18 N	46.24 E
Vetlužskij, Ross.	80	57.11 N	45.07 E
Vetlužskij, Ross.	80	58.23 N	45.26 E
Vetoškino	80	57.18 N	49.44 E
Vetovo	38	43.42 N	26.16 E
Vetralla	66	42.19 N	12.03 E
Vetren	38	42.16 N	24.03 E
Vetrino	76	55.25 N	28.28 E
Vetriolo	64	46.02 N	11.18 E
Vetrișoaia	38	46.26 N	28.13 E
Větřni	61	48.46 N	14.17 E
Vetschau	54	51.47 N	14.04 E
Vettisfossen ⌊	26	61.22 N	7.55 E
Vetto	64	44.29 N	10.20 E
Vettore, Monte ∧	66	42.49 N	13.16 E
Vetulonia	66	42.51 N	10.58 E
Veules-les-Roses	50	49.52 N	0.48 E
Veulettes-sur-Mer	50	49.51 N	0.36 E
Veurne (Furnes)	50	51.04 N	2.40 E
Vevay	218	38.44 N	85.04 W
Vevelstad	24	65.43 N	12.30 E
Veveno, Khawr ∨	140	6.40 N	32.58 E
Vevey	58	46.28 N	6.51 E
Vex	58	46.13 N	7.24 E
Veyle ≃	58	46.18 N	4.50 E
Veynes	62	44.32 N	5.49 E
Veyrier	62	45.53 N	6.10 E
Vézelay	50	47.28 N	3.44 E
Vézelise	58	48.29 N	6.05 E
Vézénobres	62	44.03 N	4.09 E
Vézère ≃	32	44.53 N	0.53 E
Vezirköprü	130	41.09 N	35.28 E
Vezouze ≃	58	48.35 N	6.29 E
Vezza d'Oglio	64	46.14 N	10.24 E
Vezzana, Cima della ∧	64	46.17 N	11.50 E
Vezzano	64	46.05 N	11.00 E
Vezzano Ligure	64	44.09 N	9.52 E
Viacha	248	16.39 S	68.18 W
Viadana	64	44.56 N	10.31 E
Viadutos	252	27.34 S	52.01 W
Viale	252	31.53 S	60.01 W
Vialonga	266c	38.52 N	9.05 W
Via Mala ∨	58	46.40 N	9.26 E
Viamão	252	30.05 S	51.02 W
Viamonte	252	33.44 S	63.06 W
Vian	196	35.29 N	94.58 W
Viana	250	3.13 S	45.00 W
Viana, Ilha do I	287a	22.52 S	43.08 W
Viana del Bollo	34	42.11 N	7.06 W
Viana do Alentejo	34	38.20 N	8.00 W
Viana do Castelo	34	41.42 N	8.50 W
Vianden	56	49.57 N	6.11 E
Vianen	52	52.00 N	5.05 E
Viangchan (Vientiane)	110	17.58 N	102.36 E
Viangphoukha	110	20.41 N	101.04 E
Viar ≃	34	37.36 N	5.50 W
Viareggio	64	43.52 N	10.14 E
Viarmes	50	49.08 N	2.22 E
Viatka → Kirov	80	58.38 N	49.42 E
Viaur ≃	32	44.08 N	2.23 E
Vibank	184	50.20 N	103.55 W
Víboras, Arroyo de las ≃	258	33.57 S	58.21 W
Viborg, Dan.	26	56.26 N	9.24 E
Viborg, S.D., U.S.	198	43.10 N	97.04 W
Viborg □[6]	41	56.18 N	9.27 E
Viborg → Vyborg	76	60.42 N	28.45 E
Vibo Valentia	68	38.40 N	16.06 E
Vibraye	50	48.03 N	0.44 E
Viburnum	194	37.42 N	91.08 W
Viby	41	55.33 N	12.02 E
Viby ◆[8]	41	56.07 N	10.10 E
Vic (Vich)	34	41.56 N	2.15 E
Vic, Étang de ⊂	62	43.29 N	3.50 E
Vicálvaro ◆[8]	266a	40.24 N	3.36 W
Vícam	232	27.35 N	110.20 W
Vicarello	66	42.10 N	12.12 E
Vicari	70	37.49 N	13.34 E
Vicchio	66	43.56 N	11.28 E
Vicco	192	37.12 N	83.03 W
Vic-en-Bigorre	32	43.23 N	0.03 E
Vicente, Point ≻	280	33.44 N	118.25 W
Vicente Casares	258	34.57 S	58.38 W
Vicente de Carvalho	256	23.56 S	46.19 W
Vicente Guerrero, Méx.	234	18.24 N	92.53 W
Vicente Guerrero, Méx.	234	23.45 N	103.59 W
Vicente Guerrero, Méx.	234	19.08 N	98.10 W
Vicente Guerrero, Presa ⊜[1]	234	24.00 N	98.45 W
Vicente López	258	34.32 S	58.28 W
Vicente López □[5]	288	34.32 S	58.30 W
Vicente Noble	238	18.23 N	71.11 W
Vicenza	64	45.33 N	11.33 E
Vicenza □[4]	64	45.40 N	11.27 E
Viceroy	184	49.27 N	105.22 W
Vichada □[5]	246	5.00 N	69.30 W
Vichada ≃	246	4.55 N	67.50 W
Vichadero	252	31.48 S	54.43 W
Vichigasta	252	29.29 S	67.31 W
Vichoreva ≃	88	56.47 N	101.22 E
Vichorevka	88	56.12 N	101.09 E
Vichra ≃	76	54.01 N	31.52 E
Vichuga → Vičuga	80	57.13 N	41.56 E
Vichuquén	252	34.53 S	72.00 W
Vichy	32	46.08 N	3.26 E
Vici	196	36.08 N	99.17 W
Vickery	214	41.23 N	82.56 W
Vicksburg, Mi., U.S.	216	42.07 N	85.31 W
Vicksburg, Ms., U.S.	194	32.21 N	90.52 W
Vicksburg, Pa., U.S.	210	40.56 N	76.59 W
Vicksburg National Military Park ♠	194	32.24 N	90.52 W
Vico	36	42.10 N	8.48 E
Vico, Lago di ⊜	66	42.19 N	12.10 E
Vico Canavese	62	45.30 N	7.47 E
Vico del Gargano	68	41.54 N	15.57 E
Vico Equense	68	40.40 N	14.25 E
Vicoforte	62	44.21 N	7.54 E
Vicopisano	66	43.42 N	10.35 E
Viçosa, Bra.	250	9.24 S	36.14 W
Viçosa, Bra.	255	20.45 S	42.53 W
Viçosa do Ceará	250	3.34 S	41.05 W
Vicosoprano	58	46.22 N	9.37 E
Vicovaro	66	42.01 N	12.54 E
Vicq	261	48.49 N	1.50 E
Vic-Sur-Aisne	50	49.24 N	3.07 E
Vic-sur-Cère	32	44.59 N	2.37 E
Vic-sur-Seille	56	48.47 N	6.32 E
Victor, Ca., U.S.	226	38.08 N	121.12 W
Victor, Id., U.S.	202	43.36 N	111.06 W
Victor, Ia., U.S.	190	41.43 N	92.17 W
Victor, Mt., U.S.	202	46.25 N	114.08 W
Victor, N.Y., U.S.	210	42.58 N	77.24 W
Victor, Lac ⊜	186	50.35 N	61.50 W
Victorbur	52	53.29 N	7.20 E
Victor Harbor	168b	35.34 S	138.37 E
Victoria, Arg.	252	32.37 S	60.10 W
Victoria, Cam.	152	4.01 N	9.12 E
Victoria, B.C., Can.	224	48.25 N	123.22 W
Victoria, P.E., Can.	186	46.13 N	63.29 W
Victoria, Chile	252	38.13 S	72.20 W
Victoria, Gren.	241k	12.12 N	61.42 W
Victoria, Guinée	150	10.50 N	14.33 W
Victoria (Xianggang), H.K.	271d	22.17 N	114.09 E
Victoria, Malay.	112	5.17 N	115.15 E
Victoria, Pil.	116	13.12 N	121.15 E
Victoria, Pil.	116	15.35 N	120.41 E
Victoria, Rom.	38	45.45 N	24.41 E
Victoria, Sey.	138	4.38 S	55.27 E
Victoria, Ks., U.S.	198	38.51 N	99.08 W
Victoria, Tx., U.S.	196	28.48 N	97.00 W
Victoria, Va., U.S.	192	36.59 N	78.13 W
Victoria □[3]	166	38.00 S	145.00 E
Victoria □[4]	154	20.54 S	31.21 E
Victoria □[6], On., Can.	212	44.35 N	78.50 W
Victoria □[6], Tx., U.S.	222	28.55 N	97.00 W
Victoria ◆[8]	288	34.28 S	58.31 W
Victoria ≃, Austl.	160	15.12 S	129.43 E
Victoria ≃, Nf., Can.	186	48.45 N	56.40 W
Victoria ≃, Méx.	234	21.02 N	99.50 W
Victoria, Isla I	254	45.18 S	73.58 W
Victoria, Lake ⊜, Afr.	154	1.00 S	33.00 E

	English	Deutsch	Español	Français	Português
≃	River	Fluß	Río	Rivière	Rio
≊	Canal	Kanal	Canal	Canal	Canal
⌊	Waterfall, Rapids	Wasserfall, Stromschnellen	Cascada, Rápidos	Chute d'eau, Rapides	Cascata, Rápidos
ʮ	Strait	Meeresstraße	Estrecho	Détroit	Estreito
⊂	Bay, Gulf	Bucht, Golf	Bahía, Golfo	Baie, Golfe	Baía, Golfo
⊜	Lake, Lakes	See, Seen	Lago, Lagos	Lac, Lacs	Lago, Lagos
≌	Swamp	Sumpf	Pantano	Marais	Pântano
⊼	Ice Features, Glacier	Eis- und Gletscherformen	Accidentes Glaciales	Formes glaciaires	Acidentes glaciares
⊤	Other Hydrographic Features	Andere Hydrographische Objekte	Otros Elementos Hidrográficos	Autres données hydrographiques	Outros acidentes hidrográficos
✢	Submarine Features	Untermeerische Objekte	Accidentes Submarinos	Formes de relief sous-marin	Acidentes submarinos
□	Political Unit	Politische Einheit	Unidad Politica	Entité politique	Unidade política
⊙	Cultural Institution	Kulturelle Institution	Institución Cultural	Institution culturelle	Instituição cultural
⊥	Historical Site	Historische Stätte	Sitio Histórico	Site historique	Sitio histórico
♠	Recreational Site	Erholungs- und Ferienort	Sitio de Recreo	Centre de loisirs	Area de Lazer
⊠	Airport	Flughafen	Aeropuerto	Aéroport	Aeroporto
■	Military Installation	Militäranlage	Instalación Militar	Installation militaire	Instalação militar
◆	Miscellaneous	Verschiedenes	Misceláneo	Divers	Diversos

ENGLISH — Name | Page | Lat.°′ | Long.°′

DEUTSCH — Name | Seite | Breite°′ | Länge°′ E = Ost

Name	Page	Lat.°′	Long.°′
Victoria, Lake ⊜, Austl.	166	34.00 S	141.16 E
Victoria, Mount ∧, Mya.	110	21.14 N	93.55 E
Victoria, Mount ∧, Pap. N. Gui.	164	8.55 S	147.35 E
Victoria, Pont ◆[5]	275a	45.29 N	73.32 W
Victoria and Albert Museum ʊ	272c	18.59 N	72.50 E
Victoria Beach	184	50.43 N	96.33 W
Victoria Beach ⊥[2]	273a	6.25 N	3.25 E
Victoria → Ciudad Victoria	234	23.44 N	99.08 W
Victoria de Durango → Durango	234	24.02 N	104.40 W
Victoria Falls	154	17.56 S	25.50 E
Victoria Falls ⌞	154	17.55 S	25.51 E
Victoria Falls National Park ♦	154	17.55 S	25.40 E
Victoria Gardens ♦	272c	18.59 N	72.50 E
Victoria Harbour	212	44.45 N	79.46 W
Victoria International Airport ⊠	224	48.39 N	123.26 W
Victoria Island I, N.T., Can.	176	71.00 N	110.00 W
Victoria Island I, Nig.	273a	6.26 N	3.26 E
Victoria Lake ⊜	273d	26.14 S	28.09 E
Victoria Lake ⊜[1]	186	48.18 N	57.30 W
Victoria Land ◆[1]	9	75.00 S	163.00 E
Victoria Lawn Tennis Association Courts ♦	274b	37.51 S	145.02 E
Victoria Memorial Hall ʊ	271c	1.17 N	103.51 E
Victoria Memorial Museum ʊ	272b	22.33 N	88.21 E
Victoria Nile ≃	154	2.14 N	31.26 E
Victoria Park	168a	31.58 S	115.55 E
Victoria Park ♦, H.K.	271d	22.17 N	114.11 E
Victoria Park ♦, Eng., U.K.	262	53.23 N	2.34 W
Victoria Peak ∧, Belize	232	16.48 N	88.37 W
Victoria Peak ∧, B.C., Can.	182	50.03 N	126.06 W
Victoria Peak ∧, H.K.	271d	22.17 N	114.08 E
Victoria Peaks ⋏	116	9.22 N	118.20 E
Victoria Point	171a	27.35 S	153.18 E
Victoria Range ⋏, N.Z.	172	42.09 S	172.08 E
Victoria Range ⋏, Pil.	116	9.32 N	118.23 E
Victoria River	164	15.37 S	131.08 E
Victoria River Downs	164	16.24 S	131.00 E
Victorias	116	10.54 N	123.05 E
Victoria State Car Club Race Circuit ♦	274b	37.45 S	145.11 E
Victoria Station ◆[5]	262	53.29 N	2.15 W
Victoria Strait ʮ	176	69.15 N	100.30 W
Victoria Terminus ◆[5]	272c	18.57 N	72.50 E
Victoria University of Manchester ʊ[2]	262	53.28 N	2.14 W
Victoriaville	206	46.03 N	71.57 W
Victoria → Vitória	255	20.19 S	40.21 W
Victoria West	158	31.25 S	23.04 E
Victorica	252	36.13 S	65.27 W
Victorino	246	2.48 N	67.50 W
Victorino de la Plaza	252	36.36 S	62.40 W
Víctor Rosales	234	22.57 N	102.42 W
Victorville	228	34.32 N	117.17 W
Victory, Mount ∧	164	9.10 S	149.05 E
Victory Gardens	276	40.52 N	74.32 W
Victory Heights	214	41.22 N	79.46 W
Victory Hills	279b	40.11 N	79.53 W
Victory Mills	210	43.05 N	73.36 W
Victory Monument ⊥	269a	13.46 N	100.33 E
Vičuga	80	57.13 N	41.56 E
Vicuña	252	30.02 S	70.44 W
Vicuña Mackenna	252	33.54 S	64.23 W
Vidal, Kaap ›	158	28.09 S	32.33 E
Vidal Gormaz, Isla I	254	52.00 S	74.45 W
Vidalia, Ga., U.S.	192	32.13 N	82.24 W
Vidalia, La., U.S.	194	31.33 N	91.25 W
Vidal Ramos	252	27.23 S	49.22 W
Vidauban	62	43.26 N	6.26 E
Videbæk	26	56.05 N	8.38 E
Videira	252	27.00 S	51.08 W
Videle	38	44.16 N	25.31 E
Vidigueira	34	38.13 N	7.48 W
Vidim, Česko.	54	50.28 N	14.31 E
Vidim, Ross.	88	56.29 N	103.09 E
Vidin	38	43.59 N	22.52 E
Vidisha	124	23.32 N	77.49 E
Vidlica	24	61.10 N	32.21 E
Vidnoje	82	55.34 N	37.41 E
Vidogošči	82	56.42 N	36.23 E
Vidor	194	30.07 N	94.00 W
Vidos ≃	267b	40.58 N	28.53 E
Vidöstern ⊜	26	57.04 N	14.01 E
Vidourle ≃	62	43.32 N	4.08 E
Vidra, Rom.	38	44.16 N	26.11 E
Vidra, Rom.	38	45.55 N	26.54 E
Vidsel	24	65.51 N	20.24 E
Vidzeme □[9]	76	57.10 N	25.30 E
Vidzy	76	55.24 N	26.38 E
Vie ≃	50	49.05 N	0.04 E
Viecht	60	48.30 N	12.04 E
Viechtach	60	49.05 N	12.53 E
Viechtwang	61	47.55 N	13.57 E
Viedma	254	40.48 S	63.00 W
Viedma, Lago ⊜	254	49.35 S	72.35 W
Viehberg ∧	61	48.33 N	14.37 E
Viehhausen	60	48.59 N	11.58 E
Vieil Armand ♦	58	47.52 N	7.10 E
Vieillard, Lac du ⊜	190	47.23 N	78.02 W
Vieille Case	240d	15.36 N	61.24 W
Vieira do Minho	34	41.39 N	8.09 W
Viejo, Cerro ∧	248	4.49 S	79.27 W
Viekšniai	76	56.16 N	22.31 E
Vielank	54	53.15 N	11.08 E
Viella	34	42.42 N	0.48 E
Vielle-Eglise-en-Yvelines	261	48.40 N	1.53 E
Vielsalm	56	50.17 N	5.55 E
Viels-Maisons	50	48.54 N	3.24 E
Viena → Vienne ≃	32	47.13 N	0.05 E
Vienenburg	54	51.57 N	10.34 E
Vienna, On., Can.	212	42.41 N	80.48 W
Vienna, Ga., U.S.	192	32.05 N	83.47 W
Vienna, Il., U.S.	194	37.25 N	88.54 W
Vienna, In., U.S.	218	38.39 N	85.46 W
Vienna, Md., U.S.	208	38.29 N	75.49 W
Vienna, Mo., U.S.	194	38.11 N	91.56 W
Vienna, N.J., U.S.	210	40.52 N	74.53 W
Vienna, Oh., U.S.	214	41.14 N	80.40 W
Vienna, S.D., U.S.	198	44.42 N	97.30 W
Vienna, Va., U.S.	208	38.54 N	77.15 W
Vienna, Va., U.S.	208	38.29 N	75.49 W
Vienna, W.V., U.S.	188	39.19 N	81.32 W
Vienna → Wien	61	48.13 N	16.20 E
Vienne	62	45.31 N	4.52 E
Vienne □[5]	32	46.35 N	0.30 E
Vienne ≃	32	47.13 N	0.05 E
Vienne-en-Arthies	261	49.04 N	1.44 E
Vienne-le-Château	56	49.11 N	4.53 E
Vienne → Wien	61	48.13 N	16.20 E
Vientiane → Viangchan	110	17.58 N	102.36 E
Vientos, Paso de los → Windward Passage ʮ	238	20.00 N	73.50 W
Vieques	240m	18.09 N	65.27 W
Vieques, Aeropuerto ⊠	240m	18.07 N	65.30 W
Vieques, Isla de I	240m	18.08 N	65.25 W
Vieques, Pasaje de ʮ	240m	18.11 N	65.37 W
Vieques, Sonda de ʮ	240m	18.15 N	65.23 W
Vière ≃	56	48.46 N	4.41 E
Viereck	54	53.32 N	14.02 E
Vieremä	26	63.45 N	27.01 E
Vierfontein	158	27.03 S	26.46 E
Vierhouten	52	52.20 N	5.50 E
Vieringhausen ◆[8]	263	51.11 N	7.10 E
Vierlande ◆[1]	52	53.26 N	10.14 E
Viernau	54	50.40 N	10.32 E
Viernheim	56	49.32 N	8.34 E
Vierraden	54	53.06 N	14.17 E
Viersen	56	51.15 N	6.23 E
Vierumäki	26	61.06 N	25.57 E
Vierwaldstättersee ⊜	58	47.00 N	8.28 E
Vierzehnheiligen ʊ[1]	56	50.08 N	11.02 E
Vierzon	50	47.13 N	2.05 E
Viesca	232	25.21 N	102.48 W
Viesecke	54	53.01 N	12.01 E
Vieselbach	54	51.00 N	11.08 E
Viesīte	76	56.21 N	25.33 E
Vieste	68	41.53 N	16.10 E
Vietgest	54	53.45 N	12.20 E
Vietnam □[1], Asia	108	16.00 N	108.00 E
Vietnam □[1], Asia	110	16.00 N	108.00 E
Vietnam Veterans Memorial ⊥	284c	38.53 N	77.03 W
Vietri di Potenza	68	40.36 N	15.30 E
Vietri sul Mare	68	40.40 N	14.44 E
Viet Tri	110	21.18 N	105.26 E
Vieux-Condé	50	50.27 N	3.34 E
Vieux-Ferette	58	47.30 N	7.18 E
Vieux-Fort, P.Q., Can.	186	51.26 N	57.49 W
Vieux-Fort, Guad.	241o	15.57 N	61.43 W
Vieux Fort, St. Luc.	241f	13.44 N	60.57 W
Vieux-Fort, Pointe du ›	241o	15.57 N	61.43 W
Vieux Fort Bay ⊂	241f	13.44 N	60.58 W
Vieux-Habitants	241o	16.04 N	61.46 W
Vieux-Thann	58	47.48 N	7.08 E
Vievis	76	54.46 N	24.48 E
View Park	280	34.00 N	118.20 W
Vieytes	258	35.16 S	57.35 W
Vif	62	45.03 N	5.40 E
Vig	41	55.51 N	11.36 E
Viga ≃	76	59.14 N	43.41 E
Vigala	76	58.43 N	24.22 E
Vigan	116	17.34 N	120.23 E
Vigarano Mainarda	64	44.50 N	11.30 E
Vigatto	64	44.43 N	10.20 E
Vigeland	26	58.05 N	7.18 E
Vigentino ◆[8]	266b	45.25 N	9.11 E
Vigersted	41	55.29 N	11.54 E
Vigese, Monte ∧	64	44.12 N	11.06 E
Vigésima Quinta de Abril, Ponte ◆[5]	266c	38.41 N	9.11 W
Vigevano	62	45.19 N	8.51 E
Viggianello	68	39.58 N	16.05 E
Viggiano	68	40.20 N	15.54 E
Viggiù	62	45.52 N	8.54 E
Vigia	250	0.48 S	48.08 W
Vigie Airport ⊠	241f	14.01 N	60.59 W
Vignacourt	50	50.01 N	2.12 E
Vignale	62	45.01 N	8.24 E
Vignanello	66	42.23 N	12.17 E
Vigneulles-lès-Hattonchâtel	56	48.59 N	5.43 E
Vigneux-sur-Seine	261	48.42 N	2.25 E
Vignola	64	44.29 N	11.00 E
Vignory	58	48.17 N	5.06 E
Vignot	56	48.46 N	5.36 E
Vigny	261	49.05 N	1.56 E
Vigo	34	42.14 N	8.43 W
Vigo, Ría de ⊂[1]	34	42.15 N	8.45 W
Vigodarzere	64	45.27 N	11.53 E
Vigo di Fassa	64	46.25 N	11.40 E
Vigolzone	62	44.55 N	9.40 E
Vigone	62	44.51 N	7.30 E
Vigonovo	64	45.23 N	12.00 E
Vigo-Rendena	64	46.05 N	10.43 E
Vigrestad	26	58.34 N	5.42 E
Viguzzolo	62	44.54 N	8.55 E
Vigy	56	49.12 N	6.18 E
Vihanti	26	64.29 N	25.00 E
Vihāri	123	30.02 N	72.21 E
Vihiers	32	47.09 N	0.32 W
Vihowa	123	31.08 N	70.30 E
Vihren ∧	38	41.46 N	23.24 E
Vihti	26	60.25 N	24.20 E
Viiala	26	61.13 N	23.47 E
Viinijärvi	26	62.39 N	29.14 E
Viinijärvi ⊜	26	62.44 N	29.17 E
Viipuri → Vyborg	76	60.42 N	28.45 E
Viitasaari	26	63.04 N	25.52 E
Viivikonna	76	59.19 N	27.42 E
Vijāpur	120	23.34 N	72.45 E
Vijayawāda	122	16.31 N	80.37 E
Vijosë (Aóös) ≃	38	40.37 N	19.20 E
Vik	40	59.44 N	17.28 E
Vik ⊥	40	59.44 N	17.27 E
Vika	40	60.31 N	15.42 E
Vikajärvi	24	66.37 N	26.12 E
Vikārābād	122	17.20 N	77.54 E
Vikbolandet ›[1]	40	58.32 N	16.40 E
Vikeke	112	8.52 S	126.22 E
Viken	41	56.09 N	12.34 E
Viken ⊜	26	58.39 N	14.20 E
Vikern ⊜	40	59.30 N	14.55 E
Vikersund	26	59.59 N	10.02 E
Vikhroli ◆[8]	272c	19.07 N	72.56 E
Viking	182	53.06 N	111.46 W
Viking Village	218	39.05 N	84.18 W
Vikmanshyttan	40	60.17 N	15.49 E
Vikna	24	64.57 N	10.58 E
Vikna I	24	64.57 N	10.58 E
Vikramasingapuram	122	8.43 N	77.24 E
Viksøyri	26	61.05 N	6.35 E
Viktor	24	66.09 N	58.07 E
Viktorovka	86	52.51 N	62.32 E
Viktring	61	46.35 N	14.16 E
Vikulovo	86	56.49 N	70.37 E
Vil'a	80	55.15 N	42.13 E
Vila Alferes Chamusca	156	24.29 S	33.00 E
Vila Augusta	287b	23.28 S	46.32 W
Vila Babi	287a	22.42 S	43.23 W
Vila Boacaya ◆[8]	287b	23.29 S	46.44 W
Vila Caldas Xavier	154	15.59 S	34.12 E
Vila da Maganja	154	17.18 S	37.30 E
Vila da Ribeira Brava	150a	16.37 N	24.18 W
Viladecans	266d	41.19 N	2.00 E
Viladecavalls del Vallès	266d	41.33 N	1.58 E
Vila de Manica	156	18.56 S	32.53 E
Vila de Rei	34	39.40 N	8.09 W
Vila Dirce	287b	23.35 S	46.48 W
Vila do Bispo	34	37.05 N	8.55 W
Vila do Conde	34	41.21 N	8.45 W
Vila do Porto	148a	36.56 N	25.09 W
Vila Embaú	256	22.37 S	45.02 W
Vila Flor	34	41.18 N	7.09 W
Vila Fontes	156	17.50 S	35.21 E
Vila Formosa ◆[8]	287b	23.34 S	46.33 W
Vilafranca del Penedès	34	41.21 N	1.42 E
Vila Franca de Xira	34	38.57 N	8.59 W
Vila Galvão	287b	23.27 S	46.33 W
Vila Gamito	154	14.12 S	33.00 E
Vila Gomes da Costa	156	24.19 S	33.38 E
Vila Gouveia	156	18.03 S	33.11 E
Vila Guilherme ◆[8]	287b	23.30 S	46.36 W
Vilaine ≃	32	47.30 N	2.27 W
Vila Isabel ◆[8]	287a	22.55 S	43.15 W
Vila Jaguára ◆[8]	287b	23.31 S	46.45 W
Viļaka	76	57.11 N	27.41 E
Vila Luísa	156	25.44 S	32.40 E
Vilama, Laguna de ⊜	252	22.36 S	66.55 W
Vila Machado	156	19.18 S	34.11 E
Vila Madalena ◆[8]	287b	23.33 S	46.42 W
Vila Maria ◆[8]	287b	23.31 S	46.34 W
Vila Mariana ◆[8]	287b	23.35 S	46.38 W
Vila Matilde ◆[8]	287b	23.32 S	46.31 W
Vilanculos	156	22.01 S	35.19 E
Viļāni	76	56.33 N	26.57 E
Vila Nova ≃	250	0.04 S	51.13 W
Vila Nova de Famalicão	34	41.25 N	8.32 W
Vila Nova de Foz Côa	34	41.05 N	7.12 W
Vila Nova de Gaia	34	41.08 N	8.37 W
Vilanova de la Roca	266d	41.33 N	2.17 E
Vilanova i la Geltrú	34	41.14 N	1.44 E
Vila Novo de Ourém	34	39.39 N	8.35 W
Vila Paiva de Andrada	156	18.44 S	34.03 E
Vila Progresso	287a	22.55 S	43.03 W
Vila Prudente ◆[8]	287b	23.35 S	46.33 W
Vila-real, Esp.	34	39.56 N	0.06 W
Vila Real, Port.	34	41.18 N	7.45 W
Vila Real de Santo António	34	37.12 N	7.25 W
Vilar Formoso	34	40.37 N	6.50 W
Vilarinho do Monte	250	1.37 S	52.01 W
Vilassar de Dalt	266d	41.31 N	2.22 E
Vilassar de Mar	266d	41.30 N	2.24 E
Vila Vasco da Gama	154	14.54 S	32.14 E
Vila Velha, Bra.	250	3.13 N	51.13 W
Vila Velha, Bra.	255	20.20 S	40.17 W
Vila Velha de Ródão	34	39.38 N	7.40 W
Vila Verde, Port.	34	41.39 N	8.26 W
Vila Verde, Port.	266c	38.50 N	9.22 W
Vila Viçosa	34	38.47 N	8.13 W
Vil'ča	78	51.22 N	29.24 E
Vilcabamba, Cordillera de ⋏	248	12.45 S	73.20 W
Vîlcea □[6]	38	45.19 N	24.00 E
Vildbjerg	41	56.12 N	8.46 E
Vilejka	76	54.30 N	26.53 E
Vilelas	252	27.57 S	62.38 W
Vilenki	82	54.16 N	38.55 E
Vil'gort, Ross.	24	61.35 N	50.40 E
Vil'gort, Ross.	24	60.34 N	56.24 E
Vilhelmina	26	64.37 N	16.39 E
Vilhena	248	12.43 S	60.07 W
Vilija (Neris) ≃	76	54.54 N	23.53 E
Viljandi	76	58.22 N	25.36 E
Viljoensdrif	158	26.44 S	27.55 E
Viljoenshof	158	34.40 S	19.42 E
Viljoenskroon	158	27.12 S	27.00 E
Viljoenspos	158	27.35 S	30.30 E
Vilkaviškis	76	54.39 N	23.02 E
Vil'kickogo, ostrov I, Ross.	72	73.29 N	75.50 E
Vil'kickogo, ostrov I, Ross.	74	75.44 N	152.20 E
Vil'kickogo, proliv ʮ	74	77.55 N	103.00 E
Vilkija	76	55.03 N	23.35 E
Vilkovo	78	45.25 N	29.35 E
Villa Abecia	248	21.00 S	65.23 W
Villa Aberastain	252	31.39 S	68.35 W
Villa Acuña → Ciudad Acuña	232	29.18 N	100.55 W
Villa Adelina ◆[8]	288	34.31 S	58.32 W
Villa Adriana ⊥	66	41.56 N	12.45 E
Villa Alejandrina	258	33.46 S	58.21 W
Villa Alemana	252	33.03 S	71.23 W
Villa Álvarez	234	19.14 N	103.43 W
Villa Ana	252	28.29 S	59.37 W
Villa Ángela	252	27.35 S	60.43 W
Villa Atamisqui	252	28.29 S	63.48 W
Villa Atuel	252	34.50 S	67.54 W
Villaba	116	11.13 N	124.23 E
Villa Ballester ◆[8]	258	34.32 S	58.33 W
Villabassa (Niederdorf)	64	46.44 N	12.10 E
Villabate	70	38.04 N	13.26 E
Villabé	261	48.35 N	2.27 E
Villa Bella	248	10.23 S	65.24 W
Villa Berthet	252	27.17 S	60.25 W
Villablino	34	42.56 N	6.19 W
Villa Borghese ʊ	267a	41.55 N	12.29 E
Villa Bosch ◆[8]	288	34.35 S	58.34 W
Villa Bruzual	246	9.20 N	69.06 W
Villa Cañás, Arg.	252	34.00 S	61.36 W
Villacañas, Esp.	34	39.38 N	3.20 W
Villa Carlos Paz	252	31.24 S	64.31 W
Villacarriedo	34	43.14 N	3.48 W
Villacarrillo	34	38.07 N	3.05 W
Villa Castelli, Arg.	252	29.00 S	68.11 W
Villa Castelli, It.	68	40.35 N	17.28 E
Villacastín	34	40.47 N	4.25 W
Villach	64	46.36 N	13.50 E
Villacidro	71	39.27 N	8.44 E
Villa Ciudadela ◆[8]	258	34.38 S	58.34 W
Villa Clara □[4]	240p	22.30 N	80.00 W
Villa Comaltitlan	236	15.13 N	92.35 W
Villa Concepción del Tío	252	31.19 S	62.50 W
Villa Constitución	252	33.14 S	60.20 W
Villa Cortese	266b	45.34 N	8.53 E
Villa Corzo	234	16.10 N	93.15 W
Villacoublay, Aérodrome de ⊠	261	48.45 N	2.10 E
Villa Creek ≃	226	35.27 N	120.58 W
Villa Cuauhtémoc, Méx.	234	19.24 N	99.34 W
Villa Cuauhtémoc, Méx.	234	22.11 N	97.50 W
Villada	34	42.15 N	4.58 W
Villa de Apaseo El Alto	234	20.27 N	100.37 W
Villa de Arista	234	22.39 N	100.50 W
Villa de Arriaga	234	21.54 N	101.23 W
Villadeati	62	45.04 N	8.10 E
Villa de Cos	234	23.17 N	102.21 W
Villa de Cura	246	10.02 N	67.29 W
Villa de Guadalupe	234	23.22 N	100.46 W
Villa del Carmen	252	32.57 S	65.03 W
Villa del Pueblito	234	20.32 N	100.27 W
Villa del Río	34	37.59 N	4.17 W
Villa del Rosario, Arg.	252	31.35 S	63.32 W
Villa del Rosario, Arg.	252	30.47 S	57.55 W
Villa de María	252	29.54 S	63.43 W
Villa de Mayo	258	34.30 S	58.41 W
Villa de Nova Sintra	150a	14.52 N	24.43 W
Villa de Reyes	234	21.48 N	100.56 W
Villa de San Antonio	236	14.16 N	87.36 W
Villa de San Francisco	236	14.10 N	86.58 W
Villa de Soto	252	30.51 S	64.59 W
Villa d'Este ⊥	267a	41.57 N	12.48 E
Villa Devoto ◆[8]	288	34.36 S	58.31 W
Villa Diamante ◆[8]	288	34.41 S	58.26 W
Villa di Chiavenna	58	46.20 N	9.29 E
Villadiego	34	42.31 N	4.00 W
Villa Dolores	252	31.56 S	65.12 W
Villa Domínico ◆[8]	258	34.41 S	58.19 W
Villadose	64	45.04 N	11.53 E
Villadossola	58	46.04 N	8.16 E
Villa Elisa	252	32.10 S	58.24 W
Villa Elisa ◆[8]	258	34.50 S	58.05 W
Villa Escalante	234	19.24 N	101.39 W
Villa Flores	234	16.14 N	93.14 W
Villa Florida	252	26.23 S	57.09 W
Villafranca d'Asti	62	44.55 N	8.02 E
Villafranca del Bierzo	34	42.36 N	6.48 W
Villafranca de los Barros	34	38.34 N	6.20 W
Villafranca di Verona	64	45.21 N	10.50 E
Villafranca in Lunigiana	64	44.17 N	9.57 E
Villafranca Piemonte	62	44.47 N	7.33 E
Villafranca Sicula	70	37.35 N	13.17 E
Villafranca Tirrena	70	38.14 N	15.26 E
Villafrati	70	37.54 N	13.29 E
Villagarcía, Esp.	34	42.36 N	8.45 W
Villa García, Méx.	234	22.10 N	101.57 W
Village	196	35.33 N	97.33 W
Village Creek ≃	194	35.28 N	91.19 W
Village Green	285	39.52 N	75.26 W
Villa General Roca	252	32.39 S	66.28 W
Village of Drummond Hill	285	39.43 N	75.42 W
Village of the Branch	276	40.51 N	73.11 W
Villa Gesell	252	37.15 S	56.55 W
Villa Giambruno	288	34.48 S	58.13 W
Villa González Ortega	234	22.30 N	101.55 W
Villagrán, Méx.	232	24.29 N	99.29 W
Villagrán, Méx.	234	20.31 N	100.59 W
Villagrande Strisaili	71	39.58 N	9.30 E
Villa Grazia	70	38.09 N	13.10 E
Villagrazia ◆[8]	70	38.05 N	13.20 E
Villa Grove	194	39.51 N	88.09 W
Villaguay	252	31.51 S	59.01 W
Villa Guerrero, Méx.	234	21.59 N	103.36 W
Villa Guerrero, Méx.	234	18.52 N	99.39 W
Villa Guillermina	252	28.14 S	59.28 W
Villa Hayes	252	25.06 S	57.34 W
Villahermosa	234	17.59 N	92.55 W
Villa Hernandarias	252	31.13 S	59.59 W
Villa Hidalgo, Méx.	204	30.59 N	116.10 W
Villa Hidalgo, Méx.	234	21.40 N	102.36 W
Villa Hidalgo, Méx.	234	21.44 N	105.15 W
Villa Hidalgo Yalalag	234	17.11 N	96.11 W
Villa Huidobro	252	34.50 S	64.35 W
Villaines-la-Juhel	32	48.21 N	0.17 W
Villa Insurgentes	232	25.12 N	111.44 W
Villa Iris	252	38.10 S	63.15 W
Villa Jiménez	234	19.55 N	101.35 W
Villa José L. Suárez ◆[8]	288	34.32 S	58.35 W
Villa Juanita	234	17.47 N	95.09 W
Villa Juárez, Méx.	232	27.10 N	109.50 W
Villa Juárez, Méx.	234	22.20 N	100.17 W
Villa Krause	252	31.34 S	68.32 W
Villa La Angostura	254	40.47 S	71.40 W
Villalago	66	41.56 N	13.50 E
Villa Larca	252	32.37 S	64.59 W
Villa La Venta	234	18.10 N	94.07 W
Villalba, Esp.	34	43.18 N	7.41 W
Villalba, It.	70	37.39 N	13.50 E
Villalba, P.R.	240m	18.08 N	66.30 W
Villaldama	232	26.30 N	100.26 W
Villa Lia	258	34.07 S	59.26 W
Villalon	116	11.31 N	124.22 E
Villalón de Campos	34	42.06 N	5.02 W
Villalonga	254	39.53 S	62.35 W
Villalpando	34	41.52 N	5.24 W
Villa Lugano ◆[8]	288	34.41 S	58.28 W
Villalvernia	62	44.49 N	8.51 E
Villa Lynch ◆[8]	288	34.36 S	58.31 W
Villa Madero, Arg.	288	34.42 S	58.30 W
Villa Madero, Méx.	234	19.24 N	101.16 W
Villa Mainero	232	24.32 N	99.38 W
Villamar	71	39.37 N	8.59 E
Villa María, Arg.	252	32.25 S	63.15 W
Villa Maria, Pa., U.S.	214	41.05 N	80.30 W
Villa Maria del Triunfo	286d	12.10 S	76.56 W
Villa María Grande	252	31.39 S	59.54 W
Villa Martín, Bol.	248	20.46 S	67.47 W
Villamartín, Esp.	34	36.52 N	5.38 W
Villamarzana	64	45.01 N	11.41 E
Villamassargia	71	39.16 N	8.38 E
Villa Matoque	252	25.49 S	63.49 W
Villa Mazán	252	28.40 S	66.34 W
Villa Media Agua	252	31.59 S	68.25 W
Villa Mercedes	252	30.07 S	68.42 W
Villa Minozzo	64	44.22 N	10.28 E
Villamontes	248	21.15 S	63.30 W
Villa Morelos	234	20.00 N	101.25 W
Villandraut	32	44.28 N	0.23 W
Villa Nova, Md., U.S.	284b	39.21 N	76.44 W
Villa Nova, Oh., U.S.	216	40.33 N	84.26 W
Villanova, Pa., U.S.	208	40.02 N	75.20 W
Villanova d'Asti	62	44.57 N	7.56 E
Villanova Mondovì	62	44.21 N	7.45 E
Villanova Monferrato	62	45.11 N	8.28 E
Villanova Monteleone	71	40.30 N	8.28 E
Villanova sull'Arda	64	45.01 N	10.00 E
Villanova Tulo	71	39.47 N	9.13 E
Villanova University ʊ[2]	285	40.02 N	75.21 W
Villa Nueva, Arg.	252	32.26 S	63.15 W
Villa Nueva, Arg.	252	32.54 S	68.47 W
Villanueva, Col.	246	10.37 N	72.59 W
Villa Nueva, Guat.	236	14.31 N	90.35 W
Villanueva, Hond.	236	15.17 N	88.00 W
Villanueva, Méx.	234	22.21 N	102.53 W
Villa Nueva, Nic.	236	12.58 N	86.49 W
Villanueva, N.M., U.S.	200	35.16 N	105.21 W
Villanueva de Córdoba	34	38.20 N	4.37 W
Villanueva de la Serana	34	38.58 N	5.48 W
Villanueva de la Sierra	34	40.12 N	6.24 W
Villanueva de los Infantes	34	38.44 N	2.59 W
Villanueva del Río y Minas	34	37.39 N	5.42 W
Villa Numancia	288	34.55 S	58.24 W
Villa Obregón	234	21.07 N	102.42 W
Villa Ocampo	252	28.28 S	59.22 W
Villa Ojo de Agua	252	29.31 S	63.42 W
Villa Oliva	252	26.01 S	57.53 W
Villa Opicina	64	45.40 N	13.49 E
Villa Oropeza	248	19.10 S	65.17 W
Villa Ottone (Uttenheim)	64	46.52 N	11.57 E
Villa Papale ʊ	267a	41.45 N	12.39 E
Villa Park, Ca., U.S.	228	33.48 N	117.48 W
Villa Park, Il., U.S.	278	41.53 N	87.59 W
Villa Park Dam ◆[6]	280	33.48 N	117.46 W
Villa Pérez	240m	18.12 N	66.47 W
Villapiana	68	39.51 N	16.28 E
Villapiana Lido	68	39.48 N	16.29 E
Villapinzón	246	5.13 N	73.36 W
Villa Potenza	66	43.19 N	13.25 E
Villaputzu	71	39.26 N	9.34 E
Villa Quinteros	252	27.14 S	65.33 W
Villa Quintilio Varo ⊥	267a	41.58 N	12.47 E
Villa Ramírez	252	32.11 S	60.12 W
Villarcayo	34	42.56 N	3.34 W
Villar-d'Arène	62	45.02 N	6.20 E
Villard-Bonnot	62	45.14 N	5.53 E
Villard-de-Lans	62	45.04 N	5.33 E
Villardefrades	34	41.43 N	5.15 W
Villar del Arzobispo	34	39.44 N	0.49 W
Villareal	116	11.34 N	124.56 E
Villa Real ◆[8]	288	34.37 S	58.31 W
Villa Regina	252	39.06 S	67.04 W
Villa Reynolds	252	33.43 S	65.23 W
Villa Rica	192	33.43 N	84.55 W
Villa Rivero	248	17.37 S	65.48 W
Villaroche	261	48.37 N	2.39 E
Villaroche ■	261	48.37 N	2.40 E
Villa Romana del Casale ⊥	70	37.22 N	14.20 E
Villa Rosa, Arg.	258	34.25 S	58.52 W
Villarosa, It.	70	37.35 N	14.10 E
Villar Pellice	62	44.48 N	7.09 E
Villar Perosa	62	44.56 N	7.15 E
Villarreales	196	26.07 N	100.20 W
Villarrica, Chile	254	39.16 S	72.13 W
Villarrica, Col.	246	3.58 N	74.37 W
Villarrica, Para.	252	25.45 S	56.26 W
Villarrica, Lago ⊜	254	39.15 S	72.06 W
Villarrobledo	34	39.16 N	2.36 W
Villarrubia de los Ojos	34	39.13 N	3.36 W
Villars, Arg.	258	34.50 S	58.56 W
Villars, Schw.	58	46.18 N	7.04 E
Villars-Colmars	62	44.10 N	6.36 E
Villars-en-Azois	58	48.04 N	4.45 E
Villars-les-Dombes	58	46.00 N	5.01 E
Villars-sur-Var	62	43.56 N	7.06 E
Villa Ruiz	258	34.25 S	59.15 W
Villas	208	39.01 N	74.56 W
Villa Sáenz Peña ◆[8]	288	34.36 S	58.31 W
Villa San Andrés ◆[8]	288	34.33 S	58.32 W
Villa Sandino	236	12.03 N	84.59 W
Villa San Giovanni	68	38.13 N	15.38 E
Villa San José	252	32.12 S	58.13 W
Villa San Martín	252	28.18 S	64.12 W
Villasanta	62	45.37 N	9.18 E
Villa Santa, Montaña ∧	236	14.12 N	86.27 W
Villa Santa Maria	66	41.57 N	14.21 E
Villa Santina	64	46.24 N	12.55 E
Villa Santo Domingo	234	23.20 N	101.44 W
Villa Santos Lugares ◆[8]	288	34.36 S	58.32 W
Villasayas	34	41.21 N	2.37 W
Villa Serrano	248	19.06 S	64.22 W
Villasimius	71	39.08 N	9.31 E
Villasis	116	15.54 N	120.35 E
Villasor	71	39.23 N	8.56 E
Villa Talavera	248	19.49 S	65.25 W
Villa Tunari	248	16.55 S	65.25 W
Villa Turdera ◆[8]	288	34.48 S	58.25 W
Villa Unión, Arg.	252	29.18 S	68.12 W
Villa Unión, Arg.	252	29.24 S	62.47 W
Villa Unión, Méx.	232	28.15 N	100.43 W
Villa Unión, Méx.	234	23.58 N	104.02 W
Villa Unión, Méx.	234	23.12 N	106.14 W
Villa Urquiza ◆[8]	288	34.34 S	58.29 W
Villa Valeria	252	34.20 S	64.55 W
Villa Vallelonga	66	41.52 N	13.37 E
Villaverde ◆[8]	266a	40.21 N	3.42 W
Villaverla	64	45.39 N	11.29 E
Villa Verona	226	39.28 N	121.33 W
Villavicencio	246	4.09 N	73.37 W
Villaviciosa	34	43.29 N	5.26 W
Villaviciosa de Córdoba	34	38.05 N	5.01 W
Villa Victoria	234	18.47 N	103.24 W
Villa Viscarra	248	17.59 S	65.36 W
Villa Vomano	66	42.37 N	13.46 E
Villazón	248	22.06 S	65.36 W
Villa Zorraquín	252	31.19 S	58.02 W
Villé	58	48.20 N	7.18 E
Villebon, Lac ⊜	190	47.58 N	77.17 W
Villebon-sur-Yvette	261	48.42 N	2.15 E
Villeconin	261	48.31 N	2.08 E
Villecresnes	261	48.43 N	2.32 E
Villecroze	62	43.35 N	6.16 E
Ville-d'Avray	261	48.50 N	2.11 E
Ville-de-Laval → Laval	206	45.35 N	73.45 W
Villedieu	32	48.50 N	1.13 W
Ville-en-Tardenois	50	49.11 N	3.48 E
Villefort	62	44.26 N	3.56 E
Villefranche	58	45.59 N	4.43 E
Villefranche-de-Rouergue	32	44.21 N	2.02 E
Villefranche-Sur-Cher	50	47.18 N	1.46 E
Villefranche-sur-Mer	62	43.42 N	7.19 E
Villejuif	50	48.48 N	2.22 E
Villejust	261	48.41 N	2.14 E
Ville-Marie	190	47.19 N	79.26 W
Villemaur-sur-Vanne	50	48.15 N	3.44 E
Villemeux-sur-Eure	50	48.40 N	1.28 E
Villemoisson-sur-Orge	261	48.40 N	2.19 E
Villemomble	261	48.53 N	2.31 E
Villena	34	38.38 N	0.51 W
Ville Nacíonal	234	17.50 N	96.14 W
Villenauxe-la-Grande	50	48.35 N	3.33 E
Villeneuve, It.	62	45.42 N	7.14 E
Villeneuve, Schw.	58	46.24 N	6.55 E
Villeneuve-d'Ascq	50	50.37 N	3.10 E
Villeneuve-d'Aveyron	32	44.26 N	2.02 E
Villeneuve-de-Berg	62	44.33 N	4.30 E
Villeneuve-la-Garenne	261	48.56 N	2.20 E
Villeneuve-la-Guyard	50	48.20 N	3.04 E
Villeneuve-l'Archevêque	50	48.14 N	3.33 E
Villeneuve-le-Comte	261	48.49 N	2.50 E
Villeneuve-le-Roi	50	48.44 N	2.25 E
Villeneuve-lès-Avignon	62	43.58 N	4.48 E
Villeneuve-lès-Maguelonne	62	43.32 N	3.52 E
Villeneuve-Saint-Denis	261	48.49 N	2.48 E
Villeneuve-Saint-Georges	50	48.44 N	2.27 E
Villeneuve-sous-Dammartin	261	49.02 N	2.39 E
Villeneuve-sur-Lot	32	44.25 N	0.42 E
Villeneuve-sur-Yonne	50	48.05 N	3.18 E
Villennes-sur-Seine	261	48.56 N	2.00 E
Villenoy	50	48.57 N	2.52 E
Villeny	50	47.37 N	1.45 E
Villeparisis	50	48.56 N	2.37 E
Villepinte	261	48.58 N	2.32 E
Ville Platte	194	30.41 N	92.16 W
Villepreux	261	48.50 N	2.01 E
Villequier	50	49.31 N	0.40 E
Villeron	261	49.03 N	2.33 E
Villeroy	50	48.59 N	2.47 E
Villers-Bocage, Fr.	32	49.05 N	0.39 W
Villers-Bocage, Fr.	50	49.59 N	2.20 E
Villers-Bretonneux	50	49.52 N	2.31 E
Villers-Carbonnel	50	49.52 N	2.54 E
Villers-Cotterêts	50	49.15 N	3.05 E
Villers-devant-Orval	56	49.37 N	5.19 E
Villers-en-Arthies	261	49.05 N	1.44 E
Villersexel	58	47.33 N	6.26 E
Villers-Farlay	58	47.00 N	5.45 E
Villers-la-Ville	50	50.35 N	4.32 E
Villers-le-Lac	58	47.04 N	6.40 E
Villers-lès-Nancy	58	48.40 N	6.09 E
Villers-lès-Pots	58	47.13 N	5.21 E
Villers-Outréaux	50	50.02 N	3.18 E
Villers-Saint-Paul	50	49.17 N	2.29 E
Villers-Semeuse	56	49.44 N	4.45 E
Villerupt	56	49.28 N	5.56 E
Villerville	50	49.24 N	0.08 E
Ville-Saint-Georges → Saint-Georges	188	46.07 N	70.40 W
Villes-sur-Auzon	62	44.03 N	5.14 E
Ville-sur-Tourbe	56	49.11 N	4.47 E
Villeta	246	5.01 N	74.28 W
Villetta Barrea	66	41.47 N	13.56 E
Villeurbanne	62	45.46 N	4.53 E
Villevaudé	261	48.55 N	2.39 E
Villeziers	261	48.40 N	2.10 E
Villiers	158	27.03 S	28.35 E
Villiers-Adam	261	49.04 N	2.14 E
Villiersdorp	158	34.00 S	19.19 E
Villiers-le-Bâcle	261	48.44 N	2.08 E
Villiers-le-Bel	261	49.00 N	2.23 E
Villiers-le-Sec	261	49.04 N	2.23 E
Villiers-Saint-Frédéric	261	48.49 N	1.54 E
Villiers-Saint-Georges	50	48.39 N	3.25 E
Villiers-sur-Marne	261	48.50 N	2.33 E
Villiers-sur-Morin	261	48.52 N	2.53 E
Villigst	263	51.26 N	7.35 E
Villingen-Schwenningen	30	48.04 N	8.28 E
Villisca	198	40.55 N	94.58 W
Villmanstrand → Lappeenranta	26	61.04 N	28.11 E
Villmergen	58	47.21 N	8.15 E
Villorba	64	45.44 N	12.14 E
Villoresi, Canale ≊	62	45.33 N	9.31 E
Villotta	64	45.52 N	12.45 E
Vilm I	54	54.19 N	13.32 E
Vilmnitz	54	54.21 N	13.31 E
Vilna	182	54.07 N	111.55 W
Vilna → Vilnius	76	54.41 N	25.19 E
Vilnius	76	54.41 N	25.19 E
Vilosnes-sur-Meuse	56	49.20 N	5.14 E
Vilppula	26	62.01 N	24.31 E
Vils	58	47.33 N	10.38 E
Vils ≃, Dtsch.	60	49.09 N	11.58 E
Vils ≃, Dtsch.	60	48.37 N	13.11 E
Vils ≃, Europe	58	47.33 N	10.40 E
Vilsandi saar I	76	58.23 N	21.52 E
Vilsbiburg	60	48.27 N	12.12 E
Vilseck	60	49.37 N	11.48 E
Vilsheim	60	48.27 N	12.07 E
Vilshofen	60	48.39 N	13.12 E
Vil'uj ≃	74	64.24 N	126.26 E
Vil'ujsk	74	63.45 N	121.35 E
Vil'ujskoje vodochranilišče ⊜[1]	74	62.30 N	111.00 E
Viluppuram	122	11.56 N	79.29 E
Vil'va	86	58.37 N	56.52 E
Vilvoorde	50	50.56 N	4.26 E
Vimercate	62	45.37 N	9.22 E
Vimianzo	34	43.07 N	9.02 W
Vimmerby	26	57.40 N	15.51 E
Vimodrone	266b	45.31 N	9.17 E
Vimoutiers	50	48.55 N	0.12 E
Vimpeli	26	63.09 N	23.48 E
Vimperk	60	49.03 N	13.47 E
Vimy	50	50.22 N	2.49 E
Vina	204	39.55 N	122.03 W
Vina ≃	146	7.45 N	15.36 E
Viñac	248	12.56 S	75.47 W
Viña del Mar	252	33.02 S	71.34 W
Vinadi	58	46.55 N	10.29 E
Vinadio	62	44.18 N	7.10 E
Viñales	240p	22.37 N	83.43 W
Vinalhaven	188	44.02 N	68.49 W
Vinalhaven Island I	188	44.05 N	68.52 W
Vinantes	261	49.01 N	2.44 E
Vina Roni, Mount ∧	175e	8.10 S	157.28 E
Vinaròs	34	40.28 N	0.29 E
Vinay	62	45.13 N	5.24 E
Vinazco ≃	234	20.56 N	97.44 W
Vincennes, Fr.	50	48.51 N	2.26 E
Vincennes, In., U.S.	194	38.40 N	87.31 W
Vincennes, Bois de ♦	261	48.50 N	2.25 E
Vincennes, Château de ⊥	261	48.51 N	2.26 E
Vincennes, Étang de ⊜	261	48.47 N	2.45 E
Vincennes Bay ⊂	9	66.30 S	109.30 E
Vincent	194	33.22 N	86.22 W
Vincent, Point ›	174c	29.00 S	167.55 E
Vincentown	208	39.56 N	74.44 W
Vinces	246	1.32 S	79.45 W
Vinchiaturo	66	41.29 N	14.35 E
Vinchina	252	28.46 S	68.10 W
Vinchos	248	13.16 S	74.21 W
Vinci	66	43.47 N	10.55 E
Vinco	214	40.25 N	78.52 W
Vindeby	41	55.03 N	10.38 E
Vindelälven ≃	24	63.54 N	19.52 E
Vindeln	26	64.12 N	19.44 E
Vinden, Mount ∧	162	27.01 S	115.38 E
Vinderslev	41	56.15 N	9.26 E
Vinderup	26	56.29 N	8.47 E
Vindhya Range ⋏	120	23.00 N	77.00 E
Vinding	41	55.41 N	9.35 E
Vindinge	41	55.19 N	10.45 E
Vine Brook ≃	283	42.27 N	71.13 W
Vinegar Hill ∧	202	44.43 N	118.34 W
Vine Grove	194	37.48 N	85.58 W
Vine Hill	282	38.00 N	122.06 W
Vineland, Mi., U.S.	216	42.03 N	86.30 W
Vineland, N.J., U.S.	208	39.29 N	75.01 W
Vinemont	194	34.14 N	86.51 W
Vine Valley	210	42.43 N	77.20 W
Vineyard Canyon V	226	35.46 N	120.41 W
Vineyard Haven	207	41.27 N	70.36 W
Vineyard Lake ⊜	216	42.05 N	84.13 W
Vineyard Sound ʮ	207	41.25 N	70.46 W
Vingåker	40	59.02 N	15.52 E
Vingeanne ≃	58	47.21 N	5.29 E
Ving Ngün	110	22.37 N	99.16 E
Vinh	110	18.40 N	105.40 E
Vinhais	34	41.50 N	7.00 W
Vinhas, Ribeira das ≃	266c	38.42 N	9.25 W
Vinh Chau	110	9.19 N	105.59 E
Vinhedo	256	23.01 S	46.59 W
Vinh Loc	269c	10.49 N	106.34 E
Vinh Long	110	10.15 N	105.58 E
Vinh Tuy, Viet	110	9.37 N	105.22 E
Vinh Tuy, Viet	110	17.24 N	106.36 E
Vinica	36	45.28 N	15.15 E
Vinita	196	36.38 N	95.09 W
Vînju Mare	38	44.26 N	22.52 E
Vinkekuil	158	32.42 S	20.27 E
Vinkeveen	52	52.13 N	4.54 E
Vinkovci	38	45.17 N	18.49 E
Vin'kovcy	78	49.02 N	27.14 E
Vinnhorst	52	52.25 N	9.43 E
Vinnica	78	49.14 N	28.29 E
Vinnica □[4]	78	49.00 N	28.45 E
Vinniki	78	49.48 N	24.08 E
Vinnitsa → Vinnica	78	49.14 N	28.29 E
Vinnum	263	51.41 N	7.24 E
Vinogradov	78	48.09 N	23.02 E
Vinogradovo, Ross.	82	55.25 N	38.32 E
Vinogradovo, Ross.	82	55.57 N	37.32 E
Vinogrobol'	78	51.51 N	36.26 E
Vinön I	40	59.12 N	15.43 E
Vinon-sur-Verdon	62	43.43 N	5.48 E
Vinovo	62	44.57 N	7.38 E
Vinslöv	26	56.06 N	13.55 E
Vinson Massif ∧	9	78.35 S	85.25 W
Vinstra	26	61.36 N	9.45 E
Vintilă Vodă	38	45.28 N	26.44 E
Vinto	248	17.58 S	67.04 W
Vinton, Ia., U.S.	190	42.10 N	92.01 W
Vinton, La., U.S.	194	30.11 N	93.34 W
Vinton, Va., U.S.	192	37.16 N	79.53 W
Vintondale	214	40.28 N	78.55 W
Vintrosa	40	59.15 N	14.57 E
Viñuelas, Arroyo de ≃	266a	40.33 N	3.33 W
Viny	76	58.22 N	32.13 E
Vinzelberg	54	52.33 N	11.40 E
Vinzili	86	56.58 N	65.46 E
Viola, Il., U.S.	190	41.12 N	90.35 W
Viola, N.Y., U.S.	276	41.08 N	74.05 W
Viola, Wi., U.S.	190	43.30 N	90.40 W
Viola, Val V	64	46.27 N	10.15 E
Violín, Isla I	236	8.51 N	83.39 W
Viols-le-Fort	62	43.45 N	3.42 E
Viosne ≃	261	49.03 N	2.06 E
Vipava	36	45.51 N	13.58 E
Vipava ≃	64	45.54 N	13.33 E
Vipiteno (Sterzing)	64	46.54 N	11.26 E
Vipos	252	26.29 S	65.22 W
Vipperow	54	53.19 N	12.41 E
Vir, Otok I	36	44.18 N	15.04 E
Vira	58	46.08 N	8.51 E
Virac	116	13.35 N	124.15 E
Viracopos, Aeroporto de ⊠	256	23.00 S	47.08 W
Virac Point ›	116	13.31 N	124.13 E
Viradouro	255	20.53 S	48.18 W
Virago Sound ʮ	182	54.00 N	132.36 W
Viramgām	120	23.07 N	72.02 E
Virandozero	24	64.05 N	35.58 E
Viranşehir	130	37.13 N	39.45 E
Vīrarājendrapet	122	12.12 N	75.48 E
Virbalis	76	54.38 N	22.49 E
Virden, Mb., Can.	184	49.51 N	100.55 W
Virden, Il., U.S.	219	39.30 N	89.46 W
Virden, N.M., U.S.	200	32.41 N	109.00 W
Vire	32	48.50 N	0.53 W
Vire ≃	32	49.20 N	1.07 W
Virelles	50	50.04 N	4.20 E
Virelles, Étang de ⊜	50	50.04 N	4.21 E
Vireux-Molhain	56	50.05 N	4.43 E
Vîrfurile	38	46.19 N	22.31 E
Virgem da Lapa	255	16.49 S	42.21 W
Virgen	64	47.00 N	12.27 E
Vírgen del San Cristóbal ʊ[1]	286e	33.26 S	70.39 W
Vírgenes, Cabo ›	254	52.22 S	68.20 W
Vírgenes, Islas → British Virgin Islands □[2]	240m	18.30 N	64.30 W
Vírgenes, Islas → Virgin Islands □[2]	240m	18.20 N	64.50 W
Virgen Tal V	64	47.00 N	12.25 E
Virgil, On., Can.	284a	43.13 N	79.08 W

Symbols in the index entries represent the broad categories identified in the key at the right. Symbols with superior numbers (⋏[1]) identify subcategories (see complete key on page *I · 1).*

Symbole im Register stellen die rechts im Schlüssel erklärten Kategorien dar. Symbole mit hochgestellten Ziffern (⋏[1]) bezeichnen Unterabteilungen einer Kategorie (vgl. vollständiger Schlüssel auf Seite *I · 1).*

Los símbolos incluídos en el texto del índice representan las grandes categorias identificadas con la clave a la derecha. Los símbolos con numeros en su parte superior (⋏[1]) identifican las subcategorías (véase la clave completa en la página *I · 1).*

Les symboles de l'index représentent les catégories indiquées dans la légende à droite. Les symboles suivis d'un indice (⋏[1]) représentent des sous-catégories (voir légende complète à la page *I · 1).*

Os símbolos incluídos no texto do índice representam as grandes categorias identificadas com a chave à direita. Os símbolos com números em sua parte superior (⋏[1]) identificam as subcategorias (veja-se a chave completa à página *I · 1).*

English	Deutsch	Español	Français	Português
∧ Mountain	Berg	Montaña	Montagne	Montanha
⋏ Mountains	Gebirge	Montañas	Montagnes	Montanhas
)(Pass	Paß	Paso	Col	Passo
V Valley, Canyon	Tal, Cañon	Valle, Cañón	Vallée, Canyon	Vale, Canhão
≃ Plain	Ebene	Llano	Plaine	Planície
› Cape	Kap	Cabo	Cap	Cabo
I Island	Insel	Isla	Île	Ilha
II Islands	Inseln	Islas	Îles	Ilhas
⊥ Other Topographic Features	Andere Topographische Objekte	Otros Elementos Topográficos	Autres données topographiques	Outros acidentes topográficos

ESPAÑOL

Nombre	Página	Lat. °′	Long. °′ W = Oeste
Virgil, Ks., U.S.	198	37.58 N	96.00 W
Virgil, N.Y., U.S.	210	42.31 N	76.12 W
Virgilina	192	36.33 N	78.52 W
Virgilio	64	45.07 N	10.47 E
Virgin ≃	200	36.31 N	114.20 W
Virgin, North Fork ≃	200	37.10 N	113.01 W
Virginal-Samme	50	50.38 N	4.12 E
Virgin Gorda I	240m	18.30 N	64.24 W
Virgin Gorda Peak ∧	240m	18.30 N	64.24 W
Virginia, Austl.	168b	34.40 S	138.34 E
Virgínia, Bra.	256	22.20 S	45.06 W
Virginia, Ire.	48	53.49 N	7.04 W
Virginia, S. Afr.	158	28.12 S	26.49 E
Virginia, Il., U.S.	219	39.57 N	90.12 W
Virginia, Mn., U.S.	190	47.31 N	92.32 W
Virginia □[3]	178	37.30 N	78.45 W
Virginia Beach	208	36.51 N	75.58 W
Virginia City, Mt., U.S.	202	45.17 N	111.56 W
Virginia City, Nv., U.S.	226	39.18 N	119.38 W
Virginia Creek ≃	226	38.13 N	119.14 W
Virginia Falls ⌊	180	61.38 N	125.42 W
Virginia Gardens	220	25.49 N	80.17 W
Virginia Hills	208	38.47 N	77.06 W
Virginia Key I	220	25.44 N	80.09 W
Virginia Peak ∧	204	39.45 N	119.28 W
Virginia Ranch Reservoir ⊜[1]	226	39.20 N	121.19 W
Virginia Range ⋀	226	39.18 N	119.30 W
Virginiatown	190	48.08 N	79.35 W
Virginia Water	260	51.24 N	0.34 W
Virginia Water ⊜[1]	260	51.24 N	0.37 W
Virginie occidentale → West Virginia □[3]	188	38.45 N	80.30 W
Virgin Islands □[2], N.A.	230	18.20 N	64.50 W
Virgin Islands □[2], N.A.	240m	18.20 N	64.50 W
Virgin Islands II	240m	18.00 N	64.40 W
Virgin Islands National Park ♠	240m	18.20 N	64.45 W
Virginópolis	255	18.45 S	42.45 W
Virgin Passage c[1]	240m	18.20 N	65.10 W
Virginville	208	40.31 N	75.52 W
Virgolândia	255	18.27 S	42.18 W
Virieu	62	45.29 N	5.28 E
Virieu-le-Grand	62	45.51 N	5.39 E
Virihaure ⊜	24	67.20 N	16.35 E
Virje	36	46.04 N	16.59 E
Virkkala	26	60.12 N	24.01 E
Virklund	41	56.07 N	9.34 E
Virneburg	56	50.20 N	7.04 E
Virôchey	110	13.59 N	106.49 E
Viroflay	50	48.48 N	2.10 E
Viroin ≃	56	50.05 N	4.43 E
Virojoki	26	60.35 N	27.42 E
Víron	267c	37.57 N	23.45 E
Vironvay	50	49.12 N	1.13 E
Viroqua	190	43.33 N	90.53 W
Virovitica	36	45.50 N	17.23 E
Virpazar	38	42.15 N	19.05 E
Virrat	26	62.14 N	23.47 E
Virsbo	40	59.52 N	16.02 E
Virserum	26	57.19 N	15.35 E
Virtaniemi	24	68.53 N	28.27 E
Virton	56	49.34 N	5.32 E
Vîrtopu	38	44.12 N	23.21 E
Virtsu	76	58.34 N	23.31 E
Virú	248	8.25 S	78.45 W
Virudunagar	122	9.36 N	77.58 E
Viru-Jaagupi	76	59.15 N	26.28 E
Virulento	196	28.52 N	104.21 W
Virunga, Parc National de ♠	154	1.00 S	29.15 E
Virungu	154	7.04 S	29.46 E
Viru-Nigula	76	59.27 N	26.41 E
Virvyčia ≃	76	56.13 N	22.34 E
Viry-Châtillon	50	48.40 N	2.23 E
Vis	36	43.03 N	16.12 E
Vis ≃, Fr.	62	43.56 N	3.42 E
Vis (Fish) ≃, Namibia	156	28.07 S	17.45 E
Vis ≃, S. Afr.	158	30.53 S	20.23 E
Vis, Otok I	36	43.02 N	16.11 E
Visale	175e	9.15 S	159.42 E
Visalia	226	36.19 N	119.17 W
Visalia Airport ⊠	226	36.19 N	119.23 W
Visayan Islands II	12	11.00 N	123.30 E
Visayan Sea ⊤[2]	116	11.35 N	123.51 E
Visbek	52	52.48 N	8.19 E
Visby	26	57.38 N	18.18 E
Viscaya, Bahía de → Biscay, Bay of c	32	44.00 N	4.00 W
Viscount	184	51.57 N	105.39 W
Viscount Melville Sound ɰ	176	74.10 N	108.00 W
Visé	56	50.44 N	5.42 E
Višegrad	38	43.47 N	19.17 E
Vis-en-Artois	50	50.15 N	2.56 E
Višera ≃	76	58.34 N	31.24 E
Viserba	66	44.05 N	12.32 E
Viseu, Bra.	250	1.12 S	46.07 W
Viseu, Port.	34	40.39 N	7.55 W
Vișeu ≃	38	47.55 N	24.09 E
Vișeu de Sus	38	47.44 N	24.22 E
Vishākhapatnam	122	17.42 N	83.18 E
Vishoek	158	34.08 S	18.26 E
Visim	86	57.39 N	59.30 E
Visingsö I	26	58.03 N	14.20 E
Visitation, Île de la I	275a	45.35 N	73.40 W
Viskafors	26	57.38 N	12.50 E
Viskan ≃	26	57.14 N	12.12 E
Viškil'	80	58.05 N	48.19 E
Viskinge	41	55.40 N	11.16 E
Visl'ajevo	82	54.25 N	36.43 E
Vislanda	26	56.47 N	14.27 E
Vislinskij zaliv c	30	54.27 N	19.40 E
Vismen ⊜	40	59.17 N	14.17 E
Visnagar	120	23.42 N	72.33 E
Višn'aki	265b	55.47 N	37.54 E
Višn'akovo	82	55.45 N	38.10 E
Višnevčik	78	49.02 N	26.28 E
Visnevo	76	54.08 N	26.14 E
Višnevoje, Ross.	80	52.38 N	43.26 E
Višnevoje, Ukr.	78	48.27 N	33.56 E
Višňové	61	48.59 N	16.09 E
Višn'ovec	78	49.54 N	25.45 E
Višn'ovka, Kaz.	86	50.49 N	72.12 E
Višn'ovka, Mol.	78	46.20 N	28.26 E
Viso, Monte ∧	62	44.40 N	7.07 E
Visoki Dečani, Manastir ♥[1]	38	42.30 N	20.31 E
Visoko	38	43.59 N	18.11 E
Visokoi Island I	18	56.42 S	27.12 W
Visp	58	46.18 N	7.53 E
Vispa ≃	58	46.18 N	7.52 E
Visrivier	158	31.55 S	25.25 E
Vissefjärda	26	56.32 N	15.35 E
Visselhövede	52	52.59 N	9.35 E
Vissenbjerg	41	55.23 N	10.08 E
Visso	66	42.56 N	13.05 E
Vissoie	58	46.13 N	7.36 E
Vista, Ca., U.S.	228	33.12 N	117.14 W
Vista, N.Y., U.S.	210	41.12 N	73.31 W
Vista Alegre, Arg.	252	38.45 S	68.11 W
Vista Alegre, Bra.	256	21.27 S	42.35 W
Vista Alegre, Chile	286e	33.30 S	70.43 W
Vista Alegre, Perú	286d	12.09 S	77.00 W
Vista Flores	252	33.38 S	69.09 W
Vistahermosa de Negrete	234	20.16 N	102.29 W
Vista La Mesa	228	32.35 N	117.01 W
Vista Park	228	35.21 N	118.55 W
Vistina	76	59.47 N	28.29 E
Vistre ≃	62	43.40 N	4.15 E
Vistula → Wisła ≃	30	54.22 N	18.55 E
Visun' ≃	78	47.07 N	32.53 E
Vit ≃	38	43.41 N	24.45 E

FRANÇAIS

Nom	Page	Lat. °′	Long. °′ W = Ouest
Vita, Mb., Can.	184	49.08 N	96.34 W
Vita, It.	70	37.52 N	12.49 E
Vita ≃	246	6.11 N	67.31 W
Vitacura	286e	33.24 S	70.36 W
Vitali	116	7.22 N	122.18 E
Vitanje	36	46.23 N	15.18 E
Vitarte	248	12.02 S	76.56 W
Vit'azevka	78	48.01 N	31.53 E
Vite	122	17.17 N	74.33 E
Vitebsk	76	55.12 N	30.11 E
Vitebsk □[8]	76	55.20 N	29.00 E
Vitebsk Station ◆[5]	265a	59.55 N	30.21 E
Vitel, Laguna ⊜	258	35.32 S	58.07 W
Viterbo	66	42.25 N	12.06 E
Viterbo □[4]	66	42.25 N	12.05 E
Vitiaz Strait ɰ	164	5.50 S	147.20 E
Vitichi	248	20.13 S	65.29 W
Vitigudino	34	41.01 N	6.26 W
Viti Levu I	175g	18.00 S	178.00 E
Vitim	74	59.28 N	112.34 E
Vitim ≃	74	59.26 N	112.34 E
Vitimskij	88	58.14 N	113.18 E
Vitimskoje ploskogorje ⋀[1]	88	54.00 N	113.30 E
Vitinia ◆[8]	267a	41.47 N	12.24 E
Vitis	61	48.45 N	15.10 E
Vítkov	30	49.46 N	17.45 E
Vito	175e	6.02 S	155.24 E
Vítor	248	16.26 S	71.49 W
Vitor ≃	248	16.37 S	72.19 W
Vitória, Bra.	250	2.54 S	52.01 W
Vitória, Bra.	255	20.19 S	40.21 W
Vitoria (Gasteiz), Esp.	34	42.51 N	2.40 W
Vitória, Ilha da I	256	23.45 S	45.01 W
Vitória da Conquista	255	14.51 S	40.51 W
Vitória de Santo Antão	250	8.07 S	35.18 W
Vitória do Mearim	250	3.28 S	44.53 W
Vitorino Freire	250	4.04 S	45.10 W
Vitravo ≃	68	39.11 N	17.05 E
Vitré	28	48.08 N	1.12 W
Vitrey-sur-Mance	58	47.49 N	5.45 E
Vitry-aux-Loges	50	47.56 N	2.16 E
Vitry-en-Artois	50	50.20 N	2.59 E
Vitry-la-Ville	50	48.50 N	4.28 E
Vitry-le-François	56	48.44 N	4.35 E
Vitry [-sur-Seine]	50	48.48 N	2.24 E
Vitshumbi	154	0.41 S	29.23 E
Vittangi	24	67.41 N	21.36 E
Vitte	54	54.34 N	13.06 E
Vitteaux	58	47.24 N	4.32 E
Vittel	58	48.12 N	5.57 E
Vittinge	40	59.54 N	17.04 E
Vittoria, On., Can.	212	42.46 N	80.19 W
Vittoria, It.	70	36.57 N	14.32 E
Vittorio Veneto	64	45.59 N	12.18 E
Vittsjö	26	56.20 N	13.40 E
Vitulano	68	41.10 N	14.38 E
Vitznau	58	47.01 N	8.29 E
Viù	62	45.14 N	7.22 E
Vivarais □[9]	62	44.40 N	4.30 E
Vivarais, Monts du ⋀	62	44.55 N	4.15 E
Viver	34	39.55 N	0.36 W
Vivero	34	43.40 N	7.35 W
Viverols	62	45.26 N	3.53 E
Viverone, Lago di ⊜	62	45.25 N	8.02 E
Vivi ≃	74	63.52 N	97.50 E
Vivian	194	32.52 N	93.59 W
Viviers	62	44.29 N	4.41 E
Viviers-du-Lac	62	45.39 N	5.54 E
Vivione, Passo del)(	64	46.02 N	10.12 E
Vivonne	32	46.26 N	0.16 E
Vivoratá	252	37.40 S	57.39 W
Vivorillo, Cayos II	236	15.50 N	83.18 W
Viwa I	175g	17.08 S	176.54 E
Vizagapatam → Vishākhapatnam	122	17.42 N	83.18 E
Vizcaíno, Desierto de ◆[2]	232	27.40 N	113.40 W
Vizcaíno, Isla I	258	33.47 S	59.15 W
Vize	130	41.34 N	27.45 E
Vize, ostrov I	72	79.30 N	77.00 E
Vizianagaram	122	18.07 N	83.25 E
Vizille	62	45.05 N	5.46 E
Vižinada	36	45.20 N	13.46 E
Vizinga	24	61.05 N	50.04 E
Vižnica	78	48.15 N	25.12 E
Vizzini	70	37.10 N	14.53 E
Vizzola	266b	45.38 N	8.42 E
Vjulka ≃	82	56.53 N	37.57 E
Vjunka ≃	265b	55.42 N	38.01 E
Vjuny	86	55.31 N	82.55 E
Vlaanderen → Flanders □[9]	50	51.00 N	3.00 E
Vlaardingen	52	51.54 N	4.21 E
Vlachovo Březí	60	49.05 N	13.57 E
Vladař ∧	54	50.05 N	13.14 E
Vlădeasa, Vîrful ∧	38	46.45 N	22.48 E
Vlădeni	38	47.25 N	27.20 E
Vladičin Han	38	42.42 N	22.04 E
Vladikavkaz	84	43.03 N	44.40 E
Vladimir	80	56.10 N	40.25 E
Vladimirec	78	51.25 N	26.08 E
Vladimir Oblast' □[4]	76	56.00 N	40.30 E
Vladimirovka, Kaz.	80	50.51 N	51.08 E
Vladimirovka, Kaz.	86	53.28 N	64.02 E
Vladimirovka, Ukr.	78	47.32 N	32.55 E
Vladimirovka, Ukr.	83	47.44 N	37.23 E
Vladimirskij Tupik	76	55.42 N	33.18 E
Vladimirskoje	80	56.49 N	45.07 E
Vladimir-Volynskij	78	50.51 N	24.20 E
Vladivostok	89	43.10 N	131.56 E
Vladyčnoje	76	58.49 N	39.29 E
Vladykino ◆[8]	265b	55.52 N	37.36 E
Vlasenica	38	44.11 N	18.56 E
Vlašim	30	49.42 N	14.54 E
Vlaskovo	82	56.11 N	36.31 E
Vlasotince	38	42.58 N	22.08 E
Vlasovo, Ross.	74	70.48 N	135.00 E
Vlasovo, Ross.	82	56.38 N	38.14 E
Vlazoviči	76	53.01 N	32.18 E
Vledder	52	52.52 N	6.12 E
Vleesbaai c	158	34.16 S	21.57 E
Vleikolk	158	29.43 S	20.50 E
Vleuten	52	52.05 N	5.02 E
Vlieland I	52	53.15 N	5.00 E
Vlijmen	52	51.42 N	5.15 E
Vlissingen (Flushing)	52	51.26 N	3.35 E
Vlodrop	52	51.08 N	6.05 E
Vloesberg → Flobecq	50	50.44 N	3.44 E
Vlonë → Vlorë	38	40.27 N	19.30 E
Vlorë	38	40.27 N	19.30 E
Vlorës, Gji i c	38	40.25 N	19.25 E
Vlotho	52	52.10 N	8.51 E
Vltava ≃	30	50.21 N	14.30 E
Vluyn	52	51.26 N	6.32 E
Vnukovo	82	55.38 N	37.16 E
Vnukovo Airport ⊠	265b	55.37 N	37.17 E
Voca	196	31.01 N	99.11 W
Vochrinka	82	55.24 N	38.18 E
Vochtoga	76	58.47 N	41.07 E
Vočin	36	45.37 N	17.32 E
Vöckla ≃	64	48.00 N	13.36 E
Vöcklabruck	60	48.01 N	13.39 E
Vöcklamarkt	60	48.00 N	13.29 E
Vodla ≃	24	61.49 N	36.00 E
Vodlozero, ozero ⊜	24	62.20 N	36.55 E
Vodňany	30	49.09 N	14.11 E
Vodnjan	36	44.57 N	13.51 E
Vodnyj	24	63.32 N	53.18 E
Vodo	64	46.25 N	12.14 E
Vodosalma	24	64.29 N	30.44 E
Vodovatovo	80	55.24 N	43.34 E
Vodzimonje	80	56.49 N	51.38 E
Voël ≃	158	33.07 S	25.07 E
Voerde, Dtsch.	52	51.35 N	6.41 E
Voerde, Dtsch.	263	51.18 N	7.24 E
Voesch	263	51.24 N	6.26 E

PORTUGUÊS

Nome	Página	Lat. °′	Long. °′ W = Oeste
Vogelenzang	52	52.19 N	4.35 E
Vogelheim ◆[8]	263	51.29 N	6.59 E
Vogelkop → Doberai, Jazirah >[1]	164	1.30 S	132.30 E
Vogel Peak → Dimlang ∧	146	8.24 N	11.47 E
Vogelsang, Dtsch.	54	53.43 N	14.09 E
Vogelsang, Dtsch.	56	50.35 N	6.27 E
Vogelsberg ⋀	56	50.30 N	9.15 E
Vogesen → Vosges ⋀	58	48.30 N	7.10 E
Voghera	62	44.59 N	9.01 E
Vognema	76	59.59 N	38.10 E
Vogogna	58	46.01 N	8.17 E
Vogtland ◆[1]	54	50.30 N	12.05 E
Voh	175f	20.58 S	164.42 E
Vohburg an der Donau	60	48.46 N	11.37 E
Vohenstrauss	60	49.37 N	12.21 E
Vohibinany	157b	18.49 S	49.04 E
Vohilava	157b	21.04 S	48.00 E
Vohimarina	157b	13.21 S	50.02 E
Vohipeno	157b	22.22 S	47.51 E
Vohitsora	157b	23.54 S	44.17 E
Võhma	76	58.38 N	25.33 E
Vöhringen, Dtsch.	58	48.02 N	8.18 E
Vöhringen, Dtsch.	58	48.16 N	10.04 E
Vöhringen, Dtsch.	58	48.20 N	8.40 E
Vöhrum	52	52.20 N	10.10 E
Vohwinkel ◆[8]	263	51.14 N	7.09 E
Voi	154	3.23 S	38.34 E
Void	58	48.41 N	5.37 E
Voight Creek ≃	224	47.06 N	122.10 W
Voikkaa	26	60.56 N	26.37 E
Voinești	38	47.05 N	27.26 E
Voinjama	150	8.25 N	9.45 W
Voinka	78	45.52 N	33.59 E
Voire ≃	58	48.27 N	4.25 E
Voiron	62	45.22 N	5.35 E
Voise	50	48.24 N	1.43 E
Voise ≃	50	48.35 N	1.35 E
Voisenon	261	48.34 N	2.40 E
Voisins-le-Bretonneux	50	48.45 N	2.03 E
Voiteur	58	46.45 N	5.37 E
Voitsberg	61	47.03 N	15.10 E
Voja ≃	80	57.23 N	49.55 E
Vojens	41	55.15 N	9.19 E
Vojevodskoje	86	52.47 N	85.35 E
Vojkovice	54	50.15 N	13.02 E
Vojkovo, Ukr.	78	45.31 N	33.52 E
Vojkovo, Ukr.	83	48.00 N	38.02 E
Vojkovskij	83	47.46 N	38.20 E
Vojmsjön ⊜	26	64.55 N	16.40 E
Vojnić	36	45.19 N	15.42 E
Vojnica	24	65.12 N	30.15 E
Vojnilov	78	49.08 N	24.30 E
Vojtanov	54	50.06 N	12.19 E
Vojvodina □[4]	38	45.00 N	20.00 E
Voj-Vož, Ross.	24	64.20 N	55.03 E
Voj-Vož, Ross.	24	62.56 N	54.56 E
Vokeo Island I	164	3.10 S	144.05 E
Volano	66	45.55 N	11.03 E
Volant	214	41.07 N	80.16 W
Volary	60	48.55 N	13.54 E
Volcán, Arg.	252	23.54 S	65.27 W
Volcán, Pan.	236	8.46 N	82.38 W
Volcán Isluga, Parque Nacional ♠	248	19.30 S	68.30 W
Volčanka	80	52.33 N	49.59 E
Volcano, Ca., U.S.	226	38.26 N	120.37 W
Volcano, Hi., U.S.	229d	19.25 N	155.14 W
Volcano Island I	116	14.00 N	121.00 E
Volcano Islands → Kazan-rettō II	14	25.00 N	141.00 E
Volcán Poás, Parque Nacional ♠	236	10.10 N	84.15 W
Volčansk, Ross.	86	59.56 N	60.04 E
Volčansk, Ukr.	78	50.18 N	36.57 E
Volčejarovka	83	48.50 N	38.22 E
Volčenskij	83	48.14 N	40.07 E
Volchonka-Zil ◆[8]	265b	55.40 N	37.37 E
Volchov	76	59.55 N	32.20 E
Volchov ≃	76	60.08 N	32.20 E
Volčicha	86	52.02 N	80.23 E
Volčij Nos, mys >	76	60.31 N	32.35 E
Volčja ≃	78	48.00 N	36.08 E
Volčje	78	49.14 N	22.53 E
Volčki	80	52.29 N	40.42 E
Volda	26	62.09 N	6.06 E
Volders	64	47.17 N	11.34 E
Volendam	52	52.30 N	5.04 E
Volga, Ross.	76	57.57 N	38.24 E
Volga, Ia., U.S.	190	42.48 N	91.32 W
Volga, S.D., U.S.	198	44.19 N	96.55 W
Volga ≃, Ross.	72	45.55 N	47.52 E
Volga ≃, Ia., U.S.	190	42.45 N	91.17 W
Volga-Baltic Canal → Volgo-Baltijskij kanal ≊	24	59.00 N	38.00 E
Volgino	76	58.27 N	33.52 E
Volgo, ozero ⊜	76	56.55 N	33.10 E
Volgo-Baltijskij kanal ≊	24	59.00 N	38.00 E
Volgodonsk	80	47.33 N	42.08 E
Volgo-Donskoj sudochodnyj kanal imeni V.I. Lenina ≊	80	48.40 N	43.37 E
Volgograd (Stalingrad)	80	48.44 N	44.25 E
Volgograd Oblast' □[4]	80	49.30 N	44.00 E
Volgogradskoje vodochranilišče ⊜[1]	80	49.20 N	45.00 E
Volgorečensk	76	57.30 N	41.02 E
Volissós	38	38.29 N	25.58 E
Vol'ka	76	52.47 N	25.39 E
Volkach	56	49.52 N	10.13 E
Volkel	52	51.38 N	5.40 E
Völkermarkt	61	46.39 N	14.38 E
Völkermarkter Stausee ⊜[1]	61	46.39 N	14.38 E
Völkerschlacht-Denkmal ⊥	54	51.18 N	12.24 E
Völklingen	56	49.15 N	6.50 E
Volkmarsen	56	51.24 N	9.07 E
Volkovincy	78	49.13 N	27.39 E
Volkovo, Ross.	76	59.15 N	41.27 E
Volkovo, Ross.	82	55.46 N	36.15 E
Volkovo Cemetery ◆	265a	59.54 N	30.22 E
Volkovskoje	82	54.49 N	37.13 E
Volkovysk	76	53.10 N	24.28 E
Volksdorf ◆[8]	52	53.39 N	10.10 E
Völksen	52	52.13 N	9.37 E
Volksrust	158	27.24 S	29.53 E
Vollenhove	52	52.41 N	5.58 E
Vollersode	52	53.18 N	8.56 E
Vollme	263	51.10 N	7.36 E
Vollore-Montagne	62	45.47 N	3.41 E
Vollore-Ville	62	45.47 N	3.36 E
Vollsjö	41	55.42 N	13.46 E
Volma ≃	76	53.35 N	28.19 E
Volmarstein	56	51.22 N	7.23 E
Volme ≃	263	51.24 N	7.27 E
Volmerange-les-Mines	56	49.27 N	6.05 E
Volmerswerth ◆[8]	263	51.11 N	6.46 E
Volmunster	56	49.07 N	7.21 E
Vol'naja Gorka	76	58.43 N	30.51 E
Volnay	58	47.00 N	4.47 E
Vol'nogorsk	78	48.29 N	34.01 E
Vol'noje, Ross.	80	47.09 N	47.38 E
Vol'noje, Ross.	86	54.17 N	71.21 E
Volnovacha	83	47.36 N	37.31 E
Vol'nyj	80	45.55 N	45.14 E
Vol'nyj, ostrov I	265a	59.58 N	30.14 E
Voločajevka Vtoraja	89	48.34 N	134.34 E
Voločanka	74	71.00 N	94.28 E
Voločisk	78	49.32 N	26.11 E
Volockaja	76	60.17 N	42.59 E
Volodarka, Ross.	86	52.43 N	83.38 E
Volodarka, Ukr.	78	49.31 N	29.55 E
Volodarsk, Ross.	76	56.13 N	43.10 E
Volodarsk, Ukr.	83	48.06 N	39.35 E
Volodarskij, Ross.	80	46.24 N	48.32 E
Volodarskij, Ross.	82	55.30 N	37.57 E
Volodarskij ◆[8]	265a	59.49 N	30.05 E
Volodarskoje, Kaz.	86	53.18 N	68.08 E
Volodarskoje, Ukr.	83	47.12 N	37.20 E
Volodarsk-Volynskij	78	50.37 N	28.25 E
Volodino	86	57.06 N	83.54 E
Vologda	76	59.12 N	39.55 E
Vologda ≃	76	59.17 N	40.13 E
Vologda Oblast' □[4]	24	60.00 N	40.00 E
Voloje	76	54.09 N	34.35 E
Volokolamsk	82	56.02 N	35.57 E
Volokonovka	78	50.29 N	37.51 E
Volokovaja	24	66.28 N	48.10 E
Volonga	24	67.07 N	47.41 E
Volonne	62	44.07 N	6.01 E
Volontirovka	78	46.26 N	29.37 E
Vólos	38	39.21 N	22.56 E
Vološino, Ross.	83	48.55 N	39.56 E
Vološino, Ross.	83	47.31 N	39.40 E
Vološka	24	61.20 N	40.06 E
Vološn'a ≃	82	55.51 N	35.54 E
Vološno	76	58.29 N	28.29 E
Volosoviči	76	54.46 N	28.50 E
Volosovo	76	59.26 N	29.29 E
Volosskaja Balaklejka	83	49.37 N	37.20 E
Volot	76	57.56 N	30.42 E
Volovec	78	48.43 N	23.11 E
Volovo, Ross.	76	53.35 N	38.02 E
Volovo, Ross.	78	52.03 N	37.53 E
Voložin	76	54.05 N	26.32 E
Volpago del Montello	64	45.47 N	12.07 E
Volpedo	62	44.53 N	8.59 E
Volpiano	62	45.12 N	7.46 E
Völpke	54	52.08 N	11.09 E
Völs → Fiè	64	46.31 N	11.30 E
Volsini, Monti ⋀	66	42.40 N	11.55 E
Vol'sk	80	52.02 N	47.23 E
Volstruisleegte	158	33.05 S	23.28 E
Volta □[4]	150	7.00 N	0.30 E
Volta ≃	150	5.46 N	0.41 E
Volta, Lake ⊜[1]	150	7.30 N	0.15 E
Volta Blanche (White Volta) ≃	150	9.10 N	1.15 W
Voltaggio	62	44.37 N	8.50 E
Voltago	64	46.16 N	12.00 E
Volta Grande	256	21.46 S	42.32 W
Voltaire, Cape >	164	14.16 S	125.35 E
Volta Mantovana	64	45.19 N	10.39 E
Volta Noire (Black Volta) ≃	150	8.41 N	1.33 W
Volta Redonda	256	22.32 S	44.07 W
Volta Rouge ≃	150	10.34 N	0.30 W
Volterra	66	43.24 N	10.51 E
Vol'teva	24	64.30 N	44.12 E
Voltri	62	44.26 N	8.45 E
Volturara Appula	68	41.30 N	15.03 E
Volturara Irpina	68	40.53 N	14.55 E
Volturino	68	41.28 N	15.07 E
Volturino, Monte ∧	68	40.25 N	15.49 E
Volturno ≃	68	41.01 N	13.55 E
Volubilis ⊥	148	34.00 N	5.30 W
Voluntown	207	41.34 N	71.52 W
Volusia □[6]	220	28.51 N	81.05 W
Vólvi, Límni ⊜	38	40.41 N	23.23 E
Volx	62	43.53 N	5.51 E
Volyn □[4]	78	51.00 N	25.00 E
Volyncy, Bela.	76	55.42 N	28.11 E
Volyncy, Ross.	80	57.48 N	45.28 E
Volyně	60	49.10 N	13.53 E
Volynka	78	51.37 N	32.26 E
Volyňka ≃	60	49.16 N	13.54 E
Volynskaja vozvyšennost' ⋀[1]	78	50.30 N	25.30 E
Volzhskiy → Volžskij	80	48.50 N	44.44 E
Volžsk	80	55.53 N	48.21 E
Volžskij, Ross.	80	53.27 N	50.07 E
Volžskij, Ross.	80	48.50 N	44.44 E
Vom	150	9.41 N	8.42 E
Vomano ≃	66	42.39 N	14.02 E
Vombsjön ⊜	41	55.41 N	13.36 E
Vomp	64	47.20 N	11.41 E
Vonavona Island I	175e	8.15 S	157.05 E
Vonda	184	52.19 N	106.06 W
Vondanka	24	59.07 N	47.49 E
Vondrozo	157b	22.49 S	47.20 E
Von Frank Mountain ∧	180	63.33 N	154.20 W
Võnnu	76	58.17 N	27.05 E
Vonozero	76	60.22 N	34.26 E
Vonsild	41	55.27 N	9.29 E
Von Treuer Tableland ⋀[1]	162	26.38 S	122.53 E
Voorburg	52	52.05 N	4.23 E
Voordeelspan	158	29.05 S	21.32 E
Voorheesville	210	42.39 N	73.56 W
Voorne I	52	51.54 N	4.08 E
Voorschoten	52	52.07 N	4.27 E
Voorst	52	52.10 N	6.09 E
Voorthuizen	52	52.12 N	5.35 E
Vop' ≃	76	54.56 N	32.44 E
Vopnafjörður	24a	65.47 N	14.44 W
Vopnafjörður c	24a	65.52 N	14.40 W
Vörå (Vöyri)	26	63.09 N	22.15 E
Vor'a ≃, Ross.	76	54.54 N	35.01 E
Vor'a ≃, Ross.	82	55.52 N	38.13 E
Vorarlberg □[3]	58	47.15 N	9.55 E
Vorau	61	47.25 N	15.54 E
Vorbach	60	49.49 N	11.45 E
Vorbasse	41	55.38 N	9.05 E
Vorbjovo	88	57.23 N	102.18 E
Vorchdorf	60	48.00 N	13.55 E
Vörden, Dtsch.	52	52.28 N	8.05 E
Vorden, Ned.	52	52.07 N	6.18 E
Vorder-Grauspitz ∧	58	47.03 N	9.36 E
Vorderkrimmi	64	47.14 N	12.12 E
Vordernberg	61	47.28 N	15.00 E
Vorderrhein ≃	58	46.49 N	9.25 E
Vorderriss	64	47.33 N	11.26 E
Vordingborg	41	55.01 N	11.55 E
Voreifel ⋀	56	50.15 N	7.10 E
Voreppe	62	45.18 N	5.38 E
Vorey	62	45.11 N	3.54 E
Vorga	76	53.45 N	32.45 E
Vorhalle ◆[8]	263	51.23 N	7.28 E
Vorhelm	52	51.48 N	7.56 E
Voríai Sporádhes II	38	39.17 N	23.23 E
Vøringsfossen ⌊	26	60.26 N	7.15 E
Vórios Evvoïkós Kólpos c	38	38.40 N	23.15 E
Vorkuta	24	67.27 N	63.58 E
Vorlich, Ben ∧, Scot., U.K.	46	56.17 N	4.46 W
Vorlich, Ben ∧, Scot., U.K.	46	56.20 N	4.14 W
Vorma ≃	26	60.09 N	11.27 E
Vormholz	263	51.24 N	7.18 E
Vormsi I	76	59.00 N	23.20 E
Vorn'any	76	54.44 N	26.01 E
Vorobjevo, Ross.	82	56.11 N	35.45 E
Vorobjevo, Ross.	86	56.08 N	76.32 E
Vorobji	82	55.09 N	36.48 E
Vorobjovka	80	50.38 N	40.56 E
Vorob'jovo, Ross.	76	59.38 N	40.55 E
Vorob'jovo, Ukr.	78	45.20 N	33.15 E
Vorochta	78	48.18 N	24.36 E
Voron'	76	55.00 N	28.39 E
Voron, porog ⌊	88	57.05 N	98.40 E
Vorona ≃	80	51.22 N	42.03 E
Voroncovka, Kaz.	86	48.49 N	81.32 E
Voroncovka, Ross.	78	50.37 N	40.21 E
Voroncovka, Ross.	86	59.39 N	60.14 E
Voroncovka, Ross.	88	58.51 N	112.56 E
Voroncovka, Ukr.	78	45.51 N	33.47 E
Voroncovo, Ross.	76	57.18 N	28.42 E
Voroncovo, Ross.	80	55.16 N	40.27 E
Voronej → Voronež	78	51.40 N	39.10 E
Voronež, Ross.	78	51.40 N	39.10 E
Voronež, Ukr.	78	51.46 N	33.28 E
Voronež ≃	76	51.56 N	39.25 E
Voronezh → Voronež	78	51.40 N	39.10 E
Voronež Oblast' □[4]	78	51.00 N	40.00 E
Voronežskij Zapovednik ◆[4]	76	51.56 N	39.37 E
Voronino	82	56.24 N	36.52 E
Voronja ≃	24	69.10 N	35.50 E
Voronjo, Ross.	24	68.27 N	35.21 E
Voronjo, Ross.	80	58.00 N	42.01 E
Voronki, Ross.	82	55.48 N	37.16 E
Voron'ki, Ukr.	78	50.14 N	33.02 E
Voronkovo	78	47.43 N	29.08 E
Voronok	76	52.23 N	32.40 E
Voronov, mys >	76	60.15 N	32.05 E
Voronovica	78	49.06 N	28.41 E
Voronovkova Niva	76	57.04 N	29.16 E
Voronovo, Bela.	76	54.09 N	25.19 E
Voronovo, Ross.	82	55.19 N	37.10 E
Voronovo, Ross.	86	56.01 N	83.52 E
Voropajevo	76	55.09 N	27.13 E
Voroshilovsk → Stavropol'	72	45.02 N	41.59 E
Voroshilov → Ussurijsk	89	43.48 N	131.59 E
Vorošilovgrad → Lugansk	83	48.34 N	39.20 E
Vorotajevka	80	51.56 N	47.16 E
Vorotynec	80	56.04 N	45.52 E
Vorotynsk	82	54.25 N	36.05 E
Vorovskolesskaja	84	44.23 N	42.25 E
Vorožba	78	51.12 N	34.14 E
Vorožejka	86	58.12 N	90.02 E
Vorpommern □[9]	54	53.40 N	13.45 E
Vorra	60	49.33 N	11.30 E
Vorsfelde	54	52.26 N	10.49 E
Vorskla ≃	78	48.53 N	34.06 E
Vorsma	80	55.59 N	43.16 E
Vorst, Bel.	56	51.04 N	5.01 E
Vorst, Dtsch.	56	51.18 N	6.25 E
Vørterkaka Nunatak ∧	9	72.20 S	27.29 E
Võrtsjärv ⊜	76	58.16 N	26.03 E
Võru	76	57.50 N	27.01 E
Voruch	85	39.52 N	70.35 E
Vorzel'	78	50.33 N	30.09 E
Vosburg	158	30.33 S	22.52 E
Voschod	80	47.24 N	41.50 E
Vösendorf	61	48.07 N	16.20 E
Vosges □[5]	58	48.10 N	6.20 E
Vosges ⋀	58	48.30 N	7.10 E
Vosja	76	59.01 N	41.11 E
Voskresenka, Ross.	80	51.01 N	46.28 E
Voskresenka, Ross.	88	53.15 N	119.31 E
Voskresenki	82	54.57 N	38.04 E
Voskresenovskoje	265a	59.43 N	30.47 E
Voskresensk	82	55.19 N	38.42 E
Voskresenskoje, Ross.	76	53.12 N	38.43 E
Voskresenskoje, Ross.	76	58.54 N	38.36 E
Voskresenskoje, Ross.	76	59.26 N	37.56 E
Voskresenskoje, Ross.	76	57.49 N	37.40 E
Voskresenskoje, Ross.	80	56.51 N	45.26 E
Voskresenskoje, Ross.	80	51.51 N	46.56 E
Voskresenskoje, Ross.	82	56.20 N	38.29 E
Voskresenskoje, Ross.	82	54.07 N	37.07 E
Voskresenskoje, Ross.	86	53.08 N	56.10 E
Voskresenskoje, Ukr.	78	47.02 N	32.09 E
Voslapp	52	53.36 N	8.05 E
Voss	26	60.39 N	6.26 E
Vosselaar	56	51.19 N	4.53 E
Vossijatskoje	78	47.41 N	32.07 E
Vossman's Beacon	158	26.11 S	30.40 E
Vostočnaja Kambal'nica	24	68.18 N	46.00 E
Vostočno-Kazachstan □[8]	86	49.00 N	84.00 E
Vostočno-Kounradskij	86	47.02 N	75.07 E
Vostočno-Sibirskoje more (East Siberian Sea) ⊤[2]	12	74.00 N	166.00 E
Vostočnyj, Ross.	82	55.47 N	37.52 E
Vostočnyj, Ross.	86	58.48 N	61.52 E
Vostočnyj, Ross.	89	53.29 N	143.03 E
Vostočnyj, Ross.	89	48.17 N	142.34 E
Vostočnyj Sajan ⋀	88	53.00 N	97.00 E
Vostok I	14	10.06 S	152.23 W
Vostok ♥[3]	9	78.30 S	106.50 E
Vostr'akovo	82	55.23 N	37.49 E
Vostrecovo	89	45.53 N	134.58 E
Vostrovo	86	52.09 N	80.38 E
Vosves	261	48.31 N	2.36 E
Votaw	222	30.26 N	94.41 W
Votice	30	49.38 N	14.39 E
Votkinsk	80	57.03 N	53.59 E
Votkinskoje vodochranilišče ⊜[1]	86	57.00 N	54.30 E
Vot'pa	86	60.13 N	62.57 E
Votuporanga	255	20.24 S	49.59 W
Voué	50	48.28 N	4.07 E
Vouga ≃	34	40.41 N	8.40 W
Vougba	152	5.10 N	23.06 E
Vougeot	58	47.10 N	4.58 E
Vouillé	32	46.39 N	0.10 E
Voujeaucourt	58	47.28 N	6.46 E
Voulangis	261	48.51 N	2.54 E
Voulou	146	8.33 N	22.36 E
Voulx	50	48.17 N	2.58 E
Voulzie ≃	50	48.25 N	3.12 E
Voutenay-sur-Cure	50	47.33 N	3.47 E
Vouvray	50	47.25 N	0.48 E
Vouvry	58	46.20 N	6.53 E
Vouziers	56	49.24 N	4.42 E
Voves	50	48.16 N	1.38 E
Vovodo ≃	140	5.40 N	24.21 E
Vowinckel	214	41.25 N	79.14 W
Voxnan ≃	26	61.17 N	16.26 E
Voyageurs National Park ♠	190	48.30 N	93.00 W
Voyeykov Ice Shelf ⩀	9	66.20 S	124.38 E
Vöyri → Vörå	26	63.09 N	22.15 E
Voža ≃	82	54.38 N	39.10 E
Vožajol'	24	62.50 N	51.17 E
Vožd' Proletariata	76	55.26 N	39.19 E
Vozdviženka, Ross.	80	53.10 N	54.14 E
Vozdviženka, Ukr.	78	47.46 N	36.05 E
Vozdviženskoje, Ross.	80	56.58 N	45.37 E
Vozdviženskoje, Ross.	80	45.50 N	43.40 E
Vozdviženskoje, Ross.	82	56.12 N	38.04 E
Vože, ozero ⊜	24	60.30 N	39.00 E
Vožega	76	60.29 N	40.12 E
Vožega ≃	76	60.33 N	39.11 E
Vožgaly	80	58.09 N	50.11 E
Vožgora	24	64.32 N	48.25 E
Voznesenje	24	61.01 N	35.27 E
Voznesenka, Kaz.	86	52.24 N	70.12 E
Voznesenka, Ukr.	78	46.51 N	35.26 E
Voznesenovka	80	46.16 N	44.21 E
Voznesensk	78	47.34 N	31.20 E
Voznesenskoje, Ross.	80	54.54 N	42.46 E
Voznesenskoje, Ross.	80	45.49 N	43.25 E
Vozroždenija, ostrov I	86	45.03 N	59.12 E
Vozroždenije	80	52.42 N	48.12 E
Vozžajevka	89	50.44 N	128.41 E
Vrå	26	57.21 N	9.57 E
Vráble	30	48.15 N	18.19 E
Vraca	38	43.12 N	23.33 E
Vračevo	82	54.53 N	39.10 E
Vrådal	26	59.20 N	8.25 E
Vrancea □[6]	38	45.45 N	27.00 E
Vrancei, Munții ⋀	38	46.00 N	26.30 E
Vrangel'a, mys >	89	54.17 N	138.39 E
Vrangel'a, ostrov I	74	71.00 N	179.30 W
Vranje	38	42.33 N	21.54 E
Vranov	61	48.54 N	15.49 E
Vranov [nad Topl'ou]	30	48.54 N	21.41 E
Vrbas	38	45.35 N	19.39 E
Vrbas ≃	36	45.06 N	17.31 E
Vrbovec	36	45.53 N	16.25 E
Vrbovsko	36	45.23 N	15.05 E
Vrchlabí	30	50.38 N	15.37 E
Vrede	158	27.30 S	29.06 E
Vredefort	158	27.05 S	27.16 E
Vreden	52	52.02 N	6.52 E
Vredenburg	158	32.54 S	17.59 E
Vredenburgh	194	31.49 N	87.19 W
Vredendal	158	31.41 S	18.35 E
Vreed en Hoop	246	6.48 N	58.11 W
Vreeswijk	52	52.01 N	5.05 E
Vrena	40	58.52 N	16.41 E
Vresse	56	49.52 N	4.56 E
Vreta kloster ♥[1]	26	58.28 N	15.29 E
Vretstorp	40	59.02 N	14.52 E
Vrginmost	36	45.21 N	15.52 E
Vrhnika	36	45.58 N	14.18 E
Vriddhāchalam	122	11.30 N	79.20 E
Vriendschaps ≃	164	5.28 S	138.53 E
Vries	52	53.04 N	6.35 E
Vriezenveen	52	52.25 N	6.38 E
Vrigne-Meuse	56	49.42 N	4.51 E
Vrigstad	26	57.21 N	14.28 E
Vrilissia	267c	38.02 N	23.50 E
Vrille ≃	50	47.31 N	2.52 E
Vrin	58	46.39 N	9.06 E
Vrin ≃	50	48.00 N	3.20 E
Vrindāvan	124	27.35 N	77.42 E
Vrlika	36	43.55 N	16.24 E
Vrnograč	36	45.10 N	15.57 E
Vroeggedeel	158	28.02 S	22.32 E
Vron	50	50.19 N	1.45 E
Vrondádhes	38	38.24 N	26.08 E
Vroomshoop	52	52.27 N	6.34 E
Vrouenspan	158	27.50 S	20.24 E
Vroutek	54	50.08 N	13.24 E
Vršac	38	45.07 N	21.18 E
Vrsar	64	45.08 N	13.37 E
Vršič)(	64	46.26 N	13.44 E
Vrubovka	83	48.44 N	38.20 E
Vrubovskij	83	48.26 N	39.07 E
Vrútky	30	49.07 N	18.55 E
Vryburg	158	26.55 S	24.45 E
Vryheid	158	27.46 S	30.48 E
Vschody	76	54.42 N	34.06 E
Vselug, ozero ⊜	76	57.03 N	32.42 E
Všepadly	60	49.28 N	13.06 E
Všeruby	60	49.50 N	13.15 E
Vsetín	30	49.21 N	17.59 E
Vsevidof, Mount ∧	180	53.07 N	168.43 W
Vsevoložsk	265a	60.01 N	30.40 E
Vtoroje Potapovo	265b	55.56 N	37.58 E
Vtoryje Levyje Lamki	80	53.17 N	41.04 E
Vuadil'	85	40.11 N	71.43 E
Vuanggava Island I	175g	18.52 S	178.54 W
Vučitrn	38	42.49 N	20.58 E
Vudor, gora ∧	85	38.13 N	71.49 E
Vue-des-Alpes)(	58	47.04 N	6.53 E
Vught	52	51.40 N	5.17 E
Vuillafans	58	47.04 N	6.13 E
Vuitebœuf	58	46.37 N	6.34 E
Vukovar	38	45.21 N	19.00 E
Vulcan, Ab., Can.	182	50.24 N	113.15 W
Vulcan, Rom.	38	45.23 N	23.17 E
Vulcan, Mi., U.S.	190	45.46 N	87.51 W
Vulcano, Bocche di ɰ	70	38.26 N	14.57 E
Vulcano, Isola I	70	38.24 N	14.58 E
Vulcano, Monte ∧	70a	35.51 N	12.52 E
Vulci ⊥	66	42.25 N	11.35 E
Vulkanešty	78	45.41 N	28.24 E
Vulkaničeskij chrebet ⋀	78	48.30 N	23.00 E
Vulture, Monte ∧	68	40.57 N	15.38 E
Vul'vyvejem ≃	180	66.58 N	179.10 W
Vung Tau	110	10.21 N	107.04 E
Vunindawa	175g	17.49 S	178.19 E
Vunisea Station	175g	19.03 S	178.09 E
Vuoggatjålme	24	66.36 N	16.22 E
Vuohijärvi	26	61.05 N	26.48 E
Vuohijärvi ⊜	26	61.12 N	26.42 E
Vuokatti ∧[2]	26	64.07 N	28.14 E
Vuoksa ≃	26	61.03 N	30.11 E
Vuoksa, ozero ⊜	76	60.40 N	29.50 E
Vuoksenniska	26	61.13 N	28.49 E
Vurnary	80	55.29 N	46.58 E
Vuturu, Pizzo ∧	70	37.56 N	14.13 E
Vuya	154	5.21 N	29.40 E
Vuyyūru	122	16.22 N	80.51 E
Vuzenica	61	46.36 N	15.10 E
Vvedenka	86	54.03 N	63.45 E
Vvedenovka	89	51.19 N	128.12 E
Vvedenskoje	82	55.42 N	36.54 E
Vyāra	120	21.07 N	73.24 E
Vyatka → Kirov	80	58.38 N	49.42 E
Vyaz'ma → V'az'ma	76	55.13 N	34.18 E
Vyazniki → V'azniki	80	56.15 N	42.10 E
Vyborg	76	60.42 N	28.45 E
Vyborgskij zaliv c	76	60.35 N	28.24 E
Výčapy	61	49.09 N	15.53 E
Vyčegda ≃	24	61.18 N	46.36 E
Vyčegodskij	24	61.16 N	46.48 E
Vychino ◆[8]	265b	55.43 N	37.48 E
Východočeský Kraj □[4]	30	50.10 N	16.00 E
Východoslovenský Kraj □[4]	30	49.00 N	21.15 E
Vydrino, Ross.	88	51.27 N	104.39 E
Vydrino, Ross.	88	56.50 N	99.02 E
Vygoda	78	48.56 N	23.55 E
Vygoniči	76	53.08 N	34.05 E
Vygoniščí	76	52.37 N	25.55 E
Vygozero, ozero ⊜	24	63.35 N	34.42 E
Vyjezdnoje	80	55.23 N	43.47 E
Vyježžij Log	86	54.58 N	93.57 E
Vyksa	80	55.18 N	42.11 E
Vylkovo	86	53.05 N	81.26 E
Vym' ≃	24	62.13 N	50.25 E
Vyntja	86	60.31 N	67.18 E
Vypolzovo	76	57.53 N	33.42 E
Vyrica	76	59.25 N	30.21 E
Vyrnwy ≃	42	52.46 N	3.00 W
Vyrnwy, Lake ⊜	42	52.47 N	3.30 W
Vyša	80	53.52 N	42.24 E
Vyša ≃	80	54.02 N	42.06 E
Vyšehrad ◆[8]	54	50.01 N	14.27 E
Vyšelej	80	53.26 N	45.29 E
Vyselki	78	45.35 N	39.38 E
Vyšesteblijevskaja	78	45.12 N	37.00 E
Vyšgorodok	76	57.02 N	28.01 E
Vyška, Ross.	76	57.31 N	35.57 E
Vyška, Turk.	128	39.20 N	54.08 E
Vyskod'	76	57.46 N	30.04 E
Vyškov, Česko.	30	49.16 N	17.00 E
Vyškov, Ross.	76	52.29 N	31.41 E
Vyškovskij, pereval)(	78	48.42 N	23.38 E
Vyšná Radvaň	30	49.07 N	21.56 E
Vyšneol'šanoje	76	52.08 N	37.39 E
Vyšnevolockoje vodochranilišče ⊜[1]	76	57.35 N	34.28 E
Vyšnij Voločok	76	57.35 N	34.34 E

≃ River	Fluß	Río	Rivière	Rio
≊ Canal	Kanal	Canal	Canal	Canal
⌊ Waterfall, Rapids	Wasserfall, Stromschnellen	Cascada, Rápidos	Chute d'eau, Rapides	Cascata, Rápidos
ɰ Strait	Meeresstraße	Estrecho	Détroit	Estreito
c Bay, Gulf	Bucht, Golf	Bahía, Golfo	Baie, Golfe	Baía, Golfo
⊜ Lake, Lakes	See, Seen	Lago, Lagos	Lac, Lacs	Lago, Lagos
⩩ Swamp	Sumpf	Pantano	Marais	Pântano
⩀ Ice Features, Glacier	Eis- und Gletscherformen	Accidentes Glaciales	Formes glaciaires	Acidentes glaciares
⊤ Other Hydrographic Features	Andere Hydrographische Objekte	Otros Elementos Hidrográficos	Autres données hydrographiques	Outros acidentes hidrográficos

✦ Submarine Features	Untermeerische Objekte	Accidentes Submarinos	Formes de relief sous-marin	Acidentes submarinos
□ Political Unit	Politische Einheit	Unidad Politica	Entité politique	Unidade política
♥ Cultural Institution	Kulturelle Institution	Institución Cultural	Institution culturelle	Institução cultural
⊥ Historical Site	Historische Stätte	Sitio Histórico	Site historique	Sitio histórico
♠ Recreational Site	Erholungs- und Ferienort	Sitio de Recreo	Centre de loisirs	Area de Lazer
⊠ Airport	Flughafen	Aeropuerto	Aéroport	Aeroporto
■ Military Installation	Militäranlage	Instalación Militar	Installation militaire	Instalação militar
◆ Miscellaneous	Verschiedenes	Misceláneo	Divers	Diversos

Name	Page	Lat.°′	Long.°′
Vysočany •8	54	50.05 N	14.31 E
Vysock, Ross.	76	60.36 N	28.34 E
Vysock, Ukr.	78	51.43 N	26.39 E
Vysokaja, gora ∧	89	45.59 N	136.35 E
Vysokaja Gora	80	55.56 N	49.19 E
Vysoké Mýto	30	49.57 N	16.10 E
Vysoké Tatry ⋏	30	49.12 N	20.05 E
Vysokiniči	82	54.54 N	36.55 E
Vysokogornyj	89	50.09 N	139.09 E
Vysokogorsk	89	44.23 N	135.23 E
Vysokoje, Bela.	76	52.22 N	23.22 E
Vysokoje, Kaz.	85	42.30 N	70.32 E
Vysokoje, Ross.	76	54.02 N	33.44 E
Vysokoje, Ross.	76	56.43 N	34.55 E
Vysokoje, Ross.	82	54.30 N	37.03 E
Vysokoje, Ross.	265b	55.59 N	37.09 E
Vysokopolje	78	47.29 N	33.32 E
Vysokovsk	82	56.19 N	36.33 E
Vysoký kámen ∧	61	49.06 N	15.13 E
Vysšaja Dubečn'a	78	50.44 N	30.40 E
Vyšší Brod	61	48.37 N	14.19 E
Vystupoviči	78	51.34 N	29.04 E
Vytebet' ≐	76	53.53 N	35.38 E
Vytegra	24	61.00 N	36.24 E
Vyževka ≐	78	51.41 N	24.35 E
Vzmorje	89	47.51 N	142.31 E
Vzvad	76	58.10 N	31.29 E
W			
W, Parc National du ♦	150	12.50 N	2.30 E
Wa	150	10.04 N	2.29 W
Waabs	41	54.32 N	9.58 E
Waackaack Creek ≐	276	40.27 N	74.08 W
Waadt → Vaud □3	58	46.40 N	6.30 E
Waajid	144	3.48 N	43.15 E
Waakirchen	64	47.46 N	11.40 E
Waal	58	48.00 N	10.46 E
Waal ≐	52	51.49 N	4.58 E
Waalre	52	51.24 N	5.26 E
Waalwijk	52	51.42 N	5.04 E
Waao	102	24.20 N	104.40 E
Waar, Meos I	164	2.05 S	134.23 E
Waarschoot	50	51.09 N	3.36 E
Waasmunster	50	51.06 N	4.05 E
Wabag	164	5.30 S	143.40 E
Wabamun	182	53.33 N	114.28 W
Wabamun Indian Reserve •4	182	53.30 N	114.30 W
Wabamun Lake ⊜	182	53.33 N	114.35 W
Waban	283	42.20 N	71.14 W
Waban, Lake ⊜	283	42.17 N	71.17 W
Wabana	186	47.38 N	52.57 W
Wabasca	182	56.00 N	113.53 W
Wabasca ≐	176	58.22 N	115.20 W
Wabasca Indian Reserve •4	182	55.53 N	113.32 W
Wabash, In., U.S.	216	40.47 N	85.49 W
Wabash, Oh., U.S.	216	40.33 N	84.45 W
Wabash □6	216	40.48 N	85.49 W
Wabash ≐	194	37.46 N	88.02 W
Wabasha	190	44.23 N	92.01 W
Wabasso, Fl., U.S.	220	27.44 N	80.26 W
Wabasso, Mn., U.S.	198	44.24 N	95.15 W
Wabatongushi Lake ⊜	190	48.26 N	84.15 W
Wabe Gestro ≐	144	4.17 N	42.02 E
Wabe Mena ≐	144	5.32 N	41.11 E
Wabeno	190	45.26 N	88.39 W
Wabera	144	6.26 N	40.42 E
Wabern	56	51.06 N	9.20 E
Wabigoon Lake ⊜	184	49.44 N	92.44 W
Wabowden	184	54.55 N	98.38 W
Wabrah ⊽4	128	27.26 N	47.22 E
Wąbrzeźno	30	53.17 N	18.57 E
Wabu	100	32.17 N	116.55 E
Wabu Hu ⊜	100	32.23 N	116.54 E
Wabuska	226	39.08 N	119.10 W
W.A.C. Bennett Dam •6	182	56.01 N	122.10 W
Waccamaw ≐	192	33.21 N	79.16 W
Waccamaw, Lake ⊜	192	34.17 N	78.30 W
Waccasassa Bay c	192	29.06 N	82.52 W
Wachapreague	208	37.36 N	75.41 W
Wachapreague Inlet c	208	37.35 N	75.36 W
Wachau •1	61	48.18 N	15.24 E
Wachenheim	56	49.26 N	8.10 E
Wachi	96	35.15 N	135.24 E
Wąchock, Klasztory ʊ1	30	51.05 N	21.01 E
Wachtberg	56	50.37 N	7.11 E
Wachtendonk	56	51.24 N	6.20 E
Wächtersbach	56	50.15 N	9.17 E
Wachusett Mountain ∧	207	42.29 N	71.53 W
Wachusett Reservoir ⊜1	207	42.23 N	71.43 W
Wacissa	192	30.21 N	83.59 W
Wackersdorf	60	49.19 N	12.11 E
Waco	222	31.32 N	97.08 W
Waco Lake ⊜1	222	31.34 N	97.13 W
Waconda Lake ⊜1	198	39.30 N	98.24 W
Waconia	190	44.51 N	93.47 W
Wacouno ≐	186	50.54 N	65.57 W
Wacousta	216	42.49 N	84.42 W
Wad	120	27.21 N	66.22 E
Wada, Nihon	94	35.02 N	140.01 E
Wada, Nihon	94	36.12 N	138.13 E
Wada, Nihon	268	35.12 N	139.38 E
Wada, Nihon	270	34.33 N	135.55 E
Wadagou	104	42.27 N	120.58 E
Wad Al-Ḥaddād	140	13.49 N	33.32 E
Wadamago	144	8.55 N	46.17 E
Wada-misaki ›	96	34.39 N	135.11 E
Wādat Ga	120	26.57 N	97.37 E
Wadayama	96	35.19 N	134.52 E
Wad Bandah	140	13.06 N	27.57 E
Wad Ban Naqa	140	16.30 N	33.08 E
Wadbilliga National Park ♦	166	36.20 S	149.35 E
Waddān	146	29.10 N	16.08 E
Waddān, Jabal ⋏2	146	29.20 N	16.20 E
Waddeneilanden II	52	53.26 N	5.30 E
Waddenzee ⊽2	52	53.15 N	5.15 E
Wadderin	162	32.00 S	118.27 E
Waddesdon	42	51.51 N	0.56 W
Waddingham	44	53.27 N	0.31 W
Waddington, Eng., U.K.	44	53.10 N	0.32 W
Waddington, N.Y., U.S.	212	44.51 N	75.12 W
Waddington, Mount ∧	182	51.23 N	125.15 W
Waddinxveen	52	52.03 N	4.40 E
Waddy	218	38.08 N	85.04 W
Wade, Mount ∧	9	84.51 S	174.15 W
Wadebridge	42	50.32 N	4.50 W
Wadena, Sk., Can.	184	51.57 N	103.47 W
Wadena, In., U.S.	216	40.43 N	87.16 W
Wadena, Mn., U.S.	198	46.26 N	95.08 W
Wädenswil	58	47.14 N	8.40 E
Wadern	56	49.32 N	6.53 E
Wadersloh	52	51.44 N	8.15 E
Wadesboro	192	34.58 N	80.04 W
Wadeville	273d	26.16 S	28.11 E
Wadeye	164	14.13 S	129.32 E
Wadgassen	56	49.16 N	6.47 E
Wad Ḥāmid	140	16.30 N	32.48 E
Wadham Islands II	186	49.34 N	53.50 W
Wadhams	182	51.30 N	127.31 W
Wadhurst	42	51.04 N	0.21 E
Wadian	100	32.48 N	112.30 E
Wādī as-Sīr	132	31.57 N	35.49 E
Wādī Ḥalfā'	140	21.56 N	31.20 E
Wādī Jimāl, Jazīrat I	140	24.40 N	35.10 E
Wādī Mūsā	132	30.19 N	35.29 E
Wading ≐, Ma., U.S.	283	41.56 N	71.13 W
Wading ≐, N.J., U.S.	208	39.33 N	74.28 W
Wading, West Branch ≐	208	39.40 N	74.32 W
Wading River	207	40.57 N	72.50 W
Wādī Rashrāsh, Bi'r ⊽4	142	29.26 N	31.31 E
Wadley, Al., U.S.	194	33.07 N	85.33 W
Wadley, Ga., U.S.	192	32.52 N	82.24 W
Wad Madanī	140	14.25 N	33.28 E
Wadowice	30	49.53 N	19.30 E
Wadsworth, Il., U.S.	216	42.26 N	87.56 W
Wadsworth, Nv., U.S.	204	39.38 N	119.17 W
Wadsworth, N.Y., U.S.	210	42.49 N	77.54 W
Wadsworth, Oh., U.S.	214	41.01 N	81.43 W
Wadsworth Moor •3	262	53.48 N	2.02 W
Wadu I	122	5.51 N	72.58 E
Waegwan	98	35.58 N	128.24 E
Waelder	222	29.42 N	97.18 W
Waenhuiskrans	158	34.41 S	20.14 E
Wafang	98	41.44 N	118.54 E
Wafania	152	1.21 S	20.20 E
Wafrah	128	28.33 N	48.02 E
Wagadugu → Ouagadougou	150	12.22 N	1.31 W
Wāgah	123	31.36 N	74.33 E
Wagait Aboriginal Reserve •4	164	13.00 S	130.20 E
Wagang	102	28.04 N	103.10 E
Wagenborgen	52	53.15 N	6.56 E
Wagenfeld-Hasslingen	52	52.33 N	8.34 E
Wageningen, Ned.	52	51.58 N	5.40 E
Wageningen, Sur.	250	5.46 N	56.41 W
Wager Bay c	176	65.26 N	88.40 W
Wagerup	168a	32.55 S	115.54 E
Waggaman Heights	284c	38.49 N	76.57 W
Wagga Wagga	171b	35.07 S	147.22 E
Waggoner	219	39.23 N	89.39 W
Waghäusel	56	49.14 N	8.31 E
Wagin	162	33.18 S	117.21 E
Waging am See	64	47.56 N	12.43 E
Waginger See ⊜	64	47.56 N	12.47 E
Wägitaler See ⊜	58	47.06 N	8.55 E
Waglan Island I	271d	22.11 N	114.18 E
Wagna	61	46.46 N	15.34 E
Wagner	198	43.04 N	98.17 W
Wagner College ʊ2	276	40.37 N	74.07 W
Wagoner	196	35.57 N	95.22 W
Wagon Mound	196	36.00 N	104.42 W
Wagontire Mountain ∧	202	43.21 N	119.53 W
Wagontown	208	40.01 N	75.51 W
Wagrain	64	47.20 N	13.18 E
Wagram → Deutsch Wagram	61	48.18 N	16.34 E
Wagrien •1	54	54.15 N	10.45 E
Wągrowiec	30	52.49 N	17.11 E
Waha	146	28.16 N	19.54 E
Wahādurgañj	124	27.32 N	82.50 E
Wahai	164	2.48 S	129.30 E
Waharoa	172	37.46 S	175.46 E
Wāh Cantonment	123	33.48 N	72.42 E
Wahiawa	229c	21.30 N	158.01 W
Wāḥid	142	30.49 N	32.20 E
Wahkiakum □6	224	46.16 N	123.28 W
Wahlen	56	49.37 N	8.51 E
Wahlstedt	54	53.57 N	10.12 E
Wahnbachstausee ⊜1	56	50.48 N	7.19 E
Wahneta	220	27.57 N	81.44 W
Wahoo	198	41.12 N	96.37 W
Wahpeton	198	46.15 N	96.36 W
Wahran (Oran)	148	35.43 N	0.43 W
Wahran □5	148	35.30 N	0.30 E
Wahrenbrück	54	51.33 N	13.22 E
Wahrenholz	54	52.36 N	10.36 E
Währing •8	264b	48.14 N	16.21 E
Wahroonga	274a	33.43 S	151.07 E
Wahweap Creek ≐	200	37.02 N	111.35 W
Wai, India	122	17.56 N	73.54 E
Wai, Indon.	164	1.42 S	127.59 E
Waialeale ∧	229b	22.04 N	159.30 W
Waialua	229c	21.34 N	158.07 W
Waialua Bay c	229c	21.36 N	158.07 W
Waianae	229c	21.26 N	158.11 W
Waianae Range ⋏	229c	21.30 N	158.10 W
Waianapanapa State Park ♦	229a	20.47 N	156.01 W
Waiapu ≐	172	37.47 S	178.29 E
Waiatoto ≐	172	43.59 S	168.47 E
Waiau	172	42.39 S	173.03 E
Waiau ≐, N.Z.	172	42.47 S	173.22 E
Waiau ≐, N.Z.	172	46.12 S	167.38 E
Waiau ≐, N.Z.	172	38.58 S	177.24 E
Waibakul	115b	9.36 S	119.35 E
Waibeem	164	0.28 S	132.58 E
Waiblingen	56	48.50 N	9.19 E
Waibstadt	56	49.18 N	8.54 E
Waichagoumen	98	40.54 N	125.45 E
Waidbruck → Ponte Gardena	64	46.36 N	11.32 E
Waidhān	124	24.04 N	82.20 E
Waidhofen an der Thaya	61	48.49 N	15.18 E
Waidhofen an der Ybbs	61	47.58 N	14.47 E
Waidmannslust •8	264a	52.36 N	13.20 E
Waidring	64	47.35 N	12.34 E
Waiehu	229a	20.55 N	156.30 W
Waigang	106	31.22 N	121.11 E
Waigatsch → Vajgač, ostrov I	72	70.00 N	59.30 E
Waigeo, Pulau I	164	0.14 S	130.45 E
Waigoumen	98	41.24 N	116.13 E
Waihao Downs	172	44.48 S	170.55 E
Waihau Bay	172	37.37 S	177.55 E
Waihee	229a	20.56 N	156.30 W
Waihee Point ›	229a	20.57 N	156.31 W
Waiheke Island I	172	36.48 S	175.06 E
Waihi	172	37.24 S	175.51 E
Waihola	172	46.02 S	170.06 E
Waihopai ≐	172	41.31 S	173.44 E
Waihou ≐	172	37.10 S	175.32 E
Waihuantan	106	30.25 N	118.40 E
Waika	154	2.21 S	25.43 E
Waikabubak	115b	9.38 S	119.25 E
Waikaia	172	45.44 S	168.51 E
Waikaia ≐	172	45.53 S	168.48 E
Waikanae	172	40.53 S	175.04 E
Waikane	229c	21.30 N	157.51 W
Waikapu	229a	20.51 N	156.30 W
Waikare, Lake ⊜	172	37.26 S	175.13 E
Waikaremoana, Lake ⊜	172	38.46 S	177.07 E
Waikari	172	42.58 S	172.41 E
Waikato ≐	172	37.23 S	174.43 E
Waikelo	115b	9.24 S	119.14 E
Waikerie	166	34.11 S	139.59 E
Waikiki Beach ♦	229c	21.17 N	157.50 W
Waikino	172	37.25 S	175.46 E
Waikouaiti	172	45.36 S	170.41 E
Waikuatang	106	31.20 N	120.41 E
Wailo	144	9.25 N	48.55 E
Wailua	229b	22.03 N	159.20 W
Wailua River State Park ♦	229b	22.02 N	159.21 W
Wailuku	229a	20.53 N	156.30 W
Waimahaka	172	46.31 S	168.49 E
Waimakariri ≐	172	43.24 S	172.42 E
Waimamaku	172	35.33 S	173.29 E
Waimana	172	38.09 S	177.05 E
Waimana ≐	172	38.04 S	177.00 E
Waimanalo	229c	21.21 N	157.43 W
Waimangaroa	172	41.43 S	171.46 E
Waimangura	115b	9.30 S	119.14 E
Waimarama	172	39.48 S	176.59 E
Waimate	172	44.44 S	171.02 E
Waimea, Hi., U.S.	229c	21.38 N	158.03 W
Waimea, Hi., U.S.	229d	21.57 N	159.40 W
Waimea Canyon V	229b	22.04 N	159.39 W
Waimea Canyon State Park ♦	229b	22.04 N	159.40 W
Waimes	56	50.25 N	6.07 E
Wainfleet All Saints	44	53.07 N	0.14 E
Wainganga ≐	122	18.50 N	79.55 E
Waingapu	115b	9.39 S	120.16 E
Waini ≐	246	8.24 N	59.51 W
Wainscott	260	51.25 N	0.31 E
Wainstalls	262	53.45 N	1.56 W
Wainuiomata	172	41.16 S	174.57 E
Wainunu Bay c	175g	16.55 S	178.53 E
Wainwright, Ab., Can.	182	52.49 N	110.52 W
Wainwright, Ak., U.S.	180	70.38 N	160.01 W
Wainwright, Oh., U.S.	214	40.25 N	81.25 W
Waiohau	172	38.14 S	176.51 E
Waiotira	172	35.56 S	174.12 E
Waiouru	172	39.29 S	175.40 E
Waipa ≐	172	37.41 S	175.09 E
Waipahi	172	46.07 S	169.15 E
Waipahu	229c	21.23 N	158.00 W
Waipaoa	172	38.32 S	177.54 E
Waipara	172	43.04 S	172.45 E
Waipara ≐	172	43.09 S	172.48 E
Waipawa	172	39.56 S	176.36 E
Waipiata	172	45.11 S	170.10 E
Waipio Acres	229c	21.28 N	158.00 W
Waipio Bay c	229a	20.55 N	156.13 W
Waipiro	172	38.01 S	178.20 E
Waipu	172	35.59 S	174.27 E
Waipukurau	172	40.00 S	176.34 E
Wairakei	172	38.38 S	176.06 E
Wairarapa, Lake ⊜	172	41.13 S	175.15 E
Wairau ≐	172	41.30 S	174.04 E
Wairau Valley	172	41.34 S	173.32 E
Wairio	172	46.00 S	168.02 E
Wairoa	172	39.02 S	177.25 E
Wairoa ≐	172	39.04 S	177.26 E
Waisanzao	106	30.57 N	121.52 E
Waischenfeld	60	49.51 N	11.21 E
Waïsisi	175f	19.30 S	169.22 E
Waitahanui	172	38.47 S	176.05 E
Waitahuna	172	45.59 S	169.46 E
Waitakaruru	172	37.15 S	175.23 E
Waitaki ≐	172	44.57 S	171.09 E
Waitara, Austl.	274a	33.43 S	151.07 E
Waitara, N.Z.	172	39.00 S	174.13 E
Waitara ≐	172	38.59 S	174.14 E
Waitarere	172	40.33 S	175.12 E
Waita Reservoir ⊜1	229b	21.55 N	159.27 W
Waitati	172	45.45 S	170.34 E
Waita-zan ∧	96	33.08 N	131.10 E
Waite Hill	214	41.37 N	81.22 W
Waitemata	172	36.56 S	174.42 E
Waite Park	190	45.33 N	94.13 W
Waitoa	172	37.37 S	175.38 E
Waitotara	172	39.48 S	174.44 E
Waitotara ≐	172	39.51 S	174.41 E
Waitpinga	168b	35.37 S	138.29 E
Waitsburg	202	46.16 N	118.09 W
Waitzen → Vác	30	47.47 N	19.08 E
Waiuku	172	37.15 S	174.45 E
Waiuta	172	42.18 S	171.49 E
Waiwera South	172	46.13 S	169.30 E
Waiwo	164	0.56 S	131.03 E
Waiya	164	3.13 S	128.55 E
Waizenkirchen	60	48.20 N	13.52 E
Wajiki	96	33.51 N	134.30 E
Wajima	92	37.24 N	136.54 E
Wajir	154	1.45 N	40.04 E
Waka, Ityo.	144	7.07 N	37.26 E
Waka, Tx., U.S.	196	36.17 N	101.03 W
Waka, Zaïre	152	1.01 N	20.13 E
Wakajabi	164	5.38 S	134.24 E
Wakakusa	94	35.36 N	138.29 E
Wakakusa-yama ∧2	270	34.42 N	135.52 E
Wakamatsu → Aizu-wakamatsu	92	37.30 N	139.56 E
Wakami ≐	190	47.43 N	82.22 W
Wakami Lake ⊜	190	47.29 N	82.51 W
Wakamiya	96	33.44 N	130.37 E
Wakano-ura ♦	96	34.11 N	135.11 E
Wakarusa	216	41.32 N	86.03 W
Wakarusa ≐	198	38.57 N	95.05 W
Wakasa	96	35.20 N	134.24 E
Wakasa-wan c	92	35.45 N	135.40 E
Wakasa-wan-kokutei-kōen ♦	96	35.35 N	135.30 E
Wakatipu, Lake ⊜	172	45.05 S	168.34 E
Wakatomika Creek ≐	214	40.07 N	82.00 W
Wakato-ōhashi •5	96	33.54 N	130.49 E
Wakaw	184	52.39 N	105.44 W
Wakaw Lake ⊜	184	52.40 N	105.35 W
Wakayama	96	34.13 N	135.11 E
Wakayama □5	96	34.00 N	135.20 E
Wakayanagi	92	38.46 N	141.08 E
Wake, Nihon	96	34.48 N	134.08 E
Wake, Zaïre	152	0.48 S	20.10 E
WaKeeney	198	39.01 N	99.53 W
Wakefield, N.Z.	172	41.24 S	173.03 E
Wakefield, Eng., U.K.	44	53.42 N	1.29 W
Wakefield, Ks., U.S.	198	39.12 N	97.00 W
Wakefield, Ma., U.S.	207	42.30 N	71.04 W
Wakefield, Ne., U.S.	198	42.16 N	96.51 W
Wakefield, Oh., U.S.	218	38.59 N	83.01 W
Wakefield, R.I., U.S.	207	41.26 N	71.30 W
Wakefield, Va., U.S.	192	36.58 N	76.59 W
Wakefield ≐	168b	34.10 S	138.10 E
Wakefield Forest	284c	38.50 N	77.14 W
Wake Forest	192	35.58 N	78.30 W
Wake Island □2, Oc.	14	19.17 N	166.36 E
Wake Island □2, Oc.	174a	19.17 N	166.36 E
Wake Island I1	174a	19.18 N	166.38 E
Wake Island Air Force Base ■	174a	19.17 N	166.37 E
Wake Lagoon c	174a	19.18 N	166.36 E
Wakema	110	16.36 N	95.11 E
Wakeman	214	41.15 N	82.23 W
Wakeman ≐	182	51.00 N	126.30 W
Wakenda Creek ≐	194	39.19 N	93.16 W
Wake Village	194	33.26 N	94.07 W
Wakhān → Vākhān •1	120	37.00 N	73.00 E
Waki	96	34.04 N	134.09 E
Wakis	164	6.13 S	150.17 E
Wakita	196	36.53 N	97.55 W
Wakkanai	92a	45.25 N	141.40 E
Wakkerstroom	158	27.24 S	30.10 E
Wakō, Nihon	268	35.47 N	139.37 E
Wako, Pap. N. Gui.	164	6.05 S	149.05 E
Wakomata Lake ⊜	190	46.34 N	83.22 W
Wakonassin ≐	190	46.28 N	81.51 W
Wakonda	198	43.00 N	97.06 W
Wakre	164	0.19 S	131.09 E
Waku Kundo	152	11.25 S	15.07 E
Wakunai	175e	5.52 S	155.13 E
Wakusimi ≐	190	49.08 N	82.17 W
Wala ≐	154	5.46 S	32.04 E
Walamba	154	13.29 S	28.45 E
Walanae ≐	112	4.08 S	119.58 E
Walang	102	28.33 N	100.54 E
Wal Athiang	140	7.42 N	29.40 E
Walawe ≐	122	6.06 N	81.01 E
Walbeck	52	51.30 N	6.15 E
Walberswick	42	52.19 N	1.39 E
Walbran Creek ≐	224	48.34 N	124.40 W
Walbridge	214	41.35 N	83.29 W
Wałbrzych (Waldenburg)	30	50.46 N	16.17 E
Walburg	222	30.44 N	97.35 W
Walbury Hill ∧2	42	51.21 N	1.30 W
Walcha	166	30.59 S	151.36 E
Walchensee ⊜	64	47.36 N	11.20 E
Walcheren I	52	51.33 N	3.35 E
Walcheren, Kanaal door ≊	50	51.26 N	3.35 E
Walchsee	64	47.39 N	12.19 E
Walcott, B.C., Can.	182	54.31 N	126.51 W
Walcott, Ia., U.S.	190	41.35 N	90.46 W
Walcott, N.D., U.S.	198	46.32 N	96.56 W
Walcott, Lake ⊜1	202	42.40 N	113.23 W
Walcourt	50	50.15 N	4.25 E
Wałcz	30	53.17 N	16.28 E
Wald	58	47.17 N	8.55 E
Wald •8	263	51.11 N	7.03 E
Waldaist ≐	61	48.19 N	14.34 E
Waldai → Valdajskaja vozvyšennost' ⋏2	24	57.00 N	33.30 E
Wald am Schoberpass	61	47.27 N	14.40 E
Waldbauer •8	263	51.18 N	7.28 E
Waldbillig	56	49.47 N	6.18 E
Waldböckelheim	56	49.49 N	7.43 E
Waldbröl	56	50.53 N	7.37 E
Waldbronn	56	48.56 N	8.29 E
Waldburg	58	47.45 N	9.43 E
Waldeck, Dtsch.	56	51.12 N	9.04 E
Waldeck, Dtsch.	60	49.52 N	11.57 E
Walden, Co., U.S.	200	40.43 N	106.16 W
Walden, N.Y., U.S.	210	41.33 N	74.11 W
Walden, Lake ⊜	281	42.39 N	83.46 W
Waldenbuch	56	48.38 N	9.07 E
Waldenburg, Dtsch.	54	50.52 N	12.36 E
Waldenburg, Dtsch.	56	49.11 N	9.38 E
Waldenburg, Schw.	58	47.23 N	7.45 E
Waldenburg → Wałbrzych	30	50.46 N	16.17 E
Walden Pond ⊜, Ma., U.S.	283	42.26 N	71.20 W
Walden Pond ⊜, Ma., U.S.	283	42.28 N	71.00 W
Walden Ridge ∧	194	35.30 N	85.15 W
Waldershof	60	49.59 N	12.04 E
Walderslade	260	51.21 N	0.32 E
Waldfischbach	56	49.17 N	7.40 E
Waldheim, Sk., Can.	184	52.37 N	106.38 W
Waldheim, Dtsch.	54	51.04 N	13.01 E
Waldighoffen	58	47.33 N	7.19 E
Wald im Pinzgau	64	47.15 N	12.14 E
Waldkappel	56	51.08 N	9.52 E
Waldkirch	58	48.05 N	7.57 E
Waldkirchen	60	48.44 N	13.37 E
Waldkirchen am Wesen	60	48.26 N	13.49 E
Waldkraiburg	60	48.12 N	12.28 E
Waldmohr	56	49.23 N	7.20 E
Waldmünchen	60	49.23 N	12.43 E
Waldnaab ≐	60	49.36 N	12.08 E
Waldo, B.C., Can.	182	49.13 N	115.13 W
Waldo, Ar., U.S.	194	33.21 N	93.17 W
Waldo, Oh., U.S.	214	40.27 N	83.04 W
Waldoboro	188	44.05 N	69.22 W
Waldo Lake ⊜	283	42.07 N	71.03 W
Waldo Lake ⊜1	202	43.44 N	122.03 W
Waldon ≐	42	50.51 N	4.15 W
Waldorf	208	38.37 N	76.56 W
Waldport	202	44.25 N	124.04 W
Waldron, Sk., Can.	184	50.51 N	102.30 W
Waldron, Ar., U.S.	194	34.53 N	94.05 W
Waldron, In., U.S.	218	39.27 N	85.40 W
Waldron, Mi., U.S.	216	41.43 N	84.25 W
Waldron Island I	224	48.43 N	123.02 W
Waldsassen	60	50.00 N	12.18 E
Waldshut	58	47.37 N	8.13 E
Waldstatt	58	47.21 N	9.17 E
Waldthurn	60	49.40 N	12.20 E
Waldviertel •1	61	48.40 N	15.15 E
Waldwick	276	41.00 N	74.07 W
Walea, Selat ʮ	112	0.40 S	122.00 E
Walembele	150	10.30 N	1.58 W
Walensee ⊜	58	47.07 N	9.12 E
Walenstadt	58	47.07 N	9.19 E
Wales, Ak., U.S.	180	65.36 N	168.05 W
Wales, Ma., U.S.	207	42.04 N	72.13 W
Wales, Wi., U.S.	216	43.00 N	88.23 W
Wales □8	28	52.30 N	3.30 W
Wales Center	210	42.46 N	78.32 W
Wales Island I, B.C., Can.	182	54.45 N	130.30 W
Wales Island I, N.T., Can.	176	68.00 N	86.43 W
Walewale	150	10.21 N	0.48 W
Walgett	166	30.01 S	148.07 E
Walgreen Coast ≗2	9	75.15 S	105.00 W
Walhachin	182	50.45 N	120.59 W
Walhalla, N.D., U.S.	198	48.55 N	97.55 W
Walhalla, S.C., U.S.	192	34.45 N	83.03 W
Walhalla ⊥	60	49.03 N	12.14 E
Walheim	56	50.42 N	6.10 E
Walhonding	214	40.22 N	82.09 W
Walhonding ≐	214	40.18 N	81.53 W
Wali	105	39.42 N	118.20 E
Walia	164	3.47 S	138.32 E
Walikale	154	1.25 S	28.03 E
Walincourt	50	50.04 N	3.20 E
Walis Island I	164	3.15 S	143.20 E
Walkaway	162	28.57 S	114.48 E
Walkden	44	53.32 N	2.24 W
Walkenried	54	51.35 N	10.37 E
Walker, Ia., U.S.	190	42.17 N	91.46 W
Walker, Mi., U.S.	216	43.00 N	85.46 W
Walker, Mn., U.S.	190	47.06 N	94.35 W
Walker, N.Y., U.S.	210	43.18 N	77.52 W
Walker □6	222	30.42 N	95.35 W
Walker ≐	204	38.54 N	118.47 W
Walker, Lac ⊜	186	50.16 N	67.09 W
Walker, Mount ∧2	171a	27.48 S	152.34 E
Walker Basin Creek ≐	228	35.20 N	118.47 W
Walker Bay c	158	34.30 S	19.20 E
Walker Creek ≐, Az., U.S.	200	36.58 N	109.42 W
Walker Creek ≐, Ma., U.S.	283	42.38 N	70.44 W
Walker Creek ≐, Wy., U.S.	198	43.09 N	104.52 W
Walker Lake ⊜, Mb., Can.	184	54.42 N	96.57 W
Walker Lake ⊜, Ak., U.S.	180	67.10 N	154.26 W
Walker Lake ⊜, Nv., U.S.	204	38.44 N	118.43 W
Walker Lake ⊜1	210	40.48 N	77.11 W
Walker Point ›	158	34.05 S	22.57 E
Walker River Indian Reservation •4	204	39.00 N	118.40 W
Walkers Mill	279b	40.24 N	80.08 W
Walkersville	208	39.29 N	77.21 W
Walkerton, On., Can.	212	44.07 N	81.09 W
Walkerton, In., U.S.	216	41.28 N	86.28 W
Walkerton, Va., U.S.	208	37.43 N	77.01 W
Walkertown	192	36.10 N	80.09 W
Walker Valley	210	41.38 N	74.23 W
Walkerville	202	46.02 N	112.32 W
Walk Mill	262	53.46 N	2.12 W
Wall, Pa., U.S.	279b	40.24 N	79.47 W
Wall, S.D., U.S.	198	43.59 N	102.14 W
Wallace, Ca., U.S.	226	38.12 N	120.59 W
Wallace, Id., U.S.	202	47.28 N	115.55 W
Wallace, Ne., U.S.	198	40.50 N	101.09 W
Wallace, N.Y., U.S.	210	42.26 N	77.28 W
Wallace, N.C., U.S.	192	34.44 N	77.59 W
Wallaceburg	214	42.36 N	82.23 W
Wallace Lake ⊜	279a	41.22 N	81.52 W
Wallaceton	214	40.57 N	78.17 W
Wallacetown	214	42.38 N	81.28 W
Wallach	263	51.35 N	6.34 E
Wallachia □9	38	44.00 N	25.00 E
Wallacia	170	33.52 S	150.39 E
Wallal Downs	162	19.47 S	120.40 E
Wallam Creek ≐	166	28.40 S	147.20 E
Wallan	169	37.25 S	144.59 E
Wallangarra	166	28.56 S	151.56 E
Wallaroo	168b	33.56 S	137.38 E
Wallaroo Mines	168b	33.57 S	137.41 E
Wallasey	44	53.26 N	3.03 W

ENGLISH

Name	Page	Lat.°′	Long.°′
Wallau	56	50.56 N	8.28 E
Walla Walla	202	46.03 N	118.20 W
Walldorf, Dtsch.	54	50.36 N	10.23 E
Walldorf, Dtsch.	56	49.18 N	8.38 E
Walldürn	56	49.35 N	9.22 E
Walled Lake	216	42.32 N	83.28 W
Walled Lake ⊜	281	42.31 N	83.29 W
Wallen	216	41.09 N	85.09 W
Wallend	260	51.27 N	0.42 E
Wallenfels	54	50.16 N	11.28 E
Wallenhorst	52	52.21 N	8.01 E
Wallenpaupack, Lake ⊜	210	41.25 N	75.12 W
Waller	222	30.04 N	95.56 W
Waller □6	222	30.00 N	96.00 W
Wallerawang	170	33.25 S	150.04 E
Wallern im Burgenland	61	47.43 N	16.56 E
Wallers	50	50.22 N	3.24 E
Wallersdorf	60	48.44 N	12.45 E
Wallersee ⊜	64	47.55 N	13.11 E
Wallerstein	56	48.53 N	10.28 E
Wallgau	64	47.31 N	11.16 E
Wallgrove	274a	33.47 S	150.51 E
Wallhead Airport ⊠	279a	41.21 N	82.09 W
Wallingford, Eng., U.K.	42	51.37 N	1.08 W
Wallingford, Ct., U.S.	207	41.27 N	72.49 W
Wallingford, Pa., U.S.	285	39.54 N	75.22 W
Wallingford, Vt., U.S.	188	43.28 N	72.58 W
Wallington	276	40.51 N	74.06 W
Wallington •8	260	51.21 N	0.09 W
Wallis	222	29.37 N	96.03 W
Wallis, Îles II	14	13.18 S	176.10 W
Wallis and Futuna □2	14	14.00 S	177.00 W
Wallisellen	58	47.25 N	8.36 E
Wallis → Valais □3	58	46.10 N	7.30 E
Wallisville	222	29.50 N	94.44 W
Wallisville Lake ⊜1	222	29.50 N	94.45 W
Wallkill	210	41.36 N	74.11 W
Wallkill ≐, U.S.	210	41.51 N	74.03 W
Wallkill ≐, U.S.	276	41.11 N	74.35 W
Wallkill, Wildcat Branch ≐	276	41.07 N	74.36 W
Wall Lake, Ia., U.S.	198	42.16 N	95.05 W
Wall Lake, Mi., U.S.	216	42.31 N	85.24 W
Wall Lake ⊜	216	42.31 N	85.23 W
Wallmer Bridge	262	53.43 N	2.48 W
Wallmerod	56	50.29 N	7.56 E
Wallops Island I	208	37.52 N	75.27 W
Wallowa	202	45.34 N	117.31 W
Wallowa ≐	202	45.43 N	117.47 W
Wallowa Mountains ⋏	202	45.10 N	117.30 W
Walls, Scot., U.K.	46a	60.14 N	1.35 W
Walls, Ms., U.S.	194	34.57 N	90.09 W
Wallsbüll	41	54.47 N	9.14 E
Wallsend, Austl.	170	32.55 S	151.40 E
Wallsend, Eng., U.K.	44	55.00 N	1.31 W
Wallstawe	54	52.47 N	11.01 E
Wall Town Drainage Ditch ≊	216	40.26 N	88.10 W
Wallula, Lake ⊜1	202	46.00 N	119.00 W
Walmer, S. Afr.	158	33.59 S	25.36 E
Walmer, Eng., U.K.	42	51.13 N	1.24 E
Walmersley	262	53.37 N	2.18 W
Walney, Isle of I	44	54.07 N	3.15 W
Walnut, Ca., U.S.	228	34.01 N	117.51 W
Walnut, Il., U.S.	190	41.33 N	89.35 W
Walnut, Ia., U.S.	198	41.28 N	95.13 W
Walnut, Ks., U.S.	198	37.36 N	95.04 W
Walnut, Ms., U.S.	194	34.56 N	88.53 W
Walnut, N.C., U.S.	192	35.50 N	82.44 W
Walnut ≐	198	37.03 N	97.00 W
Walnut Canyon National Monument ♦	200	35.10 N	111.31 W
Walnut Canyon Reservoir ⊜1	280	33.50 N	117.45 W
Walnut Cove	192	36.17 N	80.08 W
Walnut Creek, Ca., U.S.	226	37.54 N	122.03 W
Walnut Creek, Oh., U.S.	214	40.33 N	81.43 W
Walnut Creek ≐, Ca., U.S.	280	34.03 N	118.01 W
Walnut Creek ≐, Ca., U.S.	282	37.54 N	122.03 W
Walnut Creek ≐, Ks., U.S.	198	38.21 N	98.41 W
Walnut Creek ≐, Oh., U.S.	188	39.41 N	82.59 W
Walnut Creek ≐, Tx., U.S.	222	32.38 N	97.00 W
Walnut Creek, Middle Fork ≐	198	38.32 N	100.08 W
Walnut Creek, South Fork ≐	198	38.25 N	99.53 W
Walnut Grove, B.C., Can.	224	49.11 N	122.39 W
Walnut Grove, Ca., U.S.	226	38.15 N	121.31 W
Walnut Grove, Mn., U.S.	198	44.13 N	95.28 W
Walnut Grove, Ms., U.S.	194	32.35 N	89.27 W
Walnut Heights	282	37.53 N	122.08 W
Walnut Hill	219	38.29 N	89.03 W
Walnut Lake	281	42.33 N	83.19 W
Walnut Lake ⊜	281	42.33 N	83.20 W
Walnut Park	280	33.58 N	118.13 W
Walnutport	208	40.45 N	75.35 W
Walnut Ridge	194	36.04 N	90.57 W
Walnut Springs	222	32.03 N	97.45 W
Walpert Ridge ∧	282	37.38 N	122.00 W
Walpeup	166	35.08 S	142.02 E
Walpole, Austl.	162	34.57 S	116.44 E
Walpole, Ma., U.S.	207	42.08 N	71.15 W
Walpole, N.H., U.S.	188	43.04 N	72.25 W
Walpole Island I	214	42.34 N	82.30 W
Walpole Island Indian Reserve •4	214	42.32 N	82.37 W
Walpole Saint Peter	42	52.42 N	0.15 E
Walsall	42	52.35 N	1.58 W
Walschleben	54	51.04 N	10.56 E
Walsden	262	53.42 N	2.06 W
Walsenburg	200	37.37 N	104.46 W
Walsh, Austl.	164	16.39 S	143.54 E
Walsh, Ab., Can.	184	49.57 N	110.03 W
Walsh, Co., U.S.	198	37.23 N	102.16 W
Walsh, Ky., U.S.	218	38.41 N	82.58 W
Walsh ≐	164	16.31 S	143.42 E
Walshaw Dean Reservoirs ⊜1	262	53.48 N	2.03 W
Walshville	219	39.04 N	89.37 W
Walsingham	212	42.41 N	80.32 W
Walsoorden	52	51.23 N	4.02 E
Walsrode	52	52.52 N	9.35 E
Walston	214	40.58 N	79.01 W
Walsum	52	51.32 N	6.41 E
Walt Disney World ♦	220	28.26 N	81.35 W
Waltenhofen	64	47.40 N	10.17 E
Walterboro	192	32.54 N	80.40 W
Walter F. George Lake ⊜1	192	31.49 N	85.08 W
Walter Reed Army Medical Center ʊ	284c	38.58 N	77.02 W
Walters	196	34.21 N	98.18 W
Waltersdorf, Dtsch.	54	50.52 N	14.38 E
Waltersdorf, Dtsch.	264a	52.22 N	13.35 E
Waltershausen	54	50.53 N	10.33 E
Waltershofen	58	47.46 N	9.55 E
Waltersville	194	32.22 N	90.52 W
Walthall	194	33.36 N	89.16 W
Waltham, Eng., U.K.	44	53.31 N	0.06 W
Waltham, Ma., U.S.	207	42.22 N	71.14 W
Waltham Abbey	42	51.42 N	0.01 E
Waltham Forest •8	42	51.35 N	0.01 W
Waltham on the Wolds	42	52.49 N	0.49 W
Walthamstow •8	260	51.35 N	0.01 W

DEUTSCH

Name	Seite	Breite°′	Länge°′ E = Ost
Walthill	198	42.08 N	96.29 W
Walton, N.S., Can.	186	45.14 N	64.00 W
Walton, Eng., U.K.	42	51.24 N	0.25 W
Walton, Eng., U.K.	42	51.58 N	1.21 E
Walton, Fl., U.S.	220	27.17 N	80.15 W
Walton, In., U.S.	216	40.39 N	86.14 W
Walton, Ky., U.S.	218	38.52 N	84.36 W
Walton, N.Y., U.S.	210	42.10 N	75.07 W
Walton Hills	214	41.22 N	81.32 W
Walton-le-Dale	44	53.45 N	2.39 W
Walton on the Hill	260	51.17 N	0.15 W
Walton-on-the-Naze	42	51.51 N	1.16 E
Walton Run ≐	285	40.05 N	74.59 W
Waltonville	219	38.13 N	89.02 W
Waltrop	52	51.37 N	7.23 E
Walt Whitman Bridge •5	285	39.54 N	75.08 W
Walt Whitman Homes	285	39.52 N	75.11 W
Walt Whitman House State Historic Site ⊥	276	40.49 N	73.25 W
Walt Whitman Mall •9	276	40.50 N	73.25 W
Waltz	216	42.06 N	83.23 W
Walupt Lake ⊜	224	46.25 N	121.28 W
Walvisbaai (Walvis Bay)	156	22.59 S	14.31 E
Walvisbaai c	156	22.57 S	14.30 E
Walvis Bay □8	156	22.59 S	14.31 E
Walvis Bay → Walvisbaai	156	22.59 S	14.31 E
Walvis Ridge ✣3	10	28.00 S	3.00 E
Walwa	171b	35.58 S	147.45 E
Walwen	262	53.14 N	3.15 W
Walworth, N.Y., U.S.	210	43.08 N	77.17 W
Walworth, Wi., U.S.	216	42.31 N	88.35 W
Walworth □6	216	42.41 N	88.32 W
Walyunga National Park ♦	168a	31.44 S	116.04 E
Walyungup, Lake ⊜	168a	32.21 S	115.47 E
Walze	263	51.16 N	7.31 E
Walzin, Château de ⊥	56	50.13 N	4.55 E
Wama	152	12.14 S	15.33 E
Wamac	219	38.31 N	89.08 W
Wamba, Kenya	154	0.59 N	37.19 E
Wamba, Nig.	150	8.58 N	8.36 E
Wamba, Zaïre	154	2.09 N	28.00 E
Wamba (Uamba) ≐	152	3.56 S	17.12 E
Wambel •8	263	51.32 N	7.32 E
Wamego	198	39.12 N	96.18 W
Wamel	52	51.53 N	5.28 E
Wamesit	283	42.37 N	71.15 W
Wami ≐	154	6.08 S	38.49 E
Wamiao	100	30.49 N	113.02 E
Wamic	224	45.13 N	121.16 W
Wamma ≐	164	3.23 S	135.13 E
Wamme ≐	56	50.10 N	5.16 E
Wamplers Lake ⊜	216	42.05 N	84.09 W
Wampool ≐	44	54.54 N	3.14 W
Wampsville	210	43.04 N	75.42 W
Wampú	236	15.01 N	85.02 W
Wampú ≐	236	14.59 N	85.03 W
Wampum	214	40.53 N	80.20 W
Wampus ≐	276	41.07 N	73.43 W
Wampus Lake Reservoir ⊜1	276	41.09 N	73.43 W
Wamsasi	112	3.33 S	126.10 E
Wamsutter	200	41.40 N	107.58 W
Wamuran	171a	27.02 S	152.52 E
Wanaaring	166	29.42 S	144.09 E
Wanaka	172	44.42 S	169.09 E
Wanaka, Lake ⊜	172	44.30 S	169.08 E
Wanakah	210	42.45 N	78.54 W
Wanamassa	208	40.14 N	74.02 W
Wanamie	210	41.10 N	76.02 W
Wanamingo	190	44.18 N	92.47 W
Wan'an, Zhg.	100	26.56 N	117.22 E
Wan'an, Zhg.	100	26.30 N	114.49 E
Wan'an ≐	100	25.20 N	117.21 E
Wan'anchang	107	30.39 N	104.25 E
Wanapiri	164	4.33 S	135.59 E
Wanapitei ≐	190	46.02 N	80.51 W
Wanapitei Lake ⊜	190	46.45 N	80.45 W
Wanapum Lake ⊜1	202	47.00 N	120.00 W
Wanaque	210	41.02 N	74.17 W
Wanaque ≐	276	40.58 N	74.17 W
Wanaque Reservoir ⊜1	210	41.05 N	74.17 W
Wanatah	216	41.25 N	86.53 W
Wanau	164	1.22 S	132.42 E
Wanbaoshan	89	44.12 N	125.11 E
Wanbi	166	34.46 S	140.19 E
Wanblee	198	43.34 N	101.40 W
Wanborough	42	51.33 N	1.42 W
Wanchangchang	107	29.43 N	104.19 E
Wanchese	192	35.50 N	75.38 W
Wanda	158	29.36 S	24.28 E
Wandai	164	3.41 S	136.41 E
Wandana	162	32.04 S	133.49 E
Wandawega	216	42.45 N	88.40 W
Wande	98	36.21 N	116.56 E
Wanderer	154	19.37 S	29.59 E
Wandering	168a	32.40 S	116.40 E
Wandering ≐	182	55.05 N	112.30 W
Wanderup	41	54.41 N	9.20 E
Wandhofen	263	51.26 N	7.33 E
Wandingzhen	102	24.05 N	98.04 E
Wandlitz	54	52.45 N	13.26 E
Wandlitzer See ⊜	264a	52.46 N	13.27 E
Wando	98	34.18 N	126.47 E
Wan-do I	98	34.21 N	126.42 E
Wandoan	166	26.08 S	149.57 E
Wandsbek •8	52	53.34 N	10.04 E
Wandsworth •8	42	51.27 N	0.11 W
Waneta Lake ⊜	210	42.27 N	77.06 W
Wanette	196	34.57 N	97.01 W
Wanfang	104	41.57 N	122.52 E
Wanfoxia	102	40.04 N	95.55 E
Wanfried	56	51.10 N	10.10 E
Wanfu ≐	98	35.10 N	116.35 E
Wang ≐	110	17.08 N	99.02 E
Wanga	154	2.58 N	29.13 E
Wangal	164	6.10 S	134.12 E
Wanganderry, Mount ∧	170	34.20 S	150.15 E
Wanganui	172	39.56 S	175.03 E
Wanganui ≐	172	39.56 S	175.00 E
Wang'anzhen	105	39.19 N	114.54 E
Wangaratta	166	36.22 S	146.20 E
Wangary	166	34.33 S	135.29 E
Wangbaotaicun	104	41.10 N	123.18 E
Wangbenying	105	40.28 N	116.06 E
Wangbintun	104	41.58 N	123.43 E
Wangchang, Zhg.	107	28.52 N	105.55 E
Wangchang, Zhg.	107	29.05 N	104.40 E
Wangchangtuizigou	104	41.14 N	120.32 E
Wangcheng	100	28.23 N	112.48 E
Wang Chin	110	17.53 N	99.37 E
Wangcun	98	36.41 N	117.41 E
Wangcunkou	100	28.22 N	118.59 E
Wangdain	124	29.02 N	89.15 E
Wangdalong	102	29.25 N	99.03 E
Wangdian	106	30.37 N	120.44 E
Wangdu	98	38.43 N	115.09 E
Wangdu Phodrang	124	27.29 N	89.54 E
Wange	154	2.00 S	40.55 E
Wangels	54	54.16 N	10.45 E
Wangen an der Aare	58	47.14 N	7.39 E
Wangenbourg	58	48.37 N	7.19 E
Wangen im Allgäu	58	47.41 N	9.50 E
Wangerooge	52	53.48 N	7.54 E
Wangerooge I	52	53.46 N	7.55 E
Wangersen	52	53.22 N	9.25 E
Wangfu	104	42.05 N	121.29 E
Wanggameti, Gunung ∧	115b	10.07 S	120.14 E
Wanggangpu	104	41.38 N	123.09 E
Wanggao	102	24.38 N	111.30 E
Wanggezhuang	105	40.00 N	117.52 E
Wanggil-li	271b	37.36 N	126.39 E
Wanggoutun	104	41.40 N	121.53 E

Symbols in the index entries represent the broad categories identified in the key at the right. Symbols with superior numbers (⋏1) identify subcategories (see complete key on page *I* · *1*).

Symbole im Register stellen die rechts im Schlüssel erklärten Kategorien dar. Symbole mit hochgestellten Ziffern (⋏1) bezeichnen Unterabteilungen einer Kategorie (vgl. vollständiger Schlüssel auf Seite *I* · *1*).

Los símbolos incluídos en el texto del índice representan las grandes categorias identificadas con la clave a la derecha. Los símbolos con numeros en su parte superior (⋏1) identifican las subcategorías (véase la clave completa en la página *I* · *1*).

Les symboles de l'index représentent les catégories indiquées dans la légende à droite. Les symboles suivis d'un indice (⋏1) représentent des sous-catégories (voir légende complète à la page *I* · *1*).

Os símbolos incluídos no texto do índice representam as grandes categorias identificadas com a chave à direita. Os símbolos com números em sua parte superior (⋏1) identificam as subcategorias (veja-se a chave completa à página *I* · *1*).

∧ Mountain	Berg	Montaña	Montagne	Montanha
⋏ Mountains	Gebirge	Montañas	Montagnes	Montanhas
)(Pass	Paß	Paso	Col	Passo
V Valley, Canyon	Tal, Cañon	Valle, Cañón	Vallée, Canyon	Vale, Canhão
≐ Plain	Ebene	Llano	Plaine	Planície
› Cape	Kap	Cabo	Cap	Cabo
I Island	Insel	Isla	Île	Ilha
II Islands	Inseln	Islas	Îles	Ilhas
♦ Other Topographic Features	Andere Topographische Objekte	Otros Elementos Topográficos	Autres données topographiques	Outros acidentes topográficos

ESPAÑOL / FRANÇAIS / PORTUGUÊS

Nombre / Nom / Nome	Página / Page	Lat.°'	Long.°' W = Oeste / W = Ouest
Wanghai	98	40.26 N	120.30 E
Wanghai Shan ∧	104	41.37 N	121.41 E
Wanghechenggou	104	41.52 N	121.13 E
Wang Hin, Khlong ≊	269a	13.48 N	100.35 E
Wanghu	98	39.47 N	113.54 E
Wanghuzhuang	105	38.50 N	117.05 E
Wãngi	58	47.30 N	8.57 E
Wangingsha	100	22.44 N	113.33 E
Wangi Wangi	170	33.04 S	151.35 E
Wangiwangi, Pulau I	112	5.20 S	123.35 E
Wangji, Zhg.	100	34.00 N	117.46 E
Wangji, Zhg.	100	33.52 N	118.44 E
Wangjia, Zhg.	106	31.59 N	121.13 E
Wangjia, Zhg.	106	32.07 N	120.59 E
Wangjiadian, Zhg.	100	31.26 N	113.58 E
Wangjiadian, Zhg.	105	40.03 N	117.29 E
Wangjiagou	104	42.33 N	123.16 E
Wangjiajing, Zhg.	98	37.49 N	115.23 E
Wangjiajing, Zhg.	98	39.56 N	122.11 E
Wangjiang	100	30.09 N	116.41 E
Wangjiangjing	106	30.53 N	120.43 E
Wang Jian Mu (Tomb of Wang Jian) ⊥	107	30.38 N	104.04 E
Wangjiaputun	104	40.39 N	122.50 E
Wangjiapuzi, Zhg.	104	40.41 N	122.24 E
Wangjiapuzi, Zhg.	104	41.05 N	123.34 E
Wangjiaqiao	106	30.50 N	119.18 E
Wangjiashan	105	40.19 N	114.45 E
Wangjiashao	102	23.57 N	102.18 E
Wangjiatai	105	39.17 N	117.29 E
Wangjiaying, Zhg.	105	40.36 N	116.34 E
Wangjiaying, Zhg.	105	39.06 N	115.59 E
Wangjiazhai	106	31.21 N	121.37 E
Wangjiazui	106	31.16 N	120.18 E
Wangkantou	100	29.12 N	120.09 E
Wangkou	105	38.56 N	116.44 E
Wangkui	89	46.50 N	126.30 E
Wanglanzhuang	105	39.26 N	118.01 E
Wangling	100	27.13 N	113.26 E
Wangliu	100	32.25 N	115.40 E
Wangmiao	100	26.50 N	112.52 E
Wangmulazi	104	41.42 N	124.02 E
Wang Noi	110	14.13 N	100.44 E
Wangong	89	49.10 N	118.53 E
Wangpan Shan II	106	30.30 N	121.15 E
Wangpan Yang ⊂	100	30.30 N	121.46 E
Wangpingchang	107	29.17 N	105.45 E
Wangqing	89	43.20 N	129.48 E
Wangqingmen	98	41.42 N	125.23 E
Wangqingtuo	105	39.11 N	116.53 E
Wangqinzhuang	105	39.15 N	117.05 E
Wangqucun	106	31.22 N	120.19 E
Wangs	58	47.02 N	9.26 E
Wang Saphung	110	17.18 N	101.46 E
Wangshanhutun	104	42.03 N	122.37 E
Wangshi	100	33.11 N	116.04 E
Wangsi	98	38.00 N	116.55 E
Wangsim-ni ➜[8]	271b	37.36 N	127.03 E
Wangsiying	107	30.34 N	103.29 E
Wangtai, Zhg.	98	36.05 N	119.59 E
Wangtai, Zhg.	100	26.39 N	117.57 E
Wangtan	100	29.45 N	120.40 E
Wang Thong	110	16.50 N	100.26 E
Wangtian	100	25.59 N	116.04 E
Wangting	106	31.26 N	120.26 E
Wangtongshitai	104	42.05 N	123.11 E
Wangtuan, Zhg.	98	37.32 N	116.08 E
Wangtuan, Zhg.	98	37.17 N	122.04 E
Wangtuanji	100	33.12 N	116.21 E
Wangu	107	30.19 N	106.05 E
Wanguzhen	107	29.41 N	105.57 E
Wangwenzhuang	105	38.53 N	117.15 E
Wangxiangshang	106	31.29 N	120.15 E
Wangxiangtai	105	40.02 N	115.09 E
Wangxiuqiao	106	31.38 N	121.03 E
Wangyangzhen	107	29.44 N	104.14 E
Wangyedian	98	41.36 N	118.17 E
Wangyefu	98	41.50 N	118.23 E
Wangyehmiao → Horqin Youyi Qianqi	89	46.05 N	122.05 E
Wangyiguantun	104	42.36 N	123.19 E
Wangzhai	98	34.09 N	116.47 E
Wangzhimawo	105	39.39 N	117.40 E
Wangzhong	98	35.08 N	116.58 E
Wangzhuang	100	33.07 N	117.29 E
Wangzhuangbu	98	39.27 N	113.56 E
Wangzhuangji	98	34.09 N	118.23 E
Wangzhuangzi	105	39.17 N	118.14 E
Wanham	182	55.44 N	118.24 W
Wanhedian	100	32.16 N	113.16 E
Wanheimerort ➜[8]	263	51.24 N	6.46 E
Wanhsien → Wanxian	102	30.52 N	108.22 E
Wanhuyu	102	38.24 N	110.40 E
Wani	122	20.04 N	78.57 E
Wani, Gunung ∧	112	4.29 S	123.01 E
Wanica □[5]	250	5.50 N	55.10 W
Wanie-Rukula	154	0.15 N	25.32 E
Wanigela	164	9.22 S	149.10 E
Wanipigow ≏	184	51.11 N	96.18 W
Wanjiabu	100	28.51 N	115.39 E
Wanjiaqiao	106	30.25 N	119.07 E
Wanjiatun	98	40.03 N	119.51 E
Wanjindian	100	32.50 N	114.46 E
Wānkāner	120	22.37 N	70.56 E
Wankendorf	54	54.07 N	10.13 E
Wankum	56	51.24 N	6.20 E
Wanle Weyne	144	2.37 N	44.54 E
Wanli, T'aiwan	269d	25.11 N	121.41 E
Wanli, Zhg.	106	31.06 N	120.16 E
Wanna	52	53.44 N	8.46 E
Wanna Lakes ⊜	162	28.30 S	128.27 E
Wān Namton	110	22.03 N	99.33 E
Wanne-Eickel	52	51.32 N	7.09 E
Wanneroo	168a	31.45 S	115.48 E
Wannery Creek ≏	162	22.47 S	115.43 E
Wannian	100	28.42 N	117.03 E
Wanning	110	18.53 N	110.26 E
Wannsee ➜[8]	264a	52.25 N	13.09 E
Wanon Niwat	110	17.38 N	103.46 E
Wanouchi	94	35.17 N	136.38 E
Wānow	120	32.38 N	65.54 E
Wanparti	122	16.22 N	78.04 E
Wanquan	98	40.52 N	114.45 E
Wansbeck ≏	44	55.10 N	1.34 W
Wansdorf	264a	52.38 N	13.05 E
Wan-See → Van Gölü ⊜	128	38.33 N	42.46 E
Wanshan	107	30.23 N	106.06 E
Wanshouchang	107	29.26 N	105.55 E
Wanstead	172	40.08 S	176.32 E
Wanstead ➜[8]	260	51.34 N	0.02 E
Wantage	42	51.36 N	1.25 W
Wantagh	210	40.41 N	73.30 W
Wantan	102	30.03 N	110.18 E
Wantirna	274b	37.51 S	145.14 E
Wantirna South	274b	37.52 S	145.14 E
Wanxian, Zhg.	102	30.52 N	108.22 E
Wanxian, Zhg.	105	38.50 N	115.09 E
Wanyuan	102	32.04 N	108.02 E
Wanzai	100	28.06 N	114.27 E
Wanzarīk	146	27.31 N	13.29 E
Wanzhuang	105	39.34 N	116.36 E
Wanzleben	54	52.03 N	11.26 E
Wapack Range ⋏	207	42.48 N	71.52 W
Wapakoneta	216	40.34 N	84.11 W
Wapanucka	196	34.22 N	96.25 W
Wapato	202	46.26 N	120.25 W
Wapawekka Hills ⋏[2]	184	54.45 N	104.20 W
Wapawekka Lake ⊜	184	54.55 N	104.40 W
Wapella, Sk., Can.	184	50.15 N	102.00 W
Wapella, Il., U.S.	219	40.13 N	88.58 W
Wapello	190	41.10 N	91.11 W
Wapenamanda	164	5.35 S	143.55 E
Wapesi Lake ⊜	184	50.34 N	92.21 W
Wāpi	122	20.22 N	72.54 E
Wapinda	152	3.41 N	22.48 E
Wapinitia Pass)(	224	45.14 N	121.42 W
Wapisu Lake ⊜	184	55.47 N	99.11 W
Wapiti ≏	182	55.08 N	118.18 W
Wapizagonke, Lac ⊜	206	46.43 N	73.02 W
Waples	222	32.29 N	97.43 W
Wapoga ≏	164	2.42 S	136.06 E
Wappapello, Lake ⊜[1]	194	36.58 N	90.20 W
Wapping	207	41.50 N	72.33 W
Wappinger Creek ≏	210	41.35 N	73.57 W
Wappingers Falls	210	41.35 N	73.54 W
Wapsipinicon ≏	190	41.44 N	90.20 W
Waptus Lake ⊜	224	47.30 N	121.10 W
Wapus ≏	190	47.11 N	76.06 W
Wapus Lake ⊜	184	56.27 N	102.12 W
Waqf aṣ-Ṣawwān, Jibāl ⋏	132	30.53 N	36.48 E
Wāqid	142	30.42 N	30.44 E
Waqqāṣ	132	32.33 N	35.36 E
War	192	37.18 N	81.41 W
Wara	94	35.45 N	137.05 E
Warabi	94	35.49 N	139.41 E
Wārāh	120	27.27 N	67.48 E
Warakaraket I	164	2.15 S	130.36 E
Waramaug, Lake ⊜	207	41.42 N	73.22 W
Warangal	122	18.00 N	79.35 E
Wararisbari, Tanjung ›	164	1.05 S	136.23 E
Wārāseoni	120	21.45 N	80.02 E
Waratah, Austl.	166	41.27 S	145.32 E
Waratah, Austl.	170	32.54 S	151.44 E
Waratah Bay ⊂	166	38.51 S	146.04 E
Warboys	42	52.24 N	0.04 W
Warbreccan	166	24.18 S	142.51 E
Warburg	52	51.29 N	9.08 E
Warburton, Austl.	162	26.07 S	126.35 E
Warburton, Austl.	169	37.46 S	145.41 E
Warburton, Pāk.	123	31.33 N	73.50 E
Warburton, Eng., U.K.	262	53.24 N	2.27 W
Warburton Aboriginal Reserve ➜[4]	162	24.00 S	128.15 E
Warburton Bay ⊂	176	63.50 N	111.30 W
Warburton Creek ≏	166	27.55 S	137.28 E
Warchha	123	32.25 N	71.59 E
Ward, N.Z.	172	41.50 S	174.08 E
Ward, Pa., U.S.	285	39.53 N	75.31 W
Ward ≏	166	26.32 S	146.06 E
Ward, Mount ∧	172	43.52 S	169.50 E
Warda	222	30.03 N	96.55 W
Wardcliff	216	42.43 N	84.28 W
Ward Cove	182	55.24 N	131.44 W
Warden, S. Afr.	158	27.56 S	29.00 E
Warden, Wa., U.S.	202	46.58 N	119.02 W
Wardenburg	52	53.04 N	8.11 E
Warder	54	53.59 N	10.22 E
Wardersee ⊜	54	53.58 N	10.26 E
Wardha	122	20.45 N	78.37 E
Wardha ≏	122	19.38 N	79.48 E
Ward Hill ∧[2], Scot., U.K.	46	58.54 N	3.20 W
Ward Hill ∧[2], Scot., U.K.	46	58.57 N	3.09 W
Ward Hunt, Cape ›	164	8.05 S	149.55 E
Ward Hunt Strait ʊ	164	9.25 S	149.55 E
Wardle	44	53.39 N	2.08 W
Wardlow	182	50.54 N	111.33 W
Ward Mountain ∧	202	46.10 N	114.17 W
Wardner	182	49.25 N	115.26 W
Wardour, Vale of ∨	42	51.05 N	2.00 W
Wards Chapel	284b	39.24 N	76.52 W
Wards Island I	276	40.47 N	73.56 W
Ward's Stone ∧	44	54.02 N	2.38 W
Wardsville, On., Can.	214	42.39 N	81.45 W
Wardsville, Mo., U.S.	219	38.29 N	92.10 W
Wardswell Draw ∨	196	32.39 N	102.35 W
Wardt	52	51.41 N	6.25 E
Ware, Eng., U.K.	42	51.49 N	0.02 W
Ware, Ma., U.S.	207	42.15 N	72.14 W
Ware ≏	207	42.11 N	72.22 W
War Eagle Creek ≏	194	36.14 N	94.00 W
Waregem	50	50.53 N	3.25 E
Wareham, Eng., U.K.	42	50.41 N	2.07 W
Wareham, Ma., U.S.	207	41.45 N	70.43 W
Warehouse Point	207	41.55 N	72.37 W
Waremme	56	50.41 N	5.15 E
Waren, Dtsch.	54	53.31 N	12.40 E
Waren, Indon.	164	2.16 S	136.20 E
Warenai ≏	164	2.52 S	135.55 E
Warenda	166	22.37 S	140.32 E
Warendorf	52	51.57 N	7.59 E
Ware River ⊂	208	37.23 N	76.27 W
Ware Shoals	192	34.23 N	82.14 W
Waretown	208	39.47 N	74.11 W
Warffum	52	53.23 N	6.34 E
Warfusée-Abancourt	50	49.52 N	2.35 E
Warga	52	53.08 N	5.51 E
Wargalo	144	6.17 N	47.31 E
Wargla	148	31.59 N	5.25 E
Wargla □[5]	148	29.00 N	8.00 E
Warialda	166	29.32 S	150.34 E
Wariap	164	1.34 S	134.11 E
Warilau	164	5.24 S	134.30 E
Warilau, Pulau I	164	5.23 S	134.33 E
Warin	54	53.48 N	11.42 E
Warinanco Park ♦	276	40.39 N	74.14 W
Warin Chamrap	110	15.12 N	104.53 E
Waring Mountains ⋏	180	66.50 N	159.00 W
Wāris Alīganj	124	25.01 N	85.38 E
Warka	30	51.47 N	21.10 E
Warkopi	164	1.08 S	134.07 E
Warks Burn ≏	44	55.03 N	2.08 W
Warkworth, On., Can.	212	44.12 N	77.53 W
Warkworth, N.Z.	172	36.24 S	174.40 E
Warkworth, Eng., U.K.	44	55.21 N	1.36 W
Warland, Eng., U.K.	262	53.41 N	2.05 W
Warland, Mt., U.S.	182	48.30 N	115.17 W
Warland Reservoir ⊜[1]	262	53.41 N	2.04 W
Warley Moor Reservoir ⊜[1]	262	53.47 N	1.57 W
Warley → Smethwick	42	52.30 N	1.58 W
Warlingham	42	51.19 N	0.04 W
Warlington	42	51.39 N	1.01 W
Warman	184	52.20 N	106.34 W
Warmandi	164	0.22 S	132.39 E
Warmbad, Namibia	156	28.29 S	18.41 E
Warmbad, S. Afr.	156	24.55 S	28.15 E
Warm Baths → Warmbad	156	24.55 S	28.15 E
Warm Beach	224	48.10 N	122.21 W
War Memorial Cross ⊥	169	37.20 S	144.36 E
Warmenhuizen	52	52.43 N	4.44 E
Warmensteinach	60	49.59 N	11.47 E
Warmeriville	50	49.21 N	4.13 E
Warmington	42	52.08 N	1.24 W
Warminster, Eng., U.K.	42	51.13 N	2.12 W
Warminster, Pa., U.S.	208	40.12 N	75.06 W
Warminster Naval Air Development Center ■	285	40.12 N	75.09 W
Warm Springs, Ga., U.S.	192	32.53 N	84.40 W
Warm Springs, Mt., U.S.	202	46.11 N	112.48 W
Warm Springs, Or., U.S.	202	44.45 N	121.15 W
Warm Springs, Va., U.S.	192	38.02 N	79.47 W
Warm Springs ≏	202	44.52 N	121.04 W
Warm Springs Indian Reservation ➜[4]	224	45.00 N	121.25 W
Warm Springs Reservoir ⊜[1]	202	43.37 N	118.14 W
Warnbro Sound ʊ	168a	32.20 S	115.40 E
Warnemünde ➜[8]	54	54.10 N	12.04 E
Warner, Ab., Can.	182	49.17 N	112.12 W
Warner, N.H., U.S.	188	43.16 N	71.49 W
Warner, Ok., U.S.	196	35.29 N	95.18 W
Warner Lakes ⊜	202	42.25 N	119.50 W
Warner Mountains ⋏	204	41.40 N	120.20 W
Warner Peak ∧	202	42.27 N	119.44 W
Warner Ranch	228	33.56 N	117.13 W
Warner Robins	192	32.37 N	83.36 W
Warners	210	43.05 N	76.20 W
Warners Pond ⊜	283	42.28 N	71.24 W
Warnerville	210	42.34 N	74.30 W
Warnes, Arg.	252	34.55 S	60.31 W
Warnes, Bol.	248	17.30 S	63.10 W
Warnes Brook ≏	276	40.25 N	74.18 W
Warneton	50	50.45 N	2.57 E
Warngau	64	47.50 N	11.41 E
Warnicken → Primorje	76	54.57 N	20.02 E
Warnkenhagen	54	54.00 N	11.04 E
Warnow ≏	54	54.06 N	12.09 E
Warns	52	52.52 N	5.25 E
Warnsveld	52	52.08 N	6.13 E
Waroona	168a	32.50 S	115.55 E
Warpath ≏	184	52.21 N	98.26 W
Warra	166	26.56 S	150.55 E
Warrabri Aboriginal Reserve ➜[4]	162	21.00 S	134.20 E
Warracknabeal	166	36.15 S	142.24 E
Warr Acres	196	35.31 N	97.37 W
Warragamba Dam ➜[6]	170	33.54 S	150.36 E
Warragul	169	38.10 S	145.56 E
Warrandyte	274b	37.45 S	145.13 E
Warrandyte South	274b	37.46 S	145.14 E
Warrāq al-'Arab	273c	30.06 N	31.12 E
Warrāq al-Ḥaḍar, Jazīrat I	273c	30.07 N	31.13 E
Warrāq al-Hadar wa Ambūtbah wa Mīt an-Naṣārā	273c	30.06 N	31.13 E
Warrawagine	162	20.51 S	120.42 E
Warrawee	274a	33.44 S	151.07 E
Warrawolong, Mount ∧	170	33.03 S	151.15 E
Warrawong	170	34.29 S	150.53 E
Warrego ≏	166	30.24 S	145.21 E
Warrego Range ⋏	166	25.00 S	146.30 E
Warren, Austl.	166	31.42 S	147.50 E
Warren, Eng., U.K.	262	53.14 N	2.10 W
Warren, Ar., U.S.	194	33.36 N	92.03 W
Warren, Il., U.S.	190	42.29 N	89.59 W
Warren, In., U.S.	216	40.40 N	85.25 W
Warren, Ma., U.S.	207	42.12 N	72.11 W
Warren, Mi., U.S.	216	42.28 N	83.01 W
Warren, Mn., U.S.	198	48.11 N	96.46 W
Warren, Mo., U.S.	219	39.47 N	91.45 W
Warren, N.J., U.S.	276	40.37 N	74.30 W
Warren, Oh., U.S.	214	41.14 N	80.49 W
Warren, Or., U.S.	224	45.49 N	122.50 W
Warren, Pa., U.S.	214	41.50 N	79.08 W
Warren, R.I., U.S.	207	41.43 N	71.16 W
Warren □[6], In., U.S.	216	40.21 N	87.17 W
Warren □[6], Mo., U.S.	219	38.45 N	91.09 W
Warren □[6], N.J., U.S.	210	40.49 N	75.05 W
Warren □[6], N.Y., U.S.	210	43.26 N	73.43 W
Warren □[6], Oh., U.S.	218	39.26 N	84.13 W
Warren □[6], Pa., U.S.	214	41.51 N	79.08 W
Warren ≏	162	34.35 S	115.50 E
Warren City	222	32.33 N	94.54 W
Warrendale	214	40.39 N	80.04 W
Warren Dunes State Park ♦	216	41.56 N	86.36 W
Warren H. Manning State Park ♦	283	42.34 N	71.18 W
Warren Park	218	39.46 N	86.03 W
Warren Peaks ⋏	198	44.29 N	104.28 W
Warrenpoint	48	54.06 N	6.15 W
Warren Point ›	180	69.44 N	132.30 W
Warrens	190	44.07 N	90.29 W
Warrensburg, Il., U.S.	219	39.56 N	89.04 W
Warrensburg, Mo., U.S.	194	38.45 N	93.44 W
Warrensburg, N.Y., U.S.	188	43.29 N	73.46 W
Warrensville	210	41.19 N	76.57 W
Warrensville Heights	214	41.26 N	81.32 W
Warrenton, S. Afr.	158	28.09 S	24.47 E
Warrenton, Ga., U.S.	192	33.24 N	82.39 W
Warrenton, Mo., U.S.	219	38.48 N	91.08 W
Warrenton, N.C., U.S.	192	36.23 N	78.09 W
Warrenton, Or., U.S.	224	46.09 N	123.55 W
Warrenton, Tx., U.S.	222	30.01 N	96.44 W
Warrenton, Va., U.S.	188	38.42 N	77.47 W
Warrenville	216	41.49 N	88.10 W
Warrenzin	54	53.54 N	12.57 E
Warri	150	5.31 N	5.45 E
Warriedar Hill ∧[2]	162	29.06 S	117.06 E
Warriewood	274a	33.42 S	151.18 E
Warrill Creek ≏	171a	27.39 S	152.44 E
Warrington, N.Z.	172	45.43 S	170.35 E
Warrington, Eng., U.K.	44	53.24 N	2.37 W
Warrington, Fl., U.S.	194	30.23 N	87.16 W
Warrington, Pa., U.S.	285	40.15 N	75.08 W
Warrington □[8]	262	53.24 N	2.33 W
Warrington Airport ⊠	285	40.16 N	75.09 W
Warrior	194	33.48 N	86.48 W
Warrior Creek ≏	192	31.15 N	83.34 W
Warrior Reefs ✢[2]	164	9.35 S	143.10 E
Warriors Mark	214	40.42 N	78.08 W
Warrnambool	166	38.23 S	142.29 E
Warroad	198	48.54 N	95.18 W
Warrumbungle National Park ♦	166	31.20 S	149.00 E
Warsak	123	34.10 N	71.25 E
Warsaw, Il., U.S.	190	40.21 N	91.26 W
Warsaw, In., U.S.	216	41.14 N	85.51 W
Warsaw, Ky., U.S.	218	38.47 N	84.54 W
Warsaw, Mo., U.S.	194	38.14 N	93.22 W
Warsaw, N.Y., U.S.	210	42.44 N	78.07 W
Warsaw, N.C., U.S.	192	34.59 N	78.05 W
Warsaw, Oh., U.S.	214	40.20 N	82.00 W
Warsaw, Va., U.S.	208	37.57 N	76.45 W
Warsaw Station ➜[5]	265a	59.54 N	30.19 E
Warsaw → Warszawa	30	52.15 N	21.00 E
Warschau → Warszawa	30	52.15 N	21.00 E
Warscheneck ∧	61	47.39 N	14.14 E
Warshiikh	144	2.18 N	45.48 E
Warsop	44	53.13 N	1.09 W
Warspite	182	54.06 N	112.37 W
Warstein	56	51.26 N	8.21 E
Warszawa (Warsaw)	30	52.15 N	21.00 E
Warszawa □[4]	30	52.15 N	21.00 E
Warta	30	51.42 N	18.38 E
Warta ≏	30	52.35 N	14.39 E
Wartburg, S. Afr.	158	29.25 S	30.35 E
Wartburg, Tn., U.S.	192	36.06 N	84.35 W
Wartburg ⊥	54	50.58 N	10.18 E
Wartenberg	60	48.24 N	11.59 E
Wartenberg ➜[8]	264a	52.34 N	13.31 E
Warth	58	47.15 N	10.11 E
Warthan Creek ≏	226	36.08 N	120.20 W
Warthe → Warta ≏	30	52.35 N	14.39 E
Wartin	54	53.15 N	14.09 E
Warton, Eng., U.K.	44	54.09 N	2.47 W
Warton, Eng., U.K.	44	53.45 N	2.54 W
Warton Aerodrome ⊠	262	53.45 N	2.54 W
Wartrace	194	35.31 N	86.20 W
Wartsberg ∧[2]	263	51.25 N	6.29 E
Waru	164	3.24 S	130.40 E
Warud	120	21.28 N	78.16 E
Warunta, Laguna de ⊜	236	15.23 N	84.05 W
Waruta ≏	164	3.18 S	140.08 E
Warwick, Austl.	171a	28.13 S	152.02 E
Warwick, P.Q., Can.	206	45.56 N	71.59 W
Warwick, Eng., U.K.	42	52.17 N	1.34 W
Warwick, Md., U.S.	208	39.25 N	75.46 W
Warwick, N.Y., U.S.	210	41.15 N	74.21 W
Warwick, R.I., U.S.	207	41.41 N	71.22 W
Warwick ≏	208	37.05 N	76.33 W
Warwick Castle ⊥	42	52.17 N	1.34 W
Warwick Channel ʊ	164	13.51 S	136.16 E
Warwick Farm Racecourse and Motor Race Track ♦	274a	33.55 S	150.57 E
Warwickshire □[6]	42	52.13 N	1.37 W
Warza	54	51.00 N	10.41 E
Wasaga Beach	212	44.31 N	80.01 W
Wasagu	150	11.25 N	5.49 E
Wasatch Mountain State Park ♦	200	40.33 N	111.31 W
Wasatch Plateau ⋏[1]	200	39.20 N	111.30 W
Wasatch Range ⋏	200	40.40 N	111.35 W
Wasāwewāla	123	30.28 N	73.40 E
Wasbank	158	28.24 S	30.05 E
Wasbister	46	59.10 N	3.07 W
Wascana Creek ≏	184	50.39 N	104.55 W
Wäschenbeuren	56	48.46 N	9.41 E
Wasco, Ca., U.S.	226	35.35 N	119.20 W
Wasco, Or., U.S.	224	45.35 N	120.41 W
Wasco □[6]	224	45.10 N	121.12 W
Wase	150	9.06 N	9.59 E
Wase ≏	146	8.27 N	10.06 E
Waseca	190	44.04 N	93.30 W
Waseda University ⊎[2]	268	35.42 N	139.43 E
Wasekamio Lake ⊜	184	56.45 N	108.45 W
Wasen	58	47.03 N	7.48 E
Wasgomuwa National Park ♦	122	7.40 N	80.45 E
Washademoak Lake ⊜	186	45.48 N	65.58 W
Washago	212	44.45 N	79.20 W
Washburn, Il., U.S.	190	40.55 N	89.17 W
Washburn, Me., U.S.	186	46.47 N	68.09 W
Washburn, N.D., U.S.	198	47.17 N	101.01 W
Washburn, Wi., U.S.	190	46.40 N	90.53 W
Washburn ≏	44	53.54 N	1.39 W
Washburn, Mount ∧	202	44.48 N	110.25 W
Washburn Lake ⊜	176	70.03 N	106.50 W
Washdyke	172	44.21 S	171.14 E
Washicoutai	186	50.17 N	60.42 W
Washiga-take ∧	94	35.56 N	136.58 E
Wāshīm	122	20.06 N	77.09 E
Washimiya	94	36.06 N	139.40 E
Washington, Eng., U.K.	44	54.55 N	1.30 W
Washington, Ca., U.S.	226	39.22 N	120.48 W
Washington, Ct., U.S.	207	41.37 N	73.18 W
Washington, D.C., U.S.	208	38.53 N	77.02 W
Washington, D.C., U.S.	284c	38.53 N	77.02 W
Washington, Ga., U.S.	192	33.44 N	82.44 W
Washington, Il., U.S.	190	40.42 N	89.24 W
Washington, In., U.S.	194	38.39 N	87.10 W
Washington, Ia., U.S.	190	41.17 N	91.41 W
Washington, Ks., U.S.	198	39.49 N	97.03 W
Washington, Ky., U.S.	218	38.36 N	83.48 W
Washington, La., U.S.	194	30.36 N	92.03 W
Washington, Mi., U.S.	214	42.44 N	83.02 W
Washington, Mo., U.S.	219	38.33 N	91.01 W
Washington, N.J., U.S.	210	40.45 N	74.58 W
Washington, N.C., U.S.	192	35.31 N	77.01 W
Washington, Pa., U.S.	214	40.10 N	80.14 W
Washington, Tx., U.S.	222	30.20 N	96.10 W
Washington, Ut,. U.S.	200	37.07 N	113.30 W
Washington, Va., U.S.	188	38.42 N	78.09 W
Washington □[6], Il., U.S.	219	38.21 N	89.23 W
Washington □[6], In., U.S.	218	38.36 N	86.06 W
Washington □[6], N.Y., U.S.	210	43.15 N	73.27 W
Washington □[6], Or., U.S.	224	45.33 N	123.07 W
Washington □[6], Pa., U.S.	214	40.10 N	80.15 W
Washington □[6], R.I., U.S.	207	41.28 N	71.35 W
Washington □[6], Tx., U.S.	222	30.15 N	96.20 W
Washington □[6], Wi., U.S.	216	43.14 N	88.15 W
Washington □[3], U.S.	178	47.30 N	120.30 W
Washington □[3], U.S.	202	47.30 N	120.30 W
Washington, Lake ⊜, Fl., U.S.	220	28.07 N	80.45 W
Washington, Lake ⊜, Wa., U.S.	224	47.37 N	122.15 W
Washington, Mount ∧	188	44.15 N	71.15 W
Washington Court House	218	39.32 N	83.26 W
Washington Crossing	208	40.17 N	74.52 W
Washington Crossing State Historic Site ⊥	208	40.17 N	74.53 W
Washington Depot	207	41.38 N	73.18 W
Washington Heights ➜[8]	276	40.52 N	73.56 W
Washington Island	190	45.23 N	86.55 W
Washington Island I	190	45.23 N	86.55 W
Washington Memorial Chapel ⊎[1]	285	40.06 N	75.26 W
Washington Mills	210	43.03 N	75.16 W
Washington Monument ♦	284c	38.53 N	77.03 W
Washington Monument State Park ♦	208	39.30 N	77.38 W
Washington National Airport ⊠	208	38.51 N	77.02 W
Washington-on-the-Brazos State Historic Park ♦	222	30.20 N	96.09 W
Washington Park	219	38.38 N	90.05 W
Washington Park ♦, Il., U.S.	278	41.48 N	87.37 W
Washington Park ♦, Oh., U.S.	279a	41.27 N	81.40 W
Washington Pass)(	224	48.32 N	120.39 W
Washington Place	218	39.47 N	86.01 W
Washington Rock State Park ♦	276	40.37 N	74.28 W
Washington's Headquarters ⊥	285	40.06 N	75.28 W
Washington Terrace	200	41.10 N	111.58 W
Washington Township	276	40.54 N	74.00 W
Washington Valley	276	40.48 N	74.32 W
Washington Valley Reservoir ⊜[1]	276	40.36 N	74.34 W
Washingtonville, N.Y., U.S.	210	41.26 N	74.10 W
Washingtonville, Oh., U.S.	214	40.54 N	80.46 W
Washingtonville, Pa., U.S.	210	41.03 N	76.40 W
Washita ≏	196	34.12 N	96.50 W
Washoe □[6]	226	39.22 N	119.43 W
Washoe Lake ⊜	226	39.16 N	119.48 W
Washougal	224	45.34 N	122.21 W
Washougal ≏	224	45.35 N	122.23 W
Washow Bay ⊂	184	51.22 N	96.47 W
Washtenaw □[6]	216	42.15 N	83.50 W
Washtucna	202	46.45 N	118.18 W
Wāshuk	128	27.44 N	64.48 E
Wasian	164	1.54 S	133.17 E
Wasilków	30	53.12 N	23.12 E
Wasilla	180	61.35 N	149.26 W
Wasior	164	2.43 S	134.30 E
Wasiri	112	7.35 S	126.38 E
Wāsiṭ □[4]	128	32.45 N	45.25 E
Waskada	184	49.06 N	100.46 W
Waskaganish	176	51.30 N	78.45 W
Waskahigan ≏	182	54.45 N	117.12 W
Waskaiowaka Lake ⊜	184	56.30 N	96.20 W
Waskatenau	182	54.07 N	112.47 W
Waskesiu Lake ⊜	184	53.56 N	106.10 W
Waskom	194	32.29 N	94.04 W
Wąsosz	30	51.34 N	16.42 E
Waspam	236	14.44 N	83.58 W
Waspuk ≏	236	14.38 N	84.26 W
Wasquehal	50	50.40 N	3.09 E
Wassaic	210	41.48 N	73.35 W
Wasselonne	58	48.38 N	7.27 E
Wassen	58	46.42 N	8.36 E
Wassenaar	52	52.07 N	4.24 E
Wassenberg	56	51.06 N	6.08 E
Wasseralfingen	56	48.52 N	10.06 E
Wasserbillig	56	49.44 N	6.30 E
Wasserburg am Inn	60	48.04 N	12.13 E
Wasserkuppe ∧	56	50.30 N	9.56 E
Wasserkurl	263	51.33 N	7.38 E
Wasserleben	54	51.55 N	10.44 E
Wassertrüdingen	56	49.02 N	10.35 E
Wassigny	50	50.01 N	3.36 E
Wass Lake ⊜	184	53.40 N	95.25 W
Wassmannsdorf	264a	52.22 N	13.28 E
Wassou	150	10.02 N	13.39 W
Wassy	58	48.30 N	4.57 E
Wast Water ⊜	44	54.26 N	3.18 W
Wasu	164	6.00 S	147.15 E
Wasum	164	6.05 S	149.20 E
Wasungen	54	50.40 N	10.22 E
Watabeag Lake ⊜	190	48.14 N	80.32 W
Watampone (Bone)	112	4.32 S	120.20 E
Watamu Marine National Park ♦	154	3.23 S	40.00 E
Waṭan, Wādī al- ∨	142	30.26 N	31.49 E
Watansopeng	112	4.21 S	119.53 E
Watapi Lake ⊜	184	55.18 N	109.35 W
Watarai	94	34.26 N	136.37 E
Watarase ≏	94	36.13 N	139.42 E
Wataru I	122	5.43 N	73.23 E
Watatic, Mount ∧	207	42.42 N	71.53 W
Watauga	222	32.51 N	97.15 W
Watchet	42	51.12 N	3.20 W
Watch Hill	207	41.18 N	71.51 W
Watchung	276	40.38 N	74.27 W
Watchung Reservation ♦	276	40.41 N	74.23 W
Water	262	53.44 N	2.14 W
Waterbeach	42	52.16 N	0.11 E
Waterberg	156	20.28 S	17.13 E
Waterberge ⋏	156	24.30 S	28.00 E
Waterberg Plateau Park ♦	156	20.30 S	17.00 E
Waterbury, Ct., U.S.	207	41.33 N	73.02 W
Waterbury, Vt., U.S.	188	44.20 N	72.45 W
Waterdale	158	30.40 S	24.02 E
Wateree ≏	192	33.45 N	80.37 W
Wateree Lake ⊜[1]	192	34.25 N	80.50 W
Waterend, Eng., U.K.	260	51.47 N	0.30 W
Water End, Eng., U.K.	262	53.41 N	2.15 W
Waterfall, Austl.	170	34.08 S	151.00 E
Waterfall, Pa., U.S.	214	40.08 N	78.04 W
Waterford, On., Can.	212	42.56 N	80.17 W
Waterford (Port Láirge), Ire.	48	52.15 N	7.06 W
Waterford, S. Afr.	158	33.05 S	25.00 E
Waterford, Ca., U.S.	226	37.38 N	120.46 W
Waterford, Ct., U.S.	207	41.20 N	72.09 W
Waterford, In., U.S.	216	41.40 N	86.50 W
Waterford, Mi., U.S.	216	42.42 N	83.24 W
Waterford, N.Y., U.S.	210	42.47 N	73.40 W
Waterford, Pa., U.S.	214	41.56 N	79.59 W
Waterford, Wi., U.S.	216	42.45 N	88.12 W
Waterford □[6]	48	52.10 N	7.40 W
Waterford Harbour ⊂	48	52.10 N	6.55 W
Waterford Mills	216	41.33 N	85.50 W
Waterford Works	208	39.43 N	74.50 W
Watergate Bay ⊂	42	50.27 N	5.05 W
Watergrasshill	48	52.01 N	8.21 W
Watergrove Reservoir ⊜[1]	262	53.39 N	2.08 W
Waterhen ≏	184	54.38 N	107.47 W
Waterhen Lake ⊜, Mb., Can.	184	52.06 N	99.34 W
Waterhen Lake ⊜, Sk., Can.	184	54.28 N	108.25 W
Waterhouse Range ⋏	162	24.01 S	133.25 E
Wateringbury	260	51.15 N	0.25 E
Wateringen	52	52.02 N	4.16 E
Water Island	276	40.41 N	73.02 W
Waterkloof	158	30.19 S	25.18 E
Waterloo, Austl.	164	16.38 S	129.18 E
Waterloo, Austl.	168a	33.20 S	115.47 E
Waterloo, Austl.	168b	33.59 S	138.53 E
Waterloo, Bel.	50	50.43 N	4.23 E
Waterloo, On., Can.	212	43.28 N	80.31 W
Waterloo, P.Q., Can.	206	45.21 N	72.31 W
Waterloo, S.L.	150	8.20 N	13.04 W
Waterloo, Eng., U.K.	44	53.28 N	3.02 W
Waterloo, Al., U.S.	194	34.55 N	88.03 W
Waterloo, Il., U.S.	219	38.20 N	90.08 W
Waterloo, In., U.S.	216	41.25 N	85.01 W
Waterloo, Ia., U.S.	190	42.29 N	92.20 W
Waterloo, N.Y., U.S.	210	42.54 N	76.51 W
Waterloo, Wi., U.S.	216	43.11 N	88.59 W
Waterloo □[6]	212	43.30 N	80.30 W
Waterloo Bay ⊂	168b	35.08 S	137.26 E
Waterloo State Recreation Area ♦	216	42.22 N	84.20 W
Waterlooville	42	50.53 N	1.02 W
Waterman, Il., U.S.	216	41.46 N	88.46 W
Waterman, Wa., U.S.	224	47.34 N	122.35 W
Waterman Mountain ∧	228	34.20 N	117.56 W
Waterman Wash ∨	200	33.21 N	112.31 W
Water Mill	207	40.55 N	72.21 W
Waterport	210	43.20 N	78.16 W
Waterport Pond ⊜[1]	212	43.19 N	78.16 W
Waterproof	194	31.48 N	91.23 W
Waterside	214	40.11 N	78.23 W
Waterside Park	276	40.56 N	73.20 W
Watersmeet	190	46.16 N	89.10 W
Waterton ≏	182	49.32 N	113.16 W
Waterton-Glacier International Peace Park ♦	202	48.47 N	113.45 W
Waterton Lakes National Park ♦	182	49.05 N	113.50 W
Watertown, Ct., U.S.	207	41.36 N	73.07 W
Watertown, Ma., U.S.	207	42.22 N	71.11 W
Watertown, N.Y., U.S.	212	43.58 N	75.54 W
Watertown, S.D., U.S.	198	44.53 N	97.06 W
Watertown, Wi., U.S.	216	43.11 N	88.43 W
Waterval-Boven	156	25.40 S	30.20 E
Watervale	168b	33.57 S	138.38 E
Water Valley, Ms., U.S.	194	34.09 N	89.37 W
Water Valley, N.Y., U.S.	284a	42.42 N	78.51 W
Water View	208	37.43 N	76.36 W
Waterville, N.S., Can.	186	45.03 N	64.41 W
Waterville, P.Q., Can.	206	45.16 N	71.54 W
Waterville, Ire.	48	51.49 N	10.13 W
Waterville, Ks., U.S.	198	39.41 N	96.44 W
Waterville, Me., U.S.	188	44.33 N	69.37 W
Waterville, Ma., U.S.	207	42.40 N	72.04 W
Waterville, Mn., U.S.	190	44.13 N	93.34 W
Waterville, N.Y., U.S.	210	42.55 N	75.22 W
Waterville, Oh., U.S.	216	41.30 N	83.43 W
Waterville, Pa., U.S.	210	41.19 N	77.22 W
Waterville, Wa., U.S.	202	47.38 N	120.04 W
Watervliet, Mi., U.S.	216	42.11 N	86.15 W
Watervliet, N.Y., U.S.	210	42.43 N	73.42 W
Watervliet Reservoir ⊜[1]	210	42.43 N	73.58 W
Wates, Indon.	114	1.00 N	100.16 E
Wates, Indon.	115a	7.55 S	112.07 E
Wates, Indon.	115a	7.51 S	110.10 E
Watford, On., Can.	214	42.57 N	81.53 W
Watford, Eng., U.K.	42	51.40 N	0.25 W
Watford □[8]	260	51.40 N	0.25 W
Watford City	198	47.48 N	103.16 W
Wa'th	140	8.10 N	32.07 E
Wathaman ≏	184	57.16 N	102.52 W
Wathaman Lake ⊜	184	56.55 N	103.43 W
Wathena	198	39.45 N	94.56 W
Watheroo	162	30.17 S	116.04 E
Watheroo National Park ♦	162	30.14 S	115.52 E
Wathlingen	52	52.32 N	10.09 E
Wath upon Dearne	44	53.29 N	1.20 W
Wati	120	28.02 N	96.59 E
Watino	182	55.43 N	117.37 W
Watkins Glen	210	42.22 N	76.52 W
Watkins Glen International Raceway ♦	210	42.20 N	76.55 W
Watkins Glen State Park ♦	210	42.22 N	76.55 W
Watkins Island I	284c	39.02 N	77.17 W
Watkins Lake ⊜	281	42.40 N	83.22 W
Watkinsville	192	33.51 N	83.24 W
Watlaar	164	5.28 S	133.07 E
Watling Island → San Salvador I	238	24.02 N	74.28 W
Watlington	42	51.37 N	1.00 W
Watoga State Park ♦	188	38.07 N	80.05 W
Watonga	196	35.50 N	98.24 W
Watonwan ≏	198	44.04 N	94.07 W
Watopeka ≏	206	45.34 N	72.00 W
Watou	50	50.51 N	2.37 E
Wat Phai Tan, Khlong ≊	269a	13.48 N	100.33 E
Watrous, Sk., Can.	184	51.40 N	105.28 W
Watrous, N.M., U.S.	200	35.47 N	104.58 W
Watsa	154	3.03 N	29.32 E
Watseka	216	40.46 N	87.44 W
Watsi Kengo	152	0.48 S	20.33 E
Watson, Austl.	162	30.29 S	131.31 E
Watson, Sk., Can.	184	52.07 N	104.31 W
Watson, In., U.S.	218	38.22 N	85.41 W
Watsonia	274b	37.43 S	145.05 E
Watson Lake	180	60.07 N	128.48 W
Watsons Bay	274a	33.51 S	151.17 E
Watsons Creek	274b	37.40 S	145.13 E
Watsons Creek ≏	274b	37.43 S	145.16 E
Watsontown	210	41.05 N	76.51 W
Watsonville	226	36.54 N	121.45 W
Watt	222	31.39 N	96.51 W
Watten	50	50.50 N	2.13 E
Watten, Loch ⊜	46	58.29 N	3.19 W
Wattens	64	47.17 N	11.36 E
Wattenscheid	56	51.29 N	7.08 E
Wattenwil	58	46.46 N	7.30 E
Wattignies	50	50.35 N	3.03 E
Wattiwarriganna ≏	162	28.57 S	136.10 E
Wattle Flat	170	33.08 S	149.41 E
Wattle Glen	274b	37.40 S	145.11 E
Wattle Park ♦	274b	37.50 S	145.07 E
Watt Mountain ∧	240d	15.19 N	61.19 W
Watton	42	52.35 N	0.48 E
Wattrelos	50	50.42 N	3.13 E
Watts ➜[8]	280	33.56 N	118.15 W
Watts Bar Lake ⊜[1]	192	35.48 N	84.39 W
Watts Branch ≏	284c	39.03 N	77.15 W
Wattsburg	214	42.00 N	79.49 W
Watts Island I	208	37.48 N	75.53 W
Watts Mills	192	34.31 N	82.02 W
Wattville	273d	26.13 S	28.18 E
Wattwil	58	47.18 N	9.06 E
Watu	152	3.18 S	20.03 E
Watubela, Kepulauan II	164	4.35 S	131.40 E
Wat Wat	164	4.29 S	152.21 E
Watzekopf ∧	58	46.59 N	10.48 E
Watzmann ∧	64	47.33 N	12.55 E
Wau	164	7.20 S	146.45 E
Waubach	56	50.55 N	6.03 E
Waubaushene	212	44.45 N	79.42 W
Waubaushene Channel ʊ	212	44.46 N	79.45 W
Waubay	198	45.19 N	97.18 W
Waubay Lake ⊜	198	45.25 N	97.25 W
Waubesa, Lake ⊜	216	43.01 N	89.20 W
Waubra	169	37.21 S	143.39 E
Waubuno Creek ≏	212	42.58 N	81.08 W
Wauchope, Austl.	162	20.36 S	134.15 E
Wauchope, Austl.	166	31.27 S	152.44 E
Wauchula	220	27.32 N	81.48 W
Wauconda, Il., U.S.	216	42.15 N	88.08 W
Wauconda, Wa., U.S.	182	48.43 N	119.00 W
Wauconda, Wa., U.S.	202	48.43 N	119.00 W
Waugh	184	49.40 N	95.13 W
Waugh Mountain ∧	202	45.29 N	114.47 W
Waukara, Bukit ∧	112	1.15 S	119.42 E
Waukaringa	166	32.18 S	139.26 E
Waukarlycarly, Lake ⊜	162	21.25 S	121.50 E
Waukegan	216	42.21 N	87.50 W
Waukena	226	36.08 N	119.31 W
Waukesha	216	43.00 N	88.13 W
Waukesha □[6]	216	43.02 N	88.20 W
Waukomis	196	36.16 N	97.53 W
Waukon	190	43.16 N	91.28 W
Waulsort	56	50.13 N	4.52 E
Wauna	224	47.22 N	122.38 W
Waunakee	216	43.11 N	89.27 W
Wauneta	198	40.25 N	101.22 W
Waupaca	190	44.21 N	89.05 W
Waupecan Creek ≏	216	41.20 N	88.28 W
Waupoos Island I	212	43.59 N	76.58 W
Waupun	190	43.38 N	88.43 W
Wauregan	207	41.44 N	71.54 W
Waurika	196	34.10 N	97.59 W
Waurika Lake ⊜[1]	196	34.15 N	98.05 W
Wausa	198	42.29 N	97.32 W
Wausau	190	44.57 N	89.37 W
Wausaukee	190	45.22 N	87.57 W
Wauseon	216	41.32 N	84.08 W
Waushakum Pond ⊜	283	42.16 N	71.26 W
Wautoma	190	44.04 N	89.17 W
Wauwa	154	3.27 N	27.21 E
Wauwatosa	216	43.02 N	88.00 W
Wauzeka	190	43.05 N	90.52 W
Wave Hill	162	17.29 S	130.57 E
Waveland, Ma., U.S.	283	42.17 N	70.53 W
Waveland, Ms., U.S.	194	30.17 N	89.22 W
Waveney ≏	42	52.28 N	1.45 E
Waver ≏	44	54.52 N	3.17 W
Waverley, Austl.	169	37.53 S	145.10 E
Waverley, Austl.	274a	33.54 S	151.16 E
Waverley, N.Z.	172	39.46 S	174.38 E
Waverley, S. Afr.	158	31.58 S	26.28 E
Waverley, Ma., U.S.	283	42.23 N	71.11 W
Waverley ➜[8]	273d	26.08 S	28.04 E
Waverly, Al., U.S.	194	32.44 N	85.35 W
Waverly, Fl., U.S.	220	27.59 N	81.37 W
Waverly, Il., U.S.	219	39.35 N	89.57 W
Waverly, Ia., U.S.	190	42.43 N	92.28 W
Waverly, Ks., U.S.	198	38.23 N	95.36 W
Waverly, Mi., U.S.	216	42.44 N	84.33 W
Waverly, Mn., U.S.	190	45.04 N	93.57 W
Waverly, Mo., U.S.	194	39.12 N	93.31 W
Waverly, Ne., U.S.	198	40.55 N	96.31 W
Waverly, N.Y., U.S.	210	42.00 N	76.31 W
Waverly, Oh., U.S.	218	39.07 N	82.59 W
Waverly, Pa., U.S.	210	41.32 N	75.42 W
Waverly, Tn., U.S.	194	36.05 N	87.47 W

≏ River	Fluß	Río	Rivière	Rio
≊ Canal	Kanal	Canal	Canal	Canal
ʟ Waterfall, Rapids	Wasserfall, Stromschnellen	Cascada, Rápidos	Chute d'eau, Rapides	Cascata, Rápidos
ʊ Strait	Meeresstraße	Estrecho	Détroit	Estreito
⊂ Bay, Gulf	Bucht, Golf	Bahía, Golfo	Baie, Golfe	Baía, Golfo
⊜ Lake, Lakes	See, Seen	Lago, Lagos	Lac, Lacs	Lago, Lagos
≡ Swamp	Sumpf	Pantano	Marais	Pântano
⊓ Ice Features, Glacier	Eis- und Gletscherformen	Accidentes Glaciales	Formes glaciaires	Acidentes glaciares
⍑ Other Hydrographic Features	Andere Hydrographische Objekte	Otros Elementos Hidrográficos	Autres données hydrographiques	Outros acidentes hidrográficos

✢ Submarine Features	Untermeerische Objekte	Accidentes Submarinos	Formes de relief sous-marin	Acidentes submarinos
□ Political Unit	Politische Einheit	Unidad Politica	Entité politique	Unidade política
⊎ Cultural Institution	Kulturelle Institution	Institución Cultural	Institution culturelle	Instituição cultural
⊥ Historical Site	Historische Stätte	Sitio Histórico	Site historique	Sitio histórico
♦ Recreational Site	Erholungs- und Ferienort	Sitio de Recreo	Centre de loisirs	Area de Lazer
⊠ Airport	Flughafen	Aeropuerto	Aéroport	Aeroporto
■ Military Installation	Militäranlage	Instalación Militar	Installation militaire	Instalação militar
➜ Miscellaneous	Verschiedenes	Misceláneo	Divers	Diversos

Name (ENGLISH) / Name (DEUTSCH)	Page / Seite	Lat.°′ / Breite°′	Long.°′ / Länge°′ E = Ost
Waverly, Va., U.S.	208	37.02 N	77.05 W
Waverly Hall	192	32.41 N	84.44 W
Wavre	56	50.43 N	4.37 E
Wavrin	50	50.34 N	2.55 E
Wāw	140	7.42 N	28.00 E
Wāw ≃	140	7.03 N	27.13 E
Wawa, On., Can.	190	47.59 N	84.47 W
Wawa, Nig.	150	9.55 N	4.25 E
Wawa, Sūd.	140	20.26 N	30.21 E
Wawa ≃	236	13.53 N	83.28 W
Wawaka	216	41.27 N	85.28 W
Wāw al-Kabīr	146	25.20 N	16.43 E
Wawanesa	184	49.36 N	99.41 W
Wawarsing	210	41.46 N	74.21 W
Wawasee, Lake ⊜	216	41.24 N	85.41 W
Wawayanda State Park ♦	276	41.11 N	74.26 W
Wawiag ≃	190	48.25 N	91.07 W
Wawoi ≃	164	8.01 S	143.33 E
Waworada, Teluk c	115b	8.44 S	118.51 E
Wawota	184	49.55 N	102.00 W
Waxahachie	222	32.23 N	96.50 W
Waxahachie, Lake ⊜[1]	222	32.20 N	96.49 W
Waxhaw	192	34.55 N	80.44 W
Waxuecun	106	31.07 N	121.38 E
Waxweiler	56	50.05 N	6.22 E
Way, Lake ⊜	162	26.48 S	120.18 E
Waya I	175g	17.18 S	177.08 E
Wayabula	108	2.17 N	128.12 E
Wayaopu	106	30.33 N	118.53 E
Waycross	192	31.12 N	82.21 W
Wayi	154	5.11 N	30.10 E
Wayland, Ia., U.S.	190	41.08 N	91.39 W
Wayland, Ky., U.S.	192	37.26 N	82.48 W
Wayland, Ma., U.S.	283	42.21 N	71.21 W
Wayland, Mi., U.S.	216	42.40 N	85.38 W
Wayland, N.Y., U.S.	210	42.34 N	77.35 W
Wayland, Oh., U.S.	214	41.10 N	81.04 W
Waylyn	192	32.51 N	79.59 W
Waymansville	218	39.04 N	86.03 W
Waymart	210	41.34 N	75.24 W
Wayne, Ab., Can.	182	51.23 N	112.39 W
Wayne, Mi., U.S.	216	42.16 N	83.23 W
Wayne, Ne., U.S.	198	42.13 N	97.01 W
Wayne, N.J., U.S.	210	40.55 N	74.16 W
Wayne, N.Y., U.S.	210	42.28 N	77.06 W
Wayne, Oh., U.S.	214	41.18 N	83.28 W
Wayne, Ok., U.S.	196	34.55 N	97.18 W
Wayne, Pa., U.S.	208	40.02 N	75.23 W
Wayne, W.V., U.S.	188	38.13 N	82.26 W
Wayne □[6], Il., U.S.	219	38.25 N	88.40 W
Wayne □[6], In., U.S.	218	39.50 N	84.54 W
Wayne □[6], Mi., U.S.	216	42.14 N	83.12 W
Wayne □[6], N.Y., U.S.	210	43.04 N	77.00 W
Wayne □[6], Oh., U.S.	214	40.48 N	81.56 W
Wayne □[6], Pa., U.S.	210	41.34 N	75.16 W
Wayne City	194	38.20 N	88.35 W
Wayne Lakes	218	40.01 N	84.39 W
Waynesboro, Ga., U.S.	192	33.05 N	82.00 W
Waynesboro, Ms., U.S.	194	31.40 N	88.38 W
Waynesboro, Pa., U.S.	208	39.45 N	77.34 W
Waynesboro, Tn., U.S.	194	35.19 N	87.45 W
Waynesboro, Va., U.S.	192	38.04 N	78.53 W
Waynesburg, Oh., U.S.	214	40.40 N	81.15 W
Waynesburg, Pa., U.S.	188	39.53 N	80.10 W
Waynesfield	216	40.36 N	83.59 W
Wayne State University ⊍[2]	281	42.21 N	83.04 W
Waynesville, Il., U.S.	194	40.15 N	89.08 W
Waynesville, Mo., U.S.	194	37.49 N	92.12 W
Waynesville, N.C., U.S.	192	35.29 N	82.59 W
Waynesville, Oh., U.S.	218	39.32 N	84.05 W
Waynoka	196	36.34 N	98.52 W
Waynoka, Lake ⊜[1]	218	38.55 N	83.47 W
Wayoh Reservoir ⊜[1]	262	53.39 N	2.24 W
Waza	146	11.25 N	14.34 E
Waza, Parc National de ♦	146	11.20 N	13.40 E
Wazah	120	33.22 N	69.26 E
Wāzah Khwāh	120	32.12 N	68.21 E
Waziers	50	50.23 N	3.07 E
Wāzin	146	31.57 N	10.40 E
Wazīrābād	123	32.27 N	74.07 E
Wazīrābād ◆[8]	272a	28.43 N	77.14 E
Wāzirpur ◆[8]	272a	28.41 N	77.10 E
Wazuka	96	34.47 N	135.55 E
Wazuka ≃	270	34.45 N	135.53 E
Wda ≃	30	53.25 N	18.29 E
We, Pulau I	114	5.51 N	95.18 E
Wea Creek ≃	216	40.24 N	86.57 W
Weagamow Lake ⊜	184	52.53 N	91.22 W
Weald Park ♦	260	51.38 N	0.14 E
Wealdstone ◆[8]	260	51.36 N	0.20 W
Weam	164	8.40 S	141.08 E
Wear ≃	44	54.55 N	1.22 W
Wearhead	44	54.45 N	2.13 W
Wearyan ≃	164	15.57 S	136.51 E
Weatherford, Ok., U.S.	196	35.31 N	98.42 W
Weatherford, Tx., U.S.	222	32.45 N	97.47 W
Weatherford, Lake ⊜[1]	222	32.47 N	97.41 W
Weatherly	210	40.56 N	75.50 W
Weatogue	207	41.51 N	72.49 W
Weaubleau	194	37.53 N	93.32 W
Weaver, Austl.	168b	34.56 S	137.40 E
Weaver, Al., U.S.	194	33.45 N	85.48 W
Weaver, Tx., U.S.	222	33.10 N	95.25 W
Weaver ≃	44	53.18 N	2.43 W
Weaverham	44	53.16 N	2.35 W
Weaver Lake ⊜	184	52.45 N	96.35 W
Weavertown	279b	40.16 N	80.11 W
Weaverville, Ca., U.S.	204	40.43 N	122.56 W
Weaverville, N.C., U.S.	192	35.41 N	82.33 W
Webau	54	51.10 N	12.04 E
Webb, Sk., Can.	184	50.11 N	108.12 W
Webb, Ms., U.S.	194	33.56 N	90.20 W
Webb Brook ≃	283	42.32 N	71.14 W
Webb City	194	37.08 N	94.27 W
Webber Lake ⊜	184	54.28 N	94.00 W
Webberville	216	42.40 N	84.10 W
Webbwood	190	46.16 N	81.53 W
Weber ≃	200	41.13 N	112.16 W
Weber, Mount ∧	182	55.32 N	128.31 W
Weber City	192	36.37 N	82.33 W
Weber Creek ≃	226	38.46 N	121.00 W
Weber Hill	219	38.27 N	90.34 W
Weberi Bekera	144	9.39 N	39.03 E
Webster, Ab., Can.	182	55.26 N	118.42 W
Webster, Fl., U.S.	220	28.36 N	82.03 W
Webster, In., U.S.	218	39.54 N	84.57 W
Webster, Ma., U.S.	207	42.03 N	71.52 W
Webster, N.Y., U.S.	210	43.12 N	77.25 W
Webster, Pa., U.S.	214	40.11 N	79.50 W
Webster, S.D., U.S.	198	45.19 N	97.31 W
Webster, Wi., U.S.	190	45.52 N	92.22 W
Webster City	190	42.28 N	93.48 W
Webster Crossing	210	42.40 N	77.38 W
Webster Groves	219	38.35 N	90.21 W
Webster Lake ⊜	216	41.19 N	85.41 W
Websters Corners, B.C., Can.	224	49.13 N	122.30 W
Websters Corners, N.Y., U.S.	284a	41.47 N	78.45 W
Webster Springs	188	38.28 N	80.24 W
Weches	222	31.33 N	95.14 W
Wechmar	54	50.53 N	10.47 E
Wechselburg	54	51.00 N	12.47 E
Weda	108	0.21 N	127.52 E
Wedau ◆[8]	263	51.24 N	6.48 E
Wedau, Sportpark ♦	263	51.25 N	6.47 E
Weddell Island I	254	51.55 S	61.00 W
Weddell Sea ∓[2]	9	72.00 S	45.00 W
Wedderburn	166	36.25 S	143.37 E
Wedding ◆[8]	264a	52.33 N	13.22 E
Weddinghofen	263	51.36 N	7.37 E
Wedel	52	53.35 N	9.41 E
Wedemark	52	52.33 N	9.44 E
Wedge, Central Mount ∧	162	22.51 S	131.50 E
Wedge Mountain ∧	182	50.10 N	122.50 W
Wedgeport	186	43.44 N	65.59 W
Wedgewood	219	38.47 N	90.17 W
Wedmore	42	51.14 N	2.49 W
Wedowee	194	33.18 N	85.29 W
Wedron	216	41.26 N	88.46 W
Weduar, Tanjung ≻	164	6.00 S	132.50 E
Wedweil	140	9.00 N	27.12 E
Wedza	154	18.35 S	31.35 E
Weebo	162	28.01 S	121.03 E
Weed	204	41.25 N	122.23 W
Weed Heights	226	38.59 N	119.12 W
Weedon	206	45.42 N	71.28 W
Weedon Beck	42	52.14 N	1.05 W
Weedon Island I	220	27.51 N	82.36 W
Weed Patch	228	35.19 N	118.55 W
Weed Patch Hill ∧[2]	218	39.10 N	86.13 W
Weedsport	210	43.02 N	76.33 W
Weedville	214	41.17 N	78.30 W
Weehawken	276	40.46 N	74.01 W
Weeim, Pulau I	164	1.29 S	130.14 E
Wee Jasper	171b	35.09 S	148.41 E
Weekapauq	207	41.20 N	71.45 W
Weeki Wachee Spring ♦	220	28.32 N	82.35 W
Weeki Wachee Swamp ≡	220	28.31 N	82.37 W
Weeks Point ≻	276	40.53 N	73.39 W
Weekstown	208	39.35 N	74.36 W
Weelde	56	51.25 N	5.00 E
Weeley	42	51.51 N	1.07 E
Weel Shimbirro	144	2.23 N	44.16 E
Weems	208	37.39 N	76.26 W
Weende	52	51.33 N	9.55 E
Weenen	158	28.57 S	30.03 E
Weener	52	53.10 N	7.21 E
Weeney Bay c	274a	34.01 S	151.10 E
Weeping Water	198	40.52 N	96.08 W
Weequahic Lake ⊜	276	40.42 N	74.12 W
Weert	52	51.15 N	5.43 E
Weesatche	222	28.51 N	97.27 W
Weesby	41	54.50 N	9.08 E
Weesow	264a	52.39 N	13.43 E
Weesp	52	52.17 N	5.02 E
Weetfeld ◆[8]	263	51.38 N	7.49 E
Weethalle	166	33.53 S	146.38 E
Weeting	42	52.27 N	0.37 E
Weeton	262	53.48 N	2.56 W
Weetulta	168b	34.15 S	137.38 E
Wee Waa	166	30.14 S	149.26 E
Weeze	52	51.37 N	6.12 E
Wefensleben	54	52.11 N	11.09 E
Weferlingen	54	52.19 N	11.02 E
Wegberg	56	51.08 N	6.16 E
Wegdraai	158	28.50 S	21.52 E
Wegeleben	54	51.53 N	11.10 E
Wegendorf	264a	52.36 N	13.45 E
Wegenstedt	54	52.23 N	11.11 E
Wegeringhausen	56	51.02 N	7.45 E
Weggis	58	47.02 N	8.26 E
Węgliniec	30	51.17 N	15.13 E
Węgorzewo	30	54.14 N	21.44 E
Węgorzyno	30	53.32 N	15.33 E
Węgrów	30	52.25 N	22.01 E
Wegscheid	60	48.36 N	13.48 E
Wehdel	52	53.30 N	8.48 E
Wehebach Stausee ⊜[1]	56	50.45 N	6.20 E
Wehingen	58	48.08 N	8.47 E
Wehofen ◆[8]	263	51.32 N	6.46 E
Wehr	58	47.37 N	7.54 E
Wehringhausen ◆[8]	263	51.21 N	7.27 E
Wehrsdorf	54	51.03 N	14.22 E
Wei ≃, Zhg.	98	37.05 N	119.28 E
Wei ≃, Zhg.	98	36.51 N	115.43 E
Wei ≃, Zhg.	102	34.30 N	110.20 E
Weichang (Zhuizishan)	98	42.00 N	117.32 E
Weichselboden	61	47.40 N	15.10 E
Weichsel → Wisła ≃	30	54.22 N	18.55 E
Weichuan	98	34.17 N	113.58 E
Weicun	106	31.59 N	119.55 E
Weida	54	50.45 N	12.04 E
Weida ≃	54	50.47 N	12.06 E
Weiden am See	61	47.55 N	16.52 E
Weidenberg	60	49.57 N	11.43 E
Weiden in der Oberpfalz	60	49.41 N	12.10 E
Weidenstetten	56	48.33 N	9.59 E
Weiding	60	49.16 N	12.46 E
Weidling	264b	48.17 N	16.19 E
Weidlingau ◆[8]	264b	48.13 N	16.13 E
Weidlingbach	264b	48.16 N	16.15 E
Weidlingerbach ≃	264b	48.18 N	16.20 E
Weifang	98	36.42 N	119.04 E
Weigelstown	208	39.59 N	76.49 W
Weihai	98	37.28 N	122.07 E
Weihaiwei → Weihai	98	37.28 N	122.07 E
Weihmichl	60	48.36 N	12.03 E
Weihnachtsinsel → Christmas Island □[2]	112	10.30 S	105.40 E
Wei Island I	164	3.20 S	144.25 E
Weijiagou	105	40.28 N	115.08 E
Weijiatang	106	31.25 N	118.55 E
Weijiazhuang	105	39.37 N	116.22 E
Weijiazui	100	30.29 N	117.20 E
Weijingtang	106	31.27 N	120.39 E
Weikersheim	56	49.29 N	9.54 E
Weil ≃	56	50.28 N	8.16 E
Weil am Rhein	58	47.37 N	7.38 E
Weilburg	56	50.29 N	8.15 E
Weil der Stadt	56	48.45 N	8.52 E
Weiler	58	47.36 N	9.55 E
Weilerbach	56	49.29 N	7.37 E
Weilerswist	56	50.45 N	6.50 E
Weilheim	64	47.50 N	11.08 E
Weilheim an der Teck	56	48.37 N	9.32 E
Weilmoringle	166	29.15 S	146.51 E
Weilmünster	56	50.26 N	8.22 E
Weimar, Dtsch.	54	50.59 N	11.19 E
Weimar, Dtsch.	56	51.22 N	9.23 E
Weimar, Ca., U.S.	226	39.02 N	120.58 W
Weimar, Tx., U.S.	222	29.42 N	96.46 W
Weinan	102	34.29 N	109.29 E
Weinböhla	54	51.10 N	13.34 E
Weinel Cross Roads	279b	40.37 N	79.37 W
Weiner	194	35.37 N	90.53 W
Weinfelden	58	47.34 N	9.06 E
Weingarten, Dtsch.	56	49.05 N	8.31 E
Weingarten, Dtsch.	58	47.48 N	9.38 E
Weinheim	56	49.33 N	8.39 E
Weining, Zhg.	102	26.43 N	104.18 E
Weining, Zhg.	104	41.21 N	123.49 E
Weinsberg	56	49.10 N	9.17 E
Weinsberger Wald ◆[3]	61	48.30 N	14.50 E
Weinviertel ◆[1]	61	48.38 N	16.25 E
Weipa	164	12.41 S	141.52 E
Weippe	202	46.22 N	115.56 W
Weir, India	124	27.01 N	77.11 E
Weir, Ks., U.S.	198	37.18 N	94.46 W
Weir, Ms., U.S.	194	33.16 N	89.17 W
Weir ≃, Austl.	166	28.50 S	149.06 E
Weir ≃, Mb., Can.	184	56.54 N	93.21 W
Weir ≃, Ma., U.S.	283	42.16 N	70.53 W
Weir, Lake ⊜	220	29.00 N	81.57 W
Weir River	184	56.49 N	94.04 W
Weirsdale	220	28.58 N	81.55 W
Weirton	214	40.25 N	80.35 W
Weisberg → Monguelfo	64	46.45 N	12.06 E
Weisburd	252	27.18 S	62.36 W
Weisburg	218	39.13 N	85.03 W
Weischlitz	54	50.26 N	12.02 E
Weisendorf	56	49.37 N	10.49 E
Weiser	202	44.15 N	116.58 W
Weiser ≃	202	44.15 N	116.59 W
Weishan (Xiazhen), Zhg.	98	34.52 N	117.09 E
Weishan, Zhg.	100	29.20 N	120.25 E
Weishan, Zhg.	100	29.41 N	120.48 E
Weishan, Zhg.	102	25.15 N	100.20 E
Weishancheng	100	32.34 N	113.24 E
Weishanhe	104	40.47 N	123.31 E
Weishan Hu ⊜	98	34.40 N	117.15 E
Weishanzhuang	105	39.40 N	116.25 E
Weishi	98	34.25 N	114.11 E
Weismain	54	50.05 N	11.14 E
Weisner Mountain ∧	194	34.02 N	85.40 W
Weissach	56	48.50 N	8.55 E
Weissbriach	64	46.41 N	13.15 E
Weisse Elster ≃	54	51.26 N	11.57 E
Weissenbach	264b	48.05 N	16.13 E
Weissenbach am Lech	58	47.26 N	10.39 E
Weissenberg	54	51.11 N	14.40 E
Weissenborn	54	50.52 N	13.25 E
Weissenbrunn	54	50.12 N	11.20 E
Weissenburg	58	46.39 N	7.28 E
Weissenburg in Bayern	56	49.01 N	10.58 E
Weissenfels	54	51.12 N	11.58 E
Weissenhorn	58	48.18 N	10.09 E
Weissensee	54	51.11 N	11.04 E
Weissensee ◆[8]	264a	52.33 N	13.27 E
Weissensee ⊜	64	46.42 N	13.22 E
Weissenstadt	54	50.06 N	11.53 E
Weissenstein, Dtsch.	56	48.42 N	9.53 E
Weissenstein, Öst.	64	46.41 N	13.44 E
Weissenstein ∧	58	47.15 N	7.31 E
Weissenstein Tunnel ◆[5]	58	47.12 N	7.23 E
Weissenthurm	56	50.24 N	7.27 E
Weisser Main ≃	54	50.04 N	11.24 E
Weisser Nil → White Nile ≃	140	15.38 N	32.31 E
Weisser See → Beloje, ozero ⊜	76	60.11 N	37.37 E
Weisser Stein ∧	56	50.23 N	6.20 E
Weisses Meer → Beloje more ∓[2]	24	65.30 N	38.00 E
Weisse Spitze ∧	64	46.52 N	12.21 E
Weissfluh ∧	58	46.50 N	9.48 E
Weisshorn ∧	58	46.06 N	7.42 E
Weissig	54	51.05 N	13.52 E
Weisskugel (Palla Bianca) ∧	64	46.48 N	10.44 E
Weiss Lake ⊜[1]	192	34.15 N	85.35 W
Weissmeer-Ostsee Kanal → Belomorsko-Baltijskij kanal ≍	24	62.48 N	34.48 E
Weissport	210	40.50 N	75.42 W
Weisstannen	58	46.59 N	9.21 E
Weisswasser	54	51.30 N	14.38 E
Weisweiler	56	50.50 N	6.19 E
Weitang	105	40.24 N	117.24 E
Weitang ≃	104	42.19 N	122.18 E
Weitendorf	54	53.54 N	12.16 E
Weitensfeld	61	46.51 N	14.11 E
Weiterstadt	56	49.54 N	8.35 E
Weitian	100	27.43 N	118.46 E
Weitin	54	53.34 N	13.12 E
Weiting	106	31.22 N	120.47 E
Weitmar ◆[8]	263	51.27 N	7.12 E
Weitnau	58	47.38 N	10.07 E
Weitou	100	24.34 N	118.34 E
Weitra	61	48.42 N	14.54 E
Weituo	107	30.03 N	106.08 E
Weitzgrund	54	52.11 N	12.32 E
Weiwan	98	36.43 N	115.54 E
Weixdorf	54	51.09 N	13.48 E
Weixi, Zhg.	102	27.14 N	99.12 E
Weixi, Zhg.	107	30.12 N	106.39 E
Weixian, Zhg.	98	36.57 N	115.15 E
Weixian, Zhg.	98	36.22 N	114.56 E
Weixian (Hanting), Zhg.	98	36.52 N	119.07 E
Weixin	102	27.48 N	105.06 E
Weiyuan	107	29.33 N	104.39 E
Weiyuan ≃	102	22.50 N	100.20 E
Weiyuankou	100	30.09 N	115.15 E
Weiyuanpu	98	42.39 N	124.16 E
Weiz	61	47.13 N	15.37 E
Weizhen	98	37.17 N	114.44 E
Weizhou Dao I	102	21.03 N	109.04 E
Weizhou Wan c	100	24.34 N	118.30 E
Weizhuang	105	39.02 N	115.20 E
Weizi	98	40.04 N	123.10 E
Weizigou, Zhg.	104	42.25 N	122.47 E
Weizigou, Zhg.	104	41.05 N	120.38 E
Weizigou, Zhg.	104	42.05 N	120.34 E
Weizigoumen	98	41.58 N	116.49 E
Weiziyu	98	41.29 N	124.31 E
Wejherowo	30	54.37 N	18.15 E
Wekiva ≃	220	28.52 N	81.23 W
Wekiwa Springs State Park ♦	220	28.43 N	81.27 W
Wekoewa Punt ≻	241s	12.14 N	68.24 W
Wekusko Lake ⊜	184	54.45 N	99.50 W
Welaka	192	29.28 N	81.40 W
Welbourn Hill	162	27.21 S	134.06 E
Welch, Ok., U.S.	196	36.52 N	95.05 W
Welch, Tx., U.S.	196	32.56 N	102.08 W
Welch, W.V., U.S.	192	37.25 N	81.35 W
Welch Creek ≃	282	37.32 N	121.51 W
Welches	224	45.19 N	121.57 W
Welch Peak ∧	224	49.10 N	121.36 W
Welcome, On., Can.	212	43.58 N	78.21 W
Welcome, Mn., U.S.	198	43.40 N	94.37 W
Welcome, S.C., U.S.	192	34.49 N	82.26 W
Welcome Lake ⊜	212	45.25 N	78.25 W
Welcome Monument ⊥	269e	6.11 S	106.49 E
Welden	58	48.27 N	10.40 E
Weldiya	144	11.50 N	39.41 E
Weldon, Sk., Can.	184	53.00 N	105.08 W
Weldon, Il., U.S.	219	40.07 N	88.45 W
Weldon, N.C., U.S.	192	36.25 N	77.35 W
Weldon, Tx., U.S.	222	31.01 N	95.34 W
Weldon ≃	194	40.06 N	93.38 W
Weldona	198	40.20 N	103.58 W
Weldon Brook ≃	276	40.58 N	74.35 W
Weleetka	196	35.20 N	96.08 W
Welega □[4]	144	9.40 N	35.50 E
Weleri	115a	6.58 S	110.04 E
Welfare Island I	276	40.45 N	73.57 W
Welgedag	273d	26.12 S	28.30 E
Welhamgreen	260	51.44 N	0.13 W
Welheim ◆[8]	263	51.32 N	6.59 E
Weligama	122	5.58 N	80.25 E
Welikaja → Velikaja ≃	76	57.48 N	28.20 E
Welkenraedt	56	50.40 N	5.59 E
Welker Seamount ✢[3]	16	55.07 N	140.20 W
Welkite	144	8.15 N	37.50 E
Welkom	158	27.59 S	26.45 E
Well	52	51.34 N	6.06 E
Welland	212	42.59 N	79.15 W
Welland ≃, On., Can.	212	43.04 N	79.03 W
Welland ≃, Eng., U.K.	42	52.52 N	0.03 W
Welland Canal ≍	212	43.03 N	79.13 W
Welland Junction	284a	42.57 N	79.14 W
Wellard	168a	32.19 S	115.50 E
Wellaune	54	51.34 N	12.33 E
Wellborn, Fl., U.S.	192	30.13 N	82.49 W
Wellborn, Tx., U.S.	222	30.32 N	96.18 W
Wellerode	56	51.14 N	9.34 E
Wellers Bay c	212	44.00 N	77.34 W
Wellers Creek ≃	278	42.03 N	87.53 W
Wellesbourne	42	52.12 N	1.35 W
Welles Harbor c	174g	28.12 N	177.26 W
Wellesley, On., Can.	212	43.28 N	80.45 W
Wellesley, Ma., U.S.	207	42.17 N	71.17 W
Wellesley ≃	168a	33.17 S	115.44 E
Wellesley College ⊍[2]	283	42.18 N	71.19 W
Wellesley Hills	283	42.19 N	71.17 W
Wellesley Island I	212	44.19 N	75.58 W
Wellesley Islands II	164	16.42 S	139.30 E
Wellesley Island State Park ♦	212	44.19 N	76.01 W
Wellesley Lake ⊜	180	62.30 N	139.50 W
Wellfleet	207	41.56 N	70.02 W
Well Hill	260	51.21 N	0.09 E
Wellin	56	50.05 N	5.07 E
Welling ◆[8]	260	51.28 N	0.07 E
Wellingborough	42	52.19 N	0.42 W
Wellinghofen ◆[8]	263	51.28 N	7.29 E
Wellington, Austl.	166	32.33 S	148.57 E
Wellington, B.C., Can.	224	49.13 N	124.01 W
Wellington, On., Can.	212	43.57 N	77.21 W
Wellington, N.Z.	172	41.18 S	174.47 E
Wellington, S. Afr.	158	33.38 S	18.57 E
Wellington, Eng., U.K.	42	52.43 N	2.31 W
Wellington, Eng., U.K.	42	50.59 N	3.14 W
Wellington, Co., U.S.	200	40.42 N	105.00 W
Wellington, Il., U.S.	216	40.32 N	87.41 W
Wellington, Ks., U.S.	198	37.15 N	97.22 W
Wellington, Mo., U.S.	194	39.08 N	93.58 W
Wellington, Nv., U.S.	226	38.45 N	119.22 W
Wellington, Oh., U.S.	214	41.10 N	82.13 W
Wellington, Tx., U.S.	196	34.51 N	100.12 W
Wellington, Ut,. U.S.	200	39.32 N	110.44 W
Wellington □[6]	212	43.50 N	80.30 W
Wellington, Isla I	254	49.20 S	74.40 W
Wellington Bay c, N.T., Can.	176	69.30 N	106.30 W
Wellington Bay c, On., Can.	212	43.56 N	77.21 W
Wellington Channel ⊻	176	75.00 N	93.00 W
Wellington Point	171a	27.29 S	153.15 E
Wellington Reservoir ⊜[1]	168a	33.24 S	116.01 E
Wellington Station	186	46.27 N	64.00 W
Wellman, Ia., U.S.	190	41.27 N	91.50 W
Wellman, Tx., U.S.	196	33.03 N	102.26 W
Wells, B.C., Can.	182	53.06 N	121.34 W
Wells, Eng., U.K.	42	51.13 N	2.39 W
Wells, Mi., U.S.	190	45.47 N	87.04 W
Wells, Mn., U.S.	190	43.44 N	93.43 W
Wells, Nv., U.S.	204	41.06 N	114.57 W
Wells, N.Y., U.S.	210	43.24 N	74.17 W
Wells, Tx., U.S.	222	31.29 N	94.56 W
Wells □[6]	216	40.44 N	85.11 W
Wells, Lake ⊜	162	26.43 S	123.10 E
Wells, Mount ∧	168a	32.42 S	116.20 E
Wells, Mount ∧[2]	162	17.26 S	127.14 E
Wellsboro	210	41.44 N	77.18 W
Wells Bridge	210	42.22 N	75.15 W
Wellsburg, Ia., U.S.	190	42.27 N	92.56 W
Wellsburg, N.Y., U.S.	210	42.00 N	76.43 W
Wellsburg, W.V., U.S.	214	40.16 N	80.36 W
Wells Cathedral ⊍[1]	42	51.13 N	2.39 W
Wellsford	172	36.17 S	174.31 E
Wells Gray Provincial Park ♦	182	52.20 N	120.00 W
Wells Lake ⊜	184	57.15 N	101.00 W
Wells-next-the-Sea	42	52.58 N	0.51 E
Wells Point ≻	284b	39.17 N	76.23 W
Wells State Park ♦	207	42.09 N	72.05 W
Wells Tannery	214	40.05 N	78.10 W
Wellston, Oh., U.S.	188	39.07 N	82.31 W
Wellston, Ok., U.S.	196	35.41 N	97.03 W
Wellsville, Ks., U.S.	198	38.43 N	95.04 W
Wellsville, Mo., U.S.	219	39.04 N	91.34 W
Wellsville, N.Y., U.S.	210	42.07 N	77.56 W
Wellsville, Oh., U.S.	214	40.36 N	80.38 W
Wellsville, Pa., U.S.	208	40.03 N	76.56 W
Wellsville, Ut,. U.S.	200	41.38 N	111.55 W
Wellton	200	32.40 N	114.08 W
Welmel ≃	144	5.38 N	40.47 E
Welmen	263	51.39 N	6.41 E
Welney	42	52.31 N	0.15 E
Welo □[4]	144	11.50 N	40.20 E
Welper	263	51.25 N	7.12 E
Wels	61	48.10 N	14.02 E
Welschbillig	56	49.51 N	6.34 E
Welse ≃	54	53.10 N	14.18 E
Welsford	186	45.27 N	66.20 W
Welsh	194	30.14 N	92.49 W
Welshpool, Austl.	169	38.39 S	146.26 E
Welshpool, Wales, U.K.	42	52.40 N	3.09 W
Welsickendorf	54	51.54 N	13.08 E
Welsleben	54	52.00 N	11.38 E
Weltenburg	60	48.54 N	11.50 E
Welver	52	51.38 N	7.57 E
Welverdiend	158	26.23 S	27.16 E
Welwitschia	156	20.21 S	14.57 E
Welwyn Garden City	42	51.50 N	0.13 W
Welwyn Hatfield □[8]	260	51.47 N	0.12 W
Welzheim	56	48.53 N	9.38 E
Welzow	54	51.34 N	14.10 E
Wem	42	52.51 N	2.44 W
Wema	152	0.26 S	21.38 E
Wembere ≃	154	4.10 S	34.11 E
Wembley	182	55.09 N	119.08 W
Wembley ◆[8]	260	51.33 N	0.18 W
Wembley Stadium ♦, S. Afr.	273d	26.14 S	28.03 E
Wembley Stadium ♦, Eng., U.K.	260	51.33 N	0.17 W
Wembury	42	50.19 N	4.05 W
Wemding	56	48.52 N	10.43 E
Wemeldinge	52	51.31 N	4.00 E
Wemme	224	45.20 N	121.57 W
Wemperhardt	56	50.09 N	6.05 E
Wemyss Bay	46	55.53 N	4.54 W
Wen ≃, Zhg.	98	36.38 N	119.22 E
Wen ≃, Zhg.	98	35.28 N	118.32 E
Wen'an	105	38.52 N	116.28 E
Wen'an Wa ≡	105	38.54 N	116.37 E
Wenas Creek ≃	224	46.42 N	120.35 W
Wenatchee	202	47.25 N	120.18 W
Wenatchee ≃	202	47.27 N	120.19 W
Wenatchee, Lake ⊜	224	47.49 N	120.47 W
Wenatchee Mountains ⋏	202	47.20 N	120.45 W
Wenchang	110	19.41 N	110.48 E
Wencheng	100	27.50 N	120.05 E
Wenchi	150	7.42 N	2.07 W
Wenchow → Wenzhou	100	28.01 N	120.39 E
Wendaohezi	104	41.46 N	124.09 E
Wendel	279b	40.18 N	79.41 W
Wendell, Id., U.S.	202	42.46 N	114.42 W
Wendell, N.C., U.S.	192	35.46 N	78.22 W
Wendelsheim	56	49.46 N	7.59 E
Wendelstein	60	49.21 N	11.08 E
Wendelstein ∧	64	47.42 N	12.00 E
Wendelville	284a	43.04 N	78.47 W
Wenden, Dtsch.	52	52.19 N	10.30 E
Wenden, Dtsch.	56	50.57 N	7.51 E
Wenden, Az., U.S.	200	33.49 N	113.32 W
Wendeng	98	37.12 N	122.04 E
Wendesi	164	2.25 S	134.13 E
Wendilou	104	41.13 N	121.08 E
Wendisch Rietz	54	52.13 N	14.01 E
Wendish Baggendorf	54	54.04 N	12.56 E
Wendji	152	0.04 S	18.10 E
Wendland ◆[1]	54	53.00 N	11.10 E
Wendo	144	6.38 N	38.27 E
Wendover, Eng., U.K.	42	51.46 N	0.46 W
Wendover, Ut,. U.S.	200	40.44 N	114.02 W
Wenduine	50	51.18 N	3.05 E
Wenebegon ≃	190	46.53 N	83.12 W
Wenebegon Lake ⊜	190	47.24 N	83.08 W
Wenfang	100	28.02 N	117.19 E
Weng	60	48.40 N	12.23 E
Weng ≃	100	24.10 N	113.24 E
Weng'an	102	26.53 N	107.22 E
Wengbo	120	31.23 N	86.40 E
Wengcheng	100	24.23 N	113.51 E
Wengdang	124	28.50 N	90.03 E
Wenge	152	0.03 N	24.01 E
Wengen, Dtsch.	58	47.41 N	10.09 E
Wengen, Schw.	58	46.36 N	7.56 E
Wengern	263	51.24 N	7.21 E
Wengjiabu	106	30.23 N	120.21 E
Wengong	107	30.11 N	104.09 E
Wenguantun	104	41.53 N	123.30 E
Wengyang	100	28.03 N	120.58 E
Wengyuan	100	24.21 N	114.08 E
Wenham	207	42.36 N	70.53 W
Wenham Lake ⊜	283	42.35 N	70.53 W
Wenham Swamp ≡	283	42.37 N	70.55 W
Wenheng	100	25.42 N	116.45 E
Wenī	124	28.21 N	83.34 E
Wenigzell	61	47.26 N	15.47 E
Wenjiachang	107	30.41 N	103.55 E
Wenjiang	107	30.42 N	103.49 E
Wenjiangban	100	26.01 N	117.51 E
Wenjiazhen	100	28.20 N	116.05 E
Wenling	100	28.22 N	121.20 E
Wenlock	164	13.06 S	142.58 E
Wenlock ≃	164	12.02 S	141.55 E
Wenlock Edge ⩡[4]	42	52.30 N	2.40 W
Wenlong	100	24.48 N	114.54 E
Wenmingsi	100	25.33 N	113.20 E
Wennigsen	52	52.16 N	9.34 E
Wenning ≃	44	54.07 N	2.39 W
Wennington ◆[8]	260	51.30 N	0.13 E
Wenniu	102	24.18 N	104.31 E
Wenns	58	47.10 N	10.44 E
Wenona, Il., U.S.	216	41.03 N	89.03 W
Wenona, Md., U.S.	208	38.08 N	75.57 W
Wenonah	208	39.47 N	75.08 W
Wenquan, Zhg.	86	44.59 N	81.04 E
Wenquan, Zhg.	100	23.37 N	113.43 E
Wenquansi	104	41.20 N	124.04 E
Wenshan	102	23.30 N	104.20 E
Wenshang	98	35.44 N	116.29 E
Wenshui, Zhg.	102	28.28 N	106.30 E
Wenshui, Zhg.	102	37.28 N	112.01 E
Wensickendorf	264a	52.45 N	13.23 E
Wensleydale V	44	54.19 N	2.00 W
Wensum ≃	42	52.37 N	1.19 E
Went ≃	44	53.39 N	0.59 W
Wentorf	52	53.30 N	10.15 E
Wentworth, Austl.	166	34.07 S	141.55 E
Wentworth, N.C., U.S.	192	36.24 N	79.46 W
Wentworth, S.D., U.S.	198	43.59 N	96.57 W
Wentworth Falls	170	33.43 S	150.22 E
Wentworth Park	273d	26.07 S	27.48 E
Wentworthville	274a	33.48 S	150.58 E
Wentzville	219	38.48 N	90.51 W
Wenxi	102	35.26 N	111.11 E
Wenxian	102	32.58 N	104.46 E
Wenxingchang	107	29.52 N	106.29 E
Wenyu ≃	105	39.56 N	116.40 E
Wenzenbach	60	49.05 N	12.12 E
Wenzhou	100	28.01 N	120.39 E
Wenzhu	100	27.01 N	113.58 E
Wenzhuangzicun	104	42.16 N	123.51 E
Weobley	42	52.09 N	2.51 W
Weohyakapka, Lake ⊜	220	27.49 N	81.25 W
Wepener	158	29.46 S	27.00 E
Wépion	56	50.25 N	4.52 E
Weppersdorf	61	47.35 N	16.26 E
Wequetequock	207	41.21 N	71.52 W
Wera ≃	115b	8.20 S	120.43 E
Werbellin	54	52.53 N	13.41 E
Werbellinsee ⊜	54	52.54 N	13.40 E
Werben	54	52.52 N	11.58 E
Werbomont	56	50.23 N	5.41 E
Werchojansker Gebirge → Verchojanskij chrebet ⋏	74	67.00 N	129.00 E
Werda	156	25.15 S	23.16 E
Werdau	54	50.44 N	12.22 E
Werden ◆[8]	263	51.23 N	7.00 E
Werder, Dtsch.	54	52.23 N	12.56 E
Werder, Ityo.	144	6.58 N	45.20 E
Werder ◆[1]	54	53.40 N	13.25 E
Werdohl	56	51.15 N	7.45 E
Were Ilu	144	10.37 N	39.28 E
Werfen	64	47.28 N	13.11 E
Weri	164	3.12 S	132.38 E
Werkel	56	51.09 N	9.18 E
Werkendam	52	51.49 N	4.53 E
Werl	52	51.33 N	7.54 E
Werlaburgdorf	54	52.04 N	10.31 E
Werl-Aspe	52	52.04 N	8.43 E
Werleshausen	56	51.19 N	9.54 E
Werlte	52	52.51 N	7.41 E
Wermelskirchen	56	51.08 N	7.13 E
Wermsdorf	54	51.17 N	12.56 E
Wern ≃	56	50.02 N	9.44 E
Wernadinga	166	18.07 S	139.58 E
Wernberg, Dtsch.	60	49.32 N	12.10 E
Wernberg, Öst.	64	46.37 N	13.56 E
Werne	52	51.40 N	7.38 E
Werne ◆[8]	263	51.29 N	7.18 E
Werneck, Bra.	256	22.13 S	43.19 W
Werneck, Dtsch.	56	49.59 N	10.05 E
Werneuchen	54	52.38 N	13.44 E
Wernigerode	54	51.50 N	10.47 E
Wernitz	264a	52.34 N	12.55 E
Wernsdorf	264a	52.22 N	13.43 E
Wernsdorfer See ⊜	264a	52.23 N	13.42 E
Wernshausen	54	50.43 N	10.21 E
Wernstein	60	48.30 N	13.28 E
Werra ≃	30	51.26 N	9.39 E
Werribee	169	37.54 S	144.40 E
Werribee ≃	169	37.59 S	144.41 E
Werribee Gorge State Park ♦	169	37.40 S	144.21 E
Werribee South	169	37.56 S	144.42 E
Werries	52	51.41 N	7.53 E
Werrington	274a	33.45 S	150.46 E
Werris Creek	166	31.21 S	150.39 E
Werschweiler	56	49.27 N	7.13 E
Wersten ◆[8]	263	51.11 N	6.49 E
Wertach	58	47.36 N	10.25 E
Wertach ≃	58	48.24 N	10.53 E
Wertheim	56	49.46 N	9.31 E
Werther, Dtsch.	52	52.04 N	8.24 E
Werther, Dtsch.	54	51.29 N	10.46 E
Wertingen	56	48.34 N	10.41 E
Wervershoof	52	52.44 N	5.09 E
Wervik	50	50.47 N	3.02 E
Wervin	262	53.15 N	2.52 W
Werwaru	164	8.13 S	128.11 E
Weschnitz ≃	56	49.43 N	8.24 E
Weseke	52	51.54 N	6.51 E
Wesel	52	51.40 N	6.38 E
Wesel-Datteln-Kanal ≍	263	51.38 N	6.36 E
Wesenberg	54	53.17 N	12.58 E
Wesendahl	264a	52.36 N	13.49 E
Wesendorf	52	52.35 N	10.31 E
Weser ≃	52	53.32 N	8.34 E
Weser-Elbe-Kanal (Mittellandkanal) ≍	54	52.16 N	11.41 E
Weser-Ems □[5]	52	52.45 N	8.00 E
Wesergebirge ⋏	52	52.15 N	9.10 E
Wesham	262	53.48 N	2.53 W
Wesickaman Creek ≃	285	39.44 N	74.43 W
Wesī Śahar	124	28.15 N	84.23 E
Weskan	198	38.52 N	101.57 W
Weslaco	196	26.09 N	97.59 W
Weslemkoon Lake ⊜	212	45.02 N	77.25 W
Wesley, Dom.	240d	15.34 N	61.19 W
Wesley, Ia., U.S.	190	43.05 N	93.59 W
Wesleyville, Nf., Can.	186	49.09 N	53.34 W
Wesleyville, Pa., U.S.	214	42.08 N	80.00 W
Wessel, Cape ≻	164	10.59 S	136.46 E
Wesseling	56	50.49 N	6.58 E
Wessel Islands II	164	11.30 S	136.25 E
Wesselsbron	158	27.50 S	25.23 E
Wesselsvlei	158	27.23 S	23.47 E
Wessington	198	44.27 N	98.41 W
Wessington Springs	198	44.04 N	98.34 W
Wessobrunn	64	47.52 N	11.01 E
Wesson	194	31.42 N	90.23 W
Wessum	52	52.05 N	6.58 E
West, Ms., U.S.	194	33.11 N	89.46 W
West, Tx., U.S.	222	31.48 N	97.05 W
West ≃, N.Y., U.S.	210	42.41 N	77.22 W
West ≃, Vt., U.S.	188	42.52 N	72.33 W
West Abington	207	42.05 N	70.58 W
Westacres	216	42.35 N	83.26 W
West Acton	207	42.28 N	71.28 W
West Alexander	214	40.06 N	80.31 W
West Alexandria	218	39.44 N	84.31 W
Westall, Point ≻	162	32.55 S	134.04 E
West Allen ≃	44	54.55 N	2.19 W
West Allis	216	43.01 N	88.00 W
Westalton	219	38.51 N	90.13 W
West Amityville	276	40.41 N	73.26 W
West Andover	207	42.39 N	71.09 W
West Athens	280	33.55 N	118.18 W
West Atlantic City	208	39.23 N	74.28 W
West Babylon	210	40.43 N	73.21 W
Westbahnhof ◆[5]	264b	48.11 N	16.20 E
West Baines ≃	164	15.36 S	129.58 E
West Bangor	210	40.52 N	75.14 W
Westbank	182	49.50 N	119.38 W
West Bank □[9]	132	31.40 N	35.15 E
West Barnstable	207	41.42 N	70.22 W
West Barrington	207	41.44 N	71.20 W
West Bay, N.S., Can.	186	45.43 N	61.10 W
Westbay, Fl., U.S.	194	30.17 N	85.52 W
West Bay c, Fl., U.S.	194	30.16 N	85.47 W
West Bay c, Tx., U.S.	222	29.15 N	94.57 W
West Bay Shore	276	40.42 N	73.16 W
West Belmar	208	40.10 N	74.02 W
West Bend, Ia., U.S.	198	42.57 N	94.26 W
West Bend, Wi., U.S.	190	43.25 N	88.11 W
West Bengal □[3]	124	24.00 N	88.00 E
West Bergholt	42	51.55 N	0.51 E
West Berlin	208	39.48 N	74.56 W
West Bernard Creek ≃	222	29.23 N	95.58 W
Westbevern	52	52.01 N	7.47 E
West Bhāgīrath Plain ≚	126	23.30 N	88.00 E
West Bijou Creek ≃	198	39.51 N	104.08 W
West Billerica	283	42.33 N	71.19 W
West Blocton	194	33.07 N	87.07 W
West Bloomfield	210	42.54 N	77.32 W
West Bolivar	214	40.23 N	79.10 W
Westborough	207	42.16 N	71.37 W
Westbourne	184	50.09 N	98.35 W
West Bow Creek ≃	198	42.46 N	97.08 W
West Boxford	283	42.42 N	71.04 W
West Boylston	207	42.22 N	71.47 W
West Bradenton	220	27.30 N	82.37 W
West Branch, Ia., U.S.	190	41.40 N	91.20 W
West Branch, Mi., U.S.	190	44.16 N	84.14 W
West Branch Reservoir ⊜[1]	210	41.25 N	73.42 W
West Branch State Park ♦	214	41.07 N	81.05 W
Westbridge	182	49.10 N	118.59 W
West Bridgewater	207	42.01 N	71.00 W
West Bridgford	42	52.56 N	1.08 W
West Bristol	285	40.06 N	74.53 W
West Bromwich	42	52.31 N	1.56 W
Westbrook, Austl.	171a	27.36 S	151.52 E
Westbrook, On., Can.	212	44.16 N	76.38 W
Westbrook, Ct., U.S.	207	41.17 N	72.26 W
Westbrook, Me., U.S.	188	43.40 N	70.22 W
Westbrook, Mn., U.S.	198	44.02 N	95.26 W
Westbrook, Tx., U.S.	196	32.21 N	101.01 W
West Brook ≃	276	41.04 N	74.18 W
West Brookfield	207	42.14 N	72.08 W
Westbrookville	210	41.30 N	74.34 W
West Burlington, Ia., U.S.	190	40.49 N	91.09 W
West Burlington, N.Y., U.S.	210	42.42 N	75.11 W
West Burra I	46a	60.05 N	1.21 W
Westbury, Eng., U.K.	42	52.41 N	2.57 W
Westbury, Eng., U.K.	42	51.16 N	2.11 W
Westbury, N.Y., U.S.	276	40.45 N	73.35 W
Westbury-on-Severn	42	51.50 N	2.24 W
West Butte ∧	202	48.57 N	111.32 W
Westby, Austl.	171b	35.30 S	147.25 E
Westby, Mt., U.S.	198	48.52 N	104.03 W
Westby, Wi., U.S.	190	43.39 N	90.51 W
West Cache Creek ≃	196	34.13 N	98.23 W
West Caicos I	238	21.39 N	72.28 W
West Calder	46	55.52 N	3.35 W
West Caldwell	276	40.50 N	74.18 W
West Cameron	208	40.45 N	76.41 W
West Camp	210	42.07 N	73.56 W
West Canada Creek ≃	188	43.01 N	74.58 W
West Cape ≻	172	45.54 S	166.26 E
West Cape Howe ≻	162	35.08 S	117.36 E
West Cape May	208	38.56 N	74.56 W
West Carlisle	196	33.35 N	101.56 W
West Caroline Basin ✢[1]	14	4.00 N	138.00 E
West Carrollton	218	39.40 N	84.15 W
West Carson	280	33.57 N	118.23 W
West Carthage	212	43.58 N	75.36 W
West Catfish Creek ≃	212	42.46 N	81.04 W
West Channel ≃[1]	180	68.51 N	136.10 W
West Chelmsford	283	42.37 N	71.23 W
Westchester, Il., U.S.	216	41.51 N	87.52 W
West Chester, Pa., U.S.	208	39.57 N	75.36 W
Westchester, Va., U.S.	284c	38.51 N	77.16 W
Westchester □[6]	210	41.02 N	73.46 W
Westchester ◆[8], Ca., U.S.	280	33.55 N	118.25 W
Westchester ◆[8], N.Y., U.S.	276	40.51 N	73.52 W
West Chester Airport ⊠	285	39.59 N	75.35 W
Westchester County Airport ⊠	207	41.04 N	73.43 W
Westchester Creek ≃	276	40.48 N	73.51 W
Westchester Estates	284c	38.47 N	76.55 W
Westchester Station	186	45.37 N	63.40 W
West Chester University of Pennsylvania ⊍[2]	285	39.57 N	75.36 W
West Chicago	216	41.53 N	88.12 W
West Clandon	260	51.15 N	0.30 W
West Clarksville	210	42.08 N	78.15 W
West Clear Creek ≃	200	34.34 N	111.51 W
West Cleddau ≃	42	51.46 N	4.54 W
Westcliffe	200	38.08 N	105.27 W
Westcliffe ◆[8]	273d	26.11 S	28.02 E
Westcliff-on-Sea	260	51.32 N	0.41 E
West College Corner	218	39.34 N	84.48 W
West Collingswood Heights	285	39.59 N	75.07 W
West Columbia, S.C., U.S.	192	33.59 N	81.04 W

Symbols in the index entries represent the broad categories identified in the key at the right. Symbols with superior numbers (⋏[1]) identify subcategories (see complete key on page *I · 1*).

Symbole im Register stellen die rechts im Schlüssel erklärten Kategorien dar. Symbole mit hochgestellten Ziffern (⋏[1]) bezeichnen Unterabteilungen einer Kategorie (vgl. vollständiger Schlüssel auf Seite *I · 1*).

Los símbolos incluídos en el texto del índice representan las grandes categorias identificadas con la clave a la derecha. Los símbolos con numeros en su parte superior (⋏[1]) identifican las subcategorías (véase la clave completa en la página *I · 1*).

Les symboles de l'index représentent les catégories indiquées dans la légende à droite. Les symboles suivis d'un indice (⋏[1]) représentent des sous-catégories (voir légende complète à la page *I · 1*).

Os símbolos incluídos no texto do índice representam as grandes categorias identificadas com a chave à direita. Os símbolos com números em sua parte superior (⋏[1]) identificam as subcategorias (veja-se a chave completa à página *I · 1*).

∧ Mountain	Berg	Montaña	Montagne	Montanha
⋏ Mountains	Gebirge	Montañas	Montagnes	Montanhas
)(Pass	Paß	Paso	Col	Passo
V Valley, Canyon	Tal, Cañon	Valle, Cañón	Vallée, Canyon	Vale, Canhão
≚ Plain	Ebene	Llano	Plaine	Planície
≻ Cape	Kap	Cabo	Cap	Cabo
I Island	Insel	Isla	Île	Ilha
II Islands	Inseln	Islas	Îles	Ilhas
⩡ Other Topographic Features	Andere Topographische Objekte	Otros Elementos Topográficos	Autres données topographiques	Outros acidentes topográficos

ESPAÑOL

Nombre	Página	Lat.°′	Long.°′ W = Oeste
West Columbia, Tx., U.S.	222	29.08 N	95.38 W
West Concord, Ma., U.S.	207	42.27 N	71.23 W
West Concord, Mn., U.S.	190	44.09 N	92.53 W
West Conshohocken	285	40.04 N	75.19 W
West Cote Blanche Bay c	194	29.40 N	91.45 W
Westcott	260	51.13 N	0.22 W
Westcott Cove c	276	41.02 N	73.30 W
West Covina	228	34.04 N	117.56 W
West Creek	208	39.38 N	74.18 W
West Creek ≃, In., U.S.	216	41.12 N	87.30 W
West Creek ≃, Pa., U.S.	214	41.30 N	78.15 W
Westdale, Ma., U.S.	283	42.01 N	70.59 W
Westdale, N.Y., U.S.	210	43.23 N	75.49 W
West Danby	210	42.19 N	76.32 W
West Davenport	210	42.27 N	74.58 W
West Deane Park ♦	275b	43.40 N	79.34 W
West Decatur	214	40.56 N	78.17 W
West Delaware Aqueduct ≅[1]	210	41.52 N	74.31 W
Westdene ◆[8]	273d	26.11 S	27.59 E
West Dennis	207	41.39 N	70.10 W
West Derby ◆[8]	262	53.26 N	2.54 W
West Derry	214	40.20 N	79.20 W
West Des Moines	190	41.34 N	93.42 W
West Ditch ≅	276	40.56 N	74.19 W
West Dolores ≃	200	37.35 N	108.21 W
West Drayton ◆[8]	260	51.30 N	0.29 W
West Duffins Creek ≃	212	43.51 N	79.04 W
West Duxbury	283	42.03 N	70.47 W
West Easton	210	40.41 N	75.14 W
West Eaton	210	42.51 N	75.39 W
Westecunk Creek ≃	208	39.37 N	74.16 W
West Edmeston	210	42.46 N	75.17 W
West Edmondale	284b	39.18 N	76.43 W
West Elizabeth	279b	40.17 N	79.54 W
West Elk Mountains ⛰	200	38.40 N	107.15 W
West Elk Peak ∧	200	38.43 N	107.13 W
West Elkton	218	39.35 N	84.33 W
West Ellicott	214	42.05 N	79.16 W
West Elmira	210	42.04 N	76.50 W
West End, Ba.	238	26.41 N	78.58 W
West End, Eng., U.K.	260	51.44 N	0.04 W
West End, Eng., U.K.	260	51.20 N	0.38 W
West End, Ar., U.S.	194	34.13 N	92.03 W
West End, Il., U.S.	216	42.17 N	89.09 W
West End, N.Y., U.S.	210	42.28 N	75.05 W
West End, N.C., U.S.	192	35.14 N	79.34 W
West End ◆[8], Eng., U.K.	260	51.32 N	0.24 W
West End ◆[8], Pa., U.S.	279b	40.27 N	80.02 W
Westende, Bel.	50	51.10 N	2.46 E
Westende, Dtsch.	263	51.25 N	7.24 E
Westendorf	64	47.26 N	12.13 E
Westenfeld ◆[8]	263	51.28 N	7.09 E
Westenholz	52	51.45 N	8.28 E
Westenschouwen	52	51.41 N	3.42 E
Westerbauer ◆[8]	263	51.20 N	7.23 E
Westerblokker	52	52.39 N	5.08 E
Westerbönen	263	51.36 N	7.46 E
Westerbork	52	52.51 N	6.37 E
Westerburg	56	50.33 N	7.58 E
Westercelle	52	52.36 N	10.05 E
Westerdale	46	58.27 N	3.30 W
Westeregeln	54	51.57 N	11.23 E
Westerham	42	51.16 N	0.05 E
Westerhausen	54	51.48 N	11.03 E
Westerholt	52	51.36 N	7.05 E
Westerholz ◆[3]	263	51.32 N	7.28 E
Westerkappeln	52	52.18 N	7.52 E
Westerland	30	54.54 N	8.18 E
Westerlo, Bel.	56	51.05 N	4.55 E
Westerlo, N.Y., U.S.	210	42.31 N	74.03 W
Westerly	207	41.22 N	71.49 W
Western	198	40.23 N	97.11 W
Western □[4], Ghana	150	5.30 N	2.30 W
Western □[4], Kenya	154	0.30 N	34.35 E
Western □[4], Sol.Is.	175e	8.00 S	157.00 E
Western □[4], Zam.	152	16.00 S	24.00 E
Western □[5], Pap. N. Gui.	164	7.00 S	142.00 E
Western □[5], Ug.	154	1.00 N	31.00 E
Western ≃	166	22.22 S	142.25 E
Western Area □[4]	150	8.20 N	13.00 W
Western Australia □[3]	160	25.00 S	122.00 E
Western Branch ≃	284c	38.55 N	76.48 W
Western Canal ≅	226	39.28 N	121.35 W
Western Channel ʊ	98	34.40 N	129.00 E
Western Cove c	168b	35.43 S	137.38 E
Western Desert → Gharbīyah, Aṣ-Ṣaḥrā' al- ◆[2]	140	27.00 N	27.00 E
Western Division □[5]	175g	18.00 S	177.30 E
Western Ghāts ⛰	122	14.00 N	75.00 E
Western Highlands □[5]	164	5.45 S	144.30 E
Western Isles □[4]	46	57.40 N	7.00 W
Westernport	188	39.29 N	79.02 W
Western Port c	169	38.22 N	145.20 E
Western Port Bay c	169	38.15 S	145.20 E
Western Sahara □[2], Afr.	134	24.30 N	13.00 W
Western Sahara □[2], Afr.	148	24.30 N	13.00 W
Western Samoa □[1], Oc.	14	13.55 S	172.00 W
Western Samoa □[1], Oc.	175a	13.55 S	172.00 W
Western Sayans → Zapadnyj Sajan ⛰	74	53.00 N	94.00 E
Western Shore	186	44.32 N	64.19 W
Western Springs	278	41.48 N	87.54 W
Westernville	210	43.18 N	75.23 W
Westerschelde c[1]	52	51.25 N	3.45 E
Westerstede	52	53.15 N	7.55 E
Westervelt	219	39.29 N	88.52 W
Westerville	214	40.07 N	82.55 W
Westerwald ⛰	56	50.40 N	7.55 E
West European Basin ✦[1]	10	47.00 N	15.00 W
West Exeter	210	42.48 N	75.09 W
West Fairview	208	40.16 N	76.54 W
Westfalen □[9]	52	51.50 N	7.30 E
Westfalenhalle ʋ	263	51.30 N	7.27 E
West Falkland I	254	51.50 S	60.00 W
West Falls	210	42.42 N	78.41 W
West Falmouth	207	41.36 N	70.38 W
West Fargo	198	46.52 N	96.54 W
West Farleigh	260	51.15 N	0.27 E
West Farmington	214	41.23 N	80.58 W
Westfield, Eng., U.K.	42	50.55 N	0.35 E
Westfield, Il., U.S.	194	39.27 N	88.01 W
Westfield, In., U.S.	218	40.02 N	86.07 W
Westfield, Ma., U.S.	207	42.07 N	72.45 W
Westfield, N.J., U.S.	210	40.39 N	74.20 W
Westfield, N.Y., U.S.	214	42.19 N	79.34 W
Westfield, Pa., U.S.	210	41.55 N	77.32 W
Westfield, Tx., U.S.	222	30.01 N	95.24 W
Westfield, Wi., U.S.	190	43.53 N	89.29 W
Westfield ≃	207	42.05 N	72.35 W
Westfield, Middle Branch ≃	207	42.16 N	72.52 W
Westfield, West Branch ≃	207	42.13 N	72.52 W
Westfield Center	214	41.01 N	81.55 W
West Fiord c[2]	176	76.02 N	90.00 W
Westford, Ma., U.S.	283	42.34 N	71.26 W
Westford, N.Y., U.S.	210	42.39 N	74.48 W
West Fork	194	35.55 N	94.11 W
West Foxboro	283	42.05 N	71.17 W
West Frankfort	194	37.53 N	88.55 W

FRANÇAIS

Nom	Page	Lat.°′	Long.°′ W = Ouest
West Friesland ◆[1]	52	52.45 N	4.50 E
West Frisian Islands → Waddeneilanden II	52	53.26 N	5.30 E
West Fulton	210	42.34 N	74.28 W
Westgate, Austl.	166	26.35 S	146.12 E
Westgate, Mi., U.S.	216	43.03 N	85.42 W
Westgate on Sea	42	51.23 N	1.21 E
West Genesee Terrace	210	43.03 N	76.16 W
West-Ghats → Western Ghāts ⛰	122	14.00 N	75.00 E
West Gilgo Beach	276	40.37 N	73.25 W
West Glacier	202	48.29 N	113.58 W
West Glamorgan □[6]	42	51.35 N	3.35 W
West Glens Falls	210	43.18 N	73.43 W
West Glenville	210	42.56 N	74.04 W
West Goshen	207	41.49 N	73.15 W
West Granby	207	41.57 N	72.50 W
West Grand Lake ⊜	188	45.15 N	67.50 W
West Groton	207	42.36 N	71.37 W
West Grove	208	39.49 N	75.49 W
Westham	208	37.35 N	77.32 W
West Ham ◆[8]	260	51.31 N	0.01 E
West Hamburg	208	40.33 N	76.00 W
West Ham Football Club ♦	260	51.32 N	0.02 E
Westham Island I	224	49.05 N	123.10 W
West Hamlin	188	38.17 N	82.11 W
Westhampton, N.Y., U.S.	207	40.49 N	72.39 W
Westhampton, Va., U.S.	284c	38.54 N	77.11 W
West Hanningfield	260	51.40 N	0.30 E
West Hanover	283	42.07 N	70.53 W
West Harbor c	276	40.54 N	73.32 W
West Harrison	218	39.15 N	84.49 W
West Hartford	207	41.45 N	72.44 W
West Hartland	207	42.00 N	72.58 W
Westhausen	56	48.53 N	10.11 E
Westhaven, Ca., U.S.	204	41.03 N	124.06 W
West Haven, Ct., U.S.	207	41.16 N	72.57 W
Westhaven, Il., U.S.	278	41.35 N	87.51 W
West Haverstraw	210	41.12 N	73.59 W
West Hazleton	210	40.57 N	75.59 W
Westhead	262	53.34 N	2.51 W
West Hebron	210	43.14 N	73.22 W
West Heidelberg	274b	37.45 S	145.02 E
Westheim	56	49.03 N	9.44 E
West Helena	194	34.33 N	90.38 W
Westhemmerde	263	51.33 N	7.47 E
West Hempstead	276	40.42 N	73.39 W
West Henrietta	210	43.02 N	77.40 W
West Hickory	214	41.34 N	79.25 W
Westhill	46	57.09 N	2.17 W
West Hill ◆[8]	275b	43.46 N	79.11 W
Westhofen	263	51.25 N	7.31 E
Westhoff	222	29.12 N	97.28 W
Westhoffen	58	48.36 N	7.26 E
West Hollywood, Ca., U.S.	228	34.05 N	118.21 W
West Hollywood, Fl., U.S.	220	26.01 N	80.10 W
Westholme	224	49.52 N	123.42 W
West Homestead	279b	40.24 N	79.55 W
Westhope, N.D., U.S.	198	48.54 N	101.01 W
Westhope, Oh., U.S.	216	41.18 N	83.57 W
West Horndon	260	51.34 N	0.21 E
West Horsley	260	51.16 N	0.27 W
Westhoughton	262	53.33 N	2.32 W
West Hoxton	274a	33.55 S	150.49 E
West Humber ≃	212	43.44 N	79.33 W
West Humble	260	51.15 N	0.20 W
West Huntington	276	40.42 N	73.18 W
West Hurley	210	42.00 N	74.06 W
Westhuyzen	158	27.30 S	25.27 E
West Hyde	260	51.37 N	0.30 W
West Ice Shelf ⍓	9	67.00 S	85.00 E
Westick	263	51.35 N	7.38 E
Westig	263	51.22 N	7.45 E
West Indies II	230	19.00 N	70.00 W
Westindische Inseln → West Indies II	230	19.00 N	70.00 W
West Irian → Irian Jaya □[4]	164	5.00 S	138.00 E
West Island I, Austl.	164	15.36 S	136.34 E
West Island I, Ma., U.S.	207	41.36 N	70.50 W
West Islip	210	40.42 N	73.18 W
West Jan Mayen Ridge ✦[3]	10	71.00 N	13.00 W
West Jefferson, N.C., U.S.	192	36.24 N	81.29 W
West Jefferson, Oh., U.S.	218	39.56 N	83.16 W
West Jordan	200	40.36 N	111.56 W
Westkapelle, Bel.	50	51.19 N	3.18 E
Westkapelle, Ned.	52	51.32 N	3.27 E
West Keansburg	276	40.27 N	74.09 W
West Kettle ≃	182	49.07 N	119.00 W
West Kilbride	46	55.42 N	4.51 W
West Kill	210	42.13 N	74.31 W
West Kingsdown	42	51.21 N	0.17 E
West Kingston	207	41.28 N	71.33 W
West Kirby	44	53.22 N	3.10 W
Westkirchen	52	51.53 N	8.02 E
West Kittanning	214	40.49 N	79.32 W
West Lafayette, In., U.S.	216	40.25 N	86.54 W
West Lafayette, Oh., U.S.	214	40.16 N	81.45 W
Westlake, La., U.S.	194	30.15 N	93.15 W
Westlake, Oh., U.S.	214	41.27 N	81.55 W
Westlake, Tx., U.S.	222	32.59 N	97.12 W
West Lake ⊜, On., Can.	212	43.56 N	77.17 W
West Lake ⊜, Fl., U.S.	220	25.12 N	80.49 W
West Lake ⊜, N.J., U.S.	276	40.58 N	74.22 W
West Lamma Channel ʊ	271d	22.13 N	114.04 E
West Lancashire □[8]	262	53.35 N	2.50 W
Westland, Mi., U.S.	216	42.19 N	83.24 W
Westland, Pa., U.S.	214	40.17 N	80.16 W
Westland Center ◆[9]	281	42.20 N	83.23 W
Westland National Park ♦	172	43.30 S	170.10 E
Westlands	207	42.37 N	71.20 W
West Lanham Hills	284c	38.57 N	76.53 W
West Laramie	200	41.18 N	105.37 W
West Lawn	284c	38.52 N	77.11 W
West Lebanon, In., U.S.	216	40.16 N	87.23 W
West Lebanon, Pa., U.S.	214	40.35 N	79.22 W
West Leechburg	214	40.37 N	79.37 W
Westleigh, S. Afr.	158	27.31 S	27.21 E
Westleigh, Eng., U.K.	262	53.30 N	2.31 W
West Leipsic	216	41.07 N	84.00 W
Westley	226	37.33 N	121.12 W
West Leyden	212	43.28 N	75.28 W
West Liberty, Ia., U.S.	190	41.34 N	91.15 W
West Liberty, Ky., U.S.	192	37.55 N	83.15 W
West Liberty, Oh., U.S.	216	40.15 N	83.45 W
West Liberty, Pa., U.S.	214	41.00 N	80.03 W
West Liberty, W.V., U.S.	214	40.10 N	80.35 W
West Liberty ◆[8]	279b	40.24 N	80.01 W
Westliche Sahara → Western Sahara □[2]	148	24.30 N	13.00 W

PORTUGUÊS

Nome	Página	Lat.°′	Long.°′ W = Oeste
Westliche Sierra Madre → Madre Occidental, Sierra ⛰	232	25.00 N	105.00 W
Westline	214	41.47 N	78.46 W
West Linn	224	45.21 N	122.36 W
West Linton	46	55.46 N	3.22 W
West Little Owyhee ≃	202	42.28 N	117.15 W
Westlock	182	54.09 N	113.52 W
West Lorne	214	42.36 N	81.36 W
West Los Angeles ◆[8]	280	34.03 N	118.28 W
West Lulworth	42	50.38 N	2.15 W
West Lunga ≃	154	13.06 S	24.39 E
West Lunga National Park ♦	154	12.55 S	25.10 E
Westmalle	52	51.18 N	4.41 E
West Malling	42	51.18 N	0.25 E
West Malling Aerodrome ⊠	260	51.16 N	0.24 E
West Manayunk	285	40.01 N	75.14 W
West Manchester	218	39.54 N	84.37 W
West Mansfield, Ma., U.S.	207	41.59 N	71.14 W
West Mansfield, Oh., U.S.	216	40.24 N	83.32 W
West Mariana Basin ✦[1]	14	15.00 N	137.00 E
West Mayfield	214	40.47 N	80.20 W
West Meadowview	216	41.08 N	87.52 W
Westmeath □[6]	48	53.30 N	7.30 W
West Medway	207	42.08 N	71.25 W
West Melbourne	220	28.04 N	80.39 W
West Memphis	194	35.08 N	90.11 W
West Meon	42	51.01 N	1.05 W
Westmere	210	42.41 N	73.52 W
West Mersea	42	51.47 N	0.55 E
West Miami	220	25.45 N	80.17 W
West Middlesex	214	41.10 N	80.27 W
West Middletown	214	40.15 N	80.25 W
West Midlands □[6]	42	52.30 N	2.00 W
West Mifflin	214	40.22 N	79.52 W
West Milford	210	41.07 N	74.22 W
West Millbury	207	42.11 N	71.48 W
West Mill Creek ≃	222	29.55 N	96.17 W
West Milton, Oh., U.S.	218	39.57 N	84.19 W
West Milton, Pa., U.S.	210	41.01 N	76.52 W
West Milwaukee	216	43.00 N	87.58 W
West Mineola	222	32.41 N	95.31 W
Westminster, Ca., U.S.	228	33.45 N	118.02 W
Westminster, Co., U.S.	200	39.50 N	105.02 W
Westminster, Md., U.S.	208	39.34 N	76.59 W
Westminster, Ma., U.S.	207	42.32 N	71.54 W
Westminster, Oh., U.S.	216	40.42 N	83.58 W
Westminster, S.C., U.S.	192	34.39 N	83.05 W
Westminster ◆[8]	260	51.30 N	0.09 W
Westminster Abbey ʋ[1]	260	51.30 N	0.07 W
Westminster Mall ◆[9]	280	33.45 N	118.01 W
West Modesto	226	37.37 N	121.02 W
West Monroe	194	32.31 N	92.08 W
Westmont, Ca., U.S.	280	33.56 N	118.18 W
Westmont, Il., U.S.	278	41.47 N	87.58 W
Westmont, N.J., U.S.	285	39.54 N	75.02 W
Westmont, Pa., U.S.	214	40.18 N	78.57 W
West Monterey	214	41.03 N	79.39 W
West Montreal ≃	190	47.56 N	80.39 W
West Moors	42	50.49 N	1.55 W
Westmoreland, Ks., U.S.	198	39.23 N	96.24 W
Westmoreland, N.Y., U.S.	210	43.07 N	75.24 W
Westmoreland, Tn., U.S.	194	36.33 N	86.14 W
Westmoreland, Va., U.S.	208	38.04 N	76.34 W
Westmoreland □[6], Pa., U.S.	214	40.18 N	79.33 W
Westmoreland □[6], Va., U.S.	208	38.10 N	76.50 W
Westmoreland City	214	40.20 N	79.41 W
Westmoreland State Park ♦	208	38.09 N	76.50 W
Westmorland	204	33.02 N	115.37 W
Westmount	206	45.29 N	73.36 W
West Mountain ∧	188	43.51 N	74.43 W
West Mud Creek ≃	222	32.07 N	95.10 W
West Mustang Creek ≃	222	29.04 N	96.26 W
West Nab ∧	262	53.35 N	1.53 W
West Nanticoke	210	40.13 N	76.01 W
West New Britain □[5]	164	5.45 S	149.30 E
West Newbury	207	42.48 N	70.59 W
West Newton, Ma., U.S.	283	42.21 N	71.14 W
West Newton, Pa., U.S.	214	40.12 N	79.46 W
West New York	276	40.47 N	74.00 W
West Nicholson	154	21.06 S	29.25 E
West Nishnabotna ≃	198	40.39 N	95.37 W
West Nodaway ≃	194	40.38 N	95.01 W
West Norriton	208	40.08 N	75.22 W
West Norwood ◆[8]	260	51.26 N	0.06 W
West Novaya Zemlya Trough ✦[1]	10	73.30 N	50.00 E
West Nueces ≃	196	29.16 N	99.56 W
West Nyack	210	41.06 N	73.58 W
West Okaw ≃	219	39.32 N	88.42 W
Weston, Austl.	170	32.49 S	151.28 E
Weston, Malay.	112	5.13 N	115.36 E
Weston, Eng., U.K.	262	53.19 N	2.44 W
Weston, Co., U.S.	200	37.07 N	104.50 W
Weston, Ct., U.S.	207	41.12 N	73.22 W
Weston, Id., U.S.	202	42.02 N	111.58 W
Weston, Ma., U.S.	207	42.22 N	71.18 W
Weston, Mi., U.S.	216	41.46 N	84.06 W
Weston, Mo., U.S.	194	39.24 N	94.54 W
Weston, Ne., U.S.	198	41.11 N	96.44 W
Weston, Oh., U.S.	216	41.20 N	83.47 W
Weston, Or., U.S.	202	45.48 N	118.25 W
Weston, Pa., U.S.	210	40.57 N	76.09 W
Weston, W.V., U.S.	188	39.02 N	80.28 W
Weston □[8]	275b	43.43 N	79.31 W
Westonaria	273d	26.19 S	27.39 E
West Oneonta	210	42.28 N	75.07 W
Westönnen	52	51.33 N	7.58 E
Weston Reservoir ⊜[1]	283	42.21 N	71.18 W
Westons Mill Pond ⊜	276	40.28 N	74.25 W
Westons Mills	210	42.04 N	78.23 W
Weston-super-Mare	42	51.21 N	2.59 W
Weston upon Trent	42	52.45 N	2.02 W
West Orange, N.J., U.S.	276	40.47 N	74.14 W
West Orange, Tx., U.S.	194	30.05 N	93.46 W
Westover, Md., U.S.	208	38.07 N	75.42 W
Westover, Pa., U.S.	214	40.45 N	78.40 W
Westover, Tn., U.S.	194	35.36 N	88.52 W
Westover, W.V., U.S.	188	39.38 N	79.58 W
Westover Air Force Base ■	207	42.12 N	72.33 W
Westoverledingen	52	53.10 N	7.28 E
Westowne	284b	39.17 N	76.43 W
West Palm Beach	220	26.42 N	80.03 W
West Palm Beach Canal ≅	220	26.38 N	80.03 W
West Paris	188	44.19 N	70.34 W
West Park	210	41.48 N	73.58 W
West Paterson	276	40.53 N	74.11 W
West Pawlet	210	43.21 N	73.15 W
West Peckham	260	51.15 N	0.22 E
West Pensacola	194	30.25 N	87.16 W
Westphalia, Ks., U.S.	198	38.10 N	95.29 W
Westphalia, Mi., U.S.	216	42.55 N	84.47 W
Westphalia, Mo., U.S.	219	38.26 N	91.59 W
West Pittsburg, Ca., U.S.	226	38.01 N	121.56 W
West Pittsburg, Pa., U.S.	214	40.55 N	80.21 W
West Pittston	210	41.19 N	75.47 W
West Plains	194	36.43 N	91.51 W
West Point, Ca., U.S.	226	38.23 N	120.31 W
West Point, Ga., U.S.	192	32.52 N	85.11 W
Westpoint, In., U.S.	216	40.21 N	87.03 W
West Point, Ia., U.S.	190	40.43 N	91.27 W
West Point, Ky., U.S.	194	37.59 N	85.56 W
West Point, Ms., U.S.	194	33.36 N	88.39 W
West Point, Ne., U.S.	198	41.50 N	96.42 W
West Point, N.Y., U.S.	210	41.23 N	73.57 W
West Point, Oh., U.S.	214	40.43 N	80.42 W
West Point, Pa., U.S.	285	40.12 N	75.18 W
West Point, Va., U.S.	208	37.31 N	76.47 W
West Point ∧	180	64.57 N	144.40 W
West Point ›, Austl.	166	35.01 S	135.57 E
West Point ›, P.E., Can.	186	46.37 N	64.25 W
West Point Lake ⊜[1]	192	33.00 N	85.10 W
West Pond ⊜	276	40.53 N	73.38 W
Westport, Nf., Can.	186	49.47 N	56.38 W
Westport, N.S., Can.	186	44.16 N	66.21 W
Westport, On., Can.	212	44.41 N	76.26 W
Westport, Ire.	48	53.48 N	9.32 W
Westport, N.Z.	172	41.45 S	171.36 E
Westport, Ct., U.S.	207	41.08 N	73.21 W
Westport, In., U.S.	218	39.10 N	85.34 W
Westport, Ky., U.S.	218	38.28 N	85.28 W
Westport, Ma., U.S.	207	41.37 N	71.04 W
Westport, Or., U.S.	224	46.07 N	123.22 W
Westport, Pa., U.S.	214	41.18 N	77.51 W
Westport, Wa., U.S.	224	46.53 N	124.06 W
West Portland	224	45.25 N	122.45 W
West Portland Park	224	45.21 N	122.37 W
Westport Point	207	41.31 N	71.04 W
West Portsmouth	218	38.45 N	83.01 W
West Prairie ≃	182	55.30 N	116.31 W
West Puente Valley	280	34.04 N	117.59 W
West Pullman ◆[8]	278	41.41 N	87.39 W
Westpunt ›	241s	12.37 N	70.03 W
West Pymble	274a	33.46 S	151.08 E
West Quoddy Head ›	188	44.49 N	66.57 W
West Rand	273d	26.07 S	27.45 E
Westray I	46	59.18 N	3.00 W
Westray Firth ʊ	46	59.12 N	2.55 W
West Redding	207	41.19 N	73.26 W
Westrem	50	50.58 N	3.52 E
Westrich □[9]	56	49.15 N	7.20 E
West Richfield	214	41.14 N	81.39 W
West Richland	202	46.18 N	119.20 W
West River c	208	38.52 N	76.31 W
West Road ≃	182	53.19 N	122.52 W
West Rosebud Creek ≃	202	45.29 N	109.27 W
West Roxbury ◆[8]	283	42.17 N	71.09 W
West Rupert	210	43.14 N	73.14 W
West Rutland	188	43.35 N	73.02 W
West Ryde	274a	33.48 S	151.05 E
West Sacramento	226	38.34 N	121.31 W
West Saint Marys ≃	186	45.15 N	62.04 W
West Saint Modeste	186	51.36 N	56.42 W
West Salem, Il., U.S.	194	38.31 N	88.00 W
West Salem, Oh., U.S.	214	40.58 N	82.06 W
West Salem, Wi., U.S.	190	43.53 N	91.04 W
West Salt Creek ≃	200	39.13 N	108.54 W
Westsamoa → Western Samoa □[1]	175a	13.55 S	172.00 W
West Sand Lake	210	42.39 N	73.37 W
West Saugerties	210	42.07 N	74.03 W
West Sayville	276	40.43 N	73.05 W
West Sayville County Park ♦	276	40.43 N	73.06 W
West Scenic Park	220	27.55 N	81.39 W
West Scotia Basin ✦[1]	18	57.00 S	53.00 W
West Seneca	210	42.50 N	78.45 W
West Sepik □[5]	164	4.00 S	141.30 E
West Shoal Lake ⊜	184	50.20 N	97.41 W
West Siberian Plain → Zapadno-Sibirskaja ravnina ≚	72	60.00 N	75.00 E
Westsibirisches Flachland → Zapadno-Sibirskaja ravnina ≚	72	60.00 N	75.00 E
West Side Canal ≅	226	35.19 N	119.23 W
West Side Tennis Club ♦	276	40.43 N	73.51 W
West Simsbury	207	41.52 N	72.51 W
West Slope	224	45.29 N	122.45 W
West Spanish Peak ∧	200	37.23 N	104.59 W
West Springfield, Ma., U.S.	207	42.06 N	72.37 W
West Springfield, Pa., U.S.	214	41.57 N	80.29 W
West Springfield, Va., U.S.	208	38.46 N	77.13 W
West Stewartstown	206	44.59 N	71.31 W
West Stockbridge	207	42.20 N	73.22 W
West Stony Creek ≃	210	43.15 N	74.13 W
West Suffield	207	41.59 N	72.41 W
West Sunbury	214	41.00 N	79.54 W
West Sussex □[6]	42	50.55 N	0.35 W
West Swanzey	207	42.52 N	72.20 W
West Terre Haute	194	39.27 N	87.27 W
West-Terschelling	52	53.21 N	5.13 E
West Thompson Lake ⊜[1]	207	41.57 N	71.54 W
West Thurrock	260	51.29 N	0.16 E
West Tiana	207	40.52 N	72.33 W
West Tilbury	260	51.29 N	0.24 E
West Tisbury	207	41.22 N	70.40 W
West Toodyay	168a	31.33 S	116.27 E
West Torrens	168b	34.56 S	138.32 E
Westtown, N.Y., U.S.	210	41.20 N	74.32 W
Westtown, Pa., U.S.	285	39.56 N	75.33 W
West Townsend	207	42.40 N	71.44 W
West Turffontein ◆[8]	273d	26.16 S	28.02 E
West Union, Ia., U.S.	190	42.57 N	91.48 W
West Union, Oh., U.S.	218	38.47 N	83.32 W
West Union, W.V., U.S.	188	39.17 N	80.46 W
West Union Creek ≃	282	37.25 N	122.16 W
West Unity	216	41.35 N	84.26 W
West University Place	222	29.43 N	95.26 W
West Upton	207	42.10 N	71.37 W
Westvale	210	43.02 N	76.13 W
West Valley, Mt., U.S.	202	46.08 N	113.01 W
West Valley, N.Y., U.S.	210	42.24 N	78.37 W
West Valley City	200	40.42 N	111.57 W
West Vancouver	182	49.22 N	123.12 W
West View	214	40.31 N	80.02 W
West View Amusement Park ♦	279b	40.31 N	80.02 W
Westview Heights	207	41.33 N	73.05 W
Westville, N.S., Can.	186	45.34 N	62.43 W
Westville, In., U.S.	216	41.32 N	86.54 W
Westville, N.H., U.S.	207	42.49 N	71.07 W
Westville, N.J., U.S.	285	39.52 N	75.07 W
Westville, Oh., U.S.	218	40.07 N	83.51 W
Westville, Ok., U.S.	194	35.59 N	94.34 W
Westville, Pa., U.S.	214	41.13 N	78.50 W
Westville Center	206	44.57 N	74.24 W
Westville Grove	285	39.51 N	75.07 W
Westville Lake ⊜[1]	207	42.05 N	72.05 W
Westville Oaks	285	39.51 N	75.08 W
West Virginia □[3], U.S.	178	38.45 N	80.30 W
West Virginia □[3], U.S.	188	38.45 N	80.30 W
West-Vlaanderen □[4]	50	51.00 N	3.00 E
West Walker ≃	226	38.53 N	119.10 W
West Wallsend	170	32.54 S	151.35 E
Westward Ho90	42	51.02 N	4.15 W
West Wareham	207	41.47 N	70.45 W
West Warren	207	42.12 N	72.14 W
West Warwick	207	41.42 N	71.31 W
West Water ≃	46	56.47 N	2.38 W
West Webster	210	43.12 N	77.29 W
Westwego	194	29.54 N	90.08 W
West Wellow	42	50.58 N	1.35 W
West Whittier	280	33.59 N	118.03 W
West Wickham ◆[8]	260	51.22 N	0.01 W
West Willington	207	41.52 N	72.18 W
West Willow	216	42.14 N	83.34 W
West Windsor	210	42.06 N	74.46 W
West Winfield, N.Y., U.S.	210	42.53 N	75.11 W
West Winfield, Pa., U.S.	214	40.48 N	79.42 W
Westwold	182	50.28 N	119.45 W
Westwood, Ca., U.S.	204	40.18 N	121.00 W
Westwood, In., U.S.	218	39.55 N	85.25 W
Westwood, Ma., U.S.	207	42.12 N	71.14 W
Westwood, Mi., U.S.	216	42.18 N	85.38 W
Westwood, N.J., U.S.	210	40.59 N	74.01 W
Westwood, Pa., U.S.	214	40.18 N	78.56 W
Westwood ◆[8]	280	34.04 N	118.27 W
Westwood Lakes	220	25.44 N	80.22 W
Westworth Village	222	32.45 N	97.25 W
West Wyalong	166	33.55 S	147.13 E
West Wycombe	42	51.39 N	0.49 W
West Yarmouth	207	41.39 N	70.14 W
West Yegua Creek ≃	222	30.20 N	96.52 W
West Yellow Creek ≃	194	39.38 N	93.04 W
West Yellowstone	202	44.39 N	111.06 W
West York	208	39.57 N	76.45 W
West Yorkshire □[6]	44	53.45 N	1.40 W
Wetan, Pulau I	164	7.54 S	129.32 E
Wetar, Pulau I	112	7.48 S	126.18 E
Wetar, Selat ʊ	112	8.20 S	126.30 E
Wetaskiwin	182	52.58 N	113.22 W
Wete	154	5.04 S	39.43 E
Wethau	54	51.08 N	11.52 E
Wetherby	44	53.56 N	1.23 W
Wetherill Park	274a	33.51 S	150.54 E
Wethersfield	207	41.43 N	72.40 W
Wethmar	263	51.37 N	7.33 E
Wetiko Hills ⛰[2]	184	54.30 N	92.20 W
Wetluga → Vetluga ≃	80	56.18 N	46.24 E
Wetmore	198	39.38 N	95.48 W
Wet Mountains ⛰	200	38.00 N	105.10 W
Weto	152	7.57 N	7.50 E
Wetten	52	51.34 N	6.17 E
Wetter, Dtsch.	56	50.54 N	8.43 E
Wetter, Dtsch.	56	51.23 N	7.23 E
Wetter ≃	56	50.18 N	8.49 E
Wetterau □[9]	56	50.15 N	8.50 E
Wetteren	50	51.00 N	3.53 E
Wetterhorn ∧	58	46.39 N	8.08 E
Wetterstein Gebirge ⛰	64	47.25 N	11.05 E
Wettigan	110	18.57 N	95.21 E
Wettin	54	51.35 N	11.48 E
Wettingen	58	47.28 N	8.19 E
Wettringen	52	52.12 N	7.19 E
Wetumka	196	35.14 N	96.14 W
Wetumpka	194	32.32 N	86.12 W
Wetwang	44	54.01 N	0.34 W
Wetzikon	58	47.19 N	8.47 E
Wetzlar	56	50.33 N	8.29 E
Wetzstein ∧[2]	54	50.27 N	11.27 E
Wevelgem	50	50.48 N	3.10 E
Wevelinghoven	56	51.06 N	6.37 E
Wewahitchka	192	30.06 N	85.12 W
Wewak	164	3.35 S	143.40 E
Wewelsfleth	52	53.50 N	9.24 E
Wewer	52	51.41 N	8.42 E
Wewoka	196	35.09 N	96.29 W
Wexford, Ire.	48	52.20 N	6.27 W
Wexford, Pa., U.S.	214	40.38 N	80.03 W
Wexford □[6]	48	52.20 N	6.40 W
Wexford ◆[8]	275b	43.45 N	79.18 W
Wexford Harbour c	48	52.20 N	6.24 W
Wey ≃	42	51.23 N	0.28 W
Weyakwin Lake ⊜	184	54.30 N	106.00 W
Weyanoke	284c	38.48 N	77.09 W
Weyarn	64	47.51 N	11.48 E
Weyauwega	190	44.19 N	88.56 W
Weybridge	42	51.23 N	0.28 W
Weyburn	184	49.41 N	103.52 W
Weyer ◆[8]	263	51.10 N	7.01 E
Weyer Markt	61	47.52 N	14.41 E
Weyersheim	56	48.43 N	7.48 E
Weyhausen	52	52.47 N	10.23 E
Weyhe	52	52.59 N	8.52 E
Weymouth, N.S., Can.	186	44.25 N	66.00 W
Weymouth, Eng., U.K.	42	50.36 N	2.28 W
Weymouth, Ma., U.S.	207	42.13 N	70.56 W
Weymouth, N.J., U.S.	208	39.30 N	74.46 W
Weymouth, Cape ›	164	12.37 S	143.27 E
Weymouth Back ≃	283	42.15 N	70.55 W
Weymouth Fore ≃	283	42.16 N	70.56 W
Weymouth Great Pond ⊜	283	42.12 N	71.02 W
Wezemaal	56	50.57 N	4.46 E
Wezep	52	52.27 N	6.00 E
Whakatane	172	37.58 S	177.00 E
Whakatane ≃	172	37.57 S	177.00 E
Whalan	274a	33.45 S	150.49 E
Whale Creek ≃	276	40.27 N	74.13 W
Whaley Bridge	44	53.20 N	1.59 W
Whaley Lake	210	41.33 N	73.40 W
Whaleysville	208	38.23 N	75.18 W
Whaleyville	208	36.37 N	76.41 W
Whalley	44	53.50 N	2.24 W
Whalom	207	42.34 N	71.44 W
Whalsay I	46a	60.20 N	0.59 W
Whangaehu ≃	172	40.03 S	175.06 E
Whangamata	172	37.12 S	175.52 E
Whangamomona	172	39.09 S	174.44 E
Whanganui National Park ♦	172	39.20 S	175.00 E
Whangara	172	38.34 S	178.13 E
Whangarei	172	35.43 S	174.19 E
Whangaruru Harbour c	172	35.22 S	174.21 E
Whaplode	42	52.48 N	0.02 W
Wharfe ≃	44	53.51 N	1.07 W
Wharfedale V	44	54.01 N	1.56 W
Wharles	262	53.49 N	2.50 W
Wharton, N.J., U.S.	210	40.53 N	74.34 W
Wharton, Oh., U.S.	214	40.52 N	83.21 W
Wharton, Tx., U.S.	222	29.18 N	96.06 W
Wharton, W.V., U.S.	188	37.54 N	81.40 W
Wharton □[6]	222	29.17 N	96.13 W
Wharton Basin ✦[1]	12	21.00 S	100.00 E
Wharton Lake ⊜	176	64.00 N	99.55 W
Wharton State Forest ♦	285	39.45 N	74.40 W
Whataroa	172	43.17 S	170.25 E
Whatatutu	172	38.23 S	177.50 E
What Cheer	190	41.24 N	92.21 W
Whatcom □[6]	224	48.48 N	121.59 W
Whatcom, Lake ⊜	224	48.43 N	122.20 W
Whately	207	42.26 N	72.38 W
Whatley	194	31.39 N	87.42 W
Whatshan Lake ⊜	182	50.00 N	118.03 W
Whauphill	44	54.49 N	4.29 W
Wheao ≃	172	38.34 S	176.39 E
Wheatfield	216	40.33 N	87.06 W
Wheatland, Ca., U.S.	226	39.00 N	121.25 W
Wheatland, Ia., U.S.	190	41.49 N	90.50 W
Wheatland, Pa., U.S.	214	41.12 N	80.28 W
Wheatland, Wy., U.S.	200	42.03 N	104.57 W
Wheatland Hills	208	40.02 N	76.21 W
Wheatland Reservoir ⊜[1]	200	41.52 N	105.36 W
Wheatley, On., Can.	214	42.06 N	82.27 W
Wheatley, Eng., U.K.	42	51.44 N	1.08 W
Wheatley, Ar., U.S.	194	34.54 N	91.06 W
Wheatley Hill	44	54.45 N	1.23 W
Wheaton, Il., U.S.	216	41.51 N	88.06 W
Wheaton, Md., U.S.	208	39.02 N	77.03 W
Wheaton, Mn., U.S.	198	45.48 N	96.29 W
Wheaton Plaza ◆[9]	284c	39.02 N	77.03 W
Wheaton Regional Park ♦	284c	39.03 N	77.02 W
Wheat Ridge	200	39.45 N	105.04 W
Wheelbarrow Peak ∧	204	37.27 N	116.05 W
Wheeler, In., U.S.	216	41.30 N	87.10 W
Wheeler, Ms., U.S.	194	34.34 N	88.36 W
Wheeler, Tx., U.S.	196	35.26 N	100.16 W
Wheeler ≃, P.Q., Can.	176	57.02 N	67.13 W
Wheeler ≃, Sk., Can.	184	57.20 N	105.30 W
Wheeler Air Force Base ■	229c	21.29 N	158.03 W
Wheeler Dam ◆[6]	283	42.48 N	71.12 W
Wheeler Island I	282	38.05 N	121.56 W
Wheeler Lake ⊜[1]	194	34.40 N	87.05 W
Wheeler Peak ∧, Ca., U.S.	226	38.25 N	119.17 W
Wheeler Peak ∧, Nv., U.S.	204	38.59 N	114.19 W
Wheeler Peak ∧, N.M., U.S.	200	36.34 N	105.25 W
Wheeler Ridge	228	35.06 N	119.01 W
Wheelersburg	218	38.43 N	82.51 W
Wheelers Hill	274b	37.55 S	145.11 E
Wheeling, Il., U.S.	216	42.08 N	87.55 W
Wheeling, W.V., U.S.	214	40.03 N	80.43 W
Wheeling Creek ≃	214	40.03 N	80.41 W
Wheelock	222	30.54 N	96.24 W
Wheelock ≃	44	53.12 N	2.26 W
Wheelton	262	53.41 N	2.36 W
Wheelwright, Arg.	252	33.47 S	61.13 W
Wheelwright, Ky., U.S.	192	37.19 N	82.43 W
Wheelwright Park ♦	283	42.15 N	70.49 W
Wheeny Creek ≃	170	33.26 S	150.50 E
Whela Creek ≃	162	26.17 S	116.50 E
Whelan, Mount ∧[2]	166	23.25 S	138.54 E
Whelpleyhill	260	51.44 N	0.33 W
Whernside ∧	44	54.14 N	2.23 W
Whetstone Creek ≃	214	40.23 N	83.03 W
Whetstone Gulf State Park ♦	212	43.44 N	75.27 W
Whickham	44	54.56 N	1.41 W
Whidbey Island I	224	48.15 N	122.40 W
Whidbey Island Naval Air Station ■	224	48.17 N	122.37 W
Whiddon Down	42	50.43 N	3.51 W
Whigham	192	30.52 N	84.19 W
Whigville	207	41.43 N	72.56 W
Whim Creek	162	20.50 S	117.50 E
Whinham, Mount ∧	162	26.04 S	130.15 E
Whippany	210	40.49 N	74.25 W
Whippany ≃	276	40.51 N	74.21 W
Whirl Creek ≃	212	43.28 N	81.12 W
Whirlwind Reefs ✦[2]	164	4.42 S	148.16 E
Whiskey Peak ∧	200	42.18 N	107.35 W
Whiskeytown-Shasta-Trinity National Recreation Area ♦	204	40.45 N	122.15 W
Whisky Chitto Creek ≃	194	30.31 N	92.55 W
Whiston	262	53.25 N	2.50 W
Whitacres	207	41.48 N	72.39 W
Whitaker	279b	40.24 N	79.53 W
Whitakers	192	36.06 N	77.42 W
Whitbourne	186	47.25 N	53.32 W
Whitburn, Eng., U.K.	44	54.57 N	1.22 W
Whitburn, Scot., U.K.	46	55.52 N	3.42 W
Whitby, On., Can.	212	43.52 N	78.56 W
Whitby, Eng., U.K.	44	54.29 N	0.37 W
Whitby, Eng., U.K.	262	53.17 N	2.54 W
Whitby Abbey ʋ[1]	44	54.28 N	0.38 W
Whitchurch, Eng., U.K.	42	51.53 N	0.51 W
Whitchurch, Eng., U.K.	42	51.14 N	1.20 W
Whitchurch, Eng., U.K.	42	51.52 N	2.39 W
Whitchurch, Eng., U.K.	42	52.58 N	2.41 W
Whitchurch-Stouffville	212	43.58 N	79.15 W
Whitcombe, Mount ∧	172	43.13 S	170.55 E
White, Ga., U.S.	192	34.16 N	84.44 W
White, S.D., U.S.	198	44.26 N	96.38 W
White □[6]	216	40.45 N	86.46 W
White ≃, B.C., Can.	182	50.23 N	115.35 W
White ≃, On., Can.	190	48.33 N	86.16 W
White ≃, N.A.	180	63.11 N	139.36 W
White ≃, U.S.	194	33.53 N	91.03 W
White ≃, U.S.	198	43.45 N	99.30 W
White ≃, U.S.	200	40.04 N	109.41 W
White ≃, Az., U.S.	200	33.44 N	110.13 W
White ≃, In., U.S.	194	38.25 N	87.44 W
White ≃, Mi., U.S.	190	43.25 N	86.21 W
White ≃, Nv., U.S.	204	37.42 N	115.10 W
White ≃, Or., U.S.	224	45.14 N	121.04 W
White ≃, Tx., U.S.	196	33.14 N	100.56 W
White ≃, Vt., U.S.	188	43.37 N	72.20 W
White ≃, Wa., U.S.	224	47.12 N	122.15 W
White ≃, Wa., U.S.	224	47.50 N	120.49 W
White ≃, Wi., U.S.	190	46.36 N	90.42 W
White ≃, Wi., U.S.	216	42.41 N	88.17 W
White, East Fork ≃, Az., U.S.	200	33.47 N	110.00 W
White, East Fork ≃, In., U.S.	194	38.33 N	87.14 W
White, Lake ⊜	162	21.05 S	129.00 E
White, Lake ⊜[1]	218	39.07 N	83.02 W
White, North Fork ≃, Az., U.S.	200	33.47 N	110.00 W
White, North Fork ≃, Co., U.S.	200	39.58 N	107.38 W
White, South Fork ≃	200	39.58 N	107.38 W
White, West Fork ≃	224	47.07 N	121.37 W
White Bay c	186	50.00 N	56.30 W
White Bear Indian Reserve ◆[4]	184	49.45 N	102.15 W
White Bear Lake	190	45.03 N	93.00 W
Whitebear Lake ⊜	184	51.05 N	108.05 W
White Bluff	194	36.06 N	87.13 W
White Breast Creek ≃	190	41.24 N	93.02 W
White Butte ∧	198	46.23 N	103.19 W
Whitecap Lake ⊜	184	56.54 N	95.14 W
White Cap Mountain ∧	188	45.35 N	69.13 W
White Castle	194	30.10 N	91.08 W
White Center	224	47.31 N	122.21 W
White Chuck ≃	224	48.11 N	121.27 W
White City, Fl., U.S.	220	29.53 N	85.13 W
White City, Ks., U.S.	198	38.47 N	96.44 W
White City Stadium ♦	260	51.31 N	0.14 W
White Clay Creek ≃, U.S.	198	43.12 N	102.48 W
White Clay Creek ≃, U.S.	285	39.42 N	75.37 W
White Cliffs, Austl.	162	28.26 S	122.57 E
White Cliffs, Austl.	166	30.51 S	143.05 E
White Cloud	190	43.33 N	85.46 W
White Cloud Island I	212	44.50 N	80.58 W
Whitecoomb ∧, N.Z.	172	45.36 S	169.05 E
White Coomb ∧, Scot., U.K.	44	55.26 N	3.20 W
Whitecourt	182	54.09 N	115.41 W

Symbol	English	Deutsch	Español	Français	Português
≃	River	Fluß	Río	Rivière	Rio
≅	Canal	Kanal	Canal	Canal	Canal
⌊	Waterfall, Rapids	Wasserfall, Stromschnellen	Cascada, Rápidos	Chute d'eau, Rapides	Cascata, Rápidos
ʊ	Strait	Meeresstraße	Estrecho	Détroit	Estreito
c	Bay, Gulf	Bucht, Golf	Bahía, Golfo	Baie, Golfe	Baía, Golfo
⊜	Lake, Lakes	See, Seen	Lago, Lagos	Lac, Lacs	Lago, Lagos
≋	Swamp	Sumpf	Pantano	Marais	Pântano
⍓	Ice Features, Glacier	Eis- und Gletscherformen	Accidentes Glaciales	Formes glaciaires	Acidentes glaciares
⊼	Other Hydrographic Features	Andere Hydrographische Objekte	Otros Elementos Hidrográficos	Autres données hydrographiques	Outros acidentes hidrográficos
✦	Submarine Features	Untermeerische Objekte	Accidentes Submarinos	Formes de relief sous-marin	Acidentes submarinos
□	Political Unit	Politische Einheit	Unidad Politica	Entité politique	Unidade política
ʋ	Cultural Institution	Kulturelle Institution	Institución Cultural	Institution culturelle	Institução cultural
⊥	Historical Site	Historische Stätte	Sitio Histórico	Site historique	Sitio histórico
♦	Recreational Site	Erholungs- und Ferienort	Sitio de Recreo	Centre de loisirs	Area de Lazer
⊠	Airport	Flughafen	Aeropuerto	Aéroport	Aeroporto
■	Military Installation	Militäranlage	Instalación Militar	Installation militaire	Instalação militar
◆	Miscellaneous	Verschiedenes	Misceláneo	Divers	Diversos

White Creek 210 42.58 N 73.18 W
White Creek ≃, In., U.S. 218 38.58 N 86.01 W
White Creek ≃, Wa., U.S. 224 46.01 N 121.08 W
White Deer, Pa., U.S. 210 41.05 N 76.52 W
White Deer, Tx., U.S. 196 35.26 N 101.10 W
White Deer Creek ≃ 210 41.05 N 76.53 W
White Earth ≃ 198 48.09 N 102.42 W
White Earth Indian Reservation ◆⁴ 198 47.18 N 95.50 W
White Esk ≃ 44 55.12 N 3.10 W
Whiteface 196 33.36 N 102.37 W
Whiteface ≃ 190 46.58 N 92.48 W
Whiteface Mountain ∧ 188 44.22 N 73.54 W
Whitefield, Eng., U.K. 44 53.33 N 2.18 W
Whitefield, N.H., U.S. 188 44.22 N 71.36 W
Whitefish 202 48.24 N 114.20 W
Whitefish ≃ 190 45.55 N 86.57 W
Whitefish Bay 216 43.06 N 87.54 W
Whitefish Bay c, On., Can. 184 49.26 N 94.14 W
Whitefish Bay c, N.A. 190 46.40 N 84.50 W
Whitefish Lake ⊜, Ab., Can. 182 54.22 N 111.55 W
Whitefish Lake ⊜, Mb., Can. 184 55.34 N 93.13 W
Whitefish Lake ⊜, N.T., Can. 176 62.41 N 106.48 W
Whitefish Lake ⊜, On., Can. 190 48.03 N 84.29 W
Whitefish Lake ⊜, On., Can. 212 45.18 N 79.47 W
Whitefish Lake ⊜, On., Can. 212 44.31 N 76.14 W
Whitefish Lake ⊜, Ak., U.S. 180 61.21 N 160.00 W
Whitefish Lake ⊜, Mt., U.S. 202 48.27 N 114.22 W
White Fish Lake Indian Reserve ◆⁴ 182 54.20 N 111.45 W
Whitefish Point 190 46.45 N 84.59 W
Whitefish Point > 190 46.45 N 85.00 W
Whitefish Range ⩘ 202 48.40 N 114.26 W
Whiteford 208 39.42 N 76.20 W
Whiteford Point > 42 51.38 N 4.14 W
White Fox 184 53.27 N 104.05 W
White Fox ≃ 184 53.32 N 104.00 W
Whitegate 48 51.50 N 8.14 W
White Gull Creek ≃ 184 53.44 N 104.20 W
Whitehall (Paulstown), Ire. 48 52.41 N 7.01 W
Whitehall, Scot., U.K. 46 59.07 N 2.37 W
White Hall, Ar., U.S. 194 34.16 N 92.05 W
White Hall, Il., U.S. 219 39.26 N 90.24 W
White Hall, Md., U.S. 208 39.37 N 76.37 W
Whitehall, Mi., U.S. 190 43.24 N 86.20 W
Whitehall, Mt., U.S. 202 45.52 N 112.05 W
Whitehall, N.Y., U.S. 188 43.33 N 73.24 W
Whitehall, Oh., U.S. 218 39.58 N 82.53 W
Whitehall, Pa., U.S. 214 40.21 N 79.59 W
Whitehall, Wi., U.S. 190 44.22 N 91.18 W
Whitehaven, Eng., U.K. 44 54.33 N 3.35 W
White Haven, Pa., U.S. 210 41.03 N 75.46 W
Whitehead 48 54.46 N 5.43 W
White Holme Reservoir ⊜¹ 262 53.41 N 2.02 W
Whitehorse, Yk., Can. 180 60.43 N 135.03 W
White Horse, N.J., U.S. 208 40.11 N 74.42 W
White Horse, Vale of V 42 51.37 N 1.37 W
Whitehorse Hill ∧² 42 51.34 N 1.34 W
Whitehouse, Scot., U.K. 46 57.13 N 2.37 W
Whitehouse, N.J., U.S. 210 40.37 N 74.46 W
Whitehouse, Oh., U.S. 216 41.31 N 83.48 W
White House, Tn., U.S. 194 36.35 N 86.49 W
Whitehouse, Tx., U.S. 222 32.13 N 95.14 W
White House ᵾ 284c 38.54 N 77.02 W
White House Station 210 40.36 N 74.46 W
White Island I, Ant. 9 66.44 S 48.35 E
White Island I, N.T., Can. 176 65.50 N 84.50 W
White Island I, N.Z. 172 37.31 S 177.11 E
White Lake, Mi., U.S. 281 42.41 N 83.33 W
White Lake, N.Y., U.S. 210 41.40 N 74.50 W
White Lake, S.D., U.S. 198 43.43 N 98.42 W
White Lake, Wi., U.S. 190 45.09 N 88.45 W
White Lake ⊜, On., Can. 190 48.48 N 85.36 W
White Lake ⊜, On., Can. 212 44.27 N 77.03 W
White Lake ⊜, On., Can. 212 44.47 N 76.45 W
White Lake ⊜, On., Can. 212 45.18 N 76.31 W
White Lake ⊜, La., U.S. 194 29.45 N 92.30 W
White Lake ⊜, Mi., U.S. 281 42.40 N 83.34 W
Whiteland 218 39.33 N 86.05 W
Whitelaw 182 56.07 N 118.04 W
Whiteley Village 260 51.21 N 0.26 W
White Lick Creek ≃ 218 39.30 N 86.23 W
White Lick Creek, East Fork ≃ 218 39.35 N 86.22 W
White Lick Creek, West Fork ≃ 218 39.38 N 86.23 W
Whiteman Air Force Base ■ 194 38.44 N 93.34 W
Whiteman Airpark ⊠ 280 34.15 N 118.25 W
Whiteman Range ⩘ 164 5.50 S 149.55 E
Whitemans Creek ≃ 212 43.10 N 80.21 W
Whitemark 166 40.07 S 148.01 E
White Marsh 284b 39.23 N 76.26 W
Whitemarsh Run ≃ 284b 39.22 N 76.25 W
White Meadow Lake 210 40.55 N 74.31 W
White Meadow Lake ⊜ 276 40.55 N 74.31 W
White Mills 210 41.32 N 75.12 W
White Mountain 180 64.41 N 163.24 W
White Mountain Peak ∧ 204 37.38 N 118.15 W
White Mountains ⩘, U.S. 204 37.30 N 118.15 W
White Mountains ⩘, Az., U.S. 200 33.45 N 109.40 W
White Mountains ⩘, N.H., U.S. 188 44.10 N 71.35 W
Whitemouth 184 49.57 N 95.59 W
Whitemouth ≃ 184 50.07 N 96.02 W
Whitemouth Lake ⊜ 184 49.14 N 95.40 W
Whitemud ≃ 184 50.15 N 98.37 W
Whiten Head > 46 58.34 N 4.36 W
White Nile (Al-Baḥr al-Abyaḍ) ≃ 140 15.38 N 32.31 E
White Nile Dam — Jabal al-Awliyā', Khazzān ◆⁶ 140 15.14 N 32.29 E
White Oak, Md., U.S. 284c 39.02 N 77.00 W
White Oak, Pa., U.S. 279b 40.20 N 79.48 W
White Oak, Tx., U.S. 222 32.32 N 94.52 W
White Oak ≃ 192 34.40 N 77.07 W
White Oak Creek ≃, Oh., U.S. 218 38.47 N 83.57 W
White Oak Creek ≃, Tx., U.S. 194 33.16 N 94.39 W
White Oak Creek, East Fork ≃ 218 39.00 N 83.53 W
White Oak Creek, North Fork ≃ 218 39.00 N 83.53 W
White Oak Lake ⊜¹ 194 33.40 N 93.10 W
White Oak Regional Park ♦ 279a 40.21 N 79.47 W
White Pass χ, N.A. 180 59.38 N 135.05 W
White Pass χ, Wa., U.S. 224 46.38 N 121.24 W
White Pigeon 216 41.47 N 85.38 W
White Pine, Mi., U.S. 190 46.45 N 89.35 W
Whitepine, Mt., U.S. 182 47.45 N 115.29 W
White Pine, Tn., U.S. 192 36.06 N 83.17 W
White Pines, Ca., U.S. 226 38.18 N 120.21 W
White Pines, Il., U.S. 278 41.57 N 87.57 W
White Plains, Md., U.S. 208 38.35 N 76.56 W
White Plains, N.Y., U.S. 210 41.02 N 73.45 W
White Plains, N.C., U.S. 192 36.26 N 80.38 W
White Pond ⊜ 283 42.26 N 71.23 W
White River, On., Can. 190 48.35 N 85.15 W
Whiteriver, Az., U.S. 200 33.50 N 109.57 W
White River, S.D., U.S. 198 43.34 N 100.44 W
White River Junction 188 43.38 N 72.19 W
White Rock 224 49.02 N 122.49 W
White Rock Creek ≃, Ks., U.S. 198 39.55 N 97.51 W
White Rock Creek ≃, Tx., U.S. 222 32.43 N 96.44 W
White Rock Creek ≃, Tx., U.S. 222 30.54 N 95.16 W
White Rock Lake ⊜¹ 222 32.50 N 96.44 W
White Rocks ∧ 192 36.40 N 83.27 W
Whiterocks ≃ 200 40.26 N 109.55 W
White Roding 260 51.48 N 0.16 E
White Russia — Belarus □¹ 22 53.50 N 28.00 E
Whitesail Lake ⊜ 182 53.30 N 127.00 W
White Salmon 224 45.43 N 121.29 W
White Salmon ≃ 224 45.43 N 121.31 W
Whitesand ≃ 184 51.34 N 101.55 W
White Sands Beach 207 41.18 N 72.09 W
White Sands Missile Range ■ 200 32.23 N 106.28 W
White Sands National Monument ♦ 200 32.46 N 106.20 W
Whitesboro, N.J., U.S. 208 39.02 N 74.51 W
Whitesboro, N.Y., U.S. 210 43.07 N 75.17 W
Whitesboro, Tx., U.S. 196 33.39 N 96.54 W
Whitesburg 192 37.07 N 82.49 W
White Sea — Beloje more ᵀ² 24 65.30 N 38.00 E
White Settlement 222 32.45 N 97.27 W
Whiteshell Provincial Park ♦ 184 50.00 N 95.25 W
Whiteside 219 39.11 N 91.01 W
Whiteside, Canal ⊔ 254 53.55 S 70.15 W
White's Landing 214 41.25 N 82.54 W
White Springs 192 30.19 N 82.45 W
White Stone 208 37.38 N 76.23 W
Whitestone ◆⁸ 276 40.47 N 73.49 W
White Stone Lake ⊜ 184 56.25 N 97.31 W
Whitestown 218 39.59 N 86.20 W
White Sulphur Springs, Mt., U.S. 202 46.32 N 110.54 W
White Sulphur Springs, N.Y., U.S. 210 41.48 N 74.50 W
White Sulphur Springs, W.V., U.S. 192 37.47 N 80.17 W
Whites Valley 210 41.42 N 75.22 W
Whitesville, Ky., U.S. 194 37.40 N 86.52 W
Whitesville, N.Y., U.S. 210 42.02 N 77.45 W
Whitesville, W.V., U.S. 188 37.58 N 81.31 W
White Swan 224 46.22 N 120.43 W
Whiteswan Lakes ⊜ 184 54.05 N 105.10 W
Whitevale 214 43.53 N 79.09 W
White Valley 214 40.25 N 79.36 W
Whiteville, N.C., U.S. 192 34.20 N 78.42 W
Whiteville, Tn., U.S. 194 35.19 N 89.08 W
White Volta (Volta Blanche) ≃ 150 9.10 N 1.15 W
Whitewater, Ks., U.S. 198 37.57 N 97.08 W
Whitewater, Mt., U.S. 202 48.45 N 107.37 W
Whitewater, Wi., U.S. 216 42.50 N 88.43 W
Whitewater ≃, U.S. 218 39.10 N 84.47 W
Whitewater ≃, Ca., U.S. 204 33.30 N 116.03 W
Whitewater ≃, Mo., U.S. 194 37.01 N 89.43 W
Whitewater, Dry Fork ≃ 218 39.11 N 84.47 W
Whitewater, East Fork ≃ 218 39.24 N 85.01 W
Whitewater Baldy ∧ 200 33.20 N 108.39 W
Whitewater Bay c 220 25.16 N 81.00 W
Whitewater Creek ≃, N.A. 202 48.30 N 107.11 W
Whitewater Creek ≃, Ga., U.S. 192 32.21 N 84.03 W
Whitewater Creek ≃, Wi., U.S. 216 42.52 N 88.45 W
Whitewater Lake ⊜, Mb., Can. 184 49.15 N 100.20 W
Whitewater Lake ⊜, Wi., U.S. 216 42.47 N 88.42 W
Whitewater State Park ♦ 218 39.36 N 84.58 W
White Woman Creek ≃ 198 38.25 N 100.54 W
Whitewood, Austl. 166 21.28 S 143.36 E
Whitewood, Sk., Can. 184 50.20 N 102.15 W
Whitewood, S.D., U.S. 198 44.27 N 103.38 W
Whitewood, Lake ⊜ 198 44.20 N 97.18 W
Whitewright 196 33.30 N 96.23 W
Whitfield 42 51.09 N 1.18 E
Whithorn, Jam. 241q 18.15 N 78.02 W
Whithorn, Scot., U.K. 44 54.44 N 4.25 W
Whitianga 172 36.50 S 175.42 E
Whiting, In., U.S. 216 41.40 N 87.29 W
Whiting, Ia., U.S. 198 42.07 N 96.08 W
Whiting, Ks., U.S. 198 39.35 N 95.36 W
Whiting, N.J., U.S. 208 39.57 N 74.22 W
Whiting, Wi., U.S. 190 44.29 N 89.33 W
Whiting Bay 46 55.29 N 5.06 W
Whiting Field Naval Air Station ■ 194 30.43 N 87.02 W
Whitingham 207 42.47 N 72.53 W
Whitinsville 207 42.06 N 71.40 W
Whitland 42 51.50 N 4.37 W
Whitley □⁶ 216 41.10 N 85.29 W
Whitley Bay 44 55.03 N 1.25 W
Whitley City 192 36.43 N 84.28 W
Whitley Row 260 51.15 N 0.07 E
Whitman 207 42.04 N 70.56 W
Whitman Mission National Historic Site ⊥ 202 46.01 N 118.30 W
Whitmans Pond ⊜ 283 42.12 N 70.57 W
Whitman Square 208 39.45 N 75.03 W
Whitmire 192 34.30 N 81.36 W
Whitmore Lake 216 42.25 N 83.46 W
Whitmore Lake ⊜ 281 42.26 N 83.45 W
Whitmore Mountains ⩘ 9 82.35 S 104.30 W
Whitmore Village 229c 21.30 N 158.01 W
Whitner Heights 226 36.37 N 119.32 W
Whitney, On., Can. 212 45.30 N 78.14 W
Whitney, Pa., U.S. 214 40.15 N 79.24 W
Whitney, Tx., U.S. 222 31.57 N 97.19 W
Whitney, Lake ⊜¹ 222 31.55 N 97.23 W
Whitney, Mount ∧ 204 36.35 N 118.18 W
Whitney Point 210 42.19 N 75.58 W
Whitney Point Lake ⊜¹ 210 42.25 N 75.55 W
Whitney Woods Reservation ♦ 283 42.13 N 70.51 W
Whitstable 42 51.22 N 1.02 E
Whitsunday Island I 166 20.17 S 148.59 E
Whittaker 216 42.08 N 83.36 W
Whittemore, Ia., U.S. 198 43.03 N 94.25 W
Whittemore, Mi., U.S. 190 44.14 N 83.48 W
Whittier, Ak., U.S. 180 60.47 N 148.42 W
Whittier, Ca., U.S. 228 33.58 N 118.01 W
Whittier, N.C., U.S. 192 35.26 N 83.22 W
Whittier Narrows Dam ◆⁶ 280 34.01 N 118.04 W
Whittier Narrows Flood Control Basin ⊜¹ 280 34.02 N 118.04 W
Whittingham 44 55.24 N 1.54 W
Whittington 42 52.52 N 3.00 W
Whittle, Cap > 186 50.11 N 60.08 W
Whittle Hill ∧² 262 53.40 N 2.16 W
Whittle-le-Woods 262 53.41 N 2.38 W
Whittlesea, Austl. 169 37.31 S 145.07 E
Whittlesea, Ciskei 158 32.10 S 26.50 E
Whittlesey 42 52.34 N 0.08 W
Whittlesey, Mount ∧² 190 46.18 N 90.37 W
Whitwell 194 35.12 N 85.31 W
Whitwick 42 52.44 N 1.21 W
Whitworth 44 53.40 N 2.10 W
Whitworth Peak ∧ 224 49.05 N 121.13 W
Wholdaia Lake ⊜ 176 60.43 N 104.10 W
Whonock 224 49.11 N 122.28 W
W. Howard Frankland Bridge ◆⁵ 220 27.56 N 82.35 W
Whyalla 166 33.02 S 137.35 E
Whycocomagh 186 45.59 N 61.07 W
Whymper, Mount ∧ 224 48.57 N 124.10 W
Wiang Pa Pao 110 19.22 N 99.30 E
Wiang Phan 110 20.26 N 99.53 E
Wiarton 212 44.45 N 81.09 W
Wiasi 150 10.21 N 1.20 W
Wiau Lake ⊜ 182 55.23 N 111.18 W
Wiawso 150 6.12 N 2.29 W
Wiay I 46 57.23 N 7.13 W
Wiązów 30 50.49 N 17.11 E
Wibaux 198 46.59 N 104.11 W
Wiblingen ◆⁸ 58 48.21 N 9.58 E
Wichian Buri 110 15.39 N 101.07 E
Wichita 198 37.41 N 97.20 W
Wichita ≃ 196 34.07 N 98.10 W
Wichita Falls 196 33.54 N 98.29 W
Wichita Mountains ⩘ 196 34.45 N 98.40 W
Wichlinghofen ◆⁸ 263 51.27 N 7.30 E
Wick 46 58.26 N 3.06 W
Wick ≃ 46 58.27 N 3.05 W
Wickatunk 276 40.21 N 74.14 W
Wickede 56 51.29 N 7.52 E
Wickede ◆⁸ 263 51.32 N 7.37 E
Wickenburg 200 33.58 N 112.43 W
Wickepin 162 32.46 S 117.30 E
Wicker Memorial Park ♦ 278 41.34 N 87.28 W
Wickett 196 31.34 N 102.59 W
Wickford 42 51.38 N 0.31 E
Wickham, Austl. 162 20.31 S 117.08 E
Wickham, P.Q., Can. 206 45.45 N 72.30 W
Wickham, Eng., U.K. 42 50.54 N 1.10 W
Wickham ≃ 164 16.22 S 131.06 E
Wickham, Cape > 166 39.36 S 143.57 E
Wickham Bishops 260 51.47 N 0.40 E
Wickham Market 42 52.09 N 1.22 E
Wickiup Reservoir ⊜¹ 202 43.40 N 121.43 W
Wickliffe, Ky., U.S. 194 36.58 N 89.05 W
Wickliffe, Oh., U.S. 214 41.06 N 80.43 W
Wickliffe, Oh., U.S. 214 41.36 N 81.27 W
Wicklow 48 52.59 N 6.03 W
Wicklow □⁶ 48 53.00 N 6.30 W
Wicklow Head > 48 52.58 N 6.00 W
Wicklow Mountains ⩘ 48 53.02 N 6.24 W
Wickrath 56 51.07 N 6.24 E
Wicksteed Lake ⊜ 190 46.46 N 79.40 W
Wicomico 208 37.17 N 76.31 W
Wicomico □⁶ 208 38.22 N 75.36 W
Wicomico ≃ 208 38.13 N 75.55 W
Wicomico ≃ 208 38.15 N 76.51 W
Wicomico Church 208 37.49 N 76.23 W
Wiconisco 208 40.34 N 76.41 W
Wiconisco Creek ≃ 208 40.32 N 76.58 W
Wid ≃ 262 51.45 N 0.27 E
Widas ≃ 115a 7.30 S 112.08 E
Widden Brook ≃ 170 32.32 S 150.22 E
Widdern 56 49.19 N 9.25 E
Widdert ◆⁸ 263 51.08 N 7.04 E
Widdop Reservoir ⊜¹ 262 53.48 N 2.06 W
Widdrington Station 44 55.15 N 1.36 W
Wide Bay c, Pap. N. Gui. 164 5.05 S 152.05 E
Wide Bay c, Ak., U.S. 180 57.20 N 156.25 W
Widecombe in the Moor 42 50.35 N 3.48 W
Widemouth Bay 42 50.47 N 4.32 W
Widen 188 38.27 N 80.51 W
Widener College ᵾ² 285 39.52 N 75.21 W
Wide Open 44 55.03 N 1.38 W
Widerøe, Mount ∧ 9 72.08 S 23.30 E
Wide Ruin Wash V 200 35.13 N 109.52 W
Widford 260 51.43 N 0.27 E
Widgeegoara Creek ≃ 166 27.30 S 145.55 E
Widgiemooltha 162 31.30 S 121.34 E
Widnes 44 53.22 N 2.44 W
Wi-do I 98 35.36 N 126.17 E
Widodaren 115a 7.25 S 111.14 E
Widuchowa 54 53.10 N 14.25 E
Widur 124 27.55 N 85.10 E
Wiebelskirchen 56 49.22 N 7.11 E
Więcbork 30 53.22 N 17.30 E
Wieck 54 54.06 N 13.26 E
Wied ≃ 56 50.26 N 7.27 E
Wieda 58 51.38 N 10.34 E
Wiederitzsch 54 51.24 N 12.22 E
Wiedlisbach 58 47.15 N 7.39 E
Wiefelstede 52 53.15 N 8.07 E
Wiehe 54 51.16 N 11.25 E
Wiehengebirge ⩘ 52 52.20 N 8.40 E
Wiehl 56 50.57 N 7.31 E
Wiek 54 54.37 N 13.17 E
Wieleń 30 52.54 N 16.10 E
Wielichowo 30 52.08 N 16.21 E
Wieliczka 30 49.59 N 20.04 E
Wielkopolska ◆¹ 30 51.50 N 17.20 E
Wielkopolski Park Narodowy ♦ 30 52.15 N 16.50 E
Wieluń 30 51.14 N 18.34 E
Wiemelhausen ◆⁸ 263 51.28 N 7.13 E
Wien (Vienna), Öst. 61 48.13 N 16.20 E
Wien (Vienna), Öst. 264b 48.13 N 16.20 E
Wien □³ 61 48.12 N 16.22 E
Wien ≃ 264b 48.13 N 16.23 E
Wien, Universität ᵾ² 264b 48.13 N 16.21 E
Wiener Berg ∧² 264b 48.10 N 16.22 E
Wienerberg 264b 48.10 N 16.22 E
Wiener Neudorf 264b 48.05 N 16.19 E
Wiener Neustadt 61 47.49 N 16.15 E
Wiener Neustädter Kanal ≅ 61 48.05 N 16.22 E
Wienerwald ⩘ 61 48.10 N 16.00 E
Wienhagen ∧² 263 51.08 N 7.33 E
Wienhausen 52 52.35 N 10.11 E
Wien-Schwechat, Flughafen ⊠ 61 48.07 N 16.33 E
Wiepke 54 52.36 N 11.20 E
Wieprz ≃ 30 51.34 N 21.49 E
Wieprza ≃ 54 54.26 N 16.22 E
Wieprz-Krzna, Kanał ≅ 30 51.56 N 22.56 E
Wiera ≃ 56 50.55 N 9.10 E
Wierden 52 52.22 N 6.35 E
Wieren 52 52.53 N 10.39 E
Wiergate 194 31.00 N 93.42 W
Wieringermeer ◆¹ 52 52.45 N 5.00 E
Wieringerwerf 52 52.51 N 5.02 E
Wieruszów 30 51.18 N 18.08 E
Wierzyca ≃ 30 53.51 N 18.50 E
Wies 61 46.43 N 15.16 E
Wies ᵾ¹ 58 47.40 N 10.53 E
Wiesa 54 50.36 N 13.01 E
Wiesau 60 49.55 N 12.11 E
Wiesbaden 56 50.05 N 8.14 E
Wiescheid ◆⁸ 263 51.08 N 6.59 E
Wiescherhöfen ◆⁸ 263 51.39 N 7.46 E
Wiese ≃ 58 47.35 N 7.35 E
Wiesede 52 53.27 N 7.46 E
Wieselburg 61 48.08 N 15.09 E
Wiesen 58 46.43 N 9.43 E
Wiesenburg 52 52.07 N 12.26 E
Wiesenfeld 56 51.16 N 10.06 E
Wiesensteig 58 48.34 N 9.37 E
Wiesent ≃ 60 49.42 N 11.05 E
Wiesentheid 56 49.47 N 10.20 E
Wieseth ≃ 56 49.10 N 10.39 E
Wiesloch 56 49.17 N 8.42 E
Wiesmoor 52 53.25 N 7.43 E
Wieting 61 46.52 N 14.32 E
Wietmarschen 52 52.31 N 7.07 E
Wietze 52 52.39 N 9.50 E
Wietzen 52 52.43 N 9.04 E
Wigan 44 53.33 N 2.38 W
Wigan □⁸ 262 53.32 N 2.35 W
Wiggensbach 58 47.44 N 10.14 E
Wigger ≃ 58 47.18 N 7.53 E
Wiggington 260 51.47 N 0.38 W
Wiggins, Co., U.S. 198 40.13 N 104.04 W
Wiggins, Ms., U.S. 194 30.51 N 89.08 W
Wiggins Fork ≃ 202 43.27 N 109.28 W
Wigglesworth 44 54.01 N 2.17 W
Wight, Isle of I 42 50.40 N 1.20 W
Wigmore, Eng., U.K. 42 52.19 N 2.51 W
Wigmore, Eng., U.K. 260 51.21 N 0.35 E
Wignehies 50 50.01 N 4.00 E
Wigston 42 52.36 N 1.05 W
Wigton 44 54.49 N 3.09 W
Wigtown 44 54.52 N 4.26 W
Wigtown Bay c 44 54.46 N 4.15 W
Wijalpura 124 26.55 N 85.51 E
Wijchen 52 51.48 N 5.43 E
Wijhe 52 52.24 N 6.07 E
Wijk aan Zee 52 52.29 N 4.35 E
Wijk bij Duurstede 52 51.58 N 5.20 E
Wil 58 47.27 N 9.03 E
Wilbarger Creek ≃ 222 30.11 N 97.23 W
Wilber 198 40.28 N 96.57 W
Wilberforce, Austl. 170 33.33 S 150.50 E
Wilberforce, Oh., U.S. 218 39.42 N 83.52 W
Wilberforce Falls ⊔ 176 67.07 N 108.47 W
Wilbraham 207 42.07 N 72.25 W
Wilbur 202 47.45 N 118.42 W
Wilburton 196 34.55 N 95.18 W
Wilcannia 166 31.34 S 143.23 E
Wilcock, Peninsula >¹ 254 50.40 S 74.00 W
Wilcox, Sk., Can. 184 50.07 N 104.44 W
Wilcox, Ne., U.S. 198 40.21 N 99.10 W
Wilcox, Pa., U.S. 214 41.34 N 78.41 W
Wilcox, Tx., U.S. 222 30.27 N 96.22 W
Wilcox, Mount ∧ 207 42.13 N 73.16 W
Wildalpen 61 47.39 N 14.59 E
Wildau 54 52.19 N 13.38 E
Wildbad im Schwarzwald 56 48.45 N 8.32 E
Wildberg, Dtsch. 54 52.52 N 12.37 E
Wildberg, Dtsch. 56 48.37 N 8.44 E
Wildboarclough 262 53.13 N 2.02 W
Wildcat Canyon Regional Park ♦ 282 37.56 N 122.17 W
Wildcat Creek ≃, Ca., U.S. 282 37.57 N 122.23 W
Wildcat Creek ≃, In., U.S. 216 40.28 N 86.52 W
Wildcat Creek, Middle Fork ≃ 216 40.25 N 86.46 W
Wildcat Creek, South Fork ≃ 216 40.26 N 86.48 W
Wildcat Hill ∧² 184 53.17 N 102.30 W
Wild Coast ⊥² 158 32.30 S 28.45 E
Wilde ◆⁸ 288 34.42 S 58.20 W
Wildegg 58 47.25 N 8.11 E
Wildeman ≃ 164 5.33 S 139.13 E
Wildemann 56 51.49 N 10.17 E
Wildenbruch 264a 52.17 N 13.04 E
Wildenfels 54 50.40 N 12.35 E
Wildenstein 58 47.59 N 6.58 E
Wildenthal 54 50.27 N 12.37 E
Wilder 202 43.40 N 116.54 W
Wilderness 158 34.00 S 22.36 E
Wilderness of Judaea (Midbar Yehuda) ◆² 132 31.30 N 35.18 E
Wilderness State Park ♦ 190 45.42 N 84.57 W
Wildersville 194 35.46 N 88.21 W
Wildervank 52 53.04 N 6.51 E
Wildeshausen 52 52.54 N 8.26 E
Wildfield 212 43.49 N 79.44 W
Wildflecken 56 50.23 N 9.54 E
Wildfontein 158 31.04 S 24.50 E
Wildhaus 58 47.12 N 9.22 E
Wildhay ≃ 182 54.02 N 117.20 W
Wildhorn ∧ 58 46.22 N 7.22 E
Wildhorse Creek ≃, U.S. 198 40.36 N 102.00 W
Wildhorse Creek ≃, Ok., U.S. 196 34.32 N 97.10 W
Wild Horse Creek ≃, Wy., U.S. 198 44.39 N 106.08 W
Wild Horse Draw V 196 31.11 N 104.50 W
Wild Horse Hill ∧² 168a 33.12 S 116.40 E
Wild Horse Lake ⊜ 202 48.58 N 110.00 W
Wild Horse Plains 168b 34.22 S 138.17 E
Wildnest Lake ⊜ 184 55.00 N 102.20 W
Wildon 61 46.53 N 15.31 E
Wild Rice ≃, Mn., U.S. 198 47.20 N 96.50 W
Wild Rice ≃, N.D., U.S. 198 46.45 N 96.47 W
Wild Rice, South Branch ≃ 198 47.12 N 96.38 W
Wildrose, N.D., U.S. 198 48.37 N 103.11 W
Wild Rose, Wi., U.S. 190 44.10 N 89.14 W
Wildseeloder ∧ 64 47.26 N 12.32 E
Wildspitze ∧ 64 46.53 N 10.52 E
Wildstrubel ∧ 58 46.24 N 7.32 E
Wildwood, Ab., Can. 182 53.37 N 115.14 W
Wildwood, Fl., U.S. 220 28.51 N 82.02 W
Wildwood, Il., U.S. 216 42.21 N 88.00 W
Wildwood, N.J., U.S. 208 38.59 N 74.48 W
Wildwood, Pa., U.S. 214 40.36 N 79.58 W
Wildwood, Lake ⊜ 276 41.09 N 74.32 W
Wild Wood Beach 284b 39.15 N 76.25 W
Wildwood Canyon Park ♦ 280 34.13 N 118.17 W
Wildwood Crest 208 38.58 N 74.50 W
Wiley 224 46.33 N 120.39 W
Wilfersdorf 61 48.35 N 16.38 E
Wilge ≃, S. Afr. 158 25.34 S 29.10 E
Wilge ≃, S. Afr. 158 27.03 S 28.20 E
Wilgena 162 30.46 S 134.44 E
Wilgespruit ≃ 273d 26.07 S 27.52 E
Wilhelm, Lake ⊜¹ 214 41.23 N 80.08 W
Wilhelm, Mount ∧ 164 5.45 S 145.05 E
Wilhelmina Gebergte ⩘ 250 3.45 N 56.30 W
Wilhelminakanaal ≅ 52 51.47 N 4.51 E
Wilhelminaoord 52 52.53 N 6.10 E
Wilhelmina Peak — Trikora, Puncak ∧ 164 4.15 S 138.45 E
Wilhelmsburg 61 48.06 N 15.36 E
Wilhelmsburg ◆⁸ 52 53.30 N 10.00 E
Wilhelmshaven 52 53.31 N 8.08 E
Wilhelmshöhe, Schloss ⊥ 56 51.21 N 9.22 E
Wilhelmshorst 54 52.19 N 13.03 E
Wilhelmstadt ◆⁸ 264a 52.31 N 13.11 E
Wilhelmstal 156 21.54 S 16.19 E
Wilhelmstein, Schloss ⊥ 52 52.28 N 9.18 E
Wilis, Gunung ∧ 115a 7.52 S 111.48 E
Wilkau-Hasslau 54 50.40 N 12.31 E
Wilkerson Pass χ 200 39.02 N 105.32 W
Wilkes-Barre 210 41.14 N 75.52 W
Wilkes-Barre Scranton Airport ⊠ 210 41.20 N 75.45 W
Wilkesboro 192 36.08 N 81.09 W
Wilkes Island I 174a 19.18 N 166.34 E
Wilkes Land ◆¹ 9 69.00 S 120.00 E
Wilkeson 224 47.06 N 122.02 W
Wilket Creek ≃ 275b 43.43 N 79.21 W
Wilket Creek Park ♦ 275b 43.43 N 79.21 W
Wilkhaven 46 57.52 N 3.45 W
Wilkie 184 52.25 N 108.43 W
Wilkinsburg 214 40.26 N 79.51 W
Wilkinson 218 39.53 N 85.36 W
Wilkinson Lakes ⊜ 162 29.40 S 132.39 E
Wilkins Sound ⊔ 9 70.15 S 73.00 W
Wilkins Township 279b 40.25 N 79.50 W
Will □⁶ 216 41.32 N 88.05 W
Will, Mount ∧ 180 57.31 N 128.46 W
Willacoochee 192 31.20 N 83.02 W
Willamette ≃ 202 45.39 N 122.46 W
Willamette, Middle Fork ≃ 202 44.01 N 123.01 W
Willamette, North Fork ≃ 202 43.46 N 122.32 W
Willamina 224 45.04 N 123.29 W
Willamina Creek ≃ 224 45.05 N 123.28 W
Willandra Billabong Creek ≃ 166 33.08 S 144.06 E
Willapa 224 46.40 N 123.39 W
Willapa ≃ 224 46.42 N 123.50 W
Willapa Bay c 224 46.37 N 124.00 W
Willapa Hills ⩘ 224 46.35 N 123.25 W
Willard, Mo., U.S. 194 37.18 N 93.25 W
Willard, N.M., U.S. 200 34.35 N 106.01 W
Willard, N.Y., U.S. 210 42.40 N 76.52 W
Willard, Oh., U.S. 214 41.03 N 82.44 W
Willard, Ut., U.S. 200 41.24 N 112.02 W
Willard, Wa., U.S. 224 45.48 N 121.38 W
Willard, Punta > 232 28.50 N 113.15 W
Willards 208 38.23 N 75.20 W
Willaston, Austl. 168b 34.36 S 138.45 E
Willaston, Eng., U.K. 262 53.18 N 3.00 W
Willaumez Peninsula >¹ 164 5.05 S 150.05 E
Willcox 200 32.15 N 109.49 W
Willcox Playa ⊜ 200 32.08 N 109.51 W
Willebadessen 52 51.37 N 9.02 E
Willebroek 50 51.04 N 4.22 E
Willem Pretorius Game Reserve ◆⁴ 158 28.16 S 27.13 E
Willemsoord 52 52.49 N 6.05 E
Willemstad, Ned. 52 51.42 N 4.26 E
Willemstad, Ned. Ant. 241s 12.06 N 68.56 W
Willerburn Acres 284c 39.03 N 77.10 W
Willeroo 164 15.17 S 131.35 E
Willer-sur-Thur 58 47.51 N 7.05 E
Willerswalde 54 54.07 N 13.08 E
Willesden ◆⁸ 260 51.33 N 0.14 W
Willet 210 42.28 N 75.55 W
Willett Pond ⊜ 283 42.11 N 71.14 W
Willey Creek ≃ 279a 41.25 N 81.25 W
William, Lac ⊜ 206 46.07 N 71.34 W
William, Mount ∧, Austl. 166 37.17 S 142.36 E
William, Mount ∧, Austl. 169 37.13 S 144.47 E
William, Mount ∧² 168a 32.57 S 116.07 E
William Bill Dannelly Reservoir ⊜¹ 194 32.10 N 87.10 W
William Boyce Regional Park ♦ 279b 40.28 N 79.45 W
William Girling Reservoir ⊜¹ 260 51.37 N 0.02 W
William H. Harsha Lake ⊜¹ 218 39.02 N 84.07 W
William Lake ⊜ 184 53.50 N 99.25 W
Williamnagar 124 25.30 N 90.35 E
William Patterson College ᵾ² 276 40.56 N 74.12 W
William P. Gleason Park ♦ 278 41.33 N 87.21 W
William Preston Lane Jr. Memorial Bridge ◆⁵ 208 39.00 N 76.28 W
Williams, Austl. 168a 33.01 S 116.52 E
Williams, Az., U.S. 200 35.14 N 112.11 W
Williams, Ca., U.S. 226 39.09 N 122.08 W
Williams, Ia., U.S. 190 42.29 N 93.32 W
Williams, Mn., U.S. 198 48.46 N 94.57 W
Williams □⁶ 216 41.35 N 84.33 W
Williams ≃, Austl. 166 20.04 S 141.08 E
Williams ≃, Austl. 168a 32.59 S 116.24 E
Williams ≃, Austl. 170 32.45 S 151.45 E
Williams, Cape > 9 70.29 S 164.05 E
Williams Air Force Base ■ 200 33.18 N 111.40 W
Williams Bay 216 42.34 N 88.32 W
Williamsburg, On., Can. 212 44.58 N 75.15 W
Williamsburg, In., U.S. 218 39.57 N 84.59 W
Williamsburg, Ia., U.S. 190 41.39 N 92.00 W
Williamsburg, Ky., U.S. 192 36.44 N 84.09 W
Williamsburg, Ma., U.S. 207 42.23 N 72.43 W
Williamsburg, Mo., U.S. 219 38.55 N 91.42 W
Williamsburg, Oh., U.S. 218 39.03 N 84.03 W
Williamsburg, Pa., U.S. 214 40.27 N 78.12 W
Williamsburg, Va., U.S. 208 37.16 N 76.42 W
Williamsburg ◆⁸ 276 40.42 N 73.57 W
Williamsburg Bridge ◆⁵ 276 40.43 N 73.58 W
Williams Center 216 41.26 N 84.36 W
Williams Creek ≃, Austl. 274a 33.57 S 150.58 E
Williams Creek ≃, In., U.S. 218 39.36 N 85.09 W
Williamsdale 171b 35.35 S 149.09 E
Williamsfield 214 41.32 N 80.32 W
Williams Fork ≃ 200 40.26 N 107.39 W
Williams Lake 182 52.08 N 122.09 W
Williams Lake Indian Reserve ◆⁴ 182 52.07 N 122.00 W
Williams Mountain ∧² 194 34.15 N 94.33 W
Williamson, N.Y., U.S. 210 43.13 N 77.11 W
Williamson, W.V., U.S. 192 37.40 N 82.16 W
Williamson □⁶ 222 30.40 N 97.32 W
Williamson ≃ 202 42.28 N 121.57 W
Williamson Head > 9 69.09 S 157.49 E
Williamsport, Nf., Can. 186 50.32 N 56.19 W
Williamsport, In., U.S. 216 40.17 N 87.17 W
Williamsport, Oh., U.S. 214 39.35 N 83.07 W
Williamsport, Pa., U.S. 210 41.14 N 77.00 W
Williamston, Mi., U.S. 216 42.41 N 84.16 W
Williamston, N.C., U.S. 192 35.51 N 77.03 W
Williamston, S.C., U.S. 192 34.37 N 82.28 W
Williamstown, Austl. 168b 34.40 S 138.53 E
Williamstown, Austl. 169 37.52 S 144.54 E
Williamstown, On., Can. 206 45.08 N 74.35 W
Williamstown, Ky., U.S. 218 38.38 N 84.33 W
Williamstown, Ma., U.S. 207 42.42 N 73.12 W
Williamstown, N.J., U.S. 208 39.41 N 74.59 W
Williamstown, N.Y., U.S. 212 43.26 N 75.54 W
Williamstown, Pa., U.S. 208 40.34 N 76.37 W
Williamstown, Vt., U.S. 188 44.07 N 72.32 W
Williamstown, W.V., U.S. 188 39.24 N 81.27 W
Williamstown Junction 285 39.45 N 74.56 W
Williamstown Lake ⊜¹ 218 38.41 N 84.32 W
Williamsville, Il., U.S. 219 39.57 N 89.32 W
Williamsville, N.Y., U.S. 210 42.57 N 78.44 W
Williamtown 170 32.49 S 151.50 E
Willich 56 51.16 N 6.33 E
Willikies 240c 17.05 N 61.42 W
Willimantic 207 41.42 N 72.12 W
Willimantic ≃ 207 41.43 N 72.12 W
Willingale 260 51.44 N 0.19 E
Willingboro 208 40.01 N 74.52 W
Willingdon, Ab., Can. 182 53.50 N 112.08 W
Willingdon, Eng., U.K. 42 50.47 N 0.15 E
Willingdon, Mount ∧ 182 51.45 N 116.15 W
Willingen 56 51.17 N 8.37 E
Willingham 42 52.19 N 0.04 E
Willington, Eng., U.K. 42 52.50 N 1.33 W
Willington, Eng., U.K. 44 54.43 N 1.41 W
Willis, Mi., U.S. 216 42.09 N 83.33 W
Willis, Tx., U.S. 222 30.25 N 95.28 W
Willis ≃ 192 37.41 N 78.07 W
Willisau 58 47.07 N 8.00 E
Willis Group II 164 16.18 S 150.00 E
Willis Island I 186 48.48 N 53.42 W
Williston, S. Afr. 158 31.20 S 20.53 E
Williston, Fl., U.S. 192 29.23 N 82.26 W
Williston, N.D., U.S. 198 48.08 N 103.38 W
Williston, Oh., U.S. 214 41.36 N 83.20 W
Williston, S.C., U.S. 192 33.24 N 81.25 W
Williston Lake ⊜¹ 176 55.40 N 123.40 W
Williston Park 276 40.45 N 73.38 W
Willisville 194 37.59 N 89.35 W
Willis Wharf 208 37.30 N 75.48 W
Willits 204 39.24 N 123.21 W
Willmar 198 45.07 N 95.02 W
Willmersdorf 264a 52.40 N 13.41 E
Willmore Wilderness Provincial Park ♦ 182 53.45 N 119.00 W
Willoughby, Austl. 170 33.48 S 151.12 E
Willoughby, Oh., U.S. 214 41.38 N 81.25 W
Willoughby, Cape > 166 35.51 S 138.07 E
Willoughby Bay c 240c 17.02 N 61.44 W
Willoughby Hills 214 41.35 N 81.25 W
Willow, Ak., U.S. 180 61.45 N 150.03 W
Willow, Mi., U.S. 216 42.07 N 83.24 W
Willow, N.Y., U.S. 210 42.05 N 74.14 W
Willow ≃, Ab., Can. 182 55.58 N 113.55 W
Willow ≃, B.C., Can. 182 54.03 N 122.21 W
Willow ≃, Mn., U.S. 190 46.40 N 93.35 W
Willow ≃, Wi., U.S. 190 44.59 N 92.46 W
Willowbrook, Sk., Can. 184 51.13 N 102.47 W
Willow Brook, Ca., U.S. 280 33.54 N 118.13 W
Willowbrook, Il., U.S. 278 41.46 N 87.56 W
Willowbrook, Md., U.S. 284c 39.02 N 77.11 W
Willow Brook ≃, On., Can. 212 43.53 N 80.16 W
Willow Brook ≃, Eng., U.K. 42 52.32 N 0.24 W
Willow Brook ≃, N.J., U.S. 276 40.20 N 74.10 W
Willowbrook Mall ◆⁹ 276 40.53 N 74.15 W
Willowbrook Park ♦ 276 40.36 N 74.09 W
Willow Bunch 184 49.24 N 105.37 W
Willow Bunch Lake ⊜ 184 49.27 N 105.28 W
Willow City 198 48.36 N 100.17 W
Willow Creek, Ca., U.S. 204 40.56 N 123.38 W
Willow Creek, Mt., U.S. 202 45.49 N 111.38 W
Willow Creek ≃, Ab., Can. 182 49.46 N 113.21 W
Willow Creek ≃, On., Can. 212 44.25 N 79.53 W
Willow Creek ≃, Ca., U.S. 226 37.09 N 119.27 W
Willow Creek ≃, Ca., U.S. 226 39.22 N 122.05 W
Willow Creek ≃, Il., U.S. 216 41.42 N 89.10 W
Willow Creek ≃, In., U.S. 216 41.15 N 85.08 W
Willow Creek ≃, Mi., U.S. 281 42.20 N 83.25 W
Willow Creek ≃, Mt., U.S. 202 48.10 N 111.11 W
Willow Creek ≃, Mt., U.S. 202 48.09 N 106.38 W
Willow Creek ≃, Mt., U.S. 202 46.28 N 108.28 W
Willow Creek ≃, Nv., U.S. 204 38.10 N 116.35 W
Willow Creek ≃, N.D., U.S. 198 48.34 N 100.27 W
Willow Creek ≃, Oh., U.S. 279a 41.20 N 82.03 W
Willow Creek ≃, Or., U.S. 202 44.00 N 117.13 W
Willow Creek ≃, Or., U.S. 202 45.48 N 120.01 W
Willow Creek ≃, Ut., U.S. 200 40.02 N 109.45 W
Willow Creek, North Fork ≃ 226 37.13 N 119.30 W
Willow Creek, South Fork ≃ 226 39.32 N 122.10 W
Willowdale ◆⁸ 275b 43.47 N 79.26 W
Willowdale State Forest ♦ 283 42.40 N 70.54 W
Willowdene 273d 26.18 S 29.57 E
Willowemoc 210 41.55 N 74.41 W
Willowemoc Creek ≃ 210 41.53 N 74.48 W
Willow Glen ◆⁸ 282 37.18 N 121.53 W
Willow Grove 208 40.08 N 75.06 W
Willow Grove Naval Air Station ■ 208 40.12 N 75.08 W
Willow Grove Park ◆⁹ 285 40.08 N 75.08 W
Willow Hill 214 40.06 N 77.48 W
Willowick 214 41.37 N 81.28 W
Willow Lake 198 44.37 N 97.38 W
Willow Lake ⊜, N.T., Can. 176 62.11 N 119.10 W
Willow Lake ⊜, N.Y., U.S. 276 40.43 N 73.50 W
Willowlake ≃ 176 62.52 N 123.08 W
Willow Metropolitan Park ♦ 281 42.08 N 83.22 W
Willowmore 158 33.17 S 23.29 E
Willow Park 222 32.45 N 97.39 W
Willowra 162 21.15 S 132.35 E
Willowra Aboriginal Reserve ◆⁴ 162 21.15 S 132.35 E
Willow Reservoir ⊜¹ 190 45.45 N 89.50 W
Willow Ridge Estates 284a 43.01 N 78.49 W
Willow River 182 54.04 N 122.28 W
Willow Run, De., U.S. 285 39.44 N 75.37 W
Willow Run, Mi., U.S. 216 42.14 N 83.35 W
Willow Run, Va., U.S. 284c 38.49 N 77.10 W
Willow Run Airport ⊠ 281 42.14 N 83.32 W

Symbols in the index entries represent the broad categories identified in the key at the right. Symbols with superior numbers (⩘¹) identify subcategories (see complete key on page *I* · *1*).

Symbole im Register stellen die rechts im Schlüssel erklärten Kategorien dar. Symbole mit hochgestellten Ziffern (⩘¹) bezeichnen Unterabteilungen einer Kategorie (vgl. vollständiger Schlüssel auf Seite *I* · *1*).

Los símbolos incluídos en el texto del índice representan las grandes categorias identificadas con la clave a la derecha. Los símbolos con numeros en su parte superior (⩘¹) identifican las subcategorías (véase la clave completa en la página *I* · *1*).

Les symboles de l'index représentent les catégories indiquées dans la légende à droite. Les symboles suivis d'un indice (⩘¹) représentent des sous-catégories (voir légende complète à la page *I* · *1*).

Os símbolos incluídos no texto do índice representam as grandes categorias identificadas com a chave à direita. Os símbolos com números em sua parte superior (⩘¹) identificam as subcategorias (veja-se a chave completa à página *I* · *1*).

∧ Mountain	Berg	Montaña	Montagne	Montanha
⩘ Mountains	Gebirge	Montañas	Montagnes	Montanhas
χ Pass	Paß	Paso	Col	Passo
V Valley, Canyon	Tal, Cañon	Valle, Cañón	Vallée, Canyon	Vale, Canhão
≐ Plain	Ebene	Llano	Plaine	Planície
> Cape	Kap	Cabo	Cap	Cabo
I Island	Insel	Isla	Île	Ilha
II Islands	Inseln	Islas	Îles	Ilhas
⊥ Other Topographic Features	Andere Topographische Objekte	Otros Elementos Topográficos	Autres données topographiques	Outros acidentes topográficos

ESPAÑOL: Nombre | Página | Lat.°' | Long.°' W = Oeste
FRANÇAIS: Nom | Page | Lat.°' | Long.°' W = Ouest
PORTUGUÊS: Nome | Página | Lat.°' | Long.°' W = Oeste

Willows 226 39.31 N 122.11 W
Willow Springs, Ca., U.S. 228 34.53 N 118.18 W
Willow Springs, Il., U.S. 278 41.44 N 87.51 W
Willow Springs, Mo., U.S. 194 36.59 N 91.58 W
Willow Springs, Pa., U.S. 279b 40.19 N 79.44 W
Willow Street 208 39.59 N 76.17 W
Willowvale 158 32.16 S 28.30 E
Willow Woods 284c 38.50 N 77.16 W
Will Rogers Beach State Park ♠ 280 34.01 N 118.30 W
Will Rogers State Park ♠ 280 34.03 N 118.31 W
Willroth 56 50.34 N 7.31 E
Wills, Lake ⊜ 162 21.25 S 128.51 E
Wills Creek ≃, Austl. 166 22.43 S 140.02 E
Wills Creek ≃, Oh., U.S. 188 40.09 N 81.55 W
Wills Creek Lake ⊜[1] 214 40.08 N 81.45 W
Willseyville 210 42.17 N 76.23 W
Willshire 216 40.45 N 84.48 W
Wills Point 222 32.43 N 96.01 W
Willston 284c 38.52 N 77.09 W
Willunga 168b 35.17 S 138.33 E
Wilmar 194 33.37 N 91.55 W
Wilmer, Al., U.S. 194 30.49 N 88.21 W
Wilmer, Pa., U.S. 285 40.07 N 75.32 W
Wilmer, Tx., U.S. 222 32.35 N 96.41 W
Wilmerding 279b 40.23 N 79.48 W
Wilmersdorf ◆[8] 264a 52.30 N 13.19 E
Wilmette 216 42.04 N 87.43 W
Wilmington, Austl. 166 32.39 S 138.07 E
Wilmington, Eng., U.K. 260 51.26 N 0.12 E
Wilmington, De., U.S. 208 39.44 N 75.32 W
Wilmington, Il., U.S. 216 41.18 N 88.08 W
Wilmington, Ma., U.S. 207 42.32 N 71.10 W
Wilmington, N.C., U.S. 192 34.13 N 77.56 W
Wilmington, Oh., U.S. 218 39.26 N 83.49 W
Wilmington, Vt., U.S. 188 42.52 N 72.52 W
Wilmington ◆[8] 280 33.47 N 118.16 W
Wilmington Manor 285 39.41 N 75.35 W
Wilmington Manor Gardens 285 39.40 N 75.34 W
Wilmore, Ky., U.S. 192 37.51 N 84.39 W
Wilmore, Pa., U.S. 214 40.23 N 78.43 W
Wilmot, Ar., U.S. 194 33.03 N 91.34 W
Wilmot, Oh., U.S. 214 40.39 N 81.38 W
Wilmot, S.D., U.S. 198 45.24 N 96.51 W
Wilmot, Wi., U.S. 216 42.31 N 88.11 W
Wilmot Woods ♠ 278 42.18 N 87.56 W
Wilmslow 44 53.20 N 2.15 W
Wilna → Vilnius 76 54.41 N 25.19 E
Wilnecote 42 52.36 N 1.40 W
Wilnsdorf 56 50.49 N 8.09 E
Wilpattu National Park ♠ 122 8.20 N 80.00 E
Wilpen 214 40.17 N 79.12 W
Wilpshire 262 53.47 N 2.28 W
Wilsall 202 45.59 N 110.39 W
Wilsdruff 54 51.05 N 13.32 E
Wilseder Berg ∧[2] 52 53.10 N 9.56 E
Wilseyville 226 38.23 N 120.31 W
Wilshamstead 42 52.05 N 0.27 W
Wilson, Austl. 166 32.00 S 138.22 E
Wilson, Ar., U.S. 194 35.34 N 90.02 W
Wilson, Ct., U.S. 207 41.48 N 72.38 W
Wilson, Il., U.S. 278 42.21 N 87.54 W
Wilson, Ks., U.S. 198 38.49 N 98.28 W
Wilson, La., U.S. 194 30.55 N 91.06 W
Wilson, N.Y., U.S. 210 43.18 N 78.49 W
Wilson, N.C., U.S. 192 35.43 N 77.54 W
Wilson, Ok., U.S. 196 34.09 N 97.25 W
Wilson, Pa., U.S. 208 40.41 N 75.14 W
Wilson, Tx., U.S. 196 33.19 N 101.44 W
Wilson ≃, Austl. 164 16.47 S 128.17 E
Wilson ≃, Austl. 166 27.38 S 141.24 E
Wilson ≃, Or., U.S. 224 45.28 N 123.53 W
Wilson, Cape › 176 66.59 N 81.28 W
Wilson, Mount ∧, Az., U.S. 200 35.59 N 114.37 W
Wilson, Mount ∧, Ca., U.S. 280 34.13 N 118.04 W
Wilson, Mount ∧, Co., U.S. 200 37.51 N 107.59 W
Wilson, Mount ∧, Nv., U.S. 204 38.15 N 114.23 W
Wilson, Mount ∧, Or., U.S. 224 45.04 N 121.39 W
Wilson, Mount ∧[2], Austl. 162 20.14 S 127.39 E
Wilson, Mount ∧[2], Austl. 168b 35.13 S 138.38 E
Wilson, Point ›, Austl. 169 38.05 S 144.30 E
Wilson, Point ›, Wa., U.S. 224 48.08 N 122.45 W
Wilson Cliffs ≗[4] 162 22.03 S 127.09 E
Wilson Creek ≃, Tx., U.S. 222 33.07 N 96.35 W
Wilson Creek ≃, Wa., U.S. 202 47.25 N 119.07 W
Wilson Lake ⊜[1], Al., U.S. 194 34.49 N 87.30 W
Wilson Lake ⊜[1], Ks., U.S. 198 38.57 N 98.40 W
Wilson Range ⋏ 162 28.50 S 124.25 E
Wilson Run ≃, De., U.S. 285 39.48 N 75.35 W
Wilson Run ≃, Pa., U.S. 279b 40.13 N 79.37 W
Wilsons Beach 186 44.56 N 66.56 W
Wilson's Creek National Battlefield ♠ 194 37.06 N 93.27 W
Wilsons Promontory › 166 38.55 S 146.20 E
Wilsons Promontory National Park ♠ 166 39.00 S 146.25 E
Wilsonville, Il., U.S. 219 39.04 N 89.51 W
Wilsonville, Ne., U.S. 198 40.06 N 100.06 W
Wilsonville, Or., U.S. 224 45.18 N 122.46 W
Wilster 52 53.55 N 9.22 E
Wilthen 54 51.06 N 14.24 E
Wilton, Eng., U.K. 42 51.05 N 1.52 W
Wilton, Ct., U.S. 207 41.11 N 73.26 W
Wilton, Me., U.S. 188 44.35 N 70.13 W
Wilton, N.H., U.S. 207 42.50 N 71.44 W
Wilton, N.Y., U.S. 210 43.11 N 73.45 W
Wilton, N.D., U.S. 198 47.09 N 100.46 W
Wilton, Wi., U.S. 190 43.48 N 90.31 W
Wilton ≃ 164 14.45 S 134.33 E
Wilton Creek ≃ 212 44.12 N 76.56 W
Wilton Farm Acres 284b 39.18 N 76.50 W
Wilton Manors 220 26.09 N 80.08 W
Wiltshire □[6] 42 51.15 N 1.50 W
Wiltz 56 49.48 N 5.55 E
Wiluna 162 26.36 S 120.13 E
Wimapedi ≃ 184 55.27 N 99.07 W
Wimauma 220 27.42 N 82.17 W
Wimberley 196 30.00 N 98.06 W
Wimbleball Reservoir ⊜[1] 42 51.04 N 3.28 W
Wimbledon 198 47.10 N 98.27 W
Wimbledon ◆[8] 260 51.25 N 0.12 W
Wimbledon Common ♠ 260 51.26 N 0.14 W
Wimborne Minster 42 50.48 N 1.59 W
Wimereux 50 50.46 N 1.37 E
Wimmelburg 54 51.31 N 11.30 E
Wimmenau 56 48.55 N 7.25 E
Wimmera ≃ 169 36.55 S 142.56 E
Wimmis 58 46.41 N 7.38 E
Winagami Lake ⊜ 182 55.38 N 116.45 W
Winam ⊂ 154 0.15 S 34.35 E
Winamac 216 41.03 N 86.36 W
Winburg 158 28.37 S 27.00 E
Winburne 214 40.57 N 78.08 W
Wincanton 42 51.04 N 2.25 W
Wincham 262 53.16 N 2.29 W
Winchcombe 42 51.57 N 1.58 W
Winchelsea, Austl. 169 38.15 S 143.59 E
Winchelsea, Eng., U.K. 42 50.55 N 0.42 E
Winchendon 207 42.41 N 72.02 W
Winchester, On., Can. 212 45.06 N 75.21 W
Winchester, N.Z. 172 44.12 S 171.17 E
Winchester, Eng., U.K. 42 51.04 N 1.19 W
Winchester, Ca., U.S. 228 33.42 N 117.05 W
Winchester, Id., U.S. 202 46.14 N 116.37 W
Winchester, Il., U.S. 219 39.37 N 90.27 W
Winchester, In., U.S. 218 40.10 N 84.58 W
Winchester, Ky., U.S. 192 37.59 N 84.10 W
Winchester, Ma., U.S. 283 42.27 N 71.08 W
Winchester, N.H., U.S. 207 42.46 N 72.23 W
Winchester, Oh., U.S. 218 38.56 N 83.39 W
Winchester, Tn., U.S. 194 35.11 N 86.06 W
Winchester, Tx., U.S. 222 30.01 N 97.01 W
Winchester, Va., U.S. 188 39.11 N 78.10 W
Winchester Cathedral υ[1] 42 51.04 N 1.19 W
Winchmore Hill 260 51.39 N 0.39 W
Winchmore Hill ◆[8] 260 51.38 N 0.06 W
Wind ≃, Yk., Can. 180 65.49 N 135.18 W
Wind ≃, Wa., U.S. 224 45.43 N 121.47 W
Wind ≃, Wy., U.S. 202 43.35 N 108.13 W
Windang 170 34.32 S 150.53 E
Windau → Ventspils 76 57.24 N 21.36 E
Windber 214 40.14 N 78.50 W
Wind Cave National Park ♠ 198 43.32 N 103.25 W
Windeck 56 50.48 N 7.37 E
Winder 192 33.59 N 83.43 W
Winder, Lake ⊜ 220 28.15 N 80.51 W
Windera 166 26.03 S 151.50 E
Windermere, B.C., Can. 182 50.30 N 115.58 W
Windermere, Eng., U.K. 44 54.23 N 2.54 W
Windermere, Fl., U.S. 220 28.30 N 81.32 W
Windermere ⊜ 44 54.22 N 2.56 W
Windermere Lake ⊜ 190 47.56 N 83.47 W
Winder Village 285 40.06 N 74.52 W
Windfall, Ab., Can. 182 54.11 N 116.15 W
Windfall, In., U.S. 216 40.21 N 85.57 W
Windgap 210 40.51 N 75.18 W
Windham, Ct., U.S. 207 41.41 N 72.09 W
Windham, N.H., U.S. 283 42.48 N 71.18 W
Windham, N.Y., U.S. 210 42.19 N 74.15 W
Windham, Oh., U.S. 214 41.14 N 81.02 W
Windham □[6], Ct., U.S. 207 41.55 N 71.55 W
Windham □[6], Vt., U.S. 207 42.50 N 72.43 W
Windham Manor 284c 39.04 N 77.00 W
Windhoek 156 22.34 S 17.06 E
Windhoek □[5] 156 22.30 S 17.00 E
Windigo ≃ 184 53.22 N 91.48 W
Windigo Lake ⊜ 184 52.35 N 91.32 W
Windisch 58 47.29 N 8.13 E
Windischeschenbach 60 49.48 N 12.09 E
Windischgarsten 61 47.44 N 14.20 E
Wind Lake 216 42.49 N 88.09 W
Wind Lake ⊜ 216 42.50 N 88.09 W
Windlass Run ≃ 284b 39.24 N 76.24 W
Windleite ∧ 54 51.22 N 10.56 E
Windlesham 260 51.22 N 0.40 W
Windley Key ▮ 220 24.57 N 80.35 W
Windmill Point ›, On., Can. 284a 42.52 N 79.01 W
Windmill Point ›, Mi., U.S. 281 42.22 N 82.55 W
Windmill Point ›, Va., U.S. 208 37.37 N 76.17 W
Windom, Mn., U.S. 198 43.51 N 95.07 W
Windom, N.Y., U.S. 210 42.47 N 78.48 W
Windom Peak ∧ 200 37.37 N 107.35 W
Windorah 166 25.26 S 142.39 E
Windorf, Dtsch. 60 48.37 N 13.13 E
Windorf, Öst. 61 48.27 N 14.02 E
Window Rock 200 35.40 N 109.03 W
Wind Point 216 42.47 N 87.45 W
Wind River Indian Reservation ◆[4] 202 43.26 N 109.00 W
Wind River Peak ∧ 200 42.42 N 109.07 W
Wind River Range ⋏ 200 43.05 N 109.25 W
Windrush ≃ 42 51.42 N 1.25 W
Windsbach 56 49.14 N 10.50 E
Windsor, Austl. 168b 34.25 S 138.20 E
Windsor, Austl. 170 33.37 S 150.49 E
Windsor, Nf., Can. 186 48.57 N 55.40 W
Windsor, N.S., Can. 186 44.59 N 64.08 W
Windsor, On., Can. 214 42.18 N 83.01 W
Windsor, On., Can. 281 42.18 N 83.01 W
Windsor, P.Q., Can. 206 45.34 N 72.00 W
Windsor, Eng., U.K. 42 51.29 N 0.38 W
Windsor, Ca., U.S. 204 38.33 N 122.49 W
Windsor, Co., U.S. 200 40.28 N 104.54 W
Windsor, Ct., U.S. 207 41.51 N 72.38 W
Windsor, Il., U.S. 194 39.26 N 88.35 W
Windsor, In., U.S. 218 40.09 N 85.12 W
Windsor, Mo., U.S. 194 38.31 N 93.31 W
Windsor, N.J., U.S. 208 40.15 N 74.35 W
Windsor, N.Y., U.S. 210 42.05 N 75.39 W
Windsor, N.C., U.S. 192 35.59 N 76.56 W
Windsor, Oh., U.S. 214 41.32 N 80.56 W
Windsor, Pa., U.S. 208 39.54 N 76.35 W
Windsor, Vt., U.S. 188 43.29 N 72.23 W
Windsor, Va., U.S. 208 36.48 N 76.44 W
Windsor, Wi., U.S. 216 43.13 N 89.20 W
Windsor, Gare ◆[5] 275a 45.30 N 73.34 W
Windsor, University of υ[2] 281 42.18 N 83.04 W
Windsor Airport ⊠ 214 42.17 N 82.58 W
Windsor and Maidenhead □[8] 260 51.28 N 0.37 W
Windsor Castle ⊥ 42 51.29 N 0.36 W
Windsor Forest 192 31.58 N 81.07 W
Windsor Forest ◆[3] 42 51.27 N 0.43 W
Windsor Great Park ♠ 260 51.27 N 0.37 W
Windsor Heights 214 40.12 N 80.40 W
Windsor Hills 280 33.59 N 118.21 W
Windsor Locks 207 41.55 N 72.37 W
Windsor Race Course ♠ 260 51.29 N 0.39 W
Windsor Raceway ♠ 281 42.15 N 83.05 W
Windsor Terrace 284b 39.19 N 76.43 W
Windsorton 158 28.16 S 24.44 E
Windsorville 207 41.53 N 72.32 W
Windthorst 196 33.34 N 98.26 W
Windward Islands ▮▮ 238 13.00 N 61.00 W
Windward Passage ʉ 238 20.00 N 73.50 W
Windy Hills 285 39.48 N 75.35 W
Windy Lake ⊜ 184 54.22 N 102.35 W
Windy Peak ∧, Co., U.S. 200 38.21 N 106.16 W
Windy Peak ∧, Wa., U.S. 202 48.56 N 119.58 W
Windy Run ≃ 284c 38.54 N 77.05 W
Winefred ≃ 184 56.02 N 110.36 W
Winefred Lake ⊜ 182 55.30 N 110.35 W
Winejok 140 9.01 N 27.34 E
Winesburg 214 40.37 N 81.42 W
Winfield, Ab., Can. 182 52.58 N 114.26 W
Winfield, Al., U.S. 194 33.55 N 87.49 W
Winfield, Il., U.S. 216 41.52 N 88.10 W
Winfield, Ia., U.S. 190 41.07 N 91.26 W
Winfield, Ks., U.S. 198 37.14 N 96.59 W
Winfield, Mo., U.S. 219 38.59 N 90.44 W
Winfield, N.J., U.S. 276 40.38 N 74.17 W
Winfield, Tx., U.S. 222 33.10 N 95.07 W
Winfield, W.V., U.S. 188 38.31 N 81.53 W
Wing 198 47.08 N 100.16 W
Wing ≃ 198 46.29 N 94.58 W
Wingate, Eng., U.K. 44 54.44 N 1.23 W
Wingate, Md., U.S. 208 38.16 N 76.04 W
Wingate, N.C., U.S. 192 34.59 N 80.26 W
Wingate Mountains ⋏ 164 14.29 S 130.42 E
Wingates 262 53.34 N 2.32 W
Wingdale 210 41.39 N 73.34 W
Wingecarribee ≃ 170 34.23 S 150.07 E
Wingecarribee Reservoir ⊜[1] 170 34.34 S 150.30 E
Wingello 170 34.42 S 150.09 E
Wingene 50 51.04 N 3.16 E
Wingen-sur-Moder 56 48.55 N 7.22 E
Wingerworth 44 53.12 N 1.26 W
Wingham, Austl. 166 31.52 S 152.22 E
Wingham, On., Can. 212 43.53 N 81.19 W
Wingham, Eng., U.K. 42 51.17 N 1.13 E
Wing Lake Shores 281 42.33 N 83.17 W
Wingles 50 50.29 N 2.51 E
Wingo 194 36.38 N 88.44 W
Wings Field ⊠ 285 40.08 N 75.16 W
Wingst 52 53.43 N 9.03 E
Winhole Channel ʉ 276 43.37 N 73.48 W
Winhöring 60 48.16 N 12.39 E
Winifred 202 47.33 N 109.22 W
Winifreda 252 36.15 S 64.14 W
Winisk 176 55.15 N 85.12 W
Winisk ≃ 176 55.17 N 85.05 W
Winisk Lake ⊜ 176 52.55 N 87.22 W
Wink 196 31.45 N 103.06 W
Winkana 110 15.44 N 98.01 E
Winkelman 200 32.59 N 110.46 W
Winkelpos 158 27.35 S 26.49 E
Winkler, Mb., Can. 184 49.11 N 97.56 W
Winkler, Tx., U.S. 222 31.56 N 96.13 W
Winklern 64 46.52 N 12.52 E
Winlaw 182 49.37 N 117.34 W
Winlock 224 46.29 N 122.56 W
Winneba 150 5.25 N 0.36 W
Winnebago, Il., U.S. 190 42.15 N 89.14 W
Winnebago, Mn., U.S. 190 43.46 N 94.09 W
Winnebago, Ne., U.S. 198 42.14 N 96.28 W
Winnebago □[6] 216 42.17 N 89.06 W
Winnebago ≃ 190 43.03 N 92.57 W
Winnebago, Lake ⊜ 190 44.00 N 88.25 W
Winnebago Indian Reservation ◆[4], Ne., U.S. 198 42.15 N 96.31 W
Winnebago Indian Reservation ◆[4], Wi., U.S. 190 44.15 N 90.38 W
Winnecke, Mount ∧[2] 162 18.47 S 130.20 E
Winnecke Creek ≃ 162 18.35 S 131.34 E
Winneconne 190 44.06 N 88.42 W
Winneconnet 283 41.59 N 71.08 W
Winneconnet Pond ⊜ 283 41.58 N 71.08 W
Winnekendonk 52 51.36 N 6.17 E
Winnekenni Park ♠ 283 42.47 N 71.04 W
Winnemucca 204 40.58 N 117.44 W
Winnemucca Lake ⊜ 204 40.09 N 119.20 W
Winnenden 56 48.53 N 9.24 E
Winner 198 43.22 N 99.51 W
Winnetka 216 42.06 N 87.44 W
Winnetka ◆[8] 280 34.13 N 118.35 W
Winnett 202 47.00 N 108.21 W
Winnfield 194 31.55 N 92.38 W
Winnibigoshish, Lake ⊜ 190 47.27 N 94.12 W
Winnie 194 29.49 N 94.23 W
Winning 162 23.09 S 114.32 E
Winningen, Dtsch. 54 51.49 N 11.26 E
Winningen, Dtsch. 56 50.18 N 7.31 E
Winnipeg 184 49.53 N 97.09 W
Winnipeg ≃ 184 50.38 N 96.19 W
Winnipeg, Lake ⊜ 184 52.00 N 97.00 W
Winnipeg Beach 184 50.31 N 96.58 W
Winnipegosis 184 51.39 N 99.56 W
Winnipegosis, Lake ⊜ 184 52.30 N 100.00 W
Winnipesaukee, Lake ⊜ 188 43.35 N 71.20 W
Winnsboro, La., U.S. 194 32.09 N 91.43 W
Winnsboro, S.C., U.S. 192 34.22 N 81.05 W
Winnsboro, Tx., U.S. 222 32.57 N 95.17 W
Winnsboro, Lake ⊜[1] 222 32.55 N 95.21 W
Winnsboro Mills 192 34.21 N 81.05 W
Winnweiler 56 49.34 N 7.51 E
Winona, Ks., U.S. 198 39.03 N 101.14 W
Winona, Mi., U.S. 190 46.52 N 88.55 W
Winona, Mn., U.S. 190 44.03 N 91.38 W
Winona, Ms., U.S. 194 33.28 N 89.43 W
Winona, Mo., U.S. 194 37.00 N 91.19 W
Winona, Oh., U.S. 214 40.50 N 80.54 W
Winona, Tx., U.S. 222 32.29 N 95.10 W
Winona Lake, In., U.S. 216 41.13 N 85.49 W
Winona Lake, N.Y., U.S. 210 41.31 N 74.03 W
Winona Lake ⊜ 216 41.13 N 85.50 W
Winooski 188 44.29 N 73.11 W
Winooski ≃ 188 44.30 N 73.15 W
Winooski, North Branch ≃ 188 44.15 N 72.35 W
Winschoten 52 53.08 N 7.02 E
Winscombe 42 51.18 N 2.50 W
Winsen, Dtsch. 52 52.41 N 9.54 E
Winsen, Dtsch. 52 53.22 N 10.12 E
Winsford, Eng., U.K. 42 51.06 N 3.33 W
Winsford, Eng., U.K. 44 53.12 N 2.32 W
Winshill 42 52.48 N 1.36 W
Winside 198 42.10 N 97.10 W
Winslow, Eng., U.K. 42 51.57 N 0.54 W
Winslow, Az., U.S. 200 35.01 N 110.41 W
Winslow, Me., U.S. 188 44.32 N 69.37 W
Winslow, N.J., U.S. 285 39.39 N 74.52 W
Winslow Reef ✦[2] 14 1.36 S 174.57 W
Winsted, Ct., U.S. 207 41.55 N 73.03 W
Winsted, Mn., U.S. 190 44.57 N 94.02 W
Winston, Fl., U.S. 220 28.01 N 82.00 W
Winston, Or., U.S. 202 43.07 N 123.24 W
Winston Churchill Memorial υ 219 38.52 N 91.58 W
Winston Creek ≃ 224 46.30 N 122.40 W
Winston-Salem 192 36.05 N 80.14 W
Winsum 52 53.19 N 6.31 E
Wintego Lake ⊜ 184 55.33 N 102.52 W
Winter 190 45.49 N 91.00 W
Winter Beach 220 27.43 N 80.25 W
Winterberg, Dtsch. 56 51.11 N 8.32 E
Winterberg, Dtsch. 263 51.17 N 7.18 E
Winterberg ∧[2] 263 51.20 N 7.13 E
Winterberge ⋏ 158 32.28 S 26.15 E
Winterbourne Abbas 42 50.43 N 2.34 W
Winter Creek ≃ 280 34.12 N 118.02 W
Winterfeld 54 52.44 N 11.14 E
Winter Garden 220 28.33 N 81.35 W
Winter Gardens 228 32.50 N 116.56 W
Winter Harbor 188 44.23 N 68.05 W
Winter Harbour 182 50.31 N 128.02 W
Winterhaven, Ca., U.S. 204 32.44 N 114.38 W
Winter Haven, Fl., U.S. 220 28.01 N 81.43 W
Winter Hill ∧[2] 262 53.38 N 2.31 W
Wintering ≃ 198 48.12 N 100.34 W
Wintering Lake ⊜ 184 55.24 N 97.42 W
Winter Island ▮, N.T., Can. 176 66.14 N 83.04 W
Winter Island ▮, Ca., U.S. 282 38.03 N 121.51 W
Winter Island ▮, Ma., U.S. 283 42.32 N 70.52 W
Winterlingen 58 48.11 N 9.07 E
Winter Park, Fl., U.S. 220 28.35 N 81.20 W
Winter Park, N.C., U.S. 192 34.12 N 77.53 W
Winterport 188 44.38 N 68.51 W
Winters, Ca., U.S. 226 38.31 N 121.58 W
Winters, Tx., U.S. 196 31.57 N 99.57 W
Winters Bayou ≃ 222 30.22 N 95.06 W
Winters Canal ≊ 226 38.32 N 121.58 W
Wintersdorf 54 51.03 N 12.21 E
Winterset, Ia., U.S. 190 41.19 N 94.00 W
Winterset, Oh., U.S. 214 40.06 N 81.25 W
Winter Springs 220 28.41 N 81.18 W
Winters Run ≃ 208 39.26 N 76.18 W
Winterstown 208 39.50 N 76.37 W
Wintersville 214 40.22 N 80.42 W
Winterswijk 52 51.58 N 6.44 E
Winterthur, Schw. 58 47.30 N 8.43 E
Winterthur, De., U.S. 285 39.48 N 75.35 W
Winterthur Museum υ 285 39.48 N 75.36 W
Winterton, Nf., Can. 186 47.58 N 53.20 W
Winterton, S. Afr. 158 28.46 S 29.35 E
Winterton, Eng., U.K. 44 53.39 N 0.36 W
Winterton-on-Sea 42 52.43 N 1.42 E
Winterville, Ga., U.S. 192 33.58 N 83.16 W
Winterville, Ms., U.S. 194 33.30 N 91.03 W
Winterville, N.C., U.S. 192 35.31 N 77.24 W
Winthrop, Ct., U.S. 207 41.21 N 72.29 W
Winthrop, Ia., U.S. 190 42.28 N 91.44 W
Winthrop, Me., U.S. 188 44.18 N 69.58 W
Winthrop, Ma., U.S. 283 42.22 N 70.59 W
Winthrop, Mn., U.S. 190 44.32 N 94.21 W
Winthrop, Wa., U.S. 182 48.28 N 120.11 W
Winthrop, Lake ⊜ 283 42.11 N 71.25 W
Winthrop Harbor 216 42.28 N 87.49 W
Wintinna 162 27.44 S 134.07 E
Wintinna Creek ≃ 162 27.47 S 134.14 E
Winton, Austl. 166 22.23 S 143.02 E
Winton, N.Z. 172 46.09 S 168.20 E
Winton, S. Afr. 158 27.29 S 22.34 E
Winton, Ca., U.S. 226 37.23 N 120.37 W
Winton, N.C., U.S. 192 36.23 N 76.55 W
Winton, Wa., U.S. 224 47.44 N 120.44 W
Wintzenheim 58 48.04 N 7.17 E
Winwick 262 53.26 N 2.36 W
Winz 263 51.23 N 7.09 E
Winzenberg 263 51.06 N 7.38 E
Winzer 60 48.44 N 13.04 E
Winzermark 263 51.23 N 7.08 E
Wipper ≃, Dtsch. 54 51.47 N 11.42 E
Wipper ≃, Dtsch. 54 51.17 N 11.10 E
Wipper ≃, Dtsch. 263 51.07 N 7.24 E
Wipperdorf 54 51.28 N 10.42 E
Wipperfeld 263 51.05 N 7.19 E
Wipperfürth 56 51.07 N 7.23 E
Wippra 54 51.34 N 11.16 E
Wirātnagar 124 26.29 N 87.17 E
Wīrendranagar 124 28.35 N 81.38 E
Wireton, Il., U.S. 278 41.40 N 87.42 W
Wireton, Pa., U.S. 279b 40.34 N 80.14 W
Wīrgañj 124 27.00 N 84.52 E
Wiriagar ≃ 164 2.17 S 132.52 E
Wirksworth 44 53.05 N 1.34 W
Wirosari 115a 7.05 S 111.05 E
Wirral □[8] 262 53.22 N 3.05 W
Wirral ›[1] 44 53.20 N 3.03 W
Wirraminna 166 31.12 S 136.15 E
Wirrulla 162 32.24 S 134.31 E
Wisbech 42 52.40 N 0.10 E
Wisby → Visby 26 57.38 N 18.18 E
Wiscasset 188 44.00 N 69.39 W
Wischhafen 52 53.46 N 9.19 E
Wisconsin □[3], U.S. 178 44.45 N 89.30 W
Wisconsin □[3], U.S. 190 44.45 N 89.30 W
Wisconsin ≃ 190 43.00 N 91.10 W
Wisconsin, Lake ⊜[1] 190 43.24 N 89.43 W
Wisconsin Dells 190 43.37 N 89.46 W
Wisconsin Dells ∨ 190 43.41 N 89.49 W
Wisconsin Rapids 190 44.23 N 89.49 W
Wiscoy 210 42.30 N 78.05 W
Wisdom 202 45.37 N 113.27 W
Wisdom, Lake ⊜ 164 5.20 S 147.05 E
Wise 192 36.58 N 82.34 W
Wise □[6] 222 33.07 N 97.40 W
Wise ≃ 202 45.48 N 112.57 W
Wiseman 180 67.25 N 150.06 W
Wisemans Ferry 170 33.24 S 150.59 E
Wises Landing 218 38.35 N 85.25 W
Wishart 184 51.34 N 104.00 W
Wishaw 46 55.47 N 3.56 W
Wishek 198 46.16 N 99.33 W
Wishkah ≃ 224 46.58 N 123.45 W
Wishram 224 45.39 N 120.57 W
Wiske ≃ 44 54.15 N 1.26 W
Wisła 30 49.40 N 18.52 E
Wisła ≃ 30 54.22 N 18.55 E
Wisley Aerodrome ⊠ 260 51.18 N 0.28 W
Wisley Gardens ♠ 260 51.19 N 0.29 W
Wisłok ≃ 30 50.13 N 22.32 E
Wisłoka ≃ 30 50.27 N 21.23 E
Wismar, Dtsch. 54 53.53 N 11.28 E
Wismar, Guy. 246 6.00 N 58.18 W
Wismarbucht ⊂ 54 53.57 N 11.25 E
Wisner, La., U.S. 194 31.58 N 91.39 W
Wisner, Ne., U.S. 198 41.59 N 96.54 W
Wissahickon Creek ≃ 285 40.01 N 75.12 W
Wissant 50 50.53 N 1.40 E
Wissembourg 56 49.02 N 7.57 E
Wissen 56 50.47 N 7.43 E
Wissenkerke 52 51.35 N 3.45 E
Wissey ≃ 42 52.33 N 0.21 E
Wissinoming ◆[8] 285 40.01 N 75.04 W
Wissmar 56 50.38 N 8.41 E
Wissous 261 48.44 N 2.20 E
Wister 194 34.58 N 94.43 W
Wisznice 30 51.48 N 23.12 E
Witbank 158 25.56 S 29.07 E
Witberge ⋏ 158 30.45 S 27.32 E
Witbooisvlei 156 25.04 S 18.27 E
Witchekan Lake ⊜ 184 53.25 N 107.35 W
Witches Falls National Park ♠ 171a 27.56 S 153.10 E
Witch Hazel 224 45.30 N 122.46 W
Witdraai 158 26.58 S 20.45 E
Witfield 273d 26.11 S 28.12 E
Witham 42 51.48 N 0.38 E
Witham ≃ 44 53.06 N 0.13 W
Withamsville 218 39.03 N 84.16 W
Withens Clough Reservoir ⊜[1] 262 53.42 N 2.02 W
Witheridge 42 50.55 N 3.42 W
Withernsea 44 53.44 N 0.02 E
Witherspoon, Mount ∧ 180 61.23 N 147.12 W
Withington ◆[8] 262 53.26 N 2.14 W
Withington Green 262 53.14 N 2.18 W
Withlacoochee ≃, U.S. 192 30.24 N 83.10 W
Withlacoochee ≃, Fl., U.S. 192 29.00 N 82.45 W
Withnell 262 53.42 N 2.34 W
Withokspruit ≃ 273d 26.19 S 28.21 E
Witjira National Park ♠ 162 26.25 S 135.40 E
Wit-Kei ≃ 158 32.09 S 27.24 E
Witkoppies ∧ 158 27.44 S 29.20 E
Witkowo 30 52.27 N 17.47 E
Witless Bay 186 47.16 N 52.50 W
Witley 42 51.09 N 0.38 W
Wit-Mfolozi ≃ 158 28.22 S 31.58 E
Witney 42 51.48 N 1.29 W
Witnica 30 52.40 N 14.55 E
Wit Nossob ≃ 156 23.05 S 18.45 E
Witpoort 158 27.10 S 26.08 E
Witrivier 156 24.40 S 31.00 E
Witry-lès-Reims 50 49.18 N 4.07 E
Witsand 158 34.24 S 20.50 E
Witt 219 39.15 N 89.20 W
Wittabrenna Creek ≃ 166 29.20 S 142.43 E
Witteberg ⋏ 158 28.40 S 28.02 E
Witteberge ⋏ 158 33.18 S 20.36 E
Wittelsheim 58 47.49 N 7.15 E
Witten 56 51.26 N 7.20 E
Wittenau ◆[8] 264a 52.35 N 13.20 E
Wittenberg, Dtsch. 54 51.52 N 12.39 E
Wittenberg, Wi., U.S. 190 44.49 N 89.10 W
Wittenberge 54 53.00 N 11.44 E
Wittenburg 54 53.31 N 11.04 E
Wittenheim 58 47.49 N 7.20 E
Wittenoom 162 22.17 S 118.19 E
Wittensee ⊜ 41 54.23 N 9.45 E
Wittering 42 52.37 N 0.27 W
Wittgensdorf 54 50.53 N 12.52 E
Wittichenau 54 51.23 N 14.14 E
Wittingen 54 52.43 N 10.44 E
Wittislingen 56 48.37 N 10.25 E
Wittlaer 56 51.19 N 6.44 E
Wittlich 56 49.59 N 6.53 E
Wittman 208 38.47 N 76.17 W
Wittmar 54 52.07 N 10.38 E
Wittmund 52 53.34 N 7.47 E
Witton Park ♠ 262 53.45 N 2.31 W
Wittow ›[1] 54 54.38 N 13.19 E
Wittstock 54 53.10 N 12.29 E
Witu 154 2.23 S 40.26 E
Witu Islands ▮▮ 164 4.40 S 149.25 E
Witvlai 156 22.23 S 18.32 E
Witwatersrand, University of the υ[2] 273d 26.12 S 28.02 E
Witwatersrand Gold Mine ◆[7] 273d 26.12 S 28.11 E
Witwatersrant ◆[1] 158 26.00 S 27.00 E
Witzenhausen 56 51.20 N 9.51 E
Witzhelden 263 51.07 N 7.06 E
Witzputz 156 27.25 S 17.43 E
Wiveliscombe 42 51.03 N 3.19 W
Wivenhoe 42 51.52 N 0.58 E
Wivenhoe Reservoir ⊜[1] 171a 27.20 S 152.35 E
Wiwa Creek ≃ 184 50.02 N 106.31 W
Wixom 216 42.31 N 83.32 W
Wiżajny 30 54.23 N 22.51 E
Wizernes 50 50.43 N 2.14 E
Wjatka → V'atka ≃ 80 55.36 N 51.30 E
W. Kerr Scott Reservoir ⊜[1] 192 36.07 N 81.15 W
Wkra ≃ 30 52.27 N 20.44 E
Wladiwostok → Vladivostok 89 43.10 N 131.56 E
Władysławowo 30 54.49 N 18.25 E
Wleń 30 51.01 N 15.40 E
Wlingi 115a 8.05 S 112.19 E
Włocławek 30 52.39 N 19.02 E
Włocławek □[4] 30 52.30 N 19.05 E
Włodawa 30 51.34 N 23.32 E
Włoszczowa 30 50.52 N 19.59 E
Wnion ≃ 42 52.45 N 3.54 W
Woady Yaloak ≃ 169 38.06 S 143.33 E
Wobaer 85 39.19 N 75.32 E
Wöbbelin 54 53.24 N 11.30 E
Woburn 207 42.28 N 71.09 W
Woburn ◆[8] 275b 43.46 N 79.13 W
Woburn Sands 42 52.01 N 0.39 W
Woden, Austl. 171b 35.22 S 149.08 E
Woden, Tx., U.S. 222 31.30 N 94.32 W
Wodgina 162 21.11 S 118.40 E
Wodonga 166 36.07 S 146.54 E
Wodzisław Śląski 30 50.00 N 18.28 E
Woensdrecht 52 51.26 N 4.18 E
Woerdeke 85 39.41 N 77.53 E
Woerden 52 52.05 N 4.54 E
Woerth 56 48.56 N 7.45 E
Woëvre ◆[1] 56 49.05 N 5.40 E
Wofosi 105 40.09 N 115.18 E
Wo Fo Si (Temple of the Sleeping Buddha) υ[1] 105 40.01 N 116.12 E
Wognum 52 52.41 N 5.01 E
Wohlde 41 54.24 N 9.17 E
Wohlen 58 47.21 N 8.17 E
Wohlensee ⊜ 58 46.58 N 7.20 E
Wohlford, Lake ⊜[1] 228 33.10 N 116.59 W
Wohlthat Mountains ⋏ 9 71.35 S 12.20 E
Wohra ≃ 56 50.49 N 8.55 E
Woi 140 7.53 N 31.10 E
Woincourt 50 50.04 N 1.32 E
Woippy 56 49.09 N 6.09 E
Wojcieszów 30 50.58 N 15.56 E
Wokalup 168a 33.06 S 115.53 E
Wokam, Pulau ▮ 164 5.37 S 134.30 E
Wokha 120 26.06 N 94.16 E
Woking, Ab., Can. 182 55.35 N 118.46 W
Woking, Eng., U.K. 42 51.20 N 0.34 W
Woking □[8] 260 51.19 N 0.32 W
Wokingham 42 51.25 N 0.51 W
Wokingham Creek ≃ 166 22.19 S 142.30 E
Wolbach 198 41.24 N 98.24 W
Wolbeck 52 51.55 N 7.43 E
Wolbrom 30 50.24 N 19.46 E
Wolcott, Ct., U.S. 207 41.36 N 72.59 W
Wolcott, In., U.S. 216 40.45 N 87.02 W
Wolcott, N.Y., U.S. 210 43.13 N 76.48 W
Wolcott Creek ≃ 210 43.17 N 76.50 W
Wolcottsburg 210 43.04 N 78.38 W
Wolcottsville 210 43.07 N 78.31 W
Wolcottville 216 41.32 N 85.22 W
Wołcza ≃ 54 53.58 N 14.53 E
Wołczenica ≃ 54 53.52 N 14.44 E
Wołczyn 30 51.01 N 18.03 E
Woldberg ⋏[1] 52 52.25 N 5.55 E
Woldegk 54 53.27 N 13.35 E
Woldingham 260 51.17 N 0.02 W
Woleai ▮[1] 108 7.21 N 143.52 E
Woleu-Ntem □[4] 152 1.30 N 12.00 E
Wolf ≃, On., Can. 190 48.49 N 88.30 W
Wolf ≃, U.S. 194 35.09 N 90.04 W
Wolf ≃, Ks., U.S. 198 39.54 N 95.11 W
Wolf ≃, Ms., U.S. 194 30.21 N 89.18 W
Wolf ≃, Wi., U.S. 190 44.11 N 88.48 W
Wolf, Isla ▮ 246a 1.23 N 91.49 W
Wolf, Volcán ∧[1] 246a 0.02 N 91.20 W
Wolfach 58 48.17 N 8.13 E
Wolf-Bay 186 50.16 N 60.08 W
Wolf Creek, Mt., U.S. 202 47.00 N 112.04 W
Wolf Creek, Or., U.S. 202 42.41 N 123.23 W
Wolf Creek ≃, U.S. 196 36.35 N 99.30 W
Wolf Creek ≃, Ca., U.S. 226 39.02 N 121.08 W
Wolf Creek ≃, Co., U.S. 200 40.12 N 108.29 W
Wolf Creek ≃, In., U.S. 216 41.15 N 87.07 W
Wolf Creek ≃, Ia., U.S. 190 42.20 N 92.09 W
Wolf Creek ≃, Mt., U.S. 198 48.05 N 105.40 W
Wolf Creek ≃, Mt., U.S. 202 47.37 N 109.38 W
Wolf Creek ≃, Oh., U.S. 214 41.16 N 83.11 W
Wolf Creek ≃, Pa., U.S. 214 41.03 N 80.07 W
Wolf Creek ≃, S.D., U.S. 198 43.21 N 97.37 W
Wolf Creek ≃, S.D., U.S. 198 44.42 N 98.40 W
Wolf Creek Lake ⊜[1] 198 38.14 N 95.41 W
Wolf Creek Pass)(200 37.29 N 106.48 W
Wolf Creek State Park ♠ 219 39.30 N 88.41 W
Wolfdale 214 40.12 N 80.17 W
Wolfe □[6] 206 45.45 N 71.30 W
Wolfeboro 188 43.35 N 71.12 W
Wolfe City 196 33.22 N 96.04 W
Wolfegg 58 47.49 N 9.47 E
Wolfe Island 212 44.12 N 76.26 W
Wolfe Island ▮ 212 44.12 N 76.20 W
Wolfe Lake ⊜ 212 44.40 N 76.30 W
Wolfen 54 51.40 N 12.16 E
Wolfenbüttel 52 52.10 N 10.32 E
Wolfenden, Mount ∧ 182 50.26 N 127.33 W
Wolfenschiessen 58 46.55 N 8.24 E
Wolfertschwenden 58 47.53 N 10.16 E
Wolfforth 196 33.30 N 102.01 W
Wolfgangsee ⊜ 64 47.44 N 13.26 E
Wolfhagen 56 51.19 N 9.10 E
Wölfis 54 50.48 N 10.46 E
Wolf Island ▮ 212 44.33 N 78.15 W
Wolflake, In., U.S. 216 41.20 N 85.30 W
Wolf Lake, Mi., U.S. 216 43.15 N 86.06 W
Wolf Lake ⊜, Ab., Can. 182 54.42 N 110.59 W
Wolf Lake ⊜, On., Can. 212 44.44 N 78.11 W
Wolf Lake ⊜, Yk., Can. 180 60.40 N 131.40 W
Wolf Lake ⊜, U.S. 278 41.40 N 87.31 W
Wolf Lake ⊜, N.J., U.S. 276 40.57 N 74.42 W
Wolf Mountain ∧ 180 65.17 N 154.02 W
Wolfpassing 264b 48.19 N 16.11 E
Wolf Point 202 48.05 N 105.38 W
Wolframs-Eschenbach 56 49.14 N 10.43 E
Wolfratshausen 64 47.54 N 11.25 E
Wolf Rock ▮[2] 28 49.57 N 5.49 W
Wolf Run 214 40.30 N 80.54 W
Wolfsberg 61 46.51 N 14.51 E
Wolfsberg ∧[2] 263 51.38 N 6.27 E
Wolfsburg 54 52.25 N 10.47 E
Wolf's Castle 42 51.54 N 4.58 W
Wolfsegg am Hausruck 60 48.06 N 13.40 E
Wolfstein 56 49.35 N 7.36 E
Wolftrap Creek ≃ 284c 38.58 N 77.17 W
Wolf Trap Farms for the Performing Arts ♠ 284c 38.56 N 77.16 W
Wolfurt 58 47.28 N 9.45 E
Wolfville 186 45.05 N 64.22 W
Wolgan ≃ 170 33.12 S 150.28 E
Wolgast 54 54.03 N 13.46 E
Wolga → Volga ≃ 72 45.55 N 47.52 E
Wolgograder Stausee → Volgogradskoje vodochranilišče ⊜[1] 80 49.20 N 45.00 E
Wolgograd → Volgograd 80 48.44 N 44.25 E
Wolhusen 58 47.04 N 8.04 E
Wolin 30 53.50 N 14.35 E
Wolin ▮ 54 53.55 N 14.31 E
Woliński Park Narodowy ♠ 30 53.55 N 14.30 E
Wolkenstein 54 50.39 N 13.04 E
Wolkersdorf 61 48.23 N 16.31 E
Wölkisch 54 51.13 N 13.21 E
Wolkramshausen 54 51.25 N 10.44 E
Wollangambe ≃ 170 33.21 S 150.35 E
Wollaston 42 52.15 N 0.40 W
Wollaston, Islas ▮▮ 254 55.40 S 67.30 W
Wollaston Beach ≗[2] 283 42.17 N 71.01 W
Wollaston Lake ⊜, On., Can. 212 44.50 N 77.50 W
Wollaston Lake ⊜, Sk., Can. 176 58.15 N 103.20 W
Wollaston Peninsula ›[1] 176 70.00 N 115.00 W
Wollemi Creek ≃ 170 33.13 S 150.31 E
Wollemi National Park ♠ 166 32.50 S 150.30 E
Wollogorang 166 17.13 S 137.57 E
Wollombi 170 32.56 S 151.09 E
Wollombi Brook ≃ 170 32.33 S 151.04 E
Wollondilly ≃ 170 33.57 S 150.26 E
Wollongong 170 34.25 S 150.54 E
Wöllstein 56 49.49 N 7.58 E
Wolmaransstad 158 27.12 S 26.13 E
Wolmirsleben 54 51.57 N 11.29 E
Wolmirstedt 54 52.15 N 11.37 E
Wolnzach 60 48.36 N 11.37 E
Wołomin 30 52.21 N 21.14 E
Wołów 30 51.21 N 16.39 E
Wolowaru 115b 8.46 S 121.54 E
Wolseley, Sk., Can. 184 50.25 N 103.19 W
Wolseley, S. Afr. 158 33.26 S 19.12 E
Wolsey 198 44.24 N 98.28 W
Wolsingham 44 54.44 N 1.52 W
Wolsztyn 30 52.08 N 16.06 E
Wolterdingen 52 53.02 N 9.50 E
Woltersdorf, Dtsch. 54 52.24 N 12.22 E
Woltersdorf, Dtsch. 54 52.26 N 13.45 E
Woluogu 105 39.40 N 117.46 E
Woluwe-Saint-Lambert (Sint-Lambrechts-Woluwe) 56 50.51 N 4.24 E
Wolvega 52 52.53 N 6.00 E
Wolverhampton 42 52.36 N 2.08 W
Wolverine 190 45.16 N 84.36 W
Wolverine Lake 281 42.33 N 83.29 W
Wolverine Loon Lake ⊜ 281 42.33 N 83.30 W
Wolverine Mountain ∧ 180 65.20 N 149.51 W
Wolvertem 50 50.57 N 4.18 E
Wolverton 42 52.04 N 0.50 W
Wolwehoek 158 26.55 S 27.48 E
Wölzerbach ≃ 61 47.08 N 14.23 E
Wolziger See ⊜ 54 52.16 N 13.50 E
Woman ≃ 190 47.57 N 82.19 W
Wombarra 170 34.16 S 150.58 E
Wombat, Mount ∧ 169 36.51 S 145.40 E
Wombeyan Caves ≗[5] 170 34.18 S 149.56 E
Wombourne 42 52.32 N 2.11 W
Wombwell 44 53.31 N 1.24 W
Womelsdorf 208 40.22 N 76.11 W
Women's Rights National Historical Park ♠ 210 42.54 N 76.47 W
Wommels 52 53.06 N 5.36 E
Wompatuck State Park ♠ 283 42.13 N 70.51 W
Wonarah 162 19.55 S 136.20 E
Wondai 166 26.19 S 151.52 E
Wondelgem 50 51.05 N 3.43 E
Wonderfonteinspruit ≃ 273d 26.16 S 27.42 E
Wonderkop 158 27.50 S 27.26 E
Wonder Lake 216 42.25 N 88.21 W
Wonderland 204 40.24 N 121.19 W
Wonderland Center ◆[9] 281 42.22 N 83.20 W
Wonderland Dog Track ♠ 283 42.25 N 71.00 W
Wondinong 162 27.52 S 118.25 E
Wŏndong-ni 98 34.23 N 126.40 E
Wonersh 260 51.12 N 0.33 W
Wonewoc 190 43.39 N 90.13 W
Wong ≃ 124 27.10 N 89.30 E
Wongan Hills 162 30.53 S 116.42 E
Wonga Park 274b 37.44 S 145.16 E
Wonga-Wongué, Parc National de ♠ 152 0.30 S 9.30 E
Wonggarasi 112 0.33 N 121.36 E
Wong Ka Wai 271d 22.24 N 113.58 E
Woniushi 104 42.31 N 123.03 E
Wŏnjang-ni 98 39.05 N 125.32 E
Wŏnju 98 37.22 N 127.58 E
Wonogiri 115a 7.49 S 110.55 E
Wonokromo 115a 7.18 S 112.44 E
Wonosari 115a 7.58 S 110.35 E
Wonosegoro 115a 7.18 S 110.39 E
Wonosobo 115a 7.22 S 109.54 E
Wonotobo Vallen ∟ 250 4.22 N 57.58 W
Wonreli 112 8.05 S 127.09 E
Wŏnsan 98 39.09 N 127.25 E
Wonthaggi 169 38.36 S 145.35 E
Woocalla 166 31.42 S 137.13 E
Wood, Pa., U.S. 214 40.10 N 78.08 W

Symbol	English	Deutsch	Español	Français	Português
≃	River	Fluß	Río	Rivière	Rio
≊	Canal	Kanal	Canal	Canal	Canal
∟	Waterfall, Rapids	Wasserfall, Stromschnellen	Cascada, Rápidos	Chute d'eau, Rapides	Cascata, Rápidos
ʉ	Strait	Meeresstraße	Estrecho	Détroit	Estreito
⊂	Bay, Gulf	Bucht, Golf	Bahía, Golfo	Baie, Golfe	Baía, Golfo
⊜	Lake, Lakes	See, Seen	Lago, Lagos	Lac, Lacs	Lago, Lagos
≣	Swamp	Sumpf	Pantano	Marais	Pântano
⊓	Ice Features, Glacier	Eis- und Gletscherformen	Accidentes Glaciales	Formes glaciaires	Acidentes glaciares
⍑	Other Hydrographic Features	Andere Hydrographische Objekte	Otros Elementos Hidrográficos	Autres données hydrographiques	Outros acidentes hidrográficos

Symbol	English	Deutsch	Español	Français	Português
✦	Submarine Features	Untermeerische Objekte	Accidentes Submarinos	Formes de relief sous-marin	Acidentes submarinos
□	Political Unit	Politische Einheit	Unidad Politica	Entité politique	Unidade política
υ	Cultural Institution	Kulturelle Institution	Institución Cultural	Institution culturelle	Institução cultural
⊥	Historical Site	Historische Stätte	Sitio Histórico	Site historique	Sitio histórico
♠	Recreational Site	Erholungs- und Ferienort	Sitio de Recreo	Centre de loisirs	Area de Lazer
⊠	Airport	Flughafen	Aeropuerto	Aéroport	Aeroporto
■	Military Installation	Militäranlage	Instalación Militar	Installation militaire	Instalação militar
◆	Miscellaneous	Verschiedenes	Misceláneo	Divers	Diversos

Wood, S.D., U.S. 198 43.29 N 100.28 W
Wood □[6], Oh., U.S. 216 41.22 N 83.39 W
Wood □[6], Tx., U.S. 222 32.48 N 95.20 W
Wood ≃, B.C., Can. 182 52.10 N 118.30 W
Wood ≃, Sk., Can. 184 50.08 N 106.10 W
Wood ≃, U.S. 207 41.26 N 71.43 W
Wood ≃, Ak., U.S. 180 64.35 N 148.41 W
Wood ≃, Ne., U.S. 198 41.02 N 98.05 W
Wood ≃, Wy., U.S. 202 44.07 N 108.58 W
Wood, Mount ∧, Yk., Can. 180 61.14 N 140.31 W
Wood, Mount ∧, Mt., U.S. 202 45.17 N 109.49 W
Woodacre 226 38.05 N 122.36 W
Woodall Mountain ∧[2] 194 34.45 N 88.11 W
Wood Bay ⊂ 180 69.45 N 129.00 W
Woodberry Forest 284c 38.48 N 76.56 W
Woodbine, Ga., U.S. 192 30.57 N 81.43 W
Woodbine, Ia., U.S. 198 41.44 N 95.42 W
Woodbine, Md., U.S. 208 39.21 N 77.03 W
Woodbine, N.J., U.S. 208 39.14 N 74.48 W
Woodbourne, N.Y., U.S. 210 41.45 N 74.35 W
Woodbourne, Oh., U.S. 218 39.38 N 84.10 W
Woodbourne, Pa., U.S. 285 40.12 N 74.53 W
Woodbridge, Eng., U.K. 42 52.06 N 1.19 E
Woodbridge, Ca., U.S. 226 38.09 N 121.18 W
Woodbridge, Ct., U.S. 207 41.21 N 73.00 W
Woodbridge, N.J., U.S. 210 40.33 N 74.17 W
Woodbridge, Va., U.S. 208 38.39 N 77.15 W
Woodbridge Center ◆[9] 276 40.33 N 74.18 W
Woodbridge Creek ≃ 276 40.32 N 74.15 W
Woodbridge Island I 283 42.48 N 70.50 W
Woodburn, Il., U.S. 219 39.03 N 90.00 W
Woodburn, In., U.S. 216 41.07 N 84.51 W
Woodburn, Or., U.S. 224 45.08 N 122.51 W
Woodbury, Eng., U.K. 42 50.41 N 3.24 W
Woodbury, Ct., U.S. 207 41.32 N 73.12 W
Woodbury, Ga., U.S. 192 32.59 N 84.34 W
Woodbury, Mi., U.S. 216 42.46 N 85.05 W
Woodbury, N.J., U.S. 208 39.50 N 75.09 W
Woodbury, N.Y., U.S. 276 40.49 N 73.28 W
Woodbury, Pa., U.S. 214 40.14 N 78.22 W
Woodbury, Tn., U.S. 194 35.49 N 86.04 W
Woodbury Creek ≃ 285 39.52 N 75.11 W
Woodbury Heights 285 39.49 N 75.09 W
Woodchester 168b 35.13 S 138.57 E
Woodchopper 180 65.18 N 143.25 W
Woodchurch 42 51.05 N 0.46 E
Woodcliff Lake 276 41.01 N 74.04 W
Woodcliff Lake ⊜ 276 41.01 N 74.03 W
Woodcock 214 41.45 N 80.05 W
Woodcock, Mount ∧ 162 19.16 S 134.02 E
Woodcrest, Ca., U.S. 228 33.52 N 117.21 W
Woodcrest, Pa., U.S. 285 39.59 N 75.35 W
Wood Dale 278 41.57 N 87.58 W
Woodenbong 166 28.23 S 152.37 E
Woodend 169 37.22 S 144.32 E
Woodfibre 182 49.40 N 123.15 W
Woodfield ◆[9] 278 42.03 N 88.03 W
Woodford, Austl. 171a 26.57 S 152.47 E
Woodford, Ire. 48 53.03 N 8.23 W
Woodford, Eng., U.K. 262 53.21 N 2.10 W
Woodford □[6], Il., U.S. 216 40.43 N 89.16 W
Woodford □[6], Ky., U.S. 218 38.06 N 84.15 W
Woodford ◆[8] 260 51.36 N 0.02 E
Woodford Aerodrome ⊠ 262 53.20 N 2.09 W
Woodford Bridge ◆[8] 260 51.36 N 0.04 E
Woodford Halse 42 52.10 N 1.12 W
Wood Green ◆[8] 260 51.36 N 0.07 W
Woodhall Spa 44 53.09 N 0.13 W
Woodham 260 51.21 N 0.30 W
Woodham Ferrers 260 51.40 N 0.36 E
Woodham Mortimer 260 51.43 N 0.37 E
Woodham Walter 260 51.44 N 0.37 E
Woodhaven 216 42.08 N 83.14 W
Woodhaven ◆[8] 276 40.41 N 73.51 W
Woodhead Reservoir ⊜[1] 262 53.30 N 1.52 W
Woodhill 275b 43.45 N 79.41 W
Wood Hill ∧[2] 283 42.39 N 71.13 W
Woodhull, Il., U.S. 190 41.10 N 90.18 W
Woodhull, N.Y., U.S. 210 42.05 N 77.25 W
Woodinville 224 47.45 N 122.09 W
Wood Islands 186 45.58 N 62.45 W
Woodlake, Ca., U.S. 204 36.25 N 119.06 W
Wood Lake, Ne., U.S. 198 42.38 N 100.14 W
Woodlake, Tx., U.S. 222 31.01 N 95.02 W
Wood Lake ⊜, On., Can. 212 45.01 N 79.05 W
Wood Lake ⊜, Sk., Can. 184 55.17 N 103.17 W
Woodland, Ca., U.S. 226 38.40 N 121.46 W
Woodland, Ga., U.S. 192 32.47 N 84.33 W
Woodland, Il., U.S. 216 40.43 N 87.44 W
Woodland, Me., U.S. 188 45.09 N 67.24 W
Woodland, Mi., U.S. 216 42.43 N 85.08 W
Woodland, N.C., U.S. 192 36.19 N 77.12 W
Woodland, Pa., U.S. 214 40.59 N 78.20 W
Woodland, Wa., U.S. 224 45.54 N 122.44 W
Woodland Beach 216 41.57 N 83.19 W
Woodland Heights 214 41.25 N 79.43 W
Woodland Hills ◆[8] 280 34.11 N 118.35 W
Woodland Hills Park ♠ 279a 41.28 N 81.36 W
Woodland Park, Co., U.S. 200 38.59 N 105.03 W
Woodland Park, Pa., U.S. 210 41.18 N 77.03 W
Woodlands, N.Z. 172 46.22 S 168.33 E
Woodlands, Sing. 271c 1.27 N 103.46 E
Woodlands, N.Y., U.S. 276 41.01 N 73.50 W
Woodlawn, Il., U.S. 219 38.20 N 89.02 W
Woodlawn, Ky., U.S. 194 37.02 N 88.34 W
Woodlawn, Md., U.S. 284b 39.19 N 76.43 W
Woodlawn, Md., U.S. 284c 38.57 N 76.53 W
Woodlawn, Wa., U.S. 224 47.01 N 123.48 W
Woodlawn ◆[8] 278 41.47 N 87.36 W
Woodlawn Beach 210 42.48 N 78.51 W
Woodlawn Heights 284b 39.11 N 76.39 W
Woodley 42 51.28 N 0.54 W
Woodlyn 285 39.52 N 75.20 W
Woodlynne 285 39.55 N 75.05 W
Woodmansey 44 53.50 N 0.29 W
Woodmansterne 260 51.19 N 0.10 W
Woodmere, N.Y., U.S. 210 40.37 N 73.42 W
Woodmere, Oh., U.S. 279a 41.28 N 81.29 W
Woodmoor 284b 39.20 N 76.44 W
Wood Mountain ∧ 184 49.14 N 106.20 W
Wood Mountain Indian Reserve ◆[4] 184 49.21 N 106.24 W
Woodplumpton 262 53.48 N 2.47 W
Woodport 276 40.59 N 74.36 W
Woodrarung Range ⋀ 162 27.10 S 115.30 E
Woodridge, Austl. 171a 27.38 S 153.06 E
Woodridge, Mb., Can. 184 49.17 N 96.09 W
Woodridge, Il., U.S. 216 41.44 N 88.03 W
Wood-Ridge, N.J., U.S. 276 40.50 N 74.05 W
Woodridge, N.Y., U.S. 210 41.43 N 74.34 W
Wood River, Ak., U.S. 180 59.04 N 158.26 W
Wood River, Il., U.S. 219 38.51 N 90.05 W
Wood River, Ne., U.S. 198 40.49 N 98.35 W
Wood River Lakes ⊜ 180 59.30 N 158.45 W
Wood River Mountains ⋀ 180 59.32 N 159.30 W
Woodroffe ≃ 166 21.28 S 137.58 E
Woodroffe, Mount ∧ 162 26.20 S 131.45 E
Woodrow 192 35.08 N 77.05 W
Woodrow Wilson Memorial Bridge ◆[5] 284c 38.48 N 77.02 W
Woodruff, Az., U.S. 200 34.46 N 110.02 W
Woodruff, S.C., U.S. 192 34.44 N 82.02 W
Woodruff, Wi., U.S. 190 45.53 N 89.41 W
Woodruff Creek ≃ 281 42.21 N 83.43 W
Woods 168b 34.15 S 138.31 E
Woods, Lake ⊜ 162 17.50 S 133.30 E
Woods, Lake of the ⊜ 184 49.15 N 94.45 W
Woods Bay ⊂ 212 45.08 N 80.00 W
Woodsboro, Md., U.S. 208 39.31 N 77.18 W
Woodsboro, Tx., U.S. 196 28.14 N 97.19 W
Woodsburgh 276 40.37 N 73.42 W
Woods Creek ≃, N.Y., U.S. 276 40.39 N 73.24 W
Woods Creek ≃, N.Y., U.S. 284a 43.04 N 78.58 W
Woodsfield 188 39.45 N 81.06 W
Woods Hole 207 41.31 N 70.40 W
Woodside, Austl. 166 38.31 S 146.52 E
Woodside, Austl. 168b 34.57 S 138.52 E
Woodside, Eng., U.K. 260 51.45 N 0.11 W
Woodside, Ca., U.S. 226 37.25 N 122.15 W
Woodside, De., U.S. 208 39.04 N 75.34 W
Woodside, Pa., U.S. 285 40.13 N 74.53 W
Woodside ◆[8] 276 40.45 N 73.55 W
Woodside National Historic Park ♠ 212 43.26 N 80.08 W
Woodson, Il., U.S. 219 39.38 N 90.13 W
Woodson, Tx., U.S. 196 33.01 N 99.03 W
Woods Point 169 37.35 S 146.15 E
Woods Reservoir ⊜[1] 194 35.20 N 86.00 W
Woodstock, Austl. 166 22.15 S 141.57 E
Woodstock, N.B., Can. 186 46.09 N 67.34 W
Woodstock, On., Can. 212 43.08 N 80.45 W
Woodstock, Eng., U.K. 42 51.52 N 1.21 W
Woodstock, Ct., U.S. 207 41.56 N 71.58 W
Woodstock, Il., U.S. 216 42.18 N 88.26 W
Woodstock, Md., U.S. 284b 39.19 N 76.52 W
Woodstock, N.Y., U.S. 210 42.02 N 74.07 W
Woodstock, Oh., U.S. 218 40.10 N 83.32 W
Woodstock, Vt., U.S. 188 43.37 N 72.31 W
Woodstock, Va., U.S. 188 38.52 N 78.30 W
Woodstown 208 39.39 N 75.19 W
Wood Street 260 51.15 N 0.38 W
Woodsville 188 44.09 N 72.02 W
Woodvale Airfield ⊠ 262 53.35 N 3.03 W
Wood Village 224 45.32 N 122.19 W
Woodville, Austl. 168b 34.53 S 138.32 E
Woodville, On., Can. 212 44.24 N 78.59 W
Woodville, N.Z. 172 40.20 S 175.52 E
Woodville, Al., U.S. 194 34.38 N 86.16 W
Woodville, Ca., U.S. 226 36.06 N 119.12 W
Woodville, Fl., U.S. 192 30.20 N 84.15 W
Woodville, Ga., U.S. 192 33.40 N 83.06 W
Woodville, Ma., U.S. 207 42.14 N 71.33 W
Woodville, Mi., U.S. 216 43.39 N 85.40 W
Woodville, Ms., U.S. 194 31.06 N 91.17 W
Woodville, N.Y., U.S. 210 42.40 N 77.22 W
Woodville, Oh., U.S. 214 41.27 N 83.21 W
Woodville, Tx., U.S. 194 30.46 N 94.24 W
Woodward, Ia., U.S. 190 41.51 N 93.55 W
Woodward, Ok., U.S. 196 36.26 N 99.23 W
Woodward, Pa., U.S. 210 40.54 N 77.21 W
Woodward Reservoir ⊜[1] 226 37.51 N 120.52 W
Woodway, Tx., U.S. 222 31.30 N 97.12 W
Woodway, Wa., U.S. 224 47.47 N 122.23 W
Woodworth, Oh., U.S. 214 40.59 N 80.40 W
Woodworth, Wi., U.S. 216 42.34 N 88.00 W
Woody ≃ 184 52.30 N 100.51 W
Woody Creek ≃ 202 47.27 N 106.21 W
Woody Head › 166 29.22 S 153.22 E
Woody Island 180 57.47 N 152.22 W
Wool 42 50.41 N 2.14 W
Woolacombe 42 51.10 N 4.13 W
Woolamai, Cape › 169 38.34 S 145.21 E
Wool Bay 168b 35.00 S 137.45 E
Wooldridge 158 33.13 S 27.15 E
Wooler 44 55.33 N 2.01 W
Woolford 208 38.30 N 76.11 W
Woolgangie 162 31.10 S 120.32 E
Woolgoolga 166 30.07 S 153.12 E
Woollahra 274a 33.53 S 151.15 E
Woolmarket 194 30.28 N 88.59 W
Woolooware Bay ⊂ 274a 34.02 S 151.09 E
Woolpit 42 52.13 N 0.54 E
Woolrich 210 41.12 N 77.23 W
Woolsey Peak ∧ 200 33.10 N 112.53 W
Woolston 262 53.24 N 2.32 W
Woolton ◆[8] 262 53.23 N 2.52 W
Woolwich ◆[8] 260 51.29 N 0.04 E
Woomargama 171b 35.50 S 147.15 E
Woomera 166 31.31 S 137.10 E
Woomera Prohibited Area ◆[4] 162 29.45 S 134.30 E
Woonona 170 34.21 S 150.55 E
Woonsocket, R.I., U.S. 207 42.00 N 71.30 W
Woonsocket, S.D., U.S. 198 44.03 N 98.16 W
Woorabinda 166 24.08 S 149.28 E
Wooramel 162 25.44 S 114.17 E
Wooramel ≃ 162 25.47 S 114.10 E
Woorim 171a 27.08 S 153.12 E
Wooroloo 168a 31.48 S 116.19 E
Wooster 214 40.48 N 81.56 W
Wootton 42 52.11 N 0.53 W
Wootton Bassett 42 51.33 N 1.54 W
Wootton Wawen 42 52.16 N 1.47 W
Woqooyi Galbeed □[4] 144 10.00 N 44.00 E
Worb 58 46.56 N 7.34 E
Worbis 54 51.25 N 10.21 E
Worcester, S. Afr. 158 33.39 S 19.27 E
Worcester, Eng., U.K. 42 52.11 N 2.13 W
Worcester, Ma., U.S. 207 42.15 N 71.48 W
Worcester, N.Y., U.S. 210 42.35 N 74.45 W
Worcester, Pa., U.S. 285 40.12 N 75.21 W
Worcester □[6], Md., U.S. 208 38.11 N 75.24 W
Worcester □[6], Ma., U.S. 207 42.16 N 71.48 W
Worcester Municipal Airport ⊠ 207 42.16 N 71.52 W
Worden, Il., U.S. 219 38.55 N 89.50 W
Worden, Mt., U.S. 202 45.57 N 108.09 W
Worden Pond ⊜ 207 41.26 N 71.35 W
Wördern 61 48.20 N 16.13 E
Wörgl 64 47.29 N 12.04 E
Workai, Pulau I 164 6.40 S 134.40 E
Work Channel ⊔ 182 54.30 N 130.15 W
Workers' Stadium ♠ 271a 39.55 N 116.27 E
Workington 44 54.39 N 3.35 W
Worksop 44 53.18 N 1.07 W
Workum 52 52.57 N 5.26 E
Worland 202 44.01 N 107.57 W
World End Pond ⊜ 283 42.45 N 71.12 W
Worli ◆[8] 272c 19.01 N 72.50 E
Wörlitz 54 51.50 N 12.25 E
Wormerveer 52 52.28 N 4.46 E
Wormhoudt 50 50.53 N 2.28 E
Wormit 46 56.25 N 2.59 W
Wormley 260 51.44 N 0.01 W
Worms 56 49.38 N 8.22 E
Worms Head › 42 51.34 N 4.20 W
Wormshill 260 51.17 N 0.42 E
Wörnitz ≃ 56 48.42 N 10.45 E
Woronesch → Voronež 78 51.40 N 39.10 E
Woronoco 207 42.09 N 72.49 W
Woronora 274a 34.01 S 151.03 E
Woronora ≃ 274a 34.00 S 151.04 E
Woronora Reservoir ⊜[1] 170 34.08 S 150.56 E
Worplesdon 260 51.16 N 0.37 W
Worpswede 52 53.13 N 8.56 E
Wörrstadt 56 49.50 N 8.07 E
Wörsbach ≃ 56 50.22 N 8.09 E
Worsbrough 44 53.31 N 1.29 W
Worsley 262 53.30 N 2.23 W
Worsthorne 262 53.47 N 2.11 W
Wörth, Dtsch. 56 49.48 N 9.09 E
Worth, Dtsch. 263 51.13 N 7.39 E
Worth, Il., U.S. 216 41.41 N 87.47 W
Worth, Lake ⊜[1] 222 32.48 N 97.28 W
Wortham 222 31.47 N 96.27 W
Wörth am Rhein 56 49.03 N 8.16 E
Wörth an der Donau 60 49.00 N 12.25 E
Wörth an der Isar 60 48.37 N 12.24 E
Worthen 42 52.38 N 3.00 W
Wörther See ⊜ 61 46.37 N 14.10 E
Worthing 42 50.48 N 0.23 W
Worthington, In., U.S. 194 39.07 N 86.58 W
Worthington, Md., U.S. 284b 39.14 N 76.47 W
Worthington, Mn., U.S. 198 43.37 N 95.35 W
Worthington, N.Y., U.S. 276 41.02 N 73.50 W
Worthington, Oh., U.S. 214 40.05 N 83.01 W
Worthington, Pa., U.S. 214 40.50 N 79.37 W
Worthington Peak ∧ 204 37.55 N 115.37 W
Wörthsee ⊜ 60 48.03 N 11.10 E
Worthville, Ky., U.S. 218 38.36 N 85.04 W
Worthville, Pa., U.S. 214 41.02 N 79.08 W
Worton 208 39.16 N 76.05 W
Wŏrun-dong 98 39.36 N 125.20 E
Wosimi 164 2.54 S 134.31 E
Wostok → Vostok ʊ[3] 9 78.30 S 106.50 E
Wosu 112 2.21 S 121.50 E
Wotap, Pulau I 164 7.21 S 131.16 E
Wotho I[1] 14 10.06 N 165.59 E
Wotje I[1] 14 9.27 N 170.02 E
Wotton, P.Q., Can. 206 45.44 N 71.48 W
Wotton, Eng., U.K. 260 51.13 N 0.23 W
Wotton-under-Edge 42 51.39 N 2.21 W
Wotu 112 2.35 S 120.48 E
Woudenberg 52 52.05 N 5.25 E
Woudrichem 52 51.49 N 5.00 E
Woudsend 52 52.56 N 5.36 E
Wouldham 260 51.21 N 0.28 E
Wounded Knee 198 43.08 N 102.21 W
Wounded Knee Creek ≃ 198 43.26 N 102.32 W
Wounta 236 13.33 N 83.32 W
Wounta, Laguna de ⊂ 236 13.38 N 83.34 W
Wour 146 21.21 N 15.57 E
Wouri ≃ 152 4.06 N 9.43 E
Woutchaba 152 5.13 N 13.05 E
Wouw 52 51.32 N 4.24 E
Wowan 166 23.55 S 150.12 E
Wowoni, Pulau I 112 4.08 S 123.06 E
Woyla ≃ 114 4.18 N 95.56 E
Woy Woy 170 33.30 S 151.20 E
Woźniki 30 50.36 N 19.03 E
Wragby 44 53.18 N 0.19 W
Wrangel Island → Vrangel'a, ostrov I 74 71.00 N 179.30 W
Wrangell 180 56.28 N 132.23 W
Wrangell, Cape › 181a 52.50 N 172.26 E
Wrangell, Mount ∧ 180 62.00 N 144.06 W
Wrangell Island I 180 56.15 N 132.10 W
Wrangell Mountains ⋀ 180 62.00 N 143.00 W
Wrangell-Saint Elias National Park ♠ 180 61.00 N 142.00 W
Wrath, Cape › 46 58.37 N 5.01 W
Wray 198 40.04 N 102.13 W
Wraysbury 260 51.27 N 0.33 W
Wrea Green 262 53.46 N 2.55 W
Wreck Bay ⊂ 170 35.11 S 150.40 E
Wreck Island I 208 37.16 N 75.48 W
Wreck Reef ◆[2] 166 22.13 S 155.17 E
Wrecks, Bay of ⊂ 174o 1.52 N 157.17 W
Wredenhagen 54 53.17 N 12.31 E
Wremen 52 53.39 N 8.30 E
Wren 216 40.48 N 84.46 W
Wrens 192 33.12 N 82.23 W
Wrentham, Ab., Can. 182 49.32 N 112.10 W
Wrentham, Eng., U.K. 42 52.23 N 1.40 E
Wrentham, Ma., U.S. 207 42.04 N 71.19 W
Wrentham State Forest ♠ 283 42.02 N 71.20 W
Wrexham 44 53.03 N 3.00 W
Wriezen 54 52.43 N 14.08 E
Wright, Mount ∧, Austl. 166 31.12 S 142.26 E
Wright, Mount ∧, Mt., U.S. 202 47.58 N 112.49 W
Wright Brothers National Memorial ⊥ 192 35.55 N 75.50 W
Wright City, Mo., U.S. 219 38.49 N 91.01 W
Wright City, Ok., U.S. 194 34.03 N 95.00 W
Wright City, Tx., U.S. 222 32.12 N 94.59 W
Wrightington Bar 262 53.37 N 2.42 W
Wright Patman Lake ⊜[1] 194 33.16 N 94.14 W
Wright-Patterson Air Force Base ■ 218 39.49 N 84.03 W
Wright Peak ∧ 204 38.59 N 122.46 W
Wrights 219 39.23 N 90.18 W
Wrightsboro 222 29.22 N 97.34 W
Wrights Corners 210 43.13 N 78.46 W
Wrightson, Mount ∧ 200 31.42 N 110.50 W
Wrightstown, N.J., U.S. 208 40.02 N 74.37 W
Wrightstown, Pa., U.S. 208 40.17 N 74.58 W
Wrightstown, Wi., U.S. 190 44.19 N 88.09 W
Wrightsville, Ga., U.S. 192 32.43 N 82.43 W
Wrightsville, Pa., U.S. 214 40.01 N 76.31 W
Wrightsville Beach 192 34.12 N 77.47 W
Wrightwood 228 34.21 N 117.37 W
Wrigley, N.T., Can. 180 63.16 N 123.37 W
Wrigley, Tn., U.S. 194 35.54 N 87.20 W
Wrigley Field ♠ 278 41.57 N 87.39 W
Wrigley Gulf ⊂ 9 74.00 S 129.00 W
Writtle 42 51.44 N 0.26 E
Wrocław (Breslau) 30 51.06 N 17.00 E
Wrocław □[4] 30 51.15 N 17.00 E
Wrong Lake ⊜ 184 52.38 N 96.10 W
Wronki 30 52.43 N 16.23 E
Wrotham 42 51.19 N 0.19 E
Wrotham Heath 260 51.18 N 0.21 E
Wrottesley, Cape › 176 74.33 N 121.32 W
Wroughton 42 51.31 N 1.46 W
Wroxham 42 52.42 N 1.24 E
Wroxton 184 51.14 N 101.53 W
Września 30 52.20 N 17.34 E
Wschowa 30 51.48 N 16.19 E
Wu ≃, Zhg. 98 34.25 N 117.55 E
Wu ≃, Zhg. 100 28.57 N 116.39 E
Wu ≃, Zhg. 100 24.48 N 113.35 E
Wu ≃, Zhg. 102 27.03 N 109.53 E
Wu ≃, Zhg. 102 27.12 N 109.48 E
Wu ≃, Zhg. 102 29.43 N 107.24 E
Wu'an 98 36.40 N 114.12 E
Wubaozhen 107 29.14 N 104.29 E
Wubin 162 30.06 S 116.38 E
Wubu 102 37.33 N 110.39 E
Wuchagou 89 46.46 N 120.16 E
Wuchang 89 44.54 N 127.08 E
Wuchang Hu ⊜ 100 30.17 N 116.47 E
Wuchang → Wuhan 100 30.36 N 114.17 E
Wucheng, Zhg. 98 37.09 N 115.53 E
Wucheng (Jiucheng), Zhg. 98 37.13 N 116.02 E
Wucheng, Zhg. 100 29.36 N 118.10 E
Wucheng, Zhg. 100 33.28 N 113.44 E
Wucheng, Zhg. 100 29.10 N 115.59 E
Wuch'i 100 24.16 N 120.31 E
Wuchin → Changzhou 106 31.47 N 119.57 E
Wuch'iu Yü I 100 25.00 N 119.27 E
Wuchow → Wuzhou 102 23.30 N 111.27 E
Wuchuan, Zhg. 102 21.25 N 110.40 E
Wuchuan, Zhg. 102 28.25 N 107.56 E
Wuchuan, Zhg. 102 41.05 N 111.23 E
Wuchung → Wuzhong 102 37.57 N 106.10 E
Wucun 105 38.57 N 115.19 E
Wuda 102 39.30 N 106.40 E
Wudao 98 39.28 N 121.28 E
Wudaogou, Zhg. 98 41.43 N 127.05 E
Wudaogou, Zhg. 98 42.08 N 125.51 E
Wudaoliang 120 35.11 N 93.35 E
Wudaolianggou 104 40.59 N 120.35 E
Wudi 98 37.44 N 117.35 E
Wudian, Zhg. 100 31.57 N 112.46 E
Wudian, Zhg. 100 32.42 N 117.18 E
Wuding 102 25.32 N 102.23 E
Wuding ≃ 102 37.05 N 110.20 E
Wudinna 166 33.03 S 135.28 E
Wudu, Zhg. 100 28.23 N 118.14 E
Wudu, Zhg. 100 27.37 N 119.00 E
Wudu, Zhg. 102 33.24 N 104.50 E
Wuduhe 102 31.03 N 111.03 E
Wuerqihan 89 49.37 N 121.45 E
Wufeng 102 30.11 N 110.33 E
Wufeng Shan I 106 31.07 N 120.16 E
Wufengxi 107 30.37 N 104.29 E
Wufu 100 30.06 N 120.58 E
Wugang 102 26.44 N 110.38 E
Wugong 102 34.20 N 108.04 E
Wugong Shan ∧ 100 27.35 N 114.18 E
Wugong Shan ⋀ 100 27.21 N 113.50 E
Wugouying 100 33.28 N 114.08 E
Wugunuoer 89 49.10 N 119.19 E
Wuhai 102 39.39 N 106.41 E
Wuhan 100 30.36 N 114.17 E
Wuhe, Zhg. 100 33.10 N 117.54 E
Wuhe, Zhg. 100 24.26 N 115.25 E
Wuhle ≃ 264a 52.29 N 13.34 E
Wuhsing → Huzhou 106 30.52 N 120.06 E
Wuhsi → Wuxi 106 31.35 N 120.18 E
Wuhu, Zhg. 100 31.11 N 118.35 E
Wuhu, Zhg. 100 31.21 N 118.22 E
Wuhua 100 23.57 N 115.48 E
Wuhuanchi 104 42.20 N 121.51 E
Wuhuang 107 29.58 N 104.46 E
Wuhudongmiao 102 38.19 N 107.20 E
Wüjang 120 33.38 N 79.50 E
Wuji, Zhg. 98 38.13 N 114.57 E
Wuji, Zhg. 98 34.12 N 119.02 E
Wujia ≃ 102 41.10 N 108.45 E
Wujiabeigou 104 40.57 N 123.50 E
Wujiang, Zhg. 100 31.52 N 118.28 E
Wujiang, Zhg. 100 27.14 N 115.15 E
Wujiang, Zhg. 106 31.10 N 120.38 E
Wujiangdu 102 27.16 N 106.48 E
Wujianpu 107 29.10 N 105.50 E
Wujiapai 105 39.32 N 117.18 E
Wujiapu 105 38.52 N 117.07 E
Wujiazhen 107 29.38 N 105.24 E
Wujiazhuang, Zhg. 105 40.35 N 115.20 E
Wujiazhuang, Zhg. 106 32.18 N 120.10 E
Wujiazi, Zhg. 89 46.27 N 123.34 E
Wujiazi, Zhg. 104 42.13 N 122.08 E
Wujiazi, Zhg. 104 42.30 N 121.10 E
Wujing 100 25.16 N 114.36 E
Wukang 106 30.33 N 119.58 E
Wukari 150 7.51 N 9.47 E
Wukeshu, Zhg. 89 46.02 N 123.45 E
Wukeshu, Zhg. 89 44.48 N 126.08 E
Wulai 100 24.52 N 121.33 E
Wulajia 89 48.23 N 129.58 E
Wulanheduojia 102 42.40 N 113.20 E
Wulanhutong 98 41.44 N 114.49 E
Wulanmutou 104 42.23 N 121.21 E
Wulanwusu, Zhg. 86 44.20 N 85.50 E
Wulanwusu, Zhg. 102 41.39 N 107.48 E
Wular Lake ⊜ 123 34.20 N 74.33 E
Wulasitai, Zhg. 89 43.15 N 121.27 E
Wulasitai, Zhg. 89 43.28 N 122.44 E
Wulateqianqi 102 40.39 N 109.05 E
Wulaxi 102 28.38 N 101.40 E
Wuleidao Wan ⊂ 98 36.55 N 122.00 E
Wulfen 52 51.43 N 7.00 E
Wülfrath 56 51.17 N 7.02 E
Wulfsen 52 53.18 N 10.08 E
Wulfsode 52 53.04 N 10.13 E
Wulften 52 51.40 N 10.10 E
Wulian (Hongning) 98 35.47 N 119.15 E
Wulian Feng ⋀ 102 28.03 N 103.57 E
Wuliangdian 104 41.52 N 122.16 E
Wuliang Shan ⋀ 102 24.30 N 100.45 E
Wuliaru, Pulau I 164 7.27 S 131.04 E
Wulichuan 102 33.49 N 111.08 E
Wulie ≃ 105 40.54 N 117.55 E
Wuling 98 35.53 N 114.36 E
Wuling Shan ∧ 105 40.36 N 117.29 E
Wulitaizi 104 41.28 N 123.21 E
Wulizhuang 100 33.49 N 118.57 E
Wulka ≃ 61 47.52 N 16.40 E
Wüllen 52 52.04 N 6.58 E
Wullwye Creek ≃ 171b 36.30 S 148.49 E
Wulong, Zhg. 102 29.20 N 107.43 E
Wulong, Zhg. 104 41.39 N 124.13 E
Wulong ≃ 98 36.35 N 120.56 E
Wulongbei 98 40.21 N 124.16 E
Wulsdorf ◆[8] 52 53.30 N 8.35 E
Wultschau 61 48.42 N 14.50 E
Wulu ≃ 85 39.38 N 74.38 E
Wuluhan 115a 8.21 S 113.33 E
Wuluhayingzi 104 42.20 N 121.34 E
Wulumuch'i → Ürümqi 90 43.48 N 87.35 E
Wulumuqi → Ürümqi 90 43.48 N 87.35 E
Wuluo 102 26.09 N 108.15 E
Wulur 164 7.09 S 128.39 E
Wulu Station ◆[5] 271a 39.56 N 116.16 E
Wum 152 6.23 N 10.04 E
Wumang Dao I 98 39.14 N 123.03 E
Wumiaoxiang 107 30.23 N 104.17 E
Wuming 102 23.10 N 108.18 E
Wümme ≃ 52 53.10 N 8.44 E
Wunamu 86 46.06 N 85.44 E
Wundowie 168a 31.46 S 116.22 E
Wundwin 110 21.05 N 96.02 E
Wuneba 154 4.50 N 30.20 E
Wungong Brook ≃ 168a 32.06 S 115.59 E
Wuning 100 29.17 N 115.06 E
Wünnenberg 52 51.31 N 8.42 E
Wunnummin Lake ⊜ 176 52.55 N 89.10 W
Wun Rog 140 9.00 N 28.21 E
Wünschendorf 54 50.48 N 12.05 E
Wünsdorf 54 52.10 N 13.28 E
Wunsiedel 60 50.02 N 12.01 E
Wunstorf 52 52.25 N 9.26 E
Wuntho 110 23.54 N 95.41 E
Wunuer 89 48.53 N 121.15 E
Wupaowan 107 29.50 N 103.59 E
Wupatki National Monument ♠ 200 35.24 N 111.14 W
Wuping 100 25.08 N 116.06 E
Wupper ≃ 263 51.05 N 7.00 E
Wuppertal, Dtsch. 56 51.16 N 7.11 E
Wuppertal, Dtsch. 263 51.16 N 7.11 E
Wuppertal, S. Afr. 158 32.15 S 19.15 E
Wuqi, Zhg. 100 27.10 N 120.23 E
Wuqi, Zhg. 102 37.08 N 108.10 E
Wuqia 85 39.42 N 75.13 E
Wuqiang (Xiaofan) 98 38.03 N 115.58 E
Wuqing (Yangcun) 105 39.23 N 117.04 E
Wuraming 168a 32.48 S 116.16 E
Wurarga 162 28.25 S 116.17 E
Würenlingen 58 47.32 N 8.16 E
Wurgwitz 54 51.01 N 13.37 E
Würm ≃, Dtsch. 56 48.53 N 8.42 E
Wurm ≃, Dtsch. 56 51.08 N 6.10 E
Würm ≃, Dtsch. 60 48.10 N 11.28 E
Wurmannsquick 60 48.21 N 12.47 E
Wurmberg ∧ 54 51.45 N 10.37 E
Wurno 150 13.17 N 5.24 E
Wurong 164 6.07 S 140.47 E
Würselen 56 50.49 N 6.08 E
Wursten, Land ◆[1] 52 53.40 N 8.35 E
Wurtsboro 210 41.35 N 74.29 W
Wurtsboro Hills 210 41.36 N 74.30 W
Wurtsmith Air Force Base ■ 190 44.27 N 83.23 W
Wuruf 164 6.43 S 146.25 E
Wuryantoro 115a 7.54 S 110.51 E
Wurzbach 54 50.28 N 11.32 E
Würzburg 56 49.48 N 9.56 E
Wurzen 54 51.22 N 12.44 E
Wusanga 152 3.22 S 22.50 E
Wusha 100 30.39 N 117.18 E
Wushan, Zhg. 100 32.04 N 117.03 E
Wushan, Zhg. 102 34.38 N 105.04 E
Wushan, Zhg. 102 31.05 N 109.48 E
Wushan, Zhg. 106 31.44 N 118.58 E
Wusheng, Zhg. 100 29.56 N 119.25 E
Wusheng, Zhg. 107 30.21 N 106.17 E
Wushengchang 107 29.00 N 103.43 E
Wushenqi 102 38.58 N 109.01 E
Wushi, Zhg. 102 22.11 N 110.11 E
Wushi, Zhg. 106 31.44 N 120.59 E
Wushishi 150 9.46 N 6.07 E
Wushu 100 26.20 N 114.56 E
Wusi 175f 15.22 S 166.36 E
Wusih → Wuxi 106 31.35 N 120.18 E
Wuskwatim Lake ⊜ 184 55.32 N 98.32 W
Wusong 106 31.23 N 121.29 E
Wusong ≃ 106 31.15 N 121.29 E
Wust 54 52.33 N 12.07 E
Wüsten 52 52.06 N 8.47 E
Wüstensachsen 56 50.30 N 10.00 E
Wusterhausen 54 52.54 N 12.28 E
Wusterhusen 54 54.07 N 13.37 E
Wustermark 54 52.33 N 12.56 E
Wüstermarke 54 51.49 N 13.36 E
Wusterwitz 54 52.22 N 12.18 E
Wüsting 52 53.07 N 8.20 E
Wustrow, Dtsch. 54 54.05 N 11.34 E
Wustrow, Dtsch. 54 52.55 N 11.07 E
Wustrow ›[1] 54 54.05 N 11.34 E
Wusuli (Ussuri) ≃ 89 48.27 N 135.04 E
Wusuo 100 25.02 N 116.02 E
Wuta 106 31.31 N 120.39 E
Wutach ≃ 58 47.37 N 8.15 E
Wutai, Zhg. 85 39.28 N 78.09 E
Wutai, Zhg. 86 44.36 N 82.06 E
Wutai, Zhg. 98 41.18 N 113.59 E
Wutai, Zhg. 102 38.44 N 113.17 E
Wutai Shan ∧ 98 39.04 N 113.35 E
Wutai Shan ⋀ 98 39.13 N 113.45 E
Wutaizi 104 42.27 N 123.17 E
Wutan 102 28.29 N 111.40 E
Wutanchang 107 29.15 N 106.04 E
Wutang 106 31.31 N 119.10 E
Wutangdun 106 30.38 N 120.08 E
Wutangjie 100 29.59 N 122.22 E
Wuteve, Mount ∧ 150 8.09 N 9.56 W
Wutianzhen 100 30.23 N 117.12 E
Wutong 102 25.18 N 110.01 E
Wutonghaolai 89 42.55 N 120.15 E
Wutongqiao 107 29.26 N 103.51 E
Wutongwozi 102 42.27 N 95.17 E
Wutsin → Changzhou 106 31.47 N 119.57 E
Wutun 100 27.51 N 118.04 E
Wut'ungch'iao → Wutongqiao 107 29.26 N 103.51 E
Wutungkiao → Wutongqiao 107 29.26 N 103.51 E
Wutuohuo 102 40.51 N 101.48 E
Wuustwezel 50 51.23 N 4.36 E
Wuvulu Island I 164 1.45 S 142.50 E
Wuwei, Zhg. 100 31.18 N 117.54 E
Wuwei (Liangzhou), Zhg. 102 37.58 N 102.49 E
Wuxi, Zhg. 102 31.25 N 109.34 E
Wuxi, Zhg. 106 31.20 N 118.39 E
Wuxi (Wuhsi), Zhg. 106 31.35 N 120.18 E
Wuxi ≃ 100 29.00 N 118.56 E
Wuxiang 102 36.51 N 113.00 E
Wuxingchang 106 31.13 N 119.23 E
Wuxuan 102 23.36 N 109.42 E
Wuyang, Zhg. 100 33.26 N 113.34 E
Wuyang, Zhg. 100 25.41 N 115.55 E
Wuyang, Zhg. 102 26.41 N 110.20 E
Wuyi, Zhg. 98 37.49 N 115.54 E
Wuyi, Zhg. 100 32.13 N 118.26 E
Wuyi, Zhg. 100 28.54 N 119.48 E
Wuying 89 48.05 N 129.15 E
Wuyi Shan ⋀ 90 27.52 N 117.40 E
Wuyuan, Zhg. 100 29.15 N 117.49 E
Wuyuan, Zhg. 102 41.06 N 108.29 E
Wuyun 89 49.16 N 129.37 E
Wuyunqiao 100 26.02 N 114.52 E
Wuyur ≃ 89 47.00 N 124.10 E
Wuzaizi 104 42.28 N 123.57 E
Wuzhai 102 38.58 N 111.55 E
Wuzhan 89 45.51 N 126.17 E
Wuzhen 106 30.46 N 120.29 E
Wuzhi Shan ∧, Zhg. 105 40.29 N 118.00 E
Wuzhi Shan ∧, Zhg. 110 18.57 N 109.43 E
Wuzhong 102 38.00 N 106.10 E
Wuzhou (Wuchow) 102 23.30 N 111.27 E
Wuzong 106 32.14 N 121.03 E
Wyaaba Creek ≃ 164 16.27 S 141.35 E
Wyaconda 194 40.23 N 91.55 W
Wyaconda ≃ 194 40.04 N 91.30 W
Wyalkatchem 162 31.10 S 117.22 E
Wyalusing 210 41.40 N 76.15 W
Wyalusing Creek ≃ 210 41.40 N 76.16 W
Wyandanch 276 40.45 N 73.21 W
Wyandot 214 40.44 N 83.08 W
Wyandot □[6] 214 40.50 N 83.17 W
Wyandotte 216 42.12 N 83.09 W
Wyandotte Cave ⊥[5] 218 38.14 N 86.18 W
Wyandotte National Wildlife Refuge ◆[4] 281 42.14 N 83.08 W
Wyandra 166 27.15 S 145.59 E
Wyangala, Lake ⊜[1] 166 33.58 S 148.55 E
Wyano 214 40.12 N 79.42 W
Wyatt, In., U.S. 216 41.31 N 86.10 W
Wyatt, Mo., U.S. 194 36.54 N 89.13 W
Wycheproof 166 36.05 S 143.14 E
Wychwood 273d 26.12 S 28.08 E
Wyckoff 210 41.00 N 74.10 W
Wydgee 162 28.51 S 117.49 E
Wydgelee 158 34.23 S 20.26 E
Wy-Dit-Joli-Village 261 49.06 N 1.50 E
Wye 42 51.11 N 0.56 E
Wye ≃, On., Can. 212 44.44 N 79.52 W
Wye ≃, U.K. 42 51.37 N 2.39 W
Wye ≃, Eng., U.K. 44 53.12 N 1.37 W
Wyee 170 33.11 S 151.29 E
Wye Lake ⊜ 212 44.43 N 79.52 W
Wyemandoo ∧ 162 28.31 S 118.32 E
Wyeville 190 44.01 N 90.23 W
Wyhl 58 48.09 N 7.39 E
Wyhra ≃ 54 51.09 N 12.27 E
Wyk 30 54.42 N 8.34 E
Wyke Regis 42 50.36 N 2.29 W
Wykoff 190 43.42 N 92.16 W
Wylandville 279b 40.12 N 80.08 W
Wyleswood Lake ⊜ 279a 41.20 N 81.55 W
Wylie, Pa., U.S. 279b 40.27 N 79.59 W
Wylie, Tx., U.S. 222 33.01 N 96.32 W
Wylie, Lake ⊜[1] 192 35.07 N 81.02 W
Wylye ≃ 42 51.04 N 1.52 W
Wymah 171b 36.02 S 147.17 E
Wymark 184 50.07 N 107.44 W
Wymeswold 42 52.47 N 1.06 W
Wymondham 42 52.34 N 1.07 E
Wymore 198 40.07 N 96.39 W
Wynantskill 210 42.42 N 73.39 W
Wynberg 158 34.02 S 18.28 E
Wynbring 162 30.33 S 133.32 E
Wyncote 285 40.05 N 75.08 W
Wyndham, Austl. 164 15.28 S 128.06 E
Wyndham, N.Z. 172 46.20 S 168.51 E
Wyndmere 198 46.16 N 97.07 W
Wyndmoor 285 40.04 N 75.11 W
Wynigen 58 47.06 N 7.40 E
Wynndel 182 49.11 N 116.33 W
Wynne 194 35.13 N 90.47 W
Wynnewood, Ok., U.S. 196 34.38 N 97.09 W
Wynnewood, Pa., U.S. 285 40.00 N 75.16 W
Wynniatt Bay ⊂ 176 72.55 N 110.30 W
Wynnum 171a 27.27 S 153.10 E
Wynona 196 36.32 N 96.19 W
Wynoochee ≃ 224 46.58 N 123.35 W
Wynoochee Lake ⊜[1] 224 47.25 N 123.35 W
Wynot 198 42.44 N 97.10 W
Wynyard, Austl. 166 40.59 S 145.41 E
Wynyard, Sk., Can. 184 51.47 N 104.10 W
Wyocena 190 43.29 N 89.18 W
Wyodak 198 44.17 N 105.22 W
Wyola Lake ⊜ 162 29.08 S 130.17 E
Wyoming, On., Can. 190 42.57 N 82.07 W
Wyoming, De., U.S. 208 39.07 N 75.33 W
Wyoming, Il., U.S. 190 41.03 N 89.46 W
Wyoming, Ia., U.S. 190 42.03 N 91.00 W
Wyoming, Mi., U.S. 216 42.54 N 85.42 W
Wyoming, N.Y., U.S. 210 42.49 N 78.05 W
Wyoming, Oh., U.S. 218 39.13 N 84.27 W
Wyoming, Pa., U.S. 210 41.18 N 75.50 W
Wyoming, R.I., U.S. 207 41.30 N 71.42 W
Wyoming □[6], N.Y., U.S. 210 42.44 N 78.08 W
Wyoming □[6], Pa., U.S. 210 41.32 N 75.57 W
Wyoming □[3] 178 43.00 N 107.30 W
Wyoming Peak ∧ 200 42.36 N 110.37 W
Wyomissing 208 40.19 N 75.57 W
Wyong 170 33.17 S 151.25 E
Wyong ≃ 170 33.18 S 151.28 E
Wyperfield National Park ♠ 166 35.30 S 142.00 E
Wyre ≃ 44 53.55 N 3.00 W
Wyreema 171a 27.39 S 151.52 E
Wyre Forest ◆[3] 42 52.23 N 2.23 W
Wyrzysk 30 53.10 N 17.15 E
Wyśmierzyce 30 51.38 N 20.49 E
Wysoka 30 53.11 N 17.05 E
Wysokie Mazowieckie 30 52.56 N 22.32 E
Wysox 210 41.46 N 76.24 W
Wyszków 30 52.36 N 21.28 E
Wyszogród 30 52.23 N 20.11 E
Wythenshawe ◆[8] 262 53.24 N 2.17 W
Wythenshawe Hall ⊥ 262 53.24 N 2.17 W
Wytheville 192 36.56 N 81.05 W
Wytschegda → Vyčegda ≃ 24 61.18 N 46.36 E
Wyvis, Ben ∧ 46 57.42 N 4.35 W

X

Xaafuun 144 10.25 N 51.16 E
Xàbia 34 38.47 N 0.10 E
Xabregas ◆[8] 266c 38.44 N 9.07 W
Xá-Cassau 152 9.02 S 20.14 E
Xaclbal ≃ 236 16.06 N 90.58 W
Xaidulla 120 36.21 N 78.02 E
Xainza 120 30.57 N 88.38 E
Xaitongmoin 124 29.22 N 88.15 E
Xai-Xai 156 25.02 S 33.34 E
Xalapa 234 19.32 N 96.55 W
Xalin 144 9.06 N 48.37 E
Xalisco 234 21.27 N 104.54 W
Xalostoc 234 19.24 N 98.03 W
Xalpatlahuac 234 17.01 N 99.18 W
Xaltianguis 234 17.04 N 99.50 W
Xam (Chu) ≃ 110 19.53 N 105.45 E
Xambioá 250 6.25 S 48.40 W
Xambrê ≃ 255 24.02 S 53.59 W
Xam Nua 110 20.25 N 104.02 E
Xá-Muteba 152 9.34 S 17.50 E
Xan (San) ≃ 110 13.32 N 105.58 E
Xang ≃ 124 29.22 N 89.09 E
Xangongo 152 16.43 S 15.01 E
Xanten 52 51.39 N 6.26 E
Xánthi 38 41.08 N 24.53 E
Xanxerê 252 26.53 S 52.23 W
Xapecó ≃ 252 27.06 S 53.01 W
Xapuri 248 10.39 S 68.31 W
Xapuri ≃ 248 10.39 S 68.30 W
Xarardheere 144 4.39 N 47.51 E
Xar Moron ≃, Zhg. 90 43.25 N 121.41 E
Xar Moron ≃, Zhg. 102 43.02 N 111.20 E
Xarrama ≃ 34 38.14 N 8.20 W
Xàtiva (Játiva) 34 38.59 N 0.31 W
Xau, Lake ≚ 156 21.15 S 24.38 E
Xauen → Chaouen 148 35.10 N 5.16 W
Xavante ≃ 250 11.23 S 49.41 W
Xavantes ≃ 250 10.40 S 50.41 W
Xavantina 255 21.15 S 52.48 W
Xa Vo Dat 110 11.09 N 107.31 E
Xaxim 252 26.56 S 52.31 W
Xcalak 232 18.16 N 87.50 W
X-Can 232 20.50 N 87.43 W
Xelva 34 39.45 N 0.59 W
Xenia, Il., U.S. 219 38.38 N 88.38 W
Xenia, Oh., U.S. 218 39.41 N 83.55 W
Xénô 110 16.35 N 104.50 E
Xercavins, Arroyo de ≃ 266d 41.30 N 2.02 E
Xerém 256 22.33 S 43.18 W
Xeres → Jerez de la Frontera 34 36.41 N 6.08 W
Xertigny 58 48.03 N 6.24 E
Xeruã ≃ 248 6.03 S 67.50 W
Xhumo 156 21.07 S 24.42 E
Xi ≃, Zhg. 100 25.14 N 118.03 E
Xi ≃, Zhg. 100 30.21 N 115.06 E
Xi ≃, Zhg. 100 24.34 N 117.30 E
Xi ≃, Zhg. 102 22.25 N 113.23 E
Xi ≃, Zhg. 102 42.20 N 100.20 E
Xi ≃, Zhg. 104 41.15 N 123.32 E
Xi ≃, Zhg. 104 41.30 N 121.26 E
Xi ≃, Zhg. 107 30.26 N 103.48 E
Xiaang 106 30.45 N 120.07 E
Xiaba 100 24.54 N 116.06 E
Xiabai, Zhg. 106 31.12 N 119.50 E
Xiabai, Zhg. 106 30.29 N 120.00 E
Xiabanghu 100 30.31 N 112.38 E
Xiabian 104 40.51 N 120.30 E
Xiabuji 100 28.19 N 116.20 E
Xiacang 105 39.47 N 117.24 E
Xiache 100 24.40 N 115.08 E
Xiachengzi 89 44.41 N 130.27 E

Symbols in the index entries represent the broad categories identified in the key at the right. Symbols with superior numbers (⋀[1]) identify subcategories (see complete key on page *I · 1)*.

Symbole im Register stellen die rechts im Schlüssel erklärten Kategorien dar. Symbole mit hochgestellten Ziffern (⋀[1]) bezeichnen Unterabteilungen einer Kategorie (vgl. vollständiger Schlüssel auf Seite *I · 1)*.

Los símbolos incluídos en el texto del índice representan las grandes categorias identificadas con la clave a la derecha. Los símbolos con numeros en su parte superior (⋀[1]) identifican las subcategorías (véase la clave completa en la página *I · 1)*.

Les symboles de l'index représentent les catégories indiquées dans la légende à droite. Les symboles suivis d'un indice (⋀[1]) représentent des sous-catégories (voir légende complète à la page *I · 1)*.

Os símbolos incluídos no texto do índice representam as grandes categorias identificadas com a chave à direita. Os símbolos com números em sua parte superior (⋀[1]) identificam as subcategorias (veja-se a chave completa à página *I · 1)*.

∧ Mountain	Berg	Montaña	Montagne	Montanha
⋀ Mountains	Gebirge	Montañas	Montagnes	Montanhas
)(Pass	Paß	Paso	Col	Passo
V Valley, Canyon	Tal, Cañon	Valle, Cañón	Vallée, Canyon	Vale, Canhão
≚ Plain	Ebene	Llano	Plaine	Planície
› Cape	Kap	Cabo	Cap	Cabo
I Island	Insel	Isla	Île	Ilha
II Islands	Inseln	Islas	Îles	Ilhas
⊥ Other Topographic Features	Andere Topographische Objekte	Otros Elementos Topográficos	Autres données topographiques	Outros acidentes topográficos

ESPAÑOL / FRANÇAIS / PORTUGUÊS

Nombre / Nom / Nome	Página / Page	Lat.°′	Long.°′ W = Oeste / W = Ouest
Xiachuan Dao I	102	21.40 N	112.37 E
Xiacun	105	40.21 N	116.14 E
Xiadao	100	26.34 N	118.16 E
Xiadian, Zhg.	98	37.06 N	120.19 E
Xiadian, Zhg.	100	31.26 N	114.17 E
Xiadian, Zhg.	105	39.57 N	116.55 E
Xiadianjie	100	25.13 N	118.27 E
Xiafeidi	98	42.18 N	124.21 E
Xiafu, Zhg.	100	25.01 N	113.41 E
Xiafu, Zhg.	100	23.52 N	115.45 E
Xiagaixin	102	22.36 N	99.59 E
Xiagang	106	31.55 N	120.13 E
Xiagezhuang	98	36.41 N	120.25 E
Xiaguan, Zhg.	98	39.07 N	114.09 E
Xiaguan, Zhg.	102	25.34 N	100.14 E
Xiaguan, Zhg.	106	32.06 N	118.44 E
Xiaguanjunchang	104	41.28 N	121.40 E
Xiaguanpi	100	24.04 N	117.06 E
Xiagucheng	102	36.47 N	102.53 E
Xiagucun	106	30.56 N	119.09 E
Xiahada	104	41.58 N	124.08 E
Xiahailangzhai	104	41.35 N	123.46 E
Xiahe	102	35.18 N	102.30 E
Xiahuangjintun	104	41.57 N	123.48 E
Xiahuayuan	105	40.29 N	115.17 E
Xiajiabaozi	98	42.16 N	124.37 E
Xiajialou	104	42.25 N	123.39 E
Xiajiang	100	27.32 N	115.08 E
Xiajiangdun	106	31.14 N	120.24 E
Xiajiangwu	106	30.29 N	119.00 E
Xiajiayuan	106	32.13 N	120.38 E
Xiajiezi	102	27.28 N	101.35 E
Xiajin	98	36.55 N	115.57 E
Xiakou	100	28.28 N	118.31 E
Xialianggang	105	39.14 N	115.07 E
Xialufang	102	31.11 N	103.38 E
Xiamaguan	102	37.14 N	106.28 E
Xiamen (Amoy)	100	24.28 N	118.07 E
Xiamen Gang c	100	24.19 N	118.10 E
Xiamianzhen	107	30.08 N	106.32 E
Xiamin'ansutai	104	41.54 N	120.53 E
Xiamocun	106	31.09 N	119.22 E
Xi'an (Sian)	102	34.15 N	108.52 E
Xian ≏	107	29.22 N	104.44 E
Xianchenggu	98	36.53 N	115.17 E
Xiandu	100	25.04 N	117.44 E
Xianfeng, Zhg.	100	25.42 N	117.53 E
Xianfeng, Zhg.	102	29.41 N	109.02 E
Xiang ≏, Zhg.	100	25.35 N	115.49 E
Xiang ≏, Zhg.	102	29.00 N	112.56 E
Xiang'an	100	31.12 N	117.46 E
Xiangcheng, Zhg.	100	33.28 N	114.53 E
Xiangcheng, Zhg.	100	33.53 N	113.29 E
Xiangcheng, Zhg.	102	28.59 N	99.45 E
Xiangcheng, Zhg.	106	31.29 N	120.44 E
Xiangfan	102	32.03 N	112.01 E
Xiangfuguan	100	28.30 N	115.26 E
Xiangfusi	107	30.06 N	104.24 E
Xianggang → Victoria	271d	22.17 N	114.09 E
Xianggongshi	100	28.25 N	113.32 E
Xianggongzhuang	105	39.48 N	118.19 E
Xianghe	105	39.46 N	116.59 E
Xiangheguan	100	33.08 N	113.26 E
Xianghuazhen	106	31.31 N	121.43 E
Xiangjia, Zhg.	106	31.20 N	120.31 E
Xiangjia, Zhg.	106	31.19 N	120.23 E
Xiangjiachang	107	30.08 N	104.18 E
Xiangkhoang	110	19.20 N	103.22 E
Xiangkhoang, Plateau de ⋌[1]	110	19.30 N	103.10 E
Xiangning	102	36.01 N	110.45 E
Xiangride	102	36.02 N	98.08 E
Xiangshan, Zhg.	100	29.28 N	121.51 E
Xiangshan, Zhg.	105	39.59 N	116.12 E
Xiangshan Gang c	100	29.38 N	121.48 E
Xiangshizhen	107	29.17 N	105.09 E
Xiangshui, Zhg.	100	23.15 N	114.10 E
Xiangshui, Zhg.	100	34.12 N	119.34 E
Xiangtan	100	27.51 N	112.54 E
Xiangtang	100	28.26 N	115.58 E
Xiangxiang	102	27.43 N	112.27 E
Xiangyang	105	39.13 N	115.25 E
Xiangyangkou	105	40.06 N	115.47 E
Xiangyin	100	28.40 N	112.53 E
Xiangyuan	102	36.32 N	113.00 E
Xiangyun	102	25.30 N	100.30 E
Xiangzhenpu	100	30.52 N	117.21 E
Xiangzhou, Zhg.	98	36.12 N	119.24 E
Xiangzhou, Zhg.	102	23.55 N	109.49 E
Xiangzhu	100	29.02 N	120.04 E
Xianinggang	100	28.20 N	112.56 E
Xianjiang	100	27.48 N	120.30 E
Xianju	100	28.51 N	120.44 E
Xianning	100	29.53 N	114.13 E
Xiannongtan Stadium ♠	271a	39.52 N	116.23 E
Xiannübu	100	25.36 N	114.40 E
Xianru	89	43.11 N	128.02 E
Xianshichang	107	28.43 N	105.44 E
Xianshui ≏	102	30.05 N	110.59 E
Xianshuigu	105	38.59 N	117.23 E
Xiantan, Zhg.	107	29.21 N	104.53 E
Xiantan, Zhg.	107	28.50 N	106.12 E
Xiantang	100	23.48 N	114.46 E
Xianxia Ling ⋌	100	28.30 N	118.46 E
Xianxian	98	38.13 N	116.06 E
Xianyang, Zhg.	100	28.02 N	118.30 E
Xianyang, Zhg.	102	34.22 N	108.42 E
Xianyou	100	25.23 N	118.40 E
Xianzhong	100	28.36 N	113.48 E
Xiao ≏	100	28.11 N	120.14 E
Xiao'an ≏	107	29.59 N	106.13 E
Xiao'ao	100	26.14 N	119.39 E
Xiaoazhang	102	23.42 N	104.58 E
Xiaobangniulu	104	41.34 N	122.46 E
Xiaobeigou	104	41.55 N	120.46 E
Xiaobeihe, Zhg.	104	42.39 N	123.58 E
Xiaobeihe, Zhg.	104	41.22 N	122.50 E
Xiaocaohu	86	43.06 N	88.30 E
Xiaochangshan Dao I	98	39.12 N	122.41 E
Xiaocheng	100	26.20 N	119.47 E
Xiaochengdu	106	30.59 N	120.04 E
Xiaochengzi, Zhg.	89	46.33 N	122.54 E
Xiaochengzi, Zhg.	89	42.56 N	123.12 E
Xiaochi	100	30.33 N	116.23 E
Xiaochikou	100	29.46 N	115.59 E
Xiaodanyang	106	31.38 N	118.43 E
Xiaodong	102	22.14 N	108.39 E
Xiao'ergou	89	49.12 N	123.42 E
Xiaofangshen	104	42.13 N	123.54 E
Xiaofanshan	105	40.16 N	115.19 E
Xiaofen	106	31.45 N	119.39 E
Xiaofeng	106	30.36 N	119.32 E
Xiaogan	100	30.55 N	113.54 E
Xiaogangkou	100	28.14 N	115.50 E
Xiaogaojiatun	104	41.02 N	121.59 E
Xiaogencaigangzi	104	41.48 N	122.42 E
Xiaogu	107	29.08 N	104.01 E
Xiaoguai	86	45.13 N	85.02 E
Xiaogushan	98	39.49 N	123.12 E
Xiaohaizhen	106	31.58 N	120.59 E
Xiaohaladaokou	98	42.37 N	119.32 E
Xiaohan	98	35.48 N	114.52 E
Xiaohe	106	32.01 N	119.52 E
Xiaohei Shan ∧	102	24.42 N	98.55 E
Xiaohekou	102	33.19 N	107.25 E
Xiaoheyan	98	42.26 N	119.38 E
Xiaoheying	102	32.37 N	104.23 E
Xiao Hinggan Ling (Lesser Khingan Range) ⋌	89	48.45 N	127.00 E
Xiaohongmen	271a	39.49 N	116.26 E
Xiaohu	100	27.20 N	118.14 E
Xiaohuying	98	41.09 N	117.13 E
Xiaoji, Zhg.	98	36.45 N	121.01 E
Xiaoji, Zhg.	100	27.08 N	113.15 E
Xiaoji, Zhg.	100	32.38 N	119.48 E
Xiaojiachang	107	30.18 N	106.28 E
Xiaojiagang	100	31.06 N	113.55 E
Xiaojialing	100	29.35 N	116.32 E
Xiaojiang	100	25.08 N	114.59 E
Xiaojianji	100	33.23 N	116.29 E
Xiaojiawu	105	39.36 N	116.36 E
Xiaojiayingzi	98	40.17 N	118.47 E
Xiaojieling	100	31.36 N	115.09 E
Xiaojin	102	31.00 N	102.21 E
Xiaojingfang	105	39.22 N	116.34 E
Xiaojiu	89	45.15 N	127.47 E
Xiaokaoshantun	104	42.10 N	123.53 E
Xiaokuli	89	50.18 N	120.20 E
Xiaokunshan	106	31.02 N	121.07 E
Xiaolan	100	22.41 N	113.14 E
Xiaoliangshan	104	42.05 N	122.32 E
Xiaoling, Zhg.	89	45.20 N	127.18 E
Xiaoling, Zhg.	104	42.18 N	123.23 E
Xiaoling ≏	104	41.06 N	121.07 E
Xiaolingzi	104	41.07 N	123.19 E
Xiaolinzhuang	104	41.36 N	124.01 E
Xiaolipu	98	36.24 N	116.35 E
Xiaolongtan	102	23.51 N	103.10 E
Xiaoluan ≏	98	41.36 N	117.05 E
Xiaolüzhuang	106	31.57 N	119.25 E
Xiaomei	100	27.50 N	118.58 E
Xiaomei Guan Ꮃ	100	25.17 N	114.17 E
Xiaomiaozi	98	41.24 N	114.25 E
Xiaonanhai	107	29.23 N	106.27 E
Xiaopikou	98	35.47 N	115.53 E
Xiaopingyang	102	23.22 N	109.13 E
Xiao Qaidam He ⊜	102	37.30 N	95.12 E
Xiaoqiao	100	26.57 N	118.30 E
Xiaoqiaotou	106	30.43 N	119.27 E
Xiaoqing ≏	98	37.17 N	118.52 E
Xiaoqingchuizi	104	42.30 N	123.39 E
Xiaoquandong	102	41.14 N	95.26 E
Xiaosanjiazi	104	42.34 N	123.23 E
Xiaosha ≏	104	41.13 N	122.45 E
Xiaoshakou	100	29.58 N	113.16 E
Xiaoshan	106	30.10 N	120.15 E
Xiaoshangqiao	100	33.43 N	113.58 E
Xiaoshi	100	27.27 N	116.49 E
Xiaoshixiang	100	30.36 N	116.38 E
Xiaoshu	106	30.48 N	119.46 E
Xiaoshun	100	29.11 N	119.51 E
Xiaosigou	98	40.53 N	118.33 E
Xiaosijia	104	42.24 N	120.46 E
Xiaotang	98	41.38 N	119.33 E
Xiaotanghe	98	42.04 N	127.10 E
Xiaotao	100	25.46 N	117.08 E
Xiaotazi	104	42.17 N	123.08 E
Xiaotian	100	31.12 N	116.33 E
Xiaotianji	100	32.45 N	115.36 E
Xiaotun	104	42.24 N	123.44 E
Xiaotunzicun	104	41.14 N	123.20 E
Xiaowa	104	41.03 N	122.04 E
Xiaowan	100	26.53 N	116.36 E
Xiaowangmiao	100	29.41 N	121.21 E
Xiaowutai Shan ∧	105	39.51 N	115.09 E
Xiaowutai Shan ⋌	105	39.50 N	115.00 E
Xiaoxi	100	25.48 N	115.21 E
Xiaoxi ≏	106	32.15 N	120.24 E
Xiaoxian	98	34.11 N	116.56 E
Xiaoxincheng	105	39.24 N	115.11 E
Xiaoxintian	271a	39.58 N	116.22 E
Xiaoxizhen	106	30.51 N	119.50 E
Xiaoyangjiadian	104	42.23 N	122.24 E
Xiaoyangqi	89	50.48 N	124.12 E
Xiaoyantai	104	41.26 N	123.10 E
Xiaoyaozhen	100	33.46 N	114.16 E
Xiaoyi	102	37.10 N	111.46 E
Xiaoying, Zhg.	98	37.18 N	118.04 E
Xiaoying, Zhg.	105	40.12 N	116.33 E
Xiaoyingcun	105	39.28 N	116.41 E
Xiaoyuan	107	30.00 N	104.56 E
Xiaozhan	105	38.55 N	117.25 E
Xiaozhang ≏	105	39.47 N	117.22 E
Xiaozhongdian	102	27.40 N	99.46 E
Xiaozhuang	104	41.30 N	121.27 E
Xiaozhujiawan	106	31.24 N	121.01 E
Xiapu, Zhg.	100	26.52 N	120.01 E
Xiapu, Zhg.	100	27.49 N	114.26 E
Xiaqialafangzi	104	41.48 N	121.44 E
Xiaqi Dao I	100	29.42 N	122.15 E
Xiaqiubao	98	37.01 N	119.54 E
Xiasantumen	105	38.50 N	114.48 E
Xiashe	106	30.33 N	120.11 E
Xiashesi	100	27.46 N	112.57 E
Xiashi → Haining	106	30.32 N	120.41 E
Xiashu	106	32.11 N	119.10 E
Xiashuerfowei	89	50.23 N	120.47 E
Xiashuiquan	104	41.52 N	123.38 E
Xiataizi	105	40.37 N	117.45 E
Xiatang, Zhg.	100	33.45 N	112.39 E
Xiatang, Zhg.	106	31.29 N	118.41 E
Xiatangtian	106	30.55 N	120.12 E
Xiataohuatu	104	41.42 N	120.36 E
Xiawa	98	42.39 N	120.35 E
Xiawajiang	106	30.59 N	121.51 E
Xiawaziyu	104	41.15 N	123.38 E
Xiaxi	106	31.43 N	119.45 E
Xiaxian	102	35.11 N	111.15 E
Xiaxiangcheng	102	28.42 N	99.59 E
Xiaxikou	100	26.15 N	118.59 E
Xiaxinhe	106	31.40 N	119.31 E
Xiayang, Zhg.	100	28.48 N	119.41 E
Xiayang, Zhg.	100	26.46 N	117.59 E
Xiayang, Zhg.	100	24.39 N	116.52 E
Xiayi	98	34.14 N	116.06 E
Xiaying, Zhg.	98	37.03 N	119.25 E
Xiaying, Zhg.	105	40.10 N	117.25 E
Xiayunling	105	39.43 N	115.44 E
Xiazhang	98	36.08 N	116.57 E
Xiazhen	100	28.39 N	118.21 E
Xiazhuang, Zhg.	98	35.28 N	118.43 E
Xiazhuang, Zhg.	100	27.22 N	119.01 E
Xiazhuang, Zhg.	105	39.54 N	117.01 E
Xiazhuang, Zhg.	105	39.38 N	115.26 E
Xiazikou	105	39.01 N	115.25 E
Xiban	107	30.32 N	106.12 E
Xibaqianmou	104	40.59 N	121.35 E
Xibeiyingzi	104	41.55 N	121.38 E
Xibo ≏	98	42.17 N	118.57 E
Xibu	100	31.46 N	118.17 E
Xicang	106	31.34 N	120.29 E
Xichang, Zhg.	102	27.58 N	102.13 E
Xichang, Zhg.	104	42.15 N	124.12 E
Xicheng	89	48.10 N	125.29 E
Xichong	102	31.00 N	105.52 E
Xicicun	105	39.29 N	116.08 E
Xico	234	19.25 N	97.00 W
Xicoténcatl	234	23.00 N	98.56 W
Xicotepec de Juárez	234	20.17 N	97.57 W
Xictle, Volcán ∧[1]	286a	19.14 N	99.14 W
Xicun	100	27.46 N	114.14 E
Xidachuan	98	41.46 N	127.34 E
Xidapo	89	43.12 N	130.02 E
Xidaying	105	39.41 N	116.14 E
Xidian	100	29.32 N	121.26 E
Xiditou	105	39.16 N	117.23 E
Xidongting Shan ∧	106	31.07 N	120.16 E
Xié ≏	246	0.54 N	67.11 W
Xiecun	105	39.00 N	115.31 E
Xiedian	100	33.27 N	113.28 E
Xiefang	100	26.12 N	116.41 E
Xieji	98	34.32 N	115.29 E
Xiejia	98	42.24 N	125.42 E
Xiejiagangzi	104	41.55 N	122.20 E
Xiejiapu	106	31.15 N	119.09 E
Xiejunmiao	107	30.15 N	103.40 E
Xielipuke	120	31.30 N	82.45 E
Xiemachang	107	29.46 N	106.22 E
Xiemata Shan ∧	89	50.28 N	120.47 E
Xiepu	100	30.02 N	121.37 E
Xieqiao, Zhg.	106	32.03 N	120.22 E
Xieqiao, Zhg.	106	30.29 N	120.34 E
Xietang	106	31.18 N	120.44 E
Xiexi	106	31.54 N	118.54 E
Xiexinggou	104	41.51 N	121.05 E
Xifei ≏	100	32.38 N	116.39 E
Xifeng, Zhg.	98	42.43 N	124.40 E
Xifeng, Zhg.	102	27.02 N	106.30 E
Xifengkou	105	40.24 N	118.19 E
Xifocun	104	41.26 N	122.33 E
Xigangzi	89	49.58 N	127.20 E
Xigaolizhuangzi	104	41.40 N	122.55 E
Xigaotan	98	38.18 N	116.13 E
Xigaotun	98	40.27 N	122.36 E
Xigazê	120	29.17 N	88.53 E
Xiguanjiatun	104	42.35 N	123.10 E
Xiguanyingzi	104	41.50 N	120.37 E
Xihaikou	104	40.50 N	121.05 E
Xihan ≏	102	33.30 N	106.02 E
Xihe, Zhg.	100	31.01 N	118.28 E
Xihe, Zhg.	100	31.41 N	113.27 E
Xihe, Zhg.	102	34.01 N	105.17 E
Xiheying	105	39.53 N	114.42 E
Xihezhuang	105	39.20 N	118.02 E
Xi Hu ⊜	106	30.15 N	120.08 E
Xihua	100	33.47 N	114.31 E
Xihuangcang	106	31.43 N	121.40 E
Xihuanzidong	104	41.31 N	122.28 E
Xihuashan, Zhg.	100	25.28 N	114.20 E
Xihuashan, Zhg.	105	40.07 N	116.54 E
Xihuishan	104	41.41 N	122.38 E
Xiis	144	10.53 N	46.54 E
Xiji, Zhg.	102	35.58 N	105.44 E
Xiji, Zhg.	105	39.49 N	116.52 E
Xijialong	102	23.31 N	103.51 E
Xijiang	100	25.50 N	115.49 E
Xijianshanzi	104	40.47 N	120.48 E
Xi Jiao Airfield ⊠	271a	39.58 N	116.15 E
Xijiapuzitun	104	41.26 N	123.50 E
Xijir Ulan Hu ⊜	120	35.12 N	90.18 E
Xikou, Zhg.	89	46.40 N	120.40 E
Xikou, Zhg.	100	29.11 N	114.23 E
Xikou, Zhg.	100	29.44 N	118.02 E
Xikou, Zhg.	100	28.52 N	119.11 E
Xikou, Zhg.	100	25.26 N	118.45 E
Xikou, Zhg.	100	29.14 N	114.24 E
Xikou, Zhg.	106	30.40 N	118.41 E
Xikouxu	100	25.24 N	117.03 E
Xikouzi	89	53.06 N	120.40 E
Xilai	107	30.20 N	103.29 E
Xilaiqiao	106	32.03 N	119.54 E
Xilaizhen	106	32.07 N	120.25 E
Xilin	120	28.33 N	87.48 E
Xi Ling (Western Tombs) ⊥	105	39.24 N	115.18 E
Xilintuo	120	30.08 N	88.04 E
Xilitla	234	21.20 N	98.58 W
Xiliuhe	105	38.58 N	116.32 E
Xiliushuyingzi	104	42.25 N	121.54 E
Xilókastron	38	38.05 N	22.38 E
Xiluga ≏	98	42.21 N	118.38 E
Xiluncun	89	47.08 N	126.26 E
Ximagou	105	40.16 N	117.50 E
Ximakou	100	30.33 N	113.47 E
Ximalatu	89	47.00 N	122.01 E
Ximalin	98	40.48 N	114.29 E
Ximiao	102	41.09 N	100.17 E
Ximucheng	104	40.42 N	122.54 E
Xin ≏	100	28.37 N	116.40 E
Xin'an, Zhg.	89	43.46 N	125.40 E
Xin'an, Zhg.	100	23.02 N	114.56 E
Xinan, Zhg.	100	25.26 N	117.35 E
Xin'an, Zhg.	100	26.44 N	116.13 E
Xin'an, Zhg.	105	39.09 N	116.38 E
Xin'an, Zhg.	106	31.47 N	120.09 E
Xin'an, Zhg.	106	31.30 N	120.22 E
Xin'an ≏	100	29.33 N	118.58 E
Xin'andian	100	32.37 N	114.03 E
Xin'andu	100	30.52 N	116.53 E
Xin'anji	100	33.22 N	115.13 E
Xin'anjiang Shuiku ⊜[1]	100	29.27 N	119.06 E
Xin'anpu	104	42.39 N	123.27 E
Xin'anqiao	106	32.16 N	121.07 E
Xin'ansuo	102	23.16 N	103.27 E
Xin'anzhen, Zhg.	89	44.06 N	123.46 E
Xin'anzhen, Zhg.	105	39.45 N	117.32 E
Xi'nanzhuang	105	40.48 N	118.23 E
Xinavane	156	25.02 S	32.47 E
Xinba, Zhg.	98	34.27 N	119.09 E
Xinba, Zhg.	100	30.24 N	116.52 E
Xinba, Zhg.	106	32.08 N	120.39 E
Xinba, Zhg.	106	32.16 N	119.45 E
Xinbao'an	105	40.27 N	115.24 E
Xin Barag Youqi (Altan Emel)	88	48.41 N	116.53 E
Xin Barag Zuoqi (Amgalang)	88	48.14 N	118.18 E
Xinbin, Zhg.	98	41.42 N	125.02 E
Xinbin, Zhg.	106	30.56 N	121.04 E
Xinbo	98	42.19 N	117.44 E
Xincai	100	32.44 N	114.59 E
Xincang, Zhg.	106	30.25 N	120.42 E
Xincang, Zhg.	106	30.44 N	121.11 E
Xinchang, Zhg.	100	29.30 N	120.53 E
Xinchang, Zhg.	102	28.03 N	103.46 E
Xinchang, Zhg.	102	25.10 N	104.18 E
Xinchang, Zhg.	106	31.42 N	121.46 E
Xinchang, Zhg.	106	31.02 N	121.38 E
Xinchang, Zhg.	107	29.20 N	104.15 E
Xinchang, Zhg.	107	29.38 N	104.33 E
Xinchang, Zhg.	107	30.29 N	106.21 E
Xinchang, Zhg.	107	30.16 N	104.29 E
Xinchangzi	107	29.40 N	103.46 E
Xincheng, Zhg.	100	25.34 N	114.36 E
Xincheng, Zhg.	102	24.09 N	108.46 E
Xincheng (Gaobeidian), Zhg.	105	39.20 N	115.51 E
Xincheng, Zhg.	105	38.59 N	117.33 E
Xincheng, Zhg.	106	32.17 N	119.14 E
Xincheng, Zhg.	106	30.48 N	120.36 E
Xinchengzi	104	42.03 N	123.30 E
Xinchepaizi	86	44.55 N	84.30 E
Xincunji	100	32.53 N	115.31 E
Xindai	106	30.49 N	121.05 E
Xindi	104	42.21 N	120.31 E
Xindian, Zhg.	89	45.55 N	127.50 E
Xindian, Zhg.	98	37.07 N	114.49 E
Xindian, Zhg.	98	37.29 N	118.28 E
Xindian, Zhg.	100	33.07 N	112.38 E
Xindian, Zhg.	100	29.40 N	113.40 E
Xindian, Zhg.	100	31.33 N	115.16 E
Xindian, Zhg.	100	33.38 N	113.51 E
Xindian, Zhg.	105	40.11 N	116.11 E
Xindian, Zhg.	105	40.47 N	116.49 E
Xindian, Zhg.	105	39.10 N	116.27 E
Xindian, Zhg.	107	29.19 N	105.40 E
Xindianbu	100	32.24 N	116.22 E
Xindianzi, Zhg.	105	40.04 N	118.01 E
Xindianzi, Zhg.	107	28.49 N	103.35 E
Xindianzi, Zhg.	107	29.03 N	103.46 E
Xindianzi, Zhg.	107	29.52 N	106.06 E
Xindianzi, Zhg.	107	29.46 N	105.11 E
Xindianzi, Zhg.	107	29.43 N	104.01 E
Xindu	102	23.59 N	111.46 E
Xinfatuncun	104	41.13 N	122.28 E
Xinfeng, Zhg.	100	25.24 N	114.56 E
Xinfeng, Zhg.	100	27.26 N	116.40 E
Xinfeng, Zhg.	100	33.19 N	120.30 E
Xinfeng, Zhg.	100	24.04 N	114.12 E
Xinfeng, Zhg.	100	24.05 N	116.53 E
Xinfeng, Zhg.	106	31.09 N	118.40 E
Xinfeng, Zhg.	106	32.05 N	119.34 E
Xinfeng, Zhg.	106	30.43 N	120.55 E
Xinfeng ≏	100	23.42 N	114.42 E
Xinfeng Shuiku ⊜[1]	100	23.52 N	114.30 E
Xing'an, Zhg.	89	48.49 N	121.45 E
Xing'an, Zhg.	102	25.37 N	110.31 E
Xin'gang, Zhg.	106	31.56 N	120.57 E
Xingang, Zhg.	106	32.03 N	120.25 E
Xing'antun	89	51.31 N	120.08 E
Xingcheng	104	40.37 N	120.43 E
Xingguo	100	26.21 N	115.19 E
Xinghai	102	35.31 N	99.36 E
Xinghe	98	40.48 N	113.58 E
Xinghua	100	32.57 N	119.50 E
Xinghua Wan c	100	25.20 N	119.20 E
Xingjing	102	29.43 N	102.59 E
Xingkai Hu (ozero Chanka) ⊜	89	45.00 N	132.24 E
Xingliu	100	33.04 N	115.41 E
Xinglong, Zhg.	100	32.05 N	112.51 E
Xinglong, Zhg.	102	35.38 N	106.08 E
Xinglong, Zhg.	105	40.26 N	117.34 E
Xinglong, Zhg.	107	30.36 N	106.20 E
Xinglong, Zhg.	107	30.20 N	106.07 E
Xinglongchang, Zhg.	107	30.25 N	104.06 E
Xinglongchang, Zhg.	107	29.34 N	106.09 E
Xinglongchang, Zhg.	107	29.54 N	105.26 E
Xinglongcun	89	49.50 N	125.12 E
Xinglongdian, Zhg.	104	42.16 N	124.00 E
Xinglongdian, Zhg.	104	41.59 N	123.03 E
Xinglonggou, Zhg.	104	41.46 N	120.38 E
Xinglonggou, Zhg.	104	40.45 N	123.08 E
Xinglongpao	89	46.27 N	125.47 E
Xinglongtai	104	42.30 N	123.48 E
Xingning	100	24.09 N	115.45 E
Xingou, Zhg.	100	30.41 N	113.57 E
Xingou, Zhg.	100	30.08 N	112.56 E
Xingren	102	25.27 N	105.13 E
Xingrenbu	102	37.06 N	105.12 E
Xingshanbao	89	45.30 N	125.45 E
Xingtai	98	37.04 N	114.29 E
Xingtan	100	22.46 N	113.07 E
Xingtang	98	38.26 N	114.33 E
Xingtian	100	27.30 N	118.02 E
Xingu ≏	242	1.30 S	51.53 W
Xinguan	100	33.38 N	118.05 E
Xingwenping	102	29.24 N	103.23 E
Xingxian	102	38.36 N	111.15 E
Xingxing	106	30.39 N	121.09 E
Xingyi, Zhg.	98	38.18 N	115.01 E
Xingyi, Zhg.	102	25.06 N	104.58 E
Xingzhuangzi	105	40.34 N	115.00 E
Xingzi	100	29.28 N	116.01 E
Xinhe, Zhg.	98	37.32 N	115.14 E
Xinhe, Zhg.	100	28.30 N	121.27 E
Xinhe, Zhg.	105	39.03 N	117.37 E
Xinhe, Zhg.	106	31.59 N	121.21 E
Xinhekou	89	48.22 N	130.45 E
Xinheng	100	23.38 N	116.18 E
Xinhezhen	106	31.35 N	121.31 E
Xinhezhuang	106	31.10 N	118.46 E
Xinhua	102	27.37 N	111.02 E
Xinhuai ≏	100	34.23 N	120.05 E
Xinhuang	106	30.37 N	120.55 E
Xinhui	100	22.32 N	113.02 E
Xining (Sining)	102	36.38 N	101.55 E
Xiniu, Zhg.	100	24.10 N	113.07 E
Xiniu, Zhg.	106	31.25 N	120.07 E
Xiniuguchengzi	104	41.01 N	122.24 E
Xinji, Zhg.	98	35.19 N	115.36 E
Xinji, Zhg.	100	33.24 N	114.44 E
Xinji, Zhg.	105	39.52 N	117.10 E
Xinji, Zhg.	105	40.04 N	118.21 E
Xinjiaji	98	36.56 N	116.59 E
Xinjian, Zhg.	100	28.46 N	120.02 E
Xinjian, Zhg.	100	28.34 N	115.47 E
Xinjian, Zhg.	106	31.33 N	119.39 E
Xinjiang, Zhg.	100	24.29 N	113.52 E
Xinjiang, Zhg.	102	35.40 N	111.11 E
Xinjiang, Zhg.	106	32.05 N	120.40 E
Xinjianglang	106	30.58 N	120.54 E
Xinjiang Uygur Zizhiqu (Sinkiang) □[4]	90	40.00 N	85.00 E
Xinjiapu	105	40.32 N	115.57 E
Xinjiazhuang	105	40.31 N	114.58 E
Xinjie	102	26.48 N	101.15 E
Xinjieji	89	52.08 N	126.24 E
Xinjin (Pulandian), Zhg.	98	39.24 N	121.58 E
Xinjin, Zhg.	107	30.25 N	103.49 E
Xinjingzi	86	42.13 N	87.36 E
Xinjuntun	105	39.39 N	117.57 E
Xinkai ≏	89	43.37 N	123.36 E
Xinkaigang	106	31.55 N	120.56 E
Xinkengdong	100	26.09 N	113.46 E
Xinle (Dongchangshou)	98	38.24 N	114.47 E
Xinli	89	44.41 N	126.45 E
Xinlitun, Zhg.	89	43.34 N	125.18 E
Xinlitun, Zhg.	104	42.00 N	122.09 E
Xinlitun, Zhg.	104	42.15 N	122.51 E
Xinlizhuang	105	39.17 N	116.10 E
Xinmin	104	42.00 N	122.48 E
Xinmintun	104	41.39 N	123.02 E
Xinning	102	26.19 N	110.45 E
Xinping	102	24.06 N	101.58 E
Xinpu	100	24.31 N	116.08 E
Xinqianhu	98	37.59 N	118.15 E
Xinqiao, Zhg.	106	31.32 N	119.04 E
Xinqiao, Zhg.	106	31.04 N	121.18 E
Xinqiao, Zhg.	107	29.32 N	106.28 E
Xinqiao, Zhg.	107	30.10 N	103.50 E
Xinqiao, Zhg.	107	30.33 N	105.33 E
Xinqiaotou	106	31.00 N	119.24 E
Xinqiaozhen	107	29.36 N	103.39 E
Xinqiu	98	41.53 N	119.41 E
Xinqizhou	100	28.56 N	115.50 E
Xinqu	86	44.57 N	85.15 E
Xinquan	100	25.23 N	116.38 E
Xinsanyu	106	31.58 N	120.07 E
Xinshao	102	27.11 N	111.20 E
Xinshengzhen	107	29.29 N	104.39 E
Xinshi, Zhg.	106	32.04 N	120.02 E
Xinshi, Zhg.	106	30.37 N	120.19 E
Xinshizhen, Zhg.	102	28.39 N	104.02 E
Xinshizhen, Zhg.	107	30.20 N	104.35 E
Xinshu ≏	98	34.41 N	119.12 E
Xintai	98	35.54 N	117.44 E
Xintaimen	98	40.50 N	120.23 E
Xintaizi, Zhg.	104	41.06 N	122.42 E
Xintaizi, Zhg.	104	42.07 N	123.36 E
Xintang, Zhg.	100	23.08 N	113.36 E
Xintang, Zhg.	102	30.13 N	109.30 E
Xintang, Zhg.	106	31.02 N	119.59 E
Xintangcun	106	31.53 N	119.31 E
Xintanpu	100	29.43 N	114.54 E
Xintian	102	25.53 N	112.05 E
Xintun	104	42.11 N	123.45 E
Xinvi	105	40.04 N	118.21 E
Xinwei	100	25.21 N	115.48 E
Xinwen (Suncun)	98	35.53 N	117.40 E
Xinxian, Zhg.	100	31.38 N	114.51 E
Xinxian, Zhg.	102	38.25 N	112.48 E
Xinxiang	98	35.20 N	113.51 E
Xinxim ≏	250	7.57 S	53.20 W
Xinxing, Zhg.	89	43.16 N	129.48 E
Xinxing, Zhg.	100	22.40 N	112.52 E
Xinxing, Zhg.	102	19.57 N	109.32 E
Xinxu, Zhg.	100	22.52 N	114.20 E
Xinxu, Zhg.	100	24.57 N	117.34 E
Xinyang	100	32.08 N	114.04 E
Xinyao	100	27.39 N	118.52 E
Xinye	100	32.33 N	112.21 E
Xinyi (Xin'anzhen), Zhg.	98	34.22 N	118.21 E
Xinyi (Dongzhen), Zhg.	102	22.13 N	110.50 E
Xinyi ≏	100	34.29 N	119.49 E
Xinying	102	36.03 N	105.35 E
Xinyu	100	27.49 N	114.57 E
Xinyuan	86	43.08 N	82.31 E
Xinzao	100	23.02 N	113.26 E
Xinzha	102	23.41 N	101.09 E
Xinzhai, Zhg.	98	39.24 N	118.46 E
Xinzhai, Zhg.	98	36.24 N	118.37 E
Xinzhai, Zhg.	102	24.33 N	99.08 E
Xinzhan	100	33.33 N	114.50 E
Xinzhang	105	39.05 N	116.46 E
Xinzhangzi	105	40.45 N	117.50 E
Xinzhao	102	39.32 N	107.52 E
Xinzhazhen	106	31.50 N	119.52 E
Xinzhen, Zhg.	98	35.37 N	114.03 E
Xinzhen, Zhg.	105	39.01 N	116.22 E
Xinzhen, Zhg.	106	31.24 N	121.24 E
Xinzheng	100	34.25 N	113.43 E
Xinzhou, Zhg.	100	30.50 N	114.47 E
Xinzhou, Zhg.	102	19.48 N	109.18 E
Xinzhuang, Zhg.	98	35.05 N	117.56 E
Xinzhuang, Zhg.	271a	39.56 N	116.31 E
Xinzhuangtou	105	39.25 N	115.45 E
Xinzhuangzi, Zhg.	104	41.05 N	121.23 E
Xinzhuangzi, Zhg.	105	40.14 N	116.59 E
Xinzhuangzi, Zhg.	105	40.32 N	115.10 E
Xinzhuangzi, Zhg.	105	38.52 N	117.21 E
Xinzhuangzi, Zhg.	105	39.20 N	118.25 E
Xinzo de Limia	34	42.03 N	7.43 W
Xiongdi Yu II	100	23.33 N	117.40 E
Xiongjiachang	102	26.31 N	105.39 E
Xiongxian	105	38.59 N	116.05 E
Xiongyuecheng	98	40.10 N	122.08 E
Xipamanu (Chipamanu) ≏	248	10.43 S	67.50 W
Xiping, Zhg.	100	33.23 N	114.02 E
Xiping, Zhg.	100	28.27 N	119.29 E
Xiping'anhe	104	40.47 N	122.01 E
Xiqia	106	31.03 N	119.37 E
Xiqilichiquan	89	49.59 N	119.27 E
Xiqin	100	26.33 N	118.06 E
Xiqing Shan ⋌	102	35.30 N	101.30 E
Xique-Xique	250	10.50 S	42.44 W
Xisanshilipu	100	32.40 N	117.31 E
Xisantai	98	39.38 N	121.37 E
Xishan, Zhg.	100	28.34 N	115.37 E
Xishan, Zhg.	105	39.38 N	118.10 E
Xishanqiao	106	31.57 N	118.43 E
Xishanxicun	105	40.01 N	116.50 E
Xisha Qundao (Paracel Islands) II	108	16.30 N	112.15 E
Xishijiazi	104	41.46 N	120.55 E
Xishiqiao	106	31.53 N	120.06 E
Xishu	98	36.41 N	113.49 E
Xishui	100	30.27 N	115.13 E
Xishuiyu	105	40.25 N	116.16 E
Xisuhupu	104	41.41 N	123.14 E
Xitai	98	40.37 N	120.12 E
Xitan	100	23.47 N	117.08 E
Xitang	106	30.57 N	120.53 E
Xitangqiao, Zhg.	106	31.49 N	120.38 E
Xitangqiao, Zhg.	106	30.37 N	121.01 E
Xitaoyuan	104	40.57 N	122.11 E
Xiti	120	33.27 N	82.48 E
Xitianmu Shan ∧	106	30.21 N	119.25 E
Xitiao ≏	106	30.57 N	120.10 E
Xiting	106	32.07 N	121.00 E
Xitole	150	11.43 N	14.50 W
Xituan	105	39.29 N	115.47 E
Xiu ≏	100	29.13 N	115.56 E
Xiujiangpu	104	41.17 N	123.02 E
Xiuning	100	29.47 N	118.10 E
Xiushan	102	28.29 N	108.52 E
Xiushui	100	29.04 N	114.33 E
Xiushui ≏	104	42.03 N	122.58 E
Xiushuihe	104	42.22 N	123.01 E
Xiuyan	98	40.17 N	123.18 E
Xiva	34	39.28 N	0.43 W
Xiwei	100	25.22 N	117.46 E
Xiweizigou	104	42.01 N	121.59 E
Xiwenquan	107	29.42 N	106.07 E
Xiwu	100	29.40 N	121.30 E
Xiwukou	106	30.24 N	118.54 E
Xixabangma Feng ∧	124	28.22 N	85.50 E
Xixi	100	26.45 N	118.42 E
Xixia	102	33.22 N	111.28 E
Xixian, Zhg.	100	32.21 N	114.44 E
Xixian, Zhg.	102	36.43 N	110.52 E
Xixiang	102	32.48 N	107.55 E
Xixiangyang	105	39.33 N	116.02 E
Xixiaojie	104	40.42 N	122.12 E
Xixiashu	106	31.57 N	119.49 E
Xixing	106	30.11 N	120.13 E
Xixona	34	38.32 N	0.30 W
Xiyang, Zhg.	98	37.37 N	113.42 E
Xiyang, Zhg.	100	25.50 N	117.25 E
Xiyang, Zhg.	106	31.49 N	120.43 E
Xiyang, Zhg.	106	31.52 N	119.23 E
Xiyang Dao I	100	26.32 N	120.04 E
Xiyangji	100	33.25 N	116.22 E
Xiyangjiao	106	31.43 N	120.23 E
Xiyangshugou	104	40.41 N	122.44 E
Xiyangzhuang	106	31.50 N	119.22 E
Xiyingzi	104	41.55 N	122.34 E
Xiyou	98	37.24 N	119.56 E
Xiyushi	106	30.36 N	119.26 E
Xizang Zizhiqu (Tibet) □[4]	90	32.00 N	88.00 E
Xizhi ≏	100	23.04 N	114.31 E
Xizhimen Station ◆[5]	271a	39.56 N	116.21 E
Xizhong Dao I	98	39.26 N	121.17 E
Xizhou	100	29.29 N	121.39 E
Xizi	98	41.48 N	119.16 E
Xochiapa	234	17.39 N	95.46 W
Xochicalco ⊥	234	18.48 N	99.19 W
Xochimilco ◆[8]	286a	19.16 N	99.06 W
Xochimilco, Lago de ⊜	286a	19.16 N	99.06 W
Xochipala	234	17.48 N	99.39 W
Xochistlahuaca	234	16.47 N	98.15 W
Xochitlán	234	19.59 N	97.36 W
Xoka	120	29.58 N	93.48 E
Xom Binh Phuoc	269c	10.40 N	106.47 E
Xom Xoai Minh	269c	10.42 N	106.50 E
Xu ≏	100	28.17 N	116.05 E
Xuancheng	106	30.58 N	118.45 E
Xuan'en	102	30.00 N	109.20 E
Xuanfeng	100	27.42 N	114.08 E
Xuang ≏	110	19.58 N	102.15 E
Xuanhan	102	31.24 N	107.43 E
Xuanhua	105	40.37 N	115.03 E
Xuanhuadian	100	31.42 N	114.29 E
Xuanhui ≏	98	38.07 N	117.45 E
Xuanjiabao	106	32.17 N	120.01 E
Xuanjiangying	98	41.25 N	116.45 E
Xuan Loc	110	10.56 N	107.14 E
Xuantan	107	29.12 N	105.34 E
Xuan Thoi Thuong	269c	10.52 N	106.34 E
Xuanwei	102	26.07 N	104.05 E
Xuanzhuang	105	39.29 N	118.07 E
Xubu	98	40.02 N	113.43 E
Xuchang, Zhg.	100	34.03 N	113.49 E
Xuchang, Zhg.	107	29.06 N	104.31 E
Xucheng	98	35.56 N	116.27 E
Xuchilquitongo	234	17.15 N	96.53 W
Xucun	106	30.27 N	120.22 E
Xudazhuang	100	33.44 N	117.53 E
Xuddun	144	9.09 N	47.28 E
Xuddur	144	4.07 N	43.54 E
Xueao	100	29.27 N	121.30 E
Xuebu	106	31.43 N	119.22 E
Xuecheng	98	34.50 N	117.16 E
Xuedian, Zhg.	100	34.04 N	113.04 E
Xuedian, Zhg.	100	34.30 N	113.44 E
Xuefanggou	104	41.57 N	121.01 E
Xuefeng	100	33.21 N	118.22 E
Xuehu	98	34.08 N	116.27 E
Xueshan Zhang ∧	100	24.24 N	113.37 E
Xueshuiwen	89	49.10 N	129.45 E
Xuetangpuzi	104	40.38 N	123.53 E
Xueyanqiao	106	31.30 N	120.06 E
Xuezhen	106	31.35 N	118.38 E
Xuguanzhen	106	31.23 N	120.30 E
Xuguichenxiaodian	106	32.07 N	121.20 E
Xuguit Qi (Yakeshi)	89	49.17 N	120.41 E
Xuji	100	31.50 N	116.22 E
Xujiabu	100	29.27 N	116.18 E
Xujiadong	100	25.54 N	113.02 E
Xujiadu	100	28.18 N	114.44 E
Xujiagou	104	42.17 N	124.04 E
Xujiapuzi	104	40.44 N	123.18 E
Xujiatou	106	31.19 N	119.25 E
Xujiazhai, Zhg.	106	31.11 N	121.46 E
Xujiazhai, Zhg.	269b	31.23 N	121.17 E
Xuliying	105	39.28 N	116.02 E
Xun ≏, Zhg.	89	49.27 N	128.55 E
Xun ≏, Zhg.	102	23.28 N	111.18 E
Xungru	120	29.15 N	84.49 E
Xunhe	89	49.18 N	128.04 E
Xunhua	102	35.49 N	102.26 E
Xunjiansi	105	40.50 N	116.04 E
Xunke	89	49.35 N	128.25 E
Xunle	102	25.17 N	108.12 E
Xunmukou	98	34.03 N	114.42 E
Xunshansuo	98	37.10 N	122.29 E
Xunwu	100	24.58 N	115.38 E
Xunwu ≏	100	24.28 N	115.26 E
Xunxian	98	35.43 N	114.31 E
Xupu, Zhg.	102	27.44 N	110.24 E
Xupu, Zhg.	106	31.45 N	120.54 E
Xushe	106	31.24 N	119.39 E
Xushi	106	31.40 N	120.57 E
Xushui	105	39.02 N	115.39 E
Xutian	98	34.10 N	114.03 E
Xuwan	100	27.55 N	116.31 E
Xuwen	102	20.21 N	110.11 E
Xuxiandai	106	30.40 N	120.47 E
Xuxiang	106	31.33 N	120.13 E
Xuyen Moc	110	10.34 N	107.25 E
Xuyi	100	33.01 N	118.29 E
Xuyong	102	28.10 N	105.24 E
Xuzhou (Süchow)	98	34.16 N	117.11 E
Xuzhuang	106	31.09 N	120.32 E

Y

Nombre / Nom / Nome	Página / Page	Lat.°′	Long.°′ W = Oeste / W = Ouest
Yaak	182	48.50 N	115.42 W
Yaan	102	30.03 N	103.02 E
Yaapeet	166	35.46 S	142.03 E
Yaaq-Baraawe	144	1.57 N	43.11 E
Yaba ◆[8]	273a	6.30 N	3.23 E
Yaba College of Technology ⚲[2]	273a	6.32 N	3.23 E
Ya'bad	132	32.27 N	35.10 E
Yabakei	96	33.27 N	131.07 E
Yabassi	152	4.28 N	9.58 E
Yabe	96	33.09 N	130.49 E
Yabe ≏	96	33.06 N	130.26 E
Yabelo	144	4.54 N	38.05 E
Yablis	236	14.10 N	83.49 W
Yablonovy Range → Jablonovyj chrebet ⋌	88	53.30 N	115.00 E
Yabrīn ⍑[4]	128	23.17 N	48.58 E
Yabrūd	130	33.58 N	36.40 E
Yabu, Nihon	96	35.22 N	134.47 E
Yabu, Nihon	174m	26.36 N	127.57 E
Yabucoa	240m	18.03 N	65.53 W
Yabuki	94	37.12 N	140.19 E
Yabuli	89	44.55 N	128.35 E
Yacambu, Parque Nacional ♠	246	9.40 N	69.42 W
Yacaré Norte, Riacho ≏	252	22.43 S	58.14 W
Yacheng	110	18.25 N	109.11 E
Yachi ≏	102	27.18 N	107.15 E
Yachimata	94	35.39 N	140.19 E
Yachiyo, Nihon	94	35.43 N	140.07 E
Yachiyo, Nihon	94	36.10 N	139.53 E
Yacimiento Río Turbio	254	51.32 S	72.18 W
Yaco	248	17.09 S	67.24 W
Yaco (Iaco) ≏	248	9.03 S	68.34 W
Yacolt	224	45.51 N	122.24 W
Yacuiba	248	22.02 S	63.45 W
Yacuma ≏	248	13.38 S	65.23 W
Yacyretá, Isla I	252	27.25 S	56.30 W
Yada ≏	96	35.38 N	134.37 E
Yādgīr	122	16.46 N	77.08 E
Yadkin ≏	192	35.23 N	80.03 W
Yadkinville	192	36.08 N	80.39 W
Yad Mordekhay	132	31.35 N	34.34 E
Yadong	124	27.29 N	88.55 E
Yādūdah	132	32.40 N	36.04 E
Yaenengu	152	2.28 N	23.15 E
Yaeyama-rettō II	175d	24.20 N	124.00 E
Yāfā	132	32.41 N	35.17 E
Yafran	146	32.04 N	12.31 E
Yaftābād	267d	35.39 N	51.19 E
Yafuquan	85	39.12 N	76.09 E
Yagachi-shima I	174m	26.40 N	128.01 E
Yağcılar	130	39.25 N	28.23 E
Yageg	144	3.16 N	44.00 E
Yagi	96	35.04 N	135.32 E
Yagishiri-tō I	92a	44.26 N	141.25 E
Yağlıca Dağı ∧	84	40.18 N	43.18 E
Yago	234	21.50 N	105.04 W
Yagonde	152	0.02 N	22.41 E
Yagoona	274a	33.55 S	151.02 E
Yagoua	146	10.20 N	15.14 E
Yagradagzê Shan ∧	120	35.12 N	95.20 E
Yaguachi Nuevo	246	2.07 S	79.41 W
Yaguajay	240p	22.19 N	79.14 W
Yaguala ≏	236	15.25 N	86.40 W
Yaguará	246	2.40 N	75.31 W
Yaguaraparo	246	10.34 N	62.49 W
Yaguarí	252	31.31 S	54.58 W
Yaguarón (Jaguarão) ≏	252	32.39 S	53.12 W
Yaguas ≏	246	2.45 S	70.04 W
Yagur	132	32.44 N	35.04 E
Yahagi ≏	94	34.50 N	136.59 E
Yahagong	102	28.24 N	99.11 E
Yahara ≏	190	42.48 N	89.07 W
Yahata → Kitakyūshū	96	33.53 N	130.50 E
Yahe, Zhg.	89	45.24 N	130.24 E
Yahe, Zhg.	106	31.44 N	119.52 E
Yahila	152	0.13 N	24.28 E
Yahk	182	49.05 N	116.05 W
Yahmūm al-Asmar, Jabal ∧	142	29.56 N	31.38 E
Yaho	268	35.41 N	139.27 E
Yahōga-take ∧	96	33.04 N	130.50 E
Yahongqiao	105	39.45 N	117.51 E
Yahualica	234	21.08 N	102.51 W
Yahuma	152	1.05 N	23.13 E
Yahyalı	130	38.07 N	35.22 E
Yai ≏	114	5.02 N	101.47 E
Yai, Khao ∧, Asia	110	12.27 N	99.26 E
Yai, Khao ∧, Thai	110	15.25 N	99.20 E
Yainax Butte ∧	202	42.20 N	121.16 W
Yaita, Nihon	94	36.48 N	139.56 E
Yaita, Nihon	268	35.57 N	140.03 E
Yaitopya → Ethiopia □[1]	144	9.00 N	39.00 E
Yaizu	94	34.52 N	138.20 E
Yajiang	102	30.02 N	101.05 E
Yaka	130	41.15 N	34.01 E
Yakacık	130	36.47 N	36.10 E
Yakacık ◆[8]	267b	40.55 N	29.13 E
Yakage	96	34.37 N	133.35 E
Yakak, Cape ⟩	180	51.38 N	177.00 W
Yakapınar	130	37.00 N	35.36 E
Yakarta → Jakarta	115a	6.10 S	106.48 E
Yake-dake ∧	94	36.14 N	137.35 E
Yake-yama ∧	94	36.55 N	138.03 E
Yakhchāl, Afg.	120	31.47 N	64.41 E
Yakhchāl, Afg.	128	31.47 N	64.41 E
Yakima	202	46.36 N	120.30 W
Yakima □[6]	224	46.34 N	121.03 W
Yakima ≏	202	46.15 N	119.02 W
Yakima Firing Center ■	202	46.44 N	120.10 W
Yakima Indian Reservation ◆[4]	224	46.16 N	121.03 W
Yakkan ≏	96	33.34 N	131.22 E
Yakmach	128	28.45 N	63.51 E
Yako	150	12.58 N	2.16 W
Yakō ◆[8]	268	35.32 N	139.41 E
Yakobi Island I	180	58.00 N	136.30 W
Yakoma	152	4.05 N	22.27 E

≏ River	Fluß	Río	Rivière	Rio
≊ Canal	Kanal	Canal	Canal	Canal
ʟ Waterfall, Rapids	Wasserfall, Stromschnellen	Cascada, Rápidos	Chute d'eau, Rapides	Cascata, Rápidos
Ꮃ Strait	Meeresstraße	Estrecho	Détroit	Estreito
c Bay, Gulf	Bucht, Golf	Bahía, Golfo	Baie, Golfe	Baía, Golfo
⊜ Lake, Lakes	See, Seen	Lago, Lagos	Lac, Lacs	Lago, Lagos
☷ Swamp	Sumpf	Pantano	Marais	Pântano
⌂ Ice Features, Glacier	Eis- und Gletscherformen	Accidentes Glaciales	Formes glaciaires	Acidentes glaciares
⍑ Other Hydrographic Features	Andere Hydrographische Objekte	Otros Elementos Hidrográficos	Autres données hydrographiques	Outros acidentes hidrográficos
⊹ Submarine Features	Untermeerische Objekte	Accidentes Submarinos	Formes de relief sous-marin	Acidentes submarinos
□ Political Unit	Politische Einheit	Unidad Politica	Entité politique	Unidade política
⚲ Cultural Institution	Kulturelle Institution	Institución Cultural	Institution culturelle	Institução cultural
⊥ Historical Site	Historische Stätte	Sitio Histórico	Site historique	Sitio histórico
♠ Recreational Site	Erholungs- und Ferienort	Sitio de Recreo	Centre de loisirs	Area de Lazer
⊠ Airport	Flughafen	Aeropuerto	Aéroport	Aeroporto
■ Military Installation	Militäranlage	Instalación Militar	Installation militaire	Instalação militar
◆ Miscellaneous	Verschiedenes	Misceláneo	Divers	Diversos

ENGLISH — Name, Page, Lat.°′, Long.°′
DEUTSCH — Name, Seite, Breite°′, Länge°′ E = Ost

Name	Page	Lat.	Long.
Yakou	100	24.46 N	118.46 E
Yakuendai	268	35.43 N	140.03 E
Yakuluku	154	4.20 N	28.48 E
Yakumo	92a	42.15 N	140.16 E
Yakuno	96	35.19 N	135.00 E
Yakushi-dake ∧	94	36.28 N	137.33 E
Yakushi-ji ʋ[1]	94	36.25 N	139.53 E
Yaku-shima I	93b	30.20 N	130.30 E
Yakutat	180	59.33 N	139.44 W
Yakutat Bay c	180	59.40 N	140.00 W
Yakutat Seamount ✦[3]	16	35.15 N	48.00 W
Yakutia → Jakutija □[3]	74	67.00 N	125.00 E
Yakutsk → Jakutsk	74	62.00 N	129.40 E
Yala, Ghana	150	10.07 N	1.52 W
Yala, Thai	110	6.33 N	101.18 E
Yalaha	220	28.44 N	81.48 W
Yalahau, Laguna c	232	21.30 N	87.15 W
Yalakdere	130	40.36 N	29.33 E
Yalata	162	31.29 S	131.52 E
Yalata Aboriginal Reserve ◆[4]	162	31.30 S	131.45 E
Yalca, Laguna ⊜	258	35.34 S	57.55 W
Yalding	260	51.13 N	0.26 E
Yale, B.C., Can.	182	49.34 N	121.26 W
Yale, Mi., U.S.	190	43.07 N	82.47 W
Yale, Ok., U.S.	196	36.06 N	96.41 W
Yale, Va., U.S.	208	36.50 N	77.17 W
Yale, Lake ⊜	220	28.54 N	81.45 W
Yale, Mount ∧	200	38.51 N	106.18 W
Yale Lake ⊜[1]	224	46.00 N	122.12 W
Yalgar ≏	162	26.09 S	117.57 E
Yalgoo	162	28.20 S	116.41 E
Yalgorup National Park ♦	168a	32.55 S	115.41 E
Yali	152	0.04 N	21.03 E
Yaliji	98	36.06 N	114.56 E
Yalikamba	152	1.17 S	22.30 E
Yalinga	152	6.31 N	23.15 E
Yalisere	152	0.11 N	22.33 E
Yalleroi	166	24.04 S	145.45 E
Yallourn	169	38.11 S	146.21 E
Yallourn North	169	38.09 S	146.22 E
Yalnızçam Dağları ⋆	84	41.10 N	42.25 E
Yalobusha ≏	194	33.33 N	90.10 W
Yaloká	152	5.19 N	17.05 E
Yalong ≏	102	26.37 N	101.48 E
Yaloupi ≏	250	2.47 N	52.28 W
Yalova	130	40.39 N	29.15 E
Yalta → Jalta	78	44.30 N	34.10 E
Yalu	89	48.34 N	122.09 E
Yalu (Amnok-kang) ≏, Asia	98	39.55 N	124.22 E
Yalu ≏, Zhg.	89	46.56 N	123.30 E
Yalufi	152	0.45 N	24.26 E
Yalvaç	130	38.17 N	31.11 E
Yalwal Creek ≏	170	34.50 S	150.23 E
Yamachiche	206	46.16 N	72.50 W
Yamachiche ≏	206	46.16 N	72.48 W
Yamada, Nihon	92	39.28 N	141.57 E
Yamada, Nihon	94	35.49 N	140.36 E
Yamada, Nihon	94	36.34 N	137.05 E
Yamada, Nihon	96	33.33 N	130.47 E
Yamada, Nihon	174m	26.26 N	127.47 E
Yamada, Nihon	270	34.31 N	135.39 E
Yamada, Nihon	270	34.48 N	135.32 E
Yamada ≏	270	34.47 N	135.04 E
Yamada → Tosa-yamada	96	33.36 N	133.41 E
Yamaga, Nihon	96	33.01 N	130.41 E
Yamaga, Nihon	96	33.27 N	131.30 E
Yamagata, Nihon	92	38.15 N	140.20 E
Yamagata, Nihon	94	36.38 N	140.24 E
Yamagata, Nihon	94	36.10 N	137.52 E
Yamagawa	92	31.12 N	130.39 E
Yamaguchi, Nihon	94	35.33 N	137.33 E
Yamaguchi, Nihon	96	34.10 N	131.29 E
Yamaguchi, Nihon	270	34.50 N	135.15 E
Yamaguchi □[5]	96	34.20 N	131.30 E
Yamaguchi-chosuichi ⊜[1]	268	35.46 N	139.25 E
Yama-Hita-Hiko-san-kokutei-kōen ♦	96	33.25 N	131.02 E
Yamakawa	96	34.04 N	134.15 E
Yamakita	94	35.21 N	139.05 E
Yamakuni	96	33.24 N	131.02 E
Yamakuni ≏	96	33.37 N	131.12 E
Yamalia → Jamalo-Neneckij □[3]	72	67.00 N	75.00 E
Yamām, Jabal al- ∧	132	30.02 N	35.28 E
Yamamoto, Nihon	96	34.07 N	133.44 E
Yamamoto, Nihon	270	34.38 N	135.38 E
Yamanaka	94	36.15 N	136.22 E
Yamanakako	94	35.24 N	138.52 E
Yamanaka-ko ⊜	94	35.25 N	138.52 E
Yamanashi	94	35.40 N	138.40 E
Yamanashi □[5]	94	35.30 N	138.30 E
Yamanouchi	94	36.44 N	138.25 E
Yamasaki	96	35.00 N	134.33 E
Yamashina ◆[8]	270	34.58 N	135.49 E
Yamashiro, Nihon	94	34.45 N	135.49 E
Yamashiro, Nihon	96	33.57 N	133.45 E
Yamaska (Saint-Michel)	206	46.00 N	72.55 W
Yamaska □[6]	206	46.00 N	72.45 W
Yamaska ≏	206	46.06 N	72.56 W
Yamaska, Mont ∧[2]	206	45.27 N	72.52 W
Yamaska Nord ≏	206	45.17 N	72.51 W
Yamaska Sud-Est ≏	206	45.17 N	72.55 W
Yamate	270	34.30 N	135.27 E
Yamatengwumulu	102	38.38 N	97.05 E
Yamato, Nihon	94	35.48 N	136.54 E
Yamato, Nihon	94	35.29 N	139.29 E
Yamato, Nihon	94	37.10 N	138.56 E
Yamato, Nihon	96	33.08 N	130.26 E
Yamato ≏	96	34.36 N	135.26 E
Yamato-Aogaki-kokutei-kōen ♦	94	34.40 N	135.50 E
Yamato-kōriyama	96	34.38 N	135.47 E
Yamato-takada	96	34.31 N	135.45 E
Yamatsuri	94	36.52 N	140.25 E
Yamazaki	268	35.56 N	139.54 E
Yamba	166	29.26 S	153.22 E
Yambata	152	2.26 N	21.58 E
Yambéring	150	11.49 N	12.21 W
Yambio	154	4.34 N	28.23 E
Yambol → Jambol	38	42.29 N	26.30 E
Yamboyo	152	0.40 N	22.18 E
Yambrasbamba	248	5.45 S	77.54 W
Yambuya	154	1.16 N	24.33 E
Yamdena, Pulau I	164	7.36 S	131.25 E
Yame	96	33.28 N	130.34 E
Ya Men c	100	22.09 N	113.05 E
Yamenkou	105	39.53 N	116.12 E
Yamenying	89	43.25 N	122.19 E
Yamethin	110	20.26 N	96.09 E
Yamhill	224	45.21 N	123.11 W
Yamhill □[6]	224	45.15 N	123.20 W
Yamhill ≏	224	45.14 N	123.00 W
Yamia	150	13.24 N	10.18 E
Yamizo-san ∧	94	36.56 N	140.17 E
Yamma Yamma, Lake ⊜	166	26.20 S	141.25 E
Yamoussoukro	150	6.49 N	5.17 W
Yampa	200	40.09 N	106.54 W
Yampa ≏	200	40.32 N	108.59 W
Yampa Plateau ⋆[1]	200	40.25 N	109.00 W
Yamparaez	248	19.10 S	65.10 W
Yamsay Mountain ∧	202	42.56 N	121.22 W
Yamu	102	43.48 N	94.48 E
Yamuna ≏	120	25.25 N	81.50 E
Yamuna Bridge ◆[5]	272a	28.40 N	77.14 E
Yamunānagar	124	30.07 N	77.18 E
Yamzho Yumco ⊜	120	28.58 N	90.44 E
Yan	114	5.48 N	100.22 E
Yan ≏, S. Lan.	122	8.55 N	81.01 E
Yan ≏, Zhg.	102	36.24 N	110.28 E
Yanac	166	36.08 S	141.26 E
Yanacachi	248	16.23 S	67.43 W
Yanachaga-Chemillen, Parque Nacional ♦	248	10.10 S	75.20 W
Yanadani	96	33.32 N	133.01 E
Yanagawa	96	33.10 N	130.24 E
Yanagi	270	34.25 N	135.56 E
Yanagimoto	270	34.34 N	135.51 E
Yanahara	96	34.55 N	134.05 E
Yanaha-shima I	174m	26.54 N	127.56 E
Yanahuara	248	16.24 S	71.33 W
Yanai	96	33.58 N	132.07 E
Yanaka	268	35.24 N	140.01 E
Yanam	122	16.44 N	82.13 E
Yan'an	102	36.36 N	109.28 E
Yanaoca	248	14.13 S	71.26 W
Yanarsu	130	38.02 N	41.33 E
Yanbian	102	26.55 N	101.30 E
Yanbu	100	23.05 N	113.10 E
Yanbuʿ al-Baḥr	128	24.05 N	38.03 E
Yanbutou	100	29.52 N	115.04 E
Yanceyville	192	36.24 N	79.20 W
Yanchang	102	36.31 N	110.08 E
Yancheng, Zhg.	100	33.36 N	113.57 E
Yancheng, Zhg.	100	33.24 N	120.09 E
Yanchep	168a	31.33 S	115.41 E
Yanchep National Park ♦	168a	31.32 S	115.40 E
Yanchi, Zhg.	102	37.52 N	107.22 E
Yanchi, Zhg.	105	40.02 N	115.53 E
Yanchuan	102	36.56 N	110.05 E
Yanco	166	34.36 S	146.25 E
Yanco Creek ≏	166	35.16 S	145.07 E
Yanda Creek ≏	166	30.28 S	145.45 E
Yandal	162	27.33 S	121.07 E
Yandama Creek ≏	166	30.00 S	140.10 E
Yandé, Île I	175f	20.03 S	163.49 E
Yande Aboriginal Reserve ◆[4]	162	21.35 S	118.45 E
Yandev	150	7.20 N	9.01 E
Yandina	175e	9.07 S	159.13 E
Yandja	152	1.41 S	17.43 E
Yandongi	152	2.51 N	22.16 E
Yandoon	110	17.02 N	95.39 E
Yandua Island I	175g	16.49 S	178.18 E
Yandun	102	42.20 N	94.09 E
Yanfeng	102	25.53 N	101.01 E
Yanfolila	150	11.11 N	8.09 W
Yang ≏, Thai	110	15.44 N	104.00 E
Yang ≏, Zhg.	105	40.24 N	115.20 E
Yangambi	154	0.47 N	24.28 E
Yangan, Austl.	171a	28.12 S	152.13 E
Yang'an, Zhg.	98	37.38 N	117.09 E
Yan'gang	100	26.02 N	116.22 E
Yangarakata	154	3.01 N	30.28 E
Yangasa Levu I	175g	18.57 S	178.26 W
Yangbajain	120	30.06 N	90.33 E
Yangce	100	32.58 N	113.14 E
Yangcha	98	41.11 N	126.15 E
Yangchang	107	30.22 N	103.42 E
Yangcheng, Zhg.	102	35.29 N	112.25 E
Yangcheng, Zhg.	106	31.24 N	120.47 E
Yangcheng Hu ⊜	106	31.26 N	120.47 E
Yangchiang → Yangjiang	102	21.51 N	111.56 E
Yangch'ŏn ◆[8]	271b	37.34 N	126.51 E
Yangchow → Yangzhou	100	32.24 N	119.26 E
Yangchu	98	37.11 N	120.47 E
Yangch'üan → Yangquan	98	37.52 N	113.36 E
Yangchun	102	22.10 N	111.46 E
Yangcun, Zhg.	100	28.07 N	117.40 E
Yangcun, Zhg.	100	23.26 N	114.30 E
Yangcun, Zhg.	105	39.09 N	115.50 E
Yangcunqiao	100	29.36 N	119.28 E
Yangdachengzi	89	43.59 N	124.25 E
Yangdalinzi	98	42.38 N	125.07 E
Yangdang	100	32.23 N	112.39 E
Yangdian	106	31.08 N	119.45 E
Yang'erzhuang	98	38.18 N	117.30 E
Yangfang	105	40.07 N	116.07 E
Yangfangpu	105	40.48 N	115.01 E
Yangfengang	105	39.07 N	116.52 E
Yangfenzhen	106	30.28 N	120.03 E
Yanggang Do □[4]	98	41.15 N	128.00 E
Yangganzhen	106	31.00 N	119.15 E
Yanggao	98	40.25 N	113.44 E
Yanggezhuang	105	40.09 N	116.48 E
Yanggong-ni	271b	37.39 N	126.37 E
Yanggu, Taehan	98	38.06 N	127.59 E
Yanggu, Zhg.	98	34.44 N	114.48 E
Yanggu, Zhg.	98	36.08 N	115.48 E
Yangguanpu	100	32.13 N	115.31 E
Yanghang	106	31.22 N	121.26 E
Yanghe	100	33.47 N	118.23 E
Yanghexi	102	29.39 N	108.40 E
Yanghu	100	32.34 N	116.30 E
Yanghua	107	30.11 N	104.45 E
Yanghua ≏	107	30.09 N	104.42 E
Yangi-Yul' → Jangijul'	85	41.07 N	69.03 E
Yangji, Zhg.	98	36.44 N	113.56 E
Yangji, Zhg.	98	34.25 N	116.06 E
Yangji, Zhg.	100	34.19 N	119.28 E
Yangjia, Zhg.	98	34.19 N	119.28 E
Yangjia, Zhg.	106	30.41 N	120.15 E
Yangjiachang, Zhg.	107	29.23 N	104.21 E
Yangjiachang, Zhg.	107	29.45 N	105.21 E
Yangjiafeng	100	30.49 N	112.47 E
Yangjiagou	105	39.18 N	117.54 E
Yangjiajie	107	30.18 N	104.39 E
Yangjian	106	31.39 N	120.33 E
Yangjiang	102	21.51 N	111.56 E
Yangjiaogou	98	37.16 N	118.50 E
Yangjiaqiao, Zhg.	100	27.44 N	112.46 E
Yangjiaqiao, Zhg.	106	31.53 N	121.42 E
Yangjiaqiao, Zhg.	106	32.02 N	121.26 E
Yangjiatao	105	39.49 N	117.51 E
Yangjiawopu	104	42.21 N	122.57 E
Yangjiazeng	105	40.12 N	117.04 E
Yangjiazhangzi	104	40.48 N	120.33 E
Yangjie	102	24.49 N	100.22 E
Yangjishi	100	26.39 N	113.14 E
Yangkou	100	26.47 N	117.51 E
Yangkoushi	100	28.39 N	118.53 E
Yanglinjia	100	29.07 N	113.07 E
Yangliupu, Zhg.	100	30.52 N	118.37 E
Yangliupu, Zhg.	107	30.09 N	104.03 E
Yangliuqing	105	39.08 N	117.01 E
Yangloudong	100	29.31 N	113.44 E
Yangluo	100	30.41 N	114.36 E
Yangluomayu	104	40.47 N	122.54 E
Yangmachang	107	30.39 N	103.45 E
Yangma Dao I	98	37.28 N	121.37 E
Yangmahe	107	30.29 N	104.31 E
Yangmei	100	25.42 N	114.30 E
Yangmiao, Zhg.	98	34.11 N	114.53 E
Yangmiao, Zhg.	106	30.51 N	120.04 E
Yangmingshan ◆[8]	269d	25.09 N	121.33 E
Yangming Shan ∧	102	26.03 N	111.56 E
Yangmugou, Zhg.	98	40.36 N	124.28 E
Yangmugou, Zhg.	104	41.11 N	123.50 E
Yangmulin	105	40.06 N	115.12 E
Yangon (Rangoon)	110	16.47 N	96.10 E
Yangon □[8]	110	16.50 N	96.10 E
Yangor	174b	0.31 S	166.54 E
Yangpingguan	102	32.51 N	106.09 E
Yangpu	100	27.14 N	119.08 E
Yangp'yong	98	37.30 N	127.29 E
Yangp'yong-ni	98	40.53 N	127.58 E
Yangqi	106	31.23 N	119.57 E
Yangquan	98	37.52 N	113.36 E
Yangriwan	102	31.37 N	110.37 E
Yangsan	98	35.21 N	129.03 E
Yangshan, Zhg.	98	41.13 N	120.24 E
Yangshan, Zhg.	98	35.13 N	116.13 E
Yangshan, Zhg.	102	24.28 N	112.38 E
Yangshigangzi	104	41.42 N	122.59 E
Yangshitun	104	42.06 N	123.44 E
Yangshu	106	31.39 N	120.08 E
Yangshugemen	105	40.55 N	118.18 E
Yangshugoudonggou	104	41.43 N	120.41 E
Yangshuling	98	41.02 N	118.47 E
Yangshuo	102	24.45 N	110.24 E
Yangtan	106	30.42 N	119.11 E
Yangtian Zhang ∧	100	24.37 N	115.38 E
Yangting	98	37.24 N	122.07 E
Yangtou	100	23.26 N	115.24 E
Yangtze → Chang ≏	90	31.48 N	121.10 E
Yanguan	106	30.26 N	120.32 E
Yangwan, Zhg.	100	28.22 N	116.46 E
Yangwan, Zhg.	106	31.03 N	120.22 E
Yangxi, Zhg.	100	30.11 N	118.39 E
Yangxi, Zhg.	100	27.18 N	114.10 E
Yangxian	102	33.03 N	107.47 E
Yangxiang, Zhg.	106	31.29 N	119.35 E
Yangxiang, Zhg.	106	31.12 N	121.01 E
Yangxiangtun	104	40.58 N	122.48 E
Yangxiaodian	100	31.46 N	116.45 E
Yangximu ≏	104	42.04 N	123.00 E
Yangxin, Zhg.	98	37.39 N	117.34 E
Yangxin, Zhg.	100	29.51 N	115.12 E
Yangxiudian	271a	39.44 N	116.32 E
Yangyang	98	38.04 N	128.36 E
Yangyuan (Xicheng)	98	40.01 N	114.10 E
Yangze	100	26.57 N	118.23 E
Yangzhong	106	32.16 N	119.49 E
Yangzhou	100	32.24 N	119.26 E
Yangzhuang	100	33.36 N	118.58 E
Yangzhujuanzi	104	41.38 N	122.46 E
Yangzi	100	31.19 N	112.36 E
Yangzishao	98	42.28 N	126.09 E
Yanhaiyingzi	104	41.52 N	123.05 E
Yanhe, Zhg.	100	31.16 N	115.07 E
Yanhe, Zhg.	102	28.37 N	108.35 E
Yanhecheng	105	40.04 N	115.43 E
Yanheying	98	40.02 N	119.03 E
Yanhui	98	37.54 N	113.51 E
Yanina → Ioánnina	38	39.40 N	20.50 E
Yanji, Zhg.	98	34.41 N	115.27 E
Yanji, Zhg.	98	34.17 N	115.39 E
Yanji, Zhg.	98	42.57 N	129.32 E
Yanji (Longjing), Zhg.	98	42.47 N	129.26 E
Yanjia	104	40.57 N	121.41 E
Yanjiabao	106	32.19 N	120.07 E
Yanjiadian	98	39.48 N	121.49 E
Yanjiahe	100	31.48 N	114.50 E
Yanjiajie	104	41.02 N	121.32 E
Yanjiao	105	39.56 N	116.48 E
Yanjiapu	105	39.52 N	118.00 E
Yanjiatuozi	104	42.27 N	123.47 E
Yanjiawopeng	104	40.59 N	121.17 E
Yanjin	98	35.11 N	114.11 E
Yanjing, Zhg.	102	29.00 N	98.34 E
Yanjing, Zhg.	107	29.56 N	106.21 E
Yankalilla	168b	35.28 S	138.21 E
Yankalilla Bay c	168b	35.28 S	138.15 E
Yankari Game Reserve ◆[4]	146	9.45 N	10.30 E
Yankdŏk	98	39.14 N	126.41 E
Yankee Lake	210	41.35 N	74.33 W
Yankee Springs State Recreation Area ♦	216	42.38 N	85.30 W
Yankee Stadium ♦	276	40.50 N	73.56 W
Yankeetown	220	29.01 N	82.42 W
Yankton	198	42.52 N	97.23 W
Yankton Indian Reservation ◆[4]	198	43.10 N	98.22 W
Yanling, Zhg.	98	34.07 N	114.11 E
Yanling, Zhg.	106	31.54 N	119.30 E
Yanliumiao	100	32.01 N	116.52 E
Yanmeimeizi	105	39.42 N	115.03 E
Yanna	166	26.56 S	146.03 E
Yannarie ≏	162	22.28 S	114.48 E
Yanqi	90	42.00 N	86.15 E
Yanqian, Zhg.	100	24.54 N	116.14 E
Yanqian, Zhg.	100	26.15 N	117.28 E
Yanqianhu	104	42.16 N	123.12 E
Yanqiao	106	31.41 N	120.17 E
Yanqidoumen	106	31.17 N	118.42 E
Yanqing	105	40.28 N	115.58 E
Yanque	248	15.39 S	71.39 W
Yanrey	162	22.31 S	114.48 E
Yanshan, Zhg.	98	38.05 N	117.13 E
Yanshan, Zhg.	100	28.18 N	117.41 E
Yanshan, Zhg.	102	23.41 N	104.21 E
Yan Shan ⋆	105	40.20 N	117.40 E
Yanshankou	105	39.59 N	117.42 E
Yanshi	100	25.17 N	117.10 E
Yanshi ≏	100	25.20 N	117.17 E
Yanshou	89	45.28 N	128.20 E
Yansi	100	29.48 N	118.20 E
Yanṭā	132	33.36 N	35.57 E
Yantabulla	166	29.21 S	145.00 E
Yantai (Chefoo), Zhg.	98	37.33 N	121.20 E
Yantai, Zhg.	105	39.47 N	116.38 E
Yantan, Zhg.	100	28.28 N	120.44 E
Yantan, Zhg.	100	28.55 N	120.11 E
Yantan, Zhg.	107	29.17 N	104.52 E
Yantian, Zhg.	100	26.53 N	119.53 E
Yantian, Zhg.	100	27.21 N	114.22 E
Yantic ≏	207	41.31 N	72.05 W
Yantietang ≋	106	31.49 N	120.46 E
Yanting	102	31.19 N	105.23 E
Yantis	222	32.56 N	95.35 W
Yantongshan, Zhg.	89	43.17 N	126.00 E
Yantongshan, Zhg.	105	40.42 N	115.06 E
Yanu	164	9.57 S	148.25 E
Yanwangshan	104	41.36 N	123.57 E
Yanweigang	98	34.30 N	119.48 E
Yanxi	100	24.46 N	117.47 E
Yanxia	100	29.34 N	114.50 E
Yanxidu	100	26.51 N	114.58 E
Yanxing	102	25.23 N	101.42 E
Yan Yean Reservoir ⊜[1]	169	37.33 S	145.08 E
Yanyegongsi	106	32.02 N	121.41 E
Yanyuan	102	27.29 N	101.32 E
Yanzhou	98	35.33 N	116.50 E
Yanziji	106	32.09 N	118.49 E
Yanzijiao	102	23.38 N	100.12 E
Yanzikou	102	27.31 N	105.21 E
Yao, Centraf.	152	5.19 N	19.36 E
Yao, Nihon	96	34.37 N	135.36 E
Yao, Tchad	146	12.51 N	17.34 E
Yao Airport ✈	270	34.36 N	135.36 E
Yao'an	102	25.32 N	101.12 E
Yaoba	107	29.45 N	105.39 E
Yaocun, Zhg.	98	36.31 N	114.07 E
Yaocun, Zhg.	98	35.45 N	116.57 E
Yaocun, Zhg.	105	39.09 N	115.32 E
Yaodafangshen	104	42.27 N	122.59 E
Yaoerwan	105	40.49 N	115.17 E
Yaogongbu	100	29.51 N	120.18 E
Yaohongcaopao	104	40.55 N	122.26 E
Yaohuamen	106	32.08 N	118.53 E
Yaohuangdi	104	41.32 N	122.48 E
Yaojiaji	100	31.14 N	116.29 E
Yaojiaohe	106	32.10 N	119.46 E
Yaojiatun	104	41.18 N	121.57 E
Yaojiawopeng	104	41.47 N	122.25 E
Yaojie	105	40.06 N	115.12 E
Yaoling	100	24.49 N	113.58 E
Yaolugou	98	40.34 N	119.24 E
Yaoluzi	104	41.26 N	121.44 E
Yaopi	100	26.52 N	113.38 E
Yaopu	100	31.36 N	118.20 E
Yaoqianhutun	104	41.32 N	123.36 E
Yaoshizhen	107	30.11 N	105.30 E
Yaotou	98	36.34 N	114.38 E
Yaotsu	94	35.28 N	137.09 E
Yaotun, Zhg.	89	49.28 N	127.30 E
Yaotun, Zhg.	104	40.59 N	122.18 E
Yaotutun	104	42.06 N	123.29 E
Yaoundé	152	3.52 N	11.31 E
Yaowan	98	34.12 N	118.03 E
Yaowangmiao	98	40.47 N	120.10 E
Yaoxian	102	34.56 N	108.53 E
Yaoya ≏	236	13.28 N	84.14 W
Yao Yai, Ko I	110	8.00 N	98.35 E
Yaozhan	89	52.53 N	125.13 E
Yap I	174q	9.31 N	138.06 E
Yapacaní	248	16.45 S	64.18 W
Yapacani ≏	248	16.00 S	64.25 W
Yapakopra	164	4.24 S	135.05 E
Yapehe	152	0.13 S	24.27 E
Yapei (Tamale Port)	150	9.10 N	1.10 W
Yapen, Pulau I	164	1.45 S	136.15 E
Yapen, Selat ⵡ	164	1.30 S	136.10 E
Yapero	164	4.59 S	137.11 E
Yapeyú	252	29.28 S	56.49 W
Yaphank	207	40.50 N	72.56 W
Yappar ≏	166	18.22 S	141.16 E
Yapraklı	130	40.46 N	33.47 E
Yap Trench ✦[1]	14	8.30 N	138.00 E
Yaqian	100	26.38 N	114.30 E
Yaʿqūb	140	12.29 N	25.11 E
Yaque del Norte ≏	238	19.51 N	71.41 W
Yaqui ≏	232	27.37 N	110.39 W
Yaquina ≏	202	44.37 N	124.04 W
Yara	240p	20.16 N	76.57 W
Yaracuy □[3]	246	10.20 N	69.10 W
Yaraka	166	24.53 S	144.04 E
Yaratuar	164	2.58 S	134.40 E
Yarbasan	130	38.59 N	28.49 E
Yarcombe	42	50.52 N	3.05 W
Yardea	166	32.23 S	135.32 E
Yardımcı	130	37.00 N	38.59 E
Yardımcı Burnu ▸	130	36.13 N	30.25 E
Yardley	208	40.14 N	74.50 W
Yardville	208	40.10 N	74.39 W
Yare ≏	42	52.35 N	1.44 E
Yarí ≏	246	0.23 S	72.16 W
Yariga-take ∧	94	36.20 N	137.39 E
Yārik	123	32.06 N	70.47 E
Yarīm	144	14.29 N	44.21 E
Yaring	110	6.52 N	101.22 E
Yaritagua	246	10.05 N	69.08 W
Yarkand → Shache	120	38.25 N	77.16 E
Yarkand → Yarkant ≏	90	40.28 N	80.52 E
Yarkant (Yarkand) ≏	90	40.28 N	80.52 E
Yarker	212	44.23 N	76.46 W
Yarkhūn ≏	123	36.17 N	72.30 E
Yarlarweelor	162	25.35 S	117.59 E
Yarle Lakes ⊜	162	30.15 S	131.27 E
Yarloop	168a	32.57 S	115.54 E
Yarlung → Brahmaputra ≏	120	24.02 N	90.59 E
Yarma	130	37.49 N	32.54 E
Yarmouth, N.S., Can.	186	43.50 N	66.07 W
Yarmouth, Eng., U.K.	42	50.42 N	1.29 W
Yarmouth, Me., U.S.	188	43.48 N	70.11 W
Yarmouth, Ma., U.S.	207	41.42 N	70.13 W
Yarmouth → Great Yarmouth	42	52.37 N	1.44 E
Yarmu	164	4.18 S	142.17 E
Yarmūk, Nahr al- ≏	132	32.38 N	35.34 E
Yarra ≏	169	37.51 S	144.54 E
Yarra Bend Park ♦	274b	37.48 S	145.01 E
Yarra Glen	169	37.40 S	145.23 E
Yarragon	169	38.12 S	146.04 E
Yarra Junction	169	37.47 S	145.37 E
Yarraloola	162	21.34 S	115.52 E
Yarram	166	38.33 S	146.41 E
Yarraman	171a	26.50 S	151.59 E
Yarrangobilly	171b	35.39 S	148.28 E
Yarrangobilly ≏	171b	35.48 N	148.23 E
Yarrangobilly Caves ⩡[5]	171b	35.44 S	148.29 E
Yarraville	274b	37.49 S	144.53 E
Yarrawonga	166	36.01 S	146.00 E
Yarra Yarra Lakes ⊜	162	29.40 S	115.47 E
Yarrow, B.C., Can.	224	49.05 N	122.02 W
Yarrow, Scot., U.K.	46	55.32 N	3.01 W
Yarrow ≏	262	53.40 N	2.49 W
Yarrowee ≏	169	37.48 S	143.56 E
Yarrow Point	224	47.39 N	122.13 W
Yarrow Reservoir ⊜[1]	262	53.38 N	2.34 W
Yarrow Water ≏	46	55.34 N	2.51 W
Yarrunga, Lake ⊜[1]	170	34.45 S	150.20 E
Yarty ≏	42	50.47 N	3.01 W
Yarumal	246	6.58 N	75.24 W
Yasa	152	3.42 S	21.24 E
Yasaka, Nihon	96	35.39 N	135.07 E
Yasaka, Nihon	96	34.46 N	132.04 E
Yasa-Lokwa	152	5.15 S	19.24 E
Yasato	94	36.14 N	140.12 E
Yasawa I	175g	16.47 S	177.31 E
Yasawa Group II	175g	17.00 S	177.23 E
Yasendu	152	0.27 N	24.20 E
Yashanjie	106	30.51 N	119.03 E
Yashbum	144	14.19 N	46.56 E
Yashi	150	12.23 N	7.54 E
Yashikera	150	9.46 N	3.28 E
Ya-shima I	96	33.44 N	132.09 E
Yashima ♦	96	34.23 N	134.08 E
Yashio	268	35.49 N	139.51 E
Yashiro	96	34.55 N	134.58 E
Yashiro-jima I	96	33.55 N	132.15 E
Yāsīn	123	36.21 N	73.19 E
Yasku	146	12.20 N	12.30 E
Yasothon	110	15.45 N	104.08 E
Yass	166	34.50 S	148.55 E
Yassıada I	267b	40.51 N	29.00 E
Yassy → Iași	38	47.10 N	27.35 E
Yasu, Nihon	94	35.03 N	136.01 E
Yasu, Nihon	96	33.32 N	133.45 E
Yasuda	96	33.26 N	133.59 E
Yasugi	96	35.26 N	133.15 E
Yāsūj	128	30.40 N	51.36 E
Yasun Burnu ▸	130	41.08 N	37.41 E
Yasuní ≏	246	0.56 S	75.23 W
Yasuni, Parque Nacional ♦	246	0.50 S	76.15 W
Yasuoka	94	35.22 N	137.50 E
Yasuura	96	34.17 N	132.45 E
Yasuzuka	94	37.08 N	138.28 E
Yata	248	13.20 S	66.35 W
Yata ≏, Bol.	248	10.29 S	65.26 W
Yata ≏, Centraf.	146	10.23 N	22.45 E
Yatabe	94	36.02 N	140.04 E
Yatağan	130	37.20 N	28.09 E
Yatakala	150	14.48 N	0.22 E
Yata-Ngaya, Réserve de Faune de la ◆[4]	146	9.15 N	23.30 W
Yātar	132	33.09 N	35.20 E
Yatate-yama ∧	92	34.10 N	129.10 E
Yaté	175f	22.10 S	166.57 E
Yates □[6]	210	42.40 N	77.03 W
Yatesboro	214	40.48 N	79.20 W
Yates Center	198	37.52 N	95.43 W
Yates City	190	40.46 N	90.00 W
Yathata Island I	175g	17.15 S	179.32 W
Yathkyed Lake ⊜	176	62.41 N	98.00 W
Yating	102	25.03 N	106.05 E
Yatomi	94	35.06 N	136.43 E
Yatsuga-take ∧	94	35.59 N	138.23 E
Yatsuga-take-chūshin-kōgen-kokutei-kōen ♦	94	36.03 N	138.20 E
Yatsuka	96	35.17 N	133.42 E
Yatsuo	94	36.34 N	137.08 E
Yatsushiro	96	32.30 N	130.36 E
Yatsushiro-kai c	92	32.20 N	130.25 E
Yattah	132	31.27 N	35.05 E
Yatta Plateau ⋆[1]	154	2.00 S	38.00 E
Yatton	42	51.24 N	2.49 W
Yatuá ≏	246	1.43 N	66.30 W
Yatusiro → Yatsushiro	96	32.30 N	130.36 E
Yauca	248	15.40 S	74.32 W
Yauca ≏	248	15.41 S	74.31 W
Yauco	240m	18.02 N	66.51 W
Yauco ≏	240m	17.59 N	66.48 W
Yauco, Embalse de ⊜[1]	240m	18.07 N	66.50 W
Yauli	248	11.41 S	76.06 W
Yaundé → Yaoundé	152	3.52 N	11.31 E
Yaupi	246	2.59 S	77.50 W
Yauri	248	14.47 S	71.29 W
Yautepec	234	18.53 N	99.04 W
Yau Tong	271d	22.18 N	114.13 E
Yauyos	248	12.24 S	75.57 W
Yāval	120	21.10 N	75.42 E
Yavarí (Javari) ≏	242	4.21 S	70.02 W
Yavarí Mirim ≏	246	4.31 S	71.44 W
Yavaros	232	26.42 N	109.31 W
Yavatmāl	122	20.24 N	78.08 E
Yaven Yaven Creek ≏	171b	35.06 S	147.46 E
Yavero ≏	248	12.06 S	72.57 W
Yavi	130	39.48 N	36.13 E
Yaví, Cerro ∧	246	5.32 N	65.59 W
Yavita	246	2.55 N	67.26 W
Yaviza	246	8.11 N	77.41 W
Yavne	132	31.53 N	34.45 E
Yavuzeli	130	37.20 N	37.33 E
Yavuzkemal	130	40.43 N	38.21 E
Yaw ≏	110	20.55 N	94.49 E
Yawahara	268	35.59 N	140.01 E
Yawata, Nihon	96	34.52 N	135.42 E
Yawata, Nihon	268	35.32 N	140.08 E
Yawatahama	96	33.27 N	132.24 E
Yawata → Kitakyūshū	96	33.53 N	130.50 E
Yaxchilán ⊥	232	16.54 N	90.58 W
Yaxi	102	27.32 N	106.45 E
Yaxian	110	18.20 N	109.30 E
Yaxigang	106	31.23 N	119.10 E
Yaxley	42	52.31 N	0.16 W
Yayama	152	1.16 S	23.07 E
Yayladağı	130	35.56 N	36.01 E
Yayladere	130	39.14 N	40.03 E
Yaylak	130	37.23 N	38.20 E
Yayouta	150	8.11 N	8.30 W
Yayuan	98	41.47 N	126.11 E
Yazd	128	31.53 N	54.25 E
Yazd □[4]	128	32.00 N	54.30 E
Yazi	98	37.04 N	121.17 E
Yazichangcun	104	41.16 N	122.26 E
Yazıhan	130	38.36 N	38.11 E
Yazmān	123	29.08 N	71.45 E
Yazoo ≏	194	32.22 N	91.00 W
Yazoo City	194	32.51 N	90.24 W
Ybbs ≏	61	48.10 N	15.06 E
Ybbs an der Donau	61	48.11 N	15.05 E
Ybbsitz	61	47.56 N	14.53 E
Ybor City	220	27.57 N	82.27 W
Ybycuí	252	26.01 S	57.03 W
Yding Skovhøj ∧[2]	41	56.00 N	9.48 E
Ydstebøhavn	26	59.08 N	5.15 E
Ydžid Parma ⋆	24	63.06 N	58.15 E
Ye	110	15.15 N	97.51 E
Yea	169	37.13 S	145.26 E
Yea ≏	169	37.11 S	145.23 E
Yeading ◆[8]	260	51.32 N	0.24 W
Yeadon, Eng., U.K.	44	53.52 N	1.41 W
Yeadon, Pa., U.S.	285	39.56 N	75.15 W
Yeagertown	208	40.38 N	77.34 W
Yealm ≏	42	50.18 N	4.03 W
Yealmpton	42	50.21 N	3.59 W
Yebawgyi	110	18.40 N	94.35 E
Yebbi-Bou	146	20.58 N	18.04 E
Yébigué, Enneri V	146	22.04 N	17.49 E
Yèbles	261	48.38 N	2.46 E
Yebyu	110	14.15 N	98.12 E
Yecapixtla	234	18.53 N	98.52 W
Yecheng	120	37.54 N	77.25 E
Yech'ŏn	98	36.40 N	128.26 E
Yecla	34	38.37 N	1.07 W
Yécora	232	28.20 N	108.58 W
Yedashe	110	19.09 N	96.21 E
Yedi Göller Milli Parkı ♦	130	40.50 N	31.30 E
Yedikule ◆[8]	267b	40.59 N	28.55 E
Yedikule ⊥	267b	40.59 N	28.55 E
Yédinga, Ouadi V	146	15.46 N	20.05 E
Yedseram ≏	146	12.30 N	14.05 E
Yeed	144	4.33 N	43.02 E
Yeeda	162	17.36 S	123.39 E
Yeelanna	166	34.09 S	135.45 E
Yeelirrie	162	27.17 S	120.06 E
Yeernuozha Hu ⊜	120	32.30 N	89.30 E
Yegor'yevsk → Jegorjevsk	82	55.23 N	39.02 E
Yegros	252	26.24 S	56.25 W
Yegua Creek ≏	222	30.23 N	96.18 W
Yeguas, Punta ▸	258	34.55 S	56.19 W
Yeguas, Río de las ≏	34	37.22 N	4.45 W
Yehliu	269d	25.12 N	121.41 E
Yehliu Chia ▸	269d	25.13 N	121.42 E
Yehud	132	32.02 N	34.53 E
Yei	154	4.05 N	30.40 E
Yei ≏	140	6.15 N	30.13 E
Yeji, Ghana	150	8.13 N	0.39 W
Yeji, Zhg.	100	31.52 N	115.55 E
Yekaterinburg → Jekaterinburg	86	56.51 N	60.36 E
Yekaterinodar → Krasnodar	78	45.02 N	39.00 E
Yekaterinoslav → Dnepropetrovsk	78	48.27 N	34.59 E
Yekokora ≏	152	1.20 N	20.21 E
Yekumbo	152	1.02 S	23.27 E
Ye Kyun I	110	18.37 N	93.47 E
Yela Island I	160	11.21 S	154.09 E
Yelarbon	166	28.34 S	150.45 E
Yelcho, Lago ⊜	254	43.18 S	72.18 W
Yele	150	8.25 N	11.50 W
Yelets → Jelec	76	52.37 N	38.30 E
Yélimané	150	15.08 N	10.34 W
Yell I	46a	60.36 N	1.06 W
Yellandu	122	17.36 N	80.20 E
Yellow ≏, U.S.	194	30.33 N	87.00 W
Yellow ≏, In., U.S.	216	41.16 N	86.50 W
Yellow ≏, Ia., U.S.	190	43.05 N	91.11 W
Yellow ≏, Wi., U.S.	190	44.58 N	91.18 W
Yellow ≏, Wi., U.S.	190	43.59 N	90.03 W
Yellow ≏, Wi., U.S.	190	46.01 N	92.22 W
Yellow Breeches Creek ≏	208	40.13 N	76.51 W
Yellow Creek ≏, U.S.	194	33.34 N	88.20 W
Yellow Creek ≏, Co., U.S.	200	40.10 N	108.24 W
Yellow Creek ≏, Oh., U.S.	214	40.34 N	80.40 W
Yellow Creek ≏, Tn., U.S.	194	36.26 N	87.34 W
Yellow Creek, North Fork ≏	214	40.33 N	80.42 W
Yellow Creek State Park ♦	214	40.35 N	79.02 W
Yellowdine	162	31.18 S	119.39 E
Yellow Grass	184	49.49 N	104.08 W
Yellowhead Pass)(	182	52.53 N	118.28 W
Yellow House Draw V	196	33.35 N	101.50 W
Yellow → Huang ≏	90	37.32 N	118.19 E
Yellowknife	176	62.27 N	114.21 W
Yellowknife ≏	176	62.31 N	114.19 W
Yellow Lake ⊜	212	44.20 N	75.36 W
Yellow Medicine ≏	198	44.44 N	95.25 W
Yellow Mountain ∧	166	32.30 S	146.51 E
Yellow Sea ⊤[2]	90	36.00 N	123.00 E
Yellow Springs	218	39.48 N	83.53 W
Yellowstone ≏	178	47.58 N	103.59 W
Yellowstone, Clarks Fork ≏	202	45.39 N	108.43 W
Yellowstone Falls ⊥	202	44.43 N	110.30 W
Yellowstone Lake ⊜	202	44.25 N	110.22 W
Yellowstone National Park	202	44.59 N	110.42 W
Yellowstone National Park ♦	202	44.30 N	110.35 W
Yellowtail Dam ◆[6]	202	45.12 N	107.57 W
Yell Sound ⵡ	46a	60.32 N	1.15 W
Yellville	194	36.13 N	92.41 W
Yelm	224	46.56 N	122.36 W
Yelma	162	26.30 S	121.40 E
Yelvertoft	166	20.13 S	138.53 E
Yelverton	42	50.30 N	4.05 W
Yelwa	150	10.51 N	4.46 E
Yema ≏	102	41.25 N	95.10 E
Yemadu	86	43.36 N	81.50 E
Yemagong	124	29.28 N	89.06 E
Yemaotai	104	42.20 N	122.53 E
Yemassee	192	32.41 N	80.51 W
Yematan	102	34.40 N	98.16 E
Yemen (Al-Yaman) □[1], Asia	118	15.00 N	47.00 E
Yemen (Al-Yaman) □[1], Asia	144	15.00 N	47.00 E
Yemen, People's Democratic Republic of → Yemen □[1]	144	15.00 N	47.00 E
Yemen, República Popular Democrática del → Yemen □[1]	144	15.00 N	47.00 E
Yémen, République démocratique populaire du → Yemen □[1]	144	15.00 N	47.00 E
Yen	152	2.27 N	12.41 E
Yenagoa	150	4.55 N	6.19 E
Yenakiyevo → Jenakijevo	83	48.14 N	38.13 E
Yenangyaung	110	20.28 N	94.52 E
Yenanma	110	19.46 N	94.48 E
Yen Bai	110	21.42 N	104.52 E
Yen Chau	110	21.03 N	104.18 E
Yench'eng → Yancheng	100	33.24 N	120.09 E
Yenchi → Yanji	98	42.57 N	129.32 E
Yenda	166	34.15 S	146.11 E
Yende Millimou	150	8.53 N	10.11 W
Yendéré	150	10.12 N	4.58 W
Yendi	150	9.26 N	0.01 W
Ye-ngan	110	21.09 N	96.27 E
Yenge ≏	152	0.55 S	20.40 E
Yengema	150	8.43 N	11.10 W
Yengisar	85	38.57 N	76.03 E
Yengo	152	0.22 N	15.29 E
Yengo, Mount ∧	170	32.59 S	150.51 E
Yéni	150	13.26 N	2.59 E
Yeniçağa	130	40.46 N	32.02 E
Yenice, Tür.	130	39.45 N	28.55 E
Yenice, Tür.	130	41.11 N	32.19 E
Yenice, Tür.	130	39.55 N	27.18 E
Yenice, Tür.	130	36.59 N	35.03 E
Yenice ≏	130	41.35 N	32.03 E
Yenicekale	130	37.37 N	36.37 E
Yeniceoba	130	38.53 N	32.48 E
Yenierenköy	130	35.32 N	34.11 E
Yenifoça	130	38.44 N	26.51 E
Yenikapı ◆[8]	267b	41.00 N	28.57 E
Yeniköy	130	39.46 N	28.00 E
Yeniköy ◆[8]	267b	40.59 N	28.53 E
Yenimehmetli	130	39.26 N	32.10 E
Yenipazar, Tür.	130	37.48 N	28.12 E
Yenipazar, Tür.	130	40.11 N	30.31 E
Yenişehir	130	40.16 N	29.39 E
Yenisey → Jenisej ≏	72	71.50 N	82.40 E
Yennadon	224	49.14 N	122.34 W
Yenne	62	45.42 N	5.46 E
Yennora	274a	33.52 S	150.58 E
Yenshuichen	100	23.20 N	120.16 E
Yentna ≏	180	61.34 N	150.28 W
Yeo ≏, Eng., U.K.	42	51.02 N	2.49 W
Yeo ≏, Eng., U.K.	42	51.01 N	3.50 W
Yeo ≏, Eng., U.K.	42	50.45 N	3.36 W
Yeola	122	20.02 N	74.29 E
Yeo Lake ⊜	162	28.04 S	124.23 E
Yeoman	216	40.40 N	86.43 W
Yeoval	166	32.45 S	148.40 E
Yeovil	42	50.57 N	2.39 W
Yeoville ◆[8]	273d	26.12 S	28.04 E
Yepachic	232	28.26 N	108.23 W
Yeppoon	166	23.08 S	150.45 E
Yerba Buena, Montaña ∧	236	14.05 N	87.26 W
Yerba Buena Island I	282	37.48 N	122.22 W
Yères ≏	50	50.02 N	1.19 E
Yerevan → Jerevan	84	40.11 N	44.30 E
Yerilla	162	29.28 S	121.49 E
Yering	274b	37.41 S	145.23 E
Yerington	226	38.59 N	119.09 W
Yerington Indian Reservation ◆[4]	226	39.05 N	119.12 W
Yerkes	285	40.10 N	75.27 W
Yerkes Astronomical Observatory ʋ[3]	216	42.34 N	88.34 W
Yerkesik	130	37.07 N	28.17 E
Yerköy	130	39.38 N	34.29 E
Yerlisu	130	40.46 N	26.39 E
Yermasóyia	130	34.43 N	33.05 E
Yermenonville	261	48.33 N	1.37 E
Yermo	204	34.54 N	116.49 W
Yeroḥam	132	31.00 N	34.55 E
Yerolimín	38	36.28 N	22.24 E
Yèrre ≏	50	48.01 N	1.16 E
Yerres	50	48.43 N	2.30 E
Yerres ≏	50	48.43 N	2.27 E
Yerseke	52	51.29 N	4.02 E
Yerupaja, Nevado ∧	248	10.16 S	76.54 W
Yerushalayim (Al-Quds) (Jerusalem)	132	31.46 N	35.14 E
Yerushalayim □[5]	132	31.45 N	35.00 E
Yerville	50	49.40 N	0.54 E
Yesa, Embalse de ⊜[1]	34	42.36 N	1.09 W
Yesan	98	36.41 N	126.50 E
Yeshenpu	104	40.51 N	122.32 E
Yeshiva University ʋ[2]	276	40.51 N	73.55 W
Yeshvi	272c	18.55 N	73.03 E
Yeşil ≏	130	41.24 N	36.35 E
Yeşilçonlu	130	40.13 N	28.06 E
Yeşildere	130	37.09 N	33.31 E
Yeşilhisar	130	38.21 N	35.06 E
Yeşilkent	130	36.59 N	36.10 E
Yeşilköy	130	40.57 N	28.49 E
Yeşilköy Burnu ▸	267b	40.57 N	28.50 E
Yeşilova	130	37.30 N	29.46 E
Yeşiltepe	130	37.12 N	33.02 E
Yeşilyazı	130	39.20 N	39.05 E
Yeşilyurt	130	38.18 N	38.15 E
Yeso	196	34.26 N	104.36 W
Yeso Creek ≏	196	34.13 N	104.15 W
Yesŏng-gang ≏	98	37.53 N	126.24 E
Yessentuki → Jessentuki	84	44.03 N	42.51 E
Yeste	34	38.22 N	2.18 W
Yes Tor ∧	42	50.42 N	4.00 W
Yesud HaMaʿala	132	33.03 N	35.36 E
Yetholme	170	33.27 S	149.49 E
Yetman	166	28.54 S	150.46 E
Yetminster	42	50.53 N	2.33 W
Yetsou I	152	2.08 S	10.42 E
Yettem	226	36.29 N	119.16 W
Yetti	164	3.00 S	140.53 E
Yetti ◆[1]	148	26.10 N	7.50 W
Ye-u	110	22.46 N	95.26 E
Yeu, Île d' I	32	46.42 N	2.20 W
Yevpatoriya → Jevpatorija	78	45.12 N	33.22 E
Yexian, Zhg.	98	37.13 N	119.54 E
Yexian, Zhg.	100	33.37 N	113.21 E
Yexie	106	30.56 N	121.19 E
Yextla	234	18.00 N	100.06 W

Symbols in the index entries represent the broad categories identified in the key at the right. Symbols with superior numbers (⋆[1]) identify subcategories (see complete key on page *I · 1*).

Symbole im Register stellen die rechts im Schlüssel erklärten Kategorien dar. Symbole mit hochgestellten Ziffern (⋆[1]) bezeichnen Unterabteilungen einer Kategorie (vgl. vollständiger Schlüssel auf Seite *I · 1*).

Los símbolos incluidos en el texto del índice representan las grandes categorías identificadas con la clave a la derecha. Los símbolos con numeros en su parte superior (⋆[1]) identifican las subcategorías (véase la clave completa en la página *I · 1*).

Les symboles de l'index représentent les catégories indiquées dans la légende à droite. Les symboles suivis d'un indice (⋆[1]) représentent des sous-catégories (voir légende complète à la page *I · 1*).

Os símbolos incluídos no texto do índice representam as grandes categorias identificadas com a chave à direita. Os símbolos com números em sua parte superior (⋆[1]) identificam as subcategorias (veja-se a chave completa à página *I · 1*).

English	Deutsch	Español	Français	Português
∧ Mountain	Berg	Montaña	Montagne	Montanha
⋆ Mountains	Gebirge	Montañas	Montagnes	Montanhas
)(Pass	Paß	Paso	Col	Passo
V Valley, Canyon	Tal, Cañon	Valle, Cañón	Vallée, Canyon	Vale, Canhão
≐ Plain	Ebene	Llano	Plaine	Planície
▸ Cape	Kap	Cabo	Cap	Cabo
I Island	Insel	Isla	Île	Ilha
II Islands	Inseln	Islas	Îles	Ilhas
♦ Other Topographic Features	Andere Topographische Objekte	Otros Elementos Topográficos	Autres données topographiques	Outros acidentes topográficos

ESPAÑOL — Nombre / Página / Lat.°′ / Long.°′ W = Oeste
FRANÇAIS — Nom / Page / Lat.°′ / Long.°′ W = Ouest
PORTUGUÊS — Nome / Página / Lat.°′ / Long.°′ W = Oeste

Yeysk
→ Jejsk 78 46.42 N 38.16 E
Yeyuan 98 36.22 N 118.27 E
Yeywa 110 21.41 N 96.24 E
Yezd
→ Yazd 128 31.53 N 54.25 E
Yeze Hu ⊜ 106 31.08 N 120.40 E
Yezhuang 105 39.10 N 116.18 E
Yezhuhe 105 40.53 N 118.13 E
Ygatimí 252 24.05 S 55.30 W
Ygnacio Canal ≅ 282 37.55 N 122.03 W
Yguazú ≃ 252 25.20 S 55.00 W
Yhú 252 24.59 S 55.59 W
Yi 98 42.08 N 118.48 E
Yi ≃, Ur. 252 33.07 S 57.08 W
Yi ≃, Zhg. 98 34.07 N 118.15 E
Yi ≃, Zhg. 100 34.10 N 112.10 E
Yi ≃, Zhg. 105 39.14 N 115.46 E
Yi'an 89 47.55 N 125.20 E
Yiannitsá 38 40.48 N 22.25 E
Yibao 106 30.25 N 119.53 E
Yibin (Ipin) 107 28.47 N 104.38 E
Yibug Caka ⊜ 120 33.00 N 86.25 E
Yibutan 107 28.54 N 104.40 E
Yicanghe 100 32.47 N 120.43 E
Yichang (Ichang) 102 30.42 N 111.17 E
Yicheng, Zhg. 98 36.48 N 114.07 E
Yicheng, Zhg. 98 34.46 N 117.37 E
Yicheng, Zhg. 102 31.43 N 112.07 E
Yichexun 102 26.50 N 103.28 E
Yichuan, Zhg. 100 34.26 N 112.24 E
Yichuan, Zhg. 102 36.04 N 110.06 E
Yichun, Zhg. 90 47.42 N 128.55 E
Yichun, Zhg. 100 27.50 N 114.23 E
Yicun 105 38.57 N 115.37 E
Yidan 89 43.24 N 125.25 E
Yidie 102 37.08 N 110.30 E
Yidu, Zhg. 98 36.41 N 118.28 E
Yidu, Zhg. 102 30.22 N 111.22 E
Yidun 102 29.56 N 99.22 E
Yiewsley ✦[8] 260 51.31 N 0.28 W
Yifag 144 12.02 N 37.44 E
Yifeng, Zhg. 100 33.19 N 113.47 E
Yifeng, Zhg. 100 28.26 N 114.46 E
Yigaolou 106 30.56 N 120.20 E
Yığılca 130 40.58 N 31.27 E
Yigitler 130 39.52 N 26.37 E
Yigou 98 35.51 N 114.20 E
Yihe 100 23.50 N 114.53 E
Yihechang 107 30.23 N 106.24 E
Yi He Yuan (Summer Palace) ⚜ 105 40.00 N 116.16 E
Yihezhuang, Zhg. 98 37.53 N 118.23 E
Yihezhuang, Zhg. 104 41.15 N 122.57 E
Yihuang 100 27.34 N 116.10 E
Yihuang ≃ 100 28.05 N 116.18 E
Yijiangzhen 100 30.55 N 118.28 E
Yijiawan 100 27.58 N 113.01 E
Yijiazi 104 42.29 N 122.41 E
Yijingpu 105 40.08 N 117.47 E
Yijinqiao 100 30.54 N 117.12 E
Yijun 102 35.24 N 109.00 E
Yikengaolu 102 42.17 N 98.19 E
Yikou 100 26.45 N 117.00 E
Yilaha 89 48.50 N 125.10 E
Yilan 89 46.19 N 129.34 E
Yilaxi 89 43.47 N 126.08 E
Yıldız Dağı ∧ 130 40.08 N 36.56 E
Yıldız Dağları ∧ 38 41.50 N 27.30 E
Yıldızeli 130 39.52 N 36.38 E
Yilehuli Shan ∧ 89 51.20 N 124.30 E
Yili 107 30.45 N 105.58 E
Yiliang, Zhg. 102 24.58 N 103.07 E
Yiliang, Zhg. 102 27.35 N 104.01 E
Yiliekede 89 48.51 N 121.37 E
Yilin 100 33.36 N 119.37 E
Yiling 100 32.30 N 119.46 E
Yiliping 120 37.55 N 93.30 E
Yilliminning 162 32.54 S 117.22 E
Yilong, Zhg. 89 47.28 N 125.23 E
Yilong, Zhg. 102 25.20 N 103.14 E
Yilong, Zhg. 102 31.34 N 106.19 E
Yimachi 104 42.11 N 122.15 E
Yimatu 104 41.55 N 121.25 E
Yimen, Zhg. 100 33.39 N 116.02 E
Yimen, Zhg. 102 24.43 N 102.10 E
Yimuhe 89 52.45 N 120.07 E
Yin ≃, Mya. 110 20.04 N 95.01 E
Yin ≃, Zhg. 98 42.19 N 118.37 E
Yinan (Jiehu) 98 35.37 N 118.30 E
Yinbaing 110 17.25 N 97.46 E
Yinchuan 102 38.30 N 106.18 E
Yindarlgooda, Lake ⊜ 162 30.45 S 121.55 E
Yindi 154 1.35 N 27.40 E
Yinfang 105 39.07 N 114.52 E
Ying ≃ 100 32.30 N 116.32 E
Yingcheng 100 30.57 N 113.32 E
Yingchengzi, Zhg. 89 44.08 N 125.56 E
Yingchengzi, Zhg. 98 38.58 N 121.23 E
Yingchengzi, Zhg. 104 41.50 N 124.04 E
Yingchengzi, Zhg. 104 42.22 N 124.14 E
Yingde 100 24.12 N 113.24 E
Yingen 102 41.09 N 104.45 E
Yingfang 105 40.14 N 116.17 E
Yinggehai 110 18.31 N 108.44 E
Yinghe 100 32.16 N 116.31 E
Yingjin ≃ 98 42.20 N 119.19 E
Yingkoshih ≃ 269d 25.06 N 121.43 E
Yingkou, Zhg. 104 40.40 N 122.14 E
Yingkou (Dashiqiao), Zhg. 104 40.38 N 122.30 E
Yingpan, Zhg. 102 25.48 N 106.18 E
Yingpan, Zhg. 102 24.44 N 99.38 E
Yingpanjie 102 25.27 N 98.24 E
Yingqiao 100 33.58 N 113.11 E
Yingshan, Zhg. 100 30.45 N 115.39 E
Yingshan, Zhg. 100 31.38 N 113.50 E
Yingshan, Zhg. 102 31.08 N 106.31 E
Yingshang 100 32.38 N 116.15 E
Yingshouyingzi, Zhg. 105 40.33 N 117.38 E
Yingshouyingzi, Zhg. 105 40.49 N 117.55 E
Yingtan 100 28.14 N 117.00 E
Yingtaogou 104 42.08 N 121.57 E
Yingtaoyuan 104 41.10 N 123.05 E
Yingtian 100 28.50 N 112.56 E
Yingxiangjie 107 29.24 N 105.11 E
Yingxianpu 104 41.20 N 121.31 E
Yining (Kuldja) 86 43.54 N 81.21 E
Yinjiadai 106 32.03 N 120.07 E
Yinjiang 102 28.02 N 108.28 E
Yinjiawopeng 104 42.34 N 121.01 E
Yinkeng 100 26.14 N 115.34 E
Yinliu 105 39.59 N 117.23 E
Yinmabin 110 22.05 N 94.54 E
Yinmahe 89 43.58 N 126.15 E
Yinmatu ≃ 98 40.57 N 117.43 E
Yinnietharra 162 24.39 S 116.11 E
Yinnyein 110 16.48 N 97.23 E
Yinong 102 30.19 N 101.01 E
Yinping 98 34.15 N 118.39 E
Yinqiaotou 106 31.52 N 119.13 E
Yin Shan ∧ 102 41.48 N 109.00 E
Yinshanzhen 107 29.41 N 104.58 E
Yinwogou 98 41.55 N 117.55 E
Yinxian 100 29.50 N 121.38 E
Yinxiang 106 31.55 N 118.49 E
Yinxinjiali 100 32.07 N 116.32 E
Yinyangjie 104 42.16 N 121.23 E
Yinyuan 100 33.40 N 118.17 E
Yinzhan'ao 100 23.33 N 113.07 E
Yio Chu Kang 271c 1.23 N 103.51 E
Yi'ong 102 30.17 N 94.51 E
Yi'ong ≃ 120 29.56 N 95.10 E
Yi Pak 271d 22.19 N 114.00 E
Yipinchang 107 29.17 N 106.34 E
Yipinglang 102 25.11 N 101.51 E
Yiqian 100 26.34 N 116.11 E
Yirba Muda 144 6.12 N 38.42 E
Yirga Alem 144 6.52 N 38.22 E
Yirkā 132 32.57 N 35.13 E
Yirol 140 6.33 N 30.30 E
Yirrkala 164 12.14 S 136.56 E
Yirshi 89 47.20 N 119.45 E
Yirwa 140 7.47 N 27.15 E
Yisaduo 102 28.50 N 96.44 E
Yishan, Zhg. 100 27.32 N 120.32 E
Yishan, Zhg. 102 24.40 N 108.35 E
Yishui 98 35.50 N 118.41 E
Yishun 271c 1.26 N 103.50 E
Yisikan 89 49.09 N 124.47 E
Yisra'el
→ Israel □[1] 132 31.30 N 35.00 E
Yisuhe 100 27.46 N 112.54 E
Yitajing 102 42.32 N 94.12 E
Yitang, Zhg. 98 35.10 N 118.16 E
Yitang, Zhg. 100 31.06 N 113.42 E
Yíthion 38 36.45 N 22.34 E
Yiting 100 29.15 N 119.57 E
Yitm, Wādī al- ∨ 132 29.34 N 35.01 E
Yitong 89 43.40 N 125.17 E
Yitong ≃ 89 42.40 N 125.58 E
Yitulihe 89 50.38 N 121.34 E
Yiwu, Zhg. 100 29.18 N 120.04 E
Yiwu, Zhg. 102 43.15 N 94.45 E
Yiwu, Zhg. 102 22.00 N 101.28 E
Yiwulü Shan ∧ 104 41.42 N 121.42 E
Yixi 100 29.55 N 117.56 E
Yixian, Zhg. 100 30.00 N 117.55 E
Yixian, Zhg. 104 41.32 N 121.15 E
Yixian, Zhg. 105 39.21 N 115.29 E
Yixiken 89 52.57 N 125.40 E
Yixing 106 31.22 N 119.50 E
Yixingbu 105 39.12 N 117.12 E
Yixingchang 107 30.37 N 106.38 E
Yixu 100 26.02 N 119.16 E
Yixun ≃ 98 41.16 N 117.35 E
Yiyang, Zhg. 100 28.23 N 117.25 E
Yiyang, Zhg. 102 28.36 N 112.20 E
Yiyang, Zhg. 102 34.30 N 112.10 E
Yiyuan (Nanma) 98 36.11 N 118.08 E
Yiyuankou 98 40.10 N 119.35 E
Yizhang 100 25.26 N 112.56 E
Yizheng 106 32.16 N 119.12 E
Yizikong 102 25.38 N 104.28 E
Yizre'ël 132 32.33 N 35.20 E
Yizre'ël, 'Ēmeq ≅ 132 32.36 N 35.14 E
Ylakiai 76 56.17 N 21.51 E
Yläne 26 60.53 N 22.55 E
Ylihärmä 26 63.09 N 22.47 E
Yli-Kitka ⊜ 26 66.08 N 28.30 E
Ylimarkku
→ Övermark 26 62.38 N 21.30 E
Ylistaro 26 62.57 N 22.31 E
Ylivieska 26 64.05 N 24.33 E
Ylöjärvi 26 61.33 N 23.36 E
Ymeray 261 48.31 N 1.42 E
Ymir 182 49.17 N 117.13 W
Yndin 24 61.24 N 55.10 E
Yngaren ⊜ 40 58.52 N 16.35 E
Yngen ⊜ 40 59.44 N 14.18 E
Yntaly 86 48.58 N 77.55 E
Ynykčanskij 74 60.15 N 137.43 E
Yoakum 222 29.17 N 97.09 W
Yobi, Indon. 164 1.43 S 138.04 E
Yobi, Indon. 164 1.42 S 138.27 E
Yockanookany ≃ 194 32.40 N 89.40 W
Yoco 246 10.36 N 62.24 W
Yocona ≃ 194 34.11 N 90.11 W
Yōda 268 35.24 N 139.25 E
Yoder 216 40.55 N 85.10 W
Yodo ≃ 96 34.41 N 135.25 E
Yodoe 96 35.28 N 133.26 E
Yodogawa ✦[8] 270 34.42 N 135.28 E
Yoe 208 39.55 N 76.39 W
Yōga ✦[8] 268 35.38 N 139.38 E
Yogo 94 35.33 N 136.12 E
Yog Point ≻ 116 14.06 N 124.12 E
Yoğuntaş 130 41.50 N 27.04 E
Yogyakarta 115a 7.48 S 110.22 E
Yogyakarta □[4] 115a 7.45 S 110.30 E
Yoho National Park ♦ 182 51.26 N 116.30 W
Yoichi 92a 43.12 N 140.41 E
Yojoa, Lago de ⊜ 236 14.50 N 88.00 W
Yōju 98 37.18 N 127.37 E
Yōka 96 35.24 N 134.46 E
Yokadouma 152 3.31 N 15.03 E
Yōkaichi 94 35.06 N 136.12 E
Yōkaichiba 94 35.42 N 140.33 E
Yokamba 152 0.01 N 22.17 E
Yokana 152 0.45 N 22.53 E
Yokawa 96 34.52 N 135.06 E
Yokchi-do I 98 34.38 N 128.15 E
Yokkaichi, Nihon 94 34.58 N 136.37 E
Yokkaichi, Nihon 96 33.32 N 131.20 E
Yoko 152 2.36 S 20.06 E
Yokoate-jima I 93b 28.48 N 129.00 E
Yokohama, Nihon 94 35.27 N 139.39 E
Yokohama, Nihon 268 35.27 N 139.39 E
Yokohama-kō c 268 35.27 N 139.39 E
Yokohama National University ⚜[2] 268 35.25 N 139.36 E
Yokohama Park Baseball Ground ♦ 268 35.26 N 139.39 E
Yokolo 152 0.36 S 23.04 E
Yokonuma 268 35.58 N 139.27 E
Yokoshiba 94 35.40 N 140.28 E
Yokosuka 94 35.18 N 139.40 E
Yokosuka District Naval Headquarters ■ 268 35.17 N 139.39 E
Yokosuka-kō c 268 35.18 N 139.39 E
Yokosuka Naval Base ■ 94 35.18 N 139.41 E
Yokota, Nihon 96 35.10 N 133.06 E
Yokota, Nihon 268 35.23 N 140.01 E
Yokota, Nihon 270 34.40 N 135.55 E
Yokota Air Base ■ 268 35.45 N 139.21 E
Yokote 92 39.18 N 140.34 E
Yola 146 9.12 N 12.29 E
Yolaina, Serranías de ∧ 236 11.40 N 84.20 W
Yolboyu 130 37.55 N 40.00 E
Yolo 226 38.44 N 121.48 W
Yolo □[6] 226 38.41 N 121.46 W
Yolo ≃ 273b 4.19 S 15.20 E
Yolo Bypass ≅ 226 38.25 N 121.40 W
Yolombó, Col. 246 6.36 N 75.01 W
Yolombo, Zaïre 152 1.32 S 23.15 E
Yolonga 152 1.36 S 23.21 E
Yom ≃ 110 15.52 N 100.16 E
Yombi 152 1.26 S 10.37 E
Yomou 150 7.34 N 9.16 W
Yona 174p 13.25 N 144.47 E
Yonabaru 174m 26.12 N 127.45 E
Yonago 96 35.26 N 133.20 E
Yonaguni 175d 24.27 N 122.57 E
Yonaguni-shima I 175d 24.27 N 123.00 E
Yonaha-dake ∧[2] 174m 26.43 N 128.13 E
Yŏnan 98 37.55 N 126.10 E
Yoncali 130 41.16 N 32.16 E
Yoncalla 202 43.35 N 123.16 W
Yonch'ŏn ✦[8] 271b 37.38 N 127.04 E
Yoneshiro ≃ 92 40.13 N 140.01 E
Yonezawa 92 37.55 N 140.07 E
Yŏngam 98 34.48 N 126.40 E
Yongamp'o 98 39.55 N 124.24 E
Yŏngan, C.M.I.K. 98 41.15 N 129.30 E
Yong'an, Zhg. 100 25.58 N 117.22 E
Yongan, Zhg. 100 30.44 N 106.16 E
Yong'an, Zhg. 107 29.13 N 104.46 E
Yong'an, Zhg. 100 28.52 N 121.04 E
Yong'an ≃ 105 39.43 N 117.26 E
Yonganbao 98 40.15 N 119.52 E
Yong'anchang 107 30.24 N 103.58 E
Yong'anshi 100 28.13 N 113.19 E
Yongbei 102 26.41 N 100.42 E
Yongbyŏn 98 39.49 N 125.48 E
Yongchang, Zhg. 100 29.13 N 119.20 E
Yongchang, Zhg. 102 38.17 N 101.59 E
Yongchangzhen 106 31.42 N 121.44 E
Yongcheng 100 33.58 N 116.21 E
Yongch'ŏn, C.M.I.K. 98 39.59 N 124.28 E
Yŏngch'ŏn, Taehan 98 38.07 N 127.05 E
Yŏngch'ŏn, Taehan 98 35.58 N 128.56 E
Yongch'on-dong 98 41.18 N 129.40 E
Yongchuan 107 29.21 N 105.54 E
Yongchun 100 25.21 N 118.21 E
Yongdeng 102 36.48 N 103.14 E
Yongdian 98 40.34 N 124.48 E
Yongding 100 24.46 N 116.43 E
Yongding ≃, Zhg. 100 24.42 N 116.34 E
Yongding ≃, Zhg. 105 39.20 N 117.04 E
Yongdingmen Station ✦[5] 271a 39.52 N 116.23 E
Yŏngdŏk 98 36.26 N 129.23 E
Yŏngdong 98 36.10 N 127.48 E
Yŏngdŭngp'o ✦[8] 271b 37.32 N 126.54 E
Yongfeng, Zhg. 100 29.44 N 116.49 E
Yongfeng, Zhg. 100 27.19 N 115.24 E
Yongfengchang 107 30.33 N 105.05 E
Yongfu 100 25.05 N 117.20 E
Yonggang 98 38.52 N 125.21 E
Yŏnggangonch'ŏn 98 38.53 N 125.14 E
Yonggi 98 36.24 N 128.24 E
Yongguzhai 98 34.05 N 116.50 E
Yonghe 100 28.18 N 113.51 E
Yongheshi 100 28.18 N 113.51 E
Yonghung 98 39.32 N 127.13 E
Yŏnghŭng-do I 98 37.16 N 126.28 E
Yŏnghŭng-man c 98 39.15 N 127.30 E
Yongi 89 43.40 N 126.30 E
Yŏngil-man c 98 36.05 N 129.26 E
Yongji 102 34.51 N 110.29 E
Yongjia, Zhg. 100 28.11 N 120.42 E
Yongjia, Zhg. 100 29.34 N 106.01 E
Yongjing 107 37.30 N 126.31 E
Yŏngjong-do I 98 37.30 N 126.31 E
Yŏngju 98 36.50 N 128.37 E
Yongkang, Zhg. 100 32.32 N 117.24 E
Yongkang, Zhg. 100 28.53 N 120.02 E
Yongkou 100 26.16 N 118.19 E
Yongle, Zhg. 89 45.45 N 125.12 E
Yongle, Zhg. 105 39.32 N 115.59 E
Yongle ≃ 100 26.54 N 113.12 E
Yongledian 105 39.43 N 116.46 E
Yonglong 106 31.34 N 121.48 E
Yonglonghe 100 30.46 N 112.48 E
Yŏngmi-dong 98 39.40 N 125.31 E
Yongnian (Linmingguan) 98 36.47 N 114.30 E
Yongnianchang 107 29.08 N 104.51 E
Yongning, Zhg. 100 24.43 N 118.42 E
Yongning, Zhg. 102 22.42 N 108.50 E
Yongning, Zhg. 102 38.20 N 106.17 E
Yongning, Zhg. 102 27.47 N 100.38 E
Yongningcheng 105 40.34 N 116.11 E
Yongningjian 98 35.56 N 112.48 E
Yong Peng 114 2.01 N 103.04 E
Yongping, Zhg. 100 28.12 N 117.45 E
Yongping, Zhg. 102 25.28 N 99.33 E
Yongqing, Zhg. 105 39.19 N 116.29 E
Yongqing, Zhg. 107 30.00 N 105.27 E
Yongquan 100 28.46 N 121.19 E
Yongren 102 26.08 N 101.40 E
Yŏngsan-gang ≃ 98 34.54 N 126.32 E
Yŏngsan-ni 98 38.52 N 125.56 E
Yŏngsanp'o 98 34.58 N 126.44 E
Yongshan 102 28.15 N 103.24 E
Yongshanqiao 100 29.06 N 117.17 E
Yongsheng 102 26.42 N 100.42 E
Yongshou 102 34.43 N 108.05 E
Yongshun 102 28.57 N 109.41 E
Yongshunchang 107 30.06 N 105.26 E
Yongtai 100 25.54 N 118.58 E
Yŏngwŏl 98 37.12 N 128.28 E
Yŏngwŏn 98 39.49 N 126.32 E
Yŏngwŏn-ni 98 40.41 N 128.42 E
Yongxin, Zhg. 100 26.56 N 114.18 E
Yongxin, Zhg. 107 28.59 N 106.32 E
Yongxing, Zhg. 98 40.11 N 123.52 E
Yongxing, Zhg. 100 26.08 N 113.06 E
Yongxing, Zhg. 102 39.08 N 110.31 E
Yongxing, Zhg. 106 31.56 N 120.55 E
Yongxing, Zhg. 107 30.10 N 105.13 E
Yongxing, Zhg. 107 30.34 N 105.35 E
Yongxingchang, Zhg. 107 29.02 N 104.34 E
Yongxingchang, Zhg. 107 29.37 N 106.23 E
Yongxingchang, Zhg. 107 30.20 N 103.44 E
Yongxiu 100 29.04 N 115.48 E
Yŏngyang, Taehan 98 36.40 N 129.07 E
Yŏngyang, Taehan 98 26.57 N 114.46 E
Yŏngyu 98 39.18 N 125.34 E
Yongyŏn-ni 98 40.44 N 126.09 E
Yongzhai 100 27.59 N 115.26 E
Yŏnhŭi-ri 271b 37.33 N 126.41 E
Yŏnhwa-san ∧ 98 40.46 N 127.23 E
Yonibana 150 8.26 N 12.14 W
Yonkers 210 40.55 N 73.53 W
Yonkers Raceway ♦ 276 40.55 N 73.52 W
Yonne □[5] 50 47.55 N 3.45 E
Yonne ≃ 32 48.23 N 2.58 E
Yono 94 35.53 N 139.38 E
Yŏnp'yŏng-yŏlto II 98 37.38 N 125.40 E
Yonsei University ⚜[2] 271b 37.34 N 126.56 E
Yoo, Enneri ∨ 146 19.24 N 16.38 E
Yoontow 144 0.08 S 42.34 E
Yopal 246 5.21 N 72.23 W
Yop'o-ri 98 38.50 N 125.33 E
Yopurga 85 39.15 N 76.45 E
Yoqne'am 132 32.39 N 35.07 E
Yorba Linda 228 33.53 N 117.48 W
Yorii 94 36.07 N 139.12 E
Yorishima 96 34.29 N 133.35 E
York, Austl. 168a 31.53 S 116.46 E
York, On., Can. 212 43.41 N 79.29 W
York, S.L. 150 8.17 N 13.11 W
York, Eng., U.K. 44 53.58 N 1.05 W
York, Al., U.S. 194 32.29 N 88.17 W
York, In., U.S. 216 41.41 N 84.49 W
York, Ne., U.S. 198 40.52 N 97.35 W
York, N.Y., U.S. 210 42.52 N 77.53 W
York, N.D., U.S. 198 48.18 N 99.34 W
York, Pa., U.S. 208 39.57 N 76.43 W
York, S.C., U.S. 192 34.59 N 81.14 W
York □[6], On., Can. 212 43.55 N 79.25 W
York □[6], Pa., U.S. 208 39.58 N 76.44 W
York □[6], Va., U.S. 208 37.15 N 76.40 W
York ≃, On., Can. 212 45.20 N 77.35 W
York ≃, P.Q., Can. 186 48.49 N 64.34 W
York ≃, Va., U.S. 208 37.15 N 76.23 W
York, Cape ≻ 164 10.42 S 142.31 E
York, Kap ≻ 16 75.53 N 66.12 W
York, Vale of ∨ 44 54.10 N 1.20 W
Yorkana 208 39.59 N 76.35 W
York Center, Il., U.S. 278 41.52 N 87.59 W
York Center, Oh., U.S. 216 40.24 N 83.27 W
Yorkdale Centre ✦[9] 275b 43.44 N 79.27 W
Yorke Peninsula ≻[1] 166 35.00 S 137.30 E
Yorketown 168b 35.02 S 137.36 E
York Factory 184 57.00 N 92.18 W
Yorkfield 278 41.52 N 87.56 W
York Haven 208 40.06 N 76.42 W
Yorklyn 285 39.48 N 75.40 W
York Minster ⚜[1] 44 53.57 N 1.04 W
York New Salem 208 39.54 N 76.47 W
Yorkshire, N.Y., U.S. 210 42.31 N 78.28 W
Yorkshire, Pa., U.S. 208 39.59 N 76.41 W
Yorkshire, Va., U.S. 208 38.47 N 77.27 W
Yorkshire Dales National Park ♦ 44 54.13 N 2.10 W
Yorkshire Wolds ∧[2] 44 54.00 N 0.40 W
York Sound ⊔ 160 14.50 S 125.05 E
York Springs 208 40.00 N 77.07 W
Yorkton 184 51.13 N 102.28 W
Yorktown, In., U.S. 218 40.10 N 85.29 W
Yorktown, Tx., U.S. 222 28.58 N 97.30 W
Yorktown, Va., U.S. 208 37.14 N 76.30 W
Yorktown ✦[9] 278 41.51 N 88.01 W
Yorktown Battlefield ⊥ 208 37.13 N 76.31 W
Yorktown Heights 210 41.16 N 73.46 W
Yorktown Manor 207 41.38 N 71.26 W
York Township Airport ⊠ 278 41.51 N 88.02 W
York University ⚜[2] 275b 43.47 N 79.30 W
Yorkville, Il., U.S. 216 41.38 N 88.26 W
Yorkville, Mi., U.S. 216 42.23 N 85.24 W
Yorkville, N.Y., U.S. 210 43.06 N 75.16 W
Yorkville, Oh., U.S. 214 40.09 N 80.42 W
Yorkville ✦[8] 275b 43.40 N 79.24 W
Yoro, Hond. 236 15.09 N 87.07 W
Yoro, Mali 150 14.17 N 2.08 W
Yōrō, Nihon 94 35.18 N 136.33 E
Yoro □[5] 236 15.15 N 87.15 W
Yōrō ≃ 94 35.32 N 140.04 E
Yoroi-zaki ≻ 94 34.24 N 136.55 E
Yoron-jima I 93b 27.02 N 128.26 E
Yōrō-no-taki ⊾ 94 35.17 N 136.32 E
Yorosso 150 12.22 N 4.47 W
Yosemite Creek ≃ 226 37.44 N 119.36 W
Yosemite National Park 226 37.45 N 119.35 W
Yosemite National Park ♦ 226 37.51 N 119.33 W
Yoshida, Nihon 94 36.02 N 139.02 E
Yoshida, Nihon 94 34.46 N 138.15 E
Yoshida, Nihon 96 33.16 N 132.33 E
Yoshida, Nihon 96 34.40 N 132.42 E
Yoshida, Nihon 96 35.10 N 132.51 E
Yoshida ≃ 96 34.03 N 131.02 E
Yoshii, Nihon 94 36.15 N 138.59 E
Yoshii, Nihon 96 33.20 N 130.45 E
Yoshii, Nihon 96 34.38 N 133.26 E
Yoshii, Nihon 96 34.55 N 134.06 E
Yoshii, Nihon 270 34.53 N 135.01 E
Yoshii ≃ 96 34.36 N 134.03 E
Yoshikawa, Nihon 94 37.13 N 138.25 E
Yoshikawa, Nihon 94 35.53 N 139.51 E
Yoshikawa, Nihon 270 34.55 N 135.28 E
Yoshimi 94 36.02 N 139.27 E
Yoshino, Nihon 96 34.21 N 135.51 E
Yoshino, Nihon 96 34.06 N 134.23 E
Yoshino ≃, Nihon 94 34.22 N 135.40 E
Yoshino ≃, Nihon 96 34.05 N 134.36 E
Yoshinodani 94 36.17 N 136.39 E
Yoshino-Kumano-kokuritsu-kōen ♦ 92 34.07 N 135.55 E
Yoshioka 94 36.27 N 139.01 E
Yoshiumi 96 34.09 N 133.03 E
Yoshiwa 96 34.29 N 132.09 E
Yoshkar-Ola
→ Joškar-Ola 80 56.38 N 47.52 E
Yosowilangun 115a 8.15 S 113.18 E
Yos Sudarso, Pulau (Frederik Hendrikeiland) I 164 7.50 S 138.30 E
Yŏsu 98 34.46 N 127.44 E
Yotausito 248 16.03 S 63.03 W
Yōtei-zan ∧ 92a 42.49 N 140.49 E
Yotsukaidō 94 35.39 N 140.10 E
Yotvata 132 29.53 N 35.03 E
You ≃, Zhg. 100 28.46 N 110.10 E
You ≃, Zhg. 102 22.50 N 108.06 E
You ≃, Zhg. 102 28.27 N 110.24 E
Youanmi 162 28.37 S 118.49 E
Youbou 224 48.53 N 124.13 W
Youcheng 100 29.14 N 116.48 E
Youfang 106 32.09 N 119.50 E
Youghal 48 51.57 N 7.51 W
Youghal Bay c 48 51.52 N 7.50 W
Youghiogheny ≃ 214 40.22 N 79.52 W
Yougoslavie
→ Yugoslavia □[1] 22 44.00 N 21.00 E
Youhe 100 32.19 N 113.50 E
Youjidong 104 42.12 N 121.07 E
Youkounkoun 150 12.32 N 13.08 W
Youlan 100 28.34 N 116.10 E
Young, Austl. 166 34.19 S 148.18 E
Young, Sk., Can. 184 51.47 N 105.46 W
Young, Az., U.S. 200 34.06 N 110.57 W
Young, Ur. 252 32.41 S 57.38 W
Young America 216 40.34 N 86.20 W
Younghusband Peninsula ≻[1] 166 36.00 S 139.30 E
Youngs ≃ 224 46.10 N 123.49 W
Youngs, Lake ⊜ 224 47.25 N 122.07 W
Youngs Creek 218 38.29 N 86.30 W
Youngs Creek 219 39.21 N 91.51 W
Youngs Rock I[2] 174e 25.03 S 130.07 W
Youngstown, Ab., Can. 182 51.32 N 111.13 W
Youngstown, Fl., U.S. 192 30.21 N 85.26 W
Youngstown, N.Y., U.S. 210 43.14 N 79.03 W
Youngstown, Oh., U.S. 214 41.05 N 80.38 W
Youngstown Municipal Airport ⊠ 214 41.15 N 80.41 W
Youngsville, La., U.S. 194 30.05 N 91.59 W
Youngsville, N.Y., U.S. 210 41.48 N 74.54 W
Youngsville, N.C., U.S. 192 36.01 N 78.28 W
Youngsville, Pa., U.S. 214 41.51 N 79.19 W
Youngwood 214 40.14 N 79.34 W
Youngwood Park ♦ 279b 40.14 N 79.36 W
Younthville 226 38.24 N 122.22 W
Youshashan 120 38.08 N 91.10 E
Youssoufia 148 32.16 N 8.33 W
Youtingpu 107 29.26 N 105.45 E
Youville ✦[8] 275a 45.33 N 73.39 W
Youxi, Zhg. 100 28.45 N 121.06 E
Youxi, Zhg. 100 26.11 N 118.09 E
Youxi, Zhg. 100 29.12 N 106.09 E
Youxian 100 27.00 N 113.21 E
Youxizhen 107 30.35 N 106.13 E
Youyang 102 28.58 N 108.41 E
Youyi 89 46.44 N 131.44 E
Youyu 102 40.09 N 112.32 E
Youzhagou 106 31.04 N 118.46 E
Youzhuang 105 40.09 N 115.42 E
Yoweragabbie 162 28.13 S 117.39 E
Yŏyang-ni 98 37.30 N 128.43 E
Yozgat 130 39.50 N 34.48 E
Yozgat □[4] 130 39.40 N 35.10 E
Ypacaraí 252 25.23 S 57.16 W
Ypané ≃ 252 23.29 S 57.19 W
Ypé Jhú 252 23.54 S 55.20 W
Yport 50 49.44 N 0.19 E
Ypres
→ Ieper 50 50.51 N 2.53 E
Ypsilanti 216 42.14 N 83.36 W
Ypsilanti East 216 42.15 N 83.35 W
Yreka 204 41.44 N 122.38 W
Yrgajty ≃ 85 43.03 N 74.43 E
Yron ≃ 56 49.10 N 5.52 E
Ysabel Channel ⊔ 164 2.00 S 150.00 E
Ysbyty Ystwyth 42 52.20 N 3.48 W
Yser (IJzer) ≃ 50 51.09 N 2.43 E
Yssieux, Ruisseau l' ≃ 261 49.09 N 2.22 E
Yssingeaux 46 45.09 N 4.07 E
Ystad 41 55.25 N 13.49 E
Ystalyfera 42 51.47 N 3.47 W
Ysterfontein 152? 33.22 S 18.09 E
Ystrad ≃ 44 53.13 N 3.20 W
Ystrad Aeron 42 52.11 N 4.11 W
Ystradfellte 42 51.48 N 3.34 W
Ystradgynlais 42 51.47 N 3.45 W
Ystwyth ≃ 42 52.24 N 4.05 W
Ytambey ≃ 252 24.46 S 54.24 W
Ythan ≃ 46 57.18 N 2.00 W
Ytre Arna 26 60.26 N 5.30 E
Ytterhärnäs 40 60.39 N 17.21 E
Ytterhogdal 26 62.12 N 14.51 E
Yttermalung 40 60.35 N 13.50 E
Ytterseiö 40 59.23 N 17.15 E
Yttre Hållsfjärden c[2] 40 59.08 N 17.40 E
Yttygran, ostrov I 180 64.36 N 172.40 W
Yü 96 34.02 N 132.13 E
Yu ≃ 102 23.24 N 110.05 E
Yu, Pulau I 164 0.03 S 129.36 E
Yu'alliq, Jabal ∧ 140 30.22 N 33.31 E
Yuam ≃ 110 17.47 N 97.45 E
Yuan ≃, Zhg. 100 28.09 N 115.34 E
Yuan ≃, Zhg. 102 28.58 N 111.49 E
Yuan'an 102 31.04 N 111.26 E
Yuanao 100 26.29 N 119.48 E
Yuanbachang 107 29.44 N 105.27 E
Yuanhua 106 30.25 N 120.46 E
Yuanjiang 102 23.34 N 102.03 E
Yuankeng 100 26.48 N 117.44 E
Yüanli 100 24.27 N 120.39 E
Yuanlin 100 23.58 N 120.34 E
Yuanling 102 28.20 N 110.16 E
Yuanmou 102 25.38 N 101.54 E
Yuanqiao
→ Red ≃ 110 20.17 N 106.34 E
Yuanshancun 106 31.08 N 120.20 E
Yuanshi 98 37.45 N 114.32 E
Yuantan, Zhg. 100 32.47 N 112.53 E
Yuantan, Zhg. 100 23.39 N 113.12 E
Yuantongsi 107 30.13 N 104.15 E
Yuantouzhu 106 31.32 N 120.14 E
Yuanxiang 98 34.14 N 115.19 E
Yuanxiangzhen 106 31.39 N 119.15 E
Yuanxing 107 30.36 N 104.59 E
Yuanyang (Yangwu), Zhg. 98 35.04 N 113.57 E
Yuanyang, Zhg. 102 23.12 N 102.52 E
Yuanyangpu 107 30.10 N 105.15 E
Yuanyangqiao 107 29.41 N 106.33 E
Yuasa 96 34.02 N 135.11 E
Yuat ≃ 164 4.25 S 143.55 E
Yuba 102 29.27 N 97.42 E
Yuba □[6] 226 39.16 N 121.17 W
Yuba ≃ 226 39.07 N 121.36 W
Yuba City 226 39.08 N 121.36 W
Yubara 96 35.12 N 133.45 E
Yubara-chosuichi ⊜ 96 35.13 N 133.43 E
Yūbari 92a 43.04 N 141.59 E
Yūbari-sanchi ∧ 92a 43.15 N 142.20 E
Yubdo 144 9.00 N 35.22 E
Yūbetsu 92a 44.14 N 143.37 E
Yūbetsu ≃ 92a 44.14 N 143.37 E
Yucaipa 228 34.02 N 117.02 W
Yucatán □[3] 232 20.50 N 89.00 W
Yucatán, Canal de ⊔ 238 21.45 N 85.45 W
Yucatan Peninsula (Península de Yucatán) ≻[1] 232 19.30 N 89.00 W
Yucca 200 34.52 N 114.08 W
Yucca Lake ⊜ 204 36.59 N 116.01 W
Yucca Valley 204 34.07 N 116.35 W
Yuchaozhuang 105 39.35 N 117.50 E
Yucheng, Zhg. 98 36.56 N 116.39 E
Yucheng, Zhg. 100 30.32 N 120.51 E
Yuci 102 37.45 N 112.41 E
Yuda 92 39.20 N 140.50 E
Yudaokou 98 42.14 N 116.48 E
Yudi Shan ∧ 89 52.17 N 121.52 E
Yudong 106 32.02 N 121.22 E
Yudu 100 25.59 N 115.24 E
Yue ≃ 107 28.50 N 104.21 E
Yuebo 107 29.03 N 104.12 E
Yuecheng 100 32.39 N 114.49 E
Yuechi 107 30.33 N 106.26 E
Yuejiatun 104 41.10 N 120.43 E
Yuejiawopeng 104 41.35 N 122.20 E
Yuekou 100 30.32 N 113.06 E
Yuelai 106 31.56 N 120.53 E
Yuelaichang, Zhg. 107 29.44 N 106.32 E
Yuelaichang, Zhg. 107 28.53 N 106.22 E
Yuemenpu 107 30.28 N 106.34 E
Yuendumu 162 22.16 S 131.49 E
Yuendumu Aboriginal Reserve ✦[4] 162 22.20 S 131.47 E
Yuen Long 271d 22.26 N 114.02 E
Yuepu 106 31.25 N 121.26 E
Yueqing 100 28.08 N 120.58 E
Yuewang 106 31.33 N 121.29 E
Yuexi, Zhg. 100 30.50 N 116.24 E
Yuexi, Zhg. 102 28.42 N 102.28 E
Yueyang 100 29.23 N 113.06 E
Yuezi 100 24.54 N 115.02 E
Yufa 105 39.31 N 116.19 E
Yufeng 107 30.37 N 105.11 E
Yufu-dake ∧ 96 33.17 N 131.24 E
Yufuin 96 33.15 N 131.22 E
Yugan 100 28.41 N 116.41 E
Yugawara 94 35.09 N 139.04 E
Yuge 96 34.15 N 133.12 E
Yugoslavia (Jugoslavija) □[1], Europe 22 44.00 N 21.00 E
Yugoslavia (Jugoslavija) □[1], Europe 38 44.00 N 21.00 E
Yugou 100 33.42 N 118.55 E
Yuguan 98 39.56 N 119.22 E
Yuguo 104 41.52 N 123.15 E
Yuhang (Linping) 106 30.25 N 120.18 E
Yuhebu 102 38.01 N 109.27 E
Yuhu 100 27.53 N 120.08 E
Yuhuaizhuang 105 39.24 N 117.40 E
Yuhuan 100 28.10 N 121.12 E
Yuhuang Ding ∧ 98 36.16 N 117.06 E
Yui 94 35.06 N 138.34 E
Yuin 162 27.58 S 116.02 E
Yujiachang 107 29.57 N 104.04 E
Yujiacun 106 31.45 N 121.48 E
Yujiang 100 28.11 N 116.47 E
Yujiaqiao 106 31.30 N 119.25 E
Yujiawan 86 44.32 N 86.45 E
Yukarıbey 130 39.15 N 27.06 E
Yukarıdudullu ✦[8] 267b 41.02 N 29.09 E
Yuke 98 37.58 N 115.39 E
Yūki, Nihon 94 36.18 N 139.53 E
Yuki, Nihon 96 34.29 N 132.16 E
Yuki, Nihon 96 34.46 N 133.17 E
Yuki, Nihon 96 33.46 N 134.31 E
Yukon, Ok., U.S. 196 35.30 N 97.45 W
Yukon, Pa., U.S. 214 40.13 N 79.41 W
Yukon □[4], Can. 176 64.00 N 135.00 W
Yukon □[4], Can. 180 64.00 N 135.00 W
Yukon ≃ 180 62.33 N 163.59 W
Yukon Flats ⊞ 180 66.30 N 146.00 W
Yukou 98 41.17 N 117.00 E
Yukuhashi 96 33.44 N 130.59 E
Yulan 210 41.31 N 74.56 W
Yulao 100 23.31 N 111.46 E
Yulara 162 25.14 S 131.04 E
Yule ≃ 162 20.41 S 118.17 E
Yule Bay c 9 70.44 S 166.40 E
Yule Island I 164 8.50 S 146.30 E
Yuli, Nig. 146 9.42 N 10.17 E
Yüli, T'aiwan 100 23.20 N 121.18 E
Yuli, Zhg. 98 37.00 N 121.25 E
Yuliang 100 29.52 N 118.30 E
Yuliangpu 89 43.26 N 121.55 E
Yulin, Zhg. 102 38.20 N 109.29 E
Yulin, Zhg. 102 22.36 N 110.09 E
Yulin, Zhg. 110 18.16 N 109.32 E
Yulincun 106 40.12 N 116.42 E
Yul-li 98 38.52 N 126.13 E
Yulong 107 29.58 N 104.22 E
Yuma, Az., U.S. 200 32.43 N 114.37 W
Yuma, Co., U.S. 198 40.08 N 102.43 W
Yuma, Bahía de c 238 18.21 N 68.35 W
Yuma Marine Corps Air Station ■ 200 32.40 N 114.38 W
Yuma Proving Ground ■ 204 33.05 N 114.25 W
Yumare 246 10.37 N 68.41 W
Yumbel 252 37.08 S 72.32 W
Yumbi, Zaïre 152 1.53 S 16.32 E
Yumbi, Zaïre 154 1.14 S 26.14 E
Yumbo 246 3.35 N 76.28 W
Yumen (Laojunmiao) 102 39.56 N 97.51 E
Yumenzhen 102 40.17 N 97.07 E
Yumesaki 96 34.58 N 134.42 E
Yumezaki ≃ 96 34.47 N 134.39 E
Yumin 86 46.02 N 82.37 E
Yumurtalık 130 36.49 N 35.45 E
Yun ≃ 100 30.43 N 114.04 E
Yuna, Austl. 162 28.20 S 115.00 E
Yuna, Nihon 174m 26.46 N 128.12 E
Yuna ≃ 238 19.12 N 69.37 W
Yunak 130 38.49 N 31.45 E
Yunan (Ducheng) 102 23.11 N 111.29 E
Yunaska Island I 180 52.40 N 170.50 W
Yuncao 100 31.26 N 118.04 E
Yuncheng, Zhg. 98 35.35 N 115.54 E
Yuncheng, Zhg. 102 35.00 N 110.59 E
Yundamindra 162 29.07 S 122.02 E
Yundanyingzi 104 42.00 N 121.34 E
Yunderup 168a 32.35 S 115.46 E
Yunfeng Ding ∧ 106 30.56 N 120.02 E
Yungas ✦[1] 248 16.00 S 67.45 W
Yungay, Chile 252 37.07 S 72.01 W
Yungay, Perú 248 9.09 S 77.44 W
Yungchia
→ Wenzhou 100 28.01 N 120.39 E
Yungchi
→ Jilin 89 43.51 N 126.33 E
Yungho 269d 25.01 N 121.31 E
Yungning
→ Nanning 102 22.48 N 108.20 E
Yung Shue Wan 271d 22.14 N 114.06 E
Yunhe 100 28.06 N 119.34 E
Yunhe
→ Peixian 98 34.21 N 117.59 E
Yunjin 107 29.06 N 105.40 E
Yunkai Dashan ∧ 102 22.30 N 111.00 E
Yun Ling ∧ 102 27.20 N 99.20 E
Yunlong, Zhg. 102 25.50 N 99.17 E
Yunlong, Zhg. 107 30.31 N 104.46 E
Yunluchang 107 29.45 N 105.57 E
Yunmeng 100 31.02 N 113.41 E
Yunmenling 100 25.15 N 115.49 E
Yunmenzhen 107 30.06 N 106.20 E
Yunnan □[4] 102 24.00 N 101.00 E
Yunnanfu
→ Kunming 102 25.05 N 102.40 E
Yunotani 94 37.14 N 139.01 E
Yunotsu 96 35.05 N 132.21 E
Yunta 166 32.35 S 139.33 E
Yunting 106 31.53 N 120.19 E
Yunwu Shan ∧ 98 41.07 N 116.34 E
Yunxi, Zhg. 100 29.28 N 113.16 E
Yunxi, Zhg. 102 32.49 N 110.13 E
Yunxian (Yunyang), Zhg. 102 32.49 N 110.49 E
Yunxian, Zhg. 102 24.30 N 100.03 E
Yunxiao 100 24.04 N 117.20 E
Yunyan ≃ 100 34.39 N 119.18 E
Yunyang, Zhg. 100 33.28 N 112.42 E
Yunyang, Zhg. 102 30.58 N 109.05 E
Yunzalin ≃ 110 17.23 N 97.40 E
Yunzhong 100 29.13 N 117.40 E
Yunzhou 98 41.01 N 115.44 E
Yuping 102 27.07 N 108.47 E
Yuqi 106 31.43 N 120.11 E
Yuqia 102 38.07 N 94.35 E
Yuqiangou 104 41.41 N 121.28 E
Yuqiao Shuiku ⊜[1] 105 40.02 N 117.33 E
Yuqing 102 27.05 N 107.44 E
Yura, Nihon 96 33.57 N 135.07 E
Yura, Perú 248 16.11 S 71.40 W
Yura ≃ 96 35.31 N 135.17 E
Yurano-hana ≻ 96 33.01 N 132.23 E
Yurécuaro 234 20.20 N 102.18 W
Yurga
→ Jurga 86 55.42 N 84.51 E
Yuri-jima I 96 33.51 N 132.32 E
Yurimaguas 248 5.54 S 76.05 W
Yuriria 234 20.12 N 101.09 W
Yuriria, Laguna de ⊜ 234 20.15 N 101.06 W
Yuruarí ≃ 246 6.44 N 61.40 W
Yurubí, Parque Nacional ♦ 246 10.25 N 68.42 W
Yürük 130 40.56 N 27.04 E
Yurumanguí ≃ 246 3.27 N 77.21 W
Yurungkax ≃ 120 37.00 N 79.55 E
Yuryev
→ Tartu 76 58.23 N 26.43 E
Yusala, Laguna ⊜ 248 14.05 S 67.12 W
Yuşa Tepesi ∧[2] 267b 41.09 N 29.05 E
Yuscarán 236 13.55 N 86.51 W
Yushan, Zhg. 100 26.54 N 118.36 E
Yushan, Zhg. 100 28.41 N 118.15 E
Yushan, Zhg. 100 33.19 N 113.41 E
Yü Shan ∧, T'aiwan 100 23.28 N 120.57 E
Yu Shan ∧, Zhg. 100 26.06 N 115.20 E
Yushanzhen 102 29.28 N 108.19 E
Yushu, Zhg. 89 44.46 N 126.34 E
Yushu (Jiegu), Zhg. 102 33.01 N 97.00 E
Yushugou 86 44.07 N 87.05 E
Yushulinzi, Zhg. 98 41.30 N 119.07 E
Yushulinzi, Zhg. 98 40.59 N 125.57 E
Yushupu 104 41.10 N 122.08 E
Yushutai, Zhg. 89 43.30 N 124.17 E
Yushutai, Zhg. 104 41.42 N 123.26 E
Yushuwan 105 40.04 N 115.35 E
Yusichang 107 29.14 N 105.25 E
Yūsofābād ✦[8] 267d 35.44 N 51.25 E
Yuste, Monasterio de ⚜ 34 40.08 N 5.45 W
Yūsuf, Bahr ≅ 142 29.18 N 30.50 E
Yusufeli 130 40.50 N 41.33 E
Yusuhara 96 33.23 N 132.55 E
Yusuhara ≃ 96 33.11 N 132.58 E
Yutai (Guting) 98 35.02 N 116.40 E
Yutian, Zhg. 100 28.27 N 114.36 E
Yutian, Zhg. 105 39.53 N 117.45 E
Yutian, Zhg. 120 36.51 N 81.40 E
Yuting 100 29.50 N 117.57 E
Yūtō 94 34.42 N 137.38 E
Yutou 100 28.36 N 118.30 E
Yuty 252 26.32 S 56.18 W
Yutz 56 49.21 N 6.11 E
Yützu
→ Yuci 102 37.45 N 112.41 E
Yūwan-dake ∧ 93b 28.18 N 129.21 E
Yuwangcheng 100 31.31 N 114.29 E
Yüweng Tao I 100 23.36 N 119.30 E
Yuwŏnjin 98 40.18 N 126.36 E
Yuxi, Zhg. 100 25.36 N 119.18 E
Yuxi, Zhg. 102 24.23 N 102.34 E
Yuxi, Zhg. 106 32.03 N 121.11 E
Yuxi, Zhg. 107 30.19 N 105.47 E
Yuxian, Zhg. 98 39.48 N 114.33 E
Yuxian, Zhg. 100 34.10 N 113.28 E
Yuxian, Zhg. 102 38.09 N 113.26 E
Yuxiangpu 100 34.27 N 114.57 E
Yuxiangtou 106 31.14 N 120.53 E
Yuxikou 100 31.26 N 118.17 E
Yuyao 100 30.04 N 121.10 E
Yuya-wan c 96 34.23 N 130.56 E
Yuyŏn-ni 98 38.42 N 127.10 E
Yuyuan Tan ⊜ 271a 39.55 N 116.18 E
Yuza 92 39.01 N 139.54 E
Yuzawa, Nihon 92 39.10 N 140.30 E
Yuzawa, Nihon 94 36.56 N 138.49 E
Yuzhno-Sakhalinsk
→ Južno-Sachalinsk 89 46.58 N 142.42 E
Yuzhou
→ Doneck 83 48.00 N 37.48 E
Yuzuruha-san ∧ 96 34.14 N 134.49 E
Yvelines □[5] 50 48.50 N 1.50 E
Yvelines, Forêt des ♦ 261 48.40 N 1.55 E
Yverdon 58 46.47 N 6.39 E
Yvetot 50 49.37 N 0.46 E
Yvette 261 48.43 N 1.55 E
Yvette ≃ 50 48.40 N 2.20 E

Symbol	English	Deutsch	Español	Français	Português
≃	River	Fluß	Río	Rivière	Rio
≅	Canal	Kanal	Canal	Canal	Canal
⊾	Waterfall, Rapids	Wasserfall, Stromschnellen	Cascada, Rápidos	Chute d'eau, Rapides	Cascata, Rápidos
⊔	Strait	Meeresstraße	Estrecho	Détroit	Estreito
c	Bay, Gulf	Bucht, Golf	Bahía, Golfo	Baie, Golfe	Baía, Golfo
⊜	Lake, Lakes	See, Seen	Lago, Lagos	Lac, Lacs	Lago, Lagos
⊞	Swamp	Sumpf	Pantano	Marais	Pântano
⊓	Ice Features, Glacier	Eis- und Gletscherformen	Accidentes Glaciales	Formes glaciaires	Acidentes glaciares
⊼	Other Hydrographic Features	Andere Hydrographische Objekte	Otros Elementos Hidrográficos	Autres données hydrographiques	Outros acidentes hidrográficos
✦	Submarine Features	Untermeerische Objekte	Accidentes Submarinos	Formes de relief sous-marin	Acidentes submarinos
□	Political Unit	Politische Einheit	Unidad Política	Entité politique	Unidade política
⚜	Cultural Institution	Kulturelle Institution	Institución Cultural	Institution culturelle	Instituição cultural
⊥	Historical Site	Historische Stätte	Sitio Histórico	Site historique	Sitio histórico
♦	Recreational Site	Erholungs- und Ferienort	Sitio de Recreo	Centre de loisirs	Area de Lazer
⊠	Airport	Flughafen	Aeropuerto	Aéroport	Aeroporto
■	Military Installation	Militäranlage	Instalación Militar	Installation militaire	Instalação militar
✦	Miscellaneous	Verschiedenes	Misceláneo	Divers	Diversos

Name	Page	Lat.°′	Long.°′
Yvoir	56	50.20 N	4.53 E
Yvoire	58	46.22 N	6.20 E
Yvonand	58	46.48 N	6.45 E
Yvron ≃	50	48.39 N	2.56 E
Ywamun	110	20.31 N	95.25 E
Ywathagyi	110	22.18 N	95.42 E
Ywathit	110	19.10 N	97.30 E
Yxlan I	40	59.38 N	18.52 E
Yxsjöberg	40	60.03 N	14.46 E
Yzeron	62	45.42 N	4.35 E
Yzeure	32	46.34 N	3.21 E
Z			
Za ≃	102	32.00 N	96.55 E
Za, Oued ≃	148	34.34 N	3.03 W
Zaachila	234	16.57 N	96.45 W
Zaaimansdal	158	33.35 S	23.22 E
Zaajatskaja	86	52.53 N	61.35 E
Zaalajskij chrebet ⩘	85	39.20 N	72.30 E
Zaamin	85	39.58 N	68.24 E
Zaanstad	52	52.26 N	4.49 E
Žabaj ≃	86	51.42 N	68.22 E
Zabajkal'sk	88	49.38 N	117.19 E
Žabala ≃	38	45.51 N	26.46 E
Žabalj	38	46.01 N	21.55 E
Žabari	38	44.21 N	21.13 E
Zabarjad, Jazīrat I	140	23.37 N	36.12 E
Žabasak	86	50.21 N	61.40 E
Zāb-e Kūchek → Little Zab ≃	128	35.12 N	43.25 E
Zaberfeld	56	49.03 N	8.55 E
Zabīd	144	14.10 N	43.17 E
Zabīd, Wādī V	144	14.07 N	43.06 E
Žabinka	76	52.12 N	24.01 E
Zabituj	88	53.16 N	102.50 E
Ząbkowice Śląskie	30	50.36 N	16.53 E
Žabljak	38	43.09 N	19.07 E
Zabłudów	30	53.01 N	23.20 E
Žabno	30	50.09 N	20.53 E
Zābol	128	31.02 N	61.30 E
Zābol □4	120	32.00 N	67.15 E
Zābolī	128	27.07 N	61.40 E
Zabolotje, Bela.	76	52.40 N	28.34 E
Zabolotje, Bela.	76	53.56 N	24.46 E
Zabolotje, Ross.	82	56.40 N	38.06 E
Zabolotje, Ross.	82	54.24 N	38.54 E
Zabolotje, Ross.	82	55.32 N	38.12 E
Zabolotje, Ukr.	78	51.38 N	24.15 E
Zabolotov	78	48.29 N	25.16 E
Zaborje, Bela.	76	55.55 N	29.19 E
Zaborje, Ross.	76	54.51 N	32.41 E
Zaborje, Ross.	76	53.06 N	31.42 E
Zaborje, Ross.	76	55.24 N	31.34 E
Zaborje, Ross.	82	55.23 N	37.47 E
Zabory	76	55.58 N	32.17 E
Zabré	150	11.10 N	0.38 W
Zábřeh	30	49.53 N	16.52 E
Zabrze (Hindenburg)	30	50.18 N	18.46 E
Zaburunje	80	46.44 N	50.09 E
Zabyčanje	76	53.25 N	31.52 E
Zabzugu	150	9.17 N	0.22 E
Zacapa	236	14.58 N	89.32 W
Zacapa □5	236	15.00 N	89.30 W
Zacapoaxtla	234	19.53 N	97.35 W
Zacapu	234	19.50 N	101.43 W
Zacata	208	38.07 N	76.47 W
Zacatecas	234	22.47 N	102.35 W
Zacatecas □3	232	23.00 N	103.00 W
Zacatecoluca	236	13.30 N	88.52 W
Zacatepec	234	18.39 N	99.12 W
Zacatlán	234	19.56 N	97.58 W
Zacatongo	234	20.49 N	104.33 W
Začepilovka	78	49.12 N	35.14 E
Zacharias Creek ≃	285	40.11 N	75.23 W
Zacharkovo	265b	55.47 N	37.19 E
Zacharovo, Ross.	76	54.22 N	39.17 E
Zacharovo, Ross.	82	56.31 N	36.44 E
Zacharvan'	24	66.21 N	55.48 E
Zachary	194	30.38 N	91.09 W
Zachidnoje	78	51.29 N	31.15 E
Zachmet	128	37.43 N	62.30 E
Zachožje	265a	59.44 N	30.51 E
Zachrebetnoje	24	69.00 N	36.25 E
Začistje	76	54.24 N	28.45 E
Zacks Bay c	276	40.36 N	73.29 W
Zacoalco de Torres	234	20.14 N	103.35 W
Zacualpa	236	15.05 N	90.50 W
Zacualpan, Méx.	234	21.15 N	105.10 W
Zacualpan, Méx.	234	20.28 N	98.22 W
Zacualtipan	234	20.39 N	98.36 W
Zaculeu ⊥	236	15.21 N	91.29 W
Zadar	36	44.07 N	15.14 E
Zadetkale Kyun I	110	10.08 N	98.12 E
Zadetkyi Kyun I	110	9.58 N	98.13 E
Zadi (Inkisi) ≃	152	4.46 S	14.52 E
Zadní Chodov	60	49.54 N	12.44 E
Zadoi	120	33.10 N	95.05 E
Zadonsk	76	52.23 N	38.57 E
Zadorra ≃	34	42.40 N	2.54 W
Žadovo	78	52.03 N	32.39 E
Zaerap	76	59.18 N	36.37 E
Zafarabad	85	40.11 N	68.51 E
Zafar al-Qadīmah	142	30.58 N	31.37 E
Za'farānah, Bi'r ∓4	142	29.07 N	32.33 E
Za'farānah, Ra's ›	142	29.06 N	32.40 E
Zafarwāl	123	32.21 N	74.54 E
Zafer Burnu ›	130	35.42 N	34.35 E
Zafferana Etnea	70	37.41 N	15.06 E
Zafferano, Capo ›	70	38.06 N	13.30 E
Zafirovo	38	44.00 N	26.50 E
Zafra	34	38.25 N	6.25 W
Žaga	64	46.18 N	13.29 E
Zagabria → Zagreb	36	45.48 N	15.58 E
Żagań	30	51.37 N	15.19 E
Žagare	76	56.21 N	23.15 E
Zagarise	68	39.00 N	16.39 E
Zagarolo	66	41.50 N	12.50 E
Zagazig → Az-Zaqāzīq	142	30.35 N	31.31 E
Zaghouan	148	36.24 N	10.09 E
Zaghouan, Jebel ∧	36	36.21 N	10.08 E
Zagnanado	150	7.16 N	2.21 E
Zagnitkov	78	48.03 N	28.54 E
Zagora	148	30.22 N	5.50 W
Zagora ⩘	36	43.40 N	16.15 E
Zagor'anskij	265b	55.55 N	37.55 E
Zagórów	30	52.11 N	17.55 E
Zagorskij	89	47.19 N	142.28 E
Zagórz	30	49.31 N	22.17 E
Zagreb	36	45.48 N	15.58 E
Zāgros, Kūhhā-ye ⩘	128	33.40 N	47.00 E
Zagros Mountains → Zāgros, Kūhhā-ye ⩘	128	33.40 N	47.00 E
Zagryzovo	83	49.31 N	37.43 E
Žagubica	38	44.13 N	21.48 E
Zagustaj	88	51.58 N	110.45 E
Za'gya ≃	120	31.55 N	88.58 E
Zagyva ≃	30	47.10 N	20.13 E
Zahana	34	35.32 N	0.25 W
Zāhedān	128	29.30 N	60.52 E
Zahīrābād	122	17.41 N	77.37 E
Zahlah	130	33.51 N	35.53 E
Zahna	54	51.54 N	12.47 E
Zahns Airport ⊠	276	40.42 N	73.24 W
Záhony	30	48.25 N	22.11 E
Záhorská Ves	61	48.23 N	16.51 E
Zahrān	144	17.40 N	43.30 E
Zahrensdorf	54	53.45 N	11.40 E
Zaidpur	124	26.50 N	81.20 E
Zaigrajevo	88	51.50 N	108.16 E
Zaijiafangzi	104	41.17 N	122.39 E
Zailijskij-Alatau, chrebet ⩘	85	43.00 N	77.00 E
Žailma, Kaz.	85	43.46 N	69.47 E
Žailma, Kaz.	86	51.32 N	61.37 E
Zaimka	88	58.41 N	100.40 E
Zaimokuza	268	35.18 N	139.33 E
Zainsk	80	55.18 N	52.06 E
Zaire □5	152	7.00 S	13.30 E
Zaire (Zaïre) □1	138	4.00 S	25.00 E
Zaïre → Congo ≃	138	6.04 S	12.24 E
Zaizhuangzi	105	40.02 N	117.43 E
Zaj ≃	80	55.36 N	51.40 E
Zajarsk	88	56.10 N	102.52 E
Zajcevka	83	49.41 N	40.00 E
Zajcevo, Ross.	82	54.08 N	37.26 E
Zajcevo, Ross.	265b	55.39 N	37.11 E
Zajcevo, Ukr.	83	48.24 N	38.02 E
Zajcevo, Ukr.	83	48.32 N	38.04 E
Zaječar	38	43.54 N	22.17 E
Zajkany	78	47.59 N	27.22 E
Zaj-Karataj	80	54.42 N	52.22 E
Zajmo-Obryv	83	47.02 N	39.19 E
Zajsan	86	47.28 N	84.55 E
Zajsan, ozero ⊜	86	48.00 N	84.00 E
Žajsk	80	55.54 N	42.32 E
Zajukovo	84	43.37 N	43.19 E
Zaka	154	20.20 S	31.29 E
Zakamensk	88	50.23 N	103.17 E
Zakarpat □4	78	48.30 N	23.00 E
Zákas	38	40.02 N	21.16 E
Zakatal'skij zapovednik ♦	84	41.48 N	46.38 E
Zakataly	84	41.38 N	46.39 E
Zakatnyj	80	46.32 N	44.04 E
Zakfero	140	12.10 N	27.35 E
Zākhū	128	37.08 N	42.41 E
Zákinthos	38	37.47 N	20.53 E
Zákinthos I	38	37.52 N	20.44 E
Zakínthou, Porthmós ⩢	38	37.50 N	21.00 E
Zakīyah	132	33.20 N	36.08 E
Zakliczyn	30	49.51 N	20.48 E
Zaklików	30	50.47 N	22.06 E
Zákolany	54	50.10 N	14.14 E
Zakopane	30	49.19 N	19.57 E
Zakotnoje, Ukr.	83	49.28 N	38.58 E
Zakotnoje, Ukr.	83	48.54 N	37.58 E
Zakouma	146	10.54 N	19.49 E
Zakouma, Parc National de ♦	146	10.45 N	19.30 E
Zakroczym	30	52.26 N	20.37 E
Žaksy	86	51.55 N	67.20 E
Žaksybaj ≃	80	49.24 N	53.18 E
Zákupy	54	50.42 N	14.40 E
Zala	144	6.28 N	37.20 E
Zala □6	61	46.45 N	16.50 E
Zala ≃	61	46.43 N	17.16 E
Zalaegerszeg	30	46.51 N	16.51 E
Zalai-dombság ⩘2	61	46.37 N	16.48 E
Zalalövő	61	46.51 N	16.35 E
Zalamea de la Serena	34	38.39 N	5.39 W
Žalanaš	86	51.12 N	65.02 E
Zalanga	150	10.37 N	10.10 E
Žalany	54	50.35 N	13.55 E
Zalari	88	53.34 N	102.32 E
Zalaszentgrót	30	46.59 N	17.02 E
Zalatárnok	61	46.42 N	16.46 E
Zalau, Nig.	150	10.20 N	9.00 E
Zalău, Rom.	38	47.11 N	23.03 E
Žalauly, ozero ⊜	86	52.53 N	74.10 E
Zaldívar, Laguna ⊜	286b	22.58 N	82.27 W
Žalec	36	46.15 N	15.10 E
Zalegošč'	76	52.56 N	36.53 E
Zaleščiki	78	48.38 N	25.44 E
Zalesje, Ross.	76	54.51 N	21.32 E
Zalesje, Ross.	76	58.42 N	36.10 E
Zalesovo	86	54.00 N	84.47 E
Zalingei	140	12.54 N	23.29 E
Zalizničnoje	78	47.53 N	33.29 E
Záložcy	78	49.48 N	25.24 E
Zaltan	146	32.57 N	11.52 E
Zaltbommel	52	51.48 N	5.15 E
Žaltyr	86	51.40 N	69.50 E
Žaltyr, ozero ⊜	80	47.24 N	51.07 E
Zalučje	76	57.40 N	31.46 E
Zalukokoaže	84	43.54 N	43.13 E
Zalun	110	17.29 N	95.34 E
Zama, Nihon	268	35.29 N	139.24 E
Zama, Ms., U.S.	194	32.58 N	89.22 W
Zama, Camp ■	268	35.30 N	139.24 E
Zama-iriya	268	35.29 N	139.24 E
Zamakh	144	16.30 N	47.35 E
Zamālik, Jazīrat az- I	273c	30.03 N	31.13 E
Žaman-Akkol', ozero ⊜	86	48.58 N	63.30 E
Žamankak	80	48.56 N	48.45 E
Žamantau, gora ∧2	80	48.20 N	51.50 E
Zamantı ≃	130	37.36 N	35.35 E
Zamarino	82	54.18 N	37.11 E
Žambaj	80	47.11 N	50.34 E
Zambales □4	116	15.20 N	120.05 E
Zambales Mountains ⩘	116	15.45 N	120.05 E
Žamberk	30	50.05 N	16.28 E
Zambezi	152	13.33 S	23.06 E
Zambezi (Zambeze) ≃	138	18.55 S	36.04 E
Zambézia □5	154	16.15 S	37.30 E
Zambezi Escarpment ⊥4	154	16.10 S	30.30 E
Zambia □1, Afr.	138	14.30 S	27.30 E
Zambia □1, Afr.	154	14.30 S	29.00 E
Zambie → Zambia □1	154	14.30 S	27.30 E
Zamboanga	116	6.54 N	122.04 E
Zamboanga del Norte □4	116	8.15 N	123.00 E
Zamboanga del Sur □4	116	7.50 N	123.00 E
Zamboanga Peninsula ›1	116	7.32 N	122.16 E
Zamboanguita	116	9.06 N	123.12 E
Zambrano	246	9.45 N	74.49 W
Zambrone	68	38.42 N	15.59 E
Zambrów	30	53.00 N	22.15 E
Zâmbuè	154	15.10 S	30.50 E
Zambujal	266c	38.52 N	9.07 W
Zamch	30	50.20 N	23.00 E
Zamežnaja	24	65.02 N	51.50 E
Zamfara ≃	150	12.05 N	4.02 E
Zamglaj	78	51.49 N	31.13 E
Zami ≃	110	16.09 N	97.58 E
Zamjany	80	46.50 N	47.40 E
Zamkova, gora ∧2	76	53.30 N	25.43 E
Zamora, Ec.	246	4.04 S	78.58 W
Zamora, Esp.	34	41.30 N	5.45 W
Zamora, Ca., U.S.	226	38.48 N	121.53 W
Zamora □4	34	41.45 N	6.00 W
Zamora ≃	246	2.59 S	78.13 W
Zamora-Chinchipe □4	246	4.15 S	78.50 W
Zamora de Hidalgo	234	19.59 N	102.16 W
Zamość	30	50.44 N	23.15 E
Zamość □4	30	50.35 N	23.20 E
Zamožnoje	83	47.19 N	37.49 E
Zams	58	47.09 N	10.35 E
Zamševa	86	59.07 N	89.14 E
Zamuro, Punta ›	246	11.26 N	68.50 W
Zamzam, Wādī V	146	31.26 N	15.27 E
Zamzor	88	55.21 N	98.35 E
Zana ⊥	34	35.45 N	6.05 E
Žanadarja	86	44.45 N	64.40 E
Zanaga	152	2.51 S	13.50 E
Zanapa ≃	234	17.58 N	94.06 W
Žanašu	80	47.27 N	48.31 E
Žanatalap, Kaz.	86	47.11 N	61.52 E
Žanatalap, Kaz.	86	47.06 N	84.13 E
Žanatarlyk	86	44.16 N	73.12 E
Žanatas	85	43.34 N	69.45 E
Záncara ≃	34	39.18 N	3.18 W
Zanda	120	31.30 N	79.30 E
Žandov	54	50.44 N	14.24 E
Zandvoort	52	52.22 N	4.32 E
Zandvoort, Circuit Autorace ♦	52	52.24 N	4.32 E
Zane Hills ⩘2	180	66.10 N	156.00 W
Zanesfield	216	40.20 N	83.41 W
Zanesville, In., U.S.	216	41.02 N	85.00 W
Zanesville, Oh., U.S.	188	39.56 N	82.00 W
Zanevka	265a	59.56 N	30.31 E
Zangakatun	84	39.50 N	45.03 E
Zangasso	150	12.09 N	5.37 W
Zangelan	84	39.06 N	46.39 E
Zangenstein	60	49.24 N	12.19 E
Zangezurskij chrebet ⩘	84	39.30 N	45.54 E
Zanggezhuang	98	37.28 N	120.57 E
Zangguy	120	37.22 N	78.48 E
Žangiztobe	86	49.16 N	81.18 E
Zangji	100	33.01 N	113.52 E
Zangmār ≃	84	39.17 N	44.50 E
Zânguè ≃	154	17.52 S	35.20 E
Zangwan	100	29.27 N	117.23 E
Zanhuang	98	37.38 N	114.26 E
Zanjān	128	36.40 N	48.29 E
Zanjān □4	128	36.30 N	49.00 E
Zanjān ≃	128	37.08 N	47.47 E
Zanjón	252	27.55 S	64.15 W
Zanjón ≃	252	31.16 S	67.41 W
Žankala ⊥	86	44.29 N	64.05 E
Žannetty, ostrov I	74	76.43 N	158.00 E
Zannone, Isola I	66	40.58 N	13.03 E
Zanpa-misaki ›	174m	26.26 N	127.43 E
Zanri	102	28.58 N	100.50 E
Žanterek	86	47.57 N	54.21 E
Zante → Zákinthos I	38	37.52 N	20.44 E
Zanthus	162	31.02 S	123.34 E
Zantiébougou	150	11.24 N	7.15 W
Zanyang	98	34.00 N	116.13 E
Zanzibar	154	6.10 S	39.11 E
Zanzibar I	154	6.10 S	39.20 E
Zanzibar Channel ⩢	154	6.00 S	39.00 E
Zaohe	98	34.03 N	118.07 E
Zaoheshi	100	26.53 N	114.41 E
Zaojiang	98	37.30 N	115.43 E
Zaojiaochang	107	29.58 N	106.11 E
Zaojiatuo	105	39.23 N	118.11 E
Zaokskij	82	54.44 N	37.24 E
Zaolin	100	26.24 N	114.24 E
Zaorosongou	152	5.02 N	16.13 E
Zaoshi, Zhg.	100	26.22 N	112.50 E
Zaoshi, Zhg.	100	30.51 N	113.20 E
Zaostroviči	76	52.54 N	26.47 E
Zaostrovje, Ross.	24	60.50 N	30.22 E
Zaostrovje, Ross.	76	60.38 N	33.16 E
Zaouiet Azmour	36	36.55 N	11.01 E
Zaouiet el Mgaïz	36	36.56 N	10.50 E
Zaoxi	100	30.13 N	119.30 E
Zaoyang	100	32.10 N	112.43 E
Zaō-zan ∧	92	38.08 N	140.26 E
Zaozhuang	98	34.53 N	117.34 E
Zaoz'orje, Ross.	76	57.12 N	38.15 E
Zaoz'orje, Ross.	265b	55.34 N	38.02 E
Zaoz'ornyj	86	55.58 N	94.42 E
Zap	198	47.17 N	101.55 W
Zapadnaja Dvina	76	56.16 N	32.04 E
Zapadnaja Dvina (Daugava) ≃	76	57.04 N	24.03 E
Zapadna Morava ≃	38	43.42 N	21.23 E
Zapadno-Sibirskaja ravnina ≚	72	60.00 N	75.00 E
Zapadnyj Alamedin, pik ∧	85	42.32 N	74.34 E
Zapadnyj chrebet ⩘	89	50.00 N	142.25 E
Zapadnyj Karakol ≃	85	42.08 N	74.05 E
Zapadnyj Sajan ⩘	74	53.00 N	94.00 E
Západočeský Kraj □4	30	49.45 N	13.00 E
Západoslovenský Kraj □4	30	48.20 N	18.00 E
Zapala	252	38.54 S	70.04 W
Zapaleri, Cerro ∧	252	22.49 S	67.11 W
Zapardiel ≃	34	41.29 N	5.02 W
Zapata	196	26.54 N	99.16 W
Zapata, Península de ›1	240p	22.20 N	81.35 W
Zapatera, Isla I	236	11.45 N	85.50 W
Zapatoca	246	6.49 N	73.17 W
Zapato Chino Creek ≃	226	36.09 N	120.11 W
Zapatosa, Ciénaga de ⊜	246	9.05 N	73.50 W
Zapfendorf	56	50.01 N	10.56 E
Zapiola	258	35.03 S	59.03 W
Zaplavnoje, Ross.	80	52.58 N	51.44 E
Zaplavnoje, Ross.	80	48.43 N	45.01 E
Zapl'usje	76	58.26 N	29.43 E
Zapokrovskij	88	50.50 N	119.05 E
Zapol'arnyj, Ross.	24	69.26 N	30.48 E
Zapol'arnyj, Ross.	24	67.30 N	63.42 E
Zapolje	76	58.23 N	29.41 E
Zapopan	234	20.43 N	103.24 W
Zaporojie → Zaporožje	78	47.50 N	35.10 E
Zaporozh'ye → Zaporožje	78	47.50 N	35.10 E
Zaporožje, Ukr.	78	47.50 N	35.10 E
Zaporožje, Ukr.	83	48.14 N	38.41 E
Zaporožje □4	78	47.30 N	35.30 E
Zaporožskaja	78	45.23 N	36.52 E
Zapotán	234	18.41 N	103.39 W
Zapotillo	246	4.25 S	80.31 W
Zapotiltic	234	19.37 N	103.26 W
Zapotitlán	234	19.31 N	103.44 W
Zapotlán, Laguna ⊜	234	19.45 N	103.30 W
Zapotlanejo	234	20.38 N	103.04 W
Zapovednoje	76	55.04 N	21.24 E
Zapovednyj	89	42.52 N	133.45 E
Zaprudn'a	82	56.34 N	37.26 E
Zaqqūt	146	28.29 N	19.37 E
Zara	130	39.55 N	37.46 E
Zarāf, Bahr az- ≃	140	9.25 N	31.10 E
Zaragoza, Col.	246	7.30 N	74.52 W
Zaragoza, Esp.	34	41.38 N	0.53 W
Zaragoza, Méx.	232	31.39 N	106.20 W
Zaragoza, Méx.	232	28.29 N	100.55 W
Zaragoza, Méx.	234	23.58 N	99.46 W
Zaragoza, Méx.	234	19.46 N	97.33 W
Zaragoza, Méx.	234	22.02 N	100.44 W
Zaragoza □4	34	42.30 N	1.00 W
Zarajsk	82	54.46 N	38.53 E
Zaramag	84	42.43 N	43.57 E
Zarand	128	30.48 N	56.35 E
Zaranda Hill ∧2	150	10.15 N	9.35 E
Zarand-e Kohneh	128	35.17 N	50.30 E
Zarandului, Munții ⩘	38	46.10 N	22.15 E
Zaranj	128	31.06 N	61.53 E
Zarasai	76	55.44 N	26.15 E
Zárate	258	34.06 S	59.02 W
Zarautz	34	43.17 N	2.10 W
Zaraza	246	9.21 N	65.19 W
Zara → Zadar	36	44.07 N	15.14 E
Žarbulak	86	46.05 N	82.04 E
Zarcero	236	10.11 N	84.23 W
Zardaly	85	39.38 N	70.57 E
Zard Kūh ∧	128	32.22 N	50.04 E
Zardob	84	40.13 N	47.43 E
Zarečensk	24	66.40 N	31.23 E
Zarečje, Ross.	24	63.08 N	44.46 E
Zarečje, Ross.	76	56.52 N	33.50 E
Zarečje, Ross.	76	58.56 N	39.40 E
Zarečje, Ross.	265b	55.41 N	37.23 E
Zarečnoje	78	51.48 N	26.06 E
Zarečnyj, Ross.	76	53.45 N	39.35 E
Zarečnyj, Ross.	80	57.28 N	42.18 E
Zarečnyj, Ross.	80	53.13 N	45.13 E
Zarembo Island I	180	56.20 N	132.50 W
Zarephath	276	40.32 N	74.35 W
Zaresskoje, ozero ⊜	85	38.13 N	72.45 E
Zargān	128	29.46 N	52.43 E
Zarghūn Shahr	120	32.51 N	68.25 E
Zari	146	13.04 N	12.43 E
Zaria	150	11.07 N	7.44 E
Zarinskaja	86	53.43 N	84.58 E
Žarkamys	86	47.56 N	56.26 E
Żarki	30	50.38 N	19.22 E
Žarkova	86	58.00 N	87.17 E
Žarkovskij	76	55.52 N	32.17 E
Žarma	86	48.48 N	80.50 E
Zarnān	267d	35.41 N	51.09 E
Zărnești	38	45.34 N	25.19 E
Zarow ≃	54	53.46 N	14.02 E
Zarqā', Nahr az- ≃	132	32.07 N	35.33 E
Zarqā', Raqabat az- V	140	9.14 N	29.44 E
Zarqā' Mā'īn, Wādī V	132	31.37 N	35.34 E
Zarqūn	142	31.07 N	30.28 E
Zarrentin	54	53.35 N	10.55 E
Zarrīneh ≃	128	37.05 N	45.54 E
Zarrīn Shahr	128	32.32 N	51.23 E
Žarsuat	86	46.27 N	80.48 E
Zarten	58	47.58 N	7.56 E
Zarubino, Ross.	76	58.44 N	33.28 E
Zarubino, Ross.	89	42.40 N	131.04 E
Zaruma	246	3.41 S	79.37 W
Zarumilla	246	3.30 S	80.16 W
Żary (Sorau)	30	51.38 N	15.09 E
Žaryk	86	48.52 N	72.51 E
Žaryn'	76	53.47 N	33.04 E
Zarzaïtine	148	28.18 N	9.48 E
Zarzal	246	4.24 N	76.04 W
Zarzis	148	33.30 N	11.07 E
Zarzuela, Arroyo de la ≃	266a	40.29 N	3.45 W
Zarzuela, Hipodromo de la ♦	266a	40.28 N	3.45 W
Zasa	76	56.17 N	25.58 E
Zaschendorf	54	53.42 N	11.37 E
Zaschwitz	54	51.10 N	13.02 E
Zašejek	24	67.25 N	32.28 E
Zasenbeck	54	52.40 N	10.51 E
Zasieki	54	51.43 N	14.43 E
Zāskār ≃	123	34.10 N	77.20 E
Zāskār Mountains ⩘	120	33.00 N	78.00 E
Žaškov	78	49.15 N	30.06 E
Zaslavl'	76	54.01 N	27.15 E
Zaslavl'skoje vodochranilišče ⊜1	76	53.58 N	27.22 E
Zasosna	78	50.37 N	38.23 E
Žastalap	80	49.11 N	50.24 E
Zastava	24	59.12 N	46.46 E
Zastávka	61	49.11 N	16.23 E
Zastavna	78	48.31 N	25.50 E
Zastron	158	30.18 S	27.07 E
Zasulje, Bela.	76	53.34 N	26.50 E
Zasulje, Ross.	24	64.41 N	47.48 E
Za'tarī, Wādī az- V	132	32.09 N	36.15 E
Žatec	54	50.18 N	13.32 E
Zaterečnyj	84	44.48 N	45.11 E
Zatišje	78	47.19 N	29.51 E
Z'at'kovo	86	53.36 N	80.20 E
Zatobol'sk	86	53.12 N	63.43 E
Zaton	86	53.18 N	83.49 E
Zauche ◂1	54	52.15 N	12.35 E
Zauchwitz	54	52.12 N	13.02 E
Zauel	144	3.33 N	43.45 E
Zaural'skoje plato ⩘1	86	53.00 N	62.00 E
Zavalje	78	48.13 N	30.01 E
Zavalla	194	31.09 N	94.26 W
Zaval'noje	76	52.02 N	39.51 E
Zave	154	17.13 S	30.02 E
Zaventem	50	50.53 N	4.28 E
Zavet	38	43.46 N	26.40 E
Zavetnoje	80	47.07 N	43.52 E
Zavety Iljiča	89	49.02 N	140.17 E
Zavidoviči	38	44.27 N	18.09 E
Zavidovka	82	54.16 N	38.49 E
Zavidovo	82	56.32 N	36.32 E
Zavitinsk	89	50.07 N	129.27 E
Zavjalovo, Ross.	80	56.47 N	53.23 E
Zavjalovo, Ross.	86	54.30 N	82.27 E
Zavlekov	60	49.20 N	13.30 E
Zavod Michajlovskij	80	56.32 N	54.17 E
Zavodo-Petrovskij	86	56.50 N	66.45 E
Zavodoukovsk	86	56.33 N	66.32 E
Zavodouspenskoje	86	56.51 N	65.00 E
Zavodovski Island I	18	56.20 S	27.35 W
Zavodskoj, Ross.	78	48.24 N	40.19 E
Zavodskoj, Ross.	86	53.04 N	84.25 E
Zavolžje	80	56.37 N	43.26 E
Zavolžsk	80	57.30 N	42.10 E
Zavolžskoje	80	46.59 N	47.37 E
Zavoronežskoje	80	52.53 N	40.33 E
Zavorovo	82	55.20 N	38.13 E
Zāwa	120	28.04 N	66.23 E
Zawadzkie	30	50.37 N	18.29 E
Zawichost	30	50.49 N	21.52 E
Zawiercie	30	50.30 N	19.25 E
Zawīlah	146	26.10 N	15.07 E
Zāwiyat 'Abd al-Qādir	142	31.02 N	29.49 E
Zāwiyat Abū Musallum	273c	29.56 N	31.10 E
Zāwiyat al-Amwāt	142	28.04 N	30.50 E
Zawiyat al-Judhāmī	142	28.42 N	30.54 E
Zāwiyat al-Mukhaylā	146	32.09 N	22.17 E
Zāwiyat Masūs	146	31.33 N	21.03 E
Zāwiyat Nābit	273c	30.07 N	31.09 E
Zāwiyat Razīn	142	30.25 N	30.51 E
Zāwiyat Saqr	142	30.56 N	30.12 E
Zawiyat Shammās	140	31.31 N	26.24 E
Zāwiyat Sīdī Ghāzī	142	31.03 N	30.05 E
Zāwiyet an-Najjār	273c	30.11 N	31.17 E
Zawr, Ra's az- ›, Ar. Su.	128	27.25 N	49.20 E
Zawr, Ra's az- ›, Kuwayt	128	28.44 N	48.24 E
Zāyandeh ≃	128	32.16 N	52.53 E
Zaydābād	120	34.17 N	69.07 E
Zayü	102	28.48 N	97.27 E
Zayü ≃	102	28.28 N	97.03 E
Zaza ≃	240p	21.37 N	79.32 W
Zaza, Presa ⊜1	240p	21.50 N	79.23 W
Zaza del Medio	240p	22.00 N	79.23 W
Zazafotsy	157b	22.13 S	46.26 E
Zāzamt, Wādī V	146	30.58 N	14.49 E
Zazir, Oued V	148	20.25 N	5.30 E
Zban	86	48.53 N	63.58 E
Zbaraž	78	49.39 N	25.47 E
Zbąszyń	30	52.16 N	15.55 E
Zbąszynek	30	52.15 N	15.50 E
Zbečno	60	50.03 N	13.56 E
Zbiroh	60	49.52 N	13.47 E
Zborov	78	49.39 N	25.08 E
Zborovy	60	49.23 N	13.31 E
Zbraslav	30	49.59 N	14.24 E
Zbruč ≃	78	48.32 N	26.26 E
Zbůch	60	49.41 N	13.14 E
Ždanova	86	58.37 N	88.58 E
Ždanov → Mariupol'	83	47.06 N	37.33 E
Ždanovo	78	48.14 N	34.44 E
Ždany	78	50.12 N	33.13 E
Žd'ár	60	50.03 N	13.28 E
Žd'ár nad Sazavou	30	49.34 N	15.57 E
Ždiar	30	49.17 N	20.16 E
Zdice	60	49.55 N	13.59 E
Zdikovec	60	49.05 N	13.42 E
Zdolbunov	78	50.31 N	26.15 E
Zdroje ◂8	54	53.20 N	14.40 E
Zduńska Wola	30	51.36 N	18.57 E
Zduny	30	51.39 N	17.24 E
Zdviž ≃	78	51.01 N	30.02 E
Ze ≃	105	38.50 N	115.13 E
Zealandia	184	51.37 N	107.45 W
Zearing	190	42.09 N	93.17 W
Zēbāk	120	36.32 N	71.21 E
Zeballos	182	49.59 N	126.51 W
Zeballos, Monte ∧	254	47.01 S	71.42 W
Zebediela	156	24.19 S	29.21 E
Zebila	150	10.56 N	0.29 W
Zebl'aki	80	58.23 N	45.45 E
Žebrák	60	49.52 N	13.56 E
Zebulon, Ga., U.S.	192	33.06 N	84.20 W
Zebulon, N.C., U.S.	192	35.49 N	78.18 W
Zechlinerhütte	54	53.09 N	12.51 E
Zeda, Monte ∧	58	46.03 N	8.32 E
Zedang	120	29.16 N	91.46 E
Zeddine, Oued ≃	34	36.15 N	1.48 E
Zedelgem	50	51.09 N	3.08 E
Zederhaus	64	47.09 N	13.30 E
Zeebrugge	50	51.20 N	3.12 E
Zeehan	166	41.53 S	145.20 E
Zeeland, Ned.	52	51.42 N	5.40 E
Zeeland, Mi., U.S.	216	42.48 N	86.01 W
Zeeland, N.D., U.S.	198	45.58 N	99.49 W
Zeeland □4	52	51.27 N	3.45 E
Zeelandbrug ◂5	52	51.37 N	3.53 E
Zeerust	156	25.33 S	26.06 E
Zeesen	54	52.16 N	13.38 E
Zeestow	264a	52.34 N	12.58 E
Zeeuws-Vlaanderen □9	52	51.19 N	3.45 E
Zefat (Safad)	132	32.58 N	35.30 E
Žegalovo, Ross.	80	54.43 N	43.25 E
Žegalovo, Ross.	265b	55.54 N	37.59 E
Žegdoči	89	53.20 N	120.49 E
Zege	144	11.42 N	37.23 E
Zegher, Hamādat ≚	146	27.18 N	11.30 E
Zégoua	150	10.30 N	5.40 W
Zegrir, Oued V	148	32.43 N	5.00 E
Zeguo	100	28.32 N	121.20 E
Zehdenick	54	52.59 N	13.20 E
Zehlendorf	54	52.47 N	13.23 E
Zehlendorf ◂8	264a	52.26 N	13.15 E
Zeigler	194	37.53 N	89.03 W
Zeil	56	50.01 N	10.35 E
Zeil, Mount ∧	162	23.24 S	132.23 E
Zeiselmauer	264b	48.20 N	16.11 E
Zeist	52	52.05 N	5.15 E
Zeithain	54	51.19 N	13.19 E
Zeitlarn	60	49.05 N	12.06 E
Zeitz	54	51.03 N	12.08 E
Zeja	89	53.45 N	127.15 E
Zeja ≃	89	50.13 N	127.35 E
Zejskoje vodochranilišče ⊜1	89	54.28 N	127.45 E
Zekeriyaköy ◂8	267b	41.11 N	29.01 E
Zekiah Swamp Run ≃	208	38.25 N	76.57 W
Žel'abino	265b	55.52 N	37.11 E
Žel'abužskaja	82	54.36 N	36.32 E
Želannoje	83	48.13 N	37.25 E
Zelaya	258	34.21 S	58.52 W
Zelaya □5	236	13.00 N	84.00 W
Želča ≃	76	58.19 N	27.40 E
Žel'dyadyr ◂1	86	49.30 N	68.30 E
Želdybino	82	56.14 N	39.02 E
Zele	50	51.04 N	4.02 E
Żelechów	30	51.49 N	21.54 E
Zelee, Cape ›	175e	9.45 S	161.34 E
Zelená Lhota	60	49.14 N	13.10 E
Zelencovo	76	59.52 N	44.59 E
Zelenčukskaja	84	43.52 N	41.36 E
Zelenec	24	62.29 N	55.16 E
Zelenga	80	46.11 N	48.37 E
Zelengora ⩘	38	43.15 N	18.45 E
Zelenoborskij	24	66.49 N	32.18 E
Zelenogorsk	76	60.12 N	29.42 E
Zelenograd	82	56.01 N	37.11 E
Zelenogradsk	76	54.58 N	20.29 E
Zelenokumsk	84	44.24 N	43.53 E
Zelenovka	78	46.59 N	36.14 E
Želetava	61	49.09 N	15.38 E
Zeletin ≃	38	46.03 N	27.23 E
Železinka	86	53.32 N	75.18 E
Železn'a	82	54.31 N	37.28 E
Železná Ruda	60	49.09 N	13.14 E
Železnik	38	44.43 N	20.23 E
Železnodorožnyj, Ross.	24	62.35 N	50.55 E
Železnodorožnyj, Ross.	76	54.22 N	21.19 E
Železnodorožnyj, Ross.	82	55.45 N	38.01 E
Železnodorožnyj, Uzb.	86	43.04 N	58.50 E
Železnogorsk	76	52.22 N	35.23 E
Železnogorsk-Ilimskij	88	56.37 N	104.08 E
Železnoje	83	48.19 N	37.51 E
Železnovodsk	84	44.08 N	43.02 E
Zelienople	214	40.47 N	80.08 W
Zelina	36	45.58 N	16.15 E
Zell, Dtsch.	56	50.01 N	7.10 E
Zell, Dtsch.	58	47.42 N	7.51 E
Zell, Schw.	58	47.09 N	7.55 E
Zella-Mehlis	54	50.39 N	10.39 E
Zell am Harmersbach	58	48.21 N	8.04 E
Zell am Moos	64	47.54 N	13.19 E
Zell am See	64	47.19 N	12.47 E
Zell am Ziller	64	47.14 N	11.53 E
Zellersee c	58	47.42 N	9.03 E
Zeller See ⊜	64	47.19 N	12.48 E
Zellingen	56	49.53 N	9.43 E
Zellwood	220	28.44 N	81.36 W
Želnava	61	48.50 N	13.57 E
Želon' ≃	78	51.33 N	29.51 E
Zel'onaja Rošča, Ross.	76	60.10 N	29.08 E
Zel'onaja Rošča, Ross.	80	54.29 N	52.02 E
Zel'onaja Rošča, Ross.	83	47.07 N	40.13 E
Zel'onodol'sk	80	55.51 N	48.33 E
Zel'onoje	78	47.43 N	33.12 E
Zel'onoje Ozero	88	53.40 N	116.36 E
Zel'onyj, Kaz.	80	48.07 N	51.31 E
Zel'onyj, Kaz.	80	51.10 N	50.41 E
Zel'onyj, ostrov (Shibotsu-Tō) I	92a	43.30 N	146.09 E
Zel'onyj Bor	76	54.01 N	28.28 E
Zelo Surrigone	266b	45.23 N	8.59 E
Zelów	30	51.28 N	19.13 E
Žel'tau Ajtau ⩘	86	44.30 N	74.00 E
Zeltweg	61	47.11 N	14.45 E
Želudok	76	53.36 N	24.59 E
Zel'va, Bela.	76	53.09 N	24.49 E
Želva, Liet.	76	55.13 N	25.06 E
Zel'v'anka ≃	76	53.24 N	24.32 E
Zelzate	50	51.12 N	3.49 E
Žemaičių Naumiestis	76	55.22 N	21.42 E
Žemaitija □9	76	55.45 N	23.00 E
Žembejtinskij	80	50.30 N	52.39 E
Zembin	76	54.22 N	28.13 E
Zembla Septentrional → Severnaja Zeml'a II	74	79.30 N	98.00 E
Zembra, Île I	36	37.08 N	10.48 E
Žemčug	88	51.41 N	102.24 E
Zemcy	76	56.15 N	32.23 E
Zemetčino	80	53.30 N	42.38 E
Zemgale □9	76	56.30 N	25.00 E
Zémio	154	5.02 N	25.08 E
Zeml'ansk	78	51.54 N	38.44 E
Zemmer	56	49.53 N	6.41 E
Zemmora	34	35.44 N	0.45 E
Zemmour ◂1	148	24.50 N	12.15 W
Zemo-Kedi	84	41.26 N	46.24 E
Zémongo, Réserve de Faune de ◂4	140	6.45 N	25.15 E
Zemoul, Oued V	148	29.12 N	7.52 W
Žemovo	82	54.45 N	38.49 E
Zempin	54	54.04 N	13.57 E
Zempoala	234	19.24 N	96.24 W
Zempoala ≃	234	20.16 N	97.27 W
Zempoala ⊥	234	19.27 N	96.23 W
Zempoala, Punta ›	234	19.28 N	96.19 W
Zemst	50	50.59 N	4.28 E
Zemun	38	44.50 N	20.24 E
Zenas	218	39.07 N	85.29 W
Zendeh Jān	128	34.21 N	61.45 E
Zeneta	184	50.44 N	102.02 W
Zeng ≃	100	23.09 N	113.46 E
Zengcheng	100	23.19 N	113.49 E
Zengjiawan	105	39.22 N	118.24 E
Zengkou ≃	105	39.19 N	117.37 E
Zenica	38	44.12 N	17.55 E
Zenifim, Har ∧2	132	30.06 N	34.51 E
Zenith	224	47.23 N	122.19 W
Zen'kov	78	50.13 N	34.22 E
Zenn ≃	56	49.31 N	10.58 E
Zenna	58	46.06 N	8.45 E
Zenne (Senne) ≃	50	51.04 N	4.26 E
Zenon Park	184	53.04 N	103.45 W
Zenon Videla Dorna	258	35.33 S	58.53 W
Zenson di Piave	64	45.41 N	12.29 E
Zentralafrikanische Republik → Central African Republic □1	136	7.00 N	21.00 E
Zentral-Friedhof ◂	264b	48.09 N	16.27 E
Zentral-Massiv → Central, Massif ⩘	32	45.00 N	3.10 E
Zentsūji	96	34.14 N	133.47 E
Zenza do Itombe	152	9.16 S	14.13 E
Zenzeli	80	45.56 N	47.03 E
Zepernick	54	52.39 N	13.32 E
Zephyr	196	31.41 N	98.48 W
Zephyr Cove	226	39.00 N	119.57 W
Zephyrhills	220	28.14 N	82.10 W
Zepu	120	38.13 N	77.16 E
Zérab, Ouadi V	146	11.03 N	19.47 E
Zeralda	34	36.41 N	2.53 E
Zeravšan	85	39.11 N	68.40 E
Zeravšan ≃	72	39.22 N	63.45 E
Zeravšanskij chrebet ⩘	85	39.15 N	68.30 E
Zerbst	54	51.58 N	12.04 E
Žerdevka	80	51.51 N	41.28 E
Žerebec ≃	83	48.57 N	38.03 E
Zereh, Gowd-e ⊥7	128	29.45 N	61.50 E
Zerenda	86	52.55 N	69.10 E
Žerev ≃	78	51.12 N	29.04 E
Zerf	56	49.36 N	6.41 E
Zerga, Merja c	34	34.51 N	6.17 W
Zergenta	80	47.42 N	45.12 E
Zeri	62	44.21 N	9.46 E
Zerind	38	46.37 N	21.31 E
Żerków	30	52.05 N	17.34 E
Zermatt	58	46.02 N	7.45 E
Zernez	58	46.43 N	10.05 E
Zernograd	78	46.50 N	40.19 E
Žernovka	82	54.49 N	37.46 E
Zernsdorf	54	52.18 N	13.41 E
Zero ≃	64	45.32 N	12.22 E
Zeroud, Oued V	36	35.50 N	10.13 E
Zerqan	38	41.30 N	20.21 E
Žešart	24	62.05 N	49.34 E
Zestafoni	84	42.07 N	43.02 E
Žest'anka	80	51.36 N	49.24 E
Žestoki	82	56.19 N	36.22 E
Žestylevo	82	56.24 N	37.39 E
Zetel	52	53.25 N	7.58 E
Žetybaj	80	48.51 N	48.04 E
Žetykol', ozero ⊜	86	51.02 N	60.54 E
Zeulenroda	54	50.39 N	11.58 E
Zeuthen	54	52.20 N	13.37 E
Zeuthener See ⊜	264a	52.21 N	13.39 E
Zeven	52	53.18 N	9.16 E
Zevenaar	52	51.56 N	6.05 E
Zevenbergen	52	51.38 N	4.36 E
Zevenbergschen Hoek	52	51.41 N	4.40 E
Zevenwouden ◂1	52	52.57 N	6.00 E
Zevio	64	45.22 N	11.08 E
Zeyādah Kot	272b	22.27 N	88.20 E
Zeyawadi	110	18.33 N	96.26 E
Zeytinbağı	130	40.23 N	28.47 E
Zeytinburnu ◂8	267b	40.59 N	28.54 E
Zeytindağ	130	38.58 N	27.04 E
Zeyveh	84	39.07 N	47.42 E
Zeze	270	35.00 N	135.54 E
Zêzere ≃	34	39.28 N	8.20 W
Zghartā	130	34.24 N	35.54 E
Zgierz	30	51.52 N	19.25 E
Zgornje Hoče	61	46.29 N	15.38 E
Zgorzelec	30	51.12 N	15.01 E
Zgurovka	78	50.31 N	31.46 E
Zhabuchaka Hu ⊜	120	31.30 N	84.00 E
Zhage	102	26.20 N	103.51 E
Zhagenasongduo	102	33.12 N	94.33 E
Zhag'yab	102	30.32 N	98.00 E
Zhahasutai	86	42.58 N	85.20 E
Zhai ≃	100	32.19 N	115.02 E
Zhaihe	100	32.08 N	114.54 E
Zhaili	100	27.42 N	117.22 E
Zhailing	98	41.00 N	116.53 E
Zhaiqiao	106	31.35 N	119.55 E
Zhaitang	105	39.57 N	115.42 E
Zhaitun	104	41.46 N	122.06 E
Zhakou, Zhg.	102	29.59 N	112.10 E
Zhakou, Zhg.	106	30.23 N	120.47 E
Zhakou, Zhg.	106	30.13 N	120.08 E
Zhalantun → Butha Qi	89	48.02 N	122.43 E
Zhalanyingzi	104	41.29 N	120.37 E
Zhalun	120	32.25 N	81.35 E
Zhaluomude	89	49.13 N	120.22 E
Zhancheng	98	37.41 N	117.46 E
Zhang ≃, Zhg.	100	31.05 N	113.11 E
Zhang ≃, Zhg.	100	25.51 N	114.46 E
Zhang ≃, Zhg.	102	36.10 N	115.05 E
Zhangbei	98	41.04 N	114.48 E
Zhangcang	98	35.54 N	119.57 E
Zhangcun, Zhg.	100	33.20 N	115.59 E
Zhangcun, Zhg.	100	28.50 N	117.57 E
Zhangcun, Zhg.	106	30.28 N	119.22 E
Zhangcun, Zhg.	106	30.40 N	119.57 E
Zhangdang	104	41.54 N	124.05 E
Zhangde	100	34.07 N	113.27 E
Zhangdiyingzi	89	50.30 N	127.16 E
Zhangdu	100	30.38 N	118.13 E
Zhangdu Hu ⊜	100	30.40 N	114.42 E
Zhangfang	105	39.35 N	115.41 E
Zhangfengji	98	35.14 N	116.01 E
Zhanggang	100	30.34 N	112.51 E
Zhanggezhuang, Zhg.	98	36.47 N	119.47 E
Zhanggezhuang, Zhg.	105	40.08 N	116.56 E
Zhanggou	104	42.07 N	124.06 E
Zhangguangcai Ling ⩘	89	45.25 N	129.20 E
Zhangguizhuang	105	39.07 N	117.18 E
Zhanggutai	98	42.40 N	122.28 E
Zhanghezhuang	105	38.56 N	114.56 E
Zhanghuang	102	22.01 N	109.27 E
Zhanghuanggang	106	32.07 N	120.30 E
Zhanghuban	100	26.23 N	118.29 E
Zhangji	98	34.08 N	117.24 E
Zhangjiachang, Zhg.	107	29.26 N	104.34 E
Zhangjiachang, Zhg.	107	29.33 N	104.54 E
Zhangjiachang, Zhg.	107	29.57 N	103.48 E
Zhangjiadian	105	39.44 N	114.54 E
Zhangjiagou	100	30.18 N	113.22 E
Zhangjiaji	100	32.09 N	112.23 E
Zhangjiajie	104	41.28 N	124.08 E
Zhangjiakou (Kalgan)	105	40.50 N	114.53 E
Zhangjiapang	100	30.25 N	115.47 E
Zhangjiapu	104	41.18 N	122.02 E
Zhangjiaqiao, Zhg.	106	31.36 N	120.36 E
Zhangjiaqiao, Zhg.	107	30.02 N	104.15 E
Zhangjiatou	106	31.38 N	119.05 E
Zhangjiatun, Zhg.	104	41.05 N	121.44 E
Zhangjiatun, Zhg.	105	40.37 N	114.57 E
Zhangjiawa	105	40.10 N	117.52 E
Zhangjiawan	105	39.51 N	116.41 E
Zhangjiawopu	104	41.10 N	122.17 E
Zhangjiayingzi	104	42.04 N	120.57 E
Zhangjingqiao	106	31.39 N	120.27 E
Zhangjinhe	100	30.14 N	112.35 E
Zhangliangdian	100	33.42 N	113.02 E
Zhangliantang	106	31.01 N	121.02 E
Zhangling	98	36.32 N	119.29 E

Symbols in the index entries represent the broad categories identified in the key at the right. Symbols with superior numbers (⩘1) identify subcategories (see complete key on page *I · 1)*.

Symbole im Register stellen die rechts im Schlüssel erklärten Kategorien dar. Symbole mit hochgestellten Ziffern (⩘1) bezeichnen Unterabteilungen einer Kategorie (vgl. vollständiger Schlüssel auf Seite *I · 1)*.

Los símbolos incluídos en el texto del índice representan las grandes categorias identificadas con la clave a la derecha. Los símbolos con numeros en su parte superior (⩘1) identifican las subcategorías (véase la clave completa en la página *I · 1)*.

Les symboles de l'index représentent les catégories indiquées dans la légende à droite. Les symboles suivis d'un indice (⩘1) représentent des sous-catégories (voir légende complète à la page *I · 1)*.

Os símbolos incluídos no texto do índice representam as grandes categorias identificadas com a chave à direita. Os símbolos com números em sua parte superior (⩘1) identificam as subcategorias (veja-se a chave completa à página *I · 1)*.

	English	Deutsch	Español	Français	Português
∧	Mountain	Berg	Montaña	Montagne	Montanha
⩘	Mountains	Gebirge	Montañas	Montagnes	Montanhas
)(	Pass	Paß	Paso	Col	Passo
V	Valley, Canyon	Tal, Cañon	Valle, Cañón	Vallée, Canyon	Vale, Canhão
≚	Plain	Ebene	Llano	Plaine	Planície
›	Cape	Kap	Cabo	Cap	Cabo
I	Island	Insel	Isla	Île	Ilha
II	Islands	Inseln	Islas	Îles	Ilhas
⊥	Other Topographic Features	Andere Topographische Objekte	Otros Elementos Topográficos	Autres données topographiques	Outros acidentes topográficos

ESPAÑOL

Nombre	Página	Lat.°′	Long.°′ W = Oeste
Zhanglu	98	36.16 N	115.33 E
Zhangmang	100	32.03 N	114.32 E
Zhangming	102	31.49 N	104.51 E
Zhangmuqiao	100	31.26 N	116.44 E
Zhangmushi	100	27.01 N	112.38 E
Zhangmutou	100	22.55 N	114.05 E
Zhangping	100	25.19 N	117.25 E
Zhangpu, Zhg.	100	24.09 N	117.36 E
Zhangpu, Zhg.	106	31.17 N	120.57 E
Zhangqiangzhen	98	42.39 N	122.59 E
Zhangqiao	100	32.21 N	117.38 E
Zhangqiu (Mingshui)	98	36.43 N	117.30 E
Zhangsanta	102	39.37 N	110.14 E
Zhangsanying	98	41.34 N	117.39 E
Zhangshitai	104	41.50 N	122.51 E
Zhangshuping	102	31.20 N	111.02 E
Zhangshuxia	100	25.54 N	112.45 E
Zhangtaitai	104	40.59 N	121.05 E
Zhangtaizi	104	41.22 N	123.16 E
Zhangting	100	30.02 N	121.19 E
Zhangwan	100	26.43 N	119.36 E
Zhangwenpu	105	40.26 N	116.04 E
Zhangwu, Zhg.	104	42.22 N	122.31 E
Zhangwu, Zhg.	106	30.47 N	119.33 E
Zhangwutaimen	104	42.16 N	122.42 E
Zhangxinliuji	100	33.43 N	115.48 E
Zhangyan, Zhg.	106	31.48 N	119.44 E
Zhangyan, Zhg.	106	30.48 N	121.16 E
Zhangyangongtun	104	40.58 N	120.46 E
Zhangye	102	38.56 N	100.27 E
Zhangze	106	30.55 N	121.15 E
Zhangzhishan	106	31.56 N	121.01 E
Zhangzhou (Longxi)	100	24.33 N	117.39 E
Zhangzhu	106	31.16 N	119.37 E
Zhangzhuang, Zhg.	98	37.03 N	116.32 E
Zhangzhuang, Zhg.	98	36.02 N	118.01 E
Zhangzhuang, Zhg.	106	31.57 N	119.52 E
Zhangzi Dao I	98	39.00 N	122.44 E
Zhanhua (Fuguo)	98	37.42 N	118.08 E
Zhanji	98	34.14 N	115.52 E
Zhanjiajing	107	29.15 N	104.55 E
Zhanjiang	102	21.16 N	110.28 E
Zhanjiaqiao, Zhg.	100	29.19 N	113.34 E
Zhanjiaqiao, Zhg.	106	30.25 N	120.08 E
Zhanyang	100	25.30 N	119.28 E
Zhanyi	102	25.38 N	103.43 E
Zhanyu	89	44.31 N	122.37 E
Zhao'an	100	23.47 N	117.12 E
Zhao'an Wan c	100	23.38 N	117.19 E
Zhaobeikou	105	38.55 N	116.06 E
Zhaochuan	105	40.41 N	115.18 E
Zhaocun	105	39.35 N	116.14 E
Zhaodong	89	46.05 N	125.59 E
Zhaogezhuang, Zhg.	98	37.27 N	120.37 E
Zhaogezhuang, Zhg.	105	39.45 N	118.24 E
Zhaoguang	89	48.07 N	126.43 E
Zhaohe	100	33.12 N	112.49 E
Zhaohuazhen	107	29.02 N	105.08 E
Zhaojiagou	104	40.47 N	123.27 E
Zhaojiapuzi	104	40.51 N	123.49 E
Zhaojiaqiao	106	30.44 N	121.12 E
Zhaojiatangfang	104	42.07 N	122.57 E
Zhaojiatun	104	41.24 N	121.53 E
Zhaojiawopeng	104	42.30 N	123.06 E
Zhaojiaying	105	38.58 N	116.42 E
Zhaojue	102	28.15 N	102.50 E
Zhaomaozhuang	105	39.28 N	117.59 E
Zhaomutun	104	41.10 N	121.38 E
Zhaoping	102	24.03 N	110.52 E
Zhaoqiao	100	28.42 N	114.45 E
Zhaoqing (Gaoyao)	102	23.03 N	112.27 E
Zhaosu	86	43.06 N	81.08 E
Zhaotan	100	29.42 N	116.48 E
Zhaotong	102	27.19 N	103.48 E
Zhaotun	104	41.54 N	121.59 E
Zhaoxian, Zhg.	98	37.45 N	114.46 E
Zhaoxian, Zhg.	98	35.44 N	118.55 E
Zhaoxing	89	47.43 N	131.19 E
Zhaoya	107	29.00 N	105.35 E
Zhaoyi	105	39.55 N	116.43 E
Zhaoyuan, Zhg.	89	45.31 N	125.09 E
Zhaoyuan, Zhg.	98	37.22 N	120.24 E
Zhaozhou	89	45.41 N	125.21 E
Zhaozhuang, Zhg.	98	34.45 N	116.27 E
Zhaozhuang, Zhg.	98	34.14 N	116.38 E
Zhaozhuangzi	105	39.10 N	117.20 E
Zhapu	106	30.36 N	121.05 E
Zhari Namco ⊜	120	31.05 N	85.35 E
Zhashui	102	33.40 N	109.01 E
Zhaxi Co ⊜	120	32.10 N	85.05 E
Zhaxigang	120	32.32 N	79.41 E
Zhayi	102	28.34 N	99.09 E
Zhaze	106	32.09 N	119.29 E
Zhdanov → Mariupol'	83	47.06 N	37.33 E
Zhecheng	98	34.06 N	115.19 E
Zhegao	100	31.46 N	117.45 E
Zhegu	120	28.43 N	91.43 E
Zhêhor	102	31.41 N	100.24 E
Zhejiang (Chekiang) □ 4	100	29.00 N	120.00 E
Zhelang	100	22.43 N	115.32 E
Zhelin, Zhg.	100	29.14 N	115.30 E
Zhelin, Zhg.	100	23.36 N	117.06 E
Zhelin, Zhg.	106	30.50 N	121.29 E
Zhen ≃	100	24.55 N	113.44 E
Zhen'an	102	33.27 N	109.01 E
Zhenbeikou	102	39.15 N	106.17 E
Zhenbiancheng	105	40.10 N	115.49 E
Zhenchang, Zhg.	105	39.47 N	115.24 E
Zhenchang, Zhg.	106	32.04 N	121.02 E
Zhenfeng	102	25.23 N	105.41 E
Zheng'an	102	28.31 N	107.29 E
Zheng'anpu	104	41.43 N	121.56 E
Zhengcun	105	39.13 N	115.40 E
Zhengding	98	38.10 N	114.34 E
Zhengdongyu	106	31.59 N	120.10 E
Zhengfang	100	28.42 N	117.53 E
Zhengguanchang	107	29.54 N	106.35 E
Zhengguo	100	23.25 N	113.53 E
Zhenghe	100	27.22 N	118.50 E
Zhengji	98	34.26 N	117.01 E
Zhengjiadiancun	104	41.05 N	122.20 E
Zhengjiawu	100	29.29 N	120.05 E
Zhenglan Qi (Dund Hot)	98	42.16 N	115.49 E
Zhengning	102	35.22 N	108.24 E
Zhengping	100	25.22 N	114.46 E
Zhen'guosi	271a	39.51 N	116.21 E
Zhengxiangbai Qi (Qagan Nur)	98	42.16 N	114.52 E
Zhengyang	100	32.37 N	114.23 E
Zhengyangguan	100	32.28 N	116.32 E
Zhengyi	106	31.23 N	120.52 E
Zhengzhou (Chengchow)	102	34.48 N	113.39 E
Zhengzhuang	100	28.11 N	119.01 E
Zhengzi	107	29.22 N	104.16 E
Zhengzichang	107	29.08 N	106.38 E
Zhenhai, Zhg.	100	24.16 N	118.06 E
Zhenhai, Zhg.	100	29.57 N	121.42 E
Zhenhai, Zhg.	102	21.53 N	112.25 E
Zhenjiang, Zhg.	98	40.44 N	125.28 E
Zhenjiang, Zhg.	106	32.13 N	119.26 E
Zhenjiangguan	102	32.25 N	103.35 E
Zhenjiaqiao	106	32.08 N	120.49 E
Zhenjinqiao	107	30.12 N	104.22 E
Zhenkang	102	24.06 N	99.16 E
Zhenlai	89	45.52 N	123.14 E
Zhenning	102	26.05 N	105.46 E
Zhenping	102	33.08 N	112.19 E
Zhenru	106	31.15 N	121.24 E
Zhentou	100	27.04 N	114.56 E
Zhentou ≃	100	32.58 N	114.24 E
Zhentoudian	100	29.10 N	117.29 E
Zhentoushi	100	28.01 N	113.20 E
Zhenxi	107	29.29 N	104.33 E
Zhenxiaguan	100	27.12 N	120.28 E
Zhenxing	98	42.38 N	124.53 E
Zhenxiong	102	27.27 N	104.50 E

FRANÇAIS

Nom	Page	Lat.°′	Long.°′ W = Ouest
Zhenyu	100	27.08 N	120.18 E
Zhenyuan, Zhg.	102	35.46 N	107.18 E
Zhenyuan, Zhg.	102	26.53 N	108.19 E
Zhenze	106	30.55 N	120.30 E
Zhenzhumen	98	41.53 N	126.45 E
Zhenzichang, Zhg.	107	29.59 N	105.11 E
Zhenzichang, Zhg.	107	29.52 N	104.12 E
Zhenzichang, Zhg.	107	30.38 N	104.20 E
Zhenzijie	107	28.48 N	106.40 E
Zhenziling	104	42.10 N	124.12 E
Zhenzizhen	105	39.50 N	118.20 E
Zheqiao	100	26.27 N	112.48 E
Zherong	100	27.16 N	119.54 E
Zheshan	106	30.15 N	120.24 E
Zhetang	106	31.45 N	118.55 E
Zhidan	102	37.00 N	108.40 E
Zhidoi	102	33.08 N	94.50 E
Zhierling	98	40.26 N	114.16 E
Zhigou	98	35.55 N	119.13 E
Zhijiang	102	27.27 N	109.41 E
Zhijin	102	26.41 N	105.37 E
Zhili	106	30.52 N	120.16 E
Zhitan	100	29.35 N	117.16 E
Zhitang, Zhg.	106	31.33 N	121.01 E
Zhitang, Zhg.	106	31.36 N	120.58 E
Zhitomir → Žitomir	78	50.16 N	28.40 E
Zhitouji	100	33.28 N	118.18 E
Zhiwucun	106	30.38 N	119.47 E
Zhixi	100	23.57 N	114.33 E
Zhixia	100	29.42 N	119.36 E
Zhixiqiao	106	31.49 N	119.29 E
Zhiyang	100	33.47 N	113.07 E
Zhizushan	104	41.50 N	121.24 E
Zhob	120	31.20 N	69.27 E
Zhob ≃	120	32.04 N	69.50 E
Zhonganpu	104	41.37 N	121.58 E
Zhong'aozhen	107	29.46 N	105.41 E
Zhongba, Zhg.	100	23.43 N	115.22 E
Zhongba, Zhg.	120	29.38 N	84.13 E
Zhongbu, Zhg.	100	31.25 N	117.45 E
Zhongbu, Zhg.	100	31.40 N	117.45 E
Zhongbu, Zhg.	100	28.50 N	117.16 E
Zhongchuan	100	26.58 N	119.27 E
Zhongcun	102	33.27 N	110.05 E
Zhongdai	106	30.46 N	120.59 E
Zhongdian	102	27.50 N	99.40 E
Zhongdu, Zhg.	100	24.56 N	116.26 E
Zhongdu, Zhg.	100	33.04 N	118.46 E
Zhongdu, Zhg.	107	28.46 N	103.58 E
Zhongduan	100	25.17 N	116.41 E
Zhongerchong	104	41.58 N	123.58 E
Zhonggang	100	32.38 N	115.45 E
Zhonggong	98	36.30 N	117.01 E
Zhonggoumen	98	41.00 N	116.26 E
Zhonggu	104	42.27 N	124.00 E
Zhongguan	106	30.39 N	120.11 E
Zhongguo → China □ 1	90	35.00 N	105.00 E
Zhonghe	102	27.11 N	103.52 E
Zhonghechang	107	30.12 N	104.49 E
Zhongheying	102	23.48 N	103.36 E
Zhonghezhen	107	30.34 N	104.06 E
Zhonghuamen	106	32.01 N	118.46 E
Zhonghuopu	100	29.44 N	113.59 E
Zhongjianchang	107	28.46 N	106.13 E
Zhongjiang	102	31.00 N	104.18 E
Zhongjiatai	104	40.48 N	122.46 E
Zhonglou	98	35.24 N	119.02 E
Zhongluotan	100	23.23 N	113.23 E
Zhongluyantai	104	41.32 N	123.17 E
Zhongmeihe	100	31.19 N	116.45 E
Zhongmou	98	34.46 N	114.01 E
Zhongning	102	37.27 N	105.38 E
Zhongpingchang	102	31.15 N	110.10 E
Zhongqiao	106	31.11 N	119.11 E
Zhongsha	100	26.24 N	116.36 E
Zhongshan, Zhg.	100	26.12 N	117.26 E
Zhongshan (Shiqizhen), Zhg.	100	22.31 N	113.22 E
Zhongshan ᴗ 3	9	69.22 S	76.23 E
Zhongshan Park ♠	269b	31.13 N	121.25 E
Zhongtiao Shan ∧∧	102	35.12 N	111.35 E
Zhongting ≃	105	39.03 N	116.46 E
Zhongtou	100	34.00 N	113.21 E
Zhongwei	102	37.33 N	105.10 E
Zhongwopu	102	38.30 N	102.59 E
Zhongxian, Zhg.	100	27.17 N	116.47 E
Zhongxian, Zhg.	102	30.29 N	108.05 E
Zhongxiang	100	31.11 N	112.33 E
Zhongxiangzhen	107	29.50 N	104.08 E
Zhongxin, Zhg.	100	23.16 N	113.38 E
Zhongxin, Zhg.	100	24.14 N	114.44 E
Zhongxin, Zhg.	104	40.47 N	124.08 E
Zhongxing, Zhg.	106	32.17 N	119.34 E
Zhongxing, Zhg.	107	30.12 N	103.32 E
Zhongxingchang	107	29.07 N	105.18 E
Zhongxinzhen, Zhg.	107	30.16 N	106.15 E
Zhongxinzhen, Zhg.	107	30.30 N	104.03 E
Zhongyangqu	104	40.47 N	122.05 E
Zhongyaozhan	89	50.46 N	125.54 E
Zhongyi	100	31.08 N	114.52 E
Zhongying	105	39.38 N	117.06 E
Zhongzangcun	105	38.52 N	115.38 E
Zhongzhan	100	25.16 N	114.24 E
Zhongzhuang	105	39.25 N	114.47 E
Zhou ≃	105	39.47 N	117.23 E
Zhouba	107	29.06 N	103.43 E
Zhoubachang	107	28.59 N	103.52 E
Zhoucun	98	36.47 N	117.48 E
Zhoudangfan	100	31.54 N	114.31 E
Zhoujiachang	107	30.33 N	104.25 E
Zhoujiadai	106	32.12 N	120.26 E
Zhoujiadu	106	31.11 N	121.29 E
Zhoujiagou	107	30.08 N	104.30 E
Zhoujiatun, Zhg.	104	41.34 N	121.05 E
Zhoujiatun, Zhg.	104	41.29 N	121.50 E
Zhoujiatun, Zhg.	104	41.04 N	120.47 E
Zhoujiatun, Zhg.	104	41.16 N	120.58 E
Zhoujiawopu	104	42.31 N	122.45 E
Zhoujiayao	104	41.19 N	122.48 E
Zhoujingxiang	106	31.32 N	120.23 E
Zhoukoudianzhen	105	39.41 N	115.56 E
Zhoulichang	107	29.55 N	105.09 E
Zhouning	100	27.16 N	119.12 E
Zhoupo	107	29.48 N	104.01 E
Zhoupu	106	31.07 N	121.34 E
Zhouqu	102	33.43 N	104.10 E
Zhouquan	106	30.35 N	120.21 E
Zhoushan Dao I	100	30.05 N	122.10 E
Zhoushan Qundao II	100	30.00 N	122.00 E
Zhoushu	106	31.28 N	120.59 E
Zhoushuizi	98	38.57 N	121.34 E
Zhoutieqiao	106	31.26 N	120.00 E
Zhouwangmiao	106	30.28 N	120.29 E
Zhouxi	100	29.13 N	116.20 E
Zhouxiang	100	30.10 N	121.08 E
Zhouxinzhen	106	31.30 N	120.18 E
Zhouzhai	106	32.02 N	121.31 E
Zhouzhi	102	34.12 N	108.10 E
Zhouzhuang, Zhg.	105	39.09 N	115.18 E
Zhouzhuang, Zhg.	106	31.06 N	120.51 E
Zhouzhuang, Zhg.	106	32.15 N	120.08 E
Zhuanghang	106	30.54 N	121.23 E
Zhuanghe	98	39.43 N	123.01 E
Zhuangji	98	34.20 N	115.15 E
Zhuanglang	102	34.58 N	106.07 E
Zhuangtou	105	40.55 N	117.57 E
Zhuangtouyingzi, Zhg.	104	41.43 N	120.32 E
Zhuangtouyingzi, Zhg.	104	41.50 N	120.43 E
Zhuangxi	107	30.33 N	104.31 E
Zhuangyuanqiao	100	27.54 N	120.48 E
Zhuanping Shan ∧	107	29.07 N	103.37 E
Zhuanqiao	106	31.04 N	121.23 E
Zhuantouwan	100	31.29 N	112.24 E
Zhuanwantai	104	41.20 N	122.22 E
Zhuao	100	29.05 N	121.16 E
Zhucang	102	27.18 N	107.26 E

PORTUGUÊS

Nome	Página	Lat.°′	Long.°′ W = Oeste
Zhucheng	98	36.00 N	119.24 E
Zhudi	269b	31.12 N	121.18 E
Zhudian	100	30.33 N	115.12 E
Zhuergan	89	52.04 N	120.48 E
Zhufengzhen	106	30.35 N	118.56 E
Zhufuo	107	29.02 N	105.51 E
Zhugan ≃	100	32.18 N	114.42 E
Zhuganpu	100	32.13 N	114.39 E
Zhugao	107	30.37 N	104.40 E
Zhuge, Zhg.	98	36.00 N	118.32 E
Zhuge, Zhg.	100	29.15 N	119.18 E
Zhugentan	107	29.25 N	103.50 E
Zhugou	98	36.52 N	120.15 E
Zhugouzhen	100	32.47 N	113.42 E
Zhugusi	102	37.01 N	102.27 E
Zhuhai	100	22.16 N	113.33 E
Zhuhe	100	29.44 N	113.06 E
Zhuhongyu	104	40.48 N	123.00 E
Zhuji	100	29.43 N	120.14 E
Zhujiabeng	106	31.21 N	120.41 E
Zhujiabian	106	31.38 N	119.11 E
Zhujiachang, Zhg.	107	29.48 N	104.20 E
Zhujiachang, Zhg.	107	30.03 N	104.13 E
Zhujiafang	104	41.20 N	122.40 E
Zhujiahang	106	30.51 N	121.19 E
Zhujiahe	106	31.08 N	120.53 E
Zhujia Jian I	100	29.54 N	122.24 E
Zhujiajiao	106	31.06 N	121.02 E
Zhujiajiaotou	106	31.24 N	121.11 E
Zhujiang Kou c 1	100	22.36 N	113.44 E
Zhujiangqing	100	27.18 N	114.44 E
Zhujiaqiao	106	30.26 N	119.03 E
Zhujiawan, Zhg.	100	32.28 N	117.29 E
Zhujiawan, Zhg.	100	30.56 N	114.10 E
Zhujiawan, Zhg.	105	40.08 N	114.56 E
Zhujiawopeng	104	42.27 N	122.13 E
Zhujiesi	102	33.34 N	97.21 E
Zhukeng	100	23.49 N	112.55 E
Zhukou, Zhg.	98	34.07 N	115.04 E
Zhukou, Zhg.	100	27.41 N	118.53 E
Zhukou, Zhg.	100	26.58 N	117.16 E
Zhukovskiy → Žukovskij	82	55.35 N	38.08 E
Zhulanbu	100	25.36 N	115.46 E
Zhulin, Zhg.	100	32.20 N	113.38 E
Zhulin, Zhg.	106	31.45 N	119.27 E
Zhulong ≃	98	38.47 N	115.59 E
Zhulongqiao	100	32.21 N	118.09 E
Zhuluke	98	41.36 N	119.54 E
Zhumadian	100	32.58 N	114.03 E
Zhuolu	105	40.22 N	115.12 E
Zhuoni	102	34.32 N	103.24 E
Zhuotian	100	25.38 N	116.13 E
Zhuoxian	105	39.30 N	115.58 E
Zhuozi	102	40.52 N	112.33 E
Zhuqianzongpuzi	104	42.17 N	123.18 E
Zhuqiao, Zhg.	98	37.22 N	120.05 E
Zhuqiao, Zhg.	106	31.07 N	121.44 E
Zhuqiao, Zhg.	106	30.26 N	120.36 E
Zhurushan	100	30.26 N	113.48 E
Zhushan	102	32.10 N	110.19 E
Zhusigang	100	31.14 N	118.23 E
Zhutan	100	28.04 N	114.10 E
Zhutang, Zhg.	106	31.06 N	118.39 E
Zhutang, Zhg.	106	31.47 N	120.24 E
Zhutian	100	28.43 N	117.01 E
Zhuting, Zhg.	100	27.24 N	113.04 E
Zhuting, Zhg.	100	27.48 N	114.02 E
Zhuwo	105	40.02 N	115.48 E
Zhuwotuo	107	30.31 N	104.34 E
Zhuwumiao	100	30.54 N	116.19 E
Zhuxi, Zhg.	100	28.10 N	118.53 E
Zhuxi, Zhg.	102	32.09 N	109.42 E
Zhuxi, Zhg.	107	29.32 N	105.40 E
Zhuxianzhen	98	34.37 N	114.16 E
Zhuxichang	100	28.58 N	114.06 E
Zhuya	98	36.38 N	118.12 E
Zhuyang	98	36.16 N	117.22 E
Zhuyangxi	107	29.03 N	105.57 E
Zhuyangzhen	102	34.20 N	110.44 E
Zhuyuan	107	29.34 N	104.08 E
Zhuzeqiao	106	31.34 N	119.20 E
Zhuzhenji	100	32.31 N	118.42 E
Zhuzhou (Chuchow)	100	27.50 N	113.09 E
Zhuzikou	100	29.17 N	112.41 E
Zi ≃, Zhg.	98	37.12 N	118.34 E
Zi ≃, Zhg.	102	31.59 N	96.53 E
Zi ≃, Zhg.	102	28.41 N	112.43 E
Zia Indian Reservation ◆ 4	200	35.30 N	106.43 W
Zia International Airport ⊠	126	23.46 N	90.23 E
Ziama Mansouria	34	36.40 N	5.29 E
Ziano	64	46.17 N	11.34 E
Ziārat	120	30.23 N	67.43 E
Ziārat-e Shāh Maqṣūd	120	31.59 N	65.30 E
Ziārat Gali Chāh ╤ 4	128	28.20 N	63.38 E
Žiar nad Hronom	30	48.36 N	18.52 E
Zibdīn	132	33.22 N	35.28 E
Zibo (Zhangdian)	98	36.47 N	118.01 E
Zicapa	234	17.57 N	99.02 W
Zicavo	36	41.54 N	9.08 E
Zichang	102	37.19 N	109.33 E
Žichovice	60	49.16 N	13.37 E
Zichuan	98	36.38 N	117.55 E
Žičicy	76	55.07 N	31.17 E
Zickhusen	54	53.45 N	11.25 E
Židačov	78	49.23 N	24.08 E
Ziddi	85	39.03 N	68.48 E
Žideli	86	48.40 N	70.29 E
Zid'ki	78	49.42 N	36.21 E
Židlochovice	61	49.02 N	16.37 E
Ziębice	30	50.37 N	17.00 E
Ziegelroda	54	51.20 N	11.28 E
Ziegendorf	54	53.18 N	11.49 E
Ziegenhain	56	50.55 N	9.15 E
Ziegenhals	264a	52.21 N	13.40 E
Ziegenrück	54	50.37 N	11.38 E
Zielona Góra (Grünberg)	30	51.56 N	15.31 E
Zielona Góra □ 4	30	52.00 N	15.20 E
Ziemetshausen	58	48.18 N	10.31 E
Zierenberg	56	51.22 N	9.18 E
Zierikzee	52	51.38 N	3.55 E
Ziersdorf	61	48.31 N	15.55 E
Ziesar	54	52.16 N	12.17 E
Ziesendorf	54	54.00 N	12.02 E
Ziethen	54	53.53 N	13.40 E
Žiežmariai	76	54.48 N	24.27 E
Ziftā	142	30.43 N	31.15 E
Žigajlovka	78	50.38 N	35.07 E
Žigalgan	84	44.36 N	50.46 E
Žigalovo	88	54.48 N	105.08 E
Žigansk	74	66.45 N	123.20 E
Zigazinskij	86	53.50 N	57.20 E
Zigong (Tzukung)	107	29.24 N	104.47 E
Ziguéy	146	14.43 N	15.47 E
Zigui	102	31.00 N	110.31 E
Ziguinchor	150	12.35 N	16.16 W
Ziguinchor □ 4	150	12.45 N	16.20 W
Žigulevsk	80	53.25 N	49.27 E
Žiguli	80	53.22 N	49.19 E
Žiguli ∧∧	80	53.20 N	49.40 E
Zigutaicun	104	42.01 N	121.16 E
Zig Zag, Cerro ∧ 2	286d	12.12 S	76.59 W
Zihedian	98	36.48 N	118.22 E
Zihuatanejo	234	17.38 N	101.33 W
Zihukou, Zhg.	100	28.44 N	112.33 E
Zihukou, Zhg.	100	28.55 N	118.08 E
Ziiyang	102	32.31 N	108.48 E
Zijančurino	86	51.33 N	56.55 E
Žijenkum	85	42.50 N	69.00 E
Zijiao	98	37.21 N	117.25 E
Zijin	100	23.40 N	115.11 E
Zijingguan	105	39.23 N	115.12 E
Zijin Shan ∧ 2	106	32.04 N	118.51 E
Zikejevo	76	53.44 N	34.52 E
Zikhron Ya'aqov	132	32.34 N	34.57 E
Zikoufang	100	26.22 N	117.24 E

Zilair	86	52.14 N	57.30 E
Žilaja Kosa	80	46.49 N	53.12 E
Žilaja Tambica	24	62.32 N	36.09 E
Zile	130	40.18 N	35.54 E
Zili	102	26.50 N	100.27 E
Žilina	30	49.14 N	18.46 E
Žilino	76	54.54 N	21.56 E
Zillah, Lībiyā	146	28.33 N	17.35 E
Zillah, Wa., U.S.	202	46.24 N	120.15 W
Ziller ≃	64	47.24 N	11.50 E
Zillertal V	64	47.20 N	11.50 E
Zillertaler Alpen (Alpi Aurine) ∧∧	64	47.00 N	11.55 E
Zillis	58	46.38 N	9.27 E
Zillisheim	58	47.41 N	7.16 E
Zilly	54	51.56 N	10.49 E
Zilme	144	16.25 N	43.49 E
Žiloj, ostrov I	84	40.19 N	50.36 E
Žiloj Bor	76	59.06 N	34.37 E
Žil'ovo	82	54.59 N	38.02 E
Ziltendorf	54	52.12 N	14.37 E
Zilupe	76	56.23 N	28.07 E
Zilwaukee	190	43.28 N	83.55 W
Zima	88	53.55 N	102.04 E
Zima ≃	88	53.52 N	102.02 E
Žima, gora ∧	88	53.18 N	107.38 E
Zimapán	234	20.45 N	99.21 W
Zimatlán	234	16.52 N	96.47 W
Zimba	154	17.19 S	26.13 E
Zimbabwe □ 1, Afr.	138	20.00 S	30.00 E
Zimbabwe □ 1, Afr.	154	20.00 S	30.00 E
Zimbor	38	47.00 N	23.16 E
Zimella	64	45.20 N	11.22 E
Zimi	150	7.19 N	11.18 W
Zimljansker-Stausee → Ciml'anskoje vodochranilišče ⊜ 1	80	48.00 N	43.00 E
Zimmara, Monte ∧	70	37.45 N	14.16 E
Zimn'ackij	80	49.44 N	42.53 E
Zimnicea	38	43.39 N	25.21 E
Zimogorje	83	48.35 N	38.56 E
Zimonino	76	53.47 N	31.52 E
Zimovniki	80	47.08 N	42.28 E
Zimovskoje	86	57.31 N	86.52 E
Zin, Naḥal V	132	30.57 N	35.19 E
Zinal	58	46.08 N	7.38 E
Zinapécuaro [de Figueroa]	234	19.52 N	100.49 W
Zinave, Parque Nacional de ♠	156	21.35 S	33.35 E
Zinder	150	13.48 N	8.59 E
Zinder □ 5	146	15.00 N	10.30 E
Zinga	152	3.43 N	18.35 E
Zinga Mulike	154	9.09 S	38.44 E
Zingaro, Passo dello)(	70	37.43 N	14.50 E
Zingst	54	54.26 N	12.41 E
Zingst ≻ 1	54	54.25 N	12.50 E
Zingwanda	140	7.10 N	27.56 E
Ziniaré	150	12.35 N	1.18 W
Žiniške ≃	85	43.14 N	78.30 E
Zinkgruvan	40	58.49 N	15.05 E
Zin'kov	78	49.04 N	27.04 E
Zinnik → Soignies	50	50.35 N	4.04 E
Zinnowitz	54	54.04 N	13.55 E
Zinswiller	56	48.55 N	7.35 E
Zion, Il., U.S.	216	42.26 N	87.49 W
Zion, Md., U.S.	208	39.40 N	75.57 W
Zionhill	208	40.29 N	75.24 W
Zion National Park ♠	200	37.10 N	113.00 W
Zionsville	218	39.57 N	86.15 W
Zionz Lake ⊜	184	51.25 N	91.52 W
Zipaquirá	246	5.02 N	74.00 W
Žipkovšino	88	51.52 N	112.59 E
Zippori	132	32.45 N	35.17 E
Zipsendorf	54	51.02 N	12.16 E
Ziqlāb, Wādī V	132	32.30 N	35.34 E
Zir	130	39.59 N	32.31 E
Zīra	123	30.58 N	74.59 E
Žir'akovo	86	57.53 N	65.37 E
Zirándaro	234	18.27 N	100.59 W
Zirāpur	124	24.01 N	76.22 E
Žir'atino	76	53.15 N	33.44 E
Zirbitzkogel ∧	61	47.04 N	14.34 E
Zirchow	54	53.53 N	14.08 E
Zirgan	86	53.14 N	55.55 E
Žirje, Otok I	36	43.40 N	15.39 E
Zirl	64	47.17 N	11.14 E
Zirndorf	56	49.26 N	10.58 E
Žirnov	80	48.13 N	41.06 E
Žirnovsk	80	51.00 N	44.46 E
Ziro	120	27.38 N	93.42 E
Žiroškino	82	55.22 N	38.03 E
Žirovnice	30	49.15 N	15.11 E
Zishan	100	25.57 N	115.35 E
Zistersdorf	61	48.32 N	16.45 E
Zisterzienserabtei ᴗ 1	56	49.01 N	8.47 E
Zisuntang	106	30.38 N	118.42 E
Zitadelle ⊥	264a	52.33 N	13.13 E
Žiteli	24	65.04 N	47.26 E
Žitenice	54	50.35 N	14.08 E
Žitjevo	76	59.54 N	41.06 E
Žitkoviči	76	52.14 N	27.54 E
Žitkovo	76	60.42 N	29.20 E
Žitkur	80	48.57 N	46.17 E
Zitlala	234	17.38 N	99.05 W
Zitlaltepec	234	19.12 N	97.54 W
Žitnoje	80	45.49 N	47.41 E
Žitomir	78	50.16 N	28.40 E
Žitomir □ 4	78	50.30 N	28.30 E
Zitong	102	31.43 N	105.10 E
Zittau	54	50.54 N	14.47 E
Zitundo	156	26.45 S	32.50 E
Ziwa Magharibi □ 4	154	2.00 S	31.30 E
Ziway, Lake ⊜	144	8.00 N	38.50 E
Ziwuji	100	32.55 N	115.58 E
Zixi, Zhg.	100	27.42 N	117.02 E
Zixi, Zhg.	100	28.01 N	117.46 E
Zixing	100	25.58 N	113.24 E
Ziya ≃	105	39.09 N	117.10 E
Ziyamet	130	35.28 N	34.08 E
Ziyang	107	30.07 N	104.39 E
Ziyuan	102	26.01 N	110.31 E
Ziyun	102	25.43 N	106.05 E
Ziz, Oued V	148	30.39 N	4.26 W
Žizdra	76	53.45 N	34.44 E
Žizdra ≃	82	54.14 N	36.12 E
Zizers	58	46.56 N	9.34 E
Zizhong	107	29.48 N	104.50 E
Zizhou	102	37.37 N	109.41 E
Žižica	76	56.17 N	31.21 E
Žižickoje, ozero ⊜	76	56.14 N	31.15 E
Žižma ≃	76	53.54 N	25.36 E
Zlarin	36	43.42 N	15.50 E
Zlatá Koruna ᴗ 1	61	48.52 N	14.22 E
Zlatar	36	46.06 N	16.05 E
Zlaté Moravce	30	48.25 N	18.24 E
Zlatograd	38	41.23 N	25.06 E
Zlatoust	86	55.10 N	59.40 E
Zlatoustovsk	89	52.58 N	133.38 E
Zlín	30	49.13 N	17.41 E
Zlītan	146	32.28 N	14.34 E
Žlobin	76	52.54 N	30.03 E
Złocieniec	30	53.33 N	16.01 E
Złoczew	30	51.25 N	18.36 E
Zlonice	54	50.15 N	14.07 E
Złotoryja	30	51.08 N	15.55 E
Złotów	30	53.22 N	17.02 E
Žlutice	54	50.03 N	13.10 E
Zlydnev	80	48.46 N	45.48 E
Zlynka, Ross.	76	52.25 N	31.44 E
Zlynka, Ukr.	78	48.28 N	31.32 E
Zmeinogorsk	86	51.10 N	82.13 E
Zmeinyj, ostrov I	78	45.15 N	30.12 E
Žmerinka	78	49.02 N	28.06 E
Żmigród	30	51.29 N	16.55 E
Zmijev	78	49.40 N	36.19 E
Žminj	36	45.09 N	13.55 E
Zmi'ovka	76	52.40 N	36.23 E

Zna → Cna ≃	80	54.32 N	42.05 E
Znaim → Znojmo	61	48.52 N	16.02 E
Znamenka, Kaz.	86	50.05 N	79.32 E
Znamenka, Ross.	76	54.54 N	34.34 E
Znamenka, Ross.	80	52.24 N	41.26 E
Znamenka, Ross.	86	53.10 N	79.30 E
Znamenka, Ross.	86	53.32 N	91.54 E
Znamenka, Ross.	88	54.42 N	104.50 E
Znamenka, Ukr.	78	48.43 N	32.40 E
Znamenka, Ukr.	83	48.51 N	37.22 E
Znamenka Vtoraja	78	48.43 N	32.35 E
Znamensk	76	54.37 N	21.13 E
Znamenskoje, Ross.	76	53.17 N	35.41 E
Znamenskoje, Ross.	80	53.19 N	42.57 E
Znamenskoje, Ross.	86	57.08 N	73.55 E
Znamenskoje, Ross.	265b	55.45 N	37.09 E
Żnin	30	52.52 N	17.43 E
Znob'-Novgorodskoje	78	52.16 N	33.36 E
Znojmo	61	48.52 N	16.02 E
Zoagli	62	44.20 N	9.16 E
Zoar	158	33.30 S	21.28 E
Zoar Village State Memorial ⊥	214	40.36 N	81.27 W
Zoarville	214	40.35 N	81.24 W
Zobia	154	2.58 N	25.56 E
Zöblitz	54	50.39 N	13.14 E
Zóbuè	154	15.38 S	34.26 E
Zocca	64	44.21 N	10.59 E
Žochova, ostrov I	74	76.04 N	152.40 E
Zod	84	40.12 N	45.52 E
Žodino	76	54.06 N	28.21 E
Žodiški	76	54.38 N	26.26 E
Zoétélé	152	3.15 N	11.53 E
Zoetermeer	52	52.03 N	4.30 E
Zofingen	58	47.18 N	7.57 E
Zogang	102	29.55 N	97.44 E
Zogno	62	45.48 N	9.40 E
Zográfos	267c	37.59 N	23.46 E
Zohar	132	31.36 N	34.42 E
Zohar, Mizpé ∧ 2	132	31.13 N	35.14 E
Zohreh ≃	128	30.04 N	49.31 E
Zola Predosa	64	44.29 N	11.12 E
Zolder	56	51.01 N	5.18 E
Zoldo Alto	64	46.22 N	12.06 E
Zolfo Springs	220	27.29 N	81.47 W
Zolka ≃	84	44.17 N	43.51 E
Żółkiewka	30	50.55 N	22.51 E
Zollhaus	56	50.17 N	8.04 E
Zollikofen	58	47.00 N	7.28 E
Zollikon	58	47.20 N	8.35 E
Zolling	60	48.27 N	11.46 E
Zol'noje	80	53.27 N	49.48 E
Zoločov, Ukr.	78	50.17 N	35.59 E
Zoločov, Ukr.	78	49.47 N	24.52 E
Zolotaja Gora	89	54.16 N	126.36 E
Zolotaja Lipa ≃	78	48.59 N	25.04 E
Zolotari	80	49.46 N	46.21 E
Zolotar'ovka	80	53.04 N	45.20 E
Zolotkovo	80	55.32 N	41.06 E
Zolotniki	78	49.17 N	25.23 E
Zolotoje, Ross.	80	50.51 N	45.53 E
Zolotoje, Ukr.	83	48.41 N	38.31 E
Zolotoj Kolodec	83	48.32 N	37.15 E
Zolotoj Potok	78	48.54 N	25.20 E
Zolotonoša	78	49.40 N	32.02 E
Zolotucha	80	47.49 N	46.44 E
Zolotuchino	78	52.05 N	36.23 E
Žoltoje, Ukr.	78	47.47 N	33.50 E
Žoltoje, Ukr.	78	48.30 N	33.31 E
Ž'oltoje, Ukr.	83	48.39 N	39.07 E
Žoltyje Vody	78	48.21 N	33.31 E
Žolymbet	86	51.45 N	71.44 E
Zomba	154	15.23 S	35.18 E
Zomergem	50	51.07 N	3.33 E
Zone Point ≻	42	50.08 N	5.00 W
Zongchang	107	28.52 N	104.36 E
Zongjiaxiang	269b	31.12 N	121.22 E
Zongo	152	4.21 N	18.36 E
Zonguldak	130	41.27 N	31.49 E
Zonguldak □ 4	130	41.30 N	32.15 E
Zongwe	154	5.05 S	27.55 E
Zongyang	100	30.42 N	117.12 E
Zonhoven	56	50.59 N	5.21 E
Zonnebeke	50	50.52 N	2.59 E
Zons	56	51.07 N	6.50 E
Zonza	36	41.45 N	9.10 E
Zoo, Bahnhof ◆ 5	264a	52.30 N	13.20 E
Zooafskolk	158	29.56 S	20.24 E
Zoom ≃	52	51.30 N	4.14 E
Zoppot → Sopot	30	54.28 N	18.34 E
Zopui	120	23.39 N	92.14 E
Zörbig	54	51.37 N	12.07 E
Zorge	54	51.38 N	10.38 E
Zorge ≃	54	51.27 N	10.54 E
Zorgo	150	12.15 N	0.36 W
Zorgongo	150	12.16 N	0.48 W
Zorinsk	83	48.25 N	38.34 E
Zorita	34	39.17 N	5.42 W
Zorkul', ozero ⊜	120	37.27 N	73.40 E
Zorn ≃	56	48.45 N	7.55 E
Zorneding	60	48.05 N	11.49 E
Zornica	38	42.23 N	26.56 E
Zorra, Arroyo de la ≃	196	29.31 N	101.13 W
Zorritos	246	3.40 S	80.40 W
Zorzor	150	7.46 N	9.28 W
Zöschen	54	51.21 N	12.07 E
Zossen	54	52.13 N	13.27 E
Zoti	84	41.53 N	42.28 E
Zottegem	50	50.52 N	3.48 E
Zou □ 5	150	8.00 N	2.15 E
Zou ≃	150	6.28 N	2.25 E
Zouan-Hounien	150	6.55 N	8.13 W
Zouar	146	20.27 N	16.32 E
Zouérat	148	22.42 N	12.30 W
Zoug → Zug	58	47.10 N	8.31 E
Zoulabot	152	3.17 N	14.02 E
Zoumagang	107	29.28 N	106.18 E
Zoumayi	98	39.07 N	114.34 E
Zouping	98	36.53 N	117.42 E
Zourma	150	11.22 N	0.49 W
Zousfana, Oued V	148	30.29 N	2.17 W
Zoutelande	52	51.30 N	3.30 E
Zoutkamp	52	53.20 N	6.18 E
Zouxian	98	35.24 N	117.00 E
Zova	132	31.48 N	35.06 E
Zovka	76	58.26 N	28.52 E
Žovnino	78	49.23 N	32.41 E
Žovten', Ukr.	78	49.03 N	24.45 E
Žovten', Ukr.	78	47.14 N	30.20 E
Žovtnevoje, Ukr.	78	46.52 N	32.02 E
Žovtnevoje, Ukr.	78	49.39 N	34.09 E
Žovtnevoje, Ukr.	78	50.57 N	34.22 E
Žovtnevoje, Ukr.	78	51.15 N	28.07 E
Zozov	78	49.19 N	29.01 E
Zrenjanin	38	45.23 N	20.24 E
Zriba	36	36.20 N	10.16 E
Zrmanja ≃	36	44.15 N	15.32 E
Zruč nad Sázavou	30	49.45 N	15.07 E
Zscherndorf	54	51.36 N	12.15 E
Zschieren ◆ 8	54	51.00 N	13.52 E
Zschopau	54	50.44 N	13.04 E
Zschopau ≃	54	51.08 N	13.03 E
Zschorlau	54	50.34 N	12.38 E
Zschornewitz	54	51.43 N	12.25 E
Zschortau	54	51.28 N	12.21 E
Žuanbalyk	86	45.04 N	61.51 E
Žuantobe	86	44.45 N	68.54 E
Zuarungu	150	10.47 N	0.48 W
Zuata ≃	246	7.52 N	65.22 W
Zubaydīyah, Jabal az- ∧	132	33.48 N	37.02 E
Zubayr, Jazā'ir az- II	144	15.05 N	42.08 E
Zubayr, Wādī V	142	27.27 N	32.41 E
Zubcov	76	56.10 N	34.34 E
Zubkoviči	78	51.02 N	27.41 E
Zubova Pol'ana	80	54.04 N	42.51 E

Zubovka	80	54.16 N	51.06 E
Zubovo, Ross.	76	60.19 N	36.57 E
Zubovo, Ross.	76	54.33 N	35.29 E
Zubovo, Ross.	80	56.52 N	44.08 E
Zuccarello	62	44.07 N	8.07 E
Zuccone, Monte ∧	62	44.26 N	9.37 E
Zuchwil	58	47.12 N	7.33 E
Zuckerhütl ∧	64	46.58 N	11.09 E
Zudar	54	54.15 N	13.20 E
Z'udev, ostrov I	80	45.35 N	47.58 E
Zuel	64	46.31 N	12.08 E
Zuénoula	150	7.26 N	6.03 W
Zuera	34	41.52 N	0.47 W
Zufār ◆ 1	118	17.00 N	54.10 E
Zufaytat Mashtūl	142	30.20 N	31.21 E
Zug	58	47.10 N	8.31 E
Zug □ 3	58	47.00 N	8.30 E
Zugdeli	88	55.03 N	111.10 E
Zugdidi	84	42.30 N	41.53 E
Zugersee ⊜	58	47.08 N	8.30 E
Zug Island I	281	42.17 N	83.07 W
Zugló ◆ 8	264c	47.31 N	19.08 E
Zugres	83	48.01 N	38.15 E
Zugspitze ∧	64	47.25 N	10.59 E
Zugurma Game Reserve ◆ 4	150	9.55 N	5.00 E
Zühlsdorf	264a	52.44 N	13.24 E
Zui	76	57.06 N	31.37 E
Zuid-Beijerland	52	51.45 N	4.22 E
Zuid-Beveland I	52	51.25 N	3.45 E
Zuidbroek	52	53.10 N	6.52 E
Zuidelijk Flevoland ◆ 1	52	52.22 N	5.20 E
Zuiderzee → IJsselmeer ╤ 2	52	52.45 N	5.25 E
Zuid-Holland □ 4	52	52.00 N	4.30 E
Zuidhorn	52	53.14 N	6.24 E
Zuidlaren	52	53.05 N	6.41 E
Zuid-Willemsvaart ≊	52	51.12 N	5.52 E
Zuidwolde	52	53.15 N	6.35 E
Zuja	78	45.03 N	34.20 E
Žuja ≃	88	58.45 N	118.11 E
Zújar ≃	34	39.01 N	5.47 W
Zújar, Embalse del ⊜ 1	34	38.50 N	5.20 W
Zujevka, Ross.	80	58.25 N	51.10 E
Zujevka, Ukr.	83	48.04 N	38.15 E
Z'ukajka	80	58.12 N	54.43 E
Žukopa	76	56.33 N	32.42 E
Žukopa ≃	76	56.54 N	32.46 E
Žukovka, Ross.	76	53.32 N	33.44 E
Žukovka, Ross.	86	56.05 N	91.42 E
Žukovka, Ross.	265b	55.44 N	37.15 E
Žukovskaja	80	47.37 N	42.28 E
Žukovskij	82	55.35 N	38.08 E
Žukovskoje	80	46.05 N	41.21 E
Żukowo	30	54.21 N	18.22 E
Zula	144	15.11 N	39.41 E
Zula ≃	234	20.21 N	102.46 W
Žulanka	86	54.22 N	80.36 E
Zulayl, Wādī az- V	132	32.09 N	36.03 E
Žuldyz	80	49.16 N	49.30 E
Žulebino	265b	55.42 N	37.51 E
Zuli ≃	102	36.35 N	104.35 E
Zulia □ 3	246	10.00 N	72.10 W
Zulia ∧	154	4.07 N	33.58 E
Zulia ≃	246	9.04 N	72.18 W
Zülpich	56	50.41 N	6.39 E
Zulueta	240p	22.22 N	79.34 W
Zululand □ 9	158	28.10 S	32.00 E
Z'ul'z'a	88	52.33 N	116.13 E
Žumala	80	50.29 N	49.47 E
Zumar, Tur'at az- ≊	273c	29.58 N	31.15 E
Zumarraga	116	11.38 N	124.50 E
Zumba	246	4.52 S	79.09 W
Zumbo	154	15.36 S	30.25 E
Zumbro ≃	190	44.18 N	91.56 W
Zumbro, North Fork ≃	190	44.15 N	92.29 W
Zumbro, South Fork ≃	190	44.15 N	92.29 W
Zumbrota	190	44.17 N	92.40 W
Zumpango del Río	234	17.39 N	99.30 W
Zumpango de Ocampo	234	19.48 N	99.06 W
Zundert	52	51.28 N	4.40 E
Zundi	152	10.28 S	16.48 E
Zune	156	18.59 S	35.18 E
Zungeru	150	9.48 N	6.09 E
Zungri	68	38.39 N	15.59 E
Zungur	150	9.58 N	9.47 E
Zungwini	158	27.34 S	30.53 E
Zunhua	105	40.12 N	117.58 E
Zuni, N.M., U.S.	200	35.04 N	108.51 W
Zuni, Va., U.S.	208	36.51 N	76.49 W
Zuni ≃	200	34.39 N	109.40 W
Zuni Indian Reservation ◆ 4	200	35.15 N	108.20 W
Zunsuzhi	102	44.40 N	112.50 E
Zunyi	102	27.39 N	106.57 E
Zuo ≃	102	22.50 N	108.06 E
Zuo'an	100	26.10 N	114.16 E
Zuodeng	102	23.27 N	106.57 E
Zuogezhuang	105	39.01 N	116.37 E
Zuomaozigou	104	42.12 N	120.41 E
Zuomuchedong Hu ⊜	120	28.25 N	88.15 E
Zuoquan	102	37.03 N	113.30 E
Zuosuo	102	27.45 N	100.54 E
Zuotema	120	35.50 N	80.45 E
Zuowei	105	40.41 N	114.43 E
Zuoxiunulemiao	88	48.08 N	115.38 E
Zuoyun	102	40.02 N	112.54 E
Zuoz	58	46.36 N	9.58 E
Županja	38	45.04 N	18.42 E
Zūq Muṣbīḥ	132	33.58 N	35.37 E
Žura, Mol.	78	47.31 N	29.04 E
Zura, Ross.	80	57.37 N	53.26 E
Zūrābād	128	38.49 N	44.35 E
Žuraviči, Bela.	76	53.15 N	30.33 E
Žuraviči, Ukr.	78	50.59 N	25.43 E
Žuravl'ovka, Kaz.	86	51.57 N	69.56 E
Žuravl'ovka, Ukr.	83	48.13 N	38.58 E
Zurayghiṭ	128	26.29 N	40.33 E
Žurban	89	54.12 N	127.56 E
Zurich, On., Can.	190	43.26 N	81.37 W
Zurich, Ned.	52	53.06 N	5.23 E
Zürich, Schw.	58	47.23 N	8.32 E
Zürich □ 3	58	47.25 N	8.40 E
Zürich, Flughafen ⊠	58	47.27 N	8.33 E
Zurich, Lake ⊜	278	42.12 N	88.06 W
Zürichsee ⊜	58	47.13 N	8.45 E
Zurigo → Zürich	58	47.23 N	8.32 E
Zurmi	150	12.46 N	6.48 E
Żuromin	30	53.04 N	19.55 E
Zurq, Al-Qārāt az- ∧ 2	142	29.00 N	29.55 E
Zürs	58	47.10 N	10.10 E
Zuru	150	11.27 N	5.12 E
Zurzach	58	47.35 N	8.18 E
Zuša ≃	76	53.27 N	36.23 E
Zusam ≃	56	48.42 N	10.45 E
Žusandala ◆ 2	86	44.20 N	75.00 E
Zushi	94	35.18 N	139.35 E
Zusmarshausen	58	48.24 N	10.35 E
Züssow	54	53.59 N	13.32 E
Žut, Otok I	36	43.52 N	15.19 E
Zutiua ≃	250	3.43 S	45.29 W
Žutovo Vtoroje	80	47.49 N	43.51 E
Zutphen	52	52.08 N	6.12 E
Zützen	54	51.57 N	13.38 E
Zuwārah	146	32.56 N	12.06 E
Zuwayzā	132	31.42 N	35.55 E
Z'uzel'skij	86	56.29 N	60.07 E
Žužemberk	36	45.50 N	14.56 E
Z'uzino	265b	55.40 N	38.07 E
Z'uzino ◆ 8	265b	55.39 N	37.35 E
Žuzymdyk	85	43.05 N	69.08 E
Zv'agino	265b	55.59 N	37.48 E
Zvannoje	78	51.23 N	34.33 E
Zvenigorod	82	55.44 N	36.51 E

≃	River	Fluß	Río	Rivière	Rio
≊	Canal	Kanal	Canal	Canal	Canal
ʟ	Waterfall, Rapids	Wasserfall, Stromschnellen	Cascada, Rápidos	Chute d'eau, Rapides	Cascata, Rápidos
ꟺ	Strait	Meeresstraße	Estrecho	Détroit	Estreito
c	Bay, Gulf	Bucht, Golf	Bahía, Golfo	Baie, Golfe	Baía, Golfo
⊜	Lake, Lakes	See, Seen	Lago, Lagos	Lac, Lacs	Lago, Lagos
≡	Swamp	Sumpf	Pantano	Marais	Pântano
⊓	Ice Features, Glacier	Eis- und Gletscherformen	Accidentes Glaciales	Formes glaciaires	Acidentes glaciares
╤	Other Hydrographic Features	Andere Hydrographische Objekte	Otros Elementos Hidrográficos	Autres données hydrographiques	Outros acidentes hidrográficos

✣	Submarine Features	Untermeerische Objekte	Accidentes Submarinos	Formes de relief sous-marin	Acidentes submarinos
□	Political Unit	Politische Einheit	Unidad Politica	Entité politique	Unidade política
ᴗ	Cultural Institution	Kulturelle Institution	Institución Cultural	Institution culturelle	Instituição cultural
⊥	Historical Site	Historische Stätte	Sitio Histórico	Site historique	Sitio histórico
♠	Recreational Site	Erholungs- und Ferienort	Sitio de Recreo	Centre de loisirs	Area de Lazer
⊠	Airport	Flughafen	Aeropuerto	Aéroport	Aeroporto
▮	Military Installation	Militäranlage	Instalación Militar	Installation militaire	Instalação militar
◆	Miscellaneous	Verschiedenes	Misceláneo	Divers	Diversos

Name	Page	Lat. °′	Long. °′
Zvenigorodka	**78**	49.04 N	30.57 E
Zvenigovo	**80**	55.58 N	48.02 E
Zverevo	**83**	48.01 N	40.07 E
Zverinogolovskoje	**86**	54.28 N	64.50 E
Zvezdec	**38**	42.07 N	27.25 E
Zvezdnyj	**88**	56.49 N	106.27 E
Zvíkovec	**60**	49.56 N	13.42 E
Zvishavane	**154**	20.20 S	30.02 E
Zvolen	**30**	48.35 N	19.08 E
Zvon ∧	**60**	49.33 N	12.39 E
Zvornik	**38**	44.23 N	19.06 E
Zwaag	**52**	52.40 N	5.05 E
Zwaagwesteinde	**52**	53.15 N	6.04 E
Zwadība	**152**	3.04 N	14.02 E
Zwanenburg	**52**	52.23 N	4.45 E
Zwartemeer	**52**	52.43 N	7.03 E
Zwarte Meer ⊜	**52**	52.37 N	5.57 E
Zwartsluis	**52**	52.37 N	6.04 E
Zweckel ◆[8]	**263**	51.36 N	6.59 E
Zwedru	**150**	6.04 N	8.08 W
Zweibrücken	**56**	49.15 N	7.21 E
Zweifall	**56**	50.43 N	6.15 E
Zweisimmen	**58**	46.33 N	7.22 E
Zweite Wiener Hochquellenleitung ⊼[1]	**61**	48.10 N	16.14 E
Zwenkau	**54**	51.13 N	12.19 E
Zwentendorf	**61**	48.21 N	15.55 E
Zwesten	**56**	51.03 N	9.10 E
Zwettl	**61**	48.37 N	15.10 E
Zwevegem	**50**	50.48 N	3.20 E
Zwevezele	**50**	51.02 N	3.12 E
Zwickau	**54**	50.44 N	12.29 E
Zwickauer Mulde ≏	**54**	51.10 N	12.48 E
Zwiefalten	**58**	48.14 N	9.28 E
Zwiefaltendorf	**58**	48.13 N	9.31 E
Zwierzyniec	**30**	50.37 N	22.58 E
Zwiesel	**60**	49.01 N	13.14 E
Zwieselstein	**64**	46.56 N	11.02 E
Zwijndrecht	**52**	51.49 N	4.39 E
Zwillbrock	**52**	52.04 N	6.42 E
Zwingenberg, Dtsch.	**56**	49.25 N	9.02 E
Zwingenberg, Dtsch.	**56**	49.43 N	8.37 E
Zwischenahner Meer ⊜	**52**	53.12 N	8.01 E
Zwochau	**54**	51.28 N	12.16 E
Zwoleń	**30**	51.22 N	21.35 E
Zwölfaxing	**264b**	48.06 N	16.28 E
Zwolle, Ned.	**52**	52.30 N	6.05 E
Zwolle, La., U.S.	**194**	31.37 N	93.38 W
Zwönitz	**54**	50.38 N	12.49 E
Zwota	**54**	50.21 N	12.25 E
Żychlin	**30**	52.15 N	19.39 E
Zymoetz ≏	**182**	54.33 N	128.26 W
Zyr'anka	**74**	65.45 N	150.51 E
Zyr'anovsk	**86**	49.43 N	84.20 E
Zyr'anovskij	**86**	57.46 N	61.42 E
Zyr'anskoje	**86**	56.50 N	86.38 E
Żyrardów	**30**	52.04 N	20.25 E
Zyryanovsk → Zyr'anovsk	**86**	49.43 N	84.20 E
Żyrzyn	**30**	51.30 N	22.07 E
Żywiec	**30**	49.41 N	19.12 E

ENGLISH				DEUTSCH			
Name	Page	Lat. °′	Long. °′	Name	Seite	Breite °′	Länge °′ E = Ost

Symbols in the index entries represent the broad categories identified in the key at the right. Symbols with superior numbers (⋏[1]) identify subcategories (see complete key on page *I · 1).*

Symbole im Register stellen die rechts im Schlüssel erklärten Kategorien dar. Symbole mit hochgestellten Ziffern (⋏[1]) bezeichnen Unterabteilungen einer Kategorie (vgl. vollständiger Schlüssel auf Seite *I · 1).*

Los símbolos incluídos en el texto del índice representan las grandes categorias identificadas con la clave a la derecha. Los símbolos con numeros en su parte superior (⋏[1]) identifican las subcategorías (véase la clave completa en la página *I · 1).*

Les symboles de l'index représentent les catégories indiquées dans la légende à droite. Les symboles suivis d'un indice (⋏[1]) représentent des sous-catégories (voir légende complète à la page *I · 1).*

Os símbolos incluídos no texto do índice representam as grandes categorias identificadas com a chave à direita. Os símbolos com números em sua parte superior (⋏[1]) identificam as subcategorias (veja-se a chave completa à página *I · 1).*

∧ Mountain	Berg	Montaña	Montagne	Montanha
⋏ Mountains	Gebirge	Montañas	Montagnes	Montanhas
)(Pass	Paß	Paso	Col	Passo
V Valley, Canyon	Tal, Cañon	Valle, Cañón	Vallée, Canyon	Vale, Canhão
≚ Plain	Ebene	Llano	Plaine	Planície
≻ Cape	Kap	Cabo	Cap	Cabo
I Island	Insel	Isla	Île	Ilha
II Islands	Inseln	Islas	Îles	Ilhas
≛ Other Topographic Features	Andere Topographische Objekte	Otros Elementos Topográficos	Autres données topographiques	Outros acidentes topográficos